THE SOURCEBOOK

To Public Record Information

The Comprehensive Guide to County, State, & Federal Public Records Sources

Tenth Edition

BRB Publications, Inc.

www.brbpub.com

Dedicated to the Searching & Understanding of Public Records

THE SOURCEBOOK

To Public Record Information — Tenth Edition

Edited by: Peter J. Weber and Michael Sankey

©2009 by BRB Publications, Inc.
PO Box 27869
Tempe, AZ 85285
800-929-3811 Fax 800-929-4981

www.brbpub.com

Publisher's Cataloging-in-Publication
(Provided by Quality Books, Inc.)

The sourcebook to public record information : the comprehensive guide to county, state, & federal public records sources / [edited by Michael L. Sankey and Peter J. Weber]. -- 10th ed.

p. cm.
ISBN-13: 978-1-879792-92-0
ISBN-10: 1-879792-92-3

1. Public records--United States--States--Information services--Directories. 2. Courts--United States--States --Directories. 3. Public records--United States--States --Computer network resources. I. Sankey, Michael L., 1949- II. Weber, Peter J. (Peter Julius), 1952-

JK468.P76S693 2009 352.3'87'02573
QBI08-3195

Replaces *The Guide to Background Investigations*

Contents

Introduction

Over 20,000 Government Agencies at Your Fingertips

The old adage "Information is Power" is especially true today. *The Sourcebook* reveals where government records are kept, outlines the access requirements, gives searching tips, and tells which agencies offer online access to records and record indices. Over 20,000 government agencies are profiled so you can explore the depths of government maintained records.

Public records are meant to be used for the benefit of society. The public has a broad right of access to government information. As a member of the public, you or someone in authority is entitled to review the public records held by government agencies. Whether you are a business owner, a reporter, an investigator, or even a father trying to check on your daughter's first date, you can access public records to meet your needs.

Herein, we examine these paper trails that begin at or are maintained at the federal, state, county, and in certain instances, the city and town level. The *Sourcebook* is especially useful for these applications:

- Legal Research
- Pre-Employment Screening
- Background Investigation
- Tenant Screening
- Locating People
- Locating Assets
- Skiptracing
- Insurance Underwriting
- Genealogy

Equipped with the information contained in these pages, you can find the facts, gain access to the information you need, and even track your own "information trail." To that end, this book has been designed to be your tour guide and take you precisely to the location you need.

The Three Truths

There are three truths to keep in mind as you become involved with searching government records—

1. Just because records are maintained in a certain way in your state or county, do not assume that any other county or state does things the same way;
2. Not all public records are online, in fact only about 50% are; and
3. An *Information Chain* exists between the record repository and the record's end-user.

How This Book Is Organized

General Layout

The Sourcebook is organized into two Sections—

1. 51 Individual State Chapters (followed by U.S. Territories and Canadian Provinces)
2. The Appendix

Section 1: The State Chapters

Each state chapter in *The Sourcebook* has been compiled into an easy-to-use format. There are six sub-chapters organized by type of agency, and presented in this order:

1. State Public Record Agencies
2. State Licensing and Regulatory Boards
3. Federal Courts (U.S. District and Bankruptcy), shown by state
4. County, Parish, or City Courts
5. County, Parish, or City Recorder and Assessor Offices
6. County Locator

After the State Chapters is a section on Canadian Provinces and U.S. Territories.

Information in the Agency Profiles

The depth of knowledge presented about each government agency is what separates this *Sourcebook* from a typical address and telephone listing reference book or a *Google* search.

The following details have been researched and presented as applicable within each profile:

- **Agency Facts**: office hours; time zone; websites, mailing and physical addresses.
- **Searching Facts**: methods of access; indexing; search requirements; if records are available online; when free public access terminals are at the counter; personal identifiers shown on the public access terminals; turnaround times for mail requests; how far back records or record indices are kept.
- **Privacy Facts**: when restrictions are imposed on searchers or on the use of the record; when signed releases or notarized statements are required; and what specific records are not available to the public.
- **Fees**: access fees; copy fees; certification fees; expedited fees; if credit cards accepted; what types of checks accepted; to whom to make the check payable.
- **Special Attention to Online Access:** what types of records are accessible online; if free or a pay site, when subscription or registration is required, personal identifiers are needed for access, and what is shown on results.
- **Other Access:** how to purchase databases or customized lists; when more than one agency must be visited in the county to get all records; if results or specific documents will be returned by fax; when certain industries are able to access certain records or use certain access methods (i.e. attorneys, schools, etc.).

Also, be sure to check out the front portion of each State Agency, Courts, and Recorders sections. You will find a useful overview with facts and searching hints.

Using The County Locator

The *County Locato*r section in each state chapter is extremely useful when it is unclear in which county to perform a localized record search. This section contains two cross-reference indices. The City/County Cross Reference will indicate in what county(s) a "place" (city or town) is located. There are over 40,000 places referenced. The ZIP Code/City Cross Reference assists those people who have an address with ZIP Code, but are unsure in which county the ZIP in located.

Keep in mind that over 8,000 ZIP Codes cross county lines.

Note: The web version of the *Sourcebook* – called Public Record Research Systems PRRS – contains an additional 45,000 place names and has look-ups for finding adjoining counties. See below.

Section 2: The Appendix

The Appendix section of *The Sourceboo*k will assist the reader in how to search for public records. The Appendix contains many searching hints and is an excellent overall resource, especially helpful to those not familiar with searching government records.

There are four sections in the Appendix—

1. **Fundamentals of Public Record Searching**
2. **Searching Federal Courts**
3. **Searching Other Federal Records**
4. **Working with Public Record Vendors**

Each of these sections contains a wealth of information. We invite you to review this content.

What Is New in the Tenth Edition

The Tenth Edition represents an enormous amount of updated material from the last edition published 18 months ago. Over 700 online accessible sources for record searching have been added since last year. There are new fees, new addresses, and we have expanded coverage and added content to the Courts and Recorders Sections.

Specifically, within the County Courts section, additional information includes—

- When searching online, the personal identifiers shown on results.
- When searching at a public access terminal, the personal identifiers shown on results.
- When the public access terminal at the courthouse is and is not presenting the same information as provided on an online accessible system.

Within the County Recorder section, additional information includes—

- Breakout of Tax Assessor Offices, with separate addresses, phone numbers, and online access sites.

Updated Content is Available on the Web

The tenth edition of *The Sourcebook to Public Record Information* represents thousands of hours of research right up to the day of printing. We have compiled what we feel is the most up-to-date and unique compendium of its kind. However, users should also remember that the information reported in *The Sourcebook* can, and does, change.

For those of you who need to know more or need to have this information constantly updated, we recommend an expanded version of this book. ***The Public Records Research System*** (PRRS-Web) is available as a subscription service on the Internet.

Updated weekly, PRRS contains all the information found in *The Sourcebook* plus content from two CD products – *The National Directory to College and University Student Record*, and *The County Locator,* and also included are the members of the *Public Record Retrieval Network.*

For additional information, visit www.brbpub.com.

Key Abbreviations

You will find certain important abbreviations throughout *The Sourcebook.*

PAT – Refers to a Public Access Terminal. This is a computer station provided by the government agency so that a researcher may visit the agency in person and view the record index when searching for public records.

SASE – This acronym simply stands for a **S**elf **A**ddressed **S**tamped **E**nvelope. Some agencies require that a SASE is supplied with a mail request. When not required, the SASE will often speed up the turnaround time on a mail request.

DPPA – This refers to a federal law – the Driver's Privacy Protection Act. DPPA mandates who can receive personal information on motor vehicle records. DPPA denotes 14 designated permissible uses by record requesters that will permit states to place certain personal information on records. Some states are more restrictive.

FCRA – The federal Fair Credit Reporting Act is a law that covers much more than credit data. For example, the FCRA regulates governs how certain information, including criminal records, can be collected, disseminated, and reported for pre-employment screening purposes.

Thank You from the Research and Editorial Staff at BRB Publications

BRB Publications is 100% devoted to the understanding of public records. Our goal is to provide you with a valuable resource — so you can understand what you need, where it might be found, and how to access that information like a pro.

We hope you find *The Sourcebook* to be a valuable asset.

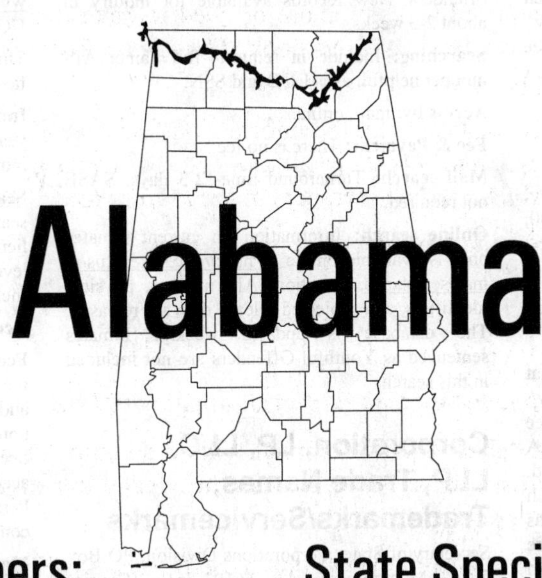

Alabama

General Help Numbers:

Governor's Office
600 Dexter Ave, #N-104 — 334-242-7100
Montgomery, AL 36130 — Fax 334-353-0004
www.governor.state.al.us — 8AM-5PM

Attorney General's Office
State House — 334-242-7300
11 S. Union Street, 3rd Fl — Fax 334-242-4891
Montgomery, AL 36130 — 8AM-5PM
www.ago.state.al.us

Legislative Records
State House — 334-242-7800 (Senate)
11 S Union St — 334-242-7600 (House)
Montgomery, AL 36130-4600 — Fax 334-242-8819
www.legislature.state.al.us — 8:30AM-4:30PM

State Archives
Archives & History Department — 334-242-4435
Reference Room, PO Box 300100 — Fax 334-240-3433
Montgomery, AL 36130-0100 — 8AM-5PM T-F,
www.archives.state.al.us — 9AM-5PM SAT

State Specifics:

Capital:	Montgomery Montgomery County
Time Zone:	CST
Number of Counties:	67
Population:	4,661,900
Website:	www.alabama.gov

State Agencies

Criminal Records

Alabama Bureau of Investigation, Identification Unit - Record Checks, PO Box 1511, Montgomery, AL 36102-1511 (Courier address- 301 S Ripley St, Montgomery, AL 36104); 334-353-4340, 334-353-7800; 8AM-5PM.

http://dps.alabama.gov/ABI/cic.aspx

Indexing & Storage: Records available from 1945 on. New records available for inquiry in about 7 days. 45% of arrests in database have final dispositions recorded, 65% for those arrests in last 5 years.

Searching: The request must be on state form ABI-46. The form can be obtained from the webpage or call to have copy sent. Include in request- notarized release from subject, date of birth, SSN, full name, race, sex. Fingerprints optional. Two witnesses may attest to signature instead of a notary. 100% of the record files have fingerprints. This data not released- juvenile records. All records or arrests are released, including those without dispositions.

Access by: mail, in person, online.

Fee & Payment: The fee is $25.00 per name. For those entities entitled by statute to an FBI fingerprint check, the fee is $49.00 per name. The FBI check is not available to the public or employers not entitled per statute. Fee payee- Alabama Bureau of Investigation. Prepayment required. Cashier checks and money orders accepted. No personal checks or cash accepted. No credit cards accepted.

Mail search: Turnaround time- 4 to 6 weeks. SASE not required.

In person search: You may bring in the required release and request form.

Online search: This agency recommends that searchers contact www.background.alabama.gov/. This is a subscription service with a $25 search fee and a $75 annual fee. Employers using a CRA must be registered first.

Statewide Court Records

Administrative Office of Courts, 300 Dexter Ave, Montgomery, AL 36104-3741; 334-954-5000, 866-954-9411; 8AM-5PM.

www.alacourt.gov

Trial court records can be obtained online.

Access by: online.

Online search: This agency recommends that searchers contact www.background.alabama.gov/. This is a subscription service with a $25 search fee and a $75 annual fee. Employers using a CRA must first registered. Another agency-supported, real time service is at www.alacourt.com/. Search fees are based on monthly volume with searches as low as $.40 each. Full identifiers are shown. There is a $150 set-up fee. Request form for case record at http://helpdesk.alacourt.gov/requestform.asp. Specific case data is needed, search is on a county basis. State Supreme Court and Appellate decisions are available at www.alalinc.net and at www.judicial.state.al.us/.

Sexual Offender Registry

Department of Public Safety, Sexual Offender Registry, PO Box 1511, Montgomery, AL 36102-1511 (Courier address- 301 S Ripley, Montgomery, AL 36102); 334-353-1172, Fax-334-353-2563; 8AM-5PM.

http://community.dps.alabama.gov/

Sections 15-20-21 to 37, defines criminal sex offenders and is part of the Alabama Community Notification Act.

Indexing & Storage: Records available from 08/01/98. New records available for inquiry in 30 days or less.

Searching: The agency indicates it will not sell or provide the database of offenders to the public or to business entities. Include in request- name, DOB, and SSN. This data not released-information on the victim or offenders who are not classified as an adult.

Access by: mail, online.

Fee & Payment: None

Mail search: Turnaround time- 7 days. A SASE is required. The agency prefers all requesters first search the web page.

Online search: Sex offender data and a felony fugitives list are available online at the home page. Search by name, ZIP, city or county. Missing persons and felony fugitives are also shown.

Incarceration Records

Alabama Department of Corrections, Central Records Office, PO Box 301501, Montgomery, AL 36130 (Courier address- 301 S. Ripley Street, Montgomery, AL 36130); 334-353-9500, 334-353-3883; 8AM-5PM.

http://doc.state.al.us

Questions regarding specific inmates can be sent to constituent.services@doc.alabama.gov.

Indexing & Storage: Records available on current and former inmates by mail; current inmates only online. No information is available on youthful offenders. New records available for inquiry in about 2-3 weeks.

Searching: Include in request- full name; AIS number helpful, as is DOB and SSN.

Access by: mail, online.

Fee & Payment: There is no fee.

Mail search: Turnaround time- 2-3 days. SASE not required.

Online search: Information on current inmates only is available online at http://doc.state.al.us/inmatesearch.asp. Location, AIS number, physical identifiers, and projected release date are released. The database is updated weekly. Inmates sentenced as Youthful Offenders are not included in this search.

Corporation, LP, LLC, LLP, Trade Names, Trademarks/Servicemarks

Secretary of State, Corporations Division, PO Box 5616, Montgomery, AL 36103-5616 (Courier address- 11 S Union St, Ste 207, Montgomery, AL 36104); 334-242-5324, 334-242-5325 (Trademarks), Fax- 334-240-3138; 8AM-5PM.

www.sos.alabama.gov/

Non-profit records here also. The office for Trademarks, Trade Names, and Servicemarks is located in Room 200.

Indexing & Storage: Records available from 1800's. Data on all above business entities mentioned, active or inactive, are available. All information here on file is considered public information. New records available for inquiry in 1 month.

Searching: Include in request- full name of business. In addition to the articles of organization, business entity records available include: Officers, Prior (Merged) names, and Reserved names.

Access by: mail, phone, fax, in person, online.

Fee & Payment: There is no search fee, but copies are $1.00 per page and $1.50 for not-for-profit records. Fee payee- Secretary of State. Prepayment required. Personal checks and credit cards accepted.

Mail search: Turnaround time- 7 to 10 days. A SASE is requested.

Phone search: Limited information is available.;

Fax search: Search requests accepted by fax.

In person search: Call first for page amount before going to their office. Expedite fees may apply.

Online search: The website has free searches of corporate and UCC records. Search individual files for Active Names at http://arc-sos.state.al.us/CGI/SOSCRP01.MBR/INPUT. Also, search securities department administrative actions lists free at http://asc.state.al.us/Issued-Orders.htm.

Expedited service: Expedited service is available for mail and phone searches, call for fees. Turnaround time- 72 hours.

Uniform Commercial Code, Federal & State Tax Liens

UCC Division - SOS, UCC Records, PO Box 5616, Montgomery, AL 36103-5616 (Courier address- 11 South Union St, Suite 200, Montgomery, AL 36104); 334-242-5231; 8AM-5PM.

www.sos.state.al.us/vb/inquiry/inquiry.aspx?area=UCC

This office will not accept any faxes, in fact all faxes are thrown away.

Indexing & Storage: Records available for one year after lapse date. New records available for inquiry in 72 hours.

Searching: Use search request form UCC-11. The search includes tax liens. Federal and state tax liens on individuals may also be filed at the county level. All tax liens on businesses are filed here. Include in request- debtor name or file number.

Access by: mail, in person, online.

Fee & Payment: In addition to the $20.00 search fee per debtor name, the copy fee is $1.00 per page and certification is $5.00 per filing. If the form is non-standard add another $5.00. Fee payee-Secretary of State. Prepayment required. Prepaid accounts available, minimum $500 deposit. Personal checks accepted. Credit cards accepted, convenience fee added.

Mail search: Turnaround time- 72 hours. SASE not required.

In person search: Turnaround time is 72 hours unless an expedited fee of $100 is paid for immediate service. However, if workload is light, they may do the search that day without the expedited fee.

Online search: The agency has UCC information available to search at www.sos.state.al.us/vb/inquiry/inquiry.aspx?area=UCC. An advanced search is offered that provides images. Use of credit card or a subscription is required. Name search is $15.00 plus $1.00 per page. Search by filing number is only $1.00 per page. Add $14.25 per transaction for misc. fees. There is no fee for the limited search. You can search by debtor's name or file number. Farm UCC filings are no longer available thru online searches.

Other access: Bulk sale by CD for $1,500 plus $300 a week for updates. No images.

Expedited service: This service is available for an additional $100.00, usually same day service.

Sales Tax Registrations

Access to Records is Restricted.

Alabama Department of Revenue, Sales, Use and Business Tax Division, PO Box 327710, Montgomery, AL 36132-7710 (Courier address-4303 Gordon Persons Bldg, 50 N Ripley St, Montgomery, AL 36104); 334-242-1490, Fax-334-353-7867; 8AM-5PM.

www.revenue.alabama.gov/salestax/menu.html

According to state law 40-2A-10, Code of Alabama 1975, this agency is unable to release any information about tax registrations. Note, their website has motor vehicle dealer regulatory license information.

Birth Certificates

Center for Health Statistics, Record Services Division, PO Box 5625, Montgomery, AL 36103-5625 (Courier address- RSA Tower Suite 1150, 201 Monroe St, Montgomery, AL 36104); 334-206-5418, Fax- 334-262-9563; 8AM-5PM.

www.adph.org/vitalrecords/

Certificates can, also, be requested in any AL County Health Department for any vital record event occurring in AL; delivery time is usually 15-30 minutes.

Indexing & Storage: Records available from 1908 to present. New records available for inquiry in 1 week or less.

Searching: Birth certificates under 125 years old may be requested by an immediate family member or person with legal right to certificate. Include in request- full name at birth, name of father, full maiden name of mother, date of birth, county or city of birth, relationship to subject, reason for request. Include a daytime phone number and a signature.

Access by: mail, phone, fax, in person, online.

Fee & Payment: Fee is $12.00 for first copy, $4.00 for each additional copy ordered at same time. Add $15.50 to expedite and use of a credit card. Fee payee- State Board of Health Prepayment required. Personal checks and major credit cards accepted.

Mail search: Turnaround time- 5 to 10 days. SASE not required.

Phone search: Telephone requests allowed using a credit card; see expedited service.

Fax search: Same criteria as phone searches.

In person search: Also, you can go to the nearest AL County Health Department to place request.

Online search: Online ordering is available from the webpage through a service provider www.vitalchek.com. Check their sites for fees and turnaround times.

Expedited service: Turnaround time- 1 day. Add $10.00 to expedite with mail return, add $5.50 for use of credit card. Overnight shipping available for additional fee, if credit card used.

Death Records

Center for Health Statistics, Record Services Division, PO Box 5625, Montgomery, AL 36103-5625 (Courier address- RSA Tower Suite 1150, 201 Monroe St, Montgomery, AL 36104); 334-206-5418, Fax- 334-262-9563; 8AM-5PM.

www.adph.org/vitalrecords/

Certificates can, also, be requested in any AL County Health Department for any vital record event occurring in AL; delivery time is usually 15-30 minutes.

Indexing & Storage: Records available from 1908 to present. New records available for inquiry in 1 week or more.

Searching: Must be immediate family or person with legal right to certificate for ordering death records less than 25 years old. Include in request- full name of decedent, date of death, DOB, parents' names, county or city of death, reason for request, relationship to subject. Include signature of requester and daytime phone number.

Access by: mail, phone, fax, in person, online.

Fee & Payment: Fee is $12.00 for first copy, $4.00 for each additional copy ordered at same time. Add $15.50 to expedite and use of a credit card. Fee payee- Vital Records Prepayment required. Personal checks and major credit cards accepted.

Mail search: Turnaround time- 5 to 10 days. SASE not required.

Phone search: Telephone requests allowed using a credit card; see expedited service.

Fax search: Same criteria as phone searches.

In person search: Also, you can go to the nearest AL County Health Department to place request.

Online search: Online ordering is available from the webpage through a service provider.

Other access: Index to records are available on microfilm for $40.00 per roll. There are 6 rolls of records for 1908 through 1959.

Expedited service: Add $10.00 to expedite with mail return, add $5.50 for use of credit card. Overnight shipping available for additional fee, if credit card used.

Marriage Certificates

Center for Health Statistics, Record Services Division, PO Box 5625, Montgomery, AL 36103-5625 (Courier address- RSA Tower Suite 1150, 201 Monroe St, Montgomery, AL 36104); 334-206-5418, Fax- 334-262-9563; 8AM-5PM.

www.adph.org/vitalrecords/

Certificates can, also, be requested in any AL County Health Department for any vital record event occurring in AL; delivery time is usually 15-30 minutes.

Indexing & Storage: Records available from August 1936 to present. New records available for inquiry in 1 week or more.

Searching: Include in request- names of husband and wife, date of marriage, county or city of license issue. Include a daytime phone number and signature of requester.

Access by: mail, phone, fax, in person, online.

Fee & Payment: Fee is $12.00 for first copy, $4.00 for each additional copy ordered at same time. Add $15.50 to expedite and use of a credit card. Fee payee- State Board of Health Prepayment required. Personal checks and major credit cards accepted.

Mail search: Turnaround time- 5 to 10 days. SASE not required.

Phone search: Telephone requests allowed using a credit card; see expedited service.

Fax search: Same criteria as phone searches.

In person search: Also, you can go to the nearest AL County Health Department to place request.

Online search: Online ordering is available from the webpage through a service provider.

Other access: Microfilm rolls are available for purchase at $40.00 each. There are 11 rolls available for an index to records for 1936 to 1969.

Expedited service: Turnaround time- 1 to 2 days. Add $10.00 to expedite with mail return, add $5.50 for use of credit card. Overnight shipping available for additional fee with credit card.

Divorce Records

Center for Health Statistics, Record Services Division, PO Box 5625, Montgomery, AL 36103-5625 (Courier address- RSA Tower Suite 1150, 201 Monroe St, Montgomery, AL 36104); 334-206-5418, Fax- 334-206-2659; 8AM-5PM.

www.adph.org/vitalrecords/

Certificates can also be requested in any AL County Health Department for any vital record event occurring in AL, delivery time is usually 15-30 minutes.

Indexing & Storage: Records available from 1950 to present. New records available for inquiry in 1 week or more.

Searching: Include in request- names of husband and wife, date of divorce, county or city of divorce. Include a daytime phone number and signature of the requester.

Access by: mail, phone, fax, in person, online.

Fee & Payment: Fee is $12.00 for first copy, $4.00 for each additional copy ordered at same time. Add $15.50 to expedite and use of a credit card. Fee payee- State Board of Health Prepayment required. Personal checks and major credit cards accepted.

Mail search: Turnaround time- 5 to 10 days. SASE not required.

Phone search: Telephone requests allowed using a credit card; see expedited service.

Fax search: Same criteria as phone searches.

In person search: Also, you can go to the nearest AL County Health Department to place request.

Online search: Online ordering is available from the webpage through a service provider.

Other access: There is one microfilm roll of index for records for 1950-59 available for $40.00.

Expedited service: Turnaround time- 1 to 2 days. Add $10.00 to expedite with mail return, add $5.50 for use of credit card. Overnight shipping available for additional fee, if credit card used.

Workers' Compensation Records

Access to Records is Restricted.

Department of Industrial Relations, C/O Central Cashier, 649 Monroe Street,, Montgomery, AL 36131; 334-353-0990, Fax- 334-242-2304; 8AM-5PM.

http://dir.alabama.gov/wc/

This agency will only release records via the legal department. There must be a subpoena. Employers may not request records when a conditional offer of employment is made. Subject may not give consent to release records.

Driver Records

Department of Public Safety, Driver Records-License Division, PO Box 1471, Montgomery, AL 36102-1471 (Courier address- 301 S Ripley St, Montgomery, 36104); 334-242-4400; 8AM-5PM.

http://dps.alabama.gov/DriverLicense/

Ticket information must be secured at the local level.

Indexing & Storage: Records available for convictions in last three years for moving violations, and accidents. New records available for inquiry immediately.

Searching: Include in request- full name, DOB and license number to obtain a record. Use Form MV-DPPA1 if you are a permissible user. The form is available from the web page. This data not released- driver's address and personal information, also certain juvenile records.

Access by: mail, in person, online.

Fee & Payment: The fee is $5.75 per record, online is higher. Fee payee- Alabama DPS, Drivers License Division. Prepayment required. Personal checks not accepted.

Mail search: Turnaround time- 3 to 5 days. Providing a self-addressed return envelope usually means quicker service.

In person search: Locations offering driving records and crash reports include Birmingham,

Dothan, Foley, Huntsville, Jacksonville, Mobile, Montgomery, Opelika, Sheffield, and Tuscaloosa.

Online search: Alabama.gov is designated the state's agent for online access of state driving records. A Subscriber Registration Agreement must be submitted. Both Alabama.gov and the Alabama DPS must approve all subscribers. There is a $75.00 annual administrative fee for new accounts and the search fee is $7.00 per record. The driver license number is needed to search. The system, open 24 hours daily, is Internet-based. Alabama.gov (Alabama Interactive) can be reached at 2 N. Jackson St, #301, Montgomery AL, 36104, (866) 353-3468.

Vehicle Ownership & Registration

Motor Vehicle Division, Alabama Dept. of Revenue, PO Box 327610, Montgomery, AL 36132-7610 (Courier address- 50 N Ripley St, 1202 Gordon Persons Bldg, Montgomery, AL); 334-242-9006, Fax- 334-353-8038; 8AM-5PM.

www.revenue.alabama.gov/motorvehicle/index.html

Email questions to titles@revenue.alabama.gov

Indexing & Storage: Records available for 24 years for title records and 10 years for registration records. New records available for inquiry in 4-6 weeks.

Searching: The restrictions specified under the DPPA (Driver's Privacy Protection Act) apply. Access is restricted to permissible users who must use Form MV-DPPA1 (found on web). Non-permissible users must have notarized release of subject. Include in request- name, specific year to search, address of the title or registration holder. VIN is helpful. Request form can be downloaded from the web. This data not released- bulk information or lists for commercial purposes.

Access by: mail, online.

Fee & Payment: Fees are $3.00 per record per year for registration records and $15.00 per year for title searches (includes lien data). Fee payee- Alabama Department of Revenue. Prepayment required. Only certified funds are accepted. No personal checks or credit cards accepted.

Mail search: Turnaround time- 1 to 2 weeks. SASE not required.

Online search: A Vehicle Information Check is at https://www.alabamainteractive.org/ador_vic/. This provides limited vehicle information, but includes lienholder data. Cost is $2.00 per record. Use of credit card is required unless requester is a subscriber to Alabama Interactive. Search using either the Title Number or VIN.

Accident Reports

Alabama Department of Public Safety, Accident Records, PO Box 1471, Montgomery, AL 36102-1471; 334-242-4241; 8AM-5PM.

Indexing & Storage: Records available from 1993.

Searching: Include in request- date of accident, location of accident, county. Also, submit names of drivers. By phone, they will search to see if a report exists, but will not give any further information. Use of request form suggested, find at dps.alabama.gov/DriverLicense/forms/DLCrashReportRequest.pdf. This data not released- SSN.

Access by: mail, in person.

Fee & Payment: The fee is $15.00 and prepayment is required. Fee payee- Alabama DPS, Accident Reports. Prepayment Certified funds accepted. Credit cards accepted.

Mail search: Turnaround time- within 2 weeks. A SASE is requested.

In person search: Locations offering driving records and crash reports include Birmingham, Dothan, Foley, Huntsville, Jacksonville, Mobile, Montgomery, Opelika, Sheffield, and Tuscaloosa. Turnaround time is while you wait.

Vessel Ownership & Registration

Dept of Conservation & Natural Resources, Marine Police Div. Boat Reg. Records, PO Box 301451, Montgomery, AL 36130 (Courier address- 64 N Union St, Montgomery, AL 36104); 334-242-3673, Fax- 334-242-3647; 8AM-5PM.

www.outdooralabama.com/boating/

Records are not freely open to the public, must give acceptable reason for record request.

Indexing & Storage: Records available from 1985 to the present. Records are indexed on computer. All mechanically propelled, sail or rental boats must be registered. New records available for inquiry in 2 months.

Searching: Vessels that have been commercially documented by the Coast Guard are not required to register with Alabama. Liens are not recorded here, but at the central state locations for UCC filings. Include in request- one of the following is required; owner's name, hull id #, current decal #, or registration #. For purged records, the registration # is required to search.

Access by: mail, phone, fax, in person.

Fee & Payment: There is no search fee, except for bulk searches (see below) or lengthy lists ($1.00 per record). Fee payee- Department of Conservation. Prepayment required. Personal checks accepted, credit cards are not.

Mail search: Turnaround time- 1 to 2 days. SASE not required.

Phone search: Records are available by phone.;

Fax search: Turnaround time is within 1 day.

In person search: Immediate records available, if list not lengthy. Request must be in writing.

Other access: This agency accepts e-mail requests for records susan.churchwell@dcnr.alabama.gov. This agency will sell all or parts of its database. Fees start at $100.00 for the first 2,500 records.

Legislation Records

Alabama Legislature, State House, 11 S Union St, Montgomery, AL 36130-4600; 334-242-7800 (Senate), 334-242-7600 (House), Fax- 334-242-8819; 8:30AM-4:30PM.

www.legislature.state.al.us

Use Room 716 for the Senate, Room 512 for the House. Fax number above is for Senate only.

Online search: There is a free service on the Internet for bill text, status, history, voting, audio of Senate, and Code of Alabama. Go to http://alisdb.legislature.state.al.us/acas/alisonstart.asp.

Voter Registration

Secretary of State-Elections Division, PO Box 5616, State Capitol E-208, Montgomery, AL 36103 (Courier address- 600 Dexter Avenue, Room E-210, Montgomery Alabama 36130); 334-242-7210, Fax- 334-242-2444; 8AM-5PM.

www.sos.alabama.gov/Elections/Default.aspx

There are no restrictions.

Indexing & Storage: New records available for inquiry immediately.

Searching: The website provides searches to Contributions & Disbursements and PAC information. This data not released- the SSN.

Access by:;

Fee & Payment: Since records are only released in bulk media format, prices are dependent upon number of names.

Other access: Bulk requests can be ordered from this office for data from all 67 counties. Call 334-242-7222 for fees and breakdowns of customized requests.

GED Certificates

State Dept of Education, GED Testing Office, 401 Adams Ave #280, Montgomery, AL 36104; 334-353-4886, Fax- 334-353-5191; 8AM-5PM.

www.acs.cc.al.us/ged/ged.aspx

Release of your GED information is prohibited without written authorization.

Searching: Requests should be writing. A signed release is necessary, even for a verification. Include in request- a signed release, name, year of test, date of birth, SSN, and city of testing. The release is required, regardless if the request is a yes/no verification or a copy of a transcript.

Access by: mail, in person.

Fee & Payment: There is a $10.00 fee for any information, including verification, copy of grades, transcript or diploma. Fee payee- GED Testing. Only cashier's checks and money orders accepted.

Mail search: Turnaround time- 1-2 days. SASE not required. Results are faxed back.

In person search: Turnaround time is a few minutes.

Hunting & Fishing License Information

Access to Records is Restricted.

Department of Conservation & Natural Resources, License Section, 64 N Union Street, Room 457, Montgomery, AL 36130-1456; 334-353-5239, Fax- 334-242-0771; 8AM-5PM.

www.outdooralabama.com/

They have a central computerized database, but record access is not available for investigation purposes or marketing purposes. Names can be sold, but no addresses or personal identifiers are reported.

Alabama State Licensing Agencies

For details about the agency responsible for licensing/certifying/registering an item below or in the Agency Quick Finder section, match an item's number with the number of the agency in the *Licensing Agency Information* section.

Alabama Licenses Searchable Online

Abortion/Reproductive Health Ctr #31 .... www.adph.org/providers/
Accountant #25 .... www.asbpa.alabama.gov/register/register.asp
Ambulatory Surgery Ctr #31 .... www.adph.org/providers/
Anesthesiologist Assistant #19 .... www.albme.org/Default.aspx?Page=LicenseeSearch
Architect #8 .... www.boa.state.al.us/rostersearch/rostersearch.asp
Assisted Living Facility/Unit #31 .... www.adph.org/providers/
Audiologist #28 .... www.abespa.org/verify.htm
Bank #5 .... www.bank.state.al.us/bank_search.aspx
Birthing Center #31 .... www.adph.org/providers/
Cerebral Palsy Center #31 .... www.adph.org/providers/
Certified Lead Firm #13 .... www.adph.org/lead/Default.asp?id=1602
Check Casher #5 .... www.bank.state.al.us/Search_All_Licences2.asp
Chiropractor #10 .... https://www.alabamainteractive.org/asbce/VerificationEntryPoint.do
Clinical Nurse Specialist #21 .... www.abn.state.al.us/Apps/Verification/Verification.aspx
Consumer Finance Company #5 .... www.bank.state.al.us/Search_All_Licences2.asp
Contractor, General #7 .... www.genconbd.state.al.us/DATABASE-SQL/roster.aspx
Cosmetologist #11 .... www.aboc.state.al.us/Search1.htm
Counselor, Professional #15 .... www.abec.state.al.us/PDFs/IndexofFinalOrders.pdf
Dietitian/Nutritionist #33 .... www.boed.alabama.gov/license_search/search_form.aspx
Electrical Contractor/Journeyman #14 .... www.aecb.state.al.us/Search/new_search.asp
Engineer/Engineer in Training #27 .... www.bels.alabama.gov/LicenseeSearch/searchmenu.asp
Esthetician/Esthetician Related #11 .... www.aboc.state.al.us/Search1.htm
Forester #26 .... http://asbrf.alabama.gov/rosterofforesters.asp
Gas Fitter #46 .... www.pgfb.state.al.us/Inquiry.aspx
Geologist #37 .... www.algeobd.state.al.us/roster_search.asp
HazMat Service #62 .... www.adem.state.al.us/LandDivision/Reports/reports.htm
Heating/Air Conditioning Contractor #38 .... www.hvacboard.state.al.us/Lic_Search/searchform.asp
Home Builder #53 .... www.hblb.state.al.us/Lic_Search/search.asp
Home Health Agency #31 .... www.adph.org/providers/
Home Medical Equip. Svcs. Provider #59 .... www.homemed.state.al.us/search.htm
Hospice #31 .... www.adph.org/providers/
Hospital #31 .... www.adph.org/providers/
Insurance Adjuster #39 .... www.aldoi.gov/SearchFor.aspx
Insurance Agent/Broker/Producer #39 .... www.aldoi.gov/SearchFor.aspx
Insurance Corp./Co./Partnership #39 .... www.aldoi.org/CompanySearch/
Interior Designer #54 .... www.idboard.alabama.gov/search/start.aspx
Interpreter #58 .... www.albit.state.al.us/INTERPRETER_ROSTERS.htm
Landscape Architect #18 .... www.abela.state.al.us/architects.html
Lender/Loan Source #5 .... www.bank.state.al.us/Search_All_Licences2.asp
LPG-Liquef'd Petrol'm Gas Broker #40 .... www.lpgb.state.al.us/Search.htm
Manicurist Salon/Sch'l/student/instruct'r #11 .... www.aboc.state.al.us/Search1.htm
Manicurist/Manicurist Appren./Exam #11 .... www.aboc.state.al.us/Search1.htm
Marriage/Family Therapist #9 .... www.mft.state.al.us/Search/search.asp
Massage Therapist #56 .... www.almtbd.state.al.us/roster_search.asp
Medical Doctor #19 .... www.albme.org/Default.aspx?Page=LicenseeSearch
Medical Gas Piper #46 .... www.pgfb.state.al.us/Inquiry.aspx
Mental Health Center #31 .... www.adph.org/providers/
Midwife Nurse #21 .... www.abn.state.al.us/Apps/Verification/Verification.aspx
Mortgage Broker #5 .... www.bank.state.al.us/Search_All_Licences2.asp
Notary Public #42 .... www.sos.state.al.us/vb/inquiry/inquiry.aspx?area=Notaries%20Public
Nurse Anesthetist #21 .... www.abn.state.al.us/Apps/Verification/Verification.aspx
Nurse-LPN/RN #21 .... www.abn.state.al.us/Apps/Verification/Verification.aspx
Nursing Disciplinary Action #21 .... www.abn.state.al.us/Apps/Verification/Verification.aspx
Nursing Home #31 .... www.adph.org/providers/
Nursing Home Administrator #22 .... www.alboenha.state.al.us/logon.html
Nutritionist #33 .... www.boed.alabama.gov/license_search/search_form.aspx
Occupational Therapist/Thera. Asst. #57 .... www.asbot.state.al.us/search.htm

Optometrist #20 .... http://optometry.alabama.gov/Search.aspx
Osteopathic Physician #19 .... www.albme.org/Default.aspx?Page=LicenseeSearch
Pawn Shop #5 .... www.bank.state.al.us/Search_All_Licences2.asp
Pharmacist #23 .... https://www.cebroker.com/public/pb_index.asp?hIndexType=alabama
Pharmacy Intern #23 .... https://www.cebroker.com/public/pb_index.asp?hIndexType=alabama
Physical Therapist/Therapist Asst #24 .... www.pt.state.al.us/License/searchform.asp
Physician #19 .... www.albme.org/Default.aspx?Page=LicenseeSearch
Physician Assistant #19 .... www.albme.org/Default.aspx?Page=LicenseeSearch
Physiological Lab, Clinical #31 .... www.adph.org/providers/
Plumber #46 .... www.pgfb.state.al.us/Inquiry.aspx
Podiatrist #4 .... www.podiatryboard.alabama.gov/current_licensees.html
Pre-Need Sales Agent #39 .... www.aldoi.gov/SearchFor.aspx
Public Account.-CPA-Non Licensee #25 .... www.asbpa.alabama.gov/register/register.asp
Real Estate Agent/Seller/Broker #2 .... www.arello.com/
Real Estate Appraiser #43 .... http://reab.state.al.us/appraisers/searchform.asp
Registered Nurse Practitioner #21 .... www.abn.state.al.us/Apps/Verification/Verification.aspx
Rehabilitation Center #31 .... www.adph.org/providers/
Renal Disease Terminal Treatment Ctr #31. www.adph.org/providers/
Rural Primary Care Hospital #31 .... www.adph.org/providers/
School Superintendent #49 .... www.alsde.edu/html/super_listing.asp?menu=none&footer=general
Senior Volunteer, Medical #19 .... www.albme.org/Default.aspx?Page=LicenseeSearch
Shampoo Assistant #11 .... www.aboc.state.al.us/Search1.htm
Sleep Disorder Center #31 .... www.adph.org/providers/
Social Worker #6 .... www.abswe.state.al.us/Lic_Search/search.asp
Social Worker, Private Practice #6 .... www.abswe.state.al.us/Lic_Search/searchpip.asp
Soil Classifier #1 .... www.swcc.state.al.us/Soil%20Roster&%20Forms.htm
Special Purpose License, Medical #19 .... www.albme.org/Default.aspx?Page=LicenseeSearch
Speech Pathologist/Audiologist #28 .... www.abespa.org/verify.htm
Sports Agent #42 .... www.sos.state.al.us/Downloads/dl1.aspx
Surgeon #19 .... www.albme.org/Default.aspx?Page=LicenseeSearch
Surgeon's Assistant #19 .... www.albme.org/Default.aspx?Page=LicenseeSearch
Surplus Line Broker #39 .... www.aldoi.gov/SearchFor.aspx
Surveyor, Land #27 .... www.bels.alabama.gov/LicenseeSearch/searchmenu.asp
Therapist, Marriage and Family #9 .... www.mft.state.al.us/Search/search.asp
Transliterator #58 .... www.albit.state.al.us/INTERPRETER_ROSTERS.htm
X-ray (Portable) Supplier #31 .... www.adph.org/providers/

Alabama Licensing Quick Finder

Abortion/Reproductive Health Ctr #31 .. 334-206-5175
Accountant #25 334-242-5700
Agric. Products Mfg/Dealer/Ship'r #30 .. 334-240-7122
Aircraft/Pilot-related Personnel #51 205-731-1557
Air-Pollution Discharger #63 334-271-7861
Ambulatory Surgery Ctr #31 334-206-5175
Anesthesiologist Assistant #19 334-242-4116
Animal Euthanasia Facility #29 256-353-3544
Apiary #30 334-242-2656
Architect #8 334-242-4179
Assisted Living Facility/Unit #31 334-206-5175
Attorney #3 334-269-1515
Audiologist #28 334-269-1434
Bank #5 334-242-3452
Beauty Shop/Booth Rental #11 334-242-1918
Beauty Shop/Salon #11 334-242-1918
Bee, Queen & Pack Shipper #30 334-240-7239
Birthing Center #31 334-206-5175
Boxer/Wrest'r (now not regulated) #52. 334-242-1380
Brand (Livestock) #30 334-240-7263
Broker/Dealer Agent #48 334-242-2984
Cerebral Palsy Center #31 334-206-5175
Certified Euthanasia Technician #29 256-353-3544
Certified Lead Firm #13 334-206-5373
Charitable Filing #48 334-242-2984
Check Casher #5 334-242-3452
Check Seller #48 334-242-2984
Chiropractor #10 205-755-8000
Clinical Nurse Specialist #21 334-242-0767
Consumer Finance Company #5 334-242-3452
Contractor, General #7 334-272-5030
Cosmetic Studio #11 334-242-1918
Cosmetologist #11 334-242-1918
Cosmetologist/Esthetic'n/Manic'r't #11 . 334-242-1918
Cosm't'l'gist/Esth'tic'n/Manic'r''t Mgr#11 334-242-1918
Cosmetology Instructor #11 334-242-1918
Cosmetology Mgr Pending Exam #11 ... 334-242-1918
Cosmetology School/Instruc/Exam #11 334-242-1918
Cosmetology Student/Apprentice #11 .. 334-242-1918
Cosmetology, Restricted Managing#11 334-242-1918
Counselor, Professional #15 205-458-8716
Dental Hygienist #12 205-985-7267
Dentist #12 205-985-7267
Dietitian/Nutritionist #33 334-242-4505
Education Administrator #49 334-242-9977
Electrical Contractor #14 334-269-9990
Electrician, Journeyman #14 334-269-9990
Electrologist #11 334-242-1918
Embalmer #17 334-242-4049
Emergency Medical Technician #50 334-206-5383
Emission Tester #63 334-271-7861
Engineer/Engineer in Training #27 334-242-5568
Esthetician School/Salon #11 334-242-1918
Esthetician/Esthetician Apprentice #11. 334-242-1918
Esthetic'n Student/Instruct/Sch'l #11 334-242-1918
Fire Boss (mining) #34 205-944-1075
Firefighter #36 205-391-3743
Forester #26 334-240-9301
Funeral Director #17 334-242-4049
Gas Fitter #46 205-945-4857
Geologist #37 .... 334-269-9990 x10
Gins/Warehouses (Agric'l) #30 .. 800-642-7761 x7223
Ginseng Dealer #30 334-240-7239
Harbor Pilot #64 251-441-7250
HazMat Service #62 334-271-7735
Hearing Instrument Dealer #35 334-242-1925
Heating/Air Conditioning Contract'r #38 334-242-5550
Hoist Cart (mine) #34 205-944-1075
Home Builder #53 334-242-2230
Home Health Agency #31 334-206-5175
Home Inspector #42 334-242-7205
Home Medic'l Equip. Svc. Provider #59 334-215-3474
Hospice #31 334-206-5175
Hospital #31 334-206-5175
Incinerator #63 334-271-7861
Industrial Revenue Bond #48 334-242-2984
Insurance Adjuster #39 334-241-4126
Insurance Agent/Broker/Producer #39. 334-241-4126
Insurance Corp./Co./Partnership #39 . 334-241-4126
Interior Designer #54 205-879-4232
Interpreter #58 334-277-8881
Investment Advisor #48 334-242-2984
Investment Advisor Rep. #48 334-242-2984
Landfill #62 334-271-7988
Landscape Architect #18 334-262-1351
Landscape Designer #55 334-240-7241
Landscape Horticulturalist/Planter #55 334-240-7241
Law Enforcement Personnel #44 334-242-4045
Lead Abatement Contractor #13 334-206-5373
Lead Abatement Professional #13 334-206-5373
Legal/Dental Svc Representative #39.. 334-241-4126
Lender/Loan Source #5 334-242-3452
Livestock Dealer/Weigher #30 334-240-7263
Livestock Market Operator #30 334-240-7263
LPG-Liquef'd Petrol'm Gas Broker #40 334-242-5649
Manicurist Salon/Sch'l/student/inst #11 334-242-1918

Manicurist/Manicur't Appren./Exam #11 334-242-1918
Marriage/Family Therapist #9 334-215-7233
Massage Therapist #56 334-269-9990
Medical Doctor #19 334-242-4116
Medical Gas Piper #46 205-945-4857
Mental Health Center #31 334-206-5175
Midwife Nurse #21 334-242-0767
Mine Worker/Electrician/Foreman #34 205-944-1075
Mine Land Reclamation #32 205-945-8671
Mine Safety and Inspection #32 205-254-1275
Mobile Home Manufacturer #41 334-242-4036
Mobile Home Set-up/Instal./Seller #41 334-242-4036
Mortgage Broker #5 334-242-3452
Motor Club Representative #39 334-241-4126
Notary Public #42 334-242-7205
Nurse Anesthetist #21 334-242-0767
Nurse-LPN/RN #21 334-242-0767
Nursing Disciplinary Action #21 334-242-0767
Nursing Home #31 334-206-5175
Nursing Home Administrator #22 334-271-6214
Nutritionist #33 334-242-4505
Occupational Therapist/Occ Asst. #57 334-353-4466
Optometrist #20 205-481-9993
Orthotist #60 334-420-1111
Osteopathic Physician #19 334-242-4116
Paramedic #50 334-206-5383
Pawn Shop #5 334-242-3452
Pest Control/Applicator/Dealer #30 334-240-7239
Petroleum Product Seller #30 334-240-7127
Pharmacist #23 205-967-0130
Pharmacy Intern #23 205-967-0130
Physical Therapist/Therapist Asst #24 334-242-4064
Physician #19 334-242-4116
Physician Assistant #19 334-242-4116
Physiological Lab, Clinical #31 334-206-5175
Pilot, Harbor #64 251-441-7250
Pilot/Bar Pilot #45 251-432-2639
Plant & Quarantine Inspector #30 334-240-7239
Plant Nursery #55 334-240-7241
Plumber #46 205-945-4857
Podiatrist #4 334-269-9990
Polygraph Examiner #47 334-353-1881
Pre-Need Sales Agent #39 334-241-4126
Prosthetist #60 334-420-1111
Psychological Technician #16 334-242-4127
Psychologist #16 334-242-4127
Public Account.-CPA-Non Licensee #25 334-242-5700
Real Estate Agent/Seller #2 334-242-5544
Real Estate Appraiser #43 334-242-8747
Real Estate Broker #2 334-242-5544
Registered Nurse Practitioner #21 334-242-0767
Rehabilitation Center #31 334-206-5175
Renal Disease Treatment Ctr #31 334-206-5175
Rural Primary Care Hospital #31 334-206-5175
School Bus Driver #49 334-242-9730
School Counselor /Superintendent #49 334-242-9977
Scrap Tire Transporter #62 334-271-7988
Securities Broker/Dealer #48 334-242-2984
Securities Salesperson #48 334-242-2984
Senior Volunteer, Medical #19 334-242-4116
Shampoo Assistant #11 334-242-1918
Sleep Disorder Center #31 334-206-5175
Social Worker #6 334-242-5860
Soil Classifier #1 334-242-2620
Special Purpose License, Medical #19 334-242-4116
Speech Pathologist/Audiologist #28 334-269-1434
Sports Agent #42 334-242-7591
Subcontractor #7 334-272-5030
Surface Mining (non-fuel) #32 334-242-8265
Surgeon/Surgeon's Assistant #19 334-242-4116
Surplus Line Broker #39 334-241-4126
Surveyor, Land #27 334-242-5568
Teacher #49 334-242-9977
Teacher, Elementary School #49 334-242-9977
Therapist, Marriage and Family #9 334-215-7233
Timeshare Real Estate Seller #43 334-242-8747
Timeshare Seller #2 334-242-5544
Transliterator #58 334-277-8881
Tree Surgeon #55 334-240-7241
U-Pick Location #30 334-240-7100
Veterinarian #29 256-353-3544
Veterinary Premise Permit #29 256-353-3544
Veterinary Technician #29 256-353-3544
Wastewater Treatment Operator #61 334-271-7796
Water Treatment Plant Operator #61 334-271-7796
Weights & Measures #30 334-240-7133
X-ray (Portable) Supplier #31 334-206-5175

Alabama Licensing Agency Information

#1 Soil and Water Conservation Committee, PO Box 304800 (100 N Union St, #334), Montgomery, AL 36130-4800; 334-242-2620, Fax- 334-242-0551. www.swcc.state.al.us

#2 Real Estate Commission, 1201 Carmichael Way, Montgomery, AL 36106; 334-242-5544, Fax- 334-270-9118. 7:30AM-4:30PM. www.arec.alabama.gov/ search at www.arello.com

#3 State Bar Association, 415 Dexter Ave, Montgomery, AL 36104; 334-269-1515, Fax- 334-261-6310. www.alabar.org

#4 Board of Podiatry, 610 S McDonough St, Montgomery, AL 36104; 334-269-9990, Fax- 334-263-6115. 8:30AM-4:30AM. www.podiatryboard.alabama.gov/board_members.html Search data at- www.podiatryboard.alabama.gov/current_licensees.html

#5 State Banking Department, Licensing and Registration, PO Box 4600 (401 Adams St, #680), Montgomery, AL 36103; 334-242-3452, Fax- 334-242-3500. www.bank.state.al.us Search data at- www.bank.state.al.us/Search_All_Licences2.asp Bureau of Loans fax number is 334-353-5961.

#6 Board of Social Work Examiners, 100 N Union St #736, Montgomery, AL 36130; 888-879-3672, 334-242-5860, Fax- 334-242-0280. www.abswe.state.al.us Search data at- www.abswe.state.al.us/Lic_Search/searchpip.asp

#7 License Board for General Contractors, 2525 Fairlane Dr, Montgomery, AL 36116; 334-272-5030, F-334-395-5336. www.genconbd.state.al.us Search data at- www.genconbd.state.al.us/DATABASE-SQL/roster.aspx

#8 Board for Registration of Architects, 770 Washington Ave, #150, Montgomery, AL 36130-4450; 334-242-4179, Fax- 334-242-4531. 7:30AM-4:30PM. www.boa.state.al.us Search data at- www.boa.state.al.us/rostersearch/rostersearch.asp

#9 Board of Examiners in Marriage & Family Therapy, PO Box 240066 (7550 Halcyon Summit Dr #125), Montgomery, AL 36124-0066; 334-215-7233, Fax- 334-215-7231. 8:30AM-4:30PM. www.mft.state.al.us

#10 Board of Chiropractic Examiners, 102 Chilton Pl, Clanton, AL 35045; 205-755-8000, Fax- 205-755-0081. 8AM-4PM. http://chiro.state.al.us Search data at- https://www.alabamainteractive.org/asbce/VerificationEntryPoint.do;jsessionid=ap_JoQrUmjsg

#11 Board of Cosmetology, PO Box 301750 (RSA Union Bldg, 100 N Union St #320), Montgomery, AL 36130; 334-242-1918, Fax- 334-242-1926. www.aboc.state.al.us Search data at- www.aboc.state.al.us/Search1.htm

#12 Board of Dental Examiners, 5346 Stadium Trace Pkwy #112, Hoover, AL 35244; 205-985-7267, Fax- 205-985-0674. 8AM-4:30PM. www.dentalboard.org Will not verify over the phone; they recommend sending a fax.

#13 Department of Public Health, Indoor Air Quality/Lead Branch, Div. of Comm. Environmental Protection - Lead Contractors, 201 Monroe St, The RSA Tower, Suite 1250, Montgomery, AL 36130-3017; 800-819-7644, 334-206-5373, Fax- 334-206-5788. www.adph.org/lead/

#14 Board of Electrical Contractors, 610 S McDonough St, Montgomery, AL 36104; 334-269-9990, Fax- 334-263-6115. 8:30AM-4:30PM. www.aecb.state.al.us Search data at- www.aecb.state.al.us/Search/new_search.asp

#15 Board of Examiners in Counseling, 950 22nd St N, #765, Birmingham, AL 35203; 205-458-8716, Fax- 205-458-8718. www.abec.state.al.us

#16 Board of Examiners in Psychology, 660 Adams Ave, #360, Montgomery, AL 36104; 334-242-4127. 8AM-1PM. www.psychology.state.al.us

#17 Board of Funeral Service, Box 309522 (50 N Ripley St, Rm 3201), Montgomery, AL 36130; 334-242-4049, Fax- 334-353-7988. www.alabamaadministrativecode.state.al.us/UpdatedMonthly/VolXXIIN8/p313.htm

#18 Board of Landscape Architects, 908 S Hull St, Montgomery, AL 36104; 334-262-1351, Fax- 334-262-1351. M,W,F. www.abela.state.al.us Search data at- www.abela.state.al.us/architects.html

#19 Board of Medical Examiners, PO Box 946 (848 Washington Ave), Montgomery, AL 36101; 334-242-4116, Fax- 334-242-4155. 8:15AM-5:15PM. www.albme.org Search data at- www.albme.org/Default.aspx?Page=LicenseeSearch Will sell Excel spreadsheet files at $.05 per record or a $50.00 minimum charge.

#20 Board of Optometry, 1431 2nd Ave, N, Bessemer, AL 35020; 205-481-9993, Fax- 205-481-9959. http://optometry.alabama.gov/

#21 Board of Nursing, PO Box 303900 (770 Washington Ave, RSA Plaza, #250), Montgomery, AL 36130-3900; 334-242-4060, Fax- 334-242-4360. www.abn.state.al.us Search data at- www.abn.state.al.us/Apps/Verification/Verification.aspx Individual verifications $30.00 each. A group online license verification is available by subscription. Also, the office sells mailing labels.

#22 Board of Nursing Home Administrators, 4156 Carmichael Rd, Montgomery, AL 36106; 334-271-6214, Fax- 334-244-6509. www.alboenha.state.al.us/ Search data at- www.alboenha.state.al.us/logon.html

#23 Board of Pharmacy, 10 Inverness Center #110, Birmingham, AL 35242; 205-981-2280, Fax- 205-981-2330. 8AM-4PM. www.albop.com

#24 Board of Physical Therapy, 100 N Union St, #724, Montgomery, AL 36130-5040; 888-726-9743; 334-242-4064, Fax- 334-240-3288. www.pt.state.al.us Search data atwww.pt.state.al.us/License/searchform.asp Will sell directories of licensees for $50.00 each.

#25 Board of Public Accountancy, PO Box 300375 (770 Washington Ave, #226), Montgomery, AL 36130-0375; 334-242-5700, Fax- 334-240-2711. www.asbpa.alabama.gov Search data at- www.asbpa.alabama.gov/register/register.asp

#26 Board of Registration for Foresters, 513 Madison Ave, Montgomery, AL 36130; 334-240-9301, Fax- 334-353-3641. http://asbrf.alabama.gov Search data at- http://asbrf.alabama.gov/rosterofforesters.asp

#27 Board of Licensure for Professional Engineers & Land Surveyors, PO Box 304451 (100 N Union St/RSA Union Bldg, #382), Montgomery, AL 36130-4451; 334-242-5568, Fax- 334-242-5105. 8AM-4:45PM. www.bels.alabama.gov Search data at- www.bels.alabama.gov/LicenseeSearch/searchmenu.asp

#28 Board of Examiners for Speech-Language Pathology & Audiology, PO Box 304760 (400 S Union St #397), Montgomery, AL 36130-4760; 334-269-1434, Fax- 334-834-9618. 8AM-4:30PM. www.abespa.org Search data at- www.abespa.org/verify.htm

#29 Board of Veterinary Medical Examiners, PO Box 1968 (2128 6th Avenue SE, Bldg 5 #501), Decatur, AL 35602-1968; 256-353-3544, Fax- 256-350-5629. 9AM-N, 1PM-5PM. http://asbvme.us For hardcopy or disk $25.00.

#30 Department of Agriculture & Industries, Executive Division - Licensing, 1445 Federal Dr, Montgomery, AL 36107; 334-240-7282, 800-642-7761, Fax- 334-240-7194. www.agi.state.al.us Fax number for the Pesticide Management Section is 334-240-7168. Weights & Measures fax is 334-240-7175. Admin Dept. fax is 334-240-7194.

#31 Department of Public Health, Provider Services Division - Licensing, 201 Monroe St, Montgomery, AL 36104; 334-206-5175, Fax- 334-206-5219. 8AM-5PM. www.adph.org Search data at- www.adph.org/providers/

#32 Department of Industrial Relations, Mining & Reclamation, 649 Monroe St, Montgomery, AL 36131-5200; 334-242-8265, Fax- 334-242-8403. http://dir.alabama.gov/mr/

#33 Dietetic/Nutrition Examiners Board, 400 S Union St #445, Montgomery, AL 36104-0500; 334-242-4505, Fax- 334-834-6398. 8:30AM-4:30PM. www.boed.alabama.gov Search data at- www.boed.alabama.gov/license_search/search_form.aspx Will sell mail list for $50.00. Verification by phone, mail no charge.

#34 Board of Mine Safety, Division of Safety and Inspection, 11 W Oxmoor Rd #201, Birmingham, AL 35209; 205-944-1075, Fax- 205-944-1078. 7:30AM-4PM.

#35 Hearing Aid Dealers, Executive Secretary, 400 S Union St, #445, Montgomery, AL 36104; 334-242-1925, Fax- 334-834-6398. 8:30AM-4:30PM. Mail lists are available for $25.00. Verifications made by phone and mail.

#36 Fire College & Personnel Standards Commission, 2501 Phoenix Dr, Tuscaloosa, AL 35405-8546; 205-391-3744, Fax- 205-391-3747. www.alabamafirecollege.org

#37 Board of Licensure of Professional Geologists, 610 S McDonough St, Montgomery, AL 36104; 866-873-4664; 334-269-9990, Fax- 334-263-6115. 8:30AM-4:30PM. www.algeobd.alabama.gov Search data at- www.algeobd.state.al.us/roster_search.asp

#38 Heating & Air Conditioning Contractors Board, 100 N Union St, #630, Montgomery, AL 36130-5025; 866-855-1912, 334-242-5550, Fax- 334-353-7050. www.hvacboard.state.al.us Search data at- www.hvacboard.state.al.us/Lic_Search/searchform.asp

#39 Department of Insurance, Agent Licensing Division, P O Box 303351 (201 Monroe St #1700), Montgomery, AL 36130; 334-269-3550, Fax- 334-241-4192. 8AM-5PM. www.aldoi.gov Search data at- www.aldoi.gov/SearchFor.aspx

#40 Liquefied Petroleum Gas Board, PO Box 1742 (818 S Perry St), Montgomery, AL 36102-1742; 334-242-5649, Fax- 334-240-3255. www.lpgb.state.al.us Search data at- www.lpgb.state.al.us/Search.htm

#41 Manufactured Housing Commission, 350 S Decatur St, Montgomery, AL 36104; 334-242-4036, Fax- 334-240-3178. www.amhc.state.al.us

#42 Registrations for Sports Agents and Notaries, Office of the Secretary of State, PO Box 5616, Montgomery, AL 36103-5616; 334-242-7205, Fax- 334-353-8993. www.sos.state.al.us/notary/index.htm

#43 Office of the Secretary of State, Real Estate Appraisers Licensing, PO Box 304355 (100 North Union St #370), Montgomery, AL 36104; 334-242-8747, Fax- 334-242-8749. http://reab.state.al.us

#44 Peace Officers Standards & Training Commission, PO Box 300075 (100 Union St, RSA Union Bldg, #600), Montgomery, AL 36130-0075; 334-242-4045, Fax- 334-242-4633. www.apostc.state.al.us

#45 Pilotage Commission, PO Box 273, Mobile, AL 36601; 251-432-2639, Fax- 251-432-9964.

#46 Plumbers & Gas Fitters Examining Board, 11 W Oxmoor, #104, Birmingham, AL 35209; 205-945-4857, Fax- 205-945-9915. http://pgfb.state.al.us/ Search data at- www.pgfb.state.al.us/Inquiry.aspx

#47 Polygraph Examiners Board, PO Box 1511 (301 S Ripley St), Montgomery, AL 36104; 334-353-1881, Fax- 334-353-2563. 1PM-5PM Wed. www.polygraph.alabama.gov

#48 Securities Commission, 770 Washington Ave, #570, Montgomery, AL 36130-4700; 334-242-2984, Fax- 334-242-0240. 8AM-5PM. www.asc.state.al.us

#49 Department of Education, Teacher Education & Certification, PO Box 302101 (50 N Ripley St), Montgomery, AL 36104; 334-242-9700, Fax- 334-242-0498. www.alsde.edu/html/home.asp

#50 Department of Health, Emergency Medical Services Division, 201 Monroe St #750, Office of EMS & Trauma, RSA Tower, Montgomery, AL 36104; 334-206-5383, Fax- 334-206-5260. www.adph.org/ems/

#51 Department of Transportation, Flight Standards District Office, 1500 Urban Center Dr #250, Vestavia Hills, AL 35242; 205-876-1300, Fax- 205-876-1358.

#53 Home Builders Licensure Board, 445 Herron St, Montgomery, AL 36130-3605; 334-242-2230, Fax- 334-263-1397. www.hblb.state.al.us Search data at- www.hblb.state.al.us/Lic_Search/search.asp Also search www.hblb.state.al.us/Lic_Search/search.asp for individual or business.

#54 Board of Registration for Interior Designers, PO Box 11026 (65 Bagby Dr #3B), Birmingham, AL 35202; 205-879-4232, Fax- 205-879-4232*51. www.idboard.alabama.gov/contact.htm

#55 Department of Agriculture & Industries, Plant Protection & Pesticide Management Division, 1445 Federal Dr, Montgomery, AL 36107; 334-240-7225, Fax- 334-240-7168. www.agi.state.al.us

#56 Board of Massage Therapy, 610 S McDonough St, Montgomery, AL 36104; 334-269-9990, Fax- 334-263-6115. 8:30AM-4:30PM. www.almtbd.state.al.us Search data at- www.almtbd.state.al.us/roster_search.asp

#57 Board of Occupational Therapy, 64 N Union St #734, Montgomery, AL 36130-4510; 334-353-4466, Fax- 334-353-4465. www.asbot.state.al.us Search data at- www.asbot.state.al.us/search.htm

#58 Licensure Board for Interpreters and Transliterators, PO Box 240187, Montgomery, AL 36124-0187; 334-277-8881, Fax- 334-277-0188. www.albit.state.al.us Search data at- www.albit.state.al.us/INTERPRETER_ROSTERS.htm

#59 Board of Home Medical Equipment Services Providers, PO Box 240636 (7550 Halcyon Summit Dr, #125), Montgomery, AL 36124-0636; 334-215-3474, Fax- 334-215-3457. www.homemed.state.al.us/ Search data at- www.homemed.state.al.us/search.htm

#60 Board of Prosthetists and Orthotists, PO Box 1052, Montgomery, AL 36101-; 334-420-1111, Fax- 334-265-1281. www.apob.alabama.gov/

#61 Water Treatment Operator Certification, Department of Environmental Management, PO Box 301463 (1400 Coliseum Blvd), Montgomery, AL 36130-1463; 334-271-7700, Fax- 334-271-7950. www.adem.state.al.us/WaterDivision/WaterDivisionPP.htm

#62 Solid Waste Branch, Department of Environmental Management, PO Box 301463 (1400 Coliseum Blvd), Montgomery, AL 36130-1463; 334-271-7700, Fax- 334-271-7950. Search data at- https://www.alabamainteractive.org/adem_loc/renewals

#63 Air Division, Department of Environmental Management, PO Box 301463 (1400 Coliseum Blvd), Montgomery, AL 36130-1463; 334-271-7861, Fax- 334-279-3044. www.adem.state.al.us/AirDivision/AirDivisionPP.htm

#64 Harbor Pilot Licensing, Alabama State Port Authority - State Docks, PO Box 1588, 250 N Water St, Mobile, AL 36633; 251-441-7250, Fax- 251-441-7255. www.asdd.com

Alabama Federal Courts

The following list indicates the district and division name for each county in the state. If the bankruptcy court location is different from the district court, then the location of the bankruptcy court appears in parentheses.

County/Court Cross Reference

County	District	Division
Autauga	Middle	Montgomery
Baldwin	Southern	Mobile
Barbour	Middle	Montgomery
Bibb	Northern	Birmingham (Tuscaloosa)
Blount	Northern	Birmingham
Bullock	Middle	Montgomery
Butler	Middle	Montgomery
Calhoun	Northern	Birmingham (Anniston)
Chambers	Middle	Opelika (Montgomery)
Cherokee	Northern	Gadsden (Anniston)
Chilton	Middle	Montgomery
Choctaw	Southern	Mobile
Clarke	Southern	Mobile
Clay	Northern	Birmingham (Anniston)
Cleburne	Northern	Birmingham (Anniston)
Coffee	Middle	Dothan (Montgomery)
Colbert	Northern	Florence (Decatur)
Conecuh	Southern	Mobile
Coosa	Middle	Montgomery
Covington	Middle	Montgomery
Crenshaw	Middle	Montgomery
Cullman	Northern	Huntsville (Decatur)
Dale	Middle	Dothan (Montgomery)
Dallas	Southern	Selma (Mobile)
De Kalb	Northern	Gadsden (Anniston)
Elmore	Middle	Montgomery
Escambia	Southern	Mobile
Etowah	Northern	Gadsden (Anniston)
Fayette	Northern	Jasper (Tuscaloosa)
Franklin	Northern	Florence (Decatur)
Geneva	Middle	Dothan (Montgomery)
Greene	Northern	Birmingham (Tuscaloosa)
Hale	Southern	Selma (Mobile)
Henry	Middle	Dothan (Montgomery)
Houston	Middle	Dothan (Montgomery)
Jackson	Northern	Huntsville (Decatur)
Jefferson	Northern	Birmingham
Lamar	Northern	Jasper (Tuscaloosa)
Lauderdale	Northern	Florence (Decatur)
Lawrence	Northern	Huntsville (Decatur)
Lee	Middle	Opelika (Montgomery)
Limestone	Northern	Huntsville (Decatur)
Lowndes	Middle	Montgomery
Macon	Middle	Opelika (Montgomery)
Madison	Northern	Huntsville (Decatur)
Marengo	Southern	Selma (Mobile)
Marion	Northern	Jasper (Tuscaloosa)
Marshall	Northern	Gadsden (Anniston)
Mobile	Southern	Mobile
Monroe	Southern	Mobile
Montgomery	Middle	Montgomery
Morgan	Northern	Huntsville (Decatur)
Perry	Southern	Selma (Mobile)
Pickens	Northern	Birmingham (Tuscaloosa)
Pike	Middle	Montgomery
Randolph	Middle	Opelika (Montgomery)
Russell	Middle	Opelika (Montgomery)
Shelby	Northern	Birmingham
St. Clair	Northern	Gadsden (Anniston)
Sumter	Northern	Birmingham (Tuscaloosa)
Talladega	Northern	Birmingham (Anniston)
Tallapoosa	Middle	Opelika (Montgomery)
Tuscaloosa	Northern	Birmingham (Tuscaloosa)
Walker	Northern	Jasper (Tuscaloosa)
Washington	Southern	Mobile
Wilcox	Southern	Selma (Mobile)
Winston	Northern	Jasper (Tuscaloosa)

Standards for Federal Courts: Fees are standard unless noted in profile. Search fee is $26.00 per item (one party name or case number). Copy fee is $.50 per page. Certification fee is $9.00 per document, double for exemplification, if available. Most courts require prepayment. Mail requests should enclose a SASE unless otherwise noted. Before releasing records, all courts require prepayment, unless noted.

District courts index by defendant and plaintiff and by case number. Bankruptcy courts usually index by debtor and case number. While most courts now have their indexes on computer, many may still maintain index card files as well. Courts will archive closed case files at different times.

There are numerous public access programs available to online subscribers. Search the U.S. Party/Case Index to find party names and case numbers among all courts. Individual case data is provided on PACER. A search of CM/ECF provides copies of cases filed electronically. For details about PACER, the US Party/Case Index, and CM/ECF see the Appendix, go to http://pacer.psc.uscourts.gov or call 800-676-6856.

US District Court
Alabama Middle District

Dothan- Southern Division c/o Montgomery Division, PO Box 711, Montgomery, AL 36101 (In person: 1 Church St, Montgomery, AL 36104), 334-954-3600; Fax- 334-954-3615. Hours- 8AM-5PM. www.almd.uscourts.gov

Counties/Note: Coffee, Dale, Geneva, Henry, Houston. Direct search requests to the Montgomery Division. Dothan Court physically located at 100 W Troy St. in Dothan.

Searches/Indexing: Include name and address in search requests and as many personal identifiers as known. Results do not include SSN or DOB. Will not fax back documents. New cases are in the index within 24 hours after filing date.

Search Access: Mail: Search usually completed within 2 days. Include SASE for return. **In person:** 1 public terminal available; records back to 1998-99. No self-serve copier.

Payment: Pay by money order, cashier's check, business check. No credit cards or personal checks accepted. Payee: US District Court.

E-Services: PACER records go back to 1994. New records online after 1 day. ECF at https://ecf.almd.uscourts.gov. **Opinions Online:** www.almd.uscourts.gov/judges/opinions.cfm.

Montgomery- Northern Division Records Search Dept, PO Box 711, Montgomery, AL 36101-0711 (In person: 1 Church St, Montgomery, AL 36104), 334-954-3600; Fax- 334-954-3615. Hours- 8AM-5PM. www.almd.uscourts.gov

Counties/Note: Autauga, Barbour, Bullock, Butler, Chilton, Coosa, Covington, Crenshaw, Elmore, Lowndes, Montgomery, Pike. There are also two add'l divisions- Dothan-Southern, and Opelika-Eastern. Search these divisions here at Montgomery. Phones and addresses are for Montgomery.

Searches/Indexing: Include name and address in search requests and as many personal identifiers as known. Results do not include SSN or DOB. Will not fax back documents. New cases are in the index within 24 hours after filing date. Computer, microfiche and card indexes maintained. Public allowed to search the microfiche index.

Search Access: Mail: Search usually completed- 48 hours. Include SASE for return. **In person:** 1 public terminal available; records back to 1998-99. No self-serve copier.

Payment: Pay by money order, cashier's check, business check. No credit cards or personal checks accepted. Payee: Clerk, US District Court.

E-Services: PACER records go back to 1994. New records online after 1 day. ECF at https://ecf.almd.uscourts.gov. **Opinions Online:** www.almd.uscourts.gov/judges/opinions.cfm.

Opelika- Eastern Division c/o Montgomery Division, PO Box 711, Montgomery, AL 36101 (In person: 1 Church St, Montgomery, AL 36104), 334-954-3600; Fax- 334-954-3615. 8AM-5PM. www.almd.uscourts.gov

Counties/Note: Chambers, Lee, Macon, Randolph, Russell, Tallapoosa. Direct search requests to the Montgomery Div. Opelika court physically located at 701 Ave A.

Searches/Indexing: Include name and address in search requests and as many personal identifiers as known. Results do not include SSN or DOB. Will not fax back documents. New cases are in the index within 24 hours after filing date.

Search Access: Mail: Search usually completed- within 2 days. SASE not required. **In person:** 1 public terminal available; records back to 1998-99. No self-serve copier.

Payment: Pay by money order, cashier's check, business check. No credit cards or personal checks accepted. Payee: US District Court.

E-Services: PACER records go back to 1994. New records online after 1 day. ECF at https://ecf.almd.uscourts.gov. **Opinions Online:** www.almd.uscourts.gov/judges/opinions.cfm.

US Bankruptcy Court Alabama Middle District

Montgomery Division Court Clerk, 1 Church St, Montgomery, AL 36104, 334-954-3800; Fax- 334-954-3819. Hours- 8:30AM-4PM. www.almb.uscourts.gov

Counties/Note: Autauga, Barbour, Bullock, Butler, Chambers, Chilton, Coffee, Coosa, Covington, Crenshaw, Dale, Elmore, Geneva, Henry, Houston, Lee, Lowndes, Macon, Montgomery, Pike, Randolph, Russell, Tallapoosa. Also has a Eastern Div. courthouse in Opelika and a Southern Div courthouse in Dothan - direct search requests here at Montgomery.

Searches/Indexing: Search request requires name only. Results include SSN number. Will fax back $.50 per page. Faxes sent out by the Records Dept. New cases are in the index immediately after filing date. Records maintained on computer back to 1980s. Case files archived 3 years after closed.

Search Access: Docket info available by phone. Voice Case Information Service available, call VCIS at 334-954-3868. **Mail:** Search usually completed- 2-3 days. Include SASE for return. **Fax:** Fax search requests accepted. **In person:** 2 public terminals available. No self-serve copier.

Payment: Pay by Visa/MC, money order, cashier's check, business check. No personal checks. Payee: Clerk of Court. Court may bill if requested to.

E-Svcs: WebPacer https://ecf.almb.uscourts.gov. Document images available. PACER records go back to 8/2000. New records online after 2-3 days. ECF at https://ecf.almb.uscourts.gov. **Opinions Online:** https://ecf.almb.uscourts.gov/cgi-bin/PublicOpinion.pl. **Online Note:** Calendars free at www.almb.uscourts.gov/calendar.htm.

US District Court Alabama Northern District

Anniston- Eastern Division c/o Birmingham Division, Hugo Black US Courthouse, 1729 5th Ave N, Rm 104, Birmingham, AL 35203, 205-278-1700 x2. Hours- 8:30AM-4:30PM. www.alnd.uscourts.gov

Counties/Note: Calhoun, Clay, Cleburne, Talladega. Search records at the Birmingham Division, address and phone given here.

Searches/Indexing: In search request include full name and case number if known. Results do not include SSN or DOB. New cases are in the index 2-3 days after filing date. Computer index back to 1992 maintained; older index on microfiche. District-wide searches available on computer. Case files sent to archives 18 months after closed.

Search Access: Mail: Search usually completed- 2 days. Include SASE for return. **In person:** Public terminals available. Self-serve copies from computer- $.10 each.

Payment: Pay by money order, cashier's or personal check. No business/personal checks or credit cards accepted.

E-Services: PACER records go back to 1994. New records online after 1 day. ECF at https://ecf.alnd.uscourts.gov. **Opinions Online:** www.alnd.uscourts.gov/judge_pages.htm.

Birmingham- Main Division Court Clerk, Hugo Black US Courthouse, 1729 5th Ave N, Rm 104, Birmingham, AL 35203, 205-278-1700 x2. Hours- 8:30AM-4:30PM. www.alnd.uscourts.gov

Counties/Note: Bibb, Blount, Fayette, Greene, Jefferson, Lamar, Marion, Pickens, Shelby, Sumter, Tuscaloosa, Walker, Winston. Has records for the Western Division (Tuscaloosa-includes 5 counties included with this Birmingham Div.) also the Eastern Division (see Anniston), also the Middle Division (see Gadsden) and the former Jasper Division. Also answers record search requests from the Northwestern Division Florence Court, see separate listing.

Searches/Indexing: In search request include full name and case number if known. Results do not include SSN or DOB. New cases are in the index immediately after filing date. Computer index back to 1992 maintained; older index on microfiche. District-wide searches available on computer. Case files archived 18 months after closed.

Search Access: Only docket info available by phone. **Mail:** Search usually completed- 24 hours. Include SASE for return. **In person:** 2 public terminals available. Self-serve copies from computer- $.10 each.

Payment: Pay by money order, cashier's check. No business/personal checks or credit cards accepted. Payee: Clerk of Court.

E-Services: PACER records go back to 1994. ECF at https://ecf.alnd.uscourts.gov. **Opinions Online:** www.alnd.uscourts.gov/judge_pages.htm.

Florence- Northwestern Division Court Clerk, 210 N Seminary St, Rm 311, Florence, AL 35630, 256-760-8415. Hours- 8:30AM-4:30PM. www.alnd.uscourts.gov

Counties/Note: Colbert, Franklin, Lauderdale. Limited public access at this court; see Birmingham Division.

Searches/Indexing: Results do not include SSN or DOB.

Search Access: In person: Self-serve copies from computer- $.10 each.

E-Services: ECF at https://ecf.alnd.uscourts.gov. **Opinions Online:** www.alnd.uscourts.gov/judge_pages.htm.

Gadsden- Middle Division c/o Birmingham Division, Hugo Black US Courthouse, 1729 5th Ave N, Rm 140, Birmingham, AL 35203, 205-278-1700 x2; Gadsden- 256-547-7301. Hours- 8:30AM-4:30PM. www.alnd.uscourts.gov

Counties/Note: Cherokee, De Kalb, Etowah, Marshall, St. Clair.

Searches/Indexing: In search request include full name and case number if known. Results do not include SSN or DOB. New cases are in the index 2-3 days after filing date. Computer index back to 1992 maintained; older index on microfiche. District-wide searches available on computer. Case files sent to archives 18 months after closed.

Search Access: Mail: Search usually completed- 2 days. Include SASE for return. **In person:** 2 public terminals available. Self-serve copies from computer- $.10 each.

Payment: Pay by money order, cashier's check. No business/personal checks/credit cards accepted.

E-Services: PACER records go back to 1994. New records online after 1 day. ECF at https://ecf.alnd.uscourts.gov. **Opinions Online:** www.alnd.uscourts.gov/judge_pages.htm.

Huntsville- Northeastern Division Clerk's Office, 302 Federal Courthouse, 101 Holmes Ave NE, Huntsville, AL 35801, 256-534-6495; Fax- 256-551-2536. Hours- 8AM-4:30PM. www.alnd.uscourts.gov

Counties/Note: Cullman, Jackson, Lawrence, Limestone, Madison, Morgan.

Searches/Indexing: In search request include full name and case number if known. Results do not include SSN or DOB. Will not fax back documents. New cases are in the index 2 days after filing date. Computer index back to 1992 maintained; older index on microfiche. District-wide searches available on computer. Case files sent to archives 18 months after closed.

Search Access: All public info is released via phone. **Mail:** Search usually completed- 24 hours. All requests for criminal searches sent to Birmingham. Include SASE for return. **In person:** 1 public terminal available. Self-serve copies from computer- $.10 each.

Payment: Pay by money order, cashier's check. No business/personal checks or credit cards accepted. Payee: US District Court Clerk.

E-Services: PACER records go back to 1994. New records online after 1 day. ECF at https://ecf.alnd.uscourts.gov. **Opinions Online:** www.alnd.uscourts.gov/judge_pages.htm.

US Bankruptcy Court Alabama Northern District

Anniston- Eastern Division Court Clerk, 1129 Noble St, #117, Anniston, AL36202-2008, 256-741-1500; Fax- 256-741-1515. Hours- 8AM-4:30PM. www.alnb.uscourts.gov

Counties: Calhoun, Cherokee, Clay, Cleburne, De Kalb, Etowah, Marshall, St. Clair, Talladega.

Searches/Indexing: In request include debtor name, SSN or the case number, helpful to provide the year the case closed and location where case filed. Results include last 4 SSN digits. Will not fax back documents. New cases are in the index immediately after filing date. Paper case files sent to archives 1 years after closed; cases kept electronically indefinitely.

Search Access: Voice Case Information Service available, call VCIS at 877-466-0795. **Mail:** Search usually completed- 1 day. Include SASE for return. **In person:** 1 public terminal available; records go back to 1970s. No self-serve copier.

Payment: Pay by money order, cashier's check. No personal checks. Payee: Clerk, US Bankruptcy Court, Northern District.

E-Services: PACER records go back to 11/1976. New records online immediately. ECF at https://ecf.alnb.uscourts.gov. Search opinions by judge name free at main website, click on Opinions. **Online Note:** Search calendars free at http://207.41.17.39/index.cfm?prg=publiccalsearch .

Birmingham- Southern Division Court Clerk, 1800 5th Ave N, Rm 120, Birmingham, AL 35203, 205-714-4000; Fax- 205-714-3913. Hours- 8AM-4:30PM. www.alnb.uscourts.gov

Counties/Note: Blount, Jefferson, Shelby.

Searches/Indexing: In request include debtor name, SSN or the case number, helpful to provide the year the case closed and location where case filed. Results include last 4 SSN digits. Will not fax back documents. New cases are in the index immediately after filing date. Paper case files sent to archives 1 years after closed; cases kept electronically indefinitely.

Search Access: Only docket info available by phone. Voice Case Information Service available, call VCIS at 877-466-0795 or 205-254-7337. **Mail:** Search usually completed- 1-2 days. Include SASE for return. **In person:** 2 public terminals available. No self-serve copier.

Payment: Pay by money order, cashier's check. No personal checks. Payee: US Bankruptcy Court.

E-Services: PACER records go back to 1992. New records online immediately. ECF at https://ecf.alnb.uscourts.gov. Search opinions by judge name free at main website, click on Opinions. **Online Note:** Search calendars free at http://207.41.17.39/index.cfm?prg=publiccalsearch

Decatur- Northern Division Court Clerk, PO Box 2748, Decatur, AL 35602 (In person: 400 Well St, Rm 220, Decatur, AL 35601), 256-584-7900; Fax- 256-584-7977. Hours- 8AM-4:30PM. www.alnb.uscourts.gov

Counties/Note: Colbert, Cullman, Franklin, Jackson, Lauderdale, Lawrence, Limestone, Madison, Morgan. The part of Winston County north of Double Springs handled by this division.

Searches/Indexing: In request include debtor name, SSN or the case number, helpful to provide the year the case closed and location where case filed. Results include last 4 SSN digits. Will not fax back documents. New cases are in the index immediately after filing date. Paper case files sent to archives 1 years after closed; cases kept electronically indefinitely.

Search Access: Voice Case Information Service available, call VCIS at 877-466-0795. **Mail:** Search usually completed- 1-2 days. Include SASE for return. **In person:** 2 public terminals available. No self-serve copier.

Payment: Pay by money order, cashier's check. No personal checks. Payee: Clerk, Bankruptcy Ct.

E-Services: PACER records go back to 1992. New records online immediately. ECF at https://ecf.alnb.uscourts.gov. Search opinions by judge name free at main website, click on Opinions. **Online Note:** Search calendars free at http://207.41.17.39/index.cfm?prg=publiccalsearch

Tuscaloosa- Western Division Court Clerk, 1118 Greensboro Ave, Rm 209, Tuscaloosa, AL 35401, 205-561-1600; Fax- 205-561-1640. Hours- 8AM-4:30PM. www.alnb.uscourts.gov

Counties/Note: Bibb, Fayette, Greene, Lamar, Marion, Pickens, Sumter, Tuscaloosa, Walker, Winston. The part of Winston County North of Double Springs is handled by Decatur Division.

Searches/Indexing: In request include debtor name, SSN or the case number, helpful to provide the year the case closed and location where case filed. Results include last 4 SSN digits. Will not fax back documents. New cases are in the index immediately after filing date. Both computer and card indexes maintained; on computer back to 10/1979. Paper case files sent to archives 1 years after closed; cases kept electronically indefinitely.

Search Access: Voice Case Information Service available, call VCIS at 877-466-0795. **Mail:** Search usually completed- 2 days. Include SASE for return. **In person:** 1 public terminal available. No self-serve copier.

Payment: Pay by money order, cashier's check, business check. No personal checks. Payee: Clerk, US Bankruptcy Court.

E-Services: PACER records go back to 1990. New records online immediately. ECF at https://ecf.alnb.uscourts.gov. Search opinions by judge name free at main website, click on Opinions. **Online Note:** Search calendars free at http://207.41.17.39/index.cfm?prg=publiccalsearch .

US District Court Alabama Southern District

Mobile- Southern Division Clerk of Court, 113 St Joseph St, Mobile, AL 36602, 251-690-2371; Fax- 251-694-4297. Hours- 8AM-5PM. www.als.uscourts.gov

Counties: Baldwin, Choctaw, Clarke, Conecuh, Escambia, Mobile, Monroe, Washington.

Searches/Indexing: To search, include full name; SSN and DOB may be helpful. Results do not include SSN or DOB. Will fax back documents for fee. New cases are in the index immediately after filing date. Computer index maintained back to 1955. The Mobile Court will accept email requests for basic case information.

Search Access: Only docket information is released over the phone. **Mail:** Search usually completed- 1-2 days, but could be more,. Include SASE for return. **In person:** 1 public terminal available. Self serve copies $.25 each.

Payment: Pay by Visa/MC/Discover/AmEx, money order, cashier's or personal check. Payee: Clerk, US District Court.

E-Services: PACER records go back to 1993 for criminal, 1991 for civil. New records online immediately. ECF at https://ecf.alsd.uscourts.gov. **Opinions Online:** www.alsd.uscourts.gov/opinions/opinions.cfm. Add'l/latest opinions are available via PACER.

Selma- Northern Division c/o Mobile Division, 113 St Joseph St, Mobile, AL 36602, 251-690-2371; Fax- 251-694-4297. 8AM-5PM. www.alsd.uscourts.gov

Counties: Dallas, Hale, Marengo, Perry, Wilcox.

Searches/Indexing: To search, include full name; SSN and DOB may be helpful. Results do not include SSN or DOB. Will fax back documents for fee. New cases are in the index immediately after filing date. Computer index back to 1955 maintained. The Mobile Court will accept email requests for basic case information.

Search Access: Only docket information is released over the phone. **Mail:** Include SASE for return. **In person:** 2 public terminals available. No self-serve copier.

Payment: Pay by Visa/MC/Discover/AmEx, money order, cashier's or personal check. Payee: Clerk, US District Court.

E-Services: PACER records go back to 1993 for criminal, 1991 for civil. New records online immediately. ECF at https://ecf.alsd.uscourts.gov. **Opinions Online:** www.alsd.uscourts.gov/opinions/opinions.cfm. Additional and latest opinions are available via PACER.

US Bankruptcy Court Alabama Southern District

Mobile Division Clerk of Court, 201 St. Louis St, Mobile, AL 36602, 251-441-5391; Fax- 251-441-6286. 8AM-5PM. www.alsb.uscourts.gov

Counties/Note: Baldwin, Choctaw, Clarke, Conecuh, Dallas, Escambia, Hale, Marengo, Mobile, Monroe, Perry, Washington, Wilcox.

Searches/Indexing: Include SSN in search request. Results include SSN info. Will not fax back documents. New cases are in the index immediately after filing date. District wide computer searches available here back to 1985.

Search Access: Only name and case number is released via phone. Voice Case Information Service available, call VCIS at 888-509-2771 or 251-441-5637. **Mail:** Search usually completed- 2-3 days. SASE not required. **In person:** 4 public terminals available. Self-serve copier available.

Payment: Pay by money order, cashier's check, business check. No personal checks. Attorney credit cards accepted. Payee: Clerk, US Bankruptcy Court.

E-Services: PACER records go back to 1993. New records online after 1 day. ECF at https://ecf.alsb.uscourts.gov. **Opinions Online:** www.alsb.uscourts.gov/opinions.htm. **Online Note:** Dockets/Calendar free at www.alsb.uscourts.gov/crtcal.htm.

Alabama County Courts

Court	Jurisdiction	No. of Courts	How Organized
Circuit Courts*	General	17	41 Circuits
District Courts*	Limited	15	67 Districts
Combined Courts*		61	
Municipal Courts	Municipal	273	
Probate Courts*	Probate	68	

* Profiled in this Sourcebook.

Court	CIVIL Tort	Contract	Real Estate	Min. Claim	Max. Claim	Small Claims	Estate	Eviction	Domestic Relations
Circuit Courts*	X	X	X	$3000	No Max				X
District Courts*	X	X	X	$3000	$10,000	$3000		X	
Municipal Courts									
Probate Courts*							X		

Court	CRIMINAL Felony	Misdemeanor	DWI/DUI	Preliminary Hearing	Juvenile
Circuit Courts*	X	X			X
District Courts*		X	X	X	X
Municipal Courts		X	X		
Family Courts					X

Administration

Director of Courts, 300 Dexter Ave, Montgomery, AL, 36104; 334-954-5000. (CST) www.alacourt.gov

Court Structure

Circuit Courts are the courts of general jurisdiction; District Courts have limited jurisdiction in civil matters. These courts are combined in all but eight larger counties. Barbour, Coffee, Jefferson, St. Clair, Talladega, and Tallapoosa Counties have two court locations within the county. Jefferson County (Birmingham), Madison (Huntsville), Marshall, and Tuscaloosa Counties have separate criminal divisions for Circuit Courts and/or District Courts. All counties have separate probate courts.

Misdemeanors committed with felonies are tried with the felony. The Circuit Courts are appeals courts for misdemeanors.

District Courts can receive guilty pleas in felony cases.

Online Access

Two sources of online access exist; both are by subscription. There are significant differences between the two; one contains almost all court record types; the second contains only criminal data.

The commercial online subscription services at www.alacourt.com draws its data from the State Judicial Information System (SJIS). This alacourt.com system is comprehensive and user friendly, includes civil, criminal, DR, traffic, warrants, and trial court dockets statewide. It also features multiple monthly payment plans. Search fees based on monthly volume with searches as low as $.40 each. Full identifers shown. There is a $150 set-up fee. A record request form is found at http://helpdesk.alacourt.gov/requestform.asp that allows you to specify case data or search on a county basis.

The second subscription service is offered by Alabama Criminal Justice Information Center (ACJIC), the state agency responsible for information sharing among the state's criminal justice community. As such, ACJIC is the official repository for all state of Alabama criminal history records and it offers an Alabama Background Check (ABC) to the public, tailored for background checkers. This is a subscription service with a $25 search fee and a $75 annual fee. Employers using a CRA must be registered first. See www.background.alabama.gov/

Also, State Supreme Court and Appellate decisions are available at www.alalinc.net and at www.judicial.state.al.us/.

Searching Tips, Fees, and Other Guidelines

Although in most counties Circuit Courts and District Courts are combined, each index may be separate. Therefore, when you request a search of both courts, be sure to state that the search is to cover "both the Circuit and District Court records." A number of courts do not perform searches, you must hire a retriever. Many courts offer public access computer terminals. Effective 01/01/07, a Directive set mandatory fees for record copies at a flate rate of $5.00 for the first 20 copies then $.50 per copy. The certification fee was set at $5.00. Also effective that date courts MAY charge $10.00 for a computerized case history check, $20.00 for a search of paper records, and $25.00 for a search of archival records.

Autauga County

Circuit & District Court 134 N Court St, #114, PO Box 681450, Prattville, AL 36068; 334-358-6800; 8AM-N, 1PM-4:30PM. ***Felony, Misdemeanor, Civil, Eviction, Small Claims.***

Civil Records: Access: Mail, in person, online. Only the court performs in person searches; visitors may not. Search fee: depends on age of case, usually $25.00. Required to search: name, years to search. Civil cases indexed by defendant, plaintiff, on computer since 1977 and in books from 1950. Mail turnaround time 1-2 weeks. The state court system offers various pay plans at www.alacourt.com subscription service; includes civil, DR, traffic, warrants, trial court dockets, and notification features.

Criminal Records: Access: Mail, online, in person. Only the court performs in person searches; visitors may not. Search fee: depends on age of case, usually $25.00. Required to search: name, years to search; also helpful: DOB, SSN. Criminal records on computer since 1977 and in books from 1950. Mail turnaround time 1-2 weeks. Access via various sub plans at www.alacourt.com court subscription service, with notification features. Also, access the state ACJIC system with sub and $25.00 pay-per-name search at http://background.alabama.gov/.

General Information: No sealed, adoptions, youthful offenders or juvenile records released. Will not fax documents. Court makes copy: $5.00 for 1st 20 pages then $.50 each add'l. Certification fee: $2.00. Payee: Circuit Court. Cashiers checks and money orders and major credit cards accepted. Prepayment required.

Probate Court 176 W 5th, Prattville, AL 36067; 334-361-3728/4842; fax: 334-361-3740; 8:30AM-5PM. ***Probate.***

Baldwin County

Circuit & District Court 312 Courthouse Sq #10, Bay Minette, AL 36507; 251-937-0370; criminal phone: 251-937-0280; civil phone: 251-937-0299; 8AM-4:30PM. ***Felony, Misdemeanor, Civil, Eviction, Small Claims, Traffic.***
http://28jc.alacourt.gov/clerk/home.aspx
Court will not do name searches. Court has satellite offices in Fairhope and Foley.

Civil Records: Access: Online, in person. Both court and visitors may perform in person searches. Search fee: $10.00 for computerized or paper records, $25.00 for archived record searches. Required to search: name, years to search. Civil cases indexed by defendant, plaintiff, indexed on computer from 1977, index books by case # to early 1900s. Civil PAT goes back to 1990 for records; 1977 for indices. The state court system offers various pay plans at www.alacourt.com subscription service; includes civil, DR, traffic, warrants, trial court dockets, and notification features.

Criminal Records: Access: Online, in person. Both court and visitors may perform in person searches. Search fee: $10.00 for computerized or paper records, $25.00 for archived record searches. Required to search: name, years to search, DOB. Criminal records indexed on computer from 1977, index books by case # to early 1900s. Criminal PAT goes back to same as civil. Access via various sub plans at www.alacourt.com court subscription service, with notification features. Also, access the state ACJIC system with sub and $25.00 pay-per-name search at http://background.alabama.gov/.

General Information: No sealed, youthful offenders or juvenile records released. Will not fax documents. Court makes copy: $5.00 for 1st 20 pages then $.50 each add'l. Self serve: $.50 per page. Certification fee: $5.00 per cert. Payee: Circuit Court Clerk. Only Cashiers checks and money orders and major credit cards accepted. Prepayment required.

Probate Court PO Box 459, 220 Courthouse Sq, Bay Minette, AL 36507; 251-937-9561; fax: 251-937-0252; 8AM-4:30PM. ***Probate.***
Online access to probate record index is free at www.deltacomputersystems.com/al/al05/probatea.html.

Barbour County

Circuit & District Court - Clayton Division PO Box 219, 1 Court Sq, Clayton, AL 36016; 334-775-8366; probate phone: 334-775-8371; fax: 334-775-1125; 8AM-4:30PM. ***Felony, Misdemeanor, Civil, Eviction, Small Claims, Probate.***
Probate court is separate from this court; probate phone number above.

Civil Records: Access: Mail, in person, online. Only the court performs in person searches; visitors may not. Search fee: $10.00 for computerized case history check; $20.00 for background check; $25.00 per case record search. Required to search: name, years to search; a release of liability is requested. Civil cases indexed by defendant. Civil records on computer back to 1993; books from 1977; archives back to 1920. Mail turnaround time 2-3 days. The state court system offers various pay plans at www.alacourt.com subscription service; includes civil, DR, traffic, warrants, trial court dockets, and notification features.

Criminal Records: Access: Mail, online, in person. Only the court performs in person searches; visitors may not. Search fee: $10.00 for computerized case history check; $20.00 for background check; $25.00 per case record search. Required to search: name, years to search, DOB; also helpful: SSN. Criminal records computerized from 1993, books from 1977; archives back to 1920. Mail turnaround time 2-3 days. Access via various sub plans at www.alacourt.com court subscription service, with notification features. Also, access the state ACJIC system with sub and $25.00 pay-per-name search at http://background.alabama.gov/.

General Information: No sealed, adoptions, youthful offenders records released. Fee to fax document $.50 per page. Court makes copy: $5.00 for 1st 20 pages then $.50 each add'l, self serve same. Certification fee: $1.50 per cert. Payee: David S Nix. Business checks accepted. No credit cards accepted. Prepayment required. Mail requests: SASE required.

Circuit & District Court - Eufaula Division 303 E Broad St, Rm 201, Eufaula, AL 36027; 334-687-1515/16; probate phone: 334-687-1530; fax: 334-687-1599; 8-4:30PM. ***Misdemeanor, Civil, Eviction, Small Claims, Probate.***
Probate court is separate from this court at Rm 101, and can be contacted at the telephone number above.

Civil Records: Access: Online, in person. Visitors must perform in person searches themselves. Required to search: name, years to search. Civil cases indexed by defendant, plaintiff, on computer from 1993. Index from 1977 to present; prior to 1977 difficult to search. Note: If case number is known, court will provide copies within 2 days. Civil PAT goes back to 1977. The state court system offers various pay plans at www.alacourt.com subscription service; includes civil, DR, traffic, warrants, trial dockets, and notification features.

Criminal Records: Access: Online, in person. Visitors must perform in person searches themselves. Required to search: name, years to search; also helpful: DOB, SSN. Criminal records computerized from 1993. Index from 1977 to present; prior to 1977 difficult to search. Note: If case number is known, will provide copies within 2 days. Criminal PAT goes back to same as civil. Access via various sub plans at www.alacourt.com court subscription service, with notification features. Also, access the state ACJIC system with sub and $25.00 pay-per-name search at http://background.alabama.gov/.

General Information: No sealed, adoptions, youthful offenders or juvenile records released. Will fax out documents. Court makes copy: $5.00 for 1st 20 pages then $.50 each add'l. Certification fee: $5.00. Payee: Clerk of Courts. No personal checks accepted. Visa/MC accepted. Prepayment required.

Bibb County

Circuit & District Court PO Box 185, Bibb County Courthouse, 35 Court Sq East, Centreville, AL 35042; 205-926-3103 Civil (Circuit); criminal phone: 205-926-3107; civil phone: 205-926-3100 (Dist); probate phone: 205-926-3108; fax: 205-926-3132; 8AM-5:00PM. ***Felony, Misdemeanor, Civil, Eviction, Small Claims, Probate.***
Probate court is separate from this court; probate phone number above.

Civil Records: Access: Mail, in person, online. Both court and visitors may perform in person searches. No search fee. Required to search: name, years to search. Civil cases indexed by defendant. Civil records on index book back to 1940s. Mail turnaround time 3-4 days. The state court system offers various pay plans at www.alacourt.com subscription service; includes civil, DR, traffic, warrants, trial dockets, and notification features.

Criminal Records: Access: Mail, online, in person. Both court and visitors may perform in person searches. No search fee. Required to search: name, years to search, DOB; also helpful: SSN. Criminal records computerized from 1995, on index books back to 1940s. Mail turnaround time 1-2 days. Access via various sub plans at www.alacourt.com court subscription service, with notification features. Also, access the state ACJIC system with sub and $25.00 pay-per-name search at http://background.alabama.gov/.

General Information: No sealed, adoptions, youthful offenders or juvenile records released. Will fax 1-2 documents to local or toll-free number. Court makes copy: $5.00 for 1st 20 pages then $.50 each add'l, self serve same. Certification fee: $5.00. Payee: Gayle S Bearden, Clerk. Business checks accepted; no personal checks. Prepayment required. Mail requests: SASE required.

Blount County

Circuit & District Court 220 2nd Ave East Rm 208, Oneonta, AL 35121; 205-625-4153; 8AM-5PM. ***Felony, Misdemeanor, Civil, Eviction, Small Claims.***

Civil Records: Access: Mail, in person, online. Both court and visitors may perform in person searches. Search fee: $10.00 for computerized case history check; $20.00 for background check; $25.00 per case record search. Required to search: name, years to search. Civil cases indexed by defendant, plaintiff, on computer from 3/1994, on index books from 1977. Mail turnaround time 7-10 days. Civil PAT goes back to 1994. The state court system offers various pay plans at www.alacourt.com subscription service; includes civil, DR, traffic, warrants, trial court dockets, and notification features.

Criminal Records: Access: Mail, online, in person. Both court and visitors may perform in person searches. Search fee: $10.00 for computerized case history check; $20.00 for background check; $25.00 per case record search. Required to search: name, years to search, DOB; also helpful: SSN. Criminal records computerized from 1998, on index books from 1977. Mail turnaround time 7-10 days. Criminal PAT goes back to same as civil. Access criminal records online same as civil, see above.

General Information: No sealed, adoptions, youthful offenders or juvenile records released. Will not fax documents. Court makes copy: $5.00 for 1st 20 pages then $.50 each add'l, self serve same. Certification fee: $5.00 per cert. Payee: Mike Chriswell. No personal checks accepted. Prepayment required. Mail requests: SASE required.

Probate Court 220 2nd Ave E, Oneonta, AL 35121; 205-625-4191/4180; fax: 205-625-4206; 8AM-5PM. ***Probate.***

Bullock County

Circuit & District Court PO Box 230, Union Springs, AL 36089; 334-738-2280; probate phone: 334-738-2250; fax: 334-738-2282; 8AM-4:30PM. ***Felony, Misdemeanor, Civil, Eviction, Small Claims, Probate.***
Probate court is separate from this court; probate phone number above.

Civil Records: Access: Phone, fax, mail, online, in person. Both court and visitors may perform in person searches. Search fee: $25.00 per name. Required to search: name, years to search. Civil cases indexed by defendant, plaintiff; index on docket books back to 1930s; on computer back to 1996. Mail

turnaround time depends on clerk availability. The state court system offers various pay plans at www.alacourt.com subscription service; includes civil, DR, traffic, warrants, trial court dockets, and notification features.
Criminal Records: Access: Phone, fax, mail, online, in person. Only the court performs in person searches; visitors may not. Search fee: $25.00 per name. Required to search: name, years to search, DOB; also helpful: SSN, signed release. Criminal records indexed in books back to 1930s; on computer back to 1996. Mail turnaround time depends on clerk availability. Public use terminal has crim records back to 1996. PAT results show name only. Access via various sub plans at www.alacourt.com court subscription service, with notification features. Also, access the state ACJIC system with sub and $25.00 pay-per-name search at http://background.alabama.gov/.
General Information: No sealed, adoptions, youthful offenders or juvenile records released. Will not fax out documents. Court makes copy: $5.00 for 1st 20 pages then $.50 each add'l. Self serve: $.50 per page. No personal checks or credit cards accepted. Prepayment required. Mail requests: SASE required.

Butler County

Circuit & District Court PO Box 236, 700 Court Sq, Greenville, AL 36037; 334-382-3521; probate phone: 334-382-3512; fax: 334-382-7488; 7:30AM-4:30PM. ***Felony, Misdemeanor, Civil, Eviction, Small Claims, Probate, Domestic, Traffic.***
Probate court is separate from this court; probate phone number above.
Civil Records: Access: Mail, in person, online. Both court and visitors may perform in person searches. Search fee: $5.00 per name. Fee is for first 2-3 years. Required to search: name, years to search. Civil cases indexed by defendant, plaintiff, on computer from 1992, books to 1979. Mail turnaround time 1-2 weeks. Civil PAT goes back to 1994. The state court system offers various pay plans at www.alacourt.com subscription service; includes civil, DR, traffic, warrants, trial court dockets, and notification features.
Criminal Records: Access: Mail, online, in person. Both court and visitors may perform in person searches. Search fee: $5.00 per name. Fee for first 2-3 years. Required to search: name, years to search; also helpful: SSN, DOB. Criminal records computerized from 1992, books to 1979. Mail turnaround time 1-2 weeks. Criminal PAT goes back to 1992. Access via various sub plans at www.alacourt.com court subscription service, with notification features. Also, access the state ACJIC system with sub and $25.00 pay-per-name search at http://background.alabama.gov/.
General Information: Online identifiers in results same as on public terminal. No sealed, adoptions, youthful offenders or juvenile records released. Fee to fax out file $1.00 per page. Court makes copy: $5.00 for 1st 20 pages then $.50 each add'l, self serve same. Certification fee: $1.50 per page. Payee: Butler County District Court. Business checks accepted. No credit cards accepted. Prepayment required. Mail requests: SASE requested.

Calhoun County

Circuit Court 25 W 11th St, #300, Anniston, AL 36201; 256-231-1750; fax: 256-231-1826; 8AM-4:30PM. ***Felony, Civil Actions over $10,000.***
www.alacourt.gov
Civil Records: Access: Online, in person. Visitors must perform in person searches themselves. Required to search: name, years to search. Civil cases indexed by defendant, plaintiff, indexed on computer from 1970s, prior in books. Civil PAT goes back to 1970. The state court system offers various pay plans at www.alacourt.com subscription service; includes civil, DR, traffic, warrants, trial court dockets, and notification features.
Criminal Records: Access: Online, in person. Visitors must perform in person searches themselves. Required to search: name, years to search, DOB; also helpful: SSN. Criminal records indexed on computer from 1970s, prior on books. Criminal PAT goes back to same as civil. Access via various sub plans at www.alacourt.com court subscription service, with notification features. Also, access the state ACJIC system with sub and $25.00 pay-per-name search at http://background.alabama.gov/. The County sex offender registry is online at www.calhouncountysheriff.org/sex_offenders.cfm.
General Information: No sealed, adoptions, youthful offenders or juvenile records released. Will not fax documents. Court makes copy: $5.00 for 1st 20 pages then $.50 each add'l. Certification fee: $1.00. Payee: Circuit/District Clerk. Personal checks accepted; credit cards are not. Prepayment required.

District Court 25 W 11th St, #260, Anniston, AL 36201; 256-231-1850; fax: 256-231-1863; 8AM-4:30PM. ***Misdemeanor, Civil Actions under $10,000, Eviction, Small Claims.***
Civil Records: Access: Mail, in person, online. Visitors must perform in person searches themselves. Search fee: $10.00 per name; if pre-1990 then add add'l $25.00 to $10.00 search fee. Required to search: name, years to search. Civil cases indexed by defendant, plaintiff, on computer from 1989, books from 1977 to 1989. Civil PAT goes back to 1977. Public terminal located in law library. The state court system offers various pay plans at www.alacourt.com subscription service; includes civil, DR, traffic, warrants, trial court dockets, and notification features.
Criminal Records: Access: Mail, online, in person. Visitors must perform in person searches themselves. Search fee: $10.00 per name; if pre-2000 then add add'l $25.00 to $10.00 search fee. Required to search: name, years to search; also helpful: SSN. Criminal records computerized from 1989, books from 1977 to 1989. Criminal PAT goes back to same as civil. Public terminal located in law library. Access via various sub plans at www.alacourt.com court subscription service, with notification features. Also, access the state ACJIC system with sub and $25.00 pay-per-name search at http://background.alabama.gov/.
General Information: No sealed, adoptions, youthful offenders or juvenile records released. Will not fax documents. Court makes copy: $5.00 for 1st 20 pages then $.50 each add'l, self serve same. Certification fee: $5.00 per doc. Payee: District Court. No personal checks or credit cards accepted. Prepayment required.

Probate Court 1702 Noble St, #102, Anniston, AL 36201; 256-241-2825; fax: 256-231-1728; 8AM-4:30PM. ***Probate.***
www.calhouncounty.org/probate/index.html

Chambers County

Circuit & District Court Chambers County Courthouse, Clerks Office, #2, Lafayette St, Lafayette, AL 36862; 334-864-4348; probate phone: 334-864-4372; fax: 334-864-4368; 8AM-N, 1-4:30PM. ***Felony, Misdemeanor, Civil, Eviction, Small Claims, Probate.***
Probate court is separate from this court; probate phone number above.
Civil Records: Access: Mail, in person, online. Both court and visitors may perform in person searches. Search fee: $10.00. Required to search: name, years to search. Civil cases indexed by defendant, plaintiff, on computer from 4/93, on index books to early 1900s. Mail turnaround time 1 week. Civil PAT goes back to 1993. The state court system offers various pay plans at www.alacourt.com subscription service; includes civil, DR, traffic, warrants, trial court dockets, and notification features.
Criminal Records: Access: Mail, online, in person. Only the court performs in person searches; visitors may not. Search fee: $10.00. Required to search: name, years to search; also helpful: DOB, SSN. Criminal records are computerized since 1993. Mail turnaround time 1 week. Criminal PAT available. Access via various sub plans at www.alacourt.com court subscription service, with notification features. Also, access the state ACJIC system with sub and $25.00 pay-per-name search at http://background.alabama.gov/.
General Information: No sealed, adoptions, youthful offenders or juvenile records released. Will not fax out documents. Court makes copy: $5.00 for 1st 20 pages then $.50 each add'l, self serve same. Certification fee: $5.00 per cert. Business checks accepted. No personal checks. Visa/MC accepted. Prepayment required. Mail requests: SASE required.

Cherokee County

Circuit & District Court 100 Main St, Rm 203, Centre, AL 35960-1532; 256-927-3340; fax: 256-927-3444; 8AM-4PM. ***Felony, Misdemeanor, Civil, Eviction, Small Claims.***
Civil Records: Access: In person, online. Visitors must perform in person searches themselves. Required to search: name, years to search. Civil cases indexed by defendant, plaintiff, on books from 1977. Civil PAT goes back to 8/1995. The state court system offers various pay plans at www.alacourt.com subscription service; includes civil, DR, traffic, warrants, trial court dockets, and notification features.
Criminal Records: Access: Online, in person. Visitors must perform in person searches themselves. Required to search: name, years to search; also helpful: DOB, SSN. Criminal docket on books from 1977. Criminal PAT goes back to same as civil. Access via various sub plans at www.alacourt.com court subscription service, with notification features. Also, access the state ACJIC system with sub and $25.00 pay-per-name search at http://background.alabama.gov/.
General Information: No sealed, adoptions, youthful offenders or juvenile records released. Court makes copy: $5.00 for 1st 20 pages then $.50 each add'l, self serve same. Certification fee: $5.00 per cert. Payee: Circuit Clerk. Business checks accepted; no personal checks or credit cards accepted. Prepayment required.

Probate Court 260 Cedar Bluff Rd, #101, Centre, AL 35960; 256-927-3363; fax: 256-927-9218; 8AM-4PM. ***Probate.***

Chilton County

Circuit & District Court PO Box 1946, 500 2nd Ave N, Clanton, AL 35046; 205-755-4275 Dist; 280-1844 Dist.; civil phone: 280-280-1844; probate phone: 205-755-1555; fax: 205-755-1387; 8AM-Noon, 1PM-5PM. ***Felony, Misdemeanor, Civil, Eviction, Small Claims, Probate.***
Search fee includes civil and criminal indexes. Probate court is separate from this court.
Civil Records: Access: Mail, in person, online. Visitors must perform in person searches themselves. Search fee: $10.00 per name. Required to search: name, years to search. Civil cases indexed by defendant, plaintiff, on computer from 9/93, on books from 1950s. Civil PAT goes back to 1994. The state court system offers various pay plans at www.alacourt.com subscription service; includes civil, DR, traffic, warrants, trial court dockets, and notification features.
Criminal Records: Access: Mail, online, in person. Visitors must perform in person searches themselves. Search fee: $10.00 per name. Required to search: name, years to search; also helpful: DOB, SSN. Criminal records on computer since 1977. Criminal PAT goes back to same as civil. Access via various sub plans at www.alacourt.com court subscription service, with notification features. Also, access the state ACJIC system with sub and $25.00 pay-per-name search at http://background.alabama.gov/.
General Information: No sealed, adoptions, youthful offenders or juvenile records released. Will not fax out documents. Court makes copy: $5.00 for 1st 20 pages then $.50 each add'l, self serve same. Certification fee: $5.00 per cert. Payee: Clerk. Business checks accepted. No personal checks or credit cards accepted. Prepayment required.

Choctaw County

Circuit & District Court Choctaw County Courthouse, #10, PO Box 428, Butler, AL 36904; 205-459-2155; probate: 205-459-2417; fax: 205-459-3218; 8AM-4:30PM. ***Felony, Misdemeanor, Civil, Eviction, Small Claims, Probate.***
Probate court is separate from this court; probate phone number above.

Civil Records: Access: Online, in person. Both court and visitors may perform in person searches. No search fee. Required to search: name, years to search. Civil cases indexed by defendant, plaintiff; index on docket books from 1940. Putting records on computer from 9/1994. Civil PAT goes back to 1994. The state court system offers various pay plans at www.alacourt.com subscription service; includes civil, DR, traffic, warrants, trial court dockets, and notification features.
Criminal Records: Access: Online, in person. Visitors must perform in person searches themselves. Required to search: name, years to search; also helpful: DOB, SSN. Criminal records indexed in books from 1940. Putting records on computer from 9/1994. Criminal PAT goes back to same as civil. Access via various sub plans at www.alacourt.com court subscription service, with notification features. Also, access the state ACJIC system with sub and $25.00 pay-per-name search at http://background.alabama.gov/.
General Information: No sealed, adoptions, youthful offenders or juvenile records released. Court makes copy: $5.00 for 1st 20 pages then $.50 each add'l. Certification fee: $5.00 per cert. Payee: Circuit Clerk. Business checks accepted. Visa/MC accepted. Prepayment required.

Clarke County

Circuit & District Court PO Box 921, Grove Hill, AL 36451; 251-275-3363; probate phone: 251-275-3251; 8AM-5PM. ***Felony, Misdemeanor, Civil, Eviction, Small Claims, Probate.***
Probate court is separate from this court; probate phone number above.
Civil Records: Access: Mail, in person, online. Both court and visitors may perform in person searches. Search fee: $5.00 per name. Required to search: name, years to search. Civil cases indexed by defendant, plaintiff; index on cards from 1977. Mail turnaround time 1 week. Civil PAT goes back to 1993. The state court system offers various pay plans at www.alacourt.com subscription service; includes civil, DR, traffic, warrants, trial court dockets, and notification features.
Criminal Records: Access: Mail, online, in person. Both court and visitors may perform in person searches. Search fee: $5.00 per name. Required to search: name, years to search; also helpful: DOB, SSN. Criminal records indexed on cards from 1977. Mail turnaround time 1 week. Criminal PAT goes back to same as civil. Access via various sub plans at www.alacourt.com court subscription service, with notification features. Also, access the state ACJIC system with sub and $25.00 pay-per-name search at http://background.alabama.gov/.
General Information: No sealed, adoptions, youthful offenders or juvenile records released. Will not fax documents. Court makes copy: $5.00 for 1st 20 pages then $.50 each add'l, self serve same. Certification fee: $5.00. Payee: Circuit Clerk. Business checks accepted. Prepayment required.

Clay County

Circuit & District Court PO Box 816, Ashland, AL 36251; 256-354-7926; probate phone: 256-354-2198; fax: 256-354-2249; 8AM-4:30PM. ***Felony, Misdemeanor, Civil, Eviction, Small Claims, Probate.***
Probate court is separate from this court, and can be reached at the telephone number given above.
Civil Records: Access: Mail, in person, online. Visitors must perform in person searches themselves. Search fee: $10.00 per name, computer index only. Required to search: name, years to search. Civil cases indexed by defendant, plaintiff. Overall records go back to 1977; computerized records go back to 1994. Mail turnaround time 10-14 days. Civil PAT goes back to 1994. PAT results show name only. The state court system offers various pay plans at www.alacourt.com subscription service; includes civil, DR, traffic, warrants, trial court dockets, and notification features.
Criminal Records: Access: Mail, online, in person. Visitors must perform in person searches themselves. Search fee: $10.00 per name, computer index only. Required to search: name, years to search; also helpful: SSN, DOB, signed release. Overall records go back to 1977; computerized records go back to 1994. Mail turnaround time 10-14 days. Criminal PAT goes back to same as civil.PAT results show name, DOB. Terminal results include SSN. Access via various sub plans at www.alacourt.com court subscription service, with notification features. Also, access the state ACJIC system with sub and $25.00 pay-per-name search at http://background.alabama.gov/. Online results show name, DOB. Terminal results include SSN.
General Information: Online identifiers in results same as on public terminal. No sealed, adoptions, youthful offenders or juvenile records released. Fee to fax out file $1.00 per page. Court makes copy: $5.00 for 1st 20 pages then $.50 each add'l. Certification fee: $5.00 per doc. Payee: Circuit Clerk. Business checks accepted. No credit cards accepted. Prepayment required. Mail requests: SASE required.

Cleburne County

Circuit & District Court 120 Vickery St, Rm 202, Heflin, AL 36264; 256-463-2651; probate phone: 256-463-5655; fax: 256-463-2257; 8AM-5PM. ***Felony, Misdemeanor, Civil, Eviction, Small Claims, Probate.***
Probate is a separate index located in Rm 101. Probate fax- 256-463-1044
Civil Records: Access: Phone, mail, online, in person. Both court and visitors may perform in person searches. No search fee. Required to search: name, years to search. Civil cases indexed by defendant, plaintiff, on computer from 1993, on books and cards from 1900. Mail turnaround time 1-2 days. The state court system offers various pay plans at www.alacourt.com subscription service; includes civil, DR, traffic, warrants, trial court dockets, and notification features.
Criminal Records: Access: Mail, online, in person. Only the court performs in person searches; visitors may not. No search fee. Required to search: name, years to search, DOB; also helpful: SSN. Criminal records computerized from 1993, on books and cards from 1900. Mail turnaround time 1-2 days. Access via various sub plans at www.alacourt.com court subscription service, with notification features. Also, access the state ACJIC system with sub and $25.00 pay-per-name search at http://background.alabama.gov/.
General Information: No sealed, adoptions, youthful offenders or juvenile records released. Will fax documents for no fee. Court makes copy: $5.00 for 1st 20 pages then $.50 each add'l, self serve same. Certification fee: $2.25. Payee: Clerk. Only cashiers checks and money orders accepted. Prepayment required. Mail requests: SASE required.

Coffee County

Circuit & District Court - Elba Division 230 M Court Ave, Elba, AL 36323; 334-897-2954; 8:30AM-N, 1-4:30PM. ***Felony, Misdemeanor, Civil, Eviction, Small Claims, Probate.***
Civil Records: Access: Mail, in person, online. Both court and visitors may perform in person searches. No search fee. Required to search: name, years to search. Civil cases indexed by defendant. Civil records on computer back to 8/1993. Mail turnaround time 3-4 days. The state court system offers various pay plans at www.alacourt.com subscription service; includes civil, DR, traffic, warrants, trial court dockets, and notification features.
Criminal Records: Access: Mail, online, in person. Only the court performs in person searches; visitors may not. No search fee. Required to search: name, years to search; also helpful: DOB. Criminal records computerized from 8/1993. Mail turnaround time varies, usually 3-4 days. Access via various sub plans at www.alacourt.com court subscription service, with notification features. Also, access the state ACJIC system with sub and $25.00 pay-per-name search at http://background.alabama.gov/.
General Information: No sealed, adoptions, youthful offenders or juvenile records released. Court makes copy: $5.00 for 1st 20 pages then $.50 each add'l, self serve same. Certification fee: $1.25 per cert includes copy. Payee: Circuit Clerk. Business checks accepted. Credit cards accepted from attorneys only. Mail requests: SASE required.

Circuit & District Court - Enterprise Division PO Box 311284, 99 Edwards, Enterprise, AL 36331; 334-347-2519; fax: 334-393-2047; 8:30AM-5PM. ***Felony, Misdemeanor, Civil, Eviction, Small Claims.***
Civil Records: Access: Mail, fax, online, in person. Visitors must perform in person searches themselves. No search fee. Required to search: name, years to search. Civil cases indexed by defendant, plaintiff, on computer since 8/1993. Civil PAT goes back to 1980. PAT results show name only. The state court system offers various pay plans at www.alacourt.com subscription service; includes civil, DR, traffic, warrants, trial court dockets, and notification features.
Criminal Records: Access: Mail, online, in person. Visitors must perform in person searches themselves. No search fee. Required to search: name, years to search, DOB; also helpful: SSN. Criminal records on computer since 8/1993. Mail turnaround time up to 1 week. Criminal PAT goes back to same as civil.PAT results show name, DOB. Access via various sub plans at www.alacourt.com court subscription service, with notification features. Also, access the state ACJIC system with sub and $25.00 pay-per-name search at http://background.alabama.gov/.
General Information: No sealed, adoptions, youthful offenders or juvenile records released. Will fax back docs no fee. Court makes copy: $5.00 for 1st 20 pages then $.50 each add'l. Certification fee: $5.00 per cert. Payee: Clerk of Courts. Only cashiers checks and money orders accepted. No credit cards accepted. Prepayment required. Mail requests: SASE required.

Probate Court - Enterprise Division PO Box 311247, 99 S Edwards, Enterprise, AL 36331; 334-347-2688; fax: 334-347-2095; 8AM-4:30PM. ***Probate.*** www.probateoffice.info/
Presided by the same judge, there is also a Probate office in Elba, 334-897-2211 or 2212, fax-334-897-2028, 230 N Court St, Elba, Al 36330.

Colbert County

Circuit and District Court - Criminal Colbert County Courthouse, 201 N Main St, Criminal Office, Tuscumbia, AL 35674; 256-386-8517; fax: 256-386-7633; 8AM-4:30PM. ***Felony, Misdemeanor, Traffic.***
For practical purposes, Circuit and District Court are virtually combined, then divided into a Civil section and a Criminal section.
Criminal Records: Access: Online, in person. Visitors must perform in person searches themselves. Required to search: name, years to search; also helpful: SSN. Criminal records computerized from 1993, prior on books. Public use terminal has crim records back to 1977. PAT results show name only. Access via various sub plans at www.alacourt.com court subscription service, with notification features. Also, access the state ACJIC system with sub and $25.00 pay-per-name search at http://background.alabama.gov/.
General Information: No sealed, adoptions, youthful offenders or juvenile records released. Will not fax documents. Court makes copy: $5.00 for 1st 20 pages then $.50 each add'l. Certification fee: $5.00 per doc. Payee: Court Clerk. No personal checks or credit cards accepted. Prepayment required.

Circuit and District Court - Civil Colbert County Courthouse, 201 N Main St, Civil Office, Tuscumbia, AL 35674; 256-386-8511; civil phone: 256-386-8513; probate phone: 256-386-8542; fax: 256-386-8505; 8AM-4:30PM. ***Civil Actions, Small Claims, Family, Eviction, Probate.***
For practical purposes, Circuit and District Court are virtually combined, then divided into a Civil section and a Criminal section. Probate court is separate from this court but at same address; probate phone above.
Civil Records: Access: Online, in person. Visitors must perform in person searches themselves. Required to search: name, years to search. Civil cases indexed by defendant, plaintiff, on computer from 1993, books from 1959. Public use terminal has civil records back to 1993. The state court system

offers various pay plans at www.alacourt.com subscription service; includes civil, DR, traffic, warrants, trial dockets, and notification features.
General Information: No sealed, youthful offenders or juvenile records released. Will not fax documents. Court makes copy: $5.00 for 1st 20 pages then $.50 each add'l, self serve same. Certification fee: $5.00 per doc. Payee: Circuit Court Clerk. Business checks accepted. No credit cards. Prepayment required.

Conecuh County

Circuit & District Court 111 Court St Rm 203, Evergreen, AL 36401; 251-578-2066; fax: 251-578-7013; 8AM-4:30PM. ***Felony, Misdemeanor, Civil, Eviction, Small Claims, Probate.***
Civil Records: Access: In person, online. Both court and visitors may perform in person searches. Search fee: $25.00. Required to search: name, years to search. Civil cases indexed by defendant, plaintiff; index on cards from 1977, on computer back to 12/1994. Civil PAT goes back to 12/1994. The state court system offers various pay plans at www.alacourt.com subscription service; includes civil, DR, traffic, warrants, trial court dockets, and notification features.
Criminal Records: Access: In person, online. Both court and visitors may perform in person searches. Search fee: $25.00. Required to search: name, years to search, DOB; also helpful: SSN. Criminal records indexed on cards from 1977, on computer back to 1994. Criminal PAT goes back to same as civil. Access via various sub plans at www.alacourt.com court subscription service, with notification features. Also, access the state ACJIC system with sub and $25.00 pay-per-name search at http://background.alabama.gov/.
General Information: No sealed, adoptions, youthful offenders or juvenile records released. Will fax out specific case files for $5.00. Court makes copy: $5.00 for 1st 20 pages then $.50 each add'l. Certification fee: $5.00. Payee: Circuit Clerk, David Jackson. Business checks accepted upon prior approval. No credit cards accepted. Prepayment required.

Coosa County

Circuit & District Court PO Box 98, 1 Main St, Rockford, AL 35136; 256-377-4988; probate phone: 256-377-4919; fax: 256-377-1599; 8AM-4:30PM. ***Felony, Misdemeanor, Civil, Eviction, Small Claims, Probate.***
Probate court is separate from this court; probate phone number above.
Civil Records: Access: Online, in person. Visitors must perform in person searches themselves. Required to search: name, years to search. Civil cases indexed by plaintiff. Civil records on books from the late 1800s, computerized records go back to 7/1994. Public use terminal has civil records back to 10 years. The state court system offers various pay plans at www.alacourt.com subscription service; includes civil, DR, traffic, warrants, trial court dockets, and notification features.
Criminal Records: Access: Online, in person, fax, mail. Visitors must perform in person searches themselves. Search fee: $5.00. Required to search: name, years to search; also helpful: DOB, SSN. Criminal docket on books from the late 1800s, computerized records go back to 7/1994. Mail turnaround time 2-3 days. Access via various sub plans at www.alacourt.com court subscription service, with notification features. Also, access the state ACJIC system with sub and $25.00 pay-per-name search at http://background.alabama.gov/.
General Information: No sealed, adoptions, youthful offenders or juvenile records released. Will not fax documents. Court makes copy: $5.00 for 1st 20 pages then $.50 each add'l. Certification fee: $5.00 per cert. Payee: Clerk of Court. Business checks accepted. Visa/MC accepted for traffic. Prepayment required.

Covington County

Circuit & District Court Covington County Courthouse, Andalusia, AL 36420; 334-428-2520; probate phone: 334-428-2510; fax: 334-428-2531; 8AM-5PM. ***Felony, Misdemeanor, Civil, Eviction, Small Claims, Probate.***
Probate court is separate from this court; probate telephone number above. For subscription service contact Administrative Office of Courts at 866-954-9411.
Civil Records: Access: Online, in person. Both court and visitors may perform in person searches. No search fee, only copy fees apply. Required to search: name, years to search. Civil cases indexed by defendant, plaintiff, on computer from 3/94; prior on books to 1920. Civil PAT goes back to 1994. The state court system offers various pay plans at www.alacourt.com subscription service; includes civil, DR, traffic, warrants, trial court dockets, and notification features.
Criminal Records: Access: Online, in person. Visitors must perform in person searches themselves. Required to search: name, years to search, DOB; also helpful: SSN. Criminal records computerized from 3/94; prior on books to 1920. Criminal PAT goes back to same as civil. Access via various sub plans at www.alacourt.com court subscription service, with notification features. Also, access the state ACJIC system with sub and $25.00 pay-per-name search at http://background.alabama.gov/.
General Information: No sealed, adoptions, youthful offenders or juvenile records released. Will not fax documents. Court makes copy: $5.00 for 1st 20 pages then $.50 each add'l, self serve same. Certification fee: $5.00 per cert. Payee: Circuit Clerk. Business checks accepted. No credit cards. Prepayment required.

Crenshaw County

Circuit & District Court PO Box 167, Luverne, AL 36049; 334-335-6575; probate phone: 334-335-6568; fax: 334-335-2076; 8AM-4:30PM. ***Felony, Misdemeanor, Civil, Eviction, Small Claims, Probate.***
Probate court is separate from this court and can be contacted at the telephone number above. Probate address is PO Box 328, Luverne, 36049.
Civil Records: Access: Mail, in person, online. Only the court performs in person searches; visitors may not. No search fee. Required to search: name, years to search. Civil cases indexed by defendant, plaintiff, on computer from 1993, on book from 1977. Mail turnaround time 2-3 days. Civil PAT goes back to 1993. PAT civil results show middle initial. The state court system offers various pay plans at www.alacourt.com subscription service; includes civil, DR, traffic, warrants, trial court dockets, and notification features.
Criminal Records: Access: Mail, online, in person. Only the court performs in person searches; visitors may not. No search fee. Required to search: name, years to search, DOB; also helpful: SSN. Criminal records computerized from 1993, on book from 1977. Mail turnaround time 2-3 days. Criminal PAT available.PAT results show name, DOB. Terminal results include SSN. Access via various sub plans at www.alacourt.com court subscription service, with notification features. Also, access the state ACJIC system with sub and $25.00 pay-per-name search at http://background.alabama.gov/. Online results show name, DOB. Terminal results include SSN.
General Information: No sealed, adoptions, youthful offenders or juvenile records released. Will fax documents. Court makes copy: $5.00 for 1st 20 pages then $.50 each add'l, self serve same. Certification fee: $1.00. Payee: Circuit Clerk. Only cashiers checks and money orders accepted. No credit cards accepted. Prepayment required. Mail requests: SASE requested.

Cullman County

Circuit Court Cullman County Courthouse, Rm 303, 500 2nd Ave SW, Cullman, AL 35055; 256-775-4654; criminal phone: 256-775-4799; civil phone: 256-775-4800; probate: 256-775-4652; 8AM-4:30. ***Felony, Civil Actions over $10,000, Probate.***
Civil Records: Access: Phone, mail, online, in person. Both court and visitors may perform in person searches. Search fee: Search fee for computerized search-$10.00; paper record search-$20.00; archived record search-$25.00. Required to search: name, years to search. Civil cases indexed by defendant, plaintiff, on computer back to 1993, index back to 1977; books from 1900s. Mail turnaround time 10 days. Civil PAT goes back to 1977. Public terminal has indices only. The state court system offers various pay plans at www.alacourt.com subscription service; includes civil, DR, traffic, warrants, trial dockets, and notification features.
Criminal Records: Access: Mail, online, in person. Both court and visitors may perform in person searches. Search fee: Search fee for computerized search-$10.00; paper record search-$20.00; archived record search-$25.00. Required to search: name, years to search, DOB; also helpful: SSN. Criminal records computerized from 1993; index back to 1977; prior in books. Mail turnaround time 10 days. Criminal PAT goes back to same as civil. Public terminal has indices only. Access via various sub plans at www.alacourt.com court subscription service, with notification features. Also, access the state ACJIC system with sub and $25.00 pay-per-name search at http://background.alabama.gov/.
General Information: No sealed, adoptions, youthful offenders or juvenile records released. Will not fax documents. Court makes copy: $5.00 for 1st 20 pages then $.50 each add'l, self serve same. Certification fee: $5.00 per doc. Payee: Robert Bates, Circuit Clerk. Business checks accepted. No credit cards accepted. Prepayment required. Mail requests: SASE required.

District Court 500 2nd Ave SW, Courthouse Rm 211, Cullman, AL 35055-4197; 256-775-4660; 8AM-4:30PM. ***Misdemeanor, Civil Actions under $10,000, Eviction, Small Claims.***
http://32jc.alacourt.gov/clerk/home.aspx
Civil Records: Access: Mail, in person, online. Both court and visitors may perform in person searches. Search fee: $10.00 for computer search; $20.00 paper search; $25.00 to search archives. Required to search: name, years to search. Civil cases indexed by defendant. Civil records on computer from 11/92, on books 10 yrs back. Mail turnaround time 1 week. Civil PAT goes back to 1992. The state court system offers various pay plans at www.alacourt.com subscription service; includes civil, DR, traffic, warrants, trial court dockets, and notification features.
Criminal Records: Access: Mail, online, in person. Both court and visitors may perform in person searches. Search fee: $10.00 for computer search; $20.00 paper search; $25.00 to search archives. Required to search: name, years to search, DOB; also helpful: SSN. Criminal records computerized from 11/92, on books 10 yrs back. Mail turnaround time 1 week. Criminal PAT goes back to same as civil. Access via various sub plans at www.alacourt.com court subscription service, with notification features. Also, access the state ACJIC system with sub and $25.00 pay-per-name search at http://background.alabama.gov/.
General Information: No sealed, adoptions, youthful offenders or juvenile records released. Will not fax documents. Court makes copy: $5.00 for 1st 20 pages then $.50 each add'l. Self serve: $.50 per page. Certification fee: $5.00 per cert. Payee: District Clerk. Only cashiers checks and money orders accepted. No credit cards accepted. Prepayment required. Mail requests: SASE required.

Dale County

Circuit & District Court PO Box 1350, Ozark, AL 36361; 334-774-5003; probate phone: 334-774-2754; 8AM-4:30PM. ***Felony, Misdemeanor, Civil, Eviction, Small Claims, Probate.***
Probate court is separate from this court; probate phone number above.
Civil Records: Access: Online, in person. Visitors must perform in person searches themselves. Required to search: name, years to search. Civil cases indexed by defendant, plaintiff, on computer from 8/92, on books and index cards from the 1920s. Civil PAT goes back to 1994. The state court system offers various pay plans at www.alacourt.com subscription service; includes civil, DR, traffic, warrants, trial dockets, and notification features.
Criminal Records: Access: Online, in person. Visitors must perform in person searches themselves. Required to search: name, years to search, DOB; also helpful: SSN. Criminal records computerized from 8/92, on books and index cards

from the 1920s. Criminal PAT goes back to same as civil. Access via various sub plans at www.alacourt.com court subscription service, with notification features. Also, access the state ACJIC system with sub and $25.00 pay-per-name search at http://background.alabama.gov/.

General Information: No sealed, adoptions, youthful offenders or juvenile records released. Will not fax documents. Court makes copy: $5.00 for 1st 20 pages then $.50 each add'l. Certification fee: $5.00 per page. Payee: Dale County Circuit Clerk. Only cashiers checks and money orders accepted. No credit cards accepted. Prepayment required.

Dallas County

Circuit Court PO Box 1148, Selma, AL 36702; 334-874-2523; criminal phone: x3; civil phone: x6; probate phone: 334-874-2500; 8AM-4:30PM. ***Felony, Civil Actions over $10,000, Probate.***
Probate court is separate from this court.

Civil Records: Access: Mail, in person, online. Both court and visitors may perform in person searches. No search fee. Required to search: name, years to search. Civil cases indexed by defendant, plaintiff, on computer from 1980, on microfiche from the late 1800s, index books prior. Mail turnaround time less than 1 week for civil cases. Civil PAT goes back to 1992. Public terminal may not include recent activity. The state court system offers various pay plans at www.alacourt.com subscription service; includes civil, DR, traffic, warrants, trial court dockets, and notification features.

Criminal Records: Access: Phone, mail, online, in person. Both court and visitors may perform in person searches. No search fee. Required to search: name, years to search, DOB; also helpful: SSN. Criminal records computerized from 1980, on microfiche from the late 1800s, index books prior. Mail turnaround time less than 1 week. Criminal PAT goes back to same as civil. Public terminal may not include recent activity. Access via various sub plans at www.alacourt.com court subscription service, with notification features. Also, access the state ACJIC system with sub and $25.00 pay-per-name search at http://background.alabama.gov/.

General Information: No sealed, adoptions, youthful offenders or juvenile records released. Will fax documents to local or toll-free number if not a lot of pages. Court makes copy: $5.00 for 1st 20 pages then $.50 each add'l. Self serve: $.10 per page. Certification fee: $1.00 per file. Payee: County Circuit Court. Personal checks accepted; credit cards are not. Prepayment required. Mail requests: SASE required.

District Court PO Box 1148, 105 Lauderdale (36701), Selma, AL 36702; 334-874-2523; fax: 334-877-0637; 9AM-4PM. ***Misdemeanor, Civil Actions under $10,000, Eviction, Small Claims.*** Probate court is separate from this court and can be reached at 334-874-2500. Traffic division phone-877-252-7294.

Civil Records: Access: Phone, mail, online, in person. Visitors must perform in person searches themselves. No search fee. Required to search: name, years to search. Civil cases indexed by defendant. Civil records on books from 1967, on computer since 1993. Civil PAT goes back to 1993. The state court system offers various pay plans at www.alacourt.com subscription service; includes civil, DR, traffic, warrants, trial court dockets, and notification features.

Criminal Records: Access: Mail, online, in person. Visitors must perform in person searches themselves. No search fee. Required to search: name, years to search; also helpful: DOB, SSN. Criminal docket on books from 1967, on computer since 1992. Mail turnaround time- varies. Criminal PAT goes back to same as civil. Access via various sub plans at www.alacourt.com court subscription service, with notification features. Also, access the state ACJIC system with sub and $25.00 pay-per-name search at http://background.alabama.gov/.

General Information: No sealed, adoptions, youthful offenders or juvenile records released. Will fax documents to local or toll-free number. Court makes copy: $5.00 for 1st 20 pages then $.50 each add'l, self serve same. Certification fee: $1.50 per cert. Payee: Circuit Clerk. Cashiers checks and money orders only. No credit cards accepted. Prepayment required. Mail requests: SASE required.

De Kalb County

Circuit & District Court PO Box 681149, Fort Payne, AL 35968; 256-845-8525; probate phone: 256-845-8510; fax: 256-845-8535; 8AM-4PM. ***Felony, Misdemeanor, Civil, Eviction, Small Claims, Probate.*** Probate court is separate from this court; probate phone number above.

Civil Records: Access: Mail, in person, online. Both court and visitors may perform in person searches. Search fee: $10.00 for a computer search, $20.00 for a paper search, and $25.00 if archival. Required to search: name, years to search. Civil cases indexed by defendant. Civil records on computer from 8/1993, on books from 1959. Mail turnaround time 1 week. Civil PAT goes back to 1993. The state court system offers various pay plans at www.alacourt.com subscription service; includes civil, DR, traffic, warrants, trial court dockets, and notification features.

Criminal Records: Access: Mail, online, in person. Both court and visitors may perform in person searches. Search fee: $10.00 for a computer search, $20.00 for a paper search, and $25.00 if archival. Required to search: name, years to search; also helpful: DOB, SSN. Criminal records computerized from 8/1993, on books from 1959. Mail turnaround time 1 week. Criminal PAT goes back to same as civil. Access via various sub plans at www.alacourt.com court subscription service, with notification features. Also, access the state ACJIC system with sub and $25.00 pay-per-name search at http://background.alabama.gov/.

General Information: No sealed, adoptions, youthful offenders or juvenile records released. Court makes copy: $5.00 for 1st 20 pages then $.50 each add'l. Certification fee: $5.00 per doc. Payee: Circuit Clerk. Business checks accepted. No credit cards accepted. Prepayment required.

Elmore County

Circuit & District Court - Civil Division PO Box 310, 8925 Hiway 213, Judicial Complex, Wetumpka, AL 36092; 334-514-4222; probate phone: 334-567-1139; fax: 334-567-5957; 8AM-4:30PM. ***Civil, Probate.***
Probate court is separate from this court but can be contacted at the telephone number above.

Civil Records: Access: Mail, in person, online. Visitors must perform in person searches themselves. Search fee: $10.00 per name for computer search; $25.00 per name if archives search is required. Required to search: name, years to search. Civil cases indexed by defendant, plaintiff, on computer from 1991, books from 1930. Mail turnaround time varies. Public use terminal has civil records back to 1991. The state court system offers various pay plans at www.alacourt.com subscription service; includes civil, DR, traffic, warrants, trial dockets, and notification features.

General Information: No sealed, adoptions, youthful offenders or juvenile records released. Will not fax out documents. Court makes copy: $5.00 for 1st 20 pages then $.50 each add'l, self serve same. Certification fee: $5.00 per doc. Payee: Circuit Court Clerk. Business checks accepted. Prepayment required.

Circuit Court - Criminal Division PO Box 310, 8935 US Hwy 23, Wetumpka, AL 36092; 334-514-4221; fax: 334-567-5957; 8AM-4:30PM. ***Felony, Misdemeanor.***

Criminal Records: Access: In person, online. Both court and visitors may perform in person searches. Search fee: Computerr check- $10.00 each; paper search $20.00; closed case search- $25.00. Required to search: name, years to search, DOB, SSN. Criminal records computerized from mid-1991, books from 1960-1992. Access via various sub plans at www.alacourt.com court subscription service, with notification features. Also, access the state ACJIC system with sub and $25.00 pay-per-name search at http://background.alabama.gov/.

General Information: No sealed, adoptions, youthful offenders or juvenile records released. Will not fax documents. Court makes copy: $5.00 for 1st 20 pages then $.50 each add'l, self serve same. Certification fee: $5.00 per cert. Payee: Circuit Court Clerk. Only cashiers checks and money orders accepted. Prepayment required. Mail requests: SASE required; use their form.

Escambia County

Circuit & District Court PO Box 856, Brewton, AL 36427; 251-867-0305; criminal phone: 251-867-0220; civil phone: 251-867-0285; probate phone: 251-867-0201; criminal fax: 251-867-0365; civil fax: same; 8AM-4PM. ***Felony, Misdemeanor, Civil, Eviction, Small Claims, Probate.***
Probate court has separate mailing address: PO Box 557. Probate fax- 251-867-0284

Civil Records: Access: Mail, fax, online, in person. Both court and visitors may perform in person searches. Search fee: $10.00 per name. Required to search: name, years to search. Civil cases indexed by defendant, plaintiff, on computer from 10/93, books and cards back to 1990. Mail turnaround time 10-14 days. Civil PAT goes back to 10/1993. The state court system offers various pay plans at www.alacourt.com subscription service; includes civil, DR, traffic, warrants, trial court dockets, and notification features.

Criminal Records: Access: Mail, fax, online, in person. Both court and visitors may perform in person searches. Search fee: $10.00 per name. Required to search: name, years to search, DOB. Criminal records computerized from 10/93, books and cards back to 1950. Mail turnaround time 10-14 days. Criminal PAT goes back to same as civil. Access via various sub plans at www.alacourt.com court subscription service, with notification features. Also, access the state ACJIC system with sub and $25.00 pay-per-name search at http://background.alabama.gov/.

General Information: No sealed, adoptions, youthful offenders or juvenile records released. Fee to fax document $1.00 each plus $.25 per page. Court makes copy: $5.00 for 1st 20 pages then $.50 each add'l, self serve same. Certification fee: $5.00 per doc. Payee: Escambia County Circuit Court. Business checks accepted. No credit cards accepted. Prepayment required. Mail requests: SASE required.

Etowah County

Circuit & District Court 801 Forrest Ave #202, Gadsden, AL 35901; 256-549-2150; criminal phone: 256-549-5437; probate phone: 256-549-5333; 8:30AM-5PM. ***Felony, Misdemeanor, Civil, Eviction, Small Claims.***
Probate court is separate from this court.

Civil Records: Access: Mail, in person, online. Both court and visitors may perform in person searches. Search fee: $10.00 for computerized records; $20.00 for paper records; $25.00 for archived/microfilmed records. Required to search: name, years to search. Civil cases indexed by defendant, plaintiff, on computer from 1984, index on computer since 1977, books prior to 1977. Mail turnaround time 4-6 weeks. Civil PAT goes back to 1984. PAT results show name only. The state court system offers various pay plans at www.alacourt.com subscription service; includes civil, DR, traffic, warrants, trial dockets, and notification features.

Criminal Records: Access: Mail, online, in person. Both court and visitors may perform in person searches. Search fee: $10.00 for computerized records; $20.00 for paper records; $25.00 for archived/microfilmed records. Required to search: name, years to search; also helpful: DOB, SSN. Criminal records computerized from 1984, index on computer since 1977, books prior to 1977. Mail turnaround time 4-6 weeks. Criminal PAT goes back to 1984. PAT results show middle initial, DOB, SSN. Access via various sub plans at www.alacourt.com court subscription service, with notification features. Also, access the state ACJIC system with sub and $25.00 pay-per-name search at http://background.alabama.gov/.

General Information: No sealed, adoptions, youthful offenders or juvenile records released. Will not fax documents. Court makes copy: $5.00 for 1st 20 pages then $.50 each add'l. Self serve: $.15 per page. Certification fee: $5.00 per doc. Payee: Clerk of Court. Only cashiers checks and money orders accepted. Visa/MC accepted. Prepayment required. Mail requests: SASE requested.

Probate Court 800 Forest Ave, #122, PO Box 187, Gadsden, AL 35901; 256-549-5340, 256-549-5341; fax: 256-546-1149; 8AM-5PM. ***Probate.***

Fayette County

Circuit & District Court PO Box 906, 113 N Temple Ave, Fayette, AL 35555; 205-932-4617; probate phone: 205-932-4519; criminal fax: 205-932-2697; civil fax: same; 8AM-4:30PM. ***Felony, Misdemeanor, Civil, Eviction, Small Claims, Probate.*** Probate court is separate from this court; mail to Probate at POBox 670. Pro, fax-205-932-7600

Civil Records: Access: Online, mail, fax, in person. Visitors must perform in person searches themselves. Search fee: $20.00 per name. Required to search: name, years to search. Civil cases indexed by defendant. Civil records on computer from 3/94, on books and cards from 1977. Civil PAT goes back to 1994. PAT results show name only. The state court system offers various pay plans at www.alacourt.com subscription service; includes civil, DR, traffic, warrants, trial court dockets, and notification features.

Criminal Records: Access: Online, mail, fax, in person. Visitors must perform in person searches themselves. Search fee: $20.00 per name. Required to search: name, years to search, DOB; also helpful: SSN. Criminal records computerized from 3/94, on books and cards from 1977. Criminal PAT goes back to same as civil. PAT results show middle initial, DOB. Terminal results include SSN. Access via various sub plans at www.alacourt.com court subscription service, with notification features. Also, access the state ACJIC system with sub and $25.00 pay-per-name search at http://background.alabama.gov/. Online results show middle initial, DOB. Terminal results include SSN.

General Information: No sealed, youthful offenders or juvenile records released. Will fax documents $.25 per page. Court makes copy: $5.00 for 1st 20 pages then $.50 each add'l, self serve same. Certification fee: $5.00 per page. Payee: Circuit Clerk. Business checks accepted, but no credit cards. Prepayment required.

Franklin County

Circuit & District Court PO Box 160, 410 N Jackson Ave, Russellville, AL 35653; 256-332-8861; probate: 256-332-8802; 8AM-5PM. ***Felony, Misdemeanor, Civil, Eviction, Small Claims, Probate.***

Probate court is separate and can be contacted at the telephone number above or PO Box 70.

Civil Records: Access: Mail, in person, online. Both court and visitors may perform in person searches. Search fee: $10.00 per name per index. Required to search: name, years to search; also helpful: address. Civil cases indexed by defendant, plaintiff, on computer from 1993, on index books prior. SSN and DOB helpful, but records are not indexed by SSN. Mail turnaround time 5-7 days. Civil PAT goes back to 1993. PAT results show name only. The state court system offers various pay plans at www.alacourt.com subscription service; includes civil, DR, traffic, warrants, trial court dockets, and notification features.

Criminal Records: Access: Mail, online, in person. Both court and visitors may perform in person searches. Search fee: $10.00 per name per index. Required to search: name, years to search, DOB; also helpful: SSN. Criminal records computerized from 1993, on index books prior. SSN and DOB helpful, but records are not indexed by SSN. Mail turnaround time 5-7 days. Criminal PAT goes back to same as civil. PAT results show name only. Access via various sub plans at www.alacourt.com court subscription service, with notification features. Also, access state ACJIC with sub and $25.00 pay-per-name search http://background.alabama.gov/.

General Information: No sealed, youthful offenders or juvenile released. Court makes copy: $5.00 for 1st 20 pages then $.50 each add'l, self serve same. Certification fee: $5.00. Payee: Circuit Court Clerk. Business checks accepted. No credit cards accepted. Prepayment required. Mail requests: SASE required.

Geneva County

Circuit & District Court PO Box 86, 200 N Commerce, Geneva, AL 36340; 334-684-5620; probate phone: 334-684-5640; fax: 334-684-5605; 8AM-5PM. ***Felony, Misdemeanor, Civil, Eviction, Small Claims, Probate.***

Probate court and records are separate form this court, but at this same general address.

Civil Records: Access: Online, in person. Visitors must perform in person searches themselves. Required to search: name, years to search; also helpful: address. Civil cases indexed by defendant, plaintiff, on computer from 1992. Civil PAT goes back to 1992. The state court system offers various pay plans at www.alacourt.com subscription service; includes civil, DR, traffic, warrants, trial court dockets, and notification features.

Criminal Records: Access: Online, in person. Visitors must perform in person searches themselves. Required to search: name, years to search, DOB; also helpful: SSN. Criminal records computerized from 1992. Criminal PAT goes back to same as civil.PAT results show name, DOB. Terminal results include SSN. Access via various sub plans at www.alacourt.com court subscription service, with notification features. Also, access the state ACJIC system with sub and $25.00 pay-per-name search at http://background.alabama.gov/.

General Information: Online identifiers in results same as on public terminal. No sealed, adoptions, youthful offenders or juvenile records released. Will not fax documents. Court makes copy: $5.00 for 1st 20 pages then $.50 each add'l, self serve same. Certification fee: $5.00 per case. Payee: Circuit Clerk. Business checks accepted. Out of state personal checks not accepted. No credit cards accepted. Prepayment required.

Greene County

Circuit & District Court PO Box 307, Eutaw, AL 35462; 205-372-3598; probate phone: 205-372-3340; criminal fax: 205-372-1510; civil fax: same; 8AM-N. 1-4:30PM. ***Felony, Misdemeanor, Civil, Eviction, Small Claims, Probate.***

Probate is a separate court.

Civil Records: Access: Mail, in person, online. Both court and visitors may perform in person searches. Search fee: $25.00 per name; $10.00 if computer only search. Required to search: name, years to search; also helpful: DOB, SSN and signed release. Civil cases indexed by defendant, plaintiff, on books from 1984. Mail turnaround time 1 week. Civil PAT goes back to 1993. PAT results show middle initial, DOB. Terminal results also show SSNs. The state court system offers various pay plans at www.alacourt.com subscription service; includes civil, DR, traffic, warrants, trial court dockets, and notification features.

Criminal Records: Access: Mail, online, in person. Visitors must perform in person searches themselves. Search fee: $25.00 per name; $10.00 if computer only search. Required to search: name, years to search; also helpful: DOB, SSN and signed release. Criminal docket on books from 1984. Mail turnaround time 1 week. Criminal PAT goes back to same as civil. PAT results show middle initial, DOB. Terminal results include SSN. Access via various sub plans at www.alacourt.com court subscription service, with notification features. Also, access state ACJIC with sub and $25.00 pay-per-name search http://background.alabama.gov/. Online results show middle initial, DOB. Terminal results include SSN.

General Information: Online identifiers in results same as on public terminal. No sealed, adoptions, youthful offenders or juvenile records released. Will fax documents. Court makes copy: $5.00 for 1st 20 pages then $.50 each add'l, self serve same. Certification fee: $1.00 per page. Payee: Circuit Clerk. Business checks accepted. No credit cards accepted. Prepayment required. Mail requests: SASE required.

Hale County

Circuit & District Court Hale County Courthouse, Rm 8, PO Drawer 99, Greensboro, AL 36744; 334-624-4334; probate phone: 334-624-8740; fax: 334-624-8064; 8AM-4:30PM. ***Felony, Misdemeanor, Civil, Eviction, Small Claims, Probate.*** Search fee includes both civil and criminal indexes. Public access terminal is no longer available. Probate court is separate from this court; probate phone number above.

Civil Records: Access: Mail, in person, online. Both court and visitors may perform in person searches. Search fee: $10.00 per name. Required to search: name, years to search. Civil cases indexed by defendant, plaintiff, on books from 1985. Mail turnaround time 1 week. The state court system offers various pay plans at www.alacourt.com subscription service; includes civil, DR, traffic, warrants, trial dockets, and notification features.

Criminal Records: Access: Mail, online, in person. Both court and visitors may perform in person searches. No search fee. Required to search: name, years to search; also helpful: DOB, SSN. Criminal docket on books from 1985. Mail turnaround time 1 week. Access via various sub plans at www.alacourt.com court subscription service, with notification features. Also, access the state ACJIC system with sub and $25.00 pay-per-name search at http://background.alabama.gov/.

General Information: No sealed, adoptions, youthful offenders or juvenile records released. Will fax documents to local and toll free numbers. Court makes copy: $5.00 for 1st 20 pages then $.50 each add'l. Certification fee: $5.00 per cert. Payee: Clerk of the Court. Business checks accepted but not personal checks. No credit cards accepted. Prepayment required. Mail requests: SASE required.

Henry County

Circuit & District Court 101 Court Square, Ste. J, Abbeville, AL 36310-2135; 334-585-2753; probate phone: 334-585-3257; fax: 334-585-5006; 8AM-4:30PM. ***Felony, Misdemeanor, Civil, Eviction, Small Claims, Probate.***

Probate court is separate from this court; probate phone number above.

Civil Records: Access: Mail, in person, online. Only the court performs in person searches; visitors may not. Search fee: $5.00 per name. There is a 30 minute or 5 name limit per order. Required to search: name, years to search. Civil cases indexed by defendant. Civil records on computer from 1994, index cards 10 yrs back. Mail turnaround time 2-3 days. Civil PAT goes back to 1994. PAT civil results show middle initial. The state court system offers various pay plans at www.alacourt.com subscription service; includes civil, DR, traffic, warrants, trial court dockets, and notification features.

Criminal Records: Access: Mail, online, in person. Only the court performs in person searches; visitors may not. Search fee: $5.00 per name. There is a 30 minute or 5 name limit per order. Required to search: name, years to search, DOB; also helpful: SSN. Criminal records computerized from 5/93, index cards 10 yrs back. Mail turnaround time 2-3 days. Criminal PAT goes back to 1993. PAT criminal results show middle initial. Access via various sub plans at www.alacourt.com court subscription service, with notification features. Also, access the state ACJIC system with sub and $25.00 pay-per-name search at http://background.alabama.gov/.

General Information: No sealed, adoptions, youthful offenders or juvenile records released. Court makes copy: $5.00 for 1st 20 pages then $.50 each add'l, self serve same. Certification fee: $5.00 per cert. Payee: Circuit Clerk. No personal checks or credit cards accepted. Prepayment required. Mail requests: SASE required.

Houston County

Circuit & District Court PO Drawer 6406, Dothan, AL 36302; 334-677-4800; criminal phone: Circ-334-677-4858; Dist-334-677-4872; civil phone: Circ-334-677-4859; Dist-334-677-4868; 7:30AM-4:30PM. ***Felony, Misdemeanor, Civil, Eviction, Small Claims, Probate.***

Probate court is separate from this court; probate phone number above. Probate fax- 334-702-0032

Civil Records: Access: Mail, in person, online. Both court and visitors may perform in person searches. No search fee. Required to search: name, years to search. Civil cases indexed by defendant. Civil

records on computer from 1977, index books from 1950s. Civil PAT goes back to 1978. The state court system offers various pay plans at www.alacourt.com subscription service; includes civil, DR, traffic, warrants, trial court dockets, and notification features.
Criminal Records: Access: Mail, online, in person. Both court and visitors may perform in person searches. No search fee. Required to search: name, years to search; also helpful: DOB, SSN. Criminal records computerized from 1977, index books from 1950s. Criminal PAT goes back to 1977. Access via various sub plans at www.alacourt.com court subscription service, with notification features. Also, access the state ACJIC system with sub and $25.00 pay-per-name search at http://background.alabama.gov/.
General Information: No sealed, adoptions, youthful offenders or juvenile records released. Will not fax documents. Court makes copy: $5.00 for 1st 20 pages then $.50 each add'l. Certification fee: $5.00. Payee: Carla Woodall. No personal checks or credit cards accepted. Prepayment required.

Jackson County

Circuit & District Court PO Box 397, 102 E Laurel St, Courthouse, Scottsboro, AL 35768; 256-574-9320; criminal: 256-574-9320; civil phone: 256-574-9320; probate phone: 256-574-9290; fax: 256-259-9981; 8AM-4:30PM. ***Felony, Misdemeanor, Civil, Eviction, Small Claims, Probate.***
Search fee includes both civil and criminal indexes. Also, probate court is at a separate office here (PO Box 128); contact probate at the phone number above or 256-574-9295. Probate fax- 256-574-9318.
Civil Records: Access: Mail, fax, online, in person. Both court and visitors may perform in person searches. Search fee: $10.00 database search; $15.00 if manual index or archives. Add'l fees is search exceeds 30 minutes. Required to search: name, years to search. Civil cases indexed by defendant. Civil records on computer from 5/1993, on cards from 1977. Mail turnaround time 1-3 weeks. Civil PAT goes back to 1993. The state court system offers various pay plans at www.alacourt.com subscription service; includes civil, DR, traffic, warrants, trial dockets, and notification features.
Criminal Records: Access: Mail, fax, online, in person. Both court and visitors may perform in person searches. Search fee: $10.00 database search; $15.00 if manual index or archives. Add'l fees is search exceeds 30 minutes. Required to search: name, years to search, DOB; also helpful: SSN. Criminal records computerized from 5/1993, on cards from 1977. Mail turnaround time 1-2 weeks. Criminal PAT goes back to 1993. Access via various sub plans at www.alacourt.com court subscription service, with notification features. Also, access the state ACJIC system with sub and $25.00 pay-per-name search at http://background.alabama.gov/.
General Information: No sealed, adoptions, youthful offenders or juvenile records released. Will fax documents only if situation urgent enough to require quick return. Court makes copy: $5.00 for 1st 20 pages then $.50 each add'l. Self serve: $.50 per page. Certification fee: $5.00 per case. Payee: Circuit Court Clerk. In-state personal checks accepted. No credit cards accepted. Prepayment required. Mail requests: SASE required.

Jefferson County

Circuit Court - Bessemer Division Rm 606, Courthouse Annex, 1801 Third Ave N, Bessemer, AL 35020; 205-481-4165; 8AM-Noon; 1PM-5PM. ***Felony, Civil Actions over $10,000.***
Civil Records: Access: Online, in person. Visitors must perform in person searches themselves. Required to search: name, years to search. Civil cases indexed by defendant, plaintiff, on computer from 1988, on index books from 1930s to 1977. Civil PAT goes back to 1985. The state court system offers various pay plans at www.alacourt.com subscription service; includes civil, DR, traffic, warrants, trial dockets, and notification features.
Criminal Records: Access: Online, in person. Visitors must perform in person searches themselves. Required to search: name, years to search, DOB; also helpful: SSN. Criminal records computerized from 1988, on index books from 1930s to 1977. Criminal PAT goes back to same as civil. PAT results show name, DOB, SSN. Access via various sub plans at www.alacourt.com court subscription service, with notification features. Also, access the state ACJIC system with sub and $25.00 pay-per-name search at http://background.alabama.gov/.
General Information: Online identifiers in results same as on public terminal. No sealed, adoptions, youthful offenders or juvenile records released. Will not fax documents. Court makes copy: $5.00 for 1st 20 pages then $.50 each add'l. Self serve: $.10 per page. Certification fee: $5.00 per case. Payee: Clerk of Circuit Court. Only cashiers checks and money orders accepted; no credit cards. Prepayment required.

District Court - Bessemer Division Rm 506, Courthouse Annex, 1801 Third Ave N, Bessemer, AL 35020; 205-481-4187; probate phone: 205-481-4100; 8AM-5PM. ***Felony, Misdemeanor, Civil Actions under $10,000, Eviction, Small Claims, Traffic.***
Civil Records: Access: Online, in person. Visitors must perform in person searches themselves. Required to search: name, years to search. Civil cases indexed by defendant, plaintiff, on computer from 1986, on index cards from 1977, prior on docket books. Civil PAT goes back to 1995. The state court system offers various pay plans at www.alacourt.com subscription service; includes civil, DR, traffic, warrants, trial court dockets, and notification features.
Criminal Records: Access: Online, in person, mail. Visitors must perform in person searches themselves. Search fee: $25.00 per name. Required to search: name, years to search, DOB; also helpful: SSN. Criminal records computerized from 1986, on index cards from 1977, prior on docket books. Mail turnaround time varies. Criminal PAT goes back to same as civil. PAT results show name, DOB, SSN. Access via various sub plans at www.alacourt.com court subscription service, with notification features. Also, access the state ACJIC system with sub and $25.00 pay-per-name search at http://background.alabama.gov/.
General Information: No sealed, adoptions, youthful offenders or juvenile records released. Will not fax documents. Court makes copy: $5.00 for 1st 20 pages then $.50 each add'l, self serve same. Certification fee: $5.00 per cert. Payee: Bessemer District Court. Business checks accepted; no personal checks. No credit cards accepted. Prepayment required.

Circuit Court - Birmingham Civil Division 716 Richard Arrington Blvd N, Rm 400, Birmingham, AL 35263; 205-325-5355; 8AM-5PM. ***Civil Actions over $10,000.***
SM & DV- 325-5331.
Civil Records: Access: Phone, mail, online, in person. Both court and visitors may perform in person searches. Search fee: $25.00 per search. Required to search: name, years to search. Civil cases indexed by defendant, plaintiff, on computer from 1976, on index books from 1976 to 1986, prior to 1976 archived. Mail turnaround time 1-2 weeks. Public use terminal has civil records back to 1976. The state court system offers various pay plans at www.alacourt.com subscription service; includes civil, DR, traffic, warrants, trial court dockets, and notification features.
General Information: No sealed, adoptions, youthful offenders or juvenile records released. Will not fax documents. Court makes copy: $5.00 for 1st 20 pages then $.50 each add'l. Certification fee: $5.00 per case. Payee: Clerk of Circuit Court. Business checks accepted, no credit cards. Prepayment required.

Circuit Court - Birmingham Criminal Division 801 Richard Arrington Blvd, Rm 901, Birmingham, AL 35203; 205-325-5285; 8AM-4:55PM. ***Felony.***
Criminal Records: Access: Online, in person. Visitors must perform in person searches themselves. Required to search: name, years to search, DOB, signed release; also helpful: address, SSN. Criminal records computerized from 1970, index books prior. Public use terminal has crim records back to 1971. Access via various sub plans at www.alacourt.com court subscription service, with notification features. Also, access the state ACJIC system with sub and $25.00 pay-per-name search at http://background.alabama.gov/.
General Information: No sealed, adoptions, youthful offenders, sex offender cases or juvenile records released. Will not fax documents. Court makes copy: $5.00 for 1st 20 pages then $.50 each add'l. Certification fee: $5.00 per case. Payee: Clerk of Court. Only cashiers checks and money orders accepted. no credit cards. Prepayment required.

District Court - Birmingham Civil Division 716 Richard Arrington Blvd N, Rm 500, Birmingham, AL 35203; 205-325-5331; probate phone: 205-325-5420; 8AM-5PM. ***Civil Actions under $10,000, Eviction, Small Claims.***
Civil Records: Access: Online, in person. Both court and visitors may perform in person searches. No search fee. Required to search: name, years to search. Civil cases indexed by defendant, plaintiff, on computer from 1977, index books stored in warehouse. Public use terminal has civil records back to 1977; also some criminal records. The state court system offers various pay plans at www.alacourt.com subscription service; includes civil, DR, traffic, warrants, trial court dockets, and notification features.
General Information: No sealed, adoptions, youthful offenders or juvenile records released. Will not fax documents. Court makes copy: $5.00 for 1st 20 pages then $.50 each add'l. Certification fee: $5.00 per case. Payee: District Court. No personal checks or credit cards accepted. Prepayment required.

District Court - Birmingham Criminal Division 801 Richard Arrington Blvd N, Rm 207, Birmingham, AL 35203; 205-325-5309; 8AM-5PM. ***Misdemeanor.***
Criminal Records: Access: Mail, online, in person. Both court and visitors may perform in person searches. No search fee. Required to search: name, DOB; also helpful: years to search, SSN, sex, date of arrest. Criminal records computerized from 1986. To search for records prior to 1987, require arrest date. Mail turnaround time 5-10 days. Public use terminal has crim records back to 1986. Access via various sub plans at www.alacourt.com court subscription service, with notification features. Also, access the state ACJIC system with sub and $25.00 pay-per-name search at http://background.alabama.gov/.
General Information: No sealed, sexual abuse, adoptions, youthful offenders or juvenile records released. Will not fax documents. Court makes copy: $5.00 for 1st 20 pages then $.50 each add'l. Certification fee: $5.00 per case. Payee: District Court. Only cashiers checks and money orders accepted. No credit cards accepted. Prepayment required. Mail requests: SASE required.

Probate Court 716 Richard Arrington Jr Blvd N., Birmingham, AL 35203; 205-325-5411; fax: 205-325-4885; 8AM-4:45PM. ***Probate.***

Lamar County

Circuit & District Court PO Box 434, Vernon, AL 35592; 205-695-7193; probate phone: 205-695-9119; fax: 205-695-0046; 8AM-4:30PM. ***Felony, Misdemeanor, Civil, Eviction, Small Claims, Probate.*** Probate court is separate from this court; probate phone number above.
Civil Records: Access: Online, in person. Visitors must perform in person searches themselves. Required to search: name, years to search; also helpful: address. Civil cases indexed by defendant, plaintiff, on books from 1900; computerized records go back to 1995. Civil PAT goes back to 1995. The state court system offers various pay plans at www.alacourt.com subscription service; includes civil, DR, traffic, warrants, trial court dockets, and notification features.
Criminal Records: Access: Online, in person. Visitors must perform in person searches themselves. Required to search: name, years to search, DOB, signed release; also helpful: SSN. Criminal docket on books from 1900; computerized records go back to 1995. Criminal PAT goes back to

1995.PAT results show name, DOB. Terminal results include SSN. Access via various sub plans at www.alacourt.com court subscription service, with notification features. Access the state ACJIC system with sub and $25.00 pay-per-name search at http://background.alabama.gov/. Online results show name, DOB. Terminal results include SSN.
General Information: Online identifiers in results same as on public terminal. No sealed, adoptions, youthful offenders or juvenile records released. Will not fax documents. Court makes copy: $5.00 for 1st 20 pages then $.50 each add'l, self serve same. Certification fee: $5.00. Payee: Circuit Clerk. Only Cashiers checks and money orders and major credit cards accepted. Prepayment required.

Lauderdale County

Circuit Court PO Box 795, Florence, AL 35631; 256-760-5710; criminal phone: 256-760-5713; probate phone: 256-760-5800; fax: 256-760-5727; 8AM-N, 1-5PM. ***Felony, Civil Actions over $10,000, Probate.*** www.alacourt.gov
Probate court is separate from this court; probate phone number above.
Civil Records: Access: Online, in person. Visitors must perform in person searches themselves. Required to search: name, years to search. Civil cases indexed by defendant, plaintiff, on computer from 1977, index books from the 1930s. Civil PAT goes back to 1985. The state court system offers various pay plans at www.alacourt.com subscription service; includes civil, DR, traffic, warrants, trial court dockets, and notification features.
Criminal Records: Access: Online, in person. Visitors must perform in person searches themselves. Required to search: name, years to search, DOB; also helpful: SSN. Criminal records computerized from 1977, index books from the 1930s. Criminal PAT goes back to same as civil. Access via various sub plans at www.alacourt.com court subscription service, with notification features. Also, access the state ACJIC system with sub and $25.00 pay-per-name search at http://background.alabama.gov/.
General Information: No sealed, adoptions, youthful offenders or juvenile records released. Will fax documents to local or toll-free number. Court makes copy: $5.00 for 1st 20 pages then $.50 each add'l, self serve same. Certification fee: $5.00. Payee: Circuit Court Clerk. Personal checks accepted; credit cards are not. Prepayment required.

District Court PO Box 776, Florence, AL 35631; 256-760-5726; criminal phone: 256-760-5724; civil phone: 256-760-5722; fax: 256-760-5727; 8AM-N, 1-5PM. ***Misdemeanor, Civil Actions under $10,000, Eviction, Small Claims.*** www.alacourt.gov
Civil Records: Access: Mail, fax, online, in person. Visitors must perform in person searches themselves. No search fee. Required to search: name, years to search. Civil cases indexed by defendant, plaintiff, on computer from 1986, books from the 1930s. Civil PAT goes back to 1985. The state court system offers various pay plans at www.alacourt.com subscription service; includes civil, DR, traffic, warrants, trial court dockets, and notification features.
Criminal Records: Access: Mail, fax, online, in person. Visitors must perform in person searches themselves. No search fee. Required to search: name, years to search, DOB; also helpful: SSN. Criminal records computerized from 1986, books from the 1930s. Mail turnaround time 1 week. Criminal PAT goes back to same as civil. Access via various sub plans at www.alacourt.com court subscription service, with notification features. Also, access the state ACJIC system with sub and $25.00 pay-per-name search at http://background.alabama.gov/.
General Information: No sealed, adoptions, youthful offenders or juvenile records released. No fee to fax documents. Court makes copy: $5.00 for 1st 20 pages then $.50 each add'l. Certification fee: $5.00. Payee: District Clerk. Personal checks accepted; credit cards are not. Prepayment required. Mail requests: SASE required.

Lawrence County

Circuit & District Court PO Box 249, Moulton, AL 35650; 256-974-2432; criminal phone: 256-974-2436; civil phone: 256-974-2435; probate phone: 256-974-2439; fax: 256-974-1118; 8AM-N, 1-4PM. ***Felony, Misdemeanor, Civil, Eviction, Small Claims, Probate.*** Probate court is separate from this court; probate phone number above.
Civil Records: Access: Online, in person. Visitors must perform in person searches themselves. Required to search: name, years to search. Civil cases indexed by defendant. Civil records on computer from mid-1994, on books and index cards from 1920s. Civil PAT goes back to 1994. The state court system offers various pay plans at www.alacourt.com subscription service; includes civil, DR, traffic, warrants, trial court dockets, and notification features.
Criminal Records: Access: Online, in person. Visitors must perform in person searches themselves. Required to search: name, years to search; also helpful: DOB, SSN. Criminal records computerized from mid-1994, on books and index cards from 1920s. Criminal PAT goes back to same as civil. Access via various sub plans at www.alacourt.com court subscription service, with notification features. Also, access the state ACJIC system with sub and $25.00 pay-per-name search at http://background.alabama.gov/.
General Information: No sealed, adoption, youthful offender, juvenile records released. Will not fax documents. Court makes copy: $5.00 for 1st 20 pages then $.50 each add'l. Certification fee: $1.00 per cert. Payee: Court clerk. No personal checks or credit cards accepted. Prepayment required.

Lee County

Circuit & District Court 2311 Gateway Dr, Rm 104, Opelika, AL 36801; 334-749-7141; fax: 334-737-3520; 8:30AM-4:30PM; no phone svc N-2PM. ***Felony, Misdemeanor, Civil, Eviction, Small Claims.*** Probate court is separate from this court, and can be contacted at 334-745-9761 or at Lee County Courthouse, 215 S 9 St, Opelika, AL 36801.
Civil Records: Access: Phone, mail, online, in person. Only the court performs in person searches; visitors may not. Search fee: $10.00 for computerized check; $20.00 for search of paper records; $25.00 for search of closed cases or otherwise archived records. Required to search: name, years to search. Civil cases indexed by defendant, plaintiff, on computer from 1980s, on index cards from 1988. Mail turnaround time 1 week. The state court system offers various pay plans at www.alacourt.com subscription service; includes civil, DR, traffic, warrants, trial court dockets, and notification features.
Criminal Records: Access: Phone, mail, online, in person. Only the court performs in person searches; visitors may not. Search fee: $10.00 for computerized check; $20.00 for search of paper records; $25.00 for search of closed cases or otherwise archived records. Required to search: name, years to search; also helpful: DOB, SSN. Criminal records computerized from 1980s, on index cards from 1988. Mail turnaround time 1 week. Access via various sub plans at www.alacourt.com court subscription service, with notification features. Also, access the state ACJIC system with sub and $25.00 pay-per-name search at http://background.alabama.gov/.
General Information: No sealed, adoptions, youthful offenders or juvenile records released. Court makes copy: $5.00 for 1st 20 pages then $.50 each add'l. Certification fee: $5.00 per page. Payee: Clerk's Office. Only Cashiers checks and money orders and major credit cards accepted. Prepayment required. Mail requests: SASE required.

Limestone County

Circuit & District Court 200 Washington St West, Athens, AL 35611; 256-233-6406; probate phone: 256-233-6427; 8AM-3:30PM. ***Felony, Misdemeanor, Civil, Eviction, Small Claims, Probate.*** Probate court is separate from this court; probate phone number above.
Civil Records: Access: In person, online. Only the court performs in person searches; visitors may not. No search fee. Required to search: name, years to search. Civil cases indexed by defendant, plaintiff, on computer since 1992; prior in docket books. Civil PAT goes back to 1900. Access by online subscription from alacourt.gov, 866-954-9411.
Criminal Records: Access: In person, online. Only the court performs in person searches; visitors may not. No search fee. Required to search: name, years to search, DOB. Criminal records on computer since 1992, prior in docket books. Note: Office is not staffed to perform full criminal background checks. Criminal PAT available. Access by online subscription from alacourt.gov, 866-954-9411.
General Information: No juvenile, youthful offender records released. Will not fax documents. Court makes copy: $5.00 for 1st 20 pages then $.50 each add'l. Self serve: $.25 per page. Certification fee: $1.00. Payee: Clerk of Court. Personal checks accepted; credit cards are not. Prepayment required.

Lowndes County

Circuit & District Court PO Box 876, 1 Washington St, Hayneville, AL 36040; 334-548-2252; probate phone: 334-548-2365; criminal fax: 334-548-2548; civil fax: same; 8AM-4:30PM. ***Felony, Misdemeanor, Civil, Eviction, Small Claims, Probate.*** Probate court is separate from this court; probate phone number above.
Civil Records: Access: Mail, in person, online. Both court and visitors may perform in person searches. Search fee: $10.00 per name. Required to search: name, years to search. Civil cases indexed by defendant, plaintiff; index on cards from 1977; computerized since 1996. Mail turnaround time up to 1 week. Civil PAT goes back to 1995. The state court system offers various pay plans at www.alacourt.com subscription service; includes civil, DR, traffic, warrants, trial court dockets, and notification features.
Criminal Records: Access: Mail, online, in person. Both court and visitors may perform in person searches. Search fee: $10.00 per name. Required to search: name, years to search; also helpful: DOB, SSN. Criminal records indexed on cards from 1977; computerized since 1996. Mail turnaround time up to 1 week. Criminal PAT goes back to same as civil. Access via various sub plans at www.alacourt.com court subscription service, with notification features. Also, access the state ACJIC system with sub and $25.00 pay-per-name search at http://background.alabama.gov/.
General Information: No sealed, adoptions, youthful offenders or juvenile records released. Will fax documents to local or toll free line. Court makes copy: $5.00 for 1st 20 pages then $.50 each add'l, self serve same. Certification fee: $5.00 per cert. Payee: District Court Clerk. Business checks accepted. Credit cards accepted for criminal searches only. Prepayment required. Mail requests: SASE required.

Macon County

Circuit & District Court PO Box 830723, Tuskegee, AL 36083; 334-724-2614; probate phone: 334-724-2611; fax: 334-727-6483; 8AM-N, 1-4:30PM. ***Felony, Misdemeanor, Civil, Eviction, Small Claims, Probate.***
Probate court is separate from this court; probate phone number above.
Civil Records: Access: Mail, in person, online. Both court and visitors may perform in person searches. Search fee: $10.00 per name. Required to search: name, years to search. Civil cases indexed by defendant, plaintiff; index on docket books from 1977; on computer back to 1993. Mail turnaround time 30 days. The state court system offers various pay plans at www.alacourt.com subscription service; includes civil, DR, traffic, warrants, trial court dockets, and notification features.
Criminal Records: Access: Mail, online, in person. Only the court performs in person searches; visitors may not. Search fee: $10.00 per name. Required to search: name, years to search; also helpful: DOB, SSN. Criminal records go back to 1977; on computer back to 1993. Mail turnaround time 30 days. Access via various sub plans at

www.alacourt.com court subscription service, with notification features. Also, access the state ACJIC system with sub and $25.00 pay-per-name search at http://background.alabama.gov/.
General Information: No sealed, adoption, youthful offender, juvenile records released. Will fax documents to local or toll free line. Court makes copy: $5.00 for 1st 20 pages then $.50 each add'l. Certification fee: $2.50 per page includes copy fee. Payee: Office of Circuit Clerk. Business checks accepted. No credit cards accepted. Prepayment required. SASE not required.

Madison County

Circuit Court - Civil 100 N Side Square, Courthouse, Huntsville, AL 35801; 256-532-3381; probate phone: 256-532-3330; fax: 256-532-3768; 8AM-5PM. ***Civil Actions over $10,000, Probate.***
www.madisoncountycircuitclerk.org
Probate court is separate from this court, and can be contacted at the telephone number above. Records before 1980 are located at Public Library in the Madison County Record Center.
Civil Records: Access: Online, in person. Visitors must perform in person searches themselves. Required to search: name, years to search; also helpful: address. Civil cases indexed by defendant, plaintiff, on computer from 1977, index books from 1937. Public use terminal has civil records back to 1977. PAT results show name only. The state court system offers various pay plans at www.alacourt.com subscription service; includes civil, DR, traffic, warrants, trial court dockets, and notification features.
General Information: No sealed, adoptions, youthful offenders or juvenile records released. Will not fax documents. Court makes copy: $5.00 for 1st 20 pages then $.50 each add'l, self serve same. Certification fee: $5.50 per cert. No personal checks or credit cards accepted. Prepayment required.

Circuit Court - Criminal 100 N Side Square, Courthouse, Huntsville, AL 35801-4820; criminal phone: 256-532-3386; fax: 256-532-3768; 8:30AM-5PM. ***Felony.***
www.madisoncountycircuitclerk.org/
Criminal Records: Access: Online, in person. Visitors must perform in person searches themselves. Required to search: name, years to search; also helpful: DOB, SSN. Criminal records computerized from 1977, books from 1937-1977 (at the Huntsville Public Library, 3rd fl archives, only). Public use terminal has crim records back to 1977.PAT results show name, DOB. SSNs appear less frequently the older the case is. Access via various sub plans at www.alacourt.com court subscription service, with notification features. Also, access the state ACJIC system with sub and $25.00 pay-per-name search at http://background.alabama.gov/. Online results show name, DOB. Criminal search results include personal physical identifiers - race, sex, eye color, height, etc. and SSN.
General Information: No sealed, adoptions, youthful offenders or juvenile records released. Court makes copy: $5.00 for 1st 20 pages then $.50 each add'l, self serve same. Certification fee: $5.00 per cert. Payee: Circuit Court Clerk. No personal checks or credit cards accepted. Prepayment required.

District Court 100 N Side Square, Rm 821 Courthouse, Huntsville, AL 35801; criminal phone: 256-532-3373; civil phone: 256-532-3622; fax: 256-532-6972; 8:30AM-5PM. ***Misdemeanor, Civil Actions under $10,000, Eviction, Small Claims.***
Civil Records: Access: Online, in person. Visitors must perform in person searches themselves. Required to search: name, years to search. Civil cases indexed by defendant, plaintiff, on computer from 1982, index books prior. Civil PAT goes back to 1980. The state court system offers various pay plans at www.alacourt.com subscription service; includes civil, DR, traffic, warrants, trial court dockets, and notification features.
Criminal Records: Access: Online, in person. Visitors must perform in person searches themselves. Required to search: name, years to search; also helpful: DOB, SSN. Criminal records computerized from 1982, index books prior since 1979. Criminal PAT goes back to 1977. Access via various sub plans at www.alacourt.com court subscription service, with notification features. Also, access the state ACJIC system with sub and $25.00 pay-per-name search at http://background.alabama.gov/.
General Information: No sealed, adoptions, youthful offenders or juvenile records released. Will not fax out documents. Court makes copy: $5.00 for 1st 20 pages then $.50 each add'l. Certification fee: $5.50 per cert. Payee: District Court. Only cashiers checks, cash or money orders accepted. Prepayment required.

Marengo County

Circuit & District Court PO Box 480566, 101 E Coats Ave #104, Linden, AL 36748; 334-295-2220; criminal phone: 334-295-2222; civil phone: 334-295-2219; probate: 334-289-4852; fax: 334-295-2092; 8-11AM, 1-4:30PM. ***Felony, Misdemeanor, Civil, Eviction, Small Claims, Probate.***
Civil Records: Access: Mail, in person, online. Both court and visitors may perform in person searches. No search fee. Required to search: name, years to search. Civil cases indexed by defendant, plaintiff, on computer from 6/94, on books and index cards from 1965. Mail turnaround time 1 week. Civil PAT goes back to 1994. The state court system offers various pay plans at www.alacourt.com subscription service; includes civil, DR, traffic, warrants, trial dockets, and notification features.
Criminal Records: Access: Mail, online, in person. Both court and visitors may perform in person searches. No search fee. Required to search: name, years to search; also helpful: DOB, SSN. Criminal records computerized from 6/94, on books and index cards from 1965. Mail turnaround time 1 week. Criminal PAT goes back to same as civil. Access via various sub plans at www.alacourt.com court subscription service, with notification features. Also, access the state ACJIC system with sub and $25.00 pay-per-name search at http://background.alabama.gov/.
General Information: No sealed, adoptions, youthful offenders or juvenile records released. Court makes copy: $5.00 for 1st 20 pages then $.50 each add'l. Self serve: none. Certification fee: $1.00 per page. Payee: Circuit Clerk. Business checks accepted. No personal checks or credit cards accepted. Prepayment required.

Marion County

Circuit & District Court PO Box 1595, 131 Military St, Hamilton, AL 35570; 205-921-7451; probate phone: 205-921-2471; fax: 205-952-9851; 8AM-5PM. ***Felony, Misdemeanor, Civil, Eviction, Small Claims, Probate.***
Probate court is separate from this court; probate phone number above.
Civil Records: Access: Mail, in person, online. Both court and visitors may perform in person searches. No search fee. Required to search: name, years to search. Civil cases indexed by defendant, plaintiff, on computer from 5/94, on books from 1950s. Mail turnaround time 7-10 days. Civil PAT goes back to 1994. PAT results show name, DOB. The state court system offers various pay plans at www.alacourt.com subscription service; includes civil, DR, traffic, warrants, trial court dockets, and notification features.
Criminal Records: Access: Mail, online, in person. Both court and visitors may perform in person searches. No search fee. Required to search: name, years to search; also helpful: DOB, SSN. Criminal records computerized from 5/94, on books from 1950s. Mail turnaround time 7-10 days. Criminal PAT goes back to same as civil.PAT results show name, DOB. Access via various sub plans at www.alacourt.com court subscription service, with notification features. Also, access the state ACJIC system with sub and $25.00 pay-per-name search at http://background.alabama.gov/.
General Information: No sealed, adoptions, youthful offenders or juvenile records released. Will fax documents for no fee. Court makes copy: $5.00 for 1st 20 pages then $.50 each add'l. Self serve: $.25 per page. Certification fee: $1.50. Payee: Circuit Clerk. Only cashiers checks and money orders accepted. No credit cards accepted. Prepayment required. Mail requests: SASE required.

Marshall County

Circuit & District Court - Albertville Division 133 S Emmet St, Albertville, AL 35950; 256-878-4522/4521/4515; criminal phone: 256-878-4522; civil phone: 256-878-4521; probate phone: 256-571-7764; 8AM-4:30PM. ***Felony, Misdemeanor, Civil, Eviction, Small Claims.***
Civil Records: Access: Mail, in person, online. Both court and visitors may perform in person searches. No search fee. Required to search: name, years to search. Civil cases indexed by defendant. Civil records on computer from 8/92, on index books from 1974. Public use terminal has civil records back to 8/1992. The state court system offers various pay plans at www.alacourt.com subscription service; includes civil, DR, traffic, warrants, trial court dockets, and notification features.
Criminal Records: Access: In person, online. Both court and visitors may perform in person searches. No search fee. Required to search: name, years to search, DOB; also helpful: SSN. Criminal records computerized from 8/92, on index books from 1974. Access via various sub plans at www.alacourt.com court subscription service, with notification features. Also, access the state ACJIC system with sub and $25.00 pay-per-name search at http://background.alabama.gov/.
General Information: No sealed, adoptions, youthful offenders or juvenile records released. Will not fax documents. Court makes copy: $5.00 for 1st 20 pages then $.50 each add'l. Self serve: $.12 per page. Certification fee: $5.00 per cert plus court copy fee. Payee: Clerk of Courts. Business checks accepted. No credit cards accepted. Prepayment required.

Circuit Court - Guntersville Civil Division 424 Blount Ave, Ste 201, Guntersville, AL 35976; 256-571-7788; civil phone: 256-571-7785; probate phone: 256-571-7764; 8AM-4:30PM. ***Civil Actions over $10,000, Small Claims, Probate.***
Probate court is separate from this court, and can be contacted at the telephone number above
Civil Records: Access: In person, online. Visitors must perform in person searches themselves. Required to search: name, years to search. Civil cases indexed by defendant, plaintiff, on computer for past 10 years, on index books early 1900s. Public use terminal has civil records back to 1992. The state court system offers various pay plans at www.alacourt.com subscription service; includes civil, DR, traffic, warrants, trial court dockets, and notification features.
General Information: No sealed, adoptions, youthful offenders or juvenile records released. Court makes copy: $5.00 for 1st 20 pages then $.50 each add'l, self serve same. Certification fee: $5.00 per cert. Payee: Circuit Clerk. Business checks accepted. No credit cards accepted. Prepayment required.

Circuit Court - Guntersville Criminal Div. 424 Blount Ave #201, Guntersville, AL 35976; 256-571-7791; 8AM-4:30PM. ***Felony, Misdemeanor.***
Criminal Records: Access: Online, in person. Visitors must perform in person searches themselves. Required to search: name, years to search; also helpful: DOB, SSN. Criminal records computerized from 1992, on index books from 1984, prior back to 1930s. Public use terminal has crim records back to 1992. Access via various sub plans at www.alacourt.com court subscription service, with notification features. Also, access the state ACJIC system with sub and $25.00 pay-per-name search at http://background.alabama.gov/.
General Information: No sealed, adoptions, youthful offenders or juvenile records released. Court makes copy: $5.00 for 1st 20 pages then $.50 each add'l. Certification fee: $5.00 per cert. Payee: Circuit Clerk. Business checks accepted. No credit cards accepted. Prepayment required.

Mobile County

Circuit Court 205 Government St #C-936, Mobile, AL 36644-2936; 251-574-8420; criminal phone: 251-574-8430; civil phone: 251-574-8526; 8AM-5PM. ***Felony, Civil Actions over $10,000.***

Courthouse information line is 251-574-4636.
Civil Records: Access: Online, in person. Visitors must perform in person searches themselves. Required to search: name, years to search. Civil cases indexed by defendant. Civil records on computer from 1977, microfiche from early 1900s. Civil PAT goes back to 1977. PAT results show name only. The state court system offers various pay plans at www.alacourt.com subscription service; includes civil, DR, traffic, warrants, trial court dockets, and notification features.
Criminal Records: Access: Online, in person. Visitors must perform in person searches themselves. Required to search: name, years to search; also helpful: DOB, SSN. Criminal records computerized from 1977, microfiche from early 1900s. Criminal PAT available. Access via various sub plans at www.alacourt.com court subscription service, with notification features. Also, access the state ACJIC system with sub and $25.00 pay-per-name search at http://background.alabama.gov/.
General Information: No sealed, adoptions, youthful offenders or juvenile records released. Will not fax documents. Court makes copy: $5.00 for 1st 20 pages then $.50 each add'l. Certification fee: $5.00 per cert. Payee: Circuit Clerk. Cashiers checks and money orders accepted. Exact change for payment is required. Major credit cards accepted for criminal searches. Prepayment required. Exact change for payments is required.

District Court 205 Government St, Mobile, AL 36644; 251-574-8786; criminal phone: 251-574-8430; civil phone: 251-574-8425; probate phone: 251-574-8502; fax: 251-574-4840; 8AM-5PM. ***Misdemeanor, Civil Actions under $10,000, Eviction, Small Claims, Probate.***
Probate court is a separate and can be reached at the phone number above. Access to Probate court recordings database is free at www.mobilecounty.org/probatecourt/recordssearch.htm. A second search is at www.mobilecounty.org/probatecourt/judicial.asp.
Civil Records: Access: Phone, fax, mail, online, in person. Both court and visitors may perform in person searches. No search fee. Required to search: name, years to search. Civil cases indexed by defendant, plaintiff, on computer from 1977, index books from 1950s. Mail turnaround time 7 days. Civil PAT goes back to 2001. PAT results show name only. The state court system offers various pay plans at www.alacourt.com subscription service; includes civil, DR, traffic, warrants, trial court dockets, and notification features.
Criminal Records: Access: Phone, mail, online, in person. Both court and visitors may perform in person searches. No search fee. Required to search: name, years to search, DOB; also helpful: SSN. Criminal records computerized from 1977, index books from 1950s. Mail turnaround time 7 days. Criminal PAT goes back to 2001.PAT results show name, DOB. Access via various sub plans at www.alacourt.com court subscription service, with notification features. Also, access the state ACJIC system with sub and $25.00 pay-per-name search at http://background.alabama.gov/.
General Information: No sealed, youthful offenders, protected files or juvenile records released. Will fax back documents for $5.00 fee. Court makes copy: $5.00 for 1st 20 pages then $.50 each add'l. Certification fee: $5.00 per cert. Payee: Clerk, District Court. Business checks accepted if pre-approved. No credit cards accepted. Prepayment required. Mail requests: SASE required.

Monroe County

Circuit & District Court County Courthouse, 65 N Alabama Ave, Monroeville, AL 36460; 251-743-2283; probate phone: 251-743-4107; 8AM-5PM. ***Felony, Misdemeanor, Civil, Eviction, Small Claims, Probate.*** Probate court is separate from this court; probate phone number above.
Civil Records: Access: Mail, in person, online. Both court and visitors may perform in person searches. Search fee: $10.00, $20.00 if by hand. Required to search: name, years to search. Civil cases indexed by defendant. Civil index on cards from 1977 and on computer since 7/1994. Mail turnaround time 1 week. Civil PAT goes back to 1977. The state court system offers various pay plans at www.alacourt.com subscription service; includes civil, DR, traffic, warrants, trial court dockets, and notification features. Online access to the probate record index is free at http://probate.mobilecountyal.gov/.
Criminal Records: Access: Mail, online, in person. Both court and visitors may perform in person searches. Search fee: $10.00, $20.00 if by hand. Required to search: name, years to search; also helpful: DOB, SSN. Criminal records indexed on cards from 1977 and on computer since 7/1994. Mail turnaround time 1 week. Criminal PAT goes back to same as civil. Access via various sub plans at www.alacourt.com court subscription service, with notification features. Also, access the state ACJIC system with sub and $25.00 pay-per-name search at http://background.alabama.gov/.
General Information: No sealed, adoptions, youthful offenders or juvenile records released. Will not fax documents. Court makes copy: $5.00 for 1st 20 pages then $.50 each add'l, self serve same. Certification fee: $5.00 per cert. Cert fee includes copies. Payee: John Sawyer, Circuit Clerk. Business checks accepted. No credit cards accepted. Prepayment required. Mail requests: SASE required.

Montgomery County

Circuit Court PO Box 1667, 251 S Lawrence, Montgomery, AL 36102-1667; criminal phone: 334-832-1289; civil phone: 334-832-1266; probate phone: 334-832-1237; 8AM-5PM. ***Felony, Civil Actions over $10,000, Probate.***
Probate court is separate from this court; probate phone number above.
Civil Records: Access: Mail, in person, online. Both court and visitors may perform in person searches. No search fee. Required to search: name, years to search. Civil cases indexed by defendant, plaintiff, on computer from 1982, microfiche from 1976. Mail turnaround time 3-4 days. Civil PAT goes back to 1985. The state court system offers various pay plans at www.alacourt.com subscription service; includes civil, DR, traffic, warrants, trial court dockets, and notification features.
Criminal Records: Access: Mail, online, in person. Both court and visitors may perform in person searches. No search fee. Required to search: name, years to search; also helpful: DOB, SSN. Criminal records computerized from 1982, microfiche from 1976. Mail turnaround time 3-4 days. Criminal PAT goes back to same as civil. Access via various sub plans at www.alacourt.com court subscription service, with notification features. Also, access the state ACJIC system with sub and $25.00 pay-per-name search at http://background.alabama.gov/.
General Information: No sealed, youthful offenders or juvenile records released. Will not fax documents. Court makes copy: $5.00 for 1st 20 pages then $.50 each add'l, self serve same. Certification fee: $1.00 per copy, plus $.25 per page. Cert fee includes copies. Payee: Circuit Clerk. Business checks accepted. No credit cards accepted. Prepayment required. Mail requests: SASE required.

District Court PO Box 1667, Montgomery, AL 36102; 334-832-4950; 8AM-5PM. ***Misdemeanor, Civil Actions under $10,000, Eviction, Small Claims.***
Civil Records: Access: Mail, in person, online. Both court and visitors may perform in person searches. No search fee. Required to search: name, years to search. Civil cases indexed by defendant. Civil records on computer from the 1980s, index books from 1977. Mail turnaround time 2 weeks. Civil PAT goes back to 1995. The state court system offers various pay plans at www.alacourt.com subscription service; includes civil, DR, traffic, warrants, trial dockets, and notification features.
Criminal Records: Access: Mail, online, in person. Both court and visitors may perform in person searches. No search fee. Required to search: name, years to search; also helpful: DOB, SSN. Criminal records computerized from the 1980s, index books from 1977. Mail turnaround time 2 weeks. Criminal PAT goes back to same as civil. Access via various sub plans at www.alacourt.com court subscription service, with notification features. Also, access the state ACJIC system with sub and $25.00 pay-per-name search at http://background.alabama.gov/.
General Information: No sealed, youthful offender, juvenile records released. Will not fax documents. Court makes copy: $5.00 for 1st 20 pages then $.50 each add'l. Certification fee: $1.00 per cert. Payee: District Court. Only cashiers checks and money orders accepted. No credit cards accepted. SASE not required.

Morgan County

Circuit Court PO Box 668, 302 Lee St, Decatur, AL 35602; 256-351-4790; criminal phone: 256-351-4792; civil phone: 256-351-4796; probate phone: 256-351-4675; fax: 256-351-4880; 8AM-4:30PM. ***Felony, Civil Actions over $10,000, Probate.***
www.morgancountycircuitclerk.org/
Probate court is separate from this court; probate phone number above.
Civil Records: Access: Mail, in person, online. Visitors must perform in person searches themselves. Search fee: $10.00 per name. Required to search: name, years to search. Civil cases indexed by defendant, plaintiff, on computer from 1994, on microfiche from 1950s, books from 1965. Public use terminal available. The state court system offers various pay plans at www.alacourt.com subscription service; includes civil, DR, traffic, warrants, trial court dockets, and notification features.
Criminal Records: Access: Mail, online, in person. Visitors must perform in person searches themselves. Search fee: $10.00 per name. Required to search: name, years to search; also helpful: DOB, SSN. Criminal records computerized from 1992. Public use terminal available. Access via various sub plans at www.alacourt.com court subscription service, with notification features. Also, access the state ACJIC system with sub and $25.00 pay-per-name search at http://background.alabama.gov/.
General Information: No sealed, adoption, youthful offender, juvenile records released. Court makes copy: $5.00 for 1st 20 pages then $.50 each add'l. Certification fee: $5.00 per page. Payee: John Pat Orr, Circuit Clerk. Only cashiers checks and money orders accepted. No credit cards accepted. Prepayment required. Mail requests: SASE required.

District Court PO Box 668, Decatur, AL 35602; 256-351-4649; fax: 256-351-4880; 8:30AM-4:30PM. ***Misdemeanor, Civil Actions under $10,000, Eviction, Small Claims.***
www.morgancountycircuitclerk.org/
Civil Records: Access: Mail, in person, online. Visitors must perform in person searches themselves. Search fee: $10.00 per name. Required to search: name, years to search. Civil cases indexed by defendant. Civil records on computer from 1992, books from 1960. Civil PAT goes back to 1992. The state court system offers various pay plans at www.alacourt.com subscription service; includes civil, DR, traffic, warrants, trial court dockets, and notification features.
Criminal Records: Access: Mail, online, in person. Visitors must perform in person searches themselves. Search fee: $10.00 per name. $25.00 for full case record. Required to search: name, years to search; also helpful: DOB, SSN. Criminal records computerized from 1992, books from 1960. Mail turnaround time varies. Criminal PAT goes back to 1992. Access via various sub plans at www.alacourt.com court subscription service, with notification features. Also, access the state ACJIC system with sub and $25.00 pay-per-name search at http://background.alabama.gov/.
General Information: No sealed, adoption, youthful offender, juvenile records released. Will fax documents to local or toll-free number. Court makes copy: $5.00 for 1st 20 pages then $.50 each add'l. Self serve: $.25 per page. Certification fee: $5.00. Payee: District Court. Only cashiers checks and money orders accepted. No credit cards accepted. Prepayment required.

Perry County

Circuit & District Court PO Box 505, Marion, AL 36756; 334-683-6106; probate phone: 334-683-2210; 8AM-4:30PM. ***Felony, Misdemeanor, Civil, Eviction, Small Claims, Probate.***

Probate court is separate from this court; probate phone number above.

Civil Records: Access: Mail, in person, online. Both court and visitors may perform in person searches. Search fee: $10.00 for computer search, $20.00 for paper check, and $25.00 to check archives. Required to search: name, years to search. Civil cases indexed by defendant, plaintiff, on books from 1900's, on computer back to 1990. Mail turnaround time 2-3 days. Civil PAT goes back to 1990. The state court system offers various pay plans at www.alacourt.com subscription service; includes civil, DR, traffic, warrants, trial court dockets, and notification features.

Criminal Records: Access: Mail, online, in person. Both court and visitors may perform in person searches. Search fee: $10.00 for computer search, $20.00 for paper check, and $25.00 to check archives. Required to search: name, years to search; also helpful: DOB, SSN. Criminal records indexed on cards back to 1900, computerized back to 1990. Mail turnaround time 2-3 days. Criminal PAT goes back to same as civil. Access via various sub plans at www.alacourt.com court subscription service, with notification features. Also, access the state ACJIC system with sub and $25.00 pay-per-name search at http://background.alabama.gov/.

General Information: No sealed, adoption, youthful offender, juvenile records released. Will not fax documents. Court makes copy: $5.00 for 1st 20 pages then $.50 each add'l. Certification fee: $5.00. Payee: District Court Clerk. Business checks accepted. No credit cards accepted. Prepayment required. Mail requests: SASE required.

Pickens County

Circuit & District Court PO Box 418, Carrollton, AL 35447; 205-367-2050 dist ct; 8AM-4:30PM. ***Felony, Misdemeanor, Civil, Eviction, Small Claims.***

Probate records at Judge of Probate Ofc, see AL recording offices. Probate phone number above.

Civil Records: Access: Mail, in person, online. Only the court performs in person searches; visitors may not. Search fee: $10.00 up to $20.00. Archived records $25.00. Required to search: name, years to search. Civil cases indexed by defendant, plaintiff, on computer from 10/93, on books and index cards from 1840s. Mail turnaround time 1-2 weeks. The state court system offers various pay plans at www.alacourt.com subscription service; includes civil, DR, traffic, warrants, trial court dockets, and notification features.

Criminal Records: Access: Mail, online, in person. Only the court performs in person searches; visitors may not. Search fee: $10.00 up to $20.00. Archived records $25.00. Required to search: name, years to search; also helpful: DOB, SSN. Criminal records on computer, on books and index cards from 1840s. Mail turnaround time 1-2 weeks. Access via various sub plans at www.alacourt.com court subscription service, with notification features. Also, access the state ACJIC system with sub and $25.00 pay-per-name search at http://background.alabama.gov/.

General Information: No sealed, adoption, youthful offender, juvenile records released. Will not fax documents. Court makes copy: $.50 per page, self serve same. Certification fee: $5.00. Payee: District Court. Business checks accepted. No credit cards accepted. Prepayment required. Mail requests: SASE required.

Pike County

Circuit & District Court 120 W Church St, Troy, AL 36081; 334-566-4622; criminal phone: 334-566-5113; civil: 334-566-5113; probate phone: 334-566-1246; 8AM-5PM. ***Felony, Misdemeanor, Civil, Eviction, Small Claims, Probate.***

Probate court is separate from this court, probate phone number above.

Civil Records: Access: Mail, in person, online. Both court and visitors may perform in person searches. Search fee: $10.00 for computer search, $20.00 for paper check, and $25.00 to check archives. Required to search: name, years to search. Civil cases indexed by defendant, plaintiff, on computer from 1977, on books from 1938. Mail turnaround time same day. Civil PAT goes back to 1993. The public terminal index goes far back but there is very little case info. The state court system offers various pay plans at www.alacourt.com subscription service; includes civil, DR, traffic, warrants, trial court dockets, and notification features.

Criminal Records: Access: Mail, online, in person. Both court and visitors may perform in person searches. Search fee: $10.00 for computer search, $20.00 for paper check, and $25.00 to check archives. Required to search: name, years to search, DOB, SSN. Criminal records computerized from 1977, on books from 1938. Mail turnaround time same day. Criminal PAT goes back to same as civil. The public terminal index goes far back but there is very little case info. Access via various sub plans at www.alacourt.com court subscription service, with notification features. Also, access the state ACJIC system with sub and $25.00 pay-per-name search at http://background.alabama.gov/.

General Information: No sealed, adoption, youthful offender, juvenile records released. Will not fax documents. Court makes copy: $5.00 for 1st 20 pages then $.50 each add'l. Certification fee: $5.00 per page. Payee: Pike County Circuit/District Court. Only cashiers checks and money orders accepted. Prepayment required. Mail requests: SASE required.

Randolph County

Circuit & District Court PO Box 328, 1 Main St, Wedowee, AL 36278; 256-357-4551; probate phone: 256-357-4933; fax: 256-357-9012; 8AM-5PM. ***Felony, Misdemeanor, Civil, Eviction, Small Claims, Probate.***

Probate court is separate from this court; probate phone number above.

Civil Records: Access: Online, in person. Visitors must perform in person searches themselves. Required to search: name, years to search. Civil cases indexed by defendant, plaintiff, on computer from 1994. The state court system offers various pay plans at www.alacourt.com subscription service; includes civil, DR, traffic, warrants, trial court dockets, and notification features.

Criminal Records: Access: Online, in person. Visitors must perform in person searches themselves. Required to search: name, years to search; also helpful: DOB, SSN. Criminal records index on computer from 1977. Access via various sub plans at www.alacourt.com court subscription service, with notification features. Also, access the state ACJIC system with sub and $25.00 pay-per-name search at http://background.alabama.gov/.

General Information: No sealed, adoption, youthful offender, juvenile records released. Will fax documents $.25 per page. Court makes copy: $5.00 for 1st 20 pages then $.50 each add'l, self serve same. Certification fee: $1.50 per page. Visitors may not make certifiable copies. Business checks accepted. No credit cards accepted. Prepayment required.

Russell County

Circuit & District Court 501 14th St, Phenix City, AL 36868; 334-298-0516; probate phone: 334-298-7979; criminal fax: 334-297-6250; civil fax: same; 8:30AM-5PM (EST). ***Felony, Misdemeanor, Civil, Eviction, Small Claims, Probate.***

www.russellcountycircuitclerk.com/Home.aspx

Probate is separate office and separate index at this same address.

Civil Records: Access: Mail, in person, online. Only the court performs in person searches; visitors may not. Search fee: $10.00 per name search back to 1/2005 on computer,. Fee is $25.00 per name if any part of search is before 1/2005,. Required to search: name, years to search; also helpful DOB, last 4 digits of SSN. Civil cases indexed by defendant, plaintiff, on computer from 1988, books from 1800s (prior to 1940 extremely difficult to find). Note: Make search requests on the court's request form only; call for form. Mail turnaround time 2 weeks. The state court system offers various pay plans at www.alacourt.com subscription service; includes civil, DR, traffic, warrants, trial court dockets, and notification features.

Criminal Records: Access: Mail, in person, online. Only the court performs in person searches; visitors may not. Search fee: $10.00 per name search back to 1/2005 on computer,. Fee is $25.00 per name if any part of search is before 1/2005,. Required to search: name, years to search, DOB, alias; also helpful: last 4 digits of SSN. Criminal records computerized from 1988, books from 1800s (prior to 1940 extremely difficult to find). Note: Make search requests on the court's request form only; call for form. Mail turnaround time 2 weeks. Cases prior to 1977 take add'l time to research. Access via various sub plans at www.alacourt.com court subscription service, with notification features. Also, access the state ACJIC system with sub and $25.00 pay-per-name search at http://background.alabama.gov/.

General Information: No sealed, adoption, youthful offender, juvenile records released. Will not fax documents. Court makes copy: $5.00 for 1st 20 pages then $.50 each add'l. Certification fee: $5.00 per cert. Payee: Clerk of Circuit Court. Business checks accepted, no credit card. Prepayment required.

Shelby County

Circuit & District Court PO Box 1810, Columbiana, AL 35051; 205-669-3760; probate phone: 205-669-3710; 8AM-4:30PM. ***Felony, Misdemeanor, Civil, Eviction, Small Claims, Probate.*** http://18jc.alacourt.gov

Probate court mailing address is PO Box 825. Probate is a separate office.

Civil Records: Access: Mail, fax, online, in person. Visitors must perform in person searches themselves. Search fee: $10.00 per name for computer search; $20.00 to search paper records; $25.00 to search archives. Required to search: name, years to search. Civil cases indexed by defendant, plaintiff, on computer from 1993, on index books from 1820s. Mail turnaround time approximately 2 weeks. Civil PAT goes back to 1993. The state court system offers various pay plans at www.alacourt.com subscription service; includes civil, DR, traffic, warrants, trial court dockets, and notification features.

Criminal Records: Access: Mail, fax, online, in person. Visitors must perform in person searches themselves. Search fee: $10.00 per name for computer search; $20.00 to search paper records; $25.00 to search archives. Required to search: name, years to search, DOB; also helpful: SSN. Criminal records computerized from 1993, on index books from 1820s. Mail turnaround time approx. 2 weeks. Criminal PAT goes back to same as civil. Access via various sub plans at www.alacourt.com court subscription service, with notification features. Also, access the state ACJIC system with sub and $25.00 pay-per-name search at http://background.alabama.gov/.

General Information: No sealed, adoption, youthful offender, juvenile records released. Will not fax documents. Court makes copy: $5.00 for 1st 20 pages then $.50 each add'l, self serve same. Certification fee: $5.00 per cert. Payee: Mary Harris, Circuit Clerk. Only cashiers checks and money orders accepted. No credit cards accepted. Prepayment required.

St. Clair County

Circuit & District Court - Ashville Division 100 6th Ave #400, Ashville, AL 35953; 205-594-2184; probate phone: 205-594-2120; fax: 205-594-2196; 8AM-5PM. ***Felony, Misdemeanor, Civil, Eviction, Small Claims, Probate.*** www.stclairco.com

Probate court is separate from this court; probate phone number above.

Civil Records: Access: Mail, in person, online. Both court and visitors may perform in person searches. No search fee. Required to search: name, years to search. Civil cases indexed by defendant, plaintiff, on computer from 1/94, in books from 1800s, no index

before 1940. Mail turnaround time 10 days. Civil PAT goes back to 1993. The state court system offers various pay plans at www.alacourt.com subscription service; includes civil, DR, traffic, warrants, trial court dockets, and notification features.
Criminal Records: Access: Mail, online, in person. Both court and visitors may perform in person searches. No search fee. Required to search: name, years to search, DOB; also helpful: SSN. Criminal records computerized from 1/94, in books from 1800s, no index before 1940. Mail turnaround time 10 days. Criminal PAT goes back to same as civil. Access via various sub plans at www.alacourt.com court subscription service, with notification features. Also, access the state ACJIC system with sub and $25.00 pay-per-name search at http://background.alabama.gov/.
General Information: No sealed, adoption, youthful offender, juvenile records released. Court makes copy: $5.00 for 1st 20 pages then $.50 each add'l, self serve same. Certification fee: $1.25. Payee: Jeff Wyatt Circuit Clerk. Business checks accepted. No credit cards accepted. Prepayment required. Mail requests: SASE required.

Circuit & District Court - Pell City Division 1815 Cogswell Ave, #217, Pell City, AL 35125; 205-338-2511; Circuit: 205-338-7224 District; probate phone: 205-338-9449; fax: 205-884-4224; 8AM-5PM. ***Felony, Misdemeanor, Civil, Eviction, Small Claims, Probate.***
Probate court is separate from this court; probate phone number above.
Civil Records: Access: Mail, in person, online. Both court and visitors may perform in person searches. No search fee. Required to search: name, years to search. Civil cases indexed by defendant, plaintiff, on computer from 11/93, on books from 1950s. Mail turnaround time 7-14 days. Civil PAT goes back to 1993. The state court system offers various pay plans at www.alacourt.com subscription service; includes civil, DR, traffic, warrants, trial court dockets, and notification features.
Criminal Records: Access: Mail, online, in person. Both court and visitors may perform in person searches. No search fee. Required to search: name, years to search, DOB; also helpful: SSN, signed release. Criminal records computerized from 11/93, on books from 1950s. Mail turnaround time 7-14 days. Criminal PAT goes back to same as civil. Access via various sub plans at www.alacourt.com court subscription service, with notification features. Also, access the state ACJIC system with sub and $25.00 pay-per-name search at http://background.alabama.gov/.
General Information: No sealed, adoption, youthful offender, juvenile records released. Will not fax documents. Court makes copy: $5.00 for 1st 20 pages then $.50 each add'l. Self serve: $.25 per page. Certification fee: $5.00 per cert. Payee: Clerk of Courts. Business checks accepted w/ phone number. No credit cards accepted. Prepayment required. Mail requests: SASE required.

Sumter County

Circuit & District Court PO Box 936, 115 Franklin St, Livingston, AL 35470; 205-652-2291; probate phone: 205-652-7281; 8AM-4:30PM. ***Felony, Misdemeanor, Civil, Eviction, Small Claims.***
Probate office address: PO Box 1040, Livingston, AL 35470-1040. Probate office hours 8AM-4PM.
Civil Records: Access: Mail, in person, online. Both court and visitors may perform in person searches. No search fee. Required to search: name, years to search. Civil cases indexed by defendant, plaintiff, on computer from early 1995, on index books from 1962. Mail turnaround time 2 weeks. Civil PAT goes back to 1980s. PAT results show name only. The state court system offers various pay plans at www.alacourt.com subscription service; includes civil, DR, traffic, warrants, trial court dockets, and notification features.
Criminal Records: Access: Mail, online, in person. Both court and visitors may perform in person searches. No search fee. Required to search: name, years to search; also helpful: DOB, SSN. Criminal records computerized from early 1995, on index books from 1962. Mail turnaround time 2 weeks. Criminal PAT goes back to 1980s. PAT results show name only. Access via various sub plans at www.alacourt.com court subscription service, with notification features. Also, access the state ACJIC system with sub and $25.00 pay-per-name search at http://background.alabama.gov/.
General Information: No sealed, adoption, youthful offender, juvenile records released. Will not fax documents. Court makes copy: $5.00 for 1st 20 pages then $.50 each add'l, self serve same. Certification fee: $1.50. Payee: Circuit Court Clerk. Business checks accepted. Visa/MC accepted. Prepayment required. Mail requests: SASE required.

Probate Court PO Box 1040, 115 Marshall St, Livingston, AL 35470; 205-652-7281; fax: 205-652-6206; 8AM-4PM. ***Probate.***

Talladega County

Circuit & District Court - Northern Division PO 6137, 148 E St N, Talladega, AL 35161; 256-761-2102; fax: 256-480-5291; 8AM-5PM. ***Felony, Misdemeanor, Civil, Eviction, Small Claims, Probate.***
Circuit & District Court phone number is 256-761-2104; 5th Division is 256-245-4352.
Civil Records: Access: Online, in person. Visitors must perform in person searches themselves. Required to search: name, years to search. Civil cases indexed by defendant, plaintiff, on computer from 1989, index books from 1970s. Civil PAT goes back to 1989. The state court system offers various pay plans at www.alacourt.com subscription service; includes civil, DR, traffic, warrants, trial court dockets, and notification features.
Criminal Records: Access: Online, in person. Visitors must perform in person searches themselves. Required to search: name, years to search; also helpful: DOB, SSN. Criminal records computerized from 1989, index books from 1970s. Criminal PAT goes back to 1985. Access via various sub plans at www.alacourt.com court subscription service, with notification features. Also, access the state ACJIC system with sub and $25.00 pay-per-name search at http://background.alabama.gov/.
General Information: No sealed, adoption, youthful offender, juvenile records released. Will not fax out documents. Court makes copy: $5.00 for 1st 20 pages then $.50 each add'l, self serve same. Certification fee: $5.00 per cert plus copy fee, $10.00 for divorce cert. Payee: Circuit Court Clerk. Business checks accepted; no personal checks. No credit cards accepted. Prepayment required.

District Court - Southern Division PO Box 183, Sylacauga, AL 35150; 256-245-4352; fax: 256-249-1013; 7:30AM-4:30AM. ***Misdemeanor, Civil Actions under $10,000, Eviction, Small Claims.***
Civil Records: Access: Mail, in person, online. Visitors must perform in person searches themselves. No search fee. Required to search: name, years to search. Civil cases indexed by defendant. Civil records on computer from 1977, on index books and cards prior to 1982 at the Northern Division District Court. Civil PAT goes back to 1989. The state court system offers various pay plans at www.alacourt.com subscription service; includes civil, DR, traffic, warrants, trial court dockets, and notification features.
Criminal Records: Access: Mail, online, in person. Visitors must perform in person searches themselves. No search fee. Required to search: name, years to search; also helpful: DOB, SSN. Criminal records computerized from 1977, on index books and cards prior to 1982 at the Northern Division District Court. Mail turnaround time up to 7-10 days. Criminal PAT goes back to same as civil.PAT results show name, DOB. Terminal results include SSN. Access via various sub plans at www.alacourt.com court subscription service, with notification features. Also, access the state ACJIC system with sub and $25.00 pay-per-name search at http://background.alabama.gov/.
General Information: No juvenile, youthful offender records released. Will fax documents to local or toll free line. Court makes copy: $5.00 for 1st 20 pages then $.50 each add'l, self serve same. Certification fee: $1.25 per page includes copy fee. Payee: Clerk of District Court. Business checks accepted, no personal checks. No credit cards accepted. Prepayment required. Mail requests: SASE required.

Probate Court PO Box 737, Talladega, AL 35161; 256-362-4175; fax: 256-761-2128; 8AM-5PM. ***Probate.***
Physical Address: #1 Court Sq, Talladega, AL 35160

Tallapoosa County

Circuit & District Court - Eastern Division Tallapoosa County Courthouse, 125 N Broadnax, Dadeville, AL 36853; 256-825-1098; x1-Dist; x2-Circ; probate phone: 256-825-4266; 8AM-5PM. ***Felony, Misdemeanor, Civil, Eviction, Small Claims, Probate.***
Probate court is separate from this court.
Civil Records: Access: Mail, in person, online. Only the court performs in person searches; visitors may not. Search fee: $3.00 per name. Required to search: name, years to search. Civil cases indexed by defendant, plaintiff, on computer from 1993, on index books from 1977. Mail turnaround time 1-2 weeks. The state court system offers various pay plans at www.alacourt.com subscription service; includes civil, DR, traffic, warrants, trial court dockets, and notification features.
Criminal Records: Access: Mail, online, in person. Only the court performs in person searches; visitors may not. Search fee: $3.00 per name. Required to search: name, years to search, DOB; also helpful: SSN. Criminal records computerized from 1993, on index books from 1977. Mail turnaround time 1-2 weeks. Access via various sub plans at www.alacourt.com court subscription service, with notification features. Also, access the state ACJIC system with sub and $25.00 pay-per-name search at http://background.alabama.gov/.
General Information: No sealed, adoption, youthful offender, juvenile records released. Will fax documents for no fee. Court makes copy: $5.00 for 1st 20 pages then $.50 each add'l. Certification fee: $1.50 per cert. Payee: Circuit Clerk. In-state business checks accepted. No credit cards accepted. Prepayment required. Mail requests: SASE required.

Circuit & District Court - Western Division PO Box 189, Alexander City, AL 35011; 205-234-4361; 8AM-5PM. ***Felony, Misdemeanor, Civil, Eviction, Small Claims.***
Civil Records: Access: Mail, in person, online. Both court and visitors may perform in person searches. Search fee: $3.00 per name. Required to search: name, years to search. Civil cases indexed by defendant, plaintiff; index on docket books from 1977, prior in docket books; on computer back to 1994. Mail turnaround time up to 2 weeks. The state court system offers various pay plans at www.alacourt.com subscription service; includes civil, DR, traffic, warrants, trial court dockets, and notification features.
Criminal Records: Access: Mail, online, in person. Both court and visitors may perform in person searches. Search fee: $3.00 per name. Required to search: name, years to search, DOB; also helpful: SSN, signed release. Criminal records indexed in books from 1977, prior in docket books; on computer back to 1994. Mail turnaround time up to 2 weeks. Access via various sub plans at www.alacourt.com court subscription service, with notification features. Also, access the state ACJIC system with sub and $25.00 pay-per-name search at http://background.alabama.gov/.
General Information: No sealed, adoption, youthful offender, juvenile records released. Will fax documents to local or toll free line. Court makes copy: $5.00 for 1st 20 pages then $.50 each add'l, self serve same. Certification fee: $1.00 per cert. Payee: Clerk of Courts. Business checks accepted, no credit cards. Prepayment required. Mail requests: SASE requested.

Tuscaloosa County

Circuit Court - Civil PO Box 038993, 714 Greensboro Ave, 2nd Fl, #214, Tuscaloosa, AL 35403; 205-349-3870; civil phone: Circuit: 205-349-3870 X260; District: x357; fax: 205-469-6590; 8:30AM-5PM. ***Civil Actions over $10,000.***

Civil Records: Access: Online, in person. Visitors must perform in person searches themselves. Required to search: name, years to search. Civil cases indexed by defendant, plaintiff, on computer from 1977, index books early 1900s. Public use terminal has civil records back to 1977. Public terminal search requires name, other names used, and DOB. The state court system offers various pay plans at www.alacourt.com subscription service; includes civil, DR, traffic, warrants, trial court dockets, and notification features.

General Information: No sealed, adoption, youthful offender, juvenile records released. Will not fax documents. Court makes copy: $5.00 for 1st 20 pages then $.50 each add'l. Self serve: $.25 per page; use copier in Law Library.Self serve copier in law library. Certification fee: $1.00. Payee: Circuit Clerk. Business checks accepted. No credit cards accepted. Prepayment required.

District Courts - Civil PO Box 2883, 714 Greensboro Ave, 6th Fl, Tuscaloosa, AL 35403; 205-349-3870; civil phone: 205-349-3870 x355; probate phone: 205-349-3870 x203; 8:30AM-4:30PM. ***Civil Actions under $10,000, Probate.***

Probate court is separate from this court and can be contacted at the telephone number above.

Civil Records: Access: Online, in person. Visitors must perform in person searches themselves. Required to search: name, years to search. Civil cases indexed by defendant, plaintiff, on computer from 1977, index books early 1965. Public use terminal has civil records back to 1977. The state court system offers various pay plans at www.alacourt.com subscription service; includes civil, DR, traffic, warrants, trial court dockets, and notification features.

General Information: No sealed records released. Court makes copy: $5.00 for 1st 20 pages then $.50 each add'l. Certification fee: $1.00 per page. Payee: District Clerk. Business checks accepted. Visa/MC accepted. Prepayment required.

Circuit Court - Criminal 714 Greensboro Ave, 3rd Fl, Tuscaloosa, AL 35401; 205-349-3870 X326; 8AM-5PM. ***Felony.***

Criminal Records: Access: Mail, online, in person. Both court and visitors may perform in person searches. Search fee: $5.00. Required to search: name, years to search, DOB; also helpful: SSN. Criminal records on computer and index books back to 1977. Mail turnaround time 1-2 days. Public use terminal has crim records back to 1977. PAT results show middle initial, DOB. Terminal results include SSN. Access via various sub plans at www.alacourt.com court subscription service, with notification features. Also, access the state ACJIC system with sub and $25.00 pay-per-name search at http://background.alabama.gov/.

General Information: Online identifiers in results same as on public terminal. No sealed, adoption, youthful offender, juvenile records released. Will not fax documents. Court makes copy: $5.00 for 1st 20 pages then $.50 each add'l, self serve same. Certification fee: $1.25 per cert. Payee: Circuit Clerk. Business checks accepted. No credit cards accepted. Prepayment required. Mail requests: SASE required.

District Court - Criminal Division PO Box 1687, 714 Greensboro Ave, 6th Fl, Tuscaloosa, AL 35403; 205-349-3870 x357; 8AM-5PM. ***Misdemeanor.***

Criminal Records: Access: Mail, online, in person. Both court and visitors may perform in person searches. Search fee: $5.00 per name. Required to search: name, years to search, signed release; also helpful: DOB, SSN. Criminal records computerized from 1985, books in storage from early 1965. Mail turnaround time 5 days. Public use terminal has crim records back to 1997. Public terminals are usually very busy. Access via various sub plans at www.alacourt.com court subscription service, with notification features. Also, access the state ACJIC system with sub and $25.00 pay-per-name search at http://background.alabama.gov/.

General Information: No sealed, youthful offender records released. Will fax documents to local or toll free line. Court makes copy: $5.00 for 1st 20 pages then $.50 each add'l. Certification fee: $5.00 per doc. Payee: District Court Clerk. Business checks accepted. Visa/MC accepted; a 4% usage fee will be added. Prepayment required. Mail requests: SASE preferred.

Walker County

Circuit & District Court PO Box 1389, Jasper, AL 35502; 205-384-7268; probate phone: 205-384-7281; fax: 205-384-7271; 8AM-2:30PM. ***Felony, Misdemeanor, Civil, Eviction, Small Claims, Probate.*** Probate court is separate from this court at PO Box 502.

Civil Records: Access: Online, in person. Visitors must perform in person searches themselves. Required to search: name, years to search. Civil cases indexed by defendant, plaintiff, on computer from 3/93, on index books from 1920s. Civil PAT goes back to 1993. The state court system offers various pay plans at www.alacourt.com subscription service; includes civil, DR, traffic, warrants, trial court dockets, and notification features.

Criminal Records: Access: Online, in person. Visitors must perform in person searches themselves. Required to search: name, years to search. Criminal records computerized from 3/93, on index books from 1920s. Criminal PAT goes back to same as civil. Access via various sub plans at www.alacourt.com court subscription service, with notification features. Also, access the state ACJIC system with sub and $25.00 pay-per-name search at http://background.alabama.gov/.

General Information: No sealed, adoption, youthful offender, juvenile records released. Will not fax documents. Court makes copy: $5.00 for 1st 20 pages then $.50 each add'l. Certification fee: $1.00 per page. Payee: Vinita Thomspon, Circuit Clerk. No personal or business checks accepted. No credit cards accepted. Prepayment required.

Washington County

Circuit & District Court PO Box 548, 1 Court St, Chatom, AL 36518; 251-847-2239; 8AM-4:30PM. ***Felony, Misdemeanor, Civil, Eviction, Small Claims, Probate.***

Probate is a separate court and separate index.

Civil Records: Access: Online, in person. Visitors must perform in person searches themselves. Required to search: name, years to search. Civil cases indexed by defendant. Civil records on computer since 9/1994; prior 7 years on index cards. Civil PAT goes back to 1994. The state court system offers various pay plans at www.alacourt.com subscription service; includes civil, DR, traffic, warrants, trial dockets, and notification features.

Criminal Records: Access: Online, in person. Visitors must perform in person searches themselves. Required to search: name, years to search, DOB; also helpful: SSN. Criminal records on computer since 9/1994; prior 7 years on index cards. Criminal PAT goes back to same as civil. Access via various sub plans at www.alacourt.com court subscription service, with notification features. Also, access the state ACJIC system with sub and $25.00 pay-per-name search at http://background.alabama.gov/.

General Information: No sealed, adoption, youthful offender, juvenile records released. Court makes copy: $5.00 for 1st 20 pages then $.50 each add'l. Certification fee: $1.00. Payee: Circuit Clerk. Only cashiers checks and money orders accepted. Visa/MC accepted. Prepayment required.

Wilcox County

Circuit & District Court PO Box 608, 12 Water St, Camden, AL 36726; 334-682-4126; probate phone: 334-682-4883; fax: 334-682-4025; 8AM-N, 1-4:30PM. ***Felony, Misdemeanor, Civil, Eviction, Small Claims, Probate.***

Probate court is separate from this court; probate phone number above.

Civil Records: Access: Online, in person. Visitors must perform in person searches themselves. Required to search: name, years to search, address. Civil cases indexed by defendant, plaintiff, on computer since 1995; prior records on index books from 1970s, prior to 1970s in vault. The state court system offers various pay plans at www.alacourt.com subscription service; includes civil, DR, traffic, warrants, trial court dockets, and notification features.

Criminal Records: Access: Online, in person. Visitors must perform in person searches themselves. Required to search: name, years to search; also helpful: DOB. Criminal records on computer since 1995; prior records on index books from 1970s, prior to 1970s in vault. Access via various sub plans at www.alacourt.com court subscription service, with notification features. Also, access the state ACJIC system with sub and $25.00 pay-per-name search at http://background.alabama.gov/.

General Information: No sealed, adoption, youthful offender, juvenile records released. Will not fax documents. Court makes copy: $5.00 for 1st 20 pages then $.50 each add'l, self serve same. Certification fee: $1.50. Payee: Circuit Clerk. Business checks accepted. No credit cards accepted. Prepayment required.

Winston County

Circuit & District Court PO Box 309, Courthouse, Main Fl, Double Springs, AL 35553; 205-489-5533; probate phone: 205-489-5219; fax: 205-489-5140; 8AM-4:30PM. ***Felony, Misdemeanor, Civil, Eviction, Small Claims, Probate.*** Probate court is separate from this court; probate phone number above.

Civil Records: Access: Mail, fax, online, in person. Visitors must perform in person searches themselves. No search fee. Required to search: name, years to search. Civil cases indexed by defendant, plaintiff; index on docket books from 1977, on computer since 6/1994 including pending cases. Civil PAT goes back to 1994. The state court system offers various pay plans at www.alacourt.com subscription service; includes civil, DR, traffic, warrants, trial court dockets, and notification features.

Criminal Records: Access: Mail, fax, online, in person. Visitors must perform in person searches themselves. No search fee. Required to search: name, years to search, DOB; also helpful: SSN. Criminal records indexed in books from 1977, on computer since 6/1994 including pending cases. Criminal PAT goes back to same as civil. Access via various sub plans at www.alacourt.com court subscription service, with notification features. Also, access the state ACJIC system with sub and $25.00 pay-per-name search at http://background.alabama.gov/.

General Information: No sealed, adoption, youthful offender, juvenile records released. Will fax back documents for legitimate purpose, but prefer not to. Court makes copy: $.50 per page; copy fee is $25.00 for older docs retrieved from archives. Self serve: $.50 per page. Certification fee: $3.00 per cert. Payee: Circuit Clerk. Business checks accepted; no personal checks. No credit cards accepted. Prepayment required. Mail requests: SASE requested.

Alabama Recording Offices

ORGANIZATION: 67 counties, 71 recording offices. The recording officer is the Judge of Probate. Four counties have two recording offices- Barbour, Coffee, Jefferson, St. Clair. See the notes under each county regarding how to determine which office is appropriate to search. Alabama is in the Central Time Zone (CST).

REAL ESTATE RECORDS: Most counties do not perform real estate searches. Copy fees vary, but usually $1.00 per page. Certification fees vary. Property tax records are located at the Assessor's Office.

UCC RECORDS: Real estate related UCCs are filed with the County Judge of Probate. Pre-Article 9 UCCs were filed with the Secretary of State. Only one-third of counties will perform searches on existing UCC records.

TAX LIEN RECORDS: Federal and state tax liens on personal property of businesses are filed with the Secretary of State. Other federal and state tax liens are filed with the County Judge of Probate. Counties do not perform separate tax lien searches although the liens are usually filed in the same index with UCC financing statements.

OTHER LIENS: Mechanics, judgment, lis pendens, hospital, vendor.

ONLINE ACCESS: There is no statewide system but a increasing number of counties offer free online access to recorded documents and tax assessor data, and property info on GIS-mapping sites. The Secretary of State's Lands and Trademarks Division does offer free access to county-by-county tract books which reflect the original ownership of Alabama lands, see www.sos.state.al.us/GovtRecords/Land.aspx. UCC information available to search at www.sos.state.al.us/vb/inquiry/inquiry.aspx?area=UCC

Autauga County

County Judge of Probate, 176 W 5th St, Prattville, AL 36067-3041. 334-361-3731, R/E recording phone-334-361-3732; fax-334-361-3740; 8:30AM-5PM (CST) www.autaugaco.org

Index: All in one. Records indexed on a public use terminal back to 10/1/1996. Only the public may search. Copy fee $1.00 per page. Fee to fax back-$5.00. Cert fee- $3.00 per doc plus copy fee. Payee-County Judge of Probate. Office does not sell bulk data. **Other phones:** Treasurer- 334-358-6701; Elections- 334-361-3728. **Property tax/Assessing-** 218 N Court, Prattville, AL 36017; 334-361-3709, assessor fax- 334-365-6985. (Appraiser/Auditor- 334-361-3712) **Online access-** Access the GIS-property info database and Tax Office free at www.emapsplus.com/ALAutauga/maps/. Click on search by name.

Baldwin County

County Judge of Probate, PO Box 459, Bay Minette, AL 36507. Recording, R/E & UCC phone-251-937-0230; fax-251-580-1883; 8AM-4:30PM (CST) www.co.baldwin.al.us/

Index: Separate indices to search include books and computer. Records indexed on a public use terminal back to 1987. Only the public may search. Copy fee $1.00 per page. Copies of subdivisin maps- $10.00. Cert fee- $3.00 per doc plus copy fee. Payee- Baldwin County Judge of Probate. **Online access to Real Estate, Deed, UCC records:** Access to recordings, deeds, and UCCs is at the website, see the "Recording" box. **Other phones:** Treasurer- 251-937-0282; Elections- 251-937-0399. **Property tax/Assessing-** 212 Courthouse Sq, Bay Minette, AL 36507; 251-937-0245. (Appraiser/Auditor- 251-937-0245) **Online access-** Property tax data is at www.deltacomputersystems.com/AL/AL05/plinkquerya.html. Search appraiser records at www.deltacomputersystems.com/AL/AL05/pappraisala.html.

Barbour County (Clayton Division)

County Judge of Probate, PO Box 158, Clayton, AL 36016. 334-775-8371; fax-334-775-1126; 8AM-4:30PM (CST)

For pre-1993 records, search for Eufaula addresses here and search for Clayton addresses there. For other county addresses, call for where to search. Index: Separate indices to search include current, older books. Records for Clayton and Eufaula indexed on a public use terminal back to 1/1993. Only the public may search. Copy fee $.50 per page. Cert fee- $2.50 per doc includes 5 copy pages; add $.50 each add'l sheet. Payee- Barbour County Judge of Probate. Office does not sell bulk data. **Other phones:** Treasurer- 334-775-3203. **Property tax/Assessing-** PO Box 267, Clayton, AL 36016; 334-775-3474. **Online access-** Access GIS-property info database and Tax Office free at www.emapsplus.com/ALBarbour/maps/. Click on search by name.

Barbour County (Eufaula Division)

County Judge of Probate, PO Box 758, Eufaula, AL 36072. 334-687-1530; fax-334-687-0921; 8AM-5PM

For pre-1993 records, search for Eufaula addresses here and search for Clayton addresses there. For other county addresses, call for where to search. Index: All in one. Records for Clayton and Eufaula indexed on a public use terminal back to 1/1993. Only the public may search. Copy fee $1.00 per page.Real estate or tax lien copy- $.50 per page. Cert fee- $3.00 per doc plus copy fee. Payee- Barbour County Judge of Probate. **Other phones:** Treasurer- 334-775-3203. **Property tax/Assessing-** 303 E Broad St, Eufaula, AL 36027; 334-687-1575, assessor fax- 334-687-1579. **Online access-** Access the GIS-property info and Tax Office free at www.emapsplus.com/ALBarbour/maps/. Click on search by name.

Bibb County

County Judge of Probate, 8 Court Sq W, #A, Centerville, AL 35042. 205-926-3104, R/E recording phone-205-926-3108; fax-205-926-3131; 8AM-5PM

Index: All in one. Records indexed on a public use terminal back to 2/95. Office will perform a UCC search but public must search other records themselves. Copy fee $3.00 per document. $1.00 each add'l page. Cert fee- $1.00 per doc plus copy fee. Payee- Bibb County Judge of Probate. Office does not sell bulk data. **Other phones:** Treasurer- 205-926-3114; Elections- 205-926-3104; Board of Registration- 205-926-3102. **Property tax/Assessing-** 8 Court Sq W, #B, Centerville, AL 35042; 205-926-3105, assessor fax- 205-926-3125. **Online access-** Access property and tax office data free at www.emapsplus.com/subscription/states/alabama/state.asp.

Blount County

County Judge of Probate, 220 2nd Ave E, Oneonta, AL 35121. 205-625-4180, R/E recording phone-205-625-4117; fax-205-625-4206; 8AM-5PM (CST)

Index: All in one. Records indexed on a public use terminal back to 1988. Only the public may search. Copy fee $1.00 per page. Cert fee- $4.00 per doc plus copy fee. Payee- Blount County Judge of Probate. Office does not sell bulk data. **Other phones:** Treasurer- 205-625-4117; Elections- 205-625-4191. **Property tax/Assessing-** 220 2nd Ave E, Rm 102, Oneonta, AL 35121; 205-625-4117, assessor fax-205-625-3992. www.blountrevenue.com **Online access-** Public records available from Commissioner's Ofc. at www.blountrevenue.com/Public_Records.htm includes property and assessment records. Also, access assessor, appraiser, real property and personal property data free at www.deltacomputersystems.com/AL/AL08/INDEX.HTML.

Bullock County

County Clerk, PO Box 71, Union Springs, AL 36089. Recording, R/E & UCC phone-334-738-2250; fax-334-738-2240; 8AM-4PM (CST)

Index: Separate indices to search. Record index not computerized. Only the public may search. Copy fee $1.00 per page.Real estate deed copy- $3.10. Cert fee- $5.00 per doc plus copy fee. Payee- Bullock County Judge of Probate. Office does not sell bulk data. **Other phones:** Elections- 334-738-2250; Vital Records- 334-738-2250. **Property tax/Assessing-** 217 N Prairie St, Rm 100, Union Springs, AL 36089; 334-738-2888 or 2750, assessor fax- 334-738-2984.

Butler County

County Judge of Probate, PO Box 756, Greenville, AL 36037. Recording, R/E & UCC phone-334-382-3512; fax-334-382-5489; 8AM-4PM M,T,Th,F; 8AM-N W. (CST)

Index: Separate indices in books by year. Record index not computerized. Only the public may search. Copy fee $1.00 per page. Cert fee- $3.00 per doc plus copy fee. Payee- Butler County Judge of Probate. Office does not sell bulk data. **Other phones:** Treasurer- 334-382-3612; Elections- 334-382-3512; Vital Records- 334-382-3512. **Property tax/ Assessing-** Revenue Commissioner, 700 Court Sq, Greenville, AL 36037; 334-382-3221, assessor fax-334-382-0385.

Calhoun County

County Judge of Probate, 1702 Noble St, #102, Anniston, AL 36201. 256-241-2825; fax-256-231-1728; 8AM-4:30PM (CST) www.calhouncounty.org

Index: All in one. Records indexed on a public use terminal back to 1954. Office will help visitors perform a UCC search but public must search other records themselves. No fee for search. Office will not search real estate records. Copy fee $1.00 per page. Cert fee- $3.00 per doc plus copy fee. Payee- Calhoun

County Judge of Probate. Office does not sell bulk data. **Other phones:** Tax Collector- 256-241-2840. **Property tax/Assessing**- 1702 Noble St, #104, Calhoun, AL 36201; 256-241-2855, assessor fax- 256-231-1890. (Appraiser/Auditor- 256-241-2870) www.calhouncounty.org/revenue/index.html **Online access**- Access the GIS-property info database and Tax Office free at www.emapsplus.com/ALCalhoun/maps/. Click on search by name.

Chambers County

County Judge of Probate, Courthouse, #2, Lafayette, AL 36862. 334-864-4384, R/E recording phone-334-864-4397, UCC recording phone-334-864-4393; fax-334-864-4394; 8AM-4:30PM (CST)
Index: Separate indices to search. Records indexed on computer back to 10/97; images back to 1985. Only the public may search. Copy fee $1.00 per page. Cert fee- $4.00 per doc plus copy fee. Payee- Chambers County Judge of Probate. Office does not sell bulk data. **Online access to Real Estate, UCC records:** Access real estate and UCC data online by subscription for $65.00 monthly fee. Records are live and go back 5 years. For info, call 706-643-1010 or 334-864-4384. **Other phones:** Elections- 334-864-4380; Vital Records- 334-864-4393; Tax Collector-334-864-4386. **Property tax/Assessing**- 2 Lafayette St, Lafayette, AL 36862; 334-864-4389, assessor fax-334-864-4387. (Appraiser/Auditor- 334-864-4379) **Online access**- Access parcel data on GIS-mapping site free at www.chamberscountymaps.com/. Must download Mapguide Viewer Software first. Password required for full data.

Cherokee County

County Judge of Probate, 260 Cedar Bluff Rd, #101; Cherokee County Admin Center, Centre, AL 35960. 256-927-3363; fax-256-927-9218; 8AM-4PM (CST)
Index: All in one since 2/1990. Records indexed on a public use terminal back to 2005. Only the public may search. Copy fee $1.00 per page. Cert fee- $3.00 per doc plus copy fee. Payee- Cherokee County Judge of Probate. Office does not sell bulk data. **Property tax/Assessing**- 260 Cedarbluff Rd, Ste 102, Centre, 35960; 256-927-5527, assessor fax- 256-927-5528.

Chilton County

County Judge of Probate, PO Box 270, Clanton, AL 35046. Recording, R/E & UCC phone-205-755-1555; fax-205-280-7219; 8AM-4PM (CST)
Index: Separate indices to search include direct index, reverse index and general index. Records indexed on a public use terminal back to 1001/1991. Only the public may search. Copy fee $1.00 per page. Cert fee-$3.00 per doc plus copy fee. Payee- Chilton County Judge of Probate. **Other phones:** Vital Records- 205-755-1555. **Property tax/Assessing**- PO Box 889, 500 2nd Ave N, Clanton, AL 35046; 205-755-0155, assessor fax- 205-280-7257. (Appraiser/Auditor- 205-755-0160) **Online access**- Access property and tax office data free at www.emapsplus.com/subscription/states/alabama/state.asp.

Choctaw County

County Judge of Probate, 117 S Mulberry; Courthouse, Butler, AL 36904. 205-459-2417; fax-205-459-4248; 8AM-4:30PM (CST)
Index: Deeds, liens, judgments, mortgages, and more - all in one. Record index not computerized. Only the public may search. Copy fee $.50 per page. Cert fee-$3.00 per doc plus copy fee. Payee- Choctaw County Judge of Probate. Office does not sell bulk data. **Other phones:** Treasurer- 205-459-2411. **Property tax/Assessing**- 117 S Mullberry, Ste 4, Butler, AL 36904; 205-459-2412, assessor fax- 205-459-4799.

Clarke County

County Judge of Probate, PO Box 10, Grove Hill, AL 36451. Recording, R/E & UCC phone-251-275-3251; fax-251-275-8427; 8AM-5PM (CST)
Index: All in one. Records indexed on a public use terminal back to 1999. Only the public may search. Copy fee $1.00 per page. Cert fee- $3.00; UCCs are $5.00 per file plus copy fee. Payee- Clarke County Judge of Probate. Office does not sell bulk data. **Other phones:** Treasurer- 251-275-3507; Elections-251-275-3251; Vital Records- 251-275-3251 (marriages); Circuit Clerk (divorce records)- 251-275-3163. **Property tax/Assessing**- PO Box 9, Grove Hill, AL 36451; 251-275-3376, assessor fax- 251-275-3498. (Appraiser/Auditor- 251-275-3010) **Online access**- Access the GIS-property info database and Tax Office free at www.emapsplus.com/ALClarke/maps/. Click on search by name.

Clay County

County Judge of Probate, PO Box 1120, Ashland, AL 36251. 256-354-3006; fax-256-354-4778; 8AM-4:30PM (CST)
Index: All in one. Records indexed on a public use terminal back to 1986. Only the public may search. Copy fee $1.00 per page. Cert fee- $5.00 per doc includes copy fee. Payee- Clay County Judge of Probate. Office does not sell bulk data. **Property tax/Assessing**- PO Box 155, Ashland, AL 36251; 256-354-2454, assessor fax- 256-354-7395. (Appraiser/Auditor- 256-354-5211)

Cleburne County

County Judge of Probate, 120 Vickery St, Rm 101, Heflin, AL 36264. Recording, R/E & UCC phone-256-463-5655; fax-256-463-1044; 8AM-5PM (CST)
Index: Separate indices to search include real estate, UCC. Records indexed on a public use terminal back to 1986. Office will perform a UCC search but public must search other records themselves. Copy fee $1.00 per page; $.50 self serve. Cert fee- $6.00 per doc includes 1 copy page. Payee- Cleburne County Judge of Probate. Office does not sell bulk data. **Other phones:** Treasurer- 256-463-2873; Elections- 256-463-5299; Vital Records- 256-463-2296. **Property tax/Assessing**- 120 Vickery St, #102, Heflin, AL 36264; 256-463-5419, assessor fax- 256-4637780. (Appraiser/Auditor- 256-463-2873);

Coffee County (Elba Division)

County Judge of Probate, 230-P N Court Ave, Elba, AL 36323. Recording, R/E & UCC phone-334-897-2211/12; fax-334-897-2028; 8AM-4:30PM (CST) www.probateoffice.info
Index: All in one. Records indexed on a public use terminal back to 1999 including both Elba and Enterprise Divisions. If from the 1990s, a record will show book & page number and the proper division. Only the public may search. Copy fee $1.00 per page if agency makes the copy. If public makes copy, fee is $.25. Cert fee- $3.00 per page includes copy fee. Payee- Coffee County Judge of Probate. Call for phone number to an outside provider. **Online access to Real Estate, Deed, Lien, Mortgage records:** Subscription access to all Judge of Probate indexes available, call Michelle at 205-758-2000 x8112; $25.00 signup fee, view images at $.75 each or less, print images $.25 each. Data is same as appears on PAT. **Other phones:** Elections- 334-897-2211/12. **Property tax/Assessing**- 230-RN Court Ave, Elba, AL 36323; 334-897-2457, assessor fax- 334-897-2481. **Online access**- Access the GIS-property info database and Tax Office free at www.emapsplus.com/ALCoffee/maps/. Click on search by name.

Coffee County (Enterprise Division)

County Judge of Probate, PO Box 311247, Enterprise, AL 36331. 334-347-2688; fax-334-347-2095; 8AM-4:30PM (CST) www.probateoffice.info
Index: All in one. Records indexed on a public use terminal back to 1999 including both Elba and Enterprise Divisions. If from the 1990s, a record will show book & page number and the proper division. Only the public may search. Copy fee $1.00 per page. Cert fee- $3.00 per doc plus copy fee. Payee- Coffee County Judge of Probate. Office does not sell bulk data. **Online access to Real Estate, Deed, Lien, Mortgage, Personal Property records:** Subscription access to all Judge of Probate indexes available, call Michelle at 205-758-2000 x8112; $25.00 signup fee, view images at $.75 each or less, print images $.25 each. Data is same as appears on PAT. **Property tax/Assessing**- PO Box 311606, 99 S Edwards, Coffee, AL 36331; 334-347-8734, assessor fax- 334-308-1220. (Appraiser/Auditor- 334-894-6085) **Online access**- Access parcel data on the GIS-property database free at www.emapsplus.com/ALCoffee/maps/. Click on Search by Name.

Colbert County

County Judge of Probate, PO Box 47, Tuscumbia, AL 35674. 256-386-8546; fax-256-386-8547; 8AM-4:30PM (CST)
Index: All in one. Records indexed on a public use terminal back to 2001. Only the public may search; office will assist. Copy fee $1.00 per page. Cert fee-$4.00 per doc plus copy fee. Payee- Colbert County Judge of Probate. Office does not sell bulk data. **Property tax/Assessing**- 201 N Main St, Tuscumbia, AL 35674; 256-386-8530, assessor fax- 256-386-8549. **Online access**- Access property tax records free at www.deltacomputersystems.com/search.html.

Conecuh County

County Judge of Probate, PO Box 149, Evergreen, AL 36401. 251-578-1221; fax-251-578-7034; 8AM-4:30PM (CST)
Index: All in one. Records indexed on a public use terminal back to 6/01. Office will perform a UCC search but public must search other records themselves. Copy fee $1.00 per page. Cert fee- $3.00 per cert plus copy fee. Payee- Conecuh County Judge of Probate. Office does not sell bulk data. **Property tax/Assessing**- PO Box 533, 111 Court St, Evergreen, AL 36401; 251-578-1890, assessor fax- 251-578-7004. (Appraiser/Auditor- 251-518-2659) **Online access**- Access to GIS/mapping for free go to www.alabamagis.com/conecuh/.

Coosa County

County Judge of Probate, PO Box 218, Rockford, AL 35136. Recording, R/E & UCC phone-256-377-4919; fax-256-377-1549; 8AM-4PM (CST)
Index: All in one. Records indexed on a public use terminal back to 99. Only the public may search. Copy fee $1.00 per page. Cert fee- $3.00 for 1st page; $1.00 each add'l, plus copy fee. Payee- Coosa County Judge of Probate. **Property tax/Assessing**- PO Box 7, Rockford, AL 35136; 256-377-4916, assessor fax-256-377-1469. (Appraiser/Auditor- 256-377-4916) **Online access**- Access property and tax office data free at www.emapsplus.com/subscription/states/alabama/state.asp.

Covington County

County Judge of Probate, PO Box 789, Andalusia, AL 36420-0789. 334-428-2518/2519, R/E recording phone-334-428-2518, fax-334-428-2563; 8AM-5PM (CST)
Index: All in one. Records indexed on a public use terminal back to 1987. Only the public may search. Copy fee $1.00 per page. Cert fee- $3.00 per doc plus copy fee. Payee- Probate Judge. Office does not sell bulk data. **Property tax/Assessing**- 1 Court Sq, Andalusia, AL 36420; 334-428-2540, assessor fax-334-428-2575. (Appraiser/Auditor- 334-428-2630);

Crenshaw County

County Judge of Probate, PO Box 328, Luverne, AL 36049-0328. 334-335-6568, R/E recording phone-x227; fax-334-335-4749; 8AM-4:30PM (CST)
Index: Separate indices to search include mortgage/deed, miscellaneous, Probate, UCC, direct and reverse. Record index not computerized. Only the public may search. Copy fee $1.00 per page. Cert fee-$3.00 per doc plus copy fee. Payee- Crenshaw County Judge of Probate. Office does not sell bulk data. **Other phones:** Treasurer- 334-335-6568 x222; Elections- 334-335-6568 x254; Vital Records- 334-335-2471. **Property tax/Assessing**- PO Box 208, Luverne, AL 36049; 334-335-6568 x231, assessor fax- 334-335-3616. (Appraiser - 334-335-6568 x236)

Cullman County

County Judge of Probate, PO Box 970, Cullman, AL 35055. Recording, R/E & UCC phone-256-775-4807; fax-256-775-4813; 8AM-4:30PM (CST)
Index: All in one. Records indexed on a public use terminal back to 4/97. Only the public may search. Copy fee $.30 per page. Cert fee- $2.00 per doc plus copy fee. Payee- Cullman County Judge of Probate. Bulk data available for purchase, contact Revenue Office. **Online access to Real Estate, Deed, Lien, Mortgage records:** Subscription access to all Judge of Probate indexes available, call Michelle at 205-758-2000 x8112; $25.00 signup fee, view images at $.75 each or less, print images $.50 each. Data is same as appears on PAT. **Other phones:** Elections- 256-775-4665. **Property tax/Assessing**- PO Box 2220, 500 2nd Ave SW, Cullman, AL 35056; 256-775-4844, assessor fax- 256-775-4863. (Appraiser/Auditor- 256-775-4825) www.cullmanrevenuecom.com/ **Online access**- Access the GIS-property info database and Tax Office free at www.emapsplus.com/ALCullman/maps/. Click on search by name.

Dale County

County Judge of Probate, PO Box 580, Ozark, AL 36361-0580. Recording, R/E & UCC phone-334-774-2754; fax-334-774-0468; 8AM-5PM (CST)
Index: Separate indices to search include books back to 1884, mtgs, deeds, misc, judgments. Records indexed on a public use terminal back to 1986. Only the public may search. Copy fee $1.00 per page, $.25 self serve. Cert fee- $4.00 per doc plus copy fee. Payee- Dale County Judge of Probate. Office does not sell bulk data. **Other phones:** Elections- 334-774-9038; Vital Records- 334-774-5146. **Property tax/Assessing**- PO Box 267, 100 E Court Sq, Ozark, AL 36360; 334-774-2226, assessor fax- 334-445-0498. (Appraiser/Auditor- 334-774-7208);

Dallas County

County Judge of Probate, PO Box 987, Selma, AL 36702-0987. 334-874-2518, R/E recording phone-334-874-2516; 8:30AM-4:30PM (CST)
Index: Separate indices to search include corporations, judgments, real property. Records indexed on a public use terminal back to 1981. Office will perform a UCC search, which includes tax liens, but public must search other records themselves. Office will find real estate record if given book and page number, $1.50 per page. UCC search per debtor name- $25.00. Separate state/federal tax lien search fee- $5.00 per debtor. Copy fee $1.50 per page. Cert fee- $3.00 per cert plus copy fee. Payee- Dallas County Judge of Probate. Office does not sell bulk data. **Other phones:** Treasurer- 334-874-2560; Elections- 334-874-2506; Vital Records- 334-874-5887; Tax Collector- 334-874-2519. **Property tax/Assessing**- PO Box 987, Selma, AL 36701; 334-874-2520, assessor fax- 334-876-4853.

De Kalb County

County Judge of Probate, 300 Grand SW, #100; Courthouse, Fort Payne, AL 35967. 256-845-8510; fax-256-845-8514; 8:00AM-4:00PM (CST)
Index: All in one. Records indexed on a public use terminal back to 5/05. Only the public may search. Copy fee $.25 per page. Cert fee- $3.00 per doc plus copy fee. Payee- De Kalb County Judge of Probate. **Other phones:** Treasurer- 256-845-8520. **Property tax/Assessing**- 206 Grand SW, Fort Payne, AL 35967; 256-845-8515, assessor fax- 256-845-8522. **Online access**- Access the GIS-property info and Tax Office at www.emapsplus.com/ALDeKalb/maps/. Click on search by name. Also, a login name and account and credit card is required to view assessment, appraisal, property tax data at. www.deltacomputersystems.com/AL/AL28/INDEX.HTML.

Elmore County

County Judge of Probate, PO Box 280, Wetumpka, AL 36092. Recording, R/E phone-334-567-1143, UCC recording phone-334-567-1143 or 1145; fax-334-567-1144; 8AM-4:30PM (CST)
Index: All in one. Records indexed on a public use terminal back to 1995. Office will perform a UCC search but public must search other records themselves. Copy fee $1.00 per page. Plats are $5.00. Cert fee- $3.00 per doc plus copy fee. Payee- Elmore County Judge of Probate. **Other phones:** Treasurer- 334-567-1156; Elections- 334-567-1140; Vital Records- 334-567-1145. **Property tax/Assessing**- 100 E Commerce St, #107, Wetumpka, AL 36092; 334-567-1118, assessor fax- 334-567-1116. (Appraiser/Auditor- 334-567-1117) **Online access**- Access the GIS-property info and Tax Office free at www.emapsplus.com/ALElmore/maps/. Click on search by name.

Escambia County

County Judge of Probate, PO Box 557, Brewton, AL 36427. 251-867-0301, R/E recording phone-251-867-0291; fax-251-867-0284; 8AM-4PM (CST) www.co.escambia.al.us/judge.html
Index: All in one. Records indexed on a public use terminal back to 10/1991. Office will perform a UCC search but public must search other records themselves. Copy fee $1.00 per page. Cert fee- $1.00 per doc plus copy fee. Payee- Escambia County Judge of Probate. **Other phones:** Elections- 251-867-0201. **Property tax/Assessing**- PO Box 556, Brewton, AL 36427; 251-867-0303, assessor fax- 251-867-0216. (Appraiser/Auditor- 251-867-9168) www.co.escambia.al.us/taxa.html **Online access**- Access to the county property appraisal data is free at www.deltacomputersystems.com/AL/AL30/INDEX.HTML . Also, access the GIS-property database and Tax Office at www.emapsplus.com/ALEscambia/maps/. Click on search by name.

Etowah County

County Judge of Probate, PO Box 187, Gadsden, AL 35902. 256-549-5329; fax-256-439-6076; 8AM-5PM (CST) www.etowahcounty.org
Index: All in one. Records indexed on a public use terminal back to 1867. Only the public may search. Copy fee $1.00 per page. Cert fee- $5.00 per doc includes copy fee. Payee- Etowah County Judge of Probate. **Property tax/Assessing**- 800 Forrest Ave, Rm 117, Gadsden, AL 35901; 256-549-8145, assessor fax- 256-549-5279. www.etowahcounty.org **Online access**- Access to property data through a private company is free at www.deltacomputersystems.com/AL/AL31/pappraisala.html. Also, tax records are free at www.deltacomputersystems.com/AL/AL31/plinkquerya.html.

Fayette County

County Judge of Probate, PO Box 670, Fayette, AL 35555. 205-932-4519; fax-205-932-7600; 8AM-4PM
Index: Separate indices to search include deed, mortgages, judgments, UCC, notaries. Records indexed on a public use terminal back to 2000. Only the public may search. Copy fee $1.00 per page. Cert fee- $2.00 per doc plus copy fee. Payee- Fayette County Judge of Probate. **Other phones:** Treasurer- 205-932-4510; Elections- 205-932-5432. **Property tax/Assessing**- 113 Temple Ave N, PO Box 307, Fayette, AL 35555; 205-932-6081, assessor fax- 205-932-7600. (Appraiser/Auditor- 205-932-6081) hours- 8AM-5PM M; 8AM-4PM T-F **Online access**- Access to property data is free at www.fayettealmaps.com; Use password "Ruby." You may have to download the map viewer. Also, access parcel data on the GIS-mapping site free at www.fayettealmaps.com/. Must download Mapguide Viewer Software first. Password required for full data.

Franklin County

County Judge of Probate, PO Box 70, Russellville, AL 35653. 256-332-8801, R/E recording phone-256-332-8804; fax-256-332-8423; 8AM-6PM (CST)
Index: All in one. Records indexed on computer. Only the public may search. Copy fee $1.00 per page. Cert fee- $4.00 per doc plus copy fee. Payee- Franklin County Judge of Probate. **Other phones:** Treasurer- 256-332-8850; Elections- 256-332-8805. **Property tax/Assessing**- 410 N Jackson St, Russellville, AL 35653; 256-332-8831, assessor fax- 256-332-8417. hours- 8AM-5PM

Geneva County

County Judge of Probate, PO Box 430, Geneva, AL 36340-0430. Recording, R/E & UCC phone-334-684-5647; fax-334-684-5723; 8AM-5PM (CST)
Index: All in one. Records indexed on a public use terminal back to 1000. Only the public may search. Copy fee $1.00 per page. Cert fee- $3.00 per doc plus copy fee. Payee- Geneva County Judge of Probate. Office does not sell bulk data. **Other phones:** Elections- 334-684-5655; Main Number -334-684-5600;. **Property tax/Assessing**- PO Box 326, Geneva, AL 36340-0325; 334-684-5650, assessor fax- 334-684-5602. (Appraiser/Auditor- 334-684-5713) **Online access**- Access the GIS-property info database and Tax Office free at www.emapsplus.com/ALGeneva/maps/. Click on search by name.

Greene County

County Judge of Probate, PO Box 790, Eutaw, AL 35462-0790. 205-372-3340, R/E recording phone-205-372-3340 or 6945; fax- 205-372-0499; 8AM-4PM (CST)
Index: Records prior to 1994 are in real estate books; 1994 to present on computer. Records indexed on a public use terminal back to 1994. Only the public may search. Copy fee $1.00 per page. Cert fee- $2.00 per page includes copy fee. Payee- Greene County Judge of Probate. Office does not sell bulk data. **Other phones:** Elections- 205-372-3340 or 6943; Vital Records- 205-372-3340 or 6945. **Property tax/Assessing**- PO Box 510, 400 Morrow Ave WM Branch Courthouse, Eutaw, AL 35462; 205-372-3202, assessor fax- 205-372-1506. (Appraiser/Auditor- 205-372-3202);

Hale County

County Judge of Probate, 1001 Main St; Courthouse, Greensboro, AL 36744. Recording, R/E & UCC phone-334-624-8740; fax-334-624-8725; 8AM-4PM
Index: All in one. Record index not computerized. Only the public may search. Copy fee $1.00 per page. Cert fee- $3.00 per doc plus copy fee. Payee- Hale County Judge of Probate. **Other phones:** Treasurer- 334-624-4257. **Property tax/Assessing**- 1001 Main St, Greensboro, AL 36744; 334-624-3854, assessor fax- 334-624-8725. (Appraiser/Auditor- 334-624-0705) hours- 8AM-4:30PM

Henry County

County Judge of Probate, 101 Court Sq, #A, Abbeville, AL 36310. Recording, R/E & UCC phone-334-585-3257; fax-334-585-3610; 8AM-4:30PM
Index: All in one. Records indexed on a public use terminal back to 11/1/1995. Only the public may search. Copy fee $1.00 per page. Cert fee- $5.00 per doc plus copy fee. Payee- Henry County Judge of Probate. **Property tax/Assessing**- 101 Court Sq, Ste C, Abbeville, AL 36310; 334-585-3043, assessor fax-334-585-3890. (Appraiser/Auditor- 334-585-1379) www.henrycountyrevenue.com **Online access**- Access tax data search database free at www.henrycountyrevenue.com/search.aspx. Also, access parcel data on the GIS-mapping site free at www.alabamagis.com/Henry/. Must download Mapguide Viewer Software first.

Houston County

County Judge of Probate, PO Drawer 6406, Dothan, AL 36302. 334-836-1302, R/E recording phone-334-677-4723; 8AM-4:30PM (CST)
Index: All in one. Records indexed on a public use terminal back to 1985. Only the public may search. Will not search UCC records. Copy fee $1.00 per page. Cert fee- $2.00 per doc plus copy fee. Payee- Houston County Judge of Probate. Office does not sell bulk data. **Online access to Real Estate, Deed, Lien, Mortgage, Personal Property records:**

Subscription access to all Judge of Probate indexes available, call Michelle at 205-758-2000 x8112; $25.00 signup fee, view images at $.75 each or less, print images $.15 each. Data is same as appears on PAT. **Property tax/Assessing**- 462 N Oates St, Dothan, AL 36303; 334-677-4714, assessor fax- 334-677-4706.

Jackson County

County Judge of Probate, PO Box 128, Scottsboro, AL 35768. 256-574-9292; fax-256-574-9318; 8AM-4:30PM http://courthouse.jacksoncountyal.com/
Index: Separate indices to search include deeds, Mortgages, Marriages, Probate, UCC. Records indexed on a public use terminal back to 1983. Office personnel or visitors may perform searches. Office personnel will only assist; they will not do search for you. Office will search real estate records. Will search UCC records, but not tax liens. Copy fee $1.00 per page. Cert fee- $3.00 per doc plus copy fee. Payee- County Judge of Probate. **Property tax/Assessing**- PO Box 307, Scottsboro, AL 35768; 256-574-9270, assessor fax- 256-574-9225. (Appraiser/Auditor- 256-574-9390) www.jacksoncountyrevenue.com/ **Online access**- Access Rev Commission property tax lookup free at www.deltacomputersystems.com/AL/AL39/pappraisala.html. Search property tax payment look up at www.jacksoncountyrevenue.com/search.aspx.

Jefferson County (Bessemer Division)

County Judge of Probate, 1801 3rd Ave, Bessemer, AL 35020. 205-481-4100; 8AM-4:30PM (CST)
Index: Separate indices to search include Real, Personal, UCCs. Records indexed on a public use terminal back to 1986, includes Birmingham and Bessemer Divisions; Older records would be at their original filing location, by zip code. Office will perform a UCC search but public must search other records themselves. Search fee $20.00 for UCC. Copy fee $1.00 per page. Cert fee- $2.00 per doc plus copy fee. Payee- Jefferson County Judge of Probate. Office does not sell bulk data. **Property tax/Assessing**- 1801 3rd Ave N, Rm 209, Bess, AL 35020; 205-481-4125, assessor fax- 205-481-4128. (Appraiser/Auditor- 205-481-4120) www.jeffcointouch.com/jeffcointouch/departments/TaxAssessor/dd11.html **Online access**- Search tax assessor name list free at www.jeffcointouch.com/ecourthouse/ta-name-search.htm. Access the Tax Due Inquiry and Tax Sales list and Insolvents list free at http://tc.jeffcointouch.com/taxcollection/HTML/index.asp. Access equalization property records free at www.jeffcointouch.com/ecourthouse/boe-search-parcel-ID.htm but no name search. Search tax collector data free at www.jeffcointouch.com/ecourthouse/tc-name-search.htm.

Jefferson County (Birmingham Division)

County Judge of Probate, 716 Richard Arrington Jr Blvd #130; Courthouse, Birmingham, AL 35203. 205-325-5512- records, R/E recording phone-205-325-5411; fax-205-325-1437; 8AM-4:45PM (CST) www.jeffcointouch.com/jeffcointouch/ieindex.asp
Index: Indices by instrument type. Records indexed on a public use terminal back to 1986, includes Birmingham and Bessemer Divisions; Older records would be at their original filing location, by zip code. Only the public may search. Copy fee $1.00 per page. Cert fee- $2.00 per doc plus copy fee. Payee- Jefferson County Judge of Probate. **Other phones:** Treasurer- 205-325-5372; Vital Records- 205-325-5182. **Property tax/Assessing**- 716 Richard Arrington, Jr Blvd N, Rm 170, Birmingham, AL 35203; 205-325-5505, assessor fax- 205-325-5297. hours- 8AM-5PM www.jeffcointouch.com/jeffcointouch/departments/TaxAssessor/dd11.html **Online access**- Search tax assessor name list free at www.jeffcointouch.com/ecourthouse/ta-name-search.htm. Access the Tax Due Inquiry and Tax Sales list and Insolvents list free at http://tc.jeffcointouch.com/taxcollection/HTML/index.asp. Access equalization property records free at www.jeffcointouch.com/ecourthouse/boe-search-parcel-ID.htm but no name searching. Also, search tax collector data by name at www.jeffcointouch.com/ecourthouse/tc-name-search.htm.

Lamar County

County Judge of Probate, PO Box 338, Vernon, AL 35592. 205-695-9119; fax-205-695-9253; 8AM-5PM M,T,TH,F; 8AM-Noon W,Sat. (CST)
Index: Separate indices to search. Record index not computerized. Only the public may search. Copy fee $.50 per page. Cert fee- $3.00 per doc plus copy fee. Payee- Lamar County Judge of Probate. Office does not sell bulk data. **Other phones:** Treasurer- 205-695-9139. **Property tax/Assessing**- PO Box 1170, 44690 Hwy 17, Vernan, AL 35592; 205-695-9139, assessor fax- 205-695-9971. hours- 8AM-5PM **Online access**- Access the GIS-property info database and Tax Office free at www.emapsplus.com/ALLamar/maps/. Click on search by name.

Lauderdale County

County Judge of Probate, PO Box 1059, Florence, AL 35631-1059. 256-760-5800; fax-256-760-5807; 8AM-5PM (CST) www.lauderdalecountyonline.com
Index: All in one. Records indexed on a public use terminal back to 2001. Only the public may search. Copy fee $1.00 per page. Cert fee- $3.00 per doc plus copy fee. Payee- Lauderdale County Judge of Probate. Office does not sell bulk data. **Other phones:** Elections- 256-760-5800; Revenue Commssioner-256-760-5875. **Property tax/Assessing**- 200 S Court St, Florence, AL 35630; 256-760-5785, assessor fax-256-760-5790. www.lauderdalecountyonline.com **Online access**- Access to property appraisal data is free at www.deltacomputersystems.com/AL/AL41/pappraisala.html.

Lawrence County

County Judge of Probate, PO Box 310, Moulton, AL 35650. Recording, R/E & UCC phone-256-974-2440; fax-256-974-3188; 8AM-4PM (CST)
Index: All in one. Records indexed on a public use terminal back to 1990. Only the public may search. Copy fee $.25 per page. Cert fee- $3.00 per doc plus copy fee. Payee- Lawrence County Judge of Probate. Office does not sell bulk data. **Other phones:** Treasurer- 256-974-2401; Elections- 256-974-2440; Vital Records- 256-974-2440. **Property tax/Assessing**- 750 Main St, #1, Moulton, AL 35650; 256-974-2429, assessor fax- 256-974-2430. (Appraiser/Auditor- 256-974-2546) hours- 8AM-5PM M; 8AM-4PM T-F **Online access**- Access property data free at www.emapsplus.com/ALLawrence/maps/ including name searching.

Lee County

County Judge of Probate, PO Drawer 2266, Opelika, AL 36803. 334-745-9761; fax-334-705-5082; 8:30AM-4:30PM (CST)
Index: Separate indices to search include books, computer. Records indexed on a public use terminal back to 6/97. Only the public may search. Copy fee $1.00 per page. Cert fee- $3.00 per doc plus copy fee. Payee- Lee County Judge of Probate. Office does not sell bulk data. **Property tax/Assessing**-, Opelika, AL 36803; 334-745-9786, assessor fax- 334-705-5080. **Online access**- Access to property appraisal records is free at www.deltacomputersystems.com/AL/AL43/pappraisala.html. View property tax data free at www.deltacomputersystems.com/AL/AL41/plinkquerya.html. Also, access parcel data on the GIS-mapping site free at www.leecountymaps.com/. Must download Mapguide Viewer Software first. Password required for full data.

Limestone County

County Judge of Probate, 100 S Clinton St, #D, Athens, AL 35612. Recording, R/E & UCC phone-256-233-6427; fax-256-233-6474; 8AM-4:30PM (CST) www.probate.limestonecounty.net/
Index: All in one. Records indexed on a public use terminal back to 3/84. Only the public may search. Copy fee $1.00 per page. Cert fee- $3.00 per doc plus copy fee. Payee- Limestone County Judge of Probate. Office does not sell bulk data. **Online access to Real Estate, Deed, Lien, Mortgage, Personal Property records:** Access to recording records by subscription to the PROMIS system; contact Michelle Wooley at Syscon at 205-758-2000 x8112. $25 signup. View images at $.75 each or less, print images $.25 each. Data is same as appears on PAT. **Other phones:** Elections- 256-233-6427. **Property tax/Assessing**- 100 S Clinton St, #A, Athens, AL 35611; 256-233-6435, assessor fax- 256-233-6692. **Online access**- Access the GIS-property database and Tax Office free at www.emapsplus.com/ALlimestone/maps/. Click on search by name.

Lowndes County

County Judge of Probate, PO Box 5, Hayneville, AL 36040-0005. 334-548-2365; fax-334-548-5399; 8AM-4:30PM (CST)
Index: All in one. Records indexed on a public use terminal back to 2002. Only the public may search. Copy fee $1.00 per page. Cert fee- $4.00 per doc plus copy fee. Payee- Lowndes County Judge of Probate. **Other phones:** Elections- 334-548-2843. **Property tax/Assessing**- PO Box 186, Hayneville, AL 36040; 334-548-2271, assessor fax- 334-548-5342. (Appraiser/Auditor- 334-548-5619);

Macon County

County Judge of Probate, 101 E Northside St, #101, Tuskegee, AL 36083-1731. 334-724-2611, R/E recording phone-334-724-2508; fax-334-724-2512; 8:30AM-4:30PM (CST)
Index: All in one. Records indexed on a public use terminal back to 6/97. Office will perform a UCC search but public must search other records themselves. Copy fee $1.00 per page. Cert fee- $5.00 per doc plus copy fee. Payee- Macon County Judge of Probate. **Other phones:** Treasurer- 334-724-5120; Elections- 334-724-2617; Vital Records- 334-724-2611. **Property tax/Assessing**- 210 N Elm St, Tuskegee, AL 36083; 334-724-2603, assessor fax-334-724-2622. (Appraiser/Auditor- 334-724-2607) **Online access**- Access property and tax office data free at www.emapsplus.com/subscription/states/alabama/state.asp.

Madison County

County Judge of Probate, 100 Northside Sq, Rm 101, Huntsville, AL 35801-4820. 256-532-3339, R/E recording- 256-532-3784/3781, fax-256-532-3338; 8:30AM-4:30PM www.co.madison.al.us/probate/home.shtml
Index: All in one. Records indexed on a public use terminal back to 1971. Only the public may search. Copy fee $1.00 per page; DD214 $2.00 regardless of pages. Cert fee- $2.00 per doc plus copy fee. Payee- Madison County Judge of Probate. Office does not sell bulk data. **Online access to Real Estate, Deed, Lien, Judgment, Marriage, Military Discharge records:** Access to the judge of probate's recording index is free at http://probate.co.madison.al.us/. Land records including images go back to 1971; marriage and military discharges back to 1976. **Other phones:** Treasurer- 256-532-3370; Elections- 256-532-3331; Vital Records- 256-532-3342. **Property tax/Assessing**- 100 Northside Sq, Rm 121, Huntsville, AL 35801; 256-532-3350, assessor fax-256-532-6942. (Appraiser/Auditor- 256-532-3350) hours- 8:30AM-5PM www.co.madison.al.us **Online access**- Access assessor, appraiser data and land and lot books free at www.deltacomputersystems.com/AL/AL47/index_assessor.html. Access the GIS-property info database and Tax Office free at www.emapsplus.com/ALMadison/maps/. Click on search by name.

Marengo County

County Judge of Probate, PO Box 480668, Linden, AL 36748. 334-295-2210, R/E recording phone-334-295-2212; fax-334-295-2254; 8AM-4:30PM (CST)
Index: All in one. Records indexed on a public use terminal back to 1995. Only the public may search. Copy fee $.50 per page.Real estate record copy- $2.00 per page includes certification. Cert fee- $2.00 per cert plus copy fee. Payee- Marengo County Judge of Probate. **Other phones:** Treasurer- 334-295-2204; Elections- 334-295-2210. **Property tax/Assessing-** PO Box 480578, Linden, AL 36748; 334-295-2215, assessor fax- 334-295-2275. (Appraiser/Auditor- 334-295-2250);

Marion County

County Judge of Probate, PO Box 1687, Hamilton, AL 35570. Recording, R/E & UCC phone-205-921-2471; fax-205-921-5109; 8AM-N, 1-5PM (CST)
Index: All in one. Records indexed on a public use terminal back to 1996. Only the public may search. Copy fee $.50 per page. Cert fee- $1.00 per copy plus $.50 per page plus copy fee. Payee- Marion County Judge of Probate. **Other phones:** Treasurer- 205-921-3561; Elections- 205-921-2471; Vital Records- 205-921-2471. **Property tax/Assessing-** 132 Military St, Hamilton, AL 35570; 205-921-2606, assessor fax-205-921-3676. (Appraiser/Auditor- 205-921-2606) hours- 8AM-4:30PM **Online access-** Access the county GIS-mapping and property data for free at www.marioncountymaps.com/FrameSet.htm. Also, access parcel data on the GIS-mapping site free at www.marioncountymaps.com/. Must download Mapguide Viewer Software first.

Marshall County

County Judge of Probate, 425 Gunter Ave, Guntersville, AL 35976. 256-571-7764, R/E recording phone-256-571-7764 x208; fax-256-571-7732; 8AM-4:30PM (CST) www.mcit.us/
Index: Separate indices to search include real estate reverse and direct, misc, UCCs. Records indexed on a public use terminal back to 10/90. Only the public may search. Copy fee $1.00 per page. Cert fee- $.50 per doc plus copy fee. Payee- Marshall County Judge of Probate. Office does not sell bulk data. **Online access to Business License records:** Search business license database free at www.mcit.us/businesslicenses/searchengine/. Search Town of Douglas licenses at www.mcit.us/businesslicenses/douglas/. **Other phones:** Treasurer- 256-571-7758; Elections-256-571-7764 x202; Vital Records- 256-582-3174. **Property tax/Assessing-** 424 Blount Ave, Guntersville, AL 35976; 256-571-7743, assessor fax-256-571-7747. www.marshallco.org **Online access-** Access property data free at www.marshallgis.org and click on Land Lookup.

Mobile County

County Judge of Probate, PO Box 7, Mobile, AL 36601. 251-574-8497, R/E recording phone-251-690-8497; fax-251-574-4939; 8AM-5PM (CST) www.probate.mobilecountyal.gov/
Records room phone numbers: 251-574-8490/fax 251-574-5580. Index: Separate indices to search include film/book-1958-1983, film-1813-1958. Records indexed on a public use terminal back to 1984. Office personnel or visitors may perform searches. Office personnel will only do one name searches, cannot do large research. No fee for search. Copy fee $1.00 1st 10 pgs, $.50 each add'l page. Incorparation copy fee $1.50 per page. Cert fee- $2.00 per doc plus copy fee; exemplification $6.00 plus copy fee. Incorporation certification fee $1.50 per cert. Payee- Mobile County Judge of Probate. **Online access to Real Estate, Grantor/Grantee, Deed, Mortgage, UCC, Incorporation, Marriage, Estate Claim, Voter Registration records:** Access real estate, grantor/grantee, deed records and more back to 2000 free at www.mobilecounty.org/probatecourt/recordssearch.htm. Also, search real and personal property, estate claims, and election results. Search marriages at http://records.mobile-county.net/Login.aspx?SessionExpired=I. **Other phones:** Treasurer- 251-690-8585; Elections- 251-574-8480; Vital Records- 251-574-8490. **Property tax/Assessing-** PO Box 1169, 3925 Michael Blvd, Ste G, Mobile, AL 36603-1169; 251-574-8530, assessor fax- 251-574-4709. (Appraiser/Auditor- 251-690-8531) www.mobilecopropertytax.com **Online access-** Access real property and personal property tax records free at http://mobilerevenue.siteonestudio.com/TaxBill/search.asp. Also, City of Mobile property ownership data is free at http://maps.cityofmobile.org/webmapping.htm. Click on Property ownership information and choose to search by name.

Monroe County

County Judge of Probate, PO Box 665, Monroeville, AL 36461-0665. 251-743-4107, R/E recording phone-251-743-4107 x121; fax-251-575-4756; 8AM-5PM M,T,W,F; 8AM-N TH. (CST)
Index: Indices for deeds, mtgs, corporation records, marriages, probate records, adoptions, and election. Records indexed on a public use terminal back to 2003. Office will perform a UCC search but public must search other records themselves. Search fee-$25.00 per name. Copy fee $1.00 per page. Cert fee-$1.00 per page plus copy fee. Payee- Monroe County Judge of Probate. **Other phones:** Elections- 251-743-4107 x120; Vital Records- 251-743-4107 x121. **Property tax/Assessing-** 65 N Alabama Ave, Monroeville, AL 36461-0665; 251-743-4107 x124, assessor fax- 251-575-3320. (Appraiser/Auditor- 251-743-4107 x124);

Montgomery County

County Judge of Probate, PO Box 223, Montgomery, AL 36195. 334-832-1237, R/E recording phone-334-832-1236/1237; fax-334-832-7137; 8AM-5PM (CST) www.mc-ala.org/Home
Index: All in one. Records indexed on a public use terminal back to 1974. Only the public may search. Copy fee $1.00 per page. Cert fee- $2.00 per doc plus copy fee. Payee- Montgomery County Judge of Probate. Office does not sell bulk data. **Property tax/Assessing-** PO Box 1667, 100 S Lawrence, Montgomery, AL 36102; 334-832-4950, assessor fax-334-832-1644. (Appraiser/Auditor- 334-832-1303) www.mc-ala.org/Home/Elected%20Officials/Revenue%20Commissioner/ **Online access-** Access the GIS-property info database and Tax Office free at www.emapsplus.com/ALMontgomery/maps/.

Morgan County

County Judge of Probate, PO Box 848, Decatur, AL 35602-0848. 256-351-4680; fax-256-351-4884; 8AM-4:30PM (CST) www.morgancountyprobate.com/DesktopDefault.aspx
Index: Separate indices to search include computer back to 1982, books by type back to 1940. Records indexed on a public use terminal back to 1982. Only the public may search. Copy fee $1.00 per page; $.25 per page if you establish an account. Cert fee- $3.00 per doc plus copy fee. Payee- Morgan County Judge of Probate. Office does not sell data on disc. **Online access to Real Estate, Deed, Lien, Marriage, Probate, Judgment records:** Access the probate office index of recordings free at www.morgancountyprobate.com/DesktopDefault.aspx?tabindex=4&tabid=8. Select to search by document type. Land records go back to 1999. **Property tax/Assessing-** PO Box 696, Decatur, AL 35602-0848; 256-351-4690, assessor fax- 256-351-4699. **Online access-** Access to the GIS-property info and Tax Office property database is free at www.emapsplus.com/ALMorgan/maps/. Click on search by name. Also, access property appraiser data free at www.deltacomputersystems.com/AL/AL52/pappraisala.html. Also, search Revenue Commissioner property tax payment search at https://secure.termnetinc.com/morgan/paymentType.jsp but no name searching.

Perry County

County Judge of Probate, PO Box 478, Marion, AL 36756. 334-683-2210; fax-334-683-2211; 8AM-4:30PM (CST)
Index: Separate indices to search. Record index not computerized. Only the public may search. Copy fee $1.00 per page. Cert fee- $3.00 per cert plus copy fee. Payee- Perry County Judge of Probate. **Other phones:** Treasurer- 334-683-2200; Elections- 334-683-2210; Revenue Commissioner- 334-683-2219. **Property tax/Assessing-** PO Box 117, Marion, AL 36756; 334-683-2219, assessor fax- 334-683-2201. (Appraiser/Auditor- 334-683-2249) **Online access-** Access property and tax office data free at www.emapsplus.com/subscription/states/alabama/state.asp.

Pickens County

County Judge of Probate, PO Box 370, Carrollton, AL 35447. Recording, R/E & UCC phone-205-367-2010; fax-205-367-2011; 8AM-4PM (CST)
Index: All in one. Records indexed on a public use terminal back to 1988. Only the public may search. Copy fee $1.00 per page. Cert fee- $3.00 per instrument plus copy fee. Payee- Pickens County Judge of Probate. Office does not sell bulk data. **Other phones:** Elections- 205-367-2010. **Property tax/Assessing-** PO Box 447, 50 Court Sq, Rm 101, Carrollton, AL 35447; 205-367-2040, assessor fax-205-367-2041. (Appraiser - 205-367-2043) http://pickensalabama.com/default.aspx **Online access-** Access parcel data on the GIS-mapping site free at www.alabamagis.com/Pickens/. Must download Mapguide Viewer Software first.

Pike County

County Judge of Probate, 120 W Church St, Troy, AL 36081. Recording, R/E & UCC phone-334-566-1246; fax-334-566-8585; 8AM-5PM (CST)
Index: Separate indices to search include deeds, mortgages, Liens, Incorp, judgment, marriage, Misc., plat, UCC, Lis pendens, advers possession, probate, and elections. Records indexed on a public use terminal back to 10/1/2003. Only the public may search. Copy fee $.50 per page. Cert fee- $3.00 per page includes copy fee. Payee- Pike County Judge of Probate. Office does not sell bulk data. **Other phones:** Elections- 334-566-1246; County Commission- 334-566-6374. **Property tax/Assessing-** Revenue Commissioner, 120 W Church St, Troy, AL 36081; 334-566-1792, assessor fax- 334-566-6382. (Appraiser/Auditor- 334-566-0706) www.pike.revenue.com **Online access-** Access to GIS/mapping property information for free at www.alabamagis.com/Pike/

Randolph County

County Judge of Probate, PO Box 249, Wedowee, AL 36278. 256-357-4933; fax-256-357-9053; 8AM-5PM (CST)
Index: Separate indices to search include deed and mortgage, judgments, liens, satisfactions. Active records indexed on a public use terminal back to 400; inactive to 1964. Only the public may search. Copy fee $.25 per page. Cert fee- $2.00 per cert plus copy fee. Payee- Randolph County Judge of Probate. Office does not sell bulk data. **Property tax/Assessing-** PO Box 310, 1 Main St, Wedowee, AL 36278; 256-357-4343, assessor fax- 256-357-4344.

Russell County

County Judge of Probate, PO Box 700, Phenix City, AL 36868-0700. Recording, R/E & UCC phone-334-298-7979; fax-334-298-7979; 8:30AM-5PM (EST)
Index: Separate indices to search include books, computer. Records indexed on a public use terminal back to 6/21/02. Only the public may search. Copy fee $1.00 per page; corporation docs- $1.50 per page. Cert fee- $3.00 per doc plus copy fee. Exemplification $10.00 per doc. Payee- Russell County Judge of Probate. Office does not sell bulk data. **Other phones:** Treasurer- 334-298-6426; Elections- 334-298-7979; Vital Records- 334-297-0251. **Property**

tax/Assessing- PO Box 669, Phenix City, AL 36868-0700; 334-298-6922, assessor fax- 334-448-4705. (Appraiser/Auditor- 334-297-8996) **Online access**- Access the GIS-property info database and Tax Office free at www.emapsplus.com/ALRussell/maps/. Click on search by name.

Shelby County

County Judge of Probate, PO Box 825, Columbiana, AL 35051. 205-669-3720; fax-205-669-3884; 8AM-4:30PM (CST) www.shelbycountyalabama.com

Index: Books, computer indexes. Records indexed on a public use terminal back to 1971. Office will perform a UCC search but public must search other records themselves. Copy fee $1.00 per page. Cert fee- $3.00 per page plus copy fee. Payee- Shelby County Judge of Probate. Office does not sell bulk data. **Online access to Real Estate, Judgment, Deed, UCC, Notary, Fictitious Name, Marriage records:** Access probate court recording data free at www.shelbycountyalabama.com/probate/default.htm. **Other phones:** Elections- 205-669-3711; Vital Records- 205-669-3711. **Property tax/Assessing**- PO Box 1269, 102 Depot St, Columbiana, AL 35051; 205-670-6900, assessor fax- 205-670-6915. www.shelbycountyalabama.com **Online access**- Search property tax records free at www.shelbycountyalabama.com/

St. Clair County (Northern Congressional District)

County Judge of Probate, PO Box 220, Ashville, AL 35953. 205-594-2434; fax-205-594-2125; 8AM-5PM (CST) www.stclairco.com/index.php

Index: All in one. Records indexed on a public use terminal back to 1977 and includes both divisional offices. Only the public may search. Copy fee $1.00 per page. Cert fee- $3.00 per doc plus copy fee. Payee- Judge of Probate. **Other phones:** Vital Records- 334-206-5418. **Property tax/Assessing**- PO Box 1129, Ashville, AL 35953; 205-594-2160, assessor fax- 205-594-2163. (Appraiser/Auditor- 205-594-2468) **Online access**- Access to the GIS-property information database and Tax Office is free at www.emapsplus.com/ALstclair/maps/. Click on search by name. Also, access property appraiser data free at www.deltacomputersystems.com/AL/AL59/pappraisala.html. Also, access county assessor data free at www.deltacomputersystems.com/AL/AL59/plinkquerya.html.

St. Clair County (Southern Congressional District)

County Judge of Probate, 1815 Cogswell Ave, #212, Pell City, AL 35125. Recording, R/E & UCC phone-205-338-9449; fax-205-884-1182; 8AM-5PM (CST)

Index: All in one, in books. Records indexed on a public use terminal back to 1977 and includes both divisional offices. Only the public may search. Copy fee $1.00 per page. Cert fee- $3.00 per doc plus copy fee. Payee- St. Clair Judge of Probate. Office does not sell bulk data. **Property tax/Assessing**- 1815 Cogswell Ave, #205, Pell City, AL 35125; 205-884-2395, assessor fax- 205-814-9541. (Appraiser/Auditor- 205-884-2395) **Online access**- Access to county assessor data is free at www.deltacomputersystems.com/AL/AL59/plinkquerya.html. Also, access property appraiser data free at www.deltacomputersystems.com/AL/AL59/pappraisala.html. Access to the GIS-property information database and Tax Office is free at www.emapsplus.com/ALstclair/maps/. Click on search by name.

Sumter County

County Judge of Probate, PO Box 1040, Livingston, AL 35470-1040. Recording, R/E & UCC phone-205-652-7281; fax-205-652-6206; 8AM-4PM (CST)

Index: All in one. Records indexed on computer back to 11/99. Only the public may search. Copy fee $1.00 per page. Cert fee- $3.00 per doc plus copy fee. Payee- Sumter County Judge of Probate. **Other phones:** Treasurer- 205-652-2731; Elections- 205-652-7281; Vital Records- 205-652-7281. **Property tax/Assessing**- PO Box 277, 115 Franklin St, Livingston, AL 35470; 205-652-2424, assessor fax-205-652-9436. (Appraiser/Auditor- 205-652-2424)

Talladega County

County Judge of Probate, PO Box 737, Talladega, AL 35161. Recording, R/E & UCC phone-256-362-4175; fax-256-761-2128; 8AM-5PM (CST)

Index: Books. Records indexed on a public use terminal back to 11/1997. Only the public may search. Copy fee $1.00 per page. Cert fee- $4.00 per page includes copy fee. Payee- Talladega County Judge of Probate. Office does not sell bulk data. **Property tax/Assessing**- PO Box 1119, 1 Courthouse Sq, Rm 200, Talladega, AL 35161; 256-761-2123, assessor fax- 256-761-2019. (Appraiser/Auditor- 256-480-7057) **Online access**- Access the GIS-property info database and Tax Office free at www.emapsplus.com/ALtalladega/maps/. Click on search by name.

Tallapoosa County

County Judge of Probate, 125 N Broadnax St, Rm 126; Courthouse, Dadeville, AL 36853. Recording, R/E & UCC phone-256-825-1090; fax-256-825-1604; 8AM-5PM (CST) www.tallaco.com

Records indexed on a public use terminal back to 10/1000. Only the public may search. Copy fee $2.00 per page. Cert fee- $3.00 per instrument plus copy fee. Payee- Tallapoosa County Judge of Probate. Office does not sell bulk data. **Property tax/Assessing**- 125 N Broadnax St, Rm 106, Dadeville, AL 36853; 256-825-7831, assessor fax- 256-825-1017. (Appraiser/Auditor- 256-825-7831) **Online access**- Access parcel data on the GIS-mapping site free at www.tallapoosacountymaps.com/. Must download Mapguide Viewer Software first. Password required for full data.

Tuscaloosa County

County Judge of Probate, PO Box 20067, Tuscaloosa, AL 35402-0067. 205-349-3870 x205/6; fax-n/a; 8:30AM-5PM (CST) www.tuscco.com

Index: Separate indices to search include deeds, mortgages, Incorporation, Bond, Judgment, Misc., Plat, and UCC. Records indexed on a public use terminal back to various years depending on records. Only the public may search. Will not search UCC records. Copy fee $1.00 per page. Cert fee- $3.00 per doc plus copy fee. Payee- Judge of Probate. Office does not sell bulk data. **Online access to Real Estate, Grantor/Grantee, Deed, Lien, Judgment, UCC, Probate, Marriage, Mortgage, Plat records:** Access to the recorders database is free at www.tuscco.com/recordroom/. Also included are incorporations, bonds, discharges, exemptions. Probate court, miscellaneous. **Property tax/Assessing**- 714 Greensboro Ave, #108, Tuscaloosa, AL 35401; 205-349-3870 x370, assessor fax- 205-758-6170. **Online access**- Access to property and assessor data is free at www.emapsplus.com/ALTuscaloosa/maps/. Click on owner search. Also, access tax sale and other records free at www.tuscco.com/recordroom/.

Walker County

County Judge of Probate, PO Box 502, Jasper, AL 35502-0502. 205-384-7282, R/E recording phone-205-384-7281; fax-205-384-7005; 8:30AM-4PM (CST) www.walkercounty.com

Index: Separate indices to search include books, computer. Records indexed on a public use terminal back to 1992. Only the public may search. Copy fee $1.00 per page. Cert fee- $3.00 per doc plus copy fee. Payee- Walker County Judge of Probate. **Online access to Real Estate, Deed, Lien, Mortgage, Personal Property records:** Access Probate office real estate/property records by subscription; $25.00 signup fee, view images at $.75 each or less, print images $1 each. Data is same as appears on PAT. Call Michelle, 205-758-200 x8112 or email mwooley@syscomonline.com. **Other phones:** Treasurer- 205-384-7276; Elections- 205-384-7284. **Property tax/Assessing**- 1803 3rd Ave, Ste 102, Jasper, AL 35501; 205-384-7265, assessor fax- 205-384-7000. (Appraiser/Auditor- 205-384-7297) hours- 8AM-4PM www.walkercountymaps.com **Online access**- Access parcel data on the GIS-mapping site free at www.walkercountymaps.com/. Must download Mapguide Viewer Software first. Password required for full data.

Washington County

County Judge of Probate, PO Box 549, Chatom, AL 36518. Recording, R/E & UCC phone-251-847-2201; fax-251-847-6450; 8AM-4:30PM (CST)

Index: Separate indices to search include corporations, judgments, will, bond, partnership, prior to 12/1995. Records indexed on a public use terminal back to 12/1995. Only the public may search. Copy fee $1.00 per page 1st 10, then $.50. Cert fee- $3.00 per doc plus copy fee. Payee- Washington County Judge of Probate. Office does not sell bulk data. **Other phones:** Treasurer- 251-847-2208; Elections- 251-847-2201. **Property tax/Assessing**- PO Box 847, 1 Court St, Chatom, AL 36518; 251-847-2780, assessor fax- 251-847-3944.

Wilcox County

County Judge of Probate, PO Box 668, Camden, AL 36726. Recording, R/E & UCC phone-334-682-4883; fax-334-682-9484; 8AM-4:30PM (CST)

Index: All in one. Records indexed on a public use terminal back to 7/01. Only the public may search; office may search UCC records if they have time. Copy fee $1.00 per page. Cert fee- $3.50 per cert plus copy fee. Payee- Wilcox County Judge of Probate. Office does not sell bulk data. **Other phones:** Treasurer- 334-682-9112. **Property tax/Assessing**- 100 Broad St, Camden, AL 36726; 334-682-4625, assessor fax- 334-682-5684.

Winston County

County Judge of Probate, PO Box 27, Double Springs, AL 35553. Recording, R/E & UCC phone-205-489-5219; fax-205-489-5135; 8AM-4:30PM (8AM-N 1st Sat of every month). (CST)

Index: All in one. Records indexed on a public use terminal back to 99. Only the public may search. Copy fee $1.00 per page, $10.00 copy of plat, $15.00 per 11 x 17 copy. Cert fee- $3.00 per includes plus copy fee. Payee- Winston County Judge of Probate. Office does not sell bulk data. **Other phones:** Vital Records- 205-489-5219 (marriages). **Property tax/Assessing**- PO Box 160, 11 Blake Dr, Rm 1, Double Springs, AL 35553; 205-489-5166, assessor fax- 205-489-8926. (Appraiser/Auditor- 205-489-5166) hours- 8AM-4:30PM **Online access**- Access parcel data on the GIS-mapping site free at www.alabamagis.com/winston/. Must download Mapguide Viewer Software first. Password required for full data.

Alabama County Locator

You will usually be able to find the city name in the City/County Cross Reference below. In that case, it is a simple matter to determine the county from the cross reference. However, only the official U.S. Postal Service city names are included in this index. There are an additional 40,000 place names that people use in their addresses. Therefore, we have also included a ZIP/City Cross Reference immediately following the City/County Cross Reference.

If you know the ZIP Code but the city name does not appear in the City/County Cross Reference index, look up the ZIP Code in the ZIP/City Cross Reference, find the city name, then look up the city name in the City/County Cross Reference. For example, you want to know the county for an address of Menands, NY 12204. There is no "Menands" in the City/County Cross Reference. The ZIP/City Cross Reference shows that ZIP Codes 12201-12288 are for the city of Albany. Looking back in the City/County Cross Reference, Albany is in Albany County.

Alabama City/County Cross Reference

ABBEVILLE Henry
ABERNANT Tuscaloosa
ADAMSVILLE Jefferson
ADDISON (35540) Winston(95), Cullman(4)
ADGER (35006) Jefferson(91), Walker(6), Tuscaloosa(2)
AKRON Hale
ALABASTER Shelby
ALBERTA Wilcox
ALBERTVILLE (35951) Marshall(73), De Kalb(26)
ALBERTVILLE Marshall
ALEXANDER CITY (35010) Tallapoosa(95), Elmore(2), Coosa(1)
ALEXANDER CITY Tallapoosa
ALEXANDRIA Calhoun
ALICEVILLE (35442) Pickens(87), Sumter(11)
ALLEN Clarke
ALLGOOD Blount
ALMA Clarke
ALPINE Talladega
ALTON Jefferson
ALTOONA (35952) Etowah(57), Blount(41)
ANDALUSIA (36420) Covington(97), Escambia(2)
ANDALUSIA (36421) Covington(98), Conecuh(1)
ANDERSON (35610) Lauderdale(74), Limestone(25)
ANNEMANIE Wilcox
ANNISTON (36203) Calhoun(79), Talladega(20)
ANNISTON Calhoun
ARAB (35016) Marshall(82), Cullman(14), Blount(2)
ARDMORE (35739) Limestone(77), Madison(22)
ARITON (36311) Dale(66), Barbour(23), Coffee(10)
ARLEY Winston
ARLINGTON (36722) Wilcox(97), Marengo(2)
ASHFORD Houston
ASHLAND Clay
ASHVILLE St. Clair
ATHENS Limestone
ATMORE (36502) Escambia(93), Monroe(4), Baldwin(2)
ATMORE Escambia
ATTALLA Etowah
AUBURN (36830) Lee(90), Macon(9)
AUBURN Lee
AUBURN UNIVERSITY Lee
AUTAUGAVILLE Autauga
AXIS Mobile
BAILEYTON (35019) Cullman(73), Morgan(26)
BANKS (36005) Pike(67), Bullock(32)
BANKSTON Fayette
BAY MINETTE Baldwin
BAYOU LA BATRE Mobile
BEAR CREEK Marion
BEATRICE Monroe
BEAVERTON Lamar
BELK Fayette
BELLAMY Sumter
BELLE MINA Limestone
BELLWOOD Geneva
BERRY (35546) Fayette(65), Tuscaloosa(31), Walker(3)
BESSEMER (35022) Jefferson(95), Shelby(4)
BESSEMER Jefferson
BIGBEE Washington
BILLINGSLEY (36006) Autauga(59), Chilton(41)
BIRMINGHAM (35244) Jefferson(53), Shelby(46)
BIRMINGHAM (35242) Shelby(90), Jefferson(9)
BIRMINGHAM Jefferson
BLACK Geneva
BLOUNTSVILLE Blount
BOAZ (35957) Marshall(78), De Kalb(18), Blount(3)
BOAZ Etowah
BOLIGEE Greene
BOLINGER Choctaw
BON AIR Talladega
BON SECOUR Baldwin
BOOTH Autauga
BOYKIN Wilcox
BRANTLEY (36009) Crenshaw(94), Coffee(5)
BREMEN (35033) Cullman(90), Walker(9)
BRENT (35034) Bibb(98), Perry(1)
BREWTON (36426) Escambia(98), Conecuh(1)
BREWTON Escambia
BRIDGEPORT Jackson
BRIERFIELD (35035) Bibb(97), Shelby(2)
BRILLIANT Marion
BROOKLYN Conecuh
BROOKSIDE Jefferson
BROOKWOOD (35444) Tuscaloosa(97), Jefferson(2)
BROWNSBORO Madison
BRUNDIDGE (36010) Pike(77), Coffee(21)
BRYANT Jackson
BUCKS Mobile
BUHL Tuscaloosa
BURNT CORN Monroe
BURNWELL Walker
BUTLER Choctaw
BYNUM Calhoun
CALERA (35040) Shelby(86), Chilton(13)
CALVERT Washington
CAMDEN Wilcox
CAMP HILL (36850) Tallapoosa(76), Chambers(19), Lee(3)
CAMPBELL Clarke
CAPSHAW Limestone
CARBON HILL (35549) Walker(83), Fayette(16)
CARDIFF Jefferson
CARLTON Clarke
CARROLLTON Pickens
CASTLEBERRY (36432) Conecuh(67), Escambia(32)
CATHERINE Wilcox
CECIL (36013) Montgomery(94), Macon(5)
CEDAR BLUFF Cherokee
CENTRE Cherokee
CENTREVILLE Bibb
CHANCELLOR (36316) Geneva(53), Coffee(46)
CHAPMAN Butler
CHATOM Washington
CHELSEA Shelby
CHEROKEE Colbert
CHILDERSBURG Talladega
CHOCCOLOCCO Calhoun
CHUNCHULA Mobile
CITRONELLE (36522) Mobile(95), Washington(4)
CLANTON (35046) Chilton(97), Coosa(2)
CLANTON Chilton
CLAY Jefferson
CLAYTON Barbour
CLEVELAND Blount
CLINTON Greene
CLIO Barbour
CLOPTON (36317) Henry(88), Barbour(6), Dale(5)
CLOVERDALE Lauderdale
COALING Tuscaloosa
CODEN Mobile
COFFEE SPRINGS (36318) Geneva(70), Coffee(29)
COFFEEVILLE Clarke
COKER Tuscaloosa
COLLINSVILLE (35961) De Kalb(79), Etowah(10), Cherokee(10)
COLUMBIA (36319) Henry(51), Houston(48)
COLUMBIANA Shelby
COOK SPRINGS St. Clair
COOSADA Elmore
CORDOVA Walker
COTTONDALE Tuscaloosa
COTTONTON Russell
COTTONWOOD Houston
COURTLAND Lawrence
COWARTS Houston
COY Wilcox
CRAGFORD (36255) Clay(97), Tallapoosa(2)
CRANE HILL Cullman
CREOLA Mobile
CROMWELL Choctaw
CROPWELL St. Clair
CROSSVILLE (35962) De Kalb(93), Marshall(6)
CUBA Sumter
CULLMAN Cullman
CUSSETA (36852) Lee(74), Chambers(25)
DADEVILLE Tallapoosa
DALEVILLE (36322) Dale(95), Coffee(2), Geneva(2)
DANVILLE (35619) Lawrence(49), Morgan(49)
DAPHNE Baldwin
DAUPHIN ISLAND Mobile
DAVISTON (36256) Tallapoosa(96), Clay(3)
DAWSON De Kalb
DAYTON Marengo
DE ARMANVILLE Calhoun
DEATSVILLE (36022) Elmore(82), Autauga(17)
DECATUR (35603) Morgan(98), Lawrence(1)
DECATUR Morgan
DEER PARK Washington
DELMAR Winston
DELTA (36258) Clay(55), Cleburne(29), Randolph(15)
DEMOPOLIS Marengo
DETROIT (35552) Marion(56), Lamar(43)
DICKINSON Clarke
DIXONS MILLS Marengo
DOCENA Jefferson
DOLOMITE Jefferson
DORA (35062) Jefferson(52), Walker(47)
DOTHAN (36303) Houston(92), Dale(7)
DOTHAN Houston
DOUBLE SPRINGS Winston
DOUGLAS Marshall
DOZIER (36028) Covington(56), Crenshaw(43)

DUNCANVILLE (35456) Tuscaloosa(98), Bibb(1)
DUTTON Jackson
EAST TALLASSEE Tallapoosa
EASTABOGA (36260) Calhoun(64), Talladega(35)
ECHOLA Tuscaloosa
ECLECTIC Elmore
EDWARDSVILLE Cleburne
EIGHT MILE Mobile
ELBA Coffee
ELBERTA Baldwin
ELDRIDGE (35554) Fayette(64), Walker(29), Marion(5)
ELKMONT Limestone
ELMORE Elmore
ELROD Tuscaloosa
EMELLE Sumter
EMPIRE (35063) Walker(72), Blount(19), Jefferson(8)
ENTERPRISE (36330) Coffee(90), Dale(9)
ENTERPRISE Coffee
EPES Sumter
EQUALITY (36026) Elmore(61), Coosa(38)
ESTILLFORK Jackson
ETHELSVILLE Pickens
EUFAULA Autauga
EUFAULA Barbour
EUTAW Greene
EVA (35621) Morgan(91), Cullman(8)
EVERGREEN Conecuh
EXCEL Monroe
FACKLER Jackson
FAIRFIELD Jefferson
FAIRHOPE Baldwin
FALKVILLE (35622) Morgan(78), Cullman(21)
FAUNSDALE Marengo
FAYETTE (35555) Fayette(92), Tuscaloosa(5), Lamar(1)
FITZPATRICK (36029) Macon(49), Bullock(32), Montgomery(18)
FIVE POINTS Chambers
FLAT ROCK (35966) Jackson(64), De Kalb(35)
FLOMATON Escambia
FLORALA Covington
FLORENCE Lauderdale
FOLEY Baldwin
FOREST HOME (36030) Butler(96), Wilcox(3)
FORKLAND Greene
FORT DAVIS Macon
FORT DEPOSIT (36032) Lowndes(75), Butler(24)
FORT MITCHELL Russell
FORT PAYNE (35967) De Kalb(96), Cherokee(3)
FORT PAYNE De Kalb
FORT RUCKER Dale
FOSTERS Tuscaloosa
FRANKLIN Monroe
FRANKVILLE Washington
FRISCO CITY Monroe
FRUITDALE Washington
FRUITHURST Cleburne
FULTON Clarke
FULTONDALE Jefferson
FURMAN Wilcox
FYFFE De Kalb
GADSDEN (35907) Etowah(98), Calhoun(1)
GADSDEN Etowah
GAINESTOWN Clarke
GAINESVILLE (35464) Sumter(86), Greene(13)
GALLANT (35972) Etowah(75), St. Clair(24)
GALLION (36742) Marengo(95), Hale(4)
GANTT Covington
GARDEN CITY Cullman
GARDENDALE Jefferson
GAYLESVILLE Cherokee
GENEVA Geneva
GEORGIANA (36033) Butler(98), Conecuh(1)
GERALDINE De Kalb
GILBERTOWN Choctaw
GLEN ALLEN Fayette
GLENWOOD (36034) Crenshaw(70), Pike(29)
GOODSPRINGS Walker
GOODWATER (35072) Clay(47), Coosa(32), Tallapoosa(18)
GOODWAY Monroe
GORDO (35466) Pickens(93), Tuscaloosa(6)
GORDON Houston
GOSHEN (36035) Pike(76), Crenshaw(23)
GRADY (36036) Montgomery(75), Crenshaw(24)
GRAHAM Randolph
GRAND BAY Mobile
GRANT Marshall
GRAYSVILLE Jefferson
GREEN POND Bibb
GREENSBORO Hale
GREENVILLE Butler
GROVE HILL Clarke
GROVEOAK (35975) De Kalb(92), Marshall(7)
GUIN (35563) Marion(91), Fayette(4), Lamar(4)
GULF SHORES Baldwin
GUNTERSVILLE (35976) Marshall(97), Blount(2)
GURLEY (35748) Madison(94), Jackson(5)
HACKLEBURG Marion
HALEYVILLE (35565) Winston(66), Marion(28), Franklin(4)
HAMILTON Marion
HANCEVILLE Cullman
HARDAWAY Macon
HARPERSVILLE Shelby
HARTFORD Geneva
HARTSELLE Morgan
HARVEST (35749) Madison(74), Limestone(25)
HATCHECHUBBEE Russell
HAYDEN Blount
HAYNEVILLE Lowndes
HAZEL GREEN Madison
HEADLAND (36345) Henry(83), Houston(10), Dale(6)
HEFLIN (36264) Cleburne(92), Randolph(7)
HELENA Shelby
HENAGAR (35978) De Kalb(79), Jackson(20)
HIGDON (35979) De Kalb(66), Jackson(33)
HIGHLAND HOME (36041) Crenshaw(97), Montgomery(2)
HILLSBORO Lawrence
HODGES (35571) Franklin(69), Marion(30)
HOLLINS Clay
HOLLY POND Cullman
HOLLYTREE Jackson
HOLLYWOOD Jackson
HOLY TRINITY Russell
HONORAVILLE (36042) Crenshaw(54), Butler(45)
HOPE HULL (36043) Montgomery(65), Lowndes(34)
HORTON (35980) Marshall(66), Blount(33)
HOUSTON Winston
HUNTSVILLE Madison
HURTSBORO (36860) Russell(86), Bullock(8), Macon(4)
HUXFORD Escambia
IDER De Kalb
IRVINGTON Mobile
JACHIN Choctaw
JACK Coffee
JACKSON Clarke
JACKSONS GAP Tallapoosa
JACKSONVILLE Calhoun
JASPER (35503) Walker(92), Winston(7)
JASPER Walker
JEFFERSON Marengo
JEMISON Chilton
JONES (36749) Dallas(53), Autauga(46)
JOPPA (35087) Cullman(50), Morgan(37), Marshall(11)
KANSAS Walker
KELLERMAN Tuscaloosa
KELLYTON (35089) Tallapoosa(60), Coosa(39)
KENNEDY (35574) Lamar(55), Pickens(33), Fayette(11)
KENT Elmore
KILLEN Lauderdale
KIMBERLY Jefferson
KINSTON (36453) Coffee(53), Geneva(42), Covington(3)
KNOXVILLE (35469) Greene(52), Tuscaloosa(47)
LACEYS SPRING (35754) Morgan(98), Marshall(1)
LAFAYETTE Chambers
LAMISON Wilcox
LANETT Chambers
LANGSTON (35755) Marshall(58), Jackson(41)
LAPINE (36046) Crenshaw(51), Montgomery(48)
LAVACA Choctaw
LAWLEY (36793) Bibb(68), Chilton(24), Perry(7)
LEEDS (35094) Jefferson(76), Shelby(13), St. Clair(10)
LEESBURG (35983) Cherokee(98), De Kalb(1)
LEIGHTON Colbert
LENOX Conecuh
LEROY Washington
LESTER Limestone
LETOHATCHEE (36047) Lowndes(68), Montgomery(31)
LEXINGTON Lauderdale
LILLIAN Baldwin
LINCOLN (35096) Talladega(89), Calhoun(10)
LINDEN Marengo
LINEVILLE (36266) Clay(82), Randolph(17)
LISMAN Choctaw
LITTLE RIVER Baldwin
LIVINGSTON Sumter
LOACHAPOKA Lee
LOCKHART Covington
LOCUST FORK Blount
LOGAN (35098) Cullman(89), Winston(10)
LOUISVILLE Barbour
LOWER PEACH TREE (36751) Monroe(47), Wilcox(28), Clarke(23)
LOWNDESBORO Lowndes
LOXLEY Baldwin
LUVERNE Crenshaw
LYNN Winston
MADISON (35756) Limestone(81), Madison(18)
MADISON Madison
MAGNOLIA Marengo
MAGNOLIA SPRINGS Baldwin
MALCOLM Washington
MALVERN Geneva
MAPLESVILLE (36750) Chilton(94), Bibb(5)
MARBURY (36051) Autauga(43), Elmore(30), Chilton(26)
MARGARET St. Clair
MARION Perry
MARION JUNCTION (36759) Dallas(94), Perry(5)
MATHEWS (36052) Montgomery(93), Bullock(6)
MAYLENE Shelby
MC CALLA (35111) Tuscaloosa(62), Jefferson(35), Bibb(1)
MC INTOSH Washington
MC KENZIE (36456) Butler(74), Covington(12), Conecuh(12)
MC SHAN Pickens
MC WILLIAMS Wilcox
MEGARGEL Monroe
MELVIN Choctaw
MENTONE (35984) De Kalb(81), Cherokee(18)
MERIDIANVILLE Madison
MEXIA Monroe
MIDLAND CITY (36350) Dale(91), Houston(8)
MIDWAY (36053) Barbour(79), Bullock(20)
MILLBROOK Elmore
MILLERS FERRY Wilcox
MILLERVILLE Clay
MILLPORT (35576) Lamar(89), Pickens(10)
MILLRY (36558) Washington(84), Choctaw(15)
MINTER (36761) Dallas(59), Lowndes(39), Wilcox(1)
MOBILE Mobile
MONROEVILLE Monroe
MONTEVALLO (35115) Shelby(83), Chilton(15), Bibb(1)
MONTGOMERY Montgomery
MONTROSE Baldwin
MOODY St. Clair
MOORESVILLE Limestone
MORRIS Jefferson
MORVIN Clarke
MOULTON Lawrence
MOUNDVILLE (35474) Hale(87), Tuscaloosa(12)
MOUNT HOPE (35651) Lawrence(98), Franklin(1)
MOUNT MEIGS Montgomery
MOUNT OLIVE Jefferson
MOUNT VERNON Mobile
MULGA Jefferson
MUNFORD Talladega
MUSCADINE Cleburne
MUSCLE SHOALS Colbert
MYRTLEWOOD Marengo
NANAFALIA Marengo
NATURAL BRIDGE Winston

NAUVOO (35578) Walker(79), Winston(20)
NEEDHAM Choctaw
NEW BROCKTON Coffee
NEW CASTLE Jefferson
NEW HOPE (35760) Madison(88), Marshall(11)
NEW MARKET Madison
NEWBERN (36765) Hale(85), Perry(14)
NEWELL Randolph
NEWTON (36352) Houston(55), Dale(42), Geneva(1)
NEWVILLE (36353) Henry(72), Dale(27)
NORMAL Madison
NORTHPORT Tuscaloosa
NOTASULGA (36866) Macon(73), Tallapoosa(20), Lee(5)
OAK HILL Wilcox
OAKMAN (35579) Walker(98), Tuscaloosa(1)
ODENVILLE St. Clair
OHATCHEE Calhoun
ONEONTA Blount
OPELIKA (36801) Lee(98), Chambers(1)
OPELIKA (36804) Lee(97), Macon(1), Russell(1)
OPELIKA Lee
OPP (36467) Covington(95), Coffee(4)
ORANGE BEACH Baldwin
ORRVILLE Dallas
OWENS CROSS ROADS Madison
OZARK Dale
PAINT ROCK Jackson
PALMERDALE Jefferson
PANOLA Sumter
PANSEY Houston
PARRISH Walker
PAUL Conecuh
PELHAM Shelby
PELL CITY St. Clair
PENNINGTON Choctaw
PERDIDO (36562) Baldwin(90), Escambia(9)
PERDUE HILL Monroe
PEROTE Bullock
PETERMAN (36471) Monroe(96), Conecuh(3)
PETERSON Tuscaloosa
PETREY Crenshaw
PHENIX CITY (36870) Lee(72), Russell(27)
PHENIX CITY (36867) Russell(90), Lee(9)
PHENIX CITY Russell
PHIL CAMPBELL (35581) Franklin(87), Marion(12)
PIEDMONT (36272) Calhoun(61), Cherokee(26), Etowah(8), Cleburne(3)
PIKE ROAD Montgomery
PINCKARD Dale
PINE APPLE Wilcox
PINE HILL Wilcox
PINE LEVEL Montgomery
PINSON (35126) Jefferson(96), Blount(3)
PISGAH (35765) Jackson(92), De Kalb(7)
PITTSVIEW Russell
PLANTERSVILLE (36758) Dallas(90), Autauga(7), Chilton(1)
PLEASANT GROVE Jefferson
POINT CLEAR Baldwin
PRAIRIE Wilcox
PRATTVILLE Autauga
PRINCETON Jackson
QUINTON (35130) Walker(65), Jefferson(34)
RAGLAND St. Clair
RAINBOW CITY Etowah
RAINSVILLE De Kalb
RALPH (35480) Tuscaloosa(97), Greene(2)
RAMER Montgomery
RANBURNE Cleburne
RANDOLPH (36792) Bibb(72), Chilton(27)
RANGE Conecuh
RED BAY Franklin
RED LEVEL (36474) Covington(97), Conecuh(2)
REFORM Pickens
REMLAP (35133) Blount(93), St. Clair(6)
REPTON (36475) Conecuh(64), Monroe(35)
RIVER FALLS Covington
RIVERSIDE St. Clair
ROANOKE (36274) Randolph(93), Chambers(6)
ROBERTSDALE Baldwin
ROCKFORD Coosa
ROGERSVILLE (35652) Lauderdale(98), Limestone(1)
RUSSELLVILLE (35654) Franklin(80), Colbert(14), Lawrence(5)
RUTLEDGE (36071) Crenshaw(97), Butler(2)
RYLAND Madison
SAFFORD (36773) Dallas(89), Marengo(10)
SAGINAW Shelby
SAINT ELMO Mobile
SAINT STEPHENS Washington
SALEM (36874) Lee(95), Russell(4)
SALITPA Clarke
SAMANTHA Tuscaloosa
SAMSON (36477) Geneva(91), Coffee(8)
SARALAND Mobile
SARDIS (36775) Dallas(81), Lowndes(18)
SATSUMA Mobile
SAWYERVILLE Hale
SAYRE Jefferson
SCOTTSBORO (35769) Jackson(70), Marshall(29)
SCOTTSBORO Jackson
SEALE Russell
SECTION (35771) Jackson(96), De Kalb(3)
SELMA (36701) Dallas(98), Perry(1)
SELMA (36703) Dallas(97), Autauga(2)
SELMA Dallas
SEMINOLE Baldwin
SEMMES Mobile
SHANNON Jefferson
SHEFFIELD Colbert
SHELBY Shelby
SHORTER Macon
SHORTERVILLE Henry
SILAS Choctaw
SILURIA Shelby
SILVERHILL Baldwin
SIPSEY Walker
SKIPPERVILLE (36374) Dale(60), Barbour(39)
SLOCOMB (36375) Geneva(84), Houston(15)
SMITHS Lee
SMITHS STATION Lee
SNOW HILL Wilcox
SOMERVILLE Morgan
SPANISH FORT Baldwin
SPRING GARDEN Cherokee
SPRINGVILLE (35146) St. Clair(81), Blount(17), Jefferson(1)
SPROTT Perry
SPRUCE PINE Franklin
STANTON Chilton
STAPLETON Baldwin
STEELE St. Clair
STERRETT Shelby
STEVENSON Jackson
STOCKTON Baldwin
SULLIGENT Lamar
SUMITON Walker
SUMMERDALE Baldwin
SUNFLOWER Washington
SWEET WATER Marengo
SYCAMORE Talladega
SYLACAUGA Talladega
SYLVANIA De Kalb
TALLADEGA (35160) Talladega(96), Clay(3)
TALLADEGA Talladega
TALLASSEE (36078) Elmore(81), Tallapoosa(18)
TANNER Limestone
THEODORE Mobile
THOMASTON Marengo
THOMASVILLE (36784) Clarke(79), Marengo(16), Wilcox(3)
THORSBY Chilton
TIBBIE Washington
TITUS (36080) Elmore(98), Coosa(1)
TONEY (35773) Madison(72), Limestone(27)
TOWN CREEK (35672) Lawrence(97), Colbert(2)
TOWNLEY Walker
TOXEY Choctaw
TRAFFORD (35172) Blount(83), Jefferson(16)
TRENTON Jackson
TRINITY (35673) Lawrence(78), Morgan(21)
TROY (36079) Pike(93), Coffee(6)
TROY (36081) Pike(98), Bullock(1)
TROY Pike
TRUSSVILLE (35173) Jefferson(81), St. Clair(18)
TUSCALOOSA Tuscaloosa
TUSCUMBIA Colbert
TUSKEGEE Macon
TUSKEGEE INSTITUTE Macon
TYLER (36785) Lowndes(75), Dallas(25)
UNION GROVE (35175) Marshall(89), Morgan(10)
UNION SPRINGS Bullock
UNIONTOWN (36786) Perry(88), Hale(5), Marengo(5)
URIAH Monroe
VALHERMOSO SPRINGS Morgan
VALLEY (36854) Chambers(74), Lee(25)
VALLEY Lee
VALLEY HEAD De Kalb
VANCE Tuscaloosa
VANDIVER Shelby
VERBENA (36091) Chilton(95), Autauga(3)
VERNON Lamar
VINA (35593) Franklin(85), Marion(14)
VINCENT (35178) Shelby(70), St. Clair(29)
VINEGAR BEND Washington
VINEMONT Cullman
VREDENBURGH Monroe
WADLEY (36276) Randolph(68), Chambers(15), Clay(11), Tallapoosa(4)
WAGARVILLE Washington
WALKER SPRINGS Clarke
WALNUT GROVE Etowah
WARD (36922) Choctaw(91), Sumter(8)
WARRIOR (35180) Jefferson(55), Blount(44)
WATERLOO Lauderdale
WATSON Jefferson
WATTSVILLE St. Clair
WAVERLY (36879) Chambers(50), Lee(49)
WEAVER Calhoun
WEBB Houston
WEDOWEE Randolph
WELLINGTON Calhoun
WEOGUFKA Coosa
WEST BLOCTON (35184) Bibb(98), Tuscaloosa(1)
WEST GREENE Greene
WESTOVER Shelby
WETUMPKA Elmore
WHATLEY (36482) Clarke(97), Monroe(2)
WILMER Mobile
WILSONVILLE Shelby
WILTON Shelby
WINFIELD (35594) Fayette(56), Marion(43)
WING (36483) Covington(63), Escambia(36)
WOODLAND Randolph
WOODSTOCK (35188) Bibb(88), Tuscaloosa(11)
WOODVILLE (35776) Jackson(82), Marshall(15), Madison(1)
YORK Sumter

Alabama ZIP/City Cross Reference

35004-35004 MOODY
35005-35005 ADAMSVILLE
35006-35006 ADGER
35007-35007 ALABASTER
35010-35011 ALEXANDER CITY
35013-35013 ALLGOOD
35014-35014 ALPINE
35015-35015 ALTON
35016-35016 ARAB
35019-35019 BAILEYTON
35020-35023 BESSEMER
35031-35031 BLOUNTSVILLE
35032-35032 BON AIR
35033-35033 BREMEN
35034-35034 BRENT
35035-35035 BRIERFIELD
35036-35036 BROOKSIDE
35038-35038 BURNWELL
35040-35040 CALERA
35041-35041 CARDIFF
35042-35042 CENTREVILLE
35043-35043 CHELSEA
35044-35044 CHILDERSBURG
35045-35046 CLANTON
35048-35048 CLAY
35049-35049 CLEVELAND
35051-35051 COLUMBIANA
35052-35052 COOK SPRINGS
35053-35053 CRANE HILL
35054-35054 CROPWELL
35055-35058 CULLMAN
35060-35060 DOCENA
35061-35061 DOLOMITE
35062-35062 DORA
35063-35063 EMPIRE
35064-35064 FAIRFIELD
35068-35068 FULTONDALE
35070-35070 GARDEN CITY
35071-35071 GARDENDALE
35072-35072 GOODWATER
35073-35073 GRAYSVILLE
35074-35074 GREEN POND
35077-35077 HANCEVILLE
35078-35078 HARPERSVILLE
35079-35079 HAYDEN
35080-35080 HELENA
35082-35082 HOLLINS
35083-35083 HOLLY POND
35085-35085 JEMISON
35087-35087 JOPPA
35089-35089 KELLYTON
35091-35091 KIMBERLY
35094-35094 LEEDS
35096-35096 LINCOLN
35097-35097 LOCUST FORK
35098-35098 LOGAN
35111-35111 MC CALLA
35112-35112 MARGARET
35114-35114 MAYLENE
35115-35115 MONTEVALLO
35116-35116 MORRIS
35117-35117 MOUNT OLIVE
35118-35118 MULGA
35119-35119 NEW CASTLE
35120-35120 ODENVILLE
35121-35121 ONEONTA
35123-35123 PALMERDALE
35124-35124 PELHAM
35125-35125 PELL CITY
35126-35126 PINSON
35127-35127 PLEASANT GROVE
35128-35128 PELL CITY
35130-35130 QUINTON
35131-35131 RAGLAND
35133-35133 REMLAP
35135-35135 RIVERSIDE
35136-35136 ROCKFORD
35137-35137 SAGINAW
35139-35139 SAYRE
35142-35142 SHANNON
35143-35143 SHELBY
35144-35144 SILURIA
35146-35146 SPRINGVILLE
35147-35147 STERRETT
35148-35148 SUMITON
35149-35149 SYCAMORE
35150-35151 SYLACAUGA
35160-35161 TALLADEGA
35171-35171 THORSBY
35172-35172 TRAFFORD
35173-35173 TRUSSVILLE
35175-35175 UNION GROVE
35176-35176 VANDIVER
35178-35178 VINCENT
35179-35179 VINEMONT
35180-35180 WARRIOR
35181-35181 WATSON
35182-35182 WATTSVILLE
35183-35183 WEOGUFKA
35184-35184 WEST BLOCTON
35185-35185 WESTOVER
35186-35186 WILSONVILLE
35187-35187 WILTON
35188-35188 WOODSTOCK
35200-35299 BIRMINGHAM
35401-35407 TUSCALOOSA
35440-35440 ABERNANT
35441-35441 AKRON
35442-35442 ALICEVILLE
35443-35443 BOLIGEE
35444-35444 BROOKWOOD
35446-35446 BUHL
35447-35447 CARROLLTON
35448-35448 CLINTON
35449-35449 COALING
35452-35452 COKER
35453-35453 COTTONDALE
35456-35456 DUNCANVILLE
35457-35457 ECHOLA
35458-35458 ELROD
35459-35459 EMELLE
35460-35460 EPES
35461-35461 ETHELSVILLE
35462-35462 EUTAW
35463-35463 FOSTERS
35464-35464 GAINESVILLE
35466-35466 GORDO
35468-35468 KELLERMAN
35469-35469 KNOXVILLE
35470-35470 LIVINGSTON
35471-35471 MC SHAN
35473-35473 NORTHPORT
35474-35474 MOUNDVILLE
35475-35476 NORTHPORT
35477-35477 PANOLA
35478-35478 PETERSON
35480-35480 RALPH
35481-35481 REFORM
35482-35482 SAMANTHA
35485-35487 TUSCALOOSA
35490-35490 VANCE
35491-35491 WEST GREENE
35501-35504 JASPER
35540-35540 ADDISON
35541-35541 ARLEY
35542-35542 BANKSTON
35543-35543 BEAR CREEK
35544-35544 BEAVERTON
35545-35545 BELK
35546-35546 BERRY
35548-35548 BRILLIANT
35549-35549 CARBON HILL
35550-35550 CORDOVA
35551-35551 DELMAR
35552-35552 DETROIT
35553-35553 DOUBLE SPRINGS
35554-35554 ELDRIDGE
35555-35555 FAYETTE
35559-35559 GLEN ALLEN
35560-35560 GOODSPRINGS
35563-35563 GUIN
35564-35564 HACKLEBURG
35565-35565 HALEYVILLE
35570-35570 HAMILTON
35571-35571 HODGES
35572-35572 HOUSTON
35573-35573 KANSAS
35574-35574 KENNEDY
35575-35575 LYNN
35576-35576 MILLPORT
35577-35577 NATURAL BRIDGE
35578-35578 NAUVOO
35579-35579 OAKMAN
35580-35580 PARRISH
35581-35581 PHIL CAMPBELL
35582-35582 RED BAY
35584-35584 SIPSEY
35585-35585 SPRUCE PINE
35586-35586 SULLIGENT
35587-35587 TOWNLEY
35592-35592 VERNON
35593-35593 VINA
35594-35594 WINFIELD
35601-35609 DECATUR
35610-35610 ANDERSON
35611-35614 ATHENS
35615-35615 BELLE MINA
35616-35616 CHEROKEE
35617-35617 CLOVERDALE
35618-35618 COURTLAND
35619-35619 DANVILLE
35620-35620 ELKMONT
35621-35621 EVA
35622-35622 FALKVILLE
35630-35634 FLORENCE
35640-35640 HARTSELLE
35643-35643 HILLSBORO
35645-35645 KILLEN
35646-35646 LEIGHTON
35647-35647 LESTER
35648-35648 LEXINGTON
35649-35649 MOORESVILLE
35650-35650 MOULTON
35651-35651 MOUNT HOPE
35652-35652 ROGERSVILLE
35653-35654 RUSSELLVILLE
35660-35660 SHEFFIELD
35661-35662 MUSCLE SHOALS
35670-35670 SOMERVILLE
35671-35671 TANNER
35672-35672 TOWN CREEK
35673-35673 TRINITY
35674-35674 TUSCUMBIA
35677-35677 WATERLOO
35699-35699 DECATUR
35739-35739 ARDMORE
35740-35740 BRIDGEPORT
35741-35741 BROWNSBORO
35742-35742 CAPSHAW
35744-35744 DUTTON
35745-35745 ESTILLFORK
35746-35746 FACKLER
35747-35747 GRANT
35748-35748 GURLEY
35749-35749 HARVEST
35750-35750 HAZEL GREEN
35751-35751 HOLLYTREE
35752-35752 HOLLYWOOD
35754-35754 LACEYS SPRING
35755-35755 LANGSTON
35756-35758 MADISON
35759-35759 MERIDIANVILLE
35760-35760 NEW HOPE
35761-35761 NEW MARKET
35762-35762 NORMAL
35763-35763 OWENS CROSS ROADS
35764-35764 PAINT ROCK
35765-35765 PISGAH
35766-35766 PRINCETON
35767-35767 RYLAND
35768-35769 SCOTTSBORO
35771-35771 SECTION
35772-35772 STEVENSON
35773-35773 TONEY
35774-35774 TRENTON
35775-35775 VALHERMOSO SPRINGS
35776-35776 WOODVILLE
35800-35899 HUNTSVILLE
35901-35905 GADSDEN
35906-35906 RAINBOW CITY
35907-35907 GADSDEN
35950-35951 ALBERTVILLE
35952-35952 ALTOONA
35953-35953 ASHVILLE
35954-35954 ATTALLA
35956-35957 BOAZ
35958-35958 BRYANT
35959-35959 CEDAR BLUFF
35960-35960 CENTRE
35961-35961 COLLINSVILLE
35962-35962 CROSSVILLE
35963-35963 DAWSON
35964-35964 DOUGLAS
35966-35966 FLAT ROCK
35967-35968 FORT PAYNE
35971-35971 FYFFE
35972-35972 GALLANT
35973-35973 GAYLESVILLE
35974-35974 GERALDINE
35975-35975 GROVEOAK
35976-35976 GUNTERSVILLE
35978-35978 HENAGAR
35979-35979 HIGDON
35980-35980 HORTON
35981-35981 IDER
35983-35983 LEESBURG
35984-35984 MENTONE
35986-35986 RAINSVILLE
35987-35987 STEELE
35988-35988 SYLVANIA
35989-35989 VALLEY HEAD
35990-35990 WALNUT GROVE
35999-35999 GADSDEN
36003-36003 AUTAUGAVILLE
36004-36004 EUFAULA
36005-36005 BANKS
36006-36006 BILLINGSLEY
36008-36008 BOOTH
36009-36009 BRANTLEY
36010-36010 BRUNDIDGE
36013-36013 CECIL
36015-36015 CHAPMAN
36016-36016 CLAYTON
36017-36017 CLIO
36020-36020 COOSADA
36022-36022 DEATSVILLE
36023-36023 EAST TALLASSEE
36024-36024 ECLECTIC
36025-36025 ELMORE
36026-36026 EQUALITY
36027-36027 EUFAULA
36028-36028 DOZIER
36029-36029 FITZPATRICK
36030-36030 FOREST HOME
36031-36031 FORT DAVIS
36032-36032 FORT DEPOSIT
36033-36033 GEORGIANA
36034-36034 GLENWOOD
36035-36035 GOSHEN
36036-36036 GRADY
36037-36037 GREENVILLE
36038-36038 GANTT
36039-36039 HARDAWAY
36040-36040 HAYNEVILLE
36041-36041 HIGHLAND HOME
36042-36042 HONORAVILLE
36043-36043 HOPE HULL
36045-36045 KENT
36046-36046 LAPINE
36047-36047 LETOHATCHEE

ZIP Range	City
36048-36048	LOUISVILLE
36049-36049	LUVERNE
36051-36051	MARBURY
36052-36052	MATHEWS
36053-36053	MIDWAY
36054-36054	MILLBROOK
36057-36057	MOUNT MEIGS
36061-36061	PEROTE
36062-36062	PETREY
36064-36064	PIKE ROAD
36065-36065	PINE LEVEL
36066-36068	PRATTVILLE
36069-36069	RAMER
36071-36071	RUTLEDGE
36072-36072	EUFAULA
36075-36075	SHORTER
36078-36078	TALLASSEE
36079-36079	TROY
36080-36080	TITUS
36081-36082	TROY
36083-36083	TUSKEGEE
36087-36088	TUSKEGEE INSTITUTE
36089-36089	UNION SPRINGS
36091-36091	VERBENA
36092-36093	WETUMPKA
36100-36199	MONTGOMERY
36201-36207	ANNISTON
36250-36250	ALEXANDRIA
36251-36251	ASHLAND
36253-36253	BYNUM
36254-36254	CHOCCOLOCCO
36255-36255	CRAGFORD
36256-36256	DAVISTON
36257-36257	DE ARMANVILLE
36258-36258	DELTA
36260-36260	EASTABOGA
36261-36261	EDWARDSVILLE
36262-36262	FRUITHURST
36263-36263	GRAHAM
36264-36264	HEFLIN
36265-36265	JACKSONVILLE
36266-36266	LINEVILLE
36267-36267	MILLERVILLE
36268-36268	MUNFORD
36269-36269	MUSCADINE
36270-36270	NEWELL
36271-36271	OHATCHEE
36272-36272	PIEDMONT
36273-36273	RANBURNE
36274-36274	ROANOKE
36275-36275	SPRING GARDEN
36276-36276	WADLEY
36277-36277	WEAVER
36278-36278	WEDOWEE
36279-36279	WELLINGTON
36280-36280	WOODLAND
36301-36305	DOTHAN
36310-36310	ABBEVILLE
36311-36311	ARITON
36312-36312	ASHFORD
36313-36313	BELLWOOD
36314-36314	BLACK
36316-36316	CHANCELLOR
36317-36317	CLOPTON
36318-36318	COFFEE SPRINGS
36319-36319	COLUMBIA
36320-36320	COTTONWOOD
36321-36321	COWARTS
36322-36322	DALEVILLE
36323-36323	ELBA
36330-36331	ENTERPRISE
36340-36340	GENEVA
36343-36343	GORDON
36344-36344	HARTFORD
36345-36345	HEADLAND
36346-36346	JACK
36349-36349	MALVERN
36350-36350	MIDLAND CITY
36351-36351	NEW BROCKTON
36352-36352	NEWTON
36353-36353	NEWVILLE
36360-36361	OZARK
36362-36362	FORT RUCKER
36370-36370	PANSEY
36371-36371	PINCKARD
36373-36373	SHORTERVILLE
36374-36374	SKIPPERVILLE
36375-36375	SLOCOMB
36376-36376	WEBB
36401-36401	EVERGREEN
36419-36419	ALLEN
36420-36421	ANDALUSIA
36425-36425	BEATRICE
36426-36427	BREWTON
36429-36429	BROOKLYN
36431-36431	BURNT CORN
36432-36432	CASTLEBERRY
36435-36435	COY
36436-36436	DICKINSON
36439-36439	EXCEL
36441-36441	FLOMATON
36442-36442	FLORALA
36444-36444	FRANKLIN
36445-36445	FRISCO CITY
36446-36446	FULTON
36449-36449	GOODWAY
36451-36451	GROVE HILL
36453-36453	KINSTON
36454-36454	LENOX
36455-36455	LOCKHART
36456-36456	MC KENZIE
36457-36457	MEGARGEL
36458-36458	MEXIA
36460-36462	MONROEVILLE
36467-36467	OPP
36469-36469	EVERGREEN
36469-36469	PAUL
36470-36470	PERDUE HILL
36471-36471	PETERMAN
36473-36473	RANGE
36474-36474	RED LEVEL
36475-36475	REPTON
36476-36476	RIVER FALLS
36477-36477	SAMSON
36480-36480	URIAH
36481-36481	VREDENBURGH
36482-36482	WHATLEY
36483-36483	WING
36501-36501	ALMA
36502-36504	ATMORE
36505-36505	AXIS
36507-36507	BAY MINETTE
36509-36509	BAYOU LA BATRE
36510-36510	BIGBEE
36511-36511	BON SECOUR
36512-36512	BUCKS
36513-36513	CALVERT
36515-36515	CARLTON
36518-36518	CHATOM
36521-36521	CHUNCHULA
36522-36522	CITRONELLE
36523-36523	CODEN
36524-36524	COFFEEVILLE
36525-36525	CREOLA
36526-36526	DAPHNE
36527-36527	SPANISH FORT
36528-36528	DAUPHIN ISLAND
36529-36529	DEER PARK
36530-36530	ELBERTA
36532-36533	FAIRHOPE
36535-36536	FOLEY
36538-36538	FRANKVILLE
36539-36539	FRUITDALE
36540-36540	GAINESTOWN
36541-36541	GRAND BAY
36542-36542	GULF SHORES
36543-36543	HUXFORD
36544-36544	IRVINGTON
36545-36545	JACKSON
36547-36547	GULF SHORES
36548-36548	LEROY
36549-36549	LILLIAN
36550-36550	LITTLE RIVER
36551-36551	LOXLEY
36553-36553	MC INTOSH
36555-36555	MAGNOLIA SPRINGS
36556-36556	MALCOLM
36558-36558	MILLRY
36559-36559	MONTROSE
36560-36560	MOUNT VERNON
36561-36561	ORANGE BEACH
36562-36562	PERDIDO
36564-36564	POINT CLEAR
36567-36567	ROBERTSDALE
36568-36568	SAINT ELMO
36569-36569	SAINT STEPHENS
36570-36570	SALITPA
36571-36571	SARALAND
36572-36572	SATSUMA
36574-36574	SEMINOLE
36575-36575	SEMMES
36576-36576	SILVERHILL
36577-36577	SPANISH FORT
36578-36578	STAPLETON
36579-36579	STOCKTON
36580-36580	SUMMERDALE
36581-36581	SUNFLOWER
36582-36582	THEODORE
36583-36583	TIBBIE
36584-36584	VINEGAR BEND
36585-36585	WAGARVILLE
36586-36586	WALKER SPRINGS
36587-36587	WILMER
36590-36590	THEODORE
36600-36612	MOBILE
36613-36613	EIGHT MILE
36614-36695	MOBILE
36701-36703	SELMA
36720-36720	ALBERTA
36721-36721	ANNEMANIE
36722-36722	ARLINGTON
36723-36723	BOYKIN
36726-36726	CAMDEN
36727-36727	CAMPBELL
36728-36728	CATHERINE
36731-36731	DAYTON
36732-36732	DEMOPOLIS
36736-36736	DIXONS MILLS
36738-36738	FAUNSDALE
36740-36740	FORKLAND
36741-36741	FURMAN
36742-36742	GALLION
36744-36744	GREENSBORO
36745-36745	JEFFERSON
36747-36747	LAMISON
36748-36748	LINDEN
36749-36749	JONES
36750-36750	MAPLESVILLE
36751-36751	LOWER PEACH TREE
36752-36752	LOWNDESBORO
36753-36753	MC WILLIAMS
36754-36754	MAGNOLIA
36756-36756	MARION
36758-36758	PLANTERSVILLE
36759-36759	MARION JUNCTION
36760-36760	MILLERS FERRY
36761-36761	MINTER
36762-36762	MORVIN
36763-36763	MYRTLEWOOD
36764-36764	NANAFALIA
36765-36765	NEWBERN
36766-36766	OAK HILL
36767-36767	ORRVILLE
36768-36768	PINE APPLE
36769-36769	PINE HILL
36771-36771	PRAIRIE
36773-36773	SAFFORD
36775-36775	SARDIS
36776-36776	SAWYERVILLE
36778-36778	SNOW HILL
36779-36779	SPROTT
36782-36782	SWEET WATER
36783-36783	THOMASTON
36784-36784	THOMASVILLE
36785-36785	TYLER
36786-36786	UNIONTOWN
36790-36790	STANTON
36792-36792	RANDOLPH
36793-36793	LAWLEY
36801-36804	OPELIKA
36830-36832	AUBURN
36849-36849	AUBURN UNIVERSITY
36850-36850	CAMP HILL
36851-36851	COTTONTON
36852-36852	CUSSETA
36853-36853	DADEVILLE
36854-36854	VALLEY
36855-36855	FIVE POINTS
36856-36856	FORT MITCHELL
36858-36858	HATCHECHUBBEE
36859-36859	HOLY TRINITY
36860-36860	HURTSBORO
36861-36861	JACKSONS GAP
36862-36862	LAFAYETTE
36863-36863	LANETT
36865-36865	LOACHAPOKA
36866-36866	NOTASULGA
36867-36870	PHENIX CITY
36871-36871	PITTSVIEW
36872-36872	VALLEY
36874-36874	SALEM
36875-36875	SEALE
36877-36877	SMITHS
36877-36877	SMITHS STATION
36879-36879	WAVERLY
36901-36901	BELLAMY
36903-36903	BOLINGER
36904-36904	BUTLER
36906-36906	CROMWELL
36907-36907	CUBA
36908-36908	GILBERTOWN
36910-36910	JACHIN
36911-36911	LAVACA
36912-36912	LISMAN
36913-36913	MELVIN
36915-36915	NEEDHAM
36916-36916	PENNINGTON
36919-36919	SILAS
36921-36921	TOXEY
36922-36922	WARD
36925-36925	YORK

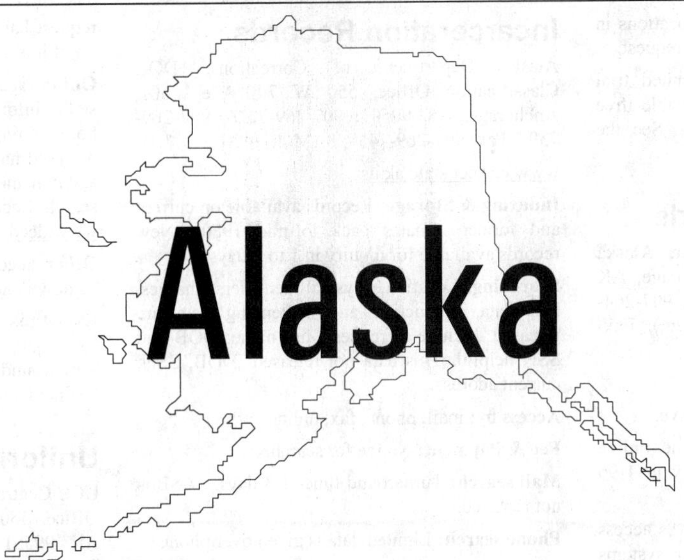

General Help Numbers:

Governor's Office
PO Box 110001 — 907-465-3500
Juneau, AK 99811-0001 — Fax 907-465-3532
www.gov.state.ak.us — 8AM-5PM

Attorney General's Office
Law Department — 907-465-3600, 465-2122
PO Box 110300 — Fax 907-465-2075
Juneau, AK 99811-0300 — 8AM-4:30PM
www.law.state.ak.us

Legislative Records
Legislative Information Office — 907-465-4648
120 4th St #111-State Capitol — Fax 907-465-2864
Juneau, AK 99801-1182 — 8AM-5PM
http://w3.legis.state.ak.us/index.php

State Archives
Alaska State Archives — 907-465-2270
141 Willoughby Ave — Fax 907-465-2465
Juneau, AK 99801-1720 — 9AM-5PM
www.archives.state.ak.us

State Specifics:

Capital: Juneau
Juneau Borough

Time Zone: AK (Alaska Standard Time)*
* Alaska's Aleutian Islands are HT (Hawaii Standard Time)

Number of Boroughs/Political Divisions: 23

Population: 686,293

Website: www.state.ak.us

State Agencies

Criminal Records

Department of Public Safety, Records and Identification, 5700 E Tudor Rd, Anchorage, AK 99507; 907-269-5767, Fax- 907-269-5091; 8AM-4:30PM. www.dps.state.ak.us

The state releases three types of records - Full Criminal History, Interested Person, and Any Person. Searches may be name-based or fingerprint-based. A Full History is only available to the subject or to government agencies.

Indexing & Storage: Records available indefinitely. Paper records available since 1959. New records available for inquiry in 5 days for arrests, 120 days for dispositions. 88% of arrests in database have final dispositions recorded; 85% for those arrests in last 5 years. Approximately 66% of records are fingerprint-supported.

Searching: "Interested Party" results are for those granting supervisory power over children or dependent adults and contain all records. "Any Person" contain past convictions and current offender information. Name searches return state records only. Include in request- set of fingerprints, full name. Fingerprints return state records and for "Interested person" requesters who so desire national results from FBI files. This data not released- sealed records. Juvenile records are not released unless adjudicated as an adult or if a serious traffic offense. All records are released, including those without final dispositions, to "Interested Person" requesters. "Any Person" requesters receive criminal records and open cases.

Access by: mail, in person.

Fee & Payment: The state name search fee is $20.00, the state fingerprint search fee is $35.00. A state and FBI combined search is $54.25 (not available for Any Person Reports). Fee payee- State of Alaska. Prepayment required. Personal Check accepted. Credit cards not accepted.

Mail search: Turnaround time- varies by volume. The fee is $5.00 for a 2nd copy.

In person search: There are 33 DPS locations in the state to process a name based-record request.

Other access: Name searching of limited trial court records and calendars are available free online at www.courtrecords.alaska.gov/. See the Statewide Court Records profile.

Statewide Court Records

Office of the Administrative Director, Alaska Court System, 820 W 4th Ave, Anchorage, AK 99501; 907-264-8232 (Administration), 907-264-0491 (Records), 907-264-8212 (IT Dept), Fax-907-264-8291; 8AM-4:30PM.

www.state.ak.us/courts/

The record center located at 825 W 4th Ave.

Indexing & Storage: Records available online only. New records available for inquiry in 1-90 days. Records are not destroyed.

Online search: The home web page gives access to Appellate opinions. There are two systems available for trial court records, both are partial; neither is statewide. Perform a name search at www.courtrecords.alaska.gov/. This is an older system with 15 jurisdictions. Records are uploaded every three months. The Alaska Court System is migrating to a newer electronic case information system called CourtView at www.courtrecords.alaska.gov/pa/pa.urd/pamw6500.display. 24 sites are active, records are real time. Search results give case number, file date, disposition date, charge, and sentence. Note that the initial index gives the only the name used on the first pleading.

Sexual Offender Registry

Department of Public Safety, Statewide Services Div-SOCKR Unit, 5700 E Tudor Rd, Anchorage, AK 99507; 907-269-0396, Fax- 907-269-0394; 8AM-4:30PM.

www.dps.state.ak.us/sorweb/Sorweb.aspx

AS 18.65.087 authorizes the Department of Public Safety to maintain a central registry of sex offenders required to register under AS 12.63.010 and to make information about the offender available to the public.

Indexing & Storage: Records available since August 10, 1994. There two levels or classes of sexual offenders in this state. All registration forms of offenders who register locally are forwarded to this address. New records available for inquiry in 24 hours.

Searching: Only offenders convicted of the sex offenses specified under AS 12.63.100 are required to register. Persons who have been arrested or charged with a sex offense are not required to register unless the arrest or charge results in a conviction. The following information about those offenders available to the public: name, address, photograph, place of employment, date of birth, crime for which convicted, date of conviction and place and court of conviction. This data not released- sealed records.

Access by: mail, in person, online.

Mail search: Turnaround time- 2-4 days.

In person: Results are usually returned by mail.

Online search: Name searching and geographic searching is available at the website. This is the primary search offered by the agency.

Incarceration Records

Alaska Department of Corrections, DOC Classification Office, 550 W 7th Ave, #601, Anchorage, AK 99501; 907-269-7426, 907-269-7397, Fax- 907-269-7439; 8AM-4:30PM.

www.correct.state.ak.us

Indexing & Storage: Records available on current and former inmates back to mid 1980s. New records available for inquiry in 1 to 2 days.

Searching: Location, physical identifiers, charges, bail data, conviction and sentencing data are released. Include in request- full name; DOB and SSN helpful. This data not released- DOB, SSN, current address.

Access by: mail, phone, fax, online.

Fee & Payment: No fee for search.

Mail search: Turnaround time- 1-3 days. SASE is not required.

Phone search: Limited data is given over phone.

Fax search: Requests accepted by fax, if not extensive in nature.

Online search: No online searching available from the agency, but it promotes a private company with a free search of DOC inmates and offenders at https://www.vinelink.com/vinelink/siteInfoAction.do?siteId=2001.

Corporation, LP, LLC, LLP, Trademarks/Servicemarks, Fictitious/Assumed Name

Corporation Section, Department of Commerce, Community & Econ Dev, PO Box 110808, Juneau, AK 99811-0808 (Courier address- 150 Third Street Rm 217, Juneau, AK 99801); 907-465-2530, Fax- 907-465-3257; 8AM-5PM.

www.commerce.state.ak.us/occ/home.htm

Non-profit records here also. Email questions to corporations@alaska.gov.

Indexing & Storage: Records available from early 1900's on. Prior to 1960, the records are kept at the State Archives. You must go through this office in order to get records. New records available for inquiry immediately.

Searching: All information contained is considered public record. Include in request- full name of business. In addition to the articles of organization, business entity records available include: Annual Reports, Officers, Directors, DBAs, Prior (Merged) names, Inactive and Reserved names.

Access by: mail, phone, fax, in person, online.

Fee & Payment: Copy fee is $1.00 per page. A copy of a document that is more than one page is $10.00. A copy of all documents pertaining to one file is $30.00 1st 50 pages then $1.00 per page. Certification is $5.00. A copy of a biennial report is $1.00. Fee payee- State of Alaska. Prepayment required. Personal checks, Visa/MCaccepted.

Mail search: Turnaround time- 1 to 2 weeks. Requested information can be placed on a CD for $25.00.

Phone search: You can make a search request only if you are local and you plan to pick-up.

Fax search: Typical fax searches involve use of a credit card.

In person search: All results are mailed unless request is being processed using expedited service. The agency will call the requester when his/her request has been processed and is ready for pick-up, if it is a local call.

Online search: At the website, one can access status information on corps, LLCs, LLP, LP (all both foreign and domestic), registered and reserved names. Search by entity name, registered agent name, or by officer name. No fee. Also, search Securities Dept. Disciplinary Actions at www.dced.state.ak.us/bsc/orders.htm.

Other access: The business license database can be downloaded from the web.

Expedited service: Expedited service is available for mail, phone and in person searches. Turnaround time- 48 hours. Add $50.00 per business name.

Uniform Commercial Code

UCC Central File Systems Office, State Recorder's Office, 550 West 7th Ave #1200A, Anchorage, AK 99501-3564; 907-269-8873, 907-269-8899, Fax- 907-269-8945; 8AM-3:30PM.

www.ucc.alaska.gov/

The statewide recording system consists of 34 separate recording districts serviced by a total of 14 separate offices.

Indexing & Storage: Records available from 1961 when the UCC system was established. Records are computerized since October 20, 1986 or earlier if with continuations. Records are kept on microfiche since 1-14-63 or prior if continuations filed. New records available for inquiry in 24 hours.

Searching: Use search request form UCC-11. Search results include all filings up to one year after lapse. All tax liens are filed at the local District Recorder offices. Direct questions to Paula_Kelsey@dnr.state.ak.us. Include in request-debtor name. All requests must be in writing.

Access by: mail, fax, in person, online.

Fee & Payment: Search by name is $15.00 per debtor name, with copies fee is $25.00 per debtor name. Certification is an additional $5.00. Document page copies are $2.00 per file. Financing Statements are $20.00 each, Amendment statements $10.00 each. Fee payee-Alaska Department of Revenue. Prepayment required. Personal checks, Visa, and MasterCard accepted.

Mail search: Turnaround time- 1 to 2 days. SASE not required.

Fax search: Credit cards accepted.

In person search: A public access terminal is available, there is no fee to use the terminal.

Online search: One can search by debtor or secured party name, date, doc number or document type at www.ucc.alaska.gov/ucc/search.cfm. There is no fee.

Other access: CDs or FTPs of document images can be purchased from the State Recorder's Office (907-269-8878).

Federal & State Tax Liens

Records not maintained by a state level agency. All tax liens are filed at local District Recorder Offices.

Sales Tax Registrations

State does not impose sales tax.

Birth Certificates

Department of Health & Social Services, Bureau of Vital Statistics, 5441 Commercial Blvd, Juneau, AK 99801; 907-465-3391, Fax- 907-465-3618; 8AM-5PM. www.hss.state.ak.us/dph/bvs/

Birth records are strictly confidential until they become public records which is 100 years after the event. The Bureau of Vital Statistics maintains offices in Anchorage, Fairbanks, and Juneau (see web page).

Indexing & Storage: Records available from 1890 to present. New records available for inquiry immediately.

Searching: Person requesting must be a parent or guardian or give a justifying reason for request. No adoption information will be given except according to statute. Include in request- full name, names of parents, mother's maiden name, date of birth, place of birth, reason for information request, relationship to person of record, and copy of requester's ID. Also, include a daytime phone number. Direct questions to BVSOFFICE@health.state.ak.us.

Access by: mail, phone, fax, in person, online.

Fee & Payment: The $20.00 search fee includes a 3 year search. Add $1.00 per year searched for each year over 3 years. Fee payee- Bureau of Vital Statistics. Prepayment required. Personal checks and major credit cards accepted.

Mail search: Turnaround time- 3-5 days. SASE not required.

Phone search: See expedited services.

Fax search: See expedited services.

In person search: Turnaround time 10 minutes.

Online search: Records may be ordered online via a state-designated vendor at www.vitalchek.com. There is a $5.50 service fee plus a $5.50 expedite fee. Use of credit card required.

Expedited service: Expedited service is available for mail, phone, online and fax searches. Turnaround time- 2 days. Add $11.00 for using a credit card and necessary fund for express mail or courier delivery.

Death Records

Department of Health & Social Services, Bureau of Vital Statistics, 5441 Commercial Blvd, Juneau, AK 99801; 907-465-3391, Fax- 907-465-3618; 8AM-5PM. www.hss.state.ak.us/dph/bvs/

The Bureau of Vital Statistics maintains offices in Anchorage, Fairbanks, and Juneau. The web page gives the address, phone number and directions for each location.

Indexing & Storage: Records available from 1913 to present. New records available for inquiry immediately.

Searching: If you are not the spouse, parent, child, or sibling of the deceased person, a letter or document from the office or the agency that needs the death certificate must be submitted with the request. Records are public after 50 years. Include in request- full name, date of death, place of death, names of parents, reason for request, relationship to person of record, copy of picture ID - government issued. Also, include a daytime phone number. Direct questions to BVSOFFICE@health.state.ak.us.

Access by: mail, phone, fax, in person, online.

Fee & Payment: The $20.00 search fee includes a 3 year search. Add $1.00 per year searched for each year over 3 years. Fee payee- Bureau of Vital Statistics. Prepayment required. Personal checks and major credit cards accepted.

Mail search: Turnaround time- 3-5 days.

Phone search: See expedited service.

Fax search: See expedited service.

In person search: Turnaround time 10 minutes.

Online search: Records may be ordered online via a state-designated vendor at www.vitalchek.com. There is a $5.50 service fee plus a $5.50 expedite fee. Use of credit card required.

Expedited service: Expedited service is available for mail, phone, online and fax searches. Turnaround time- 2 days. Add $11.00 for using a credit card and necessary fund for express mail or courier delivery.

Marriage Certificates

Department of Health & Social Services, Bureau of Vital Statistics, 5441 Commercial Blvd, Juneau, AK 99801; 907-465-3391, Fax- 907-465-3618; 8AM-5PM. www.hss.state.ak.us/dph/bvs/

The Bureau of Vital Statistics maintains offices in Anchorage, Fairbanks, and Juneau. The web page gives the address, phone number and directions for each location.

Indexing & Storage: Records available from 1913 to present. New records available for inquiry immediately.

Searching: Person requesting must be one of the registrants or an attorney representing a registrant. Records are public after 50 years. Include in request- names of husband and wife, date of marriage, place or county of marriage. All requests must include copy of government issued picture ID of the requester. Include wife's maiden name and a daytime phone number. Direct questions to BVSOFFICE@health.state.ak.us.

Access by: mail, phone, fax, in person, online.

Fee & Payment: The $20.00 search fee includes a 3 year search. Add $1.00 per year searched for each year over 3 years. Fee payee- Bureau of Vital Statistics. Prepayment required. Personal checks, Visa, and MasterCard accepted.

Mail search: Turnaround time- 3-5 days.

Phone search: See expedited service.

Fax search: See expedited service.

In person search: Turnaround time 10 minutes.

Online search: Records may be ordered online via a state-designated vendor at www.vitalchek.com. There is a $5.50 service fee. Use of credit card required.

Expedited service: Expedited service is available for mail, phone, online and fax searches. Turnaround time- 2 days. Add $11.00 for using a credit card and necessary fund for express mail or courier delivery.

Divorce Records

Department of Health & Social Services, Bureau of Vital Statistics, 5441 Commercial Blvd, Juneau, AK 99801; 907-465-3391, Fax- 907-465-3618; 8AM-5PM. www.hss.state.ak.us/dph/bvs/

The Bureau of Vital Statistics maintains offices in Anchorage, Fairbanks, and Juneau. The web page gives the address, phone number and directions for each location.

Indexing & Storage: Records available from 1950 to present. New records available for inquiry immediately.

Searching: Person requesting must be one of the registrants or an attorney representing a registrant. Records are public after 50 years. Include in request- names of husband and wife, date of divorce, place of divorce. All requests must include copy of government issued picture ID of the requester. Also, include a daytime phone number. Direct questions to BVSOFFICE@health.state.ak.us.

Access by: mail, phone, fax, in person, online.

Fee & Payment: The $20.00 search fee includes a 3 year search. Add $1.00 per year searched for each year over 3 years. Fee payee- Bureau of Vital Statistics. Prepayment required. Personal checks and major credit cards accepted.

Mail search: Turnaround time- 3-5 days. SASE not required.

Phone search: See expedited service.

Fax search: See expedited service.

In person search: Turnaround time 10 minutes.

Online search: Records may be ordered online via a state-designated vendor at www.vitalchek.com. There is a $5.50 service fee plus a $5.50 expedite fee. Use of credit card required.

Expedited service: Expedited service is available for mail, phone, online and fax searches. Turnaround time- 2 days. Add $11.00 for using a credit card and necessary fund for express mail or courier delivery.

Workers' Compensation Records

Workers' Compensation, PO Box 115512, Juneau, AK 99811-5512 (Courier address- 1111 W Eighth St, Room 307, Juneau, AK 99802); 907-465-2790, Fax- 907-465-2797; 8AM-4:30PM.

www.labor.state.ak.us/wc/wc.htm

Indexing & Storage: Records available from 1982 on the computer if active, and prior to 1982 the records are on microfilm and/or microfiche to the 1960s, and archived to statehood (1959). New records available for inquiry in one week.

Searching: All requests must be in writing. To receive a copy of a file, a signed medical release from claimant is required. Include in request- claimant name, SSN, date of accident. All requests handled on a first come first serve basis.

Access by: mail, phone, fax, in person.

Fee & Payment: Copies cost $.35 per page for active files and $.75 per page for microfilmed files. A computer printout costs $.50 per screen. There is no search fee. Fee payee- State of Alaska. Large orders require prepayment. Personal checks accepted, credit cards are not.

Mail search: Turnaround time- 10 to 14 days. SASE not required.

Phone search: The agency will let you know if a file exists.

Fax search: Fax searching available, but records returned by mail.

In person: Records are still returned by mail.

Other access: Microfiche is available at $50.00 per fiche, prepaid.

Driver Records

Division of Motor Vehicles, Attn: Research, 1300 W Benson Blvd, Ste 200, Anchorage, AK 99503; 907-269-5551, Fax- 907-269-5202; 8AM-5PM.

www.state.ak.us/dmv/

Copies of tickets are only released, in writing, to the participant, legal representative, or insurance representative.

Indexing & Storage: Records available for minor moving violations and suspensions for three years, major moving violations for five years. Convictions are automatically purged from public record by conviction date. Accidents are reported only if action is taken.

Searching: Records are considered confidential. Requester must have a signed release from the licensee, a subpoena, or show DPPA compliance. High volume requesters may maintain consent forms on file rather than send in with requests. Include in request- name, driver's license number, date of birth. Driver's residence and mailing address are included as part of the search report.

Access by: mail, fax, in person, online.

Fee & Payment: Search costs $10.00 per record. Prepayment is required. Fee payee- State of Alaska. Prepayment required. Personal checks accepted. Credit cards are accepted.

Mail search: Turnaround time- up to 30 days. SASE not required.

Fax search: One may request their own record via fax. A form is found at www.state.ak.us/dmv/forms/pdfs/faxdh.pdf.

In person: Turnaround time is while you wait.

Online search: Online access costs $10.00 per record. This is for pre-approved, ongoing requesters only. Inquiries may be made at any time, 24 hours a day. Batch inquiries may call back within thirty minutes for responses. Search by the first four letters of driver's name, license number and date of birth. Not a web-based system.

Vehicle/Vessel Registration

Division of Motor Vehicles, ATTN: Research, 1300 W Benson Blvd #200, Anchorage, AK 99503-3600; 907-269-5551; 8:30AM-4:30PM.

www.state.ak.us/dmv/

All powered boats, and all non-powered boats over 10 ft or with auxiliary power units used on any water of the state must be registered. Liens on boats are recorded at the State.

Indexing & Storage: Records available for 7 years to present. Note until Jan. 1, 2001, all boat registrations were done via the US Coast Guard.

Searching: Record requests are honored for employment, insurance, court or impound purposes. Otherwise, a signed release is required, signed by requester, attesting to purpose of request. Use of Form 851- Request for Vehicle Record is required if not a pre-approved, ongoing requester. The form may be downloaded the web.

Access by: mail, in person.

Fee & Payment: The fee is $10.00 per record. There is a $5.00 fee to do a vessel search. Fee payee- State of Alaska. Prepayment required. No credit cards accepted.

Mail search: Turnaround time- 1 to 3 weeks. SASE not required.

In person: Typically a search request is limited to three items and is a computer printout. Other research requests are mailed and can take up to 2-3 weeks to complete.

Other access: The entire master tape file of registration information is available at a cost of approximately $50.00 per 1,000 records. Call 907-269-5574 for more information.

Accident Reports

Department of Administration, Driver Services, PO Box 110221, Juneau, AK 99801; 907-465-4361, Fax- 907-465-5509; 8AM-5PM.

www.state.ak.us/dmv/

Persons involved in accidents with property damage in excess of $501, injury or death must file a report with the local police or state troopers. The information in this profile pertains to access of reports filed by law enforcement.

Indexing & Storage: Records available from seven years. New records available in 30 days.

Searching: Only legal representatives and insurance agents of the participants, or the participant him/herself may obtain copies. The lawyer or legal representative must have a notarized request, an insurance agent a signed request with reason. Include in request- names, date of incident, city, physical location of the accident, and signed release if necessary.

Access by: mail, phone, in person.

Fee & Payment: The fee is $10.00 per record. Fee payee- Div. of Motor Vehicles. Personal checks and major credit cards accepted.

Mail search: Turnaround time- 1 to 2 weeks. SASE not required. **Phone search:** Phone requests are available for pre-approved accounts.

In person: Turnaround time is while you wait.

Vessel Ownership

Records not maintained by a state level agency.

Alaska is not a title state. Liens are filed with the Department of Natural Resources, Recorder's Section at 907-269-8882. Also, until Jan. 1, 2001, all boat registrations were done through the US Coast Guard (970-463-2294).

Legislation Records

Alaska State Legislative Affairs Agency, Legislative Information Office, State Capitol Building, Ste 111, Juneau, AK 99801-1182 (Courier address- 120 4th St #111, State Capitol, Juneau, AK 99801-1182); 907-465-4648, Fax-907-465-2864; 8AM-5PM.

http://w3.legis.state.ak.us/index.php

Voter Registration

Division of Elections, PO Box 110017, Juneau, AK 99811-0017 (Courier address- Court Plaza Building, 4th Floor, 240 Main Street, Juneau, AK 99801); 907-465-4611, Fax- 907-465-3203; 8AM-5PM. www.elections.alaska.gov

There are six regional Elections Offices, besides this office. Each has access to the election records database.

Indexing & Storage: Records available from 1968. New records available for inquiry in 1 day.

Searching: Searching by name is permitted. This data not released- SSN, place or date of birth, phone number, and voter ID #.

Access by: mail, phone, fax, in person.

Fee & Payment: There is no fee for a search. There is a copy fee of $.20 per copy if request exceeds 20 copies. Fees are charged for lists, see below. Personal checks accepted.

Mail search: Turnaround time- 1 day.

Phone search: Will search if research time not lengthy. **Fax search:** Fax searching available.

In person search: Turnaround time is immediate unless extensive lists or requests for older records are presented.

Other access: The agency offers the complete record database on CD-ROM for $178. Individual districts (there are 40) can be purchased on disk for $20.00 per district.

GED Certificates

Department of Labor, Employment Security Division, PO Box 115509, Juneau, AK 99811 (Courier - 1111 8th St, #207, Juneau, 99801); 907-465-4685, Fax- 907-465-4186; 8AM-4:30PM.

www.jobs.state.ak.us/abe/ged_req.htm

The documents are referred to as GED Diplomas by this agency. Questions may be directed to ged@alaska.gov.

Indexing & Storage: Records available from 1945. New records available for inquiry in 1 day.

Searching: Include in request- full name, DOB, SSN, year of test and city of test. All requesters must include a signed release. E-mail requests accepted at ged@labor.state.ak.us.

Access by: mail, fax, in person.

Fee & Payment: There is no fee for a verification or a transcript copy. There is a $10.00 fee for a copy of a diploma. Personal checks accepted.

Mail search: Turnaround time- 1 to 2 weeks. SASE not required.

Fax search: A written release form is required.

In person search: Simple requests may be processed while you wait.

Hunting & Fishing License

Department of Fish & Game, Licensing Section, PO Box 115525, Juneau, AK 99811-5525 (Courier address- 1255 W 8th St, Juneau, AK 99802); 907-465-2376, Fax- 907-465-2440; 8AM-5PM.

www.adfg.state.ak.us

Indexing & Storage: Records available from 10 years to present. New records available for inquiry in 4 weeks.

Searching: Information used to search includes name, DOB, address, or year license issued. This data not released- SSNs or telephone numbers.

Access by: mail, phone, fax, in person.

Fee & Payment: No fee unless you request a large list. For certified copies the turnaround time is 6 weeks. Fee payee- State of Alaska. Prepayment required. Personal checks & credit cards accepted.

Mail search: Turnaround time- within 2 weeks. SASE not required.

Phone search: Limited number of requests given over phone. **Fax search:** same as phone search.

In person search: Large lists will not be processed immediately.

Other access: The vendor file is available for $25 on paper or disk. The entire license file is available for $350 on CD.

Alaska State Licensing Agencies

For details about the agency responsible for licensing/certifying/registering an item below or in the Agency Quick Finder section, match an item's number with the number of the agency in the *Licensing Agency Information* section.

Alaska Licenses Searchable Online

Acupuncturist #20	www.commerce.state.ak.us/occ/search3.htm
Anesthetist, Dental, General/Permit #20	www.commerce.state.ak.us/occ/search3.htm
Architect #20	www.commerce.state.ak.us/occ/search3.htm
Athletic Event Promoter #20	www.commerce.state.ak.us/occ/search3.htm
Athletic Trainer #20	www.commerce.state.ak.us/occ/search3.htm
Attorney #11	www.alaskabar.org/index.cfm?ID=5362
Audiologist/Hearing Aid Dealer #20	www.commerce.state.ak.us/occ/search3.htm
Bail Bondsman #13	www.commerce.state.ak.us/ins/apps/producersearch/InsLicStart.cfm
Bank #15	www.commerce.state.ak.us/bsc/pub/2007_Directory.pdf
Barber/ Shop Owner/Sch'l/Instruc #20	www.commerce.state.ak.us/occ/search3.htm
Big Game Guide/Assist/Transporter #20	www.commerce.state.ak.us/occ/search3.htm
Boxer #20	www.commerce.state.ak.us/occ/search3.htm
Boxing Physician #20	www.commerce.state.ak.us/occ/search3.htm
Boxing/Wrestling Personnel #20	www.commerce.state.ak.us/occ/search3.htm
Child Care Provider/Home/Center #16	www.hss.state.ak.us/apps/dpa/SearchFacilities.aspx
Chiropractor #20	www.commerce.state.ak.us/occ/search3.htm
Collection Agency/Operator #20	www.commerce.state.ak.us/occ/search3.htm
Concert Promoter #20	www.commerce.state.ak.us/occ/search3.htm
Construction Contractor #20	www.commerce.state.ak.us/occ/search3.htm
Contractor, Residential #20	www.commerce.state.ak.us/occ/search3.htm
Contr'r, Civil/Elect./Mech./Mining/Petrol. #20	www.commerce.state.ak.us/occ/search3.htm
Cosmetologist/Hairdresser #20	www.commerce.state.ak.us/occ/search3.htm
Cosmetology Shop Owner/school/instr #20	www.commerce.state.ak.us/occ/search3.htm
Counselor, Professional #20	www.dced.state.ak.us/occ/OccSearch/main.cfm
Defibrillator Technician #17	http://hss.state.ak.us/apps/EMSCert/portal.aspx
Dental Hygienist #20	www.commerce.state.ak.us/occ/search3.htm
Dentist/Dental Examiner #20	www.commerce.state.ak.us/occ/search3.htm
Dietitian/Nutritionist #20	www.dced.state.ak.us/occ/OccSearch/main.cfm
Drug Distributor/Drug Room #20	www.commerce.state.ak.us/occ/search3.htm
Electrical Administrator #20	www.commerce.state.ak.us/occ/search3.htm
Emergency Medical Technician #17	http://hss.state.ak.us/apps/EMSCert/portal.aspx
Employment Agency Operator #5	www.dced.state.ak.us/occ/search3.htm
Engineer #20	www.commerce.state.ak.us/occ/search3.htm
Esthetician #20	www.commerce.state.ak.us/occ/search3.htm
Funeral Director/Establishment #20	www.commerce.state.ak.us/occ/search3.htm
Geologist #20	www.commerce.state.ak.us/occ/search3.htm
Guide/Outfitter, Hunting #20	www.commerce.state.ak.us/occ/search3.htm
Hairdresser/Esthetician #20	www.commerce.state.ak.us/occ/search3.htm
Hearing Aid Dealer #20	www.commerce.state.ak.us/occ/search3.htm
Independent Adjuster #13	www.commerce.state.ak.us/ins/apps/producersearch/InsLicStart.cfm
Insurance Agent, Managing General #13	www.commerce.state.ak.us/ins/apps/producersearch/InsLicStart.cfm
Insurance Producer #13	www.commerce.state.ak.us/ins/apps/producersearch/InsLicStart.cfm
Landscape Architect #20	www.commerce.state.ak.us/occ/search3.htm
Lobbyist/Lobbyist Employer #9	www.state.ak.us/local/akpages/ADMIN/apoc/lobcov.htm
Marriage & Family Therapist #20	www.dced.state.ak.us/occ/OccSearch/main.cfm
Mechanical Administrator #20	www.commerce.state.ak.us/occ/search3.htm
Medical Doctor/Surgeon #20	www.commerce.state.ak.us/occ/search3.htm
Midwife #20	www.dced.state.ak.us/occ/OccSearch/main.cfm
Mortician/Embalmer #20	www.commerce.state.ak.us/occ/search3.htm
Naturopathic Physician #20	www.commerce.state.ak.us/occ/search3.htm
Notary Public #19	http://list.state.ak.us/guest/RemoteListSummary/AK_Notary
Nurse Anesthetist #20	www.commerce.state.ak.us/occ/search3.htm
Nurse-RN/LPN/Aide #20	www.commerce.state.ak.us/occ/search3.htm
Nursing Home Administrator #20	www.commerce.state.ak.us/occ/search3.htm
Occupational Therapist/Assistant #20	www.commerce.state.ak.us/occ/search3.htm
Optician, Dispensing #20	www.commerce.state.ak.us/occ/search3.htm
Optometrist #20	www.commerce.state.ak.us/occ/search3.htm

Osteopathic Physician #20 .... www.commerce.state.ak.us/occ/search3.htm
Paramedic #20 .... www.commerce.state.ak.us/occ/search3.htm
Parenteral Sedation (Dental) #20 .... www.commerce.state.ak.us/occ/search3.htm
Pesticide Applicator #2 .... www.dec.state.ak.us/eh/pest/certified.htm
Pesticide Permit/Registration #2 .... www.dec.state.ak.us/eh/pest/permitholders.htm
Pharmacist/Intern/Technician #20 .... www.commerce.state.ak.us/occ/search3.htm
Pharmacy #20 .... www.commerce.state.ak.us/occ/search3.htm
Physical Therapist/Assistant #20 .... www.commerce.state.ak.us/occ/search3.htm
Physician Assistant #20 .... www.commerce.state.ak.us/occ/search3.htm
Pilot, Marine #20 .... www.commerce.state.ak.us/occ/search3.htm
Podiatrist #20 .... www.commerce.state.ak.us/occ/search3.htm
Process Server #10 .... www.dps.alaska.gov/Statewide/PermitsLicensing/
Psychologist/Psycholog'l Assistant #20 .... www.commerce.state.ak.us/occ/search3.htm
Public Accountant-CPA #20 .... www.dced.state.ak.us/occ/OccSearch/main.cfm
Real Estate Agent/Broker/Assoc. #20 .... www.commerce.state.ak.us/occ/search3.htm
Real Estate Appraiser #20 .... www.commerce.state.ak.us/occ/search3.htm
Referee #20 .... www.dced.state.ak.us/occ/OccSearch/main.cfm
Reinsurance Intermediary Broker/Mgr #13 .. www.commerce.state.ak.us/ins/apps/producersearch/InsLicStart.cfm
School Administrator #1 .... www.eed.state.ak.us/TeacherCertification/CertSearchForm.cfm
School Special Service #1 .... www.eed.state.ak.us/TeacherCertification/CertSearchForm.cfm
Security Guard #10 .... www.dps.alaska.gov/Statewide/PermitsLicensing/
Social Worker/also Clinical #20 .... www.dced.state.ak.us/occ/OccSearch/main.cfm
Speech/Language Pathologist #20 .... www.commerce.state.ak.us/occ/search3.htm
Surplus Line Broker #13 .... www.commerce.state.ak.us/ins/apps/producersearch/InsLicStart.cfm
Surveyor, Land #20 .... www.commerce.state.ak.us/occ/search3.htm
Tattoo Artist/Body Piercer #20 .... www.commerce.state.ak.us/occ/search3.htm
Teacher #1 .... www.eed.state.ak.us/TeacherCertification/CertSearchForm.cfm
Transporter, Game #20 .... www.commerce.state.ak.us/occ/search3.htm
Undergr'nd Storage Tank Worker/Contr #20. www.commerce.state.ak.us/occ/search3.htm
Vessel Agent #20 .... www.commerce.state.ak.us/occ/search3.htm
Veterinarian/Veterinary Technician #20 .... www.dced.state.ak.us/occ/search3.htm
Viatical Settlement Broker #13 .... www.commerce.state.ak.us/ins/apps/producersearch/InsLicStart.cfm
Wrestler #20 .... www.dced.state.ak.us/occ/OccSearch/main.cfm

Alaska Licensing Quick Finder

Acupuncturist #20 907-465-2695
Aircraft-related Occupation #18 907-271-2158
Alcohol Establishment #21 907-269-0350
Alcohol Server #21 907-269-0350
Amusement Ride #7 907-269-4933
Anesthetist, Dental, Gen'r'l/Permit #20 907-465-2542
Architect #20 907-465-2540
Art Exhibit, Cabaret #21 907-269-0350
Asbestos Removal Worker #14 907-269-4963
Asbestos Worker #22 907-269-4960
Athletic Event Promoter #20 907-465-2695
Athletic Trainer #20 907-465-2695
Attorney #11 907-272-7469
Audiologist/Hearing Aid Dealer #20 907-465-2695
Bail Bondsman #13 907-465-2515
Bank #15 907-465-2521
Barber #20 907-465-2547
Barber Shop Owner/Sch'l/Instruc. #20 .. 907-465-2547
BIDCOS/CFAB #15 907-465-2521
Big Game Guide/Assist/Transport #20 .. 907-465-2543
Boiler Operator #7 907-269-4963
Boxer #20 907-465-2695
Boxing Physician #20 907-465-2695
Boxing/Wrestling Personnel #20 907-465-2695
Broker/Dealer #12 907-465-2521
Charter Boat, Sport Fishing #6 907-267-2369
Child Care Provider/Home/Center #16. 907-465-4756
Chiropractor #20 907-465-2589
Collection Agency/Operator #20 907-465-2695
Concealed Handgun Permit #10 907-269-0392
Concert Promoter #20 907-465-2534
Construction Contractor #20 907-465-2546
Contractor, Residential #20 907-465-2546
Contr'r, Civil/Elect./Mech./Mining/Petrol. #20 907-465-2546
Cosmetologist/Hairdresser #20 907-465-2547
Cosmetol'gy Shop Owner/sch/instr #20 907-465-2547
Counselor, Professional #20 907-465-2551
Credit Union #15 907-465-2521
Crewmember, Fishing Boat #4 907-465-2376
Defibrillator Technician #17 907-465-3029
Dental Hygienist #20 907-465-2542
Dentist/Dental Examiner #20 907-465-2542
Dietitian/Nutritionist #20 907-465-2534
Drug Distributor/Drug Room #20 907-465-2589
Electrical Administrator #20 907-465-2589
Electrician #7 907-269-4963
Elevator #7 907-269-4933
Emergency Medical Technician #17 907-465-3029
Employment Agency Operator #5 907-269-8160
Engineer #20 907-465-2540
Esthetician #20 907-465-2547
Explosives Handler #14 907-269-4963
Fisher #4 907-465-2376
Fishing Operation, Kenai #8 907-260-4882
Funeral Director/Establishment #20 607-465-2695
Fur Dealer #4 907-465-2376
Game Farm #4 907-465-2376
Geologist #20 907-465-2695
Guide, Sport Fishing #6 907-267-2369
Guide, Sport Fishing, Kenai Only #8 907-262-9368
Guide/Outfitter, Hunting #20 907-465-2543
Hairdresser/Esthetician #20 907-465-2547
Hearing Aid Dealer #20 907-465-2695
Hunter #4 907-465-2376
Hunting Guide #20 907-465-2543
Independent Adjuster #13 907-465-2515
Insurance Agent, Mgng. Generall #13 .. 907-465-2515
Insurance Occupation #13 907-465-2515
Insurance Producer #13 907-465-2515
Investment Advisor #12 907-465-2521
Investment Brok'r/Dealer/ Occup'n.#12 907-465-2521
Landscape Architect #20 907-465-2540
Lobbyist/Lobbyist Employer #9 907-465-4864
Marriage & Family Therapist #20 907-465-2551
Mechanical Administrator #20 907-465-2589
Medical Doctor/Surgeon #20 907-465-2541
Midwife #20 907-465-2580
Mobile Home Dealer #20 907-465-2547
Mortician/Embalmer #20 607-465-2695
Naturopathic Physician #20 907-465-2695
Notary Public #19 907-465-3509
Nurse Anesthetist #20 907-465-2544
Nurse-RN/LPN #20 907-465-2544
Nurses' Aide #20 907-269-8169
Nursing Home Administrator #20 907-465-2695
Occupational Therapist/Assistant #20 . 907-465-2580
Optician, Dispensing #20 907-465-5470
Optometrist #20 907-465-2580
Osteopathic Physician #20 907-465-2541
Painter #14 907-269-4963
Paramedic #20 907-465-2541
Parenteral Sedation (Dental) #20 907-465-2542
Pesticide Applicator #2 .. 907-376-1866, 800-478-2577
Pesticide Permit #2 ...... 907-376-1856, 800-478-2577
Pesticide Registr'n #2 ... 907-376-1858, 800-478-2577
Pharmacist/Pharmacist Intern #20 907-465-2589
Pharmacy #20 907-465-2589
Pharmacy Technician #20 907-465-2589
Physical Therapist/Assistant #20 907-465-2580
Physician Assistant #20 907-269-8163

Pilot, Aircraft #18 907-271-2158
Pilot, Marine #20 907-465-2548
Plumber #7 907-269-4963
Podiatrist #20 907-465-2541
Premium Finance Company #15 907-465-2521
Process Server #10 907-269-0393
Psychologist/Psycholog'l Assist'nt #20 .. 907-465-3811
Public Accountant-CPA #20 907-465-3817
Real Estate Agent/Broker/Assoc. #20 .. 907-269-8162
Real Estate Appraiser #20 907-465-2542
Referee #20 907-465-2695
Reinsurance Interm'y Broker/Mgr #13 .. 907-465-2515
School Administrator #1 907-465-2831
School Special Service #1 907-465-2831
Securities Agent #12 907-465-2521
Security Guard #10 907-269-0393
Ski Lift #7 907-269-4933
Small Loan Company #15 907-465-2521
Social Worker #20 907-465-2551
Social Worker, Clinical #20 907-465-2551
Speech/Language Pathologist #20 907-465-2534
Surplus Line Broker #13 907-465-2515
Surveyor, Land #20 907-465-2540
Tattoo Artist/Body Piercer #20 907-465-2547
Taxidermist #4 907-465-2376
Teacher #1 907-465-2831
Thrift #15 907-465-2521
Transporter, Game #20 907-465-2543
Trapper #4 907-465-2376
Trust Company #15 907-465-2521
Undergr'nd Tank Worker/Contr. #20 907-465-5470
Vessel Agent #20 907-465-2548
Veterinarian/Veterinary Technic'n #20 .. 907-465-5470
Viatical Settlement Broker #13 907-465-2515
Waste Water System Operator #3 907-465-5140
Wrestler #20 907-465-2695

Alaska Licensing Agency Information

#1 Department of Education & Early Development, Teacher Education & Certification, 801 W 10th St, #200, Box 110500, Juneau, AK 99811-0500; 907-465-2831, Fax- 907-465-2441. Hours- 8AM-4:30PM. www.eed.state.ak.us/TeacherCertification/ Search data at- www.eed.state.ak.us/TeacherCertification/CertSearchForm.cfm

#2 Department of Environmental Conservation, Div. of Environmental Health (SOA/DEC/EH), 1700 E Bogard Rd, Bldg B #103, Wasilla, AK 99654; 907-376-1870, 800-478-2577, Fax- 907-376-2382. Hours- 8AM-5PM. www.dec.state.ak.us/eh/pest/index.htm

#3 Department of Environmental Conservation, Division of Water, 410 Willoughby Ave, #303, Juneau, AK 99801-1795; 907-465-5140, Fax- 907-465-5177. www.dec.state.ak.us/water/opcert/index.htm

#4 Department of Fish & Game, Licensing Section, PO Box 15525, Juneau, AK 99802-5525; 907-465-2376, Fax- 907-465-2440. www.adfg.state.ak.us

#5 Department of Labor, Department of Commerce, Div of Occupational Licensing, 550 W 7th Ave #1500, Anchorage, AK 99501-3567; 907-269-8160, Fax- 907-261-8156. www.commerce.state.ak.us/occ/ Search data at- www.dced.state.ak.us/occ/search3.htm

#6 Department of Fish and Game, Division of Sport Fish - RTS, 333 Raspberry Rd, Anchorage, AK 99518-1599; 907-267-2369, Fax- 907-267-2422. www.sf.adfg.state.ak.us/Guides/

#7 Department of Labor, Labor & Safety Standards, Mechanical Inspection Section, 3301 Eagle St #302, Anchorage, AK 99503-4149; 907-269-4925, Fax- 907-269-4932. Hours- 8AM-4:30PM. www.labor.state.ak.us/lss/mihome.htm

#8 Department of Natural Resources, Division of Parks & Outdoor Recreation - Kenai, 514 Funny River Rd, Soldotna, AK 99669; 907-260-4882, Fax- 907-260-5992. www.dnr.state.ak.us/parks/

#9 Public Offices Commission, PO Box 110222 (240 Main St, Rm 201), Juneau, AK 99811-0222; 907-465-4864, Fax- 907-465-4832. www.state.ak.us/local/akpages/ADMIN/apoc/lobcov.htm Search data at- www.state.ak.us/local/akpages/ADMIN/apoc/lobcov.htm Download directories of licensed lobbyists at the website. Anchorage phone is 907-276-4176.

#10 Alaska State Troopers, Dept. of Public Safety/ Permits & Licensing Unit, 5700 E Tudor Rd, Anchorage, AK 99507-1225; 907-269-0392, Fax- 907-269-5609. www.dps.alaska.gov/Statewide/PermitsLicensing/

#11 Alaska Bar Association, Board of Governors, PO Box 100279 (550 W 7th Ave #1900), Anchorage, AK 99510-0279; 907-272-7469, Fax- 907-272-2932. www.alaskabar.org Search data at- www.alaskabar.org/index.cfm?ID=5362

#12 Department of Commerce Community & Economic Development, Division of Banking; Securities Section, PO Box 110807 (150 3rd St #217), Juneau, AK 99811-0807; 907-465-2521, Fax- 907-465-2549. www.commerce.state.ak.us/bsc/home.htm

#13 Department of Community & Economic Development, Division of Insurance, PO Box 110805 (333 Willoughby Ave, 9th Fl, State Office Bldg), Juneau, AK 99811-0805; 907-465-2515, Fax- 907-465-3422. Hours- 8AM-5PM. www.commerce.state.ak.us/insurance/ Search data at- www.commerce.state.ak.us/ins/apps/producersearch/InsLicStart.cfm

#14 Department of Labor, Labor & Safety Standards, Occupational Safety & Health, 3301 Eagle St #302, Anchorage, AK 99503; 907-269-4963. http://labor.state.ak.us/lss/home.htm

#15 Department of Community & Economic Development, Division of Banking; Banking Section, PO Box 110807, Juneau, AK 99811; 888-925-2521, Fax- 907-269-8146. Hours- 8AM-4:30PM. www.commerce.state.ak.us/bsc/banking.htm

#16 Department of Health & Social Services, Division of Public Asst - Child Care Licensing, SE, PO Box 110640 (SE Division Only) 150 3rd St #107, Juneau, AK 99811; 907-465-4756, Fax- 907-465-6982. www.hss.state.ak.us/dpa/ Search data at- www.hss.state.ak.us/apps/dpa/SearchFacilities.aspx 3 other divisions handle facility licensing: Anchorage Area- 907-343-4748; South Central Alaska (except Anchorage)- 907-269-4600; Fairbanks- 907-451-3198.

#17 Department of Health & Social Services, Division of Public Health/Section of Community Health and EMS, 410 Willoughby Rm 103 Box 110616, Juneau, AK 99811-0616; 907-465-6736, Fax- 907-465-4101. www.chems.alaska.gov Search data at- http://hss.state.ak.us/apps/EMSCert/portal.aspx

#18 Federal Aviation Administration, FSDO, 300 W 36th Ave, Ste #101, Anchorage, AK 99503; 907-271-2000 or 800-294-5116, Fax- 907-271-4777. Hours- 7:30AM-4PM. www.faa.gov/about/office_org/field_offices/fsdo/anc/contact/

#19 Notary Public Section, Office of Lieutenant Governor, 240 Main St #301, Juneau, AK 99801; 907-465-3509, Fax- 907-465-5400. Hours- 8:30AM-5PM. http://ltgov.state.ak.us/notary/

#20 Department of Commerce & Economic Development, Professional Licensing, PO Box 110806, Juneau, AK 99811-0806; 907-465-2550, Fax- 907-465-2974. www.dced.state.ak.us/occ/ Search data at- www.commerce.state.ak.us/occ/search3.htm Download business license lists at www.dced.state.ak.us/occ/buslic4.cfm.

#21 Department of Public Safety, Alcoholic Beverage Control Board, 5848 E Tudor Rd, Anchorage, AK 99507-1286; 907-269-0350, Fax- 907-272-9412. www.dps.state.ak.us/abc/

Alaska Federal Courts

The following list indicates the district and division name for each jurisdiction in the state. If the bankruptcy court location is different from the district court, then the location of the bankruptcy court appears in parentheses.

Alaska County/Court Cross Reference

County	Court	County	Court
Aleutian Islands, East	Anchorage	Nome	Nome (Anchorage)
Aleutian Islands, West	Anchorage	North Slope Borough	Fairbanks (Anchorage)
Anchorage Borough	Anchorage	Northwest Arctic Borough	Fairbanks (Anchorage)
Bethel	Fairbanks (Anchorage)	Prince of Wales-Outer Ketchikan	Juneau (Anchorage)
Bristol Bay Borough	Anchorage	Sitka Borough	Juneau (Anchorage)
Fairbanks North Star Borough	Fairbanks (Anchorage)	Southeast Fairbanks	Fairbanks (Anchorage)
Haines Borough	Juneau (Anchorage)	Valdez-Cordova	Anchorage
Juneau Borough	Juneau (Anchorage)	Wade Hampton	Fairbanks (Anchorage)
Kenai Peninsula Borough	Anchorage	Wrangell-Petersburg	Juneau (Anchorage)
Ketchikan Gateway Borough	Ketchikan (Anchorage)	Yakutat	Juneau (Anchorage)
Kodiak Island Borough	Anchorage	Yukon-Koyukuk	Fairbanks (Anchorage)
Matanuska-Susitna Borough	Anchorage		

Standards for Federal Courts: Fees are standard unless noted in profile. Search fee is $26.00 per item (one party name or case number). Copy fee is $.50 per page. Certification fee is $9.00 per document, double for exemplification, if available. Most courts require prepayment. Mail requests should enclose a SASE unless otherwise noted. Before releasing records, all courts require prepayment, unless noted.

District courts index by defendant and plaintiff and by case number. Bankruptcy courts usually index by debtor and case number. While most courts now have their indexes on computer, many may still maintain index card files as well. Courts will archive closed case files at different times.

There are numerous public access programs available to online subscribers. Search the U.S. Party/Case Index to find party names and case numbers among all courts. Individual case data is provided on PACER. A search of CM/ECF provides copies of cases filed electronically. For details about PACER, the US Party/Case Index, and CM/ECF see the Appendix, go to http://pacer.psc.uscourts.gov or call 800-676-6856.

US District Court District of Alaska

Anchorage Division Court Clerk, 222 W 7th Ave, #4, Anchorage, AK 99513-7564 (In person: 222 W 7th Ave, Rm 229, Anchorage, AK 99513), 907-677-6100, 866-243-3814; records- 907-677-6100. Hours- 9:00AM-12:30PM, 1:30-4:30PM. www.akd.uscourts.gov

Counties/Note: Aleutian Islands-East, Aleutian Islands-West, Anchorage Borough, Bristol Bay Borough, Dillingham, Kenai Peninsula Borough, Kodiak Island Borough, Lake and Peninsula, Matanuska-Susitna Borough, Valdez-Cordova.

Searches/Indexing: Search request requires name only. Results do not include SSN or DOB. Will not fax back documents. New cases are in the index 1-2 days after filing date. Case files indexed on computer; cards stored in file cabinets. Names and docket sheets after 5/1987 on computer. If a case was tried, file sent to Anchorage Records Center. If the case did not go to trial, file sent to Seattle Records Center.

Search Access: Only docket info available by phone. **Mail:** Search usually completed- 1-2 weeks. Include SASE for return. **Fax:** Written fax requests accepted. **In person:** 2 public terminals available. Self-serve copies $.50 each.

Payment: Pay by money order, cashier's or business checks. No personal checks or credit cards. Payee: Clerk, US District Court.

E-Services: PACER records go back to 1987. New records online after 1 day. ECF at https://ecf.akd.uscourts.gov. **Opinions Online:** www.akd.uscourts.gov/ref_mgo.htm. **Online Note:** Current and next day calendars at www.akd.uscourts.gov.

Fairbanks Division Court Clerk, 101 12th Ave, Rm 332, Fairbanks, AK 99701, 907-451-5791, 866-243-3813. Hours- 8AM-N, 1-4:30PM. www.akd.uscourts.gov

Counties/Note: Bethel, Denali, Fairbanks North Star Borough, North Slope Borough, Northwest Arctic Borough, Southeast Fairbanks, Wade Hampton, Yukon-Koyukuk.

Searches/Indexing: Search request requires name only. Results do not include SSN or DOB. Will not fax back documents. New cases are in the index 1-2 days after filing date. Case files indexed on computer; cards stored in file cabinets. Case files sent to archives 6 months after closed.

Search Access: Only docket info available by phone. **Mail:** Search usually completed- week-10 days. Include SASE for return. **Fax:** Written fax requests accepted. **In person:** No self-serve copier.

Payment: Pay by money order, cashier's or business checks. No personal checks or credit cards. Payee: Clerk, US Dist. Court. Prepayment required unless payment arrangement is made.

E-Services: PACER records go back to 1987. New records online after 1 day. ECF at https://ecf.akd.uscourts.gov. **Opinions Online:** www.akd.uscourts.gov/ref_mgo.htm. **Online Note:** Current and next day calendars at www.akd.uscourts.gov.

Juneau Division Court Clerk, PO Box 020349, Juneau, AK 99802-0349 (In person: Federal Bldg- US Courthouse, Rm 979, 709 W 9th Ave, Juneau, AK 99801), 907-586-7458, 866-243-3812; Fax- 907-586-7780. Hours- 9AM-4PM. www.akd.uscourts.gov

Counties/Note: Haines Borough, Juneau Borough, Prince of Wales-Outer Ketchikan, Sitka Borough, Skagway-Hoonah-Angoon, Wrangell-Petersburg.

Searches/Indexing: Search request requires name only. Results do not include SSN or DOB. Will not fax back documents. New cases are in the index 1-2 days after filing date. Case files indexed on computer; cards stored in file cabinets. If case was tried, file sent to division where it was filed. If the case did not go to trial, it will be sent to the Seattle Records Ctr some time after case closed.

Search Access: Only docket info available by phone. **Mail:** Search usually completed- 2 days. Include SASE for return. **Fax:** Written fax requests accepted. **In person** No self-serve copier.

Payment: Pay by money order, cashier's or business checks. No personal checks or credit cards. Payee: Clerk, US District Court.

E-Services: PACER records go back to 1987. New records online after 1 day. ECF at https://ecf.akd.uscourts.gov. **Opinions Online:** www.akd.uscourts.gov/ref_mgo.htm. **Online Note** Current and next day calendars at www.akd.uscourts.gov.

Ketchikan Div. Court Clerk, 648 Mission St, Rm 507, Ketchikan, AK 99901, 907-247-7576. Hours- 9AM-1PM. www.akd.uscourts.gov

Counties/Note: Ketchikan Gateway Borough.

Searches/Indexing: Search request requires name only. Results do not include SSN or DOB. Will not fax back documents. New cases are in the index 1-2 days after filing date. Case files indexed on computer; cards stored in file cabinets. Case files sent to archives 6 months after closed. If case was tried, file sent to Anchorage Division. If the case did not go to trial, it will be sent to the Seattle Records Center.

Search Access: Only docket info available by phone. **Mail:** Search usually completed- 2 days. Include SASE for return. **Fax:** Written fax requests accepted. **In person:** No public access terminals available. No self-serve copier.

Payment: Pay by money order, cashier's check, business check. No personal checks or credit cards. Payee: Clerk, US District Court.

E-Services: PACER records go back to 1987. New records online after 1 day. ECF at https://ecf.akd.uscourts.gov. **Opinions Online:** www.akd.uscourts.gov/ref_mgo.htm. **Online Note:** Current and next day calendars at www.akd.uscourts.gov.

Nome Division Court Clerk, PO Box 130, Nome, AK 99762 (In person: 113 Front St, 2nd Fl, Federal Bldg, #229, Nome, AK 99762), 907-443-5216; Fax- 907-443-2192. Hours- 9AM-4:30PM. www.akd.uscourts.gov

Counties/Note: Nome. Records have been retained at this court since 1960.

Searches/Indexing: Search request requires name only. Results do not include SSN or DOB. Court prefers not to fax results, but will in expedited cases at cost of fax, search, and copies. New cases are in the index 1-2 days after filing date. Case files indexed on computer; cards stored in file cabinets. Case files sent to archives 6 months after closed.

Search Access: Only docket info available by phone. Court prefers that requests be submitted in writing. **Mail:** Search usually completed- 5 day maximum. Include SASE for return. **Fax:** Written fax requests accepted. **In person:** No self-serve copier.

Payment: Pay by money order, cashier's or business check. No personal checks or credit cards . Payee: Clerk, US District Court. Prepayment is not required, but preferred. For copies, make checks payable to Alaska Court System. For searches and certified copies, make checks payable to US District Court.

E-Services: PACER records go back to 1987. New records online after 1 day. ECF at https://ecf.akd.uscourts.gov. **Opinions Online:** www.akd.uscourts.gov/ref_mgo.htm. **Online Note:** Current and next day calendars at www.akd.uscourts.gov.

US Bankruptcy Court District of Alaska

Anchorage Division Court Clerk, 605 W 4th Ave, Ste 138, Historic Courthouse, Anchorage, AK 99501-2296, 907-271-2655; 800-859-8059-AK only; Fax- 907-271-2645. Hours- 9AM-N, 1-4:30PM. www.akb.uscourts.gov

Counties/Note: All boroughs and districts in Alaska.

Searches/Indexing: Search request requires name only. Results do not include SSN or DOB. Will fax back documents for $15.00 fee. New cases are in the index 1-2 days after filing date. If a case was tried here, then file sent to Anchorage Records Center. If the case did not go to trial, file sent to Seattle Records Center. Case records sent to a Center 3 months after case closed.

Search Access: Limited search; accession number released via phone if case number is provided. If case number is unknown, info must be requested in writing along with search fee. Voice Case Information Service available, call VCIS at 888-878-3110 or 907-271-2658. **Mail:** Search usually completed- 24 hours. Include SASE for return. **Fax:** Fax search requests accepted. **In person:** 2 public terminals available. Self-serve copies $.20 each.

Payment: Pay by money order, cashier's or personal check. Payee: Clerk, US Bankruptcy Court.

E-Services: Document images available. PACER records go back to 7/1991. New records online after 1 day. ECF at https://ecf.akb.uscourts.gov. **Opinions:** www.akb.uscourts.gov/index.htm. **Online Note:** Court calendars available free at www.akb.uscourts.gov/calendars.htm.

Alaska Local Courts

Court	Jurisdiction	No. of Courts	How Organized
Superior Courts*	General	16	4 Districts
District Courts*	Limited	58	4 Districts
Combined Courts*		16	
Magistrate Courts*	Limited	24	4 Districts

* Profiled in this Sourcebook

	CIVIL								
Court	Tort	Contract	Real Estate	Min. Claim	Max. Claim	Small Claims	Estate	Eviction	Domestic Relations
Superior*	X	X	X	$0	No Max		X	X	X
District*	X	X		$0	$100,000	$10000		X	X
Magistrate*	X	X		$0	$10000	$10000			

	CRIMINAL				
Court	Felony	Misdemeanor	DWI/DUI	Preliminary Hearing	Juvenile
Superior*	X				X
District*		X	X	X	X
Magistrate*		X	X	X	

Administration

Office of the Administrative Director, 820 W 4th Ave, Anchorage, AK, 99501; Telephone: 907-264-8232; Records: 907-264-0491, Fax: 907-264-8291. www.state.ak.us/courts

Court Structure

Alaska has a unified, centrally administered, and totally state-funded judicial system with 4 Judicial Districts. Municipal governments do not maintain separate court systems. Alaska has 15 boroughs, not counties. 3 are unified home rule municipalities that are combination borough and city, and 12 boroughs. There are also 12 home rule cities which do not directly coincide with the 4 Judicial Districts. In other words, judicial boundaries cross borough boundaries.

The four levels of courts in the Alaska Court System are the Supreme Court, the Court of Appeals, the Superior Court, and the District Court. Magistrate Courts preside over certain District Court matters. The magistrate is a judicial officer of the District Court.

The Supreme Court and Court of Appeals are appellate courts, while Superior Courts and District Courts are trial courts. The Superior Court Probate is handled by Superior Courts.

The Superior Court is a trial court for both criminal and civil cases and serves as an appellate court for appeals from civil and criminal cases which have been tried in the district court and for appeals from some administrative agencies. The Superior Court hears felony and civil cases, generally involving $100,000 or more. The court also hears cases that involve children who have committed crimes or who are abused or neglected, property of deceased or incompetent persons, involuntary commitment of persons to institutions for the mentally ill, and domestic relations matters.

The District Court hears cases that involve hear state misdemeanors and violations of city and borough ordinances, first appearances and preliminary hearings in felony cases, record vital statistics (in some areas of the state), civil cases valued up to $100,000, small claims cases at $10,000 maximum, cases involving children on an emergency basis, and domestic violence cases.

Magistrates preside over certain district court matters in areas of the state where services of a full-time district court judge are not required. Some magistrates serve more than one court location. Magistrates also serve in metropolitan areas to handle routine matters and to ease the workload of the district court. Small claims cases are $10,000 maximum for most cases;, but can be $20,000 for wage claims brought by the Department of Labor.

We have listed the courts by their borough or home rule city in keeping with a convenient alphabetical format. You should search through the city court location names to determine the correct court for your search.

The 1st District encompasses all of southeast Alaska. Magistrates act as judicial officers. This 1st District has five trial/Superior Courts: Ketchikan, Wrangell, Petersburg, Sitka, Juneau. District Magistrate Courts are Haines, Skagway, Yakutat, Angoon, Kake, Hoona, Craig.

Online Access

There are two systems available for trial court records, both are partial; neither is statewide. You may do a name search at www.courtrecords.alaska.gov/. This is the older system, are uploaded every three months. 15 jurisdictions are on this system. The Court System is migrating to a newer electronic case information system at www.courtrecords.alaska.gov/pa/pa.urd/pamw6500.display. Called CourtView, 24 sites are active and records are real time. Search results give case number, file date, disposition date, charge, and sentence. Note that the initial index gives the only the name used on the first pleading.

The home web page gives access to Appellate opinions. The site at http://government.westlaw.com/akcases/ provides access to opinions of the Alaska Supreme Court and Alaska Court of Appeals.

Searching Tips, Fees, and Other Guidelines

Documents may not be filed by fax in any Alaska court without prior authorization of a judge.

The fees established by court rules for Alaska courts are: search fee- $15.00 per hour or fraction thereof; certification fee- $5.00 per document and $2.00 per additional copy of the document. Copy fee- $.25 per page. Magistrate Courts vary widely in how records are maintained and in the hours of operation – some are open only a few hours per week.

Aleutian Islands

Unalaska District Court (3rd District) PO Box 245, Unalaska, AK 99685-0245; 907-581-1266; fax: 907-581-2809; 8AM-4:30PM (AK). ***Felony, Misdemeanor, Civil.***
www.aleutianseast.org/

Civil Records: Access: In person, online. Visitors must perform in person searches themselves. Required to search: name, DOB. Civil cases indexed by defendant, plaintiff, on computer back to 1992. Civil PAT goes back to 1992. PAT results show middle initial, DOB. Search names on Trial Courts database at www.state.ak.us/courts/names.htm. Web gives basic info.

Criminal Records: Access: In person, online. Visitors must perform in person searches themselves. Required to search: name, years to search, DOB. Criminal records computerized from 1992. Criminal PAT goes back to 1992. PAT results show middle initial, DOB. Online access to criminal records is the same as civil. Online results can include DOB; most have middle initial.

General Information: Online identifiers in results same as on public terminal. Will fax documents to local or toll free line. Court makes copy: $.25 per page. Certification fee: $5.00 per doc; $2.00 for add'l cert of same doc. Payee: State of Alaska. Personal checks accepted; credit cards are not. Prepayment required.

Sand Point Magistrate Court (3rd District), AK; ***Felony, Misdemeanor, Civil Actions under $10,000, Small Claims.***
www.aleutianseast.org/

Court closed; records at Cordova Court in Valdez-Cordova District. Search court records free at new CourtView system at www.courtrecords.alaska.gov/pa/pa.urd/pamw6500.display.

St Paul Island Magistrate Court (3rd District), AK; ***Misdemeanor, Civil Actions under $10,000, Small Claims.*** www.aleutianseast.org/

Court closed. See Seward Magistrate Court in Kenai Peninsula Borough.

Anchorage Borough

Superior & District Court (3rd District) 825 W 4th, Anchorage, AK 99501-2004; 907-264-0491; probate phone: 907-264-0436; fax: 907-264-0873; 8AM-4:30PM (AK). ***Felony, Misdemeanor, Civil, Eviction, Small Claims, Probate.***
Probate fax- 907-264-0598.

Civil Records: Access: Fax, mail, in person, online. Both court and visitors may perform in person searches. Search fee: $15.00 per hour. Required to search: name, years to search; also helpful: address. Civil cases indexed by defendant, plaintiff, on computer from 1990, on microfiche and archived from 1977 to 1989, on roll index from 1940s. Mail turnaround time 2-3 weeks. Civil PAT goes back to 1990. Terminal results can include DOB; most have middle initial. Search court records free at new CourtView system at www.courtrecords.alaska.gov/pa/pa.urd/pamw6500.display.

Criminal Records: Access: Fax, mail, in person, online. Both court and visitors may perform in person searches. Search fee: $15.00 per hour. Required to search: name, years to search; also helpful: address, DOB, SSN. Criminal records computerized from 1990, on microfiche and archived from 1977 to 1989, on roll index from 1940s. Mail turnaround time 2-3 weeks. Criminal PAT goes back to 1990. Online access to criminal records is the same as civil. Online results can include DOB; most have middle initital.

General Information: Online identifiers in results same as on public terminal. No adoption, juvenile, sealed or mental records released. Will fax documents to local or toll-free number. Court makes copy: $.25 per page, self serve same. Certification fee: $5.00. Cert fee includes copies. Payee: Alaska Court System. Personal checks accepted; credit cards are not. Prepayment required. SASE not required.

Bethel District County

Superior & District Court (4th District) PO Box 130, 204 Chief Eddie Hoffman Hiway, Bethel, AK 99559-0130; 907-543-2298; fax: 907-543-4419; 8AM-4:30PM; 9AM-4:30 W (AK). ***Felony, Misdemeanor, Civil, Eviction, Small Claims, Probate.***

Civil Records: Access: Fax, mail, in person, online. Both court and visitors may perform in person searches. Search fee: $15.00 per name. Required to search: name, years to search. Civil cases indexed by defendant, plaintiff, on computer back to 1983, on microfiche, archived and on index from 1977. Mail turnaround time 2 weeks. Public use terminal available. PAT results show middle initial, DOB. Search names on the Trial Courts database at www.state.ak.us/courts/names.htm. Web gives case number only. Also, search the newer system at www.courtrecords.alaska.gov/pa/pa.urd/pamw6500.display.

Criminal Records: Access: Fax, mail, in person, online. Both court and visitors may perform in person searches. Search fee: $15.00 per name. Required to search: name, years to search, DOB; also helpful- case number. Criminal records computerized from 1983, on microfiche, archived and on index from 1977. Mail turnaround time 2 weeks. Public use terminal available. PAT results show middle initial, DOB. Online access to criminal records is the same as civil. Online results can include DOB; most have middle initial.

General Information: No adoption, juvenile, guardianship or mental records released. Fee to fax document $.25 per page. Court makes copy: $.25 per page. Certification fee: $5.00 plus $2.00 per page after first. Payee: Clerk of Court. Personal checks accepted; credit cards are not. Prepayment required. Mail requests: SASE required.

Aniak District Court (4th District) PO Box 147, Riverroad, Aniak, AK 99557-0147; 907-675-4325; criminal fax: 907-675-4278; civil fax: same; 8AM-4:30PM (AK). ***Misdemeanor, Civil Actions under $10,000, Small Claims.***

Civil Records: Access: Phone, mail, fax, in person, online. Both court and visitors may perform in person searches. Search fee: $15.00 per search. Required to search: name plus DOB, SSN, years to search. Civil records go back to 1960; on computer back to 1998. Mail turnaround time 1-2 weeks. Search the newer system at www.courtrecords.alaska.gov/pa/pa.urd/pamw6500.display.

Criminal Records: Access: Phone, mail, fax, in person, online. Both court and visitors may perform in person searches. Search fee: $15.00 per search. Required to search: name, years to search, DOB. Criminal records go back to 1960-2000 in microfilm; 2001-present in court. Mail turnaround time 1-2 weeks. Search the newer system at www.courtrecords.alaska.gov/pa/pa.urd/pamw6500.display. Online results can include DOB; most have middle initital.

General Information: Will fax documents. Court makes copy: $.25 per page. Certification fee: $5.00 per document. Payee: Aniak District Court. Personal checks accepted; credit cards are not. Prepayment required.

Quinhagak Magistrate Court (Bethel Area) c/o Bethel Clerk, PO Box 130, 204 Hoffman Hiway, Bethel, AK 99559-0130; 907-543-1105; fax: 907-543-4419; 8AM-4:30PM (AK). ***Misdemeanor, Civil Actions under $10,000, Small Claims.***

Court closed; records at Bethel Clerk of Courts at address and phone here.

Bristol Bay Borough

Naknek District Court (3rd District) PO Box 229, #1 Main St (basement in Borough Bldg), Naknek, AK 99633-0229; 907-246-4240/4224; fax: 907-246-7418; 8AM-4:30PM (AK). ***Felony, Misdemeanor, Civil Actions under $10,000, Small Claims.***

Naknek is 3NA on the state court record numbers. Some Lake and Peninsula cases heard here.

Civil Records: Access: Mail, in person, online. Only the court performs in person searches; visitors may not. Search fee: $15.00 per hour. Required to search: name. Civil cases indexed by Defendant, Plaintiff. Records go back to 1970's; computerized from 1993. Mail turnaround time same day. Search names on the Trial Courts database at www.state.ak.us/courts/names.htm. Web gives case number only.

Criminal Records: Access: Mail, in person, online. Only the court performs in person searches; visitors may not. Search fee: $15.00 per hour. Required to search: name, years to search. Records go back to 1970's; computerized from 1993. Mail turnaround time same day. Online access to criminal records is the same as civil. Online results can include DOB; most have middle initial.

General Information: Will not fax documents. Court makes copy: $.25 per page. Certification fee: $10.00 per cert. Payee: Alaska Court System. Personal checks accepted; credit cards are not. Prepayment required. Mail requests: SASE requested.

Denali Borough

Healy Magistrate Court (4th District) PO Box 298, Healy, AK 99743-0298; 907-683-2213; fax: 907-683-1383; 8AM-4:30PM (AK). ***Misdemeanor, Civil Actions under $10,000, Small Claims.***

Felony cases are at Fairbanks Superior & District Court.

Civil Records: Access: Phone, mail, fax, in person, online. Both court and visitors may perform in person searches. Search fee: $15.00 per hour. Required to search: name, years to search, DOB. Civil records indexed by defendant, plaintiff. Records on computer back to 1972. Mail turnaround time 2 weeks. Search court records free at new CourtView system at www.courtrecords.alaska.gov/pa/pa.urd/pamw6500.display.

Criminal Records: Access: Phone, mail, fax, in person, online. Both court and visitors may perform in person searches. Search fee: $15.00 per name. Required to search: name, years to search, DOB. Records on computer back to 1972. Mail turnaround time 2 weeks. Online access to criminal records is the same as civil. Felony online results can include DOB; most have middle initital.

General Information: Online identifiers in results same as on public terminal. Will fax documents to local or toll-free number. Court makes copy: $.25 per page. Certification fee: $5.00. Payee: State of Alaska. Personal check accepted. No credit cards accepted. Prepayment required. Mail requests: SASE required.

Dillingham County

Dillingham Superior Court (3rd District)

PO Box 909, Dillingham, AK 99576-0909; 907-842-5215; fax: 907-842-5746; 8AM-4:30PM (AK). *Felony, Misdemeanor, Civil, Small Claims.*

Civil Records: Access: In person, mail, online. Only the court performs in person searches; visitors may not. Search fee: $15.00. Civil records go back 7 years. Mail turnaround time 1-2 weeks. Search names on the Alaska Trial Courts database at www.state.ak.us/courts/names.htm. Web gives case number only.

Criminal Records: Access: In person, mail, online. Only the court performs in person searches; visitors may not. Search fee: $15.00 per name. Required to search: name, years to search, DOB. Mail turnaround time 1-2 weeks. Online access to criminal records is the same as civil. Online results can include DOB; most have middle initial.

General Information: Will not fax documents. Court makes copy: $.25 per page. Certification fee: $3.00 per doc. Payee: State of Alaska. Cashiers checks, money orders, personal checks accepted. No credit cards accepted. Prepayment required. Mail requests: SASE required.

Fairbanks North Star Borough

Superior & District Court (4th District)

101 Lacey St, Fairbanks, AK 99701-4761; 907-452-9277; criminal phone: 907-452-9289; civil phone: 907-452-9267; probate phone: 907-452-9256; criminal fax: 907-452-9342; civil fax: 907-452-9330; 8AM-4:30PM (AK). *Felony, Misdemeanor, Civil, Eviction, Small Claims, Probate.*

www.state.ak.us/courts/

Civil Records: Access: In person, online. Visitors must perform in person searches themselves. Required to search: name, years to search. Civil cases indexed by defendant, plaintiff, on computer from 1988, on microfiche, archived and on index from 1900s. Note: Access to closed civil cases goes back 6 months. Civil PAT goes back to 1988. Terminal results can include DOB; most have middle initial. Search court records free at CourtView system at www.courtrecords.alaska.gov/pa/pa.urd/pamw6500.display.

Criminal Records: Access: In person, online. Visitors must perform in person searches themselves. Required to search: name, years to search, DOB. Criminal records computerized from 1988, on microfiche, archived and on index from 1900s. Criminal PAT goes back to same as civil. Online access to criminal records is the same as civil. Online results can include DOB; most have middle initial.

General Information: Online identifiers in results same as on public terminal. No adoption, juvenile, guardianship or mental records released. Will not fax documents. Court makes copy: $.25 per page, self serve same. Certification fee: $5.00 plus $2.00 per copy after first. Payee: Clerk of Court. Personal checks accepted. Credit cards accepted in person only. Prepayment required.

Haines Borough

District Court (1st District)

PO Box 169, Haines, AK 99827-0169; 907-766-2801; fax: 907-766-3148; 8AM-N, 1-4:30PM (AK). *Misdemeanor, Civil Actions under $50,000, Small Claims.*

Felony cases are at Juneau Superior & District Court.

Civil Records: Access: Phone, fax, mail, in person, online. Only the court performs in person searches; visitors may not. Search fee: $15.00 per hour if time consuming. Required to search: name, years to search; also helpful: address. Civil cases indexed by defendant, plaintiff, on computer since 1993, index from 1960s. Note: Limited information is available by phone. Mail turnaround time 1-2 days. Search names on the Trial Courts database at www.state.ak.us/courts/names.htm. Web gives case number only.

Criminal Records: Access: Phone, fax, mail, in person, online. Only the court performs in person searches; visitors may not. Search fee: $15.00 per hour if time consuming. Required to search: name, years to search; also helpful: address, DOB, SSN. Criminal records on computer since 1993, index from 1960s. Mail turnaround time 1-2 days. Online access to criminal records is the same as civil. Online results show middle initial, DOB.

General Information: No juvenile records released. Will fax documents to local or toll-free number. Court makes copy: $.25 per page. Certification fee: $5.00 plus $2.00 per each add'l document requested at same time. Payee: Alaska Court System. Personal checks accepted; credit cards are not. Prepayment required. Mail requests: SASE required.

Juneau Borough & City

Superior & District Court (1st District)

Dimond Courthouse, PO Box 114100, Juneau, AK 99811-4100; 907-463-4700; probate phone: same; fax: 907-463-3788; 8AM-4:30PM M-TH, 9AM-4:30 F (AK). *Felony, Misdemeanor, Civil, Eviction, Small Claims, Probate.*

Civil Records: Access: Fax, mail, in person, online. Both court and visitors may perform in person searches. Search fee: $15.00 per hour. Required to search: name, years to search. Civil cases indexed by defendant. Civil records on computer back to 1987, on microfiche from 1960 to 1986, on index from 1959 to 1987. Mail turnaround time 2-5 days. Results include full name. Search names on Trial Courts database at www.state.ak.us/courts/names.htm. Web gives case number only. For case searches on civil go to www.courtrecords.alaska.gov.

Criminal Records: Access: Fax, mail, in person, online. Both court and visitors may perform in person searches. Search fee: $15.00 per hour. Required to search: name, years to search. Criminal records computerized from 1987, on microfiche from 1960 to 1986, on index from 1959 to 1987. Mail turnaround time 2-5 days. Results include full name. Online access to criminal records is the same as civil. For case searches on criminal use go to www.courtrecords.alaska.gov. Online results can include DOB; most have middle inititial.

General Information: No adoption, juvenile, guardianship or mental records released. Will not fax documents. Court makes copy: $.25 per page. Certification fee: $5.00 plus $2.00 per page after first. Payee: Juneau Trial Court. Personal checks accepted; credit cards are not. Prepayment required. Mail requests: SASE required.

Kenai Peninsula Borough

Superior & District Court (3rd District)

125 Trading Bay Dr, #100, Kenai, AK 99611; 907-283-3110; probate phone: same; fax: 907-283-8535; 8AM-4:30PM (AK). *Felony, Misdemeanor, Civil, Eviction, Small Claims, Probate.*

Civil Records: Access: Mail, in person, online. Both court and visitors may perform in person searches. Search fee: $15.00 per hour. Required to search: name, years to search. Civil cases indexed by defendant, plaintiff, on computer from 1982, on microfiche, archived and on index from 1959. Mail turnaround time 1 week. Civil PAT goes back to 1982. PAT results show middle initial, DOB. Search names on the Trial Courts database at www.state.ak.us/courts/names.htm. Web gives case number only.

Criminal Records: Access: Mail, in person, online. Both court and visitors may perform in person searches. Search fee: $15.00 per hour. Required to search: name, years to search, DOB. Criminal records computerized from 1982, on microfiche, archived and on index from 1959. Mail turnaround time 1 week. Criminal PAT goes back to same as civil.PAT results show name, DOB. Results include name and case number. Online access to criminal records is the same as civil. Online results can include DOB; most have middle initial.

General Information: No adoption, guardianship, children's, conservatorship or coroner records released. Will fax documents to local or toll-free number. Court makes copy: $.25 per page. Certification fee: $5.00 plus $2.00 per page after first. Payee: Clerk of Court. Personal checks accepted; credit cards are not. Prepayment required. SASE not required.

Homer District Court (3rd District)

3670 Lake St, #400, Homer, AK 99603-9647; 907-235-8171; criminal fax: 907-235-4257; civil fax: same; 8AM-4:30PM (AK). *Felony, Misdemeanor, Civil Actions under $100,000, Small Claims.*

Old felony cases could be here or at the Kenai District Court.

Civil Records: Access: Phone, fax, mail, in person, online. Visitors must perform in person searches themselves. Search fee: $15.00 per hour. Required to search: name, years to search. Civil cases indexed by defendant, plaintiff, on computer back to 1984. Mail turnaround time 5 days. Public use terminal available. PAT results show middle initial, DOB. Search names on the Trial Courts database at www.state.ak.us/courts/names.htm. Web gives case number only.

Criminal Records: Access: Phone, fax, mail, in person, online. Visitors must perform in person searches themselves. Search fee: $15.00 per hour. Required to search: name, years to search. Criminal records computerized from 1984. Mail turnaround time 5 days. Public use terminal available. PAT results show middle initial, DOB. Online access to criminal records is the same as civil. Online results show middle initial, DOB.

General Information: Online identifiers in results same as on public terminal. No confidential or sealed records released. Will fax documents free to local or toll-free number; $10.00 fax fee otherwise. Court makes copy: $.25 per page. Certification fee: $5.00. Cert fee includes copies. Payee: Alaska Court System. Personal checks accepted; credit cards are not. Prepayment required. SASE not required.

Seward Magistrate Court (3rd District)

PO Box 1929, 5th and Adams Strs, Seward, AK 99664-1929; 907-224-3075; fax: 907-224-7192; 8AM-4:30PM (AK). *Misdemeanor, Civil Actions under $10,000, Small Claims.*

Handles cases for St. Paul Island.

Civil Records: Access: In person, mail, online. Both court and visitors may perform in person searches. Search fee: $15.00 per name; may do for free as time permits. Civil records on computer since 1983. Mail turnaround time 1-2 weeks. Civil PAT goes back to 1983. Search names on the Trial Courts database at www.state.ak.us/courts/names.htm. Web gives case number and name only.

Criminal Records: Access: In person, mail, online. Both court and visitors may perform in person searches. Search fee: $15.00 per name. Required to search: name, years to search, DOB. Criminal records on computer since 1983. Mail turnaround time 1-2 weeks. Criminal PAT goes back to same as civil. Online access to criminal records is the same as civil. Online results can include DOB; most have middle initial.

General Information: Online identifiers in results same as on public terminal. Recommends against faxing documents. Court makes copy: $.25 per page. Certification fee: $5.00. Payee: State of Alaska. Personal checks accepted; credit cards are not. Prepayment required. Mail requests: SASE helpful.

Ketchikan Gateway Borough

Superior & District Court (1st District)

415 Main, Rm 400, Ketchikan, AK 99901-6399; 907-225-3195; fax: 907-225-7849; 8AM-4:30PM M-TH, 9AM-4:30PM F (AK). *Felony, Misdemeanor, Civil, Eviction, Small Claims, Probate.*

Civil Records: Access: Mail, in person, online. Both court and visitors may perform in person searches. Search fee: $15.00 per hour. Required to search: name, years to search. Civil cases indexed by defendant, plaintiff, on computer from 1983, on microfiche from 1972 to 1989, index from 1972. Mail turnaround time 2 weeks. Civil PAT goes back to 1983. PAT civil results show middle initial. Search names on the Alaska Trial Courts index free at http://orca.courts.state.ak.us/names/. Updated bi-monthly. Web gives case number only.

Criminal Records: Access: Mail, in person, online. Both court and visitors may perform in person searches. Search fee: $15.00 per hour. Required to search: name, years to search, DOB. Criminal records computerized from 1983, on microfiche from 1972 to 1989, index from 1972. Mail turnaround time 2 weeks. Criminal PAT goes back to same as civil. PAT results show middle initial, DOB. Online

access to criminal records is the same as civil. Online results show middle initial, DOB.
General Information: Online identifiers in results same as on public terminal. No confidential probate or children's records released. No fee to fax documents if toll-free. Court makes copy: $.25 per page. Certification fee: $5.00. Payee: Alaska Court System. Personal checks accepted; credit cards are not. Prepayment required. Mail requests: SASE required.

Kodiak Island Borough

Superior & District Court (3rd District)

204 Mission Rd, Rm 124, Kodiak, AK 99615-7312; 907-486-1600; fax: 907-486-1660; 8AM-4:30PM M,T,TH,F; 9AM-4:30PM W (AK). ***Felony, Misdemeanor, Civil, Eviction, Small Claims, Probate.***
Civil Records: Access: Mail, fax, in person, online. Both court and visitors may perform in person searches. Search fee: $15.00. Required to search: name, years to search; also helpful: address. Civil cases indexed by defendant, plaintiff, on computer from 1982, on microfiche, index and archived from 1959. Mail turnaround time 10 days. Civil PAT goes back to 1983. PAT results show middle initial, DOB. Search names on the Trial Courts database at www.state.ak.us/courts/names.htm. Web gives case number only.
Criminal Records: Access: Mail, fax, in person, online. Both court and visitors may perform in person searches. Search fee: $15.00. Required to search: name, years to search; also helpful: address, DOB, SSN. Criminal records computerized from 1982, on microfiche, index and archived from 1959. Mail turnaround time 10 business days. Criminal PAT goes back to same as civil. PAT results show middle initial, DOB. Online access to criminal records is the same as civil. Online results can include DOB; most have middle initial.
General Information: No adoption, juvenile, guardianship or mental records released. Will not fax documents. Court makes copy: $.25 per page. Certification fee: $5.00 plus $2.00 per add'l copy. If party to action there is no fee. Payee: Clerk of Court. Personal checks or cash accepted. No credit cards accepted. Prepayment required. Mail requests: SASE required.

Matanuska-Susitna Borough

Superior & District Court (3rd District)

435 S Denali St, Palmer, AK 99645-6437; 907-746-8181; criminal phone: x4; fax: 907-746-4151; 8AM-4:30PM, 9AM-N Sat (AK). ***Felony, Misdemeanor, Civil, Eviction, Small Claims, Probate.***
Civil Records: Access: Mail, in person, online. Both court and visitors may perform in person searches. Search fee: $15.00 per hour. Required to search: name, years to search; also helpful: address. Civil cases indexed by defendant, plaintiff, on computer from 1988, on microfiche, archived and index from 1974. Mail turnaround time 1-3 weeks. Civil PAT goes back to 1988. Terminal results can include DOB; most have middle initial. Search court records free at new CourtView system at www.courtrecords.alaska.gov/.
Criminal Records: Access: Mail, in person, online. Both court and visitors may perform in person searches. Search fee: $15.00 per hour. Required to search: name, years to search; also helpful: address, DOB, SSN. Criminal records computerized from 1988, on microfiche, archived and index from 1974. Mail turnaround time 1-3 weeks. Criminal PAT goes back to same as civil. Online access to criminal records is the same as civil. Online results show middle initial. Online results can include DOB; most have middle initial.
General Information: Online identifiers in results same as on public terminal. No adoption, juvenile, guardianship or mental records released. Will fax documents to local or toll-free number. Court makes copy: $.25 per page. Self serve: $.25 per page. Certification fee: $5.00 per document, 2nd cert copy for $2.00 if purchased at the same time. Payee: State of Alaska. Personal checks accepted. Visa/MC accepted in person only. Prepayment required. Mail requests: SASE required.

Nome

Superior & District Court (2nd District)

PO Box 1110, 113 Front St, 2nd Fl, Nome, AK 99762-1110; 907-443-5216; probate phone: same; fax: 907-443-2192; 8AM-4:30PM M,T,TH,F; 9AM-4:30 W (AK). ***Felony, Misdemeanor, Civil, Eviction, Small Claims, Probate.***
www.state.ak.us/courts/courtdir.htm
Probate fax is same as main fax number.
Civil Records: Access: Fax, mail, in person, online. Both court and visitors may perform in person searches. Search fee: $15.00 per hour or fraction of. Required to search: name, years to search; also helpful: DOB. Civil cases indexed by defendant, plaintiff, on computer from 1983, on microfiche from 1960 to 1983, on index and archived from 1960. Mail turnaround time 5 days. Civil PAT goes back to 1983. Terminal results can include DOB; most have middle initial. Search court records free at new CourtView system at www.courtrecords.alaska.gov/pa/pa.urd/pamw6500.display.
Criminal Records: Access: Fax, mail, in person, online. Both court and visitors may perform in person searches. Search fee: $15.00 per hour or fraction of. Required to search: name, years to search; also helpful: DOB, SSN. Criminal records computerized from 1983, on microfiche from 1960 to 1983, on index and archived from 1960. Mail turnaround time 5 days. Criminal PAT goes back to same as civil. Online access to criminal records is the same as civil. Online results can include DOB; most have middle initial.
General Information: Online identifiers in results same as on public terminal. No adoption, juvenile, guardianship or mental records released. Will fax documents to toll-free number. Court makes copy: $.25 per page, self serve same. Certification fee: $5.00 plus $2.00 per copy after first. Payee: Nome Trial Courts. Personal checks accepted. Visa/MC accepted. Prepayment required. Mail requests: SASE required.

Gambell Magistrate Court (2nd District)

PO Box 1110, 113 Front St, 2nd Fl, Nome, AK 99762-1110; 907-443-5216; fax: 907-443-2192; 8AM-4:30PM (AK). ***Misdemeanor, Civil Actions under $10,000, Small Claims.***
Court is vacant; records at Superior Court in Nome at address and phone here. Search court records free at new CourtView system at www.courtrecords.alaska.gov/pa/pa.urd/pamw6500.display.

Unalakleet Magistrate Court (2nd Dist.)

PO Box 250, Unalakleet, AK 99684-0250; 907-624-3015; fax: 907-624-3118; 8AM-4PM (AK). ***Misdemeanor, Civil Actions under $10,000, Small Claims.***
This is a one-person court and very quiet.
Civil Records: Access: In person, mail, fax, online. Only the court performs in person searches; visitors may not. Search fee: $15.00 per hour. Required to search: name, years to search. Civil records indexed by defendant, plaintiff. Civil records go back to 1998. Mail turnaround time 1-2 weeks. Search court records free at new CourtView system at www.courtrecords.alaska.gov/pa/pa.urd/pamw6500.display.
Criminal Records: Access: In person, mail, fax, online. Only the court performs in person searches; visitors may not. Search fee: $15.00 per hour. Required to search: name, years to search. Criminal records go back to 1998. Mail turnaround time 1-2 weeks. Online access to criminal is the same as civil, see above. Online results can include DOB; most have middle inititial.
General Information: Will fax documents for free. Court makes copy: $.25 per page. Certification fee: $5.00 per doc. Payee: Alaska Court System. Personal checks accepted; credit cards are not. Prepayment required. SASE not required.

North Slope Borough

Superior & District Court (2nd District)

PO Box 270, 1250 Agvik St, 2nd Fl, Barrow, AK 99723-0270; 907-852-4800; fax: 907-852-4804; 8AM-4:30PM except Weds 9AM-4PM (AK). ***Felony, Misdemeanor, Civil, Eviction, Small Claims, Probate.***
Civil Records: Access: Fax, mail, in person, online. Both court and visitors may perform in person searches. Search fee: $15.00 per hour. Required to search: name, years to search; also helpful: address. Civil cases indexed by defendant, plaintiff, on computer from 1983, prior on microfiche. Hard copies go back only 5 years. Mail turnaround time 3 weeks. Civil PAT goes back to 1983. Terminal results can include DOB; most have middle initial. Search court records free at new CourtView system at www.courtrecords.alaska.gov/pa/pa.urd/pamw6500.display.
Criminal Records: Access: Fax, mail, in person, online. Both court and visitors may perform in person searches. Search fee: $15.00 per hour. Required to search: name, years to search; also helpful: address, DOB, SSN. Criminal records computerized from 1983, prior on microfiche. Hard copies go back only 5 years. Mail turnaround time 3 weeks. Criminal PAT goes back to same as civil. Online access to criminal records is the same as civil. Online results can include DOB; most have middle initial.
General Information: Online identifiers in results same as on public terminal. No confidential records released. Will fax documents to local or toll-free number. Court makes copy: $.25 per page. Certification fee: $5.00 1st doc; add'l docs are $2.00. Payee: Alaska Court System. Personal checks accepted. Visa/MC accepted in person only. Prepayment required. Mail requests: SASE required.

Northwest Arctic Borough

Superior & District Court (2nd District)

PO Box 317, 605 3rd Ave, Kotzebue, AK 99752-0317; 907-442-3208; probate phone: same; fax: 907-442-3974; 8AM-4:30PM (AK). ***Felony, Misdemeanor, Civil, Eviction, Small Claims, Probate.*** This court holds records for the closed Magistrate Court formerly in Ambler, Kiana, Pt. Hope, Selawick and Noowik.
Civil Records: Access: Phone, fax, mail, in person, online. Both court and visitors may perform in person searches. Search fee: $15.00. Required to search: name, years to search. Civil cases indexed by defendant, plaintiff, on computer from 1993, prior records on microfiche archived and index from 1966 on microfilm. Note: Copy of check required before faxed requests are processed. Mail turnaround time 2 day to 3 weeks. Civil PAT goes back to 1983. Terminal results can include DOB; most have middle initial. Search court records free at new CourtView system www.courtrecords.alaska.gov/.
Criminal Records: Access: Mail, fax, in person, online. Both court and visitors may perform in person searches. Search fee: $15.00. Required to search: name, years to search, DOB; also helpful: SSN. Criminal records computerized from 1983, prior records on microfiche, archived and index from 1966 on microfilm. Mail turnaround time 2 days to 3 weeks. Criminal PAT goes back to same as civil.PAT results show name, DOB. Online access to criminal records is the same as civil. Online results can include DOB; most have middle initial.
General Information: Online identifiers in results same as on public terminal. No adoption, juvenile, guardianship or mental records released. Will fax documents to local or toll-free number. Court makes copy: $.25 per page, self serve same. Certification fee: $5.00 plus $2.00 per page after first; $15.00 for exemplification. Notary fee is $3.00. Payee: Alaska Court System. Personal checks accepted. Visa/MC in person only accepted. Prepayment required. SASE not required.

Kiana Magistrate Court (2nd District) PO Box 317, 605 Third St, Kotzebue, AK 99752-0317; 907-442-3208; ; 8AM-4:30PM (AK). ***Misdemeanor, Civil Actions under $10,000, Small Claims.***
Court is temporarily vacant; contact the Kotzebue Court for record information; Kotzebue court address and phones given here. Records available online on the new statewide Courtview system.

Selawik Magistrate Court (2nd District) PO Box 317, 605 Third St, Kotzebue, AK 99752; 907-442-3208; fax: 907-442-3974; 8AM-4:30PM (AK). ***Misdemeanor, Civil Actions under $10,000, Small Claims.***

Selawik court closed. Contact the Kotzebue Court for record information; Kotzebue court address and phones given here. Records available online on the new statewide Courtview system.

Prince of Wales - Outer Ketchikan

Craig Trial Court (1st District) PO Box 646, 1305 Craig-Klawouck Hwy, Craig, AK 99921-0646; 907-826-3316/3306; fax: 907-826-3904; 8AM-4:30PM M-TH; 9AM-4:30PM F (AK). ***Felony, Misdemeanor, Civil Actions, Small Claims.***

Prior to 7/1/2007 felony cases are at Ketchikan Superior & District Court.

Civil Records: Access: In person, phone, fax, mail, online. Only the court performs in person searches; visitors may not. Search fee: $15.00 per hour. No fee to call for the court to check index for a name and case number. Required to search: name, years to search; also helpful: DOB. Civil records go back to 1960s; on computer back to 1993. Mail turnaround time 2 weeks. Search names on the Trial Courts database at www.state.ak.us/courts/names.htm. Web gives case number only.

Criminal Records: Access: In person, phone, fax, mail, online. Only the court performs in person searches; visitors may not. Search fee: $15.00 per hour. No fee to call for the court to check index for a name and case number. Required to search: name, years to search; also helpful: DOB. Misdemeanor records go back to 1960s; on computer back to 1993. Mail turnaround time 2 weeks. Online access to criminal records is the same as civil. Online results show name only. Online results can include DOB; most have middle initial.

General Information: Will fax documents for free. Court makes copy: $.25 per page. Certification fee: $5.00 per doc; exemplification- $10.00. Payee: Alaska Court System. Personal checks accepted; credit cards are not. Prepayment required. Mail requests: SASE requested.

Sitka Borough

Superior & District Court (1st District) 304 Lake St, Rm 203, Sitka, AK 99835-7759; 907-747-3291; criminal fax: 907-747-6690; civil fax: same; 8AM-4:30PM M-TH; 9AM-4:30 F (AK). ***Felony, Misdemeanor, Civil, Eviction, Small Claims, Probate.***

Probate is in a separate index at this address. Probate fax is same as main fax number.

Civil Records: Access: Phone, fax, mail, in person, online. Both court and visitors may perform in person searches. Search fee: $15.00 per hour. No fee for info given out over the phone. Required to search: name. Civil cases indexed by defendant, plaintiff, on computer from 1983, on microfilm and archived from 1970 to 1987, on index from 1960. Mail turnaround time 1 week. Civil PAT goes back to 1980s. PAT civil results show middle initial. Search names on the Trial Courts database at www.state.ak.us/courts/names.htm. Web gives case number only.

Criminal Records: Access: Phone, fax, mail, in person, online. Both court and visitors may perform in person searches. Search fee: $15.00 per hour. No fee for info given out over the phone. Required to search: name. Criminal records computerized from 1983, on microfilm and archived from 1970 to 1987, on index from 1960. Mail turnaround time 1 week. Criminal PAT goes back to same as civil. PAT results show middle initial, DOB. Online access to criminal records is the same as civil. Online results show middle initial. Online results can include DOB; most have middle initial.

General Information: No adoption, juvenile, guardianship or mental records released. No fee to fax document to toll-free number. Court makes copy: $.25 per page. Self serve: $.10 per page. Certification fee: $5.00 per doc; exemplifications- $10.00. Payee: Alaska Court System. Personal checks accepted; credit cards are not. Prepayment required. Mail requests: SASE required.

Skagway-Yakutat-Angoon

Hoonah District Court (1st District) PO Box 430, Hoonah, AK 99829-0430; 907-945-3668; fax: 907-945-3637; 8AM-N, 1-4:30PM (AK). ***Misdemeanor, Civil Actions under $100,000, Small Claims.***

Felony cases are at Juneau Superior & District Court.

Civil Records: Access: Mail, in person, online. Only the court performs in person searches; visitors may not. No search fee. Required to search: name, years to search, case number. Civil cases indexed by defendant, plaintiff, on index from 1971 to present. Mail turnaround time 2-3 days. Search name index for limited data free at http://orca.courts.state.ak.us/names/. Data updated quarterly

Criminal Records: Access: Mail, in person, online. Only the court performs in person searches; visitors may not. Search fee: $15.00. Required to search: name, DOB, case number. Criminal records indexed from 1996 to present. Note: Older criminal records on microfilm in Juneau; research time is $15.00 per hour. Mail turnaround time 2-3 days. Search name index for limited data free at http://orca.courts.state.ak.us/names/. Updated quarterly. Online results can include DOB; most have middle initial.

General Information: No confidential, juvenile or sex related records released. Will fax documents to toll-free number. Court makes copy: $.25 per page. Certification fee: $5.00 plus $2.00 per page after first. Payee: Alaska Court System. Personal checks accepted; credit cards are not. Prepayment required. Mail requests: SASE required.

Angoon Magistrate Court (1st District) PO Box 250, Angoon, AK 99820-0123; 907-788-3229; fax: 907-788-3108; 8AM-1PM T-F; Closed M (AK). ***Misdemeanor, Civil Actions under $10,000, Small Claims.***

Felony cases are at Sitka Superior & District Court.

Civil Records: Access: Phone, mail, fax, in person. Only the court performs in person searches; visitors may not. Search fee: $15.00 per hour. Required to search: name, years to search. Records go back to 1994. Mail turnaround time 1 week.

Criminal Records: Access: Phone, mail, fax, in person. Only the court performs in person searches; visitors may not. Search fee: $15.00 per hour. Required to search: name, years to search, date of birth. Records go back to 1994. Mail turnaround time 1 week. Online results can include DOB; most have middle initial.

General Information: Fee to fax out file $5.00 per page or $15.00 per document. Court makes copy: $.25 per page. Certification fee: $5.00 per doc. Payee: Alaska Court System. Personal checks, money orders accepted. No credit cards accepted. Prepayment required. Mail requests: SASE helpful.

Pelican Magistrate Court 1st District in Sitka 304 Lake St #203, Sitka, AK 99835; 907-747-3291; fax: 907-747-6690; 8AM-4:30pm M-TH; 9AM-4:30PM F (AK). ***Misdemeanor, Civil Actions under $10,000, Small Claims.***

This Pelican court closed permanently on 12/31/99. All records are at the Sitka court, address and phone given here.

Skagway District Magistrate Court PO Box 495, 7th & Spring, McCabe Bldg, Skagway, AK 99840-0495; 907-983-2368; fax: 907-983-3801; 8AM-3PM T,W,TH; 8AM-2:30PM F; closed M (AK). ***Misdemeanor, Civil Actions under $10,000, Small Claims.***

Felony cases are at Juneau Superior & District Court.

Civil Records: Access: Mail, fax, in person, online. Only the court performs in person searches; visitors may not. Search fee: $15.00 per hour. Required to search: DOB, SSN, years to search. Civil cases indexed by defendant, plaintiff, go back to 1970 on microfilm in Anchorage; on computer back to 1998. Mail turnaround time 1-2 weeks. Search court records free at new CourtView system at www.courtrecords.alaska.gov/pa/pa.urd/pamw6500.display.

Criminal Records: Access: In person, fax, mail, online. Only the court performs in person searches; visitors may not. Search fee: $15.00 per hour. Required to search: name, years to search, DOB. Criminal records go back to 1970; on computer back to 1996. Note: No charge for a simple name search. Mail turnaround time 1-2 weeks. Online access to criminal records is the same as civil. Online results can include DOB; most have middle initial.

General Information: Will fax to toll-free numbers no charge. Court makes copy: $.25 per page. Certification fee: $5.00 per doc. Payee: State of Alaska. Personal checks accepted; credit cards are not. Prepayment required.

Yakutat Magistrate Court (1st District) PO Box 426, 508 Max Italio Dr, Yakutat, AK 99689-0426; 907-784-3274; fax: 907-784-3257; 9AM-N, 1-4:30PM M-TH, 8:30AM-N F (AK). ***Misdemeanor, Civil Actions under $10,000, Small Claims.***

Felony cases are at Juneau Superior & District Court.

Civil Records: Access: Phone, mail, fax, in person. Only the court performs in person searches; visitors may not. Search fee: $15.00 per name. Required to search: name. Civil cases indexed by defendant, plaintiff, go back to 1998; on computer back to 1976. Mail turnaround time 7-12 days.

Criminal Records: Access: Mail, fax, in person, email. Only the court performs in person searches; visitors may not. Search fee: $15.00 per name. Required to search: name and DOB or SSN. Criminal records go back to 1959; on computer back to 1998. Note: Direct email criminal record requests to yakutat@courts.state.ak.us. Mail turnaround time 7-12 days. Online results can include DOB; most have middle initial.

General Information: Will fax documents to local or toll-free number. Court makes copy: $.25 per page. Certification fee: $5.00 per doc. Payee: Alaska Court System. Personal checks accepted; credit cards are not. Prepayment required. Mail requests: SASE required.

Southeast Fairbanks

Delta Junction District Court (4th District) PO Box 401, Mile 266 Richardson Hiway, Delta Junction, AK 99737-0401; 907-895-4211; fax: 907-895-4204; 8AM-N, 1-4:30PM (AK). ***Misdemeanor, Civil Actions under $10,000, Small Claims, Eviction, Traffic.***

Felony cases are at Fairbanks Superior & District Court.

Civil Records: Access: In person, mail, online. Only the court performs in person searches; visitors may not. Search fee: $15.00 per hour. Required to search: name, years to search. Civil records go back to 2000. Mail turnaround time 1 week. Search court records free at new CourtView system at www.courtrecords.alaska.gov/pa/pa.urd/pamw6500.display.

Criminal Records: Access: phone, mail, fax, in person, online. Only the court performs in person searches; visitors may not. Search fee: $15.00 per hour. Required to search: name, years to search. Criminal records computerized go back to 1980; prior records go back to mid-70's. Mail turnaround time 1 week. Online access to criminal records is the same as civil. Online results can include DOB; most have middle initial.

General Information: Will not fax documents. Court makes copy: $.25 per page. Certification fee: $5.00 per doc. Payee: District Court. Personal checks accepted. Major credit cards accepted for traffic only. Prepayment required. Mail requests: SASE helpful.

Tok Magistrate Court (4th District) PO Box 187, 1313 S Alaska Hwy, Tok, AK 99780-0187; 907-883-5171; fax: 907-883-4367; 8AM-N; 1PM-4:30PM (AK). ***Misdemeanor, Civil Actions under $10,000, Small Claims.***

Felony cases are at Fairbanks Superior & District Court.

Civil Records: Access: In person, phone, mail, online. Visitors must perform in person searches themselves. Search fee: $15.00. Required to search: Name, DOB, SSN. Civil records computerized since 1994. Mail turnaround time 5 days. Civil PAT goes back to 1994. Terminal results can include DOB; most have middle initial. Search court records free at new CourtView system at www.courtrecords.alaska.gov/pa/pa.urd/pamw6500.display.

Criminal Records: Access: In person, phone, mail, online. Visitors must perform in person searches themselves. No search fee. Required to search: name, years to search, DOB. Criminal records computerized since 1994. Mail turnaround time 5 days. Criminal PAT goes back to same as civil. Online access to criminal records is the same as civil. Online results can include DOB; most have middle initital.

General Information: Online identifiers in results same as on public terminal. Will fax documents. Court makes copy: $.25 per page. Certification fee: $5.00 per doc. Payee: Court. Personal checks accepted. Major credit cards accepted in person only. Prepayment required. Mail requests: SASE required.

Valdez-Cordova

District Court (3rd District)
PO Box 127, 213 Meals, Valdez, AK 99686-0127; 907-835-2266; fax: 907-835-3764; 8AM-4:30PM (AK). ***Felony, Misdemeanor, Civil, Eviction, Small Claims, Probate.***

In rare instances, some of the older Valdez felony records may be found at Cordova.

Civil Records: Access: Fax, mail, in person, online. Only the court performs in person searches; visitors may not. No search fee. Required to search: name, years to search; also helpful: address. Civil cases indexed by defendant, plaintiff, on computer from 1989, on microfiche, archived and index from 1960. Mail turnaround time 1-3 weeks. Search court records free at new CourtView system at www.courtrecords.alaska.gov/pa/pa.urd/pamw6500.display.

Criminal Records: Access: Fax, mail, in person, online. Only the court performs in person searches; visitors may not. No search fee. Required to search: name, years to search; also helpful: address, DOB. Criminal records computerized from 1984, on microfiche, archived and index from 1960. Mail turnaround time 1-3 weeks. Online access to criminal records is the same as civil. Online results can include DOB; most have middle initial.

General Information: No adoption, juvenile, guardianship or mental records released. Will fax documents $15.00 fee. Court makes copy: $.25 per page. Certification fee: $5.00 per doc. Payee: Valdez Trial Court of Alaska. Personal checks accepted. Prepayment required. Mail requests: SASE required.

Cordova District Court (3rd District)
PO Box 898, 500 Water St, Cordova, AK 99574-0898; 907-424-3378; fax: 907-424-7581; 8AM-4:30PM (AK). ***Felony, Misdemeanor, Civil, Small Claims, Probate.***

Some very old Valdez court records may also reside here. Although some felony cases may be assigned to a Valdez judge or a Anchorage judge, the actual case records will be found here in Cordova.

Civil Records: Access: Phone, mail, fax, in person, online. Both court and visitors may perform in person searches. Search fee: $15.00 per name. Required to search: DOB, years to search. Civil cases indexed by defendant, plaintiff, on computer back to 1993; other records back to 1975. Note: Access by phone if time allows. Mail turnaround time 1 week. Civil PAT goes back to 7-10 years. Terminal results can include DOB; most have middle initial. Search court records free at new CourtView system at www.courtrecords.alaska.gov/pa/pa.urd/pamw6500.display.

Criminal Records: Access: Phone, mail, fax, in person, online. Both court and visitors may perform in person searches. Search fee: $15.00 per hour. Required to search: name, years to search, DOB. Criminal records computerized from 1993; other records back to 1975. Note: Will take phone requests if time allows. Results include name and address. Mail turnaround time 1 week. Criminal PAT goes back to same as civil. Online access to criminal records is the same as civil. Online results can include DOB; most have middle initital.

General Information: Online identifiers in results same as on public terminal. Will not fax documents. Court makes copy: $.25 per page. Self serve: $.25 per page. Certification fee: $5.00 per doc. Payee: State of Alaska. Personal checks accepted; credit cards are not. Prepayment required.

Glennallen District Court (3rd District)
PO Box 86, Mile 115 Richardson Hiway, Glennallen, AK 99588-0086; 907-822-3405; ; 8AM-4:30PM (AK). ***Felony, Misdemeanor, Civil, Small Claims, Probate.***

Civil Records: Access: Mail, in person, online. Only the court performs in person searches; visitors may not. Search fee: $15.00 per hour. Required to search: DOB, years to search. Civil cases indexed by defendant, plaintiff. Records go back to 1960; on computer back to 1992. Mail turnaround time 1-2 weeks. Search court records free at new CourtView system at www.courtrecords.alaska.gov/pa/pa.urd/pamw6500.display.

Criminal Records: Access: Mail, in person, online. Only the court performs in person searches; visitors may not. Search fee: $15.00 per hour. Required to search: name, years to search, DOB. Records go back to 1960; on computer back to 1992. Mail turnaround time 1-2 weeks. Online access to criminal records is the same as civil. Online results can include DOB; most have middle initital.

General Information: Online identifiers in results same as on public terminal. Will not fax documents. Court makes copy: $.25 per page. Certification fee: $5.00 per doc. Payee: Alaska Court System. No credit cards accepted. Prepayment required.

Whittier Magistrate Court (3rd District)
825 W 4th Ave, Anchorage, AK 99501-2004; 907-264-0479; ; 8AM-4:30PM (AK). ***Misdemeanor, Civil Actions under $10,000, Small Claims.***

Court closed; records available at the address and phone above. Search court records free at new CourtView system at www.courtrecords.alaska.gov/pa/pa.urd/pamw6500.display.

Wade Hampton

Chevak Magistrate Court (Bethel Area)
PO Box 238, Chevak, AK 99563-0238; 907-858-7231; criminal fax: 907-858-7230; civil fax: same; 8AM-4:30PM (AK). ***Misdemeanor, Civil Actions under $10,000, Small Claims.***

Felony cases at Bethel Superior & District Court. Indictments at Chevak District Court.

Civil Records: Access: Mail, fax, in person, online. Only the court performs in person searches; visitors may not. Search fee: $15.00. Required to search: name, years to search. Civil records go back to 1993; on computer back to 1997. Mail turnaround time 1-2 weeks. Public use terminal available, records go back to 2004. Search court records free at new CourtView system at www.courtrecords.alaska.gov/pa/pa.urd/pamw6500.display.

Criminal Records: Access: Mail, fax, in person, online. Both court and visitors may perform in person searches. Search fee: $15.00 per hour. Required to search: name, years to search, address, DOB, SSN, signed release. Criminal records go back to 1993; on computer back to 1997. Mail turnaround time 1-2 weeks. Public use terminal available, crim records go back to same. Search court records free at new CourtView system at www.courtrecords.alaska.gov/pa/pa.urd/pamw6500.display. Online results can include DOB; most have middle initital.

General Information: Will fax documents. Court makes copy: $.25 per page, self serve same. Certification fee: $3.00 per document includes copy fee. Payee: Alaska Court System. Personal checks accepted; credit cards are not. Prepayment required. Mail requests: SASE helpful.

Emmonak Magistrate Court (Bethel Area)
PO Box 176, Emmonak, AK 99581-0176; 907-949-1748; criminal fax: 907-949-1535; civil fax: same; 8AM-4:30PM (AK). ***Misdemeanor, Civil Actions under $15,000, Small Claims.***

Felony cases are at Bethel Superior & District Court.

Civil Records: Access: Mail, in person, online. Only the court performs in person searches; visitors may not. Search fee: $15.00 per hour. Required to search: name, years to search, DOB, SSN, signed release. Civil records indexed by defendant, plaintiff. Overall records go back to 1995. Computerized records go back to 2000. Mail turnaround time 1-2 weeks. Search court records free at new CourtView system at www.courtrecords.alaska.gov/pa/pa.urd/pamw6500.display.

Criminal Records: Access: Mail, in person, online. Only the court performs in person searches; visitors may not. Search fee: $15.00 per hour. Required to search: name, years to search, address, DOB, signed release; also helpful: SSN. Overall records go back to 1995. Computerized records go back to 2000. Mail turnaround time 1-2 weeks. Search court records free at CourtView system at www.courtrecords.alaska.gov/pa/pa.urd/pamw6500.display. Online results can include DOB; most have middle initital.

General Information: Will fax out documents. Court makes copy: $.25 per page. Certification fee: $5.00 includes copy fee. Payee: Emmonak Court. Personal checks accepted; credit cards are not. Prepayment required. Mail requests: SASE required.

St Mary's Magistrate Court (Bethel Area)
PO Box 269, St Mary's, AK 99658-0183; 907-438-2912; criminal fax: 907-438-2819; civil fax: 907-438-2819; 8AM-N, 1-4:30PM (AK). ***Misdemeanor, Civil Actions under $10,000, Small Claims.***

www.courtrecords.alaska.gov

Felony cases are at Bethel Superior & District Court.

Civil Records: Access: Mail, in person, online. Only the court performs in person searches; visitors may not. Search fee: $15.00 per hour. Required to search: Name, DOB, SSN, years to search 2001-2006, prior years must be requested from Bethel Court 907-543-2298. Civil records computerized go back to 1996. Mail turnaround time 3 weeks. Search names on the Trial Courts database at www.state.ak.us/courts/names.htm. Web gives case number only.

Criminal Records: Access: Mail, in person, online. Only the court performs in person searches; visitors may not. Search fee: $15.00 per hour. Required to search: name, years to search; also helpful: DOB. Criminal records computerized go back to 1996. Mail turnaround time 3 weeks. Search names on the Trial Courts database at www.state.ak.us/courts/names.htm. Web gives case number only. Online results can include DOB; most have middle initital.

General Information: Will fax documents. Court makes copy: $.25 per page, self serve same. Certification fee: $5.00 + $.25 per page copy fee. Payee: District Court. Checks accepted. No credit cards accepted. Prepayment required.

Wrangell-Petersburg

Petersburg Superior & District Court (1st District)
PO Box 1009, Petersburg, AK 99833-1009; 907-772-3824; fax: 907-772-3018; 8AM-4:30PM (AK). ***Felony, Misdemeanor, Civil, Eviction, Small Claims, Probate.***

Civil Records: Access: Phone, fax, mail, in person, online. Only the court performs in person searches; visitors may not. No search fee unless on microfilm-$15.00 per hour. Required to search: name, years to search; also helpful: address. Civil cases indexed by defendant, plaintiff, on computer from 1988, on microfiche and index from 1960s, archived from 1920s. Mail turnaround time 1 week. Search names on the Trial Courts database at www.state.ak.us/courts/names.htm. Web gives case number and disposition.

Criminal Records: Access: Phone, fax, mail, in person, online. Only the court performs in person searches; visitors may not. Search fee: $15.00 per hour fee on archive cases. Required to search: name, years to search; also helpful: address, DOB. Criminal records computerized from 1988, on microfiche and index from 1960s, archived from 1920s. Mail turnaround time 1 week. Online access to criminal records is the same as civil. Online results can include DOB; most have middle initial.

General Information: No adoption, juvenile, guardianship or mental records released. Outgoing fax limited to 10 pages; call for fee. Court makes copy: $.25 per page. Certification fee: $5.00 for 1st page, $2.00 each add'l page. Payee: Alaska Court System.

Personal checks accepted; credit cards are not. Prepayment required. Mail requests: SASE required.

Wrangell Superior & District Court (1st District)

PO Box 869, Wrangell, AK 99929-0869; 907-874-2311; fax: 907-874-3509; 8AM-4:30PM (AK). ***Felony, Misdemeanor, Civil, Eviction, Small Claims, Probate.***

The TDD office can be reached at 800-770-8255.

Civil Records: Access: Phone, fax, mail, in person, online. Only the court performs in person searches; visitors may not. Search fee: $15.00 per hour. Search fee is charged for all written responses. Required to search: name, years to search. Civil cases indexed by defendant, plaintiff, on computer from 1988, on microfiche and card files from 1959, archived from 1900s. Mail turnaround time 3 days. Civil PAT goes back to 1989. PAT results show middle initial, DOB. Search names on the Trial Courts database at www.state.ak.us/courts/names.htm. Web gives case number and court location.

Criminal Records: Access: Phone, fax, mail, in person, online. Only the court performs in person searches; visitors may not. Search fee: $15.00 per hour. Required to search: name, years to search, DOB. Criminal records computerized from 1988, on microfiche and card files from 1959, archived from 1900s. Mail turnaround time 3 days. Criminal PAT goes back to 1989. PAT results show middle initial, DOB. Online access to criminal records is the same as civil. Online results show name, DOB. Online results can include DOB; most have middle inititial.

General Information: No adoption, juvenile, guardianship or mental records released. Fee to fax out docs $15.00 each. Court makes copy: $.25 per page. Certification fee: $5.00 plus $2.00 per copy after first. Exemplification- $10.00. Payee: Alaska Court System or State of Alaska. Personal checks accepted; credit cards are not. Prepayment required. SASE not required.

Kake Magistrate Court (1st District)

PO Box 100, Kake, AK 99830-0100; 907-785-3651; fax: 907-785-3152; 8AM-Noon (AK). ***Misdemeanor, Civil Actions under $10,000, Small Claims.***

Civil Records: Access: Fax, mail, in person. Only the court performs in person searches; visitors may not. Search fee: $15.00 per name. Required to search: name. Civil cases indexed by defendant, plaintiff, go back to 1990. Mail turnaround time 1-2 weeks.

Criminal Records: Access: Fax, mail, in person. Only the court performs in person searches; visitors may not. Search fee: $15.00 per name. Required to search: name, years to search, DOB, SSN, signed release. Criminal records go back to 1990. Mail turnaround time 1-2 weeks. Online results can include DOB; most have middle inititial.

General Information: Will not fax documents. Court makes copy: $.25 per page. Certification fee: $5.00 per doc. Payee: Alaska Court System. Personal checks accepted; credit cards are not. Prepayment required.

Yukon-Koyukuk

Fort Yukon Magistrate Court (4th Dist.)

PO Box 211, Fort Yukon, AK 99740-0211; 907-662-2336; fax: 907-662-2824; 8AM-1:30PM (AK). ***Misdemeanor, Civil Actions under $10,000, Small Claims.***

Felony cases are at Fairbanks Superior & District Court.

Civil Records: Access: Fax, mail, in person, Online. Only the court performs in person searches; visitors may not. Search fee: $15.00 per name. Required to search: name, DOB. Civil cases indexed by defendant, plaintiff. Records go back to 1960s. Mail turnaround time 1-2 weeks. Search court records free at new CourtView system at www.courtrecords.alaska.gov/pa/pa.urd/pamw6500.display.

Criminal Records: Access: Fax, mail, in person, online. Only the court performs in person searches; visitors may not. Search fee: $15.00 per hour. Required to search: name, years to search, DOB. Records go back to 1960s. Mail turnaround time 1-2 weeks. Search court records free at new CourtView system at www.courtrecords.alaska.gov/pa/pa.urd/pamw6500.display. Fairbanks online results can include DOB; most have middle initial.

General Information: Will fax documents to local or toll free line. Court makes copy: $.25 per page. Certification fee: $5.00 per doc. Payee: District Court. Prepayment required.

Galena Magistrate Court (4th District)

PO Box 167, Galena, AK 99741-0167; 907-656-1322; fax: 907-656-1546; 8AM-4:30PM (AK). ***Misdemeanor, Civil Actions under $10,000, Small Claims.***

Felony cases are at Fairbanks Superior & District Court.

Civil Records: Access: Mail, in person, online. Only the court performs in person searches; visitors may not. Search fee: $15.00 per name. Required to search: name. Civil record computerized since 1995. Mail turnaround time 1-2 weeks. Search court records free at new CourtView system at www.courtrecords.alaska.gov/pa/pa.urd/pamw6500.display.

Criminal Records: Access: Mail, in person, online. Only the court performs in person searches; visitors may not. Search fee: $15.00 per hour. Required to search: name, years to search. Criminal records computerized since 1995. Mail turnaround time 1-2 weeks. Online access to civil records is the same as civil. Felony online results can include DOB; most have middle inititial.

General Information: Online identifiers in results same as on public terminal. Will not fax documents. Court makes copy: $.25 per page. Certification fee: $5.00 per doc. Payee: Magistrate Court. No credit cards accepted. Prepayment required.

McGrath Magistrate Court (4th District)

PO Box 167, Galena, AK 99741-0167; 907-656-1322; fax: 907-656-1546; 8AM-4:30PM (AK). ***Misdemeanor, Civil Actions under $10,000, Small Claims.***

McGrath Court is vacant. Court records at Galena Magistrate Court, address and phone here.

Nenana Magistrate Court (4th District)

PO Box 449, Nenana, AK 99760-0449; 907-832-5430; fax: 907-832-5841; 8AM-N, 1-4PM (AK). ***Misdemeanor, Civil Actions under $10,000, Small Claims.***

Felony cases are at Fairbanks Superior & District Court.

Civil Records: Access: Phone, fax, mail, in person, online. Both court and visitors may perform in person searches. Search fee: $15.00 per name. Required to search: name, years to search, DOB. Civil PAT goes back to 1995. Terminal results can include DOB; most have middle initial. Address appears if no attorney on case. Search court records free at www.courtrecords.alaska.gov/pa/pa.urd/pamw6500.display

Criminal Records: Access: Phone, fax, mail, in person, online. Both court and visitors may perform in person searches. No search fee. Required to search: name, years to search, DOB. Criminal records computerized from 1995. Criminal PAT goes back to same as civil. PAT criminal results show middle initial. Results may also include DL number. Online access to criminal records is same as civil, above. Online results can include DOB; most have middle initial.

General Information: Online identifiers in results same as on public terminal. Will fax back docs but only a few pages free. Court makes copy: $.25 per page. Certification fee: $5.00 per doc. Personal checks accepted; credit cards are not.

Tanana Magistrate Court (4th District)

PO Box 167, Galena, AK 99741; 907-656-1322; fax: 907-656-1546; TH-F 2nd full week monthly (AK). ***Misdemeanor, Civil Actions under $10,000, Small Claims.***

Magistrate may also be contacted by phone at 907-832-5430. Felony cases are at Fairbanks Superior & District Court. All case record files moved to Galena Court 6/2005.

Civil Records: Access: In person, phone, mail. Both court and visitors may perform in person searches. Search fee: $15.00 per name. Mail turnaround time 1-2 weeks. Civil PAT goes back to 1995.

Criminal Records: Access: In person, phone, mail. Both court and visitors may perform in person searches. Search fee: $15.00 per name. Required to search: name, years to search, DOB, signed release. Mail turnaround time 1-2 weeks. Criminal PAT goes back to same as civil. Online results can include DOB; most have middle initial.

General Information: Will not fax documents. Court makes copy: $.25 per page. Certification fee: $5.00 per doc. Payee: Magistrate Court. Prepayment required.

Alaska Recording Offices

ORGANIZATION: The 23 Alaskan counties are called boroughs. However, real estate recording is done under a system that was established at the time of the Gold Rush (1893-1916) of 34 Recording Districts. Some of the Districts are identical in geography to boroughs such as the Aleutian Islands, but other boroughs and districts overlap. Therefore, you need to know which recording district any given town or city is located in. A helpful website is http://dnr.alaska.gov/ssd/recoff/findYourDistrict.htm

The state except the Aleutian Islands is in the Alaska Time Zone (AK). The Aleutian Islands are in the Hawaiian-Aleutian Time Zone.

REAL ESTATE RECORDS: Districts do not perform real estate searches. Copies cost $1.25 for the first page, $.25 per add'l page. Certification fee is $5.00 per document.

UCC RECORDS: Real estate related collateral is filed with the District Recorder. All other UCC financing statements are filed at the Department of Natural Resources; however, prior to July, 2001 these documents were filed at the District Recorder and can be searched here if active.

TAX LIEN RECORDS: All state and federal tax liens are filed with the District Recorder. Districts do not perform separate tax lien searches.

ONLINE ACCESS: Online access to the state recorder's office www.recorder.alaska.gov database from the Dept. of Natural Resources is free at http://dnr.alaska.gov/ssd/recoff/search.cfm. This includes property data, liens, deeds, bankruptcies, surveys, plats, and more. Images go back to June, 2001; index to 2000. Also, a DNR "land records" database is searchable at http://plats.landrecords.info/.

Aleutian Islands District

District Recorder, 550 W 7th Ave, #1140; #1140, Anchorage, AK 99501. 907-269-8899/269-8872, R/E recording phone-907-762-2444; fax-907-269-6006; 8AM-3:30PM (AK)

Index: Separate indices to search. Records indexed on a public use terminal back to 2001. Only the public may search. Copy fee $1.25 1st page, $.25 each add'l. Cert fee- $5.00 per doc plus copy fee. Payee- Department of Natural Resources. Bulk data available on CD: contact Brandi Brown 907-269-8878. **Online access to Real Estate, Deed, UCC, Liens records:** Recorded documents and other public records are free on the statewide system at http://recorder.alaska.gov/search.cfm. **Property tax/Assessing**- 907-343-6770. **Online access**- Plat maps/surveys are free on the statewide system at http://recorder.alaska.gov/search.cfm.

Anchorage District

District Recorder, 550 W 7th Ave, #1200, Anchorage, AK 99501. 907-269-8879/8899, R/E recording phone-907-762-2443; fax-907-269-6912; 8AM-3:30PM (AK)

Index: All in one. Records indexed on a public use terminal back to 1984. Office personnel or visitors may perform searches. Copy fee $1.25 1st page; $.25 each add'l. UCC copy- $2.00 per financing statement. Cert fee- $5.00 per doc plus copy fee. Payee- Department of Natural Resources. Bulk data available on CD: contact Brandi Brown 907-269-8878. **Online access to Real Estate, Deed, UCC, Lien records:** Recorded documents and other public records are free on the statewide system at http://recorder.alaska.gov/search.cfm. **Property tax/Assessing**- 632 W 6th Ave, #330 907-343-6770. hours- 8AM-5PM www.muni.org/finance/paindex.cfm **Online access**- Access appraisal data free at http://redirect.muni.org/propappraisal/public.html. Access Anchorage real estate property taxes data at www.muni.org/services/departments/treasury/property/askViewer.cfm. Plat maps/surveys are free on at http://recorder.alaska.gov/search.cfm.

Barrow District

District Recorder, 1648 S Cushman St, #201, Fairbanks, AK 99701-6206. 907-452-3521, 452-2298, 451-7172, R/E recording phone-907-452-3521; 8AM-4PM (AK)

Search at Fairbanks; address and phones, etc, given here. Check coverage- www.dnr.state.ak.us/ssd/recoff/findYourDistrict.cfm. Index: All in one. Records indexed on Fairbanks 3 public use terminal back to 1971. Only the public may search. Copy fee $1.25 1st page, $.25 each add'l page. Cert fee- $5.00 per doc plus copy fee. Payee- Department of Natural Resources. Bulk data available for purchase on CD monthly, usually $25.00. **Online access to Real Estate, Deed, UCC, Liens records:** Recorded docs and other public records are free on statewide system at http://recorder.alaska.gov/search.cfm. **Property tax/Assessing**- 907-459-1000. **Online access**- Plat maps and surveys are free on the statewide system at http://recorder.alaska.gov/search.cfm.

Bethel District

District Recorder, PO Box 426, Bethel, AK 99559. 907-543-3391; fax-907-543-7053; 9:15AM-N, 1PM-3:15PM (AK)

Index: Separate indices to search include Bethel, Kuskokwim. Images on computer back to 1988 with more being added; prior in books. Records indexed on a public use terminal back to 1994. Office will perform a UCC search (active) but public must search other records themselves. Copy fee $1.25 1st page, $.25 each add'l. Cert fee- $5.00 per doc plus copy fee. Payee- Department of Natural Resouces. Contact Anchorage Office Archives Unit for bulk data purchases. **Online access to Real Estate, Deed, UCC, Liens records:** Recorded documents and other public records are free on the statewide system at http://recorder.alaska.gov/search.cfm. **Other phones:** Treasurer- 907-543-2298. **Property tax/Assessing**- Finance Dept, PO Box 1388, Bethel, AK 99559; 907-543-3150, assessor fax- 907-543-3817. **Online access**- Plat maps and surveys free on statewide system at http://recorder.alaska.gov/search.cfm.

Bristol Bay District

District Recorder, 550 W 7th Ave, #1140, Anchorage, AK 99501. 907-269-8899/269-8872, R/E recording phone-907-762-2443; fax-907-269-6006; 8AM-3:30PM (AK)

Index: All in one. Records indexed on a public use terminal back to 1991. Office personnel or visitors may perform searches. Copy fee $1.25 1st page; $.25 each add'l page. UCC copy- $2.00 per financing statement. Cert fee- $5.00 per doc plus copy fee. Payee- Department of Natural Resources. Bulk data available on CD: contact Brandi Brown 907-269-8878. **Online access to Real Estate, Deed, UCC, Liens records:** Recorded documents and other public records are free on the statewide system at http://recorder.alaska.gov/search.cfm. **Property tax/Assessing**- 907-343-6770. **Online access**- Plat maps and surveys are free on the statewide system at http://recorder.alaska.gov/search.cfm.

Cape Nome District

District Recorder, c/o Fairbanks District Recorder; 1648 S Cushman St, #201, Fairbanks, AK 99701. 907-443-5178, 907-452-3521, 452-2298, R/E recording phone-907-443-5178; 8AM-12:30PM (AK)

Cape Nome office permanently closed; Fairbanks office now processes recordings; Fairbanks address and phones given here. Check coverage- www.dnr.state.ak.us/ssd/recoff/findYourDistrict.cfm. Index: All in one. Records indexed on Fairbanks 3 public use terminal back to 1971. Only the public may search. Copy fee $1.25 1st page, $.25 each add'l page. Cert fee- $5.00 per doc plus copy fee. Payee- Department of Natural Resources. Bulk data available for purchase on CD monthly, usually $25.00. **Online access to Real Estate, Deed, UCC, Liens records:** Recorded documents and other public records are free on the statewide system at http://recorder.alaska.gov/search.cfm. **Property tax/Assessing**- . **Online access**- Plat maps and surveys are free on the statewide system at http://recorder.alaska.gov/search.cfm.

Cordova District

District Recorder, 550 W 7th Ave, #1200, #1140, Anchorage, AK 99501-3564. 907-269-8899/269-8872, R/E recording phone-907-762-2443; fax-907-269-6912; 8AM-3:30PM (AK)

Index: All in one. Records indexed on a public use terminal back to 1972. Office personnel or visitors may perform searches. Copy fee $1.25 1st page, $.25 each add'l page. UCC copy- $2.00 per financing statement. Cert fee- $5.00 per doc plus copy fee. Payee- Department of Natural Resources. Bulk data available on CD: contact Brandi Brown 907-269-

8878. **Online access to Real Estate, Deed, UCC, Liens records:** Recorded documents and other public records are free on the statewide system at http://recorder.alaska.gov/search.cfm. **Property tax/ Assessing**- 632 W 6th Ave, #330, Anchorage, AK 99501; 907-343-6770, 424-6200, assessor fax- 907-343-6761. hours- 8AM-5PM **Online access**- Plat maps and surveys are free on the statewide system at http://recorder.alaska.gov/search.cfm.

Fairbanks District

District Recorder, 1648 S Cushman St, #201, Fairbanks, AK 99701-6206. 907-452-3521, 452-2298, 451-7172, R/E recording phone-907-452-3521; fax-907-452-2951; 8AM-4PM www.co.fairbanks.ak.us
Office holds records for 10 recording areas including Fort Gibbon, Cape Nome, Manley Hot Sags, Mt McKinley, Nenana, Nulato, Rampart, Kutzebue, Nome, Barrow. Check coverage-www.dnr.state.ak.us/ssd/recoff/findYourDistrict.cfm.
Index: All in one. Records indexed on Fairbanks 3 public use terminal back to 1971. Only the public may search. Copy fee $1.25 1st page, $.25 each add'l page. Cert fee- $5.00 per doc plus copy fee. Payee- Department of Natural Resources. Bulk data available for purchase on CD monthly, usually $25.00. **Online access to Real Estate, Deed, UCC, Liens records:** Recorded documents and other public records are free on the statewide system at http://recorder.alaska.gov/search.cfm. **Property tax/Assessing**- PO Box 71267, Fairbanks, AK 99701; 907-459-1000. **Online access**- Access to the Fairbanks North Star Borough property database is free online at www.co.fairbanks.ak.us/property/. Plat maps and surveys are free on the statewide system at http://recorder.alaska.gov/search.cfm.

Fort Gibbon District

District Recorder, 1648 S Cushman St, #201, Fairbanks, AK 99701-6206. 907-452-3521, 452-2298, 451-7172, R/E recording -907-452-3521; 8AM-4PM
Search at Fairbanks; address and phones, etc, given here. Check coverage- www.dnr.state.ak.us/ssd/recoff/findYourDistrict.cfm. Index: All in one. Records indexed on Fairbanks 3 public use terminal back to 1971. Only the public may search. Copy fee $1.25 1st page, $.25 each add'l page. Cert fee- $5.00 per doc plus copy fee. Payee- Department of Natural Resources. Bulk data available for purchase on CD monthly, usually $25.00. **Online access to Real Estate, Deed, UCC, Liens records:** Recorded documents and other public records are free at http://recorder.alaska.gov/search.cfm. **Property tax/ Assessing**- 907-459-1000. **Online access**- Plat maps and surveys are free on the statewide system at http://recorder.alaska.gov/search.cfm.

Haines District

District Recorder, PO Box 111013, Juneau, AK 99811-1013. 907-465-3449 or 2514, R/E recording-907-465-2514; fax-907-465-3454; 8:30AM-4PM
Index: All in one. Records indexed on a public use terminal back to 1972. Only the public may search. Copy fee $1.25 1st page, $.25 each add'l page. Cert fee- $5.00 per doc plus copy fee. Payee- Department of Natural Resources. Bulk data available for purchase on CD, contact Paula Kelsey at 8899 or 8873. **Online access to Real Estate, Deed, UCC, Liens records:** Recorded documents and other public records are free on the statewide system at http://recorder.alaska.gov/search.cfm. **Property tax/ Assessing**- 155 S Seward St, Juneau, AK 99801; 907-586-5220, assessor fax- 907-586-5367. See Juneau for Assessor info. **Online access**- Plat maps and surveys are free on the statewide system at http://recorder.alaska.gov/search.cfm.

Homer District

District Recorder, 195 E Bunnell Ave, #A, Homer, AK 99603. 907-235-8136, 907-269-8872, R/E recording phone-907-235-8136; fax-907-235-8125; 8:30AM-N, 1-4PM (AK)
Index: All in one. Records indexed on a public use terminal. Office will perform a UCC search but public must search other records themselves. Search fee- $20.00 per name for UCC. Copy fee $1.25 1st page, $.25 each add'l page. Cert fee- $5.00 per doc plus copy fee. Payee- Department of Natural Resources. Bulk data available for purchase. **Online access to Real Estate, Deed, UCC, Liens records:** Recorded documents and other public records free on the statewide system at http://recorder.alaska.gov/search.cfm. **Other Online Records**- Access borough tax assessor rolls free at http://ak-kenai-property.governmax.com/propertymax/rover30.asp Plat maps and surveys are free on the statewide system at http://recorder.alaska.gov/search.cfm.

Iliamna District

District Recorder, 550 W 7th Ave, #1140, Anchorage, AK 99501. 907-269-8899/269-8872, R/E recording-907-762-2443; fax-907-269-6006; 8AM-3:30PM
Index: All in one. Records indexed on a public use terminal back to 1972. Office personnel or visitors may perform searches. Copy fee $1.25 1st page; $.25 each add'l page. UCC copy- $2.00 per financing statement. Cert fee- $5.00 per doc plus copy fee. Payee- Department of Natural Resources. Bulk data available on CD: contact Brandi Brown 907-269-8878. **Online access to Real Estate, Deed, UCC, Liens records:** Recorded documents and other public records are free on the statewide system at http://recorder.alaska.gov/search.cfm. **Property tax/Assessing**- 907-343-6770. **Online access**- Plat maps and surveys are free on the statewide system at http://recorder.alaska.gov/search.cfm.

Juneau District

District Recorder, PO Box 111013, Juneau, AK 99811-1013. 907-465-2514; fax-907-465-3454; 8:30AM-4PM (AK)
Index: All in one. Records indexed on a public use terminal back to 1972. Office will perform a UCC search but public must search other records themselves. Copy fee $1.25 1st page, $.25 each add'l page. Cert fee- $5.00 per doc plus copy fee. Payee- Department of Natural Resouces. Bulk data available for purchase, contact Paula Kelsey at 907-269-8882. **Online access to Real Estate, Deed, UCC, Liens records:** Recorded documents and other public records are free on the statewide system at http://recorder.alaska.gov/search.cfm. Also, a statewide recording system and the UCC Central File is found at www.juneau.org/cbj/index.php . **Property tax/Assessing**- 155 S Seward St, Juneau, AK 99801; 907-586-5220, assessor fax- 907-586-5367. **Online access**- Access to City of Juneau Property Records database is free at www.juneau.org/assessordata/sqlassessor.php. Plat maps and surveys are free at http://recorder.alaska.gov/search.cfm.

Kenai District

District Recorder, 120 Trading Bay Rd, #230, Kenai, AK 99611. 907-283-3118, R/E recording phone-907-225-3142; 8:30AM-4PM (AK)
Index: Separate indices to search physically, but all in one on the website. Records indexed on a public use terminal back to 1972. Office will perform a UCC search but public must search other records themselves. Search fee-$15.00 per name for UCC. Office will not search real estate records. Copy fee $1.25 1st page, $.25 each add'l page. Cert fee- $5.00 per doc plus copy fee. Payee- Department of Natural Resources. **Online access to Real Estate, Deed, UCC, Liens records:** Recorded documents and other public records are free on the statewide system at http://recorder.alaska.gov/search.cfm. **Property tax/Assessing**- 632 W 6th Ave, #330, Anchorage, AK 99501; 907-343-6770, assessor fax- 907-343-6599. hours- 8AM-5PM **Online access**- Access to Kenai Peninsula Borough Assessing Dept. Public Information Search Page is free at www.borough.kenai.ak.us/assessingdept/Default.htm. Plat maps and surveys are free on the statewide system at http://recorder.alaska.gov/search.cfm.

Ketchikan District

District Recorder, 415 Main St, Rm 310, Ketchikan, AK 99901. 907-225-3142; fax-907-247-3142; 8:30AM-4PM; closed for lunch hour. (AK)
Index: All in one index back to 1972. Records indexed on computer back to 1970's. Office will perform a UCC search but public must search other records themselves. Office will acknowledge existence of UCC for free. Copy fee $1.25 1st page, $.25 each add'l page. Cert fee- $5.00 per doc plus copy fee. Payee- Department of Natural Resources. Bulk data available for purchase on CD-rom, contact Brandy Brown in Archives office. **Online access to Real Estate, Deed, UCC, Liens records:** Recorded documents and other public records on the statewide system at http://recorder.alaska.gov/search.cfm. **Property tax/Assessing**- 334 Front St, Ketchikan, AK 99901; 907-225-0277. **Online access**- Plat maps and surveys are free on the statewide system at http://recorder.alaska.gov/search.cfm.

Kodiak District

District Recorder, 204 Mission Rd, Rm 110, Kodiak, AK 99615. 907-486-9432; fax-907-486-9432; 8:30AM-N, 1-4PM www.recorder.alaska.gov/info16.cfm
Index: All in one. Records indexed on a public use terminal back to 2001. Only the public may search. Copy fee $1.25 1st page, $.25 each add'l page. Cert fee- $5.00 per doc plus copy fee. Payee- Department of Natural Resources. Office does not sell bulk data. **Online access to Real Estate, Deed, UCC, Liens records:** Recorded documents and other public records are free on the statewide system at http://recorder.alaska.gov/search.cfm. **Property tax/Assessing**- 710 Millbay Rd, Kodiak, AK 99615; 907-486-9352, assessor fax- 907-486-9359. hours- 8AM-5PM **Online access**- Search property assessor real property records free at www.kib.co.kodiak.ak.us. Click on "Real Property Records." Plat maps and surveys are free on the statewide system at http://recorder.alaska.gov/search.cfm.

Kotzebue District

District Recorder, 1648 S Cushman St, #201, Fairbanks, AK 99701-6206. 907-452-3521, 452-2298, 451-7172, R/E recording-907-452-3521; 8AM-4PM
Search at Fairbanks; address and phones, etc, given here. Check coverage- www.dnr.state.ak.us/ssd/recoff/findYourDistrict.cfm. Index: All in one. Records indexed on Fairbanks 3 public use terminal back to 1971. Only the public may search. Copy fee $1.25 1st page, $.25 each add'l page. Cert fee- $5.00 per doc plus copy fee. Payee- Department of Natural Resources. Bulk data available for purchase on CD monthly, usually $25.00. **Online access to Real Estate, Deed, UCC, Liens records:** Recorded documents and other public records are free on the system at http://recorder.alaska.gov/search.cfm. **Property tax/Assessing**- 907-459-1000. **Online access**- Plat maps/surveys are free on the statewide system at http://recorder.alaska.gov/search.cfm.

Kuskokwim District

District Recorder, PO Box 426, Bethel, AK 99559. 907-543-3391; fax-907-543-7053; 9:15AM-N, 1-3:15PM (AK)
Index: All in one. Records indexed on computer back to 1975. Office will perform a UCC search but public must search other records themselves. Copy fee $1.25 1st page, $.25 each add'l page. Cert fee- $5.00 per doc plus copy fee. Payee- Department of Natural Resouces. Bulk data available for purchase, contact Paula Kelsey at 907-269-8881. **Online access to Real Estate, Deed, UCC, Liens records:** Recorded documents and other public records are free on the statewide system at http://recorder.alaska.gov/search.cfm. **Property tax/Assessing**- . **Online access**- Plat maps and surveys are free on the statewide system at http://recorder.alaska.gov/search.cfm.

Kvichak District

District Recorder, 550 W 7th Ave, #1140, Anchorage, AK 99501. 907-269-8899/269-8872, R/E recording-907-762-2443; fax-907-269-6006; 8AM-3:30PM
Index: All in one. Records indexed on a public use terminal. Office personnel or visitors may perform searches. Copy fee $1.25 1st page; $.25 each add'l page. UCC copy- $2.00 per financing statement. Cert fee- $5.00 per doc plus copy fee. Payee- Department of Natural Resources. Bulk data available on CD: contact Brandi Brown 907-269-8878. **Online access to Real Estate, Deed, UCC, Liens records:** Recorded documents and other public records are free on the statewide system at http://recorder.alaska.gov/search.cfm. **Property tax/Assessing**- 907-343-6770. **Online access**- Plat maps and surveys are free on the statewide system at http://recorder.alaska.gov/search.cfm.

Manley Hot Springs District

District Recorder, 1648 S Cushman St, #201, Fairbanks, AK 99701-6206. 907-452-3521, 452-2298, 451-7172, R/E recording phone-907-452-3521; 8AM-4PM (AK)
Search at Fairbanks; address and phones, etc, given here. Check coverage- www.dnr.state.ak.us/ssd/recoff/findYourDistrict.cfm. Index: All in one. Records indexed on Fairbanks 3 public use terminal back to 1971. Only the public may search. Copy fee $1.25 1st page, $.25 each add'l page. Cert fee- $5.00 per doc plus copy fee. Payee- Department of Natural Resources. Bulk data available for purchase on CD monthly, usually $25.00. **Online access to Real Estate, Deed, UCC, Liens records:** Recorded documents and other public records are free on the system at http://recorder.alaska.gov/search.cfm. **Property tax/Assessing**- 907-459-1000. **Online access**- Plat maps and surveys are free on statewide system at http://recorder.alaska.gov/search.cfm.

Mount McKinley District

District Recorder, 1648 S Cushman St, #201, Fairbanks, AK 99701-6206. 907-452-3521, 452-2298, 451-7172, R/E recording phone-907-452-3521; 8AM-4PM (AK) www.co.fairbanks.ak.us
Search at Fairbanks; address and phones, etc, given here. Check coverage- www.dnr.state.ak.us/ssd/recoff/findYourDistrict.cfm. Index: All in one. Records indexed on Fairbanks 3 public use terminal back to 1971. Only the public may search. Copy fee $1.25 1st page, $.25 each add'l page. Cert fee- $5.00 per doc plus copy fee. Payee- Department of Natural Resources. Bulk data available for purchase on CD monthly, usually $25.00. **Online access to Real Estate, Deed, UCC, Liens records:** Recorded documents and other public records are free on the system at http://recorder.alaska.gov/search.cfm. **Property tax/Assessing**- PO Box 71267, 809 Pioneer, Fairbanks, AK 99707; 907-459-1000, assessor fax- 907-459-1416. (Appraiser/Auditor-907-459-1429) www.co.fairbanks.ak.us/Assessing/ **Online access**- Plat maps/surveys free on the state wide system at http://recorder.alaska.gov/search.cfm.

Nenana District

District Recorder, 1648 S Cushman St, #201, Fairbanks, AK 99701-6206. 907-452-3521, 452-2298, 451-7172, R/E recording-907-452-3521; 8AM-4PM
Search at Fairbanks; address and phones, etc, given here. Check coverage- www.dnr.state.ak.us/ssd/recoff/findYourDistrict.cfm. Index: All in one. Records indexed on Fairbanks 3 public use terminal back to 1971. Only the public may search. Copy fee $1.25 1st page, $.25 each add'l page. Cert fee- $5.00 per doc plus copy fee. Payee- Department of Natural Resources. Bulk data available for purchase on CD monthly, usually $25.00. **Online access to Real Estate, Deed, UCC, Liens records:** Recorded documents and other public records are free on the statewide system at http://recorder.alaska.gov/search.cfm. **Property tax/Assessing**- 907-459-1000. **Online access**- Plat maps and surveys are free on the statewide system at http://recorder.alaska.gov/search.cfm.

Nulato District

District Recorder, 1648 S Cushman St, #201, Fairbanks, AK 99701-6206. 907-452-3521, 452-2298, 451-7172, R/E recording phone-907-452-3521; 8AM-4PM (AK)
Search at Fairbanks; address and phones, etc, given here. Check coverage- www.dnr.state.ak.us/ssd/recoff/findYourDistrict.cfm. Index: All in one. Records indexed on Fairbanks 3 public use terminal back to 1971. Only the public may search. Copy fee $1.25 1st page, $.25 each add'l page. Cert fee- $5.00 per doc plus copy fee. Payee- Department of Natural Resources. Bulk data available for purchase on CD monthly, usually $25.00. **Online access to Real Estate, Deed, UCC, Liens records:** Recorded documents and other public records are free on the system at http://recorder.alaska.gov/search.cfm. **Property tax/Assessing**- 907-459-1000. **Online access**- Plat maps and surveys free on the statewide system at http://recorder.alaska.gov/search.cfm.

Palmer District

District Recorder, 1800 Glenn Hwy, #7, Palmer, AK 99645. 907-745-3080; fax-907-745-0958; 8:30AM-4PM (AK)
Index: All in one. Records indexed on a public use terminal back to 1971. Office will perform a UCC search but public must search other records themselves. Search fee-$15.00 per name for UCC. Copy fee $1.25 1st page, $.25 each add'l page. Cert fee- $5.00 per doc plus copy fee. Payee- Department of Natural Resources. Office does not sell bulk data. **Online access to Real Estate, Deed, UCC, Liens records:** Recorded documents and other public records are free on the statewide system at http://recorder.alaska.gov/search.cfm. **Other Online Records-** Access borough property and property tax data free at www.matsugov.us/myproperty// Plat maps and surveys are free on the statewide system at http://recorder.alaska.gov/search.cfm.

Petersburg District

District Recorder, 415 Main St, Rm 310, Ketchikan, AK 99901. 907-225-3142; fax-907-247-3142; 8:30AM-4PM; closed for lunch hour. (AK)
Index: All in one. Records indexed on a public use terminal back to 1972. Only the public may search. Copy fee $1.25 1st page, $.25 each add'l page. Cert fee- $5.00 per doc plus copy fee. Payee- Department of Natural Resources. **Online access to Real Estate, Deed, UCC, Liens records:** Recorded documents and other public records are free on the statewide system at http://recorder.alaska.gov/search.cfm. **Other phones:** Elections- 907-772-4519 x23. **Property tax/Assessing-** PO Box 329, Petersburg, Alaska 99833; 907-772-4224, assessor fax- 907-247-0277. **Online access**- Plat maps and surveys are free on the statewide system at http://recorder.alaska.gov/search.cfm.

Rampart District

District Recorder, 1648 S Cushman St, #201, Fairbanks, AK 99701-6206. 907-452-3521, 452-2298, 451-7172, R/E recording-907-452-3521; 8AM-4PM
Search at Fairbanks; address and phones, etc, given here. Check coverage- www.dnr.state.ak.us/ssd/recoff/findYourDistrict.cfm. Index: All in one. Records indexed on Fairbanks 3 public use terminal back to 1971. Only the public may search. Copy fee $1.25 1st page, $.25 each add'l page. Cert fee- $5.00 per doc plus copy fee. Payee- Department of Natural Resources. Bulk data available for purchase on CD monthly, usually $25.00. **Online access to Real Estate, Deed, UCC, Liens records:** Recorded documents and other public records are free on the system at http://recorder.alaska.gov/search.cfm. **Property tax/Assessing-** 907-459-1000. **Online access**- Plat maps/surveys are free on the statewide system at http://recorder.alaska.gov/search.cfm.

Seldovia District

District Recorder, 195 E Bunnell Ave, #A, Homer, AK 99603. 907-235-8136; fax-907-235-8125; 8:30AM-N, 1-4PM (AK)
Index: All in one. Records indexed on a public use terminal back to 1974. Office will perform a UCC search for $20.00 but public must search other records themselves. Copy fee $1.25 1st page, $.25 each add'l page. Cert fee- $5.00 per doc plus copy fee. Payee- Department of Natural Resources. **Online access to Real Estate, Deed, UCC, Liens records:** Recorded documents and other public records are free on the system at http://recorder.alaska.gov/search.cfm. **Property tax/Assessing**- PO Box 3040, 144 N Binkley, Solbotna, AK 99669; 907-262-4441 x2622, assessor fax- 907-714-2393. hours- 8AM-5PM www.borough.kenai.ak.us/assessingdept/ **Online access**- Access borough tax assessor rolls is free at http://ak-kenai-property.governmax.com/propertymax/rover30.asp. Also, view Parcel Maps by pdf or tiff at www.borough.kenai.ak.us/assessingdept/maps.htm. Parcel file downloads are also available. Plat maps and surveys are free on the statewide system at http://recorder.alaska.gov/search.cfm.

Seward District

District Recorder, Box 246, Seward, AK 99664. 907-224-7032; fax-907-224-7032; 9AM-2PM (AK)
Fax number same as phone. Index: Separate indices to search; many historic records on microfilm/microfiche. Records indexed on a public use terminal back to 1978. Office personnel or visitors may perform searches. Search fee $15.00 per hour. Will search UCC records. Copy fee $1.25 1st page, $.25 each add'l page. Cert fee- $5.00 per doc plus copy fee. Payee- Department of Natural Resouces. **Online access to Real Estate, Deed, UCC, Liens records:** Recorded documents and other public records are free on the statewide system at http://recorder.alaska.gov/search.cfm. **Other Online Records-** Access borough tax assessor rolls is free at http://ak-kenai-property.governmax.com/propertymax/rover30.asp. Plat maps and surveys are free on the statewide system at http://recorder.alaska.gov/search.cfm.

Sitka District

District Recorder, 210C Lake St, Sitka, AK 99835. 907-747-3275; fax-907-747-3043; 8:30AM-N, 1PM-4PM M-Th, Closed on Fri. (AK)
Index: All in one. Records indexed on a public use terminal back to 1972. Only the public may search. Copy fee $1.25 1st page, $.25 each add'l page. Cert fee- $5.00 per doc plus copy fee. Payee- Department of Natural Resources. Office does not sell bulk data. **Online access to Real Estate, Deed, UCC, Liens records:** Recorded documents and other public records are free on the statewide system at http://recorder.alaska.gov/search.cfm. **Property tax/Assessing**- 100 Lincoln St, Sitka, AK 99835; 907-747-1822, assessor fax- 907-747-6138. hours- 8AM-5PM Sitka records located at Anchorage. www.muni.org/finance/paindex.cfm **Online access**- Plat maps and surveys are free on the statewide system at http://recorder.alaska.gov/search.cfm.

Skagway District

District Recorder, 400 Willoughby, 3rd Fl, Juneau, AK 99801. 907-465-3449; fax-907-465-3454; 8:30AM-4PM (AK)
Index: All in one. Records indexed on a public use terminal back to 1972. Only the public may search. Copy fee $1.25 1st page, $.25 each add'l page. Cert fee- $5.00 per doc plus copy fee. Payee- Department of Natural Resources. Bulk data available for purchase on CD, contact Paula Kelsey at 8899 or 8873. **Online access to Real Estate, Deed, UCC, Liens records:** Recorded documents and other public records are free on the statewide system at http://recorder.alaska.gov/search.cfm. Also, a statewide recording system and the UCC Central File is found at www.juneau.org/cbj/index.php . **Property tax/Assessing**- 155 S Seward St, Juneau, AK 99801;

907-586-5220, assessor fax- 907-586-5367. See Juneau for Assessor info. **Online access-** A citywide assessor is free at www.juneau.org/cbj/index.php. Plat maps and surveys are free on the statewide system at http://recorder.alaska.gov/search.cfm.

Talkeetna District

District Recorder, 1800 Glenn Hwy, #7, Palmer, AK 99645. 907-745-3080; fax-907-745-0958; 8:30AM-4PM (AK)

Index: All in one. Records indexed on a public use terminal back to 1972. Office will perform a UCC search but public must search other records themselves. Search fee-$15.00 per name for UCC. Copy fee $1.25 1st page, $.25 each add'l page. Cert fee- $5.00 per doc plus copy fee. Payee- Department of Natural Resources. **Online access to Real Estate, Deed, UCC, Liens records:** Recorded documents and other public records are free on the statewide system at http://recorder.alaska.gov/search.cfm. **Other Online Records-** Access borough property and property tax data free at www.matsugov.us/myproperty/. Plat maps and surveys are free on the statewide system at http://recorder.alaska.gov/search.cfm.

Valdez District

District Recorder, PO Box 2023, Valdez, AK 99686. 907-835-3153, R/E recording phone-907-835-2266; fax-907-835-3153; 8AM-1:45PM; 9AM-2PM-research. (AK) www.ci.valdez.ak.us/

Index: All in one. Records indexed on a public use terminal back to 1999. Only the public may search. Copy fee $1.25 1st page, $.25 each add'l page. Cert fee- $5.00 per doc plus copy fee. Payee- Department of Natural Resouces. Office does not sell bulk data. **Online access to Real Estate, Deed, UCC, Liens records:** Recorded documents and other public records are free on the statewide system at http://recorder.alaska.gov/search.cfm. **Other phones:** Elections- 907-834-3464. **Property tax/Assessing-** PO Box 307, 212 Chenega St, Valdez, AK 99686; 907-834-3455, assessor fax- 907-834-3403. hours- 8:30AM-5PM **Online access-** Plat maps and surveys are free on the statewide system at http://recorder.alaska.gov/search.cfm.

Valdez/Chitina District

District Recorder, PO Box 127, Valdez, AK 99686. 907-835-3153, R/E recording phone-907-745-9683, UCC recording phone-907-269-8899; fax-907-835-3764; 8:30AM-4PM (AK)

Chitina office records are now in Valdez; address and telephone given here. Index: All in one. Records indexed on a public use terminal back to 1972. Office will perform a UCC search but public must search other records themselves. Copy fee $1.25 1st page, $.25 each add'l page. UCC copy- $2.00 per financing statement. Cert fee- $5.00 per doc plus copy fee. Payee- Department of Natural Resources. **Online access to Real Estate, Deed, UCC, Liens records:** Recorded documents and other public records are free on the statewide system at http://recorder.alaska.gov/search.cfm. **Other phones:** Elections- 907-451-2835; Vital Records- 907-465-8606. **Property tax/Assessing-** PO Box 2023, 213 Meals Ave #30, Valdez, AK 99686; 907-835-3153, assessor fax- 907-835-3153. hours- 9AM-2PM **Online access-** Plat maps and surveys are free on the system at http://recorder.alaska.gov/search.cfm.

Wrangell District

District Recorder, 415 Main St, Rm 310, Ketchikan, AK 99901. 907-225-3142; fax-907-247-3142; 8:30AM-N, 1PM-4PM (AK)

Index: All in one. Records indexed on a public use terminal back to 1972. Only the public may search. Copy fee $1.25 1st page, $.25 each add'l page. UCC copy- $2.00 per financing statement. Cert fee- $5.00 per doc plus copy fee. Payee- Department of Natural Resources. **Online access to Real Estate, Deed, UCC, Liens records:** Recorded documents and other public records are free on the statewide system at http://recorder.alaska.gov/search.cfm. **Other phones:** Elections- 907-874-2381. **Property tax/Assessing-** PO Box 531, Wrangell, AK 99929; 907-874-2381, assessor fax- 907-247-0277. **Online access-** Plat maps and surveys are free on the statewide system at http://recorder.alaska.gov/search.cfm.

Alaska County Locator

You will usually be able to find the city name in the City/County Cross Reference below. In that case, it is a simple matter to determine the county from the cross reference. However, only the official US Postal Service city names are included in this index. There are an additional 40,000 place names that people use in their addresses. Therefore, we have also included a ZIP/City Cross Reference immediately following the City/County Cross Reference.

If you know the ZIP Code but the city name does not appear in the City/County Cross Reference index, look up the ZIP Code in the ZIP/City Cross Reference, find the city name, then look up the city name in the City/County Cross Reference. For example, you want to know the county for an address of Menands, NY 12204. There is no "Menands" in the City/County Cross Reference. The ZIP/City Cross Reference shows that ZIP Codes 12201-12288 are for the city of Albany. Looking back in the City/County Cross Reference, Albany is in Albany County.

Alaska City/County Cross Reference

ADAK Aleutian Islands, West
AKIACHAK Bethel
AKIAK Bethel
AKUTAN Aleutian Islands, East
ALAKANUK Wade Hampton
ALEKNAGIK Dillingham
ALLAKAKET Yukon-Koyukuk
AMBLER Northwest Arctic
ANAKTUVUK PASS North Slope Borough
ANCHOR POINT Kenai Peninsula Borough
ANCHORAGE Anchorage Borough
ANDERSON Denali
ANGOON Yakutat
ANIAK Bethel
ANVIK Yukon-Koyukuk
ARCTIC VILLAGE Yukon-Koyukuk
ATKA Aleutian Islands, West
ATQASUK North Slope Borough
AUKE BAY Juneau Borough
BARROW North Slope Borough
BEAVER Yukon-Koyukuk
BETHEL Bethel
BETTLES FIELD Yukon-Koyukuk
BIG LAKE Matanuska-Susitna Borough
BREVIG MISSION Nome
BUCKLAND Northwest Arctic
CANTWELL Denali
CENTRAL Yukon-Koyukuk
CHALKYITSIK Yukon-Koyukuk
CHEFORNAK Bethel
CHEVAK Wade Hampton
CHICKEN Southeast Fairbanks
CHIGNIK Lake & Peninsula
CHIGNIK LAGOON Lake & Peninsula
CHIGNIK LAKE Lake & Peninsula
CHITINA Valdez-Cordova
CHUGIAK Anchorage Borough
CIRCLE Yukon-Koyukuk
CLAM GULCH Kenai Peninsula Borough
CLARKS POINT Dillingham
CLEAR Denali
COFFMAN COVE Prince of Wales-Outer Ketchikan
COLD BAY Aleutian Islands, East
COOPER LANDING Kenai Peninsula Borough
COPPER CENTER Valdez-Cordova
CORDOVA Valdez-Cordova
CRAIG Prince of Wales-Outer Ketchikan
CROOKED CREEK Bethel
DEERING Northwest Arctic
DELTA JUNCTION Southeast Fairbanks
DENALI NATIONAL PARK Denali
DILLINGHAM Dillingham
DOUGLAS Juneau Borough
DUTCH HARBOR Aleutian Islands, West
EAGLE Southeast Fairbanks
EAGLE RIVER Anchorage Borough
EEK Bethel
EGEGIK Lake & Peninsula
EIELSON AFB Fairbanks North Star Borough
EKWOK Dillingham
ELFIN COVE Yakutat
ELIM Nome
ELMENDORF AFB Anchorage Borough
EMMONAK Wade Hampton
ESTER Fairbanks North Star Borough
FAIRBANKS Fairbanks North Star Borough
FALSE PASS Aleutian Islands, East
FLAT Yukon-Koyukuk
FORT GREELY Southeast Fairbanks
FORT RICHARDSON Anchorage Borough
FORT WAINWRIGHT Fairbanks North Star Borough
FORT YUKON Yukon-Koyukuk
GAKONA Valdez-Cordova
GALENA Yukon-Koyukuk
GAMBELL Nome
GIRDWOOD Anchorage Borough
GLENNALLEN Valdez-Cordova
GOODNEWS BAY Bethel
GRAYLING Yukon-Koyukuk
GUSTAVUS Yakutat
HAINES Haines Borough
HEALY Denali
HOLY CROSS Yukon-Koyukuk
HOMER Kenai Peninsula Borough
HOONAH Yakutat
HOOPER BAY Wade Hampton
HOPE Kenai Peninsula Borough
HOUSTON Matanuska-Susitna Borough
HUGHES Yukon-Koyukuk
HUSLIA Yukon-Koyukuk
HYDABURG Prince of Wales-Outer Ketchikan
HYDER Prince of Wales-Outer Ketchikan
ILIAMNA Lake & Peninsula
INDIAN Anchorage Borough
JUNEAU Juneau Borough
KAKE Wrangell-Petersburg
KAKTOVIK North Slope Borough
KALSKAG Bethel
KALTAG Yukon-Koyukuk
KARLUK Kodiak Island Borough
KASIGLUK Bethel
KASILOF Kenai Peninsula Borough
KENAI Kenai Peninsula Borough
KETCHIKAN Ketchikan Gateway Borough
KIANA Northwest Arctic
KING COVE Aleutian Islands, East
KING SALMON (99613) Bristol Bay Borough(84), Lake & Peninsula(15)
KIPNUK Bethel
KIVALINA Northwest Arctic
KLAWOCK Prince of Wales-Outer Ketchikan
KOBUK Northwest Arctic
KODIAK Kodiak Island Borough
KOTLIK Wade Hampton
KOTZEBUE Northwest Arctic
KOYUK Nome
KOYUKUK Yukon-Koyukuk
KWETHLUK Bethel
KWIGILLINGOK Bethel
LAKE MINCHUMINA Yukon-Koyukuk
LARSEN BAY Kodiak Island Borough
LEVELOCK Lake & Peninsula
LOWER KALSKAG Bethel
MANLEY HOT SPRINGS Yukon-Koyukuk
MANOKOTAK Dillingham
MARSHALL Wade Hampton
MC GRATH Yukon-Koyukuk
MEKORYUK Bethel
METLAKATLA Prince of Wales-Outer Ketchikan
MEYERS CHUCK Prince of Wales-Outer Ketchikan
MINTO Yukon-Koyukuk
MOOSE PASS Kenai Peninsula Borough
MOUNTAIN VILLAGE Wade Hampton
NAKNEK Bristol Bay Borough
NAPAKIAK Bethel
NENANA Yukon-Koyukuk
NEW STUYAHOK Dillingham
NIGHTMUTE Bethel
NIKISKI Kenai Peninsula Borough
NIKOLAI Yukon-Koyukuk
NIKOLSKI Aleutian Islands, West
NINILCHIK Kenai Peninsula Borough
NOATAK Northwest Arctic
NOME Nome
NONDALTON Lake & Peninsula
NOORVIK Northwest Arctic
NORTH POLE Fairbanks North Star Borough
NORTHWAY Southeast Fairbanks
NUIQSUT North Slope Borough
NULATO Yukon-Koyukuk
NUNAM IQUA Wade Hampton
NUNAPITCHUK Bethel
OLD HARBOR Kodiak Island Borough
OUZINKIE Kodiak Island Borough
PALMER Matanuska-Susitna Borough
PEDRO BAY Lake & Peninsula
PELICAN Yakutat
PERRYVILLE Lake & Peninsula
PETERSBURG Wrangell-Petersburg
PILOT POINT Lake & Peninsula
PILOT STATION Wade Hampton
PLATINUM Bethel
POINT BAKER Prince of Wales-Outer Ketchikan
POINT HOPE North Slope Borough
POINT LAY North Slope Borough
PORT ALEXANDER Wrangell-Petersburg
PORT ALSWORTH Lake & Peninsula
PORT HEIDEN Lake & Peninsula
PORT LIONS Kodiak Island Borough
PRUDHOE BAY North Slope Borough
QUINHAGAK Bethel
RAMPART Yukon-Koyukuk
RED DEVIL Bethel
RUBY Yukon-Koyukuk
RUSSIAN MISSION Wade Hampton
SAINT GEORGE ISLAND Aleutian Islands, West
SAINT MARYS Wade Hampton
SAINT MICHAEL Nome
SAINT PAUL ISLAND Aleutian Islands, West
SALCHA Fairbanks North Star Borough
SAND POINT Aleutian Islands, East
SAVOONGA Nome
SCAMMON BAY Wade Hampton
SELAWIK Northwest Arctic
SELDOVIA Kenai Peninsula Borough
SEWARD Kenai Peninsula Borough
SHAGELUK Yukon-Koyukuk
SHAKTOOLIK Nome
SHELDON POINT Wade Hampton
SHISHMAREF Nome
SHUNGNAK Northwest Arctic
SITKA Sitka Borough
SKAGWAY Yakutat
SKWENTNA Matanuska-Susitna Borough
SLEETMUTE Bethel
SOLDOTNA Kenai Peninsula Borough
SOUTH NAKNEK Bristol Bay Borough
STEBBINS Nome
STERLING Kenai Peninsula Borough
STEVENS VILLAGE Yukon-Koyukuk
SUTTON Matanuska-Susitna Borough
TAKOTNA Yukon-Koyukuk
TALKEETNA Matanuska-Susitna Borough
TANACROSS Southeast Fairbanks
TANANA Yukon-Koyukuk
TATITLEK Valdez-Cordova
TELLER Nome
TENAKEE SPRINGS Yakutat
TETLIN Southeast Fairbanks
THORNE BAY Prince of Wales-Outer Ketchikan
TOGIAK Dillingham
TOK Southeast Fairbanks
TOKSOOK BAY Bethel
TRAPPER CREEK Matanuska-Susitna Borough
TULUKSAK Bethel
TUNTUTULIAK Bethel
TUNUNAK Bethel
TWO RIVERS Fairbanks North Star Borough
TYONEK Kenai Peninsula Borough
UNALAKLEET Nome
UNALASKA Aleutian Islands, West
VALDEZ Valdez-Cordova
VENETIE Yukon-Koyukuk
WAINWRIGHT North Slope Borough
WALES Nome
WARD COVE Ketchikan Gateway Borough
WASILLA Matanuska-Susitna Borough
WHITE MOUNTAIN Nome
WHITTIER Valdez-Cordova
WILLOW Matanuska-Susitna Borough
WRANGELL Wrangell-Petersburg
YAKUTAT Yakutat-Not Used

Alaska ZIP/City Cross Reference

ZIP	City
99500-99504	ANCHORAGE
99505-99505	FORT RICHARDSON
99506-99506	ELMENDORF AFB
99507-99530	ANCHORAGE
99540-99540	INDIAN
99546-99546	ADAK
99547-99547	ATKA
99548-99548	CHIGNIK LAKE
99549-99549	PORT HEIDEN
99550-99550	PORT LIONS
99551-99551	AKIACHAK
99552-99552	AKIAK
99553-99553	AKUTAN
99554-99554	ALAKANUK
99555-99555	ALEKNAGIK
99556-99556	ANCHOR POINT
99557-99557	ANIAK
99558-99558	ANVIK
99559-99559	BETHEL
99561-99561	CHEFORNAK
99563-99563	CHEVAK
99564-99564	CHIGNIK
99565-99565	CHIGNIK LAGOON
99566-99566	CHITINA
99567-99567	CHUGIAK
99568-99568	CLAM GULCH
99569-99569	CLARKS POINT
99571-99571	COLD BAY
99572-99572	COOPER LANDING
99573-99573	COPPER CENTER
99574-99574	CORDOVA
99575-99575	CROOKED CREEK
99576-99576	DILLINGHAM
99577-99577	EAGLE RIVER
99578-99578	EEK
99579-99579	EGEGIK
99580-99580	EKWOK
99581-99581	EMMONAK
99583-99583	FALSE PASS
99584-99584	FLAT
99585-99585	MARSHALL
99586-99586	GAKONA
99587-99587	GIRDWOOD
99588-99588	GLENNALLEN
99589-99589	GOODNEWS BAY
99590-99590	GRAYLING
99591-99591	SAINT GEORGE ISLAND
99599-99599	ANCHORAGE
99602-99602	HOLY CROSS
99603-99603	HOMER
99604-99604	HOOPER BAY
99605-99605	HOPE
99606-99606	ILIAMNA
99607-99607	KALSKAG
99608-99608	KARLUK
99609-99609	KASIGLUK
99610-99610	KASILOF
99611-99611	KENAI
99612-99612	KING COVE
99613-99613	KING SALMON
99614-99614	KIPNUK
99615-99619	KODIAK
99620-99620	KOTLIK
99621-99621	KWETHLUK
99622-99622	KWIGILLINGOK
99624-99624	LARSEN BAY
99625-99625	LEVELOCK
99626-99626	LOWER KALSKAG
99627-99627	MC GRATH
99628-99628	MANOKOTAK
99629-99629	WASILLA
99630-99630	MEKORYUK
99631-99631	MOOSE PASS
99632-99632	MOUNTAIN VILLAGE
99633-99633	NAKNEK
99634-99634	NAPAKIAK
99635-99635	NIKISKI
99636-99636	NEW STUYAHOK
99637-99637	TOKSOOK BAY
99638-99638	NIKOLSKI
99639-99639	NINILCHIK
99640-99640	NONDALTON
99641-99641	NUNAPITCHUK
99643-99643	OLD HARBOR
99644-99644	OUZINKIE
99645-99645	PALMER
99647-99647	PEDRO BAY
99648-99648	PERRYVILLE
99649-99649	PILOT POINT
99650-99650	PILOT STATION
99651-99651	PLATINUM
99652-99652	BIG LAKE
99653-99653	PORT ALSWORTH
99654-99654	WASILLA
99655-99655	QUINHAGAK
99656-99656	RED DEVIL
99657-99657	RUSSIAN MISSION
99658-99658	SAINT MARYS
99659-99659	SAINT MICHAEL
99660-99660	SAINT PAUL ISLAND
99661-99661	SAND POINT
99662-99662	SCAMMON BAY
99663-99663	SELDOVIA
99664-99664	SEWARD
99665-99665	SHAGELUK
99666-99666	SHELDON POINT
99666-99666	NUNAM IQUA
99667-99667	SKWENTNA
99668-99668	SLEETMUTE
99669-99669	SOLDOTNA
99670-99670	SOUTH NAKNEK
99671-99671	STEBBINS
99672-99672	STERLING
99674-99674	SUTTON
99675-99675	TAKOTNA
99676-99676	TALKEETNA
99677-99677	TATITLEK
99678-99678	TOGIAK
99679-99679	TULUKSAK
99680-99680	TUNTUTULIAK
99681-99681	TUNUNAK
99682-99682	TYONEK
99683-99683	TRAPPER CREEK
99684-99684	UNALAKLEET
99685-99685	UNALASKA
99686-99686	VALDEZ
99687-99687	WASILLA
99688-99688	WILLOW
99689-99689	YAKUTAT
99690-99690	NIGHTMUTE
99691-99691	NIKOLAI
99692-99692	DUTCH HARBOR
99693-99693	WHITTIER
99694-99694	HOUSTON
99695-99695	ANCHORAGE
99697-99697	KODIAK
99701-99701	FAIRBANKS
99702-99702	EIELSON AFB
99703-99703	FORT WAINWRIGHT
99704-99704	CLEAR
99705-99705	NORTH POLE
99706-99712	FAIRBANKS
99714-99714	SALCHA
99716-99716	TWO RIVERS
99720-99720	ALLAKAKET
99721-99721	ANAKTUVUK PASS
99722-99722	ARCTIC VILLAGE
99723-99723	BARROW
99724-99724	BEAVER
99725-99725	ESTER
99726-99726	BETTLES FIELD
99727-99727	BUCKLAND
99729-99729	CANTWELL
99730-99730	CENTRAL
99731-99731	FORT GREELY
99732-99732	CHICKEN
99733-99733	CIRCLE
99734-99734	PRUDHOE BAY
99736-99736	DEERING
99737-99737	DELTA JUNCTION
99738-99738	EAGLE
99739-99739	ELIM
99740-99740	FORT YUKON
99741-99741	GALENA
99742-99742	GAMBELL
99743-99743	HEALY
99744-99744	ANDERSON
99745-99745	HUGHES
99746-99746	HUSLIA
99747-99747	KAKTOVIK
99748-99748	KALTAG
99749-99749	KIANA
99750-99750	KIVALINA
99751-99751	KOBUK
99752-99752	KOTZEBUE
99753-99753	KOYUK
99754-99754	KOYUKUK
99755-99755	DENALI NATIONAL PARK
99756-99756	MANLEY HOT SPRINGS
99757-99757	LAKE MINCHUMINA
99758-99758	MINTO
99759-99759	POINT LAY
99760-99760	NENANA
99761-99761	NOATAK
99762-99762	NOME
99763-99763	NOORVIK
99764-99764	NORTHWAY
99765-99765	NULATO
99766-99766	POINT HOPE
99767-99767	RAMPART
99768-99768	RUBY
99769-99769	SAVOONGA
99770-99770	SELAWIK
99771-99771	SHAKTOOLIK
99772-99772	SHISHMAREF
99773-99773	SHUNGNAK
99774-99774	STEVENS VILLAGE
99775-99775	FAIRBANKS
99776-99776	TANACROSS
99777-99777	TANANA
99778-99778	TELLER
99779-99779	TETLIN
99780-99780	TOK
99781-99781	VENETIE
99782-99782	WAINWRIGHT
99783-99783	WALES
99784-99784	WHITE MOUNTAIN
99785-99785	BREVIG MISSION
99786-99786	AMBLER
99788-99788	CHALKYITSIK
99789-99789	NUIQSUT
99790-99790	FAIRBANKS
99791-99791	ATQASUK
99801-99811	JUNEAU
99820-99820	ANGOON
99821-99821	AUKE BAY
99824-99824	DOUGLAS
99825-99825	ELFIN COVE
99826-99826	GUSTAVUS
99827-99827	HAINES
99829-99829	HOONAH
99830-99830	KAKE
99832-99832	PELICAN
99833-99833	PETERSBURG
99835-99835	SITKA
99836-99836	PORT ALEXANDER
99840-99840	SKAGWAY
99841-99841	TENAKEE SPRINGS
99850-99850	JUNEAU
99901-99901	KETCHIKAN
99903-99903	MEYERS CHUCK
99918-99918	COFFMAN COVE
99919-99919	THORNE BAY
99921-99921	CRAIG
99922-99922	HYDABURG
99923-99923	HYDER
99925-99925	KLAWOCK
99926-99926	METLAKATLA
99927-99927	POINT BAKER
99928-99928	WARD COVE
99929-99929	WRANGELL
99950-99950	KETCHIKAN

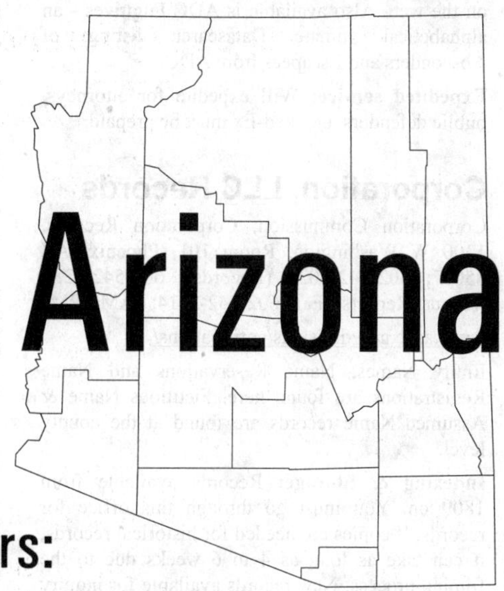

Arizona

General Help Numbers:

Governor's Office
1700 W Washington
Phoenix, AZ 85007
www.governor.state.az.us
602-542-4331
Fax 602-542-1381
8AM-5PM

Attorney General's Office
1275 W Washington
Phoenix, AZ 85007
www.azag.gov/
602-542-5025
Fax 602-542-4085
8AM-5PM

Legislative Records
Arizona Legislature
1700 W Washington
Phoenix, AZ 85007
www.azleg.gov/
602-542-3559 Senate
602-542-4221 House
Fax 602-542-4099
8AM-5PM

State Archives
1700 W Washington, Room 342
Phoenix, AZ 85007
www.lib.az.us/archives/
602-542-4159
Fax 602-542-4402
8AM-5PM

State Specifics:

Capital: Phoenix
Maricopa County

Time Zone: MST
Note that Arizona does not go on daylight Savings Time

Number of Counties: 15

Population: 6,500,180

Website: http://az.gov/webapp/portal/

State Agencies

Criminal Records

Department of Public Safety, Applicant Team One, PO Box 18430//Mail Code 2250, Phoenix, AZ 85005-8430 (Courier address- 2320 N 20th Ave, Phoenix, AZ 85009); 602-223-2223, Fax-602-223-2972; 8AM-5PM.

www.azdps.gov/

Indexing & Storage: Records available from 1983; non-automated records may go back as far as 1960's, depending on charge. New records available for inquiry in about 14 days. 58% of arrests in database have final dispositions recorded, 60% within last 5 years.

Searching: Record access is limited to agencies that have specific authorization by law including employers or employment search firms located in AZ, but results are sent to the employer. Results from out-of-state requesters can only be sent to the subject. Include in request- full set of fingerprints plus demographic information on the applicant. Be sure to address requests to Applicant Team One. Fingerprints are required for a search. 100% of arrest records are fingerprint supported. This data not released- bulk data purchase. All records are released, including those without dispositions.

Access by: mail.

Fee & Payment: The fee is $5.00 per name. Fee payee- Department of Public Safety. Prepayment required. Only cashier's checks and money orders accepted; no credit cards.

Mail search: Turnaround time- 2 to 3 days. Arizona employers may call 602-223-2223 to request fingerprint cards and forms. SASE not required.

Statewide Court Records

Administrative Offices of the Courts, Arizona Supreme Court Bldg, 1501 W Washington, Phoenix, AZ 85007-3231; 602-452-3300; 8AM-5PM. www.supreme.state.az.us

Access by: online.

Online search: Visit www.supreme.state.az.us/publicaccess/notification/default.asp. The Public Access to Court Case Information is a valuable web service providing a resource for information about court cases from 153 out of 180 courts in Arizona. Courts not covered include certain parts of Pima, Yavapai, Mohave, and Maricopa counties. Accessible information includes: detailed case information, i.e., case type, charges, filing and disposition dates; the parties in the case, not including victims and witnesses; and the court mailing address & location. Opinions from the AZ Supreme Court and Court of Appeals are available from www.supreme.state.az.us/opin/.

Sexual Offender Registry

Department of Public Safety, Sex Offender Compliance, PO Box 6638//Mail Code 9999, Phoenix, AZ 85005-6638 (Courier address- 2102 W Encanto, Phoenix, AZ 85009); 602-255-0611, Fax- 602-223-2949; 8AM-5PM.

http://az.gov/webapp/offender/main.do

The county sheriff is responsible for registering sex offenders living within their county. Arizona has approximately 15,000 registered sex offenders.

Indexing & Storage: Records available on or after June 1,1996 with risk assessment scores of Level 2 (Intermediate) or Level 3 (High). New records available for inquiry in 45 days.

Searching: The agency has a policy to assist those individuals that do not have access to the webpage and wish to do a record search. This data not released- Level 1 records and those not shown at web.

Access by: mail, phone, fax, online.

Mail search: Turnaround time- 2 to 3 days. SASE not required.

Phone search: Search requests accepted telephone.

Fax search: Fax requests accepted.

Online search: Searching of Level 2 and Level 3 offenders is available online at the website above. Search for an individual by name, or search by ZIP Code or address for known offenders. The site also lists, with pictures, absconders who are individuals whose whereabouts are unknown.

Other access: A download is available from the webpage for $25.00.

Incarceration Records

Arizona Department of Corrections, Records Department, 1601 W. Jefferson St., Phoenix, AZ 85007; 602-542-5586, Fax- 602-542-3965; 8AM-5PM. www.adc.state.az.us

Indexing & Storage: Records available on current and former inmates. New records available for inquiry in about 7 days.

Searching: Include in request- Full name, ADC number, and what you want. DOB, and SSN helpful. This data not released- medical data.

Access by: mail, phone, fax, in person, online.

Fee & Payment: Fee is $.25 for every copy. Fee payee- Arizona Department of Corrections. Business checks accepted, but not personal checks or credit cards.

Mail search: Turnaround time- 4 to 5 days. SASE is not required.

Phone search: The locator number is available 24 hours daily.

Fax search: Fax requires full name, the DOB and SSN are helpful.

In person: Visitors can fill out record request form; turnaround time is up to 7 days and office can return by mail.

Online search: For online search, you must provide last name, first initial or ADC number. Any add'l identifiers are welcomed. Location, ADC number, physical identifiers and sentencing information are released. Inmates admitted and released from 1972 to 1985 may not be searchable on the web. Also available is ADC Fugitives - an alphabetical Inmate Datasearch listing of Absconders and Escapees from ADC.

Expedited service: Will expedite for attorneys, public defenders, etc. Fed-Ex must be prepaid.

Corporation, LLC Records

Corporation Commission, Corporation Records, 1300 W Washington, Room 101, Phoenix, AZ 85007; 602-542-3026 (Records), 602-542-3285 (Annual Reports), Fax- 602-542-3414; 8AM-5PM.

www.azcc.gov/divisions/corporations/

Entity Names, Name Reservations and Name Registrations are found here. Fictitious Name & Assumed Name records are found at the county level.

Indexing & Storage: Records available from 1809 on. You must go through this office for records. If copies are needed for historical records, it can take as long as 4 to 6 weeks due to the filming process. New records available for inquiry in after 2-3 months.

Searching: Include in request- full name of business, specific records that you need copies of. In addition to the articles of organization, business entity records available include: Annual Reports, Officers, Directors, Prior (Merged) Names, Inactive and Reserved Names.

Access by: mail, in person, online.

Fee & Payment: There is no charge for a search. Uncertified LLC copies cost $5.00 plus $.50 per page; a certified copy is $10.00. A certified corporation document is $5.00 plus $.50 per page. The cost for the Good Standing is $10.00. Fee payee- Arizona Corporation Commission. Prepayment required. Personal checks and major credit cards accepted.

Mail search: Turnaround time- 3 to 5 days. Enclose a check marked "Not to exceed $10.00." A SASE is requested.

In person: Turnaround time is while you wait for up to 5 corporate names.

Online search: STARPAS, functioning 24/7 is a resource for searching the index and viewing documents (without SSNs). Go to http://starpas.azcc.gov/scripts/cgiip.exe/WService=wsbroker1/main.p. Another site, http://edocket.azcc.gov/, gives access to the Corporation Commission's official dockets and rule-making proceedings, referred herein as cases or dockets. Also, search Corp Commission's Securities Division Actions, Orders and Admin. Decisions pages at www.azcc.gov/divisions/securities/enforcement/.

Other access: To purchase the database or in bulk, see www.azcc.gov/Divisions/Corporations/starpas1/rec2003.pdf. Call 602-364-4433.

Expedited service: Expedited service is available for mail and in person searches. Turnaround time- 24 hours. Add $35.00 per request. The fee applies to large orders that must be completed within 24 hours. Generally, smaller orders or single document orders do not require this fee.

Fictitious Name, Assumed Name

Records not maintained by a state level agency.

Records are found at the county level.

Partnerships, LP, LLP, Trademarks/Servicemarks, Trade Names

Secretary of State, Trademarks/Tradenames/ Limited Partnership Division, 1700 W Washington, 7th Floor, Phoenix, AZ 85007 (Courier address- Customer Service, 14 N 18th Ave, Phoenix, AZ); 602-542-6187, Fax- 602-542-7386; 8AM-5PM.

www.azsos.gov/business_services/TNT/Default.htm

Note that corporations are filed with the Arizona Corporation Commission.

Indexing & Storage: Records available from 1984 to present on computer. LPs available to 1974 and TMs to 1968 on paper. New records available for inquiry in 1 to 3 days.

Searching: Provide the entity name, owner name or file number to search. A record request form may be downloaded from the web. This data not released- SSN.

Access by: mail, phone, in person, online.

Fee & Payment: Copies fee $.10 per page; Certified copies of Trade Name and Trademark filings $3.00. Certification of Existence for LP, FLP, LLP, LLLP $5.00. Fee payee- Secretary of State. Prepayment required. Personal checks accepted, credit cards are not.

Mail search: Turnaround time- up to 10 days. Trademarks may take longer. A SASE is requested.

Phone search: They will limited information at no charge over the phone for up to 3 searches, such as owner's name, date of application, mailing address & expiration date.

In person: If there are more than 5 pages of copies, service is overnight.

Online search: The website links to three searchable databases. One searches for Registered Names, Trade Names, and Trademarks. Also available is the full Trade Name and Trademark index in data format. Anther lists the registered names in alpha order and states the type of records available. Another way to obtain this data is from http://starpas.azcc.gov/scripts/cgiip.exe/WService=wsbroker1/main.p.

Other access: Bulk purchase is available on microfiche.

Expedited service: Expedited service is available for mail and in person searches. Turnaround time- 24-48 hours. Add $25.00 per filing.

Uniform Commercial Code, Federal & State Tax Liens

UCC Division, Secretary of State, 1700 W Washington, 7th Floor, Phoenix, AZ 85007 (Courier address- Customer Service Center, 14 North 18th Ave, Phoenix, AZ 85007); 602-542-6187, Fax- 602-542-7386; 8AM - 5PM.

www.azsos.gov/business_services/UCC/

Direct questions to ucc@sos.state.az.us.

Indexing & Storage: Records available from 3/80 to present on microfiche and from 06/95 to present on the Internet.

Searching: Use search request form UCC-11. The search includes tax liens recorded here. Please note that tax liens recorded on individuals may be filed at the county level and not here. Include in request- debtor name.

Access by: mail, phone, fax, in person, online.

Fee & Payment: The search fee is $6.00 per debtor name, except via the web which is no charge. Copies are $.10 each. Certification is an additional $3.00 plus $10.00 per page. Fee payee- Secretary of State. Prepayment required. Personal checks accepted, credit cards are not.

Mail search: Turnaround time- 5 days.

Phone search: Records are available by phone.

Fax search: Records are available by fax.

In person: They usually do not charge expedited fees for same day service, if the counter is not busy. Be sure to visit the 18th Ave address.

Online search: The UCC record index can be searched for free at www.azsos.gov/scripts/ucc_search.dll. Searching can be done by debtor, secured party name, or file number. Images are available on records since 5/1994. SSNs have been redacted. Filings that exist before May 1994 have fiche locations at the bottom of the details page.

Other access: The agency offers six options of bulk database purchases. Requests must be in writing using their request form which can be downloaded from the web.

Expedited service: Expedited service is available for mail and phone searches. Turnaround time- same day if possible. Add $25.00 per package.

Sales Tax Registrations

Revenue Department, Transaction (Sales) Tax Licenses and Registration, 1600 W Monroe, Phoenix, AZ 85007; 602-542-4565, 602 255-2060 Fax- 602-542-4772; 8AM-5PM.

www.revenue.state.az.us

Indexing & Storage: Records available from 1980.

Searching: This agency will only confirm that a business is registered and whether it is active. It will provide no other information without a power of attorney. Include in request- business name. The tax permit number is very helpful.

Access by: mail, phone, fax, in person, online.

Mail search: A SASE is requested. No fee for mail request.

Phone search: They will confirm license on phone, if given permit #.

Fax search: Records are available by fax.

In person: No fee for request.

Online search: Search sales tax registrations by tax number online free at https://www.aztaxes.gov/default.aspx?target=LicenseVerification. Must be eight digits.

Birth Certificates

Department of Health Services, Vital Records Section, PO Box 3887, Phoenix, AZ 85030 (Courier address- 1818 West Adams, Phoenix, AZ 85007); 602-364-1300 (Recording), 888-816-5907 (In-state), Fax- 602-364-1257; 8AM-5PM.

www.azdhs.gov/vitalrcd/index.htm

Arizona is a closed record state; vital records are not public record. A certificate of birth resulting in stillbirth is available as of 08/09/2001.

Indexing & Storage: Records available from late 1800's to present. Records are computerized from 1950 to present. New records available for inquiry in 10 days.

Searching: Must by 18 years of age or older to request a record and be the person named or that person's parent or legal guardian. Records 75 years or older available to the public for a $3.00 fee. Include in request- full name, names of parents, mother's maiden name, date of birth, place of birth, relationship to person of record, reason for information request. A copy of a valid government issued ID is required or the requestor signature must be notarized. This data not released- sealed records

Access by: mail, fax, in person, online.

Fee & Payment: Certified copies of birth certificates for births occurring 1990 to present are $10.00 each. Prior certified records are also $10.00 each (known as "long" records). Fee payee- Vital Records Section. Prepayment required. Personal checks are not accepted. Major credit cards accepted.

Mail search: Turnaround time- 2 weeks. SASE not required.

Fax search: See expedited services. Fax to use is 866-346-1904.

In person: Turnaround time is usually less than 1 hour if record 1950 to present.

Online search: Records may be ordered online via www.vitalchek.com, a state-endorsed vendor. Images of birth certificates from 1887 to 1929 are available free online at http://genealogy.az.gov. Death certificates 1878-1953 are also available.

Expedited service: Expedited service is available for fax and online ordering. Turnaround time- 2-3 days. There is an additional $20.50 fee to use a credit card have the results returned by courier.

Death Records

Department of Health Services, Vital Records Section, PO Box 3887, Phoenix, AZ 85030 (Courier address- 1818 West Adams, Phoenix, AZ 85007); 602-364-1300 (Recording), 888-816-5907 (In-state), Fax- 602-364-1257; 8AM-5PM.

www.azdhs.gov/vitalrcd/index.htm

Arizona is a closed record state; vital records are not public record.

Indexing & Storage: Records available from late 1800's to present. New records available for inquiry immediately.

Searching: Must have notarized release from immediate family. Only immediate family, attorney or funeral director acting for immediate family can get records. Records 50 years or older are available to the public for a $3.00 fee. Include in request- full name, date of death, place of death, relationship to person of record, reason for information request. A copy of a valid government issued ID is required or the requestor signature must be notarized. This data not released- sealed records

Access by: mail, fax, in person, online.

Fee & Payment: A certified photocopy is $10.00. Fee payee- Vital Records Section. Prepayment required. Personal checks are not accepted. Major credit cards accepted.

Mail search: Turnaround time- 2 weeks. A SASE is requested.

Fax search: See expedited services. Fax to use is 866-346-1904.

In person: Turnaround time is usually 30-50 minutes.

Online search: Death certificate images 1878-1953 are available free online at http://genealogy.az.gov. Also available are images of birth certificates from 1887 to 1928. Records may be ordered online via www.vitalchek.com, a state-endorsed vendor.

Expedited service: Expedited service is available for fax and online orders. Turnaround time- 2-3 days. There is an additional $20.50 fee to use a credit card have the results returned by courier.

Marriage Certificates, Divorce Records

Records not maintained by a state level agency.

These records are not available from this agency; records must be requested from the county or court of issue.

Workers' Compensation Records

Industrial Commission of Arizona, Claims Division, 800 West Washington Street, Phoenix, AZ 85007; 602-542-6731, Fax- 602-364-0250; 8AM-5PM.

www.ica.state.az.us/workersCompensation/index.html

Indexing & Storage: Records available from 1969. New records available for inquiry immediately.

Searching: All records are scanned and placed on the imaging system. Claim and policy records are confidential, only claimant or insured or legal representative are provided access. Include in request- signed release by claimant, SSN, claim number. A public search (post-hire check) is available, but the signed release is still required. The public search is a list of prior claims, with details. This data not released- anything beyond the employer name, carrier name, date of injury, type of injury and case number is not given.

Access by: mail, in person.

Fee & Payment: The search fee is $2.50 per person. Fee payee- ICA of Arizona Personal checks are accepted.

Mail search: Turnaround time- 2 weeks. SASE not required. If merely file copies are requested it can take 30-60 days to complete.

In person: Simple requests will receive immediate service.

Driver Records

Motor Vehicle Division, Correspondence Unit, PO Box 2100, Mail Drop 539M, Phoenix, AZ 85001-2100 (Courier address- Customer Records Services, 1801 W Jefferson, Lobby, Phoenix, AZ 85007); 602-712-8420; 8AM-5PM.

www.azdot.gov/mvd/index.asp

Indexing & Storage: Records available for either a thirty-nine month record or for a five-year record. Records may be available for ten years under special circumstances and approval. New records available for inquiry in 2 weeks.

Searching: Requesters must use Form 46-4416, which requires the reason for the request notarized signature of the requester. Casual requesters (per DPPA) must submit notarized consent from the subject. Include in request- full name, date of birth or license expiration date, driver's license number, notarized consent if necessary. Certain "exempt requesters" as identified by law need only supply 2 out of the 3 items required to search. The driver's mailing address is provided as part of the record to exempt requesters.

Access by: mail, in person, online.

Fee & Payment: The fees are $3.00 for 39 month records ($2.00 if picked up overnight at counter) and $5.00 for certified 5 year records. Electronic access fees differ. Insurers may only receive the 39 month record. All non-exempt requests must be signed and notarized. Fee payee- Motor Vehicle Division, Record Services. Prepayment required. Personal checks and major credit cards accepted.

Mail search: Turnaround time- 1 week to 10 days. If express mail is requested, then envelope must be pre-paid. If mail requester is not DPPA permissible, the requester's signature must be notarized. SASE not required.

In person: Records are available at any of the MVD field offices. There is a limit of 4 requests for immediate service. There is a $1.00 discount if requests are picked up next day.

Online search: Arizona's commercial online system is interactive and open 24 hours daily. Fee is $3.25 per record. This system is primarily for those requesters who qualify per DPPA. For more information call 602-712-7235. The site also permits licensed driver to view their own record. Fee is $3.00 and use of a credit card is required. Visit www.servicearizona.com.

Other access: Overnight cartridge ordering is available. Fee is $2.00 for 39 month record, $3.00 for 5 year record. Call 602-712-7235 for details.

Vehicle Ownership & Registration

Motor Vehicle Division - Director's Office, Record Services Section, PO Box 2100, Mail Drop 504M, Phoenix, AZ 85001-2100 (Courier address- Customer Records Services, 1801 W Jefferson, Lobby, Phoenix, AZ 85007); 602-255-0072; 8AM-5PM.

www.azdot.gov/mvd/index.asp

The Record Services Section also handles search requests for mobile homes, both attached and unattached.

Indexing & Storage: Records available for 5 years to present. New records available for inquiry in 2 weeks.

Searching: The record searcher must complete Form 46-4416, state reason for request, and have signature notarized. Ownership records are not given by merely giving a plate license number or a name. Include in request- name, plate or VIN, Form 46-4416. The vehicle owner's address is helpful. The vehicle's owner, VIN, and plate number must be submitted to receive a vehicle history.

Access by: mail, in person, online.

Fee & Payment: A lienholder record is $1.50. The fee is $3.00, $2.00 if walk-in is willing to pick up the next day, and $5.00 if the record is certified. Fee payee- Motor Vehicle Division. Prepayment required. Money orders and checks are accepted through the mail. Walk-ins may pay with cash. Personal checks accepted. Major credit cards accepted.

Mail search: Turnaround time- 1 week to 10 days.

In person: Counter service available.

Online search: Online access is offered to permissible users. Fee is $3.00 per record. The system is open 24 hours a day, seven days a week. For more information, call 602-712-7235. The MVD also offers access for vehicle owners to view and print their own title and registration records. The fee is $3.00 per record and use of a credit card is required. Visit www.servicearizona.com.

Other access: Check the attorney general's stolen vehicle list free at http://theftaz.azag.gov.

Accident Reports

Department of Public Safety, Accident Reports, PO Box 6638, Mail Drop 1110, Phoenix, AZ 85005 (Courier address- 2102 W Encanto, 1st Floor, Phoenix, AZ 85005-6638); 602-223-2230; 8AM-5PM.

www.azdps.gov/reports/collision/default.asp

If the accident was not investigated by the DPS, the investigating agency should be contacted.

Indexing & Storage: New records available for inquiry in 2 weeks.

Searching: A written request is required and the requester must state his/her connection to the incident. Records may not be used for commercial purposes. Include in request- relationship to person of record, date of accident, location of accident, full name, report number.

Access by: mail, in person.

Fee & Payment: The fee is $9.00 per record for up to first 9 pages, then $1.00 for each additional page. Fee payee- Department of Public Safety. Prepayment required. Business check or money order. No credit cards accepted.

Mail search: Turnaround time- 1 week to 14 days. A SASE is requested.

In person: Turnaround time is while you wait, provided record is on file.

Vessel Ownership & Registration

Game & Fish Dept, Watercraft Department, 5000 West Carefree Highway, Phoenix, AZ 85086; 602-942-3000; 8AM-5PM M-F.

www.azgfd.gov/outdoor_recreation/boating.shtml

Lien information is recorded at the Secretary of State.

Indexing & Storage: Records available from 1977 to present. Records are indexed on computer for the last 5 years. No titles are issued. All watercraft must be registered unless they are non-motorized. New records available for inquiry in 1 day.

Searching: Record access is governed by AZ Revised Statutes, Title 5. This agency does not recognize DPPA permissible uses. Only AZ lawyers, PIs, and financial institutions, in general and upon approval have access to records. To search, the following information is required: Arizona #, hull ID, owner's name, and picture ID.

Access by: mail, phone, fax, in person.

Fee & Payment: There is no search fee. No copy.

Mail search: Turnaround time- 1 day. SASE not required.

Phone search: Only AZ lawyers, private investigators, and government representatives can search by phone or fax.

Fax search: Same criteria as phone searching.

In person: Turnaround time is normally immediate.

Other access: Commercial records are given as bulk lists, CDs or labels.

Legislation Records

Arizona Legislature, State Senate - Room 203, 1700 W Washington, Phoenix, AZ 85007 (Courier address- Senate Wing or, House Wing, Phoenix, AZ 85007); 602-926-3559 (Senate), 602-542-4221 (House), Fax- 602-542-4099; 8AM-5PM.

www.azleg.gov/

The phone number provides information on current session bills and on some previous bills.

Indexing & Storage: Records available from 1969 to 1996 on microfilm for bill files. Committee minutes are available from 1967 to present on hard copy. New records available for inquiry in 1 to 7 business days.

Searching: Audio tapes of committee minutes and floor sessions are also available. Include in request- bill number, year.

Access by: mail, phone, fax, in person, online.

Fee & Payment: Copies are $.10 per page. Fee payee- AZ State Senate or House of Representatives. Prepayment is requested for large photocopying projects. Personal checks accepted, credit cards are not.

Mail search: Turnaround time- 1 day. All research requests are processed ASAP, determined by the demands of the legislative sessions on the staff. SASE not required.

Phone search: Search requests are accepted over the phone to be processed ASAP, but not while holding on the phone.

Fax search: Fee is $.10 per page, with a turnaround time of 1 day or sooner.

In person: A desk is provided for reviewing files, reading minutes, etc. Staff will assist if time and workload permits.

Online search: Most information, beginning with 1997, is available through the Internet (i.e. bill text, committee minutes, committee assignments, member bios, etc.). There is no fee. The AZ Revised Statutes are found at www.azleg.state.az.us/ArizonaRevisedStatutes.asp

Other access: Name, address, and office # lists are available at no charge. Roll call vote histories of individuals per year are available at $.10 per page.

Expedited service: They will ship using Federal Express, if the requester has a FedEx account.

Voter Registration

Access to Records is Restricted.

Secretary of State, Election Division, 1700 W Washington, 7th Floor, Phoenix, AZ 85007; 602-542-8683; 8AN-5PM.

www.azsos.gov/election/

The state is "HAVA compliant" with a central, computerized, statewide voter registration system. However, by state statute, the record database is not available to the public. Presently, record information can only be purchased at the county recorder offices. Their records are permitted to be sold in bulk only for political related purposes. Go to the county level to confirm names on a single inquiry basis.

GED Transcripts

Department of Education, GED Testing, 1535 W Jefferson, Phoenix, AZ 85007 (Courier address- 2005 n Central, 2nd Fl, Phoenix, AZ 85004); 602-258-2410, Fax- 602-258-4977; 8AM-5PM.

www.ade.az.gov/adult-ed/

This agency will not do a verification; they will only sell a copy of a transcript. However, the agency does send verification requesters to a third-party vendor at http://ged123.org.

Indexing & Storage: Records available from 1945 to present. New records available for inquiry in 1 to 2 weeks.

Searching: Request forms are available from the website. Include in request- name at date of test, date of birth, SSN, signed release, and year of test. All requests must be in writing, all require the signed release of the student.

Access by: mail, in person.

Fee & Payment: There is a $10.00 fee for a copy of transcript. This agency will not do a verification only; a transcript must be purchased. Fee payee- AZ Department of Education

Mail search: Turnaround time- 1 to 2 days. An SASE is strongly suggested.

In person: Counter service is available at the East Virginia Ave address. Records are available in minutes if the test was taken after 1985, otherwise research can take 1-2 hours.

Hunting & Fishing License Information

Game & Fish Department, Information & Licensing Division, 5000 W Carefree Highway, Phoenix, AZ 85086; 602-942-3000, Fax- 602-789-3924; 8AM-5PM.

www.azgfd.com/h_f/hunting_fishing.shtml

Indexing & Storage: Records available for past 3 years. New records available for inquiry in 30 days.

Searching: Records are not available to the public except as a mailing list. A Public Record Request form must be used, call to obtain. They will release certain data to attorneys or private investigators for pending litigation.

Access by: mail.

Fee & Payment: Prepayment required. Fee payee- Arizona Game & Fish. Personal checks, Visa, and MasterCard accepted.

Mail search: Turnaround time- variable. Must complete a request form. SASE not required.

Other access: There is a program to purchase the database or portions of. You can get 3 years of approximately 160,000 to 190,000 names for $.10 per name, which includes addresses. $100 minimum, can use for commercial purposes. Lists are completed within 30 days.

Arizona State Licensing Agencies

For details about the agency responsible for licensing/certifying/registering an item below or in the Agency Quick Finder section, match an item's number with the number of the agency in the *Licensing Agency Information* section.

Arizona Licenses Searchable Online

Accounting Firm, CPA/CP #7 .... www.azaccountancy.gov/scripts/BOAsearch.exe
Acupuncturist #77 .... www.azacuboard.az.gov/ASPSearch.htm
Acupuncturist Chiropractor #11 .... www.azchiroboard.com/ASPSearch.htm
Adoption Searcher #63 .... www.supreme.state.az.us/cip/directory.htm
Adult Care Home Manager #68 .... www.nciabd.state.az.us/managers.htm
Advance Fee Loan Broker #5 .... http://azdfi.gov/Lists/Lists.htm
Aerial Applicator, Pesticide #33 .... www.kellysolutions.com/az/Pilots/index.asp
Agricultural Grower Permit #33 .... www.kellysolutions.com/az/RUPBuyers/index.asp
Agricultural Grower/Seller #33 .... www.kellysolutions.com/az/RUPBuyers/index.asp
Agricultural Pest Control Advisor #33 .... www.kellysolutions.com/az/PCA/index.asp
Ambulance Service #48 .... www.azdhs.gov/bems/conmaps.htm
Ambulatory Surgical Ctr #43 .... www.azdhs.gov/als/index.htm
Applicator, Pesticide, Private/Com #33 .... www.kellysolutions.com/AZ/Applicators/index.asp
Architect #29 .... www.btr.state.az.us/listings/professional_registrant2.asp
Assayer #29 .... www.btr.state.az.us/listings/professional_registrant2.asp
Assisted Living Facility #49 .... www.azdhs.gov/als/search/index.htm
Assisted Living Facility Mgr #49 .... www.azdhs.gov/als/search/index.htm
Attorney #30 .... www.azbar.org/LegalResources/findlawyer.cfm
Audiologist #49 .... www.azdhs.gov/als/search/index.htm
Bank, State Chartered #5 .... http://azdfi.gov/Lists/BA_List.HTML
Barber School/Instruction #9 .... www.boardofbarbers.az.gov/dir.htm
Barber/Barber Shop #9 .... www.boardofbarbers.az.gov/dir.htm
Behav'l Health Emerg'y/Resi. Svcs #47 .... www.azdhs.gov/als/databases/
Behavioral Outpatient Clinic/Rehab #47 .... www.azdhs.gov/als/databases/
Bondsman (Insurance) #51 .... www.id.state.az.us/
Charity #62 .... www.azsos.gov/scripts/Charity_Search.dll
Charter School #38 .... www.ade.az.gov/charterschools/search/
Child Care #49 .... www.azdhs.gov/als/search/index.htm
Child Care Office, DES #74 .... www.de.state.az.us/childcare/office.asp
Child Residential Home #37 .... www.azdhs.gov/als/databases/providers_cc.pdf
Chiropractor #11 .... www.azchiroboard.com/ASPSearch.htm
Citrus Broker #72 .... www.azda.gov/CFV/CompaniesWithCurrentLicenses2.pdf
Clinic, Recovery Care #43 .... www.azdhs.gov/als/index.htm
Clinic, Rural Health #43 .... www.azdhs.gov/als/index.htm
Collection Agency #5 .... http://azdfi.gov/Lists/Lists.htm
Confidential Intermediary #63 .... www.supreme.state.az.us/cip/directory.htm
Consumer Lender #5 .... http://azdfi.gov/Lists/Lists.htm
Contractor #70 .... www.azroc.gov/clsc/AZROCLicenseQuery
Cosmetology/Nail Tech. Salon/Sch'l #12 .... www.beautyschoolsdirectory.com/find/index.php?search=Y&t=ALL&st=AZ
Counselor, Professional #10 .... www.bbhe.state.az.us/verifications.htm
Court Reporter #63 .... www.supreme.state.az.us/cr/pdf/3-20-08%20CR%20Directory.pdf
Credit Union, State Chartered #5 .... http://azdfi.gov/Lists/CU_List.HTML
Cremationist #15 .... www.funeralbd.state.az.us/dir.htm
Crematory #15 .... www.funeralbd.state.az.us/dir.htm
Day Care Establishment #45 .... http://hsapps.azdhs.gov/ls/sod/SearchProv.aspx?type=CC
Debt Management Company #5 .... http://azdfi.gov/Lists/Lists.htm
Defensive Driving Instructor #63 .... www.supreme.state.az.us/drive/CertifiedSchoolsList.htm
Defensive Driving School #63 .... www.supreme.state.az.us/drive/CertifiedSchoolsList.htm
Deferred Presentment Company #5 .... http://azdfi.gov/Lists/DPC_List.HTML
Detoxification Service #47 .... www.azdhs.gov/als/databases/
Development'ly Disab'd Group Home #49 .... www.azdhs.gov/als/search/index.htm
Dispensing Naturopath #19 .... www.npbomex.az.gov/directorysearch.asp
Drilling, Oil/Gas #76 .... http://azogcc.az.gov/OGpermits.htm
Drug Mfg/Wholesaler #24 .... https://az.gov/app/pharmacy/search.xhtml
Drug, Retail non-prescription #24 .... https://az.gov/app/pharmacy/search.xhtml
Dry Well Registration #41 .... www.azdeq.gov/databases/drywellsearch.html
Embalmer #15 .... www.funeralbd.state.az.us/dir.htm

Emergency Response Division #66 .... www.arra.state.az.us/
EMS ALS Base Hospital #48 .... www.azdhs.gov/bems/basehosp.htm
Engineer #29.. www.btr.state.az.us/listings/professional_registrant2.asp
Escrow Agent #5 .... http://azdfi.gov/Lists/Lists.htm
Family Day Care Home #37...................... www.azdhs.gov/als/databases/providers_cc.pdf
Feed Dealer/Wholesaler #33 .... www.kellysolutions.com/az/feeddealers/index.asp
Feed Distribution, Commercial #33........... www.kellysolutions.com/az/FeedDealers/index.asp
Fertilizer Dealer #33................................. www.kellysolutions.com/az/fertdealers/index.asp
Fertilizer Distribution, Commercial #33 ..... www.kellysolutions.com/az/FertDealers/index.asp
Fertilizer Product #33............................... www.kellysolutions.com/AZ/Fertilizer/fertilizerindex.asp
Fiduciary #63... www.supreme.state.az.us/fiduc/pdf/01-10-08%20Fiduciary%20Directory.pdf
Food Establishment #65
...... www.maricopa.gov/EnvSvc/envwebapp/business_search.aspx?as_page_title=Food%20Establishments%20Search&as_type=Food
Fruit Broker #72 .... www.azda.gov/CFV/CompaniesWithCurrentLicenses2.pdf
Funeral Director #15 .... www.funeralbd.state.az.us/dir.htm
Funeral Establishment #15 .... www.funeralbd.state.az.us/dir.htm
Funeral Pre-Need Trust Company #5....... http://azdfi.gov/Lists/Lists.htm
Geologist #29.. www.btr.state.az.us/listings/professional_registrant2.asp
Group Home, Development Disabled #49 www.azdhs.gov/als/search/index.htm
Group Home, Small #49 .... www.azdhs.gov/als/search/index.htm
Headstart Facility #45 .... http://hsapps.azdhs.gov/ls/sod/SearchProv.aspx?type=CC
Health Clinic #49.. www.azdhs.gov/als/search/index.htm
Hearing Aid Dispenser #49 .... www.azdhs.gov/als/search/index.htm
Highway Engineer #29............................... www.btr.state.az.us/listings/professional_registrant2.asp
Home Health Agency #43.......................... www.azdhs.gov/als/index.htm
Home Inspector #29.................................. www.btr.state.az.us/listings/professional_registrant2.asp
Homeopathic Physician #16 .... www.azhomeopathbd.az.gov/phy_dir.htm
Hospice #43 .... www.azdhs.gov/als/index.htm
Hospital #43 .... www.azdhs.gov/als/index.htm
Hospital, Adv'd Life Support (EMS) #48.... www.azdhs.gov/bems/basehosp.htm
Infirmary #43 .... www.azdhs.gov/als/index.htm
Insurance Producer #51............................ www.id.state.az.us/
Juvenile Group Home #37 .... www.azdhs.gov/als/search/index.htm
Landscape Architect #29 .... www.btr.state.az.us/listings/professional_registrant2.asp
Legal Document Preparer #63.................. www.supreme.state.az.us/cld/pdf/3-20-08%20LDP%20Directory.pdf
Liquor Producer/Whlse #52 .... www.azliquor.gov/query/default.asp
Liquor Retail Co-Op/Agent/Mgr. #52......... www.azliquor.gov/query/default.asp
Lobbyist #62.. www.azsos.gov/scripts/Lobbyist_Search.dll
Long Term Care Facility #49..................... www.azdhs.gov/als/search/index.htm
Marriage & Family Therapist #10.............. www.bbhe.state.az.us/verifications.htm
Massage Therapy School #19 .... www.npbomex.az.gov/directories.asp
Medical Doctor, Intern/Resident #17......... www.azmd.gov/profile/getlicense.aspx
Medical Facility #49 .... www.azdhs.gov/als/search/index.htm
Medical Gas Dist/Supplier #24.................. https://az.gov/app/pharmacy/search.xhtml
Mentally Retarded Care Facility #49......... www.azdhs.gov/als/search/index.htm
Midwife, Lay #50 .... www.azdhs.gov/als/databases/index.htm
Money Transmitter #5 .... http://azdfi.gov/Lists/Lists.htm
Mortgage Banker, Commercial #5 .... http://azdfi.gov/Lists/BK_List.HTML
Mortgage Banker/Broker #5...................... http://azdfi.gov/Lists/Lists.htm
Motor Vehicle Dealer/Sales Finance #5.... http://azdfi.gov/Lists/MVD_List.HTML
Nail Technology Instruct'r/Sch'l/Salon #12 www.beautyschoolsdirectory.com/find/index.php?search=Y&t=ALL&st=AZ
Naturopathic Medical Asst. #19 .... www.npbomex.az.gov/directories.asp
Naturopathic Physician #19 .... www.npbomex.az.gov/directorysearch.asp
Naturopathic School #19........................... www.npbomex.az.gov/directories.asp
Neuro Rehab Center #43 .... www.azdhs.gov/als/index.htm
Notary Public #62...................................... www.azsos.gov/scripts/Notary_Search.dll
Nuclear Medicine Technologist #66.......... www.arra.state.az.us/
Nurse-LPN/RN #20 .... https://www.azbn.gov/OnlineVerification.aspx
Nurses' Aide #20.. https://www.azbn.gov/OnlineVerification.aspx
Nursing Care Inst. Administrator #68........ www.nciabd.state.az.us/administrators.htm
Occupational Therapist/Assistant #21 ...... www.occupationaltherapyboard.az.gov/ASPSearch.htm
On Site Worker/Superv'r #29 .... www.btr.state.az.us/listings/professional_registrant2.asp
Optical Establishment #14 .... www.do.az.gov/directory/default.asp
Optician #14.. www.do.az.gov/directory/default.asp
Optometrist #22.. www.optometry.az.gov/directory.asp

Osteopathic Physician/Surgeon #23 .... www.azdo.gov/
Out-Patient Physical Therapy #43 .... www.azdhs.gov/als/index.htm
Out-Patient Surgical Center #43 .... www.azdhs.gov/als/index.htm
Outpatient Treatment Clinic #43 .... www.azdhs.gov/als/index.htm
P&C Managing Agent, Life/Disability #51 . www.id.state.az.us/
Packer, Fruit/Vegetable #72 .... www.azda.gov/CFV/CompaniesWithCurrentLicenses2.pdf
Pest Control Applicator/Supv./Advisor #18 www.sb.state.az.us/PCProfSearch.php
Pest Control Company #18 .... www.sb.state.az.us/PCBusSearch.php
Pesticide Custom Applicator #33 .... www.kellysolutions.com/az/CustomAppl/index.asp
Pesticide Distribution/Seller #33 .... www.kellysolutions.com/az/Dealers/index.asp
Pesticide Registration #33 .... www.kellysolutions.com/az/pesticideindex.htm
Pharmacist/Pharmacy Intern #24 .... https://az.gov/app/pharmacy/search.xhtml
Physical Therapist/Therapist Asst #25...... www.ptboard.state.az.us/public/ptays/ptSearch.asp
Physician Assistant #17 .... www.azmd.gov/profile/getlicense.aspx
Physiotherapist #11 .... www.azchiroboard.com/ASPSearch.htm
Plant Operator #41 .... www.azdeq.gov/databases/opcertsearch.html
Podiatrist #26 .... www.podiatry.state.az.us/dir.htm
Political Action Committee #62 .... www.azsos.gov/cfs/SuperPACList.aspx
Post-Secondary Educ. Institution #6 .... http://azppse.state.az.us/UserFiles/PDF/PPSEDirectory.pdf
Post-Secondary Voc. Program, Private #6 http://azppse.state.az.us/UserFiles/PDF/PPSEDirectory.pdf
Premium Finance Company #5 .... http://azdfi.gov/Lists/PF_List.HTML
Preschool #45 .... http://hsapps.azdhs.gov/ls/sod/SearchProv.aspx?type=CC
Private Investigator #53 .... http://licensing.azdps.gov/Licensesecurityguard.asp
Process Server, Private #63 .... www.supreme.state.az.us/cld/pdf/PPS%20Directory%203-6-08.pdf
Property Tax Agent #8 .... www.appraisal.state.az.us/directory/Default.aspx
Psychologist #27 .... www.psychboard.az.gov/directory.htm
Public Accountant-CPA #7 .... www.azaccountancy.gov/scripts/BOAsearch.exe
Public Accounting Firm-CPA/PA #7 .... www.azaccountancy.gov/scripts/BOAsearch.exe
Radon Mitigation Specialist #66 .... www.arra.state.az.us/
Real Estate Agent/Broker/Sales #55 .... http://159.87.254.2/publicdatabase/SearchIndividuals.aspx?mode=2
Real Estate Appraiser #8 .... www.appraisal.state.az.us/directory/Default.aspx
Real Estate School/Course #55 .... http://159.87.254.2/publicdatabase/SearchSchools.aspx?mode=3
Recovery Center #49 .... www.azdhs.gov/als/search/index.htm
Registered Medical Assistant #16 .... www.azhomeopathbd.az.gov/asst_dir.htm
Rehabilitation Agency #43 .... www.azdhs.gov/als/index.htm
Remediation Specialist #29 .... www.btr.state.az.us/listings/professional_registrant2.asp
Renal Disease Facility #43 .... www.azdhs.gov/als/index.htm
Respiratory Therapist #28 .... https://az.gov/webapp/rce/respiratorycareexaminer/licensestatus/
Risk Management Producers #51 .... www.id.state.az.us/
Sales Finance Company #5 .... http://azdfi.gov/Lists/SF_List.HTML
Sanitarian #46 .... www.azdhs.gov/phs/oeh/rs/pdf/sanreg.pdf
Security Guard #53 .... http://licensing.azdps.gov/Licensesecurityguard.asp
Seed Dealer #33 .... www.kellysolutions.com/az/SeedDealers/index.asp
Seed Labeler #33 .... www.kellysolutions.com/az/SeedLabelers/index.asp
Social Worker #10 .... www.bbhe.state.az.us/verifications.htm
Speech Pathology #43 .... www.azdhs.gov/als/index.htm
Speech-Language Pathologist #49 .... www.azdhs.gov/als/search/index.htm
Subdivision Public Report #55 .... http://159.87.254.2/publicdatabase/SearchDevelopments.aspx?mode=2
Substance Abuse Counselor #10 .... www.bbhe.state.az.us/verifications.htm
Surety #51 .... www.id.state.az.us/
Surplus Line Broker #51 .... www.id.state.az.us/
Surveyor, Land #29 .... www.btr.state.az.us/listings/professional_registrant2.asp
Telemarketing Firm #62 .... www.azsos.gov/scripts/TS_Search_engine.cgi
Travel Agent, Limited #51 .... www.id.state.az.us/
Treatment Clinic #43 .... www.azdhs.gov/als/index.htm
Trust Company #5 .... http://azdfi.gov/Lists/TC_List.HTML
Trust Div. of Chartered Financial Inst. #5 . http://azdfi.gov/Lists/Lists.htm
Veterinary Medicine/Surgery #64 .... www.vetbd.state.az.us/directory/default.aspx
Veterinary Premise (Hospital) #64 .... www.vetbd.state.az.us/directory/default.aspx
Veterinary Technician #64 .... www.vetbd.state.az.us/directory/default.aspx
Waste Water Facility Operator #41 .... www.azdeq.gov/databases/opcertsearch.html
Water Distribution System Operator #41 .. www.azdeq.gov/databases/opcertsearch.html
Well Drilling Firm #58 .... www.azwater.gov/dwr/content/Drillers/default.asp
X-ray Supplier #66 .... www.arra.state.az.us/
X-ray, Portable #43 .... www.azdhs.gov/als/index.htm

Arizona Licensing Quick Finder

Accounting Firm, CPA/CP #7 602-364-0804
Acupuncturist #77 602-542-3095
Acupuncturist Chiropractor #11 602-864-5088
Adoption Agency #74 .. 877-543-7633, 602-542-5499
Adoption Searcher #63 .... 602-364-0575, 542-9580
Adult Care Home Manager #68 602-364-2273
Advance Fee Loan Broker #5 602-255-4421
Aerial Applicator, Pesticide #33 602-542-0904
Aesthetician #12 480-784-4539
Aesthetics Instructor #12 480-784-4539
Agricultural Aircraft Pilot #33 602-542-0904
Agricultural Grower Permit /Seller #33 .. 602-542-0904
Agricultural Lab #71 602-253-1920
Agricultural Pest Control Advisor #33 ... 602-542-0904
Agricultural Seller Permit #33 602-542-0904
Air Pollution Source #39 602-771-2338
Air Quality Permit #65 602-506-6010
Aircraft Dealer/Retail #57 602-294-9144
Aircraft Mfg/Import/Dist./Transport #57 . 602-294-9144
Aircraft Owner #57 602-294-9144
Aircraft Pilot Trainer Sch'l/Instruct #57 . 602-294-9144
Aircraft Use Fuel Dealer/Mfg #56 602-542-4576
Aircraft Wrecker/Salvage #57 602-294-9144
Ambulance Service #48 602-364-3184
Ambulatory Surgical Ctr #43 602-364-3030
Amusement Park #56 602-542-4576
Amusement Printing/Advertising #56 ... 602-542-4576
Applicator, Pesticide, Private/Com #33 602-542-0904
Appraiser, Real/Personal Property #56 602-542-1539
Aquaculture Operator #34 602-542-4373
Aquatic Wildlife Stocker #59 602-942-3000
Aquifer Protection Permit #41 602-771-4644
Architect #29 602-364-4930
Assayer #29 602-364-4930
Assisted Living Facility #49 602-364-2536
Assisted Living Facility Mgr #49 602-364-2536
Attorney #30 602-252-4804
Audiologist #49 602-364-2536
Automotive Recycler #75 602-255-0072
Bait Seller, Live #59 602-942-3000
Bank, State Chartered #5 602-255-4421
Barber School/Instruction #9 602-542-4498
Barber/Barber Shop #9 602-542-4498
Bathing Place #65 602-506-6970
Bedding Seller/Mfg/Renovator #46 602-364-3118
Bedding/Furniture Mfg #65 602-506-6010
Behavioral Health Emerg'y/Resi. Svcs #47 602-364-2595
Behavioral Outpatient Clinic/Rehab #47 602-364-2595
Bingo Operation #56 602-542-4576
Biosolid Registration #39 602-771-2338
Boiler Registration #73 602-542-7117
Bondsman (Insurance) #51 602-364-4457
Bone Densitometer Operator #66 .... 602-255-4845 x242 or 243
Bottled Water Processor #65 602-506-6970
Boxer #3 602-364-1721
Boxing Physician #3 602-364-1721
Boxing Professional #3 602-364-1721
Brand, Livestock #34 602-542-0347
Building, Factorybuilt, Mfg/Dealer #36 . 602-364-1003
Campground Memb'ship Broker/Seller #55 602-468-1414
Cannabis/Control'd Substance Dealer #56 602-542-4576
CDL Examiner #75 602-255-0072
Cemetery Broker/Salesperson #55 602-468-1414
Charity #62 602-542-6670
Charter School #38 602-542-5968
Child Adoption Agency #37 602-364-2539
Child Care #49 602-364-2539
Child Care Office, DES #74 .... 800-308-9000, 602-542-4248
Child Care, 24-hour/Emergency #74 .... 877-543-7633, 602-542-5499
Child Foster Home #37 602-364-2539
Child Placing Agency #37 602-364-2539
Child Residential Home #37 602-364-2539
Children Residential Care #74 .... 877-543-7633, 602-542-5499
Children Shelter #74 .... 877-543-7633, 602-542-5499
Children's Camp #46 602-364-3118
Chiropractor #11 602-864-5088
Citrus Broker #72 602-542-0880
Clinic, Recovery Care #43 602-364-3030
Clinic, Rural Health #43 602-364-3030
Clinical Laboratory #44 602-364-0741
Collection Agency #5 602-255-4421
Commercial Leasing #56 602-542-4576
Competitive Gov't Partnership/ MVR #75602-255-0072
Concealed Weapon Permit #53 602-256-6280
Condo/Timeshare Seller #55 602-468-1414
Confidential Intermediary #63602-364-0575, 542-9580
Consumer Lender #5 602-255-4421
Contractor #70 602-542-1525
Cosmetologist #12 480-784-4539
Cosmetology Instructor #12 480-784-4539
Cosmetology/Nail Tech. Salon/School #12 480-784-4539
Counselor, Professional #10 602-542-1864
Court Reporter #63 602-364-0878
Credit Union, State Chartered #5 602-255-4421
Cremationist #15 602-542-3095
Crematory #15 602-542-3095
Dairy Farm/Facility #34 602-542-4373
Dairy Plant, Cheese/Ice Cream #34 602-542-4373
Dam #58 602-771-8500
Day Care Establishment #45 602-364-2539
Dead Game/Livestock Handler #34 602-542-6309
Debt Management Company #5 602-255-4421
Defensive Driving Instructor #63 602-364-0388
Defensive Driving School #63 602-364-0388
Deferred Presentment Company #5 602-255-4421
Degree Program, Vocational #6 602-542-5709
Dental Assistant/Hygienist #13 602-242-1492
Dentist #13 602-242-1492
Denture Technologist #13 602-242-1492
Denturist #13 602-242-1492
Detoxification Service #47 602-364-2595
Development Disab'd Group Home#49 602-364-2536
Dispensing Naturopath #19 602-542-8242
Dog Racing Kennel #54 602-364-1700
Drilling, Oil/Gas #76 520-770-3500
Driver Training School/Instructor #75 ... 602-255-0072
Drug Mfg/Wholesaler #24 623-463-2727
Drug, Retail non-prescription #24 623-463-2727
Dry Well Registration #41 602-771-4385
DUI Education Agency #47 602-364-2595
DUI Screening/Treatment Agency #47 602-364-2595
Egg Producer/Dist./Packer/Storage #34602-542-0869
Egg Product #34 602-542-0869
Elevator Registration #73 602-542-5795
Embalmer #15 602-542-3095
Embalmer Assistant #15 602-542-3095
Emergency Medical Tech. Instructor #48602-364-3150
Emergency Medical Technician #48 602-364-3186
Emergency Response Division #66602-255-4845 x239
Employment Agency #61 602-542-4515
EMS ALS Base Hospital #48 602-364-3150
Engineer #29 602-364-4930
Environmental Laboratory #44 602-364-0741
Escrow Agent #5 602-255-4421
Falconer #59 602-942-3000
Family Day Care Home #37 602-364-2539
Feed Dealer/Wholesaler #33 602-542-0814
Feed Distribution, Commercial #33 602-542-0814
Fertilizer Dealer #33 602-542-0814
Fertilizer Distribution, Commercial #33 . 602-542-0814
Fertilizer Product #33 602-542-0814
Fiduciary #63 602-363-2378
Field Trial License #59 602-942-3000
Fishing License Dealer #59 602-942-3000
Food Establishment #65 602-506-6970
Foster Care Home #49 602-364-2536
Foster Home #74 .... 877-543-7633, 602-542-5499
Fruit Broker #72 602-542-0880
Fuel User #75 602-255-0072
Funeral Director #15 602-542-3095
Funeral Establishment #15 602-542-3095
Funeral Pre-Need Trust Company #5 .. 602-255-4421
Fur Dealer #59 602-942-3000
Game Farm, Private #59 602-942-3000
Game Resident Guide #59 602-942-3000
Geologist #29 602-364-4930
Groom #54 602-364-1700
Groundwater Pumping #41 602-771-4644
Group Home, Developmentally Disabled #49 602-364-2536
Group Home, Small #49 602-364-2539
Guidance Counselor #38 602-364-2450
Guide, game/fishing #59 602-942-3000
Hazardous Waste Facility #40 602-771-4153
Headstart Facility #45 602-364-2539
Health Clinic #49 602-364-2536
Health Screening Service #44 602-364-0720
Hearing Aid Dispenser #49 602-364-2536
Highway Engineer #29 602-364-4930
Home Health Agency #43 602-364-3030
Home Inspector #29 602-364-4930
Homeopathic Physician #16 602-542-3095
Horse or Greyhound Racing #54 602-364-1700
Horse Owner/Trainer #54 602-364-1700
Hospice #43 602-364-3030
Hospital #43 602-364-3030
Hospital, Adv'd Life Support (EMS) #48602-364-3150
Hotel/Motel/Tourist Court #65 602-506-6970
Hunting & Fishing License Dealer #59. 602-942-3000
Industrial Laser #66 .... 602-255-4845 x235
Infirmary #43 602-364-3030
Insurance Producer #51 602-364-4457
Intern, Funerary Profession #15 602-542-3095
Investment Advisor #32 602-542-4242
Investment Advisor Rep. #32 602-542-4242
Jockey #54 602-364-1700
Juvenile Group Home #37 602-364-2539
Lake, Artificial #41 602-771-4644
Landscape Architect #29 602-364-4930
Laser Light Show #56 602-255-4845
Laser, Medical #66 .... 602-255-4845 x235
Legal Document Preparer #63 602-364-2378
Liquor Producer/Whlse #52 602-542-5141
Liquor Retail Co-Operative/Agent/Mgr. #52 602-542-5141
Lobbyist #62 602-542-8683
Long Term Care Facility #49 602-364-2536
Lottery Retailer #4 480-921-4400
LPG Service Agency/Rep #2 602-771-4920
Mammography Technologist #66 602-255-4845
Manufactured Home Dealer/Mfg #36 ... 602-364-1003
Marriage & Family Therapist #10 602-542-1864
Massage Therapy School #19 602-542-5709
Meat/Poultry Proces'r #34 ... 602-542-3578, 542-6398
Medical Doctor, Intern/Resident #17 480-551-2700
Medical Facility #49 602-364-2536
Medical Gas Dist/Supplier #24 623-463-2727
Medicare/Medicaid Certified #49 602-364-2536
Mental Health Screener/Eval./Treater #47 602-364-2595
Mentally Retarded Care Facility #49 602-364-2536

Metrology Certification #2 ... 602-771-4920
Midwife, Lay #50 ... 602-364-2079
Milk Dist/Whlse #34 ... 602-542-4373
Mine Inspector #67 ... 602-542-5971
Mine Reclamation Plan #67 ... 602-542-5971
Mining Elevator/Diesel #67 ... 602-542-5971
Mining Operator/Start-up #67 ... 602-542-5971
Minnow Dealer #59 ... 602-942-3000
Mobile Home Dealer/Broker/Seller #36 602-364-1003
Mobile Home Installer/Mfg. #36 ... 602-364-1003
Money Transmitter #5 ... 602-255-4421
Mortgage Banker, Commercial #5 ... 602-255-4421
Mortgage Banker/Broker #5 ... 602-255-4421
Motor Fuel Inspection #2 ... 602-771-4920
Motor Vehicle Dealer/Broker #75 ... 602-255-0072
Motor Vehicle Dealer/Sales Finance #5 602-255-4421
Motor Vehicle Dist/Import/Mfg/Whls #75 602-255-0072
Motor Vehicle Transporter #75 ... 602-255-0072
MRI License #66 ... 602-255-4845 x235
Nail Technician #12 ... 480-784-4539
Nail Technology Instruct'r/Sch'l/Salon #12 ... 480-784-4539
Native Plant Permit #33 ... 602-542-3578
Naturopathic Medical Asst. #19 ... 602-542-8242
Naturopathic Physician #19 ... 602-542-8242
Naturopathic School #19 ... 602-542-8242
Neuro Rehab Center #43 ... 602-364-3030
Notary Public #62 ... 602-542-4086
Nuclear Medicine Technologist #66 ... 602-255-4845 x242 or 243
Nurse-LPN/RN #20 ... 602-889-5150
Nurses' Aide #20 ... 602-889-5150
Nursing Care Inst. Administrator #68 ... 602-364-2273
Occupational Therapist/Assistant #21 ... 602-589-8352
Off-Track Betting Facility #54 ... 602-364-1700
On Site Worker/Superv'r #29 ... 602-364-4930
Open Burning Permit #39 ... 602-771-2338
Optical Establishment #14 ... 602-542-3095
Optician #14 ... 602-542-3095
Optometrist #22 ... 602-542-3095
Osteopathic Physician/Surgeon #23 ... 480-657-7703
Out-Patient Physical Therapy #43 ... 602-364-3030
Out-Patient Surgical Center #43 ... 602-364-3030
Outpatient Treatment Clinic #43 ... 602-364-3030
P&C Mgmt'g Agent, Life/Disability #51 ... 602-364-4457
Packer, Fruit/Vegetable #72 ... 602-542-0880
Pesticide Applicator/Supv./Advisor #18 ... 602-255-3664
Pesticide Company #18 ... 602-255-3664
Pesticide Custom Applicator #33 ... 602-542-0904
Pesticide Distribution/Registration #33 ... 602-542-0949
Pesticide Qualifying Party #18 ... 602-255-3664
Pesticide Seller #33 ... 602-542-0904
Pharmacist/Pharmacy Intern #24 ... 623-463-2727
Physical Therapist/Therapist Asst #25 ... 602-542-3095
Physician Assistant #17 ... 480-551-2700
Physiotherapist #11 ... 602-864-5088
Pipeline #56 ... 602-542-4576
Plant Operator #41 ... 602-771-4644
Podiatrist #26 ... 602-542-3095
Political Action Committee #62 ... 602-542-8683
Pollutant Discharge Permit #41 ... 602-771-4644
Post-Secondary Educ. Institution #6 ... 602-542-5709
Post-Secondary Voc. Program, Priv. #6 602-542-5709
Premium Finance Company #5 ... 602-255-4421
Pre-Need Endorsement, Establish't #15 602-542-3095
Pre-Need Salesperson #15 ... 602-542-3095
Preschool #45 ... 602-364-2539
Private Investigator #53 ... 602-223-2361
Process Server, Private #63 ... 602-364-2378
Produce Warehouse #46 ... 602-364-3118
Property Tax Agent #8 ... 602-542-1539
Psychiatric Unit #47 ... 602-364-2595
Psychologist #27 ... 602-542-8162
Public Accountant-CPA #7 ... 602-364-0804
Public Accounting Firm-CPA/PA #7 ... 602-364-0804
Radiation Handler #35 ... 602-255-4845
Radiation Machine #35 ... 602-255-4845
Radiation Machine Possession Facility #66 ... 602-255-4845 x231
Radiation Therapy Technologist #66 ... 602-255-4845 x242 or 243
Radioactive Material Possessor #66 ... 602-255-4845 x235
Radioactive Materials Lab #66 ... 602-255-4845 x246
Radiologic Techn'l'g't #66 ... 602-255-4845 x242 or 243
Radiologist #66 ... 602-255-4845 x242 or 243
Radiology Practical Technologist #66 ... 602-255-4845 x242 or 243
Radon Mitigation Specialist #66 ... 602-255-4845 x244
Real Estate Agent/Broker/Sales #55 ... 602-468-1414
Real Estate Appraiser #8 ... 602-542-1539
Real Estate Division #62 ... 602-542-1704
Real Estate Firm #55 ... 602-468-1414
Real Estate School Instructor #55 ... 602-468-1414
Real Estate School/Course #55 ... 602-468-1414
Recovery Center #49 ... 602-364-2536
Registered Medical Assistant #16 ... 602-542-3095
Rehabilitation Agency #43 ... 602-364-3030
Rehab Unit, Behavioral Health #47 ... 602-364-2595
Remediation Specialist #29 ... 602-364-4930
Renal Disease Facility #43 ... 602-364-3030
Rental of Personal Property #56 ... 602-542-4576
Respiratory Therapist #28 ... 602-542-5995
Restaurant/Bar #56 ... 602-542-4576
Retail Sales Outlet #56 ... 602-542-4576
Risk Management Producers #51 ... 602-364-4457
Sales Finance Company #5 ... 602-255-4421
Sanitarian #46 ... 602-364-3118
Savings and Loan, Chartered #5 ... 602-255-4421
Scanner, Electronic System #2 ... 602-771-4920
School Bus Driver #1 ... 602-223-2646
School Bus Driver Instructor #1 ... 602-223-2646
School Bus Transport Provider #1 ... 602-223-2646
School Librarian/Library Aide #38 ... 602-364-2450
School Psychologist #38 ... 602-364-2450
School Superintendent #38 ... 602-364-2450
School Supervisor #38 ... 602-364-2450
Scientific Collector #59 ... 602-942-3000
Securities Offering or Exemption #32 ... 602-542-4242
Securities Salesperson/Dealer #32 ... 602-542-4242
Security Guard #53 ... 602-223-2361
Seed Dealer #33 ... 602-542-0949
Seed Labeler #33 ... 602-542-0949
Self Insured Employer #60 ... 602-542-1839
Sewage/Sludge/Septic Pump Vehicle #40 ... 602-771-4153
Shooting Preserve #59 ... 602-942-3000
Slaughterhouse #34 ... 602-542-3578
Social Worker #10 ... 602-542-1864
Solar Energy Device #56 ... 602-542-4576
Solicitations by Charitable Org #62 ... 602-542-6670
Solid Waste Facility #40 ... 602-771-4153
Speech Pathology #43 ... 602-364-3030
Speech-Language Pathologist #49 ... 602-364-2536
Spray Process Applicator #65 ... 602-506-6010
Spray Process Sterilizer/Renovat'r #65 602-506-6010
Stock Pond #58 ... 602-771-8500
Subdivision Public Report #55 ... 602-468-1414
Substance Abuse Counselor #10 ... 602-542-1864
Substance Abuse Treatment Svc #47 ... 602-364-2595
Surety #51 ... 602-364-4457
Surplus Line Broker #51 ... 602-364-4457
Surveyor, Land #29 ... 602-364-4930
Tanning Facility #66 ... 602-255-4845 x235
Taxidermist #59 ... 602-942-3000
Teacher, Community College #31 ... 480-731-8437
Teacher, Elem./Sec'd'y/Special Ed #38 602-364-2450
Telemarketing Firm #62 ... 602-542-6670
Timbering #56 ... 602-542-4576
Timeshare Public Report #55 ... 602-468-1414
Timeshare/Condo Seller #55 ... 602-468-1414
Title Service Company, MVR #75 ... 602-255-0072
Tobacco Product Distributor #56 ... 602-542-4576
Traffic Survival School #75 ... 602-255-0072
Trailer Coach Park #65 ... 602-506-6970
Transporting/Towing Company #56 ... 602-542-4576
Trapper #59 ... 602-942-3000
Travel Agent, Limited #51 ... 602-364-4457
Treatment Clinic #43 ... 602-364-3030
Trust Company #5 ... 602-255-4421
Trust Div. of Chartered Financ'l Inst. #5 602-255-4421
Underground Storage/Recovery #58 ... 602-771-8500
Utility, Public #32 ... 602-542-4251
Vehicle Emission Fleet Insp. Sta. #42 ... 602-207-7007
Vehicle Emission Fleet Inspector #42 ... 602-207-7007
Vendor #56 ... 602-542-4576
Vendor/Concession on State Park Land #69 ... 602-542-4174
Veterinary Medicine/Surgery #64 ... 602-364-1738
Veterinary Premise (Hospital) #64 ... 602-364-1738
Veterinary Technician #64 ... 602-364-1738
Vocational Program #6 ... 602-542-5709
Vocational Rehabilitation #61 ... 602-542-3294
Wagering Facility #54 ... 602-364-1700
Waste Water Collect'n/Treat't/Constr'n #41 ... 602-771-4644
Waste Water Facility Operator #41 ... 602-771-4644
Waste Water Reuse #41 ... 602-771-4644
Water Collector/Dist./Treat't System #58 602-771-8500
Water Distribution Operator #41 ... 602-771-4644
Water Exchange #58 ... 602-771-8500
Water Quality Certification #41 ... 602-771-4644
Water Rights Assignment #58 ... 602-771-8500
Water Transporter, out of state #58 ... 602-771-8500
Watercraft Registration Agent #59 ... 602-942-3000
Weather Modification #58 ... 602-771-8500
Weighmaster, Public #2 ... 602-771-4920
Weights/Measure Rep./Svc. Agency #2 602-771-4920
Well Drilling Firm #58 ... 602-771-8500
Well Registration/Construction #58 ... 602-771-8500
White Amor Stocker #59 ... 602-942-3000
Wildlife Hobby License #59 ... 602-942-3000
Wildlife Holding Permit #59 ... 602-942-3000
Wildlife Rehab/Service #59 ... 602-942-3000
X-ray Supplier #66 ... 602-255-4845 x231
X-ray, Portable #43 ... 602-364-3030
Zoo #59 ... 602-942-3000

Arizona Licensing Agency Information

#1 Department of Public Safety, Student Transportation, PO Box 6638 - Mail Drop 1250, Phoenix, AZ 85005-6638; 602-223-2646, Fax- 602-223-2923. http://studenttransportation.azdps.gov/

#2 Department of Weights & Measures, 4425 W Olive, #134, Glendale, AZ 85302-3844; 602-771-4920 x7714935, Fax- 602-255-1950. http://azdwm.gov/

#3 Boxing Commission, 1110 W Washington, #260, Phoenix, AZ 85007; 602-364-1721, Fax- 602-364-1703. Hours- 8AM-5PM. http://az.gov/webapp/portal/displaycontent.jsp?id=1896

#4 Arizona State Lottery, PO Box 2913, 4740 E University Dr, Phoenix, AZ 85062-2913; 480-921-4400, Fax- 480-921-4512. www.arizonalottery.com

#5 Department of Financial institutions, 2910 N 44th St, #310, Phoenix, AZ 85018; 602-255-4421, Fax- 602-381-1225. Hours- 8AM-5PM.

http://azdfi.gov Search data at- http://azdfi.gov/Lists/Lists.htm Online or phone verifications ONLY.

#6 Board for Private Postsecondary Education, 1400 W Washington, Rm 260, Phoenix, AZ 85007; 602-542-5709, Fax- 602-542-1253. http://azppse.state.az.us

#7 Board of Accountancy, 100 N 15th Ave, #165, Phoenix, AZ 85007; 602-364-0804, Fax- 602-364-0903. www.azaccountancy.gov Search data at- www.azaccountancy.gov/scripts/BOAsearch.exe Lists of names and addresses available for $1.00 per name.

#8 Board of Appraisal, 1400 W Washington, #360, Phoenix, AZ 85007; 602-542-1539, Fax- 602-542-1598. www.appraisal.state.az.us Search data at- www.appraisal.state.az.us/directo ry/Default.aspx

#9 Board of Barbers, 1400 W Washington, #230, Phoenix, AZ 85007; 602-542-4498. http://boardofbarbers.az.gov/ Search data at- www.boardofbarbers.az.gov/dir.htm

#10 Board of Behavioral Health Examiners, 3443 N Central Ave #1700, Phoenix, AZ 85012; 602-542-1882, Fax- 602-364-0890. Hours- 8AM-5PM. www.bbhe.state.az.us Search data at- www.bbhe.state.az.us/verifications.htm A public record request form available at www.bbhe.state.az.us/public%20rec%20req.htm. Fee for verifications is $15.00; copies are $.25 each.

#11 Board of Chiropractic Examiners, 5060 N 19th Ave, #416, Phoenix, AZ 85015; 602-864-5088, Fax- 602-864-5099. Hours- 8AM-5PM. www.azchiroboard.com Search data at- www.azchiroboard.com/ASPSearch.htm Acupuncture and physiotherapy are certifications under a Chiropractic license.

#12 Board of Cosmetology, Information Services, 1721 E Broadway Rd, Tempe, AZ 85282; 480-784-4539, Fax- 480-784-4962. www.revenue.state.az.us/609/Cosmetology.html

#13 Board of Dental Examiners, 5060 N 19th Ave, #406, Phoenix, AZ 85015; 602-242-1492, Fax- 602-242-1445. Hours- 8AM-5PM. www.azdentalboard.org

#14 Board of Dispensing Opticians, 1400 W Washington, Rm 230, Phoenix, AZ 85007; 602-542-3095, Fax- 602-542-3093. Hours- 8AM-5PM. www.do.az.gov/

#15 Board of Funeral Directors & Embalmers, 1400 W Washington, #230, Phoenix, AZ 85007; 602-542-3095, Fax- 602-542-3093. www.funeralbd.state.az.us Search data at- www.funeralbd.state.az.us/dir.htm

#16 Board of Homeopathic Medical Examiners, 1400 W Washington, #230, Phoenix, AZ 85007; 602-542-3095 X4, Fax- 602-542-3093. Hours- 8AM-5PM M-TH; F by appointment. www.azhomeopathbd.az.gov A public records request must be completed.

#17 Board of Medical Examiners, 9545 E Doubletree Ranch Rd, Scottsdale, AZ 85258-5539; 480-551-2700, Fax- 480-551-2704. www.azmd.gov Search data at- www.azmd.gov/profile/getlicense.aspx Click on Doctor Search. Physician Assistant Board is also located here.

#18 Structural Pest Control Commission, 9535 E Doubletree Ranch Rd, Scottsdale, AZ 85258-5514; 602-255-3664, Fax- 602-255-1281. www.sb.state.az.us

#19 Board of Naturopathic Physicians Examiners, 1400 W Washington, #230, Phoenix, AZ 85007; 602-542-8242, Fax- 602-542-3093. www.npbomex.az.gov Licensing lookup may be under construction.

#20 Board of Nursing, 4747 N 7th St, #200, Phoenix, AZ 85014; 602-889-5150, Fax- 602-889-5155. www.azbn.gov Search data at- https://www.azbn.gov/OnlineVerification.aspx Can also find Imposter Alert at www.azbn.gov.

#21 Board of Occupational Therapy Examiners, 5060 N 19th Ave, #209, Phoenix, AZ 85015; 602-589-8352, Fax- 602-589-8354. www.occupationaltherapyboard.az.gov/ Search data at- www.occupationaltherapyboard.az.gov/ASPSearch.htm

#22 Board of Optometry, 1400 W Washington, #230, Phoenix, AZ 85007; 602-542-3095, Fax- 602-542-3093. www.optometry.az.gov

#23 Board of Osteopathic Medicine & Surgery Examiners, 9535 E Doubletree Ranch Rd, Scottsdale, AZ 85258-5539; 480-657-7703, Fax- 480-657-7715. www.azdo.gov/ Search data at- www.azdo.gov/

#24 Board of Pharmacy, 1700 W. Washington St, #250, Phoenix, AZ 85007; 602-771-2727, 866-915-7762, Fax- 602-771-2749. Hours- 8AM-5PM. www.pharmacy.state.az.us Search at- https://az.gov/app/pharmacy/search.xhtml

#25 Board of Physical Therapy, 4205 N 7th Ave, #208, Phoenix, AZ 85007; 602-274-0236, Fax- 602-274-1378. www.ptboard.state.az.us/public/ptays/home.asp

#26 Board of Podiatry Examiners, 1400 W Washington, #230, Phoenix, AZ 85007; 602-542-3095, Fax- 602-542-3093. www.podiatry.state.az.us Search data at- www.podiatry.state.az.us/dir.htm

#27 Board of Psychologist Examiners, 1400 W Washington St, #235, Phoenix, AZ 85007; 602-542-8162, Fax- 602-542-8279. Hours- 8AM-5PM. www.psychboard.az.gov Search data at- www.psychboard.az.gov/directory.htm Will sell lists.

#28 Board of Respiratory Care Examiners, 1400 W Washington, #200, Phoenix, AZ 85007; 602-542-5995, Fax- 602-542-5900. www.rb.state.az.us/ Search data at- https://az.gov/webapp/rce/respiratorycareexaminer/licensestatus/

#29 Board of Technical Registration, 1110 W Washington #240, Phoenix, AZ 85007; 602-364-4930, Fax- 602-364-4931. Hours- 8AM-5PM. www.btr.state.az.us Search data at- www.btr.state.az.us/listings/professional_registrant2.asp

#30 State Bar of Arizona, 4201 N 24th St, #200, Phoenix, AZ 85016-6288; 602-252-4804, Fax- 602-271-4930. www.azbar.org Search at- www.azbar.org/LegalResources/findlawyer.cfm

#31 Maricopa County Community College District, 2411 W 14th St, Tempe, AZ 85281; 480-731-8000, Fax- 480-731-8506. www.maricopa.edu/

#32 Registration Department, Securities Division, Corporation Commission, 1300 W Washington, 3rd Fl, Phoenix, AZ 85007; 602-542-4242, Fax- 602-594-7470. www.azcc.gov/divisions/securities/

#33 Department of Agriculture, Environmental Services Division, 1688 W Adams St, Phoenix, AZ 85007; 602-542-3578, Fax- 602-542-0466. Hours- 8AM-5PM. www.azda.gov/ESD/esd.htm Search data at- www.kellysolutions.com/az/

#34 Department of Agriculture, Animal Services Division, 1688 W Adams St, 1st Fl, Phoenix, AZ 85007; 602-542-4373. Hours- 8AM-5PM. www.azda.gov/ASD/asd.htm

#35 Radiation Regulatory Agency, 4814 S 40th St, Phoenix, AZ 85040; 602-255-4845, Fax- 602-437-0705. www.arra.state.az.us

#36 Department of Building & Fire Safety, 1110 W Washington, #100, Phoenix, AZ 85007; 602-364-1003, Fax- 602-364-1052. www.dbfs.state.az.us/

#37 Department of Health Services, Child Care Facility Licensing, 150 N 18th Ave, 4th Fl, Phoenix, AZ 85007; 602-364-2539, Fax- 602-364-4768. www.azdhs.gov/als/childcare/ Search data at- www.azdhs.gov/als/search/index.htm

#38 Department of Education, Teacher Certification Unit, PO Box 6490 (1535 W Jefferson St, Bin 34), Phoenix, AZ 85005-6490; 602-542-4367, Fax- 602-542-1141. Hours- 8AM-5PM. www.ade.az.gov/certification/ For all Verification requests except Charter Schools ask for Pat Lane.

#39 Department of Environmental Quality, Office of Air Quality, 1110 W Washington St, Phoenix, AZ 85007; 602-771-2338, Fax- 602-771-2299. www.azdeq.gov/environ/air/index.html

#40 Department of Environmental Quality, Office of Waste Programs, 1110 W Washington St, Phoenix, AZ 85007; 602-771-4208, Fax- 602-771-2302. www.azdeq.gov/environ/waste/index.html

#41 Department of Environmental Quality, Office of Water Quality, 1110 W Washington St, Phoenix, AZ 85007; 602-771-4644, Fax- 602-771-4634. www.azdeq.gov/environ/water/

#42 Department of Environmental Quality, Vehicle Emissions Section, 600 N 40th St, Phoenix, AZ 85008; 602-207-7007, Fax- 602-207-7020. www.azdeq.gov/environ/air/vei/

#43 Department of Health Services, Facilities Licensing, 150 N 18th Ave #450, Phoenix, AZ 85007-3245; 602-364-2536, Fax- 602-364-4806. www.azdhs.gov/als/ Search data at- www.azdhs.gov/als/index.htm

#44 Department of Health Services, Bureau of State Lab Services/Licensure/Cert, 250 N 17th Ave, Phoenix, AZ 85007; 602-542-1188, Fax- 602-364-0760. http://azdhs.gov/lab/

#45 Child Care Licensing, Division of Child Care, 150 N 18th Ave, 4th Fl, Phoenix, AZ 85007; 602-364-2539, Fax- 602-364-4768. www.azdhs.gov/als/childcare/ Search data at- http://hsapps.azdhs.gov/ls/sod/SearchProv.aspx?type=CC

#46 Department of Health Services, Food Safety and Environmental Services, 150 N 18th Ave, #430, Phoenix, AZ 85007; 602-364-3118, Fax- 602-364-3146. www.azdhs.gov/phs/oeh/fses/index.htm

#47 Department of Health Services, Office of Behavioral Health Licensure, 150 N18th Ave, #410, Phoenix, AZ 85007; 602-364-2595, Fax- 602-364-4801. www.azdhs.gov/als/behavior/ Search data at- www.azdhs.gov/als/databases/

#48 Department of Health Services, Bureau of EMS, 150 N 18th Ave, #540, Phoenix, AZ 85007; 602-364-3150, Fax- 602-364-3568. Hours- 8AM-5PM. www.azdhs.gov/bems/

#49 Department of Health Services, Division of Licensing Services, 150 N 18th Ave, Phoenix, AZ 85007; 602-364-2536, Fax- 602-364-4808. www.azdhs.gov/als/index.htm Search data at- www.azdhs.gov/als/search/index.htm

#50 Department of Health Services, Office of Women & Children, 150 N 18th Ave 4th Fl, Phoenix, AZ 85017-5253; 602-364-2079, Fax- 602-364-4769. www.azdhs.gov/als/midwife/ Search data at- www.azdhs.gov/als/databases/index.htm

#51 Department of Insurance, Licensing Section, 2910 N 44th St, #210, Phoenix, AZ 85018-7269; 602-364-4457, Fax- 602-364-4460. Hours- 8AM-4PM. www.id.state.az.us Lists available by completing a public records request and paying the appropriate fee.

#52 Department of Liquor License & Control, 800 W Washington, 5th Fl, Phoenix, AZ 85007; 602-542-5141, Fax- 602-542-5707. www.azliquor.gov/ Search data at- www.azliquor.gov/query/default.asp Search recently issued, expired, closed, suspended and inactive licenses at the website.

#53 Department of Public Safety, Security Guard & Private Investigator Licensing, PO Box 6328 (2102 W Encanto Blvd), Phoenix, AZ 85005-6328; 602-223-2361, Fax- 602-223-2938. www.azdps.gov/

#54 Department of Racing, Licensing Division, 1110 W Washington, #260, Phoenix, AZ 85007; 602-364-1700, Fax- 602-364-1703. www.racing.state.az.us

#55 Department of Real Estate, 2910 N 44th St, #100, Phoenix, AZ 85018; 602-771-7700, Fax- 602-468-0562. Hours- 8AM-5PM. www.re.state.az.us Search data at- http://159.87.254.2/publicdatabase/SearchIndividuals.aspx?mode=2 Download lists of RE companies and individuals free at http://159.87.254.2/publicdatabase/DownloadLists.aspx. Sites that provide information lookup and license management services is www.re.state.az.us/ONLINE_SERVICES.html.

#56 Department of Revenue, License & Registration, 1600 W Monroe, 1st Fl, Phoenix, AZ 85007-2650; 602-542-4576. www.azdor.gov/609/Revenue.html

#57 Department of Transportation, Aeronautics Division, PO Box 13588 (255 E Osborn Rd, #101), Phoenix, AZ 85002; 602-294-9144, Fax- 602-294-9141. www.azdot.gov/Aviation/

#58 Department of Water Resources, 3550 N Central Ave, Phoenix, AZ 85012; 602-771-8500, Fax- 602-771-8684. www.azwater.gov/dwr/

#59 Game & Fish Department, 5000 W Carefree Hwy, Phoenix, AZ 85086; 602-942-3000, Fax- 602-789-3921. Hours- 8AM-5PM. http://azgfd.com

#60 Division of Administration, Industrial Commission of Arizona, 800 W Washington, 3rd Fl, Phoenix, AZ 85007; 602-542-4654, Fax- 602-542-3070. www.ica.state.az.us/Divisions/adminSupport/selfInsurance.html

#61 Special Fund Division, Industrial Commission of Arizona, 800 W Washington, 4th Fl, Rm 401, Phoenix, AZ 85007; 602-542-3294, Fax- 602-542-3696. www.ica.state.az.us/Divisions/specialfund/index.html

#62 Secretary of State, 1700 W Washington St, 7th Fl, Phoenix, AZ 85007-2888; 602-542-4285, Fax- 602-542-1575. Hours- 8AM-5PM. www.azsos.gov Search lobbyists using the public body's name, the lobbyist's name or the lobbyist's employee's name.

#63 Supreme Court, Certification and Licensing Division, 1501 W Washington St, #104, Phoenix, AZ 85007-3232; 602-364-2378, Fax- 602-364-0358. Hours- 8AM-5PM. www.supreme.state.az.us/cld/

#64 Veterinary Medical Examining Board, 1400 W Washington, #240, Phoenix, AZ 85007; 602-364-1738, Fax- 602-364-1039. www.vetbd.state.az.us Search data at- www.vetbd.state.az.us/directory/default.aspx

#65 Maricopa Environmental Services, 1001 N Central, #200, Phoenix, AZ 85004; 602-506-6623, Fax- 602-506-5141. Hours- 8AM-5PM. www.maricopa.gov/envsvc/

#66 Medical Radiologic Technology Board of Examiners, AZ Radiation Regulatory Agency (ARRA), 4814 S 40th St, Phoenix, AZ 85040-2940; 602-255-4845, Fax- 602-437-0705. Hours- 8AM-5PM. www.arra.state.az.us

#67 Office of the State Mine Inspector, 1700 W Washington, 4th Fl, Phoenix, AZ 85007-2805; 602-542-5971, Fax- 602-542-5335. www.asmi.state.az.us

#68 Nursing Care Board, 1400 W Washington, #B-8, Phoenix, AZ 85007; 602-364-2273. www.nciabd.state.az.us

#69 State Parks Board, 1300 W Washington, #221, Phoenix, AZ 85007; 602-542-4174, Fax- 602-542-4180. www.pr.state.az.us

#70 Registrar of Contractors, 3838 N Central Ave, #400, Phoenix, AZ 85012; 602-542-1525, Fax- 602-542-1599. www.rc.state.az.us Search data at- www.azroc.gov/clsc/AZROCLicenseQuery

#71 Department of Agriculture, State Agricultural Lab, 2422 W Holly, Phoenix, AZ 85009; 602-253-1920. Hours- 8AM-5PM. www.azda.gov/SAL/stateag.htm

#72 Department of Agriculture, Citrus, Fruit and Vegetable Standardization, 1688 W Adams St, 3rd Fl, Phoenix, AZ 85007; 602-542-4373. Hours- 8AM-5PM. www.azda.gov/CFV/cf&v.htm

#73 Division of Occupational Safety and Health, Industrial Commission of Arizona, 800 W Washington, 2nd Fl, Phoenix, AZ 85007; 602-542-5795, Fax- 602-542-1614. Hours- 8AM-5PM. www.ica.state.az.us/Divisions/osha/index.html

#74 Department of Economic Security, Division of Children, Youth and Families- Foster Care & Adoption, PO Box 6123, 1789 W Jefferson, Site Code 940A, Phoenix, AZ 85007; 877-543-7633, 542-5499. https://www.azdes.gov/dcyf/adoption/

#75 Department of Transportation, Motor Vehicle Division, PO Box 2100, Phoenix, AZ 85001; 602-255-0072. Hours- 8AM-5PM. www.dot.state.az.us/MVD/mvd.htm

#76 Geological Survey, Department of Revenue, 416 W Congress, #100, Tucson, AZ 85701; 520-770-3500, Fax- 520-770-3505. Hours- 8AM-5PM. www.azgs.state.az.us

#77 Acupuncture Board of Examiners, 1400 W Washington, #230, Phoenix,, AZ 85007; 602-542-3095, Fax- 602-542-3093. www.azacuboard.az.gov/ Search data at- www.azacuboard.az.gov/ASPSearch.htm

Arizona Federal Courts

The following list indicates the district and division name for each county in the state. If the bankruptcy court location is different from the district court, then the location of the bankruptcy court appears in parentheses.

County/Court Cross Reference

County	Court
Apache	Prescott (Phoenix)
Cochise	Tucson
Coconino	Prescott (Phoenix)
Gila	Phoenix
Graham	Tucson
Greenlee	Tucson
La Paz	Phoenix (Yuma)
Maricopa	Phoenix
Mohave	Prescott (Yuma)
Navajo	Prescott (Phoenix)
Pima	Tucson
Pinal	Phoenix (Tucson)
Santa Cruz	Tucson
Yavapai	Prescott (Prescott Valley)
Yuma	Phoenix (Yuma)

Standards for Federal Courts: Fees are standard unless noted in profile. Search fee is $26.00 per item (one party name or case number). Copy fee is $.50 per page. Certification fee is $9.00 per document, double for exemplification, if available. Most courts require prepayment. Mail requests should enclose a SASE unless otherwise noted. Before releasing records, all courts require prepayment, unless noted.

District courts index by defendant and plaintiff and by case number. Bankruptcy courts usually index by debtor and case number. While most courts now have their indexes on computer, many may still maintain index card files as well. Courts will archive closed case files at different times.

There are numerous public access programs available to online subscribers. Search the U.S. Party/Case Index to find party names and case numbers among all courts. Individual case data is provided on PACER. A search of CM/ECF provides copies of cases filed electronically. For details about PACER, the US Party/Case Index, and CM/ECF see the Appendix, go to http://pacer.psc.uscourts.gov, or call 800-676-6856.

US District Court District of Arizona

Phoenix Division Court Clerk, 401 W Washington St, SPC 1, Ste 130, Phoenix, AZ 85003-2118, 602-322-7200; Fax- 602-322-7209. Hours- 8:30AM-5PM. www.azd.uscourts.gov

Counties/Note: Gila, La Paz, Maricopa, Pinal, Yuma. This office manages the Prescott Division records. Some Yuma cases handled by San Diego Division of the Southern District of California.

Searches/Indexing: Include name and DOB or approx. date in search request; clerk may then determine a match. Results do not include SSN or DOB. Will not fax back documents. New cases are in the index 2-3 days after filing date. Computer index maintained; criminal back to 1990. Case files sent to archives 5 years after closed.

Search Access: Only docket info available by phone. **Mail:** Search usually completed- 3-5 days. Include SASE for return. **Fax:** Fax search requests accepted. **In person:** 2 public access terminals in lobby provide docket access. No self-serve copier.

Payment: Pay by Visa/MC/AmEx/Discover, money order, cashier's check, business checks. In state personal checks also accepted. Payee: Clerk, US District Court.

E-Services: PACER records go back to 1992. New records online after 1 day. ECF at https://ecf.azd.uscourts.gov. **Opinions Online:** www.azd.uscourts.gov. Click on Cases of Interest. Published Opinions are also available via the webpage. **Online Note:** Access to court calendars at www.azd.uscourts.gov.

Prescott Division Court Clerk, 101 W Goodwin St, US Post Office Bldg, Prescott, AZ 86303, 928-445-6598; 602-322-7200-Phoenix; Phoenix recs 602-322-7205 www.azd.uscourts.gov

Counties/Note: Apache, Coconino, Mohave, Navajo, Yavapai. Currently, this is an unmanned office; direct record requests to the Phoenix Div.

Searches/Indexing: Include SSN or DOB in search request for identification. Results do not include SSN or DOB. Will not fax back documents. Open records located at Phoenix Div.

Search Access: **Mail:** SASE not required. **Fax:** Fax search requests accepted. **In person:** No self-serve copier.

Payment: Pay by Visa/MC/AmEx/Discover, money order, cashier's check, business checks. In state personal checks also accepted. Payee: Clerk, US District Court.

E-Services: ECF at https://ecf.azd.uscourts.gov. **Opinions Online:** www.azd.uscourts.gov. Click on Cases of Interest. Published Opinions are also available via the webpage. **Online Note:** Access to court calendars at www.azd.uscourts.gov.

Tucson Division Court Clerk, US Court House, 405 W Congress St, Ste 1500, Tucson, AZ 85701-5010, 520-205-4200; Fax- 520-205-4209. Hours- 8:30AM-5PM. www.azd.uscourts.gov

Counties/Note: Cochise, Graham, Greenlee, Pima, Santa Cruz. The Globe Division was closed effective 1/1994, and all case records for that division are now found at Tucson.

Searches/Indexing: Include name and DOB or approx. date in search request; clerk may then determine a match. Results do not include SSN or DOB. Will not fax back documents. New cases are in the index 2-3 days after filing date. Computer index maintained; criminal back to 1990. Electronic files might only indicate year of birth. Records available electronically only. Case files sent to archives 5 years after closed.

Search Access: Only docket info available by phone. **Mail:** Search usually completed- 1-2 days. SASE not required. **Fax:** Fax search requests accepted. **In person:** 5 public terminals available. No self-serve copier. A copy service may be used in lieu of court staff; copy service has a 1 day turnaround.

Payment: Pay by Visa/MC/AmEx/Discover, money order, cashier's check, business checks. In state personal checks also accepted. Payee: Clerk, US District Court.

E-Services: PACER records go back to 1992. New records online after 1 day. ECF at https://ecf.azd.uscourts.gov. **Opinions Online:** www.azd.uscourts.gov. Click on Cases of Interest. Published Opinions are also available via the webpage. **Online Note:** Access to court calendars at www.azd.uscourts.gov.

US Bankruptcy Court District of Arizona

Phoenix Division Court Clerk, 230 N First Ave, # 101, Phoenix, AZ 85003, 602-682-4000, 800-556-9230. 9AM-4PM. www.azb.uscourts.gov

Counties/Note: Apache, Coconino, Gila, Maricopa, Navajo.

Searches/Indexing: Include case number and name in search requests; also filing date and doc titles. Results include last 4 SSN digits only. Will not fax back documents. New cases are in the index immediately after filing date. Closed case files kept 6 months; electronic files kept indefinitely.

Search Access: Docket info available by phone. Voice Case Information Service available, call VCIS at 602-682-4001 or 888-549-5336. **Mail:** Search usually completed- 1 week. Include SASE for return. **In person:** 5 public terminals available. No self-serve copier.

Payment: Pay by money order, cashier's check, business check, debit card. No personal checks or credit cards. Payee: Clerk, US Bankruptcy Court. Copies made off of computer- $.10 each.

E-Services: PACER records go back to 1986. New records online immediately. ECF at https://ecf.azb.uscourts.gov. **Opinions Online:** www.azb.uscourts.gov/Opinions/Opinions.aspx. **Online Note:** Judge's court calendars free at www.azb.uscourts.gov. Also, search unclaimed funds list free at www.azb.uscourts.gov/UnclaimedFunds.aspx.

Prescott Valley Div Court Clerk, 3001 N. Main St, Ste 2E, Prescott Valley, AZ 86314, 602-682-4000, 800-556-9230. www.azb.uscourts.gov

Counties/Note: Yavapai County. Court is held monthly. Check the Court Calendars section for Chief Judge Redfield T Baum's Prescott calendar. Records at Phoenix Division.

Searches/Indexing: Include case number and name in search requests; also filing date and doc titles. Results include last 4 SSN digits only. Will not fax back documents. New cases are in the index immediately after filing date. Closed case files kept 6 months; electronic files kept indefinitely.

Search Access: Docket info available by phone. Voice Case Information Service available **Mail:** Search usually completed- 1 week. Include SASE for return. **In person:** No self-serve copier.

Payment: Pay by money order, cashier's check, business check, debit card. No personal checks or credit cards. Payee: Clerk, US Bankruptcy Court. Copies made off of computer- $.10 each.

E-Services: PACER records go back to 1986. New records online immediately. ECF at https://ecf.azb.uscourts.gov. **Opinions Online:** www.azb.uscourts.gov/Opinions/Opinions.aspx. **Online Note:** Judge's court calendars free at www.azb.uscourts.gov. Also, search unclaimed funds list free at www.azb.uscourts.gov/UnclaimedFunds.aspx.

Tucson Division Court Clerk, 38 S Scott Ave #100, Tucson, AZ 85701-1608, 520-202-7500, 800-556-9224. 9AM-4PM. www.azb.uscourts.gov

Counties/Note: Cochise, Graham, Greenlee, Pima, Pinal, Santa Cruz.

Searches/Indexing: Include case number and name in search requests; also filing date and doc titles. Results include last 4 SSN digits only. Will not fax back documents. New cases are in the index immediately after filing date. Records also indexed by adversary case number, if applicable. A master list of creditors available for each case back to 1995. Closed case files kept 6 months; electronic files kept indefinitely.

Search Access: Only docket and cover sheet info is released via phone. Voice Case Information Service available, call VCIS at 888-549-5336. **Mail:** Search usually completed- 24 hours. Include SASE for return. **In person:** 1 public terminal available. No self-serve copier. Copies obtained at the Office of the Bankruptcy Clerk or through an off-site copy service.

Payment: Pay by money order, cashier's check, business check, debit card. No personal checks or credit cards. Payee: Clerk, US Bankruptcy Court. Copies made off of computer- $.10 each.

E-Services: PACER records go back to 1914. New records online immediately. ECF at https://ecf.azb.uscourts.gov. **Opinions Online:** www.azb.uscourts.gov/Opinions/Opinions.aspx. **Online Note:** Judge's court calendars free at www.azb.uscourts.gov. Also, search unclaimed funds list free at www.azb.uscourts.gov/UnclaimedFunds.aspx.

Yuma Division Court Clerk, 325 W 19th St, Ste. D, Yuma, AZ 85364, 928-783-2288; records-928-783-2289; 9AM-4PM. www.azb.uscourts.gov

Counties/Note: La Paz, Mohave, Yuma.

Searches/Indexing: Include case number and name in search requests; also filing date and doc titles. Results include last 4 SSN digits only. Will not fax back documents. New cases are in the index immediately after filing date. Closed case files kept 6 months; electronic files kept indefinitely.

Search Access: Docket info available by phone. Voice Case Information Service available, call VCIS at 888-549-5336. **Mail:** Search usually completed- 1-2 days. Include SASE for return. **In person:** 1 public terminal available. No self-serve copier.

Payment: Pay by money order, cashier's check, business check, debit card. No personal checks or credit cards. Payee: Clerk, US Bankruptcy Court. Copies made off of computer- $.10 each.

E-Services: PACER records go back to the mid 1980's. New records online immediately. ECF at https://ecf.azb.uscourts.gov. **Opinions Online:** www.azb.uscourts.gov/Opinions/Opinions.aspx. **Online Note:** Judge's court calendars free at www.azb.uscourts.gov. Also, search unclaimed funds list free at www.azb.uscourts.gov/UnclaimedFunds.aspx.

Arizona County Courts

Court	Jurisdiction	No. of Courts	How Organized
Superior Courts*	General	15	15 Counties
Justice of the Peace Courts*	Limited	79	79 Precincts
Municipal Courts	Municipal	85	

* Profiled in this Sourcebook.

Court	CIVIL								
	Tort	Contract	Real Estate	Min. Claim	Max. Claim	Small Claims	Estate	Eviction	Domestic Relations
Superior Court*	X	X	X	$5000	No Max		X	X	
Justice of the Peace Courts*	X	X	X	$0	$10,000	$2500		X	X
Municipal Courts									X

Court	CRIMINAL				
	Felony	Misdemeanor	DWI/DUI	Preliminary Hearing	Juvenile
Superior Court*	X	X			X
Justice of the Peace Courts*		X	X	X	
Municipal Courts		X	X		

Administration

Administrative Office of the Courts, Arizona Supreme Court Bldg, 1501 W Washington, Phoenix, AZ, 85007; 602-452-3300. (MST - Except for a very few scattered exceptions, Arizona does not observe DST.) www.supreme.state.az.us

Court Structure

Superior Court is the court of general jurisdiction. Justice Courts and Municipal Courts generally have separate jurisdiction based on case types as indicated in the text. Estate cases are handled by Superior Court. Justice Courts accept civil actions up to $10.000 due to higher value claims in landlord/tenant cases. Civil cases between $5,000 and $10,000 may be filed at either Justice Courts or Superior Courts.

Online Access

The Public Access to Court Case Information is a valuable web service providing a resource for information about court cases from 153 of 180 courts in Arizona. Courts not covered include certain parts of Pima, Yavapai, Mohave, and Maricopa counties. Information includes detailed case information (i.e., case type, charges, filing and disposition dates), the parties in the case (not including victims and witnesses), and the court mailing address and location. Go to www.supreme.state.az.us/publicaccess/notification/default.asp.

A convenient online Maricopa County search site for free Superior Court criminal, civil, probate, and family case record, and for Justice Court case docket data is at www.superiorcourt.maricopa.gov/Docket/.

Opinions from the Supreme Court and Court of Appeals are available from the home page.

Searching Tips, Fees, and Other Guidelines

Justice Courts accept civil actions up to $10,000 due to higher value claims in landlord/tenant cases. Civil cases between $5,000 and $10,000 may be filed at either Justice Courts or Superior Courts.

Many offices do not perform searches due to personnel or budget constraints. As computerization of record offices increases across the state, more record offices are providing public access computer terminals.

Fees across all jurisdictions as established by the Arizona Supreme Court and state legislature are as follows: search- Superior Court: $26.00 per name, lower courts: $24.00 per name; certification- Superior Court: $26.00 per document, lower courts: $24.00 per document; copies- $.50 per page. Note that some courts may choose to charge no fees or a different fee.

Be aware that in some courts, when a clerk is given a specific docket or case number to pull the clerk is charging a "search fee" although no searching is performed. Useful advice from several of AZ PIs and record researchers is to bring a copy of the law in hand when visiting certain courts.

Maricopa County court case indexes is available at a central location - 1 W. Madison Ave in downtown Phoenix. The Justice Court docket index is available on public access terminals for all Justice Courts. Data can be viewed only, cannot be printed. Copies, however, must be obtained from the court where the case is heard. Most courts will search their records by plaintiff or defendant. Fees are the same as for civil and criminal case searching.

Apache County

Superior Court PO Box 365, St Johns, AZ 85936; 928-337-7550; probate phone: same; fax: 928-337-2771; 8AM-5PM. ***Felony, Civil Actions over $10,000, Probate.***
www.co.apache.az.us/clerk
Civil Records: Access: Mail, in person, online. Both court and visitors may perform in person searches. Search fee: $26.00 per name. Required to search: name, years to search; also helpful: address. Civil cases indexed by defendant, plaintiff, on computer and docket books. Mail turnaround time 3 days. Civil PAT goes back to 1995. Online access to records from 1995 forward is free at www.supreme.state.az.us/publicaccess/notification/default.asp. Also, access monthly court calendar free at www.apacheclerk.net/calendar.htm
Criminal Records: Access: Mail, in person, online. Both court and visitors may perform in person searches. Search fee: $26.00 per name. Add $5.00 if no SASE or not a toll free fax. Required to search: name, years to search, DOB; also helpful: address, SSN. Criminal records on computer and docket books. Mail turnaround time 3 days. Criminal PAT goes back to same as civil. Online access to records from 1995 forward is free at www.supreme.state.az.us/publicaccess/. Also, access monthly court calendar free at www.apacheclerk.net/calendar.htm Online results show middle initial, DOB.
General Information: No juvenile dependencies, mental health, victims, sealed or adoption records released. Will fax out docs $5.00 each. Court makes copy: $.50 per page, self serve same. Certification fee: $26.00 per doc. Payee: Clerk of the Court. Business checks accepted. Credit cards accepted. Prepayment required. Mail requests: SASE required.

Chinle Justice Court PO Box 888, US Hwy 191 MP 447, Chinle, AZ 86503; 928-674-5922; fax: 928-674-5926; 8AM-5PM. ***Misdemeanor, Civil Actions under $10,000, Eviction, Small Claims.***
Civil Records: Access: Fax, mail, in person, online. Both court and visitors may perform in person searches. Search fee: $24.00 per name. Required to search: name, years to search; also helpful: address. Civil cases indexed by defendant. Civil index in docket books from 1977, computerized back to 2000. Mail turnaround time 1-2 days. Civil PAT goes back to 2000. Access to the docket is free at www.supreme.state.az.us/publicaccess/notification/search.asp.
Criminal Records: Access: Fax, mail, in person, online. Both court and visitors may perform in person searches. Search fee: $24.00 per name. Required to search: name, years to search; also helpful: address, DOB, SSN. Criminal docket on books from 1977, computerized back to 2000. Note: Phone access is discouraged. Mail turnaround time 1-2 days. Criminal PAT goes back to same as civil. Access to the docket is free at www.supreme.state.az.us/publicaccess/notification/search.asp.
General Information: No juvenile, mental health, victims, sealed or adoption records released. Fee to fax out file $1.25 per page. Court makes copy: $.50 per page, self serve same. Certification fee: $24.00 per doc. Payee: Chinle Justice Court. Business checks accepted. No credit cards accepted. Prepayment required. Mail requests: SASE required.

Puerco Justice Court PO Box 610, Sanders, AZ 86512; 928-688-2954; fax: 928-688-2244; 8AM-N, 1-5PM. ***Misdemeanor, Civil Actions under $10,000, Eviction, Small Claims.***
Civil Records: Access: Mail, in person, online. Only the court performs in person searches; visitors may not. Search fee: $24.00 per name. Required to search: name, years to search; also helpful: address, case number. Civil cases indexed by defendant. Civil index on docket books prior to 3/1996. Mail turnaround time ASAP. Access to the docket is free at www.supreme.state.az.us/publicaccess/notification/search.asp.
Criminal Records: Access: Mail, in person, online. Only the court performs in person searches; visitors may not. Search fee: $24.00 per name. Required to search: name, years to search, DOB; also helpful: address, SSN, case number. Criminal docket on books prior to 3/1996. Mail turnaround time ASAP. Access to the docket is free at www.supreme.state.az.us/publicaccess/notification/search.asp.
General Information: No juvenile, mental health, victims, sealed or adoption records released. Court makes copy: $.50 per page. Certification fee: $24.00 per doc. Payee: Puerco Justice Court. Only cashiers checks and money orders accepted. No credit cards. Prepayment required. Mail requests: SASE required.

Round Valley Justice Court PO Box 1356, Springerville, AZ 85938; 928-333-4613; criminal fax: 928-333-4205; civil fax: same; 8AM-N, 1-5PM. ***Misdemeanor, Civil Actions under $10,000, Eviction, Small Claims.***
Civil Records: Access: Phone, fax, mail, in person, online. Both court and visitors may perform in person searches. Search fee: $24.00 per name. Required to search: name, years to search; also helpful: address. Civil cases indexed by defendant, plaintiff; index in docket books from 1990, computerized since 2/96. Mail turnaround time 5 working days. Access to the docket is free at www.supreme.state.az.us/publicaccess/notification/search.asp.
Criminal Records: Access: Phone, fax, mail, in person, online. Both court and visitors may perform in person searches. Search fee: $24.00 per name. Required to search: name, years to search; also helpful: address, DOB, SSN. Criminal docket on books from 1990, computerized since 2/96. Mail turnaround time 5 working days. Access to the docket is free at www.supreme.state.az.us/publicaccess/notification/search.asp.
General Information: No juvenile, mental health, victims, sealed or adoption records released. Will not fax documents. Court makes copy: $.50 per page, self serve same. Certification fee: $24.00 per doc. Payee: Round Valley Justice Court. Only cashiers checks and money orders accepted. No credit cards accepted. Prepayment required. Mail requests: SASE required.

St Johns Justice Court PO Box 308, St Johns, AZ 85936; 928-337-7558; criminal fax: 928-337-2683; civil fax: same; 8AM-5PM. ***Misdemeanor, Civil Actions under $10,000, Eviction, Small Claims.***
Civil Records: Access: Mail, in person, online. Only the court performs in person searches; visitors may not. Search fee: $24.00 per name. Required to search: name, years to search; also helpful: address. Civil cases indexed by defendant. Civil records on computer since 1996. Mail turnaround time 48 hours. Access to the docket is free at www.supreme.state.az.us/publicaccess/notification/search.asp.
Criminal Records: Access: Mail, in person, online. Only the court performs in person searches; visitors may not. Search fee: $24.00 per name. Required to search: name, years to search, DOB; also helpful: address, SSN. Criminal records on computer since 1996. Mail turnaround time 48 hours. Access to the docket is free at www.supreme.state.az.us/publicaccess/notification/search.asp. Online results show middle initial, DOB.
General Information: No juvenile, mental health, victims, sealed or adoption records released. Will fax documents. Court makes copy: $.50 per page. Certification fee: $24.00 per doc. Only cashiers checks and money orders accepted. No credit card. Prepayment required. Mail requests: SASE required.

Cochise County

Superior Court PO Box CK, 100 Quality Hill St, Bisbee, AZ 85603; 520-432-8604; fax: 520-432-4850; 8AM-5PM. ***Felony, Civil Actions over $5,000, Probate.*** www.co.cochise.az.us/Court/
A court records request form is available at www.co.cochise.az.us/E_Forms/Court/CourtRecordRequest.aspx. Search fee includes both civil and criminal indexes.
Civil Records: Access: Fax, mail, in person, online. Both court and visitors may perform in person searches. Search fee: $26.00 per name per year. Required to search: name, years to search. Civil cases indexed by defendant, plaintiff, on computer since 1996 and on index books from 1881 to present. Mail turnaround time 7-14 days. Civil PAT goes back to 1996. Access to the docket is free at www.supreme.state.az.us/publicaccess/notification/search.asp.
Criminal Records: Access: Fax, mail, in person, online. Both court and visitors may perform in person searches. Search fee: $26.00 per name. Per every 5 years. Required to search: name, years to search; also helpful: DOB, SSN. Criminal records on computer since 1996; prior records on index books. Mail turnaround time 7-14 days. Criminal PAT goes back to same as civil. Access docket free at www.supreme.state.az.us/publicaccess/notification/search.asp. Online results- middle initial, DOB.
General Information: No juvenile, mental health, victims, sealed or adoption records released. Fee to fax document $.50 per page. Court makes copy: $.50 per page. Certification fee: $26.00 per doc. Payee: Clerk of Superior Court. No personal checks accepted. Visa/MC accepted in person only. Prepayment required. Mail requests: SASE required.

Benson Justice Court 126 W 5th St, #1, Benson, AZ 85602; 520-586-8100; criminal phone: 520-586-8106; civil phone: 520-586-8103; criminal fax: 520-586-9647; civil fax: same; 8AM-5PM. ***Misdemeanor, Civil Actions under $10,000, Eviction, Small Claims.*** www.co.cochise.az.us/court/
Civil Records: Access: Fax, mail, in person, online. Only the court performs in person searches; visitors may not. Search fee: $24.00 per name. Required to search: name, years to search; also helpful: address. Civil cases indexed by defendant, plaintiff, go back to 1997. Mail turnaround time 7-10 days. Access the docket free at www.supreme.state.az.us/publicaccess/notification/search.asp.
Criminal Records: Access: Fax, mail, in person, online. Only the court performs in person searches; visitors may not. Search fee: $24.00 per name. Required to search: name, years to search; also helpful: address, DOB, SSN. Criminal records go back to 1997. Mail turnaround time 1-3 days. Access to the docket is free at www.supreme.state.az.us/publicaccess/notification/search.asp. Online results show middle initial, DOB.
General Information: No juvenile, mental health, victims, sealed records released. No fee to fax documents. Court makes copy: $.50 per page. Certification fee: $24.00 per doc. Payee: Benson Justice Court. No personal checks accepted without DR ID. Major credit cards accepted. Prepayment required. Mail requests: SASE required.

Bisbee Justice Court 207 N Judd Dr, Bisbee, AZ 85603; 520-432-9542; criminal: 520-432-9540; fax: 520-432-5271; 8AM-5PM. ***Misdemeanor, Civil Actions under $10,000, Eviction, Small Claims.***
www.co.cochise.az.us/court/
Civil Records: Access: Fax, mail, in person, online. Only the court performs in person searches; visitors may not. Search fee: $24.00 per name. Required to search: name, years to search; also helpful: address. Civil cases indexed by defendant, plaintiff, on computer from 1992. Some records on dockets. Mail turnaround time 1-7 days. Access to the docket is free at www.supreme.state.az.us/publicaccess/notification/search.asp.
Criminal Records: Access: Fax, mail, in person, online. Only the court performs in person searches; visitors may not. Search fee: $24.00 per name. Required to search: name, years to search; also helpful: address, DOB, SSN. Criminal records computerized from 7/92. Some records on dockets; computerized records since 1992. Mail turnaround time 1-7 days. Access to the docket is free at www.supreme.state.az.us/publicaccess/notification/search.asp.
General Information: No juvenile, mental health, victims, sealed or adoption records released. No fee to fax documents. Court makes copy: $.50 per page. Certification fee: $24.00 per doc. Payee: Bisbee Justice Court #1. No personal checks accepted. Visa/MC accepted. Prepayment required. Mail requests: SASE required.

Bowie Justice Court PO Box 317, Bowie, AZ 85605; 520-847-2303; criminal fax: 520-847-2242; civil fax: same; 8AM-5PM. ***Misdemeanor, Civil Actions under $10,000, Eviction, Small Claims.***
www.co.cochise.az.us/court/

Civil Records: Access: Phone, fax, mail, in person, online. Only the court performs in person searches; visitors may not. Search fee: $24.00 per name. Required to search: name, years to search; also helpful: address. Civil cases indexed by defendant. Civil records on computer from 7/85, some from 1994. Files maintained for 5 years after closure. Mail turnaround time 7 days. Access the docket free at www.supreme.state.az.us/publicaccess/notification/search.asp.
Criminal Records: Access: Phone, fax, mail, in person, online. Only the court performs in person searches; visitors may not. Search fee: $24.00 per name. Required to search: name, years to search, DOB; also helpful: address, SSN. Criminal records computerized from 1989. Files maintained for 5 years after closure. Mail turnaround time 1-3 days. Access to the docket is free at www.supreme.state.az.us/publicaccess/notification/search.asp.
General Information: No juvenile, mental health, victims, sealed or adoption records released. Will fax documents $2.00 per page. Court makes copy: $.50 per page. Certification fee: $24.00 per doc. Payee: Bowie Justice Court. Cashiers checks and money orders accepted. Credit cards accepted. Prepayment required. Mail requests: SASE required.

Douglas Justice Court 661 G Ave, Douglas, AZ 85607; 520-805-5640; fax: 520-364-3684; 8AM-5PM. ***Misdemeanor, Civil Actions under $10,000, Eviction, Small Claims.***
www.co.cochise.az.us/court/
Civil Records: Access: Fax, mail, in person, online. Both court and visitors may perform in person searches. Search fee: $24.00 per name. Required to search: name, years to search; also helpful: address. Civil cases indexed by defendant, plaintiff, on computer from 1991. Some records on dockets. Mail turnaround time 7-10 days. Civil PAT goes back to - traffic records 1 year, then file destroyed. PAT results show middle initial, DOB. Terminal results also show SSNs. Access to the docket is free at www.supreme.state.az.us/publicaccess/notification/search.asp.
Criminal Records: Access: Fax, mail, in person, online. Both court and visitors may perform in person searches. Search fee: $24.00 per name. Required to search: name, years to search, DOB; also helpful: address, SSN. Criminal records computerized from 1990. Some records on dockets. Mail turnaround time 7-10 days. Criminal PAT goes back to 5 years, then file destroyed. PAT results show middle initial, DOB. Terminal results include SSN. Access docket free at www.supreme.state.az.us/publicaccess/notification/search.asp. Online results show middle initial, DOB.
General Information: No juvenile, mental health, victims, sealed or adoption records released. Fee to fax out certified document is $.50 per page. Court makes copy: $.50 per page, self serve same. Certification fee: $24.00 per doc. Payee: Douglas Justice Court. Personal checks accepted. Credit cards accepted. Prepayment required. SASE not required.

Sierra Vista Justice Court 100 Colonia de Salud #108, Sierra Vista, AZ 85635; 520-803-3800/3801; criminal fax: 520-439-9106; civil fax: same; 8AM-5PM. ***Misdemeanor, Civil Actions under $10,000, Eviction, Small Claims.***
www.co.cochise.az.us/court/
Civil Records: Access: Fax, mail, in person, online. Only the court performs in person searches; visitors may not. Search fee: $24.00 per name. Required to search: name, years to search; also helpful: address. Civil cases indexed by plaintiff and defendant. Civil records on computer since 8/96. Note: In person access requires a written request. Mail turnaround time 3-7 days. PAT results show name only. Access docket free at www.supreme.state.az.us/publicaccess/notification/search.asp.
Criminal Records: Access: Fax, mail, in person, online. Only the court performs in person searches; visitors may not. Search fee: $24.00 per name. Required to search: name, years to search; also helpful: address, DOB, SSN. Criminal records by case number, on computer back to 8/1996. Note: In person access requires a written request. Mail turnaround time 3-7 days. PAT results show middle initial, DOB. Access to the docket is free at www.supreme.state.az.us/publicaccess/notification/search.asp. Online results show name, DOB.
General Information: Online identifiers in results same as on public terminal. No juvenile, mental health, victims, sealed, financial, or adoption records released. Will fax documents to local or toll free line. Court makes copy: $.50 per page. Certification fee: $24.00 per doc. Payee: Cochise County Treasurer. Personal checks accepted. Major credit cards except. Prepayment required. Mail requests: SASE required.

Willcox Justice Court 450 S Haskell, Willcox, AZ 85643; 520-384-7000; fax: 520-384-4305; 8AM-5PM. ***Misdemeanor, Civil Actions under $10,000, Eviction, Small Claims.***
www.co.cochise.az.us/court/
Civil Records: Access: Phone, fax, mail, in person, online. Both court and visitors may perform in person searches. Search fee: $24.00 per name. Required to search: name; also helpful: years to search, address. Civil cases indexed by defendant, plaintiff, index on computer from 1996. Physical records back to 2002. Mail turnaround time usually 1-5 days. Access the docket free at www.supreme.state.az.us/publicaccess/notification/search.asp.
Criminal Records: Access: Phone, fax, mail, in person, online. Both court and visitors may perform in person searches. Search fee: $24.00 per name. Required to search: name, DOB; also helpful: years to search, address, SSN. Criminal records computerized from 1996. Physical records back to 2001. Mail turnaround time usually 1-3 days. Access to the docket is free at www.supreme.state.az.us/publicaccess/notification/search.asp.
General Information: No juvenile, mental health, victims, sealed or adoption records released. No fee to fax documents. Court makes copy: $.50 per page. Certification fee: $24.00 per doc. Payee: Willcox Justice Court. Only cashiers checks and money orders accepted. Visa/MC accepted. Prepayment required. Mail requests: SASE required.

Coconino County

Superior Court 200 N San Francisco St, Flagstaff, AZ 86001; 928-779-6535; 8AM-5PM. ***Felony, Civil Actions over $5,000, Probate.***
Civil Records: Access: Mail, in person, online. Both court and visitors may perform in person searches. Search fee: $26.00 per name per year. Required to search: name, years to search; also helpful: address. Civil cases indexed by defendant. Civil records on handwritten ledger books from 1890. Some records on microfiche and dockets; computer from 1994. Mail turnaround time 2 weeks. Access to the docket is free at www.supreme.state.az.us/publicaccess/notification/search.asp.
Criminal Records: Access: Mail, in person, online. Both court and visitors may perform in person searches. Search fee: $26.00 per name per year. Required to search: name, years to search, DOB; also helpful: address, SSN. Criminal records on handwritten ledger books from 1890. Some records on microfiche and dockets; computer from 1994. Mail turnaround time 2 weeks. Access to the docket is free at www.supreme.state.az.us/publicaccess/notification/search.asp. Online results show middle initial, DOB.
General Information: No mental health, victims, sealed or adoption records released. Will not fax documents. Court makes copy: $.50 per page. Certification fee: $26.00 per doc. Payee: Clerk of Superior Court. Business checks accepted. No credit cards accepted. Prepayment required. Mail requests: SASE required.

Flagstaff Justice Court 200 N San Francisco St., Courthouse, 1st Fl, Flagstaff, AZ 86001; 928-779-6806; 8AM-5PM. ***Misdemeanor, Civil Actions under $10,000, Eviction, Small Claims.***
Civil Records: Access: Mail, fax, in person, online. Only the court performs in person searches; visitors may not. Search fee: $24.00 per name. Required to search: name, years to search; also helpful: address. Civil cases indexed by defendant, plaintiff; index on docket books. Will only maintain records for 5 years. Mail turnaround time 14-20 days. Access to the docket is free at www.supreme.state.az.us/publicaccess/notification/search.asp.
Criminal Records: Access: Mail, fax, in person, online. Only the court performs in person searches; visitors may not. Search fee: $24.00 per name per year. Required to search: name, years to search, DOB; also helpful: address, SSN. Criminal records on computer since 1987. Will only maintain records for 5 years. Mail turnaround time 14-20 days. Access to the docket is free at www.supreme.state.az.us/publicaccess/notification/search.asp.
General Information: No juvenile, mental health, victims, sealed or adoption records released. Will fax out documents no fee. Court makes copy: $.50 per page. Certification fee: $24.00 per doc. Payee: Flagstaff Justice Court. No Personal checks and major credit cards accepted. Prepayment required. Mail requests: SASE required.

Fredonia Justice Court PO Box 559, 112 N Main, Fredonia, AZ 86022-0559; 928-643-7472; fax: 928-643-7491; 8AM-5PM (closed noon hr). ***Misdemeanor, Civil Actions under $10,000, Eviction, Small Claims, Traffic.***
www.coconino.az.gov/courts.aspx?id=303
Civil Records: Access: Mail, in person, online. Only the court performs in person searches; visitors may not. Search fee: $24.00 per name. Required to search: name, years to search; also helpful: address. Civil cases indexed by number. Civil index on docket books. Will only maintain records for 5 years. Mail turnaround time 5 business days. Civil PAT available. PAT results show name, DOB. Public access terminal is located in local library adjacent to court. Access docket free at www.supreme.state.az.us/publicaccess/notification/search.asp.
Criminal Records: Access: Mail, in person, online. Only the court performs in person searches; visitors may not. Search fee: $24.00 per name. Required to search: name, years to search, DOB; also helpful: address, SSN. Criminal records for misdemeanors on computer from 1992, all others on docket books. Mail turnaround time 5 days from date received. Criminal PAT available.PAT results show name, DOB. Public access terminal is located in the local library adjacent to the court. Access to the docket is free at www.supreme.state.az.us/publicaccess/notification/search.asp. Online results show name, DOB.
General Information: Online identifiers in results same as on public terminal. No juvenile, mental health, victims, sealed or adoption records released. Will fax documents $1.00 per page. Court makes copy: $.50 per page. Certification fee: $24.00 per doc. Payee: Fredonia Justice Court. Only cashiers checks and money orders accepted. No credit cards accepted. Prepayment required. Mail requests: SASE required.

Page Justice Court PO Box 1565, Page, AZ 86040; 928-645-8871; criminal fax: 928-645-1869; civil fax: same; 8AM-5PM. ***Misdemeanor, Civil Actions under $10,000, Eviction, Small Claims.***
www.coconino.az.gov/courts.aspx
Civil Records: Access: Mail, in person, online. Only the court performs in person searches; visitors may not. Search fee: $24.00 per name. Required to search: name, years to search; also helpful: address. Civil cases indexed by defendant. Civil records on computer since 9/96; prior on docket books. Will only maintain records for 5 years. Mail turnaround time 5 days. Access to the docket is free at www.supreme.state.az.us/publicaccess/notification/search.asp.
Criminal Records: Access: Mail, in person, online. Only the court performs in person searches; visitors may not. Search fee: $24.00 per name. Required to search: name, years to search, DOB; also helpful: address, SSN. Criminal records for misdemeanors on computer from 1987, felony since 1991, all others on docket books. Mail turnaround time 5 days. Access to the docket is free at www.supreme.state.az.us/publicaccess/notification/search.asp.
General Information: No juvenile, mental health, victims, sealed or adoption records released. Will fax documents. Court makes copy: $.50 per page. Certification fee: $24.00 per doc. Payee: Page Justice Court. Cashiers checks and money orders accepted. Visa/MC accepted. Prepayment required. Mail requests: SASE required.

Williams Justice Court 700 W Railroad Ave, Williams, AZ 86046; 928-635-2691; fax: 928-635-4463; 8AM-N; 1-5PM. ***Misdemeanor, Civil Actions under $10,000, Eviction, Small Claims.*** www.coconino.az.gov/courts.aspx?id=311

Civil Records: Access: Mail, in person, online. Both court and visitors may perform in person searches. Search fee: $24.00 per name. Required to search: name, years to search; also helpful: address. Civil cases indexed by defendant, plaintiff; index on docket books. Will only maintain records for 5 years. Mail turnaround time 2-3 weeks. Civil PAT goes back to 3 years. Access to the docket is free at www.supreme.state.az.us/publicaccess/notification/search.asp.

Criminal Records: Access: Mail, in person, online. Both court and visitors may perform in person searches. Search fee: $24.00 per name. Required to search: name, years to search, DOB; also helpful: address, SSN. Criminal docket on books. Mail turnaround time 2-3 weeks. Criminal PAT goes back to 5 years. Access to the docket is free at www.supreme.state.az.us/publicaccess/notification/search.asp.

General Information: No juvenile, mental health, victims, sealed or adoption records released. Will not fax documents. Court makes copy: $1.25 per page. Certification fee: $24.00 per doc. Payee: Williams Justice Court. Only cashiers checks and money orders accepted. No credit cards accepted. Prepayment required. Mail requests: SASE required.

Gila County

Superior Court 1400 E Ash, Globe, AZ 85501; 928-425-3231 X8553; fax: 928-425-7802; 8AM-5PM. ***Felony, Civil Actions over $5,000, Probate.*** www.co.gila.az.us

Civil Records: Access: Mail, in person, online. Both court and visitors may perform in person searches. Search fee: $26.00 per name per year. Required to search: name, years to search; also helpful: address. Civil cases indexed by defendant, plaintiff, indexed on computer from 1982. On microfiche from 1913 to 1982. Some records on docket books and index cards. Mail turnaround time 10 days to 2 weeks. Access to the docket is free at www.supreme.state.az.us/publicaccess/notification/search.asp.

Criminal Records: Access: Mail, in person, online. Both court and visitors may perform in person searches. Search fee: $26.00 per name. Required to search: name, years to search, DOB; also helpful: address, SSN. Criminal records computerized from 1913. Mail turnaround time 10 days to 2 weeks. Access to the docket is free at www.supreme.state.az.us/publicaccess/notification/search.asp. Online results show middle initial, DOB.

General Information: Online identifiers in results same as on public terminal. No juvenile prior to June 1996, mental health, victims, sealed or adoption records released. Will not fax documents. Court makes copy: $.50 per page. Certification fee: $26.00 per doc. Exemplification- $36.00, Authentication- $54.00. Payee: Clerk of Superior Court. Personal checks accepted; credit cards are not. Prepayment required. Mail requests: SASE required.

Northern Regional Justice Court 714 S Beeline Hwy, #103, Payson, AZ 85541; 928-474-5267; criminal fax: 928-474-6214; civil fax: same; 8AM-5PM. ***Misdemeanor, Civil Actions under $10,000, Eviction, Small Claims.*** This court holds the records for the Pine Justice Court which is closed.

Civil Records: Access: Fax, mail, in person, online. Only the court performs in person searches; visitors may not. Search fee: $24.00 per name. Required to search: name, years to search; also helpful: address. Civil cases indexed by party names; defendant and plaintiff. Civil records on computer since 1992. Records on dockets. Will retain for 5 years. Mail turnaround time 10 days. Civil PAT goes back to 1992. PAT results show middle initial, DOB, SSN. Access to the docket is free at www.supreme.state.az.us/publicaccess/notification/search.asp.

Criminal Records: Access: Fax, mail, in person, online. Only the court performs in person searches; visitors may not. Search fee: $24.00 per name. Required to search: name, years to search, DOB; also helpful: address, SSN. Criminal records on computer since 1992. Records on dockets. Will retain for 5 years. Mail turnaround time 10 days. Criminal PAT goes back to 1992. PAT results show middle initial, DOB, SSN. Access to the docket is free at www.supreme.state.az.us/publicaccess/notification/search.asp.

General Information: No juvenile, mental health, victims, sealed or adoption records released. Will not fax documents. Court makes copy: $.50 per page. Certification fee: $24.00 per doc. Payee: Payson Justice Court. No personal checks or credit cards accepted. Prepayment required. Mail requests: SASE required.

Southern Regional Justice Court Globe/Miami Magistrate Court, 1400 E Ash, Globe, AZ 85501; 928-425-3231 x8545; fax: 928-425-4773; 8AM-5PM. ***Misdemeanor, Civil Actions under $10,000, Eviction, Small Claims.***

This courts holds the records for the justice courts formerly located in Miami and Hayden/Winkelman.

Civil Records: Access: Mail, fax, in person, online. Both court and visitors may perform in person searches. Search fee: $24.00 per name. Required to search: name, years to search. Civil cases indexed by defendant, plaintiff, on computer from 2000. Some records on dockets. Will retain for 5 years. Mail turnaround time 2-4 days. Civil PAT goes back to 1997. PAT results show middle initial, DOB. Public access terminal in Law Library on 1st fl. Access to the docket is free at www.supreme.state.az.us/publicaccess/notification/search.asp.

Criminal Records: Access: Mail, fax, in person, online. Both court and visitors may perform in person searches. Search fee: $24.00 per name. Required to search: name, years to search; also helpful: SSN, DOB, signed release. Criminal records computerized from 1997. Some records on dockets. Will retain for 5 years. Mail turnaround time 2-4 days. Criminal PAT goes back to 1997. PAT results show middle initial, DOB. Public access terminal in Law Library on 1st Fl. Access to the docket is free at www.supreme.state.az.us/publicaccess/notification/search.asp.

General Information: No juvenile, mental health, victims, sealed or adoption records released. Will fax documents to local or toll free line. Court makes copy: $.50 per page. Certification fee: $24.00 per doc. Payee: Globe Regional Justice Court. Business checks accepted. No credit cards accepted. Prepayment required. Mail requests: SASE required.

Winkleman Justice Court 1400 E Ash St, c/o Globe Regional Justice Court, Globe, AZ 85501-1414; ***Misdemeanor, Civil Actions under $10,000, Eviction, Small Claims.***

Now part of the Globe Regional Justice Court.

Graham County

Superior Court 800 Main St, Safford, AZ 85546-3803; 928-428-3100; criminal fax: 928-428-0061; civil fax: same; 8AM-5PM. ***Felony, Civil Actions over $5,000, Probate.***

Probate fax is same as main fax number.

Civil Records: Access: Fax, mail, in person, online. Both court and visitors may perform in person searches. Search fee: $26.00 per name. Required to search: name, years to search. Civil cases indexed by defendant, plaintiff, on dockets. Mail turnaround time 3 days minimum. Civil PAT goes back to 9/1995. PAT results show middle initial, DOB. Access docket free at www.supreme.state.az.us/publicaccess/notification/search.asp.

Criminal Records: Access: Phone, fax, mail, in person, online. Both court and visitors may perform in person searches. Search fee: $26.00 per name per year. Required to search: name, years to search. Criminal records on dockets. Mail turnaround time 3 days minimum. Criminal PAT goes back to same as civil. PAT results show middle initial, DOB. Access docket free at www.supreme.state.az.us/publicaccess/notification/search.asp. Online results show middle initial, DOB.

General Information: Online identifiers in results same as on public terminal. No mental health, victims, sealed or adoption records released. Will fax documents $5.00 fee. Court makes copy: $.50 per page, self serve same. Certification fee: $26.00 per doc. Payee: Clerk of Superior Court. No personal checks. Visa/MC accepted. Prepayment required. Mail requests: SASE required.

Justice Court Precinct #1 800 W Main St, Safford, AZ 85546; 928-428-1210; fax: 928-428-3523; 8AM-5PM. ***Misdemeanor, Civil Actions under $10,000, Eviction.*** www.graham.az.gov/county_offices.asp?id=1391&sub_id=1478

Civil Records: Access: Mail, in person, online. Both court and visitors may perform in person searches. Search fee: $24.00 per name. Required to search: name, years to search; also helpful: address. Civil cases indexed by case number. Civil records on computer from 1995, on dockets prior. Mail turnaround time 3-4 days. Access docket is free at www.supreme.state.az.us/publicaccess/notification/search.asp.

Criminal Records: Access: Mail, in person, online. Both court and visitors may perform in person searches. Search fee: $24.00 per name. Required to search: name, years to search, DOB; also helpful: address, SSN. Criminal records computerized from 1995, on dockets prior. Mail turnaround time 2-3 days. Access to the docket is free at www.supreme.state.az.us/publicaccess/notification/search.asp.

General Information: No juvenile, mental health, victims, sealed or adoption records released. Will fax documents to local or toll free line. Court makes copy: $.50 per page. Certification fee: $24.00 per doc. Payee: Safford Justice Court. Cashiers checks and money orders accepted. Major credit cards accepted. Prepayment required. Mail requests: SASE required.

Pima Justice Court Precinct #2 PO Box 1159, 136 W Center St, Pima, AZ 85543; 928-485-2771; fax: 928-485-9961; 8AM-5PM. ***Misdemeanor, Civil Actions under $10,000, Eviction, Small Claims.*** www.supreme.state.az.us

They also handle criminal traffic.

Civil Records: Access: Fax, mail, in person, online. Both court and visitors may perform in person searches. Search fee: $24.00 per name. Required to search: name, years to search; also helpful: address, docket number. Civil cases indexed by defendant. Civil records on dockets back to 1985; on computer back to 1995. Retained for 5 years. Mail turnaround time 2 weeks. Access to the docket is free at www.supreme.state.az.us/publicaccess/notification/search.asp.

Criminal Records: Access: Fax, mail, in person, online. Both court and visitors may perform in person searches. Search fee: $24.00 per name. Required to search: name, years to search, DOB; also helpful: address, SSN, docket number. Criminal records on dockets back to 1985; on computer back to 1995. Retained for 5 years. Mail turnaround time 2 weeks. Access to the docket is free at www.supreme.state.az.us/publicaccess/notification/search.asp.

General Information: No juvenile, mental health, victims, sealed or adoption records released. Will fax documents $17.00 per doc. Court makes copy: $.50 per page, self serve same. Certification fee: $24.00 per doc. Payee: Graham Justice Court. Cashiers checks and money orders and major credit cards accepted. Prepayment required. Mail requests: SASE required.

Greenlee County

Superior Court PO Box 1027, 223 Fifth St, Clifton, AZ 85533; 928-865-4242; fax: 928-865-5358; 8AM-5PM. ***Felony, Civil Actions over $5,000, Probate.***

Search fee includes both civil and criminal index.

Civil Records: Access: Mail, in person, online. Both court and visitors may perform in person searches. Search fee: $26.00 per name per year. Required to search: name, years to search. Civil cases indexed by defendant, plaintiff, in docket books from 1911; on computer from 12/97. Mail turnaround time 3 days. Access to the docket is free at www.supreme.state.az.us/publicaccess/notification/search.asp.

Criminal Records: Access: Mail, in person, online. Both court and visitors may perform in person searches. Search fee: $26.00 per name per year. Required to search: name, years to search. Criminal

records on computer since 12/97; on books from 1911. Mail turnaround time 7 days. Access to the docket is free at www.supreme.state.az.us/publicaccess/notification/search.asp. Online results show middle initial, DOB.
General Information: Online identifiers in results same as on public terminal. No adoption released. Will fax documents to local or toll free line. Court makes copy: $.50 per page. Certification fee: $26.00 per doc. Payee: Clerk of Superior Court. Personal checks accepted; credit cards are not. Prepayment required. Mail requests: SASE required.

Justice Court Precinct #1 PO Box 517, Clifton, AZ 85533; 928-865-4312; fax: 928-865-5644; 8AM-5PM. ***Misdemeanor, Civil Actions under $10,000, Eviction, Small Claims.***
Civil Records: Access: Mail, in person, online. Only the court performs in person searches; visitors may not. Search fee: $24.00 per name. Required to search: name, years to search. Civil cases indexed by defendant, plaintiff, on computer Aztec System. Mail turnaround time 1 week. Access docket is free at www.supreme.state.az.us/publicaccess/notification/search.asp.
Criminal Records: Access: Mail, in person, online. Only the court performs in person searches; visitors may not. Search fee: $24.00 per name. Required to search: name, years to search; also helpful: DOB, SSN. Criminal records on computer Aztec System. Mail turnaround time 1 week. Access to the docket is free at www.supreme.state.az.us/publicaccess/notification/search.asp.
General Information: No juvenile, sealed, victims, mental health or adoption records released. Will fax documents to local or toll-free number. Court makes copy: $.50 per page. Certification fee: $24.00 per doc. Payee: Justice of the Peace. Only cashiers checks and money orders accepted. No credit cards accepted. Prepayment required. SASE not required.

Justice Court Precinct #2 PO Box 208, Duncan, AZ 85534; 928-359-2536; fax: 928-359-1936; 8AM-5PM. ***Misdemeanor, Civil Actions under $10,000, Eviction, Small Claims.***
Civil Records: Access: Mail, in person, online. Both court and visitors may perform in person searches. Search fee: $24.00 per name. Required to search: name, years to search. Civil cases indexed by defendant, plaintiff, on computer since 1996. Documents retained for 5 years. Mail turnaround time 2 days. Civil PAT goes back to 1996-97. Access to the docket is free at www.supreme.state.az.us/publicaccess/notification/search.asp.
Criminal Records: Access: Mail, in person, online. Both court and visitors may perform in person searches. Search fee: $24.00 per name. Required to search: name, years to search. Criminal Records computerized since 1996. Mail turnaround time 2 days. Criminal PAT goes back to same as civil. Access to the docket is free at www.supreme.state.az.us/publicaccess/notification/search.asp.
General Information: No juvenile, victims, sealed, mental health or adoption records released. Will fax documents for no fee. Court makes copy: $.50 per page, self serve same. Certification fee: $24.00 per doc. Payee: Justice Court. No personal checks or credit cards accepted. Prepayment required. Mail requests: SASE required.

La Paz County

Superior Court 1316 Kofa Ave, #607, Parker, AZ 85344; 928-669-6131; fax: 928-669-2186; 8AM-5PM. ***Felony, Civil Actions over $5,000, Probate.*** www.co.la-paz.az.us/courts.htm
Civil Records: Access: Mail, in person, online. Both court and visitors may perform in person searches. Search fee: $26.00 per name per year. Required to search: name, years to search; also helpful: address. Civil cases indexed by defendant, plaintiff, computerized since 1996, to 1983 on docket books. For records prior to 1983, check with Yuma County Superior Court. Mail turnaround time 2-3 days. Civil PAT goes back to 1996. PAT results show middle initial, DOB. Access to the docket is free at www.supreme.state.az.us/publicaccess/notification/search.asp.
Criminal Records: Access: Mail, in person, online. Both court and visitors may perform in person searches. Search fee: $26.00 per name per year. Required to search: name, years to search; also helpful: address, DOB, SSN. Criminal records computerized since 1996, to 1983 on docket books. For records prior to 1983, check with Yuma County Superior Court. Mail turnaround time 2-3 days. Criminal PAT goes back to same as civil. PAT results show middle initial, DOB. Access to the docket is free at www.supreme.state.az.us/publicaccess/notification/search.asp. Online results show middle initial, DOB.
General Information: Online identifiers in results same as on public terminal. No dependency or adoption records released. Will fax documents for certification fee. Court makes copy: $.50 per page. Certification fee: $26.00 per doc. Payee: Clerk of Superior Court. Business checks accepted, but no personal. Major credit cards accepted. Prepayment required. Mail requests: SASE required.

Parker Justice Court 1105 Arizona Ave, Parker, AZ 85344; 928-669-2504; fax: 928-669-2915; 8AM-5PM. ***Misdemeanor, Civil Actions under $10,000, Eviction, Small Claims.***
Civil Records: Access: Mail, in person, online. Only the court performs in person searches; visitors may not. Search fee: $24.00 per name. Required to search: name, years to search; also helpful: address. Civil cases indexed by defendant. Civil records on dockets back to 1800s, computerized since 1996. Mail turnaround time 2-3 weeks. Access docket free at www.supreme.state.az.us/publicaccess/notification/search.asp.
Criminal Records: Access: Mail, in person, online. Only the court performs in person searches; visitors may not. Search fee: $24.00 per name. Required to search: name, years to search, DOB; also helpful: address, SSN. Criminal records on dockets back to 1800s, computerized since 1996. Mail turnaround time 2-3 weeks. Access docket free at www.supreme.state.az.us/publicaccess/notification/search.asp.
General Information: No juvenile, mental health, victims or sealed records released. Will not fax documents. Court makes copy: $.50 per page. Certification fee: $24.00 per doc. Payee: Clerk of Justice Court. Only cashiers checks and money orders accepted. No credit cards accepted. Prepayment required. Mail requests: SASE required.

Quartzsite Justice Court PO Box 580, Quartzsite, AZ 85346; 928-927-6313; criminal fax: 928-927-4842; civil fax: same; 8AM-5PM. ***Misdemeanor, Civil Actions under $10,000, Eviction, Small Claims.***
Civil Records: Access: Fax, mail, in person, online. Both court and visitors may perform in person searches. Search fee: $24.00 per name/year. Required to search: name, years to search. Civil cases indexed by defendant, plaintiff, computerized since 7/96. Files retained for 5 yrs after final disposition. Mail turnaround time within 3 weeks. Access docket free at www.supreme.state.az.us/publicaccess/notification/search.asp.
Criminal Records: Access: Fax, mail, in person, online. Both court and visitors may perform in person searches. Search fee: $24.00 per name. Required to search: name, years to search, date of offense; also helpful: DOB, SSN, offense. Criminal records computerized since 7/96. Files retained for 5 yrs after final disposition. Mail turnaround time within 3 weeks. Access to the docket is free at www.supreme.state.az.us/publicaccess/notification/search.asp.
General Information: No juvenile, mental health, victims, sealed or adoption records released. Will fax documents to local or toll-free number. Court makes copy: $.50 per page. Certification fee: $24.00 per doc. Payee: Quartsite Justice Court. Cashiers checks and money orders accepted. Visa/MC accepted. Prepayment required. Mail requests: SASE required.

Salome Justice Court PO Box 661, Salome, AZ 85348; 928-859-3871; fax: 928-859-3709; 8AM-5PM. ***Misdemeanor, Civil Actions under $10,000, Eviction, Small Claims.***
Civil Records: Access: Mail, in person, online. Only the court performs in person searches; visitors may not. Search fee: $24.00 per name. Required to search: name, years to search; also helpful: address. Civil cases indexed by defendant. Civil records on dockets from mid-1960s. Records destroyed after 5 years. Computerized back to 1996. Note: Civil traffic records destroyed after 1 year. Mail turnaround time 2-3 days. Access to the docket is free at www.supreme.state.az.us/publicaccess/notification/search.asp.
Criminal Records: Access: Mail, in person, online. Only the court performs in person searches; visitors may not. Search fee: $24.00 per name. Required to search: name, years to search, DOB; also helpful: address, SSN. Criminal docket index from mid-1960s. Records destroyed after 5 years. Computerized back to 1996. Mail turnaround 2-3 days. Access docket is free at www.supreme.state.az.us/publicaccess/notification/search.asp.
General Information: No juvenile, mental health, victims, sealed or adoption records released. Will not fax documents. Court makes copy: $.50 per page. Certification fee: $24.00 per doc. Payee: Salome Justice Court. Only cashiers checks and money orders accepted. No business or personal checks. Visa/MC accepted. Prepayment required. SASE not required.

Maricopa County

Superior Court 201 W Jefferson - Correspondence, 601 W Jackson St., Phoenix, AZ 85003; 602-506-3360; fax: 602-506-7619; 8AM-5PM. ***Felony, Civil Actions over $5,000, Probate.*** www.clerkofcourt.maricopa.gov/
Civil Records: Access: Fax, mail, online, in person. Both court and visitors may perform in person searches. Search fee: $26.00 per name. Required to search: name, years to search. Civil cases indexed by defendant, plaintiff, on computer from 7/87, on microfiche from 1969 to present. Some records on docket books. Mail turnaround time 2 weeks. Civil PAT goes back to 7/1987. PAT civil results show middle initial. Access to civil case dockets free at www.superiorcourt.maricopa.gov/docket/index.asp. Case file docket can be printed. Search by first and last name or by business name or by case number. DOB not shown. Also, access to probate court dockets is at www.superiorcourt.maricopa.gov/docket/ProbateCourtCases/. Family court filings are at www.superiorcourt.maricopa.gov/docket/FamilyCourtCases/
Criminal Records: Access: Fax, mail, online, in person. Both court and visitors may perform in person searches. Search fee: $26.00 per name. Required to search: name, years to search; also helpful: DOB. Criminal records computerized from 7/87, on microfiche from 1969 to present. Some records on docket books. Note: DOB not provided on civil. Mail turnaround time 2 weeks. Criminal PAT goes back to same as civil. PAT results show middle initial, DOB. Access to criminal case dockets is free at www.superiorcourt.maricopa.gov/docket/CriminalCourtCases/. Search by first and last name or by initials of first and last name with DOB, or by case number. Results list shows DOB.
General Information: Online identifiers in results same as on public terminal. No mental health, victims, sealed or adoption records released. Will fax documents $5.00 plus $.50 per page. Court makes copy: $.50 per page. Certification fee: $26.00 per doc; Exemplification fee $36.00 per doc. Payee: Clerk of Superior Court. Personal checks accepted. Visa/MC accepted. Prepayment required. SASE not required. If not included $5.00 shipping & handling.

Agua Fria (Tolleson) Justice Court 9550 W Van Buren, #6, Tolleson, AZ 85353; 623-936-1449; fax: 623-936-4859; 8-5PM. ***Misdemeanor, Civil Actions under $10,000, Eviction, Small Claims.*** www.superiorcourt.maricopa.gov/justiceCourts/
Countywide Justice Court docket information is sold on disk. Data on disks and countywide terminals may be 2-3 months old.
Civil Records: Access: Mail, in person, online. Only the court performs in person searches; visitors may

not. Search fee: $24.00 per name. Required to search: name, years to search; also helpful: address. Civil cases indexed by defendant, plaintiff, on computer since 1993. Mail turnaround time 1-2 weeks. Access court index free on countywide site at www.superiorcourt.maricopa.gov/docket/JusticeCourtCases/caseSearch.asp.
Criminal Records: Access: Mail, in person, online. Only the court performs in person searches; visitors may not. Search fee: $24.00 per name. Required to search: name, years to search, DOB; also helpful: address, SSN. Criminal records on computer since 1993. Mail turnaround time 1-2 weeks. Online access same as civil. Online results show middle initial, DOB.
General Information: No juvenile, mental health, victims, sealed or adoption records released. Will not fax documents. Court makes copy: $.50 per page. Certification fee: $24.00 per doc. Payee: Agua Fria Justice Court. Personal checks accepted. Credit cards accepted. Prepayment required. Mail requests: SASE required.

Arcadia Biltmore (East Phoenix #2) Justice Court 620 W Jackson St, Phoenix, AZ 85003; 602-372-6300; fax: 602-372-6412; 8AM-5PM. ***Misdemeanor, Civil Actions under $10,000, Eviction, Small Claims.***
www.superiorcourt.maricopa.gov/justiceCourts/
Countywide Justice Court docket information is sold on disk. Data on disks and countywide terminals may be 2-3 months old.
Civil Records: Access: Mail, in person, online. Both court and visitors may perform in person searches. Search fee: $24.00 per name. Required to search: name, years to search. Civil cases indexed by defendant, plaintiff, on computer since 1981. Mail turnaround time 1-2 weeks. Civil PAT available. PAT results show name only. Countywide dockets on iCIS system; no print outs. Access court index free on countywide site at www.superiorcourt.maricopa.gov/docket/JusticeCourtCases/caseSearch.asp.
Criminal Records: Access: Mail, in person, online. Both court and visitors may perform in person searches. Search fee: $24.00 per name. Required to search: name, years to search, DOB. Criminal records computerized since 1991. Mail turnaround time 1-2 weeks. Criminal PAT available. PAT results show name only. Countywide dockets on iCIS system; no print outs. Online access same as civil. Online results show middle initia and usually the DOB.
General Information: No juvenile, mental health, victims, sealed or adoption records released. Will not fax documents. Court makes copy: $.50 per page. Self serve: is available. Certification fee: $24.00 per doc. Payee: Arcadia Biltmore Justice Court. Personal checks accepted. Credit cards accepted. Prepayment required. Mail requests: SASE required.

Downtown (East Phoenix #1) Justice Court 620 W Jackson St, Phoenix, AZ 85003; 602-372-6300; fax: 602-372-6406; 8AM-5PM. ***Misdemeanor, Civil Actions under $10,000, Eviction, Small Claims.***
www.superiorcourt.maricopa.gov/justiceCourts/
Countywide Justice Court docket information is sold on disk. Data on disks and countywide terminals may be 5-6 months old.
Civil Records: Access: Mail, in person, online. Visitors must perform in person searches themselves. Search fee: $24.00 per name. Required to search: name, years to search. Civil cases indexed by defendant, plaintiff, on dockets by number; computerized records since 1990's. Mail turnaround time 1-2 weeks. Civil PAT available. Countywide dockets on iCIS system; no print outs. Access court index free on countywide site at www.superiorcourt.maricopa.gov/docket/JusticeCourtCases/caseSearch.asp.
Criminal Records: Access: Mail, in person, online. Visitors must perform in person searches themselves. Search fee: $24.00 per name. Required to search: name, years to search, DOB. Criminal dockets by number; computerized records since 1990's. Mail turnaround time 1-2 weeks. Criminal PAT available. Countywide dockets on iCIS system; no print outs. Online access same as civil. Online results show middle initial, DOB.

General Information: No mental health, victims or sealed records released. Will not fax documents. Court makes copy: $.50 per page. Certification fee: $24.00 per doc. Payee: East Phoenix #1 Justice Court. Personal checks accepted. Credit cards accepted in person only. Prepayment required. Mail requests: SASE required.

Dreamy Draw (Northeast Phoenix) Justice Court 18380 N 40th St, #130, Phoenix, AZ 85032; 602-372-7000; fax: 602-372-7911; 8AM-5PM. ***Misdemeanor, Civil Actions under $10,000, Eviction, Small Claims.***
www.superiorcourt.maricopa.gov/justiceCourts/
Now co-located with the McDowell Mtn (Scottsdale) and Moon Valley (Northwest) Justice Courts in the Northeast Regional Justice Court Center. Countywide Justice Court docket information is sold on disk, data on disks and terminals may be 8-9 months old.
Civil Records: Access: Phone, mail, in person, online. Only the court performs in person searches; visitors may not. Search fee: $24.00 per name. Required to search: name, years to search. Civil cases indexed by defendant, plaintiff, on computer since 1985. Records kept for 5 years on closed cases. Mail turnaround time 2-3 weeks. Civil PAT available. PAT results show name only. Countywide dockets on iCIS system; no print outs. Access court index free on countywide site at www.superiorcourt.maricopa.gov/docket/JusticeCourtCases/caseSearch.asp.
Criminal Records: Access: Phone, mail, in person, online. Only the court performs in person searches; visitors may not. Search fee: $24.00 per name. Required to search: name, years to search. Criminal records on computer since 1985. Records kept for 5 years on closed cases. Mail turnaround time 2-3 weeks. Criminal PAT available. PAT results show name only. Countywide dockets on iCIS system; no print outs. Online access same as civil. Online results show middle initial, DOB.
General Information: No juvenile, mental health, victims, sealed or adoption records released. Court makes copy: $.50 per page. Certification fee: $24.00 per doc. Payee: Scottsdale Justice Court. Personal checks accepted. Credit cards accepted. Prepayment required. Mail requests: SASE required.

East Mesa Justice Court 4811 E Julep, #128, Mesa, AZ 85205; 480-985-0188; fax: 480-396-6327; 8AM-5PM. ***Misdemeanor, Civil Actions under $10,000, Eviction, Small Claims.***
www.superiorcourt.maricopa.gov/justiceCourts/
Countywide Justice Court docket information is sold on disk. Data on disks and countywide terminals may be 2-3 months old.
Civil Records: Access: Mail, in person, online. Only the court performs in person searches; visitors may not. Search fee: $24.00 per name. Required to search: name, years to search; also helpful: address. Civil cases indexed by defendant, plaintiff, on computer since 1990. Prior records in docket books by number. Mail turnaround time 1-2 weeks. Nearest public terminal located at San Tan JC, 201 E Chicago in Chandler.
Access court index free on countywide site at www.superiorcourt.maricopa.gov/docket/JusticeCourtCases/caseSearch.asp.
Criminal Records: Access: Mail, in person, online. Only the court performs in person searches; visitors may not. Search fee: $24.00 per name. Required to search: name, years to search, DOB; also helpful: address, SSN. Criminal records on computer since 1990. Prior records in docket books by number. Mail turnaround time 1-2 weeks. Nearest public terminal located at San Tan JC, 201 E Chicago in Chandler. Online access same as civil. Online results show middle initial, DOB.
General Information: No juvenile, mental health, victims, sealed or adoption records released. Will not fax documents. Court makes copy: $.50 per page. Certification fee: $24.00 per doc. Payee: East Mesa Justice Court. Personal checks accepted. Credit cards accepted. Prepayment required. Mail requests: SASE required.

Encanto (Central Phoenix) Justice Court 620 W Jackson St, Phoenix, AZ 85003; 602-372-6300; fax: 602-372-6414; 8AM-5PM. ***Misdemeanor, Civil Actions under $10,000, Eviction, Small Claims.***
www.superiorcourt.maricopa.gov/justiceCourts/
Countywide Justice Court docket information is sold on disk. Data on disks and countywide terminals may be 8-9 months old.
Civil Records: Access: Phone, fax, mail, in person, online. Visitors must perform in person searches themselves. Search fee: $24.00 per name. Required to search: name, years to search. Civil cases indexed by defendant, plaintiff, on computer since 1985. Mail turnaround time 1-2 weeks. Civil PAT goes back to 1985. Countywide dockets on iCIS system; no print outs. Access court index free on countywide site at www.superiorcourt.maricopa.gov/docket/JusticeCourtCases/caseSearch.asp.
Criminal Records: Access: Mail, fax, in person, online. Visitors must perform in person searches themselves. Search fee: $24.00 per name. Required to search: name, years to search, DOB, SSN. Criminal records on computer since 1985. Mail turnaround time 1-2 weeks. Criminal PAT goes back to same as civil. Countywide dockets on iCIS system; no print outs. Online access same as civil. Online results show middle initial, DOB.
General Information: No sealed records released. Will fax documents to local or toll-free number; will not fax certified copies. Court makes copy: $.50 per page. Certification fee: $24.00 per doc. Payee: Encanto Justice Court. Personal checks accepted with DL. Visa/MC accepted. Prepayment required. Mail requests: SASE required.

Estrella Mountain (Buckeye Precinct) Justice Court 100 N Apache Rd, #C, Buckeye, AZ 85326; 623-386-4822; fax: 623-386-5796; 8AM-5PM. ***Misdemeanor, Civil Actions under $10,000, Eviction, Small Claims.***
www.superiorcourt.maricopa.gov/justiceCourts/
Countywide Justice Court docket information is sold on disk. Data on disks and countywide terminals may be 2-3 months old.
Civil Records: Access: Mail, in person, online. Only the court performs in person searches; visitors may not. Search fee: $24.00 per name. Required to search: name, years to search. Civil cases indexed by defendant, plaintiff, on dockets by number, computerized since 1990. Mail turnaround time 1-2 weeks. Civil PAT available. PAT results show name only. Countywide dockets on iCIS system; no print outs. Access court index free on countywide site at www.superiorcourt.maricopa.gov/docket/JusticeCourtCases/caseSearch.asp.
Criminal Records: Access: Mail, in person, online. Only the court performs in person searches; visitors may not. Search fee: $24.00 per name. Required to search: name, years to search, DOB. Criminal dockets by number, computerized since 1990. Mail turnaround time 1-2 weeks. Criminal PAT available. PAT results show name only. Countywide dockets on iCIS system; no print outs. Online access same as civil. Online results show middle initial, DOB.
General Information: No juvenile, mental health, victims, sealed or adoption records released. Will fax documents to local or toll free line. Court makes copy: $.50 per page. Certification fee: $24.00 per doc. Payee: Estrella Mountain Justice Court. Personal checks accepted. Visa/MC accepted. Prepayment required. Mail requests: SASE required.

Hassayampa (Wickenburg) Justice Court 14264 W Tierra Buena Ln, Surprise, AZ 85374; 602-372-2000; fax: 602-372-2620; 8AM-5PM. ***Misdemeanor, Civil Actions under $10,000, Eviction, Small Claims.***
www.superiorcourt.maricopa.gov/justiceCourts/
Wickenburg Town Court phone is 928-684-5451. Countywide Justice Court docket info is sold on disk. Data on disks and countywide terminals may be 5-6 months old.
Civil Records: Access: Mail, in person, online. Only the court performs in person searches; visitors may not. Search fee: $24.00 per name. Required to search:

name, years to search; also helpful: address. Civil cases indexed by defendant, plaintiff, on computer since 1994. Mail turnaround time 1-2 weeks. Civil PAT available. PAT results show name only. Countywide dockets on iCIS system; no print outs. Access court index free on countywide site at www.superiorcourt.maricopa.gov/docket/JusticeCourtCases/caseSearch.asp.
Criminal Records: Access: Mail, in person, online. Only the court performs in person searches; visitors may not. Search fee: $24.00 per name. Required to search: name, years to search, DOB; also helpful: SSN. Criminal records on computer by name and case number. Mail turnaround time 1-2 weeks. Criminal PAT available. PAT results show name only. Countywide dockets on iCIS system; no print outs. Online access same as civil. Online results show middle initial, DOB.
General Information: No juvenile, mental health, victims, sealed records released. Court makes copy: $.50 per page. Certification fee: $24.00 per doc. Payee: Wickenburg Justice Court. Personal checks accepted. Credit cards accepted. Prepayment required. Mail requests: SASE required.

Ironwood (Gila Bend) Justice Court PO Box 648, 209 E Pima St, Gila Bend, AZ 85337; 928-683-2651; fax: 928-683-6412; 8AM-5PM. ***Misdemeanor, Civil Actions under $10,000, Eviction, Small Claims.***
www.superiorcourt.maricopa.gov/justiceCourts/
Countywide Justice Court docket information is sold on disk. Data on disks and countywide terminals may be 2-3 months old.
Civil Records: Access: Mail, in person, online. Only the court performs in person searches; visitors may not. Search fee: $24.00 per name. Required to search: name, years to search. Civil cases indexed by defendant, plaintiff, on computer since 1987. Mail turnaround time 1-2 weeks. Access court index free at www.superiorcourt.maricopa.gov/docket/JusticeCourtCases/caseSearch.asp.
Criminal Records: Access: Mail, in person, online. Only the court performs in person searches; visitors may not. Search fee: $24.00 per name. Required to search: name, years to search; also helpful: DOB. Criminal records on computer since 1987. Mail turnaround time 1-2 weeks. Online access same as civil. Online results show middle initial, DOB.
General Information: No juvenile, mental health, victims, sealed or adoption records released. Will fax documents to local or toll-free number. Court makes copy: $.50 per page. Certification fee: included in search fee. Payee: Gila Bend or Ironwood Justice Court. Personal checks accepted. Visa/MC accepted. Prepayment required. Mail requests: SASE required.

Kyrene (West Tempe) Justice Court 201 E Chicago St, #104, Chandler, AZ 85225; 602-372-3400; fax: 602-372-3494; hours- 8AM-5PM. ***Misdemeanor, Civil Actions under $10,000, Eviction, Small Claims, Traffic.***
www.superiorcourt.maricopa.gov/justiceCourts/
Formerly known as the West Tempe Justice Court. Countywide Justice Court docket information is sold on disk. Data on disks and countywide terminals may be 2-3 months old.
Civil Records: Access: Mail, in person, online. Only the court performs in person searches; visitors may not. Search fee: $24.00 per name. Required to search: name, years to search. Civil cases indexed by defendant, plaintiff, on computer by case number. Mail turnaround time 5 days Civil PAT available. PAT results show name only. Countywide dockets on iCIS system; no print outs. Access court index free at www.superiorcourt.maricopa.gov/docket/JusticeCourtCases/caseSearch.asp.
Criminal Records: Access: Mail, in person, online. Only the court performs in person searches; visitors may not. Search fee: $24.00 per name. Required to search: name, years to search, DOB. Criminal records on computer by case number. Mail turnaround time 5 days. Criminal PAT available. PAT results show name only. Countywide dockets on iCIS system; no print outs. Online access same as civil. Online results show middle initial, DOB.
General Information: No juvenile, mental health, victims, sealed records released. Will not fax documents. Court makes copy: $.50 per page. Certification fee: $24.00 per doc. Payee: Kyrene Justice Court. Personal checks/credit cards accepted. Prepayment required. Mail requests: SASE required.

Lake Pleasant (Peoria) Justice Court 14264 W Tierra Buena Ln, Surprise, AZ 85374; 602-372-2000; fax: 602-372-2620; 8AM-5PM. ***Misdemeanor, Civil Actions under $10,000, Eviction, Small Claims.***
www.superiorcourt.maricopa.gov/justiceCourts/
Countywide Justice Court docket information is sold on disk. Data on disks and countywide terminals may be 5-6 months old.
Civil Records: Access: Phone, mail, in person, online. Only the court performs in person searches; visitors may not. Search fee: $24.00 per name. Required to search: name, years to search. Civil cases indexed by defendant, plaintiff, on computer by casc number. Mail turnaround time 1-2 weeks. Civil PAT available. PAT results show name only. Countywide dockets on iCIS system; no print outs. Access court index free on countywide site at www.superiorcourt.maricopa.gov/docket/JusticeCourtCases/caseSearch.asp.
Criminal Records: Access: Phone, mail, in person, online. Only the court performs in person searches; visitors may not. Search fee: $24.00 per name. Required to search: name, years to search; also helpful: DOB. Criminal records on computer by case number. Mail turnaround time 1-2 weeks. Criminal PAT available. PAT results show name only. Countywide dockets on iCIS system; no print outs. Online access same as civil. Online results show middle initial, DOB.
General Information: No juvenile, mental health, victims, sealed or adoption records released. Will fax documents to 602, 480, 623 area codes only- $1.25 per page. Court makes copy: $.50 per page. Certification fee: $24.00 per doc. Payee: Peoria Justice Court. Personal checks/credit cards accepted. Prepayment required. Mail requests: SASE required.

Manistee (Glendale) Justice Court 14264 W Tierra Buena Ln, Surprise, AZ 85374; 602-372-2000; fax: 602-372-2620; 8-5PM. ***Misdemeanor, Civil Actions under $10,000, Eviction, Small Claims.***
www.superiorcourt.maricopa.gov/justiceCourts/
Countywide Justice Court docket information is sold on disk. Data on disks and countywide terminals may be 5-6 months old.
Civil Records: Access: Mail, in person, online. Only the court performs in person searches; visitors may not. Search fee: $24.00 per name. Required to search: name, years to search. Civil cases indexed by defendant, plaintiff, on dockets by case number, computerized since 1993. Mail turnaround time 1-2 weeks. Civil PAT available. PAT results show name only. Countywide dockets on iCIS system; no print outs. Access court index free on countywide site at www.superiorcourt.maricopa.gov/docket/JusticeCourtCases/caseSearch.asp.
Criminal Records: Access: Mail, in person, online. Only the court performs in person searches; visitors may not. Search fee: $24.00 per name. Required to search: name, years to search, DOB; also helpful: SSN. Criminal dockets by case number, computerized since 1992. Note: The DOB shows approx 50% of the time on search results. Mail turnaround time 1-2 weeks. Criminal PAT available. PAT results show name only. Countywide dockets on iCIS system; no print outs. Online access same as civil. The DOB shows approx 50% of the time on search results. Online results show middle initial, DOB.
General Information: No juvenile, mental health, victims, sealed or adoption records released. Will not fax documents. Court makes copy: $.50 per page. Certification fee: $24.00 per doc. Payee: Glendale Justice Court. Personal checks/Visa/MC accepted. Prepayment required. Mail requests: SASE required.

Maryvale Justice Court 4622 W Indian School Rd, Bldg D10, Phoenix, AZ 85031; 623-245-0432; probate phone: same; criminal fax: 623-245-1216; civil fax: same; 8AM-5PM. ***Misdemeanor, Civil Actions under $10,000, Eviction, Small Claims.***
www.superiorcourt.maricopa.gov/justiceCourts/
Countywide Justice Court docket information is sold on disk. Data on disks and countywide terminals may be 2-3 months old.
Civil Records: Access: Mail, in person, online. Only the court performs in person searches; visitors may not. Search fee: $24.00 per name. Required to search: name, years to search, address. Civil cases indexed by defendant, plaintiff, on dockets by number. Mail turnaround time 1-2 weeks. Nearest public terminal located downtown Phoenix. Access court index free on countywide site at www.superiorcourt.maricopa.gov/docket/JusticeCourtCases/caseSearch.asp.
Criminal Records: Access: Mail, in person, online. Only the court performs in person searches; visitors may not. Search fee: $24.00 per name. Required to search: name, years to search, address, DOB; also helpful: SSN, aliases. Criminal dockets by number. Mail turnaround time 1-2 weeks. Nearest public terminal located downtown Phoenix. Online access same as civil, however chance of DOB appearing is greater. Online results show middle initial, DOB.
General Information: No juvenile, mental health, victims, sealed or adoption records released. Will not fax documents. Court makes copy: $.50 per page. Certification fee: $24.00 per doc. Payee: Maryvale Justice Court. Personal checks accepted if preprinted. major credit cards accepted. Prepayment required. Mail requests: SASE required.

McDowell Mountain (Scottsdale) 18380 N 40th St, Phoenix, AZ 85032; 602-372-7000; fax: 602-372-7910; 8AM-5PM. ***Misdemeanor, Civil Actions under $10,000, Eviction, Small Claims.***
www.superiorcourt.maricopa.gov/justiceCourts/
Now co-located with the Moon Valley and Dreamy Draw. Countywide Justice Court docket information is sold on disk. Data on disks and countywide terminals may be 2-3 months old.
Civil Records: Access: Mail, in person, online. Only the court performs in person searches; visitors may not. Search fee: $24.00 per name. Required to search: name, years to search; also helpful: address. Civil cases indexed by defendant, plaintiff, on computer since 1993. Records on dockets by name and case number. Mail turnaround time 1-2 weeks. Civil PAT available. PAT results show name only. Countywide dockets on iCIS system; no print outs. Access court index free on countywide site at www.superiorcourt.maricopa.gov/docket/JusticeCourtCases/caseSearch.asp.
Criminal Records: Access: Mail, in person, online. Only the court performs in person searches; visitors may not. Search fee: $24.00 per name. Required to search: name, years to search, DOB; also helpful: address, SSN. Criminal dockets by name and case number. Mail turnaround time 1-2 weeks. Criminal PAT available. PAT results show name only. Countywide dockets on iCIS system; no print outs. Online access same as civil. Online results show middle initial, DOB.
General Information: No juvenile, mental health, victims, sealed or adoption records released. Will not fax documents. Court makes copy: $.50 per page. Certification fee: $24.00 per doc. Payee: Clerk of Justice Court. Personal checks accepted; cashier's check or money orders only for traffic. Visa/MC accepted only from person named on card. Prepayment required. Mail requests: SASE required.

Moon Valley (Northwest Phoenix) Justice Court 18380 N 40th St, Phoenix, AZ 85032; 602-372-7000; fax: 602-372-7910; 8AM-5PM. ***Misdemeanor, Civil Actions under $10,000, Eviction, Small Claims.***
www.superiorcourt.maricopa.gov/justiceCourts/
Now co-located with the McDowell Mt (Scottsdale) and Dreamy Draw (Northeast) Justice Courts. Countywide Justice Court docket information is sold on disk. Data on disks and countywide terminals may be 8-9 months old.
Civil Records: Access: Mail, in person, online. Only the court performs in person searches; visitors may not. Search fee: $24.00 per name. Required to search: name, years to search. Civil cases indexed by defendant, plaintiff, on dockets. Will retain for 5 years, computerized records since 1987. Mail turnaround time 1-2 weeks. Civil PAT available.

PAT results show name only. Countywide dockets on iCIS system; no print outs. Access court index free at www.superiorcourt.maricopa.gov/docket/JusticeCourtCases/caseSearch.asp.
Criminal Records: Access: Mail, in person, online. Only the court performs in person searches; visitors may not. Search fee: $24.00 per name. Required to search: name, years to search. Criminal records on dockets. Will retain for 5 years, computerized records since 1987. Mail turnaround time 1-2 weeks. Criminal PAT available. PAT results show name only. Countywide dockets on iCIS system; no print outs. Online access same as civil. Online results show middle initial, DOB.
General Information: Will not fax documents. Court makes copy: $.50 per page. Self serve: available at the regional center only. Certification fee: $24.00 per doc. Payee: Northwest Phoenix Justice Court. Personal checks accepted. Credit/Debit cards accepted only by person named on card. Prepayment required. Mail requests: SASE required.

North Mesa Justice Court 1837 S Mesa Dr, #B-103, Mesa, AZ 85210; 480-926-9731; fax: 480-926-7763; 8AM-5PM. ***Misdemeanor, Civil Actions under $10,000, Eviction, Small Claims.***
www.superiorcourt.maricopa.gov/justiceCourts/
Countywide Justice Court docket information is sold on disk. Data on disks and countywide terminals may be 2-3 months old.
Civil Records: Access: Mail, in person, online. Only the court performs in person searches; visitors may not. Search fee: $24.00 per name, limit 3 names. Required to search: name, years to search. Civil cases indexed by defendant, plaintiff, on computer by case number. Mail turnaround time 1-2 weeks. Nearest public terminal located at San Tan JC, 201 E Chicago in Chandler. Access court index free on at www.superiorcourt.maricopa.gov/docket/JusticeCourtCases/caseSearch.asp.
Criminal Records: Access: Mail, in person, online Mail, in person. Only the court performs in person searches; visitors may not. Search fee: $24.00 per name, limit 3 names. Required to search: name, years to search, offense; also helpful: DOB. Criminal records on computer by case number. Mail turnaround time 1-2 weeks. Nearest public terminal located at San Tan JC, 201 E Chicago in Chandler. Online access same as civil. Online results show middle initial, DOB.
General Information: No juvenile, mental health, victims or sealed records released. Will not fax documents. Court makes copy: $.50 per page. Certification fee: $24.00 per doc. Payee: North Mesa Justice Court. Personal checks/credit cards accepted. Prepayment required. Mail requests: SASE required.

North Valley Justice Court 14264 W Tierra Buena Ln, Surprise, AZ 85374; 602-372-2000; fax: 602-372-2620; 8AM-5PM. ***Misdemeanor, Civil Actions under $10,000, Eviction, Small Claims.***
www.superiorcourt.maricopa.gov/justiceCourts/
Countywide Justice Court docket information is sold on disk. Data on disks and countywide terminals may be 5-6 months old.
Civil Records: Access: Mail, in person, online. Only the court performs in person searches; visitors may not. Search fee: $24.00 per name. Required to search: name, years to search. Civil cases indexed by defendant, plaintiff, on dockets by case number; on computer back to 1999. Mail turnaround time 1-2 weeks. Civil PAT available. PAT results show name only. Countywide dockets on iCIS system; no print outs. Access court index free on countywide site at www.superiorcourt.maricopa.gov/docket/JusticeCourtCases/caseSearch.asp.
Criminal Records: Access: Mail, in person, online. Only the court performs in person searches; visitors may not. Search fee: $24.00 per name. Required to search: name, years to search, DOB; also helpful: SSN. Criminal dockets by case number; on computer back to 1999. Mail turnaround time 1-2 weeks. Criminal PAT available. PAT results show name only. Countywide dockets on iCIS system; no print outs. Online access same as civil. Online results show middle initial, DOB.
General Information: No juvenile, mental health, victims, sealed or adoption records released. Will not fax documents. Court makes copy: $.50 per page. Certification fee: $24.00 per doc. Payee: North Valley Justice Court. Personal checks/Credit cards accepted. Prepayment required. Mail requests: SASE required.

San Marcos (Chandler) Justice Court 201 E Chicago St, #103, Chandler, AZ 85225-8502; 602-372-3400 x3; fax: 602-372-3468; 8AM-5PM. ***Misdemeanor, Civil Actions under $10,000, Eviction, Small Claims.***
www.superiorcourt.maricopa.gov/justiceCourts/
Formerly known as Chandler Justice Court. There are 3 other Justice Courts co-located at this address, separate phones. Countywide Justice Court docket information is sold on disk.
Civil Records: Access: Mail, in person, online. Only the court performs in person searches; visitors may not. Search fee: $24.00 per name. Required to search: name, years to search; also helpful: address. Civil cases indexed by defendant, plaintiff, on dockets by number; records go back 5 years; on computer back to 1991. Mail turnaround time 1-2 weeks. Civil PAT available. PAT results show name only. Countywide dockets on iCIS system; no print outs. Access court index free on countywide site at www.superiorcourt.maricopa.gov/docket/JusticeCourtCases/caseSearch.asp.
Criminal Records: Access: Mail, in person, online. Only the court performs in person searches; visitors may not. Search fee: $24.00 per name. Required to search: name, years to search, DOB; also helpful: address, SSN. Criminal docket by number; records on computer go back to 1991. Mail turnaround time 1-2 weeks. Criminal PAT available. PAT results show name only. Countywide dockets on iCIS system; no print outs. Online access same as civil. Online results show middle initial, DOB.
General Information: No juvenile, mental health, victims, sealed or adoption records released. Will not fax documents. Court makes copy: $.50 per page. Certification fee: $24.00 per doc. Payee: San Marcos Justice Court. Personal checks/credit cards accepted. Prepayment required. Mail requests: SASE required.

San Tan (South Mesa/Gilbert) Justice Court 201 E Chicago St, #102, Chandler, AZ 85225-8502; 602-372-3400; criminal fax: 602-372-3441; civil fax: same; 8AM-5PM. ***Misdemeanor, Civil Actions under $10,000, Eviction, Small Claims.***
www.superiorcourt.maricopa.gov/justiceCourts/
Formerly known as South Mesa./Gilbert Justice Court. Countywide Justice Court docket information is sold on disk. Data on disks and countywide terminals may be 2-3 months old.
Civil Records: Access: Mail, in person, online. Only the court performs in person searches; visitors may not. Search fee: $24.00 per name. Required to search: name, years to search, DOB, SSN, signed release. Civil cases indexed by defendant, plaintiff, on computer by case number back to 1994. Mail turnaround time 1-2 weeks. Civil PAT available. PAT results show name only. Countywide dockets on iCIS system; no print outs. Access court index free at www.superiorcourt.maricopa.gov/docket/JusticeCourtCases/caseSearch.asp.
Criminal Records: Access: Mail, in person, online. Only the court performs in person searches; visitors may not. Search fee: $24.00 per name. Required to search: name, years to search, DOB, SSN, signed release. Criminal records on computer by case number; computerized back to 1994. Mail turnaround 1-2 weeks. Criminal PAT available. PAT results show name only. Countywide dockets on iCIS system; no print outs. Online access same as civil. Online results show middle initial, DOB.
General Information: No juvenile, mental health, victims, sealed or adoption records released. Will not fax documents. Court makes copy: $.50 per page. Certification fee: $24.00 per doc. Payee: San Tan Justice Court. Cashiers checks and money orders accepted. Visa/MC accepted. Prepayment required. Mail requests: SASE required.

South Mountain (South Phoenix) Justice Court 620 W Jackson St, M/S 1044, Phoenix, AZ 85003; 602-372-6300; fax: 602-372-6410; 8AM-5PM. ***Misdemeanor, Civil Actions under $10,000, Eviction, Small Claims.***
www.superiorcourt.maricopa.gov/justiceCourts/
Countywide Justice Court docket information is sold on disk. Data on disks and countywide terminals may be 2-3 months old.
Civil Records: Access: Mail, in person, online. Visitors must perform in person searches themselves. Search fee: $24.00 per name. Required to search: name, years to search; also helpful: address. Civil cases indexed by defendant, plaintiff, on computer since 1990, on dockets by number. Mail turnaround time 1-2 weeks. Civil PAT available. PAT results show name only. Countywide dockets on iCIS system; no print outs. Access court index free at www.superiorcourt.maricopa.gov/docket/JusticeCourtCases/caseSearch.asp.
Criminal Records: Access: Mail, in person, online. Visitors must perform in person searches themselves. Search fee: $24.00 per name. Required to search: name, years to search; also helpful: DOB. Criminal dockets by number. Mail turnaround time 1-2 weeks. Criminal PAT available. PAT results show name only. Countywide dockets on iCIS system; no print outs. Online access same as civil. Online results show middle initial, DOB.
General Information: No juvenile, mental health, victims, sealed or adoption records released. Will not fax documents. Court makes copy: $.50 per page, self serve same. Certification fee: $24.00 per doc. Payee: South Mountain Justice Court. Personal checks accepted. Credit cards accepted. Prepayment required. Mail requests: SASE required.

University Lakes (East Tempe) Justice Court 201 E Chicago St, #101, Chandler, AZ 85225-8502; 602-372-3400; fax: 602-372-3414; 8AM-5PM. ***Misdemeanor, Civil Actions under $10,000, Eviction, Small Claims.***
www.superiorcourt.maricopa.gov/justiceCourts/
Formerly known as East Tempe Justice Court. Countywide Justice Court docket information is sold on disk. Data on disks and countywide terminals may be 2-3 months old.
Civil Records: Access: Mail, in person, online. Only the court performs in person searches; visitors may not. Search fee: $24.00 per name. Required to search: name, years to search. Civil cases indexed by defendant, plaintiff, on computer by case number. Mail turnaround time 1-2 weeks Civil PAT available. PAT results show name only. Countywide dockets on iCIS system; no print outs. Access court index free on countywide site at www.superiorcourt.maricopa.gov/docket/JusticeCourtCases/caseSearch.asp.
Criminal Records: Access: Mail, in person, online. Only the court performs in person searches; visitors may not. Search fee: $24.00 per name. Required to search: name, years to search, DOB. Criminal records on computer by case number. Mail turnaround time is 1-2 weeks. Criminal PAT available. PAT results show name only. Countywide dockets on iCIS system; no print outs. Online access same as civil.
General Information: No juvenile, mental health, victims, sealed records released. Will not fax documents. Court makes copy: $.50 per page. Certification fee: $24.00 per doc. Payee: Tempe Justice Court. Personal checks/Visa/MC accepted. Prepayment required. Mail requests: SASE required.

West McDowell (West Phoenix) Justice Court 620 W Jackson St, #1038, Courtroom 200, Phoenix, AZ 85003; 602-372-6300; fax: 602-372-6408; 8AM-5PM. ***Misdemeanor, Civil Actions under $10,000, Eviction, Small Claims.***
www.superiorcourt.maricopa.gov/justiceCourts/
Countywide Justice Court docket information is sold on disk. Data on disks and countywide terminals may be 6-7 months old.
Civil Records: Access: Mail, in person, online. Both court and visitors may perform in person searches. Search fee: $24.00 per name. Required to search: name, years to search. Civil cases indexed by defendant, plaintiff. Some but not all civil records on computer since 1993. Note: Records 8/31/2005 forward are not on public access system. Mail turnaround time varies. Civil PAT available. PAT results show name only. Countywide dockets on iCIS system; no print outs. Access court index free on at www.superiorcourt.maricopa.gov/docket/JusticeCourtCases/caseSearch.asp.

Criminal Records: Access: In person, online. Both court and visitors may perform in person searches. Search fee: $24.00 per name. Required to search: name, years to search, DOB. Some but not all criminal records on computer since 1993 by case number. Note: Records 8/31/2005 forward are not on public access system. Criminal PAT available. PAT results show name only. Countywide dockets on iCIS system; no print outs. Online access same as civil. Online results show middle initial, DOB.
General Information: No juvenile, mental health, victims, sealed or adoption records released. Will not fax documents. Court makes copy: $.50 per page. Certification fee: $24.00 per doc. Payee: West McDowell Justice Court. Personal checks and major credit cards accepted. Prepayment required. Mail requests: SASE required for civil.

West Mesa Justice Court 2050 W University Dr, Mesa, AZ 85201; 480-964-2958; fax: 480-969-1098; 8AM-5PM. ***Misdemeanor, Civil Actions under $10,000, Eviction, Small Claims.*** www.superiorcourt.maricopa.gov/justiceCourts/
Countywide Justice Court docket information is sold on disk. Data on disks and countywide terminals may be 2-3 months old.
Civil Records: Access: Mail, in person, online. Only the court performs in person searches; visitors may not. Search fee: $24.00 per name. Required to search: name, years to search. Civil cases indexed by defendant, plaintiff, on computer since 1990 by case number. Mail turnaround time 1-2 weeks Nearest public terminal located at San Tan JC, 201 E Chicago in Chandler, or downtown Phoenix. Access court index free on countywide site at www.superiorcourt.maricopa.gov/docket/JusticeCourtCases/caseSearch.asp.
Criminal Records: Access: Mail, in person, online. Only the court performs in person searches; visitors may not. Search fee: $24.00 per name. Required to search: name, years to search, DOB; also helpful: SSN. Criminal records on computer since 1990 by case number. Mail turnaround time is 1-2 weeks. Nearest public terminal located at San Tan JC, 201 E Chicago in Chandler, or downtown Phoenix. Online access same as civil. Online results show middle initial, DOB.
General Information: No juvenile, mental health, victims, sealed or adoption records released. Will not fax documents. Court makes copy: $.50 per page. Certification fee: $24.00 per doc. Payee: West Mesa Justice Court. Personal checks accepted. Credit cards accepted. Prepayment required.

Mohave County

Superior Court PO Box 7000, Kingman, AZ 86402-7000; 928-753-0713; fax: 928-753-0781; 8AM-5PM. ***Felony, Civil Actions over $5,000, Probate.*** www.mohavecourts.com
Civil Records: Access: Phone, fax, mail, in person, online. Both court and visitors may perform in person searches. Search fee: $26.00 per name per year per index. Required to search: name, years to search. Civil cases indexed by defendant, plaintiff, on computer since 11/95; prior records on microfiche and index books. Mail turnaround time 5 days. Civil PAT goes back to 1995. PAT results show middle initial, DOB, SSN. Online access to index or register of action for case files except probate is free at www.supreme.state.az.us/publicaccess/notification/search.asp
Criminal Records: Access: Phone, fax, mail, in person, online. Both court and visitors may perform in person searches. Search fee: $26.00 per name (increases to $26 effective 09/26/08) per yr. Required to search: name, years to search; also helpful: DOB, SSN. Criminal records on computer since 11/95; prior records on microfiche and index books. Mail turnaround time 5 days. Criminal PAT goes back to same as civil. PAT results show middle initial, DOB, SSN. Online access to criminal is the same as civil. Online results show middle initial, DOB.
General Information: No mental health, victims, sealed or adoption records released. Will fax documents $18.00. Court makes copy: $.50 per page, self serve same. Certification fee: $26.00 per doc. Payee: Clerk of Superior Court. Business checks accepted. Major credit cards accepted. Prepayment required. Mail requests: SASE required.

Bullhead City Justice Court 2225 Trane Rd, Bullhead City, AZ 86442; 928-758-0709; fax: 928-758-2644; 8AM-5PM. ***Misdemeanor, Civil Actions under $10,000, Eviction, Small Claims.*** www.mohavecourts.com
Civil Records: Access: Phone, fax, mail, in person, online. Only the court performs in person searches; visitors may not. Search fee: $24.00 per name. Required to search: name, years to search. Civil cases indexed by defendant, plaintiff, on computer from 1988. Some records on docket books. Records retained for 5 years. Will only search back to 1988 unless w/docket number. Mail turnaround time 2-3 days. Civil PAT goes back to 1997. PAT results show name only. Access court data free at www.supreme.state.az.us/publicaccess/notification/search.asp.
Criminal Records: Access: Mail, in person, online. Only the court performs in person searches; visitors may not. Search fee: $17.00 per 10 names. Required to search: name, years to search; also helpful: DOB, SSN. Criminal records computerized from 1988. Some records on docket books. Records retained for 5 years. Will only search back to 1988 unless w/docket numb. Mail turnaround time 2-3 days. Criminal PAT available. PAT results show middle initial, DOB. Online access to criminal same as civil. Online results- middle initial, DOB.
General Information: Online identifiers in results same as on public terminal. No juvenile, mental health, victims, sealed or adoption records released. Will fax documents to local or toll-free number; long distance faxing depends on shortness of document. Court makes copy: $.50 per page. Certification fee: $24.00 per doc. Payee: Bullhead City Justice Court. Personal checks accepted. Major credit cards accepted up to $50.00; minimum $17.00. Prepayment required. Mail requests: SASE requested.

Kingman/Cerbat Justice Court 524 W Beale St, PO Box 29, Kingman, AZ 86401-0029; 928-753-0710; fax: 928-753-7840; 8AM-5PM. ***Misdemeanor, Civil Actions under $10,000, Eviction, Small Claims.*** www.mohavecourts.com
Civil Records: Access: Phone, fax, mail, in person, online. Only the court performs in person searches; visitors may not. Search fee: $24.00 per name. Required to search: name, years to search. Civil cases indexed by defendant, plaintiff, on computer from 1988. Some records on docket books. Records retained for 5 years. Mail turnaround time 2-3 days. Public access at www.supreme.state.az.us/publicaccess/notification/search.asp
Criminal Records: Access: Phone, fax, mail, in person, online. Only the court performs in person searches; visitors may not. Search fee: $24.00 per name. Required to search: name, years to search; also helpful: DOB, SSN. Criminal records computerized from 1988. Some records on docket books. Records retained for 5 years. Mail turnaround time 2-3 days. Public access at www.supreme.state.az.us/publicaccess/notification/search.asp
General Information: No juvenile, mental health, victims, sealed or adoption records released. Will fax documents $.50 per page. Court makes copy: $.50 per page. Certification fee: $24.00 per doc. Payee: Kingman/Cerbat Justice Court. Personal checks accepted. Credit cards accepted. Prepayment required. Mail requests: SASE required.

Lake Havasu Consolidated Court 2001 College Dr, #148, Lake Havasu City, AZ 86403; 928-453-0705; fax: 928-680-0193; 8AM-5PM. ***Misdemeanor, Civil Actions under $10,000, Eviction, Small Claims.*** www.mohavecourts.com
Civil Records: Access: Mail, fax, in person. Only the court performs in person searches; visitors may not. Search fee: $24.00 per name. Required to search: name, years to search. Civil cases indexed by defendant, plaintiff, on computer from 1983. Some records on docket books. Records retained for 5 years after closed/satisfied. Mail turnaround time 3 days.
Criminal Records: Access: Fax, mail, in person. Only the court performs in person searches; visitors may not. Search fee: $24.00 per name. Required to search: name, years to search; also helpful: DOB. Criminal records computerized from 1983. Some records on docket books. Records retained for 5 years after closed/satisfied. Mail turnaround time 3 days.
General Information: No juvenile or victims records released. Will fax non-certified documents. Court makes copy: $.50 per page. Certification fee: $24.00 per doc. Payee: Lake Havasu Consolidated Court. Personal checks and major credit cards accepted. Prepayment required. Mail requests: SASE required.

Moccasin Justice Court HC-65, PO Box 90, Moccasin, AZ 86022; 928-643-7104; fax: 928-643-6206; 8AM-5PM. ***Misdemeanor, Civil Actions under $10,000, Eviction, Small Claims.*** www.mohavecourts.com This court is also the Magistrate Court for Colorado City.
Civil Records: Access: Mail, in person. Only the court performs in person searches; visitors may not. Search fee: $24.00 per name. Required to search: name, years to search. Civil cases indexed by defendant, plaintiff; index on docket books. Records retained for 5 years. Mail turnaround 7-30 days.
Criminal Records: Access: Mail, in person. Only the court performs in person searches; visitors may not. Search fee: $24.00 per name. Required to search: name, years to search. Criminal docket on books. Records retained for 5 years. Mail turnaround time 14-30 days.
General Information: No juvenile, mental health, victims, sealed or adoption records released. Will fax documents $17.00. Court makes copy: $.50 per page. Certification fee: $24.00 per doc. Payee: Moccasin Justice Court. Personal checks accepted. Visa/MC accepted. Prepayment required. SASE not required.

Navajo County

Superior Court PO Box 668, Holbrook, AZ 86025; 928-524-4188; fax: 928-524-4261; 8AM-5PM. ***Felony, Civil Actions over $5,000, Probate.***
Civil Records: Access: Phone, fax, mail, in person, online. Both court and visitors may perform in person searches. Search fee: $26.00 per name. Required to search: name, years to search. Civil cases indexed by defendant, plaintiff; index on docket books, index cards and microfiche back to 1890; computerized back to 1994. Mail turnaround time ASAP. Civil PAT goes back to 1994. PAT results show middle initial, DOB. Access docket free at www.supreme.state.az.us/publicaccess/notification/search.asp.
Criminal Records: Access: Phone, fax, mail, in person, online. Both court and visitors may perform in person searches. Search fee: $26.00 per name. Required to search: name, years to search; also helpful: DOB, SSN. Criminal docket on books, index cards and microfiche back to 1890; computerized back to 1994. Mail turnaround time ASAP. Criminal PAT goes back to same as civil. PAT results show middle initial, DOB. Access docket free at www.supreme.state.az.us/publicaccess/notification/search.asp. Online results show middle initial, DOB.
General Information: Online identifiers in results same as on public terminal. No mental health, victims, sealed or adoption records released. Fee to fax out doc $18.00. Court makes copy: $.50 per page, self serve same. Certification fee: $26.00 per doc. Payee: Clerk of Superior Court. Only cashiers checks and money orders accepted. Prepayment required. Mail requests: SASE required.

Holbrook Justice Court PO Box 366, 121 W Buffalo, Holbrook, AZ 86025; 928-524-4720; fax: 928-524-4725; 8AM-5PM. ***Misdemeanor, Civil Actions under $10,000, Eviction, Small Claims.*** www.navajocountyjusticecourts.org/holbrook.htm
Civil Records: Access: Mail, in person, online. Both court and visitors may perform in person searches. Search fee: $24.00 per name. Required to search: name, years to search. Civil cases indexed by defendant, plaintiff, on computer since 1994. Records on dockets and index cards back for 5 years. Mail turnaround time 1 week. Civil PAT goes back to 1994. Access docket free at www.supreme.state.az.us/publicaccess/notification/search.asp.
Criminal Records: Access: Mail, in person, online. Both court and visitors may perform in person

searches. Search fee: $24.00 per name. Required to search: name, years to search. Criminal records on computer since 1992. Records on dockets and stat books back for 5 years. Mail turnaround time 1 week. Criminal PAT goes back to 1992. Access to the docket is free at www.supreme.state.az.us/publicaccess/notification/search.asp.
General Information: No victim names or sealed records released. Will not fax documents. Court makes copy: $.50 per page. Certification fee: $24.00 per doc. Payee: Holbrook Justice Court. Business checks accepted. No personal checks accepted. Prepayment required. Mail requests: SASE required.

Kayenta Justice Court PO Box 38, Kayenta, AZ 86033; 928-697-3522; fax: 928-697-3528; 8AM-N,1-5PM. ***Misdemeanor, Civil Actions under $10,000, Eviction, Small Claims.***
www.navajocountyjusticecourts.org/kayenta.htm
In-person search, call to make an appointment.
Civil Records: Access: Mail, in person, online. Only the court performs in person searches; visitors may not. Search fee: $24.00 per name. Required to search: name, years to search, address. Civil cases indexed by defendant, plaintiff; index on docket books and index cards; on computer back to 1994. Mail turnaround 1 week. Public terminal available. PAT results show name, DOB. Access docket free at www.supreme.state.az.us/publicaccess/notification/search.asp.
Criminal Records: Access: Mail, in person, online. Only the court performs in person searches; visitors may not. Search fee: $24.00 per name. Required to search: name, years to search, address, DOB, SSN, signed release. Criminal docket on books and index cards; on computer back to 1994. Mail turnaround time 1 week. Public use terminal available.PAT results show name, DOB. Access to docket is free at www.supreme.state.az.us/publicaccess/notification/search.asp.
General Information: No victim's names released. Will not fax documents. Court makes copy: $.50 per page. Certification fee: $24.00 per doc. Payee: Kayenta Justice Court. Only cashiers checks and money orders accepted. No credit cards accepted. Prepayment required. Mail requests: SASE required.

Pinetop-Lakeside Justice Court PO Box 2020, 1360 Neils Hansen Dr, Lakeside, AZ 85929; 928-368-6200; fax: 928-368-8674; 8AM-5PM. ***Misdemeanor, Civil Actions under $10,000, Eviction, Small Claims, Traffic.***
www.navajocountyjusticecourts.org/pinetop.htm
Civil Records: Access: Fax, mail, in person, online. Only the court performs in person searches; visitors may not. Search fee: $24.00 per name per year. Required to search: name, years to search. Civil cases indexed by case number. Civil records on electronic dockets by case number and case files by numeric. Mail turnaround time 7-10 days. Access docket free at www.supreme.state.az.us/publicaccess/notification/search.asp.
Criminal Records: Access: Fax, mail, in person, online. Only the court performs in person searches; visitors may not. Search fee: $24.00 per name per year. Required to search: name, years to search. Criminal records on electronic dockets by case number and case files by alpha back to 1970. Computerized back to 1996. Mail turnaround time 7-10 days. Access docket free at www.supreme.state.az.us/publicaccess/notification/search.asp.
General Information: No victim's names released. No fee to fax documents. Court makes copy: $.50 per page. Certification fee: $24.00 per doc. Payee: Pinetop-Lakeside Justice Court. No personal checks or credit cards accepted. Mail: SASE requested.

Show Low Justice Court PO Box 3085, 620 E McNeil, Show Low, AZ 85902-3085; 928-532-6030; fax: 928-532-6035; 8-5PM. ***Misdemeanor, Civil Actions under $10,000, Eviction, Small Claims.***
www.navajocountyjusticecourts.org/show_low.htm
Civil Records: Access: Mail, in person, online. Only the court performs in person searches; visitors may not. Search fee: $24.00 per name. Required to search: name, years to search. Civil cases indexed by plaintiff. Civil records on computer. Note: In person access requires a written request. Mail turnaround time 48 hours. PAT results show name, DOB. Access to the docket is free at www.supreme.state.az.us/publicaccess/notification/search.asp.
Criminal Records: Access: Mail, in person, online. Only the court performs in person searches; visitors may not. Search fee: $24.00 per name per year. Required to search: name, years to search; also helpful: DOB, SSN. Criminal records on computer for five years. Note: In person must be written request. Mail turnaround- 48 hours. PAT results show name, DOB. Access docket free at www.supreme.state.az.us/publicaccess/notification/search.asp.
General Information: No victim's names released. Will fax documents if fees prepaid. Court makes copy: $.50 per page. Certification fee: $24.00 per doc. Payee: Show Low Justice Court. Personal checks accepted; credit cards are not. Prepayment required. Mail requests: SASE required.

Snowflake Justice Court 145 S Main #D, Snowflake, AZ 85937; 928-536-4141; fax: 928-536-3511; 8AM-5PM. ***Misdemeanor, Civil Actions under $10,000, Eviction, Small Claims.***
www.navajocountyjusticecourts.org/snowflake.htm
Civil Records: Access: Phone, fax, mail, in person, online. Only the court performs in person searches; visitors may not. Search fee: $24.00 per name. Required to search: name, years to search. Civil cases indexed by defendant, plaintiff, on computer back to 6/96, prior on docket books and index cards. Misdemeanors, DUI's and traffic records kept for 3 years, others held f. Mail turnaround time 2 weeks. Access docket free at www.supreme.state.az.us/publicaccess/notification/search.asp.
Criminal Records: Access: Fax, mail, in person, online. Only the court performs in person searches; visitors may not. Search fee: $24.00 per name. Required to search: name, years to search; also helpful: DOB, SSN. Criminal records computerized from 6/96, prior on docket books and index cards. Misdemeanors, DUI's and traffic records kept for 3 years, others held. Mail turnaround time 2 weeks. Access docket free at www.supreme.state.az.us/publicaccess/notification/search.asp.
General Information: No victim's names or search warrants released, no juvenile records released. Court makes copy: $.50 per page. Certification fee: $24.00 per doc. Payee: Snowflake Justice Court. Only cashiers checks and money orders accepted. Prepayment required. Mail requests: SASE required.

Winslow Justice Court Box 808, Winslow, AZ 86047; 928-289-6840; fax: 928-289-6847; 8AM-5PM. ***Misdemeanor, Civil Actions under $10,000, Eviction, Small Claims.***
www.navajocountyjusticecourts.org/winslow.htm
Civil Records: Access: Fax, mail, in person, online. Only the court performs in person searches; visitors may not. Search fee: $24.00 per name. Required to search: name, years to search. Civil cases indexed by defendant, plaintiff; index on docket books; on computer since 1994. Mail turnaround time 1 week. Access docket free at www.supreme.state.az.us/publicaccess/notification/search.asp.
Criminal Records: Access: Fax, mail, in person, online. Only the court performs in person searches; visitors may not. Search fee: $24.00 per name. Required to search: name, years to search; also helpful: DOB, SSN. Criminal docket on books; on computer since 1995. Mail turnaround time 1 week. Access to the docket is free at www.supreme.state.az.us/publicaccess/notification/search.asp.
General Information: No victim's names released. Will fax documents to local or toll free line. Court makes copy: $.50 per page. Certification fee: $24.00 per doc. Payee: Winslow Courts. Only cash or money order accepted. No credit cards accepted. Prepayment required. Mail requests: SASE required.

Pima County

Superior Court 110 W Congress, Tucson, AZ 85701; 520-740-3200; criminal phone: 520-740-3228; civil phone: 520-740-3210; fax: 520-798-3531; 8AM-5PM. ***Felony, Civil Actions over $5,000, Probate.*** www.cosc.co.pima.az.us
Address correspondence to attention of civil or criminal section. Superior Court, general phone 520-740-4200. **Civil Records:** Access: Phone, mail, in person, online. Both court and visitors may perform in person searches. Search fee: $26.00 per name. Required to search: name, years to search, DOB. Civil cases indexed by defendant, plaintiff, on computer since 1980s, on microfilm since late 1800s. Mail turnaround time 14 days; include $5.00 mailing fee. Civil PAT goes back to 1970s. PAT results show name, DOB. Access superior court records free at www.agave.cosc.pima.gov/PublicDocs/. Search by name, biz name, or by case number. Online results show middle initial, DOB. Images are shown.
Criminal Records: Access: Mail, in person. Both court and visitors may perform in person searches. Search fee: $26.00 per name. Add $5.00 for postage and handling. Required to search: name, years to search, DOB. Criminal records on computer since 1980s, on microfilm since late 1800s. Mail turnaround time 14 days; include $5.00 mailing fee. Criminal PAT goes back to 1983.PAT results show name, DOB.
General Information: Online identifiers in results same as on public terminal. No juvenile, mental health, adoption, victims or sealed records released. Fee to fax out file $5.00 plus $.50 per page. Court makes copy: $.50 per page. Cert fee: $26.00 per doc. Payee: Clerk of Superior Court. Cashiers checks/ money orders accepted. Visa/MC accepted in person only. Prepayment required. SASE not required.

Ajo Justice Court 111 La Mina Ave, Ajo, AZ 85321; 520-387-7684; fax: 520-387-6028; 8AM-5PM. ***Misdemeanor, Civil Actions under $10,000, Eviction, Small Claims.***
Civil and criminal search treated as one.
Civil Records: Access: Mail, in person, online. Only the court performs in person searches; visitors may not. Search fee: $24.00 per name. Required to search: name, years to search. Civil cases indexed by defendant, plaintiff, on computer since 1997, prior in docket books. Mail turnaround time 2 weeks. Access docket is free at www.supreme.state.az.us/publicaccess/notification/search.asp.
Criminal Records: Access: Mail, in person, online, fax. Only the court performs in person searches; visitors may not. Search fee: $24.00 per name. Required to search: name, years to search. Criminal records on computer since 1987, prior in docket books. Mail turnaround time 2 weeks. Access to the docket is free at www.supreme.state.az.us/publicaccess/notification/search.asp.
General Information: No juvenile, sealed, victim records released. Will fax documents to local or toll-free number. Court makes copy: $.50 per page. Certification fee: $24.00 per doc. Payee: Ajo Justice Court. Personal checks accepted; credit cards are not. Prepayment required. SASE not required.

Green Valley Justice Court 601 N La-Canada, Green Valley, AZ 85614; 520-648-0658; fax: 520-648-2235; 8AM-5PM. ***Misdemeanor, Civil Actions under $10,000, Eviction, Small Claims.***
Civil Records: Access: Mail, in person, online. Only the court performs in person searches; visitors may not. Search fee: $24.00 per name. Required to search: name, years to search. Civil cases indexed by defendant, plaintiff, on computer back to 1996; card files prior. Note: Clerk will only search computerized records. Mail turnaround time 2 weeks. Access to the docket is free at www.supreme.state.az.us/publicaccess/notification/search.asp. **Criminal Records:** Access: Mail, in person, online. Only the court performs in person searches; visitors may not. Search fee: $24.00 per name. Required to search: name, years to search, DOB. Criminal records computerized from 1996; card files prior. Note: Clerk will only search computerized records. Mail turnaround time 14 days. Access docket free at www.supreme.state.az.us/publicaccess/notification/search.asp.
General Information: No juvenile, mental health, victims, sealed or adoption records released. Will not fax documents. Court makes copy: $.50 per page. Certification fee: $24.00 per doc. Payee: Green Valley Justice Court. Personal check - Visa/MC accepted. Prepayment required. Mail requests: SASE required.

Pima County Consolidated Justice Ct 115 N Church Ave, Tucson, AZ 85701; 520-740-3171; fax: 520-884-0346; 8AM-4:30PM. ***Misdemeanor, Civil Actions under $10,000, Eviction, Small Claims, Traffic.*** www.jp.pima.gov/

Civil Records: Access: Fax, mail, in person, online. Both court and visitors may perform in person searches. Search fee: $24.00 per name. Required to search: name, years to search, DOB and/or SSN. Civil cases indexed by defendant, plaintiff, on computer since 1988, on docket books prior. Mail turnaround time 2 days. Public use terminal available. Online access free http://jp.co.pima.az.us/casesearch/index.php. You can search docket info for civil, crim or traffic cases by name, docket or citation.

Criminal Records: Access: Fax, mail, online, in person. Both court and visitors may perform in person searches. Search fee: $24.00 per name. Required to search: name, years to search, DOB, SSN. Criminal records on computer since 1988, on docket books prior. Mail turnaround time 2 days. Public use terminal available. PAT results show middle initial, DOB. Online access to criminal records is the same as civil. Online results show middle initial, DOB.

General Information: No information about set-aside judgments, unserved search warrants or felony warrants released. Will not fax documents. Court makes copy: $.50 per page. Certification fee: $24.00 per doc. Payee: Pima County Consolidated Justice Court. Personal checks accepted. Credit cards accepted. Prepayment required. Mail requests: SASE required.

Pinal County

Superior Court PO Box 2730, Florence, AZ 85232-2730; 520-866-5300; probate phone: same; fax: 520-866-5320; 8AM-5PM. ***Felony, Civil Actions over $5,000, Probate.*** www.co.pinal.az.us/clerksc/

Probate fax is same as main fax number.

Civil Records: Access: Phone, mail, in person, online. Both court and visitors may perform in person searches. Search fee: $26.00 per name. Required to search: name, years to search. Civil cases indexed by defendant, plaintiff, on computer from 1993. Some records on docket books back to 1775. Mail turnaround time 7 days. Civil PAT goes back to 1993. Access to the docket is free at www.supreme.state.az.us/publicaccess/notification/search.asp.

Criminal Records: Access: Phone, mail, in person, online. Both court and visitors may perform in person searches. Search fee: $26.00 per name. Required to search: name, years to search. Criminal records computerized from 1987. Some records on docket books back to 1875. Mail turnaround time 7 days. Criminal PAT goes back to 1987. PAT results show middle initial, DOB. Access to the docket is free at www.supreme.state.az.us/publicaccess/notification/search.asp. Online results show middle initial, DOB.

General Information: Online identifiers in results same as on public terminal. No victim names, adoption records released. Fee to fax document $.50 per page. Court makes copy: $.50 per page. Certification fee: $26.00 per doc. Payee: Clerk of Superior Court. Business checks accepted. No credit cards accepted. Prepayment required. Mail requests: SASE required.

Apache Junction Justice Court 575 N Idaho, #200, Apache Junction, AZ 85219; 480-982-2921; criminal fax: 520-866-6153; civil fax: same; 8AM-5PM. ***Misdemeanor, Civil Actions under $10,000, Eviction, Small Claims.*** http://co.pinal.az.us/JusticeCourts Yes, the area code for the fax number is different than the voice number.

Civil Records: Access: Fax, mail, in person, online. Both court and visitors may perform in person searches. Search fee: $24.00 per name. Required to search: name, years to search. Civil cases indexed by defendant, plaintiff, on computer since 1999. Records retained for 5 years. Mail turnaround time varies. Access docket free at www.supreme.state.az.us/publicaccess/notification/search.asp.

Criminal Records: Access: Fax, mail, in person, online. Only the court performs in person searches; visitors may not. Search fee: $24.00 per name. Required to search: name, years to search. Criminal records on computer since 1993. Records retained for 5 years. Mail turnaround time varies. Access docket free at www.supreme.state.az.us/publicaccess/notification/search.asp.

General Information: Will fax documents $1.25 per page. Court makes copy: $.50 per page. Certification fee: $24.00 per doc. Payee: Apache Junction Justice Court. No personal checks or credit cards accepted. Prepayment required. Mail requests: SASE required.

Casa Grande Justice Court 820 E Cottonwood Ln, Bldg B, Casa Grande, AZ 85222; 520-836-5471; criminal fax: 520-866-7404; civil fax: same; 8AM-5PM. ***Misdemeanor, Civil Actions under $10,000, Eviction, Small Claims.*** http://co.pinal.az.us/JusticeCourts

Civil Records: Access: Mail, in person, online. Only the court performs in person searches; visitors may not. Search fee: $24.00 per name. Required to search: name, years to search. Civil cases indexed by defendant, plaintiff, on computer since 1999, index back to 1999. Mail turnaround time 1 day. Access docket free at www.supreme.state.az.us/publicaccess/notification/search.asp.

Criminal Records: Access: Mail, in person, online. Only the court performs in person searches; visitors may not. Search fee: $24.00 per name. Required to search: name, years to search, DOB; also helpful: SSN. Criminal records on computer since 1999, index back to 2000. Mail turnaround time 1 day. Access docket free at www.supreme.state.az.us/publicaccess/notification/search.asp.

General Information: No juvenile, mental health, victims, sealed or adoption records released. Will fax documents. Court makes copy: $.50 per page, self serve same. Certification fee: $24.00 per doc. Payee: Casa Grande Justice Court. Business checks must be pre-approved. Visa/MC by phone at Official Payments 800-847-4567. Prepayment required. Mail requests: SASE required.

Eloy Justice Court PO Box 586, Eloy, AZ 85231; 520-466-9221; fax: 520-466-4473; 8AM-N, 1-5PM. ***Misdemeanor, Civil Actions under $10,000, Eviction, Small Claims.*** http://co.pinal.az.us/JusticeCourts

Civil Records: Access: Mail, in person, online. Only the court performs in person searches; visitors may not. Search fee: $18.00 per name. Required to search: name, years to search. Civil cases indexed by defendant, plaintiff, on computer since 8/92. On docket books and index cards from 1981. Mail turnaround time 1-2 weeks. Access to the docket is free at www.supreme.state.az.us/publicaccess/notification/search.asp.

Criminal Records: Access: Mail, in person, online. Only the court performs in person searches; visitors may not. Search fee: $24.00 per name. Required to search: name, years to search, DOB. Criminal records on computer since 8/92. On docket books and index cards from 1981. Mail turnaround time 1-2 weeks. Access to the docket is free at www.supreme.state.az.us/publicaccess/notification/search.asp.

General Information: No juvenile, mental health, victims, sealed or adoption records released. Will not fax documents. Court makes copy: $.50 per page. Certification fee: $24.00 per doc. Payee: Eloy Justice Court. No personal checks accepted. Visa/MC accepted. Prepayment required. Mail: SASE required.

Florence Justice Court PO Box 1818, Florence, AZ 85232; 520-866-7194; civil phone: 520-886-7195; fax: 520-866-7190; 8AM-5PM. ***Misdemeanor, Civil Actions under $10,000, Eviction, Small Claims.*** http://co.pinal.az.us/JusticeCourts

Civil Records: Access: Mail, in person, online. Only the court performs in person searches; visitors may not. Search fee: $24.00 per name. Required to search: name, years to search. Civil cases indexed by defendant, plaintiff, are on computer since 1/1999. Mail turnaround time 1 week. Access docket info free at www.supreme.state.az.us/publicaccess/notification/search.asp.

Criminal Records: Access: Mail, in person, online. Only the court performs in person searches; visitors may not. Search fee: $24.00 per name. Required to search: name, years to search. Criminal records are on computer since 1/1999. Mail turnaround time 1 week. Access to the docket is free at www.supreme.state.az.us/publicaccess/notification/search.asp. Online results show middle initial, DOB.

General Information: No juvenile, mental health, victims, sealed or adoption records released. Will fax documents no fee. Court makes copy: $.50 per page. Certification fee: $24.00 per doc. Payee: Florence Justice Court. Only cashiers checks and money orders accepted. No credit cards accepted. Prepayment required. Mail requests: SASE required.

Mammoth Justice Court PO Box 777, Mammoth, AZ 85618; 520-487-2262; fax: 520-866-7839; 8AM-5PM. ***Misdemeanor, Civil Actions under $10,000, Eviction, Small Claims.*** http://co.pinal.az.us/JusticeCourts

Civil Records: Access: Mail, fax, in person, online. Both court and visitors may perform in person searches. Search fee: $24.00 per name. Required to search: name, years to search. Civil cases indexed by defendant, plaintiff; index on docket books. Civil records retained for 7 years; on computer back 5 years. Mail turnaround time 2 days. Civil PAT goes back to 5 years. Access docket free at www.supreme.state.az.us/publicaccess/notification/search.asp.

Criminal Records: Access: Mail, in person, online. Both court and visitors may perform in person searches. Search fee: $24.00 per name. Required to search: name, years to search, DOB. Criminal docket on books. Misdemeanor records retained for 7 years; on computer back 5 years. Mail turnaround time 2 days. Criminal PAT goes back to same as civil. Access docket free at www.supreme.state.az.us/publicaccess/notification/search.asp.

General Information: No juvenile, mental health, victims, sealed or adoption records released. Will fax documents to local or toll free line. Court makes copy: $.50 per page. Certification fee: $24.00 per doc. Cert fee includes copies. Payee: Mammoth Justice Court. Personal checks accepted; credit cards are not. Prepayment required. Mail requests: SASE required.

Maricopa Justice Court PO Box 201, 44625 W Garvey Rd, Maricopa, AZ 85239; 520-568-2451; fax: 520-568-2924; 8AM-5PM. ***Misdemeanor, Civil Actions under $10,000, Eviction, Small Claims.*** http://co.pinal.az.us/JusticeCourts

Civil Records: Access: Fax, mail, in person, online. Only the court performs in person searches; visitors may not. Search fee: $24.00 per name. Required to search: name, years to search. Civil cases indexed by defendant. Civil records on computer since 1999; on dockets to 1993. Mail turnaround time 7 days. Access to the docket is free at www.supreme.state.az.us/publicaccess/notification/search.asp.

Criminal Records: Access: Fax, mail, in person, online. Only the court performs in person searches; visitors may not. Search fee: $24.00 per name. Required to search: name, years to search. Criminal records on computer since 1999; on dockets to 1993. Mail turnaround time 7 days. Access docket free at www.supreme.state.az.us/publicaccess/notification/search.asp.

General Information: No juvenile, mental health, victims, sealed or adoption records released. Will fax documents to local or toll-free number. Court makes copy: $.50 per page. Certification fee: $24.00 per doc. Payee: Maricopa Justice Court. Personal checks accepted; credit cards are not. Prepayment required. Mail requests: SASE required.

Oracle Justice Court PO Box 3924, Oracle, AZ 85623; 520-896-9250; fax: 520-866-7812; 8AM-5PM. ***Misdemeanor, Civil Actions under $10,000, Eviction, Small Claims, Traffic.*** http://pinalcountyaz.gov/Departments/JudicialBranch/Pages/Home.aspx

Civil Records: Access: Mail, in person, online. Both court and visitors may perform in person searches. Search fee: $24.00 per name. Required to search: name, years to search; also helpful: address. Civil cases indexed by defendant. Civil index on docket books and computer back to 1991. Mail turnaround

time 5 days Civil PAT goes back to 1991. Access docket free at www.supreme.state.az.us/publicaccess/notification/search.asp.
Criminal Records: Access: Mail, in person, online. Both court and visitors may perform in person searches. Search fee: $24.00 per name. Required to search: name, years to search, DOB; also helpful: address, SSN. Criminal docket on books and computer back to 1991. Mail turnaround time 5 days. Criminal PAT goes back to same as civil. Access to the docket is free at www.supreme.state.az.us/publicaccess/notification/search.asp.
General Information: No juvenile, mental health, victims, sealed, adoption records released. Fee to fax out file $1.00 per page. Court makes copy: $.50 per page, self serve same. Certification fee: $24.00 per doc. Payee: Oracle Justice Court. No personal checks; money orders, cashier's checks or cash only. Prepayment required. Mail requests: SASE required.

Superior/Kearny Justice Court 60 E Main St, Superior, AZ 85273; 520-689-5871; criminal fax: 520-689-2369; civil fax: same; 8AM-N, 1-5PM. ***Misdemeanor, Civil Actions under $10,000, Eviction, Small Claims.***
http://co.pinal.az.us/JusticeCourts
Civil Records: Access: Fax, mail, in person, online. Only the court performs in person searches; visitors may not. Search fee: $24.00 per name. Required to search: name, years to search. Civil cases indexed by defendant, plaintiff, go back 5 years; computerized records go back 5 years. Mail turnaround time 3 days. Access docket is free at www.supreme.state.az.us/publicaccess/notification/search.asp.
Criminal Records: Access: Fax, mail, in person, online. Only the court performs in person searches; visitors may not. Search fee: Justice- $24.00 per name Superior - $18.00 per name (increases to $26 effective 09/26/08). Required to search: name, years to search, DOB; also helpful: SSN. Criminal records go back 5 years; computerized records go back 5 years. Mail turnaround time 3 days. Access docket free at www.supreme.state.az.us/publicaccess/notification/search.asp.
General Information: No juvenile, mental health, victims, sealed or adoption records released. No fee to fax documents. Court makes copy: $.50 per page. Certification fee: $26.00 per doc; $24 for Justice Court. Payee: Superior/Kearny Justice Court. No personal checks accepted. Cash, money order or cashier's check accepted only. Prepayment required. Mail requests: SASE required.

Santa Cruz County

Superior Court PO Box 1265, Nogales, AZ 85628; 520-375-7700; criminal phone: 520-375-7700; fax: 520-375-7703; 8AM-5PM. ***Felony, Civil Actions over $5,000, Probate.*** http://sccazcourts.org
Civil Records: Access: Mail, fax, in person, online. Both court and visitors may perform in person searches. Search fee: $26.00 per name per year per index. Required to search: name, years to search. Civil cases indexed by defendant, plaintiff, on microfiche from 1898 to 1950. Records on docket books from 1950 to 1996; on computer after 1996. Mail turnaround time 10 days. Civil PAT goes back to 1996. Access civil records free at www.supreme.state.az.us/publicaccess/notification/default.asp.
Criminal Records: Access: Mail, fax, in person, online. Both court and visitors may perform in person searches. Search fee: $26.00 per name. Required to search: name, years to search, DOB; also helpful: SSN. Criminal records archived on microfiche from 1898 to 1995. Records on docket books from 1977 to 1996; on computer after 1996. Mail turnaround time 1 1/2 weeks. Criminal PAT goes back to same as civil. Access criminal records free at www.supreme.state.az.us/publicaccess/. Online results show middle initial, DOB.
General Information: Online identifiers in results same as on public terminal. No mental health, victims, sealed or adoption records released. Fee to fax document $.50 per page. Court makes copy: $.50 per page, self serve same. Certification fee: $26.00 per doc. Payee: Clerk of Superior Court. Personal checks and major credit cards accepted. Prepayment required. Mail requests: SASE required.

East Santa Cruz County Justice Court - Precinct #2 PO Box 1330, 3147 State Rte 83, #103, Sonoita, AZ 85637-1330; 520-455-5796; criminal fax: 520-455-5133; civil fax: same; 8:30AM-5PM. ***Misdemeanor, Civil Actions under $10,000, Eviction, Small Claims.***
Send fax requests to Attention: Justice Court.
Civil Records: Access: Mail, fax, in person, online. Only the court performs in person searches; visitors may not. Search fee: $24.00 per name. Required to search: name, years to search; also helpful: address. Civil cases indexed by plaintiff. Civil index on docket books. Mail turnaround time 3-5 days. Access civil records free at www.supreme.state.az.us/publicaccess/notification/default.asp
Criminal Records: Access: Mail, fax, in person, online. Only the court performs in person searches; visitors may not. Search fee: $24.00 per name. Required to search: name, years to search, DOB, SSN, signed release; also helpful: address. Criminal docket on books. Mail turnaround time 3-5 days. Access docket free at www.supreme.state.az.us/publicaccess/notification/search.asp.
General Information: No juvenile, mental health, victims, sealed or adoption records released. Will fax documents to local or toll free line. Court makes copy: $.50 per page. Certification fee: $24.00 per doc. Payee: East Santa Cruz County Justice Court. Personal checks and major credit cards accepted. Prepayment required. SASE not required.

Santa Cruz Justice Court PO Box 1150, Nogales, AZ 85628; 520-375-7762; fax: 520-375-7759; 8AM-5PM. ***Misdemeanor, Civil Actions under $10,000, Eviction, Small Claims.***
www.sccazcourts.org
Civil Records: Access: Fax, mail, in person, online. Both court and visitors may perform in person searches. Search fee: $24.00 per name. Required to search: name, years to search; also helpful: address. Civil cases indexed by defendant, plaintiff, go back to 1975; on computer back to 2/96. Mail turnaround time 1-3 weeks. Civil PAT goes back to 1996. Access civil records free at www.supreme.state.az.us/publicaccess/notification/default.asp. Also, weekly court calendars are at www.sccazcourts.org/court_calendars.htm.
Criminal Records: Access: Fax, mail, in person, online. Both court and visitors may perform in person searches. Search fee: $24.00 per name. Required to search: name, years to search, DOB; also helpful: address, SSN. Criminal records go back to 1975; on computer back to 2/96. Mail turnaround time 1-3 weeks. Criminal PAT goes back to same as civil. Access to the docket is free at www.supreme.state.az.us/publicaccess/notification/search.asp. Also, weekly court calendars are at www.sccazcourts.org/court_calendars.htm.
General Information: No juvenile, mental health, victims, sealed or adoption records released. Will fax documents. Court makes copy: $.50 per page, self serve same. Certification fee: $24.00 per doc. Payee: Santa Cruz Justice Court. Personal checks accepted. Credit cards accepted. Prepayment required. Mail requests: SASE required.

Yavapai County

Superior Court Yavapai County Courthouse, Court Clerk, 120 S Cortez, Prescott, AZ 86303; 928-771-3312, 928-777-7934; fax: 928-771-3111; 8AM-5PM. ***Felony, Civil Actions over $10,000, Probate.*** www.co.yavapai.az.us/supct.aspx
Direct search requests to the record room.
Civil Records: Access: Fax, mail, in person, online. Both court and visitors may perform in person searches. Search fee: $26.00 per name. Required to search: name, years to search. Civil cases indexed by defendant, plaintiff, archived from 1900s. Some records on handwritten index book. Mail turnaround time 10 days. Civil PAT goes back to 1992. PAT results show name only. Access to Superior Court records is free at www.supreme.state.az.us/publicaccess/notification/default.asp.
Criminal Records: Access: Fax, mail, in person, online. Both court and visitors may perform in person searches. Search fee: $26.00 per name. Required to search: name, years to search, offense. Criminal records archived from 1900s. Some records on handwritten index book. Mail turnaround time 10 days. Criminal PAT goes back to 1992. PAT results show middle initial, SSN; DOB, middle initial and/or address may appear on crim results, but not always on newer records. Free online access to Superior Court records is at www.supreme.state.az.us/publicaccess/. Online results show middle initial, DOB. PAT has images, online system does not.
General Information: No juvenile, mental health, victims, sealed or adoption records released. Will fax documents $5.00 per doc. Court makes copy: $.50 per page. Cert fee: $26.00 per doc. Authentification of all pages- $54.00. Payee: Clerk of Superior Court. Personal checks and major credit cards accepted. Prepayment required. Mail requests: SASE required.

Bagdad Justice Court PO Box 243, Bagdad, AZ 86321; 928-633-2141; criminal fax: 928-633-4451; civil fax: same; 8AM-5PM M; 8:00AM-4:00PM T-TH. ***Misdemeanor, Civil Actions under $10,000, Eviction, Small Claims.***
www.co.yavapai.az.us/LawandJustice.aspx
Civil Records: Access: Mail, in person, online. Only the court performs in person searches; visitors may not. Search fee: $24.00 per name. Required to search: name, years to search; also helpful: address. Records indexed by plaintiff name. Civil records on computer since 3/94. Records on docket books and index cards. Records purged after 10 years. Mail turnaround time 2 days. Access to the docket is free at www.supreme.state.az.us/publicaccess/notification/search.asp.
Criminal Records: Access: Mail, in person, online. Only the court performs in person searches; visitors may not. Search fee: $24.00 per name. Required to search: name, years to search, DOB; also helpful: address, SSN. Criminal records on computer since 3/94. Records on docket books and index cards. Records purged after 5 years. Mail turnaround time 2 days. Access to the docket is free at www.supreme.state.az.us/publicaccess/notification/search.asp.
General Information: No juvenile, mental health, victims, sealed or adoption records released. Will not fax documents. Court makes copy: $.50 per page. Certification fee: $24.00 per doc. Payee: Bagdad Justice Court. Only cashiers checks and money orders accepted. Visa/MC accepted. Prepayment required. Mail requests: SASE required.

Mayer Justice Court PO Box 245, 12840 Central Ave, Mayer, AZ 86333; 928-771-3355; fax: 928-771-3356; 8AM-5PM. ***Misdemeanor, Civil Actions under $10,000, Eviction, Small Claims.***
www.co.yavapai.az.us/LawandJustice.aspx
Search fee includes civil and criminal indexes.
Civil Records: Access: Mail, in person, online. Only the court performs in person searches; visitors may not. Search fee: $24.00 per name. Required to search: name, years to search. Civil cases indexed by defendant, plaintiff, on computer back to 1989. Records purged after 5 years. Mail turnaround time 4 days. Access to the docket is free at www.supreme.state.az.us/publicaccess/notification/search.asp.
Criminal Records: Access: Mail, in person, online. Only the court performs in person searches; visitors may not. Search fee: $24.00 per name. Required to search: name, years to search; also helpful: DOB. Criminal records computerized from 1989. Records purged after 5 years. Mail turnaround time 4 days. Access to the docket is free at www.supreme.state.az.us/publicaccess/notification/search.asp.
General Information: No juvenile, mental health, victims, sealed or adoption records released. Will not fax documents. Court makes copy: $.50 per page. Certification fee: $24.00 per doc. Payee: Mayer Justice Court. Only cashiers checks and money orders accepted. No credit cards accepted. Prepayment required. Mail requests: SASE required.

Prescott Justice Court Yavapai County Courthouse, 120 S Cortez, Rm 103, Prescott, AZ 86301; 928-771-3300; criminal fax: 928-771-3302; civil fax: same; 8AM-5PM. ***Misdemeanor, Civil Actions under $10,000, Eviction, Small Claims.***
www.prescottjpcourt.com

Civil Records: Access: Fax, mail, in person, online. Both court and visitors may perform in person searches. Search fee: $24.00 per name. Required to search: name, years to search; also helpful: address. Civil cases indexed by defendant, plaintiff, are indexed on computer then purged after 5 years. Note: Court only provides searches for past 5 years. Mail turnaround time 2 days. PAT results show name only. Access to City and Justice court records is free at http://71.216.160.127/csp/pcc/csp1.csp.

Criminal Records: Access: Fax, mail, in person, online. Both court and visitors may perform in person searches. Search fee: $17.00. Required to search: name, years to search, DOB; also helpful: address, SSN. Criminal records are indexed on computer then purged after 5 years. Note: Court only provides searches for past 5 years. Mail turnaround time 2 days. PAT results show name only. Access to City Court and Justice Court records is free at http://71.216.160.127/csp/pcc/csp1.csp. Online results show middle initial, DOB.

General Information: No juvenile, victims or sealed records released. Will fax documents $17.00 per doc. Court makes copy: $.50 per page. Certification fee: $24.00 per doc. Payee: City of Prescott. No 2-party checks accepted. Visa/MC/AmEx accepted. Prepayment required. Mail requests: SASE required.

Seligman Justice Court PO Box 56, 54150 N Floyd St, Seligman, AZ 86337-0056; 928-422-3281; fax: 928-442-5982; 8AM-5PM. ***Misdemeanor, Civil Actions under $10,000, Eviction, Small Claims.***
www.co.yavapai.az.us/LawandJustice.aspx

Civil Records: Access: Phone, fax, mail, in person, online. Both court and visitors may perform in person searches. No search fee. Required to search: name, years to search; also helpful: address. Civil cases indexed by defendant, plaintiff, on computer. Records purged after 5 years. Mail turnaround time 2 days. Access to the docket is free at www.supreme.state.az.us/publicaccess/notification/search.asp.

Criminal Records: Access: Phone, fax, mail, in person, online. Both court and visitors may perform in person searches. No search fee. Required to search: name, years to search, DOB; also helpful: address, SSN. Criminal records on computer. Records purged after 5 years. Mail turnaround time 2 days. Access docket is free at www.supreme.state.az.us/publicaccess/notification/search.asp.

General Information: No juvenile or victims records released. Will fax back documents no add'l fee. Court makes copy: $.10 per page. Certification fee: $24.00 per doc. Payee: Seligman Justice Court. Business checks accepted. Visa/MC and other cards accepted. Prepayment required. Mail requests: SASE required.

Verde Valley Justice Court 10 S 6th St, Cottonwood, AZ 86326; 928-639-5820; criminal fax: 928-639-5828; civil fax: same; 8AM-5PM. ***Misdemeanor, Civil Actions under $10,000, Eviction, Small Claims.***
www.co.yavapai.az.us/VVJC.aspx

Civil Records: Access: Mail, in person, online. Both court and visitors may perform in person searches. Search fee: $24.00 per name. Required to search: name, years to search; also helpful: DOB. Civil cases indexed by plaintiff. Civil records on computer from 6/99. Records purged after 5 years. Mail turnaround time 2 days. Access to the docket is free at www.supreme.state.az.us/publicaccess/notification/search.asp.

Criminal Records: Access: Mail, in person, online. Both court and visitors may perform in person searches. Search fee: $17.00. Required to search: name, years to search, DOB; also helpful: address, SSN. Criminal records computerized since 6/99. Records purged after 5 years. Mail turnaround time 2 days. Access to the docket is free at www.supreme.state.az.us/publicaccess/notification/search.asp.

General Information: No juvenile, mental health, victims, sealed records released. Will not fax documents. Court makes copy: $.50 per page. Certification fee: $24.00 per doc. Payee: Verde Valley Justice Court. Personal checks accepted. Credit cards accepted. Prepayment required. Mail requests: SASE required.

Yarnell Justice Court PO Box 65, Justice Court Bldg, Yarnell, AZ 85362; 928-427-3318; fax: 928-771-3362; 8AM-5PM. ***Misdemeanor, Civil Actions under $10,000, Eviction, Small Claims.***
www.co.yavapai.az.us/LawandJustice.aspx

Civil Records: Access: Mail, in person, online. Only the court performs in person searches; visitors may not. Search fee: $24.00 per name. Required to search: name, years to search. Civil cases indexed by defendant, plaintiff, on computer from 1989. Prior records on docket books. Records purged after 10 years. Mail turnaround time 5 days. Access to the docket is free at www.supreme.state.az.us/publicaccess/notification/search.asp.

Criminal Records: Access: Mail, in person, online. Only the court performs in person searches; visitors may not. Search fee: $24.00 per name. Required to search: name, years to search. Criminal records computerized from 1989, prior on docket books. Records purged after 5 years. Mail turnaround time 5 days. Access to the docket is free at www.supreme.state.az.us/publicaccess/notification/search.asp. Also, view current warrants, sentencing's and felony complaints at www.co.yavapai.az.us/VVJC.aspx.

General Information: No juvenile, mental health, victims, sealed or adoption records released. Will fax out documents $.50 per page. Court makes copy: $.50 per page. Certification fee: $24.00 per doc. Payee: Yarnell Justice Court. Only cashiers checks and money orders accepted. Visa/MC accepted. Prepayment required. Mail requests: SASE required.

Yuma County

Superior Court 250 W 2nd St, #B, Yuma, AZ 85364; 928-817-4210; fax: 928-817-4211; 8AM-5PM. ***Felony, Civil Actions over $5,000, Probate.***
www.co.yuma.az.us/courts

Civil Records: Access: Fax, mail, in person, online. Both court and visitors may perform in person searches. Search fee: $26.00 per name per year. Required to search: name, years to search. Civil cases indexed by defendant, plaintiff; index in docket books from 1900s, new and pending cases from 11/1994 on computer. Mail turnaround time 7-10 days. Civil PAT goes back to 1995. PAT results show name, DOB. Results include name (first, last) and case number. Access to the docket is free at www.supreme.state.az.us/publicaccess/notification/search.asp.

Criminal Records: Access: Fax, mail, in person, online. Both court and visitors may perform in person searches. Search fee: $26.00 per name. Required to search: name, years to search. Criminal docket on books from 1900s, new and pending cases from 11/1994 on computer. Mail turnaround time 1 week to 10 days. Criminal PAT goes back to same as civil.PAT results show name, DOB. Results include name (first, last) and case number. Access to the docket is free at www.supreme.state.az.us/publicaccess/notification/search.asp. Online results show middle initial, DOB.

General Information: No adoption, mental health records released. Will fax documents $18.00 per doc. Court makes copy: $.50 per page. Certification fee: $26.00 per doc. Payee: Clerk of Superior Court. Business checks and money orders accepted. Visa/MC accepted. Prepayment required. Mail requests: SASE not required, but $5.00 shipping & handling fee.

Somerton Justice Court PO Box 458, 350 W Main St, Somerton, AZ 85350; 928-627-2722; criminal fax: 928-627-1076; civil fax: same; 8AM-5PM. ***Misdemeanor, Civil Actions under $10,000, Eviction, Small Claims.***
www.somertoncourts.com

Civil Records: Access: Phone, fax, mail, in person, online. Both court and visitors may perform in person searches. Search fee: $24.00 per name. Required to search: name, years to search. Civil cases indexed by defendant. Civil records on computer. Mail turnaround time 7-10 days. Online access to records is free the website above as well as at www.supreme.state.az.us/publicaccess/notification/default.asp.

Criminal Records: Access: Phone, fax, mail, in person, online. Only the court performs in person searches; visitors may not. Search fee: $24.00 per name. Required to search: name, years to search, DOB, SSN, offense, date of offense. Criminal records on computer. Mail turnaround time 2-4 days. Access records free at the website above as well as at www.supreme.state.az.us/publicaccess/.

General Information: No set aside judgment records released. Will fax documents $.50 per page. Court makes copy: $.50 per page. Certification fee: $24.00 per doc. Payee: Somerton Justice Court. Business checks accepted. Visa/MC accepted. Prepayment required. Mail requests: SASE required.

Wellton Justice Court PO Box 384, Wellton, AZ 85356; 928-785-3321; fax: 928-785-4933; 8AM-5PM. ***Misdemeanor, Civil Actions under $10,000, Eviction, Small Claims.***

Civil Records: Access: Phone, fax, mail, in person, online. Only the court performs in person searches; visitors may not. No search fee. Required to search: name, years to search. Civil cases indexed by defendant, plaintiff, on computer to 1992. Mail turnaround time same day. Access to the docket is free at www.supreme.state.az.us/publicaccess/notification/search.asp.

Criminal Records: Access: Phone, fax, mail, in person, online. Only the court performs in person searches; visitors may not. No search fee. Required to search: name, years to search, offense, date of offense. Criminal records on computer to 1992. Mail turnaround time same day. Access to the docket is free at www.supreme.state.az.us/publicaccess/notification/search.asp.

General Information: No set aside judgment records released. Will fax documents to local or toll free line. Court makes copy: $.50 per page. Certification fee: $24.00 per doc. Payee: Wellton Justice Court. Personal checks accepted. All major credit cards accepted. Prepayment required. SASE not required.

Yuma Justice Court 250 W 2nd St, #A, Yuma, AZ 85364; 928-817-4100; fax: 928-817-4101; 8AM-5PM. ***Misdemeanor, Civil Actions under $10,000, Eviction, Small Claims.***

The office hopes to have a public access terminal available for the public in early 2006.

Civil Records: Access: Mail, in person, online. Both court and visitors may perform in person searches. Search fee: $24.00 per name. Required to search: name, years to search. Civil cases indexed by defendant. Civil records on computer. Purged after 5 years. Info available only for cases after 9/01/97; computerized records since 1997. Mail turnaround time 2-4 days. Civil PAT goes back to 1994. Access to the docket is free at www.supreme.state.az.us/publicaccess/notification/search.asp.

Criminal Records: Access: Mail, in person, online. Only the court performs in person searches; visitors may not. Search fee: $24.00 per name. Required to search: name, years to search. Criminal records on computer. Purged after 5 years. Info available only for cases after 9/01/97; computerized records since 1997. Mail turnaround time 2-4 days. Criminal PAT available. Access to the docket is free at www.supreme.state.az.us/publicaccess/notification/search.asp.

General Information: Court will not release victim's names. Will not fax documents. Court makes copy: $.50 per page. Certification fee: $24.00 per doc. Payee: Justice Court #1. No personal checks accepted. Credit cards accepted. Prepayment required. Mail requests: SASE required.

Arizona Recording Offices

ORGANIZATION: 15 counties, 16 recording offices (the Navajo Nation Recorder is the 16th office and covers northern parts of Apache and Navajo Counties). Recording officer is the County Recorder. Recordings are usually placed in a Grantor/Grantee index. Arizona is in the Mountain Time Zone and does not change to Daylight Savings Time.

REAL ESTATE RECORDS: Most counties do not perform real estate searches. Copy fee is usually $1.00 per page. Certification fee is usually $3.00 per document.

UCC RECORDS: Only real estate related collateral isfiled with the County Recorder. However, prior to July, 2001, consumer goods and farm collateral were filed at the County Recorder and these older records can be searched there, if active. UCC search fee is generally $10.00 per debtor name.

TAX LIEN RECORDS: Federal and state tax liens on personal property of businesses are filed with the Secretary of State. Federal and state tax liens on individuals are filed with the County Recorder.

ONLINE ACCESS: A number of county assessor offices offer online access.

Apache County

County Recorder, PO Box 425, St. Johns, AZ 85936. 928-337-7514, R/E phone-928-337-7515; fax-928-337-7676; 8-5PM www.co.apache.az.us/Recorder/

Index: Separate indices to search. Records indexed on a public use terminal back to 1986. Office will perform a UCC search but public must search other records themselves. Search fee $10.00 per name. Office will not search real estate records. Copy fee $1.00 per page. Cert fee- $3.00 per doc plus copy fee. Payee- Apache County Recorder. **Online access to Real Estate, Deed, Judgment, Lien records:** Access to the recorder is free at www.thecountyrecorder.com/(zln0ur55nfvssi55tboxw245)/Search.aspx?CountyKey=5. Index back to 1985. **Other phones:** Treasurer- 928-337-7513; Elections- 928-337-7537.

Property tax/Assessing- PO Box 770, St. Johns, AZ 85936; 928-337-7521, fax- 928-337-3386. www.co.apache.az.us/Departments/Assessor/Assessor.htm **Online access-** Access assessor search page free at www.co.apache.az.us/parcelsearch/parcelsearch.aspx.

Cochise County

County Recorder, 1415 Melody Ln, Bldg B, Bisbee, AZ 85603. 520-432-8350; fax-520-432-8368; 8AM-5PM www.co.cochise.az.us/recorders/Default.htm

Index: All in one. Records indexed on public access terminal back to 1987. Office will perform a UCC search but public must search other records themselves. Search fee $10.00 per name. Office will do a simple real estate name search no charge. Copy fee $1.00 per page. Cert fee- $3.00 per cert plus copy fee. Payee- Cochise County Recorder. Bulk data available for purchase, contact Sylvia Gruhn. **Online access to Real Estate, Deed, Lien, Judgment, Mortgage records:** Access the recorder office document search site free at www.thecountyrecorder.com/(g5ze11rp4f5xuc2y2xsl4245)/Default.aspx. **Other phones:** Treasurer- 520-432-8400; Elections- 520-432-8970; Voter Registration- 520-432-8354. **Property tax/Assessing-** PO Box 168, 1415 Melody Ln, Bldg B, Bisbee, AZ 85603; 520-432-8650, assessor fax- 520-432-8698. Also has offices in Sierra Vista, Benson, Douglas, Willcox. **Online access-** Access treasurer's back tax list free at www.cochise.az.gov/cochise_treasurer.aspx?id=68&ekmensel=c580fa7b_148_0_68_4.

Coconino County

County Recorder, 110 E Cherry Ave, Flagstaff, AZ 86001. 928-779-6585; fax-928-779-6739; 8AM-5PM (MST) www.coconino.az.gov/recorder/

Index: All in one. Records indexed on a public use terminal back to 1983. Office personnel or visitors may perform searches. Search fee $10.00 per name. Copy fee $1.00 per page. Cert fee- $3.00 per doc plus copy fee. Payee- Coconino County Recorder. Bulk data available for purchase $.01 per image, contact office. **Online access to Real Estate, Grantor/Grantee, Deed, Owner History, Plat, Map records:** Access the recorder system free at http://eaglerecorder.coconino.az.gov/recorder/web/ . Documents are $1.00 to print; online records go back to 1983; images back to 3/1999. For official or certified copies or inquiries on documents prior to 1983 please contact office at 928-779-6585 or 1-800-793-6181. **Other phones:** Treasurer- 928-779-6615; Elections- 928-779-6589; Vital Records- 602-364-1300. **Property tax/Assessing-** 110 E Cherry Ave, Flagstaff, AZ 86001; 928-679-7962, assessor fax-926-679-7977. (Appraiser/Auditor- 928-679-7962) www.coconino.az.gov/assessor.aspx?id=9902 **Online access-** Search owner histories at www.coconino.az.gov/assessor/ASPublic/Search.aspx. Access property owner site for free at http://gis-map.coconino.az.gov/PropertySearch/PropertySearch.aspx.

Gila County

County Recorder, 1400 E Ash St, Globe, AZ 85501. 928-425-3231, R/E recording phone-928-425-3231 x8738; fax-928-425-9270; 8AM-5PM (MST) www.gilacountyaz.gov/recorder/default.html

Index: All in one. Records indexed on a public use terminal back to 1985. Office personnel or visitors may perform searches. General index search fee $10.00 per hour for searches 1985 to present; $15 per hour if prior to 1985. UCC search per debtor name- $18.00. Copy fee $1.00 per page. Cert fee- $3.00 per doc plus copy fee. Payee- Gila County Recorder. Bulk data available for purchase, contact Vicki Pena at 928-402-8732 for microfiche & CD's. **Online access to Real Estate, Grantor/Grantee, Deed, Lien records:** Access to the recorder's index are free at http://recorder.gilacountyaz.gov/recorder/web/. Search for free, but official copies are $1.00 per page. Records go back to 1985, images back to 1998. **Other phones:** Treasurer- 928-425-3231 x8701; Elections- 928-425-3231 x8740; Vital Records- 602-364-1300. **Property tax/Assessing-** 1400 E Ash St, Globe, AZ 85501; 928-425-3231 x8720, assessor fax- 928-425-0408. www.gilacountyaz.gov/assessor/default.html **Online access-** Search assessor property data free at www.co.gila.az.us/parcelsearch/parcelsearch.aspx

Graham County

County Recorder, 921 Thatcher Blvd, Safford, AZ 85546. Recording, R/E & UCC phone-928-428-3560; fax-928-428-8829; 8AM-5PM www.graham.az.gov

Index: All in one. Records indexed on a public use terminal back to 1984. Office will perform a UCC search but public must search other records themselves. Search fee $10.00 per name. Copy fee $1.00 per finding. Cert fee- $3.00 per instrument plus copy fee. Payee- Graham County Recorder. **Online access to Real Estate, Deed, Divorce, Judgment, Lien records:** Access to recorder records is at www.thecountyrecorder.com/(tftb2c55gxt51pz3lhdlsn45)/Search.aspx?CountyKey=1; index goes back to 1984. **Other phones:** Treasurer- 928-428-3440; Elections- 928-428-3930; Vital Records- 928-428-0110. **Property tax/Assessing-** 921 Thatcher Blvd, Safford, AZ 85546; 928-428-2828, assessor fax- 928-428-5849. (Appraiser/Auditor- 928-428-2828) www.graham.az.gov **Online access-** Access the assessor database of property and assessments free at http://72.165.8.78/parcelsearch/parcelsearch.aspx.

Greenlee County

County Recorder, PO Box 1625, Clifton, AZ 85533-1625. 928-865-2632; fax-928-865-4417; 8AM-5PM www.co.greenlee.az.us/Recorder/RecorderHomePage.aspx Index: All in one. (Divorces included in index. Divorce records located here) Records indexed on a public use terminal back to 1/1978. Only the public may search. Copy fee $1.00 per page. Cert fee- $3.00 per doc plus copy fee. Payee- Greenlee County Recorder. Bulk county data avaiable through Saul's Creek Engineering, 888-608-8565, Bayfield, CO. , Box 1520, Bayfield, CO 81122. **Online access to Real Estate, Deed, Lien, Judgment, Vital Statistic records:** Access to recorder records is free at www.thecountyrecorder.com/(iudkas45oort5iucbx3ckzbj)/Search.aspx?CountyKey=2. Index back to 1/1/1978. **Other phones:** Treasurer- 928-865-3422; Elections- 928-865-1717. **Property tax/Assessing-** PO Box 777, 253 5th St, Clifton, AZ 85533; 928-865-5302, assessor fax- 928-865-4417. www.co.greenlee.az.us/Assessor/AssessorHomePage.aspx **Online access-** Search treasurer's tax lien sale list free at www.co.greenlee.az.us/treasurer/taxlien.pdf.

La Paz County

County Recorder, 1112 Joshua Ave, #201, Parker, AZ 85344. 928-669-6136; fax-928-669-5638; 8AM-5PM www.co.la-paz.az.us/

Index: All in one. Records indexed on a public use terminal back to 1985. Only the public may search. Copy fee $1.00 per page. Maps are $3.00 and up depending on size. Postage fee per doc- $1.00. Cert fee- $3.00 per doc plus copy fee. Payee- La Paz County Recorder. **Online access to Real Estate, Deed, Judgment, Lien records:** Access to the recorder document index only back to 1986 is free at www.thecountyrecorder.com/(jl14cu55x2riwz45rlfcieyq)/default.aspx. **Other phones:** Treasurer- 928-669-6145; Elections- 928-669-6115; Vital Records- 928-669-6131 (marriages only). **Property tax/Assessing-** 1112 Joshua Ave, #204, Parker, AZ 85344; 928-669-6165, assessor fax- 928-669-9747.

Maricopa County

County Recorder, 111 S 3rd Ave, #103, Phoenix, AZ 85003. 602-506-3535; fax-602-506-3273; 8AM-5PM (MST) http://recorder.maricopa.gov

Also, branch office at 202 E Havelina Ave. in Mesa. Index: All in one. Records indexed on a public use terminal back to 1991. Office personnel or visitors may perform searches. Office will not search real estate records except in person; in person search fee- $9.00 1st 5 pages, $1.00 handling fee. UCC and tax lien search per debtor name- $10.00 plus $1.00 for each found page. Copy fee $1.00 per page. Cert fee- $3.00 per doc plus copy fee. Payee- Maricopa County Recorder. **Online access to Real Estate, Deed,**

Mortgage, Lien, Plat, Death, Divorce records: Access recordings by direct dial-up or the Internet. Dial-up access requires one-time $300 set-up fee plus $.06 per minute. Dial-up hours are 8am-10pm, 8-5 Sat-Sun. Records date to 1983. For add'l info, contact Linda Kinchloe, 602-506-3637. Access to Recorder's database at http://recorder.maricopa.gov/recdocdata/. Index back to 1871, images to 9/91. Search data back to 2002 free at the clerk's office. **Property tax/Assessing**- 301 W Jefferson St, Phoenix, AZ 85003; 602-506-3406, fax- 602-506-7620. www.maricopa.gov/assessor/ **Online access**- Assessor database is at www.maricopa.gov/assessor/. Residential data available. Also, perform tax appeal lookups at SBOE site at www.sboe.state.az.us/cgi-bin/name_lookup.pl. Search treasurers tax data free at http://treasurer.maricopa.gov/parcels/.

Mohave County

County Recorder, PO Box 70, Kingman, AZ 86402-0070. Recording, R/E & UCC phone-928-753-0701; fax-928-753-0727; 8AM-5PM www.co.mohave.az.us
Index: Separate indices to search include deeds, mortgages, misc. (Divorces included in index. Divorce records located here) Records indexed on a public use terminal back to 1990. Pre-1990 in books and microfiche. Only the public may search. Will search UCC records. Copy fee $1.00 per page. Cert fee- $3.00 per doc plus copy fee. Payee- Mohave County Recorder. To discuss bulk data purchases, please contact Robert Ballard at x4597. **Online access to Real Estate, Grantor/Grantee, Deed, Lien, Judgment, Death records:** Access the Recorder's System free at http://eagleweb.co.mohave.az.us/recorder/web/login.jsp. Registration-password required; sign-up with IT Dept, x4357. **Other phones:** Treasurer- 928-753-0737; Elections- 928-753-0733; Vital Records- 602-364-1300 (Phoenix); Billing-Susan Huffine- 928-753-0701 x4003; Purchasing-Robert Ballard -928-753-0701 x4597;. **Property tax/Assessing**- 700 Beale St, Kingman, AZ 86401; 928-753-0703, assessor fax- 928-753-0749. (Appraiser/Auditor- 928-753-0703) **Online access**- Online access the Assessor's property database free at http://legacy.co.mohave.az.us/depts/assessor/prop_info.asp. A sales history also available. Tax maps at http://legacy.co.mohave.az.us/taxmaps/. Property sales history back to 2000 free at http://legacy.co.mohave.az.us/1moweb/depts_files/assessor_files/saleshist.asp. Also, the treasurer's tax sale parcel search is at http://legacy.co.mohave.az.us/depts/treas/tax_sale.asp.

Navajo County

County Recorder, PO Box 668, Holbrook, AZ 86025-0668. 928-524-4194; fax-928-524-4308; 8AM-5PM (MST) www.navajocountyaz.gov/recorder/
Index: All in one. Records indexed on a public use terminal back to 1989; images back to 4/1995. Only the public may search. Copy fee $1.00 per page. Cert fee- $3.00 per seal plus copy fee. Payee- Navajo County Recorder. Various bulk data available, call Saul's Creek at 970-884-6115. **Online access to Real Estate, Grantor/Grantee, Deed, UCC, Death records:** Access to the recorder's database of land data, UCCs, Liens, and Grantor/Grantee indices free at www.thecountyrecorder.com/(gdzvqy55ijfb0h550lajpg55)/default.aspx. Documents go back to 1989; images to 1995. **Other phones:** Treasurer- 928-524-4172. **Property tax/Assessing**- PO Box 668, 100 E Carter Dr, S Hwy 77, Holbrook, AZ 86025-0668; 928-524-4086, assessor fax- 928-524-4291. www.navajocountyaz.gov/assessor/ **Online access**- Access property assessor database free at www.navajocountyaz.gov/parcelsearch.aspx. Also, the county GIS-mapping site allows manual parcel searching at http://navcogis.co.navajo.az.us/website/NavajoCountyGIS.htm. Also, a Tax Lien Auction list is at found at www.navajocountyaz.gov/treasurer/.

Navajo Nation

Recorder, PO Box 663, Division of Economic Development, Window Rock, AZ 86515. 928-871-7365, R/E recording phone-928-871-6544, UCC recording phone-928-871-7365; fax-928-871-7381; 8AM-N, 1-5PM (MST) www.navajobusiness.com/
Navajo Nation UCCs are here. Land recording is handled by Navajo County. All in one. Records indexed on computer; no public use terminal available. Office personnel or visitors may perform searches. Search fee $.50 per name. Office will not search real estate records. UCC search per debtor name- $.50 per page found. Copy fee $.50 per page. Cert fee- $5.00 per page plus copy fee. Payee- Navajo Nation Business Regulatory Dept. Office does not sell bulk data. **Online access to Real Estate, Grantor/Grantee, Deed, UCC, Death records:** Access to the county recorder's database of land data, UCCs, Liens, and Grantor/Grantee indices is free at www.thecountyrecorder.com/(gdzvqy55ijfb0h550lajpg55)/default.aspx. Documents go back to 1989; images to 1995. **Other phones:** Treasurer- 928-524-4172; Elections- 928-871-6367; Vital Records- 928-871-6386. **Property tax/Assessing**- PO Box 1903, Navajo Tax Commission, Window Rock, AZ 86515; 928-871-6681, fax- 928-871-7608, hours- 8AM-5PM Physical Address: Hwy 264, 100 Taylor Rd, Karigan Professional Bldg, #115, St. Michales, AZ 86511. www.navajotax.org **Online access**- Search property tax data and also sales at www.navajocountyaz.gov/parcelsearch.aspx. Also, the county GIS-mapping site allows manual parcel searching at http://navcogis.co.navajo.az.us/website/NavajoCountyGIS.htm.

Pima County

County Recorder, PO Box 3145, Tucson, AZ 85702. 520-740-4350; fax-520-623-1785; 8AM-5PM (MST) www.recorder.pima.gov
Index: All in one. Records indexed on a public use terminal back to 4/87. Office personnel or visitors may perform searches. Search fee $10.00 per name. Copy fee $1.00 per page. Cert fee- $3.00 per doc plus copy fee. Payee- Pima County Recorder. **Online access to Real Estate, Deed, Lien, Mortgage, Fictitious Name, UCC records:** Access recorder records index free at http://doc.recorder.pima.gov/search/login.htm. Full image access is available as a subscription service only. Also, a name/parcel/property tax lookup may be performed free on the SBOE site at www.sboe.state.az.us/cgi-bin/name_lookup.pl. **Property tax/Assessing**- 115 N Church Ave, Tucson, AZ 85701; 520-740-8630, assessor fax- 520-792-9825. www.asr.co.pima.az.us/ **Online access**- Records on the Pima County Tax Assessor database are free at www.asr.co.pima.az.us/links/frm_AdvancedSearch_v2.aspx?search=Parcel. Also, search the property tax inquiry database at www.to.co.pima.az.us/property_search.html. Also, search tax lien sale, bankruptcies, and expiring liens free at www.to.co.pima.az.us/tax_lien_sale.html. There is also a real estate property tax search at www.to.co.pima.az.us/tax_lien_sale.html but no name searching.

Pinal County

County Recorder, PO Box 848, Florence, AZ 85232-0848. Recording, R/E & UCC phone-520-866-6830; fax-520-866-6831; 8AM-5PM (MST) http://pinalcountyaz.gov/Pages/Home.aspx
Has branch offices in Casa Grande (520-866-7488, contact Donna Diaz) and Apache Junction (480-983-7038, contact Teresa Barr). Public access terminals available. Index: Separate indices to search include grantor/grantee, fee number. (Divorces included in index. Divorce records located here) Records indexed on a public use terminal back to 05/1980. Office will perform a UCC search but public must search other records themselves. Search fee-$10.00 per name. Copy fee $1.00 per page. Cert fee- $3.00 per doc plus copy fee. Payee- Pinal County Recorder. **Online access to Real Estate, Grantor/Grantee, Deed records:** Access to the recorder's index is free at http://pinalcountyaz.gov/Pages/Home.aspx. **Other phones:** Treasurer- 520-866-6425; Elections- 520-866-7550; Voter Registration- 520-866-6850. **Property tax/Assessing**- PO Box 709, Florence, AZ 85232-0848; 520-866-6361, assessor fax- 520-866-6353. (Appraiser/Auditor- 520-866-6361) **Online access**- Search the assessor's property tax database free at http://pinalcountyaz.gov/Pages/Home.aspx. Also, access to the county treasurer's database of tax liens, tax bills, and tax sales is free at http://pinalcountyaz.gov/Pages/Home.aspx. Click on appropriate "Tax Searches" button.

Santa Cruz County

County Recorder, 2150 N Congress, #101; County Complex, Nogales, AZ 85621. Recording, R/E & UCC phone-520-375-7990; 8AM-5PM (MST) www.co.santa-cruz.az.us/recorder/index.html
Index: All in one. Records indexed on a public use terminal back to 4/87. Only the public may search. Copy fee $1.00 per page. Cert fee- $3.00 per doc plus $1.00 per page, plus copy fee. Payee- Santa Cruz County Recorder. **Online access to Real Estate, Deed, Lien, Judgment, Marriage records:** Access to recording index is free at www.thecountyrecorder.com/(zq1bs155v24ag545wiy24p55)/default.aspx. Index goes back to 1986. **Other phones:** Treasurer-520-375-7980; Elections- 520-375-7808; Court house Operator -520-375-7800;. **Property tax/Assessing**- PO Box 1150, 2150 N Congress Dr, #102, Nogales, AZ 85621; 520-375-8030, fax- 520-375-8045. (Appraiser/Auditor- 520-375-8030) www.co.santa-cruz.az.us/assessor/index.html **Online access**- Access County Assessor data at www.sccaz-assessor.org/SCCAssessorPropertySearch/.

Yavapai County

County Recorder, 1015 Fair St, Rm 228, Prescott, AZ 86305. 928-771-3244; fax-928-771-3258; 8AM-5PM (MST) www.co.yavapai.az.us
2nd office located at 10 S 6th St, Cottonwood AZ 86326, phone- 928-639-5807, fax- 928-639-5812. Index: Separate indices to search. Records indexed on a public use terminal back to 1976. Office will perform a UCC search but public must search other records themselves. Office will not perform open-ended real estate records searches. Copy fee $1.00 per page. Cert fee- $3.00 per seal plus copy fee. Payee-Yavapai County Recorder. Bulk data is available for purchase, contact Jessica Manley for info. **Online access to Real Estate, Deed records:** Access to the recording office iCRIS database is free at www.co.yavapai.az.us/Content.aspx?id=19122
Records from 1976 to present; images from 1976 to present. **Other phones:** Treasurer- 928-771-3233; Elections- 928-771-3250; Voter Registration- 928-771-3248. **Property tax/Assessing**- 1015 Fair St, Rm 228, Prescott, AZ 86305; 928-771-3220, assessor fax-928-771-3181. www.co.yavapai.az.us/Assessor.aspx **Online access**- Assessor and land records on County GIS database free at http://mapserver.co.yavapai.az.us/interactive/map.asp. Data also at http://mapserver.co.yavapai.az.us/parcelinfo/map.asp. Also, the board of supervisors tax sale list is at www.co.yavapai.az.us/Content.aspx?id=18198.

Yuma County

County Recorder, 410 S Maiden Ln, Yuma, AZ 85364-2311. 928-373-6020, R/E recording phone-928-373-6029, UCC recording phone-928-373-6028; fax-928-373-6024; 8AM-5PM www.co.yuma.az.us
Index: All in one. Records indexed on a public use terminal back to 9/93. Office will perform a UCC search but public must search other records themselves. Search fee-$10.00 per name. Copy fee $1.00 per page. Cert fee- $3.00 per doc plus copy fee. Payee- Yuma County Recorder. Day's recordings and aff. of property value available for purchase; call Ed Garcia at 928-373-6026. **Other phones:** Treasurer-928-539-7781; Elections- 928-373-1014; Vital Records- 928-317-4530. **Property tax/Assessing**-410 S Maiden Ln, Yuma, AZ 85364-2311; 928-373-6040, assessor fax- 928-373-6041. www.co.yuma.az.us/assr/index.htm **Online access**-Access county property data free at http://itax.co.yuma.az.us:8080/itax/taxSplash.jsp; registration required.

Arizona County Locator

You will usually be able to find the city name in the City/County Cross Reference below. In that case, it is a simple matter to determine the county from the cross reference. However, only the official US Postal Service city names are included in this index. There are an additional 40,000 place names people use in their addresses. We have included a ZIP/City Cross Reference following the City/County Cross Reference.

If you know the ZIP Code but the city name does not appear in the City/County Cross Reference index, look up the ZIP Code in the ZIP/City Cross Reference, find the city name, then look up the city name in the City/County Cross Reference.

Arizona City/County Cross Reference

AGUILA Maricopa
AJO Pima
ALPINE Apache
AMADO (85645) Pima(90), Santa Cruz(9)
ANTHEM Maricopa
APACHE JUNCTION (85220) Pinal(85), Maricopa(14)
APACHE JUNCTION Pinal
ARIVACA Pima
ARIZONA CITY Pinal
ARLINGTON Maricopa
ASH FORK Yavapai
AVONDALE Maricopa
BAGDAD Yavapai
BAPCHULE Pinal
BELLEMONT Coconino
BENSON (85602) Cochise(93), Pima(6)
BISBEE Cochise
BLACK CANYON CITY Yavapai
BLUE Greenlee
BLUE GAP Navajo
BOUSE La Paz
BOWIE Cochise
BUCKEYE Maricopa
BULLHEAD CITY Mohave
BYLAS Graham
CAMERON Coconino
CAMP VERDE Yavapai
CAREFREE Maricopa
CASA GRANDE Pinal
CASHION Maricopa
CATALINA Pima
CAVE CREEK Maricopa
CENTRAL Graham
CHAMBERS Apache
CHANDLER Maricopa
CHANDLER HEIGHTS Maricopa
CHINLE Apache
CHINO VALLEY Yavapai
CHLORIDE Mohave
CIBICUE Navajo
CIBOLA La Paz
CLARKDALE Yavapai
CLAY SPRINGS Navajo
CLAYPOOL Gila
CLIFTON Greenlee
COCHISE Cochise
COLORADO CITY Mohave
CONCHO Apache
CONGRESS Yavapai
COOLIDGE Pinal
CORNVILLE Yavapai
CORTARO Pima
COTTONWOOD Yavapai
CROWN KING Yavapai
DATELAND Yuma
DENNEHOTSO Apache
DEWEY Yavapai
DOLAN SPRINGS Mohave
DOUGLAS Cochise
DRAGOON Cochise
DUNCAN Greenlee
EAGAR Apache
EDEN Graham
EHRENBERG La Paz
EL MIRAGE Maricopa
ELFRIDA Cochise
ELGIN Santa Cruz
ELOY Pinal
FLAGSTAFF Coconino
FLORENCE Pinal
FOREST LAKES Coconino
FORT APACHE Navajo
FORT DEFIANCE Apache
FORT HUACHUCA Cochise
FORT MCDOWELL Maricopa
FORT MOHAVE Mohave
FORT THOMAS Graham
FOUNTAIN HILLS Maricopa
FREDONIA Coconino
GADSDEN Yuma
GANADO Apache
GILA BEND Maricopa
GILBERT Maricopa
GLENDALE Maricopa
GLOBE Gila
GOLDEN VALLEY Mohave
GOODYEAR Maricopa
GRAND CANYON Coconino
GRAY MOUNTAIN Coconino
GREEN VALLEY Pima
GREER Apache
HACKBERRY Mohave
HAPPY JACK Coconino
HAYDEN Gila
HEBER Navajo
HEREFORD Cochise
HIGLEY Maricopa
HOLBROOK Navajo
HOTEVILLA Navajo
HOUCK Apache
HUACHUCA CITY Cochise
HUALAPAI Mohave
HUMBOLDT Yavapai
INDIAN WELLS Navajo
IRON SPRINGS Yavapai
JEROME Yavapai
JOSEPH CITY Navajo
KAIBITO Coconino
KAYENTA Navajo
KEAMS CANYON Navajo
KEARNY Pinal
KINGMAN Mohave
KIRKLAND Yavapai
KYKOTSMOVI VILLAGE Navajo
LAKE HAVASU CITY Mohave
LAKE MONTEZUMA Yavapai
LAKESIDE Navajo
LAVEEN Maricopa
LEUPP Coconino
LITCHFIELD PARK Maricopa
LITTLEFIELD Mohave
LUKACHUKAI Apache
LUKE AFB Maricopa
LUKEVILLE Pima
LUPTON Apache
MAMMOTH Pinal
MANY FARMS Apache
MARANA (85653) Pima(84), Pinal(15)
MARBLE CANYON Coconino
MARICOPA Pinal
MAYER Yavapai
MC NARY Apache
MC NEAL Cochise
MEADVIEW Mohave
MESA (85212) Maricopa(92), Pinal(7)
MESA Maricopa
MIAMI Gila
MOHAVE VALLEY Mohave
MORENCI Greenlee
MORMON LAKE Coconino
MORRISTOWN Maricopa
MOUNT LEMMON Pima
MUNDS PARK Coconino
NACO Cochise
NAZLINI Apache
NEW RIVER Maricopa
NOGALES Santa Cruz
NORTH RIM Coconino
NUTRIOSO Apache
OATMAN Mohave
ORACLE Pinal
OVERGAARD Navajo
PAGE Coconino
PALO VERDE Maricopa
PARADISE VALLEY Maricopa
PARKER La Paz
PARKS Coconino
PATAGONIA Santa Cruz
PAULDEN Yavapai
PAYSON Gila
PEACH SPRINGS Mohave
PEARCE Cochise
PEORIA Maricopa
PERIDOT Gila
PETRIFIED FOREST NATL PK Apache
PHOENIX Maricopa
PICACHO Pinal
PIMA Graham
PINE Gila
PINEDALE Navajo
PINETOP Navajo
PINON Navajo
PIRTLEVILLE Cochise
POLACCA Navajo
POMERENE Cochise
POSTON La Paz
PRESCOTT Yavapai
PRESCOTT VALLEY Yavapai
QUARTZSITE La Paz
QUEEN CREEK (85242) Maricopa(61), Pinal(38)
RED ROCK Pinal
RED VALLEY Apache
RILLITO Pima
RIMROCK Yavapai
RIO RICO Santa Cruz
RIO VERDE Maricopa
ROCK POINT Apache
ROLL Yuma
ROOSEVELT Gila
ROUND ROCK Apache
SACATON Pinal
SAFFORD Graham
SAHUARITA Pima
SAINT DAVID Cochise
SAINT JOHNS Apache
SAINT MICHAELS Apache
SALOME La Paz
SAN CARLOS Gila
SAN LUIS Yuma
SAN MANUEL Pinal
SAN SIMON Cochise
SANDERS Apache
SASABE Pima
SAWMILL Apache
SCOTTSDALE Maricopa
SECOND MESA Navajo
SEDONA (86336) Yavapai(67), Coconino(32)
SEDONA Coconino
SEDONA Yavapai
SELIGMAN Yavapai
SELLS Pima
SHONTO Navajo
SHOW LOW Navajo
SIERRA VISTA Cochise
SKULL VALLEY Yavapai
SNOWFLAKE Navajo
SOLOMON Graham
SOMERTON Yuma
SONOITA (85637) Santa Cruz(82), Pima(17)
SPRINGERVILLE Apache
STANFIELD Pinal
SUN CITY Maricopa
SUN CITY WEST Maricopa
SUN VALLEY Navajo
SUPAI Coconino
SUPERIOR Pinal
SURPRISE Maricopa
TACNA Yuma
TAYLOR Navajo
TEEC NOS POS Apache
TEMPE Maricopa
TEMPLE BAR MARINA Mohave
THATCHER Graham
TOLLESON Maricopa
TOMBSTONE Cochise
TONALEA Coconino
TONOPAH Maricopa
TONTO BASIN Gila
TOPAWA Pima
TOPOCK Mohave
TORTILLA FLAT Maricopa
TSAILE Apache
TUBA CITY Coconino
TUBAC Santa Cruz
TUCSON (85739) Pima(57), Pinal(42)
TUCSON Pima
TUMACACORI Santa Cruz
VAIL Pima
VALENTINE Mohave
VALLEY FARMS Pinal
VERNON Apache
WADDELL Maricopa
WELLTON Yuma
WENDEN La Paz
WHITE MOUNTAIN LAKE Navajo
WHITERIVER Navajo
WICKENBURG Maricopa
WIKIEUP Mohave
WILLCOX (85643) Cochise(98), Graham(1)
WILLCOX Cochise
WILLIAMS Coconino
WILLOW BEACH Mohave
WINDOW ROCK Apache
WINKELMAN (85292) Pinal(54), Gila(45)
WINSLOW Navajo
WITTMANN Maricopa
WOODRUFF Navajo
YARNELL Yavapai
YOUNG Gila
YOUNGTOWN Maricopa
YUCCA Mohave
YUMA Yuma

Arizona ZIP/City Cross Reference

85000-85086 PHOENIX
85086-85086 ANTHEM
85087-85087 NEW RIVER
85098-85099 PHOENIX
85201-85216 MESA
85217-85220 APACHE JUNCTION
85221-85221 BAPCHULE
85222-85222 CASA GRANDE
85223-85223 ARIZONA CITY
85224-85226 CHANDLER
85227-85227 CHANDLER HEIGHTS
85228-85228 COOLIDGE
85230-85230 CASA GRANDE
85231-85231 ELOY
85232-85232 FLORENCE
85233-85234 GILBERT
85235-85235 HAYDEN
85236-85236 HIGLEY
85237-85237 KEARNY
85239-85239 MARICOPA
85240-85240 MESA
85241-85241 PICACHO
85242-85243 QUEEN CREEK
85244-85244 CHANDLER
85245-85245 RED ROCK
85246-85246 CHANDLER
85247-85247 SACATON
85248-85249 CHANDLER
85250-85252 SCOTTSDALE
85253-85253 PARADISE VALLEY
85254-85262 SCOTTSDALE
85263-85263 RIO VERDE
85264-85264 FORT MCDOWELL
85266-85267 SCOTTSDALE
85268-85269 FOUNTAIN HILLS
85271-85271 SCOTTSDALE
85272-85272 STANFIELD
85273-85273 SUPERIOR
85274-85277 MESA
85278-85278 APACHE JUNCTION
85279-85279 FLORENCE
85280-85289 TEMPE
85290-85290 TORTILLA FLAT
85291-85291 VALLEY FARMS
85292-85292 WINKELMAN
85296-85299 GILBERT
85301-85308 GLENDALE
85309-85309 LUKE AFB
85310-85318 GLENDALE
85320-85320 AGUILA
85321-85321 AJO
85322-85322 ARLINGTON
85323-85323 AVONDALE
85324-85324 BLACK CANYON CITY
85325-85325 BOUSE
85326-85326 BUCKEYE
85327-85327 CAVE CREEK
85328-85328 CIBOLA
85329-85329 CASHION
85331-85331 CAVE CREEK
85332-85332 CONGRESS
85333-85333 DATELAND
85334-85334 EHRENBERG
85335-85335 EL MIRAGE
85336-85336 GADSDEN
85337-85337 GILA BEND
85338-85338 GOODYEAR
85339-85339 LAVEEN
85340-85340 LITCHFIELD PARK
85341-85341 LUKEVILLE
85342-85342 MORRISTOWN
85343-85343 PALO VERDE
85344-85344 PARKER
85345-85345 PEORIA
85346-85346 QUARTZSITE
85347-85347 ROLL
85348-85348 SALOME
85349-85349 SAN LUIS
85350-85350 SOMERTON
85351-85351 SUN CITY
85352-85352 TACNA
85353-85353 TOLLESON
85354-85354 TONOPAH
85355-85355 WADDELL
85356-85356 WELLTON
85357-85357 WENDEN
85358-85358 WICKENBURG
85359-85359 QUARTZSITE
85360-85360 WIKIEUP
85361-85361 WITTMANN
85362-85362 YARNELL
85363-85363 YOUNGTOWN
85364-85369 YUMA
85371-85371 POSTON
85372-85373 SUN CITY
85374-85374 SURPRISE
85375-85376 SUN CITY WEST
85377-85377 CAREFREE
85378-85379 SURPRISE
85380-85385 PEORIA
85387-85388 SURPRISE
85388-85388 SUN CITY
85390-85390 WICKENBURG
85396-85396 BUCKEYE
85501-85502 GLOBE
85530-85530 BYLAS
85531-85531 CENTRAL
85532-85532 CLAYPOOL
85533-85533 CLIFTON
85534-85534 DUNCAN
85535-85535 EDEN
85536-85536 FORT THOMAS
85539-85539 MIAMI
85540-85540 MORENCI
85541-85541 PAYSON
85542-85542 PERIDOT
85543-85543 PIMA
85544-85544 PINE
85545-85545 ROOSEVELT
85546-85546 SAFFORD
85547-85547 PAYSON
85548-85548 SAFFORD
85550-85550 SAN CARLOS
85551-85551 SOLOMON
85552-85552 THATCHER
85553-85553 TONTO BASIN
85554-85554 YOUNG
85601-85601 ARIVACA
85602-85602 BENSON
85603-85603 BISBEE
85605-85605 BOWIE
85606-85606 COCHISE
85607-85608 DOUGLAS
85609-85609 DRAGOON
85610-85610 ELFRIDA
85611-85611 ELGIN
85613-85613 FORT HUACHUCA
85614-85614 GREEN VALLEY
85615-85615 HEREFORD
85616-85616 HUACHUCA CITY
85617-85617 MC NEAL
85618-85618 MAMMOTH
85619-85619 MOUNT LEMMON
85620-85620 NACO
85621-85621 NOGALES
85622-85622 GREEN VALLEY
85623-85623 ORACLE
85624-85624 PATAGONIA
85625-85625 PEARCE
85626-85626 PIRTLEVILLE
85627-85627 POMERENE
85628-85628 NOGALES
85629-85629 SAHUARITA
85630-85630 SAINT DAVID
85631-85631 SAN MANUEL
85632-85632 SAN SIMON
85633-85633 SASABE
85634-85634 SELLS
85635-85636 SIERRA VISTA
85637-85637 SONOITA
85638-85638 TOMBSTONE
85639-85639 TOPAWA
85640-85640 TUMACACORI
85641-85641 VAIL
85643-85644 WILLCOX
85645-85645 AMADO
85646-85646 TUBAC
85648-85648 RIO RICO
85650-85650 SIERRA VISTA
85652-85652 CORTARO
85653-85653 MARANA
85654-85654 RILLITO
85655-85655 DOUGLAS
85662-85662 NOGALES
85670-85670 FORT HUACHUCA
85671-85671 SIERRA VISTA
85700-85737 TUCSON
85738-85738 CATALINA
85739-85777 TUCSON
85901-85902 SHOW LOW
85911-85911 CIBICUE
85912-85912 WHITE MOUNTAIN LAKE
85920-85920 ALPINE
85922-85922 BLUE
85923-85923 CLAY SPRINGS
85924-85924 CONCHO
85925-85925 EAGAR
85926-85926 FORT APACHE
85927-85927 GREER
85928-85928 HEBER
85929-85929 LAKESIDE
85930-85930 MC NARY
85931-85931 FOREST LAKES
85932-85932 NUTRIOSO
85933-85933 OVERGAARD
85934-85934 PINEDALE
85935-85935 PINETOP
85936-85936 SAINT JOHNS
85937-85937 SNOWFLAKE
85938-85938 SPRINGERVILLE
85939-85939 TAYLOR
85940-85940 VERNON
85941-85941 WHITERIVER
85942-85942 WOODRUFF
86001-86011 FLAGSTAFF
86015-86015 BELLEMONT
86016-86016 GRAY MOUNTAIN
86017-86017 MUNDS PARK
86018-86018 PARKS
86020-86020 CAMERON
86021-86021 COLORADO CITY
86022-86022 FREDONIA
86023-86023 GRAND CANYON
86024-86024 HAPPY JACK
86025-86025 HOLBROOK
86028-86028 PETRIFIED FOREST NATL PARK
86029-86029 SUN VALLEY
86030-86030 HOTEVILLA
86031-86031 INDIAN WELLS
86032-86032 JOSEPH CITY
86033-86033 KAYENTA
86034-86034 KEAMS CANYON
86035-86035 LEUPP
86036-86036 MARBLE CANYON
86038-86038 MORMON LAKE
86039-86039 KYKOTSMOVI VILLAGE
86040-86040 PAGE
86042-86042 POLACCA
86043-86043 SECOND MESA
86044-86044 TONALEA
86045-86045 TUBA CITY
86046-86046 WILLIAMS
86047-86047 WINSLOW
86052-86052 NORTH RIM
86053-86053 KAIBITO
86054-86054 SHONTO
86301-86305 PRESCOTT
86312-86312 PRESCOTT VALLEY
86313-86313 PRESCOTT
86314-86314 PRESCOTT VALLEY
86320-86320 ASH FORK
86321-86321 BAGDAD
86322-86322 CAMP VERDE
86323-86323 CHINO VALLEY
86324-86324 CLARKDALE
86325-86325 CORNVILLE
86326-86326 COTTONWOOD
86327-86327 DEWEY
86329-86329 HUMBOLDT
86330-86330 IRON SPRINGS
86331-86331 JEROME
86332-86332 KIRKLAND
86333-86333 MAYER
86334-86334 PAULDEN
86335-86335 RIMROCK
86336-86336 SEDONA
86337-86337 SELIGMAN
86338-86338 SKULL VALLEY
86339-86341 SEDONA
86342-86342 LAKE MONTEZUMA
86343-86343 CROWN KING
86351-86351 SEDONA
86401-86402 KINGMAN
86403-86406 LAKE HAVASU CITY
86409-86409 KINGMAN
86411-86411 HACKBERRY
86412-86412 HUALAPAI
86413-86413 GOLDEN VALLEY
86426-86427 FORT MOHAVE
86429-86430 BULLHEAD CITY
86431-86431 CHLORIDE
86432-86432 LITTLEFIELD
86433-86433 OATMAN
86434-86434 PEACH SPRINGS
86435-86435 SUPAI
86436-86436 TOPOCK
86437-86437 VALENTINE
86438-86438 YUCCA
86439-86439 BULLHEAD CITY
86440-86440 MOHAVE VALLEY
86441-86441 DOLAN SPRINGS
86442-86442 BULLHEAD CITY
86443-86443 TEMPLE BAR MARINA
86444-86444 MEADVIEW
86445-86445 WILLOW BEACH
86446-86446 MOHAVE VALLEY
86502-86502 CHAMBERS
86503-86503 CHINLE
86504-86504 FORT DEFIANCE
86505-86505 GANADO
86506-86506 HOUCK
86507-86507 LUKACHUKAI
86508-86508 LUPTON
86509-86509 CHAMBERS
86510-86510 PINON
86511-86511 SAINT MICHAELS
86512-86512 SANDERS
86514-86514 TEEC NOS POS
86515-86515 WINDOW ROCK
86520-86520 BLUE GAP
86535-86535 DENNEHOTSO
86538-86538 MANY FARMS
86540-86540 NAZLINI
86544-86544 RED VALLEY
86545-86545 ROCK POINT
86547-86547 ROUND ROCK
86549-86549 SAWMILL
86556-86556 TSAILE

Arkansas

General Help Numbers:

Governor's Office

State Capitol, #250
Little Rock, AR 72201
www.governor.arkansas.gov/
501-682-2345
Fax 501-682-3597
8AM-5PM

Attorney General's Office

323 Center St #200
Little Rock, AR 72201
www.ag.state.ar.us
501-682-2007
Fax 501-682-8084
8AM-5PM

Legislative Records

Elections Department
State Capitol, Room 026
Little Rock, AR 72201
www.arkleg.state.ar.us
501-682-5070
Fax 501-682-3408
8AM-5PM

State Archives

State Archives
One Capitol Mall
Little Rock, AR 72201
www.ark-ives.com/
501-682-6900
8AM-4:30PM M-SAT

State Specifics:

Capital: Little Rock
Pulaski County

Time Zone: CST

Number of Counties: 75

Population: 2,855,390

Website: www.arkansas.gov

State Agencies

Criminal Records

Arkansas State Police, Identification Bureau, #1 State Police Plaza Dr, Little Rock, AR 72209; 501-618-8500, Fax- 501-618-8404; 7:30AM-4:30PM.

www.asp.arkansas.gov

The public may obtain criminal history records, including third parties on behalf of employers. A signed, notarized release form must be on file with the requesting entity.

Indexing & Storage: Records available for the past 25 years. Older records are located in the off-site State Archives. New records available for inquiry in 2-3 weeks. 81% of arrests in database have final dispositions recorded, 79% for those arrests in last 5 years.

Searching: Manual requests will not include pending arrests or records without dispositions, unless the requester is entitled to federally disqualifying arrests. Online records will show records w/o dispositions. Include in request-notarized release from subject, name, date of birth, sex, SSN, driver's license number. Fingerprints are not required, but may be included. 100% of the arrest records are fingerprint supported. Is it suggested to use the Bureau's request form (ASP-122) for manual requests. This data not released-pardons and juvenile records. Felony records without dispositions are released only to employers and licensing boards, otherwise all records without disposition are not released.

Access by: mail, in person, online.

Fee & Payment: The fee is $25.00 per record, $22.00 if online. Certain entities required by statute to obtain criminal record checks have a different fee schedule in place. Fee payee-Arkansas State Police. Prepayment required. Personal checks accepted, credit or debit cards are not.

Mail search: Turnaround time- 5 to 7 days. A SASE is required. As mentioned above, only convictions are shown.

In person: Bring in signed, notarized release. Results of less than 10 requests can usually be done as you wait.

Online search: Online access available to only employers or their agents, and professional licensing boards. A subscriber account with the Information Network of Arkansas (INA) is required, a $75 annual fee is imposed. The search fee is $22.00. Searches are conducted by name. Search results includes registered sex offenders. For more info on this online service, see https://www.ark.org/criminal/index.php. Accounts must maintain the signed release documents in-house for three years. Visit https://www.ark.org/ina/sub/bgcheck_agreement.php for an excellent overview of record release provisions.

Statewide Court Records

Administrative Office of Courts, 625 Marshall Street, Ste 1100, Little Rock, AR 72201-1078; 501-682-9400, 501-682-6849, Fax- 501-682-9410; 8AM-5PM.

www.courts.state.ar.us

There is no statewide access to county court records from this office. Except for certain online research capabilities, all court record access must be done at the local level.

Access by: online.

Online search: The home web page gives online access to Supreme Court Opinions and Appellate Court dockets, or access via www.courts.state.ar.us/dockets/docket_search.cfm. Must have name and case number. This docket search includes all active cases; it also includes any closed case that has had activity within ninety (90) days previous. Also find Court of Appeals dockets, corrected opinions, and parallel citations, an attorney search, and search of court rules and administrative orders.

Other access: A CD of felony records and misdemeanor records for cases appealed is available for $100. The data does not contain SSNs or driver license numbers. Note that this agency makes a point to provide no warranties on the accuracy of the data.

Sexual Offender Registry

Arkansas Crime Information Center, Sexual Offender Registry, One Capitol Mall, 4D200, Little Rock, AR 72201; 501-682-7441, Fax- 501-683-5592; 8:30AM-4:30PM.

www.acic.org/Registration/index.htm

Based on information obtained from the risk assessment process, offenders are assigned the following levels: Level 1: Low Risk; Level 2: Moderate Risk; Level 3: High Risk; Level 4: Sexually Violent Predator.

Indexing & Storage: Records available from August 1, 1997 forward. There are over 6,100 registered sex offenders in the database.

Searching: ACIC provides information on registered sex offenders to all law enforcement agencies in the county where the offender resides. Local law enforcement agencies release names of those determined most likely to re-offend. Arkansas Code Annotated 12-12-913 requires the Arkansas Crime Information Center to maintain a registry. All Level 3 and Level 4 offenders are made available to the public via the Internet. This data not released- Level 1 and 2. See local law enforcement for those names.

Access by: mail, phone, online.

Mail search: Turnaround time- 1 -2 weeks. There is no fee.

Phone search: Records available by telephone for requesters without.

Online search: Searching is available at www.acic.org/soff/index.php. Search by name or location (county). Includes Level 3 and Level 4 offenders. Also, registered sex offenders are indicated on the criminal record online system maintained by the State Police; however, this system is only available to employers and professional licensing boards.

Incarceration Records

Arkansas Department of Corrections, Records Supervisor, PO Box 8707, Pine Bluff, AR 71611-8707; 870-267-6424, 870-267-6999; 8AM-4:30PM.

www.adc.arkansas.gov/

Direct questions to adc.inmate.info@arkansas.gov.

Indexing & Storage: Records available on current and former inmates; however, the online access is limited to current inmates. New records available for inquiry in 2-3 weeks.

Searching: Include in request- first and last name or ADC number. Location, ADC number, physical Identifiers and sentencing information, release dates are released.

Access by: mail, online.

Fee & Payment: There is no fee.

Mail search: Turnaround time- 5 to 7 days. A mail search can also be directed through the Attorney General's office (phone 510-682-2007).

Online search: The online access at www.adc.arkansas.gov/inmate_info/index.html has many search criteria capabilities.

Other access: The inmate access web page offers a download of the inmate database. Fee includes an annual INA subscription of $75.00 plus $0.10 per record enhanced access fee.

Corporation, Fictitious Name, LLC, Partnerships (LP, LLP LLLP, Foreign)

Secretary of State, Business & Commercial Service Division, State Capitol Bldg, Little Rock, AR 72201 (Courier address- Business & Commercial Service Division, 1401 W Capitol Ave Ste 250, Little Rock, AR 72201); 501-682-3409, 888-233-0325, Fax- 501-682-3437; 8AM-5PM (4:30 on F).

www.sos.arkansas.gov/corps/

Non-profit records here also.

Indexing & Storage: Records available from late 1800's on. Corporation records are on computer from 1987 on. Prior records, such as dissolved corporations, may be in paper files or scanned. New records available for inquiry immediately.

Searching: Franchise tax information is not released except for names and addressees of parties involved and certain information about the shares of stock. Include in request- full name of business. In addition to the articles of organization, business entity records available include: Prior (Merged) names, Reserved names, Good standing. Officers listed on franchise tax form is now public information. This data not released- members of LLC

Access by: mail, phone, in person, online.

Fee & Payment: There are no search fees. Copies are $.50 a page. Certification of records is an additional $5.00. Fee payee- Secretary of State. Prepayment required. Personal checks accepted. Credit cards accepted, $2.50 fee plus 4% of total.

Mail search: Turnaround time- same day if possible. Call first for copy fees. Records prior to 1988 will take longer to search. SASE not required. Minimum copy fee for mail service is $2.50.

Phone search: They will give incorporation dates, history, agent name, and status over the phone.

In person: Copies cost $.50 per page.

Online search: The Internet site permits free searching of corporation records. You can search by name, registered agent, or filing number. Also, search securities companies registered with the state at www.securities.arkansas.gov/starsqldb/asdsecifs/.

Other access: Bulk release of records is available for $.50 per page. Contact Records Dept. 501-682-3409 or visit website for details.

Trademarks/Servicemarks

Secretary of State, Trademarks Section, State Capitol Bldg, Little Rock, AR 72201 (Courier address- Business & Commercial Services Div, 1401 W Capitol Ave #250, Little Rock, AR 72201); 501-682-3409, 888-233-0325, Fax- 501-682-3437; 8AM-5PM (4:30PM on F).

www.sos.arkansas.gov/corps/trademk/

Indexing & Storage: Records available from the 1950s. New records available for inquiry in minutes.

Searching: Include in request- name.

Access by: mail, phone, in person, online.

Fee & Payment: There is no search fee, copy fees are $.50 per copy. Fee payee- Secretary of State. Prepayment required. Personal checks accepted, credit cards are not.

Mail search: Turnaround time- 24-48 hours. Minimum fee for copies by mail is $2.50. SASE not required.

Phone search: They will give information over the phone.

In person: Turnaround time is within a few minutes.

Online search: Searching is available at no fee over the Internet site. Search by name, owner, city, or filing number. Search via email at corprequest@sosmail.state.ar.us.

Other access: Records can be provided in bulk for $.50 per page. Call 501-682-3409 or visit website for details.

Uniform Commercial Code, Federal Tax Liens

UCC Division - Commercial Svcs, Secretary of State, State Capitol Bldg, Little Rock, AR 72201 (Courier address- Commercial Business & Service Division, 1401 W Capitol Ave Rm 250, Little Rock, AR 72201); 501-682-5078, Fax- 501-682-3500; 8AM-5PM.

www.sos.arkansas.gov

Indexing & Storage: Records available from 1962. You can make requests by fax, but they will be returned by mail. Records are not searched by phone, but they will inform if there is anything on file. New records available for inquiry in minutes.

Searching: Use search request form UCC-11. A search includes federal tax liens on businesses, via a lien search certificate. Federal tax liens on individuals and all state tax liens (AKA municipal judgments before 1978) are filed at the county. Include in request- debtor name.

Access by: mail, fax, in person, online.

Fee & Payment: A lien search certificate is $6.00. Photostat copies of financing statements are $6.00 for the first page, $.50 each additional, maximum $100.00. The fee for certification of a copy of a filed financing statement is $.50 Fee payee- Secretary of State. Personal checks and credit cards accepted.

Mail search: Turnaround time- 1 to 2 days. SASE not required.

Fax search: There is no additional fees.

In person: Requesters can leave request and pick up the next day.

Online search: Subscribers of INA (Information Network of Arkansas) can search by file number or debtor name; subscription fees and search fees involved. See https://www.ark.org/sos/ucc/index.php for details. UCC Download is available via the Internet, but only to subscribers. Fee is $2,000.00 per month for weekly, bi-weekly or monthly downloads. Watch notifications are available for a $35.00 monthly fee.

Other access: A download of UCC data is available via the Internet, but only to subscribers. Fee is $2,000.00 per month for weekly, bi-weekly or monthly downloads.

State Tax Liens

Records not maintained by a state level agency.

Records are at the county level.

Sales Tax Registrations

Finance & Administration Department, Sales & Use Tax Office - Reg. Dept, PO Box 1272, Little Rock, AR 72203; 501-682-1895, Fax- 501-682-7904; 8AM-4:30PM.

www.state.ar.us/dfa/excise_tax_v2/st_index.html

The records and files of taxpayers are confidential and privileged. Arkansas law requires that the Director of the Department of Finance and Administration as the official custodian keep records, files, and information in his possession confidential.

Indexing & Storage: Records available from the 1940s.

Searching: DFA will only confirm that a business is registered with the State of Arkansas to collect and remit sales and use taxes. If the permit number is provided over the telephone or e-mail, we will verify if the account is registered with the State of Arkansas. This data not released- tax returns, audits

Access by: mail, phone, fax, in person.

Mail search: Turnaround time- 3 to 5 days. A SASE is requested. No fee for mail request.

Phone search: No fee for telephone request. This is the recommended search request method.

Fax search: Fax searching available.

In person: No fee for request.

Birth Certificates

Arkansas Department of Health, Division of Vital Records, PO Box 8184, Little Rock, AR 72203-8184 (Courier address- 4815 W Markham St, Slot 44, Little Rock, AR 72205); 501-661-2174, 501-661-2336 (Message Number), 866-209-9482 (Credit Card), 800-637-9314 (Toll Free), Fax-501-661-2717; 8AM-4:30PM.

www.healthyarkansas.com

Three types of records are available; certification copy, actual copy, and wallet size copy.

Indexing & Storage: Records available from 02/01/1914 to present. New records available for inquiry immediately.

Searching: Must have a signed release from person of record if requester is not a member of parents, grandparents or spouse. Include your name, address and signature on the request. Include in request- full name, names of parents, mother's maiden name, date of birth, place of birth, relationship to person of record, reason for information request. Also include your phone number.

Access by: mail, phone, fax, in person, online.

Fee & Payment: The fee is $12.00 for the first copy and $10.00 for each add'l of same record. Fee payee- Division of Vital Records. Prepayment required. Personal checks and major credit cards accepted.

Mail search: Turnaround time- 4 weeks. SASE not required.

Phone search: See expedited service. You must use a credit card. Turnaround time is 1 week.

Fax search: See expedited service.

In person: Turnaround time while you wait.

Online search: Orders can be placed via a state designated vendor. Go to www.vitalchek.com. Extra fees are involved.

Other access: Research projects require the approval of the director.

Expedited service: Expedited service is available for phone, online, and fax requests. Turnaround time- 1-5 days. Add additional fees for use of credit card and funds for the delivery method desired, fees per vendor www.vitalchek.com.

Death Records

Arkansas Department of Health, Division of Vital Records, PO Box 8184, Little Rock, AR 72203-8184 (Courier address- 4815 W Markham St, Slot 44, Little Rock, AR 72205); 501-661-2174, 501-661-2336 (Message number), 866-209-9482 (Credit Card Line), Fax- 501-661-2717; 8AM-4:30PM.

www.healthyarkansas.com

This agency does not hold the actual records, but does have an index of all deaths since 1914 and some death index records for Fort Smith and Little Rock prior to 1914.

Indexing & Storage: Records available from 02/01/1914 to present. New records available for inquiry immediately.

Searching: Must have a signed release from immediate family member if requester is not a member of family, unless record is over 50 years old. Include in request- full name, date of death, place of death, relationship to person of record, reason for information request, wife's maiden name. Include requester's signature and phone number.

Access by: mail, phone, fax, in person, online.

Fee & Payment: The fee is $10.00 for the first copy and $8.00 for each add'l of same record. Add $6.00 if you use a credit card. Fee payee- Division of Vital Records. Prepayment required. Personal checks and major credit cards accepted.

Mail search: Turnaround time- 4 weeks. Turnaround time with a credit card is 1 week. SASE not required.

Phone search: You must use a credit card.

Fax search: You must use a credit card or prepay before record is sent.

In person: Turnaround time is usually 1 hour.

Online search: Orders can be placed via a state designated vendor. Go to www.vitalchek.com. Extra fees are involved.

Expedited service: Expedited service is available for online, phone and fax searches. Turnaround time- 1-5 days. Add additional fees for use of credit card and funds for the delivery method desired, fees per vendor www.vitalchek.com.

Marriage Certificates

Arkansas Department of Health, Division of Vital Records, PO Box 8184, Little Rock, AR 72203-8184 (Courier address- 4815 W Markham St, Slot 44, Little Rock, AR 72205); 501-661-2174, 501-661-2336 (Message Number), 866-209-9482 (Credit Card Line), Fax- 501-661-2717; 8AM-4:30PM.

www.healthyarkansas.com

Customers who want a copy of the actual license or decree must contact the County Clerk or Circuit Clerk office where the record was recorded.

Indexing & Storage: Records available from 1917 on. The Division of Vital Records issues a certified copy of the coupon of marriage or divorce in paper form. New records available for inquiry immediately.

Searching: Must have a signed release from person of record if requester is not a member of immediate family. Include in request- full names of husband and wife, registration number, date of marriage, place or county of marriage, wife's maiden name. Requester must sign request and provide phone number. You must know the county name and/or date of event.

Access by: mail, phone, fax, in person, online.

Fee & Payment: The fee is $10.00 to search either three counties and one year, or three years and one county. Fee payee- Division of Vital Records. Prepayment required. Personal checks and major credit cards accepted.

Mail search: Turnaround time- 4 weeks. Turnaround time with a credit card is 1 week. SASE not required.

Phone search: You may call in your request, but you must use a credit card. Turnaround time is 1 week.

Fax search: A credit card is required or must prepay before records sent.

In person: Turnaround time is 30 minutes to an hour.

Online search: Records may requested from www.vitalchek.com, a state-endorsed vendor. Expedited service fees apply.

Expedited service: Expedited service is available for online, phone and fax searches. Turnaround time- 1-5 days. Add additional fees for use of credit card and funds for the delivery method desired, fees per vendor www.vitalchek.com.

Divorce Records

Arkansas Department of Health, Division of Vital Records, PO Box 8184, Little Rock, AR 72203-8184 (Courier address- 4815 W Markham St, Slot 44, Little Rock, AR 72205); 501-661-2174, 501-661-2336 (Message Number), 866-209-9482 (Credit Card Line), 800-637-9314, Fax- 501-661-2717; 8AM-4:30PM.

www.healthyarkansas.com

Customers who want a copy of the actual license or decree must contact the County Clerk or Circuit Clerk office where the record was recorded.

Indexing & Storage: Records available from 1923 to present. The Division of Vital Records issues a certified copy of the coupon of marriage or divorce in paper form. New records available for inquiry in 30 days.

Searching: Must have a signed release from person of record if requester is not a member of the immediate family. Include in request- names of husband and wife, date of divorce, place of divorce. Requester must sign request and provide phone number. You must know the county name and/or date of event.

Access by: mail, phone, fax, in person, online.

Fee & Payment: The fee is $10.00 to search either three counties and one year, or three years and one county. Fee payee- Division of Public Records. Prepayment required. Personal checks and major credit cards accepted.

Mail search: Turnaround time- 4 weeks. Turnaround time with a credit card is 1 week. SASE not required.

Phone search: See expedited service. You must use a credit card. Turnaround time is 1 week.

Fax search: See expedited service.

In person: Turnaround time is within 1 hour.

Online search: Records may requested from www.vitalchek.com, a state-endorsed vendor. See expedited service.

Expedited service: Expedited service is available for online, phone and fax searches. Turnaround time- 1-5 days. Add additional fees for use of credit card and funds for the delivery method desired, fees per vendor www.vitalchek.com.

Workers' Compensation Records

Workers Compensation Commission, Operations/Compliance, 324 Spring Street, PO Box 950, Little Rock, AR 72203-0950; 501-682-3930, 800-622-4472, Fax- 501-682-6761; 8AM-4:30PM M-F.

www.awcc.state.ar.us

The electronic database of claims includes employee claims for compensation and employer reports of injury resulting in lost time of more than seven days or resulting in permanent disability or death, regardless whether benefits were paid.

Indexing & Storage: Records available from 1940s on. New records available for inquiry immediately.

Searching: Only written requests are accepted. You may fax a request, but it is returned by mail. Include in request- claimant name, SSN, place of employment at time of accident, file number (if known). This data not released- SSNs or medical information.

Access by: mail, phone, fax, in person, online.

Fee & Payment: Copies must be requested are not automatically part of a search. Reportedly, the fee is $5.00 per name searched and $.50 per page for copies, but each requester is asked to contact the Clerk's office prior to requesting information. Fee payee- Workers' Compensation Commission. An invoice is mailed with the results of the request. Personal checks accepted, credit cards are not.

Mail search: Turnaround time- 7-10 days. SASE not required.

Phone search: Records are available by phone.

Fax search: Search requests should be faxed to 501-682-2494. Copy requests should be faxed to 501-682-2042.

In person: You may make copies at $.50 per page. You are allowed to look through the files without charge.

Online search: To perform an online claim search, one must be a subscriber to the Information Network of Arkansas (INA). Records are from May 1, 1997 forward. There is an annual $75 subscriber fee to INA. Each record request is $3.50; if more than 20 are ordered in one month, the fee is $2.50 each request over 20. For more info, visit www.awcc.state.ar.us/electron.html.

Driver Records

Department of Driver Services, Driving Records Division, PO Box 1272, Room 1130, Little Rock, AR 72203-1272 (Courier address- 1900 W 7th, #1130, Little Rock, AR 72201); 501-682-7207, 501-682-7908, Fax- 501-682-2075; 8AM-4:30PM.

www.accessarkansas.org/dfa/driver_services/ds_index.html

Copies of tickets must be requested from the local jurisdiction where the ticket was issued.

Indexing & Storage: Records available for 3 years for moving violations and are retained per federal retention period. DWI and suspensions show until all requirements are met. New records available for inquiry in less than 1 day.

Searching: Arkansas requires signed authorization by the driver to obtain a driving record. Volume requesters must have these authorizations on file. Violations on an interstate highway not exceeding 75 mph won't show on records requested for insurance purposes. Include in request- full name, driver's license number, date of birth. Race and sex on listed on insurance-requested records. Driver's address is included as part of the search report for permissible requesters.

Access by: mail, in person, online.

Fee & Payment: Fees are $7.00 for an insurance record and $10.00 for record on a commercial driver, online is higher. There is a full charge for a "no record found." Fee payee- State of Arkansas, Driver Services. Prepayment required. Personal checks accepted, credit cards are not.

Mail search: Turnaround time- 24 hours. Requester must enclose written release, full name, DOB, driver's license number, and proper fees. SASE not required.

In person: The state will process up to 5 requests while you wait.

Online search: Access is available through the Information Network of Arkansas (INA). The system offers both batch and interactive service. The system is only available to INA subscribers who have statutory rights to the data. The record fee is $8.50, or $11.50 for commercial drivers. Visit www.arkansas.gov/sub_services.php. The annual subscription fee is $75.00, other record services are available.

Vehicle Ownership & Registration

Office of Motor Vehicles, MV Title Records, PO Box 1272, Room 1100, Little Rock, AR 72203 (Courier address- 7th & Battery Sts, Ragland Bldg, Room 1100, Little Rock, AR 72201); 501-682-4692, 800-662-8247, Fax- 501-682-4756; 8AM-4:30PM.

www.accessarkansas.org/dfa/

Indexing & Storage: Records available from license plate records from 1968 on microfilm; plate number and name from 1981 on microfiche. All records are kept on film, not paper. New records available for inquiry in 4 to 6 weeks.

Searching: Vehicle registration information cannot be sold or used for solicitation purposes. Requesters that do not have DPPA approved purpose, cannot receive records with personal information, unless consent of subject is given. Include in request- vehicle make and VIN. Approved account holders may request via e-mail. This data not released- SSNs or date of birth.

Access by: mail, phone, fax, in person, online.

Fee & Payment: The fee for vehicle and/or ownership searches is $1.00 per copy and $1.00 per search. Fee payee- Department of Finance and Administration. Prepayment required. If mailing a check to open a new account, place "Attn: Search Account" on the request. If mailing an information request, place "Attn: Correspondence Desk" on the request. Personal checks accepted, credit cards are not.

Mail search: Turnaround time- 2-3 days. SASE not required.

Phone search: Searching by phone is available for established accounts. A $125.00 deposit required.

Fax search: For approved account holders only.

In person: Turnaround time while you wait.

Online search: Approved, DPPA compliant accounts may access records online by VIN, plate, or title number. The fee is $1.50. Name searches and certificated documents may be ordered. For further info, go to www.arkansas.gov/sub_services.php.

Other access: The bulk purchase of records, except for recall or statistical purposes, is prohibited.

Accident Reports

Arkansas State Police, Crash Records Section, 1 State Police Plaza Dr, Little Rock, AR 72209; 501-618-8130, Fax- 501-618-8131; 8AM-5PM.

www.asp.state.ar.us/divisions/rs/rs_crash.html

Indexing & Storage: Records available from 2001 to present. New records available for inquiry in 5 to 10 business days.

Searching: Include in request- date of accident, location, name of at least on driver. Records 1995 through 1999 have been destroyed.

Access by: mail, phone, in person, online.

Fee & Payment: The fee is $10.00 per record, $2.00 more if ordered online. There is no charge for a "no record found." Payment will be refunded. Fee payee- Arkansas State Police, Accident Records. Prepayment required. Personal checks and money orders accepted. Credit cards accepted only online.

Mail search: Turnaround time- 4 to 6 weeks. A SASE is requested.

Phone search: Limited information is available.

In person: Turnaround time is while you wait, if staffing available.

Online search: Limited information is available from the webpage for no charge (names involved), date, county but full record copy may be purchased for $12.00. Search by name, license number and/or date range. Once purchased, reports will be available for 30 days and may be repeatedly accessed with an Order ID. For further information regarding the contents of the report, please contact the Arkansas State Police at 501-618-8130. Credit card is required, unless requester is member of INA. Available records date back to 01/02/01.

Vessel Ownership & Registration

Office of Motor Vehicles, Boat Registration, PO Box 1272, Little Rock, AR 72203; 501-682-4692, Fax- 501-682-4756; 8AM-4:30PM.

www.arkansas.gov/dfa/motorvehicle/index.html

Lien information is filed at the Secretary of State.

Indexing & Storage: Records available for 25 years. All boats propelled by sail or machinery must be registered. Vessels are not titled in this state. New records available for inquiry immediately.

Searching: Motor vehicle title, registration and lien information is available for users that qualify under DPPA. Ongoing requesters should become account holders. Include in request- name and address of requester and account number if applicable. Search by name or registration number or hull number.

Access by: mail, phone, fax, in person.

Fee & Payment: The search fee is $1.00 per search and $1.00 per copy of a record. Fee payee- Office of Motor Vehicles. Prepayment required. Personal checks accepted, credit cards are not.

Mail search: Turnaround time- 2 weeks. SASE not required.

Phone search: Requests only accepted for account holders.

Fax search: Requests only accepted for account holders.

In person: Records are usually obtained at once, unless they require extensive research.

Other access: Bulk access to approved users is available via FTP.

Legislation Records

Elections Department, State Capitol, Room 026, Little Rock, AR 72201; 501-682-5070, Fax- 501-682-3408; 8AM-5PM.

www.arkleg.state.ar.us

This agency will do simple research; they will respond to requests by act number or code number.

Indexing & Storage: Records available from 1909 to present.

Access by: mail, phone, fax, in person, online.

Fee & Payment: One may purchase copies of bills or Acts for $.25 per page. They will return copies by Federal Express if you give your billing number. Fee payee- Secretary of State. Prepayment required. Personal checks accepted, credit cards are not.

Mail search: Turnaround time- 1 day. SASE not required.

Phone search: Simple requests are available only.

Fax search: Fax searching available.

In person: Simple requests may be processed while you wait.

Online search: Probably the best way to search is through the Internet site listed above. You may also search by subject matter. Legislative acts from 1997 are available online. There is also a tracking service to track up to 40 bills at once. The Arkansas Code is found at www.arkleg.state.ar.us/SearchCenter/Pages/ArkansasCodeSearchResultPage.aspx.

Voter Registration

Secretary of State, Voter Services, State Capitol, Room 026, Little Rock, AR 72201; 501-682-3204, Fax- 501-682-3548; 8AM-5PM.

www.sosweb.state.ar.us/elections.html

The state will sell the voter database data, there are no commercial restrictions. All individual search requests should be done at the local County Clerk's office. The SSN will not be released.

Indexing & Storage: Records available from 1995.

Searching: The agency produces a new CD monthly that contains names, addresses and phone numbers of all registered voters.

Access by: mail, in person, online.

Fee & Payment: There is no fee for individual searches, if permitted. Bulk records require a fee.

Mail search: Record requests are available by mail, please state the purpose

In person: The reason for the request must be given.

Online search: Search one's voter registration information at https://www.voterview.ar-nova.org/. Name and DOB required.

Other access: The CD as described above is available for $2.50. If bulk data is requested on other formats, including paper, the cost is considerably higher.

GED Certificates

GED Testing, Dept of Workforce Education, #3 Capitol Mall, Room 305D, Little Rock, AR 72201; 501-682-1978 (Main Number), Fax- 501-682-1982; 8AM-4:30PM.

http://dwe.arkansas.gov/ged.htm

Indexing & Storage: Records available from 1970's forward. New records available for inquiry in one month.

Searching: For verification or for a copy of a transcript, all of the following is required: a signed release, name, year of test, date of birth, and SSN.

Access by: mail, fax, in person.

Fee & Payment: There is no fee.

Mail search: Turnaround time- 2 to 3 days. SASE is helpful.

Fax search: Will return fax requests immediately but only for employers, military, or schools.

In person: Records can be accessed immediately.

Expedited service: Will provide expedited service if needed for immediate hiring or enrollment in college, and documented by signature of company/school official. Turnaround time- 1 day or less.

Hunting & Fishing License Information

Access to Records is Restricted.

Game & Fish Commission, Attn: Licensing & FOIA Legal Div., 2 Natural Resources Dr, Little Rock, AR 72205; 501-223-6300, 800-364-4263, Fax- 501-223-6425; 8AM-4:30PM.

www.agfc.com

Requests for records are only processed in accordance with the Arkansas Freedom of Information Act. Must mention request is under the Freedom of Information Act.

Arkansas State Licensing Agencies

For details about the agency responsible for licensing/certifying/registering an item below or in the Agency Quick Finder section, match an item's number with the number of the agency in the *Licensing Agency Information* section.

Arkansas Licenses Searchable Online

Acupuncturist #9 .... www.accessarkansas.org/asbce/acupuncture_roster.html
Aesthetician #49........ www.arkansas.gov/cos/search.php
Agriculture Educator #32........ http://arkedu.state.ar.us/teachers/accessing_licensure_info.html
Architect #6 .... www.arkansas.gov/arch/search_ind.php
Asbestos Inspector/Planner #28 .... www.adeq.state.ar.us/compsvs/webmaster/databases.htm
Asbestos Removal Worker #28........ www.adeq.state.ar.us/compsvs/webmaster/databases.htm
Asbestos Training Provider #28 .... www.adeq.state.ar.us/compsvs/webmaster/databases.htm
Athletic Trainer (Health) #24 .... www.aratb.org/search.php
Attorney #43........ http://courts.arkansas.gov/attorneys/attorney_search.cfm
Auctioneer #5........ https://www.ark.org/auct_ds/app/index.html
Audiologist #41........ www.arkansas.gov/abespa_licv/app/enter.html
Bank #38 .... www.sos.arkansas.gov/corps/search_all.php
Boiler Inspector/Installer/Repairer #27........ www.arkansas.gov/labor/online_services/online_services_p1.html
Boiler Operator #27........ www.arkansas.gov/labor/online_services/online_services_p1.html
Business Education Teacher #32 .... http://arkedu.state.ar.us/teachers/accessing_licensure_info.html
Career Orientation Teacher #32 .... http://arkedu.state.ar.us/teachers/accessing_licensure_info.html
Cemetery, Perpetual Care #39 .... www.securities.arkansas.gov/starsqldb/asdcsifs/
Charitable Annuity #2........ http://insurance.arkansas.gov/is/companysearch/cosearch.asp
Check Casher #10 .... www.asbca.org/check_search/
Check Seller #39........ www.securities.arkansas.gov/starsqldb/asdcsifs/
Chemical, List 1, Wholesale Distr. #17 .... www.ark.org/asbp/roster/index.php
Child Care Provider #26........ www.arkansas.gov/childcare/licensing/newweb.html
Chiropractor #9 .... www.accessarkansas.org/asbce/search.html
Collection Agency #10 .... www.asbca.org/collect_search/
Collection Agency Collector/Mgr. #10........ www.asbca.org/collect_search/
Contractor #23 .... www.accessarkansas.org/clb/search.html
Cosmetologist/Cosmetology Instr. #49 .... www.arkansas.gov/cos/search.php
Counselor, Professional #51 .... www.accessarkansas.org/abec/search.php
Court Reporter #8 .... www.arkansas.gov/court_reporters/search/index.php
Dental Hygienist #11 .... www.asbde.org/rdhroster/search.php
Dentist #11 .... www.asbde.org/ddsroster/search.php
Drugs, Legend, Wholesale Distr. #17 .... www.ark.org/asbp/roster/index.php
Electrical Contractor #27........ www.arkansas.gov/labor/online_services/online_services_p1.html
Electrician Journeyman/ Master #27........ www.arkansas.gov/labor/online_services/online_services_p1.html
Electrologist/Electrolysis Instructor #49 .... www.arkansas.gov/cos/search.php
Embalmer/Embalmer Apprentice #12 .... www.arkansas.gov/fdemb/
Emergency Med. Tech.-Paramedic #25........ https://www.ark.org/dhhsems/index.php
Emergency Medical Technician #25 .... https://www.ark.org/dhhsems/index.php
Employee Leasing Firm #2 .... http://insurance.arkansas.gov/is/companysearch/cosearch.asp
Engineer/Engineer in Training #19........ www.arkansas.gov/pels/search/search.php
Farm Mutual Aid Assoc #2 .... http://insurance.arkansas.gov/is/companysearch/cosearch.asp
Fire Equipment Inspector/Repairer #47 .... www.arfireprotection.org/roster/index.html
Fire Extinguisher Sprinkler Inspect'r #47 .... www.arfireprotection.org/roster/index.html
Forester #20........ https://www.ark.org/foresters_rsearch/app/enter.html
Funeral Director/Apprentice #12 .... www.arkansas.gov/fdemb/
Funeral Home/Crematory #12........ www.arkansas.gov/fdemb/
Geologist #21 .... www.pgboard.ar.gov/
HMO Medicare #2........ http://insurance.arkansas.gov/is/companysearch/cosearch.asp
Home Inspector #38........ www.ahib.org/
Hospital Medical Service #2........ http://insurance.arkansas.gov/is/companysearch/cosearch.asp
Insurance Agency #2 .... http://insurance.arkansas.gov/is/Agency/agency.asp

Insurance Agency #38 .... www.sos.arkansas.gov/corps/search_all.php
Insurance Company #2 .... http://insurance.arkansas.gov/is/companysearch/cosearch.asp
Insurance Sales Agent #2 .... http://insurance.arkansas.gov/is/agentsearch/agent.asp
Investment Advisor #39 .... www.securities.arkansas.gov/starsqldb/asdsecifs/
Landscape Architect #6 .... www.arkansas.gov/asbla/find_landscape_architect.html
Life Care #2 .... http://insurance.arkansas.gov/is/companysearch/cosearch.asp
Lobbyist #38 .... www.sosweb.state.ar.us/elections/elections_pdfs/lobby_lists/2005/2005list.pdf
Manicurist #49 .... www.arkansas.gov/cos/search.php
Marriage & Family Therapist #51 .... www.accessarkansas.org/abec/search.php
Medicaid Provider #52 .... https://www.medicaid.state.ar.us/InternetSolution/
Medical Corporation #31 .... https://www.armedicalboard.org/licenseverf/
Medical Doctor/Surgeon #31 .... https://www.armedicalboard.org/licenseverf/
Midwife Nurse #15 .... www.arsbn.org/registry/index.html
Mortgage Loan Broker/Company #39 .... www.securities.arkansas.gov/starsqldb/asdcsifs/
Motor Club #2 .... http://insurance.arkansas.gov/is/companysearch/cosearch.asp
Motor Vehicle Dealer/Distributor #35 .... www.armvc.com/licensee_search/index.html
Motor Vehicle Mfg/Rep, New #35 .... www.armvc.com/licensee_search/index.html
Multiple Employee Welfare Assoc #2 .... http://insurance.arkansas.gov/is/companysearch/cosearch.asp
Notary Public #38 .... www.sos.arkansas.gov/corps/notary/index.php
Nurse #15 .... www.arsbn.org/registry/index.html
Nurse Anesthetist #15 .... www.arsbn.org/registry/index.html
Nurse-LPN #15 .... www.arsbn.org/registry/index.html
Nursing Home Facility #52 .... www.arhspa.org/agency_decisions.html
Occupational Therapist/Assistant #31 .... https://www.armedicalboard.org/licenseverf/
Optician #50 .... www.ark.org/directory/detail2.cgi?ID-1050
Optometrist #16 .... www.arbo.org/index.php?action=findanoptometrist
Osteopathic Physician #31 .... https://www.armedicalboard.org/licenseverf/
P & C Company #2 .... http://insurance.arkansas.gov/pclh/pcweb.asp
Pharmacist #17 .... www.ark.org/asbp/roster/index.php
Pharmacy Technician #17 .... www.ark.org/asbp/roster/index.php
Pharmacy, Hospital/Institution #17 .... www.ark.org/asbp/roster/index.php
Pharmacy, Specialty #17 .... www.ark.org/asbp/roster/index.php
Pharmacy-In-State, Retail #17 .... www.ark.org/asbp/roster/index.php
Pharmacy-Out-of-State, Retail #17 .... www.ark.org/asbp/roster/index.php
Physical Therapist #3 .... www.arptb.org/ptroster/search.php
Physician Assistant #31 .... https://www.armedicalboard.org/licenseverf/
Political Action Committee #38 .... www.sosweb.state.ar.us/elections/elections_pdfs/pac_lists/pac_list_02-03-05.pdf
Pre-Need Seller #2 .... http://insurance.arkansas.gov/is/companysearch/cosearch.asp
Psychological Examiner #13 .... www.arkansas.gov/abep/Licensees.htm
Psychologist #13 .... www.arkansas.gov/abep/Licensees.htm
Public Accountant-CPA #18 .... www.arkansas.gov/asbpa/
Real Estate Agent/Broker/Sales #37 .... https://www.ark.org/arec_renewals/index.php/search/agent
Real Estate Appraiser #37 .... www.arkansas.gov/alcb/search.php
Reins Intermediary #2 .... http://insurance.arkansas.gov/is/companysearch/cosearch.asp
Reinsurer #2 .... http://insurance.arkansas.gov/is/companysearch/cosearch.asp
Respiratory Care Practitioner #31 .... https://www.armedicalboard.org/licenseverf/
School Principal/Admin/Super #32 .... http://arkedu.state.ar.us/teachers/accessing_licensure_info.html
Securities Agent #39 .... www.securities.arkansas.gov/starsqldb/asdsecifs/
Securities Broker/Dealer/Exemption #39 .... www.securities.arkansas.gov/starsqldb/asdsecifs/
Security Mutual Fund #39 .... www.securities.arkansas.gov/starsqldb/asdsecifs/
Service Contract Provider #2 .... http://insurance.arkansas.gov/is/companysearch/cosearch.asp
Social Worker #40 .... www.accessarkansas.org/swlb/search/index.html
Solid Waste Facility Operator #28 .... www.adeq.state.ar.us/compsvs/webmaster/databases.htm
Speech Pathologist #41 .... www.arkansas.gov/abespa_licv/app/enter.html
Supplier- Legend Device/Med Gas #17 .... www.ark.org/asbp/roster/index.php
Supplier of Med Equipment #17 .... www.ark.org/asbp/roster/index.php
Surplus Lines Insurer #2 .... http://insurance.arkansas.gov/is/companysearch/cosearch.asp
Surveyor, Land #19 .... www.arkansas.gov/pels/search.php
Teacher #32 .... http://arkedu.state.ar.us/teachers/accessing_licensure_info.html

Arkansas Licensing Quick Finder

Abstractor #48 870-942-8064
Acupuncturist #9 501-682-9015
Aesthetician #49 501-682-2168
Agricultural Consultant #33 501-225-1598
Agriculture Educator #32 501-682-4695
Alcohol/Drug Abuse Program #25 501-661-2000
Anesthetician #15 501-682-2200
Announcer, Athletic Event/Ring #4 501-687-1038
Architect #6 501-682-3171
Armored Car Guard #42 501-618-8600
Asbestos Inspector/Planner #28 501-682-0718
Asbestos Removal Worker #28 501-682-0718
Asbestos Training Provider #28 501-682-0718
Athlete Agent #38 501-682-5070
Athletic Manager #4 501-687-1038
Athletic Promoter/Matchmaker #4 501-687-1038
Athletic Trainer (Health) #24 501-683-4076
Athletic Trainer (Sports) #4 501-687-1038
Attorney #43 501-682-6849
Auction, Charitible w/Alcohol #1 501-682-1105
Auctioneer #5 501-682-1156
Audiologist #41 501-682-9180
Bail Bondsman #2 501-682-9050
Bank #38 501-682-3409
Barber Instructor #7 501-682-4035
Barber/Barber Technician #7 501-682-4035
Bed & Breakfast w/Alcohol #1 501-682-1105
Beer Festival #1 501-682-1105
Beer Mfg./Seller #1 501-682-1105
Birthing Center #25 501-661-2518
Boiler Inspector/Installer/Repairer #27 501-682-4513
Boiler Operator #27 501-682-4513
Boxer #4 501-687-1038
Boxing/Wrestling Referee #4 501-687-1038
Brandy, Native #1 501-682-1105
Brewer, Native #1 501-682-1105
Burglar Alarm System Agent/Mgr #42 501-618-8600
Business Education Teacher #32 501-682-4695
Career Education Coordinator #32 501-682-4695
Career Orientation Teacher #32 501-682-4695
Caterer, w/Alcohol #1 501-682-1105
Cemetery, Perpetual Care #39 501-324-9260
Charitable Annuity #2 501-371-2750
Check Casher #10 501-376-1434
Check Seller #39 501-324-9260
Chemical, List 1, Wholesale Distr. #17 501-682-0190
Child Care Provider #26 501-682-8590
Chiropractor #9 501-682-9015
Claims Adjuster #2 501-371-2750
Clinics, Health #25 501-661-2518
Collection Agency #10 501-376-1438
Collection Agency Collector/Mgr. #10 501-376-1438
Contractor #23 501-372-4661
Cosmetologist/Cosmetology Instr. #49 501-682-2168
Counselor, Professional #51 870-901-7055
Court Reporter #8 501-682-6850
Dental Assistant #11 501-682-2085
Dental Hygienist #11 501-682-2085
Dentist #11 501-682-2085
Dietitian #29 .... 501-221-0566, 580-9294
Distiller #1 501-682-1105
Drugs, Legend, Wholesale Distr. #17 501-682-0190
Egg Grader #53 501-907-2400
Electrical Contractor #27 501-682-4549
Electrician Journeyman/ Master #27 501-682-4549
Electrologist/Electrolysis Instructor #49 501-682-2168
Elevator/Lifting Device Inspector #27 501-682-4531
Embalmer/Embalmer Apprentice #12 501-682-0574
Emergency Med. Tech.-Paramedic #25 501-661-2262
Emergency Medical Technician #25 501-661-2262
Employee Leasing Firm #2 501-371-2750
Employment Agency Manager #27 501-682-4505
Employment Agent/Counselor #27 501-682-4505
Engineer/Engineer in Training #19 501-682-2824
Exterminator #33 501-225-1598
Farm Mutual Aid Assoc #2 501-371-2750
Fire Equipment Inspector/Repairer #47 501-661-7903
Fire Extinguisher Sprinkler Inspector #47 501-661-7903
Forester #20 501-296-1998
Funeral Director/Apprentice #12 501-682-0574
Funeral Home/Crematory #12 501-682-0574
Gas Fitter/Trainee #25 501-661-2242
Geologist #21 501-683-0150
Grain Warehouseman #33 501-225-1598
Greyhound Racing #36 501-682-1467
Handgun, Concealed #42 501-618-8600
Health Facility #25 501-661-2201
Hearing Instrument Dispenser #14 501-663-5869
HMO #25 501-661-2518
HMO Medicare #2 501-371-2750
H-M-R Maximum/Minimum #1 501-682-1105
Home Health Agency #25 501-661-2518
Home Inspector #38 501-683-3710
Homebuilders #23 501-372-4661
Horse Racing #36 501-682-1467
Hospice Facility #25 501-661-2518
Hospital Maintenance Plumber #25 501-661-2698
Hospital Medical Service #2 501-371-2750
Industrial Maintenance Electrician #27 501-682-4549
Insurance Agency #38 501-682-3409
Insurance Agency #2 501-371-2750
Insurance Company #2 501-371-2750
Insurance Sales Agent #2 501-371-2750
Investment Advisor #39 501-324-9260
Laboratory #25 501-661-2191
Landscape Architect #6 501-682-3112
Life Care #2 501-371-2750
Liquor Distiller #1 501-682-1105
Liquor Distributor #1 501-682-1105
Liquor Sampling #1 501-682-1105
Liquor, Vinous #1 501-682-1105
Livestock Brand #53 501-907-2400
Livestock Dealer #53 501-907-2400
Lobbyist #38 501-682-5070
LPG Safety Supervisor #30 501-683-4100
Manicurist #49 501-682-2168
Manufactured Home Dealer/Mfg #54 501-324-9032
Manufactured Home Installer #54 501-324-9032
Manufactured Home Salesperson #54 501-324-9032
Marriage & Family Therapist #51 870-901-7055
Martial Arts #4 501-687-1038
Massage Therapy Tech/masseur/m'use #22 501-520-0555
Medicaid Provider #52 800-482-5431
Medical Corporation #31 501-296-1802
Medical Doctor/Surgeon #31 501-296-1802
Medicare Certified Facility #25 501-661-2201
Microbrewery #1 501-682-1105
Midwife Nurse #15 501-682-2200
Military Service Club Alcol. Permit #1 501-682-1105
Mortgage Loan Broker/Company #39 501-324-9260
Motor Club #2 501-371-2750
Motor Vehicle Dealer/Distributor #35 501-682-1428
Motor Vehicle Dealer/Seller, Used #42 501-618-8600
Motor Vehicle Mfg/Rep, New #35 501-682-1428
Multiple Employee Welfare Assoc #2 501-371-2750
Notary Public #38 501-682-3409
Nurse #15 501-682-2200
Nurse Anesthetist #15 501-682-2200
Nurse-LPN #15 501-682-2200
Nurseryman #33 501-225-1598
Nursing Home Administrator #52 501-682-1873
Nursing Home Facility #52 501-682-1873
Occupational Therapist/Assistant #31 501-296-1802
Optician #50 870-572-2847
Optometrist #16 501-268-4351
Osteopathic Physician #31 501-296-1802
P & C Company #2 501-371-2750
Permanent Cosmetic/Tattoo Artist #25 501-661-2171
Pesticide Applicator #33 501-225-1598
Petroleum Dealer #30 501-683-4100
Pharmacist #17 501-682-0190
Pharmacist Intern #17 501-682-0190
Pharmacy Technician #17 501-682-0190
Pharmacy, Hospital/Institution #17 501-682-0190
Pharmacy, Specialty #17 501-682-0190
Pharmacy-In-State, Retail #17 501-682-0190
Pharmacy-Out-of-State, Retail #17 501-682-0190
Physical Therapist #3 501-228-7100
Physician Assistant #31 501-296-1802
Podiatrist #34 501-664-3668
Political Action Committee #38 501-682-5070
Polygraph Examiner #42 501-618-8600
Post Exchange w/Alcohol #1 501-682-1105
Precious Metals Dealer #42 501-618-8600
Pre-Need Seller #2 501-371-2750
Private Club #1 501-682-1105
Private Investigator #42 501-618-8600
Psychological Examiner #13 501-682-6167
Psychologist #13 501-682-6167
Public Accountant-CPA #18 501-682-1520
Pump Installer #45 501-682-1025
Radiologic Technician #25 501-661-2306
Real Estate Agent/Broker/Sales #37 501-683-8010
Real Estate Appraiser #37 501-683-8010
Reins Intermediary #2 501-371-2750
Reinsurer #2 501-371-2750
Residential Journeyman #27 501-682-4549
Respiratory Care Practitioner #31 501-296-1802
Restaurant Wine #1 501-682-1105
Restaurant, w/Wine #1 501-682-1105
Retail Beer/Liquor/Wine #1 501-682-1105
School Counselor #32 501-682-4344
School Principal/Admin/Super #32 501-682-4344
Securities Agent #39 501-324-9260
Securities Broker/Dealer #39 501-324-9260
Securities Exemption #39 501-324-9260
Security Guard #42 501-618-8600
Security Mutual Fund #39 501-324-9260
Seed Dealer #33 501-225-1598
Septic Tank Cleaner #25 501-661-2171
Service Contract Provider #2 501-371-2750
Social Worker #40 501-372-5071
Solid Waste Facility Operator #28 501-682-0585
Speech Pathologist #41 501-682-9180
State Trooper #42 501-618-8282
Sunday Alcohol Permit #1 501-682-1105
Supplier: Legend Device/Med Gas #17 501-682-0190
Supplier of Med Equipment #17 501-682-0190
Surplus Lines Insurer #2 501-371-2750
Surveyor, Land #19 501-682-2824
Surveyor-in-Training #19 501-682-2824
Teacher #32 501-682-4695
Temporary Alcohol Permit #1 501-682-1105
Veterinarian #44 501-224-2836
Veterinary Technician #44 501-224-2836
Waste Water Plant Operator #28 501-682-0998
Water Supply Operator #25 501-661-2623
Water Well Driller #45 501-682-1025
Wine Permit #1 501-682-1105
Winery Farm/Mfg/Wholse #1 501-682-1105
Wrestler #4 501-687-1038

Arkansas Licensing Agency Information

#1 Alcoholic Beverage Control Division, 1515 W 7th St #503, Little Rock, AR 72201; 501-682-1105, Fax- 501-682-2221. Agency will sell lists of permit holders by category.

#2 Department of Insurance, Licensing Division, 1200 W 3rd St, Little Rock, AR 72201; 800-282-9134, Fax- 501-371-2618. http://insurance.arkansas.gov/

#3 Board of Physical Therapy, 9 Shackleford Plaza, #3, Little Rock, AR 72211; 501-228-7100, Fax- 501-228-0294. Hours- 8AM-4:30PM. www.arptb.org Search data at- www.arptb.org/ptroster/search.php

#4 Athletic Commission, 9110 Lew Dr, Little Rock, AR 72209; 501-687-1038, Fax- 501-568-0731. www.asac.arkansas.gov/

#5 Auctioneers Licensing Board, 101 E Capitol, #112B, Little Rock, AR 72201; 501-682-1156, Fax- 501-682-1158. www.aralb.com/ Search data at- https://www.ark.org/auct_ds/app/index.html

#6 State Board of Architects, 101 E Capitol Ave, Ste #110, Little Rock, AR 72201-3822; 501-682-3171, Fax- 501-682-3172. www.arkansas.gov/arch/

#7 Board of Barber Examiners, 103 E 7th St, Rm 212, Donaghey Plaza South, Little Rock, AR 72201-4512; 501-682-4035, Fax- 501-682-5073. www.state.ar.us/directory/detail2.cgi?ID=1044

#8 Board of Certified Court Reporter Examiners, 625 Marshall St, Justice Bldg, Little Rock, AR 72201; 501-682-6850. www.arcrb.com Search data at- www.arkansas.gov/court_reporters/search/index.php

#9 Board of Chiropractic Examiners, 101 E Capital Ave, #209, Little Rock, AR 72201; 501-682-9015, Fax- 501-682-9016. Hours- 8:30AM-4:30PM. www.accessarkansas.org/asbce/ Search data at- www.accessarkansas.org/asbce/search.html

#10 Board of Collection Agencies, 523 Louisiana St, #460, Little Rock, AR 72201; 501-376-1438, Fax- 501-372-5383. www.asbca.org

#11 Board of Dental Examiners, 101 E Capitol Ave, #111, Little Rock, AR 72201; 501-682-2085, Fax- 501-682-3543. Hours- 8AM-4:30PM. www.asbde.org

#12 Board of Embalmers & Funeral Directors, 101 E Capitol Ave, #113, Little Rock, AR 72201; 501-682-0574, Fax- 501-682-0575. Hours- 8AM-4:30PM. www.arkansas.gov/fdemb/

#13 Board of Examiners in Psychology, 101 E Capitol Ave, #415, Little Rock, AR 72201; 501-682-6167, Fax- 501-682-6165. Hours- 8AM-4:30PM. www.arkansas.gov/abep/ Search- www.arkansas.gov/abep/Licensees.htm Accepts verifications by phone or fax. They require a written request only plus a $10.00 per verification. A form may be downloaded from their website to fill out and return.

#14 Board of Hearing Instrument Dispensers, 305 N Monroe, Little Rock, AR 72205; 501-663-5869, Fax- 501-663-6359. www.arkansas.gov/government_details_expanded.php?id=92

#15 Board of Nursing, 1123 S University, University Tower Bldg, #800, Little Rock, AR 72204-1619; 501-686-2700, Fax- 501-686-2714. www.arsbn.org Search data at- www.arsbn.org/registry/index.html An account with the Information Network of Arkansas (INA) is required to access services such as TVR's, TRL's, searching the Board of Nursing registry or licenses & workers' compensation claims & opinions go to www.arkansas.gov/sub_services.php.

#16 Board of Optometry, 407 N Elm St, Searcy, AR 72143; 501-268-4351, Fax- 501-268-4361. www.aroptometry.org Search data at- www.arbo.org/index.php?action=findanoptometrist

#17 Board of Pharmacy, 101 E Capitol, #218, Little Rock, AR 72201; 501-682-0190, Fax- 501-682-0195. www.arkansas.gov/asbp/ Search data at- www.ark.org/asbp/roster/index.php

#18 Board of Public Accountancy, 101 E Capitol, #450, Little Rock, AR 72201; 501-682-1520, Fax- 501-682-5538. www.arkansas.gov/asbpa/

#19 Board of Registration for Engineers/Land Surveyors, PO Box 3750 (623 Woodlane Ave), Little Rock, AR 72203; 501-682-2824, Fax- 501-682-2827. www.state.ar.us/pels/ Search data at- www.arkansas.gov/pels/search/search.php

#20 Board of Registration for Foresters, 3821 W Roosevelt Rd, Little Rock, AR 72204; 501-296-1998, Fax- 501-296-1949. www.arkansas.gov/abof/contact_us.html

#21 Geological Commission, Board of Registration for Professional Geologists, 3815 W Roosevelt Rd, Little Rock, AR 72204; 501-683-0150, Fax- 501-683-2192. Hours- 8AM-04:30PM. www.pgboard.ar.gov/ Search data at- www.pgboard.ar.gov/ Geologist directory available in xls or pdf format.

#22 Board of Massage Therapy, PO Box 20739, Hot Springs, AR 71903-0739; 501-520-0555, Fax- 501-623-4130. www.arkansasmassagetherapy.com

#23 Contractors Licensing Board, 4100 Richards Rd, North Little Rock, AR 72117; 501-372-4661, Fax- 501-372-2247. www.accessarkansas.org/clb/ Search data at- www.state.ar.us/clb/search.html

#24 State Board of Athletic Training, 9 Shackleford Plaza #3, Little Rock, AR 72211; 501-683-4076, Fax- 501-228-0294. Hours- 8AM-4:30PM. www.aratb.org Search data at- www.aratb.org/search.php

#25 Division of Health, Bureau of Health Resources; Administration/Licensing, 4815 W Markham, Little Rock, AR 72205-3867; 501-661-2000, Fax- 501-280-4901. Hours- 8AM-4:30PM. www.healthyarkansas.com Search data at- www.healthyarkansas.com/permits/permits.html

#26 Department of Human Services, Division of Child Care & Early Childhood Education, PO Box 1437 Slot S140 (700 Main St), Little Rock, AR 72203; 501-682-4891, Fax- 501-682-2317. www.arkansas.gov/childcare/ Search data at- www.arkansas.gov/childcare/licensing/newweb.html

#27 Department of Labor, 10421 W Markham, Little Rock, AR 72205; 501-682-4500, Fax- 501-682-4535. www.arkansas.gov/labor/ Online rosters available.

#28 Department of Environmental Quality, 5301 Northshore Dr, North Little Rock, AR 72118-5317; 501-682-0744, Fax- 501-682-0707. www.adeq.state.ar.us Search data at- www.adeq.state.ar.us/compsvs/webmaster/databases.htm

#29 Dietetics Licensing Board, PO Box 1016, Little Rock, AR 72115; 501-221-0566, Fax- 501-843-0878. www.ardieteticslicbrd.net/ Verification of Licensure form at www.ardieteticslicbrd.net/adlbs/ADLB-4.htm.

#30 Liquefied Petroleum Gas Board, 3800 Richards Rd, North Little Rock, AR 72117; 501-683-4100, Fax- 501-683-4110. www.arkansaslpgasboard.com/

#31 Medical Board, 2100 Riverfront Dr, Little Rock, AR 72202-1435; 501-296-1802, Fax- 501-296-1972. www.armedicalboard.org/Info/ Search data at- https://www.armedicalboard.org/licenseverf/ Offers online verification system that includes additional professional information. Must use Internet Explorer 5.0 or greater.

#32 Department of Education, Office of Teacher Education & Licensure, #4 State Capitol Mall, Little Rock, AR 72201; 501-682-4342, Fax- 501-682-4898. http://arkedu.state.ar.us/teachers/teachers_licensure.html Search data at- http://arkedu.state.ar.us/teachers/accessing_licensure_info.html

#33 State Plant Board, PO Box 1069 (One Natural Resources Dr), Little Rock, AR 72205; 501-225-1598, Fax- 501-225-3590. Hours- 8AM-4:30PM. www.plantboard.org

#34 Board of Podiatric Medicine, 2001 Georgia Ave, Little Rock, AR 72207-5114; 501-207-5014, Fax- 501-666-3338. Hours- 7AM-11AM M-F; closed 2nd Thurs. Verification requests in writing are free if a toll free fax number is provided, and/or a SASE provided. Fax written confirmation is accepted if provided a toll-free fax number.

#35 Motor Vehicle Commission, 101 E Capitol #212, Little Rock, AR 72201-3826; 501-682-1428, Fax- 501-682-5573. www.armvc.com Search data at- www.armvc.com/licensee_search/index.html

#36 Racing Commission, PO Box 3076, (1515 W 7th St Ste 505), Little Rock, AR 72203; 501-682-1467, Fax- 501-682-5273. www.arkansas.gov/dfa/racing/

#37 Real Estate Commission, 612 S Summit St, Little Rock, AR 72201; 501-683-8010, Fax-501-682-8020. Hours- 8AM-4:30PM. www.arkansas.gov/arec/

#38 Secretary of State, State Capitol #256, Little Rock, AR 72201; 501-682-3409, Fax-501-682-3437. Hours- 8AM-5PM M-Th; 8AM-4:30PM F. www.sos.arkansas.gov Search data at- www.sos.arkansas.gov/corps/

#39 Securities Department, 201 E Markham St, Heritage West Bldg, #300, Little Rock, AR 72201; 501-324-9260, Fax- 501-324-9268. Hours- 8AM-4:30PM. www.securities.arkansas.gov

#40 Social Work Licensing Board, PO Box 250381 (2020 W 3rd, #503), Little Rock, AR 72225; 501-372-5071, Fax- 501-372-6301. www.accessarkansas.org/swlb/ Search data at- www.accessarkansas.org/swlb/search/index.html

#41 Board of Examiners of Speech Language and Audiology, 101 E Capitol, Ste 211, Little Rock, AR 72201; 501-682-9180, Fax- 501-682-9181. Hours- 9AM-5PM. www.abespa.com/index.html

#42 Regulatory Service Section, State Police Admin. Svcs., #1 State Police Plaza Dr, Little Rock, AR 72209; 501-618-8600, Fax- 501-618-8621. www.asp.state.ar.us Direct polygraph questions to Board of Private Investigators and Private Security Agencies at this address and phone.

#43 Supreme Court, State Board of Law Examiners, 625 Marshall, Justice Bldg, Little Rock, AR 72201; 501-682-6849. Hours- 8AM-5PM. http://courts.state.ar.us Search data at- http://courts.arkansas.gov/attorneys/attorney_search.cfm

#44 Veterinary Medical Examining Board, One Natural Resources Dr, Little Rock, AR 72205; 501-224-2836, Fax- 501-224-1100. www.state.ar.us/directory/detail2.cgi?ID=1137 Hard copy of Veterinary/Tech Roster each year- $25.00.

#45 Water Well Construction Commission, 101 E Capitol #350, Little Rock, AR 72201; 501-682-1025, Fax- 501-682-3991. www.arkansas.gov/awwcc/

#46 Board of Acupuncture & Related Techniques, 1401 W 6th St, Little Rock, AR 72207; 501-687-1396, Fax- 501-372-4505. www.asbart.org/

#47 Fire Protection Licensing Board, 7509 Cantrell Rd #103-A, Little Rock, AR 72207; 501-661-7903, Fax- 501-603-3540. www.arfireprotection.org Search data at- www.arfireprotection.org/roster/index.html

#48 Abstractors Board of Examiners, PO Box 166006, Little Rock, AR 72216; 501-246-1622. www.arkansas.gov/directory/detail2.cgi?ID=1014

#49 Board of Cosmetology, 101 E Capitol Ave #108, Little Rock, AR 72201; 501-682-2168, Fax- 501-682-5640. www.arkansas.gov/cos/ Search data at- www.arkansas.gov/cos/search.php

#50 Board of Dispensing Opticians, Box 627, Helena, AR 72342; 870-572-2847, Fax- 870-572-2847. www.abdo.arkansas.gov/

#51 Board of Examiners for Counselors & Marriage/Family Therapists, PO Box 70 (124 S Jackson, #312), Magnolia, AR 71754-0070; 870-901-7055, Fax- 870-234-1842. www.accessarkansas.org/abec/ Search data at- www.accessarkansas.org/abec/search.php They provide lists in email, fax, land line and written requests.

#52 Department of Human Services, Office of Long Term Care, 7th & Main Streets, Little Rock, AR 72203; 501-682-8487, Fax- 501-682-8551. https://www.medicaid.state.ar.us/InternetSolution/General/units/oltc/index.aspx

#53 Livestock & Poultry Commission, 1 Natural Resources Dr, Little Rock, AR 72205; 501-907-2400, Fax- 501-907-2425. Hours- 8AM-4:30PM. www.arlpc.org

#54 Manufactured Home Commission, 523 South Louisiana, Suite 500, Little Rock, AR 72201; 501-324-9032, Fax- 501-324-9034.

Arkansas Federal Courts

The following list indicates the district and division name for each county in the state. If the bankruptcy court location is different from the district court, then the location of the bankruptcy court appears in parentheses.

County/Court Cross Reference

County	District	Division
Arkansas	Eastern	Pine Bluff (Little Rock)
Ashley	Western (Eastern)	El Dorado (Little Rock)
Baxter	Western	Harrison (Fayetteville)
Benton	Western	Fayetteville
Boone	Western	Harrison (Fayetteville)
Bradley	Western (Eastern)	El Dorado (Little Rock)
Calhoun	Western (Eastern)	El Dorado (Little Rock)
Carroll	Western	Harrison (Fayetteville)
Chicot	Eastern	Pine Bluff (Little Rock)
Clark	Western (Eastern)	Hot Springs (Little Rock)
Clay	Eastern	Jonesboro (Little Rock)
Cleburne	Eastern	Batesville (Little Rock)
Cleveland	Eastern	Pine Bluff (Little Rock)
Columbia	Western (Eastern)	El Dorado (Little Rock)
Conway	Eastern	Little Rock
Craighead	Eastern	Jonesboro (Little Rock)
Crawford	Western	Fort Smith (Fayetteville)
Crittenden	Eastern	Jonesboro (Little Rock)
Cross	Eastern	Helena (Little Rock)
Dallas	Eastern	Pine Bluff (Little Rock)
Desha	Eastern	Pine Bluff (Little Rock)
Drew	Eastern	Pine Bluff (Little Rock)
Faulkner	Eastern	Little Rock
Franklin	Western	Fort Smith (Fayetteville)
Fulton	Eastern	Batesville (Little Rock)
Garland	Western (Eastern)	Hot Springs (Little Rock)
Grant	Eastern	Pine Bluff (Little Rock)
Greene	Eastern	Jonesboro (Little Rock)
Hempstead	Western (Eastern)	Texarkana (Little Rock)
Hot Spring	Western (Eastern)	Hot Springs (Little Rock)
Howard	Western (Eastern)	Texarkana (Little Rock)
Independence	Eastern	Batesville (Little Rock)
Izard	Eastern	Batesville (Little Rock)
Jackson	Eastern	Batesville (Little Rock)
Jefferson	Eastern	Pine Bluff (Little Rock)
Johnson	Western	Fort Smith (Fayetteville)
Lafayette	Western (Eastern)	Texarkana (Little Rock)
Lawrence	Eastern	Jonesboro (Little Rock)
Lee	Eastern	Helena (Little Rock)
Lincoln	Eastern	Pine Bluff (Little Rock)
Little River	Western (Eastern)	Texarkana (Little Rock)
Logan	Western	Fort Smith (Fayetteville)
Lonoke	Eastern	Little Rock
Madison	Western	Fayetteville
Marion	Western	Harrison (Fayetteville)
Miller	Western (Eastern)	Texarkana (Little Rock)
Mississippi	Eastern	Jonesboro (Little Rock)
Monroe	Eastern	Helena (Little Rock)
Montgomery	Western (Eastern)	Hot Springs (Little Rock)
Nevada	Western (Eastern)	Texarkana (Little Rock)
Newton	Western	Harrison (Fayetteville)
Ouachita	Western (Eastern)	El Dorado (Little Rock)
Perry	Eastern	Little Rock
Phillips	Eastern	Helena (Little Rock)
Pike	Western (Eastern)	Hot Springs (Little Rock)
Poinsett	Eastern	Jonesboro (Little Rock)
Polk	Western	Fort Smith (Fayetteville)
Pope	Eastern	Little Rock
Prairie	Eastern	Little Rock
Pulaski	Eastern	Little Rock
Randolph	Eastern	Jonesboro (Little Rock)
Saline	Eastern	Little Rock
Scott	Western	Fort Smith (Fayetteville)
Searcy	Western	Harrison (Fayetteville)
Sebastian	Western	Fort Smith (Fayetteville)
Sevier	Western (Eastern)	Texarkana (Little Rock)
Sharp	Eastern	Batesville (Little Rock)
St. Francis	Eastern	Helena (Little Rock)
Stone	Eastern	Batesville (Little Rock)
Union	Western (Eastern)	El Dorado (Little Rock)
Van Buren	Eastern	Little Rock
Washington	Western	Fayetteville
White	Eastern	Little Rock
Woodruff	Eastern	Helena (Little Rock)
Yell	Eastern	Little Rock

Standards for Federal Courts: Fees are standard unless noted in profile. Search fee is $26.00 per item (one party name or case number). Copy fee is $.50 per page. Certification fee is $9.00 per document, double for exemplification, if available. Most courts require prepayment. Mail requests should enclose a SASE unless otherwise noted. Before releasing records, all courts require prepayment, unless noted. District courts index by defendant and plaintiff and by case number. Bankruptcy courts usually index by debtor and case number. While most courts now have their indexes on computer, many may still maintain index card files as well. Courts will archive closed case files at different times. There are numerous public access programs available to online subscribers. Search the U.S. Party/Case Index to find party names and case numbers among all courts. Individual case data is provided on PACER. A search of CM/ECF provides copies of cases filed electronically. For details about PACER, the US Party/Case Index, and CM/ECF see the Appendix, go to http://pacer.psc.uscourts.gov or call 800-676-6856.

US District Court Eastern District of Arkansas

Batesville Division c/o Little Rock Division, 600 W Capitol, Rm A-149, Little Rock, AR 72201, 501-604-5351. Hours- 8AM-5PM. www.are.uscourts.gov

Counties/Note: Cleburne, Fulton, Independence, Izard, Jackson, Sharp, Stone. Clerk's office in Batesville is unstaffed.

Searches/Indexing: Only full name required in search request. Results do not include SSN or DOB. Will not fax back documents. New cases are in the index immediately after filing date. Case files sent to archives 4 years after closed.

Search Access: Docket info available via phone. **Mail:** Search usually completed- 1-2 weeks. Include SASE for return. **In person:** 5 public terminals available. No self-serve copier.

Payment: Pay by Visa/MC, money order or cashier's check. No personal checks accepted. Payee: Clerk, US District Court.

E-Services: Search records on the Internet using ECF at https://ecf.ared.uscourts.gov/cgi-bin/login.pl. Fees now apply; document images available. PACER records go back to 1987-89. New records online after 1 day. ECF at https://ecf.ared.uscourts.gov. **Opinions Online:** www.are.uscourts.gov/mdl/index.cfm?fuseaction=DFNTCase. Opinions can be searched by report-defendant, plaintiff, firm or filing date. Also, written opinions can be searched from the CM/ECF reports menu via PACER; fees apply.

Helena Division c/o Little Rock Division, 600 W Capital, Rm 402, Little Rock, AR 72201-3325, 501-604-5351. 8AM-5PM. www.are.uscourts.gov

Counties/Note: Cross, Lee, Monroe, Phillips, St. Francis, Woodruff. Clerk's office in Helena is unstaffed.

Searches/Indexing: Only full name required in search request. Results do not include SSN or DOB. Will not fax back documents. New cases are in the index immediately after filing date. Computer index back to 1993 maintained. Case files sent to archives 4 years after closed.

Search Access: Docket info available via phone. **Mail:** Search usually completed- 1-2 weeks. Include SASE for return. **In person:** 2 public terminals available. No self-serve copier.

Payment: Pay by Visa/MC, money order, cashier's, business checks. Payee: Clerk, US District Court.

E-Services: Search records on the Internet using ECF at https://ecf.ared.uscourts.gov/cgi-bin/login.pl. Fees now apply; document images available. PACER records go back to 1987-89. New records online after 1 day. ECF at https://ecf.ared.uscourts.gov. **Opinions Online:** www.are.uscourts.gov/mdl/index.cfm?fuseaction=DFNTCase. Opinions can be searched by report-defendant, plaintiff, firm or filing date. Also, written opinions can be searched from the CM/ECF reports menu via PACER; fees apply.

Jonesboro Division Court Clerk, Federal Office Bldg, Rm 312, 615 S Main St, Jonesboro, AR 72401, 870-972-4610; Fax- 870-972-4612. Hours- 8AM-5PM. www.are.uscourts.gov

Counties/Note: Clay, Craighead, Crittenden, Greene, Lawrence, Mississippi, Poinsett, Randolph.

Searches/Indexing: Only full name required in search request. Results do not include SSN or DOB. Will not fax back documents. New cases are in the index immediately after filing date. Computer index maintained back to 1993. Case files sent to archives 4 years after closed.

Search Access: Docket info available via phone. **Mail:** Search usually completed- 1-2 weeks. Include SASE for return. **In person:** 2 public terminals available. No self-serve copier.

Payment: Pay by Visa/MC, money order, cashier's check. Payee: Clerk, US District Court.

E-Services: Search records on the Internet using ECF at https://ecf.ared.uscourts.gov/cgi-bin/login.pl. Fees now apply; document images available. PACER records go back to 1987-89. New records online after 1 day. ECF at https://ecf.ared.uscourts.gov. **Opinions Online:** www.are.uscourts.gov/mdl/index.cfm?fuseaction=DFNTCase. Opinions can be searched by report-defendant, plaintiff, firm or filing date. Also, written opinions can be searched from the CM/ECF reports menu via PACER; fees apply.

Little Rock Division Court Clerk, 600 W Capitol, Rm 402, Little Rock, AR 72201, 501-604-5351. Hours- 8AM-5PM. www.are.uscourts.gov

Counties: Conway, Faulkner, Lonoke, Perry, Pope, Prairie, Pulaski, Saline, Van Buren, White, Yell.

Searches/Indexing: Only full name required in search request. Results do not include SSN or DOB. Will not fax back documents. New cases are in the index immediately after filing date. Computer, microfiche and card indexes maintained, computer back to 3/92. Case files sent to archives 4 years after closed.

Search Access: Docket info available via phone. **Mail:** Search usually completed- 1-2 weeks. Include SASE for return. **In person:** 2 public terminals available. No self-serve copier.

Payment: Pay by Visa/MC, money order, cashier's or personal check. Payee: Clerk, US District Court.

E-Services: Search records on the Internet using ECF at https://ecf.ared.uscourts.gov/cgi-bin/login.pl. Fees now apply; document images available. PACER records go back to 1987-89. New records online after 1 day. ECF at https://ecf.ared.uscourts.gov. **Opinions Online:** www.are.uscourts.gov/mdl/index.cfm?fuseaction=DFNTCase. Opinions can be searched by report-defendant, plaintiff, firm or filing date. Also, written opinions can be searched from the CM/ECF reports menu via PACER; fees apply.

Pine Bluff Division Court Clerk, US Post Office & Courthouse, 100 E 8th St, Rm 3103, Pine Bluff, AR 71601, 870-536-1190; Fax- 870-536-6330. 8AM-4:30PM. www.are.uscourts.gov

Counties/Note: Arkansas, Chicot, Cleveland, Dallas, Desha, Drew, Grant, Jefferson, Lincoln.

Searches/Indexing: Only full name required in search request. Results do not include SSN or DOB. Will not fax back documents. New cases are in the index immediately after filing date. Computer index back to 1993 maintained; also on microfiche. Case files sent to archives 4 years after closed.

Search Access: Docket info available via phone. **Mail:** Search usually completed- 1-2 weeks. Include SASE for return. **In person:** 2 public terminals available. No self-serve copier.

Payment: Pay by Visa/MC, money order, cashier's or personal check. Payee: Clerk, US District Court.

E-Services: Search records on the Internet using ECF at https://ecf.ared.uscourts.gov/cgi-bin/login.pl. Fees now apply; document images available. PACER records go back to 1987-89. New records online after 1 day. ECF at https://ecf.ared.uscourts.gov. **Opinions Online:** www.are.uscourts.gov/mdl/index.cfm?fuseaction=DFNTCase. Opinions can be searched by report-defendant, plaintiff, firm or filing date. Also, written opinions can be searched from the CM/ECF reports menu via PACER; fees apply.

US Bankruptcy Court Arkansas Eastern District

Little Rock Division Court Clerk, 300 W 2nd St, Little Rock, AR 72203, 501-918-5500; Fax-501-918-5520 8AM-5PM. www.areb.uscourts.gov

Counties/Note: Same counties as included in Eastern District of Arkansas, plus the counties included in the Western District divisions of El Dorado, Hot Springs and Texarkana. All bankruptcy cases in Arkansas prior to mid-1993 were heard at Little Rock.

Searches/Indexing: Include last four SSN digits in search request; phone and address for pro se debtors is helpful. Results include last 4 SSN digits. Will fax back docs to toll-free or local number if fees paid. New cases are in the index immediately after filing date. Computer, microfiche and card indexes maintained. Case files sent to archives 6 month to a year after closed.

Search Access: Voice Case Information Service available, call VCIS at 800-891-6741 or 501-918-5555. **Mail:** Search usually completed- 1-2 weeks. Include SASE for return. **In person:** 4 public terminals available. No self-serve copier.

Payment: Pay by Visa/MC, money order, cashier's or personal check. No debtor checks accepted. Payee: Clerk, US Bankruptcy Court.

E-Services: PACER records go back to 5/1989. New records online after 1 day. ECF at https://ecf.areb.uscourts.gov. **Opinions Online:** www.arb.uscourts.gov/orders-rules-opinions/opinions.html. **Online Note:** Calendars at www.arb.uscourts.gov/calendars/calendars.html.

US District Court Arkansas Western District

El Dorado Division Court Clerk, PO Box 1566, El Dorado, AR 71731 (In person: 101 S Jackson, Rm 205, El Dorado, AR 71730), 870-862-1202; Fax- 870-863-4880. Hours- 8AM-4:30PM. www.arwd.uscourts.gov

Counties/Note: Ashley, Bradley, Calhoun, Columbia, Ouachita, Union. This is a one clerk office; please call in advance for clerk availability.

Searches/Indexing: Only the full name required in search request. Results do not include SSN or DOB. New cases are in the index immediately after filing date. Computer index back to 1992 maintained. Files maintained numerically by year. Closed cases sent to archives after 5 years.

Search Access: Only docket info is available by phone. **Mail:** Search usually completed- 1 week. Include SASE for return. **Fax:** Fax search requests accepted if results do not have to be in writing.

In person: 1 public terminal available. No self-serve copier.

Payment: Pay by money order, cashier's or personal check. Payee: Clerk, US District Court. Prepayment required for out of state searchers.

E-Services: PACER account required for ECF. PACER records go back to 9/1990. New records online after 1 day. ECF at https://ecf.arwd.uscourts.gov. **Opinions Online:** www.arwd.uscourts.gov/go/online-documents.

Fayetteville Division Court Clerk, 35 E Mountain St, #510, Fayetteville, AR 72701, 479-521-6980; Fax- 479-575-0774. Hours- 8AM-5PM. www.arwd.uscourts.gov

Counties/Note: Benton, Madison, Washington. Fayetteville also holds records for Harrison Div.

Searches/Indexing: Only the full name required in search request. Results do not include SSN or DOB. Will fax back documents; fee may apply. New cases are in the index immediately after filing date. Computer index back to 1992 maintained. Files maintained numerically by year. Closed cases sent to archives after 5 years.

Search Access: Only docket info is available by phone. **Mail:** Search usually completed- 24 hours. SASE not required. **Fax:** Fax search same as mail. **In person:** 1 public terminal available. No self-serve copier available.

Payment: Pay by money order, cashier's or personal check. No credit cards accepted. Payee: Clerk, Western District of Arkansas. Prepayment required for out of state searchers.

E-Services: PACER account required for ECF. PACER records go back to 9/1990. New records online immediately. ECF at https://ecf.arwd.uscourts.gov. **Opinions Online:** www.arwd.uscourts.gov/go/online-documents.

Fort Smith Division Court Clerk, PO Box 1547, Fort Smith, AR 72902 (In person: Judge Isaac C. Parker Federal Bldg #1038, 30 S 6th St, Fort Smith, AR 72901), 479-783-6833; Fax- 479-783-6308. 8AM-5PM. www.arwd.uscourts.gov

Counties/Note: Crawford, Franklin, Johnson, Logan, Polk, Scott, Sebastian.

Searches/Indexing: Only the full name required in search request. Results do not include SSN or DOB. Will not fax back documents. New cases are in the index immediately after filing date. Computer index back to 1992 maintained. Files maintained numerically by year. Closed cases sent to archives after 5 years.

Search Access: Only docket info is available by phone. **Mail:** Search usually completed- week-10 days. SASE required. **In person:** 1 public terminal available. Self-serve copies $.50 each.

Payment: Pay by money order, cashier's or personal check. Payee: Clerk of Court. Prepayment required for out of state searchers.

E-Services: PACER account required for ECF. PACER records go back to 9/1990. New records online after 1 day. ECF at https://ecf.arwd.uscourts.gov. **Opinions Online:** www.arwd.uscourts.gov/go/online-documents.

Hot Springs Division Court Clerk, Federal Bldg, Rm 347, 100 Reserve St, Hot Springs, AR 71901-4141 (In person: Federal Bldg, Rm 347, 100 Reserve St, Hot Springs, AR 71901), 501-623-6411; Fax- 501-623-8606. Hours- 8AM-4:30PM. www.arwd.uscourts.gov

Counties/Note: Clark, Garland, Hot Springs, Montgomery, Pike.

Searches/Indexing: Only the full name required in search request. Results do not include SSN or DOB. New cases are in the index immediately after filing date. Computer index back to 1992 maintained. Files maintained numerically by year. Closed cases sent to archives after 5 years.

Search Access: Only docket info is available by phone. **Mail:** Search usually completed- 2 days. Include SASE for return. **In person:** 1 public terminal available. No self-serve copier.

Payment: Pay by money order, cashier's or personal check. Payee: Clerk, Western District of Arkansas. Prepayment required for out of state searchers.

E-Services: PACER account required for ECF. PACER records go back to 9/1990. New records online after 1 day. ECF at https://ecf.arwd.uscourts.gov. **Opinions Online:** www.arwd.uscourts.gov/go/online-documents.

Texarkana Division Court Clerk, 500 N State Line Ave, Rm 302, Texarkana, AR 71854 (In person: 500 N State Line Ave, Rm 302, Texarkana, AR 71854), 870-773-3381; Fax- 870-772-4802. 8AM-4:30PM. www.arwd.uscourts.gov

Counties/Note: Hempstead, Howard, Lafayette, Little River, Miller, Nevada, Sevier.

Searches/Indexing: Only the full name required in search request. Results do not include SSN or DOB. New cases are in the index immediately after filing date. Computer index back to 1992 maintained. Files maintained numerically by year. Closed cases sent to archives after 5 years.

Search Access: Case numbers are released via phone; anything else depends on workload of deputy clerk. **Mail:** Search usually completed- 24 hours. SASE not required. **In person:** 1 public terminal available. Self-serve copies $.50 each.

Payment: Pay by money order, cashier's or personal check. Payee: Clerk of the Court. Prepayment required for out of state searchers.

E-Services: PACER account required for ECF. PACER records go back to 9/1990. New records online after 1 day. ECF at https://ecf.arwd.uscourts.gov. **Opinions Online:** www.arwd.uscourts.gov/go/online-documents.

US Bankruptcy Court Arkansas Western District

Fayetteville Division Court Clerk, 35 E Mountain, Rm 316, Fayetteville, AR 72701, 479-582-9800; Fax- 479-582-9825. Hours- 8AM-5PM. www.arb.uscourts.gov

Counties/Note: Same counties as included in US District Court - Western District of Arkansas except that counties included in El Dorado and Texarkana Divisions are heard in Little Rock.

Searches/Indexing: Include full name and SSN in search request. Results include last 4 SSN digits. Will not fax back documents. New cases are in the index immediately after filing date. All records now maintained on computer back to 2002. All paper files have been sent to archives.

Search Access: Only docket info provided released via phone; includes case number, chapter, judge, attorney, trustee. Also check VCIS for more. Voice Case Information Service available, call VCIS at 800-891-6741 or 501-918-5555. **Mail:** Search usually completed- 1 day. Include SASE for return. **Fax:** No fax requests accepted; best to phone. **In person:** 2 public terminals available. No self-serve copier.

Payment: Pay by Visa/MC, money order, cashier's or personal check. No debtor checks accepted. Payee: Clerk, US Bankruptcy Court. Licensed attorneys may be invoiced for copy work.

E-Services: PACER records go back to 5/1989. New records online after 1 day. ECF at https://ecf.arwb.uscourts.gov. **Opinions Online:** www.arb.uscourts.gov/orders-rules-opinions/opinions.html.

Arkansas County Courts

Court	Jurisdiction	No. of Courts	How Organized
Circuit Courts*	General	38	28 Circuits
District Courts*	Limited	130	
City Courts	Limited	115	

* Profiled in this Sourcebook.

Court	CIVIL								
	Tort	Contract	Real Estate	Min. Claim	Max. Claim	Small Claims	Estate	Eviction	Domestic Relations
Circuit Courts*	X	X	X	$5000	No Max		X		X
District Courts*		X	X	$0	$5000	$5000		X	
City Courts		X	X	$0	$300				

Court	CRIMINAL				
	Felony	Misdemeanor	DWI/DUI	Preliminary Hearing	Juvenile
Circuit Courts*	X				X
District Courts*		X	X	X	
City Courts		X		X	

Administration

Administrative Office of Courts, 625 Marshall St, Ste 1100, Little Rock, AR, 72201; 501-682-9400, 501-682-6849, Fax: 501-682-9410. www.courts.state.ar.us

Court Structure

Circuit Courts are the courts of general jurisdiction and are arranged in 28 circuits. Circuit Courts consist of five subject matter divisions: criminal, civil, probate, domestic relations, and juvenile. The Circuit Clerks are the keepers of records for the Circuit Courts, they also serve as the country recorder of deeds and other instruments; however some counties have a County Clerk that handles probate. District Courts, formerly known as Municipal Courts before passage of Amendment 80 to the Arkansas Constitution, exercise countywide jurisdiction over misdemeanor cases, preliminary felony cases, and civil cases in matters of less than $5,000, including small claims. The City Courts exercise citywide jurisdiction and operate in smaller communities where District Courts do not exist. All courts are in the Central Time Zone (CST)

Online Access

The home web page gives online access to Supreme Court Opinions and Appellate Court dockets. Must have name and case number. This docket search includes all active cases and includes any closed cases with activity within ninety (90) days previous. Also find Court of Appeals dockets, corrected opinions, and parallel citations, an attorney search, and search of court rules and administrative orders.

Online access to courts at the county level remains almost non-existant.

Searching Tips, Fees, and Other Guidelines

Many courts that allow written search requests require an SASE. Fees vary widely across jurisdictions as do prepayment requirements.

Arkansas County

Circuit Court - Northern District 302 S College St, Stuttgart, AR 72160; 870-673-2056; probate phone: 870-673-7311; fax: 870-673-3869; 8AM-4:30PM. ***Felony, Civil Actions, Probate.***
The court is not bonded to search Civil or Chancery records. Probate has a different Clerk.
Civil Records: Access: In person only. Visitors must perform in person searches themselves. Required to search: name, years to search. Civil cases indexed by defendant, plaintiff, in files from 1913. Civil PAT goes back to 2004. PAT civil results show middle initial.
Criminal Records: Access: In person only. Visitors must perform in person searches themselves. Required to search: name, years to search, DOB. Criminal records in files from 1913, earlier records located in DeWitt. Criminal PAT goes back to same as civil. PAT criminal results show middle initial.
General Information: No juvenile records released. Will fax documents $1.00 fee per page. Court makes copy: $.50 per page, self serve same. Certification fee: $5.00 per doc includes copy fee. Payee: Arkansas Circuit Court. Personal checks accepted; credit cards are not. Prepayment required.

Circuit Court - Southern District 101 Courthouse Sq, De Witt, AR 72042; 870-946-4219; fax: 870-946-1394; 8AM-4:30PM. ***Felony, Civil Actions over $5,000.***
No longer performs current records searches. Court will honor written requests to do searches for genealogy purposes for $10.00 base rate per search.
Civil Records: Access: In person only. Visitors must perform in person searches themselves. Required to search: name, years to search. Civil cases indexed by defendant, plaintiff, in files from 1923, computerized since 1995, prior records (the two other courts in this county also) located at this court. Civil PAT goes back to 1996.
Criminal Records: Access: In person only. Visitors must perform in person searches themselves. Required to search: name, DOB; also helpful: SSN. Criminal records in files from 1923, computerized since 1995, prior records (the two other courts in this county also) located at this court. Criminal PAT goes back to same as civil. Results include name and case number.
General Information: No juvenile, expunged records released. Will not fax documents. Court makes copy: $.50 per page, self serve same. Certification fee: $5.00 per doc. Payee: Arkansas County Circuit Clerk. Personal checks accepted; credit cards are not. Prepayment required.

Stuttgart District Court 304 S Maple, Stuttgart, AR 72160; 870-673-7951; fax: 870-673-6522; 8AM-4:30PM. ***Misdemeanor, Civil Actions under $5,000, Eviction, Small Claims.***
Civil Records: Access: Phone, mail, fax, in person. Both court and visitors may perform in person

searches. No search fee. Required to search: name plus SSN. Records go back to 1990; on computer back to 1991. Mail turnaround time 3 days.
Criminal Records: Access: Phone, mail, fax, in person. Both court and visitors may perform in person searches. No search fee. Required to search: name, years to search, SSN; also helpful: DOB. Records go back to 1990; on computer back to 1991. Mail turnaround time 3 days.
General Information: Will fax documents. Court makes copy: $.25 per page. No certification fee. Payee: City of Stuttgart. Personal checks accepted; credit cards are not. Mail requests: SASE required.

Ashley County

Circuit Court Ashley County Courthouse, 205 E Jefferson, Hamburg, AR 71646; 870-853-2030; probate: 870-853-2020; fax: 870-853-2034; 8AM-4:30PM. ***Felony, Civil Actions over $5,000, Probate.***
Probate records managed by the county clerk office
Civil Records: Access: Mail, in person. Visitors must perform in person searches themselves. Search fee: $5.00 per name. Required to search: name, years to search. Civil cases indexed by defendant, plaintiff, on files and index cards from 1950s. Mail turnaround time 2 days.
Criminal Records: Access: Mail, in person. Visitors must perform in person searches themselves. Search fee: $5.00 per name. Required to search: name, years to search; also helpful: DOB, SSN. Criminal records on files and index cards from 1950s. Mail turnaround time 2 days.
General Information: No juvenile records released. Fee to fax out file $1.00 per page. Court makes copy: $.50 per page, self serve same. Certification fee: $2.50 per doc plus copy fee per page. Payee: Circuit Clerk's Office. Personal checks accepted; credit cards are not. Prepayment required. Mail requests: SASE required.

Hamburg District Court PO Box 72, 305 W Adams, Hamburg, AR 71646; 870-853-8326; fax: 870-853-5433; 8AM-4:30PM. ***Misdemeanor, Civil Actions under $5,000, Eviction, Small Claims.***
Civil Records: Access: Mail, in person. Both court and visitors may perform in person searches. No search fee. Required to search: name. Civil cases indexed by Defendant. Plaintiff. Civil records go back 10 years; on computer back to 2000. Mail turnaround time 1-2 days. Civil PAT goes back to 1989.
Criminal Records: Access: Mail, in person. Both court and visitors may perform in person searches. No search fee. Required to search: name, years to search, DOB. Criminal records go back to 1976; on computer back to 1989. Mail turnaround time 1-2 days. Criminal PAT goes back to same as civil.
General Information: Will not fax documents. Court makes copy: $.50 per page, self serve same. Certification fee: $10.00 per doc. Payee: District Court. No personal checks or credit cards accepted. Prepayment required.

Baxter County

Circuit Court 1 E 7th St, Rm 103, Courthouse Square, Mountain Home, AR 72653; 870-425-3475; probate phone: same; fax: 870-424-5105; 8AM-4:30PM. ***Felony, Civil Actions over $5,000, Probate.***
Civil Records: Access: In person. Both court and visitors may perform in person searches. No search fee. Required to search: name, years to search. Civil cases indexed by defendant, plaintiff, on computer from 1982, on criminal fee book from early 1900s. Civil PAT goes back to 1995. PAT results show name only.
Criminal Records: Access: In person. Both court and visitors may perform in person searches. No search fee. Required to search: name, years to search, SSN. Criminal records computerized from 1982, on criminal fee book from early 1900s. Criminal PAT goes back to same as civil. PAT results show name only. Results include case number.
General Information: No adoption or juvenile records released. Will fax documents $5.00 per page. Court makes copy: $.25 per page. Certification fee: $5.00 per doc. Payee: Baxter County Clerk. Personal checks accepted; credit cards are not. Prepayment required.

District Court 301 E 6th St #130, Mountain Home, AR 72653; 870-425-3140; criminal phone: 870-425-3140; civil phone: 870-425-8910; criminal fax: 870-425-8470; civil fax: same; 8AM-4:30PM. ***Misdemeanor, Civil Actions under $5,000, Eviction, Small Claims.***
Civil Records: Access: Mail, in person. Only the court performs in person searches; visitors may not. Search fee: $6.00 per name; no fee if you are AR resident. Required to search: name, years to search, also helpful-DOB, SSN, signed release. Civil cases indexed by defendant, plaintiff, go back to 1980's; computerized records back to 8/1/08. Mail turnaround time 3 days.
Criminal Records: Access: Mail, in person. Only the court performs in person searches; visitors may not. Search fee: $6.00 per name; no fee if you are AR resident. Required to search: name, years to search, DOB, SSN. Criminal records go back to 1980's; computerized since 1995. Mail turnaround- 3 days.
General Information: Will not fax documents. Court makes copy: $.25 per page. Certification fee: $5.00 per doc. Payee: Baxter County District Court. Personal checks accepted; credit cards are not. Prepayment required.

Benton County

Circuit Court 102 NE "A" St, Bentonville, AR 72712; 479-271-1015; probate phone: 479-271-5727; criminal fax: 479-271-5719; civil fax: same; 8AM-5PM. ***Felony, Civil Actions over $5,000, Probate.***
www.co.benton.ar.us
Probate records managed by the County Clerk.
Civil Records: Access: Mail, in person, online. Visitors must perform in person searches themselves. No search fee. Required to search: name, years to search. Civil cases indexed by defendant, plaintiff, on computer from 1991, on dockets from 1880s. Civil PAT goes back to 1987. PAT results show name only. Search civil court dockets free at http://records.co.benton.ar.us:5061/
Criminal Records: Access: Mail, online, in person. Visitors must perform in person searches themselves. No search fee. Required to search: name, years to search. Criminal records computerized from 1991, on dockets from 1880s. Note: This court suggests to direct search requests to AR State Police. Mail turnaround time in 24 hours. Criminal PAT goes back to same as civil. PAT results show middle initial, DOB. Terminal results include SSN. Search criminal court docket information free at http://records.co.benton.ar.us:5061/ Online results show middle initial, DOB. Terminal results include SSN.
General Information: Online identifiers in results same as on public terminal. No juvenile records released. Will fax documents to local or toll free line. Court makes copy: $.25 per page, self serve same. Certification fee: $5.00. Payee: Benton County Circuit Clerk. Personal checks accepted; credit cards are not. Prepayment required. Mail requests: SASE required.

District Court 117 W Central, Bentonville, AR 72712; criminal phone: 479-271-3120; civil phone: 479-271-3121; fax: 479-271-3134; 8AM-4:30PM. ***Misdemeanor, Civil Actions under $5,000, Small Claims.***
www.bentonvillear.com/district_court_main.html
Civil Records: Access: Mail, in person. Only the court performs in person searches; visitors may not. No search fee. Required to search: name, address, DOB, SSN. Civil records on computer back to 1996; other records go back to 1985. Mail turnaround time 5 days.
Criminal Records: Access: Mail, in person. Only the court performs in person searches; visitors may not. No search fee. Required to search: name, years to search, DOB. Criminal records computerized from 1992; other records go back to 1982. Mail turnaround time 5 days.
General Information: Will fax documents to local or toll free line. Court makes copy: $5.00; only certified copies released. Certification fee: $5.00 per doc includes copies. Payee: Bentonville District Court. Personal checks accepted. No out of state checks accepted. No credit cards accepted. Prepayment required. Mail requests: SASE required.

Boone County

Circuit Court 100 N Main St #200, Harrison, AR 72601; 870-741-5560; fax: 870-741-4335; 8AM-4:30PM. ***Felony, Civil Actions over $5,000.***
Probate records are in the County Clerk's office, 870-741-8428.
Civil Records: Access: In person. Visitors must perform in person searches themselves. Required to search: name, years to search. Civil cases indexed by defendant, plaintiff, archived from 1940, index from 1977, computerized from 1990. Civil PAT goes back to 1997. PAT results show name only.
Criminal Records: Access: In person. Both court and visitors may perform in person searches. No search fee. Required to search: name, years to search. Criminal records archived from 1940, index from 1977, computerized from 1990. Criminal PAT goes back to same as civil. PAT results show name only. Online results show name only.
General Information: Online identifiers in results same as on public terminal. No indictments or juvenile records released. Fee to fax out file $5.00 each. Court makes copy: $.25 per page, self serve same. Certification fee: $5.00. Payee: Circuit Clerk. Personal checks accepted; credit cards are not. Prepayment required. Mail requests: SASE required for mail return of any copies.

District Court PO Box 968, Harrison, AR 72602; 870-741-2788; fax: 870-741-4329; 8AM-4:30PM. ***Misdemeanor, Civil Actions under $25,000, Eviction, Small Claims.***
Civil Records: Access: Mail, in person. Both court and visitors may perform in person searches. No search fee. Required to search: name and years to search. Civil cases indexed by Defendant, Plaintiff. Records indexed since 1997. Mail turnaround time 2 weeks.
Criminal Records: Access: Mail, fax, in person. Both court and visitors may perform in person searches. No search fee. Required to search: name, years to search; also helpful: DOB. Records indexed since 1997 on computer. Mail turnaround 2 weeks.
General Information: Will fax documents $1.00 per page. Court makes copy: $.25 per page. Self serve: $.25 per copy. Certification fee: $5.00 per doc. Payee: Boone County District Court. No personal checks or credit cards accepted. Prepayment required. Mail requests: SASE required.

Bradley County

Circuit Court Bradley County Courthouse - Records, 101 E Cedar, Warren, AR 71671; 870-226-2272; probate phone: 870-226-3464; fax: 870-226-8404; 8AM-4:30PM. ***Felony, Civil Actions over $5,000, Probate.***
Civil Records: Access: In person only. Visitors must perform in person searches themselves. Required to search: name, years to search. Civil cases indexed by defendant, plaintiff, (active cases) on dockets, retired cases on indexes from 1880, no computerization.
Criminal Records: Access: In person only. Visitors must perform in person searches themselves. Required to search: name, years to search; also helpful: DOB, SSN. Criminal records (active cases) on dockets, retired cases on indexes from 1880, no computerization.
General Information: No juvenile released. Will not fax documents. Court makes copy: $.50 per page. Self serve: $.50 per page. Certification fee: $3.00. Payee: Circuit Court. Personal checks accepted; credit cards are not.

District Court PO Box 352, 101 Myrtle, City Hall, Warren, AR 71671; 870-226-2567; criminal fax: 870-226-8305; civil fax: same; 8AM-4:30PM. ***Misdemeanor, Civil Actions under $5,000, Eviction, Small Claims.*** Search fee includes both the civil and criminal indexes.
Civil Records: Access: Mail, in person. Both court and visitors may perform in person searches. Search fee: $6.00 per name. Required to search: name; also helpful address, other names used, case number. Computerized records since 1993. Note: Only the court may search on computer; visitors may hand-search indexed records indexed by case number only. Mail turnaround time 2-3 days.

Criminal Records: Access: Mail, in person. Only the court performs in person searches; visitors may not. Search fee: $6.00 per name. Required to search: name, years to search, DOB; searcher may be required to provide DR number. Computerized records since 1993. Mail turnaround time 3-5 days.
General Information: Will fax back documents for no fee. Court makes copy: included in serch fee. Certification fee: Search fee includes certification. Payee: District Court. No personal checks or credit cards accepted. Prepayment required. Mail requests: SASE required.

Calhoun County

Circuit Court PO Box 1175, Hampton, AR 71744; 870-798-2517; fax: 870-798-2428; 8AM-4:30PM. ***Felony, Civil Actions over $5,000, Probate.***
Civil Records: Access: Mail, in person. Only the court performs in person searches; visitors may not. Search fee: $6.00. Required to search: name, years to search. Civil cases indexed by defendant, plaintiff, on dockets from 1851. Mail turnaround time 1-3 days.
Criminal Records: Access: Mail, in person. Only the court performs in person searches; visitors may not. Search fee: $6.00. Required to search: name, years to search, DOB; also helpful: SSN. Criminal docket index from 1851. Mail turnaround 1-3 days.
General Information: No juvenile or adoption released. Will fax documents $2.00. Court makes copy: $.25 per page, self serve same. Certification fee: $5.00. Payee: Calhoun County Clerk. Personal checks accepted; credit cards are not. Prepayment required. Mail requests: SASE required.

District Court PO Box 783, 121 N 2nd St, Courthouse, Hampton, AR 71744; 870-798-2753; criminal: 870-798-4610; civil phone: 870-798-2165; fax: 870-798-3201; 8AM-4:30PM. ***Misdemeanor, Civil Actions under $5,000, Eviction, Small Claims.*** Separate PO Box for civil court - PO Box 864. Archives located across street. Phone city's Municipal Clerk at 870-798-3201.
Civil Records: Access: Mail, in person. Both court and visitors may perform in person searches. Search fee: $5.00 per name. Required to search: name, years to search; SSN helpful. Records on computer back to 1998. Mail turnaround 2 days.
Criminal Records: Access: Mail, in person. Both court and visitors may perform in person searches. Search fee: $5.00 per name. Required to search: name, years to search; SSN helpful. Records on computer back to 1998. Mail turnaround 2 days.
General Information: Will fax documents. Court makes copy: $10.00 per document. Certification fee: $5.00 per doc. Payee: Hampton Police Dept. No personal checks or credit cards accepted. Mail requests: SASE requested.

Carroll County

Berryville Circuit Court - Eastern District Carroll County Circuit Court, PO Box 71, Berryville, AR 72616; 870-423-2422; probate phone: 870-423-2022; criminal fax: 870-423-4796; civil fax: same; 8:30AM-4:30PM. ***Felony, Civil Actions over $5,000, Eviction, Probate*** Probate located at 210 W Church Ave. Probate fax- 870-423-7400.
Civil Records: Access: Mail, in person. Both court and visitors may perform in person searches. Search fee: $6.00 per name. Required to search: name, years to search. Civil cases indexed by defendant, plaintiff, on computer from 1997, on index books since 1869. Mail turnaround time same or next day. Civil PAT goes back to 1997.
Criminal Records: Access: Fax, mail, in person. Both court and visitors may perform in person searches. Search fee: $6.00 per name. Required to search: name, years to search, DOB, SSN. Criminal records computerized from 1997, on index books since 1869. Mail turnaround time 1-2 days. Criminal PAT goes back to same as civil. PAT results and Online results show name only.
General Information: No juvenile records released. Fee to fax out file $1.00 per page for either receiving or sending. Court makes copy: $.25 per page; $.50 per page if mailed. Self serve: $.25 per page. Certification fee: $5.00 per doc. Payee: Circuit Clerk of Carroll County. Personal checks accepted; credit cards are not. Prepayment required. Mail requests: SASE required.

Eureka Springs Circuit Court - Western District 44 S Main, PO Box 109, Eureka Springs, AR 72632; 479-253-8646; fax: 479-253-6013; 8:30AM-4:30PM. ***Felony, Civil Actions over $5,000, Eviction, Probate.***
Civil Records: Access: In person only. Visitors must perform in person searches themselves. Required to search: name, years to search. Civil cases indexed by defendant, plaintiff, on indexes from 1883.
Criminal Records: Access: Phone, mail, in person. Both court and visitors may perform in person searches. Search fee: $6.00 per name. Required to search: name, years to search; also helpful: DOB. Criminal records on indexes from 1883, computerized since 2/21/02. Mail turnaround time varies. Public use terminal has crim records. PAT results show middle initial, DOB. Public terminal has recent criminal cases only.
General Information: No expunged criminal records released. Fee to fax out file $1.00 per page. Court makes copy: $.50 per page. Self serve: $.25 per page. Certification fee: $5.00 per doc. Payee: Circuit Clerk of Carroll County or County Clerk. Personal checks accepted; credit cards are not. Prepayment required. Mail requests: SASE required for criminal.

Berryville District Court 103 S Springs, Berryville, AR 72616; 870-423-6247; fax: 870-423-7069; 8AM-4:30PM. ***Misdemeanor, Civil Actions under $5,000, Small Claims.***
Civil Records: Access: Mail, fax, in person. Both court and visitors may perform in person searches. No search fee. Required to search: name, DOB. Records computerized since 1987. Mail turnaround time 1-2 days.
Criminal Records: Access: Mail, in person. Both court and visitors may perform in person searches. No search fee. Required to search: name, years to search; also helpful: DOB. Records computerized since 1987. Mail turnaround time 1-2 days.
General Information: Will fax documents to local or toll-free number. Court makes copy: $.25 per page. No personal checks or credit cards accepted. Prepayment required.

Eureka Springs District Court Courthouse, 44 S Main, Eureka Springs, AR 72632; 479-253-8574; fax: 479-253-6887; 8-5PM. ***Misdemeanor, Civil Actions under $5,000, Small Claims.*** www.cityofeurekasprings.org/muncourt.html
Civil Records: Access: Phone, mail, in person. Both court and visitors may perform in person searches. No search fee. Required to search: name. Civil cases indexed by defendant, plaintiff. Records on computer back to 1990. Mail turnaround time 1 week.
Criminal Records: Access: Phone, mail, in person. Both court and visitors may perform in person searches. No search fee. Required to search: name, years to search. Criminal records computerized from 1990. Mail turnaround time 1 week.
General Information: Will fax documents to local or toll-free number. Court makes copy for no fee.Self serve: Civil self serve copy- $1.00 each. No certification fee. Payee: District Court. Personal checks accepted; credit cards are not. Mail requests: SASE required.

Chicot County

Circuit Court 108 Main St, County Courthouse, Lake Village, AR 71653; 870-265-8010; probate phone: 870-265-8000; 8AM-4:30PM. ***Felony, Civil Actions over $5,000, Probate.***
Probate is located here in a separate office.
Civil Records: Access: In person only. Both court and visitors may perform in person searches. No search fee. Required to search: name, years to search. Civil cases indexed by defendant, plaintiff, on dockets and files from 1900s.
Criminal Records: Access: In person only. Both court and visitors may perform in person searches. No search fee. Required to search: name, years to search. Criminal records on dockets and files from 1900s. Court suggest to search at the State Police.
General Information: No juvenile records released. Will fax out docs $1.00 per page. Court makes copy: $.50 per page, self serve same. Certification fee: $2.00 per doc. Payee: Circuit Clerk. Personal checks accepted; credit cards are not. Prepayment required.

Lake Village District Court PO Box 832, Lake Village, AR 71653; 870-265-3283; criminal fax: 870-265-5668; civil fax: same; 9AM-4:30PM. ***Misdemeanor, Civil Actions under $5,000, Eviction, Small Claims.***
Civil Records: Access: Mail, fax, in person. Both court and visitors may perform in person searches. Search fee: $5.00 per name. Required to search: name, years to search, other names used; also helpful-DOB, SSN, address, signed release. Civil cases indexed by defendant, plaintiff, on computer go back to 10/02; other records go back to 1977. Mail turnaround time ASAP.
Criminal Records: Access: Mail, in person. Both court and visitors may perform in person searches. Search fee: $5.00 per name. Required to search: name, years to search; also helpful: DOB, SSN. Criminal records on computer go back to 8/2000; other records go back to 1977. Mail turnaround time ASAP.
General Information: Will fax documents. Court makes copy for no fee. Certification fee: $5.00 per doc. Payee: Lake Village District Court. No personal checks or credit cards accepted. Prepayment required. Mail requests: SASE required.

Clark County

Circuit Court PO Box 576, Arkadelphia, AR 71923; 870-246-4281; probate phone: 870-246-4491; criminal fax: 870-246-1419; civil fax: same; 8:30AM-4:30PM. ***Felony, Civil Actions over $5,000, Probate.*** Probate is a separate index, separate address
Civil Records: Access: Mail, in person. Both court and visitors may perform in person searches. Search fee: $5.00 per name. Required to search: name, years to search. Civil cases indexed by defendant, plaintiff, on computer since 1985. Mail turnaround time 1-2 days. Civil PAT goes back to 1985. PAT results show name only.
Criminal Records: Access: Mail, in person. Both court and visitors may perform in person searches. Search fee: $5.00 per name. Required to search: name, years to search. Criminal records on computer since 1985. Mail turnaround time 1-2 days. Criminal PAT goes back to same as civil. PAT results show name only.
General Information: No juvenile records released. Will fax documents $1.00 per page. Court makes copy: $.50 per page, self serve same. Certification fee: $5.00 per document includes copies. Payee: Penny R Ross Circuit Clerk. Personal checks accepted; credit cards are not. Prepayment required. Mail requests: SASE required.

District Court PO Box 449, 419 Clay St, Arkadelphia, AR 71923; 870-246-9552; fax: 870-246-1415; 8:30AM-4:30PM. ***Misdemeanor, Civil Actions under $5,000, Eviction, Small Claims.***
Civil Records: Access: In person only. Both court and visitors may perform in person searches. No search fee. Required to search: name, DOB, SSN, signed release, other names used; also helpful-DL number. Civil cases indexed by defendant, plaintiff. Records go back to 1980; on computer since 1990.
Criminal Records: Access: In person. Both court and visitors may perform in person searches. No search fee. Required to search: name, years to search; also helpful: DOB. Records go back to 1980; on computer since 1990.
General Information: Will fax documents to local or toll-free number. Court makes copy for no fee. No cert fee. No personal checks/credit cards accepted.

Clay County

Corning Circuit Court 800 SW 2nd St, Corning, AR 72422-2715; 870-857-3271; probate phone: 870-857-3480; criminal fax: 870-857-9201; civil fax: same; 8AM-4:30PM. ***Felony, Civil Actions over $5,000, Probate.*** Probate is a separate office and separate index at this same address.
Civil Records: Access: In person only. Visitors must perform in person searches themselves. Required to

search: name, years to search. Civil cases indexed by defendant, plaintiff, on books from 1893. Public use terminal available, records go back to 2005-06 only.
Criminal Records: Access: In person only. Visitors must perform in person searches themselves. Required to search: name, years to search. Criminal docket on books from 1893. Note: Court personnel will not do a name search, but will pull specific case data if docket number given. Public use terminal available, crim records go back to 2005-06.
General Information: No juvenile records released. Will not fax out case files. Court makes copy: $1.00 per page if mailed, $.25 if in person. Self serve: $.25 per page. Certification fee: $5.00 per document. Payee: Circuit Clerk. Personal checks accepted; credit cards are not. Prepayment required.

Piggott Circuit Court 151 S 2nd, Piggott, AR 72454; 870-598-2524; probate phone: 870-598-2813; fax: 870-598-1107; 8AM-4:30PM. ***Felony, Civil Actions over $5,000.***
Civil Records: Access: In person only. Visitors must perform in person searches themselves. Required to search: name, years to search. Civil cases indexed by defendant, plaintiff, on books from 1893.
Criminal Records: Access: In person only. Visitors must perform in person searches themselves. Required to search: name, years to search, DOB, SSN. Criminal docket on books from 1893.
General Information: No expunged criminal records released. Will fax documents $5.00 per doc. Court makes copy: $.25 per page, self serve same. Certification fee: $5.00 per doc. Payee: Circuit Clerk. Personal checks accepted; credit cards are not. Prepayment required.

District Court 151 S 2nd Ave, Piggott, AR 72454; 870-598-2265; fax: 870-598-2229; 8AM-4:30PM. ***Misdemeanor, Civil Actions under $5,000, Eviction, Small Claims.***
Office is open 20 hours per week only. For eviction information the court says to contact Clay County Sheriff, 151 S 2nd St, Piggott, 72454, 870-598-2266.
Civil Records: Access: Mail, in person. Only the court performs in person searches; visitors may not. Search fee: $8.00. Required to search: name, DOB, years. Civil cases indexed by Defendant, Plaintiff. Records on computer back to 1998. Mail turnaround time 3-4 days.
Criminal Records: Access: Mail, in person. Only the court performs in person searches; visitors may not. Search fee: $8.00. Required to search: name, years to search, SSN; also helpful: DOB. Records on computer back to 1998. Mail turnaround 3-4 days.
General Information: Will fax documents to local or toll free line. Court makes copy: $.25 per page. Certification fee: $5.00 per docket. Payee: District Court. No personal checks or credit cards accepted. Prepayment required. Mail requests: SASE required.

Cleburne County

Circuit Court PO Box 543, Heber Springs, AR 72543; 501-362-8149; criminal fax: 501-362-4650; civil fax: same; 8:30AM-4:30PM. ***Felony, Civil Actions over $5,000, Probate.***
Probate is on a separate index at this address. Probate fax is same as main fax number.
Civil Records: Access: Fax, mail, in person. Both court and visitors may perform in person searches. Search fee: $6.00 per name. Required to search: name, years to search. Civil cases indexed by defendant, plaintiff, on dockets from 1883. Mail turnaround 1-2 days. Civil PAT goes back to 1997.
Criminal Records: Access: Phone, mail, in person. Both court and visitors may perform in person searches. Search fee: $6.00 per name. Required to search: name, years to search. Criminal docket index from 1883. Mail turnaround time 1-2 days. Criminal PAT goes back to 1997. PAT results show middle initial, DOB.
General Information: No juvenile records released. Will fax documents $4.00 1st page; $1.00 each add'l page. Court makes copy: $.50 per page, self serve same. Certification fee: $1.00 per document. Payee: Circuit Clerk. Personal checks accepted; credit cards are not. Prepayment required. Mail requests: SASE required.

District Court 102 E Main, Heber Springs, AR 72543; 501-362-6585; fax: 501-362-4661; 8:30AM-4:30PM. ***Misdemeanor, Civil Actions under $5,000, Small Claims, Eviction.***
Civil Records: Access: Phone, mail, fax, in person. Both court and visitors may perform in person searches. No search fee. Civil records on computer back to 1989. Mail turnaround time 10 working days.
Criminal Records: Access: Phone, mail, fax, in person. Both court and visitors may perform in person searches. No search fee. Required to search: name, years to search, offense, DOB. Criminal records computerized from 1989. Mail turnaround time 10 working days.
General Information: Court makes copy for no fee. No certification fee. No personal checks or credit cards accepted. Mail requests: SASE required.

Cleveland County

Circuit Court PO Box 368, Rison, AR 71665; 870-325-6521; criminal fax: 870-325-6144; civil fax: same; 8AM-4:30PM. ***Felony, Civil Actions over $5,000, Probate.***
Probate is a separate office and separate index at this same address. Probate fax is same as main fax number.
Civil Records: Access: Mail, in person. Visitors must perform in person searches themselves. No search fee. Required to search: name, years to search. Civil cases indexed by defendant, plaintiff, from 1980.
Criminal Records: Access: Mail, in person. Both court and visitors may perform in person searches. No search fee. Required to search: name, years to search, DOB. Criminal records from 1980. Mail turnaround time same day, if possible.
General Information: No juvenile or adoption records released. Fee to fax out file $1.00 per page. Court makes copy: $.25 per page, self serve same. Certification fee: $5.00 per document. Payee: Clerk of Circuit Court. Personal checks accepted; credit cards are not. Prepayment required.

District Court PO Box 405, City Hall, 405 Main St, Rison, AR 71665; 870-325-7382; fax: 870-325-6152; 8AM-4PM. ***Misdemeanor, Civil Actions under $5,000, Eviction, Small Claims.***
Civil Records: Access: In person only. Both court and visitors may perform in person searches. No search fee; court will charge for multiple records. Computerized records go back 1 year.
Criminal Records: Access: In person only. Both court and visitors may perform in person searches. No search fee, but court will charge for multiple records. Required to search: name, years to search, SSN. Computerized records go back 1 year.
General Information: Will not fax documents. Court makes copy: Court makes no copies. No certification fee. No personal checks or credit cards accepted.

Columbia County

Circuit Court 1 Court Sq #3, Magnolia, AR 71753-3595; 870-235-3700; probate phone: 870-235-3774; fax: 870-235-3786; 8AM-4:30PM. ***Felony, Civil Actions over $5,000, Probate.***
Probate is a separate office and separate index at this same address.
Civil Records: Access: In person. Visitors must perform in person searches themselves. Required to search: name, years to search. Civil cases indexed by defendant, plaintiff, on dockets and index cards; computerized since 8/97. Civil PAT available.
Criminal Records: Access: In person. Visitors must perform in person searches themselves. Required to search: name, years to search, DOB, SSN. Criminal records on dockets and index cards; computerized records since 8/97. Criminal PAT available.
General Information: No juvenile or adoption. Will fax documents. Court makes copy: $1.00 per page. Self serve: $.50 per page. Certification fee: $5.00 per document. Payee: Circuit Clerk. Personal checks accepted; credit cards are not. Prepayment required.

Magnolia District Court 216 S Washington, Magnolia, AR 71753; 870-234-7312; fax: 870-234-7312; 8AM-5PM. ***Misdemeanor, Civil Actions under $5,000, Eviction, Small Claims.***
Civil Records: Access: In person only. Visitors must perform in person searches themselves. Required to search: Name, plus DOB or SSN. Civil cases indexed by case number. Civil records available since 1993. Civil PAT goes back to 2003. PAT results show name only.
Criminal Records: Access: In person only. Visitors must perform in person searches themselves. Required to search: name, DOB and SSN, years to search; also helpful: address. Criminal records available sine 1987. Note: Court does not do criminal searches except for Law Enforcement Agencies. Criminal PAT goes back to 1987.PAT results show name, DOB.
General Information: Will fax documents to local or toll-free number. Court makes copy: $1.00 per page, self serve same. Certification fee: $5.00 includes copy fee. Payee: District Court Clerk. No credit cards accepted. Prepayment required.

Conway County

Circuit Court Conway County Courthouse, Rm 206, 115 S Moose, Morrilton, AR 72110; 501-354-9617; probate: 501-354-9621; fax: 501-354-9612; 8-5PM. ***Felony, Civil Actions over $5,000, Probate***
Probate is a separate office at this same address.
Civil Records: Access: In person only. Visitors must perform in person searches themselves. Required to search: name, years to search. Civil cases indexed by defendant, plaintiff, indexed back to 1900's.
Criminal Records: Access: In person only. Both court and visitors may perform in person searches. No search fee. Required to search: name, years to search, DOB; also helpful: sex, SSN. Criminal records indexed in books back to 1900's.
General Information: No juvenile records released. Fee to fax out file $1.00 per page. Court makes copy: $1.00 per page, self serve same. Certification fee: $5.00 per doc includes copies. Payee: Circuit Clerk. Personal checks accepted; credit cards are not. Prepayment required.

District Court Conway County Courthouse, PO Box 127, 117 S Moose, Morrilton, AR 72110; 501-354-9615; fax: 501-354-9633; 8AM-4:30PM. ***Misdemeanor, Civil Actions under $5,000, Eviction, Small Claims.***
Civil Records: Access: Mail, in person. Both court and visitors may perform in person searches. No search fee. Computerized records since 1994. Mail turnaround time 1-2 days. Civil PAT available. PAT results show name, DOB. Terminal results include driver's license number.
Criminal Records: Access: Mail, in person. Only the court performs in person searches; visitors may not. No search fee. Required to search: name, years to search; also helpful: DOB. Computerized records since 1994. Mail turnaround time 1-2 days. Criminal PAT available.
General Information: Will fax documents. Court makes copy: $1.00 per page, self serve same. Certification fee: $5.00. Payee: District Court Clerk. No personal checks or credit cards accepted. Prepayment required. Mail requests: SASE required.

Craighead County

Jonesboro Circuit Court PO Box 120, 511 S Main, Jonesboro, AR 72403; 870-933-4530; probate phone: 870-933-4520; criminal fax: 870-933-4534; civil fax: same; 8AM-5PM. ***Felony, Civil Actions over $5,000, Probate.*** www.craigheadcounty.org
Probate fax- 870-933-4514
Civil Records: Access: Fax, mail, in person. Both court and visitors may perform in person searches. Search fee: $6.00 per name. Required to search: name, years to search. Civil cases indexed by defendant, plaintiff, on computer from 1972, on microfiche from 1800s. Mail turnaround time 1-2 days. Civil PAT goes back to 1997.
Criminal Records: Access: Fax, mail, in person. Both court and visitors may perform in person searches. Search fee: $6.00 per name. Required to search: name, years to search, DOB; also helpful: address, SSN. Criminal records computerized from 1972, on microfiche from 1800s. Mail turnaround time 1-2 days. Criminal PAT goes back to 1997.

General Information: No juvenile records released. Will fax documents $1.00 per page. Court makes copy: $.25 per page, self serve same. Certification fee: $3.00 per document. Payee: Circuit Clerk. Personal checks accepted; credit cards are not. Prepayment required. Mail requests: SASE required.

Lake City Circuit Court - Eastern District PO Box 537, Lake City, AR 72437; 870-237-4342; fax: 870-237-8174; 8AM-5PM. ***Felony, Civil Actions over $5,000, Probate.***
Civil Records: Access: Mail, fax, in person. Both court and visitors may perform in person searches. No search fee. Required to search: name, years to search, address. Civil cases indexed by defendant, plaintiff, on computer from 1976. Civil PAT goes back to 1976. PAT results show name only.
Criminal Records: Access: Mail, fax, in person. Both court and visitors may perform in person searches. No search fee. Required to search: name, years to search, address, DOB; also helpful: SSN. Criminal records computerized from 1976. Criminal PAT goes back to same as civil. PAT results show name only.
General Information: No adoption records released. Will fax documents to local or toll free line. Court makes copy: $.25 per page, self serve same. Certification fee: $3.00 per doc. Payee: Circuit Clerk. Business checks accepted. No credit cards accepted. Prepayment required. Mail requests: SASE required.

District Court 410 W Washington, Jonesboro, AR 72401; 870-933-4508; criminal phone: x1; criminal fax: 870-933-4582; civil fax: same; 8AM-5PM. ***Misdemeanor, Civil Actions under $5,000, Eviction, Small Claims.*** www.craigheadcounty.org/
Civil Records: Access: Mail, in person. Only the court performs in person searches; visitors may not. Search fee: $4.00 per name. Required to search: name, DOB. Civil cases indexed by defendant, plaintiff. Computerized records go back 10 years. Mail turnaround time 1-2 days.
Criminal Records: Access: Mail, in person. Only the court performs in person searches; visitors may not. Search fee: $4.00 per name. Required to search: name, years to search, SSN. Computerized records go back 10 years. Mail turnaround time 1-2 days.
General Information: Will fax documents to local or toll-free number; fee may apply otherwise. Court makes copy: $.20 per page. Certification fee: $2.00 each usually includes copy fee. Payee: District Court. Personal checks accepted; credit cards are not. Prepayment required. Mail requests: SASE required.

Crawford County

Circuit Court 300 Main St, Rm 22, Van Buren, AR 72956; 479-474-1821; probate phone: 479-474-1312; fax: 479-471-0622; 8AM-5PM. ***Felony, Civil Actions over $5,000, Probate.***
www.crawford-county.org/circuit_court.htm
Probate is a separate office, separate index.
Civil Records: Access: Mail, in person. Both court and visitors may perform in person searches. Search fee: $6.00 per name, if written response needed. Required to search: name, years to search. Civil cases indexed by defendant, plaintiff, on computer from 1988, on dockets from 1877. Mail turnaround time same day. Civil PAT goes back to 1992. PAT civil results show middle initial.
Criminal Records: Access: Mail, in person. Both court and visitors may perform in person searches. Search fee: $6.00 per name, if written response needed. Required to search: name, years to search. Criminal records computerized from 1992, on dockets from 1877. Mail turnaround time 1-2 days. Criminal PAT goes back to same as civil. PAT criminal results show middle initial. Online results show middle initial.
General Information: Online identifiers in results same as on public terminal. No juvenile records released. Will fax documents to toll-free number. Court makes copy: $1.00 per page if mailed, otherwise $.50. Self serve: $.50 per page. Certification fee: $5.00. Payee: Circuit Clerk. Personal checks accepted; credit cards are not. Prepayment required. Mail requests: SASE required.

District Court 1003 Broadway, Van Buren, AR 72956; 479-474-1671; fax: 479-471-5005; 8AM-5PM,. ***Misdemeanor, Civil Actions under $5,000, Eviction, Small Claims.***
Civil Records: Access: Mail, in person. Both court and visitors may perform in person searches. No search fee. Civil cases indexed by defendant, plaintiff. Records available from 1975, computerized from 2000. Mail turnaround time 2-3 days. Civil PAT goes back to 2000. Public terminal only available Fridays.
Criminal Records: Access: Mail, in person. Both court and visitors may perform in person searches. No search fee. Required to search: name, years to search; also helpful: DOB, SSN. Specific court cases prior to 2000 need the conviction date. Records available from 1975, computerized from 2000. Mail turnaround time 2-3 days. Criminal PAT goes back to same as civil. Public terminal only available Fridays.
General Information: Will fax documents to local or toll-free number. Court makes copy: $.50 per page. Certification fee: $10.00 per document. Payee: Crawford County District Court. Personal checks accepted; credit cards are not. Prepayment required. Mail requests: SASE required.

Crittenden County

Circuit Court 100 Court St, Marion, AR 72364; 870-739-3248; probate phone: 870-739-4434; criminal fax: 870-739-3287; civil fax: same; 8AM-4:30PM. ***Felony, Civil Actions over $5,000, Probate.*** Probate is not in the Circuit Clerk's office and is managed by the County Clerk office. The phone number is given above.
Civil Records: Access: Mail, in person. Both court and visitors may perform in person searches. Search fee: $6.00 per name. Required to search: name, years to search. Civil cases indexed by plaintiff only. Civil records on dockets from 1930s; manual lookups.
Criminal Records: Access: In person only. Visitors must perform in person searches themselves. Required to search: name, case number. Criminal docket index from 1930s; manual lookups. Note: The court suggests to send criminal record inquiries to Ark. State Police, 501-681-8100.
General Information: No juvenile records released. Fee to fax out file $4.50 per document. Court makes copy: $.25 per page, self serve same. Certification fee: $3.00. Payee: Circuit Court. Personal checks accepted; credit cards are not. Prepayment required. Mail requests: SASE required for civil.

District Court PO Box 766, West Memphis, AR 72303; 870-732-7560; civil phone: 870-732-7563; fax: 870-732-7566; 8AM-4:30PM. ***Misdemeanor, Civil Actions under $5,000, Eviction, Small Claims.*** Court #12 can be reached at 870-732-7566.
Civil Records: Access: Phone, fax, mail, in person. Both court and visitors may perform in person searches. No search fee. Required to search: name, years to search, DOB or SSN. Civil records on computer back to 1989; other records go back to 1945. Mail turnaround time 2-3 days.
Criminal Records: Access: Phone, mail, in person. Both court and visitors may perform in person searches. No search fee. Required to search: name, years to search; also helpful: SSN, racc, sex, DOB. Criminal records computerized from 1989; other records go back to 1945. Mail turnaround 2-3 days.
General Information: No fee to fax documents. Court makes copy: $.25 per page. Self serve: no copy fee. No certification fee. Payee: District Court. Personal checks and major credit cards accepted. Prepayment required.

Cross County

Circuit Court County Courthouse, 705 E Union, Rm 9, Wynne, AR 72396; 870-238-5720; probate phone: 870-238-5735; fax: 870-238-5722; 8AM-4PM. ***Felony, Civil Actions over $5,000, Probate.***
Civil Records: Access: In person only. Visitors must perform in person searches themselves. Required to search: name, years to search. Civil cases indexed by defendant. Civil records (child support) on computer. All on dockets from 1800s. Civil PAT goes back to 2001. PAT results show middle initial, DOB.
Criminal Records: Access: In person only. Visitors must perform in person searches themselves. Required to search: name, years to search; SSN helpful. Criminal records (child support) on computer. All on dockets from 1800s. Criminal PAT goes back to same as civil. PAT results show middle initial, DOB.
General Information: No juvenile records released. Will not fax documents. Court makes copy: $.25 per page. Self serve: $.25 per page. Certification fee: $3.00 per doc. Payee: Cross County Circuit Court. Personal checks accepted; credit cards are not. Prepayment required.

District Court 205 Mississippi St, Wynne, AR 72396; 870-238-9171; fax: 870-238-3930; 8AM-4PM. ***Misdemeanor, Civil Actions under $5,000, Eviction, Small Claims.***
Civil Records: Access: Mail, in person. Only the court performs in person searches; visitors may not. Search fee: $10.00. Required to search: name, years to search. Records on computer back to 1986. Mail turnaround time 5-7 days.
Criminal Records: Access: Mail, in person. Only the court performs in person searches; visitors may not. Search fee: $10.00. Required to search: name, years to search, signed release; also helpful: SSN. Records on computer back to 1986. Mail turnaround time 5-7 days.
General Information: Will fax documents to local or toll-free number. Court makes copy for no fee. Certification fee: $5.00 per doc. Payee: Cross County Court. Personal checks accepted; credit cards are not. Prepayment required. Mail requests: SASE required.

Dallas County

Circuit Court Dallas County Courthouse, Fordyce, AR 71742; 870-352-2307; fax: 870-352-7179; 8:30AM-4:30PM. ***Felony, Civil Actions over $5,000, Probate.***
Civil Records: Access: Phone, fax, mail, in person. Both court and visitors may perform in person searches. No search fee. Required to search: name, years to search. Civil cases indexed by defendant, plaintiff, go back to 1863; on computer back to 8/1997. Civil PAT goes back to 8/1997. PAT results show name only.
Criminal Records: Access: In person only. Visitors must perform in person searches themselves. Required to search: name, years to search, DOB; SSN helpful. Criminal records go back to 1863; on computer back to 8/1997. Criminal PAT goes back to same as civil. PAT results show name only.
General Information: No juvenile records released. Will fax documents $2.00 plus $.25 per page. Court makes copy: $.50 per page, self serve same. Certification fee: $5.00. Payee: Circuit Clerk. Business checks, money orders or cashiers checks accepted; Law firm accounts allowed. No credit cards accepted. Prepayment required. Mail requests: SASE required for civil.

District Court 206 W 3rd St, Fordyce, AR 71742; 870-352-2332; fax: 870-352-3414; 8AM-4PM. ***Misdemeanor, Civil Actions under $5,000, Eviction, Small Claims.***
Civil Records: Access: In person, mail. Only the court performs in person searches; visitors may not. No search fee. Required to search: name. Computerized records since 1997. Mail turnaround time 1-2 days.
Criminal Records: Access: In person, mail. Only the court performs in person searches; visitors may not. No search fee. Required to search: name, years to search, SSN; also helpful: DOB. Computerized records since 1997.
General Information: Will fax documents. Court makes copy: $.25 per page. No certification fee. Payee: Dallas County District Court. Checks or cash accepted. No credit cards accepted. Prepayment required.

Desha County

Circuit Court PO Box 309, 604 President St, Arkansas City, AR 71630; 870-877-2411; probate phone: 870-877-2323; fax: 870-877-3407; 8AM-4PM. ***Felony, Civil Actions over $5,000, Probate.***

Civil Records: Access: Fax, mail, in person. Both court and visitors may perform in person searches. No search fee. Required to search: name, years to search. Civil cases indexed by defendant, plaintiff, on dockets from 1920s; on computer back to 1997. Mail turnaround time 1-2 days. Public use terminal has civil records back to 1965. PAT results show middle initial, DOB, SSN. Public terminal may only have deeds, mortgages, judgments.
Criminal Records: Access: Fax, mail, in person. Both court and visitors may perform in person searches. No search fee. Required to search: name, years to search, SSN. Criminal docket index from 1920s, on computer back to 1997. Mail turnaround time 1-2 days.
General Information: No juvenile records released. No fee to fax documents. Court makes copy: $.50 per page. Self serve: $.25 per page. Certification fee: $3.00 per doc. Payee: Skippy Leek, Circuit Court Clerk. Personal checks accepted; credit cards are not. Prepayment required. Mail requests: SASE required.

District Court PO Box 157, Dumas, AR 71639-2226; 870-382-6972; criminal phone: 870-382-6862; civil phone: 870-382-6972; criminal fax: 870-382-1106; civil fax: same; 8AM-4:30PM. ***Misdemeanor, Civil Actions under $5,000, Eviction, Small Claims.***
Civil Records: Access: Mail, in person. Only the court performs in person searches; visitors may not. Search fee: $5.00 per name. Required to search: name, years to search, signed release; also helpful: address. Civil records go back to 1988. Note: search fee includes copy fee if record found Mail turnaround time 1-2 days.
Criminal Records: Access: Mail, in person. Only the court performs in person searches; visitors may not. Search fee: $5.00 per name. Required to search: name, years to search, signed release; also helpful: address. Criminal records go back to 1988. Mail turnaround time 1-2 days.
General Information: Will fax documents for no fee. Court makes copy: search fee includes copy fee if record found. Certification fee: $5.00 per record includes copy fee. Payee: Dumas District Court. Personal checks accepted; credit cards are not. Prepayment required. Mail requests: SASE required.

Drew County

Circuit Court 210 S Main, Monticello, AR 71655; 870-460-6250; probate phone: 870-460-6260; fax: 870-460-6255; 8AM-4:30PM. ***Felony, Civil Actions over $5,000, Probate.***
Civil Records: Access: In person only. Both court and visitors may perform in person searches. No search fee. Required to search: name, years to search. Civil cases indexed by defendant, plaintiff, on dockets from 1846; on computer back to 1996 approx. Civil PAT goes back to 1996.
Criminal Records: Access: In person only. Visitors must perform in person searches themselves. Required to search: name, years to search. Criminal docket index from 1846; on computer back to 1997 approx. Criminal PAT goes back to 1997.
General Information: No juvenile or expunged records released. Will fax documents $1.25 1st page, $1.00 each add'l. Court makes copy: $.75 per page. Self serve: $.50 per page. Certification fee: $2.50 per doc. Payee: Drew County Circuit Clerk. Personal checks accepted; credit cards are not. Prepayment required.

District Court PO Box 505, Monticello, AR 71655; 870-367-4420; criminal fax: 870-460-9056; civil fax: same; 8AM-4:30PM. ***Misdemeanor, Civil Actions under $5,000, Eviction, Small Claims.***
Civil Records: Access: Mail, fax, in person. Both court and visitors may perform in person searches. No search fee. Required to search: name, years to search, DOB, SSN, signed release. Name or case number. Records overall since 1980, on computer since 1987. Mail turnaround time 1-2 days.
Criminal Records: Access: Mail, fax, in person. Only the court performs in person searches; visitors may not. No search fee. Required to search: name, years to search, DOB; also helpful: SSN. DL#, sex, signed release. Records overall since 1980, on computer since 1987. Mail turnaround time 1-2 days.
General Information: Will fax documents to local or toll free line. Court makes copy for no fee. No certification fee. Payee: Drew County District Court. No personal checks or credit cards accepted. Mail requests: SASE required.

Faulkner County

Circuit Court Circuit Clerk, PO Box 9, Conway, AR 72033; 501-450-4911; probate phone: 501-450-4909; fax: 501-450-4948; 8AM-4:30PM. ***Felony, Civil Actions over $5,000, Probate.***
Probate handled at different office, number above.
Civil Records: Access: Fax, mail, in person. Both court and visitors may perform in person searches. Search fee: $6.00 per name. Required to search: name, years to search. Civil cases indexed by defendant, plaintiff, on computer back to 1987; on docket from 1800s. Mail turnaround time 1-2 days. Civil PAT goes back to 1987. Not all cases will show DOB, SSN, full name.
Criminal Records: Access: Fax, mail, in person. Both court and visitors may perform in person searches. Search fee: $6.00 per name. Required to search: name, years to search. Criminal records computerized from 1987; on docket from 1800s. Note: Effective 3/1/08 the court no longer performs searches for prospective employers. Mail turnaround time 1-2 days. Criminal PAT goes back to 1987. Not all cases will show DOB, SSN, full name.
General Information: No juvenile records released. Will fax documents $1.00 if local, $3.50 plus $.25 per page if long distance. Court makes copy: $.25 per page, self serve same. Certification fee: $3.00 per doc. Payee: Faulkner County Circuit Clerk. Personal checks accepted; credit cards are not. Prepayment required. Mail requests: SASE required.

District Court 810 Parkway, Conway, AR 72034; 501-450-6112; criminal phone: ext 5302; civil phone: ext 5304; fax: 501-450-6184; 8AM-4:30PM. ***Misdemeanor, Civil Actions under $5,000, Small Claims.***
Civil Records: Access: Mail, fax, in person. Both court and visitors may perform in person searches. No search fee. Required to search: name, years to search, DOB, signed release; also helpful: address. Computerized records go back to 2005. Mail turnaround time 2 days.
Criminal Records: Access: Mail, fax, in person. Both court and visitors may perform in person searches. No search fee. Required to search: name, years to search, DOB, signed release; also helpful: address. Computerized records go back to 1993. Mail turnaround time 2 days. PAT results show name, DOB. Terminal results include SSN.
General Information: Will fax documents to local or toll free number. Court makes copy: $.25 per page. Certification fee: $5.00 per doc. Payee: Conway District Court. Personal checks accepted. Visa/MC accepted. Prepayment required. Mail requests: SASE required.

Franklin County

Charleston Circuit Court 607 E main, Charleston, AR 72933; 479-965-7332; probate phone: 479-965-2129; fax: 479-965-9322; 8AM-4:30PM. ***Felony, Civil Actions over $5,000, Probate.***
Civil Records: Access: Mail, in person. Both court and visitors may perform in person searches. Search fee: $6.00 per name. Required to search: name, years to search, DOB. Civil cases indexed by defendant, plaintiff, on dockets from 1900s. Mail turnaround time 1-2 days.
Criminal Records: Access: Mail, in person. Both court and visitors may perform in person searches. Search fee: $6.00 per name. Required to search: name, years to search, DOB. Criminal docket index from 1900s. Mail turnaround time 1-2 days.
General Information: No juvenile records released. Will fax documents $1.00 per page. Court makes copy: $.25 per page, self serve same. Certification fee: $5.00. Payee: Franklin County. Personal checks accepted; credit cards are not. Prepayment required. Mail requests: SASE required.

Ozark Circuit Court PO Box 1112, 211 W Commercial, Ozark, AR 72949; 479-667-3818; probate phone: 479-667-3607; fax: 479-667-5174; 8AM-4:30PM. ***Felony, Civil Actions over $5,000, Probate.***
Probate is maintained at the County Clerk's Office. Court personnel will NOT perform name searches.
Civil Records: Access: In person only. Visitors must perform in person searches themselves. Required to search: name, years to search. Civil cases indexed by plaintiff. Civil records on dockets from 1900s.
Criminal Records: Access: In person only. Visitors must perform in person searches themselves. Required to search: name, years to search. Criminal docket index from 1900s.
General Information: No juvenile records released. Will fax documents $1.00 per page. Court makes copy: $.25 per page, self serve same. Certification fee: $5.00. Payee: Circuit Clerk. Personal checks accepted; credit cards are not. Prepayment required.

District Court PO Box 426, 503 E Main St, Charleston, AR 72933; 479-965-7455; fax: 479-965-9980; 8AM-5PM. ***Misdemeanor, Civil Actions under $5,000, Small Claims.***
Civil Records: Access: Mail, fax, in person. Both court and visitors may perform in person searches. No search fee. Civil cases indexed by defendant, plaintiff, are not computerized, records index in docket books. Mail turnaround time 3-4 days.
Criminal Records: Access: Mail, fax, in person. Both court and visitors may perform in person searches. No search fee. Required to search: name, years to search, DOB; also helpful-SSN, signed release. Criminal records computerized from 1/2000. Mail turnaround time 3-4 days.
General Information: Will fax back documents. Court makes copy for no fee. No certification fee. Personal checks accepted; credit cards are not.

Fulton County

Circuit Court PO Box 219, Salem, AR 72576; 870-895-3310; criminal fax: 870-895-3383; civil fax: same; 8AM-4:30PM. ***Felony, Civil Actions over $5,000, Probate.***
Probate fax is same as main fax number.
Civil Records: Access: Mail, in person. Both court and visitors may perform in person searches. Search fee: $6.00 per name. Required to search: name, years to search. Civil cases indexed by defendant, plaintiff, on dockets from 1900s; on computer back to 2000. Mail turnaround time 1-2 days.
Criminal Records: Access: Mail, in person. Both court and visitors may perform in person searches. Search fee: $6.00 per name. Required to search: name, years to search. Criminal docket index from 1900s; on computer back to 2000. Note: Only the court can search on the computer terminal. Mail turnaround time 1-2 days.
General Information: No juvenile records released. Will fax documents. Court makes copy: $.20 per page, self serve same. No certification fee. Payee: Fulton County Clerks. Personal checks accepted; credit cards are not. Prepayment required. Mail requests: SASE required.

District Court PO Box 928, Salem, AR 72576; 870-895-4136; fax: 870-895-4137; 8AM-4:30PM. ***Misdemeanor, Civil Actions under $5,000, Eviction, Small Claims.***
Civil Records: Access: Mail, in person. Only the court performs in person searches; visitors may not. No search fee. Required to search: name. Computerized records since 1995. Mail turnaround time 1 week.
Criminal Records: Access: Phone, mail, in person. Both court and visitors may perform in person searches. No search fee. Required to search: name, years to search, DOB. Computerized records since 1995. Mail turnaround time 1 week.
General Information: Will fax documents to local or toll-free number. Court makes copy for no fee. No certification fee. Payee: Fulton County District Court. Personal checks accepted; credit cards are not. Mail requests: SASE required.

Garland County

Circuit Court Garland County Courthouse, 501 Ouachita Ave, Rm 207, Hot Springs, AR 71901; 501-622-3630; criminal phone: 501-622-3640; probate phone: 501-622-3610; criminal fax: 501-609-9043; civil fax: same; 8AM-5PM. ***Felony, Civil Actions over $5,000, Probate.***
www.garlandcounty.org/circuit_clerk.htm
Criminal searches performed by the court for Law enforcement personnel only. Probate records are handled by the County Clerk, phone number above.
Civil Records: Access: In person only. Visitors must perform in person searches themselves. Required to search: name; also helpful: years to search. Civil cases indexed by defendant, plaintiff, on microfiche and docket from 1900s; on computer back to 1989. Note: Index is in book form for the public. Computer index for Court Orders available to public.
Criminal Records: Access: In person only. Visitors must perform in person searches themselves. Required to search: name, years to search; also helpful: DOB, SSN, maiden name, race, aliases, sex. Criminal records on microfiche and docket from 1900s; on computer back to 1989. Note: Index is in book form for the public. Computer index for Court Orders available to public.
General Information: No expunged, sealed records released. Fee to fax out file $2.00 plus $.25 per page. Court makes copy: $.25 per page, self serve same. Certification fee: $.50 per doc. Payee: Garland County Circuit Clerk. Personal checks accepted; credit cards are not. Prepayment required.

District Court 607 Ouachita, Rm 150, Hot Springs, AR 71901; 501-321-6765; fax: 501-321-6764; 8AM-4:30PM. ***Misdemeanor, Civil Actions under $5,000, Eviction, Small Claims.***
Civil Records: Access: In person only. Both court and visitors may perform in person searches. No search fee. Required to search: name, DOB, SSN, years to search. Civil cases indexed by both defendant/plaintiff. Civil record on computer back to 2000. Public use terminal available.
Criminal Records: Access: In person only. Only the court performs in person searches; visitors may not. Required to search: name, years to search, offense. Criminal records computerized from 1990. Public use terminal available.
General Information: Will not fax documents. Court makes copy: $.25 per page. Certification fee: $5.00 per doc. Payee: HSDC. Personal checks accepted. Visa/MC accepted. Prepayment required.

Grant County

Circuit Court Grant County Courthouse, 101 W Center, Rm 106, Sheridan, AR 72150; 870-942-2631; criminal fax: 870-942-3564; civil fax: same; 8AM-4:30PM. ***Felony, Civil Actions over $5,000, Probate.***
Probate fax is same as main fax number.
Civil Records: Access: In person only. Visitors must perform in person searches themselves. Required to search: name, years to search. Civil cases indexed by defendant, plaintiff, on dockets and index from 1877.
Criminal Records: Access: In person only. Visitors must perform in person searches themselves. Required to search: name, years to search. Criminal records on dockets and index from 1982.
General Information: No juvenile, probate or adoption records released. Will fax specific case docs for $3.00 fee. Court makes copy: $.25 per page, self serve same. Certification fee: $2.00 per cert. Payee: Circuit Clerk. Personal checks accepted; credit cards are not. Prepayment required.

District Court PO Box 603, Sheridan, AR 72150; 870-942-3464; criminal fax: 870-942-8885; civil fax: same; 8AM-N, 1-4:15PM. ***Misdemeanor, Civil Actions under $5,000, Small Claims, Eviction.***
Probate is a separate index, separate court
Civil Records: Access: Mail, in person. Only the court performs in person searches; visitors may not. No search fee. Required to search: name. Computerized records since 1992. Mail turnaround time 3 days.
Criminal Records: Access: Mail, in person. Only the court performs in person searches; visitors may not. No search fee. Required to search: name, years to search, DOB, also DL# or SSN. Computerized records since 1992. Mail turnaround time 3 days.
General Information: Will fax documents $3.00 per fax. Court makes copy: $.25 per page, self serve same. Certification fee: $5.00. Payee: Grant County District Court. Personal checks accepted; credit cards are not. Prepayment required. Mail requests: SASE required.

Greene County

Circuit Court 320 W Court #124, Paragould, AR 72450; 870-239-6330; fax: 870-239-3550; 8AM-4:30PM. ***Felony, Civil Actions over $5,000, Probate.***
Searching is done by viewing the printouts.
Civil Records: Access: Fax, mail, in person. Both court and visitors may perform in person searches. Search fee: $6.00 per name. Required to search: name, years to search. Civil cases indexed by plaintiff. Civil records on index from 1830. Mail turnaround time 1-2 days.
Criminal Records: Access: Fax, mail, in person. Both court and visitors may perform in person searches. Search fee: $6.00 per name. Required to search: name, years to search; also helpful: DOB, SSN. Criminal records indexed since 1876. Mail turnaround time 1-2 days.
General Information: No juvenile records released. For fax return, $1.00 for first 3 pages then $.25 per page. Court makes copy: $.20 per page, self serve same. Certification fee: $5.00 per doc. Payee: Greene County Circuit Clerk. Personal checks accepted; credit cards are not. Prepayment required. Mail requests: SASE required.

District Court 320 W Court, Rm 227, Paragould, AR 72450; 870-239-7507; fax: 870-239-7506; 8AM-4:30PM. ***Misdemeanor, Civil Actions under $5,000, Eviction, Small Claims.***
www.gccourt.com
Civil Records: Access: Mail, in person. Only the court performs in person searches; visitors may not. No search fee. Required to search: name, years to search, DOB or SSN. Civil cases indexed by Defendant/Plaintiff. Records on computer back to 1989. Mail turnaround time 2 days.
Criminal Records: Access: Mail, in person. Only the court performs in person searches; visitors may not. Search fee: $5.00 per name. Required to search: name, years to search, DOB or SSN. Records on computer back to 1989. Mail turnaround time 2 days.
General Information: Will fax documents to local or toll-free number. Court makes copy: $.50 per page. Certification fee: $5.00 per doc. Payee: District Clerk. Only cashiers checks and money orders accepted. No credit cards accepted. Prepayment required. Mail requests: SASE required.

Hempstead County

Circuit Court PO Box 1420, Hope, AR 71802; 870-777-2384; probate phone: 870-777-2241; fax: 870-777-7827; 8AM-4PM. ***Felony, Civil Actions over $5,000, Probate.***
Probate is handled by the County Clerk at same address.
Civil Records: Access: Phone, fax, mail, in person. Both court and visitors may perform in person searches. Search fee: $6.00 per name. Required to search: name, years to search. Civil cases indexed by defendant, plaintiff, on dockets from 1910. Mail turnaround time 1-2 days.
Criminal Records: Access: Phone, fax, mail, in person. Both court and visitors may perform in person searches. Search fee: $6.00 per name. Required to search: name, years to search, DOB, SSN. Criminal docket index from 1910; computerized since 1975. Mail turnaround time 1-2 days.
General Information: No juvenile records released. Will fax documents $.50 per page. Court makes copy: $.50 per page. Self serve: $.25 per page. Certification fee: $5.00. Payee: Circuit Clerk. Personal checks accepted; credit cards are not. Prepayment required. Mail requests: SASE required.

District Court PO Box 1420, Hope, AR 71802-1420; 870-777-2525; fax: 870-777-7830; 8AM-4PM. ***Misdemeanor, Civil Actions under $5,000, Small Claims.***
Civil Records: Access: Mail, in person. Both court and visitors may perform in person searches. Search fee: $5.00 per name includes copies. Required to search: name, years to search. Civil cases indexed by defendant, plaintiff, not computerized. Mail turnaround time less than 1 week.
Criminal Records: Access: Mail, in person. Both court and visitors may perform in person searches. Search fee: $5.00 per name includes copies. Required to search: name, years to search, SSN, DOB. Criminal records computerized from 1987. Mail turnaround time less than 1 week.
General Information: Will not fax documents. Court makes copy: $1.00 per page. Certification fee: $5.00 per doc includes copies. Payee: District Court. Personal checks accepted; credit cards are not. Prepayment required. Mail requests: SASE required.

Hot Spring County

Circuit Court PO Box 1220, 210 Locust St, Malvern, AR 72104; 501-332-2281; probate phone: 501-332-2291; 8AM-4:30PM. ***Felony, Civil Actions over $5,000.***
Civil Records: Access: Mail, in person. Both court and visitors may perform in person searches. Search fee: $5.00. Required to search: name, years to search, plaintiff's name. Civil cases indexed by plaintiff. Civil records on dockets from 1980. Mail turnaround time 1-2 days.
Criminal Records: Access: Mail, in person. Both court and visitors may perform in person searches. Search fee: $5.00. Required to search: name, years to search, DOB or SSN. Criminal docket index from 1980. Mail turnaround time 1-2 days.
General Information: No juvenile records released. Will not fax documents. Court makes copy: $.50 per page, self serve same. Certification fee: $5.00 per doc. Payee: Circuit Clerk. No personal checks or credit cards accepted. Prepayment required. Mail requests: SASE required.

Malvern District Court 305 Locust St, Rm 201, Malvern, AR 72104; 501-332-7604; criminal phone: 501-332-7606; fax: 501-332-3144; 8AM-4:30PM. ***Misdemeanor, Civil Actions under $5,000, Eviction, Small Claims.***
Formerly known as Malvern Municipal Court before 7/1/01.
Civil Records: Access: Mail, fax, in person. Visitors must perform in person searches themselves. No search fee. Required to search: name, years to search and DOB or SSN, case number. Civil cases indexed by Defendant, Plaintiff. Records computerized back to 1994.
Criminal Records: Access: Mail, fax, in person. Visitors must perform in person searches themselves. No search fee. Required to search: name, years to search, DOB; also helpful: address, SSN. Records computerized back to 1994. Mail turnaround time 3 days.
General Information: Will fax documents $.25 per record. Court makes copy: $.25 per page. No certification fee. No personal checks or credit cards accepted. Prepayment required. Mail requests: SASE required.

Howard County

Circuit Court 421 N Main, Rm 7, Nashville, AR 71852; 870-845-7506; probate phone: 870-845-7503; 8AM-4:30PM. ***Felony, Civil Actions over $5,000, Probate.***
Probate is handled by the County Clerk at this address in Room 10.
Civil Records: Access: Phone, mail, in person. Both court and visitors may perform in person searches. Search fee: $6.00. Required to search: name, years to search. Civil cases indexed by defendant, plaintiff, on dockets from 1873. Mail turnaround time 2 days. Civil PAT goes back to 7/2003.
Criminal Records: Access: In person only. Visitors must perform in person searches themselves. Required to search: name, years to search, DOB. Criminal docket index from 1873. Criminal PAT goes back to same as civil.
General Information: No juvenile or sealed records released. Will fax documents $1.00 per page; incoming fax also $1.00. Court makes copy: $.25 per

page, self serve same. Certification fee: $5.00. Payee: Circuit Clerk. Personal checks accepted; credit cards are not. Prepayment required. Mail requests: SASE required for civil.

District Court 426 N Main, ##7, Nashville, AR 71852-2009; 870-845-7522; criminal fax: 870-845-3705; civil fax: same; 8AM-4:30PM. ***Misdemeanor, Civil Actions under $5,000, Eviction, Small Claims.***
Civil Records: Access: Mail, in person. Visitors must perform in person searches themselves. No search fee. Required to search: name, years to search. Civil cases indexed by defendant, plaintiff, viewable back to 1989.
Criminal Records: Access: Mail, in person. Both court and visitors may perform in person searches. No search fee. Required to search: name, years to search, DOB; also helpful: address, SSN. Criminal records viewable past 7 years. Mail turnaround time 1-3 days.
General Information: Will fax documents to local or toll free line. Court makes copy for no fee. Certification fee: $5.00 per doc. Payee: Howard County District Court. Personal checks accepted; credit cards are not. Prepayment required. Mail requests: SASE required.

Independence County

Circuit Court PO Box 2155, 192 E Main at Broad St, Batesville, AR 72503; 870-793-8833; fax: 870-793-8888; 8AM-4:30PM. ***Felony, Civil Actions over $5,000.***
Civil Records: Access: In person only. Visitors must perform in person searches themselves. Required to search: name, years to search; also helpful: address. Civil cases indexed by defendant, plaintiff. Civil judgments on computer from 1980, all others on index books from 1970s.
Criminal Records: Access: In person only. Visitors must perform in person searches themselves. Required to search: name, years to search, DOB; also helpful: address. Criminal records indexed in books from 1970s.
General Information: No juvenile records released. Will fax documents $3.50 1st page; $.25 ea add'l. Court makes copy: $.50 per page. Self serve: $.50 per page. Certification fee: $3.00 per instrument. Payee: Circuit Clerk. Personal checks accepted; credit cards are not. Prepayment required.

District Court 549 W Main, Batesville, AR 72501; 870-793-8817; fax: 870-793-8875; 8AM-4:30PM. ***Misdemeanor, Civil Actions under $5,000, Eviction, Small Claims.***
Civil Records: Access: Mail, in person. Both court and visitors may perform in person searches. No search fee. Civil cases indexed by defendant, plaintiff, go back to 1975. Mail turnaround time 1-2 days.
Criminal Records: Access: Mail, in person. Both court and visitors may perform in person searches. No search fee. Required to search: name, years to search. Criminal records go back to 1975. Mail turnaround time 1-2 days.
General Information: Will fax documents. Court makes copy for no fee. No certification fee. Payee: District Court. Only cashiers checks and money orders accepted. No credit cards accepted. Prepayment required. Mail requests: SASE required.

Izard County

Circuit Court PO Box 95, Main St, Courthouse, Melbourne, AR 72556; 870-368-4316; fax: 870-368-4748; 8:30AM-4:30PM. ***Felony, Civil Actions over $5,000, Probate.***
Civil Records: Access: Fax, mail, in person. Visitors must perform in person searches themselves. Search fee: $6.00 per name. Required to search: name, years to search. Civil cases indexed by plaintiff. Civil records on judgment books from 1889. Mail turnaround time 2 weeks.
Criminal Records: Access: Fax, mail, in person. Both court and visitors may perform in person searches. Search fee: $6.00 per name. Required to search: name, years to search, DOB; also helpful: address. Criminal records on judgment books from 1889. Mail turnaround time 2 weeks.
General Information: No juvenile records released. No fee to fax documents locally; is $1.00 per page if long distance. Court makes copy: $.20 per page, self serve same. Certification fee: $5.00 per document. Payee: Izard County and Circuit Clerk. Personal checks accepted; credit cards are not. Prepayment required. Mail requests: SASE required.

District Court PO Box 337, Melbourne, AR 72556; 870-368-4390; fax: 870-368-2267; 8:30AM-4:30PM. ***Misdemeanor, Civil Actions under $5,000, Small Claims.***
Civil Records: Access: Mail, fax, in person. Only the court performs in person searches; visitors may not. Search fee: $6.00. Required to search: name, years to search, Case #. Civil cases indexed by defendant, plaintiff, go back to 1977. Mail turnaround time varies.
Criminal Records: Access: Mail, fax, in person. Only the court performs in person searches; visitors may not. Search fee: $6.00. Required to search: name, years to search, DOB. Criminal records go back to 1977; on computer back to 1997. Mail turnaround time varies.
General Information: Will fax documents $1.00 per page. Court makes copy: $.25 per page, self serve same. Certification fee: $6.00 per doc. Payee: District Court. Personal checks accepted; credit cards are not. Prepayment required. Mail requests: SASE required.

Jackson County

Circuit Court Jackson County Courthouse, 208 Main St, Newport, AR 72112; 870-523-7423; fax: 870-523-3682; 8AM-4:30PM. ***Felony, Civil Actions over $5,000, Probate.***
Civil Records: Access: In person only. Visitors must perform in person searches themselves. Required to search: name, years to search. Civil cases indexed by defendant, plaintiff, on dockets from 1800s. Civil PAT goes back to 1997.
Criminal Records: Access: In person only. Visitors must perform in person searches themselves. Required to search: name, years to search. Criminal docket index from 1800s, computerized back to 1997. Criminal PAT goes back to 1997. Public terminal has name index.
General Information: No juvenile records released. Will fax back $1.00 per page. Court makes copy: $.25 per page, self serve same. Certification fee: $3.00 per doc. Payee: Circuit Clerk. Personal checks accepted; credit cards are not. Prepayment required.

District Court 615 3rd St, Newport, AR 72112; 870-523-9555; criminal phone: x118; civil phone: Ext 120; fax: 870-523-4365; 8AM-4:30PM. ***Misdemeanor, Civil Actions under $5,000, Eviction, Small Claims.***
Civil Records: Access: Phone, mail, fax, in person. Both court and visitors may perform in person searches. No search fee. Records indexed by defendant only. Civil records go back to 1987. Mail turnaround time 5-7 days.
Criminal Records: Access: Mail, fax, in person. Both court and visitors may perform in person searches. No search fee. Required to search: name, years to search, DOB. Criminal records go back to 1993 on computer, searchable to 1950. Mail turnaround time 5-7 days.
General Information: Will fax documents to local or toll free line. Court makes copy: $5.00 for 10+ pages. No certification fee. Payee: Newport District Court. No personal checks or credit cards accepted. Prepayment required. Mail requests: SASE required.

Jefferson County

Circuit Court PO Box 7433, 101 W Barkque, Pine Bluff, AR 71611; criminal phone: 870-541-5307; civil phone: 870-541-5306; 8:30AM-5PM. ***Felony, Civil Actions over $5,000, Probate.***
Civil Records: Access: In person only. Visitors must perform in person searches themselves. Required to search: name, years to search. Civil cases indexed by defendant, plaintiff, on dockets from 1950. Civil PAT goes back to 1991. Results include name and case number.
Criminal Records: Access: In person only. Visitors must perform in person searches themselves. Required to search: name, years to search, DOB. Criminal docket index from 1950. Criminal PAT goes back to same as civil. Results include name and case number.
General Information: No juvenile records released. Court makes copy: $.50 per page, self serve same. Certification fee: $.50 per page. Payee: Circuit Clerk. Only cashiers checks and money orders accepted. No credit cards accepted. Prepayment required.

District Court 200 E 8th Ave, Pine Bluff, AR 71601; 870-543-1860 Div.I; 850-7584 Div. II; criminal phone: 870-543-1869; fax: 870-543-1889; 8AM-5PM. ***Misdemeanor, Civil Actions under $5,000, Eviction, Small Claims.***
Civil Records: Access: Mail, in person. Both court and visitors may perform in person searches. Search fee: $5.00 per name. Required to search: name. Civil records go back to 1994. Mail turnaround time 3 days.
Criminal Records: Access: Mail, in person. Both court and visitors may perform in person searches. Search fee: $5.00 per name. Required to search: name, years to search; also helpful: DOB, SSN. Criminal records go back to 1989; computerized records since 1997. Mail turnaround time 3 days.
General Information: Will fax documents for fee, takes 3 days for return. Court makes copy: $1.00 per page. Certification fee: $5.00 per doc. Payee: District Court. Only cashiers checks and money orders and. Visa/MC accepted. Mail requests: SASE required.

Johnson County

Circuit Court PO Box 189, 215 Main St, Clarksville, AR 72830-0189; 479-754-2977; probate phone: 479-754-3967; fax: 479-754-4235; 8AM-4:30PM. ***Felony, Civil Actions over $5,000, Probate.***
Probate records handled by County Clerk, PO Box 57, 479-754-3967.
Civil Records: Access: Fax, mail, in person. Both court and visitors may perform in person searches. No search fee. Required to search: name, years to search. Civil cases indexed by defendant, plaintiff, on index from 1900s. Mail turnaround time 1-2 days.
Criminal Records: Access: Mail, in person. Both court and visitors may perform in person searches. No search fee. Required to search: name, years to search, DOB; also helpful: SSN. Criminal records indexed from 1900s. Mail turnaround time 1-2 days.
General Information: No juvenile records released. Will fax to 800 numbers only. Court makes copy: $.50 per page. Self serve: $.50 per page. Certification fee: $1.00 per cert. Personal checks accepted; credit cards are not. Prepayment required. Mail requests: SASE required.

District Court PO Box 581, 301 Porter Industrial Rd, Clarksville, AR 72830; 479-754-8533; fax: 479-754-6014; 8AM-4:30PM. ***Misdemeanor, Civil Actions under $5,000, Eviction, Small Claims.***
Civil Records: Access: Mail, in person. Both court and visitors may perform in person searches. No search fee. Required to search: name. Civil cases indexed by defendant, plaintiff, go back 10 years. Mail turnaround time 2-3 days.
Criminal Records: Access: Mail, in person. Both court and visitors may perform in person searches. No search fee. Required to search: name, years to search; also helpful: DOB, SSN. Records not computerized. Mail turnaround time 2-3 days.
General Information: Will fax documents if only a page or 2. Court makes copy: no charge for 1st 10 pages, self serve same. No certification fee. Payee: Dist Ct of Johnson County. Will accept checks, but prefer not to. Major credit cards accepted. Prepayment required. Mail requests: SASE required.

Lafayette County

Circuit Court #3 Courthouse Square, Lewisville, AR 71845; 870-921-4878; probate phone: 870-921-4633; fax: 870-921-4879; 8AM-4:30PM. ***Felony, Civil Actions over $5,000, Probate.***
Probate is located at #2 Courthouse Square.
Civil Records: Access: Phone, mail, in person. Both court and visitors may perform in person searches. No search fee. Required to search: name, years to search. Civil cases indexed by defendant, plaintiff, on dockets from 1950s. Mail turnaround time 2 days.
Criminal Records: Access: Mail, in person. Visitors must perform in person searches themselves. No

search fee. Required to search: name, years to search. Criminal docket index from 1950s. Mail turnaround time 2 days.
General Information: No juvenile records released without written order form the judge. Will fax documents to local or toll-free number. Court makes copy: $.50 per page, self serve same. Certification fee: $5.00 per doc. Payee: Circuit Clerk. Personal checks accepted; credit cards are not. Prepayment required. Mail requests: SASE required.

District Court 110 E Fourth, #1, Lewisville, AR 71845; 870-921-5555; fax: 870-921-4256; 8AM-4:30PM. ***Misdemeanor, Civil Actions under $5,000, Eviction, Small Claims.***
Civil Records: Access: In person only. Visitors must perform in person searches themselves. Required to search: name; helpful- SSN.
Criminal Records: Access: Phone, In person. Both court and visitors may perform in person searches. No search fee. Required to search: name, years to search, DOB; helpful- SSN. Records on computer back to 1994. Note: Office may do a name lookup via phone, but only back to 4/1996. Public use terminal has crim records back to 1996.
General Information: Will fax docs no add'l fee. Court makes copy: $.25 per page, self serve same. Certification fee: $5.00 per doc. Payee: District Court. No credit cards accepted.

Lawrence County

Circuit Court PO Box 581, 315 W Main St, Rm 7, Walnut Ridge, AR 72476; 870-886-1112; probate phone: 870-886-1111; fax: 870-886-1128; 8AM-4:30PM. ***Felony, Civil Actions over $5,000, Probate.*** Probate is a separate index, separate mailing address.
Civil Records: Access: In person only. Visitors must perform in person searches themselves. Required to search: name, years to search. Civil cases indexed by defendant, plaintiff, on index from 1981, on docket sheets from 1960s.
Criminal Records: Access: In person only. Visitors must perform in person searches themselves. Required to search: name, years to search. Criminal records indexed from 1981, docket sheets from 1960s.
General Information: No juvenile records released. Will fax documents $1.00 per page. Court makes copy: $.20 per page, self serve same. Certification fee: $3.00 per document. Payee: Circuit Clerk. Personal checks accepted; credit cards are not. Prepayment required.

Walnut Ridge District Court 210 W Main, Walnut Ridge, AR 72476; 870-886-1140; fax: 870-886-3905; 8AM-4:30PM. ***Misdemeanor, Civil Actions under $5,000, Small Claims.***
Civil Records: Access: Mail, in person. Both court and visitors may perform in person searches. No search fee. Civil cases indexed by Defendant, Plaintiff, Case #. Computerized records since 1992. Mail turnaround time 2-3 days.
Criminal Records: Access: Mail, in person. Both court and visitors may perform in person searches. No search fee. Required to search: name, years to search, offense. Computerized records since 1992. Mail turnaround time 2-3 days.
General Information: Will fax documents to local or toll free line. Court makes copy for no fee.Self serve: same. No certification fee. No credit cards accepted.

Lee County

Circuit Court 15 E Chestnut, Marianna, AR 72360; 870-295-7710; probate phone: 870-295-7715; fax: 870-295-7712; 8:30AM-4:30PM. ***Felony, Civil Actions over $5,000, Probate.***
Probate fax- 870-295-7766
Civil Records: Access: In person only. Visitors must perform in person searches themselves. Required to search: name, years to search. Civil cases indexed by defendant, plaintiff; index on docket books from 1873; computerized records since 1/2002. Civil PAT goes back to 2002.
Criminal Records: Access: In person only. Visitors must perform in person searches themselves. Required to search: name, years to search, DOB. Criminal records indexed in books from 1873; computerized records since 1/2002. Criminal PAT goes back to same as civil.
General Information: No juvenile records released. Will fax documents $1.00 per page. Court makes copy: $.25 per page, self serve same. Certification fee: $5.00. Payee: Circuit Court. Personal checks accepted; credit cards are not. Prepayment required.

District Court 15 E Chestnut, Rm 9, Marianna, AR 72360; 870-295-7730; fax: 870-295-7788; 8:30AM-4:30PM. ***Misdemeanor, Civil Actions under $5,000, Eviction, Small Claims.***
Civil Records: Access: Mail, in person. Only the court performs in person searches; visitors may not. Search fee: $5.00. Civil records go back to 1995; on Computer back to 1995. Mail turnaround 5 days.
Criminal Records: Access: Mail, in person. Only the court performs in person searches; visitors may not. Search fee: $5.00. Required to search: name, years to search. Computerized records since 1994. Mail turnaround time 5 days.
General Information: Court makes copy: $.25 per page. Certification fee: $5.00 per doc. Payee: Lee County District Court. Personal checks accepted; credit cards are not. Mail requests: SASE requested.

Lincoln County

Circuit Court Courthouse, 300 S Drew, Star City, AR 71667; 870-628-3154; probate phone: 870-628-5114; criminal fax: 870-628-5546; civil fax: same; 8AM-4:30PM. ***Felony, Civil Actions over $5,000, Probate.*** Probate is a separate index and separate office at this address.
Civil Records: Access: In person only. Both court and visitors may perform in person searches. No search fee. Required to search: name, years to search. Civil cases indexed by defendant, plaintiff, on index from 1920, archived from 1920.
Criminal Records: Access: In person only. Visitors must perform in person searches themselves. Required to search: name, years to search. Criminal records indexed from 1920, archived from 1920.
General Information: No sealed records released. Will fax documents $1.00 per page. Court makes copy: $.50 per page, self serve same. Certification fee: $3.00 per document. Payee: Lincoln County Circuit Court. Personal checks accepted; credit cards are not. Prepayment required.

District Court 300 S Drew St, Rm 201, Star City, AR 71667; 870-628-4904; civil phone: 870-628-4166; fax: 870-628-6442; 8-4:30PM. ***Misdemeanor, Civil Actions under $5,000, Eviction, Small Claims.***
Civil Records: Access: Mail, in person. Both court and visitors may perform in person searches. Search fee: $6.00 per name. Required to search: name, years to search, DOB. Civil records go back to 1980. Mail turnaround time 3-5 days.
Criminal Records: Access: Mail, in person. Both court and visitors may perform in person searches. Search fee: $6.00 per name. Required to search: name, years to search, DOB, signed release; also helpful: address, SSN, DL#. Criminal records go back to 1980; on computer back to 1991. Mail turnaround time 3-5 days.
General Information: No fee to fax 5 pages or less; $.50 per page if more. Court makes copy: $.50 per page, self serve same. Certification fee: $25.00 includes copies. Payee: District Court of Star City. Personal checks accepted but money orders preferred. No credit cards accepted. Prepayment required.

Little River County

Circuit Court PO Box 575, Ashdown, AR 71822; 870-898-7212; probate phone: 870-898-7210; criminal fax: 870-898-5783; civil fax: same; 8AM-4:30PM. ***Felony, Civil Actions over $5,000, Probate.*** Probate fax is same as main fax number.
Civil Records: Access: in person only. Both court and visitors may perform in person searches. No search fee. Required to search: name, years to search. Civil cases indexed by plaintiff. Civil records docket books back to 1868.
Criminal Records: Access: In person only. Visitors must perform in person searches themselves. Required to search: name. Criminal docket on books back to 1893. Note: Direct criminal records searches to AR state police; 870-777-4641.
General Information: No juvenile records released. Will not fax documents. Court makes copy: $.50 per page, self serve same. Certification fee: $5.00 per document. Payee: Circuit Clerk. Personal checks accepted; credit cards are not. Prepayment required.

District Court 351 N 2nd St, #8, Ashdown, AR 71822; 870-898-7230; fax: 870-898-3109; 8:30AM-4:30PM. ***Misdemeanor, Civil Actions under $5,000, Eviction, Small Claims.***
Civil Records: Access: Mail, in person. Both court and visitors may perform in person searches. Search fee: $5.00. Civil records on computer since 1987. Mail turnaround time 1 week.
Criminal Records: Access: Mail, in person. Both court and visitors may perform in person searches. Search fee: $5.00. Required to search: name, years to search; also helpful: DOB, SSN. Criminal records on computer since 1987. Mail turnaround time 1 week. Public use terminal has crim records back to 10 years. PAT results show name only. Results include driver's license number.
General Information: Will fax documents. Court makes copy: $.50 per page. Certification fee: $5.00 per doc. Payee: District Court. Only cashiers checks and money orders accepted. No credit cards accepted. Mail requests: SASE required.

Logan County

Circuit Court Courthouse, 25 W Walnut, Paris, AR 72855; 479-963-2164; probate phone: 479-963-2618; fax: 479-963-3304; 8AM-4:30PM. ***Felony, Civil Actions over $5,000, Probate.***
Probate is handled by the county clerk in Rm #25. Probate fax- 479-963-9017
Civil Records: Access: In person only. Visitors must perform in person searches themselves. Required to search: name, years to search. Civil cases indexed by defendant, plaintiff, on criminal index from 1901, on computer back to 1991-92.
Criminal Records: Access: In person only. Visitors must perform in person searches themselves. Required to search: name, years to search. Criminal records on criminal index from 1901.
General Information: Will fax documents for $1.00 per page fee. Court makes copy: $.50 per page, self serve same. Certification fee: $5.00. Payee: Circuit Clerk. Personal checks accepted; credit cards are not. Prepayment required.

Paris District Court Paris Courthouse, 25 W Walnut, Paris, AR 72855; 479-963-3792; fax: 479-963-2762; 8:30AM-4:30PM. ***Misdemeanor, Civil Actions under $5,000, Eviction, Small Claims.***
Civil Records: Access: Mail, in person. Both court and visitors may perform in person searches. No search fee. Civil records go back to the 1970's; computerized records since 1994. Mail turnaround time 1-2 days.
Criminal Records: Access: Mail, in person. Both court and visitors may perform in person searches. No search fee. Required to search: name, years to search; also helpful: DOB. Criminal records go back to 1970's; computerized records since 1994. Mail turnaround time 1-2 days.
General Information: Will fax documents to local or toll free line. Court makes copy for no fee. No certification fee. Payee: District Court. Mail requests: SASE required.

Lonoke County

Circuit Court PO Box 219, Attn: Circuit Clerk, 301 N Center St, Lonoke, AR 72086; 501-676-2316; probate phone: 501-676-2368; 8AM-4:30PM. ***Felony, Civil Actions over $5,000, Probate.***
Civil Records: Access: in person only. Visitors must perform in person searches themselves. Required to search: name, years to search. Civil cases indexed by defendant. Civil records on computer from 1989, on dockets from 1918's. Civil PAT available. PAT results show name only.
Criminal Records: Access: Mail, in person. Both court and visitors may perform in person searches. Search fee: $6.00 per name. Required to search: name, years to search, SSN. Criminal records computerized from 1989, on dockets from 1918's (not for public use). Mail turnaround time 1-2 days. Criminal PAT available. PAT results show middle initial, DOB.

General Information: No juvenile records released. Will fax documents $1.00 per page. Court makes copy: $.25 per page, self serve same. Certification fee: $6.00. Payee: Circuit Clerk. Personal checks accepted; credit cards are not. Prepayment required. Mail requests: SASE required for criminal.

Lonoke District Court 107 W 2nd St, Lonoke, AR 72086-2701; 501-676-3585; fax: 501-676-4316; 8AM-4:30PM. ***Misdemeanor, Civil Actions under $5,000, Eviction, Small Claims.***
Civil Records: Access: Mail, in person. Both court and visitors may perform in person searches. Search fee: $5.00. Computerized records since 1999. Mail turnaround time 1-2 days.
Criminal Records: Access: Mail, in person. Both court and visitors may perform in person searches. No search fee. Required to search: name, years to search. Computerized records since 1999. Mail turnaround time 1-2 days.
General Information: Will fax documents for no fee. Court makes copy for no fee. No certification fee. Payee: District Court. No personal checks or credit cards accepted. Prepayment required. Mail requests: SASE required.

Madison County

Circuit Court PO Box 626, Courthouse, Huntsville, AR 72740; 479-738-2215; probate phone: 479-738-2747; fax: 479-738-1544; 8AM-4:30PM. ***Felony, Civil Actions over $5,000, Probate.*** Probate is in the County Clerk's office, PO Box 37. Probate fax- 479-738-2735
Civil Records: Access: In person only. Visitors must perform in person searches themselves. Required to search: name, years to search; also helpful: address. Civil cases indexed by defendant, plaintiff, on dockets back to 1892. Civil PAT goes back to 1994. PAT results show name only. PAT index includes only court orders and judgments.
Criminal Records: Access: In person only. Visitors must perform in person searches themselves. Required to search: name, years to search; also helpful: DOB, SSN. Criminal records on dockets back to 1906. Criminal PAT goes back to 1994.PAT results show name, DOB. PAT index includes only court orders and judgments.
General Information: No juvenile records released. Will fax specific doc for $1.00 per page. Court makes copy: $.25 per page, self serve same. Certification fee: $5.00 per doc. Payee: Circuit Clerk. Personal checks accepted; credit cards are not. Prepayment required.

District Court PO Box 549, 208 E War Eagle, Huntsville, AR 72740; 479-738-2911; fax: 479-738-6846; 8AM-4:30PM. ***Misdemeanor, Civil Actions under $5,000, Eviction, Small Claims.***
Civil Records: Access: Mail, fax, in person. Both court and visitors may perform in person searches. No search fee. Records go back to 1991; computerized records since 1999. Note: Court will search only if time permits. Mail turnaround time 1 week. Civil PAT goes back to 1999. PAT results show name only.
Criminal Records: Access: In person, mail, fax. Both court and visitors may perform in person searches. No search fee. Required to search: name, years to search, DOB, SSN. Criminal records go back to 1991; on computer back to 1999. Note: Court will in person criminal search only if time permits. Mail turnaround time 1 week. Criminal PAT goes back to same as civil. PAT results show middle initial, DOB. Terminal results include SSN.
General Information: Will not fax documents. Court makes copy: $.25 per page. Self serve: $.25 per page.If citation is in Madison County payments are sent to: The Madison County Sheriff's Dept, PO Box 476, Huntsville, AR 72740. Certification fee: $5.00 per doc. Payee: Huntsville Police Dept. No personal checks or credit cards accepted. Mail requests: SASE required.

Marion County

Circuit Court PO Box 385, Yellville, AR 72687; 870-449-6226; fax: 870-449-4979; 8AM-4:30PM. ***Felony, Civil Actions over $5,000, Probate.*** Probate is separate index as this same address. Might be the smallest county courthouse in the US.
Civil Records: Access: In person only. Visitors must perform in person searches themselves. Required to search: name, years to search. Civil cases indexed by plaintiff. Civil records on dockets from 1956, records are not computerized.
Criminal Records: Access: In person only. Visitors must perform in person searches themselves. Required to search: name, years to search. Criminal docket index from 1956, records are not computerized.
General Information: No juvenile or adoption records released. Will fax specifically-requested case file for $1.00 per page. Court makes copy: $.25 per page, self serve same. Certification fee: $5.00 per document includes copies. Payee: Marion County Circuit Clerk. Personal checks accepted; credit cards are not. Prepayment required.

District Court PO Box 301, 105 S Berry St, Yellville, AR 72687; 870-449-6030; fax: 870-449-1177; 8AM-4:30PM. ***Misdemeanor, Civil Actions under $5,000, Small Claims.***
Civil Records: Access: Mail, in person. Both court and visitors may perform in person searches. Search fee: $6.00 per name. Required to search: name. Civil records go back to 1985. Mail turnaround time 1-2 days.
Criminal Records: Access: Mail, in person. Both court and visitors may perform in person searches. Search fee: $6.00 per name. Required to search: name, years to search, DOB. Criminal records go back to 1985; on computer back to 1996. Mail turnaround time 1-2 days.
General Information: Will fax documents to local or toll free line. Court makes copy: $.25 per page, self serve same. Certification fee: $5.00 per doc. Payee: Marion County Court. Personal checks accepted; credit cards are not. Prepayment required.

Miller County

Circuit Court 412 Laurel St, Rm 109, Texarkana, AR 71854; 870-774-4501; probate phone: 870-774-1501; criminal fax: 870-772-5293; civil fax: same; 8AM-4:30PM. ***Felony, Civil Actions over $5,000, Probate.***
Probate is at the County Clerk's office and not part of the Circuit Court.
Civil Records: Access: Phone, mail, in person, online. Both court and visitors may perform in person searches. Search fee: $8.00 per name. Required to search: name, years to search. Civil cases indexed by defendant, plaintiff, on index from 1850s. Mail turnaround time 1-3 days. Civil PAT goes back to 2003. PAT results show name only. Online access to circuit court dockets by subscription through RecordsUSA.com. Credit card, username and password is required; choose either monthly or per-use plan. Visit the website for sign-up or call Lisa at 601-264-7701 for information.
Criminal Records: Access: Mail, in person, online. Both court and visitors may perform in person searches. Search fee: $8.00 per name. Required to search: name, years to search. Criminal records indexed from 1850s; computerized records since 2000. Note: Clerk will only perform your criminal search if you have a case number; clerk will certify the disposition on that case. Or, direct search to AR State Police or the ACIC. Mail turnaround time 1-2 days. Criminal PAT goes back to same as civil. PAT results show name only. Online access to criminal dockets is the same as civil. Online results show name only.
General Information: No expunged records released. Will fax documents to local or toll free line. Court makes copy: $1.00 per page, self serve same. Certification fee: $3.50 per doc. Payee: Miller County Circuit Clerk. Personal checks accepted; credit cards are not. Prepayment required and SASE required.

District Court 100 N Stateline #2, Texarkana, AR 75501; 903-798-3016; fax: 903-798-3588; 8AM-5PM. ***Misdemeanor, Civil Actions under $5,000, Small Claims, Eviction.*** www.txkusa.org/
Civil Records: Access: Mail, in person. Both court and visitors may perform in person searches. Search fee: $6.00 per name. Required to search: name, SSN, DOB. Civil cases indexed by defendant, plaintiff, on docket index, year not given. Mail turnaround time 2 days.
Criminal Records: Access: Mail, in person. Only the court performs in person searches; visitors may not. No search fee, unless extensive searching involved. Required to search: name, years to search, DOB. Criminal records on computer back to 1997. Mail turnaround time 2 days.
General Information: Will fax documents to local or toll free line. Court makes copy: $1.00 each from computer screen. Certification fee: $10.00 per transcript. Payee: Miller District Court. Only cashiers checks and money orders accepted. No credit cards accepted. Prepayment required and SASE required.

District Court 2300 East St, Texarkana, AR 71854; 870-772-2780; fax: 870-773-3595; 8AM-4:30PM. ***Misdemeanor, Eviction.***
Criminal Records: Access: Mail, in person. Only the court performs in person searches; visitors may not. No search fee. Required to search: name, years to search, DOB. Criminal records on computer back to 1997. Mail turnaround time 2 days.
General Information: Will fax documents to local or toll free line. Court makes copy for no fee. No certification fee. No credit cards accepted. Mail requests: SASE required.

Mississippi County

Blytheville Circuit Court PO Box 1498, Blytheville, AR 72316; 870-762-2332; fax: 870-762-8148; 9AM-4:30PM. ***Felony, Civil Actions over $5,000.***
Civil Records: Access: In person only. Visitors must perform in person searches themselves. Required to search: name, years to search. Civil cases indexed by plaintiff. Civil records prior on index from 1940; court orders on imaging computer back to 1/2003.
Criminal Records: Access: In person only. Visitors must perform in person searches themselves. Required to search: name, years to search, DOB, SSN. Criminal records prior on index for 7 years, in storage from 1940; court orders on imaging computer back to 1/2003. Note: The court refers all criminal record name searches to AR State Police.
General Information: No juvenile records released. Will fax specific case file $1.00 per page. Court makes copy: $.50 per page, self serve same. Certification fee: $3.00 includes copy fee. Court may add add'l copy fee is document is lengthy. Payee: Circuit Clerk. No personal checks or credit cards accepted. Prepayment required.

Osceola Circuit Court PO Box 466, 200 W Hale, County Courthouse, Osceola, AR 72370; 870-563-6471; fax: 870-563-5063; 9AM-4:30PM. ***Felony, Civil Actions over $5,000, Probate.***
Civil Records: Access: In person only. Visitors must perform in person searches themselves. Required to search: name, years to search. Civil cases indexed by plaintiff. Civil records computerized since 1992, on index from 1940. Civil PAT goes back to 1992. PAT results show name only. Results include plaintiff's name.
Criminal Records: Access: In person only. Both court and visitors may perform in person searches. No search fee. Required to search: name, years to search, DOB, charge; also helpful: SSN. Criminal records on computer since 1992. Note: Court directs criminal search requests to the AR State Police. Criminal PAT goes back to 1988. PAT results show name only. Results include plaintiff's name.
General Information: No juvenile records released. Will fax documents $1.00 per page. Court makes copy: $.50 per page, self serve same. Certification fee: $5.00 per document. Payee: Circuit Clerk. Personal checks accepted; credit cards are not. Prepayment required.

Blytheville District Court 121 N 2nd St, #104, Blytheville, AR 72315; 870-763-7513; fax: 870-762-0433; 8AM-5PM. ***Misdemeanor, Civil Actions under $5,000, Small Claims.***
Civil Records: Access: Mail, fax, in person. Only the court performs in person searches; visitors may not. Search fee: $4.00 per name. Civil cases indexed by defendant, plaintiff, go back to 1960; on computer back to 1987. Mail turnaround time 1 day, sometimes 2.

Criminal Records: Access: Mail, fax, in person. Only the court performs in person searches; visitors may not. Search fee: $4.00 per name. Required to search: name, years to search; also helpful: DOB, SSN. Criminal records go back to 1960; on computer back to 1987. Mail turnaround time 1-2 days.
General Information: Will fax documents to local or toll free line. Court makes copy: $.50 per page. Self serve: $.25 per page. Certification fee: $5.00. Payee: City of Blytheville. Personal checks accepted; credit cards are not. Prepayment required. Mail requests: SASE required.

Osceola District Court 397 W Keiser, Osceola, AR 72370; 870-563-1303; fax: 870-563-8439; 8AM-4PM. ***Misdemeanor, Civil Actions under $5,000, Small Claims.***
Civil Records: Access: Mail, in person, fax. Only the court performs in person searches; visitors may not. Search fee: $10.00. Required to search: name, DOB and SSN. Records computerized for at least 7 years. Mail turnaround time 1-2 days.
Criminal Records: Access: Mail, in person. Only the court performs in person searches; visitors may not. Search fee: $10.00. Required to search: name, years to search; also helpful: address, DOB, SSN. Records computerized for at least 7 years. Mail turnaround time 1-2 days.
General Information: Will fax documents to local or toll free line. Court makes copy: $1.00 per page, self serve same. Certification fee: $2.00 per page. Payee: Osceola District Court. Personal checks accepted; credit cards are not. Prepayment required. Mail requests: SASE required.

Monroe County

Circuit Court 123 Madison St, Courthouse, Clarendon, AR 72029; 870-747-3615; probate phone: 870-747-3632; fax: 870-747-3710; 8AM-4:30PM. ***Felony, Civil Actions over $5,000, Probate.*** Probate is managed by the County Clerk office.
Civil Records: Access: Fax, mail, in person. Both court and visitors may perform in person searches. No search fee. Required to search: name, years to search. Civil cases indexed by defendant, plaintiff; index on docket books from 1931.
Criminal Records: Access: In person only. Visitors must perform in person searches themselves. Required to search: name, years to search. Criminal records indexed in books from 1933.
General Information: No juvenile records released. Will fax documents $2.50 per page and $2.50 per doc. Add $.50 per page if more than 4. Court makes copy: $.25 per page, self serve same. Certification fee: $2.50. Payee: Monroe County Circuit Clerk. Personal checks accepted; credit cards are not. Prepayment required. Mail requests: SASE required for civil.

District Court City Hall, 270 Madison St, Clarendon, AR 72029; 870-747-5200; criminal fax: 870-747-9969; civil fax: same; 8AM-5PM. ***Misdemeanor, Civil Actions under $5,000, Small Claims, Traffic.***
Civil Records: Access: Mail, in person. Both court and visitors may perform in person searches. No search fee. Required to search: name, years to search, DOB. Records go back to 1988, on computer since 1994. Mail turnaround time 1-2 days.
Criminal Records: Access: Mail, in person. Both court and visitors may perform in person searches. No search fee. Required to search: name, years to search, DOB, SSN. Records go back to 1988, on computer since 1994. Mail turnaround 1-2 days.
General Information: Will fax documents to local or toll free line. Court makes copy: $.25 per page, self serve same. Certification fee: $5.00 per doc includes copy fee. Payee: Clarendon District Court. Personal checks accepted; credit cards are not. Prepayment required.

Montgomery County

Circuit Court 105 Hwy 270 E, #10, Courthouse, Mount Ida, AR 71957; 870-867-3521; criminal fax: 870-867-2177; civil fax: same; 8AM-4:30PM. ***Felony, Civil Actions over $5,000, Probate.***
Probate is a separate index at the courthouse. Probate fax is same as main fax number.
Civil Records: Access: Phone, fax, mail, in person. Both court and visitors may perform in person searches. Search fee: $6.00 per name. Required to search: name, years to search; also helpful: address. Civil cases indexed by defendant, plaintiff, on card files from 1960s. Mail turnaround time same day. Civil PAT goes back to 6/2006. PAT results show middle initial, DOB, SSN.
Criminal Records: Access: In person only. Visitors must perform in person searches themselves. Required to search: name, years to search; also helpful: DOB, SSN. Criminal records on card files from 1960s. Criminal PAT goes back to 6/2006. PAT results show middle initial, DOB, SSN.
General Information: No juvenile or adoption records released. Will fax out docs for $3.00 per each 5 pages; call office to confirm. Court makes copy: $.50 per page. Self serve: $.25 per page. Certification fee: $5.00. Payee: Circuit Clerk. Personal checks accepted; credit cards are not. Prepayment required. Mail requests: SASE required for civil.

District Court PO Box 548, Mount Ida, AR 71957; 870-867-2221; fax: 870-867-3695; 8AM-4:30PM. ***Misdemeanor, Civil Actions under $5,000, Eviction, Small Claims.***
Civil Records: Access: Mail, in person. Both court and visitors may perform in person searches. No search fee. Required to search: name, years to search, DOB, SSN. Records indexed by plaintiff and defendant. Records go back to 1973; computerized records go back to 1993. Mail turnaround 1-2 days.
Criminal Records: Access: Mail, in person. Both court and visitors may perform in person searches. No search fee. Required to search: name, years to search, DOB, SSN. Records go back to 1973; computerized records go back to 1993. Mail turnaround time 1-2 days.
General Information: No fee to fax documents. Court makes copy for no fee.Self serve: none. No certification fee. Payee: Montgomery County Sheriff Office. Personal checks accepted; credit cards are not. Prepayment required. Mail requests: SASE required.

Nevada County

Circuit Court PO Box 204, Prescott, AR 71857; 870-887-2511; fax: 870-887-1911; 8AM-4:30PM. ***Felony, Civil Actions over $5,000.***
Civil Records: Access: Phone, fax, mail, in person. Both court and visitors may perform in person searches. Search fee: $6.00 per name. Required to search: name, years to search. Civil cases indexed by defendant, plaintiff, on index since 1850. Mail turnaround time 1-2 days.
Criminal Records: Access: In person only. Visitors must perform in person searches themselves. Required to search: name, years to search, DOB. Criminal records on index since 1850.
General Information: No juvenile records released. Will fax documents $1.00 per page. Court makes copy: $1.00 per page, self serve same. Certification fee: $2.00. Payee: Nevada County Circuit Clerk. Personal checks accepted; credit cards are not. Prepayment required. Mail requests: SASE required.

District Court 215 E 2nd St S, #104, Prescott, AR 71857; 870-887-6016; fax: 870-887-3244; 8:30AM-4:30PM. ***Misdemeanor, Civil Actions under $5,000, Small Claims.***
Civil Records: Access: Phone, mail, fax, in person. Only the court performs in person searches; visitors may not. Search fee: $6.00 per name. Records on computer go back to 1997. Mail turnaround time 2-5 days.
Criminal Records: Access: Phone, mail, fax, in person. Only the court performs in person searches; visitors may not. Search fee: $6.00 per name. Required to search: name, years to search, DOB, SSN. Records on computer go back to 1997. Mail turnaround time 2-5 days.
General Information: Will fax documents to local or toll free line. Court makes copy: $6.00 per page. Certification fee: $6.00. Will only certify civil records, not criminal. Payee: District Court. No personal checks or credit cards accepted. Prepayment required. Mail requests: SASE requested.

Newton County

Circuit Court PO Box 410, Jasper, AR 72641; 870-446-5125; probate phone: same; fax: 870-446-5755; 8AM-4:30PM. ***Felony, Civil Actions over $5,000, Probate.***
Civil Records: Access: Fax, mail, in person. Both court and visitors may perform in person searches. Search fee: $6.00 per name. Required to search: name, years to search. Civil cases indexed by defendant, plaintiff, on dockets from 1800s. Mail turnaround time varies.
Criminal Records: Access: Fax, mail, in person. Both court and visitors may perform in person searches. Search fee: $6.00 per name. Required to search: name, years to search, DOB. Criminal docket index from 1800s. Mail turnaround time varies.
General Information: No juvenile records released. Will fax documents $2.50 1st page, $.50 each add'l. Court makes copy: $.25 per page, self serve same. Certification fee: $5.00. Payee: Circuit Clerk. Personal checks accepted; credit cards are not. Prepayment required. Mail requests: SASE required.

District Court PO Box 550, 100 E Court St, 2nd Fl, Jasper, AR 72641; 870-446-5335; fax: 870-446-2234; 8AM-4:30PM. ***Misdemeanor, Civil Actions under $5,000, Eviction, Small Claims.***
Civil Records: Access: Mail, fax, in person. Only the court performs in person searches; visitors may not. No search fee. Required to search: name plus years to search, and DOB or SSN. Civil cases indexed by defendant, plaintiff. Records go back to 1984, civil records not computerized. Mail turnaround 24 hours.
Criminal Records: Access: Mail, fax, in person. Only the court performs in person searches; visitors may not. No search fee. Required to search: name plus years to search, and DOB or SSN. Records go back to 1972, on computer back to 1997. Mail turnaround time 24 hours.
General Information: Will fax documents to local or toll free line. Court makes copy: $.25 per page, self serve same. Certification fee: $10.00. Payee: Newton County District Court. Personal checks accepted; credit cards are not. Prepayment required.

Ouachita County

Circuit Court PO Box 667, Camden, AR 71701; 870-837-2230 (Circuit); probate phone: 870-837-2220; criminal fax: 870-837-2252; civil fax: same; 8AM-4:30PM. ***Felony, Civil Actions over $5,000, Probate.*** Probate is a separate index c/o County Clerk, PO Box 1041. Probate fax- 870-837-2251.
Civil Records: Access: In person only. Visitors must perform in person searches themselves. Required to search: name, years to search. Civil cases indexed by defendant, plaintiff, archived from 1950s; on computer back to 3/1999. Civil PAT goes back to 1999. PAT results show name only.
Criminal Records: Access: In person only. Visitors must perform in person searches themselves. Required to search: name, years to search; also helpful: DOB, SSN. Criminal records archived from 1950s; on computer back to 3/1999. Criminal PAT goes back to same as civil. PAT results show name only.
General Information: No juvenile records released. Will fax specific case file $3.00 per fax. Court makes copy: $.50 per page, self serve same. Certification fee: $2.50 per cert. Payee: Circuit Clerk of Ouachita County. Personal checks accepted; credit cards are not. Prepayment required.

District Court 213 Madison St, Camden, AR 71701; 870-836-0331; criminal fax: 870-837-5530; civil fax: same; 8AM-4:30PM. ***Misdemeanor, Civil Actions under $5,000, Eviction, Small Claims.***
Civil Records: Access: Mail, fax, in person. Both court and visitors may perform in person searches. Search fee: $5.00 per name. Required to search: name, years to search, also helpful Case #. Civil records are indexed by Plaintiff, Defendant. Records go back to 1950; computerized since 1987. Mail turnaround time 1-2 days.
Criminal Records: Access: Mail, fax, in person. Both court and visitors may perform in person searches. Search fee: $5.00 per name. Required to search: name, years to search, DOB; also helpful:

SSN. Records go back to 1950; computerized since 1987. Mail turnaround time 1-2 days.
General Information: Will fax documents to local or toll free line. Court makes copy: $.25 per page, self serve same. Certification fee: $5.00 per document. Payee: District Court. No personal checks accepted. Business check and money orders accepted. No credit cards accepted. Prepayment required.

Perry County

Circuit Court PO Box 358, Perryville, AR 72126; 501-889-5126; criminal fax: 501-889-5759; civil fax: same; 8AM-4:30PM. ***Felony, Civil Actions over $5,000, Probate.***
Civil Records: Access: In person only. Both court and visitors may perform in person searches. No search fee. Required to search: name, years to search. Civil cases indexed by defendant, plaintiff, on computer from 1997, on dockets from 1916. Civil PAT back to 1997. PAT results show name only.
Criminal Records: Access: Phone, mail, in person. Both court and visitors may perform in person searches. No search fee. Required to search: name, years to search, DOB. Criminal records computerized from 1997, on dockets from 1916. Note: The court's phone search is a quick index search. Criminal PAT goes back to same as civil. PAT results show name only.
General Information: No juvenile or adoption records released. Will fax specific case file $2.00 per page. Court makes copy: $.50 first page, $.25 each add'l, self serve same. Certification fee: $5.00 per document. Payee: Circuit Clerk. Personal checks accepted; credit cards are not. Prepayment required. Mail requests: SASE required for criminal.

District Court PO Box 186, Perryville, AR 72126; 501-889-5296; fax: 501-889-5835; 8AM-4:30PM. ***Misdemeanor, Civil Actions under $5,000, Eviction, Small Claims, Traffic.***
Civil Records: Access: Mail, fax, in person. Only the court performs in person searches; visitors may not. Search fee: $2.00 per name. Required to search: name. Records back to 1993. Mail turnaround time 3-5 days.
Criminal Records: Access: Mail, in person. Only the court performs in person searches; visitors may not. Search fee: $2.00 per name. Required to search: name, years to search, DOB, SSN. Computerized records back to 1997, prior on hard copy back to 1993. Mail turnaround time 3-5 days.
General Information: Will fax documents. Court makes copy: $.25 per page. Certification fee: $2.00 per doc. Payee: District Court. Personal checks accepted; credit cards are not. Prepayment required.

Phillips County

Circuit Court 620 Cherry St #206, Courthouse, Helena, AR 72342; 870-338-5515; probate phone: 870-338-5505; criminal fax: 870-338-5513; civil fax: same; 8AM-4:30PM. ***Felony, Civil Actions over $5,000, Probate.***
Probate records located in the County Clerk office.
Civil Records: Access: In person. Visitors must perform in person searches themselves. Required to search: name, years to search, DOB. Civil cases indexed by plaintiff. Civil records on fee books from 1970; on computer back to 1998. Civil PAT goes back to 2000 (orders only). PAT civil results show middle initial.
Criminal Records: Access: In person. Visitors must perform in person searches themselves. Required to search: name, years to search; also helpful-DOB. Criminal records on fee books from 1970; on computer back to 2000. Note: Court suggests Arkansas State Police for criminal search. Criminal PAT goes back to 2000. PAT criminal results show middle initial.
General Information: No juvenile records released. Fee to fax document $1.00 each. Court makes copy: $.25 per page, self serve same. Certification fee: $3.00 per cert. Payee: Circuit Clerk. Personal checks accepted; credit cards are not. Prepayment required.

District Court 226 Perry ST, City Hall, Helena, AR 72342; 870-338-8825; fax: 870-338-9832; 8AM-4:30PM. ***Misdemeanor, Civil Actions under $5,000, Eviction, Small Claims.***
Civil Records: Access: Mail, in person. Both court and visitors may perform in person searches. Search fee: $5.00. Civil cases indexed by case number. Computerized from 1993-2000. Mail turnaround time 3 days.
Criminal Records: Access: Mail, in person. Both court and visitors may perform in person searches. Search fee: $5.00 per name. Required to search: name, years to search, address, DOB, SSN. Computerized back to 1993. Mail turnaround 3 days.
General Information: Will fax documents if prepaid. Court makes copy: $.25 per page. Certification fee: $5.00 per page. Payee: City of Helena District Court. No personal checks or credit cards accepted. Prepayment required.

Pike County

Circuit Court PO Box 219, Murfreesboro, AR 71958; 870-285-2231; fax: 870-285-3281; 8AM-4:30PM. ***Felony, Civil Actions over $5,000, Probate.***
Probate at County Clerk's office at 870-285-2743.
Civil Records: Access: In person only. Visitors must perform in person searches themselves. Required to search: name, years to search. Civil cases indexed by defendant. Civil records archived from 1895. Some records on dockets books, computerized since 1989. Civil PAT goes back to 2008. PAT results show name only.
Criminal Records: Access: In person only. Visitors must perform in person searches themselves. Required to search: name, years to search, DOB. Criminal records archived from 1895. Some records on dockets, fee books. Computerized records from 1992. Criminal PAT goes back to 2008. PAT results show name only.
General Information: No juvenile or adoption records released. Will fax documents $1.50 1st 3 pages, $.50 ea add'l. Court makes copy: $.50 per page, self serve same. Certification fee: $5.00 per doc. Payee: Pike County Clerk. Personal checks accepted; credit cards are not. Prepayment required.

District Court PO Box 197, Courthouse Sq, Murfreesboro, AR 71958; 870-285-3865; fax: 870-285-3540; 8AM-4:30PM. ***Misdemeanor, Civil Actions under $5,000, Eviction, Small Claims.***
Civil Records: Access: Phone, fax, mail, in person. Both court and visitors may perform in person searches. No search fee. Required to search: name, years to search. Civil records on computer back to 1997; prior on index books. Mail turnaround time 2-3 days.
Criminal Records: Access: Phone, fax, mail, in person. Both court and visitors may perform in person searches. Required to search: name, years to search, offense. Criminal records computerized from 1997; prior on index books. Mail turnaround time 2-3 days.
General Information: Will fax documents. Court makes copy: $.50 per page. No certification fee. Payee: Pike County District Court. Prepayment required. Mail requests: SASE helpful.

Poinsett County

Circuit Court PO Box 46, Harrisburg, AR 72432; 870-578-4420; fax: 870-578-4427; 8:30AM-4:30PM. ***Felony, Civil Actions over $5,000, Probate.***
Civil Records: Access: Mail, in person. Only the court performs in person searches; visitors may not. Search fee: $6.00 per name. Required to search: name, years to search. Civil cases indexed by defendant, plaintiff, on computer from 1985. Some records on dockets. Note: All requests must be in writing. Mail turnaround time 1-2 days.
Criminal Records: Access: Mail, in person. Only the court performs in person searches; visitors may not. Search fee: $6.00 per name. Required to search: name, years to search, DOB. Criminal records computerized from 1985. Some records on dockets. Note: All requests must be in writing. Mail turnaround time 1-2 days.
General Information: No juvenile records released. Will fax documents to toll-free number for no fee. Court makes copy: $.50 per page. Certification fee: $2.00 per doc. Payee: Circuit Clerk. Personal checks accepted; credit cards are not. Prepayment required. Mail requests: SASE required.

Harrisburg District Court 202 N East St, Harrisburg, AR 72432; 870-578-4110; fax: 870-578-4123; 7:30AM-4:30PM. ***Misdemeanor, Civil Actions under $5,000, Eviction, Small Claims.***
Civil Records: Access: Mail, in person. Both court and visitors may perform in person searches. Search fee: $2.00. Required to search: name, DOB, SSN, signed release. Civil records go back to 1978. Note: Mail requests must include SASE. Mail turnaround time 1 day.
Criminal Records: Access: Mail, in person. Both court and visitors may perform in person searches. Search fee: $2.00. Required to search: name, years to search; also helpful: DOB, SSN, signed release. Criminal records computerized from 1987. Mail turnaround time 1 day.
General Information: Will not fax documents. Court makes copy: $.25 per page. Certification fee: $5.00. Payee: Harrisburg District Court. Attorney checks accepted. No credit cards accepted. Prepayment required. Mail requests: SASE required.

Lepanto District Court PO Box 610, 117 Greenwood, Lepanto, AR 72354; 870-475-2415; fax: 870-475-3161; 8AM-4PM. ***Misdemeanor, Civil Actions under $5,000, Eviction, Small Claims.***
Civil Records: Access: Mail, in person. Both court and visitors may perform in person searches. Search fee: $2.00. Required to search: name, DOB, SSN, signed release. Civil cases indexed by Defendant. Civil records go back to 1978. Mail turnaround time 1-2 days.
Criminal Records: Access: Mail, in person. Both court and visitors may perform in person searches. Search fee: $2.00. Required to search: name, years to search; also helpful: DOB, SSN, signed release. Criminal records computerized from 2003. Note: All requests must be in writing. Mail turnaround time 1-2 days.
General Information: Will not fax documents. Court makes copy: $.25 per page. Certification fee: $5.00 per doc. Payee: District Court. No personal checks or credit cards accepted. Prepayment required.

Marked Tree District Court #1 Elm St, Marked Tree, AR 72365; 870-358-2024; fax: 870-358-7867; 8AM-4:30PM. ***Misdemeanor, Civil Actions under $5,000, Eviction, Small Claims.***
Civil Records: Access: Mail, in person. Both court and visitors may perform in person searches. No search fee. Required to search: name, DOB, SSN, signed release. Civil records go back to 1978. Mail turnaround time 1-2 days.
Criminal Records: Access: Mail, in person. Only the court performs in person searches; visitors may not. No search fee. Required to search: name, years to search; also helpful: DOB, SSN, signed release. Criminal records computerized from 1987. Mail turnaround time 1-2 days.
General Information: Will fax documents for fee. Court makes copy: $.25 per page. Certification fee: $5.00 per doc. Payee: District Court. No personal checks or credit cards accepted. Prepayment required. Mail requests: SASE required.

Trumann District Court 221 S Melton, Trumann, AR 72472; 870-483-7771; criminal fax: 870-483-2620; civil fax: same; 8AM-4:30PM. ***Misdemeanor, Civil Actions under $5,000, Eviction, Small Claims.***
Civil Records: Access: Mail, in person. Only the court performs in person searches; visitors may not. Required to search: name, DOB, SSN, signed release. Civil cases indexed by defendant, plaintiff, go back to 1978. Mail turnaround time 3 days.
Criminal Records: Access: Mail, in person. Only the court performs in person searches; visitors may not. Required to search: name, years to search; also helpful: DOB, SSN, signed release. Criminal records computerized from 1999. Mail turnaround 3 days.
General Information: Will fax documents. Court makes copy: $.25 per page, self serve same. Certification fee: $5.00 per doc includes copies. Payee: District Court. No personal checks or credit cards accepted. Prepayment required. Mail requests: SASE required.

Tyronza District Court PO Box 275, 143 EN Main, Tyronza, AR 72386; 870-487-2168; criminal

fax: 870-487-2729; civil fax: same; 8AM-5PM. ***Misdemeanor, Civil Actions under $5,000, Eviction, Small Claims.***
Civil Records: Access: Mail, in person. Both court and visitors may perform in person searches. Search fee: $2.00. Required to search: name, DOB, SSN, signed release. Civil records go back to 1994.
Criminal Records: Access: Mail, in person. Both court and visitors may perform in person searches. Search fee: $2.00. Required to search: name, years to search; also helpful: DOB, SSN, signed release. Criminal records computerized from 1994. Note: All requests must be in writing. Mail turnaround time is 2 days.
General Information: Will fax documents. Court makes copy: $.25 per page. Certification fee: $10.00 per doc includes copy fee. Payee: District Court. Personal checks (in-state) accepted. No credit cards accepted. Prepayment required.

Polk County

Circuit Court 507 Church St, Mena, AR 71953; 479-394-8100; probate phone: 479-394-8123; fax: 479-394-8170; 8AM-4:30PM. ***Felony, Civil Actions over $5,000, Probate, Domestic Relations.***
Probate is handled separately from the court by the County Clerk's Office. Probate fax- 479-394-8115
Civil Records: Access: Mail, in person, online. Both court and visitors may perform in person searches. Search fee: $6.00 per name. Required to search: name, years to search. Civil cases indexed by defendant, plaintiff, on dockets and index from late 1800s. Mail turnaround time 1-2 days. Civil PAT goes back to 7/03. PAT results show name only. Online access to circuit court dockets by subscription through RecordsUSA.com. Credit card, username and password is required; choose either monthly or per-use plan. Visit the website for sign-up or call 601-264-7701 for information.
Criminal Records: Access: Mail, in person, online. Both court and visitors may perform in person searches. Search fee: $6.00 per name. Required to search: name, years to search, DOB. Criminal records on dockets and index from late 1800s. Mail turnaround time 1-2 days. Criminal PAT goes back to same as civil. Online access to criminal dockets is the same as civil.
General Information: Online identifiers in results same as on public terminal. No juvenile records released. Will fax documents to local or toll free line. Court makes copy: $.25 per page; $.50 legal size, self serve same. Certification fee: $5.00. Payee: Circuit Clerk. Personal checks accepted. Prepayment required. Mail requests: SASE required.

District Court 507 Church Ave, Courthouse, Mena, AR 71953; 479-394-8140; criminal fax: 479-394-6199; civil fax: same; 8AM-4:30PM. ***Misdemeanor, Civil Actions under $5,000, Eviction, Small Claims.***
Civil Records: Access: In person only. Visitors must perform in person searches themselves. Civil cases indexed by defendant, plaintiff, go back 10 years; computerized records go back 10 years. Note: Court will assist visitors with search.
Criminal Records: Access: In person only. Visitors must perform in person searches themselves. Required to search: name, years to search, DOB; SSN helpful. Criminal records go back 10 years; computerized records go back 10 years. Note: Court will assist visitors with search.
General Information: Will not fax documents. Court makes copy for no fee. No certification fee. No credit cards accepted.

Pope County

Circuit Court 100 W Main, Russellville, AR 72801; 479-968-7499; probate phone: 479-968-6064; fax: 479-880-8463; 8AM-4PM. ***Felony, Civil Actions over $5,000.***
Probate is a separate office at this same address.
Civil Records: Access: In person. Visitors must perform in person searches themselves. Required to search: name, years to search. Civil cases indexed by defendant, plaintiff, on dockets from early 1900s; on computer back to 1998. Civil PAT goes back to 1998. PAT results show name only.
Criminal Records: Access: In person. Visitors must perform in person searches themselves. Required to search: name, years to search, DOB; also helpful: SSN. Criminal docket index from early 1900s; on computer back to 1998. Criminal PAT goes back to same as civil.PAT results show name, DOB.
General Information: No juvenile records released. Will not fax documents. Court makes copy: $1.00 per page. Self serve: $.25 per page. Certification fee: $3.00. Payee: Pope County. Personal checks accepted; credit cards are not. Prepayment required.

District Court 205 W Second, Russellville, AR 72801; 479-968-1393; fax: 479-968-4166; 8AM-5PM. ***Misdemeanor, Civil Actions under $5,000, Small Claims.***
Civil Records: Access: Phone, fax, mail, in person. Both court and visitors may perform in person searches. No search fee. Required to search: name, DOB, years to search. cases indexed by defendant names. Civil records go back to 1970s. Mail turnaround time 2-3 days.
Criminal Records: Access: Phone, fax, mail, in person. Both court and visitors may perform in person searches. No search fee. Required to search: name, years to search; also helpful: DOB. Criminal records go back to 1970s; on computer back to 1991. Mail turnaround time 2-3 days.
General Information: Will fax documents to local or toll free line. Court makes copy: $.25 per page. Certification fee: $5.00 per doc. Cert fee includes copies. Payee: District Court. Personal checks accepted; credit cards are not. Prepayment required. Mail requests: SASE required.

Prairie County

Circuit Court - Southern District PO Box 283, De Valls Bluff, AR 72041; 870-998-2314; fax: 870-998-2314; 8AM-4:30PM. ***Felony, Civil Actions over $5,000, Probate.***
Civil Records: Access: Phone, fax, mail, in person. Both court and visitors may perform in person searches. Search fee: $6.00. Required to search: name, years to search. Civil cases indexed by defendant, plaintiff, on dockets from 1885. Mail turnaround time 1 day. Civil PAT goes back to 1885.
Criminal Records: Access: Phone, fax, mail, in person. Both court and visitors may perform in person searches. Search fee: $6.00. Required to search: name, years to search, DOB, SSN. Criminal docket index from 1885. Mail turnaround time 1 day. Criminal PAT goes back to 1885.
General Information: No juvenile or adoption records released. Will fax documents $1.00 per page. Court makes copy: $.50 per page, self serve same. Certification fee: $5.00 per doc. Payee: Circuit Clerk. Personal checks accepted; credit cards are not. Prepayment required. Mail requests: SASE required.

Circuit Court - Northern District 200 Courthouse Sq, #140, Des Arc, AR 72040; 870-256-4434; criminal fax: 870-256-4434; civil fax: same; 8AM-4:30PM. ***Felony, Civil Actions over $5,000, Probate.***
Probate is a separate index at this same address. Probate fax is same as main fax number.
Civil Records: Access: Mail, in person. Both court and visitors may perform in person searches. Search fee: $6.00 per name. Required to search: name, years to search. Civil cases indexed by defendant, plaintiff, on dockets from 1800s. Mail turnaround time 1 day.
Criminal Records: Access: Mail, in person. Both court and visitors may perform in person searches. Search fee: $6.00 per name. Required to search: name, years to search. Criminal docket index from 1800s. Mail turnaround time 1 day.
General Information: No juvenile, adoption records released. Fee to fax out file $1.00 per page. Court makes copy: $1.00 per page. Self serve: $.50 per page. Certification fee: $5.00 per cert. Payee: Circuit Clerk. Personal checks accepted; credit cards are not. Prepayment required. Mail requests: SASE required.

Des Arc District Court PO Box 389, 107 S 3rd St, Des Arc, AR 72040; 870-256-3011; fax: 870-256-4612; 8AM-4:30PM. ***Misdemeanor, Civil Actions under $5,000, Small Claims.***
Civil Records: Access: Mail, in person. Both court and visitors may perform in person searches. No search fee. Civil records available since 1988. Mail turnaround time 1-2 days.
Criminal Records: Access: Mail, in person. Both court and visitors may perform in person searches. No search fee. Required to search: name, years to search. Criminal records available since 1988. Mail turnaround time 1-2 days.
General Information: Will fax documents to local or toll-free number. Court makes copy: $.50 per page. Self serve: $.25 per page. No certification fee. Payee: Des Arc District Court. No personal checks or credit cards accepted. Prepayment required.

Pulaski County

District Court 3001 W Roosevelt, Little Rock, AR 72204; 501-340-6824; fax: 501-340-6899; 7AM-5:30PM. ***Misdemeanor, Civil Actions under $5,000, Eviction, Small Claims.***
Civil Records: Access: Phone, mail, in person. Both court and visitors may perform in person searches. No search fee. Required to search: DOB, SSN, case number. Overall records and computerized records go to 1988. Mail turnaround time 2-3 days.
Criminal Records: Access: Phone, mail, in person. Both court and visitors may perform in person searches. No search fee. Required to search: name, years to search; also helpful: SSN. Overall records and computerized records go to 1988. Mail turnaround time 2-3 days.
General Information: Will fax documents to local or toll-free number only if time permits. Court makes copy: $.50 per page. Certification fee: $1.00 per page. Payee: County District Court. Personal checks accepted; credit cards are not.

Circuit Court Courthouse, Rm 102, 401 W Markham St, #102, Little Rock, AR 72201; 501-340-8431; fax: 501-340-8884; 8:30-4:30PM. ***Felony, Civil Actions over $5,000, Probate.*** Probate was handled by the Chancery Court #12 until July 1, 2001.
Civil Records: Access: In person, online. Visitors must perform in person searches themselves. Required to search: name, years to search. Civil cases indexed by defendant, plaintiff, on computer from 1982, on microfiche from 1974 to 1982, archived from 1900. Civil PAT goes back to early 1990s. PAT results show name only. Access court records free at www.pulaskiclerk.com/Archives.html - civil back to 4/2005; Probate back to 1/2006; domestic back to 1/2007.
Criminal Records: Access: In person, online. Visitors must perform in person searches themselves. Required to search: name, years to search, DOB, SSN. Criminal records computerized from 1982, on microfiche from 1974 to 1982, archived from 1900. Criminal PAT goes back to mid-1980s. PAT results show name only. PAT results include alias. Access court records free at www.pulaskiclerk.com/Archives.html - criminal back to 4/2005.
General Information: No expunged records released. Will fax documents to local or toll-free number. Court makes copy: $.50 1st page; $.25 per each add'l page, self serve same. Certification fee: $5.00 per cert. Payee: Circuit Clerk. Personal checks accepted; credit cards are not. Prepayment required. SASE required for mail return of any copies.

Randolph County

Circuit Court 107 W Broadway, Pocahontas, AR 72455; 870-892-5522 or 0289; probate phone: 870-892-5822; fax: 870-892-8794; 8AM-4:30PM. ***Felony, Civil Actions over $5,000, Probate.***
Probate records are located at the same address, right down the hall.
Civil Records: Access: Mail, in person. Visitors must perform in person searches themselves. Search fee: $6.00 per name. Required to search: name, years to search. Civil cases indexed by defendant, plaintiff, on criminal index from 1836. Mail turnaround time same day.
Criminal Records: Access: In person. Visitors must perform in person searches themselves. Required to search: name, years to search, DOB. Criminal records on criminal index from 1836.

General Information: No juvenile records released. Will not fax documents. Court makes copy: $.25 per page. Self serve: $.20 per page. Certification fee: $2.00. Payee: Circuit Clerk. Personal checks accepted; credit cards are not. Prepayment required. Mail requests: SASE required for mail return of any copies.

District Court 1510 Pace Rd, Pocahontas, AR 72455; 870-892-4033; criminal fax: 870-892-4392; civil fax: same; 8AM-4:30PM. ***Misdemeanor, Civil Actions under $5,000, Eviction, Small Claims.***
Civil Records: Access: Mail, in person. Both court and visitors may perform in person searches. Search fee: $6.00. Required to search: name, years to search, DOB, SSN. Records maintained since 1980s. Mail turnaround time 1 day.
Criminal Records: Access: Mail, in person. Both court and visitors may perform in person searches. Search fee: $6.00. Required to search: name, years to search, DOB, SSN. Records maintained since 1986. Mail turnaround time 1 day.
General Information: Will fax documents to local or toll free line. Court makes copy for no fee. Certification fee: $5.00 per cert includes copies. Payee: District Court. No personal checks or credit cards accepted. Prepayment required. Mail requests: SASE required.

Saline County

Circuit Court 200 N Main St, Benton, AR 72015; 501-303-5615; probate phone: 501-303-5630; 8AM-4:30PM. ***Felony, Civil Actions over $5,000, Probate.*** Probate records located at 215 N Main St. at County Court. Probate fax- 501-303-5684
Civil Records: Access: In person, online. Visitors must perform in person searches themselves. Required to search: name, years to search. Civil cases indexed by defendant, plaintiff, on computer since 1991, prior on docket books. Civil PAT goes back to 1991. Court records index search is free at https://www.ark.org/grs/app/saline but records are $12 each or you may subscribe monthly.
Criminal Records: Access: In person, online. Visitors must perform in person searches themselves. Required to search: name, years to search. Criminal records on computer since 1991, prior on docket books. Criminal PAT goes back to same as civil. Online access to criminal is same as civil.
General Information: No juvenile records released. Will not fax documents. Court makes copy: $.25 per page, self serve same. Certification fee: $5.00. Payee: Circuit Court. Personal checks accepted. Prepayment required.

Benton District Court 1605 Edison Ave #19, Benton, AR 72015; 501-303-5670/1; fax: 501-303-5696; 8AM-4:30PM. ***Misdemeanor, Civil Actions under $5,000, Eviction, Small Claims.***
Search fee includes both civil and criminal index.
Civil Records: Access: Mail, in person. Only the court performs in person searches; visitors may not. Search fee: $5.00 per name. Required to search: name. Civil cases indexed by defendant, plaintiff, go back to 1982. Mail turnaround time 72 hours.
Criminal Records: Access: Mail, in person. Only the court performs in person searches; visitors may not. Search fee: $5.00 per name. Required to search: name, years to search, DOB; also helpful: DOB, SSN, DL. Criminal records go back to 1994 on computer. Mail turnaround time 72 hours.
General Information: Will fax back documents for no fee. Court makes copy: $.50 per page. Certification fee: $5.00 per doc. Payee: Benton District Court. No Personal checks and major credit cards accepted. Prepayment required.

Scott County

Circuit Court PO Box 2165, 190 W First St Box 10, Waldron, AR 72958; 479-637-2642; criminal fax: 479-637-0124; civil fax: same; 8AM-4:30PM. ***Felony, Civil Actions over $5,000, Probate.*** Probate fax is same as main fax number.
Civil Records: Access: Phone, mail, fax, in person. Both court and visitors may perform in person searches. No search fee. Required to search: name, years to search. Civil cases indexed by defendant, plaintiff; index on docket books from 1882. Mail turnaround time 1 week.
Criminal Records: Access: Mail, fax, in person. Both court and visitors may perform in person searches. No search fee. Required to search: name, years to search, DOB, SSN. Criminal records indexed in books from 1882. Mail turnaround time 1 week.
General Information: No juvenile or adoption records released. Will fax documents for no fee. Court makes copy: $.50 per page. Self serve: $.50 per page. Certification fee: $5.00 per cert includes copies. Payee: Scott County Clerk. Personal checks accepted; credit cards are not. Prepayment required. Mail requests: SASE required.

District Court 190 W 1st St, Box 15, Waldron, AR 72958; 479-637-4694; criminal fax: 479-637-4712; civil fax: same; 8AM-4:30PM. ***Misdemeanor, Civil Actions under $5,000, Eviction, Small Claims.***
Civil Records: Access: Mail, in person. Both court and visitors may perform in person searches. No search fee. Required to search: name, years to search, DOB; also helpful-other names used, SSN. Records on computer to 1998. Mail turnaround 1-2 days.
Criminal Records: Access: Mail, in person. Both court and visitors may perform in person searches. No search fee. Required to search: name, years to search. Records go back to 1998; on computer back to 10/1998. Mail turnaround time 1-2 days.
General Information: Will fax documents to local or toll-free number. Court makes copy for no fee. No certification fee. Payee: District Court of Scott County. No personal checks accepted. Money order and cash accepted. No credit cards accepted. Mail requests: SASE required.

Searcy County

Circuit Court PO Box 998, Marshall, AR 72650; 870-448-3807; fax: 870-448-5005; 8AM-4:30PM. ***Felony, Civil Actions over $5,000, Probate.***
Civil Records: Access: Mail, in person. Visitors must perform in person searches themselves. Search fee: $6.00 per name. Required to search: name, years to search, written request. Civil cases indexed by defendant, plaintiff, archived from 1881. Some records on dockets. Mail turnaround 1 day.
Criminal Records: Access: Mail, in person. Visitors must perform in person searches themselves. Search fee: $6.00 per name. Required to search: name, years to search, offense; also helpful: DOB, SSN. Criminal records archived from 1881. Some records on dockets. Note: Court may try to direct you to the state police.
General Information: No juvenile or adoption records released. Will fax documents $1.00 per page. Court makes copy: $.25 per page, self serve same. Cert fee: $5.00 per document. Payee: Searcy County Clerk. Personal checks accepted; credit cards are not. Prepayment required. Mail requests: SASE required.

District Court PO Box 885, Marshall, AR 72650; 870-448-5411; fax: 870-448-5927; 9AM-5PM. ***Misdemeanor, Civil Actions under $5,000, Eviction, Small Claims.***
Civil Records: Access: Mail, in person. Both court and visitors may perform in person searches. Search fee: $6.00 per name. Required to search: name. Civil records go back to 1992. Mail turnaround time 1 week.
Criminal Records: Access: Mail, in person. Both court and visitors may perform in person searches. No search fee. Required to search: name, years to search, DOB, SSN. Criminal records go back to 1992. Mail turnaround time 1 week.
General Information: Will fax documents to local or toll-free number. Court makes copy: $.25 per page. Certification fee: $5.00 per doc. Payee: Court. No personal checks or credit cards accepted. Prepayment required. Mail requests: SASE helpful.

Sebastian County

Circuit Court - Greenwood Division PO Box 310, County Courthouse, Greenwood, AR 72936; 479-996-4175; fax: 479-996-6885; 8AM-5PM. ***Felony, Civil Actions over $5,000, Probate.***
www.sebastiancountyonline.com
Records from both Circuit Courts - Fort Smith and Greenwood Division - are on the same computer system, but copies of case files must be pulled from individual courts.
Civil Records: Access: Mail, in person. Both court and visitors may perform in person searches. Search fee: $6.00 per name. Required to search: name, years to search. Civil cases indexed by defendant, plaintiff, on computer from 10/87, on dockets from 1900. Mail turnaround time 1-2 weeks. Civil PAT goes back to 1988. PAT results show name only.
Criminal Records: Access: In person only. Both court and visitors may perform in person searches. No search fee. Required to search: name, years to search; also helpful: SSN. Criminal records computerized from 10/87, on dockets from 1900. Criminal PAT goes back to same as civil. PAT results show middle initial, DOB. Terminal results include SSN.
General Information: No juvenile records released. Will fax documents $1.00 per page. Court makes copy: $1.00 per page by mail; $.50 in person. Self serve: $.50 per page. Certification fee: $5.00 per cert. Payee: Circuit Clerk. Personal checks accepted; credit cards are not. Prepayment required. Mail requests: SASE required for civil.

Circuit Court - Fort Smith 35 S 6th St, Rm 203, PO Box 1179, Fort Smith, AR 72902; 479-782-1046; fax: 479-784-1580; 8AM-5PM. ***Felony, Civil Actions over $5,000, Probate.***
www.sebastiancountyonline.com
Records from both Circuit Courts-Fort Smith and Greenwood Districts-are on the same computer system, but copies of case files must be pulled from the individual Districts. Closed files in this Circuit are maintained in Fort Smith and Greenwood.
Civil Records: Access: Mail, in person. Visitors must perform in person searches themselves. Search fee: $6.00 per name. Required to search: name, years to search; also helpful: address. Civil cases indexed by defendant, plaintiff, computerized from 1988, on dockets from 1900. Mail turnaround time 1-2 days. Civil PAT goes back to 1988. PAT civil results show middle initial.
Criminal Records: Access: Mail, in person. Visitors must perform in person searches themselves. Search fee: $6.00 per name. Required to search: name, years to search; also helpful: address, DOB, SSN. Criminal records computerized from 1988, on dockets from 1900. Note: Court will only perform searches for criminal justice purposes. Mail turnaround time 1-2 days. Criminal PAT goes back to same as civil. PAT results- middle initial, DOB.
General Information: No juvenile records released. Will fax documents $1.00 per page. Court makes copy: $1.00 per page if mailed, otherwise $.50. Self serve: $.50 per page. Cert fee: $5.00. Payee: Circuit Clerk. Personal checks accepted; credit cards are not. Prepayment required. Mail requests: SASE required.

Fort Smith District Court Courthouse, 35 S 6th St, Fort Smith, AR 72901; 479-784-2420; fax: 479-784-2438; 8:30AM-5PM. ***Misdemeanor, Civil Actions under $25,000, Traffic, Small Claims.***
www.districtcourtfortsmith.org
Civil Records: Access: Phone, fax, mail, in person, online. Both court and visitors may perform in person searches. No search fee. Required to search: full name, years to search. Record stored from 1984. Note: If copies are required, then your request must be in writing. Mail turnaround time 1-2 days. Civil PAT goes back to 1993. PAT results show name only. Access court records free at www.districtcourtfortsmith.org/ and click on Online Records Search.
Criminal Records: Access: Phone, fax, mail, in person, online. Both court and visitors may perform in person searches. No search fee. Required to search: name, years to search, DOB; also helpful: SSN. Records are computerized since 1993. Note: If copies are required, then your request must be in writing. Mail turnaround time 1-2 days. Criminal PAT goes back to same as civil. PAT results show middle initial, DOB. Terminal results include SSN. Access court records free at www.districtcourtfortsmith.org/ and click on Online Records Search.
General Information: Fee to fax document $.25 per page. Court makes copy: $.25 per page. Certification

fee: $5.00 per doc. Payee: Fort Smith District Court. Personal checks accepted. Major credit cards accepted in person only, by person named. Prepayment required. Mail requests: SASE required for mail return of any copies.

Sevier County

Circuit Court 115 N 3rd, Courthouse, De Queen, AR 71832; 870-584-3055; probate phone: 870-642-2852; fax: 870-642-3119; 8AM-4:30PM. ***Felony, Civil Actions over $5,000, Probate.***
Probate index in the same building at County Clerk.
Civil Records: Access: In person only. Visitors must perform in person searches themselves. Required to search: name, years to search. Civil cases indexed by defendant, plaintiff, archived from 1900. Civil PAT goes back to 2003.
Criminal Records: Access: In person only. Visitors must perform in person searches themselves. Required to search: name, years to search. Criminal records index goes back to 1961, prior back to 1912. Criminal PAT goes back to same as civil.
General Information: No juvenile records released. Fee to fax out file $5.00 each; free if to a toll-free number. Court makes copy: $.25 per page, self serve same. Certification fee: $5.00 per document. Payee: Circuit Clerk. Personal checks accepted; credit cards are not. Prepayment required.

District Court 115 N 3rd St, Rm 215, De Queen, AR 71832; 870-584-7311; criminal fax: 870-642-6651; civil fax: same; 8AM-4:30PM. ***Misdemeanor, Civil Actions under $5,000, Eviction, Small Claims.***
Civil Records: Access: Mail, in person. Both court and visitors may perform in person searches. No search fee. Required to search: name, DOB, SSN, address. Records available since 1991. Mail turnaround time 1-2 weeks.
Criminal Records: Access: Mail, in person. Both court and visitors may perform in person searches. No search fee. Required to search: name, years to search, DOB. Records available since 1991. Mail turnaround time 1-2 weeks.
General Information: Will fax documents. Court makes copy for no fee. No cert fee. Payee: District Court. Personal checks accepted; credit cards are not.

Sharp County

Circuit Court PO Box 307, Ash Flat, AR 72513; 870-994-7361; fax: 870-994-7712; 8AM-4PM. ***Felony, Civil Actions over $5,000, Probate.***
Civil Records: Access: Fax, mail, in person, online. Both court and visitors may perform in person searches. Search fee: $6.00 per name. Required to search: name, years to search. Civil cases indexed by defendant, plaintiff, on card files from 1970s. Some records on dockets, computerized since 1986. Mail turnaround time 1 week Civil PAT goes back to 1986. Court has outsourced online access to probate and court orders to www.etitlesearch.com/. data is mostly recorded documents, fees involved.
Criminal Records: Access: In person. Visitors must perform in person searches themselves. Required to search: name, years to search; also helpful: DOB, SSN. Criminal records on card files from 1970s. Some records on dockets, computerized since 1986. Criminal PAT goes back to same as civil.
General Information: No juvenile or expunged records released. No fee to fax documents to toll free numbers only. Court makes copy: $.25 per page. Cert fee: $5.00 per doc. Payee: Sharp County Clerk. Personal checks accepted; credit cards are not. Prepayment required. Mail: SASE required for civil.

District Court PO Box 2, Ash Flat, AR 72513; 870-994-2745; fax: 870-994-7901; 8AM-4PM. ***Misdemeanor, Civil Actions under $5,000, Eviction, Small Claims.***
Civil Records: Access: Mail, in person. Both court and visitors may perform in person searches. No search fee. Records stored from 1991. Mail turnaround time 1 day. Civil PAT goes back to 1991. PAT results show name only.
Criminal Records: Access: Mail, in person. Both court and visitors may perform in person searches. Search fee: $6.00 per name. Required to search: name, years to search; also helpful: DOB, SSN. Records searchable back to 1999. Mail turnaround time 1 day. Criminal PAT goes back to 1999. PAT results show middle initial, DOB. Results may also include DL number and SSN.
General Information: Will fax documents to local or toll-free number. Court makes copy: $.50 per page, self serve same. Certification fee: $2.00 per page. Payee: Sharp County District Court. Personal checks accepted; credit cards are not. Prepayment required. Mail requests: SASE required.

St. Francis County

Circuit Court PO Box 1775, 313 S Izard St #8, Forrest City, AR 72336; 870-261-1715; criminal fax: 870-261-1723; civil fax: same; 8AM-4:30PM. ***Felony, Civil Actions over $5,000, Probate.***
Probate is a separate index at this same address. Probate fax- 870-630-1210.
Civil Records: Access: Fax, mail, in person. Both court and visitors may perform in person searches. Search fee: $5.00 per name. Required to search: name, years to search. Civil cases indexed by defendant, plaintiff, on index from 1982, archived from 1920s. Mail turnaround time same day. Civil PAT available. PAT results show name only.
Criminal Records: Access: In person only. Visitors must perform in person searches themselves. Required to search: name, years to search, DOB, SSN. Criminal records indexed from 1982, archived from 1920s. Note: Court directs criminal searches to AR State Police, phone 501-618-8500. Criminal PAT available. PAT results show name only.
General Information: No juvenile records released. Will fax documents $5.00 fee. Court makes copy: $.25 per page, self serve same. Cert fee: $3.00 per cert includes copy fee. Payee: Circuit Clerk. Personal checks accepted; credit cards are not. Prepayment required. Mail requests: SASE required for civil.

District Court 615 E Cross, Forrest City, AR 72335; 870-261-1410; fax: 870-261-1411; 8AM-4:30PM. ***Misdemeanor, Civil Actions under $5,000, Eviction, Small Claims.***
Civil Records: Access: Mail, in person. Only the court performs in person searches; visitors may not. Search fee: $5.00 per name. Required to search: Name, DOB, also helpful- SSN. Civil cases indexed by defendant, plaintiff, on computer since 1994. Mail turnaround time 5 days.
Criminal Records: Access: Mail, in person. Only the court performs in person searches; visitors may not. Search fee: $5.00 per name. Required to search: name, years to search. Criminal records on computer since 1990. Mail turnaround time 5 days.
General Information: Will fax documents. Court makes copy: $.25 per page. Certification fee: $5.00 per doc. Payee: District Court. No Personal checks and major credit cards accepted. Prepayment required. Mail requests: SASE required.

Stone County

Circuit Court 107 W Mail #D, Mountain View, AR 72560; 870-269-3271; fax: 870-269-2303; 8AM-4:30PM. ***Felony, Civil Actions over $5,000, Probate.*** www.16thdistrictark.org
Civil Records: Access: In person only. Visitors must perform in person searches themselves. Required to search: name, years to search. Civil cases indexed by defendant, plaintiff, on dockets from 1960s; computerized records since 1992. Note: Mountain View Abstract Corp does searches by mail. Call 870-269-3470. Civil PAT goes back to 1992.
Criminal Records: Access: In person only. Visitors must perform in person searches themselves. Required to search: name, years to search, DOB; SSN helpful. Criminal docket index from 1960s; computerized records since 1992. Criminal PAT goes back to same as civil.
General Information: No juvenile or adoption records released. Court makes copy: $.25 per page, self serve same. Certification fee: $5.00 per document. Payee: Stone County Clerk. Personal checks accepted; credit cards are not. Prepayment required.

District Court 107 W Main, #H, Mountain View, AR 72560; 870-269-3465; fax: same; 8AM-4:30PM. ***Misdemeanor, Civil Actions under $5,000, Eviction, Small Claims.***
Civil Records: Access: Phone, fax, mail, in person. Both court and visitors may perform in person searches. No search fee. Required to search: names used, years to search. Civil cases indexed by case number. Records available since 1984, not computerized. Mail turnaround time varies.
Criminal Records: Access: Phone, fax, mail, in person. Both court and visitors may perform in person searches. No search fee. Required to search: name, years to search; also helpful: DOB, SSN. Records on computer since 1990. Mail turnaround time varies.
General Information: Will fax documents to local or toll-free number. Court makes copy: $.50 per page, self serve same. Certification fee: $5.00 per doc. Payee: District Court. No personal checks or credit cards accepted. Prepayment required.

Union County

Circuit Court PO Box 1626, El Dorado, AR 71730; 870-864-1940; probate phone: 870-864-1910; fax: 870-864-1994; 8:30AM-5PM. ***Felony, Civil Actions over $5,000, Probate.***
Civil Records: Access: In person, online. Visitors must perform in person searches themselves. Required to search: name, years to search. Civil cases indexed by defendant, plaintiff, on computer back to 1996 on dockets from 1800s. Civil PAT goes back to 1999. PAT results show name only. Online access to circuit court dockets by subscription through RecordsUSA.com. Credit card, username and password is required; choose either monthly or per-use plan. Visit the website for sign-up or call Lisa at 601-264-7701 for information.
Criminal Records: Access: In person, online. Visitors must perform in person searches themselves. Required to search: name, years to search, DOB; also helpful: SSN. Criminal records computerized from 1996 on dockets from 1800s. Criminal PAT goes back to same as civil. PAT results show name only. Online access to criminal dockets is the same as civil. Online results show name only.
General Information: Online identifiers in results same as on public terminal. No juvenile records released. Will fax out specific case files for $1.00 per page. Court makes copy: $.50 per page, self serve same. Certification fee: $3.00. Payee: Circuit Clerk. Personal checks accepted; credit cards are not. Prepayment required.

District Court 250 American #A, El Dorado, AR 71730; 870-864-1950; fax: 870-864-1955; 8:30AM-5PM. ***Misdemeanor, Civil Actions under $5,000, Eviction, Small Claims.***
Civil Records: Access: In person, fax, mail. Both court and visitors may perform in person searches. No search fee. Required to search: name. Computerized records since 1987. Mail turnaround time 1-2 days. Civil PAT goes back to 1987.
Criminal Records: Access: In person, fax, mail. Both court and visitors may perform in person searches. No search fee. Required to search: name, years to search, DOB; also helpful: SSN. Computerized records since 1987. Mail turnaround 1-2 days. Criminal PAT goes back to same as civil.
General Information: Will fax back documents. Court makes copy for no fee. No certification fee. No personal checks or credit cards accepted.

Van Buren County

Circuit Court 451 Main St, Clinton, AR 72031; 501-745-4140; fax: 501-745-7400; 8AM-5PM. ***Felony, Civil Actions over $5,000, Probate.***
Civil Records: Access: Mail, in person. Visitors must perform in person searches themselves. Search fee: $1.00. Required to search: name, years to search; also helpful: address. Civil cases on computer from 1987, archived from 1900s. Mail turnaround time 7-10 days. Civil PAT goes back to 1987. PAT results show name only.
Criminal Records: Access: Mail, in person. Both court and visitors may perform in person searches. Search fee: $1.00 per name. Required to search: name, years to search; also helpful: address, DOB, SSN. Criminal records computerized from 1987, archived from 1900s. Mail turnaround time 7-10

days. Criminal PAT goes back to 1987. PAT results show name only.
General Information: No juvenile or adoption records released. Will fax documents to local or toll free line. Court makes copy: $.50 per page, self serve same. Certification fee: $5.00. Payee: Van Buren County Clerk's Office. Personal checks accepted; credit cards are not. Prepayment required. Mail requests: SASE required.

District Court 339 Boykin St, Clinton, AR 72031; 501-745-8894; criminal fax: 501-745-5810; civil fax: same; 8AM-5PM. ***Misdemeanor, Civil Actions under $5,000, Small Claims.***
Civil Records: Access: Phone, mail, fax, in person. Visitors must perform in person searches themselves. No search fee. Required to search: name, years to search, DOB. Civil records on computer back to 1992; in books back to 1992.
Criminal Records: Access: Phone, mail, fax, in person. Both court and visitors may perform in person searches. Search fee: $5.00 per name. Required to search: name, years to search, DOB, SSN; also helpful-docket or ticket number. Criminal records computerized from 1992; in books back to 1992; computerized since 1992. Mail turnaround time is 1 week.
General Information: Will fax documents. Certification fee: $5.00 per doc. Payee: Clinton District Court. Personal checks accepted; credit cards are not. Prepayment required.

Washington County

Circuit Court 280 N College, #302, Fayetteville, AR 72701; 479-444-1538; probate phone: 479-444-1711; fax: 479-444-1537; 8AM-4:30PM. ***Felony, Civil Actions over $5,000, Probate.*** www.co.washington.ar.us Probate is a separate index in the County Clerk's office.
Civil Records: Access: Fax, mail, in person, online. Visitors must perform in person searches themselves. No search fee. Required to search: name, years to search. Civil cases indexed by defendant, plaintiff, on computer from 1992, on index from 1950. Civil PAT goes back to 1992. Online case index at www.co.washington.ar.us/resolution/. Civil cases indexed from 1992 forward. This is a commercial system, fee is $50.00 per month prepaid. Search pre-1973 court indices free at www.co.washington.ar.us/ArchiveSearch/CourtRecordSearch.asp.
Criminal Records: Access: In person, online. Visitors must perform in person searches themselves. Required to search: name, years to search. Criminal records computerized from 1992, on index from 1950. Note: This court will not do criminal record name searches and refers requests to the state police. Criminal PAT goes back to 1992. Online case index at www.co.washington.ar.us/resolution/. Criminal cases indexed from 1992 forward. This is a commercial system, fee is $50.00 per month prepaid. Pre-1933 criminal court indices free at www.co.washington.ar.us/ArchiveSearch/CourtRecordSearch.asp. Note that these cases are very old.
General Information: No juvenile records released. Will fax documents $5.00 per doc. Court makes copy: $.15 per page, self serve same. Certification fee: $5.00 per document includes copy fee. Payee: Circuit Clerk. Personal checks accepted; credit cards are not. Prepayment required. Mail requests: SASE required.

Fayetteville District Court 100 B W Rock, Fayetteville, AR 72701; 479-587-3596; fax: 479-444-3480; 8AM-5PM. ***Misdemeanor, Civil Actions under $5,000, Small Claims.*** www.co.washington.ar.us
Civil Records: Access: Phone, mail, fax, in person. Both court and visitors may perform in person searches. Search fee: $5.00 per name. Required to search: name, years to search. Civil records on computer go back to 1984. Mail turnaround 1 week.
Criminal Records: Access: Mail, in person. Only the court performs in person searches; visitors may not. Search fee: $5.00 per name. Required to search: name, years to search, DOB, SSN, signed release; also helpful: address. Criminal records on computer go back to 1984. Mail turnaround time 1 week.
General Information: Will fax documents no charge. Court makes copy: $5.00 per document. No certification fee. Payee: City of Fayetteville. Personal checks accepted. SASE not required.

White County

Circuit Court 301 W Arch, Searcy, AR 72143; 501-279-6223; probate phone: 501-279-6204; criminal fax: 501-279-6218; civil fax: same; 8AM-4:30PM. ***Felony, Civil Actions over $5,000, Probate.*** Probate is a separate office, address is Courthouse Sq, Searcy, AR 72143. Records in this court are not computerized.
Civil Records: Access: Mail, in person. Both court and visitors may perform in person searches. Search fee: $6.00 per name. Required to search: name, years to search; also helpful: address. Records book indexed back to 2000. Mail turnaround 1 day.
Criminal Records: Access: Mail, in person. Both court and visitors may perform in person searches. Search fee: $6.00 per name. Required to search: name, years to search, DOB, SSN; also helpful: address. Criminal docket on books back to 1982. Note: All requests must be in writing, even if in person. Mail turnaround time 1 day.
General Information: No juvenile records released. Will fax documents $1.00 per page. Court makes copy: $.50 per page, self serve same. Certification fee: $2.50 per certification. Payee: Circuit Clerk. Personal checks accepted; credit cards are not. Prepayment required. Mail requests: SASE required.

Searcy District Court PO Box 958, 1600 E Booth Rd, Searcy, AR 72145; 501-279-1040, 268-7622; fax: 501-305-4638; 8AM-4:30PM. ***Misdemeanor, Civil Actions under $5,000, Small Claims.*** www.cityofsearcy.org
On 1/27/05 the courthouse burned down and a significant amount of records were lost. Clerk now located in White County Law Enforcement Bldg.
Civil Records: Access: Mail, fax, phone, in person. Only the court performs in person searches; visitors may not. Search fee: $6.00 per name. Required to search: name plus SSN, years to search. Records on computer back to 6/1995; older records destroyed by fire. Mail turnaround time 5 days.
Criminal Records: Access: In person, phone, fax, mail. Only the court performs in person searches; visitors may not. Search fee: $6.00 per name. Required to search: name, years to search, DOB, SSN. Records on computer back to 6/1995; older records destroyed by fire. Mail turnaround 5 days.
General Information: Will fax documents. Court makes copy: $.50 per page. No certification fee. Payee: Searcy District Court for civil; City of Searcy for criminal. Instate personal checks accepted. No credit cards accepted. Prepayment required. Mail requests: SASE requested.

Woodruff County

Circuit Court PO Box 492, 500 N 3rd St, Augusta, AR 72006; 870-347-2391; probate phone: 870-347-2871; fax: 870-347-8703; 8AM-4PM. ***Felony, Civil Actions over $5,000.***
Probate is handled by the County Clerk.
Civil Records: Access: In person only. Both court and visitors may perform in person searches. No search fee. Required to search: name, years to search. Civil cases indexed by defendant, plaintiff, on dockets from 1982.
Criminal Records: Access: In person only. Both court and visitors may perform in person searches. No search fee. Required to search: name, years to search, DOB. Criminal docket index from 1980.
General Information: No juvenile records released. Will fax documents $1.00 per page. Court makes copy: $1.00 per page. Self serve: $.50 per page. Cert fee: $5.00. Payee: Circuit Clerk. Personal checks accepted; credit cards are not. Prepayment required.

District Court PO Box 381, Augusta, AR 72006; 870-347-2790; fax: 870-347-2436; 8:30AM-5PM. ***Misdemeanor, Civil Actions under $5,000, Eviction, Small Claims.***
Civil Records: Access: Mail, in person. Only the court performs in person searches; visitors may not. No search fee. Required to search: name. Civil cases indexed by defendant, plaintiff. Computerized records go back to 1995. Mail turnaround 10 days.
Criminal Records: Access: Mail, in person. Only the court performs in person searches; visitors may not. No search fee. Required to search: name, years to search, DOB, signed release. Computerized records go back to 1995. Mail turnaround time 10 days.
General Information: No fee to fax documents. Court makes copy: $.25 per page. No certification fee. Payee: Woodruff District Court. Personal checks accepted; credit cards are not. Prepayment required. Mail requests: SASE required.

Yell County

Danville Circuit Court PO Box 219, Danville, AR 72833; 479-495-4850; criminal fax: 479-495-4875; civil fax: same; 8AM-4PM. ***Felony, Civil Actions over $5,000, Probate.***
Probate is a separate index at this same address. Probate fax is same as main fax number.
Civil Records: Access: Mail, fax, in person. Both court and visitors may perform in person searches. Search fee: $6.00 per name. Required to search: name, years to search; also helpful: address. Civil cases indexed by defendant. Civil records on dockets from 1900s. Mail turnaround time 1 day. Civil PAT goes back to 1946. PAT results show middle initial, DOB, SSN.
Criminal Records: Access: Mail, fax, in person. Both court and visitors may perform in person searches. Search fee: $6.00 per name. Required to search: name, years to search, DOB; also helpful: address. Criminal docket index from 1900s. Mail turnaround time 1 day. Criminal PAT goes back to 1918. PAT results show middle initial, DOB, SSN.
General Information: No juvenile or adoption records released. Will fax documents $3.00 if file is lengthy. Court makes copy: $.25 per page, self serve same. Certification fee: $5.00 per document. Payee: Circuit Clerk of Yell County. Personal checks accepted; credit cards are not. Prepayment required. Mail requests: SASE required.

Dardanelle Circuit Court County Courthouse, 108 Union St, #105, Dardanelle, AR 72834; 479-229-4404; fax: 479-229-5634; 8AM-4PM. ***Felony, Civil Actions over $5,000, Probate.***
Civil Records: Access: Mail, in person. Both court and visitors may perform in person searches. Search fee: $6.00 per name. Required to search: name, years to search. Civil cases indexed by defendant. Civil records on dockets from 1800s. Mail turnaround time 1 day. Civil PAT goes back to - cases currently being scanned; incomplete.
Criminal Records: Access: Mail, in person. Both court and visitors may perform in person searches. Search fee: $6.00 per name. Required to search: name, years to search; also helpful: DOB. Criminal docket index from 1800s. Mail turnaround time 1 day. Criminal PAT goes back to - cases currently being scanned; incomplete.
General Information: No adoption or juvenile records released. Will fax documents $3.00 each. Court makes copy: $.25 per page, self serve same. Certification fee: $5.00 per doc. Payee: Circuit Clerk of Yell County. Personal checks accepted; credit cards are not. Prepayment required. SASE required.

District Court County Courthouse, Dardanelle, AR 72834; 479-229-1389; fax: 479-229-5740; 8AM-4PM. ***Misdemeanor, Civil Actions under $5,000, Eviction, Small Claims.***
Civil Records: Access: Mail, in person. Both court and visitors may perform in person searches. Search fee: $3.00 per name. Civil records go back to 1982. Mail turnaround time 2-4 days.
Criminal Records: Access: Mail, in person. Both court and visitors may perform in person searches. Search fee: $3.00 per name. Required to search: name, years to search, signed release; also helpful: address, DOB, SSN. Criminal records go back to 1982, on computer back to 1994. Mail turnaround time 2-4 days.
General Information: Will fax documents to local or toll free line. Court makes copy: $.25 per page. No certification fee. Payee: District Court. No credit cards accepted. Prepayment required.

Arkansas Recording Offices

ORGANIZATION: 75 counties, 85 recording offices. The recording officer is the Clerk of Circuit Court who is Ex Officio Recorder. Ten counties have two recording offices - Arkansas, Carroll, Clay, Craighead, Franklin, Logan, Mississippi, Prairie, Sebastian, Yell; see notes for each county for how to determine which office to search. Arkansas is in the Central Time Zone.

REAL ESTATE RECORDS: Most counties do not perform real estate searches. Copy fees fees vary but certification fee is usually $5.00 per doc.

UCC RECORDS: Prior to July, 2001 Arkansas was a dual filing state. Financing statements were filed at the state level and with the Circuit Clerk, except for consumer goods, farm and real estate related collateral which were filed only with the Circuit Clerk. Now all financing statements are filed at the state level except for real estate related collateral which is still filed with the Circuit Clerk. Fewer and fewer counties will perform UCC searches. Use search request form UCC-11. UCC search fees are usually $6.00 per debtor name. Copy fees vary.

TAX LIEN RECORDS: Federal tax liens on personal property of businesses are filed with the Secretary of State. Other federal and all state tax liens are filed with the Circuit Clerk. Many counties will perform separate tax lien searches. Tax lien search fees are usually $6.00 per name.

OTHER LIENS: Mechanics, lis pendens, judgments, hospital, child support, materialman.

ONLINE ACCESS: Statewide access to UCC info is at https://www.ark.org/sos/ucc/index.php. There is no statewide access to assessor data; however, all counties cooperate with at least one commercial vendor. Registration and login is required to search assessor records for 41 counties at www.arcountydata.com. Signup fee is $200 plus $.10 per minute usage but 15 counties offers some free access. For signup or information call 479-631-8054 or visit at the web. Also, several counties are now on the new Citrix system - registration and logon is required to search assessor records on Citrix. Also, access property data free for 25 counties at www.actdatascout.com. Subscription for deeper info is $20 per month. 50% discount on add'l counties. Also, 53 counties are available at www.datascoutpro.com/ by various subscription plans up to $150 monthly for all.

Arkansas County (Northern District)

County Circuit Clerk, 302 S College St., Stuttgart, AR 72160. Recording, R/E & UCC phone-870-673-2056; fax-870-673-3869; 8AM-4:30PM (CST)

Index: Separate indices to search include computer, books if before 1996. Records indexed on a public use terminal back to 1996. Office will perform a UCC search but public must search other records themselves. Office will not search real estate records. UCC search per debtor name- $6.00. Copy fee $.50 per page. Will fax back for $1.00 per page. Cert fee- $5.00 per doc includes copy fee. Payee- Arkansas County Circuit Clerk. **Property tax/Assessing**- 312 S College, Stuttgart, AR 72160; 870-673-6586, assessor fax- 870-673-0044. **Online access**- Registration and logon is required to search assessor records at www.arcountydata.com. Signup fee is $200 plus $.10 per minute usage. For signup or info call 479-631-8054 or visit the website.

Arkansas County (Southern District)

County Circuit Clerk, 101 Court Sq, De Witt, AR 72042. Recording, R/E & UCC phone-870-946-4219; fax-870-946-1394; 8AM-4:30PM (CST)

Index: Books, computer. Records indexed on a public use terminal back to 1996. Office will perform a UCC search (only current/active) but public must search other records themselves. No fee for search. Copy fee $.50 per copy. $1.00 for fax copy. Cert fee- $5.00 plus copy fee. Payee- Arkansas County Circuit Clerk. **Other phones:** Treasurer- 870-946-4210; Elections- 870-846-4349; Tax Collector- 870-946-2911. **Property tax/Assessing**- 101 Court Sq, De Witt, AR 72042; 870-946-1795. hours- 8AM-N, 12:30-4:30PM **Online access**- Registration and logon is required to search assessor records at www.arcountydata.com. Signup fee is $200 plus $.10 per minute usage. For signup or info call 479-631-8054 or visit the website.

Ashley County

County Circuit Clerk, 205 E Jefferson St; Courthouse, Hamburg, AR 71646. Recording, R/E & UCC phone- 870-853-2030; fax-870-853-2034; 8AM-4:30PM (CST)

Index: All in one. Record index not computerized. Only the public may search. Copy fee $.50 per page. Cert fee- $5.00 per doc plus copy fee. Payee- Ashley County Circuit Clerk. Office does not sell bulk data. **Other phones:** Treasurer- 870-853-2010; Elections- 870-853-2020; Tax Collector- 870-853-2050. **Property tax/Assessing**- 205 E Jefferson, Box #2, Hamburg, AR 71646; 870-853-2060, assessor fax- 870-853-2002. **Online access**- Access property data free at www.actdatascout.com. Subscription for deeper info is $20 per month.

Baxter County

County Circuit Clerk, 1 E 7th St, #103; Courthouse Sq, Mountain Home, AR 72653. 870-425-3475; fax- 870-424-5105; 8AM-4:30PM (CST)

Index: All in one. Records indexed on a public use terminal back to 9/95. Office will perform a UCC search but public must search other records themselves. Search fee-$6.00 per name. Copy fee $1.00 per page. Cert fee- $5.00 per doc plus copy fee. Payee- Baxter County Circuit Clerk. Office does not sell bulk data. **Online access to Real Estate, Deed records:** Access recording office land data at www.etitlesearch.com; registration required, fee based on usage. **Other phones:** Tax Collector- 870-425-3444. **Property tax/Assessing**- 6 E 7th St, Mountain Home, AR 72653; 870-425-3453. **Online access**- Registration and logon is required to search assessor records on Citrix system at www.arcountydata.com. Signup fee is $200 plus $.10 per minute usage. For signup or info call 479-631-8054 or visit the website.

Benton County

County Circuit Clerk, 215 E Central St, #6, Bentonville, AR 72712. Recording, R/E & UCC phone-479-271-1015; fax-479-271-5719; 8AM-5PM (CST) www.co.benton.ar.us

Index: Separate indices to search include deed, mortgage books. Records indexed on a public use terminal back to 1990. Only the public may search. Copy fee $.25 per page. Cert fee- $5.00 per page includes copy fee. Payee- Benton County Circuit Clerk. Office does not sell bulk data. **Online access to Real Estate, Deed, Lien, Plat, Judgment, Medical Lien records:** County recorder, medical liens, plats and circuit court data is free at www.benton.ar.us.landata.com/default.asp or phone 888-85-IMAGE. $49.95/$79.90 or monthly. Also, land records at http://etitlesearch.com; call 870-856-3055 for subscription info. **Other phones:** Treasurer- 479-271-1018; Elections- 479-271-1013; Tax Collector- 479-271-1040. **Property tax/Assessing**- 215 E Central, Bentonville, AR 72712; 479-271-1037. www.co.benton.ar.us **Online access**- Search property and personal property tax data free at www.countyservice.net/bentax.asp. Search and pay taxes free at http://collector.co.benton.ar.us/searchpay.html#. Also,search index free at www.arcountydata.com/county.asp?county=Benton. Also, register and logon required to search full assessor records, for info, call 479-631-8054.

Boone County

County Circuit Clerk, 100 N Main, #200; Courthouse, Harrison, AR 72601. Recording, R/E & UCC phone- 870-741-5560; fax-870-741-4335; 8AM-4:30PM

Index: Separate indices to search include land & court records are indexed on the computer as of mid 1990. UCCs in a card index file. Older records for land & court are indexed in books. Records indexed on a public use terminal back to 1990. Only the public may search. Copy fee $.25 per page. Cert fee- $5.00 per doc includes copy fee. Payee- Boone County Circuit Clerk. **Online access to Real Estate, Deed records:** Land records are at http://etitlesearch.com. You can do a name search; choose from $45.00 monthly subscription or per click account. **Other phones:** Treasurer- 870-741-3068; Elections- 870-741-8428; Tax Collector- 870-741-6646; Marriages -870-741-8428;. **Property tax/Assessing**- PO Box 2425, Harrison, AR 72602; 870-741-3783, assessor fax-870-741-2937. A public access terminal available. **Online access**- Registration and logon is required to search all participating counties' assessor records at www.arcountydata.com. Signup fee is $200 minimum plus $.10 per minute usage. For signup or info call 479-631-8054 or visit www.arcountydata.com.

Bradley County

County Circuit Clerk, 101 E Cedar St; Courthouse, Warren, AR 71671. Recording, R/E & UCC phone-870-226-2272; fax-870-226-8401; 8AM-4:30PM

Index: Separate indices to search include mortgages, deeds. Record index not computerized. Only the public may search. Copy fee $.50 per page. Cert fee-$5.00 per doc plus copy fee. Payee- Bradley County Circuit Clerk. **Other phones:** Treasurer- 870-226-8402; Elections- 870-226-3464. **Property tax/Assessing**- 101 E Cedar St, #8, Warren, AR 71671; 870-226-2211, assessor fax- 870-226-5179. **Online access**- Registration and logon is required to search assessor records at www.arcountydata.com. Signup fee is $200 plus $.10 per minute usage. For signup or info call 479-631-8054 or visit the website.

Calhoun County

County Circuit Clerk, PO Box 1175, Hampton, AR 71744. Recording, R/E & UCC phone-870-798-2517; fax-870-798-2428; 8AM-4:30. (CST)

Index: Separate indices to search. Records indexed on a public use terminal back to 0501/1975. Office personnel or visitors may perform searches. General search fee $.50 per name. Will search UCC records at $6.00 per name. Copy fee $.25 per page. Cert fee-$5.00 per doc includes copy fee. Payee- Calhoun County Circuit Clerk. Office does not sell bulk data. **Other phones:** Treasurer- 870-798-2827; Tax Collector- 870-798-2357. **Property tax/Assessing**- PO Box 276, Hampton, AR 71744; 870-798-2740, assessor fax- 870-798-2352. **Online access**- Search property database at www.arcountydata.com. Login and password required. There is a one-time, $200 setup charge to create a new account, access is charged at 10¢ per minute.

Carroll County (Eastern District)

County Circuit Clerk, PO Box 71, Berryville, AR 72616. Recording, R/E & UCC phone-870-423-2422; fax-870-423-4796; 8:30AM-4:30PM (CST)

Index: Separate indices to search include deeds, mortgages, UCCs, judgments, liens. Records indexed on a public use terminal back to 1997. Deeds and mortgage go back to 1989. Office will perform a UCC search but public must search other records themselves. Search fee $6.00 per name. Copy fee $.25 per page. If typing is required, fee is $5.00 per page. Cert fee- $5.00 per doc; if exceeds 2 pages, add $.25 per page copy fee. Payee- Carroll County Circuit Clerk. Office does sell bulk data on CD's, contact Bob. **Other phones:** Treasurer- 870-423-3189; Elections- 870-423-2022; Vital Records- 870-423-2022; Tax Collector- 870-423-2867. **Property tax/Assessing**- 108 Spring St, Berryville, AR 72616; 870-423-2388, assessor fax- 870-423-2529. (Appraiser/Auditor- 870-423-3991) **Online access**- Access property data free at www.actdatascout.com. Subscription for deeper info is $20 per month. Also, with registration and logon you may search assessor records on Citrix system at www.arcountydata.com. Signup fee is $200 plus $.10 per minute usage. For signup or info call 479-631-8054 or visit the website.

Carroll County (Western District)

County Circuit Clerk, PO Box 109, Eureka Springs, AR 72632. 479-253-8646, R/E recording phone-870-423-2422; fax-479-253-6013; 8:30AM-4:30PM

Index: Separate indices to search. Records indexed on a public use terminal back to 10/1997. Office will perform a UCC or tax lien search but public must search other records themselves. Search fee $6.00. Copy fee $.25 per page. Cert fee- $5.00 per doc. Payee- Carroll County Circuit Clerk. Office does not sell bulk data. **Other phones:** Treasurer- 870-423-3189; Elections- 870-423-2022; Vital Records- 870-423-2022 (marriage); Tax Collector- 870-423-2867. **Property tax/Assessing**- 108 Spring St, Berryville, AR 72616; 870-423-6400, 423-2388, assessor fax-870-423-2529. (Appraiser/Auditor- 870-423-3991) **Online access**- Access property data free at www.actdatascout.com. Subscription for deeper info is $20 per month. Also, with registration and logon you may search assessor records on Citrix system at www.arcountydata.com. Signup fee is $200 plus $.10 per minute usage. For signup or info call 479-631-8054 or visit website.

Chicot County

County Circuit Clerk, 108 Main St; Courthouse, Lake Village, AR 71653. 870-265-8010, R/E recording phone-870-265-236; fax-870-265-8012; 8AM-4:30PM (CST)

Index: All in one. Record index not computerized. Office will perform a UCC and Tax lien search but public must search other records themselves. Search fee-$6.00 per name. Office will not search real estate records. Copy fee $.50 per page. Cert fee- $5.00 per doc plus copy fee. Payee- Chicot County Circuit Clerk. Office does not sell bulk data. **Other phones:** Tax Collector- 870-265-8040. **Property tax/Assessing**- 108 Main St, Courthouse, Lake Village, AR 71653; 870-265-8025, assessor fax- 870-265-8046. **Online access**- Registration and logon is required to search assessor records on Citrix system at www.arcountydata.com. Signup fee is $200 plus $.10 per minute usage. For signup or info call 479-631-8054 or visit the website.

Clark County

County Circuit Clerk, PO Box 576, Arkadelphia, AR 71923. Recording, R/E & UCC phone-870-246-4281; fax-870-246-1419; 8:30AM-4:30PM (CST) www.clarkcountyarkansas.com

Index: All in one. Records indexed on a public use terminal back to 1985; paper index back to 1821. Office personnel or visitors may perform searches. Search fee $5.00 per name payable in advance. Office will not search real estate records. Office will not search UCC records. Copy fee $1.00 per page, $.25 self serve. Will fax back copy for $1.00 per page. Cert fee- $5.00 per doc includes copy fee. Payee- Clark County Circuit Clerk. Office does not sell bulk data. **Other phones:** Treasurer- 870-246-4361; Elections-870-246-4491; Tax Collector- 870-246-2211. **Property tax/Assessing**- 401 Clay St, Arkadelphia, AR 71923; 870-246-4431, assessor fax- 870-246-1421. www.clarkcountyarkansas.com **Online access**- Access property data free at www.actdatascout.com/default.aspx?ci=3. Subscription required for deeper info is $20 per month. Search by: Property ID, Parcel, Name, Property Address, Subdivision, S-T-R.

Clay County (Eastern District)

County Circuit Clerk, 151 S 2nd St, Piggott, AR 72454. Recording, R/E & UCC phone-870-598-2524; fax-870-598-1107; 8AM-N, 1-4:30PM (CST)

Index: Separate indices to search include real estate, judgments. Records indexed on a public use terminal back to 2005. Only the public may search. General search fee $6.00 per name, but no RE or UCCs. Copy fee $.25 per page. Cert fee- $5.00 per doc includes copies. Payee- Clay County Circuit Clerk. Office does not sell bulk data. **Other phones:** Treasurer- 870-598-3879; Elections- 870-598-2813; Vital Records- 870-598-2813. **Property tax/Assessing**- 151 S 2nd St, Piggott, AR 72454; 870-598-3870, assessor fax- 870-598-5609. **Online access**- Registration and logon is required to search assessor records on Citrix system at www.arcountydata.com. Signup fee is $200 plus $.10 per minute usage. For signup or info call 479-631-8054 or visit the website.

Clay County (Western District)

County Circuit Clerk, 800 SW 2nd St, Corning, AR 72422. 870-857-3271; fax-870-857-9201; 8AM-N, 1PM-4:30PM (CST)

Index: Separate indices to search include books, computer. Records indexed on a public use terminal back to 1/2005. Only the public may search. Copy fee $1.00 per page, self serve $.25. Cert fee- $5.00 per doc plus copy fee. Payee- Clay County Circuit Clerk. **Other phones:** Tax Collector- 870-855-3011. **Property tax/Assessing**- 800 W 2nd St, Corning, AR 72422; 870-857-3133, assessor fax- 870-857-0096. **Online access**- Search at www.arcountydata.com. Login and password required. There is a one-time, $200 setup charge to create a new account, access is charged at 10¢ per minute.

Cleburne County

County Circuit Clerk, PO Box 543, Heber Springs, AR 72543. Recording, R/E & UCC phone-501-362-8149; fax-501-362-4681; 8:30AM-4:30PM (CST)

Index: All in one. Records indexed on a public use terminal back to 1994. Office will perform a UCC search but public must search other records themselves. Search fee $6.00. Copy fee $.50 per page. Fax fee $4.00 1st page, $1.00 each add'l. Cert fee-$5.00 per doc plus copy fee. Payee- Cleburne County Circuit Clerk. Old deed books back to 1/19988 available to purchase, contact Deputy Clerk Donna Powell. **Other phones:** Treasurer- 501-362-8124; Elections- 501-362-4620; Tax Collector- 501-362-8145. **Property tax/Assessing**- 320 W Main St, Heber Springs, AR 72543; 501-362-8147, assessor fax- 501-362-4651. **Online access**- Access property data free at www.actdatascout.com. Subscription for deeper info is $20 per month.

Cleveland County

County Circuit Clerk, PO Box 368, Rison, AR 71665. Recording, R/E & UCC phone-870-325-6521; fax-870-325-6144; 8AM-4:30PM (CST)

Index: Separate indices to search include deeds and mortgages. Records indexed on a public use terminal back to 1990 for deeds and 1994 for mortgages. Only the public may search. Copy fee $.25 per page. Cert fee- $5.00 per doc plus copy fee. Payee- Cleveland County Circuit Clerk. Office does not sell bulk data. **Other phones:** Treasurer- 870-325-6681; Elections-870-325-6521; Tax Collector- 870-325-6681. **Property tax/Assess-ing**- PO Box 391, Rison, AR 71665; 870-325-6695.

Columbia County

County Circuit Clerk, PO Box 327, Magnolia, AR 71754. Recording, R/E & UCC phone-870-235-3700; fax-870-235-3786; 8AM-4:30PM (CST) www.countyofcolumbia.net/circuit-clerk/

Index: All in one except for juvenile. Records indexed on a public use terminal back to 1997. Only the public may search. Copy fee $1.00 per page. Cert fee- $5.00 per page plus copy fee. For UCC's $12.00 plus $.50 each add'l page. Deeds and mortgages $15.00. Payee- Columbia County Circuit Clerk. Office does not sell bulk data. **Other phones:** Treasurer- 870-235-3704; Elections- 870-235-3774; Vital Records- Little Rock; Tax Collector- 870-235-4171. **Property tax/Assessing**- 101 County Annex, S Court Sq, Magnolia, AR 71753; 870-234-4380. (Appraiser/Auditor- 870-234-4380) **Online access**- Search at www.arcountydata.com. Login and password required. There is a one-time, $200 setup charge to create a new account, access is charged at 10¢ per minute. Also, search property and tax records free at www.countyofcolumbia.net/circuit-clerk/.

Conway County

County Circuit Clerk, 115 S Moose St, Rm 206; County Courthouse, Morrilton, AR 72110. Recording, R/E & UCC phone-501-354-9617; fax-501-354-9612; 8AM-4:30PM (CST)

Index: Separate indices to search include deeds, Mtgs, misc, oil and gas, UCCs. Records indexed on a public use terminal back to 1994. Only the public may search. Copy fee $1.00 per page. Cert fee- $5.00 per doc includes copy fee. Payee- Conway County Circuit Clerk. Bulk data available for purchase through the Circuit Clerk office. **Other phones:** Treasurer- 501-354-9623; Elections- 501-354-9621; Tax Collector- 501-354-9600. **Property tax/Assessing**- 117 S Moose St, Morrilton, AR 72110; 501-354-9622, assessor fax- 501-354-9605. **Online access**- Access property data free at www.actdatascout.com. Subscription for deeper info is $20 per month.

Craighead County (Eastern District)

County Circuit Clerk, PO Box 537, Lake City, AR 72437. Recording, R/E & UCC phone-870-237-4342; fax-870-237-8174; 8AM-5PM (CST)
Index: Separate indices to search include deeds, mtgs. Records indexed on a public use terminal back to 1979. Office will perform a UCC search but public must search other records themselves. Search fee $6.00. Office will not search real estate records. Copy fee $.25 per page. UCC copies- $5.00 per instrument. Cert fee- $5.00 per doc plus copy fee. Payee- Craighead County Circuit Clerk. **Online access to Real Estate, Deed, Property records:** Access recording office land data at www.etitlesearch.com; registration required, fee based on usage. **Property tax/Assessing**- 511 Union, Ste 130, Jonesboro, AR 72401; 870-933-4572, assessor fax- 870-933-4522. **Online access**- Search property and personal property data free at www.countyservice.net/assess.asp?id=cratax. Also, with address, search property tax records free at www.arcountydata.com/county.asp?county=Craighead. Or, registration and logon is required to search assessor records at www.arcountydata.com. Signup fee is $200 plus $.10 per minute usage. For signup or info call 479-631-8054 or visit the website.

Craighead County (Western District)

County Circuit Clerk, PO Box 120, Jonesboro, AR 72401. 870-933-4530; fax-870-933-4534; 8AM-5PM (CST) www.craigheadcounty.org
Index: All in one. Records indexed on a public use terminal back to 1974. Deeds from 1985 to present. Only the public may search. Copy fee $.25 per page. Cert fee- $5.00 per doc includes copy fee. Payee- Craighead County Circuit Clerk. Office does sell bulk data on CD's, contact Ann Hudson. **Online access to Real Estate, Deed, Lien records:** Access recording office land data at www.etitlesearch.com; registration required, fee based on usage. **Other phones:** Treasurer- 870-933-4549; Elections- 870-933-4520; Tax Collector- 870-933-4560. **Property tax/Assessing**- 511 Union St, Jonesboro, AR 72401; 870-933-4570, assessor fax- 870-933-4522. **Online access**- Search property and personal property data free at www.countyservice.net/assess.asp?id=cratax. Also, with address, search property tax records free at www.arcountydata.com/county.asp?county=Craighead. Or, registration and logon is required to search assessor records at www.arcountydata.com. Signup fee is $200 plus $.10 per minute usage. For signup or info call 479-631-8054 or visit the website.

Crawford County

County Circuit Clerk, 300 Main, Rm 22; Courthouse, Van Buren, AR 72956-5799. Recording, R/E & UCC phone-479-474-1821; fax-479-471-0622; 8AM-5PM (CST) www.crawford-county.org/
Index: Separate indices to search include computer index and non-computer index. Records indexed on a public use terminal back to 1988. Office personnel or visitors may perform searches. Office will search real estate records. Copy fee $1.00 per page by fax, $.50 per page if picked up in person. Cert fee- $5.00 per doc plus copy fee. Payee- Crawford County Circuit Clerk. **Online access to Real Estate, Deed records:** Land records are at http://etitlesearch.com. You can do a name search; choose from $30.00 monthly subscription or per click account. **Other phones:** Treasurer- 479-474-6641; Vital Records- 501-661-2000; Tax Collector- 479-474-1111. **Property tax/Assessing**- 300 Main, Rm 8 & 8-b, Van Buren, AR 72956-5799; 479-474-1751, assessor fax- 479-471-3225. www.crawford-county.org/ **Online access**- Access property data free at www.actdatascout.com. Subscription for deeper info is $20 per month.

Crittenden County

County Circuit Clerk, 100 Court St, Marion, AR 72364. Recording, R/E & UCC phone-870-739-3248; fax-870-739-3287; 8AM-4:30PM (CST)
Index: All in one. Records indexed on computer back to 1998. Office will perform a UCC search but public must search other records themselves. Search fee- $6.00 per name. Copy fee $.25 per page. Cert fee- $5.00 per doc plus copy fee. Exemplification fee $6.50. Payee- Crittenden County Circuit Clerk. **Other phones:** Treasurer- 870-739-4112; Elections- 870-739-4434. **Property tax/Assessing**- 100 Court St, Marion, AR 72364; 870-739-3606, assessor fax- 870-739-1181. (Appraiser/Auditor- 870-739-3606) hours- 8AM-4:30PM **Online access**- Registration and logon is required to search assessor records at www.arcountydata.com. Signup fee is $200 plus $.10 per minute usage. For signup or info call 479-631-8054 or visit the website.

Cross County

County Circuit Clerk, 705 E Union, Rm 9, Wynne, AR 72396. Recording, R/E & UCC phone-870-238-5720; fax-870-238-5722; 8AM-4PM (CST)
Index: Books, computer. Deeds only indexed on a public use terminal back to 1992. Only the public may search. Copy fee $.25 per page. Cert fee- $5.00 per doc includes copy fee. Payee- Cross County Circuit Clerk. Office does not sell bulk data. **Other phones:** Treasurer- 870-238-5725; Elections- 870-238-5735; Vital Records- 870-238-5735; Tax Collector- 870-238-5710. **Property tax/Assessing**- 705 E Union, #5715, Wynne, AR 72396; 870-238-5715, assessor fax- 870-238-5714. (Appraiser/Auditor- 870-238-5715) **Online access**- Access property data free at www.actdatascout.com. Subscription for deeper info is $20 per month.

Dallas County

County Circuit Clerk, 206 W 3rd St; Courthouse, Fordyce, AR 71742-3299. Recording, R/E & UCC phone-870-352-2307; fax-870-352-7179; 8:30AM-4:30PM (CST)
Index: All in one. Records indexed on computer back to 8/26/97. Only the public may search. Copy fee $.50 per page. Cert fee- $5.00 per doc plus copy fee. Payee- Dallas County Circuit Clerk. **Other phones:** Treasurer- 870-352-2333; Elections- 870-352-3965; Vital Records- 870-352-7688; Tax Collector- 870-352-5181. **Property tax/Assessing**- 206 W 3rd St, Courthouse, Fordyce, AR 71742-3299; 870-352-7983, assessor fax- 870-352-7259. (Appraiser/Auditor- 870-352-3342) **Online access**- Registration and logon is required to search assessor records at www.arcountydata.com. Signup fee is $200 plus $.10 per minute usage. For signup or info call 479-631-8054 or visit the website.

Desha County

County Circuit Clerk, PO Box 309, Arkansas City, AR 71630. 870-877-2411; fax-870-877-3407; 8AM-4PM (CST)
Index: All in one since 1998. Records indexed on a public use terminal. Only the public may search. Copy fee $.50 per page. Cert fee- $5.00 per doc plus copy fee. Payee- Circuit Clerk of Desha County. Office does not sell bulk data. **Other phones:** Treasurer- 870-877-2353; Elections- 870-877-2353; Tax Collector- 870-877-2353. **Property tax/Assessing**- 604 President St, Arkansas City, AR 71630; 870-877-2431, assessor fax- 870-877-3408. **Online access**- Registration and login is required to search assessor records at www.arcountydata.com. Signup fee is $200 plus $.10 per minute usage. For signup or info call 479-631-8054 or visit the website.

Drew County

County Circuit Clerk, 210 S Main, Monticello, AR 71655. Recording, R/E & UCC phone-870-460-6250; fax-870-460-6246; 8AM-4:30PM (CST)
Index: All in one. Records indexed on a public use terminal back to 2001. Only the public may search. Copy fee $.75 per page, $.50 self serve. Cert fee- $5.00 per doc plus copy fee. Payee- Drew County Circuit Clerk. **Other phones:** Treasurer- 870-460-6225; Elections- 870-460-6220; Tax Collector- 870-460-6225. **Property tax/Assessing**- 210 S Main, Monticello, AR 71655; 870-460-6240, assessor fax- 870-460-6246. A public access terminal available. **Online access**- Search property data at www.actdatascout.com/default.aspx?ci=9. 4 levels of pricing starting at $10 for 24 hrs, to $150 per month.

Faulkner County

County Circuit Clerk, PO Box 9, Conway, AR 72033. Recording, R/E & UCC phone-501-450-4911; fax-501-450-4948; 8AM-4:30PM (CST) www.faulknercc.org
Index: Separate indices to search include books, computer. Records indexed on a public use terminal back to 6/89; real estate records back to 1970s. Office personnel or visitors may perform searches. Real estate or tax lien copy- $.25 per copy. UCC copy fee $6.00 per name plus $2.00 each add'l page includes copy fee. Cert fee- $3.00 per doc plus copy fee. Payee- Faulkner County Circuit Clerk. **Other phones:** Treasurer- 501-450-4902; Elections- 501-450-4909; Tax Collector- 501-450-4921. **Property tax/Assessing**- 806 Faulkner, Conway, AR 72034; 501-450-4905, assessor fax- 501-450-4908. **Online access**- Registration and logon is required to search assessor tax and personal property tax records at www.arcountydata.com. Free search but fee for full data- signup fee is $200 plus $.10 per minute usage. For signup or info call 479-631-8054 or visit website. Also, search property tax data free at https://www.ark.org/faulknercounty/index.php. At 2nd page you may search by name.

Franklin County (Charleston District)

County Circuit Clerk, 607 E Main St, Charleston, AR 72933. Recording, R/E & UCC phone-479-965-7332; fax-479-965-9322; 8AM-N, 12:30-4:30PM (CST)
Index: All in one. Records indexed on a public use terminal back to 2003. Only the public may search. Office will not search real estate records. Office will not search UCC records or tax liens. Copy fee $.25 per page. Cert fee- $5.00 per doc includes copy fee. Payee- Franklin County Circuit Clerk. Office does not sell bulk data. **Other phones:** Treasurer- 479-965-2333; Elections- 479-965-2129. **Property tax/Assessing**- PO Box 152, 607 E Main St, Charleston, AR 72933; 479-965-7797.

Franklin County (Ozark District)

County Circuit Clerk, PO Box 1112, Ozark, AR 72949. 479-667-3818; fax-479-667-5174; 8AM-4:30PM (CST)
Index: All in one. Record index not computerized. Only the public may search. Copy fee $.25 per page. Cert fee- $5.00 per instrument plus copy fee. Payee- Franklin County Circuit Clerk. **Other phones:** Treasurer- 479-667-2427; Elections- 479-667-3607; Vital Records- 479-965-2129. **Property tax/Assessing**- PO Box 152, 219 W Main, Ozark, AR 72949; 479-667-2415, assessor fax- 479-667-3266. A public access terminal available. **Online access**- Search at www.arcountydata.com. Login and password required. There is a one-time, $200 setup charge to create a new account, access is charged at 10¢ per minute.

Fulton County

County Circuit Clerk, PO Box 219, Salem, AR 72576. 870-895-3310; fax-870-895-3383; 8AM-4:30PM (CST)

Index: Before year 2000 each book has own grantor/grantee index. Records indexed on computer name search since 2000. Office will perform a UCC search but public must search other records themselves. Search fee $6.00 per name. Copy fee $.20 per page. Cert fee- $5.00 per page includes copy fee. Payee- Fulton County Circuit Clerk. **Other phones:** Treasurer- 870-895-3522; Vital Records- 501-661-2336; Tax Collector- 870-895-2457. **Property tax/Assessing**- PO Box 586, Salem, AR 72576; 870-895-3592, assessor fax- 870-895-3362. **Online access**- Registration and logon is required to search assessor records at www.arcountydata.com. Signup fee is $200 plus $.10 per minute usage. For signup or info call 479-631-8054 or visit the website.

Garland County

County Circuit Clerk, Courthouse, Rm 207, Hot Springs, AR 71901. Recording, R/E & UCC phone-501-622-3630; fax-501-609-9043; 8AM-5PM (CST)
Index: All in one. Records indexed on a public use terminal back to 1980's. Office will perform a UCC search but public must search other records themselves. Search fee-$6.00 for UCC. Copy fee $.25 per page. Cert fee- $.50 per doc plus copy fee. Exemplification fee- $2.50 per doc plus copy fee. Payee- Garland County Circuit Clerk. Office does not sell bulk data. **Other phones:** Treasurer- 501-622-3650; Elections- 501-622-3610; Vital Records- 501-661-2336 (Little Rock); Tax Collector- 501-622-3710. **Property tax/Assessing**- 200 Woodbine St, #123, Hot Springs, AR 71901; 501-622-3730, assessor fax- 501-622-3739. A public access terminal available. **Online access**- Access property data free at www.actdatascout.com. Subscription for deeper info is $20 per month.

Grant County

County Circuit Clerk, 101 W Center, Rm 106; Courthouse, Sheridan, AR 72150. Recording, R/E & UCC phone-870-942-2631; fax-870-942-3564; 8AM-4:30PM (CST)
Index: Separate indices to search include mortgages/deeds, power of attorney, plats/surveys. Records indexed on a public use terminal back to 2001. Only the public may search. Copy fee $.50 per page. Cert fee- $5.00 per doc includes copy fee. Payee- Grant County Circuit Clerk. Office does not sell bulk data. **Other phones:** Treasurer- 870-942-2031; Elections- 870-942-4363; Tax Collector- 870-942-4315. **Property tax/Assessing**- 101 W Center, Rm 106, Courthouse, Sheridan, AR 72150; 870-942-3711, assessor fax- 870-942-8928. **Online access**- Registration and logon is required to search assessor records at www.arcountydata.com. Signup fee is $200 plus $.10 per minute usage. For signup or info call 479-631-8054 or visit the website.

Greene County

County Circuit Clerk, 320 W Court St, Rm 124, Paragould, AR 72450. Recording, R/E & UCC phone-870-239-6330; fax-870-239-3550; 8AM-4:30PM (CST)
Index: All in one. Records indexed on a public use terminal back to 1963, Deeds,1987, Mtg. Office personnel or visitors may perform searches. Search fee $6.00. Office will not search real estate records. Copy fee $.20 per page. Cert fee- $5.00 per doc includes copy fee. Payee- Greene County Circuit Clerk. **Other phones:** Treasurer- 870-239-6304; Elections- 870-239-6311. **Property tax/Assessing**- 320 W Court St, #101, Paragould, AR 72450; 870-239-6303, assessor fax- 870-239-6303. A public access terminal available. **Online access**- Registration and logon is required to search assessor records at www.arcountydata.com. Signup fee is $200 plus $.10 per minute usage. For signup or info call 479-631-8054 or visit the website.

Hempstead County

County Circuit Clerk, PO Box 1420, Hope, AR 71802. Recording, R/E & UCC phone-870-777-2384; fax-870-777-7827; 8AM-4PM (CST)
Index: All in one. Records indexed on computer back to 1991. Office will perform a UCC search but public must search other records themselves. Copy fee $.50 per page, self serve $.25 per page. Cert fee- $5.00 per page includes copy fee. Payee- Hempstead County Circuit Clerk. Office does not sell bulk data. **Other phones:** Treasurer- 870-777-3141; Elections- 870-777-2241; Vital Records- 501-661-2000; Tax Collector- 870-777-4103. **Property tax/Assessing**- PO Box 1420, 402 Washington St, Hope, AR 71802; 870-777-6190, assessor fax- 870-777-7834. (Appraiser/Auditor- 870-777-6190) A public access terminal available. **Online access**- Access property data free at www.actdatascout.com. Subscription for deeper info is $20 per month.

Hot Spring County

County Circuit Clerk, PO Box 1220, Malvern, AR 72104. 501-332-2281; 8AM-4:30PM (CST)
Index: All in one. Records indexed on computer back to 1994. Only the public may search. Copy fee $.50 per page. Cert fee- $5.00 per doc plus copy fee. Payee- Hot Spring County Circuit Clerk. Office does not sell bulk data. **Other phones:** Treasurer- 501-337-7411; Elections- 501-332-2291; Tax Collector- 501-332-7211. **Property tax/Assessing**- 210 Locust St, Courthouse, Malvern, AR 72104; 501-332-2461, assessor fax- 501-332-2221. **Online access**- Access property data free at www.actdatascout.com. Subscription for deeper info is $20 per month.

Howard County

County Circuit Clerk, 421 N Main St, Rm 7, Nashville, AR 71852. Recording, R/E & UCC phone-870-845-7506; 8AM-4:30PM (CST)
Index: All in one. Records indexed on a public use terminal back to 1984 or so. Office will perform a UCC or tax lien search but public must search other records themselves. Search fee-$6.00. Office will not search real estate records. Copy fee $.50 per page; UCC copy $5.00. Cert fee- $5.00 plus $.50 per page. Payee- Howard County Circuit Clerk. Bulk data of daily zip disk for abstract companies available for purchase. Contact Bobbie Jo Green. **Other phones:** Treasurer- 870-845-7504; Elections- 870-845-7503. **Property tax/Assessing**- 421 N Main St, #4, Nashville, AR 71852; 870-845-7511, assessor fax-870-845-1986. A public access terminal available. **Online access**- Registration and logon is required to search assessor records at www.arcountydata.com. Signup fee is $200 plus $.10 per minute usage. For signup or info call 479-631-8054 or visit the website.

Independence County

County Circuit Clerk, PO Box 2155, Batesville, AR 72503. Recording, R/E & UCC phone-870-793-8865; fax-870-793-8888; 8AM-4:30PM (CST)
Index: All in one. Records indexed on computer, liens and UCCs back to 1980; deeds back to 1967; deed of trust back to March, 1992. Office will perform a UCC search but public must search other records themselves. Copy fee $.50 per page. Cert fee- $3.00 per doc plus copy fee. Payee- Independence County Circuit Clerk. **Online access to Real Estate, Deed records:** Land records available via a private contractor at http://etitlesearch.com. You can do a name search; choose from $200.00 monthly subscription or per click account. **Other phones:** Treasurer- 870-793-8899. **Property tax/Assessing**-110 Broad St, Batesville, AR 72501; 870-793-8842. www.independencecounty.com/county_assessor.htm **Online access**- Access property data free at www.actdatascout.com. Subscription for deeper info is $20 per month.

Izard County

County Circuit Clerk, PO Box 95, Melbourne, AR 72556. Recording, R/E & UCC phone-870-368-4316; fax-870-368-4748; 8:30AM-4:30PM (CST)
Index: All in one. Records indexed on computer back to 2000. Deeds back to 1977, mortgages back to 1998. Office personnel or visitors may perform searches. Search fee $6.00 per name. Office will not search real estate records. Copy fee $.20 per page, $.25 for 11x17. Cert fee- $5.00 per doc includes copy fee. Payee- Izard County Circuit Clerk. **Other phones:** Treasurer- 870-368-4394; Elections- 870-368-4316; Vital Records- 501-661-2726; Tax Collector- 870-368-7247. **Property tax/Assessing**- PO Box 131, Melbourne, AR 72556; 870-368-7810, assessor fax-870-368-3183. (Appraiser/Auditor- 870-368-5594) **Online access**- Search free at www.arcountydata.com/county.asp?county=Izard but registration and logon is required to search full assessor records at www.arcountydata.com. Signup fee is $200 plus $.10 per minute usage. For signup or info, call 479-631-8054 or visit the website. Also, visit www.countyservice.net/assess.asp?id=izatax for free look-ups but address is required.

Jackson County

County Circuit Clerk, 208 Main St; Courthouse, Newport, AR 72112. 870-523-7423, R/E recording phone-870-523-3826; fax-870-523-3682; 8AM-4:30PM (CST)
Index: Separate indices to search include books by type. Records indexed on a public use terminal back to 1985. Deeds back to 1982, judgments and liens back to 1988. Only the public may search. Copy fee $.25 per page. Cert fee- $5.00 per doc plus copy fee. Payee- Jackson County Circuit Clerk. Office does not sell bulk data. **Other phones:** Tax Collector- 870-523-7401. **Property tax/Assessing**- 208 Main St, Courthouse, 2nd Fl, Newport, AR 72112; 870-523-7410, assessor fax- 870-523-7440. A public access terminal is available. **Online access**- Access property data free at www.actdatascout.com. Subscription for deeper info is $20 per month.

Jefferson County

County Circuit Clerk, PO Box 7433, Pine Bluff, AR 71611. 870-541-5309, R/E recording phone-870-541-5344, UCC recording phone-870-541-5304; fax-none; 8:30AM-5PM (CST)
Index: All in one. Records indexed on a public use terminal back to 1991. Office will perform a UCC search but public must search other records themselves. Copy fee $.50 per page. Cert fee- $5.00 per doc plus copy fee. Payee- Jefferson County Circuit Clerk. **Other phones:** Elections- 870-541-5323; Tax Collector- 870-541-5313. **Property tax/Assessing**- 101 W Barroque, Pine Bluff, AR 71601; 870-541-5338, assessor fax- 870-541-5335. **Online access**- Search property and personal property data free at www.countyservice.net. Also, subscription access to property data available at www.actdatascout.com; subscription is $20 per month, 50% discount on add'l counties.

Johnson County

County Circuit Clerk, PO Box 189, Clarksville, AR 72830-0189. Recording, R/E & UCC phone-479-754-2977; fax-479-754-4235; 8AM-4:30PM (CST)
Index: Separate indices to search include books by type. Record index not computerized. Only the public may search. Copy fee $.50 per page. Cert fee- $5.00 per doc plus copy fee. Payee- Johnson County Circuit Clerk. Office does not sell bulk data. **Other phones:** Tax Collector- 479-754-3056. **Property tax/Assessing**- 215 Main St, Clarksville, AR 72830; 479-754-8839, assessor fax- 479-754-5705. (Appraiser/Auditor- 479-754-8839) **Online access**- Registration and logon is required to search all participating counties on the Citrix system at www.arcountydata.com. Signup fee is $200 minimum plus $.10 per minute usage. For signup or info call 479-631-8054 or visit www.arcountydata.com.

Lafayette County

County Circuit Clerk, 3 Courthouse Sq; 3rd & Spruce, Lewisville, AR 71845. Recording, R/E & UCC phone-870-921-4878; fax-870-921-4879; 8AM-4:30PM (CST)
Index: Books, computer. Records indexed on a public use terminal back to 2001. Office personnel or visitors may perform searches. Search fee $6.00. Office will

search real estate records if enough information is given to them by the customer. Will search UCC records. Copy fee $.50 per page. Cert fee- $5.00 per doc includes copy fee. Payee- Lafayette County Circuit Clerk. **Other phones:** Treasurer- 870-921-4755; Tax Collector- 870-921-4755; County Clerk - 870-921-4633;. **Property tax/Assessing-** #7 Courthouse Sq, Lewisville, AR 71845; 870-921-4808, assessor fax- 870-921-4505. A public access terminal available. **Online access-** Access property data free at www.actdatascout.com. Subscription for deeper info is $20 per month.

Lawrence County

County Circuit Clerk, PO Box 581, Walnut Ridge, AR 72476. Recording, R/E & UCC phone-870-886-1112; fax-870-886-1128; 8AM-4:30PM (CST)
Index: Separate indices to search include books, misc, deeds, mtgs, Lis Pendens. Records indexed on a public use terminal back to 1990. Office will perform a UCC search but public must name search other records themselves. Search fee $6.00. Copy fee $.20 per page. Cert fee- $5.00 per doc plus copy fee. Payee- Lawrence County Circuit Clerk. **Other phones:** Treasurer- 870-886-1116; Elections- 870-866-1111; Tax Collector- 870-886-1114. **Property tax/ Assessing-** PO Box 187, 315 W Main, #14, Walnut Ridge, AR 72476; 870-886-1135, assessor fax- 870-886-5904. **Online access-** Access property data free at www.actdatascout.com. Subscription for deeper info is $20 per month.

Lee County

County Circuit Clerk, 15 E Chestnut St; Courthouse, Marianna, AR 72360. Recording, R/E & UCC phone-870-295-7710; fax-870-295-7712; 8:30AM-4:30PM
Index: Separate indices to search include deeds, judgments, mortgages. Records indexed on a public use terminal back to 2002. Office will perform a UCC search (5 years) but public must search other records themselves. Search fee $6.00. Copy fee $.25 per page. Cert fee- $5.00 per doc plus copy fee. Payee- Lee County Circuit Clerk. **Other phones:** Treasurer- 870-295-2588; Elections- 870-295-7715; Tax Collector-870-295-7752. **Property tax/Assessing-** 15 E Chestnut St, Courthouse, Marianna, AR 72360; 870-295-7750, assessor fax- 870-295-7705. No public terminal. **Online access-** Registration and logon is required to search assessor records at www.arcountydata.com. Signup fee is $200 plus $.10 per minute usage. For signup or info call 479-631-8054 or visit the website.

Lincoln County

County Circuit Clerk, 300 S Drew St, Rm 103, Star City, AR 71667. Recording, R/E & UCC phone-870-628-3154; fax-870-628-5546; 8AM-4:30PM (CST)
Include a SASE with all mailed-in requests. Index: Separate indices to search include deeds, mortgages together; all others in separate books. Record index not computerized. Office will perform a UCC search but public must search other records themselves. Search fee $6.00 per name. Copy fee $.50 per page. Cert fee- $5.00 per doc plus copy fee. Payee- Lincoln County Circuit Clerk. Office does not sell bulk data. **Other phones:** Treasurer- 870-628-4816; Elections-870-628-5114; Tax Collector- 870-628-5320. **Property tax/Assessing-** 300 S Drew St, Star City, AR 71667; 870-628-4401, assessor fax- 870-628-6595. A public access terminal is available. **Online access-** Subscription access to property data available at www.actdatascout.com; subscription is $20 per month, 50% discount on add'l counties.

Little River County

County Circuit Clerk, PO Box 575, Ashdown, AR 71822-0575. Recording, R/E & UCC phone-870-898-7211; fax-870-898-5783; 8AM-4:30PM (CST)
Index: Separate indices to search include prior to 2003, direct and indirect indexes for real estate, UCC records are in cards and in a separate index book. Records indexed on a public use terminal back to 2003. Office will perform a tax lien search (5 year only) and real estate (but no mortgages) but public must search other records themselves. Search fee $6.00 per name. Copy fee $.50 per page. Cert fee- $5.00 per doc plus copy fee. Payee- Little River County Circuit Clerk. **Other phones:** Treasurer- 870-898-7215; Elections- 870-898-7210. **Property tax/Assessing-** 351 N 2nd, #3, Ashdown, AR 71822; 870-898-7204, assessor fax- 870-898-7207. **Online access-** Access property data free at www.actdatascout.com. Subscription for deeper info is $20 per month.

Logan County (Northern District)

County Circuit Clerk, 24 W Walnut, Courthouse, Paris, AR 72855. 479-963-2164; fax-479-963-3304; 8AM-4:30PM (CST)
Index: All in one handwritten index. Records indexed on a public use terminal back to 1991. Office will perform a UCC search but public must search other records themselves. Search fee $6.00 per name. Copy fee $.25 per page; $.50 per page if mailed. Cert fee- $5.00 per doc includes copy fee. Payee- Logan County Circuit Clerk. **Other phones:** Tax Collector-479-963-2038. **Property tax/Assessing-** 24 W Walnut, Courthouse, Paris, AR 72855; 479-963-2716, assessor fax- 479-963-8197. Computer terminal available for public use. **Online access-** Registration and logon is required to search assessor records on the Citrix system at www.arcountydata.com. Signup fee is $200 plus $.10 per minute usage. For signup or info, call 479-631-8054 or visit the website. Also, visit www.countyservice.net/assess.asp?id=logtax for free look-ups but address is required.

Logan County (Southern District)

County Circuit Clerk, 366 N Broadway, #2; Courthouse, Booneville, AR 72927. 479-675-2894; fax-479-675-0577; 8AM-4:30PM (CST)
Index: All in one. Records indexed on a public use terminal back to 1998. Only the public may search. Copy fee $.25 per page. Cert fee- $5.00 per doc plus copy fee. Payee- Logan County Circuit Clerk. Office does not sell bulk data. **Other phones:** Tax Collector-479-675-5131. **Property tax/Assessing-** 366 N. Broadway, Rm 8, Booneville, AR 72927; 479-675-3942, assessor fax- 479-675-3741. **Online access-** Registration and logon is required to search assessor records on the Citrix system at www.arcountydata.com. Signup fee is $200 plus $.10 per minute usage. For signup or info, call 479-631-8054 or visit the website. Also, visit www.countyservice.net/assess.asp?id=logtax for free look-ups but address is required.

Lonoke County

County Circuit Clerk, PO Box 219, Lonoke, AR 72086-0219. 501-676-2316, R/E recording phone-501-676-3043, UCC recording phone-501-676-2316; fax-501-676-3014; 8AM-4:30PM (CST)
Index: Separate indices to search. Records indexed on a public use terminal back to 5/99 for real estate. 2006 for court records. Office will perform a UCC search but public must search other records themselves. Copy fee $.25 per page. Cert fee- $6.00 per doc plus copy fee. Payee- Lonoke County Circuit Clerk. Office does not sell bulk data. **Other phones:** Treasurer- 501-676-3019; Elections- 501-676-3098. **Property tax/Assessing-** 212 N Center St, PO Box 237, Lonoke, AR 72086; 501-676-6938, assessor fax-501-676-3099. A public access terminal is available. **Online access-** Registration and logon is required to search assessor records at www.arcountydata.com. Signup fee is $200 plus $.10 per minute usage. For signup or info call 479-631-8054 or visit the website.

Madison County

County Circuit Clerk, PO Box 626, Huntsville, AR 72740. Recording, R/E & UCC phone-479-738-2215; fax-479-738-1544; 8AM-4:30PM (CST)
Index: All recorded docs in a separate index. Records indexed on a public use terminal back 13 years. Office will perform a UCC search but public must search other records themselves. Copy fee $.25 per page. Cert fee- $5.00 per doc includes free copies. Payee- Madison County Circuit Clerk. Bulk data of recorded images available for purchase. **Other phones:** Treasurer- 479-738-6514; Elections- 479-738-2747; Vital Records- 501-661-2726; Tax Collector- 479-738-6673. **Property tax/Assessing-** PO Box 334, 201 W Main, Rm 206, Huntsville, AR 72740; 479-738-2325, assessor fax- 479-738-1788. **Online access-** Access property data free at www.actdatascout.com. Subscription for deeper info is $20 per month.

Marion County

County Circuit Clerk, PO Box 385, Yellville, AR 72687. Recording, R/E & UCC phone-870-449-6226; fax-870-449-4979; 8AM-4:30PM (CST)
Index: Separate indices to search include real estate in computer since 1998, everything else in individual books. Records indexed on a public use terminal back to 1998 (real estate only). Office will perform a UCC search but public must search other records themselves. Search fee-$6.00 per name for UCC. Copy fee $.25 per page. Cert fee- $5.00 per doc includes copy fee. Payee- Marion County Circuit Clerk. **Other phones:** Treasurer- 870-449-6331; Tax Collector- 870-449-6253. **Property tax/Assessing-** PO Box 532, 301 E. Main St, Yellville, AR 72687; 870-449-4113, assessor fax- 870-449-6056. **Online access-** Registration and logon is required to search assessor records on the Citrix system at www.arcountydata.com. Signup fee is $200 plus $.10 per minute usage. For signup or info call 479-631-8054 or visit the website.

Miller County

County Circuit Clerk, 412 Laurel St, #109; County Courthouse, Texarkana, AR 71854. 870-774-4501; fax-870-772-5293; 8AM-4:30PM (CST)
Index: Separate indices to search. Records indexed on a public use terminal back to 2000. Only the public may search. Copy fee $1.00 per page. Cert fee- $5.00 per doc plus copy fee. Payee- Miller County Circuit Clerk. Office does not sell bulk data. **Other phones:** Treasurer- 870-774-0003; Elections- 870-774-1501; Tax Collector- 870-772-0003. **Property tax/Assessing-** 400 Laurel St, #109, Texarkana, AR 71854; 870-774-1502, assessor fax- 870-773-0923. **Online access-** Access property data free at www.actdatascout.com. Subscription for deeper info is $20 per month.

Mississippi County (Chickasawba District)

County Circuit Clerk, PO Box 1498, Blytheville, AR 72316-1498. 870-762-2332; fax-870-762-8148; 9AM-4:30PM (CST)
Index: Separate indices to search include cott indexes and Computer. Records indexed on a public use terminal back to 1991. Office will perform a UCC search but public must search other records themselves. Search fee $6.00. Copy fee $.25 per page. Cert fee- $5.00 per doc includes copy fee if not over 8 pages. Payee- Mississippi County Circuit Clerk. Office does not sell bulk data. **Other phones:** Tax Collector- 870-762-2152. **Property tax/Assess-ing-** 200 W Walnut, Ste 101, Blytheville, AR 72315; 870-763-6860, assessor fax- 870-763-5151.

Mississippi County (Osceola District)

County Circuit Clerk, PO Box 466, Osceola, AR 72370. 870-563-6471; fax-870-563-5063; 9AM-4:30PM (CST)
Index: Separate indices to search include deed, O&G, Mortgage, Misc. in books. Records indexed on computer back to 01/08. Office will perform a UCC search but public must search other records themselves. Copy fee $.50 per page. Cert fee- $5.00 per doc plus copy fee. Payee- Mississippi County Circuit Clerk. Office does not sell bulk data. **Other phones:** Tax Collector- 870-762-2152. **Property tax/Assessing-** PO Box 466, Osceola, AR 72370; 870-563-2683, assessor fax- 870-563-2543. **Online**

access- Access to property assessment records is free at www.dsmone.com/missco/.

Monroe County

County Circuit Clerk, 123 Madison St, Clarendon, AR 72029. Recording, R/E & UCC phone-870-747-3615; fax-870-747-3710; 8AM-4:30PM (CST)
Index: Separate indices to search include books, computer. Real estate records indexed on computer back to 3/1/2005. Office personnel or visitors may perform searches. No fee for search. UCC only- $6.00 per name. Office will not search mortgage records. Copy fee $.25 per page. Cert fee- $5.00 per doc includes copies. Payee- Monroe County Circuit Clerk. **Other phones:** Treasurer- 870-747-3722; Elections- 870-747-3632; Tax Collector- 870-747-3819. **Property tax/Assessing**- 123 Madison St, Clarendon, AR 72029; 870-747-3847, assessor fax- 870-747-5907. Computer terminal available for public use.

Montgomery County

County Circuit Clerk, 105 Hwy 270 E, #10, Mount Ida, AR 71957-0369. 870-867-3521; fax-870-867-2177; 8AM-4:30PM (CST)
Index: All in one. Records indexed on a public use terminal. Only the public may search. Copy fee $.50 per page, $1.00 if from vault. Cert fee- $5.00 per doc includes copy fee. Payee- Montgomery County Circuit Clerk. Office does sell bulk data, contact Debbie Baxter. **Other phones:** Treasurer- 870-867-3411; Tax Collector- 870-867-3155. **Property tax/Assessing**- 105 Hwy 270 E, #8, Mt Ida, AR 71957; 870-867-3271, assessor fax- 870-867-3485. **Online access**- Access property data free at www.actdatascout.com. Subscription for deeper info is $20 per month.

Nevada County

County Circuit Clerk, PO Box 204, Prescott, AR 71857. Recording, R/E & UCC phone-870-887-2511; fax-870-887-1911; 8AM-4:30PM (CST)
Index: All in one. Record index not computerized. Only the public may search. Copy fee $1.00 per page. Cert fee- $2.00 per doc plus copy fee. Payee- Nevada County Circuit Clerk. **Other phones:** Treasurer- 870-887-2811; Tax Collector- 870-887-2811. **Property tax/Assessing**- PO Box 45, 100 E Court St, Jasper, AR 72641; 870-887-3410. **Online access**- Subscription access to property data available at www.actdatascout.com; subscription is $20 per month, 50% discount on add'l counties.

Newton County

County Circuit Clerk, PO Box 410, Jasper, AR 72641. 870-446-5125; fax-870-446-5755; 8AM-4:30PM
Index: All in one. Record index not computerized. Only the public may search. Copy fee $.25 per page. Cert fee- $5.00 per doc includes copy fee. Payee- Newton County Circuit Clerk. Office does not sell bulk data. **Other phones:** Treasurer- 870-446-2936; Tax Collector- 870-446-2936. **Property tax/Assessing**- PO Box 45, 100 E Court St, Jasper, AR 72641; 870-446-2937, assessor fax- 870-446-2937. Computer terminal available for public use. **Online access**- Registration and logon is required to search assessor records at www.arcountydata.com. Signup fee is $200 plus $.10 per minute usage. For signup or info call 479-631-8054 or visit the website.

Ouachita County

County Circuit Clerk, PO Box 667, Camden, AR 71701. Recording, R/E & UCC phone-870-837-2230; fax-870-837-2252; 8AM-4:30PM (CST)
Index: All in one since 1999. Records indexed on a public use terminal back to 99. Only the public may search. Copy fee $.50 per page. Cert fee- $2.50 per doc plus copy fee; exemplification fee $5.00. Payee- Ouachita County Circuit Clerk. **Other phones:** Treasurer- 870-837-2250; Elections- 870-837-2220; Vital Records- 501-661-2336. **Property tax/Assessing**- 145 Jefferson St, Camden, AR 71701; 870-837-2240, assessor fax- 870-837-2242. (Appraiser/Auditor- 870-837-2240) A public access terminal is available. **Online access**- Access property data free at www.actdatascout.com. Subscription for deeper info is $20 per month.

Perry County

County Circuit Clerk, PO Box 358, Perryville, AR 72126. 501-889-5126; fax-501-889-5759; 8AM-4:30PM (CST)
Index: All in one. Records indexed on computer back to 7/97. Only the public may search. Copy fee $1.00 per page. Cert fee- $5.00 per doc includes copy fee of $.50 first page, $.25 each add'l page. Payee- Perry County Circuit Clerk. **Other phones:** Treasurer- 501-889-2710; Tax Collector- 501-889-5285. **Property tax/Assessing**- PO Box 6, 310 Main St, Perryville, AR 72126; 501-889-2865, assessor fax- 501-889-5974. Computer terminal available for public use. **Online access**- Access property data free at www.actdatascout.com. Subscription for deeper info is $20 per month.

Phillips County

County Circuit Clerk, 620 Cherry St, #206; Courthouse, Helena, AR 72342. Recording, R/E & UCC phone-870-338-5515; fax-870-338-5513; 8AM-4:30PM (CST)
Index: Separate indices to search. Records indexed on a public use terminal back to 1998. Office will perform a UCC/lien search but public must search other records themselves. Search fee-$6.00 per name. Copy fee $.25 per page. Cert fee- $5.00 per doc plus copy fee. Payee- Phillips County Circuit Clerk. Office does not sell bulk data. **Online access to Real Estate, Deed records:** Access land records at http://etitlesearch.com. You can do a name search; choose from $25.00 monthly subscription or per-click account. **Other phones:** Treasurer- 870-338-5510; Tax Collector- 870-338-5580. **Property tax/Assessing**- 620 Cherry St, #100, Helena, AR 72342; 870-338-5535, assessor fax- 870-338-5586.

Pike County

County Circuit Clerk, PO Box 219, Murfreesboro, AR 71958. Recording, R/E & UCC phone-870-285-2231; fax-870-285-3281; 8AM-4:30PM (CST) www.pikecountyarkansas.org
Index: All in one. Records indexed on a public use terminal back to 1993. Only the public may search. Copy fee $.50 per page. Cert fee- $5.00 per doc plus copy fee. Payee- Pike County Circuit Clerk. Office does not sell bulk data. **Other phones:** Treasurer- 870-285-2422; Elections- 870-285-2743; Vital Records- In Little Rock; Tax Collector- 870-285-3121; County Clerk -870-285-2743;. **Property tax/Assessing**- PO Box 356, 1 Courthouse Sq, Murfreesboro, AR 71958; 870-285-3316, assessor fax- 870-285-3281. **Online access**- Registration and logon is required to search assessor records at www.arcountydata.com. Signup fee is $200 plus $.10 per minute usage. For signup or info call 479-631-8054 or visit the website.

Poinsett County

County Circuit Clerk, PO Box 46, Harrisburg, AR 72432-0046. 870-578-4420, R/E recording phone-870-578-4422, UCC recording phone-870-578-4420; fax-870-578-4427; 8:30AM-4:30PM (CST)
Index: Books, computer. Records indexed on a public use terminal back to 1998. Office personnel or visitors may perform searches. Search fee $6.00 per name. Office will not search real estate records. Office will search active UCC records. Copy fee $.50 per page. Cert fee- $5.00 per doc. Payee- Poinsett County Circuit Clerk. **Other phones:** Treasurer- 870-578-4405; Elections- 870-578-4410; Tax Collector- 870-578-4415. **Property tax/Assessing**- PO Box 543, Harrisburg, AR 72432; 870-578-4430, 4435. **Online access**- Registration and logon is required to search assessor records at www.arcountydata.com. Signup fee is $200 plus $.10 per minute usage. For signup or info call 479-631-8054 or visit the website.

Polk County

County Circuit Clerk, 507 Church St; Courthouse, Mena, AR 71953. Recording, R/E & UCC phone-479-394-8100; fax-479-394-8170; 8AM-4:30PM
Index: Separate indices to search include deed, mortgages, liens, judgments, UCCs. Records indexed on a public use terminal back to 7/02, deeds back to 7/03. Only the public may search. Copy fee $.25 per page; $.50 if legal size.Real estate record copy- $.50 per page. Cert fee- $5.00 per doc includes copy fee. UCC cert-$6.00. Payee- Polk County Circuit Clerk. **Online access to Deed Records:** Online access to land records is by subscription through RecordsUSA.com. Images are available. Visit the website for sign-up or call Rob at 888-633-4748 x17 for info. **Other phones:** Treasurer- 479-394-8150; Elections- 479-394-8123; Tax Collector- 479-394-8110. **Property tax/Assessing**- 507 Church St, Courthouse, Mena, AR 71953; 479-394-8121, assessor fax- 479-394-8168. (Appraiser/Auditor- 479-394-8121) **Online access**- Access property data free at www.actdatascout.com. Subscription for deeper info is $20 per month.

Pope County

County Circuit Clerk, 100 W Main, 3rd Fl; County Courthouse, Russellville, AR 72801. Recording, R/E & UCC phone-479-968-7499, UCC recording phone-479-968-6989; fax-479-880-8463; 8AM-4PM (CST)
Index: Separate indices to search. Records indexed on a public use terminal back to 1987. Only the public may search. Copy fee $.25 per page, for fax or mailing $1.00 per page. Cert fee- $5.00 per doc plus copy fee. Payee- Pope County Circuit Clerk. Office does not sell bulk data. **Online access to Real Estate, Deed, Lien records:** Access recording office land data and liens at www.etitlesearch.com; registration required, fee based on usage. **Other phones:** Treasurer- 479-968-7016; Tax Collector- 479-968-7016. **Property tax/Assessing**- 100 W Main, Russellville, AR 72801; 479-968-7418, assessor fax-479-968-4571. Computer terminal available for public use. **Online access**- Search assessor property data free at www.arcountydata.com/county.asp?county=Pope. Registration and logon is required to search deeper assessor records at www.arcountydata.com. Signup fee is $200 plus $.10 per minute usage. For signup or info call 479-631-8054 or visit the website. Also, free access assessor data at www.countyservice.net/assess.asp?id=poptax - address is required.

Prairie County (Northern District)

County Circuit Clerk, 200 Courthouse Sq #104, Des Arc, AR 72040. 870-256-4434; fax-870-256-4434; 8AM-4:30PM (CST)
Index: Separate indices to search include deed and mortgage indexes. Record index not computerized. Office will perform a UCC search, no tax liens, but public must search other records themselves. Search fee $6.00 per name. Copy fee $.50 per page. Fax fee $1.00 per page. Cert fee- $5.00 per doc plus copy fee. Payee- Prairie County Circuit Clerk. Bulk data available for purchase, contact County Clerk. **Online access to Real Estate, Deed records:** Access recording office land data at www.etitlesearch.com; registration required, fee based on usage. **Other phones:** Treasurer- 870-256-4786; Tax Collector-870-256-4764. **Property tax/Assessing**- PO Box 436, 204 Courthouse Sq, Des Arc, AR 72040; 870-256-4692, assessor fax- 870-256-4308. **Online access**- Subscription access to property data available at www.actdatascout.com; subscription is $20 per month, 50% discount on add'l counties.

Prairie County (Southern District)

County Circuit Clerk, PO Box 283, De Valls Bluff, AR 72041-0283. Recording, R/E & UCC phone-870-998-2314; fax-870-998-2314; 8AM-N, 1-4:30PM
Index: Separate indices to search. Record index not computerized. Office will perform a UCC search but public must search other records themselves. Search fee $6.00 per name. Copy fee $.50 per page. Cert fee- $5.00 per doc plus copy fee. Payee- Prairie County

Circuit Clerk. **Online access to Real Estate, Deed records:** Access recording office land data at www.etitlesearch.com; registration required, fee based on usage. **Other phones:** Treasurer- 870-256-4786; Tax Collector- 870-256-4764. **Property tax/Assessing**- PO Box 436, 204 Courthouse Sq, Des Arc, AR 72040; 870-256-4692, assessor fax- 870-256-4308. Direct requests to the main office in Des Arc; Des Arc address given here. **Online access**- Subscription access to property data available at www.actdatascout.com; subscription is $20 per month, 50% discount on add'l counties.

Pulaski County

County Circuit Clerk, 401 W Markham St, Rm S216, Little Rock, AR 72201. 501-340-8433; fax-501-340-8889; 8:30AM-4:30PM (CST) www.co.pulaski.ar.us
Index: Separate indices to search include computer, pre-1994 on microfilm. Records indexed on a public use terminal back to 1994. Only the public may search. Copy fee $.50 per page. Cert fee- $5.00 per doc plus copy fee. Payee- Pulaski County Circuit Clerk. **Online access to Real Estate, Deed, Lien, Mortgage, Judgment, Plat, Voter Registration, Marriage records:** At the main web page, Click on Online Services for the free search of voter registration, real estate, courts, marriages, ministers at www.pulaskiclerk.com/SearchChoiceMain.html. Real estate may be temp suspended. Also, access recording office land data at www.etitlesearch.com; registration required, fee based on usage. **Other phones:** Treasurer- 501-340-8345; Elections- 501-340-8683 (Vote); Tax Collector- 501-340-8345. **Property tax/Assessing**- 201 S Broadway, Little Rock, AR 72201; 501-340-6170. **Online access**- Registration and logon is required to search assessor and personal property records on the Citrix system at www.arcountydata.com. Signup fee is $200 plus $.10 per minute usage. For signup or info call 479-631-8054 or visit www.arcountydata.com. Data is no longer being updated as of 12/2005. Also, search current Personal Property - vehicles - free at http://vehicles.pulaskicountyassessor.net/webware/MotorVehicle/VehicleLogin.aspx.

Randolph County

County Circuit Clerk, 107 W Broadway, Pocahontas, AR 72455. Recording, R/E & UCC phone-870-892-5522; fax-870-892-8794; 8AM-4:30PM (CST)
Index: Separate indices to search include deeds, mortgages, misc. Records indexed on a public use terminal back to 1836. Office will perform a UCC search but public must search other records themselves. Search fee $6.00. Copy fee $.25 per page. Cert fee- $2.00 per doc plus copy fee. Payee- Randolph County Circuit Clerk. **Other phones:** Treasurer- 870-892-5238; Elections- 870-892-5822; Tax Collector- 870-892-5491. **Property tax/Assessing**- 107 W Broadway, Pocahantas, AR 72455; 870-892-3200, assessor fax- 870-892-3204. A public access terminal is available. www.actdatascout.com/default.aspx?ci=29 **Online access**- Search property and personal property data free at www.countyscrvice.net. Also, access property data free at www.actdatascout.com. Subscription for deeper info is $20 per month.

Saline County

County Circuit Clerk, 200 N Main St, #113, Benton, AR 72018. 501-303-5615; 8AM-4:30PM (CST) www.salinecounty.org
Index: Separate indices to search include 1991 to present on computer; prior separate books for deeds, mortgages, etc. Records indexed on a public use terminal back to 1991. Office will perform a UCC search but public must search other records themselves. UCC search per debtor name- $6.00. Copy fee $.25 per page. Cert fee- $5.00 per doc plus copy fee. Payee- Saline County Circuit Clerk. **Other phones:** Treasurer- 501-303-5633; Tax Collector- 501-303-5620. **Property tax/Assessing**- 215 N Main St, Ste 7, Benton, AR 72015; 501-303-5622. **Online access**- Search assessor data free at www.arcountydata.com/county.asp?county=Saline but Registration and logon is required to search full assessor records. Signup is $200 plus $.10 per minute usage. Call 479-631-8054 or visit the website. Search assessor records free at www.countyservice.net/assess.asp?id=saltax, free search requires address. Search tax collector records free at https://www.ark.org/salinecounty/index.php.

Scott County

County Circuit Clerk, PO Box 2165, Waldron, AR 72958. Recording, R/E & UCC phone-479-637-2642; fax-479-637-0124; 8AM-4:30PM (CST)
Index: Separate indices to search arranged by years. Records indexed on a public use terminal back to 11/2002. Office will perform a UCC search but public must search other records themselves. Search fee- UCC only- $6.00 per name. Office will retrieve real estate record back up to 7 years but not search. Copy fee $.50 per page. Cert fee- $5.00 per doc includes copy fee. Payee- Scott County Circuit Clerk. Bulk data available for purchase; $700 per year on weekly CDs; contact Sandy. **Other phones:** Treasurer- 479-637-2780; Tax Collector- 479-637-4156. **Property tax/Assessing**- PO Box 12, 190 W First St, Waldron, AR 72958; 479-637-2666, assessor fax- 479-637-8816. **Online access**- Registration and logon is required to search assessor records on the Citrix system at www.arcountydata.com. Signup fee is $200 plus $.10 per minute usage. For signup or info call 479-631-8054 or visit the website.

Searcy County

County Circuit Clerk, PO Box 998, Marshall, AR 72650. 870-448-3807; fax-870-448-5005; 8AM-4:30PM (CST)
Index: Separate indices to search. Record index not computerized. Office personnel or visitors may perform searches. Office will not search real estate records. UCC search per debtor name- $8.00. Tax lien search fee- $6.00 per search. Copy fee $.50 per copy. Cert fee- $5.00 per doc plus copy fee. Payee- Searcy County Circuit Clerk. Office does not sell bulk data. **Other phones:** Treasurer- 870-448-3828; Tax Collector- 870-448-5050. **Property tax/Assessing**- PO Box 1335, 106 W Nome St, Marshall, AR 72650; 870-448-2464, assessor fax- 870-448-2496. (Appraiser/Auditor- 870-448-2464) **Online access**- Subscription access to property data available at www.actdatascout.com; subscription is $20 per month, 50% discount on add'l counties.

Sebastian County (Fort Smith District)

County Clerk and Recorder, PO Box 1089, Fort Smith, AR 72902-1089. Recording, R/E & UCC phone-479-782-5065; fax-479-784-1567; 8AM-5PM www.sebastiancountyonline.com
Sebastian County has 2 courthouses for recordings. Index: All in one. Records indexed on a public use terminal back to 1988. Office will perform a UCC search but public must search other records themselves. Search fee $6.00. Copy fee $.50 each 1st 10 pages $.25 add'l per page. Cert fee- $5.00 per doc plus copy fee. Payee- Sebastian County Clerk and Recorder. Office does sell bulk data, contact Angie Carter. **Other phones:** Elections- 479-782-5065. **Property tax/Assessing**- 35 S 6th St, Rm 105, Fort Smith, AR 72901; 479-783-8948, assessor fax- 479-784-1522. **Online access**- Registration and logon is required to search assessor records up to 1/2006 only is at www.arcountydata.com. Signup fee is $200 plus $.10 per minute usage. For signup or info call 479-631-8054 or visit the website which is not updated. Also, search tax payment data free at https://www.ark.org/sebastiancounty/index.php. Also, access property data free at www.actdatascout.com. Subscription for deeper info is $20 per month.

Sebastian County (Southern District)

County Clerk, PO Box 428, Greenwood, AR 72936. Recording, R/E & UCC phone- 479-996-4195; fax-479-996-4165; hours- 8AM-5PM (CST) www.sebastiancountyonline.com
Sebastian County has 2 courthouses for recordings. Records indexed on computer back to 1984, on index books from 1983 to 1882. Office will perform a UCC search but public must search other records themselves. Search fee $6.00. Office will not search real estate records. Office will not search tax liens. Copy fee $.50 each 1st 10 copies. $.25 add'l per page. If attained by mail $1.00 each. Cert fee- $5.00 per doc plus copy fee. Payee- Sebastian County Clerk-Doris Tate. **Other phones:** Elections- 479-996-4195; Vital Records- 479-996-4195 (marriages). **Property tax/Assessing**- PO Box 357, 113 E. Center St, Greenwood, AR 72936; 479-996-6591, assessor fax- 479-996-7045. (Appraiser/Auditor- 479-996-7045) www.sebastiancountyonline.com **Online access**- Registration and logon is required to search assessor records at www.arcountydata.com. Signup fee is $200 plus $.10 per minute usage. For signup or info call 479-631-8054 or visit the website. Also, search property and personal property data free at www.countyservice.net. Also, access property data free at www.actdatascout.com. Subscription for deeper info is $20 per month.

Sevier County

County Circuit Clerk, 115 N 3rd St, De Queen, AR 71832. Recording, R/E & UCC phone-870-584-3055; fax-870-642-3119; 8AM-4:30PM (CST)
Index: All in one. Records indexed on a public use terminal back to 1985. Only the public may search. Copy fee $.25 per page. Cert fee- $5.00 per doc plus copy fee. Payee- Sevier County Circuit Clerk. Office does not sell bulk data. **Other phones:** Treasurer- 870-642-2358; Tax Collector- 870-642-2358. **Property tax/Assessing**- 115 N. 3rd St, Rm 117, DeQueen, AR 71832; 870-584-3182, assessor fax- 870-642-9638. **Online access**- Access property data free at www.actdatascout.com. Subscription for deeper info is $20 per month.

Sharp County

County Circuit Clerk, PO Box 307, Ash Flat, AR 72513. Recording, R/E & UCC phone-870-994-7361; fax-870-994-7712; 8AM-4PM (CST)
Index: All in one. Records indexed on a public use terminal back to 1998. Only the public may search. Copy fee $.25 per page. Cert fee- $5.00 per page includes copy fee. Payee- Sharp County Circuit Clerk. Office does not sell bulk data. **Online access to Real Estate, Deed records:** Access land records at http://etitlesearch.com. You can do a name search; choose from $25.00 monthly subscription or per-click account. **Other phones:** Treasurer- 870-994-7347; Elections- 870-994-7361; Tax Collector- 870-994-7347. **Property tax/Assessing**- PO Box 101, Ash Flat, AR; 870-994-7328, assessor fax- 870-994-7708. **Online access**- Registration and logon is required to search assessor records at www.arcountydata.com. Signup fee is $200 plus $.10 per minute usage. For signup or info call 479-631-8054 or visit the website.

St. Francis County

County Circuit Clerk, PO Box 1775, Forrest City, AR 72336-1775. Recording, R/E & UCC phone-870-261-1715, fax-870-261-1723; 8AM-4:30PM (CST)
Index: All in one. Records indexed on a public use terminal back to 2003. Office will perform a UCC search but public must search other records themselves. Search fee-$6.00 per name. Copy fee $.25 per page. Cert fee- $5.00 per doc includes copy fee. Payee- St. Francis County Circuit Clerk. **Other phones:** Treasurer- 870-261-1705; Elections- 870-261-1725; Tax Collector- 870-261-1792. **Property tax/Assessing**- 313 S Izard St, Forrest City, AR 72336-1775; 870-261-1710, assessor fax- 870-261-1714. A public access terminal available. **Online access**- Search assessor data free at www.arcountydata.com/county.asp?county=St.%20Francis but Registration and logon is required to search full assessor records at www.arcountydata.com. Signup fee is $200 plus $.10 per minute usage. For

signup or info call 479-631-8054 or visit the website. Also, search assessor real estate and personal property records free at www.countyservice.net/stftax.asp but free search requires address.

Stone County

County Circuit Clerk, 107 W Main, #D, Mountain View, AR 72560. Recording, R/E & UCC phone-870-269-3271; fax-870-269-2303; 8AM-4:30PM

Index: Separate indices to search include Land, Court, UCC, Marriage. Records indexed on a public use terminal back to 1972. Only the public may search. Real estate or tax lien copy- $.25 per page. Cert fee- $5.00 per doc plus copy fee up to 10 pages. Payee- Stone County Circuit Clerk. Office does not sell bulk data. **Other phones:** Treasurer- 870-269-8426; Elections- 870-269-5550; Tax Collector- 870-269-2211. **Property tax/Assessing**- 108 W Washington, Mountain View, AR 72560; 870-269-3524, assessor fax- 870-269-9798. (Appraiser/Auditor- 870-269-5521) Computer terminal available for public use. **Online access**- Registration and logon is required to search assessor records on the Citrix system at www.arcountydata.com. Signup fee is $200 plus $.10 per minute usage. For signup or info call 479-631-8054 or visit the website.

Union County

County Circuit Clerk, PO Box 1626, El Dorado, AR 71731-1626. 870-864-1940; fax-870-864-1994; 8:30AM-5PM (CST)

Index: All in one. Records indexed on a public use terminal back to 2001. Office personnel or visitors may perform searches. Search fee $6.00 per name. Office will not search real estate records. Office will search UCC records; search includes tax liens if requested. Real estate or tax lien copy- $.50 per page. Cert fee- $5.00 per page. Payee- Union County Circuit Clerk. Office will sell data in bulk, contact Cheryl 870-864-1945. **Online access to Real Estate, Deed, Land Records:** Online access to land records is by subscription through RecordsUSA.com. Images are available. Visit the website for sign-up or call Rob at 888-633-4748 x17 for info. **Other phones:** Treasurer- 870-864-1928; Tax Collector- 870-864-1930. **Property tax/Assessing**- 101 N Washington, Courthouse, Rm 107, El Dorado, AR 71731-1626; 870-864-1920, assessor fax- 870-864-1926. **Online access**- Subscription access to property data available at www.actdatascout.com; subscription is $20 per month, 50% discount on add'l counties.

Van Buren County

County Circuit Clerk, 451 Main St, #2, Clinton, AR 72031-9806. Recording, R/E & UCC phone-501-745-4140; fax-501-745-7400; 8AM-5PM M; 8AM-4:30PM T-F. (CST)

Recording ends 4:30 PM. Index: All in one. Records indexed on a public use terminal back to 1917 for deeds, 1974 for mortgages and Misc. Office personnel or visitors may perform searches. Search fee-$1.00 per search. Office will search real estate records. Office will not search UCC records or tax liens. Copy fee $.50 per page. Cert fee- $5.00 per doc includes copy fee. If document is over 5 pgs-add'l fee of $.50 per page. Payee- Van Buren County Circuit Clerk. Bulk data available for purchase, images only, contact Ester Bass. **Online access to Real Estate, Deed records:** Access land records at http://etitlesearch.com. You can do a name search; call 870-856-3055 for subscription info. **Other phones:** Treasurer- 501-745-2400; Elections- 501-745-8683. **Property tax/Assessing**- 1414 Hwy 65 S, Ste 117, Clinton, AR 72031; 501-745-2464. (Appraiser/Auditor- 501-745-2474) **Online access**- Access assessor date free at www.arcountydata.com/county.asp?county=Van%20Buren but registration and logon is required to search full assessor records on the Citrix system at www.arcountydata.com. Signup fee is $200 plus $.10 per minute usage. For signup or info call 479-631-8054 or visit the website. Also, search tax payments free at https://www.ark.org/vanburencounty/index.php and use name search to locate property owner.

Washington County

County Circuit Clerk, 280 N College, #302; Courthouse, Fayetteville, AR 72701. 479-444-1538; fax-479-444-1537; hours- 8AM-4:30PM (CST) www.co.washington.ar.us

Archived records pre-1992 found at 479-444-1543. Index: All in one. Records indexed on a public use terminal back to 1992. Only the public may search. Copy fee $.15 per page. Cert fee- $5.00 per doc plus copy fee. Payee- Washington County Circuit Clerk. Office does not sell bulk data. **Online access to Real Estate, Deed, Lien, UCC, Court, Vital Statistic records:** Search Clerk's index of real estate, liens, and UCCs (to '92) at www.co.washington.ar.us/resolution/. Username, password and $50.00 subscription required. Also, search property records for free at www.co.washington.ar.us/PropertySearch/MapSearch.asp. Also, search court record archives at www.co.washington.ar.us/ArchiveSearch/CourtRecordSearch.asp. Also, access land records at http://etitlesearch.com. You can do a name search, fees involved, call 870-856-3055 for info. **Other phones:** Treasurer- 479-444-1526; Tax Collector- 479-444-1526. **Property tax/Assessing**- 280 N College, #250, Fayetteville, AR 72701; 479-444-1520, assessor fax- 479-444-1501. **Online access**- Search property records for free at www.co.washington.ar.us/PropertySearch/MapSearch.asp.

White County

County Circuit Clerk, 300 N Spruce; County Courthouse, Searcy, AR 72143. 501-279-6203; 8AM-4:30PM (CST)

Index: Separate indices to search. Records indexed on a public use terminal back to 1998. Office personnel or visitors may perform searches. Search fee $6.00 per name. Office will not search real estate records. Copy fee $.50 per page. Cert fee- $5.00 per doc plus copy fee. Payee- White County Circuit Clerk. Office does not sell bulk data. **Other phones:** Treasurer- 501-279-6206; Tax Collector- 501-279-6206. **Property tax/Assessing**- 119 W Arch Ave, Searcy, AR 72143; 501-279-6205, assessor fax- 501-279-6258. Computer terminal available for public use. **Online access**- Registration and logon is required to search assessor records at www.arcountydata.com. Signup fee is $200 plus $.10 per minute usage. For signup or info call 479-631-8054 or visit the website. Also, free access to assessor records at www.countyservice.net/assess.asp?id=whitax. Address required.

Woodruff County

County Circuit Clerk, PO Box 492, Augusta, AR 72006. Recording, R/E & UCC phone-870-347-2391; fax-870-347-8703; 8AM-4PM (CST)

Index: Separate indices to search. Records indexed on a public use terminal back to 1998. Office will perform a UCC search but public must search other records themselves. Search fee $9.00. Copy fee $.50 per page. Cert fee- $5.00 per doc plus copy fee. Payee- Woodruff County Circuit Clerk. Office does not sell bulk data. **Online access to Real Estate, Deed records:** Access land records at http://etitlesearch.com. You can do a name search; choose from $25.00 monthly subscription or per-click account. **Other phones:** Treasurer- 870-347-5416; Tax Collector- 870-347-5152. **Property tax/Assessing**- 500 N 3rd St, Augusta, AR 72006; 870-347-5151, assessor fax- 870-347-5901. **Online access**- Subscription access to property data available at www.actdatascout.com; subscription is $20 per month, 50% discount on add'l counties.

Yell County (Danville District)

County Circuit Clerk, PO Box 219, Danville, AR 72833. Recording, R/E & UCC phone-479-495-4850; fax-479-495-4875; 8AM-4PM (CST)

Index: All in one. Record index not computerized. Only office personnel may search. Search fee $6.00 per name. Office will not search real estate records. Copy fee $.25 per page. Cert fee- $5.00 per doc includes copy fee. Payee- Yell County Circuit Clerk. **Other phones:** Treasurer- 479-495-2933; Elections- 479-495-4850; Vital Records- 479-495-4850. **Property tax/Assessing**- PO Box 607, 101 E 5th, Danville, AR 72833; 479-495-2940, assessor fax- 479-495-3171.

Yell County (Dardanelle District)

County Circuit Clerk, 108 Union St Rm 105, Dardanelle, AR 72834. 479-229-4404; fax-479-229-5634; 8AM-4PM (CST)

Index: Separate indices to search include computer, books, UCCs, judgments. Records indexed on a public use terminal back to 1998. Office personnel or visitors may perform searches. Search fee $6.00 per name. Office will not search real estate records. Copy fee $.25 per page. Cert fee- $5.00 per doc includes copy fee. Payee- Yell County Circuit Clerk. Office does not sell bulk data. **Property tax/Assessing**- PO Box 607, 101 E 5th, Danville, AR 72833; 479-229-2693, assessor fax- 479-495-3171. Search at the Danville office; Danville address given here.

Arkansas County Locator

You will usually be able to find the city name in the City/County Cross Reference below. In that case, it is a simple matter to determine the county from the cross reference. However, only the official US Postal Service city names are included in this index. There are an additional 40,000 place names that people use in their addresses. Therefore, we have also included a ZIP/City Cross Reference immediately following the City/County Cross Reference.

If you know the ZIP Code but the city name does not appear in the City/County Cross Reference index, look up the ZIP Code in the ZIP/City Cross Reference, find the city name, then look up the city name in the City/County Cross Reference. For example, you want to know the county for an address of Menands, NY 12204. There is no "Menands" in the City/County Cross Reference. The ZIP/City Cross Reference shows that ZIP Codes 12201-12288 are for the city of Albany. Looking back in the City/County Cross Reference, Albany is in Albany County.

Arkansas City/County Cross Reference

ADONA (72001) Perry(53), Conway(46)
ALCO (72610) Stone(95), Searcy(4)
ALEXANDER (72002) Saline(93), Pulaski(6)
ALICIA Lawrence
ALIX Franklin
ALLEENE Little River
ALMA Crawford
ALMYRA Arkansas
ALPENA (72611) Boone(50), Carroll(49)
ALPINE Clark
ALTHEIMER Jefferson
ALTUS (72821) Franklin(75), Johnson(24)
AMAGON Jackson
AMITY (71921) Clark(54), Pike(29), Hot Spring(16)
ANTOINE Pike
ARKADELPHIA (71923) Clark(96), Hot Spring(3)
ARKADELPHIA Clark
ARKANSAS CITY Desha
ARMOREL Mississippi
ASH FLAT (72513) Fulton(48), Sharp(45), Izard(6)
ASHDOWN Little River
ATKINS (72823) Pope(97), Conway(2)
ATKINS Pope
AUBREY Lee
AUGUSTA Woodruff
AUSTIN Lonoke
AVOCA Benton
BALCH Jackson
BALD KNOB White
BANKS Bradley
BARLING Sebastian
BARTON Phillips
BASS Newton
BASSETT Mississippi
BATES Scott
BATESVILLE Independence
BAUXITE Saline
BAY Craighead
BEARDEN (71720) Ouachita(85), Dallas(11), Calhoun(3)
BEAVER Carroll
BEE BRANCH (72013) Van Buren(96), Conway(3)
BEEBE White
BEECH GROVE Greene
BEEDEVILLE Jackson
BEIRNE Clark
BELLA VISTA Benton
BELLEVILLE Yell
BEN LOMOND Sevier
BENTON (72015) Saline(98), Grant(1)
BENTON Saline
BENTONVILLE Benton
BERGMAN Boone
BERRYVILLE Carroll
BEXAR Fulton
BIG FLAT (72617) Baxter(75), Searcy(18), Stone(6)
BIGELOW (72016) Perry(52), Pulaski(47)
BIGGERS (72413) Randolph(92), Clay(7)
BIRDEYE Cross
BISCOE Prairie
BISMARCK Hot Spring
BLACK OAK Craighead
BLACK ROCK Lawrence
BLAKELY Garland
BLEVINS Hempstead
BLUE MOUNTAIN Logan
BLUFF CITY Nevada
BLUFFTON (72827) Yell(89), Scott(10)
BLYTHEVILLE Mississippi
BOARD CAMP Polk
BOLES Scott
BONNERDALE (71933) Hot Spring(46), Garland(35), Montgomery(17)
BONO (72416) Craighead(77), Greene(22)
BOONEVILLE (72927) Logan(85), Scott(8), Sebastian(5)
BOSWELL Izard
BRADFORD (72020) Jackson(48), White(37), Independence(13)
BRADLEY Lafayette
BRANCH Franklin
BRICKEYS Lee
BRIGGSVILLE Yell
BRINKLEY (72021) Monroe(98), Woodruff(1)
BROCKWELL Izard
BROOKLAND Craighead
BRUNO Marion
BRYANT (72022) Saline(96), Pulaski(3)
BRYANT Saline
BUCKNER (71827) Lafayette(78), Nevada(21)
BULL SHOALS Marion
BURDETTE Mississippi
CABOT (72023) Lonoke(75), Pulaski(23)
CADDO GAP Montgomery
CALDWELL St. Francis
CALE Nevada
CALICO ROCK (72519) Baxter(66), Stone(18), Izard(14)
CALION Union
CAMDEN (71701) Ouachita(97), Calhoun(2)
CAMDEN Ouachita
CAMP Fulton
CANEHILL Washington
CARAWAY (72419) Craighead(94), Poinsett(5)
CARLISLE (72024) Lonoke(96), Prairie(3)
CARTHAGE (71725) Dallas(92), Cleveland(7)
CASA (72025) Perry(80), Conway(18), Yell(2)
CASH (72421) Craighead(77), Poinsett(19), Jackson(2)
CASSCOE Arkansas
CAVE CITY (72521) Sharp(69), Independence(30)
CAVE SPRINGS Benton
CECIL (72930) Franklin(80), Sebastian(19)
CEDARVILLE Crawford
CENTER RIDGE (72027) Conway(97), Faulkner(1)
CENTERTON Benton
CENTERVILLE Yell
CHARLESTON (72933) Franklin(83), Sebastian(16)
CHARLOTTE Independence
CHATFIELD Crittenden
CHEROKEE VILLAGE (72529) Sharp(77), Fulton(22)
CHEROKEE VILLAGE Sharp
CHERRY VALLEY (72324) Cross(90), Poinsett(9)
CHESTER Crawford
CHIDESTER Ouachita
CHOCTAW Van Buren
CLARENDON Monroe
CLARKEDALE Crittenden
CLARKRIDGE Baxter
CLARKSVILLE Johnson
CLEVELAND (72030) Conway(52), Van Buren(47)
CLINTON (72031) Van Buren(95), Stone(2), Conway(1)
COAL HILL Johnson
COLLEGE STATION Pulaski
COLLINS Drew
COLT (72326) St. Francis(87), Cross(12)
COLUMBUS (71831) Hempstead(60), Howard(40)
COMBS Madison
COMPTON (72624) Newton(83), Carroll(16)
CONCORD (72523) Cleburne(87), Independence(12)
CONWAY Faulkner
CORD Independence
CORNING Clay
COTTER Baxter
COTTON PLANT (72036) Woodruff(88), Monroe(11)
COVE Polk
COY Lonoke
CRAWFORDSVILLE Crittenden
CROCKETTS BLUFF Arkansas
CROSSETT Ashley
CRUMROD Phillips
CURTIS Clark
CUSHMAN Independence
DAMASCUS (72039) Van Buren(71), Faulkner(28)
DANVILLE Yell
DARDANELLE (72834) Yell(98), Logan(1)
DATTO Clay
DE QUEEN Sevier
DE VALLS BLUFF Prairie
DE WITT Arkansas
DECATUR Benton
DEER Newton
DELAPLAINE Greene
DELAWARE Logan
DELIGHT Pike
DELL Mississippi
DENNARD Van Buren
DERMOTT (71638) Chicot(84), Drew(12), Desha(3)
DES ARC Prairie
DESHA Independence
DIAMOND CITY Boone
DIAZ Jackson
DIERKS (71833) Howard(94), Sevier(5)
DODDRIDGE Miller
DOLPH Izard
DONALDSON Hot Spring
DOVER Pope
DRASCO (72530) Cleburne(94), Stone(5)
DRIVER Mississippi
DUMAS (71639) Desha(97), Lincoln(2)
DYER Crawford
DYESS Mississippi
EARLE (72331) Crittenden(95), Cross(4)
EDGEMONT (72044) Cleburne(80), Stone(19)
EDMONDSON Crittenden
EGYPT Craighead
EL DORADO Union
EL PASO (72045) White(98), Faulkner(1)
ELAINE Phillips
ELIZABETH (72531) Baxter(53), Fulton(46)
ELKINS (72727) Madison(50), Washington(49)
ELM SPRINGS Washington
EMERSON Columbia
EMMET (71835) Nevada(78), Hempstead(21)
ENGLAND (72046) Lonoke(81), Pulaski(10), Jefferson(7)
ENOLA Faulkner
ETHEL Arkansas
ETOWAH Mississippi
EUDORA Chicot
EUREKA SPRINGS Carroll
EVANSVILLE Washington
EVENING SHADE Sharp
EVERTON (72633) Boone(59), Marion(37), Searcy(3)
FAIRFIELD BAY (72088) Van Buren(91), Cleburne(8)
FARMINGTON Washington
FAYETTEVILLE Washington
FERNDALE Pulaski
FIFTY SIX Stone
FISHER (72429) Poinsett(97), Cross(3)
FLIPPIN Marion
FLORAL (72534) Independence(86), Cleburne(13)
FORDYCE (71742) Dallas(96), Calhoun(3)
FOREMAN Little River
FORREST CITY St. Francis
FORT SMITH Sebastian
FOUKE Miller

FOUNTAIN HILL (71642) Ashley(82), Drew(17)
FOX Stone
FRANKLIN Izard
FRENCHMANS BAYOU Mississippi
FRIENDSHIP Hot Spring
FULTON Hempstead
GAMALIEL Baxter
GARFIELD Benton
GARLAND CITY (71839) Miller(96), Lafayette(4)
GARNER White
GASSVILLE Baxter
GATEWAY Benton
GENOA Miller
GENTRY Benton
GEPP (72538) Fulton(94), Baxter(5)
GILBERT Searcy
GILLETT (72055) Arkansas(89), Jefferson(10)
GILLHAM (71841) Sevier(89), Polk(10)
GILMORE Crittenden
GLENCOE Fulton
GLENWOOD (71943) Pike(56), Montgomery(39), Hot Spring(4)
GOODWIN St. Francis
GOSHEN Washington
GOSNELL Mississippi
GOULD (71643) Lincoln(88), Desha(11)
GRADY (71644) Jefferson(64), Lincoln(35)
GRANNIS Polk
GRAPEVINE Grant
GRAVELLY (72838) Yell(93), Scott(6)
GRAVETTE Benton
GREEN FOREST Carroll
GREENBRIER Faulkner
GREENLAND Washington
GREENWAY Clay
GREENWOOD Sebastian
GREGORY Woodruff
GRIFFITHVILLE (72060) White(70), Prairie(29)
GRUBBS Jackson
GUION Izard
GURDON Clark
GUY Faulkner
HACKETT Sebastian
HAGARVILLE (72839) Johnson(97), Pope(2)
HAMBURG Ashley
HAMPTON Calhoun
HARDY (72542) Sharp(86), Fulton(13)
HARRELL Calhoun
HARRIET (72639) Searcy(95), Marion(4)
HARRISBURG Poinsett
HARRISON Boone
HARTFORD Sebastian
HARTMAN Johnson
HARVEY (72841) Scott(81), Yell(18)
HASTY Newton
HATFIELD Polk
HATTIEVILLE (72063) Conway(94), Pope(5)
HATTON Polk
HAVANA (72842) Yell(98), Logan(1)
HAYNES Lee
HAZEN Prairie
HEBER SPRINGS Cleburne
HECTOR Pope
HELENA Phillips
HENDERSON Baxter
HENSLEY (72065) Saline(84), Pulaski(11), Grant(4)
HERMITAGE Bradley
HETH (72346) St. Francis(94), Cross(4), Crittenden(1)
HICKORY PLAINS Prairie
HICKORY RIDGE (72347) Cross(80), Jackson(18)
HIGDEN (72067) Cleburne(89), Van Buren(10)
HIGGINSON White
HINDSVILLE (72738) Madison(80), Washington(12), Benton(6)
HIWASSE Benton
HOLLY GROVE (72069) Monroe(91), Phillips(8)
HOPE Hempstead
HORATIO Sevier
HORSESHOE BEND Izard
HOT SPRINGS NATIONAL PARK Garland
HOT SPRINGS VILLAGE (71909) Garland(74), Saline(25)
HOT SPRINGS VILLAGE Garland
HOUSTON Perry
HOWELL Woodruff
HOXIE Lawrence
HUGHES (72348) St. Francis(48), Crittenden(45), Lee(5)
HUMNOKE (72072) Lonoke(90), Jefferson(9)
HUMPHREY (72073) Arkansas(77), Jefferson(22)
HUNT Johnson
HUNTER Woodruff
HUNTINGTON Sebastian
HUTTIG Union
IDA Cleburne
IMBODEN (72434) Randolph(71), Lawrence(28)
IVAN Dallas
JACKSONPORT Jackson
JACKSONVILLE (72076) Pulaski(95), Lonoke(4)
JACKSONVILLE Pulaski
JASPER Newton
JEFFERSON (72079) Jefferson(85), Grant(14)
JENNIE Chicot
JEROME Drew
JERSEY Bradley
JERUSALEM (72080) Van Buren(48), Conway(41), Pope(10)
JESSIEVILLE Garland
JOHNSON Washington
JOINER Mississippi
JONES MILLS Hot Spring
JONESBORO (72401) Craighead(98), Greene(1)
JONESBORO Craighead
JUDSONIA White
JUNCTION CITY Union
KEISER Mississippi
KENSETT White
KEO Lonoke
KINGSLAND Cleveland
KINGSTON (72742) Madison(91), Newton(8)
KIRBY Pike
KNOBEL (72435) Clay(93), Greene(6)
KNOXVILLE Johnson
LA GRANGE Lee
LAFE (72436) Greene(84), Clay(15)
LAKE CITY Craighead
LAKE VILLAGE Chicot
LAKEVIEW Baxter
LAMAR (72846) Johnson(97), Pope(2)
LAMBROOK Phillips
LANEBURG Nevada
LANGLEY Pike
LAVACA Sebastian
LAWSON Union
LEACHVILLE (72438) Mississippi(87), Craighead(12)
LEAD HILL (72644) Boone(89), Marion(10)
LEOLA (72084) Grant(54), Hot Spring(27), Dallas(18)
LEPANTO (72354) Poinsett(78), Mississippi(21)
LESLIE (72645) Van Buren(42), Searcy(34), Stone(22)
LETONA White
LEWISVILLE Lafayette
LEXA (72355) Phillips(88), Lee(11)
LIGHT Greene
LINCOLN Washington
LITTLE ROCK (72210) Pulaski(92), Saline(7)
LITTLE ROCK Pulaski
LITTLE ROCK AIR FORCE BASE Pulaski
LOCKESBURG Sevier
LOCUST GROVE (72550) Independence(56), Cleburne(28), Stone(14)
LONDON (72847) Pope(62), Johnson(37)
LONOKE Lonoke
LONSDALE (72087) Saline(57), Garland(42)
LOUANN Ouachita
LOWELL Benton
LUXORA Mississippi
LYNN Lawrence
MABELVALE (72103) Saline(79), Pulaski(20)
MADISON St. Francis
MAGAZINE Logan
MAGNESS Independence
MAGNOLIA (71753) Columbia(98), Union(1)
MAGNOLIA Columbia
MALVERN (72104) Hot Spring(98), Saline(1)
MAMMOTH SPRING (72554) Fulton(68), Sharp(31)
MANILA Mississippi
MANSFIELD (72944) Sebastian(59), Scott(40)
MARBLE FALLS Newton
MARCELLA Stone
MARIANNA Lee
MARION Crittenden
MARKED TREE Poinsett
MARMADUKE Greene
MARSHALL (72650) Searcy(90), Stone(9)
MARVELL (72366) Phillips(96), Monroe(1), Lee(1)
MAUMELLE Pulaski
MAYFLOWER Faulkner
MAYNARD Randolph
MAYSVILLE Benton
MC CASKILL Hempstead
MC CRORY (72101) Woodruff(89), Jackson(8), Cross(2)
MC CRORY Cross
MC CRORY Woodruff
MC DOUGAL Clay
MC GEHEE Desha
MC NEIL Columbia
MC RAE White
MELBOURNE Izard
MELLWOOD Phillips
MENA Polk
MENIFEE Conway
MIDLAND Sebastian
MIDWAY Baxter
MINERAL SPRINGS Howard
MINTURN Lawrence
MOKO Fulton
MONETTE Craighead
MONROE Monroe
MONTICELLO Drew
MONTROSE Ashley
MORO (72368) Lee(90), Monroe(9)
MORRILTON Conway
MORROW Washington
MOSCOW Jefferson
MOUNT HOLLY Union
MOUNT IDA Montgomery
MOUNT JUDEA Newton
MOUNT PLEASANT Izard
MOUNT VERNON (72111) Faulkner(64), White(35)
MOUNTAIN HOME (72653) Baxter(98), Marion(1)
MOUNTAIN HOME Baxter
MOUNTAIN PINE Garland
MOUNTAIN VIEW (72560) Stone(98), Izard(1)
MOUNTAINBURG Crawford
MULBERRY (72947) Crawford(61), Franklin(38)
MURFREESBORO Pike
NASHVILLE (71852) Howard(87), Hempstead(6), Pike(6)
NATURAL DAM (72948) Crawford(95), Washington(4)
NEW BLAINE Logan
NEW EDINBURG (71660) Cleveland(96), Bradley(3)
NEWARK Independence
NEWHOPE (71959) Pike(60), Howard(39)
NEWPORT Jackson
NORFORK Baxter
NORMAN Montgomery
NORPHLET Union
NORTH LITTLE ROCK Pulaski
O KEAN Randolph
OAK GROVE Carroll
OAKLAND Marion
OARK (72852) Johnson(90), Newton(5), Madison(4)
ODEN Montgomery
OGDEN Little River
OIL TROUGH Independence
OKOLONA Clark
OLA (72853) Perry(64), Yell(35)
OMAHA (72662) Boone(98), Carroll(1)
ONEIDA Phillips
ONIA Stone
OSCEOLA Mississippi
OXFORD Izard
OZAN Hempstead
OZARK (72949) Franklin(97), Johnson(1), Logan(1)
OZONE (72854) Johnson(94), Newton(5)
PALESTINE (72372) St. Francis(85), Lee(14)
PANGBURN (72121) White(69), Cleburne(30)
PARAGOULD Greene
PARIS Logan
PARKDALE (71661) Ashley(88), Chicot(11)
PARKIN Cross
PARKS Scott
PARON (72122) Saline(69), Pulaski(30)
PARTHENON Newton
PATTERSON Woodruff
PEA RIDGE Benton
PEACH ORCHARD (72453) Greene(89), Clay(10)
PEARCY (71964) Garland(90), Hot Spring(9)
PEEL Marion
PELSOR (72856) Pope(52), Newton(47)
PENCIL BLUFF Montgomery
PERRY (72125) Perry(71), Conway(28)
PERRYVILLE (72126) Perry(96), Pulaski(3)
PETTIGREW (72752) Madison(84), Johnson(14)
PICKENS (71662) Lincoln(53), Desha(46)
PIGGOTT Clay
PINDALL Searcy
PINE BLUFF (71602) Jefferson(98), Grant(1)
PINE BLUFF Jefferson
PINEVILLE Izard
PLAINVIEW (72857) Yell(70), Perry(29)
PLEASANT GROVE Stone
PLEASANT PLAINS (72568) Independence(92), White(7)
PLUMERVILLE Conway
POCAHONTAS Randolph
POLLARD Clay
PONCA Newton
POPLAR GROVE (72374) Phillips(98), Lee(1)
PORTIA Lawrence
PORTLAND (71663) Ashley(65), Chicot(34)

POTTSVILLE Pope
POUGHKEEPSIE Sharp
POWHATAN Lawrence
POYEN (72128) Grant(98), Hot Spring(1)
PRAIRIE GROVE Washington
PRATTSVILLE Grant
PRESCOTT (71857) Nevada(96), Hempstead(3)
PRIM Cleburne
PROCTOR (72376) Crittenden(98), St. Francis(1)
PYATT Marion
QUITMAN (72131) Cleburne(82), Faulkner(9), Van Buren(7)
RATCLIFF (72951) Logan(58), Franklin(41)
RAVENDEN (72459) Lawrence(50), Randolph(35), Sharp(13)
RAVENDEN SPRINGS Randolph
RECTOR (72461) Clay(91), Greene(8)
REDFIELD (72132) Jefferson(84), Grant(15)
REYDELL Jefferson
REYNO Randolph
RISON (71665) Cleveland(98), Jefferson(1)
RIVERVALE Poinsett
ROE (72134) Monroe(82), Arkansas(13), Prairie(3)
ROGERS Benton
ROLAND Pulaski
ROMANCE White
ROSE BUD (72137) White(58), Cleburne(41)
ROSIE Independence
ROSSTON Nevada
ROUND POND St. Francis
ROVER Yell
ROYAL Garland
RUDY Crawford
RUSSELL White
RUSSELLVILLE Pope
SAFFELL (72572) Lawrence(66), Independence(33)
SAGE Izard
SAINT CHARLES Arkansas
SAINT FRANCIS Clay
SAINT JOE (72675) Marion(60), Searcy(39)
SAINT PAUL Madison
SALADO Independence
SALEM Fulton
SARATOGA (71859) Hempstead(60), Howard(40)
SCOTLAND Van Buren
SCOTT (72142) Pulaski(62), Lonoke(37)
SCRANTON Logan
SEARCY White
SEDGWICK Lawrence
SHERIDAN (72150) Grant(98), Jefferson(1)
SHERRILL Jefferson
SHERWOOD (72120) Pulaski(96), Faulkner(3)
SHIRLEY (72153) Van Buren(93), Stone(6)
SIDNEY (72577) Sharp(73), Izard(26)
SILOAM SPRINGS Benton
SIMS Montgomery
SMACKOVER (71762) Union(96), Ouachita(3)
SMITHVILLE (72466) Lawrence(63), Sharp(36)
SNOW LAKE Desha
SOLGOHACHIA Conway
SPARKMAN (71763) Dallas(92), Ouachita(4), Clark(2)
SPRINGDALE (72764) Washington(97), Benton(2)
SPRINGDALE Washington
SPRINGFIELD Conway
SPRINGTOWN Benton
STAMPS (71860) Lafayette(94), Columbia(5)
STAR CITY (71667) Lincoln(97), Cleveland(1)
STATE UNIVERSITY Craighead
STEPHENS (71764) Ouachita(57), Columbia(35), Nevada(5), Union(1)
STEPROCK White
STORY Montgomery
STRAWBERRY (72469) Lawrence(80), Sharp(19)
STRONG Union
STURKIE Fulton
STUTTGART (72160) Arkansas(96), Prairie(1), Jefferson(1)
SUBIACO Logan
SUCCESS Clay
SULPHUR ROCK (72579) Independence(94), Sharp(5)
SULPHUR SPRINGS Benton
SUMMERS Washington
SUMMIT Marion
SWEET HOME Pulaski
SWIFTON Jackson
TAYLOR (71861) Columbia(63), Lafayette(36)
TEXARKANA Miller
THIDA Independence
THORNTON (71766) Calhoun(97), Ouachita(2)
TICHNOR Arkansas
TILLAR (71670) Desha(81), Drew(18)
TILLY (72679) Pope(61), Van Buren(25), Searcy(12)
TIMBO Stone
TOMATO Mississippi
TONTITOWN Washington
TRASKWOOD (72167) Saline(80), Hot Spring(14), Grant(4)
TRUMANN Poinsett
TUCKER Jefferson
TUCKERMAN Jackson
TUMBLING SHOALS Cleburne
TUPELO Jackson
TURNER Phillips
TURRELL Crittenden
TWIST Cross
TYRONZA (72386) Poinsett(63), Mississippi(18), Crittenden(17)
ULM Prairie
UMPIRE (71971) Howard(78), Pike(21)
UNIONTOWN Crawford
URBANA Union
VALLEY SPRINGS (72682) Marion(83), Boone(16)
VAN BUREN Crawford
VANDERVOORT Polk
VANNDALE Cross
VENDOR Newton
VILLAGE Columbia
VILONIA Faulkner
VIOLA Fulton
VIOLET HILL Izard
WABASH Phillips
WABBASEKA (72175) Jefferson(98), Arkansas(1)
WALCOTT Greene
WALDENBURG Poinsett
WALDO (71770) Columbia(88), Nevada(11)
WALDRON Scott
WALNUT RIDGE (72476) Lawrence(91), Randolph(3), Craighead(2), Greene(2)
WARD (72176) Lonoke(98), Prairie(1)
WARM SPRINGS Randolph
WARREN (71671) Bradley(97), Cleveland(2)
WASHINGTON Hempstead
WATSON Desha
WAVELAND Yell
WEINER (72479) Poinsett(85), Jackson(9), Craighead(4)
WESLEY (72773) Madison(98), Washington(1)
WEST FORK Washington
WEST HELENA Phillips
WEST MEMPHIS Crittenden
WEST POINT White
WEST RIDGE Mississippi
WESTERN GROVE (72685) Newton(92), Searcy(4), Boone(2)
WHEATLEY (72392) St. Francis(78), Monroe(14), Woodruff(5), Lee(1)
WHEELER Washington
WHELEN SPRINGS Clark
WHITE HALL Jefferson
WICKES (71973) Polk(93), Howard(6)
WIDEMAN Izard
WIDENER St. Francis
WILBURN Cleburne
WILLIFORD Sharp
WILLISVILLE Nevada
WILMAR (71675) Drew(92), Bradley(7)
WILMOT (71676) Ashley(94), Chicot(5)
WILSON Mississippi
WILTON Little River
WINCHESTER Drew
WINSLOW (72959) Washington(87), Crawford(12)
WINTHROP Little River
WISEMAN (72587) Izard(94), Fulton(5)
WITTER Madison
WITTS SPRINGS (72686) Searcy(90), Pope(9)
WOODSON Pulaski
WOOSTER Faulkner
WRIGHT Jefferson
WRIGHTSVILLE Pulaski
WYNNE Cross
YELLVILLE Marion
YORKTOWN Lincoln

Arkansas ZIP/City Cross Reference

71601-71612 PINE BLUFF
71612-71612 WHITE HALL
71613-71613 PINE BLUFF
71630-71630 ARKANSAS CITY
71631-71631 BANKS
71634-71634 COLLINS
71635-71635 CROSSETT
71638-71638 DERMOTT
71639-71639 DUMAS
71640-71640 EUDORA
71642-71642 FOUNTAIN HILL
71643-71643 GOULD
71644-71644 GRADY
71646-71646 HAMBURG
71647-71647 HERMITAGE
71649-71649 JENNIE
71650-71650 JEROME
71651-71651 JERSEY
71652-71652 KINGSLAND
71653-71653 LAKE VILLAGE
71654-71654 MC GEHEE
71655-71657 MONTICELLO
71658-71658 MONTROSE
71659-71659 MOSCOW
71660-71660 NEW EDINBURG
71661-71661 PARKDALE
71662-71662 PICKENS
71663-71663 PORTLAND
71665-71665 RISON
71666-71666 MC GEHEE
71667-71667 STAR CITY
71670-71670 TILLAR
71671-71671 WARREN
71674-71674 WATSON
71675-71675 WILMAR
71676-71676 WILMOT
71677-71677 WINCHESTER
71678-71678 YORKTOWN
71701-71711 CAMDEN
71720-71720 BEARDEN
71721-71721 BEIRNE
71722-71722 BLUFF CITY
71724-71724 CALION
71725-71725 CARTHAGE
71726-71726 CHIDESTER
71728-71728 CURTIS
71730-71731 EL DORADO
71740-71740 EMERSON
71742-71742 FORDYCE
71743-71743 GURDON
71744-71744 HAMPTON
71745-71745 HARRELL
71747-71747 HUTTIG
71748-71748 IVAN
71749-71749 JUNCTION CITY
71750-71750 LAWSON
71751-71751 LOUANN
71752-71752 MC NEIL
71753-71754 MAGNOLIA
71758-71758 MOUNT HOLLY
71759-71759 NORPHLET
71762-71762 SMACKOVER
71763-71763 SPARKMAN
71764-71764 STEPHENS
71765-71765 STRONG
71766-71766 THORNTON
71767-71767 HAMPTON
71768-71768 URBANA
71769-71769 VILLAGE
71770-71770 WALDO
71772-71772 WHELEN SPRINGS
71801-71802 HOPE
71820-71820 ALLEENE
71822-71822 ASHDOWN
71823-71823 BEN LOMOND
71825-71825 BLEVINS
71826-71826 BRADLEY
71827-71827 BUCKNER
71828-71828 CALE
71831-71831 COLUMBUS
71832-71832 DE QUEEN
71833-71833 DIERKS
71834-71834 DODDRIDGE
71835-71835 EMMET
71836-71836 FOREMAN
71837-71837 FOUKE
71838-71838 FULTON
71839-71839 GARLAND CITY
71840-71840 GENOA
71841-71841 GILLHAM
71842-71842 HORATIO
71844-71844 LANEBURG
71845-71845 LEWISVILLE
71846-71846 LOCKESBURG
71847-71847 MC CASKILL
71851-71851 MINERAL SPRINGS
71852-71852 NASHVILLE
71853-71853 OGDEN
71854-71854 TEXARKANA
71855-71855 OZAN
71857-71857 PRESCOTT
71858-71858 ROSSTON
71859-71859 SARATOGA
71860-71860 STAMPS
71861-71861 TAYLOR
71862-71862 WASHINGTON
71864-71864 WILLISVILLE
71865-71865 WILTON

71866-71866	WINTHROP
71901-71903	HOT SPRINGS NATIONAL PARK
71909-71910	HOT SPRINGS VILLAGE
71913-71914	HOT SPRINGS NATIONAL PARK
71920-71920	ALPINE
71921-71921	AMITY
71922-71922	ANTOINE
71923-71923	ARKADELPHIA
71929-71929	BISMARCK
71931-71931	BLAKELY
71932-71932	BOARD CAMP
71933-71933	BONNERDALE
71935-71935	CADDO GAP
71937-71937	COVE
71940-71940	DELIGHT
71941-71941	DONALDSON
71942-71942	FRIENDSHIP
71943-71943	GLENWOOD
71944-71944	GRANNIS
71945-71945	HATFIELD
71946-71946	HATTON
71949-71949	JESSIEVILLE
71950-71950	KIRBY
71951-71951	HOT SPRINGS NATIONAL PARK
71952-71952	LANGLEY
71953-71953	MENA
71956-71956	MOUNTAIN PINE
71957-71957	MOUNT IDA
71958-71958	MURFREESBORO
71959-71959	NEWHOPE
71960-71960	NORMAN
71961-71961	ODEN
71962-71962	OKOLONA
71964-71964	PEARCY
71965-71965	PENCIL BLUFF
71966-71966	ODEN
71968-71968	ROYAL
71969-71969	SIMS
71970-71970	STORY
71971-71971	UMPIRE
71972-71972	VANDERVOORT
71973-71973	WICKES
71998-71999	ARKADELPHIA
72001-72001	ADONA
72002-72002	ALEXANDER
72003-72003	ALMYRA
72004-72004	ALTHEIMER
72005-72005	AMAGON
72006-72006	AUGUSTA
72007-72007	AUSTIN
72009-72009	BALCH
72010-72010	BALD KNOB
72011-72011	BAUXITE
72012-72012	BEEBE
72013-72013	BEE BRANCH
72014-72014	BEEDEVILLE
72015-72015	BENTON
72016-72016	BIGELOW
72017-72017	BISCOE
72018-72018	BENTON
72020-72020	BRADFORD
72021-72021	BRINKLEY
72022-72022	BRYANT
72023-72023	CABOT
72024-72024	CARLISLE
72025-72025	CASA
72026-72026	CASSCOE
72027-72027	CENTER RIDGE
72028-72028	CHOCTAW
72029-72029	CLARENDON
72030-72030	CLEVELAND
72031-72031	CLINTON
72032-72035	CONWAY
72036-72036	COTTON PLANT
72037-72037	COY
72038-72038	CROCKETTS BLUFF
72039-72039	DAMASCUS
72040-72040	DES ARC
72041-72041	DE VALLS BLUFF
72042-72042	DE WITT
72043-72043	DIAZ
72044-72044	EDGEMONT
72045-72045	EL PASO
72046-72046	ENGLAND
72047-72047	ENOLA
72048-72048	ETHEL
72051-72051	FOX
72052-72052	GARNER
72053-72053	COLLEGE STATION
72055-72055	GILLETT
72057-72057	GRAPEVINE
72058-72058	GREENBRIER
72059-72059	GREGORY
72060-72060	GRIFFITHVILLE
72061-72061	GUY
72063-72063	HATTIEVILLE
72064-72064	HAZEN
72065-72065	HENSLEY
72066-72066	HICKORY PLAINS
72067-72067	HIGDEN
72068-72068	HIGGINSON
72069-72069	HOLLY GROVE
72070-72070	HOUSTON
72071-72071	HOWELL
72072-72072	HUMNOKE
72073-72073	HUMPHREY
72074-72074	HUNTER
72075-72075	JACKSONPORT
72076-72078	JACKSONVILLE
72079-72079	JEFFERSON
72080-72080	JERUSALEM
72081-72081	JUDSONIA
72082-72082	KENSETT
72083-72083	KEO
72084-72084	LEOLA
72085-72085	LETONA
72086-72086	LONOKE
72087-72087	LONSDALE
72088-72088	FAIRFIELD BAY
72089-72089	BRYANT
72099-72099	LITTLE ROCK AIR FORCE BASE
72100-72100	NORTH LITTLE ROCK
72101-72101	MC CRORY
72102-72102	MC RAE
72103-72103	MABELVALE
72104-72104	MALVERN
72105-72105	JONES MILLS
72106-72106	MAYFLOWER
72107-72107	MENIFEE
72108-72108	MONROE
72110-72110	MORRILTON
72111-72111	MOUNT VERNON
72112-72112	NEWPORT
72113-72113	MAUMELLE
72114-72119	NORTH LITTLE ROCK
72120-72120	SHERWOOD
72121-72121	PANGBURN
72122-72122	PARON
72123-72123	PATTERSON
72124-72124	NORTH LITTLE ROCK
72125-72125	PERRY
72126-72126	PERRYVILLE
72127-72127	PLUMERVILLE
72128-72128	POYEN
72129-72129	PRATTSVILLE
72130-72130	PRIM
72131-72131	QUITMAN
72132-72132	REDFIELD
72133-72133	REYDELL
72134-72134	ROE
72135-72135	ROLAND
72136-72136	ROMANCE
72137-72137	ROSE BUD
72139-72139	RUSSELL
72140-72140	SAINT CHARLES
72141-72141	SCOTLAND
72142-72142	SCOTT
72143-72149	SEARCY
72150-72150	SHERIDAN
72152-72152	SHERRILL
72153-72153	SHIRLEY
72156-72156	SOLGOHACHIA
72157-72157	SPRINGFIELD
72158-72158	BENTON
72159-72159	STEPROCK
72160-72160	STUTTGART
72164-72164	SWEET HOME
72165-72165	THIDA
72166-72166	TICHNOR
72167-72167	TRASKWOOD
72168-72168	TUCKER
72169-72169	TUPELO
72170-72170	ULM
72173-72173	VILONIA
72175-72175	WABBASEKA
72176-72176	WARD
72178-72178	WEST POINT
72179-72179	WILBURN
72180-72180	WOODSON
72181-72181	WOOSTER
72182-72182	WRIGHT
72183-72183	WRIGHTSVILLE
72189-72189	MC CRORY
72190-72199	NORTH LITTLE ROCK
72200-72207	LITTLE ROCK
72208-72208	FERNDALE
72209-72297	LITTLE ROCK
72301-72303	WEST MEMPHIS
72310-72310	ARMOREL
72311-72311	AUBREY
72312-72312	BARTON
72313-72313	BASSETT
72314-72314	BIRDEYE
72315-72317	BLYTHEVILLE
72319-72319	GOSNELL
72320-72320	BRICKEYS
72321-72321	BURDETTE
72322-72322	CALDWELL
72323-72323	CHATFIELD
72324-72324	CHERRY VALLEY
72325-72325	CLARKEDALE
72326-72326	COLT
72327-72327	CRAWFORDSVILLE
72328-72328	CRUMROD
72329-72329	DRIVER
72330-72330	DYESS
72331-72331	EARLE
72332-72332	EDMONDSON
72333-72333	ELAINE
72335-72336	FORREST CITY
72338-72338	FRENCHMANS BAYOU
72339-72339	GILMORE
72340-72340	GOODWIN
72341-72341	HAYNES
72342-72342	HELENA
72346-72346	HETH
72347-72347	HICKORY RIDGE
72348-72348	HUGHES
72350-72350	JOINER
72351-72351	KEISER
72352-72352	LA GRANGE
72353-72353	LAMBROOK
72354-72354	LEPANTO
72355-72355	LEXA
72358-72358	LUXORA
72359-72359	MADISON
72360-72360	MARIANNA
72364-72364	MARION
72365-72365	MARKED TREE
72366-72366	MARVELL
72367-72367	MELLWOOD
72368-72368	MORO
72369-72369	ONEIDA
72370-72370	OSCEOLA
72372-72372	PALESTINE
72373-72373	PARKIN
72374-72374	POPLAR GROVE
72376-72376	PROCTOR
72377-72377	RIVERVALE
72378-72378	ROUND POND
72379-72379	SNOW LAKE
72381-72381	TOMATO
72383-72383	TURNER
72384-72384	TURRELL
72385-72385	TWIST
72386-72386	TYRONZA
72387-72387	VANNDALE
72389-72389	WABASH
72390-72390	WEST HELENA
72391-72391	WEST RIDGE
72392-72392	WHEATLEY
72394-72394	WIDENER
72395-72395	WILSON
72396-72397	WYNNE
72397-72397	MC CRORY
72401-72404	JONESBORO
72410-72410	ALICIA
72411-72411	BAY
72412-72412	BEECH GROVE
72413-72413	BIGGERS
72414-72414	BLACK OAK
72415-72415	BLACK ROCK
72416-72416	BONO
72417-72417	BROOKLAND
72419-72419	CARAWAY
72421-72421	CASH
72422-72422	CORNING
72424-72424	DATTO
72425-72425	DELAPLAINE
72426-72426	DELL
72427-72427	EGYPT
72428-72428	ETOWAH
72429-72429	FISHER
72430-72430	GREENWAY
72431-72431	GRUBBS
72432-72432	HARRISBURG
72433-72433	HOXIE
72434-72434	IMBODEN
72435-72435	KNOBEL
72436-72436	LAFE
72437-72437	LAKE CITY
72438-72438	LEACHVILLE
72439-72439	LIGHT
72440-72440	LYNN
72441-72441	MC DOUGAL
72442-72442	MANILA
72443-72443	MARMADUKE
72444-72444	MAYNARD
72445-72445	MINTURN
72447-72447	MONETTE
72449-72449	O KEAN
72450-72451	PARAGOULD
72453-72453	PEACH ORCHARD
72454-72454	PIGGOTT
72455-72455	POCAHONTAS
72456-72456	POLLARD
72457-72457	PORTIA
72458-72458	POWHATAN
72459-72459	RAVENDEN
72460-72460	RAVENDEN SPRINGS
72461-72461	RECTOR
72462-72462	REYNO
72464-72464	SAINT FRANCIS
72465-72465	SEDGWICK
72466-72466	SMITHVILLE
72467-72467	STATE UNIVERSITY
72469-72469	STRAWBERRY
72470-72470	SUCCESS
72471-72471	SWIFTON
72472-72472	TRUMANN
72473-72473	TUCKERMAN
72474-72474	WALCOTT
72475-72475	WALDENBURG
72476-72476	WALNUT RIDGE
72478-72478	WARM SPRINGS
72479-72479	WEINER
72482-72482	WILLIFORD
72501-72503	BATESVILLE
72512-72512	HORSESHOE BEND
72513-72513	ASH FLAT
72515-72515	BEXAR
72516-72516	BOSWELL
72517-72517	BROCKWELL
72519-72519	CALICO ROCK

72520-72520	CAMP
72521-72521	CAVE CITY
72522-72522	CHARLOTTE
72523-72523	CONCORD
72524-72524	CORD
72525-72525	CHEROKEE VILLAGE
72526-72526	CUSHMAN
72527-72527	DESHA
72528-72528	DOLPH
72529-72529	CHEROKEE VILLAGE
72530-72530	DRASCO
72531-72531	ELIZABETH
72532-72532	EVENING SHADE
72533-72533	FIFTY SIX
72534-72534	FLORAL
72536-72536	FRANKLIN
72537-72537	GAMALIEL
72538-72538	GEPP
72539-72539	GLENCOE
72540-72540	GUION
72542-72542	HARDY
72543-72543	HEBER SPRINGS
72544-72544	HENDERSON
72545-72545	HEBER SPRINGS
72546-72546	IDA
72550-72550	LOCUST GROVE
72553-72553	MAGNESS
72554-72554	MAMMOTH SPRING
72555-72555	MARCELLA
72556-72556	MELBOURNE
72557-72557	MOKO
72560-72560	MOUNTAIN VIEW
72561-72561	MOUNT PLEASANT
72562-72562	NEWARK
72564-72564	OIL TROUGH
72565-72565	OXFORD
72566-72566	PINEVILLE
72567-72567	PLEASANT GROVE
72568-72568	PLEASANT PLAINS
72569-72569	POUGHKEEPSIE
72571-72571	ROSIE
72572-72572	SAFFELL
72573-72573	SAGE
72575-72575	SALADO
72576-72576	SALEM
72577-72577	SIDNEY
72578-72578	STURKIE
72579-72579	SULPHUR ROCK
72581-72581	TUMBLING SHOALS
72583-72583	VIOLA
72584-72584	VIOLET HILL
72585-72585	WIDEMAN
72587-72587	WISEMAN
72601-72602	HARRISON
72610-72610	ALCO
72611-72611	ALPENA
72612-72612	BASS
72613-72613	BEAVER
72615-72615	BERGMAN
72616-72616	BERRYVILLE
72617-72617	BIG FLAT
72618-72618	BRUNO
72619-72619	BULL SHOALS
72623-72623	CLARKRIDGE
72624-72624	COMPTON
72626-72626	COTTER
72628-72628	DEER
72629-72629	DENNARD
72630-72630	DIAMOND CITY
72631-72632	EUREKA SPRINGS
72633-72633	EVERTON
72634-72634	FLIPPIN
72635-72635	GASSVILLE
72636-72636	GILBERT
72638-72638	GREEN FOREST
72639-72639	HARRIET
72640-72640	HASTY
72641-72641	JASPER
72642-72642	LAKEVIEW
72644-72644	LEAD HILL
72645-72645	LESLIE
72648-72648	MARBLE FALLS
72650-72650	MARSHALL
72651-72651	MIDWAY
72653-72654	MOUNTAIN HOME
72655-72655	MOUNT JUDEA
72657-72657	TIMBO
72658-72659	NORFORK
72660-72660	OAK GROVE
72661-72661	OAKLAND
72662-72662	OMAHA
72663-72663	ONIA
72666-72666	PARTHENON
72668-72668	PEEL
72669-72669	PINDALL
72670-72670	PONCA
72672-72672	PYATT
72675-72675	SAINT JOE
72677-72677	SUMMIT
72679-72679	TILLY
72680-72680	TIMBO
72682-72682	VALLEY SPRINGS
72683-72683	VENDOR
72685-72685	WESTERN GROVE
72686-72686	WITTS SPRINGS
72687-72687	YELLVILLE
72701-72704	FAYETTEVILLE
72711-72711	AVOCA
72712-72712	BENTONVILLE
72714-72715	BELLA VISTA
72716-72716	BENTONVILLE
72717-72717	CANEHILL
72718-72718	CAVE SPRINGS
72719-72719	CENTERTON
72721-72721	COMBS
72722-72722	DECATUR
72727-72727	ELKINS
72728-72728	ELM SPRINGS
72729-72729	EVANSVILLE
72730-72730	FARMINGTON
72732-72732	GARFIELD
72733-72733	GATEWAY
72734-72734	GENTRY
72735-72735	GOSHEN
72736-72736	GRAVETTE
72737-72737	GREENLAND
72738-72738	HINDSVILLE
72739-72739	HIWASSE
72740-72740	HUNTSVILLE
72741-72741	JOHNSON
72742-72742	KINGSTON
72744-72744	LINCOLN
72745-72745	LOWELL
72747-72747	MAYSVILLE
72749-72749	MORROW
72751-72751	PEA RIDGE
72752-72752	PETTIGREW
72753-72753	PRAIRIE GROVE
72756-72758	ROGERS
72760-72760	SAINT PAUL
72761-72761	SILOAM SPRINGS
72762-72766	SPRINGDALE
72767-72767	SPRINGTOWN
72768-72768	SULPHUR SPRINGS
72769-72769	SUMMERS
72770-72770	TONTITOWN
72773-72773	WESLEY
72774-72774	WEST FORK
72775-72775	WHEELER
72776-72776	WITTER
72801-72812	RUSSELLVILLE
72820-72820	ALIX
72821-72821	ALTUS
72822-72823	ATKINS
72824-72824	BELLEVILLE
72826-72826	BLUE MOUNTAIN
72827-72827	BLUFFTON
72828-72828	BRIGGSVILLE
72829-72829	CENTERVILLE
72830-72830	CLARKSVILLE
72832-72832	COAL HILL
72833-72833	DANVILLE
72834-72834	DARDANELLE
72835-72835	DELAWARE
72837-72837	DOVER
72838-72838	GRAVELLY
72839-72839	HAGARVILLE
72840-72840	HARTMAN
72841-72841	HARVEY
72842-72842	HAVANA
72843-72843	HECTOR
72844-72844	HUNT
72845-72845	KNOXVILLE
72846-72846	LAMAR
72847-72847	LONDON
72851-72851	NEW BLAINE
72852-72852	OARK
72853-72853	OLA
72854-72854	OZONE
72855-72855	PARIS
72856-72856	PELSOR
72857-72857	PLAINVIEW
72858-72858	POTTSVILLE
72860-72860	ROVER
72863-72863	SCRANTON
72865-72865	SUBIACO
72867-72867	WAVELAND
72901-72919	FORT SMITH
72921-72921	ALMA
72923-72923	BARLING
72924-72924	BATES
72926-72926	BOLES
72927-72927	BOONEVILLE
72928-72928	BRANCH
72930-72930	CECIL
72932-72932	CEDARVILLE
72933-72933	CHARLESTON
72934-72934	CHESTER
72935-72935	DYER
72936-72936	GREENWOOD
72937-72937	HACKETT
72938-72938	HARTFORD
72940-72940	HUNTINGTON
72941-72941	LAVACA
72943-72943	MAGAZINE
72944-72944	MANSFIELD
72945-72945	MIDLAND
72946-72946	MOUNTAINBURG
72947-72947	MULBERRY
72948-72948	NATURAL DAM
72949-72949	OZARK
72950-72950	PARKS
72951-72951	RATCLIFF
72952-72952	RUDY
72955-72955	UNIONTOWN
72956-72957	VAN BUREN
72958-72958	WALDRON
72959-72959	WINSLOW

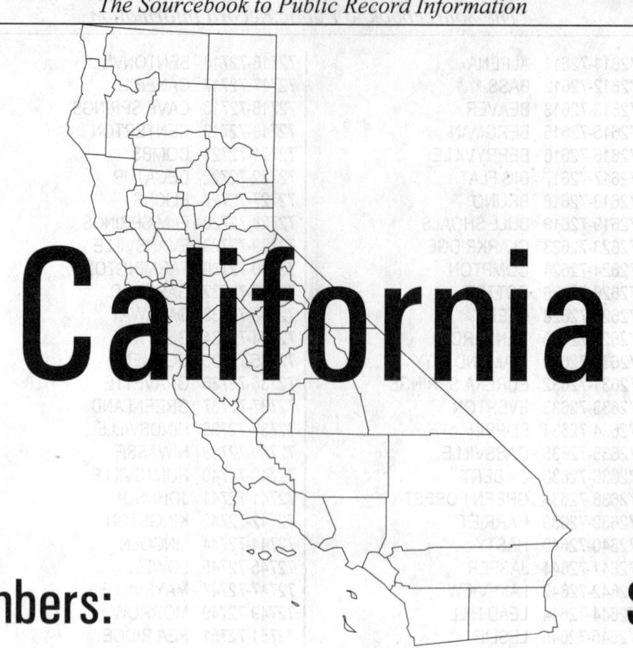

California

General Help Numbers:

Governor's Office

State Capitol, 1st Floor — 916-445-2841
Sacramento, CA 95814 — Fax 916-558-3160
http://gov.ca.gov/ — 8:30AM-5PM

Attorney General's Office

Justice Department — 916-445-9555,445-3360
PO Box 944255 — Fax 916-323-5341
Sacramento, CA 94244-2550 — 8AM-5PM
http://caag.state.ca.us

Legislative Records

State Capitol, Room B-32 — 916-445-2323
Sacramento, CA 95814 — Fax 916-322-1257
www.leginfo.ca.gov — 8AM-5PM

State Archives

1020 "O" St — 916-653-7715/2246
Sacramento, CA 95814 — Fax 916-653-7363
www.sos.ca.gov/archives/archives.htm — 9:30AM-4PM

State Specifics:

Capital:	Sacramento Sacramento County
Time Zone:	PST
Number of Counties:	58
Population:	36,756,666
Website:	www.ca.gov/

State Agencies

Criminal Records

Access to Records is Restricted.

Department of Justice, Records Security Section, PO Box 903417, Sacramento, CA 94203-4170 (Courier address- 4949 Broadway, Sacramento, CA 95820); 916-227-3460 (Dept of Justice), 916-227-3849 (General Information), Fax- 916-227-4815; 8AM-5PM.

www.caag.state.ca.us

Penal Code Sec. 11105.3 limits access to searches involving child care, the elderly, the handicapped and mentally impaired. The subject can obtain their own copy, but the record cannot be used for employment or licensing. Entities must be authorized before records can be requested. 99% of arrest records are fingerprint supported, entered from final disposition.

Statewide Court Records

Administration Office of Courts, Office of Communications, 455 Golden Gate Ave, San Francisco, CA 94102-3660; 415-865-4200, 415-865-7740, Fax- 415-865-4334; 8AM-5PM.

www.courtinfo.ca.gov

All trial court record access must be done at the local level. Email questions to pubinfo@jud.ca.gov.

Access by: online.

Online search: The home page provides access to all opinions from the Supreme and Appeals courts from 1850 to present. The site is an extensive resource for matters of court administration and court procedures.

Sexual Offender Registry

Department of Justice, Sexual Offender Program, PO Box 903387, Sacramento, CA 94203-3870 (Courier address- 4949 Broadway, Rm H-216, Sacramento, CA 95820); 916-227-4974, 916-227-4199 (Tracking), Fax- 916-227-4345; 8AM-5PM.

www.meganslaw.ca.gov/

There are over 85,000 registered sexual offenders in CA.

Indexing & Storage: New records available for inquiry in 48 hours or less.

Searching: The agency refers all requesters to the web page. Email questions to MegansLaw@doj.ca.gov. Include in request- full name; also helpful DOB and SSN.

Access by: online.

Online search: The web page offers online searching by a sex offender's specific name or by geographic location including ZIP Code, county or within a predetermined radius of a selected address, park, or school. This site will provide access to information on more than 63,000 persons required to register in California as sex offenders. Specific home addresses are displayed on more than 33,500 offenders.

Incarceration Records

Dept of Corrections, Corrections & Rehabilitation ID Unit, PO Box 942883, Sacramento, CA 94283-0001; 916-557-5933 (Inmate Check Line (Media Only)), 916-445-6713 (Ident Unit (Public Inquiry)), 916-445-7682 (Dept. of Corrections Main #), Fax- 916-327-1988; 8AM-5PM.

www.cdcr.ca.gov

The state provides no online searching, however a private company offers free web access to some county DOC records, www.vinelink.com/index.jsp

Indexing & Storage: Records available on current and former inmates. New records available for inquiry in about 7 days.

Searching: Include in request- full name, DOB, your fax and phone numbers; also helpful: inmate number. Location, conviction and sentencing information, and county of conviction are released. Agency prefers to return results via fax. This data not released- case specifics, which should be acquired from the courts.

Access by: mail, phone, fax.

Fee & Payment: There is no fee.

Mail search: Turnaround time- 4-6 days.

Phone search: The Inmate Locator help line at 916-445-6713 is open the same hours as mentioned above. Provides an inmate's location, mailing addresses and relevant phone numbers.

Fax search: Records are available by fax.

Corporation, LLC, LP, LLP

Secretary of State, Information Retrieval/ Certification Unit, PO Box 944260, Sacramento, CA 94244-2600 (Courier address- 1500 11th Street, 3rd Fl, Sacramento, CA 95814); 916-657-5448 x1; 8AM-4:30PM.

www.sos.ca.gov/business/business.htm

Indexing & Storage: New records available for inquiry immediately.

Searching: Include in request- full name of business. Business entity records include: formation documents, statements of information and change documents (including, but not limited to amendments, mergers, conversions, dissolutions, and cancellations).

Access by: mail, phone, fax, in person, online.

Fee & Payment: Reproductions of copies of records is $1.00 first page, $.50 each add'l. Copies can be certified for an add'l $5.00. A certification of filing or status is $5.00 A report of status with agent for service of process is $4.00. Fee payee- Secretary of State. Prepayment required. Personal checks accepted. Credit cards accepted for over-the-counter inquiries.

Mail search: Turnaround time- varies. The web page also provides latest processing timelines; A SASE is requested. Request forms may be downloaded form the web.

Phone search: Only pre-paid accounts have telephone access to corporate status and name availability/reservation. Fee is $4.00 per name searched. Call 916-653-1233 for details on establishing an account.

Fax search: Return of documents and/or status information is an additional $5.00 per document, $10.00 if international.

In person: Turnaround time is while you wait for computer printouts of status reports, but a $10.00 expedite fee is charged for counter service. This office provides all services, but the four regional offices can provide certificates of status for active corporations.

Online search: The website at http://kepler.ss.ca.gov/list.html offers access to more than 2 million records including corporation, LLC, and LP. Information available includes status, file number, date of registration, jurisdiction and agent for service of process. The file is updated weekly. Also, search securities companies registered with the state at http://134.186.208.228/caleasi/pub/exsearch.htm.

Other access: Information regarding bulk lists and other forms of records access is available by contacting the Sec. of State's Information Technology Division at 916-653-8905.

Trademarks/Servicemarks

Secretary of State, Trademark Unit, PO Box 942877, Sacramento, CA 94277-0001 (Courier address- 1500 11th Street, 2nd Fl, Sacramento, CA 95814); 916-653-3984 x320 (Trademark/Servicemarks); 8AM-5PM.

www.sos.ca.gov/business/ts/ts.htm

California is the busiest state registration office in the country and has the largest number of registrations of any state, consisting of approx. 80,000 active marks.

Indexing & Storage: Records available for active and expired records. Records are microfilmed monthly. New records available for inquiry in 3 to 4 weeks.

Searching: Include in request- trademark/ servicemark name. Information returned includes name of trademark, name of owner and address, and date of filing.

Access by: mail, phone, in person.

Fee & Payment: Copies are $1.00 per page and $.50 each add'l. Certification is $5.00 per document. A Certificate of Status is $5.00. Fee payee- Secretary of State. Prepayment required. Personal checks accepted, credit cards are not.

Mail search: Turnaround time- 3 to 4 weeks. A SASE is requested. No fee for mail request.

Phone search: No fee for telephone request of a name search. There is a limit of 2 searches per call.

In person: You can wait for results. If lists are presented, then the results are returned by mail.

Other access: Microfilm is sold on monthly basis with year contract.

Assumed Name, Fictitious Name

Records not maintained by a state level agency.

Records are found at the county level.

Uniform Commercial Code, Federal & State Tax Liens

Business Programs Division, UCC Section, PO Box 942835, Sacramento, CA 94235 (Courier address- 1500 11th St, Room 255, Sacramento, CA 95814); 916-651-9885; 8AM-5PM.

www.sos.ca.gov/business/ucc/ucc.htm

Indexing & Storage: Records available for current records and expired records up to 1 year after lapse. New records available for inquiry immediately.

Searching: Use search request form UCC-11; one form per debtor name. The search includes federal and some state tax liens on businesses. Federal tax liens on individuals are filed at the county level, state tax liens are filed at either location. Include in request- debtor name. Item 3b-3d on the UCC-11 provide fields for narrowing the search by a specific address or by a date range, but this is not recommended by this agency. This data not released- SSN.

Access by: mail, in person, online.

Fee & Payment: The search fee is $10.00 per debtor name. The copy fee is $1.00 for the first page of the document and $.50 each additional page. There is a certification fee of $5.00 if the state seal is needed. Note that fees are different for the online system, Fee payee- Secretary of State. Prepayment required. Those conducting business frequently with this office may utilize a prepaid account option. Personal checks accepted. Major credit cards accepted.

Mail search: Turnaround time- 2-3 days.

In person: There is an additional $6.00 special handling fee for each document received over the counter.

Online search: UCC Connect provides an online service at https://uccconnect.sos.ca.gov/acct/acct-login.asp to conduct a variety of inquiries and place orders for copies and debtor search certificates on records and submit UCC filings. Ongoing requesters can become subscribers. Fees are based on name inquires ($5.00 per name) and images viewed ($1.00). The web page has a complete list of fees and excellent FAQ section. Click on the Help tab.

Other access: The database is available for purchase, daily updates are available for an additional fee on a yearly subscription basis. The web page has prices.

Sales Tax Registrations

Board of Equalization, Sales and Use Tax Department, PO Box 942879, Sacramento, CA 94279-0001; 916-445-6362, 800-400-7115 (In California Only), Fax- 916-324-4433; 8AM-5PM.

www.boe.ca.gov

A list of the field offices is available at www.boe.ca.gov/info/phone.htm.

Searching: This Board will provide owners' name, firm name, business address, account number, starting date, whether account is active or closed and, if closed, the closing date. The responsibility of assisting taxpayers in verifying the validity of resale certificates is primarily at the District level, but this office will provide search services. Requesters must provide name of the business, its location, and permit number.

Access by: mail, phone, fax, online.

Fee & Payment: No charge is required for verification of resale certificates and permits. However, a fee for other requests, such as those received from attorneys and collection agencies, is $3.00 per name searched. Fee payee- Board of Equalization. Prepayment required. Monthly billing is available for ongoing requesters. Personal checks accepted, credit cards are not.

Mail search: Turnaround time- 2 weeks. A SASE is requested.

Phone search: No fee for telephone request. The 24 hour phone service is offered to verify a seller's permit is valid. Calls are not limited to number of requests.

Fax search: Generally, turnaround time is 2 weeks.

Online search: The Internet site provides a permit verification service. Permit number is needed. System is open 5AM to midnight.

Other access: Lists, available for a fee, are sorted in a number of ways including CA Industry Code. For further information and fees, call the Technical Services Division at 916-445-5848

Birth Certificates

State Department of Health Svcs, Office of Vital Records - MS 5103, PO Box 997410, Sacramento, CA 95899-7410 (Courier address- 1501 Capitol Ave, Rm 71-1110, Sacramento, CA 95814); 916-445-2684 (Recording); 8AM-noon.

www.cdph.ca.gov/Pages/default.aspx

If requesting an Authorized Certified Birth or Death certificate online or by fax, applicants must complete a Sworn Statement and a notarized Certificate of Acknowledgment in the presence of a Notary Public.

Indexing & Storage: Records available from July 1905 on. New records available for inquiry in up to 6 months.

Searching: Certified records are not open to the public. Requester must be related to the subject or attorney representing subject or subject's family. However, persons who are not eligible to receive a Certified Copy can receive a Certified Informational Copy. Include in request- full name, mother's full maiden name, date of birth, place of birth, father's full name is optional. Certified copy must included notarized statement of requester. If you do not use their form, the search may be delayed 2-3 weeks.

Access by: mail, fax.

Fee & Payment: The fee for a certified copy is $14.00, if the birth date is not known, a fee of $14.00 is charged for each decade searched. Fee payee- Office of Vital Records. Prepayment required. Personal checks and money orders accepted. Credit cards accepted only by the vendors.

Mail search: Turnaround time- may exceed 3 months. Always include your daytime phone number. SASE not required. Download and use the request form at the website.

Fax search: Applicant must complete a Sworn Statement and a notarized Certificate of Acknowledgment in the presence of a Notary Public.

Expedited service: A vendor (www.vitalchek.com) processes online orders via the appropriate county agency. The fee is $29.95.

Death Records

State Department of Health Svcs, Office of Vital Records - MS 5103, PO Box 997410, Sacramento, CA 95899-7410 (Courier address- 1501 Capitol Ave, Rm 71-1110, Sacramento, CA 95814); 916-445-2684; 8AM-noon.

www.cdph.ca.gov/Pages/default.aspx

Indexing & Storage: Records available from July 1905 to present. New records available for inquiry in up to 6 months.

Searching: Certified records are not open to the public. Requester must be related to the subject or attorney representing subject or subject's family. However, persons who are not eligible to receive a Certified Copy can receive a Certified Informational Copy. Include in request- full name, date of death, date of birth, place of death, SSN. Certified copy must included notarized sworn statement of requester. There will be a 2-3 week delay if you do not use their form.

Access by: mail, online.

Fee & Payment: Search fee is $12.00 per name for each decade searched, the fee is $9.00 for a fetal death certificate. Fee payee- Office of Vital Records. Prepayment required. Personal checks accepted. Credit cards accepted only by the vendors.

Mail search: Turnaround time- 3 months or more. Download and use the request form at the website.

Online search: Access death records 1940 thru 1997 at http://vitals.rootsweb.ancestry.com/ca/death/search.cgi.

Other access: A vendor (www.vitalchek.com) processes online orders via the appropriate county agency. The fee is $29.95.

Marriage Certificates, Divorce Certificates

Access to Records is Restricted.

State Department of Health Svcs, Office of Vital Records - MS 5103, PO Box 997410, Sacramento, CA 95899-7410 (Courier address- 1501 Capitol Ave, Rm 71-1110, Sacramento, CA 95814); 916-445-2684; 8AM-noon.

www.cdph.ca.gov/Pages/default.aspx

It can take from 6 months to 2 years for this agency to process requests. Plus the divorce record index at the location has only 1962 through June 1984. Therefore it is strongly urged to search at the county level.

Workers' Compensation Records

Division of Workers' Compensation, Headquarters, 1515 Clay Street, 17th Fl, Oakland, CA 94612; 510-286-7100, Fax- 510-286-3470; 8AM-5PM.

www.dir.ca.gov/dwc/dwc_home_page.htm

Per law, no addresses of any injured workers are given out. Request for public records should be sent to a local district office. The list of offices is found at www.dir.ca.gov/dwc/dir2.htm.

Indexing & Storage: Records available for varying periods depending on injury and if case files sent to State Records Center.

Searching: Using the proper forms, one can either view a file or ask if records exist. This authorization process does not require the signature or approval of the claimant. Forms may be faxed. Include in request- name, address and phone of requestor, purpose of request. Use form found at www.dir.ca.gov/dwc/forms.html. Email questions to DWC_PRA@dir.ca.gov This data not released- residence address, SSNs, sealed records.

Access by: mail, fax, in person.

Fee & Payment: There is no search fee, there is a copy fee. The agency will quote a fee upon order.

Mail search: Turnaround time- variable. Use the request form, the agency will let you know if there is a record. The agency suggests that out-of-state requesters use a local CA retriever who already has the necessary authorization to search. SASE not required.

Fax search: Turnaround is usually 10 days.

In person: With a case number, requester can visit any of the 25 district offices.

Driver Records

Department of Motor Vehicles, Information Services Branch, PO Box 944247, Mail Station G199, Sacramento, CA 94244-2470 (Courier address- 2415 First Ave, Sacramento, CA 95818); 916-657-8098, 916-657-5564 (Requester Accounts), Fax- 916-657-8098; 8AM-5PM.

www.dmv.ca.gov

The public counter is closed for record access by walk-in requesters, unless subject wishes to obtain own record. Copies of tickets are not available at the state level and must be ordered from the courts.

Indexing & Storage: Records available for 3 years from accidents and minor moving violations dates, 7 years for major violations, and 10 years (since 01/01/07 only) for DUIs. A Failure to Appear is reported for 5 years, and 10 years if for a DUI offense. New records available for inquiry in 10 days or more (as received from the courts).

Searching: Commercial requesters/users who meet certain criteria must maintain a Commercial Requester Account, which may require a $50,000 bond if confidential address information is released. For more details call 916-657-5564 or visit www.dmv.ca.gov. Include in request- driver's license number, full name, date of birth. Non-commercial requesters are known as "casual requesters." These requests may be held for 10 days and the state notifies the licensee of each release. If released, address is shielded unless a permissible use shown. This data not released- mental health records, medical records, pending records, and SSNs.

Access by: mail, online.

Fee & Payment: Manual searches are $5.00; electronic MVRs are $2.00; guarantor's signature- $20.00; license status only $1.00 via an approved vendor. Fee payee- California Department of Motor Vehicles. Prepayment required. Personal checks accepted, credit cards are not.

Mail search: Turnaround time- 1 to 2 weeks. An SASE is not requested.

Online search: The department offers online access, but a $10,000 one-time setup fee may be required. Entities who order from an online vendor must also be pre-approved and fees are involved.

The fee is $2.00 per record. The system is available 24 hours, 7 days a week. For more information call 916-657-5582.

Other access: Employers may monitor their drivers in the Pull Notice Program. The DMV informs the organization when there is activity on enrolled drivers. Call 916-657-6346 for details.

Vehicle, Vessel Ownership & Registration

Department of Motor Vehicle, Office of Information Services, PO Box 944247, MS-G199, Sacramento, CA 94244-2470 (Courier address- 2415 First Ave, Sacramento, CA 95818); 916-657-8098, 916-657-5564 (Commercial Accounts), 916-657-6893 (Vessel Registration), Fax- 916-657-7243; 8AM-5PM.

www.dmv.ca.gov

All motorized and sail, and watercraft over 8 ft (except rowboats) must be registered.

Indexing & Storage: Records available for current plus three years when microfilmed. New records available for inquiry in up to 10 days.

Searching: It is suggested to use departmental forms, which can be obtained the webpage or fax request to 916-657-7243. Include in request- license plate, CF number, VIN or vessel hull number. There are two types of requesters: "casual requesters" and "requester account holders." For those businesses and entities who need to access on a regular basis, call 916-657-5564. A bond may be required. This data not released- confidential or suppressed records per the Vehicle Code.

Access by: mail, in person, online.

Fee & Payment: Current record by license, VIN or CF#, by registration owner name and address- $5.00; owner as of data by license, VIN or CF#- $5.00; current automated history data-$5.00; photocopies-$20.00 per year. Fee payee- California Department of Motor Vehicles. Prepayment required. Personal checks accepted, credit cards are not.

Mail search: Turnaround time- 1 to 2 weeks. A SASE is not requested.

In person: Only the registered, owner, spouse, or minor child (with same address) can purchase a copy of their vehicle/vessel record at any DMV field office.

Online search: 24 hour online access is limited to certain Authorized Vendors. Requesters may not use data for direct marketing, solicitation, nor resell for those purposes. A bond is required and a $10,000 one-time permit fees is required. Then records are $2.00 ea. For more information, call the Electronic Access Administration Section at 916-657-5582.

Other access: California offers delivery of registration information on FTP VPN, magnetic tape, disk or paper within special parameters. Release of information is denied for commercial marketing purposes.

Accident Reports

Department of Motor Vehicles, Accident Reports, PO Box 942884, Sacramento, CA 94284; 800-777-0133; 8AM-5PM (open at 9AM of F).

www.dmv.ca.gov

Most accident reports are held by the California Highway Patrol or local law enforcement agency that filed the report. There are 115 area offices of the California Highway Patrol. Fees vary. Limited reports are held by this office.

Indexing & Storage: New records available for inquiry in 30 to 60 days.

Searching: Reports are made if there was property damage of more than $750 ($500 for accidents prior to January 1, 2003), bodily injury or death. Include in request- name and DOB of driver, location, date, and name of requester. Copies of SR-1 accident reports are provided to limited requesters by the Department of Motor Vehicles.

Access by: mail.

Fee & Payment: The fee is $20.00.

Mail search: SR-1 accident reports are available by mail from this office.

Legislation Records

California State Legislature, State Capitol, Room B-32 (Legislative Bill Room), Sacramento, CA 95814; 916-445-2323 (Current/Pending Bills), 916-653-7715 (State Archives), Fax- 916-322-1257; 8AM-5PM.

www.leginfo.ca.gov

This office carries only latest amended versions (last 2 years). The agency recommends that any California law library would have complete copies of all bills for other years and may be easier to search.

Indexing & Storage: Records available for three years on paper. New records available for inquiry in 1 day.

Searching: Include in request- bill number, year. Author's name helpful.

Access by: mail, phone, in person, online.

Fee & Payment: There is no charge for up to 5 bills. They will compute copy charges, if needed. Fee payee- Legislative Bill Room. Personal checks and major credit cards accepted.

Mail search: Turnaround time- 5 to 7 days. Must first know what the copies will be prior to ordering. SASE not required.

Phone search: You may call for bill copies.

In person: You may request copies in person.

Online search: The Internet site has all legislative information back to 1993. The site also gives access to state statutes.

Voter Registration

Access to Records is Restricted.

Secretary of State, Elections Division, 1500 11th Street, 5th Fl, Sacramento, CA 95814; 916-657-2166, Fax- 916-653-3214; 8AM-5PM.

www.sos.ca.gov/elections/elections.htm

Records are not open and cannot be viewed at this agency. Individual verification must be done at the local level. The state will sell CDs with all or portions of the statewide database for political or pre-approved purposes. Call for details.

GED Certificates

ETS - GED Records Center, PO Box 4005, Concord, CA 94524-4005; 866-370-4740; 8AM-5PM.

www.cde.ca.gov/ta/tg/gd/

A verification by itself is not available. Requester must purchase the Score Report.

Indexing & Storage: Records available from July 1990, prior are archived. New records available for inquiry in 2 months.

Searching: Include in request- a signed, notarized release with a name, DOB, date/year of test, SSN, and city of test. This applies to either a verification or if obtaining a transcript copy. E-signatures not accepted.

Access by: mail.

Fee & Payment: Score reports are provided for $5.00; there is a $12.00 fee (money order only) for a High School Equivalency certificate. Fee payee- CA Dept of Ed Prepayment required. Personal and business checks not accepted. Credit cards not accepted.

Mail search: Turnaround time- 10 business days. SASE is suggested.

Hunting & Fishing License Information

Access to Records is Restricted.

Department of Fish & Game, License & Revenue Branch, 1740 N Market Blvd, Sacramento, CA 95834-1997; 916-928-5805, 916-928-6899, Fax- 916-419-7587; 9AM-5PM.

www.dfg.ca.gov/licensing/

Records are not available to the public.

California State Licensing Agencies

For details about the agency responsible for licensing/certifying/registering an item below or in the Agency Quick Finder section, match an item's number with the number of the agency in the *Licensing Agency Information* section.

California Licenses Searchable Online

Acupuncturist #1 .... www.acupuncture.ca.gov
Adoption Agency #50 .... www.ccld.ca.gov/docs/ccld_search/ccld_search.aspx
Agricultural Engineer #10 .... www.pels.ca.gov/consumers/lic_lookup.shtml
Air Conditioning Contractor #28 .... http://www2.cslb.ca.gov/OnlineServices/CheckLicense/NameRequest.asp
Alarm Firm/Employee/Mngr #22 .... www.bsis.ca.gov/online_services/verify_license.shtml
Appraiser, Real Estate #53 .... www.orea.ca.gov/html/lic_appraisers.asp
Apprentice Program, Skilled Labor #48 .... www.dir.ca.gov/databases/das/aigstart.asp
Architect #7 .... www.cab.ca.gov/consumers/license_verification.shtml
Asbestos Consultant/Surveillance #52 .... www.dir.ca.gov/databases/doshcaccsst/caccsst_query_1.html
Asbestos Contractor #52 .... www.dir.ca.gov/databases/doshacru/acrusearch.html
Asbestos Trainer #52 .... www.dir.ca.gov/databasedown.asp
Asbestos Worker/Trainee #52 .... www.dir.ca.gov/DOSH/ACRU/TP_AsbestosTrainingCertificates.html
Attorney #23 .... http://members.calbar.ca.gov/search/member.aspx
Audiologist #42 .... www.slpab.ca.gov/consumers/verify.shtml
Automobile Dealer/Repair #19 .... www.bar.ca.gov/70_SiteWideInfo/02_Tools/03_VerifyLicense.html
Bank Agencies/Branches, Foreign #11 .... www.dfi.ca.gov/licensees/otherstate/default.asp
Bank, State Chartered #11 .... www.dfi.ca.gov/licensees/
Bank, State Chartered, Industr'l #11 .... www.dfi.ca.gov/directory/regulate.asp
Bar Association #23 .... http://members.calbar.ca.gov/search/ba_search.aspx
Barber Instructor/School #4 .... http://www2.dca.ca.gov/pls/wllpub/wllqryna$lcev2.startup?p_qte_code=FRM&p_qte_pgm_code=3300
Barber/Barber Shop/Apprentice #4 .... http://www2.dca.ca.gov/pls/wllpub/wllqryna$lcev2.startup?p_qte_code=IND&p_qte_pgm_code=3300
Baton Training Facility/Instruct. #22 .... www.bsis.ca.gov/online_services/verify_license.shtml
Brake & Lamp Adjuster/Brake Station #19 .... www.bar.ca.gov/70_SiteWideInfo/02_Tools/03_VerifyLicense.html
Building Contr., General-Class B #28 .... http://www2.cslb.ca.gov/OnlineServices/CheckLicense/NameRequest.asp
Cabinet/Millwork Contractor #28 .... http://www2.cslb.ca.gov/OnlineServices/CheckLicense/NameRequest.asp
Car Washing/Polishing #48 .... www.dir.ca.gov/databases/dlselr/carwash.html
Care Facility for Chronically Ill #50 .... www.ccld.ca.gov/docs/ccld_search/ccld_search.aspx
Care Facility, Children, Transitional #50 .... www.ccld.ca.gov/docs/ccld_search/ccld_search.aspx
Cemetery, Cemetery Broker/Seller #25 .... www.cfb.ca.gov/consumer/lookup.shtml
Child Care Center #50 .... www.ccld.ca.gov/docs/ccld_search/ccld_search.aspx
Chiropractic Corporation/Satellite #46 .... www.chiro.ca.gov/onlineservices/licsearch.html
Chiropractic Referral Service #46 .... www.chiro.ca.gov/onlineservices/licsearch.html
Chiropractor #46 .... www.chiro.ca.gov/onlineservices/licsearch.html
Clinic Pharmaceutical Permit #13 .... www.pharmacy.ca.gov/online/verify_lic.shtml
Community Treatment Facility #50 .... www.ccld.ca.gov/docs/ccld_search/ccld_search.aspx
Concrete Contractor/Company #28 .... http://www2.cslb.ca.gov/OnlineServices/CheckLicense/NameRequest.asp
Conscious Sedation Permit #9 .... http://www2.dca.ca.gov/pls/wllpub/wllquery$.startup
Construction Permit, Excava'n/Shoring #52 .... www.dir.ca.gov/dosh/PermitHolder/PermitHolder.asp
Continuing Education Provider #8 .... www.bbs.ca.gov/quick_links/weblookup.shtml
Contractor, Business/Individual #28 .... http://www2.cslb.ca.gov/OnlineServices/CheckLicense/NameRequest.asp
Cosmetician/Cosmetologist #4 .... http://www2.dca.ca.gov/pls/wllpub/wllqryna$lcev2.startup?p_qte_code=IND&p_qte_pgm_code=3300
Cosmetology School #4 .... http://www2.dca.ca.gov/pls/wllpub/wllqryna$lcev2.startup?p_qte_code=FRM&p_qte_pgm_code=3300
Cosmetology/Electrology Firm/Instr. #4 .... http://www2.dca.ca.gov/pls/wllpub/wllqryna$lcev2.startup?p_qte_code=IND&p_qte_pgm_code=3300
Court Reporter/Shorthand Reporter #29 .... http://www2.dca.ca.gov/pls/wllpub/wllqryna$lcev2.startup?p_qte_code=CSR&p_qte_pgm_code=8100
CPA/CPA Firm #6 .... http://www2.dca.ca.gov/pls/wllpub/wllquery$.startup
Crane Operator #52 .... www.dir.ca.gov/databases/crane/cranesearch.html
Credit Union #11 .... www.dfi.ca.gov/licensees/cu/default.asp
Cremated Remains Disposer #25 .... www.cfb.ca.gov/consumer/lookup.shtml
Crematory #25 .... www.cfb.ca.gov/consumer/lookup.shtml
Day Care, Adult/Child #50 .... www.ccld.ca.gov/docs/ccld_search/ccld_search.aspx
Dental Anesthesia Permit #9 .... http://www2.dca.ca.gov/pls/wllpub/wllquery$.startup
Dental Assistant #27 .... www.comda.ca.gov/verification/index.shtml
Dental Hygienist #27 .... www.comda.ca.gov/verification/index.shtml
Dental Registered Provider #9 .... http://www2.dca.ca.gov/pls/wllpub/wllquery$.startup
Dentist #9 .... http://www2.dca.ca.gov/pls/wllpub/wllquery$.startup
Dentist Fictitious Name #9 .... http://www2.dca.ca.gov/pls/wllpub/wllquery$.startup

Development Corporation #11 .... www.dfi.ca.gov/directory/bidco.asp
Driving School/Instructor #49 .... https://mv.dmv.ca.gov/olinq2/welcome.do
Drug Wholesaler/Drug Room #13 .... www.pharmacy.ca.gov/online/verify_lic.shtml
Drywall Contractor #28 .... http://www2.cslb.ca.gov/OnlineServices/CheckLicense/NameRequest.asp
Earthwork/Paving Contractor #28 .... http://www2.cslb.ca.gov/OnlineServices/CheckLicense/NameRequest.asp
Electrical Contr. & Electric Sign Contr. #28 .. http://www2.cslb.ca.gov/OnlineServices/CheckLicense/NameRequest.asp
Electrologist #4 .... http://www2.dca.ca.gov/pls/wllpub/wllqryna$lcev2.startup?p_qte_code=IND&p_qte_pgm_code=3300
Electrology School #4 .... http://www2.dca.ca.gov/pls/wllpub/wllqryna$lcev2.startup?p_qte_code=FRM&p_qte_pgm_code=3300
Electronic & Appliance Repair #20 .... www.bear.ca.gov/consumer/look_up.shtml
Elevator Installation Contractor #28 .... http://www2.cslb.ca.gov/OnlineServices/CheckLicense/NameRequest.asp
Embalmer/Embalmer Apprentice #25 .... www.cfb.ca.gov/consumer/lookup.shtml
Engineer (various disciplines) #10 .... www.pels.ca.gov/consumers/lic_lookup.shtml
Esthetician #4 .... http://www2.dca.ca.gov/pls/wllpub/wllqryna$lcev2.startup?p_qte_code=IND&p_qte_pgm_code=3300
Family Child Care Home #50 .... www.ccld.ca.gov/docs/ccld_search/ccld_search.aspx
Farm Labor Contractor #48 .... www.dir.ca.gov/databases/dlselr/Farmlic.html
Fencing Contractor #28 .... http://www2.cslb.ca.gov/OnlineServices/CheckLicense/NameRequest.asp
Firearm Permit #22 .... www.bsis.ca.gov/online_services/verify_license.shtml
Firearm Training Facility/Instr. #22 .... www.bsis.ca.gov/online_services/verify_license.shtml
Flooring/Floor Covering Contractor #28 .... http://www2.cslb.ca.gov/OnlineServices/CheckLicense/NameRequest.asp
Foster Family Agency #50 .... www.ccld.ca.gov/docs/ccld_search/ccld_search.aspx
Funeral Director/Establishment #25 .... www.cfb.ca.gov/consumer/lookup.shtml
Funerary Training Establ./Apprentice #25 ... www.cfb.ca.gov/consumer/lookup.shtml
Garment Manufacturer #48 .... www.dir.ca.gov/databases/dlselr/Garmreg.html
Geologist #18 .... http://www2.dca.ca.gov/pls/wllpub/wllqryna$lcev2.startup?p_qte_code=GEO&p_qte_pgm_code=5100
Geologist, Engineering/Geophysicist #18 .... http://www2.dca.ca.gov/pls/wllpub/wllqryna$lcev2.startup?p_qte_code=GEO&p_qte_pgm_code=5100
Glazier #28 .... http://www2.cslb.ca.gov/OnlineServices/CheckLicense/NameRequest.asp
Group Home #50 .... www.ccld.ca.gov/docs/ccld_search/ccld_search.aspx
Healing Art Supervisor #31 .... www.applications.dhs.ca.gov/rhbxray/
Hearing Aid Dispenser #34 .... http://www2.dca.ca.gov/pls/wllpub/wllqryna$lcev2.startup?p_qte_code=HA&p_qte_pgm_code=6700
Heating & Warm-Air Vent. Contr. #28 .... http://www2.cslb.ca.gov/OnlineServices/CheckLicense/NameRequest.asp
Home Furnishings #21 .... http://www2.dca.ca.gov/pls/wllpub/wllqryna$lcev2.startup?p_qte_code=LIC&p_qte_pgm_code=5710
Horse Racing Entity #24 .... www.chrb.ca.gov/license_search.htm
Horse Racing Occupation #24 .... www.chrb.ca.gov/license_search.htm
Hospital Pharmaceutical Exemptee #13 ...... www.pharmacy.ca.gov/online/verify_lic.shtml
Hydrogeologist #18 .... http://www2.dca.ca.gov/pls/wllpub/wllqryna$lcev2.startup?p_qte_code=GEO&p_qte_pgm_code=5100
Hypodermic Needle & Syringe Dist. #13 ..... www.pharmacy.ca.gov/online/verify_lic.shtml
Infant Center #50 .... www.ccld.ca.gov/docs/ccld_search/ccld_search.aspx
Insulation/Acoustical Contractor #28 .... http://www2.cslb.ca.gov/OnlineServices/CheckLicense/NameRequest.asp
Insurance Adjuster #32 .... www.insurance.ca.gov/0200-industry/0200-prod-licensing/0200-current-lic-info/
Insurance Agent/Broker/Producer #32 .... www.insurance.ca.gov/license-status/index.cfm
Insurance Company #32 .... www.insurance.ca.gov/0200-industry/0070-check-license-status/index.cfm
Insurance2 Agent/Broker #32 .... www.insurance.ca.gov/0200-industry/0070-check-license-status/index.cfm
Investment Advisor #30 .... http://search.dre.ca.gov/integrationaspcode/
Lamp Station #19 .... www.bar.ca.gov/70_SiteWideInfo/02_Tools/03_VerifyLicense.html
Land Surveyor-in-Training #10 .... www.pels.ca.gov/consumers/lic_lookup.shtml
Landscape Architect #35 .... www.latc.ca.gov/consumers/search.shtml
Landscaping Contractor #28 .... http://www2.cslb.ca.gov/OnlineServices/CheckLicense/NameRequest.asp
Legal Specialist #23 .... http://members.calbar.ca.gov/search/ls_search.aspx
Legal Specialization Provider #23 .... http://members.calbar.ca.gov/search/cert.aspx
Lobbyist/Lobbying Firm/Employer #47 .... http://cal-access.ss.ca.gov/Lobbying/
Locksmith/Locksmith Company #22 .... www.bsis.ca.gov/online_services/verify_license.shtml
Mammographic Facility #31 .... www.applications.dhs.ca.gov/rhbxray/
Manicurist #4 .... http://www2.dca.ca.gov/pls/wllpub/wllqryna$lcev2.startup?p_qte_code=IND&p_qte_pgm_code=3300
Marriage & Family Therapist #8 .... www.bbs.ca.gov/quick_links/weblookup.shtml
Masonry Contractor #28 .... http://www2.cslb.ca.gov/OnlineServices/CheckLicense/NameRequest.asp
Medical Doctor, Enforcem't Document #36 . www.medbd.ca.gov/lookup.html
Medical Doctor/Surgeon #36 .... www.medbd.ca.gov/lookup.html
Medical Evaluator #52 .... www.dir.ca.gov/databases/dwc/qmestartnew.asp
Midwife, Midwife Nurse #36 .... http://www2.dca.ca.gov/pls/wllpub/wllqryna$lcev2.startup?p_qte_code=LM&p_qte_pgm_code=6200
Money Order Issuer #11 .... www.dfi.ca.gov/licensees/moneytransmitters/default.asp
Notary Education Vendor #37 .... http://notaryeducation.sos.ca.gov/
Nuclear Medicine Technologist #31 .... www.applications.dhs.ca.gov/rhbxray/
Nurse Registered #16 .... http://www2.dca.ca.gov/pls/wllpub/wllqryna$lcev2.startup?p_qte_code=RN&p_qte_pgm_code=7800
Nursing Continued Edu. Provider #16 .... http://www2.dca.ca.gov/pls/wllpub/wllqryna$lcev2.startup?p_qte_code=RN&p_qte_pgm_code=7800
Nursing Home Administrator #5 .... www.applications.dhs.ca.gov/cvl/

Occupational Therapist #51	http://www2.dca.ca.gov/pls/wllpub/wllqryna$lcev2.startup?p_qte_code=OT&p_qte_pgm_code=1475
Occupational Therapist Assistant #51	http://www2.dca.ca.gov/pls/wllpub/wllqryna$lcev2.startup?p_qte_code=OT&p_qte_pgm_code=1475
Ornamental Metal Contractor #28	http://www2.cslb.ca.gov/OnlineServices/CheckLicense/NameRequest.asp
Osteopath #36	www.opsc.org/displaycommon.cfm?an=1&subarticlenbr=9
Painting/Decorating Contractor #28	http://www2.cslb.ca.gov/OnlineServices/CheckLicense/NameRequest.asp
Parking/Highway Improvement Contr. #28	http://www2.cslb.ca.gov/OnlineServices/CheckLicense/NameRequest.asp
Patrol Operator, Private #22	www.bsis.ca.gov/online_services/verify_license.shtml
Payment Instrument Issuer #11	www.dfi.ca.gov/directory/pi.asp
Pesticide Applicator/Operator #44	www.pestboard.ca.gov/license.shtml
Pesticide Field Representative #44	www.pestboard.ca.gov/license.shtml
Pharmaceutical Dist/Whlse./Exemptee #13	www.pharmacy.ca.gov/online/verify_lic.shtml
Pharmacist/Pharmacist Intern #13	www.pharmacy.ca.gov/online/verify_lic.shtml
Pharmacy/Pharmacy Technician #13	www.pharmacy.ca.gov/online/verify_lic.shtml
Photogrammetrist #10	www.pels.ca.gov/consumers/lic_lookup.shtml
Physical Therapist/Assistant #38	http://www2.dca.ca.gov/pls/wllpub/wllqryna$lcev2.startup?p_qte_code=PT&p_qte_pgm_code=6800
Physician Assistant #39	www.pac.ca.gov/forms_pubs/online_services/license_lookup.shtml
Plastering Contractor #28	http://www2.cslb.ca.gov/OnlineServices/CheckLicense/NameRequest.asp
Plumber #28	http://www2.cslb.ca.gov/OnlineServices/CheckLicense/NameRequest.asp
Podiatrist #14	www.bpm.ca.gov/licensing/index.shtml
Premium Finance Company #11	http://search.dre.ca.gov/integrationaspcode/
Private Investigator #22	www.bsis.ca.gov/online_services/verify_license.shtml
Psychiatric Technician #17	www.bvnpt.ca.gov/License_Verification.asp
Psychological Assistant #15	http://www2.dca.ca.gov/pls/wllpub/wllqryna$lcev2.startup?p_qte_code=PSX&p_qte_pgm_code=7300
Psychologist #15	http://www2.dca.ca.gov/pls/wllpub/wllqryna$lcev2.startup?p_qte_code=PSX&p_qte_pgm_code=7300
Psychologist, Educational #8	www.bbs.ca.gov/quick_links/weblookup.shtml
Public Accountant-CPA #6	http://www2.dca.ca.gov/pls/wllpub/wllquery$.startup
Public Works Trainer #48	www.dir.ca.gov/databases/das/pwaddrstart.asp
Radioactive Material Licensee #31	www.applications.dhs.ca.gov/rhbxray/
Radiologic Technologist #31	www.applications.dhs.ca.gov/rhbxray/
Real Estate Agent/Seller #33	http://search.dre.ca.gov/integrationaspcode/
Real Estate Appraiser #53	www.orea.ca.gov/html/lic_appraisers.asp
Real Estate Broker/Corporation #33	http://search.dre.ca.gov/integrationaspcode/
Refrigeration Contractor #28	http://www2.cslb.ca.gov/OnlineServices/CheckLicense/NameRequest.asp
Repossessor Agency/Mgr./Employee #22	www.bsis.ca.gov/online_services/verify_license.shtml
Representative (Banking) Foreign #11	www.dfi.ca.gov/licensees/otherstate/default.asp
Residential Care for Elderly #50	www.ccld.ca.gov/docs/ccld_search/ccld_search.aspx
Residential Facility, Adult #50	www.ccld.ca.gov/docs/ccld_search/ccld_search.aspx
Respiratory Care Practitioner #41	http://www2.dca.ca.gov/pls/wllpub/wllqryna$lcev2.startup?p_qte_code=RCP&p_qte_pgm_code=7600
Roofing Contractor #28	http://www2.cslb.ca.gov/OnlineServices/CheckLicense/NameRequest.asp
Sanitation System Contractor #28	http://www2.cslb.ca.gov/OnlineServices/CheckLicense/NameRequest.asp
Savings & Loan Association #11	http://search.dre.ca.gov/integrationaspcode/
School Administrative Service #26	www.ctc.ca.gov/credentials/default.html
Securities Broker/Dealer #30	http://search.dre.ca.gov/integrationaspcode/
Security Guard #22	www.bsis.ca.gov/online_services/verify_license.shtml
Service Contract Seller, Appliance #20	www.bear.ca.gov/consumer/look_up.shtml
Sheet Metal Contractor #28	http://www2.cslb.ca.gov/OnlineServices/CheckLicense/NameRequest.asp
Shelter, Temporary #50	www.ccld.ca.gov/docs/ccld_search/ccld_search.aspx
Smog Check Station/Technician #19	www.bar.ca.gov/70_SiteWideInfo/02_Tools/03_VerifyLicense.html
Social Rehabilitation Facility #50	www.ccld.ca.gov/docs/ccld_search/ccld_search.aspx
Social Worker, Clinical #8	www.bbs.ca.gov/quick_links/weblookup.shtml
Solar Energy Contractor #28	http://www2.cslb.ca.gov/OnlineServices/CheckLicense/NameRequest.asp
Specialty Contractor-Class C #28	http://www2.cslb.ca.gov/OnlineServices/CheckLicense/NameRequest.asp
Speech Pathologist/Audiologist Aide #42	www.slpab.ca.gov/consumers/verify.shtml
Speech-Language Pathologist #42	www.slpab.ca.gov/consumers/verify.shtml
Steel Contractor #28	http://www2.cslb.ca.gov/OnlineServices/CheckLicense/NameRequest.asp
Studio Teacher #48	www.dir.ca.gov/databases/dlselr/StudTch.html
Support Center, Adult #50	www.ccld.ca.gov/docs/ccld_search/ccld_search.aspx
Surgical Clinic Pharm., Nonprofit #13	www.pharmacy.ca.gov/online/verify_lic.shtml
Surplus Lines Brokers #32	www.insurance.ca.gov/0100-consumers/0030-licensee-info/0030-lesli/
Surveyor, Land #10	www.pels.ca.gov/consumers/lic_lookup.shtml
Swimming Pool Contractor #28	http://www2.cslb.ca.gov/OnlineServices/CheckLicense/NameRequest.asp
Talent Agency #48	www.dir.ca.gov/databases/dlselr/Talag.html
Tax Education Provider #45	https://secure.ctec.org/provider/logon.asp
Tax Preparer #45	http://ctec.org/verify.asp
Thrift & Loan Company #11	http://search.dre.ca.gov/integrationaspcode/

Tile Contractor, Ceramic/Mosaic #28 ....http://www2.cslb.ca.gov/OnlineServices/CheckLicense/NameRequest.asp
Trainer, Public Works #48 ....www.dir.ca.gov/databases/das/pwaddrstart.asp
Travelers Checks Issuer #11 ....www.dfi.ca.gov/licensees/moneytransmitters/default.asp
Trust Company #11 ....www.dfi.ca.gov/licensees/trust/default.asp
Veterinarian #40 ....www.vmb.ca.gov/consumers/licverif.shtml
Veterinary Food/Animal Drug Retailer #13 ..www.pharmacy.ca.gov/online/verify_lic.shtml
Veterinary Premise/Technician #40........www.vmb.ca.gov/consumers/licverif.shtml
Viatical Settlement Insurer #32........www.insurance.ca.gov/0100-consumers/0030-licensee-info/0040-viatical-settlements/
Vocational Nurse #17 ....www.bvnpt.ca.gov/License_Verification.asp
Water Well Driller #28........http://www2.cslb.ca.gov/OnlineServices/CheckLicense/NameRequest.asp
X-ray Machine Registration #31 ....www.applications.dhs.ca.gov/rhbxray/
X-ray Technician #31........www.applications.dhs.ca.gov/rhbxray/

California Licensing Quick Finder

Acupuncturist #1 916-445-3021
Adoption Agency #50 916-274-6200
Agricultural Engineer #10 916-263-2222
Air Conditioning Contractor #28 800-321-2752
Alarm Firm/Employee/Mngr #22........800-952-5210
Amusement Ride #52........714-567-7211
Announcer, Athletic Event/Ring #3........916-263-2195
Appraiser, Real Estate #53........916-552-9000
Apprentice Program, Skilled Labor #48.415-703-5100
Arbitrator, Consumer (Lemon Law) #2.916-323-3406
Architect #7........916-574-7220
Asbestos Consultant/Surveillance #52.510-286-7362
Asbestos Contractor #52........510-286-7362
Asbestos Trainer #52........510-286-7362
Asbestos Worker/Trainee #52........510-286-7362
Athletic Event Ticket Seller #3........916-263-2195
Athletic Event-related Occupation #3...916-263-2195
Athletic Gym #3........916-263-2195
Athletic Mgr/Promot'r/Matchmaker #3..916-263-2195
Athletic Trainer/Second #3........916-263-2195
Attorney #23........415-538-2577
Audiologist #42........916-263-2666
Auto Mfg. Arbitration Program #2........916-323-3406
Automobile Dealer/Repair #19........916-255-3145
Bank Agencies/Branches, Foreign #11.800-622-0620
Bank Facility, Foreign #11........800-622-0620
Bank, State Chartered #11........800-622-0620
Bank, State Chartered, Industr'l #11....800-622-0620
Bar Association #23........415-538-2577
Barber Instructor/School #4........916-445-7061
Barber/Barber Shop/Apprentice #4........916-445-7061
Baton Training Facility/Instruct. #22.....800-952-5210
Bedding Mfg./Renovate/Ret./Whls #21.800-952-5210
Boiler, Hot Water/Steam Fitting #28.....800-321-2752
Boxer #3........916-263-2195
Boxing Second #3........916-263-2195
Brake & Lamp Adjuster #19........916-255-3145
Brake Station #19........916-255-3145
Building Contr., General-Class B #28..800-321-2752
Building Moving/Demolition #28........800-321-2752
Bungee Jump #52........714-567-7211
Business/Industrial Developm't Firm #11
........213-897-2085
Cabinet/Millwork Contractor #28........800-321-2752
Car Washing/Polishing #48........415-703-5640
Carcinogen Use, Construction #52......714-567-7211
Care Facility for Chronically Ill #50........916-274-6200
Care Facility, Children, Transition'l #50.916-274-6200
Cemetery, Cemetery Broker/Seller #25 916-574-7870
Child Care Center #50........916-274-6200
Child Development Specialist #26........916-445-7254
Chiropractic Corporation/Satellite #46..916-263-5355
Chiropractic Referral Service #46........916-263-5355
Chiropractor #46........916-263-5355
Clinic Pharmaceutical Permit #13........916-445-5014
Clinical Education Specialist #26........916-445-7254
Community Treatment Facility #50......916-274-6200
Concrete Contractor/Company #28......800-321-2752
Conscious Sedation Permit #9........916-263-2300
Construction Permit, Excava'n/Shoring #52
........714-567-7211
Continuing Education Provider #8........916-574-7830
Contractor, Business/Individual #28.....800-321-2752
Cosmetician/Cosmetologist #4........916-445-7061
Cosmetology School #4........916-445-7061
Cosmetology/Electrol'gy Firm/Instr. #4 . 916-445-7061
Court Reporter/Shorthand Report'r #29 916-263-3660
CPA/CPA Firm #6........916-263-3680
Crane Operator #52........415-567-7142
Credit Union #11........800-622-0620
Cremated Remains Disposer #25........916-574-7870
Crematory #25........916-574-7870
Day Care, Adult/Child #50........916-274-6200
Dental Anesthesia Permit #9........916-263-2300
Dental Assistant #27........916-263-2595
Dental Assistant, Extend Function #27 . 916-263-2595
Dental Hygienist #27........916-263-2595
Dentist/Dental Registered Provider #9. 916-263-2300
Dentist Fictitious Name #9........916-263-2300
Development Corporation #11
........800-622-0620, 916-322-5966
Driving School/Instructor #49........916-229-3127
Drug Wholesaler/Drug Room #13........916-445-5014
Drywall Contractor #28........800-321-2752
Earthwork/Paving Contractor #28........800-321-2752
Edu. Specialist (Special Ed) Speaking #26
........916-445-7254
Electrical Contr. & Electric Sign Contr. #28
........800-321-2752
Electrologist #4........916-445-7061
Electrology School #4........916-445-7061
Electroneuromyographer #38........916-561-8200
Electronic & Appliance Repair #20........916-574-2069
Elementary School Teacher #26........916-445-7254
Elevator Inspection #52........714-567-7211
Elevator Installation Contractor #28.....800-321-2752
Embalmer/Embalmer Apprentice #25..916-574-7870
Engineer (various disciplines) #10........916-263-2222
Esthetician #4........916-445-7061
Family Child Care Home #50........916-274-6200
Farm Labor Contractor #48........415-703-4854
Fencing Contractor #28........800-321-2752
Fire Protection #28........800-321-2752
Firearm Permit #22........800-952-5210
Firearm Training Facility/Instr. #22........800-952-5210
Flooring/Floor Covering Contract'r #28 800-321-2752
Foster Family Agency #50........916-274-6200
Fundraiser to establish training school #43
........916-574-7825
Funeral Director/Establishment #25.....916-574-7870
Funerary Training Establ./Apprentice #25
........916-574-7870
Furniture and Bedding Retailer #21.....800-952-5210
Furniture Mfg./Retailer/Whlse. #21.....800-952-5210
Garment Manufacturer #48........415-703-4848
Geologist #18........916-263-2113
Geologist, Engineering #18........916-263-2113
Geophysicist #18........916-263-2113
Glazier #28........800-321-2752
Group Home #50........916-274-6200
Healing Art Supervisor #31........916-327-5106
Hearing Aid Dispenser #34........916-263-2288
Heating & Warm-Air Vent. Contr. #28..800-321-2752
Helicopter, Use in Construction #52....714-567-7211
Home Furnishings #21........800-952-5210
Home Improvement Salesperson #28 . 800-321-2752
Horse Racing Entity #24........916-263-6000
Horse Racing Occupation #24........916-263-6000
Hospital Pharmaceut'l Exemptee #13..916-445-5014
Hydrogeologist #18........916-263-2113
Hypodermic Needle/Syringe Dist. #13 . 916-445-5014
Industrial Loan Company, Premium #11
........800-622-0620, 916-322-5966
Infant Center #50........916-274-6200
Insulation/Acoustical Contractor #28...800-321-2752
Insurance Adjuster #32........916-492-3085
Insurance Agent/Broker #32........916-322-3555
Insurance Company #32........916-322-3555
Insurance Producer #32........916-322-3555
Insurance2 Agent/Broker #32........916-322-3555
Investment Advisor #30........916-445-3062
Kickboxer, Amateur #3........916-263-2195
Kickboxer/Full Contact Karate #3........916-263-2195
Kinesiological Electromyographer #38. 916-561-8200
Lamp Station #19........916-255-3145
Land Surveyor-in-Training #10........916-263-2222
Landscape Architect #35........916-575-7230
Landscaping Contractor #28........800-321-2752
Lathing Contractor #28........800-321-2752
Lawyer Referral Service #23........415-538-2577
Legal Specialist #23........415-538-2577
Legal Specialization Provider #23........415-538-2577
Lobbying Firm/Employer #47........916-653-6224
Lobbyist #47........916-653-6224
Locksmith/Locksmith Company #22....800-952-5210
Mammographic Facility #31........916-327-5106
Manicurist #4........916-445-7061
Manufactured Housing Contractor #28 800-321-2752
Marriage & Family Therapist #8........916-574-7830
Masonry Contractor #28........800-321-2752
Medical Doctor, Enforcement Document #36
........916-263-2382
Medical Doctor/Surgeon #36........916-263-2382
Medical Evaluator #52........415-703-5070
Midwife, Midwife Nurse #36........916-263-2393
Money Order Issue #11.800-622-0620, 916-322-5966
Notary Education Vendor #37........916-653-3595
Notary Public #37........916-653-3595
Nuclear Medicine Technologist #31........916-327-5106
Nurse Registered #16..800-838-6828, 916-322-3350
Nurse Temporary or Intern #16
........800-838-6828, 916-322-3350
Nursing Continued Edu. Provider #16
........800-838-6828, 916-322-3350
Nursing Home Administrator #5........916-552-8780
Occupational Therapist #51........916-322-3394
Occupational Therapist Assistant #51 . 916-322-3394

Optician, Dispensing #36..................916-263-2634
Optometrist/Otpometric Corp #12.........916-575-7170
Optometry Practice/Branch Office #12..916-575-7170
Ornamental Metal Contractor #28........800-321-2752
Osteopath #36..................916-263-3100
Painting/Decorating Contractor #28.....800-321-2752
Parking/Highway Improvement Contr. #28 800-321-2752
Patrol Operator, Private #22..................800-952-5210
Payment Instrument Issuer #11 ....800-622-0620, 916-322-5966
Pesticide Applicator/Operator #44........916-561-8704
Pesticide Field Representative #44.......916-561-8704
Pharmaceutical Dist., Out-of-State #13 916-445-5014
Pharmaceutical Whlse./Exemptee #13 916-445-5014
Pharmacist/Pharmacist Intern #13.......916-445-5014
Pharmacy/Pharmacy Technician #13...916-445-5014
Photogrammetrist #10..................916-263-2222
Physical Therapist/Assistant #38.........916-561-8200
Physician Assistant #39..................916-561-8780
Pipeline Contractor #28..................800-321-2752
Plastering Contractor #28..................800-321-2752
Plumber #28..................800-321-2752
Podiatrist #14..................916-263-2382
Premium Finance Company #11 ....800-622-0620, 916-322-5966
Pressure Vessel #52 ... 510-622-3066, 714-567-7208
Private Investigator #22..................800-952-5210
Psychiatric Technician #17..................916-263-7800
Psychoanalyst, Research #36..................916-263-2370
Psychological Assistant #15..................916-263-2699
Psychologist #15..................916-263-2699
Psychologist, Educational #8..................916-574-7830
Public Accountant-CPA #6..................916-263-3680
Public Works Trainer #48..................415-703-5100
Radioactive Material Licensee #31......916-327-5106
Radiologic Technologist #31..................916-327-5106
Reading Specialist #26..................916-445-7254
Real Estate Agent/Seller #33..................916-227-0931
Real Estate Appraiser #53..................916-552-9000
Real Estate Broker/Corporation #33....916-227-0931
Refrigeration Contractor #28..................800-321-2752
Rehabilitative Education Special't #26..916-445-7254
Repossessor Agency/Mgr./Employee #22 800-952-5210
Representative (Banking) Foreign #11.800-622-0620
Residential Care for Elderly #50.........916-274-6200
Residential Facility, Adult #50..................916-274-6200
Respiratory Care Practitioner #41 ....916-323-9983/866-375-0386
Roofing Contractor #28..................800-321-2752
Sanitation System Contractor #28.........800-321-2752
Sanitizer of Home Furnishings #21......800-952-5210
Savings & Loan Association #11 ....800-622-0620, 916-322-5966
School Administrative Service #26.......916-445-7254
School Counselor #26..................916-445-7254
School Nurse #26..................916-445-7254
School Psychologist/Social Worker #26 916-445-7254
School Teacher #26..................916-445-7254
Securities Broker/Dealer #30..................916-445-3062
Security Guard #22..................800-952-5210
Service Contract Seller, Appliance #20. 916-574-2069
Sheet Metal Contractor #28..................800-321-2752
Shelter, Temporary #50..................916-274-6200
Ski Lift #52..................714-567-7211
Smog Check Station/Technician #19...916-255-3145
Social Rehabilitation Facility #50.........916-274-6200
Social Worker, Clinical #8..................916-574-7830
Solar Energy Contractor #28..................800-321-2752
Sparring Permit #3..................916-263-2195
Specialty Contractor-Class C #28........800-321-2752
Specialty Sublicenses, Limited #28......800-321-2752
Speech Patholog't/Audiologist Aid #42. 916-263-2666
Speech Pathology Assistant #42..........916-263-2666
Speech-Language Pathologist #42......916-263-2666
Steel Contractor #28..................800-321-2752
Studio Teacher #48..................415-703-4854
Substitute Teacher #26..................916-445-7254
Support Center, Adult #50..................916-274-6200
Surgical Clinic Pharm., Nonprofit #13..916-445-5014
Surplus Lines Brokers #32..................916-322-3555
Surveyor, Land #10..................916-263-2222
Swimming Pool Contractor #28..........800-321-2752
Talent Agency #48..................415-703-4846
Tax Education Provider #45..................877-850-2832
Tax Interviewer /Tax Preparer #45.......877-850-2832
Thermal Insulation Manufacturer #21..800-952-5210
Thrift & Loan Company #11 ....800-622-0620, 916-322-5966
Tile Contractor, Ceramic/Mosaic #28...800-321-2752
Tower Crane #52..................714-567-7211
Trainer, Public Works #48..................415-703-5100
Tramway #52..................714-567-7211
Travelers Checks Issuer #11 ....800-622-0620, 916-322-5966
Trust Company #11......800-622-0620, 916-322-5966
Tunnel/Mine Operation #52..................714-567-7211
Upholsterer, Custom #21..................800-952-5210
Veterinarian #40..................916-263-2610
Veterinary Food/Animal Drug Retailer #13 916-445-5014
Veterinary Premise/Technician #40.....916-263-2610
Viatical Settlement Insurer #32..........916-322-3555
Vocational Nurse #17..................916-263-7800
Water Well Driller #28..................800-321-2752
X-ray Machine Registration #31..........916-327-5106
X-ray Technician #31..................916-327-5106

California Licensing Agency Information

#1 Acupuncture Lisensing Board, 444 N. 3rd Street, #260, Sacramento, CA 95811; 916-445-3021, Fax- 916-445-3015. Hours- 8AM-5PM. www.acupuncture.ca.gov

#2 Arbitration Certification Program, 1625 N Market Blvd #N112, Sacramento, CA 95834; 916-574-7350, Fax- 916-574-8638. www.dca.ca.gov/acp/

#3 Athletic Commission, 2005 Evergreen St #2010, Sacramento, CA 95815; 916-263-2195, Fax- 916-263-2197. www.dca.ca.gov/csac/

#4 Board of Barbering & Cosmetology, 2420 Del Paso Road, #100, Sacramento, CA 95834; 916-445-1254, 800-952-5210, Fax- 916-323-5037. Hours- 8AM-5PM. www.barbercosmo.ca.gov Search data at- http://www2.dca.ca.gov/pls/wllpub/wllqryna$lcev2.startup?p_qte_code=IND&p_qte_pgm_code=3300 800-952-5210 is number when calling in-state.

#5 Nursing Home Administrator Program, PO Box 997416, MS 3302 (1800 3rd St #162), Sacramento, CA 95899-7416; 916-552-8780, Fax- 916-552-8777. www.cdph.ca.gov/certlic/occupations/Pages/NursingHomeAdministrator.aspx Search data at- www.applications.dhs.ca.gov/cvl/

#6 Board of Accountancy, 2000 Evergreen St, #250, Sacramento, CA 95815-3832; 916-263-3680, Fax- 916-263-3675. Hours- 8AM-5PM. www.dca.ca.gov/cba/ Search data at- http://www2.dca.ca.gov/pls/wllpub/wllquery$.startup Search either individual or company names.

#7 Architects Board, 2420 Del Paso Road #105, Sacramento, CA 95834; 916-574-7220, Fax- 916-575-7283. www.cab.ca.gov Search at- www.cab.ca.gov/consumers/license_verification.shtml

#8 Board of Behavioral Sciences, 1625 North Market Blvd. S-200, Sacramento, CA 95834; 916-574-7830, Fax- 916-574-8625. Hours- 8AM-5PM. www.bbs.ca.gov Search data at- www.bbs.ca.gov/quick_links/weblookup.shtml

#9 Dental Board, 2005 Evergreen St #1550, Sacramento, CA 95815; 916-263-2300, Fax- 916-263-2140. Hours- 8AM-5PM. www.dbc.ca.gov/ Search data at- http://www2.dca.ca.gov/pls/wllpub/wllquery$.startup

#10 Board of Professional Engineers & Land Surveyors, 2535 Capitol Oaks Dr #300, Sacramento, CA 95833-2944; 916-263-2222, Fax- 916-263-2246. Hours- 8AM-5PM. www.pels.ca.gov/ Member lists at Dept of Consumer Affairs, Public Info Unit, 916-574-8150. Engineers- civil, fire protect, electrical, mech, geotech, structural, traffic, oil, nuclear, control, chemical, industrial, mfg, metallurg'l petroleum, corrosion, quality, safety.

#11 Department of Financial Institutions, Consumer Services, 1801 13th Street, Sacramento, CA 95814; 916-322-5966, Fax- 916-445-2123. Hours- 8AM-5PM. www.dfi.ca.gov/consumers/

#12 Board of Optometry, 2420 Del Paso Rd, #255, Sacramento, CA 95834; 916-575-7170, Fax- 916-575-7292. Hours- 8AM-5PM. www.optometry.ca.gov Search data at- http://www2.dca.ca.gov/pls/wllpub/wllqryna$lcev2.startup?p_qte_code=GEN&p_qte_pgm_code=6900 Access the license search from the home page, www.optometry.ca.gov.

#13 Board of Pharmacy, 1625 N Market Blvd, N219, Sacramento, CA 95834; 916-574-7900, Fax- 916-574-8618. www.pharmacy.ca.gov Search at- www.pharmacy.ca.gov/online/verify_lic.shtml

#14 Board of Podiatric Medicine, 2005 Evergreen St #1300, Sacramento, CA 95815-3831; 916-263-2647, Fax- 916-263-2651. Hours- 8AM-5PM. www.bpm.ca.gov

#15 Board of Psychology, 2005 Evergreen St #1400, Sacramento, CA 95815-3831; 916-263-2699, Fax- 916-263-2697. Hours- 8AM-5PM. www.psychboard.ca.gov Search data at- http://www2.dca.ca.gov/pls/wllpub/wllqryna$lcev2.startup?p_qte_code=PSX&p_qte_pgm_code=7300

#16 Board of Registered Nursing, 1625 N Market Blvd, N217, Sacramento, CA 95834-1924; 916-322-3350, Fax- 916-574-7699. www.rn.ca.gov/ Search data at- http://www2.dca.ca.gov/pls/wllpub/wllqryna$lcev2.startup?p_qte_code=RN&p_qte_pgm_code=7800 Toll free number is available 24 hours a day.

#17 Board of Vocational Nursing & Psychiatric Technicians, 2535 Capitol Oaks Dr, #205, Sacramento, CA 95833; 916-263-7800, Fax- 916-263-7855. www.bvnpt.ca.gov/ Search data at- www.bvnpt.ca.gov/License_Verification.asp

#18 Board for Geologists & Geophysicists, 1625 N Market Blvd, N-324, Sacramento, CA 95834; 916-574-7749, Fax- 916-574-7791. www.geology.ca.gov

#19 Bureau of Automotive Repair, PO Box 989001 (10240 Systems Pky), West Sacramento, CA 95798-9001; 916-255-3145, 800-952-5210. Hours- 8AM-5PM. www.bar.ca.gov/ Search data - www.bar.ca.gov/70_SiteWideInfo/02_Tools/03_VerifyLicense.html

#20 Department of Consumer Affairs, Bureau of Electronic & Appliance Repair, 3485 Orange Grove Ave, #A, North Highlands, CA 95660; 916-574-2069, Fax- 916-574-2120. Hours- 8AM-5PM. www.bear.ca.gov Search data at- www.bear.ca.gov/consumer/look_up.shtml

#21 Department of Consumer Affairs, Bureau of Home Furnishings & Thermal Insulation, 3485 Orange Grove Ave, North Highlands, CA 95660; 916-574-2041, Fax- 916-574-2043. Hours- 7:30AM-4PM. www.bhfti.ca.gov

#22 Bureau of Security & Investigative Services, 2420 Del Paso Rd, #270, Sacramento, CA 95834; 916-322-4000, Fax- 916-575-7290. www.dca.ca.gov/bsis/ Search data at- www.bsis.ca.gov/online_services/verify_license.shtml

#23 State Bar of California, California Committee of Bar Examiners, 180 Howard St, San Francisco, CA 94105; 415-538-2300, Fax- 415-538-2361. www.calbar.ca.gov/state/calbar/calbar_home.jsp Search data at- http://calbar.ca.gov/state/calbar/calbar_generic.jsp?cid=10114 The member online database does not include judges or deceased former members.

#24 Horse Racing Board, 1010 Hurley Way, #300, Sacramento, CA 95825; 916-263-6000, Fax- 916-263-6042. www.chrb.ca.gov Search data at- www.chrb.ca.gov/license_search.htm

#25 Cemetery and Funeral Bureau, 1625 N Market Blvd #S208, Sacramento, CA 95834; 916-574-7870, Fax- 916-574-8620. Hours- 8AM-5PM. www.cfb.ca.gov Search data at- www.cfb.ca.gov/consumer/lookup.shtml

#26 Commission on Teacher Credentialing, PO Box 944270 (1900 Capitol Ave), Sacramento, CA 94244-2700; 916-445-7254, 888-921-2682, Fax- 916-327-3166. www.ctc.ca.gov Search at- https://teachercred.ctc.ca.gov/teachers/PublicSearchProxy

#27 Committee on Dental Auxiliaries, 2005 Evergreen St, #15050, Sacramento, CA 95815; 916-263-2595, Fax- 916-263-2709. www.comda.ca.gov Search data at- www.comda.ca.gov/verification/index.shtml

#28 Contractors License Board, PO Box 26000 (9821 Business Park Dr), Sacramento, CA 95826; 916-255-3900, 800-321-2752, Fax- 916-255-4535. Hours- 8AM-5PM. www.cslb.ca.gov Search data - http://www2.cslb.ca.gov/OnlineServices/CheckLicense/NameRequest.asp

#29 Court Reporters Board of California, 2535 Capitol Oaks Dr, #230, Sacramento, CA 95833; 916-263-3660, Fax- 916-263-3664. www.courtreportersboard.ca.gov To search website, click on "License Verification.".

#30 Department of Corporations, 1515 K St #200, Sacramento, CA 95814; 916-445-7205. Hours- 8AM-5PM. www.corp.ca.gov Search data at- http://search.dre.ca.gov/integrationaspcode/

#31 Department of Health Services, Radiological Health Branch, PO Box 997414, MS 7610, Sacramento, CA 95899-7414; 916-327-5106, Fax- 916-440-7999. Hours- 8AM-5PM. www.cdph.ca.gov/programs/Pages/RadiologicHealthBranch.aspx Search data at- www.applications.dhs.ca.gov/rhbxray/

#32 Department of Insurance, Producer Licensing Bureau, 320 Capitol Mall, Sacramento, CA 95814; 916-322-3555, Fax- 916-327-6907. Hours- 8AM-5PM. www.insurance.ca.gov Search data at- www.insurance.ca.gov/license-status/index.cfm

#33 Department of Real Estate, 2201 Broadway, Sacramento, CA 95818-2500; 916-227-0931, Fax- 916-227-0925. Hours- 8AM-5PM. www.dre.ca.gov Search data at- http://search.dre.ca.gov/integrationaspcode/

#34 Hearing Aid Dispensers Bureau, 1625 N Market Blvd, #-S-202, Sacramento, CA 95834; 916-574-7990, Fax- 916-574-8645. www.dca.ca.gov/hearingaid/ Search data at- http://www2.dca.ca.gov/pls/wllpub/wllqryna$lcev2.startup?p_qte_code=HA&p_qte_pgm_code=6700

#35 Landscape Architects Technical Committee, 2420 Del Paso Road #105, Sacramento, CA 95834; 916-575-7230, Fax- 916-575-7285. www.latc.dca.ca.gov Search data at- www.latc.ca.gov/consumers/search.shtml

#36 Medical Board, 2005 Evergreen St #1200, Sacramento, CA 95815; 916-263-2382, Fax- 916-263-2944. www.medbd.ca.gov

#37 Office of the Secretary of State, PO Box 942877 (1500 11th St, 2nd Fl), Sacramento, CA 94277-0001; 916-653-3595, Fax- 916-653-9580. www.sos.ca.gov/business/notary/notary.htm

#38 Physical Therapy Board, 2005 Evergreen St, #1350, Sacramento, CA 95815; 916-561-8200, Fax- 916-263-2560. Hours- 8AM-5PM. www.ptb.ca.gov

#39 Department of Consumer Affairs, Physician Assistant Committee, 2005 Evergreen St #1100, Sacramento, CA 95815; 916-561-8780, Fax- 916-263-2671. www.pac.ca.gov/ Search data at- www.pac.ca.gov/forms_pubs/online_services/license_lookup.shtml

#40 Veterinary Medical Board, Registered Veterinary Technician Committee, 2005 Evergreen St #2250, Sacramento, CA 95815-3831; 916-263-2610, Fax- 916-263-2621. www.vmb.ca.gov Search data at- www.vmb.ca.gov/consumers/licverif.shtml Anyone can call or write the VMB to learn whether a vet is currently licensed. Before you call have as much info as you can about the vet, including full name, office address of practice. Many vets in CA have the same or similar names.

#41 Respiratory Care Board of California, 444 N 3rd St, #270, Sacramento, CA 95814; 916-323-9983, Fax- 916-323-9999. Hours- 8AM-5PM. www.rcb.ca.gov Search data at- http://www2.dca.ca.gov/pls/wllpub/wllqryna$lcev2.startup?p_qte_code=RCP&p_qte_pgm_code=7600

#42 Speech Language Pathology & Audiology Board, 2005 Evergreen St #2100, Sacramento, CA 95815; 916-263-2666, Fax- 916-263-2668. Hours- 8AM-5PM. www.slpab.ca.gov

#43 Board of Guide Dogs for the Blind, 1625 N Market Blvd, S-202, Sacramento, CA 95834; 916-574-7825, Fax- 916-574-8619. www.guidedogboard.ca.gov/

#44 Structural Pest Control Board, 2005 Evergreen St, #1500, Sacramento, CA 95815; 916-561-8704, Fax- 916-263-2469. Hours- 8AM-5PM. www.pestboard.ca.gov Search data at- www.pestboard.ca.gov/license.shtml

#45 Tax Preparer Program, CA Tax Education Council, PO Box 2890, Sacramento, CA 95812-2840; 877-850-2832, Fax- 877-850-2832. Hours- 8AM-5PM. www.ctec.org Search data at- www.ctec.org/verify.asp

#46 Board of Chiropractic Examiners, 2525 Natomas Park Dr #260, Sacramento, CA 95833-2931; 916-263-5355, Fax- 916-263-5369. Hours- 8AM-5PM. www.chiro.ca.gov/ Search data at- www.chiro.ca.gov/onlineservices/licsearch.html

#47 Secretary of State, Political Reform Division, 1500 11th Street, Rm 495, Sacramento, CA 95814; 916-653-6224, Fax- 916-653-5045. http://cal-access.ss.ca.gov Search data at- http://cal-access.ss.ca.gov/Lobbying/

#48 Division of Labor Standards Enforcement, Licensing and Registration Unit, PO Box 420603, San Francisco, CA 94142; 415-703-5100, Fax- 415-703-4808. www.dir.ca.gov Search data at- www.dir.ca.gov/dirdatabases.html

#49 Driving School Complaint Unit, Occupational Licensing, PO Box 932342 L224, Sacramento, CA 94232-3420; 916-229-3127. www.dmv.ca.gov/vehindustry/ol/drschool.htm Search data at- https://mv.dmv.ca.gov/olinq2/welcome.do

#50 Department of Social Services, Community Care Licensing Division, 744 P St, Sacramento, CA 95814; 916-274-6200, Fax- 916-274-6205. http://ccld.ca.gov Search data at- www.ccld.ca.gov/docs/ccld_search/ccld_search.aspx

#51 Board of Occupational Therapy, 2005 Evergreen St, #2050, Sacramento, CA 95815; 916-263-2294, Fax- 916-263-2701 ww.bot.ca.gov Search data at- http://www2.dca.ca.gov/pls/wllpub/wllqryna$lcev2.startup?p_qte_code=OT&p_qte_pgm_code=1475 Will provide certification/letter of good standing.

#52 Department of Industrial Relations, Division of Occupational Safety & Health, 455 Golden Gate Ave, 10th Fl, San Francisco, CA 94102; 415-703-5070, Fax- 415-703-5135. www.dir.ca.gov/occupational_safety.html Search data at- www.dir.ca.gov/dirdatabases.html

#53 Office of Real Estate Appraisers, 1102 Q St, #4100, Sacramento, CA 95811; 916-552-9000. Hours- 8AM-5PM. www.orea.ca.gov/ Search data at- http://search.dre.ca.gov/integrationaspcode

California Federal Courts

The following list indicates the district and division name for each county in the state. If the district or division name of the bankruptcy court is different from the civil/criminal court, it appears in parentheses.

For California counties of Alameda, Contra Costa, Del Norte, Humboldt, Lake, Marin, Mendocino, Napa, San Francisco, San Mateo, and Sonoma in the Northern District of California District Court, cases may be filed at either the San Francisco Division or Oakland Division. From there a case may be assigned to either division. Records are available electronically or on public access terminals at either Division, and at the San Jose Division. To find the actual locations of records, first search by name to find case numbers; the first number of the case number indicates the file location: 3~=San Francisco, 4~=Oakland., 5~=San Jose.

County/Court Cross Reference

County	District	Division
Alameda	Northern	Oakland/SF (Oakland)
Alpine	Eastern	Sacramento
Amador	Eastern	Sacramento
Butte	Eastern	Sacramento
Calaveras	Eastern	Sacramento (Modesto)
Colusa	Eastern	Sacramento
Contra Costa	Northern	Oakland/SF (Oakland)
Del Norte	Northern	San Francisco/Oakland (Santa Rosa)
El Dorado	Eastern	Sacramento
Fresno	Eastern	Fresno
Glenn	Eastern	Sacramento
Humboldt	Northern	San Francisco/Oakland (Santa Rosa)
Imperial	Southern	San Diego
Inyo	Eastern	Fresno
Kern	Eastern	Fresno
Kings	Eastern	Fresno
Lake	Northern	San Francisco/Oakland (Santa Rosa)
Lassen	Eastern	Sacramento
Los Angeles	Central	Los Angeles (Western)
Madera	Eastern	Fresno
Marin	Northern	San Francisco/Oakland (Santa Rosa)
Mariposa	Eastern	Fresno
Mendocino	Northern	San Francisco/Oakland (Santa Rosa)
Merced	Eastern	Fresno
Modoc	Eastern	Sacramento
Mono	Eastern	Sacramento
Monterey	Northern	San Jose
Napa	Northern	San Francisco/Oakland (Santa Rosa)
Nevada	Eastern	Sacramento
Orange	Central	Santa Ana (Southern)
Placer	Eastern	Sacramento
Plumas	Eastern	Sacramento
Riverside	Central	Riverside (Eastern)
Sacramento	Eastern	Sacramento
San Benito	Northern	San Jose
San Bernardino	Central	Riverside (Eastern)
San Diego	Southern	San Diego
San Francisco	Northern	San Francisco/Oakland (San Francisco)
San Joaquin	Eastern	Sacramento (Sacramento- Modesto to 11/04)
San Luis Obispo	Central	Los Angeles (Western)
San Mateo	Northern	San Francisco/Oakland (San Francisco)
Santa Barbara	Central	Los Angeles (Western)
Santa Clara	Northern	San Jose
Santa Cruz	Northern	San Jose
Shasta	Eastern	Sacramento
Sierra	Eastern	Sacramento
Siskiyou	Eastern	Sacramento
Solano	Eastern	Sacramento
Sonoma	Northern	San Francisco/Oakland (Santa Rosa)
Stanislaus	Eastern	Fresno (Modesto)
Sutter	Eastern	Sacramento
Tehama	Eastern	Sacramento
Trinity	Eastern	Sacramento
Tulare	Eastern	Fresno
Tuolumne	Eastern	Fresno (Modesto)
Ventura	Central	Los Angeles (Western)
Yolo	Eastern	Sacramento
Yuba	Eastern	Sacramento

Standards for Federal Courts: Fees are standard unless noted in profile. Search fee is $26.00 per item (one party name or case number). Copy fee is $.50 per page. Certification fee is $9.00 per document, double for exemplification, if available. Most courts require prepayment. Mail requests should enclose a SASE unless otherwise noted. Before releasing records, all courts require prepayment, unless noted.

District courts index by defendant and plaintiff and by case number. Bankruptcy courts usually index by debtor and case number. While most courts now have their indexes on computer, many may still maintain index card files as well. Courts will archive closed case files at different times.

There are numerous public access programs available to online subscribers. Search the U.S. Party/Case Index to find party names and case numbers among all courts. Individual case data is provided on PACER. A search of CM/ECF provides copies of cases filed electronically. For details about PACER, the US Party/Case Index, and CM/ECF see the Appendix, go to http://pacer.psc.uscourts.gov or call 800-676-6856.

US District Court
California Central District

Los Angeles (Western) Division Attn: Correspondence Section, US Courthouse, 312 N Spring St, Rm G-8, Los Angeles, CA 90012, 213-894-1565, 894-2215; records- 213-894-2742, 894-2714, 894-3863; crim dockets- 213-894-3642; civil dockets- 213-894-3751; Fax- 213-894-4422; records room fax- 213-894-2607; fax record requests to- 213-894-2607. Hours- 10AM-4PM Records Rm. www.cacd.uscourts.gov

Counties/Note: Los Angeles, San Luis Obispo, Santa Barbara, Ventura. An add'l Los Angeles courtroom is located in the Roybal Federal Bldg at 255 E Temple, 213-894-1565, for criminal intake.

Searches/Indexing: Include full name in search request. Results do not include SSN or DOB. Will not fax back documents. New cases are in the index 1 day after filing date. Computer index goes back to 1992. Records Rm staff will assist you to search microfiche for older records. District-wide searches available here. Case files sent to archives 2-3 years after closed.

Search Access: Docket info is released over phone; search fee applies. **Mail:** Search usually completed- 2-4 days. Include prepaid FexEd envelope for expedited return. Include SASE for return. **Fax:** Fax search requests accepted with payment. **In person:** 6 public terminals available. No self-serve copier.

Payment: Pay by money order, cashier's check, business check. No personal checks. Will accept attorney credit cards. Payee: Clerk, US District Court. An outside copy service is available.

E-Services: Document images available. PACER records go back to 1993. New records online after 1 day. ECF at https://ecf.cacd.uscourts.gov. **Opinions Online:** www.cacd.uscourts.gov. Click on Recent Opinions. **Online Note:** Limited calendars at main website.

Riverside (Eastern) Division US District Court Clerk, 3470 12th St, Rm 134, Riverside, CA 92501, 951-328-4451 clerk; records- 213-328-4450; Fax- 951-328-4468. Hours- 10AM-4PM. www.cacd.uscourts.gov

Counties/Note: Riverside, San Bernardino.

Searches/Indexing: Include full name in search request. Results do not include SSN or DOB. Will not fax back documents. New cases are in the index 1 day after filing date. Computer index goes back to 1992 and older card indexes maintained. District-wide searches available here. Case files sent to archives 2-3 years after closed.

Search Access: Only docket info available by phone. **Mail:** Search usually completed- 4-7 days. Include prepaid FexEd envelope for expedited return. Include SASE for return. **Fax:** Fax search requests accepted with payment; call for fax number. **In person:** 2 public terminals available. No self-serve copier.

Payment: Pay by money order, cashier's check, business check. No personal checks. Will accept attorney credit cards. Payee: Clerk, US District Court. An outside copy service is available.
E-Services: Document images available. PACER records go back to 1993. New records online after 1 day. ECF at https://ecf.cacd.uscourts.gov. **Opinions Online:** www.cacd.uscourts.gov. Click on Recent Opinions. **Online Note:** Limited calendars at main website.

Santa Ana (Southern) Division Court Clerk, 411 W 4th St, Rm 1053, Santa Ana, CA 92701-4516, 714-338-4750, 714-338-4764 clerk; records- 714-338-4768; Fax- 714-338-4778. Hours- 10AM-4PM. www.cacd.uscourts.gov
Counties/Note: Orange.
Searches/Indexing: Include full name in search request. Results do not include SSN or DOB. Will not fax back documents. New cases are in the index 1 day after filing date. Computer index goes back to 1992 and older card indexes maintained. District-wide searches available here. Case files sent to archives 2-3 years after closed.
Search Access: Only docket info available by phone. **Mail:** Search usually completed- 4-7 days. Include prepaid FexEd envelope for expedited return. Include SASE for return. **Fax:** Fax search requests accepted with payment; call for fax number. **In person:** 2 public terminals available. No self-serve copier.
Payment: Pay by money order, cashier's check, business check. No personal checks. Will accept attorney credit cards. Payee: Clerk, US District Court. An outside copy service is available.
E-Services: Document images available. PACER records go back to 1993. New records online after 1 day. ECF at https://ecf.cacd.uscourts.gov. **Opinions Online:** www.cacd.uscourts.gov. Click on Recent Opinions. **Online Note:** Limited calendars at main website.

US Bankruptcy Court California Central District

Los Angeles Division Court Clerk, 255 E Temple St, Roybal Bldg, #940, Los Angeles, CA 90012, 213-894-3118 (long wait times), 213-894-6751 Public Info; Fax- 213-894-1261. Hours- 9AM-4PM. www.cacb.uscourts.gov
Counties/Note: Los Angeles (cases filed in certain northern Los Angeles County ZIP Codes may be shared with the San Fernando Valley Division.) A useful Zip Code Locator at the website allows you to determine which court to search. Los Angeles Division (only) cases that were closed 1/ 2001 or prior now accessed at https://pacer.login.uscourts.gov/cgi-bin/login.pl?court_id=CACBLA.
Searches/Indexing: Search request requires name only. Results include last 4 SSN digits. Will not fax back documents. New cases are in the index immediately after filing date. Records indexed on computer back to 1990s, earlier on microfiche, cards. District-wide searches available at all 5 locations. Los Angeles Div uses case prefix #2. Case files sent to archives 1 year after closed.
Search Access: Voice Case Information Service available, call VCIS at 866-522-6053 or 213-894-4111. **Mail:** Search usually completed- 2 days. Include SASE for return. **In person:** 2 public terminals available. No self-serve copier. Copy Svc available $.14 per page.
Payment: Pay by Visa/MC (attorneys only), money order, cashier's check. No business or personal checks accepted. Payee: Clerk, US Bankruptcy Court.
E-Services: PACER online at https://pacer.login.uscourts.gov/cgi-bin/login.pl?court_id=CACBLA. Document images available. Cases closed 1/2001 or prior can now be accessed here as well. PACER records go back to 1992. New records online after 1 day. ECF at https://ecf.cacb.uscourts.gov. **Opinions Online:** www.cacb.uscourts.gov/cacb/Welcome.nsf/NNP-Publications-WrittenOpinions?OpenPage. Select written opinions only.

Riverside (East) Division Court Clerk, 3420 12th St #125, Riverside, CA 92501-3819, 951-774-1000, 951-774-1107; Fax- 951-276-1709, 951-276-2908. 9am-4pm. www.cacb.uscourts.gov
Counties/Note: Riverside, San Bernardino.
Searches/Indexing: Search request requires name only. Results include last 4 SSN digits. Will not fax back documents. New cases are in the index immediately after filing date. Computer index maintained back to early 1990s. District-wide searches available at all 5 locations. Riverside Div uses case prefix number 6. No set time for sending records to archives.
Search Access: Only docket info is available by phone. Voice Case Information Service available, call VCIS at 866-522-6053 or 213-894-4111. **Mail:** Search usually completed- 24 hours. Include case number, document title, document number (if known), your phone number and any applicable fees. Include SASE for return. **In person:** 2 public terminals available. No self-serve copier. Copy Svc available $.14 per page.
Payment: Pay by Visa/MC (attorneys only), money order, cashier's check. Payee: US Bankruptcy Court.
E-Services: PACER-https://pacer.login.uscourts.gov/cgi-bin/login.pl?court_id=CACBRS. Document images available. PACER records go back to 1992. New records online after 1 day. ECF at https://ecf.cacb.uscourts.gov. **Opinions Online:** www.cacb.uscourts.gov/cacb/Welcome.nsf/NNP-Publications-WrittenOpinions?OpenPage. Select written opinions only.

San Fernando Valley Division Court Clerk, 21041 Burbank Blvd, Woodland Hills, CA 91367, 818-587-2900, 818-587-2805 Operations; Fax- 818-587-2953. Hours- 9AM-4PM. www.cacb.uscourts.gov
Counties/Note: Los Angeles, Ventura. (Cases filed in certain northern Los Angeles County ZIP Codes are shared with the Los Angeles Division, and cases filed in certain eastern Ventura County ZIP Codes are shared with the Ventura Division). A useful Zip Code Locator at the website allows you to determine which court to search.
Searches/Indexing: Search request requires name only. Results include last 4 SSN digits. Will not fax back documents. New cases are in the index immediately after filing date. Computer index maintained back to early 1990s. District-wide searches available at all 5 locations. San Fernando Valley Div uses case prefix number 1. No set time for sending records to archives.
Search Access: Voice Case Information Service available, call VCIS at 866-522-6053 or 213-894-4111. **Mail:** Search usually completed- 2 days. Include SASE for return. **In person:** Public terminals available. No self-serve copier. Copy Svc available $.14 per page.
Payment: Pay by Visa/MC (attorneys only), money order, cashier's check. Payee: Clerk, US Bankruptcy Court.
E-Services: PACER at https://pacer.login.uscourts.gov/cgi-bin/login.pl?court_id=CACBSV. Document images available. PACER records go back to 1992. New records online after 1 day. ECF at https://ecf.cacb.uscourts.gov. **Opinions Online:** www.cacb.uscourts.gov/cacb/Welcome.nsf/NNP-Publications-WrittenOpinions?OpenPage. Select written opinions only.

Santa Ana Division Court Clerk, 411 W 4th St, #2030, Ronald Reagan Federal Bldg and US Courthouse, Santa Ana, CA 92701-4593, 714-338-5300; 714-338-5348 Deputy in Charge; Fax- 714-338-5393. 9AM-4PM. www.cacb.uscourts.gov
Counties/Note: Orange.
Searches/Indexing: Search request requires name only. Results include last 4 SSN digits. Will not fax back documents. New cases are in the index 24-48 hours after filing date. Computer index maintained back to early 1990s. District-wide searches available at all 5 locations. Santa Ana Div uses case prefix number 8. No set time for sending records to archives.
Search Access: Docket info available via phone. Voice Case Information Service available, call VCIS at 866-522-6053 or 213-894-4111. **Mail:** Search usually completed- 1 week. Include SASE for return. **In person:** Public terminals available. No self-serve copier. Copy Svc- $.14 per page.
Payment: Pay by Visa/MC (attorneys only), money order, cashier's check. No personal or debtor checks. Payee: US Bankruptcy Court.
E-Services: PACER online at https://pacer.login.uscourts.gov/cgi-bin/login.pl?court_id=CACBSA. Document images available. PACER records go back to 6/3/1991. New records online after 1 day. ECF at https://ecf.cacb.uscourts.gov. **Opinions Online:** www.cacb.uscourts.gov/cacb/Welcome.nsf/NNP-Publications-WrittenOpinions?OpenPage. Select written opinions only.

Santa Barbara (Northern) Division Court Clerk, 1415 State St, Santa Barbara, CA 93101, 805-884-4800; Fax- 805-963-4068. Hours- 9AM-4PM. www.cacb.uscourts.gov
Counties/Note: San Luis Obispo, Santa Barbara, Ventura. Certain Ventura County ZIP Codes are assigned to the new office in San Fernando Valley.
Searches/Indexing: Search request requires name only. Results include last 4 SSN digits. Will not fax back documents. New cases are in the index immediately after filing date. Computer index maintained back to early 1990s. District-wide searches available at all 5 locations. Northern Div uses case prefix number 9. No set time for sending records to archives.
Search Access: Voice Case Information Service available, call VCIS at 866-522-6053 or 213-894-4111. **Mail:** Search usually completed- 24 hours. Include case number, document title, document number (if known), your phone number and any applicable fees. Include SASE for return. **In person:** Public terminals available. No self-serve copier. Copy Svc available $.14 per page.
Payment: Pay by Visa/MC (attorneys only), money order, cashier's check. Payee: US Bankruptcy Court.
E-Services: PACER at https://pacer.login.uscourts.gov/cgi-bin/login.pl?court_id=CACBND. Document images available. PACER records go back to 6/1992. New records online after 1 day. ECF at https://ecf.cacb.uscourts.gov. **Opinions:** www.cacb.uscourts.gov/cacb/Welcome.nsf/NNP-Publications-WrittenOpinions?OpenPage. Select written opinions only.

US District Court California Eastern District

Fresno Division Court Clerk, 2500 Tulare St, Rm 1501, Fresno, CA 93721, 559-499-5600; Fax-559-499-5992. 9am-4pm. www.caed.uscourts.gov

Counties/Note: Calaveras, Fresno, Inyo, Kern, Kings, Madera, Mariposa, Merced, Stanislaus, Tulare, Tuolumne. There is a Bakersfield location that hears civil, criminal and miscellaneous actions arising primarily in Kern and Inyo counties. Bakersfield hears cases monthly; cases at 1200 Truxton Ave, #1200, 661-326-6624. There is also offices at Edwards AFB and at Independence.

Searches/Indexing: Include full name and DOB in search requests. Results do not include SSN or DOB. Will not fax back documents. New cases are in the index 24 hours after filing date. Computer index back to 1991 maintained. Records stored by case type and case number. Case files sent to archives as time permits.

Search Access: Only docket info is available by phone. **Mail:** Search usually completed- 2 days. SASE not required. **In person:** 3 public access terminals available. No self-serve copier. Court will copy a maximum of 20 pages, otherwise searchers must contact an outside copy service.

Payment: Pay by major credit cards, money order, cashier's or personal check. Payee: Clerk, US District Court.

E-Services: PACER records go back to 1990, some earlier. New records online after 1 day. ECF at https://ecf.caed.uscourts.gov. **Opinions Online:** www.caed.uscourts.gov. Opinions are now located on the CM/ECF system. **Note:** Judges calendars free at http://207.41.19.127/caed/staticOther/page_460.htm.

Sacramento Division Court Clerk, 501 I St, 4th Fl, Sacramento, CA 95814, 916-930-4000. Hours- 9AM-4PM. www.caed.uscourts.gov

Counties/Note: Alpine, Amador, Butte, Colusa, El Dorado, Glenn, Lassen, Modoc, Mono, Nevada, Placer, Plumas, Sacramento, San Joaquin, Shasta, Sierra, Siskiyou, Solano, Sutter, Tehama, Trinity, Yolo, Yuba. A Yosemite office is located near the Yosemite Valley Visitors Ctr at 9004 Castle Cliffs Court, Yosemite, CA 95389, 209-372-0320; another is located at South Lake Tahoe, 916-930-4583. There is also a closed location in Redding, phone 530-246-5416.

Searches/Indexing: Include full name and DOB in search requests. Results do not include SSN or DOB. Will not fax back documents. New cases are in the index immediately after filing date. Computer index maintained back to 1990. Archived case records indexed on microfiche by case number. Case files sent to archives at varying intervals, usually as time permits.

Search Access: Only docket info is available by phone. **Mail:** Search usually completed- 1-2 days. Include SASE for return. **In person:** 2 public terminals available. Self-serve copier available. Court can recommend outside vendor for copies.

Payment: Pay by credit cards, money order, cashier's check, business check. Payee: Clerk, US District Court.

E-Services: PACER records go back to 1990, some earlier. New records online after 1 day. ECF at https://ecf.caed.uscourts.gov. **Opinions Online:** www.caed.uscourts.gov. Opinions are now located on the CM/ECF system. **Online Note:** Judges calendars free at http://207.41.19.127/caed/staticOther/page_460.htm.

US Bankruptcy Court California Eastern District

Fresno Division Court Clerk, 2500 Tulare St #2501, Fresno, CA 93721, 559-499-5800. Hours-9AM-4PM. www.caeb.uscourts.gov

Counties/Note: Fresno, Inyo, Kern, Kings, Madera, Mariposa, Merced, Mono, Tulare. Three Kern ZIP Codes - 93243, 93523, 93524 - are handled by San Fernando Valley in Central Dist.

Searches/Indexing: Include full name and SSN in search request. Results include last 4 SSN digits. Will not fax back documents. New cases are in the index immediately after filing date. Computer index back to 1979. Fresno Div uses case prefix number 1 or 6. Cases before 3/99 sent to archives.

Search Access: Only docket info is available by phone. **Mail:** Search usually completed- 1 day. SASE required. **In person:** 4 public terminals.

Payment: Pay by money order, cashier's check, business check. No personal checks or credit cards. Payee: Clerk, US Bankruptcy Court.

E-Services: Document images available. PACER records go back to 8/1990. New records online after 1 day. ECF at https://ecf.caeb.uscourts.gov. **Opinions:** www.caeb.uscourts.gov/cortinfo/opinions.asp. Opinions after 2/16/2005 at www.caeb.uscourts.gov/search/search.asp. Calendars free at www.caeb.uscourts.gov/calendar/calendar.asp.

Modesto Division Court Clerk, 1200 I St, Suite 4, Modesto, CA 95354, 209-521-5160. Hours- 9AM-4PM. www.caeb.uscourts.gov

Counties/Note: Calaveras, Stanislaus, Tuolumne. Pre-11/2004 San Joaquin records are all now in Sacramento. Mariposa and Merced counties were transferred to the Fresno Division as of 1/1995.

Searches/Indexing: Include full name and last 4 digits of SSN in search request. Results include last 4 SSN digits. Will not fax back documents. New cases are in the index immediately after filing date. Modesto Div uses case prefix number 9.

Search Access: Only docket info is available by phone. **Mail:** Search usually completed- within 1 week. SASE required. **In person:** 2 public terminals available. Self-serve copies from the lobby computer- $.10 each.

Payment: Pay by money order, cashier's check. No personal checks or credit cards. Payee: Clerk, US Bankruptcy Court. Copies printed from public computer- $.10 each.

E-Services: Document images available. PACER records go back to 8/1990. New records online after 1 day. ECF at https://ecf.caeb.uscourts.gov. **Opinions:** www.caeb.uscourts.gov/cortinfo/opinions.asp. Opinions after 2/16/2005 at www.caeb.uscourts.gov/search/search.asp. Calendars free at www.caeb.uscourts.gov/calendar/calendar.asp.

Sacramento Division Court Clerk, US Courthouse Rm 3-200, 501 I St, Sacramento, CA 95814, 916-930-4400. Hours- 9AM-4PM. www.caeb.uscourts.gov

Counties/Note: Alpine, Amador, Butte, Colusa, El Dorado, Glenn, Lassen, Modoc, Nevada, Placer, Plumas, Sacramento, San Joaquin, Shasta, Sierra, Siskiyou, Solano, Sutter, Tehama, Trinity, Yolo, Yuba. There is a hearing location in Bakersfield at 1300 18th St, but no cases or case records there. Pre-11/2004 San Joaquin county records are at Modesto Division for these ZIP Codes: 95220, 95227, 95234, 95237, 95240-95242, 95253, 95258, 95286.

Searches/Indexing: Include full name and SSN in search request. Results include last 4 SSN digits. Will not fax back documents. New cases are in the index immediately after filing date. Sacramento Div uses case prefix number 2, 3, or 4. Make an appointment in order to conduct a search yourself.

Search Access: Only docket info is available by phone. **Mail:** Search usually completed- 24-48 hours. SASE required. **In person:** 2 public terminals available. Computer copies $.10 each.

Payment: Pay by money order, cashier's check, business or attorney check. No personal checks or credit cards. Payee: Clerk, US Bankruptcy Court.

E-Services: Document images available. PACER records go back to 8/1990. New records online after 1 day. ECF at https://ecf.caeb.uscourts.gov. **Opinions:** www.caeb.uscourts.gov/cortinfo/opinions.asp. Opinions after 2/16/2005 at www.caeb.uscourts.gov/search/search.asp. Calendars free at www.caeb.uscourts.gov/calendar/calendar.asp.

US District Court California Northern District

Oakland Division Court Clerk, 1301 Clay St, Ste 400S, Oakland, CA 94612-5212, 510-637-3530. Hours- 9AM-4PM. www.cand.uscourts.gov

Counties/Note: Alameda, Contra Costa. (Note: Cases may be filed Oakland or at San Francisco Div.; records available electronically at either; the 1st number of the case number indicates the file location: 3=SF, 4=Oak, 5=SJ.

Searches/Indexing: Search request requires full name, SSN and DOB. Results do not include SSN or DOB. Will not fax back documents. Computer and microfiche indexes maintained; computer back to 1990. Records stored by case number; use plaintiff or defendant name to find case number. Case files sent to archives 6 months after closed.

Search Access: Only docket info available by phone. **Mail:** Search usually completed- 7 days. Include SASE for return. **In person:** 2 public terminals available. Self-serve copier available.

Payment: Pay by money order, cashier's and personal checks. No credit cards accepted. Payee: Clerk, US District Court.

E-Services: PACER records go back to 1984. New records online after 1 day. ECF at https://ecf.cand.uscourts.gov. ECF includes civil cases filed after 4/1/2001 and criminal and miscellaneous cases after 1/1/2004. For opinions, click on Opinions at main website. Access to court calendars at www.cand.uscourts.gov.

San Francisco Division Court Clerk, 450 Golden Gate Ave, 16th Fl, San Francisco, CA 94102, 415-522-2000. Hours- 9AM-4PM. www.cand.uscourts.gov

Counties/Note: Del Norte, Humboldt, Lake, Marin, Mendocino, Napa, San Francisco, San Mateo, Sonoma. (Note: Cases may be filed at San Francisco or at Oakland Div; records available electronically at either; the 1st number of the case indicates the file location: 3=SF, 4=Oak, 5=SJ.

Searches/Indexing: Search request requires full name, SSN and DOB. Results do not include SSN or DOB, but office can confirm or deny. Will not fax back documents. New cases are in the index immediately after filing date. Computer and microfiche indexes maintained; computer back to 1990. Records stored by case number; Case files sent to archives 6 months after closed.

Search Access: Only docket info available by phone. **Mail:** Search usually completed- 7 days. Include SASE for return. **In person:** 3 public terminals available. Self-serve copier available.

Payment: Pay by money order, cashier's and personal checks. No credit cards accepted. Payee: Clerk, US District Court.

E-Services: PACER records go back to 1984. New records online after 1 day. ECF at https://ecf.cand.uscourts.gov. ECF includes civil cases filed after 4/1/2001 and criminal and miscellaneous cases after 1/1/2004. For opinions, click on Opinions at main website. **Online Note:** Court calendars at www.cand.uscourts.gov.

San Jose Division Court Clerk, 280 S 1st St, Rm 2112, San Jose, CA 95113, 408-535-5364/5363. 9AM-4PM. www.cand.uscourts.gov Monterey, San Benito, Santa Clara, Santa Cruz.

Searches/Indexing: Search request requires full name, SSN and DOB. Results do not include SSN or DOB. Older cases may have DOB or SSN but they will not show on computer. New cases are in the index immediately after filing date. Computer and microfiche indexes maintained. Records stored by case number; use plaintiff or defendant name to find case number. Case files sent to archives 6 months after closed.

Search Access: Only docket info available by phone. **Mail:** Search usually completed- 7 days. Include SASE for return. **In person:** Public terminals available. Self-serve copier available.

Payment: Pay by money order, cashier's or personal checks. No credit cards accepted. Payee: Clerk, US District Court.

E-Services: PACER records go back to 1984. New records online after 1 day. ECF at https://ecf.cand.uscourts.gov. ECF includes civil cases filed after 4/1/2001 and criminal and miscellaneous cases after 1/1/2004. For opinions, click on Opinions at main website. **Online Note:** Court calendars at www.cand.uscourts.gov.

US Bankruptcy Court California Northern District

Oakland Division Court Clerk, 1300 Clay St, Rm 300, Oakland, CA 94612, 510-879-3600; help desk- 510-879-3554; Fax- 510-879-3556. Hours- 9AM-4:30PM. www.canb.uscourts.gov

Counties/Note: Alameda, Contra Costa.

Searches/Indexing: Include SSN in search request. Results include last 4 SSN digits. Will not fax back documents. New cases are in the index immediately after filing date. Computer index is maintained. Oakland Div uses case prefix number 4. Files sent to archives up to 1 year after closed.

Search Access: Only basic docket data is released via phone. Voice Case Information Service available, call VCIS at 888-457-0604. **Mail:** Search usually completed- 2-4 days. Include SASE for return. **In person:** 2 public terminals available. Self-serve copies $.25 each.

Payment: Pay by money order, cashier's check, business check. No personal checks. Attorney credit cards OK. Payee: Clerk, Bankruptcy Court.

E-Services: PACER records go back to 1993. New records online after 1 day. ECF at https://ecf.canb.uscourts.gov. **Opinions Online:** www.canb.uscourts.gov. Click on Judges Decisions. Click on Calendars at main website.

San Francisco Division Court Clerk, PO Box 7341, San Francisco, CA 94120-7341 (In person: 235 Pine St, 19th Fl, San Francisco, CA 94104), 415-268-2300; help desk- 415-268-2368; Fax- 415-268-2302. Hours- 9AM-4:30PM. www.canb.uscourts.gov

Counties/Note: San Francisco, San Mateo.

Searches/Indexing: Include SSN in search request. Searches conducted by a copy service. Results include last 4 SSN digits. Will not fax back documents. New cases are in the index immediately after filing date. Computer index back to 1984 maintained, also on microfiche. San Francisco Div uses case prefix number 3. Case files sent to archives up to 1 year after closed.

Search Access: Only data from dockets of open cases is released via phone. Voice Case Information Service available, call VCIS at 888-457-0604. **Mail:** Search usually completed- 1-2 weeks. Include SASE for return. **In person:** Self-serve copies $.25 each.

Payment: Pay by money order, cashier's check, business check. No personal checks. Attorney credit cards accepted. Payee: Clerk of the Court.

E-Services: PACER records go back to 1993. New records online after 1 day. ECF at https://ecf.canb.uscourts.gov. **Opinions Online:** www.canb.uscourts.gov. Click on Judges Decisions. Click on Calendars at main website.

San Jose Division Court Clerk, 280 S 1st St, Rm 3035, San Jose, CA 95113-3099, 408-535-5118; help desk- 408-0535-5471; records- 408-535-5445; Fax- 408-535-5132. 9AM-4:30PM. www.canb.uscourts.gov **Counties:** Monterey, San Benito, Santa Clara, Santa Cruz.

Searches/Indexing: Include SSN in search request. Results include last 4 SSN digits. Will not fax back documents. New cases are in the index immediately after filing date. Computer index back to 1980 maintained. San Jose Div uses case prefix number 5. Case files sent to archives yearly around September/October.

Search Access: Only basic docket data, such as date of filing, is released via phone. Voice Case Information Service available, call VCIS at 888-457-0604. **Mail:** Search usually completed- 2-3 days. Include SASE for return. **In person:** 2 public terminals available. Computer copies $.10 each.

Payment: Pay by money order, cashier's check, business check. No personal checks. Attorney credit cards OK. Payee: Clerk, Bankruptcy Court.

E-Services: PACER records go back to 1993. New records online after 1 day. ECF at https://ecf.canb.uscourts.gov. **Opinions Online:** www.canb.uscourts.gov. Click on Judges Decisions. **Online Note:** For calendars, click on Calendars at main website.

Santa Rosa Division Court Clerk, 99 South E St, Santa Rosa, CA 95404, 707-525-8539; help desk- 707) 525-8539 x236; Fax- 707-579-0374. Hours- 9AM-4:30PM. www.canb.uscourts.gov

Counties/Note: Del Norte, Humboldt, Lake, Marin, Mendocino, Napa, Sonoma.

Searches/Indexing: Include SSN in search request. Results include last 4 SSN digits. Will not fax back documents. New cases are in the index immediately after filing date. Computer index is maintained. Santa Rosa Div uses case prefix #1. Files sent to archives up to 1 year after closed.

Search Access: Names and accession numbers released via phone. Voice Case Information Service available, call VCIS at 888-457-0604. **Mail:** Search usually completed- 5 days. Include SASE for return. **In person:** Self-serve copier available. Court can recommend an outside vendor to search and make copies.

Payment: Pay by money order, cashier's check, business check. No personal checks. Attorney credit cards OK. Payee: Clerk - Bankruptcy Court.

E-Services: PACER records go back to 1993. New records online after 1 day. ECF at https://ecf.canb.uscourts.gov. **Opinions Online:** www.canb.uscourts.gov. Click on Judges' Decisions. Click on Calendars at main website.

US District Court California Southern District

San Diego Division Clerk of Court, 880 Front St, Rm 4290, San Diego, CA 92101-8900, 619-557-5600; records- 619-557-7362 file review ofc.; Fax- 619-557-6684; records room fax- 619-702-9941; fax record requests to- 619-702-9941. Hours- 8:30AM-4:30PM. www.casd.uscourts.gov

Counties/Note: Imperial, San Diego. Court also handles some cases from Yuma County, AZ. San Diego office also holds records for the El Centro Ct, 2003 W Adams Ave #220, 760-353-1271.

Searches/Indexing: Search request requires name only. Clerk's Office can perform party name searches for $15 per name. Results do not include SSN or DOB. Will not fax back documents. New cases are in the index 24 hours after filing date. Docket sheets of criminal cases filed in or after 7/1991 and civil cases filed in or after 5/1989 can be reviewed via WebPACER in office. Older records 1953-1995 available in card files in the File Retrieval Rm of the Clerk's Office Lobby or on microfiche there. When local space becomes unavailable, closed cases are transferred to Record Ctr archives.

Search Access: Mail: Search usually completed- 7-10 days. SASE not required. **In person:** 4 public terminals available. Self serve computer copies- $.10 per page.

Payment: Pay by Visa/MC, money order, cashier's or personal check. Payee: US District Court.

E-Services: PACER online at http://pacer.casd.uscourts.gov. Document images available. PACER records go back to 1990. New records online after 1 day. ECF at https://ecf.casd.uscourts.gov. Noteworthy Filings accessed free at www.casd.uscourts.gov/index.php?page=noteworthy-filings. **Online Note:** Calendars are posted on the website daily. Access a computer bulletin board at 619-557-6779.

US Bankruptcy Court California Southern District

San Diego Division Office of the Clerk, 325 West F St, US Courthouse, San Diego, CA 92101, 619-557-5620; records- x0; Fax- 619-557-5536. Hours- 9AM-4PM. www.casb.uscourts.gov

Counties/Note: Imperial, San Diego.

Searches/Indexing: To search, include full name; SSN and DOB may be helpful. Results do not include SSN or DOB. Computer index maintained back to 1998. San Diego Div uses case prefix # 0 or #1. Files sent to archives after 6 months.

Search Access: Only docket info available by phone. Voice Case Information Service available, call VCIS at 619-557-6521. **Mail:** Search usually completed- 7 days. Court can recommend a vendor to handle copy and fax requests. SASE not required. **In person:** No self-serve copier.

Payment: Pay by money order, cashier's check. Payee: Clerk, US Bankruptcy Court.

E-Services: PACER online at http://pacer.casb.uscourts.gov. Document images available. PACER records go back to 1989. New records online after 1 day. ECF at https://ecf.casb.uscourts.gov. **Opinions Online:** www.casb.uscourts.gov/html/body_opinions.htm. View recent opinions free by judge name. **Online Note:** Unpublished decisions listed by judge at www.casb.uscourts.gov/html/unpublished.htm

California County Courts

Court	Jurisdiction	No. of Courts	How Organized
Superior Courts*	General	29	
Limited Superior Courts*	Limited	122	
Combined Superior Courts*	Limited & General	58	

* Profiled in this Sourcebook.

Court	CIVIL								
	Tort	Contract	Real Estate	Min. Claim	Max. Claim	Small Claims	Estate	Eviction	Domestic Relations
General Jurisdiction*	X	X	X	$25,000	No Max		X		X
Limited Jurisdiction*	X	X	X	$0	$25,000	$5000		X	

Court	CRIMINAL				
	Felony	Misdemeanor	DWI/DUI	Preliminary Hearing	Juvenile
General Jurisdiction*	X	X	X		X
Limited Jurisdiction*		X	X	X	

Administration

Administrative Office of Courts, 455 Golden Gate Ave, San Francisco, CA, 94102; 415-865-4200 or 865-7740, Fax: 415-865-4334. (PST) www.courtinfo.ca.gov

Court Structure

Between 1998 and 2000 individual counties unified the Superior Courts and Municipal Courts within their respective counties. Some courts that were formerly Municipal Courts became Limited Jurisdiction Superior Courts. In some counties the Superior Courts and Municipal Courts were combined into one Superior Court. Civil cases under $25,000 can be heard by a Limited Civil Court, if over $25,000then an Unlimited Civil Court, if no distinction then the court is a Combined Civil Court. Appeals in limited civil cases (where $25,000 or less is at issue) and misdemeanors are heard by the appellate division of the superior court. When a small claims case is appealed, a superior court judge decides the case.

It is important to note that Limited Courts may try minor felonies.

Due to its large number of courts, the Los Angeles County section is arranged uniquely in this book. Each branch or "Division" of the Los Angeles Superior Court is given by name, which usually indicates a court's general jurisdictional and geographic boundary. The court name is followed by the District it is located in — South Central, West, Northeast, Central, etc. Also, a court name may mention whether its jurisdiction is "Civil only" or "Criminal only."

Online Access

The website at www.courtinfo.ca.gov offers access to all opinions from the Supreme Court and Appeals Courts from 1850 to present. Opinions not certified for publications are available for the last 60 days. This site also contains very useful information about the state court system, including opinions from the Supreme Court and Appeals Courts.

There is no statewide online computer access available. However, a number of counties have developed their own online access sytems and provide internet access at no fee. Los Angeles County has an extensive free and fee-based online system at www.lasuperiorcourt.org.

Searching Tips, Fees, and Other Guidelines

If there is more than one court of a type within a county, where the case is tried and where the record is held depends on how a citation is written, where the infraction occurred, or where the filer chose to file the case. Case file information may need to be found from the exact court of record.

Fees are set by statute, the last change was in early 2006. There is no search fee unless the search takes more than 10 minutes, in which case the fee is $15.00, but some courts charge the fee regardless of the time involved. Certification is $15.00 per document plus copy fee; copies are $.50 per page. Most courts follow these quidelines, but not all do.

Alameda County

Superior Court - Criminal 1225 Fallon St, Rm 107, Oakland, CA 94612; 510-891-6009; 8:30AM-4PM. ***Felony.*** www.alameda.courts.ca.gov/courts
Located at the Rene C Davidson Alameda County Courthouse.
Criminal Records: Access: Mail, in person. Both court and visitors may perform in person searches. Search fee: $15.00 per name if search exceeds 10 minutes. Required to search: name, years to search, signed release; also helpful: DOB, SSN. Criminal records on computer back 10 years; on microfiche from 1940, archived and indexed from 1880. Mail turnaround time 1 week. Public use terminal has crim records back to 1998. PAT results show middle initial, DOB. At the website, search "Find Your Court Date" to determine if a name has an upcoming court date.
General Information: No probation, medical, adoption, juvenile or sealed records released. Will fax documents. Court makes copy: $.50 per page. Certification fee: $15 per doc. Payee: Clerk of Superior Court. Personal checks accepted; credit cards are not. Prepayment required. Mail requests: SASE required.

Oakland/Piedmont/Emeryville Superior Court - Civil Allen E Broussard Justice Center, 600 Washington St, Rm 4020, Oakland, CA 94607; 510-268-4222; civil phone: 51-268-7724; 8:30AM-4PM. ***Civil Actions under $25,000, Eviction, Small Claims.*** www.alameda.courts.ca.gov/courts
Comprises the cities of Oakland, Piedmont and Emeryville. Located at Allen E Broussard Justice Ctr.
Civil Records: Access: Mail, in person, online. Both court and visitors may perform in person searches. Search fee: $15.00 per name if search exceeds 10 minutes. Required to search: name, years to search. Civil cases indexed by defendant, plaintiff, on computer from 1990. Mail turnaround time 2-3 weeks. Public use terminal has civil records back to 10 years. PAT results show name only. Online access to calendars, limited civil case summaries and complex litigations are free from Domain Web at the website. Search limited cases by number; litigations by case name or number. At the website, search "Find Your Court Date" to determine if a name has an upcoming court date.
General Information: No sealed or confidential records released. Court makes copy: $.50 per page. Certification fee: $20.00 per doc. Payee: Clerk of Court, Alameda Superior Court. Personal checks accepted. Visa/MC accepted. Prepayment required. Mail requests: SASE required.

Superior Court - Civil 1225 Fallon St, Rm 109, Oakland, CA 94612; 510-272-6763; probate phone: 510-647-4439; 8:30AM-4:00PM. ***Civil Actions over $25,000, Probate.*** www.alameda.courts.ca.gov/courts
Located at the Rene C Davidson Courthouse. Research and copy work--570-272-6799.
Civil Records: Access: Mail, in person, online. Both court and visitors may perform in person searches. Search fee: $15.00 per name if search exceeds 10 minutes. Required to search: name, years to search. Civil cases indexed by defendant, plaintiff, on computer from 1974, on microfiche and archived from 1900s. Note: Court prefers you use their "consent form." Mail turnaround time 2 weeks. Public use terminal has civil records back to 1998. PAT civil results show middle initial. Online access to calendars, limited civil case summaries and complex litigations back to 2000 are free from Domain Web at the website. Search limited cases by number; litigations by case name or number. At the website, search "Find Your Court Date" to determine if a name has an upcoming court date. Online results show middle initial.
General Information: No sealed records nor adoption records released unless court ordered. Will not fax documents. Court makes copy: $.50 per page. Certification fee: $15 per doc. Payee: Superior Court. Personal checks accepted; credit cards are not. Prepayment required. Mail requests: SASE required.

Superior Court South Branch/Hayward - Civil 24405 Amador St, Rm 108, Hayward, CA 94544; 510-690-2705; fax: 510-690-2773; 8:30AM-4PM. ***Civil, Small Claims, Probate.*** www.alameda.courts.ca.gov/courts
Located at the Hayward Hall of Justice.
Civil Records: Access: Mail, in person, online. Visitors must perform in person searches themselves. Search fee: $15.00 per name if search exceeds 10 minutes. Required to search: name, years to search. Civil cases indexed by defendant, plaintiff, on computer from 1974, on microfiche and archived from 1900s. Mail turnaround time 2-3 weeks. Public use terminal has civil records back to 1974. PAT results show name only. Online access to calendars, limited civil case summaries and complex litigations are free from Register of Actions/Domain Web at the website. Search limited cases by number; litigations by case number. At the website, search "Find Your Court Date" to determine if a name has an upcoming court date.
General Information: No sealed files, paternity or adoption records released. Will fax documents $.50 per page. Court makes copy: $.50 per page. Certification fee: $15 per doc. Payee: Clerk of Superior Court. Personal checks accepted. Credit cards accepted. Prepayment required. Mail requests: SASE required.

Alameda Branch Superior Court 2233 Shoreline Dr, George E McDonald Hall of Justice, Alameda, CA 94501; 510-263-4300; criminal phone: 510-263-4330; civil phone: 510-263-4304; fax: 510-263-4330; 8:30AM-4:00PM; phones- 8:30AM-5PM. ***Felony, Misdemeanor, Civil Actions under $25,000, Eviction, Small Claims.*** www.alameda.courts.ca.gov/courts
Co-extensive with the city limits of Alameda only. The fax number is not for public use.
Civil Records: Access: Mail, in person, online. Both court and visitors may perform in person searches. Search fee: $15.00 per name if search exceeds 10 minutes. Required to search: name, years to search. Civil cases indexed by defendant, plaintiff, on computer since 1987. Mail turnaround time 3 days to 1 week. Civil PAT goes back to at least 7 years, some 10. PAT results show name only. Online access to calendars, limited civil case summaries and complex litigations are free from Domain Web at the website. Search limited cases by number; litigations by case number.
Criminal Records: Access: Mail, in person. Both court and visitors may perform in person searches. Search fee: $15.00 per name if search exceeds 10 minutes. Required to search: name, years to search, DOB, signed release; also helpful: SSN. Criminal records on computer 10 years back. Mail turnaround time 1 week. Criminal PAT goes back to same as civil. PAT results show name only. Court will not verify personal identifiers. At the website, search "Find Your Court Date" to determine if a name has an upcoming court date.
General Information: No confidential records released. Will not fax documents. Court makes copy: $.50 per page. Certification fee: $15 per doc. Payee: Alameda Superior Court. Personal checks accepted. Accepts credit cards in person only. Prepayment required. Mail requests: SASE required.

Berkeley/Albany Superior Court - Civil 2120 Martin Luther King Jr Way, Berkeley Courthouse, Berkeley, CA 94704; 510-647-4423, 510-647-4426; fax: 510-883-9359; 8:30AM-4:00PM. ***Civil Actions under $25,000, Eviction, Small Claims.*** www.alameda.courts.ca.gov/courts
Co-extensive with the city limits of Berkeley and Albany.
Civil Records: Access: Mail, in person, online. Both court and visitors may perform in person searches. Search fee: $15.00 per name if search exceeds 10 minutes. Required to search: name, years to search. Civil cases indexed by defendant, plaintiff, on computer from 1986. Mail turnaround time 1 week. Public use terminal has civil records back to 1986. Online access to calendars, limited civil case summaries and complex litigations are free from Domain Web at the website. Search limited cases by number; litigations by case number. At the website, search "Find Your Court Date" to determine if a name has an upcoming court date.
General Information: Online identifiers in results same as on public terminal. No sealed, judge's notes or confidential records released. Will not fax documents. Court makes copy: $.50 per page. Certification fee: $15 per doc. Payee: Superior Court. Personal checks and major credit cards accepted. Prepayment required. Mail requests: SASE required.

Fremont Superior Court 39439 Paseo Padre Pky, Fremont Hall of Justice, Fremont, CA 94538; criminal phone: 510-818-7501; civil phone: 510-818-7503; criminal fax: 510-818-7601; civil fax: 510-818-7564; 8:30AM-4PM. ***Felony, Misdemeanor, Civil Actions under $25,000, Eviction, Small Claims.*** www.alameda.courts.ca.gov/courts
Jurisdiction includes Fremont, Newark, and Union City. Located at the Fremont Hall of Justice.
Civil Records: Access: Fax, mail, in person, online. Both court and visitors may perform in person searches. Search fee: $15.00 per name if search exceeds 10 minutes. Required to search: name, years to search. Civil cases indexed by defendant, plaintiff, on computer from 1990. Note: 3 file limit at counter. Mail turnaround time 1 week. Civil PAT goes back to 15 years. PAT results show name only. Online access to calendars, limited civil case summaries and complex litigations are free at the DomainWeb section at the website. Search limited cases by number; litigations by case name or number.
Criminal Records: Access: Mail, in person. Both court and visitors may perform in person searches. Search fee: $15.00 per name if search exceeds 10 minutes. Required to search: name, years to search, DOB, signed release. Criminal records on computer only go back 7 years. Note: 5 file limit at counter. Mail turnaround time 1 week. Criminal PAT goes back to 7 years. PAT results show name only. At the website, search "Find Your Court Date" to determine if a name has an upcoming court date.
General Information: No sealed or confidential records released. Will fax civil documents only, $1.00 per page. Court makes copy: $.50 per page. Certification fee: $15 per doc. Payee: Fremont Superior Court. Personal checks accepted; credit cards are not. Prepayment required. Mail requests: SASE required.

Hayward Superior Court 24405 Amador St, Hayward, CA 94544; 510-690-2700; criminal phone: 510-690-2703; civil phone: 510-690-2705; fax: 510-690-2824; 8:30AM-4PM. ***Misdemeanor, Civil Actions, Eviction, Small Claims.*** www.alameda.courts.ca.gov/courts
Formerly San Leandro/Hayward Superior Ct. Includes the cities of San Leandro, Hayward and adjoining unincorporated areas of Castro Valley and San Lorenzo. Located at the Hayward Hall of Justice.
Civil Records: Access: Mail, in person, online. Both court and visitors may perform in person searches. Search fee: $15.00 per name if search exceeds 10 minutes. Required to search: name, years to search. Civil cases indexed by defendant, plaintiff, on computer back 20 years; also on paper index. Mail turnaround time 2-3 days. Civil PAT goes back to at 1998 or older. PAT civil results show middle initial. Online access to calendars, civil case summaries and complex litigations are free from Domain Web at the website. Search civil cases by number; litigations by case name or number. Online results show middle initial.
Criminal Records: Access: Mail, in person. Both court and visitors may perform in person searches. Search fee: $15.00 per name if search exceeds 10 minutes. Will only search back 7 years. Required to search: name, years to search, DOB. Signed release is required if court does name search. Criminal records on computer back at least 20 years; also on paper index. Mail turnaround time 2-3 days. Criminal PAT goes back to same as civil. PAT results show middle initial, DOB. At the website, search "Find Your Court Date" to determine if a name has an upcoming court date.
General Information: No sealed or confidential records released. No fee to fax documents. Court makes copy: $.50 per page. Certification fee: $15 per doc. Payee: Clerk of the Court. Local personal checks

accepted. ATM and credit cards accepted in person. Prepayment required. Mail requests: SASE required.

Oakland/Piedmont/Emeryville Superior Court - Criminal 661 Washington St, 2nd Fl, Oakland, CA 94607; 510-268-7700; 8:30AM-4PM. ***Felony, Misdemeanor.*** www.alameda.courts.ca.gov/courts

Comprises the cities of Oakland, Piedmont and Emeryville, Albany and Berkeley. Located at the Wiley W Manuel Courthouse.

Criminal Records: Access: Mail, in person. Both court and visitors may perform in person searches. Search fee: $15.00 per name if search exceeds 10 minutes. Required to search: name, years to search. Criminal records computerized from 1994, maintained since 1972. Mail turnaround time 1 week. Public use terminal has crim records back to 1998. At the website, search "Find Your Court Date" to determine if a name has an upcoming court date.

General Information: No sealed or confidential records released. Will not fax documents. Court makes copy: $.50 per page. Certification fee: $15 per doc. Payee: Clerk of Superior Court. Personal checks accepted. Visa/MC accepted in person only. Prepayment required. Mail requests: SASE required.

Pleasanton Superior Court 5672 Stoneridge Dr, Gale/Schenone Hall of Justice, Pleasanton, CA 94588; 925-227-6700; fax: 925-227-6772; 8:30AM-4PM. ***Misdemeanor, Civil Actions over $25,000, Eviction, Small Claims, Probate.*** www.alameda.courts.ca.gov/courts

Includes the cities of Livermore, Dublin, Sunol and Pleasanton and all areas east to San Joaquin County line, north of Highway 580 to Contra Costa line.

Civil Records: Access: Mail, in person, online. Both court and visitors may perform in person searches. Search fee: $15.00 per name if search exceeds 10 minutes. Required to search: name, years to search. Civil cases indexed by defendant, plaintiff, on computer from 1990. Mail turnaround time 4-6 weeks. Civil PAT goes back to 1998. PAT civil results show middle initial. Online access to calendars, civil case summaries, probate, family law, and complex litigations are free from Domain Web at the website. Search all by case number.

Criminal Records: Access: Mail, in person. Both court and visitors may perform in person searches. Search fee: $15.00 per name if search exceeds 10 minutes. Required to search: name, years to search; also helpful: address, DOB. Criminal records computerized from 1990. Note: Court prefers that you use their "consent form." Mail turnaround time 4-6 weeks. Criminal PAT goes back to same as civil. PAT criminal results show middle initial. At the website, search "Find Your Court Date" to determine if a name has an upcoming court date within five days.

General Information: Online identifiers in results same as on public terminal. No records older than 10 years are released. Will not fax documents. Court makes copy: $.50 per page. Certification fee: $15 per doc. Payee: Alameda County Superior Court. Personal checks accepted. Credit card accepted in person only. Prepayment required. Mail requests: SASE required.

Berkeley/Albany Superior Court - Traffic, Berkeley, CA 94704; ***Traffic.***

This traffic court has been transferred to Wiley W Manuel Courthouse in Oakland, see Superior Ct-Oakland. This court no longer handles Misdemeanor cases; records at Oakland/Piedmont/Emeryville Superior Ct Crim Div at 661 Washington St, Oakland.

Alpine County

Superior Court PO Box 518, Markleeville, CA 96120; 530-694-2113; probate phone: same; fax: 530-694-2119; 8AM-4:30PM. ***Felony, Misdemeanor, Civil, Eviction, Small Claims, Probate.*** www.alpine.courts.ca.gov

Civil Records: Access: Mail, in person. Both court and visitors may perform in person searches. Search fee: $15.00 per name if search exceeds 10 minutes. Required to search: name, years to search. Civil cases indexed by defendant, plaintiff, on index file from 1981, closed files archived from 1800s to 1998. Computer records go back 10 years. Mail turnaround time 2-3 days.

Criminal Records: Access: Mail, in person. Only the court performs in person searches; visitors may not. Search fee: $15.00 per name if search exceeds 10 minutes. Required to search: name, years to search; also helpful-SSN. Criminal records on index file from 1981, archived from 1800s. Computer records go back 10 years. Mail turnaround time 1-3 days.

General Information: No juvenile, paternity, adoption or sealed released. Fee to fax out file $1.00 per page. Court makes copy: $.50 per page, self serve same. Certification fee: $15 per doc. Payee: Alpine County Superior Court. Personal checks accepted; credit cards no. Prepayment required. Mail requests: SASE required or toll-free number for return.

Amador County

Superior Court 500 Argonaut Ln, Jackson, CA 95642-9534; criminal phone: 209-257-2604; civil phone: 209-257-2603; fax: 209-257-2676; 9:30AM-4PM. ***Felony, Misdemeanor, Civil, Eviction, Small Claims, Probate.*** www.amadorcourt.org

Civil Records: Access: Mail, in person. Only the court performs in person searches; visitors may not. Search fee: $15.00 per name if search exceeds 10 minutes. Required to search: name, years to search. Civil cases indexed by defendant, plaintiff, on computer back to 1989. Archived and indexed in books from 1800s. Note: Names searches go back to 1989 only. Mail turnaround time 7-14 days. Court calendars are by date up to 7 days ahead at www.amadorcourt.org/courtcal/courtcal.html. Personal identifiers are name and case number.

Criminal Records: Access: Mail, in person. Only the court performs in person searches; visitors may not. Search fee: $15.00 per name if search exceeds 10 minutes. Names searches go back to 1989 only. Required to search: name, years to search. Criminal records computerized from 1989. Felonies are archived and indexed in books from 1800s; misdemeanors retained 2-10 years depending on offense. Note: Visitors may search pre-1989 records themselves. Fax access limited to public agency searches. Mail turnaround time 4-6 weeks. Court calendars are by date up to 10 days ahead at www.amadorcourt.org/courtcal/courtcal.html. Personal identifiers are name and case number.

General Information: No adoption, juvenile or paternity records released. Unlawful detainee released after 60 days of filing. Will not fax documents. Court makes copy: $.50 per page. Certification fee: $15 per doc. Payee: Amador Superior Court. Personal checks accepted for correct amount only. No credit cards accepted. Prepayment required. Mail requests: SASE required for private agencies.

Butte County

Superior Court One Court St, Oroville, CA 95965; 530-532-7002 Admin; criminal phone: 530-532-7011; civil phone: 530-532-7009; probate phone: 530-532-7017; fax: 530-538-9017; 8:30AM-4PM. ***Felony, Misdemeanor, Small Claims, Eviction, Traffic, Probate, Family.*** www.buttecourt.ca.gov

Civil fax- 530-892-8516. Courthouse physically holds most criminal court files for the county, including Gridley, Chico, Paradise Branches; however, search countywide computer index at any court. Civil cases were transferred to the Chico court in 2003.

Civil Records: Access: Mail, in person, online. Both court and visitors may perform in person searches. Search fee: $15.00 per name if search exceeds 10 minutes. Required to search: name, years to search; also helpful: address. Civil cases indexed by defendant, plaintiff, on computer from 1988, on microfiche from 1983 thru 1988. Mail turnaround time 2-5 days. Civil PAT goes back to 1990. PAT results show name only. Limited case index searching by name is free at www.buttecourt.ca.gov/online_index/cmssearch.cfm. There is also a calendar lookup at www.buttecourt.ca.gov/calendarlookup/cmscalendarlookup.cfm.

Criminal Records: Access: Mail, in person, online. Both court and visitors may perform in person searches. Search fee: $15.00 per name if search exceeds 10 minutes. Required to search: name, years to search; also helpful: DOB. Criminal records computerized from 1988, on microfiche from 1983 thru 1988. Mail turnaround time 1-2 weeks. Criminal PAT goes back to same as civil. PAT results show name only. 2 terminals available. Limited case index search by name free online at www.buttecourt.ca.gov/online_index/cmssearch.cfm. There is also a calendar lookup, see above.

General Information: No juvenile, paternity or adoption records released. Will fax documents $5.00 1st page, $1.00 each add'l. Court makes copy: $.50 per page, self serve same. Certification fee: $15 per doc. Payee: Butte County Superior Court. Personal checks accepted. Visa/MC accepted. Prepayment required. Mail requests: SASE required.

Chico Branch - Superior Court 655 Oleander Ave, Chico, CA 95926; 530-892-9407 (Traffic); civil phone: 530-532-7009; probate phone: 530-532-7017; fax: 530-892-8516; 8:30AM-4PM. ***Civil Actions, Eviction, Small Claims, Probate.*** www.buttecourt.ca.gov

Traffic phone- 530-892-9407. This court handles civil cases previously handled by Oroville court. All misdemeanor cases now at Oroville. Active probate case records located here at Chico; closed cases archived in basement of the main Court in Oroville.

Civil Records: Access: Mail, in person, online. Both court and visitors may perform in person searches. Search fee: $15.00 per name if search exceeds 10 minutes. Required to search: name, years to search. Civil cases indexed by defendant, plaintiff, in index files. Records destroyed after 10 years. Mail turnaround time 4 weeks. Public use terminal has civil records back to 1986. PAT results show name only. Limited case index searching by name is free www.buttecourt.ca.gov/online_index/cmssearch.cfm. There is also a calendar lookup at www.buttecourt.ca.gov/calendarlookup/cmscalendarlookup.cfm. Online results show name only.

General Information: No sealed records released. Will not fax documents. Court makes copy: $.50 per page. Certification fee: $15 per doc. Payee: Superior Court. Personal checks accepted. Visa/MC accepted. Prepayment required. Mail requests: SASE required.

Gridley Branch - Superior Court 1 Court St, Oroville, CA 95965; 530-532-7002; ***Misdemeanor-Traffic, Eviction, Small Claims.*** www.buttecourt.ca.gov

Court closed. Closed cases must be searched at Oroville court, address and phone given here.

Paradise Branch - Superior Court 747 Elliott Rd, Paradise, CA 95969; 530-532-7018; civil phone: 530-532-7009; probate phone: 530-532-7017; fax: 530-872-2614; 8AM-1PM T-F; 8AM-5PM M. ***Small Claims, Eviction, Misdemeanor Traffic, Infraction.*** www.buttecourt.ca.gov

Probate fax- 530-538-8516. This branch is now largely a data center. See Oroville Court for this court's old misdemeanor records. Most copy work done at the main branch in Oroville.

Civil Records: Access: Mail, in person, online. Only the court performs in person searches; visitors may not. Search fee: $15.00 per name if search exceeds 10 minutes. Required to search: name; also helpful: years to search. Civil cases indexed by defendant, plaintiff, are located in The Chico Superior Court. Records go back to 1980; on computer back to 1997. PAT results show name only. Limited case index searching by name free at www.buttecourt.ca.gov/online_index/cmssearch.cfm. There is a calendar lookup at www.buttecourt.ca.gov/calendarlookup/cmscalendarlookup.cfm. Online results show name only.

General Information: No sealed records released. Court makes copy: $.50 per page. Certification fee: $15 per doc. Payee: Superior Court. Personal checks accepted. Visa/MC accepted. Prepayment required. Mail requests: SASE required for civil.

Calaveras County

Superior Court 891 Mt Ranch Rd, San Andreas, CA 95249; 209-754-6311 info; criminal phone: 209-754-6338; civil phone: 209-754-6310; probate phone: 209-754-6310; criminal fax: 209-754-6689; civil fax: same; 8AM-4PM. ***Felony, Misdemeanor, Civil, Small Claims, Probate, Infractions.*** www.calaveras.courts.ca.gov

Civil Records: Access: Mail, in person. Both court and visitors may perform in person searches. Search fee: $15.00 per name if search exceeds 10 minutes. Required to search: name, years to search. Civil cases indexed by defendant, plaintiff, on computer since 6/96; in index books and microfiche from 1975. Mail turnaround time 1-2 weeks.
Criminal Records: Access: Mail, in person. Both court and visitors may perform in person searches. Search fee: $15.00 per name if search exceeds 10 minutes. Required to search: name, years to search, DOB; also helpful: aliases. Criminal records on computer since 6/96; in index books and microfiche from 1975. Mail turnaround time 1-2 weeks.
General Information: No juvenile or confidential records released. Will not fax documents. Court makes copy: $.50 per page. Certification fee: $15 per doc. Payee: Calaveras Superior Court. Personal checks accepted; credit cards are not. Prepayment required. Mail requests: SASE required.

Colusa County

Superior Court - Dept 1 532 Oak St, Colusa, CA 95932; 530-458-5149; fax: 530-458-2230; 8:30AM-5PM. ***Felony, Civil Actions over $25,000, Probate.*** www.colusa.courts.ca.gov
Since 1995, the records have been combined for both courts in this county; prior records must be searched at the individual courts. Dept. 1's courtroom is at 547 Market St. Weekly calendars available at the website.
Civil Records: Access: Mail, in person. Both court and visitors may perform in person searches. Search fee: $15.00 per name if search exceeds 10 minutes. Required to search: name, years to search. Civil cases indexed by defendant, plaintiff, on computer from 1986, in index files from 1800s. Mail turnaround 7 days. Civil PAT goes back to 1995.
Criminal Records: Access: Mail, in person. Both court and visitors may perform in person searches. Search fee: $15.00 per name if search exceeds 10 minutes. Required to search: name, years to search. Criminal records computerized from 1986, in index files from 1800s. Mail turnaround time 7 days. Criminal PAT goes back to same as civil.
General Information: No juvenile, paternity (except Judgment) or adoption records released. Will not fax documents. Court makes copy: $.50 per page. Certification fee: $15 per doc. Payee: Colusa County Superior Court. Personal checks accepted. No credit cards accepted for fees. Prepayment required. Mail requests: SASE required.

Superior Court - Dept 2 532 Oak St, Colusa, CA 95932; 530-458-5149; fax: 530-458-2230; 8:30AM-5PM. ***Felony, Misdemeanor, Civil, Eviction, Small Claims.*** www.colusa.courts.ca.gov
Records from both courts in this county have been combined. Weekly calendars available at the website.
Civil Records: Access: Mail, in person. Both court and visitors may perform in person searches. Search fee: $15.00 per name if search exceeds 10 minutes. Required to search: name, years to search. Civil cases indexed by defendant, plaintiff, on computer from 1994, index books prior. Mail turnaround time up to 2 weeks. Civil PAT goes back to 1995.
Criminal Records: Access: Mail, in person. Both court and visitors may perform in person searches. Search fee: $15.00 per name if search exceeds 10 minutes. Required to search: name, years to search, DOB. Criminal records computerized from 1994, index books prior. Mail turnaround time up to 2 weeks. Criminal PAT goes back to same as civil.
General Information: No sealed records released. Will not fax documents. Court makes copy: $.50 per page, self serve same. Certification fee: $15 per doc. Payee: Colusa Superior Court. Personal checks accepted; credit cards are not. Prepayment required. Mail requests: SASE required.

Contra Costa County

Superior Court PO Box 991, 725 Court St, Wafefield Taylor Courthouse, Rm 100, Martinez, CA 94553; 925-646-2950; criminal phone: 925-646-2440; civil phone: 925-646-2951; 8AM-3PM. ***Felony, Civil Actions over $25,000, Probate.*** www.cc-courts.org
Civil and Probate cases heard at the Wakefield Taylor Courthouse (address above); Criminal at AF Bray Bldg., 1020 Ward St. The Family Law Center can be reached at 925-957-7866. Traffic and Small Claims cases from this area are heard in the Concord Court.
Civil Records: Access: Mail, in person, online. Both court and visitors may perform in person searches. Search fee: $15.00 per name if search exceeds 10 minutes. Required to search: name, years to search. Civil cases indexed by defendant, plaintiff, on computer from 1987, on microfiche from 1900s. Note: Court visitors can view microfiche. Mail turnaround time 7-10 days With registration, use Open Access to view Civil case, Probate, Family and Small Claims information is free at http://icms.cc-courts.org/iotw/. Also, lookup your court case info free at http://icms.cc-courts.org/tellme/. Online civil search results include month/year of birth.
Criminal Records: Access: Mail, in person. Both court and visitors may perform in person searches. Search fee: $15.00 per name if search exceeds 10 minutes. Required to search: name, DOB. Criminal records computerized from 1987, on microfiche from 1900s. Note: Send written requests to Room 127. Visitors can view microfiche. Mail turnaround time 7-10 days.
General Information: No adoption, juvenile or sealed records released. Will not fax documents. Court makes copy: $.50 per page per side. Certification fee: $15 per doc plus copy fee, exemplification fee $20.00. Payee: Clerk of the Superior Court. Business checks accepted. No credit cards accepted. Prepayment required. Mail requests: SASE required.

Walnut Creek Branch - Superior Court 640 Ygnacio Valley Rd, Walnut Creek, CA 94596-3820; 925-646-6578; criminal phone: 925-646-6763; civil phone: 925-646-6579; 8AM-3PM. ***Felony, Misdemeanor, Eviction, Small Claims, Traffic.*** www.cc-courts.org
Includes Alamo, Canyon, Danville, Lafayette, Moraga, Orinda, Rheem, San Ramon, St Mary's College, Walnut Creek and Ygnacio Valley. Effective 01/01/99, this court has all civil records formerly at the municipal court in Concord.
Civil Records: Access: Phone, mail, online, in person. Both court and visitors may perform in person searches. Search fee: $15.00 per name if search exceeds 10 minutes. Add $5.00 archive retrieval fee for older cases. In person searching of microfiche is free. Required to search: name; also helpful: years to search. Civil cases indexed by defendant, plaintiff, on computer from 1991. Records are destroyed after 10 years. Mail turnaround time 1 week. Civil PAT available. With registration, use Open Access to view Civil case, Probate, Family and Small Claims information is free at http://icms.cc-courts.org/iotw/. Also, lookup your court case info free at http://icms.cc-courts.org/tellme/. Online civil search results include month/year of birth.
Criminal Records: Access: Mail, in person, online. Both court and visitors may perform in person searches. Search fee: $15.00 per name if search exceeds 10 minutes. Add $5.00 archive retrieval fee for older cases. In person microfiche searching is free. Required to search: name, years to search, DOB. Criminal records go back 10 years. Mail turnaround time 1 week. Criminal PAT available. Lookup your court case info free at www.cc-courts.org/ and click on Case Info or Tell Me About My Case.
General Information: No probation reports or sealed case records released. Will not fax documents. Court makes copy: $.50 per page. Certification fee: $15 per doc. Payee: Walnut Creek Superior Court. Personal checks accepted; credit cards are not. Prepayment required. Mail requests: SASE required.

Concord Branch - Superior Court 2970 Willow Pass Rd, Concord, CA 94519; 925-646-5410; 8AM-3PM. ***Eviction, Small Claims, Traffic.*** www.cc-courts.org
Includes Avon, Clayton, Clyde, Concord, Martinez, Pacheco, Pleasant Hill. This court serves as the lowest court for the Main Court in Martinez. Probate, Family and Small Claims information free at www.cc-courts.org/index.cfm.

Pittsburg Branch - Superior Court 45 Civic Ave, Pittsburg, CA 94565-0431; criminal phone: 925-427-8173; civil phone: 925-427-8159; 8AM-3PM. ***Felony, Misdemeanor, Eviction, Small Claims, Traffic.*** www.cc-courts.org
Includes Antioch, Bay Pt., Bethel Is, Bradford Is, Brentwood, Byron, Holland Tract, Jersey Is, Knightsen, Oakley, Pittsburg, Quimby Is, Shore Acres, Webb Tract and parts of Clayton.
Civil Records: Access: Mail, in person, online. Both court and visitors may perform in person searches. Search fee: $15.00 per name if search exceeds 15 minutes. Required to search: name, years to search. Civil cases indexed by defendant, plaintiff, on computer from 1991. Records are destroyed after 10 years. Mail turnaround time 1 week. Civil PAT goes back to 1989. With registration, use Open Access to view Civil case, Probate, Family and Small Claims information is free at http://icms.cc-courts.org/iotw/. Also, lookup your court case info free at http://icms.cc-courts.org/tellme/. Online civil search results include month/year of birth.
Criminal Records: Access: Mail, in person. Both court and visitors may perform in person searches. Search fee: $15.00 per name if search exceeds 15 minutes. Required to search: name, years to search, DOB. Criminal records computerized from 1991, index files for 10 years. Records are destroyed after 10 years. Note: Visitor may search microfiche only. Mail turnaround time 1 week. Criminal PAT goes back to 1994.
General Information: No probation reports released. Will not fax documents. Court makes copy: $.50 per page. Certification fee: $15 per doc. Payee: Superior Court. Personal checks accepted; credit cards are not. Prepayment required. Mail requests: SASE required.

Richmond Superior Court 100 37th St, Richmond, CA 94805; 510-374-3138; criminal phone: 510-374-3156; civil phone: 510-374-3137; 8AM-3PM. ***Felony, Misdemeanor, Eviction, Small Claims, Traffic.*** www.cc-courts.org
Includes Crockett, El Cerrito, El Sobrante, Hercules, Kensington, North Richmond, Pinole, Point Richmond, Port Costa, Richmond, Rodeo, Rollingwood, San Pablo, Tilden North Pk. Traffic phone- 510-374-3171
Civil Records: Access: Mail, in person, online. Both court and visitors may perform in person searches. Search fee: $15.00 per name if search exceeds 10 minutes. Required to search: name. Civil cases indexed by defendant, plaintiff, on computer from 1991. Records are destroyed after 10 years unless renewal of judgment filed. Mail turnaround time 5 days. With registration, use Open Access to view Civil case, Probate, Family and Small Claims information is free at http://icms.cc-courts.org/iotw/. Also, lookup your court case info free at http://icms.cc-courts.org/tellme/. Online civil search results include month/year of birth.
Criminal Records: Access: Mail, in person. Only the court performs in person searches; visitors may not. Search fee: $15.00 per name if search exceeds 10 minutes. There is an additional fee for retrieval of archive files. Required to search: name, years to search; also helpful: address, DOB, SSN. Criminal records maintained for 10 years, but can be destroyed after 2 years depending on violation code. Mail turnaround time 5 days.
General Information: No probation reports released. Will not fax documents. Court makes copy: $.50 per page. Certification fee: $15 per doc. Payee: Richmond Superior Court. Personal checks accepted. No credit cards accepted in person; cards accepted for full payment on internet. Prepayment required. Mail requests: SASE required.

Del Norte County

Superior Court 450 "H" St, Rm 209, Crescent City, CA 95531; 707-464-8115; criminal phone: x4; civil phone: x4; criminal fax: 707-465-4005; civil fax: 707-464-8115; 8AM-5PM. ***Felony, Misdemeanor, Civil, Eviction, Small Claims, Probate.*** www.delnorte.courts.ca.gov
Civil Records: Access: Fax, mail, in person. Only the court performs in person searches; visitors may not. Search fee: $15.00 per name if search exceeds 10 minutes. Required to search: name, years to search,

DOB. Civil cases indexed by defendant, plaintiff, in index files and on microfiche back to 1975. Mail turnaround time 1 week.
Criminal Records: Access: Mail, fax, in person. Only the court performs in person searches; visitors may not. Search fee: $15.00 per name if search exceeds 10 minutes. Required to search: name, years to search, DOB, middle name; also helpful-SSN. Criminal records in index files and microfiche back to 1975. Mail turnaround time 1 week.
General Information: No adoption, juvenile, probate, LPS conservatorship released. Will not fax documents. Court makes copy: $.50 per page. Certification fee: $15 per doc. Payee: Superior Court. Personal checks accepted; credit cards are not. Prepayment required. Mail requests: SASE required.

El Dorado County

Placerville Branch - Superior Court 495 Main St, Placerville, CA 95667; 530-621-6426; criminal phone: 530-621-6716; fax: 530-622-9774; 8AM-3PM. ***Felony.*** www.eldoradocourt.org/
Criminal Records: Access: Mail, in person, online. Both court and visitors may perform in person searches. Search fee: $15.00 per name if search exceeds 10 minutes. Fee is $4.00 to request a file from archives. Required to search: name, years to search. Criminal records computerized from 2000, in hardbound books from 1979 to 1999, prior archived in Placerville. Mail turnaround time 2 weeks. Access alpha Case Index lists back to year 2000 free at www.eldoradocourt.org/caseindex/case_index.aspx. Search monthly calendars free at http://eldocourtweb.eldoradocourt.org/calendar.aspx. Online results show name only.
General Information: No adoption, juvenile, mental or confidential released. Will not fax documents. Court makes copy: $.50 per page. Self serve: $.15 per page. Certification fee: $15 per doc. Payee: Superior Court. Personal checks accepted; credit cards are not. Prepayment required. Mail requests: SASE required.

South Lake Tahoe Branch - Superior Court - Civil 1354 Johnson Blvd, #2, South Lake Tahoe, CA 96150; 530-573-3075; fax: 530-544-6532; 8AM-3PM. ***Civil, Eviction, Probate.*** www.eldoradocourt.org/
Civil Records: Access: Mail, in person, online. Both court and visitors may perform in person searches. Search fee: $15.00 per name if search exceeds 10 minutes. Required to search: name, years to search; also helpful-case number. Civil cases indexed by defendant, plaintiff, on computer from 1989, in hardbound books from 1979 to 1989, prior archived in Placerville. Mail turnaround time 2 weeks. Access alpha Case Index lists back to year 2000 free at www.eldoradocourt.org/caseindex/case_index.aspx. Judge's weekly tentative rulings may be free at the website. Search monthly calendars free at http://eldocourtweb.eldoradocourt.org/calendar.aspx. Online results show name only.
General Information: No adoption, juvenile, mental or confidential released. Court makes copy: $.50 per page. Certification fee: $15 per doc. Payee: Superior Court. Personal checks accepted; credit cards are not. Prepayment required. Generally, submit a 'not to exceed' $30.00 check. Mail requests: SASE required for civil.

South Lake Tahoe Branch - Superior Court - Criminal 1354 Johnson Blvd, #1, South Lake Tahoe, CA 96150; 530-573-3044; fax: 530-542-9102; 8AM-2PM; till 4:30PM TH. ***Felony, Misdemeanor.*** www.eldoradocourt.org/
Criminal Records: Access: Mail, in person, online. Both court and visitors may perform in person searches. Search fee: $15.00 per name if search exceeds 10 minutes. Required to search: name, years to search; also helpful: DOB, SSN. Criminal records computerized from 2000, index files from 1983. Records are destroyed after 10 years. Mail turnaround time 2 weeks. Public use terminal has crim records. Access alpha Case Index lists back to year 2000 free at www.eldoradocourt.org/caseindex/case_index.aspx. Search monthly calendars free at http://eldocourtweb.eldoradocourt.org/calendar.aspx. Online results show name only.

General Information: No probation reports released. Faxed record request must be prepaid. Court makes copy: $.50 per page. Certification fee: $15 per doc. Payee: El Dorado Superior Court. Personal checks accepted. Credit cards only accepted at www.paybill.com/eldoradocourt. Prepayment required. Mail requests: SASE required.

Cameron Park Branch - Superior Court 3321 Cameron Park Dr, Cameron Park, CA 95682; 530-621-5867; probate phone: same; fax: 530-672-2413; 8AM-3PM. ***Civil, Probate.*** www.eldoradocourt.org/
This is a Trial and Law & Motion court. Only records after 2004 are housed here. Records from 1999 and prior are available at the Placerville Branch Superior Court OR at record storage location in Sacramento.
Civil Records: Access: Mail, in person, online. Both court and visitors may perform in person searches. Search fee: $15.00 per name if search exceeds 10 minutes. Required to search: name, years to search. Civil records on computer from 2000, index cards prior. Records are destroyed after 10 years. Mail turnaround time 1 week. Access alpha Case Index lists back to year 2000 free at www.eldoradocourt.org/caseindex/case_index.aspx. Judge's weekly tentative rulings may be free at the website. Search monthly calendars free at http://eldocourtweb.eldoradocourt.org/calendar.aspx. Online results show name only.
General Information: Will not fax documents. Court makes copy: $.50 per page. Certification fee: $15 per doc plus copy fee; Exemplification fee $20.00. Payee: Superior Court. Personal checks accepted; credit cards are not. Prepayment required. Mail requests: SASE required.

West Slope Branch Superior Court 2850 Fairlane Ct, Bldg C, Placerville, CA 95667; criminal phone: 530-621-7464; civil phone: 530-621-7470; criminal fax: 530-626-0656; civil fax: 530-295-2536; 8AM-3PM. ***Misdemeanor, Small Claims, Evictions, Traffic.*** www.eldoradocourt.org/
Also known as the Fairlane Branch. Also hears felony arraignments.
Civil Records: Access: Mail, in person, online. Both court and visitors may perform in person searches. Search fee: $15.00 per name if search exceeds 10 minutes. Required to search: name, years to search. Civil cases indexed by defendant, plaintiff, on computer from 2000. Note: Address search requests to Dept. 8. Mail turnaround time 2 weeks. Civil PAT goes back to 2000. Access alpha Case Index lists back to year 2000 free at www.eldoradocourt.org/caseindex/case_index.aspx. Judge's weekly tentative rulings may be free at the website. Search monthly calendars at http://eldocourtweb.eldoradocourt.org/calendar.aspx.
Criminal Records: Access: Mail, in person, online. Both court and visitors may perform in person searches. Search fee: $15.00 per name if search takes 10 minutes or more. $4.00 retrieval fee for records in storage. Required to search: name, years to search; also helpful: DOB. Criminal records computerized from 2000, prior on index books, index files from 1983. Records are destroyed after 10 years. Note: Address search requests to Dept 7. Mail turnaround time 2 weeks. Criminal PAT goes back to 2000. Access alpha Case Index lists back to year 2000 free at www.eldoradocourt.org/caseindex/case_index.aspx. Search monthly calendars free at http://eldocourtweb.eldoradocourt.org/calendar.aspx. Online results show name only.
General Information: No probation reports released. Will not fax documents. Court makes copy: $.50 per page. Certification fee: $15 per doc. Payee: El Dorado County Superior Courts. Personal checks accepted; credit cards are not. Prepayment required. Mail requests: SASE required.

Fresno County

Superior Court - Criminal 1100 Van Ness Ave, #401, Fresno, CA 93724; 559-488-1825; criminal phone: 559-488-3142 misd.; 559-488-3388 felony; fax: 559-488-3433; 8AM-4PM. ***Felony, Misdemeanor, Traffic, Family.*** www.fresnosuperiorcourt.org

Felony address is B-102; Misdemeanor address is Rm 402; Fax for misdemeanors is 599-488-3334. Civil court main office is at 2317 Tuolumne St.
Criminal Records: Access: Phone, fax, mail, in person. Both court and visitors may perform in person searches. Search fee: $15.00 per name if search exceeds 10 minutes. Required to search: name, years to search. Criminal records computerized from 1976; microfiche, index files and archived from 1800s. Mail turnaround time 3-5 days. Public use terminal has crim records back to 1976.PAT results show name, DOB.
General Information: No confidential, adoption or juvenile records released. Will not fax documents. Court makes copy: $.50 per page. Certification fee: $15 per doc. Payee: Superior Court Clerk's Office. Personal checks accepted. Visa/MC accepted. Prepayment required. Mail requests: SASE required.

Superior Court - Civil 2317 Tuolumne St, M Street Civil Courthouse, Fresno, CA 93721-1220; 559-497-4100; fax: 559-497-4290; 8AM-5PM. ***Civil, Small Claims, Eviction.***
The civil court was separated from the criminal court location in about 2007.
Civil Records: Access: Phone, fax, mail, in person, online. Only the court performs in person searches; visitors may not. Search fee: $15.00 per name if search exceeds 10 minutes. Required to search: name, years to search. Civil cases indexed by defendant, plaintiff, on computer back to 1976; on microfiche, index files and archived from 1800s. Mail turnaround time 3-5 days. Public use terminal has civil records back to 1976. PAT results show name, DOB. Access to civil, probate, family, small claims cases is free at www.fresnosuperiorcourt.org/case_info/.
General Information: No confidential, adoption or juvenile records released. Will not fax documents. Court makes copy: $.50 per page. Certification fee: $15 per doc. Payee: Superior Court Clerk's Office. Personal checks accepted. Visa/MC accepted. Prepayment required. Mail requests: SASE required.

Clovis Division - Superior Court 1011 5th St, Clovis, CA 93612; 559-299-4964; fax: 559-299-2595; 8AM-4PM. ***Misdemeanor, Civil Actions under $25,000, Eviction, Small Claims, Traffic.*** www.fresnosuperiorcourt.org
Includes Alder Springs, Auberry, Big Creek, Burroughs Valley, Clovis, Friant, Huntington Lake, Millerton Lake, Pine Ridge, Prather, Shaver, Tollhouse, Watts. Felony welfare fraud cases only.
Civil Records: Access: Mail, in person, online. Only the court performs in person searches; visitors may not. Search fee: $15.00 per name if search exceeds 10 minutes. Required to search: name, years to search. Civil cases indexed by defendant, plaintiff, on computer and index files from 1983. Records destroyed after 10 years. Mail turnaround time 2 weeks. Access to civil, probate, family, small claims cases is free at www.fresnosuperiorcourt.org/case_info/.
Criminal Records: Access: Mail, in person. Only the court performs in person searches; visitors may not. Search fee: $15.00 per name if search exceeds 10 minutes. Required to search: name, years to search, DOB. Criminal records on computer and index files from 1983. Records destroyed after 10 years. Mail turnaround time 2 weeks.
General Information: No probation reports released. Will not fax documents. Court makes copy: $.50 per page. Certification fee: $15 per doc. Payee: Clovis Superior Court. Personal checks accepted. Visa/MC accepted in person only. Prepayment required. Mail requests: SASE required.

Coalinga Division - Superior Court 160 W Elm St, Coalinga, CA 93210; 559-935-2017/2018; fax: 559-935-5324; 8AM-4PM. ***Misdemeanor, Civil Actions under $25,000, Eviction, Small Claims.*** www.fresnosuperiorcourt.org
Includes Coalinga and Huron.
Civil Records: Access: Mail, in person, online. Only the court performs in person searches; visitors may not. Search fee: $15.00 per name if search exceeds 10 minutes. Required to search: name, years to search; also helpful: address. Civil cases indexed by defendant, plaintiff; index on cards and are computerized since 1990. Will only search back 10

years. Mail turnaround time 1 week. Access to civil, probate, family, small claims cases is free at www.fresnosuperiorcourt.org/case_info/.
Criminal Records: Access: Mail, in person. Only the court performs in person searches; visitors may not. Search fee: $15.00 per name if search exceeds 10 minutes. Required to search: name, years to search, DOB; also helpful: address. Criminal records computerized from 1990, on index cards prior. Will only search back 10 years, Traffic 10 years. Mail turnaround time 1 week.
General Information: No confidential records or cases not finished released. Will not fax documents. Court makes copy: $.50 per page. Certification fee: $15 per doc. Payee: Superior Court. Personal checks accepted. Credit cards accepted at the counter, but not over on phone. Prepayment required. Mail requests: SASE required.

Firebaugh Division - Superior Court 1325 "O" St, Firebaugh, CA 93622; 559-659-2011/2012; fax: 559-659-6228; 8AM-4PM. ***Misdemeanor, Civil Actions under $25,000, Eviction, Small Claims.***
www.fresnosuperiorcourt.org
Includes Firebaugh and Mendota. Now also houses Chowchilla Division.
Civil Records: Access: Phone, fax, mail, in person, online. Only the court performs in person searches; visitors may not. Search fee: $15.00 per name if search exceeds 10 minutes. Required to search: name, years to search. Civil cases indexed by defendant, plaintiff, on computer from 1990, index cards prior. Will only search back 7 years. Note: 5 name limit at counter. Mail turnaround time 1 week. Civil PAT available. Public terminal available at the Fresno main Superior Court. Access to civil, probate, family, small claims cases is free at www.fresnosuperiorcourt.org/case_info/.
Criminal Records: Access: Phone, fax, mail, in person. Only the court performs in person searches; visitors may not. Search fee: $15.00 per name if search exceeds 10 minutes. Required to search: name, years to search, DOB. Criminal records computerized from 1990. Will only search back 7 years. Note: 5 name limit at counter. Mail turnaround time 1 week. Criminal PAT available. Public terminal available at the Fresno main Superior Court.
General Information: No confidential records released. Will not fax documents. Court makes copy: $.50 per page. Certification fee: $15 per doc. Payee: Firebaugh Superior Court. Personal checks accepted. Visa/MC accepted. Prepayment required. Mail requests: SASE required.

Fowler Division - Superior Court 127 E Merced St, Fowler, CA 93625; 559-834-3215; fax: 559-834-1645; 8AM-4PM. ***Civil Actions under $25,000, Eviction, Small Claims.***
www.fresnosuperiorcourt.org This court holds the records for the closed courts in Caruthers, Parlier, as well as cases from the cities of Bowles, Del Rey, Fowler, Kingsburg, Monmouth, and Raisin City. Selma case records are now back at Selma.
Civil Records: Access: Mail, in person, online. Only the court performs in person searches; visitors may not. Search fee: $15.00 per name if search exceeds 10 minutes. Required to search: name, years to search. Civil cases indexed by defendant, plaintiff; index on cards. Will only search back 7 years. Mail turnaround time 1 week. Access to civil, probate, family, small claims cases is free at www.fresnosuperiorcourt.org/case_info/.
General Information: No confidential records released. Will not fax documents. Court makes copy: $.50 per page, self serve same. Certification fee: $15 per doc. Payee: Fowler Superior Court. Personal checks accepted. Visa/MC accepted. Prepayment required. Mail requests: SASE required.

Kerman Division - Superior Court 719 S Madera Ave, Kerman, CA 93630; 559-846-7371; fax: 559-846-5751; 8AM-4PM. ***Misdemeanor, Civil Actions under $25,000, Eviction, Small Claims.***
www.fresnosuperiorcourt.org
Includes Biola, Biola Junction, Cantua, Five Points, Helm, Kerman, Rolinda, San Joaquin, and Tranquillity. The court holds preliminary hearings for felonies.
Civil Records: Access: Phone, mail, in person, online. Only the court performs in person searches; visitors may not. Search fee: $15.00 per name if search exceeds 10 minutes. Required to search: name, years to search. Civil cases indexed by defendant, plaintiff; index on cards, computerized since 1994. Court will only search back 7 years. Mail turnaround time 1 week. Public use terminal has civil records back to 1976. Access to civil, probate, family, small claims cases is free at www.fresnosuperiorcourt.org/case_info/.
Criminal Records: Access: Phone, mail, in person. Only the court performs in person searches; visitors may not. Search fee: $15.00 per name if search exceeds 10 minutes. Required to search: name, years to search. Criminal records computerized from 1994 index cards prior. Court will only search back 7 years. Note: May have terminals available at archives location; 1963 E St, Kerman, CA, Ph-559-233-2800. Mail turnaround time 1 week.
General Information: No confidential records released. Will fax documents. Court makes copy: $.50 per page. Certification fee: $15 per doc. Payee: Superior Court. Personal checks accepted. Visa/MC, ATM accepted in person only. Prepayment required. Mail requests: SASE required.

Kingsburg Division - Superior Court 1600 California St, Kingsburg, CA 93631; 559-897-2241; fax: 559-897-1419; 8AM-4PM. ***Felony, Misdemeanor, Civil (Limited), Traffic.***
www.fresnosuperiorcourt.org
This court includes criminal case records from the branch courts closed in Riverdale, Selma/Parlick/Fowler, and cases from the cities of Burrel, Camden, Kingsburg, Lanare, Laton, and Riverdale. Civil records kept at Fowler Division.
Civil Records: Access: Mail, in person, online. Only the court performs in person searches; visitors may not. Search fee: $15.00 per name if search exceeds 10 minutes. Required to search: name, years to search. Mail turnaround time 1 week. Access to civil, probate, family, small claims cases is free at www.fresnosuperiorcourt.org/case_info/.
Criminal Records: Access: Mail, in person. Only the court performs in person searches; visitors may not. Search fee: $15.00 per name if search exceeds 10 minutes. Required to search: name, years to search, DOB. Criminal records computerized from 4/1994, index cards prior. Mail turnaround time 1 week.
General Information: No confidential records released. Will not fax documents. Court makes copy: $.50 per page. Certification fee: $15 per doc. Payee: Superior Court. Personal checks accepted. Prepayment required. Mail requests: SASE required.

Reedley Division - Superior Court 815 "G" St, Reedley, CA 93654; 559-638-3114; fax: 559-637-1534; 8AM-4PM. ***Misdemeanor, Civil Actions under $25,000, Eviction, Small Claims.***
www.fresnosuperiorcourt.org
Includes Badger, Cedarbrook, Cedar Pines, Dunlap, Hume, Kings River Canyon, Navalencia, Minkler, Miramonte, Orange Cove, Piedra, Reedley, Sanger (only criminal cases), Squaw Valley, Trimmer Springs and Wahtoke.
Civil Records: Access: Mail, in person, online. Only the court performs in person searches; visitors may not. Search fee: $15.00 per name if search exceeds 10 minutes. Required to search: name, years to search. Civil cases indexed by defendant, plaintiff, on computer back 10 years, index cards prior. Will only search back 7 years. Mail turnaround time 1 week. Access to civil, probate, family, small claims cases is free at www.fresnosuperiorcourt.org/case_info/.
Criminal Records: Access: Mail, in person. Only the court performs in person searches; visitors may not. Search fee: $15.00 per name if search exceeds 10 minutes. Required to search: name, years to search, DOB. Criminal records on computer back 10 years, index cards prior. Will only search back 7 years. Mail turnaround time 1 week.
General Information: No confidential records released. Will not fax documents. Court makes copy: $.50 per page. Certification fee: $15 per doc. Payee: Reedley Superior Court. Personal checks accepted. Visa/MC accepted. Prepayment required. Mail requests: SASE required.

Sanger Division - Superior Court 619 N St, Sanger, CA 93657; 559-876-6000; fax: 559-875-8609; 8AM-4PM. ***Civil Actions under $25,000, Eviction, Small Claims, Traffic, Ordinance.***
www.fresnosuperiorcourt.org
This court closed as of 07/03, then, re-opened for civil cases. Misdemeanor cases files are still in Reedley. This Sanger court had jurisdiction over Centerville and Sanger.

Probate Court 1999 Tuolumne St, 5th Fl, #501, Trade Center Bldg, Fresno, CA 93721; 559-263-8700; fax: 559-263-8710; 8AM-4PM. ***Probate.***
www.fresnosuperiorcourt.org/probate/
Access to civil, probate, family, small claims cases is free at www.fresnosuperiorcourt.org/case_info/.

Selma Division - Superior Court 2424 McCall Ave, Selma, CA 93662; 559-891-3120; fax: 559-891-3128. ***Civil Actions under $25,000, Eviction, Small Claims.***
www.fresnosuperiorcourt.org
This court was closed 06/03 thru 04/06. Criminal case files went to the Court in Kingsburg. Civil and small claims cases were tried in Fowler.
Civil Records: Access: Mail, in person, online. Only the court performs in person searches; visitors may not. Search fee: $15.00 per name if search exceeds 10 minutes. Required to search: name, years to search. Civil cases indexed by defendant, plaintiff; index on cards. Note: Court will only search back 7 years. Mail turnaround time 1 week. Access to civil, probate, family, small claims cases is free at www.fresnosuperiorcourt.org/case_info/.
General Information: No confidential records released. Will not fax documents. Court makes copy: $.50 per page. Certification fee: $15 per doc. Payee: Fresno Superior Court. Personal checks accepted. Prepayment required. Mail requests: SASE required.

Glenn County

Superior Court 526 W Sycamore, Willows, CA 95988; 530-934-6446; fax: 530-934-6728; 8AM-5PM. ***Felony, Misdemeanor, Civil, Small Claims, Probate, Family*** www.glenncourt.ca.gov
Records from the municipal court were combined with this court when the courts were consolidated. Records-530-934-6446.
Civil Records: Access: Mail, in person, online. Both court and visitors may perform in person searches. Search fee: $15.00 per name if search exceeds 10 minutes. Required to search: name, years to search. Civil cases indexed by defendant, plaintiff, on computer back to 1996, on microfiche, archived and in index file from 1894. Mail turnaround time 1 day. Civil PAT goes back to 1996. Search case index at www.glenncourt.ca.gov/online_index/.
Criminal Records: Access: Mail, in person, online. Both court and visitors may perform in person searches. Search fee: $15.00 per name if search exceeds 10 minutes. Required to search: name, years to search; also helpful: DOB. Criminal records computerized from 1996, on microfiche, archived and in index file from 1894. Mail turnaround time 1 day. Criminal PAT goes back to same as civil. Search index at www.glenncourt.ca.gov/online_index/.
General Information: No adoption, juvenile or paternity released. Will not fax documents. Court makes copy: $.50 per page, self serve same. Certification fee: $15 per doc. Payee: Superior Court. Personal checks accepted; credit cards are not. Prepayment required. Mail requests: SASE required.

Humboldt County

Superior Court 825 5th St, Eureka, CA 95501; 707-445-7256; fax: 707-445-7041; 10AM-4PM. ***Felony, Civil, Small Claims, Eviction, Probate.***
www.courtinfo.ca.gov/courts/trial/humboldt/
Address for civil window is 421 I St. Do countywide search from this court, records computerized back 10 years. Former Eureka, Eel River, and N Humboldt Muni. Court Divisions part of this court. Hoopa Tribal & Garberville Branches here except on Fridays.
Civil Records: Access: Mail, in person. Both court and visitors may perform in person searches. Search fee: $15.00 per name if search exceeds 10 minutes. Required to search: name, years to search. Civil cases indexed by defendant, plaintiff, on

computer back to 1993; on microfiche and archived from 1964. Note: Phone requests are limited to 2 names only. Mail turnaround time 2 weeks.
Criminal Records: Access: Mail, in person, phone. Both court and visitors may perform in person searches. Search fee: $15.00 per name if search exceeds 10 minutes. Required to search: name, years to search; also helpful: DOB. Criminal records computerized from 1985; on microfiche and archived from 1964. Note: Phone requests are limited to 2 names only. Mail turnaround time 2 weeks.
General Information: No probation, medical, adoption, juvenile or sealed records released. Will not fax documents. Court makes copy: $.50 per page. Certification fee: $15 per doc. Payee: Humboldt Superior Court. Personal checks accepted; credit cards are not. Prepayment required. Mail requests: SASE required.

Garberville Branch - Superior Court c/o Eureka Superior Court, 825 5th St, Eureka, CA 95501; 707-445-7256, Fridays- 707-923-2141; fax: 707-445-7041; 9AM-3PM Fri only. ***Misdemeanor, Eviction, Small Claims.***
Court is open one day a week at 483 Conger St; no longer opens new civil cases. All mail inquires or research are directed to the Superior Court in Eureka. Garberville fax number Fridays only is 707-923-3133.

Klamath/Trinity Branch - Superior Court 825 5th St, c/o Eureka Superior Court, Eureka, CA 95501; ***Misdemeanor, Civil Actions under $25,000, Eviction, Small Claims.*** Records for this branch are housed at main court in Eureka, address given here.

Imperial County

Imperial Branch - Superior Court 939 W Main St, El Centro, CA 92243; 760-482-4374; criminal phone: 760-482-4256; civil phone: 760-482-4217; criminal fax: 760-482-4219; civil fax: 760-482-4219; 8AM-4PM. ***Felony, Misdemeanor, Civil, Eviction, Small Claims, Probate.***
www.imperial.courts.ca.gov/
All in person record searching for Imperial county must be done at each location. Only court can use the countywide system. However, if case is 10 years or older, it can be found on the books here.
Civil Records: Access: Mail, in person. Only the court performs in person searches; visitors may not. Search fee: $15.00 per name if search exceeds 10 minutes. Required to search: name, years to search. Civil cases indexed by defendant, plaintiff, on microfiche from 1972, in index file from 1917. Mail turnaround time 2-4 days.
Criminal Records: Access: Mail, in person. Only the court performs in person searches; visitors may not. Search fee: $15.00 per name if search exceeds 10 minutes. Required to search: name, years to search, year action filed. Criminal records on microfiche from 1972, index file from 1917. Mail turnaround time 2-4 days.
General Information: No adoption, juvenile, medical, probation or sealed records released. Court makes copy: $.50 per page. Certification fee: $15 per doc. Payee: Imperial County Superior Court. Personal checks accepted. Prepayment required. Mail requests: SASE required.

Brawley Branch - Superior Court 220 Main St., Brawley, CA 92227; 760-351-2840; criminal phone: x3; civil phone: x2; fax: 760-351-7703; 8AM-4PM. ***Misdemeanor, Civil Actions under $25,000, Eviction, Small Claims, Traffic.***
www.imperial.courts.ca.gov/
Traffic phone- ext1. There is no countywide public access database in this county. However, if case is 10 years or older, it can be found on the books at the main court in El Centro.
Civil Records: Access: Fax, mail, in person. Both court and visitors may perform in person searches. Search fee: $15.00 per name if search exceeds 10 minutes. Required to search: name, years to search. Civil cases indexed by defendant, plaintiff, on computer from 09/93 (traffic from 1991), in index files from 1983. Records destroyed after 10 years. Mail turnaround time 1 week.
Criminal Records: Access: Fax, mail, in person. Only the court performs in person searches; visitors may not. Search fee: $15.00 per name if search exceeds 10 minutes. Required to search: name, years to search, DOB. Criminal records on computer back about 5 years (traffic only from 1991), in index files from 1983. Records destroyed after 10 years. Mail turnaround time 1 week.
General Information: No probation reports released. Will not fax documents. Court makes copy: $.50 per page. Certification fee: $15 per doc. Payee: Brawley Superior Court. Personal checks accepted. Visa/MC accepted. Prepayment required. Mail requests: SASE required.

Calexico Branch - Superior Court 415 4th St, Calexico, CA 92231; 760-357-3727; fax: 760-357-6571; 8AM-4PM. ***Misdemeanor, Civil Actions under $25,000, Eviction, Small Claims, Traffic.***
www.imperial.courts.ca.gov/
Traffic phone- 760-357-3726. There is no countywide public access database in this county. Only court can use the countywide system. However, if case is 10 years or older, it can be found on the books at the main court in El Centro.
Civil Records: Access: Fax, mail, in person. Both court and visitors may perform in person searches. Search fee: $15.00 per name if search exceeds 10 minutes. Required to search: name, years to search. Civil cases indexed by defendant, plaintiff, on computer from 1991, index files from 1983. Records destroyed after 10 years. Note: Civil search fee is separate from the criminal search fee. Mail turnaround time 1-2 weeks. Civil PAT goes back to 1998.
Criminal Records: Access: Fax, mail, in person. Only the court performs in person searches; visitors may not. Search fee: $15.00 per name if search exceeds 10 minutes. Required to search: name, years to search. Criminal records computerized from 1991, index files from 1983. Records destroyed after 10 years. Mail turnaround time 1-2 weeks. Criminal PAT goes back to 1998.
General Information: No probation reports released. Will not fax out documents. Court makes copy: $.50 per page. Certification fee: $15 per doc. Payee: Superior Court. Personal checks accepted. Write case number on check. Visa/MC accepted. Prepayment required. Mail requests: SASE required.

Winterhaven Branch - Superior Court PO Box 1087, 2124 Winterhaven Dr, Winterhaven, CA 92283-1087; 760-572-0354; fax: 760-572-2683; 8AM-N, 1-4PM. ***Small Claims, Traffic.***
www.imperial.courts.ca.gov/ Misdemeanor and civil records have been moved to the Calexico Branch. Only small claims and traffic records remain here.

Inyo County

Superior Court PO Drawer U, 168 N Edwards St, Independence, CA 93526; 760-878-0218; fax: 760-878-2298; 8AM-4PM. ***Felony, Civil Actions over $25,000, Probate.***
www.inyocourt.ca.gov
At this Superior court, there is a Independence Dept. and a Bishop Dept. In name search requests, specify to search both. The fax for the Bishop Dept. is 760-872-1067. There is no countywide database; branch courts must be searched separately.
Civil Records: Access: Mail, in person. Both court and visitors may perform in person searches. Search fee: $15.00 per name if search exceeds 10 minutes. Required to search: name, years to search. Civil cases indexed by defendant, plaintiff, on computer to mid-1999, on microfiche and in index files from 1800s. Mail turnaround time 1 week.
Criminal Records: Access: Mail, in person. Both court and visitors may perform in person searches. Search fee: $15.00 per name if search exceeds 10 minutes. Required to search: name, years to search. Criminal records computerized from 1993, on microfiche and in index files from 1800s. Mail turnaround time 1 week.
General Information: No adoption, juvenile, medical, probation or sealed records released. Will fax to 800 number no fee; otherwise $1.00 per page. Court makes copy: $.50 per page. Certification fee: $15 per doc. Payee: Inyo Superior Court. Personal checks accepted; credit cards are not. Prepayment required. Mail requests: SASE required.

Bishop Branch - Superior Court 301 W Line St, Bishop, CA 93514; 760-872-4971; fax: 760-872-1067; 8AM-4PM. ***Misdemeanor, Civil Actions under $25,000, Eviction, Small Claims.***
www.inyocourt.ca.gov There is no countywide database, each branch court must be searched. The phone will not be answered except between 2-5PM.
Civil Records: Access: Mail, in person. Only the court performs in person searches; visitors may not. Search fee: $15.00 per name if search exceeds 10 minutes. Required to search: name, years to search. Civil cases indexed by defendant, plaintiff; index on cards. Will only search back 7 years. Mail turnaround time 1 week.
Criminal Records: Access: Mail, in person. Only the court performs in person searches; visitors may not. Search fee: $15.00 per name if search exceeds 10 minutes. Required to search: name, years to search. Criminal records computerized from 1993, index cards prior. Mail turnaround time 1 week.
General Information: No confidential records released. Will fax to 800 number no fee; otherwise $1.00 per page. Court makes copy: $.50 per page. Certification fee: $15 per doc. Payee: Superior Court. Personal checks accepted; credit cards are not. Prepayment required. Mail requests: SASE required.

Independence Limited Branch - Superior Court PO Drawer 518, 168 N Edwards St, Independence, CA 93526; 760-878-0319; fax: 760-878-0334; 8AM-4PM. ***Misdemeanor, Civil Actions under $25,000, Eviction, Small Claims.***
www.inyocourt.ca.gov There is no countywide database, each branch court must be searched.
Civil Records: Access: Mail, in person. Both court and visitors may perform in person searches. Search fee: $15.00 per name if search exceeds 10 minutes. Required to search: name, years to search. Civil cases indexed by defendant, plaintiff, on computer back to 1999, in index books and index cards. Will only search back 7 years. Mail turnaround time 1 week.
Criminal Records: Access: Mail, in person. Both court and visitors may perform in person searches. Search fee: $15.00 per name if search exceeds 10 minutes. Required to search: name, years to search, DOB. Criminal records computerized from 2/1993, index books and index cards prior. Will only search back 7 years. Mail turnaround time 1 week.
General Information: No confidential records released. Will fax to 800 number no fee; otherwise $1.00 per page. Court makes copy: $.50 per page, self serve same. Certification fee: $15 per doc. Payee: Inyo County Court. Personal checks accepted; credit cards are not. Prepayment required. Mail requests: SASE required.

Kern County

Superior Court 1415 Truxtun Ave, Bakersfield, CA 93301; 661-868-5393; criminal fax: 661-868-4883; civil fax: 661-868-4883; 8AM-5PM. ***Felony, Civil Actions, Eviction, Small Claims, Probate.***
www.kern.courts.ca.gov
Has electronic access to all divisions. Felonies in Rm 111. Misdemeanors at separate address - see separate listing. No faxing to criminal record section. Probate at #100, 1st Fl.
Civil Records: Access: Mail, fax, in person, online. Both court and visitors may perform in person searches. Search fee: $15.00 per name if search exceeds 10 minutes. Required to search: name, years to search. Civil cases indexed by defendant, plaintiff, on microfiche from 1964, archived and in index file from 1800s. Mail turnaround time 1 day to 1 week. Civil PAT available. PAT civil results show middle initial. Terminal in 3rd Fl law library. Search civil records free at www.kern.courts.ca.gov/home.aspx. Civil case info and calendars on special kiosk computers located at every court location and at website.
Criminal Records: Access: Mail, in person, online. Both court and visitors may perform in person searches. Search fee: $15.00 per name if search exceeds 10 minutes. Required to search: name, years to search, DOB. Criminal records computerized from 1989, also microfiche, archived, and in index files. Note: Visitors may search court counter index which excludes identifiers; court searches

electronically with identifiers. Mail turnaround time up to 2 weeks. Criminal PAT goes back to 1989. PAT results show middle initial, DOB. Terminal in 3rd Fl law library. Access defendant database free at www.co.kern.ca.us/courts/crimcal/crim_index_def.asp; Results show year of birth only; old records being added. Current court calendars free at www.co.kern.ca.us/courts/crim_index_case_info_cal.asp. Access defendant hearings schedule at www.co.kern.ca.us/courts/crimcal/crim_hearing_srch.asp. Also, search sheriff inmate list at www.kern.courts.ca.gov/case-menu-main.asp. Click on "inmate search." Online results show middle initial, DOB. Terminal results show year of birth only.

General Information: Online identifiers in results same as on public terminal. No adoption, juvenile, medical, probation or sealed records released. Will not fax out docs. Court makes copy: $.50 per page. Certification fee: $15 per doc. Exemplification- $20.00. Payee: Kern Superior Court. Personal checks accepted; credit cards are not. Prepayment required. Mail requests: SASE required.

Delano/McFarland Branch Superior Court - North Division 1122 Jefferson St, Delano, CA 93215; 661-720-5800; criminal phone: x3; civil phone: x4; criminal fax: 661-721-1237; civil fax: same; 8AM-4PM. ***Misdemeanor, Civil Actions under $25,000, Eviction, Small Claims.*** www.kern.courts.ca.gov/

Access all recent court division criminal defendant records from this division computer.

Civil Records: Access: Fax, mail, in person, online. Both court and visitors may perform in person searches. Search fee: $15.00 per name if search exceeds 10 minutes. Required to search: name, years to search. Civil cases indexed by defendant, plaintiff, in index files from 1983. Records destroyed after 10 years. Mail turnaround time 2 days. Civil PAT goes back to 1988. PAT civil results show middle initial. Search civil records free at www.kern.courts.ca.gov/home.aspx. Civil case info and calendars on special kiosk computers located at every court location and at website.

Criminal Records: Access: Mail, in person, online. Both court and visitors may perform in person searches. Search fee: $15.00 per name if search exceeds 10 minutes. Required to search: name, years to search; also helpful: DOB. Criminal records computerized from 1988, in index files from 1983. Records destroyed after 10 years. Note: Visitors may search counter index which excludes identifiers; court searches electronically with identifiers. Mail turnaround time 2 days. Criminal PAT goes back to 1988. Access defendant search database free at www.co.kern.ca.us/courts/crimcal/crim_index_def.asp; new system with old records being added. Current court calendars are free at www.co.kern.ca.us/courts/crim_index_case_info_cal.asp. Also, access court defendant hearings schedule by name at www.co.kern.ca.us/courts/crimcal/crim_hearing_srch.asp. Also, search county sheriff inmate list at www.kern.courts.ca.gov/case-menu-main.asp. Click on "inmate search." Online results show middle initial, DOB. Terminal results show year of birth only.

General Information: No probation reports released. Will not fax documents. Court makes copy: $.50 per page. Certification fee: $15 per doc. Payee: Superior Court Kern County-Delano/McFarland Branch. Personal checks and major credit cards accepted. Prepayment required. Mail requests: SASE required.

Kern River Branch Superior Court - East Division 7046 Lake Isabella Blvd, Lake Isabella, CA 93240; 760-549-2000; fax: 760-549-2120; 8AM-4PM M,T,W,F; 8AM-4PM TH. ***Misdemeanor, Civil Actions under $25,000, Eviction, Small Claims.*** www.kern.courts.ca.gov/

Includes the communities of Lake Isabella, Kern River, Weldon, Onyx, and Mt Mesa. You should be able to access all recent court division criminal defendant records from this division computer.

Civil Records: Access: Phone, fax, mail, in person, online. Only the court performs in person searches; visitors may not. Search fee: $15.00 per name if search exceeds 10 minutes. Required to search: name, DOB, years to search. Civil cases indexed by defendant, plaintiff, on computer from 1991, in index files from 1983. Records destroyed after 10 years. Mail turnaround time 2 days. PAT civil results show middle initial. Search civil records free at www.kern.courts.ca.gov/home.aspx. Civil case info and calendars on special kiosk computers located at every court location and at website.

Criminal Records: Access: Phone, mail, in person, online. Both court and visitors may perform in person searches. Search fee: $15.00 per name if search exceeds 10 minutes. Required to search: name, years to search. Criminal records computerized from 1991, in index files from 1983. Records destroyed after 10 years. Mail turnaround time 2 days. Public use terminal has crim records back to 1987. Access defendant search database free at www.co.kern.ca.us/courts/crimcal/crim_index_def.asp; new system with old records being added. Current court calendars are free at www.co.kern.ca.us/courts/crim_index_case_info_cal.asp. Also, access court defendant hearings schedule by name at www.co.kern.ca.us/courts/crimcal/crim_hearing_srch.asp. Search county sheriff inmate list at www.kern.courts.ca.gov/case-menu-main.asp. Click on "inmate search." Online results show middle initial, DOB. Terminal results show year of birth only.

General Information: No probation reports released. Will not fax documents. Court makes copy: $.50 per page. Certification fee: $15 per doc. Payee: East Kern Superior Court. Personal checks accepted. Visa, AmEx accepted. Prepayment required. Mail requests: SASE required.

Lamont/Arvin Branch Superior Court - South Division 12022 Main St, Lamont, CA 93241; 661-868-5800; fax: 661-845-9142; 8AM-5PM. ***Misdemeanor, Civil Actions under $25,000, Eviction, Small Claims.*** www.kern.courts.ca.gov/

Access all recent court division criminal defendant records from this division computer.

Civil Records: Access: Mail, in person, online. Both court and visitors may perform in person searches. Search fee: $15.00 per name if search exceeds 10 minutes. Required to search: name, years to search. Civil cases indexed by defendant, plaintiff, on computer from 1989. Records destroyed after 10 years. Mail turnaround time 2 days. Civil PAT goes back to 1989. PAT civil results show middle initial. Search civil records free at www.kern.courts.ca.gov/home.aspx. Civil case info and calendars on special kiosk computers located at every court location and at website.

Criminal Records: Access: Fax, mail, in person, online. Both court and visitors may perform in person searches. Search fee: $15.00 per name if search exceeds 10 minutes. Required to search: name, years to search, DOB; also helpful CA DL#, SSN, signed release. Criminal records computerized from 1989. Records destroyed after 10 years. Note: Visitors may search court counter index which excludes identifiers; court searches electronically with identifiers. Results include name, entity name, case number and calendar. Mail turnaround time 2 days. Criminal PAT goes back to same as civil. Results include year of DOB, filing date and arrest date. Access defendant search database free www.co.kern.ca.us/courts/crimcal/crim_index_def.asp; new system with old records being added. Current court calendars are free at www.co.kern.ca.us/courts/crim_index_case_info_cal.asp. Also, access court defendant hearings schedule by name at www.co.kern.ca.us/courts/crimcal/crim_hearing_srch.asp. Also, search county sheriff inmate list at www.kern.courts.ca.gov/case-menu-main.asp. Click on "inmate search." Online results show middle initial, DOB. Terminal results show year of birth only.

General Information: No probation reports released. No fee to fax documents. Court makes copy: $.50 per page. Certification fee: $15 per doc. Payee: Superior Court Lamont Branch. Personal checks accepted. Visa/MC, AmEx accepted. Prepayment required. Mail requests: SASE required.

Mojave Branch Superior Court - East Division 1773 Hwy 58, Mojave, CA 93501; 661-824-7100; criminal phone: x3; civil phone: x4; criminal fax: 661-824-7089; civil fax: 661-824-7084; 8AM-5PM M,T,W,F; 8AM-4PM TH. ***Misdemeanor, Civil Actions under $25,000, Eviction, Small Claims.***

www.kern.courts.ca.gov/

Includes California City, Edwards AFB, Mojave, Boron, Rosemond, Cantil, and Tehachapi. You should be able to access all recent court division criminal defendant records from this division computer.

Civil Records: Access: Mail, fax, in person, online. Both court and visitors may perform in person searches. Search fee: $15.00 per name if search exceeds 10 minutes. Required to search: name, years to search. Civil cases indexed by defendant, plaintiff, on computer from 1991, in index files from 1983. Records destroyed after 10 years. Mail turnaround time up to 1 week. Civil PAT goes back to 1991. PAT results show name only. Search civil records free at www.kern.courts.ca.gov/home.aspx. Civil case info and calendars on special kiosk computers located at every court location and at website.

Criminal Records: Access: Mail, fax, in person, online. Both court and visitors may perform in person searches. Search fee: $15.00 per name if search exceeds 10 minutes. Required to search: name, years to search, DOB. Criminal records computerized from 1991, in index files from 1983. Mail turnaround time up to 10 days. Criminal PAT goes back to same as civil. PAT results show middle initial, DOB. Access defendant search database free at www.co.kern.ca.us/courts/crimcal/crim_index_def.asp; new system with old records being added. Current court calendars are free at www.co.kern.ca.us/courts/crim_index_case_info_cal.asp. Also, access court defendant hearings schedule by name at www.co.kern.ca.us/courts/crimcal/crim_hearing_srch.asp. Also, search county sheriff inmate list at www.kern.courts.ca.gov/case-menu-main.asp. Click on "inmate search." Online results show middle initial, DOB. Terminal results show year of birth only.

General Information: Online identifiers in results same as on public terminal. No probation reports released. Will not fax documents. Court makes copy: $.50 per page. Certification fee: $15 per doc. Payee: East Kern Superior Court. Personal checks accepted. Visa, AmEx accepted; a $7.50 credit card charge. Prepayment required. Mail requests: SASE required.

Ridgecrest Branch Superior Court - East Division 132 E Coso St, Ridgecrest, CA 93555; 760-384-5900; civil phone: 760-384-5986; fax: 760-384-5899; 8AM-5PM, TH til 4PM. ***Misdemeanor, Civil Actions under $25,000, Eviction, Small Claims.*** www.kern.courts.ca.gov/

Includes the communities of Ridgecrest, Inyokern, China Lake, Johannesburg, and Randsburg. You should be able to access all recent court division criminal defendant records from division computer.

Civil Records: Access: Mail, in person, online. Both court and visitors may perform in person searches. Search fee: $15.00 per name if search exceeds 10 minutes. Required to search: name, years to search. Civil cases indexed by defendant, plaintiff, on computer from 1990, in index files from 1983. Records destroyed after 10 years. Mail turnaround time 2 days. Civil PAT goes back to 1990. PAT civil results show middle initial. Search civil records at www.kern.courts.ca.gov/home.aspx. Civil case info and calendars on special kiosk computers at every court location and at website.

Criminal Records: Access: Phone, fax, mail, in person, online. Both court and visitors may perform in person searches. Search fee: $15.00 per name if search exceeds 10 minutes. Required to search: name, years to search; also helpful: DOB, SSN. Criminal records computerized from 1990, in index files from 1983. Records destroyed after 5 years. Mail turnaround time 2 days. Criminal PAT goes back to same as civil. Access defendant database free at www.co.kern.ca.us/courts/crimcal/crim_index_def.asp; new system with old records being added. Current court calendars are free at www.co.kern.ca.us/courts/crim_index_case_info_cal.asp. Also, access court defendant hearings schedule by name at www.co.kern.ca.us/cou

rts/crimcal/crim_hearing_srch.asp. Also, search county sheriff inmate list at www.kern.courts.ca.gov/case-menu-main.asp. Click on "inmate search." Online results show middle initial, DOB. Terminal results show year of birth only.
General Information: No probation reports released. Will not fax documents. Court makes copy: $.50 per page. Certification fee: $15 per doc. Payee: Kern County Superior Court. Personal checks accepted. Visa, AmEx accepted. Prepayment required. Mail requests: SASE required.

Shafter/Wasco Branch Superior Court - North Division 325 Central Valley Hwy, Shafter, CA 93263; 661-746-7500; fax: 661-746-0545; 8AM-5PM. ***Misdemeanor, Civil Actions under $25,000, Eviction, Small Claims.***
www.kern.courts.ca.gov/ Access all recent court division criminal records from this division computer.
Civil Records: Access: Phone, fax, mail, in person, online. Both court and visitors may perform in person searches. Search fee: $15.00 per name if search exceeds 10 minutes. Required to search: name, years to search; also helpful: address. Civil cases indexed by defendant, plaintiff, go back to 1994. Note: Visitors may search counter index that excludes identifiers; court searches electronically with identifiers. Mail turnaround time 2 days. Civil PAT available. PAT results show name only. Search civil records free at www.kern.courts.ca.gov/home.aspx. Civil case info and calendars on special kiosk computers located at every court location and at website.
Criminal Records: Access: Mail, in person, online. Both court and visitors may perform in person searches. Search fee: $15.00 per name if search exceeds 10 minutes. Required to search: name, years to search, DOB; also helpful: address, SSN. Criminal records on computer since 1988, traffic since 1991. Note: Visitors may search court counter index which excludes identifiers; court searches electronically with identifiers. Phone searches limited to a few names only. Mail turnaround time 2 days. Criminal PAT goes back to 1988. Access defendant search database free at www.co.kern.ca.us/courts/crimcal/crim_index_def.asp; new system with old records being added. Current court calendars are free at www.kern.courts.ca.gov/case-menu-main.aspx. Also, search county sheriff inmate list at same site. Online results show middle initial, DOB. Terminal results show year of birth only.
General Information: No probation reports released. No fee to fax documents. Court makes copy: $.50 per page. Certification fee: $15 per doc. Payee: Superior Court North Division. Personal checks accepted. Visa/Amex/Discover accepted. Prepayment required. Mail requests: SASE required.

Superior Court Metropolitan Division 1215 Truxtun Ave, Bakersfield, CA 93301; 661-868-2482; 868-2534 search requests; fax: 661-868-2695; 8AM-5PM. ***Misdemeanor, Traffic.***
www.kern.courts.ca.gov/
Formerly Bakersfield Municipal Court. Includes Bakersfield, Oildale, Edison, Glenville, Woody. Access all recent court division criminal defendant records from this division computer.
Criminal Records: Access: Mail, in person, online. Both court and visitors may perform in person searches. Search fee: $15.00 per name if search exceeds 10 minutes. Required to search: name, years to search. Criminal records on computer since 1988, microfilm since 1988. Note: Visitors may search court counter index which excludes identifiers; court searches electronically with identifiers. Mail turnaround time 10 days. Criminal PAT goes back to 1988. Public access terminal results show middle initial, DOB birth year. Access defendant search database free at www.co.kern.ca.us/courts/crimcal/crim_index_def.asp; new system with old records being added. Current court calendars are free at www.co.kern.ca.us/courts/crim_index_case_info_cal.asp. Also, access court defendant hearings schedule by name at www.co.kern.ca.us/courts/crimcal/crim_hearing_srch.asp. Also, search county sheriff inmate list at www.kern.courts.ca.gov/case-menu-main.asp. Click on "inmate search." Online results show middle initial, DOB. Terminal results show year of birth only. **General Information:** Online identifiers in results same as on public terminal. No probation reports, rap sheets, medical or financial released. No fee to fax document. Will only fax one or two pages due to time constraints. Court makes copy: $.50 per page. Cert fee: $15 per doc. Payee: Superior Court of California. Personal checks accepted; credit cards not. Prepayment required. Mail request: SASE helpful.

Taft Branch Superior Court - South Division 311 N Lincoln St, Taft, CA 93268; 661-763-8531; fax: 661-763-2439; 8AM-4PM. ***Misdemeanor, Civil Actions under $25,000, Eviction, Small Claims.*** www.kern.courts.ca.gov/
Access all recent court division criminal defendant records from this division's computer.
Civil Records: Access: Phone, mail, in person, online. Both court and visitors may perform in person searches. Search fee: $15.00 per name if search exceeds 10 minutes. Required to search: name, years to search; also helpful: address. Civil cases indexed by defendant, plaintiff, on computer from 1988, in index files from 1983. Records destroyed after 10 years. Mail turnaround time 2 days. Civil PAT goes back to 1988. PAT civil results show middle initial. Search civil records free at www.kern.courts.ca.gov/home.aspx. Civil case info and calendars on special kiosk computers located at every court location and at website.
Criminal Records: Access: Phone, mail, in person, online. Both court and visitors may perform in person searches. Search fee: $15.00 per name if search exceeds 10 minutes. Purchase of complaint and docket required. Required to search: name, years to search, DOB; also helpful: address, SSN. Criminal records computerized from 1988, in index files from 1983. Records destroyed after 10 years. Mail turnaround time 2 days. Criminal PAT goes back to same as civil. Access defendant database free at www.co.kern.ca.us/courts/crimcal/crim_index_def.asp; new system with old records being added. Current court calendars are free at www.co.kern.ca.us/courts/crim_index_case_info_cal.asp. Also, access court defendant hearings schedule by at www.co.kern.ca.us/courts/crimcal/crim_hearing_srch.asp. Also, search county sheriff inmate list at www.co.kern.ca.us/courts/caseinfo_menu.asp. Click on "inmate search." Online results show middle initial, DOB. Terminal results show year of birth only.
General Information: No probation reports released. Will fax documents to local or toll-free number. Court makes copy: $.50 per page. Certification fee: $15 per doc. Payee: South Taft Court. Personal checks accepted. Credit cards accepted. Prepayment required. Mail requests: SASE required.

Kings County

Superior Court - Criminal 1426 South Dr, Hanford, CA 93230; 559-582-1010 x3042; fax: 559-585-3267; 8AM-5PM. ***Felony, Misdemeanor.*** www.kings.courts.ca.gov
Criminal Records: Access: Mail, in person. Both court and visitors may perform in person searches. Search fee: $15.00 per name if search exceeds 10 minutes. Required to search: name, years to search, DOB. Criminal records computerized from 1991, in index files from 1983. Records destroyed after 10 years. Mail turnaround time 10 days. Public use terminal has crim records back to 1991. PAT results show middle initial, DOB.
General Information: No probation or police reports released. Will not fax documents. Court makes copy: $.50 per page. Certification fee: $15 per doc. Payee: Kings County Superior Court. Personal checks accepted; credit cards are not. Prepayment required. Mail requests: SASE required.

Superior Court - Civil 1426 South Dr, Hanford, CA 93230; 559-582-1010; probate phone: x3083; fax: 559-585-3242; 8AM-5PM. ***Civil Actions, Eviction, Small Claims, Probate.***
www.kings.courts.ca.gov
Civil Records: Access: Mail, in person. Both court and visitors may perform in person searches. Search fee: $15.00 per name if search exceeds 10 minutes. Required to search: name, years to search. Civil cases indexed by defendant, plaintiff, on computer from 1989, on microfiche and archived from 1970s, in index file from 1914. Mail turnaround time 4 weeks. Public use terminal has civil records back to 1989. PAT results show name only. Access 30-day calendars free at www.kings.courts.ca.gov/Calinfo/Calendar.asp.
General Information: No adoption, juvenile, medical, probation or sealed records released. Will not fax documents. Court makes copy: $.50 per page. Certification fee: $15 per doc. Payee; Superior Court of the State of California. Business checks accepted. Checks accepted with proper identification. No credit cards accepted. Prepayment required. Mail requests: SASE required.

Avenal Division Superior Court 501 E Kings St, Avenal, CA 93204; 559-582-1010 x4094; 559-386-5225; fax: 559-585-3269; 8AM-5PM. ***Misdemeanor, Civil Actions under $25,000, Eviction, Small Claims.*** www.kings.courts.ca.gov
Civil Records: Access: Phone, fax, mail, in person. Both court and visitors may perform in person searches. Search fee: $15.00 per name if search exceeds 10 minutes. Required to search: name, years to search. Civil index on cards, computerized. Mail turnaround time 10 working days Public use terminal has civil records back to 1990. Access 30-day calendars free at www.kings.courts.ca.gov/Calinfo/Calendar.asp.
Criminal Records: Access: Fax, mail, in person. Both court and visitors may perform in person searches. Search fee: $15.00 per name if search exceeds 10 minutes. Required to search: name, years to search, DOB. Criminal records computerized from 1991, index cards prior. Mail turnaround time 10 working days.
General Information: No juvenile or adoption records released. Court makes copy: $.50 per page. Certification fee: $15 per doc. Payee: Superior Court. Personal checks accepted; credit cards are not. Prepayment required. Mail requests: SASE required.

Corcoran Division Superior Court 1000 Chittenden Ave, Corcoran, CA 93212; 559-582-1010 x3004; 559-992-5193; fax: 559-585-3270; 8AM-5PM. ***Misdemeanor, Civil Actions under $25,000, Eviction, Small Claims.*** www.kings.courts.ca.gov
Civil Records: Access: Mail, in person
Mail, in person. Only the court performs in person searches; visitors may not. Search fee: $15.00 per name if search exceeds 10 minutes. Required to search: name, years to search; also helpful: address. Civil cases indexed by defendant, plaintiff, on computer from 1990, index cards to 1974. Will only search back 7 years. Mail turnaround time 1 week. Access 30-day calendars free at www.kings.courts.ca.gov/Calinfo/Calendar.asp.
Criminal Records: Access: Mail, in person. Only the court performs in person searches; visitors may not. Search fee: $15.00 per name if search exceeds 10 minutes. Required to search: name, years to search, DOB; also helpful: address, aka's. Criminal records computerized from 1990, index cards to 1974. Will only search back 7 years. Mail turnaround 1 week.
General Information: No juvenile or adoption records released. Will not fax documents. Court makes copy: $.50 per page. Certification fee: $15 per doc. Payee: Superior Court of California. Personal checks accepted. Prepayment required. Mail requests: SASE required.

Lemoore Division Superior Court 449 "C" St, Lemoore, CA 93245; 559-582-1010 x3014; 559-924-7757; criminal phone: x3034; civil phone: x3073; 8AM-5PM. ***Misdemeanor, Civil Actions under $25,000, Eviction, Small Claims.***
www.kings.courts.ca.gov
Court says to search records at Hanford court; 1426 South Dr, Hanford, CA 93230, Ph-559-582-1010 x3034 Criminal; x2075 Civil.
Civil Records: Access: Fax, mail, in person. Both court and visitors may perform in person searches. Search fee: $15.00 per name if search exceeds 10 minutes. Required to search: name, years to search. Civil cases indexed by defendant, plaintiff, computerized since 1990, on index cards back to 1977. Note: In person access limited. Fax requests are accepted, though the court will recommend a fax processing service; add'l charge for fax

requests. Mail turnaround time 10 days. Access 30-day calendars free at www.kings.courts.ca.gov/Calinfo/Calendar.asp. **Criminal Records:** Access: in person only. Only the court performs in person searches; visitors may not. Search fee: $15.00 per name if search exceeds 10 minutes. Crims on computer since 1990, index cards back to 1977. **General Information:** Will not fax documents. Court makes copy: $.50 per page. Certification fee: $15 per doc. Payee: Clerk of Courts. Personal checks accepted; credit cards are not. Prepayment required. Mail requests: SASE required.

Lake County

Superior Court - Lakeport Division 255 N Forbes St, 4th Fl, Lakeport, CA 95453; 707-262-4279; fax: 707-262-1327; 8-4. ***Felony, Misdemeanor, Civil, Eviction, Small Claims, Probate.***
www.courtinfo.ca.gov/courts/trial/lake/lakeport.htm
This court holds the records for the former Northlake Municipal Court. Please note that there are also felony records at the South Lake Div, and both courts should be checked when doing a criminal record search.
Civil Records: Access: Mail, in person. Both court and visitors may perform in person searches. Search fee: $15.00 per name if search exceeds 10 minutes. Required to search: name, years to search. Civil cases indexed by defendant, plaintiff, on computer from 1991, on microfiche, archived, and in index files from 1800s. Mail turnaround time 1-3 weeks. Civil PAT goes back to 1991. PAT results show name only. Public access terminal is at the Lake Port Courthouse.
Criminal Records: Access: Mail, in person. Both court and visitors may perform in person searches. Search fee: $15.00 per name if search exceeds 10 minutes. Required to search: name, years to search, DOB. Criminal records computerized from 1991, on microfiche, archived, and in index files from 1800s. Mail turnaround time 1-3 weeks. Criminal PAT goes back to same as civil. PAT results show name only. Public terminal at Lake Port Courthouse.
General Information: No adoption, juvenile, medical, probation or sealed records released. Will not fax documents. Court makes copy: $.50 per page. Cert fee: $15 per doc. Payee: Lake County Superior Court. Personal checks accepted; credit cards are not. Prepayment required. Mail requests: SASE required.

Superior Court - South Lake Division 7000A S Center Dr, Clearlake, CA 95422; 707-994-6598; fax: 707-994-1625; 8AM-4PM. ***Felony, Misdemeanor, Civil Actions under $25,000, Eviction, Small Claims, Traffic.***
www.courtinfo.ca.gov/courts/trial/lake/clearlake.htm
To contact the Records Dept directly call 707-262-4279. Some felony cases here will not be on the computer index at the Superior Court in Lakeport.
Civil Records: Access: Mail, in person, phone. Both court and visitors may perform in person searches. Search fee: $15.00 per name if search exceeds 10 minutes. Required to search: name, years to search. Civil cases indexed by defendant, plaintiff; index on docket books. Mail turnaround 1-2 weeks. Civil PAT back to 1990. PAT results show name only.
Criminal Records: Access: Mail, in person, phone. Both court and visitors may perform in person searches. Search fee: $15.00 per name if search exceeds 10 minutes. Required to search: name, years to search, DOB. Criminal records computerized from 1990, index books prior. Mail turnaround time 1-2 weeks for criminal. Criminal PAT goes back to 1990. PAT results show name only. Some records prior to 1990 also available on public terminal.
General Information: No police reports or sealed records released. Will not fax documents. Court makes copy: $.50 per page. Certification fee: $15 per doc. Payee: Lake County Superior Court. Personal checks accepted; credit cards are not. Prepayment required. Mail requests: SASE required.

Lassen County

Superior Court 220 S Lassen St, #2, Susanville, CA 96130; 530-251-8205; fax: 530-257-9061; 7:30AM-5:30PM. ***Felony, Misdemeanor, Civil, Eviction, Small Claims, Probate.***
www.lassencourt.ca.gov
Probate fax is same as main fax number.
Civil Records: Access: Mail, in person. Only the court performs in person searches; visitors may not. Search fee: $15.00 per name if search exceeds 10 minutes. Required to search: name, years to search. Civil cases indexed by defendant, plaintiff, on computer from 11/89, archived and in index files from 1900s. Mail turnaround time 5-10 days.
Criminal Records: Access: Mail, in person. Only the court performs in person searches; visitors may not. Search fee: $15.00 per request if search exceeds 10 minutes. No hit, no fee. Required to search: name, years to search. Criminal records computerized from 11/89, archived and in index files from 1900s. Mail turnaround time 5-10 days.
General Information: No adoption, juvenile, medical, probation or sealed records released. Will fax documents if all fees prepaid. Court makes copy: $.50 per page, self serve same. Certification fee: $15 per doc. Payee: Lassen County Superior Court. Business checks accepted. Major credit cards accepted. Prepayment required. Pay via the Official Payments at 800-272-9829 using jurisdiction code 1506. Or, pay online at www.officialpayments.com. Mail requests: SASE required.

Los Angeles County

Los Angeles Superior Court - Central District - Civil Stanley Mosk Courthouse, 111 N Hill St, Rm 102, Los Angeles, CA 90012; 213-974-6135 (974-5171 if Civil over $25,000); probate phone: 213-974-5471; fax: 213-621-2701; 8:30AM-4:30PM. ***Civil Actions, Eviction, Small Claims, Probate.*** www.lasuperiorcourt.org
Any civil cases here under $25,000 are co-extensive with the city limits of Los Angeles and includes the City of San Fernando and sections designated as San Pedro, West Los Angeles, Van Nuys, Venice and the unincorporated county area known as Florence.
Civil Records: Access: Phone, mail, online, in person. Both court and visitors may perform in person searches. Search fee: $15.00 per name if search exceeds 10 minutes. Required to search: name, years to search. Civil cases indexed by defendant, plaintiff, on computer from 1991, index files from 1983. Records destroyed after 10 years. Note: Small Claims (213-974-6350) and Probate (213-974-5471) and Family Law are located at 110 N Grand Ave. Mail turnaround time 24 hours, more if busy. Public use terminal has civil records back to 1991. For cases over $25,000 there is a fee-based lookup for case images at https://www.lasuperiorcourt.org/OnlineServices/CivilImages/index.asp. Search fee is $4.75, case document file is $7.50. There is a free case summary lookup for cases under $25,000 at this site but lookup is by case number, not name. Includes probate from 1/97.
General Information: No probation reports released. Will not fax documents. Court makes copy: $.50 per page. Certification fee: $15 per doc plus copy fee; Exemplification fee- $10.00. Payee: Los Angeles Superior Court. Personal checks/credit cards accepted. Prepayment required. Mail requests: SASE required.

Los Angeles Superior Court - Central District - Felony Clara Shortridge Foltz Criminal Justice Center, 210 W Temple St, Rm M-6, Los Angeles, CA 90012; 213-974-6141; criminal phone: 213-974--6141/42; Felon Recs- 213-974-6147; fax: 213-617-1224; 8:30AM-4:30PM. ***Felony, Misdemeanor.*** www.lasuperiorcourt.org
This court now handles felonies and misdemeanors; they can do misdemeanor searches for the Central District area of downtown LA, East LA, and Hollywood. Fax number above is for government agencies only.
Criminal Records: Access: Mail, in person, online. Only the court performs in person searches; visitors may not. Search fee: $15.00 per name if search exceeds 10 minutes. Required to search: name, years to search, DOB, sex. Criminal records on microfiche and index files since 1956, computerized misdemeanors since 1988; felonies since 1996. Note: In requests, court suggests to include full spelling of middle name. 5 name limit at counter. Mail turnaround time 24 hours; up to 3 weeks if busy. Felony and misdemeanor defendant records are online at https://www.lasuperiorcourt.org/OnlineServices/criminalindex/index.asp. Search fee is $4 to $4.75. **General Information:** No adoption, juvenile, medical, probation or sealed records released. Will not fax out docs. Court makes copy: $.50 per page. Certification fee: $15 per doc. Certification clerk phone- 213-974-6141. Payee: Los Angeles Superior Court. Personal checks and major credit cards accepted. Prepayment required. Mail requests: SASE required.

Los Angeles Superior Court - Probate Department 111 N Hill St, Rm 258, Los Angeles, CA 90012; 213-974-5471; 8:15AM-4:30PM. ***Probate.*** www.lasuperiorcourt.org/probate
Case summaries-notes available free at website; search by case number. Also, probate for current cases in Central Dist. including Burbank, Compton, Glendale, Lancaster, Long Beach, Pasadena, Pomona, San Fernando, Santa Monica, Torrance Dist. Courts.

Airport Superior Court - West District 11701 S La Cienega Blvd, Los Angeles, CA 90045; 310-727-6020- Misdemeanors; criminal phone: 310-727-6100- Felony; 8:30AM-4:30PM. ***Felony, Misdemeanor.***
www.lasuperiorcourt.org/Locations/LAX.htm
New court in 2000; includes the areas of Palms, Mar Vista, Rancho Park, Marina del Rey, Venice, Playa del Rey, Sawtelle. Holds records for the former West LA Court covering Culver, El Segundo, Hawthorne.
Criminal Records: Access: Mail, in person, online. Only the court performs in person searches; visitors may not. Search fee: $15.00 per name if search exceeds 10 minutes. Required to search: name, years to search; helpful: DOB, address. Criminal records computerized from 1991, index files from 1983. Records destroyed after 10 years. Note: Will do search if you have a case number. Felony and misdemeanor defendant records for a fee at https://www.lasuperiorcourt.org/OnlineServices/criminalindex/index.asp. Search fee is $4 to $4.75.
General Information: No probation reports released. Will not fax documents. Court makes copy: $.50 per page. Certification fee: $15 per doc. Payee: Los Angeles Superior Court. Personal checks accepted. Visa/MC accepted. Prepayment required. Mail requests: SASE required.

Alhambra Superior Court - Northeast District 150 W Commonwealth Ave, 2nd Fl, Rm 200, Alhambra, CA 91801; criminal phone: 626-308-5525; civil phone: 626-308-5521; fax: 626-570-4667; 8:15AM-4:30PM. ***Misdemeanor, Civil Actions under $25,000, Eviction, Small Claims.***
www.lasuperiorcourt.org
Includes cities of Alhambra, Monterey Park, San Gabriel, Temple City and the unincorporated County area known as South San Gabriel. Address the specific division (criminal, civil, small claims) in correspondence. Traffic phone- 213-742-1928.
Civil Records: Access: Mail, in person, online. Only the court performs in person searches; visitors may not. Search fee: $15.00 per name if search exceeds 10 minutes. Required to search: name, years to search. Civil cases indexed by defendant, plaintiff, on computer back to 1991, index files from 1983. Records destroyed after 10 years. Mail turnaround time 2 days. Free case summary lookup at https://www.lasuperiorcourt.org/OnlineServices/CivilImages/index.asp, but the lookup is by case number, not name. There is a fee-based name search for records back to 1991 (if Small Claims 1992) at this site. Fee is $4.75 per search.
Criminal Records: Access: Mail, in person, online. Only the court performs in person searches; visitors may not. Search fee: $15.00 per name if search exceeds 10 minutes. Required to search: name, years to search, DOB; also helpful: CDL. Criminal records computerized from 1996, index files from 1991. Records destroyed after 10 years. Mail turnaround time 2 days. Felony and misdemeanor defendant records are online for a fee at https://www.lasuperiorcourt.org/OnlineServices/criminalindex/index.asp. Search fee is $4 to $4.75.
General Information: No probation records released. Will not fax documents. Court makes copy: $.50 per page. Certification fee: $15 per doc. Payee: Los Angeles Superior Court. Personal checks accepted. Credit cards accepted. Prepayment required. Mail requests: SASE required.

Bellflower Superior Court - Southeast District 10025 E Flower St, Bellflower, CA 90706; 562-804-8025; criminal phone: 562-804-8018/19; civil phone: 562-804-8009; 8AM-4:30PM. ***Misdemeanor, Civil Actions under $25,000, Eviction, Small Claims.*** www.lasuperiorcourt.org/Locations/LosCerritos.htm
Includes Artesia, Bellflower, Hawaiian Gardens, Lakewood, Cerritos. Also includes Norwalk for criminal cases only. Sm claims phone- 562-804-8011.
Civil Records: Access: Mail, in person, online. Both court and visitors may perform in person searches. Search fee: $15.00 per name if search exceeds 10 minutes. Required to search: name, years to search. Civil cases indexed by defendant, plaintiff, on computer from 1991, index files from 1983. Records destroyed after 10 years. Note: Specify it is a "civil records" search request. Mail turnaround time 2-3 days. Public use terminal has civil records back to 10 years. Free summary lookup by case number at https://www.lasuperiorcourt.org/OnlineServices/CivilImages/index.asp. Also, a fee-based name search for records back to 1991 (if Small Claims 1992) at this site. Fee is $4.75 per search.
Criminal Records: Access: Mail, in person, online. Only the court performs in person searches; visitors may not. Search fee: $15.00 per name if search exceeds 10 minutes. Required to search: name, years to search, DOB. Criminal records computerized from 1991, index files from 1983. Records destroyed after 10 years. Note: Specify it is a "criminal records" search request. Mail turnaround time 2-3 days. Criminal defendant records for a fee at https://www.lasuperiorcourt.org/OnlineServices/criminalindex/index.asp/. Search fee $4 to $4.75.
General Information: No probation reports released. Will not fax documents. Court makes copy: $.50 per page. Certification fee: $15 per doc. Payee: Los Angeles Superior Court. Personal checks accepted. Credit cards accepted. Prepayment required. Mail requests: SASE required.

Beverly Hills Superior Court - West District 9355 Burton Way, Beverly Hills, CA 90210; 310-860-0070; criminal phone: 310-288-1309; civil phone: 310-288-1308; fax: 310-275-5224; 8AM-4:30PM. ***Misdemeanor, Civil Actions under $25,000, Eviction, Small Claims.*** www.lasuperiorcourt.org Includes cities of Beverly Hills and West Hollywood. Small Claims phone- 310-288-1305. Traffic phone- 213-742-6648.
Civil Records: Access: Phone, mail, online, in person. Both court and visitors may perform in person searches. Search fee: $15.00 per name if search exceeds 10 minutes. Fee is per data bank per year. Required to search: name, years to search; also helpful: address. Civil cases indexed by defendant, plaintiff, on computer from 1991, index files from 1983. Records destroyed after 10 years. Note: 5 name limit at counter. Mail turnaround time 2 days. Free case summary lookup at https://www.lasuperiorcourt.org/OnlineServices/CivilImages/index.asp but lookup is by case number, not by name. There is a fee-based name search for records back to 1991 (if Small Claims 1992) at this site. Fee is $4.75 per search.
Criminal Records: Access: Phone, mail, in person, online. Only the court performs in person searches; visitors may not. Search fee: $15.00 per name if search exceeds 10 minutes. Fee is per database per year. Required to search: name, years to search, DOB; also helpful: address, sex, signed release. Criminal records computerized from 1991, index files from 1983. Records destroyed after 10 years. Note: 5 name limit at counter. Mail turnaround time 2 days. Felony and misdemeanor defendant records are online for a fee at https://www.lasuperiorcourt.org/OnlineServices/criminalindex/index.asp. Search fee $4 to $4.75.
General Information: No probation, arrest records released. Will not fax documents. Court makes copy: $.50 per page. Certification fee: $15 per doc. Payee: Los Angeles Superior Court. Personal checks accepted. Credit cards accepted. Prepayment required. Mail requests: SASE required.

Burbank Superior Court - North Central District 300 E Olive Ave, Burbank, CA 91502-1215; criminal phone: 818-557-3466; civil phone: 818-557-3482; 818-557-3461 Sm Claims; criminal fax: 818-569-7413; civil fax: 818-953-9455; 8:30AM-4:30PM. ***Felony, Misdemeanor, Civil Actions, Eviction, Small Claims, Older Probate.*** www.lasuperiorcourt.org
Civil Records: Access: Mail, in person, online. Both court and visitors may perform in person searches. Search fee: $15.00 per name if search exceeds 10 minutes. Required to search: name, years to search. Civil cases indexed by defendant, plaintiff, on computer from 1991. Limited hard copy civil records, destroyed 10 years after judgment. Mail turnaround time 3-5 days. Public use terminal has civil records back to 1977. PAT civil results show middle initial. Public terminal has Courtney; includes probate records. Free summary lookup by case number at https://www.lasuperiorcourt.org/OnlineServices/CivilImages/index.asp. Includes probate from 3/98. There is a fee-based name search for records back to 1991 (if Small Claims 1992) at this site. Fee is $4.75 per search.
Criminal Records: Access: Mail, in person, online, phone. Only the court performs in person searches; visitors may not. Search fee: $15.00 per name if search exceeds 10 minutes. Required to search: name, years to search, DOB. Criminal records computerized from 1991, index files from 1983. Records destroyed after 10 years. Note: Supply case number and they give case info over phone. 5 name limit at counter. Mail turnaround time 3-5 days. Access criminal records for fee at https://www.lasuperiorcourt.org/OnlineServices/criminalindex/index.asp. Search fee $4 to $4.75.
General Information: No probation reports released. Will fax documents $3.37 per page. Court makes copy: $.50 per page. Certification fee: $15 per doc plus copy fee, Exemplification fee $20.00 & copy fee. Payee: Los Angeles Superior Court. Personal checks accepted. Visa/MC accepted. Prepayment required. Mail requests: SASE required.

Chatsworth Courthouse 9425 Penfield Avenue, Chatsworth, CA 91311; 818-576-8595-Civil Unlimited; 576-8575- Limited; 8:30AM-4:30PM. ***Civil, Small Claims, Traffic.*** www.lasuperiorcourt.org
Phone for small claims- 818-576-8586.
Civil Records: Access: Mail, in person, online. Both court and visitors may perform in person searches. Search fee: $15.00 per name if search exceeds 10 minutes. Civil cases indexed by defendant, plaintiff, on computer from 1991, index files from 1983. Records destroyed after 10 years. Mail turnaround time 1-3 days. A fee-based name search for records back to 1991 (if Small Claims 1992) at https://www.lasuperiorcourt.org/OnlineServices/CivilImages/index.asp is $4.75 per search.
General Information: No probation reports released. Will not fax documents. Court makes copy: $.50 per page. Certification fee: $15 per doc. Payee: Los Angeles Superior Court. Major credit cards accepted. Prepayment required. Mail requests: SASE requested.

Compton Superior Court - South Central District 200 W Compton Blvd, Compton, CA 90220; 310-762-9100; criminal phone: 310-603-7112; civil phone: 310-603-7842; probate phone: 310-603-7842; criminal fax: 310-223-5941; civil fax: 310-639-8724; 8:30AM-4:30PM; clerks- 9-11AM, 2-4PM. ***Felony, Misdemeanor, Civil Actions, Eviction, Small Claims, Probate.*** www.lasuperiorcourt.org
Includes cities of Carson, Compton, Lynwood, Paramount and unincorporated county areas around them. Civil Div- 9th Fl; Criminal in Rm 403. Traffic Clerk's Office open for Night Court until 6:30PM 1st & 3rd Wed each month. Traffic-213-763-1644.
Civil Records: Access: Mail, in person, online. Both court and visitors may perform in person searches. Search fee: $15.00 per name if search exceeds 10 minutes. Required to search: name, years to search. Civil cases indexed by defendant, plaintiff, on computer from 1991, index files from 1983. Records destroyed after 10 years. Mail turnaround time 7 days. Public use terminal has civil records back to 1991. PAT civil results show middle initial. Free summary lookup by case number (not name) at https://www.lasuperiorcourt.org/OnlineServices/CivilImages/index.asp. Includes probate from 09/99. There is a fee-based name search for records back to 1991 (Small Claims to 1992) at this site. Fee is $4.75 per search.
Criminal Records: Access: Mail, in person, online. Only the court performs in person searches; visitors may not. Search fee: $15.00 per name if search exceeds 10 minutes. Required to search: name, years to search, DOB. Criminal records computerized from 1991, index files from 1983. Records destroyed after 10 years. Mail turnaround time 7 days. Felony & misdemeanor defendant records for a fee at https://www.lasuperiorcourt.org/OnlineServices/criminalindex/index.asp. Search fee is $4 to $4.75. Online results show middle initial.
General Information: No complaint records released. Will not fax documents. Court makes copy: $.50 per page. Certification fee: $15 per doc. Payee: Los Angeles Superior Court-Compton. Personal checks accepted. Credit cards accepted. Prepayment required. Mail requests: SASE required.

Culver City Superior Ct - West District 1725 Main St, Rm224, Santa Monica, CA 90401; 310-260-3522 Admin; civil phone: 310-206-1876 Unlimited; 1886 Limited; probate phone: 310-260-1876; fax: 310-576-1399; 8AM-4:30PM. ***Civil Actions under $25,000, Eviction, Small Claims, Probate.*** www.lasuperiorcourt.org Now combined with Santa Monica; new phone and address given here. Small Claims- 310-260-1886. Culver City did include Angelus Vista, portions of Marina del Rey, View Park and Windsor Hills, all surrounded by City of LA, on south bounded by Inglewood.

Downey Superior Ct - Southeast District 7500 E Imperial Hwy, Downey, CA 90242; criminal phone: 562-803-7049; civil phone: 562-803-7052; fax: 562-803-6392; 8:30AM-4:30PM; 8:30AM-6PM 2nd & 4th M. ***Misdemeanor, Civil Actions under $25,000, Eviction, Small Claims.*** www.lasuperiorcourt.org
Comprised of the cities of Downey, Norwalk, La Mirada. Sm Claims phone- 562-803-7053/54.
Civil Records: Access: Mail, in person, online. Both court and visitors may perform in person searches. Search fee: $15.00 per name if search exceeds 10 minutes. Required to search: name, years to search. Civil cases indexed by defendant, plaintiff, on computer from 1991, index files from 1983. Records destroyed after 10 years. Mail turnaround time 5 days. Free summary lookup by case number at https://www.lasuperiorcourt.org/OnlineServices/CivilImages/index.asp. There is a fee-based name search for records back to 1991 (if Small Claims 1992) at this site. Fee is $4.75 per search.
Criminal Records: Access: Mail, in person, online. Only the court performs in person searches; visitors may not. Search fee: $15.00 per name if search exceeds 10 minutes. Required to search: name, years to search; also helpful: DOB. Criminal records computerized from 1989, on microfiche, archived, and index files. Note: Mail or in person - court may choose not to run lists of names. Mail turnaround time 5 days. Felony and misdemeanor defendant records are online for a fee at https://www.lasuperiorcourt.org/OnlineServices/criminalindex/index.asp. Search fee is $4 to $4.75.
General Info: No adoption, juvenile, medical, probation or sealed records released. Will not fax documents. Court makes copy: $.50 per page. Certification fee: $15 per doc. Payee: Los Angeles Superior Court. Personal checks/credit cards accepted. Prepayment required. Mail requests: SASE required.

East Los Angeles Superior Court - Central District 4848 E Civic Center Way, Los Angeles, CA 90022; criminal: 323-780-2025 (2-4PM only); civil: 323-780-2017 (2-4 PM only); fax: 323-780-3538; 8:30-4:30PM. ***Misdemeanor, Eviction, Small Claims, Traffic.*** www.lasuperiorcourt.org
Includes cities of Montebello, Commerce, and adjacent unincorporated area bordering Monterey Park to north and Los Angeles to the west. Civil actions discontinued as of 5/2003. Court offers night court 2nd & 4th Monday each month. Traffic- 323-780-2086

Civil Records: Access: Mail, in person, online. Search fee: $15.00 per name if search exceeds 10 minutes. Required to search: name, years to search. Civil cases indexed by defendant, plaintiff, on computer from 1991, index files from 1983. Records destroyed after 10 years. Note: No civil actions since 5/03, however, there are eviction and small claims records. A fee-based name search for Small Claims back to 1992 available at https://www.lasuperiorcourt.org/OnlineServices/CivilImages/index.asp is $4.75 per search.
Criminal Records: Access: Mail, in person, online. Only the court performs in person searches; visitors may not. Search fee: $15.00 per name if search exceeds 10 minutes. Required to search: name, years to search; also helpful: DOB. Criminal records computerized from 1991, index files from 1983. Records destroyed after 10 years. Mail turnaround time 2 days. Felony and misdemeanor defendant records are online for a fee at https://www.lasuperiorcourt.org/OnlineServices/criminalindex/index.asp. Search fee is $4 to $4.75.
General Information: No probation reports released. Will not fax documents. Court makes copy: $.50 per page. Certification fee: $15 per doc. Payee: Superior Court of East Los Angeles. Personal checks accepted. Accepts Visa/MC/Discover cards. Prepayment required. Mail requests: SASE required.

El Monte Superior Court - East District

11234 E Valley Blvd, El Monte, CA 91731; criminal phone: 626-575-4121; civil phone: 626-575-4117; fax: 626-444-9029; 8AM-4:30PM. ***Misdemeanor, Civil Actions under $25,000, Eviction, Small Claims.***
www.lasuperiorcourt.org Includes cities of El Monte, South El Monte, La Puente, Rosemead and adjacent unincorporated county area.
Civil Records: Access: Mail, in person, online. Only the court performs in person searches; visitors may not. Search fee: $15.00 per name if search exceeds 10 minutes. Required to search: name, years to search. Civil cases indexed by defendant, plaintiff, on computer since 1989, microfiche since 1980. Records destroyed after 10 years. Mail turnaround time 5 days. Free case summary lookup at https://www.lasuperiorcourt.org/OnlineServices/CivilImages/index.asp; lookup is by case number, not name. There is a fee-based name search for records back to 1991 (Small Claims 10 1992) at this site. Fee- $4.75 per search.
Criminal Records: Access: Mail, in person, online. Only the court performs in person searches; visitors may not. Search fee: $15.00 per name if search exceeds 10 minutes. Required to search: name, years to search; also helpful: DOB. Criminal records computerized from 1985, microfiche to 1980. Mail turnaround time 5 days. Search felony & misdemeanor defendant records for a $5 fee at https://www.lasuperiorcourt.org/OnlineServices/criminalindex/index.asp.
General Information: Will not release unlawful detainer for 60 days. No probation reports, med records, search warrants, rap sheet, CLETS's, transcripts or sealed records released. Will fax docs for fee. Court makes copy: $.50 per page. Certification fee: $15 per doc. Payee: Los Angeles Superior Court. 2-party checks not accepted. Write "not to exceed $x.xx" on check. Major credit cards accepted. Prepayment required. Mail requests: SASE required.

Glendale Superior Court - North Central District

600 E Broadway, Glendale, CA 91206; criminal phone: 818-500-3530; civil phone: 818-500-3551; criminal fax: 818-241-3735; civil fax: 818-548-0486; 8:15AM-4:30PM. ***Misdemeanor, Civil Actions under $25,000, Eviction, Small Claims.***
www.lasuperiorcourt.org
Includes cities of Glendale, LaCanada-Flintridge and county areas known as Montrose, La Crescenta, Verdugo City, Highway Highlands, Kogel Canyon.
Civil Records: Access: Mail, in person, online. Both court and visitors may perform in person searches. Search fee: $15.00 per name if search exceeds 10 minutes. Required to search: name, years to search. Civil cases indexed by defendant, plaintiff. On computer from 1990, small claims from 7/92, index files from 1983. Records destroyed after 10 years. Note: 5 name limit at counter. Free summary lookup by case number (not name) at https://www.lasuperiorcourt.org/OnlineServices/CivilImages/index.asp. Includes probate cases from 1/6/98. There is a fee-based name search for records back to 1991 (if Small Claims 1992) at this site. Fee is $4.75 per search.
Criminal Records: Access: Mail, in person, online. Only the court performs in person searches; visitors may not. Search fee: $15.00 per name if search exceeds 10 minutes. Required to search: name, years to search. On computer from 1990, microfilm past 10 years. Note: 5 name limit at counter. Mail turnaround time 2 days. Felony & misdemeanor defendant records are online at https://www.lasuperiorcourt.org/OnlineServices/criminalindex/index.asp. Search fee $4 to $4.75.
General Information: No probation, police, CII reports released. Will not fax out docs. Court makes copy: $.50 per page. Certification fee: $20 per doc. Payee: Los Angeles Superior Court. Personal checks accepted. Visa/MC accepted. Prepayment required. Mail requests: SASE required.

Hollywood Superior Court - Central Dist

5925 Hollywood Blvd, Los Angeles, CA 90028; 323-856-5747; fax: 323-962-6157; 8:30AM-4:30PM. ***Misdemeanor.*** www.lasuperiorcourt.org Handles high-grade and low-grade Misdemeanors for the Hollywood area. Fax used strictly for business.
Criminal Records: Access: Mail, in person, online. Only the court performs in person searches; visitors may not. Search fee: $15.00 per name if search exceeds 10 minutes. Required to search: name, years to search, DOB. Criminal records on computer go back 10 years, prior on microfiche. Note: Mail or in person request will be expedited if a SASE provided. Mail turnaround time 2-3 days. Felony and misdemeanor defendant records for a fee at https://www.lasuperiorcourt.org/OnlineServices/criminalindex/index.asp. Search fee is $4 to $4.75.
General Information: No probation, driver's license, medical, arrest report or confidential reports released. Will not fax documents. Court makes copy: $.50 per page, self serve same. Certification fee: $15 per doc. Payee: Los Angeles Superior Court. Personal checks accepted. Credit cards accepted except AMEX. Prepayment required. Mail requests: SASE required.

Huntington Park Superior Ct- Southeast District

6548 Miles Ave, Huntington Park, CA 90255; 323-586-6365; civil phone: Sm Claims- 323-586-6359; fax: 323-589-6769; 8AM-4:30PM. ***Civil Actions under $25,000, Eviction, Small Claims, Traffic Pre-8/2004 Misdemeanor.***
www.lasuperiorcourt.org Includes Bell, Bell Gardens, Cudahy, Huntington Park, Maywood, Vernon. Also includes South Gate, Hollydale and unincorporated area of Walnut Park from closed court at South Gate. Court no longer handles criminal cases as 8/2004.
Civil Records: Access: Mail, in person, online. Only the court performs in person searches; visitors may not. Search fee: $15.00 per name if search exceeds 10 minutes. Required to search: name, years to search. Civil cases indexed by defendant, plaintiff. Civil on computer from 1991, index files from 1983. Records destroyed after 10 years. Mail turnaround time 2 days. Free case summary lookup at https://www.lasuperiorcourt.org/OnlineServices/CivilImages/index.asp but lookup is by case number, not name Also, search records back to 1991 (if Small Claims 1992) at this site. $4.75 per search.
General Information: No probation reports released. Will not fax out docs. Court makes copy: $.50 per page. Certification fee: $15 per doc. Payee: LA Superior Court. Personal checks accepted. Credit cards accepted. Prepayment required. Mail requests: SASE required.

Inglewood Superior Ct - Southwest Dist

1 Regent St, Inglewood, CA 90301; 310-419-5132; criminal fax: 310-680-7053; civil fax: 310-680-7055; 8AM-4:30PM. ***Felony, Misdemeanor, Civil Actions under $25,000, Eviction, Small Claims,***
www.lasuperiorcourt.org Includes cities of Inglewood, Lennox and adjoining unincorporated area. Felony cases are only from these areas. Administration "clarification" fax-310-674-4862.
Civil Records: Access: Mail, in person, online. Only the court performs in person searches; visitors may not. Search fee: $15.00 per name if search exceeds 10 minutes. Required to search: name, years to search. Civil cases indexed by defendant, plaintiff, on computer from 1991, index files from 1983. Records destroyed after 10 years. Mail turnaround time 2 days. Free summary lookup by case number at https://www.lasuperiorcourt.org/OnlineServices/CivilImages/index.asp. There is a fee-based name search for records back to 1991 (if Small Claims 1992) at this site. Fee is $4.75 per search.
Criminal Records: Access: Mail, in person, online. Only the court performs in person searches; visitors may not. Search fee: $15.00 per name if search exceeds 10 minutes. Required to search: name, years to search; also helpful: DOB. Criminal records computerized from 1991, index files from 1983. Records destroyed after 10 years. Mail turnaround time 2 days. Felony and misdemeanor defendant records are online for a fee at https://www.lasuperiorcourt.org/OnlineServices/criminalindex/index.asp. Search fee is $4 to $4.75.
General Information: No probation reports released. Will not fax out docs. Court makes copy: $.50 per page, self serve same. Certification fee: $15 per doc. Payee: Los Angeles Superior Court. Personal checks accepted. Credit cards accepted. Prepayment required. Mail requests: SASE required.

Lancaster Superior Court - North District

Antelope Valley Courthouse, 42011 4th St West, Lancaster, CA 93534; 661-974-7200; probate phone: 661-974-7200; 8AM-4:30PM. ***Felony, Misdemeanor, Civil, Small Claims, Probate, Family.***
www.lasuperiorcourt.org Formerly Antelope; includes Lancaster, City of Palmdale, and unincorporated County territory including Acton, Agua Dulce, Fairmont, Lake Hughes, Llano, Leona Valley, Littlerock, Pearblossom, Quartz Hill, Roosevelt, Green Valley Big Pines, Lake Elizabeth
Civil Records: Access: Phone, mail, online, in person. Only the court performs in person searches; visitors may not. Search fee: $15.00 per name if search exceeds 10 minutes. Required to search: name, years to search. Civil cases indexed by defendant, plaintiff, on computer since 1989, index books since 1983. Records destroyed after 10 years. Mail turnaround time 2 days. Free summary lookup by case number at https://www.lasuperiorcourt.org/OnlineServices/CivilImages/index.asp. Includes probate cases from 06/05. $4.75 per name.
Criminal Records: Access: Mail, in person, online. Only the court performs in person searches; visitors may not. Search fee: $15.00 per name if search exceeds 10 minutes. Required to search: name, years to search; also helpful: case number. Criminal records on computer since 1989, index books since 1983. Records destroyed after 10 years. Mail turnaround time 2 days. A fee-based docket look-up is at https://www.lasuperiorcourt.org/OnlineServices/criminalindex/index.asp. Fees range from $4.00 to $4.75 depending on volume.
General Information: No probation reports released. Will not fax documents. Court makes copy: $.50 per page. Certification fee: $15 per doc. Payee: Los Angeles Superior Court. Personal checks accepted; must be pre-imprinted. Prepayment required. Mail requests: SASE required.

Long Beach Superior Court - South District

415 W Ocean Blvd, Long Beach, CA 90802; 562-491-6201; criminal phone: 562-491-6226/6227; civil phone: 562-491-6234 Limited; 562-491-5925- unlimited; 562-491-6235 Sm Claims; probate phone: 562-491-5928; 8:30AM-4:30PM; phones- 8:30-10:30AM & 1:30-3:30PM. ***Felony, Misdemeanor, Civil Actions under $25,000, Eviction, Small Claims, Probate.***
www.lasuperiorcourt.org Includes cities of Long Beach and Signal Hill and adjoining unincorporated area. Address requests to civil or criminal division. Criminal on 4th Fl; Civil on 2nd Fl.
Civil Records: Access: Mail, in person, online. Both court and visitors may perform in person searches. Search fee: $15.00 per name if search exceeds 10 minutes. Required to search: name, years to search. Civil cases indexed by defendant, plaintiff, on computer from 1991, index files from 1983. Records destroyed after 10 years. Note: Traffic division phone is 562-491-6284. Mail turnaround time 2

days. Civil PAT goes back to 1991; index files back to 1983. Public terminals on 1st Fl as well as ROMs #207 and #401. Free summary lookup by case number at https://www.lasuperiorcourt.org/OnlineServices/CivilImages/index.asp. Has probate from 01/97. There is a fee-based name search for records at this site.
Criminal Records: Access: Mail, in person, online. Both court and visitors may perform in person searches. Search fee: $15.00 per name if search exceeds 10 minutes. Required to search: name, years to search, DOB. Criminal records computerized from 1991, index files from 1983. Records destroyed after 10 years. Mail turnaround time 2 days. Criminal PAT goes back to same as civil. Public terminals on 1st Fl as well as Rms #207 and #401. Felony & misdemeanor records at https://www.lasuperiorcourt.org/OnlineServices/criminalindex/index.asp, search fee online depends on volume.
General Information: No probation reports released. Will fax documents for fee. Court makes copy: $.50 per page, self serve same. Certification fee: $15 per doc plus ciopy fee. Payee: Los Angeles Superior Court. Personal checks accepted. Visa/MC, Discover accepted, in person only. Prepayment required. Mail requests: SASE required.

Malibu Superior Court - West District 23525 W Civic Center Way, Malibu, CA 90265; criminal phone: 310-317-1335; civil phone: 310-317-1331; fax: 310-456-0194; 8:30AM-4:30PM. ***Misdemeanor, Civil Actions under $25,000, Eviction, Small Claims.*** www.lasuperiorcourt.org
Includes Malibu, Agoura Hills, Calabasas, Westlake Village, Hidden Hills and unincorporated areas known as Topanga and Chatsworth Lake, bounded by Ventura County on the west and north, Pacific Ocean on the south and City of Los Angeles on the east.
Civil Records: Access: Mail, in person, online. Only the court performs in person searches; visitors may not. Search fee: $15.00 per name if search exceeds 10 minutes. Required to search: name, years to search. Civil cases indexed by defendant, plaintiff, on computer from 1991, index files from 1983. Records destroyed after 10 years. Mail turnaround time 1-5 days. Free summary lookup by case number at https://www.lasuperiorcourt.org/OnlineServices/CivilImages/index.asp. There is a fee-based name search for records back to 1991 (if Small Claims 1992) at this site. Fee is $4.75 per search.
Criminal Records: Access: Mail, in person, online. Only the court performs in person searches; visitors may not. Search fee: $15.00 per name if search exceeds 10 minutes. Required to search: name, years to search; also helpful: DOB. Criminal records computerized from 1991, index files from 1983. Records destroyed after 10 years. Mail turnaround time 1-5 days. Felony and misdemeanor defendant records are at https://www.lasuperiorcourt.org/OnlineServices/criminalindex/index.asp. Search fee is $4 to $4.75.
General Information: No probation reports released. Will not fax out docs. Court makes copy: $.50 per page. Certification fee: $15 per doc. Payee: Los Angeles Superior Court. Personal checks and major credit cards accepted. Prepayment required. Mail requests: SASE required.

Metropolitan Branch Superior Court - Central District 1945 S Hill St, Rm 200, Los Angeles, CA 90007; 213-744-4023/4022; fax: 213-744-1879; 8AM-4:30PM. ***Misdemeanor, Traffic.***
www.lasuperiorcourt.org Vehicle Code misdemeanor and traffic citations for the incorporated City of Los Angeles excluding the areas known as San Pedro, W. Los Angeles and communities of San Fernando Valley and the unincorporated County area more commonly known as Florence.
Criminal Records: Access: Mail, in person, online. Only the court performs in person searches; visitors may not. Search fee: $15.00 per name if search exceeds 10 minutes. Required to search: name, years to search, DOB. Criminal records computerized from 1991. Records destroyed after 10 years. Mail turnaround time 2-3 days. Felony & misdemeanor defendant records are at https://www.lasuperiorcourt.org/OnlineServices/criminalindex/index.asp. Search fee is $4 to $4.75.

General Information: No probation, driver's license, medical, arrest report or confidential reports released. Will not fax documents. Court makes copy: $.50 per page. Certification fee: $15 per doc. Payee: Los Angeles Superior Court. Personal checks and major credit cards accepted. Prepayment required. Mail requests: SASE requested.

Norwalk Superior Ct - Southeast District 12720 Norwalk Blvd, Norwalk, CA 90650; 562-807-7266; probate phone: 562-807-7263; fax: 562-863-8757; 8:30AM-4:30PM. ***Felony, Civil Actions over $25,000, Probate.*** www.lasuperiorcourt.org
Civil Records: Access: Mail, in person, online. Both court and visitors may perform in person searches. Search fee: $15.00 per name if search exceeds 10 minutes. Required to search: name, years to search. Civil cases indexed by defendant, plaintiff, on computer from 1991, index files from 1983. Mail turnaround time 2-10 days. Civil PAT available. Use public terminal to find case number only. Free summary lookup by case number (not name) at https://www.lasuperiorcourt.org/OnlineServices/CivilImages/index.asp. Also includes probate cases from 02/11/03. There is a fee-based name search for records back to 1991 (if Small Claims 1992) at this site. Fee is $4.75 per search.
Criminal Records: Access: Mail, in person, online. Both court and visitors may perform in person searches. Search fee: $15.00 per name if search exceeds 10 minutes. Required to search: name, years to search, DOB; also helpful: sex. Criminal records computerized from 1991, index files from 1983. Mail turnaround time 2-10 days. Criminal PAT available. Use public terminal to find case number only. Felony and misdemeanor defendant records at https://www.lasuperiorcourt.org/OnlineServices/criminalindex/index.asp. Search fee $4 to $4.75.
General Information: No probation reports released. Will not fax out docs. Court makes copy: $.50 per page. Certification fee: $15 per doc. Payee: Los Angeles Superior Court. Personal checks and major credit cards accepted. Prepayment required. Mail requests: SASE required.

Pasadena Superior Ct - Northeast Dist. 300 E Walnut, Pasadena, CA 91101; 626-356-5689; criminal: 626-356-5254; civil phone: 626-356-5415; probate: 626-356-5683; fax: 626-568-3903; 8:30AM-4:30PM. ***Misdemeanor, Civil Actions under $25,000, Civil Actions over $25,000, Eviction, Small Claims, Probate.*** www.lasuperiorcourt.org
Includes cities of Pasadena, South Pasadena, San Marino, Sierra Madre and the area of Altadena. Traffic phone- 626-356-5265. Some older probate records may be found in the Burbank Court.
Civil Records: Access: Mail, in person, online. Both court and visitors may perform in person searches. Search fee: $15.00 per name if search exceeds 10 minutes. Required to search: name, years to search. Civil cases indexed by defendant, plaintiff, on computer from 1991, index files from 1983. Limited Juris records destroyed after 10 years; General Juris are not. Mail turnaround time 2 days. Public use terminal has civil records. Free summary lookup by case number (not name) at https://www.lasuperiorcourt.org/OnlineServices/CivilImages/index.asp. Also includes probate cases from 06/97. There is a fee-based name search for records back to 1991 (if Small Claims 1992) at this site. Fee is $4.75 per search.
Criminal Records: Access: Mail, in person, online. Only the court performs in person searches; visitors may not. Search fee: $15.00 per name if search exceeds 10 minutes. Required to search: name, years to search. Criminal records computerized from 1991, index files from 1983. Mail turnaround time 2 days. Felony & misdemeanor defendant records are online for a fee at https://www.lasuperiorcourt.org/OnlineServices/criminalindex/index.asp. Search fee is $4 to $4.75.
General Information: No probation reports released. Will fax out docs to local or toll-free number. Court makes copy: $.50 per page. Certification fee: $15.00; exemplification fee- $20.00. Payee: Los Angeles Superior Court. Personal checks and major credit cards accepted. Prepayment required. Mail requests: SASE required.

Pomona Superior Court - North 350 W Mission Blvd, Pomona, CA 91766; 909-802-9944; probate phone: 909-620-3023; criminal fax: 909-865-6767; civil fax: 909-620-6143; 8AM-4:30PM. ***Misdemeanor, Civil Actions under $25,000, Eviction, Small Claims, Probate.***
www.lasuperiorcourt.org Includes cities of Pomona, Claremont, La Verne, Walnut, San Dimas and unincorporated area including Diamond Bar. There is another court in Pomona on 400 Civic Center that deals with family and juvenile matters.
Civil Records: Access: Fax, mail, online, in person. Only the court performs in person searches; visitors may not. Search fee: $15.00 per name if search exceeds 10 minutes. Required to search: name, years to search. Civil cases indexed by defendant, plaintiff, on computer from 1990, index files from 1983. Records destroyed after 10 years. Mail turnaround time 1-2 days. Free summary lookup by case number at https://www.lasuperiorcourt.org/OnlineServices/CivilImages/index.asp. Also includes probate cases from 01/95. There is a fee-based name search for records back to 1991 (if Small Claims 1992). Fee is $4.75 per search.
Criminal Records: Access: Mail, in person, online. Only the court performs in person searches; visitors may not. Search fee: $15.00 per name if search exceeds 10 minutes. Required to search: name, years to search, DOB. Criminal records computerized from 1990, index files from 1983. Records destroyed after 10 years. Note: Drop box available. Mail turnaround time 2-4 days. Felony & misdemeanor defendant records are online for a fee at https://www.lasuperiorcourt.org/OnlineServices/criminalindex/index.asp. Search fee is $4 to $4.75.
General Information: No probation, mental health or police reports released. Will not fax documents. Court makes copy: $.50 per page. Certification fee: $15 per doc. Payee: Los Angeles Superior Court. Personal checks accepted. Visa/MC accepted. Prepayment required. Mail requests: SASE required.

Redondo Beach Superior Court - Southwest District 117 W Torrance Blvd, Redondo Beach, CA 90277-3638; 310-798-6875; fax: 310-376-4051; 8:30AM-4:30PM. ***Civil Actions over $25,000.*** www.lasuperiorcourt.org
Closed cases located at Torrance Courthouse.
Civil Records: Access: Mail, in person, online. Only the court performs in person searches; visitors may not. Search fee: $15.00 per name if search exceeds 10 minutes. If case closed, direct search request to the Torrance Courthouse, Civil Div. Required to search: name, years to search. Civil cases indexed by defendant, plaintiff, on computer from 1991, closed cases at Torrance Court; index files from 1983. Records destroyed after 10 years. Mail turnaround time 3-4 days. Free summary lookup by case number at https://www.lasuperiorcourt.org/OnlineServices/CivilImages/index.asp. There is a fee-based name search for records back to 1991 (if Small Claims 1992. Fee is $4.75 per search.
General Information: Unlawful detainers held for 60 days. Will not fax documents. Court makes copy: $.50 per page. Certification fee: $15 per doc. Payee: Los Angeles Superior Court. Personal checks and major credit cards accepted. Prepayment required. Mail requests: SASE required.

San Fernando Superior Court - North Valley District 900 3rd St, #1135 or #1137, San Fernando, CA 91340; 818-898-2401 Admin.; criminal phone: 818-898-2655, 818-898-2407 Misc.; civil phone: Sm Claims- 818-898-2425; fax: 818-837-7297; 8:30AM-4:30PM. ***Felony, Misdemeanor, Small Claims.*** www.lasuperiorcourt.org
Includes Granada Hills, Northridge, Chatsworth, Sunland, Tujunga, Pacoima, Mission Hills, Sylmar, Arleta, Lake View Terrace, Sun Valley, San Fernando. Court merged with Newhall Court to become North Valley Court. Traffic - 818-898-2405.
Civil Records: Access: Mail, in person, online. Search fee: $15.00 per name if search exceeds 10 minutes. Required to search: name, years to search. Civil cases indexed by defendant, plaintiff, on computer from 1991, index files from 1983. Records destroyed after 10 years. Note: Probate at Van Nuys Courthouse. Online access is free at www.lasuperiorcourt.org. Court location, case

number required to search. Includes civil, small claims, probate and unlawful detainer records; includes probate cases from 06/98. There is a fee-based name search for records back to 1991 (if Small Claims 1992) at this site. $4.75 per search.

Criminal Records: Access: Mail, online, in person. Only the court performs in person searches; visitors may not. Search fee: $15.00 per name if search exceeds 10 minutes. Required to search: name, years to search; also helpful: DOB. Criminal records computerized from 1988. Records destroyed after 10 yrs. Note: Misdemeanor clerk's office is Rm 1137. Sheriff's Department (Court Services)- 818-898-2436. Mail turnaround time 2 days. Public use terminal has crim records back to 1996. Felony and misdemeanor defendant records online at https://www.lasuperiorcourt.org/OnlineServices/criminalindex/index.asp. Search fee is $4 to $4.75.

General Information: No probation reports or arrest reports released. Will not fax out docs. Court makes copy: $.50 per page. Certification fee: $15 per doc. Payee: Los Angeles Superior Court. Personal checks accepted. No 3rd party checks. Major credit cards accepted. Prepayment required. SASE required.

San Pedro Superior Court - South District 505 S Centre St, Rm 202, San Pedro, CA 90731; 310-519-6018- general civil; civil phone: 310-519-6015 Limited Civil; 310-519-6014- Sm Claims; fax: 310-514-0314; 8:30AM-4:30PM; Traffic- 8AM-4:30PM. ***Civil Actions, Eviction, Small Claims, Traffic.*** www.lasuperiorcourt.org

Includes San Pedro, Wilmington, and a county strip in Torrance extending up to Western Ave. Traffic phone- 213-742-1884. The San Pedro Courthouse Annex is located at 638 S. Beacon St, phone-310-519-6018 for clerk's office

Civil Records: Access: Mail, in person, online. Only the court performs in person searches; visitors may not. Search fee: $15.00 per name if search exceeds 10 minutes. Required to search: name, years to search. Civil cases indexed by defendant, plaintiff, on computer go back 10 years; on index files from 1984. Records destroyed after 10 years. Mail turnaround time 2 days. Free summary lookup by case number at https://www.lasuperiorcourt.org/OnlineServices/CivilImages/index.asp. There is a fee-based name search for records back to 1991 (if Small Claims 1992) at this site. Fee is $4.75 per search.

General Information: No probation, arrest, records released. Will fax documents $3.37 per page. Court makes copy: $.50 per page. Certification fee: $15 per doc. Payee: Los Angeles Superior Court. Personal checks accepted. Accepts Visa cards plus 6% surcharge. Prepayment required. SASE required.

Santa Clarita Superior Court - North Valley District 23747 W Valencia Blvd, Santa Clarita, CA 91355; 661-253-7316; criminal phone: 661-253-7384; civil phone: 661-253-7309, 253-7313; criminal fax: 661-254-4107; civil fax: 661-286-1546; 8:30AM-4:30PM. ***Misdemeanor, Civil Actions under $25,000, Eviction, Small Claims.*** www.lasuperiorcourt.org

Formerly Newhall Sup. Ct. Includes Saugus, Canyon Country, Valencia, Santa Clarita and open area bound by Ventura County, Kern County line, Agua Dulce, and Glendale/Los Angeles city limits (south). Sm Claims - 661-253-7311/12. Traffic- 213-742-6648.

Civil Records: Access: Mail, in person, online. Both court and visitors may perform in person searches. Search fee: $15.00 per name if search exceeds 10 minutes. Required to search: name, years to search. Civil cases indexed by defendant, plaintiff, on computer from 1991, in files from 1983. Records destroyed after 10 years; Many records on microfiche. Note: Visitors may view microfiche record index. Mail turnaround time 7-10 days. Free summary lookup by case number (not name) at https://www.lasuperiorcourt.org/OnlineServices/CivilImages/index.asp. Name search for records to 1991 (if Small Claims 1992) - $4.75 per search.

Criminal Records: Access: Mail, in person, online. Only the court performs in person searches; visitors may not. Search fee: $15.00 per name if search exceeds 10 minutes. Required to search: name, years to search; also helpful: DOB. Records on computer from 1991, indices from 1983. Records destroyed after 10 years, many records on microfiche. Note: Visitors may view microfiche index. Mail turnaround time 7-10 days. Search at https://www.lasuperiorcourt.org/OnlineServices/criminalindex/index.asp. Search fee- $4 to $4.75.

General Information: No probation, or police reports w/out court approval released. Will fax civil docs for $3.37 per doc. Court makes copy: $.50 per page. Certification fee: $15 per doc. Payee: Los Angeles Superior Court. Personal checks accepted. Credit cards accepted. Prepayment required. Mail requests: SASE required.

Santa Monica Superior Ct - West Dist. 1725 Main St, Rm 224, Santa Monica, CA 90401; 310-260-3522; civil phone: 310-260-1876 unlimited; 260-1886 limited; probate phone: 310-260-3521; fax: 310-576-1399; 8:30AM-4:30PM. ***Civil Actions under $25,000, Eviction, Small Claims, Probate.*** www.lasuperiorcourt.org

Includes Santa Monica City and unincorporated area of Veteran's Admin. facilities in West LA. Now has Culver City records. Small claims-310-260-1886. Probate- 260-1876, Rm 101. Criminal section moved to LAX-Airport Courthouse, 2004, 310-727-6020.

Civil Records: Access: Mail, in person, online. Both court and visitors may perform in person searches. Search fee: $15.00 per name if search exceeds 10 minutes. Required to search: name, years to search. Civil cases indexed by defendant, plaintiff, on computer from 1991, files from 1983. Records destroyed after 10 yrs. Mail turnaround time 1-2 days. Free summary lookup by case number at https://www.lasuperiorcourt.org/OnlineServices/CivilImages/index.asp. Includes probate from 7/2/04. A fee-based name search for records back to 1991 (if Small Claims 1992) at site is $4.75 per search.

General Information: No probation reports or unlawful detainer records released. Will not fax out docs. Court makes copy: $.50 per page. Certification fee: $15 per doc. Payee: Los Angeles Superior Court. Personal checks and major credit cards accepted. Prepayment required. Mail requests: SASE required.

Torrance Superior Ct - Southwest Dist. 825 Maple Ave, Torrance, CA 90503-5058; 310-222-6505, 222-6501 Admin.; criminal phone: 310-222-6506; civil: 310-222-8801/09; 222-6400 Sm Claims; probate phone: 310-222-8802/8809; criminal fax: 310-783-5108; civil fax: 310-782-7326; 8:15AM-4:30PM. ***Misdemeanor, Civil, Traffic, Eviction, Small Claims, Probate.*** www.lasuperiorcourt.org Includes cities of Torrance, Gardena, Rolling Hills/Estates, Manhattan Beach, Lomita, Redondo Beach, Hermosa Beach, Palos Verdes Estates, Rancho Palos Verdes & Lawndale.

Civil Records: Access: Mail, in person, online. Both court and visitors may perform in person searches. Search fee: $15.00 per name if search exceeds 10 minutes. Required to search: name. Civil cases indexed by defendant, plaintiff, on computer from 1991, index files from 1983. Records destroyed after 10 yrs. Mail turnaround time 5 days. Public use terminal available. Public terminal in Rm 100. Free case summary lookup at https://www.lasuperiorcourt.org/OnlineServices/CivilImages/index.asp , search by case # but not name. Includes probate cases back to 2/97. A fee-based name search for records back to 1991 (if Small Claims 1992) at this site is $4.75 per search.

Criminal Records: Access: Mail, in person, online. Only the court performs in person searches; visitors may not. Search fee: $15.00 per name if search exceeds 10 minutes. Required to search: name, years to search, DOB. Criminal records computerized from 1991, index files from 1983. Records destroyed after 10 yrs. Mail turnaround time 5 days. Public use terminal available. Criminal defendant records at https://www.lasuperiorcourt.org/OnlineServices/criminalindex/index.asp. Search fee is $4 to $4.75.

General Information: No probation reports, medical or psychiatric reports, criminal history rap sheets released. Will not fax out docs. Court makes copy: $.50 per page. Certification fee: $15 per doc. Payee: LA Superior Court. Personal checks and major credit cards accepted. Prepayment required. Mail requests: SASE required.

Van Nuys Superior Court - East - Civil 6230 Sylmar St, Van Nuys, CA 91401; 818-374-2208; civil phone: 818-374-2208- Unlimited; 818-374-2904- Limited; probate phone: 818-374-2199; Sm Claims- 374-2901; fax: 818-779-7713; 8:30AM-4:30PM. ***Civil Actions, Eviction, Small Claims, Family Law, Probate.*** www.lasuperiorcourt.org

Small Claims 818-374-2208. Includes Sherman Oaks, Van Nuys, Reseda, North Hollywood, Woodland Hills, Canoga Park, Tarzana, Porter Ranch, Winnetka and Panorama City. Civil jurisdiction depends on whether limited or general.

Civil Records: Access: Mail, in person, online. Both court and visitors may perform in person searches. Search fee: $15.00 per name if search exceeds 10 minutes. Required to search: name, years to search. Civil cases indexed by defendant, plaintiff, on computer from 1991, index files from 1983. Records destroyed after 10 years. Mail turnaround time 2-3 days. Public use terminal has civil records back to 1991. Free summary lookup by case number at https://www.lasuperiorcourt.org/OnlineServices/CivilImages/index.asp. Also includes probate cases from 02/01. A fee-based name search for records back to 1991 (if Small Claims 1992) at this site is $4.75 per search.

General Information: No probation reports or arrest reports released. Will not fax documents. Court makes copy: $.50 per page. Certification fee: $15 per doc; exemplification- $20.00 plus copies. Payee: Los Angeles Superior Court or LASC. Personal checks accepted; write 'not to exceed" and the amount on the check. Major credit cards accepted. Prepayment required. Mail requests: SASE required.

Van Nuys Superior Ct - West - Criminal 14400 Erwin St, Mall, Rm 200, Van Nuys, CA 91401; 818-374-2903; fax: 818-904-0534; 8:30AM-4:30PM. ***Felony, Misdemeanor.*** www.lasuperiorcourt.org

Misdemeanors for that part of city known as Sherman Oaks, Van Nuys, Reseda, North Hollywood, Woodland Hills, Canoga Park, Tarzana, Porter Ranch, Winnetka and Panorama City.

Criminal Records: Access: Phone, mail, in person, online. Only the court performs in person searches; visitors may not. Search fee: $15.00 per name if search exceeds 10 minutes. Required to search: name, years to search, sex; also helpful: DOB. Criminal records computerized from 1991, index files from 1983. Mail turnaround time 2-3 days. Felony and misdemeanor defendant records are online at https://www.lasuperiorcourt.org/OnlineServices/criminalindex/index.asp. Search fee is $4 to $4.75.

General Information: No probation reports or arrest reports released. Will not fax documents. Court makes copy: $.50 per page. Certification fee: $15 per doc. Payee: Los Angeles Superior Court. Personal checks and major credit cards accepted. Prepayment required. Mail requests: SASE required.

West Covina Superior Ct - East District 1427 W Covina Pky, West Covina, CA 91790; criminal phone: 626-813-3239; civil phone: 626-813-3236 Civil; 626-813-3226 Sm Claims; fax: 626-338-7364; 8:30AM-4:30PM. ***Misdemeanor, Civil Actions under $25,000, Eviction, Small Claims.*** www.lasuperiorcourt.org Formerly known as Citrus Court. Includes cities of Azusa, Baldwin Pk, Covina, Glendora, Industry, Irwindale, Valinda, West Covina and surrounding unincorporated county area. Traffic phone- 213-742-1928.

Civil Records: Access: Mail, in person, online. Both court and visitors may perform in person searches. Search fee: $15.00 per name if search exceeds 10 minutes. Required to search: name, years to search. Civil cases indexed by defendant, plaintiff, on computer from 1991, index files from 1983. Records destroyed after 10 years. Mail turnaround time 2 weeks Civil PAT goes back to 1996. Free summary lookup by case number (not name) at https://www.lasuperiorcourt.org/OnlineServices/CivilImages/index.asp. A fee-based name search for records back to 1991 (if Small Claims 1992) at this site is $4.75 per search.

Criminal Records: Access: Mail, in person, online. Only the court performs in person searches; visitors may not. Search fee: $15.00 per name if search exceeds 10 minutes. Required to search: name,

years to search; also helpful: DOB. Criminal records computerized from 1991, index files from 1983. Records destroyed after 10 years. Note: Direct criminal searches to; LA County Court, Felony; phone-213-974-6145, address-210 W Temple St, LA, CA. Mail turnaround time is 2 weeks. Criminal PAT available. Felony & misdemeanor defendant records are online at https://www.lasuperiorcourt.org/OnlineServices/criminalindex/index.asp. Search fee- $4 to $4.75.
General Information: No probation reports released. Will not fax out docs. Court makes copy: $.50 per page. Certification fee: $15 per doc. Payee: Los Angeles Superior Court. Personal checks accepted. Credit cards accepted. Prepayment required. Mail requests: SASE required.

West Los Angeles Superior Court - West District 1633 Purdue Ave, Los Angeles, CA 90025; 310-312-6545; civil phone: 310-312-6550 Sm Claims; fax: 310)-478-1275; 8:30AM-4:30PM. ***Civil Actions under $25,000, Eviction, Small Claims.*** www.lasuperiorcourt.org Includes the areas of Palms, Mar Vista, Rancho Park, Marina del Rey, Venice, Playa del Rey and Sawtelle. Holds records for the former Robertson branch. Criminal felony and misdemeanors are at the new Airport Court.
Civil Records: Access: Phone, mail, online, in person. Both court and visitors may perform in person searches. Search fee: $15.00 per name if search exceeds 10 minutes. Required to search: name, years to search. Civil cases indexed by defendant, plaintiff, on computer from 1991, index files from 1983. Records destroyed after 10 years. Mail turnaround time 1-5 days. Public use terminal has civil records. Free summary lookup by case number at https://www.lasuperiorcourt.org/OnlineServices/CivilImages/index.asp. A fee-based name search for records back to 1991 (if Small Claims 1992) at this site is $4.75 per search.
General Information: No probation records released. Will not fax documents. Court makes copy: $.50 per page. Certification fee: $15 per doc. Payee: Los Angeles Superior Court. Personal checks and major credit cards accepted. Prepayment required. Mail requests: SASE required.

Whittier Superior CT - Southeast Dist. 7339 S Painter Ave, Whittier, CA 90602; criminal phone: 562-907-3113; civil phone: 562-907-3127; fax: 562-464-2825; 8AM-4:30PM. ***Misdemeanor, Civil Actions under $25,000, Eviction, Small Claims.*** www.lasuperiorcourt.org Includes cities of Whittier, Santa Fe Springs, Pico Rivera, La Habra Heights plus unincorporated territory in the Whittier area including areas designated as Los Nietos and South Whittier.
Civil Records: Access: Mail, in person, online. Both court and visitors may perform in person searches. Search fee: $15.00 per name if search exceeds 10 minutes. Required to search: name, years to search. Civil cases indexed by defendant, plaintiff, on computer from 1991, index files from 1983. Records destroyed after 10 years. Note: Civil and small claims in basement. Mail turnaround time 2 days. Free summary lookup by case number at https://www.lasuperiorcourt.org/OnlineServices/CivilImages/index.asp. A fee-based name search for records back to 1991 (if Small Claims 1992) at this site is $4.75 per search.
Criminal Records: Access: Mail, in person, online. Only the court performs in person searches; visitors may not. Search fee: $15.00 per name if search exceeds 10 minutes. Required to search: name, years to search; also helpful: DOB. Criminal records computerized since 1987. Note: Criminal in Rm 100. Mail turnaround time 2 days. Felony & misdemeanor defendant records for a fee at https://www.lasuperiorcourt.org/OnlineServices/criminalindex/index.asp. Search fee is $4 to $4.75.
General Information: No probation reports released. Will not fax documents. Court makes copy: $.50 per page. Certification fee: $15 per doc. Payee: Los Angeles Superior Court. Personal checks accepted. Credit cards accepted. Prepayment required. Mail requests: SASE required.

Santa Anita Superior Ct - Northeast Dist 150 W Commonwealth Ave, Alhambra, CA 91801; criminal: 626-308-5525; civil: 626-308-5521; fax: 626-570-4667; 8AM-4:30PM. ***Civil Actions under $25,000, Eviction, Small Claims.*** Court closed - merged with Alhambra Court; phone and address given above. Formerly included cities of Monrovia, Arcadia, Duarte, Bradbury and unincorporated county territory in surrounding area.

Madera County

Superior Court 209 W Yosemite Ave, Madera, CA 93637; 559-675-7944; criminal phone: 559-675-7734; civil phone: 559-675-7995; probate phone: 559-675-7795; criminal fax: 559-675-7618; civil fax: 559-675-6565; 8AM-4PM. ***Felony, Civil, Probate, Eviction, Small Claims.*** www.madera.courts.ca.gov
The Superior and Municipal courts located in the City of Madera have combined into a consolidated court. There is a countywide index of criminal records.
Civil Records: Access: Mail, fax, in person. Both court and visitors may perform in person searches. Search fee: $15.00 per name if search exceeds 10 minutes. Required to search: name, years to search. Civil cases indexed by defendant, plaintiff, on microfiche, archived and index file from 1893. Mail turnaround time 2-3 weeks. Civil PAT goes back to 2003. PAT results show name only.
Criminal Records: Access: Mail, fax, in person. Only the court performs in person searches; visitors may not. Search fee: $15.00 per name if search exceeds 10 minutes. Required to search: name, years to search, DOB, signed release. Criminal records on microfiche, archived and index file. Mail turnaround time 2-3 weeks. Criminal PAT goes back to 2003. PAT results show name only.
General Information: No adoption, juvenile, medical, probation or sealed records released. Will not fax documents. Court makes copy: $.50 per page. Certification fee: $15 per doc. Payee: Madera Superior Court. Only business checks accepted. No credit cards accepted. Prepayment required. Mail requests: SASE required.

Sierra Division - Superior Court 40601 Road 274, Bass Lake, CA 93604; 559-642-3235; probate phone: same; fax: 559-642-3445; 8:30AM-12:30PM, 1:30-4:00PM. ***Felony, Misdemeanor, Civil Actions, Eviction, Small Claims, Probate.*** www.madera.courts.ca.gov
There is a countywide index database of court records.
Civil Records: Access: Mail, in person. Both court and visitors may perform in person searches. Search fee: $15.00 per name if search exceeds 10 minutes. Required to search: name, years to search. Civil cases indexed by defendant, plaintiff, on computer back to 3/30/03 prior on index cards. Will only search back 7 years. Mail turnaround time 1-2 weeks. Public use terminal available.
Criminal Records: Access: Mail, in person. Both court and visitors may perform in person searches. Search fee: $15.00 per name if search exceeds 10 minutes. Required to search: name, years to search; also helpful: DOB. Criminal records computerized from 3/30/03 prior on index cards for criminal. Mail turnaround 1-2 weeks. Public use terminal available.
General Information: No adoption, juvenile, medical, probation or sealed records released. Will not fax documents. Court makes copy: $.50 per page. Certification fee: $15 per doc. Payee: Madera Superior Court. Personal checks accepted; credit cards are not. Prepayment required. Mail requests: SASE required.

Traffic Division - Superior Court 209 W. Yosemite Ave, Madera, CA 93637; 559-675-7944; fax: 559-675-7618; 8AM-4PM. ***Misdemeanor Traffic.*** www.madera.courts.ca.gov
Formerly located at 141 S 2nd. St. in Chowchilla. Now at the main courthouse in Madera.

Marin County

Superior Court PO Box 4988, San Rafael, CA 94913-4988; 415-473-4131; criminal phone: 415-473-6225; civil phone: 415-473-6407; 8:30AM-4PM. ***Felony, Misdemeanor, Civil, Eviction/Family, Small Claims, Probate.*** www.co.marin.ca.us/courts
Civil Records: Access: Phone, mail, in person, online. Both court and visitors may perform in person searches. Search fee: $15.00 per name if search exceeds 10 minutes. Required to search: name, years to search, case number if known. Civil cases indexed by defendant, plaintiff, on computer from 1986, on microfiche from 1973 to 1985, archived from 1900 to 1972, on reel from 1900. Note: Phone requests are limited to one name. Mail turnaround time 3 weeks. Civil PAT goes back to 1980. Access court index back to 1970s free at www.marincourt.org/PublicIndex/Default.aspx or http://public.marincourt.org/publicindex/default.aspx.
Criminal Records: Access: Mail, in person, online, phone. Both court and visitors may perform in person searches. Search fee: $15.00 per name if search exceeds 10 minutes. Required to search: name, years to search, case number if known. Criminal records computerized from 1986, on microfiche from 1973 to 1985, archived from 1900 to 1972, on reel from 1900. Note: Phone requests are limited to one name. 5 name limit at counter. Mail turnaround time 3 weeks. Criminal PAT goes back to 1976. Online access to criminal index is same as civil.
General Information: No adoption, paternity, sole custody, juvenile, medical, probation or sealed records released. Will not fax documents. Court makes copy: $.50 per page. Certification fee: $15 per doc. Payee: Marin County Superior Court. Personal checks accepted. Out-of-state checks not accepted. Write "not to exceed $x.xx" on check. Call first. Major credit cards accepted. Prepayment required. Mail requests: SASE required.

Mariposa County

Superior Court PO Box 28, 5088 Bullion St, Mariposa, CA 95338; 209-966-2005; criminal phone: 209-966-2005; civil phone: 209-966-6599; probate phone: 209-966-6599; fax: 209-742-6860; 8:30AM-4PM. ***Felony, Misdemeanor, Civil, Small Claims, Eviction, Probate.*** www.mariposacourt.org/
Include fax return number with any faxed requests.
Civil Records: Access: Mail, fax, in person. Only the court performs in person searches; visitors may not. Search fee: $15.00 per name if search exceeds 10 minutes. Required to search: name, DOB, years to search. Civil cases indexed by defendant, plaintiff, on computer from 1999, on microfiche and index files from 1800s. Note: 5 name limit at counter. Mail turnaround time 5 days. Civil PAT goes back to 1999. PAT results show name, DOB. PAT terminals are offsite at Self Help Ctr. Case number needed to access PAT records.
Criminal Records: Access: Mail, fax, in person. Only the court performs in person searches; visitors may not. Search fee: $15.00 per name if search exceeds 10 minutes. Required to search: name, DOB, years to search. Criminal records computerized from 1999, on microfiche and index files from 1800s. Note: 5 name limit at counter. Mail turnaround time 5 days. Criminal PAT goes back to 1999.PAT results show name, DOB. PAT terminals are offsite at Self Help Ctr. Case number needed to access PAT records.
General Information: No adoption, juvenile, medical, probation or sealed records released. Will fax documents for no add'l fee. Court makes copy: $.50 per page. Certification fee: $15 per doc plus copy fee' exemplification- $20.00. Payee: Mariposa Superior Court. Personal checks accepted; credit cards are not. Prepayment required. Mail requests: SASE required.

Mendocino County

Superior Court 100 N State St, #108, Ukiah, CA 95482; 707-463-4661; criminal phone: 707-463-4766; civil phone: 707-463-4481; probate phone: 707-468-2005; criminal fax: 707-463-4655; civil fax: 707-463-6850; 8AM-4PM. ***Felony, Civil Actions over $25,000, Probate.*** www.mendocino.courts.ca.gov
Mailing address is for the Criminal Div. Mailing for Civil Div is Rm 107. Anderson Branch/Boonville closed permanently 6/26/2003. Most of Anderson Judicial District merged into Ukiah. MP marker 13.6 on Hiway 128 is the new western district boundary.
Civil Records: Access: Mail, in person, online. Both court and visitors may perform in person searches. Search fee: $15.00 per name if search exceeds 10 minutes. Fee for mail search only. Required to search: name, years to search. Civil cases indexed by

defendant, plaintiff, on computer from 1990s, on microfilm from 1800 to 1940. Mail turnaround time 1-2 weeks. Civil PAT goes back to 1996. Search index at www.mendocino.courts.ca.gov/caseindex.html. Online index may be up to 2 months behind.
Criminal Records: Access: Mail, in person, online. Both court and visitors may perform in person searches. Search fee: $15.00 per name if search exceeds 10 minutes. Required to search: name, years to search. Criminal records computerized from 1990s, on microfilm from 1800 to 1940. Mail turnaround time -12 weeks. Criminal PAT goes back to same as civil. Search index at www.mendocino.courts.ca.gov/caseindex.html. Online index may be up to 2 months behind. Online results show middle initial.
General Information: No adoption, juvenile, medical, probation or sealed records released. Will not fax documents. Court makes copy: $.50 per page. Certification fee: $15 per doc. Payee: Mendocino Superior Court. Personal checks accepted. Prepayment required. Mail requests: SASE required.

Ten Mile Branch - Superior Court 700 S Franklin St, Fort Bragg, CA 95437; 707-964-3192; fax: 707-961-2611; 8AM-2:30PM M-TH; 8AM-N F. ***Felony, Misdemeanor, Civil Actions, Eviction, Small Claims.***
www.mendocino.courts.ca.gov/fortbragg.html
Records of the Port Arean Branch are now located here at Ft Bragg. The court hearing address in Port Arena 24000 S Highway One; Pr Arean court days are only once a month.
Civil Records: Access: Mail, in person, online. Only the court performs in person searches; visitors may not. Search fee: $15.00 per case if search exceeds 10 minutes. Required to search: name, years to search. Civil cases indexed by defendant, plaintiff. Will only search back 10 years. Mail turnaround time 2 weeks. Search index at www.mendocino.courts.ca.gov/caseindex.html.
Criminal Records: Access: Mail, in person, online. Only the court performs in person searches; visitors may not. Search fee: $15.00 per case if search exceeds 10 minutes. Required to search: name, years to search, DOB. Criminal records go back to 1990; on computer back 1995; will only search back 10 years. Mail turnaround 2 weeks. Search index at www.mendocino.courts.ca.gov/caseindex.html. Online results show middle initial.
General Information: No juvenile or probation records released. Will not fax documents. Court makes copy: $.50 per page. Certification fee: $15 per doc. Payee: Superior Court. Personal checks accepted; credit cards are not. Prepayment required. Mail requests: SASE required.

Willits Branch - Superior Court 125 E Commercial St, Rm 100, Willits, CA 95490; 707-459-5554; fax: 707-459-7818; 8AM-4PM. ***Felony, Misdemeanor, Civil Actions under $25,000, Eviction, Small Claims.***
www.mendocino.courts.ca.gov
Records of the Round Valley/Covelo Branch now located here at Willits. The court hearing address in Covelo is 76270 Grange St. but Covelo court days are only once a month. On 6/30/03, operations for the Long Valley Branch merged with Willits Court.
Civil Records: Access: Mail, in person, online. Only the court performs in person searches; visitors may not. Search fee: $15.00 per name if search exceeds 10 minutes. Required to search: name, years to search. Civil cases indexed by defendant, plaintiff, on computer since 1992, index files prior. Mail turnaround time 1 week. Search index at www.mendocino.courts.ca.gov/caseindex.html.
Criminal Records: Access: Mail, in person, online. Both court and visitors may perform in person searches. Search fee: $15.00 per name if search exceeds 10 minutes. Required to search: name, years to search, DOB. Criminal records on computer since 1992, index files prior. Mail turnaround time 1 week. Search index at www.mendocino.courts.ca.gov/caseindex.html. Online results show middle initial.
General Information: No probation reports released. Will not fax documents. Court makes copy: $.50 per page. Certification fee: $15 per doc. Payee: MCSC. Personal checks accepted. Visa/MC accepted in person only. Prepayment required. Mail requests: SASE required.

Anderson Branch in Boonville - Superior Court, CA; ***Misdemeanor, Civil Actions under $25,000, Eviction, Small Claims.***
This court is closed. Records transferred to Ukiah. Everything east of Mile Post marker 13.6 on Highway 128 is now in Ukiah; everything west is in Ft Bragg.

Round Valley Branch - Superior Court, CA; ***Misdemeanor, Civil Actions under $25,000, Eviction, Small Claims.***
This court has merged with the Willits Division.

Arena Branch - Superior Court, CA;
Effective June 30, 2003, operations for the Arena Branch of the Superior Court have been merged with the Ten Mile Court in Fort Bragg.

Merced County

Superior Court 627 W 21st St, Merced, CA 95340; 209-725-4100; criminal phone: 209-725-4113; civil phone: 209-725-4111; criminal fax: 209-725-4112; civil fax: 209-725-4112; 8AM-4PM. ***Felony, Civil Actions over $25,000, Probate.***
www.mercedcourt.org
Civil Records: Access: Mail, in person. Both court and visitors may perform in person searches. Search fee: $15.00 per name if search exceeds 10 minutes. Required to search: name, years to search. Civil cases indexed by defendant, plaintiff. Mail turnaround time 1 week. Civil PAT goes back to 1979. Results include case number.
Criminal Records: Access: Mail, in person. Both court and visitors may perform in person searches. Search fee: $15.00 per name if search exceeds 10 minutes. Required to search: name, years to search. Criminal records in index files from 1900s, computer from 1979, on microfiche from 1900s. Mail turnaround time 1 week. Criminal PAT goes back to 1986.
General Information: No juvenile nor adoption records released. Court makes copy: $.50 per page. Certification fee: $15 per doc. Payee: Merced County Superior Court. Business checks and money orders accepted. No credit cards accepted. Prepayment required. Mail requests: SASE required.

Los Banos Branch - Superior Court 445 "I" St, Los Banos, CA 93635; 209-725-4124; fax: 209-725-4125; 7:30AM-4PM. ***Misdemeanor, Civil Actions under $25,000, Eviction, Small Claims.***
www.mercedcourt.org
This court was combined with the old Dos Palos and Gustine Municipal Courts.
Civil Records: Access: Mail, in person. Only the court performs in person searches; visitors may not. Search fee: $15.00 per name if search exceeds 10 minutes. Required to search: name, years to search. Civil cases indexed by defendant, plaintiff, on microfiche. Mail turnaround time 2-3 days. PAT results show name only.
Criminal Records: Access: Mail, in person. Only the court performs in person searches; visitors may not. Search fee: $15.00 per name if search exceeds 10 minutes. Required to search: name, years to search; also helpful: DOB. Criminal records on microfiche. Mail turnaround time 2-3 days. PAT results show name only.
General Information: No juvenile or probation records released. Will fax documents to local or toll free line. Court makes copy: $.50 per page. Certification fee: $15 per doc. Payee: Superior Court. Personal checks accepted; credit cards are not. Prepayment required. Mail requests: SASE required.

Merced Superior Court 2260 N St, Merced, CA 95340; 209-725-4113; fax: 209-725-4114; 7:45AM-4PM. ***Misdemeanor.*** www.mercedcourt.org
Criminal Records: Access: Mail, in person. Only the court performs in person searches; visitors may not. No search fee; $15.00 per name fee may apply if search exceeds 10 minutes. Required to search: name, years to search. Criminal records computerized from 1992; prior on microfiche. Will only search back 7 years. Mail turnaround time 1 week. Criminal PAT available.PAT results show name, DOB.
General Information: No juvenile or probation records released. Will fax documents. Court makes copy: $.50 per page. Certification fee: $15 per doc. Payee: Merced County Superior Court. Only cashiers checks and money orders accepted. No credit card. Prepayment required. Mail requests: SASE required.

Merced Superior Court Civil Limited 627 W 21st St, Merced, CA 95340; 209-725-4109; fax: 209-725-4110; 8AM-4PM. ***Civil Actions under $25,000, Eviction, Small Claims.***
www.mercedcourt.org
Deliveries to 670 W 22nd St, Rm 15.
Civil Records: Access: Mail, in person. Search fee: $15.00 per name if search exceeds 10 minutes. Required to search: name, years to search. Civil cases indexed by defendant, plaintiff, on microfiche, computer. Mail turnaround time 2-3 days.
General Information: Court makes copy: $.50 per page. Certification fee: $15 per doc. Payee: Merced Superior Court. No credit cards accepted. Prepayment required. Mail requests: SASE required.

Modoc County

Superior Court 205 S East St, Alturas, CA 96101; criminal phone: 530-233-6515; civil phone: 530-233-6516; fax: 530-233-6500; 8:30AM-5PM. ***Felony, Misdemeanor, Civil, Small Claims, Eviction, Probate.*** www.modocsuperiorcourt.ca.gov/
Civil Records: Access: Mail, in person. Only the court performs in person searches; visitors may not. Search fee: $15.00 per name if search exceeds 10 minutes. Required to search: name, years to search, DOB. Civil cases indexed by plaintiff. Civil records in index file from 1874, computerized since 7/25/95. Mail turnaround 1-2 weeks. Civil PAT available.
Criminal Records: Access: Fax, mail, in person. Only the court performs in person searches; visitors may not. Search fee: $15.00 per name if search exceeds 10 minutes. Required to search: name, years to search, DOB. Criminal records computerized since 1991. Mail turnaround time 1-2 weeks. Criminal PAT available.
General Information: No adoption, juvenile, medical, probation or sealed records released. Will fax documents to local or toll-free number. Court makes copy: $.50 per page. Certification fee: $15 per doc. Payee: Modoc County Superior Courts. Personal checks accepted. Visa/MC accepted. Prepayment required. Mail requests: SASE required.

Mono County

Mammoth Lakes Division - Superior Court PO Box 1037, Mammoth Lakes, CA 93546; 760-924-5444; criminal fax: 760-924-5419; civil fax: same; 9AM-5PM. ***Felony, Misdemeanor, Civil, Eviction, Small Claims.*** www.monocourt.org/
This court performs all record searches for the Bridgeport Branch.
Civil Records: Access: Mail, in person. Only the court performs in person searches; visitors may not. Search fee: $15.00 per name if search exceeds 10 minutes. Required to search: name, years to search. Civil cases indexed by defendant, plaintiff; index on cards. Will only search back 10 years. Mail turnaround time 1 week.
Criminal Records: Access: Mail, in person. Only the court performs in person searches; visitors may not. Search fee: $15.00 per name if search exceeds 10 minutes. Required to search: name, years to search, DOB. Criminal records computerized from 1989, index cards prior. Will only search back 7 years. Mail turnaround time 1 week.
General Information: No juvenile or probation records released. Will fax documents to local or toll-free number. Court makes copy: $.50 per page. Certification fee: $15 per doc plus $1.00 per page copy fee. Payee: Mono Superior Court. Personal checks accepted; credit cards are not. Prepayment required. Mail requests: SASE required.

Superior Court - Bridgeport Branch PO Box 537, Hiway 395, School St, Bridgeport, CA 93517; 760-932-5239; fax: 760-932-7520; 8:30AM-5PM. ***Felony, Misdemeanor, Civil, Small Claims, Probate.***
www.monocourt.org/

All record searches are directed to the court in Mammoth Lakes. There are only 2 staff people at this court. Older records are stored in another building which is hard to access.

Monterey County

Superior Court - Monterey Branch 1200 Aguajito Rd, 2nd Fl, Monterey, CA 93940; 831-647-5800; criminal phone: x3002; civil phone: x3008; 8AM-4PM; make file requests before 3:30PM. ***Civil, Probate, Small Claims.*** www.monterey.courts.ca.gov Court holds the civil records from the city of Salinas. Criminal records for Monterey are held in Salinas.

Civil Records: Access: Mail, in person. Visitors must perform in person searches themselves. Search fee: $15.00 per name. Required to search: name, years to search. Civil cases indexed by defendant, plaintiff. Some civil records computerized since 7/03, on microfiche from 1973, index books prior. Mail turnaround time 2-3 weeks. Public use terminal has civil records. PAT results show middle initial, DOB, SSN. Terminal results may also show SSN. Access court data free at https://www.justicepartners.monterey.courts.ca.gov/Public/JPPublicIndex.aspx, Search calendars at https://www.justicepartners.monterey.courts.ca.gov/Public/JPPublicCalendarSearch.aspx, Online results show middle initial.

General Information: No juvenile or probation records released. Will not fax documents. Court makes copy: $.50 per page. Certification fee: $15 per doc. Payee: Superior Court. Personal checks accepted; credit cards are not. Prepayment required. Mail requests: SASE required.

Superior Court - Salinas Division 240 Church St, Rm 318, Salinas, CA 93901; 831-775-5400; criminal phone: 831-775-5400 x302; fax: 831-775-5497; 9:30AM-4PM. ***Felony, Misdemeanor.*** www.monterey.courts.ca.gov

All criminal records are filed at the Salinas courthouse. All civil, probate, and family law cases are files at the Monterey courthouse.

Criminal Records: Access: Mail, in person, online. Both court and visitors may perform in person searches. Search fee: $15.00 per name if search exceeds 10 minutes. Required to search: name, years to search; also helpful: DOB. Felony records computerized since 1998, on microfiche to 1940s. Misdemeanor records computerized since 1992, on microfiche since 1986. Mail turnaround time 2 weeks. Public use terminal has crim records back to 1990. PAT results show middle initial, DOB, SSN. Access court data free at https://www.justicepartners.monterey.courts.ca.gov/Public/JPPublicIndex.aspx, Search calendars at https://www.justicepartners.monterey.courts.ca.gov/Public/JPPublicCalendarSearch.aspx. Online results show middle initial, DOB.

General Information: No adoption, juvenile, medical, probation or sealed records released. Will not fax documents. Court makes copy: $.50 per page. Certification fee: $15 per doc. Payee: Monterey Superior Court. Personal checks and major credit cards accepted. Add'l fees apply to credit card payments. Prepayment required. Mail requests: SASE required.

King City Div. - Consolidated Trial Court 250 Franciscan Way, King City, CA 93930; 831-386-5200; 8AM-5PM; Public hrs: 9:30AM-4PM. ***Felony, Misdemeanor, Civil Actions under $25,000, Eviction, Small Claims.*** www.monterey.courts.ca.gov Encompasses the cities of King City, Greenfield, Soledad, areas south of King City to the San Luis Obispo County line.

Civil Records: Access: Mail, in person, online. Both court and visitors may perform in person searches. Search fee: $15.00 per name if search exceeds 10 minutes. Required to search: name, years to search. Civil cases indexed by defendant, plaintiff, on computer from 1992, index files from 1983. Records destroyed after 10 years. Mail turnaround time 2-4 weeks. Access court data free at https://www.justicepartners.monterey.courts.ca.gov/Public/JPPublicIndex.aspx, Search calendars at https://www.justicepartners.monterey.courts.ca.gov/Public/JPPublicCalendarSearch.aspx,

Criminal Records: Access: Mail, in person, online. Both court and visitors may perform in person searches. Search fee: $15.00 per name if search exceeds 10 minutes. Required to search: name, years to search; also helpful: DOB. Criminal records computerized from 1992, index files from 1983. Records destroyed after 10 years. Mail turnaround time 2-4 week. Access court data free at https://www.justicepartners.monterey.courts.ca.gov/Public/JPPublicIndex.aspx, Calendar search-same as civil. Online results show middle initial.

General Information: No probation reports released. Will not fax documents. Court makes copy: $.75 per page. Certification fee: $15 per doc. Payee: Monterey County Courts. Personal checks accepted. Visa, AmEx cards accepted; add'l fee charged for credit card. Prepayment required. Mail requests: SASE requested.

Superior Court - Marina Division 3180 Del Monte Blvd, Marina, CA 93933; 831-883-5300; 8AM-2:30PM-M,T,W,F; Closed TH. ***Traffic.*** www.monterey.courts.ca.gov

Access court data free at https://www.justicepartners.monterey.courts.ca.gov/Public/JPPublicIndex.aspx, Search calendars at https://www.justicepartners.monterey.courts.ca.gov/Public/JPPublicCalendarSearch.aspx,

Napa County

Superior Court - Civil 825 Brown St, Napa, CA 94559; 707-299-1130; fax: 707-253-4229; 8AM-5PM. ***Civil, Eviction, Small Claims, Probate.*** www.napa.courts.ca.gov

Civil Records: Access: Mail, in person. Both court and visitors may perform in person searches. Search fee: $15.00 per name if search exceeds 10 minutes. Required to search: name, years to search. Civil cases indexed by defendant, plaintiff, on computer since 1989; prior records on index books or microfilm back to 1800s. Mail turnaround time 2 weeks. Public use terminal has civil records back to 1989. Access to tentative rulings is free at www.napa.courts.ca.gov/Civil/civil_tentative.asp. These only go back about 1 week.

General Information: No adoption, juvenile, medical, probation or sealed records released. Will not fax documents. Court makes copy: $.50 per page. Certification fee: $15 per doc. Payee: Superior Court. Personal checks and major credit cards accepted. Prepayment required. Mail requests: SASE required.

Superior Court - Criminal 1111 3rd St, Napa, CA 94559; 707-299-1180; fax: 707-253-4673; 8AM-5PM. ***Felony, Misdemeanor.*** www.napa.courts.ca.gov

Criminal Records: Access: Mail, in person, fax, online. Both court and visitors may perform in person searches. Search fee: $15.00 per name if search exceeds 10 minutes. Required to search: name, years to search, DOB; also helpful: address. Records on computer back to 1990. Note: There is no fee to search by case number. Mail turnaround time 2 weeks. Public use terminal has crim records back to 1990. Online access at www.napa.courts.ca.gov. A DOB and search fee payment required. An AKA constitutes an add'l separate name search request.

General Information: No adoption, juvenile, medical, probation or sealed records released. Court makes copy: $.50 per page, self serve same. Certification fee: $15 per doc. Payee: Napa Superior Court. Personal checks accepted. Visa/MC accepted. Prepayment required. Mail requests: SASE required.

Nevada County

Superior Court - Civil 201 Church St, #5, Nevada City, CA 95959; 530-265-1294; probate phone: 530-265-1293; fax: 530-478-5627; 8AM-4PM. ***Civil, Eviction, Small Claims, Family.*** http://court.co.nevada.ca.us/

Phone number for Evictions and Small Claims is 530-265-1294 or 530-265-1318.

Civil Records: Access: Mail, in person, online. Both court and visitors may perform in person searches. Search fee: $15.00 per name if search exceeds 10 minutes. Required to search: name or case number. Civil cases indexed by defendant, plaintiff, on computer back to 1990. Cases with dispositions available on microfilm in most cases, also some Limited Civil, Small Claims. Mail turnaround time 5 days. Public use terminal has civil records back to 1990. PAT results show name only. Access calendar free at www.court.co.nevada.ca.us/cgi/dba/casecal/db.cgi. Online results show name only.

General Information: No probation reports released. Will not fax documents. Court makes copy: $.50 per page. Certification fee: $15 per doc. Payee: Nevada County Superior Court. Personal checks accepted; credit cards are not. Prepayment required. Mail requests: SASE required.

Superior Court - Criminal 201 Church St, #7, Nevada City, CA 95959; 530-265-1311; criminal phone: 530-265-1311; fax: 530-478-1938; 8AM-4PM. ***Felony, Misdemeanor.*** http://court.co.nevada.ca.us/

Criminal Records: Access: Phone, mail, in person, online. Only the court performs in person searches; visitors may not. Search fee: $15.00 per name if search exceeds 10 minutes. Required to search: name, years to search; also helpful: DOB. Criminal records computerized from 1987, felony only prior to 1987; felony in books back to 1800s. Mail turnaround time 2 weeks. Access to case calendar is free at www.court.co.nevada.ca.us/cgi/dba/casecal/db.cgi.

General Information: No adoption, paternity, juvenile, medical, probation or sealed records released. Will fax documents to local or toll free line. Court makes copy: $.50 per page. Certification fee: $6.60 per doc. Payee: Nevada County Superior Courts. Personal checks accepted; credit cards are not. Prepayment required. Mail requests: SASE required.

Truckee Branch - Superior Court 10075 Levon Ave, #301, Truckee, CA 96161; criminal phone: 530-582-7835; civil phone: 530-582-7835; criminal fax: 530-582-7875; civil fax: same; 8AM-4PM. ***Misdemeanor, Civil, Eviction, Small Claims.*** http://court.co.nevada.ca.us/

Civil Records: Access: Mail, in person, online. Both court and visitors may perform in person searches. Search fee: $15.00 per name if search exceeds 10 minutes. Required to search: name, years to search. Civil cases indexed by defendant, plaintiff, on computer from 1991, index files from 1983. Records destroyed after 10 years. Mail turnaround time 1 week. Civil PAT goes back to 1989. Access to case calendar is free at www.court.co.nevada.ca.us/cgi/dba/casecal/db.cgi.

Criminal Records: Access: Mail, in person, online. Both court and visitors may perform in person searches. Search fee: $15.00 per name if search exceeds 10 minutes. Required to search: name, years to search. Criminal records computerized from 1991, index files from 1983. Records destroyed after 10 years. Mail turnaround time 1 week. Criminal PAT goes back to 1992. Access case calendarsfree at www.court.co.nevada.ca.us/cgi/dba/casecal/db.cgi.

General Information: No probation reports released. Will not fax documents. Court makes copy: $.50 per page. Certification fee: $15 per doc. Payee: Superior Court. Personal checks accepted; credit cards are not. Prepayment required. Mail requests: SASE required.

Orange County

Superior Court - Civil 700 Civic Center Dr W, Santa Ana, CA 92701; 714-834-2200; fax: 714-834-5589; 8AM-4PM. ***Civil Actions, Small Claims.*** www.occourts.org This court handles civil actions over $25,000 countywide, but holds only limited civil and small claims cases for this central jurisdiction venue (Santa Ana area).

Civil Records: Access: Mail, in person, online. Both court and visitors may perform in person searches. Search fee: $15.00 per name if search exceeds 10 minutes. Required to search: name, years to search. Civil cases indexed by defendant, plaintiff, on computer from mid 1980s, partial prior to 1986, microfiche and index file from 1900s. Note: This court's fax back service fee is $1.00 per page. Mail turnaround time 1-2 weeks. Public use terminal has civil records back to 9/2003. PAT civil results show middle initial. Access civil case index and calendars free at www.occourts.org/online-services/case-access/. Family court calendars also shown. Civil, small claims, probate cases index for

the county can be purchased on CD; index goes back to 12/31/01 or can be purchased on monthly basis.Online results show middle initial.
General Information: No adoption, juvenile, medical, probation or sealed records released. Will fax back documents. Court makes copy: $.50 per page. Certification fee: $15 per doc. Payee: Clerk of the Court. Personal checks accepted. Visa/MC accepted. Prepayment required. Mail requests: SASE required.

Superior Court - Criminal Operations 700 Civic Center Dr W, Santa Ana, CA 92701; 714-834-2200; 834-5334- info; criminal phone: 714-834-2266; 8AM-4PM. ***Felony, Misdemeanor.*** www.occourts.org
Criminal Records: Access: Mail, in person, online. Both court and visitors may perform in person searches. Search fee: $15.00 per name if search exceeds 10 minutes. Required to search: name, years to search, DOB. Criminal records computerized from 1988, on microfiche and archived from 1966. Note: Dockets in storage may take add'l 5-6 days to retrieve. Mail turnaround time 1-2 weeks. Public use terminal has crim records back to 1995. 8 public access terminals available. Online access to criminal, traffic and calendars free at http://visionweb.occourts.org/Vision_Public/Index.do, click on Cases. Search result includes dispositions, dismissals, sentences, and participants, but no DOB. Index rarely goes back beyond 2002. Also shows names, aliases, and Court True name. The case index can be purchased on CD; index goes back to 12/31/01 or can be purchased on monthly basis. Online results show middle initial. Online results include aliases and physical demographics.
General Information: No adoption, juvenile, medical, probation or sealed records released. Will not fax documents. Court makes copy: $.50 per page. Certification fee: $15 per doc. Payee: Clerk of the Court. Personal checks accepted. Visa/MC accepted. Prepayment required. Mail requests: SASE required.

Central Orange County Superior Court - Limited Jurisdiction PO Box 1138, 700 Civic Ctr Dr W, Santa Ana, CA 92702; criminal phone: 714-834-3575; civil phone: 714-834-3580; fax: 714-834-5589; 8AM-5PM. ***Misdemeanor, Civil Actions under $25,000, Eviction, Small Claims.*** www.occourts.org Includes cities of Santa Ana, Orange, Tustin and surrounding unincorporated territories including Cowan Heights, El Modena, Tustin Marine Air Base, Lemon Heights, Modjeska, Orange Park Acres, Silverado Canyon and Villa Park.
Civil Records: Access: Mail, in person, online. Both court and visitors may perform in person searches. Search fee: $15.00 per name if search exceeds 10 minutes. Required to search: name, years to search, DOB. Civil cases indexed by defendant, plaintiff, on index files and microfiche from 1985. Records destroyed after 10 years. Mail turnaround time 2-4 days. Civil PAT goes back to 1995. Public access terminal is in Rm K107. Access civil case index and calendars free at www.occourts.org/online-services/case-access/. Family court calendars also shown. Civil, small claims, probate cases index for the county can be purchased on CD; index goes back to 12/31/01 or can be purchased on monthly basis.Online results show middle initial.
Criminal Records: Access: Mail, in person, online. Only the court performs in person searches; visitors may not. Search fee: $15.00 per name if search exceeds 10 minutes. Required to search: name, years to search, DOB. Criminal records on index files and microfiche from 1986; on computer since 1995. Records destroyed after 10 years. Mail turnaround time 2-4 days. Criminal PAT available.PAT results show name, DOB. Public access terminal is in Rm K107. Free access to criminal and traffic at http://visionweb.occourts.org/Vision_Public/Index.do, click on Cases. Search result includes dispositions, dismissals, sentences, and participants, but no DOB. Index rarely goes back beyond 2002. Also shows names, aliases, and Court True name. The case index can be purchased on CD; index goes back to 12/31/01 or can be purchased on monthly basis. Online results show middle initial. Online results include aliases and physical demographics.
General Information: No probation reports released. Will not fax documents. Court makes copy: $.50 per page. Cert fee: $15 per case number. Payee: Clerk of Court. Personal checks accepted. Credit cards accepted. Prepayment required. Mail requests: SASE required.

Harbor - Laguna Hills Superior Court - Civil Division 23141 Moulton Pky, Laguna Hills, CA 92653; 949-472-6964; civil phone: 949-472-6968- Sm Claims; 8AM-5PM. ***Civil Actions under $25,000, Eviction, Small Claims.*** www.occourts.org/ Formerly known as South Orange, this includes Aliso Viejo, Capistrano Bch, Coto De Caza, Dana Pt, Laguna (various), Lake Forest, Mission Viejo, Rancho St. Margarita, San Clemente, San Juan Capistrano, Trabuco Canyon.
Civil Records: Access: Mail, in person, online. Both court and visitors may perform in person searches. Search fee: $15.00 per name if search exceeds 10 minutes. Required to search: name, years to search. Civil cases indexed by defendant, plaintiff, in index files and on microfiche back to 1987; on computer back to 2000. Mail turnaround time 2-3 days. Public use terminal has civil records back to 12/1989. Access civil case index and calendars free at www.occourts.org/online-services/case-access/. Family court calendars also shown. Civil, small claims, probate cases index for the county can be purchased on CD; index goes back to 12/31/01 or can be purchased on monthly basis.Online results show middle initial.
General Information: No unlawful detainer records released for 60 days. Will not fax documents. Court makes copy: $.50 per page. Certification fee: $15 per doc. Payee: Clerk of Court. Personal checks accepted. Credit cards accepted. Prepayment required. Mail requests: SASE required.

Harbor - Newport Beach Superior Court Justice Center, 4601 Jamboree Rd, Newport Beach, CA 92660-2595; 866-901-3011, 714-449-8100 x3; civil phone: 949-476-4765 x5; 8AM-5PM. ***Misdemeanor, Civil Actions under $25,000, Eviction, Small Claims.*** www.occourts.org Includes Balboa Island, Corona Del Mar, Costa Mesa, Newport Beach, Irvine, Santa Ana Heights, John Wayne/Orange Co Airport, Lido Isle and surrounding unincorporated areas. Mention issues about criminal division phone service to 714-834-7413.
Civil Records: Access: Mail, in person, online. Both court and visitors may perform in person searches. Search fee: $15.00 per name if search exceeds 10 minutes. Required to search: name, years to search, DOB. Civil cases indexed by defendant, plaintiff, go back 10 years. Mail turnaround time 5-10 days. Civil PAT goes back to 1999. Access civil case index and calendars free at www.occourts.org/online-services/case-access/. Family court calendars also shown. Civil, small claims, probate cases index for the county can be purchased on CD; index goes back to 12/31/01 or can be purchased on monthly basis.Online results show middle initial.
Criminal Records: Access: Mail, in person, online. Only the court performs in person searches; visitors may not. Search fee: $15.00 per name if search exceeds 10 minutes. Required to search: name, years to search, DOB. Criminal records on computer go back 10 years; on microfiche -- felonies kept 75 years, misdemeanors 5 years. Mail turnaround time 5-10 days. Criminal PAT goes back to 1999. PAT results show middle initial, DOB. Online access to criminal, traffic and calendars free at http://visionweb.occourts.org/Vision_Public/Index.do, click on Cases. Search result includes dispositions, dismissals, sentences, and participants, but no DOB. Index rarely goes back beyond 2002. Also shows names, aliases, and Court True name. The case index can be purchased on CD; index goes back to 12/31/01 or can be purchased on monthly basis. Online results show middle initial. Online results include aliases and physical demographics.
General Information: No probation reports nor police reports released. Court makes copy: $.50 per page. Certification fee: $15 per doc. Payee: Clerk of Court. Personal checks accepted; checks must be in-state and be imprinted with name and address. Major credit cards accepted. Prepayment required. Mail requests: SASE required.

Harbor Justice Center - Criminal Division 23141 Moulton Pkwy, Laguna Hills, CA 92653; 949-449-8100; 7:30AM-5PM. ***Felony, Misdemeanor.*** www.occourts.org
Also known as South Justice Center. Includes Capistrano Bch, Coto De Caza, Dana Pt, Laguna Hills, Laguna Niguel, Mission Viejo, Rancho St. Margarita, San Clemente, San Juan Capistrano, Trabuco Canyon.
Criminal Records: Access: Mail, in person, online. Both court and visitors may perform in person searches. Search fee: $15.00 per name if search exceeds 10 minutes. Required to search: name, DOB. Criminal records on computer since 1987; prior records on books. Mail turnaround time 2-3 days. Online access to criminal and traffic free at http://visionweb.occourts.org/Vision_Public/Index.do, click on Cases. Search result includes dispositions, dismissals, sentences, and participants, but no DOB. Index rarely goes back beyond 2002. Also shows names, aliases, and Court True name. The case index can be purchased on CD; index goes back to 12/31/01 or can be purchased on monthly basis. Online results show middle initial. Online results include aliases and physical demographics.
General Information: No probation report, unlawful detainer records released. Will fax out documents. Court makes copy: $.50 per page. Certification fee: $15 per doc. Payee: Clerk of Court. Personal checks accepted. Credit cards accepted. Prepayment required. Mail requests: SASE required.

North Orange County Superior Court PO Box 5000, 1275 N Berkeley Ave, Fullerton, CA 92832-0500; 714-773-4555; 773-4667 (Small Claims); criminal phone: 714-773-4668; civil phone: 714-773-4664 x4; 7:30AM-5PM. ***Felony, Misdemeanor, Civil Actions under $25,000, Eviction, Small Claims.*** www.occourts.org/
Traffic phone- 714-773-4615. Includes the cities of Anaheim, Brea, Buena Park, Fullerton, La Habra, La Palma, Placentia, Yorba Linda and surrounding unincorporated area including Anaheim Hills.
Civil Records: Access: Mail, in person, online. Both court and visitors may perform in person searches. Search fee: $15.00 per name if search exceeds 10 minutes. Required to search: name, also helpful: years to search. Civil cases indexed by defendant, plaintiff. Records destroyed after 10 years. Mail turnaround time 5 days. Civil PAT available. PAT results show name only. Access the PAT at kiosk out front. Access civil case index and calendars free at www.occourts.org/online-services/case-access/. Family court calendars also shown. Civil, small claims, probate cases index for the county can be purchased on CD; index goes back to 12/31/01 or can be purchased on monthly basis.Online results show middle initial.
Criminal Records: Access: Mail, in person, online. Only the court performs in person searches; visitors may not. Search fee: $15.00 per name if search exceeds 10 minutes. Required to search: name, years to search, DOB. All Criminal records are on computer. Records destroyed after 5-7 years from date of conviction. Mail turnaround time 1-10 working days. Criminal PAT available. Access the PAT at kiosk out front. Online access to criminal, traffic and calendars free at http://visionweb.occourts.org/Vision_Public/Index.do, click on Cases. Search result includes dispositions, dismissals, sentences, and participants, but no DOB. Index rarely goes back beyond 2002. Also shows names, aliases, and Court True name. The case index can be purchased on CD; index goes back to 12/31/01 or can be purchased on monthly basis. Online results show middle initial. Online results include aliases and physical demographics.
General Information: No probation reports or UD's for 60 days released. Will not fax documents. Court makes copy: $.50 per page. Certification fee: $15 per doc. Payee: Clerk of Court. Personal checks accepted with proper ID. Major credit cards accepted. Prepayment required. Mail requests: SASE required.

West Orange County Superior Court 8141 13th St, Westminster, CA 92683; 714-896-7181; criminal phone: 714-896-7351; civil phone: 714-896-7191; criminal fax: 714-896-7404; civil fax: 714-896-7404; 8AM-5PM. ***Misdemeanor, Civil Actions under $25,000, Eviction, Small Claims.***
www.occourts.org Includes the cities of Cypress, Fountain Valley, Garden Grove, Huntington Beach, Los Alamitos, Rossmore, Seal Beach, Stanton, Sunset Beach, Surfside, Westminster and adjoining and unincorporated territory.
Civil Records: Access: Mail, in person, online. Both court and visitors may perform in person searches. Search fee: $15.00 per name if search exceeds 10 minutes. Required to search: name, years to search. Civil cases indexed by defendant, plaintiff, on computer back to 1992, microfiche from 1983. Records destroyed after 10 years. Mail turnaround time 2 days. Public use terminal has civil records. Not all civil data on terminal; some restrictions. Access civil case index and calendars free at www.occourts.org/online-services/case-access/. Family court calendars also shown. Civil, small claims, probate cases index for the county can be purchased on CD; index goes back to 12/31/01 or can be purchased on monthly basis.Online results show middle initial.
Criminal Records: Access: Mail, in person, online. Both court and visitors may perform in person searches. Search fee: $15.00 per name if search exceeds 10 minutes. Required to search: name, years to search, DOB. Criminal records computerized from 1996, microfiche from 1983. Most misdemeanor records destroyed after 5 years. Mail turnaround time approx. 4 days. Online access to criminal, traffic and calendars free at http://visionweb.occourts.org/Vision_Public/Index.do, click on Cases. Search result includes dispositions, dismissals, sentences, and participants, but no DOB. Index rarely goes back beyond 2002. Also shows names, aliases, and Court True name. The case index can be purchased on CD; index goes back to 12/31/01 or can be purchased on monthly basis. Online results show middle initial. Online results include aliases and physical demographics.
General Information: No probation reports, unlawful detainer (under 60 days old) records released. Will not fax documents. Court makes copy: $.50 per page. Certification fee: $15 per doc. Payee: Clerk of Court. Personal check/Credit cards accepted. Prepayment required. Mail requests: SASE required.

Orange County Probate Court 341 The City Dr, Orange, CA 92868; 714-935-6061; 8AM-5PM. ***Probate.*** www.occourts.org/probate
Jurisdiction includes juvenile, family law, and mental health filings. Search court calendars free at www.occourts.org/online-services/calendars/; indices at https://ocapps.occourts.org/ProbPubv2/Home.do

Placer County

Superior Court - Civil PO Box 619072, 10820 Justice Center Dr, Roseville, CA 95661; 530-745-2210-info, 916-408-6000; 8AM-3PM (9AM on some W). ***Civil, Eviction, Small Claims, Probate.***
www.placercourts.org The $5.00 computer search by mail request at this office gives access to all county court record types including criminal.
Civil Records: Access: Mail, in person. Both court and visitors may perform in person searches. Search fee: $15.00 per name if search exceeds 10 minutes. Required to search: name, years to search. Civil cases indexed by defendant, plaintiff, on computer from 1992, on microfiche from 1974, archived and index file from 1800s. Mail turnaround time 2 weeks. Public use terminal has civil records back to 1992.
General Information: No adoption, juvenile, medical, paternity, probation or sealed records released. Will fax documents for fee. Court makes copy: $.50 per page. Certification fee: $15 per doc. Payee: Clerk of the Court. Personal checks and major credit cards accepted. Prepayment required. Mail requests: SASE required.

Superior Court - Criminal PO Box 619072, 10820 Justice Center Dr, Roseville, CA 95661; 916-408-6000, 530-745-2210-info, 530-886-1200; 8AM-3PM. ***Felony, Misdemeanor.***
www.placercourts.org Includes Auburn, Penryn, Newcastle, Bowman, Colfax, Weimar, Alta, Dutch Flat, Loomis -- Roseville, Rocklin, Lincoln criminal as of 12/8/97. Has most all county criminal records except Tahoe Department 14.
Criminal Records: Access: Mail, in person. Both court and visitors may perform in person searches. Search fee: $15.00 per name if search exceeds 10 minutes. Required to search: name, years to search, DOB. Criminal Records indexed on computer back to 1992; felonies back to 1999; records go back 10 years. Note: A felony name search here includes all of Placer County computer system records, including the Tahoe Court felony cases. Mail turnaround time 2 weeks. Criminal PAT back to mid-1999.
General Information: No probation reports or copies of warrants released. Will not fax documents. Court makes copy: $.50 per page, self serve same. Certification fee: $15 per doc. Payee: Clerk of the Court. Personal checks accepted. Prepayment required. Mail requests: SASE required.

Tahoe Division - Superior Court PO Box 5669, 2501 N Lake Blvd, Tahoe City, CA 96145; 530-584-3460; criminal: 530-584-3463; civil: 530-584-3464; fax: 530-584-3471; 8AM-3PM. ***Felony (Limited), Misdemeanor, Civil, Eviction, Small Claims, Traffic.*** www.placercourts.org
This court does all areas of law (including felony prelims and guilty pleas) with the exception of Adoptions and Probate and felony trials.
Civil Records: Access: Mail, in person. Only the court performs in person searches; visitors may not. Search fee: $15.00 per name. Required to search: name, years to search, DOB. Civil cases indexed by defendant, plaintiff, computerized since 1999, previous on index cards. Note: Will accept fax search requests under agreement. Mail turnaround time 1 week. Public access terminal only available in Roseville court.
Criminal Records: Access: Mail, in person. Only the court performs in person searches; visitors may not. Search fee: $15.00 per name. Required to search: name, years to search, DOB. Criminal records indexed on cards. Will only search back 10 years; computerized records since 1999. Note: Will accept fax search requests under agreement. A felony name search here includes all of Placer County computer system records. Mail turnaround time 1 week. Public access terminal only available in Roseville court.
General Information: No probation reports released. Will not fax documents. Court makes copy: $.50 per page. Certification fee: $15 per doc. Payee: Clerk of Court. Personal checks accepted. Write "not to exceed $x.xx" on check. No credit cards accepted. Prepayment required. Mail requests: SASE required.

Lincoln Division - Superior Court, CA;
This Lincoln Division is now fully consolidated with the Roseville Court. All traffic cases have been transferred to Roseville custody.

Roseville Division - Superior Court 300 Taylor St, Roseville, CA 95678; 916-783-1600; fax: 916-783-1690; 8AM-3PM. ***Traffic.***
www.placercourts.org This court holds the records for the Foresthill Division Court which has closed, also Lincoln Court Traffic only.

Plumas County

Superior Court - Civil 520 Main St, Rm 104, Quincy, CA 95971; 530-283-6305; probate phone: same; fax: 530-283-6415; 8AM-5PM. ***Civil, Small Claims, Probate.*** www.plumascourt.ca.gov
Civil Records: Access: Phone, fax, mail, in person. Both court and visitors may perform in person searches. Search fee: $15.00 per name if search exceeds 10 minutes. Required to search: name, years to search. Civil cases indexed by defendant, plaintiff, on computer from 1993, archived from 1980, index file from 1850. Mail turnaround time 1 week.
General Information: No adoption, juvenile, confidential, medical, probation or sealed records released. Will fax documents $5.00 per doc. Court makes copy: $.50 per page. Certification fee: $15 per doc. Payee: Plumas County Courts. Personal checks accepted; credit cards are not. Prepayment required. Mail requests: SASE required.

Superior Court - Criminal 520 Main St, Rm 104, Quincy, CA 95971; 530-283-6232; fax: 530-283-6415; 8AM-5PM. ***Felony, Misdemeanor.***
http://plumascourt.ca.gov
Criminal Records: Access: Mail, in person, fax. Only the court performs in person searches; visitors may not. Search fee: $15.00 per name if search exceeds 10 minutes. Required to search: name, years to search, DOB; also, signed release if juvenile. Criminal records indexed on computer back to 1989. Mail turnaround time 1-2 days.
General Information: No probation reports, financial statements or juvenile released. Will fax documents. Court makes copy: $.50 per page. Certification fee: $15 per doc. Payee: Superior Court. Personal checks accepted; credit cards are not. Prepayment required. Mail requests: SASE required.

Chester Branch - Superior Court PO Box 722, 1st & Willow Way, Chester, CA 96020; 530-258-2646; fax: 530-258-2652; 8AM-4PM. ***Civil Actions under $25,000, Eviction, Small Claims.***
www.plumascourt.ca.gov
Civil Records: Access: Phone, mail, in person. Only the court performs in person searches; visitors may not. Search fee: $15.00 per name if search exceeds 10 minutes. Required to search: name, years to search. Civil cases indexed by defendant, plaintiff. Traffic on computer, index cards for civil records. Will only search back 7 years. Records on computer back 13 years. Mail turnaround time 1-2 days.
General Information: No probation reports released. Fee to fax out file $5.00 each. Court makes copy: $1.00 per page. Certification fee: $15 per doc. Payee: Superior Court. Personal checks accepted; credit cards are not. Prepayment required. Mail requests: SASE required.

Portola Branch - Superior Court PO Box 1054, 161 Nevada St, Portola, CA 96122; 530-832-4286; fax: 530-832-5838; 8AM-4PM. ***Civil Actions under $25,000, Eviction, Small Claims, Traffic.***
www.plumascourt.ca.gov
Civil Records: Access: Phone, fax, mail, in person. Only the court performs in person searches; visitors may not. Search fee: $15.00 per name if search exceeds 10 minutes. Required to search: name, years to search. Civil cases indexed by defendant, plaintiff. Traffic on computer, computer for civil records. Court will only search back 10 years. Mail turnaround time ASAP.
Criminal Records: Access: Phone, mail, in person. Only the court performs in person searches; visitors may not. Search fee: $15.00 per name if search exceeds 10 minutes. Required to search: name, years to search. Traffic on computer, computer for criminal records. Court will only search back 10 years. Mail turnaround time ASAP.
General Information: No probation reports released. Will not fax documents. Court makes copy: $1.00 per page. Certification fee: $15 per doc. Payee: Superior Court. Personal checks accepted; credit cards are not. Prepayment required. Mail requests: SASE required.

Greenville Branch - Superior Court PO Box 706, 115 Crescent St, Hiway 89, Greenville, CA 95947; 530-284-7213; fax: 530-284-0857; 8AM-4:30PM. ***Misdemeanor, Small Claims, Eviction, Ordinance.*** www.plumascourt.ca.gov

Riverside County

Superior Court - Civil 4050 Main St, Historic Courthouse, Riverside, CA 92501; 951-955-1960; probate phone: 951-955-1970; fax: 951-955-1751; 8AM-4PM. ***Civil Actions, Small Claims, Probate. Eviction.*** www.riverside.courts.ca.gov/
Has Superior Court and Limited Jurisdiction files except for those cases filed within Mt. San Jacinto Judicial Dist. and Three Lakes Judicial Dist. Includes case records from closed branch in Lake Elsinore, Moreno Valley, Perris, Hemet, Corona.
Civil Records: Access: Phone, fax, mail, online, in person. Both court and visitors may perform in person searches. Search fee: $15.00 per name if

search exceeds 10 minutes. Required to search: name, years to search. Civil cases indexed by defendant, plaintiff, on computer and microfiche from 1970, index file from 1956, archived from 1900s. Mail turnaround time 3 days. Public use terminal has civil records back to 1991. Access to civil records is free at www.riverside.courts.ca.gov/pubacc.htm. Online records date back to 1991 for Riverside, 1994 for Corona, 1996 forward for most remaining limited court cases. Also, civil indexes on CD-Rom; fee is $25.00 per month per dept. Civil index back to 1993; Criminal index back to 1990; Family & Probate index back to 1992. Complete name index history is $300 per dept. Online results show name only.
General Information: Online identifiers in results same as on public terminal. No adoption, juvenile, medical, probation, unlawful detainers for 60 days or sealed records released. Will fax docs $1.00 per page. Court makes copy: $.50 per page, self serve same. Certification fee: $15 per doc. Payee: Riverside County Superior Court. Personal checks accepted. Credit cards accepted. Prepayment required. Mail requests: SASE required.

Superior Court - Criminal 4100 Main St, Riverside Hall of Justice, Riverside, CA 92501; 951-955-2300; fax: 951-955-4007; 7:30AM-4PM. ***Felony, Misdemeanor.*** www.riverside.courts.ca.gov/ Criminal indexes available on CD-Rom, but no DOBs. CD-Rom fee is $25.00 per month per department. Overall index goes back to 6/90. Complete name index history is $300.00 per department. For info, contact 951-955-1431.
Criminal Records: Access: Phone, fax, mail, online, in person. Both court and visitors may perform in person searches. Search fee: $15.00 per name if search exceeds 10 minutes. Required to search: name, years to search, DOB; also helpful: SSN. Criminal records on microfiche and computer since 1970, index file from 1956. Mail turnaround time 2 to 4 weeks. Public use terminal has crim records back to 1989. Access criminal records free at www.riverside.courts.ca.gov/pubacc.htm or logon as GUEST at http://75.28.114.12/OpenAccess/. Identifiers- month and year of birth. Online records go back to 1990. Includes Desert and Riverside felony, misdemeanor, & traffic; and misdemeanor from Corona, Palm Springs, Indio and Blythe. Review dates of criminal record indexes at www.riverside.courts.ca.gov/openaccess_criminal.pdf. DOBs on online results show month and year only.
General Information: No adoption, juvenile, medical, probation, unlawful detainers for 60 days or sealed records released. Will not fax out documents. Court makes copy: $.50 per page. Certification fee: $15 per doc. Payee: Clerk of the Court. Personal checks accepted. Visa/MC accepted. Prepayment required. Mail requests: SASE required.

Blythe Division - Superior Court 265 N Broadway, Blythe, CA 92225; criminal phone: 760-921-7828; civil phone: 760-921-7981; criminal fax: 760-921-5936; civil fax: 760-921-7941; 7:30AM-4PM. ***Felony, Misdemeanor, Civil Actions, Eviction, Small Claims, Traffic.***
www.riverside.courts.ca.gov/
Includes Blythe, Ripley. Phone for Family Law is 760-921-7982. Traffic phone is 760-921-7828.
Civil Records: Access: Phone, fax, mail, online, in person. Both court and visitors may perform in person searches. Search fee: $15.00 per name if search exceeds 10 minutes. Required to search: name, years to search. Civil cases indexed by defendant, plaintiff, on computer from 1991, index files from 1983. Records destroyed after 10 years. Mail turnaround time 2 days. Civil PAT goes back to 1994. See Riverside Division location for online information. Blythe online civil court and sc court go back to 1994. Also, see Riverside Civil Division for info on name indexes back to 3/89 on CD-rom.
Criminal Records: Access: Phone, fax, mail, online, in person. Both court and visitors may perform in person searches. Search fee: $15.00 per name if search exceeds 10 minutes. Required to search: name, years to search; also helpful: DOB, sex. Criminal records computerized from 1991, index files from 1983. Records destroyed after 10 years. Note: See Riverside Division for information on name indexes on CD-rom. Mail turnaround time 2 days. Criminal PAT goes back to 11/1992. Access criminal records free at www.riverside.courts.ca.gov/pubacc.htm or logon as GUEST at http://75.28.114.12/OpenAccess/. Identifiers- birth month, year. Online records go back to 1990 for felony, 1991-1993 for misd., 1998 for traffic. Review dates of criminal record indexes at www.riverside.courts.ca.gov/openaccess_criminal.pdf. Also, see Riverside Criminal Division for information on name indexes back to 11/89 on CD-rom. DOBs on online results show month and year only.
General Information: No probation reports released. $1.00 per page to fax in or fax out. Court makes copy: $.50 per page. Certification fee: $15 per doc. Payee: Clerk of the Court. Personal checks accepted. Visa/MC accepted. Prepayment required. Mail requests: SASE required.

Banning Division - Superior Court 135 N Allesandro Rd, Banning, CA 92220; criminal phone: 951-922-7145; civil phone: 951-922-7155; criminal fax: 951-922-7150; civil fax: 951-922-7160; 7:30AM-4PM. ***Felony, Misdemeanor, Civil Actions under $25,000, Eviction, Small Claims, Traffic.***
www.riverside.courts.ca.gov/ Includes Banning, Cabazon, Highland Springs, Poppet Flatt, Silent Valley, Beaumont, Calimesa, Cherry Valley and Whitewater. **Civil Records:** Access: Phone, mail, online, in person. Both court and visitors may perform in person searches. Search fee: $15.00 per name if search exceeds 10 minutes. Required to search: name, years to search; also helpful-case number. Civil cases indexed by defendant, plaintiff, on computer from 1991, index files from 1983. Records destroyed after 10 years. Note: Phone access limited to short searches. Mail turnaround time 2 days. Public use terminal has civil records back to 1997. PAT results show middle initial, DOB. See Riverside Division location for online information. It is assumed that Banning civil and small claims online records go back to 1994. Also, see Riverside Civil Division for info on name indexes back to 3/89 on CD-rom.
Criminal Records: Access: Phone, mail, online, in person. Only the court performs in person searches; visitors may not. Search fee: $15.00 per name if search exceeds 10 minutes. Required to search: name, years to search; also helpful-case number. Criminal records computerized from 1992, index files from 1983. Records destroyed after 10 years. Note: Will perform phone searches for one or two names only. Mail turnaround time 2 days. Access criminal records free at www.riverside.courts.ca.gov/pubacc.htm or logon as GUEST at http://75.28.114.12/OpenAccess/. Identifiers- month and year of birth. Banning criminal records go back to 11/1996. Review dates of criminal record indexes at www.riverside.courts.ca.gov/openaccess_criminal.pdf. Also, see Riverside Criminal Division for information on name indexes back to 11/89 on CD-rom. DOBs on online results show month and year only.
General Information: No probation reports released. Will not fax out documents. Court makes copy: $.50 per page. Certification fee: $15 per doc. Payee: Clerk of the Court. Personal checks and Visa/MC accepted. Prepayment required. Mail requests: SASE required.

Hemet Division - Superior Court 880 N State St, Hemet, CA 92543; civil phone: 951-766-2321; fax: 951-766-2317; 7:30AM-4PM. ***Civil Actions under $25,000, Eviction, Small Claims, Traffic.*** www.riverside.courts.ca.gov/ Includes Aguanga, Anza, Gilman Hot Springs, Hemet, Idylwild, Mountain Ctr, Pine Cove, Redec, Sage, San Jacinto, Sobba Hot Spring, Valle Vista, Winchester.
Civil Records: Access: Mail, in person, online. Both court and visitors may perform in person searches. Search fee: $15.00 per name if search exceeds 10 minutes. Required to search: name, years to search. Civil cases indexed by defendant, plaintiff, on computer from 1996, index files from 1983. Records destroyed after 10 years. Public use terminal has civil records. PAT civil results show middle initial. See Riverside Division location for online information. Hemet civil online records go back to 10/1996, small claims online to 9/1996. Also, see Riverside Civil Division for info on name indexes back to 3/89 on CD-rom. Online results show name only.
General Information: Online identifiers in results same as on public terminal. Will not fax out documents. Court makes copy: $.50 per page. Certification fee: $15 per doc. Payee: Clerk of the Court. Personal checks accepted. Visa/MC accepted. Prepayment required. Mail requests: SASE required.

Indio Division - Superior Court 46-200 Oasis St, Justice Center, Indio, CA 92201; 760-863-8426; 863-7585-post court svcs; criminal phone: 760-863-8206; civil phone: 760-863-8208; probate phone: 760-863-8207; fax: 760-863-8909; 7:30AM-4PM. ***Misdemeanor, Civil Actions under $25,000, Eviction, Small Claims, Probate, Traffic.***
www.riverside.courts.ca.gov/
Includes Desert Center, Eagle Mountain, Indio, La Quinta, Coachella, Bermuda Dunes, Mecca, North Shore, Pinyon Pines, Palm Springs, Salton Sea, Oasis, Thermal. Most Palm Springs records here.
Civil Records: Access: Phone, fax, mail, online, in person. Visitors must perform in person searches themselves. No search fee. Required to search: name, years to search. Civil cases indexed by defendant, plaintiff, on computer from 1993, index files from 1983. Records destroyed after 10 years. Note: Phone and fax access limited to short searches. Civil PAT goes back to 1993. PAT results show name only. See Riverside Division location for online information. Indio online civil records go back to 5/1991 (Palm Springs to 9/1993), online small claims to 4/1994 (Palm Spring sc's to 9/1993). Also, see Riverside Civil Division for info on name indexes back to 3/89 on CD-rom.
Criminal Records: Access: Phone, fax, mail, online, in person. Visitors must perform in person searches themselves. No search fee. Required to search: name, years to search, signed release. Criminal records computerized from 1993, index files from 1983. Records destroyed after 10 years. Mail turnaround time 2 days. Criminal PAT goes back to same as civil.PAT results show name, DOB. Access criminal records free at www.riverside.courts.ca.gov/pubacc.htm or logon as GUEST at http://75.28.114.12/OpenAccess/. Identifiers- month and year of birth. Online felony records go back to 1990. 1991-1993 for misd.; 1998 for traffic Review dates of criminal record indexes at www.riverside.courts.ca.gov/openaccess_criminal.pdf. Also, see Riverside Criminal Division for information on name indexes back to 11/89 on CD-rom. DOBs on online results show month and year only.
General Information: Online identifiers in results same as on public terminal. No probation reports released. Will fax documents $1.00 per page. Court makes copy: $.50 per page, self serve same. Certification fee: $15 per doc. Payee: Clerk of the Court. Personal checks accepted. Credit cards accepted. Prepayment required. Mail requests: SASE required.

Southwest Justice Center - Superior Court 30755 "D" Auld Rd, #1226, Murrieta, CA 92563; 951-304-5000; fax: 951-304-5250; 7:30AM-4PM. ***Felony, Misdemeanor, Family Law.***
www.riverside.courts.ca.gov/ This is a new court as of 1/21/03 that took in the criminal court cases from the closed Superior Courts in Hemet and Perris.
Criminal Records: Access: Fax, mail, online, in person. Both court and visitors may perform in person searches. Search fee: $15.00 per name if search exceeds 10 minutes. Required to search: name, years to search. Criminal records on computer since 1992; prior records on fiche. Note: Phone and fax access limited to short searches. Mail turnaround time 1 week. Public use terminal has crim records. Access criminal records free at www.riverside.courts.ca.gov/pubacc.htm or logon as GUEST at http://75.28.114.12/OpenAccess/. Identifiers- month and year of birth. Records go back to 1990. Review dates of criminal record indexes at www.riverside.courts.ca.gov/openaccess_criminal.pdf. See Riverside Criminal Division for

information on name indexes back to 11/89 on CD-Rom. DOBs on online results show month and year only.
General Information: No adoption, juvenile, medical, probation or sealed records released. Will not fax out documents. Court makes copy: $.50 per page. Certification fee: $15 per doc. Payee: Clerk of the Court. Personal checks accepted. Visa/MC accepted. Prepayment required. Mail requests: SASE required.

Temecula Branch - Superior Court 41002 County Center Dr, Temecula, CA 92591; 951-600-6400; criminal fax: 951-600-6423; civil fax: 951-304-5178; 7:30AM-4PM. ***Civil Actions under $25,000, Eviction, Small Claims, Traffic.***
www.riverside.courts.ca.gov/
Includes Alberhill, Canyon Lk, Perris, Lake Elsinore, Lakeland Village, Sun City, Romoland, Homeland, Lakeview, Glenn Valley, Mead Valley, Murrieta Hot Spgs, Menifee, Meadowbrook, Sedco Hills, Quail Valley, Nuevo, Temecula, Wildonar, Vail Lk.
Civil Records: Access: Phone, mail, online, in person. Both court and visitors may perform in person searches. Search fee: $15.00 per name if search exceeds 10 minutes. Required to search: name, years to search, DOB. Civil cases indexed by defendant, plaintiff, on computer go back 10-12 years; records held for 10 years. Note: Visitors may search on computer only. Mail turnaround time 7 days. Public use terminal has civil records back to at least 3 years. See Riverside Division location for online information. Temecula online civil goes back to 10/1996, small claims online to 9/1996. Also, see Riverside Civil Division for info on name indexes back to 3/89 on CD-rom. Online results show name only.
General Information: Online identifiers in results same as on public terminal. No confidential, adoption or sealed records released. Unlawful detainers not released for 60 days. Will not fax documents. Court makes copy: $.50 per page. Cert fee: $20 per doc. Payee: Clerk of the Court. Personal checks accepted. Credit cards accepted. Prepayment required. Mail requests: SASE required.

Corona Branch - Superior Court, CA; 909-272-5620; ***Felony, Misdemeanor, Civil Actions under $25,000, Eviction, Small Claims.***
This court closed as of 7/03. See Riverside for record files and online access.

Lake Elsinore Division - Superior Court
This court closed 01/01/03. See the Riverside Superior Court for case files and online access.

Palm Springs Division - Superior Court, ***Misdemeanor, Evictions, Traffic.***
This Court closed as of 07/03. See Indio court for court files and online access.

Perris Branch - Superior Court
This court closed 01/01/03. See Riverside Superior Court for case files and online access.

Sacramento County

Superior Court 720 9th St, #102/#101, Sacramento, CA 95814; 916-874-5522; criminal phone: 916-874-5744; civil phone: 916-874-7186; fax: 916-874-5620; 8:30AM-4:30PM. ***Felony, Misdemeanor, Civil Limited/Unlimited.***
www.saccourt.com Includes Galt, Elk Grove, and Walnut Grove branches are closed; this court now holds their Misd. records. Probate, Family Law, Juvenile at Family Relations Courthouse. Small Claims and Unlawful Detainers at Carol Miller Ctr.
Civil Records: Access: Phone, mail, online, in person. Both court and visitors may perform in person searches. Search fee: $15.00 per name if search exceeds 10 minutes. Required to search: name, years to search; also helpful: address, add'l parties to the action. Civil cases indexed by defendant, plaintiff, on microfiche and archived from 1937, index books from 1800s. Mail turnaround time 2-4 weeks. Public use terminal available. PAT results show name only. Access court records back to 1993 free at https://services.saccourt.com/indexsearchnew/. Includes civil, probate, small claims, unlawful detainer, family as well as criminal.
Criminal Records: Access: Phone, mail, online, in person. Both court and visitors may perform in person searches. Search fee: $15.00 per name if search exceeds 10 minutes. Required to search: name, DOB; also helpful: address, years to search, SSN, OLN. Criminal records on computer since 1989 (Superior & Muni), on microfiche and archived from 1962 (Superior only). Mail turnaround time 2-4 weeks. Public use terminal available. PAT criminal results show middle initial. Access criminal records back to 1989 free at https://services.saccourt.com/indexsearchnew/. May also search using DOB. Online results show middle initial.
General Information: Online identifiers in results same as on public terminal. No adoption, juvenile, medical, probation or sealed records released. Will not fax out documents. Court makes copy: $.50 per page. Self serve: $.15 per page. Certification fee: $15 per doc. Payee: Superior Court. Personal checks accepted. Visa/Amex accepted. Prepayment required. Mail requests: SASE required.

Carol Miller Justice Center 301 Bicentennial Circle, Sacramento, CA 95826; 916-875-7354; Traffic- 916-875-7800; civil phone: Sm Claims-916-875-7514; 8:30AM-4:30PM. ***Small Claims, Evictions, Traffic.***
www.saccourt.com/geninfo/location/cmjc.asp
Access court records back to 1993 free at https://services.saccourt.com/indexsearchnew/. Online includes civil, probate, small claims, unlawful detainer, family as well as criminal.

Galt Division - Superior Court, ***Misdemeanor, Small Claims.***
This court is closed as of 03/03. Misdemeanor records and files are now housed at the Sacramento Superior Court. Traffic records were sent to the Carol Miller Justice Center, 916-875-7354/7800.

South Sacramento Superior Court - Elk Grove Branch, ***Misdemeanor, Civil Actions under $25,000, Eviction, Small Claims.***
This court has been closed. All records are located at the Superior Court in Sacramento.

Walnut Grove Branch - Superior Court,
This court was closed, records are now at the Superior Court in Sacramento.

Family Relations Courthouse 3341 Power Inn Rd, Sacramento, CA 95826; 916-875-3400; 8:30AM-4:30PM. ***Probate, Family, Juvenile.***
www.saccourt.com/geninfo/location/wrrfrc.asp
Probate ph-x2; Family Law-x1. Access records back to 1993 free at https://services.saccourt.com/indexsearchnew/. Includes civil, probate, sm claims, unlawful detainer, family. Search also at https://services.saccourt.com/publicdms2/DefaultDMS.aspx.

San Benito County

Superior Court 440 Fifth St, Courthouse Rm 205, Hollister, CA 95023; 831-636-4057; civil phone: 831-636-4057- Ltd civil; fax: 831-636-2046; 8AM-4PM. ***Felony, Misdemeanor, Civil, Small Claims, Eviction, Probate.***
www.sanbenito.courts.ca.gov
Court calendar for the week at the website. Family Court located at 390 Fifth St.
Civil Records: Access: Mail, in person. Both court and visitors may perform in person searches. Search fee: $15.00 per name if search exceeds 10 minutes. Required to search: name, years to search. Civil cases indexed by defendant, plaintiff, on computer since 1990, index books and archived from 1873. Mail turnaround time 1-2 weeks. Civil PAT goes back to 1990.
Criminal Records: Access: Mail, in person. Both court and visitors may perform in person searches. Search fee: $15.00 per name if search exceeds 10 minutes. Required to search: name, years to search. Criminal records on computer since 1989, index books and archived from 1900. Mail turnaround time 1-2 weeks. Criminal PAT goes back to same as civil.
General Information: No adoption, juvenile, medical, probation or sealed records released. Will not fax documents. Court makes copy: $.50 per page. Certification fee: $15 per doc. Payee: Superior Court. Personal checks accepted; credit cards are not. Prepayment required. Mail requests: SASE required.

San Bernardino County

Central District - Superior Court 351 N Arrowhead Ave, San Bernardino, CA 92415; 909-885-0139; criminal phone: 909-384-1888; civil phone: 909-387-3922; criminal fax: 909-387-4993; civil fax: 909-387-4428; 8AM-4PM. ***Felony, Misdemeanor, Civil Actions, Small Claims, Eviction.***
www.sbcounty.gov/courts Civil Division is at 303 W Third ST. Small claims phone- 909-885-0139. Probate cases for this jurisdiction are handled by the Redlands District Superior Court.
Civil Records: Access: Mail, fax, in person, online. Both court and visitors may perform in person searches. Search fee: $15.00 per name if search exceeds 10 minutes. Required to search: name, years to search. Civil cases indexed by defendant, plaintiff, on computer from 1992, microfiche from 1972, archived and index file from 1856. Note: Address mail search access requests to Research Dept. Mail turnaround time 7-10 days. Civil PAT goes back to 1998. PAT results show name only. Online access to civil cases is free at www.sbcounty.gov/courts/genInfo/openaccess.htm. Includes calendars. Online access to "Probate Notes" is free at www.co.san-bernardino.ca.us/courts/ Click on Probate.
Criminal Records: Access: Mail, in person, online. Both court and visitors may perform in person searches. Search fee: $15.00 per name if search exceeds 10 minutes. Required to search: name, years to search, DOB, SSN. Criminal records computerized from 1996, microfiche from 1972, index files from 1983, archived back to 1856. Mail turnaround time 7-10 days. Criminal PAT goes back to same as civil. PAT results show name only. Online access to criminal cases and traffic is free at www.sbcounty.gov/courts/genInfo/openaccess.htm Includes calendars. Also, the daily criminal docket is free at the court main website. Online results show DOB month and year only.
General Information: Online identifiers in results same as on public terminal. No adoption, juvenile, medical, probation or sealed records released. Will not fax documents. Court makes copy: $.50 per page. Certification fee: $15 per doc. Payee: Superior Court. Business and personal checks accepted. Visa/MC accepted. Prepayment required. Mail requests: SASE required.

Barstow District - Superior Court 235 E Mountain View Ave, Barstow, CA 92311; 760-256-4814; criminal phone: 760-256-4758; civil phone: 760-256-4910; fax: 760-256-4884; 7:30AM-4PM. ***Felony, Misdemeanor, Civil, Eviction, Small Claims.***
www.sbcounty.gov/courts
Includes the City of Barstow and the unincorporated areas of Yermo, Lenwood, Daggett, Hinkley and Baker. Probate filings after 10/23/2006 can be found at Redlands District.
Civil Records: Access: Mail, in person, online. Both court and visitors may perform in person searches. Search fee: $15.00 per name if search exceeds 10 minutes. Required to search: name, years to search. Civil cases indexed by defendant, plaintiff, on computer from 1991, index books and microfilm. Microfilm is 3 to 4 weeks current. Records destroyed after 10 years. Mail turnaround time 2-5 days. Civil PAT goes back to 1999. PAT results show name, DOB. Online access to civil cases is free at www.sbcounty.gov/courts/genInfo/openaccess.htm Includes calendars. Access to limited Probate Notes is free at www.co.san-bernardino.ca.us/courts/ Click on Probate.
Criminal Records: Access: Mail, in person, online. Both court and visitors may perform in person searches. Search fee: $15.00 per name if search exceeds 10 minutes. Required to search: name, years to search. Criminal records computerized from 1999, index books and microfilm. Microfilm is 3 to 4 weeks current. Records destroyed after 10 years. Mail turnaround time 2-5 days. Criminal PAT goes back to same as civil.PAT results show name, DOB. Online access to criminal cases and traffic free at www.sbcounty.gov/courts/genInfo/openaccess.htm

. Includes calendars. Also, the daily criminal docket is free at the court main website. Online results show DOB month and year only.
General Information: No probation or confidential reports released. Will not fax documents. Court makes copy: $.50 per page. Certification fee: $15 per doc. Payee: Clerk of the Court. Cashiers checks and money orders accepted. Major credit cards accepted. Prepayment required. Mail requests: SASE required.

Joshua Tree District - Superior Court 6527 White Feather Rd, Joshua Tree, CA 92252; 760-366-5770; criminal phone: 760-366-5775; civil phone: 760-366-5770; fax: 760-366-4156; 8AM-4PM. ***Felony, Misdemeanor, Civil, Eviction, Small Claims.*** www.sbcounty.gov/courts
Includes the incorporated area of City of Twenty-Nine Palms, Town of Yucca Valley and unincorporated areas of Morongo Valley, Pioneertown, Landers, Johnson Valley, Joshua Tree, and Wonder Valley. Probate now at Redlands.
Civil Records: Access: Mail, in person, online. Both court and visitors may perform in person searches. Search fee: $15.00 per name if search exceeds 10 minutes. Required to search: name, years to search. Civil cases indexed by defendant, plaintiff, on computer from 1991, index books from 1983. Records destroyed after 10 years. Mail turnaround time 1 week. Civil PAT goes back to 1998. Online access to civil cases is free at www.sbcounty.gov/courts/genInfo/openaccess.htm Includes calendars. Access to limited Probate Notes is free at www.co.san-bernardino.ca.us/courts/ Click on Probate.
Criminal Records: Access: Mail, in person, online. Both court and visitors may perform in person searches. Search fee: $15.00 per name if search exceeds 10 minutes. Required to search: name, years to search, DOB. Criminal records computerized from 1991, index books from 1983. Records destroyed after 10 years. Mail turnaround time 1 week. Criminal PAT goes back to same as civil. Online access to criminal cases and traffic is free at www.sbcounty.gov/courts/genInfo/openaccess.htm Includes calendars. Also, the daily criminal docket is free at the court main website. Online results show DOB month and year only.
General Information: No probation reports, confidential records released. Will not fax documents. Court makes copy: $.50 per page. Certification fee: $15 per doc. Payee: Joshua Tree Superior Court. Personal checks accepted. Visa/MC accepted. Prepayment required. Mail requests: SASE required.

Rancho Cucamonga District - Superior Court 8303 N Haven Ave, Rancho Cucamonga, CA 91730; criminal phone: 909-350-9764; civil phone: 909-945-4131; fax: 909-945-4154; 8AM-4PM. ***Felony, Misdemeanor, Civil, Eviction, Small Claims, Probate, Traffic.*** www.co.san-bernardino.ca.us/courts
Formerly West District Superior Ct. Includes cities of Montclair, Ontario, Upland, Rancho Cucamonga, Alta Loma, Etiwanda, Guasti and unincorporated area near Mt Baldy. Probate filings after 10/23/2006 can be found at Redlands District.
Civil Records: Access: Phone, fax, mail, in person, online. Both court and visitors may perform in person searches. Search fcc: $15.00 per name if search exceeds 10 minutes; $5.00 if less then 10. Required to search: name, years to search. Civil cases indexed by defendant, plaintiff, on computer since 4/1994, index cards prior. Records destroyed after 10 years. Mail turnaround time 1 week. Civil PAT goes back to 1998. PAT results show name only. Access civil cases free at www.sbcounty.gov/courts/genInfo/openaccess.htm. Includes calendars. Access to limited Probate Notes is free at www.co.san-bernardino.ca.us/courts/ Click on Probate.
Criminal Records: Access: Phone, mail, in person, online. Both court and visitors may perform in person searches. Search fee: $15.00 per name if search exceeds 10 minutes. Required to search: name, years to search; also helpful: DOB. Criminal records computerized since 1994, prior on index cards and microfiche. Mail turnaround time 2-4 weeks. Criminal PAT goes back to 1994. PAT results show name, DOB year of birth only. Access to criminal cases and traffic is free at www.sbcounty.gov/courts/genInfo/openaccess.htm Includes calendars. Also, daily criminal docket is free at court main website. DOB on internet results shows year of birth only.
General Information: No probation reports released. Will not fax out docs. Court makes copy: $.50 per page. Certification fee: $15 per doc. Payee: Superior Court. Personal checks not accepted for criminal records. Visa/MC accepted for civil records. Prepayment required. Mail requests: SASE required.

Victorville District - Superior Court 14455 Civic Dr, Victorville, CA 92392; 760-245-6215; criminal phone: x2; civil phone: x7, sm claims/evict-x7; criminal fax: 760-243-8794; civil fax: 760-243-8790; 8AM-4PM. ***Felony, Misdemeanor, Civil, Eviction, Small Claims, Probate.***
www.sbcounty.gov/courts
Includes the Cities of Victorville, Adelanto Hesperia and the areas of Apple Valley, El Mirage, Helendale, Lucerne Valley, Oro Grande, Phelan, Pinon Hill, Oakhills and Wrightwood. Probate filings after 10/23/2006 can be found at Redlands District.
Civil Records: Access: Mail, in person, online. Both court and visitors may perform in person searches. Search fee: $15.00 per name if search exceeds 10 minutes. Required to search: name, years to search. Civil cases indexed by defendant, plaintiff, on microfiche from 1982 to 7/1999, on computer from 1989 to present, index books prior. Records destroyed after 10 years. Note: 10/03/2008, selected Law & Motion matters filed in the Victorville Court will be heard by videoconferencing or CourtCall by Judge Joseph Brisco in Needles. Mail turnaround time within 2 weeks. Civil PAT goes back to 1984. Online access to civil cases is free at www.sbcounty.gov/courts/genInfo/openaccess.htm Includes calendars. Access to limited Probate Notes is free at www.co.san-bernardino.ca.us/courts/ Click on Probate.
Criminal Records: Access: Mail, in person, online. Both court and visitors may perform in person searches. Search fee: $15.00 per name if search exceeds 10 minutes. Required to search: name, years to search; also helpful: DOB, date of offense. Criminal index books by defendant 1986 - present. Note: Only court allowed to search computer index. Mail turnaround time within 2 weeks. Criminal PAT goes back to 1998. Online access to criminal cases and traffic is free at www.sbcounty.gov/courts/genInfo/openaccess.htm . Includes calendars. Also, the daily criminal docket is free at the court main website. Online results show DOB month and year only.
General Information: No probation reports released. Will not fax documents. Court makes copy: $.50 per page. Certification fee: $15 per doc. Payee: Superior Court. Personal checks accepted. $5.00 minimum for credit card payment. Prepayment required. Mail requests: SASE required.

Big Bear Lake District - Superior Court 477 Summit Blvd, Big Bear Lake, CA 92315; 909-866-0150; fax: 909-866-0160; 8AM-4PM. ***Misdemeanor, Civil Actions under $25,000, Eviction, Small Claims.*** www.sbcounty.gov/courts
Probate filings after 10/23/2006 can be found at Redlands District.
Civil Records: Access: Mail, in person, online. Both court and visitors may perform in person searches. Search fee: $15.00 per name if search exceeds 10 minutes. Required to search: name, years to search. Civil cases indexed by defendant, plaintiff, on computer since 9/1/96; prior on index books. Will only search back 7 years. Mail turnaround time 1 week. Civil PAT goes back to 10 years. Public terminals are found in the lobby of the courthouse. Online access to civil cases is free at www.sbcounty.gov/courts/genInfo/openaccess.htm . Includes calendars. Access to limited Probate Notes is free at www.co.san-bernardino.ca.us/courts/ Click on Probate.
Criminal Records: Access: Mail, in person, online. Both court and visitors may perform in person searches. Search fee: $15.00 per name if search exceeds 10 minutes. Required to search: name, years to search, DOB; also helpful: SSN. Criminal records indexed in books. Will only search back 7 years. Mail turnaround time 1 week. Criminal PAT goes back to 10 years. Public terminals are found in the lobby of the courthouse. Online access to criminal cases and traffic is free at www.sbcounty.gov/courts/genInfo/openaccess.htm . Includes calendars. Also, the daily criminal docket is free at the court main website. Online results show DOB month and year only.
General Information: No probation reports released. Will not fax documents. Court makes copy: $.50 per page. Certification fee: $15 per doc. Payee: Superior Court. Personal checks accepted. Visa/MC accepted. Prepayment required. Mail requests: SASE required.

Chino Division - Superior Court 13260 Central Ave, Chino, CA 91710; 909-356-5337; fax: 909-465-5221; 8AM-4PM. ***Felony, Misdemeanor, Eviction, Small Claims.***
www.sbcounty.gov/courts
Includes City of Chino and surrounding unincorporated area. Rancho Cucamonga Courts handles all civil cases since 01/01/99.
Civil Records: Access: Mail, in person, online. Only the court performs in person searches; visitors may not. Search fee: $5.00 per name. Required to search: name, years to search; also helpful: address. Civil cases indexed by defendant, plaintiff, on computer from 1991, index books from 1983. Records destroyed after 10 years. Mail turnaround time 2 days. Public use terminal has civil records. Online access to civil cases is free at www.sbcounty.gov/courts/genInfo/openaccess.htm
Criminal Records: Access: Mail, in person, online. Only the court performs in person searches; visitors may not. Search fee: $5.00 per name. Required to search: name, years to search, DOB; also helpful: address. Criminal records computerized from 1991, index books from 1983. Records destroyed after 10 years. Mail turnaround time 2 days. Online access to criminal cases and traffic is free at www.sbcounty.gov/courts/genInfo/openaccess.htm . Includes calendars. Also, the daily criminal docket is free at the court main website. Online results show DOB month and year only.
General Information: Online identifiers in results same as on public terminal. No probation reports released. Will not fax documents. Court makes copy: $.50 per page. Certification fee: $15 per doc. Payee: Chino Superior Court. Personal checks and major credit cards accepted. Prepayment required. Mail requests: SASE required.

Fontana District - Superior Court 17780 Arrow Blvd, Fontana, CA 92335; 909-350-9322; 8AM-4PM. ***Felony, Misdemeanor, Civil Actions under $25,000, Eviction, Small Claims, Traffic.*** www.sbcounty.gov/courts Includes the Cities of Fontana, Rialto, Crestmore and the unincorporated areas of Lytle Creek Canyon and Bloomington.
Civil Records: Access: Mail, in person, online. Only the court performs in person searches; visitors may not. Search fee: $15.00 per name if search exceeds 10 minutes. Required to search: name, years to search; also helpful: address. Civil cases indexed by defendant, plaintiff, on computer from 1987, microfilm prior. Mail turnaround time 2-5 days. Online access to civil cases is free at www.sbcounty.gov/courts/genInfo/openaccess.htm . Includes calendars.
Criminal Records: Access: Mail, in person, online. Both court and visitors may perform in person searches. Search fee: $15.00 per name if search exceeds 10 minutes. Required to search: name, years to search; also helpful: DOB. Criminal records computerized from 1987, microfilm prior. Mail turnaround time 2-5 days. Online access to criminal cases and traffic is free at www.sbcounty.gov/courts/genInfo/openaccess.htm . Includes calendars. Also, the daily criminal docket is free at the court main website. Online results show DOB month and year only.
General Information: No probation reports or police records released. Will not fax documents. Court makes copy: $.50 per page. Cert fee: $15 per doc. Payee: Fontana Courts. Personal checks accepted. Prepayment required. Mail requests: SASE required.

Needles District - Superior Court 1111 Bailey Ave, Needles, CA 92363; 760-326-9245; criminal fax: 760-326-9254; civil fax: same; 8AM-4PM. ***Felony, Misdemeanor, Civil Actions under $25,000, Eviction, Small Claims.***
www.sbcounty.gov/courts
Selected Law & Motion matters filed in the Victorville Court will be heard by videoconferencing or CourtCall by Judge Joseph Brisco here.
Civil Records: Access: Mail, in person, online. Only the court performs in person searches; visitors may not. Search fee: $15.00 per name if search exceeds 10 minutes. Required to search: name, years to search. Civil cases indexed by plaintiff. Civil records in index books. Will only search back 7 years. Mail turnaround time 1-2 weeks. Civil PAT goes back to 10 years. Online access to civil cases is free at www.sbcounty.gov/courts/genInfo/openaccess.htm . Includes calendars.
Criminal Records: Access: Mail, in person, online. Only the court performs in person searches; visitors may not. Search fee: $15.00 per name if search exceeds 10 minutes. Required to search: name, years to search. Criminal records computerized from 1990, index books prior. Will only search back 7 years. Mail turnaround time 1-2 weeks. Criminal PAT available. Access criminal cases and traffic free www.sbcounty.gov/courts/genInfo/openaccess.htm. Includes calendars. Also, the daily criminal docket is free at the court main website. Online results show DOB month and year only.
General Information: No probation reports released. Will not fax documents. Court makes copy: $.50 per page. Certification fee: $15 per doc. Payee: Superior Court. Personal checks accepted. Visa/MC cards accepted but not over phone. Prepayment required. Mail requests: SASE required.

Redlands District - Superior Court 216 Brookside Ave, Redlands, CA 92373; criminal phone: 909-885-1269 (traffic); civil phone: 909-888-4260 (probate); fax: 909-798-8588; 8AM-4PM. ***Traffic Infractions, Probate.*** www.sbcounty.gov/courts
Countywide Probate/ Conservatorships here. Felonies/misdemeanors now filed at Central Dist. Court. This Court's district includes traffic violations only for Redlands, Yucaipa, Mentone and unincorporated areas of Angeles Oaks, Barton Flats, Forest Home.
Civil Records: Access: Mail, in person, online. Visitors must perform in person searches themselves. Search fee: $15.00 per name if search exceeds 10 minutes. Required to search: name, years to search, DOB. Civil cases indexed by defendant, plaintiff, on computer from 1998, index books prior. Records destroyed after 10 years. Mail turnaround time 1 week. Civil PAT goes back to 1998. PAT civil results show middle initial. Probate and daily calendars free online at www.sbcounty.gov/courts/genInfo/openaccess.htm . Access to limited Probate Notes is free at www.co.san-bernardino.ca.us/courts/ Click on Probate. Online results show name, DOB.
General Information: Online identifiers in results same as on public terminal. No probation reports released. Will not fax documents. Court makes copy: $.50 per page.Exemplified copy $20.00. Certification fee: $15.00 per doc plus copy fee; exemplification - $20.00. Payee: Superior Court. Personal checks accepted. Visa/MC accepted. Prepayment required. Mail requests: SASE required.

Twin Peaks District - Superior Court 26010 State Hwy 189, Twin Peaks, CA 92391; 909-336-0620; ***Traffic Misdemeanor, Civil under $25,000, Eviction, Small Claims.***
www.sbcounty.gov/courts
Court Closed 10/2/2006; cases now heard at the San Bernardino District Courthouse, 351 N Arrowhead Ave, San Bernardino, 909-885-0139. For traffic- 909-384-1888; Civil- 909-387-3922; Small Claims- 909-387-3170.

San Diego County

Superior Court - Civil PO Box 120128, 330 W Broadway, San Diego, CA 92112-0128; 619-531-3141; civil phone: 619-531-3141; probate: 619-450-7676; fax: 619-515-8997; 8:30AM-3:30PM; records- 9AM-4PM. ***Civil, Probate, Eviction, Small Claims, Probate.*** www.sdcourt.ca.gov
Has Central Div. Ltd Jurisdiction civil cases. For any San Diego County request, always specify which division - Central, East, North or South. Central Records is in the basement, phone- 619-450-7361. Probate at Madge Bradley Bldg, 1409 4th Ave.
Civil Records: Access: Mail, in person, online. Both court and visitors may perform in person searches. Search fee: $15.00 per name if search exceeds 10 minutes. Required to search: name, years to search. Civil cases indexed by defendant, plaintiff, index on computer from 1974 to present. Mail turnaround time 1 day. Public use terminal has civil records back to 1974. Online search of indexes, new filings, calendars and probate examiner notes is free at www.sdcourt.ca.gov/. Click on Online Services. Also, civil records online for fee from Accurint, Courtlink, OpenOnline, or Westlaw. Also, the court sells a county-wide CD-ROM of civil, domestic, mental health, and probate indices, generally from 1974 to 1999, for $25.00. Online results show name only.
General Information: Will not fax documents. Court makes copy: $.50 per copy. Certification fee: $15 per doc. Payee: San Diego Superior Court. Personal checks accepted. Major credit cards accepted, in person only. Prepayment required. Mail requests: SASE required.

Superior Court - Criminal PO Box 120128, 220 W Broadway, San Diego, CA 92112-0128; 619-450-5400, 531-3040; 8:30AM-3:30PM; records- 9AM-4PM. ***Felony, Misdemeanor.***
www.sdcourt.ca.gov
Both General and Limited Criminal records are located here. Central Records is in the basement, phone is 619-450-7361.
Criminal Records: Access: Mail, in person, online. Both court and visitors may perform in person searches. Search fee: $15.00 per name if search exceeds 10 minutes. Required to search: name, years to search, DOB. Felony records on index from 1974 to present, paper ledgers from 1880s. Mail turnaround time 1-2 weeks. Public use terminal has crim records back to 25 yrs for felony, 10 for misd. Online search for case information, calendars, and new filings is free at www.sdcourt.ca.gov/. Click on Online Services. The CD-rom of county criminal records is no longer available Online results show name only.
General Information: No adoption, juvenile, medical, probation or sealed records released. Will not fax documents. Court makes copy: $.50 per page. Certification fee: $15 per doc. Payee: San Diego Superior Court. No out of state personal checks. Major credit cards accepted in person only. Prepayment required. Mail requests: SASE required.

East County Division - Superior Court 250 E Main St, El Cajon, CA 92020; 619-456-4100; 8AM-3:30PM crim; 8:30AM-3:30PM civil. ***Felony, Misdemeanor, Civil, Small Claims, Eviction, Traffic.***
www.sdcourt.ca.gov Court now houses the former municipal court records. Includes El Cajon, La Mesa, Lemon Grove, Santee and unincorporated towns of Alpine, Boulevard, Campo, Dulzura, Grossmont, Jacumba, Jamul, Julian, Lakeside, Mesa Grande, Ramona, Spring Valley, Tecate.
Civil Records: Access: Mail, in person, online. Both court and visitors may perform in person searches. Search fee: $15.00 per name if search exceeds 10 minutes. Required to search: name, years to search. Civil cases indexed by defendant, plaintiff, on computer since 1974; microfilm prior. Mail turnaround time 3-5 days. Civil PAT goes back to 1974. PAT results show name only. Online search of indexes, new filings, calendars and probate examiner notes is free at www.sdcourt.ca.gov/. Click on Online Services. There is a free party name case search from the home page.
Criminal Records: Access: Mail, in person, online. Both court and visitors may perform in person searches. Search fee: $15.00 per name if search exceeds 10 minutes. Required to search: name, years to search; also helpful: DOB. Criminal records on computer since 1974; microfilm prior. Mail turnaround time 3-5 days. Criminal PAT goes back to 1974. Terminal results may or may not include middle initial. Online search for case information, calendars and new filings is free at www.sdcourt.ca.gov/. Click on Online Services. The county system sells a CD-ROM of criminal records; felonies from 6/1974 to 1999; misdemeanors back 10 years. Online results show name only.
General Information: No confidential or sealed records released. Will not fax documents. Court makes copy: $.50 per page. Certification fee: $15 per doc. Payee: Clerk of Superior Court. Personal checks accepted. Law firm and Calif. checks with preprinted name and address accepted only. Major credit cards accepted. Prepayment required. Mail requests: SASE required.

North County Branch - Superior Court 325 S Melrose Dr, Vista, CA 92081; 760-201-8600; 8:30AM-3:30PM. ***Felony, Misdemeanor, Civil Actions, Eviction, Small Claims, Probate, Traffic.***
www.sdcourt.ca.gov
Includes Cities of Oceanside, Del Mar, Carlsbad, Solana Beach, Encinitas, Escondido, San Marcos, Vista and unincorporated towns of Del Dios, Olivehain, San Luis Rey, San Pasqual, Rancho Santa Fe, Valley Ctr., Bonsall, Palomar Mt., Borrego Spr., Pala, etc.
Civil Records: Access: Mail, in person, online. Both court and visitors may perform in person searches. Search fee: $15.00 per name if search exceeds 10 minutes. Required to search: name, years to search. Civil cases indexed by defendant, plaintiff, on computer back to 1993; prior on microfiche and index books. Mail turnaround time 2-3 days. Civil PAT goes back to 10 years. Online search of indexes, new filings, calendars and probate examiner notes is free at www.sdcourt.ca.gov/. Click on Online Services.
Criminal Records: Access: Mail, in person, online. Both court and visitors may perform in person searches. Search fee: $15.00 per name if search exceeds 10 minutes. Required to search: name, years to search. Criminal records computerized from 1993; prior on microfiche and index books. Mail turnaround time 2-3 days. Criminal PAT goes back to same as civil. Online search for case information, calendars and new filings is free at www.sdcourt.ca.gov/. Click on Online Services. The county system sells a CD-ROM of criminal records; felonies from 6/1974 to 1999; misdemeanors back 10 years. Online results show name only.
General Information: No sealed or confidential documents released. Will not fax documents. Court makes copy: $.50 per page. Certification fee: $15 per doc. Payee: Clerk of the Superior Court. Personal checks accepted. Out of state checks not accepted. Major credit cards accepted. Prepayment required. Mail requests: SASE required.

South County Branch - Superior Court 500-C 3rd Ave, Chula Vista, CA 91910; 619-456-4100; 8:30AM-3:30PM civil; 7:30AM-3:30PM crim. ***Felony, Misdemeanor, Civil Actions, Eviction, Small Claims.*** www.sdcourt.ca.gov
Includes National City, Chula Vista, Coronado, Imperial Beach and that portion of the City of San Diego lying south of the City of Chula Vista and contiguous unincorporated areas.
Civil Records: Access: Mail, in person, online. Both court and visitors may perform in person searches. Search fee: $15.00 per name per year. No fee for small claims searches. Required to search: name, years to search. Civil cases indexed by defendant, plaintiff, on computer; for case files prior to 1991, contact Superior Court's Main Records Division, Downtown. Mail turnaround time up to 1 week. Civil PAT goes back to 10 years. Online search of indexes, new filings, calendars and probate examiner notes is free at www.sdcourt.ca.gov/. Click on Online Services.
Criminal Records: Access: Phone, fax, mail, in person, online. Both court and visitors may perform in person searches. Search fee: $15.00 per name if search exceeds 10 minutes. Required to search: name, years to search, DOB. Criminal records on computer, cases files in or before 1986 on microfiche. Mail turnaround time depends on clerk availability. Criminal PAT goes back to same as civil. Online

search for case information, calendars and new filings is free at www.sdcourt.ca.gov/. Click on Online Services. The county system sells a CD-ROM of criminal records; felonies from 6/1974 to 1999; misdemeanors back 10 years. Online results show name only.
General Information: No confidential or sealed records released. Will fax documents to local or toll-free number. Court makes copy: $.50 per page. Certification fee: $15 per doc. Payee: Superior Court (Civil)-Clerk of the Court (Criminal). Personal checks and major credit cards accepted. Prepayment required. Mail requests: SASE required.

Kearny Mesa Branch - Central Division 8950 Clairemont Mesa Blvd, San Diego, CA 92123; 858-634-1919 Small Claims; fax: 858-694-2252; 8:30AM-3:30PM. ***Small Claims, Traffic, Infractions.*** www.sdcourt.ca.gov Traffic phone is 858-634-1800. Some minor infractions are heard at this court.

Ramona Branch - East Division 1428 Montecito Rd, Ramona, CA 92065; 760-738-2435, 760-738-2400; 8AM-3:30PM crim; 8:30AM-3:30PM civil. ***Misdemeanor, Civil Actions under $25,000, Eviction, Small Claims, Traffic.*** www.sdcourt.ca.gov
Jurisdiction over the northeast area of the county.
Civil Records: Access: Mail, in person, online. Only the court performs in person searches; visitors may not. Search fee: $15.00 per name if search exceeds 10 minutes. Required to search: name, years to search. Civil cases indexed by defendant, plaintiff, on computer from 1991, index files since 1983. Files destroyed after 10 years. Mail turnaround time 2-3 days. Online search of indexes, new filings, calendars and probate examiner notes is free at www.sdcourt.ca.gov/. Click on Online Services.
Criminal Records: Access: Mail, in person, online. Only the court performs in person searches; visitors may not. Search fee: $15.00 per name if search exceeds 10 minutes. Required to search: name, years to search; also helpful: DOB. Criminal records computerized from 1991, index files since 1983. Files destroyed after 10 years. Mail turnaround time 2-3 days. Online search for case information, calendars and new filings is free at www.sdcourt.ca.gov/. The county system sells a CD-ROM of criminal records; felonies from 6/1974 to 1999; misdemeanors back 10 years. Online results show name only.
General Information: No probation reports or DMV records released. Will not fax documents. Court makes copy: $.50 per page. Certification fee: $15 per doc. Payee: Clerk of the Court. Personal checks accepted. Credit cards accepted. Prepayment required. Mail requests: SASE required.

San Marcos Branch - North Division ***Misdemeanor, Traffic.*** On July 14, 2003, they moved into the North County Branch in Vista at 325 S Melrose Dr, #350, Annex Bldg, 92081.

San Francisco County

Superior Court - Criminal 850 Bryant St, Rm 101, Hall of Justice, San Francisco, CA 94103; 415-553-9394, 415-553-1159; 8AM-4:30PM. ***Felony, Misdemeanor.*** http://sfgov.org/site/courts_index.asp
Records Dept- 415-553-1665. Court Mgr phone- 415-553-1897.
Criminal Records: Access: Mail, in person. Both court and visitors may perform in person searches. Search fee: $15.00 per name if search exceeds 10 minutes. Add warehouse retrieval fee of $5.00 for archived records. Required to search: name, years to search, DOB. Criminal records go back to the beginning. Note: If searching by mail, direct your request to "Prior Convictions" Mail turnaround time 1 week.
General Information: No medical, probation or sealed records released. No fee to fax documents if prepaid. Court makes copy: $.50 per page. Certification fee: $15 per doc. Payee: Clerk of the Superior Court. Personal checks accepted with ID. Cashier checks and money orders accepted. Visa/MC cards accepted in person only. Prepayment required. Mail requests: SASE required.

Superior Court - Civil 400 McAllister St, #103, San Francisco, CA 94102; 415-551-4000 (general info); 415-551-3802 records section; civil phone: 415-551-3888; probate: 415-551-3892/3891/3893; fax: 415-551-3801; 8AM-4PM; records Rm- 10AM-4PM. ***Civil, Small Claims, Eviction, Probate.*** http://sfgov.org/site/courts_index.asp
Civil Limited and Civil Unlimited sections are now combined. Includes all of San Francisco County, including former municipal court on Folsom St. Small Claims phone- 415-551-3955.
Civil Records: Access: Mail, in person, online. Both court and visitors may perform in person searches. Search fee: $15.00 per name if search exceeds 10 minutes. No charge if easily pulled from computer after 1987. Required to search: name, years to search. Civil cases indexed by defendant, plaintiff, on computer since 1987 for limited and unlimited jurisdiction; indexes on microfilm and microfiche for prior years. Mail turnaround time 7 business days; in person turnaround is 3-5 days. Public use terminal has civil records back to 1987. PAT civil results show middle initial. Public terminal available starting at 8AM. Older records may contain DOB. The San Francisco Superior Court offers online queries by case number, name search, and tentative rulings. You can find the Register of Actions and documents for cases in the following departments: Civil, Family Law, Probate, and Small Claims. Visit www.sfgov.org/site/courts_index.asp. Online results show middle initial.
General Information: Online identifiers in results same as on public terminal. No medical, probation or sealed records released without court order. Will not fax documents. Court makes copy: $.50 per page.If doc is 5 pages or less, it is copied same day. If over 5, it is sent out to be copies and is delayed. Certification fee: $15 per doc. Payee: San Francisco Superior Court. Personal checks accepted. Visa/MC accepted in person only. Prepayment required. Mail requests: SASE required.

San Joaquin County

Superior Court - Criminal 222 E Weber Ave, Rm 101, Stockton, CA 95202; 209-468-2935; fax: 209-468-8577; 7:30AM-4PM. ***Felony, Misdemeanor.*** www.stocktoncourt.org/courts
Criminal Records: Access: Mail, fax, in person, online. Both court and visitors may perform in person searches. Search fee: $15.00 per name if search exceeds 10 minutes. Required to search: name, years to search; also helpful: DOB, SSN. Criminal Records on computer since 1990, on microfiche since 1972, older records archived to 1800s. Mail turnaround time 1-2 weeks. Public use terminal has crim records to 1991. PAT criminal results show middle initial. Access court calendars at www.stocktoncourt.org/stkcrtwwwV5web/SCCalDayIndex.html.
General Information: No juvenile, medical, probation, sealed records released. Will not fax back to the public. Court makes copy: $.50 per page. Certification fee: $15 per doc. Payee: San Joaquin Superior Court. Personal checks and money orders accepted. No credit cards accepted. Prepayment required. Mail requests: SASE required.

Superior Court - Civil 222 E Weber Ave, Rm 303, Stockton, CA 95202-2709; 209-468-2355; civil phone: 209-468-2933; probate phone: 209-468-2843; fax: 209-468-0539; 7:30AM-4PM. ***Civil Actions, Eviction, Small Claims, Probate.*** www.stocktoncourt.org/courts
Includes City of Stockton and suburban areas Farmington and Linden, Delta area and surrounding unincorporated areas. Samll claims phone is 209-468-2949. Family Court is now located at 540 E Main St. Courthouse.
Civil Records: Access: Mail, in person, online. Both court and visitors may perform in person searches. Search fee: $15.00 per name if search exceeds 10 minutes. Required to search: name, years to search. Civil cases indexed by defendant, plaintiff, on computer from 1996; indices/books from 1850-1977; Microfiche 1977-1996. Note: Case inquiry phone numbers when online access is down are- Civil tentative rulings- 209-468-2827; Probate Tentative- 209-468-2866; Probate Notes- 209-468-9895. Mail turnaround time 5-7 days. Public use terminal has civil records back to 1996. PAT civil results show middle initial. Free access to civil case summaries, with name searching, at www.stocktoncourt.org/courts/caseinfo.htm. Also, access court calendars free at www.stocktoncourt.org/stkcrtwwwV5web/SCCalDayIndex.html. Online results show name only.
General Information: Online identifiers in results same as on public terminal. No probation, confidential records released. Will not fax documents. Court makes copy: $.50 per page. Certification fee: $20 per doc plus copy fee; Exemplification- $15.00. Payee: Superior Court. Personal checks accepted. Major credit cards accepted in person only. Prepayment required. Mail requests: SASE required.

Lodi Division - Superior Court - Civil 315 W Elm St, Lodi, CA 95240; 209-331-2101; fax: 209-331-2133; 8AM-4PM. ***Misdemeanor Traffic, Civil Actions under $25,000, Eviction, Small Claims.*** www.stocktoncourt.org/courts
Includes City of Lodi, eight mile road to Sacramento County line, towns of Acampo, Clements, Lockeford, Terminous, Thornton, Woodbridge.
Civil Records: Access: Phone, mail, fax, in person, online. Both court and visitors may perform in person searches. Search fee: $15.00 per name if search exceeds 10 minutes. Required to search: name, years to search. Civil cases indexed by defendant, plaintiff, on computer from 1994, index files from 1989. Records destroyed after 10 years. Note: Case inquiry phone numbers when online access is down are- Civil tentative rulings- 209-468-2827; Probate Tentative- 209-468-2866; Probate Notes- 209-468-9895. Mail turnaround time 5 days. Free access to civil case summaries, with name search, www.stocktoncourt.org/courts/caseinfo.htm. Also, access court calendars free at www.stocktoncourt.org/stkcrtwwwV5web/SCCalDayIndex.html. Online results show name only.
General Information: No probation reports released. Will not fax documents. Court makes copy: $.50 per page. Certification fee: $15 per doc. Payee: Superior Court. Personal checks/major credit cards accepted. Prepayment required. Mail requests: SASE required.

Lodi Division - Superior Court - Criminal 230 W Elm St, Lodi, CA; 209-331-2121; fax: 209-331-2135; 8AM-4PM. ***Felony, Misdemeanor.*** www.stocktoncourt.org/courts
Includes City of Lodi, eight mile road to Sacramento County line, towns of Acampo, Clements, Lockeford, Terminous, Thornton, Woodbridge.
Criminal Records: Access: Phone, mail, fax, in person. Both court and visitors may perform in person searches. Search fee: $15.00 per name if search exceeds 10 minutes. Required to search: name, years to search, DOB; also helpful: address, SSN, sex. Criminal records computerized from 1991, index files from 1983. Records destroyed after 10 years. Mail turnaround time 5 days. Public use terminal has crim records back to 1991. PAT results show middle initial, DOB. Access court calendars free at www.stocktoncourt.org/stkcrtwwwV5web/SCCalDayIndex.html.
General Information: No probation reports released. Will not fax documents. Court makes copy: $.50 per page. Certification fee: $15 per doc. Payee: Superior Court. Personal checks accepted only for payments above $10.00. Visa/MC accepted. Prepayment required. Mail requests: SASE required.

Manteca Branch - Superior Court 315 E Center St, Manteca, CA 95336; criminal phone: 209-239-1316; civil phone: 209-239-9188; 8AM-4PM. ***Felony, Misdemeanor, Civil Actions under $25,000, Eviction, Small Claims.*** www.stocktoncourt.org/courts
Includes Cities of Manteca, Ripon, Escalon, French Camp, Lathrop and surrounding unincorporated areas.
Civil Records: Access: Mail, in person, online. Only the court performs in person searches; visitors may not. Search fee: $15.00 per name if search exceeds 10 minutes. Required to search: name, years to search. Civil cases indexed by defendant, plaintiff. Records on microfiche since 1986, index files from 1983. Records destroyed after 10 years. Note: Case inquiry phone numbers when online access is down are-

Civil tentative rulings- 209-468-2827; Probate Tentative- 209-468-2866; Probate Notes- 209-468-9895. Mail turnaround time 1-2 weeks. Civil PAT goes back to 1996. Free access to civil case summaries, with name searching, at www.stocktoncourt.org/courts/caseinfo.htm. Also, access court calendars free at www.stocktoncourt.org/stkcrtwwwV5web/SCCalDayIndex.html.

Criminal Records: Access: Mail, in person, online. Only the court performs in person searches; visitors may not. Search fee: $15.00 per name if search exceeds 10 minutes. Required to search: name, years to search; also helpful: DOB. Criminal records on computer since 1990, microfiche since 1986, index files from 1983. Records destroyed after 10 years. Note: Use of special request form required to view files in person. Mail turnaround time 1-2 weeks. Criminal PAT available. Access court calendars at www.stocktoncourt.org/stkcrtwwwV5web/SCCalDayIndex.html. Online results show name only.

General Information: No judge's notes, probation or police reports released. Will not fax documents. Court makes copy: $.50 per page. Certification fee: $15 per doc. Payee: Superior Court. Personal checks accepted. Visa/MC accepted. Prepayment required. Mail requests: SASE required.

Tracy Branch - Superior Court 475 E 10th St, Tracy, CA 95376; criminal phone: 209-831-5900; civil phone: 209-831-5902; fax: 209-831-5919; 8AM-4PM. ***Felony, Misdemeanor, Civil Actions under $25,000, Eviction, Small Claims.*** www.stocktoncourt.org/courts All closed cases are located at the Manteca court; search there. This Tracy Court includes Cities of Tracy, Banta, portion of Vernalis and surrounding unincorporated area.

Civil Records: Access: Phone, mail, in person, online. Only the court performs in person searches; visitors may not. Search fee: $15.00 per name if search exceeds 10 minutes. Required to search: name, years to search. Civil cases indexed by defendant, plaintiff, on computer since 3/95; on index files from 1983. Records destroyed after 10 years. Note: Case inquiry phone numbers when online access is down are- Civil tentative rulings- 209-468-2827; Probate Tentative- 209-468-2866; Probate Notes- 209-468-9895. Mail turnaround time 5-10 days. Free access to civil case summaries, with name searching, at www.stocktoncourt.org/courts/caseinfo.htm. Also, access court calendars free at www.stocktoncourt.org/stkcrtwwwV5web/SCCalDayIndex.html.

Criminal Records: Access: Mail, in person, online. Only the court performs in person searches; visitors may not. Search fee: $15.00 per name if search exceeds 10 minutes. Required to search: name, years to search, DOB. Criminal records computerized from 1991; on index files from 1983. Records destroyed after 10 years. Mail turnaround time 5-10 days. Access court calendars free at www.stocktoncourt.org/stkcrtwwwV5web/SCCalDayIndex.html. Online results show name only.

General Information: No probation reports, DMV history and criminal history records released. Will not fax documents. Court makes copy: $.50 per page. Certification fee: $15 per doc. Payee: Tracy Superior Court. Personal checks accepted. Visa/MC accepted. Prepayment required. Mail requests: SASE required.

San Luis Obispo County

Superior Court - Civil 1035 Palm St, Rm 385, Government Ctr, San Luis Obispo, CA 93408; 805-781-5677; probate phone: 805-781-5242; 8:30AM-4PM. ***Civil Actions, Small Claims, Eviction, Probate, Family Law.*** www.slocourts.net This Court has jurisdiction over all of San Luis Obispo County for Civil actions over $25,000, and also the current and former "limited jurisdiction" (under $25,000) civil cases and small claims in the immediate area.

Civil Records: Access: Mail, in person. Both court and visitors may perform in person searches. Search fee: $15.00 per name if search exceeds 10 minutes. Required to search: name, years to search. Civil cases indexed by defendant, plaintiff, on computer from 1975, index files from 1865. Records destroyed after 10 years. Mail turnaround time 2-5 days. Public use terminal has civil records back to 1975. PAT civil results show middle initial. Access daily calendars from the website.

General Information: No probation reports released. Will not fax documents. Court makes copy: $.50 per page. Cert fee: $15 per doc. Payee: Superior Court. Personal checks and major credit cards accepted. Prepayment required. Mail requests: SASE required.

Superior Court - Criminal Government Center, Rm 220, 1050 Monterey St., San Luis Obispo, CA 93408; 805-781-5143; criminal phone: 805-781-5670; 8:30AM-4PM. ***Felony, Misdemeanor, Traffic.*** www.slocourts.net

Criminal Records: Access: Mail, in person. Both court and visitors may perform in person searches. Search fee: $15.00 if search exceeds 10 minutes; limit 5 names per contact. Required to search: name, years to search. Criminal records on computer and microfiche from 1975, archived and index felony files from late 1800s. Note: A "11 search" is for 1985 to present for Misd, felonies, and non-traffic infractions; a name search of 1975-1985 misd. Records is a "10 search,' or a electronic felony index 1975-1995. Mail turnaround time 7-10 days. Public use terminal has crim records back to 1975-felony; 1985-misdemeanors. Access daily calendar from their website.

General Information: No adoption, juvenile, medical, probation or sealed records released. Will not fax documents. Court makes copy: $.50 per page. Certification fee: $15 per doc. Payee: Superior Court Criminal Court Operations. Personal checks and major credit cards accepted. Prepayment required. Mail requests: SASE required.

Grover Beach Branch - Superior Court 214 S 16th St, Grover Beach, CA 93433-2299; criminal phone: 805-473-7072; civil phone: 805-473-7077; 8:30AM-4PM. ***Misdemeanor, Civil Actions under $25,000, Eviction, Small Claims.*** www.slocourts.net ncludes Nipomo, Grover Beach, Arroyo Grande, Pismo Beach, Oceano, South Coast unincorporated areas.

Civil Records: Access: Phone, mail, in person. Both court and visitors may perform in person searches. Search fee: $15.00 per name if search exceeds 10 minutes. Required to search: name, years to search. Civil cases indexed by defendant, plaintiff; index on cards to 1976; on computer back to 1998 Records destroyed after 10 years. Mail turnaround time 2-3 weeks. Civil PAT goes back to 10 years. PAT results show name only. Access daily calendar from the website.

Criminal Records: Access: Phone, mail, in person. Both court and visitors may perform in person searches. Search fee: $15.00 per name if search exceeds 10 minutes. Required to search: name, years to search. Criminal records indexed on cards to 1976; on computer back to 1986. Records destroyed after 10 years. Mail turnaround time 1 week. Criminal PAT goes back to same as civil. Access daily calendar from their website.

General Information: No probation reports released. Will not fax documents. Court makes copy: $.50 per page. Certification fee: $15 per doc. Payee: Superior Court. Personal checks/major credit cards accepted. Prepayment required. Mail requests: SASE required.

Paso Robles Branch - Superior Court 549 10th St, Paso Robles, CA 93446-2593; criminal phone: 805-237-3080; civil phone: 805-237-3079; 8:30AM-4PM. ***Misdemeanor, Civil Actions under $25,000, Eviction, Small Claims, Traffic.*** www.slocourts.net Includes Atascadero, Templeton, Paso Robles, San Miguel, Shandon, Cholame, areas north and east of the Cuesta Grade.

Civil Records: Access: Phone, mail, in person. Both court and visitors may perform in person searches. Search fee: $15.00 per name if search exceeds 10 minutes. Required to search: name, years to search. Civil cases indexed by defendant, plaintiff, on computer from 1975, index files from 1983. Records destroyed after 10 years. Note: Mail requests limited to 5 at a time. Mail turnaround time 1-7 days. Civil PAT goes back to 10 years. Access daily calendar from the website.

Criminal Records: Access: Phone, mail, in person. Both court and visitors may perform in person searches. Search fee: $15.00 per name if search exceeds 10 minutes. Required to search: name, years to search; also helpful: DOB. Criminal records computerized from 1975, index files from 1983. Records destroyed after 10 years. Note: Mail requests limited to 5 at a time. Mail turnaround time 1-7 days. Criminal PAT goes back to same as civil. Access daily calendar from their website.

General Information: No driving histories, rap sheets, sealed or probation reports released. Will not fax documents. Court makes copy: $.50 per page. Certification fee: $15 per doc. Payee: Superior Court. Personal checks and major credit cards accepted. Prepayment required. Mail requests: SASE required.

San Mateo County

Superior Court 400 County Center, Redwood City, CA 94063; 650-363-4711; criminal phone: 650-599-1170; civil phone: 650-363-4576; probate phone: 650-363-1267; fax: 650-363-4914; 8AM-4PM. ***Felony, Civil Actions over $25,000, Probate.*** www.sanmateocourt.org

Southern Area Limited Criminal, lower-value civil actions, evictions and small claims also located here, but shown in a separate listing.

Civil Records: Access: Mail, in person, online. Both court and visitors may perform in person searches. Search fee: $15.00 per name if search exceeds 10 minutes. Required to search: name, years to search. Civil cases indexed by defendant, plaintiff, and Family Law on computer from 1978; index books prior. Mail turnaround time 1 week. Civil PAT goes back to 1978. PAT results show name only. Public terminal has probate records back to 1972. Online access is free at www.sanmateocourt.org/midx/. Includes probate and small claims.

Criminal Records: Access: Mail, in person, online. Both court and visitors may perform in person searches. Search fee: $15.00 per name if search exceeds 10 minutes. Required to search: name, DOB, SSN, CADL#. Criminal records on computer since 1964; prior on books. Note: Criminal matters only filed by Belmont, Foster City, Half Moon Bay, San Carlos, Menlo Pk, East Palo Alto and unincorporated areas are heard at the Southern Branch. Mail turnaround time 1 week. Criminal PAT goes back to 1964. PAT results show name only. Search all county case records including criminal for free at www.sanmateocourt.org/midx/. Online results show middle initial.

General Information: No confidential jackets on conservatorships & guardianships, adoptions, juvenile, medical, probation or sealed records released. Will fax out documents for $1.00 for 1-10 pages. Court makes copy: $.50 per page. Certification fee: $15 per doc. Payee: Superior Court. Personal checks accepted. Visa/MC accepted. Prepayment required. Mail requests: SASE required.

San Mateo Central Branch 800 N Humboldt St, San Mateo, CA 94401; 650-573-2628; 650-573-2616 Traf.; fax: 650-342-5438; 8AM-4PM. ***Small Claims, Traffic, Infractions.*** www.sanmateocourt.org Small claims phone is 650-573-2628. Includes small claims for Belmont, Burlingame, El Granada, Foster City, Half Moon Bay, Hillsborough, Millbrae, Miramar, Montara, Moss Beach, San Mateo and adjoining unincorporated areas.

Superior Court - Northern Branch 1050 Mission Rd, South San Francisco, CA 94080; 650-877-5773; criminal phone: 650-877-5771; civil phone: 650-877-5705; criminal fax: 650-877-5703; civil fax: 650-615-0875; 8AM-4PM. ***Misdemeanor, Small Claims, Traffic.*** www.sanmateocourt.org Includes Brisbane, Daly City (including Westlake), Pacifica, San Bruno, South San Francisco, the northern coastal towns and all unincorporated areas in the north end of the county including Colma, Bart and Broadmoor. Small Claims phone is 650-877-5778.

Civil Records: Access: Mail, in person, online. Both court and visitors may perform in person searches. Search fee: $15.00 per name if search exceeds 10 minutes. Required to search: name, years to search. Civil cases indexed by defendant, plaintiff, go back to 1959 by name index. Note: Probate filings are accepted here, but there are no probate records to search here. Mail turnaround time 2 days to 2 weeks. Civil PAT goes back to 1978. Online

access is free at www.sanmateocourt.org/midx/. Includes probate and small claims.
Criminal Records: Access: In person, online. Both court and visitors may perform in person searches. Search fee: $15.00 per name if search exceeds 10 minutes. Required to search: name, years to search; also helpful: DOB. Criminal records computerized from 1991, index files from 1983. Records destroyed after 10 years. Criminal PAT goes back to 1964. PAT results show name only. Search all county case records including criminal for free at www.sanmateocourt.org/midx/. Also, search traffic citations at https://www.sanmateocourt.org/traffic/. Online results show middle initial.
General Information: Online identifiers in results same as on public terminal. No probation reports or confidential information records released. Will fax documents to local or toll free line, limit 3-5 pages. Court makes copy: $.50 per page. Certification fee: $15 per doc. Payee: Superior Court. Personal checks and major credit cards accepted. Prepayment required. Mail requests: SASE required for civil.

Superior Ct - Southern Branch Limited
400 County Center, Redwood City, CA 94063; criminal phone: 650-363-4302; civil: 650-363-4576; fax: 650-363-4976; 8AM-4PM. ***Misdemeanor, Civil, Eviction, Small Claims.***
www.sanmateocourt.org Limited Criminal/Civil (former Muni Ct) - Includes Atherton, Belmont, Foster City, Half Moon Bay, Menlo Park, Portola Valley, Redwood City, San Carlos, Woodside, East Palo Alto and unincorporated areas including La Honda, Pescadera, and San Gregorio.
Civil Records: Access: Mail, fax, in person, online. Both court and visitors may perform in person searches. Search fee: $15.00 per name if search exceeds 10 minutes. Required to search: name, years to search. Civil cases indexed by defendant, plaintiff, on computer back to 1959. Mail turnaround time 1-2 weeks. Civil PAT goes back to 1959. Online access is free at www.sanmateocourt.org/midx/.
Criminal Records: Access: Mail, fax, in person, online. Both court and visitors may perform in person searches. Search fee: $15.00 per name if search exceeds 10 minutes. Required to search: name, years to search. Limited Criminal records computerized from 1991, index files from 1983. Records destroyed after 10 years. Note: Only limited criminal cases for the Southern District can be found at this location. Mail turnaround time 1-2 weeks. Criminal PAT goes back to 1991. Search all county case records including criminal for free at www.sanmateocourt.org/midx/. Also, search traffic citations at https://www.sanmateocourt.org/traffic/. Online results show middle initial.
General Information: No probation reports or confidential information records released. Court makes copy: $.50 per side. Certification fee: $15 per doc. Payee: Superior Court. Personal checks accepted. Write "not to exceed $x.xx" on check. Visa/MC accepted in person only. Prepayment required. Mail requests: SASE required.

Santa Barbara County

Superior Ct - Civil - Anacapa Division
Box 21107, 1100 Anacapa St, Santa Barbara, CA 93121; 805-882-4520; civil phone: 805-882-4550; probate phone: 805-882-4520; fax: 805-882-4519; 8AM-4PM. ***Civil Actions, Eviction, Small Claims, Probate.*** www.sbcourts.org/index.asp
Also known as the Anacapa Division. Includes the City of Santa Barbara, Goleta, and adjacent unincorporated areas, Carpenteria and Montecito. Daily calendars free at www.sbcourts.org/pubcal/.
Civil Records: Access: Fax, mail, in person, online. Both court and visitors may perform in person searches. Search fee: $15.00 per name if search exceeds 10 minutes. Required to search: name, years to search. Civil cases indexed by defendant, plaintiff, on computer and microfiche from 1975, archived and index file from 1920. Mail turnaround time 1 week. Public use terminal has civil records back to 1977. PAT civil results show middle initial. Search general civil index 1975 to present or limited civil back to 1977 free at www.sbcourts.org/pubindex/. Online results show name only.
General Information: Online identifiers in results same as on public terminal. No adoption, juvenile, medical, probation or sealed records released. Will not fax documents. Court makes copy: $.50 per page. Certification fee: $15 per doc. Payee: Superior Court. Personal checks, Visa/MC/Discover accepted. Prepayment required. Mail requests: SASE required.

Superior Ct - Criminal - Figueroa Div.
118 E Figueroa St, Santa Barbara, CA 93101; 805-568-3959; 802-882-4735; criminal phone: 805-882-4778-records; fax: 805-882-4647; 7:45AM-4PM; phones- 9AM-N, 1:30-4PM. ***Felony, Misdemeanor, Small Claims.*** www.sbcourts.org/
Includes the City of Santa Barbara, Goleta and adjacent unincorporated areas, Carpenteria, Montecito. For civil cases call Anacapa Division at 805-882-4520. Daily calendars free at www.sbcourts.org/pubcal/.
Criminal Records: Access: Mail, in person. Both court and visitors may perform in person searches. Search fee: $15.00 per name if search exceeds 10 minutes. Add $15 fee if records in storage. Required to search: name, years to search; also helpful: DOB. Criminal records computerized from 1991, index files from 1983, microfiche from 1975. Records destroyed after 10 years. Note: Will accept fax requests from gov't agencies only. A CD-Rom of monthly court indices from all divisions is $40.00. Mail turnaround time 3-5 days. Public use terminal has crim records back to 1991.
General Information: No probation reports released. Will not fax documents. Court makes copy: $.50 per page. cert fee: $15 per doc. Payee: Clerk of the Court. Personal checks and major credit cards accepted. Prepayment required. Mail requests: SASE required.

Santa Maria Cook Div. - Superior Court
PO Box 5369, 312-C E Cook St, Santa Maria, CA 93454-5369; 805-614-6414; fax: 805-614-6616; 8AM-4PM. ***Civil Actions, Probate, Eviction, Small Claims.*** www.sbcourts.org/index.asp
The Cook Division handles Civil; its sister court (Miller Division) handles Criminal. Cook includes Betteravia, Casmalia, Cuyama, Guadalupe, Gary, Los Alamos, New Cuyama, Orcutt, Santa Maria, Sisquoc, Tepusquet and sections of Vandenburg AFB.
Civil Records: Access: Mail, in person, online. Both court and visitors may perform in person searches. Search fee: $15.00 per name if search exceeds 10 minutes. Required to search: name, years to search. Civil cases indexed by defendant, plaintiff, in index files from 1964. Records destroyed after 10 years. Note: Also, a CD-Rom of monthly court indices from all divisions is for $40.00. Mail turnaround time 5 days. Public use terminal has civil records back to 2000. PAT civil results show middle initial. Search general civil index 1975 to present or limited civil back to 1977 free at www.sbcourts.org/pubindex/. Daily calendars free at www.sbcourts.org/pubcal/. Online results show name only.
General Information: No probation reports, financial, judges notes, confidential or sealed records released. Will fax documents $1.00 per page fee. Court makes copy: $.50 per page. Certification fee: $15 per doc. Payee: Clerk of Court. Personal checks accepted. Visa/MC accepted; include name address of card holder. Prepayment required. Mail requests: SASE required.

Santa Maria Miller Division - Superior Court
312-M E Cook St, Bldg E, Santa Maria, CA 93454-5165; 805-614-6590; fax: 805-614-6591; 8AM-4PM. ***Felony, Misdemeanor, Traffic.*** www.sbcourts.org/index.asp
Miller Division is in the same building complex as the Cook Division, which handles civil, small claims, family cases. Miller includes the same jurisdictional area as Cook Division. A CD-Rom of monthly court indices from all divisions is for $40.00.
Criminal Records: Access: Mail, fax, in person. Both court and visitors may perform in person searches. Search fee: $15.00 per name per birthdate if search exceeds 10 minutes. Required to search: complete name and alias, years to search, DOB; also helpful- driver license number. Criminal records in index files from 7/1964. Note: A CD-Rom of monthly court indices from all divisions is $40.00. Mail turnaround time 5 days. Public use terminal has crim records back to 1990, some back to 1980. PAT criminal results show middle initial. Public record terminal has index only.
General Information: No probation reports, financial, judges notes, confidential or sealed records released. Will fax documents $1.00 per page. Court makes copy: $.50 per page. Cert fee: $15 per doc. Payee: Clerk of Court. Personal checks accepted. Visa/MC accepted if you provide name and mailing address. Prepayment required. Mail requests: SASE required.

Lompoc Division - Superior Court
115 Civic Center Plz, Lompoc, CA 93436; 805-737-7789; criminal phone: 805-737-5390; civil phone: 805-737-5452; criminal fax: 805-737-5440; civil fax: same; 8AM-4PM. ***Felony. Misdemeanor, Civil Actions under $25,000, Eviction, Small Claims.***
www.sbcourts.org/ Includes Lompoc and adjacent unincorporated areas including sections of Vandenburg Air Force Base. Daily calendars free at www.sbcourts.org/pubcal/. A CD-Rom of monthly court indices from all divisions is $40.00.
Civil Records: Access: Mail, in person, online. Both court and visitors may perform in person searches. Search fee: $15.00 per name if search exceeds 10 minutes. Required to search: name, years to search. Civil cases indexed by defendant, plaintiff, on computer from 1991, index files from 1983. Records destroyed after 10 years. Mail turnaround time 1 week. Public use terminal available. Search general civil index 1975 to present or limited civil back to 1977 free at www.sbcourts.org/pubindex/. Online results show name only.
Criminal Records: Access: Mail, in person. Both court and visitors may perform in person searches. Search fee: $15.00 per name if search exceeds 10 minutes. Required to search: name, years to search, DOB; also helpful: address. Criminal records computerized from 1991, index files from 1983. Records destroyed after 10 years. Note: Includes Solvang jurisdiction filings from 1997 to present. Mail turnaround time 1 week. Public use terminal available. A CD-Rom of monthly court indices from all divisions is $40.00.
General Information: No probation reports released. Will fax documents $1.00 per page. Court makes copy: $.50 per page. Cert fee: $15 per doc. Payee: Clerk of the Superior Ct. Personal checks accepted. Prepayment required. Mail requests: SASE required.

Solvang Division - Superior Court
1745 Mission Dr, #C, Solvang, CA 93463; 805-686-5040; criminal phone: 805-686-7482; civil phone: 805-686-7499; criminal fax: 805-686-7491; civil fax: same; 8AM-4PM. ***Misdemeanor, Small Claims, Traffic.***
www.sbcourts.org/index.asp
Includes the City of Solvang, Buellton, and adjacent unincorporated areas, Los Olivos and Santa Ynez. Daily calendars free at www.sbcourts.org/pubcal/. A CD-Rom of monthly court indices from all divisions is $40.00.
Civil Records: Access: Phone, mail, in person, online. Both court and visitors may perform in person searches. Search fee: $15.00 per name if search exceeds 10 minutes. Required to search: name, years to search. Civil cases indexed by defendant, plaintiff, on computer from 1997 to present, index lists prior. Mail turnaround time 1 week. Civil PAT goes back to 1976. Search general civil index 1975 to present or limited civil back to 1977 free at www.sbcourts.org/pubindex/. Online results show name only. Also, a CD-Rom of monthly court indices from all divisions is for $40.00.
Criminal Records: Access: Mail, in person. Both court and visitors may perform in person searches. Search fee: $15.00 per name if search exceeds 10 minutes. Required to search: name, years to search, DOB. Criminal records computerized from 1988 to 1996. Note: There are no criminal filings at this court since 1/1997. Court has misdemeanors prior to 1996 only. Mail turnaround time 1 week. Criminal PAT goes back to 1987.
General Information: Online identifiers in results same as on public terminal. No sealed or confidential records released. Will not fax documents. Court makes copy: $.50 per page. Self serve: Self-serve copier across the hall. Certification fee: $15 per

doc. Payee: Superior Court. Personal checks accepted. Visa/MC only accepted at the counter and by phone. Prepayment required. Mail requests: SASE required.

Santa Clara County

Superior Court - Civil 191 N 1st St, San Jose, CA 95113; 408-882-2100; probate phone: 408-882-2100; 8:30AM-4PM. ***Civil, Eviction, Probate, Family.*** www.sccsuperiorcourt.org

Handles cases for San Jose, Milpitas, Santa Clara, Los Gatos and Campbell areas. Santa Clara Courthouse at 1095 Homestead Rd, Santa Clara, but records here, ditto for Family Court, 170 Park Center Plaza (408-481-3500).

Civil Records: Access: Mail, in person, online. Both court and visitors may perform in person searches. Search fee: $15.00 per name if search exceeds 10 minutes. Required to search: name, years to search. Civil cases indexed by defendant, plaintiff, on computer 1993 to present; prior on books to 1800s. Mail turnaround time 2 weeks. Public use terminal has civil records back to 1993. PAT results show name only. Civil, Family, Probate, and Small Claims case records and court calendars are free online at www.sccaseinfo.org. CD-rom is also available, fee-$150.00. Online results show middle initial.

General Information: No probation reports or confidential records released. Will not fax documents. Court makes copy: $.50 per page. Certification fee: $15 per doc. Payee: Clerk of Superior Court. Personal checks and major credit cards accepted. Prepayment required. Mail requests: SASE required.

Superior Court - Criminal 191 N 1st St, 190 W Hedding, Hall of Justice, San Jose, CA 95113-1001; 408-808-6600; 8:30AM-4PM. ***Felony, Misdemeanor.*** www.sccsuperiorcourt.org

Includes the Cities of Alviso, Campbell, Los Gatos, Milpitas, Monte Sereno, San Jose, Santa Clara, and Saratoga. Terraine Courthouse Drug Court, 115 Terraine St (408-491-4700), records also here.

Criminal Records: Access: Mail, in person. Both court and visitors may perform in person searches. Search fee: $15.00 per name if search exceeds 10 minutes. Required to search: name, years to search, DOB. Criminal indexes on microfiche from 1975-present. Old files are kept in archives or on microfilm to 1954. Note: 5 name limit for counter service. Mail turnaround time 3-7 days. Public use terminal has crim records. Criminal case access may be available at the web at some future date.

General Information: No probation, confidential or sealed records released. Will not fax documents. Court makes copy: $.50 per page plus postage charge based on number of copies. Certification fee: $15 per doc. Payee: Santa Clara Superior Court. Personal checks accepted. Visa/MC/Discover/AmEx accepted with $12.95 usage fee. Prepayment required. Mail requests: SASE required.

South County Facility - Superior Court 12425 Monterey Rd, San Martin, CA 95046-9590; 408-695-5000; criminal phone: 408-695-5014; civil phone: 408-695-5012; 8:30AM-4PM. ***Felony, Misdemeanor, Civil Actions under $25,000, Eviction, Small Claims, Traffic.*** http://sccsuperiorcourt.org

Jurisdiction includes the Cities of Gilroy, Morgan Hill, San Martin and surrounding unincorporated areas. Traffic case phone number is 408-695-5011.

Civil Records: Access: Mail, in person, online. Both court and visitors may perform in person searches. Search fee: $5.00 per name if search exceeds 10 minutes. Required to search: name, years to search. Civil cases indexed by defendant, plaintiff, on microfiche. Mail turnaround time 1 week. Civil, Family, Probate, and Small Claims case records and court calendars are free online at www.sccaseinfo.org. CD-rom is also available, fee-$150.00. **Criminal Records:** Access: Mail, in person. Both court and visitors may perform in person searches. Search fee: $5.00 per name if search exceeds 10 minutes. Required to search: name, years to search; also helpful: DOB. Same record keeping as civil. Mail turnaround time 1 week. Criminal case access may be available at the web at some future date.

General Information: No adoption, juvenile, medical, probation or sealed records released. Will not fax documents. Court makes copy: $.50 per page. Certification fee: $15 per doc. Payee: Superior Court. Personal checks accepted. Credit cards accepted. Prepayment required. Mail requests: SASE required.

Palo Alto Facility - Superior Court 270 Grant Ave, Palo Alto, CA 94306; 650-462-3800; 8:30AM-4PM. ***Felony, Misdemeanor, Small Claims, Traffic.*** www.sccsuperiorcourt.org

Includes Palo Alto, Mountain View, Los Altos, Los Altos Hills, Stanford University, Sunnyvale and the surrounding unincorporated areas.

Civil Records: Access: Mail, in person, online. Both court and visitors may perform in person searches. Search fee: $15.00 per name if search exceeds 10 minutes. Required to search: name, years to search. Mail turnaround time 1 week. Civil PAT available. Civil, Family, Probate, and Small Claims case records and court calendars are free online at www.sccaseinfo.org. CD-rom is also available, fee-$150.00.

Criminal Records: Access: Mail, in person. Both court and visitors may perform in person searches. Search fee: $15.00 per name if search exceeds 10 minutes. Required to search: name, years to search; also helpful: DOB. Criminal records on microfiche. Mail turnaround time 1 week. Criminal PAT available.PAT results show name, DOB. Criminal case access may be available at the web at some future date.

General Information: No probation, doctor report, pretrial report records released. Will not fax documents. Court makes copy: $.50 per page. Certification fee: $15 per doc. Payee: Superior Court. Personal checks accepted. Credit cards accepted. Prepayment required. Mail requests: SASE required.

Notre Dame, Sunnyvale, Los Gatos - Superior Court 191 N 1st St, (99 Notre Dame Ave), San Jose, CA 95113; 408-882-2900 N.D.; 408-481-3500 Sunny; 408-370-4440 Los Gat; 8:30AM-4PM. ***Misdemeanor, Family.*** http://sccsuperiorcourt.org

Includes Los Gatos, Monte Sereno towns; Campbell, Saratoga cities; surrounding unincorporated areas; also San Jose, Milpitas, Santa Clara. This is also the mailing address for Los Gatos (14205 Capri Dr) and Sunnyvale Courthouses (605 W El Camino Real).

Civil Records: Access: Phone, mail, in person, online. Both court and visitors may perform in person searches. Search fee: $15.00 per name if search exceeds 10 minutes. Required to search: name, years to search. Civil cases indexed by defendant, plaintiff. Civil record index on microfiche. Public use terminal has civil records. PAT civil results show middle initial. Civil, Family, Probate, and Small Claims case records and court calendars are free online at www.sccaseinfo.org. Name and address appear on online civil search results. CD-rom is also available, fee-$150.00.

Criminal Records: Access: Mail, in person. Both court and visitors may perform in person searches. Search fee: $15.00 per name if search exceeds 10 minutes. Required to search: name, years to search. Criminal records index on microfiche.

General Information: Will not fax documents. Court makes copy: $.50 per page. Certification fee: $15 per doc. Payee: Superior Court. Personal checks accepted. Credit cards accepted, but $12.95 service charge added. Prepayment required.

Santa Cruz County

Superior Court - Civil 701 Ocean St, Rm 110, Santa Cruz, CA 95060; 831-454-2020, 831-420-2200; 8AM-4PM. ***Civil, Probate.*** www.santacruzcourt.org

This court also handles Family Law.

Civil Records: Access: Phone, mail, in person, online. Both court and visitors may perform in person searches. Search fee: $15.00 per name if search exceeds 10 minutes. Required to search: name, years to search. Civil cases indexed by defendant, plaintiff, on computer back to 6/1985; microfiche, archived and index books from 1880. Mail turnaround time 10-15 days. Public use terminal has civil records back to 1985. PAT results show name only. Access civil records free at www.santacruzcourt.org/Case%20Info/index.htm. Includes civil, small claims, family law, probate. Access using case number or party name. Online results show name only.

General Information: No adoption, juvenile, medical, probation or sealed records released. Will not fax documents. Court makes copy: $.50 per page. Cert fee: $15 per doc. Payee: Superior Court. Personal checks accepted. Visa/Amex/Discover accepted. Prepayment required. Mail requests: SASE required.

Superior Court - Criminal 701 Ocean St, Rm 120, Santa Cruz, CA 95060; 831-420-2200 x2; fax: 831-454-2265; 8AM-4PM. ***Felony, Misdemeanor.*** www.santacruzcourt.org

Criminal Records: Access: Fax, mail, in person. Only the court performs in person searches; visitors may not. Search fee: $15.00 per name if search exceeds 10 minutes. Required to search: name; also helpful: years to search, DOB. Criminal records on computer since 1994; older records on microfiche index by party name back to 1972. Mail turnaround time 2-4 weeks. Public use terminal has crim records back to 1994.

General Information: No juvenile, probation or sealed records released. Will fax documents to local or toll free line. Court makes copy: $.50 per page. Certification fee: $15 per doc plus $1.00 per page. Payee: Superior Court. Personal checks and major credit cards accepted. Prepayment required. Mail requests: SASE required.

Watsonville Division - Superior Court 1 2nd St #300, Watsonville, CA 95076; 831-786-7200; fax: 831-782-7250; 8AM-4PM. ***Misdemeanor, Civil Actions under $25,000, Eviction, Small Claims.*** www.santacruzcourt.org

Includes all of Santa Cruz County. Wireless internet available at courthouse for fee.

Civil Records: Access: Mail, in person, online. Both court and visitors may perform in person searches. Search fee: $15.00 per name if search exceeds 10 minutes. Required to search: name, years to search. Civil cases indexed by defendant, plaintiff, on computer from 1992, index books prior. Records destroyed after 10 years. Mail turnaround time 2-5 days. Civil PAT goes back to 2004. PAT results show name only. Search the index at www.santacruzcourt.org/Case%20Info/index.htm. Includes small claims, family law, probate.

Criminal Records: Access: Mail, in person. Both court and visitors may perform in person searches. Search fee: $15.00 per name if search exceeds 10 minutes. Required to search: name, years to search; also helpful: DOB. Criminal records computerized from 1994, microfilm to 1993, index books prior. Records destroyed after 10 years. Note: In person searchers may use microfilm - records back to 1993. Mail turnaround time 2-5 days. Criminal PAT goes back to 1993-2002.

General Information: No probation or juvenile records released. Will not fax documents. Court makes copy: $.50 per page. Self serve: $.15 per page. Certification fee: $15 per doc. Payee: Superior Court. Personal checks accepted. Visa/MC/AmEx accepted. Prepayment required. Mail requests: SASE required.

Shasta County

Superior Court 1500 Court St, Redding, CA 96001; 530-245-6789; criminal fax: 530-245-6483; civil fax: 530-225-5564; 8:30AM-4:30PM. ***Felony, Misdemeanor, Civil, Small Claims, Eviction, Probate.*** www.shastacourts.com

Address #319 for civil division and #219 for criminal division.

Civil Records: Access: Phone, mail, in person, online. Both court and visitors may perform in person searches. Search fee: $15.00 per name if search exceeds 10 minutes. Required to search: name, years to search. Civil cases indexed by defendant, plaintiff, on computer from 1992, index books prior. Mail turnaround time 2-7 days. Civil PAT goes back to 1992. Access to civil division index free back to 1993 at www.shastacourts.com/indexes/index_menu.php.

Criminal Records: Access: Mail, in person, online. Both court and visitors may perform in person

searches. Search fee: $15.00 per name if search exceeds 10 minutes. Required to search: name, years to search. Criminal records computerized from 1992, index books prior. Mail turnaround time 2-7 days. Criminal PAT goes back to same as civil. Access the criminal division index free back to 1993 at www.shastacourts.com/indexes/index_menu.php. Also, access via the Integrated Justice System. Online results show name only.

General Information: No probation or confidential records released. Will fax documents to local or toll free line. Court makes copy: $.50 per page. Certification fee: $15 per doc. Payee: Superior Court. Personal checks accepted. Cash not accepted. Credit cards accepted. Prepayment required. Mail requests: SASE required.

Burney Branch - Superior Court 20509 Shasta St, Burney, CA 96013; 530-335-3571; fax: 530-225-5684; 8AM-N, 1-4:30PM. ***Misdemeanor, Eviction, Small Claims.***
www.shastacourts.com Civil actions handled by Redding Branch since 1992. Prior civil limited jurisdiction records maintained here.

Civil Records: Access: Mail, in person, online. Only the court performs in person searches; visitors may not. Search fee: $15.00 per name if search exceeds 10 minutes. Required to search: name, years to search. Civil cases indexed by defendant, plaintiff, on computer from 1992, index books prior. Mail turnaround time 2-14 days. Access to county civil division index free back to 1993 at www.shastacourts.com/indexes/index_menu.php.

Criminal Records: Access: Mail, in person, online. Only the court performs in person searches; visitors may not. Search fee: $15.00 per name if search exceeds 10 minutes. Required to search: name, years to search, DOB. Criminal records computerized from 1993, index books prior. Mail turnaround time 2-14 days. Online access to criminal division index is free back to 1993 at www.shastacourts.com/indexes/index_menu.php. Also, access via the Integrated Justice System. While there is no public access terminal at this court, there is access at the office next door. Online results show name only.

General Information: No probation, juvenile, or DMV reports released. Will not fax documents. Court makes copy: $.50 per page. Certification fee: $15 per doc. Payee: Superior Court. Personal checks accepted. Write 'not to exceed' a dollar amount on checks. No credit cards accepted at this branch. Prepayment required. Mail requests: SASE required.

Sierra County

Superior Court PO Box 476, 100 Courthouse Sq, 2nd Fl, Downieville, CA 95936; 530-289-3698; fax: 530-289-0205; 8AM-N, 1-5PM. ***Felony, Misdemeanor, Civil, Eviction, Small Claims, Probate.*** www.sierracourt.org
Probate is a separate index at this same address. Probate fax is same as main fax number. There is no court in Loyalton.

Civil Records: Access: Phone, fax, mail, in person. Only the court performs in person searches; visitors may not. Search fee: $15.00 per name if search exceeds 10 minutes. Required to search: name, years to search. Civil cases indexed by defendant, plaintiff, on computer from 1985, index books from 1852. Mail turnaround time 2-4 days.

Criminal Records: Access: Phone, fax, mail, in person. Only the court performs in person searches; visitors may not. Search fee: $15.00 per name if search exceeds 10 minutes. Required to search: name, years to search. Criminal records computerized from 1985, index books from 1852. Mail turnaround time 2-4 days. **General Information:** No adoption, juvenile, medical, probation or sealed records released. Will fax documents $1.00 per page. Court makes copy: $.50 per page. Certification fee: $15 per doc. Payee: Superior Court. Personal checks and major credit cards accepted. Prepayment required. Mail requests: SASE required.

Siskiyou County

Superior Court PO Box 1026, 311 4th St, Yreka, CA 96097; criminal phone: 530-842-8195; civil phone: 530-842-8238; criminal fax: 530-842-8339; civil fax: 530-842-0164; 8AM-4PM; phones- 8AM-3PM. ***Felony, Misdemeanor, Civil, Probate.***
www.siskiyou.courts.ca.gov
The phone number for research is 530-842-8390. Most branch electronic records indexed here, but branches can be searched manually for paper records, except Happy Camp court which is temporarily closed and records are here.

Civil Records: Access: Phone, mail, in person, online. Both court and visitors may perform in person searches. Search fee: $15.00 per name if search exceeds 10 minutes. Required to search: name, years to search. Civil cases indexed by defendant, plaintiff, on computer since 1991, archived and index book from 1900 for felonies. Mail turnaround time 1 week. Civil PAT goes back to 1998. PAT civil results show middle initial. Public terminal here includes case indexes from all four courts. Access to county superior court records is free at www.siskiyou.courts.ca.gov/CaseHistory.asp. Includes traffic but no juvenile/confidential cases.

Criminal Records: Access: Mail, in person, online. Both court and visitors may perform in person searches. Search fee: $15.00 per name if search exceeds 10 minutes. Required to search: name, years to search. Criminal records on computer since 1991, archived and index book from 1900. Mail turnaround time 1 week. Criminal PAT goes back to same as civil. PAT criminal results show middle initial. Online access to criminal records is same as civil

General Information: No adoption, juvenile, medical, probation or sealed records released. Will fax documents to local or toll free line. Court makes copy: $.50 per page. Certification fee: $15 per doc. Payee: Siskiyou Superior Court. Personal checks accepted; credit cards are not. Prepayment required. Mail requests: SASE required.

Weed Branch - Superior Court 550 Main St, Weed, CA 96094; 530-938-2483; civil phone: 530-842-0107; fax: 530-842-0109; 8AM-4PM, phones- 8AM-3PM. ***Misdemeanor, Small Claims.***
www.siskiyou.courts.ca.gov

Civil Records: Access: Mail, fax, in person, online. Both court and visitors may perform in person searches. Search fee: $15.00 per name if search exceeds 10 minutes. Required to search: full name, years to search. Civil cases indexed by defendant, plaintiff, go back to 1980; on computer since 1995. Mail turnaround time 10 days. Public use terminal has civil records back to 1998. PAT civil results show middle initial. Public access terminal available at the Yreka Main court only. Access to county superior court records is free at www.siskiyou.courts.ca.gov/CaseHistory.asp. Includes traffic but not juvenile.

Criminal Records: Access: Mail, fax, in person, online. Both court and visitors may perform in person searches. Search fee: $15.00 per name if search exceeds 10 minutes. Required to search: full name, years to search, DOB, SSN. Criminal records go back to 1994; computerized records back 7 years. Mail turnaround time 10 days. Online access to criminal records is same as civil. Online results show middle initial, DOB.

General Information: Fee to fax out file $1.00 per page. Court makes copy: $.50 per page. Certification fee: $15 per doc. Payee: Siskiyou Superior Court. Personal checks accepted only from party to the case. No credit cards accepted. Prepayment required. Mail requests: SASE required.

Dorris/Tulelake Branch - Superior Court 324 N Pine St, Dorris, CA 96023; 530-397-3161; fax: 530-397-3169; 8-11AM, N-4PM. ***Civil Actions under $25,000, Eviction, Small Claims.***
www.siskiyou.courts.ca.gov
This court only maintains a few misdemeanor records for a year. Most new misdemeanor cases are referred to Weed, CA Branch. This Dorris branch jurisdiction includes the Tulelake court sessions at 591 Main St., Tulelake.

Civil Records: Access: Mail, in person, online. Only the court performs in person searches; visitors may not. Search fee: $15.00 per name. Required to search: name, years to search. Civil records on computer back to 1998; prior on books back to 1992. Mail turnaround time 1 week. Public use terminal has civil records back to 1998. PAT civil results show middle initial. Public access terminal available at the Yreka Main court only. Access to county superior court records is free at www.siskiyou.courts.ca.gov/CaseHistory.asp. Includes traffic but not juvenile.

General Information: No probation reports released. Will not fax documents. Court makes copy: $.50 per page. Certification fee: $15 per doc. Payee: Siskiyou Superior Court. Personal checks accepted. Visa/MC accepted, but not for search fee. Prepayment required. Mail requests: SASE required.

Happy Camp Branch - Superior Court c/o PO Box 1026, c/o 311 4th St, Yreka, CA 96097; 530-493-2327; (at Yreka- 8AM-4PM; phones- 8AM-3PM). ***Civil Actions under $25,000, Eviction, Small Claims.*** www.siskiyou.courts.ca.gov
Closed until further notice; cases now managed by Yreka court, address and phone given here. Happy Camp Branch was located at 28 Fourth St, Happy Camp, CA, 96039.

Solano County

Superior Court - Civil 600 Union Ave, Hall of Justice, Fairfield, CA 94533; 707-207-7330; probate phone: 707-207-7341; fax: 707-435-2950; 8AM-4PM. ***Civil, Eviction, Probate.***
www.solanocourts.com/
Includes Fairfield, Suisun, Vacaville, Dixon, Rio Vista, and surrounding area. Northern Solano Muni. Ct. has been combined with this Court. Probate is a separate office at this same address. Small claims phone-707-207-7335.

Civil Records: Access: Mail, in person, online. Both court and visitors may perform in person searches. Search fee: $15.00 per name if search exceeds 10 minutes. Required to search: name, years to search. Civil cases indexed by defendant, plaintiff, on computer since 1992, microfiche since 1971, archived and index files since 1800s. Note: Phone access limited to short searches. Mail turnaround time 2-3 days. Public use terminal has civil records back to 1992. PAT civil results show middle initial. Online access to civil records is free at http://courtconnect.solanocourts.com/courtconnect/ Also, civil tentative rulings and probate notes are free at www.solanocourts.com/civil_tent.htm. Online results show middle initial.

General Information: No sealed records released. Will not fax documents. Court makes copy: $.50 per page. Certification fee: $15 per doc. Payee: Solano County Courts. Personal checks accepted. Prepayment required. Mail requests: SASE required.

Superior Court - Criminal 530 Union Ave, #200, law and Justice Bldg, Fairfield, CA 94533; 707-207-7380; fax: 707-421-7439; 8AM-4PM. ***Felony, Misdemeanor.*** www.solanocourts.com
The Northern Solano Municipal Court has been combined with the Superior Court. This court includes Fairfield, Suisun City, Vacaville, Dixon, Rio Vista Village and the adjacent unincorporated areas.

Criminal Records: Access: Mail, in person, online. Visitors must perform in person searches themselves. Search fee: $15.00 per name if search exceeds 10 minutes. Required to search: name, years to search; also helpful: DOB, SSN. Superior Court records on computer since 1992, microfiche since 1971; Municipal Court records on computer for past 10 years. Note: Phone questions can only be answered during noon hour. Records from this court found here only, not at other divisions. 5 name limit at counter. Mail turnaround time 1 week. Public use terminal has crim records back to 1999. PAT criminal results show middle initial. Online access to misdemeanor index is free at http://courtconnect.solanocourts.com/courtconnect/. Online results show middle initial.

General Information: Online identifiers in results same as on public terminal. No probation reports released. Will fax out docs to gov't agencies only. Court makes copy: $.50 per page. Certification fee: $15 per doc. Payee: Solano Superior Court. Personal checks and major credit cards accepted. Prepayment required. Mail requests: SASE required.

Vallejo Branch - Superior Court 321 Tuolumne St, Solano Justice Bldg, Vallejo, CA 94590; 707-561-7800; criminal phone: 707-561-7880; civil: 707-561-7830; fax: 707-648-8101; 8AM-4PM. ***Felony, Misdemeanor, Civil, Eviction, Small Claims, Probate.*** www.solanocourts.com

Includes Cities of Vallejo and Benicia and the adjacent unincorporated areas.

Civil Records: Access: Mail, in person, online. Only the court performs in person searches; visitors may not. Search fee: $15.00 per name if search exceeds 10 minutes. Required to search: name, years to search. Civil cases indexed by defendant, plaintiff, on computer from 1/1992, index files from 1983 for Fairfield only. Records destroyed after 10 years. Mail turnaround time 2 days. Public use terminal has civil records back to 1991. PAT civil results show middle initial. Online access to civil records free at http://courtconnect.solanocourts.com/courtconnect/. Also, civil tentative rulings and probate notes are free at www.solanocourts.com/civil_tent.htm.

Criminal Records: Access: Mail, in person, online. Only the court performs in person searches; visitors may not. Search fee: $15.00 per name if search exceeds 10 minutes. Required to search: name, years to search. Criminal records computerized from 1996; index files from 1998. Records destroyed after 5 years. Mail turnaround time 2 days. PAT criminal results show middle initial. Online access to misdemeanor index is free at http://courtconnect.solanocourts.com/courtconnect/ Online results show middle initial.

General Information: No probation reports released. Will fax documents for fee. Court makes copy: $.50 per page. Certification fee: $15 per doc. Payee: Superior Court. Personal checks accepted. Visa, AmEx accepted. Prepayment required. Mail requests: SASE required.

Sonoma County

Superior Court - Criminal 600 Administration Dr, Rm 105J, Hall of Justice, Santa Rosa, CA 95403; 707-521-6500; fax: 707-521-6763; 8AM-4PM M,T,W,F; 8AM-6PM TH; phone- 8AM-N. ***Felony, Misdemeanor.***

www.sonomasuperiorcourt.com/index.php

Archived/older records are located here in Rm 110J.

Criminal Records: Access: Phone, mail, in person, online. Both court and visitors may perform in person searches. Search fee: $15.00 per name if search exceeds 10 minutes. Required to search: name, years to search, DOB. Criminal records computerized from 1985, microfiche and index books 1850 to 1984. Note: Misdemeanor records can be destroyed after 10 years. Mail turnaround time 2-3 weeks. Public use terminal available, crim records go back to 10/1984. Search free calendars directly at www.sonomasuperiorcourt.com/index.php. Online index does not provide register of actions, just case number and parties. Goes back 3 months.

General Information: No adoption, juvenile, medical, probation or sealed records released. Will not fax documents. Court makes copy: $.50 per page.Copy fee $2.25 minimum if copies to be mailed back. Cert fee: $15 per doc plus copy fee; exemplification- $20.00. Payee: Superior Court. No out of state personal checks accepted. No credit cards. Prepayment required. Mail requests: SASE required.

Superior Court - Civil 600 Administration Dr, Rm 107J, hall of Justice, Santa Rosa, CA 95403; 707-565-1100; probate phone: 707-521-6893; 8AM-4PM M,T,W,F; till 6PM TH; phones- 8AM-N. ***Civil, Eviction, Small Claims, Probate.***

www.sonomasuperiorcourt.com/index.php

Archived/older records are located here in Rm 110J.

Civil Records: Access: Mail, in person, online. Both court and visitors may perform in person searches. Search fee: $15.00 per name per each 10 minutes. Required to search: name, years to search. Civil cases indexed by defendant, plaintiff, on computer to 10/84, index files prior. Judgment records destroyed after 10 years, dismissals after 1. Computer index include criminal. Mail turnaround time 3 days to 2 weeks. Public use terminal has civil records back to 1984. Public access terminal includes probate records. If terminal search exceeds 10 minutes, court may charge you $15.00. Search free at www.sonomasuperiorcourt.com/index.php for court calendars, cases recently filed, tentative rulings.

General Information: No probation reports or sealed records released. Will not fax documents. Court makes copy: $.50 per page.Copy fee $2.25 minimum if copies to be mailed back. Certification fee: $15 per doc plus copy fee; exemplification- $20.00. Payee: Superior Court. Personal checks accepted. Write 'not to exceed' or 'NTE' and the estimated amount for copy cost and search cost. No credit cards accepted. Prepayment required. Mail requests: SASE required.

Stanislaus County

Superior Court - Criminal PO Box 1098, 800 11 St, Rm 140, Modesto, CA 95353; 209-558-6000; 8AM-3PM. ***Felony, Misdemeanor.***

www.stanct.org/

Criminal Records: Access: Phone, mail, in person, online. Both court and visitors may perform in person searches. Search fee: $15.00 per name if search exceeds 10 minutes. Required to search: name, years to search, DOB; also helpful- charges, felony/or/misd. Criminal Records on microfiche since 1974, archived back to 1800s. Mail turnaround time 6-8 weeks. Public use terminal has crim records back to 1995. PAT results show name only. Index and case numbers only on public terminal; some records go back further than 1995. Access the yearly case indices free at www.stanct.org/Case_Index/index.html Superior Court Case Index is available alphabetically in a 2-CD set. Case Index is updated quarterly and includes cases filed 1900-1999, and 2000-present day. Cost is $15.00 per each 2-CD set, which includes S&H. Online results show name only.

General Information: No adoption, juvenile, medical, probation or sealed records released. Court makes copy: $.50 per page. Certification fee: $15 per doc. Payee: Superior Court Clerk. Personal checks accepted. Visa/MC accepted. Prepayment required. Mail requests: SASE required.

Superior Court - Civil 801 Tenth St, 4th Fl, Modesto, CA 95354; 209-530-3102; probate phone: 209-525-4432; 8AM-4PM. ***Civil, Eviction, Small Claims, Probate.*** www.stanct.org/

Ceres Branch is operational, but all filings are here. Small Claims is located at 2260 Floyd Ave.

Civil Records: Access: Mail, in person, online. Both court and visitors may perform in person searches. Search fee: $15.00 per name if search exceeds 10 minutes. Required to search: name, years to search. Civil cases indexed by defendant, plaintiff, on computer from 1991, in index files from 1983, microfilm to 1974. Records destroyed after 10 years. Mail turnaround time varies. Public use terminal has civil records. PAT civil results show middle initial. Results include year case was filed. Search yearly case index by name and year at www.stanct.org/Case_Index/index.html. Superior Court Case Index is available alphabetically in a 2-CD set. Case Index is updated quarterly and includes cases filed 1900-1999, and 2000-present day. Cost is $15.00 per each 2-CD set, which includes S&H. Online results show name only.

General Information: No probation or juvenile records released. Will not fax documents. Court makes copy: $.50 per side. Certification fee: $15 per doc. Payee: Superior Court. Personal checks accepted. Visa/MC accepted. Prepayment required. Mail requests: SASE required.

Turlock Division - Superior Court 300 Starr Ave, Turlock, CA 95380; 209-558-6000; fax: 209-664-8009; 8AM-N, 12:30-3PM. ***Small Claims, Traffic, Ordinances, Infractions.***

www.stanct.org/

Sutter County

Superior Court - Civil 463 2nd St, Rm 211, Courthouse East, 2nd Fl, Yuba City, CA 95991; 530-822-3304; probate phone: same; fax: 530-822-3504; 8AM-5PM. ***Civil, Eviction, Small Claims, Probate.***

www.suttercourts.com

Civil Records: Access: Mail, in person. Both court and visitors may perform in person searches. Search fee: $15.00 per name if search exceeds 10 minutes. Required to search: name, years to search, type of case. Civil cases indexed by defendant, plaintiff, in index books and archived from 1800s, on computer back to 1/95. Mail turnaround time 2 days if records on site. Public use terminal has civil records back to 1995. PAT civil results show middle initial. Access calendars at www.suttercourts.com/unprotected/Calendar/themed.asp.

General Information: No adoption, juvenile, medical, probation or sealed records released. Will not fax documents. Court makes copy: $.50 per page. Certification fee: $15 per doc. Payee: Superior Court. Personal checks accepted. Visa/MC accepted. Prepayment required. Mail requests: SASE required.

Superior Court - Criminal 446 2nd St, Yuba City, CA 95991; 530-822-3306; fax: 530-822-3506; 8AM-5PM. ***Felony, Misdemeanor.***

www.suttercourts.com

Criminal Records: Access: Fax, mail, in person. Both court and visitors may perform in person searches. Search fee: $15.00 per name if search exceeds 15 minutes, or the case is pre-1994. Required to search: name, years to search. Criminal docket on books and archived from 1800s, computerized since 1995. Mail turnaround time 1 week. Public use terminal has crim records back to 1995. PAT results show middle initial, DOB. Access calendars free at www.suttercourts.com/unprotected/Calendar/themed.asp.

General Information: No police reports or probation records released. Will fax documents to local or toll free line. Court makes copy: $.50 per page. Cert fee: $15 per doc. Payee: Sutter County Superior Court. Personal checks accepted. Visa/MC accepted. Prepayment required. Mail requests: SASE required.

Tehama County

Superior Court - Civil PO Box 310, 633 Washington St, Rm 17, Red Bluff, CA 96080; 530-527-6441; fax: 530-527-0984; 8AM-5PM. ***Civil, Small Claims, Eviction, Probate, Family Law.***

www.tehamacourt.ca.gov

Civil Records: Access: Mail, in person. Only the court performs in person searches; visitors may not. Search fee: $15.00 per name if search exceeds 10 minutes. Required to search: name, years to search. Civil cases indexed by defendant, plaintiff, on computer back to 1991, archived and index books from 1900s. Note: Tentative rulings back 3 weeks available at the website. Mail turnaround time same day.

General Information: No adoption, juvenile, mental, probation or sealed records released. Will not fax documents. Court makes copy: $.50 per page. Certification fee: $15 per doc. Payee: Tehama County Superior Court Clerk. Personal checks accepted. Major credit cards currently accepted. Prepayment required. Mail requests: SASE required.

Superior Court - Criminal PO Box 1170, 445 Pine St, Red Bluff, CA 96080; 530-527-3563; criminal phone: 530-527-7314; fax: 530-527-0956; 8AM-5PM. ***Felony, Misdemeanor.***

www.tehamacourt.ca.gov

Criminal Records: Access: Mail, in person. Both court and visitors may perform in person searches. Search fee: $15.00 per name if search exceeds 10 minutes. Required to search: name, years to search; also helpful: DOB. Criminal records computerized from 1991, index cards prior. Will only search back 7 years. Mail turnaround time within 1 week.

General Information: No probation reports released. Will not fax documents. Court makes copy: $.50 per page. Certification fee: $15 per doc. Payee: Superior Court. Personal checks accepted; credit cards are not. Prepayment required. Mail requests: SASE required.

Corning Branch - Superior Court 720 Hoag St, Corning, CA 96021; 530-824-4601; fax: 530-824-6457; 8AM-5PM. ***Misdemeanor, Civil Actions under $25,000, Eviction, Small Claims.***

Civil Records: Access: Mail, in person. Both court and visitors may perform in person searches. Search fee: $15.00 per name if search exceeds 10 minutes. Required to search: name, years to search.

Civil cases indexed by defendant, plaintiff; index on cards. Will only search back 7 years; records on computer since 1990. Note: Requests must be in writing. Mail turnaround time 1 week.
Criminal Records: Access: Mail, in person. Only the court performs in person searches; visitors may not. Search fee: $15.00 per name if search exceeds 10 minutes. Required to search: name, years to search; also helpful: DOB. Criminal records computerized from 1990, index cards prior. Will only search back 7 years. Note: Requests must be in writing. Mail turnaround time 1 week.
General Information: No probation reports released. Will fax documents to local or toll free line, if prepaid. Court makes copy: $.50 per page. Certification fee: $15 per doc. Payee: Tehama Superior Court. Personal checks accepted. Visa/MC accepted. Prepayment required. Mail requests: SASE required.

Trinity County

Superior Court PO Box 1258, 11 Court St, Weaverville, CA 96093; 530-623-1208; criminal fax: 530-623-3762; civil fax: same; 8AM-5PM. ***Felony, Misdemeanor, Civil, Eviction, Small Claims, Probate.*** www.trinity.courts.ca.gov/
Probate fax is same as main fax number.
Civil Records: Access: Mail, in person. Only the court performs in person searches; visitors may not. Search fee: $15.00 per name if search exceeds 10 minutes. Required to search: name, years to search. Civil cases indexed by defendant, plaintiff, on microfiche, archived and index files from 1900s. Note: 1-2 names only counter service. Mail turnaround time 1-5 days.
Criminal Records: Access: Mail, in person. Only the court performs in person searches; visitors may not. Search fee: $15.00 per name if search exceeds 10 minutes. Required to search: name, years to search. Criminal records on microfiche, archived and index files from 1900s. Note: 1-2 names only counter service. Mail turnaround time 1-5 days.
General Information: No adoption, juvenile, medical, probation or sealed records released. Will not fax documents. Court makes copy: $.50 per page. Certification fee: $15 per doc. Payee: Superior Court. Personal checks accepted; credit cards are not. Prepayment required. Mail requests: SASE required.

Tulare County

Superior Court Courthouse, 221 S Mooney Blvd, Visalia, CA 93291; 559-730-5000, 559-733-6561; fax: 559-737-4547; 8AM-4PM. ***Felony, Civil, Eviction, Small Claims, Probate.***
www.tularesuperiorcourt.ca.gov This court has records from Exeter, Woodlake, Farmersville, Goshen and Three Rivers. Address criminal record requests to Rm. 124 and civil to Rm. 201.
Civil Records: Access: Mail, in person. Both court and visitors may perform in person searches. Search fee: $15.00 per name if search exceeds 10 minutes. Required to search: name, years to search. Civil cases indexed by defendant, plaintiff, on computer back to 2/1986; microfiche and index books from 1800s. Mail turnaround time 3 weeks. Civil PAT goes back to 1986. PAT results show name only. Daily calendar and civil tentative rulings and probate recommendations at www.tularesuperiorcourt.ca.gov.
Criminal Records: Access: Mail, in person. Both court and visitors may perform in person searches. Search fee: $15.00 per name if search exceeds 10 minutes. Required to search: name, years to search, DOB or SSN. Criminal records computerized from 2/1986; microfiche and index books from 1800s. Mail turnaround time 1 week. Criminal PAT goes back to same as civil.PAT results show name, DOB. Daily calendar at www.tularesuperiorcourt.ca.gov.
General Information: No adoption, juvenile, mental, probation reports or sealed records released. Will not fax documents. Court makes copy: $.50 per page. Certification fee: $15 per doc. Payee: Tulare County Superior Court. Personal checks accepted. Prepayment required. Mail requests: SASE required.

Dinuba Division - Superior Court 640 S Alta Ave, Dinuba, CA 93618; 559-595-6400; 559-591-5815; fax: 559-591-5871; 8AM-4PM. ***Felony, Misdemeanor, Civil Actions under $25,000, Eviction, Small Claims.***
www.tularesuperiorcourt.ca.gov
Includes Dinuba, Cutler, Orosi, Seville, Traver, London, Delf, Orange Cove.
Civil Records: Access: Mail, in person. Both court and visitors may perform in person searches. Search fee: $15.00 per name if search exceeds 10 minutes. Required to search: name, years to search; helpful- case number. Civil cases indexed by defendant, plaintiff, on computer from 1993, index files from 1983. Records destroyed after 10 years. Mail turnaround time 2-3 days. Civil PAT goes back to 1993. PAT results show name, DOB. Daily calendar and civil tentative rulings and probate recommendations at www.tularesuperiorcourt.ca.gov.
Criminal Records: Access: Mail, in person. Both court and visitors may perform in person searches. Search fee: $15.00 per name if search exceeds 10 minutes. Required to search: name, years to search, DOB. Criminal records computerized from 1993, index files from 1983. Records destroyed after 10 years. Mail turnaround time 2-6 days. Criminal PAT goes back to same as civil.PAT results show name, DOB. Daily calendar at www.tularesuperiorcourt.ca.gov.
General Information: No probation reports released. Will not fax documents. Court makes copy: $.50 per page. Certification fee: $15 per doc. Payee: Dinuba Superior Court. In state checks accepted. No credit cards accepted. Prepayment required. Mail requests: SASE required.

Porterville Division - Superior Court 87 E Morton Ave, Porterville, CA 93257; 559-782-4710, 782-3700; fax: 559-782-4805; 8AM-4PM. ***Felony, Misdemeanor, Civil Actions under $25,000, Eviction, Small Claims.***
Includes Porterville, Springville, Camp Nelson, Johnsondale, Terra Bella, Ducor, Richgrove, Poplar, Strathmore and surrounding areas.
Civil Records: Access: Mail, in person. Both court and visitors may perform in person searches. Search fee: $15.00 per name if search exceeds 10 minutes. Required to search: name, years to search, DOB, SSN, case #. Civil cases indexed by defendant, plaintiff, on computer from 2/1992, index book prior. Records destroyed after 10 years. Mail turnaround time 3-5 days. Civil PAT goes back to 2/1992. Daily calendar and civil tentative rulings and probate recommendations at www.tularesuperiorcourt.ca.gov.
Criminal Records: Access: Mail, in person. Both court and visitors may perform in person searches. Search fee: $15.00 per name if search exceeds 10 minutes. Required to search: name, years to search; also helpful: DOB, SSN, case #. Criminal records computerized from 2/1992, index book prior. Records destroyed after 10 years. Mail turnaround time 3-5 days. Criminal PAT goes back to same as civil. Daily calendar at www.tularesuperiorcourt.ca.gov.
General Information: No probation reports released. Court makes copy: $.50 per page. Certification fee: $15 per doc. Payee: Porterville Superior Court. Personal checks and major credit cards accepted. Prepayment required. Mail requests: SASE required.

Tulare/Pixley Division - Superior Court PO Box 1136, 425 E Kern St, Tulare, CA 93275; 559-685-5500; 559-685-2556; fax: 559-685-2663; 8AM-5PM, lobby closed at 4PM. ***Misdemeanor, Civil Actions under $25,000, Eviction, Small Claims.*** Includes Tulare, Pixley, Tipton, Earlimart, Alpaugh, Allensworth, Woodville, Waukena and surrounding areas.
Civil Records: Access: Mail, fax, in person. Both court and visitors may perform in person searches. Search fee: $15.00 per name if search exceeds 10 minutes. Required to search: name, years to search. Civil cases indexed by defendant, plaintiff, in index books. Records destroyed after 10 years; on computer back to 1992. Mail turnaround time 2 days. Civil PAT goes back to 1992. PAT results show name only. Daily calendar and civil tentative rulings and probate recommendations at www.tularesuperiorcourt.ca.gov.
Criminal Records: Access: Mail, fax, in person. Both court and visitors may perform in person searches. Search fee: $15.00 per name if search exceeds 10 minutes. Required to search: name, years to search, DOB; also helpful: address, SSN. Criminal index in books. Records destroyed after 10 years; on computer back to 1992. Mail turnaround time 2 days. Criminal PAT goes back to same as civil. PAT results show name only. Daily calendar at www.tularesuperiorcourt.ca.gov.
General Information: No probation reports released. Will not fax documents. Court makes copy: $.50 per page. Certification fee: $15 per doc. Payee: Superior Court. Personal checks accepted. Visa/MC accepted. Prepayment required. Mail requests: SASE required.

Tuolumne County

Superior Court - Civil 41 W Yaney Ave, Sonora, CA 95370; 209-533-5555; 8AM-4PM. ***Civil, Eviction, Small Claims, Probate.***
www.tuolumne.courts.ca.gov Departments 1, 2, and 5. The small claims court can be reached at 209-533-6509. Unlawful detainer clerk- 209-533-5555.
Civil Records: Access: Mail, in person. Both court and visitors may perform in person searches. Search fee: $15.00 per name if search exceeds 10 minutes. Required to search: name, years to search. Civil cases indexed by defendant, plaintiff, on computer back to 1994, microfiche and archived from 1900, index files from 1800s. Mail turnaround time 1 week. Public use terminal has civil records back to 1994.
General Information: No adoption, juvenile, medical, probation or sealed records released. Will not fax documents. Court makes copy: $.50 per page. Certification fee: $15 per doc. Payee: Superior Court. Personal checks accepted but not out of state checks. Major credit cards accepted, in person only. Prepayment required. Mail requests: SASE required.

Superior Court - Criminal 60 N Washington St, Sonora, CA 95370; 209-533-5563; fax: 209-533-5581; 8AM-4PM. ***Felony, Misdemeanor, Traffic.***
www.tuolumne.courts.ca.gov
Departments 3 and 4. Traffic court can be reach at 209-533-5671.
Criminal Records: Access: Mail, in person, online. Both court and visitors may perform in person searches. Search fee: $15.00 per name if search exceeds 10 minutes. Required to search: name, years to search, DOB. Felony records on computer from 1993; misdemeanors from 1999; index files prior. Will only search back 7 years. Mail turnaround time 14 days. Public use terminal has crim records back to 1993. PAT criminal results show middle initial. Results include case number. Access criminal records by case number of DR# at www.tuolumne.courts.ca.gov; click on "Criminal Division." Online results show middle initial.
General Information: No sealed records released. Most records are public. Will only fax to public agencies. Court makes copy: $.50 per page. Certification fee: $15 per doc. Payee: Tuolumne County Superior Court. Personal checks accepted. Visa/MC accepted, in person only. Prepayment required. Mail requests: SASE required.

Ventura County

Ventura Superior Court PO Box 6489, 800 S Victoria Ave, #218, Ventura, CA 93006-6489; criminal phone: 805-654-2611; civil phone: 805-654-2609; probate phone: 805-654-2264; fax: 805-650-4032; 8AM-5PM. ***Felony, Misdemeanor, Civil, Eviction, Small Claims, Probate.***
www.ventura.courts.ca.gov
Records Division phone- 805-654-2880. Sm Claims- 805-654-2610. Search request can include civil and criminal if you specify. Court record indexes also available in bulk format.
Civil Records: Access: Phone, mail, online, in person. Both court and visitors may perform in person searches. Search fee: $15.00 per name if search exceeds 10 minutes. Required to search: name, years to search. Civil cases indexed by defendant, plaintiff, prior to 10/93 are on microfiche, after are on

computer. Mail turnaround time 5-10 days; archived records require longer. Civil PAT goes back to 1993. PAT results show name only. Access case information, calendars and dockets at www.ventura.courts.ca.gov/via/CaseSearch.aspx. Search by defendant or plaintiff name, case number, or date. Search probate at www.venturacogensoc.org/Probate.html. Search family cases but case number required at www.ventura.courts.ca.gov/civcase/case_home.asp.
Criminal Records: Access: Phone, mail, online, in person. Both court and visitors may perform in person searches. Search fee: $15.00 per name if search exceeds 10 minutes. Required to search: name, years to search, DOB. Criminal records go back to 1893; Criminal records computerized from 1989, prior on microfiche. Mail turnaround time 5-10 days; records from archives require longer. Criminal PAT goes back to same as civil. PAT results show name only. Access case information back to 1995, calendars and dockets is free at www.ventura.courts.ca.gov/vent_frameset_puba.htm. DOB required for crim name search at https://public.courts.ventura.org/casehome.htm. Online results show name only.
General Information: No adoption, mental health, paternity actions, juvenile, medical, probation or sealed records released. Will not fax out documents. Court makes copy: $.50 per page. Certification fee: $15 per doc. Payee: Superior Court. Personal checks accepted. Credit cards accepted; a surcharge is added. Prepayment required. Mail requests: SASE required.

East County Superior Court PO Box 1200, 3855F Alamo St, Simi Valley, CA 93063; 805-582-8086; civil- 8AM-11:30AM; 1:30PM-5PM. ***Civil, Eviction, Small Claims, Family Law, Misdemeanor***
www.ventura.courts.ca.gov
Other phones- Eviction 582-8086; Small Claims 582-8078; Family Law 582-8086; Traffic 582-8080.
Civil Records: Access: Phone, mail, online, in person. Both court and visitors may perform in person searches. Search fee: $15.00 per name if search exceeds 10 minutes. Required to search: name, years to search. Civil cases indexed by defendant, plaintiff, go back to 4/92. Mail turnaround time 5 days. Civil PAT goes back to 10/1993. PAT results show may show partial SSN. Access to civil court records 10/93-present is free at the www.ventura.courts.ca.gov/via/CaseSearch.aspx. Search by defendant or plaintiff name, case number, or date. Also, search family cases but case number required at www.ventura.courts.ca.gov/civcase/case_home.asp.
Criminal Records: Access: Phone, mail, in person, online. Both court and visitors may perform in person searches. Search fee: $15.00 per name if search exceeds 10 minutes. Required to search: name, years to search, DOB. Same record keeping as civil. Mail turnaround time 5 days. Criminal PAT available. PAT results show name only. Access to case information back to 1995, calendars and dockets is free at webpage. DOB required for crim name search at https://public.courts.ventura.org/casehome.htm. Online results show name only.
General Information: Online identifiers in results same as on public terminal. No adoption, mental health, paternity actions, juvenile, medical, probation or sealed records released. Court makes copy: $.50 per page. Self serve: $.15 per page. Certification fee: $15 per doc. Payee: Ventura County Superior Courts. Personal checks accepted. All major credit cards accepted; add'l transaction fee for credit card. Prepayment required. Mail requests: SASE required.

Yolo County

Superior Court 725 Court St, Woodland, CA 95695; 530-406-6700; criminal phone: 530-406-6705; civil phone: 530-406-6704; criminal fax: 530-406-6763; civil fax: 530-406-6734; 8AM-4PM Crim; 8:30AM-4PM civil. ***Felony, Misdemeanor, Civil, Eviction, Small Claims, Probate.***
www.yolo.courts.ca.gov/
Identify specific dept room number when mailing requests. Address: civil requests #103 and criminal #111. Small claims phone is 530-406-6706.
Civil Records: Access: Phone, mail, in person. Both court and visitors may perform in person searches. Search fee: $15.00 per name if search exceeds 10 minutes. Required to search: name, years to search. Civil cases indexed by defendant, plaintiff, on computer from 1995, microfiche, archived and index files from 1800s. Mail turnaround time 2 weeks. Calendars are online free at www.yolocourts.com/calendar_daily.html. Search Probate Notes at www.yolocourts.com/probate_notes.html.
Criminal Records: Access: Phone, mail, in person, online. Both court and visitors may perform in person searches. Search fee: $15.00 per name if search exceeds 10 minutes. Required to search: name, years to search; also helpful: DOB. Criminal records computerized from 1995, microfiche, archived and index files from 1800s. Mail turnaround time 2 weeks. Access criminal and traffic records free at http://secure.yolo.courts.ca.gov:80/GetWeb/YoloCrimTrafStart.html but no name searching; search by case number or DL only. Also, calendars are free at www.yolocourts.com/calendar_daily.html.
General Information: No adoption, juvenile, medical, probation or sealed records released. Will not fax documents. Court makes copy: $.50 per page. Self serve: $.25 per page. Certification fee: $15 per doc. Payee: Yolo Superior Court. Personal checks accepted. Prepayment required. Mail requests: SASE required.

Yuba County

Superior Court 215 5th St, #200, Marysville, CA 95901; 530-749-7600; criminal phone: x3; fax: 530-749-7351; 8:30AM-4:30PM. ***Felony, Misdemeanor, Civil, Small Claims, Probate.***
www.yubacourts.org
Civil Records: Access: Mail, in person. Both court and visitors may perform in person searches. Search fee: $15.00 per name if search exceeds 10 minutes. Required to search: name, years to search. Civil cases indexed by defendant, plaintiff, on computer from 1992, index books through 1962, archives and index files from 1854. Mail turnaround time 1-2 weeks. Civil PAT goes back to 1993. PAT civil results show middle initial. Results may include DOB.
Criminal Records: Access: Mail, in person. Both court and visitors may perform in person searches. Search fee: $15.00 per name if search exceeds 10 minutes. Required to search: name, years to search. Criminal records computerized from 1992, index books through 1962, archives and index files from 1854. Mail turnaround time 1-2 weeks. Criminal PAT goes back to same as civil. PAT results show middle initial, DOB.
General Information: No adoption, paternity, juvenile, medical, probation or sealed records released. Will not fax out documents. Court makes copy: $.50 per page. Certification fee: $15 per doc. Payee: Yuba County Superior Court. Personal checks accepted; credit cards are not. Prepayment required. Mail requests: SASE required.

Yuba County Superior Court 215 5th St, #200, Marysville, CA 95901; 530-749-7600; fax: 530-749-7351; 8:30AM-4:30PM. ***Civil Actions under $25,000, Eviction, Small Claims.***
www.yubacourts.org
Civil Records: Access: Mail, in person. Both court and visitors may perform in person searches. Search fee: $15.00 per name if search exceeds 10 minutes. Required to search: name, years to search, DOB. Civil cases indexed by defendant, plaintiff, on computer through 1992, index books prior back to 1850's. Mail turnaround time 1-2 weeks. Public use terminal has civil records back to 1993. PAT civil results show middle initial. Probate Notes arranged by session back 4 months are available free at www.yubacourts.org/probate.html
General Information: No labor commissioner judgment, juvenile, or judge's records released. Will not fax documents. Court makes copy: $.50 per page. Certification fee: $15 per doc. Payee: Yuba County Superior Court. Personal checks accepted; credit cards are not. Prepayment required. Mail requests: SASE required.

California Recording Offices

ORGANIZATION: 58 counties, 58 recording offices. The recording officer is the County Recorder. Recordings are usually located in a Grantor/Grantee or General Index. All California offices are in the Pacific Time Zone (PST).

REAL ESTATE RECORDS: Most California counties do not perform real estate name searches. Copy fees and certification fees vary. Copy fee for the 1st page is usually a dollar or so more than add'l pages.

UCC RECORDS: Financing statements are filed at the state level except for real estate related collateral which are filed with the County Recorder. Prior to July, 2001, consumer goods and farm collateral were also filed at the County Recorder and these older records can be searched here. Few will perform UCC searches. Use search request form UCC-11. Copy costs vary.

TAX LIEN RECORDS: Federal and state tax liens on personal property of businesses are filed with the Secretary of State. Other federal and state tax liens are filed with the County Recorder, and state tax liens on individuals can be found at both the Secretary of State and the county level. A few counties will perform separate tax lien searches.

OTHER LIENS: Judgment (note- many judgments are also filed at the Sec. of State), child support, mechanic.

ONLINE ACCESS: A number of California counties offer online access to assessor and real estate information. The assessor's system in Los Angeles County is now free online, but no name searching. There is also a subscription Online Property Database for LA County - $100 monthly for maintaining the account, plus $1.00 per inquiry/screen, and $75.00 signup fee - and name searching. UCC Connect provides an online UCC service at https://uccconnect.sos.ca.gov/acct/acct-login.asp.

Alameda County

County Recorder, 1106 Madison St, 1st Fl, Oakland, CA 94607. 510-272-6362; fax-510-208-9957; 8:30AM-4:30PM (PST) www.acgov.org

Index: Separate indices to search. Records indexed on a public use terminal back to 1970. Only the public may search. Copy fee $1.50 per page; UCC copy-$2.00 per page. Cert fee- $12.00 per doc plus copy fee. Payee- Alameda County Recorder. Office does not sell bulk data. **Online access to Real Estate, Deed, Lien, Fictitious Name, Voter Status records:** Access the clerk-recorder's official public records and fictitious name databases for free at http://rechart1.co.alameda.ca.us/ Also, check voter registration status at www.acgov.org/rov/voter_reg_lookup.htm. **Other phones:** Treasurer- 510-272-6800; Elections- 510-272-6933. **Property tax/Assessing**- 1221 Oak St, Oakland, CA 94612; 510-272-3755, assessor fax- 510-208-3970. hours- 8:30AM-5PM A public access terminal available. **Online access**- Access to the Property Assessment database is free at www.acgov.org/MS/prop/index.aspx but no name searching. Also, property tax data is at www.acgov.org/prop_tax_info_app/index.jsp.

Alpine County

County Recorder, PO Box 217, Markleeville, CA 96120. Recording, R/E & UCC phone-530-694-2286; fax-530-694-2491; 9AM-N,1-4PM (PST) www.alpinecountyca.gov/departments/treasurer

Index: All in one. Record index not computerized. Office personnel or visitors may perform searches. Search fee $5.00 per name per year. Office will not search real estate records. Will search limited UCC records. Copy fee $1.00 1st page, $.50 each add'l page plus 7.25% tax. Cert fee- $1.75 per cert plus copy fee. Payee- Alpine County Recorder. Bulk data is available for purchase, contact Deb or Tina at Recorder office. **Other phones:** Treasurer- 530-694-2286; Elections- 530-694-2281; Vital Records- 530-694-2286. **Property tax/Assessing**- PO Box 155, 99 Water St, Markleeville, CA 96120; 530-694-2283, assessor fax- 530-694-2491. hours- 8AM-N, 1-5PM A public access terminal available. www.alpinecountyca.gov/departments/assessor

Amador County

County Recorder, 810 Court St, Jackson, CA 95642-2132. Recording, R/E & UCC phone-209-223-6468; fax-209-223-6204; 8AM-5PM (PST) www.co.amador.ca.us/depts/recorder/index.htm

Index: Grantor/grantee on public computer 1991 to current; Cott Indexes-1935 to 1990; General Index-1887 to 1935. Deeds back to 8/4/1854. Records indexed on a public use terminal back to 1991. Only the public may search. Copy fee $2.00 for 1st page, $1 each add'l. Cert fee- $4.00 per cert plus copy fee. Payee- Amador County Recorder. Bulk data available for purchase in 16mm film format or on CD; Contact PFA INC 818-504-1996, Attn: Jim Harper. **Online access to All Recorded Documents records:** Access to the county's recorded documents is free at www.co.amador.ca.us/depts/recorder/criis.htm or www.criis.com/amador/recorded.htm. **Other phones:** Treasurer- 209-223-6364; Elections- 209-223-6465; Vital Records- 209-223-6468. **Property tax/Assessing**- 810 Court St, Jackson, CA 95642-2132; 209-223-6351, assessor fax- 209-223-6721. (Appraiser/Auditor- 209-223-6351) A public access terminal available. www.co.amador.ca.us/depts/assessor/ **Online access**- Access online property records at www.co.amador.ca.us/depts/assessor/inquery1.cfm. Also, tax sale data is at www.co.amador.ca.us/depts/treasurer/index.htm; search by year.

Butte County

County Recorder, 25 County Ctr Dr, Oroville, CA 95965-3375. Recording, R/E & UCC phone-530-538-7691; fax-530-538-7975; 9AM-5PM; Recording hours: 9AM-4PM (PST) http://clerk-recorder.buttecounty.net

Index: All in one. Records indexed on a public use terminal back to 1/1/1988. Only the public may search. Copy fee $2.00 per page. Cert fee- $2.00 per cert plus copy fee. Payee- Butte County Recorder. **Online access to Real Estate, Fictitious Business Name records:** Access to the recorder's database of official documents is free at http://clerk-recorder.buttecounty.net/Riimsweb/Asp/ORInquiry.asp. Records go back to 1988. Marriages, births and deaths are no longer available. **Other phones:** Treasurer- 530-538-7576; Elections- 530-538-7761; Vital Records- 530-538-7690. **Property tax/Assessing**- 25 County Ctr Dr, Oroville, CA 95965-3375; 530-538-7721, assessor fax- 530-538-7991. (Appraiser/Auditor- 530-538-7721) hours- 9AM-5PM A public access terminal available. http://buttecounty.net **Online access**- View property tax data free at http://ttc.buttecounty.net/Default.aspx?tabid=63 but no name searching. Also, access to tax sales lists is free through a private company at www.bid4assets.com.

Calaveras County

County Recorder, 891 Mountain Ranch Rd; Government Ctr, San Andreas, CA 95249. 209-754-6372; fax-209-754-6733; 8AM-4PM (PST) www.co.calaveras.ca.us/cc/Departments/ClerkRecorder.aspx

Index: All in one. Records indexed on computer back to 9/95. Only the public may search. Copy fee $1.00 1st page; $.50 each add'l. Cert fee- $1.00 per cert plus copy fee. Payee- Calaveras County Recorder. **Other phones:** Treasurer- 209-754-6350; Elections- 209-754-6376; Vital Records- 209-754-6372. **Property tax/Assessing**- 891 Mountain Ranch Rd, San Andreas, CA 95249; 209-754-6356, assessor fax- 209-754-6739. (Appraiser/Auditor- 209-754-6356) A public access terminal is available. www.co.calaveras.ca.us/cc/Departments/Assessor.aspx **Online access**- Access property data free at www.co.calaveras.ca.us/parcelsearch.asp. No name searching. Also, access GIS Project of property data at www.co.calaveras.ca.us/departments/gisproj.asp. Click on "The Parcel Information System." No name searching.

Colusa County

County Recorder, 546 Jay St, #200, Colusa, CA 95932. Recording, R/E & UCC phone-530-458-0500; fax-530-458-0512; 8:30AM-4PM (PST) www.colusacountyclerk.com/recorder/Default.asp

Index: All in one. Records indexed on a public use terminal back to 1989. Office personnel or visitors may perform searches. Search fee $5.00 per name plus $1.00 per page. Office will not search real estate records. Office will not search UCC records or tax liens. Copy fee $1.00 per page. Cert fee- $1.00 per doc plus copy fee; maps $2.00 per page. Payee- Colusa County Recorder. Bulk data available for purchase of monthly index of records on CD for $70.00, monthly images of records on CD for $130.00, contact Rose Gallo-Vasquez, Asst Recorder.

Other phones: Treasurer- 530-458-0440; Elections- 530-458-0500; Vital Records- 530-458-0500. **Property tax/ Assessing**- 547 Market St, Colusa, CA 95932; 530-458-0450, assessor fax- 530-458-0461. (Appraiser/Auditor- 530-458-0450) A public access computer terminal is available.

Contra Costa County

County Recorder, PO Box 350, Martinez, CA 94553. 925-335-7900; hours - 8AM-4PM (PST) http://contra.napanet.net/depart/elect/clerk/
County Clerk located at 555 Escober St, Martinez, CA 94553. Index: All in one. Records indexed on a public use terminal back to 1849. Only the public may search. Will not search UCC records. Copy fee $1.00 per page. Cert fee- $2.50 per cert plus copy fee. Payee- Contra Costa County Recorder. **Online access to Real Estate, Deed, Lien, Judgment, Fictitious Business Names records:** Recorder office records including marriage records back to 1992 are free at www.criis.com/contracosta/official.shtml. By order of governor, birth and death records have been removed from the internet. Fictitious Business names are at www.criis.com/contracosta/sfictitious.shtml. **Other phones:** Elections- 925-335-7800; Vital Records- 925-335-7900. **Property tax/Assessing**- 2530 Arnold Dr, #100, Martinez, CA 94553; 925-313-7400, assessor fax- 925-313-7488. hours- 8AM-4:30PM M-TH; 8AM-4PM F www.co.contra-costa.ca.us/index.asp?nid=191

Del Norte County

County Recorder, 981 H St, #160, Crescent City, CA 95531. Recording, R/E & UCC phone-707-464-7216; fax-707-465-0321; hours - 8AM-N,1-5PM (PST) www.co.del-norte.ca.us
Index: All in one. Records indexed on a public use terminal back to 1973. Only the public may search. Copy fee $2.00 1st page, $1.00 each add'l. Cert fee- $2.00 per seal plus copy fee. Payee- Del Norte County Recorder. Bulk data available for purchase, contact Vicki Frazier or Alissia Northrup. **Other phones:** Treasurer- 707-464-7283; Elections- 707-465-0383; Vital Records- 707-464-7216. **Property tax/Assessing**- 981 H St, #120, Crescent City, CA 95531; 707-464-7200, assessor fax- 707-464-6215. hours- 8AM-5PM A public access terminal is available. http://co.del-norte.ca.us

El Dorado County

County Recorder, 360 Fair Lane, Placerville, CA 95667-4197. Recording, R/E & UCC phone-530-621-5490; fax-530-621-2147; 8AM-5PM (No recordings after 4PM). www.co.el-dorado.ca.us/countyclerk/
Index: All in one. Records indexed on computer back to 1850 (excluding 1911-1948). Only the public may search. Copy fee $1.00 1st page, $.50 each add'l. Vital records and maps copy fee is more. Cert fee- $1.00 per cert plus copy fee. Payee- El Dorado County Recorder. **Online access to Real Estate, Deed, Lien, Mortgage, Vital Statistic, Fictitious Names records:** Access Recorder's index free at http://main.co.el-dorado.ca.us/CGI/WWB012/WWM501/R. Records go back to 1850. Search business licenses free at http://main.co.el-dorado.ca.us/CGI/WWB012/WWM200/T?S=A. Search recorder's Official Records index free at http://main.co.el-dorado.ca.us/CGI/WWB012/WWM501/C. Search by date range, name or doc number. Search county non-confidential marriages and fictitious names for free at http://main.co.el-dorado.ca.us/CGI/WWB012/WWM500/C. Births and deaths have been removed. **Other phones:** Treasurer- 530-621-5800; Elections- 530-621-7480; Vital Records- 530-621-5490. **Property tax/Assessing**- 360 Fair Lane, Placerville, CA 95667-4197; 530-621-5719, assessor fax- 530-642-8148. hours- 8AM-5PM A public access computer terminal is available in office for index and records searches. www.co.el-dorado.ca.us/assessor/ **Online access**- Parcel, tax, and personal property information available free at http://main.co.el-dorado.ca.us/CGI/WWB012/WWM400/A.

Fresno County

County Recorder, PO Box 766, Fresno, CA 93712. Recording, R/E & UCC phone-559-488-3471; fax-559-488-6774; hours- 9AM-4PM (PST) www.co.fresno.ca.us/Departments.aspx?id=186
Husband and wife count as one search, if so indicated. Index: All in one. Records indexed on a public use terminal back to 1981. Only the public may search. Copy fee $1.50 1st page; $.50 each add'l. Cert fee- $9.00 1st page,$3.00 per cert plus copy fee. Payee- Fresno County Recorder. Bulk data available for purchase, contact Gilbert Carter. **Online access to Real Estate, Deed, Lien, Mortgage, Birth, Death, Marriage records:** Access to the recorder database is free at www.criis.com/fresno/srecord.shtml. Marriage records are at www.criis.com/fresno/smarriage.shtml. County Birth Records and death records have been removed from the internet. **Other phones:** Vital Records- 559-488-3476. **Property tax/Assessing**- PO Box 1146, 2281 Tulare St, Rm 201, Fresno, CA 93715; 559-488-3534, assessor fax- 559-488-6774. hours- 8AM-5PM www.co.fresno.ca.us/Departments.aspx?id=116

Glenn County

County Recorder, 526 W Sycamore St, Willows, CA 95988. Recording, R/E & UCC phone-530-934-6412; fax-530-934-6305; hours- 8AM-5PM (PST) www.countyofglenn.net/govt/departments/recorder/
Index: All in one. Records indexed on a public use terminal back to 7/89. Only the public may search. Copy fee $1.50 per page. Cert fee- $2.00 per cert plus copy fee. Payee- Glenn County Recorder. Bulk data of images and indexes on CD are available for purchase, please contact Debbie LaGrande. **Other phones:** Treasurer- 530-934-6410; Elections- 530-934-6414; Vital Records- 530-934-6412. **Property tax/Assessing**- 516 W Sycamore St, Willows, CA 95988; 530-934-6402, assessor fax- 530-934-6571. (Appraiser/Auditor- 530-934-6402) A public access terminal is available. www.countyofglenn.net/govt/departments/assessor/

Humboldt County

County Recorder, 825 5th St, 5th Fl, Eureka, CA 95501. Recording, R/E & UCC phone-707-445-7593; fax-707-445-7324; hours- 8:30AM-5PM (PST) http://co.humboldt.ca.us/recorder/
Index: Separate indices to search include 1854-1988 and 1989 to present. Records indexed on a public use terminal back to 1989. Only the public may search. Copy fee $2.00 1st page; $1.00 each add'l; double for maps and surveys. Cert fee- $2.00 per cert plus copy fee. Payee- Humboldt County Recorder. Bulk data available for purchase, contact Ben Hershberger for details, 707-445-7593. **Other phones:** Treasurer- 707-445-7331; Elections- 707-445-7481; Vital Records- 707-445-7382. **Property tax/Assessing**- 825 5th St, Rm 300, Eureka, CA 95501; 707-445-7663, assessor fax- 707-445-7410. http://co.humboldt.ca.us/assessor/

Imperial County

County Recorder, 940 Main St, Rm 202, El Centro, CA 92243-2865. 760-482-4272, R/E recording phone-760-482-4275; fax-760-482-4271; 9AM-4:30 www.imperialcounty.net/Recorder/Default.htm
Index: All in one. Records indexed on a public use terminal back to 00. Only the public may search. Copy fee $1.00 per page; $.50 each add'l. Cert fee- $1.00 per cert plus copy fee. Payee- Imperial County Clerk/Recorder. **Online access to Real Estate, Grantor-Grantee, Deed, Lien, Marriage records:** Access the Recorder's Official records index free at http://implookup.imperialcounty.net/. Index goes back to 4/1/1986, but no images available. Fictitious business names are at www.imperialcounty.net/Recorder/FBN/Fbn_Page.htm. **Other phones:** Treasurer- 760-482-6281; Elections- 760-482-4226; Vital Records- 760-482-4272. **Property tax/Assessing**- 940 Main, #115, El Centro, CA 92243; 760-482-4244, assessor fax- 760-482-4243. Bulk assessor property data available for purchase. www.imperialcounty.net/assessor/ **Online access**- A GIS-mapping site can assist you in finding parcel data free at www.geovieweronline.net/website/icpublic/viewer.htm but no name searching.

Inyo County

County Recorder, PO Box F, Independence, CA 93526. Recording, R/E & UCC phone-760-878-0222; fax-760-878-1805; hours- 8AM-N, 1-5PM (PST) www.countyofinyo.org
Index: All in one. Records indexed on a public use terminal back to 1982. Office personnel or visitors may perform searches. Search fee $.50 per name per year. Office will not search real estate records. UCC search per debtor name- $15.00. Copy fee $1.00 per page. Cert fee- $3.00 for 1st page; $1.00 each add'l, plus copy fee. Payee- Inyo County Recorder. Bulk data availablefor purchase on CD. Contact Merie Hannah. **Other phones:** Treasurer- 760-878-0333; Elections- 760-878-0223; Vital Records- 760-878-0410. **Property tax/Assessing**- PO Drawer J, 168 S Edwards, Independence, CA 93526; 760-878-0302, assessor fax- 760-878-0307. (Appraiser/Auditor- 760-878-0302) Public access computer terminal available. www.countyofinyo.org/inyo_county_assessor.htm

Kern County

County Recorder, 1655 Chester Ave; Hall of Records, Bakersfield, CA 93301. Recording, R/E & UCC phone-661-868-6448; fax-661-868-6401; 8AM-5PM; recording 8AM-2PM; Copy Svc 8AM-4:30PM (PST) http://recorder.co.kern.ca.us
Index: All in one. Records indexed on a public use terminal back to 1974. Only the public may search. Copy fee $3.00 1st page, $.50 each add'l. Cert fee- $.50 per doc plus copy fee. Payee- Kern County Recorder. **Online access to Real Estate, Deed, Fictitious Business Name records:** Search recorders database of deeds free at http://recorderonline.co.kern.ca.us/. Also, search county clerk's fictitious business name database free at www.co.kern.ca.us/ctyclerk/dba/default.asp. Search county recent sales data at http://kerndata.com. **Other phones:** Treasurer- 661-868-3490; Elections- 661-868-3590; Vital Records- 661-868-6449. **Property tax/Assessing**- 1115 Truxtun Ave, Bakersfield, CA 93301; 661-868-3485, assessor fax- 661-868-3303. (Appraiser/Auditor- 661-868-3485) hours- 8AM-5PM **Online access**- Assessor database records available free at http://assessor.co.kern.ca.us/propertysearch/index.php. Search tax collector data at www.kcttc.co.kern.ca.us/payment/mainsearch.aspx.

Kings County

County Recorder, 1400 W Lacey Blvd, Hanford, CA 93230. Recording, R/E & UCC phone-559-582-3211 x2470; fax-559-582-6639; 8AM-3PM (PST) www.countyofkings.com
Index: All in one. Records indexed on a public use terminal back to 1977. Only the public may search. Will not search UCC records. Copy fee $2.60 per page. Cert fee- $2.60 per cert plus copy fee. Payee- Kings County Clerk Recorder. **Other phones:** Treasurer- 559-582-3211 x2477; Elections- 559-582-3211 x2439; Vital Records- 559-582-3211 x2470. **Property tax/Assessing**- 1400 W Lacey Blvd, Hanford, CA 93230; 559-582-3211 x2486, assessor fax- 559-582-2794. hours- 8AM-5PM www.countyofkings.com/acr/Assessor/index.html

Lake County

County Recorder, 255 N Forbes, Rm 223, Lakeport, CA 95453. Recording, R/E & UCC phone-707-263-2293; fax-707-263-3703; 9AM-5PM (PST) www.co.lake.ca.us/Government/Directory/Assessor-Recorder.htm
Index: All in one. Records indexed on a public use terminal back to 1975. Office will perform a UCC search but public must search other records themselves. Search fee $15.00 per debtor. Copy fee $1.00 for 1st page; $.50 each add'l. Cert fee- $1.00 per cert plus copy fee. Payee- Lake County Recorder. Bulk data is available for purchase, please contact

Assessor-Recorder Doug Wacker for info. **Online access to Real Estate, Grantor/Grantee, Deed, Lien, Mortgage records:** Access limited index display of official records at http://acm.co.lake.ca.us/recorder/cms_recordssearch.asp. **Other phones:** Treasurer- 707-263-2236; Elections- 707-263-2372; Vital Records- 707-263-2293. **Property tax/Assessing**- 255 N Forbes, Rn 223, Lakeport, CA 95453; 707-263-2302, assessor fax- 707-263-3703. A public access computer terminal is available for index and records searches. www.co.lake.ca.us/Government/Directory/Assessor-Recorder.htm **Online access**- Parcel records on the GIS Mapping site available by clicking on Lake County Base Maps free at http://gis.co.lake.ca.us/. No name searching.

Lassen County

County Recorder, 220 S Lassen St, #5, Susanville, CA 96130. Recording, R/E & UCC phone-530-251-8234; fax-530-257-3480; 10AM-N, 1-3PM; Phone hours- 8AM-4PM (PST) www.lassencounty.org
Index: All in one. Records indexed on a public use terminal back to 1985. Only the public may search. Copy fee $1.50 per page; $.50 each add'l. Cert fee- $1.75 1st page plus copy fee. Payee- Lassen County Recorder. Office does not sell bulk data. **Online access to Real Estate, Deed records:** Access to the recorder database is free at http://icris.lassencounty.org. Registration is required. Recorded documents go back to 7/1985. **Other phones:** Treasurer- 530-251-8220; Elections- 530-251-8217; Vital Records- 530-251-8234. **Property tax/Assessing**- 220 S Lassen St, #4, Susanville, CA 96130; 530-251-8241; 251-8242, assessor fax- 530-251-8245. hours- 9PM-N, 1-4PM A public access terminal is available. http://co.lassen.ca.us **Online access**- Access to tax sales lists is free through a private company at www.bid4assets.com.

Los Angeles Recorder/County Clerk

County Recorder, PO Box 53195; Real Estate Records Section, Los Angeles, CA 90053-0195. 562-462-2133, 800-815-2666; fax-562-864-1250; 8AM-5PM, till 7PM on 3rd Thursday every month. (PST) http://regrec.co.la.ca.us
Alternative fax #- 562-929-5086. Real estate related documents at Real Estate Records Sec, info given here. Also, a Document Analysis & Recording Sec, POB 53115, LA, CA 90053, 562-462-2125. Records for both sections physically at Imperial Hiway location. Index: Separate indices arranged by year. Records indexed on a public use terminal back to 1992. Office personnel or visitors may perform searches, but no telephone requests for index searches accepted. Search fee with document number- $.50 per name per year; this only applies if you cannot supply the exact year of the document. Real Estate Records Section will not name search real estate records. An application for real estate record form is at www.lavote.net/RECORDER/PDFS/REAL_ESTATE.pdf. For credit card order by telephone, call the RE Records Section at 562-462-2133. Office will not search tax liens. UCC search per debtor name- $.50 per year with $1.00 minimum. Real Estate record copy fee $5.00 per doc, uncertified. Fictitious name copy- $2.00 per doc. Express mail delivery- $16.95. Cert fee- $6.00 for 1st page; $3.00 each add'l page, copies included. Payee- Los Angeles County Recorder; out of state checks accepted. Credit card orders-add $6.00. All major cards accepted. The county sells a variety of data; view list and details at http://assessor.lacounty.gov/extranet/Outsidesales/catalog.aspx. **Online access to Fictitious Business Names records:** Search fictitious business names at http://regrec.co.la.ca.us/CLERK/FBN_Search.cfm. **Property tax/Assessing**- 500 W Temple St, Rm 225, Los Angeles, CA 90012; 213-974-3211, assessor fax-213-633-4705. 8-5PM www.assessor.lacounty.gov **Online access**- For assessments use the PDB Inquiry System dial-up svc. for $100 monthly plus $1.00 per inquiry, also $75 sign-up fee for 3-year dial-up with usage fee of $6.50 per hr or $.11 per minute. PDB registration at. http://assessor.lacounty.gov/extranet/outsidesales/online.aspx. Tax info line- 213-974-3838. Also search property/assessor data (no name searching) free at http://assessormap.co.la.ca.us/mapping/viewer.asp.

Madera County

County Recorder, 200 W 4th St, Madera, CA 93637. Recording, R/E & UCC phone-559-675-7724; fax-559-675-7870; 8AM-3:30PM (PST) www.madera-county.com
Index: Separate indices to search include computer, roll film. Records indexed on a public use terminal back to 9/90. Only the public may search. Copy fee $1.00 1st page; $.50 each add'l. Cert fee- $1.75 per cert plus copy fee. Payee- Madera County Recorder. Bulk data is available for purchase; contact the recording office. **Other phones:** Treasurer- 559-675-7713; Elections- 559-675-7720; Vital Records- 559-675-7724. **Property tax/Assessing**- 200 W 4th St, Madera, CA 93637; 559-675-7710, assessor fax- 559-675-7654. hours- 8AM-5PM A public access terminal is available. www.madera-county.com/assessor/ **Online access**- Access parcel and ownership data free on the GIS-mapping site free at www.madera-county.com/rma/parcelmap.html -no name searching.

Marin County

County Recorder, PO Box C, San Rafael, CA 94913. Recording, R/E & UCC phone-415-499-6092; fax-415-499-7893; 8AM-4PM research & copies; 8AM-3PM are hours for recording. (PST) www.co.marin.ca.us/depts/AR/main/index.cfm
Index: All in one. Records indexed on a public use terminal back to 1974. Only the public may search. Copy fee $4.00 1st page, $2.00 each add'l page. Cert fee- $4.00 per cert plus copy fee. Payee- Marin County Recorder. **Online access to Real Estate, Grantor/Grantee, Deed, Marriage records:** Search the county Grantor/Grantee index free at www.co.marin.ca.us/depts/AR/RiiMs/index.asp. Also, search the real estate sales lists by month and year by selecting the year. Also, search the marriage records by document index number at www.co.marin.ca.us/depts/AR/VitalStatistics/index.asp. Marriage records go back to 1948. Search business names by type at www.marin.org/bizmo/. **Other phones:** Treasurer- 415-499-6145; Elections- 415-499-6456; Vital Records- 415-499-6094. **Property tax/Assessing**- PO Box C, Civic Center Branch, Rm 208, San Rafael, CA 94913; 415-499-7215, assessor fax- 415-499-6542. hours- 9AM-4PM A public access terminal available. www.co.marin.ca.us **Online access**- Search the property tax database at www.co.marin.ca.us/depts/AR/COMPASS/index.asp but there is no name searching.

Mariposa County

County Recorder, PO Box 35, Mariposa, CA 95338. 209-966-5719 or 2332, R/E recording phone-209-966-5719; 8AM-5PM (recording 8AM-3:30PM). (PST) www.mariposacounty.org/index.asp?NID=64
Index: All in one. Records indexed on a public use terminal back to 1988, prior records in books back to 1850's. Only the public may search. Copy fee $1.00 per page, $1.50 for legal size. Cert fee- $1.00 per doc plus copy fee. Payee- Mariposa County Recorder. **Other phones:** Treasurer- 209-966-2621; Elections-209-966-2007. **Property tax/Assessing**- PO Box 35, 4982 10th St, Mariposa, CA 95338; 209-966-2332, assessor fax- 209-966-6496. hours- 8AM-5PM www.mariposacounty.org/index.asp?NID=64

Mendocino County

County Recorder, 501 Low Gap Rd, Rm 1020, Ukiah, CA 95482. Recording, R/E & UCC phone-707-463-4376; fax-707-463-4257; 8AM-5PM (PST) www.co.mendocino.ca.us
Index: All in one. Records indexed on a public use terminal back to 1966. Office will honor mailed in requests for real estate records searches, otherwise the public must search for themselves. Search fee $5.00 per name. Copy fee $2.50 1st page, $.50 each add'l. Cert fee- $1.00 per cert plus copy fee. Payee- Mendocino County Recorder. **Other phones:** Treasurer- 707-463-4388; Elections- 707-463-4374; Vital Records- 707-463-4371. **Property tax/Assessing**- 501 Low Gap Rd, #1020, Ukiah, CA 95482; 707-463-4311, assessor fax- 707-463-6597. (Appraiser/Auditor- 707-463-4311) www.co.mendocino.ca.us/acr/assessor.htm

Merced County

County Recorder, 2222 M St, Merced, CA 95340. 209-385-7627; fax-209-385-7626; 8AM-4:30PM (PST) www.co.merced.ca.us/index.asp?NID=239
Index: All in one. Records indexed on a public use terminal back to 1963. Only the public may search. Copy fee $3.00 for 1st page; $1 each add'l. Cert fee-$2.00 1st page plus copy fee. Payee- Merced County Recorder. Office does sell bulk data CD's and maps, contact Connie Hamilton. **Online access to Real Estate, Grantor/Grantee, Deed records:** Access to the recorder official records index PARIS system is free at www.recorder.merced.ca.us/. **Other phones:** Treasurer- 209-385-7307; Elections- 209-385-7541. **Property tax/Assessing**- 2222 M St, Merced, CA 95340; 209-385-7631, assessor fax- 209-725-3956. 8AM-5PM www.co.merced.ca.us/assessor/index.html **Online access**- Search parcel maps at www.co.merced.ca.us/index.asp?NID=196. Search by fee parcel number or assessment number at www.co.merced.ca.us/index.asp?NID=193 but no name searching.

Modoc County

County Recorder, 204 Court St, Alturas, CA 96101. Recording, R/E & UCC phone-530-233-6205; fax-530-233-6666; 8:30AM-N, 1PM-5PM (PST)
Index: Separate indices to search. Records indexed on a public use terminal back to 1987. Only the public may search. Copy fee $1.00 for 1st page; $.50 each add'l. Cert fee- $2.00 per cert plus $.50 each add'l. Payee- Modoc County Recorder. Office does not sell bulk data. **Online access to Real Estate, Deed, Fictitious Business Name records:** Access to the county clerk recording database soon to be free at www.criis.com/modoc/official.shtml. Fictitious business names may also be found. **Other phones:** Treasurer- 530-233-6223; Elections- 530-233-6201; Vital Records- 530-233-6205. **Property tax/Assessing**- 204 S Court St, Rm 106, Alturas, CA 96101; 530-233-6217; 233-6218, assessor fax- 530-233-6237. (Appraiser/Auditor- 530-233-6221) A public access computer terminal is available in office for searches. www.modoccounty.us/dept/assessor/

Mono County

County Recorder, PO Box 237, Bridgeport, CA 93517. Recording, R/E & UCC phone-760-932-5530; fax-760-932-5531; 8AM-5PM (PST) www.monocounty.ca.gov/departments.html
Index: All in one. Records indexed on a public use terminal back to 1990. Office personnel or visitors may perform searches. General index search fee $2.00 per year per name. Real estate record owner searches available. UCC search does not include tax liens. UCC search per debtor name- $15.00 per name per 5 years. Tax lien search fee- $2.00 per year per debtor. Copy fee $.05 per page. Cert fee- $1.75 per cert plus copy fee. Payee- Mono County Recorder. Office does sell bulk data, contact Linda Roberts. **Other phones:** Treasurer- 760-932-5480; Elections- 760-932-5537; Vital Records- 760-932-5535. **Property tax/Assessing**- PO Box 456, 25 Bryant St, Bridgeport, CA 93517; 760-932-5510, assessor fax-760-932-5511. A public access terminal available. www.monocounty.ca.gov/departments/assessor/assessor.html **Online access**- Access property data free at http://gis.mono.ca.gov/IMS/PublicPV/ but no name searching.

Monterey County

County Recorder, 168 W Alisal St, 1st Fl, Salinas, CA 93901. Recording, R/E & UCC phone-831-755-5041; fax-831-755-5064; hours- 8AM-5PM (PST) www.co.monterey.ca.us./recorder/
Index: All in one. Records indexed on computer back to 1978. Only the public may search. Copy fee $2.00 per page. Cert fee- $2.00 per cert plus copy fee. Payee- Monterey County Recorder. **Online access to Real Estate, Grantor/Grantee, Deed, Lien records:** Access the county PARIS system including official records and fictitious business names free at http://65.249.61.8/. Official records go back to 1978. **Other phones:** Treasurer- 831-755-5015; Elections- 831-796-1499; Vital Records- 831-755-5041. **Property tax/Assessing**- PO Box 579, 168 W Alisal, Salinas, CA 93902; 831-755-5035, assessor fax- 831-755-5320. **Online access**- Search assessment data free at http://000sweb.co.monterey.ca.us/assessor/asmt-query.htm but no name searching. The county tax defaulted property list is at www.co.monterey.ca.us/taxcollector/Auction_Internet.html.

Napa County

County Recorder, PO Box 298, Napa, CA 94559-0298. 707-253-4246, R/E recording phone-707-253-4105; fax-707-259-8149; 8AM-5PM (PST) www.co.napa.ca.us
Index: All in one. Records indexed on a public use terminal back to 1986. Office will perform a UCC search but public must search other records themselves. Search fee $5.00 per name, per year. Copy fee $2.00 per page. Cert fee- $3.00 per doc plus copy fee. Fee to fax results is $3 for 1st page, $1 each add'l. Payee- Napa County Recorder. Bulk data available for purchase, contact Vicki Poli. **Online access to Real Estate, Grantor/Grantee, Deed, Judgment, Lien, Voter Registration records:** Access "Official Records" by subscription; fee- $3600 per year. Index goes back to 5/1986; images back to 5/1986. Also, search Official Records Inquiry site for real estate and Grantor/Grantee index back to 5/1986 free at www.co.napa.ca.us/orpublic/ORInquiry.asp. Also, with name and DOB search voter registration at https://commerce.co.napa.ca.us/VoterAccess/. **Other phones:** Treasurer- 707-253-4311; Elections- 707-253-4321; Vital Records- 707-253-4247. **Property tax/Assessing**- 1127 1st St, #128, Napa, CA 94559; 707-253-4466, assessor fax- 707-253-6171. A public access terminal available. **Online access**- Search assessor's property tax payments free at www.co.napa.ca.us/propertypayments/ but no name searching. Also, search for property data by address for free at www.co.napa.ca.us/MyProperty/. Also search for property data on the GIS-mapping site free at http://gis.napa.ca.gov/Prcl_Smry/dyn_search.asp.

Nevada County

County Recorder, 950 Maidu Ave, Nevada City, CA 95959. 530-265-1221; fax-530-478-1275; 8AM-5PM (PST) www.mynevadacounty.com/recorder/
Index: All in one. Records indexed on a public use terminal back to 1987. Only the public may search. Copy fee $3.00 for 1st page; $.50 each add'l. Will fax results for $2.00 per page fee. Cert fee- $1.00 per cert plus copy fee. Payee- Nevada County Recorder. Daily/weekly/monthly CD-roms available, contact Christine or Angie. **Online access to Real Estate, Deed, Judgment, Fictitious Name, Property Tax, GIS-mapping records:** Access to the county clerk database of recordings and assumed names is free at www.criis.com/nevada/official.shtml. Subscription access to the recorders full database is $200 per month fee. **Other phones:** Treasurer- 530-265-1285; Elections- 530-265-1298; Vital Records- 530-265-1221. **Property tax/Assessing**- 950 Maidu Ave, Eric Rood Admin Bldg, Nevada City, CA 95959; 530-265-1232. **Online access**- Search the GIS mapping site by address for property info for free at http://63.205.214.10:1711. Also, search property tax payment records at http://treas-tax.co.nevada.ca.us/searchtax.php; no name searching.

Orange County

County Clerk Recorder, PO Box 238, Santa Ana, CA 92702-0238. 714-834-2500 (questions), R/E recording phone-714-834-2500 (recorded info only); fax-714-834-2575; 8AM-4:30PM (PST) www.ocrecorder.com
For questions about requesting documents, call Tom Daly, 714-834-2500. Fax requests not accepted. Index: All in one. Records indexed on a public use terminal back to 1982. Office will perform a UCC search but public must search other records themselves. Office will not search real estate records. Copy fee $1.00 per page. Cert fee- $1.00 per doc plus copy fee. Payee- Orange County Clerk-Recorder. **Online access to Real Estate, Grantor/Grantee, Deed, Lien, Judgment, Fictitious Business Name records:** Orange County Grantor/Grantee index is free at http://cr.ocgov.com/grantorgrantee/index.asp. Also, search fictitious business names at http://cr.ocgov.com/fbn/index.asp. **Other phones:** Treasurer- 714-834-2682; Vital Records- 714-834-2568. **Property tax/Assessing**- PO Box 149, 630 N Broadway, Bld. 12, Rm 142, Santana, CA 92702; 714-834-2727, assessor fax- 714-834-3934. **Online access**- Search property tax records at http://tax.ocgov.com/tcweb/search_page.asp; no name searching. Also, search tax parcel data, aircraft, and vessels at http://tax.ocgov.com/tcweb/search_page.asp but no name searching.

Placer County

County Recorder, 2954 Richardson Dr, Auburn, CA 95603. Recording, R/E & UCC phone-530-886-5600; fax-530-886-5687; 8AM-5PM (recording 9-4PM). www.placer.ca.gov/Departments/Recorder.aspx
Index: All in one. Records indexed on a public use terminal back to 1972. Only the public may search. Copy fee $2.00 1st page, $1.00 each add'l page. Cert fee- $2.00 per doc plus copy fee. Payee- Placer County Recorder. **Online access to Real Estate, Deed, Fictitious Name, Marriage records:** Recorder office index records are free at www.criis.com/placer/srecord_current.shtml. Marriage records are at www.criis.com/placer/smarriage.shtml. Search county Fictitious Business Names at www.criis.com/placer/sfictitious.shtml. **Other phones:** Elections- 530-886-5650; Vital Records- 530-886-5600. **Property tax/Assessing**- 2980 Richardson Dr, Auburn, CA 95603; 530-889-4300, assessor fax- 530-889-4305. www.placer.ca.gov/Departments/Assessor.aspx
Online access- Assessor's property assessment data free at www.placer.ca.gov/Departments/Assessor/Assessment%20Inquiry/Assessment%20Inquiry%20Iframe.aspx. Also, search GIS data at http://lis.placer.ca.gov/gis.asp?s=1000&h2=545.

Plumas County

County Recorder, 520 Main St, Rm 102, Quincy, CA 95971. 530-283-6218; fax-530-283-6155; 8AM-5PM (PST) www.countyofplumas.com
Index: All in one. Records indexed on a public use terminal back to 1986, previous to 1986 in books. Only the public may search. Will not search UCC records. Copy fee $1.00 1st page, $.50 each add'l. Large books $1.50 1st page, $.80 each add'l. Cert fee- $1.00 per cert plus copy fee. Payee- Plumas County Recorder. Office does sell bulk data, contact Debra Housen at 530-283-6218. **Other phones:** Treasurer- 530-283-6260; Elections- 530-283-6256. **Property tax/Assessing**- #1 Crescent St, Quincy, CA 95971; 530-283-6380, assessor fax- 530-283-6195. www.countyofplumas.com/assessor/index.htm

Riverside County

County Recorder, PO Box 751; Attn: County Recorder/Clerk, Riverside, CA 92502-0751. Recording, R/E & UCC phone-951-486-7000; fax-951-486-7047; 8AM-4:30PM (recording hours 8AM-2PM). (PST) http://riverside.asrclkrec.com
Index: Separate indices to search. Records indexed on a public use terminal back to 1998. Office personnel or visitors may perform searches. Search fee $2.00 1st page found, $1.00 each add'l page. Office will not search real estate records. Office will not search UCC records. Copy fee $2.00 1st page, $1.00 each add'l. Cert fee- $1.00 per cert plus copy fee. Payee- Riverside County Recorder. **Online access to Real Estate, Grantor/Grantee, Deed, Lien, Judgment, Mortgage, Divorce, Fictitious Name records:** Search Grantor/Grantee index and recorded data at www.enetwizard.com/shop/affiliates/11467_01/pre.asp. Also, access to county fictitious name database is free at http://riverside.asrclkrec.com/ACR/OSfbn.asp. **Other phones:** Treasurer- 951-955-3900; Vital Records- 951-486-7000. **Property tax/Assessing**- PO Box 12004, Riverside, CA 92500-2204; 951-955-6250. **Online access**- Access property tax data free at http://pic.asrclkrec.com/Default.aspx but no name searching.

Sacramento County

County Recorder, PO Box 839, Sacramento, CA 95812-0839. 916-874-6334; 800-313-7133, R/E recording phone-916-874-6334; fax-916-874-8012; 8AM-5PM (recording 8AM-3PM). (PST) www.ccr.saccounty.net
Index: Separate indices to search include grantor and grantee. 0lder indexes from 1850-1909. Records indexed on computer back to 1965. Only the public may search. Copy fee $11.00 for 1st page; $2.00 each add'l. Cert fee- $1.00 per cert plus copy fee. Payee- Sacramento County Clerk/Recorder. **Online access to Real Estate, Grantor/Grantee, Deed, Fictitious Names, Business License, Voter Registration records:** Access Clerk-recorder Grantee/Grantor index back to 1965 for free at www.erosi.saccounty.net/Inputs.asp. Also, search registered voters by DOB at https://shadow.saccounty.net/pollingplacelookupen/. Search fictitious names at www.efbn.saccounty.net. Also, search City of West Sacramento business licenses at www.cityofwestsacramento.org/cityhall/departments/finance/buslic/blfind.cfm. **Other phones:** Treasurer- 916-874-6725; Elections- 916-874-6451; Vital Records- 916-874-7850. **Property tax/Assessing**- 3701 Power Inn Rd, Ste 3000, Sacramento, CA 95826-4329; 916-875-0700, assessor fax- 916-875-0705. (Appraiser/Auditor- 916-875-0700) hours- 8AM-5PM; phone- 9AM-4PM **Online access**- Search property tax & parcels at www.eproptax.saccounty.net; no name searching. Also, find property data at http://assessorparcelviewer.saccounty.net/GISViewer/Default.aspx; no name searching. Search treasurer tax sale, tax bill, and fictitious names free at www.finance.saccounty.net/tax/Default.asp.

San Benito County

County Recorder, 440 5th St, Rm 206, Hollister, CA 95023. Recording, R/E & UCC phone-831-636-4046; fax-831-636-2939; 8AM-5PM (recording 9:30AM-4PM). (PST) www.san-benito.ca.us
Index: Separate indices to search include computer back to 1989, microfilm back to 1984, prior in index books. Records indexed on a public use terminal. Only the public may search. Copy fee $2.00 1st page; $1.00 each add'l. Cert fee- $3.00 per doc plus copy fee. Payee- San Benito County Clerk. Bulk data available for purchase; contact Lillian Pereira, Asst Co Clerk/Recorder. **Other phones:** Treasurer- 831-636-4043; Elections- 831-636-4016; Vital Records-831-636-4029. **Property tax/Assessing**- 440 5th St, 1st Fl, Rm 107, Hollister, CA 95023; 831-636-4030, assessor fax- 831-636-4033. hours- 8AM-5PM A public access terminal available.

San Bernardino County

County Recorder, 222 W Hospitality Ln, 1st Fl, San Bernardino, CA 92415-0022. Recording, R/E & UCC phone-909-387-8306; fax-909-386-9050; 8AM-4:30PM (PST) www.co.san-bernardino.ca.us
Automated call distribution- 909-387-8306; for fictitious names- 909-386-8970. Index: All in one. Records indexed on a public use terminal back to 1980. Only the public may search. Copy fee $2.00 1st page, $1.25 each add'l. Cert fee- $5.25 per doc plus

copy fee. Payee- San Bernardino County Recorder. Office does not sell bulk data. **Online access to Real Estate, Grantor/Grantee, Deed records:** Auditor/Controller Grantor/Grantee recording index back to 1980 is free at http://acrparis.co.san-bernardino.ca.us/cgi-bin/odsmnu1.html/input. Search fictitious business names at http://170.164.50.51/fbn/index.html. **Other phones:** Treasurer- 909-387-8308; Elections- 909-387-8300; Vital Records- 909-387-8314; Admin- 909-387-8924. **Property tax/Assessing**- 172 W 3rd St, San Bernardino, CA 92415; 909-387-6730, assessor fax- 909-387-6781. (Appraiser/Auditor- 909-387-6730) A public access terminal available. **Online access**- Records on the County Assessor database are free at www.mytaxcollector.com/trSearch.aspx. No name searching. Property can also be searched on PIMS at https://nppublic.co.san-bernardino.ca.us/newpims/.

San Diego County

County Recorder, PO Box 121750, San Diego, CA 92112. Recording, R/E & UCC phone-619-238-8158; fax-619-557-4155; 8AM-5PM (PST) http://arcc.co.san-diego.ca.us/arcc/default.aspx

Index: Separate indices to search. Records indexed on a public use terminal back to 1982. Office will perform a UCC search but public must search other records themselves. General search fee $15.00 per name. UCC search per debtor name- $10.00. General copy fee- $2.00 per page. Cert fee- $1.00 per cert plus copy fee. Payee- San Diego Recorder/Clerk. Office does not sell bulk data. **Online access to Real Estate, Grantor/Grantee, Deed, Property Sale, Fictitious Name records:** From the home page above or at http://arcc.co.san-diego.ca.us/services/grantorgrantee/search.aspx search for recorded documents and property sales. Search fictitious names at https://arcc.co.san-diego.ca.us/services/fbn/search.aspx **Other phones:** Treasurer- 619-236-3121; Vital Records- 619-237-0502. **Property tax/Assessing**- 1600 Pacific Hwy, #103, San Diego, CA 92101; 619-236-3771, assessor fax- 619-685-2338. **Online access**- From the county home page above or at https://arcc.co.san-diego.ca.us/services/parcelmap/search.aspx search for assessor data on the parcel mapping site. Search for property sales data at http://arcc.co.san-diego.ca.us/services/propsales/propsales_search.aspx; no name searching. Assessor date also available in bulk, see https://arcc.co.san-diego.ca.us/subscription/login.aspx or call 619-685-2455.

San Francisco County

County Recorder, 1 Dr Carlton E Goodlet Pl, Rm 190; City Hall, San Francisco, CA 94102. 415-554-4176, R/E recording phone-415-554-4579; fax-415-554-4179; 8AM-4PM (PST) www.sfgov.org

Index: Indices on computer, microfilm, microfiche. Records indexed on public access terminal back to 1990. Only the public may search. Copy fee $3.00 for 1st 3 pages; $.50 after 3rd page. Cert fee- $1.00 per doc plus copy fee. Payee- San Francisco County Assessor-Recorder. Bulk data available for purchase on microfilm. **Online access to Real Estate, Deed, Real Estate, Lien, Judgment, Fictitious Business Name, Birth, Death records:** Search recorders database free at www.criis.com/sanfrancisco/srecord.shtml. Fictitious business names are also searchable at http://services.sfgov.org/bns/start.asp. Limited vital statistic data is searchable at www.sfgenealogy.com/sf/, a privately operated site. **Property tax/Assessing**- Same address as recording office. 415-554-5516. **Online access**- Access the City Property Tax database free at https://services.sfgov.org/ptx/intro.asp. Click on begin. No name searching; address or block/lot number required.

San Joaquin County

County Recorder, PO Box 1968, Stockton, CA 95201. 209-468-3939; fax-209-468-8040; 8AM-5PM (PST) www.co.san-joaquin.ca.us

Index: All in one. Records indexed on a public use terminal back to 1968. Only the public may search. Copy fee $2.00 per page staff assisted, $1.00 per page self assisted. Cert fee- $2.00 per doc includes copy fee. Payee- San Joaquin County Recorder. **Other phones:** Treasurer- 209-468-2133; Vital Records- 209-468-8075. **Property tax/Assessing**- 24 S Hunter, Rm 303, Stockton, CA 95202; 209-468-2630, assessor fax- 209-468-8383. A public access terminal available. A property information line is available at 209-468-2652 from 10AM-1PM. **Online access**- Access property data on the GIS-mapping site free at www.sjmap.org/mapapps.asp; no name searching.

San Luis Obispo County

County Recorder, 1055 Monterey St, Rm D120, San Luis Obispo, CA 93408. Recording, R/E & UCC phone-805-781-5080; fax-805-781-1111; 8AM-5PM (PST) www.slocounty.ca.gov/Page113.aspx

Also a North County office at 5955 Capistrano, #B, Atascadero CA 93422, 805-461-6041. Index: All in one. Records indexed on a public use terminal back to 1924, books back to late 1800's. Office will perform a UCC search but public must search other records themselves. Search fee- UCC only $10.00. Copy fee $1.00 per page. Cert fee- $1.00 per doc plus copy fee. Payee- San Luis Obispo County Recorder. Office does sell bulk data, contact D. Graton. **Online access to Real Estate, Grantor/Grantee, Deed, Judgment, Lien, Mortgage, Fictitious Business Name, records:** Search the recorder database for free at http://services.sloclerkrecorder.org/officials/searchform.cfm. (Index only). **Other phones:** Treasurer- 805-781-5843; Elections- 805-781-5228; Vital Records- 805-781-5080. **Property tax/Assessing**- 1055 Monterey, Ste D360, San Luis Obispo, CA 93408; 805-781-5643, assessor fax- 805-788-2041. www.slocounty.ca.gov/assessor **Online access**- Access property information search free at www.slocounty.ca.gov/Assessor/Property_Information_Search.htm but no name searching. Also, parcel map records free at www.slocounty.ca.gov/Assessor/Parcel_Maps_Online.htm but name searching.

San Mateo County

County Recorder, 555 County Ctr, 1st Fl, Redwood City, CA 94063. 650-363-4713, 363-4500, R/E recording phone-650-363-4713; fax-650-363-4843; 8AM-5PM (PST) www.smcare.org

Index: All in one. Records indexed on a public use terminal back to 1985. Only the public may search. Copy fee $2.00 1st page, $1.00 each add'l. Cert fee- $1.00 per cert plus copy fee. Payee- San Mateo County Recorder. Bulk data available for purchase, contact Penny. **Online access to Real Estate, Grantor/Grantee, Deed, Property Tax, Fictitious Name records:** Access the recorder's grantor/grantee index free at www.smcare.org/records/recording/search_database.asp. Also, search fictitious names at www.smcare.org/business/fictitious/default.asp. **Other phones:** Treasurer- 650-363-4840; Elections- 650-312-5222; Vital Records- 650-363-4500. **Property tax/Assessing**- 555 County Ctr, Redwood City, CA 94063; 650-363-4500, assessor fax- 650-599-7435. (Appraiser/Auditor- 650-363-4500) www.smcare.org **Online access**- Records on county property tax data site is free at http://smctweb1.co.sanmateo.ca.us/index.html, view secured or unsecured.

Santa Barbara County

County Recorder, PO Box 159, Santa Barbara, CA 93102-0159. Recording, R/E & UCC phone-805-568-2250; fax-805-568-2266; 8AM-4:30PM (PST) www.sbcrecorder.com/Home.aspx

County also has a branch in Santa Maria at 511 E Lakeside Pkwy, #115, 93455, 805-346-8370. Index: All in one. Records indexed on a public use terminal back to 1989. Only the public may search. Copy fee $1.00 for 1st page, $.50 each add'l. Cert fee- $3.00 per cert plus copy fee. Payee- Santa Barbara County Recorder. **Online access to Real Estate, Grantor/Grantee, Deed, Lien records:** Search the recorder's grantor/grantee index at www.sbcrecorder.com/ClerkRecorder/GrantorGranteeIndex.aspx. **Other phones:** Treasurer- 805-568-2490; Elections- 805-568-2200; Vital Records- 805-568-2257. **Property tax/Assessing**- 105 E Anapamu, Rm 204, Santa Barbara, CA 93102; 805-568-2550, assessor fax- 805-568-3247. (Appraiser/Auditor- 805-568-2550) 8-5PM Public access terminal available. www.sbcrecorder.com/Assessor/Assessor.aspx **Online access**- Access to assessor online property info system (OPIS) in free at www.sbcrecorder.com/assessor/search.aspx but no name searching. Records go back 10 years. Full access requires registration. Subscribers may download data. Also, search property tax bills at http://taxes.co.santa-barbara.ca.us/propertytax.asp; click on View/Search Secured Property Tax Bills. No name searching.

Santa Clara County

County Clerk Recorder, 70 W Hedding St, 1st Fl; County Gov't Ctr, East Wing, San Jose, CA 95110. 408-299-5670, R/E recording phone-408-299-5667; fax-408-280-1768; 8AM-4:30PM (PST) www.clerkrecordersearch.org

Index: Separate indices to search include computer; microfiche/film for pre-1981. Records indexed on a public use terminal back to 1981. Office will perform a tax lien search but public must search other records themselves. Search fee $.50 per name per year. Office will search real estate records if given specific names and date range. General copy fee-$10.00 first page, $3.00 each add'l page. Cert fee- $2.00 per cert plus copy fee. Payee- Santa Clara County Recorder. **Online access to Real Estate, Grantor/Grantee, Deed, Fictitious Business Name, Birth records:** Access to the County Clerk-Recorder database is free at www.clerkrecordersearch.org/cgi-bin/odsmnu1.html/input. Search births 1905-1995 free at www.mariposaresearch.net/php/. Also, search fictitious business names for free at www.clerkrecordersearch.org/cgi-bin/FBNSearch.html/input. Also, search the tax collector database at http://payments.scctax.org/payment/jsp/startup.jsp. No name searching. **Other phones:** Vital Records- 408-299-5669; Official Record Copies- 408-299-5670. **Property tax/Assessing**- 70 W Hedding St, East Wing, San Jose, CA 95110; 408-299-5500, assessor fax- 408-297-9526. www.sccassessor.org/ **Online access**- Search the assessment roll free a www.sccassessor.org/ari/home.do but no name searching.

Santa Cruz County

County Recorder, 701 Ocean St, Rm 230, Santa Cruz, CA 95060. 831-454-2800; fax-831-454-3169; 8AM-4PM (PST) www.co.santa-cruz.ca.us/rcd/

Index: All in one. Records indexed on computer. Only the public may search. Copy fee $2.00 per page. Cert fee- $2.50 per cert plus copy fee. Payee- Santa Cruz County Recorder. Official records are available for purchase on CD-rom, contact Carol Sutherland. **Online access to Real Estate, Deed records:** Access to the recorder's official records is free at http://sccounty01.co.santa-cruz.ca.us/clerkrecorder/Asp/ORInquiry.asp. Online indexes go back to 1978. **Other phones:** Treasurer- 831-454-2510; Elections- 831-454-2060; Vital Records- 831-454-2800. **Property tax/Assessing**- 701 Ocean St, Rm 130, Santa Cruz, CA 95060; 831-454-2002, assessor fax- 831-454-2495. **Online access**- Access the assessor's parcel data free at http://sccounty01.co.santa-cruz.ca.us/ASR/. No name searching. Also, search for property data using the GIS map at http://gis.co.santa-cruz.ca.us.

Shasta County

County Recorder, 1450 Court St, Rm 208, Redding, CA 96001. 530-225-5671; fax-530-225-5152; 8AM-5PM (PST) www.co.shasta.ca.us

Index: All in one. Records indexed on a public use terminal back to 1925. Only the public may search. General copy fee $1.00 1st page, $.50 each add'l. Cert fee- $1.00 per doc plus copy fee. Payee- Shasta County Recorder. Office does sell bulk data by subscription, contact Debbie. **Online access to Vital**

Records records: A private site lists various birth, death, and marriage records of the county and more at http://myclouds.tripod.com/shasta/shastaco.html. **Other phones:** Treasurer- 530-225-5511; Elections- 530-225-5730; Vital Records- 530-225-5678. **Property tax/Assessing**- 1450 Court St, Rm 208A, Redding, CA 96001; 530-225-3600, assessor fax- 530-225-5673. (Appraiser/Auditor- 530-225-3600) A public access terminal is available. www.co.shasta.ca.us/Departments/AssessorRecorder/index.shtml **Online access**- Search assessor and recorded documents for free at www.co.shasta.ca.us/Departments/AssessorRecorder/PublicInquiry.shtml. Records on the City of Redding Parcel Search By Parcel Number Server are free at http://cor400.ci.redding.ca.us/nd/gow3lkap.ndm/input. CA state law has removed owner names.

Sierra County

County Recorder, PO Drawer D, Downieville, CA 95936. Recording, R/E & UCC phone-530-289-3295; fax-530-289-2830; hours- 8AM-N,1-4PM (PST) www.sierracounty.ws
Index: All in one. Records indexed on computer back to 1985. Office will perform a UCC search back to 1985 but public must search other records themselves. UCC search per debtor name- $5.00. Copy fee $1.00 per page. Cert fee- $1.75 per cert plus copy fee. Payee- Sierra County Recorder. Bulk index and images on CD, $125.00 per month. **Other phones:** Treasurer- 530-289-3286; Elections- 530-289-3295; Vital Records- 530-289-3295. **Property tax/Assessing**- PO Box 8, Downieville, CA 95936; 530-289-3283, assessor fax- 530-289-2801. (Appraiser/Auditor- 530-289-3283) hours- 8AM-N, 1-5PM A public access terminal available. **Online access**- Access to tax sales lists is free through a private company at www.bid4assets.com

Siskiyou County

County Recorder, PO Box 8, Yreka, CA 96097. 530-842-8065; fax-530-842-8077; 8AM-4PM (PST)
Index: All in one. Records indexed on a public use terminal back to 1975. Only the public may search. Copy fee $1.00 1st page, $.50 each add'l. Cert fee- $1.00 per doc plus copy fee. Payee- Siskiyou County Recorder. **Online access to Real Estate, Deed, Lien, Fictitious Business Name records:** Access to the Recorder records database is free at www.criis.com/siskiyou/srecord_current.shtml. Also, access to the fictitious names database is at www.criis.com/siskiyou/sfictitious.shtml. **Other phones:** Vital Records- 530-842-8065. **Property tax/Assessing**- 311 4th St, Rm 108, Yreka, CA 96097-2984; 530-842-8036, assessor fax- 530-842-8059. www.co.siskiyou.ca.us/assessor/index.htm **Online access**- Access to tax sales lists is free through a private company at www.bid4assets.com.

Solano County

County Recorder, 675 Texas St, #2700, Fairfield, CA 94533-6338. Recording, R/E & UCC phone-707-784-6290; fax-707-784-6911; 8AM-4PM; 8AM-3:30PM recording hours; copies 8AM-4PM (PST) www.solanocounty.com
Index: Separate indices to search. Records indexed on a public use terminal back to 1990; images back to 1998. Only the public may search. Office will honor copy requests for search real estate records. Will search UCC records for $.50 per name, per year. No over the phone research. Copy fee $5.00 for 1st page; $1.00 each add'l for official record. Cert fee- $3.00 per cert plus copy fee. Payee- Solano County Recorders Office. Bulk official records and maps are available for purchase, contact Jan Phelps Supvr of Scanning an Vital Units. **Online access to Real Estate, Grantor/Grantee, Deed, Judgment, Lien records:** Access recorder's indexes free at http://recorderonline.solanocounty.com. Access recorded data free at http://recorderonline.solanocounty.com/cgi-bin/odsmnu1.html/input. **Other phones:** Treasurer- 707-784-7485; Elections- 707-784-7485; Vital Records- 707-784-6294. **Property tax/Assessing**- 675 Texas St, #2700, Fairfield, CA 94533; 707-784-6210, assessor fax- 707-784-7046. (Appraiser/Auditor- 707-784-6210) hours- 8AM-5PM A public access terminal available from 8AM-4PM. **Online access**- See the treasurer/tax collector search above for add'l property data. Also, search the treasurer/tax collector/county clerk property tax database free at www.solanocounty.com/depts/treasurer_clerk/onlinetaxinfo.asp. No name searching. Also, search the treasurer/tax collector/county clerk property tax database free at www.solanocounty.com/depts/treasurer_clerk/onlinetaxinfo.asp. No name searching.

Sonoma County

County Recorder, PO Box 1709, Santa Rosa, CA 95402-1709. 707-565-2651; fax-707-565-3905; 8-4:30 www.sonoma-county.org/recorder/aboutus.asp
Index: All in one. Records indexed on computer back to 1/1/64. Only the public may search. Copy fee $1.75 per page up to 11" x 17" (over 11" x 17" - $2.50 per page. Cert fee- $2.00 per doc plus copy fee. Payee- Sonoma County Recorder. Recorded data available for sale on CD and DVD; contact Karen Lukas. **Online access to Real Estate, Deed, Lien, UCC, Voter Registration records:** Access recorder index records free at http://deeds.sonoma-county.org/search.asp?cabinet=opr. No images on this system. Also, with address, ZIP, and DOB search voter registration records free at www.co.sonoma.ca.us/RegVoter/RegVoterLookup.htm. **Other phones:** Treasurer- 707-565-2281; Elections- 707-565-6800; Vital Records- 707-565-2645. **Property tax/Assessing**- 585 Fiscal Dr, Rm 104F, Santa Rosa, CA 95403; 707-565-1888, assessor fax- 707-565-3317. hours- 8AM-5PM A public access terminal available. http://sonoma-county.org **Online access**- Access assessor information free at www.sonoma-county.org/Assessor/.

Stanislaus County

County Recorder, PO Box 1008, Modesto, CA 95353. Recording, R/E & UCC phone-209-525-5260; fax-209-525-5207; hours- 8AM-N,1-4PM (PST) www.co.stanislaus.ca.us
Index: All in one. Records indexed on a public use terminal back to 4/93. Only the public may search. Copy fee $3.00 1st page, $2.00 each add'l. Cert fee- $2.00 per doc plus copy fee. Payee- Stanislaus County Recorder. Bulk data available for purchase, contact Bonnie. **Online access to Real Estate, Deed, Lien, Land, Fictitious Name records:** Recorder office records index of recent records are free at www.criis.com/stanislaus/srecord_current.shtml. Birth, death and marriage records have been removed from the Internet. County Fictitious Name records are at www.criis.com/stanislaus/sfictitious.shtml. **Other phones:** Elections- 209-525-5200; Vital Records- 209-525-5291. **Property tax/Assessing**- 1010 10th St, #2400, Modesto, CA 95354; 209-525-6461, assessor fax- 209-525-6586. hours- 7:30AM-5PM www.co.stanislaus.ca.us/assessor/ **Online access**- Access property assessment data free at www.co.stanislaus.ca.us/assessor/assessor-disclaimer2.shtm but no name searching. Fuller data for profess'l service companies available by subscription.

Sutter County

County Recorder, PO Box 1555, Yuba City, CA 95992-1555. Recording, R/E & UCC phone- 530-822-7134; fax-530-822-7214; 8AM-5PM (PST) www.suttercounty.org
Index: All in one. Records indexed on a public use terminal back to 1995. Office personnel or visitors may perform searches. Search fee $.50 per name per year, but office will not search RE or UCCs. Copy fee $1.25 per page. Cert fee- $2.25 per doc plus copy fee. Payee- Sutter County Recorder. Bulk data available for purchase online; contact Cindy McMIllan Asst. Clerk-Recorder. **Online access to Real Estate, Grantor/Grantee, Deed, Fictitious Name records:** Access the recorder database free at www.suttercounty.org/apps/recordsquery/clerk/. Records go back to 12/29/1994. **Other phones:** Treasurer- 530-822-7117; Elections- 530-822-7122; Vital Records- 530-822-7134. **Property tax/Assessing**- 1160 Civic Center Blvd, Yuba City, CA 95993; 530-822-7160, assessor fax- 530-822-7198. (Appraiser/Auditor- 530-822-7160) A public access terminal available. **Online access**- Access assessment and property tax records free at www.suttercounty.org/doc/apps/recordsquery/recordsquery but no name searching.

Tehama County

County Recorder, PO Box 250, Red Bluff, CA 96080. Recording, R/E & UCC phone-530-527-3350; fax-530-527-1745; 8AM-5PM www.co.tehama.ca.us
Index: Separate indices to search include various document types. Records indexed on a public use terminal back to 1975. Only the public may search. Copy fee $1.50 per page. Cert fee- $2.00 per cert plus copy fee. Payee- Tehama County Recorder. Official records available for bulk purchase on CD for $300.00 per month; contact Jennifer Vise at 530-527-3350. **Online access to Real Estate, Grantor/Grantee, Deed, Lien records:** Search recorder's official public records free at http://tehamapublic.countyrecords.com/ . **Other phones:** Treasurer- 530-527-4535; Elections- 530-527-8190; Vital Records- 530-527-3350; Auditor- 530-527-3474. **Property tax/Assessing**- PO Box 428, Red Bluff, CA 96080; 530-527-5931, assessor fax- 530-529-4019. (Appraiser/Auditor- 530-527-5931) A public access terminal available. **Online access**- Search property tax data on the county unsecured tax information lookup at www.co.tehama.ca.us/index.php?option=com_chronocontact&chronoformname=view_pay_taxes&Itemid=122.

Trinity County

County Recorder, PO Box 1215, Weaverville, CA 96093-1215. 530-623-1215; fax-530-623-8398; 8AM-5PM (PST) www.trinitycounty.org/Departments/assessor-clerk-elect/clerkrecorder.htm
Index: Books, microfiche, computer. Records indexed on a public use terminal back to 10/1994. Only the public may search. Copy fee $1.25 per page. Cert fee- $2.00 per cert plus copy fee. Payee- Trinity County Recorder. Office does not sell bulk data. **Online access to Fictitious Business Name records:** Access to the Recorder's fictitious business names database is free at http://halfile.trinitycounty.org. For user name, enter "fbn"; leave password field empty. **Other phones:** Treasurer- 530-623-1251; Elections- 530-623-1220; Vital Records- 530-623-1215. **Property tax/Assessing**- PO Box 1255, Weaverville, CA 96093-1215; 530-623-1257, assessor fax- 530-623-8398. A public access terminal available.

Tulare County

County Recorder, 221 S Mooney Blvd, Rm 103; County Civic Ctr, Visalia, CA 93291-4593. 559-636-5050; fax-559-740-4329; 8AM-5PM (recording 8AM-3PM). (PST) www.co.tulare.ca.us
Index: All in one. Records indexed on a public use terminal back to 1987. Only the public may search. Search fee for special information requests- $53.00 per hour. Will not search UCC records. Copy fee $3.00 1st page; $1.00 each add'l page. Conformed copy- $1.00 per doc and include SASE. Film images of records are $.06 each. Will fax back results for $3.00 add'l. Cert fee- $2.00 per page plus copy fee. Payee- Tulare County Recorder. A monthly CD-rom of Official Record Images is available for $400.00. **Online access to Real Estate, Deed, Judgment, Lien, Vital Statistic, Fictitious Name records:** Search the recorders database including births, marriages, deaths free at http://209.78.90.65/riimsweb/orinquiry.asp. A monthly subscription for full data and information services is $600.00. **Other phones:** Elections- 559-733-6377; Vital Records- 559-636-5051. **Property tax/Assessing**- 221 S Mooney Blvd, Rm 102 E, Visalia, CA 93291; 559-636-5100, assessor fax- 559-737-4468. www.co.tulare.ca.us/government/assessor/default.asp **Online access**- Search treasurer/tax collector property data free at

www.co.tulare.ca.us/government/treasurertax/mytaxes/default.asp; no name searching.

Tuolumne County

County Recorder, 2 S Green St; County Admin Ctr, Sonora, CA 95370. 209-533-5531; fax-209-533-6543; 8AM-5PM (PST) www.tuolumnecounty.ca.gov
Index: All in one. Records indexed on a public use terminal back to 1972. Only the public may search. General copy fee $3.00 1st page, $1.00 per add'l page. Cert fee- $1.00 per doc plus copy fee. Payee- Tuolumne County Recorder. **Online access to Real Estate, Deed, Lien, Judgment records:** Access the recorder grantor/grantee index at https://www.records.co.tuolumne.ca.us/. Logon using 'web' for free access; turn off your pop-up blocker. **Other phones:** Treasurer- 209-533-5544; Elections- 209-533-5570; Vital Records- 209-533-5531. **Property tax/Assessing-** 2 S Green St, County Admin Ctr, Sonora, CA 95370; 209-533-5535, assessor fax- 209-533-5674. (Appraiser/Auditor- 209-533-5535) A public access terminal is available.

Ventura County

County Recorder, 800 S Victoria Ave; Government Ctr, Ventura, CA 93009. 805-654-2292, R/E recording phone-805-654-3665; fax-805-654-2392; 8AM-4PM (PST)
http://recorder.countyofventura.org/venclrk.htm
Index: All in one. Records indexed on a public use terminal back to 1900. Birth or death records cannot be viewed on access terminal. Only the public may search. Copy fee $2.00 1st page, $1.00 each add'l. Cert fee- $3.00 for 1st page; $1.00 each add'l, plus copy fee. Payee- Ventura County Recorder. Bulk data available for purchase, contact Jeff Innes 805-654-2297. **Online access to Real Estate, Grantor/Grantee, Deed, Lien, Judgment, Fictitious Name records:** Access the county clerk & recorder database free at http://recorder.countyofventura.org/venclrk.htm. **Other phones:** Treasurer- 805-654-3735; Elections- 805-654-2664; Vital Records- 805-654-3666. **Property tax/Assessing-** 800 S Victoria Ave, Government Ctr, Ventura, CA 93009; 805-654-2181, assessor fax- 805-645-1305. hours- 8AM-5PM Public access terminal available. **Online access-** Search property tax data for free at http://prop-tax.countyofventura.org/ but no name searching.

Yolo County

County Recorder, PO Box 1130, Woodland, CA 95776-1130. 530-666-8130; fax-530-666-8109; 8AM-4PM (PST) www.yolorecorder.org
Index: All in one. Records indexed on a public use terminal back to 1970. Office will perform a 10-yr Tax lien search but public must search other records themselves. Will not search UCC records. Copy fee $3.50 for 1st page; $.50 each add'l. Cert fee- $3.00 per cert plus copy fee. Payee- Yolo County Clerk/Recorder. Bulk data available for purchase, contact Cyndi Stiles or Barbara Patenaude. **Online access to Real Estate, Deed, Lien, Birth, Death, Fictitious Business Name, Marriage records:** Access to recordings on the county clerk database are free at www.yolorecorder.org/recsearch and at www.criis.com/yolo/srecord_current.shtml. Marriage records are at www.criis.com/yolo/smarriage.shtml. County Fictitious Business Name at www.yolorecorder.org/recording/fictitious/lookup. Also look up fictitious names at www.criis.com/yolo/sfictitious.shtml. Search City of Davis business licenses free at http://cityofdavis.org/ed/business/. **Other phones:** Treasurer- 530-666-8625; Elections- 530-666-8133; Vital Records- 530-666-8130; Planning & Public Works- 530-666-8775. **Property tax/Assessing-** 625 Court St, Rm 104, Woodland, CA 95695; 530-666-8135, assessor fax- 530-666-8213. hours- 8AM-5PM Bulk parcel data can be downloaded from the GIS site. **Online access-** With an address, look up parcel numbers free at www.yolocounty.org/Index.aspx?page=344. Search for parcels free at www.yolocounty.org/index.aspx?page=587.

Yuba County

County Recorder, 915 8th St, #107, Marysville, CA 95901. 530-749-7850; fax-530-749-7854; 8AM-5PM (PST) www.co.yuba.ca.us/departments/clerk/
Index: All indexes are searchable except vital records. Records indexed on a public use terminal back to 1989. Only the public may search. Copy fee $2.00 1st page, $.50 each add'l. Cert fee- $2.50 per doc plus copy fee. Payee- Yuba County Recorder. Bulk data available for purchase, contact Fayo Martin or Terry Hansen. **Online access to Real Estate, Deed, Judgment, Lien records:** Access recorded document index free at www.co.yuba.ca.us/services/Land%20Records/. Online records go back to 1989. **Other phones:** Treasurer- 530-749-7840; Elections- 530-749-7855; Vital Records- 530-749-7851; Clerk- 530-749-7851. **Property tax/Assessing-** 915 8th St, #101, Marysville, CA 95901; 530-749-7820, assessor fax- 530-749-7824. A public access terminal is available. www.co.yuba.ca.us/departments/assessor/ **Online access-** Access to property records is free at www.co.yuba.ca.us/services/Parcel%20Search/ but no name searching.

California County Locator

You will usually be able to find the city name in the City/County Cross Reference below. In that case, it is a simple matter to determine the county from the cross reference. However, only the official US Postal Service city names are included in this index. There are an additional 40,000 place names that people use in their addresses. Therefore, we have also included a ZIP/City Cross Reference immediately following the City/County Cross Reference.

If you know the ZIP Code but the city name does not appear in the City/County Cross Reference index, look up the ZIP Code in the ZIP/City Cross Reference, find the city name, then look up the city name in the City/County Cross Reference. For example, you want to know the county for an address of Menands, NY 12204. There is no "Menands" in the City/County Cross Reference. The ZIP/City Cross Reference shows that ZIP Codes 12201-12288 are for the city of Albany. Looking back in the City/County Cross Reference, Albany is in Albany County.

California City/County Cross Reference

ACAMPO San Joaquin
ACTON Los Angeles
ADELANTO San Bernardino
ADIN (96006) Modoc(66), Lassen(33)
AGOURA HILLS Los Angeles
AGUANGA Riverside
AHWAHNEE (93601) Madera(96), Mariposa(3)
ALAMEDA Alameda
ALAMO Contra Costa
ALBANY Alameda
ALBION Mendocino
ALDERPOINT Humboldt
ALHAMBRA Los Angeles
ALISO VIEJO Orange
ALLEGHANY Sierra
ALPAUGH Tulare
ALPINE San Diego
ALTA Placer
ALTA LOMA San Bernardino
ALTADENA Los Angeles
ALTAVILLE Calaveras
ALTURAS Modoc
ALVISO Santa Clara
AMADOR CITY Amador
AMBOY San Bernardino
AMERICAN CANYON Napa
ANAHEIM Orange
ANDERSON Shasta
ANGELS CAMP Calaveras
ANGELUS OAKS San Bernardino
ANGWIN Napa
ANNAPOLIS Sonoma
ANTELOPE Sacramento
ANTIOCH Contra Costa
ANZA Riverside
APPLE VALLEY San Bernardino
APPLEGATE Placer
APTOS Santa Cruz
ARBUCKLE (95912) Colusa(98), Yolo(1)
ARCADIA Los Angeles
ARCATA Humboldt
ARMONA Kings
ARNOLD Calaveras
AROMAS (95004) Monterey(53), San Benito(46)
ARROYO GRANDE San Luis Obispo
ARTESIA Los Angeles
ARTOIS Glenn
ARVIN Kern
ATASCADERO San Luis Obispo
ATHERTON San Mateo
ATWATER Merced
ATWOOD Orange
AUBERRY Fresno
AUBURN (95602) Placer(73), Nevada(26)
AUBURN Placer
AVALON Los Angeles
AVENAL Kings
AVERY Calaveras
AVILA BEACH San Luis Obispo
AZUSA Los Angeles
BADGER Tulare
BAKER San Bernardino
BAKERSFIELD Kern
BALDWIN PARK Los Angeles
BALLICO Merced
BANGOR (95914) Butte(90), Yuba(10)
BANNING Riverside
BANTA San Joaquin
BARD Imperial
BARSTOW San Bernardino
BASS LAKE Madera
BAYSIDE Humboldt
BEALE AFB Yuba
BEAUMONT Riverside
BECKWOURTH Plumas
BELDEN Plumas
BELL Los Angeles
BELL GARDENS Los Angeles
BELLA VISTA Shasta
BELLFLOWER Los Angeles
BELMONT San Mateo
BELVEDERE TIBURON Marin
BEN LOMOND Santa Cruz
BENICIA Solano
BENTON Mono
BERKELEY (94708) Alameda(83), Contra Costa(16)
BERKELEY Alameda
BERRY CREEK Butte
BETHEL ISLAND Contra Costa
BEVERLY HILLS Los Angeles
BIEBER Lassen
BIG BAR Trinity
BIG BEAR CITY San Bernardino
BIG BEAR LAKE San Bernardino
BIG BEND Shasta
BIG CREEK Fresno
BIG OAK FLAT Tuolumne
BIG PINE Inyo
BIG SUR Monterey
BIGGS Butte
BIOLA Fresno
BIRDS LANDING Solano
BISHOP (93514) Inyo(93), Mono(6)
BISHOP Inyo
BLAIRSDEN-GRAEAGLE Plumas
BLOCKSBURG Humboldt
BLOOMINGTON San Bernardino
BLUE JAY San Bernardino
BLUE LAKE Humboldt
BLYTHE Riverside
BODEGA Sonoma
BODEGA BAY Sonoma
BODFISH Kern
BOLINAS Marin
BONITA San Diego
BONSALL San Diego
BOONVILLE Mendocino
BORON (93516) Kern(93), San Bernardino(6)
BORON Kern
BORREGO SPRINGS (92004) San Diego(94), Imperial(5)
BOULDER CREEK Santa Cruz
BOULEVARD San Diego
BOYES HOT SPRINGS Sonoma
BRADLEY (93426) Monterey(69), San Luis Obispo(30)
BRANDEIS Ventura
BRANSCOMB Mendocino
BRAWLEY Imperial
BREA Orange
BRENTWOOD Contra Costa
BRIDGEPORT Mono
BRIDGEVILLE (95526) Humboldt(90), Trinity(10)
BRISBANE San Mateo
BROOKDALE Santa Cruz
BROOKS Yolo
BROWNS VALLEY Yuba
BROWNSVILLE Yuba
BRYN MAWR San Bernardino
BUELLTON Santa Barbara
BUENA PARK Orange
BURBANK Los Angeles
BURLINGAME San Mateo
BURNEY Shasta
BURNT RANCH Trinity
BURREL Fresno
BURSON Calaveras
BUTTE CITY Glenn
BUTTONWILLOW Kern
BYRON (94514) Contra Costa(89), Alameda(9), San Joaquin(1)
CABAZON Riverside
CADIZ San Bernardino
CALABASAS Los Angeles
CALEXICO Imperial
CALIENTE Kern
CALIFORNIA CITY Kern
CALIFORNIA HOT SPRINGS Tulare
CALIMESA Riverside
CALIPATRIA Imperial
CALISTOGA (94515) Napa(88), Sonoma(11)
CALLAHAN Siskiyou
CALPELLA Mendocino
CALPINE Sierra
CAMARILLO Ventura
CAMBRIA San Luis Obispo
CAMINO El Dorado
CAMP MEEKER Sonoma
CAMP NELSON Tulare
CAMP PENDLETON San Diego
CAMPBELL Santa Clara
CAMPO San Diego
CAMPO SECO Calaveras
CAMPTONVILLE (95922) Yuba(85), Sierra(14)
CANBY Modoc
CANOGA PARK Los Angeles
CANTIL Kern
CANTUA CREEK Fresno
CANYON Contra Costa
CANYON COUNTRY Los Angeles
CANYONDAM Plumas
CAPAY Yolo
CAPISTRANO BEACH Orange
CAPITOLA Santa Cruz
CARDIFF BY THE SEA San Diego
CARLOTTA Humboldt
CARLSBAD San Diego
CARMEL Monterey
CARMEL VALLEY Monterey
CARMICHAEL Sacramento
CARNELIAN BAY Placer
CARPINTERIA Santa Barbara
CARSON Los Angeles
CARUTHERS Fresno
CASMALIA Santa Barbara
CASPAR Mendocino
CASSEL Shasta
CASTAIC Los Angeles
CASTELLA Shasta
CASTRO VALLEY Alameda
CASTROVILLE Monterey
CATHEDRAL CITY Riverside
CATHEYS VALLEY Mariposa
CAYUCOS San Luis Obispo
CAZADERO Sonoma
CEDAR GLEN San Bernardino
CEDAR RIDGE Nevada
CEDARPINES PARK San Bernardino
CEDARVILLE Modoc
CERES Stanislaus
CERRITOS Los Angeles
CHALLENGE (95925) Butte(56), Yuba(43)
CHATSWORTH (91311) Los Angeles(98), Ventura(1)
CHATSWORTH Los Angeles
CHESTER Plumas
CHICAGO PARK Nevada
CHICO Butte
CHILCOOT Plumas
CHINESE CAMP Tuolumne
CHINO San Bernardino
CHINO HILLS San Bernardino
CHOLAME San Luis Obispo
CHOWCHILLA (93610) Madera(97), Merced(2)
CHUALAR Monterey
CHULA VISTA San Diego
CIMA San Bernardino
CITRUS HEIGHTS Sacramento
CITY OF INDUSTRY Los Angeles
CLAREMONT Los Angeles
CLARKSBURG Yolo
CLAYTON Contra Costa
CLEARLAKE Lake
CLEARLAKE OAKS Lake
CLEARLAKE PARK Lake
CLEMENTS San Joaquin
CLIO Plumas
CLIPPER MILLS Butte
CLOVERDALE (95425) Sonoma(98), Mendocino(1)
CLOVIS Fresno
COACHELLA Riverside
COALINGA Fresno
COARSEGOLD Madera
COBB Lake
COLEVILLE Mono
COLFAX Placer
COLLEGE CITY Colusa

COLOMA El Dorado
COLTON (92324) San Bernardino(96), Riverside(3)
COLUMBIA Tuolumne
COLUSA Colusa
COMPTCHE Mendocino
COMPTON Los Angeles
CONCORD Contra Costa
COOL El Dorado
COPPEROPOLIS Calaveras
CORCORAN (93212) Kings(97), Tulare(2)
CORNING Tehama
CORONA (92880) Riverside(98), San Bernardino(1)
CORONA Riverside
CORONA DEL MAR Orange
CORONADO San Diego
CORTE MADERA Marin
COSTA MESA Orange
COTATI Sonoma
COTTONWOOD (96022) Tehama(51), Shasta(48)
COULTERVILLE (95311) Mariposa(92), Tuolumne(7)
COURTLAND Sacramento
COVELO Mendocino
COVINA Los Angeles
COYOTE Santa Clara
CRESCENT CITY Del Norte
CRESCENT MILLS Plumas
CRESSEY Merced
CREST PARK San Bernardino
CRESTLINE San Bernardino
CRESTON San Luis Obispo
CROCKER NAT BANK San Francisco
CROCKETT Contra Costa
CROWS LANDING Stanislaus
CULVER CITY Los Angeles
CUPERTINO Santa Clara
CUTLER Tulare
CUTTEN Humboldt
CUYAMA Santa Barbara
CYPRESS Orange
DAGGETT San Bernardino
DALY CITY San Mateo
DANA POINT Orange
DANVILLE Contra Costa
DARDANELLE Tuolumne
DARWIN Inyo
DAVENPORT Santa Cruz
DAVIS Yolo
DAVIS CREEK Modoc
DEATH VALLEY Inyo
DEER PARK Napa
DEL MAR San Diego
DEL REY Fresno
DELANO (93215) Kern(92), Tulare(7)
DELANO Kern
DELHI Merced
DENAIR Stanislaus
DESCANSO San Diego
DESERT CENTER Riverside
DESERT HOT SPRINGS Riverside
DI GIORGIO Kern
DIABLO Contra Costa
DIAMOND BAR Los Angeles
DIAMOND SPRINGS El Dorado
DILLON BEACH Marin
DINUBA (93618) Tulare(98), Fresno(1)
DIXON Solano
DOBBINS Yuba
DORRIS Siskiyou
DOS PALOS (93620) Merced(85), Fresno(14)
DOS RIOS Mendocino
DOUGLAS CITY Trinity
DOUGLAS FLAT Calaveras
DOWNEY Los Angeles
DOWNIEVILLE Sierra
DOYLE Lassen
DRYTOWN Amador
DUARTE Los Angeles
DUBLIN Alameda
DUCOR Tulare
DULZURA San Diego
DUNCANS MILLS Sonoma
DUNLAP Fresno
DUNNIGAN Yolo
DUNSMUIR (96025) Siskiyou(93), Shasta(6)
DURHAM Butte
DUTCH FLAT Placer
EAGLEVILLE Modoc
EARLIMART Tulare
EARP San Bernardino
EAST IRVINE Orange
ECHO LAKE El Dorado
EDISON Kern
EDWARDS Kern
EL CAJON San Diego
EL CENTRO Imperial
EL CERRITO Contra Costa
EL DORADO El Dorado
EL DORADO HILLS El Dorado
EL GRANADA San Mateo
EL MACERO Yolo
EL MONTE Los Angeles
EL NIDO Merced
EL PORTAL Mariposa
EL SEGUNDO Los Angeles
EL SOBRANTE Contra Costa
EL TORO Orange
EL VERANO Sonoma
ELDRIDGE Sonoma
ELK Mendocino
ELK CREEK (95939) Glenn(94), Colusa(5)
ELK GROVE Sacramento
ELMIRA Solano
ELVERTA (95626) Sacramento(84), Placer(12), Sutter(2)
EMERYVILLE Alameda
EMIGRANT GAP Placer
EMPIRE Stanislaus
ENCINITAS San Diego
ENCINO Los Angeles
ESCALON San Joaquin
ESCONDIDO San Diego
ESPARTO Yolo
ESSEX San Bernardino
ETNA Siskiyou
EUREKA Humboldt
EXETER Tulare
FAIR OAKS Sacramento
FAIRFAX Marin
FAIRFIELD Solano
FALL RIVER MILLS Shasta
FALLBROOK San Diego
FARMERSVILLE Tulare
FARMINGTON (95230) Stanislaus(34), San Joaquin(33), Calaveras(28), Tuolumne(2)
FAWNSKIN San Bernardino
FEATHER FALLS Butte
FELLOWS Kern
FELTON Santa Cruz
FERNDALE Humboldt
FIDDLETOWN (95629) El Dorado(75), Amador(24)
FIELDS LANDING Humboldt
FILLMORE Ventura
FINLEY Lake
FIREBAUGH (93622) Fresno(89), Madera(8), Merced(2)
FISH CAMP (93623) Mariposa(81), Madera(18)
FIVE POINTS Fresno
FLORISTON Nevada
FLOURNOY Tehama
FOLSOM Sacramento
FONTANA San Bernardino
FOOTHILL RANCH Orange
FORBESTOWN (95941) Butte(84), Yuba(15)
FOREST FALLS San Bernardino
FOREST KNOLLS Marin
FOREST RANCH Butte
FORESTHILL Placer
FORESTVILLE Sonoma
FORKS OF SALMON Siskiyou
FORT BIDWELL Modoc
FORT BRAGG Mendocino
FORT DICK Del Norte
FORT IRWIN San Bernardino
FORT JONES Siskiyou
FORT ORD Monterey
FORTUNA Humboldt
FOUNTAIN VALLEY Orange
FOWLER Fresno
FRAZIER PARK Kern
FREEDOM Santa Cruz
FREMONT Alameda
FRENCH CAMP San Joaquin
FRENCH GULCH Shasta
FRESNO Fresno
FRIANT (93626) Fresno(58), Madera(41)
FT ORD Monterey
FULLERTON Orange
FULTON Sonoma
GALT (95632) Sacramento(95), San Joaquin(4)
GARBERVILLE Humboldt
GARDEN GROVE Orange
GARDEN VALLEY El Dorado
GARDENA Los Angeles
GASQUET (95543) Del Norte(98), Trinity(2)
GAZELLE Siskiyou
GEORGETOWN El Dorado
GERBER Tehama
GEYSERVILLE Sonoma
GILROY Santa Clara
GLEN ELLEN Sonoma
GLENCOE Calaveras
GLENDALE Los Angeles
GLENDORA Los Angeles
GLENHAVEN Lake
GLENN Glenn
GLENNVILLE Kern
GOLD RUN Placer
GOLETA Santa Barbara
GONZALES Monterey
GOODYEARS BAR Sierra
GOSHEN Tulare
GRANADA HILLS Los Angeles
GRAND TERRACE San Bernardino
GRANITE BAY Placer
GRASS VALLEY Nevada
GRATON Sonoma
GREEN VALLEY LAKE San Bernardino
GREENBRAE Marin
GREENFIELD Monterey
GREENVIEW Siskiyou
GREENVILLE Plumas
GREENWOOD El Dorado
GRENADA Siskiyou
GRIDLEY Butte
GRIMES Colusa
GRIZZLY FLATS El Dorado
GROVELAND (95321) Tuolumne(97), Mariposa(2)
GROVER BEACH San Luis Obispo
GUADALUPE Santa Barbara
GUALALA Mendocino
GUASTI San Bernardino
GUATAY San Diego
GUERNEVILLE Sonoma
GUINDA Yolo
GUSTINE Merced
HACIENDA HEIGHTS Los Angeles
HALF MOON BAY San Mateo
HAMILTON CITY Glenn
HANFORD Kings
HAPPY CAMP Siskiyou
HARBOR CITY Los Angeles
HARMONY San Luis Obispo
HAT CREEK Shasta
HATHAWAY PINES Calaveras
HAWAIIAN GARDENS Los Angeles
HAWTHORNE Los Angeles
HAYFORK Trinity
HAYWARD Alameda
HEALDSBURG Sonoma
HEBER Imperial
HELENDALE San Bernardino
HELM Fresno
HEMET Riverside
HERALD Sacramento
HERCULES Contra Costa
HERLONG Lassen
HERMOSA BEACH Los Angeles
HESPERIA San Bernardino
HICKMAN Stanislaus
HIDDEN VALLEY LAKE Lake
HIGHLAND San Bernardino
HILMAR Merced
HINKLEY San Bernardino
HOLLISTER San Benito
HOLT San Joaquin
HOLTVILLE Imperial
HOLY CITY Santa Clara
HOMELAND Riverside
HOMEWOOD Placer
HONEYDEW Humboldt
HOOD Sacramento
HOOPA Humboldt
HOPLAND Mendocino
HORNBROOK Siskiyou
HORNITOS Mariposa
HORSE CREEK Siskiyou
HUGHSON Stanislaus
HUME Fresno
HUNTINGTON BEACH Orange
HUNTINGTON LAKE Fresno
HUNTINGTON PARK Los Angeles
HURON Fresno
HYAMPOM Trinity
HYDESVILLE Humboldt
IDYLLWILD Riverside
IGO Shasta
IMPERIAL Imperial
IMPERIAL BEACH San Diego
INDEPENDENCE Inyo
INDIAN WELLS Riverside
INDIO Riverside
INGLEWOOD Los Angeles
INVERNESS Marin
INYOKERN (93527) Kern(93), Inyo(3), Tulare(2)
IONE Amador
IRVINE Orange
ISLETON Sacramento
IVANHOE Tulare
JACKSON Amador
JACUMBA San Diego
JAMESTOWN Tuolumne
JAMUL San Diego
JANESVILLE Lassen
JENNER Sonoma
JOHANNESBURG Kern
JOLON Monterey
JOSHUA TREE San Bernardino
JULIAN San Diego
JUNCTION CITY Trinity
JUNE LAKE Mono
KAWEAH Tulare
KEELER Inyo
KEENE Kern
KELSEYVILLE Lake
KENTFIELD Marin
KENWOOD Sonoma
KERMAN Fresno
KERNVILLE (93238) Kern(89), Tulare(10)
KETTLEMAN CITY Kings
KEYES Stanislaus
KING CITY Monterey
KINGS BEACH Placer
KINGS CANYON NATIONAL PK Tulare
KINGSBURG (93631) Fresno(83), Tulare(11), Kings(4)

KIRKWOOD Alpine
KIT CARSON Amador
KLAMATH Del Norte
KLAMATH RIVER Siskiyou
KNEELAND Humboldt
KNIGHTS LANDING (95645) Sutter(84), Yolo(15)
KNIGHTSEN Contra Costa
KORBEL Humboldt
KYBURZ El Dorado
LA CANADA FLINTRIDGE Los Angeles
LA COUNTY TAX COLLECTOR Los Angeles
LA CRESCENTA Los Angeles
LA GRANGE (95329) Tuolumne(57), Mariposa(34), Stanislaus(8)
LA HABRA (90631) Orange(87), Los Angeles(12)
LA HABRA Orange
LA HONDA San Mateo
LA JOLLA San Diego
LA MESA San Diego
LA MIRADA (90638) Los Angeles(98), Orange(1)
LA MIRADA Los Angeles
LA PALMA Orange
LA PUENTE Los Angeles
LA QUINTA Riverside
LA VERNE Los Angeles
LADERA RANCH Orange
LAFAYETTE Contra Costa
LAGUNA BEACH Orange
LAGUNA HILLS Orange
LAGUNA NIGUEL Orange
LAGUNITAS Marin
LAKE ARROWHEAD San Bernardino
LAKE CITY Modoc
LAKE ELSINORE Riverside
LAKE FOREST Orange
LAKE HUGHES Los Angeles
LAKE ISABELLA Kern
LAKEHEAD Shasta
LAKEPORT Lake
LAKESHORE Fresno
LAKESIDE San Diego
LAKEVIEW Riverside
LAKEWOOD Los Angeles
LAMONT Kern
LANCASTER Los Angeles
LANDERS San Bernardino
LARKSPUR Marin
LATHROP San Joaquin
LATON (93242) Fresno(84), Kings(15)
LAWNDALE Los Angeles
LAYTONVILLE Mendocino
LE GRAND Merced
LEBEC (93243) Kern(73), Los Angeles(26)
LEE VINING Mono
LEGGETT Mendocino
LEMON COVE Tulare
LEMON GROVE San Diego
LEMOORE Kings
LEWISTON Trinity
LIKELY Modoc
LINCOLN Placer
LINCOLN ACRES San Diego
LINDEN (95236) San Joaquin(95), Calaveras(4)
LINDSAY Tulare
LITCHFIELD Lassen
LITTLE LAKE Inyo
LITTLERIVER Mendocino
LITTLEROCK Los Angeles
LIVE OAK Sutter
LIVERMORE (94551) Alameda(97), Contra Costa(2)
LIVERMORE Alameda
LIVINGSTON Merced
LLANO Los Angeles
LOCKEFORD San Joaquin
LOCKWOOD Monterey
LODI San Joaquin
LOLETA Humboldt
LOMA LINDA San Bernardino
LOMA MAR San Mateo
LOMITA Los Angeles
LOMPOC Santa Barbara
LONE PINE Inyo
LONG BARN Tuolumne
LONG BEACH Los Angeles
LOOKOUT Modoc
LOOMIS Placer
LOS ALAMITOS Orange
LOS ALAMOS Santa Barbara
LOS ALTOS Santa Clara
LOS ANGELES Los Angeles
LOS BANOS Merced
LOS GATOS (95033) Santa Cruz(66), Santa Clara(33)
LOS GATOS Santa Clara
LOS MOLINOS Tehama
LOS OLIVOS Santa Barbara
LOS OSOS San Luis Obispo
LOST HILLS Kern
LOTUS El Dorado
LOWER LAKE Lake
LOYALTON Sierra
LUCERNE Lake
LUCERNE VALLEY San Bernardino
LUDLOW San Bernardino
LYNWOOD Los Angeles
LYOTH San Joaquin
LYTLE CREEK San Bernardino
MACDOEL Siskiyou
MAD RIVER Trinity
MADELINE Lassen
MADERA Madera
MADISON Yolo
MAGALIA Butte
MALIBU (90265) Los Angeles(94), Ventura(5)
MALIBU Los Angeles
MAMMOTH LAKES Mono
MANCHESTER Mendocino
MANHATTAN BEACH Los Angeles
MANTECA San Joaquin
MANTON (96059) Tehama(67), Shasta(32)
MARCH AIR FORCE BASE Riverside
MARICOPA (93252) Kern(60), Santa Barbara(24), Ventura(12), San Luis Obispo(2)
MARINA Monterey
MARINA DEL REY Los Angeles
MARIPOSA Mariposa
MARKLEEVILLE Alpine
MARSHALL Marin
MARTELL Amador
MARTINEZ Contra Costa
MARYSVILLE Yuba
MATHER Sacramento
MAXWELL Colusa
MAYWOOD Los Angeles
MC FARLAND Kern
MC KITTRICK Kern
MCARTHUR (96056) Lassen(54), Shasta(31), Modoc(14)
MCARTHUR Lassen
MCCLELLAN Sacramento
MCCLELLAN AFB Sacramento
MCCLOUD Siskiyou
MCKINLEYVILLE Humboldt
MEADOW VALLEY Plumas
MEADOW VISTA Placer
MECCA Riverside
MENDOCINO Mendocino
MENDOTA Fresno
MENIFEE Riverside
MENLO PARK San Mateo
MENTONE San Bernardino
MERCED Merced
MERIDIAN (95957) Sutter(97), Colusa(2)
MI WUK VILLAGE Tuolumne
MIDDLETOWN Lake
MIDPINES Mariposa
MIDWAY CITY Orange
MILFORD Lassen
MILL CREEK Tehama
MILL VALLEY Marin
MILLBRAE San Mateo
MILLVILLE Shasta
MILPITAS Santa Clara
MINERAL Tehama
MIRA LOMA Riverside
MIRAMONTE (93641) Fresno(90), Tulare(10)
MIRANDA Humboldt
MISSION HILLS Los Angeles
MISSION VIEJO Orange
MOBIL OIL CREDIT CORPORATION Contra Costa
MOCCASIN Tuolumne
MODESTO Stanislaus
MOJAVE Kern
MOKELUMNE HILL Calaveras
MONO HOT SPRINGS Fresno
MONROVIA Los Angeles
MONTAGUE Siskiyou
MONTARA San Mateo
MONTCLAIR San Bernardino
MONTE RIO Sonoma
MONTEBELLO Los Angeles
MONTEREY Monterey
MONTEREY PARK Los Angeles
MONTGOMERY CREEK Shasta
MONTGOMERY WARD Contra Costa
MONTROSE Los Angeles
MOORPARK Ventura
MORAGA Contra Costa
MORENO VALLEY Riverside
MORGAN HILL Santa Clara
MORONGO VALLEY San Bernardino
MORRO BAY San Luis Obispo
MOSS BEACH San Mateo
MOSS LANDING Monterey
MOUNT AUKUM El Dorado
MOUNT HAMILTON Santa Clara
MOUNT HERMON Santa Cruz
MOUNT LAGUNA San Diego
MOUNT SHASTA Siskiyou
MOUNT WILSON Los Angeles
MOUNTAIN CENTER Riverside
MOUNTAIN PASS San Bernardino
MOUNTAIN RANCH Calaveras
MOUNTAIN VIEW Santa Clara
MT BALDY Los Angeles
MURPHYS Calaveras
MURRIETA Riverside
MYERS FLAT Humboldt
NAPA Napa
NATIONAL CITY San Diego
NAVARRO Mendocino
NEEDLES San Bernardino
NELSON Butte
NESTOR San Diego
NEVADA CITY Nevada
NEW ALMADEN Santa Clara
NEW CUYAMA Santa Barbara
NEWARK Alameda
NEWBERRY SPRINGS San Bernardino
NEWBURY PARK Ventura
NEWCASTLE Placer
NEWHALL Los Angeles
NEWMAN Stanislaus
NEWPORT BEACH Orange
NEWPORT COAST Orange
NICASIO Marin
NICE Lake
NICOLAUS Sutter
NILAND Imperial
NIPOMO San Luis Obispo
NIPTON San Bernardino
NORCO Riverside
NORDEN Nevada
NORTH FORK Madera
NORTH HIGHLANDS Sacramento
NORTH HILLS Los Angeles
NORTH HOLLYWOOD Los Angeles
NORTH PALM SPRINGS Riverside
NORTH SAN JUAN (95960) Nevada(61), Sierra(31), Yuba(6)
NORTHRIDGE Los Angeles
NORWALK Los Angeles
NOVATO Marin
NUBIEBER Lassen
NUEVO Riverside
O NEALS Madera
OAK PARK Ventura
OAK RUN Shasta
OAK VIEW Ventura
OAKDALE Stanislaus
OAKHILLS San Bernardino
OAKHURST Madera
OAKLAND Alameda
OAKLEY Contra Costa
OAKVILLE Napa
OBRIEN Shasta
OCCIDENTAL Sonoma
OCEANO San Luis Obispo
OCEANSIDE San Diego
OCOTILLO Imperial
OJAI Ventura
OLANCHA Inyo
OLD STATION Shasta
OLEMA Marin
OLIVEHURST Yuba
OLYMPIC VALLEY Placer
ONTARIO San Bernardino
ONYX Kern
ORANGE Orange
ORANGE COVE (93646) Fresno(90), Tulare(10)
ORANGEVALE Sacramento
OREGON HOUSE Yuba
ORICK Humboldt
ORINDA Contra Costa
ORLAND Glenn
ORLEANS Humboldt
ORO GRANDE San Bernardino
OROSI Tulare
OROVILLE Butte
OXNARD Ventura
PACIFIC GROVE Monterey
PACIFIC PALISADES Los Angeles
PACIFICA San Mateo
PACOIMA Los Angeles
PAICINES San Benito
PALA San Diego
PALERMO Butte
PALM DESERT Riverside
PALM SPRINGS Riverside
PALMDALE Los Angeles
PALO ALTO (94303) Santa Clara(51), San Mateo(48)
PALO ALTO San Mateo
PALO ALTO Santa Clara
PALO CEDRO Shasta
PALO VERDE Imperial
PALOMAR MOUNTAIN San Diego
PALOS VERDES PENINSULA Los Angeles
PANORAMA CITY Los Angeles
PARADISE Butte
PARAMOUNT Los Angeles
PARKER DAM San Bernardino
PARLIER Fresno
PASADENA Los Angeles
PASKENTA Tehama
PASO ROBLES San Luis Obispo
PATTERSON Stanislaus
PATTON San Bernardino
PAUMA VALLEY San Diego
PAYNES CREEK Tehama
PEARBLOSSOM Los Angeles
PEBBLE BEACH Monterey
PENN VALLEY Nevada
PENNGROVE Sonoma
PENRYN Placer
PERRIS Riverside

PESCADERO San Mateo
PETALUMA Sonoma
PETROLIA Humboldt
PHELAN San Bernardino
PHILLIPSVILLE Humboldt
PHILO Mendocino
PICO RIVERA Los Angeles
PIEDMONT Alameda
PIEDRA Fresno
PIERCY Mendocino
PILOT HILL El Dorado
PINE GROVE Amador
PINE VALLEY San Diego
PINECREST Tuolumne
PINOLE Contra Costa
PINON HILLS San Bernardino
PIONEER Amador
PIONEERTOWN San Bernardino
PIRU Ventura
PISMO BEACH San Luis Obispo
PITTSBURG Contra Costa
PIXLEY Tulare
PLACENTIA Orange
PLACERVILLE El Dorado
PLANADA Merced
PLATINA (96076) Tehama(46), Trinity(27), Shasta(25)
PLAYA DEL REY Los Angeles
PLEASANT GROVE (95668) Sutter(72), Placer(27)
PLEASANT HILL Contra Costa
PLEASANTON Alameda
PLEASANTON Contra Costa
PLYMOUTH Amador
POINT ARENA Mendocino
POINT MUGU NAWC Ventura
POINT REYES STATION Marin
POLLOCK PINES El Dorado
POMONA (91766) Los Angeles(95), San Bernardino(4)
POMONA Los Angeles
POPE VALLEY Napa
PORT COSTA Contra Costa
PORT HUENEME Ventura
PORT HUENEME CBC BASE Ventura
PORTERVILLE Tulare
PORTOLA Plumas
PORTOLA VALLEY San Mateo
POSEY Tulare
POTRERO San Diego
POTTER VALLEY Mendocino
POWAY San Diego
PRATHER Fresno
PRINCETON (95970) Glenn(79), Colusa(20)
PROBERTA Tehama
QUINCY Plumas
RACKERBY Yuba
RAIL ROAD FLAT Calaveras
RAISIN Fresno
RAMONA San Diego
RANCHITA San Diego
RANCHO CORDOVA Sacramento
RANCHO CUCAMONGA San Bernardino
RANCHO MIRAGE Riverside
RANCHO PALOS VERDES Los Angeles
RANCHO SANTA FE San Diego
RANCHO SANTA MARGARITA Orange
RANDSBURG Kern
RAVENDALE Lassen
RAYMOND (93653) Madera(79), Mariposa(20)
RED BLUFF Tehama
RED MOUNTAIN Kern
REDCREST Humboldt
REDDING Shasta
REDLANDS (92373) San Bernardino(96), Riverside(3)
REDLANDS San Bernardino
REDONDO BEACH Los Angeles
REDWAY Humboldt
REDWOOD CITY San Mateo
REDWOOD ESTATES Santa Clara
REDWOOD VALLEY Mendocino
REEDLEY (93654) Fresno(97), Tulare(2)
REPRESA Sacramento
RESCUE El Dorado
RESEDA Los Angeles
RIALTO San Bernardino
RICHGROVE Tulare
RICHMOND Contra Costa
RICHVALE Butte
RIDGECREST (93555) Kern(98), San Bernardino(1)
RIDGECREST Kern
RIMFOREST San Bernardino
RIO DELL Humboldt
RIO LINDA Sacramento
RIO NIDO Sonoma
RIO OSO Sutter
RIO VISTA (94571) Solano(94), Sacramento(5)
RIPLEY (92272) Riverside(98), San Diego(1)
RIPON San Joaquin
RIVER PINES Amador
RIVERBANK Stanislaus
RIVERDALE (93656) Fresno(88), Kings(11)
RIVERSIDE Riverside
ROBBINS Sutter
ROCKLIN Placer
RODEO Contra Costa
ROHNERT PARK Sonoma
ROSAMOND (93560) Kern(98), Los Angeles(1)
ROSEMEAD Los Angeles
ROSEVILLE Placer
ROSS Marin
ROUGH AND READY Nevada
ROUND MOUNTAIN Shasta
ROWLAND HEIGHTS Los Angeles
RUMSEY Yolo
RUNNING SPRINGS San Bernardino
RUTHERFORD Napa
RYDE Sacramento
SACRAMENTO (95837) Sacramento(70), Sutter(29)
SACRAMENTO Sacramento
SAINT HELENA Napa
SALIDA Stanislaus
SALINAS Monterey
SALTON CITY Imperial
SALYER Trinity
SAMOA Humboldt
SAN ANDREAS Calaveras
SAN ANSELMO Marin
SAN ARDO Monterey
SAN BERNARDINO San Bernardino
SAN BRUNO San Mateo
SAN CARLOS San Mateo
SAN CLEMENTE Orange
SAN DIEGO San Diego
SAN DIMAS Los Angeles
SAN FERNANDO Los Angeles
SAN FRANCISCO San Francisco
SAN FRANCISCO San Mateo
SAN GABRIEL Los Angeles
SAN GERONIMO Marin
SAN GREGORIO San Mateo
SAN JACINTO Riverside
SAN JOAQUIN Fresno
SAN JOSE Santa Clara
SAN JUAN BAUTISTA San Benito
SAN JUAN CAPISTRANO Orange
SAN LEANDRO Alameda
SAN LORENZO Alameda
SAN LUCAS Monterey
SAN LUIS OBISPO San Luis Obispo
SAN LUIS REY San Diego
SAN MARCOS San Diego
SAN MARINO Los Angeles
SAN MARTIN Santa Clara
SAN MATEO San Mateo
SAN MIGUEL (93451) San Luis Obispo(58), Monterey(41)
SAN PABLO Contra Costa
SAN PEDRO Los Angeles
SAN QUENTIN Marin
SAN RAFAEL Marin
SAN RAMON Contra Costa
SAN SIMEON San Luis Obispo
SAN YSIDRO San Diego
SANGER Fresno
SANTA ANA Orange
SANTA BARBARA Santa Barbara
SANTA CLARA Santa Clara
SANTA CLARITA Los Angeles
SANTA CRUZ Santa Cruz
SANTA FE SPRINGS Los Angeles
SANTA MARGARITA San Luis Obispo
SANTA MARIA (93454) Santa Barbara(98), San Luis Obispo(1)
SANTA MARIA Santa Barbara
SANTA MONICA Los Angeles
SANTA PAULA Ventura
SANTA RITA PARK Merced
SANTA ROSA Sonoma
SANTA YNEZ Santa Barbara
SANTA YSABEL San Diego
SANTEE San Diego
SARATOGA Santa Clara
SAUSALITO Marin
SCOTIA Humboldt
SCOTT BAR Siskiyou
SCOTTS VALLEY Santa Cruz
SEAL BEACH Orange
SEASIDE Monterey
SEBASTOPOL Sonoma
SEELEY Imperial
SEIAD VALLEY Siskiyou
SELMA Fresno
SEQUOIA NATIONAL PARK Tulare
SHAFTER Kern
SHANDON San Luis Obispo
SHASTA Shasta
SHASTA LAKE Shasta
SHAVER LAKE Fresno
SHEEP RANCH Calaveras
SHERIDAN Placer
SHERMAN OAKS Los Angeles
SHINGLE SPRINGS El Dorado
SHINGLETOWN Shasta
SHOSHONE Inyo
SIERRA CITY Sierra
SIERRA MADRE Los Angeles
SIERRAVILLE Sierra
SIGNAL HILL Los Angeles
SILVERADO Orange
SIMI VALLEY Ventura
SKYFOREST San Bernardino
SLOUGHHOUSE Sacramento
SMARTVILLE (95977) Nevada(62), Yuba(37)
SMITH RIVER Del Norte
SNELLING Merced
SODA SPRINGS Nevada
SOLANA BEACH San Diego
SOLEDAD Monterey
SOLVANG Santa Barbara
SOMERSET El Dorado
SOMES BAR Siskiyou
SOMIS Ventura
SONOMA Sonoma
SONORA Tuolumne
SOQUEL Santa Cruz
SOULSBYVILLE Tuolumne
SOUTH DOS PALOS Merced
SOUTH EL MONTE Los Angeles
SOUTH GATE Los Angeles
SOUTH LAKE TAHOE El Dorado
SOUTH PASADENA Los Angeles
SOUTH SAN FRANCISCO San Mateo
SPRECKELS Monterey
SPRING VALLEY San Diego
SPRINGVILLE Tulare
SQUAW VALLEY Fresno
STANDARD Tuolumne
STANDISH Lassen
STANTON Orange
STEVENSON RANCH Los Angeles
STEVINSON Merced
STEWARTS POINT Sonoma
STINSON BEACH Marin
STIRLING CITY Butte
STOCKTON San Joaquin
STONYFORD Colusa
STORRIE Plumas
STRATFORD Kings
STRATHMORE Tulare
STRAWBERRY Tuolumne
STRAWBERRY VALLEY (95981) Yuba(66), Plumas(33)
STUDIO CITY Los Angeles
SUGARLOAF San Bernardino
SUISUN CITY Solano
SULTANA Tulare
SUMMERLAND Santa Barbara
SUN CITY Riverside
SUN VALLEY Los Angeles
SUNLAND Los Angeles
SUNNYVALE Santa Clara
SUNOL Alameda
SUNSET BEACH Orange
SURFSIDE Orange
SUSANVILLE Lassen
SUTTER Sutter
SUTTER CREEK Amador
SYLMAR Los Angeles
TAFT Kern
TAHOE CITY Placer
TAHOE VISTA Placer
TAHOMA El Dorado
TALMAGE Mendocino
TARZANA Los Angeles
TAYLORSVILLE Plumas
TECATE San Diego
TECOPA Inyo
TEHACHAPI Kern
TEHAMA Tehama
TEMECULA Riverside
TEMPLE CITY Los Angeles
TEMPLETON San Luis Obispo
TERMO Lassen
TERRA BELLA Tulare
THE SEA RANCH Sonoma
THERMAL (92274) Riverside(65), Imperial(34)
THORNTON San Joaquin
THOUSAND OAKS (91362) Ventura(83), Los Angeles(16)
THOUSAND OAKS Ventura
THOUSAND PALMS Riverside
THREE RIVERS Tulare
TIPTON Tulare
TOLLHOUSE Fresno
TOLUCA LAKE Los Angeles
TOMALES Marin
TOPANGA Los Angeles
TOPAZ Mono
TORRANCE Los Angeles
TRABUCO CANYON Orange
TRACY (95391) San Joaquin(88), Alameda(11)
TRACY San Joaquin
TRANQUILLITY Fresno
TRAVER Tulare
TRAVIS AFB Solano
TRES PINOS San Benito
TRINIDAD Humboldt
TRINITY CENTER (96091) Trinity(56), Siskiyou(43)
TRONA San Bernardino
TRUCKEE (96161) Nevada(89), Placer(10)
TRUCKEE Nevada
TUJUNGA Los Angeles
TULARE Tulare

TULELAKE (96134) Modoc(71), Siskiyou(28)
TUOLUMNE Tuolumne
TUPMAN Kern
TURLOCK Stanislaus
TUSTIN Orange
TWAIN Plumas
TWAIN HARTE Tuolumne
TWENTYNINE PALMS San Bernardino
TWIN BRIDGES El Dorado
TWIN PEAKS San Bernardino
UKIAH Mendocino
UNION CITY Alameda
UNIVERSAL CITY Los Angeles
UPLAND San Bernardino
UPPER LAKE Lake
VACAVILLE Solano
VALENCIA Los Angeles
VALLECITO Calaveras
VALLEJO Solano
VALLEY CENTER San Diego
VALLEY FORD Sonoma
VALLEY HOME Stanislaus
VALLEY SPRINGS Calaveras
VALLEY VILLAGE Los Angeles
VALYERMO Los Angeles
VAN NUYS Los Angeles
VENICE Los Angeles
VENTURA Ventura
VERDUGO CITY Los Angeles
VERNALIS (95385) Stanislaus(76), San Joaquin(23)
VICTOR San Joaquin
VICTORVILLE San Bernardino
VIDAL San Bernardino
VILLA GRANDE Sonoma
VILLA PARK Orange
VINA Tehama
VINEBURG Sonoma
VINTON Plumas
VISALIA Tulare
VISTA San Diego
VOLCANO Amador
WALLACE Calaveras
WALNUT Los Angeles
WALNUT CREEK Contra Costa
WALNUT GROVE (95690) Sacramento(73), Solano(17), San Joaquin(8)
WARNER SPRINGS San Diego
WASCO Kern
WASHINGTON Nevada
WATERFORD Stanislaus
WATSONVILLE (95076) Santa Cruz(86), Monterey(13)
WATSONVILLE Santa Cruz
WAUKENA Tulare
WEAVERVILLE Trinity
WEED Siskiyou
WEIMAR Placer
WELDON Kern
WENDEL Lassen
WEOTT Humboldt
WEST COVINA Los Angeles
WEST HILLS (91307) Los Angeles(94), Ventura(5)
WEST HILLS Los Angeles
WEST HOLLYWOOD Los Angeles
WEST POINT Calaveras
WEST SACRAMENTO Yolo
WESTLAKE VILLAGE (91361) Ventura(74), Los Angeles(25)
WESTLAKE VILLAGE Los Angeles
WESTLAKE VILLAGE Ventura
WESTLEY Stanislaus
WESTMINSTER Orange
WESTMORLAND Imperial
WESTPORT Mendocino
WESTWOOD (96137) Plumas(70), Lassen(29)
WHEATLAND Yuba
WHISKEYTOWN Shasta
WHITE WATER Riverside
WHITETHORN (95589) Humboldt(95), Mendocino(4)
WHITMORE Shasta
WHITTIER Los Angeles
WILDOMAR Riverside
WILLIAMS Colusa
WILLITS Mendocino
WILLOW CREEK Humboldt
WILLOWS Glenn
WILMINGTON Los Angeles
WILSEYVILLE Calaveras
WILTON Sacramento
WINCHESTER Riverside
WINDSOR Sonoma
WINNETKA Los Angeles
WINTERHAVEN Imperial
WINTERS (95694) Yolo(85), Solano(14)
WINTON Merced
WISHON Madera
WITTER SPRINGS Lake
WOFFORD HEIGHTS Kern
WOODACRE Marin
WOODBRIDGE San Joaquin
WOODLAKE Tulare
WOODLAND Yolo
WOODLAND HILLS Los Angeles
WOODY Kern
WRIGHTWOOD San Bernardino
YERMO San Bernardino
YETTEM Tulare
YOLO Yolo
YORBA LINDA Orange
YORKVILLE Mendocino
YOSEMITE NATIONAL PARK Mariposa
YOUNTVILLE Napa
YREKA Siskiyou
YUBA CITY Sutter
YUCAIPA (92399) San Bernardino(98), Riverside(1)
YUCCA VALLEY San Bernardino
ZAMORA Yolo
ZENIA Trinity

California ZIP/City Cross Reference

90000-90068 LOS ANGELES
90069-90069 WEST HOLLYWOOD
90070-90189 LOS ANGELES
90201-90201 BELL
90202-90202 BELL GARDENS
90209-90213 BEVERLY HILLS
90220-90224 COMPTON
90230-90233 CULVER CITY
90239-90242 DOWNEY
90245-90245 EL SEGUNDO
90247-90249 GARDENA
90250-90251 HAWTHORNE
90254-90254 HERMOSA BEACH
90255-90255 HUNTINGTON PARK
90260-90261 LAWNDALE
90262-90262 LYNWOOD
90263-90265 MALIBU
90266-90267 MANHATTAN BEACH
90270-90270 MAYWOOD
90272-90272 PACIFIC PALISADES
90274-90274 PALOS VERDES PENINSULA
90275-90275 RANCHO PALOS VERDES
90277-90278 REDONDO BEACH
90280-90280 SOUTH GATE
90290-90290 TOPANGA
90291-90291 VENICE
90292-90292 MARINA DEL REY
90293-90293 PLAYA DEL REY
90294-90294 VENICE
90295-90295 MARINA DEL REY
90296-90296 PLAYA DEL REY
90300-90398 INGLEWOOD
90400-90411 SANTA MONICA
90500-90510 TORRANCE
90601-90612 WHITTIER
90620-90622 BUENA PARK
90623-90623 LA PALMA
90624-90624 BUENA PARK
90630-90630 CYPRESS
90631-90633 LA HABRA
90637-90639 LA MIRADA
90640-90640 MONTEBELLO
90650-90659 NORWALK
90660-90665 PICO RIVERA
90670-90671 SANTA FE SPRINGS
90680-90680 STANTON
90701-90702 ARTESIA
90703-90703 CERRITOS
90704-90704 AVALON
90706-90707 BELLFLOWER
90710-90710 HARBOR CITY
90711-90715 LAKEWOOD
90716-90716 HAWAIIAN GARDENS
90717-90717 LOMITA
90720-90721 LOS ALAMITOS
90723-90723 PARAMOUNT
90731-90734 SAN PEDRO
90740-90740 SEAL BEACH
90742-90742 SUNSET BEACH
90743-90743 SURFSIDE
90744-90744 WILMINGTON
90745-90747 CARSON
90748-90748 WILMINGTON
90749-90749 CARSON
90755-90755 SIGNAL HILL
90800-90899 LONG BEACH
90895-90895 CARSON
91001-91003 ALTADENA
91006-91007 ARCADIA
91009-91010 DUARTE
91011-91012 LA CANADA FLINTRIDGE
91016-91017 MONROVIA
91020-91021 MONTROSE
91023-91023 MOUNT WILSON
91024-91025 SIERRA MADRE
91030-91031 SOUTH PASADENA
91040-91041 SUNLAND
91042-91043 TUJUNGA
91046-91046 VERDUGO CITY
91050-91051 PASADENA
91052-91052 LA COUNTY TAX COL'R
91066-91077 ARCADIA
91100-91107 PASADENA
91108-91108 SAN MARINO
91109-91117 PASADENA
91118-91118 SAN MARINO
91121-91191 PASADENA
91200-91210 GLENDALE
91214-91214 LA CRESCENTA
91221-91222 GLENDALE
91224-91224 LA CRESCENTA
91225-91226 GLENDALE
91301-91301 AGOURA HILLS
91302-91302 CALABASAS
91303-91305 CANOGA PARK
91306-91306 WINNETKA
91307-91308 WEST HILLS
91309-91309 CANOGA PARK
91310-91310 CASTAIC
91311-91313 CHATSWORTH
91316-91316 ENCINO
91319-91320 NEWBURY PARK
91321-91322 NEWHALL
91324-91330 NORTHRIDGE
91331-91334 PACOIMA
91335-91337 RESEDA
91340-91341 SAN FERNANDO
91342-91342 SYLMAR
91343-91343 NORTH HILLS
91344-91344 GRANADA HILLS
91345-91346 MISSION HILLS
91350-91350 SANTA CLARITA
91351-91351 CANYON COUNTRY
91352-91353 SUN VALLEY
91354-91355 VALENCIA
91356-91357 TARZANA
91358-91358 THOUSAND OAKS
91359-91359 WESTLAKE VILLAGE
91360-91360 THOUSAND OAKS
91361-91361 WESTLAKE VILLAGE
91362-91362 THOUSAND OAKS
91363-91363 WESTLAKE VILLAGE
91364-91371 WOODLAND HILLS
91372-91372 CALABASAS
91375-91376 AGOURA HILLS
91377-91377 OAK PARK
91380-91380 SANTA CLARITA
91381-91381 STEVENSON RANCH
91382-91383 SANTA CLARITA
91384-91384 CASTAIC
91385-91385 VALENCIA
91386-91387 CANYON COUNTRY
91388-91388 VAN NUYS
91390-91390 SANTA CLARITA
91392-91392 SYLMAR
91393-91393 NORTH HILLS
91394-91394 GRANADA HILLS
91395-91395 MISSION HILLS
91396-91396 WINNETKA
91399-91399 WOODLAND HILLS
91400-91401 VAN NUYS
91402-91402 PANORAMA CITY
91403-91403 SHERMAN OAKS
91404-91411 VAN NUYS
91412-91412 PANORAMA CITY
91413-91413 SHERMAN OAKS
91416-91416 ENCINO
91423-91423 SHERMAN OAKS
91426-91436 ENCINO
91461-91494 VAN NUYS
91495-91495 SHERMAN OAKS
91496-91499 VAN NUYS
91500-91526 BURBANK
91600-91603 NORTH HOLLYWOOD
91604-91604 STUDIO CITY
91605-91606 NORTH HOLLYWOOD
91607-91607 VALLEY VILLAGE
91608-91608 UNIVERSAL CITY
91609-91609 NORTH HOLLYWOOD
91610-91610 TOLUCA LAKE
91611-91612 NORTH HOLLYWOOD
91614-91614 STUDIO CITY
91615-91616 NORTH HOLLYWOOD
91617-91617 VALLEY VILLAGE
91618-91618 UNIVERSAL CITY
91618-91618 NORTH HOLLYWOOD
91701-91701 ALTA LOMA
91702-91702 AZUSA
91706-91706 BALDWIN PARK
91708-91708 CHINO
91709-91709 CHINO HILLS
91710-91710 CHINO
91711-91711 CLAREMONT
91714-91716 CITY OF INDUSTRY
91718-91720 CORONA
91722-91724 COVINA
91729-91730 RANCHO CUCAMONGA
91731-91732 EL MONTE
91733-91733 SOUTH EL MONTE
91734-91735 EL MONTE
91737-91737 ALTA LOMA
91739-91739 RANCHO CUCAMONGA
91740-91741 GLENDORA

91743-91743 GUASTI
91744-91744 LA PUENTE
91745-91745 HACIENDA HEIGHTS
91746-91747 LA PUENTE
91748-91748 ROWLAND HEIGHTS
91749-91749 LA PUENTE
91750-91750 LA VERNE
91752-91752 MIRA LOMA
91754-91756 MONTEREY PARK
91758-91758 ONTARIO
91759-91759 MT BALDY
91760-91760 NORCO
91761-91762 ONTARIO
91763-91763 MONTCLAIR
91764-91764 ONTARIO
91765-91765 DIAMOND BAR
91766-91769 POMONA
91770-91772 ROSEMEAD
91773-91773 SAN DIMAS
91775-91778 SAN GABRIEL
91780-91780 TEMPLE CITY
91784-91786 UPLAND
91788-91789 WALNUT
91790-91793 WEST COVINA
91795-91795 WALNUT
91797-91797 BALDWIN PARK
91797-91797 POMONA
91798-91798 ONTARIO
91799-91799 POMONA
91800-91899 ALHAMBRA
91901-91901 ALPINE
91902-91902 BONITA
91903-91903 ALPINE
91905-91905 BOULEVARD
91906-91906 CAMPO
91908-91908 BONITA
91909-91915 CHULA VISTA
91916-91916 DESCANSO
91917-91917 DULZURA
91921-91921 CHULA VISTA
91931-91931 GUATAY
91932-91933 IMPERIAL BEACH
91934-91934 JACUMBA
91935-91935 JAMUL
91941-91944 LA MESA
91945-91946 LEMON GROVE
91947-91947 LINCOLN ACRES
91948-91948 MOUNT LAGUNA
91950-91951 NATIONAL CITY
91962-91962 PINE VALLEY
91963-91963 POTRERO
91976-91979 SPRING VALLEY
91980-91987 TECATE
91990-91995 POTRERO
92003-92003 BONSALL
92004-92004 BORREGO SPRINGS
92007-92007 CARDIFF BY THE SEA
92008-92013 CARLSBAD
92014-92014 DEL MAR
92018-92018 CARLSBAD
92019-92022 EL CAJON
92023-92024 ENCINITAS
92025-92027 ESCONDIDO
92028-92028 FALLBROOK
92029-92033 ESCONDIDO
92036-92036 JULIAN
92037-92039 LA JOLLA
92040-92040 LAKESIDE
92046-92046 ESCONDIDO
92049-92052 OCEANSIDE
92053-92053 NESTOR
92054-92054 OCEANSIDE
92055-92055 CAMP PENDLETON
92056-92058 OCEANSIDE
92059-92059 PALA
92060-92060 PALOMAR MOUNTAIN
92061-92061 PAUMA VALLEY
92064-92064 POWAY
92065-92065 RAMONA
92066-92066 RANCHITA
92067-92067 RANCHO SANTA FE
92068-92068 SAN LUIS REY

92069-92069 SAN MARCOS
92070-92070 SANTA YSABEL
92071-92072 SANTEE
92073-92073 SAN DIEGO
92074-92074 POWAY
92075-92075 SOLANA BEACH
92078-92079 SAN MARCOS
92081-92081 VISTA
92082-92082 VALLEY CENTER
92083-92085 VISTA
92086-92086 WARNER SPRINGS
92088-92088 FALLBROOK
92090-92090 EL CAJON
92091-92091 RANCHO SANTA FE
92092-92093 LA JOLLA
92096-92096 SAN MARCOS
92100-92117 SAN DIEGO
92118-92118 CORONADO
92119-92142 SAN DIEGO
92143-92143 SAN YSIDRO
92145-92172 SAN DIEGO
92173-92173 SAN YSIDRO
92174-92177 SAN DIEGO
92178-92178 CORONADO
92179-92199 SAN DIEGO
92201-92203 INDIO
92210-92210 INDIAN WELLS
92211-92211 PALM DESERT
92220-92220 BANNING
92222-92222 BARD
92223-92223 BEAUMONT
92225-92226 BLYTHE
92227-92227 BRAWLEY
92230-92230 CABAZON
92231-92232 CALEXICO
92233-92233 CALIPATRIA
92234-92235 CATHEDRAL CITY
92236-92236 COACHELLA
92239-92239 DESERT CENTER
92240-92241 DESERT HOT SPRINGS
92242-92242 EARP
92243-92244 EL CENTRO
92247-92248 LA QUINTA
92249-92249 HEBER
92250-92250 HOLTVILLE
92251-92251 IMPERIAL
92252-92252 JOSHUA TREE
92253-92253 LA QUINTA
92254-92254 MECCA
92255-92255 PALM DESERT
92256-92256 MORONGO VALLEY
92257-92257 NILAND
92258-92258 NORTH PALM SPRINGS
92259-92259 OCOTILLO
92260-92261 PALM DESERT
92262-92264 PALM SPRINGS
92266-92266 PALO VERDE
92267-92267 PARKER DAM
92268-92268 PIONEERTOWN
92270-92270 RANCHO MIRAGE
92272-92272 RIPLEY
92273-92273 SEELEY
92274-92274 THERMAL
92275-92275 SALTON CITY
92276-92276 THOUSAND PALMS
92277-92278 TWENTYNINE PALMS
92280-92280 VIDAL
92281-92281 WESTMORLAND
92282-92282 WHITE WATER
92283-92283 WINTERHAVEN
92284-92284 YUCCA VALLEY
92285-92285 LANDERS
92286-92286 YUCCA VALLEY
92292-92292 PALM SPRINGS
92301-92301 ADELANTO
92304-92304 AMBOY
92305-92305 ANGELUS OAKS
92307-92308 APPLE VALLEY
92309-92309 BAKER
92310-92310 FORT IRWIN
92311-92312 BARSTOW
92313-92313 GRAND TERRACE

92314-92314 BIG BEAR CITY
92315-92315 BIG BEAR LAKE
92316-92316 BLOOMINGTON
92317-92317 BLUE JAY
92318-92318 BRYN MAWR
92319-92319 CADIZ
92320-92320 CALIMESA
92321-92321 CEDAR GLEN
92322-92322 CEDARPINES PARK
92323-92323 CIMA
92324-92324 COLTON
92325-92325 CRESTLINE
92326-92326 CREST PARK
92327-92327 DAGGETT
92328-92328 DEATH VALLEY
92329-92329 PHELAN
92332-92332 ESSEX
92333-92333 FAWNSKIN
92334-92337 FONTANA
92338-92338 LUDLOW
92339-92339 FOREST FALLS
92340-92340 HESPERIA
92341-92341 GREEN VALLEY LAKE
92342-92342 HELENDALE
92344-92345 HESPERIA
92346-92346 HIGHLAND
92347-92347 HINKLEY
92350-92350 LOMA LINDA
92351-92351 BAKER
92352-92352 LAKE ARROWHEAD
92353-92353 LAKEVIEW
92354-92354 LOMA LINDA
92356-92356 LUCERNE VALLEY
92357-92357 LOMA LINDA
92358-92358 LYTLE CREEK
92359-92359 MENTONE
92363-92363 NEEDLES
92364-92364 NIPTON
92365-92365 NEWBERRY SPRINGS
92366-92366 MOUNTAIN PASS
92368-92368 ORO GRANDE
92369-92369 PATTON
92371-92371 PHELAN
92372-92372 PINON HILLS
92373-92375 REDLANDS
92376-92377 RIALTO
92378-92378 RIMFOREST
92382-92382 RUNNING SPRINGS
92384-92384 SHOSHONE
92385-92385 SKYFOREST
92386-92386 SUGARLOAF
92389-92389 TECOPA
92391-92391 TWIN PEAKS
92392-92395 VICTORVILLE
92397-92397 WRIGHTWOOD
92398-92398 YERMO
92399-92399 YUCAIPA
92400-92427 SAN BERNARDINO
92500-92517 RIVERSIDE
92518-92518 MARCH AIR FORCE BASE
92519-92522 RIVERSIDE
92530-92532 LAKE ELSINORE
92536-92536 AGUANGA
92539-92539 ANZA
92543-92546 HEMET
92548-92548 HOMELAND
92549-92549 IDYLLWILD
92551-92557 MORENO VALLEY
92561-92561 MOUNTAIN CENTER
92562-92564 MURRIETA
92567-92567 NUEVO
92570-92572 PERRIS
92581-92583 SAN JACINTO
92584-92584 MENIFEE
92585-92587 SUN CITY
92589-92593 TEMECULA
92595-92595 WILDOMAR
92596-92596 WINCHESTER
92599-92599 PERRIS
92601-92601 ATWOOD
92602-92604 IRVINE
92605-92605 HUNTINGTON BEACH

92606-92606 IRVINE
92607-92607 LAGUNA NIGUEL
92609-92609 EL TORO
92610-92610 FOOTHILL RANCH
92612-92612 IRVINE
92613-92613 ORANGE
92614-92614 IRVINE
92615-92615 HUNTINGTON BEACH
92616-92620 IRVINE
92621-92622 BREA
92623-92623 IRVINE
92624-92624 CAPISTRANO BEACH
92625-92625 CORONA DEL MAR
92626-92628 COSTA MESA
92629-92629 DANA POINT
92630-92630 LAKE FOREST
92631-92631 BREA
92632-92635 FULLERTON
92637-92637 LAGUNA HILLS
92640-92640 FULLERTON
92641-92645 GARDEN GROVE
92646-92649 HUNTINGTON BEACH
92650-92650 EAST IRVINE
92651-92652 LAGUNA BEACH
92653-92654 LAGUNA HILLS
92655-92655 MIDWAY CITY
92656-92656 ALISO VIEJO
92657-92657 NEWPORT COAST
92658-92663 NEWPORT BEACH
92664-92669 ORANGE
92670-92670 PLACENTIA
92672-92674 SAN CLEMENTE
92675-92675 SAN JUAN CAPISTRANO
92676-92676 SILVERADO
92677-92677 LAGUNA NIGUEL
92678-92679 TRABUCO CANYON
92680-92681 TUSTIN
92683-92685 WESTMINSTER
92686-92687 YORBA LINDA
92688-92688 RANCHO SANTA MARGARITA
92690-92692 MISSION VIEJO
92693-92693 SAN JUAN CAPISTRANO
92694-92694 MISSION VIEJO
92694-92694 LADERA RANCH
92697-92698 IRVINE
92698-92698 ALISO VIEJO
92701-92707 SANTA ANA
92708-92708 FOUNTAIN VALLEY
92709-92710 IRVINE
92711-92712 SANTA ANA
92713-92720 IRVINE
92725-92725 SANTA ANA
92728-92728 FOUNTAIN VALLEY
92730-92730 IRVINE
92735-92735 SANTA ANA
92780-92782 TUSTIN
92799-92799 SANTA ANA
92800-92809 ANAHEIM
92811-92811 ATWOOD
92812-92817 ANAHEIM
92821-92823 BREA
92825-92825 ANAHEIM
92831-92838 FULLERTON
92840-92846 GARDEN GROVE
92850-92850 ANAHEIM
92856-92859 ORANGE
92860-92860 NORCO
92861-92861 VILLA PARK
92862-92869 ORANGE
92870-92871 PLACENTIA
92877-92883 CORONA
92885-92887 YORBA LINDA
92899-92899 ANAHEIM
93001-93009 VENTURA
93010-93012 CAMARILLO
93013-93014 CARPINTERIA
93015-93016 FILLMORE
93020-93021 MOORPARK
93022-93022 OAK VIEW
93023-93024 OJAI
93030-93036 OXNARD
93040-93040 PIRU

Zip Range	City
93041-93041	PORT HUENEME
93042-93042	POINT MUGU NAWC
93043-93043	PORT HUENEME CBC BASE
93044-93044	PORT HUENEME
93060-93061	SANTA PAULA
93062-93063	SIMI VALLEY
93064-93064	BRANDEIS
93065-93065	SIMI VALLEY
93066-93066	SOMIS
93067-93067	SUMMERLAND
93093-93099	SIMI VALLEY
93101-93111	SANTA BARBARA
93116-93118	GOLETA
93120-93190	SANTA BARBARA
93199-93199	GOLETA
93201-93201	ALPAUGH
93202-93202	ARMONA
93203-93203	ARVIN
93204-93204	AVENAL
93205-93205	BODFISH
93206-93206	BUTTONWILLOW
93207-93207	CALIFORNIA HOT SPRINGS
93208-93208	CAMP NELSON
93210-93210	COALINGA
93212-93212	CORCORAN
93214-93214	CUYAMA
93215-93216	DELANO
93217-93217	DI GIORGIO
93218-93218	DUCOR
93219-93219	EARLIMART
93220-93220	EDISON
93221-93221	EXETER
93222-93222	FRAZIER PARK
93223-93223	FARMERSVILLE
93224-93224	FELLOWS
93225-93225	FRAZIER PARK
93226-93226	GLENNVILLE
93227-93227	GOSHEN
93230-93232	HANFORD
93234-93234	HURON
93235-93235	IVANHOE
93237-93237	KAWEAH
93238-93238	KERNVILLE
93239-93239	KETTLEMAN CITY
93240-93240	LAKE ISABELLA
93241-93241	LAMONT
93242-93242	LATON
93243-93243	LEBEC
93244-93244	LEMON COVE
93245-93246	LEMOORE
93247-93247	LINDSAY
93249-93249	LOST HILLS
93250-93250	MC FARLAND
93251-93251	MC KITTRICK
93252-93252	MARICOPA
93254-93254	NEW CUYAMA
93255-93255	ONYX
93256-93256	PIXLEY
93257-93258	PORTERVILLE
93260-93260	POSEY
93261-93261	RICHGROVE
93262-93262	SEQUOIA NATIONAL PARK
93263-93263	SHAFTER
93265-93265	SPRINGVILLE
93266-93266	STRATFORD
93267-93267	STRATHMORE
93268-93268	TAFT
93270-93270	TERRA BELLA
93271-93271	THREE RIVERS
93272-93272	TIPTON
93274-93275	TULARE
93276-93276	TUPMAN
93277-93279	VISALIA
93280-93280	WASCO
93282-93282	WAUKENA
93283-93283	WELDON
93285-93285	WOFFORD HEIGHTS
93286-93286	WOODLAKE
93287-93287	WOODY
93290-93292	VISALIA
93300-93399	BAKERSFIELD
93401-93401	SAN LUIS OBISPO
93402-93402	LOS OSOS
93403-93410	SAN LUIS OBISPO
93412-93412	LOS OSOS
93420-93421	ARROYO GRANDE
93422-93423	ATASCADERO
93424-93424	AVILA BEACH
93426-93426	BRADLEY
93427-93427	BUELLTON
93428-93428	CAMBRIA
93429-93429	CASMALIA
93430-93430	CAYUCOS
93431-93431	CHOLAME
93432-93432	CRESTON
93433-93433	GROVER BEACH
93434-93434	GUADALUPE
93435-93435	HARMONY
93436-93438	LOMPOC
93440-93440	LOS ALAMOS
93441-93441	LOS OLIVOS
93442-93443	MORRO BAY
93444-93444	NIPOMO
93445-93445	OCEANO
93446-93447	PASO ROBLES
93448-93449	PISMO BEACH
93450-93450	SAN ARDO
93451-93451	SAN MIGUEL
93452-93452	SAN SIMEON
93453-93453	SANTA MARGARITA
93454-93458	SANTA MARIA
93460-93460	SANTA YNEZ
93461-93461	SHANDON
93463-93464	SOLVANG
93465-93465	TEMPLETON
93475-93475	OCEANO
93483-93483	GROVER BEACH
93501-93502	MOJAVE
93504-93505	CALIFORNIA CITY
93510-93510	ACTON
93512-93512	BENTON
93513-93513	BIG PINE
93514-93515	BISHOP
93516-93516	BORON
93517-93517	BRIDGEPORT
93518-93518	CALIENTE
93519-93519	CANTIL
93522-93522	DARWIN
93523-93524	EDWARDS
93526-93526	INDEPENDENCE
93527-93527	INYOKERN
93528-93528	JOHANNESBURG
93529-93529	JUNE LAKE
93530-93530	KEELER
93531-93531	KEENE
93532-93532	LAKE HUGHES
93534-93539	LANCASTER
93541-93541	LEE VINING
93542-93542	LITTLE LAKE
93543-93543	LITTLEROCK
93544-93544	LLANO
93545-93545	LONE PINE
93546-93546	MAMMOTH LAKES
93549-93549	OLANCHA
93550-93552	PALMDALE
93553-93553	PEARBLOSSOM
93554-93554	RANDSBURG
93555-93556	RIDGECREST
93558-93558	RED MOUNTAIN
93560-93560	ROSAMOND
93561-93561	TEHACHAPI
93562-93562	TRONA
93563-93563	VALYERMO
93570-93570	KEENE
93581-93582	TEHACHAPI
93584-93586	LANCASTER
93590-93591	PALMDALE
93592-93592	TRONA
93596-93596	BORON
93599-93599	PALMDALE
93601-93601	AHWAHNEE
93602-93602	AUBERRY
93603-93603	BADGER
93604-93604	BASS LAKE
93605-93605	BIG CREEK
93606-93606	BIOLA
93607-93607	BURREL
93608-93608	CANTUA CREEK
93609-93609	CARUTHERS
93610-93610	CHOWCHILLA
93611-93613	CLOVIS
93614-93614	COARSEGOLD
93615-93615	CUTLER
93616-93616	DEL REY
93618-93618	DINUBA
93619-93619	CLOVIS
93620-93620	DOS PALOS
93621-93621	DUNLAP
93622-93622	FIREBAUGH
93623-93623	FISH CAMP
93624-93624	FIVE POINTS
93625-93625	FOWLER
93626-93626	FRIANT
93627-93627	HELM
93628-93628	HUME
93629-93629	HUNTINGTON LAKE
93630-93630	KERMAN
93631-93631	KINGSBURG
93633-93633	KINGS CANYON NAT PK
93634-93634	LAKESHORE
93635-93635	LOS BANOS
93637-93639	MADERA
93640-93640	MENDOTA
93641-93641	MIRAMONTE
93642-93642	MONO HOT SPRINGS
93643-93643	NORTH FORK
93644-93644	OAKHURST
93645-93645	O NEALS
93646-93646	ORANGE COVE
93647-93647	OROSI
93648-93648	PARLIER
93649-93649	PIEDRA
93650-93650	FRESNO
93651-93651	PRATHER
93652-93652	RAISIN
93653-93653	RAYMOND
93654-93654	REEDLEY
93656-93656	RIVERDALE
93657-93657	SANGER
93660-93660	SAN JOAQUIN
93661-93661	SANTA RITA PARK
93662-93662	SELMA
93664-93664	SHAVER LAKE
93665-93665	SOUTH DOS PALOS
93666-93666	SULTANA
93667-93667	TOLLHOUSE
93668-93668	TRANQUILLITY
93669-93669	WISHON
93670-93670	YETTEM
93673-93673	TRAVER
93675-93675	SQUAW VALLEY
93700-93888	FRESNO
93901-93915	SALINAS
93920-93920	BIG SUR
93921-93923	CARMEL
93924-93924	CARMEL VALLEY
93925-93925	CHUALAR
93926-93926	GONZALES
93927-93927	GREENFIELD
93928-93928	JOLON
93930-93930	KING CITY
93932-93932	LOCKWOOD
93933-93933	MARINA
93940-93940	MONTEREY
93941-93941	FT ORD
93941-93941	FORT ORD
93941-93944	MONTEREY
93950-93950	PACIFIC GROVE
93953-93953	PEBBLE BEACH
93954-93954	SAN LUCAS
93955-93955	SEASIDE
93960-93960	SOLEDAD
93962-93962	SPRECKELS
94002-94003	BELMONT
94005-94005	BRISBANE
94010-94012	BURLINGAME
94013-94017	DALY CITY
94018-94018	EL GRANADA
94019-94019	HALF MOON BAY
94020-94020	LA HONDA
94021-94021	LOMA MAR
94022-94024	LOS ALTOS
94025-94026	MENLO PARK
94027-94027	ATHERTON
94028-94028	PORTOLA VALLEY
94029-94029	MENLO PARK
94030-94031	MILLBRAE
94035-94035	MOUNTAIN VIEW
94037-94037	MONTARA
94038-94038	MOSS BEACH
94039-94043	MOUNTAIN VIEW
94044-94045	PACIFICA
94059-94059	REDWOOD CITY
94060-94060	PESCADERO
94061-94065	REDWOOD CITY
94066-94067	SAN BRUNO
94070-94071	SAN CARLOS
94074-94074	SAN GREGORIO
94080-94083	SOUTH SAN FRANCISCO
94085-94091	SUNNYVALE
94096-94098	SAN BRUNO
94099-94099	SOUTH SAN FRANCISCO
94100-94199	SAN FRANCISCO
94203-94299	SACRAMENTO
94300-94310	PALO ALTO
94400-94497	SAN MATEO
94501-94502	ALAMEDA
94503-94503	AMERICAN CANYON
94504-94504	MOBIL OIL CREDIT CORP
94506-94506	DANVILLE
94507-94507	ALAMO
94508-94508	ANGWIN
94509-94509	ANTIOCH
94510-94510	BENICIA
94511-94511	BETHEL ISLAND
94512-94512	BIRDS LANDING
94513-94513	BRENTWOOD
94514-94514	BYRON
94515-94515	CALISTOGA
94516-94516	CANYON
94517-94517	CLAYTON
94518-94522	CONCORD
94523-94523	PLEASANT HILL
94524-94524	CONCORD
94525-94525	CROCKETT
94526-94526	DANVILLE
94527-94527	CONCORD
94528-94528	DIABLO
94529-94529	CONCORD
94530-94530	EL CERRITO
94531-94531	ANTIOCH
94533-94534	FAIRFIELD
94535-94535	TRAVIS AFB
94536-94539	FREMONT
94540-94545	HAYWARD
94546-94546	CASTRO VALLEY
94547-94547	HERCULES
94548-94548	KNIGHTSEN
94549-94549	LAFAYETTE
94550-94551	LIVERMORE
94552-94552	CASTRO VALLEY
94553-94553	MARTINEZ
94555-94555	FREMONT
94556-94556	MORAGA
94557-94557	HAYWARD
94558-94559	NAPA
94560-94560	NEWARK
94561-94561	OAKLEY
94562-94562	OAKVILLE
94563-94563	ORINDA
94564-94564	PINOLE
94565-94565	PITTSBURG
94566-94566	PLEASANTON
94567-94567	POPE VALLEY
94568-94568	DUBLIN
94569-94569	PORT COSTA
94570-94570	MORAGA
94571-94571	RIO VISTA

ZIP Range	City
94572-94572	RODEO
94573-94573	RUTHERFORD
94574-94574	SAINT HELENA
94575-94575	MORAGA
94576-94576	DEER PARK
94577-94579	SAN LEANDRO
94580-94580	SAN LORENZO
94581-94581	NAPA
94582-94582	PLEASANTON
94582-94583	SAN RAMON
94585-94585	SUISUN CITY
94586-94586	SUNOL
94587-94587	UNION CITY
94588-94588	PLEASANTON
94589-94592	VALLEJO
94593-94593	CROCKER NAT BANK
94594-94594	MONTGOMERY WARD
94595-94598	WALNUT CREEK
94599-94599	YOUNTVILLE
94601-94607	OAKLAND
94608-94608	EMERYVILLE
94609-94619	OAKLAND
94620-94620	PIEDMONT
94621-94661	OAKLAND
94662-94662	EMERYVILLE
94666-94666	OAKLAND
94701-94705	BERKELEY
94706-94706	ALBANY
94707-94720	BERKELEY
94801-94802	RICHMOND
94803-94803	EL SOBRANTE
94804-94805	RICHMOND
94806-94806	SAN PABLO
94807-94808	RICHMOND
94820-94820	EL SOBRANTE
94850-94875	RICHMOND
94901-94903	SAN RAFAEL
94904-94904	GREENBRAE
94911-94913	SAN RAFAEL
94914-94914	KENTFIELD
94915-94915	SAN RAFAEL
94920-94920	BELVEDERE TIBURON
94922-94922	BODEGA
94923-94923	BODEGA BAY
94924-94924	BOLINAS
94925-94925	CORTE MADERA
94926-94926	COTATI
94927-94928	ROHNERT PARK
94929-94929	DILLON BEACH
94930-94930	FAIRFAX
94931-94931	COTATI
94933-94933	FOREST KNOLLS
94937-94937	INVERNESS
94938-94938	LAGUNITAS
94939-94939	LARKSPUR
94940-94940	MARSHALL
94941-94942	MILL VALLEY
94945-94945	NOVATO
94946-94946	NICASIO
94947-94949	NOVATO
94950-94950	OLEMA
94951-94951	PENNGROVE
94952-94955	PETALUMA
94956-94956	POINT REYES STATION
94957-94957	ROSS
94960-94960	SAN ANSELMO
94963-94963	SAN GERONIMO
94964-94964	SAN QUENTIN
94965-94966	SAUSALITO
94970-94970	STINSON BEACH
94971-94971	TOMALES
94972-94972	VALLEY FORD
94973-94973	WOODACRE
94974-94974	SAN QUENTIN
94975-94975	PETALUMA
94976-94976	CORTE MADERA
94977-94977	LARKSPUR
94978-94978	FAIRFAX
94979-94979	SAN ANSELMO
94998-94998	NOVATO
94999-94999	PETALUMA
95001-95001	APTOS
95002-95002	ALVISO
95003-95003	APTOS
95004-95004	AROMAS
95005-95005	BEN LOMOND
95006-95006	BOULDER CREEK
95007-95007	BROOKDALE
95008-95009	CAMPBELL
95010-95010	CAPITOLA
95011-95011	CAMPBELL
95012-95012	CASTROVILLE
95013-95013	COYOTE
95014-95016	CUPERTINO
95017-95017	DAVENPORT
95018-95018	FELTON
95019-95019	FREEDOM
95020-95021	GILROY
95023-95024	HOLLISTER
95026-95026	HOLY CITY
95030-95033	LOS GATOS
95035-95036	MILPITAS
95037-95038	MORGAN HILL
95039-95039	MOSS LANDING
95041-95041	MOUNT HERMON
95042-95042	NEW ALMADEN
95043-95043	PAICINES
95044-95044	REDWOOD ESTATES
95045-95045	SAN JUAN BAUTISTA
95046-95046	SAN MARTIN
95050-95056	SANTA CLARA
95060-95065	SANTA CRUZ
95066-95067	SCOTTS VALLEY
95070-95071	SARATOGA
95073-95073	SOQUEL
95075-95075	TRES PINOS
95076-95077	WATSONVILLE
95100-95139	SAN JOSE
95140-95140	MOUNT HAMILTON
95141-95196	SAN JOSE
95201-95219	STOCKTON
95220-95220	ACAMPO
95221-95221	ALTAVILLE
95222-95222	ANGELS CAMP
95223-95223	ARNOLD
95224-95224	AVERY
95225-95225	BURSON
95226-95226	CAMPO SECO
95227-95227	CLEMENTS
95228-95228	COPPEROPOLIS
95229-95229	DOUGLAS FLAT
95230-95230	FARMINGTON
95231-95231	FRENCH CAMP
95232-95232	GLENCOE
95233-95233	HATHAWAY PINES
95234-95234	HOLT
95236-95236	LINDEN
95237-95237	LOCKEFORD
95240-95242	LODI
95245-95245	MOKELUMNE HILL
95246-95246	MOUNTAIN RANCH
95247-95247	MURPHYS
95248-95248	RAIL ROAD FLAT
95249-95249	SAN ANDREAS
95250-95250	SHEEP RANCH
95251-95251	VALLECITO
95252-95252	VALLEY SPRINGS
95253-95253	VICTOR
95254-95254	WALLACE
95255-95255	WEST POINT
95257-95257	WILSEYVILLE
95258-95258	WOODBRIDGE
95267-95296	STOCKTON
95296-95296	LYOTH
95297-95298	STOCKTON
95301-95301	ATWATER
95303-95303	BALLICO
95304-95304	BANTA
95305-95305	BIG OAK FLAT
95306-95306	CATHEYS VALLEY
95307-95307	CERES
95309-95309	CHINESE CAMP
95310-95310	COLUMBIA
95311-95311	COULTERVILLE
95312-95312	CRESSEY
95313-95313	CROWS LANDING
95314-95314	DARDANELLE
95315-95315	DELHI
95316-95316	DENAIR
95317-95317	EL NIDO
95318-95318	EL PORTAL
95319-95319	EMPIRE
95320-95320	ESCALON
95321-95321	GROVELAND
95322-95322	GUSTINE
95323-95323	HICKMAN
95324-95324	HILMAR
95325-95325	HORNITOS
95326-95326	HUGHSON
95327-95327	JAMESTOWN
95328-95328	KEYES
95329-95329	LA GRANGE
95330-95330	LATHROP
95333-95333	LE GRAND
95334-95334	LIVINGSTON
95335-95335	LONG BARN
95336-95337	MANTECA
95338-95338	MARIPOSA
95340-95341	MERCED
95342-95342	ATWATER
95343-95344	MERCED
95345-95345	MIDPINES
95346-95346	MI WUK VILLAGE
95347-95347	MOCCASIN
95348-95348	MERCED
95350-95358	MODESTO
95360-95360	NEWMAN
95361-95361	OAKDALE
95363-95363	PATTERSON
95364-95364	PINECREST
95365-95365	PLANADA
95366-95366	RIPON
95367-95367	RIVERBANK
95368-95368	SALIDA
95369-95369	SNELLING
95370-95370	SONORA
95372-95372	SOULSBYVILLE
95373-95373	STANDARD
95374-95374	STEVINSON
95375-95375	STRAWBERRY
95376-95378	TRACY
95379-95379	TUOLUMNE
95380-95382	TURLOCK
95383-95383	TWAIN HARTE
95384-95384	VALLEY HOME
95385-95385	VERNALIS
95386-95386	WATERFORD
95387-95387	WESTLEY
95388-95388	WINTON
95389-95389	YOSEMITE NATIONAL PARK
95390-95390	RIVERBANK
95391-95391	TRACY
95397-95397	MODESTO
95401-95409	SANTA ROSA
95410-95410	ALBION
95412-95412	ANNAPOLIS
95415-95415	BOONVILLE
95416-95416	BOYES HOT SPRINGS
95417-95417	BRANSCOMB
95418-95418	CALPELLA
95419-95419	CAMP MEEKER
95420-95420	CASPAR
95421-95421	CAZADERO
95422-95422	CLEARLAKE
95423-95423	CLEARLAKE OAKS
95424-95424	CLEARLAKE PARK
95425-95425	CLOVERDALE
95426-95426	COBB
95427-95427	COMPTCHE
95428-95428	COVELO
95429-95429	DOS RIOS
95430-95430	DUNCANS MILLS
95431-95431	ELDRIDGE
95432-95432	ELK
95433-95433	EL VERANO
95435-95435	FINLEY
95436-95436	FORESTVILLE
95437-95437	FORT BRAGG
95439-95439	FULTON
95441-95441	GEYSERVILLE
95442-95442	GLEN ELLEN
95443-95443	GLENHAVEN
95444-95444	GRATON
95445-95445	GUALALA
95446-95446	GUERNEVILLE
95448-95448	HEALDSBURG
95449-95449	HOPLAND
95450-95450	JENNER
95451-95451	KELSEYVILLE
95452-95452	KENWOOD
95453-95453	LAKEPORT
95454-95454	LAYTONVILLE
95456-95456	LITTLERIVER
95457-95457	LOWER LAKE
95458-95458	LUCERNE
95459-95459	MANCHESTER
95460-95460	MENDOCINO
95461-95461	MIDDLETOWN
95462-95462	MONTE RIO
95463-95463	NAVARRO
95464-95464	NICE
95465-95465	OCCIDENTAL
95466-95466	PHILO
95467-95467	HIDDEN VALLEY LAKE
95468-95468	POINT ARENA
95469-95469	POTTER VALLEY
95470-95470	REDWOOD VALLEY
95471-95471	RIO NIDO
95472-95473	SEBASTOPOL
95476-95476	SONOMA
95480-95480	STEWARTS POINT
95481-95481	TALMAGE
95482-95482	UKIAH
95485-95485	UPPER LAKE
95486-95486	VILLA GRANDE
95487-95487	VINEBURG
95488-95488	WESTPORT
95490-95490	WILLITS
95492-95492	WINDSOR
95493-95493	WITTER SPRINGS
95494-95494	YORKVILLE
95497-95497	THE SEA RANCH
95501-95503	EUREKA
95511-95511	ALDERPOINT
95514-95514	BLOCKSBURG
95518-95518	ARCATA
95519-95519	MCKINLEYVILLE
95521-95521	ARCATA
95524-95524	BAYSIDE
95525-95525	BLUE LAKE
95526-95526	BRIDGEVILLE
95527-95527	BURNT RANCH
95528-95528	CARLOTTA
95531-95532	CRESCENT CITY
95534-95534	CUTTEN
95536-95536	FERNDALE
95537-95537	FIELDS LANDING
95538-95538	FORT DICK
95540-95540	FORTUNA
95542-95542	GARBERVILLE
95543-95543	GASQUET
95545-95545	HONEYDEW
95546-95546	HOOPA
95547-95547	HYDESVILLE
95548-95548	KLAMATH
95549-95549	KNEELAND
95550-95550	KORBEL
95551-95551	LOLETA
95552-95552	MAD RIVER
95553-95553	MIRANDA
95554-95554	MYERS FLAT
95555-95555	ORICK
95556-95556	ORLEANS
95558-95558	PETROLIA
95559-95559	PHILLIPSVILLE
95560-95560	REDWAY
95562-95562	RIO DELL
95563-95563	SALYER

95564-95564 SAMOA
95565-95565 SCOTIA
95567-95567 SMITH RIVER
95568-95568 SOMES BAR
95569-95569 REDCREST
95570-95570 TRINIDAD
95571-95571 WEOTT
95573-95573 WILLOW CREEK
95585-95585 LEGGETT
95587-95587 PIERCY
95589-95589 WHITETHORN
95595-95595 ZENIA
95601-95601 AMADOR CITY
95602-95604 AUBURN
95605-95605 WEST SACRAMENTO
95606-95606 BROOKS
95607-95607 CAPAY
95608-95609 CARMICHAEL
95610-95611 CITRUS HEIGHTS
95612-95612 CLARKSBURG
95613-95613 COLOMA
95614-95614 COOL
95615-95615 COURTLAND
95616-95617 DAVIS
95618-95618 EL MACERO
95619-95619 DIAMOND SPRINGS
95620-95620 DIXON
95621-95621 CITRUS HEIGHTS
95622-95622 NICOLAUS
95623-95623 EL DORADO
95624-95624 ELK GROVE
95625-95625 ELMIRA
95626-95626 ELVERTA
95627-95627 ESPARTO
95628-95628 FAIR OAKS
95629-95629 FIDDLETOWN
95630-95630 FOLSOM
95631-95631 FORESTHILL
95632-95632 GALT
95633-95633 GARDEN VALLEY
95634-95634 GEORGETOWN
95635-95635 GREENWOOD
95636-95636 GRIZZLY FLATS
95637-95637 GUINDA
95638-95638 HERALD
95639-95639 HOOD
95640-95640 IONE
95641-95641 ISLETON
95642-95642 JACKSON
95643-95643 PLACERVILLE
95644-95644 KIT CARSON
95645-95645 KNIGHTS LANDING
95646-95646 KIRKWOOD
95648-95648 LINCOLN
95650-95650 LOOMIS
95651-95651 LOTUS
95652-95652 MCCLELLAN AFB
95652-95652 MCCLELLAN
95653-95653 MADISON
95654-95654 MARTELL
95655-95655 MATHER
95656-95656 MOUNT AUKUM
95658-95658 NEWCASTLE
95659-95659 NICOLAUS
95660-95660 NORTH HIGHLANDS
95661-95661 ROSEVILLE
95662-95662 ORANGEVALE
95663-95663 PENRYN
95664-95664 PILOT HILL
95665-95665 PINE GROVE
95666-95666 PIONEER
95667-95667 PLACERVILLE
95668-95668 PLEASANT GROVE
95669-95669 PLYMOUTH
95670-95670 RANCHO CORDOVA
95671-95671 REPRESA
95672-95672 RESCUE
95673-95673 RIO LINDA
95674-95674 RIO OSO
95675-95675 RIVER PINES
95676-95676 ROBBINS
95677-95677 ROCKLIN
95678-95678 ROSEVILLE
95679-95679 RUMSEY
95680-95680 RYDE
95681-95681 SHERIDAN
95682-95682 SHINGLE SPRINGS
95683-95683 SLOUGHHOUSE
95684-95684 SOMERSET
95685-95685 SUTTER CREEK
95686-95686 THORNTON
95687-95688 VACAVILLE
95689-95689 VOLCANO
95690-95690 WALNUT GROVE
95691-95691 WEST SACRAMENTO
95692-95692 WHEATLAND
95693-95693 WILTON
95694-95694 WINTERS
95695-95695 WOODLAND
95696-95696 VACAVILLE
95697-95697 YOLO
95698-95698 ZAMORA
95699-95699 DRYTOWN
95701-95701 ALTA
95703-95703 APPLEGATE
95709-95709 CAMINO
95712-95712 CHICAGO PARK
95713-95713 COLFAX
95714-95714 DUTCH FLAT
95715-95715 EMIGRANT GAP
95717-95717 GOLD RUN
95720-95720 KYBURZ
95721-95721 ECHO LAKE
95722-95722 MEADOW VISTA
95724-95724 NORDEN
95726-95726 POLLOCK PINES
95728-95728 SODA SPRINGS
95735-95735 TWIN BRIDGES
95736-95736 WEIMAR
95741-95743 RANCHO CORDOVA
95746-95746 GRANITE BAY
95747-95747 ROSEVILLE
95757-95759 ELK GROVE
95762-95762 EL DORADO HILLS
95763-95763 FOLSOM
95765-95765 ROCKLIN
95776-95776 WOODLAND
95798-95799 WEST SACRAMENTO
95800-95842 SACRAMENTO
95843-95843 ANTELOPE
95851-95899 SACRAMENTO
95901-95901 MARYSVILLE
95903-95903 BEALE AFB
95910-95910 ALLEGHANY
95912-95912 ARBUCKLE
95913-95913 ARTOIS
95914-95914 BANGOR
95915-95915 BELDEN
95916-95916 BERRY CREEK
95917-95917 BIGGS
95918-95918 BROWNS VALLEY
95919-95919 BROWNSVILLE
95920-95920 BUTTE CITY
95922-95922 CAMPTONVILLE
95923-95923 CANYONDAM
95924-95924 CEDAR RIDGE
95925-95925 CHALLENGE
95926-95929 CHICO
95930-95930 CLIPPER MILLS
95931-95931 COLLEGE CITY
95932-95932 COLUSA
95934-95934 CRESCENT MILLS
95935-95935 DOBBINS
95936-95936 DOWNIEVILLE
95937-95937 DUNNIGAN
95938-95938 DURHAM
95939-95939 ELK CREEK
95940-95940 FEATHER FALLS
95941-95941 FORBESTOWN
95942-95942 FOREST RANCH
95943-95943 GLENN
95944-95944 GOODYEARS BAR
95945-95945 GRASS VALLEY
95946-95946 PENN VALLEY
95947-95947 GREENVILLE
95948-95948 GRIDLEY
95949-95949 GRASS VALLEY
95950-95950 GRIMES
95951-95951 HAMILTON CITY
95953-95953 LIVE OAK
95954-95954 MAGALIA
95955-95955 MAXWELL
95956-95956 MEADOW VALLEY
95957-95957 MERIDIAN
95958-95958 NELSON
95959-95959 NEVADA CITY
95960-95960 NORTH SAN JUAN
95961-95961 OLIVEHURST
95962-95962 OREGON HOUSE
95963-95963 ORLAND
95965-95966 OROVILLE
95967-95967 PARADISE
95968-95968 PALERMO
95969-95969 PARADISE
95970-95970 PRINCETON
95971-95971 QUINCY
95972-95972 RACKERBY
95973-95973 CHICO
95974-95974 RICHVALE
95975-95975 ROUGH AND READY
95976-95976 CHICO
95977-95977 SMARTVILLE
95978-95978 STIRLING CITY
95979-95979 STONYFORD
95980-95980 STORRIE
95981-95981 STRAWBERRY VALLEY
95982-95982 SUTTER
95983-95983 TAYLORSVILLE
95984-95984 TWAIN
95986-95986 WASHINGTON
95987-95987 WILLIAMS
95988-95988 WILLOWS
95991-95993 YUBA CITY
96001-96003 REDDING
96006-96006 ADIN
96007-96007 ANDERSON
96008-96008 BELLA VISTA
96009-96009 BIEBER
96010-96010 BIG BAR
96011-96011 BIG BEND
96013-96013 BURNEY
96014-96014 CALLAHAN
96015-96015 CANBY
96016-96016 CASSEL
96017-96017 CASTELLA
96019-96019 SHASTA LAKE
96020-96020 CHESTER
96021-96021 CORNING
96022-96022 COTTONWOOD
96023-96023 DORRIS
96024-96024 DOUGLAS CITY
96025-96025 DUNSMUIR
96027-96027 ETNA
96028-96028 FALL RIVER MILLS
96029-96029 FLOURNOY
96031-96031 FORKS OF SALMON
96032-96032 FORT JONES
96033-96033 FRENCH GULCH
96034-96034 GAZELLE
96035-96035 GERBER
96037-96037 GREENVIEW
96038-96038 GRENADA
96039-96039 HAPPY CAMP
96040-96040 HAT CREEK
96041-96041 HAYFORK
96044-96044 HORNBROOK
96045-96045 HORSE CREEK
96046-96046 HYAMPOM
96047-96047 IGO
96048-96048 JUNCTION CITY
96049-96049 REDDING
96050-96050 KLAMATH RIVER
96051-96051 LAKEHEAD
96052-96052 LEWISTON
96053-96053 MCARTHUR
96054-96054 LOOKOUT
96055-96055 LOS MOLINOS
96056-96056 MCARTHUR
96057-96057 MCCLOUD
96058-96058 MACDOEL
96059-96059 MANTON
96061-96061 MILL CREEK
96062-96062 MILLVILLE
96063-96063 MINERAL
96064-96064 MONTAGUE
96065-96065 MONTGOMERY CREEK
96067-96067 MOUNT SHASTA
96068-96068 NUBIEBER
96069-96069 OAK RUN
96070-96070 OBRIEN
96071-96071 OLD STATION
96073-96073 PALO CEDRO
96074-96074 PASKENTA
96075-96075 PAYNES CREEK
96076-96076 PLATINA
96078-96078 PROBERTA
96079-96079 SHASTA LAKE
96080-96080 RED BLUFF
96084-96084 ROUND MOUNTAIN
96085-96085 SCOTT BAR
96086-96086 SEIAD VALLEY
96087-96087 SHASTA
96088-96088 SHINGLETOWN
96089-96089 SHASTA LAKE
96090-96090 TEHAMA
96091-96091 TRINITY CENTER
96092-96092 VINA
96093-96093 WEAVERVILLE
96094-96094 WEED
96095-96095 WHISKEYTOWN
96096-96096 WHITMORE
96097-96097 YREKA
96099-96099 REDDING
96101-96101 ALTURAS
96103-96103 BLAIRSDEN-GRAEAGLE
96104-96104 CEDARVILLE
96105-96105 CHILCOOT
96106-96106 CLIO
96107-96107 COLEVILLE
96108-96108 DAVIS CREEK
96109-96109 DOYLE
96110-96110 EAGLEVILLE
96111-96111 FLORISTON
96112-96112 FORT BIDWELL
96113-96113 HERLONG
96114-96114 JANESVILLE
96115-96115 LAKE CITY
96116-96116 LIKELY
96117-96117 LITCHFIELD
96118-96118 LOYALTON
96119-96119 MADELINE
96120-96120 MARKLEEVILLE
96121-96121 MILFORD
96122-96122 PORTOLA
96123-96123 RAVENDALE
96124-96124 CALPINE
96125-96125 SIERRA CITY
96126-96126 SIERRAVILLE
96127-96127 SUSANVILLE
96128-96128 STANDISH
96129-96129 BECKWOURTH
96130-96130 SUSANVILLE
96132-96132 TERMO
96133-96133 TOPAZ
96134-96134 TULELAKE
96135-96135 VINTON
96136-96136 WENDEL
96137-96137 WESTWOOD
96140-96140 CARNELIAN BAY
96141-96141 HOMEWOOD
96142-96142 TAHOMA
96143-96143 KINGS BEACH
96145-96145 TAHOE CITY
96146-96146 OLYMPIC VALLEY
96148-96148 TAHOE VISTA
96150-96158 SOUTH LAKE TAHOE
96160-96162 TRUCKEE
96635-96688 FPO

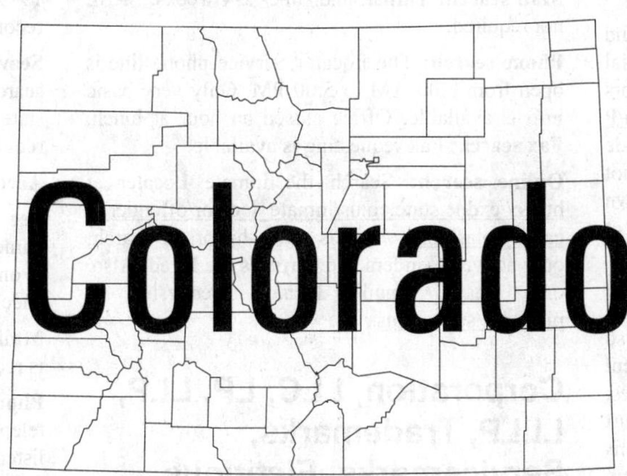

Colorado

General Help Numbers:

Governor's Office

136 State Capitol Bldg — 303-866-2471
Denver, CO 80203-1792 — Fax 303-866-2003
www.colorado.gov/governor — 8AM-5PM

Attorney General's Office

Department of Law — 303-866-4500
1525 Sherman St, 5th Floor — Fax 303-866-5691
Denver, CO 80203 — 8AM-5PM
www.ago.state.co.us/index.cfm.html

Legislative Records

Legislative Council Library
State Capitol, 200 E Colfax Ave, Rm 029 — 303-866-3521
Denver, CO 80203-1776 — Fax 303-866-2218
www.leg.state.co.us/ — 8AM-5PM

State Archives

Archives & Public Records — 303-866-2555
1313 Sherman St, Room 1B-20 — Fax 303-866-2257
Denver, CO 80203 — 8AM-4:30PM
http://statearchives.us/colorado.htm

State Specifics:

Capital:	Denver Denver County
Time Zone:	MST
Number of Counties:	64
Population:	4,939,456
Website:	www.colorado.gov

State Agencies

Criminal Records

Bureau of Investigation, State Repository, Identification Unit, 690 Kipling St, Suite 3000, Denver, CO 80215; 303-239-4208, Fax- 303-239-5858; 8AM-4:30PM. http://cbi.state.co.us

Indexing & Storage: Records available from early 1950s. Records prior to 1967 are in on-site computer archives. New records available for inquiry in less than 72 hours. 17% of all arrests in database have final dispositions recorded, over 78% for those arrests within last 5 years.

Searching: The requester must sign a disclaimer stating "This record shall not be used for the direct solicitation of business for pecuniary gain." Include in request- full name, date of birth, and disclaimer. The SSN, race, and gender are optional. Fingerprints are optional unless statutorily-required. Records are 100% fingerprint supported. If charged after fingerprinted, the practice of notifying the state is becoming more common, though this not yet statewide. All records or arrests are released, including those without dispositions, except sealed records, juvenile records and pending mental comps.

Access by: mail, in person, online.

Fee & Payment: Name check-$13.00 per name; fingerprint search-$16.50 per fingerprint. A state mandated fingerprint search plus notification of subsequent arrest in CO-$17.50; or nationwide fingerprint search-$39.50. Internet searches are $6.85 each. Fee payee- Colorado Bureau of Investigations (CBI). Prepayment required. No Personal checks, Visa, and MasterCard accepted.

Mail search: Turnaround time- 3 days. SASE not required. **In person:** You may request information in person; responses normally returned by mail.

Online search: There is an Internet access at https://www.cbirecordscheck.com/CBI_New/CBI_newIndex.asp. Requesters must use a credit card, an account does not need to be established. However, account holders may set up a batch system. The fee is $6.85 per record.

Statewide Court Records

State Court Administrator, 1301 Pennsylvania St, Ste 300, Denver, CO 80203-2416; 303-861-1111, 800-888-0001, Fax- 303-837-2340; 8AM-5PM.

www.courts.state.co.us

Online search: Trial court case documents and files are not available directly through the Judicial Branch website, but there are 4 designated vendors found at www.courts.state.co.us/Administration/Program.cfm/Program/11 who provide a statewide search. Fees may vary. Denver County data is not in the statewide system; Denver has its own separate free online access system at www.denvergov.org/apps/newcourt/court_select.aspx. Current dockets free; includes case, party and action information, possibly DOB. The 4 vendors providing statewide access by subscription also include a separate search of Denver. Document copies are not available from any of the websites; only through the actual court. Daily trial court dockets free at www.courts.state.co.us/. Opinions from the Court of Appeals are also available from the court homepage.

Sexual Offender Registry

Colorado Bureau of Investigation, SOR Unit, 690 Kipling St, Suite 3000, Denver, CO 80215; 303-239-4222, Fax- 303-239-4661; 8AM-5PM.

http://sor.state.co.us

Each local police or sheriff's agency is required to maintain a list of convicted sex offenders in their jurisdiction and may release that info to the public.

Indexing & Storage: New records available for inquiry in one hour.

Searching: Requesters are screened for purpose, they must be at least 18 years of age. Include in request- name, address. Requester should include DL# and phone number. This data not released- victim information, case details, sale of bulk data.

Access by: mail, in person, online.

Fee & Payment: The CBI may assess reasonable fees for the search, retrieval, and copying of information requested. Fee payee- CBI Personal checks are not accepted. Credit cards are accepted.

Mail search: Turnaround time- 10 days. Lists of names can be ordered by city or by ZIP Code.

In person: Lists of names can be ordered by city or by ZIP Code, or complete state.

Online search: The website gives access to only certain high-risk registered sex offenders in the following categories: Sexually Violent Predator (SVP), Multiple Offenses, Failed to Register, and adult felony conviction.

Incarceration Records

Colorado Department of Corrections, Offender Records, 2862 South Circle Dr. #418, Colorado Springs, CO 80906-4195; 719-226-4880 (Locator Service), Fax- 719-226-4899; 8AM-5PM.

www.doc.state.co.us

Indexing & Storage: Records available on current and former inmates to 1976. This office can release: sentence information (crime/sentencing court/docket #); location of incarceration; parole eligibility date/approved parole date; and mandatory release date. New records available for inquiry in 4 weeks.

Searching: Include in request- full name, date of birth, DOC # if available. Include signed release form subject, if subject no longer incarcerated.

Access by: mail, phone, fax, online.

Fee & Payment: Fee is $1.00 per page. Prepayment required. No credit cards or personal checks accepted.

Mail search: Turnaround time- 2-4 weeks. SASE not required.

Phone search: The Locator Service phone line is open from 8:00 AM to 5:00 PM. Only very basic info is available. Office closed an hour at lunch. **Fax search:** Fax requesting is available.

Online search: Search the Inmate Locater at https://exdoc.state.co.us/inmate_locator/offender_search_splash.php. This is not a historical search; only active offenders and parolees are listed. Also, one may email locator requests to pio@doc.state.co.us.

Corporation, LLC, LP, LLP, LLLP, Trademarks, Servicemarks, Fictitious, Assumed, Trade Name

Secretary of State, Business Division, 1700 Broadway, Suite 200, Denver, CO 80290; 303-894-2200 x2 (Business Entities), Fax- 303-869-4864; 7:30AM-5PM. www.sos.state.co.us

Indexing & Storage: Records available for all active companies. Some inactive company records are archived. New records available immediately.

Searching: Include in request- business full name.

Access by: mail, phone, fax, in person, online.

Fee & Payment: There is no fee for searching active companies online. There is a $25.00 per business name searched via paper request, $25.00 fee for archived records. The copy fee is $2.00 per certified document. Fee payee- Secretary of State. Personal checks accepted, credit cards are not.

Mail search: Turnaround time- 2 to 3 days. An SASE is not required.

Phone search: Limit of 3 names. **Fax search:** Orders requested by fax are processed the same as other searches. **In person:** A public access terminal offers free searching.

Online search: The Sec. of State's Business Record Search page offers free searching of corporate names, trade names and associate info at www.sos.state.co.us/pubs/business/main.htm. Since 07/04, some e-filing documents are available. Click on Business Center. Also, search for charitable nonprofit members of CANPO - Colorado Association of Nonprofit Organizations - at www.coloradononprofits.org/member.cfm. Also, search securities dept. enforcement actions at www.dora.state.co.us/securities/enforcement.htm.

Other access: Various information is available as a one time order or via subscription. Transmittal can be through CDs, tapes or FTP.

Expedited service: available for mail, in person and fax searches. Turnaround time- up to 3 days. Add $150.00 per business name.

Uniform Commercial Code, Federal Tax Liens

Secretary of State, UCC Division, 1700 Broadway, Suite 200, Denver, CO 80290; 303-894-2200 x2, Fax- 303-869-4864; 7:30AM-5PM.

www.sos.state.co.us

State tax liens are handled by the Department of Revenue. These liens can be filed at any one of the state's county recording offices, and so should be searched as such.

Indexing & Storage: Records available from 1966. Records are indexed on computer from 1979, and on microfiche from 1987 to 1997. New records available for inquiry in 2-5 days.

Searching: Use search request form UCC-11. The search includes all federal tax liens recorded at the state level. This includes all IRS liens. Include in request- debtor name. SSN data not released.

Access by: mail, phone, fax, in person, online.

Fee & Payment: The search fee is $13.00 per name searched. Copies are $1.25 per page but free if online. Fee payee- Secretary of State. Personal checks accepted, credit cards are not.

Mail search: Turnaround time- 10 days. A SASE is requested.

Phone search: The latest 4 liens are available by telephone, press 2 when connected using number listed above. **Fax search:** Fax searching available.

In person: Simple requests may be processed while you wait.

Online search: There is free record searching of the index at this agency's website. Registration is required. See www.sos.state.co.us/pubs/business/search_records.htm. More extensive data is also available via subscription for ongoing business requesters.

Other access: Various information is available as a one time order or via subscription. Transmittal can be through CDs, tapes or FTP. The program may be delayed due to the redaction of SSNs.

Expedited service: Expedited service is available for mail, phone and in person searches. Turnaround time- 1-3 days. There is a $150.00 fee per debtor name to expedite search.

Sales Tax Registrations

Revenue Department, Taxpayers Services Office, 1375 Sherman St, Denver, CO 80261; 303-238-7378, 303-238-3278 (Verifications), Fax- 303-866-3211; 8AM-4:30PM.

www.colorado.gov/revenue

Indexing & Storage: Records available from 1988 and are computerized. New records available for inquiry in 2 weeks.

Searching: This agency will confirm that a business is registered. Include in request- business name. They will also search by tax permit number.

Access by: phone, in person, online.

Fee & Payment: There is no search fee.

Phone search: No fee for telephone request, the license number must be requested.

In person: They will release the owner's name if petitioned in writing.

Online search: verify a sales tax license or exemption # at https://www.taxview.state.co.us/.

Birth Certificates

Department of Public Health & Environment, Vital Records Section HSVR-A1, 4300 Cherry Creek Dr S, Denver, CO 80246-1530; 303-756-4464 (Recorded Message), 866-300-8540 (Credit Card Ordering), 303-692-2224 (General Information), Fax- 800-423-1108; 8:30AM-4:30PM. www.cdphe.state.co.us/certs/index.html

Certified copies for birth years 1910 to present can also be ordered at most county health departments.

Indexing & Storage: Records available from 1910 to present. New records available for inquiry immediately.

Searching: The person named on the record, members of the immediate family, legal representatives of those named above, and others demonstrating a direct and tangible interest in the record may request a copy. Include in request- full name, names of parents, mother's maiden name, date of birth, place of birth, proof of relationship to person of record, reason for information request. Birth Certificates are filed under person of record's last name. Email questions to vital.records@state.co.us.

Access by: mail, phone, fax, in person, online.

Fee & Payment: Search fee is $17.00 per name. Add $9.00 if you use a credit card. Add $10.00 per name requested for additional copies. You can order by fax using a credit card. Also include copy of requester's ID (government issued). Fee payee- Vital Records. Prepayment required. Personal checks and major credit cards accepted.

Mail search: Turnaround time- 2 weeks. Include a daytime telephone number. SASE not required.

Phone search: You must use a credit card for an additional $6.00 fee. Turnaround time is 5 working days. **Fax search:** Turnaround time 5 days, credit card required.

In person: Turnaround time is 30-45 minutes.

Online search: Records can be ordered online from state designated vendors. Go to https://www.vitalchek.com/default.aspx.

Expedited service: available for online searches. Turnaround time- next day. Add credit card fee ($9.00) and express delivery fee.

Death Records

Department of Public Health & Environment, Vital Records Section HSVR-A1, 4300 Cherry Creek Dr S, Denver, CO 80246-1530; 303-756-4464 (Recorded Message), 866-300-8540 (Credit Card Ordering), 303-692-2224, Fax- 800-423-1108; 8:30AM-4:30PM.

www.cdphe.state.co.us/certs/index.html

Email questions to vital.records@state.co.us.

Indexing & Storage: Records available from 1900 to present. New records available for inquiry in within 4 weeks.

Searching: Certified copies may be issued to: parents; grandparents; stepparents; siblings; spouse; adult children, stepchildren or grandchildren of the deceased; legal representatives of above; genealogists, probate researchers or those with a tangible interest. Include in request- full name, date of death, place of death, names of parents, proof of relationship to person of record, reason for information request. Death certificates are indexed by decedent's last name and the year of death. Include date of birth or age at death.

Access by: mail, phone, fax, in person, online.

Fee & Payment: Search fee is $17.00 per name. Add $9.00 if you use a credit card. Add $10.00 per name requested for an additional copy. Also include copy of requester's ID (government issued). Fee payee- Vital Records. Personal checks and major credit cards accepted.

Mail search: Turnaround time- 3 weeks. Also include a day time phone number.

Phone search: You must use a credit card. Turnaround time is 5 working days.

Fax search: Same criteria as phone searching.

In person: You may request records in person for same day service. Turnaround time 30-45 minutes.

Online search: Records can be ordered online from state designated vendors. Go to https://www.vitalchek.com/default.aspx.

Expedited service: Available for fax searches. Turnaround time- next day. Add use of credit card fee ($9.00) and express delivery fee.

Marriage Certificates

Department of Public Health & Environment, Vital Records Section, 4300 Cherry Creek Dr S, Denver, CO 80246-1530; 303-756-4464 (Recorded Message), 866-300-8540 (Credit Card Ordering), 303-692-2224, Fax- 800-423-1108; 8:30AM-4:30PM.

www.cdphe.state.co.us/certs/index.html

Records available include 1900 to 1939, and 1975 to present. Verifications for the years 1940 to 1974 are not available from this office and must be obtained from county where license was obtained.

Indexing & Storage: New records available for inquiry in 3 months.

Searching: Records are not open to the public. This agency refers to the record checks as "verifications." Include in request- date of marriage, county of license issue. Also include copy of requester's ID (government issued). Email questions to vital.records@state.co.us.

Access by: mail, phone, fax, in person, online.

Fee & Payment: The state fee for a marriage verification is $17.00. If the year is not known and the entire index is searched, there is an additional $5.00. Fee payee- Vital Records. Prepayment required. Credit card use is only for fax, phone, and Internet searches. Personal checks accepted. Major credit cards accepted.

Mail search: Turnaround time- 2 weeks.

Phone search: Turnaround time is 5 days. There is an additional $9.00 fee for use of a credit card.

Fax search: Use of credit card (extra $9.00) required, turnaround time 5 days.

In person: Turnaround time is 30 to 45 minutes.

Online search: An index of older records is found at www.cdphe.state.co.us/certs/genealogy.html. There is no fee. Records can be ordered online from state designated vendors. https://www.vitalchek.com/default.aspx.

Expedited service: Expedited service is available. Use of credit card is required (extra $9.00 fee). Total fee depends on delivery service requested.

Divorce Records

Department of Public Health & Environment, Vital Records Section, 4300 Cherry Creek Dr S, Denver, CO 80246-1530; 303-756-4464 (Recorded Message), 866-300-8540 (Credit Card Ordering), 303-692-2224, Fax- 800-423-1108; 8:30AM-4:30PM.

www.cdphe.state.co.us/certs/index.html

Email questions to vital.records@state.co.us.

Indexing & Storage: Records from 1851 to 1939 and 1968 to current at this office. Searches must be performed at the county level for all other years. Records include annulments and separations. New records available for inquiry in 6 months.

Searching: Include in request- names of parties, date of action, county. Also include copy of requester's ID (government issued). The agency only has an INDEX of the records and will provide a certified verification. Actual copies of the dissolution must be obtained from the county where the event was finalized.

Access by: mail, phone, fax, in person, online.

Fee & Payment: The state fee for a divorce verification is $17.00. If the year is not known and the entire index is searched, there is an additional $5.00. Fee payee- Vital Records. Personal checks and major credit cards accepted.

Mail search: Turnaround time- 2-3 weeks.

Phone search: A credit card is required with an additional fee of $9.00. Turnaround time is 5 business days. **Fax search:** Same criteria as phone searching, but turnaround time is 5 business days.

In person: Records can be obtained across the counter within 30 to 45 minutes.

Online search: A vendor offers online ordering, go to https://www.vitalchek.com/default.aspx.

Expedited service: Expedited service is available for online searches. Turnaround time- 1 day. Use of credit card is required (extra $9.00 fee). Total fee depends on delivery service requested.

Workers' Compensation

Division of Workers' Compensation, Customer Service, 633 17th Street 400, Denver, CO 80202-3660; 303-318-8700, Fax- 303-318-8710; 8AM-5PM. www.coworkforce.com/DWC/

Indexing & Storage: Records available as far back 1979, many records have been scanned and are stored electronically. If the physical records have been destroyed, the wage information is still on computer. New records available immediately.

Searching: If you are not a party to the claim, you must have a notarized release from claimant not older than 90 days. Judges notes, transcripts and depositions are not released. Older purged files will get a screen print only. Include in request- claimant name, SSN, DOB. There is a search form that is suggested. The form is not yet available from the web page.

Access by: mail, phone, fax, in person.

Fee & Payment: There is no search fee, copies are $.25 per page, rush copies are $.50 per page, the fee to return via fax is $1.00 per page. Certification is $2.00. Fee payee- Division of Workers' Compensation. Prepayment required. Approved accounts are billed monthly. No personal checks or credit cards accepted.

Mail search: Turnaround time- 1 to 2 days. A SASE is requested.

Phone search: Limited information is given over the phone only if caller is a party to the case. **Fax search:** Turnaround time is 1-2 days, unless otherwise requested. **In person:** call first so that they can locate records. Bring ID and notarized statement.

Other access: Lists and/or labels of carriers, adjusting companies, and attorneys are available upon request. Fees range from $3.00 to $7.00 (for list, not per name) plus postage.

Driver Records

Division of Motor Vehicles, Driver Control, Denver, CO 80261-0016 (Courier address- 1881 Pierce Street, Lakewood, CO 80214); 303-205-5613, Fax- 303-205-5990; 8AM-5PM.

www.colorado.gov/revenue/dmv

Copies of tickets may be obtained at this address for a fee of $2.20 per record. All requests must be submitted in writing and include the driver's name, DOB, and the specific ticket number.

Indexing & Storage: Records available for up to 7 years. Dl records maintained back to 1983 on microfilm. New records available for inquiry in 3 to 12 days.

Searching: Address and personal data is given to certain pre-approved, permissible requesters per the DPPA. The "Requester Release and Affidavit of Intended Use" form must be signed by requester. Include in request- name, date of birth, driver's license number. The middle initial and DL are optional, but suggested. Data not released-SSN

Access by: mail, in person, online.

Fee & Payment: The fee for manually processed records from the state is $2.20 per record, $2.70 if certified. Online access from Colorado Interactive is $2.00. Fee payee- Department of Revenue. Prepayment required. Personal checks accepted, credit cards are not.

Mail search: Turnaround time- 24 hours. SASE not required.

In person: Turnaround time is immediate. Up to 50 records may be processed while you wait, depending on staff availability.

Online search: Colorado Interactive, 600 17th Street, Ste. 2150 South, Denver, CO 80202 800-970-3468, www.colorado.gov is the entity designated by the state to provide online access to driving records to registered users. Both interactive and batch processing is offered. Requesters must be approved per state compliance requirements with DPPA. There is an annual $75.00 registration fee, records are $2.00 each. Submit DL and either last name or DOB. For more information call or visit the web page and click on "Registered Services Center." For questions about this service one may also call the MVD; contact Mary Tuttle at 303-205-5762. **Other access:** A driver monitoring program is offered by Colorado Interactive.

Vehicle Ownership & Registration

Division of Motor Vehicles, Title and Registration Section, Denver, CO 80261-0016 (Courier address- 1881 Pierce Street, Lakewood, CO 80214); 303-205-5608 (Titles), 303-205-5607 (Registration), Fax- 303-205-5765; 8AM-5PM.

www.colorado.gov/revenue/dmv

Indexing & Storage: Records available for 10 years back plus the current year. New records available for inquiry in (varies - depend on when county submits record).

Searching: Handicap and disabled vet plate data are not released. Include in request- Vehicle Identification Number. To obtain vehicle or ownership information, or for title and lien records, the requester's driver license number, and the Requestor Release and Affidavit of Intended Use Form and permission for Release of Individual Record Form DR2559 are required.

Access by: mail, in person.

Fee & Payment: The fee for searches is $2.20 per record. Fee payee- Department of Revenue. Prepayment required. Personal checks accepted, credit cards are not.

Mail search: Turnaround time- 24 hours. SASE not required.

In person: Turnaround time is while you wait.

Other access: Bulk requests of vehicle information on magnetic tape, computer paper, and on microfiche are available. Direct inquires to the Data Services Section, Motor Vehicle Extractions, DMV, Driver Control, Denver, CO 80261-0016.

Accident Reports

Motor Vehicle Division, Driver Control, Denver, CO 80261-0016 (Courier address- 1881 Pierce Street, Lakewood, CO 80214); 303-205-5613, Fax- 303-205-5990; 8AM-5PM.

www.mv.state.co.us

Indexing & Storage: Records available for 6 years plus current year from date of the accident. 10 years of records are microfilmed. New records available for inquiry in 30 to 60 days.

Searching: Use of "Requestor Release and Information Request" Form DR 2559 is required. If requester is not involved in accident, permission must be given by one of involved drivers; otherwise data is not released. Include in request- full name, date of accident, location of accident, and requester's mailing address.

Access by: mail, in person.

Fee & Payment: The fee is $2.20 per record for walk-in or mail-in searches. Fee payee- Department of Revenue. Prepayment required. Personal checks accepted, credit cards are not.

Mail search: Turnaround time- variable. SASE not required.

In person: Turnaround time depends on availability of report.

Vessel Ownership & Registration

Colorado State Parks, Registration, 13787 S Highway 85, Littleton, CO 80125; 303-791-1920, Fax- 303-470-0782; 8AM-5PM.

www.parks.state.co.us/

Records are open. Liens must be searched at the Secretary of State.

Indexing & Storage: Records available since 1994. Current year on paper, rest scanned. Older records are available on microfiche. All sail and motorized vessels must be registered. New records available for inquiry in 24 hours or less.

Searching: Include in request- name or boat registration. To search, a Release of Registration Records Form must be completed and signed. This data not released- registrant's DOB. SSNs are not recorded on the system.

Access by: mail, fax.

Fee & Payment: There is a $2.00 search fee plus a $1.00 charge per page for copies. Fee payee- Colorado State Parks. Prepayment required. Personal checks accepted, credit cards are not.

Mail search: Turnaround time- 1-3 weeks. SASE not required. **Fax search:** Turnaround time varies. Results are faxed or mailed back.

Legislation Records

Legislative Council Library, State Capitol, 200 E Colfax Ave, Rm 029, Denver, CO 80203; 303-866-2045 (Legal Services), 303-866-3055, 303-866-2390 (Archives), Fax- 303-866-2218; 8AM-5PM. www.leg.state.co.us

Voter Registration

Department of State, Elections Department, 1700 Broadway #270, Denver, CO 80290; 303-894-2200 x6307, Fax- 303-869-4861; 7:30AM-5PM.

www.elections.colorado.gov/DDefault.aspx

Indexing & Storage: Records available for the current year only. New records available for inquiry in 1-2 days.

Searching: Voters may request not to have their information released. Provide name and address or DOB to search. This data not released- SSNs.

Access by: mail, fax, in person, online.

Fee & Payment: The fee is $.50 per name. Fee payee- Department of State. Prepayment required. No credit cards accepted.

Mail search: Turnaround time- 2 to 3 days. A SASE is requested. **Fax search:** Same criteria as mail searching.

In person: Availability depends on how extensive search is.

Online search: Verify voter registration status at https://www.sos.state.co.us/Voter/secuVoterHome.do. Search campaign finance information and registered lobbyists through links at the home page listed above. **Other access:** The entire database is available on tape or CD-ROM. The cost is $500. No customization is available.

GED Certificates

GED Testing Program, 201 E Colfax Ave Rm 100, Denver, CO 80203; 303-866-6613, Fax- 303-866-6947; 8AM-4:55PM.

www.cde.state.co.us/cdeadult/GEDindex.htm

Indexing/Storage: Records available from 1946.

Searching: All written requests must have a yes or no answer to the following question in the upper right hand corner of the request: Did the person who received the GED ever attend a Colorado public school (as in elementary or high school)? All of the following are required to search: a signed release, name, date/year of test, date of birth, SSN, and location of testing.

Access by: mail, fax, in person.

Fee & Payment: There is no fee for a "yes or no" verification. The search fee $15.00 per transcript. Fee payee- GED Testing. Prepayment required. Money orders & Personal checks accepted, credit cards are not.

Mail search: Turnaround time- up to 14 days. The agency requests use of their request form, which can be downloaded from the web site. SASE not required.

Fax search: One may do a verification by fax. The signed release is still needed.

In person: Turnaround time is same day.

Hunting & Fishing License

Access to Records is Restricted.

Department of Natural Resources, Division of Wildlife, 6060 Broadway, Denver, CO 80216; 303-297-1192, Fax- 303-291-7106; 8AM-5PM.

www.wildlife.state.co.us

The state attorney general has decided that no information on holders of individual hunting and fishing licenses can be given to the public. It is only available to law enforcement officials or to the licensed individual.

Colorado State Licensing Agencies

For details about the agency responsible for licensing/certifying/registering an item below or in the Agency Quick Finder section, match an item's number with the number of the agency in the *Licensing Agency Information* section.

Colorado Licenses Searchable Online

Accident & Health Insurer #10 .... http://cdilookup.asisvcs.com/CompanySearch.aspx
Acupuncturist #14 .... https://www.doradls.state.co.us/alison.php
Addiction Counselor #20 .... https://www.doradls.state.co.us/alison.php
Architect #15 .... https://www.doradls.state.co.us/alison.php
Asbestos Abatement Contr'r #5 .... www.cdphe.state.co.us/ap/asbestos/AsGenAbatCont.pdf
Asbestos Disposal Site #5 .... www.cdphe.state.co.us/ap/asbestos/ASBESTOSDISPOSAL.pdf
Attorney #4 .... www.coloradosupremecourt.com/Search/AttSearch.asp
Audiologist #14 .... https://www.doradls.state.co.us/alison.php
Bail Bond Agent #10 .... http://cdilookup.asisvcs.com/IndividualSearch.aspx
Barber #16 .... https://www.doradls.state.co.us/lic_database_req.php
Bus, Charter/Scenic/Children's #30 .... www.dora.state.co.us/pls/real/puc_permit.search_form
Casualty Company #10 .... http://cdilookup.asisvcs.com/CompanySearch.aspx
CDL Third-Party Tester #7 .... www.colorado.gov/cs/Satellite/Revenue-MV/RMV/1186129986882?rendermode=preview
Charitable Organization #37 .... www.sos.state.co.us/ccsa/CcsaInquiryMain.do
Chiropractor #17 .... https://www.doradls.state.co.us/alison.php
Collection Agency #3 .... www.ago.state.co.us/CADC/CADCmain.cfm.html
Commercial Driving School #7 .... www.colorado.gov/cs/Satellite/Revenue-MV/RMV/1186129986882?rendermode=preview
Common Carrier/Contract Carrier #30 .... www.dora.state.co.us/pls/real/puc_permit.search_form
Contractor Registration #41 .... https://www.doradls.state.co.us/alison.php
Cosmetologist #16 .... https://www.doradls.state.co.us/lic_database_req.php
Counselor, Professional #20 .... https://www.doradls.state.co.us/alison.php
Credit Union #9 .... www.dora.state.co.us/financial-services/homeregu.html
Dental Hygienist #18 .... https://www.doradls.state.co.us/lic_database_req.php
Dentist #18 .... https://www.doradls.state.co.us/lic_database_req.php
Drug Company (DRU) Mfg/Dist/Whlse #26 .... https://www.doradls.state.co.us/alison.php
Electrical Contractor #41 .... https://www.doradls.state.co.us/alison.php
Electrician Journeyman/Master #41 .... https://www.doradls.state.co.us/alison.php
Engineer/Engineer Intern #19 .... https://www.doradls.state.co.us/alison.php
Fundraising Consultant #37 .... www.sos.state.co.us/ccsa/PfcInquiryCriteria.do
HazMat Carrier #30 .... www.dora.state.co.us/pls/real/puc_permit.search_form
Hearing Aid Dealer #14 .... https://www.doradls.state.co.us/alison.php
Household Goods/Property Carrier #30 .... www.dora.state.co.us/pls/real/puc_permit.search_form
Insurance Agency/Agent #10 .... http://cdilookup.asisvcs.com/IndividualSearch.aspx
Insurance Company #10 .... http://cdilookup.asisvcs.com/CompanySearch.aspx
Land Surveyor/Land Surveyor Intern #19 .... https://www.doradls.state.co.us/alison.php
Lead Abatement Worker/Supervisor #5 .... www.cdphe.state.co.us/ap/asbestos/AsGenAbatCont.pdf
Life Care Institution #9 .... www.dora.state.co.us/financial-services/homeregu.html#life
Life Insurance Company #10 .... http://cdilookup.asisvcs.com/CompanySearch.aspx
Limousine #30 .... www.dora.state.co.us/pls/real/puc_permit.search_form
Lobbyist #37 .... www.elections.colorado.gov/WWW/default/Lobbyists/prof_lobrpt.pdf
Lobbyist Volunteer #37 .... www.elections.colorado.gov/WWW/default/Lobbyists/vol%20lobby%202005.pdf
Manicurist #16 .... https://www.doradls.state.co.us/lic_database_req.php
Manufactured Housing Dealer/Mfg #22 .... http://dola.colorado.gov/cdh/codes/index.htm
Manufacturer Housing Inspector #22 .... http://dola.colorado.gov/cdh/codes/index.htm
Manufacturer Housing Installer #22 .... http://dola.colorado.gov/cdh/codes/index.htm
Marriage & Family Therapist #20 .... https://www.doradls.state.co.us/alison.php
Medical Doctor #21 .... https://www.doradls.state.co.us/alison.php
Mental H. Psychotherap't, Unlicensed #20 .... https://www.doradls.state.co.us/alison.php
Midwife #28 .... https://www.doradls.state.co.us/lic_database_req.php
Milk Shipper #6 .... www.cdphe.state.co.us/cp/dairy/Othe_rlinks.html
Nurse #1 .... https://www.doradls.state.co.us/alison.php
Nursery #2 .... www.colorado.gov/cs/Satellite/CO-Portal/CXP/1206035635118
Nurses' Aide #1 .... https://www.doradls.state.co.us/alison.php
Nursing Home Administrator #23 .... https://www.doradls.state.co.us/alison.php
Off-Road Charter #30 .... www.dora.state.co.us/pls/real/puc_permit.search_form
Optometrist #33 .... https://www.doradls.state.co.us/alison.php
Outfitter #24 .... https://www.doradls.state.co.us/alison.php
Pesticide Applicator #2 .... www.colorado.gov/cs/Satellite/CO-Portal/CXP/1206035635118

Pharmacist/Pharmacist Intern #26 .... https://www.doradls.state.co.us/alison.php
Pharmacy #26 .... https://www.doradls.state.co.us/alison.php
Pharmacy Limited License #26 .... https://www.doradls.state.co.us/alison.php
Pharmacy, Out-of-State/In-State/PDO #26 .. https://www.doradls.state.co.us/alison.php
Physical Therapist #32 .... https://www.doradls.state.co.us/alison.php
Physician Assistant #21 .... https://www.doradls.state.co.us/alison.php
Plumber Journeyman/Master/Resid'l #35 .... https://www.doradls.state.co.us/alison.php
Podiatrist #27 .... https://www.doradls.state.co.us/alison.php
Psychiatric Technician #1 .... https://www.doradls.state.co.us/alison.php
Psychologist #20 .... https://www.doradls.state.co.us/alison.php
Public Accountant-CPA #13 .... https://www.doradls.state.co.us/alison.php
Public Adjuster #10 .... http://cdilookup.asisvcs.com/IndividualSearch.aspx
Real Estate Agent/Broker/Seller #12 .... http://eservices.psiexams.com/crec/search.jsp
Real Estate Appraiser #12 .... http://eservices.psiexams.com/crec/search.jsp
Reinsurance Intermediary Manager #10 ...... http://cdilookup.asisvcs.com/IndividualSearch.aspx
Respiratory Therapist #16 .... https://www.doradls.state.co.us/lic_database_req.php
River Outfitter #24 .... https://www.doradls.state.co.us/alison.php
Savings & Loan Association #9 .... www.dora.state.co.us/financial-services/homeregu.html
School Administrator/Principal #40 .... https://forms.cde.state.co.us/pes/FirstLastSearch.jsp
School Special Service Associate #40 .... https://forms.cde.state.co.us/pes/FirstLastSearch.jsp
Securities Broker/Dealer #34 .... www.finra.org/Investors/ToolsCalculators/BrokerCheck/index.htm
Ski Lift #25 .... https://www.doradls.state.co.us/lic_database_req.php
Social Work #20 .... https://www.doradls.state.co.us/alison.php
Solicitor, Paid #37 ....
www.sos.state.co.us/cgi-forte/fortecgi?serviceName=ccsaprodaccess&templateName=/sessauto/mainMenu_outer_form.forte&hasr=T&hast=T
Stock Broker #34 .... www.finra.org/Investors/ToolsCalculators/BrokerCheck/index.htm
Substitute Teacher #40 .... https://forms.cde.state.co.us/pes/FirstLastSearch.jsp
Surplus Lines Seller #10 .... http://cdilookup.asisvcs.com/IndividualSearch.aspx
Teacher #40 .... https://forms.cde.state.co.us/pes/FirstLastSearch.jsp
Towing Carrier #30 .... www.dora.state.co.us/pls/real/puc_permit.search_form
Tramway #25 .... https://www.doradls.state.co.us/lic_database_req.php
Travel Ticker Seller #10 .... http://cdilookup.asisvcs.com/IndividualSearch.aspx
Veterinarian #31 .... https://www.doradls.state.co.us/alison.php.
Vocational Education Teacher #40 .... https://forms.cde.state.co.us/pes/FirstLastSearch.jsp
Wireman, Residential #41 .... https://www.doradls.state.co.us/alison.php

Colorado Licensing Quick Finder

Accident & Health Insurer #10 800-275-8247
Acupuncturist #14 303-894-2464
Addiction Counselor #20 303-894-7800
Architect #15 303-894-7801
Asbestos Abatement Contr'r/Supvr #5 . 303-692-3100
Asbestos Air Monitor Specialist #5 303-692-3100
Asbestos Disposal Site #5 303-692-3100
Attorney #4 303-866-6626
Audiologist #14 303-894-2464
Bail Bond Agent #10 800-275-8247
Bank, Commercial/Industrial #8 303-894-7575
Barber #16 303-894-7545
Bulk Milk Hauler #6 303-692-3633
Bus, Charter/Scenic/Children's #30 303-894-2867
Casualty Company #10 800-275-8247
CDL Third-Party Tester #7 303-205-5635
Charitable Organization #37 303-894-2200
Child Care Facility #29 303-866-5700
Chiropractor #17 303-894-7762
Collection Agency #3 303-866-5706
Commercial Driving School #7 303-205-5635
Common Carrier/Contract Carrier #30 . 303-894-2870
Contractor Registration #41 303-894-2300
Cosmetologist #16 303-894-7772
Counselor, Professional #20 303-894-7800
Court Reporter #36 303-837-3695
Credit Union #9 303-894-2336
Dairy Farm #6 303-692-3633
Dairy Plant #6 303-692-3633
Debt Management Company #8 303-894-7575
Dental Hygienist #18 303-894-7758
Dentist #18 303-894-7758
Drug Company Mfg/Dist/Whlse #26 303-894-7800
Egg Seller #2 303-477-0093
Electrical Contractor #41 303-894-2300
Electrician Journeyman/Master #41 303-894-2300
Engineer/Engineer Intern #19 303-894-7788
Family Care Home #29 303-866-5958
Food Plant Operator #2 303-477-0093
Fundraising Consultant #37 303-894-2200
Greyhound Racing #11 303-205-2990
HazMat Carrier #30 303-894-2868
Hearing Aid Dealer #14 303-894-2464
Horse Racing #11 303-205-2990
Household Goods/Property Carrier #30 303-894-2868
Insurance Agency/Agent #10 800-275-8247
Insurance Company #10 800-275-8247
Investment Advisor #34 303-894-2320
Kennel #2 303-239-4167
Land Surveyor/ Surveyor Intern #19 303-894-7788
Lead Abatement Firm #5 303-692-3100
Lead Abatement Inspector #5 303-692-3100
Lead Abatement Project Designer #5 .. 303-692-3100
Lead Abatement Risk Assessor #5 303-692-3100
Lead Abatement Worker/Supervisor #5 303-692-3100
Lead Abatem't Inspec./Risk Asses'r #5. 303-692-3100
Lead Evaluation Firm #5 303-692-3100
Life Care Institution #9 303-894-2336
Life Insurance Company #10 800-275-8247
Limousine #30 303-894-2867
Liquor Control #39 303-205-2300
Lobbyist #37 303-894-2200
Lobbyist Volunteer #37 303-894-2200
Manicurist #16 303-894-7772
Manufactured Housing Dealer/Mfg #22 303-866-2033
Manufacturer Housing Inspector #22 303-866-2033
Manufacturer Housing Installer #22 303-866-2033
Marriage & Family Therapist #20 303-894-7800
Medical Doctor #21 303-894-7690
Mental Health Psychotherap't, Unlicensed #20
.... 303-894-7800
Midwife #28 303-894-2464
Milk Shipper #6 303-692-3633
Milk/Cream Sampler/Tester #6 303-692-3633
Money Order Company #8 303-894-7575
Motor Vehicle Buyer/Whlse/Seller #38 303-205-5604
Motor Vehicle Dealer, Franchised #38. 303-205-5604
Motor Vehicle Dealer, Used #38 303-205-5604
Motor Vehicle Manufacturer Rep. #38 . 303-205-5604
Notary Public #37 .... 303-894-2200 x6405
Nurse #1 303-894-2430
Nursery #2 303-239-4154
Nurses' Aide #1 303-894-2816
Nursing Home Administrator #23 303-894-7760
Off-Road Charter #30 303-894-2867
Optometrist #33 303-894-7750
Outfitter #24 303-894-7778
Pesticide Applicator #2 303-239-4148
Pet Animal/Bird Dealer #2 303-239-4167
Pharmacist/Pharmacist Intern #26 303-894-7800
Pharmacy #26 303-894-7800
Pharmacy Limited License #26 303-894-7800

Pharmacy, Out-of-State/In-State/PDO #26 303-894-7800
Physical Therapist #32 303-894-7800
Physician Assistant #21 303-894-7690
Physiotherapist #32 303-894-7800
Plumber Journey'n/Master/Resid'l #35. 303-894-2300 x110
Podiatrist #27 303-894-2464
Psychiatric Technician #1 303-894-2430
Psychologist #20 303-894-7800
Public Accountant-CPA #13 303-894-7441
Public Adjuster #10 800-275-8247
Real Estate Agent/Broker/Seller #12.... 303-894-2166
Real Estate Appraiser #12 303-894-2166
Reinsurance Intermediary Mgr. #10..... 303-894-2419
Respiratory Therapist #16 303-894-7789
River Outfitter #24 303-894-7772
Savings & Loan Association #9 303-894-2336
School Administrator/Principal #40 303-866-6628
School Special Service Associate #40. 303-866-6628
Securities Broker/Dealer #34 303-894-2320
Securities Sales Promoter #34 303-894-2320
Ski Lift #25 303-894-7785
Social Work #20 303-894-7766
Solicitor, Paid #37 303-894-2200
Solicitor/Telemarketer #3 303-866-5079
Stock Broker #34 303-894-2320
Substitute Teacher #40 303-866-6628
Surplus Lines Seller #10 800-275-8247
Teacher #40 303-866-6628
Towing Carrier #30 303-894-2846
Trainer for Childcare Workers #29....... 303-866-5700
Trainer, First Aid/CPR #29 303-866-5700
Tramway #25 303-894-7785
Travel Ticker Seller #10 800-275-8247
Trust Company #8 303-894-7575
Veterinarian #31 303-894-7755
Vocational Education Teacher #40...... 303-866-6628
Wireman, Residential #41 303-894-2300

Colorado Licensing Agency Information

#1 Board of Nursing, 1560 Broadway, #1350, Denver, CO 80202; 303-894-2430, Fax- 303-894-2821. www.dora.state.co.us/nursing/ Search data at- https://www.doradls.state.co.us/alison.php

#2 Agriculture Department, 700 Kipling St, #4000, Lakewood, CO 80215-8000; 303-239-4100, Fax- 303-239-4125. www.ag.state.co.us/privacy.html

#3 Attorney General's Office, 1525 Sherman St, 7th Fl, Denver, CO 80203; 303-866-4500, Fax-303-866-5691. Hours- 8AM-5PM. www.ago.state.co.us/consumer_protection.cfmMenuPage=True.html

#4 Supreme Court, Board of Law Examiners, 1560 Broadway, Suite 1820, Denver, CO 80202; 303-866-6626, Fax- 303-866-6630. www.coloradosupremecourt.com/BLE/Contacts.htm Search data at- www.coloradosupremecourt.com/Search/AttSearch.asp

#5 Department of Public Health & Environment, Air Pollution Control Division, 4300 Cherry Creek Dr S, Denver, CO 80246; 303-692-3100, Fax-303-782-0278. Hours- 8AM-5PM. www.cdphe.state.co.us/ap/index.html

#6 Consumer Protection Division, Department of Public Health and Environment, 4300 Cherry Creek Dr S, Denver, CO 80246-1530; 303-692-3620, Fax- 303-753-6809. Hours- 8:30AM-5PM. www.cdphe.state.co.us/cp/dairy/dairy.html

#7 Department of Revenue, Div or Motor Vehicles, Drivers License - Driver Education, 1375 Sherman St, Rm 409, Denver, CO 80261; 303-205-5635, Fax- 303-205-5634. www.revenue.state.co.us/main/home.asp Search data at- www.colorado.gov/cs/Satellite/Revenue-MV/RMV/1186129986882?rendermode=preview

#8 Division of Banking, 1560 Broadway, #975, Denver, CO 80202; 303-894-7575, Fax- 303-894-7570. www.dora.state.co.us/Banking/

#9 Division of Financial Services, 1560 Broadway, #950, Denver, CO 80202; 303-894-2336, Fax- 303-894-7886. Hours- 8AM-5PM. www.dora.state.co.us/financial-services/ Search data at- www.dora.state.co.us/financial-services/homeregu.html

#10 Division of Insurance, 1560 Broadway, #850, Denver, CO 80202; 303-894-7499, Fax- 303-894-7455. www.dora.state.co.us/insurance/ Search data at- http://cdilookup.asisvcs.com/

#11 Division of Racing Events, 1881 Pierce St, #108, Lakewood, CO 80214-1494; 303-205-2990, Fax- 303-205-2950. Hours- 8AM-5PM. www.colorado.gov/revenue/racing

#12 Division of Real Estate, Real Estate Commission, 1560 Broadway, Suite 925, Denver, CO 80202; 303-894-2166, Fax- 303-894-2683. www.dora.state.co.us/real-estate/ Search data at- http://eservices.psiexams.com/crec/search.jsp Download Division of Registrations licensee data in Excel format at https://www.doradls.state.co.us/lic_database_req.php.

#13 Division of Registrations, Board of Accountancy, 1560 Broadway, #1350, Denver, CO 80202; 303-894-7800, Fax- 303-894-2310. Hours- 8AM-5PM. www.dora.state.co.us/Accountants/ Search data at- https://www.doradls.state.co.us/alison.php Download Division of Registrations licensee data in Excel format at https://www.doradls.state.co.us/lic_database_req.php.

#14 Division of Registrations, Audiology Registration Ofc / Acupuncture Licensing, 1560 Broadway, #1350, Denver, CO 80202; 303-894-7800, Fax- 303-894-7764. 8AM-5PM. www.dora.state.co.us/audiologists/aud/licensing.htm Search data at- https://www.doradls.state.co.us/alison.php Download Division of Registrations licensee data in Excel format at https://www.doradls.state.co.us/lic_database_req.php.

#15 Division of Registrations, Board of Examiners of Architects, 1560 Broadway, #1350, Denver, CO 80202; 303-894-7801, Fax- 303-894-7790. www.dora.state.co.us/aes/index.htm Search data at- https://www.doradls.state.co.us/alison.php Download Division of Registrations licensee data in Excel format at https://www.doradls.state.co.us/lic_database_req.php.

#16 Division of Registrations, Office of Barber & Cosmetologist Licensing, 1560 Broadway, #1350, Denver, CO 80202; 303-894-7772, Fax- 303-894-7764. Hours- 8AM-5PM. www.dora.state.co.us/Barbers_Cosmetologists/ Search data at- https://www.doradls.state.co.us/lic_database_req.php Download Division of Registrations licensee data in Excel format at https://www.doradls.state.co.us/lic_database_req.php.

#17 Division of Registrations, Board of Chiropractors, 1560 Broadway, #1350, Denver, CO 80202; 303-894-7800, Fax- 303-894-7764. www.dora.state.co.us/chiropractic/ Search data at- https://www.doradls.state.co.us/alison.php Download Division of Registrations licensee data in Excel format at https://www.doradls.state.co.us/lic_database_req.php.

#18 Division of Registrations, Board of Dental Examiners, 1560 Broadway, #1350, Denver, CO 80202; 303-894-7758, Fax- 303-894-7764. Hours- 8AM-4PM. www.dora.state.co.us/dental/ Search data at- https://www.doradls.state.co.us/lic_database_req.php Download Division licensee data in Excel format at https://www.doradls.state.co.us/lic_database_req.php.

#19 Division of Registrations, Board of Reg for Prof Engineers and Land Surveyors, 1560 Broadway, #1350, Denver, CO 80202; 303-894-7788, Fax- 303-894-7790. www.dora.state.co.us/aes/index.htm Search data at- https://www.doradls.state.co.us/alison.php Download Division of Registrations licensee data in Excel format at https://www.doradls.state.co.us/lic_database_req.php.

#20 Division of Registrations, Mental Health Licensing Section, 1560 Broadway, #880, Denver, CO 80202; 303-894-7800, Fax- 303-894-7747. www.dora.state.co.us/Mental-Health/ Search data at- https://www.doradls.state.co.us/alison.php Download Division of Registrations licensee data in Excel format at https://www.doradls.state.co.us/lic_database_req.php.

#21 Div of Registrations, Dept of Regulatory Agencies, Board of Medical Examiners, 1560 Broadway, #1350, Denver, CO 80202-5140; 303-894-7690, Fax- 303-894-7692. www.dora.state.co.us/medical/ Search data at- https://www.doradls.state.co.us/alison.php Download Division of Registrations licensee data in Excel format at https://www.doradls.state.co.us/lic_database_req.php.

#22 Division of Housing, 1313 Sherman St #518, Denver, CO 80203; 303-866-2033, Fax- 303-866-4077. http://dola.colorado.gov/cdh/index.html

#23 Division of Registrations, Board of Examiners of Nursing Home Administrators, 1560 Broadway, #1350, Denver, CO 80202; 303-894-7760, Fax- 303-894-7764. Hours- 8AM-5PM. www.dora.state.co.us/nursing-home-administrators/ Search data at- https://www.doradls.state.co.us/alison.php. Download Division of Registrations licensee data in Excel format at https://www.doradls.state.co.us/lic_database_req.php.

#24 Division of Registrations, Office of Outfitters Registration, 1560 Broadway, #1350, Denver, CO 80202; 303-894-7778, Fax- 303-894-7692. www.dora.state.co.us/Outfitters/ Search data at- https://www.doradls.state.co.us/alison.php Download Division of Registrations licensee data in Excel format at https://www.doradls.state.co.us/lic_database_req.php.

#25 Division of Registrations, Colorado Tramway Passenger Safety Board, 1560 Broadway, #1350, Denver, CO 80202; 303-894-7785, Fax- 303-894-

7790. www.dora.state.co.us/Tramway/ Download Division of Registrations licensee data in Excel format at https://www.doradls.state.co.us/lic_database_req.php.

#26 Division of Registrations, Board of Pharmacy, 1560 Broadway, #1315 (Board- #1310), Denver, CO 80202-5146; 303-894-7800, Regis- 303-894-7750, Fax- 303-894-7692, Regis- 303-894-9693. Hours- 8AM-5PM. www.dora.state.co.us/Pharmacy/ Search data at- www.dora.state.co.us/pls/real/ARMS_Search.Disclaimer_Page Download Division of Registrations licensee data in Excel format at https://www.doradls.state.co.us/lic_database_req.php.

#27 Division of Registrations, Podiatry Board, 1560 Broadway, #1350, Denver, CO 80202; 303-894-7690, Fax- 303-894-7692. www.dora.state.co.us/Podiatrists/ Search data at- https://www.doradls.state.co.us/alison.php Download Division of Registrations licensee data in Excel format at https://www.doradls.state.co.us/lic_database_req.php.

#28 Division of Registrations, Midwives Registration, 1560 Broadway, #1350, Denver, CO 80202; 303-894-7800, Fax- 303-894-7764. Hours- 8AM-5PM. www.dora.state.co.us/Midwives/ Search data at- https://www.doradls.state.co.us/lic_database_req.php Download Division licensee data in Excel format at https://www.doradls.state.co.us/lic_database_req.php.

#29 Department of Human Services, Division of Child Care, 1575 Sherman St, Denver, CO 80202; 800-799-5700, Fax- 303-866-4047. www.cdhs.state.co.us/childcare/

#30 Public Utilities Commission, Department of Regulatory Agencies, 1560 Broadway, #250, Denver, CO 80202; 800-888-0170, 303-894-2070, Fax- (303) 894-2071. www.dora.state.co.us/puc/ Search at- www.dora.state.co.us/pls/real/puc_permit.search_form

#31 Division of Registrations, Board of Veterinary Medicine, 1560 Broadway, #1350, Denver, CO 80202; 303-894-7800, Fax- 303-894-7764. Hours- 8AM-5PM. www.dora.state.co.us/Veterinarians/ Search data at- https://www.doradls.state.co.us/alison.php. Download Division of Registrations licensee data in Excel format at https://www.doradls.state.co.us/lic_database_req.php.

#32 Division of Registrations, Physical Therapy Registration, 1560 Broadway, #1350, Denver, CO 80202; 303-894-7800, Fax- 303-894-7764. Hours- 8AM-5PM. www.dora.state.co.us/Physical-Therapy/ Search data at- https://www.doradls.state.co.us/alison.php Download Division of Registrations licensee data in Excel format at https://www.doradls.state.co.us/lic_database_req.php.

#33 Division of Registrations, Board of Optometry Examiners, 1560 Broadway, #1350, Denver, CO 80202-5146; 303-894-7800, Fax- 303-894-7764. Hours- 8AM-5PM. www.dora.state.co.us/Optometry/ Search data at- https://www.doradls.state.co.us/alison.php Download Division of Registrations licensee data in Excel format at https://www.doradls.state.co.us/lic_database_req.php.

#34 Department of Regulatory Agencies, Division of Securities, 1560 Broadway, #900, Denver, CO 80202; 303-894-2320, Fax- 303-861-2126. Hours-8AM-5PM. www.dora.state.co.us/Securities/brokers.htm Search data at- www.finra.org/Investors/ToolsCalculators/BrokerCheck/index.htm

#35 Division of Registrations, Examining Board of Plumbers, 1560 Broadway, #1350, Denver, CO 80202; 303-894-2300, Fax- 303-894-2310. www.dora.state.co.us/Plumbing/ Search data at- https://www.doradls.state.co.us/alison.php Download Division of Registrations licensee data in Excel format at https://www.doradls.state.co.us/lic_database_req.php.

#36 Judicial Department, Human Resources Office, 1301 Pennsylvania St, #300, Denver, CO 80203; 970-351-7300, Fax- 303-837-2340. www.courts.state.co.us

#37 Licensing Division, Office of Secretary of State, 1700 Broadway, #300, Denver, CO 80202; 303-894-2200, Fax- 303-869-4871. www.sos.state.co.us/pubs/bingo_raffles/main.htm Search data at- www.sos.state.co.us/pubs/bingo_raffles/main.htm Colorado Assoc. of Nonprofit Organizations member list is available free at www.coloradononprofits.org/member.cfm.

#38 Motor Vehicle Dealer Board, 1881 Pierce St, #142, Lakewood, CO 80215; 303-205-5604, Fax- 303-205-5977. Hours- 8AM-5PM. www.colorado.gov/revenue/dmv All requests have to come to the department through the Public Information Act.

#39 Revenue Department, Alcohol Control Division, 1881 Pierce St, #108A, Lakewood, CO 80214; 303-205-2300, Fax- 303-205-2341. Hours- 8AM-5PM. www.colorado.gov/revenue/liquor Search data at- www.ttb.gov/foia/frl.shtml

#40 State Board of Education, Department of Education, 201 E Colifax Ave, Denver, CO 80203-1799; 303-866-6628, Fax- 303-866-6761. www.cde.state.co.us/index_license.htm Search data at- https://forms.cde.state.co.us/pes/FirstLastSearch.jsp

#41 Division of Registrations, Electrical Board, 1560 Broadway, #1500, Denver, CO 80203-1939; 303-894-2300, Fax- 303-894-2310. www.dora.state.co.us/Electrical/ Search data at- https://www.doradls.state.co.us/alison.php Download Division of Registrations licensee data in Excel format at https://www.doradls.state.co.us/lic_database_req.php.

Colorado Federal Courts

The following list indicates the district and division name for each county in the state.

County/Court Cross Reference

County	Court	County	Court	County	Court
Adams	Denver	Fremont	Denver	Montrose	Denver
Alamosa	Denver	Garfield	Denver	Morgan	Denver
Arapahoe	Denver	Gilpin	Denver	Otero	Denver
Archuleta	Denver	Grand	Denver	Ouray	Denver
Baca	Denver	Gunnison	Denver	Park	Denver
Bent	Denver	Hinsdale	Denver	Phillips	Denver
Boulder	Denver	Huerfano	Denver	Pitkin	Denver
Chaffee	Denver	Jackson	Denver	Prowers	Denver
Cheyenne	Denver	Jefferson	Denver	Pueblo	Denver
Clear Creek	Denver	Kiowa	Denver	Rio Blanco	Denver
Conejos	Denver	Kit Carson	Denver	Rio Grande	Denver
Costilla	Denver	La Plata	Denver	Routt	Denver
Crowley	Denver	Lake	Denver	Saguache	Denver
Custer	Denver	Larimer	Denver	San Juan	Denver
Delta	Denver	Las Animas	Denver	San Miguel	Denver
Denver	Denver	Lincoln	Denver	Sedgwick	Denver
Dolores	Denver	Logan	Denver	Summit	Denver
Douglas	Denver	Mesa	Denver	Teller	Denver
Eagle	Denver	Mineral	Denver	Washington	Denver
El Paso	Denver	Moffat	Denver	Weld	Denver
Elbert	Denver	Montezuma	Denver	Yuma	Denver

US District Court
District of Colorado

Colorado Division Court Clerk, 901 19th St, US Courthouse, Denver, CO 80294-3589, 303-335-2075; records- 303-844-3433; crim dockets- 303-844-2115; civil dockets- 303-844-3433; Fax- 303-335-2714. 8AM-5PM. www.co.uscourts.gov

Counties/Note: All counties in Colorado.

Searches/Indexing: Include full name in search request. Results do not include SSN or DOB. Will fax back documents for $.50 per page. New cases are in the index immediately after filing date. Index on computer back to 1990. Closed records sent to archives at irregular intervals.

Search Access: Court accepts certificate of search requests via telephone. **Mail:** Search usually completed- 1 day. Include SASE for return. **Fax:** Fax search requests accepted, if prepaid. Fax to attention Joe or David. **In person:** 3 public terminals available. No self-serve copier.

Payment: Pay by Visa/MC, money order, cashier's or personal check. Payee: Clerk, US District Court. No prepayment required unless bill over $100.00.

E-Services: PACER records go back to 1990. New records online after 1 day. ECF at www.co.uscourts.gov/CMECF/CMECF.aspx. **Opinions Online:** www.co.uscourts.gov/Judges/Opinions.aspx. **Online Note:** Current and next week judges' calendars at www.co.uscourts.gov/Judges/Calendars.aspx.

US Bankruptcy Court
District of Colorado

Colorado Division Court Clerk, US Custom House, Rm 114, 721 19th St, Denver, CO 80202-2508, 720-904-7300; records- 303-904-7407. Hours- 8AM-5PM. www.cob.uscourts.gov

Counties/Note: All counties in Colorado. View records from 8:00AM-4:45PM in Rm 114.

Searches/Indexing: Include last 4 digits of SSN in search request. Results do not include SSN or DOB. Docket sheet includes last 4 digits of SSN. Will not fax back documents. New cases are in the index 24-48 hours after filing date. Records on computer back to 1996; pre-6/1996 on microfilm. Closed electronic cases not purged.

Search Access: Voice Case Information Service available, call VCIS at 720-904-7419. **Mail:** Search usually completed- within 7 days. SASE required. **In person:** 2 public terminals available. Computer generated copies- $.10 each.

Payment: Pay by credit cards, money order, cashier's or attorney checks. No debtor personal checks accepted. Payee: Clerk, US Bankruptcy Court. Exemplification fee- $18.00.

E-Services: PACER records go back to 7/1981. New records online immediately. ECF at https://ecf.cob.uscourts.gov. **Opinions Online:** www.cob.uscourts.gov/opinions.asp. **Online Note:** Calendars free at www.cob.uscourts.gov/calendar.asp. Search the court's unclaimed funds list at www.cob.uscourts.gov/ucfunds_a.asp.

Standards for Federal Courts: Fees are standard unless noted in profile. Search fee is $26.00 per item (one party name or case number). Copy fee is $.50 per page. Certification fee is $9.00 per document, double for exemplification, if available. Most courts require prepayment. Mail requests should enclose a SASE unless otherwise noted. Before releasing records, all courts require prepayment, unless noted.

District courts index by defendant and plaintiff and by case number. Bankruptcy courts usually index by debtor and case number. While most courts now have their indexes on computer, many may still maintain index card files as well. Courts will archive closed case files at different times.

There are numerous public access programs available to online subscribers. Search the U.S. Party/Case Index to find party names and case numbers among all courts. Individual case data is provided on PACER. A search of CM/ECF provides copies of cases filed electronically. For details about PACER, the US Party/Case Index, and CM/ECF see the Appendix or go to http://pacer.psc.uscourts.gov or call 800-676-6856.

Colorado County Courts

Court	Jurisdiction	No. of Courts	How Organized
District Courts*	General	14	22 Districts
County Courts*	Limited	17	64 Counties
Combined Courts*		49	
Denver Probate Courts*	Probate	1	
Municipal Courts	Municipal	206	
Denver Juvenile Courts	Special	1	
Water Courts	Special	7	7 Districts

* Profiled in this Sourcebook.

Court	CIVIL								
	Tort	Contract	Real Estate	Min. Claim	Max. Claim	Small Claims	Estate	Eviction	Domestic Relations
District Courts*	X	X	X	$0	No Max		X		X
County Courts*	X	X	X	$0	$15,000	$7500		X	
Denver Probate*							X		
Water Courts			X	$0	No Max				

Court	CRIMINAL				
	Felony	Misdemeanor	DWI/DUI	Preliminary Hearing	Juvenile
District Courts*	X				X
County Courts*		X	X	X	
Denver Probate*					
Denver Juvenile					X

Administration

State Court Administrator, 1301 Pennsylvania St, Suite 300, Denver, CO, 80203; 303-861-1111, Fax: 303-837-2340. (MST) www.courts.state.co.us

Court Structure

The District and County Courts have overlapping jurisdiction over civil cases involving less than $15,000 ($10,000 prior to 9/1/2001). Fortunately, District and County Courts are combined in most counties. Combined courts usually search both civil or criminal indexes for a single fee, except as indicated in the profiles. Co-located with seven district courts are divisions known as Water Courts located in Weld, Pueblo, Alamosa, Montrose, Garfield, Routt, and La Platta counties.

The Denver Court System differs from those in the rest of the state, in part because Denver is both a city and a county. The Denver County Court functions as a municipal and a county court and is paid for entirely by Denver taxes, rather than by state taxes. The Denver County Court is not part of the state court system; the District Court is.

On November 15, 2001, Broomfield City & County came into existence, derived from parts of counties of Adams, Boulder, Jefferson, and Weld. A District and County Court (in 17th Judicial District) was established.

Colorado municipal courts only have jurisdiction over traffic, parking, and ordinance violations. Denver is the only county where the Probate Court and Juvenile Court is separate from the District Court.

Online Access

Trial court case documents and files are not available directly through the Colorado Judicial Branch website, but there are 4 designated vendors found at www.courts.state.co.us/Administration/Program.cfm/Program/11 who provide a statewide search. Fees will vary. Denver County data is not in the statewide system; Denver has its own separate free online access system at www.denvergov.org/apps/newcourt/court_select.aspx. Current dockets free; includes case, party and action information, possibly DOB. The 4 vendors providing statewide access by subscription also include a separate search of Denver. Document copies not available from any of the websites; only through the actual court.

Daily trial court dockets free at www.courts.state.co.us/. Opinions from the Court of Appeals also are available from the website.

Searching Tips, Fees, and Other Guidelines

Most courts charge $5.00 per name for a name search and the copy fee is $.75, $.25 if self serve. Some courts charge $25.00 per hour. Certification is set at $20.00 per document. See fees at www.courts.state.co.us/userfiles/File/Self_Help/fees.pdf. Nearly every court requires a self-addressed, stamped envelope (SASE) for return of information.

Water Court records are maintained by the Water Clerk and fees are similar to those for other court records. To retrieve a Water Court record, one must furnish the case number or the legal description (section, township, and range) or the full name of the respondent (case number or legal description are preferred).

Adams County

17th District Court 1100 Judicial Center Dr, Brighton, CO 80601; 303-659-1161; criminal phone: 303-654-3314; civil phone: 303-654-3237; probate phone: 303-654-3237; criminal fax: 303-654-3216; civil fax: same; 8AM-5PM. ***Felony, Civil Actions over $10,000, Probate.***
www.17thjudicialdistrict.com
District and County courts have combined but records are searched separately unless you ask the court to search both courts for no extra fee). Probate is in a separate index. Probate fax is same as main fax number.
Civil Records: Access: Mail, in person, online. Both court and visitors may perform in person searches. Search fee: $5.00 per name. Fee is $10.00 for cases before 1990. There is no fee if search done by party of case. Required to search: name, years to search. Civil cases indexed by defendant, plaintiff, on computer from 1990, index books back to early 1900s. Mail turnaround time 3 days. Pay service to civil case look-up at www.courts.state.co.us; click on Court Records Search.
Criminal Records: Access: Mail, in person, online. Both court and visitors may perform in person searches. Search fee: $5.00 per name. Fee is $10.00 for cases before 1990. Required to search: name, years to search, DOB. Criminal records computerized from 1990, index books back to early 1900s. Mail turnaround time 3 days. Criminal case index at www.courts.state.co.us. Current dockets free, records not- click on Court Records Search.
General Information: No adoption, sealed, juvenile, mental health or expunged cases released. Will not fax documents. Court makes copy: $.75 per page. Self serve: $.25 per page. Certification fee: $20.00 per doc. Payee: Clerk of the District Court. Personal checks accepted. Accepts credit cards in person only. Prepayment required. Mail requests: SASE required.

County Court 1100 Judicial Center Dr, Brighton, CO 80601; 303-659-1161; criminal phone: 303-654-3314; civil phone: 303-654-3335; fax: 303-654-3216; 8AM-5PM; Lunch hour- slow. File Rm open till 4PM. ***Misdemeanor, Civil Actions under $15,000, Eviction, Small Claims.***
www.17thjudicialdistrict.com
The District and County courts have combined, but records are searched separately unless you specifically ask the court to search both courts for no add'l fee.
Civil Records: Access: Mail, in person, online. Both court and visitors may perform in person searches. Search fee: $5.00 per name. $10.00 per name for pre-computer records. Required to search: name, years to search. Civil cases indexed by defendant, plaintiff, on computer from 1/1990, index books back to 1965. Mail turnaround time 3 working days. Civil PAT goes back to 2007. Still in development, the public terminals are not recommended as reliable or complete. Pay service to civil case look-up at www.courts.state.co.us; click on Court Records Search.
Criminal Records: Access: Mail, in person, online. Both court and visitors may perform in person searches. Search fee: $5.00 per name. $10.00 per name for pre-computer records. Required to search: name, years to search, DOB. Criminal records computerized from 1/1990, index books back to 1965. Mail turnaround time 3 working days. Criminal PAT goes back to 2008. Still in development, the public terminals are not recommended as reliable or complete. Criminal case index at www.courts.state.co.us. Current dockets free, records not- click on Court Records Search.
General Information: No adoption, sealed, juvenile, mental health or expunged cases released. Will not fax documents. Court makes copy: $.75 per page. Self serve: $.25 per page. Certification fee: $20.00 per doc. Payee: Adams County Combined Court. Personal checks accepted. Credit cards accepted. Prepayment required. Mail requests: SASE required.

Alamosa County

Alamosa Combined Court 702 4th St, Alamosa, CO 81101; 719-589-4996; fax: 719-589-4998; 8AM-5PM. ***Felony, Misdemeanor, Civil, Eviction, Small Claims, Probate, Traffic.***
www.courts.state.co.us/Courts/County/Choose.cfm
Civil Records: Access: Phone, mail, in person, online. Only the court performs in person searches; visitors may not. Search fee: $5.00 per name. $25.00 per hour if extensive research is needed. Required to search: name, years to search. Civil cases indexed by defendant, plaintiff, on computer from 1993, index cards from 5/1978, index books back to 1913. Mail turnaround time 10 days. Civil PAT goes back to 1993. PAT results show name, DOB. Pay service to civil case look-up at www.courts.state.co.us; click on Court Records Search.
Criminal Records: Access: Phone, mail, in person, online. Only the court performs in person searches; visitors may not. Search fee: $5.00 per name. $25.00 per hour if extensive research is needed. Required to search: name, years to search, DOB. Criminal records computerized from 1993, index cards from 5/1978, index books back to 1913. Mail turnaround time 10 days. Criminal PAT goes back to 1993.PAT results show name, DOB. Criminal case index at www.courts.state.co.us. Current dockets free, records not- click on Court Records Search. Online results show middle initial, DOB.
General Information: No adoption, juvenile, mental health, sealed or expunged cases released. Will not fax documents. Court makes copy: $.75 per page. Certification fee: $20.00. Payee: Clerk, Combined Court. Personal checks and major credit cards accepted. Prepayment required. Mail requests: SASE required.

Arapahoe County

18th District Court 7325 S Potomac St, Centennial, CO 80112; 303-649-6355; 8AM-4PM. ***Felony, Civil Actions over $15,000, Probate.***
www.courts.state.co.us/Courts/County/Choose.cfm
Civil Records: Access: Phone, mail, in person, online. Both court and visitors may perform in person searches. Search fee: $5.00 per name. $25.00 per hour if extensive research is needed. Required to search: name, years to search. Civil cases indexed by defendant, plaintiff, on computer from 1985, microfiche back to 1903. Mail turnaround time 10 working days. Pay service to civil case look-up at www.courts.state.co.us; click on Court Records Search.
Criminal Records: Access: Phone, mail, in person, online. Both court and visitors may perform in person searches. Search fee: $5.00 per name. $25.00 per hour if extensive research is needed. Required to search: name, years to search, DOB. Criminal records computerized from 1985, microfiche back to 1903. Mail turnaround time 7-10 days. Criminal case index at www.courts.state.co.us. Current dockets free, records not- click on Court Records Search.
General Information: No adoption, sealed, juvenile, mental health or expunged cases released. Will not fax documents. Court makes copy: $.75 per page. Self serve: $.25 per page. Certification fee: $20.00. Payee: Clerk of District Court. Personal checks accepted. Credit cards accepted in person. Prepayment required. Mail requests: SASE required.

Arapahoe County Court Division A 1790 W Littleton Blvd, Littleton, CO 80120-2060; 303-798-4591; fax: 303-798-0524; 8AM-N-1:15-4PM. ***Misdemeanor, Civil Actions under $15,000, Eviction, Small Claims, Traffic.***
www.courts.state.co.us/Courts/County/Choose.cfm
Civil Records: Access: Mail, in person, online. Only the court performs in person searches; visitors may not. Search fee: $5.00 per name. $25.00 per hour if extensive research is needed. Required to search: name, years to search. Civil cases indexed by defendant, plaintiff, on computer from 1986, index cards from 1965, microfiche from 1861 in District Court. Note: Only court performs searches of files prior to March 1986. Mail turnaround time 5-10 business days. Pay service to civil case look-up at www.courts.state.co.us; click on Court Records Search.
Criminal Records: Access: Mail, in person, online. Only the court performs in person searches; visitors may not. Search fee: $5.00 per name. $25.00 per hour if extensive research is needed. Required to search: name, years to search, DOB. Criminal records computerized from 1986, index cards from 1965, microfiche from 1861 in District Court. Note: Only court performs searches prior to March 1986. Mail turnaround time 5-10 business days. Criminal case index at www.courts.state.co.us. Current dockets free, records not- click on Court Records Search.
General Information: No adoption, sealed, juvenile, mental health or expunged cases released. Will not fax documents. Court makes copy: $.75 per page. Certification fee: $20.00 per document. Payee: Clerk of County Court. Personal checks accepted. Credit cards accepted. Prepayment required. Mail requests: SASE required.

Arapahoe County Court Division B 15400 E 14th Pl, Aurora, CO 80011; 303-363-8004; fax: 303-363-7155; 8AM-5PM. ***Misdemeanor, Civil Actions under $15,000, Eviction.***
www.courts.state.co.us/Courts/County/Choose.cfm
Search fee includes both civil and criminal indexes. Small Claims cases now at Littleton.
Civil Records: Access: Phone, mail, in person, online. Only the court performs in person searches; visitors may not. Search fee: $5.00 per name or $25.00 per hour. Required to search: name, years to search. Civil cases indexed by defendant, plaintiff, on computer from 4/1986, microfiche from 1980-1983, index cards from 1980. Mail turnaround time 5-10 days. Pay service to civil case look-up at www.courts.state.co.us; click on Court Records Search.
Criminal Records: Access: Phone, mail, in person, online. Only the court performs in person searches; visitors may not. Search fee: $5.00 per name $25.00 per hour. Required to search: name, years to search, DOB. Criminal records computerized from 4/1986, microfiche from 1980-1983, index cards from 1980. Mail turnaround time 5-10 days. Criminal case index at www.courts.state.co.us. Current dockets free, records not- click on Court Records Search.
General Information: No adoption, sealed, juvenile, mental health or expunged cases released. Will not fax documents. Court makes copy: $.75 per page. Self serve: $.25 per page. Certification fee: $20.00 per doc. Payee: Clerk of County Court. Personal checks accepted. Visa/MC accepted over the phone. Prepayment required. Mail requests: SASE required.

Archuleta County

Combined Courts PO Box 148, Pagosa Springs, CO 81147; 970-264-5932; fax: 970-264-2407; 8AM-4PM. ***Felony, Misdemeanor, Civil, Eviction, Small Claims, Probate.***

www.courts.state.co.us/Courts/County/Choose.cfm

Civil Records: Access: Mail, in person, online. Only the court performs in person searches; visitors may not. Search fee: $5.00 per name. Specific case information $5.00 per file after 1st file. Required to search: name, years to search. Civil cases indexed by defendant, plaintiff; index on cards from 1976, index books back to 1885, on computer since 8/95. Mail turnaround time 1-2 weeks. Pay service to civil case look-up at www.courts.state.co.us; click on Court Records Search.

Criminal Records: Access: Mail, in person, online. Only the court performs in person searches; visitors may not. Search fee: $5.00 per name. Specific case information $5.00 per file after 1st file. Required to search: name, years to search, DOB. Criminal records indexed on cards from 1976, index books back to 1885, on computer since 8/95. Mail turnaround time 1-2 weeks. Criminal case index at www.courts.state.co.us. Current dockets free, records not- click on Court Records Search.

General Information: No adoption, sealed, juvenile, mental health or expunged cases released. Will fax documents to local or toll free line, otherwise $1.00 per page. Court makes copy: $.75 per page. Certification fee: $20.00 per doc. Payee: Archuleta Combined Court. Personal checks accepted. Major credit cards accepted in person only. Prepayment required. Mail requests: SASE required.

Baca County

Baca County District & County Courts 741 Main St, Springfield, CO 81073; 719-523-4555; fax: 719-523-4552; 8AM-5PM. ***Felony, Misdemeanor, Civil, Eviction, Small Claims, Probate.***

www.courts.state.co.us/Courts/County/Choose.cfm

Civil Records: Access: Mail, in person, online. Only the court performs in person searches; visitors may not. Search fee: $5.00 per name. $25.00 per hour if extensive research is needed. Required to search: name, years to search. Civil cases indexed by defendant, plaintiff; index on cards from 1945, index books back to 1910, computerized since 1995. Mail turnaround time 1-2 days. Pay service to civil case look-up at www.courts.state.co.us; click on Court Records Search.

Criminal Records: Access: Mail, in person, online. Only the court performs in person searches; visitors may not. Search fee: $5.00 per name. $25.00 per hour if extensive research is needed. Required to search: name, years to search, DOB. Criminal records indexed on cards from 1945, index books back to 1910, computerized since 1995. Mail turnaround time 1-2 days. Criminal case index at www.courts.state.co.us. Current dockets free, records not- click on Court Records Search.

General Information: No adoption, sealed, juvenile, mental health or expunged cases released. Will fax documents $1.00 per page only two pages. Will not fax back lengthy docs. Court makes copy: $.75 per page. Certification fee: $20.00 per doc. Payee: Baca County Combined Courts. Personal checks accepted; credit cards are not. Prepayment required. Mail requests: SASE required.

Bent County

16th District Court Bent County Courthouse, 725 Bent, Las Animas, CO 81054; 719-456-1353; probate phone: same; fax: 719-456-0040; 8AM-N, 1-5PM. ***Felony, Misdemeanor, Civil, Eviction, Small Claims, Probate.***

www.courts.state.co.us/Courts/County/Choose.cfm

Civil Records: Access: Mail, in person, online. Only the court performs in person searches; visitors may not. Search fee: $5.00 per name. $25.00 per hour if extensive research is needed. Required to search: name, years to search. Civil cases indexed by defendant, plaintiff; index on cards to 1976, some on microfilm, on computer from 11/95 forward- all indexes available at this office. Mail turnaround time 4-5 days. Pay service to civil case look-up at www.courts.state.co.us; click on Court Records Search.

Criminal Records: Access: Mail, in person, online. Only the court performs in person searches; visitors may not. Search fee: $5.00 per name. $25.00 per hour if extensive research is needed. Required to search: name, years to search, DOB. Criminal records indexed on cards to 1976, some on microfilm, on computer from 11/95 forward- all indexes available at this office. Mail turnaround time 4-5 days. Criminal case index at www.courts.state.co.us. Current dockets free, records not- click on Court Records Search.

General Information: No adoption, sealed, juvenile, mental health or expunged cases released. Will fax documents to local or toll free line. Court makes copy: $.75 per page. Self serve: $.15 per page. Certification fee: $20.00. Payee: Clerk of Combined Court. Personal checks accepted; credit cards are not. Prepayment required. Mail requests: SASE required.

Boulder County

20th District & County Courts 6th & Canyon, 1777 6th St, Boulder, CO 80306; 303-441-3750; probate phone: 303-441-4740; fax: 303-441-3737; 9AM-4PM. ***Felony, Misdemeanor, Civil, Eviction, Small Claims, Probate.***

www.courts.state.co.us/Courts/County/Choose.cfm

Research Dept. phone- 303-441-4860. Probate fax- 303-441-4750.

Civil Records: Access: Mail, in person, online. Only the court performs in person searches; visitors may not. Search fee: $5.00 per name. $25.00 per hour if extensive research is needed. Required to search: name, years to search. Civil cases indexed by defendant, plaintiff, on computer from 1983, microfiche prior from 1977, all prior records in books. Mail turnaround time 5 days. Pay service to civil case look-up at www.courts.state.co.us; click on Court Records Search.

Criminal Records: Access: Mail, in person, online. Only the court performs in person searches; visitors may not. Search fee: $5.00 per name. $25.00 per hour if extensive research is needed. Required to search: name, years to search, DOB, signed release. Criminal records computerized from 1983, microfiche prior from 1977, all prior records in books. Mail turnaround time 5 days. Criminal case index at www.courts.state.co.us. Current dockets free, records not- click on Court Records Search.

General Information: No adoption, sealed, juvenile, mental health or expunged cases released. Will fax documents to local or toll-free number. Court makes copy: $.75 per page. Self serve: $.25 per page. Certification fee: $20.00. Payee: 20th Judicial District. Business checks or attorney checks accepted. Visa/MC accepted. Prepayment required. Mail requests: SASE required.

Broomfield County

Broomfield Combined Court District, County & Municipal, 17 DesCombes Dr, Broomfield, CO 80020; 720-887-2100; fax: 720-887-2122; 8AM-5PM. ***Felony, Misdemeanor, Civil, Eviction, Small Claims, Probate.***

www.broomfield.org/courts/

County created on Nov. 15, 2001. Older records should be searched in Adams, Boulder, Jefferson or Weld counties. This court holds Municipal court records prior to county organization.

Civil Records: Access: Mail, in person, online. Only the court performs in person searches; visitors may not. Search fee: $5.00 per name. $25.00 per hour if extensive research is needed. Civil cases indexed by defendant, plaintiff, on computer since 11/15/01. Mail turnaround time 3 days. Pay service to civil case look-up at www.courts.state.co.us; click on Court Records Search.

Criminal Records: Access: Mail, in person, online. Only the court performs in person searches; visitors may not. Search fee: $5.00 per name. $25.00 per hour if extensive research is needed. Required to search: name, also helpful: address, DOB. Criminal records computerized from 11/15/01. Mail turnaround time 3 days. Criminal case index at www.courts.state.co.us. Current dockets free, records not- click on Court Records Search.

General Information: No Juvenile or protective custody records released. Will not fax documents. Court makes copy: $.75 per page. Self serve: $.25 per page. Certification fee: $20.00. Payee: Broomfield Combined Courts. Will accept checks. Major credit cards accepted. Prepayment required. Mail requests: SASE required.

Chaffee County

11th District & County Courts PO Box 279, Salida, CO 81201; 719-539-2561/6031; fax: 719-539-6281; 8AM-5PM. ***Felony, Misdemeanor, Civil, Eviction, Small Claims, Probate.***

www.courts.state.co.us/Courts/County/Choose.cfm

This court combined in 2002; formerly two courts: one county court, one district court. Probate fax is same as main fax number.

Civil Records: Access: Phone, mail, in person, online. Only the court performs in person searches; visitors may not. Search fee: $5.00 per name. $25.00 per hour if extensive research is needed. Required to search: name, years to search. Civil cases indexed by defendant, plaintiff, on computer back to 1995; index cards from 4/1976, index books back to late 1800s. Mail turnaround time ASAP. Pay service to civil case look-up at www.courts.state.co.us; click on Court Records Search.

Criminal Records: Access: Phone, mail, in person, online. Only the court performs in person searches; visitors may not. Search fee: $5.00 per name. Fee applies if 3 or more files involved. Required to search: name, years to search, DOB. Criminal records computerized from 1995; index cards back to 4/1976, index books back to late 1800s. Mail turnaround time 2-3 days. Criminal case index at www.courts.state.co.us. Current dockets free, records not- click on Court Records Search.

General Information: No adoption, sealed, juvenile, mental health or expunged cases released. Fee to fax document $.50 per page. Court makes copy: $.75 per page. Certification fee: $20.00 per certification. Payee: Clerk of District Court. Personal checks accepted; credit cards are not. Prepayment required. Mail requests: SASE required.

Cheyenne County

District & County Courts PO Box 696, 51 S First St, Cheyenne Wells, CO 80810; 719-767-5649; fax: 719-767-5671; 8AM-4PM M-TH; till noon F. ***Felony, Misdemeanor, Civil, Eviction, Small Claims, Probate.***

www.courts.state.co.us/Courts/County/Choose.cfm

Civil Records: Access: Mail, in person, online. Only the court performs in person searches; visitors may not. Search fee: $5.00 per name. $25.00 per hour if extensive research is needed. Required to search: name, years to search. Civil cases indexed by defendant, plaintiff, on computer since 11/1/95, index cards from 1960, index books back to early 1900s. Mail turnaround time 5-7 days. Pay service to civil case look-up at www.courts.state.co.us; click on Court Records Search.

Criminal Records: Access: Mail, in person, online. Only the court performs in person searches; visitors may not. Search fee: $5.00 per name. $25.00 per hour if extensive research is needed. Required to search: name, years to search, DOB, notarized signed release. Criminal records on computer since 11/1/95, index cards from 1960, index books back to early 1900s. Mail turnaround time 5-7 days. Criminal case index at www.courts.state.co.us. Current dockets free, records not- click on Court Records Search.

General Information: No adoption, sealed, juvenile, mental health or expunged cases released. Will fax documents $1.00 per page. Court makes copy: $.75 per page. Certification fee: $20.00 per document. Payee: Cheyenne County Combined Court. Business checks accepted. No credit cards accepted. Prepayment required. Will bill attorneys only. Mail requests: SASE required.

Clear Creek County

Clear Creek Combined Courts PO Box 367, 405 Argentine St, Georgetown, CO 80444; 303-569-3273; fax: 303-569-3274; 8AM-5PM. ***Felony, Misdemeanor, Civil, Eviction, Small Claims, Probate.***

www.courts.state.co.us/Courts/County/Choose.cfm

No searches done on records prior to 1976.

Civil Records: Access: Mail, in person, online. Both court and visitors may perform in person searches. Search fee: $5.00 per name. $25.00 per hour if extensive research is needed. Required to search: name, years to search. Civil cases indexed by defendant, plaintiff; index on cards from 1976, ledger books back to late 1800. Mail turnaround time 1 week. Pay service to civil case look-up at www.courts.state.co.us; click on Court Records Search.

Criminal Records: Access: Mail, in person, online. Both court and visitors may perform in person searches. Search fee: $5.00 per name. $25.00 per hour if extensive research is needed. Required to search: name, years to search, DOB. Criminal records indexed on cards from 1976, ledger books back to late 1800, computerized since 9/95. Mail turnaround time 1 week. Criminal case index at www.courts.state.co.us. Current dockets free, records not- click on Court Records Search. Online results show middle initial, DOB.

General Information: No adoption, sealed, juvenile, mental health or expunged cases released. Will not fax documents. Court makes copy: $.75 per page. Certification fee: $20.00 per doc does not include copies. Payee: Clerk of Combined Court. Personal checks accepted. Visa/MC accepted. Prepayment required. Mail requests: SASE required.

Conejos County

12th District & County Courts PO Box 128, 6683 County Road 13, Conejos, CO 81129; 719-376-5466; probate phone: 719-376-5465; fax: 719-376-5939; 8AM-4PM. ***Felony, Misdemeanor, Civil, Eviction, Small Claims, Probate.***

www.courts.state.co.us/Courts/County/Choose.cfm

Civil Records: Access: Mail, in person, online. Only the court performs in person searches; visitors may not. Search fee: $5.00 per name. $25.00 per hour if extensive research is needed. Required to search: name, years to search. Civil cases indexed by defendant, plaintiff, on computer since 6/94, on index cards from 1980. Mail turnaround time 2 weeks. Pay service to civil case look-up at www.courts.state.co.us; click on Court Records Search.

Criminal Records: Access: Mail, in person, online. Only the court performs in person searches; visitors may not. Search fee: $5.00 per name. $25.00 per hour if extensive research is needed. Required to search: name, years to search, DOB. Criminal records on computer since 6/94, on index cards from 1980. Mail turnaround time 2 weeks. Criminal case index at www.courts.state.co.us. Current dockets free, records not- click on Court Records Search.

General Information: No adoption, sealed, juvenile, mental health or expunged cases released. Will not fax documents. Court makes copy: $.75 per page. Certification fee: $20.00. Payee: Conejos Combined Court. Personal checks and major credit cards accepted. Prepayment required. Mail requests: SASE required.

Costilla County

12th District & County Courts PO Box 301, 401 S Church Pl, San Luis, CO 81152; 719-672-3681; criminal fax: 719-672-4493; civil fax: same; 8AM-N, 1-4PM. ***Felony, Misdemeanor, Civil, Eviction, Small Claims, Probate.***

www.courts.state.co.us/Courts/County/Choose.cfm

Probate fax is same as main fax number. They no longer accept faxes.

Civil Records: Access: Mail, in person, online. Both court and visitors may perform in person searches. Search fee: $5.00 per name. Records prior to 1994 are $25.00 per hour. Required to search: name, years to search; also helpful: address. Civil cases indexed by defendant, plaintiff; index on cards from 1970, index books back to 1865, indexed on computer since 1994. In CO state archives prior to 1970. Mail turnaround time 1-2 weeks. Pay service to civil case look-up at www.courts.state.co.us; click on Court Records Search.

Criminal Records: Access: Mail, in person, online. Only the court performs in person searches; visitors may not. Search fee: $5.00 per name, records prior to 1994 are $25.00 per hour. Required to search: name, years to search, DOB; also helpful: address, SSN. Criminal records indexed on cards from 1970, index books back to 1865, indexed on computer since 1994. In CO state archived prior to 1970. Mail turnaround time 1-2 weeks. Criminal case index at www.courts.state.co.us. Current dockets free, records not- click on Court Records Search. Online results show middle initial, DOB.

General Information: No adoption, sealed, juvenile, mental health, certain criminal cases or expunged cases released. Court makes copy: $.75 per page. Self serve: $.25 per page. Certification fee: $20.00 per document. Payee: Costilla Combined Courts. Personal checks and major credit cards accepted. Prepayment required. Mail requests: SASE required.

Crowley County

Combined Courts 110 E 6th St, #303, Ordway, CO 81063; 719-267-4468; fax: 719-267-3753; 8AM-N, 1-5PM. ***Felony, Misdemeanor, Civil, Eviction, Small Claims, Probate.***

www.courts.state.co.us/Courts/County/Choose.cfm

Search fee includes civil and criminal indexes.

Civil Records: Access: Phone, mail, fax, in person, online. Only the court performs in person searches; visitors may not. Search fee: $5.00 per name. $25.00 per hour if extensive research is needed. Required to search: name, years to search. Civil cases indexed by defendant, plaintiff, on computer back to 1993, fiche since 1980s, index books back to 1925. Mail turnaround time 3-5 days. Pay service to civil case look-up at www.courts.state.co.us; click on Court Records Search.

Criminal Records: Access: Mail, fax, in person, online. Only the court performs in person searches; visitors may not. Search fee: $5.00 per name. $25.00 per hour if extensive research is needed. Required to search: name, years to search, DOB, SSN. Criminal records computerized from 1993, fiche since 1980's, index books back to 1925. Mail turnaround time 3-5 days. Criminal case index at www.courts.state.co.us. Current dockets free, records not- click on Court Records Search.

General Information: No adoption, sealed, juvenile, mental health or expunged cases released. Will fax documents for $1.00 per page fee. Court makes copy: $.75 per page. Certification fee: $20.00 per doc. Payee: Crowley Combined Court. Personal checks accepted; credit cards are not. Prepayment required. Mail requests: SASE required.

Custer County

11th District & County Courts PO Box 60, 205 S 6th St, Westcliffe, CO 81252; 719-783-2274; fax: 719-783-2995; 8AM-4PM. ***Felony, Misdemeanor, Civil, Eviction, Small Claims, Probate, Traffic.***

www.courts.state.co.us/Courts/County/Choose.cfm

Civil Records: Access: Mail, in person, online. Only the court performs in person searches; visitors may not. Search fee: $5.00 per name. $25.00 per hour if extensive research is needed. Required to search: name, years to search. Civil cases indexed by defendant, plaintiff; index on cards from 1973, ledger books back to 1965, on computer since 1993, archived 1879-1972. Mail turnaround 3-4 days. Pay service to civil case look-up at www.courts.state.co.us; click on Court Records Search.

Criminal Records: Access: Mail, in person, online. Only the court performs in person searches; visitors may not. Search fee: $5.00 per name. $25.00 per hour if extensive research is needed. Required to search: name, years to search, DOB. Criminal records indexed on cards from 1973, ledger books back to 1965, on computer since 1993, archived from 1879-1972. Mail turnaround time 3-4 days. Criminal index at www.courts.state.co.us. Current dockets free, records not. Click court records search.

General Information: No adoption, sealed, juvenile, mental health or expunged cases released. Will fax documents $1.00 per page. This fee applies to incoming faxes too. Court makes copy: $.75 per page. Certification fee: $20.00. Payee: Custer Combined Court. Personal checks accepted; credit cards are not. Prepayment required. Mail requests: SASE required.

Delta County

Combined Courts 501 Palmer St, Rm 338, Delta, CO 81416; 970-874-6280; fax: 970-874-4306; 9AM-5PM. ***Felony, Misdemeanor, Civil, Eviction, Small Claims, Probate.***

www.courts.state.co.us/Courts/County/Choose.cfm

Civil Records: Access: Mail, fax, in person, online. Only the court performs in person searches; visitors may not. Search fee: $5.00 per name. $25.00 per hour if extensive research is needed. Required to search: name, years to search. Civil cases indexed by defendant, plaintiff, on computer back to 10/1994, index cards from 1972, index books back to 1900. Mail turnaround time 10 days. Pay service to civil case look-up at www.courts.state.co.us; click on Court Records Search. Also, weekly dockets for the 7th district courts are at www.7thjudicialdistrictco.org/docket.html.

Criminal Records: Access: Mail, fax, in person, online. Only the court performs in person searches; visitors may not. Search fee: $5.00 per name. $25.00 per hour if extensive research is needed. Required to search: name, years to search, DOB, signed release. Criminal records computerized from 10/1994, index cards from 1972, index books back to 1900. Mail turnaround time 10 days. Criminal case index at www.courts.state.co.us. Current dockets free, records not- click on Court Records Search. Also, weekly dockets are available, see civil, above.

General Information: No adoption, sealed, juvenile, mental health or expunged cases released. Will fax documents $1.00 per page. Court makes copy: $.75 per page. Certification fee: $20.00 per cert. Payee: Clerk of Court. Personal and business checks accepted. Visa/MC accepted. Prepayment required. Mail requests: SASE required.

Denver County

2nd District Courts 1437 Bannock, Rm 256, Office of the Court Clerk, Denver, CO 80202; 720-865-8301; 7:30AM-4:30PM. ***Felony, Civil Actions over $15,000, Domestic.***

www.courts.state.co.us/Courts/County/Choose.cfm

This court will not process written requests for information. You must use the Internet or hire a retriever, or visit in person. Case files in Rm 38.

Civil Records: Access: In person, online. Both court and visitors may perform in person searches. No search fee. Required to search: name, years to search. Civil cases indexed by defendant, plaintiff, on computer from 1974, index books back to the late 1800s if convicted of criminal charges. Online search of Denver County Civil Division court cases is at www.denvergov.org/apps/newcourt/court_select.aspx. Search by name, business name, or case number. A subscription account is also available via www.courts.state.co.us where daily trial court dockets can be searched free.

Criminal Records: Access: In person, online. Both court and visitors may perform in person searches. No search fee. Required to search: name, years to search, DOB. Criminal records computerized from 1974, index books back to the late 1800s if convicted of criminal charges. PAT results show name, DOB. Criminal case index at www.denvergov.org/apps/newcourt/court_select.aspx where Denver case histories go back at least 5 years; results include case, party and action information. A subscription account is also available via www.courts.state.co.us where daily trial court dockets can be searched free. Online results show middle initial, DOB. DOBs do not always appear on Denver online results.

General Information: No sealed or expunged cases released. Will not fax documents. Court makes copy: $.75 per page. Self serve: $.25 per page. Certification fee: $20.00 per cert. Payee: Denver District Court. Personal checks accepted. Visa/MC accepted. Prepayment required.

County Court - Civil Division 1515 Cleveland Pl, 4th Fl, Denver, CO 80202; 303-640-5161; fax: 303-640-4730; 8AM-5PM. ***Civil Actions under $15,000, Eviction, Small Claims.***
www.courts.state.co.us/Courts/County/Choose.cfm
Civil Records: Access: Mail, in person, online. Only the court performs in person searches; visitors may not. No search fee. Required to search: name, years to search. Civil cases indexed by defendant, plaintiff, on computer from 1987, microfiche since 1965. Mail turnaround time 1 week. Online search of Denver County Civil Division court cases is at www.denvergov.org/apps/newcourt/court_select.aspx. Search by name, business name, or case number. A subscription account is also available via www.courts.state.co.us where daily trial court dockets can be searched free. Online results show middle initial, DOB.
General Information: No adoption, sealed, juvenile, mental health or expunged cases released. Will not fax documents. Court makes copy: $.75 per page. Self serve: $.25 per page. Certification fee: $20.00. Payee: Denver County Court. Personal checks accepted; credit cards are not. Prepayment required. Mail requests: SASE required.

County Court - Criminal Division 1437 Bannock St, Rm 111A, Denver, CO 80202; 720-865-7820; fax: 720-865-7865; 8-5PM. ***Misdemeanor.***
www.courts.state.co.us/Courts/County/Choose.cfm
Criminal Records: Access: Mail, in person, online. Only the court performs in person searches; visitors may not. No search fee, until after 2nd request then $5.00. Required to search: name, years to search, DOB; also helpful: address. Criminal records computerized since 1978. Mail turnaround time 1 week. PAT results show name, DOB. Criminal case index at www.denvergov.org/apps/newcourt/court_select.aspx where Denver case histories go back at least 5 years; results include case, party and action information. A subscription account is also available via www.courts.state.co.us where daily trial court dockets can be searched free. Online results show name, DOB. DOBs do not always appear on Denver online results.
General Information: Online identifiers in results same as on public terminal. No adoption, sealed, juvenile, mental health or expunged cases released. Will fax documents $5.00 per name plus $.75 per page. Court makes copy: $.75 per page. Certification fee: $20.00. Payee: Denver County Court. Personal checks and major credit cards accepted. Prepayment required. Mail requests: SASE required.

Probate Court 1437 Bannock St, Rm 230, Denver, CO 80202; 720-865-8310; fax: 720-865-8329; 8AM-4:30PM. ***Probate.***
www.denverprobatecourt.org
Online access to selected opinions is available free at www.denverprobatecourt.org/selectedopinions.htm.

Dolores County

22nd District & County Courts PO Box 511, Dove Creek, CO 81324; 970-677-2258; fax: 970-677-4156; 8AM-5PM M, T; 8AM-N F. ***Felony, Misdemeanor, Civil, Eviction, Small Claims, Probate.***
www.courts.state.co.us/Courts/County/Choose.cfm
Office is closed on Wednesday & Thursday.
Civil Records: Access: Phone, mail, in person, online. Only the court performs in person searches; visitors may not. No search fee. Required to search: name, years to search. Civil cases indexed by defendant, plaintiff; index on cards from 1972, index books back to 1895, on computer from 6/95 to present. Mail turnaround time 1 week. Pay service to civil case look-up at www.courts.state.co.us; click on Court Records Search.
Criminal Records: Access: Phone, mail, in person, online. Only the court performs in person searches; visitors may not. No search fee. Required to search: name, years to search, DOB. Criminal records indexed on cards from 1972, index books back to 1895, on computer from 6/95 to present. Mail turnaround time 1 week. Criminal case index at www.courts.state.co.us. Current dockets free, records not- click on Court Records Search.
General Information: No adoption, sealed, juvenile, mental health or expunged cases released. Will not fax documents. Court makes copy: $.75 per page. Certification fee: $20.00. Payee: Dolores County Combined. Only cashiers checks and money orders accepted. No credit cards accepted. Prepayment required. Mail requests: SASE required.

Douglas County

Douglas County Combined Court 4000 Justice Way, #2009, Castle Rock, CO 80109; 303-663-7200; fax: 303-688-1962; 8AM-N; 1:15-4PM. ***Felony, Misdemeanor, Civil, Eviction, Small Claims, Probate.***
www.courts.state.co.us/Courts/County/Choose.cfm
Probate fax is same as main fax number.
Civil Records: Access: Mail, in person, online. Both court and visitors may perform in person searches. Search fee: $5.00 per name. $25.00 per hour for extensive search for records 1996 and prior. Required to search: name, years to search, case number if available. Civil cases indexed by defendant, plaintiff, on computer back to 1/1988, index cards from 1975, index books to 1880s. Note: Only the court personnel may search microfilm and CDs. Mail turnaround time 1-2 weeks. Public use terminal has civil records back to 2003. Includes e-filed records only. Pay service to civil case look-up at www.courts.state.co.us; click on Court Records Search.
Criminal Records: Access: Mail, in person, online. Both court and visitors may perform in person searches. Search fee: $5.00 per name. $25.00 per hour for extensive search for records 1996 and prior. Required to search: name, years to search, case number if available. Criminal records computerized from 1/1994 (in fee cases to 1988 with limited data), index cards from 1975, index books to 1880s. Note: Only the court personnel may search microfilm and CDs. Mail turnaround time 1-2 weeks. Criminal case index at www.courts.state.co.us. Current dockets free, records not- click on Court Records Search.
General Information: No adoption, sealed, juvenile, mental health or expunged cases released. Will not fax documents. Court makes copy: $.75 per page. Self serve: $.25 per page. Certification fee: $20.00 per cert. Payee: Clerk of Court. No out of state checks accepted. Credit cards accepted in person. Prepayment required. Mail requests: SASE required.

Eagle County

Eagle Combined Court PO Box 597, 0885 Chambers Ave, Eagle, CO 81631; 970-328-6373; fax: 970-328-6328; 8AM-Noon; 1-4PM. ***Felony, Misdemeanor, Civil, Eviction, Small Claims, Probate.***
www.courts.state.co.us/Courts/County/Choose.cfm
Civil Records: Access: Fax, mail, in person, online. Both court and visitors may perform in person searches. Search fee: $5.00 per name. $25.00 per hour if extensive research is needed. Required to search: name, years to search. Civil cases indexed by defendant, plaintiff, on computer since 9/95; prior on fiche to 1970, books to 1930. Mail turnaround time 5-7 days. Pay service to civil case look-up at www.courts.state.co.us; click on Court Records Search.
Criminal Records: Access: Fax, mail, in person, online. Both court and visitors may perform in person searches. Search fee: $5.00 per name. $25.00 per hour if extensive research is needed. Required to search: name, years to search, DOB. Criminal records on computer since 9/95; prior on fiche to 1970, books to 1930. Mail turnaround time 5-7 days. Criminal case index at www.courts.state.co.us. Current dockets free, records not- click on Court Records Search.
General Information: No adoption, sealed, juvenile, mental health or expunged cases released. Will fax documents $1.00 per page; pay fax fee with credit card. Court makes copy: $.75 per page. Certification fee: $20.00 per doc. Payee: Eagle Combined Courts. Personal checks accepted. Visa/MC accepted. Prepayment required. Mail requests: SASE required.

El Paso County

El Paso Combined Court PO Box 2980, 270 S Tejon, Colorado Springs, CO 80901-2980; 719-448-7599, record search- 448-7700; fax: 719-448-7695; 8AM-N, 1PM-4PM. ***Felony, Misdemeanor, Civil Actions, Probate.***
www.gofourth.org/clerkoffelp.htm
Request form available at website. Records Center is located in the basement.
Civil Records: Access: Fax, mail, in person, online. Both court and visitors may perform in person searches. Search fee: $5.00 per name, if records prior to 1988 then $5.00 each 15 minutes. Add $1.00 to fax or mail. Required to search: name, years to search. Civil cases indexed by defendant, plaintiff, on computer from 1/1975, index cards to 1975, index books to 1861. Mail turnaround time 5-7 days. Pay service to civil case look-up at www.courts.state.co.us; click on Court Records Search.
Criminal Records: Access: Fax, mail, in person, online. Both court and visitors may perform in person searches. Search fee: $5.00 per name; if pre-1988, fee is $20.00 per hour. Add $1.00 to fax or mail. Required to search: name, years to search, DOB; also helpful: SSN. Criminal records computerized from 1/1975, index cards to 1975, index books to 1861. Mail turnaround time 5-7 days. Criminal case index at www.courts.state.co.us. Current dockets free, records not- click on Court Records Search. Online results show middle initial, DOB.
General Information: No adoption, sealed, juvenile, mental health, expunged cases or other access restricted cases released. Fee to fax document $1.00 per page. Court makes copy: $.75 per page. Certification fee: $20.00 per doc. Payee: Clerk of District Court. Personal checks and major credit cards accepted. Prepayment required. Mail requests: SASE required.

Elbert County

Elbert District & County Courts PO Box 232, Kiowa, CO 80117; 303-663-7238 (Douglas Court); probate phone: same; fax: 303-688-1962; 8AM-4PM. ***Felony, Misdemeanor, Civil, Eviction, Small Claims, Probate.***
www.courts.state.co.us/Courts/County/Choose.cfm
Court closed until 01/09. All court proceedings are heard at Douglas County Combined Ct, 4000 Justice Way, Castle Rock, 303-663-7200. (Douglas fax given here) To order a file not on computer, the Douglas Clerk will retrieve the file for next day viewing.
Civil Records: Access: Mail, in person, online. Only the court performs in person searches; visitors may not. Search fee: $5.00 per name. $25.00 per hour if extensive research is needed. Required to search: full name, years to search. Civil cases indexed by defendant, plaintiff, on computer back to 1995, index cards from 1978-1994, index books from 1920s, archived prior to 1920. Mail turnaround time 1-2 weeks. Public use terminal has civil records. Public access terminal available for mandatory e-file cases. Pay service to civil case look-up at www.courts.state.co.us; click on Court Records Search.
Criminal Records: Access: Mail, in person, online. Only the court performs in person searches; visitors may not. Search fee: $5.00 per name. $25.00 per hour if extensive research is needed. Required to search: full name, years to search, DOB, signed release. Criminal records computerized from 1995, index cards from 1978, index books from 1920s. Mail turnaround time 1-2 weeks. Criminal case index at www.courts.state.co.us. Current dockets free, records not- click on Court Records Search.
General Information: No adoption, sealed, juvenile, mental health or expunged cases released. Will not fax documents. Court makes copy: $.75 per page. Certification fee: $20.00. Payee: Elbert Combined Courts. Business checks accepted. Visa/MC accepted in person only. Prepayment required. Mail requests: SASE required.

Fremont County

District & County Courts 136 Justice Center Rd, Rm 103, Canon City, CO 81212; 719-269-0100; fax: 719-269-0134; 8AM-4PM. ***Felony, Misdemeanor, Civil, Eviction, Small Claims, Probate, Traffic.***

www.courts.state.co.us/Courts/County/Choose.cfm

Civil Records: Access: Mail, fax, in person, online. Only the court performs in person searches; visitors may not. Search fee: $5.00 per name. $25.00 per hour if extensive research is needed. Required to search: name, years to search; also helpful: address. Civil cases indexed by defendant, plaintiff, computerized since 1995, on index cards from 1978, index books at archives in Denver back to 1861. Mail turnaround time up to 14 working days. Pay service to civil case look-up at www.courts.state.co.us; click on Court Records Search.

Criminal Records: Access: Mail, in person, online. Only the court performs in person searches; visitors may not. Search fee: $5.00 per name. $25.00 per hour if extensive research is needed. Required to search: name, years to search; also helpful: address, DOB. Criminal records computerized since 1995, on index cards from 1978. Mail turnaround time up to 14 working days. Criminal case index at www.courts.state.co.us. Current dockets free, records not- click on Court Records Search. Online results show middle initial, DOB.

General Information: No adoption, sealed, juvenile, mental health or expunged cases released; dissolutions and probate only released to the parties. Will not fax documents. Court makes copy: $.75 per page. Certification fee: $20.00. Payee: Clerk of the Combined Courts. Personal checks accepted. Visa/MC accepted. Prepayment required. Mail requests: SASE required.

Garfield County

9th District & County Courts 109 8th St, #104, Glenwood Springs, CO 81601; 970-945-5075; fax: 970-945-8756; 8AM-4:55PM. ***Felony, Misdemeanor, Civil, Eviction, Small Claims, Probate.***

www.courts.state.co.us/Courts/County/Choose.cfm

Civil Records: Access: Mail, in person, online. Only the court performs in person searches; visitors may not. Search fee: $5.00 per name. $25.00 per hour if extensive research is needed. Required to search: name, years to search. Civil cases indexed by defendant, plaintiff, on computer from 1992, on fiche from 1970, index books back to late 1800s. Mail turnaround time 1-2 weeks. Pay service to civil case look-up at www.courts.state.co.us; click on Court Records Search.

Criminal Records: Access: Mail, in person, online. Only the court performs in person searches; visitors may not. Search fee: $5.00 per name. $25.00 per hour if extensive research is needed. Required to search: name, years to search. Criminal records computerized from 1992, on fiche from 1970, index books back to late 1800s. Mail turnaround time 1-2 weeks. Criminal case index at www.courts.state.co.us. Current dockets free, records not- click on Court Records Search.

General Information: No adoption, sealed, juvenile, mental health or expunged cases released. Will fax back documents $1.00 per page. Court makes copy: $.75 per page. Self serve: $.25 per page. Certification fee: $20.00 per doc includes copy fee. Payee: Garfield Combined Courts. Personal checks accepted. Visa/MC accepted. Prepayment required. Mail requests: SASE required.

County Court - Rifle 200 E 18th St, Ste. 103, Rifle, CO 81650; 970-625-5100; fax: 970-625-1125; 8AM-5PM. ***Misdemeanor, Civil Actions under $15,000, Eviction, Small Claims, Traffic.***

www.courts.state.co.us/Courts/County/Choose.cfm

This court handles cases in the county for the area from New Castle to the west.

Civil Records: Access: Phone, fax, mail, in person, online. Only the court performs in person searches; visitors may not. No search fee. Required to search: name, years to search. Civil cases indexed by defendant, plaintiff; index on cards from 1965, computerized since 1994. Mail turnaround time 1 week. Results include name and case number. Pay service to civil case look-up at www.courts.state.co.us; click on Court Records Search.

Criminal Records: Access: Phone, fax, mail, in person, online. Only the court performs in person searches; visitors may not. No search fee. Required to search: name, years to search, DOB. Criminal records indexed on cards from 1965, computerized since 1994. Mail turnaround time 1 week. PAT results show middle initial, DOB. Criminal case index at www.courts.state.co.us. Current dockets free, records not- click on Court Records Search.

General Information: No adoption, sealed, juvenile, mental health or expunged cases released. Will fax documents $1.00 per page to send or receive. Court makes copy: $.75 per page. Certification fee: $20.00 per page. Payee: Associate County Court. Personal checks accepted. Credit cards accepted. Prepayment required. Mail requests: SASE required.

Gilpin County

1st District & County Courts 2960 Dory Hill Rd, #200, Black Hawk, CO 80422; 303-582-5522; fax: 303-582-3112; 9AM-4PM. ***Felony, Misdemeanor, Civil, Eviction, Small Claims, Probate.***

www.courts.state.co.us/Courts/County/Choose.cfm

Civil Records: Access: Mail, in person, online. Only the court performs in person searches; visitors may not. Search fee: $5.00 per name. Fee is for past 7 years. Required to search: name, years to search. Civil cases indexed by defendant, plaintiff, on computer (County-1993, District-1994), on index cards from 1970s, index books from 1950s. Mail turnaround time 5 days. Pay service to civil case look-up at www.courts.state.co.us; click on Court Records Search.

Criminal Records: Access: Mail, in person, online. Only the court performs in person searches; visitors may not. Search fee: $10.00 per name. Fee is for past 7 years. Required to search: name, years to search, DOB. Criminal records on computer (County-1993, District-1994), on index cards from 1970s, index books from 1950s. Mail turnaround time 5 days. Criminal case index at www.courts.state.co.us. Current dockets free, records not- click on Court Records Search.

General Information: No adoption, sealed, juvenile, mental health or expunged cases released. Will fax documents to local or toll free line. Court makes copy: $.75 per page. Certification fee: $20.00 per doc. Payee: Clerk of the Combined Courts. Personal checks and major credit cards accepted. Prepayment required. Mail requests: SASE required.

Grand County

14th District & County Courts PO Box 192, Hot Sulphur Springs, CO 80451; 970-725-3357; 8AM-5PM. ***Felony, Misdemeanor, Civil, Eviction, Small Claims, Probate.***

www.courts.state.co.us/Courts/County/Choose.cfm

Civil Records: Access: Phone, mail, in person, online. Only the court performs in person searches; visitors may not. Search fee: $5.00 per name if 1976-1991; $20.00 if pre-1976; No fee 1992-present. Required to search: name, years to search. Civil cases indexed by defendant, plaintiff, on computer from 7/1991, fiche from 1970, index books from 1900. Note: Phone requests accepted only if no fees involved. Mail turnaround time 1 week. Pay service to civil case look-up at www.courts.state.co.us; click on Court Records Search.

Criminal Records: Access: Phone, mail, in person, online. Only the court performs in person searches; visitors may not. Search fee: $5.00 per name if 1976-1991; $20.00 if pre-1976; No fee 1992-present. Required to search: name, years to search, DOB. Criminal records computerized from 7/1991, fiche from 1970, index books from 1900. Note: Phone requests accepted only if no fees involved. Mail turnaround time 1 week. Criminal case index at www.courts.state.co.us. Current dockets free, records not- click on Court Records Search.

General Information: No adoption, sealed, juvenile, mental health or expunged cases released. Will not fax documents. Court makes copy: $.75 per page. Certification fee: $20.00. Payee: Grand County Combined Court. Personal checks and major credit cards accepted. Prepayment required. Mail requests: SASE required.

Gunnison County

7th District & County Courts 200 E Virginia Ave, Gunnison, CO 81230; 970-641-3500; fax: 970-641-6876; 8AM-5PM. ***Felony, Misdemeanor, Civil, Eviction, Small Claims, Probate.***

www.courts.state.co.us/Courts/County/Choose.cfm

Search fee includes civil and criminal indexes of both courts. Fax requests should include credit card for payment. Phone requests are usually limited to those with a need to know.

Civil Records: Access: Phone, fax, mail, in person, online. Only the court performs in person searches; visitors may not. Search fee: $5.00 per name. $25.00 per hour if extensive research is needed. Required to search: name, years to search. Civil cases indexed by defendant. Civil records on computer from 1994, index cards from 1977, index books back to 1877. Mail turnaround time 1-2 days. Pay service to civil case look-up at www.courts.state.co.us; click on Court Records Search.

Criminal Records: Access: Phone, fax, mail, in person, online. Only the court performs in person searches; visitors may not. Search fee: $5.00 per name. $25.00 per hour if extensive research is needed. Required to search: name, years to search, DOB. Criminal records computerized from 1994, index cards from 1977, index books back to 1877. Mail turnaround time 1-2 days. Criminal case index at www.courts.state.co.us. Current dockets free, records not- click on Court Records Search. Online results show middle initial, DOB. Terminal results include SSN.

General Information: No adoption, sealed, juvenile, mental health or expunged cases released. Will fax documents $1.00 per page. Court makes copy: $.75 per page. Certification fee: $20.00 per doc. Payee: Gunnison Combined Courts. Personal checks accepted. Visa/MC accepted. Prepayment required. Payments may be made online via www.courts.state.co.us. Mail requests: SASE required.

Hinsdale County

7th District & County Courts PO Box 245, Lake City, CO 81235; 970-944-2227; criminal fax: 970-944-2289; civil fax: same; 8:30AM-1:30PM W,F. ***Felony, Misdemeanor, Civil, Eviction, Small Claims, Probate.***

www.courts.state.co.us/Courts/County/Choose.cfm

Probate fax is same as main fax number.

Civil Records: Access: Phone, fax, mail, in person, online. Only the court performs in person searches; visitors may not. No search fee. Required to search: name, years to search. Civil cases indexed by defendant, plaintiff; index on cards from 1975, index books back to 1900. Mail turnaround time 2-4 weeks. Pay service to civil case look-up at www.courts.state.co.us; click on Court Records Search.

Criminal Records: Access: Phone, fax, mail, in person, online. Only the court performs in person searches; visitors may not. Search fee: Fee depends on time required for search. Required to search: name, years to search, DOB. Criminal records indexed on cards from 1975, index books back to 1900. Mail turnaround time 2-4 weeks. Criminal case index at www.courts.state.co.us. Current dockets free, records not- click on Court Records Search.

General Information: No adoption, sealed, juvenile, mental health or expunged cases released. Will fax out docs $1.00 per page. Incoming faxes are 1-10 pgs- $10; 6-10 pgs-$20; 11-15 pgs $30; 16-20 pgs- $40. Court makes copy: $.75 per page. Certification fee: $20.00 per cert. Payee: Clerk of the Combined Courts. Personal checks accepted; credit cards are not. Prepayment required. Mail requests: SASE required.

Huerfano County

3rd District & County Courts 401 Main St, #304, Walsenburg, CO 81089; 719-738-1040; fax: 719-738-1267; 8AM-4PM. ***Felony, Misdemeanor, Civil, Eviction, Small Claims, Probate.***
www.courts.state.co.us/Courts/County/Choose.cfm
Civil Records: Access: Mail, in person, online. Only the court performs in person searches; visitors may not. Search fee: $5.00 per name. $25.00 per hour if extensive research is needed. Required to search: name, years to search. Civil cases indexed by defendant, plaintiff, on computer from 1995 (county court only), index cards from 1978, index books from 1861. Mail turnaround time 2 weeks. Pay service to civil case look-up at www.courts.state.co.us; click on Court Records Search.
Criminal Records: Access: Mail, in person, online. Only the court performs in person searches; visitors may not. Search fee: $5.00 per name. $25.00 per hour if extensive research is needed. Required to search: name, years to search, DOB. Criminal records computerized from 1995 (county court only), index cards from 1978, index books from 1861. Mail turnaround time 2 weeks. Criminal case index at www.courts.state.co.us. Current dockets free, records not- click on Court Records Search. Online results show middle initial, DOB.
General Information: No adoption, sealed, juvenile, mental health or expunged cases released. Will fax documents $1.00 per page. Court makes copy: $.75 per page. Certification fee: $20.00. Payee: Huerfano County Combined Courts. No personal checks accepted. Visa/MC accepted. Prepayment required. Mail requests: SASE required.

Jackson County

8th District & County Courts PO Box 308, Walden, CO 80480; 970-723-4363; fax: 970-723-4337; 9AM-1PM. ***Felony, Misdemeanor, Civil, Eviction, Small Claims, Probate.***
www.courts.state.co.us/Courts/County/Choose.cfm
Civil Records: Access: Mail, in person, online. Both court and visitors may perform in person searches. No search fee. Required to search: name, years to search. Civil cases indexed by defendant, plaintiff, on computer since 1994; prior on index cards from 1974, index books from the 1900s. Mail turnaround time 2 weeks. Pay service to civil case look-up at www.courts.state.co.us; click on Court Records Search.
Criminal Records: Access: Mail, in person, online. Both court and visitors may perform in person searches. Required to search: name, years to search, DOB. Criminal records on computer since 1994; prior on index cards from 1974, index books from the 1900s. Mail turnaround time 2 weeks. Criminal case index at www.courts.state.co.us. Current dockets free, records not- click on Court Records Search.
General Information: No adoption, sealed, juvenile, mental health or expunged cases released. Will not fax documents. Court makes copy: $.75 per page, self serve same. Certification fee: $20.00. Payee: Clerk of the Combined Courts. Personal checks accepted; credit cards are not. Prepayment required. Mail requests: SASE required.

Jefferson County

1st District & County Courts 100 Jefferson County Pky, Golden, CO 80401-6002; 303-271-6215; criminal phone: 303-271-6237; civil phone: 303-271-6228; probate phone: 303-271-6135; criminal fax: 303-271-6188; civil fax: same; 8AM-4PM. ***Felony, Misdemeanor, Civil, Eviction, Small Claims, Probate, Traffic.***
www.courts.state.co.us/Courts/County/Choose.cfm
Probate fax is same as main fax number.
Civil Records: Access: Mail, in person, online. Both court and visitors may perform in person searches. Search fee: $5.00 per name. Fee is per case. Add $5.00 if search includes microfilm records. Required to search: name, years to search; also helpful: DOB. Civil cases indexed by defendant, plaintiff, on computer from 1985, microfiche from 1975, index books from 1963-1974, archived prior to 1963. Mail turnaround time 1 week. Pay service to civil case look-up at www.courts.state.co.us; click on Court Records Search.
Criminal Records: Access: Mail, in person, online. Both court and visitors may perform in person searches. Search fee: $5.00 per name. Fee varies depending on number of years searched. Add $5.00 if search includes microfilm records. Required to search: name, years to search, DOB; also helpful: address. Criminal records computerized from 1985, microfiche from 1975, index books from 1963-1974, archived prior to 1963. Mail turnaround time 1 week. Criminal case index at www.courts.state.co.us. Current dockets free, records not- click on Court Records Search. Online results show middle initial, DOB.
General Information: No adoption, sealed, juvenile, mental health or expunged cases released. Will not fax documents. Court makes copy: $.75 per page. Self serve: $.25 per page. Certification fee: $20.00 per document. Payee: Clerk of Combined Courts. Personal checks accepted. Visa/MC accepted in person only. Prepayment required. Mail requests: SASE required.

Kiowa County

15th District & County Courts PO Box 353, Eads, CO 81036; 719-438-5558; fax: 719-438-5300; 9AM-4PM. ***Felony, Misdemeanor, Civil, Eviction, Small Claims, Probate.***
www.courts.state.co.us/Courts/County/Choose.cfm
Civil Records: Access: Phone, fax, mail, in person, online. Only the court performs in person searches; visitors may not. Search fee: $5.00 per name. $25.00 per hour if extensive research is needed. Required to search: name, years to search. Civil cases indexed by defendant, plaintiff; index on cards from the 1960s, index books from 1889. Recent records are computerized. Mail turnaround time 1 week. Pay service to civil case look-up at www.courts.state.co.us; click on Court Records Search.
Criminal Records: Access: Phone, fax, mail, in person, online. Only the court performs in person searches; visitors may not. Search fee: $5.00 per name. $25.00 per hour if extensive research is needed. Required to search: name, years to search, DOB. Criminal records indexed on cards from the 1960s, index books from 1889. Recent records are computerized. Mail turnaround time 1 week. Criminal case index at www.courts.state.co.us. Current dockets free, records not- click on Court Records Search.
General Information: No adoption, sealed, juvenile, mental health or expunged cases released. Will fax documents $1.00 each. Court makes copy: $.75 per page. Certification fee: $20.00 per doc. Payee: Kiowa County Court. Business checks accepted. No credit cards accepted. Prepayment required. Mail requests: SASE required.

Kit Carson County

Kit Carson Combined Court 251 16th St, #301, Burlington, CO 80807; 719-346-5524; fax: 719-346-7805; 8AM-4PM. ***Felony, Misdemeanor, Civil, Eviction, Small Claims, Probate.***
www.courts.state.co.us/Courts/County/Choose.cfm
Civil Records: Access: Mail, in person, online. Only the court performs in person searches; visitors may not. Search fee: $5.00 per name. $25.00 per hour if extensive research is needed. Required to search: name, years to search. Civil cases indexed by defendant, plaintiff; index on cards from 1910, index books from 1889. Mail turnaround time 1 week. Pay service to civil case look-up at www.courts.state.co.us; click on Court Records Search.
Criminal Records: Access: Mail, in person, online. Only the court performs in person searches; visitors may not. Search fee: $5.00 per name. $25.00 per hour if extensive research is needed. Required to search: name, years to search, DOB. Criminal records indexed on cards from 1910, index books from 1889. Mail turnaround time 1 week. Criminal case index at www.courts.state.co.us. Current dockets free, records not- click on Court Records Search.
General Information: No adoption, sealed, juvenile, mental health or expunged cases released. Will fax documents $5.00 per doc. Court makes copy: $.75 per page. Certification fee: $20.00. Payee: Combined Courts. No personal checks accepted. Visa/MC accepted. Prepayment required. Mail requests: SASE required.

La Plata County

La Plata Combined Courts 1060 E 2nd Ave #106, Durango, CO 81301; 970-247-2304; criminal fax: 970-247-4348; civil fax: 970-259-0258; 8AM-4PM. ***Felony, Misdemeanor, Civil, Small Claims, Probate.***
www.courts.state.co.us/Courts/County/Choose.cfm
Civil Records: Access: Mail, in person, online. Only the court performs in person searches; visitors may not. Search fee: $5.00 per name. Fee is per case and can be as much as $20.00. Required to search: name, years to search. Civil cases indexed by defendant, plaintiff, on computer from 1990, index cards from 1976, index books from 1874. Mail turnaround time 3-7 days. Pay service to civil case look-up at www.courts.state.co.us; click on Court Records Search.
Criminal Records: Access: Mail, in person, online. Only the court performs in person searches; visitors may not. Search fee: $5.00 per name. $25.00 per hour if extensive research is needed. Required to search: name, years to search, DOB. Criminal records computerized from 1996, index cards from 1976, index books from 1874. Mail turnaround time 3-7 days. Criminal case index at www.courts.state.co.us. Current dockets free, records not- click on Court Records Search.
General Information: No adoption, sealed, juvenile, mental health or expunged cases released. Fee to fax out file $3.00 each. Court makes copy: $.75 per page. Certification fee: $20.00. Payee: Clerk of the Combined Courts. Personal checks and major credit cards accepted. Prepayment required. Mail requests: SASE required.

Lake County

Lake County Combined Courts PO Box 55, 505 Harrison St, Leadville, CO 80461; 719-486-0535; fax: 719-486-5006; 8AM-N, 1-4PM. ***Felony, Misdemeanor, Civil, Eviction, Small Claims, Probate.***
www.courts.state.co.us/Courts/County/Choose.cfm
Civil Records: Access: Phone, mail, in person, online. Only the court performs in person searches; visitors may not. Search fee: $20.00 per name. Required to search: name, years to search. Civil cases indexed by defendant, plaintiff; index on cards from 1988 (District), 1970 (County), index books from 1865. Note: Court may do a phone search for no fee if the request is simple - for a recent record. Mail turnaround time 7 days. Pay service to civil case look-up at www.courts.state.co.us; click on Court Records Search.
Criminal Records: Access: Phone, mail, in person, online. Only the court performs in person searches; visitors may not. Search fee: $20.00 per name. Required to search: name, years to search, DOB. Criminal records indexed on cards from 1988 (District), 1970 (County), index books from 1865. Note: Court may do a phone search for no fee if the request is simple - for a recent record. Mail turnaround time 7 days. Criminal case index at www.courts.state.co.us. Current dockets free, records not- click on Court Records Search.
General Information: No adoption, sealed, juvenile, mental health or expunged cases released. Will fax documents $1.00 per page. Court makes copy: $.75 per page. Certification fee: $20.00 per cert. Payee: Lake County Court. Business checks accepted. Visa/MC accepted. Prepayment required. Mail requests: SASE required.

Larimer County

8th District Court 201 La Porte Ave, #100, Ft Collins, CO 80521; 970-498-6100; probate phone: 970-498-6111; fax: 970-498-6110; 8AM-4PM. ***Felony, Civil Actions over $10,000, Probate.***
www.courts.state.co.us/Courts/County/Choose.cfm

Civil Records: Access: Phone, mail, in person, online. Both court and visitors may perform in person searches. Search fee: $5.00 per name. $25.00 per hour if extensive research is needed. Required to search: name; also helpful: years to search. Civil cases indexed by defendant, plaintiff, on computer from 1976, index books back to 1861. Mail turnaround time 1-2 weeks. Pay service to civil case look-up at www.courts.state.co.us; click on Court Records Search.
Criminal Records: Access: Mail, in person, online. Only the court performs in person searches; visitors may not. Search fee: $5.00 per name. $25.00 per hour if extensive research is needed. Required to search: name; also helpful: years to search, DOB, SSN. Criminal records computerized from 1976, index books back to 1861. Mail turnaround time 7-10 days. Criminal case index at www.courts.state.co.us. Current dockets free, records not- click on Court Records Search.
General Information: No adoption, sealed, juvenile, mental health or expunged cases released. Will not fax documents. Court makes copy: $.75 per page. Self serve: $.25 per page. Certification fee: $20.00. Payee: Clerk of District Court. Personal checks accepted. Visa/MC accepted. Prepayment required. Mail requests: SASE required.

County Court 201 La Porte Ave, #100, Ft Collins, CO 80521; 970-498-6100; fax: 970-498-6110; 8AM-4PM. ***Misdemeanor, Civil Actions under $15,000, Eviction, Small Claims.***
www.courts.state.co.us/Courts/County/Choose.cfm
Civil Records: Access: Mail, in person, online. Both court and visitors may perform in person searches. Search fee: $5.00 per name. $25.00 per hour if extensive research is needed. Required to search: name, years to search; also helpful: address. Civil cases indexed by defendant, plaintiff. Some records on computer from 1986, index cards from 1965. Note: Daily dockets found online by link at court main website. Mail turnaround time 1-2 weeks. Pay service to civil case look-up at www.courts.state.co.us; click on Court Records Search.
Criminal Records: Access: Mail, in person, online. Both court and visitors may perform in person searches. Search fee: $5.00 per name. $25.00 per hour if extensive research is needed. Required to search: name, years to search, DOB, signed release, offense; also helpful: address. Some records on computer from 1986, index cards from 1965. Note: Daily dockets found online by link at court main website. Mail turnaround time 1-2 weeks. Criminal case index at www.courts.state.co.us. Current dockets free, records not- click on Court Records Search.
General Information: No sealed cases released. Will not fax documents. Court makes copy: $.75 per page. Self serve: $.25 per page. Certification fee: $20.00. Payee: Larimer County Combined Court. Personal checks accepted. Visa/MC accepted. Prepayment required. Mail requests: SASE required.

Las Animas County

3rd District Court 200 E 1st St, Rm 304, Trinidad, CO 81082; 719-846-3316/2221; probate phone: 719-846-3316; fax: 719-846-9367; 8AM-N; 1-4PM. ***Felony, Misdemeanor, Civil, Eviction, Small Claims, Probate.***
www.courts.state.co.us/Courts/County/Choose.cfm
Civil Records: Access: Mail, in person, online. Both court and visitors may perform in person searches. Search fee: $5.00 per name. $25.00 per hour if extensive research is needed. Required to search: name, years to search. Civil cases indexed by defendant, plaintiff; index on cards from 1976, index books to 1950. Mail turnaround time 1 week. Pay service to civil case look-up at www.courts.state.co.us; click on Court Records Search.
Criminal Records: Access: Mail, in person, online. Both court and visitors may perform in person searches. Search fee: $5.00 per name. $25.00 per hour if extensive research is needed. Required to search: name, years to search, DOB; also helpful: SSN. Criminal records indexed on cards from 1976, index books to 1950. Mail turnaround time 1 week. Criminal case index at www.courts.state.co.us. Current dockets free, records not- click on Court Records Search.
General Information: No adoption, sealed, juvenile, mental health or expunged cases released. Fee to fax out file $1.00 per page. Court makes copy: $.75 per page. Cert fee: $20.00. Payee: Combined Courts. Personal checks and major credit cards accepted. Prepayment required. Mail requests: SASE required.

Lincoln County

18th District & County Courts PO Box 128, Hugo, CO 80821; 719-743-2455; 8AM-5PM. ***Felony, Misdemeanor, Civil, Eviction, Small Claims, Probate.***
www.courts.state.co.us/Courts/County/Choose.cfm
Civil Records: Access: Phone, mail, in person, online. Only the court performs in person searches; visitors may not. Search fee: $5.00 per name. $25.00 per hour if extensive research is needed. Required to search: name, years to search. Civil cases indexed by defendant, plaintiff, on computer since 12/94, index cards from 1977, index books back to 1889, archived 10 years back. Mail turnaround time within 10 days. Pay service to civil case look-up at www.courts.state.co.us; click on Court Records Search.
Criminal Records: Access: Phone, mail, in person, online. Only the court performs in person searches; visitors may not. Search fee: $5.00 per name. $25.00 per hour if extensive research is needed. Required to search: name, years to search, DOB. Criminal records on computer since 12/94, index cards from 1977, index books back to 1889, archived 10 years back. Mail turnaround within 10 days. Criminal case index at www.courts.state.co.us. Current dockets free, records not- click on Court Records Search.
General Information: No adoption, sealed, juvenile, mental health or expunged cases released. Will not fax documents. Court makes copy: $.75 per page. Certification fee: $20.00 per document. Payee: Lincoln County Combined Courts. Personal checks and major credit cards accepted. Prepayment required. Mail requests: SASE required.

Logan County

Combined Court 110 N Riverview Rd, Rm 205, Sterling, CO 80751; 970-522-6565 District; 970-522-1572 County Ct; fax: 970-522-6566; 8AM-4PM. ***Felony, Misdemeanor, Civil Actions, Eviction, Small Claims, Probate.***
www.courts.state.co.us/Courts/County/Choose.cfm
County Court Fax is 970-526-5359. In search request, specify to search both court indexes; fee is $5.00 for the combined search. Access to Domestic Relations and Probate cases are limited to those involved unless petitioned in writing.
Civil Records: Access: Mail, fax, in person, online. Only the court performs in person searches; visitors may not. Search fee: $5.00 per name. $25.00 per hour if extensive research is needed. Required to search: name, years to search. Civil cases indexed by defendant, plaintiff, computerized since 8/95, on index cards from 1973, index books back to 1887. Mail turnaround time 1 week. Pay service to civil case look-up at www.courts.state.co.us; click on Court Records Search. Public can only view redacted information.
Criminal Records: Access: Mail, fax, in person, online. Only the court performs in person searches; visitors may not. Search fee: $5.00 per name. $25.00 per hour if extensive research is needed. Required to search: name, years to search, DOB. Criminal records computerized since 8/95, on index cards from 1973, index books back to 1887. Mail turnaround time 1 week. Criminal case index at www.courts.state.co.us. Current dockets free, records not- click on Court Records Search. Public can only view redacted information.
General Information: No adoption, sealed, juvenile, mental health or expunged cases released. Fee to fax out file $1.00 per page local; $2.00 per page long-distance. Court makes copy: $.75 per page. Certification fee: $20.00 per doc. Payee: Logan District Court. Personal checks accepted. Visa/MC accepted. Prepayment required. Mail requests: SASE required.

Mesa County

Mesa County Combined Court PO Box 20000-5030, 125 N Spruce, County District Court, Grand Junction, CO 81502; 970-257-3640; probate phone: 970-257-3640; fax: 970-257-8776; 8AM-4PM. ***Felony, Civil Actions over $10,000, Small Claims, Probate, Traffic.***
www.mesacourt.org/
Domestic and Probate records open to parties only.
Civil Records: Access: Phone, mail, in person, online. Only the court performs in person searches; visitors may not. Search fee: $5.00 per name. $25.00 per hour if extensive research is needed. Required to search: name, years to search, DOB. Civil cases indexed by defendant, plaintiff, on computer since 1989, on microfiche to 1970s. Mail turnaround time 1-2 days, often same day. Pay service to civil case look-up at www.courts.state.co.us; click on Court Records Search.
Criminal Records: Access: Mail, in person, online. Only the court performs in person searches; visitors may not. Search fee: $5.00 per name. $25.00 per hour if extensive research is needed. Required to search: name, years to search, DOB. Criminal records on computer since 1989, on microfiche to 1970s. Mail turnaround time 1-2 days, often same day. Criminal case index at www.courts.state.co.us. Current dockets free, records not- click on Court Records Search. Online results show name, DOB.
General Information: No adoption, sealed, juvenile, mental health or expunged cases released. Will not fax documents. Court makes copy: $.75 per page. Certification fee: $20.00 per doc. Payee: Mesa County Combined Court. Business checks accepted. Visa/MC accepted. Prepayment required. Mail requests: SASE required.

Mineral County

12th District & County Courts PO Box 337, Creede, CO 81130; 719-658-2575; fax: 719-658-0507; 8AM-N, 1-3PM. ***Felony, Misdemeanor, Civil, Eviction, Small Claims, Probate.***
www.courts.state.co.us/Courts/County/Choose.cfm
Civil Records: Access: Mail, in person, online. Only the court performs in person searches; visitors may not. Search fee: $5.00 per name. $25.00 per hour if extensive research is needed. Required to search: name, years to search. Civil cases indexed by defendant, plaintiff, on computer since 7/1993, on index cards from 1977, index books back to 1893. Mail turnaround time 2-3 days. Pay service to civil case look-up at www.courts.state.co.us; click on Court Records Search.
Criminal Records: Access: Mail, in person, online. Only the court performs in person searches; visitors may not. Search fee: $5.00 per name. $25.00 per hour if extensive research is needed. Required to search: name, years to search, DOB. Criminal records on computer since 7/1993, on index cards from 1977, index books back to 1893. Mail turnaround time 2-3 days. Criminal case index at www.courts.state.co.us. Current dockets free, records not- click on Court Records Search.
General Information: No adoption, sealed, juvenile, mental health or expunged cases released. Will not fax documents. Court makes copy: $.75 per page. Certification fee: $20.00 per doc. Payee: Mineral Combined Courts. Personal checks accepted; credit cards are not. Prepayment required. Mail requests: SASE required.

Moffat County

Moffat County Combined Court 221 W Victory Wy, #300, Craig, CO 81625; 970-824-8254; 8AM-4PM. ***Felony, Misdemeanor, Civil, Eviction, Small Claims, Probate.***
www.courts.state.co.us/Courts/County/Choose.cfm
Civil Records: Access: Phone, mail, in person, online. Only the court performs in person searches; visitors may not. Search fee: $5.00 for records 1976-91; $20.00 prior to 1976. $25.00 per hour search fee for lengthy search projects. Required to search: name, years to search. Civil cases indexed by defendant, plaintiff, on computer from 1992, index cards from 1976, either microfilmed or archived back to 1911. Mail turnaround time 1-2 weeks. Pay service to

civil case look-up at www.courts.state.co.us; click on Court Records Search.
Criminal Records: Access: Mail, in person, online. Only the court performs in person searches; visitors may not. Search fee: $5.00 1976-1991; $20.00 prior to 1976. $25.00 per hour search fee for lengthy search projects. Required to search: name, years to search, DOB. Criminal records computerized from 1992, index cards from 1976, either microfilmed or archived back to 1911. Mail turnaround time 1-2 weeks. Criminal case index at www.courts.state.co.us. Current dockets free, records not- click on Court Records Search.
General Information: No adoption, sealed, juvenile, mental health or expunged cases released. Will not fax documents. Court makes copy: $.75 per page. Certification fee: $20.00 per document. Payee: Moffat County Combined Courts. Personal checks and major credit cards accepted. Prepayment required. Mail requests: SASE required.

Montezuma County

22nd District Court 109 W Main St, #210, Cortez, CO 81321; 970-565-1111; fax: 970-565-8516; 8AM-5PM. ***Felony, Civil Actions over $15,000, Probate.***
www.courts.state.co.us/Courts/County/Choose.cfm
Fax requests must be pre-approved. Search fee includes civil and criminal indexes.
Civil Records: Access: Mail, in person, online. Only the court performs in person searches; visitors may not. Search fee: $5.00 per name or case number, or $20.00 per hour to search. Required to search: name, years to search. Civil cases indexed by defendant, plaintiff, on computer back to 6/95, microfiche up to 1988, index cards from 1975, index books back to late 1890s. Mail turnaround 1-2 weeks. Pay service to civil case look-up at www.courts.state.co.us; click on Court Records Search.
Criminal Records: Access: Mail, in person, online. Only the court performs in person searches; visitors may not. Search fee: $5.00 per name or case number, or $20.00 per hour to search. Required to search: name, years to search, DOB. Criminal records computerized from 6/95, microfiche up to 1988, index cards from 1975, index books back to late 1890s. Mail turnaround time 1-2 weeks. Criminal case index at www.courts.state.co.us. Current dockets free, records not- click on Court Records Search.
General Information: No adoption, sealed, juvenile, mental health or expunged cases released. Will not fax documents. Court makes copy: $.75 per page. Certification fee: $20.00 per doc. Payee: Montezuma District Court. Personal checks accepted; credit cards are not. Prepayment required. Will bill mailing and copy costs. Mail requests: SASE required.

County Court 601 N Mildred Rd, Cortez, CO 81321; 970-565-7580; fax: 970-565-8798; 8AM-4:30PM. ***Misdemeanor, Civil Actions under $15,000, Eviction, Small Claims, Traffic.***
www.courts.state.co.us/district/22nd/22distindex.htm
Civil Records: Access: Mail, in person, online. Only the court performs in person searches; visitors may not. Search fee: $5.00 per name. $25.00 per hour if extensive research is needed. Required to search: name, years to search. Civil cases indexed by defendant, plaintiff, on computer since 1993. Note: All requests must be in writing. Mail turnaround time 7-10 days. Pay service to civil case look-up at www.courts.state.co.us; click on Court Records Search.
Criminal Records: Access: Mail, in person, online. Only the court performs in person searches; visitors may not. Search fee: $5.00 per name. $25.00 per hour if extensive research is needed. Required to search: name, years to search, DOB. Criminal records indexed on cards from 1975, index books prior. Note: Search requests must be in writing. Mail turnaround time 5-7 days. Criminal case index at www.courts.state.co.us. Current dockets free, records not- click on Court Records Search.
General Information: No adoption, sealed, juvenile, mental health or expunged cases released. Will fax documents for $1.00 per page fee, prepaid only. Court makes copy: $.75 per page. Certification fee: $20.00 per doc. Payee: Montezuma County Court. Personal checks accepted; credit cards are not. Prepayment required. Mail requests: SASE required.

Montrose County

Montrose County Combined Court 1200 N Grand Ave, Bin A, Montrose, CO 81401-3164; 970-252-4300; fax: 970-252-4309; 9AM-4PM. ***Felony, Misdemeanor, Civil, Eviction, Small Claims, Probate.***
www.courts.state.co.us/Courts/County/Choose.cfm
Civil Records: Access: Mail, in person, online. Only the court performs in person searches; visitors may not. Search fee: $5.00 per name plus $25.00 per hour. Required to search: name, years to search. Civil cases indexed by defendant, plaintiff; index on cards from 1975, index books back to 1890. Mail turnaround time 10 days. Pay service to civil case look-up at www.courts.state.co.us; click on Court Records Search. Also, weekly dockets available free at www.7thjudicialdistrictco.org/docket.html.
Criminal Records: Access: Mail, fax, in person, online. Only the court performs in person searches; visitors may not. Search fee: $5.00 per name plus $25.00 per hour. Required to search: name, years to search, DOB. Criminal records indexed on cards from 1975, index books back to 1890. Mail turnaround time 10 days. Criminal case index at www.courts.state.co.us. Current dockets free, records not- click on Court Records Search.
General Information: No adoption, sealed, juvenile, mental health or expunged cases released. Will fax documents $1.00 per page. Court makes copy: $.75 per page. Certification fee: $20.00 per doc. Payee: Montrose Combined Courts. Personal checks and major credit cards accepted. Prepayment required. Mail requests: SASE required.

Morgan County

13 Judicial District Combined Court 400 Warner St, Ft Morgan, CO 80701; 970-542-3435 Dist; 970-542-3414 County; criminal fax: 970-542-3436; civil fax: same; 8AM-4PM. ***Felony, Misdemeanor, Civil, Probate, Eviction, Small Claims, Traffic.***
www.courts.state.co.us/Courts/County/Choose.cfm
District and County Court combined as of 2006. Fax for County Court Division (Misdemeanor, Civil Actions Under $15,000, Eviction, Small Claims, Traffic) is 970-542-3416.
Civil Records: Access: Fax, mail, in person, online. Only the court performs in person searches; visitors may not. Search fee: $5.00 per name. $25.00 per hour if extensive research is needed. Required to search: name, years to search. Civil cases indexed by defendant, plaintiff; index on cards from 1967 for District Court (County court back to 1980), index books back to 1906; computerized since 8/95. Mail turnaround time 1 week. Pay service to civil case look-up at www.courts.state.co.us; click on Court Records Search. In person searching must look at both indices, the District and County Court records are not commingled.
Criminal Records: Access: Fax, mail, in person, online. Only the court performs in person searches; visitors may not. Search fee: $5.00 per name. $25.00 per hour if extensive research is needed. Required to search: name, years to search, DOB, SSN; also helpful: signed release. Criminal records indexed on cards from 1967 for District Court (County court back to 1980), index books back to 1906, computerized since 8/95. Mail turnaround time 1 week. Criminal case index at www.courts.state.co.us. Current dockets free, records not- click on Court Records Search. In person searching must look at both indices, the District and County Court records are not commingled.
General Information: No adoption, sealed, juvenile, mental health or expunged cases released. Will fax documents if less than 5 pages for $1.00 per page if local or toll-free call. Court makes copy: $.75 per page. Certification fee: $20.00. Payee: Morgan District Court. Personal checks accepted. Credit cards accepted. Prepayment required. Will bill copy fees to attorneys. Mail requests: SASE required.

Otero County

District & County Courts Courthouse, Rm 207, 13 W 3rd St, La Junta, CO 81050; 719-384-4951 district; -4721 County; fax: 719-384-4991; 8AM-5PM. ***Felony, Misdemeanor, Civil, Eviction, Small Claims, Probate.***
www.courts.state.co.us/Courts/County/Choose.cfm
While these courts have been "combined" for certain practical purposes, there are separate offices and record databases, although the search fee covers both courts. But Probate is also a separate index; Probate fax is same as main fax number.
Civil Records: Access: Mail, in person, online. Only the court performs in person searches; visitors may not. Search fee: $5.00 per name. $25.00 per hour if extensive research is needed. Required to search: name, years to search. Civil cases indexed by defendant, plaintiff; index on cards from 1978, index books back to 1889, microfiche from 1889-1992. Mail turnaround time 5-8 days. Pay service to civil case look-up at www.courts.state.co.us; click on Court Records Search.
Criminal Records: Access: Mail, in person, online. Only the court performs in person searches; visitors may not. Search fee: $5.00 per name. $25.00 per hour if extensive research is needed. Required to search: name, years to search, DOB. Criminal records indexed on cards from 1978, index books back to 1889, microfiche from 1889-1992. Mail turnaround time 5-8 days. Criminal case index at www.courts.state.co.us. Current dockets free, records not- click on Court Records Search.
General Information: No adoption, sealed, juvenile, mental health or expunged cases released. Will fax documents $1.00 per page. Court makes copy: $.75 per page, self serve same. Certification fee: $20.00 per document. Payee: Otero County Combined Courts. Personal checks accepted; credit cards are not. Prepayment required. Mail requests: SASE required.

Ouray County

7th District & County Courts PO Box 643, Ouray, CO 81427; 970-325-4405; criminal fax: 970-325-7364; civil fax: same; 9AM-N, 1-4PM M-TH; Closed F. ***Felony, Misdemeanor, Civil, Eviction, Small Claims, Probate.***
www.courts.state.co.us/Courts/County/Choose.cfm
Probate fax is same as main fax number.
Civil Records: Access: Mail, in person, online. Only the court performs in person searches; visitors may not. Search fee: $5.00 per name. $25.00 per hour if extensive research is needed. Required to search: name, years to search, case type if known. Civil cases indexed by defendant, plaintiff, on computer since 1994, index cards from 1976, index books back to 1876, archived prior to 1925. Mail turnaround time 1 week. Pay service to civil case look-up at www.courts.state.co.us; click on Court Records Search.
Criminal Records: Access: Mail, in person, online. Only the court performs in person searches; visitors may not. Search fee: $5.00 per name. $25.00 per hour if extensive research is needed. Required to search: name, years to search, DOB, case type if known. Criminal records on computer since 1994, index cards from 1976, index books back to 1876, archived prior to 1925. Mail turnaround time 1 week. Criminal case index at www.courts.state.co.us. Current dockets free, records not- click on Court Records Search.
General Information: No adoption, sealed, juvenile, financial, drug/alcohol evaluations, mental health or expunged cases released. Fee to fax out file $1.00 per page. Court makes copy: $.75 per page. Self serve: $.25 per page. Certification fee: $20.00. Payee: Ouray Combined Courts. Personal checks accepted. Visa/MC accepted. Prepayment required. Mail requests: SASE requested.

Park County

Park County Combined Courts PO Box 190, 300 4th St, Fairplay, CO 80440; 719-836-2940; fax: 719-836-2892; 7:30AM-4:30PM. ***Felony, Misdemeanor, Civil, Eviction, Small Claims, Probate.***
www.courts.state.co.us/Courts/County/Choose.cfm

Civil Records: Access: Mail, online. Only the court performs in person searches; visitors may not. Search fee: $5.00 per name. $25.00 per hour if extensive research is needed. Required to search: name, years to search. Civil cases indexed by defendant, plaintiff, computerized since 1995, on index cards from 1978, index books back to 1950, archived prior to 1950. Mail turnaround time within 1 week. Pay service to civil case look-up at www.courts.state.co.us; click on Court Records Search.

Criminal Records: Access: Mail, online. Only the court performs in person searches; visitors may not. Search fee: $5.00 per name. $25.00 per hour if extensive research is needed. Required to search: name, years to search, DOB, signed release. Criminal records computerized since 1995, on index cards from 1978, index books back to 1950, archived prior to 1950. Mail turnaround time within 1 week. Criminal case index at www.courts.state.co.us. Current dockets free, records not- click on Court Records Search.

General Information: No adoption, sealed, juvenile, mental health or expunged cases released. Will not fax documents. Court makes copy: $.75 per page. Certification fee: $20.00. Payee: Park County Combined Court. Personal checks accepted; credit cards are not. Prepayment required. Mail requests: SASE required.

Phillips County

13th District & County Combined Court 221 S Interocean, Holyoke, CO 80734; 970-854-3279; fax: 970-854-3179; 8AM-1PM. ***Felony, Misdemeanor, Civil, Eviction, Small Claims, Probate.***

www.courts.state.co.us/Courts/County/Choose.cfm

Civil Records: Access: Phone, fax, mail, in person, online. Only the court performs in person searches; visitors may not. Search fee: $5.00 per name. $25.00 per hour if extensive research is needed. Required to search: name, years to search. Civil cases indexed by defendant, plaintiff, on computer since 1995; records go back to 1880. Mail turnaround time 1-3 days. Pay service to civil case look-up at www.courts.state.co.us; click on Court Records Search.

Criminal Records: Access: Phone, fax, mail, in person, online. Only the court performs in person searches; visitors may not. Search fee: $5.00 per name. $25.00 per hour if extensive research is needed. Required to search: name, years to search, DOB. Criminal records on computer since 1995; records go back to 1880. Mail turnaround time 1-3 days. Criminal case index at www.courts.state.co.us. Current dockets free, records not- click on Court Records Search.

General Information: No adoption, sealed, juvenile, mental health or expunged cases released. Will fax documents $2.00 each, prepaid. Court makes copy: $.75 per page. Certification fee: $20.00 per document. Payee: Phillips County Combined Court. Personal checks accepted; credit cards are not. Prepayment required. Mail requests: SASE required.

Pitkin County

9th District & County Courts 506 E Main St, #300, Aspen, CO 81611; 970-925-7635; probate phone: x2; fax: 970-925-6349; 8AM-N, 1-5PM. ***Felony, Misdemeanor, Civil, Eviction, Small Claims, Probate.***

www.courts.state.co.us/Courts/County/Choose.cfm

Civil Records: Access: Phone, mail, fax, in person, online. Both court and visitors may perform in person searches. Search fee: No fee for computer search. Required to search: name, years to search. Civil cases indexed by defendant. Civil records on computer back to 1990, microfiche from 1940-1970, index cards from 1975. Mail turnaround time 1 week. Pay service to civil case look-up at www.courts.state.co.us; click on Court Records Search. Search probate 1881-1953 at www.colorado.gov/dpa/doit/archives/probate/pitkin_probate.htm.

Criminal Records: Access: Mail, fax, in person, online. Both court and visitors may perform in person searches. Search fee: There is no fee for searching computer, otherwise rate determined by time and volume. Required to search: name, years to search, DOB, SSN. Criminal records computerized from 1990, microfiche from 1940-1970, index cards from 1975. Mail turnaround time 1 week. Criminal case index at www.courts.state.co.us. Current dockets free, records not- click on Court Records Search.

General Information: No adoption, sealed, juvenile, mental health or expunged cases released. Fee to fax out file $1.00 per page. Court makes copy: $.75 per page. Cert fee: $20.00 per doc. Payee: Pitkin County Combined Court. Cashiers checks and money orders accepted. Visa/MC accepted. Prepayment required.

Prowers County

15th District and County Court 301 S Main St, #300, Lamar, CO 81052-2834; 719-336-7424; fax: 719-336-9757; 8AM-5PM. ***Felony, Misdemeanor, Civil Actions, Eviction, Small Claims, Traffic, Probate.***

www.courts.state.co.us/Courts/County/Choose.cfm

Search fee includes both civil and criminal indexes, and includes both courts. County court phone-719-336-7416.

Civil Records: Access: Fax, mail, in person, online. Only the court performs in person searches; visitors may not. Search fee: $5.00 per name. $25.00 per hour if extensive research is needed. Required to search: name, years to search. Civil cases indexed by defendant, plaintiff, computerized since 1995, on microfiche from 1920, index books from the late 1800s. Mail turnaround time 1 week. Pay service to civil case look-up at www.courts.state.co.us; click on Court Records Search.

Criminal Records: Access: Fax, mail, in person, online. Only the court performs in person searches; visitors may not. Search fee: $5.00 per name. $25.00 per hour if extensive research is needed. Required to search: name, years to search, DOB. Criminal records computerized since 1995, on microfiche from 1920, index books from the late 1800s. Mail turnaround time 1 week. Criminal case index at www.courts.state.co.us. Current dockets free, records not- click on Court Records Search.

General Information: No adoption, sealed, juvenile, mental health or expunged cases released. Will fax documents $1.00 per page. Court makes copy: $.75 per page. Certification fee: $20.00 per doc. Payee: Clerk of District Court. Business checks accepted. No credit cards accepted. Prepayment required. Mail requests: SASE required.

Pueblo County

Combined Courts 320 W 10th St, Pueblo, CO 81003; 719-583-7000; civil phone: 719-583-7026; probate phone: 719-583-7030; 8AM-4PM. ***Felony, Misdemeanor, Civil, Eviction, Small Claims, Probate.***

www.courts.state.co.us/Courts/County/Choose.cfm

Civil Records: Access: Mail, in person, online. Only the court performs in person searches; visitors may not. Search fee: $5.00 per name. $25.00 per hour if extensive research is needed. Required to search: name, years to search; also helpful: address. Civil cases indexed by defendant, plaintiff, on computer from 1976, index books back to the 1890s. Mail turnaround time 3-5 days. Pay service to civil case look-up at www.courts.state.co.us; click on Court Records Search.

Criminal Records: Access: Mail, in person, online. Only the court performs in person searches; visitors may not. Search fee: $5.00 per name. $25.00 per hour if extensive research is needed. Required to search: name, years to search, DOB; also helpful: address. Criminal records computerized from 1976, index books back to the 1890s. Mail turnaround time 3-5 days, longer if archived. Criminal case index at www.courts.state.co.us. Current dockets free, records not- click on Court Records Search.

General Information: No adoption, sealed, juvenile, mental health or expunged cases released. Will fax documents $1.00 per page. Court makes copy: $.75 per page. Certification fee: $20.00 per doc. Payee: Clerk of Court. Personal checks accepted. Visa/MC accepted in person only. Prepayment required. Mail requests: SASE required.

Rio Blanco County

9th District & County Courts PO Box 1150, 555 Main St, Rm 303, Meeker, CO 81641; 970-878-5622; fax: 970-878-4295; 8AM-N, 1-5PM. ***Felony, Misdemeanor, Civil, Eviction, Small Claims, Probate.***

www.courts.state.co.us/Courts/County/Choose.cfm

You may fax in after agreeing to $1.00 per page fax fee. The search fee includes both civil and criminal indexes. Phoned-in search requests may or may not be acceptable - depends on clerk availability and your friendly demeanor.

Civil Records: Access: Phone, fax, mail, in person, online. Only the court performs in person searches; visitors may not. Search fee: $5.00 per name. May charge for lengthy in-person search request. Required to search: name; also helpful: years to search. Civil cases indexed by defendant, plaintiff, on computer since 8/1994, on index cards from 4/1976, index books back to 1889. Mail turnaround time 2 days. Pay service to civil case look-up at www.courts.state.co.us; click on Court Records Search.

Criminal Records: Access: Phone, fax, mail, in person, online. Only the court performs in person searches; visitors may not. Search fee: $5.00 per name. May charge for lengthy in-person search request. Required to search: name, years to search; also helpful: DOB. Criminal records on computer since 8/1994, on index cards from 4/1976, index books back to 1889. Mail turnaround time 2 days. Criminal case index at www.courts.state.co.us. Current dockets free, records not- click on Court Records Search.

General Information: No adoption, sealed, juvenile, mental health or expunged cases released. Fee to fax out file $1.00 per page. Court makes copy: $.75 per page. Certification fee: $20.00 per doc. Payee: Clerk of the Combined Courts. Business checks accepted, no personal. Visa/MC accepted. Prepayment required. Mail requests: SASE required.

Rio Grande County

12th District & County Courts 6th & Cherry, PO Box 427, Del Norte, CO 81132; 719-657-3394; fax: 719-657-2636; 8AM-N, 1-4PM. ***Felony, Misdemeanor, Civil, Eviction, Small Claims, Probate.***

www.courts.state.co.us/Courts/County/Choose.cfm

Civil Records: Access: Mail, in person, online. Only the court performs in person searches; visitors may not. Search fee: $5.00 per name, additional $25.00 to search archived records. Required to search: name, years to search. Civil cases indexed by defendant, plaintiff, on computer from 5/95, County on index cards from 1950s, District from 1977. All on index books from the 1800s. Mail turnaround time 2-4 days. Pay service to civil case look-up at www.courts.state.co.us; click on Court Records Search.

Criminal Records: Access: Mail, in person, online. Only the court performs in person searches; visitors may not. Search fee: $5.00 per name, additional $25.00 to search archived records. Required to search: name, DOB; also helpful: years to search. Criminal records computerized from 5/95, County on index cards from 1950s, District from 1977. All on index books from the 1800s. Mail turnaround time 2-4 days. Criminal case index at www.courts.state.co.us. Current dockets free, records not- click on Court Records Search.

General Information: No adoption, sealed, juvenile, mental health or expunged cases released. Will fax documents $1.00 per page. Court makes copy: $.75 per page. Certification fee: $20.00. Payee: Rio Grande Combined Court. Personal and business checks accepted. Visa/MC accepted. Prepayment required. Mail requests: SASE required.

Routt County

Routt Combined Courts PO Box 773117, 222 Lincoln Ave, 3rd Fl, Steamboat Springs, CO 80477; 970-879-5020; fax: 970-879-3531; 8AM-N, 1-4PM. ***Felony, Misdemeanor, Civil, Eviction, Small Claims, Probate.***

www.courts.state.co.us/Courts/County/Choose.cfm

Civil Records: Access: Mail, in person, online. Both court and visitors may perform in person searches. Search fee: $5.00 for 1976-1991; prior to 1976 $20.00. There is no fee to search computerized records. Required to search: name, years to search. Civil cases indexed by defendant. Civil records on computer back to 1994, on index cards from 1977, microfiche from 1/1977 to 12/1990, archived from 1877. Mail turnaround time 7-10 days. Pay service to civil case look-up at www.courts.state.co.us; click on Court Records Search.
Criminal Records: Access: Mail, in person, online. Both court and visitors may perform in person searches. Search fee: $5.00 for 1976-1991; prior to 1976 $20.00. There is no fee to search computerized records. Required to search: name, years to search, DOB, maiden name, aliases. Criminal records computerized from 1994, on index cards from 1977, microfiche from 1/1977 to 12/1990, archived from 1877. Mail turnaround time 7-10 days. Criminal case index at www.courts.state.co.us. Current dockets free, records not- click on Court Records Search.
General Information: No adoption, sealed, juvenile, mental health or expunged cases released. Will not fax documents. Court makes copy: $.75 per page. Certification fee: $20.00 per doc. Payee: Routt Combined Court. Personal checks accepted. Visa/MC accepted. Prepayment required. Mail requests: SASE required.

Saguache County

12th District & County Courts PO Box 197, 4th and Christy Sts, Courthouse, Saguache, CO 81149; 719-655-2522; fax: 719-655-0109; 8AM-N, 1-4PM, phones til 5PM. ***Felony, Misdemeanor, Civil, Eviction, Small Claims, Probate.***
www.courts.state.co.us/Courts/County/Choose.cfm
Probate fax is same as main fax number.
Civil Records: Access: Mail, in person, online. Only the court performs in person searches; visitors may not. Search fee: $5.00 per name. Required to search: name, years to search. Civil cases indexed by defendant, plaintiff, on computer since 6/94, on index cards from 1980s, index books back to 1866. Note: Civil records containing financial information are not available by mail. Mail turnaround time 1 week. Pay service to civil case look-up at www.courts.state.co.us; click on Court Records Search.
Criminal Records: Access: Mail, in person, online. Only the court performs in person searches; visitors may not. Search fee: $5.00 per name. $25.00 per hour if extensive research is needed. Required to search: name, years to search, DOB. Criminal records on computer since 6/94, on index cards from 1980s, index books back to 1866. Note: Criminal record search at this office will reveal dispositions only, generally. Mail turnaround time 1 week. Criminal case index at www.courts.state.co.us. Current dockets free, records not- click on Court Records Search.
General Information: No adoption, sealed, juvenile, mental health or expunged cases released. Will not fax documents. Court makes copy: $.75 per page. Certification fee: $20.00 per doc. Payee: Saguache Combined Courts. Personal checks accepted. Visa/MC accepted. Prepayment required. Mail requests: SASE required.

San Juan County

6th District & County Courts PO Box 900, 1557 Greene St, Silverton, CO 81433; 970-387-5790; fax: 970-387-0295; 8AM-4PM T & TH. ***Felony, Misdemeanor, Civil, Eviction, Small Claims, Probate.***
www.courts.state.co.us/Courts/County/Choose.cfm
Civil Records: Access: Phone, fax, mail, in person, online. Only the court performs in person searches; visitors may not. Search fee: $9.00 per name. Fee is $20.00 for lengthy search. Required to search: name, years to search. Civil cases indexed by defendant, plaintiff, on computer since 1995; prior on index cards from 1975, index books back to 1876. Mail turnaround time 1 week. Pay service to civil case look-up at www.courts.state.co.us; click on Court Records Search.
Criminal Records: Access: Mail, fax, in person, online. Only the court performs in person searches; visitors may not. Search fee: $9.00 per name. Required to search: name, years to search, DOB, signed release. Criminal records on computer since 1995; prior on index cards from 1975, index books back to 1876. Mail turnaround time 1 week. Criminal case index at www.courts.state.co.us. Current dockets free, records not- click on Court Records Search.
General Information: No adoption, sealed, juvenile, mental health, open domestic, probate or expunged cases released. Will fax documents to local numbers only. Court makes copy: $.75 per page. Certification fee: $20.00 per doc. Payee: San Juan County Court. Business checks accepted. No credit cards accepted. Prepayment required. Mail requests: SASE required.

San Miguel County

7th District & County Courts PO Box 919, 305 W Colorado St, Telluride, CO 81435; 970-728-3891; fax: 970-728-6216; 9AM-N, 1-4PM. ***Felony, Misdemeanor, Civil, Eviction, Small Claims, Probate.*** www.7thjudicialdistrictco.org
Civil Records: Access: Phone, mail, in person, online. Only the court performs in person searches; visitors may not. Search fee: $5.00 per name if after 1994. Required to search: name, years to search. Civil cases indexed by defendant, plaintiff; index on cards from 1970, index books back to 1861, archived back to 1880; on computer back to 1994. Note: Will do very limited phone searches back to 1994. Mail turnaround time 30 days. Pay service to civil case look-up at www.courts.state.co.us; click on Court Records Search.
Criminal Records: Access: Phone, mail, in person, online. Only the court performs in person searches; visitors may not. Search fee: $5.00 per name if after 1994. Required to search: name, years to search, DOB. Criminal records indexed on cards from 1970, index books back to 1861, archived back to 1880; on computer back to 1994. Note: Will do very limited phone searches back to 1994. Mail turnaround time 30 days. Criminal case index at www.courts.state.co.us. Current dockets free, records not- click on Court Records Search.
General Information: No adoption, sealed, juvenile, mental health or expunged cases released. Will fax documents if prepaid. Court makes copy: $.75 per page. Certification fee: $20.00 per doc. Payee: Combined Courts. Personal checks accepted. Visa/MC accepted. Prepayment required. Mail requests: SASE required.

Sedgwick County

13th District & County Courts 3rd & Pine, Julesburg, CO 80737; 970-474-3627; criminal fax: 970-474-2026; civil fax: same; 8AM-1PM. ***Felony, Misdemeanor, Civil, Eviction, Small Claims, Probate.***
www.courts.state.co.us/Courts/County/Choose.cfm
Probate fax is same as main fax number.
Civil Records: Access: Fax, mail, in person, online. Both court and visitors may perform in person searches. Search fee: The court reserves the right to charge if an extensive search is required. Required to search: name; also helpful: years to search. Civil cases indexed by defendant, plaintiff; index on cards from early 1970s, index books back to 1889; on computer back to 8/1995. Mail turnaround time 1-2 days. Pay service to civil case look-up at www.courts.state.co.us; click on Court Records Search.
Criminal Records: Access: Fax, mail, in person, online. Only the court performs in person searches; visitors may not. Search fee: The court reserves the right to charge if an extensive search is required. Required to search: name, DOB; also helpful: years to search. Criminal records indexed on cards from early 1970s, index books back to 1889; on computer back to 8/1995. Mail turnaround time 1-3 days. Criminal case index at www.courts.state.co.us. Current dockets free, records not- click on Court Records Search.
General Information: No adoption, sealed, juvenile, mental health or expunged cases released. Fee to fax out file $2.00 each. Court makes copy: $.75 per page. Certification fee: $20.00 per doc. Payee: Sedgwick County Combined Court. Personal checks accepted; credit cards are not. Prepayment required. Mail requests: SASE required.

Summit County

Summit Combined Courts PO Box 185, Breckenridge, CO 80424; 970-453-2241 District; 970-453-2272 County; fax: 970-453-1134; 8AM-4PM. ***Felony, Misdemeanor, Civil, Eviction, Small Claims, Probate.***
www.courts.state.co.us/Courts/County/Choose.cfm
District Court uses PO Box 269.
Civil Records: Access: In person, online. Only the court performs in person searches; visitors may not. Required to search: name. Civil cases indexed by defendant, plaintiff, on computer back to 1995, index cards from the early 1970s, index books back to 1861, archived from 1980 and prior. Note: Records prior to 2003 in storage; request must be in writing and fee paid prior to court providing record. Pay service to civil case look-up at www.courts.state.co.us; click on Court Records Search.
Criminal Records: Access: Mail, in person, online. Only the court performs in person searches; visitors may not. Search fee: $5.00 per name. $25.00 per hour if extensive research is needed. Required to search: name, DOB, signed release. Criminal records name index on computer as of 9/95. Note: Records prior to 2003 in storage; request must be in writing and fee paid prior to court providing record. Criminal case index at www.courts.state.co.us. Current dockets free, records not- click on Court Records Search.
General Information: No adoption, sealed, juvenile, mental health or expunged cases released. Will not fax documents. Court makes copy: $.75 per page. Cert fee: $20.00. Payee: County Clerk. Only cashiers checks and money orders accepted; cash accepted in person. Visa/MC accepted. Prepayment required.

Teller County

Teller Combined Courts PO Box 997, Cripple Creek, CO 80813; 719-689-2574; fax: 719-686-8000; 9AM-N; 1PM-4PM. ***Felony, Misdemeanor, Civil, Eviction, Small Claims, Probate.***
www.tellercountycourts.com
Civil Records: Access: Mail, in person, online. Only the court performs in person searches; visitors may not. Search fee: $5.00 per name. If not on computer, fee is $20.00 per hour. Fee is $15.00 to retrieve file from offsite. Required to search: name, years to search. Civil cases indexed by defendant, plaintiff, computerized back to 1988, on index cards from 1960, index books back to 1899. Note: Download a record request form at https://33.securedata.net/gofourth/pub_data_req_form.htm. Mail turnaround time 5-7 days; 4-6 weeks if not on computer. Pay service to civil case look-up at www.courts.state.co.us; click on Court Records Search.
Criminal Records: Access: Mail, in person, online. Only the court performs in person searches; visitors may not. Search fee: $5.00 per name. If records not on computer, fee is $20.00 per hour. Fee is $15.00 to retrieve file from offsite. Required to search: name, years to search, DOB; also helpful: address, SSN. Criminal records computerized back to 1988, on index cards from 1960, index books back to 1899. Mail turnaround time 5-7 days; 4-6 weeks if file not on computer. Criminal case index at www.courts.state.co.us. Current dockets free, records not- click on Court Records Search.
General Information: No adoption, sealed, juvenile, mental health or expunged cases released. Will fax documents $1.00 per page. Court makes copy: $.75 per page. Certification fee: $20.00. Payee: Teller County Combined Courts. Personal and business checks accepted. Credit cards accepted. Prepayment required. Mail requests: SASE required.

Washington County

Washington County Combined Court 26861 Hwy 34, PO Box 455, Akron, CO 80720; 970-345-2756; fax: 970-345-2829; 8AM-N, 1-5PM. ***Felony, Misdemeanor, Civil, Eviction, Small Claims, Probate.***

www.courts.state.co.us/district/13th/13dist.htm

Civil Records: Access: Phone, mail, in person, online. Only the court performs in person searches; visitors may not. No search fee. Required to search: name, years to search. Civil cases indexed by defendant. Civil index on cards from 1970, index books back to 1887; computerized since 1995. Mail turnaround time 2-3 days. Pay service to civil case look-up at www.courts.state.co.us; click on Court Records Search.

Criminal Records: Access: Phone, mail, in person, online. Only the court performs in person searches; visitors may not. No search fee. Required to search: name, years to search, DOB. Criminal records indexed on cards from 1970, index books back to 1887; computerized since 1995. Note: Criminal case index available for a fee via a choice of 3 private providers. Mail turnaround time 2-3 days. Criminal case index at www.courts.state.co.us. Current dockets free, records not- click on Court Records Search.

General Information: No adoption, sealed, juvenile, mental health or expunged cases released. Will fax documents $5.00 fee. Court makes copy: $.75 per page. Certification fee: $20.00. Payee: Washington County Combined Court. Personal checks accepted; credit cards are not. Prepayment required. Mail requests: SASE required.

Weld County

19th District & County Courts PO Box 2038, 915 10th St, Centennial Bldg, Greeley, CO 80632; 970-351-7300; criminal phone: x5597 (Lisa); civil phone: x5596; probate phone: x5400; fax: 970-336-7245; 7:30AM-4:30PM. ***Felony, Misdemeanor, Civil, Eviction, Small Claims, Probate.***

www.courts.state.co.us/Courts/County/Choose.cfm

Civil Records: Access: Mail, in person, online. Only the court performs in person searches; visitors may not. Search fee: $5.00 per name. $25.00 per hour if extensive research is needed. Required to search: name, years to search. Civil cases indexed by defendant, plaintiff, on computer from 1975 (District), 1990 (County), index cards from 1958, index books back to 1876. Mail turnaround time ASAP. Pay service to civil case look-up at www.courts.state.co.us; click on Court Records Search.

Criminal Records: Access: Mail, in person, online. Only the court performs in person searches; visitors may not. Search fee: $5.00 per name. $25.00 per hour if extensive research is needed. Required to search: name, years to search; also helpful: DOB. Criminal records computerized from 1975 (District), 1990 (County), index cards from 1958, index books back to 1876. Mail turnaround time ASAP. Criminal case index at www.courts.state.co.us. Current dockets free, records not- click on Court Records Search.

General Information: No adoption, sealed, juvenile, mental health or expunged cases released. Will fax out documents $1.00 per page; written request required. Court makes copy: $.75 per page. Certification fee: $20.00 per doc. Payee: Clerk of Combined Court. Personal checks and major credit cards accepted. Prepayment required. Mail requests: SASE required.

Yuma County

13th District & County Courts PO Box 347, 310 Ash St, Wray, CO 80758; 970-332-4118; fax: 970-332-4119; 8AM-4PM. ***Felony, Misdemeanor, Civil, Eviction, Small Claims, Probate.***

www.courts.state.co.us/Courts/County/Choose.cfm

Civil Records: Access: Mail, in person, online. Only the court performs in person searches; visitors may not. Search fee: $5.00 per name. $25.00 per hour if extensive research is needed. Required to search: name, years to search. Civil cases indexed by defendant. Civil records on computer back to 3/1996; on index cards from 1982, index books back to 1889. Mail turnaround time 2-5 days. Pay service to civil case look-up at www.courts.state.co.us; click on Court Records Search.

Criminal Records: Access: Mail, in person, online. Only the court performs in person searches; visitors may not. Search fee: $5.00 per name. May be no charge if it is an in person search and for only a couple years. Required to search: name. Criminal records computerized from 3/1996; on index cards from 1982, index books back to 1889. Mail turnaround time 2-5 days. Criminal case index at www.courts.state.co.us. Current dockets free, records not- click on Court Records Search.

General Information: No adoption, sealed, juvenile, mental health or expunged cases released. Will fax documents $1.00 per page. Fee applies incoming fax as well. Court makes copy: $.75 per page. Certification fee: $20.00 per cert. Payee: Yuma County Combined Court. Personal checks accepted; credit cards are not. Prepayment required. Mail requests: SASE required.

Colorado Recording Offices

ORGANIZATION: 63 counties, 63 recording offices. The recording officer is the County Clerk and Recorder. Colorado is in the Mountain Time Zone.

November 15, 2001, Broomfield City and County came into existence, derived from portions of Adams, Boulder, Jefferson, and Weld counties. To determine if an address is in Broomfield County, you may parcel search by address at the Broomfield County Assessor search site at www.co.broomfield.co.us/centralrecords/assessor.shtml or www.broomfield.org/maps/IMS.shtml

REAL ESTATE RECORDS: Counties do not perform real estate searches. Copy fee is usually $1.25 per page and certification fee is usually $1.00 per document. Tax records are located in Assessor's Office.

UCC RECORDS: Financing statements are filed at the state level - Secretary of State - except for real estate related collateral which are filed with the County Clerk & Recorder. However, prior to July, 2001, Colorado was a dual filing state. Consumer goods and farm collateral were could be filed at the state or the County Clerk & Recorder and some older records can be searched here. At the few counties where UCC searches are still performed, a UCC search is usually $5.00 per debtor name and $2.00 for each additional year searched.

TAX LIEN RECORDS: Federal and some state tax liens on personal property are filed with the Secretary of State. However, some federal and state tax liens are filed with the County Clerk and Recorder..

OTHER LIENS: Judgments, motor vehicle, mechanics.

ONLINE ACCESS: At least 18 Colorado counties offer free access to property assessor basic tax roll records and sometimes sales via www.qpublic.net/. A 3-level subscription service plan is also offered.

At the state level, the Secretary of State offers web access to UCCs, and the Department of Revenue offers trade name searches. Search Colorado statewide UCCs and Liens free at http://www.sos.state.co.us/pubs/business/search_records.htm after registration. Also, the state archives provides limited "inheritance tax" records for 15 Colorado counties at www.colorado.gov/dpa/doit/archives/inh_tax/index.html. Generally, these records extend forward only to the 1940s.

Adams County

County Clerk & Recorder, 450 S 4th Ave; Admin Bldg, Brighton, CO 80601-3197. Recording, R/E & UCC phone-303-654-6020; fax-303-654-6009; 8AM-4:30PM (MST) www.co.adams.co.us

County public trustee address is 1000 Judicial Ctr Dr, #200, Brighton, CO 80601. Index: All in one. Records indexed on a public use terminal back to 1960. Office personnel or visitors may perform searches. Search fee $5.00 per name. Copy fee $1.25 per page. Cert fee- $1.00 per doc plus copy fee. Payee- Adams County Clerk and Recorder. **Online access to Real Estate, Deed, Lien, Marriage, Death, Judgment, Mortgage, UCC records:** Search recorded documents free at www.co.adams.co.us/oncoreweb/. **Other phones:** Treasurer- 303-654-6160; Elections- 303-920-7850; Vital Records- 303-654-6020. **Property tax/Assessing**- Same address as recording office. 303-654-6038, assessor fax- 303-654-6037. **Online access**- Records from the Adams County Assessor database are free at http://co.adams.co.us/gis/quicksearch/.

Alamosa County

County Clerk & Recorder, PO Box 630, Alamosa, CO 81101. 719-589-6681; fax-719-589-6118; (MST) www.alamosacounty.org

Index: All in one. Records indexed on a public use terminal back to 1984. Only the public may search. Copy fee $.25 per page. Cert fee- $1.00 per doc plus copy fee. Payee- Alamosa County Clerk and Recorder. A CD of plats is available for purchase for $650.00; contact recording office. **Online access to Real Estate, Grantor/Grantee, Deed, Lien, Judgment, Marriage records:** Access to recording data back to 1985 is by subscription to Image Silo; fee is $200.00 per month; for info and sign up, contact the Recording office. **Other phones:** Treasurer- 719-589-3626; Elections- 719-589-6681; Vital Records- 719-589-6681. **Property tax/Assessing**- PO Box 638, Alamosa, CO 81101; 719-589-6365, assessor fax-719-589-6118. 8-4:30PM www.alamosacounty.org **Online access**- Access property data free at www.qpublic.net/co/alamosa/search.html. Subscription required for full data. Also, search via www.alamosacounty.org/depts/Assessor/records.html

Arapahoe County

County Clerk & Recorder, 5334 S Prince St; Admin Bldg, Littleton, CO 80166. 303-795-4200, R/E recording phone-303-795-4520; fax-303-794-4625; 7AM-4:30PM www.co.arapahoe.co.us/Departments/CR/index.asp

Index: All in one. Records indexed on a public use terminal back to 1979. Office personnel or visitors may perform searches. Office will not search real estate records. Office will not search UCC records. Copy fee $1.25 per page. Cert fee- $1.00 per doc plus copy fee. Payee- Arapahoe County Clerk and Recorder. **Online access to Real Estate, Deed, Judgment, Lien records:** Access to the recorders database is free at www.co.arapahoe.co.us/Apps/LegalDocuments/default.aspx. **Other phones:** Treasurer- 303-795-4550; Elections- 303-795-4511; Vital Records- 303-756-4464. **Property tax/Assessing**- 5334 S Prince St, Adminstration Bldg, Littleton, CO 80166; 303-738-4600, assessor fax-303-797-1295. (Appraiser/Auditor- 303-795-4611) **Online access**- Centrally assessed tax data is available at www.co.arapahoe.co.us/Apps/Tax/Default.aspx but no name searching. Search business personal property free at www.co.arapahoe.co.us/apps/PersProp/PersPropForm.asp. Search other tax/parcel data by category free at www.co.arapahoe.co.us/ and click on Online Tools. Search county foreclosures free at www.co.arapahoe.co.us/Apps/ForeClosure/index.aspx.

Archuleta County

County Clerk & Recorder, PO Box 2589, Pagosa Springs, CO 81147-2589. 970-264-8310, R/E recording phone-970-264-8350; fax-970-264-8319; 8AM-4PM (MST) http://archuletacounty.org

Index: All in one. Records indexed on computer 1985 to current; prior is a book search. Office will perform a UCC search (5 years to current) but public must search other records themselves. Copy fee $.25 per page. Marriage license copy- $1.25. Cert fee- $1.00 per cert plus copy fee. Payee- Archuleta County Clerk and Recorder. Office does not sell bulk data. **Online access to Real Estate, Deed, Lien records:** Access to record data is by internet subscription, fee is $250 monthly. Call Recording office for further info and sign-up. **Other phones:** Treasurer- 970-264-8325; Elections- 970-264-8350; Vital Records- 970-264-2673. **Property tax/Assessing**- PO Box 1089, 449 San Juan St, Pagosa Springs, CO 81147; 970-264-8310, assessor fax- 970-264-8319. **Online access**- Search assessment property records at www.qpublic.net/co/archuleta/index.html for a fee for full data; a basic search is free. Also search index data free at http://64.234.218.210/cgi-bin/colorado_links.cgi?county=archuleta.

Baca County

County Clerk & Recorder, 741 Main St; Courthouse, Springfield, CO 81073. Recording, R/E & UCC phone-719-523-4372; fax-719-523-4881; 8:30AM-4:30PM (MST) www.bacacounty.net

Index: All in one. Records indexed on a public use terminal back to 1997. Only the public may search. Copy fee $.25 per page. Cert fee- $1.00 per cert plus copy fee. Payee- Baca County Clerk and Recorder. **Online access to Real Estate, Deed, Lien, Vital Statistic, UCC, Judgment records:** Search recorded documents at www.thecountyrecorder.com/(vv5dpfytud3jdv55a5o3et45)/default.aspx. Online records go back to 1997. No name searching. **Other phones:** Treasurer- 719-523-4262; Elections- 719-523-4372; Vital Records-719-523-6665. **Property tax/Assessing**- Baca County

Assessing Office, 741 Main St, Courthouse, Springfield, CO 81073; 719-523-4332, assessor fax-719-523-4735. (Appraiser/Auditor- 719-523-4332) Computer terminal available for public use.

Bent County

County Clerk & Recorder, PO Box 350, Las Animas, CO 81054. 719-456-2009; fax-719-456-0375; (MST)
Index: All in one. Records indexed on a public use terminal back to 1995. Only the public may search. Copy fee $1.25 per page. Marriage license copy-$2.00. Cert fee- $1.00 per doc plus copy fee. Payee-Bent County Clerk and Recorder. **Online access to Real Estate, Deed, Lien, Judgment, Vital Statistic records:** Access to recorded data is available by subscription. Fee is $200 per month. To print documents, an add'l fee of $.25 per page applies. To sign-up, contact Patti Nickell; a sign up form will be faxed to you.tn046 . **Other phones:** Treasurer- 719-456-2211; Elections- 719-456-2009; Vital Records-719-456-6042. **Property tax/Assessing**- 725 Bent Ave, Las Animas, CO 81054; 719-456-2010, assessor fax- 719-456-3108. hours- 8:30AM-4:30PM Public access computer in office for index and records searching. **Online access**- Access assessor property records free at www.qpublic.net/co/lasanimas/search.html. Search by parcel number, location, or owner name.

Boulder County

County Clerk & Recorder, 1750 33rd St, #201, Boulder, CO 80301-2549. 303-441-3530, R/E recording phone-303-413-7770; fax-303-441-4996; 8AM-4:30PM (MST) www.bouldercounty.org/clerk/
Index: Military records are the only confidential index. Records indexed on a public use terminal back to 1862. Office will perform a UCC search but public must search other records themselves. Search fee $5.00 for 5-year search. Copy fee $.25 per page. Cert fee- $1.00 per doc plus copy fee. Payee- Boulder County Clerk and Recorder. **Online access to Real Estate, Grantor/Grantee, Deed, Judgment, Lien records:** Recorder data is on the iCris system at http://icris.co.boulder.co.us/splash.jsp. To search free, login as public, password public. Also, search voter registration at https://www.bouldercounty.org/clerk/elections/voterreg/promptforname.aspx. Name and DOB required. **Other phones:** Treasurer- 303-441-3520; Elections- 303-413-7740. **Property tax/Assessing**- PO Box 471, Boulder, CO 80306-0471; 303-441-3530, asscssor fax- 303-441-4996. hours- 8AM-5PM www.bouldercounty.org/assessor/ **Online access**- Search the assessor's property database for free at www.bouldercounty.org/assessor/disclaimer.htm. No name searching. Also, search property tax records at www.bouldercounty.org/treas/disclaim.htm. No name searching. Also, the county treasurer offers data electronically and on microfiche. Alpha index by owner name is $25.00 per set.

Broomfield County

County/City Clerk & Recorder, One DesCombes Dr, Broomfield, CO 80020. 303-469-3301; fax-303-438-6252; 8AM-5PM (MST) www.broomfield.org/centralrecords/clerk_and_recorder.shtml
Became a county in 2001; further info at website. Includes Zip Codes 80020, 80021, 80038. Index: All in one. Records indexed on a public use terminal back to 2001. Only the public may search. Copy fee $.25 (Broomfield records) per page, $1.25 (other county records) per page. Cert fee- $1.00 per doc plus copy fee. Payee- City and County of Broomfield. **Online access to Voter Registration records:** Verify voter registration records at www.broomfield.org/elections/voter_inquiry/. House number and registrant name both required. **Other phones:** Central Records, all departments- 303-464-5819. **Property tax/Assessing**- PO Box 1149, One Des Combes Dr, Broomfield, CO 80038; 303-464-5819, assessor fax-303-438-6252. Public access computer in office for index and records searching. www.broomfield.org/centralrecords/asrfaq.shtml **Online access**- Access to the property database portal is free at www.ci.broomfield.co.us/maps/IMS.shtml. Search by address or parcel ID only. Also, search property and tax assessment data free at https://info.ci.broomfield.co.us/Tax/Default.asp but no name searching. Also, you may download the GIS/Assessor 'Broomfield Parcels' database free at www.broomfield.org/maps/Data.shtml. Also, search tax sales list free at www.ci.broomfield.co.us/centralrecords/TaxSale.shtml.

Chaffee County

County Clerk & Recorder, PO Box 699, Salida, CO 81201. 719-539-6913, R/E recording phone-719-539-4004; fax-719-539-8588; 8AM-4PM Recording; 8AM-5PM Researching. www.chaffeecounty.org/
Index: All in one. Records indexed on a public use terminal. Only the public may search. Copy fee $1.25 per page. Cert fee- $1.00 per doc plus copy fee. Payee- Chaffee County Clerk and Recorder. **Other phones:** Treasurer- 719-539-6808; Elections- 719-539-6913. **Property tax/Assessing**- 104 Crestone Ave, Salida, CO 81201; 719-539-4016, assessor fax-719-539-8513. hours- 9AM-5PM www.chaffeecounty.org/Pa ge.aspx?PageID=255 **Online access**- Search assessor database free at http://annex.chaffeecounty.org/assessorsearch/searchhome.aspx.

Cheyenne County

County Clerk & Recorder, PO Box 567, Cheyenne Wells, CO 80810. Recording, R/E & UCC phone-719-767-5685; fax-719-767-5540; 8AM-4PM (MST) www.co.cheyenne.co.us/countydepartments/clerkandrecorder.htm
Index: All in one. Records indexed on a public use terminal back to 7/3/95. Only the public may search. Copy fee $1.25 per page. Cert fee- $1.00 per doc plus copy fee. Payee- Cheyenne County Clerk and Recorder. To inquire about bulk data sale please contact couty clerk's office. **Online access to Real Estate, Grantor/Grantee, Deed, Lien, Mortgage, Judgment, Marriage records:** Access recorded documents online free at www.thecountyrecorder.com/(g5ze11rp4f5xuc2y2xsl4245)/Default.aspx and choose Cheyenne, CO from the drop-down list. **Other phones:** Treasurer- 719-767-5657; Elections-719-767-5685; Vital Records- 719-767-5661. **Property tax/Assessing**- PO Box 36, 51 S 1st St, Cheyenne Wells, CO 80810; 719-767-5664, assessor fax- 719-767-5540. Public access computer in office for index and records searches. **Online access**- Search the county property sales lists free at www.co.cheyenne.co.us/countydepartments/assessor.htm. Lookups at bottom of webpage.

Clear Creek County

County Clerk & Recorder, PO Box 2000, Georgetown, CO 80444-2000. Recording, R/E & UCC phone-303-679-2339; fax-303-679-2416; 7AM-4:30PM www.co.clear-creek.co.us/depts/clerk.htm
Index: All in one. Records indexed on a public use terminal back to 1983. Only the public may search. Copy fee $.25 per page. Plats $5.00. Cert fee- $1.00 per doc plus copy fee. Payee- Clear Creek County Clerk and Recorder. Bulk data available for purchase, images and voter lists. **Other phones:** Treasurer- 303-679-2353; Elections- 303-679-2339; Vital Records-303-679-2357. **Property tax/Assessing**- Clear Creek County Assessing Office, 405 Argentine St, PO Box 2000, Georgetown, CO 80444-2000; 303-679-2322, assessor fax- 303-679-2441. (Appraiser/Auditor- 303-679-2322) hours- 8:30AM-4:30PM Public access computer in office for index and records searches. http://co.clear-creek.co.us **Online access**- Limited assessor information free at www.co.clear-creek.co.us/Depts/assess.htm.

Conejos County

County Clerk & Recorder, PO Box 127, Conejos, CO 81129-0127. Recording, R/E & UCC phone-719-376-5422; fax-719-376-5997; 8AM-4:30PM (MST)
Index: All in one. Records indexed on a public use terminal back to 1994. Office personnel or visitors may perform searches. Search fee $5.00 for 1st year, $1.00 each add'l year. Office will search real estate records. Will search UCC records. Copy fee $.25 per page. Cert fee- $1.00 per doc plus copy fee. Payee-Conejos County Clerk and Recorder. Bulk data available for purchase, contact Lawrence D Gallegos, Clerk & Recorder. **Online access to Real Estate, Grantor/Grantee, Deed, Lien, Judgment, UCC records:** Access to recorder office index back to 1978 is by subscription, $100 per month. Call recorder for signup and info. Fee is $150.00 per month. **Other phones:** Treasurer- 719-376-5919; Elections- 719-376-5422; Vital Records- 719-589-6681 (birth & death). **Property tax/Assessing**- PO Box 67, Conejos, CO 81129; 719-376-5585, assessor fax-719-376-2442. **Online access**- Access data from the final tax roll free at http://qpublic.net/co/conejos/. There are also 3 levels of subscription service based on your needs.

Costilla County

County Clerk & Recorder, PO Box 308, San Luis, CO 81152. Recording, R/E & UCC phone-719-672-3301; fax-719-672-3781; 8AM-12:30, 1-4:30PM (MST) www.costilla-county.com
Index: Separate indices to search include books, microfiche. Records indexed on a public use terminal back to 1997. Only the public may search. Copy fee $1.25 per page. Cert fee- $1.00 per page plus copy fee. Payee- Costilla County Clerk and Recorder. Bulk data available for purchase on CD, $1.00 per image. Contact: Charlene. **Other phones:** Treasurer- 719-672-3342; Elections- 719-672-3301; Vital Records-719-672-3301. **Property tax/Assessing**- PO Box 344, San Luis, CO 81152; 719-672-3642, assessor fax-719-672-3206. **Online access**- Access assessor property data free at http://64.234.218.210/cgi-bin/colorado_links.cgi?county=costilla. Also, access data from the final tax roll free at http://qpublic.net/co/costilla/. There are also 3 levels of subscription service based on your need.

Crowley County

County Clerk & Recorder, 631 Main, #104, Ordway, CO 81063-1092. 719-267-5229, R/E recording phone-719-267-5225; fax-719-267-4608; 8AM-4PM
Index: All in one. Records indexed on a public use terminal back to 1954. Only the public may search. Will not search UCC records. Copy fee $.25 per page. Plats- $5.00 each. Cert fee- $1.00 per doc plus copy fee. Payee- Crowley County Clerk and Recorder. **Other phones:** Treasurer- 719-267-5232; Elections-719-267-5225. **Property tax/Assessing**- 631 Main, Ordway, CO 81063; 719-267-5229, assessor fax-719-267-4608. **Online access**- Access data from the final tax roll free at http://qpublic.net/co/crowley/. There are also 3 levels of subscription service based on your needs. Also, access property assessment data by sub at http://64.234.218.210/cgi-bin/colorado.pl.

Custer County

County Clerk & Recorder, PO Box 150, Westcliffe, CO 81252. Recording, R/E & UCC phone-719-783-2441; fax-719-783-2885; 8AM-4PM (MST)
Index: All in one. Records indexed on a public use terminal back to 1986. Only the public may search. Copy fee $1.25 per page. $1.50 per page faxed back. Cert fee- $1.00 per doc plus copy fee. Payee- Custer County Clerk and Recorder. **Other phones:** Treasurer- 719-783-2341; Elections- 719-783-2441; Vital Records- 719-783-2441. **Property tax/Assessing**- PO Box 518, Westcliffe, CO 81252; 719-783-2218, assessor fax- 719-783-2885. (Appraiser/Auditor- 719-783-2218) **Online access**- Access assessor final tax roll data free at www.qpublic.net/co/custer/search.html. Full property data is available by subscription as well.

Delta County

County Clerk & Recorder, 501 Palmer St, #211, Delta, CO 81416. 970-874-2150; fax-970-874-2161; 8AM-4:30PM (MST) www.deltacounty.com

Index: All in one. Records indexed on a public use terminal back to 1988. Only the public may search. Copy fee $.25 per page. Cert fee- $1.00 per doc plus copy fee. Payee- Delta County Clerk and Recorder. **Online access to Real Estate, Deed, Lien, Judgment, Death, Marriage, DOT Release records:** Access recorder records free at http://clerk.deltacounty.com/Search.aspx. **Other phones:** Treasurer- 970-874-2135; Elections- 970-874-2150; Vital Records- 970-874-2152. **Property tax/Assessing**- 501 Palmer St, #210, Delta, CO 81416; 970-874-2120, assessor fax- 970-874-2482. (Appraiser/Auditor- 970-874-2120) hours- 8AM-5PM **Online access**- Access Assessor data on the GIS site for free at http://itax.deltacounty.com/assessor/web/ .

Denver County

County Clerk & Recorder, 201 W Colfax Ave, Dept 101, Denver, CO 80202. 720-913-4162, R/E recording phone-720-865-8400; 9AM-4PM (MST) www.denvergov.org

Index: All in one. Records indexed on computer back to 1980. Only office personnel may search. Office will not name search real estate records. Tax liens not included in UCC search. UCC search per debtor name-$5.00 per name, 1st year, $2.00 add'l 1 year. Separate tax lien searches performed at same cost as UCC search. Copy fee $1.00 per page.Real estate or tax lien copy- $1.25 per page. Cert fee- $1.00 per doc plus copy fee. Payee- Denver County Clerk and Recorder. **Other phones:** Treasurer- 720-865-7070; Elections- 720-913-8683; Vital Records- 303-436-7350. **Property tax/Assessing**- 201 W Colfax Ave, Dept. 406, Denver, CO 80202; 720-913-4162, assessor fax- 720-913-4103. (Appraiser/Auditor- 720-913-4032) **Online access**- Records on the Denver City and Denver County Assessor database are free at www.denvergov.org/realproperty.asp. With address, search business personal property at www.denvergov.org/apps/perspropertyapplication/persproperty.asp. Also, search real estate property tax data for free at www.denvergov.org/treasurypt/PropertyTax.asp. Address or parcel number required to search. Search foreclosures at www.denvergov.org/TabId/37910/TopicId/1313/default.aspx.

Dolores County

County Clerk & Recorder, PO Box 58, Dove Creek, CO 81324-0058. Recording, R/E & UCC phone-970-677-2381; fax-970-677-4144; 8:30AM-4:30PM

Index: All in one. Records indexed on a public use terminal back to 11/15/1996. Office personnel or visitors may perform searches. Search fee $15.00 for 1st year; $5.00 each add'l year. Office will search real estate records. Will search UCC records. Copy fee $.25 per page. Cert fee- $1.00 per doc plus copy fee. Payee- Dolores County Clerk and Recorder. Office does not sell bulk data. **Other phones:** Treasurer- 970-677-2386; Elections- 970-677-2381; Vital Records- 970-677-2381. **Property tax/Assessing**- PO Box 478, Dove Creek, CO 81324; 970-677-2385, assessor fax- 970-677-3068. (Appraiser/Auditor- 970-677-2385) **Online access**- Assessor information and free search at www.qpublic.net/co/dolores/index.html. Subscription and log-on required for legal information, go to http://64.234.218.210/cgi-bin/colorado.pl for new subscriber sign-up.

Douglas County

County Clerk & Recorder, PO Box 1360, Castle Rock, CO 80104. Recording, R/E & UCC phone-303-660-7446; fax-303-814-2776; 8:AM-5PM (MST) www.douglas.co.us

Index: All in one. Records indexed on a public use terminal back to 1983. Office will perform a UCC search but public must search other records themselves. Search fee $5.00. Standard copy fee $.25 per page. per page; plats- $.65 1st page; $.40 each add'l. Cert fee- $1.00 per doc plus copy fee. Payee- Douglas County Clerk and Recorder. Bulk data (images back to 1994, indexes to 1983) available for purchase at www.douglas.co.us/clerk/recording/busingess_services. **Online access to Real Estate, Grantor/Grantee, Deed, Judgment, Lien, Mortgage, UCC, Vital Statistic records:** Access to recorders data is free at http://apps.douglas.co.us/apps/pubdocaccess/simpleSearch.do. **Other phones:** Treasurer- 303-660-7455; Elections- 303-660-7444. **Property tax/Assessing**- 301 Wilcox, #201, Castle Rock, CO 80104; 303-660-7450, assessor fax- 303-660-1429. (Appraiser/Auditor- 303-660-7450) **Online access**- Records on the county assessor database are free at www.douglas.co.us/assessor/. Also, download related list data from the site. Locate parcels free at http://publicstaging.douglas.co.us/website/default.htm .

Eagle County

County Clerk & Recorder, PO Box 537, Eagle, CO 81631. Recording, R/E & UCC phone-970-328-8723; fax-970-328-8716; 7:30-5PM www.eaglecounty.us

Index: All in one. Records indexed on a public use terminal back to 1/1984. Only the public may search. Office will search real estate records. Copy fee $.25 per page. Cert fee- $1.00 per doc plus copy fee. Payee- Eagle County Clerk and Recorder. Bulk data available to purchase, contact Karen Valas. **Online access to Real Estate, Grantor/Grantee, Deed, Judgment, Lien, Vital Statistic, UCC records:** Search clerk and recorder data at www.eaglecounty.us/cloe/search.cfm. Search index free, fee for images. **Other phones:** Treasurer- 970-328-8860; Elections- 970-328-8715. **Property tax/Assessing**- PO Box 449, Eagle, CO 81631; 970-328-8640, assessor fax- 970-328-8679. hours- 8AM-5PM **Online access**- Access the County Assessor and treasurer databases free at www.eaglecounty.us/patie/index_content.cfm. Comps sales at www.eaglecounty.us/Assessor/saleslist.cfm.

El Paso County

County Clerk & Recorder, PO Box 2007, Colorado Springs, CO 80901-2007. Recording, R/E & UCC phone-719-520-6200; fax-719-520-6230; 8AM-5PM (MST) http://car.elpasoco.com

Index: Separate indices to search include marriages, main index. Records indexed on a public use terminal back to 1986. Office will perform a UCC search but public must search other records themselves. Copy fee $.25 per page. Plat maps are $3.00 per page. Cert fee- $1.00 per doc plus copy fee. Payee- El Paso County Clerk and Recorder. Recorded images and index available for bulk purchase; contact Sandy Hook, 719-520-6208. **Online access to Real Estate, Grantor-Grantee, Deed, Lien Judgment records:** Search the grantor/grantee index at http://car2.elpasoco.com/rcdquery.asp. Search marriages back to 5/1/1991 on a separate lookup page. Also, search marriages 1/1985 to 5/1991 free on the OPR - Official Public Records - search page. **Other phones:** Treasurer- 719-520-6666; Elections- 719-520-8683; Vital Records- 719-520-7475. **Property tax/Assessing**- 27 E Vermijo Ave, Colorado Springs, CO 80903; 719-520-6600, assessor fax- 719-520-6635. hours- 8:30AM-4:30PM **Online access**- Records on the county Assessor database are free at http://land.elpasoco.com.

Elbert County

County Clerk & Recorder, PO Box 37, Kiowa, CO 80117. 303-621-3129, 303-621-3116, R/E recording phone-303-621-3128; fax-303-621-3168; 8AM-4:30PM (MST) www.elbertcounty-co.gov

Index: All in one. Records indexed on computer back to 1985. Only the public may search. Will not search UCC records. Copy fee $.25 per page.Real estate or tax lien copy- $1.25 per page. Cert fee- $1.00 per doc plus copy fee. Payee- Elbert County Clerk and Recorder. Bulk data available for purchase, contact Clerk/Recording at 303-621-3128. **Other phones:** Treasurer- 303-621-3117; Elections- 303-621-3127. **Property tax/Assessing**- PO Box 26, Kiowa, CO 80117; 303-621-3101, assessor fax- 303-621-3173. www.elbertcounty-co.gov **Online access**- Search Assessor data free at http://elbertco.tyler-esubmittal.com/assessor/web/ but no name searching; free registration required. Parcel and GIS-Map search free at http://projects.thetsrgroup.com/elbert/members/index.asp but no name searching.

Fremont County

County Clerk & Recorder, 615 Macon Ave, Rm 102, Canon City, CO 81212-3311. 719-276-7336; fax-719-276-7338; hours- 8:30AM-4:30PM (MST) www.fremontco.com/clerkandrecorder/index.shtml

Index: All in one. Records indexed back to 1/1987. Only the public may search. Will not search UCC records. Copy fee $1.25 per page.$10.00 for one or two pages. $15.00 for three or more pages. Cert fee- $1.00 per doc plus copy fee. Certified copies requested for military benefits are free of charge. Payee- Fremont County Clerk and Recorder. **Online access to Real Estate, Deed, Lien, Will, Mortgage, Death, Divorce, Marriage records:** Search recorded documents free at www.fremontco.com/clerkandrecorder/aptitude/oncoreweb/Search.aspx. **Other phones** Treasurer- 719-276-7380; Elections- 719-276-7332; Vital Records- 719-276-1556. **Property tax/Assessing**- Fremont County Assessing Office, 615 Macon Ave, Rm 102, Canon City, CO 81212-3311; 719-276-7310, assessor fax- 719-276-7311. **Online access**- Access the assessors property and sales database free at http://qpublic.net/fremont/. There are also 3 levels of subscription service for your needs.

Garfield County

County Clerk & Recorder, 109 8th St, #200, Glenwood Springs, CO 81601. 970-945-2377 x1840, R/E recording phone-970-945-2377 x1845; fax-970-947-1078; 8:30AM-5PM www.garfield-county.com

Index: All in one. Records indexed on a public use terminal back to 1982. Only the public may search. Copy fee $.25 per page for up to 8 1/2 x 14; $5.00 up to 11 x 17; $6.00 for larger. Cert fee- $1.00 per doc plus copy fee. Payee- Garfield County Clerk and Recorder. Office does not sell bulk data. **Online access to Real Estate, Deed, Lien, Judgment, Mortgage, GIS-mapping records:** Access recording data free at www.garcoact.com/clerk/search.asp?. Also, access to maps for free go to www.garfield-county.com/Index.aspx?page=651 . **Other phones:** Treasurer- 970-945-6382; Elections- 970-945-2377 x1770; Vital Records- 970-945-2377 x1950; Other Real Estate- 970-384-3700 x3. **Property tax/Assessing**- 109 8th St #200, Glenwood Springs, CO 81601; 970-945-9134, assessor fax- 970-945-3953. **Online access**- Search the assessor and treasurer property and tax data free at www.garcoact.com/assessor/search.asp. Also, you may search assessor sales data by subscription at www.garcoact.com/assessor/Login.asp. Fee is $300 per year or $35 per month. Also, access PDF parcel maps and property information free at www.garfield-county.com/Index.aspx?page=990.

Gilpin County

County Clerk & Recorder, PO Box 429, Central City, CO 80427. 303-582-5321; fax-303-565-1797; 7:30AM-5:30PM (MST) www.co.gilpin.co.us

Index: All in one. Records indexed on a public use terminal back to 1988. Only the public may search. Will not search UCC records. Copy fee $.25 per page. Cert fee- $1.00 per doc plus copy fee. Payee- Gilpin County Clerk and Recorder. Bulk data available for purchase, contact Jessica D Lotingier. **Online access to Marriage records:** Access to county marriage records from 1864 to 1944 is free at www.colorado.gov/dpa/doit/archives/marriage/gilpin_index.htm. **Other phones:** Treasurer- 303-582-5222; Elections- 303-582-5321. **Property tax/Assessing**- PO Box 338, 203 Eureka St, Central City, CO 80427; 303-582-5451, assessor fax- 303-582-3086. (Appraiser/Aud.- 303-582-5451) 8:30AM-12:30PM, 1-5PM www.co.gilpin.co.us/Assessor/default.htm

Online access- Assessor data and research of property at http://64.78.150.78/gilpincounty/web/login.jsp.

Grand County

County Clerk & Recorder, PO Box 120, Hot Sulphur Springs, CO 80451. 970-725-3347 x273, R/E recording phone-970-725-3347 x115; fax-970-725-0100; 8:30AM-5PM (MST) http://co.grand.co.us/Clerk/clerkand.htm

Index: All in one. Records indexed on a public use terminal back to 1997. Only the public may search. Copy fee $1.25 per page. Cert fee- $1.00 per doc plus copy fee. Payee- Grand County Clerk and Recorder. **Online access to Real Estate, Grantor/Grantee, Deed, Lien, Birth, Death, Marriage records:** Access to Clerk-Recorder index is free at http://co.grand.co.us/aptitude/oncoreweb/. **Other phones:** Treasurer- 970-725-3347 x131; Elections- 970-725-3347 x114; Vital Records- 970-725-3347 x113. **Property tax/Assessing-** PO Box 302, Hot Sulphur Springs, CO 80451; 970-725-3347 x119, assessor fax- 970-725-3505. **Online access**- Access assessor data free at http://www2.co.grand.co.us/assessor_lookup/. Access the assessor database free at http://co.grand.co.us/Assessor/Download_Page.html.

Gunnison County

County Clerk & Recorder, 221 N Wisconsin, #C; Courthouse, Gunnison, CO 81230. 970-641-1516, R/E recording phone-970-641-2038; fax-970-641-7956; 8AM-5PM (MST) www.co.gunnison.co.us

Index: All in one. Records indexed on a public use terminal back to 1992. Only the public may search. Copy fee $.25 per page. Cert fee- $1.00 per doc plus copy fee. Payee- Gunnison County Clerk and Recorder. Office will sell data in bulk; contact Susan McIntosh 970-641-7938. **Other phones:** Treasurer- 970-641-2231; Elections- 970-641-7927; Vital Records- 970-641-0209. **Property tax/Assessing-** 221 N Wisconsin, #C, Courthouse, Gunnison, CO 81230; 970-641-1085, assessor fax- 970-641-7920.

Hinsdale County

County Clerk & Recorder, PO Box 9, Lake City, CO 81235. 970-944-2228; fax-970-944-2202; 8AM-5:30PM (MST)

Index: All in one. Records indexed on a public use terminal back to 1997. Only the public may search. General copy fee $.25 per page. Cert fee- $1.00 per doc includes copy fee. Payee- Hinsdale County Clerk and Recorder. **Other phones:** Treasurer- 970-944-2223; Elections- 970-944-2228. **Property tax/Assessing-** PO Box 28, Lake City, CO 81235; 970-944-2224, assessor fax- 970-944-2202.

Huerfano County

County Clerk & Recorder, 401 Main St, #204; Courthouse, Walsenburg, CO 81089. 719-738-2380; fax-719-738-2364; 8AM-4PM (MST)

Treasurer performs tax lien searches. Index: Separate indices to search include microfiche is before 1995. Records indexed on a public use terminal back to 1995. Only the public may search. Copy fee $.25 per page. Cert fee- $1.00 per doc plus copy fee. Payee- Huerfano County Clerk and Recorder. Abstract office will sell bulk data, please call 719-738-1730 for info. **Other phones:** Treasurer- 719-738-1280. **Property tax/Assessing-** 401 Main St, #205, Courthouse, Walsenburg, CO 81089; 719-782-1191 (call ahead to fax), assessor fax- 719-782-1191.

Jackson County

County Clerk & Recorder, PO Box 337, Walden, CO 80480-0337. 970-723-4334; fax-970-723-3214; 8AM-5PM, closed N-1PM (MST)

Index: All in one. Records indexed on a public use terminal back to 1996. Only the public may search. Copy fee $.25 per page. Cert fee- $1.00 per doc plus copy fee. Payee- Jackson County Clerk and Recorder. Office does not sell bulk data. **Other phones:** Treasurer- 970-723-4220; Elections- 970-723-4334; Vital Records- 970-723-4334. **Property tax/Assessing-** PO Box 813, Walden, CO 80480; 970-723-4751.

Jefferson County

County Clerk & Recorder, 100 Jefferson County Pky, #2530, Golden, CO 80419-2530. 303-271-8121; fax-303-271-8180; 7:30AM-5:30PM-Office; 8:30 AM-4:30 PM (phone hrs). (MST) https://cr-web.co.jefferson.co.us/

Index: All in one. Records indexed on a public use terminal back to 1963. Office will perform a UCC search but public must search other records themselves. UCC search per debtor name- $5.00 per 1st year. Copy fee $.25 per page, $5.00 for large format copies. Cert fee- $1.00 per doc plus copy fee. Payee- Jefferson County Clerk and Recorder. **Online access to Real Estate, Grantor/Grantee, Deed, Judgment records:** Search the recorder's Grantor/Grantee index for free at https://cr-web.co.jefferson.co.us. Index goes back to 1963; images to 1994. **Other phones:** Treasurer- 303-271-8330; Elections- 303-271-8111; Vital Records- 303-271-6450. **Property tax/Assessing-** 100 Jefferson City Pky, #2500, Golden, CO 80419; 303-271-8666, assessor fax- 303-271-8674. **Online access**- Records on the Assessor database are free at www.co.jefferson.co.us/ats/splash.do. No name searching.

Kiowa County

County Clerk & Recorder, PO Box 37, Eads, CO 81036-0037. Recording, R/E & UCC phone-719-438-5421; fax-719-438-5327; 7:30AM-5PM (MST)

Index: All in one. Records indexed on a public use terminal. Only the public may search. Copy fee $1.25 per page. Cert fee- $1.00 per doc plus copy fee. Payee- Kiowa County Clerk and Recorder. **Online access to Real Estate, Deed, Lien, Judgment, Marriage records:** Access to recording index is free from a 3rd party company at www.thecountyrecorder.com/(g5ze11rp4f5xuc2y2xsl4245)/Default.aspx. Select Kiowa from the county list. Index goes back only to 2006. **Other phones:** Treasurer- 719-438-5831; Elections- 719-438-5421; Vital Records- 719-438-5590. **Property tax/Assessing-** PO Box 295, 1305 Goff St, Eads, CO 81036; 719-438-5521, assessor fax- 719-438-5614. hours- 8AM-4:30PM

Kit Carson County

County Clerk & Recorder, PO Box 249, Burlington, CO 80807-0249. 719-346-8638; fax-719-346-7242; 8AM-4PM (MST) www.kitcarsoncounty.org

Index: All in one. Records indexed on a public use terminal back to 1994. Only the public may search. Copy fee $.25 per page. Cert fee- $1.00 per doc plus copy fee. Payee- Kit Carson County Clerk & Recorder. **Other phones:** Treasurer- 719-346-8434; Elections- 719-346-8638; Vital Records- 719-346-8133. **Property tax/Assessing-** 251 16th St, Burlington, CO 80807; 719-346-8946, assessor fax-719-346-6017. **Online access**- Access data from the final tax roll free at http://qpublic.net/co/kitcarson/. There are also 3 levels of subscription service.

La Plata County

County Clerk & Recorder, 1060 E 2nd Ave, Rm 134; Courthouse, Durango, CO 81301. 970-382-6294, R/E recording phone-970-382-6280/6281; fax-970-382-6285; 8AM-5PM (MST) http://co.laplata.co.us

Index: All in one. Records indexed on a public use terminal back to 1800's. Only the public may search. Will not search UCC records. Copy fee $.25 per page. Cert fee- $1.00 per doc plus copy fee. Payee- La Plata County Clerk and Recorder. Bulk data available for purchase, contact Linda Daley for info. **Other phones:** Treasurer- 970-382-6245; Elections- 970-247-5702. **Property tax/Assessing-** PO Box 3339, Durango, CO 81301; 970-382-6221, 970-382-6235, assessor fax- 970-382-6299. hours- 8AM-4:30PM http://co.laplata.co.us/asr/asr.htm **Online access**- Property information is available at http://eagleweb.laplata.co.us/assessor/web/. Also, records on the county Real Estate Parcel Search Page are free at www.laplatainfo.com/search2.html. This is basic property data but for sales and tax data, there is a subscription service for $20.00 per month, credit cards accepted.

Lake County

County Clerk & Recorder, PO Box 917, Leadville, CO 80461. Recording, R/E & UCC phone-719-486-4131, UCC recording phone-719-894-2200; fax-719-486-3972; 9AM-5PM www.lakecountyco.com

Index: All in one. Records indexed on computer 1981 forward, prior in vault. Office will perform a UCC search but public must search other records themselves. Copy fee $1.25 per page. Cert fee- $1.00 per doc plus copy fee. Payee- Lake County Clerk and Recorder. Office does not sell bulk data. **Other phones:** Treasurer- 719-486-0530; Elections- 719-486-1410; Vital Records- 719-486-0708. **Property tax/Assessing-** PO Box 28, Leadville, CO 80461; 719-486-0413 x6, 486-4110, assessor fax- 719-486-3725. **Online access**- Access county assessor property data free at http://64.234.218.210/cgi-bin/colorado_links.cgi?county=lake or at http://qpublic.net/co/lake/index.html. Also, registration and password is required to search at www.coassessors.com; fee is $275.00 per year.

Larimer County

County Clerk & Recorder, PO Box 1280, Fort Collins, CO 80522-1280. Recording, R/E & UCC phone-970-498-7860; fax-970-498-7830; 7:30AM-5PM (MST) www.larimer.org

Index: All in one. Records indexed on a public use terminal back to 1971. Office personnel will provide directions for searching so visitors may perform searches. No fee for search. Office will not search real estate records. UCC search includes tax liens. Separate tax lien search fee same as UCC search. Copy fee $.25 per page. Marriage license copy- $3.00 each. Large plats- $5.00 per page. Cert fee- $1.00 per doc plus copy fee. Payee- Larimer County Clerk and Recorder. Bulk data available for purchase, contact Sherrie Swisher- Recording Manager. **Online access to Real Estate, Deed, UCC, Lien, Judgment, Voter Registration records:** Search the county Public Record Databases (indexing only-no images) for free at www.larimer.org/databases/index.htm. Search registered voter list free at www.co.larimer.co.us/depts/clerkr/elections/voter_inquiry.cfm. **Other phones:** Treasurer- 970-498-7020; Elections- 970-498-7820; Vital Records- 970-498-5710. **Property tax/Assessing-** 200 W Oak, #2000, Ft Collins, CO 80521; 970-498-7050, assessor fax- 970-498-7070. hours- 7:30AM-4:30PM Public use terminal available. **Online access**- Search assessor and property data free at www.larimer.org/assessor/propertyExplorer/propertyexplorer.html. Also, search assessor and property data at www.co.larimer.co.us/assessor/query/search.cfm. Search treasurer data free at www.larimer.org/treasurer/query/search.cfm but no name searching.

Las Animas County

County Clerk & Recorder, PO Box 115, Trinidad, CO 81082. 719-846-3314; fax-719-845-2573; 8AM-4PM

Index: Separate indices to search include grantor/grantee, reception #, book/page, name. Records indexed on a public use terminal back to 1993. Only the public may search. Copy fee $1.25 per page. Cert fee- $1.00 per doc plus copy fee. Payee- Las Animas County Clerk and Recorder. **Other phones:** Treasurer- 719-846-2295; Elections- 719-846-3314; Vital Records- 719-846-2213. **Property tax/Assessing-** 200 E 1st St, Rm 203, Trinidad, CO 81082; 719-846-2295, assessor fax- 719-846-7061. **Online access**- Access data from the final tax roll free at http://qpublic.net/co/lasanimas/. There are also 3 levels of subscription service based on your needs.

Lincoln County

County Clerk & Recorder, PO Box 67, Hugo, CO 80821-0067. 719-743-2358; fax-719-743-2524; 8am-4:30PM http://lincolncountyco.us/county_clerk.htm

Index: All in one. Records indexed on a public use terminal back to 4/27/97. Only the public may search. Copy fee $.25 per page; fax back- $1.00 per page. Cert fee- $1.00 per doc plus copy fee. Payee- Lincoln County Clerk and Recorder. **Other phones:** Treasurer- 719-743-2633; Elections- 719-743-2444; Vital Records- 719-743-2444. **Property tax/ Assessing-** PO Box 277, 103 3rd Ave, Hugo, CO 80821; 719-743-2358, assessor fax- 719-743-2838. **Online access-** Access data from the final tax roll free at http://qpublic.net/co/lincoln/. There are also 3 levels of subscription service based on your needs.

Logan County

County Clerk & Recorder, 315 Main St, Ste. 3; Logan County Courthouse, Sterling, CO 80751. Recording, R/E & UCC phone-970-522-1544; fax-970-522-2063; 8AM-5PM (MST) www.loganco.gov/
Index: Separate indices to search include grantor/grantee, marriage licenses. (Divorces included in index. Divorces show up only if real estate involved.) Records indexed on a public use terminal back to 1/21/1997. Office will perform a UCC search but public must search other records themselves. Office will not search real estate records, but can retrieve them by request. UCC search per debtor name- $5.00 per name per year; $2.00 each add'l year. Copy fee $.25 per page. Plat copy $6.50 each. Cert fee- $1.00 per doc plus copy fee. Payee- Logan County Clerk and Recorder. **Online access to Real Estate, Deed, Mortgage, Lien, Judgment, Birth, Death, Marriage, Will, UCC records:** Enter the recorder's database site free at https://64.187.69.141/recorder/web/ and click on Public Login button to search index, otherwise registration and username/password required to view and print images, Sub fee is $300 per month. **Other phones:** Treasurer- 970-522-2462; Elections- 970-522-1544; Vital Records- 970-522-1544 (marriage); Birth & Death Certificates- 970-522-3741. **Property tax/Assessing-** 315 Main St, #1, Sterling, CO 80751; 970-522-2797, assessor fax- 970-522-1987. www.logancountyco.gov/assessor/ **Online access-** Access to assessor property data is free at http://logancountyco.gov/assessor/PropertySearch.aspx.

Mesa County

County Clerk & Recorder, PO Box 20000-5003, Grand Junction, CO 81502-5007. Recording, R/E & UCC phone-970-244-1679; fax-970-256-1588; 8AM-5PM (MST) www.mesacounty.us
An interactive Voice Response System lets callers access real property data at 970-256-1563. Fax back service available for minimum $2.00 fax fee. Index: All in one. Records indexed on a public use terminal back to 1978. Only the public may search. Copy fee $.25 per page; $5.00 for plats. Cert fee- $1.00 per doc plus copy fee. Payee- Mesa County Clerk and Recorder. Bulk data available for purchase, contact 970-244-1679 for information. **Online access to Real Estate, Grantor/Grantee, Deed, Judgment, Mortgage, Lien, UCC, Will, Parcel, GIS-mapping records:** Search the recorder's Grantor/Grantee index free at http://apps.mesacounty.us/oncore/Search.aspx. GIS-mapping and property data at http://gis.mesacounty.us/interactive.aspx. **Other phones:** Treasurer- 970-244-1824; Elections- 970-244-1662; Vital Records- 970-248-6900 (birth/death); Marriage Records -970-244-1679;. **Property tax/Assessing-** PO Box 20000-5003, Grand Junction, CO 81502-5007; 970-244-1610, assessor fax- 970-244-1790. Public use terminal available. **Online access-** Records on the county Assessor database and sales are free at http://assessor.mesacounty.us/parsearch.aspx. Click on Assessor lookup and search by address or parcel.

Mineral County

County Clerk & Recorder, PO Box 70, Creede, CO 81130. Recording, R/E & UCC phone-719-658-2440; fax-719-658-0358; 8AM-N, 1PM-4PM (MST) http://mineralcountycolorado.com/clerkrecorder.html
Index: All in one. Records indexed on a public use terminal back to 12/1995. Office personnel or visitors may perform searches. Search fee $50.00 per name. Copy fee $1.25 per page. Cert fee- $1.00 per doc plus copy fee. Payee- Mineral County Clerk and Recorder. Bulk data available for purchase on CD's, contact Eryn Follmana. Voter Reg rolls available. **Online access to Real Estate, Deed records:** Public online search coming soon; see website. **Other phones:** Treasurer- 719-658-2325; Elections- 719-658-2440; Vital Records- 719-658-2497. **Property tax/Assessing-** PO Box 574, Creede, CO 81130; 719-658-2669, assessor fax- 719-658-2931. **Online access-** Access data from the final tax roll free at http://qpublic.net/co/mineral/. There are also 3 levels of subscription service based on your needs.

Moffat County

County Clerk & Recorder, 221 W Victory Way, #200, Craig, CO 81625-2716. Recording, R/E & UCC phone-970-824-9104; fax-970-826-3413; 8AM-4:45PM (MST)
Index: Separate indices to search include in books by Marriage, Real Estate, UCCs, and liens. Records indexed on a public use terminal back to 1996. Only the public may search. Copy fee $.25 per page. Cert fee- $1.00 per doc plus copy fee. Payee- Moffat County Clerk and Recorder. Bulk data available for purchase, $250.00 per month for CD. **Other phones:** Treasurer- 970-824-9111; Elections- 970-824-9104; Vital Records- 970-824-8233. **Property tax/ Assessing-** 221 W Victory Way, #200, Craig, CO 81625-2716; 970-824-9102, assessor fax- 970-824-9189. hours- 8AM-5PM Public use terminal available. **Online access-** Access to assessor property data free at http://co.moffat.co.us/assessor/default.htm but may not be available at this time. Also, search the treasurer's tax database free at http://moffat.visualgov.com/SearchSelect.aspx.

Montezuma County

County Clerk & Recorder, 109 W Main St, Rm 108, Cortez, CO 81321. Recording, R/E & UCC phone-970-565-3728, UCC phone-303-894-2200; fax-970-564-0215; 8:30-4:30PM www.co.montezuma.co.us
Records indexed from 6/3/96 are on Crist Plus system before that are in Grantor/Grantee book indexes. Only the public may search books; office will try to help on computer, time permitting. Office will not search real estate records. Office will not search UCC records or tax liens. Copy fee $.25 per page. Marriage license copy- $1.25. Cert fee- $1.00 per doc plus copy fee. Payee- Montezuma County Clerk and Recorder. **Online access to Real Estate, Deed, Lien, Judgment, UCC, Marriage, Death, Divorce records:** Access recorded records back to 6/3/1996 at http://eagleweb.co.montezuma.co.us/recorder/web/. **Other phones:** Treasurer- 970-565-7550; Elections- 970-565-3728; Vital Records- 970-565-3728. **Property tax/Assessing-** 109 W Main St, Rm 310, Cortez, CO 81321; 970-565-3428, assessor fax- 970-565-1247. **Online access-** Access county property tax data back to June, 1996 and property sales free at http://eagleweb.co.montezuma.co.us/recorder/web/ .

Montrose County

County Clerk & Recorder, PO Box 1289, Montrose, CO 81402. 970-249-3362, R/E recording phone-970-249-3362 x2; fax-970-249-0757; 8:30AM-4:30PM (MST) www.montrosecounty.net/clerkrecorder/
Index: All in one. Records indexed on a public use terminal back to 1996. Only the public may search. General copy fee $1.00 per page.Real estate or tax lien copy- $1.25 per page. Cert fee- $1.00 per doc plus copy fee. Payee- Montrose County Clerk and Recorder. **Other phones:** Treasurer- 970-249-3565; Elections- 970-249-3362 x3; Vital Records- 970-249-3362 x0. **Property tax/Assessing-** PO Box 1186, 320 S 1st St, Montrose, CO 81402; 970-249-3753, assessor fax- 970-252-4559. hours- 8AM-4:30PM www.montrosecounty.net/assessor/ **Online access-** Access to Property Information EagleWeb System is free at http://eagleweb.co.montrose.co.us/eagleassessor/web/splash.jsp.

Morgan County

County Clerk & Recorder, PO Box 1399, Fort Morgan, CO 80701. Recording, R/E & UCC phone-970-542-3521; fax-970-542-3525; 8AM-4PM (MST) www.co.morgan.co.us/index.html
Index: All in one. Records indexed on a public use terminal back to 1994. Only the public may search. Copy fee $.25 per page. Cert fee- $1.00 per page plus copy fee. Payee- Morgan County Clerk and Recorder. **Online access to Real Estate, Grantor/Grantee, Deed, Lien, Judgment, Marriage records:** Access the recorder's online index free or by subscription for images for $300 per year at www.co.morgan.co.us:8080/recorder/web/splash.jsp. **Other phones:** Treasurer- 970-542-3518; Elections-970-542-3521; Vital Records- 970-867-4918. **Property tax/Assessing-** PO Box 892, Ft Morgan, CO 80701; 970-542-3512, assessor fax- 970-542-3502. (Appraiser/Auditor- 970-542-3512) **Online access-** Search the assessor database free at www.co.morgan.co.us/itax/TaxLogin.jsp. Username and password are both "Public".

Otero County

County Clerk & Recorder, PO Box 511, La Junta, CO 81050-0511. 719-383-3020, R/E recording phone-719-383-3023; fax-719-383-3026; 8AM-5PM (MST)
Index: All in one. Images go back to 1966. Records indexed on a public use terminal back to 1993. Office will perform a UCC search but public must search other records themselves. Copy fee $.25 per page plus $1.00 per doc admin fee. Cert fee- $1.00 per doc plus copy fee. Payee- Otero County Clerk and Recorder. Title companies may purchase bulk data, contact County Clerk. **Online access to Real Estate, Deed, Lien records:** Access to recorded data is by subscription only. Fee is $200 per month but you may signup for a free 15-day trial. Contact the Clerk/Recorder office for more info and sign-up. **Other phones:** Treasurer- 719-383-3030; Elections-719-383-3024; Vital Records- 719-383-3040. **Property tax/Assessing-** 13 W 3rd St, Rm 211, La Junta, CO 81050; 719-383-3010, assessor fax- 719-383-3019. **Online access-** Access property data free at www.oterocountyassessor.net.

Ouray County

County Clerk & Recorder, PO Box C, Ouray, CO 81427. Recording, R/E & UCC phone-970-325-4961, UCC recording phone-970-894-2200; fax-970-325-0452; 9AM-4PM (MST) www.ouraycountyco.gov
Index: All in one. Records indexed on a public use terminal back to 1887. Office personnel or visitors may perform searches. Search fee $25.00 per name. Office will search RE records, but not UCCs. Copy fee $.25 per page. Marriage license- $.25 per copy. Cert fee- $1.00 per doc plus copy fee. Payee- Ouray County Clerk and Recorder. Office does not sell bulk data. **Online access to Real Estate, Deed, Lien, Judgment, UCC, Marriage, Death records:** Access the record data free at http://ouraycountyco.gov/recording/oncoreweb/Search.aspx. **Other phones:** Treasurer- 970-325-4487; Elections- 970-325-4961; Vital Records- 970-325-4487. **Property tax/Assessing-** PO Box 665, Ouray, CO 81427; 970-325-4371, assessor fax- 970-325-4611. **Online access-** Access recorder data free at http://ouraycountyco.gov:8090/assessor/web/login.jsp With registration, you may also create and print reports for properties free of charge.

Park County

County Clerk & Recorder, PO Box 220, Fairplay, CO 80440. 719-836-4333, R/E recording phone-719-836-4225/26, UCC recording phone-719-836-4235; fax-719-836-4348; 8AM-5PM, til 4PM for recording. (MST) www.parkco.org
Index: All in one. Records indexed on a public use terminal back to 1989. Pre-1990 images not on system. Only the public may search. Copy fee $.25 (1990 to present); $1.25 if prior. Plats- $7.50 each. Fee to fax back- $2.00 per page. Postage- 1-10 pgs =$1.00; 11+ = $2.00. Cert fee- $1.00 per doc plus

copy fee. Payee- Park County Clerk and Recorder. Office does not sell bulk data. **Online access to Divorce records:** County divorce records from 1957 to 1974 free at www.colorado.gov/dpa/doit/archives/divorce/1park.htm. **Other phones:** Treasurer- 719-836-2771 x242; Elections- 719-836-4223; Vital Records- 719-836-4225; 719-836-4333. **Property tax/Assessing-** Park County Assessing Office, PO Box 636, Fairplay, CO 80440; 719-836-4189, assessor fax- 719-836-4193. hours- 8AM-N, 1-5PM **Online access-** Records on the county Assessor database are free at www.parkco.org/Search2.asp? including tax data, owner, address, building characteristics, legal and deed information.

Phillips County

County Clerk & Recorder, 221 S Interocean, Holyoke, CO 80734. Recording, R/E & UCC phone- 970-854-3131; fax-970-854-4745; 8AM-4:30PM
Index: Separate indices to search include books and computer. Records indexed on a public use terminal back to 1997. Only the public may search. Copy fee $.25 per page. Cert fee- $1.00 per doc plus copy fee. Payee- Phillips County Clerk and Recorder. Office does not sell bulk data. **Other phones:** Treasurer- 970-852-2822; Elections- 970-854-3131; Vital Records- 970-854-3350. **Property tax/Assessing-** Phillips County Assessing Office, 221 S Interocean, Holyoke, CO 80734; 970-854-3151, assessor fax- 970-854-3151. (Appraiser/Auditor- 970-854-3151);

Pitkin County

County Clerk & Recorder, 530 E Main St, #101, Aspen, CO 81611. 970-920-5180; fax-970-920-5196; 8:30AM-4:30PM (MST) www.aspenpitkin.com
Index: All in one. Records indexed on a public use terminal back to 11/77. Images available to view from 1992 to present. Only the public may search. Copy fee $.25 per page. Cert fee- $1.00 per doc plus copy fee. Payee- Pitkin County Clerk and Recorder. Bulk recorded document data 6/2007 to current available via FTP. Older data also available in bulk. **Online access to Real Estate, Grantor/Grantee, Deed, Lien, UCC, Mortgage, Judgment, Divorce, Probate records:** Search recorded documents free at www.pitkinclerk.org/oncoreweb/. Also, probate records from 1881 to 1953 are at www.colorado.gov/dpa/doit/archives/probate/pitkin_probate.htm. Divorce records 1931 to 1964 are at www.colorado.gov/dpa/doit/archives/divorce/1pitkin.htm. **Other phones:** Treasurer- 970-920-5170; Elections- 970-920-5180. **Property tax/Assessing-** 506 E Main, #202, Aspen, CO 81611; 970-920-5160, assessor fax- 970-920-5174. **Online access-** Records on the county Assessor database are free at www.pitkinassessor.org/Assessor/.

Prowers County

County Clerk & Recorder, 301 S Main St, #210, Lamar, CO 81052. Recording, R/E & UCC phone- 719-336-8011; fax-719-336-5306; 8:30AM-4:30PM
Index: Separate indices to search include grantor/grantee & general reception book (numeric order). Records indexed on a public use terminal back to 7/1/94. Only the public may search. Copy fee $1.25 per page. Plats- $5.00; marriage license copy- $.25. Cert fee- $1.00 per doc plus copy fee. Payee- Prowers County Clerk and Recorder. Bulk data available for purchase-real estate image can be put on CD's, contact Dottie McCaslin or Jana Coen. **Other phones:** Treasurer- 719-336-8081; Elections- 719-336-8011; Vital Records- 719-336-2606. **Property tax/Assessing-** 301 S Main St, #205, Lamar, CO 81052; 719-336-8000, assessor fax- 719-336-7232. (Appraiser/Auditor- 719-336-8000) hours- 8AM-5PM

Pueblo County

County Clerk & Recorder, PO Box 878, Pueblo, CO 81002-0878. 719-583-6625, R/E recording phone- 719-583-6629, UCC recording phone-719-583-6625; fax-719-583-4625; 8AM-4:30PM (MST) www.co.pueblo.co.us/clerk/
Index: All in one. Records indexed on a public use terminal back to 5/1/91. Only the public may search. Copy fee $.25 per page. Cert fee- $1.00 per doc plus copy fee. Payee- Pueblo County Clerk and Recorder. Bulk data available on an online FTP site, $275.00 per month for images of documents, data recording starts at time of purchase. **Online access to Real Estate, Grantor/Grantee, Deed, Mortgage, Lien, Marriage, UCC, Judgment, Registered Voter records:** Access clerk & recorder index of recorded docs at http://erecording.co.pueblo.co.us/recorder/web/ but no images. Also, access voter registration data free at www.co.pueblo.co.us/clerk/elections/ and click on Confirm. **Other phones:** Treasurer- 719-583-6015; Elections- 719-583-6620; Vital Records- 719-583-4555; Main switchboard -719-583-6000;. **Property tax/Assessing-** 215 W 10th St, Pueblo, CO 81003; 719-583-6564, 583-6563, assessor fax- 719-583-6600. (Appraiser/Auditor- 719-583-6596) **Online access-** Access county assessor data free at http://assessor.co.pueblo.co.us.

Rio Blanco County

County Clerk & Recorder, PO Box 1067, Meeker, CO 81641. 970-878-9460; fax-970-878-3587; 8:30-4:30PM www.co.rio-blanco.co.us/clerkandrecorder/
Index: All in one. Records indexed on a public use terminal back to 6/1/83. Only the public may search. Copy fee $.25 per page. Cert fee- $1.00 per doc plus copy fee. Payee- Rio Blanco County Clerk and Recorder. Will sell bulk data, paper copy or CD available, contact Nancy Emick. **Other phones:** Treasurer- 970-878-9660; Elections- 970-878-9460; Vital Records- 970-878-9460. **Property tax/Assessing-** PO Box 508, 555 Main St, Meeker, CO 81641; 970-878-9410, assessor fax- 970-878-5701. hours- 8AM-5PM www.co.rio-blanco.co.us/assessor/ **Online access-** Access assessor property data at www.co.rio-blanco.co.us/assessor/.

Rio Grande County

County Clerk & Recorder, PO Box 160, Del Norte, CO 81132. Recording, R/E & UCC phone-719-657-3334, UCC recording phone-719-657-3334 real estate only; fax-719-657-2621; 8AM-4PM (MST) www.riograndecounty.org/depts/clerkrecorder/
Index: All in one. Records indexed on a public use terminal back to 1985. Office will perform a UCC search but public must search other records themselves. Copy fee $1.25 per page. Cert fee- $1.00 per doc plus copy fee. Payee- Rio Grande County Clerk and Recorder. **Other phones:** Treasurer- 719-657-2747; Elections- 719-657-3334; Vital Records- 719-657-3334. **Property tax/Assessing-** 925 6th St #105, Del Norte, CO 81132; 719-657-3326, assessor fax- 719-657-4006. (Appraiser - 719-657-3326) **Online access-** Access property assessor's data free at www.qpublic.net/riogrande/. A property sale search is available. For full data, there is 3 subscription levels.

Routt County

County Clerk & Recorder, PO Box 773598, Steamboat Springs, CO 80477. Recording, R/E & UCC phone-970-870-5556; fax-970-870-1329; 8AM-4:30PM (MST) www.co.routt.co.us
Index: All in one. Records indexed on computer back to 1983. Only the public may search. Copy fee $.25 per page. Plats- $7.00 per page. Cert fee- $1.00 per doc plus copy fee. Payee- Routt County Clerk and Recorder. **Online access to Real Estate, Deed, Judgment, Property Sale records:** Search records free on the County Clerk & Recorder Reception Search database at www.co.routt.co.us/clerk.html. **Other phones:** Treasurer- 970-870-5555; Elections- 970-870-5558; Vital Records- 970-879-1632. **Property tax/Assessing-** PO Box 773210, 522 Lincoln Ave, Steamboat Springs, CO 80477; 970-870-5544, assessor fax- 970-870-5461. (Appraiser/Auditor- 970-870-5554) **Online access-** Records on the county Assessor/Treasurer Property Search database are free at www.co.routt.co.us/assessor.html. Also, a gis-mapping site has property data for free at http://maps.co.routt.co.us/website/parcels/index.asp. Search by name.

Saguache County

County Clerk & Recorder, PO Box 176, Saguache, CO 81149-0176. Recording, R/E & UCC phone-719-655-2512; fax-719-655-2730; 8AM-4PM (MST) www.saguachecounty.net
Index: All in one. Records indexed on a public use terminal back to 10/1994. Only the public may search. Copy fee $1.25 per page. Cert fee- $1.00 per doc plus copy fee. Payee- Saguache County Clerk and Recorder. **Online access to Real Estate, Deed, Lien, Death, Marriage records:** Access Recorder database free at www.thecountyrecorder.com/(2taror55j1fchl45xgn5agjt)/default.aspx. Index goes back to 1994; images back to 1994. **Other phones:** Treasurer- 719-655-2656; Elections- 719-655-2512; Vital Records- 719-655-2559. **Property tax/Assessing-** PO Box 38, Saguache, CO 81149; 719-655-2521, assessor fax- 719-655-0152. **Online access-** Search Assessor tax roll database free at www.qpublic.net/co/saguache/. Also 3 levels of subscription service based on your needs.

San Juan County

County Clerk & Recorder, PO Box 466, Silverton, CO 81433-0466. Recording, R/E & UCC phone-970-387-5671; fax-970-387-5671; 9AM-5PM (MST) www.sanjuancountycolorado.us/
Index: All in one. Records indexed on a public use terminal back to 1997. Only the public may search. Copy fee $1.25 per page. Cert fee- $1.00 per page. Payee- San Juan County Clerk and Recorder. **Online access to Real Estate, Deed, Lien, Judgment, Marriage records:** Access to recording index is free from a 3rd party company at www.thecountyrecorder.com/(g5ze11rp4f5xuc2y2xsl4245)/Default.aspx. Select San Juan from county list. Index goes back to 1997. **Other phones:** Treasurer- 970-389-5488; Elections- 970-387-5671; Vital Records- 970-387-5488; Admin- 970-387-5766. **Property tax/Assessing-** 1557 Greene, Silverton, CO 81433; 970-387-5632. **Online access-** Access data from the final tax roll free at www.qpublic.net/co/sanjuan/. There are also 3 levels of subscription service based on your needs.

San Miguel County

County Clerk & Recorder, PO Box 548, Telluride, CO 81435-0548. Recording, R/E & UCC phone-970-728-3954; fax-970-728-4808; 8:30AM-4:30PM (MST) www.sanmiguelcounty.org
Index: Separate indices to search include computer, microfiche, older grantor/grantee books. Records indexed on a public use terminal back to 1998. Only the public may search. Copy fee $1.25 per page. Cert fee- $1.00 per doc plus copy fee. Payee- San Miguel County Clerk and Recorder. Office does not sell bulk data. **Online access to Real Estate, Deed, Lien, Mortgage, Judgment, Marriage records:** Access to recording index is free from a 3rd party company at www.thecountyrecorder.com/(g5ze11rp4f5xuc2y2xsl4245)/Default.aspx. Choose San Miguel County from the county list. Index goes back to 1998. **Other phones:** Treasurer- 970-728-4451; Elections- 970-728-3954; Vital Records- 970-728-4451. **Property tax/Assessing-** PO Box 506, 333 W Colorado Ave, Telluride, CO 81435-0506; 970-728-3174, assessor fax- 970-369-1007. (Appraiser/Aud.- 970-728-3174)

Sedgwick County

County Clerk & Recorder, 315 Cedar St, #220, Julesburg, CO 80737. Recording, R/E & UCC phone-970-474-3346; fax-970-474-0954; 8AM-4PM (MST) http://sedgwickcountygov.net/
Index: Separate indices to search include from 1997 forward index in computer, prior to 1997 in books in vault. Records indexed on a public use terminal back to 11/97. Only the public may search. Copy fee $.25 per page. Cert fee- $1.00 per doc plus copy fee. Payee- Sedgwick County Clerk and Recorder. **Other phones:** Treasurer- 970-474-3473; Elections- 970-

474-3346; Vital Records- 970-474-3473. **Property tax/Assessing-** 315 Cedar St, #200, Julesburg, CO 80737; 970-474-2531, assessor fax- 970-474-3507. **Online access-** Access data from the final tax roll free at http://qpublic.net/co/sedgwick/. There are also 3 levels of subscription service based on your needs.

Summit County

County Clerk & Recorder, PO Box 1538, Breckenridge, CO 80424. Recording, R/E & UCC phone-970-453-3475; fax-970-453-3540; 8AM-5PM (MST) www.co.summit.co.us/Clerk/index.htm
Index: All in one. Records indexed on a public use terminal back to 1990. Office will perform a UCC search but public must search other records themselves. Search fee- depends on amount of time spent searching. Office will not search real estate records. Copy fee $1.25 per page. Cert fee- $1.00 per doc plus copy fee. Payee- Summit County Clerk and Recorder. Bulk data available for purchase. **Other phones:** Treasurer- 970-453-3440; Elections- 970-453-3479; Vital Records- 970-453-3472. **Property tax/Assessing-** PO Box 276, Breckenridge, CO 80424; 970-453-3480, assessor fax- 970-453-3481. (Appraiser/Auditor- 970-453-3480) **Online access-** Access to the GIS-mapping site property data is free at www.co.summit.co.us/disclaimlive.htm.

Teller County

County Clerk & Recorder, PO Box 1010, Cripple Creek, CO 80813-1010. 719-689-2951, R/E recording phone-719-686-8035; fax-719-686-8030; 8AM-4:30PM (MST) www.co.teller.co.us
Index: All in one. Records indexed on a public use terminal back to 1980. Only the public may search. Copy fee $.25 per page. Cert fee- $1.00 per doc plus copy fee. Payee- Teller County Clerk and Recorder. Bulk data available on CD; contact Juliana Mestas, Chief Deputy. **Online access to Real Estate, Grantor/Grantee, Deed records:** Access the county clerk real estate database free at http://data.co.teller.co.us/AsrData/wc.dll?Doc~GrantSearch. Records go back to 1978; fee for documents $.25 per page. **Other phones:** Treasurer- 719-689-2985; Elections- 719-686-8032; Vital Records- 719-686-8035. **Property tax/Assessing-** PO Box 1008, Cripple Creek, CO 80813; 719-689-2941, assessor fax- 719-689-0988. **Online access-** Search the assessor database free at http://data.co.teller.co.us/AsrData/wc.dll?AsrDataProc~OwnerNameSearch.

Washington County

County Clerk & Recorder, PO Box L, Akron, CO 80720-0380. Recording, R/E & UCC phone-970-345-6565, UCC recording phone-303-894-2200; fax-970-345-6607; 8AM-4:30PM (MST)
Index: All in one. Records indexed on a public use terminal back to 9/96. Only the public may search. Copy fee $.25 per page. Cert fee- $1.00 per doc plus copy fee. Payee- Washington County Clerk. Bulk data is available for purchase, please contact Garland Wahl for info. **Other phones:** Treasurer- 970-345-6601; Elections- 970-345-6565; Vital Records- 970-345-6562. **Property tax/Assessing-** 150 Ash, Courthouse, Akron, CO 80720; 970-345-6662, assessor fax- 970-345-2329. (Appraiser/Auditor- 970-345-6662) **Online access-** Access data from the final tax roll free at http://qpublic.net/co/washington/. There are also 3 levels of subscription service based on your needs.

Weld County

County Clerk & Recorder, PO Box 459, Greeley, CO 80632-0459. 970-304-6530; fax-970-353-1964; 8AM-5PM (MST) www.co.weld.co.us
Index: All in one. Records indexed on computer back to 1982. Office will perform a tax lien search but public must search other records themselves. No fee for search. Office will not search real estate records. Will not search UCC records. Copy fee $.25 per page. Cert fee- $1.00 per doc plus copy fee. Payee- Weld County Clerk and Recorder. Bulk data available for purchase of FTP for $500.00 monthly, ICRIS for $300.00, CD's daily-$10.0, weekly-$25.00 and monthly-$100.00. **Other phones:** Treasurer- 970-353-3845 x3260; Elections- 970-304-6525 x3070; Vital Records- 970-304-6510. **Property tax/Assessing-** 1400 N 17th Ave, Greeley, CO 80631; 970-353-3845 x3650, assessor fax- 970-304-6433. www.co.weld.co.us/departments/assessor.html
Online access- Access assessor data, property sales, ownership listings, transfers, property cards free at www.co.weld.co.us/departments/assessor.html. Search property data on the map server database free at http://maps2.merrick.com/website/Weld/. Search treasurer's property database free at https://www.weldtax.com/treasurer/web/.

Yuma County

County Clerk & Recorder, 310 Ash St, #F, Wray, CO 80758. 970-332-5809; fax-970-332-5919; 8:30AM-4:30PM www.yumacounty.net/clerk_recorder.html
Index: All in one. Records indexed on a public use terminal back to 1/28/1997. Only the public may search. Copy fee $.25 per page. Marriage license copy- $.25. Cert fee- $1.00 per doc plus copy fee. Payee- Yuma County Clerk and Recorder. Bulk data available for purchase, contact Cindy Taylor or Carrie Sharp. **Other phones:** Treasurer- 970-332-4965; Elections- 970-332-5809; Vital Records- 970-332-4431; Birth/Death Records- 970-332-4431/970- 848-3878. **Property tax/Assessing-** 310 Ash St, #D, Wray, CO 80758; 970-332-5032, assessor fax- 970-332-3373. (Appraiser/Auditor- 970-332-5032) A public access terminal is available. **Online access-** Access data from the final tax roll free at http://qpublic.net/co/yuma/. There are also 3 levels of subscription service based on your needs.

Colorado County Locator

You will usually be able to find the city name in the City/County Cross Reference below. In that case, it is a simple matter to determine the county from the cross reference. However, only the official US Postal Service city names are included in this index. There are an additional 40,000 place names that people use in their addresses. Therefore, we have also included a ZIP/City Cross Reference immediately following the City/County Cross Reference.

If you know the ZIP Code but the city name does not appear in the City/County Cross Reference index, look up the ZIP Code in the ZIP/City Cross Reference, find the city name, then look up the city name in the City/County Cross Reference. For example, you want to know the county for an address of Menands, NY 12204. There is no "Menands" in the City/County Cross Reference. The ZIP/City Cross Reference shows that ZIP Codes 12201-12288 are for the city of Albany. Looking back in the City/County Cross Reference, Albany is in Albany County.

Colorado City/County Cross Reference

AGATE Elbert
AGUILAR Las Animas
AKRON Washington
ALAMOSA (81101) Alamosa(98), Conejos(1)
ALAMOSA Alamosa
ALLENSPARK (80510) Boulder(95), Larimer(4)
ALMA Park
ALMONT Gunnison
AMHERST Phillips
ANTON Washington
ANTONITO Conejos
ARAPAHOE Cheyenne
ARBOLES Archuleta
ARLINGTON (81021) Kiowa(80), Lincoln(19)
ARRIBA Lincoln
ARVADA (80003) Jefferson(86), Adams(13)
ARVADA Jefferson
ASPEN Pitkin
ATWOOD Logan
AULT Weld
AURORA (80010) Adams(52), Arapahoe(47)
AURORA (80011) Arapahoe(61), Adams(38)
AURORA (80014) Arapahoe(91), Denver(8)
AURORA Adams
AURORA Arapahoe
AUSTIN Delta
AVON Eagle
AVONDALE Pueblo
BAILEY Park
BASALT (81621) Eagle(68), Pitkin(31)
BATTLEMENT MESA Garfield
BAYFIELD La Plata
BEDROCK Montrose
BELLVUE Larimer
BENNETT (80102) Adams(51), Arapahoe(44), Elbert(3)
BERTHOUD (80513) Larimer(90), Weld(9)
BETHUNE Kit Carson
BEULAH Pueblo
BLACK HAWK Gilpin
BLANCA Costilla
BONCARBO Las Animas
BOND Eagle
BOONE Pueblo
BOULDER Boulder
BOYERO Lincoln
BRANSON Las Animas
BRECKENRIDGE Summit
BRIGGSDALE Weld
BRIGHTON (80603) Weld(54), Adams(45)
BRIGHTON Adams
BRISTOL Prowers
BROOMFIELD (80020) Broomfield(77), Jefferson(11), Adams(8), Boulder(2)
BROOMFIELD (80021) Jefferson(84), Broomfield(15)
BROOMFIELD Boulder
BRUSH (80723) Morgan(98), Washington(1)
BUENA VISTA Chaffee
BUFFALO CREEK Jefferson
BURLINGTON Kit Carson
BURNS Eagle
BYERS (80103) Arapahoe(87), Adams(12)
CAHONE Dolores
CALHAN (80808) El Paso(97), Elbert(2)
CAMPO Baca
CANON CITY Fremont
CAPULIN Conejos
CARBONDALE (81623) Garfield(62), Eagle(15), Pitkin(11), Gunnison(9)
CARR (80612) Weld(95), Larimer(4)
CASCADE El Paso
CASTLE ROCK Douglas
CEDAREDGE Delta
CENTER (81125) Saguache(67), Rio Grande(31), Alamosa(1)
CENTRAL CITY Gilpin
CHAMA Costilla
CHERAW Otero
CHEYENNE WELLS Cheyenne
CHIMNEY ROCK Archuleta
CHROMO Archuleta
CIMARRON (81220) Gunnison(81), Montrose(18)
CLARK Routt
CLIFTON Mesa
CLIMAX Lake
COAL CREEK Fremont
COALDALE Fremont
COALMONT Jackson
COKEDALE Las Animas
COLLBRAN Mesa
COLORADO CITY Pueblo
COLORADO SPRINGS (80926) El Paso(98), Fremont(1)
COLORADO SPRINGS El Paso
COMMERCE CITY Adams
COMO Park
CONEJOS Conejos
CONIFER Jefferson
COPE Washington
CORTEZ Montezuma
CORY Delta
COTOPAXI Fremont
COWDREY Jackson
CRAIG Moffat
CRAWFORD (81415) Delta(80), Montrose(19)
CREEDE Mineral
CRESTED BUTTE Gunnison
CRESTONE Saguache
CRIPPLE CREEK Teller
CROOK Logan
CROWLEY Crowley
DACONO Weld
DE BEQUE (81630) Mesa(63), Garfield(36)
DEER TRAIL (80105) Arapahoe(63), Elbert(26), Adams(9)
DEL NORTE (81132) Rio Grande(88), Saguache(11)
DELTA (81416) Delta(96), Montrose(3)
DENVER (80221) Adams(87), Denver(12)
DENVER (80234) Adams(97), Broomfield(2)
DENVER (80212) Denver(77), Jefferson(18), Adams(3)
DENVER (80216) Denver(60), Adams(39)
DENVER (80222) Denver(94), Arapahoe(5)
DENVER (80230) Denver(98), Adams(1)
DENVER (80247) Denver(69), Arapahoe(27), Adams(3)
DENVER (80249) Denver(96), Adams(3)
DENVER (80235) Jefferson(61), Denver(38)
DENVER Adams
DENVER Denver
DENVER Jefferson
DILLON Summit
DINOSAUR Moffat
DIVIDE Teller
DOLORES Montezuma
DOVE CREEK (81324) Dolores(98), San Miguel(1)
DRAKE Larimer
DUMONT Clear Creek
DUPONT Adams
DURANGO La Plata
EADS Kiowa
EAGLE Eagle
EASTLAKE Adams
EATON Weld
ECKERT Delta
ECKLEY Yuma
EDWARDS Eagle
EGNAR (81325) Dolores(85), San Miguel(14)
EL JEBEL Eagle
ELBERT (80106) El Paso(60), Elbert(37), Douglas(2)
ELDORADO SPRINGS Boulder
ELIZABETH Elbert
EMPIRE Clear Creek
ENGLEWOOD (80110) Arapahoe(98), Denver(1)
ENGLEWOOD (80112) Arapahoe(90), Douglas(5), Denver(4)
ENGLEWOOD Arapahoe
ERIE (80516) Weld(59), Boulder(40)
ESTES PARK Larimer
EVANS Weld
EVERGREEN (80439) Jefferson(88), Clear Creek(11)
EVERGREEN Jefferson
FAIRPLAY Park
FIRESTONE Weld
FLAGLER (80815) Kit Carson(86), Washington(13)
FLEMING Logan
FLORENCE Fremont
FLORISSANT (80816) Teller(78), Park(21)
FORT COLLINS Larimer
FORT GARLAND Costilla
FORT LUPTON Weld
FORT LYON Bent
FORT MORGAN Morgan
FOUNTAIN El Paso
FOWLER (81039) Otero(91), Pueblo(6), Crowley(1)
FOXTON Jefferson
FRANKTOWN Douglas
FRASER Grand
FREDERICK Weld
FRISCO Summit
FRUITA Mesa
GALETON Weld
GARCIA Costilla
GARDNER Huerfano
GATEWAY Mesa
GENOA (80818) Lincoln(83), Washington(16)
GEORGETOWN Clear Creek
GILCREST Weld
GILL Weld
GLADE PARK Mesa
GLEN HAVEN Larimer
GLENWOOD SPRINGS Garfield
GOLDEN (80403) Jefferson(74), Gilpin(21), Boulder(4)
GOLDEN Jefferson
GRANADA (81041) Prowers(92), Baca(7)
GRANBY Grand
GRAND JUNCTION Mesa
GRAND LAKE Grand
GRANITE (81228) Lake(62), Chaffee(37)
GRANT Park
GREELEY Weld
GREEN MOUNTAIN FALLS El Paso
GROVER Weld
GUFFEY Park
GULNARE Las Animas
GUNNISON Gunnison
GYPSUM (81637) Eagle(91), Garfield(8)
HAMILTON (81638) Moffat(59), Routt(30), Rio Blanco(9)
HARTMAN Prowers
HARTSEL Park
HASTY Bent
HASWELL (81045) Kiowa(63), Lincoln(20), Cheyenne(16)
HAXTUN (80731) Phillips(55), Logan(23), Yuma(21)
HAYDEN Routt
HENDERSON Adams
HEREFORD Weld
HESPERUS La Plata
HILLROSE Morgan
HILLSIDE Fremont
HOEHNE Las Animas
HOLLY (81047) Prowers(92), Kiowa(4), Baca(2)
HOLYOKE (80734) Phillips(95), Yuma(4)
HOMELAKE Rio Grande
HOOPER (81136) Alamosa(94), Saguache(5)

HOT SULPHUR SPRINGS Grand
HOTCHKISS Delta
HOWARD Fremont
HUDSON (80642) Weld(67), Adams(32)
HUGO Lincoln
HYGIENE Boulder
IDAHO SPRINGS Clear Creek
IDALIA Yuma
IDLEDALE Jefferson
IGNACIO La Plata
ILIFF Logan
INDIAN HILLS Jefferson
JAMESTOWN Boulder
JAROSO Costilla
JEFFERSON Park
JOES Yuma
JOHNSTOWN Weld
JULESBURG Sedgwick
KARVAL Lincoln
KEENESBURG (80643) Weld(88), Adams(11)
KERSEY Weld
KIM Las Animas
KIOWA Elbert
KIRK Yuma
KIT CARSON Cheyenne
KITTREDGE Jefferson
KREMMLING (80459) Grand(98), Summit(1)
LA JARA Conejos
LA JUNTA Otero
LA SALLE Weld
LA VETA Huerfano
LAFAYETTE Boulder
LAKE CITY Hinsdale
LAKE GEORGE (80827) Teller(71), Park(28)
LAKEWOOD (80226) Jefferson(98), Denver(1)
LAKEWOOD Jefferson
LAMAR (81052) Prowers(98), Bent(1)
LAPORTE Larimer
LARKSPUR Douglas
LAS ANIMAS Bent
LAZEAR Delta
LEADVILLE Lake
LEWIS Montezuma
LIMON (80828) Lincoln(70), Elbert(29)
LIMON Lincoln
LINDON Washington
LITTLETON (80128) Jefferson(94), Arapahoe(5)
LITTLETON Arapahoe
LITTLETON Douglas
LITTLETON Jefferson
LIVERMORE Larimer
LOG LANE VILLAGE Morgan
LOMA Mesa
LONGMONT (80504) Weld(75), Boulder(22), Larimer(1)
LONGMONT Boulder
LOUISVILLE Boulder
LOUVIERS Douglas
LOVELAND (80537) Larimer(98), Weld(1)
LOVELAND Larimer
LUCERNE Weld
LYONS (80540) Larimer(53), Boulder(46)
MACK Mesa
MAHER Delta
MANASSA Conejos
MANCOS (81328) Montezuma(96), La Plata(3)
MANITOU SPRINGS El Paso
MANZANOLA (81058) Otero(78), Crowley(21)
MARVEL La Plata
MASONVILLE Larimer
MATHESON Elbert
MAYBELL Moffat
MC CLAVE Bent
MC COY (80463) Eagle(80), Routt(20)
MEAD Weld
MEEKER (81641) Rio Blanco(93), Moffat(4), Garfield(1)
MEREDITH Pitkin
MERINO (80741) Logan(90), Washington(7), Morgan(1)
MESA Mesa
MESA VERDE NATIONAL PARK Montezuma
MILLIKEN Weld
MINTURN Eagle
MODEL (81059) Las Animas(77), Otero(22)
MOFFAT Saguache
MOLINA Mesa
MONARCH Chaffee
MONTE VISTA (81144) Rio Grande(96), Alamosa(3)
MONTROSE (81401) Montrose(96), Ouray(3)
MONTROSE Montrose
MONUMENT El Paso
MORRISON Jefferson
MOSCA Alamosa
NATHROP Chaffee
NATURITA Montrose
NEDERLAND Boulder
NEW CASTLE Garfield
NEW RAYMER (80742) Weld(66), Morgan(33)
NIWOT Boulder
NORWOOD San Miguel
NUCLA Montrose
NUNN Weld
OAK CREEK Routt
OHIO CITY Gunnison
OLATHE Montrose
OLNEY SPRINGS (81062) Crowley(94), Pueblo(5)
OPHIR San Miguel
ORCHARD (80649) Morgan(55), Weld(44)
ORDWAY (81063) Crowley(95), Lincoln(4)
OTIS (80743) Washington(97), Logan(2)
OURAY Ouray
OVID Sedgwick
PADRONI Logan
PAGOSA SPRINGS Archuleta
PALISADE Mesa
PALMER LAKE El Paso
PAOLI Phillips
PAONIA Delta
PARACHUTE Garfield
PARADOX Montrose
PARKER Douglas
PARLIN Gunnison
PARSHALL Grand
PEETZ Logan
PENROSE Fremont
PEYTON El Paso
PHIPPSBURG Routt
PIERCE Weld
PINE (80470) Jefferson(69), Park(30)
PINECLIFFE Boulder
PITKIN Gunnison
PLACERVILLE San Miguel
PLATTEVILLE Weld
PLEASANT VIEW Montezuma
PONCHA SPRINGS Chaffee
POWDERHORN Gunnison
PRITCHETT (81064) Baca(77), Las Animas(22)
PRYOR Huerfano
PUEBLO (81008) Pueblo(84), El Paso(15)
PUEBLO Pueblo
RAMAH (80832) Elbert(48), El Paso(46), Lincoln(5)
RAND Jackson
RANGELY Rio Blanco
RED CLIFF Eagle
RED FEATHER LAKES Larimer
RED WING Huerfano
REDVALE Montrose
RICO Dolores
RIDGWAY Ouray
RIFLE (81650) Garfield(96), Rio Blanco(3)
ROCKVALE Fremont
ROCKY FORD Otero
ROGGEN Weld
ROLLINSVILLE Gilpin
ROMEO Conejos
RUSH (80833) El Paso(49), Lincoln(40), Elbert(10)
RYE Pueblo
SAGUACHE Saguache
SALIDA Chaffee
SAN ACACIO Costilla
SAN LUIS Costilla
SAN PABLO Costilla
SANFORD (81151) Conejos(77), Costilla(21), Rio Grande(1)
SARGENTS Saguache
SEDALIA Douglas
SEDGWICK Sedgwick
SEGUNDO Las Animas
SEIBERT (80834) Kit Carson(90), Washington(9)
SEVERANCE Weld
SHAWNEE Park
SHERIDAN LAKE Kiowa
SILT Garfield
SILVER CLIFF Custer
SILVER PLUME Clear Creek
SILVERTHORNE Summit
SILVERTON San Juan
SIMLA (80835) Elbert(89), El Paso(10)
SLATER Moffat
SLICK ROCK San Miguel
SNOWMASS Pitkin
SNOWMASS VILLAGE Pitkin
SNYDER Morgan
SOMERSET (81434) Gunnison(90), Delta(9)
SOUTH FORK Rio Grande
SPRINGFIELD Baca
STARKVILLE Las Animas
STEAMBOAT SPRINGS Routt
STERLING Logan
STONEHAM Weld
STONINGTON Baca
STRASBURG (80136) Adams(66), Arapahoe(33)
STRATTON Kit Carson
SUGAR CITY (81076) Crowley(94), Lincoln(3), Kiowa(1)
SWINK Otero
TABERNASH Grand
TELLURIDE San Miguel
TIMNATH Larimer
TOPONAS Routt
TOWAOC Montezuma
TRINCHERA Las Animas
TRINIDAD Las Animas
TWIN LAKES Lake
TWIN LAKES CPO Lake
TWO BUTTES (81084) Baca(89), Prowers(10)
U S A F ACADEMY El Paso
VAIL Eagle
VERNON Yuma
VICTOR Teller
VILAS Baca
VILLA GROVE Saguache
VIRGINIA DALE Larimer
VONA Kit Carson
WALDEN Jackson
WALSENBURG Huerfano
WALSH Baca
WARD Boulder
WATKINS (80137) Arapahoe(59), Adams(40)
WELDONA Morgan
WELLINGTON (80549) Larimer(95), Weld(4)
WESTCLIFFE Custer
WESTMINSTER (80031) Adams(93), Jefferson(6)
WESTMINSTER Adams
WESTON Las Animas
WETMORE (81253) Custer(69), Fremont(26), Pueblo(4)
WHEAT RIDGE Jefferson
WHITEWATER Mesa
WIGGINS (80654) Morgan(92), Weld(4), Adams(2)
WILD HORSE Cheyenne
WILEY (81092) Prowers(60), Bent(36), Kiowa(3)
WINDSOR (80550) Weld(94), Larimer(5)
WINDSOR Weld
WINTER PARK Grand
WOLCOTT Eagle
WOODLAND PARK Teller
WOODROW Washington
WOODY CREEK Pitkin
WRAY Yuma
YAMPA Routt
YELLOW JACKET Montezuma
YODER El Paso

Colorado ZIP/City Cross Reference

80001-80007 ARVADA
80010-80019 AURORA
80020-80021 BROOMFIELD
80022-80022 COMMERCE CITY
80024-80024 DUPONT
80025-80025 ELDORADO SPRINGS
80026-80026 LAFAYETTE
80027-80028 LOUISVILLE
80030-80031 WESTMINSTER
80033-80034 WHEAT RIDGE
80035-80036 WESTMINSTER
80037-80037 COMMERCE CITY
80038-80038 BROOMFIELD
80040-80047 AURORA
80101-80101 AGATE
80102-80102 BENNETT
80103-80103 BYERS
80104-80104 CASTLE ROCK
80105-80105 DEER TRAIL
80106-80106 ELBERT
80107-80107 ELIZABETH
80108-80109 CASTLE ROCK
80110-80113 ENGLEWOOD
80116-80116 FRANKTOWN
80117-80117 KIOWA
80118-80118 LARKSPUR
80120-80130 LITTLETON
80131-80131 LOUVIERS
80132-80132 MONUMENT
80133-80133 PALMER LAKE
80134-80134 PARKER
80135-80135 SEDALIA
80136-80136 STRASBURG
80137-80137 WATKINS
80138-80138 PARKER
80150-80155 ENGLEWOOD
80160-80166 LITTLETON
80201-80214 DENVER
80215-80215 LAKEWOOD
80216-80225 DENVER
80226-80226 LAKEWOOD
80227-80227 DENVER
80228-80228 LAKEWOOD
80229-80231 DENVER
80232-80232 LAKEWOOD
80233-80299 DENVER
80301-80329 BOULDER
80401-80419 GOLDEN
80420-80420 ALMA
80421-80421 BAILEY
80422-80422 BLACK HAWK
80423-80423 BOND
80424-80424 BRECKENRIDGE
80425-80425 BUFFALO CREEK
80426-80426 BURNS
80427-80427 CENTRAL CITY
80428-80428 CLARK
80429-80429 CLIMAX
80430-80430 COALMONT
80432-80432 COMO
80433-80433 CONIFER
80434-80434 COWDREY
80435-80435 DILLON
80436-80436 DUMONT
80437-80437 EVERGREEN
80438-80438 EMPIRE
80439-80439 EVERGREEN
80440-80440 FAIRPLAY
80441-80441 FOXTON
80442-80442 FRASER
80443-80443 FRISCO
80444-80444 GEORGETOWN
80446-80446 GRANBY
80447-80447 GRAND LAKE
80448-80448 GRANT
80449-80449 HARTSEL
80451-80451 HOT SULPHUR SPRINGS
80452-80452 IDAHO SPRINGS
80453-80453 IDLEDALE
80454-80454 INDIAN HILLS
80455-80455 JAMESTOWN
80456-80456 JEFFERSON
80457-80457 KITTREDGE
80459-80459 KREMMLING
80461-80461 LEADVILLE
80463-80463 MC COY
80465-80465 MORRISON
80466-80466 NEDERLAND
80467-80467 OAK CREEK
80468-80468 PARSHALL
80469-80469 PHIPPSBURG
80470-80470 PINE
80471-80471 PINECLIFFE
80473-80473 RAND
80474-80474 ROLLINSVILLE
80475-80475 SHAWNEE
80476-80476 SILVER PLUME
80477-80477 STEAMBOAT SPRINGS
80478-80478 TABERNASH
80479-80479 TOPONAS
80480-80480 WALDEN
80481-80481 WARD
80482-80482 WINTER PARK
80483-80483 YAMPA
80487-80488 STEAMBOAT SPRINGS
80497-80498 SILVERTHORNE
80501-80504 LONGMONT
80510-80510 ALLENSPARK
80511-80511 ESTES PARK
80512-80512 BELLVUE
80513-80513 BERTHOUD
80514-80514 DACONO
80515-80515 DRAKE
80516-80516 ERIE
80517-80517 ESTES PARK
80520-80520 FIRESTONE
80521-80528 FORT COLLINS
80530-80530 FREDERICK
80532-80532 GLEN HAVEN
80533-80533 HYGIENE
80534-80534 JOHNSTOWN
80535-80535 LAPORTE
80536-80536 LIVERMORE
80537-80539 LOVELAND
80540-80540 LYONS
80541-80541 MASONVILLE
80542-80542 MEAD
80543-80543 MILLIKEN
80544-80544 NIWOT
80545-80545 RED FEATHER LAKES
80546-80546 SEVERANCE
80547-80547 TIMNATH
80548-80548 LAPORTE
80548-80548 VIRGINIA DALE
80549-80549 WELLINGTON
80550-80551 WINDSOR
80553-80553 FORT COLLINS
80601-80603 BRIGHTON
80610-80610 AULT
80611-80611 BRIGGSDALE
80612-80612 CARR
80614-80614 EASTLAKE
80615-80615 EATON
80620-80620 EVANS
80621-80621 FORT LUPTON
80622-80622 GALETON
80623-80623 GILCREST
80624-80624 GILL
80631-80639 GREELEY
80640-80640 HENDERSON
80642-80642 HUDSON
80643-80643 KEENESBURG
80644-80644 KERSEY
80645-80645 LA SALLE
80646-80646 LUCERNE
80648-80648 NUNN
80649-80649 ORCHARD
80650-80650 PIERCE
80651-80651 PLATTEVILLE
80652-80652 ROGGEN
80653-80653 WELDONA
80654-80654 WIGGINS
80701-80701 FORT MORGAN
80705-80705 LOG LANE VILLAGE
80720-80720 AKRON
80721-80721 AMHERST
80722-80722 ATWOOD
80723-80723 BRUSH
80726-80726 CROOK
80727-80727 ECKLEY
80728-80728 FLEMING
80729-80729 GROVER
80731-80731 HAXTUN
80732-80732 HEREFORD
80733-80733 HILLROSE
80734-80734 HOLYOKE
80735-80735 IDALIA
80736-80736 ILIFF
80737-80737 JULESBURG
80740-80740 LINDON
80741-80741 MERINO
80742-80742 NEW RAYMER
80743-80743 OTIS
80744-80744 OVID
80745-80745 PADRONI
80746-80746 PAOLI
80747-80747 PEETZ
80749-80749 SEDGWICK
80750-80750 SNYDER
80751-80751 STERLING
80754-80754 STONEHAM
80755-80755 VERNON
80757-80757 WOODROW
80758-80758 WRAY
80759-80759 YUMA
80801-80801 ANTON
80802-80802 ARAPAHOE
80804-80804 ARRIBA
80805-80805 BETHUNE
80806-80806 BOYERO
80807-80807 BURLINGTON
80808-80808 CALHAN
80809-80809 CASCADE
80810-80810 CHEYENNE WELLS
80812-80812 COPE
80813-80813 CRIPPLE CREEK
80814-80814 DIVIDE
80815-80815 FLAGLER
80816-80816 FLORISSANT
80817-80817 FOUNTAIN
80818-80818 GENOA
80819-80819 GREEN MOUNTAIN FALLS
80820-80820 GUFFEY
80821-80821 HUGO
80822-80822 JOES
80823-80823 KARVAL
80824-80824 KIRK
80825-80825 KIT CARSON
80826-80826 LIMON
80827-80827 LAKE GEORGE
80828-80828 LIMON
80829-80829 MANITOU SPRINGS
80830-80830 MATHESON
80831-80831 PEYTON
80832-80832 RAMAH
80833-80833 RUSH
80834-80834 SEIBERT
80835-80835 SIMLA
80836-80836 STRATTON
80840-80841 U S A F ACADEMY
80860-80860 VICTOR
80861-80861 VONA
80862-80862 WILD HORSE
80863-80863 WOODLAND PARK
80864-80864 YODER
80866-80866 WOODLAND PARK
80900-80997 COLORADO SPRINGS
81001-81015 PUEBLO
81019-81019 COLORADO CITY
81020-81020 AGUILAR
81021-81021 ARLINGTON
81022-81022 AVONDALE
81023-81023 BEULAH
81024-81024 BONCARBO
81025-81025 BOONE
81026-81026 EADS
81027-81027 BRANSON
81028-81028 BRISTOL
81029-81029 CAMPO
81030-81030 CHERAW
81032-81032 COKEDALE
81033-81034 CROWLEY
81036-81036 EADS
81038-81038 FORT LYON
81039-81039 FOWLER
81040-81040 GARDNER
81041-81041 GRANADA
81042-81042 GULNARE
81043-81043 HARTMAN
81044-81044 HASTY
81045-81045 HASWELL
81046-81046 HOEHNE
81047-81047 HOLLY
81049-81049 KIM
81050-81050 LA JUNTA
81052-81052 LAMAR
81054-81054 LAS ANIMAS
81055-81055 LA VETA
81057-81057 MC CLAVE
81058-81058 MANZANOLA
81059-81059 MODEL
81062-81062 OLNEY SPRINGS
81063-81063 ORDWAY
81064-81064 PRITCHETT
81065-81065 PRYOR
81066-81066 RED WING
81067-81067 ROCKY FORD
81069-81069 RYE
81070-81070 SEGUNDO
81071-81071 SHERIDAN LAKE
81073-81073 SPRINGFIELD
81074-81074 STARKVILLE
81075-81075 STONINGTON
81076-81076 SUGAR CITY
81077-81077 SWINK
81081-81081 TRINCHERA
81082-81082 TRINIDAD
81084-81084 TWO BUTTES
81087-81087 VILAS
81089-81089 WALSENBURG
81090-81090 WALSH
81091-81091 WESTON
81092-81092 WILEY
81101-81102 ALAMOSA
81120-81120 ANTONITO
81121-81121 ARBOLES
81122-81122 BAYFIELD
81123-81123 BLANCA
81124-81124 CAPULIN
81125-81125 CENTER
81126-81126 CHAMA
81127-81127 CHIMNEY ROCK
81128-81128 CHROMO
81129-81129 CONEJOS
81130-81130 CREEDE
81131-81131 CRESTONE
81132-81132 DEL NORTE
81133-81133 FORT GARLAND
81134-81134 GARCIA
81135-81135 HOMELAKE
81136-81136 HOOPER
81137-81137 IGNACIO
81138-81138 JAROSO
81140-81140 LA JARA
81141-81141 MANASSA
81143-81143 MOFFAT

81144-81144 MONTE VISTA
81146-81146 MOSCA
81147-81147 PAGOSA SPRINGS
81148-81148 ROMEO
81149-81149 SAGUACHE
81150-81150 SAN ACACIO
81151-81151 SANFORD
81152-81152 SAN LUIS
81153-81153 SAN PABLO
81154-81154 SOUTH FORK
81155-81155 VILLA GROVE
81157-81157 PAGOSA SPRINGS
81201-81201 SALIDA
81210-81210 ALMONT
81211-81211 BUENA VISTA
81212-81215 CANON CITY
81220-81220 CIMARRON
81221-81221 COAL CREEK
81222-81222 COALDALE
81223-81223 COTOPAXI
81224-81225 CRESTED BUTTE
81226-81226 FLORENCE
81227-81227 MONARCH
81228-81228 GRANITE
81230-81231 GUNNISON
81232-81232 HILLSIDE
81233-81233 HOWARD
81235-81235 LAKE CITY
81236-81236 NATHROP
81237-81237 OHIO CITY
81239-81239 PARLIN
81240-81240 PENROSE
81241-81241 PITKIN
81242-81242 PONCHA SPRINGS
81243-81243 POWDERHORN
81244-81244 ROCKVALE
81246-81246 CANON CITY
81247-81247 GUNNISON
81248-81248 SARGENTS
81249-81249 SILVER CLIFF
81250-81250 COTOPAXI
81251-81251 TWIN LAKES
81251-81251 TWIN LAKES CPO
81252-81252 WESTCLIFFE
81253-81253 WETMORE
81290-81290 FLORENCE
81301-81303 DURANGO
81320-81320 CAHONE
81321-81321 CORTEZ
81323-81323 DOLORES
81324-81324 DOVE CREEK
81325-81325 EGNAR
81326-81326 HESPERUS
81327-81327 LEWIS
81328-81328 MANCOS
81329-81329 MARVEL
81330-81330 MESA VERDE NATIONAL PARK
81331-81331 PLEASANT VIEW
81332-81332 RICO
81333-81333 SLICK ROCK
81334-81334 TOWAOC
81335-81335 YELLOW JACKET
81401-81402 MONTROSE
81410-81410 AUSTIN
81411-81411 BEDROCK
81413-81413 CEDAREDGE
81414-81414 CORY
81415-81415 CRAWFORD
81416-81416 DELTA
81418-81418 ECKERT
81419-81419 HOTCHKISS
81420-81420 LAZEAR
81421-81421 MAHER
81422-81422 NATURITA
81423-81423 NORWOOD
81424-81424 NUCLA
81425-81425 OLATHE
81426-81426 OPHIR
81427-81427 OURAY
81428-81428 PAONIA
81429-81429 PARADOX
81430-81430 PLACERVILLE
81431-81431 REDVALE
81432-81432 RIDGWAY
81433-81433 SILVERTON
81434-81434 SOMERSET
81435-81435 TELLURIDE
81501-81506 GRAND JUNCTION
81520-81520 CLIFTON
81521-81521 FRUITA
81522-81522 GATEWAY
81523-81523 GLADE PARK
81524-81524 LOMA
81525-81525 MACK
81526-81526 PALISADE
81527-81527 WHITEWATER
81601-81602 GLENWOOD SPRINGS
81610-81610 DINOSAUR
81611-81612 ASPEN
81615-81615 SNOWMASS VILLAGE
81620-81620 AVON
81621-81621 BASALT
81623-81623 CARBONDALE
81624-81624 COLLBRAN
81625-81626 CRAIG
81628-81628 EL JEBEL
81630-81630 DE BEQUE
81631-81631 EAGLE
81632-81632 EDWARDS
81633-81633 DINOSAUR
81635-81635 PARACHUTE
81636-81636 BATTLEMENT MESA
81637-81637 GYPSUM
81638-81638 HAMILTON
81639-81639 HAYDEN
81640-81640 MAYBELL
81641-81641 MEEKER
81642-81642 MEREDITH
81643-81643 MESA
81645-81645 MINTURN
81646-81646 MOLINA
81647-81647 NEW CASTLE
81648-81648 RANGELY
81649-81649 RED CLIFF
81650-81650 RIFLE
81652-81652 SILT
81653-81653 SLATER
81654-81654 SNOWMASS
81655-81655 WOLCOTT
81656-81656 WOODY CREEK
81657-81658 VAIL

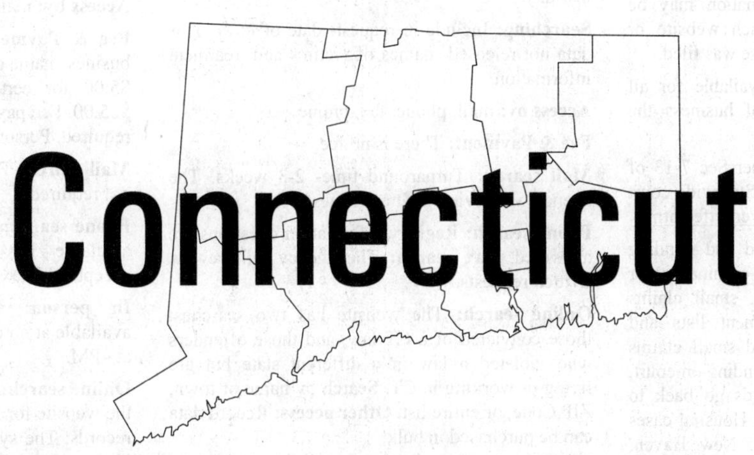

Connecticut

General Help Numbers:

Governor's Office

State Capitol, 210 Capitol Ave — 860-566-4840
Hartford, CT 06106 — Fax 860-566-4677
www.ct.gov/governorrell/site/default.asp — 8AM-5PM

Attorney General's Office

PO Box 120 — 860-808-5318
Hartford, CT 06141-0120 — Fax 860-808-5387
www.ct.gov/ag/site/default.asp — 8:30AM-4:30PM

Legislative Records

State Library, Bill Room 231 — 860-757-6550
Hartford, CT 06106 — Fax 860-757-6594
www.cga.ct.gov — 9AM-5PM

State Archives

History & Genealogy Unit — 860-757-6580
231 Capitol Ave — Fax 860-757-6677
Hartford, CT 06106 — 9AM-5PM M-F; 9AM-2PM SAT
www.cslib.org/archives/

State Specifics:

Capital:	**Hartford**
	Hartford County
Time Zone:	**EST**
Number of Counties:	**8**
Population:	**3,501,252**
Website:	**www.ct.gov**

State Agencies

Criminal Records

Department of Public Safety, Bureau of Identification, 1111 Country Club Rd, Middletown, CT 06457; 860-685-8480, Fax- 860-685-8361; 8:30AM-4:30PM.

www.ct.gov/dps/site/default.asp

DPS-846-C Form "State Police Bureau of Identification Request" can be downloaded from the website.

Indexing & Storage: Records available from the 1950's on. Records were first computerized in 1983. New records available for inquiry in about 30 days.

Searching: Records are open to the public using a name search. Fingerprint searches are not available to the public. Pending case information is available. Include in request- date of birth. Request forms may be downloaded from the website. Approximately 90% of the records on file are fingerprint supported. This data not released- dismissals or juvenile records. The records released to the public contain guilty pending and nolles if the nolle has not reached 13 months. Nolle over 13 months can appear if part of an indictment that contains a disposition.

Access by: mail, in person.

Fee & Payment: The fee is $25.00 per request. Fee payee- Commissioner of Public Safety. Prepayment required. Personal checks accepted, credit cards are not.

Mail search: Turnaround time- 7 to 10 days. Records must be in writing. SASE helpful.

In person: Request must be on agency form; results are mailed only. If you come in-person, the results are still mailed.

Statewide Court Records

Chief Court Administrator, 231 Capitol Ave, Hartford, CT 06106; 860-757-2100, 860-757-2270

(External Affairs), Fax- 860-757-2130; 8AM-5PM. www.jud.ct.gov/

Requests for specific case information may be requested from the Judicial Branch website or from the clerk's office where the case was filed.

Indexing & Storage: Records available for all data entry completed by close of business the previous day.

Searching: Records are retained per Sec 7-13 of Superior Court General provision. Statewide court fees www.jud.ct.gov/external/super/courtfee.htm.

Online search: Look up disposed and pending docket information for civil/family, criminal/motor vehicle, housing (landlord-tenant), small claims www.jud.ct.gov/jud2.htm. Assignment lists and calendars also available. Civil and small claims records go back 1 to 10 years, depending on court. Criminal and motor vehicle records go back to 01/01/2000 for date of disposition. Housing cases only available from the Hartford, New Haven, New Britain, Bridgeport, Norwalk and Waterbury districts. Opinions from Supreme and Appellate courts at www.jud.state.ct.us/opinions.htm.

Other access: Information may be purchased in bulk through the Information Technology Division - 860-282-6403.

Statewide Court Records - Records Center

Connecticut Record Center, 111 Phoenix Ave, Enfield, CT 06082; 860-741-3714; 9AM-5PM.

www.jud.state.ct.us

Case records are sent to the Record Center from 3 months to 5 years after disposition by the courts. These records are then maintained 10 years for misdemeanors and 20+ years for felonies.

Indexing & Storage: Records available for all data entry completed by close of business the previous day.

Searching: This agency only pulls case files; it does NOT do name searches. If a requester is certain that the record is at the Record Center, it is quicker to direct the request here rather than to the original court of record. Include in request- full defendant name, docket number, disposition date, and court action. Requests are only accepted in writing or in person.

Access by: mail, in person.

Fee & Payment: Fee is $3.00 for each docket, $5.00 if certified. If in person, the fee is $1.00 per page plus certification. Fee payee- Treasurer-State of Connecticut Personal checks must have name and address printed on the check; if requesting in person, check must have same address as drivers' license.

Mail search: Need either docket number or case number. **In person:** Counter service is available for simple search requests.

Sexual Offender Registry

Department of Public Safety, Sex Offender Registry Unit, 1111 Country Club Rd, Middletown, CT 06457; 860-685-8060, Fax- 860-685-8349; 8:30AM-4:30PM.

www.ct.gov/dps/cwp/view.asp?a=2157&Q=294474&dpsNav=|

It is suggested to visit local law enforcement if you cannot search online. Email questions to sex.offender.registry@po.state.ct.us.

Indexing & Storage: Records available from October 1, 1988. New records available for inquiry in 1 day.

Searching: Include in request- date of birth. This data not released- names of victims and treatment information.

Access by: mail, phone, fax, online.

Fee & Payment: There is no fee.

Mail search: Turnaround time- 2-3 weeks. The agency will review written requests.

Phone search: Registry information questions are answered. **Fax search:** The agency will review written requests.

Online search: The website has two searches: those convicted of a CT law, and those offenders who violated a law in a different state but are living or working in CT. Search by name or town, ZIP Code, or entire list. **Other access:** Record data can be purchased in bulk.

Incarceration Records

Connecticut Department of Corrections, Public Information Office, 24 Wolcott Hill Rd, Wethersfield, CT 06109; 860-692-7780 (Locater), Fax- 860-692-7783; 8:30AM-4:30PM.

www.ct.gov/doc/site/default.asp

Direct questions to DOC.PIO@po.state.ct.us.

Indexing & Storage: Records available on current and former inmates, except for the website which is current only. Computerized records go back to 1974. Paper record kept from 1983. Prior records in state archives. New records available for inquiry in about 30 days.

Searching: Records are open to the public using a name search. Location, conviction and sentencing information, bond, and release dates are released. An FOI request must be submitted to access records for inmates not currently incarcerated. Include in request- name; DOB and SSN are helpful. This data not released- visiting lists,

Access by: mail, phone, online.

Fee & Payment: There is a $.25 fee to mail a search request. Fee payee- CT Department of Corrections Prepayment Required.

Mail search: Turnaround time- 7 to 10 days.

Phone search: For phone search, use the "Locater" number listed above.

Online search: Current inmates may be searched at www.ctinmateinfo.state.ct.us/searchop.asp.

Corporation, LP, LLC, LLP, Statutory Trust, Trademarks/Servicemarks

Secretary of State, Commercial Recording Division, 30 Trinity St, Hartford, CT 06106; 860-509-6002 (Research & Response Unit), 860-509-6003 (Document Review), Fax- 860-509-6069; 8:30AM-4:30PM.

www.sots.ct.gov/sots/site/default.asp

Assumed names and trade names are found at the town level.

Indexing & Storage: New records available for inquiry immediately.

Searching: Include in request- full name of business, specific records that you need copies of. In addition to the articles of organization, business entity records available include: Annual Reports, Officers, Directors, Prior (merged) names, Inactive and Reserved names.

Access by: mail, phone, fax, in person, online.

Fee & Payment: The search fee is $20.00 per business name document for copies on record. Add $5.00 for certification. A trademark search is $25.00. Fee payee- Secretary of State. Prepayment required. Personal checks, Visa/MC accepted.

Mail search: Turnaround time- 2 to 3 days. SASE not required.

Phone search: Only limited, basic information is available by phone. **Fax search:** Requests accepted by fax.

In person: Certain, limited information is available at no charge. Counter closes to the public at 4PM.

Online search: Click on the CONCORD option at the website for free access to corporation and UCC records. The system is open from 7AM to 11PM. You can search by business name, business ID or by filing number. The web also offers online filing. Go to www.concord-sots.ct.gov/CONCORD/index.jsp. Search securities division enforcement actions at www.ct.gov/dob/cwp/view.asp?a=2246&q=401762.

Expedited service: Expedited service is available on limited filings for an add'l $25.00 per business name. Turnaround time- 24 hours. The fee is per transaction requested; review is one transaction, copy is another, etc.

Uniform Commercial Code, Federal & State Tax Liens

UCC Division, Secretary of State, PO Box 150470, Hartford, CT 06115-0470 (Courier address- 30 Trinity St, Hartford, CT 06106); 860-509-6002, Fax- 860-509-6057; 8:30AM-4PM.

www.concord-sots.ct.gov/CONCORD/index.jsp

Also, this website is used: www.concord.sots.ct.gov/CONCORD/index.jsp

Indexing & Storage: Records available from 8/94 on computer, earlier records are on microfilm from 10/80. New records available for inquiry in one month or less.

Searching: Use search request form UCC-11. The search includes tax liens. Include in request- debtor name or original.

Access by: mail, fax, in person, online.

Fee & Payment: UCC searches include tax liens and are free if requested in person, $25.00 per name by mail. Copies are additional and are $20.00 for a plain copy or $25.00 for a certified copy. Fee payee- Secretary of State. Prepayment required. Credit cards are accepted for in-person searching only. Personal checks, Visa, and MasterCard accepted.

Mail search: Turnaround time- 3 to 5 days. SASE not required.

Fax search: Use of credit card required.

In person: A public access terminal for record look-up is available.

Online search: An free index search is offered at www.concord-sots.ct.gov/CONCORD/index.jsp.

Other access: Bulk lists and CDs are available for purchase. Call the Financial Area at 860-509-6165.

Sales Tax Registrations

Dept of Revenue - Taxpayer Services Division, Sales Tax Registrations, 25 Sigourney St, Hartford, CT 06106; 860-297-4885, Fax- 860-297-5714; 8AM-5PM.

www.ct.gov/drs/site/default.asp

Indexing & Storage: New records available for inquiry in up to 3 weeks.

Searching: This agency will only confirm that the business is registered and active. They will provide no other information. Include in request- business name. They will also search by tax permit number. Authorized business representatives may request copies of their records only by mail, fax, or in person.

Access by: mail, phone, fax, in person.

Fee & Payment: There is no search fee

Mail search: Turnaround time- 1 day.

Phone search: Records available by phone only to verify a permit was issued.

Fax search: Same criteria as mail searches.

In person: If the question is more than "has a permit been issued," the requester must have documents completed and have legal authority to make request.

Death Records

Department of Public Health, Vital Records Section MS# 11VRS, PO Box 340308, Hartford, CT 06134-0308 (Courier address- 410 Capitol Ave, Hartford, CT 06134); 860-509-7897, 860-509-7700, Fax- 860-509-7964; 8AM-4PM M-F.

www.ct.gov/dph/site/default.asp

Vital Records offices are located in each of the 169 towns in Connecticut. Certificate requests for events that occurred in Hartford must be directed to the City of Hartford Vital Records Registrar.

Indexing & Storage: Records available from 1897 to present.

Searching: Connecticut death certificates are available to the general public. Anyone over 18 years of age may request a copy of any Connecticut death certificate. Include in request- name of the decedent, the approximate date of death, and the town where the death occurred. The state indicates records may be obtained from this office or from the town/city clerk of occurrence for $10.00 each.

Access by: mail, in person.

Mail search: Turnaround time- 10-12 weeks.

In person: Counter gives immediate record services.

Expedited service: Expedited service is available for mail searches if sent overnight and overnight return supplied. You go to the top of the list. Turnaround time- 24-48 hours.

Birth Certificates

Department of Public Health, Vital Records Section MS# 11VRS, PO Box 340308, Hartford, CT 06134-0308 (Courier address- 410 Capitol Ave, Hartford, CT 06134); 860-509-7897, 860-509-7700, Fax- 860-509-7964; 8AM-4PM M-F.

www.ct.gov/dph/site/default.asp

Vital Records offices are located in each of the 169 towns in Connecticut. Certificate requests for events that occurred in Hartford must be directed to the City of Hartford Vital Records Registrar.

Indexing & Storage: Records available from 1897 to present are at this office.

Searching: Records 100 years or older are available to the public. If less than 100 years, requester must be registrant, family, attorney with authorization, or member of an incorporated genealogical society. Include in request- mother's name (include maiden), father's name, place of birth, date of birth. The state indicates records may be obtained from the town/city clerk of occurrence for $10.00 each, $5.00 for wallet size. The fee to obtain a birth record from this office is $15.00 per record. This data not released- paternity, adoption, gender change, gestational agreements not released without court order.

Access by: mail, in person.

Mail search: Turnaround time- 6 months.

In person: Counter gives immediate record services.

Expedited service: Expedited service is available for mail searches if sent overnight and overnight return supplied. You go to the top of the list. Turnaround time- 24-48 hours.

Marriage Certificates

Department of Public Health, Vital Records Section MS# 11VRS, PO Box 340308, Hartford, CT 06134-0308 (Courier address- 410 Capitol Ave, Hartford, CT 06134); 860-509-7897, 860-509-7700, Fax- 860-509-7964; 8AM-4PM M-F.

www.ct.gov/dph/site/default.asp

Vital Records offices are located in each of the 169 towns in Connecticut. Certificate requests for events that occurred in Hartford must be directed to the City of Hartford Vital Records Registrar.

Indexing & Storage: Records available from 1897 to present.

Searching: Marriage certificates and civil union certificates are open to the general public. Anyone over 18 years of age may request a copy of any certificate. Include in request- names of the wife and husband, the approximate date of marriage, and the town in which the marriage took place. The state indicates records may be obtained from this office or from the town/city clerk of occurrence for $10.00 each.

Access by: mail.

Mail search: Turnaround time- 10-12 weeks.

Expedited service: Expedited service is available for mail searches if sent overnight and overnight return supplied. You go to the top of the list. Turnaround time- 24-48 hours.

Divorce Records

Access to Records is Restricted.

Department of Public Health, Vital Records Section MS# 11VRS, PO Box 340308, Hartford, CT 06134-0308 (Courier address- 410 Capitol Ave, Hartford, CT 06134); 860-509-7897, 860-509-7700, Fax- 860-509-7964; 8AM-4PM M-F.

www.ct.gov/dph/site/default.asp

To obtain a copy of a Divorce Decree or Dissolution of Civil Union Decree, one must request it from the Superior Court where the divorce or dissolution was granted. The state agency only has an index of records; copies of the original certificates must be obtained from the town or city where the divorce was recorded.

Workers' Compensation Records

Workers Compensation Commission, 21 Oak Street, Hartford, CT 06106; 860-493-1500, Fax-860-247-1361; 7:45AM-4:30PM.

http://wcc.state.ct.us

All files are kept at one of the eight district offices. This agency will forward the request to the proper district office, or you can order direct from the D. Office. Requesters with authorization may email requests to peter.miecznikowski@ct.gov

Indexing & Storage: Records available on microfilm from 1914 thru 1985 and computerized from 1985 forward, for insurance coverage files. The case files since 1995 are indexed on computer. Records are not destroyed. New records available for inquiry in 1 month.

Searching: Include in request- claimant name, SSN (if available), date of injury, name and address of employer. Include as much information as possible. This data not released- medical records, commissioner's notes.

Access by: mail, phone, fax, in person.

Fee & Payment: Fees vary depending upon the nature of the request and are determined at that time. Fee payee- Workers Compensation Commission. Personal checks accepted, credit cards are not.

Mail search: Turnaround time- variable. A SASE is requested.

Phone search: You may call for information.

Fax search: Fax requests are accepted.

In person: Counter service available.

Other access: The agency will sell self-insured lists for $5.00.

Driver Records

Department of Motor Vehicles, Copy Records Unit, 60 State St., Wethersfield, CT 06161-0503; 860-263-5154; 8:30AM-4:30PM T-F.

www.ct.gov/dmv/site/default.asp

Copies of tickets may be obtained from the Superior Court Records Center, 860-741-3714 for a fee of $3.00, or $5.00 for certified copy.

Indexing & Storage: Records available for 3/5/10 years to present, dependent upon the type of violation. New records available for inquiry in 5 to 7 days.

Searching: Mail and in person requesters must complete Form J-23 and state permissible use. Casual requests must include evidence of the individual's consent and form. The form can be ordered from the web or by calling 860-263-5700. Include in request- two forms of ID (one with photo), signed Form J-23. The driver's license number, name and address are needed when searching, the DOB is optional. A DWI first offense violation will not appear if the offender attends an "Accelerated Alcohol Class." This data not released- address

Access by: mail, in person, online.

Fee & Payment: The fee for walk-in or mail-in driving records is $20.00 per record (the highest fee in the US for a driving record). The fee for ordering online is $15.00. The fee for a license status check is $20.00. Fee payee- Department of Motor Vehicles. Prepayment required. Personal checks accepted, credit cards are not.

Mail search: Turnaround time- 2 weeks. A SASE is suggested for faster turnaround time.

In person: The state will process up to 3 requests (at one time) for walk-in requesters who have a permissible use as stipulated in C.G.S.#14-10. Please note the office is closed on Mondays.

Online search: Electronic access is provided to approved businesses that enter into written contract. The contract requires a $37,500 prepayment deposit for the first 2,500 records. Fee is $15.00 per record. The address is part of the record. For more information, call 203-805-6093. Also, search disposed conviction and bond forfeitures at www.jud2.ct.gov/crdockets/SearchByDefDisp.aspx by Geographical Area court. Links include pending case lookup pages and docket/calendar lookup pages.

Other access: Batch requests are available for approved users, call 203-805-6093 for details.

Vehicle Ownership & Registration

Department of Motor Vehicles, Copy Record Unit, 60 State St,, Wethersfield, CT 06161-1896; 860-263-5154; 8:AM-4:30PM T- F.

www.ct.gov/dmv/site/default.asp

Section 14-10 of the Connecticut General Statutes regulates the release of record information in accordance with federal DPPA guidelines.

Indexing & Storage: Records available for 3 years to present. Any records prior to this period may be destroyed at the discretion of the commissioner. New records available for inquiry in six weeks.

Searching: Permissible users of the information are listed on back of Form J-23. Otherwise, requester must include evidence of subject's written consent. Form J-23 can be ordered from the website or obtained by calling 860-263-5700. Include in request- name and plate number, or plate number and description (VIN is helpful). Requester must submit two forms of ID and one must contain a photo of the person signing the Form. Name searches and license plate searches are available to J-23 approved requesters.

Access by: mail, in person.

Fee & Payment: Record searches are $20.00 each, including title, lien, and current owner searches. Certification is an additional $20.00. A full charge is for a "no record found." Fee payee- Department of Motor Vehicles. Prepayment required. Personal checks accepted, credit cards are not.

Mail search: Turnaround time- 3 to 4 working days. The agency requests that you use their Form J-23. A SASE is not requested.

In person: The state will process up to 3 requests (file information only) for walk-in customers. Drop off requests accepted. Please note the office is closed on Mondays.

Other access: Vehicle record information is available on a volume basis to approved businesses that enter into a written agreement. The contract requires an annual fee and a surety bond. For more information, call 203-805-6093.

Accident Reports

Department of Public Safety, Reports and Records Unit, 1111 Country Club Rd, Middletown, CT 06457; 860-685-8250; 8:30AM-4:30PM.

www.ct.gov/dps/cwp/view.asp?a=2154&Q=294426&dpsNav=|

Indexing & Storage: Records available from 10 years to present. Searching by name only goes back 5 years.

Searching: Include in request- date and location of incident, names of operators, and the 8 digit case number (if known). Use Form DPS-96-C "Request for Copy of Report." This is found on the web. This data not released- pending cases or sealed records.

Access by: mail.

Fee & Payment: Prepayment of the $8.00 search fee per uncertified record is required. The fee for a certified record is $9.00. Fee payee- Commissioner of Public Safety. Personal checks accepted, credit cards are not.

Mail search: Turnaround time- 4 to 6 weeks. A SASE is requested.

Vessel Ownership & Registration

Department of Motor Vehicles, Marine Vessel Section, 60 State Street, Wethersfield, CT 06161-3032; 860-263-5151, Fax- 860-263-5555; 8AM-5PM T-F; til 12:30 PM Sat.

www.ct.gov/dmv/cwp/view.asp?A=818&Q=245044

Lien information is found at the Secretary of State.

Indexing & Storage: Records available from 1982, records are maintained on computer for 4 years then placed on microfiche. All motorized boats any length, and all vessels over 19.5 ft without motor must be registered. New records available for inquiry in within minutes.

Searching: All requests must be in writing. Requests follow requirements of DPPA. Use Form J-23B. Include in request- photo ID and money. Either the name, CT registration number or hull number is needed to do a search. This data not released- SSN

Access by: mail, in person.

Fee & Payment: The fee is $20.00 for a current owner search or for a copy of the registration for a complete boat history. Certification is an additional $20.00. Fee payee- Department of Motor Vehicles. Prepayment required. Personal checks accepted, credit cards are not.

Mail search: Turnaround time- 1 to 2 weeks. SASE not required.

In person: In some instances, results are returned by mail. The agency is closed to the public on Mondays.

Other access: Bulk list information is available by contract and DPPA standards. The fee depends on data requested. Call 860-263-5241 for ordering procedures.

Legislation Records

Connecticut General Assembly, State Library, Bill Room at State Library, 231 Capitol Ave, Hartford, CT 06106; 860-757-6550, Fax- 860-757-6594; 9AM-5PM. www.cga.ct.gov

Indexing & Storage: Records available from 1991 on the web, older records are archived. New records available for inquiry in 2 weeks.

Voter Registration

Secretary of State, Election Services Division, 30 Trinity Street, 2nd Fl, Hartford, CT 06106; 860-509-6100.

www.sots.ct.gov/sots/site/default.asp

A statewide database is available to the public. Presently records are open at the town level. There are 169 towns.

Searching: This data not released- DOB, SSN.

Access by: mail, in person.

Mail search: Name requests are accepted if list not extensive.

In person: Same day counter service available.

Other access: An electronic file of all registered voters is available for $300. The agency does not offer geographic customization.

GED Certificates

Department of Education, GED Records, 25 Industrial Park Rd, Middletown, CT 06457; 860-807-2110, 860-807-2111+, Fax- 860-807-2112; 8AM-5PM.

www.sde.ct.gov/sde/site/default.asp

Indexing & Storage: New records available for inquiry in 6 weeks.

Searching: Include in request- signed release, SSN; date of birth is helpful. The year of the test is helpful. For records prior to 1982, the location of the test is needed.

Access by: mail, fax, in person.

Fee & Payment: There is no search fee.

Mail search: Turnaround time- 2 to 3 days. SASE not required.

Fax search: There is no fee to fax back to a local phone number. For Transcript Request form go to www.sde.ct.gov/sde/cwp/view.asp?a=2620&Q=320688&dsftns=45490

In person: Photo ID is required.

Hunting & Fishing License Information

Department of Environmental Protection, License Division, 79 Elm St, Hartford, CT 06106; 860-424-3105, Fax- 860-424-4122; 9AM-4PM.

www.ct.gov/dep/site/default.asp

Indexing & Storage: Records available for 5 years to present to present. New records available for inquiry in 1 day.

Searching: Only deer and turkey tag information is released. Include in request- full name, address. All requests must be in writing.

Access by: mail, in person.

Fee & Payment: There is no search fee. Copies are $.25 per page. Fee payee- Department of Environmental Protection. Prepayment required. Personal checks accepted, credit cards are not.

Mail search: Turnaround time- 1 to 3 days. SASE not required.

In person: Must have the request in writing.

Other access: CDs are available, usually $50.00 per disk.

Connecticut State Licensing Agencies

For details about the agency responsible for licensing/certifying/registering an item below or in the Agency Quick Finder section, match an item's number with the number of the agency in the *Licensing Agency Information* section.

Connecticut Licenses Searchable Online

Accounting Firm #16 .... www.sboalicense.ct.gov/cpalookup/Default.aspx
Acupuncturist #11 .... www.dir.ct.gov/dph/Scripts/hlthprof.asp
Alcohol/Drug Counselor #11 .... www.dir.ct.gov/dph/Scripts/hlthprof.asp
Antenna Svcs Dealer/Technician #5 .... https://www.ask-dcp.ct.gov/lookup/default.asp
Apple Product Mfg #8 .... https://www.ask-dcp.ct.gov/lookup/default.asp
Appraiser, MVPD/MVR #2 .... www.ct-clic.com
Architect #3 .... https://www.ask-dcp.ct.gov/lookup/default.asp
Architectural Firm #3 .... https://www.ask-dcp.ct.gov/lookup/default.asp
Asbestos Consultant/Contractor #30 .... www.dir.ct.gov/dph/Scripts/hlthprof.asp
Asbestos Worker/Supvr. #30 .... www.dir.ct.gov/dph/Scripts/hlthprof.asp
Association Manager #17 .... https://www.ask-dcp.ct.gov/lookup/default.asp
Athletic Promoter #7 .... https://www.ask-dcp.ct.gov/lookup/default.asp
Attorney/Attorney Firm #1 .... http://civilinquiry.jud.ct.gov/AttorneyFirmInquiry.aspx
Audiologist #11 .... www.dir.ct.gov/dph/Scripts/hlthprof.asp
Automobile Glass Technician #4 .... https://www.ask-dcp.ct.gov/lookup/default.asp
Automobile Insurance Adjuster #2 .... www.ct-clic.com
Bail Bond Agent #2 .... www.ct-clic.com
Bail Bondsman #13 .... www.ct.gov/dps/lib/dps/special_licensing_and_firearms/licensed_bondsman.pdf
Bail Enforcement Agent #13 .... www.ct.gov/dps/lib/dps/special_licensing_and_firearms/licensed_bea.pdf
Bail Enforcement Instructor #13 .... www.ct.gov/dps/lib/dps/special_licensing_and_firearms/bea_instructors.pdf
Bakery #8 .... https://www.ask-dcp.ct.gov/lookup/default.asp
Bank and/or Trust Company #6 .... www.ct.gov/dob/cwp/view.asp?a=2239&Q=298138&dobNAV_GID=1659&dobNav=|
Bank Branch #6 .... www.ct.gov/dob/cwp/view.asp?a=2239&Q=298138&dobNAV_GID=1659&dobNav=|
Bank CEO #6 .... www.ct.gov/dob/cwp/view.asp?a=2239&Q=298138&dobNAV_GID=1659&dobNav=|
Banking Office, Non-depository #6 .... www.ct.gov/dob/cwp/view.asp?a=2239&Q=298138&dobNAV_GID=1659&dobNav=|
Barber #11 .... www.dir.ct.gov/dph/Scripts/hlthprof.asp
Bazaar/Raffle Permit #12 .... www.ct-clic.com/
Bedding Mfg/Renovation #4 .... https://www.ask-dcp.ct.gov/lookup/default.asp
Bedding Supply/Sterilizer #4 .... https://www.ask-dcp.ct.gov/lookup/default.asp
Beekeeper #14 .... www.ct.gov/caes/site/default.asp
Beverage/Water Bottler #4 .... https://www.ask-dcp.ct.gov/lookup/default.asp
Bingo Registration #12 .... www.ct-clic.com/
Bottler, Non-Alcohol #8 .... https://www.ask-dcp.ct.gov/lookup/default.asp
Boxer/Boxing Professional #7 .... https://www.ask-dcp.ct.gov/lookup/default.asp
Building Contractor #7 .... https://www.ask-dcp.ct.gov/lookup/default.asp
Casino #12 .... www.ct-clic.com/
Casino Occupation #12 .... www.ct-clic.com/
Casualty Adjuster #2 .... www.ct-clic.com
Caterer/Concessioner, Liquor #15 .... https://www.ask-dcp.ct.gov/lookup/default.asp
Check Cashing Service #6 .... www.ct.gov/dob/cwp/view.asp?a=2239&Q=298138&dobNAV_GID=1659&dobNav=|
Chiropractor #11 .... www.dir.ct.gov/dph/Scripts/hlthprof.asp
Closing Out Sale #4 .... https://www.ask-dcp.ct.gov/lookup/default.asp
Collection Agency #6 .... www.ct.gov/dob/cwp/view.asp?a=2239&Q=298138&dobNAV_GID=1659&dobNav=|
College/University #28 .... www.ctdhe.org/database/default.htm
Contractor, Major #4 .... https://www.ask-dcp.ct.gov/lookup/default.asp
Contractor, Mechanical #4 .... https://www.ask-dcp.ct.gov/lookup/default.asp
Controlled Substance Lab #44 .... https://www.ask-dcp.ct.gov/lookup/default.asp
Cosmetologist #11 .... www.ct.gov/dph/site/default.asp
Counselor, Professional #11 .... www.ct.gov/dph/site/default.asp
Credit Union #6 .... www.ct.gov/dob/cwp/view.asp?a=2239&Q=298138&dobNAV_GID=1659&dobNav=|
Debt Adjuster #6 .... www.ct.gov/dob/cwp/view.asp?a=2239&Q=298138&dobNAV_GID=1659&dobNav=|
Dental Anes./Sedation Permittee #11 .... www.dir.ct.gov/dph/Scripts/hlthprof.asp
Dentist/Dental Hygienist #11 .... www.dir.ct.gov/dph/Scripts/hlthprof.asp
Dessert Mfg, Frozen #8 .... https://www.ask-dcp.ct.gov/lookup/default.asp
Dietician/Nutritionist #11 .... www.dir.ct.gov/dph/Scripts/hlthprof.asp
Dog Racing Owner/Trainer #12 .... www.ct-clic.com/

Drug/Cosmetic Whlse/Mfg #44 .... https://www.ask-dcp.ct.gov/lookup/default.asp
Druggist Liquor Permittee #15 .... https://www.ask-dcp.ct.gov/lookup/default.asp
Electrical Contr./Inspector #7 .... https://www.ask-dcp.ct.gov/lookup/default.asp
Electrical Journeyman/Apprentice #4 .... https://www.ask-dcp.ct.gov/lookup/default.asp
Electrical Sign Installer #7 .... https://www.ask-dcp.ct.gov/lookup/default.asp
Electrician #7 .... https://www.ask-dcp.ct.gov/lookup/default.asp
Electrologist/Hypertricologist #11 .... www.dir.ct.gov/dph/Scripts/hlthprof.asp
Electronics Service Dealer/Tech. #5 .... https://www.ask-dcp.ct.gov/lookup/default.asp
Elevator Inspector/Mechanic #4 .... https://www.ask-dcp.ct.gov/lookup/default.asp
Embalmer #11 .... www.dir.ct.gov/dph/Scripts/hlthprof.asp
Emergency Med. Svc Professional #11 .... www.dir.ct.gov/dph/Scripts/hlthprof.asp
EMS First Responder #11 .... www.dir.ct.gov/dph/Scripts/hlthprof.asp
EMS Instructor #11 .... www.dir.ct.gov/dph/Scripts/hlthprof.asp
Engineer #4 .... https://www.ask-dcp.ct.gov/lookup/default.asp
Engineer-in-Training #4 .... https://www.ask-dcp.ct.gov/lookup/default.asp
Fire Protection Inspector/Contractor #4 .... https://www.ask-dcp.ct.gov/lookup/default.asp
Fire Sprinkler Technician #4 .... https://www.ask-dcp.ct.gov/lookup/default.asp
Funeral Director/Home #11 .... www.dir.ct.gov/dph/Scripts/hlthprof.asp
Gasoline Dealer, Retail #8 .... https://www.ask-dcp.ct.gov/lookup/default.asp
Glazier #4 .... https://www.ask-dcp.ct.gov/lookup/default.asp
Hairdresser #11 .... www.dir.ct.gov/dph/Scripts/hlthprof.asp
Health Care Center Insurer #2 .... www.ct-clic.com
Health Club #4 .... https://www.ask-dcp.ct.gov/lookup/default.asp
Hearing Instrument Specialist #11 .... www.dir.ct.gov/dph/Scripts/hlthprof.asp
Heating/Piping/Cooling Cont./Journ'y'n #4 https://www.ask-dcp.ct.gov/lookup/default.asp
Home Heating Oil Seller #8 .... https://www.ask-dcp.ct.gov/lookup/default.asp
Home Improvement Contr./Seller #4 .... https://www.ask-dcp.ct.gov/lookup/default.asp
Home Inspector #4 .... https://www.ask-dcp.ct.gov/lookup/default.asp
Homemaker Companion #4 .... https://www.ask-dcp.ct.gov/lookup/default.asp
Homeopathic Physician #11 .... www.dir.ct.gov/dph/Scripts/hlthprof.asp
Honey Bee Registration #14 .... www.ct.gov/caes/site/default.asp
Hypnotist #4 .... https://www.ask-dcp.ct.gov/lookup/default.asp
Insurance Adjuster/Public Adjuster #2 ...... www.ct-clic.com
Insurance Agent, Fraternal #2 .... www.ct-clic.com
Insurance Appraiser #2 .... www.ct-clic.com
Insurance Company/Producer #2 .... www.ct-clic.com
Insurance Consultant #2 .... www.ct-clic.com
Interior Designer #4 .... https://www.ask-dcp.ct.gov/lookup/default.asp
Interstate Land Sale #17 .... https://www.ask-dcp.ct.gov/lookup/default.asp
Investment Advisor/Agent #6 .... www.ct.gov/dob/cwp/view.asp?a=2239&Q=298138&dobNAV_GID=1659&dobNav=|
Juice Producer #8 .... https://www.ask-dcp.ct.gov/lookup/default.asp
Land Sale, Interstate #17 .... https://www.ask-dcp.ct.gov/lookup/default.asp
Land Surveyor/Surveyor Firm #3 .... https://www.ask-dcp.ct.gov/lookup/default.asp
Landscape Architect #3 .... https://www.ask-dcp.ct.gov/lookup/default.asp
Lead Consultant #30 .... www.dir.ct.gov/dph/Scripts/hlthprof.asp
Legalized Gaming Occupation #12 .... www.ct-clic.com/
Liquor License/Permittee #15 .... https://www.ask-dcp.ct.gov/lookup/default.asp
Liquor Mfg/Dist/Whlse #15 .... https://www.ask-dcp.ct.gov/lookup/default.asp
Liquor Store/Broker/Shipper #15 .... https://www.ask-dcp.ct.gov/lookup/default.asp
Loan Company, Small #6 .... www.ct.gov/dob/cwp/view.asp?a=2239&Q=298138&dobNAV_GID=1659&dobNav=|
Lottery/Lottery Sales Agent #12 .... www.ct-clic.com/
Marriage & Family Therapist #11 .... www.dir.ct.gov/dph/Scripts/hlthprof.asp
Marshall, State #33 .... www.jud.ct.gov/faq/marshals.htm
Martial Arts Facility #4 .... https://www.ask-dcp.ct.gov/lookup/default.asp
Massage Therapist #11 .... www.dir.ct.gov/dph/Scripts/hlthprof.asp
Mausoleum #11 .... www.dir.ct.gov/dph/Scripts/hlthprof.asp
Medical Doctor #11 .... www.dir.ct.gov/dph/Scripts/hlthprof.asp
Medical Gas/Vacuum System #4 .... https://www.ask-dcp.ct.gov/lookup/default.asp
Medical Response Technician #11 .... www.dir.ct.gov/dph/Scripts/hlthprof.asp
Midwife #11 .... www.dir.ct.gov/dph/Scripts/hlthprof.asp
Midwife Nurse #11 .... www.dir.ct.gov/dph/Scripts/hlthprof.asp
Mobile Home Park/Seller #17 .... https://www.ask-dcp.ct.gov/lookup/default.asp
Money Forwarder #6 .... www.ct.gov/dob/cwp/view.asp?a=2239&Q=298138&dobNAV_GID=1659&dobNav=|
Money Order/Travelers Check Issuer #6 .. www.ct.gov/dob/cwp/view.asp?a=2233&q=297862&dobNAV_GID=1663
Mortgage Broker/Lender #6 .... www.ct.gov/dob/cwp/view.asp?a=2239&Q=298138&dobNAV_GID=1659&dobNav=|

Naturopathic Physician #11 .... www.dir.ct.gov/dph/Scripts/hlthprof.asp
New Home Construction Contr. #4 .... https://www.ask-dcp.ct.gov/lookup/default.asp
Nurse #11 .... www.dir.ct.gov/dph/Scripts/hlthprof.asp
Nurse, Advance Registered Practice #11 . www.dir.ct.gov/dph/Scripts/hlthprof.asp
Nurse-LPN #11 .... www.dir.ct.gov/dph/Scripts/hlthprof.asp
Nursery Plant Dealer #14 .... www.ct.gov/caes/site/default.asp
Nursery, Plant #14 .... www.ct.gov/caes/site/default.asp
Nursing Home Administrator #11 .... www.dir.ct.gov/dph/Scripts/hlthprof.asp
Occupational Therapist/Assistant #11 .... www.dir.ct.gov/dph/Scripts/hlthprof.asp
Off-Track Betting #12 .... www.ct-clic.com/
Optical Shop #11 .... www.dir.ct.gov/dph/Scripts/hlthprof.asp
Optician #11 .... www.dir.ct.gov/dph/Scripts/hlthprof.asp
Optometrist #11 .... www.dir.ct.gov/dph/Scripts/hlthprof.asp
Osteopathic Physician #11 .... www.dir.ct.gov/dph/Scripts/hlthprof.asp
Paramedic #11 .... www.dir.ct.gov/dph/Scripts/hlthprof.asp
Perfusionist #11 .... www.dir.ct.gov/dph/Scripts/hlthprof.asp
Pesticide Applicator #25 .... www.kellysolutions.com/CT/Applicators/index.htm
Pesticide-related Business #25 .... www.kellysolutions.com/CT/Business/index.htm
Pharmacist/Pharmacist Intern #44 .... https://www.ask-dcp.ct.gov/lookup/default.asp
Pharmacy/Pharmacy Technician #44 .... https://www.ask-dcp.ct.gov/lookup/default.asp
Physical Therapist/Assistant #11 .... www.dir.ct.gov/dph/Scripts/hlthprof.asp
Physician #11 .... www.dir.ct.gov/dph/Scripts/hlthprof.asp
Physician Assistant #11 .... www.dir.ct.gov/dph/Scripts/hlthprof.asp
Pipefitter #7 .... https://www.ask-dcp.ct.gov/lookup/default.asp
Plumber #4 .... https://www.ask-dcp.ct.gov/lookup/default.asp
Podiatrist #11 .... www.dir.ct.gov/dph/Scripts/hlthprof.asp
Premium Finance Company #2 .... www.ct-clic.com
Private Detective Company #13 .... www.ct.gov/dps/lib/dps/special_licensing_and_firearms/licensed_pi_security_companies.pdf
Private Investigator #13 .... www.ct.gov/dps/lib/dps/special_licensing_and_firearms/licensed_pi_security_companies.pdf
Private Occupational School #28 .... www.ctdhe.org/database/default.htm
Psychologist #11 .... www.dir.ct.gov/dph/Scripts/hlthprof.asp
Public Accountant-CPA #16 .... www.sboalicense.ct.gov/cpalookup/Default.aspx
Public Service Technician #4 .... https://www.ask-dcp.ct.gov/lookup/default.asp
Radiographer #11 .... www.dir.ct.gov/dph/Scripts/hlthprof.asp
Real Estate Agent/Broker/Sales #17 .... https://www.ask-dcp.ct.gov/lookup/default.asp
Real Estate Appraiser #17 .... https://www.ask-dcp.ct.gov/lookup/default.asp
Real Estate Educ. Provider #17 .... https://www.ask-dcp.ct.gov/lookup/default.asp
Reinsurance Intermediary #2 .... www.ct-clic.com
Rental Car Company #2 .... www.ct-clic.com
Respiratory Care Practitioner #11 .... www.dir.ct.gov/dph/Scripts/hlthprof.asp
Risk Purchasing/Retention Group #2 .... www.ct-clic.com
Sales Finance Company #6 .... www.ct.gov/dob/cwp/view.asp?a=2239&Q=298138&dobNAV_GID=1659&dobNav=|
Sanitarian #11 .... www.dir.ct.gov/dph/Scripts/hlthprof.asp
Savings & Loan Association Bank #6 .... www.ct.gov/dob/cwp/view.asp?a=2239&Q=298138&dobNAV_GID=1659&dobNav=|
Savings Bank #6 .... www.ct.gov/dob/cwp/view.asp?a=2239&Q=298138&dobNAV_GID=1659&dobNav=|
School Principal/Superintendent #9 .... www.csde.state.ct.us/public/csde/reports/SuperintendentContacts.asp
Securities Agent #6 .... www.finra.org/index.htm
Securities Broker/Dealer #6 .... www.finra.org/index.htm
Security Company Firearms Instructor #1
... www.ct.gov/dps/lib/dps/special_licensing_and_firearms/certified_security_officers_firearms_instructors-blue_cards.pdf
Security Company, Private #13 .... www.ct.gov/dps/lib/dps/special_licensing_and_firearms/licensed_pi_security_companies.pdf
Security Officer Instructor #13
... www.ct.gov/dps/lib/dps/special_licensing_and_firearms/approved_cj_security_instructor_(public).pdf
Security Service #13 .... www.ct.gov/dps/lib/dps/special_licensing_and_firearms/licensed_pi_security_companies.pdf
Sheet Metal Contr./Journeyman #4 .... https://www.ask-dcp.ct.gov/lookup/default.asp
Shorthand Court Reporter #4 .... https://www.ask-dcp.ct.gov/lookup/default.asp
Social Worker #11 .... www.dir.ct.gov/dph/Scripts/hlthprof.asp
Solar Energy Contr./Journeyman #4 .... https://www.ask-dcp.ct.gov/lookup/default.asp
Speech Pathologist #11 .... www.dir.ct.gov/dph/Scripts/hlthprof.asp
Sprinkler Layout Technician #4 .... https://www.ask-dcp.ct.gov/lookup/default.asp
Student Athlete Agent #4 .... https://www.ask-dcp.ct.gov/lookup/default.asp
Surplus Lines Broker #2 .... www.ct-clic.com
Surveyor, Land #3 .... https://www.ask-dcp.ct.gov/lookup/default.asp
Telecommunication Technician #4 .... https://www.ask-dcp.ct.gov/lookup/default.asp
Television/Radio License #4 .... https://www.ask-dcp.ct.gov/lookup/default.asp

Utilization Review Company #2	www.ct-clic.com
Vehicle Dealer/Repairer #26	www.ct.gov/dmv/cwp/view.asp?a=799&q=401814&dmvPNavCtr=|#48712
Vending Machine Operator #8	https://www.ask-dcp.ct.gov/lookup/default.asp
Vendor, Itinerant #4	https://www.ask-dcp.ct.gov/lookup/default.asp
Veterinarian #11	www.dir.ct.gov/dph/Scripts/hlthprof.asp
Viatical Settlement Broker/Provider #2	www.ct-clic.com
Water Bottler #8	https://www.ask-dcp.ct.gov/lookup/default.asp
Water Distribution System Operator #11	www.dir.ct.gov/dph/Scripts/hlthprof.asp
Water Treatment Plant Operator #11	www.dir.ct.gov/dph/Scripts/hlthprof.asp
Weigher #8	https://www.ask-dcp.ct.gov/lookup/default.asp
Weights/Measures Dealer/Repair/Reg'r #8	https://www.ask-dcp.ct.gov/lookup/default.asp
Well Driller #7	https://www.ask-dcp.ct.gov/lookup/default.asp
Winery Farm #15	https://www.ask-dcp.ct.gov/lookup/default.asp
Wrestler/Wrestling Manager #7	https://www.ask-dcp.ct.gov/lookup/default.asp

Connecticut Licensing Quick Finder

Accounting Firm #16	860-509-6179
Acupuncturist #11	860-509-7603
Air Emission Permittee #29	860-424-4152
Airport/Heliport #42	860-594-2000
Alcohol/Drug Counselor #11	860-509-7603
Ambulance #11	860-509-7603
Amusement Park #24	860-685-8470
Antenna Svcs Dealer/Technician #5	860-713-6000
Apple Product Mfg #8	860-713-6160
Appraiser, MVPD/MVR #2	860-297-3954
Aquaculture Operation #19	203-874-0696
Arborist #25	860-424-3369
Architect #3	860-713-6145
Architectural Firm #3	860-713-6145
Asbestos Consultant/Contractor #30	860-509-7559
Asbestos Worker/Supvr. #30	860-509-7559
Assisted Living Service #11	860-509-7400
Association Manager #17	860-713-6150
Athletic Promoter #7	860-566-6980
Attorney/Attorney Firm #1	860-568-5157
Audiologist #11	860-509-7603
Automobile Auction #43	203-805-6307
Automobile Glass Technician #4	860-713-6100
Automobile Insurance Adjuster #2	860-297-3954
Automobile Parts Mfg'r #26	860-263-5057
Automobile Racing Permit #26	860-263-5057
Automobile Renter/Leaser #26	860-263-5057
Backflow Tester #11	860-509-7333
Bail Bond Agent #2	860-297-3844
Bail Bondsman #13	860-685-8046
Bail Enforcement Agent #13	860-685-8046
Bail Enforcement Instructor #13	860-685-8046
Bait Seller, Live #10	860-424-3474
Bakery #8	860-713-6160
Bank and/orTrust Company #6	860-240-8299
Bank Branch #6	860-240-8299
Bank CEO #6	860-240-8299
Banking Office, Non-depository #6	860-240-8299
Barber #11	860-509-7603
Bazaar/Raffle Permit #12	860-594-5480
Bedding Mfg/Renovation #4	860-713-6100
Bedding Supply/Sterilizer #4	860-713-6123
Beekeeper #14	203-974-8500
Beverage/Water Bottler #4	860-713-6100
Bingo Registration #12	860-594-5480
Bird/Poultry Permit/Buyer #21	860-713-2512
Bottler, Non-Alcohol #8	860-713-6160
Boxer/Boxing Professional #7	860-713-6135
Building Contractor #7	860-566-2825
Building Inspector #32	860-685-8330
Building Official #24	860-685-8330
Bus Driver #22	860-263-5720
Business Opportunity Offering #6	860-240-8299
Car Dealer #26	860-263-5056
Carnival/Circus Operator #24	860-685-8470
Casino #12	860-594-0643
Casino Occupation #12	860-594-0643
Casualty Adjuster #2	860-297-3954
Caterer/Concessioner, Liquor #15	860-713-6200
Cattle/Swine Dealer #21	860-713-2512
Charitable Solicitor #35	860-808-5030
Charter Fishing Vessel #41	860-434-6043
Chauffeur/Livery Company #23	860-594-2916
Check Cashing Service #6	860-240-8299
Cheese Dealer #21	860-713-2512
Child Caring Agency/Facility #36	860-550-6445
Child Clinic (Well Child) #11	860-509-7444
Child Placing Agency #36	860-550-6445
Child Psychiatric Clinic #36	860-550-6445
Chiropractor #11	860-509-7603
Cigarette Seller/Distributor #20	860-297-5962
Closing Out Sale #4	860-713-6100
Coach, High/Grade School #9	860-713-6969
Coast/Tidal/Naviga'ble Waters Permit #31	860-424-3034
Collection Agency #6	860-240-8299
College/University #28	860-947-1822
Community Assoc. Manager #7	860-713-6150
Community Living for Ment'y Retarded #37	860-418-6081
Conch/Depuration/Oyster License #19	203-874-0696
Construction Inspector #24	860-685-8310
Contractor, Major #4	860-713-6100
Contractor, Mechanical #4	860-713-6135
Controlled Substance Lab #44	860-713-6070
Controlled Substance License #7	860-713-6065
Convalescent Nursing Home #11	860-509-7400
Cosmetologist #11	860-509-7603
Counselor, Professional #11	860-509-7603
Crane Operator #24	860-685-8470
Cranes/Hoisting Equipment #24	860-685-8470
Credit Union #6	860-240-8299
Crematorium #11	860-509-7296
Cross-Connection Survey Inspect'r #11	860-509-7333
Dairy Laboratory Analyst #21	860-713-2512
Dairy Sample Collector #21	860-713-2512
Dairy Transporter #21	860-713-2512
Day Care Provider #11	860-509-8045
Day Treatment Facility, Extended #36	860-550-6445
Debt Adjuster #6	860-240-8299
Demolition Operator #24	860-685-8470
Dental Anes./Sedation Permittee #11	860-509-7603
Dentist/Dental Hygienist #11	860-509-7603
Dessert Mfg, Frozen #8	860-713-6160
Diesel Fuel Distributor #20	860-297-5962
Dietician/Nutritionist #11	860-509-7603
Digger of Shellfish #19	203-874-0696
Dog Racing Owner/Trainer #12	860-594-0643
Dog Training Facility #21	860-713-2512
Driver Education Instr/School #26	860-263-5057
Driving Instructor #22	860-263-5720/5442
Driving School #22	860-263-5442
Drug/Cosmetic Whlse/Mfg #44	860-713-6070
Druggist Liquor Permittee #15	860-713-6200
Egg Grader #21	860-713-2513
Electrical Contr./Inspector #7	860-713-6135
Electrical Journeyman/Apprentice #4	860-713-6100
Electrical Sign Installer #7	860-713-6135
Electrician #7	860-713-6135
Electrologist/Hypertricologist #11	860-509-7603
Electronics Service Dealer/Tech. #5	860-713-6000
Elevator Inspector/Mechanic #4	860-713-6100
Embalmer #11	860-509-7603
Emergency Med. Svc Professional #11	860-509-7552
Emissions Technician #34	203-805-6244
Employment Agency #38	860-263-6790
EMS First Responder #11	860-509-7552
EMS Instructor #11	860-509-7975
Engineer #4	860-713-6100
Engineer-in-Training #4	860-713-6100
Environmental Lab Director #11	860-509-7389
Environmental Professional #39	860-424-3705
Explosive Handler #24	860-685-8470
Explosive Hauler #24	860-685-8470
Family Planning Clinic #11	860-509-8045
Family Residence, Permanent #36	860-550-6445
Fire Investigator, PI #13	860-685-8046
Fire Officer/Driver/Instructor #40	860-627-6363 x225
Fire Protection Inspector/Contract'r #4	860-713-6100
Fire Sprinkler Technician #4	860-713-6100
Fire/Life Safety Educator #40	860-627-6363 x225
Firearms Registration #13	860-685-8290
Firefighter #40	860-627-6363 x225
Fireworks Display Operator #24	860-685-8470
Fireworks Occupation/Permit #24	860-685-8470
Fisher #10	860-424-3105
Fishery #10	860-424-3474
Food Service Inspector #11	860-509-7297
Food Tester #11	860-509-7297
Forest Product Harvest'r/Practit'n'r #10	860-424-3630
Fruit Storage #21	860-713-2548
Fund Raiser, Paid #35	860-808-5030
Funeral Director/Home #11	860-509-7603
Fur Breeder #21	860-713-2512
Fur Buyer #10	860-424-3011
Game Breeder #10	860-424-3011
Gasoline Dealer, Retail #8	860-713-6160
Glazier #4	860-713-6100
Gun Dealer #13	860-685-8290
Hairdresser #11	860-509-7603
Hatchery #19	203-874-0696
Hazardous Material Tech'c'n #40	860-627-6363 x225
Hazardous Waste Disposer #39	860-424-3372
Hazardous Waste Transporter #39	860-424-3372
Health Care Center Insurer #2	860-297-3814
Health Club #4	860-713-6100
Hearing Instrument Specialist #11	860-509-7603

Heating/Piping/Cooling Cont./Journey'n #4 860-713-6100
Home Health Aide Agency #11 860-509-7400
Home Health Aide Homemaker #11 860-509-7400
Home Heating Oil Seller #8 860-713-6160
Home Improvement Contr./Seller #4 860-713-6110
Home Inspector #4 860-713-6145
Homemaker Companion #4 860-713-6100
Homeopathic Physician #11 860-509-7603
Honey Bee Registration #14 203-974-8500
Hospice #11 860-509-7400
Hospital #11 860-509-7400
Hypertrichologist #11 860-509-7603
Hypnotist #4 860-713-6100
Insurance Adjuster/Public Adjuster #2 860-297-3954
Insurance Agent, Fraternal #2 860-297-3954
Insurance Appraiser #2 860-297-3954
Insurance Company/Producer #2 860-297-3845
Insurance Consultant #2 860-297-3954
Interior Designer #4 860-566-2825
Interstate Land Sale #17 860-713-6150
Investment Advisor/Agent #6 860-240-8299
Issuer Agent (Financial) #6 860-240-8299
Juice Producer #8 860-713-6160
Junkyard Operator #26 860-263-5057
Kennel #21 860-713-2512
Laboratory, Animal #11 860-509-7400
Laboratory, Clinical #11 860-509-7400
Land Sale, Interstate #17 860-713-6150
Land Surveyor/Surveyor Firm #3 860-713-6145
Landscape Architect #3 860-713-6145
Lead Consultant #30 860-509-7559
Legalized Gaming Occupation #12 860-594-0643
Lender #6 860-240-8200
Lender, Correspondent #6 860-240-8299
Liquor License #15 860-713-6200
Liquor Mfg/Dist/Whlse #15 860-713-6200
Liquor Permittee #15 860-713-6200
Liquor Store/Broker/Shipper #15 860-713-6200
Livestock Dealer #21 860-713-2512
Loan Broker/Originator #6 860-240-8299
Loan Company, Small #6 860-240-8299
Lobbyist #18 860-566-4472
Lobster Seller #10 860-424-6043
Lottery #12 860-594-0643
Lottery Sales Agent #12 860-594-0643
Marine Fisher #41 860-434-6043
Marriage & Family Therapist #11 860-609-7603
Marshall, State #33 860-566-7109
Martial Arts Facility #4 860-713-6100
Massage Therapist #11 860-509-7603
Materialman #20 860-297-5962
Maternity Home #11 860-509-7400
Mausoleum #11 860-509-7603
Medical Doctor #11 860-509-7603
Medical Gas/Vacuum System #4 860-713-6135
Medical Response Technician #11 860-509-7603
Medication Admin. for Ment'y Retarded #37 860-418-6081
Mental Health Facility/Clinic #11 860-509-7400
Midwife #11 860-509-7603
Midwife Nurse #11 .... 860-509-7603/7570
Milk Dealer/Producer #21 860-713-2512
Milk/Cream Weigher #21 860-713-2512
Mobile Home Park/Seller #17 860-713-6150
Money Forwarder #6 860-240-8299
Money Order/Travelers Check Issuer #6 860-240-8299
Mooring Space #42 860-594-2000
Mooring/Swim Float #31 860-424-3034
Mortgage Broker/Lender #6 860-240-8299

Motion Picture Theater #24 860-685-8470
Motion Picture Theater Mgr #24 860-685-8470
Motor Bus Company #23 860-594-2849
Motor Vehicle Recycler #26 860-263-5056
Mover, Household Goods #23 860-594-2780
Naturopathic Physician #11 860-509-7603
New Home Construction Contr. #4 860-713-6100
Notary Public #16 860-509-6200
Nurse #11 .... 860-509-7603/7570
Nurse, Advance Registered Practice #11 .... 860-509-7603/7570
Nurse-LPN #11 860-509-7603
Nursery Plant Dealer #14 203-974-8500
Nursery, Plant #14 203-974-8500
Nurses' Aide #11 860-509-7603
Nursing Home #11 860-509-7400
Nursing Home Administrator #11 860-509-7603
Occupational Therapist/Assistant #11 860-509-7603
Off-Track Betting #12 860-594-0643
Optical Shop #11 860-509-7603
Optician #11 860-509-7603
Optometrist #11 860-509-7603
Osteopathic Physician #11 860-509-7603
Outpatient Clinic #11 860-509-7400
Parachute Jump Area #42 860-594-2000
Paramedic #11 860-509-7603
Pawnbroker #20 860-297-4874
Perfusionist #11 860-509-7603
Pesticide Applicator #25 860-424-3369
Pesticide-related Business #25 860-424-3369
Pet Groomer #21 860-713-2512
Pet Store Operator #21 860-713-2512
Pharmacist/Pharmacist Intern #44 860-713-6070
Pharmacy #44 860-713-6070
Pharmacy Technician #44 860-713-6070
Physical Therapist/Assistant #11 860-509-7603
Physician #11 860-509-7603
Physician Assistant #11 860-509-7603
Pilot, Marine #42 860-443-3856
Pipefitter #7 860-713-6135
Plan Review Technician #24 860-685-8310
Plumber #4 860-713-6100
Plumbing Inspector #24 860-685-8310
Podiatrist #11 860-509-7603
Police Officer #27 203-238-6694
Poultry Buyer #21 860-713-2512
Premium Finance Company #2 860-297-3916
Private Detective Company #13 860-685-8046
Private Investigator #13 860-685-8046
Private Occupational School #28 860-947-1822
Psychologist #11 860-509-7603
Public Accountant-CPA #16 860-509-6179
Public Service Technician #4 860-713-6100
Radiation Permittee #29 860-424-3029
Radiographer #11 860-509-7603
Real Estate Agent/Broker/Sales #17 860-713-6150
Real Estate Appraiser #17 860-713-6150
Real Estate Educ. Provider #17 860-713-6150
Recycler #39 860-424-3365
Reinsurance Intermediary #2 860-297-3955
Rental Car Company #2 860-297-3953
Residence for Mentally Retarded #37 860-418-6081
Residential Care Home #11 860-509-7400
Respiratory Care Practitioner #11 860-509-7603
Rest Home #11 860-509-7400
Risk Purchasing/Retention Group #2 860-297-3880
Safety Officer #40 .... 860-627-6363 x225
Sales Finance Company #6 860-240-8299
Sanitarian #11 860-509-7603
Savings & Loan Association Bank #6 860-240-8299
Savings Bank #6 860-240-8299

School Administrator/Supervisor #9 860-713-6969
School Bus Driver #22 860-263-5720
School Guidance Counselor #9 860-713-6969
School Library Media Specialist #9 860-713-6969
School Principal/Superintendent #9 860-713-6969
School Psychologist #9 860-713-6969
School Social Worker #9 860-713-6969
Scientific Collector #10 860-424-3589
SCOR #6 860-240-8299
Seafood Dealer #41 860-434-6043
Securities Agent #6 860-240-8299
Securities Broker/Dealer #6 860-240-8299
Security Company Firearms Instructor #13 860-685-8046
Security Company, Private #13 860-685-8046
Security Guard #13 860-685-8046
Security Officer Instructor #13 860-685-8046
Security Service #13 860-685-8046
Septic Tank Cleaner #11 860-509-8000
Sewage Disposal System Installer #11 860-509-8000
Sheet Metal Contr./Journeyman #4 860-713-6100
Shellfish Professional #19 203-874-0696
Shorthand Court Reporter #4 860-713-6100
Social Worker #11 860-509-7603
Solar Energy Contr./Journeyman #4 860-713-6100
Solid Waste Facility Operator #39 860-424-3705
Special Effects Permit #24 860-685-8470
Speech Pathologist #11 860-509-7603
Speech/Language Pathologist #9 860-713-6969
Sprinkler Layout Technician #4 860-713-6100
Student Athlete Agent #4 860-713-6100
Substance Abuse Clinic #11 860-509-7400
Surplus Lines Broker #2 860-297-3868
Surveyor, Land #3 860-713-6145
Tattoo Artist #11 860-509-8000
Taxable Entity #20 860-297-4874
Taxi Company #23 860-594-2849
Taxidermist #10 860-424-3105
Teacher #9 860-713-6969
Telecommunication Technician #4 860-713-6100
Television/Radio License #4 860-713-6100
Theatre Manager #24 860-685-8470
Tobacco Products Permit #20 860-297-5962
Towing Operator #26 860-263-5056
Training Home for Mentally Retarded #37 860-418-6081
Trapper #10 860-424-3105
Tree Surgeon #7 860-713-6135
Truck Driver #22 860-263-5720
Underground Storage Tank #39 860-424-3374
Utilization Review Company #2 860-297-3862
Vehicle Dealer #26 860-263-5056
Vehicle Repairer #26 860-263-5057
Vending Machine Operator #8 860-713-6160
Vendor, Itinerant #4 860-713-6100
Veterinarian #11 860-509-7603
Viatical Settlement Broker/Provider #2 860-297-3955
Waste Disposal Permittee #39 860-424-3705
Water Bottler #8 860-713-6160
Water Distribut'n System Operat'r #11 860-509-8000
Water Treatment Plant Operator #11 860-509-8000
Weigher #8 860-713-6000
Weights/Measures Dealer/Repair/Regul'r #8 860-713-6000
Well Driller #7 860-713-6135
Wildlife Control Operator #10 860-424-3011
Wildlife Rehabilitator #10 860-424-3011
Winery Farm #15 860-713-6200
Winery, Small #20 860-297-5962
Wrestler/Wrestling Manager #7 860-713-6135
Youth Camp #11 .... 860-509-8045, 800-282-6063

Connecticut Licensing Agency Information

#1 Attorney Registration, Statewide Grievance Committee, 287 Main St, 2nd Fl #2, East Hartford, CT 06118-; 860-568-5157, Fax- 860-568-4953. www.jud.state.ct.us/SGC/ Search data at- http://civilinquiry.jud.ct.gov/AttorneyFirmInquiry.aspx

#2 Department of Insurance, Licensing Division, PO Box 816 (153 Market St), Hartford, CT 06142-; 860-297-3845, Fax- 860-297-3978. Hours- 8AM-5PM. www.ct.gov/cid/site/default.asp Search data at- www.ct-clic.com Fees for pre-programmed lists: printed report-$7.88 + $.25 per page, labels-$7.88 + $.25 per 100 labels, Diskette-$7.88 + $.17 per diskette, CD-ROM-$7.88 + $.57 per CD, email-$7.88. Programmer time of $108.75 per hr.

#3 Department of Consumer Protection, Board of Architects, 165 Capitol Ave, Hartford, CT 06106-; 860-713-6050, Fax- 860-713-7243. www.ct.gov/dcp/site/default.asp Search data at- https://www.ask-dcp.ct.gov/lookup/SearchCriteria.asp Download lists at https://www.ask-dcp.ct.gov/roster/default.asp?dcpNav=|.

#4 Department of Consumer Protection, Board of Trades Division, 165 Capitol Ave, Hartford, CT 06106-; 860-713-6100, Fax- 860-713-7229. Hours- 8:30AM-4:30PM. www.ct.gov/dcp/cwp/view.asp?a=1625&q=274454&dcpNav=|&dcpNav_GID=1546 Search data at- https://www.ask-dcp.ct.gov/lookup/SearchCriteria.asp Download lists at https://www.ask-dcp.ct.gov/roster/default.asp?dcpNav=|.

#5 Department of Consumer Protection/Occupational Licensing, Board of Television & Radio Service Examiners, 165 Capitol Ave, Hartford, CT 06106-; 860-713-6000, Fax- 860-713-7239. www.ct.gov/dcp/cwp/view.asp?a=1624&Q=290382&PM=1 Search data at- https://www.ask-dcp.ct.gov/lookup/SearchCriteria.asp

#6 Department of Banking, 260 Constitution Plaza, Hartford, CT 06103-1800; 860-240-8299, Fax- 860-240-8178. Hours- 8AM-5PM. www.ct.gov/dob/site/default.asp Search data at- www.ct.gov/dob/cwp/view.asp?a=2233&q=297862&dobNAV_GID=1663

#7 Department of Consumer Protection, Occupational Licensing Division, 165 Capitol Ave, Hartford, CT 06106-; 860-713-6135, Fax- 860-713-7239. Hours- 8:30AM-4:30PM. www.ct.gov/dcp/site/default.asp Search data at- https://www.ask-dcp.ct.gov/lookup/SearchCriteria.asp Download lists at https://www.ask-dcp.ct.gov/roster/default.asp?dcpNav=|.

#8 Department of Consumer Protection, Food and Standards Division, 165 Capitol Ave, State Office Bldg, Hartford, CT 06106-1630; 860-713-6160, Fax- 860-713-7237. www.ct.gov/dcp/cwp/view.asp?a=1621&q=273706 Search data at- https://www.ask-dcp.ct.gov/lookup/SearchCriteria.asp Download lists at https://www.ask-dcp.ct.gov/roster/default.asp?dcpNav=|.

#9 Department of Education, Bureau of Educator Preparation, Certification, Support & Certification, PO Box 150471, Rm 243, Hartford, CT 06115-0471; 860-713-6969, Fax- 860-713-7017. Hours- 8AM-4:45PM. www.sde.ct.gov/sde/site/default.asp License verification through "Freedom of Information Act" (FOIA). Request must be submitted in writing.

#10 Department of Environmental Protection, Bureau of Natural Resources, 79 Elm St, Hartford, CT 06106-; 860-424-3010, Fax- 860-424-4078. www.ct.gov/dep/site/default.asp

#11 Department of Public Health, Health Care or Environmental Health Licensing, PO Box 340308 (410 Capital Ave, MS 12MQA), Hartford, CT 06134-0308; 860-509-7603, Fax- 860-509-7607. www.ct.gov/dph/ Search data at- www.dir.ct.gov/dph/Scripts/hlthprof.asp

#12 Division of Special Revenue, Licensing Section, PO Box 310424 (555 Russell Rd), Newington, CT 06131-; 860-594-0643, 800-519-6697, Fax- 860-594-0696. Hours- 8AM-5PM. www.ct.gov/dosr/site/default.asp Search data at- www.ct-clic.com

#13 Department of Public Safety, Division of State Police, Special Licensing & Firearms Division, 1111 Country Club Rd, Middletown, CT 06457-; 860-685-8290, Fax- 860-685-8496. www.ct.gov/dps/cwp/view.asp?a=2158&Q=294512&dpsNav_GID=1658&dpsNav=| Search data at- www.ct.gov/dps/cwp/view.asp?a=2158&Q=294512&dpsNav_GID=1658&dpsNav=|

#14 Office of the State Entomologist, Agricultural Experiment Station, 123 Huntington St, New Haven, CT 06511-; 203-974-8500, Fax- 203-974-8502. Hours- 8:30AM-4:30PM. www.ct.gov/caes/site/default.asp

#15 Department of Consumer Protection, Liquor Control Division, 165 Capitol Ave, Hartford, CT 06106-; 860-713-6200, Fax- 860-713-7235. www.ct.gov/dcp/site/ Search data at- https://www.ask-dcp.ct.gov/lookup/default.asp Download lists at https://www.ask-dcp.ct.gov/roster/default.asp?dcpNav=|.

#16 Office of the Secretary of the State, Recording Division, 30 Trinity St, Hartford, CT 06106-; 860-509-6200, Fax- 860-509-6230. Hours- 8:30AM-4:30PM. http://ct.gov:80/sboa/site/default.asp Search data - www.sboalicense.ct.gov/cpalookup/Default.aspx Click on Downloadable Data Files on main webpage to access lists of accountants and firms.

#17 Department of Consumer Protection, Real Estate Division, 165 Capitol Ave, Rm 110, Hartford, CT 06106-; 860-713-6150, Fax- 860-713-7230. www.ct.gov/dcp/cwp/view.asp?a=1622&Q=287752&PM=1 Search data at- https://www.ask-dcp.ct.gov/lookup/SearchCriteria.asp Download lists at https://www.ask-dcp.ct.gov/roster/default.asp?dcpNav=|.

#18 Office of State Ethics, 18-20 Trinity St #205, Hartford, CT 06106-; 860-566-4472, Fax- 860-566-3806. www.ct.gov/ethics/site/default.asp May not have full lobbyist rosters. Also search reports and enforcement actions.

#19 Dept. of Agriculture, Bureau of Aquaculture, PO Box 97 (190 Rogers Ave), Milford, CT 06460-; 203-874-0696, Fax- 203-783-9976. www.ct.gov/doag/cwp/view.asp?a=1369&q=259168&doagNav=|

#20 Department of Revenue Svcs, Audit Unit (Licensing), 25 Sigourney St, Hartford, CT 06106-; 860-297-5962, Fax- 860-297-4797. http://ct.gov/drs/site/

#21 Department of Agriculture, Bureau of Regulation & Inspection, 165 Capitol Ave, Hartford, CT 06106-; 860-713-2504, Fax- 860-713-2514. www.ct.gov/doag/cwp/view.asp?a=1367&q=259106&doagNav=|

#22 Department of Motor Vehicles, Specialized Licenses & Permits, 60 State St, Wethersfield, CT 06109-; 860-263-5720. www.ct.gov/dmv/site/default.asp

#23 Department of Transportation, Regulatory & Compliance Unit, PO Box 317546 (2800 Berlin Turnpike), Newington, CT 06131-7546; 860-594-2865, Fax- 860-594-2859. Hours- 8AM-4:30PM. www.ct.gov/dot/cwp/view.asp?a=1386&q=415026

#24 Department of Public Safety, Division of Fire, Emergency & Building Svcs, 1111 Country Club Rd, Middletown, CT 06457-9294; 860-685-8300, Fax- 860-685-8363. www.ct.gov/dps/cwp/view.asp?a=2142&Q=294116&dpsNav_GID=1672&dpsNav=|

#25 Department of Environmental Protection, Pesticide Division, Bureau of Waste Management, 79 Elm St, Hartford, CT 06106-; 860-424-3369, Fax- 860-424-4060. www.ct.gov/dep/site/default.asp Search data at- www.kellysolutions.com/CT/

#26 Department of Motor Vehicles, Dealer and Repairer Division, 60 State St, Wethersfield, CT 06109-; 860-263-5057, Fax- 860-263-5554. www.ct.gov/dmv/taxonomy/ct_taxonomy.asp?DLN=30152&dmvNav=|30152| Licenses cannot be verified by phone; must use form J23 available at all DMV offices.

#27 Police Officers Standards & Training Council, Certification, Assessment & Audit Unit, 285 Preston Ave, Meriden, CT 06450-; 203-238-6505, Fax- 203-238-6643. www.ct.gov/post/site/default.asp

#28 Department of Higher Education, Academic Affairs, 61 Woodland St, Hartford, CT 06105-2326; 860-947-1801, Fax- 860-947-1310. www.ctdhe.org

#29 Department of Environmental Protection, Bureau of Air Mgmt; Compliance & Filed Ops Div., 79 Elm St, Hartford, CT 06106-; 860-424-4152, Fax- 860-424-4064. www.ct.gov/dep/site/

#30 Department of Public Health, Asbestos Licensure, PO Box 340308 (410 Capitol Ave, MS # 51EPL, Hartford, CT 06134-0308; 860-509-7559, Fax- 860-509-7378. www.dph.state.ct.us Search data at- www.dph.state.ct.us/scripts/hlthprof.asp

#31 Department of Environmental Protection, Office of Long Island Sound Programs, 79 Elm St, Hartford, CT 06106-; 860-424-3034, Fax- 860-424-4045. www.ct.gov/dep/site/default.asp

#32 Department of Public Safety, Office of Education & Data Management, PO Box 2794 (1111 County Club Rd), Middletown, CT 06457-9294; 860-685-8330, Fax- 860-685-8611. www.ct.gov/dps/cwp/view.asp?a=2147&Q=294160&dpsNav_GID=1677&dpsNav=| Search data atwww.ct.gov/dps/cwp/view.asp?a=2148&Q=294206&dpsNav=|

#33 State Marshall Commission, State of Connecticut Judicial Branch, 765 Asylum Ave, Hartford, CT 06105-; 860-566-7109, Fax- 860-566-3743. www.jud.ct.gov Search data at- www.jud.ct.gov/faq/marshals.htm

#34 Department of Motor Vehicles, Emissions Division, 55 West Main St, Rowland State Gov Ctr, #400, Waterbury, CT 06072-; 203-805-6244. www.ct.gov/dmv/cwp/view.asp?a=800&Q=244982

#35 Department of Consumer Protection, Public Charities Unit - Ofc. of the Attorney General, PO Box 120 (55 Elm St), Hartford, CT 06141-0120; 860-808-5030, Fax- 860-808-5347. www.ct.gov/dcp/cwp/view.asp?a=1629&q=274418

#36 DCF Licensing, Department of Children & Families, 505 Hudson St, Hartford, CT 06106-; 860-550-6445, Fax- 860-550-6665. Hours- 8AM-5PM. www.ct.gov/dcf/site/default.asp

#37 Department of Developmental Services, 460 Capitol Ave, Hartford, CT 06106-; 860-418-6000, Fax- 860-418-6079. www.ct.gov/dds/site/default.asp Formerly known as Department of Mental Retardation.

#38 Department of Labor, Wage and Workplace Standards, 200 Folly Brook Blvd, Wethersfield, CT 06109-1114; 860-263-6790, Fax- 860-263-6541. www.ctdol.state.ct.us/index.htm

#39 Department of Environmental Protection, Bureau of Waste Management, 79 Elm St, 2nd Fl, Hartford, CT 06106-; 860-424-3705. Hours- 8:30AM-4:30PM. www.ct.gov/dep/site/default.asp

#40 Commission on Fire Prevention & Control, Director of Certification, 34 Perimeter Rd, Windsor Locks, CT 06096-; 860-627-6363 x225, Fax- 860-654-1889. Hours- 7:30AM-4PM. www.ct.gov/cfpc/taxonomy/ct_taxonomy.asp

#41 Department of Environmental Protection, Marine Fisheries Division, PO Box 719 (333 Ferry Rd), Old Lyme, CT 06371-; 860-434-6043, Fax- 860-434-6150. www.ct.gov/dep/site/default.asp

#42 Department of Transportation, Bureau of Aviation and Ports, 2800 Berlin Turnpike, Newington, CT 06131-7546; 860-594-2000, Fax- 860-437-7251. www.ct.gov/dot/site/default.asp

#43 Department of Motor Vehicles, Fiscal Services Division, 55 W Main St, Waterbury, CT 06702-; 203-805-6307, Fax- 203-805-6161. Hours- 9AM-5PM. Dealer license required to host licensed vehicle auctions.

#44 Department of Consumer Protection, Commission of Pharmacy, 165 Capitol Ave. #147, Hartford, CT 06106-; 860-713-6070, Fax- 860-713-7242. www.ct.gov/dcp/cwp/view.asp?a=1620&Q=273844&PM=1 Search data at- https://www.ask-dcp.ct.gov/lookup/SearchCriteria.asp

Connecticut Federal Courts

The following list indicates the district and division name for each county in the state. If the bankruptcy court location is different from the district court, then the location of the bankruptcy court appears in parentheses. **See the Appendix for addition info on standardized Federal Court searching and fees.**

County/Court Cross Reference

County	Court	County	Court
Fairfield	Bridgeport	New Haven	New Haven
Hartford	Hartford	New London	New Haven
Litchfield	New Haven (Hartford)	Tolland	Hartford
Middlesex	New Haven (Hartford)	Windham	Hartford

US District Court

Bridgeport Division Court Clerk, McMahon Federal Building, 915 Lafayette Blvd, Rm 400, Bridgeport, CT 06604, 203-579-5861. Hours-9AM-4PM. www.ctd.uscourts.gov

Counties/Note: Litchfield (after 2004), Fairfield (prior to 1993). Since 1/1993, cases from any county may be assigned to any district division.

Searches/Indexing: Include full name only in search request. Results do not include SSN or DOB. Will not fax back documents. New cases are in the index immediately after filing date. Computer index back to 2003 maintained. Records kept where the assigned judge sits, then stored by the federal record number system.

Search Access: Only docket info is available by phone. **Mail:** Search usually completed- 7 days. SASE not required. **In person:** 1 public terminal available. Copy fee from CM/ECF public terminal $.10 per page. Copy machine- $.25 each.

Payment: Pay by money order, cashier's check. Business and personal checks accepted with address and phone number on check. No credit cards. Payee: Clerk, US District Court.

E-Services: PACER records go back to 11/1991. New records online after 1 day. ECF at https://ecf.ctd.uscourts.gov. Copies off the ECF terminal are $.10 per page. **Opinions Online:** www.ctd.uscourts.gov/opinions.html. Judges' selected opinions only, back to 5/2006. Also, more recent opinions available free at www.nysd.uscourts.gov/courtweb/public.htm.

Hartford Division Court Clerk, Ribicoff Federal Bldg, 450 Main St, Hartford, CT 06103, 860-240-3200. 9AM-4PM. www.ctd.uscourts.gov

Counties/Note: Hartford, Tolland, Windham (prior to 1993). Since 1993, cases from any county may be assigned to any district division.

Searches/Indexing: Include full name only in search request. Results do not include SSN or DOB. Will not fax back documents. New cases are in the index immediately after filing date. Computer index back to 2003 maintained. Records kept where the assigned judge sits, then stored by the federal record number system.

Search Access: Only docket info is available by phone. **Mail:** Search usually completed- 2 weeks. Include SASE for return. **In person:** 2 public terminals available. Self-serve copies $.25 each.

Payment: Pay by money order, cashier's or personal check. No credit cards. Payee: Clerk, US District Court.

E-Services: PACER records go back to 11/1991. New records online after 1 day. ECF at https://ecf.ctd.uscourts.gov. Copies off the ECF terminal are $.10 per page. **Opinions Online:** www.ctd.uscourts.gov/opinions.html. Judges' selected opinions only, back to 5/2006. Also, more recent opinions available free at www.nysd.uscourts.gov/courtweb/public.htm.

New Haven Division Court Clerk, US Courthouse, 141 Church, New Haven, CT 06510, 203-773-2140. 9AM-4PM. www.ctd.uscourts.gov

Counties/Note: Middlesex, New Haven, New London (prior to 1993), Litchfield (prior to 2004). Since 1993, cases from any county may be assigned to any district division.

Searches/Indexing: Include full name only in search request. Results do not include SSN or DOB. Will not fax back documents. New cases are in the index immediately after filing date. Computer index back to 2003 maintained. Older records indexed on microfiche. District-wide searches available here back to 1982. Records kept where the assigned judge sits, then stored by the federal record number system.

Search Access: Only docket info is available by phone. **Mail:** Search usually completed- 3-4 days. Include SASE for return. **In person:** 1 public terminal available. Self-serve copies $.25 each.

Payment: Money order, cashier's check, business check, no credit cards. Payee: District Court Clerk.

E-Services: PACER records go back to 11/1991. New records online after 1 day. ECF at https://ecf.ctd.uscourts.gov. Copies off the ECF terminal are $.10 per page. **Opinions Online:** www.ctd.uscourts.gov/opinions.html. Judges' selected opinions only, back to 5/2006. Also, more recent opinions available free at www.nysd.uscourts.gov/courtweb/public.htm.

US Bankruptcy Court

Bridgeport Div. Court Clerk, 915 Lafayette Blvd, Bridgeport, CT 06604, 203-579-5808; Fax-203-579-5827. 9AM-4PM. www.ctb.uscourts.gov

Counties/Note: Fairfield.

Searches/Indexing: Include name, SSN in search request, also case number if known. Results include last 4 SSN digits, also address. Will not fax back documents. New cases are in the index immediately after filing date. Records indexed on computer back to mid-1991. District-wide searches available here. Files sent to archives 1 year later.

Search Access: Only docket info is available by phone. Voice Case Information Service available, call VCIS at 800-800-5113. **Mail:** Search usually completed- up to 2 weeks. Include SASE for return. **Fax:** Fax search requests accepted with prepayment. **In person:** 2 public terminals available. Self-serve copies- $.25 each.

Payment: Pay by Visa/MC, money order, cashier's or business checks. No personal checks. Payee: Clerk, US Bankruptcy Court.

E-Services: Document images available. PACER records go back to 1979. New records online after 1 day. ECF at https://ecf.ctb.uscourts.gov. **Opinions Online:** www.ctb.uscourts.gov. Click on Opinions. Search calendars at https://ecf.ctb.uscourts.gov/cgi-bin/PublicCalendar.pl. Unclaimed Funds free at www.ctb.uscourts.gov/search_unclaimed_funds.htm.

Hartford Division Court Clerk, 450 Main St, 7th Fl, Hartford, CT 06103, 860-240-3675. Hours-9AM-4PM. www.ctb.uscourts.gov

Counties/Note: Hartford, Tolland, Windham.

Searches/Indexing: Include name, SSN in search request, also case number if known. Results include last 4 SSN digits, also address. Will not fax back documents. New cases are in the index 1 day after filing date. Records indexed on computer back to mid-1991. District-wide searches available here. Case files sent to archives 1 year after closed.

Search Access: Only docket info is available by phone. Voice Case Information Service available, call VCIS at 800-800-5113. **Mail:** Search usually completed- week-10 days. Include SASE for return. **Fax:** Fax search requests accepted with prepayment. **In person:** 2 public terminals available. Self-serve copies- $.25 each.

Payment: Pay by Visa/MC, money order, cashier's or business checks. No personal checks. Payee: Clerk, US Bankruptcy Court.

E-Services: Document images available. PACER records go back to 1979. New records online after 1 day. ECF at https://ecf.ctb.uscourts.gov. **Opinions Online:** www.ctb.uscourts.gov. Click on Opinions. Search calendars at https://ecf.ctb.uscourts.gov/cgi-bin/PublicCalendar.pl.

New Haven Division Court Clerk, 157 Church St, 18th Fl, Connecticut Financial Ctr, New Haven, CT 06510, 203-773-2009. Hours-9AM-4PM. www.ctb.uscourts.gov

Counties/Note: Litchfield, Middlesex, New Haven, New London.

Searches/Indexing: Include name, SSN in search request, also case number if known. Results include last 4 SSN digits, also address. Will not fax back documents. New cases are in the index 1 week after filing date. Records indexed on computer back to mid-1991. District-wide searches available here. Files sent to archives after 1 year.

Search Access: Only docket info is available by phone. Voice Case Information Service available, call VCIS at 800-800-5113. **Mail:** Search usually completed- week-10 days. Include SASE for return. **Fax:** Fax search requests accepted with prepayment. **In person:** Public terminal available. Self-serve copies- $.25 each.

Payment: Pay by Visa/MC, money order, cashier's or business check. No personal checks. Payee: Clerk, US Bankruptcy Court.

E-Services: Document images available. PACER records go back to 1979. New records online after 1 day. ECF at https://ecf.ctb.uscourts.gov. **Opinions Online:** www.ctb.uscourts.gov. Click on Opinions. Search calendars at https://ecf.ctb.uscourts.gov/cgi-bin/PublicCalendar.pl. Unclaimed Funds free at www.ctb.uscourts.gov/search_unclaimed_funds.htm.

Connecticut County Courts

Court	Jurisdiction	No. of Courts	How Organized
Judicial District Courts*	General	15	13 Districts
Geographic Area Courts*	Limited	20	20 Geographic Areas
Probate Courts*	Probate	129	

• Profiled in this Sourcebook.

Court	CIVIL								
	Tort	Contract	Real Estate	Min. Claim	Max. Claim	Small Claims	Estate	Eviction	Domestic Relations
Judicial District Courts*	X	X	X	No Min	No Max				X
Geographic Area Courts*						$5000		X	
Probate Courts*							X		

Court	CRIMINAL				
	Felony	Misdemeanor	DWI/DUI	Preliminary Hearing	Juvenile
Judicial District Courts*	X				X
Geographic Area Courts*		X	X	X	
Probate Courts*					

Administration

Chief Court Administrator, 231 Capitol Av, Hartford, CT, 06106; 860-757-2100, Fax: 860-757-2130. (EST) www.jud.ct.gov/

Court Structure

The Superior Court is the sole court of original jurisdiction for all causes of action, except for matters over which the Probate Courts have jurisdiction as provided by statute. The state is divided into 13 Judicial Districts, 20 Geographic Area Courts, and 13 Juvenile Districts. The Superior Court - comprised primarily of the Judicial District Courts and the Geographical Area Courts - has 5 divisions: Criminal, Civil, Family, Juvenile, and Administrative Appeals. When not combined, the Judicial District Courts handle felony and civil cases while the Geographic Area Courts handle misdemeanors, and most handle small claims. Divorce records are maintained by the Chief Clerk of the Judicial District Courts. Probate is handled by city Probate Courts and are not part of the state court system.

Online Access

The Judicial Branch offers web look-up to docket information for civil, family, criminal, motor vehicle, housing, and small claims cases at www.jud.ct.gov/jud2.htm. Case look-ups are segregated into four types- civil/family, criminal/motor vehicle, housing, and small claims. For civil/family and small claims cases statewide are available from one to 10 years after the disposition date, depending on location. Search statewide or by location. The criminal and motor vehicle case docket data is available on cases where a disposition or bond forfeiture occurred on or after 01/01/2000. To search statewide, leave the location field blank. For housing (landlord/tenant) cases, search by name, address, or docket number. Housing case records are only available from the Hartford, New Haven, New Britain, Bridgeport, Norwalk and Waterbury districts. Also access all Probate Judges free at www.ctprobatejudges.org/

Opinions from the Supreme and Appellate courts are available at www.jud.state.ct.us/opinions.htm.

Searching Tips, Fees, and Other Guidelines

Certain fees are set by statute; $1.00 for a copy and $2.00 to certify a copy page. A certified copy of a judgment file is $25.00.

The Superior Court Record Center in Enfield, CT is the repository for criminal and some civil records, open 9AM-5PM M-F. Case records are sent to the Enfield Record Center from 3 months to 5 years after disposition by the courts. Records are maintained 10 years for misdemeanors and 20+ years for felonies. If a requester is certain that the record is at the Record Center, it is quicker to direct the request here rather than to the original court of record. Only written requests are accepted. Enfield does not do name searches. Search requirements– full defendant name, docket number, disposition date, and court action. Fee is $3.00 for each docket, $5.00 if certifed. Fee payee is Treasurer, State of Connecticut. Direct Requests to: Connecticut Record Center, 111 Phoenix Avenue, Enfield, CT 06082, telephone 860-741-3714.

Personal checks must have name and address printed on the check. If requesting in person, your check must have same address as your drivers' license.

Probate information request requirements are consistent across the state – requesters must provide full name of decedent, year and place of death, and SASE. There is no search fee. The certification fee is $5.00 for 1st 2 pages and $2.00 for each additional page. The probate copy fee is $5.00 for each five pages or or fraction thereof. Fees are set by statute.

Fairfield County

Bridgeport Judicial District Court 1061 Main St, Attn: criminal or civil, Bridgeport, CT 06604; 203-579-6527; fax: 203-382-8406; 9AM-5PM. ***Felony, Civil Actions, Divorce.***

Civil Records: Access: Mail, in person, online. Both court and visitors may perform in person searches. No search fee. Required to search: name, years to search. Civil cases indexed by defendant, plaintiff, on computer from 1990, on microfiche from 1975 to 1990, prior on index cards. After 5 years sent to Records Center at Enfield, CT. Mail turnaround time 2-3 weeks. Civil PAT available. Access civil case index free at http://civilinquiry.jud.ct.gov/.

Criminal Records: Access: Mail, in person, online. Only the court performs in person searches; visitors may not. No search fee. Required to search: name, years to search, DOB. Criminal records on computer since 1997, on microfiche from 1975 to 1996. Mail turnaround time 4 weeks. Criminal PAT available. Pending, current and disposed criminal and motor vehicle dockets back to 2000 free at www.jud.ct.gov/jud2.htm. Online results show name also show year of birth.

General Information: Online identifiers in results same as on public terminal. No sealed, adoption records released. Court makes copy: $1.00 per page. Self serve: $.25 per page if cutomer researches. Certification fee: $2.00 per cert; Exemplification fee-$20.00; judgment copy- $15.00, $25 if certified. Payee: Clerk Superior Court. Personal checks accepted; proper ID required. Visa/MC accepted. Prepayment required. Mail requests: SASE requested.

Danbury Judicial District Court 146 White St, Danbury, CT 06810; 203-207-8600; criminal phone: 203-207-8666; civil phone: 203-207-8642; 9AM-5PM. ***Felony, Misdemeanor, Civil Actions, Eviction, Small Claims, Divorce.***

Civil Records: Access: Mail, in person, online. Only the court performs in person searches; visitors may not. No search fee. Required to search: name, years to search. Civil cases indexed by plaintiff and defendant. Civil records on microfilm from 11-87, prior on index cards. Mail turnaround time 2-4 days. Access civil case index free at http://civilinquiry.jud.ct.gov/; also access small claims index by hearing date, party name, or docket number free at www.jud2.ct.gov/Small_Claims/. Also, eviction case data free at www.jud.ct.gov/housing.htm.

Criminal Records: Access: Mail, in person, online. Only the court performs in person searches; visitors may not. No search fee. Required to search: name, years to search, DOB. Criminal records on microfilm from 11-87, prior on index cards but only list docket number and disposal date. Mail turnaround time 3-4 days. Pending, current and disposed criminal and motor vehicle dockets back to 2000 free at www.jud.ct.gov/jud2.htm. Online results show name also show year of birth.

General Information: Online identifiers in results same as on public terminal. No sealed records released. Will not fax documents. Court makes copy: $1.00 per page. Certification fee: $2.00 per cert plus copy fee or per statute. Will not certify unless copies are made by the court personnel. Payee: Clerk of Superior Court. ID required with personal check. Visa/MC accepted in person. Prepayment required.

Stamford-Norwalk Judicial District Ct. 123 Hoyt St, Stamford, CT 06905; criminal phone: 203-965-5208 x4016; civil phone: 203-965-5307; criminal fax: 203-965-5355; civil fax: 203-965-5370; 9AM-5PM. ***Felony, Misdemeanors, Civil Actions, Divorce, Eviction, Small Claims.***

This court also includes Geographical Area Court #1. Family court- 203-965-0368.

Civil Records: Access: Mail, in person, online. Both court and visitors may perform in person searches. No search fee. Required to search: name, years to search. Civil cases indexed by defendant, plaintiff. Only pending civil cases on computer, on microfiche from 1970s, on index cards from 1958. Public use terminal has civil records. PAT results show name only. Public terminal has pending cases only. Access civil case index free at http://civilinquiry.jud.ct.gov/; also access small claims index by hearing date, party name, or docket free at www.jud2.ct.gov/Small_Claims/. Also, eviction case data free at www.jud.ct.gov/housing.htm.

Criminal Records: Access: Mail, in person, online. Both court and visitors may perform in person searches. No search fee. Required to search: name, years to search. Only pending cases on computer, on microfiche from 1970s, on index cards from 1962. Pending, current and disposed criminal and motor vehicle dockets back to 2000 free at www.jud.ct.gov/jud2.htm. Online results show name also show year of birth.

General Information: Online identifiers in results same as on public terminal. No sealed records released. Will not fax documents. Court makes copy: $1.00 per page. Certification fee: $2.00. Payee: Clerk of Superior Court. Personal checks accepted. Prepayment required.

Geographical Area Court #2 1051 Main St, Bridgeport, CT 06604; criminal phone: 203-579-6560; civil: 203-579-6527; fax: 203-382-8406; 9AM-5PM. ***Misdemeanor, Eviction, Small Claims.*** Serves the towns of Bridgeport, Easton, Fairfield, Monroe, Stratford and Trumbull.

Civil Records: Access: In person, online. Both court and visitors may perform in person searches. No search fee. Required to search: name, years to search. Civil cases indexed by defendant. Civil records pending and from 1990 on computer, on microfiche from 1982 to 1990, prior on index cards. After are microfilmed and entered on index cards. Civil PAT goes back to 2001. Access small claims index by hearing date, party name, or docket number free at www.jud2.ct.gov/Small_Claims/. Also, eviction case data free at www.jud.ct.gov/housing.htm.

Criminal Records: Access: In person, online. Visitors must perform in person searches themselves. Required to search: name, years to search. Criminal records pending and from 1990 on computer, on microfiche from 1982. Note: Refer mail requests to the state criminal records agency, PO Box 2794, Middletown CT 06457. For access via the state Dept of Public Safety system, see www.ct.gov/dps and click on Reports And Records. Criminal PAT goes back to 2001. Pending, current and disposed criminal and motor vehicle dockets back to 2000 free at www.jud.ct.gov/jud2.htm. Online results show name also show year of birth.

General Information: Online identifiers in results same as on public terminal. No sealed records released. Court makes copy: $1.00 per page. Certification fee: $3.00. Payee: Clerk of Superior Court. In-state personal checks accepted. Visa/MC accepted. Prepayment required.

Geographical Area Court #20 17 Belden Ave, Norwalk, CT 06850; 203-846-3237; criminal phone: 203-846-3237; civil phone: 203-846-4206; fax: 203-847-8710; 9AM-5PM. ***Misdemeanor, Eviction, Small Claims.*** Serving the towns of New Canaan, Norwalk, Weston, Westport, and Wilton.

Civil Records: Access: Online, in person. Visitors must perform in person searches themselves. Required to search: name, years to search. Civil cases indexed by defendant, plaintiff, on computer from 1986. Access civil case index free at http://civilinquiry.jud.ct.gov/; also access small claims index by hearing date, party name, or docket free at www.jud2.ct.gov/Small_Claims/. Also, eviction case data free at www.jud.ct.gov/housing.htm.

Criminal Records: Access: In person, online. Visitors must perform in person searches themselves. Required to search: name, years to search; also helpful: DOB. Criminal records computerized from 1986, prior records on index cards. Pending, current and disposed criminal and motor vehicle dockets back to 2000 free at www.jud.ct.gov/jud2.htm. Online results show name, also show year of birth.

General Information: Online identifiers in results same as on public terminal. Will fax back doc for no fee. Court makes copy: $1.00 per page. Certification fee: $2.00 per cert. Payee: Superior Court GA #20. Only cashiers checks and money orders accepted. Visa/MC accepted. Prepayment required.

Geographical Area Court #3 146 White St, Danbury, CT 06810; 203-207-8600; fax: 203-207-8666; 9AM-5PM. ***Misdemeanor, Eviction, Small Claims.*** Serving the towns of Bethel, Brookfield, Danbury, New Fairfield, Newtown, Redding, Ridgefield, Sherman.

Civil Records: Access: Mail, in person, online. Only the court performs in person searches; visitors may not. No search fee. Required to search: name, years to search. Civil cases indexed by defendant. Civil records on microfilm from 11-87, prior on index cards, but only list docket number and disposal date, then referred to Records Center at Enfield. Note: In person searches are returned by mail. Civil PAT available. Access small claims index by hearing date, party name, or docket number free at www.jud2.ct.gov/Small_Claims/. Also, eviction case data free at www.jud.ct.gov/housing.htm.

Criminal Records: Access: In person, online. Visitors must perform in person searches themselves. Required to search: name, years to search; also helpful: DOB. Criminal records computerized from 11/9/87. Criminal PAT available. Pending, current and disposed criminal and motor vehicle dockets back to 2000 free at www.jud.ct.gov/jud2.htm. Online results show name also show year of birth.

General Information: Online identifiers in results same as on public terminal. No youthful offender or dispositions by dismissal after 20 days from date of judgment records released. Court makes copy: $1.00 per page. Certification fee: $2.00 per cert. Payee: Clerk of Superior Court. Personal checks accepted. Visa/MC accepted. Prepayment required. Mail requests: SASE required for civil.

Bethel Probate Court 1 School St, PO Box 144, Bethel, CT 06801; 203-794-8508; fax: 203-794-8587; 9AM-1:00PM. ***Probate.***

Bridgeport Probate District 202 State St, McLevy Hall, 3rd Fl, Bridgeport, CT 06604; 203-576-3945; fax: 203-576-7898; 8:30AM-5PM M-TH; 8:30AM-4PM F. ***Probate.***

Brookfield Probate Court PO Box 5192, 100 Pocono Rd, Brookfield, CT 06804; 203-775-3700; fax: 203-775-5246; 9AM-3:30PM T-F; 9AM-1PM Mon. ***Probate.***

Danbury Probate Court 155 Deer Hill Ave, Danbury, CT 06810; 203-797-4521; 8:30AM-4:30PM. ***Probate.***

Darien Probate Court Town Hall, 2 Renshaw Rd, Darien, CT 06820; 203-656-7342; fax: 203-656-0774; 8:30AM-12:30, 1:30-4:30PM; Sum'r-8:30-12:30, 1:30-4:30PM M,T. ***Probate.*** Also open Fridays 8:30AM-12:30PM in Summer.

Fairfield Probate Court Independence Hall, 725 Old Post Rd, Fairfield, CT 06824; 203-256-3041; fax: 203-256-3044; 8:30-4:30PM. ***Probate.***

Greenwich Probate Court 101 Field Point Rd, Greenwich, CT 06836; 203-622-7879; fax: 203-622-6451; 8AM-4PM M-TH; 8AM-N F July-Aug. ***Probate.*** www.greenwichct.org/Probate/Probate.asp

New Canaan Probate Court 77 Main St, New Canaan, CT 06840; 203-594-3050; fax: 203-594-3128; 8:30AM-4:30PM; 8:30AM-1PM F July-Aug. ***Probate.***

New Fairfield Probate Court 4 Brush Hill Rd, Town Hall, New Fairfield, CT 06812; 203-312-5627; 9AM-5PM T-W-Th; closed 12:30-3:30PM TH; also by app't. ***Probate.***

Newtown Probate Court Edmond Town Hall, 45 Main St, Newtown, CT 06470; 203-270-4280; fax: 203-270-4283; 8:30AM-N, 1-4:30PM. ***Probate.***

Norwalk Probate Court 125 East Ave, PO Box 2009, Norwalk, CT 06852-2009; 203-854-7737; fax: 203-854-7825; 9AM-4:30PM. ***Probate.*** District includes Town of Wilton.

Redding Probate Court Town Hall, 100 Lonetown Rd, PO Box 1125, Redding, CT 06875-1125; 203-938-2326; fax: 203-938-8816; 9AM-1PM. ***Probate.***

Ridgefield Probate Court Town Hall, 400 Main St, Ridgefield, CT 06877; 203-431-2776; fax: 203-431-2722; 8:30AM-4:30PM. ***Probate.***

Shelton Probate Court PO Box 127, 40 White St, Shelton, CT 06484; 203-924-8462; fax: 203-924-8943; 9AM-5PM. ***Probate.***

Sherman Probate Court 4 Brush Hill Rd, NewFairfield, CT 06812; 203-312-5627; fax: same; 9AM-5PM T W TH. ***Probate.***
Records now located at New Fairfield.

Stamford Probate Court 888 Washington Blvd, 8th Fl, PO Box 10152, Stamford, CT 06904-2152; 203-323-2149; fax: 203-964-1830; 9AM-4PM. ***Probate.***

Stratford Probate Court 468 Birdseye St, 2nd Fl, Stratford, CT 06615; 203-385-4023; fax: 203-375-6253; 9:30AM-4:30PM. ***Probate.***

Trumbull Probate Court Town Hall, 5866 Main St, Trumbull, CT 06611-5416; 203-452-5068; fax: 203-452-5092; 9AM-4:30PM. ***Probate.***
District includes Town of Easton, and Monroe.

Westport Probate Court Town Hall, 110 Myrtle Ave, Westport, CT 06880; 203-341-1100; fax: 203-341-1102; 9AM-4:30PM. ***Probate.***
District includes Town of Weston.

Hartford County

Hartford Judicial District Court - Civil 95 Washington St, Hartford, CT 06106; 860-548-2700; fax: 860-548-2711; 9-5. ***Civil Actions.***
Hartford Family Court located at 90 Washington St, 860-706-5100.
Civil Records: Access: Mail, in person, online. Both court and visitors may perform in person searches. No search fee. Required to search: name, years to search. Civil cases indexed by defendant, plaintiff, on computer if active, older on microfiche, older records at Enfield Records Center. Mail turnaround time 7-10 days. Public use terminal has civil records. PAT results show name only. Access civil case index free at http://civilinquiry.jud.ct.gov/. Online results show name only.
General Information: Online identifiers in results same as on public terminal. Will not fax documents. Court makes copy: $1.00 per page. Certification fee: $2.00 per doc. Payee: Clerk of Superior Court. Personal checks accepted. Credit cards accepted in person only; $10.00 minimum. Prepayment required. Mail requests: SASE required.

Hartford Judicial Dist Court - Criminal 101 LaFayette St, Hartford, CT 06106; 860-566-1630; fax: 860-566-1983; 9AM-5PM. ***Felony.***
This court shares phone line and address with Geographical Court #14.
Criminal Records: Access: In person, online. Only the court performs in person searches; visitors may not. Required to search: name, years to search; also helpful: DOB. Criminal records computerized from 1989. Mail turnaround time 7-10 days. Pending, current and disposed criminal and motor vehicle dockets back to 2000 free at www.jud.ct.gov/jud2.htm. Online results show name also show year of birth.
General Information: Online identifiers in results same as on public terminal. No youthful offender records or dismissals released. Will fax documents. Court makes copy: $1.00 per page. Certification fee: $2.00 per doc. Payee: Clerk of Superior Court. Personal checks accepted. Visa/MC accepted, $10.00 minimum. Prepayment required. Mail requests: SASE required.

New Britain Judicial District Court 20 Franklin Square, New Britain, CT 06051; 860-515-5080; fax: 860-515-5185; 9AM-5PM. ***Felony, Civil Actions, Small Claims, Divorce.***
Civil is on 2nd Floor.
Civil Records: Access: Phone, mail, online, in person. Both court and visitors may perform in person searches. No search fee. Required to search: name, years to search. Civil cases indexed by plaintiff. Civil records on computer up to one year after closing, index cards back to 1989, prior in Hartford. Mail turnaround time 1-3 days. Public use terminal available. Access civil case index free at http://civilinquiry.jud.ct.gov/; also access small claims index by hearing date, party name, or docket free at www.jud2.ct.gov/Small_Claims/.
Criminal Records: Access: Mail, in person, online. Both court and visitors may perform in person searches. No search fee. Required to search: name, years to search. Criminal records on computer for 2 years, then purged when cases sent to State Record Center. Note: This court prefers that you search at Enfield Mail turnaround time 3 days. Public use terminal available. Pending, current and disposed criminal and motor vehicle dockets back to 2000 free at www.jud.ct.gov/jud2.htm. Online results show name also show year of birth.
General Information: Online identifiers in results same as on public terminal. Certain paternity, family case studies and sealed records not released. Will not fax out documents. Court makes copy: $1.00 per page. Self serve: Court Srvs lets you have 1st 10 pages free, then $.10 per page. Certification fee: $2.00 per cert. Payee: Clerk of Superior Court. No personal checks accepted. Visa/MC accepted; $10 minimum. Prepayment required. Mail requests: SASE required.

Geographic Area Court #15 20 Franklin Square, New Britain, CT 06051; criminal phone: 860-515-5080; civil phone: 860-515-5180; criminal fax: 860-515-5103; civil fax: 860-515-5185; 9AM-5PM. ***Misdemeanor, Eviction, Small Claims.***
Serving the towns of Berlin, New Britain, Newington, Rocky Hill and Wethersfield.
Civil Records: Access: Mail, in person, online. Only the court performs in person searches; visitors may not. No search fee. Required to search: name, years to search. Civil cases indexed by defendant, plaintiff, on computer for 3 years, then on microfiche. All info in archives at Record Center at Enfield, CT. Mail turnaround time 1 month. Access small claims index by hearing date, party name, or docket number free at www.jud2.ct.gov/Small_Claims/. Also, eviction case data free at www.jud.ct.gov/housing.htm.
Criminal Records: Access: Mail, in person, online. Only the court performs in person searches; visitors may not. No search fee. Required to search: name, years to search, DOB. Data is purged every two years. Criminal records computerized from 1985, then on microfiche. All info in archives at Enfield Record Center. Mail turnaround time 1 month. Pending, current and disposed criminal and motor vehicle dockets back to 2000 free at www.jud.ct.gov/jud2.htm. Online results show name also show year of birth.
General Information: Online identifiers in results same as on public terminal. No sealed records released. Court makes copy: $1.00 per page. Certification fee: $2.00 per cert. Payee: Clerk of Superior Court. No out-of-state checks accepted. Major credit cards accepted with proper ID; $10.00 minimum. Prepayment required. Mail requests: SASE required.

Geographical Area Court #12 410 Center St, Manchester, CT 06040; 860-647-1091; fax: 860-645-7540; 9AM-5PM; Phone Hours: 9AM-4PM. ***Misdemeanor, Eviction, Small Claims.***
Evictions are handled by a special Housing Court, 80 Washington St, Hartford, CT, 860-756-7920. Serving the towns of East Hartford, Glastonbury, Manchester, Marlborough and South Windsor.
Civil Records: Access: Mail, in person, online. Both court and visitors may perform in person searches. No search fee. Required to search: name, years to search. Civil cases indexed by defendant. Civil records on computer for 3 years. Mail turnaround time 1-2 weeks. Access civil case index free at http://civilinquiry.jud.ct.gov/; also access small claims index back to 2000 by hearing date, party name, or docket number free at www.jud2.ct.gov/Small_Claims/. Also, eviction case data free at www.jud.ct.gov/housing.htm.
Criminal Records: Access: Mail, in person, online. Only the court performs in person searches; visitors may not. No search fee. Required to search: name, years to search, DOB. Criminal records on computer since 2002, available since 1979. Note: In person search results returned by mail only. The court urges requesters to go to the State Police for criminal record searches. Mail turnaround time 1-2 weeks. Pending, current and disposed criminal and motor vehicle dockets back to 2000 free at www.jud.ct.gov/jud2.htm. Online results show name also show year of birth.
General Information: Online identifiers in results same as on public terminal. No non disclosable records released. Will not fax documents. Court makes copy: $1.00 per page. Certification fee: $2.00 per doc. Payee: Clerk of Superior Court. Personal checks accepted. Visa/MC accepted; $10.00 minimum. Prepayment required. Mail requests: SASE required.

Geographical Area Court #13 111 Phoenix Ave, Enfield, CT 06082; 860-741-3727 x2; fax: 860-741-3474; hours -9AM-5PM. ***Misdemeanor.***
Eviction cases are handled by Hartford Housing, 860-756-7920. Serving the towns of East Granby, East Windsor, Enfield, Granby, Simsbury, Suffield, Windsor and Windsor Locks.
Criminal Records: Access: Mail, in person, online. Visitors must perform in person searches themselves. No search fee. Required to search: name, years to search, DOB. Criminal records on computer for 3 years, microfiche by year. Archived at Record Center which is also here in Enfield, CT. Mail turnaround time 1-2 weeks. PAT results show name, DOB. Pending, current and disposed criminal and motor vehicle dockets back to 2000 free at www.jud.ct.gov/jud2.htm. Online results show name also show year of birth.
General Information: Online identifiers in results same as on public terminal. Will not fax out documents. Court makes copy: $1.00 per page. Certification fee: $2.00 per doc. Payee: Clerk of Superior Court. Will take personal check with ID. Major credit cards accepted with proper ID; $10.00 minimum. Prepayment required.

Geographical Area Court #17 131 N Main St, Bristol, CT 06010; 860-582-8111; fax: 860-585-8799; 9AM-5PM. ***Misdemeanor, Some Felony.***
www.jud.ct.gov
Serving the towns of Bristol, Burlington, Plainville, Plymouth, Southington.
Criminal Records: Access: Mail, in person, online. Only the court performs in person searches; visitors may not. No search fee. Required to search: name, years to search, DOB, date of arrest. Criminal records computerized from 1986, on microfiche from 1982, prior on index cards from 1979-1992, microfiche 1988-1996 and docket books; records o. Note: Photo ID required for records search. Most convictions and older records are stored off-site. Mail turnaround time 1-2 days. Pending, current and disposed criminal and motor vehicle dockets back to 2000 free at www.jud.ct.gov/jud2.htm. Online results show name also show year of birth.
General Information: Online identifiers in results same as on public terminal. No dismissals, not guilty, youthful offender or NOLLE records released. Will fax documents. Court makes copy: $3.00 per disposition; $1.00 per page. Certification fee: $5.00. Payee: Clerk of Superior Court. Personal checks accepted with ID. Visa/MC accepted; $10.00 mimimum. Prepayment required. Mail requests: SASE required.

Geographical Area Court #14 101 LaFayette St, Hartford, CT 06106; 860-566-1630; fax: 860-566-1983; 9AM-5PM. ***Misdemeanor.***
Serving the towns of Avon, Bloomfield, Canton, Farmington, Hartford and West Hartford.
Criminal Records: Access: In person, online. Only the court performs in person searches; visitors may not. Required to search: name, years to search, DOB. Criminal records on computer for 3 years, microfiche by year. Archived at Record Center which is also here in Enfield, CT. PAT results show name, DOB. Pending, current and disposed criminal and motor

vehicle dockets back to 2000 free at www.jud.ct.gov/jud2.htm. Online results show name also show year of birth.
General Information: Online identifiers in results same as on public terminal. Will fax documents. Court makes copy: $1.00 per page. Certification fee: $2.00 per doc. Payee: Clerk of Superior Court. Only cashiers checks and money orders accepted. No credit cards accepted. Prepayment required. Mail requests: SASE required.

Avon Probate Court 60 W Main St, Avon, CT 06001-0578; 860-409-4348; fax: 860-409-4368; 9:15AM-3:30 M,TH; 9:15AM-2:15PM T,W,F. ***Probate.***

Berlin Probate Court 1 Liberty Square, PO Box 400, New Britain, CT 06050-0400; 860-826-2696/860-515-5200; fax: 860-826-2695; 9AM-4PM. ***Probate.***
District includes towns of New Britain, Kennsington, East Berlin.

Bloomfield Probate Court 800 Bloomfield Ave, Town Hall, Bloomfield, CT 06002; 860-769-3548; fax: 860-242-1167; 9AM-4:30PM. ***Probate.*** www.bloomfieldct.org/Pages/BloomfieldCT_Probate/index

Bristol Probate Court 111 N Main St, City Hall, 3rd Fl, Bristol, CT 06010; 860-584-6230; fax: 860-584-3818; 9AM-5PM. ***Probate.***

Burlington Probate Court 200 Spielman Hwy, Burlington, CT 06013; 860-673-2108 x213; fax: 860-673-1527; 8:30AM-12:30PM M; 8:30AM-2:30PM TH. ***Probate.***

Canton Probate Court 4 Market St, Canton Town Hall, 3rd Fl, PO Box 175, Collinsville, CT 06022-0175; 860-693-7851; fax: 860-693-7889; 8:30AM-2PM M,T,TH; 8:30AM-N, 1-4PM W; 9AM-N F. ***Probate.***

East Granby-Suffield Probate Court PO Box 542, 9 Center St, East Granby, CT 06026-0542; 860-653-3434; fax: 860-653-7085; 9AM-N T-W-TH (and by app't). ***Probate.***

East Hartford Probate Court Town Hall, 740 Main St, East Hartford, CT 06108; 860-291-7278; fax: 860-291-7211; 9AM-4PM M,T,TH; 9AM-? Wed; 9AM-3PM F. ***Probate.***

East Windsor Probate Court Town Hall, 1540 Sullivan Ave, South Windsor, CT 06074; 860-644-2511 X270; fax: 860-648-5047; 8AM-3PM. ***Probate.***
District also includes Town of South Windsor.

Enfield Probate Court 820 Enfield St, Enfield, CT 06082; 860-253-6305; fax: 860-253-6388; 9AM-4:30PM. ***Probate.***

Farmington Probate Court One Monteith Dr, Farmington, CT 06032; 860-675-2360; fax: 860-673-8262; 8:30-9:30AM. ***Probate.***

Glastonbury Probate Court PO Box 6523, 2155 Main St, Glastonbury, CT 06033-6523; 860-652-7629; fax: 860-368-2520; 9:30AM-4:30PM (7PM on T). ***Probate.***

Granby Probate Court 15 N Granby Rd, Town Hall, Granby, CT 06035-0240; 860-844-5314; fax: 860-653-4769; 8:30AM-1PM Mon; 9AM-1PM T,W,TH; 9AM-12:30PM F. ***Probate.***

Hartford Probate Court 250 Constitution Plaza, 3rd Fl, Hartford, CT 06103; 860-757-9150; fax: 860-724-1503; 9AM-4PM M-F; 4-6:30PM Mon by app't. ***Probate.***

Manchester Probate Court 66 Center St, Manchester, CT 06040; 860-647-3227; fax: 860-647-3236; 8:30AM-N, 1-4:30PM. ***Probate.***

Marlborough Probate Court 26 N Main St, PO Box 29, Marlborough, CT 06447; 860-295-6239; fax: 860-295-6122; 8-11AM M,F; 10AM-N Wed; 8AM-3:00PM T,T. ***Probate.***

New Hartford Probate Court 530 Main St, PO Box 308, New Hartford, CT 06057; 860-379-3254; fax: 860-379-0940; 8:30AM-3PM M,T,TH; 8:30AM-N W; 8AM-N F. ***Probate.***
Also serving Barkhamsted and Hartland.

Newington Probate Court 66 Cedar St, Rear, Newington, CT 06111; 860-665-1285; fax: 860-665-1331; 9AM-4PM M-W, F; 9AM-6PM TH. ***Probate.***
District includes towns of Rocky Hill, Wethersfield, Newington.

Plainville Probate Court 1 Central Square, Plainville, CT 06062; 860-793-0221 x250; fax: 860-793-2424; 8:30AM-N, 1-3:30PM M-TH; 8AM-N F. ***Probate.***

Simsbury Probate Court 933 Hopmeadow St, PO Box 495, Simsbury, CT 06070; 860-658-3277; fax: 860-658-3204; 8:30AM-1, 2-4:30PM. ***Probate.***

Southington Probate Court Town Hall, 75 Main St, PO Box 165, Southington, CT 06489; 860-276-6253; fax: 860-276-6255; 8:30AM-4:30PM; 8:30AM-7PM TH. ***Probate.***

Suffield- East Granby Probate Court 83 Mountain Rd, Town Hall, Suffield, CT 06078; 860-668-3835; fax: 860-668-3029; 8AM-1PM. ***Probate.***
Passport applications by appointment.

West Hartford Probate Court 50 S Main St, West Hartford, CT 06107; 860-561-7940; fax: 860-561-7591; 8:30AM-4:30PM. ***Probate.***

Windsor Locks Probate Court Town Office Bldg, 50 Church St, Windsor Locks, CT 06096; 860-627-1450; fax: 860-654-8919; 9AM-2PM M-TH. ***Probate.***

Windsor Probate Court 275 Broad St, PO Box 342, Windsor, CT 06095; 860-285-1976; fax: 860-285-1909; 8:30AM-4:30PM M-TH; 8:30AM-N F. ***Probate.***

Litchfield County

Litchfield Judicial District Court PO Box 247, Litchfield, CT 06759; 860-567-0885; fax: 860-567-4779; 9AM-5PM. ***Felony, Civil Actions, Divorce.***
Civil Records: Access: Fax, mail, online, in person. Only the court performs in person searches; visitors may not. No search fee. Required to search: name, years to search. Civil cases indexed by defendant, plaintiff. Pending cases only on computer, on index cards from 1972. Note: Must make search request in writing. Mail turnaround time 3-4 weeks. Access civil case index free at http://civilinquiry.jud.ct.gov/.
Criminal Records: Access: Fax, mail, in person, online. Only the court performs in person searches; visitors may not. No search fee. Required to search: name, years to search; also helpful: DOB. Pending cases only on computer, on index cards from 1972. Note: Must make requests in writing. Mail turnaround time 3-4 weeks. Pending, current and disposed criminal and motor vehicle dockets back to 2000 free at www.jud.ct.gov/jud2.htm. Online results show name also show year of birth.
General Information: Online identifiers in results same as on public terminal. No sealed files released. No fee to fax documents. Court makes copy: $1.00 per page. Certification fee: $2.00 per cert. Payee: Clerk of Superior Court. Personal checks accepted. Visa/MC accepted in person only. Prepayment required. Mail requests: SASE required.

Geographical Area Court #18 PO Box 667, 80 Doyle Rd, Bantam, CT 06750; 860-567-3942; fax: 860-567-3934; 9AM-5PM. ***Misdemeanor, Eviction, Small Claims.***
Serving Barkhamsted, Bethlehem, Bridgewater, Canaan, Colebrook, Cornwall, Goshen, Hartland, Harwinton, Kent, Litchfield, Morris, New Hartford, New Milford, Norfolk, North Canaan, Roxbury, Salisbury, Sharon, Thomaston, Torrington, Warren, Wash & Winchester
Civil Records: Access: Mail, in person, online. Both court and visitors may perform in person searches. No search fee. Required to search: name, years to search. Civil cases indexed by defendant. Civil records on computer for 2 years, on microfiche from 1986. Mail turnaround time 1 week. Access small claims index by hearing date, party name, or docket number free at www.jud2.ct.gov/Small_Claims/. Also, eviction case data free at www.jud.ct.gov/housing.htm.
Criminal Records: Access: Mail, in person, online. Only the court performs in person searches; visitors may not. No search fee. Required to search: name, years to search, DOB; also helpful: address. Criminal records on computer for 1 year, microfiche from 1986, on index cards for 40 years. Archived at Records Center at Enfield, CT. Mail turnaround time 1 week. Pending, current and disposed criminal and motor vehicle dockets back to 2000 free at www.jud.ct.gov/jud2.htm. Online results show name also show year of birth.
General Information: Online identifiers in results same as on public terminal. No youthful offender or non-disclosable records released. Court makes copy: $1.00 per page. Certification fee: $2.00 per doc. Payee: Clerk of Superior Court. Personal checks accepted. Visa/MC accepted. Prepayment required. Mail requests: SASE required.

Barkhamsted Probate Court, CT 06063; ***Probate.*** Merged with New Hartford- 860-379-3254.

Cornwall Probate Court, CT; 860-824-7012; fax: 860-824-7428; 9AM-4PM M-TH. ***Probate.***
See Northwest Corner Probate District Court. Phone, fax and hours given here.

Harwinton Probate Court Town Hall, 100 Bentley Dr, Harwinton, CT 06791; 860-485-1403; fax: 860-485-2716; 8AM-1PM Tu,W,TH; 9-10AM M,F. ***Probate.***

Kent Probate Court - Litchfield PO Box 505, 74 West St, Litchfield, CT 06759; 860-567-8065; fax: 860-567-2538; 9AM-4PM (and by app't). ***Probate.***
Kent Probate Court Is now consolidated (1/3/2007) with the Litchfield District Probate Court.

Litchfield Probate Court PO Box 505, 74 West St, Litchfield, CT 06759; 860-567-8065; fax: 860-567-2538; 9AM-4PM and by app't. ***Probate.***
District includes towns of Morris, Warren, Kent, Litchfield.

New Hartford Probate Court Town Hall, 530 Main St, PO Box 308, New Hartford, CT 06057; 860-379-3254; fax: 860-379-0940; 8:30AM-3PM M,T,TH; 8AM-N W,F. ***Probate.***
Includes towns of New Hartford, Barkhamsted, and Hartland

New Milford/Bridgewater Probate Court 10 Main St, Town Hall, New Milford, CT 06776; 860-355-6029; fax: 860-355-6024; 9AM-N 1-5PM T-TH; 9AM-N 1-4PM M; 8:30AM-N F. ***Probate.*** www.newmilford.org/content/240/
District includes Town of Bridgewater.

Norfolk Probate Court, CT; 860-824-7012; fax: 860-824-7428; 9AM-4PM M-TH. ***Probate.***
See Northwest Corner Probate District Court. Phone, fax and hours given here.

Northwest Corner Probate District Court PO Box 849, 100 Pease St, #100, Canaan, CT 06018; 860-824-7012; fax: 860-824-7428; 9AM-4PM M-TH. ***Probate.***
Formerly known as Canaan Probate Court. This court is now home to 5 probate court, combined: Canaan, Cornwall, Salisbury, Sharon, and Norfolk

Plymouth Probate Court 80 Main St, Terryville, CT 06786; 860-585-4014; fax: 860-585-4099; 9AM-1PM M,T,W,F, 1-5PM TH; Summer-8:30AM-4:30PM T,TH. ***Probate.***

Roxbury Probate Court Town Hall, 29 North St, PO Box 203, Roxbury, CT 06783; 860-354-1184; fax: 860-355-3091; Noon-2PM M,Wed; 8:30AM-N Tues; 8:30AM-2:30PM TH,F. ***Probate.*** www.roxburyct.com/probate.html

Salisbury Probate Court, CT; 860-824-7012; fax: 860-824-7428; 9AM-4PM M-TH. ***Probate.***
See Northwest Corrner Probate District Court. Phone, fax and hours given here.

Sharon Probate Court, CT; 860-824-7012; fax: 860-824-7428; 9AM-4PM M-TH. ***Probate.***
See Northwest Corrner Probate District Court. Phone, fax and hours given here.

Thomaston Probate Court 158 Main St, Town Hall Bldg, PO Box 136, Thomaston, CT 06787; 860-283-4874; fax: 860-283-1013; 12-3PM M, 3-6PM T-TH, 1-5PM F, and by app't. ***Probate.***

Torrington Probate Court Municipal Bldg, 140 Main St, Torrington, CT 06790; 860-489-2215; fax: 860-496-5910; 8:30AM-4:00PM, M-W; 8:30AM-6:30PM T; 8:30AM-12:30PM F. ***Probate.***
District includes Town of Goshen.

Washington Probate Court Town Hall, 2 Bryan Mem. Plaza, PO Box 295, Washington Depot, CT 06794; 860-868-7974; fax: 860-868-0512; 9AM-N, 1-5PM M,W,F and by app't. ***Probate.*** www.washingtonct.org/probate.html

Watertown Probate Court PO Box 843, 281 Main St South, Woodbury, CT 06798; 203-263-2417; fax: 203-263-2748; 9AM-N, 1-4PM M-TH, 9AM-N F. ***Probate.***
Merged with Woodbury Probate Court on 01/08/03.

Winchester Probate Court 338 Main St, PO Box 625, Winsted, CT 06098; 860-379-5576; fax: 860-738-7053; 9AM-12,1-4PM M-W, 9AM-N, 1-7PM TH; 9AM-noon F. ***Probate.***
District includes towns of Colebrook, Winsted.

Woodbury Probate Court 281 Main St S, PO Box 843, Woodbury, CT 06798; 203-263-2417; fax: 203-263-2748; 9AM-N, 1PM-4PM M; 9AM-N, 1-3PM T,W,TH; 9AM-N F. ***Probate.***
District includes Town of Bethlehem, Watertown, Woodbury, and Oakville.

Middlesex County

Middlesex District Court - Criminal & GA Court #9 1 Court St, 1st Fl, Middletown, CT 06457-3348; 860-343-6445; fax: 860-343-6566; 9AM-5PM. ***Felony, Misdemeanor.***
Serving the towns of Chester, Clinton, Cromwell, Deep River, Durham, East Haddam, East Hampton, Essex, Haddam, Killingworth, Middlefield, Middletown, Old Saybrook, Portland and Westbrook.
Criminal Records: Access: Mail, in person, online. Only the court performs in person searches; visitors may not. No search fee. Required to search: name, years to search, DOB, signed release; also helpful: address, SSN. Criminal records on computer for 1 year from disposition or sentence, on microfiche prior to 1984, prior on index cards to 1961. Mail turnaround time 3-4 days. Pending, current and disposed criminal and motor vehicle dockets back to 2000 free at www.jud.ct.gov/jud2.htm. Online results show name also show year of birth.
General Information: Online identifiers in results same as on public terminal. No youthful offender records or dismissals released. Will not fax documents. Court makes copy: $1.00 per page. Certification fee: $2.50. Payee: Clerk, Superior Court. Personal checks accepted. Visa/MC accepted in person only. Prepayment required. Mail requests: SASE required.

Middlesex Judicial District Court - Civil 1 Court St, 2nd Fl, Middletown, CT 06457-3374; 860-343-6400; fax: 860-343-6423; 9AM-5PM. ***Civil Actions, Divorce, Eviction, Small Claims.***
Civil Records: Access: Mail, in person, online. Only the court performs in person searches; visitors may not. No search fee. Required to search: name, years to search; also helpful: type of case, docket number. Civil cases indexed by defendant, plaintiff, on computer 1 year post-judgment; on index card back 15 years, prior on docket books, microfiche. Mail turnaround time 1 week. Public use terminal has civil records back to 1997. PAT results show name only. Access civil case index free at http://civilinquiry.jud.ct.gov/; also access small claims index by hearing date, party name, or docket number free at www.jud2.ct.gov/Small_Claims/. Also, eviction case data free at www.jud.ct.gov/housing.htm. Online results show name only.
General Information: Online identifiers in results same as on public terminal. No sealed records released. Will not fax documents. Court makes copy: $1.00 per page. Self serve: $.10 per page, but you cannot copy court papers. Certification fee: $2.00; judgment file copy-$15.00 ($25 if certified); Cert. Judgment in Foreclosure action-$25.00. Exemplification copies-$20.00. Payee: Clerk, Superior Court. Personal checks accepted; name and address must be on pre-printed check. Credit cards accepted if payment over $10.00. Prepayment required. Mail requests: SASE required.

Clinton Probate Court 50 E Main St, PO Box 130, Clinton, CT 06413-0130; 860-669-6447; fax: same; 10AM-3PM M-TH; closed F. ***Probate.***
Call before faxing.

Deep River Probate Court PO Box 391, Town Hall, 171B Main St, Deep River, CT 06417; 860-526-6026; fax: 860-526-6094; 9AM-1PM M,F; 9AM-5PM T,TH; 9AM-12:3PM & 2-5PM W, by App't. ***Probate.***

East Haddam Probate Court PO Box 217, 7 Main St, East Haddam, CT 06423; 860-873-5028; fax: 860-873-5025; 10AM-2PM and by app't. ***Probate.***

East Hampton Probate Court 20 E High St, Annex, East Hampton, CT 06424; 860-267-9262; fax: 860-267-6453; 9AM-2PM M-TH. ***Probate.***

Essex Probate Court Town Hall, 29 West Ave, Essex, CT 06426; 860-767-4340 X125; fax: 860-767-2538; 9AM-3PM (and by app't). ***Probate.***

Haddam Probate Court 30 Field Park Dr, Haddam, CT 06438; 860-345-8531; probate phone: 860-345-8531 x210; fax: 860-345-3730; 9AM-2PM M-TH. ***Probate.***

Killingworth Probate Court 323 Rte 81, Killingworth, CT 06419; 860-663-2304; fax: 860-663-3305; 9-11AM M,F; 8AM-1PM T,TH; 9-3PM W; Summer- 9-3PM T,W,TH. ***Probate.***
Additional hours by appointment.

Middletown Probate Court 94 Court St, Middletown, CT 06457; 860-347-7424; fax: 860-346-1520; 8:30AM-4:30PM. ***Probate.***
District includes towns of Cromwell, Durham, Middlefield, Middletown.

Old Saybrook Probate Court 302 Main St, Old Saybrook, CT 06475-2384; 860-510-5028; 9AM-3PM. ***Probate.***
Court is open on Wed. evenings, also

Portland Probate Court 33 E Main St, PO Box 71, Portland, CT 06480; 860-342-6739; fax: 860-342-6755; 9AM-2PM M,W,TH; 2-6PM T; 9AM-N Fri. ***Probate.*** www.portlandct.org/portland/departments/probate.htm

Saybrook Probate Court 203 Middlesex Ave, Chester, CT 06412; 860-526-0013 x221; fax: 860-526-0004; 8AM-1PM M-TH; and by app't. ***Probate.***
District includes Town of Chester

Westbrook Probate Court 866 Boston Post Rd, Westbrook, CT 06498; 860-399-5661; fax: 860-399-3092; 1-4:30PM. ***Probate.***

New Haven County

Ansonia-Milford Judicial District Court PO Box 210, 14 W River St, 1st Fl, Milford, CT 06460; 203-877-4293; fax: 203-876-8640; 9AM-5PM. ***Felony (higher), Civil Actions, Divorce, Eviction.*** www.ctd.uscourts.gov/NewHaven.htm
Civil Records: Access: Mail, fax, online, in person. Only the court performs in person searches; visitors may not. No search fee. Required to search: name, years to search. Civil cases indexed by defendant, plaintiff, on computer back to 1993, on index cards from 1978. Purged computer records are on microfilm. Maintained 75 years at Records Center at E. Mail turnaround time 1-2 days. Access civil case index free at http://civilinquiry.jud.ct.gov/. Also, eviction case data free at www.jud.ct.gov/housing.htm.
Criminal Records: Access: Mail, in person, online. Only the court performs in person searches; visitors may not. No search fee. Required to search: name, years to search, DOB; also helpful-SSN. Criminal records computerized from 1993, on index cards from 1978. Purged computer records are on microfilm. Maintained 75 years at Records Center a. Mail turnaround time 1-2 days. Pending, current and disposed criminal and motor vehicle dockets back to 2000 free at www.jud.ct.gov/jud2.htm. Online results show name also show year of birth.
General Information: Online identifiers in results same as on public terminal. Will fax documents only to toll-free or local numbers. Court makes copy: $1.00 per page. Certification fee: $2.00 per cert plus copy fee; Exemplification is $20.00 add'l. Judgment file- $25.00. Payee: Clerk of Superior Court. Personal checks accepted if proper ID provided. Visa/MC accepted. Prepayment required. Mail requests: SASE required.

Meriden Judicial District Court 54 W Main St, Meriden, CT 06451; 203-238-6666; fax: 203-238-6322; 9AM-5PM. ***Civil Actions, Divorce, Eviction, Housing, Small Claims.***
Civil Records: Access: Mail, in person, online. Only the court performs in person searches; visitors may not. No search fee. Required to search: name, years to search. Civil cases indexed by defendant, plaintiff. Pending and 1 yr after disposed cases on computer, on microfiche from 1984, prior on index cards. Mail turnaround time 1-2 days. Public use terminal has civil records. Access civil case index free at http://civilinquiry.jud.ct.gov/; also access small claims index by hearing date, party name, or docket number free at www.jud2.ct.gov/Small_Claims/. Also, eviction case data free at www.jud.ct.gov/housing.htm. Online results show name only.
General Information: Online identifiers in results same as on public terminal. No acknowledgments of paternity, agreements to support prior to 10/01/95 records released. Will not fax documents. Court makes copy: $1.00 per page. Certification fee: $2.00 per doc. Payee: Clerk of Superior Court. In state Personal checks and major credit cards accepted. Prepayment required. Mail requests: SASE required.

New Haven Judicial District Court 235 Church St, New Haven, CT 06510; 203-503-6800; fax: 203-789-6424; 9AM-5PM. ***Felony, Civil Actions, Family, Divorce, Small Claims.*** www.jud.state.ct.us/directory/directory/location/newhaven.htm
Civil Records: Access: Mail, in person, online. Only the court performs in person searches; visitors may not. No search fee. Required to search: name, years to search. Civil cases indexed by defendant, plaintiff. Pending cases on computer, disposed cases deleted after 1 year, on microfiche from 1972, prior on index cards. Note: Visits may search live cases only in person. Mail turnaround time 2-5 weeks. Public use terminal has civil records back to 1991. PAT results show name only. Access civil case index free at http://civilinquiry.jud.ct.gov/; also access small claims index by hearing date, party name, or docket number free at www.jud2.ct.gov/Small_Claims/.
Criminal Records: Access: Mail, in person, online. Only the court performs in person searches;

visitors may not. No search fee. Required to search: name, years to search, DOB. Pending criminal cases on computer, disposed deleted after 1 year, prior on index cards. Mail turnaround time 2-5 weeks. Pending, current and disposed criminal and motor vehicle dockets back to 2000 free at www.jud.ct.gov/jud2.htm. Online results show name also show year of birth.
General Information: Online identifiers in results same as on public terminal. No sealed records released. Will not fax documents. Court makes copy: $1.00 per page.No pro se personal checks for copies. Certification fee: $2.00. Payee: Clerk of Superior Court. CT personal checks accepted if address on check matches address on drivers license. Visa/MC accepted. Prepayment required. Mail requests: SASE required.

Waterbury Judicial District Court 300 Grand St, Waterbury, CT 06702; 203-591-3300; civil phone: small claims- 203-591-3320; fax: 203-596-4032; 9AM-5PM. ***Civil Actions, Small Claims, Divorce, Eviction.***
Address mail requests for Misdemeanor searches to 400 Grand St. (Geographical Area Court #4).
Civil Records: Access: Fax, mail, online, in person. Only the court performs in person searches; visitors may not. No search fee. Required to search: name, years to search. Civil cases indexed by defendant. Civil records on computer back to 1990; none-computer records go back to 1900. Note: Phone access limited to one search. Mail turnaround time 1-2 weeks. Public use terminal has civil records back to about 10 years. PAT results show name only. Access civil case index free at http://civilinquiry.jud.ct.gov/; also access small claims index by hearing date, party name, or docket number free at www.jud2.ct.gov/Small_Claims/. Also, eviction case data free at www.jud.ct.gov/housing.htm. Online results show name only.
General Information: Online identifiers in results same as on public terminal. Will not fax documents. Court makes copy: $1.00 per page. Certification fee: $2.00 per page. Payee: Clerk of Superior Court. Personal checks accepted. Major credit cards accepted, in person only. Prepayment required. Mail requests: SASE requested.

Geographical Area Court #22 14 W River St, 2nd Fl, Milford, CT 06460; criminal phone: 203-874-1116; civil phone: 203-877-4293; fax: 203-874-5233; 9AM-5PM. ***Felony (lower), Misdemeanor, Small Claims, Traffic.***
Serving the towns of Milford and West Haven. This court handles lower-grade felonies; see the Judicial district court for other felonies.
Civil Records: Access: Mail, in person, online. Only small claims cases maintained here, no civil. Access small claims index by hearing date, party name, or docket number free at www.jud2.ct.gov/Small_Claims/.
Criminal Records: Access: Mail, in person, online. Only the court performs in person searches; visitors may not. No search fee. Required to search: name, years to search; also helpful: DOB, town where offense occurred. Criminal records on computer for 6 months, after disposal, on microfiche from 1986, prior on index cards and docket books. Mail turnaround time 1 week. Pending, current and disposed criminal and motor vehicle dockets back to 2000 free at www.jud.ct.gov/jud2.htm. Online results show name also show year of birth.
General Information: Online identifiers in results same as on public terminal. Will fax out documents in emergency situations only. Court makes copy: $1.00 per page. Certification fee: $2.00 per cert. Payee: Clerk of Superior Court. Personal checks accepted. Visa/MC accepted. Prepayment required. Mail requests: SASE required.

Geographical Area Court #23 121 Elm St, New Haven, CT 06510; 203-789-7461; fax: 203-789-7492; 9AM-5PM. ***Misdemeanor, Eviction.***
Serving towns of Bethany, Branford, E Haven, Guilford, Madison, New Haven, North Branford, Woodbridge. Small claims is located at 235 Church St, Clerk's Office, New Haven, CT 06510, 860-756-7800, instate-866-383-5927; Evictions phone- 203-789-7937.
Criminal Records: Access: Mail, in person, online. Only the court performs in person searches; visitors may not. No search fee. Required to search: name, years to search, DOB. Criminal records on computer back 13 months, microfiche from 1986, prior archived for criminal and motor vehicle. Note: In person search results mailed back. Mail turnaround time 2-3 weeks. Public use terminal has crim records back to 2004.PAT results show name, DOB. Public terminal located at information desk. Pending, current and disposed criminal and motor vehicle dockets back to 2000 free at www.jud.ct.gov/jud2.htm. Also, eviction case data free at www.jud.ct.gov/housing.htm. Online results show name, DOB. Online criminal results show year of birth only.
General Information: Online identifiers in results same as on public terminal. No dismissals, juvenile records released. Will not fax documents. Court makes copy: $1.00 per page. Certification fee: $2.00 per cert. Payee: Superior Court. Personal checks and major credit cards accepted. Prepayment required. Mail requests: SASE required.

Geographical Area Court #4 400 Grand St, Waterbury, CT 06702; 203-236-8100; fax: 203-236-8099; 9AM-5PM. ***Felony, Misdemeanor, Traffic.***
Serving the towns of Middlebury, Naugatuck, Prospect, Southbury, Waterbury, Watertown, Wolcott and Woodbury.
Criminal Records: Access: Phone, mail, in person, online. Only the court performs in person searches; visitors may not. No search fee. Required to search: name, years to search; also helpful: DOB. Criminal records on computer since 1985. Mail turnaround time 1-2 weeks. Pending, current and disposed criminal and motor vehicle dockets back to 2000 free at www.jud.ct.gov/jud2.htm. Online results show name also show year of birth.
General Information: Online identifiers in results same as on public terminal. No youthful offenders records or dismissals released. Court makes copy: $1.00 per page. Certification fee: $2.00; certifications are made by the record center. Payee: Clerk of Superior Court. Personal checks/Visa/MC accepted. Prepayment required. Mail requests: SASE required.

Geographical Area Court #5 106 Elizabeth St, Derby, CT 06418; 203-735-7438; criminal phone: 203-735-7438; civil phone: 203-735-9654; fax: 203-735-2047; 9AM-5PM. ***Misdemeanor, Eviction, Small Claims.***
Serving the towns of Ansonia, Beacon Falls, Derby, Orange, Oxford, Seymour and Shelton.
Civil Records: Access: Mail, in person, online. Only the court performs in person searches; visitors may not. No search fee. Required to search: name, years to search. Civil cases indexed by defendant, plaintiff. Pending and records for 1 yr after disposal on computer, prior on index cards. Note: They only hold small claims civil records in this office. In person search results are mailed back. Mail turnaround time 1-2 weeks. Access small claims index by hearing date, party name, or docket number free at www.jud2.ct.gov/Small_Claims/. Also, eviction case data free at www.jud.ct.gov/housing.htm.
Criminal Records: Access: Mail, in person, online. Only the court performs in person searches; visitors may not. No search fee. Required to search: name, years to search, DOB. Pending and records for 1 yr after disposal on computer, on microfiche from 1986, prior on index cards. Note: In person search results returned by mail only. Mail turnaround time 1-2 weeks. Pending, current and disposed criminal and motor vehicle dockets back to 2000 free at www.jud.ct.gov/jud2.htm. Online results show name also show year of birth.
General Information: Online identifiers in results same as on public terminal. No sealed records released. Will not fax documents. Court makes copy: $1.00 per page. Certification fee: $2.00 per cert. Payee: Clerk of Superior Court. Personal checks accepted. Visa/MC accepted. Prepayment required. SASE not required.

Geographical Area Court #7 54 W Main St, Meriden, CT 06451; criminal phone: 203-238-6130; civil phone: 203-238-6128; criminal fax: 203-238-6016; civil fax: same; 9AM-5PM. ***Misdemeanor, Small Claims.*** Serving the towns of Cheshire, Hamden, Meriden, North Haven and Wallingford.
Civil Records: Access: Mail, in person, online. Only the court performs in person searches; visitors may not. No search fee. Required to search: name, years to search. Civil cases indexed by defendant, plaintiff. Pending and 1 yr after disposed cases on computer, on microfiche from 1985, prior on index cards. All manual records by docket number. Mail turnaround time 1-2 days. Civil PAT available. Access small claims index by hearing date, party name, or docket number free at www.jud2.ct.gov/Small_Claims/.
Criminal Records: Access: Phone, mail, in person, online. Only the court performs in person searches; visitors may not. No search fee. Required to search: name, years to search, DOB. Criminal records on computer since 1986, purged every 6 months and maintained in Enfield, CT. Mail turnaround time 1-2 days. Criminal PAT available. Pending, current and disposed criminal and motor vehicle dockets back to 2000 free at www.jud.ct.gov/jud2.htm. Online results show name also show year of birth.
General Information: Online identifiers in results same as on public terminal. No sealed records released. Will not fax documents. Court makes copy: $1.00 per page. Certification fee: $10.00. Payee: Clerk of Superior Court. Personal checks accepted. Visa/MC accepted. Prepayment required. Mail requests: SASE required.

Bethany Probate Court Town Hall, 40 Peck Rd, Bethany, CT 06524; 203-393-3744; fax: 203-393-0821; 9AM-1PM and by appt. ***Probate.***

Branford Probate Court PO Box 638, 1019 Main St, Branford, CT 06405-0638; 203-488-0318; fax: 203-315-4715; 8:30AM-4:30PM, till 12:30PM F in Summer. ***Probate.***
www.branford-ct.gov/Probate%20Court.htm

Cheshire Probate Court 84 S Main St, Cheshire, CT 06410; 203-271-6608; 8:30AM-1PM, 1:30-4PM M-TH; 9AM-N F. ***Probate.***
District includes Town of Prospect.

Derby Probate Court 253 Main St, 2nd Fl, Ansonia, CT 06401; 203-734-1277; fax: 203-736-1434; 8:30AM-5PM M-TH; 8:30AM-4PM F. ***Probate.*** District includes towns of Ansonia, Seymour & Derby.

East Haven Probate Court 250 Main St, Town Hall, East Haven, CT 06512; 203-468-3895; fax: 203-468-5155; 9:30-4:30 M; 9:30-3:30 T; 8:30-3:30 W; 8:30-4:30 TH; 9-1 F. ***Probate.***

Guilford Probate Court Town Hall, 31 Park St, Guilford, CT 06437; 203-453-8006; fax: 203-453-8132; 9AM-N,1-4PM M,T,TH,F; 9AM-N W. ***Probate.***

Hamden Probate Court Gov't Center, 2750 Dixwell Ave, Hamden, CT 06518; 203-287-7082; fax: 203-287-7087; 9AM-4:30PM. ***Probate.***

Madison Probate Court 8 Campus Dr, Madison, CT 06443; 203-245-5661; fax: 203-245-5653; 9AM-3PM and by app't. ***Probate.***

Meriden Probate Court City Hall, 142 E Main St, Rm 113, Meriden, CT 06450; 203-630-4150; fax: 203-630-4043; 8:30AM-7PM M; 8:30-4:30 T-F. ***Probate.***

Milford Probate Court PO Box 414, 70 W River St, Parsons Government Office Complex, Milford, CT 06460; 203-783-3205; fax: 203-783-3364; 8:30AM-4:30PM. ***Probate.***

Naugatuck Probate Court Town Hall, 229 Church St, Naugatuck, CT 06770; 203-720-7046; fax: 203-720-5476; 8:30AM-4PM M-TH; 8:30AM-2PM F. ***Probate.***
District includes Town of Beacon Falls.

New Haven Probate Court 200 Orange St, 1st Fl, PO Box 905, New Haven, CT 06504; 203-946-4880; fax: 203-946-5962; 9AM-4PM. ***Probate.***

North Branford Probate Court 909 Foxon Rd, PO Box 214, North Branford, CT 06471; 203-484-6007; fax: 203-484-6017; 8:30AM-1PM. ***Probate.***

North Haven Probate Court PO Box 175, 18 Church St, North Haven, CT 06473-0175; 203-239-5321 x775; fax: 203-239-1874; 8:30AM-4:30PM M-TH; 8:30AM-12:30PM F; and by app't. ***Probate.***

Orange Probate Court 525 Orange Center Rd, Orange, CT 06477; 203-891-2160; fax: 203-891-2161; 8:30AM-1PM. ***Probate.***

Oxford Probate Court 486 Oxford Rd, Oxford Town Hall, Oxford, CT 06478; 203-888-2543 x3014; fax: 203-888-2136; 7-9PM Mon; 11:45AM-5PM T,W; 9AM-5PM, 7-9PM TH. Closed F. ***Probate.***

Southbury Probate Court PO Box 674, 501 Main St S, Town Hall, Southbury, CT 06488; 203-262-0641; fax: 203-264-9310; 9AM-4:30PM (and by app't). ***Probate.***

Wallingford Probate Court Town Hall, 45 S Main St, Rm 114, Wallingford, CT 06492; 203-294-2100; fax: 203-294-2109; 9AM-5PM. ***Probate.***

Waterbury Probate Court 49 Leavenworth St, Waterbury, CT 06702; 203-755-1127; fax: 203-597-0824; 8:45AM-4:45PM. ***Probate.***
District includes towns of Middlebury, Wolcott.

West Haven Probate Court 355 Main St, PO Box 127, West Haven, CT 06516; 203-937-3552/3/4/5; fax: 203-937-3556; 9AM-4PM. ***Probate.***

Woodbridge Probate Court Town Hall, 11 Meetinghouse Ln, Woodbridge, CT 06525; 203-389-3410; fax: 203-387-5878; 8:30AM-1:30PM T,W,TH. ***Probate.***

New London County

New London Judicial District Court 70 Huntington St, New London, CT 06320; 860-443-5363; criminal phone: 860-443-6016; fax: 860-442-7703; 9AM-5PM. ***Felony, Civil Actions, Divorce.***
Civil Records: Access: Mail, in person, online. No search fee. Required to search: exact name, years to search. Civil cases indexed by defendant, plaintiff, pending and 1 yr after disposed on computer, on microfiche from mid-70s. Note: In person access limited to five names. Mail turnaround time 2 weeks. Public use terminal has civil records. Access civil case index free at http://civilinquiry.jud.ct.gov/.
Criminal Records: Access: Mail, in person, online. Both court and visitors may perform in person searches. No search fee. Required to search: name, years to search; also helpful: DOB. Criminal records computerized from 1991, prior on index cards. Note: Results include name and address. Mail turnaround time 2 weeks. Pending, current and disposed criminal and motor vehicle dockets back to 2000 free at www.jud.ct.gov/jud2.htm. Online results show name also show year of birth.
General Information: Online identifiers in results same as on public terminal. No sealed or youthful offender records released. Will not fax documents. Court makes copy: $1.00 per page. Certification fee: $2.00. Payee: Clerk of Superior Court. Personal checks accepted. Visa/MC accepted. Prepayment required. Mail requests: SASE required.

Norwich Judicial District Court 1 Courthouse Sq, Norwich, CT 06360; 860-887-3515; fax: 860-887-8643; 9AM-5PM. ***Civil Actions, Family.***
Civil Records: Access: Phone, mail, fax, online, in person. Both court and visitors may perform in person searches. No search fee. Required to search: name, years to search. Civil cases indexed by defendant, plaintiff. Pending and disposed cases on computer from 1992, on microfiche from 1975, prior on index cards. Mail turnaround time up to 2 months. Public use terminal has civil records back to 1992. PAT results show name only. Access civil case index free at http://civilinquiry.jud.ct.gov/. Online results show name only.
General Information: Online identifiers in results same as on public terminal. No criminal search warrant, acknowledgment of paternity prior to 1995, sealed records released. Will fax documents $1.00 per page. Court makes copy: $1.00 per page. Judgment copies $15.00. Self serve: no fee. Certification fee: $2.00 per doc. Certified copy of Judgment $25.00. Payee: Clerk of Superior Court. Personal checks accepted; checks must have imprinted name and address and match valid CT driver license or picture ID. Visa/MC accepted in person only. Prepayment required. SASE not required.

Geographical Area Court #10 112 Broad St, New London, CT 06320; 860-443-8343; civil phone: 860-443-8346; 9AM-5PM. ***Misdemeanor, Eviction, Small Claims.***
Serving the towns of East Lyme, Groton, Ledyard, Lyme, New London, North Stonington, Old Lyme, Stonington and Waterford.
Civil Records: Access: Mail, in person, online. Both court and visitors may perform in person searches. No search fee. Required to search: name, years to search. Civil cases indexed by defendant. Civil index on cards and docket books. Mail turnaround time up to 2 months. Access small claims index by hearing date, party name, or docket number free at www.jud2.ct.gov/Small_Claims/. Also, eviction case data free at www.jud.ct.gov/housing.htm.
Criminal Records: Access: Mail, in person, online. Only the court performs in person searches; visitors may not. No search fee. Required to search: name, years to search, DOB. Criminal records on computer for 2 years; on microfiche back to 1962. Mail turnaround time up to 2 months. Pending, current and disposed criminal and motor vehicle dockets back to 2000 free at www.jud.ct.gov/jud2.htm. Online results show name also show year of birth.
General Information: Online identifiers in results same as on public terminal. No sealed, dismissed, youth or program records released. Court makes copy: $1.00 per page. Certification fee: $2.00 per page. Payee: Clerk, Superior Court. Personal checks accepted. Visa/MC accepted. Prepayment required. Mail requests: SASE required.

Geographical Area Court #21 1 Courthouse Sq, Norwich, CT 06360; criminal phone: 860-889-7338; civil phone: 860-887-3515; fax: 860-885-0509; 9AM-5PM. ***Misdemeanor, Eviction, Small Claims.***
Serving the towns of Bozrah, Colchester, Franklin, Griswold, Lebanon, Lisbon, Montville, Norwich, Preston, Salem, Sprague and Voluntown.
Civil Records: Access: Online, in person. Visitors must perform in person searches themselves. Required to search: name, years to search. Civil cases indexed by defendant. Pending and 2-4 years history of disposed on computer, on microfiche from 1986, prior on index cards and docket books. Small claims, evictions not on. Civil PAT available. Also access small claims index by hearing date, party name, or docket number free at www.jud2.ct.gov/Small_Claims/.
Criminal Records: Access: In person, online. Visitors must perform in person searches themselves. Required to search: name, years to search, DOB. Pending and 2-4 years history of disposed on computer, on microfiche from 1986, prior on index cards and docket books. Small claims, evictions not on. Note: Mail requests are referred to the Judicial Records Center in Enfield. Criminal PAT available. Pending, current and disposed criminal and motor vehicle dockets back to 2000 free at www.jud.ct.gov/jud2.htm. Online results show name also show year of birth.
General Information: Online identifiers in results same as on public terminal. No youthful offender or dismissed/erased records released. Court makes copy: $1.00 per page. Certification fee: $2.00 per cert. Certified copy of Judgment $15.00. Payee: Superior Court GA #21. Personal checks accepted. Visa/MC accepted. Prepayment required.

Bozrah Probate Court Town Hall, 2nd Fl, One River Rd, Bozrah, CT 06334; 860-889-2958; fax: 860-887-7571; 10AM-2PM except T 1-5PM. ***Probate.***

Colchester Probate Court Town Hall, 127 Norwich Ave, Colchester, CT 06415; 860-537-7290; fax: 860-537-7298; 12:30PM-4:30PM M,F; 9AM-4:30PM T,W,T. ***Probate.***
www.colchesterct.net/probate.html
The court also holds records for former probate court in Lebanon from Jan '03 to present.

East Lyme Probate Court PO Box 519, 118 Pennsylvania Ave, Niantic, CT 06357; 860-739-6052; fax: 860-739-6738; 8:30AM-12:30PM. ***Probate.***

Griswold Probate Court Town Hall, 28 Main St, PO Box 369, Jewett City, CT 06351; 860-376-7060 x213; fax: 860-376-6628; 9AM-4PM T; 11:30AM-5:30PM W; 9AM-4PM TH, Closed Monday & Fri. ***Probate.***

Lebanon Probate Court, CT; ***Probate.***
Court records now located at Colchester Probate Court at 860-537-7290.

Ledyard Probate Court 741 Colonel Ledyard Hwy, Rte 17, Ledyard, CT 06339; 860-464-3219; fax: 860-464-8531; 8:30AM-1:30PM M-TH. ***Probate.***
www.jud.ct.gov/scripts/protest.asp

Lyme Probate Court 480 Hamburg Rd, Town Hall, Lyme, CT 06371; 860-434-7733; fax: 860-434-2989; 9AM-3PM M; 9AM-N T,TH; N-4PM W,F. ***Probate.***
www.ctprobatejudges.org/

Montville Probate Court 310 Norwich-New London Turnpike, Uncasville, CT 06382; 860-848-3030 x319; fax: 860-848-2116; 9AM-1PM M,T,TH,F; 9AM-4PM W. ***Probate.***
www.montville-ct.org/CMS/default.asp?CMS_AreaID=139

New London Probate Court PO Box 148, 181 State St, Municipal Bldg, New London, CT 06320; 860-443-7121; fax: 860-437-8155; 8:30AM-4PM. ***Probate.***
District includes City of New London and Town of Waterford.

North Stonington Probate Court 391 Norwich Westerly Rd, Rte #2, PO Box 204, North Stonington, CT 06359; 860-535-8441; fax: same; 9AM-N M & W; 1-4PM T; N-5:30PM TH. ***Probate.***
Call before faxing.

Norwich Probate Court PO Box 38, 100 Broadway, Rm 122, Norwich, CT 06360; 860-887-2160; fax: 860-887-2401; 9AM-4:30PM. ***Probate.***
District includes Towns of Franklin, Lisbon, Norwich, Preston, Sprague, Voluntown

Old Lyme Probate Court 52 Lyme St, Memorial Town Hall, Old Lyme, CT 06371; 860-434-1605 x222; fax: 860-434-1400; 9AM-N, 1-4PM. ***Probate.***
www.oldlyme-ct.gov/Pages/OldlymeCT_Probate/index

Salem Probate Court 270 Hota Rd, Salem, CT 06420; 860-859-3873; 10:00AM-N F and by app't. ***Probate.***
www.ctprobatejudges.org/

Stonington Probate Court 152 Elm St, PO Box 312, Stonington, CT 06378; 860-535-5090; fax: 860-535-0520; 9AM-N, 1-4PM. ***Probate.***
District includes Town of Mystic.

Tolland County

Tolland Judicial District Court - Civil 69 Brooklyn St, Rockville, CT 06066; 860-896-4920; fax: 860-875-0777; 9AM-5PM. ***Civil Actions, Family.***
Civil Records: Access: Mail, in person, online. Only the court performs in person searches; visitors may

not. No search fee. Required to search: name, years to search. Civil cases indexed by defendant, plaintiff, on computer from 2003, on microfiche from 1980, all prior on index cards. Mail turnaround time 1-2 weeks. Access civil case index free at http://civilinquiry.jud.ct.gov/. Online results show name only.
General Information: Online identifiers in results same as on public terminal. No youthful offender, dismissed or not guilty verdict records released. Will not fax documents. Court makes copy: $1.00 per page; Copy of Judgment- $15.00. Exemplification fee- $20.00. Certification fee: $2.00. A full Certified Copy of Judgment is $25.00 including copy fee. Payee: Clerk of Superior Court. Personal checks accepted. Visa/MC accepted. Prepayment required. Mail requests: SASE required.

Tolland Judicial District Court - Criminal 20 Park St, Vernon, CT 06066; 860-870-3200; fax: 860-870-3290; 9AM-5PM. ***Felony.***
The address can use either Rockville or Vernon, but the US Postal Service will sometimes return mail addressed to Rockville.
Criminal Records: Access: In person, online. Only the court performs in person searches; visitors may not. No search fee. Required to search: name, years to search; also helpful: DOB. Criminal records are for active cases only. Completed cases must be searched State Police. Note: Mail requests should be sent to the State Police Bureau in Middletown, CT. Pending, current and disposed criminal and motor vehicle dockets back to 2000 free at www.jud.ct.gov/jud2.htm. Online results show name also show year of birth.
General Information: Online identifiers in results same as on public terminal. No youthful offender, dismissed or not guilty verdict records released. Will not fax documents. Court makes copy: $1.00 per page. No certification fee. Payee: Clerk of Superior Court. Personal checks accepted. Visa/MC accepted. Prepayment required.

Geographical Area Court #19 PO Box 980, 20 Park St, Rockville, CT 06066-0980; 860-870-3200; fax: 860-870-3290; 9-5PM. ***Misdemeanor.***
Serving the towns of Andover, Bolton, Columbia, Coventry, Ellington, Hebron, Mansfield, Somers, Stafford, Tolland, Union, Vernon and Willington.
Criminal Records: Access: Mail, in person, online. Only the court performs in person searches; visitors may not. No search fee. Required to search: name, years to search, DOB. Criminal records on computer approx. 2 yrs from disposition, on microfiche from 1985, prior on index cards. Mail turnaround time 7-14 days. Pending, current and disposed criminal and motor vehicle dockets back to 2000 free at www.jud.ct.gov/jud2.htm. Online results show name also show year of birth.
General Information: Online identifiers in results same as on public terminal. No youthful offender records released. Will not fax documents. Court makes copy: $1.00 per page. Certification fee: $2.00. Payee: Clerk of Superior Court. Personal checks accepted. Visa/MC accepted. Prepayment required. Mail requests: SASE required.

Hebron Probate Court 15 Gilead St, Hebron, CT 06248; 860-228-5971 x127; fax: 860-228-4859; 8:30AM-12:30PM and by app't. ***Probate.***

Andover Probate Court 222 Bolton Center Rd, Bolton, CT 06043; 860-647-7979; fax: 860-649-8674; 8:30AM-4:30PM M; 8:30AM-4PM T-TH; 8:30-1PM F. ***Probate.***
District includes towns of Andover, Bolton and Columbia. The physical address is Notch Road Muni Ctr, 104 Notch Rd.

Ellington Probate Court PO Box 268, 14 Park Pl, Rockville, CT 06066; 860-872-0519; fax: 860-870-5140; 8:30AM-4:30PM M-W; 8:30AM-7PM TH; 8:30AM-1PM F. ***Probate.***
District includes Towns of Vernon, Ellington.

Mansfield Probate Court 4 S Eagleville Rd, Storrs, CT 06268; 860-429-3313; fax: 860-429-4088; 8AM-12PM, 1-4:30PM T; 1-4:30PM W; 1PM-6:30PM TH; 8AM-N M,F. ***Probate.***

Stafford Probate Court Town Hall, 1 Main St, PO Box 63, Stafford Springs, CT 06076; 860-684-1783; fax: 860-684-1797; 9AM-N, 1-4:30PM M; 9AM-12:30 Tu-TH; 9AM-N F. ***Probate.***
District includes towns of Union, Stafford and Somers. Somers Probate Court merged with this court in Jan. 1999.

Tolland Probate Court 21 Tolland Green, Tolland, CT 06084; 860-871-3640; fax: 860-871-3641; 9AM-2:30 M-W; 4-7:30PM TH, and by app't. ***Probate.***
District includes Town of Willington.

Windham County

Windham Judicial District Court 155 Church St, Putnam, CT 06260; 860-928-7749; civil phone: 860-756-7800-small claims; fax: 860-928-7076; 9AM-5PM. ***Civil Actions, Divorce.***
www.jud.ct.gov
Civil Records: Access: Phone, mail, online, in person. Only the court performs in person searches; visitors may not. No search fee. Required to search: name, years to search. Civil cases indexed by defendant, plaintiff, on computer for 1 year, prior on index cards, prior to 70s archived. Note: The court must look up records for searches of records over 1 year old. Mail turnaround time 1-2 days. Public use terminal has civil records back to 1 year only. Access civil case index free at http://civilinquiry.jud.ct.gov/. Online results show name only.
General Information: Online identifiers in results same as on public terminal. No sealed, dismissed records released. Will not fax documents. Court makes copy: $1.00 per page. Certification fee: $2.00 per cert. Payee: Clerk of Superior Court. Personal checks accepted. Visa/MC accepted. Prepayment required. Mail requests: SASE required for civil.

Geographical Area Court #11 120 School St, #110, Danielson, CT 06239-3024; 860-779-8480; fax: 860-779-8488; 9AM-5PM. ***Felony, Misdemeanor, Eviction, Small Claims.***
Serving the towns of Ashford, Brooklyn, Canterbury, Chaplin, Eastford, Hampton, Killingly, Plainfield, Pomfret, Putnam, Scotland, Sterling, Thompson, Windham and Woodstock.
Civil Records: Access: Phone, mail, online, in person. Both court and visitors may perform in person searches. No search fee. Required to search: name, years to search. Civil cases indexed by defendant. Small claims records on computer since 8/96; all other records on index cards. Mail turnaround time 1-2 weeks. Public use terminal has civil records back to 8/1996. PAT results show name only. Terminal results include hearing date, charges and bond information. Also access small claims index by hearing date, party name, or docket number free at www.jud2.ct.gov/Small_Claims/. Also, eviction case data free at www.jud.ct.gov/housing.htm.
Criminal Records: Access: Mail, in person, online. Only the court performs in person searches; visitors may not. No search fee. Required to search: name, years to search, DOB, dates of disposition. Pending criminal and 1 year after disposed on computer, on microfiche from 1986, prior on index cards. Mail turnaround time 1-2 weeks. Pending, current and disposed criminal and motor vehicle dockets back to 2000 free at www.jud.ct.gov/jud2.htm. Online results show name also show year of birth.
General Information: Online identifiers in results same as on public terminal. No sealed records released. Will not fax documents. Court makes copy: $1.00 per page. Certification fee: $2.00 per page. Payee: Clerk of Superior Court. Personal checks and major credit cards accepted. Prepayment required. Mail requests: SASE required.

Ashford Probate Court 5 Town Hall Rd, PO Box 61, Ashford, CT 06278; 860-487-4408; fax: 860-487-4436; 8:30AM-3:30PM Mon; 8:30-11AM T; 8:30AM-4:30PM & 7-9PM W. ***Probate.***

Brooklyn Probate Court 69 S Main St, Ste. 22, Brooklyn, CT 06234; 860-774-5973; fax: 860-779-5675; 8AM-N. ***Probate.***

Canterbury Probate Court, CT; ***Probate.***
Closed. See Plainfield Probate District.

Chaplin Probate Court c/o Eastford Probate District Court, PO Box 98, Eastford, CT 06278-0061; 860-974-3024; fax: 860-974-0624. ***Probate.***
Physical address is: c/o Eastford Probate District, 16 Westford Rd, Eastford, CT, 06242. See Eastford probate Court; Champlin Court merged with Eastford in late 1990's.

Eastford Probate Court PO Box 98, 16 Westford Rd, Eastford, CT 06242-0207; 860-974-3024; fax: 860-974-0624; 9AM-N M-W, 1-5PM M & Wed, 2-5PM Tues, and by app't. ***Probate.***

Hampton Probate Court Town Hall, 164 Main St, PO Box 143, Hampton, CT 06247; 860-455-9132 x8; fax: 860-455-0517; 9AM-4PM T,TH. ***Probate.***
http://hamptonct.org/probate.htm

Killingly Probate Court 172 Main St, Danielson, CT 06239; 860-779-3074; fax: 860-779-3074; 9AM-1PM. ***Probate.***
Also handles marriages, guardianships, adoptions, name changes, trusts.

Plainfield Probate Court Town Hall, 8 Community Ave, Plainfield, CT 06374; 860-230-3031; fax: 860-230-3033; 8:30AM-3:30PM M-Th; 8:30AM-N F. ***Probate.***
The Probate Court merged into this court Jan. 2003.

Pomfret Probate Court 5 Haven Rd, Rt. 44, Pomfret Center, CT 06259; 860-974-0186; fax: 860-974-3950; 8:30AM-12:30PM. ***Probate.***

Putnam Probate Court PO Box 548, 126 Church St, Putnam, CT 06260; 860-963-6868; fax: 860-963-6817; 1-4PM. ***Probate.***

Sterling Probate Court, CT; ***Probate.***
This court merged into the Plainfield Probate Court.

Thompson Probate Court 815 Riverside Dr, Town Hall, PO Box 74, North Grosvenordale, CT 06255; 860-923-2203; fax: 860-923-9105; Mornings, on W to 3:15 PM and TH to 5PM. ***Probate.***

Windham Probate Court 979 Main St, PO Box 34, Willimantic, CT 06226; 860-465-3049; fax: 860-465-2162; 9AM-2PM M-TH; 9AM-N F. ***Probate.***
District includes only Towns of Willimanitc, Scotland and Windham.

Woodstock Probate Court 415 Rte 169, Woodstock, CT 06281; 860-928-2223; fax: 860-963-7557; 9AM-4:30PM T,TH; 1-6PM W, and by app't. ***Probate*** www.woodstockct.gov.

Connecticut Recording Offices

ORGANIZATION: 8 counties and 169 towns/cities. There is no county recording in Connecticut, all recording is at the town/city level. The recording officer is the Town/City Clerk. Be careful not to confuse searching in the following towns/cities as equivalent to a countywide search (since they have the same names): Fairfield, Hartford, Litchfield, New Haven, New London, Tolland, and Windham. Connecticut is in the Eastern Time Zone (EST).

REAL ESTATE RECORDS: Most towns do not perform real estate searches. Copy fee is usually $1.00 per page. Certification fee is usually $2.00 per cert plus copy fee. Copies of Vital Records are $5.00, $10.00 certified.

UCC RECORDS: Connecticut adopted Revised Article 9 on October 1, 2001. Financing statements are filed at the state level except for real estate related collateral which are filed only with the Town/City Clerk. A few towns will perform UCC searches of older records. UCC copy fee is usually $1.00 per page.

TAX LIEN RECORDS: All federal and state tax liens on personal property are filed with the Secretary of State. Federal and state tax liens on real property are filed with the Town/City Clerk. Towns will not perform tax lien searches.

OTHER LIENS: Mechanics, judgments, lis pendens, municipal, welfare, carpenter, sewer & water, city/town.

ONLINE ACCESS: A number of towns offer free access to assessor information. The State's Municipal Public Access Initiative has produced a website of Town and Municipality general information at www.munic.state.ct.us. Also, a private vendor has placed assessor records from a number of New England towns on the Internet, visit http://data.visionappraisal.com. A free statewide UCC index search is offered at www.concord-sots.ct.gov/CONC ORD/index.jsp

Andover Town

Town Clerk, 17 School Rd, Andover, CT 06232-0328. Recording, R/E & UCC phone-860-742-0188; fax-860-742-7535; 8:15AM-7PM M; 8:15AM-4PM T-TH; Closed on Fri. (EST) www.andoverct.org

Index: Separate indices to search include day book, grantor/grantee. Records indexed on computer back to 1848. Public access terminal available. Only the public may search. Copy fee $1.00 per page. Cert fee- $2.00 per doc plus copy fee. Payee- Andover Town Clerk. **Other phones:** Treasurer- 860-742-4035; Elections- 860-742-7305; Vital Records- 860-742-0188; Tax Collector- 860-742-4035. **Property tax/Assessing**- 17 School Rd, Andover, CT 06232-0328; 860-742-4035, assessor fax- 860-742-7535. Self addressed stamped envelope must be included with search request. Public terminal available. **Online access**- Search town assessor database at http://data.visionappraisal.com/AndoverCT/. Free registration for full data.

Ansonia City

City Clerk, 253 Main St; City Hall, Ansonia, CT 06401. 203-736-5980; fax-203-736-5982; 8AM-5:30PM, M, T, W, F; 8AM-6:30PM, TH. (EST)

Index: All in one. Records indexed on computer back to 1968. Only the public may search. Copy fee $1.00 per page. Cert fee- $1.00 per cert plus copy fee. Payee- Ansonia City Clerk. **Other phones:** Treasurer- 203-734-5920; Elections- 203-736-5970; Vital Records- 203-736-5980. **Property tax/Assessing**- 253 Main St, Ansonia, CT 06401; 203-736-5950, assessor fax- 203-736-5959. **Online access**- Access assessor property data at http://data.visionappraisal.com/AnsoniaCT/.

Ashford Town

Town Clerk, 5 Town Hall, Ashford, CT 06278. 860-487-4401; fax-860-487-4431; 8:30-3PM M-W & F; 7-9PM Wed, Closed Th. www.ashfordtownhall.org

Index: All in one. Record index partially computerized back to 600. Only the public may search. Copy fee $1.00 per page. Maps- $3.00 per page. Cert fee- $2.00 per doc plus copy fee. Payee- Town of Ashford. **Other phones:** Treasurer- 860-487-4410; Elections- 860-487-4410; Vital Records- 860-487-4401. **Property tax/Assessing**- 5 Town Hall Rd, Ashford, CT 06278; 860-487-4403, assessor fax- 860-487-4432. hours- 8:30AM-3PM M,T,W,F www.ashfordtownhall.org/tile.ez?pageId=28&action Name=display **Online access**- Access to property assessment free after registration at http://data.visionappraisal.com/AshfordCT/DEFAULT.asp

Avon Town

Town Clerk, 60 W Main St, Avon, CT 06001. 860-409-4310; fax-860-677-8428; 8:30AM-4:30PM (Summer- 8AM-4:45PM M-Th; 8-N Fri. (EST) www.town.avon.ct.us

Records indexed on a public use terminal back to 1961. Only the public may search. Copy fee $1.00 per page. Cert fee- $2.00 per cert plus copy fee. Payee- Avon Town Clerk. **Online access to Real Estate, Grantor/Grantee, Deed, Mortgage, Lien, Judgment, Trade Name records:** Access land data and trade names free at http://landrecords.town.avon.ct.us/. **Other phones:** Elections- 860-409-4350; Vital Records- 860-409-4310. **Property tax/Assessing**- 60 W Main St, Avon, CT 06001; 860-409-4335, assessor fax- 860-409-4366. **Online access**- Access to property data is free at www.avonassessor.com/index.shtml.

Barkhamsted Town

Town Clerk, 67 Ripley Hill Rd, Barkhamsted, CT 06063. Recording, R/E & UCC phone-860-379-8665; fax-860-379-9284; 9AM-4PM M,T,TH; 10AM-6PM W; 9AM-N F. (EST)

Index: All in one. Records indexed on computer back to 1957. Only the public may search. Copy fee $1.00 per page. Cert fee- $2.00 per doc plus copy fee. Payee- Town of Barkhamsted. **Other phones:** Treasurer- 860-379-8285; Elections- 860-738-4695; Vitals- 860-379-8665. **Property tax/Assessing**- PO Box 558, Pleasant Valley, CT 06063; 860-379-3600, assessor fax- 860-379-9284. **Online access**- Access to property assessment free at http://data.vision appraisal.com/BarkhamstedCT/DEFAULT.asp.

Beacon Falls Town

Town Clerk, 10 Maple Ave, Beacon Falls, CT 06403. Recording, R/E & UCC phone-203-729-8254; fax-203-720-1078; 9-12:30, 1-4 M,T,W; 9-12:30-1-8PM Th; 9-12:30-1-2:30PM F. (EST) www.beaconfalls.us

Index: All in one. Record index not computerized. Only the public may search. Copy fee $1.00 per page. Cert fee- $2.00 per cert plus copy fee. Payee- Beacon Falls Town Clerk. Office does not sell bulk data. **Other phones:** Treasurer- 203-729-4340; Elections- 203-729-4216; Vital Records- 203-729-8254. **Property tax/Assessing**- 10 Maple Ave, Beacon Falls, CT 06403; 203-723-5253, assessor fax- 203-720-1078. hours- 9AM-4:30PM M-W; 9AM-8PM Th; 9AM-2:30PM Fri

Berlin Town

Town Clerk, 240 Kensington Rd, Berlin, CT 06037. Recording, R/E & UCC phone-860-828-7035; fax-860-828-8628; 8:30AM-4:30PM M-W; TH 8:30AM-7PM; F 8:30AM-1PM (EST) www.town.berlin.ct.us

Index: Separate indices to search include grantor/grantee. Records indexed on a public use terminal back to 1972. Only the public may search. Copy fee $1.00 per page. Cert fee- $2.00 per cert plus copy fee. Payee- Berlin Town Clerk. **Online access to Real Estate, Deed, Maps records:** Access the recorders index only free at www.town.berlin.ct.us/resolution/. **Other phones:** Treasurer- 860-828-7023; Elections- 860-828-7020; Vital Records- 860-828-7035. **Property tax/Assessing**- 240 Kensington Rd, Kensington, CT 06037; 860-828-7039, assessor fax- 860-828-7110. **Online access**- Search town assessor database at http://data.visionappraisal.com/BerlinCT/.

Bethany Town

Town Clerk, 40 Peck Rd, Bethany, CT 06524-3338. 203-393-2100 x104, x105, R/E recording phone-203-393-2100 x104,x105,x106; fax-203-393-0821; 9AM-4:30PM (No copying or recording after 4PM). (EST)

Index: All in one. Records indexed on computer back to 1981. Only the public may search. Copy fee $1.00 per page. Cert fee- $1.00 per cert plus copy fee. Payee- Bethany Town Clerk. Office does not sell bulk data. **Other phones:** Treasurer- 203-393-2100 x100; Vital Records- 203-393-2100 x104, x105, x106. **Property tax/Assessing**- 40 Peck Rd, Bethany, CT 06524-3338; 203-393-2100 x112, assessor fax- 203-393-0828. hours- 9AM-4:30PM

Bethel Town

Town Clerk, 1 School St, Bethel, CT 06801. Recording, R/E & UCC phone-203-794-8505; fax-203-794-8588; 8:30AM-4:30PM www.bethelct.org
Index: Separate indices to search include computer, paper. Records indexed on computer back to 1973. Only the public may search. Copy fee $1.00 per page. Cert fee- $2.00 per cert plus copy fee. Payee- Bethel Town Clerk. Office does not sell bulk data. **Online access to GIS-mapping records:** Access to GIS parcel information for free go to www.bethelct.org/assessor/assessor_field_map.html . **Other phones:** Vital Records- 203-794-8505. **Property tax/Assessing**- 1 School St, Bethel, CT 06801; 203-794-8507.

Bethlehem Town

Town Clerk, PO Box 160, Bethlehem, CT 06751. Recording, R/E & UCC phone-203-266-7510; fax-203-266-7670; 9AM-N T,W,Th,F,Sat. (EST) www.ci.bethlehem.ct.us
Index: All in one. Record index not computerized. Only the public may search. Will not search UCC records. Copy fee $1.00 per page. Cert fee- $1.00 per page plus copy fee. Payee- Bethlehem Town Clerk. Office does not sell bulk data. **Other phones:** Treasurer- 203-266-7677; Elections- 203-266-7961; Vital Records- 203-266-7510. **Property tax/Assessing**- PO Box 160, 36 Main St, S, Bethlehem, CT 06751; 203-266-5479, assessor fax-203-266-7670. A public access terminal available. **Online**- Access property data free at http://data.visionappraisal.com/BethlehemCT/DEFAULT.asp.

Bloomfield Town

Town Clerk, PO Box 337, Bloomfield, CT 06002. 860-769-3507; fax-860-769-3597; 9AM-5PM (EST) www.bloomfieldct.org
Index: All in one. Records indexed on a public use terminal back to 1988. Only the public may search. Copy fee $1.00 per page. Cert fee- $2.00 per cert plus copy fee. Payee- Town of Bloomfield. **Other phones:** Elections- 860-769-3507; Vital Records- 860-769-3507. **Property tax/Assessing**- 800 Bloomfield Ave, Bloomfield, CT 06002; 860-769-3530, assessor fax-860-769-3597. **Online access**- Access property data free at www.prophecyone.us/index_prophecy.php?town=Bloomfield. No name searching. Also, Access property data free at http://data.visionappraisal.com/BloomfieldCT/DEFAULT.asp.

Bolton Town

Town Clerk, 222 Bolton Ctr Rd, Bolton, CT 06043-7698. 860-649-8066, R/E recording phone-860-649-8066 x106, UCC recording phone-860-649-8066 x107; fax-860-643-0021; 8:30AM-4PM M,W,TH; 8:30A-6:30PM, T; 8:30AM-1PM Fri. (EST) http://bolton.govoffice.com
Index: All in one. Records indexed on a public use terminal back to 1961. Only the public may search. Copy fee $1.00 per page. Cert fee- $1.00 per cert plus copy fee. Payee- Bolton Town Clerk. Treasurer- 860-649-7780; Elections- 860-649-8066 x116; Vital Records- 860-649-8066 x106. **Property tax/Assessing**- 222 Bolton Ctr Rd, Bolton, CT 06043; 860-649-8066 x100, assessor fax- 860-643-0021.

Bozrah Town

Town Clerk, 1 River Rd, Bozrah, CT 06334. 860-889-2689 x2, R/E recording phone-860-889-2689; fax-860-887-5449; 9AM-4PM M,T,W; 9AM-4PM TH; 9AM-N F. (EST)
Index: Separate land indices are 3 years each. Records indexed on computer back to 1/02; computer is not for public use. Only the public may search. Copy fee $1.00 per page. Cert fee- $3.00 1st page plus $1.00 each add'l, includes copy fee. Payee- Bozrah Town Clerk. **Other phones:** Treasurer- 860-889-2689; Elections- 860-889-2689; Vital Records- 860-889-2689 x2. **Property tax/Assessing**- 1 River Rd, Bozrah, CT 06334; 860-889-2689, assessor fax- 860-887-5449. hours- 9AM-4PM T,W,TH

Branford Town

Town Clerk, PO Box 150, Branford, CT 06405. 203-488-6305, R/E recording phone-203-315-0678; fax-203-481-5561; 8:30AM-4:30PM (9AM-4PM recordings). www.branford-ct.gov
Index: All in one. Records indexed on a public use terminal back to 7/94. Images start 11/22/04. Only the public may search. Copy fee $1.00 per page for land records & maps, $5.00 for full size maps, and general copies $.25 per page. Cert fee- $2.00 per cert plus copy fee. Payee- Branford Town Clerk. **Online access to Real Estate, Deed, Trade Name records:** Access to town clerk's recording records is free at http://deeds.branford-ct.gov/resolution/. Land records go back to 7/1/1994; maps and trade names to 1/18/2005. **Other phones:** Treasurer- 203-488-8394; Elections- 203-483-3998; Vital Records- 203-315-0678. **Property tax/Assessing**- 1019 Main St, Branford, CT 06405; 203-488-2039, assessor fax-203-315-3334. hours- 8:30AM-4:30PM www.branford-ct.gov/Assessor.htm **Online access**- Search the town assessor database at http://data.visionappraisal.com/BranfordCT/.

Bridgeport Town

Town Clerk, 45 Lyon Terrace, Rm 124; City Hall, Bridgeport, CT 06604. 203-576-7208, R/E recording phone-203-576-7207; 9am-4:30pm; Recording until 4
Index: Separate indices to search include tax liens, trade names, military discharges, maps of land records. Records indexed on a public use terminal back to 1980. Only the public may search. Will not search UCC records. Copy fee $1.00 per page. Cert fee- $2.00 per page plus copy fee. Payee- Bridgeport Town Clerk. **Other phones:** Treasurer- 203-576-7286; Elections- 203-576-7281; Vital Records- 203-576-7445 or 576-7208; City Hall Information- 203-576-7200. **Property tax/Assessing**- 45 Lyon Terrace, Rm 105, Bridgeport, CT 06604; 203-576-7241, assessor fax- 203-332-5521. (Appraiser/Auditor- 203-576-7241) hours- 9AM-4PM **Online access**- Access assessor data free at www.ci.bridgeport.ct.us/newdepartments/tax_assessor/assessorspro.aspx. Also, access property data free at http://data.visionappraisal.com/BridgeportCT/.

Bridgewater Town

Town Clerk, PO Box 216, Bridgewater, CT 06752-0216. Recording, R/E & UCC phone-860-354-5102; fax-860-350-5944; 8AM-N M,W,F; 8AM-5PM T. (EST) www.bridgewatertownhall.org
Index: Separate indices to search include indexes from 1856-1958, 1959-1984, 6/1/84-6/30/97, 7/1/97-12/31/02, 1/1/03-12/31/04, 1/1/05 to present. Records indexed on computer. Only the public may search. Copy fee $1.00 per page. Cert fee- $1.00 per cert plus copy fee. Payee- Bridgewater Town Clerk. **Other phones:** Treasurer- 860-354-2683; Elections- 860-354-5102; Vital Records- 860-354-5102. **Property tax/Assessing**- PO Box 171, Bridgewater, CT 06752; 860-355-9379, assessor fax- 860-350-5944. **Online access**- Access assessor data free at http://data.visionappraisal.com/BridgewaterCT/.

Bristol City

Town Clerk, PO Box 114, Bristol, CT 06011-0114. 860-584-6100, R/E recording phone-860-584-6200; 8:30AM-5PM (EST) www.ci.bristol.ct.us
Index: Separate indices to search include trade names, land records, maps. Records indexed on computer back to 1975. Only the public may search. Will not search UCC records. Copy fee $1.00 per page. Cert fee- $2.00 per cert plus copy fee. Payee- Bristol Town Clerk. Office does not sell bulk data. **Online access to Parcel, Maps records:** Also, access to City of Bristol Zoning Map for free at www.ci.bristol.ct.us/content/3326/3370/default.aspx. **Other phones:** Treasurer- 860-584-6285; Elections- 860-584-6165; Vital Records- 860-584-6200. **Property tax/Assessing**- 111 N Main St, Bristol, CT 06011-0114; 860-584-6240, fax- 860-584-6151.

Brookfield Town

Town Clerk, PO Box 5106, Brookfield, CT 06804-5106. 203-775-7313; fax-203-775-5231; 8:30AM-4:30PM; Most Th to 7PM (EST) www.brookfield.org
Index: All in one. Records indexed on a public use terminal back to 7/73. Only the public may perform title searches. Office will not search UCC records. Copy fee $1.00 per page. Map pages- $3.00 each. Cert fee- $1.00 per cert plus copy fee. Payee- Brookfield Town Clerk. Office does not sell bulk data. **Other phones:** Treasurer- 203-775-7308; Elections- 203-775-7343; Vital Records- 203-775-7313. **Property tax/Assessing**- 100 Pocono Rd, Brookfield, CT 06804-5106; 203-775-7302, assessor fax- 203-775-5317. **Online access**- Search town assessor field cards at http://data.visionappraisal.com/BrookfieldCT/. Free registration for full data.

Brooklyn Town

Town Clerk, PO Box 356, Brooklyn, CT 06234. Recording, R/E & UCC phone-860-774-9543; fax-860-774-5732; 8AM-5PM M,T,W; 8AM-6PM TH; Closed Fri. (EST) www.brooklynct.org
Index: All in one. Records indexed on a public use terminal back to 1920. Only the public may search. Copy fee $1.00 per page. Cert fee- $2.00 per cert plus copy fee. Payee- Town of Brooklyn. **Other phones:** Treasurer- 860-779-3411; Elections- 860-779-3411; Vital Records- 860-774-9543. **Property tax/Assessing**- PO Box 356, 4 Wolf Den Rd, Brooklyn, CT 06234; 860-774-5611, assessor fax-860-779-7853. www.brooklynct.org/home.htm **Online access**- Access assessor database records free at www.rmsreval.com/login.asp?town=Brooklyn. Free email registration required. No name searching. Data may be old.

Burlington Town

Town Clerk, 200 Spielman Hwy, Burlington, CT 06013. Recording, R/E & UCC phone-860-673-2108; fax-860-675-9312; 8:30AM-4PM M,T,TH; 8:30AM-6:30PM W; 8:30AM-1:30PM F. (EST)
Index: Separate indices to search include grantor/grantee. Records indexed on a public use terminal back to 1990. Only the public may search. Copy fee $1.00 per page. Cert fee- $2.00 per cert plus copy fee. Payee- Burlington Town Clerk. **Other phones:** Treasurer- 860-673-6789; Elections- 860-673-2108; Vital Records- 860-673-2108; Tax Collector- 860-673-0717. **Property tax/Assessing**- 200 Spielman Hwy, Burlington, CT 06013; 860-673-3901, assessor fax- 860-675-9312. **Online access**- Search assessor database free after registration at http://data.visionappraisal.com/BurlingtonCT/DEFAULT.asp.

Canaan Town

Town Clerk, PO Box 47, Falls Village, CT 06031. 860-824-0707; fax-860-824-4506; 9AM-3PM M-TH. (EST) www.canaanfallsvillage.org/
Index: All in one. Records indexed on a public use terminal back to 2000. Only the public may search. Copy fee $1.00 per page. Cert fee- $2.00 per doc plus copy fee. Payee- Town of Canaan. **Other phones:** Treasurer- 860-824-0707; Elections- 860-824-0707; Vital Records- 860-824-0707. **Property tax/Assessing**- PO Box 47, 108 Main St, Falls Village, CT 06031; 860-824-0707, assessor fax- 860-824-4506. (Appraiser/Auditor- 860-824-0707) **Online access**- Access assessor data free at http://data.visionappraisal.com/CanaanCT/DEFAULT.asp.

Canterbury Town

Town Clerk, PO Box 27, Canterbury, CT 06331-0027. Recording, R/E & UCC phone-860-546-9377; fax-860-546-9295; 9AM-4PM M-W; 9AM-6:30PM TH; 9AM-1:30PM F. (EST)
Index: All in one. Records indexed on a public use terminal back to 2000. Only the public may search. Copy fee $1.00 per page. Cert fee- $2.00 per cert plus copy fee. Payee- Canterbury Town Clerk. Office does not sell bulk data. **Other phones:** Treasurer- 860-546-2089; Elections- 860-546-9377; Vital Records- 860-546-9377. **Property tax/Assessing**- 1 Municipal Dr,

Canterbury, CT 06331-0027; 860-546-6035, assessor fax- 860-546-7805. **Online access**- Access assessor property data free at http://data.visionappraisal.com/CanterburyCT/DEFAULT.asp

Canton Town

Town Clerk, PO Box 168, Collinsville, CT 06022. Recording, R/E & UCC phone-860-693-7870; fax-860-693-7840; 8:15AM-1PM 2PM-4:30PM M,T,TH; to 6:45PM W; to Noon F. www.townofcantonct.org
Index: All in one. Records indexed on a public use terminal back to 1976. Only the public may search. Copy fee $1.00 per page. Cert fee- $2.00 per cert plus copy fee. Payee- Town of Canton. Office does not sell bulk data. **Other phones:** Treasurer- 860-693-7852; Elections- 860-693-7870; Vital Records- 860-693-7870. **Property tax/Assessing**- PO Box 168, 4 Market St, Collinsville, CT 06022; 860-693-7842, assessor fax- 860-693-7840. hours- 8:15AM-1PM, 2-4:30PM M,T,Th; 8:15AM-1PM, 2-6:45PM W; 8:15AM-N F **Online access**- Search of property address, search by owner name, or search sales at www.cantonassessor.com.

Chaplin Town

Town Clerk, PO Box 286, Chaplin, CT 06235. Recording, R/E & UCC phone-860-455-9455; fax-860-455-0027; 9AM-3PM M, W, Th; 1-7PM Tues; Closed Fri. (EST) www.chaplinct.org/
Index: Separate indices to search include 1970-1983, 1984-1993, 1994-1999, etc. A public use terminal to be available. Only the public may search. Copy fee $1.00 per page. Cert fee- $2.00 per cert plus copy fee. Payee- Town of Chaplin. **Other phones:** Treasurer- 860-455-2170; Elections- 860-455-9455; Vital Records- 860-455-9455. **Property tax/Assessing**- PO Box 286, Chaplin, CT 06235; 860-455-9333, assessor fax- 860-455-0027. (Appraiser/Auditor- 860-455-9333) hours- 4-7PM Tu **Online access**- Access property data free after registration at http://data.visionappraisal.com/. Coming soon.

Cheshire Town

Town Clerk, 84 S Main St; Town Hall, Cheshire, CT 06410. Recording, R/E & UCC phone-203-271-6601; fax-203-271-6615; 8:30AM-4PM (Recording until 3:30PM). (EST) www.cheshirect.org
Index: All in one. Records indexed on a public use terminal back to 1932. Only the public may search. Copy fee $1.00 per page. Cert fee- $2.00 per cert plus copy fee. Payee- Cheshire Town Clerk. **Other phones:** Treasurer- 203-271-6610; Elections- 203-271-6680; Vital Records- 203-271-6601. **Property tax/Assessing**- 84 S Main St, Cheshire, CT 06410; 203-271-6620, assessor fax- 203-271-6615. hours- 8:30AM-4PM **Online access**- Access property data free at www.prophecyone.us/index_prophecy.php?town=Cheshire. No name searching.

Chester Town

Town Clerk, 203 Middlesex Ave, Chester, CT 06412-1200. Recording, R/E & UCC phone-860-526-0013 x511; fax-860-526-0004; 9AM-N, 1-4PM M,W,Th; 9AM-N, 1-7PM T; 9AM-N Fri. (EST) www.chesterct.org/departments/townclerk.htm
Index: All in one. Only the public may search. Copy fee $1.00 per page. Cert fee- $2.00 per cert plus copy fee. Payee- Chester Town Clerk. Office does not sell bulk data. **Other phones:** Treasurer- 860-526-0013 x214; Elections- 860-526-0013 x211; Vital Records- 860-526-0013 x511. **Property tax/Assessing**- 203 Middlesex Ave, Chester, CT 06412-1200; 860-526-0013 x512, assessor fax- 860-526-0004. hours- 9AM-N, 1-4PM M-TH; 9AM-N Fri www.chesterct.org/departments/assessor.htm

City of New London

City Clerk, 181 State St, New London, CT 06320. Recording, R/E & UCC phone-860-447-5205; fax-860-447-1644; 8:30-4PM www.ci.new-london.ct.us
File here for City of New London, not for county. No county filing in CT. Index: All in one. Records indexed on a public use terminal back to 1/1/1969. Only the public may search. Copy fee $1.00 per page. Cert fee- $2.00 per cert plus copy fee. Payee- New London City Clerk. Office does not sell bulk data. **Other phones:** Treasurer- 860-447-5209; Elections- 860-447-5206; Vital Records- 860-447-5205; Tax Collector- 860-447-5208. **Property tax/Assessing**- PO Box 92, New London, CT 06320; 860-447-5216, assessor fax- 860-447-5225. (Appraiser/Auditor- 860-447-5216) **Online access**- Search the city assessor's database free at http://data.visionappraisal.com//NewLondonCT/.

Clinton Town

Town Clerk, 54 E Main St, Clinton, CT 06413. Recording, R/E & UCC phone-860-669-9101; fax-860-669-0890; 9AM-4PM www.clintonct.org/townclerk.htm
Index: All in one. Records indexed on a public use terminal back to 1/1977. Only the public may search. Copy fee $1.00 per page. Cert fee- $2.00 per cert plus copy fee. Payee- Clinton Town Clerk. Office does not sell bulk data. **Other phones:** Treasurer- 860-669-9465; Elections- 860-669-6436; Vital Records- 860-669-9101. **Property tax/Assessing**- 54 E Main St, Clinton, CT 06413; 860-669-9269, assessor fax- 860-664-4469. hours- 9AM-4PM M-W, 9AM-7PM Th; 9AM-N F **Online access**- Search Assessor records at http://data.visionappraisal.com/ClintonCT/.

Colchester Town

Town Clerk, 127 Norwich Ave, Colchester, CT 06415. Recording, R/E & UCC phone-860-537-7215; fax-860-537-0547; 8:30AM-4:30PM M-W & F; 8:30AM-7PM Th. (EST) www.colchesterct.gov/Pages/ColchesterCT_Dept/CTC/index
Index: All in one. Records indexed on computer back to 1933. Only the public may search. Copy fee $1.00 per page. Cert fee- $2.00 per doc plus copy fee. Payee- Town of Colchester. **Other phones:** Treasurer- 860-537-7225; Elections- 860-537-7204; Vital Records- 860-537-7215. **Property tax/Assessing**- 127 Norwich Ave, Colchester, CT 06415; 860-537-7205, assessor fax- 860-537-1147. www.colchesterct.gov/Pages/ColchesterCT_Dept/TA/index **Online access**- Search the town assessor database at http://data.visionappraisal.com/ColchesterCT/. Free registration for full data.

Colebrook Town

Town Clerk, PO Box 5, Colebrook, CT 06021. 860-379-3359 ext 213, R/E recording phone-860-379-3359 x213; fax-860-379-2342; 9AM-N, 1PM-4:30PM (EST)
Index: All in one. Record index not computerized. Office personnel will perform small searches or visitors may perform searches. Office will not search real estate records. Office will not search UCC records or tax liens. Copy fee $1.00 per page. Large maps- $5.00. Cert fee- $2.00 per cert plus copy fee. Payee- Colebrook Town Clerk. Office does not sell bulk data. **Other phones:** Treasurer- x212; Elections- x211; Vital Records- x213. **Property tax/Assessing**- PO Box 5, Colebrook, CT 06021; 860-379-3359 x206, assessor fax- 860-379-7215. **Online access**- Access assessor records free at http://data.visionappraisal.com/ColebrookCT/.

Columbia Town

Town Clerk, 323 Jonathan Trumbull Hwy, Columbia, CT 06237. 860-228-3284; fax-860-228-2335; 8AM-4PM M-W; 8AM-6PM Th; 8AM-N Fri. (EST) www.columbiact.org
Index: All in one. Record index not computerized. Only the public may search. Copy fee $1.00 per page. Cert fee- $2.00 per cert plus copy fee. Payee- Columbia Town Clerk. **Other phones:** Vital Records- 860-228-3284. **Property tax/Assessing**- 323 Rte 87, Columbia, CT 06237; 860-228-9555, assessor fax- 860-228-2335.

Cornwall Town

Town Clerk, PO Box 97, Cornwall, CT 06753-0097. Recording, R/E & UCC phone-860-672-2709; fax-860-672-4069; 9AM-N, 1-4PM M-Th. (EST)
Index: All in one. Record index not computerized. Only the public may search. Will not search UCC records. Copy fee $1.00 per page. Cert fee- $2.00 per cert plus copy fee. Payee- Town of Cornwall. Office does not sell bulk data. **Other phones:** Treasurer- 860-672-2707; Elections- 860-672-4070; Vital Records- 860-672-2709; Tax Collector- 860-672-2705. **Property tax/Assessing**- PO Box 178, Cornwall, CT 06754; 860-672-2703, assessor fax- 860-672-4069. hrs- 1-4PM Tu-Th; 9-N, 1-4PM Wed

Coventry Town

Town Clerk, 1712 Main St, Coventry, CT 06238. 860-742-7966; fax-860-742-8911; 8:30AM-4:30PM M-W; 8:30AM-6:30PM Th; 8:30AM-1:30PM Fri. (EST) www.coventryct.org
Index: All in one. Records indexed on a public use terminal back to 7/83; prior were only in grantor/grantee index books. Only the public may search. General copy fee- $1.00 per page for land record books; $7.00 each for full maps. Cert fee- $1.00 per cert plus copy fee. Payee- Town of Coventry. Office does not sell bulk data. **Other phones:** Treasurer- 860-742-3528; Elections- 860-742-4061; Vital Records- 860-742-7966. **Property tax/Assessing**- 1712 Main St, Coventry, CT 06238; 860-742-4067, assessor fax- 860-742-8911. Public use terminal available. **Online access**- Access assessor and property data free at http://ceo.fando.com/coventry/.

Cromwell Town

Town Clerk, 41 West St, Cromwell, CT 06416-2100. Recording, R/E & UCC phone-860-632-3440; fax-860-632-3425; 8:30AM-4PM www.cromwellct.com
Index: All in one. Records indexed on a public use terminal back to 1851. Only the public may search. Will not search UCC records. Copy fee $1.00 per page. Cert fee- $2.00 per cert plus copy fee. Payee- Town of Cromwell. Office does not sell bulk data. Please contact ACS, P.O. Box 4889, Syracuse, NY 13221 ph: 1-800-800-7009. **Other phones:** Treasurer- 860-632-3440; Elections- 860-632-3418; Vital Records- 860-632-3440. **Property tax/Assessing**- 41 West St, Cromwell, CT 06416-2100; 860-632-3442, assessor fax- 860-632-1548. **Online access**- Access property and GIS-mapping records free at http://hosting.tighebond.com/cromwellct/main.htm.

Danbury City

Town Clerk, 155 Deer Hill Ave; City Hall, Danbury, CT 06810. 203-797-4531; 8:30AM-4:30PM (EST) www.ci.danbury.ct.us
Index: All in one. Records indexed on a public use terminal back to 1968. Only the public may search. Will not search UCC records. Copy fee $1.00 per page. Cert fee- $2.00 per cert plus copy fee. Payee- City of Danbury. Office does not sell bulk data. **Other phones:** Treasurer- 203-797-4650; Elections- 203-797-4531; Vital Records- 203-797-4531. **Property tax/Assessing**- 155 Deer Hill Ave, Danbury, CT 06810; 203-797-4556, assessor fax- 203-796-1651. **Online access**- Search the city assessor database at http://data.visionappraisal.com/DanburyCT/.

Darien Town

Town Clerk, 2 Renshaw Rd, Darien, CT 06820-5397. 203-656-7307; 8:30AM-4:30PM www.darienct.gov
Index: All in one. Records indexed on computer back to June, 1983. Only the public may search. Will not search UCC records. Copy fee $1.00 per page. Cert fee- $2.00 per cert plus copy fee. Payee- Town of Darien. **Other phones:** Treasurer- 203-656-7334; Elections- 203-656-7316; Vital Records- 203-656-7307. **Property tax/Assessing**- 2 Renshaw Rd, Darien, CT 06820-5397; 203-656-7310, assessor fax-203-656-7380. A public access terminal available.

Deep River Town

Town Clerk, 174 Main St; Town Hall, Deep River, CT 06417. Recording, R/E & UCC phone-860-526-6024; fax-860-526-6023; 9AM-4PM (EST) www.deeprivercet.us
Index: All in one. Record index not computerized. Only the public may search. Copy fee $1.00 per page. Cert fee- $2.00 per cert plus copy fee. Payee- Deep River Town Clerk. **Other phones:** Elections- 860-526-6024; Vital Records- 860-526-6024. **Property tax/Assessing**- 174 Main St, Deep River, CT 06417; 860-526-6029, assessor fax- 860-526-6023. hours- 9AM-N, 1PM-4PM

Derby City

Town Clerk, 1 Elizabeth St, Derby, CT 06418. Recording, R/E & UCC phone-203-736-1462; fax-203-736-1458; hours- 9AM-5PM (EST) http://electronicvalley.org/derby/
Index: All in one. Records indexed on a public use terminal back to 2003. Only the public may search. Copy fee $1.00 per page. Cert fee- $2.00 per cert plus copy fee. Payee- Derby Town Clerk. Office does not sell bulk data. **Other phones:** Treasurer- 203-736-1452; Elections- 203-736-1462; Vital Records- 203-736-1462. **Property tax/Assessing**- 1 Elizabeth St, Derby, CT 06418; 203-736-1455, assessor fax- 203-736-1480. (Appraiser/Auditor- 203-736-1452);

Durham Town

Town Clerk, PO Box 428, Durham, CT 06422. Recording, R/E & UCC phone-860-349-3453; fax-860-349-0547; 8:30AM-4:30PM M,W,TH,F; 8:30AM-8PM T. (EST) http://townofdurhamct.org
Index: Separate indices to search include land, maps. Records indexed on a public use terminal back to 1967. Only the public may search. Copy fee $1.00 per page. Cert fee- $2.00 per cert plus copy fee. Payee- Durham Town Clerk. Office does not sell bulk data. **Other phones:** Treasurer- 860-349-3625; Elections- 860-349-3452; Vital Records- 860-349-3453. **Property tax/Assessing**- PO Box 428, Durham, CT 06422; 860-349-3452 x1, assessor fax- 860-349-8391. hours- 8:30AM-4:30PM **Online access**- Access the assessor's database at http://durham.univers-clt.com. Also, Assessor maps access free at www.townofdurhamct.org/content/18701/18791/.

East Granby Town

Town Clerk, PO Box TC, East Granby, CT 06026-0459. Recording, R/E & UCC phone-860-653-6528; fax-860-653-4017; 8:30AM-N, 1-4PM M-Th; 8:30AM-1PM Fri. (EST) www.eastgranby.net
Index: All in one. Records indexed on computer. Only the public may search. Copy fee $1.00 per page. Cert fee- $2.00 per doc plus copy fee. Payee- Town of East Granby. Office does not sell bulk data. **Other phones:** Treasurer- 860-653-0096; Elections- 860-653-0097; Vital Records- 860-653-6528; Selectmen-860-653-2576. **Property tax/Assessing**- PO Box 1858, East Granby, CT 06026; 860-653-2852, assessor fax- 860-653-4017. hours- 8AM-N, 1-4PM M-TH; 8AM-1PM F **Online access**- Access to property tax for free go to www.eastgranby.net/index.php?option=com_content&task=view&id=2.

East Haddam Town

Town Clerk, PO Box K; Town Office Bldg, East Haddam, CT 06423. 860-873-5027; fax-860-873-5042; 8AM-4PM M,W,TH; 8AM-7PM T; Closed Fri. http://easthaddam.org
Index: All in one. Records indexed on computer. Only the public may search. Copy fee $1.00 per page. Cert fee- $2.00 plus copy fee. Payee- East Haddam Town Clerk. Office does not sell bulk data. **Other phones:** Treasurer- 860-873-5022; Elections- 860-873-5027; Vital Records- 860-873-5027. **Property tax/Assessing**- PO Box K, East Haddam, CT 06423; 860-873-5026, assessor fax- 860-873-5042. **Online access**- Access property data free at http://easthaddam.org/property_value.htm.

East Hampton Town

Town Clerk, 20 E High St, East Hampton, CT 06424. 860-267-2519; fax-860-267-1027; 8AM-4PM M,W,TH; 8AM-7:30PM T; 8AM-12:30PM F. (EST) www.easthamptonct.org
Index: All in one. Records indexed on a public use terminal back to 1/1974. Only the public may search. Copy fee $1.00 per page. Cert fee- $2.00 per doc plus copy fee. Payee- East Hampton Town Clerk. Office does not sell bulk data. **Online access to Real Estate, Deed, Lien, Judgment, UCC records:** Access to recorded land records for free go to www.rmsreval.com/selection.html . **Other phones:** Treasurer- 860-267-7548 x322; Elections- 860-267-2519 x321; Vital Records- 860-267-2519. **Property tax/Assessing**- 20 E High St, East Hampton, CT 06424; 860-267-2510, assessor fax- 860-267-1027. www.easthamptonct.org/Pages/EastHamptonCT_Assessor/Index **Online access**- Access assessor database at www.rmsreval.com/login.asp?town=East%20Hampton after email registration. Data may be old.

East Hartford Town

Town Clerk, 740 Main St, East Hartford, CT 06108-3126. 860-291-7230; fax-860-289-0831; 8:30AM-4:30PM (EST) www.ci.east-hartford.ct.us
Index: All in one. Records indexed on a public use terminal back to 1967. Only the public may search. Copy fee $1.00 per page. Cert fee- $1.00 per cert includes copy fee. Payee- Town Clerk, East Hartford. **Other phones:** Treasurer- 860-291-7240; Elections-860-291-7230; Vital Records- 860-291-7230. **Property tax/Assessing**- 740 Main St, East Hartford, CT 06108; 860-291-7260 x268, assessor fax- 860-291-7308. www.ci.east-hartford.ct.us/Public_Documents/EastHartfordCT_Assessor/index

East Haven Town

Town Clerk, 250 Main St, East Haven, CT 06512-3034. 203-468-3201; 8:30AM-4:15PM (EST) www.townofeasthavenct.org
Index: All in one except for municipal liens. Records indexed on a public use terminal back to 1977. Only the public may search. Will not search UCC records. Copy fee $1.00 per page. Cert fee- $2.00 per cert plus copy fee. Payee- East Haven Town Clerk. Office does not sell bulk data. **Other phones:** Elections- 203-468-3320; Vital Records- 203-468-3201. **Property tax/Assessing**- 250 Main St, East Haven, CT 06512-3034; 203-468-3996, assessor fax- 203-468-3851. hours- 8:30AM-4:30PM **Online access**- Access property data free at www.prophecyone.us/index_prophecy.php?town=East%20Haven no name searches.

East Lyme Town

Town Clerk, PO Box 519, Niantic, CT 06357. Recording, R/E & UCC phone-860-739-6931; fax-860-739-6930; 8AM-4PM www.eltownhall.com
Index: All in one. Records indexed on a public use terminal back to 1975. Only the public may search. Will not search UCC records. Copy fee $1.00 per page. Maps- $5.00 per page. Cert fee- $2.00 per cert plus copy fee. Payee- East Lyme Town Clerk. Office does not sell bulk data. **Other phones:** Treasurer-860-739-6931; Vital Records- 860-739-6931. **Property tax/Assessing**- PO Box 519, Niantic, CT 06357; 860-739-6931, assessor fax- 860-739-6930. **Online access**- Search the town assessor database free at http://data.visionappraisal.com/EastLymeCT/.

East Windsor Town

Town Clerk, PO Box 213, Broad Brook, CT 06016-0213. Recording, R/E & UCC phone-860-292-8255; fax-860-623-4798; 8:30AM-4:30PM M,T,W; 8:30AM-7PM Th; 8:30AM-1PM Fri. (EST) www.eastwindsorct.com/Home/
Index: All in one. Records indexed on a public use terminal back to 1/1/1978. Office will perform minimal UCC searches but public must search other records themselves. Copy fee $1.00 per page. Cert fee- $2.00 per cert plus copy fee. Payee- Town of East Windsor. Office does not sell bulk data. **Other phones:** Treasurer- 860-292-5909; Elections- 860-292-5915; Vital Records- 860-292-8255; Selectmen-860-623-8122. **Property tax/Assessing**- PO Box 51, 11 Rye St, Broad Brook, CT 06016; 860-623-8878, assessor fax- 860-623-4798. www.eastwindsorct.com/ **Online access**- Access property data free at www.prophecyone.us/index_prophecy.php?town=East%20Windsor. No name searching.

Eastford

Town Clerk, PO Box 98, Eastford, CT 06242-0098. 860-974-1885; fax-860-974-0624; 10AM-N 1PM-4PM T,W; 5:30PM-7:30PM 2nd & 4th T. (EST) www.munic.state.ct.us/eastford/townclerk.htm
Index: All in one. Record index not computerized. Only the public may search. Copy fee $1.00 per page. Vital records- $10.00 each for certified copies. Cert fee- $1.00 per page plus copy fee. Payee- Eastford Town Clerk. **Other phones:** Treasurer- 860-974-0133; Elections- 860-974-1885; Vital Records- 860-974-1885. **Property tax/Assessing**- PO Box 98, 16 Westford Rd, Eastford, CT 06242-0098; 860-974-1291 x7, assessor fax- 860-974-0624. hours- 10AM-N, 1PM-4PM T,W www.munic.state.ct.us/eastford/assessor.html **Online access**- Access assessor data free after registration at http://data.visionappraisal.com/EastfordCT/DEFAULT.asp.

Easton Town

Town Clerk, PO Box 61, Easton, CT 06612. 203-268-6291; fax-203-261-6080; 9AM-2PM (EST) http://eastonct.gov/address.htm
Index: All in one. Book and Page numbers indexed on computer. Only the public may search. General copy fee $1.00 per page. Map copy $20.00. Cert fee- $1.00 per cert includes copy fee. Payee- Town of Easton. **Other phones:** Treasurer- 203-268-6291; Elections-203-268-6291; Vital Records- 203-268-6291. **Property tax/Assessing**- 325 Center Rd, Easton, CT 06612; 203-268-6291, assessor fax- 203-268-4928. (Appraiser/Auditor- 203-268-6291) hours- 8:30AM-4:30PM **Online access**- Access property data free at www.prophecyone.us/index_prophecy.php?town=Easton. No name searching.

Ellington Town

Town Clerk, PO Box 187, Ellington, CT 06029-0187. Recording, R/E & UCC phone-860-870-3105; fax-860-870-3158; 8:30AM-6PM M; 8:30AM-4PM T,W,TH; 8:30AM-1:30PM Fri. www.ellington-ct.gov
Index: All in one. Records indexed on a public use terminal back to 1963. Only the public may search. Will not search UCC records. Copy fee $1.00 per page. Cert fee- $2.00 per cert plus copy fee. Payee- Ellington Town Clerk. **Online access to Real Estate, Deed, Mortgage, Map records:** Access land records (indexes only) back to 1963 free at http://landrecords.ellington-ct.gov/. Also, search maps and surveys back to 2005. **Other phones:** Treasurer-860-870-3115; Elections- 860-870-3107; Vital Records- 860-870-3105; Tax Collector- 860-870-3113. **Property tax/Assessing**- PO Box 187, Ellington, CT 06029-0187; 860-870-3109, assessor fax- 860-870-3197. **Online access**- Online access to assessor records at http://data.visionappraisal.com/EllingtonCT/DEFAULT.asp.

Enfield Town

Town Clerk, 820 Enfield St, Enfield, CT 06082-2997. 860-253-6440, R/E recording phone-860-253-6435; 9-5 http://enfield-ct.gov/content/91/148/default.aspx
Index: All in one. Records indexed on a public use terminal back to 7/1/79. Only the public may search. Will not search UCC records. Copy fee $1.00 per page. Cert fee- $2.00 per doc plus copy fee. Payee-Town of Enfield. **Online access to Real Estate, Deed records:** Access real estate records free at https://app7.enfield.org/. **Other phones:** Treasurer-860-253-6330; Elections- 860-253-6320; Vital Records- 860-253-6440. **Property tax/Assessing**-820 Enfield St, Enfield, CT 06082-2997; 860-253-6339, assessor fax- 860-253-6331. http://enfield-ct.gov/content/91/803/785/default.aspx **Online access**- Access assessor's parcel data free at

https://app6.enfield.org/Find_a_Parcel.htm but no name searching. Also, search for parcel data free on the GIS-mapping site at http://gis.cdm.com/enfieldct/map.htm. Use 'Search For' feature to name search.

Essex Town

Town Clerk, 29 West Ave, Essex, CT 06426. Recording, R/E & UCC phone-860-767-4340 x129, UCC recording phone-860-767-4344 x129; fax-860-767-4560; 9AM-4PM (EST) www.essexct.gov/departments/townclerk.html
Index: All in one. Records indexed on a public use terminal back to 1982. Only the public may search. Copy fee $1.00 per page. Cert fee- $2.00 per page plus copy fee. Payee- Essex Town Clerk. Bulk data available for purchase, info phone- 860-767-4340 x129. **Online access to Real Estate, Deed, Lien, Mortgage, Death, Trade Name records:** Access land records back to 1982 free at http://landrecords.essexct.gov/. Other records go back to 6/16/2004. **Other phones:** Treasurer- 860-767-4340 x127; Elections- 860-767-4340 x129; Vital Records- 860-767-4340 x129. **Property tax/Assessing**- 29 West Ave, Essex, CT 06426; 860-767-4340 x124, assessor fax- 860-767-8509. **Online access**- Access to property data is free at http://data.visionappraisal.com/EssexCT/.

Fairfield Town

Town Clerk, 611 Old Post Rd, Fairfield, CT 06824. Recording, R/E & UCC phone-203-256-3090; 8:30AM-4:30PM (EST) www.fairfieldct.org
Index: All in one. Records indexed on a public use terminal back to 1984. Only the public may search. Will not search UCC records. Copy fee $1.00 per page. Cert fee- $2.00 per doc plus copy fee. Payee- Fairfield Town Clerk. **Other phones:** Elections- 203-256-3090; Vital Records- 203-256-3090. **Property tax/Assessing**- 611 Old Post Rd, Fairfield, CT 06824; 203-256-3110, assessor fax- 203-256-3114. **Online access**- Search the town assessor database at http://data.visionappraisal.com/FairfieldCT/.

Farmington Town

Town Clerk, 1 Monteith Dr, Farmington, CT 06032. 860-675-2380; fax-860-675-2389; 8:30AM-4:30PM www.farmington-ct.org/TownServices/TownClerk/
Index: All in one. Records indexed on a public use terminal back to 1984. Only the public may search. Copy fee $1.00 per page. Cert fee- $2.00 per cert plus copy fee. Payee- Farmington Town Clerk. Office does not sell bulk data. **Other phones:** Vital Records- 860-675-2380. **Property tax/Assessing**- One Monteith Dr, Farmington, CT 06032; 860-675-2370, assessor fax- 860-675-2376. **Online access**- Access property assessor data free at www.farmington-ct.org/TownServices/Assessor//LandRecord.aspx.

Franklin Town

Town Clerk, 7 Meeting House Hill Rd; Town Hall, Franklin, CT 06254. 860-642-7352; fax-860-642-6606; 8:30AM-3PM M-Th; 6PM-8PM T. (EST) www.franklinct.com
Index: All in one. Records indexed on computer back to 1989. Only the public may search. Copy fee $1.00 per page. Cert fee- $2.00 per cert plus copy fee. Payee- Franklin Town Clerk. **Other phones:** Treasurer- 860-642-6055. **Property tax/Assessing**- 7 Meeting House Hill Rd, Franklin, CT 06254; 860-642-6475 x19, assessor fax- 860-642-6606. hours-9AM-3PM, 6-8PM Tu; 9AM-3PM W

Glastonbury Town

Town Clerk, PO Box 6523; 2155 Main St, Glastonbury, CT 06033. Recording, R/E & UCC phone-860-652-7616; fax-860-652-7639; 8AM-4:30PM (EST) www.glastonbury-ct.gov
Index: All in one. Records indexed on computer back to 1/1/73. Only the public may search. Copy fee $1.00 per page. Cert fee- $2.00 per doc plus copy fee. Payee- Glastonbury Town Clerk. Office does not sell bulk data. **Online access to Real Estate, Deed, Lien, Mortgage, Judgment, Birth, Death records:** Access town clerks recorded document index free at http://town.glasct.org/wb_or1/or_sch_1.asp. **Other phones:** Treasurer- 860-652-7586; Elections- 860-652-7627/28; Vital Records- 860-652-7616. **Property tax/Assessing**- 2155 Main St, Glastonbury, CT 06033; 860-652-7600, assessor fax- 860-652-7610. **Online access**- Search town assessment data free on the GIS Mapping site at http://gis.glastonbury-ct.gov/ceo/.

Goshen Town

Town Clerk, PO Box 54, Goshen, CT 06756-0054. Recording, R/E & UCC phone-860-491-3647; 9AM-N,1-4PM M-Th; 9AM-1PM F. (EST) http://goshenct.gov
Index: Separate indices to search include maps, trade names, grantor/grantee. Records indexed on a public use terminal back to 8/87. Only the public may search. Will not search UCC records. Copy fee $1.00 per page. Cert fee- $2.00 per doc plus copy fee. Maps may vary depending on size-up to $5.00. Payee- Town Clerk. Bulk data available in paper format only. ACS is current vender. **Other phones:** Treasurer- 860-491-2308; Elections- 860-491-2308 x236; Vital Records- 860-491-3647; Tax Office- 860-491-3275 x226. **Property tax/Assessing**- PO Box 187, Goshen, CT 06756; 860-491-2115, assessor fax- 860-491-6028. 9AM-N, 1-4PM Tu-W **Online**- Search assessor data at http://data.visionappraisal.com/goshenCT/.

Granby Town

Town Clerk, 15 N Granby Rd, Granby, CT 06035. 860-844-5308; fax-860-653-4769; 8AM-N,1-4PM M,T,W; 8AM-N, 1-6:30PM Th; 8AM-12:30PM F. (EST) www.granby-ct.gov
Index: Separate indices to search include books. Records indexed on computer back to 7/30/84. Only the public may search. Will not search UCC records. Copy fee $1.00 per page. Cert fee- $2.00 per cert plus copy fee. Payee- Town of Granby. Office does not sell bulk data. **Other phones:** Elections- 860-84405308; Vital Records- 860-844-5308. **Property tax/Assessing**- Granby Town Assessing Office, 15 N Granby Rd, Granby, CT 06035; 860-844-5311, assessor fax- 860-653-4769. **Online access**- Search the town assessor's database free at http://data.visionappraisal.com/GranbyCT/.

Greenwich Town

Town Clerk, PO Box 2540, Greenwich, CT 06836. 203-622-7897; fax-203-622-3767; 8AM-4PM (EST) www.greenwichct.org/Home/default.asp
Index: All in one. Records indexed on a public use terminal back to 1960. Only the public may search. Copy fee $1.00 per page. Cert fee- $2.00 per cert plus copy fee. Payee- Town of Greenwich. Office does not sell bulk data. **Other phones:** Elections- 203-662-7897; Vital Records- 203-662-7869; Main switchboard -203-622-7700;. **Property tax/Assessing**- PO Box 2540, Greenwich, CT 06836; 203-622-7885, assessor fax- 203-618-7655. hours-8:30AM-3:30PM **Online access**- Search current tax records free at www.greenwichct.org/ServicesOnline/services_online.asp#. You may also search real estate, personal property, and motor vehicles.

Griswold Town

Town Clerk, PO Box 369, Jewett City, CT 06351. 860-376-7060 x100, R/E recording phone-860-376-7060 x101; fax-860-376-7070; 8:30AM-4PM M,T,W, 8:30AM-6:30PM Th, 8:30AM-1:30PM Fr. (EST) www.griswold-ct.org
Index: All in one. Records indexed on a public use terminal back to 1984. Only the public may search. Will not search UCC records. Copy fee $1.00 per page. Cert fee- $1.00 per page plus copy fee. Payee- Town of Griswold. Office does not sell bulk data. **Other phones:** Treasurer- 860-376-7060 x205; Elections- 860-376-7060 x208; Vital Records- 860-376-7060 x101. **Property tax/Assessing**- PO Box 369, Jewett City, CT 06351; 860-376-7060 x103, assessor fax- 860-376-7070. (Appraiser/Auditor- 860-376-7060 x105);

Groton Town

Town Clerk, 45 Fort Hill Rd, Groton, CT 06340. Recording, R/E & UCC phone-860-441-6642; fax-860-441-6703; 8:30AM-4:30PM M-W & F; 9AM-4:30PM Th. (EST) www.town.groton.ct.us
Index: All in one. Records indexed on a public use terminal back to 1964. Only the public may search. Copy fee $1.00 per page. Cert fee- $2.00 per cert plus copy fee. Payee- Groton Town Clerk. Office does sell bulk data, contact Janet Downs. **Other phones:** Treasurer- 860-441-6609; Elections- 860-441-6640; Vital Records- 860-441-6640. **Property tax/Assessing**- 45 Fort Hill Rd, Groton, CT 06340; 860-441-6660, assessor fax- 860-441-6678. hours-8:30AM-4:30PM Public access terminal available. www.town.groton.ct.us/depts/finance/assessment.asp **Online access**- Access property data free at http://grotongis.town.groton.ct.us. Click on Interactive Mapping, then Property Viewer, then owner name. Records back to 1990. Search list of tax payments for 2005 free at www.town.groton.ct.us/taxes/listing.asp.

Guilford Town

Town Clerk, 31 Park St; Town Hall, Guilford, CT 06437. 203-453-8001; 8:30AM-4:30PM (EST) www.ci.guilford.ct.us
Index: All in one. Record index not computerized. Only the public may search. Copy fee $1.00 per page. Cert fee- $2.00 per cert plus copy fee. Payee- Guilford Town Clerk. Office does not sell bulk data. **Other phones:** Treasurer- 203-453-8022; Elections- 203-453-8028; Vital Records- 203-453-8001. **Property tax/Assessing**- 31 Park St, Guilford, CT 06437; 203-453-8010, assessor fax- 203-453-8017. **Online access**- Access property data by owner name, address, or legal free at www.prophecyone.us/index_prophecy.php?town=Guilford.

Haddam Town

Town Clerk, PO Box 87, Haddam, CT 06438. 860-345-8531 x212, R/E recording phone-860-345-8531; fax-860-345-3730; 9AM-4PM M,T,W,; 9AM-7PM Th; 9AM-N F. (EST) www.haddam.org
Index: All in one. Records indexed on a public use terminal back to 1979. Office will perform a UCC search but public must search other records themselves. Copy fee $1.00 per page. Cert fee- $2.00 per cert plus copy fee. Office does not sell bulk data. **Other phones:** Treasurer- 860-345-8531; Elections- 860-345-8531; Vital Records- 860-345-8531 x212. **Property tax/Assessing**- 30 Field Pk Dr, Haddam, CT 06438; 860-345-8531, assessor fax- 860-345-3730. **Online access**- Access Assessor data free after email registration at http://rmsreval.com/login.asp?town=Haddam. Data may be old.

Hamden Town

Town Clerk, 2750 Dixwell Ave, Hamden, CT 06518. 203-287-7029, R/E phone-203-287-7112; fax-203-287-7095; 8:45AM-4:15PM www.hamden.com
Index: Separate indices to search include grantor/grantee, Tax Lien, Sewer Lien. Records indexed on a public use terminal back to 1968, also 1920 to 1948. 1948-68 handwritten. Office will perform a UCC search but public must search other records themselves. Copy fee $1.00 per page. Cert fee- $2.00 per page plus copy fee. Payee- Hamden Town Clerk. Office does not sell bulk data. **Other phones:** Treasurer- 203-387-7007; Elections- 203-287-7081; Vital Records- 203-287-7112. **Property tax/Assessing**- 2750 Dixwell Ave, Hamden, CT 06518; 203-287-7128, assessor fax- 203-287-7125. (Appraiser/Auditor- 203-287-7128) **Online access**- Search the town assessor's database free at http://data.visionappraisal.com/hamdenct/.

Hampton Town

Town Clerk, PO Box 143, Hampton, CT 06247-0143. 860-455-9132, R/E recording phone-860-455-9132 x10; fax-860-455-0517; 9AM-4PM T,TH; 6-8PM TH. www.hamptonct.org/TownHall/town_clerk.htm
Index: All in one. Records (land records from 8/1/08) indexed on computer. Only the public may search.

Copy fee $1.00 per page. Cert fee- $2.00 per cert plus copy fee. Payee- Hampton Town Clerk. **Other phones:** Treasurer- 860-455-9132 x7; Elections- 860-455-9132 x10; Vital Records- 860-455-9132 x10. **Property tax/Assessing**- 164 Main St, Hampton, CT 06247-0143; 860-455-9132 x5, assessor fax- 860-455-0517. hours- 9AM-3PM T; N-4PM, 6PM-8PM TH www.hamptonct.org/TownHall/tax_assessor.htm **Online access**- Access property data free after registration at http://data.visionappraisal.com/.

Hartford City

City Clerk, 550 Main St, Hartford, CT 06103-2992. 860-543-8580, R/E recording phone-860-722-8040; fax-860-722-8041; 8:30AM-4:30 PM (EST)
Index: All in one. Records indexed on a public use terminal back to 192; limited images back to 2000. Only the public may search. Copy fee $1.00 per page. Cert fee- $2.00 per doc plus copy fee. Payee- Hartford City Clerk. Office does not sell bulk data. **Other phones:** Treasurer- 860-543-8530. **Property tax/Assessing**- 550 Main St, Hartford, CT 06103; 860-757-9311, assessor fax- 860-722-6142. **Online access**- Search city assessor data free at http://assessor.hartford.gov/Default.asp?br=exp&vr=6 .

Hartland Town

Town Clerk, PO Box 297, East Hartland, CT 06027. 860-653-0285; fax-860-653-0452; 10AM-N, 1-4PM M,T,W. www.munic.state.ct.us/hartland/hartland.htm
Index: Separate indices to search. Records indexed on computer back to 2001. Office personnel or visitors may perform searches. Office will do short search as time allows only. Office will not search UCC or real estate records. Copy fee $1.00 per page; $5.00 for map fee. Cert fee- $2.00 per cert. Payee- Hartland Town Clerk. Office does sell bulk data, contact Gloria Nelson. **Other phones:** Treasurer- 860-653-6800; Elections- 860-653-0285; Vital Records- 860-653-0285; Tax Collector- 860-653-0609 x105. **Property tax/Assessing**- 22 South Rd, East Hartland, CT 06027; 860-653-0287, assessor fax- 860-653-7919.

Harwinton Town

Town Clerk, 100 Bentley Dr; Town Hall, Harwinton, CT 06791. Recording, R/E & UCC phone-860-485-9613; fax-860-485-0051; 8:30AM-4PM M,T,Th; 8:30AM-6PM W; 8:30AM-12:30PM Fri. (EST) www.harwinton.us
Index: All in one. Records indexed on computer back to 1975. Only the public may search. Copy fee $1.00 per page. Cert fee- $1.00 per cert plus copy fee. Payee- Harwinton Town Clerk. Office does not sell bulk data. **Other phones:** Treasurer- 860-485-9051; Elections- 860-485-9613; Vital Records- 860-485-9613; Tax Collector- 860-485-0446. **Property tax/Assessing**- 100 Bentley Dr, Harwinton, Ct 06791; 860-485-0898, assessor fax- 860-485-0051.

Hebron Town

Town Clerk, PO Box 156, Hebron, CT 06248. 860-228-5971 x124, R/E recording phone-860-228-5971; fax-860-228-4859; 8AM-4PM M-W; 8AM-6PM Th; 8AM-1PM F. (EST) www.hebronct.com
Index: All in one. Records indexed on a public use terminal back to 1698. Only the public may search. Copy fee $1.00 per page. Cert fee- $2.00 per cert plus copy fee. Payee- Town of Hebron. Paper copies of land records available; contact town manager. **Other phones:** Treasurer- 860-228-5971; Elections- 860-228-5971; Vital Records- 860-228-5971. **Property tax/Assessing**- 15 Gilead St, Hebron, CT 06248; 860-228-5971 x5, assessor fax- 860-228-4859. (Appraiser/Auditor- 860-228-5971) **Online access**- property data free at www.prophecyone.us/index_prophecy.php?town=Hebron. No name searching.

Kent Town

Town Clerk, PO Box 843, Kent, CT 06757-0678. 860-927-3433; fax-860-927-4541; 9AM-4PM; Jul-Aug 9-4 M-Th, 9AM-N Fri. (EST) www.kentct.org/townclerk.htm
Index: Separate indices to search include grantor/grantee. Records indexed on computer back to 1971. Only the public may search. Copy fee $1.00 per page. Cert fee- $2.00 per page. Payee- Kent Town Clerk. Office does not sell bulk data. **Other phones:** Treasurer- 860-927-1313; Vital Records- 860-927-3433. **Property tax/Assessing**- PO Box 678, 41 Kent Green Blvd, Kent, CT 06757-0678; 860-927-3160, assessor fax- 860-927-4541. hours- 9AM-N, 1PM-4PM M,W A public access terminal available. www.kentct.org/kent.htm#tax_assessor **Online access**- Access to property assessor data is at http://data.visionappraisal.com/KentCT/.

Killingly Town

Town Clerk, PO Box 6000, Danielson, CT 06239. Recording, R/E & UCC phone-860-779-5307; fax-860-779-5394; 8:30AM-4:30PM www.killinglyct.gov
Index: Separate indices to search include 1939-2004 history, and 2005-present current. Records indexed on a public use terminal back to 1939. Only the public may search. Copy fee $1.00 per page. Cert fee- $2.00 per page plus copy fee. Payee- Killingly Town Clerk. **Other phones:** Treasurer- 860-779-5337; Elections- 860-779-5346; Vital Records- 860-779-5307. **Property tax/Assessing**- PO Box 6000, Danielson, CT 06239; 860-779-5323, assessor fax- 860-779-5370. hours- 8AM-4:30PM **Online access**- Access assessor records free at www.killinglyct.gov/index.asp?Type=B_BASIC&SEC={1EB50B8D-0530-4765-937E-F2C174D7B8AA}.

Killingworth Town

Town Clerk, 323 Rte 81, Killingworth, CT 06419-1298. 860-663-1616; fax-860-663-4050; 8AM-N,1-4PM (EST)
Index: Recorded by years or groups of years. Records indexed on a public use terminal back to 1965. Only the public may search. Copy fee $1.00 per page. Cert fee- $2.00 per cert plus copy fee. Payee- Town of Killingworth. Office does not sell bulk data. **Other phones:** Vital Records- 860-663-1616. **Property tax/Assessing**- Killingworth Town Assessing Office, 323 Rte 81, Killingworth, CT 06419-1298; 860-663-2002, assessor fax- 860-663-4050. hours- 9AM-N, 1-4PM Computer terminal available for public use. **Online access**- Access property data free at www.prophecyone.us/index_prophecy.php?town=Killingworth. No name searching.

Lebanon Town

Town Clerk, 579 Exeter Rd; Town Hall, Lebanon, CT 06249. 860-642-7319; fax-860-642-7716; 8AM-4PM M,Th,F; 8AM-6PM T. (EST) www.lebanontownhall.org
Index: All in one. Record index not computerized. Only the public may search. Copy fee $1.00 per page. Cert fee- $2.00 per cert plus copy fee. Payee- Town of Lebanon. **Other phones:** Treasurer- 860-642-3572; Vital Records- 860-642-7319. **Property tax/Assessing**- 579 Exeter Rd, Town Hall, Lebanon, CT 06249; 860-642-6141, assessor fax- 860-642-2022. hours- 9AM-4PM M,Th,F; 9AM-6PM Tu A public access terminal is available.

Ledyard Town

Town Clerk, 741 Col Ledyard Hwy, Ledyard, CT 06339. 860-464-3257, R/E recording phone-860-464-3259; fax-860-464-1126; 8:30AM-4:30PM (EST) www.town.ledyard.ct.us/index.asp?nid=74
Records indexed on a public use terminal back to 1962. Only the public may search. Copy fee $1.00 per page. Cert fee- $2.00 per cert plus copy fee. Payee- Town of Ledyard. Office does not sell bulk data. **Other phones:** Treasurer- 860-464-3228; Vital Records- 860-464-3259. **Property tax/Assessing**- 741 Colonel Ledyard Hwy, Ledyard, CT 06339; 860-464-3237, assessor fax- 860-464-1126. www.town.ledyard.ct.us/index.asp?nid=75 **Online access**- Search the assessor database at www.visionappraisal.com/databases/index.htm. Free registration required.

Lisbon Town

Town Clerk, 1 Newent Rd; RD 2 Town Hall, Lisbon, CT 06351-9802. 860-376-2708; fax-860-376-6545; 9AM-3PM M-Th; 6PM-8PM W; 9AM-1PM F; 9AM-N Sat. (EST)
Index: All in one. Record index not computerized. Only the public may search. Copy fee $1.00 per page. Cert fee- $2.00 per cert plus copy fee. Payee- Lisbon Town Clerk. **Other phones:** Treasurer- 860-376-3400. **Property tax/Assessing**- 1 Newent Rd, Lisbon, CT 06351; 860-376-5115, assessor fax- 860-376-6545. hours- 9AM-3PM

Litchfield Town

Town Clerk, PO Box 488, Litchfield, CT 06759-0488. Recording, R/E & UCC phone-860-567-7561; fax-860-567-7552; 9AM-4:30PM (EST)
Index: Separate indices to search. Record index not computerized. Only the public may search. Copy fee $1.00 per page. Cert fee- $1.00 per cert plus copy fee. Payee- Litchfield Town Clerk. Office does not sell bulk data. **Other phones:** Treasurer- 860-567-7554; Vital Records- 860-567-7561; Registrar- 860-567-7558. **Property tax/Assessing**- PO Box 488, 74 West St, Litchfield, CT 06759-0488; 860-567-7559, fax-860-567-7552. www.litchfieldct.com/gvt/govt.html

Lyme Town

Town Clerk, 480 Hamburg Rd; Town Hall, Lyme, CT 06371. Recording, R/E & UCC phone-860-434-7733; fax-860-434-2989; 9AM-4PM www.townlyme.org/
Index: All in one. Record index not computerized. Only the public may search. Copy fee $1.00 per page. Cert fee- $2.00 per page plus copy fee. Payee- Lyme Town Clerk. **Other phones:** Treasurer- 860-434-7733; Elections- 860-434-7733; Vital Records- 860-434-7733. **Property tax/Assessing**- Lyme Town Assessing Office, 480 Hamburg Rd, Town Hall, Lyme, CT 06371; 860-434-8092, assessor fax- 860-434-2989. (Appraiser/Auditor- 860-434-8094)

Madison City

Town Clerk, 8 Campus Dr, Madison, CT 06443-2538. Recording, R/E phone-203-245-5672; fax-203-245-5675; 8:30AM-4PM www.madisonct.org
Index: All in one. Records indexed on a public use terminal back to 7/1/79. Only the public may search. Copy fee $1.00 per page. Cert fee- $2.00 per cert plus copy fee. Payee- Madison Town Clerk. Office does not sell bulk data. **Other phones:** Elections- 203-245-5671; Vital Records- 203-245-5672. **Property tax/Assessing**- 8 Campus Dr, Madison, CT 06443; 203-245-5652, assessor fax- 2203-245-5639. Public access terminal available. **Online access**- Search the city assessor database at http://data.visionappraisal.com/MadisonCT/. Free registration required for full access. Also, access property data at www.appraisalresource.com/Search.aspx?town=Madison.

Manchester Town

Town Clerk, PO Box 191, Manchester, CT 06045-0191. Recording, R/E & UCC phone-860-647-3037; fax-860-647-3029; 8:30AM-5PM (EST) www.townofmanchester.org/Town_Clerk/
Index: All in one. Records indexed on a public use terminal back to 1823. Only the public may search. Copy fee $1.00 per page. Cert fee- $1.00 per cert includes copy fee. Payee- Manchester Town Clerk. Office does not sell bulk data. **Other phones:** Treasurer- 860-647-3023; Elections- 860-647-3037; Vital Records- 860-647-3037. **Property tax/Assessing**- PO Box 191, 31 Center St, Manchester, CT 06045-0191; 860-647-3016, assessor fax- 860-647-3099. (Appraiser/Auditor- 860-647-3017) **Online access**- Search town assessor database at http://data.visionappraisal.com/ManchesterCT/. Also, click on TOMnet Public parcel viewer to search property free at www.manchestergis.com/ but no name searching.

Mansfield Town

Town Clerk, 4 S Eagleville Rd, Mansfield, CT 06268. 860-429-3302; fax-860-429-7785; 8:15AM-4:30PM M-W; 8:15AM-6:30PM Th; 8AM-N Fri. (EST) www.mansfieldct.org
Index: All in one. Records indexed on a public use terminal back to 1984. Only the public may search. Office will not search real estate records. Will not search UCC records. Copy fee $1.00 per page. Cert fee- $1.00 per page plus copy fee. Payee- Town of Mansfield. **Online access to Parcel, GIS-Mapping records:** Access GIS-Mapping and parcels free at www.mainstreetmaps.com/CT/Mansfield/. **Other phones:** Elections- 860-429-3369. **Property tax/Assessing**- Mansfield Town Assessing Office, 4 S Eagleville Rd, Mansfield, CT 06268; 860-429-3327, assessor fax- 860-429-7785. hours- 8:15AM-4:30PM M-W www.mansfieldct.org/town/departments/finance/assessor/index.php **Online access**- Access property and GIS-Mapping free at www.mainstreetmaps.com/CT/Mansfield/.

Marlborough Town

Town Clerk, PO Box 29, Marlborough, CT 06447. Recording, R/E & UCC phone-860-295-6206; fax-860-295-0317; 8AM-4:30PM M-TH; 8AM-7PM T; 8AM-N F. (EST) www.marlboroughct.net
Index: All in one. Records indexed on a public use terminal back to 6/30/50. Only the public may search. Copy fee $1.00 per page. Cert fee- $2.00 per doc plus copy fee. Payee- Marlborough Town Clerk. **Other phones:** Treasurer- 860-295-6165; Elections- 860-295-6166; Vital Records- 860-295-6206. **Property tax/Assessing**- Marlborough Town Assessing Office, PO Box 29, Marborough, CT 06447; 860-295-6201, assessor fax- 860-295-6167. **Online access**- Search the assessor database free at http://data.visionappraisal.com/M arlboroughCT/.

Meriden City

City Clerk, 142 E Main St, Meriden, CT 06450-8022. Recording, R/E & UCC phone-203-630-4030; fax-203-630-4059; 8AM-7PM M; 8AM-5PM T-F. (EST) www.cityofmeriden.org
Index: All in one. Records indexed on a public use terminal back to 1983. Only the public may search. Copy fee $1.00 per page. Cert fee- $2.00 per cert plus copy fee. Payee- Meriden City Clerk. Office does not sell bulk data. **Other phones:** Treasurer- 203-630-4134; Elections- 203-630-4075; Vital Records- 203-630-4030. **Property tax/Assessing**- Same address as recording office. 203-630-4065, assessor fax- 203-630-4068. hours- 8AM-5PM, til 7PM 1st & 3rd Monday **Online access**- Search by parcel ID or address for property assessor data at www.cityofmeriden.org. Click on Property Searches. Also, search property data free on a private site at www.appraisalresource.com/Search.aspx?town=Meriden but no searching. Also, access parcel data free at http://gis.ci.meriden.ct.us/website/default.asp.

Middlebury Town

Town Clerk, PO Box 392, Middlebury, CT 06762-0392. Recording, R/E & UCC phone-203-758-2557; fax-203-758-2915; 9-5PM www.middlebury-ct.org
Index: All in one. Records indexed on a public use terminal back to 1920. Only the public may search. Copy fee $1.00 per page. Minutes-$.50 per page, full maps-$5.00, section of map-$1.00 per page. Cert fee- $2.00 per cert plus copy fee. Payee- Middlebury Town Clerk. **Other phones:** Treasurer- 203-758-1770; Elections- 203-758-2557; Vital Records- 203-758-2557. **Property tax/Assessing**- Same address as recording office. 203-758-1447, assessor fax- 203-758-2915. **Online access**- Access assessor and property data free at http://data.visionappraisal.com/MiddleburyCT/DEFAULT.asp.

Middlefield Town

Town Clerk, 393 Jackson Hill Rd, Middlefield, CT 06455. Recording, R/E & UCC phone-860-349-7116; fax-860-349-7115; 9AM-5PM M; 9AM-4PM T-TH; 9AM-3PM F. (EST)
Index: Separate indices to search include grantor/grantee. Record index not computerized. Only the public may search. Copy fee $1.00 per page. Cert fee- $1.00 per cert includes copy fee. Payee- Middlefield Town Clerk. **Other phones:** Treasurer- 860-349-7114; Elections- 860-349-7119; Vital Records- 860-349-7116. **Property tax/Assessing**- Middlefield Town Assessing Office, 393 Jackson Hill Rd, PO Box 179, Middlefield, CT 06455; 860-349-7111, assessor fax- 860-349-7115. hours- 9AM-4PM **Online access**- Search the town assessor database free at http://data.visionappraisal.com/MiddlefieldCT/.

Middletown City

City Clerk, PO Box 1300, Middletown, CT 06457. Recording, R/E & UCC phone-860-344-3459; fax-860-344-3591; 8:30AM-4:30PM (EST) www.cityofmiddletown.com/
Index: Separate indices arranged by 10 to 20 year increments. Records indexed on computer from 5/24/07 to present. Only the public may search. Copy fee $1.00 per page. Cert fee- $2.00 per cert plus copy fee. Payee- Middletown Town Clerk. Bulk data available for purchase from IT department, call 860-344-3500 for information. **Other phones:** Treasurer- 860-344-3438; Elections- 860-344-3485; Vital Records- 860-344-3474. **Property tax/Assessing**- PO Box 1300, 245 DeKoven Dr, Middletown, CT 06457; 860-344-3454, assessor fax- 860-344-3563. **Online access**- Access property data free at http://host.appgeo.com/MiddletownCT/Default.aspx but no name searching.

Milford City

City Clerk, 70 W River St, Milford, CT 06460-3364. Recording, R/E & UCC phone-203-783-3210; fax-203-783-3362; 8:30AM-5PM www.ci.milford.ct.us
Index: All in one. Records indexed on a public use terminal back to 12/3100. Only the public may search; office will search for a particular book/page. Office will not search UCC records. Copy fee $1.00 per page. Cert fee- $2.00 per cert plus copy fee. Payee- Milford City Clerk. **Other phones:** Treasurer- 203-783-3257; Elections- 203-783-3339 (DEM); 203-783-3242 (REP); Vital Records- 203-783-3210; Tax Collector- 203-783-3217 or 3218. **Property tax/Assessing**- 70 W River St, Milford, CT 06460; 203-783-3215, assessor fax- 203-878-2609. (Appraiser/Auditor- 203-783-3215) hours- 8:30AM-4:30PM **Online access**- Search the city assessor's database at http://data.visionappraisal.com/milfordct/.

Monroe Town

Town Clerk, 7 Fan Hill Rd, Monroe, CT 06468-1800. 203-452-2811, R/E recording phone-203-452-2800; fax-203-452-6581; 9AM-5PM www.monroect.org
Index: All in one. Records indexed on computer back to 1968. Only the public may search. Copy fee $1.00 per page. Cert fee- $2.00 per cert plus copy fee. Payee- Town of Monroe. **Other phones:** Treasurer-203-452-2802; Elections- 203-452-2820; Vital Records- 203-452-2800. **Property tax/Assessing**- 7 Fan Hill Rd, Monroe, CT 06468; 203-452-2803, assessor fax- 203-261-6197. (Appraiser/Auditor- 203-452-2803);

Montville Town

Town Clerk, 310 Norwich-New London Tpke; Town Hall, Uncasville, CT 06382. 860-848-3030; fax-860-848-9784; 8AM-4:30PM www.townofmontville.org
Index: All in one. Records indexed on computer back to 1950. Office will not search UCC records. Copy fee $1.00 per page. Cert fee- $2.00 per cert plus copy fee. Payee- Montville Town Clerk. Office does not sell bulk data. **Online access to Real Estate, Grantor/Grantee, Deed, Death, Marriage, Civil Union, Trade Name, Map records:** Access to recorders databases are available free at http://66.212.195.75/resolution/. Land records go back to 1/1950; marriage and death back to 10/30/1870; trade names to 2/11/1938; civil unions back to 10/6/2005. **Other phones:** Treasurer- 860-848-0139; Vital Records- 860-848-3030. **Property tax/Assessing**- 310 Norwich New London Turnpike, Uncasville, CT 06832; 860-848-8221 #5, assessor fax- 860-848-4078. **Online access**- Access assessor data free with registration at http://data.visionappraisal.com/MontvilleCT/DEFAULT.asp.

Naugatuck Town

Town Clerk, 229 Church St; Town Hall, Naugatuck, CT 06770. 203-720-7000, R/E recording phone-203-720-7055; fax-203-720-7099; 8:30AM-4PM (EST)
Index: Separate indices to search include grantor/grantee. Records indexed on a public use terminal from 1991 to present. Only the public may search. Copy fee $1.00 per page. Cert fee- $2.00 per cert plus copy fee. Payee- Naugatuck Town Clerk. **Other phones:** Treasurer- 203-720-7021; Elections- 203-720-7047; Vital Records- 203-720-7055. **Property tax/Assessing**- 229 Church St, Town Hall, Naugatuck, CT 06770; 203-720-7016, assessor fax-203-720-7207. **Online access**- Search assessor data free at http://data.visionappraisal.com/NaugatuckCT/.

New Britain Town

Town Clerk, 27 W Main St, New Britain, CT 06051. 860-826-3344; fax-860-826-3348; 8:15AM-3:45PM; 8:15AM-6:45PM Last Th. www.new-britain.net
Index: All in one. Records indexed on a public use terminal back to 10/1/58. Only the public may search. Copy fee $1.00 per page. Cert fee- $2.00 per cert plus copy fee. Payee- New Britain Town Clerk. Office does not sell bulk data. **Property tax/Assessing**- 27 W Main St, New Britain, CT 06051; 860-826-3323, assessor fax- 860-612-5013. hours- 8:15AM-3:45PM Public access terminal available. **Online access**- Search the city assessor database at http://data.visionappraisal.com/NewbritainCT/.

New Canaan Town

Town Clerk, 77 Main St, 1st Fl; Town Hall, New Canaan, CT 06840. 203-594-3073, R/E recording phone-203-594-3070; 8:30AM-4:30PM (EST) www.newcanaan.info
Index: All in one. Records indexed on computer back to 1981. Only the public may search. Copy fee $1.00 per page if court copies, $.25 per page if self copy. Cert fee- $2.00 per cert plus copy fee. Payee- New Canaan Town Clerk. Office does not sell bulk data. **Other phones:** Treasurer- 203-594-3024; Elections-203-594-3060; Vital Records- 203-594-3070. **Property tax/Assessing**- 77 Main St, New Canaan, CT 06840; 203-594-3005, assessor fax- 203-594-3130. **Online access**- Access to property data is at http://data.visionappraisal.com/NewCanaanCT/. Free registration required.

New Fairfield Town

Town Clerk, 4 Brushhill Rd, New Fairfield, CT 06812. 203-312-5616; 8:30AM-5PM T-F; 8:30AM-N Sat. (EST) www.newfairfield.org
Index: Separate indices to search. Records indexed on a public use terminal back to 1972. Only the public may search. Copy fee $1.00 per page. Cert fee- $2.00 per cert plus copy fee. Payee- New Fairfield Town Clerk. Office does not sell bulk data. **Other phones:** Elections- 203-312-5614; Vital Records- 203-312-5616. **Property tax/Assessing**- New Fairfield Town Assessing Office, 4 Brushhill Rd, New Fairfield, CT 06812; 203-312-5625, assessor fax- 203-312-5612. hours- 8:30AM-5PM T-F, 8:30-12PM Sat **Online access**- Access the assessor database free at http://data.visionappraisal.com/NewfairfieldCT/.

New Hartford Town

Town Clerk, PO Box 426, New Hartford, CT 06057. Recording, R/E & UCC phone-860-379-5037; fax-860-379-0614; 9AM-N, 12:40-4PM M,T,Th; 9AM-N, 1PM-6PM W;. www.town.new-hartford.ct.us
Index: All in one. Records indexed on a public use terminal back to 1977. Only the public may search. Will not search UCC records. Copy fee $1.00 per page. Cert fee- $2.00 per cert plus copy fee. Payee- New Hartford. Office does not sell bulk data. **Online access to Real Estate, Grantor/Grantee, Deed,**

Lien, Judgment, Assumed Name records: Access real estate, assumed names records for free at http://landrecords.town.new-hartford.ct.us/. **Other phones:** Treasurer- 860-379-3389; Elections- 860-738-9721; Vital Records- 860-379-5037. **Property tax/Assessing-** PO Box 316, New Hartford, CT 06057; 860-379-5235, assessor fax- 860-379-1367. **Online access-** Access to property data is at http://data.visionappraisal.com/NewhartfordCT/.

New Haven City

City Clerk, 200 Orange St, Rm 202, New Haven, CT 06510. 203-946-8339, R/E recording phone-203-946-8344; fax-203-946-6974; 9AM-5PM (EST) www.cityofnewhaven.com
Index: All in one. Records indexed on a public use terminal back to 1959. Only the public may search. Copy fee $.50 per page. Cert fee- $2.00 per page plus copy fee. Payee- New Haven City Clerk. Office does not sell bulk data. **Other phones:** Treasurer- 203-946-8300; Elections- 203-946-8346; Vital Records- 203-946-8084. **Property tax/Assessing-** 165 Church St., New Haven, CT 06510; 203-946-4800, assessor fax- 203-946-7122. **Online access-** Search the city assessor database at http://data.visionappraisal.com/NewhavenCT/.

New Milford Town

Town Clerk, 10 Main St, New Milford, CT 06776. 860-355-6020; fax-860-210-2096; 8:30AM-4:30PM (EST) www.newmilford.org/
Index: All in one. Records indexed on a public use terminal back to 1963. Only the public may search. Copy fee $1.00 per page. Cert fee- $2.00 per cert plus copy fee. Payee- New Milford Town Clerk. **Other phones:** Vital Records- 860-355-6020. **Property tax/Assessing-** 10 Main St, New Milford, CT 06776; 860-355-6070, assessor fax- 860-355-6032. hours- 8AM-4PM **Online access-** Search town assessor data at http://data.visionappraisal.com/NewMilfordCT/.

Newington Town

Town Clerk, 131 Cedar St, Newington, CT 06111-2696. Recording, R/E & UCC phone-860-665-8545; fax-860-665-8551; 8:30-4:30 www.newingtonct.gov
Index: All in one. Records indexed on a public use terminal back to 1984. Only the public may search. Copy fee $1.00 per page. Cert fee- $2.00 per doc plus copy fee. Payee- Newington Town Clerk. **Other phones:** Elections- 860-665-8516; Vital Records- 860-665-8545. **Property tax/Assessing-** Same address as recording office. 860-665-8530, assessor fax- 860-665-8531. **Online access-** Access assessor property data free http://newington.univers-clt.com.

Newtown Town

Town Clerk, 45 Main St, Newtown, CT 06470. 203-270-4210; fax-203-270-4205; 8-4:30 www.newtown-ct.gov/Public_Documents/NewtownCT_Clerk/index
Index: All in one. Records indexed on a public use terminal back to 1900. Only the public may search. Copy fee $1.00 per page. Cert fee- $2.00 per cert plus copy fee. Payee- Town of Newtown. Office does not sell bulk data. **Other phones:** Treasurer- 203-270-4221; Elections- 203-270-4250; Vital Records- 203-270-4210. **Property tax/Assessing-** 45 Main St, Newtown, CT 06470; 203-270-4240, assessor fax- 203-270-4243. www.newtown-ct.gov/Public_Documents/NewtownCT_Assessor/index **Online access-** Access property data free at www.prophecyone.us/index_prophecy.php?town=Newtown. No name searching. Also, other site for property search for free go to www.totalvaluation.com/tvweb/mainsearch.aspx?city=newtown.

Norfolk Town

Town Clerk, PO Box 552, Norfolk, CT 06058-0552. 860-542-5679; fax-860-542-5274; 8:30AM-N, 1-4PM M-TH, 8:30AM-N Fri. (EST)
Index: All in one. Record index not computerized. Only the public may search. All land records copy fee $1.00 per page. Cert fee- $2.00 per doc plus copy fee. Payee- Town of Norfolk. Office does not sell bulk data. **Other phones:** Elections- 860-542-5679; Vital Records- 860-542-5679. **Property tax/Assessing-** PO Box 552, 19 Maple Ave, Norfolk, CT 06058; 860-542-5287, assessor fax- 860-542-5274. 9AM-N

North Branford Town

Town Clerk, PO Box 287, North Branford, CT 06471-0287. 203-484-6015; fax-203-484-6025; 8:30AM-4:30PM www.townofnorthbranfordct.com/town_services/town_clerk.htm
Index: All in one. Records indexed on a public use terminal back to 1985. Only the public may search. Copy fee $1.00 per page. Cert fee- $2.00 per cert plus copy fee. Payee- North Branford Town Clerk. Office does not sell bulk data. **Other phones:** Treasurer- 203-484-6002; Elections- 203-484-1033; Vital Records- 203-484-6015. **Property tax/Assessing-** 909 Foxon Rd, North Branford, CT 06471; 203-484-6013, assessor fax- 203-484-6025. www.townofnorthbranfordct.com/town_services/assessor.htm **Online access-** Search assessor records at http://data.visionappraisal.com/NorthBranfordCT/DEFAULT.asp.

North Canaan Town

Town Clerk, PO Box 338, North Canaan, CT 06018. 860-824-3138; fax-860-824-3139; 9:30AM-N, 1-4PM; Closed Fri. (EST)
Index: All in one. Record index not computerized. Only the public may search. Copy fee $1.00 per page. Cert fee- $1.00 per cert plus copy fee. Payee- North Canaan Town Clerk. **Other phones:** Treasurer- 860-824-3144. **Property tax/Assessing-** North Canaan Town Assessing Office, PO Box 907, North Canaan, CT 06018; 860-824-3137, assessor fax- 860-824-3146. hours- 9AM-N 1PM-4PM

North Haven Town

Town Clerk, 18 Church St; Town Hall, North Haven, CT 06473. 203-239-5321 x541; fax-203-234-2130; 8:30AM-4:30PM (EST) www.town.north-haven.ct.us
Index: Separate indices to search include liens, etc. Records indexed on computer back to 1965. Only the public may search. Copy fee $.50 per page. Cert fee- $2.00 per cert plus copy fee. Payee- North Haven Town Clerk. Office does not sell bulk data. **Other phones:** Elections- 203-239-5321 x755; Vital Records- 203-239-5321 x541. **Property tax/Assessing-** 18 Church St, Town Hall, North Haven, CT 06473; 203-239-5321 x700, assessor fax- 203-234-2130. www.town.north-haven.ct.us/TownHallDepts/Assessor.asp **Online access-** Access property data free at http://north-haven.univers-clt.com.

North Stonington Town

Town Clerk, 40 Main St, North Stonington, CT 06359. 860-535-2877 x21, R/E recording phone-860-535-2877 x32, UCC recording phone-860-535-2877 x21; fax-860-535-4554; 9AM-4PM (EST) www.munic.state.ct.us/N_Stonington/
Index: All in one. Records indexed on a public use terminal back to 010100. Only the public may search. Copy fee $1.00 per page for land records; $.25 per page all other copies. Cert fee- $2.00 per cert plus copy fee. Payee- Town of North Stonington. **Other phones:** Treasurer- 860-535-2877 x10; Elections- 860-535-2877 x28; Vital Records- 860-535-2877 x21. **Property tax/Assessing-** PO Box 263, North Stonington, CT 06359; 860-535-2877 x23, assessor fax- 860-535-4554. 8AM-4PM www.northstoningtonct.gov/Pages/index **Online access-** Access GIS/mapping free at www.northstoningtongis.com/

Norwalk City

Town Clerk, PO Box 5125, Norwalk, CT 06856-5125. 203-854-7746; fax-203-854-7802; 8:30AM-4:30PM M,T,W,F; 8:30AM-7PM TH. (EST) www.norwalkct.org
Index: Separate indices to search include computer, books. Records indexed on computer back to 1974. Also all map indexes and images are now included in computer. Only the public may search. Copy fee $2.00 per page. Cert fee- $1.00 per cert plus copy fee. Payee- Town Clerk of Norwalk. Office does not sell bulk data. **Online access to Real Estate, Deed, Lien, Marriage, UCC records:** Access to the town clerk's Official Records is free at www.norwalkct.org/TownClerk/landrecords/default.asp . **Other phones:** Elections- 203-854-7746; Vital Records- 203-854-7746. **Property tax/Assessing-** 125 East Ave, Rm 106, Norwalk, CT 06851; 203-854-7887, assessor fax- 203-854-7986. **Online access-** Access to Norwalk property records is free at www.norwalkct.org/norwalk/pckls.asp.

Norwich City

City Clerk, 100 Broadway, Rm 215; City Hall, Norwich, CT 06360. 860-823-3732; fax-860-823-3790; 8:30AM-4:30PM (EST) www.norwichct.org
Index: All in one. Records (land) indexed on index books back to 1928. Only the public may search. Copy fee $1.00 per page. Cert fee- $2.00 per cert plus copy fee. Payee- Norwich City Clerk. Office does not sell bulk data. **Online access to Real Estate, Deed records:** Also, access to the clerk's town land records is online by subscription. Index goes back to 1929 and images to 1997. Fee is $350.00 per year; sign-up at www.norwichct.org/content/43/280/81/249.aspx or call 860-823-3734. **Other phones:** Treasurer- 860-823-3712; Vital Records- 860-823-3734. **Property tax/Assessing-** 100 Broadway, Norwich, CT 06360; 860-823-3723, assessor fax- 860-823-3719. **Online access-** Search the city assessor's database at http://data.visionappraisal.com/NorwichCT/. Also, access to property data to be available soon at www.appraisalresource.com/OnlineDatabases.aspx.

Old Lyme Town

Town Clerk, 52 Lyme St, Old Lyme, CT 06371. Recording, R/E & UCC phone-860-434-1605 x221; fax-860-434-1400; 9AM-N,1-4PM www.oldlyme-ct.gov
Index: All in one. Records indexed on computer back to 0801/87. Only the public may search. Copy fee $1.00 per page. For copies of minutes fee $.25 per page. Cert fee- $1.00 per cert plus copy fee. Payee- Old Lyme Town Clerk. **Other phones:** Treasurer- 860-434-1605 x232; Elections- 860-434-1605 x230; Vital Records- 860-434-1605 x221. **Property tax/Assessing-** 52 Lyme St, Town Hall, Old Lyme, CT 06371; 860-434-1605 x218, assessor fax- 860-434-1400. (Appraiser/Auditor- 860-434-1605 x218) 9AM-4PM **Online access-** Search town Assessor's data http://data.visionappraisal.com/OLDLYMECT/.

Old Saybrook Town

Town Clerk, 302 Main St, Old Saybrook, CT 06475. Recording, R/E & UCC phone-860-395-3135; fax-860-395-5014; 8:30-4:30PM www.oldsaybrookct.org
Index: All in one. Records indexed on a public use terminal back to 0101/1966. Only the public may search. Copy fee $1.00 per page. No photocopies after 4PM. Cert fee- $2.00 per doct plus copy fee. Payee- Old Saybrook Town Clerk. **Other phones:** Treasurer- 860-395-3073; Elections- 860-395-3135; Vital Records- 860-395-3135. **Property tax/Assessing-** Old Saybrook Town Assessing Office, 302 Main St, Old Saybrook, CT 06475; 860-395-3137, assessor fax- 860-395-5014.

Orange Town

Town Clerk, 617 Orange Center Rd; Town Hall, Orange, CT 06477. 203-891-2122 x4, R/E recording phone-203-891-2122 x730; fax-203-891-2185; 8:30AM-4:30PM (EST) www.orange-ct.gov
Index: All in one. Records indexed on a public use terminal back to 1972. Only the public may search. Copy fee $1.00 per page. Cert fee- $2.00 per cert plus copy fee. Payee- Orange Town Clerk. Office does not sell bulk data. **Other phones:** Treasurer- 203-891-2122 x734; Elections- 203-891-2122 x715; Vital Records- 203-891-2122 x734; First Selectman- 203-891-2122 x737. **Property tax/Assessing-** 617 Orange Center Rd, Orange, CT 06477; 203-891-2122 x722, assessor fax- 203-891-2185.

Oxford Town

Town Clerk, 486 Oxford Rd, Oxford, CT 06478. 203-888-2543; fax-203-888-2136; 9AM-5PM M-TH; 7PM-9PM M & TH. (EST) www.oxford-ct.gov
Index: All in one. Records indexed on a public use terminal back to 1978. Only the public may search. Copy fee $1.00 per page. Cert fee- $1.00 per cert plus copy fee. Payee- Oxford Town Clerk. **Other phones:** Treasurer- 203-888-2543; Elections- 203-888-2543; Vital Records- 203-888-2543. **Property tax/Assessing**- 486 Oxford Rd, Oxford, CT 06478; 203-888-2543 x3055, assessor fax- 203-888-2136. **Online access**- Access property data free at www.prophecyone.us/index_prophecy.php?town=Oxford. No name searching.

Plainfield Town

Town Clerk, 8 Community Ave; Town Hall, Plainfield, CT 06374. Recording, R/E & UCC phone-860-230-3009; fax-860-230-3011; 8:30AM-4:30PM (EST) www.plainfieldct.org/
Index: Separate indices to search. Records indexed on a public use terminal back to 1937. Only the public may search. Copy fee $1.00 per page. Cert fee- $1.00 per cert plus copy fee. Payee- Town of Plainfield. **Other phones:** Treasurer- 860-230-3003; Elections-860-230-3009; Vital Records- 860-230-3009. **Property tax/Assessing**- 8 Community Ave, Plainfield, CT 06374; 860-230-3006, assessor fax-860-230-3033. _**Online access**- Search maps free at www.plainfieldct.org/index_files/Page2267.htm and perform a property assessor search at http://plainfield.ias-clt.com/parcel.list.php.

Plainville Town

Town Clerk, 1 Central Sq; Municipal Ctr, Plainville, CT 06062. 860-793-0221 x4, x2, R/E recording phone-860-793-0221; fax-860-793-2285; 8AM-4PM M,T,W; 8AM-7PM TH; 8AM-Noon F. (EST) www.plainvillect.com
Index: All in one. Records indexed on a public use terminal back to 1/1989. Only the public may search. Copy fee $1.00 per page. Cert fee- $2.00 per page plus copy fee. Payee- Town of Plainville. Office does not sell bulk data. **Property tax/Assessing**- 1 Central Sq, Plainville, CT 06062; 860-793-0221 x244, assessor fax- 860-793-2285. www.plainvillect.com **Online access**- Access town assessor property data free at http://plainville.univers-clt.com.

Plymouth Town

Town Clerk, 80 Main St; Town Hall, Terryville, CT 06786. Recording, R/E & UCC phone-860-585-4039; fax-860-585-4015; 8:30-4:30 www.plymouthct.us
Index: All in one. Records indexed on a public use terminal back to the 1960's. Only the public may search. Copy fee $1.00 per page. Cert fee- $2.00 cert fee plus $1.00 per page copy fee. Payee- Plymouth Town Clerk. **Other phones:** Treasurer- 860-585-4009; Elections- 860-585-4033; Vital Records- 860-585-4039. **Property tax/Assessing**- 80 Main St, Town Hall, Terryville, CT 06786; 860-585-4006, assessor fax- 860-585-4005.

Pomfret Town

Town Clerk, PO Box 286, Pomfret Center, CT 06259. Recording, R/E & UCC phone-860-974-0343; fax-860-974-3950; 9AM-4PM M,T,Th; 9AM-6PM W; 9AM-2PM F. (EST) http://pomfretct.org
Index: Separate indices to search include trade names, vitals, armed forces discharges, land maps. Records indexed on a public use terminal back to 1985. Only the public may search. Copy fee $1.00 per page. Cert fee- $1.00 per doc plus copy fee. Payee- Town of Pomfret. **Other phones:** Treasurer- 860-974-0343; Elections- 860-974-0343; Vital Records- 860-974-0343. **Property tax/Assessing**- 5 Haven Rd, PO Box 286, Pomfret Center, CT 06259; 860-974-1674, assessor fax- 860-974-3950. **Online access**- Search town assessor database at http://data.visionappraisal.com/PomfretCT/. Search for land data such as subdivisions, wetlands and zoning regulations at http://pomfretct.org.

Portland Town

Town Clerk, PO Box 71, Portland, CT 06480. Recording, R/E & UCC phone-860-342-6743; fax-860-342-0001; 9AM-4:30PM (EST)
Index: All in one. Records indexed on a public use terminal back to 1923. Office will perform a UCC search but public must search other records themselves. Copy fee $1.00 per page. Cert fee- $1.00 per doc includes copy fee. Payee- Portland Town Clerk. **Other phones:** Treasurer- 860-342-6726; Elections- 860-342-6743; Vital Records- 860-342-6743. **Property tax/Assessing**- PO Box 71, 33 E Main St, Portland, CT 06480; 860-342-6744, assessor fax- 860-342-6738. 9AM-4PM M-TH; 9AM-N F

Preston Town

Town Clerk, 389 Rte 2; Town Hall, Preston, CT 06365-8830. 860-887-9821 x2, R/E recording phone-860-887-9821; fax-860-885-0171; 9AM-4:30PM T-F; TH until 6:30PM (EST) www.preston-ct.org/
Index: All in one. Records indexed on a public use terminal back to 1978. Only the public may search. Copy fee $1.00 per page. Cert fee- $2.00 per cert plus copy fee. Payee- Preston Town Clerk. Office does not sell bulk data. **Other phones:** Treasurer- X5; Elections- X7; Tax Collector- X2. **Property tax/Assessing**- 389 Rte 2, Preston, CT 06365; 860-889-2529 x3, assessor fax- 860-885-0171. **Online access**- Access assessor data after free registration at http://data.visionappraisal.com/PrestonCT/DEFAULT.asp.

Prospect Town

Town Clerk, 36 Center St, Prospect, CT 06712-1699. 203-758-4461; fax-203-758-7230; 8:30AM-4PM (EST)
Index: All in one. Record index not computerized. Only the public may search. Copy fee $1.00 per page. Records of minutes $.50 per page. Cert fee- $2.00 per page plus copy fee. Payee- Prospect Town Clerk. Office does not sell bulk data. **Other phones:** Vital Records- 203-758-4461. **Property tax/Assessing**- 36 Center St, Prospect, CT 06712-1699; 203-758-4461. **Online access**- Access property data free at www.prophecyone.us/index_prophecy.php?town=Prospect. No name searching.

Putnam Town

Town Clerk, 126 Church St, Putnam, CT 06260. Recording, R/E & UCC phone-860-963-6807; fax-860-963-5360; 8:30AM-N; 1PM-4:15PM (EST) www.putnamct.us
Index: All in one. Records indexed on a public use terminal back to 1960. Only the public may search. Copy fee $1.00 per page. Cert fee- $2.00 per cert plus copy fee. Payee- Town of Putnam. **Other phones:** Treasurer- 860-963-6809; Vital Records- 860-963-6807. **Property tax/Assessing**- 126 Church St, Putnam, CT 06260; 860-963-6802, assessor fax- 860-963-5369. hours- 8:30AM-4:30PM **Online access**- Access assessor property data free after registration at http://data.visionappraisal.com/PutnamCT/.

Redding Town

Town Clerk, PO Box 1028, Redding, CT 06875-1028. Recording, R/E & UCC phone-203-938-2377; fax-203-938-5000; 8:30AM-5:30PM M-W; 8:30AM-6PM TH; Closed Fri. (EST) www.townofreddingct.org/Public_Documents/ReddingCT_Clerk/index
Index: All in one. Records indexed on computer back to 1971. Only the public may search. Copy fee $1.00 per page; map copies $3.00 per page. Cert fee- $2.00 per cert plus copy fee. Payee- Redding Town Clerk. **Other phones:** Treasurer- 203-938-3616; Elections-203-938-5012; Vital Records- 203-938-2377; Tax Collector- 203-938-2706. **Property tax/Assessing**-PO Box 1028, 100 Hill Rd, Redding, CT 06875; 203-938-2626, assessor fax- 203-938-8816. (Appraiser/Auditor- 203-938-2626) hours- 9AM-4PM www.townofreddingct.org/Public_Documents/ReddingCT_Assessor/index

Ridgefield Town

Town Clerk, 400 Main St, Ridgefield, CT 06877. 203-431-2783; fax-203-431-2722; 8:30AM-4:30PM (EST) www.ridgefieldct.org/
Index: All in one. Records indexed on a public use terminal back to 1960. Only the public may search. Copy fee $1.00 per page. Cert fee- $2.00 per instrument plus copy fee. Payee- Ridgefield Town Clerk. Office does not sell bulk data. **Other phones:** Treasurer- 203-431-2763; Elections- 203-431-2771/2772; Vital Records- 203-431-2783. **Property tax/Assessing**- 400 Main St, Ridgefield, CT 06877; 203-431-2706, assessor fax- 203-431-2340. A public access terminal available. **Online access**- For property assessments free go to www.prophecyone.us/ridgefield/index_prophecy.php?town=Ridgefield

Rocky Hill Town

Town Clerk, 761 Old Main St., Rocky Hill, CT 06067. 860-258-2705; 8:30AM-4:30PM M-W; 8:30-7PM Th; 8:30AM-12:30PM F. (EST) www.ci.rocky-hill.ct.us
Index: All in one. Records indexed on a public use terminal back to 1973. Only the public may search. Will not search UCC records. Copy fee $1.00 per page. Cert fee- $2.00 per cert plus copy fee. Payee- Rocky Hill Town Clerk. **Online access to Land, Marriage, Death, Trade Name, Map records:** Access to the Town Clerk's Index Search is free at www.ci.rocky-hill.ct.us/resolution/. Land records go back to 1973; Marriages/Deaths to 1990; trade names to 1987; maps to 1982. **Other phones:** Elections-860-258-2715. **Property tax/Assessing**- 761 Old Main St, Rocky Hill, CT 06067; 860-258-2722, assessor fax- 860-258-2708.

Roxbury Town

Town Clerk, 29 North St, Roxbury, CT 06783-1405. Recording, R/E & UCC phone-860-354-3328; fax-860-354-0560; 9AM-N, 1-4PM T Th; 9AM-N W; 9AM-N F. (EST) www.roxburyct.com
Index: Separate indices to search include grantor/grantee. Records indexed on a public use terminal back to 1999. Office will perform a UCC search but public must search other records themselves. Copy fee $1.00 per page. Cert fee- $1.00 per page plus copy fee. Payee- Roxbury Town Clerk. **Other phones:** Treasurer- 860-354-9938; Elections-860-354-3328; Vital Records- 860-354-3328. **Property tax/Assessing**- PO Box 203, 29 North St, Roxbury, CT 06783; 860-354-2634, assessor fax-860-354-0560. hours- 9AM-N, 1-4PM T Th; 9AM-N F **Online access**- Access to property data is free at http://data.visionappraisal.com/RoxburyCT/.

Salem Town

Town Clerk, 270 Hartford Rd; Town Office Bldg, Salem, CT 06420. Recording, R/E & UCC phone-860-859-3873 x170; fax-860-859-1184; 8AM-4PM M-W; 8AM-5PM Th; 8AM-N Fri. (EST) www.salemct.gov
Index: Separate indices to search by years. Records computerized and indexed on a public use terminal back to 1987. Office will perform a UCC search but public must search other records themselves. Copy fee $1.00 per page (land records). Large maps (2'x3')-$5.00, minutes-$.50 per page/document, maps (11x17)-$1.00, maps (8 1/2 x 11)-$.50. Cert fee-$2.00 per doc plus copy fee. Payee- Town of Salem. Office does not sell bulk data. **Other phones:** Treasurer- 860-859-3873 x125; Elections- 860-859-3873 x230; Vital Records- 860-859-3873 x170; Tax Collector- 860-859-3873 x150. **Property tax/Assessing**- 270 Hartford Rd, Salem, CT 06420; 860-859-3873 x130/140, assessor fax- 860-859-1184.

Salisbury Town

Town Clerk, PO Box 548, Salisbury, CT 06068. 860-435-5182; fax-860-435-5172; 9AM-4PM (EST) www.salisburyct.us
Index: All in one. Record index not computerized. Only the public may search. Copy fee $1.00 per page. Cert fee- $2.00 per cert plus copy fee. Payee-

Salisbury Town Clerk. **Other phones:** Treasurer- 860-435-5174; Elections- 860-435-5175; Vital Records- 860-435-5182. **Property tax/Assessing**- PO Box 548, Salisbury, CT 06068; 860-435-5176, assessor fax- 860-435-5172.

Scotland Town

Town Clerk, PO Box 122, Scotland, CT 06264. Recording, R/E & UCC phone-860-423-9634; fax-860-423-3666; 9AM-3PM M,T,TH; Noon-8PM W; closed Fri. (EST)
Index: Separate indices to search. Record index not computerized. Only the public may search. Copy fee $1.00 per page. Cert fee- $2.00 per cert plus copy fee. Payee- Scotland Town Clerk. Office does not sell bulk data. **Other phones:** Treasurer- 860-423-9634; Elections- 860-423-9634; Vital Records- 860-423-9634. **Property tax/Assessing**- 9 Devotion Rd, PO Box 122, Scotland, CT 06264; 860-423-9634, assessor fax- 860-423-3666.

Seymour Town

Town Clerk, 1 -1st St; Town Hall, Seymour, CT 06483-2817. 203-888-0519; fax-203-881-5005; 9AM-5PM, no recording after 4:15PM (EST) www.seymourct.org/Departments/town_clerk.htm
Index: Indices arranged by years. Records indexed on computer back to 1975. Only the public may search. Copy fee $1.00 per page. Cert fee- $1.00 per cert plus copy fee. Payee- Seymour Town Clerk. Office does not sell bulk data. **Other phones:** Treasurer- 203-888-0581; Elections- 203-881-5039; Vital Records- 203-888-0519. **Property tax/Assessing**- 1 -1st St, Town Hall, Seymour Town, New Haven CT 06483; 203-881-5013, fax- 203-881-5005. 8AM-5:30PM M-TH www.seymourct.org/Departments/assessor.htm

Sharon Town

Town Clerk, PO Box 224, Sharon, CT 06069. 860-364-5224; fax-same; 8:30AM-N, 1-4PM M-Th ; Fri 8:30AM-N. (EST) www.sharonct.org
Index: All in one. Records indexed on computer back to 2005. Only the public may search. Copy fee $1.00 per page. Cert fee- $1.00 per cert plus copy fee. Payee- Sharon Town Clerk. Office does not sell bulk data. **Other phones:** Treasurer- 860-364-5789; Elections- 860-364-5789; Vital Records- 860-364-5224. **Property tax/Assessing**- Sharon Town Assessing Office, PO Box 224, Sharon, CT 06069; 860-364-0205, assessor fax- 860-364-5224. www.sharonct.org **Online access**- Access assessor data free at http://data.visionappraisal.com/SharonCT/.

Shelton City

City Clerk, PO Box 364, Shelton, CT 06484-0364. 203-924-1555, R/E recording phone-203-924-1555 x377, UCC recording phone-203-924-1555 x323; fax-203-924-1721; 8AM-5:30PM www.cityofshelton.org
Index: All in one. Records indexed on a public use terminal back to 1944. Only the public may search. Copy fee $1.00 per page. Cert fee- $3.00 per cert plus copy fee. Payee- Shelton City Clerk. **Other phones:** Treasurer- 203-924-1555 x318; Elections- 203-924-1555 x337; Vital Records- 203-924-1555 x321. **Property tax/Assessing**- 54 Hill St, Shelton, CT 06484-0364; 203-924-1555 x335, assessor fax- 203-924-4865. A public access terminal available.

Sherman Town

Town Clerk, PO Box 39, Sherman, CT 06784-0039. Recording, R/E & UCC phone-860-354-5281; fax-860-350-5041; 9AM-N, 1PM-4PM T,W,TH,F; 9AM-N Sat. (EST)
Index: All in one. Records indexed on office computer back to 1976. Only the public may search. Copy fee $2.00 per page. Cert fee- $1.00 per cert plus copy fee. Payee- Town of Sherman. **Other phones:** Treasurer- 860-355-1139; Elections- 860-350-4694; Vital Records- 860-354-5281. **Property tax/Assessing**- PO Box 29, 9 Rte 39 N, Sherman, CT 06784-0039; 860-355-0376, assessor fax- 860-350-5041. hours- 9AM-N, 1PM-4PM T-F Field cards available for public access.

Simsbury Town

Town Clerk, PO Box 495, Simsbury, CT 06070. 860-658-3243; fax-860-658-3206; 8:30AM-4:30PM (EST) www.simsbury-ct.gov/townclerk.htm
Index: All in one. Records indexed on a public use terminal back to 1976. Only the public may search. Copy fee $1.00 per page. Cert fee- $2.00 per cert plus copy fee. Payee- Town of Simsbury. **Property tax/Assessing**- PO Box 495, 933 Hopmeadow St, Simsbury, CT 06070; 860-658-3251, assessor fax-860-658-3285. www.simsbury-ct.gov/Public_Documents/SimsburyCT_Assessment/index **Online access**- Access property data free at www.prophecyone.us/index_prophecy.php?town=Simsbury. Also, search pdf files of property sales by name and by address free at www.simsbury-ct.gov/Public_Documents/Departments/SimsburyCT_Assessment/index.

Somers Town

Town Clerk, PO Box 308, Somers, CT 06071. 860-763-8206; fax-860-763-8228; 8:30AM-4:30PM M-W; 8:30AM-7PM Th; 8:30-1PM F. (EST) www.somersnow.com/Town/TownClerk.htm
Index: Separate indices to search. Records indexed on computer from 6/04 to current. Only the public may search. Copy fee $1.00 per page. Cert fee- $2.00 per doc plus copy fee. Payee- Town of Somers. **Other phones:** Treasurer- 860-763-8204; Elections- 860-763-8211; Vital Records- 860-763-8206. **Property tax/Assessing**- PO Box 308, 600 Main St, Somers, CT 06071; 860-763-8203, fax- 860-763-8228.

South Windsor Town

Town Clerk, 1540 Sullivan Ave, South Windsor, CT 06074. 860-644-2511 x225, R/E recording phone-860-644-2511 x225/226/227; fax-860-644-3781; 8AM-4:30PM (EST) www.southwindsor.org
Index: All in one. Records indexed on a public use terminal back to 1845. Only the public may search. Will not search UCC records. Copy fee $1.00 per page. Cert fee- $2.00 per cert plus copy fee. Payee- Town of South Windsor. **Other phones:** Treasurer- 860-644-2511 x261; Elections- 860-644-2511 x275, x276; Vital Records- 860-644-2511 x225/226/227; Tax Collector- 860-644-2511 x220/221/222. **Property tax/Assessing**- 1540 Sullivan Ave, South Windsor, CT 06074; 860-644-2511 x213, assessor fax- 860-644-3781. Public access terminal available.

Southbury Town

Town Clerk, 501 Main St S, Southbury, CT 06488-2295. Recording, R/E & UCC phone-203-262-0657; fax-203-264-9762; 8:30AM-4:30PM (EST)
Index: All in one. Records indexed on a public use terminal back to 1787. Only the public may search. Copy fee $1.00 per page. Cert fee- $2.00 per cert plus copy fee. Payee- Southbury Town Clerk. Contact Town Clerk with request. **Other phones:** Treasurer- 203-262-0663; Elections- 203-262-0644; Vital Records- 203-262-0657. **Property tax/Assessing**- 501 Main St S, Southbury, CT 06488-2295; 203-262-0674, assessor fax- 203-264-9762. A public access terminal available.

Southington Town

Town Clerk, PO Box 152, Southington, CT 06489. 860-276-6211; fax-860-276-6229; 8:30AM-4PM M, T, W, F; 8:30AM-7PM TH. www.southington.org
Index: All in one. Records indexed on a public use terminal back to 1926. Only the public may search. Land record copy fee $1.00 per page; other records $.25 per page. Cert fee- $2.00 per cert plus copy fee. Payee- Southington Town Clerk. **Online access to Real Estate, Grantor/Grantee, Deed, Map/Survey, Voter Registration records:** Access to county land index back to 1926 at http://townclerk.southington.org/resolution/ and also includes maps and surveys back to 1847. Access the voter registration lookup free at http://registrars.southington.org/voterlist/voters.php. **Other phones:** Treasurer- 860-276-6228; Elections-860-276-6268; Vital Records- 860-276-6211. **Property tax/Assessing**- 75 Main St, Town Office Bldg, Southington, CT 06489; 860-276-6205, assessor fax- 860-628-4727. hours- 8:30AM-4:30PM M,T,W,F; 8:30AM-7PM TH www.southington.org/content/50/2424/68/default.aspx **Online access**- Access town assessor records free at http://assessor.southington.org/Main/Home.aspx then click on Property Records.

Sprague Town

Town Clerk, PO Box 162, Baltic, CT 06330. 860-822-3000 x220, R/E recording phone-x220; fax-860-822-3016; 8AM-4:30PM M-T; W till 5:30PM (EST) www.ctsprague.org
Recording done on Town level not County. Index: All in one. Record index not computerized. Only the public may search. Copy fee $1.00 per page. Cert fee- $2.00 per cert plus copy fee. Payee- Town of Sprague. **Other phones:** Treasurer- x209; Elections- x220; Vital Records- x220; Tax Collector- x224. **Property tax/Assessing**- PO Box 162, 1 Main St, Baltic, CT 06330; 860-822-3000 x222, assessor fax- 860-822-3016. hours- 6AM-6PM M; 7AM-Noon T. A public access terminal available.

Stafford Town

Town Clerk, PO Box 11, Stafford Springs, CT 06076. Recording, R/E & UCC phone-860-684-1765; fax-860-684-1795; 8:15AM-4:30PM M-W; 8:15AM-6:30PM Th; 8AM-N F. (EST) www.staffordct.org
Records indexed on a public use terminal back to 1977. Only the public may search. Copy fee $1.00 per page. Cert fee- $2.00 per doc plus copy fee. Payee- Stafford Town Clerk. **Online access to Real Estate, Deed, Lien records:** Access town clerk land records back to 1/03/1977 free at http://records.staffordct.org/Resolution/search_menu.asp but free registration is required. **Other phones:** Treasurer- 860-684-1772; Elections- 860-684-1765; Vital Records- 860-684-1765. **Property tax/Assessing**- 1 Main St, Warren Memorial Town Hall, Stafford Springs, CT 06076; 860-684-1786, assessor fax- 860-684-1785. www.staffordct.org **Online access**- Access assessor property data free at http://stafford.univers-clt.com.

Stamford City

City Clerk, PO Box 10152, Stamford, CT 06904. Recording, R/E & UCC phone-203-977-4054, UCC recording phone-203-977-4707; fax-203-977-4943; 8AM-3:45PM (EST) www.cityofstamford.org/
Index: All in one. Records indexed on a public use terminal back to 1967. Office personnel or visitors may perform searches. No fee for search. Office will not search UCC or real estate records. Copy fee $1.00 per page.Real estate or tax lien copy- $.50 per page. Cert fee- $1.00 per cert plus copy fee. Payee- City of Stamford. Office does not sell bulk data. **Online access to Trade Name, City Businesses records:** Search the city registry of trade names for free at http://cityofstamford.org/apps/tradenames/. **Other phones:** Elections- 203-977-4011; Vital Records-203-977-4054. **Property tax/Assessing**- PO Box 10152, 888 Washington Blvd (06904), Stamford, CT 06904-2152; 203-977-5888, assessor fax- 203-977-5898. hours- 8:30AM-4:30PM www.cityofstamford.org/content/25/52/131/144/152/default.aspx **Online access**- Access assessor tax data free at www.cityofstamford.org/apps/tax/default.htm. Also, search sales data by type for free at www.cityofstamford.org/content/25/52/131/144/152/2482.aspx

Sterling Town

Town Clerk, PO Box 157, Oneco, CT 06373-0157. Recording, R/E & UCC phone-860-564-2657; 8:30AM-3:30PM-M,T,TH; 8AM-6PM-W; 8AM-N Fri. (EST) www.sterlingct.us
Index: All in one. Records indexed on a public use terminal back to 1980. Only the public may search. Will not search UCC records. Copy fee $1.00 per

page. Survey maps- $5.00. Cert fee- $2.00 per cert plus copy fee. Payee- Sterling Town Clerk. Office does not sell bulk data. **Other phones:** Treasurer- 860-564-8488; Elections- 860-564-2657; Vital Records- 860-564-2657; Tax Collector- 860-564-7563. **Property tax/Assessing-** Sterling Town Assessing Office, PO Box 157, Oneco, CT 06373; 860-564-3030 x16, assessor fax- 860-564-1660. Computer terminal available for public use. www.sterlingct.us/services.htm

Stonington Town

Town Clerk, 152 Elm St, Stonington, CT 06378. Recording, R/E & UCC phone-860-535-5060; fax-860-535-5062; hours 8:30AM-4PM (EST) www.townofstonington.com
Index: All in one. Records indexed on a public use terminal back to 1948. Only the public may search. Copy fee $1.00 per page. Cert fee- $2.00 per cert plus copy fee. Payee- Stonington Town Clerk. **Other phones:** Elections- 860-535-5047; Vital Records- 860-535-5060; Finance Phone- 860-535-5070; Tax Collector -860-535-5080;. **Property tax/Assessing-** 152 Elm St, Stonington, CT 06378; 860-535-5098, assessor fax- 860-535-5052. A public access terminal available. **Online access-** Access property data free at http://data.visionappraisal.com/StoningtonCT/DEFAULT.asp. Access parcel and mapping data free at http://ceo.fando.com/stonington/.

Stratford Town

Town Clerk, 2725 Main St, Rm 106, Stratford, CT 06615. 203-385-4020; fax-203-385-4005; 8AM-4PM (EST) www.townofstratford.com
Index: All in one. Records indexed on computer back to 1984. Only the public may search. Copy fee $1.00 per page. Cert fee- $1.00 per doc plus copy fee. Payee- Town of Stratford. **Other phones:** Treasurer- 203-385-4040; Elections- 203-385-4048; Vital Records- 203-385-4020. **Property tax/Assessing-** 2725 Main St, Stratford, CT 06615; 203-385-4025, assessor fax- 203-385-4067. hours- 8AM-4:30PM www.townofstratford.com/content/1302/402/635/default.aspx
Online access- Search town assessor database free at http://data.visionappraisal.com/StratfordCT/.

Suffield Town

Town Clerk, 83 Mountain Rd; Town Hall, Suffield, CT 06078. 860-668-3880; fax-860-668-3898; 8AM-4:30PM M; 8AM-6PM Th; 8AM-1PM F. (EST) www.suffieldtownhall.com
Open Thursday evenings to 6PM year around. Index: All in one. Records indexed on computer back to 1984. Only the public may search. Copy fee $1.00 per page. Cert fee- $1.00 per doc plus copy fee. Payee- Town of Suffield. **Other phones:** Treasurer- 860-668-3851; Elections- 860-668-3880; Vital Records- 860-668-3880. **Property tax/Assessing-** Suffield Town Assessing Office, 83 Mountain Rd, Town Hall, Suffield, CT 06078; 860-668-3866, assessor fax- 860-668-3315. (Appraiser/Auditor- 860-668-3850) **Online access-** Search the town assessor's database at http://data.visionappraisal.com/SuffieldCT/.

Thomaston Town

Town Clerk, 158 Main St, Thomaston, CT 06787. Recording, R/E & UCC phone-860-283-4141; fax-860-283-1013; 9AM-4:30PM (EST) http://thomastonct.org/Content/Town_Clerk_.asp
Index: All in one. Record index not computerized. Only the public may search. Copy fee $1.00 per page. Cert fee- $10.00 per cert plus copy fee. Payee- Thomaston Town Clerk. **Other phones:** Treasurer- 860-283-9678. **Property tax/Assessing-** PO Box 136, 158 Main St, Level 3, Thomaston, CT 06787; 860-283-0305, assessor fax- 860-283-2893. 8AM-4PM http://thomastonct.org/Content/Thomaston_CT_Tax_Assessor.asp **Online access-** Search property data free at www.prophecyone.us/index_prophecy.php?town=Thomaston but no name searching.

Thompson Town

Town Clerk, PO Box 899, No. Grosvenor Dale, CT 06255. 860-923-9900; fax-860-923-7426; 8:30AM-4:30PM M-W, till 6PM Th; till 3PM F. (EST) www.thompsonct.org
Index: All in one. Records indexed on a public use terminal back to 1938. Office will perform a UCC search but public must search other records themselves. Copy fee $1.00 per page. Fee to fax docs- $2.50 per doc. Cert fee- $2.00 per cert plus copy fee. Payee- Town of Thompson. Office does not sell bulk data. **Other phones:** Treasurer- 860-923-3593; Elections- 860-923-9900; Vital Records- 860-923-9900. **Property tax/Assessing-** PO Box 899, 815 Riverside Dr, North Grosvenordale, CT 06255; 860-923-2259, assessor fax- 860-923-9897. hours- 9AM-4:30PM M,T,W,F; 9AM-6PM TH http://s113439721.onlinehome.us/33901.html **Online access-** Search the town assessor database free at http://data.visionappraisal.com/ThompsonCT/. Free registration required.

Tolland Town

Town Clerk, 21 Tolland Green; Hicks Memorial Muni Ctr, Tolland, CT 06084. Recording, R/E & UCC phone-860-871-3630; fax-860-871-3663; 8:30AM-4PM MTW; 8:30AM-7:30PM TH; 8:30AM-N Fri. (EST) www.tolland.org/
Do not confuse this town with the County of Tolland. Only Town of Tolland filings here. Index: All in one. Records indexed on a public use terminal back to 07/1977. Only the public may search. Copy fee $1.00 per page. Cert fee- $2.00 per doc plus copy fee. Payee- Tolland Town Clerk. **Other phones:** Treasurer- 860-871-3658; Elections- 860-871-3634; Vital Records- 860-871-3630. **Property tax/Assessing-** 21 Tolland Green, 5th Level, Tolland, CT 06084; 860-871-3650, assessor fax- 860-871-3667. hours- 8:30AM-4PM M-W; 8:30AM-7:30PM Th; 8:30am-N Fri www.tolland.org/ **Online access-** Search assessor data free at http://data.visionappraisal.com/TollandCT/.

Torrington City

Town Clerk, 140 Main St; City Hall, Torrington, CT 06790. 860-489-2236, R/E recording phone-860-489-2238, UCC recording phone-860-489-2237; fax-860-489-2548; 8AM-4:30PM M-W; 8:30AM-6:30PM TH; 8-1PM F. (EST) www.torringtonct.org
Index: All in one. Records indexed on a public use terminal back to 1955. Office will perform a UCC search but public must search other records themselves. Copy fee $1.00 per page. Cert fee- $1.00 per cert plus copy fee. Payee- City of Torrington. **Other phones:** Treasurer- 860-489-2334; Elections- 860-489-2226; Vital Records- 860-489-2236. **Property tax/Assessing-** 140 Main St, City Hall, Torrington, CT 06790; 860-489-2222, assessor fax- 860-496-5907. hours- 8:30AM-4PM M-W, 8:30AM-6:30PM TH, 8:30AM-12:30PM F **Online access-** Access property data for free after registration at http://data.visionappraisal.com/TorringtonCT/.

Town of Morris

Town Clerk, PO Box 66, Morris, CT 06763-0066. Recording, R/E & UCC phone-860-567-7433; fax-860-567-7432; 9AM-N, 1-4PM M T F; 9AM-N, 1PM-5PM W TH. (EST) www.townofmorrisct.org
Index: All in one. Records indexed on a public use terminal back to Vol. 86, Page 345. Office will perform a UCC search but public must search other records themselves. Copy fee $1.00 per page of land records, map fees higher. Cert fee- $2.00 per cert includes copy fee. Payee- Town of Morris Clerk. Bulk data available for purchase from IMAS LLC. **Other phones:** Treasurer- 860-567-6094; Elections- 860-567-7433 x121; Vital Records- 860-567-7433; Tax Collector- 860-567-7435; Tax Assessment -860-567-6096;. **Property tax/Assessing-** PO Box 66, 3 East St, Morris, CT 06763-0066; 860-567-7435, assessor fax- 860-567-7432. hours- 9AM-N W, 2-5PM TH **Online access-** Access assessor data free at http://data.visionappraisal.com/MorrisCT/DEFAULT.asp

Trumbull Town

Town Clerk, 5866 Main St, Trumbull, CT 06611. 203-452-5035; fax-203-452-5094; 9AM-5PM (EST) www.trumbull-ct.gov
Index: All in one. Records indexed on a public use terminal back to 1950. Only the public may search. Copy fee $1.00 per page. Cert fee- $2.00 per cert plus copy fee. Payee- Trumbull Town Clerk. Office does not sell bulk data. **Online access to Real Estate, Grantor/Grantee, Deed, Lien, UCC Judgment, Fictitious Name records:** Search land records free at http://209.244.152.236/resolution/login.asp but registration and username required. **Other phones:** Treasurer- 203-452-5014; Elections- 203-452-5058; Vital Records- 203-452-5035. **Property tax/Assessing-** 5866 Main St, Trumbull, CT 06611; 203-452-5016, assessor fax- 203-452-5082. **Online access-** Search the assessor database free at http://data.visionappraisal.com/TrumbullCT/.

Union Town

Town Clerk, 1043 Buckley Hwy, Rte 171, Union, CT 06076-9520. Recording, R/E & UCC phone-860-684-3770; fax-860-684-8830; 9AM-N T,Th; 9AM-N, 1-3PM W. (EST) www.unionconnecticut.org/
Index: All in one. Records index computerized back 12 years. Only the public may search; office may search UCCs as time allows. Copy fee $1.00 per page. Cert fee- $2.00 per cert plus copy fee. Payee- Union Town Clerk. Office does not sell bulk data. **Other phones:** Treasurer- 860-684-8831; Elections- 860-684-3770; Vital Records- 860-684-3770; Tax Collector- 860-684-8834. **Property tax/Assessing-** Union Town Assessing Office, 1043 Buckley Hwy, Rte 171, Union, CT 06076-9520; 860-684-5705, assessor fax- 860-684-8830. 9AM-N, 1-3PM W

Vernon Town

Town Clerk, 14 Park Pl, Vernon, CT 06066. Recording, R/E & UCC phone-860-870-3662; fax-860-870-3683; 8:30AM-4:30PM M-W; 8:30AM-7PM Th; 8:30AM-1PM F. www.vernon-ct.gov/
Index: Separate indices to search include grantor/grantee. Records indexed on a public use terminal back to 0101/1978. Only the public may search. Will not search UCC records. Copy fee $1.00 per page. Cert fee- $2.00 per cert plus copy fee. Payee- Town of Vernon. **Other phones:** Treasurer- 860-870-3660 (Tax Collector); Elections- 860-870-3685 (Reg of Voters); Vital Records- 860-870-3662. **Property tax/Assessing-** 8 Park Pl, Vernon, CT 06066; 860-870-3625, assessor fax- 860-870-3586.

Voluntown Town

Town Clerk, PO Box 96, Voluntown, CT 06384-0096. Recording, R/E & UCC phone-860-376-4089; fax-860-376-3295; 9AM-4PM; 6PM-8PM T. (EST) www.voluntown.gov
Index: All in one. Record index not computerized. Only the public may search. Copy fee $2.00 per page. Cert fee- $1.00 per cert plus copy fee. Payee- Town of Voluntown. Office does not sell bulk data. **Other phones:** Treasurer- 860-376-3927; Elections- 860-376-4089; Vital Records- 860-376-4089. **Property tax/Assessing-** PO Box 96, Voluntown, CT 06384; 860-376-3927, assessor fax- 860-376-3295. hours- 9AM-2PM

Wallingford Town

Town Clerk, 45 S Main St, Rm 108; Municipal Bldg, Wallingford, CT 06492. Recording, R/E & UCC phone-203-294-2145; fax-203-294-2150; 9AM-5PM
Index: All in one. Records indexed on a public use terminal back to 1963. Office will perform a UCC search but public must search other records themselves. Copy fee $1.00 per page. Cert fee- $2.00 per cert plus copy fee. Payee- Wallingford Town Clerk. Bulk data available for purchase (voter lists, dog owners). **Other phones:** Treasurer- 203-294-2042; Elections- 203-294-2125; Vital Records- 203-

294-2145. **Property tax/Assessing-** 45 S Main St, Wallingford, CT 06492; 203-294-2001, assessor fax-203-294-2003. (Appraiser/Auditor- 203-294-2001);

Warren Town

Town Clerk, 7 Sackett Hill Rd; Town Hall, Warren, CT 06754. 860-868-7881 x101, R/E recording phone-860-868-0090; fax-860-868-7746; 9AM-1PM M F; 9AM-4PM W TH. (EST) www.warrenct.org/
Index: All in one. Records indexed on computer back to 1996. Only the public may search. Will not search UCC records. Copy fee $1.00 per page. Survey map fee $2.00. Cert fee- $2.00 per cert plus copy fee. Payee- Warren Town Clerk. **Property tax/Assessing-** 7 Sackett Hill Rd, Warren, CT 06754; 860-868-7881 x105, assessor fax- 860-868-7746. hours- 9AM-N Wed A public access terminal available. **Online access-** Access assessor property data at http://data.visionappraisal.com/warrenct/DEFAULT.asp

Washington Town

Town Clerk, PO Box 383, Washington Depot, CT 06794. 860-868-2786; fax-860-868-3103; 9AM-N, 1PM-4:45PM (EST) www.washingtonct.org
Index: All in one. Record index not computerized. Only the public may search. Copy fee $1.00 per page. Cert fee- $2.00 per doc plus copy fee. Payee- Town of Washington. **Other phones:** Treasurer- 860-868-2259; Elections- 860-868-2786; Vital Records- 860-868-2786. **Property tax/Assessing-** PO Box 383, Washington Depot, CT 06794; 860-868-0398, assessor fax- 860-868-3103. Public terminal available.

Waterbury City

Town Clerk, 235 Grand St; City Hall, Waterbury, CT 06702. Recording, R/E & UCC phone-203-574-6806; fax-203-574-6887; 8:30AM-4:30PM (EST) www.waterburyct.org
Index: All in one. Records indexed on a public use terminal back to 1984. Only the public may search. Copy fee $1.00 per page. Cert fee- $2.00 per doc plus copy fee. Payee- Waterbury Town Clerk. **Online access to Real Estate, Grantor/Grantee, Deed, Lien, Mortgage records:** Real Estate records and lien lists can be accessed at free www.waterburyct.org/content/609/648/652/default.aspx . **Other phones:** Elections- 203-574-6751; Vital Records- 203-574-6801. **Property tax/Assessing-** 26 Kenderick Ave, Waterbury, CT 06702; 203-574-6821, assessor fax- 203-574-6992. hours- 8.50AM-4:50PM **Online access-** Access assessor property data free at www.totalvaluation.com/tvweb/mainsearch.aspx?city=waterbury.

Waterford Town

Town Clerk, 15 Rope Ferry Rd, Waterford, CT 06385. Recording, R/E & UCC phone-860-444-5831; fax-860-437-0352; 8AM-4PM www.waterfordct.org
Index: All in one. Records indexed on computer back to 1959. Only the public may search. Copy fee $1.00 per page. Cert fee- $2.00 per cert plus copy fee. Payee- Waterford Town Clerk. **Other phones:** Vital Records- 860-444-5831. **Property tax/Assessing-** 15 Rope Ferry Rd, Waterford, CT 06385; 860-444-5820, assessor fax- 860-437-0352. **Online access-** Access property data free at www.prophecyone.us/index_prophecy.php?town=Waterford but no name searching.

Watertown Town

Town Clerk, 37 DeForest St, Watertown, CT 06795. Recording, R/E & UCC phone-860-945-5230; fax-860-945-2706; 9AM-5PM www.watertownct.org
Index: All in one. Records indexed on a public use terminal back to 7/1/03. Only the public may search. Copy fee $1.00 per page. Cert fee- $2.00 per doc plus copy fee. Payee- Watertown Town Clerk. Office does not sell bulk data. **Other phones:** Treasurer- 860-945-5261; Elections- 860-945-5230; Vital Records- 860-945-5230; Town Manager- 860-945-5255. **Property tax/Assessing-** 37 DeForest St, Watertown, CT 06795; 860-945-5235, assessor fax- 860-945-4741. **Online access-** Access property data free at http://data.visionappraisal.com/watertownct/.

West Hartford Town

Town Clerk, 50 S Main St, Rm 313; Town Hall Common, West Hartford, CT 06107-2431. 860-561-7430; fax-860-561-7438; 8:30AM-4:30PM (EST) www.west-hartford.com
Index: All in one. Records indexed on a public use terminal back to 1963. Only the public may search. Copy fee $1.00 per page. Cert fee- $2.00 per cert plus copy fee. Payee- Town of West Hartford. Office does not sell bulk data. **Other phones:** Treasurer- 860-561-7474; Elections- 860-561-7450; Vital Records- 860-561-7431. **Property tax/Assessing-** 50 S. Main St, Rm 142, West Hartford, CT 06107; 860-561-7414, assessor fax- 860-561-7590. (Appraiser/Auditor- 860-561-7414) **Online access-** Access to the assessor property records on the GIS-mapping site is free, or by subscription for name searching. Details and sign-up are at www.westhartford.org/whprs/, and option to free search. Also, lookup property tax data using address (no name searching) free at www.westhartford.org/taxestimator/index.aspx.

West Haven City

City Clerk, PO Box 526, West Haven, CT 06516. 203-937-3534, R/E recording phone-203-937-3535; fax-203-937-3504; hours- 9AM-5PM (EST) www.cityofwesthaven.com/
Index: All in one. Records indexed on a public use terminal back to 1968. Only the public may search. Copy fee $1.00 per page. Cert fee- $1.00 per cert plus copy fee. Payee- West Haven City Clerk. **Other phones:** Vital Records- 203-937-3536. **Property tax/Assessing-** 355 Main St, 1st Fl, West Haven, CT 06516; 203-937-3515, assessor fax- 203-937-3544. **Online access-** Search the town assessor's database free at http://data.visionappraisal.com/Westhavenct/.

Westbrook Town

Town Clerk, 866 Boston Post Rd, Westbrook, CT 06498-1881. 860-399-3044; fax-860-399-3092; 9AM-4PM M-W & F; 9AM-7PM Th; 9AM-Noon F. www.westbrookct.us
Index: All in one back to 1972. Record index not computerized. Only the public may search. Copy fee $1.00 per page. Cert fee- $2.00 per cert plus copy fee. Payee- Westbrook Town Clerk. **Other phones:** Treasurer- 860-399-3040; Elections- 860-399-3042; Town Clerk- 860-399-3044. **Property tax/Assessing-** Westbrook Town Assessing Office, 866 Boston Post Rd, Westbrook, CT 06498-1881; 860-399-3045, assessor fax- 860-399-3092. Computer terminal available for public use. www.westbrookct.us/

Weston Town

Town Clerk, PO Box 1007, Weston, CT 06883. 203-222-2616, R/E recording phone-203-222-2617, UCC recording phone-203-222-2616; fax-203-222-8871; 9AM-4:30PM (EST) www.weston-ct.com
Index: All in one. Records indexed on a public use terminal back to 1950. Only the public may search. General copy fee $1.00 per page if court copies, $.50 if self copy. Cert fee- $2.00 per cert plus copy fee. Payee- Weston Town Clerk. **Online access to Real Estate, Grantor/Grantee, Marriage, Death, Trade Name, UCC records:** Access the Town Clerk's index records free at www.weston-ct.com/resolution/. For username and password use cott, cott. **Other phones:** Elections- 203-222-2616; Vital Records- 203-222-2616; General Information -203-222-2500;. **Property tax/Assessing-** PO Box 1007, 56 Norfield Rd, Weston, 06883; 203-222-2606, fax- 203-222-8871.

Westport Town

Town Clerk, PO Box 549, Westport, CT 06881. Recording, R/E & UCC phone-203-341-1110; fax-203-341-1112; 8:30AM-4:30PM www.westport.gov/agencies/townmanagement/clerk/
Index: All in one. Land records indexed on a public use terminal back to 1900. Only the public may search. Will not search UCC records. Copy fee $1.00 per page. Cert fee- $2.00 per cert plus copy fee. Payee- Westport Town Clerk. **Online access to Real Estate, Deed, Lien, Map, Death, Marriage, Civil Union, Trade Name, Burial records:** Search a variety of public record indexes only at http://publicrecords.westportct.gov/ including land records back to 1900, Civil unions back to 2005, deaths and marriages to 1949, maps/surveys to 1886, trade names to 1924, burials back to 2006. **Other phones:** Treasurer- 203-341-1080; Elections- 203-341-1115; Vital Records- 203-341-1110; Main Number -203-341-1000;. **Property tax/Assessing-** 110 Myrtle Ave, Westport, CT 06881; 203-341-1070, assessor fax- 203-341-1136. www.westportct.gov/agencies/financesandtaxes/assessor/ **Online access-** Search assessor data free at http://data.visionappraisal.com/WestportCT/DEFAULT.asp. Also, lookup assessment data on the town lookup site at www.westportct.gov/residents/assessments/default.htm. Also, search property data free on the GIS-mapping site at http://webmap.jws.com/website4/ccbviewer1.14.4/viewer_2.jsp.

Wethersfield Town

Town Clerk, 505 Silas Deane Hwy, Wethersfield, CT 06109. Recording, R/E & UCC phone-860-721-2880; fax-860-721-2994; 8AM-4:30PM http://wethersfieldct.com/government/contacts/town-clerk
Index: All in one. Records indexed on a public use terminal back to 10/1/1991. Only the public may search. Copy fee $1.00 per page. Cert fee- $1.00 per cert plus copy fee. Payee- Wethersfield Town. **Other phones:** Treasurer- 860-721-2861; Elections- 860-721-2819; Vital Records- 860-721-2880. **Property tax/Assessing-** Wethersfield Town Assessing Office, 505 Silas Deane Hwy, Wethersfield, CT 06109; 860-721-2810, assessor fax- 860-721-2813. http://wethersfieldct.com/government/contacts/assessor **Online access-** Access to property data is free at http://data.visionappraisal.com/WethersfieldCT/.

Willington Town

Town Clerk, 40 Old Farms Rd, Willington, CT 06279. Recording, R/E & UCC phone-860-487-3121; fax-860-487-3103; 9AM-2PM T-F; 12:30-7:30PM Mon. (EST) http://willingtonct.virtualtownhall.net/
Index: All in one. Records indexed on a public use terminal back to 1982. Only the public may search. Copy fee $1.00 per page. Cert fee- $2.00 per cert plus copy fee. Payee- Willington Town Clerk. **Other phones:** Treasurer- 860-487-3133; Elections- 860-487-3120; Vital Records- 860-487-3121. **Property tax/Assessing-** 40 Old Farms Road, Willington, CT 06279; 860-487-3121, assessor fax- 860-487-3103. hours- 12:30-7PM M; 9AM-2PM T-F http://willingtonct.virtualtownhall.net/Public_Documents/WillingtonCT_Assess/assessor **Online access-** Access Property Assessment data free at www.visionappraisal.com/databases/.

Wilton Town

Town Clerk, 238 Danbury Rd, Wilton, CT 06897. Recording, R/E & UCC phone-203-563-0106; fax-203-563-0130; 8:30AM-4:30PM (EST) www.wiltonct.org/departments/clerk.html
Index: All in one. Records indexed on a public use terminal back to 1942. Only the public may search. Copy fee $1.00 per page. Cert fee- $2.00 per page plus copy fee. Payee- Town of Wilton. **Other phones:** Treasurer- 203-563-0114; Elections- 203-563-0112; Vital Records- 203-563-0106. **Property tax/Assessing-** 238 Danbury Rd, Wilton, CT 06897; 203-563-0121, assessor fax- 203-563-0293. www.wiltonct.org/departments/assessor.html **Online access-** Search the town assessor database free at http://data.visionappraisal.com/WiltonCT/.

Winchester Town

Town Clerk, 338 Main St; Town Hall, Winsted, CT 06098-1697. Recording, R/E & UCC phone-860-738-6963; fax-860-738-6595; 8AM-4PM M-W, 8AM-7PM TH, 8AM-N F. www.townofwinchester.org

Index: All in one, arranged by year. Records indexed on a public use terminal back to 1/1/1963. Only the public may search. Copy fee $1.00 per page. Cert fee- $2.00 per cert plus copy fee. Payee- Town of Winchester. **Other phones:** Treasurer- 860-738-6961; Elections- 860-379-2713 x355; Vital Records- 860-738-6963; Appraiser- 860-379-5461. **Property tax/Assessing**- 338 Main St, Town Hall, Winstead, CT 06098-1697; 860-379-5461, assessor fax- 860-738-6595. (Appraiser/Auditor- 860-379-5461) hours- 8:00AM-4:00PM M-W; 8:00AM-7:00PM Th; 8:00AM-N Fri. Computer terminal available for public use. **Online**- Access town property tax data free at http://data.visionappraisal.com/WinchesterCT/.

Windham Town

Town Clerk, PO Box 94, Willimantic, CT 06226. 860-465-3013; fax-860-465-3012; 8AM-5PM M-W; 8AM-7:30PM Th; 8AM-N Fri. www.windhamct.com
Index: All in one. Records indexed on a public use terminal back to 1966. Only the public may search. Copy fee $1.00 per page. Cert fee- $2.00 per cert plus copy fee. Payee- Windham Town Clerk. **Other phones:** Treasurer- 860-465-3013. **Property tax/Assessing**- Windham Town Assessing Office, 979 Main St, Willimantic, CT 06226; 860-465-3025, assessor fax- 860-465-2180. www.windhamct.com/department.htm?id=o5ljy6b0&m=boards **Online access**- Access assessor valuation data free at http://windham.univers-clt.com/.

Windsor Locks Town

Town Clerk, 50 Church St; Town Office Bldg, Windsor Locks, CT 06096. Recording, R/E & UCC phone-860-627-1441; 8AM-4PM M-W; 8AM-6PM Th; 8AM-1PM F. (EST)
Index: All in one. Records indexed on a public use terminal back to 1987. Only the public may search. Will not search UCC records. Copy fee $1.00 per page. Cert fee- $2.00 per cert plus copy fee. Payee- Town of Windsor Locks. **Other phones:** Treasurer- 860-627-1449; Elections- 860-654-1619; Vital Records- 860-627-1441; Tax Collector- 860-627-1415. **Property tax/Assessing**- 50 Church St, Windsor Locks, CT 06096; 860-627-1448, assessor fax- 860-292-1121. **Online access**- Search assessor data free at http://data.visionappraisal.com/WINDSORLOCKSCT/.

Windsor Town

Town Clerk, PO Box 472, Windsor, CT 06095-0472. Recording, R/E & UCC phone-860-285-1902; fax-860-285-1909; hours- 8AM-5PM (EST) www.townofwindsorct.com
Index: All in one. Records indexed on a public use terminal back to 1970. Only the public may search. Copy fee $1.00 per page. Cert fee- $2.00 per cert plus copy fee. Payee- Town of Windsor. **Online access to Real Estate, Grantor/Grantee, Deed records:** Search the town clerk's land records index for free at www.townofwindsorct.com/records.htm. Index goes back to 1970. Town services search page at www.townofwindsorct.com. **Other phones:** Treasurer- 860-285-1890; Elections- 860-285-1902; Vital Records- 860-285-1902. **Property tax/Assessing**- 275 Broad St, Windsor, CT 06095; 860-285-1817, assessor fax- 860-285-1820. **Online access**- Search the town GIS database at http://info.townofwindsorct.com/gis/.

Wolcott Town

Town Clerk, 10 Kenea Ave; Town Hall, Wolcott, CT 06716. Recording, R/E & UCC phone-203-879-8100; fax-203-879-8105; 8:30AM-4:30PM (Recording until 4PM). (EST) www.wolcottct.org
Index: Separate indices to search include sewer, sewer usage, water, water usage & municipal tax liens. Records indexed on computer back to 1960. Only the public may search. Copy fee $1.00 per page. Cert fee- $2.00 per cert plus copy fee. Vitals-Certified copies only-$10.00 each with restrictions. Payee- Wolcott Town Clerk. **Other phones:** Treasurer- 203-879-8100; Elections- 203-879-8100; Vital Records- 203-879-8100. **Property tax/Assessing**- 10 Kenea Ave, Wolcott, CT 06716; 203-879-8100 x111, assessor fax- 203-879-8105. hours- 8:30AM-5PM M-W; 8:30AM-6:30PM Th; 8:30AM-N Fri **Online access**- Access property data free at www.prophecyone.us/index_prophecy.php?town=Wolcott. No name searching.

Woodbridge Town

Town Clerk, 11 Meetinghouse Ln, Woodbridge, CT 06525. Recording, R/E & UCC phone-203-389-3422; fax-203-389-3473; 8:30AM-4PM (office hrs) 8:30AM-3:30PM (recording hrs). (EST) www.woodbridgect.org/
Index: All in one. Records indexed on a public use terminal back to 1/1/1970. Only the public may search. Copy fee $1.00 per page. Cert fee- $2.00 per cert includes copy fee. Payee- Woodbridge Town Clerk. **Other phones:** Treasurer- 203-389-3414; Elections- 203-389-3408; Vital Records- 203-389-3424. **Property tax/Assessing**- Woodbridge Town Assessing Office, 11 Meetinghouse Ln, Woodbridge, CT 06525; 203-389-3416, assessor fax- 203-389-3480. (Appraiser/Auditor- 203-389-3414) **Online access**- Search the town assessor's database at http://data.visionappraisal.com/woodbridgeCT/.
Assessor email: bquist@ci.woodbridge.ct.us

Woodbury Town

Town Clerk, PO Box 369, Woodbury, CT 06798-3407. 203-263-2144; fax-203-263-4755; 8AM-4PM (EST) www.woodburyct.org
Index: All in one. Records indexed on a public use terminal back to 1984. Only the public may search. Copy fee $1.00 per page. Cert fee- $2.00 per cert plus copy fee. Payee- Woodbury Town Clerk. **Other phones:** Treasurer- 203-263-2449; Elections- 203-263-4750; Vital Records- 203-263-2144. **Property tax/Assessing**- PO Box 369, 275 Main St S, Woodbury, CT 06798-3407; 203-263-2435, assessor fax- 203-263-2948. Public access terminal available.

Woodstock Town

Town Clerk, 415 Rte 169; Town Hall, Woodstock, CT 06281. 860-928-6595; fax-860-963-7557; 8:30AM-4:30PM M,T,TH; 8:30AM-6PM W; 8:30AM-3PM Fri.
www.woodstockct.gov/Default.aspx?tabid=215
Index: All in one. Records indexed on a public use terminal back to 1984. Only the public may search. Copy fee $1.00 per page. Cert fee- $2.00 per cert plus copy fee. Payee- Town of Woodstock. **Property tax/Assessing**- 415 Rte 169, Woodstock, CT 06281; 860-928-6929 x326, assessor fax- 860-963-7557. www.woodstockct.gov/ **Online access**- Search assessor property database at http://data.visionappraisal.com/WoodstockCT/.

Connecticut County Locator

You will usually be able to find the city name in the City/County Cross Reference below. In that case, it is a simple matter to determine the county from the cross-reference. However, only the official US Postal Service city names are included in this index. Included is a ZIP/City Cross Reference following the City/County Cross Reference. If you know the ZIP Code but the city name does not appear in the City/County Cross list, look up the ZIP Code in the ZIP/City Cross Reference, find the city name, then look up the city in the City/County Cross Reference.

Connecticut City/County Cross Reference

ABINGTON Windham
AMSTON Tolland
ANDOVER Tolland
ANSONIA New Haven
ASHFORD Windham
AVON Hartford
BALLOUVILLE Windham
BALTIC (06330) New London(92), Windham(7)
BANTAM Litchfield
BARKHAMSTED Litchfield
BEACON FALLS New Haven
BETHANY New Haven
BETHEL Fairfield
BETHLEHEM Litchfield
BLOOMFIELD Hartford
BOLTON Tolland
BOTSFORD Fairfield
BOZRAH New London
BRANFORD New Haven
BRIDGEPORT Fairfield
BRIDGEWATER Litchfield
BRISTOL Hartford
BROAD BROOK Hartford
BROOKFIELD Fairfield
BROOKLYN Windham
BURLINGTON Hartford
CANAAN Litchfield
CANTERBURY Windham
CANTON Hartford
CANTON CENTER Hartford
CENTERBROOK Middlesex
CENTRAL VILLAGE Windham
CHAPLIN Windham
CHESHIRE New Haven
CHESTER Middlesex
CLINTON Middlesex
COBALT Middlesex
COLCHESTER (06415) New London(90), Middlesex(9)
COLEBROOK Litchfield
COLLINSVILLE Hartford
COLUMBIA Tolland
CORNWALL Litchfield
CORNWALL BRIDGE Litchfield
COS COB Fairfield
COVENTRY Tolland
CROMWELL Middlesex
DANBURY Fairfield
DANIELSON Windham
DARIEN Fairfield
DAYVILLE Windham
DEEP RIVER Middlesex
DERBY New Haven
DURHAM Middlesex
EAST BERLIN Hartford
EAST CANAAN Litchfield
EAST GLASTONBURY Hartford
EAST GRANBY Hartford
EAST HADDAM Middlesex
EAST HAMPTON Middlesex
EAST HARTFORD Hartford
EAST HARTLAND Hartford
EAST HAVEN New Haven
EAST KILLINGLY Windham
EAST LYME New London
EAST WINDSOR Hartford
EAST WINDSOR HILL Hartford
EAST WOODSTOCK Windham
EASTFORD (06242) Windham(96), Tolland(3)
EASTON Fairfield
ELLINGTON Tolland
ENFIELD Hartford
ESSEX Middlesex
FABYAN Windham
FAIRFIELD Fairfield
FALLS VILLAGE Litchfield
FARMINGTON Hartford
GALES FERRY New London
GAYLORDSVILLE Litchfield
GEORGETOWN Fairfield
GILMAN New London
GLASGO New London
GLASTONBURY Hartford
GOSHEN Litchfield
GRANBY Hartford
GREENS FARMS Fairfield
GREENWICH Fairfield
GROSVENOR DALE Windham
GROTON New London
GUILFORD New Haven
HADDAM Middlesex
HADLYME New London
HAMDEN New Haven
HAMPTON Windham
HANOVER New London
HARTFORD Hartford
HARWINTON Litchfield
HAWLEYVILLE Fairfield
HEBRON Tolland
HIGGANUM Middlesex
IVORYTON Middlesex
JEWETT CITY New London
KENSINGTON Hartford
KENT Litchfield
KILLINGWORTH Middlesex
LAKESIDE Litchfield
LAKEVILLE Litchfield
LEBANON New London
LEDYARD New London
LITCHFIELD Litchfield
MADISON New Haven
MANCHESTER (06040) Hartford(98), Tolland(1)
MANCHESTER Hartford
MANSFIELD CENTER (06250) Tolland(97), Windham(2)
MANSFIELD DEPOT Tolland
MARION Hartford
MARLBOROUGH Hartford
MASHANTUCKET New London
MELROSE Hartford
MERIDEN New Haven
MIDDLE HADDAM Middlesex
MIDDLEBURY New Haven
MIDDLEFIELD Middlesex
MIDDLETOWN Middlesex
MILFORD New Haven
MILLDALE Hartford
MONROE Fairfield
MONTVILLE New London
MOODUS Middlesex
MOOSUP Windham
MORRIS Litchfield
MYSTIC New London
NAUGATUCK New Haven
NEW BRITAIN Hartford
NEW CANAAN Fairfield
NEW FAIRFIELD Fairfield
NEW HARTFORD Litchfield
NEW HAVEN New Haven
NEW LONDON New London
NEW MILFORD Litchfield
NEW PRESTON MARBLE DALE Litchfield
NEWINGTON Hartford
NEWTOWN Fairfield
NIANTIC New London
NORFOLK Litchfield
NORTH BRANFORD New Haven
NORTH CANTON Hartford
NORTH FRANKLIN New London
NORTH GRANBY Hartford
NORTH GROSVENORDALE Windham
NORTH HAVEN New Haven
NORTH STONINGTON New London
NORTH WESTCHESTER New London
NORTH WINDHAM Windham
NORTHFIELD Litchfield
NORTHFORD New Haven
NORWALK Fairfield
NORWICH New London
OAKDALE New London
OAKVILLE Litchfield
OLD GREENWICH Fairfield
OLD LYME New London
OLD MYSTIC New London
OLD SAYBROOK Middlesex
ONECO Windham
ORANGE New Haven
OXFORD New Haven
PAWCATUCK New London
PEQUABUCK Litchfield
PINE MEADOW Litchfield
PLAINFIELD Windham
PLAINVILLE Hartford
PLANTSVILLE Hartford
PLEASANT VALLEY Litchfield
PLYMOUTH Litchfield
POMFRET Windham
POMFRET CENTER Windham
POQUONOCK Hartford
PORTLAND Middlesex
PRESTON New London
PROSPECT New Haven
PUTNAM Windham
QUAKER HILL New London
QUINEBAUG Windham
REDDING Fairfield
REDDING CENTER Fairfield
REDDING RIDGE Fairfield
RIDGEFIELD Fairfield
RIVERSIDE Fairfield
RIVERTON Litchfield
ROCKFALL Middlesex
ROCKY HILL Hartford
ROGERS Windham
ROXBURY Litchfield
SALEM New London
SALISBURY Litchfield
SANDY HOOK Fairfield
SCOTLAND Windham
SEYMOUR New Haven
SHARON Litchfield
SHELTON Fairfield
SHERMAN (06784) Fairfield(98), Litchfield(1)
SIMSBURY Hartford
SOMERS Tolland
SOMERSVILLE Tolland
SOUTH BRITAIN New Haven
SOUTH GLASTONBURY Hartford
SOUTH KENT Litchfield
SOUTH LYME New London
SOUTH WILLINGTON Tolland
SOUTH WINDHAM Windham
SOUTH WINDSOR Hartford
SOUTH WOODSTOCK Windham
SOUTHBURY New Haven
SOUTHINGTON Hartford
SOUTHPORT Fairfield
STAFFORD Tolland
STAFFORD SPRINGS (06076) Tolland(93), Windham(6)
STAFFORDVILLE Tolland
STAMFORD Fairfield
STERLING Windham
STEVENSON Fairfield
STONINGTON New London
STORRS MANSFIELD Tolland
STRATFORD Fairfield
SUFFIELD Hartford
TACONIC Litchfield
TAFTVILLE New London
TARIFFVILLE Hartford
TERRYVILLE Litchfield
THOMASTON Litchfield
THOMPSON Windham
TOLLAND Tolland
TORRINGTON Litchfield
TRUMBULL Fairfield
UNCASVILLE New London
UNIONVILLE Hartford
VERNON ROCKVILLE Tolland
VERSAILLES New London
VOLUNTOWN (06384) New London(97), Windham(2)
W HARTFORD Hartford
WALLINGFORD New Haven
WASHINGTON DEPOT Litchfield
WATERBURY New Haven
WATERFORD New London
WATERTOWN Litchfield
WAUREGAN Windham
WEATOGUE Hartford
WEST CORNWALL Litchfield
WEST GRANBY Hartford
WEST HARTFORD Hartford
WEST HARTLAND Hartford
WEST HAVEN New Haven
WEST MYSTIC New London
WEST SIMSBURY Hartford
WEST SUFFIELD Hartford
WESTBROOK Middlesex
WESTON Fairfield
WESTPORT Fairfield
WETHERSFIELD Hartford
WILLIMANTIC Windham
WILLINGTON Tolland
WILTON Fairfield
WINCHESTER CENTER Litchfield
WINDHAM Windham
WINDSOR Hartford
WINDSOR LOCKS Hartford
WINSTED Litchfield
WOLCOTT New Haven
WOODBRIDGE New Haven
WOODBURY Litchfield
WOODSTOCK Windham
WOODSTOCK VALLEY Windham
YANTIC New London

Connecticut ZIP/City Cross Reference

ZIP	City
06001-06001	AVON
06002-06002	BLOOMFIELD
06006-06006	WINDSOR
06010-06011	BRISTOL
06013-06013	BURLINGTON
06016-06016	BROAD BROOK
06018-06018	CANAAN
06019-06019	CANTON
06020-06020	CANTON CENTER
06021-06021	COLEBROOK
06022-06022	COLLINSVILLE
06023-06023	EAST BERLIN
06024-06024	EAST CANAAN
06025-06025	EAST GLASTONBURY
06026-06026	EAST GRANBY
06027-06027	EAST HARTLAND
06028-06028	EAST WINDSOR HILL
06029-06029	ELLINGTON
06030-06030	FARMINGTON
06031-06031	FALLS VILLAGE
06032-06032	FARMINGTON
06033-06033	GLASTONBURY
06034-06034	FARMINGTON
06035-06035	GRANBY
06037-06037	KENSINGTON
06039-06039	LAKEVILLE
06040-06042	MANCHESTER
06043-06043	BOLTON
06045-06045	MANCHESTER
06049-06049	MELROSE
06050-06053	NEW BRITAIN
06057-06057	NEW HARTFORD
06058-06058	NORFOLK
06059-06059	NORTH CANTON
06060-06060	NORTH GRANBY
06061-06061	PINE MEADOW
06062-06062	PLAINVILLE
06063-06063	PLEASANT VALLEY
06063-06063	BARKHAMSTED
06064-06064	POQUONOCK
06065-06065	RIVERTON
06066-06066	VERNON ROCKVILLE
06067-06067	ROCKY HILL
06068-06068	SALISBURY
06069-06069	SHARON
06070-06070	SIMSBURY
06071-06071	SOMERS
06072-06072	SOMERSVILLE
06073-06073	SOUTH GLASTONBURY
06074-06074	SOUTH WINDSOR
06075-06075	STAFFORD
06076-06076	STAFFORD SPRINGS
06077-06077	STAFFORDVILLE
06078-06078	SUFFIELD
06079-06079	TACONIC
06080-06080	SUFFIELD
06081-06081	TARIFFVILLE
06082-06083	ENFIELD
06084-06084	TOLLAND
06085-06087	UNIONVILLE
06088-06088	EAST WINDSOR
06089-06089	WEATOGUE
06090-06090	WEST GRANBY
06091-06091	WEST HARTLAND
06092-06092	WEST SIMSBURY
06093-06093	WEST SUFFIELD
06094-06094	WINCHESTER CENTER
06095-06095	WINDSOR
06096-06096	WINDSOR LOCKS
06098-06098	WINSTED
06100-06106	HARTFORD
06107-06107	W HARTFORD
06107-06107	WEST HARTFORD
06108-06108	EAST HARTFORD
06109-06109	WETHERSFIELD
06110-06110	W HARTFORD
06110-06110	WEST HARTFORD
06111-06111	NEWINGTON
06112-06115	HARTFORD
06117-06117	W HARTFORD
06117-06117	WEST HARTFORD
06118-06118	EAST HARTFORD
06119-06119	W HARTFORD
06119-06119	WEST HARTFORD
06120-06126	HARTFORD
06127-06127	W HARTFORD
06127-06127	WEST HARTFORD
06128-06128	EAST HARTFORD
06129-06129	WETHERSFIELD
06131-06131	NEWINGTON
06132-06132	HARTFORD
06133-06133	W HARTFORD
06133-06133	WEST HARTFORD
06134-06134	HARTFORD
06137-06137	W HARTFORD
06137-06137	WEST HARTFORD
06138-06138	EAST HARTFORD
06140-06199	HARTFORD
06226-06226	WILLIMANTIC
06230-06230	ABINGTON
06231-06231	AMSTON
06232-06232	ANDOVER
06233-06233	BALLOUVILLE
06234-06234	BROOKLYN
06235-06235	CHAPLIN
06237-06237	COLUMBIA
06238-06238	COVENTRY
06239-06239	DANIELSON
06241-06241	DAYVILLE
06242-06242	EASTFORD
06243-06243	EAST KILLINGLY
06244-06244	EAST WOODSTOCK
06245-06245	FABYAN
06246-06246	GROSVENOR DALE
06247-06247	HAMPTON
06248-06248	HEBRON
06249-06249	LEBANON
06250-06250	MANSFIELD CENTER
06251-06251	MANSFIELD DEPOT
06254-06254	NORTH FRANKLIN
06255-06255	NORTH GROSVENORDALE
06256-06256	NORTH WINDHAM
06258-06258	POMFRET
06259-06259	POMFRET CENTER
06260-06260	PUTNAM
06262-06262	QUINEBAUG
06263-06263	ROGERS
06264-06264	SCOTLAND
06265-06265	SOUTH WILLINGTON
06266-06266	SOUTH WINDHAM
06267-06267	SOUTH WOODSTOCK
06268-06269	STORRS MANSFIELD
06277-06277	THOMPSON
06278-06278	ASHFORD
06279-06279	WILLINGTON
06280-06280	WINDHAM
06281-06281	WOODSTOCK
06282-06282	WOODSTOCK VALLEY
06320-06320	NEW LONDON
06330-06330	BALTIC
06331-06331	CANTERBURY
06332-06332	CENTRAL VILLAGE
06333-06333	EAST LYME
06334-06334	BOZRAH
06335-06335	GALES FERRY
06336-06336	GILMAN
06337-06337	GLASGO
06338-06338	MASHANTUCKET
06339-06339	LEDYARD
06340-06349	GROTON
06350-06350	HANOVER
06351-06351	JEWETT CITY
06353-06353	MONTVILLE
06354-06354	MOOSUP
06355-06355	MYSTIC
06357-06357	NIANTIC
06359-06359	NORTH STONINGTON
06360-06360	NORWICH
06365-06365	PRESTON
06370-06370	OAKDALE
06371-06371	OLD LYME
06372-06372	OLD MYSTIC
06373-06373	ONECO
06374-06374	PLAINFIELD
06375-06375	QUAKER HILL
06376-06376	SOUTH LYME
06377-06377	STERLING
06378-06378	STONINGTON
06379-06379	PAWCATUCK
06380-06380	TAFTVILLE
06382-06382	UNCASVILLE
06383-06383	VERSAILLES
06384-06384	VOLUNTOWN
06385-06386	WATERFORD
06387-06387	WAUREGAN
06388-06388	WEST MYSTIC
06389-06389	YANTIC
06401-06401	ANSONIA
06403-06403	BEACON FALLS
06404-06404	BOTSFORD
06405-06405	BRANFORD
06408-06408	CHESHIRE
06409-06409	CENTERBROOK
06410-06411	CHESHIRE
06412-06412	CHESTER
06413-06413	CLINTON
06414-06414	COBALT
06415-06415	COLCHESTER
06416-06416	CROMWELL
06417-06417	DEEP RIVER
06418-06418	DERBY
06419-06419	KILLINGWORTH
06420-06420	SALEM
06422-06422	DURHAM
06423-06423	EAST HADDAM
06424-06424	EAST HAMPTON
06426-06426	ESSEX
06430-06432	FAIRFIELD
06436-06436	GREENS FARMS
06437-06437	GUILFORD
06438-06438	HADDAM
06439-06439	HADLYME
06440-06440	HAWLEYVILLE
06441-06441	HIGGANUM
06442-06442	IVORYTON
06443-06443	MADISON
06444-06444	MARION
06447-06447	MARLBOROUGH
06450-06454	MERIDEN
06455-06455	MIDDLEFIELD
06456-06456	MIDDLE HADDAM
06457-06459	MIDDLETOWN
06460-06460	MILFORD
06461-06461	BRIDGEPORT
06466-06466	MILFORD
06467-06467	MILLDALE
06468-06468	MONROE
06469-06469	MOODUS
06470-06470	NEWTOWN
06471-06471	NORTH BRANFORD
06472-06472	NORTHFORD
06473-06473	NORTH HAVEN
06474-06474	NORTH WESTCHESTER
06475-06475	OLD SAYBROOK
06477-06477	ORANGE
06478-06478	OXFORD
06479-06479	PLANTSVILLE
06480-06480	PORTLAND
06481-06481	ROCKFALL
06482-06482	SANDY HOOK
06483-06483	SEYMOUR
06484-06484	SHELTON
06487-06487	SOUTH BRITAIN
06488-06488	SOUTHBURY
06489-06489	SOUTHINGTON
06490-06490	SOUTHPORT
06491-06491	STEVENSON
06492-06495	WALLINGFORD
06497-06497	STRATFORD
06498-06498	WESTBROOK
06500-06511	NEW HAVEN
06512-06512	EAST HAVEN
06513-06513	NEW HAVEN
06514-06514	HAMDEN
06515-06515	NEW HAVEN
06516-06516	WEST HAVEN
06517-06518	HAMDEN
06519-06521	NEW HAVEN
06524-06524	BETHANY
06525-06525	WOODBRIDGE
06530-06540	NEW HAVEN
06600-06610	BRIDGEPORT
06611-06611	TRUMBULL
06612-06612	EASTON
06614-06615	STRATFORD
06650-06699	BRIDGEPORT
06701-06710	WATERBURY
06712-06712	PROSPECT
06716-06716	WOLCOTT
06720-06749	WATERBURY
06750-06750	BANTAM
06751-06751	BETHLEHEM
06752-06752	BRIDGEWATER
06753-06753	CORNWALL
06754-06754	CORNWALL BRIDGE
06755-06755	GAYLORDSVILLE
06756-06756	GOSHEN
06757-06757	KENT
06758-06758	LAKESIDE
06759-06759	LITCHFIELD
06762-06762	MIDDLEBURY
06763-06763	MORRIS
06770-06770	NAUGATUCK
06776-06776	NEW MILFORD
06777-06777	NEW PRESTON MARBLE DALE
06778-06778	NORTHFIELD
06779-06779	OAKVILLE
06781-06781	PEQUABUCK
06782-06782	PLYMOUTH
06783-06783	ROXBURY
06784-06784	SHERMAN
06785-06785	SOUTH KENT
06786-06786	TERRYVILLE
06787-06787	THOMASTON
06790-06790	TORRINGTON
06791-06792	HARWINTON
06792-06792	TORRINGTON
06793-06794	WASHINGTON DEPOT
06795-06795	WATERTOWN
06796-06796	WEST CORNWALL
06798-06798	WOODBURY
06801-06801	BETHEL
06804-06804	BROOKFIELD
06807-06807	COS COB
06810-06811	DANBURY
06812-06812	NEW FAIRFIELD
06813-06817	DANBURY
06820-06820	DARIEN
06824-06828	FAIRFIELD
06829-06829	GEORGETOWN
06830-06836	GREENWICH
06838-06838	GREENS FARMS
06840-06842	NEW CANAAN
06850-06860	NORWALK
06870-06870	OLD GREENWICH
06875-06875	REDDING CENTER
06876-06876	REDDING RIDGE
06877-06877	RIDGEFIELD
06878-06878	RIVERSIDE
06879-06879	RIDGEFIELD
06880-06881	WESTPORT
06883-06883	WESTON
06888-06889	WESTPORT
06890-06890	SOUTHPORT
06896-06896	REDDING
06897-06897	WILTON
06900-06928	STAMFORD

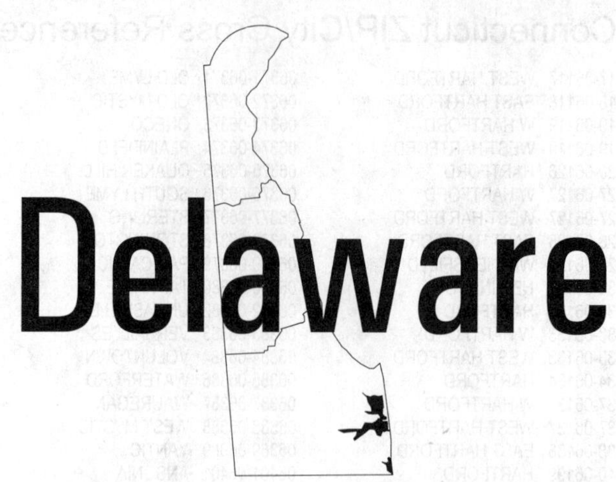

Delaware

General Help Numbers:

Governor's Office

820 N. French St — 302-577-3210
Wilmington, DE 19801 — Fax 302-577-3118
http://governor.delaware.gov/index.shtml — 8AM-5:30PM

Attorney General's Office

Carvel State Office Bldg — 302-577-8400
820 N French St — Fax 302-577-6630
Wilmington, DE 19801 — 8AM-5PM
www.state.de.us/attgen

Legislative Records

Division of Research — 302-744-4114
PO Box 1401 — Fax 302-739-5318
Wilmington, DE 19903 — 8AM-5:30PM
http://attorneygeneral.delaware.gov/

State Archives

121 Duke of York St — 302-744-5000
Dover, DE 19901 — Fax 302-739-6710
http://archives.delaware.gov/ — 8:30AM-4:15PM M-F
(till 8PM on W, 5PM on SAT)

State Specifics:

Capital:	Dover Kent County
Time Zone:	EST
Number of Counties:	3
Population:	873,092
Website:	http://delaware.gov

State Agencies

Criminal Records

Delaware State Police, State Bureau of Identification, PO Box 430, Dover, DE 19903-0430 (Courier address- 1407 N Dupont Highway, Dover, DE 19901); 302-739-2134, Fax- 302-739-5888; 8AM-4PM.

http://dsp.delaware.gov/default.shtml

Indexing & Storage: Records available from 1935. New records available for inquiry in up to 3 days. 94% of all arrests in database have final dispositions recorded, 92% for those arrests within last 5 years.

Searching: Must have a signed release from the subject for the fingerprint search and release of information. You do not need to use the state's forms. Include in request- fingerprints, full name, signed release. Will not expedite requests; their policy is first come first served. Data not released- traffic ticket information. If the disposition is not known by this agency, the record will say "disposition not known." Will only release records with dispositions to pre-employment screeners.

Access by: mail, in person.

Fee & Payment: The search fee is $45.00 per request. Fee payee- Delaware State Police. Prepayment required. Funds must be certified or money order. Personal checks not accepted. Credit cards accepted for in person searches only.

Mail search: Turnaround time- 4 to 6 weeks. Must have a signed release and full set of fingerprints. A SASE is requested.

In person: Records can be requested, but results are mailed.

Statewide Court Records

Administrative Office of the Courts, Supreme Court of Delaware, 500 N King St, #11600, Wilmington, DE 19801; 302-255-0090, Fax- 302-255-2217; 8:30AM-5PM.

http://courts.delaware.gov

All trial court record access must be done at the local level. There is a second office in Georgetown, DE.

Access by: online.

Online search: Chancery, Superior, Common Pleas, and Supreme Courts opinions and orders are available free online at http://courts.delaware.gov/opinions/. Supreme, Superior, and Common Pleas Courts calendars are available free at http://courts.delaware.gov/calendars/. Chancery Courts and Supreme Courts filings are available from a vendor at www.virtualdocket.com. Registration and fees required.

Sexual Offender Registry

Delaware State Police, Sex Offender Central Registry, PO Box 430, Dover, DE 19903-0430 (Courier address- 1407 N Dupont Highway, Dover, DE 19901); 302-672-5306, Fax- 302-739-5888; 8AM-4PM.

http://sexoffender.dsp.delaware.gov/

There are three Tiers or Levels of offenders in the state. The public is only made aware of Tiers 2 and 3 via the Internet through public notification programs by local law enforcement. Door-to-door is used for Tier 3 notification.

Indexing & Storage: Records available from 06/24/94. New records available for inquiry in up to 3 days.

Searching: Name searching is not available in the state except through the web page. Email questions to soffender@state.de.us. This data not released- victim data

Access by: online.

Online search: Statewide registry can be searched at the website. The site gives the ability to search by last name, Development, and city or Zip Code. Any combination of these fields may be used; however, a search cannot be performed if both a city and Zip Code are entered.

Incarceration Records

Delaware Department of Corrections, Director of Central Offender Records, 245 McKee Rd, Dover, DE 19904; 302-857-5490, Fax- 302-739-7486; 8AM-4PM.

http://doc.delaware.gov/

The Department of Correction does not offer the public access to an automated database of offender information. But escapees and death row convicts are listed.

Indexing & Storage: Records available on current and former inmates. Records are archived after two years. Paper records maintained to 1989. New records available for inquiry in only minutes.

Searching: However, the public may receive basic information about an offender, including whether the individual is incarcerated in Delaware, where the individual is incarcerated and, how to contact an offender, by calling the number above. Include in request- name and DOB.

Access by: mail, fax.

Mail search: Turnaround time- 1 week. An SASE is not required.

Fax search: Fax requests are accepted, the agency will only give out information that is public record.

Other access: Escapees and death penalty lists are available online at http://doc.delaware.gov/escapees/escapees.shtml.

Corporation, LLC, LP, LLP, General Partnerships, Trademarks/Servicemarks

Secretary of State, Corporation Records, PO Box 898, Dover, DE 19903 (Courier address- 401 Federal Street #4, Dover, DE 19901); 302-739-3073, Fax- 302-739-3812; 8AM-4:30PM.

www.corp.delaware.gov/

DBA's or Doing Business As names are registered in the Prothonotary's office at the county.

Indexing & Storage: Records available from the formation of the Division. Indexes are maintained on imaging system and in-house computer. Delaware Registered Agents have online access. New records available for inquiry immediately.

Searching: Include in request- full name of business. In addition to the articles of organization, business entity records available include: Annual Reports, Officers, Directors, Prior (merged) names, Inactive and Reserved names.

Access by: mail, phone, fax, in person, online.

Fee & Payment: Record search is $30.00. Certification is $30.00 (plus $2.00 per page if annual report), $20.00 for trademarks. Plain copies are $10.00 first page and $2.00 each additional. Fee payee- Delaware Secretary of State. Prepayment required. Personal checks accepted. Visa/MC/Discover accepted.

Mail search: Turnaround time- 3 - 5 days. SASE not required.

Phone search: There is no fee for general information given over the phone.

Fax search: Fax requests can be received by fax, but are not returned by fax.

In person: Requests are returned by regular mail unless a courier account # is provided.

Online search: Check status on the web free for entity name, file number, incorporation/formation date, registered agent name, address, phone number and residency.

Expedited service: Expedited services available for mail, fax, phone, and in person. Add $20.00 for 24 hour service for plain copies. Same day service is $40.00. The rates quoted include $1,000 for one hour service. $500 for 2 hour service.

Uniform Commercial Code, Federal Tax Liens

UCC Division, Secretary of State, PO Box 793, Dover, DE 19903 (Courier address- Townsend Bldg, 401 Federal Street #4, Dover, DE 19901); 302-739-3077, Fax- 302-739-3813; 8:30AM-4:30PM.

www.corp.delaware.gov/ucc.shtml

All non "Search to Reflect" UCC Searches are outsourced to a Delaware Authorized Searcher, who performs the search. The website maintains a list of these private vendors. All UCC searches performed by these agents are Certified UCC Searches.

Indexing & Storage: Records available from 1967. Records are computerized since 1992. New records available for inquiry immediately.

Searching: Use search request form UCC-11, downloadable from web. The search includes federal tax liens since 1976. All state tax liens are filed at the county level. Include in request- debtor name.

Access by: mail, phone, in person.

Fee & Payment: Search to Reflect fee is $25.00 Plain copies are $10.00 first page, $2.00 each additional. Certified copies are $30.00 for first page and $2.00 each add'l. Fee payee- Delaware Secretary of State. Prepayment required. Volume users may establish an account. Personal checks accepted. Visa/MC/Discover accepted.

Mail search: Turnaround time- 5-7 days.

Phone search: Use a Delaware Authorized Searcher (see website for list).

In person: Immediate counter service is considered expedited and entails extra fee.

Other access: Bulk purchase of copies of financing statements is $2.00 per page.

Expedited service: available for mail searches for $25.00. Turnaround time- 24 hours.

State Tax Liens

Records not maintained by a state level agency.

Records are at the county level.

Sales Tax Registrations

Finance Department - Div. Rev., Gross Receipt Tax Registration, PO Box 8750, Wilmington, DE 19899-8750 (Courier address- Carvel State Office Bldg, 820 N French St, 9th Fl, Wilmington, DE 19801); 302-577-8230, Fax- 302-577-8203; 8AM-4:30PM.

http://revenue.delaware.gov/

This state has a gross receipts tax, not a sales tax per se. They will release the information found on the face of the business licensee issued to the business.

Indexing & Storage: Records available for the past 3-5 years. New records available for inquiry in seconds.

Searching: This agency will do an alpha search for a business name and will provide the business name, address and business license number, type of business, and amount of license fee paid. They will not release business owner or officer names. Include in request- business name. The federal tax ID can also be used. This data not released- financial records, delinquencies.

Access by: mail, phone, fax, in person.

Mail search: Turnaround time- 1 week. A SASE is requested. No fee for mail request.

Phone search: No fee for telephone request. There is a limit of 3 searches per phone call. **Fax search:** There is no fee for fax searches. Turnaround time is 2 days.

In person: No fee for request.

Birth Certificates

Department of Health, Office of Vital Statistics, 417 Federal St, Dover, DE 19901 (Courier address- William Penn & Federal Sts, Jesse Cooper Bldg, Dover, DE 19901); 302-744-4549, 877-888-0248 (Order); 8AM-4:30PM (Counter closes at 4:15 PM).

www.dhss.delaware.gov/dhss/dph/ss/vitalstats.html

The agency will also release an adoptee birth certificate.

Indexing & Storage: Records available from 1932 to present. Prior records are at the State Archives. New records available for inquiry in 1 month.

Searching: Must have a signed release from person of record or immediate family member. Others may only obtain records if they demonstrate the record is needed for the determination or protection of their personal property rights or for genealogical uses. Include in request- full name, names of parents, mother's maiden name, date of birth, place of birth, reason for information request, relationship to person of record, photo ID.

Access by: mail, phone, in person, online.

Fee & Payment: Search fee is $10.00 per name for every 5 years searched. Add $12.95 if you use a credit card via vitalchek.com. Fee payee- Office of Vital Statistics. Prepayment required. Personal checks accepted. Major credit cards accepted by VitalChek (not state).

Mail search: Turnaround time- 1 day to 1 week. SASE not required.

Phone search: Records may be ordered using the toll-free number above.

In person: Records may be ordered in person at this agency or at the local county agency in New Castle or Sussex counties. The addresses are found on the web. Turnaround time is generally 10 minutes or less.

Online search: Access available at vitalchek.com, a state designated vendor.

Expedited service: VitalChek offers expedited services when ordered online or by fax. Turnaround time- 3 to 5 days. Add $12.95 to the $10.00 record fee as well as courier fee if you wish records expressed.

Death Records

Department of Health, Office of Vital Statistics, 417 Federal St, Dover, DE 19901 (Courier address- William Penn & Federal Sts, Jesse Cooper Bldg, Dover, DE 19901); 302-744-4549, 877-888-0248 (Order); 8AM-4:15PM.

www.dhss.delaware.gov/dhss/dph/ss/vitalstats.html

Indexing & Storage: Records available from 1964 to present. Prior records are at the State Archives. New records available for inquiry in 3 days.

Searching: Must have a signed release from immediate family member. Include in request- full name, date of death, place of death, names of parents, reason for information request, relationship to person of record, photo ID.

Access by: mail, phone, in person, online.

Fee & Payment: The search fee is $10.00 per name for every 5 years searched. Add $12.95 if you use a credit card via vitalchek.com. Fee payee- Office of Vital Statistics. Prepayment required. Personal checks accepted. Major credit cards accepted by VitalChek (not state).

Mail search: Turnaround time- 1 day. SASE not required.

Phone search: Records may be ordered using the toll-free number above.

In person: Records may be ordered in person at this agency or at the local county agency in New Castle or Sussex counties. The addresses are found on the web. Turnaround time is 10 to 15 minutes.

Online search: Access available at vitalchek.com, a state designated vendor.

Expedited service: VitalChek offers expedited services when ordered online or by fax. Turnaround time- 3 to 5 days. Add $12.95 to the $10.00 record fee as well as courier fee if you wish records expressed.

Marriage Certificates

Department of Health, Office of Vital Statistics, 417 Federal St, Dover, DE 19901 (Courier address- William Penn & Federal Sts, Jesse Cooper Bldg, Dover, DE 19901); 302-744-4549, 877-888-0248 (Order); 8AM-4:15PM.

www.dhss.delaware.gov/dhss/dph/ss/vitalstats.html

Indexing & Storage: Records available from 1964 to present. Prior records are in the State Public Archives. New records available for inquiry in 1 month.

Searching: Must have a signed release from person or persons of record or immediate family member. Include in request- names of husband and wife, date of marriage, place or county of marriage, relationship to person of record, reason for information request, wife's maiden name, photo ID.

Access by: mail, phone, in person, online.

Fee & Payment: The search fee is $10.00 per name for every 5 years searched. Add $12.95 if you use a credit card via vitalchek.com. Fee payee- Office of Vital Statistics. Prepayment required. Personal checks accepted. Major credit cards accepted by VitalChek (not state).

Mail search: Turnaround time- 1 day. SASE not required.

Phone search: Records may be ordered using the toll-free number above.

In person: Records may be ordered in person at this agency or at the local county agency in New Castle or Sussex counties. The addresses are found on the web. Turnaround time is 10 to 15 minutes.

Online search: Access is available via VitalChek.com, a state designated vendor.

Expedited service: VitalChek offers expedited services when ordered online or by fax. Turnaround time- 3 to 5 days. Add $12.95 to the $10.00 record fee as well as courier fee if you wish records expressed.

Divorce Records

Records not maintained by a state level agency.

The Office of Vital Statistics will verify whether a divorce occurred after 1935, but will not issue record copies. For records 1976 to present, go to the Family Court at the county; prior to 1976, go to the Prothonotary at the county level.

Workers' Compensation Records

Labor Department, Industrial Accident Board, 4425 N Market Street, 3rd Fl, Wilmington, DE 19802; 302-761-8200 x2, Fax- 302-761-6601; 8AM-4:30PM.

www.delawareworks.com/industrialaffairs/services/workerscomp.shtml

Case records must have been adjudicated to be considered public. First reports of injury only (non-adjudicated) are not covered under FOIA.

Indexing & Storage: Records available from 1985. New records available for inquiry immediately.

Searching: Include in request- use copy request form which requires claimant name, SSN, employer, and date of accident. Call or write for the request form, it is not available on the web.

Access by: mail, fax, online.

Fee & Payment: There is no fee. Copies are $.25 each. Fee payee- DOL/IA. Prepayment required. Payment is for copies only. Personal checks accepted, credit cards are not.

Mail search: Turnaround time- 2 to 5 days. A SASE is requested.

Fax search: Requests accepted by fax if requester meets the criteria.

Online search: To check on an employers and employer's name and the insurance history visit www.delawareworks.com/industrialaffairs/compsearch.shtml.

Driver Records

Division of Motor Vehicles, Driver's License Unit, PO Box 698, Dover, DE 19903 (Courier address- 303 Transportation Circle, Dover, DE 19901); 302-744-2506, Fax- 302-739-2602; 8AM-4:30PM (12-8PM W).

www.dmv.de.gov/

Indexing & Storage: Records available for 3 years to present for public record purposes. New records available for inquiry in 2 to 3 weeks.

Searching: Records cannot be sold from one vendor to another unless approved. Casual requesters can obtain records only with MV703 Form requiring notarized signature of requester. Include in request- full name, driver's license number, date of birth, Form MV703. Authorized account holders must complete an Application and a Contract for Direct Access. This data not released- SSNs or medical information.

Access by: mail, in person, online.

Fee & Payment: The fee for all search modes is $15.00 per request. Fee payee- Division of Motor Vehicles. Prepayment required. Personal checks and money orders accepted. No credit cards accepted.

Mail search: Turnaround time- 3 to 5 days. A SASE is requested.

In person: Three requests will be processed while you wait, additional requests are processed overnight. Walk-in requesters may obtain records from centers in Wilmington, New Castle, Dover, and Georgetown.

Online search: The Direct Access Program is provided 24 hours via the web. The fee is $15.00 per name. Searches are done by submitting the driver's license number. Requesters must be pre-approved, a signed contract application is required. Online searching is by single inquiry only; no batch request mode is offered. For more information about establishing an account, call Mr. Larry Bryant at 302-744-2596.

Vehicle Ownership & Registration

DMV - Administration, Vehicle Records, PO Box 698, Dover, DE 19903 (Courier address- 303 Transportation Circle, Dover, DE 19901); 302-744-2596, Fax- 302-739-3152; 8AM-4:30PM M-T-TH-F; 12-8PM W.

www.dmv.de.gov/

Indexing & Storage: Records available for 3 years to present. New records available for inquiry in 2 to 3 weeks.

Searching: Those routinely seeking information must complete an Application and Contract for Direct Access to become an account holder. Casual requesters must use Form MV703 which requires notarized signature of subject.

Access by: mail, in person, online.

Fee & Payment: The fee for ownership, plate, and registration searches is $15.00 per record, $20.00 if certified. Fee payee- Division of Motor Vehicles. Prepayment required. Personal checks accepted, credit cards are not.

Mail search: Turnaround time- 3 to 5 days. A SASE is requested.

In person: Turnaround time is while you wait.

Online search: The Direct Access Program is provided 24 hours via the web. The fee is $15.00 per name. Requesters must be pre-approved; a signed contract application is required. Online searching is by single inquiry only; no batch request mode is offered. For more information about establishing an account, call Larry Bryant at 302-744-2596. This program is strictly monitored and not available for non-permissible uses.

Accident Reports

Delaware State Police, Traffic Control Section, PO Box 430, Dover, DE 19903 (Courier address- 1441 N Dupont Hwy, Dover, DE 19901); 302-739-5931, Fax- 302-739-5936; 8AM-4PM.

http://dsp.delaware.gov/default.shtml

Indexing & Storage: Records available from 1984. New records available for inquiry in 2 weeks.

Searching: Include in request- full names, date of accident, location of accident. If known, please give the Compliant Number.

Access by: mail, phone.

Fee & Payment: The fee is $25.00 per report, $60.00 if fatal accident report. Fee payee- Delaware State Police. Prepayment required. Personal checks accepted, credit cards are not.

Mail search: Turnaround time- 5 to 10 days. A SASE is requested.

Phone search: You can only verify if a report exists.

Vessel Ownership & Registration

Division of Fish & Wildlife, Delaware Boat Registration Office, 89 Kings Highway, Dover, DE 19901; 302-739-9916, Fax- 302-739-6157; 8AM-4:30PM.

www.fw.delaware.gov/Services/Pages/Licenses.aspx

Records are confidential and not released to general public per DPPA. No name searching of records is allowed. The information below only pertains to those who have legal right to access.

Indexing & Storage: Records available from 1979 to present. Records are registration only, no titles, and are indexed on microfiche from 1978 to 1989. Records are computer indexed from 1990 to the present. All motorized craft are registered. New records available for inquiry in one month or less.

Searching: Liens are filed with UCC filings, not at this location. Either the owner's name, hull ID# or registration number must be submitted for a verification.

Access by: mail, phone, fax, in person.

Fee & Payment: There is no fee.

Mail search: Turnaround time- 3 days. Records are available by mail.

Phone search: They will verify information over the phone using "yes" and "no" only.

Fax search: If DPPA approved.

In person: Verification only.

Legislation Records

Legislative Hall, Division of Research, PO Box 1401, Dover, DE 19903; 302-744-4114, 302-739-5318 (Archives for old bills), 800-282-8545 (In-state), Fax- 302-739-5318; 8AM-4:30PM.

http://legis.delaware.gov/

Direct questions to LIS.Webmaster@state.de.us.

Indexing & Storage: Records available from 1973 forward. Prior bills are archived.

Searching: Include in request- bill number.

Access by: mail, phone, fax, in person, online.

Fee & Payment: There is no charge unless you want many copies or a copy of a large document. They will compute the charges. Fee payee- State of Delaware. Personal checks accepted, credit cards are not.

Mail search: Turnaround time- variable. SASE not required.

Phone search: You may call for copies.

Fax search: Records are available by fax if under 10 pages.

In person: You may request copies in person.

Online search: Access bill information and bill tracking at the Internet site, no fee. State statutes and codes may be found at http://delcode.delaware.gov/.

Voter Registration

Access to Records is Restricted.

Commissioner of Elections, Voter Registration Records, 111 S West St #10, Dover, DE 19904; 302-739-4277, Fax- 302-739-6794; 8AM-4:30PM.

http://elections.delaware.gov/

There is no individual record searching permitted, except in person. Lists may be only purchased for political purposes. The entire state database is available on CD for $250. Individual districts (432) are available on disk for $2.00 per district or $.025 per name on labels. Also, there are several different types of printed lists available. Disks are encrypted.

GED Certificates

Department of Education, Adult Education - GED Testing, 35 Commerce Way #1, Dover, DE 19904; 302-857-3348, Fax- 302-739-1770; 8AM-4:30PM.

www.doe.state.de.us

The office is located in the John W Collette Educational Resource Center.

Indexing & Storage: Records available since inception. New records available for inquiry in 8-12 weeks.

Searching: Consent of subject is needed for all third-party searches. Include in request- signed release, name, date of birth, SSN, location of test center. Requests must be in writing. The year of the test is very helpful.

Access by: mail, fax, in person.

Fee & Payment: There is no fee for a verification. A duplicate certificate is available for $5.00. Fee payee- Department of Education Must use a money order. Personal checks not accepted.

Mail search: Turnaround time- 2 to 3 weeks. SASE not required.

Fax search: Same criteria as mail searching.

In person: Requester must present a photo ID.

Hunting & Fishing License Information

Access to Records is Restricted.

Division of Fish & Wildlife, License Records, 89 Kings Hwy, Dover, DE 19901; 302-739-5296, 302-739-9911, Fax- 302-739-6157; 8AM-4:30PM.

www.fw.delaware.gov/Pages/FWPortal.aspx

Records are not on a computerized database, but kept on paper and filed alphabetically. Per Delaware Code, license holder information is restricted and not available for public access.

Delaware State Licensing Agencies

For details about the agency responsible for licensing/certifying/registering an item below or in the Agency Quick Finder section, match an item's number with the number of the agency in the *Licensing Agency Information* section.

Delaware Licenses Searchable Online

Adult Entertainment #11 .... https://dpronline.delaware.gov/mylicense%20weblookup/Search.aspx
Aesthetician #11 .... https://dpronline.delaware.gov/mylicense%20weblookup/Search.aspx
Amateur Boxing-related #11 .... https://dpronline.delaware.gov/mylicense%20weblookup/Search.aspx
Architect #11 .... https://dpronline.delaware.gov/mylicense%20weblookup/Search.aspx
Athletic Agent /Trainer #11 .... https://dpronline.delaware.gov/mylicense%20weblookup/Search.aspx
Audiologist #11 .... https://dpronline.delaware.gov/mylicense%20weblookup/Search.aspx
Barber #11 .... https://dpronline.delaware.gov/mylicense%20weblookup/Search.aspx
Bodyworker #11 .... https://dpronline.delaware.gov/mylicense%20weblookup/Search.aspx
Boxer/Boxing Professional #11 .... https://dpronline.delaware.gov/mylicense%20weblookup/Search.aspx
Charitable Gaming Permittee #11 .... https://dpronline.delaware.gov/mylicense%20weblookup/Search.aspx
Chiropractor #11 .... https://dpronline.delaware.gov/mylicense%20weblookup/Search.aspx
Cosmetologist #11 .... https://dpronline.delaware.gov/mylicense%20weblookup/Search.aspx
Counselor, Elem./Second'y School #4 .... https://deeds.doe.k12.de.us/public/deeds_pc_findeducator.aspx
Counselor, Professional #11 .... https://dpronline.delaware.gov/mylicense%20weblookup/Search.aspx
Deadly Weapons Dealer #11 .... https://dpronline.delaware.gov/mylicense%20weblookup/Search.aspx
Dentist, Dental Hygienist #11 .... https://dpronline.delaware.gov/mylicense%20weblookup/Search.aspx
Dietician/Nutritionist #11 .... https://dpronline.delaware.gov/mylicense%20weblookup/Search.aspx
Electrical Inspector #11 .... https://dpronline.delaware.gov/mylicense%20weblookup/Search.aspx
Electrician #11 .... https://dpronline.delaware.gov/mylicense%20weblookup/Search.aspx
Electrologist #11 .... https://dpronline.delaware.gov/mylicense%20weblookup/Search.aspx
Emergency Medical Tech/Paramedic #11 .... https://dpronline.delaware.gov/mylicense%20weblookup/Search.aspx
Engineer/Engineering Firm #12 .... www.dape.org/App/peRoster.asp
Funeral Director #11 .... https://dpronline.delaware.gov/mylicense%20weblookup/Search.aspx
Gaming Control #11 .... https://dpronline.delaware.gov/mylicense%20weblookup/Search.aspx
Geologist #11 .... https://dpronline.delaware.gov/mylicense%20weblookup/Search.aspx
Hearing Aid Dealer/Fitter #11 .... https://dpronline.delaware.gov/mylicense%20weblookup/Search.aspx
Insurance-Related Profession/Firm #8 .... https://sbs-de.naic.org/Lion-Web/jsp/sbsreports/AgentLookup.jsp
Landscape Architect #11 .... https://dpronline.delaware.gov/mylicense%20weblookup/Search.aspx
Library/Media Specialist #4 .... https://deeds.doe.k12.de.us/public/deeds_pc_findeducator.aspx
Liquid Waste Hauler #17 .... www.dnrec.state.de.us/water2000/Sections/GroundWat/GWDSLicenses.htm
Lobbyist #9 .... www.delawaregov.us/pic/index.cfm?ref=74391
Massage #11 .... https://dpronline.delaware.gov/mylicense%20weblookup/Search.aspx
Medical Doctor/Surgeon/Practice #11 .... https://dpronline.delaware.gov/mylicense%20weblookup/Search.aspx
Mental Health Counselor #11 .... https://dpronline.delaware.gov/mylicense%20weblookup/Search.aspx
Midwife Nurse #11 .... https://dpronline.delaware.gov/mylicense%20weblookup/Search.aspx
Nail Technician #11 .... https://dpronline.delaware.gov/mylicense%20weblookup/Search.aspx
Nurse #11 .... https://dpronline.delaware.gov/mylicense%20weblookup/Search.aspx
Nursing Home Administrator #11 .... https://dpronline.delaware.gov/mylicense%20weblookup/Search.aspx
Nutritionist #11 .... https://dpronline.delaware.gov/mylicense%20weblookup/Search.aspx
Occupational Therapist/Assistant #11 .... https://dpronline.delaware.gov/mylicense%20weblookup/Search.aspx
Optometrist #11 .... www.arbo.org/index.php?action=findanoptometrist
Osteopathic Physician #11 .... https://dpronline.delaware.gov/mylicense%20weblookup/Search.aspx
Pesticide Applicator #10 .... www.kellysolutions.com/de/Applicators/index.htm
Pesticide Business #10 .... www.kellysolutions.com/de/Business/index.htm
Pesticide Dealer #10 .... www.kellysolutions.com/de/Dealers/index.htm
Pharmacist #11 .... https://dpronline.delaware.gov/mylicense%20weblookup/Search.aspx
Pharmacy/Pharmacy-related Business #11 .... https://dpronline.delaware.gov/mylicense%20weblookup/Search.aspx
Physical Therapist/Assistant #11 .... https://dpronline.delaware.gov/mylicense%20weblookup/Search.aspx
Physician Assistant #11 .... https://dpronline.delaware.gov/mylicense%20weblookup/Search.aspx
Pilot, River #11 .... https://dpronline.delaware.gov/mylicense%20weblookup/Search.aspx
Plumber #11 .... https://dpronline.delaware.gov/mylicense%20weblookup/Search.aspx
Podiatrist #11 .... https://dpronline.delaware.gov/mylicense%20weblookup/Search.aspx
Psychologist/ Psychological Asst. #11 .... https://dpronline.delaware.gov/mylicense%20weblookup/Search.aspx
Public Accountant-CPA #11 .... https://dpronline.delaware.gov/mylicense%20weblookup/Search.aspx
Real Estate Agent/Broker #11 .... https://dpronline.delaware.gov/mylicense%20weblookup/Search.aspx
Real Estate Appraiser #11 .... www.asc.gov/content/category1/nr_intro.aspx?id=10
Respiratory Care Practitioner #11 .... https://dpronline.delaware.gov/mylicense%20weblookup/Search.aspx
School-Related Professional #4 .... https://deeds.doe.k12.de.us/public/deeds_pc_findeducator.aspx
Social Worker #11 .... https://dpronline.delaware.gov/mylicense%20weblookup/Search.aspx
Speech Pathologist/Audiologist #11 .... https://dpronline.delaware.gov/mylicense%20weblookup/Search.aspx
Surplus Lines Broker #8 .... https://sbs-de.naic.org/Lion-Web/jsp/sbsreports/AgentLookup.jsp

Surveyor, Land #11 ...... https://dpronline.delaware.gov/mylicense%20weblookup/Search.aspx
Teacher #4 ...... https://deeds.doe.k12.de.us/public/deeds_pc_findeducator.aspx
Veterinarian #11 ...... https://dpronline.delaware.gov/mylicense%20weblookup/Search.aspx

Delaware Licensing Quick Finder

Adult Entertainment #11 302-744-4500
Aesthetician #11 302-744-4500
Alarm Firm/Employee #3 302-739-5991
Alcoholic Bev. Establishment #1 302-577-5222
Amateur Boxing-related #11 320-744-4500
Ambulance Attendant #13 302-739-4773
Architect #11 302-744-4500
Armored Car Agency/Employee #3 302-739-5991
Athletic Agent/Trainer #11 302-744-4500
Attorney #2 302-739-4155
Attorney, 2005 New #2 302-577-7038
Audiologist #11 302-744-4500
Bail Enforcement Agent #3 302-739-5991
Barber #11 302-744-4500
Bodyworker #11 302-744-4500
Boiler Inspector #14 302-744-2735
Boxer/Boxing Professional #11 302-787-5720
Charitable Gaming Permittee #11 302-744-4500
Chiropractor #11 302-744-4500
Contractor/Worker/Supervisor #15 302-739-5644
Constable #3 302-739-5991
Contractor, General #5 302-577-8778
Cosmetologist #11 302-744-4500
Counselor, Elem./Second'y School #4 888-759-9133
Counselor, Professional #11 302-744-4500
Deadly Weapons Dealer #11 302-744-4500
Dental Assistant #16 302-744-4556
Dentist/Dental Hygienist #11 302-744-4500
Dental Radiation Technician #16 302-744-4556
Dietician/Nutritionist #11 302-744-4500
Electrical Inspector #11 302-744-4500
Electrician #11 302-744-4500
Electrologist #11 302-744-4500
Emergency Med. Tech/Paramedic #11 302-739-6637
EMT-B #13 302-739-4773
Engineer #12 302-577-6500
Engineering Firm #12 302-577-6500
Fire Company #13 302-739-4773
Funeral Director #11 302-744-4500
Gaming Control #11 302-744-4500
Geologist #11 302-744-4500
Harness Racing #6 302-698-4500
Hearing Aid Dealer/Fitter #11 302-744-4500
Horse Racing (Thorobred) #6 302-698-4500
Insurance-Related Professional/Firm#8 302-739-4254
Landscape Architect #11 302-744-4500
Library/Media Specialist #4 888-759-9133
Liquid Waste Hauler #17 302-739-9950
Lobbyist #9 302-739-2399
Massage #11 302-744-4500
Medical Doctor/Surgeon #11 302-744-4500
Medical Practice #11 302-744-4500
Mental Health Counselor #11 302-744-4500
Midwife Nurse #11 302-744-4500
Nail Technician #11 302-744-4500
Notary Public #9 302-739-3073
Nuclear Medicine Technologist #16 302-744-4556
Nurse #11 302-744-4500
Nursing Home Administrator #11 302-744-4500
Nutritionist #11 302-744-4500
Occupational Therapist/Assistant #11 302-744-4500
Optometrist #11 302-744-4500
Osteopathic Physician #11 302-744-4500
Pesticide Appl/DealerFirm/Course #10 302-698-4570
Pesticide, Registered #10 302-698-4570
Pharmacist #11 302-744-4500
Pharmacy/Pharmacy-related Firm #11 320-744-4500
Physical Therapist/Assistant #11 302-744-4500
Physician Assistant #11 302-744-4500
Pilot, River #11 302-744-4500
Plumber #11 302-744-4500
Podiatrist #11 302-744-4500
PI Agency/Employee #3 302-739-5991
Private Security Agency/Employee #3 302-739-5991
Professional Services Firm #15 302-739-5644
Project Monitor (Construction) #15 302-739-5644
Psychological Assistant #11 302-744-4500
Psychologist #11 302-744-4500
Public Accountant-CPA #11 302-744-4500
Radiation Therapist/Technician #16 302-744-4556
Radiologic Technologist #16 302-744-4556
Real Estate Agent/Broker #11 302-744-4500
Real Estate Appraiser #11 302-744-4500
Rental Car Insurer #8 302-739-4254
Respiratory Care Practitioner #11 302-744-4500
School-related Profession #4 888-759-9133
Securities Agent #8 302-739-4254
Social Worker #11 302-744-4530
Speech Pathologist/Audiologist #11 302-744-4500
Surplus Lines Broker #8 302-739-4254
Surveyor, Land #11 302-744-4500
Teacher #4 888-759-9133
Veterinarian #11 302-744-4500
Waste Water Operator #17 302-739-9950
Water Supply Operator #7 302-741-8630
X-ray Technician #7 302-744-4546

Delaware Licensing Agency Information

#1 Alcoholic Beverage Control Division, 820 N French St, 3rd Fl, Carvel State Office Bldg, Wilmington, DE 19801; 302-577-5222, Fax- 302-577-3204. http://date.delaware.gov/dabcpublic/index.jsp

#2 Board of Bar Examiners, 820 N French St. 11th Fl, Carvel State Office Bldg, Wilmington, DE 19801-3545; 302-577-7038, Fax- 302-577-7037. http://courts.delaware.gov/bbe/

#3 State Police, State Bureau of Identification, Detective Licensing, PO Box 430, Dover, DE 19903; 302-739-5991, Fax- 302-739-5888. Hours- 8AM-4PM. http://dsp.delaware.gov/

#4 Department of Education, Certification Division, 401 Federal St, #2, Dover, DE 19903; 888-759-9133, 302-739-4120, Fax- 302-739-3092. Hours- 8AM-4:30PM. https://deeds.doe.k12.de.us/default.aspx Search data at- https://deeds.doe.k12.de.us/public/deeds_pc_findeducator.aspx

#5 Division of Revenue, 820 N French St, Carvel State Office Bldg, Wilmington, DE 19801; 302-577-8200, Fax- 302-577-8202. http://revenue.delaware.gov/

#6 Harness Racing Commission, 2320 S DuPont Hwy, Dover, DE 19901; 302-698-4500, Fax- 302-697-4748. http://dda.delaware.gov/harness/index.shtml

#7 Health & Social Services Department, Division of Public Health, PO Box 637 (Federal & Water Sts), Dover, DE 19903; 302-744-4701, Fax- 302-739-6659. Hours- 8AM-4:30PM. www.dhss.delaware.gov/dhss/dph/

#8 Insurance Department, Producer Licensing, 841 Silver Lake Blvd, Dover, DE 19904; 302-674-7390, Fax- 302-739-5280. www.delawareinsurance.gov/departments/licensing/licensing.shtml Search at- https://sbs-de.naic.org/Lion-eb/jsp/sbsreports/AgentLookup.jsp

#9 Notary Division, Office of Secretary of State, 401 Federal St, #3, Dover, DE 19901; 302-739-4111, Fax- 302-739-3812. http://sos.delaware.gov/nphome.shtml

#10 Dept. of Agriculture, Pesticide Section, 2320 S DuPont Hwy, Dover, DE 19901; 302-698-4571, Fax- 302-697-4483. 8AM-4:30PM. http://dda.delaware.gov/pesticides/index.shtml

#11 Division of Professional Regulations, Department of Admin. Svcs., 861 Silver Lake Blvd, Cannon Bldg #203, Dover, DE 19904; 302-739-4500, Fax- 302-739-2711. http://dpr.delaware.gov Search data at- https://dpronline.delaware.gov/mylicense%20weblookup/Search.aspx

#12 Assoc. of Professional Engineers, Engineering Licensing Board, 56 W Main St, #208, Plaza 273, Christiana, DE 19702-1500; 302-368-6708, Fax- 302-368-6710. https://www.dape.org/index.asp? Search data at- www.dape.org/App/peRoster.asp Searchable rosters link is on left hand margin of web page.

#13 Fire Prevention Commission, 1463 Chestnut Grove Rd, Dover, DE 19904; 302-739-3160, Fax- 302-739-4436. http://statefirecommission.delaware.gov

#14 Department of Public Safety, Division of Boiler Safety, 303 Transportation Cir, Dover, DE 19901; 302-744-2735, Fax- 302-739-2526. www.dnrec.delaware.gov/BoilerSafety/Pages/Default.aspx

#15 Division of Facilities Mgmt, 540 S DuPont Hwy, Thomas Collins Building, #1, Dover, DE 19901; 302-739-5644, Fax- 302-739-3037/6148. Hours- 8AM-4:30PM. http://dfm.delaware.gov

#16 Division of Public Health, Office of Radiation Control, 417 Federal St, Dover, DE 19901; 302-744-4556, Fax- 302-739-3839. Hours- 8AM-4:30PM. http://dhss.delaware.gov/dhss/dph/hsp/orc.html

#17 Department of Natural Resources & Environmental Control, Division of Water Resources, 89 Kings Hwy, Dover, DE 19901; 302-739-9950, Fax- 302-739-8369. Hours- 8AM-4:30PM. www.dnrec.state.de.us/water2000/

Delaware Federal Courts

The following list indicates the district and division name for each county in the state.

County/Court Cross Reference

Kent	Wilmington
New Castle	Wilmington
Sussex	Wilmington

US District Court District of Delaware

Wilmington Division Court Clerk, US Courthouse, 844 N King St, Lock Box 18, Wilmington, DE 19801 (In person: US Courthouse, Clerk's Office, 844 N King St, 4th Fl, Rm 4209, Wilmington, DE 19801), 302-573-6170; records- 302-573-6158. Hours- 8:30AM-4:30PM. www.ded.uscourts.gov

Counties/Note: All counties in Delaware.

Searches/Indexing: Include full name, years to search, type (party, judgment, or all). Results do not include SSN or DOB. Will not fax back documents. New cases are in the index 1 day after filing date. Closed cases not sent to the archives for a minimum of 6 months.

Search Access: Via phone, this court will search civil cases back to 1991 and criminal cases back to 1993; will only say if a case was found and a case number. **Mail:** Search usually completed- 2-3 days. Search can include all computer, microfiche and judgment indexes. SASE not required. **In person:** 2 public terminals available. No self-serve copier. For civil court document copies - court can recommend an outside vendor to so searches and copies.

Payment: Pay by money order, cashier's or personal check. No credit cards accepted. Payee: Clerk, US District Court.

E-Services: PACER records go back to 1/1991 (civil) and 1/1993 (crim). New records online after 1 day. ECF at https://ecf.ded.uscourts.gov. CM/ECF dockets and documents available on PACER. **Opinions Online:** www.ded.uscourts.gov/CLKmain.htm. Opinions are for last 30 days only. Search recent Standing Orders at www.ded.uscourts.gov/StandingOrdersMain.htm. **Online Note:** Search the Judgment Index 1980 through 1/31/2005 free at www.ded.uscourts.gov/JdgmtCards/judgsearch.asp Search the Party Index 1982 through 1990 free at www.ded.uscourts.gov/JdgmtCards/partysearch.asp.

US Bankruptcy Court District of Delaware

Wilmington Division Court Clerk, 824 N Market St, 3rd Fl, Wilmington, DE 19801, 888-667-5530, 302-252-2900; records- 302-252-2887-helpdesk. 8AM-4PM. www.deb.uscourts.gov

Counties/Note: All counties in Delaware.

Searches/Indexing: Search request requires name, SSN helpful. Results include last 4 SSN digits. Will not fax back documents. New cases are in the index 1 day after filing date. All records on computer back to 2001 for images; back to 1990s for index. Case files sent to archives when court has collected 150 records boxes.

Search Access: Via telephone, this court will only confirm case exists and releases case number. Voice Case Information Service available, call VCIS at 302-252-2560. **Mail:** Search usually completed- 1-2 days. Include SASE for return. **In person:** 8-9 public terminals available. Computer generated copies $.10 each. An in-house private copy service available.

Payment: Pay by money order, cashier's or personal check. Payee: Clerk, US Bankruptcy Court.

E-Services: PACER records go back to 1991. New records online after 1 day. ECF at https://ecf.deb.uscourts.gov. **Opinions Online:** www.deb.uscourts.gov/Opinions/opinions_cover.htm. **Online Note:** Chapter 11 filing monthly lists are free at www.deb.uscourts.gov/Chapter11/chapter11_filings.htm.

Standards for Federal Courts: Fees are standard unless noted in profile. Search fee is $26.00 per item (one party name or case number). Copy fee is $.50 per page. Certification fee is $9.00 per document, double for exemplification, if available. Most courts require prepayment. Mail requests should enclose a SASE unless otherwise noted. Before releasing records, all courts require prepayment, unless noted.

District courts index by defendant and plaintiff and by case number. Bankruptcy courts usually index by debtor and case number. While most courts now have their indexes on computer, many may still maintain index card files as well. Courts will archive closed case files at different times.

There are numerous public access programs available to online subscribers. Search the U.S. Party/Case Index to find party names and case numbers among all courts. Individual case data is provided on PACER. A search of CM/ECF provides copies of cases filed electronically. For details about PACER, the US Party/Case Index, and CM/ECF see the Appendix or go to http://pacer.psc.uscourts.gov or call 800-676-6856.

Delaware County Courts

Court	Jurisdiction	No. of Courts	How Organized
Superior Courts*	General	3	
Chancery Courts*	General	3	
Court of Common Pleas*	Limited	3	
Justice of the Peace Courts*	Municipal	17	
Alderman's Courts	Municipal	7	
Family Courts	Special	3	

* Profiled in this Sourcebook.

Court	CIVIL								
	Tort	Contract	Real Estate	Min. Claim	Max. Claim	Small Claims	Estate	Eviction	Domestic Relations
Superior Courts*	X	X	X	$50,000	No Max				
Chancery Courts*	X	X	X	$0	No Max		X		
Court of Common Pleas*	X	X	X	$0	$5,000				
Justice of the Peace Courts*			X	$0	$15,000	same		X	
Alderman's Courts									
Family Courts									X

Court	CRIMINAL				
	Felony	Misdemeanor	DWI/DUI	Preliminary Hearing	Juvenile
Superior Courts*	X	X			
Chancery Courts*					
Court of Common Pleas*		X		X	
Justice of the Peace Courts*		X	X		
Alderman's Courts		X	X		
Family Courts		X			X

Administration

Administrative Office of the Courts, Supreme Court of Delaware, 500 N King St, #11600, Wilmington, DE, 19801; 302-255-0090, Fax: 302-255-2217. 8:30AM-5PM. (EST). http://courts.delaware.gov

Court Structure

The Superior Court has original jurisdiction over criminal and civil cases except equity cases.The Superior Court has exclusive jurisdiction over felonies and almost all drug offenses. The Court of Common Pleas has jurisdiction in civil cases where the amount in controversy, exclusive of interest, does not exceed $50,000. In criminal cases, the Court of Common Pleas handles all misdemeanors occurring in the state except certain drug-related offenses and traffic offenses. Appeals may be taken to the Superior Court. The Court of Chancery has jurisdiction to hear all matters relating to equity – litigation in this tribunal deals largely with corporate issues, trusts, estates, other fiduciary matters, disputes involving the purchase of land, and questions of title to real estate as well as commercial and contractual matters. The Justice of the Peace Court has jurisdiction over civil cases in which the disputed amount is less than $15,000. In criminal cases, the Justice of the Peace Court hears certain misdemeanors and most motor vehicle cases (excluding felonies) and the Justices of the Peace may act as committing magistrates for all crimes. Alderman's Courts handle traffic matters.

Online Access

Chancery, Superior, Common Pleas, and Supreme Courts opinions and orders are available free online at http://courts.state.de.us/opinions. Supreme, Superior, and Common Pleas Courts calendars are available free at http://courts.delaware.gov/calendars. Chancery Courts and Supreme Courts filings are available from a vendor at www.virtualdocket.com. Registration and fees required.

Searching Tips, Fees, and Other Guidelines

Search fees and copy fees vary widely. A fee schedule provides limits on fees rather than specific fees.

Kent County

Superior Court Office of Prothonotary, 38 The Green, Dover, DE 19901; 302-739-3184; criminal: x6; civil: x7; fax: 302-739-6717; 8AM-4:30PM. ***Felony, Misdemeanor, Civil Actions over $50,000.*** http://courts.delaware.gov/Courts/Superior%20Court/ Court refers records request to State Agency-302-739-5961.
Civil Records: Access: In person only. Visitors must perform in person searches themselves. Required to search: name, years to search. Civil cases indexed by defendant, plaintiff. Judgments on computer from 1996, on books from 1918. Civil PAT goes back to 7/1996. PAT results show name only.
Criminal Records: Access: In person only. Both court and visitors may perform in person searches. No search fee, but $25.00 search fee for retrieval of closed cases. Required to search: name, years to search, DOB. Judgments on computer from 1996, on microfiche from 1918. Note: Contact Dept of Records for search assistance. Criminal PAT goes back to 1987. PAT results show middle initial, DOB.
General Information: No sealed or psychological evaluation records released. Will not fax documents. Court makes copy: $1.50 per page; same for copies off the computer, self serve same. Certification fee: $6.00 fee for 3 pages; add copy fee for add'l pages. Exemplification fee- $10.00. Payee: Prothonotary. Personal checks and major credit cards accepted. Prepayment required.

Chancery Court 38 The Green, Dover, DE 19901; 302-736-2242; probate phone: 302-744-2330; fax: 302-736-2240; 8AM-4:30PM. ***Civil, Probate.*** http://courts.delaware.gov/Courts/Court%20of%20Chancery/ This is an equity court only.
Civil Records: Access: In person, online. Visitors must perform in person searches themselves. Required to search: name, years to search. Civil cases indexed by defendant, plaintiff; index on docket books. The Court of Chancery oversees corporate and equity matters and guardianship. The Register of Wills oversees estate, and. Public use terminal has civil records back to 1999. PAT results show name only. Access to civil records online is available by subscription through LexisNexis efiling company.
General Information: No juvenile, sealed or mental health records released. Fee to fax out file $10.00 1st page, $2.00 each add'l. Court makes copy: $1.50 per page. Certification fee: $25.00 per doc. Payee: Register in Chancery (Register of Wills for Probate). Personal checks accepted; credit cards are not. Prepayment required.

Court of Common Pleas 38 The Green, Dover, DE 19901; 302-739-4618; criminal: x3; civil: x4; criminal fax: 302-739-4501; civil fax: 302-739-8100; 8AM-4:30PM. ***Misdemeanor, Civil Actions under $50,000.*** http://courts.delaware.gov/Courts/Court%20of%20Common%20Pleas/ Superior Court has most records.
Civil Records: Access: In person only. Visitors must perform in person searches themselves. Required to search: name, years to search. Civil cases indexed by defendant, plaintiff, on computer from 1992, on microfiche from 10/85, archived prior. Civil PAT goes back to 1992. PAT results show name only.
Criminal Records: Access: In person. Visitors must perform in person searches themselves. Required to search: name, years to search, DOB, offense, date of offense. Criminal records computerized from 1980, on microfiche from 10/85, archived prior. Criminal PAT goes back to 1980. PAT results show name only. **General Information:** No sealed records released. Will fax documents to local or toll free line. Court makes copy: $1.00 per page for docket copy. Certification fee: $10.00. Payee: Court of Common Pleas. No personal checks or credit cards accepted. Prepayment required.

Dover Justice of the Peace #16 480 Bank Ln, Dover, DE 19904; 302-739-4316; fax: 302-739-6797; 8AM-4PM. ***Civil Actions under $15,000, Eviction, Small Claims.*** http://courts.delaware.gov/jpcourt
Civil Records: Access: Mail, in person. Only the court performs in person searches; visitors may not. No search fee. Required to search: name, years to search. Civil cases indexed by defendant, plaintiff, computerized since 10/98. Mail turnaround time varies. **General Information:** Will not fax documents. Court makes copy: $.25 per page. Certification fee: $10.00 per doc. Payee: JCP Court 16. Personal checks and major credit cards accepted. Prepayment required. Mail: SASE requested for civil.

Dover Justice of the Peace #7 480 Bank Ln, Dover, DE 19903; 302-739-4554; fax: 302-739-6797; Open 24 hours. ***Misdemeanor.*** http://courts.delaware.gov/jpcourt
Search requests must include charge/or/disposition; name searches without charge are referred to the State Bureau of Investigation.
Criminal Records: Access: Mail, fax, in person. Only the court performs in person searches; visitors may not. Search fee: $7.00 per charge. Fee includes copy certification. Required to search: name, charge info, DOB, signed release, offense, date of offense; also helpful: address. Record computerized since 1992, manually searched 1967-1992.
General Information: Will not fax documents. Court makes copy: $.25 per page. Certification fee: $7.00 per charge. Payee: State of Delaware. Personal checks and major credit cards accepted. Prepayment required.

Harrington Justice of the Peace #6 35 Cams Fortune Way, Harrington, DE 19952; 302-422-5922; fax: 302-422-1527; 8-4PM. ***Misdemeanor.*** http://courts.delaware.gov/jpcourt
Also holds records for JP #5 which has been closed.
Criminal Records: Access: In person only. Only the court performs in person searches; visitors may not. No search fee. Required to search: name, years to search, DOB. Criminal records go back to 2004. Note: Court form required for all searches.
General Information: Will fax out documents no fee. Court makes copy: $1.00 per page. Certification fee: $7.00 per doc includes copies. Payee: State of Delaware. Visa/MCDiscover accepted. Prepayment required.

Smyrna Justice of the Peace #8 100 Monrovia Ave, Smyrna, DE 19977; 302-653-7083; fax: 302-653-2888; 8AM-4PM. ***Misdemeanor.*** http://courts.delaware.gov/jpcourt
Criminal Records: Access: Mail, in person. Only the court performs in person searches; visitors may not. No search fee. Required to search: name, years to search; also helpful: DOB. Criminal records go back to 1992. Note: Search requests must be on court's form. Mail turnaround time is 1 week.
General Information: Will fax documents to local or toll-free number. Court makes copy: $.30 per page. Certification fee: $7.00 per doc includes copies. Payee: State of Delaware. Personal checks accepted. Visa/MC accepted. Prepayment required.

New Castle County

Superior Court Office of the Prothonotary, 500 N King St, #500, Wilmington, DE 19801; 302-255-0800; fax: 302-255-2264; 8:30AM-5PM. ***Felony, Misdemeanor, Civil Actions over $50,000.*** http://courts.delaware.gov/Courts/Superior%20Court/
Civil Records: Access: In person only. Visitors must perform in person searches themselves. Required to search: name, years to search. Civil cases indexed by defendant, plaintiff, on computer from 1991, prior in docket books or on microfiche. Civil PAT goes back to 1991. PAT results show name only. Results include case number.
Criminal Records: Access: In person only. Visitors must perform in person searches themselves. Required to search: name, DOB, years to search. Criminal records computerized from 4/80, prior on microfiche. Criminal PAT goes back to 1980. PAT results show middle initial, DOB, SSN.
General Information: No psychological evaluation, sealed records released. Will fax documents $6.00 for 1st 3 pages, $1.00 each add'l page. Court makes copy: $1.50 per page. Certification fee: $6.00 for 1st 3 pages; $1.50 each add'l. Exemplification fee- $10.00 for 1st pages; $1.50 each add'l. Payee: Prothonotary's Office. Personal checks accepted; credit cards are not. Prepayment required.

Chancery Court 500 N King St, #1551, Attn: Register in Chancery, Wilmington, DE 19801; 302-255-0544; probate phone: 302-395-7800; fax: 302-255-2213; 8:30AM-5PM. ***Civil, Probate.*** http://courts.delaware.gov/Courts/Court%20of%20Chancery/
Probate records in a separate index in separate office. Probate fax- 302-395-7801.
Civil Records: Access: Phone, fax, mail, in person. Both court and visitors may perform in person searches. No search fee. Required to search: name; also helpful: years to search. Civil cases indexed by defendant, plaintiff, indexed on computer since 1963, in books prior to 1963. The civil records for the Court of Chancery deal with corporate and equity matte. Mail turnaround time 2 days. Public terminal has civil records back to 1963. PAT shows name only.
General Information: No guardianship records released. Will fax documents $10.00 1st page, $2.00 each add'l. Court makes copy: $1.50 per page. $2.00 if from microfilm, self serve same. Certification fee: $25.00. Payee: Register in Chancery (Register of Wills for Probate). Personal checks accepted; credit cards are not. Prepayment required. Will bill fax requests. SASE not required.

Court of Common Pleas 500 N King St, Wilmington, DE 19801-3704; 302-255-0900; criminal phone: x3; civil phone: x4; criminal fax: 302-255-2244; civil fax: 302-255-2245; 8:30AM-4:30PM. ***Misdemeanor, Civil Actions under $50,000.*** http://courts.delaware.gov/Courts/Court%20of%20Common%20Pleas/
Civil Records: Access: Phone, fax, mail, in person. Both court and visitors may perform in person searches. No search fee. Required to search: name, years to search. Civil cases indexed by defendant, plaintiff, on computer from 1989; prior records on docket books. Mail turnaround time up to 3 weeks. Civil PAT goes back to 1974.
Criminal Records: Access: In person only. Both court and visitors may perform in person searches. No search fee. Required to search: name, charge year of offense; also helpful: DOB. Criminal records computerized from 1993; prior records on docket books. Note: Court does not do name searches; you must know the charge or arrest date for court response. Criminal PAT goes back same as civil.
General Information: No closed records released. Will fax documents $1.00 per page. Court makes copy: $1.00 per page. Certification fee: $10.00. Payee: Court of Common Pleas. No personal checks accepted. Prepayment required. Mail requests: SASE required for civil.

Middletown Justice of the Peace #9 757 N Broad St, Middletown, DE 19709; 302-378-5221; fax: 302-378-5220; 8AM-4PM M,T,TH,F, N-8PM W. ***Civil Actions under $15,000, Misdemeanor, Eviction, Small Claims.*** http://courts.delaware.gov/jpcourt
Due to a court fire, criminal cases 7/24/2000 to 5/1/2001 are heard at New Castle JP Court 11, 323-4450. Civil cases were heard at Prices Corner JP Court 12, 995-8646. Now, all new cases are back here at Middletown.
Civil Records: Access: In person only. Both court and visitors may perform in person searches. No search fee. Required to search: name, years to search. Civil cases indexed by defendant. Due to fire, records on computer only back to mid-1990s. Note: The Court said they will not do name searches, but will search if a civil action # is presented.
Criminal Records: Access: In person only. Both court and visitors may perform in person searches. No search fee. Required to search: name, years to search, DOB. Due to fire, records on computer only back to mid-1990s. Note: This office prefers that you search through the state agency, but they did not say they would refuse all search requests.
General Information: Will fax documents to local or toll-free number. Court makes copy: $.25 per page. Certification fee: $10.00 per Civil doc includes copies; $7.00 per criminal doc. Payee: State of Delaware. Cashiers checks, money orders and major credit cards accepted. Prepayment required.

New Castle Justice of the Peace #11 61 Christiana Rd, New Castle, DE 19720; 302-323-4450; fax: 302-323-4452; Open 24 hours. ***Misdemeanor.*** http://courts.delaware.gov/jpcourt
Criminal Records: Access: In person only. Visitors must perform in person searches themselves. Required to search: name, years to search. Records indexed on computer to 1966, older records hand written in log book.
General Information: Court makes copy: $.25 per page. Certification fee: $10.00 per doc. Cert fee includes copies. Payee: State of Delaware. Cashiers checks and money orders and credit cards accepted.

Prices Corner Justice of the Peace #10 210 Greenbank Rd, Wilmington, DE 19808; 302-995-8640; fax: 302-995-8642; 8AM-10PM. ***Misdemeanor Traffic.*** http://courts.delaware.gov/jpcourt Court refers records request to State Agency-302-739-5961.

Prices Corner Justice of the Peace #12 - Prices Corner, Greenbank Rd, DE 19808; ***Civil Actions under $15,000, Eviction, Small Claims.*** This court and records is now located at Justice of the Peace Court #13.

Wilmington Justice of the Peace #13 1010 Concord Ave, Concord Professional Ctr, Wilmington, DE 19802; 302-577-2550; fax: 302-577-2526; 8AM-4PM. ***Civil Actions under $15,000, Eviction, Small Claims.***
http://courts.delaware.gov/jpcourt
Justice of the Peace Court #12 is now located here.
Civil Records: Access: In person only. Visitors must perform in person searches themselves. Required to search: name, years to search. Civil cases indexed by defendant, plaintiff, are computerized since 9/01/99. Note: The court will pull specific case data if CA# given, if and when time permitting.
General Information: No sealed, juvenile, adoption or mental health records released. Will fax documents to local or toll-free number. Court makes copy: $.25 per page. Certification fee: $10.00 per case includes copies. Payee: Justice of the Peace Court #13. Personal checks and major credit cards accepted. Prepayment required.

Wilmington Justice of the Peace #15 130 Hickman Rd, #13, Claymont, DE 19703; 302-798-5327; fax: 302-798-4508; 8-4PM. ***Misdemeanor.***
http://courts.delaware.gov/jpcourt
Criminal Records: Access: Mail, in person. Only the court performs in person searches; visitors may not. Search fee: $7.00 per name. Required to search: name, years to search, DOB; also helpful: offense. Mail turnaround time 2-4 weeks.
General Information: Will fax back documents; a fee may be charged for certain case types. Court makes copy: $.25 per page. Certification fee: $7.00 per case. Payee: State of Delaware. Personal checks and major credit cards accepted. Prepayment required. Mail requests: SASE helpful.

Wilmington Justice of the Peace #20 Public Safety Bldg, 300 N Walnut St, Wilmington, DE 19801; 302-577-7234; fax: 302-577-7237; open 24 hours. ***Misdemeanor.***
http://courts.delaware.gov/jpcourt
This court now also maintains the case records from the former JP Court #18. Records department phone is 302-255-0000. Search requests may also be directed to Dover - 800-464-4557 for information.
Criminal Records: Access: In person only. Visitors must perform in person searches themselves. Required to search: name, years to search.
General Information: Will not fax documents. Court makes copy: $7.00 per disposition. Certification fee: Copies include certification. Payee: Justice of the Peace Court #13. Cashiers checks and money orders and major credit cards accepted. Prepayment required.

Sussex County

Superior Court 1 The Circle #2, Georgetown, DE 19947; criminal phone: 302-856-5741; civil phone: 302-856-5742; fax: 302-856-5739; 8:30AM-4:30PM. ***Felony, Misdemeanor, Civil Actions.***
http://courts.delaware.gov/Courts/Superior%20Court/
Civil Records: Access: In person only. Visitors must perform in person searches themselves. Required to search: name, years to search. Civil cases indexed by defendant, plaintiff, on computer from 6/91 or as far back as 1980 if case was pending in 1991; microfiche prior. Civil PAT goes back to 1980s. PAT civil results show middle initial.
Criminal Records: Access: In person only. Visitors must perform in person searches themselves. Required to search: name, years to search, DOB. Criminal records on manual index; computerized records since 1983. Criminal PAT goes back to 1983. PAT criminal results show middle initial.
General Information: No divorce, victim info, sealed records, expungments, or CCDW permit records released. Will not fax documents. Court makes copy: $.50 per page, self serve same. Certification fee: $6.00 plus $1.00 per page after 1st three. Payee: Prothonotary. Personal checks accepted; credit cards are not. Prepayment required.

Chancery Court Register in Chancery, 34 The Circle, Georgetown, DE 19947; 302-856-5775; probate phone: 302-855-7875; fax: 302-856-5778; 8:30AM-4:30PM. ***Civil, Probate*** .http://courts.delaware.gov/Courts/Court%20of%20Chancery/ Fees charged by Register of Wills for Probate are separate.
Civil Records: Access: Phone, mail, in person, online. Both court and visitors may perform in person searches. No search fee. Required to search: name, years to search. Civil cases indexed by defendant, plaintiff; index on docket books; on computer back to 1999. Mail turnaround time 1-3 days. Public use terminal has civil records back to 1999. PAT civil results show middle initial. Access to civil records online is available by subscription through LexisNexis efiling company.
General Information: All records public. Will fax documents $10.00 plus $2.00 each add'l page. Court makes copy: $1.50 per page, self serve same. Certification fee: $25.00 per cert. Exemplifications fee- $50.00 per doc. Payee: Register in Chancery (or Register of Wills for Probate). Personal checks accepted; credit cards are not. Prepayment required. Mail requests: SASE required.

Court of Common Pleas 1 The Circle #1, Georgetown, DE 19947; 302-856-5333; fax: 302-856-5056; 8:30AM-4:30PM. ***Misdemeanor, Civil Actions under $50,000.*** http://courts.delaware.gov/Courts/Court%20of%20Common%20Pleas/
Fees for archive or closed file retrieval is $25.00.
Civil Records: Access: Phone, fax, mail, in person. Both court and visitors may perform in person searches. No search fee. Required to search: name, years to search. Civil cases indexed by defendant. Civil records on computer from 1993, on microfiche from 9/53, archived prior. Mail turnaround time 1-2 weeks. Civil PAT goes back to 1993.
Criminal Records: Access: Phone, fax, mail, in person. Both court and visitors may perform in person searches. No search fee. Required to search: name, years to search, DOB, offense, date of offense. Criminal records computerized from 1994, on microfiche from 10/65, archived prior. Mail turnaround time 1-2 weeks. Criminal PAT goes back to 1994. Criminal PAT results include name and case number only.
General Information: No closed case records released. No fee to fax documents. Court makes copy: $5.00 (maximum per page). Certification fee: $10.00. Payee: Court of Common Pleas. Personal checks accepted. Visa/MC, Discover accepted. Prepayment required. Mail requests: SASE required.

Georgetown Justice of the Peace #17 23730 Shortly Rd, Georgetown, DE 19947; 302-856-1447; fax: 302-856-4654; 8AM-4PM. ***Civil Actions under $15,000, Eviction, Small Claims.***
http://courts.delaware.gov/jpcourt
See also Court 19 in Seaford.
Civil Records: Access: Mail, in person. Only the court performs in person searches; visitors may not. No search fee. Required to search: name, years to search, parties in case. Civil cases indexed by defendant, plaintiff; index on docket books from 1966 to present. Mail turnaround time 1-2 days. PAT results show name only. **General Information:** Will fax documents to local or toll-free number. Court makes copy: $.25 per page. Certification fee: $10.00. Payee: State of Delaware. Personal checks accepted; credit cards are not. Prepayment required. Mail requests: SASE requested.

Georgetown Justice of the Peace #3 23730 Shortly Rd, Georgetown, DE 19947; 302-856-1445; fax: 302-856-5844; 24 hours daily. ***Misdemeanor.*** http://courts.delaware.gov/jpcourt
In 2008, the actual court proceedings will be in Seaford due to construction in the Georgetown court. However, all contact information for Georgetown remains the same. **Criminal Records:** Access: Mail, in person. Only the court performs in person searches; visitors may not. Search fee: $7.00 per case. Search fee includes certification. Required to search: name, years to search, DOB; also helpful: SSN. Records are here from 2001 to present. On microfilm 1966-1983. From 1984-2000 records archived. Mail turnaround time 3-10 days.
General Information: Will fax documents to local or toll-free number. Court makes copy: $.25 per page. Certification fee: $7.00 per case. Payee: State of Delaware. Personal checks accepted. Debit cards accepted in person only. Visa/MC, Discover accepted. Prepayment required. Mail requests: SASE requested.

Justice of the Peace #1 9 Main St, Frankford, DE 19945; 302-732-9580; fax: 302-732-9586; 8AM-4PM. ***Misdemeanor.*** http://courts.state.de.us/Courts/Justice%20of%20the%20Peace%20Court/
This court also handles traffic.
Criminal Records: Access: Mail, in person. Only the court performs in person searches; visitors may not. No search fee. Required to search: name, years to search, DOB. Records available from 1983, computerized since '90. Mail turnaround same day.
General Information: Will fax documents to local or toll-free number only if an emergency situation. Court makes copy: $.25 per page. Certification fee: $7.00 per case. Payee: State of Delaware. Personal checks accepted. Credit cards accepted. Prepayment required. Personal and business checks accepted.

Rehoboth Beach Justice of the Peace #2 35252 Hudson Way, #1, Rehoboth Beach, DE 19971-9738; 302-645-6163; fax: 302-645-8842; 8AM-Midnight. ***Misdemeanor, Traffic.***
http://courts.delaware.gov/jpcourt
Criminal Records: Access: Mail, in person. Both court and visitors may perform in person searches. No search fee. Required to search: name, years to search, DOB. Records available since 1990, computerized since 1992. Mail turnaround 3 weeks.
General Information: Will fax documents to local or toll-free number. Court makes copy: $1.00 per page. Certification fee: $7.00. Payee: State of Delaware. Personal checks and major credit cards accepted. Prepayment required. Mail requests: SASE required.

Seaford Justice of the Peace #19 408 Stein Hwy, Seaford, DE 19973; 302-629-5433; fax: 302-628-6517; 8AM-4PM. ***Civil Actions under $15,000, Eviction, Small Claims.***
http://courts.delaware.gov/jpcourt
Civil Records: Access: In person, mail. Only the court performs in person searches; visitors may not. Search fee: $.25 per page. Required to search: name, years to search; case number helpful. Civil cases indexed by defendant, plaintiff, in docket books since 1985; computerized records since 9/98. Note: In person access requires identification. Mail turnaround time 5 days. **General Information:** Will fax documents to local or toll-free number. Court makes copy: $.25 per page. Certification fee: $10.00. Payee: State of Delaware. Personal checks accepted. Visa/MC accepted. Prepayment required.

Seaford Justice of the Peace #4 408 Stein Hwy, Seaford, DE 19973; 302-323-4531; 8AM - Midnight. ***Misdemeanor.***
http://courts.delaware.gov/jpcourt Court refers records request to State Agency-302-739-5961.
Criminal Records: Access: In person only. Visitors must perform in person searches themselves. Required to search: name, years to search. Criminal records go back to 2000. **General Information:** Will not fax documents. Court makes copy: $.25 per page. Certification fee: $7.00 per cert. Payee: JP Court 4. Prepayment required.

Delaware Recording Offices

ORGANIZATION: Delaware has 3 counties and 3 recording offices. The recording officer is the County Recorder. Delaware is in the Eastern Time Zone (EST).

REAL ESTATE RECORDS: Counties do not perform real estate searches but will provide copies. If the office makes your copies, expect to pay at least $1.00 per page. Certification fee usually $5.00 per document.

UCC RECORDS: Financing statements are filed at the state level - Secretary of State, UCC Division - except for real estate related collateral which are filed only with the County Recorder. All counties perform UCC searches. Copy fees vary. Each of the 3 Delaware counties handle UCC search fees differently.

TAX LIEN RECORDS: Federal tax liens on personal property of businesses are filed with the Secretary of State. Other federal and all state tax liens on personal property are filed with the County Recorder.

ONLINE ACCESS: There is no statewide online system for county recorded documents.

Kent County

County Recorder of Deeds, 555 Bay Rd, Rm 160; County Complex, Dover, DE 19901. 302-744-2314; fax-302-736-2035; 8AM-5PM www.co.kent.de.us/Departments/RowOffices/Recorder/index.htm

Index: Separate indices to search include Real property, financial statements. Records indexed on a public use terminal back to 1873. Office will perform a UCC search but public must search other records themselves. No fee for search. Copy fee $1.00 per page. Cert fee- $5.00 per page includes copy fee. Payee- Kent County Recorder of Deeds. **Online access to Property, Land Record records:** Land/Deed Record Data available by subscription at https://de.uslandrecords.com/delr/DelrApp/index.jsp; fee is $10.00 per 30 days. **Other phones:** Treasurer- 302-744-2341; Prothonotary- 302-739-5328. **Property tax/Assessing**- 555 Bay Rd, Dover, DE 19901; 302-744-2401 or 744-1915, assessor fax- 302-736-2271. www.co.kent.de.us/Departments/Finance/assessment.htm **Online access**- Access Kent county property data free at http://400.co.kent.de.us/PropInfo/PIName.HTM. Also locate parcels on the GIS-mapping site free at http://66.173.241.168/kent_co/ but no name searching and you must chose a 'hundred.'

New Castle County

County Recorder of Deeds, 800 French St, 4th Fl, Wilmington, DE 19801. Recording, R/E & UCC phone-302-395-7700; fax-302-395-7712; 9AM-4:45PM www.ncc-deeds.com/recclkshr/default.asp

Index: Separate indices to search include deed, mortgage, assignments, fed liens, UCCs, satisfactions. Records indexed on computer back to 1945. Office will perform a UCC search but public must search other records themselves. UCC search per debtor name- $16.00. Copy fee $1.00 per page if mailed; $.50 for print-out. Cert fee- $2.00 per page; $5.00 if pages supplied by office, plus copy fee. Payee- New Castle County Recorder of Deeds. Bulk data available for purchase of recorded dockets for a monthly subscription for $100.00. **Online access to Real Estate, Deed, Marriage, Corporation records:** Access to the Recorder of Deeds database is free at www.ncc-deeds.com/recclkshr/. **Other phones:** Treasurer- 302-395-5177; Elections- 302-577-3464; Prothonotary- 302-255-0800. **Property tax/Assessing**- Receiver of Taxes, 87 Reads Way, New Castle, DE 19720; 302-395-5400, assessor fax- 302-395-5544. (Appraiser/Auditor- 302-395-5400) **Online access**- County property data is found at www.nccde.org/parcelview/. No name searching.

Sussex County

County Recorder of Deeds, PO Box 827, Georgetown, DE 19947-0827. 302-855-7785; fax-302-855-7787; 8:30AM-4:30PM (EST) www.sussexcountyde.gov/dept/rod/

Index: All in one. Records indexed on a public use terminal back to 1952. Office will perform a UCC search but public must search other records themselves. Search fee $10.00 per hour plus $5.00 each add'l hour. General copy fee $2.00. Mailed real estate record copy $5.00 1st page; $.50 each add'l page. Self serve copy- $.30 per page. Will expedite document return for add'l $25.00 per instrument. Cert fee- $5.00 per cert plus copy fee. Payee- Sussex County Recorder of Deeds. **Other phones:** Treasurer- 302-855-7763; Prothontary- 302-856-5740. **Property tax/Assessing**- PO Box 589, 2 The Circle, Rms 270 & 249, Georgetown, DE 19947; 302-855-7824, assessor fax- 302-855-7828. www.sussexcountyde.gov/dept/assessment/ **Online access**- Access tax info free at www.sussexcounty.net/e-service/propertytaxes/. Search parcels on GIS-mapping site free at http://map.sussexcountyde.gov/. Search current sheriff sale list at www.sussexcountyde.gov/dept/sheriff/. Search county tax data free at www.sussexcountyde.gov/e-service/propertytaxes/index.cfm?resource=search_page

Delaware County Locator

You will usually be able to find the city name in the City/County Cross Reference below. In that case, it is a simple matter to determine the county from the cross reference. However, only the official US Postal Service city names are included in this index. There are an additional 40,000 place names that people use in their addresses. Therefore, we have also included a ZIP/City Cross Reference immediately following the City/County Cross Reference.

If you know the ZIP Code but the city name does not appear in the City/County Cross Reference index, look up the ZIP Code in the ZIP/City Cross Reference, find the city name, then look up the city name in the City/County Cross Reference. For example, you want to know the county for an address of Menands, NY 12204. There is no "Menands" in the City/County Cross Reference. The ZIP/City Cross Reference shows that ZIP Codes 12201-12288 are for the city of Albany. Looking back in the City/County Cross Reference, Albany is in Albany County.

Delaware City/County Cross Reference

BEAR New Castle
BETHANY BEACH Sussex
BETHEL Sussex
BRIDGEVILLE Sussex
CAMDEN WYOMING Kent
CHESWOLD Kent
CLAYMONT New Castle
CLAYTON (19938) Kent(89), New Castle(10)
DAGSBORO Sussex
DELAWARE CITY New Castle
DELMAR Sussex
DOVER Kent
DOVER AFB Kent
ELLENDALE Sussex
FARMINGTON Kent
FELTON Kent
FENWICK ISLAND Sussex
FRANKFORD Sussex
FREDERICA Kent
GEORGETOWN Sussex
GREENWOOD (19950) Sussex(65), Kent(34)
HARBESON Sussex
HARRINGTON Kent
HARTLY Kent
HOCKESSIN New Castle
HOUSTON Kent
KENTON Kent
KIRKWOOD New Castle
LAUREL Sussex
LEWES Sussex
LINCOLN Sussex
LITTLE CREEK Kent
MAGNOLIA Kent
MARYDEL Kent
MIDDLETOWN New Castle
MILFORD (19963) Sussex(61), Kent(38)
MILLSBORO Sussex
MILLVILLE Sussex
MILTON Sussex
MONTCHANIN New Castle
NASSAU Sussex
NEW CASTLE New Castle
NEWARK New Castle
OCEAN VIEW Sussex
ODESSA New Castle
PORT PENN New Castle
REHOBOTH BEACH Sussex
ROCKLAND New Castle
SAINT GEORGES New Castle
SEAFORD Sussex
SELBYVILLE Sussex
SMYRNA (19977) Kent(89), New Castle(10)
TOWNSEND New Castle
VIOLA Kent
WILMINGTON New Castle
WINTERTHUR New Castle
WOODSIDE Kent
YORKLYN New Castle

Delaware ZIP/City Cross Reference

19701-19701 BEAR
19702-19702 NEWARK
19703-19703 CLAYMONT
19706-19706 DELAWARE CITY
19707-19707 HOCKESSIN
19708-19708 KIRKWOOD
19709-19709 MIDDLETOWN
19710-19710 MONTCHANIN
19711-19718 NEWARK
19720-19721 NEW CASTLE
19725-19726 NEWARK
19730-19730 ODESSA
19731-19731 PORT PENN
19732-19732 ROCKLAND
19733-19733 SAINT GEORGES
19734-19734 TOWNSEND
19735-19735 WINTERTHUR
19736-19736 YORKLYN
19800-19899 WILMINGTON
19901-19901 DOVER
19902-19902 DOVER AFB
19903-19906 DOVER
19930-19930 BETHANY BEACH
19931-19931 BETHEL
19933-19933 BRIDGEVILLE
19934-19934 CAMDEN WYOMING
19936-19936 CHESWOLD
19938-19938 CLAYTON
19939-19939 DAGSBORO
19940-19940 DELMAR
19941-19941 ELLENDALE
19942-19942 FARMINGTON
19943-19943 FELTON
19944-19944 FENWICK ISLAND
19945-19945 FRANKFORD
19946-19946 FREDERICA
19947-19947 GEORGETOWN
19950-19950 GREENWOOD
19951-19951 HARBESON
19952-19952 HARRINGTON
19953-19953 HARTLY
19954-19954 HOUSTON
19955-19955 KENTON
19956-19956 LAUREL
19958-19958 LEWES
19960-19960 LINCOLN
19961-19961 LITTLE CREEK
19962-19962 MAGNOLIA
19963-19963 MILFORD
19964-19964 MARYDEL
19966-19966 MILLSBORO
19967-19967 MILLVILLE
19968-19968 MILTON
19969-19969 NASSAU
19970-19970 OCEAN VIEW
19971-19971 REHOBOTH BEACH
19973-19973 SEAFORD
19975-19975 SELBYVILLE
19977-19977 SMYRNA
19979-19979 VIOLA
19980-19980 WOODSIDE

District of Columbia

General Help Numbers:

Mayor's Office

1350 Pennsylvania Ave NW 202-727-2980
Washington, DC 20004 Fax 202-727-0505
http://dc.gov/mayor/index.shtm 8:30AM-6:00PM

Attorney General

441 4th St NW, Suite 1060 N 202-727-3400
Washington, DC 20001 Fax 202-347-8922
http://occ.dc.gov/occ/site/default.asp 8:30AM-5:00PM

Legislative Records

Council of the District of Columbia 202-724-8050
1350 Pennsylvania Ave NW, Rm 10 Fax 202-347-3070
Washington, DC 20004 9AM-5:30PM
www.dccouncil.us/legislation

District Archives

Office of Archives/Public Records 202-671-1105
1300 Naylor Ct NW Fax 202-727-6076
Washington, DC 20001-4225; 9AM-4:00PM research hrs
http://os.dc.gov/os/cwp/view,a,1207,q,585889.asp

District Specifics:

Time Zone: EST

Population: 591,833

Website: www.dc.gov/index.asp

District Agencies

Criminal Records

Metropolitan Police Dept., Henry J Daley Bldg, Identification and Records Section, 300 Indiana Ave NW, Rm 3055, Washington, DC 20001; 202-727-4245, 202-727-4357, Fax- 202-442-4247; 9AM-5PM.

http://mpdc.dc.gov/mpdc/site/default.asp

Records are also available with less restrictions from the Superior Court, Criminal Div. at 500 Indiana NW, Rm 4001, phone 202-879-1373. The court record mail/fax search fee is $10.00; a signed release not required there.

Indexing & Storage: Records available for 10 years. New records available for inquiry in 1 day. 46% of all arrests in database have final dispositions recorded, 84% for those arrests within last 5 years.

Searching: Records are referred to as Police Clearances. Include in request- signed, notarized release from subject, full name (middle initial), date and place of birth, year. Use of the PD70 Application (Criminal History Request) is suggested. The SSN, race, current address and case number, if known, are helpful. Although 80% of the records are fingerprint supported, fingerprints searches are not available. This data not released-pending cases. The only records released to the public contain convictions.

Access by: mail, in person.

Fee & Payment: A Police Clearance is $7.00, a Police Report of an incident is $3.00. Fee payee-Superior Court, Criminal Division Personal checks not accepted. Make money order or cashier check payable to DC Treasurer. No credit cards accepted.

Mail search: Turnaround time- 2 to 4 weeks. Clearances on individuals for employment purposes must include signed, notarized authorization by the subject. A SASE is required. Send to Attn: Police Clearances.

In person: Counter service for a Police Clearance is available at this address at Arrest and Criminal History Sect, 3rd Fl. Wait is usually less than 1 hr. If you are the subject, you most provide a gov't-issed photo ID or original birth certificate and SSN card.

Sexual Offender Registry

Metropolitan Police Department, Sex Offender Registry Unit, 300 Indiana Ave NW, Rm 3009, Washington, DC 20001; 202-727-4407, Fax- 202-727-9292; 8AM-4PM.

http://mpdc.dc.gov/mpdc/site/default.asp

In general, an offense requiring registration is a felony sexual assault (regardless of the age of the victim); an offense involving sexual abuse or exploitation of minors; or sexual abuse of wards, patients, or clients.

Indexing & Storage: Records available from 1996. New records available for inquiry in 1 day.

Searching: Searchers can visit any police station and inspect a public registry that will contain current information on all registered sex offenders in the District of Columbia. Include in request- name, DOB. This data not released- pending cases.

Access by: fax, in person, online.

Fax search: Records may be requested by fax.

In person: Records for all classes may be searched at this office and all local police stations in DC.

Online search: A list of Class A & B registered sex offenders is provided on the website. Under "Services" click on Sex Offender Registry.

Incarceration Records

District of Columbia Department of Corrections, DC Jail Records Office, 1901 D Street SE, Washington, DC 20003; 202-673-8257, Fax- 202-671-2043; 8AM-5PM.

www.doc.dc.gov/doc/site/default.asp

The administrative headquarters is located at 1923 Vermont Ave, NW, Washington, DC 20001; the telephone number is (202) 673-7316.

Indexing & Storage: Records available on current and former inmates. New records available for inquiry in 1 day.

Searching: For full information, a subpoena or signed release is required. The reason for the search must be stated in your request. For general "public" information, this agency prefers that you access the VINE telephone locator system. Include in request- full name, and DOB. SSN, inmate number, PVID or case number helpful and requested. Type of data released varies depending on request.

Access by: mail, online.

Mail search: Turnaround time- 2 to 4 weeks minimum. For a search, you must provide first and last name, DOB; SSN and/or PVID number helpful.

Online search: The agency directs online searching to a third party at https://www.vinelink.com/vinelink/siteInfoAction.do?siteId=9900.

Corporation, LP, LLC, Trade Name, Fictitious Name

Department of Consumer & Regulatory Affairs, Corporations Division, 941 N Capitol St NE, Washington, DC 20002; 202-442-4432, Fax- 202-442-4523; 8:30AM-4PM.

http://dcra.dc.gov/dcra/site/default.asp

Indexing & Storage: Records available from 1794. There is no trademark or servicemark statute. New records available for inquiry in 1-2 days.

Searching: Include in request- full name of business. The website provides download capability of forms.

Access by: mail, phone, in person, online.

Fee & Payment: The fee is $35.00 per certified legal document, plain copies are not available. A Good Standing is $15.00, $18.00 for partnerships, and $30.00 if a not-for-profit. Fee payee- DC Treasury. Prepayment required. Personal checks accepted. Credit cards accepted for in person searches only.

Mail search: Turnaround time- 5 to 10 days.

Phone search: They will release agent's name and address, date of incorporation, and status over the phone at no fee. Names and addresses of Officers and Directors will not be released over the phone, unless time permits.

In person: You may request information in person. There is no fee unless copies of documents are needed. You may use a credit card.

Online search: No online access to corporation or business entities filing records but agency enables one to search for and reserve business names at http://mblr.dc.gov/corp/reservation/index.asp or simply search at http://mblr.dc.gov/corp/lookup/index.asp.

Other access: For information concerning lists and bulk file purchases, contact the Office of Information Services.

Uniform Commercial Code, Federal & State Tax Liens

UCC Recorder, District of Columbia Recorder of Deeds, 515 D Street NW, Washington, DC 20001; 202-727-5374; 8:30AM-4:30PM.

http://otr.cfo.dc.gov/otr/cwp/view,a,1330,q,594562.asp

Records from 1983 forward are located in Room 101, prior records are in Room 304. This agency will not perform name searches (you must do yourself or hire someone).

Indexing & Storage: Records available from the 1900's; 1979 from the online system.

Searching: Local tax liens are called district tax liens. Include in request- debtor name. Searches from 1973 forward are not performed by state personnel. Use the in-house terminal or the website. Searches prior to 1973 need a book and page number.

Access by: mail, in person, online.

Fee & Payment: Copies cost $2.25 per page. Fee payee- DC Treasurer. Prepayment required. Personal checks accepted. Credit cards accepted for online service only.

Mail search: Turnaround time- 2 weeks. No name searches.

In person: There is a public access terminal available to look up names to find instrument numbers.

Online search: Search index by name or doc number at www.washington.dc.us.landata.com/. Registration is required. There are two commercial plans to purchase images. Note this for all recorded documents, not just UCC. A subscriber pays $175 per month for unlimited views of images and $2.00 per document image downloaded. Accounts are also available for larger firms with multiple users. A registered "non-subscriber" pays no fee to view documents and $4.00 per document mage downloaded.

Sales Tax Registrations

Office of Tax and Revenue, Sales Tax Certificates, 941 N. Capitol Street NE, Washington, DC 20002; 202-727-4829; 8:15AM-4:30PM.

http://brc.dc.gov/tax/tax.asp

Indexing & Storage: Records available from the 1980's. Records are computerized since 1990, otherwise are hard copies.

Searching: This agency will only confirm that a tax certificate number is registered. If a request is made to search by company name, requester should talk to the agency's legal department. They will provide no other information. Include in request- business name, tax certification number, federal employer identification number, address.

Access by: mail, phone, fax, in person.

Mail search: Turnaround time- 3 to 5 days. A SASE is requested. No fee for mail request.

Phone search: No fee for telephone request.

Fax search: Same criteria as mail searches.

In person: Immediate turnaround time. The Customer Service Center is on the 1st Fl.

Birth Certificates

Department of Health, Vital Records Division, 825 North Capitol St NE, 1st Fl, Washington, DC 20002; 202-442-9303, 877-572-6332 (Order), Fax-202-442-4848; 8:30AM-3:30PM.

http://doh.dc.gov/doh/site/default.asp

Indexing & Storage: Records available from 1874 to present. New records available for inquiry immediately.

Searching: Records less than 100 years old are only released to person of record or immediate family members or to legal representative of family. Requester should include a copy of photo ID and daytime phone number. Include in request- full name, date of birth, place of birth, names of parents, name of the hospital.

Access by: mail, phone, fax, in person, online.

Fee & Payment: The $18.00 fee is for the short form of birth certificate for every consecutive 3 years searched. The archival long form costs $23.00. All copies are certified. Fee payee- DC Treasurer. Prepayment required. Credit cards are only accepted for expedited services. Personal checks accepted. Major credit cards accepted.

Mail search: Turnaround time- 2 weeks. All genealogical searches must be done by mail and cannot be expedited. SASE not required.

Phone search: phone requests are through VitalChek, are considered expedited and extra fees are involved.

Fax search: Order from VitalChek at 202-783-0136.

In person: Simple requests may be processed while you wait.

Online search: Orders may be placed online via a state designated vendor at www.vitalchek.com.

Expedited service: Expedited service is available for phone, fax and online orders. Expedited service is available from VitalChek 800-255-2414 and requires a credit card and additional $12.95 for 7-10 day delivery or $29.95 for 3-5 day service.

Death Records

Department of Health, Vital Records Division, 825 North Capitol St NE, 1st Fl, Washington, DC 20002; 202-671-5000, 877-572-6332 (Order); 8:30AM-3:30PM.

http://doh.dc.gov/doh/site/default.asp

Request forms are available from the website.

Indexing & Storage: Records available from August 1874 on. New records available for inquiry immediately.

Searching: Records up to 50 years old are only released to immediate family members of person of record or to legal representative of family. Requester should include copy of a photo ID and daytime phone number. Include in request- full name, date of death, SSN.

Access by: mail, phone, fax, in person, online.

Fee & Payment: The fee is $18.00 per record. All copies are certified. Fee payee- DC Treasurer. Prepayment required. Credit cards are only accepted for expedited services. Personal checks accepted. Major credit cards accepted.

Mail search: Turnaround time- 2 weeks. Genealogical searches must be in writing and cannot be expedited. SASE not required.

Phone search: phone requests are through VitalChek, are considered expedited and extra fees are involved.

Fax search: Order from VitalChek at 202-783-0136.

In person: Turnaround time is 1/2 hour unless extensive search required.

Online search: Orders may be placed online via a state designated vendor at www.vitalchek.com. Also, a Nationwide Gravesite Locator is located at http://gravelocator.cem.va.gov/j2ee/servlet/NGL_v1. Includes VA, national, state, military, veteran, DOI, and where grave is marked with a government grave marker.

Expedited service: Expedited service is available for phone, fax and online orders. Expedited service is available from VitalChek 800-255-2414 and requires a credit card and additional $12.95 for 7-10 day delivery or $29.95 for 3-5 day service.

Marriage Certificates

Superior Court House, Marriage Bureau, 500 Indiana Ave, NW, Room 4485, Washington, DC 20001; 202-879-4840, Fax- 202-879-1280; 8:30AM-5PM.

Indexing & Storage: Records available from 1811 on. New records available for inquiry immediately.

Searching: Include in request- both names, wife's maiden name, date of marriage. This data not released- SSN

Access by: mail, in person.

Fee & Payment: Search fee is $10.00. Extra copies are $.50 per page. To search prior to 1921 there is an additional $10.00 per year charge to search. Fee payee- Clerk of DC Superior Court. Prepayment required. Only money orders are accepted unless requester is an attorney or a minister/priest/rabbi. No personal checks or credit cards accepted.

Mail search: Turnaround time- 2 weeks. A SASE is requested.

In person: Unless the request is a simple search, the results are mailed within 15 days. Turnaround time is within the same day.

Divorce Records

Superior Court House, Divorce Records, 500 Indiana Ave, NW, Room 4230, Washington, DC 20001; 202-879-1261, Fax- 202-879-1572; 8:30AM-5PM.

Indexing & Storage: Records available from 1956 on. Records prior to 1956 are located at the US District Court at 202-273-0520. New records available for inquiry immediately.

Searching: Include in request- names of husband and wife, date of divorce, year divorce case began, case number (if known). This data not released- sealed records.

Access by: mail, in person.

Fee & Payment: Search fee is $10.00. Certification is $6.50. Copy fee is $.50 per page. Fee payee- Clerk of the Superior Court. Prepayment required. Use either a money order or a cashier's check if ordering by mail. No personal checks or credit cards accepted.

Mail search: Turnaround time- 3-6 weeks. Written requests must include requester's phone number so the court can call back with the charge. A SASE is requested.

In person: Turnaround time is same day for record after 1996. Prior records are kept off site and will take longer to retrieve.

Workers' Compensation Records

Office of Workers' Compensation, Records, 64 New York Avenue, NE, 2nd floor, Washington, DC 20002; 202-671-1000, Fax- 202-671-1929; 8:30AM-5PM.

http://does.dc.gov/does/cwp/view,a,1232,q,537428.asp

Indexing & Storage: Records available from June 1982 on. Records are archived after a year and will take longer to locate. Records are only from private employers. New records available for inquiry immediately.

Searching: Only claimant or parties to claim can access records. An employer may request a post-hire record check, but must submit a signed release from the employee. Include in request- claimant release, SSN, employer. An employer may request

Access by: mail, fax, in person.

Fee & Payment: There is no search fee, copies are $.25 per page. Fee payee- DC Treasurer. Prepayment required. Personal checks accepted, credit cards are not.

Mail search: Turnaround time- 2 to 3 days. A SASE is requested.

Fax search: Limit 2 pages, turnaround time is 2-3 days.

In person: Limited to interested parties or with signed release from claimant.

Driver Records

Department of Motor Vehicles, Driver Records Division, PO Box 90120, Washington, DC 20090; 202-737-4404, 202-737-4400 (General); 8:15AM-4PM.

www.dmv.dc.gov/serv/dlicense.shtm

Copies of tickets are available from the Bureau of Traffic Adjudication, same address. The fee is $1.00 per ticket.

Indexing & Storage: Records available for 3 years for moving violations, suspensions/revocations for 5 years, and DWIs for an indefinite period. Accidents are listed on the record if there is a conviction, but fault is not indicated.

Searching: The agency's policy is stricter than DPPA. Personal information is suppressed unless authority is granted by subject. Include in request- name and DL number; DOB is optional. Online requesters must submit DL, name and DOB; the sex and middle initial is optional. This data not released- SSN, height, and weight

Access by: mail, in person, online.

Fee & Payment: The cost for a driving record is $7.00 for a three or five-year record and $13.00 for a ten-year record. Since 7/1/2008, only the ten-year record is sold online. Fee payee- DC Treasurer. Prepayment required. Personal checks accepted. Credit cards accepted for in person requests.

Mail search: Turnaround time- 5 to 10 days. SASE not required.

In person: Walk-in requesters may obtain up to 5 records at once. Additional records are available the next day. The counter is located at 301 "C" St NW. There are also three other locations in the city that will process records.

Online search: Online requests are taken throughout the day and are available in batch the next morning after 8:15 am. There is no minimum order requirement. Fee is $13.00 per record; only the ten-year record is sold. Requesters are restricted to high volume, ongoing users. Each requester must be approved, sign a contract and pay a $3,500 annual fee. Billing is a "bank" system which draws from pre-paid account. For more information, call 202-727-5692.

Vehicle Ownership & Registration

Department of Motor Vehicles, Vehicle Records, 95 M Street SW, Washington, DC 20024; 202-737-4400; 8:15AM-5PM M-F; 8PM Wed.

www.dmv.dc.gov

Indexing & Storage: New records available for inquiry in 24 hours.

Searching: Records are classified as either "Authorized" or "General." Authorized is for law enforcement. General records (DPPA permissible use purposes) suppress the SSN but show personal information. Casual requesters must have permission of the subject. This data not released- SSNs or financial information.

Access by: mail, in person.

Fee & Payment: The current fee is $7.00 per request for VIN, registration or lien information. Fee payee- DC Treasurer. Prepayment required. Cash is accepted for in person transactions. Personal checks and credit cards accepted.

Mail search: Turnaround time- 10 days. SASE not required.

In person: Counter service available.

Other access: Bulk requests can be obtained for commercial purposes upon approval by the Director, Department of Motor Vehicles if it is determined that the requested use "is for the public interest." Commercial purposes are not permitted.

Accident Reports

Metro. Police Dept., Accident Report Section, 300 Indiana Ave NW, Room 3075, Washington, DC 20001; 202-727-4357, 202-727-4245, Fax- 202-727-4467; 9AM-5PM.

http://mpdc.dc.gov/mpdc/site/default.asp

This office holds the officer investigated accident reports known as PD-10s and incident reports.

Indexing & Storage: New records available for inquiry in 14 days.

Searching: Include in request- full name and either date of accident and location of accident or the six-digit report number. The agency will not perform a "name only" search. This data not released- reports that have not been validated by staff review.

Access by: mail, phone, in person.

Fee & Payment: The fee is $3.00 per report, non-refundable if no record found. There is no charge for complainants, their spouses, and parents/guardians. Fee payee- DC Treasurer. Prepayment required. Personal checks not accepted, corporate checks are. No credit cards accepted.

Mail search: Turnaround time- 2 weeks. A SASE is requested.

Phone search: No searching by telephone.

In person: Counter service available.

Vessel Ownership & Registration

Access to Records is Restricted.

Metropolitan Police Dept, Harbor Patrol, 550 Water St SW, Washington, DC 20024; 202-727-4582, 202-727-4383, Fax- 202-727-3663; 7AM-3PM.

http://mpdc.dc.gov/mpdc/site/default.asp

All vessels regardless of size, with or without mechanical propulsion, must be registered and titled. Liens are shown here. Coast Guard documented vessels must register, but will not be titled. Information is not open to the public. Record verifications are handled on a case-by-case basis. The agency uses discretion in release of data for lawful purposes, but does not follow DPPA.

Legislation Records

Council of the District of Columbia, Legislative Services Division, 1350 Pennsylvania Ave NW, Grd Fl Rm 10, Washington, DC 20004; 202-724-8050, Fax- 202-347-3070; 9AM-5:30PM.

www.dccouncil.us/legislation

Indexing & Storage: Records available from 1975 to present on microfilm.

Searching: Include in request- bill number.

Access by: mail, phone, fax, in person, online.

Fee & Payment: 1993-2000 bills are considered current and are on paper. 1975 through 1988 are on microfilm, and you must do your own copying at $.10 per page. 1989-1992 are stored offsite at archives. Fee payee- DC Treasurer. Prepayment required. Personal checks accepted, credit cards are not.

Mail search: Turnaround time- 1 to 4 days. SASE not required.

Phone search: No fee for telephone request. Bill status is given over the phone.

Fax search: Same criteria as phone searching.

In person: You may request copies in person.

Online search: Bill text and status may be reviewed at the Internet site. The District's Official Code can be viewed at http://government.westlaw.com/linkedslice/default.asp?SP=DCC-1000.

Voter Registration

DC Board of Elections and Ethics, Voter Registration Records, 441 4th St NW, #250 North, Washington, DC 20001; 202-727-2525, Fax- 202-347-2648; 9AM-4PM.

www.dcboee.org

Indexing & Storage: Records available for active records. The database is updated every four months.

Searching: Records are open to the public. This data not released- SSNs or date of birth.

Access by: mail, phone, fax, in person, online.

Fee & Payment: There is no fee for a search, but there is a $.25 copy fee. Fee payee- DC Treasurer. Prepayment required. If purchasing the database, certified funds are required. No credit cards accepted.

Mail search: Turnaround time- 7 to 10 days.

Phone search: For verification purposes only.

Fax search: Fax searching available.

In person: Information is available immediately.

Online search: One may check voter registration status at www.dcboee.org/voter_info/reg_status/. Name, DOB and ZIP are required.

Other access: Records can be purchased on CD or printed lists. A variety of data is available from party registration to voter history. Minimum fee $50 plus $10 for CD. Call 202-727-2525 for details. Form at www.dcboee.org/pdf_files/Data_Request_Form.pdf.

GED Certificates

GED Testing Center, State Education Agency, Washington, DC 20004; 202-274-7173, Fax- 202-274-6507; 9AM-1PM.

www.dcged.org/

A request form available from the web page at http://dcged.org/documents/GEDTranscriptRequestForm1.pdf.

Indexing & Storage: Records available from 1940 to present. Test records for the years 1997 - 2002 are maintained under SSN. Records prior to 1997 are filed by year. New records available for inquiry in 4 weeks.

Searching: An examinee must request in writing that an official score report or verification be sent to a specific institution, employer, or other organization. Include in request- a signed release, name at time of test, DOB, date/year test, SSN, and city of test. Test records for the years 1997 - 2002 are maintained under SSN. Records prior to 1997 are filed by year. The requester can submit a "Fax Waiver" form so that the transcript copy can be sent to a designated third party.

Access by: mail, in person.

Fee & Payment: All verifications and transcript copy requests are $10.00. Fee payee- UDC - GED Testing Center Money orders are accepted. No credit cards accepted.

Mail search: Turnaround time is 7-10 days if record is after 1994, 2-3 weeks if prior to 1994.

In person: Results are mailed or can be picked up.

Fishing & Hunting License Information

Access to Records is Restricted.

Environmental Health Regulation, Fisheries & Wildlife Division, 51 N Street NE - 5th Fl, Washington, DC 20002-3323; 202-535-2260, Fax-202-535-1359; 8AM-5PM.

http://doh.dc.gov/doh/cwp/view,a,1374,Q,584468,dohNav_GID,1810,.asp

Hunting of any kind is prohibited within the District of Columbia. Fishing records are not available to the public, they are only released as a Freedom of Information Act request. Certain data may be released to attorneys for pending litigation or statistical use with a written request.

District of Columbia Licensing Agencies

For details about the agency responsible for licensing/certifying/registering an item below or in the Agency Quick Finder section, match an item's number with the number of the agency in the *Licensing Agency Information* section.

Licenses Searchable Online

Acupuncturist #2 .... http://app.hpla.doh.dc.gov/weblookup/
Addiction Counselor #2 .... http://app.hpla.doh.dc.gov/weblookup/
Alcohol Mfg./Vendor/Dist. #1 .... http://abra.dc.gov/abra/site/default.asp
Alcohol Server/Seller #1 .... http://abra.dc.gov/abra/site/default.asp
Alcohol Susp'd/Revk'd License #1 .... http://abra.dc.gov/abra/site/default.asp
Appraiser, Real Estate #5 .... www.asc.gov/content/category1/nr_intro.aspx?id=10
Attorney #3 .... www.dcbar.org/find_a_member/index.cfm
Bank #10 .... http://dbfi.dc.gov/dbfi/cwp/view,a,3,q,585840,dbfiNav,|31299|.asp
Barber #5 .... www.asisvcs.com/indhome_fs.asp?CPCAT=1309STATEREG
Bingo Operation #13 .... www.dclottery.com
Boxing Event/Professional #5 .... www.asisvcs.com/indhome_fs.asp?CPCAT=BX09STATEREG
Card Tournament #13 .... www.dclottery.com
Check Casher #10 .... http://app.dbfi.dc.gov/ifs/default.asp
Chiropractor #2 .... http://app.hpla.doh.dc.gov/weblookup/
Cosmetologist #5 .... www.asisvcs.com/indhome_fs.asp?CPCAT=2009STATEREG
Counselor, Professional #2 .... http://app.hpla.doh.dc.gov/weblookup/
Dance Therapist #2 .... http://app.hpla.doh.dc.gov/weblookup/
Dentist/Dental Hygienist #2 .... http://app.hpla.doh.dc.gov/weblookup/
Dietitian/Nutritionist #2 .... http://app.hpla.doh.dc.gov/weblookup/
Electrician #5 .... www.asisvcs.com/indhome_fs.asp?CPCAT=3609STATEREG
Engineer #5 .... www.asisvcs.com/indhome_fs.asp?CPCAT=EN09STATEREG
Funeral Director #5 .... www.asisvcs.com/indhome_fs.asp?CPCAT=FN09STATEREG
Gambling Party/Event #13 .... www.dclottery.com
Insurance Broker/Agent/Firm #12 .... http://disb.dc.gov/disr/cwp/view,a,1299,Q,638165,disrNav,%7C32821%7C.asp
Lobbyist #9 .... http://ocf.dc.gov/WebsiteReports/repperiod_lob.asp
Lottery Retailer #13 .... www.dclottery.com
Massage Therapist #2 .... http://app.hpla.doh.dc.gov/weblookup/
Medical Doctor #2 .... http://app.hpla.doh.dc.gov/weblookup/
Midwife Nurse #2 .... http://app.hpla.doh.dc.gov/weblookup/
Money Lender/Transmitter #10 .... http://app.dbfi.dc.gov/ifs/default.asp
Mortgage Broker/Lender #10 .... http://app.dbfi.dc.gov/ifs/default.asp
Naturopath #2 .... http://app.hpla.doh.dc.gov/weblookup/
Nurse Anesthetist #2 .... http://app.hpla.doh.dc.gov/weblookup/
Nurse, Clinical/LPN/RN #2 .... http://app.hpla.doh.dc.gov/weblookup/
Nursing Home Administrator #2 .... http://app.hpla.doh.dc.gov/weblookup/
Occupational Therapist #2 .... http://app.hpla.doh.dc.gov/weblookup/
Optometrist #2 .... http://app.hpla.doh.dc.gov/weblookup/
Osteopath #2 .... http://app.hpla.doh.dc.gov/weblookup/
Pharmacist/Pharmacy #2 .... http://app.hpla.doh.dc.gov/weblookup/
Physical Therapist #2 .... http://app.hpla.doh.dc.gov/weblookup/
Physician Assistant #2 .... http://app.hpla.doh.dc.gov/weblookup/
Plumber #5 .... www.asisvcs.com/indhome_fs.asp?CPCAT=4909STATEREG
Podiatrist #2 .... http://app.hpla.doh.dc.gov/weblookup/
Political Campaign Contributor #9 .... http://ocf.dc.gov/dsearch/dsearch.asp
Psychologist #2 .... http://app.hpla.doh.dc.gov/weblookup/
Raffle #13 .... www.dclottery.com
Real Estate Agent/Broker/Seller #5 .... https://www.asisvcs.com/services/licensing/Dcopla/LicRenewals/LrIndex.asp?CBCAT=0909BR
Real Estate Appraiser #5 .... www.asc.gov/content/category1/nr_intro.aspx?id=10
Real Estate School #5 .... http://dcra.dc.gov/dcra/cwp/view,a,1342,q,600757,dcraNav_GID,1697,dcraNav,|33466|.asp
Recreational Therapist #2 .... http://app.hpla.doh.dc.gov/weblookup/
Respiratory Care #2 .... http://app.hpla.doh.dc.gov/weblookup/
Sales Finance Company #10 .... http://app.dbfi.dc.gov/ifs/default.asp
Social Worker #2 .... http://app.hpla.doh.dc.gov/weblookup/
Taxi Dispatch #6 .... www.dctaxi.dc.gov/dctaxi/cwp/view.asp?a=1187&q=487917
Taxi Fleet/Company #6 .... www.dctaxi.dc.gov/dctaxi/cwp/view.asp?a=1187&q=487910
Taxi Insurer #6 .... www.dctaxi.dc.gov/dctaxi/cwp/view.asp?a=1187&q=487938

District of Columbia Licensing Quick Finder

Acupuncturist #2 ... 202-724-4900
Addiction Counselor #2 ... 202-724-4900
Air Conditioning/Refrigeration #5 ... 202-442-4459
Alarm Technician #14 ... 410-799-0191 x340
Alcohol Mfg./Vendor/Dist. #1 ... 202-442-4423
Alcohol Permit #1 ... 202-442-4423
Alcohol Server/Seller #1 ... 202-442-4423
Alcohol Susp'd/Revk'd License #1 ... 202-442-4423
Appraiser, Real Estate #5 ... 202-442-4472
Architect #5 ... 202-442-4461
Asbestos Contractor/Worker #5 ... 202-442-4459
Attorney #3 ... 202-626-3475
Attorney Discipline Case #3 ... 202-638-1501
Auctioneer #5 ... 202-442-9200
Audiologist #8 ... 202-442-5377
Automobile Repossessor #5 ... 202-442-9200
Bank #10 ... 202-727-8000
Barber #5 ... 202-442-4459
Bingo Operation #13 ... 202-645-8041
Boxing Event/Professional #5 ... 202-442-4472
Card Tournament #13 ... 202-645-8041
Check Casher #10 ... 202-727-8000
Chiropractor #2 ... 202-724-4900
Contractor, Mechanical/Resident'l #5 ... 202-442-4459
Cosmetologist #5 ... 202-442-4459
Counselor, Professional #2 ... 202-724-4900
Credit Union #10 ... 202-727-8000
Dance Therapist #2 ... 202-724-4900
Dentist/Dental Hygienist #2 ... 202-724-4900
Dietitian/Nutritionist #2 ... 202-724-4900
Educational Institution, Higher #8 ... 202-442-5377
Electrician #5 ... 202-442-4459
Emergency Medical Technician #11 ... 202-671-4222
Engineer #5 ... 202-442-4459
Engineer, Steam #5 ... 202-442-4459
Fair Housing Provider #5 ... 202-442-4400
Firearms Instructor #14 ... 410-799-0191 x341
Firearms Permit #14 ... 410-799-0191 x341
Firearms Registration Section #14 ... 410-799-0191 x324
Funeral Director #5 ... 202-442-4461
Gambling Party/Event #13 ... 202-645-8041
Gas Fitter #5 ... 202-442-4459
Hearing Aid Dispenser #2 ... 202-724-4900
Insurance Broker/Agent #12 ... 202-442-7813
Insurance Company #12 ... 202-727-7425
Interior Designer #5 ... 202-442-4461
Investment Advisor #7 ... 202-442-4934
Investment Advisor Rep. #7 ... 202-442-4934
K-9 Unit #14 ... 410-799-0191 x334
Lobbyist #9 ... 202-671-0550
Lottery Retailer #13 ... 202-645-8041
Massage Therapist #2 ... 202-724-4900
Mechanic, Master #5 ... 202-442-9200
Medical Doctor #2 ... 202-724-4900
Midwife Nurse #2 ... 202-724-4900
Money Lender #10 ... 202-727-8000
Money Transmitter #10 ... 202-727-8000
Mortgage Broker/Lender #10 ... 202-727-8000
Motor Vehicle Dealer/Salesperson #5 ... 202-442-9200
Naturopath #2 ... 202-724-4900
Notary Public #15 ... 202-727-3117
Nurse Anesthetist #2 ... 202-724-4900
Nurse, Clinical #2 ... 202-724-4900
Nurse-LPN/RN #2 ... 202-724-4900
Nursing Home Administrator #2 ... 202-724-4900
Occupational Therapist #2 ... 202-724-4900
Optometrist #2 ... 202-724-4900
Osteopath #2 ... 202-724-4900
Parking Lot Attendant #5 ... 202-442-9200
Pesticide Applicator #4 ... 202-535-2299
Pesticide Dealer #4 ... 202-535-2299
Pesticide Employee/Operator #4 ... 202-535-2299
Pharmacist/Pharmacy #2 ... 202-724-4900
Physical Therapist #2 ... 202-724-4900
Physician Assistant #2 ... 202-724-4900
Plumber #5 ... 202-727-1000
Podiatrist #2 ... 202-724-4900
Political Campaign Contributor #9 ... 202-671-0550
Private Investigator #14 ... 410-799-0191 x331
Property Manager #5 ... 202-442-9200
Psychologist #2 ... 202-724-4900
Psychometrist/School Psychologist #8 202-442-5377
Public Accountant #5 ... 202-442-4461
Raffle #13 ... 202-645-8041
Real Estate Agent/Broker/Seller #5 ... 202-442-4400
Real Estate Appraiser #5 ... 202-442-4472
Real Estate School #5 ... 202-442-4400
Recreational Therapist #2 ... 202-724-4900
Respiratory Care #2 ... 202-724-4900
Sales Finance Company #10 ... 202-727-8000
Savings & Loan Company #10 ... 202-727-8000
School Athletic Trainer/Coach #8 ... 202-442-5377
School Attendance Officer/Worker #8 ... 202-442-5377
School Counselor #8 ... 202-442-5377
School Librarian/Media Specialist #8 ... 202-442-5377
School Social Worker #8 ... 202-442-5377
School, Degree/Non-Degree Granting #5 ... 202-442-4314/4465
Securities Agent #7 ... 202-442-4934
Securities Broker/Dealer #7 ... 202-442-4934
Security Agency/Guard #14 ... 410-799-0191 x340
Security Alarm Dealer/Agent #5 ... 202-442-9200
Social Worker #2 ... 202-724-4900
Solicitor #5 ... 202-442-9200
Solid Waste Collector #5 ... 202-442-9200
Speech Language Pathologist #8 ... 202-442-5377
Steam Fitter #5 ... 202-442-4459
Surveyor, Land #5 ... 202-442-4459
Taxi Dispatch #6 ... 202-645-6018
Taxi Fleet/Company #6 ... 202-645-6018
Taxi Insurer #6 ... 202-645-6018
Teacher/Teacher Trainer #8 ... 202-442-5377
Tour Guide #5 ... 202-442-9200
Trust Company #10 ... 202-727-8000
Veterinarian #5 ... 202-442-9200
Wrestling Event/Professional #5 ... 202-442-4472

Licensing Agency Information

#1 Department of Consumer Regulatory Affairs, Alcohol & Beverage Control Division, 941 N Capitol St NE #7200, Washington, DC 20002-4259; 202-442-4423, Fax- 202-442-9563. www.abra.dc.gov/abra/site/default.asp

#2 Department of Health, Health Professional Licensing, 717 14th Street NW, #600, Washington, DC 20005; 202-724-4900, Fax- 202-727-8471. Hours- 8:15AM-4:45PM. http://hpla.doh.dc.gov/hpla/site/default.asp Search data at- http://app.hpla.doh.dc.gov/weblookup/

#3 District of Columbia Bar Association, 1250 H St NW, 6th Fl, Washington, DC 20005; 202-737-4700, Fax- 202-626-3471. www.dcbar.org Search data at- www.dcbar.org/find_a_member/index.cfm

#4 Department of Health, Bureau of Hazardous & Toxic Substances, 51 N St NE, 3rd Fl, #3032, Washington, DC 20002; 202-535-2299, Fax- 202-535-2483. http://doh.dc.gov/doh/cwp/view,a,1374,Q,585693,dohNav_GID,1814,.asp Also, check licensees via the Dept. of Consumer Affairs at 202-442-4400.

#5 Department of Consumer & Regulatory Affairs, License & Certification Division - Central Verifications, 941 N Capitol St NE, Washington, DC 20002-4259; 202-442-4400. http://dcra.dc.gov/dcra/site/

#6 DC Taxicab Commission, 2041 Martin Luther King Jr Ave, SE, #204, Washington, DC 20020-7024; 202-645-6018, Fax- 202-889-3604. Hours- 8:15AM-4:45PM. www.dctaxi.dc.gov/dctaxi/site/default.asp Search data at- www.dctaxi.dc.gov/dctaxi/site/default.asp

#7 Department of Insurance & Securities Regulation, Securities Bureau, 810 1st St NE #610, Washington, DC 20002-4227; 202-727-8000, Fax- 202-442-0661. www.disr.dc.gov/disr/site/default.asp

#8 District of Columbia Public Schools, Licensure & Credentials, 825 N Capitol St NE, 6th Floor, Washington, DC 20002; 202-442-5377, Fax- 202-442-5311. www.k12.dc.us/dcsea/certification/

#9 Director of Campaign Finance, Office of Campaign Finance, 2000 14th St NW, #433, Frank D Reeves Municipal Bldg, Washington, DC 20009; 202-671-0550, Fax- 202-671-0658. http://ocf.dc.gov

#10 Economic Development, Banking & Financial Institutions Office, 810 1st St NE #701, Washington, DC 20002; 202-727-8000, Fax- 202-535-1196. Hours- 8:15AM-4:45PM. http://dbfi.dc.gov/dbfi/site/default.asp Search data at- http://app.disb.dc.gov/ifs/default.asp

#11 Emergency, Health & Medical Svcs. Office, 1923 Vermont Ave NW, #201, Washington, DC 20001; 202-673-3331, Fax- 202-673-3188. http://dc.gov/agencies/detail.asp?id=38

#12 Department of Insurance & Securities Regulation, Insurance Licensing Division, 810 1st St NE #701, Washington, DC 20002; 202-727-8000. http://disb.dc.gov/disr/site/default.asp Search data at- http://disb.dc.gov/disr/cwp/view,a,1299,Q,638165,disrNav,%7C32821%7C.asp

#13 Lottery & Charitable Games Control Board, 2101 Martin Luther King Jr Ave SE, Washington, DC 20020-5731; 202-645-7900 or 645-8000, Fax- 202-645-0006. Hours- 8:15AM-4:45PM. www.dclottery.com

#14 State Police, Licensing Division, 1111 Reisterstown Rd, Pikesville, MD 21208; 410-653-4500, 800-525-5555. Hours- 8AM-5PM. www.mdsp.org/

#15 Notary Commissions & Authentications Section, Office of the Secretary, 1350 Pennsylvania Ave NW, #419, Washington, DC 20004; 202-727-3117, Fax- 202-727-3582. Hours- 9AM-1PM. http://os.dc.gov/os/cwp/view%2Ca%2C1206%2Cq%2C522329.asp

District of Columbia Federal Courts

US District Court District of Columbia

Washington DC Division Clerk's Office, US Courthouse, Rm 1225, 333 Constitution Ave NW, Washington, DC 20001, 202-354-3000; records- 202-354-3080; crim dockets- 202-354-3060; civil dockets- 202-354-3120; Fax- 202-354-3524. Hours- 9AM-4PM. www.dcd.uscourts.gov

Counties/Note: District of Columbia.

Searches/Indexing: Search request requires name; helpful- DOB, SSN, address. Criminal search results include DOB; civil returns name only. Will fax back documents no add'l fee, but only a couple pages only. New cases are in the index 48 hours after filing date. Both computer back to 1991 and card indexes maintained. Records on computer back to 1991, includes an archive program of some older cases; microfiche for crim cases from 1932 to mid-1991; from 1950 for civil. Divorce cases up to 1956 are still here. Case files sent to archives 5 years after closed.

Search Access: Searchers calling locally are not given info via phone. Out of state calls are given the 3 most current docket entries only. Archived records not available via phone. **Mail:** Search usually completed- 7 days. Include SASE for return. **Fax:** Fax search requests accepted; include names, parties, civil/criminal, your phone, etc and case number if known. **In person:** 4 public terminals available. Court will make up to 20 copies only. No self serve copier at court. Court can recommend an outside vendor to make copies.

Payment: Pay by money order or cashier's or personal check. No credit cards accepted. Payee: Clerk, US District Court. Include a prepaid FedEx envelope for expedited return.

E-Services: ECF at https://ecf.dcd.uscourts.gov. **Opinions Online:** www.dcd.uscourts.gov/court-opinions.html. **Online Note:** Weekly court schedules at www.dcd.uscourts.gov/court-schedules.html.

US Bankruptcy Court District of Columbia

Washington DC Division Court Clerk, E Barrett Prettyman Courthouse, Rm 1225, 333 Constitution Ave NW, Washington, DC 20001, 202-565-2500. 9AM-4PM. www.dcb.uscourts.gov

Counties/Note: District of Columbia.

Searches/Indexing: Search request requires name only. Results include last 4 SSN digits. Will not fax back documents. New cases are in the index immediately after filing date. Computer and card indexes maintained; after 10/6/03 records on computer only. Indexed on computer back to 1990. Case files sent to archives 1 year after closed.

Search Access: Voice Case Information Service available, call VCIS at 202-208-1365. **Mail:** Search usually completed- within 7 days. Include SASE for return. **In person:** 4 public terminals available. No self-serve copier. Court can recommend an outside vendor to make copies.

Payment: Pay by money order, cashier's check. No personal checks or credit cards. Payee: Clerk, US Bankruptcy Court. Cash accepted in person.

E-Services: PACER records go back to 1991. New records online after 1 day. ECF at https://ecf.dcb.uscourts.gov. **Opinions Online:** https://ecf.dcb.uscourts.gov/cgi-bin/Opinions.pl.

Standards for Federal Courts: Fees are standard unless noted in profile. Search fee is $26.00 per item (one party name or case number). Copy fee is $.50 per page. Certification fee is $9.00 per document, double for exemplification, if available. Most courts require prepayment. Mail requests should enclose a SASE unless otherwise noted. Before releasing records, all courts require prepayment, unless noted.

District courts index by defendant and plaintiff and by case number. Bankruptcy courts usually index by debtor and case number. While most courts now have their indexes on computer, many may still maintain index card files as well. Courts will archive closed case files at different times.

There are numerous public access programs available to online subscribers. Search the U.S. Party/Case Index to find party names and case numbers among all courts. Individual case data is provided on PACER. A search of CM/ECF provides copies of cases filed electronically. For details about PACER, the US Party/Case Index, and CM/ECF see the Appendix or go to http://pacer.psc.uscourts.gov or call 800-676-6856.

District of Columbia Courts

Court	Jurisdiction	No. of Courts	How Organized
Superior Courts*	General	1	3 Divisions
Probate/Tax Court*	Special	1	

* Profiled in this Sourcebook.

Court	CIVIL								
	Tort	Contract	Real Estate	Min. Claim	Max. Claim	Small Claims	Estate	Eviction	Domestic Relations
Superior Courts*	X	X	X	$5000	No Max	$5000		X	X
Probate Court*							X		

Court	CRIMINAL				
	Felony	Misdemeanor	DWI/DUI	Preliminary Hearing	Juvenile
Superior Courts*	X	X	X	X	X
Probate Court*					

Administration

Executive Office, 500 Indiana Av NW, Room 1500, Washington, DC, 20001; 202-879-1700, Fax: 202-879-4829. (EST) www.dccourts.gov/dccourts/index.jsp

Court Structure

The Superior Court handles all local trial matters. The Civil Division is divided into four branches: the Civil Actions Branch, the Quality Review Branch, the Landlord and Tenant Branch and the Small Claims Branch. The Criminal Division hears all local criminal matters including felony, misdemeanor, and serious traffic cases. The Family Court is divided into six branches: the Domestic Relations Branch, the Juvenile and Neglect Branch, the Paternity and Child Support Branch, the Marriage Bureau Branch, the Mental Health and Mental Retardation Branch, and the Counsel for Child Abuse and Neglect Branch. The Probate Division has jurisdiction over estates of those who have passed away, trusts, guardianships of minors, and guardianships and conservatorships of incapacitated adults.

Online Access

The Superior Court and Court of Appeals offer access to opinions at the main web page above.

Superior Court - Criminal 500 Indiana Ave NW, Rm 4001, Washington, DC 20001; 202-879-1373; fax: 202-879-0146; 8:30AM-5PM (EST). ***Felony, Misdemeanor.*** www.dccourts.gov/dccourts/ The court is selective of type of document they will make copies.

Criminal Records: Access: Mail, fax, in person. Visitors must perform in person searches themselves. Search fee: $10.00 per name. Required to search: name, years to search, DOB. Criminal records computerized from 1978, on microfiche from 1974, on index from 1970, archived from 1962. Note: This court recommends that you contact the Metro DC Police to perform a "police clearance" record check for $7.00. ID and signed release is required. Metro Police is at 202-727-4245, ID & Records Sec., Mail Correspondence Sec., 300 Indiana Av NW, DC 20001 Mail turnaround time depends on case involved. Public use terminal has crim records back to 1978. Three public access terminals available, includes Traffic cases index.

General Information: No sealed records released. Will not fax documents. Court makes copy: $.25 per page. Self serve: $.25 per page. No certification fee. Payee: DC Superior Court. Personal checks accepted; credit cards are not.

Superior Court - Civil 500 Indiana Ave NW, JM 170, Washington, DC 20001; 202-879-1133; fax: 202-879-8335; 8:30AM-5PM ***Civil Actions.*** www.dccourts.gov/dccourts/superior/civil/index.jsp As of 2005, Small Claims is a separate branch that handles claims of $5,000 or less.

Civil Records: Access: Mail, in person, online. Both court and visitors may perform in person searches. Search fee: $10.00 per name. Required to search: name. Civil cases indexed by defendant, plaintiff, on computer from 1983, on microfiche, archived and on index from 1976. Mail turnaround time depends on case involved. Public use terminal has civil records back to 1983. Access civil records free at https://www.dccourts.gov/pa/. Attorneys and legal professionals participating in the e-Filing Project must register for the CaseFileXpress eFile service either by logging onto www.lexisnexis.com/courtlink/online/ or calling 1-877-433-4533.

General Information: Online identifiers in results same as on public terminal. No sealed records released. Will not fax documents. Court makes copy: $.50 per page. Self serve: $.25 per page. Certification fee: $5.00. Payee: Clerk-Superior Court of DC. Only cashiers checks and money orders accepted. No credit cards accepted. Prepayment required. Mail requests: SASE required.

Superior Court - Small Claims Division 510 Fourth St #120, Washington, DC 20001; 202-879-1120; fax: 202-508-1696; 8:30AM-5PM (EST). ***Small Claims.***

Civil Records: Access: In person, online. Visitors must perform in person searches themselves. Required to search: name. Small Claims records on computer back to 1986; non-computer records go back to 1998; 1987-97 some, not all, records in archives. Public use terminal has civil records back to 2000. Access civil records free at https://www.dccourts.gov/pa/. Online results show name only.

General Information: Will not fax documents. Court makes copy: $.50 per page, self serve same. Certification fee: $5.00 per doc includes copy fee. Payee: The Clerk of DC Superior Court. No personal checks accepted. Will accept checks from members of the DC Bar. No credit cards accepted. Prepayment required.

Superior Court - Landlord & Tenant Branch 409 E Street NW Rm110, Washington, DC 20001; 202-879-4879; 8:30AM-5PM; 9AM-N Sat; 6:30-8PM W eve (EST). ***Eviction.*** www.dccourts.gov/dccourts/ This information applies to the Landlord & Tenant Branch only.

Civil Records: Access: Mail, In person, online. Both court and visitors may perform in person searches. Search fee: $10.00. Required to search: name, years to search; also helpful-case number. Civil records go back to 1994; computerized records go back 5 years. Note: No out of district inquires taken by phone. Mail turnaround time depends on case involved. Public use terminal back to 2002. Access civil records free at https://www.dccourts.gov/pa/.

General Information: Will fax documents to local or toll-free number. Court makes copy: $.50 per page. Certification fee: $5.00. Payee: Clerk-Superior Court of DC. No personal checks or credit cards accepted. Prepayment required.

Superior Court - Probate Division 500 Indiana Ave NW, #5000, Washington, DC 20001; 202-879-1499; 8:30AM-5PM (EST). ***Probate***

District of Columbia Recording Offices

ORGANIZATION: Recording officer is the Recorder of Deeds. District of Columbia is in the Eastern Time Zone (EST).

REAL ESTATE RECORDS: The District does not perform real estate searches.

UCC RECORDS: Financing statements are filed with the Recorder, including real estate related collateral.

TAX LIEN RECORDS: Federal tax liens on personal property of businesses are filed with the Secretary of State. Other federal and all state tax liens on personal property are filed with the Recorder. Note- a taxpayer who resides outside the U.S.A. is deemed to be a resident of D.C.

ONLINE ACCESS: Search the Recorder's database at www.washington.dc.us.landata.com. Registration is required; images are available for free, fee is charged to purchase images. Also, search the real property database and real estate sales database at http://otr.cfo.dc.gov/otr/cwp/view,a,1330,q,594345.asp.

District of Columbia

Recorder of Deeds, 515 D St, Washington, DC 20001. 202-727-5374; fax-202-727-9629; 8:15AM-4:30PM. (EST) www.dc.gov Recorder of Deeds also has a branch office located at 320 Pennsylvania Ave SE. The mayor's citywide call center is suggested to quickly find phone number info- 202-727-1000. Index: All in one. Records indexed on a 20 public use terminals back to 1972. Search pre-1972 manually in Rm #304. Only the public may search. Copy fee $2.25 per page. Cert fee- $2.25 per page plus copy fee; example- 2 page certified doc would be $6.75. Payee- D.C. Treasurer. **Online access to Real Estate, Deed, Judgment, Lien, UCC records:** Search the recorders database at www.washington.dc.us.landata.com. Registration is required; search index for free; $4.00 fee to view and copy. Subscribe for $175.00 per month or per use, and get docs for $2.00 per page. Records go back to 1973. **Other phones:** Treasurer- 202-727-6055. **Property tax/Assessing**- 941 N Capitol St NE, Tax and Revenue Ofc, Washington, DC 20002; 202-442-7024, assessor fax- 202-442-6796. hours- 8:15AM-4:45PM http://cfo.dc.gov/cfo/site/default.asp **Online access**- Search the real property database at https://www.taxpayerservicecenter.com/RP_Search.jsp?search_type=Assessment. Search the real estate sales database at https://www.taxpayerservicecenter.com/RP_Search.jsp?search_type=Sales. Also, search the tax sales list at http://otr.cfo.dc.gov/otr/frames.asp?doc=/otr/lib/otr/532250601.pdf.

District of Columbia County Locator

You will usually be able to find the city name in the City/County Cross Reference below. In that case, it is a simple matter to determine the county from the cross reference. We have also included a ZIP/City Cross Reference immediately following the City/County Cross Reference.

If you know the ZIP Code but the city name does not appear in the City/County Cross Reference index, look up the ZIP Code in the ZIP/City Cross Reference, find the city name, then look up the city name in the City/County Cross Reference. For example, you want to know the county for an address of Menands, NY 12204. There is no "Menands" in the City/County Cross Reference. The ZIP/City Cross Reference shows that ZIP Codes 12201-12288 are for the city of Albany. Looking back in the City/County Cross Reference, Albany is in Albany County.

District of Columbia City/County Cross Reference

ANACOSTIA ANNEX - District of Columbia
NAVAL ANACOST ANNEX - District of Columbia
WASHINGTON - District of Columbia
WASHINGTON NAVY YARD - District of Columbia

District of Columbia ZIP/City Cross Reference

20000-20099 WASHINGTON
20201-20330 WASHINGTON
20332-20373 WASHINGTON
20373-20373 ANACOSTIA ANNEX
20373-20373 NAVAL ANACOST ANNEX
20374-20374 WASHINGTON
20374-20374 WASHINGTON NAVY YARD
20375-20376 WASHINGTON
20376-20376 WASHINGTON NAVY YARD
20380-20388 WASHINGTON
20388-20388 WASHINGTON NAVY YARD
20389-20391 WASHINGTON
20391-20391 WASHINGTON NAVY YARD
20392-20398 WASHINGTON
20398-20398 WASHINGTON NAVY YARD
20401-20599 WASHINGTON
20511-20511 WASHNGTON, DIR NATIONAL INTELLIGENCE
56901-56920 WASHINGTON

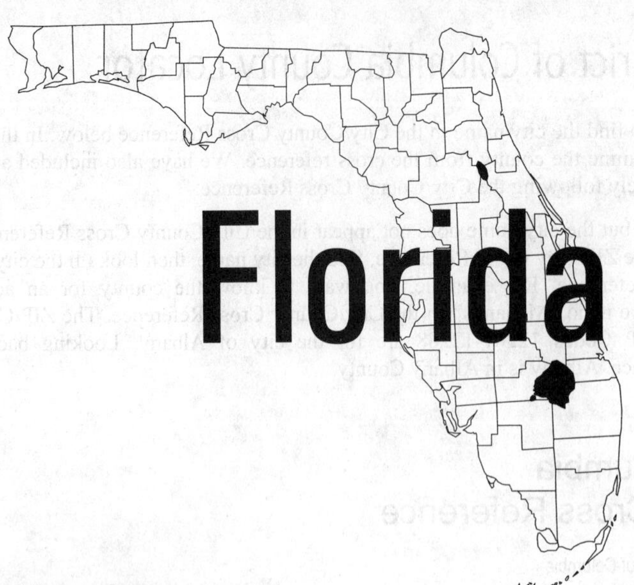

Florida

General Help Numbers:

Governor's Office

The Capitol,PL05 400 S Monroe St — 850-488-4441
Tallahassee, FL 32399-0001 — Fax 850-487-0801
www.flgov.com/ — 8AM-5PM

Attorney General's Office

Legal Affairs Department — 850-414-3300
The Capitol, PL-01 — Fax 850-410-1630
Tallahassee, FL 32399-1050 — 8AM-5PM
http://myfloridalegal.com/

Legislative Records

Division of Legislative Information Srvs — 850-488-4371
111 W Madison St, Rm 704 — Fax 850-921-5334
Tallahassee, FL 32399-1400 — 8AM-5PM
www.leg.state.fl.us/

State Archives

Archives & Records — 850-245-6700
R A Gray Bldg, 500 S Bronough — Fax 850-488-4894
Tallahassee, FL 32399-1400 — 8AM-5PM
http://dlis.dos.state.fl.us/index_researchers.cfm

State Specifics:

Capital:	Tallahassee Leon County
Time Zone:	EST*
Number of Counties:	67
Population:	18,328,340
Website:	www.myflorida.com/

* Florida's ten western-most counties are CST: They are: Bay, Calhoun, Escambia, Gulf, Holmes, Jackson, Okaloosa, Santa Rosa, Walton, Washington.

State Agencies

Criminal Records

Florida Department of Law Enforcement, User Services Bureau/Public Records, PO Box 1489, Tallahassee, FL 32302 (Courier address- 2331 Phillip Rd, Tallahassee, FL 32308); 850-410-8109, 850-410-8107, Fax- 850-410-8201; 8AM-5PM.

www.fdle.state.fl.us

A great webpage profiling this agency's various records and services is at www.fdle.state.fl.us/criminalhistory/.

Indexing & Storage: Records available from the early 1930's. New records available for inquiry in 1 day. 70% of all felony arrests in database have final dispositions recorded; 63% of misdemeanors. 68% of all records within last 5 years include dispositions.

Searching: The SSN is suppressed except for the last 4 digits. Include in request- date of birth, race, sex, name. SSN is helpful. One can submit fingerprints, for the same fee, but it is not required. 100% of the arrest records are fingerprint-supported. This data not released- sealed or expunged records, juvenile records prior to 10/94 if felony, 06/30/96 if misdemeanor. All records are released, including those without dispositions.

Access by: mail, in person, online.

Fee & Payment: The fee is $24.00 per individual. Pre-paid accounts receive turnaround time of two to five working days. Fee payee- Department of Law Enforcement. Prepayment required. Personal checks accepted. Credit cards accepted only for online requests.

Mail search: Turnaround time- 5 working days. SASE not required.

In person: in person requests are treated the same as mail requests; processing takes 5 working days.

Online search: Criminal history information may be ordered over the Department Program Internet site at https://www2.fdle.state.fl.us/cchinet/. The $24.00 fee applies. Juvenile records from 10/1994 forward are also available. Credit card ordering will return records to your screen or via email. Search state's wanted list at www3.fdle.state.fl.us/fdle/wpersons_search.asp.

Statewide Court Records

State Courts Administrator, 500 S Duval, Supreme Court Bldg, Tallahassee, FL 32399-1900; 850-922-5081, Fax- 850-488-0156; 8AM-5PM.

www.flcourts.org

Except for certain online research capabilities, all trial court record access must be done at the local level.

Searching: The Clerk of the Circuit Court cannot place an image or copy of the certain documents on a publicly available Internet website for general public display.

Online search: Supreme Court dockets are available online at http://jweb.flcourts.org/pls/docket/ds_docket_search. A large number of the courts do offer online access to the public, usually through the Clerk of the Circuit Court. Also, there is an index of judgments, liens, recorded documents at www.myfloridacounty.com. Fees are involved to order copies; save $1.50 per record by becoming a subscriber.

Sexual Offender Registry

Florida Department of Law Enforcement, Offender Registration and Tracking Svcs, PO Box 1489, Tallahassee, FL 32302 (Courier address- 2331 Phillips Rd, Tallahassee, FL 32308); 888-357-7332, 850-410-8572, Fax- 850-410-8599; 8AM-6:30PM.

http://offender.fdle.state.fl.us/offender/homepage.do

Chapter 97-299, Laws of Florida, requires certain sex offenders to directly register with law enforcement or to have information compiled by the Department of Corrections, with the information to be provided to FDLE.

Indexing & Storage: Records available from 10/01/97. New records available for inquiry in 1 day.

Searching: Under Chapter 119, Florida Statutes, the Public Records Law, any of the public records of the Department of Law Enforcement are available for review upon request, subject to statutorily-authorized editing of exempt or confidential information. Include in request- name and address. This data not released- data about victims.

Access by: mail, phone, fax, online.

Fee & Payment: If documents need printing or are substandard forms, then fees may be involved. Fee payee- FDLE Prepayment required. Personal checks accepted. Credit cards not accepted.

Mail search: Turnaround time- 5 working days. No SASE required.

Phone search: The toll free number is manned 24 hours daily.

Fax search: Search criteria is the same phone search.

Online search: Search the registry from the web page. Searching can be done by name or by geographic area.

Incarceration Records

Florida Department of Corrections, Central Records Office, 2601 Blair Stone Rd, Tallahassee, FL 32399-2500; 850-488-2533, 850-488-1503 (Records), 850-922-0000 (Parole Commission), Fax- 850-413-8302; 8AM-5PM.

www.dc.state.fl.us

Full records are housed at the individual institutions, though inmate information available through this agency and the website should sufficiently fulfill most searches.

Indexing & Storage: Records available on current and former inmates. New records available for inquiry in 1 day (if paper).

Searching: Location, DOC number, physical identifiers, conviction information, and release dates released. Include in request- first and last name and DOB. The SSN and DOC number are helpful. This data not released- medical data, SSN, post-sentence and pre-sentence investigations

Access by: mail, phone, fax, in person, online.

Fee & Payment: Fee is $.15 per copy. A staff fee may be involved if extensive research is involved. Fee payee- Florida Department of Corrections

Mail search: Turnaround time- 30-60 working days. SASE not required.

Phone search: Searching limited to general "public" information is available by phone.

Fax search: Fax requesting available.

In person: in person requesters must call for appointment for a Public File Review; please call two weeks in advance.

Online search: Extensive search capabilities are offered at www.dc.state.fl.us/inmateinfo/inmateinfomenu.asp . Click on Inmate Population Information Search.

Other access: Bulk data may be purchased on a CD.

Corporation, LP, LLC, Trademarks/Servicemarks, Fictitious Names, Federal Tax Liens

Division of Corporations, Department of State, PO Box 6327, Tallahassee, FL 32314; 850-245-6053 (Copy Certification), 850-245-6056 (Annual Reports); 8AM-5PM.

www.sunbiz.org

This agency recommends accessing the Internet site. Send requests for Judgment Lien Filings to PO Box 6250, Tallahassee 32314.

Indexing & Storage: Records available from the late 1800's. New records available for inquiry immediately.

Searching: Other fees note - LLC status is $5.00, LLC certified copy of record is $30.00. Include in request- full name of business. In addition to the articles of organization, business entity records available include: Annual Reports (date of filing and updates), Officers, Directors, Prior (merged) names, Inactive names, and US Tax ID number. This data not released- addresses of judges and police.

Access by: mail, in person, online.

Fee & Payment: In person copies are $1.00 per page, certified copies are $8.75 for the first 8 pages and $1.00 for each additional page, not to exceed $52.50. By mail, a flat fee of $8.75 for certification and $10.00 for copies of complete record. Fict. name is $30. Fee payee- Secretary of State. Prepayment required. Personal checks accepted. Accepts credit cards for online filing of annuals, only.

Mail search: Turnaround time- 3 to 5 days. SASE not required.

In person: Limited searches available at the counter.

Online search: The state's excellent Internet site gives detailed information on all corporate, trademark, limited liability company and limited partnerships; fictitious names; and lien records. Images of filed documents are available from 1996/7 to present.

Other access: This agency offers record purchases on microfiche sets and on CD disks.

Uniform Commercial Code

UCC Filings, FLORIDAUCC, Inc, PO Box 5588, Tallahassee, FL 32314 (Courier address- 2670 Executive Center Circle West, #100, Tallahassee, FL 32301); 850-222-8526; 8AM-5PM.

www.floridaucc.com

The Secretary of State privatized the filing and searching of UCC. The vendor, FLORIDAUCC, is responsible for all filings, photocopy and certification requests, forms, and database availability for searches. Direct questions to help@FLORIDAUCC.com.

Indexing & Storage: Records available from 1966, if active, 1997 forward on the web. Records are on computer and microfiche. Records filed by electronic process are available in image format. New records available for inquiry immediately.

Searching: Information on Tax Liens is maintained at the Department of State, Division of Corporations. Tax liens are not filed here, unless filed as a UCC. It is suggested to search tax liens at the county level. Include in request- debtor name. The agency will not do a search. You must hire an outside firm, the web page, or use the state designated vendor.

Access by: in person, online.

Fee & Payment: Fees are $1.00 per page for mail searching. Fee payee- FLORIDAUCC Inc or Secretary of State; Prepayment required. Personal checks accepted, credit cards are not.

In person: Counter service available, but you must perform the search yourself.

Online search: The Internet site www.floridaucc.com/UCCWEB/Search.aspx allows access for no charge. Search by name or document number, for records 1997 to present. TIFF images of Florida UCC filings can be downloaded from the Internet for all filings from 1997 to present. Tax Liens are not included with UCC filing information.

Other access: Microfilm reels and CD's of images are available for bulk purchase requesters. Call for more information.

State Tax Liens

Records not maintained by a state level agency.

These records are filed and found at the county level.

Sales Tax Registrations

Florida Department of Revenue, Sales Tax Registration Records, 168 Blountstown Highway #C, Tallahassee, FL 32304-3702; 850-488-9925, Fax- 850-922-5936; 8AM-7PM.

http://dor.myflorida.com/dor/

Indexing & Storage: Records available for 5 years, then they are purged.

Searching: This agency will confirm that a business is registered and has filed returns with the department. The following are required to search; business name, tax ID number, and business location. Federal ID is helpful. They can also search by the owner's name.

Access by: mail, fax, in person.

Fee & Payment: There is no fee.

Mail search: The turnaround time is 7-10 days.

Fax search: Same criteria as mail searching.

In person: Records are still returned by mail.

Birth Certificates

Department of Health, State Office of Vital Statistics, PO Box 210, Jacksonville, FL 32231-0042 (Courier address- 1217 Pearl St, Jacksonville, FL 32202); 904-359-6900 x9000, 877-550-7330 (Order Line), 877-550-7428 (Fax Order Line), Fax- 904-359-6633; 8AM-5PM.

www.doh.state.fl.us/Planning_eval/Vital_Statistics/index.html

The website includes general information and ordering instructions. The vendor www.vitalchek.com also can process orders via online or by fax. Service fees involved.

Indexing & Storage: Records available from 1865 to present, however few records were filed prior to 1917. Birth registration was not required until 1917. New records available for inquiry in 4 weeks after birth.

Searching: Certified copies released only to individual named, if of legal age, or to parents or legal guardians. Include in request- full name, names of parents including mother's maiden name, date of birth, county. Include relationship of requester to subject and copy of valid picture ID. Legal guardian or representative must submit a notarized affidavit along with current government issued valid photo ID. Note that records over 100 years old are open to the public and do not require the notarized statements.

Access by: mail, phone, fax, in person.

Fee & Payment: Fee is $9.00 for a certified computer copy or $14.00 for a certified photocopy. Extra fees involved for expedited services. $4.00 per copy when ordering additional same name at the same time. Fee payee- Office of Vital Statistics. Prepayment required. Personal checks accepted. Major credit cards only accepted by the vendor.

Mail search: Turnaround time- 10 to 15 days. SASE not required.

Phone search: See expedited services. This is an automated phone service open 24 hours daily.

Fax search: See expedited services.

In person: Turnaround time is normally the same day. The lobby closes at 4:30 pm.

Other access: Commemorative birth certificates in large size, signed by the governor, and suitable for framing are available. The fee is $34.00 or $25.00 when ordered in conjunction with other certified copies of the same record. Allow 4 to 6 weeks for delivery.

Expedited service: Expedited service is available for mail, phone and fax searches. Fax phone is 877-550-7428. Add $10.00 for "2 to 3 day rush service" plus pre-paid express delivery service. If you wish to use the vendor www.vitalchek.com there are additional fees for use of a credit card.

Death Records

Department of Health, State Office of Vital Statistics, PO Box 210, Jacksonville, FL 32231-0042 (Courier address- 1217 Pearl St, Jacksonville, FL 32202); 904-359-6900 x9000, 877-550-7330 (Order Line), 877-550-7428 (Fax Order Line), Fax- 904-359-6633; 8AM-5PM.

www.doh.state.fl.us/Planning_eval/Vital_Statistics/index.html

The website contains general information, ordering instructions, and forms. The vendor www.vitalchek.com also can process orders via online or by fax.

Indexing & Storage: Records available from 1877 to present. Note that death registration was not required by state law until 1917. New records available for inquiry in 4 -6 weeks after death.

Searching: The death certificate minus cause of death is public information. Certification with cause of death is released after 50 years to public. Include in request- full name, sex, date of death, county of death. Valid photo ID required if cause of death information released. If record less than 50 years old, requester must show proof of being a family member or have copy of will or document demonstrating interest in the estate, or provide documentation of acting on behalf of an entitled person.

Access by: mail, phone, fax, in person.

Fee & Payment: Fee is $5.00 for the first year searched. If the specific year is not known, additional years may be searched for $2.00 per year with a maximum fee of $55.00. Add $4.00 per copy when ordering additional copies at the same time. Fee payee- Office of Vital Statistics. Prepayment required. Personal checks accepted. Major credit cards only accepted by the vendor.

Mail search: Turnaround time- 10 to 15 days. SASE not required.

Phone search: See expedited service. Order line is open 24 hours daily.

Fax search: See expedited service.

In person: Turnaround time is normally the same day. The lobby closes at 4:30 pm.

Expedited service: Expedited service is available for mail, phone and fax searches. Fax phone is 877-550-7428. Add $10.00 for "2 to 3 day rush service" plus pre-paid express delivery service. If you wish to use the vendor www.vitalchek.com there are additional fees for use of a credit card.

Marriage Certificates

Department of Health, State Office of Vital Statistics, PO Box 210, Jacksonville, FL 32231-0042 (Courier address- 1217 Pearl St, Jacksonville, FL 32202); 904-359-6900 x9000, 877-550-7330, Fax- 904-359-6633; 8AM-5PM.

www.doh.state.fl.us/Planning_eval/Vital_Statistics/index.html

The website contains general information, ordering instructions and order forms to download. The vendor www.vitalchek.com also can process orders via online or by fax with use of a credit card.

Indexing & Storage: Records available from June 1927 to present on microfiche, from 1970 to present on computer. New records available for inquiry in 6 weeks.

Searching: Include in request- full names, including maiden name, date and county of occurrence. Records are indexed by husband's name and/or by wife's maiden name. This data not released- SSNs.

Access by: mail, phone, fax, in person.

Fee & Payment: The fee is $5.00 per name for the first year searched. Additional years may be searched for $2.00 per year with a maximum fee of $55.00. Add $4.00 per copy when ordering additional copies at the same time. Fee payee- Office of Vital Statistics. Prepayment required. Personal checks accepted. Major credit cards only accepted by the vendor.

Mail search: Turnaround time- 15 to 20 days. SASE not required.

Phone search: See expedited service.

Fax search: See expedited service.

In person: Turnaround time is same day. The lobby closes at 4:30 pm.

Other access: A large size, commemorative marriage certificate signed by the governor is available for $30.00 or $25.00 when ordered in conjunction with other certified copies of the same record. Allow 4 to 6 weeks for delivery.

Expedited service: Expedited service is available for mail, phone and fax searches. Use 904-359-6633 for the fax number. Add $10.00 for "2 to 3 day rush service" plus pre-paid express delivery service. If you wish to use the vendor www.vitalchek.com there are additional fees for use of a credit card.

Divorce Records

Department of Health, State Office of Vital Statistics, PO Box 210, Jacksonville, FL 32231-0042 (Courier address- 1217 Pearl St, Jacksonville, FL 32202); 904-359-6900 x9000, 877-550-7330, Fax- 904-359-6633; 8AM-5PM.

www.doh.state.fl.us/Planning_eval/Vital_Statistics/index.html

The website provides general information and ordering instructions. The vendor www.vitalchek.com also can process orders via online or by fax with use of a credit card.

Indexing & Storage: Records available from June 1927 to present. New records available for inquiry in 6-8 weeks after divorce.

Searching: Include in request- full names, date and county of occurrence. Records are indexed by husband's name and wife's first name only.

Access by: mail, phone, fax, in person.

Fee & Payment: Fees are $5.00 per request for the first year and $2.00 per year for each additional search year, with a maximum search fee of $55.00. Add $4.00 per copy per name when ordering additional copies at the same time. Fee payee- Office of Vital Statistics. Prepayment required. Personal checks accepted. Major credit cards only accepted by the vendor.

Mail search: Turnaround time- 15 to 20 days. SASE not required.

Phone search: See expedited service.

Fax search: See expedited service.

In person: The fee is nonrefundable. Turnaround time is same day. The lobby closes at 4:30 pm.

Expedited service: Expedited service is available for mail, phone and fax searches. Use 904-359-6633 for the fax number. Turnaround time- 2 days. Add $10.00 for "2 to 3 day rush service" plus pre-paid express delivery service. If you wish to use the vendor www.vitalchek.com there are additional fees for use of a credit card.

Workers' Compensation Records

Workers Compensation Division, Data Quality Section, 200 E Gaines St, Tallahassee, FL 32399-4226; 850-413-1607, 850-413-1905 (Claims Database), Fax- 850-414-7341; 8AM-5PM.

www.fldfs.com/wc/

All information that would identify an ill or injured worker contained on the first notice of injury (DWC-1) is confidential and may not be disclosed to the public. However, the web has access to a variety of data.

Indexing & Storage: Records available from 1970's. New records available for inquiry in 3 days (imaged).

Searching: To get medical or financial information, a properly served subpoena is required. Include in request- claimant name, SSN, date of accident. To receive medical records, a signed release is needed unless requester is an insurance company or a legal representative. Direct questions to wchelp@fldfs.com. This data not released- SSN

Access by: mail, fax, in person, online.

Fee & Payment: There is no search fee, but copies are $.50 per page plus an additional $.55 per page for "special service" if 9 pages and more. Fee payee- Workers Compensation Administrative Trust Fund. Prepayment required. Personal checks accepted, credit cards are not.

Mail search: Turnaround time- 1 week. They will send an invoice, and will send you the copies after they receive the check. SASE not required.

Fax search: Same turnaround as mail requests.

In person: Requests are still returned by mail, unless you have a subpoena.

Online search: A myriad of information is available at www.fldfs.com/wc/databases.html. Access to the claims history database is provided, all personal information has been redacted.

Driver Records

Division of Drivers Licenses, Bureau of Records, PO Box 5775, Tallahassee, FL 32314-5775 (Courier address- 2900 Apalachee Pky, MS90, Neil Kirkman Bldg, Tallahassee, FL 32399); 850-617-2000; 8AM-5PM.

www.flhsmv.gov/

Copies of tickets may be obtained from the same address listed above for $2.00 per ticket plus $;50 copy fee or $1.00 for certified copies.

Indexing & Storage: Records available as a 3-year record or as a 7-year record. Accidents will appear only if convicted of a violation.

Searching: Florida adopted the amendment to DPPA. Casual requesters can obtain personal information only with consent of the subject. Either the driver license number or the name, DOB and sex are required for ordering.

Access by: mail, in person, online.

Fee & Payment: The fee is $2.10 for a three-year record. Add $1.00 for certification. A seven-year record or a complete record (8+ years) is available for $3.10. There is a full charge for a "no record found." Fee payee- Division of Drivers Licenses. Prepayment required. Personal checks accepted, credit cards are not.

Mail search: Turnaround time- 10 days. SASE not required.

In person: Normally, up to 50 requests will be processed while you wait, time permitting. Some county Clerks of Courts will also provide driving records.

Online search: Record access online has been privatized through Network Providers. Requesters with 5,000 or more records per month are considered Network Providers. Requesters with less than 5,000 requests per month (called Individual Users) are directed to a Provider. Call 850-617-2014 to become a Provider. A list of providers is found at the website. The state fee is as stated above; Providers add a service fee, which varies by vendor. Online requests are processed on an interactive basis. Check the status of any Florida driver license free at https://www6.hsmv.state.fl.us/dlcheck/dlchecking. Simply enter the driver license number.

Other access: This agency will process batch data via FTP or tape cartridge for approved users. Call 850-617-2634 for more details.

Vehicle Ownership & Registration

Division of Motor Vehicles, Information Research Unit - MS73, Neil Kirkman Bldg, A-126, Tallahassee, FL 32399; 850-617-2000, 850-617-3001, Fax- 850-488-8983; 8AM-4:30PM.

www.flhsmv.gov/html/titlinf.html

The state's policy is in compliance with the DPPA.

Indexing & Storage: Records available for 10 years. New records available for inquiry in 6 weeks.

Searching: Non-DPPA compliant requesters cannot obtain personal information without the specific consent of subject. Forms are found at www.flhsmv.gov/html/forms.html. Please submit the city (residence) and DOB if doing a name search.

Access by: mail, in person, online.

Fee & Payment: The fee for a computer printout of information is $.50, $1.00 per page copy fee, add $3.00 if certification is needed. The current license plate registration or copy of title is $2.00. A complete 10 year history is $15.00. Fee payee- Division of Motor Vehicles. Prepayment required. Personal checks accepted, credit cards are not.

Mail search: Turnaround time- 2 to 3 weeks. SASE not required.

In person: In cases when the information is not readily available the wait is 2 to 3 days. Also, one may do a plate search at a local tax Collector's Office.

Online search: For a free vehicle status check enter the title # or VIN to check vehicle status at https://www6.hsmv.state.fl.us/rrdmvcheck/mvchecking. Florida has contracted to release detailed vehicle information through approved Network Providers. Accounts must first be approved by the state. For each record accessed, the charge is $.50 plus a transactional fee, and the subscriber fee. Users must work from an estimated 2 1/2 month pre-paid bank. New subscribers must complete an application with Department, call 850-617-2634.

Accident Reports

DHSMV-, Crash Records-MS-28, 2900 Apalachee Parkway, Tallahassee, FL 32399-0537; 850-617-3416, Fax- 850-617-5134; 8AM-4:30PM.

www.flhsmv.gov/

The agency will not provide homicide reports, which must come from the investigating agency.

Indexing & Storage: Records available from 1942 to the present. Records are stored on microfilm from 1983 forward. New records available for inquiry in 12 weeks.

Searching: Records sealed by court order and juvenile information cannot be accessed. Homicide reports less than 5 years old should be requested from the local law enforcement agency that wrote the report, if over 5 years call 850-617-2306. Include in request- the full name of driver, exact date of crash (after 1983), county and city, local agency that investigated. For reports prior to 1983 the exact date, county, location and if crash involved a fatality must be supplied with request.

Access by: mail, in person.

Fee & Payment: The cost is $2.00 per report, $25.00 if homicide. You cannot search by phone; however, you can call to determine if report is available. Fee payee- Department of Highway Safety and Motor Vehicles. Prepayment required. Personal checks accepted, credit cards are not.

Mail search: Turnaround time- 2 to 4 weeks. A SASE is requested.

In person: You may request information in person at the customer service counter on 1st floor (Room B-133).

Other access: List or bulk purchase is available by special request.

Vessel Ownership & Registration

Dept of Highway Safety and Motor Vehicles, Bureau of Titles & Registrations, 2900 Apalachee Parkway, MS 68, Tallahassee, FL 32399; 850-617-2000, 850-617-3001, Fax- 850-921-1935; 8AM-5PM.

www.flhsmv.gov/dmv/faqboat.html

The state does not offer online access, but has outsourced some online access via approved vendors. Check the web page for details.

Indexing & Storage: Records available for 10 yrs to present. Records indexed on computer. Motorized vessels must be titled and registered. Registration of non-powered vessels is not required, but non-powered vessels 16 ft and over must be titled. Liens show on records. New records available for inquiry in 6 weeks.

Searching: A written request is required for all searches. Include in request- Florida registration #, title #, hull id #, or the exact name. If doing name search, submit DOB and city. This data not released- address, SSN, DL#.

Access by: mail, in person.

Fee & Payment: $.50 per page for computer print-out. $1.00 per photocopy of record. Additional $3.00 for each item to be certified. Fee payee- Dept of Highway Safety. Prepayment required. Personal checks accepted, credit cards are not.

Mail search: Turnaround time- 1-2 weeks. SASE not required.

In person: Simple requests may be processed while you wait.

Other access: A bulk purchase program is available for electronic media, labels or printed list. There is a $50.00 deposit required and a fee of $.01 per record.

Legislation Records

Office of Legislative Services, Division of Legislative Information Services, 111 W Madison St, Pepper Bldg, Rm 704, Tallahassee, FL 32399-1400; 850-488-4371, 850-487-5915 (Senate Bills), 850-488-7475 (House Bills), 850-245-6270 (Session Laws), Fax- 850-921-5334; 8AM-5PM.

www.leg.state.fl.us

Visit the "Legistore" at website to purchase a variety of related items.

Indexing & Storage: Records available from 1965 to present in book format, from 1972 to present on microfiche, and current and prior year on computer. New records available for inquiry in 30-90 days.

Searching: Include in request- bill number. Search by subject also.

Access by: mail, phone, in person, online.

Mail search: Turnaround time- 3 days. SASE not required.

Phone search: You may call for copies. There is an in-state toll-free line, 800-342-1827, for bill information.

In person: You may request copies in person.

Online search: Their Internet site contains full text of bills and a bill history session outlining actions taken on bills as well as a link to the state statutes. The site is updated throughout the day. Records go back to 1998. There is a more extensive online information service available. This system also includes information on lobbyists. Fees are involved.

Expedited service: Express mail is available at the requester's expense.

Voter Registration

Dept of State - Division of Elections, 500 South Bronough St, RA Gray Building, Room 316, Tallahassee, FL 32399-0250; 850-245-6200, Fax-850-245-6217; 8AM-5PM.

http://election.dos.state.fl.us

The state maintains a central voter file and sells a statewide disk, updated monthly. All individual searching must be done at the county level or at the state library.

Access by:;

Other access: The only format for bulk release is via DVD for $10.00. The content includes name, address, party, gender, voting history, and the telephone if provided on registration or if not marked confidential.

GED Certificates

GED Transcripts/Certificates, 325 W Gaines St Rm 634, Tallahassee, FL 32399; 850-245-0449, Fax- 850-245-0990; 8AM-5PM.

www.fldoe.org/workforce/ged/gedover.asp

Indexing & Storage: New records available for inquiry in 24 hours or less.

Searching: To verify, the following is required: name, date of birth, year of test, SSN, and county/city of test. If known, the GED Diploma number is helpful. A signed release is needed to get a copy of a transcript or diploma. This data not released- test scores.

Access by: mail, fax, in person.

Fee & Payment: The fee is $4.00 per copy of transcript or diploma. There is no fee for verification. Fee payee- FDOE Prepayment required. Money orders and cashiers' checks are required. Personal checks and credit cards are not accepted.

Mail search: Turnaround time- 5-7 business days. A SASE is required.

Fax search: Verification requests are accepted via fax, returned in 2-3 days.

In person: Must call and arrange before pick-up.

Hunting & Fishing License Information

Fish & Wildlife Cons. Comm., Licensing & Permit Board, 2590 Executive Center Circle, #200, Tallahassee, FL 32301; 850-488-3641, Fax- 850-414-8212; 8AM-5PM.

www.floridaconservation.org

Indexing & Storage: Records available from 2/97 forward.

Searching: Requests are preferred in writing. The agency will release address, telephone number, and type of license. Include in request- name, date of birth. This data not released- SSN, DOB

Access by: mail, in person.

Fee & Payment: There is no search fee with individual search, fees required for database sales.

Mail search: Turnaround time- 2 to 4 days. SASE not requested.

In person: Records may be view, but must be redacted first. It is suggested to send requests by mail.

Other access: Will sell entire database of records. Request must be in writing. Fees are associated with this service. Call the department for more information.

Florida State Licensing Agencies

For details about the agency responsible for licensing/certifying/registering an item below or in the Agency Quick Finder section, match an item's number with the number of the agency in the *Licensing Agency Information* section.

Florida Licenses Searchable Online

Acupuncturist #1 .... http://ww2.doh.state.fl.us/irm00praes/praslist.asp
Air Ambulance #20........ www.doh.state.fl.us/demo/ems/Providers/Providers.html
Air Conditioning Contractor/Svc #16........ https://www.myfloridalicense.com/wl11.asp
Alcoholic Beverage Permit #6........ https://www.myfloridalicense.com/wl11.asp
Ambulance Service #20........ www.doh.state.fl.us/demo/ems/Providers/Providers.html
Architect/Architectural Firm #11........ https://www.myfloridalicense.com/wl11.asp
Athletic Agent #6........ https://www.myfloridalicense.com/wl11.asp
Athletic Trainer #1........ http://ww2.doh.state.fl.us/irm00praes/praslist.asp
Attorney #23........ www.floridabar.org/names.nsf/MESearch?OpenForm
Auctioneer/Auction Firm #22........ https://www.myfloridalicense.com/wl11.asp
Audiologist #1........ http://ww2.doh.state.fl.us/irm00praes/praslist.asp
Automobile Repossessor #18........ http://licgweb.doacs.state.fl.us/access/individual.html
Barber/Barber Assist./Shop #6........ https://www.myfloridalicense.com/wl11.asp
Boxer #6........ https://www.myfloridalicense.com/wl11.asp
Building Code Administrator #6........ https://www.myfloridalicense.com/wl11.asp
Building Contractor #16........ https://www.myfloridalicense.com/wl11.asp
Building Inspector #6........ https://www.myfloridalicense.com/wl11.asp
Cemetery #29........ https://apps.fldfs.com/fclicense/searchpage.aspx
Cemetery Lot Salesperson #29........ https://apps.fldfs.com/fclicense/searchpage.aspx
Child Care Center #10........ www.dcf.state.fl.us/childcare/
Chiropractic-related Occupation #1........ http://ww2.doh.state.fl.us/irm00praes/praslist.asp
Chiropractor #1........ http://ww2.doh.state.fl.us/irm00praes/praslist.asp
Clinical Lab Personnel #1........ http://ww2.doh.state.fl.us/irm00praes/praslist.asp
Community Assoc. Manager #6........ https://www.myfloridalicense.com/wl11.asp
Company in Receivership #14........ www.fldfs.com/Receiver/receivership_list.asp
Construction Qualified Business #16........ https://www.myfloridalicense.com/wl11.asp
Continuing Edu. Provider, Medical #1........ http://ww2.doh.state.fl.us/irm00praes/praslist.asp
Contractor, General #16........ https://www.myfloridalicense.com/wl11.asp
Contractor, Residential #16........ https://www.myfloridalicense.com/wl11.asp
Cosmetologist, Nails/Salon #6........ https://www.myfloridalicense.com/wl11.asp
Crematory #29........ https://apps.fldfs.com/fclicense/searchpage.aspx
Day Care/Child Care Ctr/NurserySch'l #10 www.dcf.state.fl.us/childcare/
Dentist/Dental Assistant #1........ http://ww2.doh.state.fl.us/irm00praes/praslist.asp
Dietician/Nutritionist #1........ http://ww2.doh.state.fl.us/irm00praes/praslist.asp
Doctor, Limited #1........ http://ww2.doh.state.fl.us/irm00praes/praslist.asp
Drywall/Gypsum Specialty Contr. #16........ https://www.myfloridalicense.com/wl11.asp
Electrical Contractor #16........ https://www.myfloridalicense.com/wl11.asp
Electrologist/Electrologist Facility #1........ http://ww2.doh.state.fl.us/irm00praes/praslist.asp
Elevator Certificates of Operation #6........ https://www.myfloridalicense.com/wl11.asp
Embalmer #29........ https://apps.fldfs.com/fclicense/searchpage.aspx
Emergency Medical Technician #20........ www.doh.state.fl.us/demo/ems/Providers/Providers.html
Employee Leasing Company #16........ https://www.myfloridalicense.com/wl11.asp
Engineer #17........ www.fbpe.org/engineeringdirectory.asp
Engineering Firm #17........ www.fbpe.org/engineeringdirectory.asp
Finance Company, Consumer #30........ www.flofr.com/
Firearm Instructor/School/Agency #15........ https://licgweb.doacs.state.fl.us/account_maintenance/index.html
Firearms Instructor #18........ http://licgweb.doacs.state.fl.us/access/individual.html
Firearms License, Statewide #18........ http://licgweb.doacs.state.fl.us/access/individual.html
Food Services Establishment #6........ https://www.myfloridalicense.com/wl11.asp
Fumigation Performance Special ID #4........ www.flaes.org/aes%2Dent/
Funeral Director #29........ https://apps.fldfs.com/fclicense/searchpage.aspx
Funeral Home #29........ https://apps.fldfs.com/fclicense/searchpage.aspx
Gas Line Specialty Contractor #16........ https://www.myfloridalicense.com/wl11.asp
Geologist/Geology Firm #6........ https://www.myfloridalicense.com/wl11.asp
Hair Braider #6........ https://www.myfloridalicense.com/wl11.asp
Hearing Aid Specialist #1........ http://ww2.doh.state.fl.us/irm00praes/praslist.asp

Home Improvement Financer #30 .... www.flofr.com/
Hotel/Restaurant #6 .... https://www.myfloridalicense.com/wl11.asp
In Home Family Day Care Center #10 ..... www.dcf.state.fl.us/childcare/
Insect Sting Treatment Specialist #20 ..... www.doh.state.fl.us/demo/ems/Providers/Providers.html
Installment Seller, Retail #30 .... www.flofr.com/
Insurance Adjuster/Agent/Title Agent #14 www.fldfs.com/data/aar_alis1/
Insurance-related Company #14 .... www.floir.com/companysearch/
Interior Design Business/Individual #11 https://www.myfloridalicense.com/wl11.asp
Investment Advisor #30 .... www.flofr.com/
Kickboxer #6 .... https://www.myfloridalicense.com/wl11.asp
Land Sale, Condominiums #6 .... https://www.myfloridalicense.com/wl11.asp
Landscape Architecture Firm/Individ'l #11 https://www.myfloridalicense.com/wl11.asp
Landscape Maint./Pest Mgmt Co. #4 .... www.flaes.org/aes%2Dent/
Liquor Store #6 .... https://www.myfloridalicense.com/wl11.asp
Lobby Principal (Miami-Dade) #28 .... www.miamidade.gov/govaction/lbRegByPrinc.asp?Action=lbRegByPrinc
Lobbyist (Miami-Dade only) #28 .... www.miamidade.gov:80/govaction/lbRegByLob.asp?Action=lbRegByLob
Lobbyist/Principal #28 .... www.leg.state.fl.us/lobbyist/
Lodging Establishment #6 .... https://www.myfloridalicense.com/wl11.asp
Marriage & Family Therapist #1 .... http://ww2.doh.state.fl.us/irm00praes/praslist.asp
Massage Therapist/School/Facility #1 ...... http://ww2.doh.state.fl.us/irm00praes/praslist.asp
Mechanical Contractor #16 .... https://www.myfloridalicense.com/wl11.asp
Medical Doctor #1 .... http://ww2.doh.state.fl.us/irm00praes/praslist.asp
Medical Faculty Member #1 .... http://ww2.doh.state.fl.us/irm00praes/praslist.asp
Mental Health Counselor #1 .... http://ww2.doh.state.fl.us/irm00praes/praslist.asp
Midwife #1 .... http://ww2.doh.state.fl.us/irm00praes/praslist.asp
Mobile Home #6 .... https://www.myfloridalicense.com/wl11.asp
Money Transmitter #30 .... www.flofr.com/
Monument Dealer #29 .... https://apps.fldfs.com/fclicense/searchpage.aspx
Mortgage Broker #30 .... www.flofr.com/
Mortgage Broker Firm #30 .... www.flofr.com/
Mortgage Business School #30 .... www.flofr.com/
Motel/Restaurant #6 .... https://www.myfloridalicense.com/wl11.asp
Nail Specialist #6 .... https://www.myfloridalicense.com/wl11.asp
Naturopath #1 .... http://ww2.doh.state.fl.us/irm00praes/praslist.asp
Naturopathic Physician #1 .... http://ww2.doh.state.fl.us/irm00praes/praslist.asp
Notary Public #19 .... http://notaries.dos.state.fl.us/not001.html
Nuclear Radiology Physicist #1 .... http://ww2.doh.state.fl.us/irm00praes/praslist.asp
Nurse, Practical #1 .... http://ww2.doh.state.fl.us/irm00praes/praslist.asp
Nurse/Nursing Assistant #1 .... http://ww2.doh.state.fl.us/irm00praes/praslist.asp
Nursing Home Administrator #1 .... http://ww2.doh.state.fl.us/irm00praes/praslist.asp
Nutrition Counselor #1 .... http://ww2.doh.state.fl.us/irm00praes/praslist.asp
Occupational Therapist #1 .... http://ww2.doh.state.fl.us/irm00praes/praslist.asp
Optician/Optician Apprentice #1 .... http://ww2.doh.state.fl.us/irm00praes/praslist.asp
Optometrist #1 .... http://ww2.doh.state.fl.us/irm00praes/praslist.asp
Orthotist/Prosthetist #1 .... http://ww2.doh.state.fl.us/irm00praes/praslist.asp
Osteopathic Physician #1 .... http://ww2.doh.state.fl.us/irm00praes/praslist.asp
Paramedic #20 .... www.doh.state.fl.us/demo/ems/Providers/Providers.html
Pari-Mutuel Wagering #6 .... https://www.myfloridalicense.com/wl11.asp
Pedorthist #1 .... http://ww2.doh.state.fl.us/irm00praes/praslist.asp
Pest Control Operator #4 .... www.flaes.org/aes%2Dent/
Pest Control, Structural #4 .... www.flaes.org/aes%2Dent/
Pesticide Applicator #4 .... www.flaes.org/aes%2Dent/
Pharmacist, Consulting #1 .... http://ww2.doh.state.fl.us/irm00praes/praslist.asp
Pharmacist/Pharmacist Intern #1 .... http://ww2.doh.state.fl.us/irm00praes/praslist.asp
PHPC Public Health Pest Control #4 .... www.flaes.org/aes%2Dent/
Physical Therapist/Assistant #1 .... http://ww2.doh.state.fl.us/irm00praes/praslist.asp
Physician Assistant #1 .... http://ww2.doh.state.fl.us/irm00praes/praslist.asp
Physicist, Medical #1 .... http://ww2.doh.state.fl.us/irm00praes/praslist.asp
Pilot, State/Deputy #6 .... https://www.myfloridalicense.com/wl11.asp
Plumbing Contractor #16 .... https://www.myfloridalicense.com/wl11.asp
Pollutant Storage System Contr. #16 .... https://www.myfloridalicense.com/wl11.asp
Polygraph Assn Member #27 .... www.floridapolygraph.org/directory/
Polygraph Examiner #27 .... www.floridapolygraph.org/directory/
Precision Tank Tester #16 .... https://www.myfloridalicense.com/wl11.asp
Preneed Seller, Funeral #29 .... https://apps.fldfs.com/fclicense/searchpage.aspx

Private Investigator/Agency #18 .... http://licgweb.doacs.state.fl.us/access/individual.html
Psychologist/Ltd License Psycholog't #1 .. http://ww2.doh.state.fl.us/irm00praes/praslist.asp
Public Accountant-CPA #21 .... https://www.myfloridalicense.com/wl11.asp
Racing, Dog/Horse #6 .... https://www.myfloridalicense.com/wl11.asp
Radiologic Physician #1 .... http://ww2.doh.state.fl.us/irm00praes/praslist.asp
Radiologist #1 .... http://ww2.doh.state.fl.us/irm00praes/praslist.asp
Real Estate Agent/Broker/Sales #24 .... https://www.myfloridalicense.com/wl11.asp
Real Estate Appraiser #24 .... https://www.myfloridalicense.com/wl11.asp
Recovery Agent School/Instrct./Mgr. #18 . http://licgweb.doacs.state.fl.us/access/agency.html
Recovery Agent/Agency/Intern #18 .... http://licgweb.doacs.state.fl.us/access/agency.html
Respiratory Care Therapist/Provider #1 ... http://ww2.doh.state.fl.us/irm00praes/praslist.asp
Roofing Contractor #16 .... https://www.myfloridalicense.com/wl11.asp
Sales Finance Company #30 .... www.flofr.com/
School Psychologist #1 .... http://ww2.doh.state.fl.us/irm00praes/praslist.asp
Securities Agent/Dealer #30 .... www.flofr.com/
Securities Broker Dealer/Branch Ofc #30 . www.flofr.com/
Securities Broker/Seller/Associate #30 ..... www.flofr.com/
Securities Registration #30 .... www.flofr.com/
Security Officer School #18 .... http://licgweb.doacs.state.fl.us/access/agency.html
Security Officer/Instructor #18 .... http://licgweb.doacs.state.fl.us/access/individual.html
Sheet Metal Contractor #16 .... https://www.myfloridalicense.com/wl11.asp
Social Worker, Clinical/Master #1 .... http://ww2.doh.state.fl.us/irm00praes/praslist.asp
Solar Contractor #16 .... https://www.myfloridalicense.com/wl11.asp
Solid Waste Facility Operator #8 .... http://landfill.treeo.ufl.edu/Reports.aspx
Specialty Structure Contractor #16 .... https://www.myfloridalicense.com/wl11.asp
Speech-Language Pathologist #1 .... http://ww2.doh.state.fl.us/irm00praes/praslist.asp
Surveyor, Mapping #6 .... https://www.myfloridalicense.com/wl11.asp
Swimming Pool/Spa Contr./Svc #16 .... https://www.myfloridalicense.com/wl11.asp
Talent Agency #6 .... https://www.myfloridalicense.com/wl11.asp
Teacher #2 .... www.fldoe.org/edcert/
Therapeutic Radiologic Physician #1 .... http://ww2.doh.state.fl.us/irm00praes/praslist.asp
Tobacco Wholesale #6 .... https://www.myfloridalicense.com/wl11.asp
Underground Utility Contractor #16 .... https://www.myfloridalicense.com/wl11.asp
Veterinarian/Veterinary Establishment #6. https://www.myfloridalicense.com/wl11.asp
Visiting Mental Health Faculty #1 .... http://ww2.doh.state.fl.us/irm00praes/praslist.asp
X-ray, Pod, Assistant #1 .... http://ww2.doh.state.fl.us/irm00praes/praslist.asp
Yacht & Ship Broker/Salesman #6 .... https://www.myfloridalicense.com/wl11.asp

Florida Licensing Quick Finder

Acupuncturist #1 850-488-0595
Adoption Service #9 850-922-6656
Adult & Foster Care #9 850-487-2383
Air Ambulance #20 850-245-4440
Air Conditioning Contractor/Svc #16 850-487-1395
Alcoholic Beverage Permit #6 850-487-1395
Ambulance Service #20 850-245-4440
Animal Registra'n (Marks/Brands) #3 ... 850-922-0187
Architect/Architectural Firm #11 850-487-1395
Assisted Living Facility #26 850-487-2515
Athletic Agent #6 850-488-8500
Athletic Trainer #1 850-488-0595
Attorney #23 850-561-5832
Auctioneer/Auction Firm #22 850-487-1395
Audiologist #1 850-488-0595
Automobile Dealer, New #13 850-617-3003
Automobile Dealer/Seller #13 850-617-3003
Automobile Repossessor #18 850-488-5381
Bail Bondsman #14 850-413-3137
Bank #5 850-410-9800
Barber/Barber Assist./Shop #6 850-487-1395
Boxer #6 850-488-8500
Building Code Administrator #6 850-487-1395
Building Contractor #16 850-487-1395
Building Inspector #6 850-487-1395
Cemetery #29 .... 800-323-2627, 850-413-3039
Cemetery Lot Seller #29 800-323-2627, 850-413-3039
Child Care Center #10 850-488-4900
Child Care/Child Placing Facility #9 850-922-6656
Chiropractic-related Occupation #1 850-488-0595
Chiropractor #1 850-488-0595
Clinical Lab Personnel #1 850-488-0595
Clinical Laboratory #26 850-487-3109
Community Assoc. Manager #6 850-487-1395
Company in Receivership #14 800-882-3054
Concealed Weapon #15 850-245-5691
Concealed Weapon License #18 850-488-5381
Construction Qualified Business #16 ... 850-487-1395
Continuing Edu. Provider, Medical #1 .. 850-488-0595
Contractor, General #16 850-487-1395
Contractor, Residential #16 850-487-1395
Cosmetologist, Nails/Salon #6 850-487-1395
Credit Union #5 850-410-9800
Crematory #29 .... 800-323-2627, 850-413-3039
Day Care/Child Care Ctr/Nursery Sch'l #10 850-488-4900
Dentist/Dental Assistant #1 850-488-0595
Dietician/Nutritionist #1 850-488-0595
Doctor, Limited #1 850-488-0595
Drywall/Gypsum Specialty Contr. #16 .. 850-487-1395
Electrical Contractor #16 850-488-3109
Electrologist/Electrologist Facility #1 850-488-0595
Elevator Certificates of Operation #6 ... 850-487-1395
Embalmer #29 .... 800-323-2627, 850-413-3039
Emergency Medical Technician #20 850-245-4440
Employee Leasing Company #16 850-487-1395
Engineer/Engineering Firm #17 850-521-0500
Finance Company, Consumer #30 850-410-9895
Financial Institution #5 850-410-9800
Firearm Instructor/School/Agency #15. 850-245-5691
Firearms Instructor #18 850-488-5381
Firearms License, Statewide #18 850-488-5381
Fishing, Commercial Fresh Water #25 . 850-487-0554
Food Services Establishment #6 850-487-1395
Foster Family Home #9 850-922-6656
Fumigation Performance Spec'l ID #4 . 850-921-4177
Funeral Director #29 .... 800-323-2627, 850-413-3039
Funeral Home #29 .... 800-323-2627, 850-413-3039
Gas Line Specialty Contractor #16 850-487-1395
Geologist/Geology Firm #6 850-488-1105
Guidance Counselor #2 800-445-6739
Hair Braider #6 850-487-1395
Health Facility #26 850-922-5455
Hearing Aid Specialist #1 850-488-0595
Home Health Care Agency #26 850-414-6010
Home Improvement Financer #30 850-410-9895
Hospital #26 850-487-2717
Hotel/Restaurant #6 850-488-7891
In Home Family Day Care Center #10. 850-488-4900
Insect Sting Treatment Specialist #20 . 850-245-4440
Installment Seller, Retail #30 850-410-9895
Insurance Adjuster/Agent/Title Agent #14 850-413-3137
Insurance-related Company #14 850-413-3137
Interior Design Firm/Individual #11 850-487-1395
Internal Pollutant Storage Tank Lining #16 850-487-1395

International Bank Office #5 850-410-9800
Investment Advisor #30 850-410-9893
Kickboxer #6 850-488-8500
Lab License #26 850-487-3109
Labor Org Business Agent #7 850-488-3131
Labor Organization #7 850-488-3131
Land Sale, Condominiums #6 850-488-1636
Landscape Architecture Firm/Individ'l #11 850-487-1395
Landscape Maint./Pest Mgmt Co. #4 ... 850-921-4177
Liquor Store #6 850-488-8288
Livestock Hauler #3 850-922-0187
Lobby Principal (Miami-Dade) #28 305-375-5137
Lobbyist (Miami-Dade only) #28 305-375-5137
Lobbyist/Principal #28 850-922-4990
Lodging Establishment #6 850-487-1395
Marriage & Family Therapist #1 850-488-0595
Massage Therapist/School/Facility #1 .. 850-488-0595
Mechanical Contractor #16 850-487-1395
Medical Doctor #1 850-488-0595
Medical Faculty Member #1 850-488-0595
Mental Health Counselor #1 850-488-0595
Midwife #1 850-488-0595
Milk Hauler/Tester #12 850-487-1450
Mobile Home #6 850-488-1636
Mobile Home Dealer/Broker/Mfg #13 ... 850-617-3003
Money Transmitter #30 850-410-9805
Monument Dealer #29 . 800-323-2627, 850-413-3039
Mortgage Broker #30 850-410-9895
Mortgage Broker Firm #30 850-410-9895
Mortgage Business School #30 850-410-9895
Motel/Restaurant #6 904-488-1133
Nail Specialist #6 850-487-1395
Naturopath #1 850-488-0595
Naturopathic Physician #1 850-488-0595
Notary Public #19 850-245-6975
Nuclear Radiology Physicist #1 850-488-0595
Nurse, Practical #1 850-488-0595
Nurse/Nursing Assistant #1 850-488-0595
Nursing Home Administrator #1 850-488-0595
Nutrition Counselor #1 850-488-0595
Occupational Therapist #1 850-488-0595
Optician/Optician Apprentice #1 850-488-0595
Optometrist #1 850-488-0595
Orphanage #9 850-922-6656
Orthotist/Prosthetist #1 850-488-0595
Osteopathic Physician #1 850-488-0595
Paramedic #20 850-245-4440
Pari-Mutuel Wagering #6 850-488-9161
Pedorthist #1 850-488-0595
Pest Control Operator #4 850-921-4177
Pest Control, Structural #4 850-921-4177
Pesticide Applicator #4 850-921-4177
Pet Shop #25 850-487-0554
Pharmacist, Consulting #1 850-488-0595
Pharmacist/Pharmacist Intern #1 850-488-0595
PHPC Public Health Pest Control #4 ... 850-921-4177
Physical Therapist/Assistant #1 850-488-0595
Physician Assistant #1 850-488-0595
Physicist, Medical #1 850-488-0595
Pilot, State/Deputy #6 850-488-0698
Plumbing Contractor #16 850-487-1395
Pollutant Storage System Contr. #16 ... 850-487-1395
Polygraph Assn Member #27 954-321-4264
Polygraph Examiner #27 954-321-4264
Precision Tank Tester #16 850-487-1395
Preneed Seller, Funeral #29 .... 800-323-2627, 850-413-3039
Private Investigator #15 850-245-5691
Private Investigator/Agency #18 850-488-5381
Psychologist/Ltd Psycholog't #1 850-488-0595
Public Accountant-CPA #21 850-487-1395
Racing, Dog/Horse #6 850-488-9130
Radiologic Physician #1 850-488-0595
Radiologist #1 850-488-0595
Real Estate Agent/Broker/Sales #24 407-245-0800
Real Estate Appraiser #24 407-245-0800
Recovering Agent #15 850-245-5691
Recovery Agent Sch'l/Instrct./Mgr. #18. 850-488-5381
Recovery Agent/Agency/Intern #18 850-488-5381
Recreational Vehicle Dealer #13 850-617-3003
Respiratory Care Therap'st/Provider #1 850-488-0595
Retail Installment Seller #5 850-410-9800
Roofing Contractor #16 850-487-1395
Sales Finance Company #30 850-410-9895
Savings & Loan Assn, Charter #5 850-410-9800
School Admin./Supervisor #2 800-445-6739
School Educ. Media Specialist #2 800-445-6739
School Principal #2 800-445-6739
School Psychologist #1 850-488-0595
Securities Agent #30 850-410-9893
Securities Broker Dealer/Branch #30.... 850-410-9893
Securities Broker/Seller/Associate #30. 850-410-9893
Securities Dealer #30 850-410-9935
Securities Registration #30 850-410-9805
Security Officer #15 850-245-5691
Security Officer School #18 850-488-5381
Security Officer/Instructor #18 850-488-5381
Sheet Metal Contractor #16 850-487-1395
Social Worker, Clinical/Master #1 850-488-0595
Solar Contractor #16 850-487-1395
Solid Waste Facility Operator #8 . 352-392-9570 x227
Specialty Structure Contractor #16 850-487-1395
Speech-Language Pathologist #1 850-488-0595
Surveyor, Mapping #6 850-487-1395
Sweepstakes Operator (game promo) #18 850-488-5381
Swimming Pool/Spa Contr./Svc #16 850-487-1395
Talent Agency #6 850-487-1395
Teacher #2 800-445-6739
Therapeutic Radiologic Physician #1 ... 850-488-0595
Tobacco Wholesale #6 850-487-6793
Trust Company #5 850-410-9800
Underground Utility Contractor #16 850-487-1395
Veterinarian/Vet Establishment #6 850-487-1395
Visiting Mental Health Faculty #1 850-488-0595
X-ray, Pod, Assistant #1 850-488-0595
Yacht & Ship Broker/Salesman #6 850-488-1636
Zoo #25 850-487-0554

Florida Licensing Agency Information

#1 Dept. of Health, Division of Medical Quality Assurance, 4052 Bald Cypress Way, Tallahassee, FL 32399; 850-488-0595. www.doh.state.fl.us/mqa/ Search at- http://ww2.doh.state.fl.us/irm00praes/praslist.asp

#2 Dept. of Education, Bureau of Educator Certification, 325 W Gaines St, #201, Turlington Bldg, Tallahassee, FL 32399; 800-445-6739, Fax- 850-245-9667. 8AM-5PM. www.fldoe.org Search data at- www.fldoe.org/edcert/public.asp

#3 Dept. of Agriculture & Consumer Services, Division of Animal Industry, 407 S Calhoun St, MS: M7, Tallahassee, FL 32399-0800; 850-410-0900, Fax- 850-410-0957. www.doacs.state.fl.us/ai/

#4 Dept. of Agriculture & Consumer Services, Bureau of Entomology & Pest Control, 3125 Conner Blvd, #F, Tallahassee, FL 32399-1650; 850-921-4177, Fax- 850-410-0724. www.flaes.org/aes-ent/ Search data at- www.flaes.org/aes%2Dent/

#5 Financial Regulation, Financial Institutions Division, 200 E Gaines St, Larsen Bldg, Tallahassee, FL 32399-0371; 850-410-9800, Fax- 850-410-9548. www.flofr.com/banking/index.htm Formerly the Dept of Banking and Finance.

#6 Dept. of Business & Professional Regulation, DBPR Licensing, 1940 N Monroe St, #300, Tallahassee, FL 32399; 850-487-1395, Fax- 850-921-4216. www.myflorida.com/dbpr/ Search data at- https://www.myfloridalicense.com/wl11.asp

#7 Dept. of Business & Professional Regulation, Farm and Child Labor Program, PO Box 1698, Tallahassee, FL 32302-1698; 850-488-3131, Fax- 850-488-0512.

#8 Dept. of Environmental Protection, Division of Waste Management, 2600 Blair Stone Rd, M/S 3500, Tallahassee, FL 32399-2400; 850-245-8734, Fax- 850-245-8811. Hours- 8AM-5PM. www.dep.state.fl.us Search data at- http://landfill.treeo.ufl.edu/Reports.aspx The voluntary database for solid waste facility operators is maintained by The Univ. of FL for the Dept of Environmental Protection. Since it is voluntary it may not contain data for 100% of the operators.

#9 Dept. of Children & Families, Interstate Corporate Office, 1317 Winewood Blvd, Bldg 1, #202, Tallahassee, FL 32399-0700; 850-487-2383, Fax- 850-488-0751. www.state.fl.us/cf_web/ Agency provides an informative searchable online list of children available for adoption through them.

#10 Dept. of Children & Families, Child Care Program Office, 1317 Winewood Blvd, Tallahassee, FL 32399-0700; 850-488-4900, Fax- 850-414-7974. Hours- 8AM-5PM. www.dcf.state.fl.us/childcare/

#11 Dept. of Professional Regulation, Board of Architecture and Interior Design, 1940 N Monroe St, Tallahassee, FL 32399-1027; 850-487-1395, Fax- 850-922-4191. 8AM-5PM. www.myflorida.com/dbpr/pro/arch/index.html Search data at- https://www.myfloridalicense.com/wl11.asp

#12 Dept. of Agriculture & Consumer Services, Division of Dairy Industry, 3125 Conner Blvd, M/S C-27, Tallahassee, FL 32399-1650; 850-487-1450, Fax- 850-922-9444. http://doacs.state.fl.us/dairy/

#13 Dept. of Highway Safety & Motor Vehicles, Bureau of Field Operations, 2900 Apalachee Pky, MS65, Tallahassee, FL 32399-0500; 850-617-3171, Fax- 850-922-9840. Hours- 8AM-5PM. www.flhsmv.gov/html/records.html List available $25.00 each. Request must be in writing.

#14 Dept. of Financial Services, Office of Insurance Regulation; Agents & Agency Licensing, 200 E Gaines St, Larsen Bldg,

Tallahassee, FL 32399; 850-413-3140, Fax-850-488-3334. Hours- 8AM-4PM. www.fldfs.com Search data at- www.fldfs.com/data/aar_alis1/ Formerly the Dept. of Insurance.

#15 Agriculture and Consumer Services, Division of Licensing, PO Box 6687, Tallahassee, FL 32314-6687; 850-245-5499, Fax- 850-245-5505. Hours- 8AM-5PM. http://licgweb.doacs.state.fl.us

#16 Dept. of Professional Regulation, Construction Industry Licensing Board, 1940 N Monroe St, Tallahassee, FL 32399; 850-487-1395, Fax- 850-921-4216. Hours- 8AM-6PM M-F, 10AM-2PM Sat. www.myflorida.com/dbpr/pro/cilb/index.html Search data at- https://www.myfloridalicense.com/wl11.asp

#17 Board of Professional Engineers, 2507 Calloway Rd #200, Tallahassee, FL 32303-5267; 850-521-0500, Fax- 850-521-0521. www.fbpe.org Search data at- www.fbpe.org/engineeringdirectory.asp Roster lists are also available on CD-rom for $5.00.

#18 Division of Licensing, Bureau of License Issuance, PO Box 6687, Tallahassee, FL 32314-6687; 850-488-5381, Fax- 850-487-7950. 8AM-5PM. http://licgweb.doacs.state.fl.us Search data at- http://licgweb.doacs.state.fl.us

#19 Dept. of State, Division of Corporations, Notary Commision, PO Box 6327, Tallahassee, FL 32314; 850-245-6975, Fax- 850-245-6966. http://notaries.dos.state.fl.us Search data at- http://notaries.dos.state.fl.us/not001.html

#20 Emergency Medical Services, 4025 Bald Cypress Way, Bin #C18, Tallahassee, FL 32311; 850-245-4440, Fax- 850-488-9408. www.doh.state.fl.us/demo/ems/Providers/Providers.html Search data at- www.doh.state.fl.us/demo/ems/Providers/Providers.html

#21 Dept. of Business & Professional Regulation, Board of Accountancy, 240 NW 76th Dr, #A, Gainesville, FL 32607; 850-487-1395, Fax- 352-333-2508. Hours- 8AM-5PM. www.myflorida.com/dbpr/cpa/index.html Search data at- https://www.myfloridalicense.com/wl11.asp

#22 Dept. of Business & Professional Regulation, Board of Auctioneers, 1940 N Monroe St, Tallahassee, FL 32399; 850-487-1395. www.myfloridalicense.com/dbpr/pro/auct/index.html Search data at- https://www.myfloridalicense.com/wl11.asp

#23 Bar Membership Records Dept, Board of Bar Examiners, 651 E Jefferson St, Tallahassee, FL 32399-2300; 850-561-5832, Fax- 850-561-1141. www.floridabarexam.org Search data at- www.floridabar.org/names.nsf/MESearch?OpenForm

#24 Dept. of Business & Professional Regulation, Division of Real Estate, 400 W Robinson St, N801, Orlando, FL 32801; 850-487-1395, Fax- 407-317-7245. www.myflorida.com/dbpr/re/freab.html Search data at- https://www.myfloridalicense.com/wl11.asp

#25 Fish & Wildlife Conservation Commission, 2590 Executive Center Cir E, #201, Tallahassee, FL 32301; 850-487-0554, Fax- 850-487-4847. www.marinefisheries.org

#26 Facilities Licensing, Agency for Health Care Administration (AHCA), 2727 Mahan Dr, Tallahassee, FL 32308-5401; 850-414-9796, Fax- 850-487-6240. www.oppaga.state.fl.us/profiles/5048/

#27 Florida Polygraph Association, 1937 Vineland Dr, Tallahassee, FL 32317; 850-617-3286, Fax- 850-922-9051. www.floridapolygraph.org

#28 The Florida Legislature, Lobbyist Registration, 111 W Madison St, Rm G-68, Tallahassee, FL 32399-1425; 850-922-4990. www.leg.state.fl.us/lobbyist/ Search data at- www.leg.state.fl.us/lobbyist/

#29 Funeral, Cemetery & Consumer Services Board, Dept. of Financial Services, 200 E Gaines St, Tallahassee, FL 32399-0300; 850-413-3039, Fax- 850-413-4087. www.fldfs.com/FuneralCemetery/ Search at- https://apps.fldfs.com/fclicense/searchpage.aspx

#30 Office of Financial Regulation, Securities & Finance Division, 200 E Gaines St, Tallahassee, FL 32399; 850-410-9805, Fax-850-410-9748. Hours- 8AM-5PM. www.flofr.com/Securities/index.htm Search data at- www.flofr.com/ Formerly the Dept of Banking and Finance.

Florida Federal Courts

The following list indicates the district and division name for each county in the state. If the bankruptcy court location is different from the district court, then the location of the bankruptcy court appears in parentheses.

County/Court Cross Reference

County	District	Division
Alachua	Northern	Gainesville (Tallahassee)
Baker	Middle	Jacksonville
Bay	Northern	Panama City (Tallahassee)
Bradford	Middle	Jacksonville
Brevard	Middle	Orlando
Broward	Southern	Fort Lauderdale (Miami)
Calhoun	Northern	Panama City (Tallahassee)
Charlotte	Middle	Fort Myers (Tampa)
Citrus	Middle	Ocala (Jacksonville)
Clay	Middle	Jacksonville
Collier	Middle	Fort Myers (Tampa)
Columbia	Middle	Jacksonville
Dade	Southern	Miami
De Soto	Middle	Fort Myers (Tampa)
Dixie	Northern	Gainesville (Tallahassee)
Duval	Middle	Jacksonville
Escambia	Northern	Pensacola
Flagler	Middle	Jacksonville
Franklin	Northern	Tallahassee
Gadsden	Northern	Tallahassee
Gilchrist	Northern	Gainesville (Tallahassee)
Glades	Middle	Fort Myers (Tampa)
Gulf	Northern	Panama City (Tallahassee)
Hamilton	Middle	Jacksonville
Hardee	Middle	Tampa
Hendry	Middle	Fort Myers (Tampa)
Hernando	Middle	Tampa
Highlands	Southern	Fort Pierce (Miami)
Hillsborough	Middle	Tampa
Holmes	Northern	Panama City (Tallahassee)
Indian River	Southern	Fort Pierce (Miami)
Jackson	Northern	Panama City (Tallahassee)
Jefferson	Northern	Tallahassee
Lafayette	Northern	Gainesville (Tallahassee)
Lake	Middle	Ocala (Orlando)
Lee	Middle	Fort Myers (Tampa)
Leon	Northern	Tallahassee
Levy	Northern	Gainesville (Tallahassee)
Liberty	Northern	Tallahassee
Madison	Northern	Tallahassee
Manatee	Middle	Tampa
Marion	Middle	Ocala (Jacksonville)
Martin	Southern	Fort Pierce (Miami)
Monroe	Southern	Key West (Miami)
Nassau	Middle	Jacksonville
Okaloosa	Northern	Pensacola
Okeechobee	Southern	Fort Pierce (Miami)
Orange	Middle	Orlando
Osceola	Middle	Orlando
Palm Beach	Southern	W. Palm Beach (Miami)
Pasco	Middle	Tampa
Pinellas	Middle	Tampa
Polk	Middle	Tampa
Putnam	Middle	Jacksonville
Santa Rosa	Northern	Pensacola
Sarasota	Middle	Tampa
Seminole	Middle	Orlando
St. Johns	Middle	Jacksonville
St. Lucie	Southern	Fort Pierce (Miami)
Sumter	Middle	Ocala (Jacksonville)
Suwannee	Middle	Jacksonville
Taylor	Northern	Tallahassee
Union	Middle	Jacksonville
Volusia	Middle	Orlando (Jacksonville)
Wakulla	Northern	Tallahassee
Walton	Northern	Pensacola
Washington	Northern	Panama City (Tallahassee)

Standards for Federal Courts: Fees are standard unless noted in profile. Search fee is $26.00 per item (one party name or case number). Copy fee is $.50 per page. Certification fee is $9.00 per document, double for exemplification, if available. Most courts require prepayment. Mail requests should enclose a SASE unless otherwise noted. Before releasing records, all courts require prepayment, unless noted.

District courts index by defendant and plaintiff and by case number. Bankruptcy courts usually index by debtor and case number. While most courts now have their indexes on computer, many may still maintain index card files as well. Courts will archive closed case files at different times.

There are numerous public access programs available to online subscribers. Search the U.S. Party/Case Index to find party names and case numbers among all courts. Individual case data is provided on PACER. A search of CM/ECF provides copies of cases filed electronically. For details about PACER, the US Party/Case Index, and CM/ECF see the Appendix or go to http://pacer.psc.uscourts.gov or call 800-676-6856.

US District Court
Florida Middle District

Fort Myers Division Court Clerk, US Courthouse & Federal Building, 2110 First St, Rm 2-194, Fort Myers, FL 33901, 239-461-2000. Hours-8:30AM-4PM. www.flmd.uscourts.gov

Counties/Note: Charlotte, Collier, De Soto, Glades, Hendry, Lee.

Searches/Indexing: To search, include full name only; SSN and DOB may be helpful for older cases. Results do not include SSN or DOB. Will not fax back documents. New cases are in the index immediately after filing date. Computer index goes back to 1995. Civil case index is computerized; criminal index is not. Case files sent to archives 3 years after closed.

Search Access: Limited docket info available by phone. **Mail:** Search usually completed- 3 days. Include SASE for return. **Fax:** Written fax requests accepted, prepaid. **In person:** 2 public terminals available; index back to 1999. Self-serve copier available.

Payment: Pay by money order, cashier's or personal check. Payee: Clerk, US District Court.

E-Services: Document images available. PACER records go back to 1989-90. ECF at https://ecf.flmd.uscourts.gov. **Opinions Online:** www.flmd.uscourts.gov. Selected notable opinions only. **Online Note:** Calendars free at www.flmd.uscourts.gov.

Jacksonville Division Court Clerk, Bryan Simpson US Courthouse, 300 N Hogan St, Ste. 9-150, Jacksonville, FL 32202, 904-549-1900. Hours-8:30AM-4PM. www.flmd.uscourts.gov

Counties/Note: Baker, Bradford, Clay, Columbia, Duval, Flagler, Hamilton, Nassau, Putnam, St. Johns, Suwannee, Union.

Searches/Indexing: To search, include full name only; SSN and DOB may be helpful for older cases. Results do not include SSN or DOB. Will not fax back documents. New cases are in the index 1 day after filing date. Computer index goes back to 1995. Case files sent to archives 3 years after closed.

Search Access: Mail: Search usually completed- 3-5 days. Include SASE for return. **In person:** 3 public terminals available; index back to 1999. Self-serve copies $.50 each.

Payment: Pay by money order, cashier's or personal checks. No credit cards accepted. Payee: Clerk, US District Court.

E-Services: Document images available. PACER records go back to 1989-90. ECF at https://ecf.flmd.uscourts.gov. **Opinions Online:** www.flmd.uscourts.gov. Selected notable opinions only. **Online Note:** Calendars free at www.flmd.uscourts.gov.

Ocala Division Court Clerk, Federal Building and US Courthouse, 207 NW Second St, Rm 337, Ocala, FL 34475, 352-369-4860. 9AM-4:30PM. www.flmd.uscourts.gov

Counties/Note: Citrus, Lake, Marion, Sumter.

Searches/Indexing: To search, include full name only; SSN and DOB may be helpful for older cases. Results do not include SSN or DOB. Will not fax back documents. New cases are in the index 1 day after filing date. Computer index goes back to 1995. Open records located at Jacksonville Div. Files sent to archives 3 years after closed.

Search Access: Mail: Include SASE for return. **In person:** 1 public terminal available; index back to 1999. No self-serve copier.

Payment: Pay by money order, cashier's or personal checks. No credit cards accepted.

E-Services: Document images available. PACER records go back to 1989-90. ECF at https://ecf.flmd.uscourts.gov. **Opinions Online:** www.flmd.uscourts.gov. Selected notable opinions only. **Online Note:** Calendars free at www.flmd.uscourts.gov.

Orlando Div. Court Clerk, US Courthouse, 401 W Central Blvd, Ste 1200, Orlando, FL 32801, 407-835-4200; records- 407-835-4216. Hours- 8:30AM-4PM. www.flmd.uscourts.gov

Counties/Note: Brevard, Orange, Osceola, Seminole, Volusia.

Searches/Indexing: To search, include full name only; SSN and DOB may be helpful for older cases. Results do not include SSN or DOB. Will not fax back documents. New cases are in the index immediately after filing date. Computer index back to 1995 maintained. Records available electronically only. Case files sent to archives 3 years after closed.

Search Access: Limited docket info available by phone. **Mail:** Search usually completed- 3 days. Include SASE for return. **In person:** 1 public terminal available; index back to 1999. Self-serve copies $.50 each.

Payment: Pay by money order, cashier's or personal checks. No foreign checks and no credit cards accepted. Payee: Clerk, US District Court.

E-Services: Document images available. PACER records go back to 1995. New records online after 2000. ECF at https://ecf.flmd.uscourts.gov. **Opinions Online:** www.flmd.uscourts.gov. Selected notable opinions only. **Online Note:** Calendars free at www.flmd.uscourts.gov.

Tampa Division Office of the Clerk, Sam M Gibbons US Courthouse, 801 N Florida Ave #218, Tampa, FL 33602-4500, 813-301-5400. Hours- 9AM-4:30PM. www.flmd.uscourts.gov

Counties/Note: Hardee, Hernando, Hillsborough, Manatee, Pasco, Pinellas, Polk, Sarasota.

Searches/Indexing: To search, include full name only; SSN and DOB may be helpful for older cases. Results do not include SSN or DOB. Will not fax back documents. New cases are in the index 1 day after filing date. Computer index goes back to 1995. Records available electronically only. Files sent to archives 3 years after closed.

Search Access: Limited docket info available by phone. **Mail:** Search usually completed- 3-5 days. Include SASE for return. **In person:** 1 public terminal available; index back to 1999. Self-serve copies $.25 each.

Payment: Pay by money order, cashier's or personal check. Payee: Clerk, US District Court.

E-Services: Document images available. PACER records go back to 1989-90. ECF at https://ecf.flmd.uscourts.gov. **Opinions Online:** www.flmd.uscourts.gov. Selected notable opinions only. **Online Note:** Calendars free at www.flmd.uscourts.gov.

US Bankruptcy Court Florida Middle District

Jacksonville Div. Court Clerk, 300 N Hogan St #3-350, Jacksonville, FL 32202, 904-301-6490. Hours-8:30AM-4PM. www.flmb.uscourts.gov

Counties: Baker, Bradford, Citrus, Clay, Columbia, Duval, Flagler, Hamilton, Marion, Nassau, Putnam, St. Johns, Sumter, Suwannee, Union, Volusia.

Searches/Indexing: Include SSN and full name in search request; helpful to use Search Application form. Results include last 4 SSN digits. New cases are in the index immediately after filing date. No specific time when closed records sent to Archive.

Search Access: Voice Case Information Service available, call VCIS at 866-879-1286 or 904-301-6490. **Mail:** Search usually completed- 1-2 days. SASE not required. **In person:** 2 public terminals available. No self-serve copier.

Payment: Pay by money order, cashier's check, business check. No personal checks. Attorney Visa/MC cards accepted. Payee: Clerk, US Bankruptcy Court.

E-Services: PACER online at http://pacer.flmb.uscourts.gov. PACER records go back to 1981. New records online after 1 day. ECF at https://ecf.flmb.uscourts.gov. **Opinions Online:** http://pacer.flmb.uscourts.gov/fwxflmb/opn/dcs.fwx. Also, search the Judgment Order Book back to 1/2006 at http://pacer.flmb.uscourts.gov/judgments/book.asp. **Online Note:** Search the Bench database back to 1/1/1988 free at http://pacer.flmb.uscourts.gov/judges/search.asp. Use judge name or case number, dates, keyword, or header title. Search Unclaimed Funds free at http://pacer.flmb.uscourts.gov/fwxflmb/fud/fud.fwx

Orlando Division Court Clerk, 135 W Central Blvd, Ste 950, Orlando, FL 32801, 407-648-6365; records- x6200. Hours- 8:30AM - 4PM. www.flmb.uscourts.gov

Counties: Brevard, Lake, Orange, Osceola, Seminole.

Searches/Indexing: Include SSN and full name in search request; helpful to use Search Application form. Results do not include SSN or DOB. New cases are in the index immediately after filing date. No specific time when closed records sent to Atlanta Records Center.

Search Access: Voice Case Information Service available, call VCIS at 866-879-1286. **Mail:** Search usually completed- 1-2 days. Include SASE for return. **In person:** Public terminals available. No self-serve copier. There may be a 5 page photocopy limit at court.

Payment: Pay by money order, cashier's check, business check. No personal checks. Attorney Visa/MC accepted. Payee: Clerk, Bankruptcy Ct.

E-Services: PACER online at http://pacer.flmb.uscourts.gov. PACER records go back to 1986. New records online after 1 day. ECF at https://ecf.flmb.uscourts.gov. **Opinions Online:** http://pacer.flmb.uscourts.gov/fwxflmb/opn/dcs.fwx. Also, search the Judgment Order Book back to 1/2006 free at http://pacer.flmb.uscourts.gov/judgments/book.asp. **Online Note:** Search the Bench database back to 1/1/1988 free at http://pacer.flmb.uscourts.gov/judges/search.asp. Use judge name or case number, dates, keyword, or header title. Search Unclaimed Funds free at http://pacer.flmb.uscourts.gov/fwxflmb/fud/fud.fwx

Tampa Division Court Clerk, 801 N Florida Ave, #727, Court Clerk Office Intake, Tampa, FL 33602, 813-301-5065, 813-301-5162; records- 813-228-7200. Hours- 8:30AM - 4PM. www.flmb.uscourts.gov

Counties/Note: Charlotte, Collier, De Soto, Glades, Hardee, Hendry, Hernando, Hillsborough, Lee, Manatee, Pasco, Pinellas, Polk, Sarasota. A Fort Myers branch is located at 2110 1st St, Ft Myers; records are managed by the Tampa Court.

Searches/Indexing: Include SSN and full name in search request; helpful to use Search Application form. Results do not include SSN or DOB. New cases in the index immediately after filing date. No specific time when closed records sent to archives.

Search Access: Voice Case Information Service available, call VCIS at 866-879-1286 or 813-301-5210. **Mail:** Search usually completed- 1-2 days. Include SASE for return. **In person:** Public terminals available. No self-serve copier.

Payment: Pay by money order, cashier's check, business check. No personal checks. Attorney Visa/MC cards accepted. Payee: Clerk, US Bankruptcy Court.

E-Services: PACER online at http://pacer.flmb.uscourts.gov. PACER records go back to 1992. New records online after 1 day. ECF at https://ecf.flmb.uscourts.gov. **Opinions Online:** http://pacer.flmb.uscourts.gov/fwxflmb/opn/dcs.fwx. Search Judgment Order Book back to 1/2006 free at http://pacer.flmb.uscourts.gov/judgments/book.asp. **Online Note:** Search the Bench database back to 1/1/1988 free at http://pacer.flmb.uscourts.gov/judges/search.asp. Use judge name or case number, dates, keyword, or header title. Search Unclaimed Funds free at http://pacer.flmb.uscourts.gov/fwxflmb/fud/fud.fwx

US District Court Florida Northern District

Gainesville Division Court Clerk, 401 SE First Ave, Rm 243, Gainesville, FL 32601, 352-380-2400; Fax- 352-380-2424. Hours- 8:30AM-5:00PM. www.flnd.uscourts.gov

Counties/Note: Alachua, Dixie, Gilchrist, Lafayette, Levy. Records for cases prior to 7/1996 are maintained at the Tallahassee Division.

Searches/Indexing: Search request requires name only. Results do not include SSN or DOB. Will fax back documents for fee. New cases are in the index 3 days after filing date. Both computer and card indexes maintained. District-wide searches available back to 8/1992. Closed cases sent to archives depending on case type.

Search Access: Only 1-3 names may be searched via phone, and only docket info is released. **Mail:** Search usually completed- 2-3 days. Include SASE for return. **Fax:** Fax search requests accepted. **In person:** 2 public terminals available. Computer generated copies- $.10 each.

Payment: Pay by Visa/MC, money order, cashier's or personal check. Payee: Clerk, US District Court.

E-Services: PACER records go back to 1992. New records online after 1 day. ECF at https://ecf.flnd.uscourts.gov. Opinions available on ECF PACER system.

Panama City Division Court Clerk, 30 W Government St, Panama City, FL 32401, 850-769-4556; Fax- 850-769-7528. Hours-8AM-4:30PM. www.flnd.uscourts.gov

Counties/Note: Bay, Calhoun, Gulf, Holmes, Jackson, Washington.

Searches/Indexing: Search request requires name only. Results do not include SSN or DOB. Will fax back documents for fee. New cases are in the index 2-3 days after filing date. Records on computer back to 1995, also card indexes. District-wide searches available back to 8/1992. Case files sent to archives 3 years after closed; electronic versions kept indefinitely.

Search Access: Only basic info is released via phone. **Mail:** Search usually completed- 2-3 days. Include SASE for return. **Fax:** Fax search requests accepted. **In person:** 1 public terminal available. No self-serve copier.

Payment: Pay by Visa/MC, money order, cashier's or personal check. No business checks accepted. Payee: Clerk, US District Court.

E-Services: PACER records go back to 1992. New records online after 1 day. ECF at https://ecf.flnd.uscourts.gov. Opinions available on ECF PACER system.

Pensacola Division Court Clerk, US Courthouse #226, 1 N Palafox St, Pensacola, FL 32502, 850-435-8440; Fax- 850-433-5972. Hours-8AM-4:30AM. www.flnd.uscourts.gov

Counties/Note: Escambia, Okaloosa, Santa Rosa, Walton.

Searches/Indexing: Search request requires name only. Results do not include SSN or DOB. Will fax back documents for fee. New cases are in the index 2-3 days after filing date. Both computer and card indexes maintained; computer back to 8/1992. District-wide searches available back to 8/1992. Case files sent to archives 3 years after closed; electronic versions kept indefinitely.

Search Access: Only basic info is released via phone. Court will not release all docket data via phone. **Mail:** Search usually completed- 2-3 days. Include SASE for return. **Fax:** Fax search requests accepted. **In person:** 2 public terminals available. No self-serve copier.

Payment: Pay by Visa/MC, money order, cashier's or personal check. Payee: Clerk, US District Court.

E-Services: PACER records go back to 1992. New records online after 1 day. ECF at https://ecf.flnd.uscourts.gov. Opinions available on ECF PACER system.

Tallahassee Division Court Clerk, 111 N Adams St, Suite 322, Tallahassee, FL 32301, 850-521-3501; Fax- 850-521-3656. Hours-8AM-4:30PM. www.flnd.uscourts.gov

Counties/Note: Franklin, Gadsden, Jefferson, Leon, Liberty, Madison, Taylor, Wakulla.

Searches/Indexing: Search request requires name only. Results do not include SSN or DOB. Will fax back documents for fee. New cases are in the index 2-3 days after filing date. Both computer and card indexes maintained. Records indexed by year closed. District-wide searches available back to 8/1992. Case files sent to archives 3 years after closed; electronic versions kept indefinitely.

Search Access: Basic case info requested by name (reveals case number) or by case number (reveals names of parties or their attorneys, date of complaint, general status) is available free by phone. **Mail:** Search usually completed- 2-3 days. Include SASE for return. **Fax:** Fax search requests accepted. **In person:** 1 public terminal available. No self-serve copier.

Payment: Pay by Visa/MC, money order, cashier's or personal check. Payee: Clerk, US District Court.

E-Services: PACER records go back to 1992. New records online after 1 day. ECF at https://ecf.flnd.uscourts.gov. Opinions available on ECF PACER system.

US Bankruptcy Court Florida Northern District

Pensacola Division Court Clerk, 220 W Garden St, Suite 700, Pensacola, FL 32502, 866-639-4615 (is Tallahassee ct). Hours-9AM-4PM. www.flnb.uscourts.gov

Counties/Note: Escambia, Okaloosa, Santa Rosa, Walton. You may search at either division.

Searches/Indexing: Include name and SSN in search request. Results do not include SSN or DOB. Will not fax back documents. New cases are in the index immediately after filing date. Both computer and card indexes maintained. All case files are electronicly stored.

Search Access: Only docket info is available by phone. Voice Case Information Service available, call VCIS at 888-765-1751. **Mail:** Search usually completed- 1-2 days. Include SASE. **In person:** 2 public terminals available. No self-serve copier.

Payment: Pay by credit cards, money order, cashier's check, business check. No personal checks accepted. Payee: Clerk, Bankruptcy Court.

E-Services: PACER records go back to 9/1985. ECF at https://ecf.flnb.uscourts.gov. **Opinions:** www.flnb.uscourts.gov/webapps/opinions/.
Online Note: Calendars available free at www.flnb.uscourts.gov/.

Tallahassee Division Court Clerk, 110 E Park Ave #100, Tallahassee, FL 32301-7726, 850-521-5001, 850-521-5001; Fax- 850-521-5004. Hours-9AM-4PM. www.flnb.uscourts.gov

Counties/Note: Alachua, Bay, Calhoun, Dixie, Franklin, Gadsden, Gilchrist, Gulf, Holmes, Jackson, Jefferson, Lafayette, Leon, Levy, Liberty, Madison, Taylor, Wakulla, Washington. You may search at either division.

Searches/Indexing: Include name and SSN in search request. Results do not include SSN or DOB. Will not fax back documents. New cases are in the index immediately after filing date. Both computer and card indexes maintained. All case files are electronicly stored.

Search Access: Only docket info is available by phone. Voice Case Information Service available, call VCIS at 888-765-1751 or 850-521-5040 (Tallahassee only). **Mail:** Search usually completed- 1-2 days. Include SASE for return. **In person:** 2 public terminals available. No self-serve copier.

Payment: Pay by credit cards, money order, cashier's check, business check. No personal checks accepted. Payee: Clerk, Bankruptcy Court.

E-Services: PACER records go back to 9/23/1985. New records online after 1 day. ECF at https://ecf.flnb.uscourts.gov. **Opinions Online:** www.flnb.uscourts.gov/webapps/opinions/.
Online Note: Calendars available free at www.flnb.uscourts.gov/.

US District Court Florida Southern District

Fort Lauderdale Division Court Clerk, 299 E Broward Blvd, #108, Fort Lauderdale, FL 33301, 954-769-5400. Hours-8:30AM-4:30PM; phones til 5PM. www.flsd.uscourts.gov

Counties/Note: Broward.

Searches/Indexing: Full name of any party, case type required to search; include DOB. Recent cases do not include SSN or DOB. Will not fax back documents. New cases are in the index immediately after filing date. Civil cases on computer back to 8/1990; criminal to 1/1992. Cases from 1983 on microfiche; prior on microfilm. Case files sent to Atlanta Records Center 5 years after closed.

Search Access: Only docket info available by phone. **Mail:** Search usually completed- 10 working days. Include SASE for return. **In person:** 2 public terminals available. Self-serve copier available in lobby, $.25 each. Court can recommend a vendor to search and make copies.

Payment: Pay by Visa/MC, money order, cashier's check, business check, local personal check. No out of state personal checks accepted. Payee: US Courts.

E-Services: PACER online at http://pacer.flsd.uscourts.gov. Document images available. PACER records go back to 8/1990. New records online after 1 day. ECF at https://ecf.flsd.uscourts.gov. **Opinions:** www.flsd.uscourts.gov/default.asp?file=cases/pressDocs.asp. Filings and verdicts free at www.flsd.uscourts.gov/default.asp?file=fileverdicts.html.

Fort Pierce Division Court Clerk, 300 S Sixth St, US Courthouse, Fort Pierce, FL 34950, 772-467-2300. Hours- 8:30AM-4:30PM; phones til 5PM. www.flsd.uscourts.gov

Counties/Note: Highlands, Indian River, Martin, Okeechobee, St. Lucie.

Searches/Indexing: Full name of any party, case type required to search; include DOB. Recent cases do not include SSN or DOB. Will not fax back documents. New cases are in the index immediately after filing date. Computer index maintained; civil back to 1985, criminal to 1990. Open records located at Miami Division. Files sent to Atlanta Records Center 5 years after closed.

Search Access: Only docket info available by phone. **Mail:** Search usually completed- 10

working days. Include SASE for return. **In person:** No self-serve copier.

Payment: Pay by Visa/MC, money order, cashier's or personal check. Payee: US Courts.

E-Services: PACER online at http://pacer.flsd.uscourts.gov. Document images available. PACER records go back to 8/1990. New records online after 1 day. ECF at https://ecf.flsd.uscourts.gov. **Opinions Online:** www.flsd.uscourts.gov/default.asp?file=cases/pressDocs.asp. Filings and verdicts free at www.flsd.uscourts.gov/default.asp?file=fileverdicts.html.

Key West Division c/o Miami District Court, Wilkie D. Ferguson, Jr. United State Courthouse, 400 N Miami Ave, 8th Fl, Miami, FL 33128 (In person: 301 Simonton St, Key West, FL 33040), 305-295-8100; records- 305-523-5210. Hours-8:30AM-4PM. www.flsd.uscourts.gov

Counties/Note: Monroe. The Key West Courthouse observes irregular hours.

Searches/Indexing: Full name of any party, case type required to search; include DOB. Recent cases do not include SSN or DOB. Will not fax back documents. New cases are in the index immediately after filing date. Computer index back to 1991 maintained. Case files sent to Atlanta Record Ctr archives 5 years after closed.

Search Access: Only docket info available by phone. **Mail:** Search usually completed- 10 working days. Include SASE for return. **In person:** No public access terminals available. Self-serve copies $.50 each. A copy service will pull records and make copies for a fee.

Payment: Pay by Visa/MC, money order, cashier's or personal check. Payee: US Courts.

E-Services: PACER http://pacer.flsd.uscourts.gov. Document images available. PACER records go back to 8/1992. New records online after 1 day. ECF at https://ecf.flsd.uscourts.gov. **Opinions:** www.flsd.uscourts.gov/default.asp?file=cases/pressDocs.asp. Filings and verdicts free at www.flsd.uscourts.gov/default.asp?file=fileverdicts.html.

Miami Division Court Clerk, Wilkie D. Ferguson, Jr. United State Courthouse, 400 N Miami Ave, 8th Fl, Miami, FL 33128, 305-523-5100; records- 305-523-5210; Hours-8:30AM-4:30PM; phones til 5PM. www.flsd.uscourts.gov

Counties/Note: Dade, Miami-Dade.

Searches/Indexing: Full name of any party, case type required to search; include DOB. Results have SSN on criminal, DOB on judgments. Will not fax back documents. New cases are in the index 1 day after filing date. Computer index back to 1990 maintained. Case files sent to Atlanta Records Center 5 years after closed.

Search Access: Only docket info available by phone. **Mail:** Search usually completed- 10 working days. Include SASE for return. **In person:** 3 public terminals available. Self-serve $.25 copier available in the lobby area of Records and Docketing Section. Court can recommend an outside vendor to search and make copies.

Payment: Pay by Visa/MC, money order, cashier's check. Payee: US Courts.

E-Services: PACER online at http://pacer.flsd.uscourts.gov. Document images available. PACER records go back to 8/1990. New records online after 1 day. ECF at https://ecf.flsd.uscourts.gov. **Opinions Online:** www.flsd.uscourts.gov/default.asp?file=cases/pressDocs.asp. Filings and verdicts free at www.flsd.uscourts.gov/default.asp?file=fileverdicts.html.

West Palm Beach Division Court Clerk, 701 Clematis St, Rm 402, West Palm Beach, FL 33401, 561-803-3400. Hours-8:30AM-4:30PM; phones til 5PM. www.flsd.uscourts.gov

Counties/Note: Palm Beach.

Searches/Indexing: Full name of any party, case type required to search; include DOB. Recent cases do not include SSN or DOB. Will not fax back documents. New cases are in the index immediately after filing date. Computer index back to 1990 maintained. Case files sent to archives 5 years after closed, then sent to Atlanta Records Center.

Search Access: Only docket info available by phone. **Mail:** Search usually completed- 1-2 days. Include SASE for return. **In person:** 2 public terminals available. Self-serve copies $.50 each. A copy service is available to pull records and copy.

Payment: Pay by Visa/MC, money order, cashier's check, business check. No personal checks. Payee: US Courts.

E-Services: PACER online at http://pacer.flsd.uscourts.gov. Document images available. PACER records go back to 8/1990. New records online after 1 day. ECF at https://ecf.flsd.uscourts.gov. **Opinions Online:** www.flsd.uscourts.gov/default.asp?file=cases/pressDocs.asp. Filings and verdicts free at www.flsd.uscourts.gov/default.asp?file=fileverdicts.html.

US Bankruptcy Court Florida Southern District

Fort Lauderdale Division Court Clerk, 299 E Broward Blvd, Rm 112, Fort Lauderdale, FL 33301, 954-769-5700. Hours- 9AM-4:30PM. www.flsb.uscourts.gov

Counties/Note: Broward. Records may also include some older records from Miami-Dade County, particularly Chapter 13s.

Searches/Indexing: Include SSN or EIN with full name in search request. Results do not include SSN or DOB. Will not fax back documents. New cases are in the index immediately after filing date. Computer index includes dockets from the 3 division courts; older records also on books and microfiche. Case files sent to archives 6 months after closed.

Search Access: Voice Case Information Service available, call VCIS at 800-473-0226 or 305-536-5979. **Mail:** Search usually completed- 3-5 days. Include SASE for return. **In person:** 2 public terminals available.

Payment: Pay by credit cards, money order, cashier's check, and law firm check accepted. Payee: US Courts.

E-Services: PACER now on ECF. PACER records go back to 1986. New records online after 1 day. ECF at https://ecf.flsb.uscourts.gov. **Opinions Online:** www.flsb.uscourts.gov/FRAMES/court_opi.pl. **Online Note:** Judges calendars at www.flsb.uscourts.gov/FRAMES/judge_cal.pl.

Miami Division Court Clerk, 51 SW 1st Ave, Rm 1517, Miami, FL 33130, 305-714-1800. Hours-9AM-4:30PM. www.flsb.uscourts.gov

Counties/Note: Dade, Miami-Dade, Monroe.

Searches/Indexing: Include SSN or EIN with full name in search request. Results do not include SSN or DOB. Will not fax back documents. New cases are in the index immediately after filing date. Computer index includes dockets from the 3 division courts; older records also on books and microfiche. Case files sent to archives 6 months after closed.

Search Access: Voice Case Information Service available, call VCIS at 800-473-0226 or 305-536-5979. **Mail:** Search usually completed- 3-5 days. Include SASE for return. **In person:** 4 public terminals available. No self-serve copier.

Payment: Pay by money order, cashier's check, and law firm check accepted. No credit cards or personal checks accepted. Payee: Clerk, US Courts.

E-Services: PACER now on ECF. PACER records go back to 1986. New records online after 1 day. ECF at https://ecf.flsb.uscourts.gov. **Opinions Online:** www.flsb.uscourts.gov/FRAMES/court_opi.pl. **Online Note:** Judges calendars at www.flsb.uscourts.gov/FRAMES/judge_cal.pl.

West Palm Beach Division Court Clerk, 1515 N Flagler Dr, 8th Fl, West Palm Beach, FL 33401, 561-514-4100. Hours- 9AM-4:30PM. www.flsb.uscourts.gov

Counties/Note: Highlands, Indian River, Martin, Okeechobee, Palm Beach, St. Lucie. Records may also include some older records from Miami-Dade County, particularly Chapter 13s.

Searches/Indexing: Include SSN or EIN with full name in search request. Results include last 4 SSN digits. Will not fax back documents. New cases are in the index immediately after filing date. Computer index includes dockets from the 3 division courts. Case files sent to archives 6 months after closed.

Search Access: Voice Case Information Service available, call VCIS at 800-473-0226 or 305-536-5979. **Mail:** Search usually completed- 3-5 days. Include SASE for return. **In person:** 2 public terminals available.

Payment: Pay by money order, cashier's check, and law firm check accepted. No credit cards or personal checks accepted. Payee: Clerk, US Courts.

E-Services: PACER now on ECF. PACER records go back to 1986. New records online after 1 day. ECF at https://ecf.flsb.uscourts.gov. **Opinions Online:** www.flsb.uscourts.gov/FRAMES/court_opi.pl. **Online Note:** Judges calendars at www.flsb.uscourts.gov/FRAMES/judge_cal.pl.

Florida County Courts

Court	Jurisdiction	No. of Courts	How Organized
Circuit Courts*	General	10	20 Circuits
County Courts*	Limited	13	
Combined Courts*		81	

* Profiled in this Sourcebook.

Court	CIVIL Tort	Contract	Real Estate	Min. Claim	Max. Claim	Small Claims	Estate	Eviction	Domestic Relations
Circuit Courts*	X	X	X	$15,000	No Max		X		X
County Courts*	X	X	X	$0	$15,000	$5000		X	

Court	CRIMINAL Felony	Misdemeanor	DWI/DUI	Preliminary Hearing	Juvenile
Circuit Courts*	X				X
County Courts*		X	X	X	

Administration

Office of State Courts Administrator, Supreme Court Bldg, 500 S Duval, Tallahassee, FL, 32399-1900; All counties except the far-westernmost are in Easter Time Zone. Those western county in CST are so marked. 850-922-5081, Fax: 850-488-0156. www.flcourts.org

Court Structure

Circuit courts have general trial jurisdiction over matters not assigned by statute to the county courts and also hear appeals from county court cases. Thus, circuit courts are simultaneously the highest trial courts and the lowest appellate courts in Florida's judicial system.

The trial jurisdiction of Circuit Courts includes, among other matters, original jurisdiction over civil disputes involving more than $15,000; controversies involving the estates of decedents, minors, and persons adjudicated as incapacitated; cases relating to juveniles; criminal prosecutions for all felonies; tax disputes; actions to determine the title and boundaries of real property; suits for declaratory judgments that is, to determine the legal rights or responsibilities of parties under the terms of written instruments, laws, or regulations before a dispute arises and leads to litigation; and requests for injunctions to prevent persons or entities from acting in a manner that is asserted to be unlawful. The trial jurisdiction of County Courts is established by statute. The jurisdiction of county courts extends to civil disputes involving $15,000 or less.

Many counties have combined Circuit and County Courts. The Circuit Court is the court of general jurisdiction. The bulk of trial court decisions that are appealed are never heard by the Supreme Court. Rather, they are reviewed by three-judge panels in one of the five District Courts of Appeal.

Online Access

Search Supreme Court dockets online at http://jweb.flcourts.org/pls/docket/ds_docket_search. Thee is no statewide access to trial court data. A number of courts offer online access of recorded civil judgment liens via www.myfloridacountycom. Fees are involved when ordering copies; subscribers save $1.50 per record. Visit www.flcourts.org/gen_public/stratplan/privacy.shtml for the latest information regarding the electronic release and privacy of court records in Florida.

Searching Tips, Fees, and Other Guidelines

All courts have one address and switchboard, however the divisions within a court are completely separate. Requesters should specify which court and which division – e.g., Circuit Civil, County Civil, etc. – to direct the request, even though some counties will automatically check both with one request. Most courts have very lengthy phone recording systems.

Fees are set by statute and are as follows as of July 1, 2008: search fee - $2.00 per name per year; certification fee - $1.50 per document plus copy fee; copy fee - $1.50 per page. Most courts follow this schedule.

Alachua County

Circuit & County Courts - Criminal 220 S Main St, Gainesville, FL 32602; 352-374-3636 x3; records- 352-374-3657; criminal: 352-374-3681; fax: 352-377-6158; 8-5PM. ***Felony, Misdemeanor.***
www.clerk-alachua-fl.org/Clerk/index.cfm

Criminal Divisions are now in a separate building from the civil; county Official Records court records and recorder. etc., are located at Civil Court Clerk Office, 201 E University Ave. Telephone for ancient (older, pre-1950s) records- 352-384-3174.

Criminal Records: Access: Fax, mail, in person. Search fee: $2.00 per name per year. Required to search: name, years to search, DOB; also helpful-address, SSN, race, sex. Criminal records on computer since 1990. Mail turnaround time 1-3 days. PAT results show middle initial, DOB. Criminal records are no longer available online.

General Information: No juvenile, child abuse or sexual battery records released. Will fax documents $1.00 per page. Court makes copy: $1.00 per page. Certification fee: $2.00 per doc. Payee: Clerk of Circuit Court. Personal checks accepted. Visa/MC accepted; a $2.50 usage fee may apply. Prepayment required. SASE not required.

Circuit & County Courts - Civil PO Box 600, 201 E University Ave, Gainesville, FL 32602; 352-374-3657, 352-374-3636; criminal phone: x1; civil phone: x2; fax: 352-338-3207; 8:15AM-5PM. ***Civil, Eviction, Small Claims, Probate, Civil Traffic.***
www.clerk-alachua-fl.org/Clerk/index.cfm

The county Official Records court records and recorder. etc., are located at this address. There is a separate phone for ancient (older, pre-1950s) records-352-384-3174.

Civil Records: Access: Fax, mail, in person, online. Both court and visitors may perform in person searches. Search fee: $2.00 per name per year. Required to search: name, years to search; also helpful: address. Civil cases indexed by defendant, plaintiff, on computer from 1979, some records on docket books. Mail turnaround time 24 hours. Civil PAT goes back to 1979. PAT results show middle initial, SSN. Results that show index may or may not have DOB, address; usually, records do show DOB, address, DL number, and other identifiers. Search civil records free at www.alachuacounty.us/government/clerk/records/civildept.aspx. This connects to the Clerk's LINDAS System. Acess an index of judgments & recorded documents at www.myfloridacoun ty.com. Fees involved to order copies; subscribers save $1.50 per record. Search civil traffic citations free at http://assets.alachuacounty.us/ws/a pplications-asp/Traffic/. Also, search probate and other ancient records free at www.clerk-alachua-fl.org/archive/default.cfm.
General Information: No juvenile records released. Will fax documents $1.00 per page. Court makes copy: $1.00 per page.Computer printouts of civil records are $1.00 per page Certification fee: $2.00 per doc. Payee: Clerk of Circuit Court. Personal checks accepted. Visa/MC accepted; a $2.50 usage fee may apply. Prepayment required. SASE not required.

Baker County

Circuit & County Courts - Civil
339 E Macclenny Ave, Macclenny, FL 32063; civil phone: 904-259-0209; probate phone: 904-259-8449; fax: 904-259-4176; 8:30AM-5PM. ***Civil, Eviction, Small Claims, Probate.*** http://bakercountyfl.org/clerk
Civil Records: Access: Mail, in person, online. Both court and visitors may perform in person searches. Search fee: $2.00 per name per year. Required to search: name, years to search; also helpful: address. Civil cases indexed by defendant, plaintiff, on computer back to 1996; prior on index cards and docket books. Mail turnaround time 2 days. Public use terminal has civil records back to 2000. Access an index of judgments, liens, recorded documents at www.myfloridacounty.com. Fees involved to order copies; subscribers save $1.50 per record.
General Information: No juvenile, child abuse or sexual battery records released. Will fax documents $3.00 each. Court makes copy: $1.00 per page, self serve same. Certification fee: $2.00. Payee: Clerk of Circuit Court. Business checks accepted. No credit cards accepted. Prepayment required. Mail requests: SASE preferred.

Circuit & County Courts - Criminal
339 E Macclenny Ave, Macclenny, FL 32063; 904-259-0206/0274; fax: 904-259-4176; 8:30AM-5PM. ***Felony, Misdemeanor.*** http://bakercountyfl.org/clerk
County Court Misdemeanor phone number is 904-259-0204 and 0212.
Criminal Records: Access: Mail, in person, online. Both court and visitors may perform in person searches. Search fee: $2.00 per name per year. Required to search: name, years to search, DOB. Criminal records on computer since 1989. Some records on docket books. Mail turnaround time 1-2 days. Public use terminal has crim records back to 1989. Access the circuit-wide criminal quick lookup at http://circuit8.org. Account and password is required; restricted usage. Call the court for details. Online results show name only.
General Information: No juvenile or guardianship records released. Court makes copy: $1.00 per page, self serve same. Certification fee: $2.00. Payee: Clerk of Circuit Court. Business checks accepted. No credit cards accepted. Prepayment required. Mail requests: SASE required.

Bay County

Circuit Court - Civil
PO Box 2269, 300 E 4th St, Panama City, FL 32402; civil phone: 850-747-5715; probate phone: 850-747-5118; fax: 850-747-5249; 8AM-4:30PM (CST). ***Civil Actions over $15,000, Probate.*** www.baycoclerk.com
Civil Records: Access: Fax, mail, in person, online. Both court and visitors may perform in person searches. Search fee: $2.00 per name per year. Required to search: name, years to search. Civil cases indexed by defendant, plaintiff, on computer from 1984, on microfiche and books from 1950 to 1980, archived from 1913 to 1979. Some records on dockets. Mail turnaround time varies. Public use terminal has civil records back to 1984. PAT results show name only. PATs located in Rm 110 or in 3rd Fl law library. Search the court cases, including traffic and probate, for free at www.clerk.co.bay.fl.us/index.cfm?FuseAction=CaseSearch.Home. Access an index of judgments, liens, recorded docs at www.myfloridacounty.com. Fees involved to order copies; subscribers save $1.50 per record.
General Information: No juvenile, adoption, child abuse or sexual battery records released. Will not fax documents. Court makes copy: $1.00 per page. Certification fee: $2.00. Payee: Clerk of Circuit Court. No personal checks. Credit cards accepted in person only. Prepayment required. Mail requests: SASE required.

Circuit Court - Criminal
300 E 4th St, Rm 111, Panama City, FL 32401; 850-763-9061; fax: 850-747-5263; 8AM-4:30PM (CST). ***Felony.*** www.baycoclerk.com
Criminal Records: Access: Mail, fax, in person, online. Both court and visitors may perform in person searches. Search fee: $2.00 per year. Required to search: name, years to search, DOB; also helpful: SSN, signed release. Criminal records computerized from 1986, on microfilm from 1938 to 1982, prior archived. Mail turnaround time 3-7 days. Public use terminal has crim records. Search court cases free at www.clerk.co.bay.fl.us/index.cfm?FuseAction=CaseSearch.Home
General Information: No sealed, juvenile or expunged records released. Will not fax documents. Court makes copy: $1.00 per page. Certification fee: $1.50 per cert. Payee: Clerk of Circuit Court. No personal checks or credit cards accepted. Prepayment required. Mail requests: SASE requested.

County Court - Civil
300 E 4th St, Rm 105, Panama City, FL 32401; 850-763-9061; fax: 850-747-5249; 8AM-4:30PM (CST). ***Civil Actions under $15,000, Eviction, Small Claims.*** www.baycoclerk.com
Civil Records: Access: Phone, fax, mail, in person, online. Both court and visitors may perform in person searches. Search fee: $2.00 per name per year. Required to search: name, years to search. Civil cases indexed by defendant, plaintiff, on computer from 1986, on microfiche from 1950 to 1980, archived from 1913 to 1979. Some records on docket books. Mail turnaround time 2 days. Search the court cases, including traffic and probate, free at www.clerk.co.bay.fl.us/index.cfm?FuseAction=CaseSearch.Home. Also, access an index of judgments, liens, recorded docs at www.myfloridacounty.com. Fees involved to order copies; subscribers save $1.50 per record.
General Information: No juvenile, child abuse or sexual battery records released. Will fax documents $1.00 per page local, $1.50 per page long distance. Court makes copy: $1.00 per page. Certification fee: $2.00 per page. Payee: Clerk of Circuit Court. No personal checks. Credit cards accepted. Prepayment required. Mail requests: SASE requested.

County Court - Misdemeanor
PO Box 2269, 300 E 4th St, Rm 109, Panama City, FL 32402; 850-747-5146; fax: 850-747-5164; 8AM-4:30PM (CST). ***Misdemeanor.*** www.baycoclerk.com
Criminal Records: Access: Phone, fax, mail, in person, online. Both court and visitors may perform in person searches. Search fee: $2.00 per name per year. Required to search: name, years to search; also helpful: DOB, SSN. Criminal records computerized from 1984, felonies on microfilm from 1950 to 1987, archived from 1913. Misdemeanors from 1996-present; pending cases back. Mail turnaround time 7-10 days. Search courts case database for free at www.clerk.co.bay.fl.us/index.cfm?FuseAction=CaseSearch.Home Online results show middle initial, DOB. **General Information:** No sealed or expunged records released. Will fax documents $2.00 each. Court makes copy: $1.00 per page, self serve same. Certification fee: $2.00. Payee: Clerk of Circuit Court. No personal checks accepted. Visa/MC accepted. Prepayment required. Mail requests: SASE requested.

Circuit Court - Probate Division
300 E 4th St, Rm 205, Panama City, FL 32402; 850-763-9061, 747-5118; fax: 850-742-5260; 8AM-4:30PM (CST). ***Probate.*** www.baycoclerk.com
Search probate records free at www.clerk.co.bay.fl.us/index.cfm?FuseAction=CaseSearch.Home.

Bradford County

Circuit Court
PO Drawer B, 945 N Temple Ave, Starke, FL 32091; criminal phone: 904-966-6255; civil phone: 904-966-6282; probate phone: 904-966-6297; fax: 904-964-4454; 8AM-5PM. ***Felony, Civil Actions over $15,000, Probate.*** http://circuit8.org
Civil Records: Access: Mail, fax, in person, online. Both court and visitors may perform in person searches. Search fee: $2.00 per name per year. Required to search: name, years to search. Civil cases indexed by defendant, plaintiff, on computer since late 1987, others on index books. Mail turnaround time 1 week. Access an index of judgments, liens, recorded docs at www.myfloridacounty.com. Fees involved to order copies; subscribers save $1.50 per record.
Criminal Records: Access: Mail, fax, in person, online. Both court and visitors may perform in person searches. Search fee: $2.00 per name per year. Required to search: name, years to search, DOB, SSN. Criminal records on computer since 1989, others on index books. Mail turnaround time 1 week. Access to the circuit-wide criminal quick lookup is at http://circuit8.org. Account and password is required; restricted usage.
General Information: No juvenile, child abuse or sexual battery records released. Court makes copy: $1.00 per page, self serve same. Certification fee: $2.00 per document. Payee: Clerk at Circuit Court. Business and personal checks and Visa/MC accepted. Prepayment required. Mail requests: SASE required.

County Court
PO Drawer B, 945 N Temple Ave, Starke, FL 32091; 904-966-6280; criminal phone: 904-966-2264; civil phone: 904-966-6297; criminal fax: 904-964-4454; civil fax: same; 8AM-5PM. ***Misdemeanor, Civil Actions under $15,000, Eviction, Small Claims.*** www.bradford-co-fla.org
Send mail requests to "Attention Records" and mention the case type: civil, sm claims, Misd., etc.
Civil Records: Access: Mail, in person, online. Only the court performs in person searches; visitors may not. Search fee: $2.00 per name per year. Required to search: name, years to search. Civil cases indexed by defendant, plaintiff, on computer back to 1989. Some records on docket books, some microfilm. Mail turnaround time up to 1 week. Access an index of judgments, liens, recorded documents at www.myfloridacounty.com. Online results show name only. Fees involved to order copies; subscribers save $1.50 per record.
Criminal Records: Access: Mail, in person. Only the court performs in person searches; visitors may not. Search fee: $2.00 per name per year. Required to search: name, years to search, DOB, SSN. Criminal records computerized from 1988. Records back to 1970's on docket books. Mail turnaround time up to 1 week.
General Information: No juvenile records released. Will not fax documents. Court makes copy: $1.00 per page, self serve same. Certification fee: $2.50 per doc; exemplification- $7.00. Payee: Clerk of Court. Personal checks accepted with valid driver's license for ID. Credit cards accepted in person only, with valid driver's license for ID. Prepayment required. Mail requests: SASE required.

Brevard County

Circuit Court - Civil
PO Box 2767, Official Records Copy Desk, Titusville, FL 32781-2767; 321-637-2004; fax: 321-264-5246; 8AM-5PM. ***Civil, Eviction, Small Claims, Probate, Family.*** www.brevardclerk.us
Civil Records: Access: Phone, fax, mail, online, in person. Both court and visitors may perform in person searches. Search fee: $2.00 per name per year. Required to search: name, years to search. Civil cases indexed by defendant, plaintiff, on computer

since 1987, on microfiche since early 1900s. Some records on docket books. Mail turnaround time 1-2 weeks. Public use terminal has civil records back to 1987. Access records index free at http://webinfo4.brevardclerk.us/facts/facts_search.cfm. Online records back to 1988 can be searched by name, case number or citation number.
General Information: No juvenile, child abuse or sexual battery victim records released. Will fax documents $2.00 per page, no fee if local. Court makes copy: $1.00 per page, self serve same. Certification fee: $2.00 per doc. Payee: Circuit Clerk. Personal checks and major credit cards accepted. Prepayment required. SASE not required.

Circuit Court - Felony PO Box 2767, Titusville, FL 32781-2767; 321-637-2004; fax: 321-264-5246; 8AM-5PM. ***Felony.*** www.brevardclerk.us
Criminal Records: Access: Phone, fax, mail, online, in person. Both court and visitors may perform in person searches. Search fee: $2.00 per name per year. Required to search: name, DOB. Criminal records on computer since 1989, on microfiche from early 1900s. Some records on docket books. Mail turnaround time 1 week. Public use terminal has crim records back to 1989. PAT results show middle initial, DOB. Access records index free at http://webinfo4.brevardclerk.us/facts/facts_search.cfm. Online records back to 1989 can be searched by name, case number or citation number. Online results show middle initial, DOB.
General Information: Online identifiers in results same as on public terminal. No juvenile, child abuse, sexual battery or adoption records released. Will fax documents $2.00 per page. Court makes copy: $1.00 per page, self serve same. Certification fee: $2.00. Payee: Circuit Clerk. Personal checks accepted. Credit cards accepted. Prepayment required. SASE not required.

County Court - Misdemeanor PO Box 2767, 700 S Park Ave, Bldg B, Titusville, FL 32781; 321-637-20045445; fax: 321-264-5246; 8AM-5PM. ***Misdemeanor.*** www.brevardclerk.us
Criminal Records: Access: Phone, fax, mail, online, in person. Only the court performs in person searches; visitors may not. Search fee: $2.00 per name per year. Required to search: name, years to search, DOB. Criminal records on computer since 1989, on microfiche from early 1900s. Mail turnaround time up to 10 days; phone turnaround 1-10 days. Public use terminal has crim records back to 1989. PAT results show middle initial, DOB. Access records index free at http://webinfo4.brevardclerk.us/facts/facts_search.cfm. Online records back to 1989 can be searched by name, case number or citation number. Online results show middle initial, DOB.
General Information: Online identifiers in results same as on public terminal. No juvenile, child abuse, sexual battery or adoption records released. Will fax documents $2.00 per doc long distance; no charge to fax out to 321 local area code. Court makes copy: $1.00 per page. Certification fee: $2.00 per doc. Payee: Brevard County Clerk. Personal checks accepted. Credit cards accepted. Prepayment required. SASE not required.

Broward County

Circuit & County Courts 201 SE 6th St, Ft Lauderdale, FL 33301; 954-831-6565; criminal phone: 954-831-6565; civil phone: 954-831-7196 Circuit CT; County civil- 831-5622; probate phone: 954-831-7154; criminal fax: 954-831-5661; civil fax: 954-831-6572 Circuit; 831-7059 County Ct; 8AM-4:30PM. ***Felony, Misdemeanor, Civil, Eviction, Small Claims, Probate.*** www.clerk-17th-flcourts.org/
Civil circuit- Rm 230; civil- Rm 120; Misd Dept- Rm 130; Probate- Rm 252. The Correspondence Clerk handles searches. There is a free dial-up case records system (Chips) for phone access to case files; case # or name required- 954-712-7899.
Civil Records: Access: Phone, fax, mail, online, in person, email. Both court and visitors may perform in person searches. Search fee: $2.00 per name per year. Add $4.00 for written response (affidavit). Required to search: name, years to search. Written requests may be submitted to Rm 230 for Circuit Civil; use Rm 120 for County Ct Civil Div searches. Civil cases indexed by defendant, plaintiff, on computer from 1986. Some records on dockets. Will search back 10 years. Chips free dial-up system is 954-712-7899; civil- x5; probate- x4. Mail turnaround time 1-14 days. Civil PAT goes back to 2003. Address sometimes appears on results. Basic info is free at www.clerk-17th-flcourts.org/BCCOC2/Pubsearch/CaseSearch.aspx. Search by name, case number or case type. There is also a premium case subscription service available to registered users and free to one-time users. Direct email record requests to eclerk@browardclerk.org.
Criminal Records: Access: Mail, online, in person, email. Both court and visitors may perform in person searches. Search fee: $2.00 per name per year. Add $4.00 for written response (affidavit). Required to search: name, years to search, DOB. Criminal records on computer since 1980. Chips free dial-up system is 954-712-7899; criminal- x1, x2. Requests can be made in writing at #160 Central Courthouse. Mail turnaround time 1-14 days. Criminal PAT goes back to 2003. PAT results show name only. 3 public terminals available in Rm 230. Address sometimes appears on results. Basic info free at www.clerk-17th-flcourts.org/BCCOC2/Pubsearch/CaseSearch.aspx. Search by name. case number or case type. Also, there is a "Premium Access" for detailed case information; requires a fee, registration and password. Call 954-831-5654 for information or visit the website. Also, direct email record requests to eclerk@browardclerk.org. Online results show middle initial and DOBs for criminal defendants only.
General Information: Court makes copy: $1.00 per page. Certification fee: $2.00; Exemplification is-$7.00 each. Payee: Clerk of the Court. Only cashiers checks and money orders accepted. No credit cards accepted. Prepayment required.

Calhoun County

Circuit & County Court 20859 E Central Ave, #130, Blountstown, FL 32424; 850-674-4545; fax: 850-674-5553; 8AM-4PM (CST). ***Felony, Misdemeanor, Civil, Eviction, Small Claims, Probate.*** www.calhounclerk.com
Civil Records: Access: Phone, mail, in person, online. Both court and visitors may perform in person searches. Search fee: $7.00 per name. Required to search: name, years to search. Civil cases indexed by defendant, plaintiff, on computer back to 1986, books from 1970s. Mail turnaround time 2 days. Civil PAT goes back to 1986. Access an index of judgments, liens, recorded documents at www.myfloridacounty.com. Fees involved to order copies; subscribers save $1.50 per record.
Criminal Records: Access: Phone, mail, in person. Both court and visitors may perform in person searches. Search fee: $7.00 per name. Required to search: name, years to search. Criminal records computerized from 1986, on docket books from 1970s. Mail turnaround time 2 days. Criminal PAT goes back to 1986.
General Information: No juvenile, child abuse or sexual battery records released. Will not fax documents. Court makes copy: $.15 per page. Certification fee: $2.00. Cert fee includes copy fee. Payee: Clerk of Court. Personal checks and major credit cards accepted. Prepayment required. Mail requests: SASE required.

Charlotte County

Circuit & County Courts - Civil Division PO Box 511687, 350 E Marion, Justice Center, Punta Gorda, FL 33951-1687; 941-505-4751 rec ctr; 941-639-3111 x1, then x1, x3; probate: 941-637-2210; 8AM-5PM. ***Civil, Eviction, Small Claims, Probate.*** http://co.charlotte.fl.us/clrkinfo/clerk_default.htm
Civil Records: Access: Mail, in person, online. Both court and visitors may perform in person searches. Search fee: $2.00 per name per year. Required to search: name, years to search. Civil cases indexed by defendant, plaintiff, on computer back to 1982, on microfiche since 1987. Mail turnaround time 1-2 days. Public use terminal has civil records back to 1982. PAT results show middle initial, SSN; not all terminal results show a DOB or an address. Public terminals located on 1st Fl and in Murdock Ofc. Access civil court records free at http://208.47.160.68/Magic94Scripts/mgrqispi94.dll?APPNAME=civ_casweb&PRGNAME=PUBSEARCHF. Also, online access to civil and probate records is by subscription, see the website. First payment is $186.00 ($150 refundable) plus a usage fee based on # of transactions. Allows copy printing. For info, call 941-637-4848. Also, access an index of judgments, liens, recorded documents at www.myfloridacounty.com fees for copies.
General Information: No juvenile, child abuse, sexual battery, adoption records released. Will fax documents for $2.00 fee. Court makes copy: $1.00 per page. Certification fee: $2.00 per doc plus copy fee; Exemplification fee $6.00. Payee: Clerk of Circuit Court. Personal checks accepted. Visa/MC accepted. Prepayment required. Mail requests: SASE requested.

Circuit & County Courts - Criminal Div. PO Box 511687, Punta Gorda, FL 33951-1687; 941-637-2269; fax: 941-637-2159; 8AM-5PM. ***Felony, Misdemeanor, Traffic.*** http://co.charlotte.fl.us/clrkinfo/clerk_default.htm
Criminal Records: Access: Phone, mail, in person, online. Both court and visitors may perform in person searches. Search fee: $2.00 per name per year. Required to search: name, years to search, DOB; also helpful: address, SSN, race, sex. Criminal records on computer since 1985, misdemeanors on index cards, felonies on judgment books, imaging on disc from 1993. Mail turnaround time 1 week. Public use terminal has crim records back to 1985.PAT results show name, DOB. Terminal results include SSN. Access index free at https://www.co.charlotte.fl.us/scripts/mgrqispi.dll?appname=MPI%20Criminal&prgname=PUBSEARCHF. Name and birthdate required to search. Online results show name, DOB. Terminal results include SSN.
General Information: No juvenile, child abuse or sexual battery records released. Fee to fax out file $2.00 per page. Court makes copy: $1.00 per page, self serve same. Certification fee: $2.00. Payee: Clerk of Circuit Court. Personal checks accepted. Visa/MC accepted. Prepayment required. SASE not required.

Citrus County

Circuit Court 110 N Apopka, Rm 101, Inverness, FL 34450-4299; 352-341-6400; fax: 352-341-6413; 8AM-5PM. ***Felony, Civil Actions over $15,000, Probate.*** www.clerk.citrus.fl.us/home.jsp
Marriage license data is found online at the website.
Civil Records: Access: Phone, fax, mail, in person, online. Both court and visitors may perform in person searches. Search fee: $2.00 per name per year. Required to search: name, years to search; also helpful: address. Indicate on search request type of cases to search. Civil cases indexed by defendant, plaintiff, on computer from 1989, archived from 1940 to 1991. Some records on docket books. By phone only back to 1989. Mail turnaround time 1-2 days. Civil PAT goes back to 1989. PAT results show name only. View court record index (no images) at http://search.clerk.citrus.fl.us/courts/login.asp; Subscription system giving full identifiers also available. Also there is an index of judgments, liens, official docs at www.myfloridacounty.com. Fees involved to order copies; subscribers save $1.50 per record.
Criminal Records: Access: Phone, fax, mail, in person, online. Both court and visitors may perform in person searches. Search fee: $2.00 per name per year. Required to search: name, years to search, DOB; also helpful: address, SSN, race, sex. Criminal records computerized from 1989, on microfiche from 1948 to 1987, archived from 1940-1991. By phone only back to 1989. Mail turnaround time 1 week. Criminal PAT goes back to same as civil. PAT results show middle initial, DOB. Terminal results sometimes include SSN and address. Free court record index (no images) at www.clerk.citrus.fl.us/home.jsp; Subscription system giving full address and DOB identifiers also available. Online results show middle initial, DOB. Terminal results include SSN.

General Information: Online identifiers in results same as on public terminal. No juvenile, adoption, child abuse or sexual battery records released. Will fax documents $1.00 per page if local; $2.00 per page long distance. Court makes copy: $1.00 per page. Certification fee: $2.00. Payee: Clerk of Circuit Court. Personal checks and major credit cards accepted. Prepayment required. Mail requests: SASE required.

County Court 110 N Apopka, Rm 101, Inverness, FL 34450; 352-341-6400; fax: 352-341-6413; 8AM-5PM. ***Misdemeanor, Civil Actions under $15,000, Eviction, Small Claims.***
www.clerk.citrus.fl.us/home.jsp
Civil Records: Access: Phone, fax, mail, in person, online. Both court and visitors may perform in person searches. Search fee: $2.00 per name per year. Required to search: name, years to search; also helpful: address. Civil cases indexed by defendant, plaintiff, on computer from 1990, prior records on docket books. Mail turnaround time 1-3 days. Civil PAT goes back to 1990. View court record index (no images) free at http://search.clerk.citrus.fl.us/courts/login.asp; Subscription system with identifiers also available. Access an index of judgments, liens, recorded documents at www.myfloridacounty.com/services/officialrecords_intro.shtml; Fees involved to order copies; subscribers save $1.50 per record.
Criminal Records: Access: Phone, fax, mail, in person, online. Both court and visitors may perform in person searches. Search fee: $2.00 per name per year. Required to search: name, years to search, DOB; also helpful: address, SSN, race, sex. Criminal records computerized from 1990, prior records on docket books. Mail turnaround time 1-3 days. Criminal PAT goes back to same as civil. PAT results show name and may include address. View court record index (no images) free at www.clerk.citrus.fl.us/home.jsp; Subscription system with identifiers also available. Online results show name only. Free index search does not give DOB or full address, subscription system does.
General Information: Online identifiers in results same as on public terminal. No juvenile, child abuse or sexual battery records released. Will fax documents $1.00 per page; $2.00 per page for long distance. Court makes copy: $1.00 per page. Certification fee: $2.00 per cert. Payee: Clerk of Circuit Court. Personal checks and major credit cards accepted. Prepayment required. Mail requests: SASE required.

Clay County

Circuit Court PO Box 698, Green Cove Springs, FL 32043; 904-284-6302; probate phone: ext 6516; fax: 904-284-6390; 8:15AM-4:30PM. ***Felony, Civil Actions over $15,000, Probate.***
http://clerk.co.clay.fl.us
Civil Records: Access: Mail, in person, online. Both court and visitors may perform in person searches. Search fee: $2.00 per name per year. Required to search: name, years to search; also helpful: address. Civil cases indexed by defendant, plaintiff, on computer from 1985, prior records on docket books. Mail turnaround time 1-3 days. Public use terminal available, records go back to 1983. PAT results show middle initial, DOB, SSN. Clerk of the circuit court provides free access to records at http://clayclerk.com/OdysseyPA/default.aspx. Access an index of judgments, liens, recorded documents at www.myfloridacounty.com. Fees involved to order copies; subscribers save $1.50 per record.
Criminal Records: Access: Mail, in person, online. Both court and visitors may perform in person searches. Search fee: $1.00 per name per year. $6.00 for clerk certification. Required to search: name, years to search, DOB; also helpful: address, SSN, race, sex. Criminal records (felony) on microfiche in recording department from 1967, prior records on docket books. Mail turnaround time 1-3 days. Public use terminal available. PAT results show middle initial, DOB, SSN. Access to criminal record index is free at http://clayclerk.com/OdysseyPA/default.aspx.
General Information: Online identifiers in results same as on public terminal. No juvenile, child abuse or sexual battery records released. Will not fax documents. Court makes copy: $1.00 per page. Certification fee: $2.00. Payee: Clerk of Circuit Court. Only cashiers checks and money orders accepted. Major credit cards accepted. Prepayment required. Mail requests: SASE required.

County Court PO Box 698, 825 N Orange, Green Cove Springs, FL 32043; 904-284-6316; criminal phone: 904-269-6337; civil: 904-278-3695; fax: 904-278-3670; 8:30AM-4:30PM. ***Misdemeanor, Civil Actions under $15,000, Eviction, Small Claims.***
http://clayclerk.com/default.html
Civil Records: Access: Mail, in person, online. Both court and visitors may perform in person searches. Search fee: $2.00 per name per year. $6.00 for 3 years if search is pre-1986. Required to search: name, years to search; also helpful: address. Civil cases indexed by defendant, plaintiff, on computer back to 1986, prior records on docket books. Mail turnaround time 1-2 days. Civil PAT goes back to 1980s. PAT results show name, DOB. Access civil records back to 1992 free at http://clayclerk.com/OdysseyPA/default.aspx. Also, access an index of judgments, liens, recorded documents at www.myfloridacounty.com. Fees involved to order copies; subscribers save $1.50 per record.
Criminal Records: Access: Mail, in person, online. Both court and visitors may perform in person searches. Search fee: $2.00 per name per year. Required to search: name, years to search, DOB, SSN; also helpful: address, race, sex. Criminal records computerized from 1992, prior records on docket books. Mail turnaround time 1 week. Criminal PAT goes back to same as civil. PAT results show middle initial, DOB. Access criminal records free at http://clayclerk.com/OdysseyPA/default.aspx. Online results show middle initial, DOB.
General Information: Online identifiers in results same as on public terminal. No juvenile, child abuse or sexual battery records released. Fee to fax out file $1.00 per page. Court makes copy: $1.00 per page. Certification fee: $2.00 per cert. Payee: Clerk of Circuit Court. No personal checks accepted. Credit cards accepted; $2.50 convenience fee applies. Prepayment required. Mail requests: SASE required.

Collier County

Circuit Court PO Box 413044, 3301 Tamiami Trail East, Naples, FL 34101-3044; 239-252-2646; criminal phone: 239-252-2648; civil: 239-252-2646; 8AM-5PM. ***Felony, Civil Actions over $15,000, Probate.*** www.clerk.collier.fl.us
Traffic phone- 239-252-2646. Traffic Div located on 1st Fl. Civil is in Bldg L on 6th Fl; Criminal also on 6th Fl.
Civil Records: Access: Mail, in person, online. Both court and visitors may perform in person searches. Search fee: $1.00 per name per year. Required to search: name, years to search. Civil cases indexed by defendant, plaintiff, on computer from 1990, all on microfiche back to 1922. Mail turnaround time within 1 week. Civil PAT goes back to 1988. PAT civil results show middle initial. Public access terminal is on the 6th Fl. Some records may show SSN. Online access is free at http://apps.collierclerk.com/public_inquiry/. Records include probate, traffic and domestic. Access an index of judgments, liens, recorded documents at www.myfloridacounty.com. Fees involved to order copies; subscribers save $1.50 per record.
Criminal Records: Access: Phone, mail, online, in person. Both court and visitors may perform in person searches. Search fee: $2.00 per name per year. Required to search: name, years to search, DOB; also helpful: SSN, add your phone number. Criminal records computerized from 1990, on microfiche from 1922 to 1994, archived from 1922. Clerk often refers full background check requests to the County Sheriff's Ofc. Mail turnaround time within 1 week. Criminal PAT goes back to same as civil. PAT results show name only. Public access terminal is on the 6th Fl. Criminal records access is free at www.collierclerk.com/ Online results show name only.
General Information: No sealed by court or statute records released. Will fax documents $3.00 per page if long distance. Court makes copy: $1.00 per page. Certification fee: $2.00 per doc. Payee: Clerk of Circuit Court. Personal checks accepted. Credit cards accepted for traffic payments only. Prepayment required. Mail requests: SASE required.

County Court PO Box 413044, 3301 Tamiami Trail East, Naples, FL 34101-3044; 239-252-2646; 8AM-5PM. ***Misdemeanor, Civil Actions under $15,000, Eviction, Small Claims.***
www.collierclerk.com/
Civil Records: Access: Mail, in person, online. Both court and visitors may perform in person searches. Search fee: $2.00 per name per year. Required to search: name, years to search; also helpful: address. Civil cases indexed by defendant, plaintiff, on computer from 1990, on microfiche from 1922 to 1995. Mail turnaround time 1 week. Civil PAT goes back to 1990. PAT results show name, DOB. Online access is free at http://apps.collierclerk.com/public_inquiry/. Records include probate, traffic and domestic.
Criminal Records: Access: Mail, online, in person. Both court and visitors may perform in person searches. Search fee: $2.00 per name per year. Required to search: name, years to search, DOB; also helpful: address, SSN, race, sex. Criminal records computerized from 1988; felony on microfiche from 1922 to 1999 - misdemeanors to 2000. Mail turnaround time 1 week. Criminal PAT goes back to 1988.PAT results show name, DOB. Criminal records access is free at http://apps.collierclerk.com/public_inquiry/.
General Information: No juvenile, child abuse or sexual battery records released. Will fax documents; $1.00 if local, $3.00 if long distance. Court makes copy: $1.00 per page. Certification fee: $2.00 per doc. Payee: Clerk of County Court. Personal checks and major credit cards accepted. Prepayment required. Mail requests: SASE required.

Columbia County

Circuit & County Courts PO Drawer 2069, Lake City, FL 32056; 386-719-7403; criminal phone: 386-758-1164; civil phone: 386-758-1036; probate phone: 386-758-1054; fax: 386-719-7539; 8AM-5PM. ***Felony, Misdemeanor, Civil, Eviction, Small Claims, Probate.*** http://www2.myfloridacounty.com/wps/wcm/connect/columbiaclerk
Civil Records: Access: Mail, in person, online. Both court and visitors may perform in person searches. Search fee: $2.00 per name per year per department. Required to search: name, years to search. Civil cases indexed by defendant, plaintiff, on computer from 1990, archived from 1800s. DOB and SSN also helpful for searching. Mail turnaround time 48 hours. Civil PAT goes back to 1990. Access Clerk of Circuit Court records at https://www2.myfloridacounty.com/ccm/?county=12
Criminal Records: Access: In person, online. Both court and visitors may perform in person searches. Search fee: $2.00 per name per year per department. Required to search: name, years to search, DOB; SSN helpful. Criminal records computerized from 1989, archived from 1800s. Criminal PAT goes back to 1989. Online access to criminal is same as civil.
General Information: Online identifiers in results same as on public terminal. No names of victims of sex related offenses, juveniles, incompetence or mental health records released. Fee to fax out file $3.00 per page. Court makes copy: $1.00 per page, self serve same. Certification fee: $2.00 per cert. Payee: Clerk of Circuit Court. Cashiers check or money order only. Major credit cards accepted. Prepayment required. Mail requests: SASE required for civil.

Dade County

Circuit & County Courts - Civil 73 W Flagler St, #242, Miami, FL 33130; 305-275-1155; 9AM-4PM. ***Civil under $15,000, Eviction, Small Claims, Probate.***
www.miami-dadeclerk.com/dadecoc/
Better known as Miami-Dade County.
Civil Records: Access: Mail, in person, online. Both court and visitors may perform in person searches. Search fee: $2.00 per name per year. Required to search: name, years to search. Civil and domestic

relations cases indexed by plaintiff/petitioner, defendant/respondent. Civil and domestic relations records on computer back to 1973; archives from 1836; microfilm in county recorder office. Mail turnaround time 10 days. Public use terminal has civil records back to 1973. Clerk of Court's online services- choose between Standard (free) and Premier fee-based services. Subscribers to the Premier service may access 3 advanced options: Civil/Family/Probate, Public Records, Traffic. Fees based on # of units purchased; minimum $5.00 in advance. Also, though limited, search felony, misdemeanor, civil and county ordinance violations free at http://www2.miami-dadeclerk.com/CJIS/CaseSearch.aspx. Search Civil/Family/Probate free at www.miami-dadeclerk.com/dadecoc/.
General Information: No juvenile, adoption, mental health records releases. Will not fax documents. Court makes copy: $1.00 per page. Certification fee: $2.00 per cert. Payee: Clerk of Circuit & County Courts. Personal checks and money orders accepted. Credit cards accepted. Prepayment required. Mail requests: SASE requested.

Circuit & County Courts - Criminal 1351 NW 12th St, #9000, Miami, FL 33125; 305-275-1155; criminal phone: 305-548-5527; fax: 305-548-5526; 9AM-4PM. ***Felony, Misdemeanor.***
www.miami-dadeclerk.com/dadecoc/
Better known as Miami-Dade County. Although located in the same building, the records of the felony and the misdemeanor courts are not co-mingled. Search the Circuit Court for felony and the County Court for misdemeanor records.
Criminal Records: Access: Mail, online, in person. Both court and visitors may perform in person searches. Search fee: $1.50 per year. Required to search: name, years to search, DOB; also helpful: address, SSN, race, sex. Criminal records computerized from 1971, on microfiche from 1975, archived from 1836. Mail turnaround time 10-15 days. Public use terminal has crim records back to 1970.PAT results show name, DOB. Race and sex also appear on terminal search results. Free and Premier fee-based online services available. Though limited, search felony, misdemeanor, civil and county ordinance violations free at http://www2.miami-dadeclerk.com/CJIS/CaseSearch.aspx. Subscribers to the Clerk's Premier Services may Access advanced options in 3 of the Clerk's internet-based systems: Civil/Family /Probate, Public Records, Traffic. $.25 per search, in advance. Search traffic free at www.miami-dadeclerk.com/spirit/publicsearch/defnamesearch.asp.
General Information: No juvenile, child abuse or sexual battery records released. Will not fax documents. Court makes copy: $1.00 per page. Certification fee: $2.00. Payee: Clerk of Circuit and County Court. Personal checks accepted. Credit cards accepted in person only. Prepayment required. Mail requests: SASE required.

De Soto County

Circuit & County Courts 115 E Oak St, Arcadia, FL 34266; 863-993-4876; criminal phone: 863-993-4876; civil phone: 863-993-4880; probate phone: 863-993-4880; fax: 863-993-4669; 8AM-4:45PM. ***Felony, Misdemeanor, Civil, Eviction, Small Claims, Probate.*** www.desotoclerk.com
Misdemeanors 863-993-4880. County Court & Evictions 863-993-4880. Probate fax is same as main fax number.
Civil Records: Access: Mail, in person, online. Both court and visitors may perform in person searches. Search fee: $2.00 per name per year. Required to search: name, years to search. Civil cases indexed by defendant, plaintiff, on computer from 1986, on microfiche from 1974, archived from 1887. Mail turnaround time 2 days. Civil PAT goes back to 1984. PAT results show middle initial, DOB. Free access to civil, marriage/divorce, small claims, traffic/parking, Muni ordinances, domestic relations, name changes, foreclosures at www.desotoclerk.com. Also, access an index of judgments, liens, recorded documents at www.myfloridacounty.com. Fees involved to order copies; subscribers save $1.50 per record.
Criminal Records: Access: Mail, in person, online. Both court and visitors may perform in person searches. Search fee: $2.00 per name per year. Required to search: name, years to search, DOB; also helpful: SSN, aliases. Criminal records on computer since 1986, archived since 1887. Mail turnaround time 2 days. Criminal PAT goes back to same as civil. PAT results show middle initial, DOB. Terminal results include SSN. Access to records at www.myfloridacounty.com. Fees involved to order copies. Online results show middle initial, DOB.
General Information: Online identifiers in results same as on public terminal. No juvenile or sex related records released. Will fax documents $1.00 per page. Court makes copy: $1.00 per page, self serve same. Certification fee: $2.00. Payee: Clerk of the Court. Personal checks accepted. Credit cards accepted. Prepayment required. Mail requests: SASE requested.

Dixie County

Circuit & County Courts PO Drawer 1206, Cross City, FL 32628-1206; 352-498-1200; fax: 352-498-1201; 8:30AM-5:30PM. ***Felony, Misdemeanor, Civil, Eviction, Small Claims, Probate.*** http://www2.myfloridacounty.com/wps/wcm/connect/dixieclerk
Civil Records: Access: Mail, in person, online. Only the court performs in person searches; visitors may not. Search fee: $2.00 per name per year. Required to search: name, years to search; also helpful: address. Civil cases indexed by defendant, plaintiff, on computer since 1987, archived to 1920's. Mail turnaround time 1 week. Access to Clerk of Circuit Court records at https://www2.myfloridacounty.com/ccm/?county=12
Criminal Records: Access: Mail, in person, online. Only the court performs in person searches; visitors may not. Search fee: $2.00 per name per year. Required to search: name, years to search, DOB; also helpful: address, SSN, race, sex. Criminal records on computer since 1989, archived to 1920's. Mail turnaround time 1 week. Online access is the same as civil, see above.
General Information: No juvenile, child abuse or sexual battery records released. Fee to fax out file $1.00 per page. Court makes copy: $1.00 per page. Certification fee: $2.00 per doc. Payee: Clerk of Circuit Court. Personal checks accepted. No credit cards accepted at present time. Prepayment required. Mail requests: SASE required.

Duval County

Circuit & County Courts - Civil Division 330 E Bay St, 2nd Fl Copy Center, Jacksonville, FL 32202; 904-630-1276; civil phone: 904-630-2031; probate phone: 904-630-2053; fax: 904-630-7506; 8:30AM-5PM. ***Civil, Eviction, Small Claims, Probate.*** www.duvalclerk.com/ccWebsite/
Direct search requests to the Copy Center; phone number given above. Separate search fee for each court, and for each division. Probate is Rm #101, probate fax- 904-630-0493.
Civil Records: Access: Fax, mail, online, in person. Both court and visitors may perform in person searches. Search fee: $2.00 per name per year. Required to search: name, years to search; also helpful: address. Civil cases indexed by defendant, plaintiff, (Circuit) on computer from 1968, county from 1984. County civil on index books from 1975 to 1986, prior on docket books. Circuit civil o. Mail turnaround time for county records 5-7 days; circuit 2-4 days. Public use terminal has civil records back to 1968. PAT results show middle initial, DOB. Two sources are available. First, access court records free at https://showcase.duvalclerk.com/Login.aspx?ReturnUrl=%2fDefault.aspx. Login is Public, password is Public. Access an index of judgments, liens, recorded documents at www.myfloridacounty.com. Fees involved to order copies; subscribers save $1.50 per record. Online results show middle initial, DOB.
General Information: Online identifiers in results same as on public terminal. No juvenile, child abuse or sexual battery records released. Will fax documents for $1.00 per page fee. Court makes copy: $1.00 per page. Certification fee: $2.00 per doc. Payee: Clerk of Circuit Court. Business checks accepted. Major credit cards except AmEx accepted; a $2.50 courtesy fee applies. Prepayment required. Mail requests: SASE required.

Circuit & County Courts - Criminal Div Attn: Copy Center, 501 E Bay St, 2nd Fl, Jacksonville, FL 32202; 904-630-1276 Copy Ctr; 904-630-2065 felony; fax: 904-630-1115; 8:30AM-5PM. ***Felony, Misdemeanor.*** www.duvalclerk.com
Direct search requests to the Copy Center, or alternatively make a search request to the County Sheriff Office (JSO) Records Dept at 501 E Bay St, or phone 904-630-2209; search fee is $5.00.
Criminal Records: Access: Mail, in person, online. Visitors must perform in person searches themselves. Search fee: $2.00 per name, per year, per court. Required to search: name, years to search, DOB; also helpful: address, SSN, race, sex. Criminal records (Circuit) on computer from 1982, county from 1988. Search request must be in writing. Court sometimes recommends to contact JSO Records, see note above. Mail turnaround time 2-3 days. Public use terminal has crim records back to 1988.PAT results show name, DOB. Not all court records have correct names or DOBs. Contact Sheriff office for alias and fingerprint checks. Access court records free at https://showcase.duvalclerk.com/Login.aspx?ReturnUrl=%2fDefault.aspx. Login is Public, password is Public. Online results show name, DOB.
General Information: Online identifiers in results same as on public terminal. No juvenile, child abuse or sexual battery records released. Will not fax documents. Court makes copy: $1.00 per page. Certification fee: $2.00 per doc. Payee: Clerk of the Court. Business checks accepted. Major credit cards except AmEx accepted; a $2.50 courtesy fee applies. Prepayment required. Mail requests: SASE helpful.

Escambia County

Circuit & County Courts - Civil Division PO Box 333, 190 Governmental Ctr, Pensacola, FL 32591-0333; 850-595-4170; civil phone: 850-595-4130 (Circ Ct. Civil); probate phone: 850-595-4300; fax: 850-595-4176; 8AM-5PM (CST). ***Civil, Eviction, Small Claims, Probate.***
www.escambiaclerk.com/
Archive Dept. performs searches.
Civil Records: Access: Phone, fax, mail, in person, online. Both court and visitors may perform in person searches. Search fee: $1.50 per year per name. $6.00 for cover letter response (no record found, etc). Required to search: name, years to search; also helpful: address. Civil cases indexed by defendant, plaintiff. County civil records on computer from mid 1986; Circuit Court civil on computer from mid 1987. Prior on index books. Judgments/small claims on microfilm. Mail turnaround time 1-5 days. Public use terminal has civil records back to 1986. Online access to county clerk records is free at http://public.escambiaclerk.com/cv_web_1a.asp. Search by name, citation, or case number. Small claims, traffic, and marriage data also available. Access an index of judgments, liens, recorded documents at www.myfloridacounty.com. Fees involved to order copies; subscribers save $1.50 per record.
General Information: No juvenile, child abuse, adoption, mental health or sexual battery records released. Will fax documents $1.10 per page if local, $1.25 per page long distance. Court makes copy: $1.00 per page. Certification fee: $2.00 per page. Payee: Clerk of Circuit Court. Personal checks accepted. Credit cards accepted. Prepayment required. Mail requests: SASE requested for civil.

Circuit & County Courts - Criminal Div. 190 Governmental Ctr, Pensacola, FL 32501; 850-595-4150; criminal phone: 850-595-4185 County; fax: 850-595-4198; 8AM-5PM (CST). ***Felony, Misdemeanor.*** www.escambiaclerk.com/
Misdemeanor records phone is 850-595-4185.
Criminal Records: Access: Fax, mail, in person, online. Both court and visitors may perform in person searches. Search fee: $2.00 per name per year. Required to search: name, years to search, DOB;

also helpful: address, SSN, race, sex. Criminal records on computer and microfiche from 1973, archived from 1940 to 1972. Mail turnaround time within 1 week. Public use terminal has crim records back to 1984. PAT results show middle initial, DOB. Online access to criminal records is free at http://public.escambiaclerk.com/cv_web_1a.asp. Search by name, citation, or case number. Online results show middle initial, DOB. On search results, the middle initial will only appear if on the original arrest report; also, address may appear.
General Information: Online identifiers in results same as on public terminal. No juvenile, child abuse, mental health, adoption or sexual battery records released. Will fax documents $1.00 per page; over 5 pages $2.00; each add'l group of 5 pages charge increases by $1.00, plus phone charge. Court makes copy: $1.00 per page. Self serve: $1.00 per page. Certification fee: $2.00; Exemplification fee-$7.00. Payee: Clerk of Circuit Court. Personal checks accepted. Credit cards accepted by phone. Prepayment required. SASE not required.

Flagler County

Circuit & County Courts Attn: Records Management, 1769 E Moody Blvd., Bldg. 1, Bunnell, FL 32110; criminal phone: 386-313-4472; civil phone: 386-313-4495 (Circ), 386-313-4483 (Cty); probate phone: 386-313-4486; criminal fax: 386-437-5603; civil fax: 386-437-1928; 8:30AM-5PM. ***Felony, Misdemeanor, Civil, Eviction, Small Claims, Probate.*** www.flaglerclerk.com/
Direct search requests to Records Management; Records Mgmt fax is above. The criminal court department fax is-386-437-2681. Misdemeanor phone- 386-313-4476.
Civil Records: Access: Mail, in person, email. Both court and visitors may perform in person searches. Search fee: $2.00 per name per year. Required to search: name, years to search; also helpful: address. Civil cases indexed by defendant, plaintiff, on computer from 1990. All archived from 1917, some on index books. Mail turnaround time 2-7 days. Civil PAT goes back to 1990. PAT results show middle initial, DOB. Access clerk's civil records free at www.flaglerclerk.com/courtrecords.htm. Also, access an index of judgments, liens, recorded documents at www.myfloridacounty.com. Fees involved to order copies. Also, you may email record requests to rmld@flaglerclerk.com.
Criminal Records: Access:
ail, in person, email. Both court and visitors may perform in person searches. Search fee: $2.00 per name per year. Required to search: name, years to search, DOB; also helpful: address, SSN, race, sex. Felony records on computer back to 1999; misdemeanors back to 1988. All archived from 1917, some on index books. Email record requests to rmld@flaglerclerk.com Mail turnaround time 2-7 days. Criminal PAT goes back to 1999 felony; 1988 misdemeanor. PAT results show middle initial, DOB. Access clerk's criminal records free at www.flaglerclerk.com/courtrecords.htm. Also, email record requests to rmld@flaglerclerk.com. Online results show middle initial, DOB.
General Information: No juvenile, adoption, child abuse or sexual battery records released. Will fax documents $1.00 per page plus a fax usage fee. Court makes copy: $1.00 per page. Certification fee: $2.00 per doc. Payee: Clerk of Court. Local business checks, money orders, or cashiers checks accepted. Major credit cards accepted in person only; $2.50 courtesy fee applies. Prepayment required. Mail requests: SASE required.

Franklin County

Circuit & County Courts 33 Market St, #203, Apalachicola, FL 32320; 850-653-8861; criminal phone: x166 or x107; civil phone: x106 or x149; probate: x106; fax: 850-653-2261; 8:30AM-4:30PM. ***Felony, Misdemeanor, Civil, Eviction, Small Claims, Probate.*** www.franklinclerk.com
Probate is a separate index at this courthouse. Probate fax is same as main fax number.
Civil Records: Access: Mail, in person, online. Both court and visitors may perform in person searches. Search fee: $2.00 per name per year. Required to search: name, years to search; also helpful: address. Civil cases indexed by defendant, plaintiff, on computer from 3/92. Mail turnaround time 2-5 days. Civil PAT goes back to 1992. Access index and records free at https://www2.myfloridacounty.com/ccm/?county=19. Circuit goes back to 3/1997; County to 10/1998; Probate back to 2/1982. Also, access an index of judgments and recorded documents at www.myfloridacounty.com. Fees involved to order copies; subscribers save $1.50 per record.
Criminal Records: Access: Mail, in person, online. Both court and visitors may perform in person searches. Search fee: $2.00 per name per year. Required to search: name, years to search, DOB; also helpful: address, race, sex. Criminal records on computer since 1989. Mail turnaround time 2-5 days. Criminal PAT goes back to 1989. Access index and records free at https://www2.myfloridacounty.com/ccm/?county=19. Felony goes back to 3/4/1984; Misdemeanors back to 8/18/1978. Also, access criminal records by subscription at https://www.myfloridacounty.com/subscription/. Fees are involved.
General Information: No juvenile, child abuse or sexual battery records released. Will fax documents if prepaid. Court makes copy: $1.00 per page, self serve same. Certification fee: $2.00. Payee: Clerk of Circuit Court. In county personal checks accepted. No credit cards accepted. Prepayment required. Mail requests: SASE requested.

Gadsden County

Circuit & County Courts - Criminal Div. 24 N Adams, Quincy, FL 32351; 850-875-8601; fax: 850-875-7265; 8:30AM-5PM. ***Felony, Misdemeanor.*** www.clerk.co.gadsden.fl.us
Requests may be sent to PO Box 1649, ZIP is 32353. Email addresses are Felony@clerk.co.gadsden.fl.us and Misdemeanor@clerk.co.gadsden.fl.us. The misdemeanor department fax is 850-875-4083
Criminal Records: Access: Mail, in person. Only the court performs in person searches; visitors may not. Search fee: $2.00 per name per year. Required to search: name, years to search, DOB; also helpful: SSN. Criminal records computerized from 1984, some on index books and cards. Mail turnaround time 3-5 days. Public use terminal has crim records back to 2000.
General Information: No juvenile or sex offender records released. Will fax documents $1.00 per page. Court makes copy: $.25 per page. Certification fee: $2.00. Payee: Clerk of Circuit Court. Personal checks accepted. Visa/MC, Discover accepted. Prepayment required. SASE not required.

Circuit & County Courts - Civil Division PO Box 1649, 10 E Jefferson St, Quincy, FL 32353; 850-875-8601; civil phone: x231; probate phone: 850-875-8601 x232; fax: 850-627-6925; 8:30AM-5PM. ***Civil, Eviction, Small Claims, Probate.*** www.clerk.co.gadsden.fl.us Extension 246 is County Civil Clerk- Marsha Moore; fax-850-875-3253.
Civil Records: Access: Phone, fax, mail, in person, online, email. Both court and visitors may perform in person searches. Search fee: $2.00 per name, per yr. Required to search: name, years to search. Civil cases indexed by defendant, plaintiff, on computer since 1984. Mail turnaround time 1 week. Public use terminal has civil records back to 1964. Search for judgments only on the Official Records Index. Access to the index of civil court judgments, etc. is free from the County Clerk at www.clerk.co.gadsden.fl.us. Direct email civil requests to clerkofcourt@clerk.co.gadsden.fl.us. Also, access an index of judgments, liens, recorded documents at www.myfloridacounty.com. Fees involved to order copies; subscribers save $1.50 per record.
General Information: No juvenile, child abuse or sexual battery records released. Will fax documents $1.00 per page. Court makes copy: $1.00 per page for official; $.25 regular, self serve same. Certification fee: $2.00. Payee: Clerk of Circuit Court. Only cashiers checks and money orders accepted. Major credit cards accepted; photo ID required. Prepayment required. Mail requests: SASE required.

Gilchrist County

Circuit & County Courts PO Box 37, Trenton, FL 32693; 352-463-3170; probate phone: same; fax: 352-463-3166; 8:30AM-5PM. ***Felony, Misdemeanor, Civil, Eviction, Small Claims, Probate.*** http://gilchrist.fl.us/
Civil Records: Access: Mail, in person, online. Only the court performs in person searches; visitors may not. Search fee: $2.00 per name per year. Required to search: name, years to search; also helpful: address. Civil cases indexed by defendant, plaintiff, on computer from 1987, prior on index books. Mail turnaround time 2-3 days. Search judgments and liens online at http://records.gilchrist.fl.us/oncoreweb/. Access to County Clerk of Circuit Court records is at https://www2.myfloridacounty.com/ccm/?county=21
Criminal Records: Access: Mail, in person, online. Only the court performs in person searches; visitors may not. Search fee: $2.00 per name per year. Required to search: name, years to search, DOB; also helpful: address, SSN, race, sex. Criminal records on computer since 1989, prior on index books. Mail turnaround time 2-3 days. Access to County Clerk of Circuit Court records is at https://www2.myfloridacounty.com/ccm/?county=12
General Information: No juvenile, child abuse or sexual battery records released. Will fax documents $1.00 per page; available for civil only. Court makes copy: $1.00 per page, self serve same. Certification fee: $2.00. Payee: Clerk of Circuit Court. Personal checks accepted; credit cards are not. Prepayment required. Mail requests: SASE required.

Glades County

Circuit & County Courts PO Box 10, Moore Haven, FL 33471; 863-946-6011; criminal fax: 863-946-0560; civil fax: same; 8AM-5PM. ***Felony, Misdemeanor, Civil, Eviction, Small Claims, Probate.*** http://gladesclerk.com
Probate is separate index at this same address. Probate fax is same as main fax number.
Civil Records: Access: Mail, in person, online. Only the court performs in person searches; visitors may not. Search fee: $2.00 per name per year. Required to search: name, years to search; also helpful: address. Civil cases indexed by defendant, plaintiff, on computer from 1991. Mail turnaround time 2-3 days. Access an index of judgments only available at www.myfloridacounty.com. Fees involved to order copies; subscribers save $1.50 per record.
Criminal Records: Access: Mail, in person. Only the court performs in person searches; visitors may not. Search fee: $2.00 per name per year. Required to search: name, years to search, DOB; also helpful: address, SSN, race, sex. Criminal records computerized from 1991. Mail turnaround 2-3 days.
General Information: No juvenile, child abuse or sexual battery records released. Will fax documents $3.00 per page. Court makes copy: $1.00 per page, self serve same. Certification fee: $2.00 per doc. Payee: Clerk of Circuit Court. Personal checks and major credit cards accepted. Prepayment required. Mail requests: SASE required.

Gulf County

Circuit & County Courts 1000 Cecil Costin Blvd, Port St Joe, FL 32456; 850-229-6112; fax: 850-229-6174; 9AM-5PM. ***Felony, Misdemeanor, Civil, Eviction, Small Claims, Probate.*** www.gulfclerk.com
Civil Records: Access: Fax, mail, in person, online. Only the court performs in person searches; visitors may not. Search fee: $2.00 per name per year. Required to search: name, years to search. Civil cases indexed by defendant, plaintiff, on computer from 1990; archived to 1925. Mail turnaround time 1-3 days. Access an index of judgments, liens, recorded documents at www.myfloridacounty.com. Fees involved to order copies; subscribers save $1.50 per record.
Criminal Records: Access: Fax, mail, in person. Only the court performs in person searches; visitors may not. Search fee: $2.00 per name per year. Required to search: name, years to search, DOB; also helpful: SSN. Criminal records computerized

from 1990; archived to 1925. Mail turnaround time 1-3 days.

General Information: No juvenile, adoption, child abuse or sexual battery records released. Will fax documents $1.50 per page. Court makes copy: $.15 per page. Certification fee: $2.00 per cert. Payee: Clerk of Circuit Court. Personal checks and major credit cards accepted. Prepayment required. Mail requests: SASE requested.

Hamilton County

Circuit & County Courts 207 NE 1st St, #106, Jasper, FL 32052; 386-792-1288; fax: 386-792-3524; 8:30AM-4:30PM. ***Felony, Misdemeanor, Civil, Eviction, Small Claims, Probate.***

Civil Records: Access: Mail, in person, online. Both court and visitors may perform in person searches. Search fee: $2.00 per name per year. Required to search: name, years to search; also helpful: address. Civil cases indexed by defendant, plaintiff, on computer from 1/91, county civil from 3/91. Mail turnaround time 2-3 days. Access an index of judgments, liens, recorded documents at www.myfloridacounty.com. Fees involved to order copies; subscribers save $1.50 per record.

Criminal Records: Access: Mail, in person. Both court and visitors may perform in person searches. Search fee: $2.00 per name per year. Required to search: name, years to search, DOB; also helpful: address, SSN, race, sex. Criminal records on computer since 1/89. Mail turnaround time 2-3 days.

General Information: No juvenile, child abuse or sexual battery records released. Will fax documents $2.00 per page. Court makes copy: $1.00 per page, self serve same. Certification fee: $2.00. Payee: Clerk of Circuit Court. No personal checks. Major credit cards accepted, but only in person. Prepayment required. Mail requests: SASE requested.

Hardee County

Circuit & County Courts PO Drawer 1749, Wauchula, FL 33873-1749; 863-773-4174; 8AM-5PM. ***Felony, Misdemeanor, Civil, Eviction, Small Claims, Probate.*** www.hardeeclerk.com/

Main fax number is: 863-773-4422.

Civil Records: Access: Mail, in person, online. Both court and visitors may perform in person searches. Search fee: $2.00 per name per year. Required to search: name, years to search; also helpful: address. Civil cases indexed by defendant, plaintiff, on computer from 1984. Mail turnaround time 2 days. Civil PAT goes back to 1984, PAT results show name only. Access index of judgments, liens, recorded docs at www.myfloridacounty.com. Fees involved to order copies; subscribers save $1.50 per record. Online results show name only.

Criminal Records: Access: Mail, in person. Both court and visitors may perform in person searches. Search fee: $2.00 per name per year. Required to search: name, years to search, DOB; also helpful: address, race, sex. Criminal records computerized from 1984. Mail turnaround time 3 days. Criminal PAT goes back to same as civil. PAT results show name only.

General Information: No juvenile, child abuse or sexual battery records released. Fee to fax out file $1.00 per page. Court makes copy: $1.00 per page. Certification fee: $2.00 per instrument. Exemplification fee is $6.00 (is different from certification). Payee: B Hugh Bradley, Clerk of Court. Business checks accepted. Cash, money orders, cashier checks. Visa/MC accepted. Prepayment required. Mail requests: SASE requested.

Hendry County

Circuit & County Courts PO Box 1760, 25 E Hickpoochee Ave - SR 80 corner SR 29 (33935), LaBelle, FL 33975; 863-675-5369; criminal phone: 863-675-5214; civil phone: 863-675-5206; criminal fax: 863-612-4748; civil fax: 863-612-5299; 8:30AM-5PM. ***Felony, Misdemeanor, Civil, Eviction, Small Claims, Probate.***

www.hendryclerk.org/

Civil Records: Access: Mail, fax, in person, online. Both court and visitors may perform in person searches. Search fee: $2.00 per name per year plus cert fee. Required to search: name, years to search, DOB, SSN or DL, specify index to search; also helpful: address. Civil cases indexed by defendant, plaintiff, on computer since 5/92; on microfiche prior to 1989 if filed. Fax search requests must include credit card payment. Mail turnaround time varies. Access an index of judgments, liens, recorded docs at www.myfloridacounty.com. Fees involved to order copies; subscribers save $1.50 per record.

Criminal Records: Access: Mail, in person. Both court and visitors may perform in person searches. Search fee: $2.00 per name per year plus cert fee. Required to search: name, years to search, DOB, SSN or DL, specify index to search; also helpful: address, race, sex. Misdemeanor records on computer since 1989, felony back to 1986; prior on microfiche. Mail turnaround time varies.

General Information: No juvenile, child abuse or sexual battery records released. Will fax documents to local or toll-free number. Court makes copy: $1.00 per page. Certification fee: $6.00 per document if they do search; $2.00 for simple cert seal per page. Payee: Clerk of Circuit Court. Cashiers checks and money orders accepted. Visa/MC accepted. Prepayment required. Pay as you go plan. Mail requests: SASE requested.

Hernando County

Circuit & County Courts 20 N Main St, Brooksville, FL 34601; 352-754-4201; criminal phone: 352-540-6444; civil phone: 352-540-6377; probate phone: 352-540-6366; fax: 352-754-4247; 8AM-5PM. ***Felony, Misdemeanor, Civil, Eviction, Small Claims, Probate.*** www.clerk.co.hernando.fl.us

Civil Records: Access: Mail, in person, online. Both court and visitors may perform in person searches. Search fee: $2.00 per name per year. Required to search: name, years to search. Civil cases indexed by defendant, plaintiff, on computer from 1982, archived from late 1800s. Mail turnaround time approx. 5 days. Civil PAT goes back to 1983. PAT civil results show middle initial. Access court records free www.clerk.co.hernando.fl.us/SearchType.asp. Online records may go as far back as 1/1983. Your browser must be JavaScript enables (MS Explorer 4.0 or above). Access an index of judgments, liens, recorded docs at www.myfloridacounty.com. Fees involved to order copies; subscribers save $1.50 per record.

Criminal Records: Access: Mail, online, in person. Both court and visitors may perform in person searches. Search fee: $2.00 per name per year. Required to search: name, years to search, DOB; also helpful: SSN. Criminal records computerized from 1982, archived from late 1800s. Index and docket information is available for felony and misdemeanor records. Mail turnaround time approx. 5 days. Criminal PAT goes back to same as civil. PAT results show middle initial, DOB. Online access to criminal records is the same as civil. Online results show middle initial, DOB.

General Information: Online identifiers in results same as on public terminal. No juvenile, child abuse or sexual battery records released. Will fax documents $1.25 per page, $1.00 if local. Court makes copy: $1.00 per page, self serve same. Certification fee: $2.00. Payee: Clerk of Circuit Court. Personal checks and major credit cards accepted. Prepayment required.

Highlands County

Circuit & County Courts 430 S Commerce Ave, Sebring, FL 33870-3867; 863-402-6595; criminal phone: 863-402-6594; civil phone: 863-402-6591; fax: 863-402-6575; 8AM-5PM. ***Felony, Misdemeanor, Civil, Eviction, Small Claims, Probate.*** www.hcclerk.org

Probate fax- 863-402-6903

Civil Records: Access: Mail, in person, online. Only the court performs in person searches; visitors may not. Search fee: $2.00 per name per year. Required to search: name, years to search. Civil cases indexed by defendant, plaintiff, on computer since 1992, prior on microfiche and film. Mail turnaround time 1 week. Civil PAT goes back to 1991. PAT results show name, DOB. Access to county clerk civil and probate records is free at http://courts.hcclerk.org/iquery/ back to 1991. Also includes small claims, probate, and tax deeds. Access an index of judgments, liens, recorded documents at www.myfloridacounty.com. Fees involved to order copies; subscribers save $1.50 per record.

Criminal Records: Access: Mail, in person, online. Only the court performs in person searches; visitors may not. Search fee: $2.00 per name per year. Required to search: name, years to search; also helpful: SSN. Criminal records on computer since 1991, prior on microfiche and film. Mail turnaround time 1 week. Criminal PAT available. PAT results show middle initial, DOB. Subscribe for access to court records at http://courts.hcclerk.org/iquery/. Online results show name, DOB. Search results may also include race, sex.

General Information: No juvenile, child abuse or sexual battery records released. Will fax documents $1.00 per page. Court makes copy: $1.00 per page. Certification fee: $2.00. Payee: Clerk of Courts. Personal checks and major credit cards accepted. Prepayment required. SASE not required.

Hillsborough County

Circuit & County Courts 800 E Twiggs, 1st Fl, Tampa, FL 33602; 813-276-8100; criminal phone: 813-276-8100 x4368; civil phone: 813-276-8100 x4382; 8AM-5PM. ***Felony, Misdemeanor, Civil, Eviction, Small Claims, Probate.***

www.hillsclerk.com/publicweb/home.aspx

Civil Records: Access: Fax, mail, in person, online. Both court and visitors may perform in person searches. Search fee: $2.00 per name per year. Required to search: name, years to search; also helpful: address. Civil cases indexed by defendant, plaintiff, on computer since 5/85, prior on microfiche. Mail turnaround time 1-2 days. Civil PAT available. Online access to records at http://publicrecord.hillsclerk.com/. Search the Court Progress Dockets free at http://publicrecord.hillsclerk.com/oridev/criminal_pack.ins. A subscription service is also available for records; visit the home page for details and fees. Also, access an index of judgments, liens, recorded docs at www.myfloridacounty.com. Fees involved to order copies; subscribers save $1.50 per record.

Criminal Records: Access: Fax, mail, online, in person. Both court and visitors may perform in person searches. Search fee: $2.00 per name per year. Required to search: name, years to search, DOB; also helpful: address, SSN, race, sex. Criminal records on computer since 1989, prior on microfiche to 1975, archived 1953 to 1974. Mail turnaround time 1-2 days. Criminal PAT available. Online access to Criminal Court Dockets Search is same as civil.

General Information: No juvenile, child abuse or sexual battery records released. No fee to fax documents. Fax account required. Court makes copy: $1.00 per page. Certification fee: $2.00 per cert. Payee: Clerk of Circuit Court. Local personal checks accepted. Visa/MC accepted. Prepayment required.

Holmes County

Circuit & County Courts PO Box 397, Bonifay, FL 32425; 850-547-1100; fax: 850-547-6630; 8AM-4PM (CST). ***Felony, Misdemeanor, Civil, Eviction, Small Claims, Probate.***

www.holmesclerk.com/

Civil Records: Access: Mail, in person, online. Both court and visitors may perform in person searches. Search fee: $2.00 per name per year. Required to search: name, years to search; also helpful: address. Civil cases indexed by defendant, plaintiff, on computer from 10/91, archived from early 1900s. Mail turnaround time 1 week. Civil PAT goes back to 1983. Access to County Clerk of Circuit Court records is at https://www2.myfloridacounty.com/ccm/?county=30

Criminal Records: Access: Mail, in person, online. Both court and visitors may perform in person searches. Search fee: $2.00 per name per year. Required to search: name, years to search, DOB; also helpful: address, SSN, race, sex. Criminal records on computer since 1989, prior archived since early 1900s. Mail turnaround time 1 week. Criminal

PAT goes back to same as civil. Online access to criminal is the same as civil, see above.
General Information: Online identifiers in results same as on public terminal. No juvenile, child abuse or sexual battery records released. Will fax documents $2.00 1st page, $1.00 each add'l. Court makes copy: $1.00 per page. Certification fee: $2.00. Payee: Holmes County Clerk of Court. Personal checks and major credit cards accepted. Prepayment required. Mail requests: SASE required.

Indian River County

Circuit & County Courts PO Box 1028, Vero Beach, FL 32961; 772-770-5185; fax: 772-770-5008; 8:30AM-5PM. ***Felony, Misdemeanor, Civil, Eviction, Small Claims, Probate.***
www.clerk.indian-river.org
Civil Records: Access: Mail, in person, online. Both court and visitors may perform in person searches. Search fee: $2.00 per name per year. Required to search: name, years to search; also helpful: address. Civil cases indexed by defendant, plaintiff, on computer since 1984, prior on microfiche. Mail turnaround time 2 days. Civil PAT goes back to 1983. PAT results show middle initial, DOB. Online access to county recordings index is free at www.clerk.indian-river.org/recordssearch/ori.asp. Records go back to 1983. Full access to court records is via the clerk's subscription service. Fee is $25.00 per month, with onetime $100 setup fee. For information about free and fee access, call Gary at 772-567-8000 x1216.
Criminal Records: Access: Mail, in person, online. Both court and visitors may perform in person searches. Search fee: $2.00 per name per year. Required to search: name, years to search, DOB; also helpful: address, SSN, race, sex. Criminal records on computer (Felony since 1986, Misdemeanor since 1983), both archived since 1925. Mail turnaround time 2 days. Criminal PAT goes back to same as civil. PAT results show middle initial, DOB. Online access to criminal records is the same as civil. Online results show middle initial, DOB.
General Information: No juvenile, child abuse or sexual battery records released. Will not fax documents. Court makes copy: $1.00 per page. Certification fee: $2.00. Payee: Clerk of Circuit Court. Cashiers checks and money orders accepted. Credit cards accepted in person. Prepayment required. Mail requests: SASE helpful.

Jackson County

Circuit & County Courts PO Box 510, Marianna, FL 32447; 850-482-9552; fax: 850-482-7849; 8AM-4:30PM (CST). ***Felony, Misdemeanor, Civil, Eviction, Small Claims, Probate.***
www.jacksonclerk.com
Civil Records: Access: Fax, mail, in person, online. Both court and visitors may perform in person searches. Search fee: $2.00 per name per year. Required to search: name, years to search; also helpful: address. Civil cases indexed by defendant, plaintiff, go back to 1900; computerized records go back to 1992. Mail turnaround time 1-5 days. Civil PAT goes back to 1992. PAT results show middle initial, DOB, SSN. Access an index of judgments, liens, recorded documents at www.myfloridacounty.com. Fees involved to order copies; subscribers save $1.50 per record.
Criminal Records: Access: Fax, mail, in person. Both court and visitors may perform in person searches. Search fee: $2.00 per name per year. Required to search: name, years to search, DOB; also helpful: address, SSN, race, sex. Criminal records go back to 1900; computerized records since 1989. Mail turnaround time 1-5 days. Criminal PAT goes back to same as civil. PAT results show middle initial, DOB, SSN.
General Information: Online identifiers in results same as on public terminal. No juvenile, child abuse or sexual battery records released. Will fax documents $3.00 1st page, $1.00 each add'l. Court makes copy: $1.00 per page, self serve same. Certification fee: $2.00. Payee: Clerk of Circuit Court. Personal checks accepted only if it is a local bank in Marianna. Credit cards accepted. Prepayment required. Mail requests: SASE helpful.

Jefferson County

Circuit & County Courts Jefferson County Courthouse, Rm 10, Monticello, FL 32344; 850-342-0218; criminal phone: x226; civil phone: x228; fax: 850-342-0222; 8AM-5PM. ***Felony, Misdemeanor, Civil, Eviction, Small Claims, Probate.*** www.jeffersonclerk.com
Civil Records: Access: Mail, in person, online. Only the court performs in person searches; visitors may not. Search fee: $2.00 per name per year. Required to search: name, years to search; also helpful: address. Civil cases indexed by defendant, plaintiff, on computer since 7/90, prior on dockets. Mail turnaround time 1 week. Access to County Clerk of Circuit Court records is at https://www2.myfloridacounty.com/ccm/?county=33
Criminal Records: Access: Fax, mail, in person, online. Only the court performs in person searches; visitors may not. Search fee: $2.00 per name per year. Required to search: name, years to search, DOB; also helpful: address, SSN, race, sex. Criminal records on computer since 1989, prior on microfiche from 1969 to 1980, archived since 1950s, prior to 1950 on dockets. Mail turnaround time 1 week. Online access to criminal same as civil.
General Information: No juvenile, child abuse or sexual battery records released. Fee to fax out file $2.00 per page. Court makes copy: $1.00 per page. Certification fee: $2.00. Payee: Clerk of Circuit Court. Personal checks accepted. Visa/MC cards accepted in person, surcharges apply. Prepayment required.

Lafayette County

Circuit & County Courts PO Box 88, 120 W Main St, Mayo, FL 32066; 386-294-1600; fax: 386-294-4231; 8AM-5PM. ***Felony, Misdemeanor, Civil, Eviction, Small Claims, Probate.***
www.lafayetteclerk.com
Civil Records: Access: Phone, mail, fax, in person, online. Both court and visitors may perform in person searches. No search fee. Required to search: name, years to search; also helpful: address. Civil cases indexed by defendant, plaintiff, on computer since 1997, on books back to early 1900s. Mail turnaround time 5-7 days. Public use terminal available, records go back to 11 years. PAT results show name, DOB. Results include case number. Access an index of judgments, liens, recorded documents at www.myfloridacounty.com. Fees involved to order copies; subscribers save $1.50 per record.
Criminal Records: Access: Phone, mail, fax, in person. Both court and visitors may perform in person searches. Search fee: $2.00 per name per yr. Required to search: name, years to search, DOB; also helpful: address, SSN, race, sex. Criminal records computerized since 1989. Mail turnaround time 5-7 days. Public use terminal available, crim records go back to 18 years. PAT results show middle initial, DOB.
General Information: No juvenile, child abuse or sexual battery records released. Court makes copy: $1.00 per page, self serve same. Certification fee: $2.00. Payee: Clerk of Circuit Court. Personal checks accepted; credit cards are not. Prepayment required. Mail requests: SASE required.

Lake County

Circuit & County Courts PO Box 7800, 550 W Main St, Tavares, FL 32778; 352-742-4100; criminal phone: 352-742-4126(Felony) 352-742-4128(Misdemeanor); civil phone: 352-742-4145 County; 352-742-4148 Circuit; probate phone: 352-742-4122; fax: 352-742-4166; 8:30AM-5PM. ***Felony, Misdemeanor, Civil, Eviction, Small Claims, Probate.***
www.lakecountyclerk.org/default1.asp
Civil Records: Access: Fax, mail, in person, online. Both court and visitors may perform in person searches. Search fee: $2.00 per name per year. Required to search: name, years to search. Civil cases indexed by defendant, plaintiff, on computer since 1984, county civil on index books since 11/51, circuit civil since 1888. Mail turnaround time 7-10 days. Civil PAT goes back to 1985. PAT civil results show middle initial. Online access to Clerk of Court records is free at www.lakecountyclerk.org/services.asp?subject=Online_Court_Records. County civil records go back to 1985; Circuit records go back to 9/84. Also, previous 2-weeks civil records and divorces on a private site at http://extra.orlandosentinel.com/publicrecords/search.asp.
Criminal Records: Access: Fax, mail, in person, online. Both court and visitors may perform in person searches. Search fee: $2.00 per name per year. Required to search: name, years to search, DOB; also helpful: SSN, sex. Criminal records on computer since 1989, archived since 1888. Some on index books. Mail turnaround time 7-10 days. Criminal PAT goes back to 1989. PAT criminal results show middle initial. Online access is the same as civil, see above. Online results show middle initial.
General Information: Expunged or sealed records not released. No mental health, juvenile, child abuse or sexual battery records released. Will fax documents $1.00 per page. Court makes copy: $1.00 per page. Certification fee: $2.00. Payee: Clerk of Circuit Court. Personal checks accepted; credit cards are not. Prepayment required. Mail requests: SASE helpful.

Lee County

Circuit & County Courts PO Box 2469, 2115 Second St, Justice Ctr, 2nd Fl, Ft Myers, FL 33902; 239-533-5000; 7:45-5PM. ***Felony, Misdemeanor, Civil, Eviction, Small Claims, Probate, Traffic.***
www.leeclerk.org
A second location is at Cape Coral Branch Office (Lee County Gov't Ctr): 1039 SE 9th Pl, Cape Coral, FL 33990, near Cape Coral City Hall and Post Office.
Civil Records: Access: Mail, in person, online. Both court and visitors may perform in person searches. Search fee: $2.00 per name per year. Required to search: name, years to search. Civil cases indexed by defendant, plaintiff, on computer since 1988, prior on microfilm and dockets. Mail turnaround 5 days. Civil PAT goes back to 1990. Access records free at www.leeclerk.org/court_inquiry_disclaimer.htm Online records go back to 1988. Includes traffic, felony, misdemeanor, civil, small claims and probate. Access an index of judgments, liens, recorded documents at www.leeclerk.org or www.myfloridacounty.com. Search free but fees involved to order certified copies; save the per-record copy fee by becoming a subscriber; sub fee is $25.00 per month.
Criminal Records: Access: Mail, online, in person. Both court and visitors may perform in person searches. Search fee: $2.00 per name per year. Required to search: name, years to search, DOB; also helpful: address, SSN, race, sex. Criminal records on computer-(Felony since 1978, Misdemeanor since 1986), prior on microfilm. Mail turnaround time 5 days. Criminal PAT goes back to same as civil. Online access to criminal records is the same as civil. Online results show middle initial, DOB.
General Information: No juvenile, child abuse or sexual offense records released. Will not fax documents. Court makes copy: $1.00 per page. Certification fee: $2.00 per doc. Payee: Clerk of Circuit Court. Personal checks accepted. Credit cards accepted; $2.50 transaction fee added. Prepayment required. Mail requests: SASE required.

Leon County

Circuit & County Courts 301 S Monroe St, #100, PO Box 726, Tallahassee, FL 32301; 850-577-4000; criminal phone: 850-577-4070; civil phone: 850-577-4170; probate phone: 850-577-4180; criminal fax: 850-577-8012; civil fax: 850-577-8012; 8AM-5PM. ***Felony, Misdemeanor, Civil, Eviction, Small Claims, Probate.***
www.clerk.leon.fl.us
Address above is for felony cases. Misdemeanor at PO Box 105; Probate at PO Box 1024, both use 32302.
Civil Records: Access: Mail, fax, online, in person. Both court and visitors may perform in person searches. Search fee: $2.00 per name per year. Required to search: name, years to search; also helpful: address, other identifiers. Civil cases indexed by defendant, plaintiff, on computer since 8/86, prior

on docket books. Mail turnaround time 1-5 days. Civil PAT goes back to 1990. PAT results show middle initial, DOB. Public terminal civil results may include SSN and other personal identifiers. Search all types of civil and traffic cases free at http://cvweb.clerk.leon.fl.us/index.asp. Access an index of judgments, liens, recorded documents at www.myfloridacounty.com. Fees involved to order copies; subscribers save $1.50 per record.
Criminal Records: Access: Mail, fax, in person. Both court and visitors may perform in person searches. Search fee: $2.00 per name per year. Required to search: name, years to search, DOB; also helpful: address, SSN, race, sex. Criminal records on computer since 1976, on microfiche since 1937, archived since late 1800s/early 1900s. Mail turnaround time 1-5 days. Criminal PAT goes back to 1990. PAT results show middle initial, DOB. Terminal results may include add'l identifiers. Search all types traffic cases free at http://cvweb.clerk.leon.fl.us/index.asp. Also county inmate search only at http://lcso.leonfl.org/jailinfo/inmate_search.asp. Criminal searching online is not available at publication time. When available, online results show middle initial, DOB.
General Information: No juvenile, child abuse or sexual battery records released. Will not fax out documents. Court makes copy: $1.00 per page. Certification fee: $2.00 per doc. Payee: Clerk of Circuit Court. Personal checks and major credit cards accepted. Prepayment required. Mail requests: SASE helpful.

Levy County

Circuit & County Courts PO Box 610, Bronson, FL 32621; 352-486-5266; criminal phone: x256; civil phone: x238; probate phone: x259; 8AM-5PM. ***Felony, Misdemeanor, Civil, Eviction, Small Claims, Probate.***
www.levyclerk.com
Civil Records: Access: Mail, in person, online. Both court and visitors may perform in person searches. Search fee: $2.00 per name per year. Required to search: name, years to search; also helpful: address. Civil cases indexed by defendant, plaintiff, on computer from 1986, microfiche to 1981 (in process), prior on docket books. Mail turnaround time 1-2 days. Public use terminal has civil records back to 1986. Judgments available on the Clerk of the Circuit Court Official Records Index free at http://oncore.levyclerk.com/oncoreweb/.
Criminal Records: Access: Mail, in person. Only the court performs in person searches; visitors may not. Search fee: $2.00 per name per year. Required to search: name, years to search, DOB, signed release; also helpful: address, SSN, race, sex. Criminal records computerized from 1986 to present, prior on docket books. Mail turnaround time 2-3 days.
General Information: No juvenile, child abuse or sexual battery records released. Court makes copy: $1.00 per page, self serve same. Certification fee: $2.00. Payee: Clerk of Circuit Court. Business checks accepted. Credit cards accepted. Prepayment required. Mail requests: SASE required.

Liberty County

Circuit & County Courts PO Box 399, Bristol, FL 32321; 850-643-2215; probate phone: same; fax: 850-643-2866; 8AM-5PM. ***Felony, Misdemeanor, Civil, Eviction, Small Claims, Probate.*** www.libertyclerk.com
Civil Records: Access: Mail, in person, online. Both court and visitors may perform in person searches. Search fee: $2.00 per name per year. Required to search: name, years to search; also helpful: address. Civil cases indexed by defendant, plaintiff; index on docket books. Mail turnaround time 1 week. Civil PAT goes back to 2002. PAT results show name only. Access an index of judgments, liens, and civil court-related documents at www.myfloridacounty.com. Fees involved to order copies; subscribers save $1.50 per record.
Criminal Records: Access: Mail, in person. Both court and visitors may perform in person searches. Search fee: $2.00 per name per year. Required to search: name, years to search, DOB; also helpful: address, SSN, race, sex. Criminal docket on books. Mail turnaround time 1 week. Criminal PAT goes back to 1998. PAT results show name only.
General Information: No juvenile, child abuse or sexual battery records released. Will fax documents to local or toll-free number. Court makes copy: $1.00 per page. Certification fee: $2.00. Payee: Clerk of Circuit Court. Business checks accepted. Major credit cards accepted. Prepayment required. Mail requests: SASE required.

Madison County

Circuit & County Courts PO Box 237, Madison, FL 32341; 850-973-1500; fax: 850-973-2059; 8AM-5PM. ***Felony, Misdemeanor, Civil, Eviction, Small Claims, Probate.***
Civil Records: Access: Phone, mail, in person, online. Both court and visitors may perform in person searches. Search fee: $2.00 per name per year. Required to search: name, years to search; also helpful: address. Civil cases indexed by defendant, plaintiff, on computer since 1988, prior on docket books. Mail turnaround time 1-3 days. Access an index of judgments, liens, recorded documents at www.myfloridacounty.com. Fees involved to order copies; subscribers save $1.50 per record.
Criminal Records: Access: Phone, mail, in person. Both court and visitors may perform in person searches. Search fee: $2.00 per name per year. Required to search: name, years to search, DOB; also helpful: address, SSN, race, sex. Criminal records on computer since 1988, prior on docket books. Mail turnaround time 1-3 days.
General Information: No juvenile, child abuse or sexual battery records released. Will not fax documents. Court makes copy: $1.00 per page, self serve same. Certification fee: $2.00. Payee: Clerk of Circuit Court. Personal checks and major credit cards accepted. Prepayment required. Mail requests: SASE requested.

Manatee County

Circuit & County Courts PO Box 25400, Bradenton, FL 34206; 941-749-1800; criminal phone: 941-741-4019; civil phone: 941-741-4025; probate phone: 941-741-4021; criminal fax: 941-741-4082; civil fax: 941-741-4093; 8AM-4:30PM. ***Felony, Misdemeanor, Civil, Eviction, Small Claims, Probate.***
www.manateeclerk.com
Probate fax- 941-741-4093
Civil Records: Access: Phone, fax, mail, online, in person, email. Both court and visitors may perform in person searches. Search fee: $2.00 per name per year. Required to search: name, years to search; also helpful: address. Civil cases indexed by defendant, plaintiff, on computer since 9/80, prior on microfilm back to 1972. Mail turnaround time 2 days. Civil PAT goes back to 9/1980. Access court records at Circuit clerk's office free at www.manateeclerk.org/ but subscription required for images; before 3/1/2004 are not available. Also, you may direct email record requests to lori.tolksdorf@manateeclerk.com. Access an index of judgments, liens, recorded documents at www.myfloridacounty.com. Fees involved to order copies; subscribers save $1.50 per record.
Criminal Records: Access: Phone, fax, mail, online, in person, email. Both court and visitors may perform in person searches. Search fee: $2.00 per name per year. Required to search: name, years to search, DOB; also helpful: address, charge, race, sex. Criminal records on computer since 1981, prior on docket books back to 1972. Mail turnaround time 2 days. Criminal PAT goes back to 1981. Online access to criminal records is the same as civil. Online results show name, DOB. Results include gender and race.
General Information: No juvenile, adoption, child abuse or sexual battery victim records released. Will fax documents $1.00 per page. Court makes copy: $1.00 per page, self serve same. Certification fee: $2.00. Payee: Clerk of Circuit Court. Personal checks accepted. Credit cards accepted. Prepayment required. Mail requests: SASE helpful.

Marion County

Circuit & County Courts PO Box 1030, Ocala, FL 34478-1030; 352-671-5604; criminal phone: 352-671-5674; civil phone: 352-671-5610 (Circ); probate phone: 352-671-5658; criminal fax: 352-671-5600; civil fax: 352-671-5519; 8AM-5PM. ***Felony, Misdemeanor, Civil, Eviction, Small Claims, Probate, Traffic.***
www.marioncountyclerk.org
Civil Records: Access: Fax, mail, in person, online. Both court and visitors may perform in person searches. Search fee: $2.00 per name per year. Required to search: name, years to search; also helpful: address. Civil cases indexed by defendant, plaintiff, on computer since 1983, on microfiche since 1958. Mail turnaround time 1-2 weeks. Civil PAT goes back to 1983. PAT results show middle initial, DOB. Online access to county clerk records is free at www.marioncountyclerk.org/. Click on 'Case Search' found under Courts section. Also, access an index of judgments, liens, recorded documents at www.myfloridacounty.com. Fees involved to order copies; subscribers save $1.50 per record.
Criminal Records: Access: Fax, mail, in person, online. Both court and visitors may perform in person searches. Search fee: $2.00 per name per year. Required to search: name, years to search, DOB; also helpful: address, SSN, race, sex. Criminal records on computer. Felonies since 1984, on microfiche from 1950 to 1979, prior on index cards. Misdemeanors since 1983, on microfiche from. Mail turnaround time 1-2 weeks. Criminal PAT goes back to same as civil. PAT results show middle initial, DOB. Online access to criminal same as civil.
General Information: No juvenile records released. Will fax documents to local or toll free line, otherwise fee involved. Court makes copy: $1.00 per page. Certification fee: $2.00 per cert; exemplification-$6.00. Payee: Clerk of Court. Personal checks accepted. In person requester may use credit card, surcharge applies. Prepayment required. Mail requests: SASE requested.

Martin County

Circuit & County Courts PO Box 9016, Stuart, FL 34995; 772-288-5736; criminal phone: 772-288-5536; civil phone: 772-288-5717; probate phone: 772-288-5540; criminal fax: 772-288-5548; civil fax: 772-288-5991; 8AM-5PM. ***Felony, Misdemeanor, Civil, Eviction, Small Claims, Probate.*** http://clerk-web.martin.fl.us/ClerkWeb
Probate fax- 772-221-2388
Civil Records: Access: Phone, fax, mail, online, in person. Both court and visitors may perform in person searches. Search fee: $2.00 per name per year. Required to search: name, years to search; also helpful: address. Civil cases indexed by defendant, plaintiff, on computer since 10/86, prior on microfiche, microfilm and archived. Mail turnaround time 1 week. Civil PAT goes back to 1984. Search all court records free at http://clerk-web.martin.fl.us/ClerkWeb/ccis_disclaimer.htm. Also includes small claims, recordings, other document types. Search online by name or SSN.
Criminal Records: Access: Phone, fax, mail, in person, online. Both court and visitors may perform in person searches. Search fee: $2.00 per name per year prior to 1990. Required to search: name, years to search, DOB; also helpful: address, SSN. Criminal records on computer, felonies to 1986 (misdemeanors since 1985), on microfiche since 1956, prior on index cards/docket books. Mail turnaround time 1 week. Criminal PAT goes back to 1989. Search all court records free at http://clerk-web.martin.fl.us/ClerkWeb/ccis_disclaimer.htm. Search online by name or SSN. Online results show name only. Online results include partial address, sex, race, alias.
General Information: No juvenile, child abuse or sexual battery records released. Will fax documents $1.25 per page. Court makes copy: $1.00 per page. Certification fee: $2.00. Payee: Clerk of Circuit Court. Personal checks and major credit cards accepted. Prepayment required. Mail requests: SASE required.

Monroe County

Circuit & County Courts Clerk of the Court, 500 Whitehead St, Key West, FL 33040; 305-294-4641 x3342; criminal phone: 305-294-4641 x3970; civil phone: 305-294-4641 x3310; fax: 305-295-3623; 8:30AM-5PM. ***Felony, Misdemeanor, Civil, Eviction, Small Claims, Probate.***
www.monroe.fl.us.landata.com/default.asp
Civil Records: Access: Mail, fax, in person, online. Both court and visitors may perform in person searches. Search fee: $2.00 per name per year. Required to search: name, years to search; also helpful: address. Civil cases indexed by defendant, plaintiff, on computer since 1983, on microfiche since 1972, prior on docket books. Some records purged after 2 years. Probate from 1972. Mail turnaround time 1-2 weeks. Civil PAT goes back to 1982. Online access to civil cases is free at www.clerk-of-the-court.com/searchCivilCases.asp. Subscription is required for viewing full document library. Search probate cases free at www.clerk-of-the-court.com/searchProbateCases.asp.
Criminal Records: Access: Mail, fax, in person, online. Both court and visitors may perform in person searches. Search fee: $2.00 per name per year. Required to search: name, years to search, DOB; also helpful: address, SSN, race, sex. Criminal records (pending felony and misdemeanors) on computer, others since 1992, non-pending on microfiche since 1945. Mail turnaround time 1-2 weeks. Criminal PAT goes back to same as civil. Online access to criminal records is free at www.clerk-of-the-court.com/searchTrafficCriminalCases.asp. Includes traffic cases online. Subscription is required for viewing full document library. Online results show name, DOB.
General Information: No juvenile, child abuse or sexual battery records released. Fee to fax out file $1.00 per page. Court makes copy: $1.00 per page. Certification fee: $2.00. Payee: Clerk of Circuit Court. Personal checks accepted; credit cards are not. Prepayment required. Mail requests: SASE helpful.

Nassau County

Circuit & County Courts PO Box 456, 76347 Veterans Way, Fernandina Beach, FL 32035; criminal phone: 904-548-4613; civil phone: 904-548-4606; probate phone: 904-548-4606; fax: 904-548-4529; 8:30AM-5PM. ***Felony, Misdemeanor, Civil, Eviction, Small Claims, Probate.***
www.nassauclerk.com
Civil Records: Access: Phone, fax, mail, in person, online. Only the court performs in person searches; visitors may not. Search fee: $2.00 per name per year. Required to search: name, years to search; also helpful: address. Civil cases indexed by defendant, plaintiff, on computer since 1993, on microfiche since 1982, prior on docket books. Mail turnaround time 1 week. Search civil cases free back to 1989 and perhaps earlier at www.nassauclerk.com/cocoa/cocoa.index.cfm. Access an index of judgments, sentences, county commitments, uniform state commitments, disposition notices and nolle prosequi only at www.myfloridacounty.com. Fees involved to order copies; subscribers save $1.50 per record.
Criminal Records: Access: Phone, fax, mail, in person, online. Only the court performs in person searches; visitors may not. Search fee: $2.00 per name per year. Required to search: name, years to search, DOB; also helpful: address, SSN, race, sex. Criminal records on computer since 1985, on microfiche since 1982, prior on docket books. Past 10 years only can be done on the phone. Mail turnaround time 1 week. Search criminal and traffic cases free at www.nassauclerk.com/cocoa/cocoa.index.cfm
General Information: No juvenile, child abuse or sexual battery records released. Will fax documents to local or toll-free number. Court makes copy: $1.00 per page. Certification fee: $2.00. Payee: Clerk of Circuit Court. Personal checks and major credit cards accepted. Prepayment required. Mail requests: SASE required.

Okaloosa County

Circuit & County Courts 1250 N Eglin Pky, Shalimar, FL 32579; 850-651-7200; fax: 850-651-7230; 8AM-5PM (CST). ***Felony, Misdemeanor, Civil, Eviction, Small Claims, Probate.***
www.clerkofcourts.cc
Civil Records: Access: Mail, in person, online. Both court and visitors may perform in person searches. Search fee: $2.00 per year per name. Required to search: name, years to search; also helpful: address. Civil cases indexed by defendant, plaintiff, on computer from 1/86; archives from 1915; prior on microfilm. Mail turnaround time 1 day. Civil PAT goes back to 6/1986. Civil records are free at www.clerkofcourts.cc/court/courtsearch.htm. Records go back to 1/83. Search civil index by defendant or plaintiff, date, or file type. Also, access an index of judgments, liens, recorded documents back to 1/1983 at www.myfloridacounty.com. Fees involved to order copies; subscribers save $1.50 per record.
Criminal Records: Access: Mail, online, in person. Both court and visitors may perform in person searches. Search fee: $2.00 per year per name. Required to search: name, years to search, DOB; also helpful: address, SSN, race, sex. Criminal records computerized from 1/89; archives from 1915; prior on microfilm. Mail turnaround time 1 day to 1 week. Criminal PAT goes back to 1/1989. County clerk criminal records some back to 1980s free at www.clerkofcourts.cc/court/courtsearch.htm.
General Information: No juvenile, child abuse or sexual battery records released. Will fax documents $1.00 per page. Court makes copy: $1.00 per page. Certification fee: $2.00 per doc. Payee: Clerk of Circuit Court. Personal checks accepted. Prepayment required. Mail requests: SASE required.

Okeechobee County

Circuit & County Courts Okeechobee County Judicial Center, 312 NW Third Street, Okeechobee, FL 34972; 863-763-2131; fax: 863-763-1258; 8:30AM-5PM. ***Felony, Misdemeanor, Civil, Eviction, Small Claims, Probate.***
www.clerk.co.okeechobee.fl.us/
Civil Records: Access: Mail, in person, online. Both court and visitors may perform in person searches. Search fee: $2.00 per name per year. Required to search: name, years to search; also helpful: address. Civil cases indexed by defendant, plaintiff, on computer since 1990, on index cards from 1983 to 1988. Mail turnaround time 1 week. Civil PAT goes back to 1990. Index of judgments and recorded documents can be searched at http://204.215.37.218/wb_or1/. Also, access to County Clerk of Circuit Court records is at https://www2.myfloridacounty.com/ccm/?county=47
Criminal Records: Access: Mail, in person, online. Both court and visitors may perform in person searches. Search fee: $2.00 per name per year. Required to search: name, years to search, DOB; also helpful: address, SSN, race, sex. Criminal records on computer since 1989, on index cards from 1932 to 1988. Mail turnaround time 1 week. Criminal PAT goes back to 1985. Online access to criminal is same as civil.
General Information: No confidential, adoption, records released. Will fax documents for fee varying on number of pages sent, basically $.25 per page. Court makes copy: $1.00 per page. Certification fee: $2.00. Payee: Clerk of Circuit Court. Personal checks accepted; credit cards are not. Prepayment required. Mail requests: SASE required.

Orange County

Circuit & County Courts PO Box 4994, 425 N Orange Ave, Rm 310, Orlando, FL 32801-1544; 407-836-2060; civil phone: 407-836-2065; fax: 407-836-2225; 8AM-5PM. ***Felony, Misdemeanor, Civil, Eviction, Small Claims, Probate.***
http://myorangeclerk.com/
Mail requests should use room numbers; civil circuit-310; civil county-350; crim circuit-210; crim county-250.
Civil Records: Access: Mail, in person, online, email. Both court and visitors may perform in person searches. Search fee: $2.00 per name per year. Required to search: name, years to search. Civil cases indexed by defendant, plaintiff, are on computer as follows: Circuit civil-1992; Domestic civil-1992; Probate-1993; Traffic-1980. Mail turnaround time 2 days. Civil PAT goes back to 2000. Public terminal available in Records Management Division. Free Myclerk Case Inquiry System is at http://myorangeclerk.com/criminal/iclerk_disclaimer.shtml. Civil and Probate records available. Also, previous 2-weeks civil records on a private site at http://extra.orlandosentinel.com/publicrecords/search.asp. This court also accepts email requests at hr@orange-clerk.org.
Criminal Records: Access: Mail, online, in person, email. Both court and visitors may perform in person searches. Search fee: $2.00 per name per year. Required to search: name, years to search, DOB. Criminal records on computer go back to 1990; prior records go back to 1987. This court also accepts email requests at hr@orange-clerk.org. Mail turnaround time 2 days. Criminal PAT goes back to same as civil. Public terminal available in Records Management Division. Access criminal records free on Myclerk Case Inquiry System at http://myorangeclerk.com/criminal/iclerk_disclaimer.shtml. Online results show name, DOB.
General Information: No sex-related or adoption records released. Court makes copy: $1.00 per page. Certification fee: $2.00. Payee: Orange County Clerk of Courts. Personal checks accepted from Orange County only. No credit cards accepted. Prepayment required. Mail requests: SASE helpful.

County Court - Apopka Branch 1111 N Rock Springs Rd, Apopka, FL 32712; 407-836-2007; criminal phone: 407-836-2056; civil phone: 407-836-2065; criminal fax: 407-836-2306; civil fax: 407-836-2099; 8AM-5PM. ***Misdemeanor, Civil Actions under $15,000, Eviction, Small Claims.***
http://orangeclerk.ocfl.net
Records also maintained at Orlando office; Orlando address and phones given here.
Civil Records: Access: Mail, in person, online. Both court and visitors may perform in person searches. Search fee: $2.00 per name per year. Required to search: name, years to search. Civil cases indexed by defendant, plaintiff. Pending civil records on computer. All dockets on microfilm or microfiche; some records on index cards. Mail turnaround time 2 days. PAT civil results show middle initial. The free myclerk Case Inquiry System is at http://myorangeclerk.com/criminal/iclerk_disclaimer.shtml. Civil and Probate records available. Also, previous 2-weeks civil records on a private site at http://extra.orlandosentinel.com/publicrecords/search.asp.
Criminal Records: Access: Mail, online, in person. Both court and visitors may perform in person searches. Search fee: $2.00 per name per year. Required to search: name, years to search, DOB; also helpful: SSN. Criminal records (Pending) on computer. All dockets on microfilm or microfiche. Some records on index cards. Mail turnaround time 2 days. PAT criminal results show middle initial. Acccss criminal rccords free on the Myclerk Case Inquiry System at http://myorangeclerk.com/criminal/iclerk_disclaimer.shtml. Online results show name, DOB.
General Information: No sex related or adoption records released. Court makes copy: $1.00 per page. Certification fee: $2.00. Payee: Clerk of County Court. Personal checks accepted for traffic only. Visa/MC accepted. Prepayment required. Mail requests: SASE helpful.

County Court - NE Orange Division PO Box 4994, 425 N Orange, Ste 250, Winter Park, FL 32801; 407-836-2007; criminal phone: 407-836-2056; civil phone: 407-836-2065; fax: 407-671-4837; 8AM-5:30PM. ***Misdemeanor, Civil Actions under $15,000, Eviction, Small Claims.***
http://orangeclerk.ocfl.net
Civil Records: Access: Phone, mail, online, in person. Only the court performs in person searches; visitors may not. Search fee: $2.00 per name per year. Required to search: name, years to search. Civil

cases indexed by defendant, plaintiff, (Pending) on computer. All dockets on microfilm or microfiche. Mail turnaround time 2 days. The free myclerk Case Inquiry System is at http://myorangeclerk.com/criminal/iclerk_disclaimer.shtml. Civil and Probate records available. Also, previous 2-weeks civil records on a private site at http://extra.orlandosentinel.com/publicrecords/search.asp.
Criminal Records: Access: Phone, mail, online, in person. Only the court performs in person searches; visitors may not. Search fee: $2.00 per name per year. Required to search: name, years to search, DOB; also helpful: SSN. Criminal records (Pending) on computer. All dockets on microfilm or microfiche. Results include address. Mail turnaround time 2 days. Access criminal records free on the myclerk Case Inquiry System at http://myorangeclerk.com/criminal/iclerk_disclaimer.shtml. Online results show name, DOB.
General Information: No sex related or adoption records released. Will fax documents to local or toll-free number. Court makes copy: $1.00 per page. Certification fee: $2.00. Payee: Clerk of County Court. Only cashiers checks and money orders accepted. No credit cards accepted. Prepayment required. Mail requests: SASE helpful.

County Court #3 Clerk of Courts, 475 W Story Rd, Ocoee, FL 34761; 407-836-2007; criminal phone: 407-836-2066; civil phone: 407-836-2065; fax: 407-836-2306; 8AM-5PM. ***Misdemeanor, Civil Actions under $15,000, Eviction, Small Claims.***
http://orangeclerk.ocfl.net
Incoming calls are handled by the Branch Call Center, which is very helpful.
Civil Records: Access: Mail, fax, online, in person. Both court and visitors may perform in person searches. Search fee: $5.00 per name. Required to search: name, years to search. Civil cases indexed by defendant, plaintiff, go back to 1890; on computer back to 1990. All dockets are on microfilm or microfiche. Mail turnaround time 2 days depending on file availability. Free Myclerk Case Inquiry System is at http://myorangeclerk.com/criminal/iclerk_disclaimer.shtml. Civil and Probate records available. Also, previous 2-weeks civil records on a private site at http://extra.orlandosentinel.com/publicrecords/search.asp.
Criminal Records: Access: Mail, fax, online, in person. Both court and visitors may perform in person searches. Search fee: $5.00 per name. Required to search: name, years to search, DOB; also helpful: SSN. Criminal records go back to 1890; on computer back to 1990. All dockets are on microfilm or microfiche. Mail turnaround time 2 days depending on file. Access criminal records free on the myclerk Case Inquiry System at http://myorangeclerk.com/criminal/iclerk_disclaimer.shtml. Online results show name, DOB.
General Information: No sex related or adoption records released. Will not fax documents. Court makes copy: $1.50 per page. Certification fee: $2.00 per cert. Payee: Clerk of County Court. Personal checks accepted; credit cards are not. Prepayment required. Mail requests: SASE helpful.

Osceola County

Circuit Court - Civil 2 Courthouse Sq, Kissimmee, FL 34741; 407-742-3500; civil phone: 407-742-3479; probate phone: 407-343-3506; 8:30AM-5PM. ***Civil Actions over $5,000, Probate.***
www.ninthcircuit.org/
Civil Records: Access: Mail, in person, online. Both court and visitors may perform in person searches. Search fee: $2.00 per name per year per division. Required to search: name, years to search. Civil cases indexed by defendant, plaintiff, on computer from 1990, on docket books from 1800s to 1990. Mail turnaround time 1-2 days. Public use terminal has civil records back to 1990. Online access to court records on the Clerk of Circuit Court database are free at www.osceolaclerkcourt.org/genrlmnu.htm. Also, access an index of judgments, liens, recorded documents at www.myfloridacounty.com. Fees involved to order copies; subscribers save $1.50 per record. Also, previous 2-weeks civil records on a private site at http://extra.orlandosentinel.com/publicrecords/search.asp.
General Information: No appeal records released. Will fax documents if prepaid. Court makes copy: $1.00 per page. Certification fee: $2.00 per cert. Payee: Clerk of Court. Business checks accepted. Visa/MC accepted. Prepayment required. Mail requests: SASE required.

County Court - Civil 2 Courthouse Sq, #2000, Kissimmee, FL 34741; 407-742-3500; fax: 407-742-3652; 8:30AM-5PM. ***Civil Actions under $5,000, Eviction, Small Claims, Family.***
www.osceolaclerk.com
Civil Records: Access: Mail, in person, online. Both court and visitors may perform in person searches. Search fee: $2.00 per name per year per division. Required to search: name, years to search. Civil cases indexed by defendant, plaintiff, on computer from 1991, on index cards from 1972 to 1991, on docket books from 1800s to 1972. Mail turnaround time 1 week. Public use terminal has civil records back to 1990. PAT results show name only. Terminal is located on 2nd floor. Online access to court records on the Clerk of Circuit Court database are free at http://198.140.240.34/pa/ or at www.osceolaclerkcourt.org.
General Information: No juvenile records released. Will not fax out documents. Court makes copy: $1.00 per page. Certification fee: $2.00 per doc. Payee: Clerk of Court. Local business checks accepted. No personal checks. Credit cards accepted in the office only, no mail or phone use. Prepayment required. Mail requests: SASE helpful.

Circuit & County Courts - Criminal Div. 2 Courthouse Square, #200, Kissimmee, FL 34741; 407-742-3566, 407-742-3500; 8:30AM-5PM. ***Felony, Misdemeanor, Traffic.***
www.osceolaclerk.com
Misdemeanors fax 407-742-3563.
Criminal Records: Access: Mail, in person, online. Both court and visitors may perform in person searches. Search fee: $2.00 per name per year. Required to search: name, years to search, DOB, SSN. Criminal records computerized from 1990, on index since 1978, prior on docket books 1800s to 1978. Both the court and visitors may perform in person searches as long as the case occurred 1990 or after. Mail turnaround time 1 week. Public use terminal has crim records back to 1990. PAT results show middle initial, DOB. The most reliable public terminal is in the Public Information Room, #2800. Online access to criminal records is free at https://www.co.charlotte.fl.us/scripts/mgrqispi.dll?appname=MPI%20Criminal&prgname=PUBSEARCHF. Includes party index and case summary searching. Search county inmates at www.osceola.org/index.cfm?lsFuses=inmates.
General Information: No juvenile or sealed records released. Will fax documents to local or toll free line. Court makes copy: $1.00 per page, self serve same. Certification fee: $2.00 per doc. Payee: Clerk of the Court. Business checks accepted. Credit cards accepted; a surcharge is added. Prepayment required. Mail requests: SASE requested.

Palm Beach County

Circuit Court - Civil Division PO Box 4667, 205 N Dixie Highway, 3rd Fl, Rm 3.23, West Palm Beach, FL 33402; 561-355-2986; fax: 561-355-4643; 8AM-5PM. ***Civil.***
www.pbcountyclerk.com
Civil Records: Access: Mail, in person, online. Both court and visitors may perform in person searches. Search fee: $2.00 per exact name per year (mail requests accepted on at the Official Records Serv Section). Required to search: name, years to search; also helpful: address. Civil cases indexed by defendant, plaintiff, (Circuit) on computer from 1982, prior records on microfiche and dockets. County on computer from 1987, prior on microfilm. Mail turnaround time 1 week. Public use terminal has civil records back to 2000. Access to the countywide online remote system is free. Civil index goes back to '88. Records also include probate, traffic and domestic. Also, civil records are free at http://courtcon.co.palm-beach.fl.us/pls/jiwp/ck_public_qry_main.cp_main_idx. Records include criminal and traffic.
General Information: No juvenile, child abuse or sexual battery records released. Court makes copy: $1.00 per page. Certification fee: $2.00 per doc. Payee: Clerk and Comptroller. Personal checks accepted. Prepayment required. Mail requests: SASE required.

County Court - Civil Division 205 N Dixie Hwy, West Palm Beach, FL 33402; 561-355-2500, records- 561-355-2932; fax: 561-355-6211; 8AM-5PM. ***Civil Actions under $15,000, Eviction, Small Claims.*** www.pbcountyclerk.com
Direct mail requests to the Official Records Svcs Section, Rm 4.25 - for judgments and court paper searches.
Civil Records: Access: Mail, in person, online. Both court and visitors may perform in person searches. Search fee: $2.00 per exact name per year (mail requests accepted on at the Official Records Serv Section). Required to search: name, years to search; also helpful: address. Civil cases indexed by defendant, plaintiff, (Circuit) on computer from 1982, prior records on microfiche and dockets. County on computer from 1987, prior on microfilm. Mail turnaround time 1 week. Public use terminal has civil records back to 2000. PAT results show name only. Access to the countywide remote online system requires $145 setup and $65 per month fees. Civil index goes back to '88. Records also include probate, traffic and domestic. Also, civil records are free at http://courtcon.co.palm-beach.fl.us/pls/jiwp/ck_public_qry_main.cp_main_idx.
General Information: No juvenile, child abuse or sexual battery records released. Will not fax out documents. Records Services will expedite doc return by Fed Ex if prepaid. Court makes copy: $1.00 per page. Certification fee: $2.00 per doc. Payee: Clerk and Comptroller. Personal checks accepted; credit cards are not. Prepayment required. Mail requests: SASE required.

Circuit & County Courts - Criminal Div. PO Box 2906, 205 N Dixie Hwy, 3rd Fl, Rm 3.24, West Palm Beach, FL 33401; 561-355-2519; local toll free- 888-760-9167; fax: 561-355-3802; 8AM-5PM. ***Felony, Misdemeanor.***
www.pbcountyclerk.com
Faxes can only be received from state agencies. Misdemeanor are in County Court, 2nd Fl, Rm 2.23. Mail address for Circuit Felony Division is PO Box 2906, 33402. County Court Misdemeanor mailing address is PO Box 3544.
Criminal Records: Access: Phone, fax, mail, online, in person. Both court and visitors may perform in person searches. Search fee: $2.00 per exact name per year. Required to search: name, years to search, DOB, aliases. Criminal records on computer & microfiche (some files) from 1970s, archived from 1920s. Mail turnaround time 5-7 days. Public use terminal has crim records back to varies by type. PAT results show middle initial, DOB. Includes microfiche and on-demand access. Access to the countywide criminal system is at http://courtcon.co.palm-beach.fl.us/pls/jiwp/ck_public_qry_main.cp_main_idx. Records also include civil, probate, traffic and domestic. Online results show middle initial, DOB.
General Information: No juvenile, child abuse or sexual battery records released. Will not fax documents. Court makes copy: $1.00 per page. Certification fee: $2.00 per doc. Payee: Clerk and Comptroller. Personal checks accepted. Visa/MC accepted. Prepayment required. Mail requests: SASE required.

Circuit Court - Probate Division PO Box 4667, 205 N Dixie Hwy, 3rd Fl, Rm 3.23, West Palm Beach, FL 33402; 561-355-2986; Fla. toll tree- 888-760-9208; fax: 561-355-4643; 8AM-5PM. ***Probate.***
www.pbcountyclerk.com Access countywide court online system at http://courtcon.co.palm-beach.fl.us/pls/jiwp/ck_public_qry_main.cp_main_idx.
Public access terminals in Rm 2.22 and File Rm 3.23 - probate records on terminal go back to 1990.

Pasco County

Circuit & County Courts - Civil Division
38053 Live Oak Ave, Dade City, FL 33523; 352-521-4517; probate phone: 352-521-4563; 8:30AM-5PM. ***Civil, Eviction, Small Claims, Probate.*** www.pascoclerk.com/

A branch court at West Pasco Judicial Ctr, 7530 Little Rd, New Port Richey, 34654.

Civil Records: Access: Mail, in person, online. Both court and visitors may perform in person searches. Search fee: $2.00 per name per year. Required to search: name, years to search. Civil cases indexed by defendant, plaintiff, on computer from 1985, on docket cards and docket books from 1900s. Mail turnaround time 2-4 days. Public use terminal has civil records back to 3/1985. Results include aliases. Access court records free at www.pascoclerk.com/public-online-services-disclaimer-courts-search.asp. Also, access to County Clerk of Circuit Court records is at https://www2.myfloridacounty.com/ccm/?county=51

General Information: Online identifiers in results same as on public terminal. No adoption records released. Will not fax documents. Court makes copy: $1.00 per page. Certification fee: $2.00. Payee: Clerk of Court. Personal Florida checks and Attorney's offices personal checks accepted only. Major credit cards accepted; small fee added if you use credit card. Prepayment required.

Circuit & County Courts - Criminal Division
38053 Live Oak Ave, Dade City, FL 33523-3894; 352-521-4503; 8:30AM-5PM. ***Felony, Misdemeanor.*** www.jud6.org

Circuit Court at 352-521-4517. A branch court at West Pasco Judicial Ctr, 7530 Little Rd, New Port Richey, 34654.

Criminal Records: Access: Mail, online, in person. Both court and visitors may perform in person searches. Search fee: $2.00 per name per year. Required to search: name, years to search, address, DOB; also helpful: SSN. Criminal records on computer since 1978. Mail turnaround time 2-4 days. Public use terminal has crim records back to 1979. PAT results show middle initial, DOB, SSN. Access court records free at www.pascoclerk.com/public-online-services-disclaimer-courts-search.asp. Also, access to County Clerk of Circuit Court records is at https://www2.myfloridacounty.com/ccm/?county=51

General Information: No confidential, sealed or juvenile records released. Court makes copy: $1.00 per page. Certification fee: $2.00. Payee: Clerk of Courts. No personal checks accepted. Local residents may use credit card. Visa only nationwide. Prepayment required.

Pinellas County

Circuit Court - Criminal
Criminal Justice Center, Circuit Court, 14250 49th St N, Clearwater, FL 34722; 727-464-6793; fax: 727-464-6233; 8AM-5PM. ***Felony.*** www.jud6.org

Criminal Records: Access: Fax, mail, online, in person. Both court and visitors may perform in person searches. Search fee: $2.00 per name per year. Required to search: name, years to search, DOB. Criminal records computerized from 1977, on microfilm from 1912 to 1976, on docket books from 1912. Mail turnaround time 1 week. Public use terminal has crim records back to 1977. PAT results show middle initial, DOB. Access the clerk's criminal and other data free at https://pubtitles.co.pinellas.fl.us/login/loginx.jsp. Criminal index goes back to 1972.

General Information: Online identifiers in results same as on public terminal. Will fax documents $1.00 per page. Court makes copy: $1.00 per page. Certification fee: $2.00. Payee: Clerk of Circuit Court. Personal checks and major credit cards accepted. Prepayment required.

Circuit & County Courts - Civil Division
315 Court St, Rm170, Clearwater, FL 33756; 727-464-3267; probate phone: 727-464-3321; fax: 727-464-4070; 8AM-5PM. ***Civil, Eviction, Small Claims, Probate, Traffic.*** www.jud6.org

There are also branches in St Petersburg, 545 1st Ave N, and North County, 29582 US Hiway 19 N, Clearwater. Probate Court located at 315 Court St, Clearwater

Civil Records: Access: Fax, mail, online, in person. Both court and visitors may perform in person searches. Search fee: $2.00 per name per year. Required to search: name, years to search. Civil cases indexed by defendant, plaintiff, on computer from 1980, on microfiche from 1900s to 1982, older data in warehouse. Mail turnaround time 1 week. Public use terminal has civil records back to 1972. PAT results show middle initial, DOB, SSN. Access to the countywide civil system requires $60 fee plus $5.00 a month & $.05 per screen over 100. Index back to 1972. Includes probate & traffic records. Contact Sue Maskeny-727-464-3779. Also, access clerk's criminal & other data free as a non-subscriber at https://pubtitles.co.pinellas.fl.us/login/loginx.jsp. You're on the clock, may be booted. Also, access index of judgments and recorded docs at www.myfloridacounty.com. Fees to order copies; subscribers save $1.50 per record. Online results show name only.

General Information: No adoption or juvenile records released. Will fax documents $1.00 per page. Court makes copy: $1.00 per page. Certification fee: $2.00 per page. Payee: Clerk of the Court. Personal checks accepted. Major credit cards accepted; a $2.50 convenience fee is added. Prepayment required. Mail requests: SASE helpful.

County Court - Criminal Division
14250 49th St N, Clearwater, FL 34762; 727-464-7000; fax: 727-464-7040; 8AM-5PM. ***Misdemeanor, Ordinances, Citations.*** www.jud6.org

Criminal Records: Access: Mail, online, in person. Both court and visitors may perform in person searches. Search fee: $2.00 per name per year. Required to search: name, years to search; also helpful: address, DOB, SSN. Criminal records on computer since 10/77, prior on index books. Prior to 1993 on microfilm. Mail turnaround time 3-5 days. Public use terminal has crim records back to 1980. PAT results show middle initial, DOB. Access to the countywide criminal online system requires $60 fee plus $5.00 a month and $.05 per screen over 100. Criminal index goes back to 1972. Contact Sue Maskeny at 727-464-3779 for information. Also, you can access the clerk's criminal and other data as a free non-subscriber at https://pubtitles.co.pinellas.fl.us/login/loginx.jsp. However, you are on the clock and may be booted if you overuse the system. Online results show middle initial, DOB.

General Information: Online identifiers in results same as on public terminal. No sealed or non-arrested case records released. Court makes copy: $1.00 per page. Certification fee: $2.00. Payee: Clerk of Courts. Personal checks accepted. Major credit cards accepted except Discover. Prepayment required.

Polk County

Circuit & County Courts - Felony Div.
PO Box 9000, Drawer CC9, Bartow, FL 33830; 863-534-4000; fax: 863-534-4457; 8AM-5PM. ***Felony.*** www.polk-county.net/clerk/clerk.html

Criminal Records: Access: Phone, mail, in person, online. Both court and visitors may perform in person searches. Search fee: $2.00 per name. Required to search: name, years to search, DOB. Criminal records on computer-felonies since 1977, misdemeanors purged periodically. Both on microfiche and archived since 1800s. Mail turnaround time varies. Indicate date on request when record is needed. Public use terminal has crim records back to 1977. Access to County Clerk of Circuit Court records is free at www.polkcountyclerk.net/. Criminal index goes back to 1991; Records may also be accessed at https://www2.myfloridacounty.com/ccm/?county=53. Online results show middle initial.

General Information: No sex related cases, victims or child abuse released. Will not fax documents. Court makes copy: $1.00 per page, self serve same. Certification fee: $2.00 per page; Exemplified cert fee- $7.00. Payee: Clerk of Circuit Court. Personal checks accepted. Visa/MC accepted. Prepayment required. Mail requests: SASE required.

Circuit Court - Civil Division
PO Box 9000, Drawer CC2, 255 N Broadway, Bartow, FL 33831-9000; 863-534-4488; probate phone: 863-534-4478; fax: 863-534-5835; 8AM-5PM. ***Civil Actions over $15,000, Probate.*** www.polkcountyclerk.net/

Civil Records: Access: Phone, mail, online, in person. Both court and visitors may perform in person searches. Search fee: $2.00 per name per year. Required to search: name, years to search; also helpful: DOB, SSN, address. Civil cases indexed by defendant, plaintiff, on computer since 1978; on microfiche from 1800s to 1978. Mail turnaround time 2-3 days. Public use terminal has civil records back to 1978, but not complete. PAT results show name only. Free online access to dockets at www.polkcountyclerk.net/RecordsSearch/disclaimer.aspx. A subscription account for attorneys only for complete database access requires $150 setup fee, but there is no monthly fees. Call 863-534-7575 for more information. Also, access to County Clerk of Circuit Court records is at https://www2.myfloridacounty.com/ccm/?county=53.

General Information: No sex related cases, adoption, confidential, victims or child abuse records released. Will fax documents to local or toll free line if copies prepaid; out of state faxes add $1.00 per fax. Court makes copy: $1.00 per page if image on computer; $2.00 if not. Certification fee: $2.00 per cert. Payee: Clerk of Court. Personal checks accepted. Major credit cards accepted in person only. Prepayment required. Mail requests: SASE required.

County Court - Civil Division
PO Box 9000, Drawer CC12, Bartow, FL 33830-9000; 863-534-4556; fax: 863-534-4045; 8AM-5PM. ***Civil Actions under $15,000, Eviction, Small Claims.*** www.polkcountyclerk.net

Civil Records: Access: Phone, mail, online, in person. Both court and visitors may perform in person searches. Search fee: $2.00 per name per year. Required to search: name, years to search. Civil cases indexed by defendant, plaintiff, on computer from 1983, on microfiche from 1961 to 1995. Mail turnaround time 1-5 days. Public use terminal has civil records back to 1983. PAT civil results show middle initial. Results include date filed. Case index information back to 1983 is free from the County Clerk's website at www.polkcountyclerk.net. Also, access to County Clerk of Circuit Court records is at https://www2.myfloridacounty.com/ccm/?county=53. Online results show middle initial.

General Information: Online identifiers in results same as on public terminal. Will not fax documents. Court makes copy: $1.00 per page. Certification fee: $2.00. Payee: Clerk of Court. Checks, cash, cashiers checks and money orders accepted. Visa/MC/Discover/AmEx accepted. Prepayment required. Credit card fee- add $2.50 to cover transaction cost. Mail requests: SASE required.

Circuit & County Courts - Misdemeanor Division
PO Box 9000, Drawer CC10, Bartow, FL 33831-9000; 863-534-4446; fax: 863-534-4137; 8AM-5PM. ***Misdemeanor, Traffic.*** www.polkcountyclerk.net

Criminal Records: Access: Mail, in person, online. Both court and visitors may perform in person searches. Search fee: 3 year search: $4.10; lifetime: $5.10. Required to search: name, years to search, DOB; also helpful: SSN. Criminal records on computer; felonies since 1977, misdemeanors purged periodically. Both on microfiche and archived since 1800s. Mail turnaround time varies. Indicate date on request when record is needed. Public use terminal has crim records back to 1977. PAT results show middle initial, DOB. Access to County Clerk of Circuit Court records is at https://www2.myfloridacounty.com/ccm/?county=53. Online results show middle initial, DOB.

General Information: No sex related cases, victims or child abuse released. Will not fax documents. Court makes copy: $1.00 per page. Certification fee: $2.00 per cert. Payee: Clerk of Circuit Court. Personal checks accepted. Visa/MC accepted. Prepayment required. Mail requests: SASE required.

Putnam County

Circuit & County Courts - Civil Division

PO Box 758, 410 St. Johns Ave (32177), Palatka, FL 32178; 386-329-0361; civil phone: 386-329-0251; probate phone: 386-329-0251; fax: 386-329-0888; 8:30AM-5PM. ***Civil, Eviction, Small Claims, Probate.*** www.putnam-fl.com

Civil Records: Access: Mail, fax, in person, email, online. Both court and visitors may perform in person searches. Search fee: $2.00 per name per year. Required to search: name, years to search. Civil cases indexed by defendant, plaintiff, on computer from 1984, on microfiche from 1973 to 1984, on index cards and docket books from 1900s to 1973. Mail turnaround time 2-3 days. Public use terminal has civil records back to 1984. Access to the countywide remote online system requires $400 setup fee and $40. monthly charge plus $.05 per minute over 20 hours. Civil records go back to 1984. System includes criminal and real property records. Contact Putnam County IT Dept at 386-329-0390 to register. Also, access an index of judgments, liens, recorded documents at www.myfloridacounty.com. Fees involved to order copies; subscribers save $1.50 per record.

General Information: No juvenile or incompetency records released. Fee to fax out file $2.25 per page. Court makes copy: $1.00 per page. Self serve: $.15 per page. Certification fee: $2.00. Payee: Clerk of Court. Personal checks and major credit cards accepted. Prepayment required. Mail requests: SASE requested.

Circuit & County Courts - Criminal Div.

PO Box 758, Palatka, FL 32178; 386-329-0255; fax: 386-329-1223; 8:30AM-5PM. ***Felony, Misdemeanor.*** www.putnam-fl.com

Criminal Records: Access: Mail, fax, in person, email, online. Both court and visitors may perform in person searches. Search fee: $2.00 per name per year. Required to search: name, years to search; also helpful: DOB. Criminal records computerized from 1988, in files from 1930s to 1988. Mail turnaround time 2-3 days. Public use terminal has crim records back to 1972. Access to the countywide criminal online system requires $400 setup fee and $40. monthly charge plus $.05 per minute over 20 hours. Criminal records go back to 1972. System includes civil and real property records. Contact 386-329-0390 to register. Also, you may direct email criminal record requests to putn.clerk@co.putnam.fl.us. Online results show name only.

General Information: Online identifiers in results same as on public terminal. No juvenile records released. Fee to fax out file $2.25 per page. Court makes copy: $1.00 per page. Self serve: $.15 per page. Certification fee: $2.00. Payee: Clerk of Circuit Court. Personal checks accepted; credit cards are not. Prepayment required. Mail requests: SASE required.

Santa Rosa County

Circuit & County Courts - Civil Division

PO Box 472, Milton, FL 32572; 850-983-4625; probate phone: 850-981-5584; fax: 850-983-1990; 8AM-4:30PM (CST). ***Civil, Eviction, Small Claims, Probate.*** www.santarosaclerk.com

Small claims at 850-983-4661.

Civil Records: Access: Fax, mail, in person, online. Both court and visitors may perform in person searches. Search fee: $2.00 per name per year. Required to search: name, years to search. Civil cases indexed by defendant, plaintiff, (Circuit) on computer from 1990, archived and on docket books from 1900s. County on computer from 1989, on microfiche from 1900s, on doc. Mail turnaround time ASAP. Public use terminal has civil records back to 1991. Access index of judgments, liens, and court records free at http://www2.myfloridacounty.com/ccm/?county=57. Also, access to County Clerk of Circuit Court records is at https://www2.myfloridacounty.com/ccm/?county=57

General Information: No adoption records released. Will fax documents $2.00 per page. Court makes copy: $1.00 per page. Certification fee: $2.00 per instrument. Payee: Clerk of Courts. Personal checks accepted. Credit cards accepted. Prepayment required. Mail requests: SASE required.

Circuit & County Courts - Criminal Division

PO Box 472, Milton, FL 32572; 850-981-5579; fax: 850-626-0346; 8AM-4:30PM (CST). ***Felony, Misdemeanor.*** www.santarosaclerk.com

Misdemeanor phone number is 850-981-5562

Criminal Records: Access: Mail, fax, in person, online. Both court and visitors may perform in person searches. Search fee: $2.00 per name per year. Required to search: name, years to search, DOB. Criminal records computerized from 1989; felonies on index cards from 1925, misdemeanors on docket books from 1900s. Mail turnaround time 1 week. Public use terminal has crim records back to 1989. PAT results show middle initial, DOB. Access an index of judgments, liens, and court records free at http://oncoreweb.srccol.com/oncoreweb4101/Search.aspx Also, access to County Clerk of Circuit Court records is at http://www2.myfloridacounty.com/ccm/?county=57 Online results show name only.

General Information: No records released before sentencing. Fee to fax out file $2.00 per page. Court makes copy: $1.00 per page. Certification fee: $2.00 per page. Payee: Clerk's Office (include Division/Department name). Personal checks accepted. Credit cards accepted. Prepayment required. Mail requests: SASE required.

Sarasota County

Circuit & County Courts - Civil

PO Box 3079, Attn: Clerk of the Circuit Court, 2000 Main St, Sarasota, FL 34230; 941-861-7400; fax: 941-861-7453; 8:30AM-5PM. ***Civil, Eviction, Small Claims, Probate.*** www.sarasotaclerk.com

Civil Records: Access: Mail, in person, online. Both court and visitors may perform in person searches. Search fee: $2.00 per name per year. Required to search: name, years to search. Civil cases indexed by defendant, plaintiff, on computer from 1983, circuit & county on docket books from 1900s to 1983. Mail turnaround time 1 week. Public use terminal has civil records back to 1984. Civil and DV case dockets from the Clerk of Circuit Court database are free at www.clerk.co.sarasota.fl.us/srqapp/civilinq.asp. Probate court dockets are at www.clerk.co.sarasota.fl.us/srqapp/probinq.asp. Also see the clerk's judgment/official document search for images back 10 years. Also, access an index of judgments, liens, recorded documents at www.myfloridacounty.com. Fees involved to order copies; subscribers save $1.50 per record.

General Information: No adoption, mental health, or sealed records released. Will fax out documents no fee. Court makes copy: $1.00 per page. Certification fee: $2.00 per instrument; Exemplification fee- $7.00. Payee: Clerk of Circuit Court. Personal checks accepted. Visa/MC accepted. Prepayment required. Mail requests: SASE helpful.

Circuit & County Courts - Criminal Div.

PO Box 3079, 2000 Main St, Sarasota, FL 34230; 941-861-7400; 8:30-5PM. ***Felony, Misdemeanor.*** www.sarasotaclerk.com

Criminal Records: Access: Phone, mail, online, in person. Both court and visitors may perform in person searches. Search fee: $2.00 per name per year. Required to search: name, years to search, DOB, SSN. Criminal records on computer since 1983, (circuit) on docket books from 1900s to 1983, (county) on docket books from 1960s to 1983. Results include address. Mail turnaround time 1 week. Public use terminal has crim records back to 1995. PAT criminal results show middle initial. Criminal and traffic case dockets from the Clerk of the Circuit Court database are free online at http://clerk.co.sarasota.fl.us/cvdisclaim.htm. Civil, probate and domestic dockets are also available. Online results show middle initial.

General Information: Online identifiers in results same as on public terminal. No juvenile records released. Court makes copy: $1.00 per page. Certification fee: $2.00 per instrument; Exemplification fee- $7.00. Payee: Clerk of Circuit Court. Personal checks accepted. Visa/MC accepted. Prepayment required. Mail requests: SASE helpful.

Seminole County

Circuit & County Courts - Civil Division

PO Box 8099, 301 N Park Ave, Sanford, FL 32771; 407-665-4330; civil phone: 407-665-4378 Circ; 665-4361 Count Civil; Sm Claims 665-4362; probate phone: 407-665-4328; fax: 407-330-7193; 8AM-4:30PM. ***Civil, Eviction, Small Claims, Probate.*** www.seminoleclerk.org

Civil Records: Access: Mail, in person, online. Both court and visitors may perform in person searches. Search fee: $2.00 per name per year. Required to search: name, years to search. Civil cases indexed by defendant, plaintiff, on computer since 1986, on microfiche since 1913. Mail turnaround time 1 week. Public use terminal has civil records back to 1986. PAT civil results show middle initial. Images related to Probate cases are not available on the Clerk's website. Access to judgment and probate records is free at http://officialrecords.seminoleclerk.org/.

General Information: No confidential files pursuant to law or sealed records released. Will fax documents $1.00 per page local or $2.00 per page long-distance. Court makes copy: $1.00 per page. Certification fee: $2.00 per doc; Exemplification certificate $6.00 (includes signing and sealing). Payee: Clerk of the Circuit Court. Personal checks accepted; credit cards are not. Prepayment required. Mail requests: SASE required.

Circuit & County Courts - Criminal Div.

101 Bush Blvd, 1st Fl, Sanford, FL 32773; 407-665-4450; fax: 407-665-4545; 8AM-4:30PM. ***Felony, Misdemeanor.*** www.seminoleclerk.org

Criminal Records: Access: Mail, in person, online. Both court and visitors may perform in person searches. Search fee: $2.00 per name per year. Required to search: name, years to search, DOB; also helpful: race, sex. Criminal records computerized from 1983; prior on microfiche. Mail turnaround time 2-4 days for felonies, no set time for misdemeanors. Public use terminal has criminal records back to 1983. PAT results show name, partial DOB. Access criminal dockets free at www.seminoleclerk.org click on Criminal Dockets Search.

General Information: No records of investigations which have not resulted in an arrest released. Local faxes $1.00 per page; out of state faxes $2.00 per page. Court makes copy: $1.00 per page. Certification fee: $2.00 per doc; $7.00 to sign and seal. Payee: Clerk of Courts. Local personal and company checks accepted. No credit cards accepted. Prepayment required. SASE not required.

St. Johns County

Circuit & County Courts - Civil Division

4010 Lewis Speedway, St Augustine, FL 32084; 904-819-3600; civil phone: 904-819-3652/51; probate phone: 904-819-3654; fax: 904-819-3661; 8AM-5PM. ***Civil, Eviction, Small Claims, Probate.*** www.co.st-johns.fl.us

Civil Records: Access: Fax, mail, online, in person. Both court and visitors may perform in person searches. Search fee: $2.00 per name per year. Required to search: name, years to search. Civil cases indexed by defendant, plaintiff, on computer from 1984, on microfiche from 1976 to 1986, on docket books from 1820 to 1983. County on computer from 1991, microfiche from. Mail turnaround time 4-5 days. Public use terminal has civil records back to 1986. Also, access the county Clerk of Circuit Court recording data free at http://doris.clk.co.st-johns.fl.us/oncoreweb/Search.aspx. Access an index of judgments, liens, recorded documents at www.myfloridacounty.com. Fees involved to order copies; subscribers save $1.50 per record at $25.00 per month.

General Information: No confidential or sealed records released. Will not fax out documents. Court makes copy: $1.00 per page. Certification fee: $2.00. Payee: Clerk of Circuit Court. Personal checks accepted. Visa/MC accepted. Prepayment required. Mail requests: SASE required.

Circuit & County Courts - Criminal Division 4010 Lewis Speedway, St Augustine, FL 32084; 904-819-3615; criminal phone: 904-819-3625; fax: 904-819-3666; 8AM-5PM. ***Felony, Misdemeanor.*** www.co.st-johns.fl.us

Criminal Records: Access: Fax, mail, online, in person. Both court and visitors may perform in person searches. Search fee: $1.00 per name per year. Required to search: name, years to search, DOB; also helpful: address, SSN. Criminal Records on computer. Felony since 1986, Misdemeanor since 1984. Felony on log books from 1950 to 1984. Mail turnaround time 4-5 days. Public use terminal has crim records back to Felony 1986; Misd.-2000. Access to the countywide criminal online system requires $200 setup fee plus a monthly fee of $50. Searching is by name or case number. Call Mark Dearing at 904-819-3611 for more information. (Not setting up new accounts at this time).

General Information: Online identifiers in results same as on public terminal. No juvenile or sexual offense records released. Fee to fax out file $1.00 per page. Court makes copy: $1.00 per page. Certification fee: $2.00 per doc. Payee: Clerk of Circuit Court. Personal checks accepted. Credit cards accepted. Prepayment required. Escrow/billing accounts available to government agencies. Mail requests: SASE required.

St. Lucie County

Circuit & County Courts - Civil Division PO Drawer 700, 218 S 2nd St, Ft Pierce, FL 34954; 772-462-6976 (Circuit); civil phone: 772-785-5884 (County); criminal fax: 772-462-1774; civil fax: 772-462-1998; 8AM-5PM. ***Civil, Eviction, Small Claims.***

www.slcclerkofcourt.com/circuitcivil/circuitcivil.htm

Small claims phone is 772-785-5880; Small Claims and County Civil files and microfiche are located at the Courthouse Annex, 250 NW County Club Dr, Pt St. Lucie, FL 34986.

Civil Records: Access: Mail, in person, online. Both court and visitors may perform in person searches. Search fee: $2.00 per name per year. Required to search: name, years to search. Civil cases indexed by defendant, plaintiff. Circuit records on computer back to 1992. Circuit on microfiche from 1981 to 1992, County from 1981 to 1992. Circuit on docket books from 1900s to 198. Mail turnaround time 1 day. Public use terminal has civil records back to 10 years. PAT results show name only. Online access to civil records at http://public.slcclerkofcourt.com. Case tracking and bond record tracking are available. Access an index of judgments, liens, recorded documents at www.myfloridacounty.com. Fees involved to order copies; subscribers save $1.50 per record. Online results show name only.

General Information: No sealed cases or adoption records released. Will fax documents to local or toll free line. Court makes copy: $1.00 per page, self serve same. Certification fee: $2.00 per doc. Payee: Clerk of Court. No personal checks accepted. Visa/MC accepted. Prepayment required.

Circuit & County Courts - Criminal Division PO Drawer 700, 218 S 2nd St, Ft Pierce, FL 34954; 772-462-6900; criminal phone: 772-462-3228; fax: 772-462-2833; 8AM-5PM. ***Felony, Misdemeanor.***

www.slcclerkofcourt.com/felony/felony.htm

County Misdemeanor and criminal traffic phone is 772-462-6954 or 772-462-6958; fax number is 772)-462-6868.

Criminal Records: Access: Fax, mail, in person, online. Both court and visitors may perform in person searches. Search fee: $2.00 per name per year. Required to search: name, years to search, DOB, signed release; also helpful: SSN, race, sex. Criminal records computerized from 1982, on microfiche to 1960, on books prior to 1900s. Mail turnaround time 1-2 weeks; fax turnaround time 1-5 days. Public use terminal has crim records back to 1983. PAT results show middle initial, DOB. Print docs off the PAT. Online access to bonds, traffic and misdemeanor records is free at http://public.slcclerkofcourt.com. Online records go back to 7/6/1992. Felony records only available to government agencies. Online results show middle initial, DOB.

General Information: No sealed or expunged records released. Fee to fax out file $1.25 per page. Court makes copy: $1.00 per page. Certification fee: $2.00. Payee: Clerk of Court. Cashiers checks and money orders accepted. Credit cards accepted; 3.2% fee added. Prepayment required. SASE not required.

Probate Court Clerk of Circuit. Ct; Attn: Probate Dept, PO Box 700, Ft Pierce, FL 34954; 772-462-6920; fax: 772-462-6984; 8AM-5PM. ***Probate.***

www.slcclerkofcourt.com/probate/probate.htm

Physical Address: 201 S Indian River Dr, Fort Pierce, Fl, 34950.

Sumter County

Circuit & County Courts - Civil Division 209 N Florida St, Bushnell, FL 33513; 352-793-0211; fax: 352-568-6608; 8:30AM-5PM. ***Civil, Eviction, Small Claims, Probate.***

www.sumterclerk.com/public/

Civil Records: Access: Fax, mail, in person, online. Both court and visitors may perform in person searches. Search fee: $2.00 per name per year. Required to search: name, years to search. Civil cases indexed by defendant, plaintiff, go back to 1800s; on computer go back to 12/1999; in docket books from 1986 to 11/30/99 (circuit only). Faxes accepted if only pre-paid. Mail turnaround time 1 week. Access an index of civil, probate and domestic relationship records at https://www2.myfloridacounty.com/ccm/?county=60.F

General Information: No juvenile or adoption records released. Will fax documents $1.00 per page. Court makes copy: $1.00 per page. Certification fee: $2.00 per doc. Payee: Clerk of Circuit Court. No personal checks accepted. Visa/MC accepted in person. Prepayment required. Mail requests: SASE requested.

Circuit & County Courts - Criminal Division 209 N Florida St, Bushnell, FL 33513; 352-793-0211; fax: 352-568-6608; 8:30AM-5PM. ***Felony, Misdemeanor.***

www.sumterclerk.com/public/

Criminal Records: Access: Mail, in person, online. Both court and visitors may perform in person searches. Search fee: $2.00 per name per year. Required to search: name, years to search, DOB. Criminal records (circuit) on computer since 2000, on index books from 1965 to 1999, prior in vaults. County on computer since 1982, on microfiche fro. Mail turnaround time 1 week. Access index of felony, criminal traffic, misdemeanor records at https://www2.myfloridacounty.com/ccm/?county=60. Race, sex, city and ZIP Shown.

General Information: No juvenile records released. Fee to fax out file $1.00 per page. Court makes copy: $1.00 per page. Certification fee: $2.00. Payee: Clerk of Court. Only cashiers checks and money orders accepted. Prepayment required. Mail requests: SASE requested.

Suwannee County

Circuit & County Courts 200 S Ohio Ave, Live Oak, FL 32064; civil phone: 386-362-0517; criminal fax:; civil fax: 386-362-0577; 8AM-4:30PM. ***Felony, Misdemeanor, Civil, Eviction, Small Claims, Probate.***

www.suwclerk.org/mambo/

Civil Records: Access: Mail, in person, online. Both court and visitors may perform in person searches. Search fee: $2.00 per name per year. Fee is per index. Required to search: name, years to search; also helpful: address. Civil cases indexed by defendant, plaintiff, on computer from 1983, archived from 1859 to 1983. Written requests require prepayment. Mail turnaround time 1 week. Access to County Clerk of Circuit Court records is at https://www2.myfloridacounty.com/ccm/?county=61. Also court records on recording index free at http://151.213.249.227/oncoreweb/ which includes county Official Records.

Criminal Records: Access: Mail, in person, online. Both court and visitors may perform in person searches. Search fee: $2.00 per name per year. Fee is per index. Required to search: name, years to search, DOB, signed release; also helpful: address. Criminal records computerized from 1983, archived from 1859 to 1983. Written requests require prepayment. Mail turnaround time 1 week. Online access to criminal is the same as civil.

General Information: No juvenile or adoption records released. Will fax documents $3.00 1st page, $.50 each add'l. Court makes copy: $1.00 per page, self serve same. Certification fee: $2.00. Payee: Suwannee Court Clerk. Personal checks and major credit cards accepted. Prepayment required. Mail requests: SASE required.

Taylor County

Circuit & County Courts PO Box 620, Perry, FL 32348; 850-838-3506; probate phone: x110; fax: 850-838-3549; 8-5PM. ***Felony, Misdemeanor, Civil, Eviction, Small Claims, Probate.***

http://www2.myfloridacounty.com/wps/wcm/connect/taylorclerk

Civil Records: Access: Mail, in person, online. Only the court performs in person searches; visitors may not. Search fee: $2.00 per name per year. Required to search: name, years to search. Civil cases indexed by defendant, plaintiff, on computer back to 1982; on index from 1973 to 1991, prior on index books to 1856. Mail turnaround time 1 week. Access an index of judgments, liens, recorded documents at www.myfloridacounty.com. Fees involved to order copies; subscribers save $1.50 per record.

Criminal Records: Access: Mail, in person. Only the court performs in person searches; visitors may not. Search fee: $2.00 per name per year. Required to search: name, years to search, DOB; also helpful: SSN, race, sex. Criminal records computerized from 1982; on index from 1973 to 1991, prior on index books to 1950. Mail turnaround time 1 week.

General Information: No juvenile records released. Will fax documents $1.00 per fax. Court makes copy: n/a. Self serve: $1.00 per page. Certification fee: $2.00. Payee: Taylor County Clerk of Court. Business checks accepted. No credit cards accepted. Prepayment required. Mail requests: SASE helpful.

Union County

Circuit & County Courts 55 W Main, Rm 103, Lake Butler, FL 32054; 386-496-3711; probate phone: same; fax: 386-496-1718; 8AM-5PM. ***Felony, Misdemeanor, Civil, Eviction, Small Claims, Probate.*** http://circuit8.org

Civil Records: Access: Fax, mail, in person, online. Only the court performs in person searches; visitors may not. Search fee: $2.00 per name per year. Required to search: name, years to search. Civil cases indexed by defendant, plaintiff; index in docket books from 1921. Mail turnaround time 2-3 days. Public use terminal has civil records. Civil PAT includes judgments, liens and other recorded documents generally. Access an index of judgments, liens, recorded documents at www.myfloridacounty.com. Fees involved to order copies; subscribers save $1.50 per record.

Criminal Records: Access: Fax, mail, in person, online. Only the court performs in person searches; visitors may not. Search fee: $2.00 per name per year. Required to search: name, years to search, DOB; also helpful: SSN. Criminal docket on books from 1921. Mail turnaround time 2-3 days. Access the circuit-wide criminal quick lookup at http://circuit8.org. Account and password is required; restricted usage.

General Information: No juvenile records released. Will fax documents $1.00 per page. Court makes copy: $1.00 per page, self serve same. Certification fee: $2.00. Payee: Clerk of Court. Personal checks accepted. Visa/MC accepted. Prepayment required. Mail requests: SASE preferred.

Volusia County

Circuit & County Courts - Civil Division PO Box 6043, 101 N Alabama Ave., De Land, FL 32721; 386-736-5915; civil phone: 386-736-5907; probate phone: 386-736-5914; fax: 386-740-5294; 8AM-4:30PM. ***Civil, Eviction, Small Claims, Probate.*** www.clerk.org

Civil Records: Access: Fax, mail, online, in person. Both court and visitors may perform in person searches. Search fee: $2.00 per name per year. Required to search: name, years to search. Civil cases indexed by defendant, plaintiff, on computer from 1986, on docket books from 1863 to 1986. Mail turnaround time 1 week. Public use terminal has civil records back to 1986. PAT civil results show middle initial. Online access available free at www.clerk.org/cm/publicrecords/publicrecords.jsp. Also, access an index of judgments, liens, recorded documents at www.myfloridacounty.com with fees for copies. Also, previous 2-weeks civil records on a private site at http://extra.orlandosentinel.com/publicrecords/search.asp. Online results show name only.

General Information: Online identifiers in results same as on public terminal. No sealed records released. Fee to fax out file $1.00 per page. Court makes copy: $1.00 per page. Certification fee: $2.00 per doc. Payee: Clerk of Circuit Court. Personal checks accepted. Major credit cards accepted; service fee applies, fee depends on size of doc. Prepayment required. Mail requests: SASE requested.

Circuit & County Courts - Criminal Division PO Box 6043, De Land, FL 32721-6043; 386-736-5915; fax: 386-740-5175; 8AM-4:30PM. ***Felony, Misdemeanor.*** www.clerk.org

Criminal Records: Access: Mail, online, in person. Both court and visitors may perform in person searches. Search fee: $2.00 per name per year. Required to search: name, years to search, DOB; also helpful: SSN, race, sex. Criminal records 1982 to present on computer, on microfiche from 1856 to 1988, on docket books prior to 1983. Mail turnaround time up to 1 week. Public use terminal has crim records back to 2000. PAT criminal results show middle initial. Access the countywide Clerk of Circuit Ct court records is free at www.clerk.org/cm/publicrecords/publicrecords.jsp. Access to the Clerk of Circuit Courts database of Citation Violations and 24-hour Arrest Reports is free at www.clerk.org/index.html. Online results show middle initial.

General Information: No confidential, sexual battery and juvenile records released. Will fax documents $1.00 per page. Court makes copy: $1.00 per page. Self serve: $.25 per page. Certification fee: $2.00. Payee: Clerk of Court. Personal and out of state checks accepted with proper ID. No credit cards accepted. Prepayment required. Mail requests: SASE required.

Wakulla County

Circuit & County Courts 3056 Crawfordville Hwy, Crawfordville, FL 32327; 850-926-0905; criminal phone: 850-926-0324; civil phone: 850-926-0323; criminal fax: 850-926-0936; civil fax: 850-926-0938; 8AM-5PM. ***Felony, Misdemeanor, Civil, Eviction, Small Claims, Probate.*** www.wakullaclerk.com

Felony/Misdemeanor court can be reached at 850-926-0324, for records searches.

Civil Records: Access: Phone, fax, mail, in person, online. Both court and visitors may perform in person searches. Search fee: $2.00 per name per year. Required to search: name, years to search. Civil cases indexed by defendant, plaintiff, on computer since 1990, on docket books from 1800s. Fax requests must be pre-paid. Mail turnaround time 3-4 days. Access to County Clerk of Circuit Court records is at https://www2.myfloridacounty.com/ccm/?county=65

Criminal Records: Access: Fax, mail, in person, online. Only the court performs in person searches; visitors may not. Search fee: $2.00 per name per year. Required to search: name, years to search, DOB; also helpful: SSN. Criminal records on computer since 1990, on docket books from 1800s. Visitors may review docket books, only court performs name searches. Faxes must be pre-paid. Mail turnaround time 3-4 days. Online access to criminal is same as civil.

General Information: No juvenile, adoption records released. Will fax prepaid documents to toll-free number. Court makes copy: $1.00 per page. Certification fee: $2.00. Payee: Clerk of Court. Personal checks accepted; credit cards are not. Prepayment required. Mail requests: SASE required.

Walton County

Circuit & County Courts PO Box 1260, De Funiak Springs, FL 32435; 850-892-8115; criminal fax: 850-892-8017; civil fax: 850-892-7551; 8AM-4:30PM (CST). ***Felony, Misdemeanor, Civil, Eviction, Small Claims, Probate.*** http://clerkofcourts.co.walton.fl.us

Probate is a separate index at this same address. Probate fax- 850-892-7551

Civil Records: Access: Fax, mail, online, in person. Only the court performs in person searches; visitors may not. Search fee: $2.00 per name per year. Required to search: name, years to search. Civil cases indexed by defendant, plaintiff, on computer from 1988, on dockets from 1900s. You may deposit money into an escrow account for future record searches. Contact any of the personnel for add'l information. Mail turnaround time same day if received before 3PM. Public use terminal has civil records back to mid-1980s. Results include specified date range search. Access final judgments or orders on closed cases at http://clerkofcourts.co.walton.fl.us/ORSearch/. Also, access County Clerk of Circuit Court records at https://www2.myfloridacounty.com/ccm/?county=66.

Criminal Records: Access: Fax, mail, online, in person. Only the court performs in person searches; visitors may not. Search fee: $2.00 per name per year. Required to search: name, years to search, DOB. Criminal records computerized from 1988, on dockets from 1900s. You may deposit money into an escrow account for future record searches. Contact any of the personnel for add'l information. Mail turnaround time 24 hours. Results include specified date range search. Access felony judgments of guilt only at http://clerkofcourts.co.walton.fl.us/ORSearch/. Also, access to Clerk of Circuit Court records at https://www2.myfloridacounty.com/ccm/?county=66.

General Information: Online identifiers in results same as on public terminal. No sealed, expunged, or pre-sentence investigation records released. Will fax documents $1.00 per page. Court makes copy: $1.00 per page, self serve same. Certification fee: $2.00 per instrument. Payee: Clerk of Courts. Personal checks and major credit cards accepted. Prepayment required. Mail requests: SASE helpful.

Washington County

Circuit & County Courts PO Box 647, 1293 Jackson Ave, #100, Chipley, FL 32428-0647; 850-638-6285; criminal phone: x229; civil phone: x226; probate phone: x225; fax: 850-638-6297; 8AM-4PM (CST). ***Felony, Misdemeanor, Civil, Eviction, Small Claims, Probate.*** www.washingtonclerk.com

Small Claims phone- x246.

Civil Records: Access: Phone, fax, mail, in person, online. Both court and visitors may perform in person searches. Search fee: $2.00 per name per year. Required to search: name, years to search. Civil cases indexed by defendant, plaintiff, on computer from 1990; on docket books from 1940. Mail turnaround time 1 day. Public use terminal has civil records back to 1990. Access an index of judgments, liens, recorded documents at www.myfloridacounty.com. Fees involved to order copies; subscribers save $1.50 per record.

Criminal Records: Access: Phone, fax, mail, in person. Only the court performs in person searches; visitors may not. Search fee: $2.00 per name per year. Required to search: name, years to search. Criminal records computerized from 1990, felonies on docket books from 1900. Mail turnaround 1 day.

General Information: Online identifiers in results same as on public terminal. No adoption or juvenile records released. Will fax documents to local or toll free line no fee; fee charged otherwise. Court makes copy: $1.00 per page, self serve same. Certification fee: $2.00. Payee: Clerk of Court. Business checks accepted. Local personal checks accepted. No credit cards accepted. Prepayment required. Mail requests: SASE requested.

Florida Recording Offices

ORGANIZATION: 67 counties, 67 recording offices. The recording officer is the Clerk of the Circuit Court. All transactions are recorded in the "Official Record," a grantor/grantee index. Some counties will search by type of transaction while others will return everything on the index. 57 Florida counties are in the Eastern Time Zone (EST) and the 10 westernmost "panhandle counties" are in the Central Time Zone (CST).

Clerk of the Circuit Court office manages both the Circuit Court's records and the county's recorded documents. In smaller Florida counties these records are managed by a single "records office." Larger Florida counties may have court records and recordings at separate offices, or separate buildings, but all are under the umbrella of the county's Clerk of the Circuit Court. Divorce record keeping is a function of the court records section, and divorce case information and paper can be found there, but a copy of the Divorce Final Decree is recorded in the recording records section, usually indexed in the Official Records Index.

REAL ESTATE RECORDS: Any name searched in the "Official Records" will usually include all types of liens and property transfers for that name. A majority of Florida counties will perform searches. In addition to the usual $1.00 per page copy fee, certification of a doc is either $1.50 or $2.00. Tax records are located at the Property Appraiser Office.

A growing number of Florida counties make their real estate records available online; see Online Access below.

UCC RECORDS: Financing statements are filed at the state level, and real estate related collateral at the Clerk of the Circuit Court. Until 1/1/2002, farm related financing were also filed at the clerk's office. Fewer and fewer counties will now perform UCC searches. Search fees are usually $1.50 per debtor name per year searched and include all lien and real estate transactions on record. UCC copy fee is usually $1.00 per page.

TAX LIEN RECORDS: Federal tax liens on personal property of businesses are filed with the Secretary of State. All other federal and state tax liens on personal property are filed with the county Clerk of Circuit Court. Usually tax liens on personal property are filed in the same index with UCC financing statements and real estate transactions. Most counties will perform a tax lien as part of a UCC search. Tax lien copy fee is usually $1.00 per page.

OTHER LIENS: Judgments, hospital, mechanics, sewer, ambulance. Divorce actions are often indexed with judgments.

ONLINE ACCESS: There are numerous county agencies that provide online access to records, but the statewide system MyFlorida.com predominates. My Florida offers free access to the over 60 counties Circuit Clerks of Court recorded document indexes, including real estate records liens, judgments, marriages, and deaths at www.myfloridacounty.com/services/officialrecords_intro.shtml. Fees involved to order copies; save $1.50 per record by becoming a subscriber. Subscription fee is $120.00 per year plus any transaction fees for copies.

Since October 1, 2002, any person preparing or filing a document for recording in the Official Record may not include a Social Security Number in such document unless required by law. The Clerk of the Circuit Court cannot place an image or copy of the following documents on a publicly available website for general public display: military discharges; death certificates; court files, records or papers relating to Family Law, Juvenile Law, or Probate Law cases.

Any person has the right to request the Clerk/County Recorder to redact/remove his or her Social Security Number from an image or copy of an Official Record that has been placed on such Clerk/County Recorder's publicly available website.

www.floridaucc.com/UCCWEB/Search.aspx allows access to statewide UCCs for no charge.

Alachua County

County Clerk of the Circuit Court, PO Box 600, Gainesville, FL 32602. 352-374-3625; fax-352-491-4649; 8:15AM-5PM (EST) www.alachuacounty.us/government/clerk/

Index: All in one. Records indexed on a public use terminal back to 1971. Office personnel or visitors may perform searches. No title searches. Search fee $2.00 per name per year. Office will search real estate records. Copy fee $1.00 per page. Cert fee- $2.00 per doc plus copy fee. Payee- Alachua County Clerk of Circuit Court. Bulk data available for purchase, index and images at $42.00 per book. Index only can be purchased for $15.00, contact Karen Kenniston at 352-374-3625. **Online access to Real Estate, Deed, Lien, Judgment, Vital Statistic records:** Access Clerk's recording database free at alachuaclerk.org. Index goes back to 1971; images to 1990. Also, search county property by various methods free at www.acpafl.org. Search ancient records -pre-1940 plats, pre-1970 marriages, deeds, transcriptions, more- free at www.alachuaclerk.org/archive/default.cfm but may be temporarily unavailable. Access index of recordings at www.myfloridacounty.com but registration and fees required for images. **Other phones:** Treasurer- 352-374-3605; Finance Director- 352-374-3605. **Property tax/Assessing**- 12 SE 1st St, Rm 213, Gainesville, FL 32601; 352-374-5236, assessor fax- 352-374-5281. (Appraiser/Auditor- 352-374-5230) hours- 8AM-5:30PM www.acpafl.org **Online access**- Search Appraiser's Property pages free at www.acpafl.org. Tax Deed Sales search and GIS search also here. Property also at www.emapsplus.com/FLAlachua/maps/. Sales data free at www.acpafl.org/salessearch.asp. Tax deed sales- www.alachuacounty.us/government/clerk/taxdeed/. Tax rolls- http://alachuataxcollector.governmax.com/collectmax/collect30.asp.

Baker County

County Clerk of the Circuit Court, 339 E MacClenny Ave, MacClenny, FL 32063. 904-259-0208; fax-904-259-4176; hours- 8:30AM-5PM (EST) www.bakercountyfl.org/clerk/

Index: All in one. Records indexed on a public use terminal back to 1985. Office personnel or visitors may perform searches. Search fee $1.50 per name per year. Office will not search real estate or tax lien records. Copy fee $1.00 per page. Cert fee- $1.50 per doc plus copy fee. Payee- Baker County Clerk of Circuit Court. **Online access to Real Estate, Deed, Lien records:** Access an index of recorded documents at www.myfloridacounty.com. Fees involved to order copies; save $1.50 per record by becoming a subscriber. **Other phones:** Treasurer- 904-259-6880; Elections- 904-259-6339; Tax Collector- 904-653-4518. **Property tax/Assessing**- 32 N 5th St #B, Macclenny, FL, 32063; 904-259-3191, assessor fax- 904-259-8221. (Appraiser/Auditor- 904-259-3191) www.bakerpa.com/index.asp **Online access**- assessor data free at www.emapsplus.com/FLBaker/maps/. Also, search appraiser data free at www.bakerpa.com/index_disclaimer.asp. Also, name search the Tax Collector database free at http://70.84.137.66/~baker/search.html. Also, create county sales reports free at www.bakerpa.com/GIS/Search_F.asp?SalesReport.

Bay County

County Clerk of the Circuit Court, PO Box 2269, Panama City, FL 32402. 850-747-5104; fax-850-747-5199; 8AM-4:30PM (CST) www.baycoclerk.com

Index: All in one. Records indexed on a public use terminal back to 1913. Office will perform a UCC search but public must search other records themselves. Copy fee $1.00 per page. Cert fee- $1.50 per doc plus copy fee. Payee- Bay County Clerk of Circuit Court. **Online access to Real Estate, Deed, Lien, Judgment, Death, Marriage, Plat records:** Access to the Clerk of the Circuit Court Recordings database is free at www.baycoclerk.com/index.cfm. Records go back to 1/1987. Search court judgments and probate free at www.clerk.co.bay.fl.us/index.cfm?FuseAction=CaseSearch.Home. Also, access an index of recorded documents at www.myfloridacounty.com. Fees involved to order copies; save $1.50 per record by becoming a subscriber. **Property tax/Assessing**- 658 Mulberry Ave, Panama City, FL 32401; 850-784-4095, assessor fax- 850-784-6128. (Appraiser/Auditor- 850-784-4095) No public terminal. **Online access**- Search property appraiser data free at www.qpublic.net/bay/ or at www.qpublic.net/bay/search1.html. Tax collector data is at http://bctc.elementaldata.com/disclaimer.asp.

Bradford County

County Clerk of the Circuit Court, PO Drawer B, Starke, FL 32091. Recording, R/E & UCC phone-904-966-6283; fax-904-964-4454; 8AM-5PM (EST) www.bradford-co-fla.org

Index: All in one. Records indexed on a public use terminal back to 1986. Only the public may search. Copy fee $1.00 per page. Cert fee- $2.00 per doc plus copy fee. Payee- Bradford County Clerk of Circuit Court. **Online access to Real Estate, Deed, Lien, Judgment, Marriage, Court records:** Access an index of recorded documents at www.myfloridacounty.com. Fees involved to order copies; save $1.50 per record by becoming a subscriber. **Other phones:** Treasurer- 904-966-6246; Elections- 904-966-6236; Vital Records- 904-966-7383. **Property tax/Assessing**- PO Box 250, Starke, FL 32091; 904-966-6217, assessor fax- 904-966-6167. (Appraiser/Auditor- 904-964-6260) www.bradfordappraiser.com **Online access**- Search the property appraiser database at www.bradfordappraiser.com/Search_F.asp. Also, search county assessor data free at www.emapsplus.com/FLBradford/maps/.

Brevard County

County Clerk of the Circuit Court, PO Box 2767, Titusville, FL 32781. 321-637-2006, 264-5350; fax-321-264-5246; 8AM-5PM http://199.241.8.125/

Commercial Entity Affidavits now available due to recent legislative changes regarding Public Record Laws. For a fee, this provides access to information no longer available to the general public. See below.

Index: All in one. Records indexed on a public use terminal back to 1981. Office will perform a UCC search but public must search other records themselves. Copy fee $1.00 per page. Cert fee- $1.00 per page plus $2.00 per instrument. Payee- Brevard County Clerk of Circuit Court. **Online access to Real Estate, Deed, Lien, Marriage, Mortgage records:** For all records, visit http://199.241.8.125/index.cfm?FuseAction=OfficialRecords.Home. Also, the clerk offers a public system at http://webfyi.clerk.co.brevard.fl.us/netfyi/instruct.html that includes plats, traffic, courts, and more. Also, access clerk's tax lien (1981-95), land records (1995-) & indexed records 1981 - 9/30/1995; Registration/password required for full data. Access marriage indexes 1938 to 10/2006 free at http://199.241.8.125/index.cfm?FuseAction=MarriageLicenses.Home . **Property tax/Assessing**- 400 South St, 5th Fl, Brevard County Gov't Complex N, Titusville, FL 32780; 321-264-6700, assessor fax-321-264-5187. (Appraiser/Auditor- 321-264-6700) www.brevardpropertyappraiser.com/mainhtml/mapsdata.asp **Online access**- Access property tax and personal property records free at http://brevardpropertyappraiser.com/asp/disclaimer.asp. Access parcels and property/GIS free at www.emapsplus.com/FLBrevard/maps/. Property sales & tax records at http://brevardpropertyappraiser.com/asp/disclaimer.asp. Also, tax deed sale lists free at http://199.241.8.125/index.cfm?FuseAction=TaxDeedAuctions.TaxDeedSales.

Broward County

Director of County Records, 115 S Andrews Ave, Rm 114; Records Division, Fort Lauderdale, FL 33301. Recording, R/E & UCC phone-954-357-7281; fax-954-357-7267; hours - 7:30AM-5PM (EST) www.broward.org/records/

Caution: recorder web page allows people to block their public records from being displayed. Index: All in one. Records indexed on a public use terminal back to 1978. Office will search all records upon payment of statutorily mandated fees. Office personnel or visitors may perform searches. Search fee $1.00 per name. Office will search real estate records. UCC search per debtor name- $1.50 per name per year. Copy fee $1.00 per page. Cert fee- $1.50 per doc plus copy fee. Payee- Broward County Board of County Commissioners. **Online access to Real Estate, Deed, Lien, Mortgage records:** Access to the county records Public Search database 1978-present is free at http://205.166.161.12/oncoreV2/. **Other phones:** Elections- 954-357-7050; Vital Records- Birth 954-467-4413/Death records 954-467-4424; Revenue Collector- 954-531-4000. **Property tax/Assessing**- Property Appraisor, 115 S Andrews Ave, Rm 111, Ft. Lauderdale, FL 33301; 954-357-6830, assessor fax-954-357-8474. hours- 7AM-6PM www.bcpa.net **Online access**- Access assessor and property/GIS free at www.emapsplus.com/FLBroward/maps/. Also, access property appraisal data and property/Gis images free at www.bcpa.net/search.asp. Also, search property tax data for free at http://bcegov.co.broward.fl.us/revenue/nameform.asp.

Calhoun County

County Clerk of the Circuit Court, 20859 Central Ave, #E, Rm 107, Blountstown, FL 32424. Recording, R/E & UCC phone-850-674-4545; fax-850-674-5553; 8AM-4PM (CST) http://www2.myfloridacounty.com/wps/wcm/connect/calhounclerk

Index: All in one. Records indexed on computer back to 09/85. Office personnel or visitors may perform searches. Search fee $1.00 per name. Office will not search real estate records. Will not search UCC records. Will not perform tax lien searches. Copy fee $1.00 per page. Cert fee- $1.50 per doc plus copy fee. Payee- Calhoun County Clerk of Circuit Court. **Online access to Real Estate, Deed, Lien, Judgment records:** Access an index of recorded documents at www.myfloridacounty.com. Fees involved to order copies; save $1.50 per record by becoming a subscriber. **Property tax/Assessing**- Calhoun County Assessing Office, 20859 Central Ave, Rm 107, Blountstown, FL 32424; 850-674-8242, assessor fax- 850-674-5611. (Appraiser/Auditor- 850-674-8242) http://calhouncountytaxcollector.com **Online access**- Search assessor's data free at http://calhounpa.net and click on "Search Records."

Charlotte County

County Clerk of the Circuit Court, PO Box 510156, Punta Gorda, FL 33951-0156. 941-637-2245; fax-941-637-2172; 8AM-5PM www.co.charlotte.fl.us

Index: All in one. Records indexed on a public use terminal back to 1977. Office personnel or visitors may perform searches. Search fee $2.00 per year. Office will search real estate records (fee must be prepaid). Will search UCC records (fee must be prepaid). Copy fee $1.00 per page. Cert fee- $2.00 per doc plus copy fee. Payee- Clerk of Circuit Court. Bulk data available for purchase, contact the IT Dept. **Online access to Real Estate, Deed, Lien, Marriage, Mortgage records:** Search recorded data and marriages free at http://208.47.160.77/or/Search.aspx. Access index of recorded documents at www.myfloridacounty.com. Fees involved to order copies; subscribers save $1.50 per record. **Property tax/Assessing**- 18500 Murdock Cir, Port Charlotte, FL 33948; 941-743-1498, assessor fax- 941-743-1499. (Appraiser/Auditor- 941-743-1488) hours- 8AM-4:45PM www.cctaxcol.com, www.ccappraiser.com **Online access**- Property records are free at www.ccappraiser.com/record.asp. Search Assessor and property/GIS free at www.emapsplus.com/FLCharlotte/maps/. Sales records are on the tax collector database free at www.cctaxcol.com/record.asp?.

Citrus County

County Clerk of the Circuit Court, 110 N Apopka Ave,. Rm 101, Inverness, FL 34450-4299. 352-341-6475; fax-352-341-6477; 8AM-5PM (EST) www.clerk.citrus.fl.us

Index: All in one. Records indexed on a public use terminal back to 1980. Office personnel or visitors may perform searches. Search fee $2.00 per name per year. Office will search real estate records (a name search for requested years). Copy fee $1.00 per page. Cert fee- $2.00 per doc plus copy fee. Payee- Citrus County Clerk of Circuit Court. **Online access to Real Estate, Deed, Lien, Marriage, Probate, Military Discharge, Tax Deed Sale records:** Access to the Clerk of Circuit Court recording records is free at http://search.clerk.citrus.fl.us/. Also, download county land sales data free at www.pa.citrus.fl.us/sales_download.html. Access recorded documents index at www.myfloridacounty.com. Fees involved to order copies; save $1.50 per record by becoming a subscriber. View tax deed sales at www.clerk.citrus.fl.us/nws/home.jsp?section=8&item=88. **Other phones:** Elections- 352-341-6470; Tax Collector- 352-341-6600. **Property tax/Assessing**- 210 N Apopka Ave, #200, Inverness, Fl 34450; 352-341-6600, assessor fax- 352-341-6660. (Appraiser/Auditor- 352-341-6600) **Online access**- Search property appraiser and personal property records free at www.pa.citrus.fl.us/pls/apex/f?p=100:1:2625091711388720. Click on Search Parcel Database. Also, download land sales data by year free. Search property and other related-tax records free at https://www.citrus.county-taxes.com/tcb/app/main/home.

Clay County

County Clerk of the Circuit Court, PO Box 698, Green Cove Springs, FL 32043-0698. Recording, R/E & UCC phone-904-284-6362; fax-904-278-3641; 8:30AM-4:30PM (EST) www.clayclerk.com

Index: All in one. Records indexed on a public use terminal back to 1983. Only the public may search. Office will help lookup real estate records in official records, but no title searches. Copy fee $1.00 per page. Cert fee- $2.00 per doc plus copy fee. Payee- Clay County Clerk of Circuit Court. **Online access to Real Estate, Deed, Lien, Mortgage records:** County Clerk of Circuit Court allows free access to recording records at http://clerk.co.clay.fl.us/oncoreweb42/. Records go back to 1981. Also, access an index of recorded documents at www.myfloridacounty.com. Fees involved to order copies; save $1.50 per record by becoming a subscriber. **Other phones:** Elections-904-269-6350. **Property tax/Assessing**- PO Box 38, 477 Houston St, Green Cove Springs, FL 32043-0038; 904-284-6305, assessor fax- 904-284-2923. (Appraiser/Auditor- 904-284-6320) hours- 8AM-4:30PM Computer terminal available for in person search. www.ccpao.com/ **Online access**- Access property appraiser records free at www.ccpao.com/search1.html; tangible property at http://64.148.133.165/tpp/srchasmt.asp. Also, search assessor data free at www.emapsplus.com/FLClay/maps/. Search treasurer RE & tangible personal property at www.claycountytax.com/Tax_Searchr/porr.html. Tax search free at www.claycountytax.com/Tax_Searchr/taxsearch.cgi.

Collier County

County Clerk of the Circuit Court, PO Box 413044, Naples, FL 34101-3044. 239-252-2646; fax-239-252-8003; 8AM-5PM; no recording after 4:30. (EST) www.collierclerk.com/

Index: All in one. Records indexed on a public use terminal back to 1981. Office will perform a UCC and Tax lien search but public must search other records themselves. General index search fee $2.00 per name per year. Copy fee $1.00 per page. Cert fee- $2.00 per doc plus copy fee. Payee- Collier County Clerk of Circuit Court. **Online access to Real Estate, Deed, Lien, UCC, Vital Statistic records:** Access court, lien, real estate, UCCs and vital records free at www.collierclerk.com/. Lending agency data available. Also, access recorded document index at www.myfloridacounty.com. Fees involved to order copies; save $1.50 per record by becoming a subscriber. Also, the tax deeds sales data is free at www.collierclerk.com/RecordsSearch/TaxDeeds. **Other phones:** Treasurer- 239-732-6179; Elections- 239-732-8450; Vital Records- 239-732-8205. **Property tax/Assessing**- Collier County PA, 3285 Tamiami Tr E, Naples, FL 34112-5758; 239-774-8141, assessor fax- 239-774-2071. (Appraiser/Auditor- 239-774-8175) www.collierappraiser.com/ **Online access**- Access Property Appraiser data free at www.collierappraiser.com/Search.asp. Also property assessor/ GIS free at www.emapsplus.com/FLCollier/maps/. Also, search property tax roll at www.colliertax.com/search/.

Columbia County

County Clerk of the Circuit Court, PO Box 2069, Lake City, FL 32056-2069. 386-758-1342, R/E recording phone-386-758-1031, UCC recording phone-386-758-1053; fax-386-758-1337; 8AM-5PM (EST) http://www2.myfloridacounty.com/wps/wcm/connect/columbiaclerk
Index: All in one. Records indexed on a public use terminal back to 1987. Office personnel or visitors may perform searches. Search fee $2.00 per name per year. Office will not search real estate records. Will search UCC records. Copy fee $1.00 per page. Cert fee- $2.00 per doc plus copy fee. Payee- Columbia County Clerk of Circuit Court. Bulk data available for purchase, contact Katrina Vercher at 386-719-7580. **Online access to Real Estate, Deed, Lien records:** Access Clerk of Circuit Courts recording database index at http://www2.myfloridacounty.com/wps/wcm/connect/columbiaclerk. Click on Order Official Records. Search by name, book/page, file number of document type. This is a www.myfloridacounty.com website; fees are involved to order copies; save $1.50 per record by becoming a subscriber. **Other phones:** Treasurer- 386-758-1042; Elections- 386-758-1028; Vital Records- 386-758-1150. **Property tax/Assessing**- Columbia County Tax Collector, 135 NE Hernando Ave, #125, Lake City, FL 32055-4006; 386-758-1077, assessor fax- 386-758-1340. (Appraiser/Auditor- 386-758-1087) hours- 8AM-4:30PM http://columbia.floridapa.com/, www.columbiataxcollector.com **Online access**- Search county property appraiser records free at http://columbia.floridapa.com/GIS/Search_F.asp. Also, search property assessor data free at www.emapsplus.com/FLColumbia/maps/. Search property/GIS free at www.emapsplus.com/FLColumbia/maps/. Also, search the tax rolls and occupational licenses for free at http://fl-columbia-taxcollector.governmax.com/collectmax/collect30.asp

Dade County (Miami City)

County Clerk of the Circuit Court, PO Box 011711; Flagler Station, Miami, FL 33101. 305-275-1155; fax-305-679-1044; 9AM-4PM (EST) www.miami-dadeclerk.com/dadecoc/
No phone and no fax search requests accepted. Elections Dept located at 2700 NW 87th Ave. Index: Separate indices to search include deed/mortgage, lien, satisfactions, financing statements, court orders. Records indexed on a public use terminals back to 3/74. Office personnel or visitors may perform searches. General index search fee $1.00 per year. Copy fee $1.00 per page. Cert fee- $1.00 per doc plus copy fee. Payee- Dade County Clerk of Circuit Court. **Online access to Real Estate, Deed, Lien, Judgment, Marriage, Voter Registration records:** Access records and index free at http://miamidade.gov/wps/portal. Recorded docs at www.miami-dadeclerk.com/public-records/. Access voter registration check site free at www.miamidade.gov/elections/ab-status.asp. **Other phones:** Elections- 305-499-VOTE (8683). **Property tax/Assessing**- 111 NW 1st St, 7th Fl, Miami, FL 33128; 305-375-4099, assessor fax- 305-375-4491. (Appraiser/Auditor- 305-375-5447) **Online access**- Access assessor data free at www.miamidade.gov/pa/property_search.asp. Also, lookup property tax free at www.miamidade.gov/proptax/home.asp. Search assessor property and GIS site free at www.emapsplus.com/FLDade/maps/. Tax collector records free at www.co.miami-dade.fl.us/proptax/.

De Soto County

County Clerk of the Circuit Court, 115 E Oak St, Arcadia, FL 34266. Recording, R/E & UCC phone-863-993-4876; fax-863-993-4669; 8AM-4:45PM (EST) www.desotoclerk.com
Index: Separate indices to search. Records indexed on a public use terminal back to 1974. Office personnel or visitors may perform searches. Search fee $1.50 per name per year. Office will search real estate records. Copy fee $1.00 per page. Cert fee- $1.50 per doc plus copy fee. Payee- De Soto County Clerk of Circuit Court. **Online access to Real Estate, Deed, Lien, Mortgage records:** Access an index of recorded documents at www.myfloridacounty.com. Fees involved to order copies; save $1.50 per record by becoming a subscriber. **Property tax/Assessing**- 101 E Oak St, PO Box 729, Arcadia, FL 34266; 863-993-4861, assessor fax- 863-993-4863. (Appraiser/Auditor- 863-993-4866) **Online access**- Access the property appraiser data free at http://qpublic.net/desoto/search.html. Also, search property assessor/GIS free at www.emapsplus.com/FLdesoto/maps/.

Dixie County

County Clerk of the Circuit Court, PO Box 1206, Cross City, FL 32628. Recording, R/E & UCC phone-352-498-1200; fax-352-498-1201; 8:30AM-5PM (EST)
Index: All in one. Records indexed on a public use terminal back to 1983. Office will perform a UCC search but public must search other records themselves. Copy fee $1.00 per page. Cert fee- $1.50 per doc plus copy fee. Payee- Dixie County Clerk of Circuit Court. **Online access to Real Estate, Deed, Lien, Mortgage records:** Access an index of recorded documents at www.myfloridacounty.com. Fees involved to order copies; save $1.50 per record by becoming a subscriber. **Other phones:** Elections- 352-498-1216. **Property tax/Assessing**- PO Box 260, 214 NE 351 Hwy #G, Cross City, FL 32628; 352-498-1212, assessor fax- 352-498-1211. (Appraiser/Auditor- 352-498-1212) hours- 9AM-N 1PM-5PM **Online access**- Access assessor's property data free at www.qpublic.net/dixie/.

Duval County

County Clerk of the Circuit Court, 330 E Bay St, #103; Courthouse, Jacksonville, FL 32202. 904-630-2043; fax-904-630-2959; 8:30AM-4:30PM (EST) www.duvalclerk.com/ccWebsite/
Index: Separate indices to search. Records indexed on a public use terminal back to 1985. Office personnel or visitors may perform searches. Search fee $1.50 per name per year. Office will not search real estate records. Copy fee $1.00 per page. Cert fee- $1.50 per doc plus copy fee. Payee- Duval County Clerk of Circuit Court. **Online access to Real Estate, Grantor/Grantee, Deed, Lien, Judgment, Vital Statistic records:** Access Clerk of Circuit Court and City of Jacksonville Official Records index free at www.duvalclerk.com/ccWebsite/recordSearch.page. Access an index of recorded documents at www.myfloridacounty.com. Fees involved to order copies. **Other phones:** Treasurer- 904-630-2068. **Property tax/Assessing**- 231 E Forsyth St, #270, (Admin Division), Jacksonville, FL 32202; 904-630-2011, assessor fax- 904-630-2922. (Appraiser/Auditor- 904-630-2020) hours- 8AM-5PM Residential Div- Rm 360, 904-630-2037 (fax-904-630-2590); Land Rcs- Rm 230, 904-630-2019 (fax-904-630-59170); Tangible Prop- Rm 330, 904-630-1964; Commcial Div- Rm 350, 904-630-2600. www.coj.net/Departments/Property+Appraiser/default.htm **Online access**- Search Property Appraiser records free at http://apps.coj.net/pao_propertySearch/Basic/Search.aspx. Search personal property records free at http://apps.coj.net/PAO/tppf/. Search parcel data free at http://maps.coj.net/jaxgis/ click on Duval Maps. Also, access county Property Assessor/GIS-mapping data free at www.emapsplus.com/Flduval/maps/. Search tax collector real estate, personal property data free and Oc licensing at http://fl-duval-taxcollector.governmax.com/collectmax/collect30.asp.

Escambia County

County Clerk of the Circuit Court, 223 Palafox Pl, #110; Official Records Division, Pensacola, FL 32502. Recording, R/E & UCC phone-850-595-3930; fax-850-595-4827; 8AM-5PM (CST) http://public.escambiaclerk.com/home/index.html
Index: All in one. Records indexed on a public use terminal back to 1982. Office personnel or visitors may perform searches. Search fee $1.50 per name per year. Office will not search real estate records. Copy fee $1.00 per page. Cert fee- $1.50 per doc plus copy fee. Payee- Escambia Clerk of Circuit Court. **Online access to Real Estate, Grantor/Grantee, Deed, Lien, Vital Statistic records:** Access to the Clerk of Court Public Records database is free at http://public.escambiaclerk.com/home/index.html. This includes grantor/grantee index and marriage, traffic, court records, tax sales. Access an index of recorded documents at www.myfloridacounty.com. Fees involved to order copies; save $1.50 per record by becoming subscriber. **Other phones:** Treasurer- 850-436-5200. **Property tax/Assessing**- 221 Palafox Pl, Old Courthouse, Penascola, FL 32502; 850-434-2735, assessor fax- 850-435-9526. (Appraiser/Auditor- 850-434-2735) **Online access**- Search the property appraiser records and sales, condos and subdivisions free at www.escpa.org/search.aspx. Find tax sale info at http://ectc.co.escambia.fl.us/Pageview.asp?edit_id=103. Also, access the tax collector's Property database free at http://escambiataxcollector.governmaxa.com/collectmax/collect30.asp.

Flagler County

County Clerk of the Circuit Court, 1769 E Moody Blvd, Bldg 1; Recording Division, Bunnell, FL 32110. 386-313-4360, R/E recording phone-386-313-4380; 8AM-4:30PM (EST) www.flaglerclerk.com
Index: All in one. Records indexed on a public use terminal back to 9/1/88; overall index goes back to 1917; also on microfilm. Office personnel or visitors may perform searches. Search fee $1.50 per name per year. Office will search for any real estate or UCC records in general index. Copy fee $1.00 per page. Oversize pages are $5.00 each. Cert fee- $1.50 per doc plus copy fee. Payee- Flagler County Clerk of Circuit Court. No credit cards accepted. Recording index on CD-rom $25 per O.R. book; for info call Vickie Hunter 386-437-7396. **Online access to Real Estate, Deed, Lien, Probate, Judgment, Marriage, Death, Military Discharge, Property Sale records:** Search recording records free at www.flaglerclerk.com/oncoreweb/Search.aspx. Also, name search the tax collector tax records site free at http://fl-flagler-taxcollector.governmax.com/collectmax/collect30.asp Check property sales at www.qpublic.net/flagler/flaglersearch.html. The state recorders' meta-search site is free at www.myflaglercounty.com. Click on Official Records. Also, access an index of recorded documents at www.myfloridacounty.com. Fees involved to order copies; save $1.50 per record by becoming a subscriber. **Other phones:** Treasurer- 386-313-4160; Elections- 386-313-4170; Tax Deeds- 386-313-4375; Marriages -386-313-4360;. **Property tax/Assessing**- PO Box 936, 1769 E Moody Blvd, Bldg 2 #201, Bunnell, FL 32110; 386-313-4150, assessor fax- 386-313-4151. (Appraiser/Auditor- 386-313-4150) hours- 8AM-5PM www.flaglerpa.com **Online access**- Search appraiser property data free at www.qpublic.net/flagler/search.html or free at http://flaglerpa.com. Also, search Property Assessor/GIS free at www.emapsplus.com/FLflagler/maps/.

Franklin County

County Clerk of the Circuit Court, 33 Market St, #203, Apalachicola, FL 32320. 850-653-8861 x108 or x109; fax-850-653-2261; 8:30AM-4:30PM (EST) http://www2.myfloridacounty.com/wps/wcm/connect/franklinclerk

Also an office at Carrabelle Annex,1647 Hwy 98 E, Carrabelle, FL 32322; 850-697- 3263. Index: All in one. Records indexed on a public use terminal back to 1986. Only the public may search. Copy fee $1.00 per page. Cert fee- $1.50 per doc plus copy fee. Payee- Franklin County Clerk of Circuit Court. **Online access to Real Estate, Deed, Lien records:** Access an index of recorded documents at www.myfloridacounty.com. Fees involved to order copies; save $1.50 per record by becoming a subscriber. **Other phones:** Treasurer- 850-653-8861; Elections- 850-653-9520. **Property tax/Assessing-** 33 Market St, #202, Apalachicola, FL 32320; 850-653-9323, assessor fax- 850-653-2529. (Appraiser/Auditor- 850-653-9236) **Online access-** Property record search is free at http://qpublic.net/franklin/.

Gadsden County

County Clerk of the Circuit Court, PO Box 1649, Quincy, FL 32353-1649. 850-875-8601; fax-850-875-8612; 8:30AM-5PM (EST) www.clerk.co.gadsden.fl.us

Index: All in one. Records indexed on a public use terminal back to 1985. Office personnel or visitors may perform searches. Search fee $2.00 per year. Will search UCC records. Copy fee $1.00 per page. Cert fee- $2.00 per doc plus copy fee. Payee- Gadsden County Clerk of Circuit Court. **Online access to Real Estate, Deed, Lien, Judgment records:** Access to official records index is free at http://69.21.116.234/chronicleweb/. Index records go back to 1990. Provides index numbers only. **Other phones:** Elections- 850-627-9910. **Property tax/Assessing-** 16 S Calhoun St, Quincy, FL 32351; 850-627-7168, assessor fax- 850-627-0396. (Appraiser/Auditor- 850-627-7168) **Online access-** Access to the property appraiser database is free at www.qpublic.net/gadsden/search.html. Search property sales at www.qpublic.net/gadsden/gadsdensearch.html. No name searching. Also, search tax collector records at http://fl-gadsden-taxcollector.governmax.com/collectmax/collect30.asp.

Gilchrist County

County Clerk of the Circuit Court, PO Box 37, Trenton, FL 32693. Recording, R/E & UCC phone-352-463-3170; fax-352-463-3166; 8:30AM-5PM (EST) http://gilchrist.fl.us/

Index: All in one. Records indexed on a public use terminal back to 1983. Only the public may search. Copy fee $1.00 per page. Cert fee- $1.50 per doc plus copy fee. Payee- Gilchrist County Clerk of Circuit Court. **Online access to Real Estate, Deed, Lien, Judgment, Marriage, Death records:** Access is free to recorded documents generally and some courts records at records.gilchrist.fl.us. Images available for deeds, mortgages, and some other document types. Access an index of recorded docs at http://mygilchristcounty.com or www.myfloridacounty.com. Fees involved to order copies. **Other phones:** Elections-352-463-3194. **Property tax/Assessing-** 112 S Main St, Trenton, FL 32693; 352-463-3190, assessor fax-352-463-3193. (Appraiser/Auditor- 352-463-3190) www.gcpaonline.net **Online access-** Access to the property appraiser database is free at www.qpublic.net/gilchrist/search.html. Property sales searches at www.gcpaonline.net; click on Search.

Glades County

County Clerk of the Circuit Court, PO Box 10, Moore Haven, FL 33471. Recording, R/E & UCC phone-863-946-6010; fax-863-946-0560; 8AM-5PM (EST) http://www2.myfloridacounty.com/wps/wcm/connect/gladesclerk

Index: All in one. Records indexed on computer back to 1/89. Office personnel or visitors may perform searches. Search fee $2.00 per name per year. Office will search real estate records (name searches). Will search UCC records. Copy fee $1.00 per page. Cert fee- $2.00 per doc plus copy fee. Payee- Glades County Clerk of Circuit Court. Bulk data available for purchase, microfilm or TIFF images on CD's. **Online access to Real Estate, Deed, Lien records:** Access an index of recorded documents at www.myfloridacounty.com. View docs back to 1/1990 without ordering. Fees involved to order copies; save $1.50 per record by becoming a subscriber. **Other phones:** Elections- 863-946-6005. **Property tax/Assessing-** PO Box 1106, US 27th & 6th St, Rm 202, Moore Haven, FL 33471; 863-946-0818, assessor fax- 863-946-3359. (Appraiser/Auditor- 863-946-6025) **Online access-** Search Property Assessor/GIS free at www.emapsplus.com/FLglades/maps/. Also, sales searches are at www.gcpaonline.net; click on Search.

Gulf County

County Clerk of the Circuit Court, 1000 Cecil G Costin Sr Blvd, Rm 148, Port St. Joe, FL 32456. 850-229-6112, R/E recording phone-850-229-6113; fax-850-229-6174; 9AM-5PM (EST) http://www2.myfloridacounty.com/wps/wcm/connect/gulfclerk

Index: All in one. Records indexed on a public use terminal back to 1986. Office will perform a UCC search but public must search other records themselves. Search fee $1.00 per name per year. Copy fee $1.00 per page. Cert fee- $1.50 per doc plus copy fee. Payee- Gulf County Clerk of Circuit Court. Bulk data available for purchase, official records can be purchased on a CD and consists of 2 books. Fee $20.00. Contact Tina Shearer at 850-229-6113. **Online access to Real Estate, Deed, Judgment, Marriage, Death records:** Access an index of recorded documents at www.myfloridacounty.com. Fees involved to order copies; save $1.50 per record by becoming a subscriber. **Other phones:** Treasurer-850-229-6116; Elections- 850-229-6117; Vital Records- 850-227-1276. **Property tax/Assessing-** 1000 Cecil G Costin Sr Blvd, Port St. Joe, FL 32456; 850-229-6115, assessor fax- 850-229-6661. (Appraiser/Auditor- 850-229-6115) www.gulfpa.com **Online access-** Access to the property appraiser database is free at www.gulfpa.com

Hamilton County

County Clerk of the Circuit Court, 207 NE 1st St, Rm 106, Jasper, FL 32052. Recording, R/E & UCC phone-386-792-1288; fax-386-792-3524; 8:30AM-4:30PM (EST) www.hamiltoncountyflorida.com/cd_clerk.aspx

Index: All in one. Records indexed on a public use terminal back to 1984. Only the public may search. Copy fee $1.00 per page. Cert fee- $1.50 per doc plus copy fee. Payee- Hamilton County Clerk of Circuit Court. Bulk data (books on CD) available for purchase for $37.50 per book. Contact Vanessa Hill. **Online access to Real Estate, Deed, Lien records:** Access an index of recorded documents at www.myfloridacounty.com. Fees involved to order copies; save $1.50 per record by becoming a subscriber. **Other phones:** Treasurer- 386-792-1288; Elections- 386-792-1426; Vital Records- 386-792-1288. **Property tax/Assessing-** 207 NE 1st St, Rm 106, Jasper, FL 32052; 386-792-1284, assessor fax-386-792-0878. (Appraiser/Auditor- 386-792-2791) www.hamiltoncountytaxcollector.com **Online access-** Access to the property appraiser database is free at www.hamiltoncountytaxcollector.com

Hardee County

County Clerk of the Circuit Court, PO Drawer 1749, Wauchula, FL 33873. 863-773-4174; fax-863-773-3295; 8AM-5PM; 8AM-3:30PM recording hours. (EST) www.hardeeclerk.com

Index: All in one. Records indexed on a public use terminal back to 1984. Office personnel or visitors may perform searches. Search fee $1.50 per name per year. Office will search real estate records. Will search UCC records. Copy fee $1.00 per page. Cert fee- $1.50 per doc plus copy fee. Payee- Hardee County Clerk of Circuit Court. **Online access to Real Estate, Deed, Lien, Judgment records:** Access an index of recorded documents at www.myfloridacounty.com. Fees involved to order copies; save $1.50 per record by becoming a subscriber. **Property tax/Assessing-** PO Box 877, 110 W Oak St, Wachula, FL 33873; 863-773-9144, assessor fax- 863-773-0954. (Appraiser - 863-773-2196) www.hardeepa.net **Online access-** Access to the property appraiser data is free at www.hardeecounty.net/cfaps/appraiser/propform.cfm. Search assessor data on the GIS site free at www.emapsplus.com/Flhardee/maps/.

Hendry County

County Clerk of the Circuit Court, PO Box 1760, La Belle, FL 33975-1760. Recording, R/E & UCC phone-863-675-5217, UCC recording phone-863-675-5202; fax-863-675-5238; 8:30AM-5PM (EST) www.hendryclerk.org

Index: All in one. Records indexed on a public use terminal back to 1980. Office personnel or visitors may perform index searches. General index search fee $2.00 per name per year. Real estate owner, mortgage, and property transfer searches available. Will search UCC records. Copy fee $1.00 per page. Cert fee- $2.00 per doc plus copy fee. Payee- Hendry County Clerk of Circuit Court. **Online access to Real Estate, Deed, Lien records:** Access an index of recorded documents at www.myfloridacounty.com. Also, access Official Records Data free at www.hendryclerk.org/officialrecords.htm - has images from 12/30/1988 - Book 450 Page 1 to latest available. Web records updated daily. **Other phones:** Elections- 863-675-5230; Tax Collector- 863-675-5280. **Property tax/Assessing-** PO Box 1840, 25 E Hickpochee, Labelle, FL 33975; 863-675-5270, assessor fax- 863-675-5254. hours- 8AM-5PM www.hendryprop.org **Online access-** Access the property appraiser database at www.hendryprop.com/GIS/Search_F.asp. Also, search Property Assessor/GIS free at www.emapsplus.com/FLhendry/maps/.

Hernando County

County Clerk of the Circuit Court, 20 N Main, Rm 215, Brooksville, FL 34601. 352-540-6768; fax-352-754-4243; hours- 8AM-5PM (EST) www.clerk.co.hernando.fl.us

Index: All in one. Records indexed on a public use terminal back to 1983. Office will perform a UCC search but public must search other records themselves. Copy fee $1.00 per page. Cert fee- $2.00 per doc plus copy fee. Payee- Hernando County Clerk of Circuit Court. **Online access to Real Estate, Deed, Lien, Marriage, Judgment records:** Access to the clerk's Official Records database is now free at www.clerk.co.hernando.fl.us/disclaimer.asp. Your browser must be JavaScript enabled. Includes recordings, marriages, and court records. Also, access recorded document index at www.myfloridacounty.com. Fees involved to order copies. **Other phones:** Treasurer- 352-754-4190; Tax Collector- 352-754-4180. **Property tax/Assessing-** 201 Howell Ave, #300, Brooksville, FL 34601-2041; 352-754-4190, assessor fax- 352-754-4198. (Appraiser 352-754-4190) www.co.hernando.fl.us/pa/ **Online access-** Search 2 levels of the Public Inquiry System Property Appraiser Real Estate database - Easy Search and Real Time Search - free at www.hernandocounty.us/pa/propertysearch.asp. Search by owner, address, or parcel key.

Highlands County

County Clerk of the Circuit Court, 590 S Commerce Ave, Sebring, FL 33870. Recording, R/E & UCC phone-863-402-6590, UCC recording phone-800-822-5436; 8AM-5PM (EST) www.hcclerk.org

Index: All in one. Records indexed on a public use terminal back to 1983. Only the public may search. Copy fee $1.00 per page. Cert fee- $1.50 per doc plus copy fee. Payee- Clerk of Court. **Online access to Real Estate, Deed, Lien records:** Online access to the recorders' meta-search site is at www.myflorida.com. Click on Official Records. Free search; fee for documents. Also, online access to official records -deeds, mortgages, judgments, etc - from the county recording database is free at www.hcclerk.org/SearchOfficialRecords.aspx. Records go back to 1983. **Other phones:** Treasurer- 863-402-6685; Elections- 863-402-6654; Vital Records- 863-386-6040. **Property tax/Assessing-** 560 S Commerce Ave, Sebring, FL 33870; 863-402-6659, assessor fax- 863-402-6765. (Appraiser/Auditor- 863-402-6661) hours- 9AM-5PM www.appraiser.co.highlands.fl.us **Online access-** Search Property Assessor/GIS free at www.emapsplus.com/FLhighlands/maps/. Also, property appraiser records are free at www.appraiser.co.highlands.fl.us/search.html; tangible personal property records available. Also, search tax deed sales by date free at www.hcclerk.org/TaxDeedsSales.aspx. Also, county tax collector database free at https://www.highlands.county-taxes.com/tcb/app/re/accounts. Also, search the Property/GIS mapping site free at www.emapsplus.com/FLhighlands/maps/.

Hillsborough County

County Clerk of the Circuit Court, PO Box 3249, Tampa, FL 33601-1110. 813-276-8100 x4367, R/E recording phone-813-276-8100; fax-813-276-2114; 8AM-5PM (EST) www.hillsclerk.com

Index: All in one. Records indexed on computer back to 1965. Office will perform a UCC search but public must search other records themselves. General index search fee $1.00 per year. Copy fee $1.00 per page. Cert fee- $1.50 per doc plus copy fee. Payee- Hillsborough County Clerk of Circuit Court. **Online access to Real Estate, Deed, Lien, Judgment, Mortgage records:** Search clerk's recordings index at http://publicrecord.hillsclerk.com. Images of official records from 1990 to present. Also, access recorded document index at www.myfloridacounty.com; fees involved to order copies; subscribers save $1.50 per record. Call 813-276-8100 x4444 for info. **Other phones:** Treasurer- 813-635-5200. **Property tax/Assessing-** 601 E Kennedy St, 16th Fl, Tampa, FL 33602-4932; 813-272-6100, assessor fax- 813-272-5519. (Appraiser/Auditor- 813-272-6100) www.hcpafl.or g/www/index.shtml **Online access-** Search county property appraiser records free at www.hcpafl.org/www/search/index.shtml. Receive owner data, legal, sales, value summaries. Also, search for similar tax data free on the tax collector site at www.hillstax.org/taxapp/property_information.asp. Search property on GIS site at http://propmap3.hcpafl.org/main.asp?cmd=ZOOMFOLIO&folio=.

Holmes County

County Clerk of the Circuit Court, PO Box 397, Bonifay, FL 32425. Recording, R/E & UCC phone-850-547-1100; fax-850-547-6630; 8AM-4PM (CST) http://www2.myfloridacounty.com/wps/wcm/connect/holmesclerk

Index: All in one. Records indexed on a public use terminal back to 1982. Office will perform a UCC search but public must search other records themselves. UCC search per debtor name $1.00 per year. Copy fee $1.00 per page. Cert fee- $1.50 per doc plus copy fee. Payee- Holmes County Clerk of Circuit Court. Bulk data available for purchase- official records images; contact Recording Dept. **Online access to Real Estate, Deed, Lien records:** Access an index of recorded documents at www.myfloridacounty.com. Fees involved to order copies; save $1.50 per record by becoming a subscriber. **Other phones:** Treasurer- 850-547-1115; Elections- 850-547-1107. **Property tax/Assessing-** 226 N Waukesha St, Bonifay, FL 32425; 850-547-1113, assessor fax- 850-547-2445. (Appraiser/Auditor- 850-547-1113) **Online access-** Access property appraiser data free including property, sales and sales lists free at http://qpublic.net/holmes/.

Indian River County

County Clerk of the Circuit Court, PO Box 1028, Vero Beach, FL 32961-1028. 772-770-5185 x3105; fax-772-770-5008; hourss - 8AM-5PM (EST) www.clerk.indian-river.org

Index: All in one. Records indexed on a public use terminal back to 20/3/83. Office personnel or visitors may perform searches. Search fee $1.50 per name plus $1.50 per add'l year. Copy fee $1.00 per page. Cert fee- $1.50 per doc plus copy fee. Payee- Indian River County Clerk of Circuit Court. **Online access to Real Estate, Deed, Lien, Mortgage records:** Access to Clerk's recording indices are free at www.clerk.indian-river.org/recordssearch/ori.asp. Records go back to 1983. Full real estate, lien and court and vital records from the Clerk of the Circuit Court is at their fee site; subscriptions start at $25.00 per month, increasing with amount of access. For info about free and fee access, call 772-567-8000 x216. **Other phones:** Vital Records- 772-794-7460; Tax Collector- 772-567-8000. **Property tax/Assessing-** 1840 25th St, Vero Beach, FL 32960; 772-567-8000 x1469, assessor fax- 772-770-5087. www.ircpa.org **Online access-** Appraiser records free at www.ircpa.org. Also, search Property Assessor/GIS free at www.emapsplus.com/FLindianriver/maps/.

Jackson County

County Clerk of the Circuit Court, PO Drawer 510, Marianna, FL 32447. Recording, R/E & UCC phone-850-482-9552; fax-850-482-7849; 8AM-4:30PM (CST) http://www2.myfloridacounty.com/wps/wcm/connect/jacksonclerk

Index: All in one. Records indexed on a public use terminal back to 1990. Indexed in books from 1848 to current. Office will perform a UCC search but public must search other records themselves. Will search UCC records on computer from 1990 to current. Copy fee $1.00 per page. Cert fee- $1.50 per doc plus copy fee. Payee- Jackson County Clerk of Circuit Court. Bulk data available for purchase in copies, CD's and maps. Contact Stephanie M Edenfield. **Online access to Real Estate, Lien, Deed, Marriage, Probate records:** Access an index of recorded documents at www.myfloridacounty.com. Fees involved to order copies; save $1.50 per record by becoming a subscriber. Images will go back to 5/1990. **Other phones:** Treasurer- 850-482-9653; Elections- 850-482-9652; Vital Records- 850-482-9552 (marriage only). **Property tax/Assessing-** PO Box 1526, 4445 Lafayette St, Marianna, FL 32447; 850-482-9653, assessor fax- 850-526-3821. (Appraiser/Auditor- 850-482-9646) **Online access-** Search property tax data for free at www.jacksoncountytaxcollector.com/SearchSelect.aspx.

Jefferson County

County Clerk of the Circuit Court, Courthouse, Rm 10, Monticello, FL 32344. 850-342-0218 x227, R/E recording phone-850-342-0218 x 227; fax-850-342-0222; 8AM-5PM (EST) http://jeffersonclerk.com

Index: All in one. Records indexed on a public use terminal back to 1973. Office will perform a UCC search but public must search other records themselves. General index search fee $1.50 per year per name. Copy fee $1.00 per page. Cert fee- $1.50 per doc plus copy fee. Payee- Jefferson County Clerk of Circuit Court. **Online access to Property, Real Estate, Lien, UCC, Marriage records:** Access an index of recorded documents at www.myfloridacounty.com. Fees involved to order copies; save $1.50 per record by becoming a subscriber. Also, access the Clerk of Circuit Court recordings database free at www.myjeffersoncounty.com. **Other phones:** Treasurer- 850-342-0218 x 232; Elections- 850-997-3348. **Property tax/Assessing-** Property Appraiser's Office, 480 W Walnut St, Monticello, FL 32345; 850-997-3356, assessor fax- 850-997-0988. (Appraiser/Auditor- 850-997-3356) hours- 7:30AM-5:30PM **Online access-** Access Property Appraiser data free at http://qpublic.net/jefferson/search.html. Sales searches are also available. Search assessor parcel map at http://archie.co.jefferson.co.us/website/aspin/disclaimer.htm. Also, search property records free at www.co.jefferson.co.us/ats/splash.do. Search the tax collector database free at www.jeffersoncountytaxcollector.com/SearchSelect.aspx.

Lafayette County

County Clerk of the Circuit Court, PO Box 88, Mayo, FL 32066. 386-294-1600; fax-386-294-4231; 8AM-5PM (EST) http://www2.myfloridacounty.com/wps/wcm/connect/lafayetteclerk

Index: All in one. Records indexed on a public use terminal back to 1988. Only the public may search. Copy fee $1.00 per page. Cert fee- $2.00 per doc plus copy fee. Payee- Lafayette County Clerk of Circuit Court. **Online access to Real Estate, Deed, Lien records:** Access an index of recorded documents at www.myfloridacounty.com. Fees involved to order copies; save $1.50 per record by becoming a subscriber. **Other phones:** Treasurer- 386-294-1961; Elections- 386-294-1261. **Property tax/Assessing-** PO Box 6, 120 W Main St, Mayo, FL 32066; 386-294-1991, assessor fax- 386-294-1106. (Appraiser - 386-294-1991) www.lafayettepa.com **Online access-** Search appraiser's property data free at www.lafayettepa.com/GIS/Search_F.asp. Also, search county property sales free at www.lafayettepa.com/GIS/Search_F.asp?SalesReport

Lake County

County Clerk of the Circuit Court, PO Box 7800, Tavares, FL 32778-7800. Recording, R/E & UCC phone-352-253-2600; fax-352-253-2616; 8:30AM-5PM; recording- 8:30AM-4:30PM (EST) www.lakecountyclerk.org

Index: All in one. Records indexed on a public use terminal back to 1957. Office personnel or visitors may perform searches. General index search fee $2.00 per name/year. Office will search real estate records (general name searches only). Will search UCC records (general name searches only). Copy fee $1.00 per page. Cert fee- $2.00 per doc plus copy fee. Payee- Lake County Clerk of Circuit Court. Bulk information available for purchase on microfilm; contact Renita Herbison. **Online access to Real Estate, Deed, Lien, Marriage records:** Access to the new county clerk official records database is free at www.lakecountyclerk.org/services.asp?subject=Online_Official_Records. Records go as far back as 1957. Includes court records. Also, marriage records back to 11/2000 are at www.lakecountyclerk.org/departments.asp?subject=Marriage_Licenses. Also, access to state recorders' meta-search site is free at www.myfloridacounty.com. Click on Official records. **Other phones:** Elections- 352-343-9734; Vital Records- 352-589-6424; Tax Collector- 352-343-9622. **Property tax/Assessing-** Property Appraiser, 317 W Main St 3rd Fl, Tavares, FL 32778-4027; 352-343-9748, assessor fax- 352-343-9894. (Appraiser/Auditor- 352-343-9748) hours- 8:30AM-5PM www.lakecopropappr.com **Online access-** Search the County Property Assessor parcel and tax data also property sales free at www.lakecopropappr.com/. Also, search property on the tax collector site free at http://laketaxcollector.governmax.com/collectmax/collect30.asp. Also, access to tax search for free go to www.laketax.com/.

Lee County

County Clerk of the Circuit Court, PO Box 2278, Fort Myers, FL 33902-2278. 239-533-5000; fax-239-485-2170; 8AM-5PM (EST) www.leeclerk.org

Also a Cape Coral Branch Office - Lee County Gov't Ctr., 1039 SE 9th PL, Cape Coral, FL 33990. Index: All in one. Records indexed on a public use terminal back to 1988. Office personnel or visitors may perform searches. General search fee $2.00 per year. Real estate owner, mortgage, and property transfer searches available. UCC search includes tax liens if requested. UCC search per debtor name- $1.50 per name per year. Copy fee $1.00 per page. Cert fee- $2.00 per doc plus copy fee. Payee- Lee County Clerk of Circuit Court. **Online access to Real Estate, Deed, Lien, Judgment, Mortgage records:** Search the recorders index free at www.leeclerk.org/OR/Search.aspx or other indexes (subject to change) at www.leeclerk.org/SearchOfficialRecords.htm. Also, obtain certified copies at the Clerk's office or order certified copies online and search other Florida Counties' Official Records at www.myfloridacounty.com and click on Order Official Records. **Other phones:** Elections- 239-533-8683. **Property tax/Assessing-** PO Box 1546, 2480 Thompson St, Fort Meyers, FL 33902; 239-533-6100, assessor fax- 239-533-6160. (Appraiser/Auditor- 239-533-6100 (866-673-2868)) hours- 8:30AM-5PM www.leepa.org **Online access-** Search tangible business property at www.leepa.org/Tangible/Business%20Search.htm. The online property info inquiry is at www.leepa.org/Queries/SearchCriteria.htm. A generic tax search page for tax rolls,. certificates, mobiles, vessels, vehicles is free at www.leetc.com/search_criteria.asp.Search .Property assessor/GIS mapping free at www.emapsplus.com/FLlee/maps/.

Leon County

County Clerk of the Circuit Court, PO Box 726, Tallahassee, FL 32302. 850-577-4030, R/E recording phone-850-577-4050; fax-850-577-4235; 8:30AM-5PM (EST) www.clerk.leon.fl.us

Online records at www.clerk.leon.fl.us MAY have personal identifiers removed; records MAY have been removed from this online service, though this is rare. Index: All in one. Records indexed on a public use terminal back to 1966. Only the public may search. Copy fee $1.00 per page. Cert fee- $1.50 per doc plus copy fee. Payee- Leon County Clerk of Circuit Court. **Online access to Real Estate, Deed, Lien, Mortgage, Marriage records:** Real Estate, lien, and foreclosure records from the County Clerk are free at www.clerk.leon.fl.us. Lending agency data is also available. Also, access to full document images requires user name and password, plus $100 per month. Marriages data is available at http://cvweb.clerk.leon.fl.us/index_marriage.html. Also, access recorded documents index at www.myfloridacounty.com. Fees involved to order copies. **Other phones:** Elections- 850-606-8683; Tax Collector- 850-488-4735. **Property tax/Assessing-** Property Appraiser--PO Box 1750, 315 S Calhoun St 3 Fl, Tallahassee, FL 32302; 850-488-6102, assessor fax- 850-922-7238. (Appraiser/Auditor- 850-488-6102) hours- 8AM-5PM www.leonpa.org **Online access-** Search Property Appraiser database records free at www.co.leon.fl.us/propappr/search.cfm. Search tax collector rolls at http://dta.co.leon.fl.us/tax/default.asp.

Levy County

County Clerk of the Circuit Court, PO Drawer 610, Bronson, FL 32621. Recording, R/E & UCC phone-352-486-5229; 8AM-5PM (EST) www.levyclerk.com

Index: All in one. Records indexed on a public use terminal back to 1983. Only the public may search. Real estate owner, mortgage, and property transfer records available if you provide book and page number; fee is $1.00 per page. Copy fee $1.00 per page. Cert fee- $1.50 per doc plus copy fee. Payee- Levy County Clerk of Circuit Court. **Online access to Real Estate, Deed, Lien records:** Access the Clerk of Circuit Court recording database free at http://oncore.levyclerk.com/oncoreweb/Search.aspx. Search by name, book/page, file number or document type. Access an index of recorded documents at www.myfloridacounty.com. Fees involved to order copies; save $1.50 per record by becoming a subscriber. Also, search county warrants list for free at www.levyso.com. **Other phones:** Elections- 352-486-5163; Vital Records- 352-486-5274. **Property tax/Assessing-** PO Drawer 100, Bronson, DL 32621; 352-486-5222, assessor fax- 352-486-5187. (Appraiser/Auditor- 352-486-5222) hours- 8:30AM-5PM www.levypa.com/ **Online access-** Access to the property appraiser data is free at www.levypa.com/CamaDisplay.aspx?OutputMode=Input&SearchType=RealEstate&Page=SalesSearch. Also search tax collector and property data free at http://fl-levy-taxcollector.governmax.com/collectmax/collect30.asp and click on Tax Search; also has tax sales.

Liberty County

County Clerk of the Circuit Court, PO Box 399, Bristol, FL 32321. 850-643-2215; fax-850-643-2866; 8AM-5PM (EST) http://www2.myfloridacounty.com/wps/wcm/connect/libertyclerk

Index: All in one. Records indexed on a public use terminal back to 1990. Only the public may search. Copy fee $1.00 per page. Cert fee- $2.00 per doc plus copy fee. Exemplification fee- $7.00 plus copy fee. Payee- Liberty County Clerk of Circuit Court. **Online access to Real Estate, Deed, Lien records:** Access an index of recorded documents at www.myfloridacounty.com. Fees involved to order copies; save $1.50 per record by becoming a subscriber. **Other phones:** Treasurer- 850-643-2442; Elections- 850-643-5226. **Property tax/Assessing-** PO Box 580, County Courthouse, Bristol, FL 32321; 850-643-2279, assessor fax- 850-643-4193. (Appraiser/Auditor- 850-643-2279) **Online access-** Access assessor property records free at www.qpublic.net/liberty/.

Madison County

County Clerk of the Circuit Court, PO Box 237, Madison, FL 32341-0237. 850-973-1500, R/E recording phone-850-973-1500 x236; fax-850-973-2059; 8AM-5PM (EST) http://www2.myfloridacounty.com/wps/wcm/connect/madisonclerk

Index: All in one. Records indexed on a public use terminal back to 1990. Office will perform a UCC search but public must search other records themselves. Search fee $1.00 per year. Copy fee $1.00 per page. Cert fee- $2.00 per doc plus copy fee. Payee- Madison County Clerk of Circuit Court. **Online access to Real Estate, Deed, Lien records:** Access an index of recorded documents at www.myfloridacounty.com. Fees involved to order copies; save $1.50 per record by becoming a subscriber. Official Records indexes are for past 10 years. **Other phones:** Treasurer- 850-973-1500; Elections- 850-973-6507. **Property tax/Assessing-** Property Appraiser, 229 SW Pinckney St, Rm 201, Madison, FL 32340; 850-973-6133, assessor fax-850-973-8928. (Appraiser/Auditor- 850-973-6133) www.madisonpa.com/General_Info.asp **Online access-** Access property assessor and sale data free at www.madisonpa.com/GIS/Search_F.asp.

Manatee County

County Clerk of the Circuit Court, PO Box 25400, Bradenton, FL 34206. 941-741-4041, R/E recording phone-941-741-4040 or 4041; 8:30AM-5PM (EST) www.manateeclerk.com

Index: All in one. Records indexed on a public use terminal back to 1978. Office will perform a UCC or RE search but public must search other records themselves. General index search fee $1.00 per year per name. Copy fee $1.00 per page. Cert fee- $2.00 per doc plus copy fee. Payee- Manatee County Clerk of Circuit Court. Bulk data available for purchase, index and images. **Online access to Real Estate, Deed, Lien, Judgment, Death, Marriage, Condominium records:** Several sources exist. Search and view real estate and recordings records free from the Clerk of Circuit Court and Comptroller's database at www.manateeclerk.com. **Other phones:** Treasurer- 941-748-4800; Elections- 941-741-3823; Vital Records- 941-748-0747. **Property tax/Assessing-** PO Box 1338, Bradenton, FL 34206; 941-748-8208, assessor fax- 941-742-5664. (Appraiser/Auditor- 941-748-8208) www.manateepao.com/ **Online access-** Search Property Assessor/GIS data free at www.emapsplus.com/FLmanatee/maps/. Also, access index of recorded docs at www.myfloridacounty.com. Fees involved to order copies. Property Appraiser records free at www.manateepao.com/Search/GenericSearch.aspx. Tax deed sales at www.clerkofcourts.com/Sales/TaxDeeds/taxdeed.pdf. Also, property tax records are at www.taxcollector.com/dataaccess/design/1owner.asp. Search foreclosure sales at www.manateeclerk.com.

Marion County

County Clerk of the Circuit Court, PO Box 1030, Ocala, FL 34478-1030. 352-671-5630; fax-352-671-5629; 8AM-5PM (EST) www.marioncountyclerk.org

Index: All in one. Records indexed on a public use terminal back to 1984. Office personnel or visitors may perform searches. Search fee $2.00 per name per year. Copy fee $1.00 per page. Cert fee- $2.00 per doc plus copy fee. Payee- Marion County Clerk of Circuit Court. **Online access to Real Estate, Deed, Lien, Judgment, Death, Marriage records:** Search recorded records free at http://216.255.240.38/wb_or1/or_sch_1.asp. Also, access an index of recorded documents at www.myfloridacounty.com. Fees involved to order copies; save $1.50 per record by becoming a subscriber. **Property tax/Assessing-** 110 NW 1st Ave, Ocala, FL 34475; 352-671-5630, assessor fax-352-671-5629. (Appraiser/Auditor- 352-368-8300) **Online access-** Access property appraiser data free at www.propappr.marion.fl.us/MCPASCH.HTML. Search county tax rolls free at https://www.mariontax.com/itm.asp. Also, access county property data free at www.marioncountyfl.org/MSTU/assessment.aspx.

Martin County

County Clerk of the Circuit Court, PO Box 9016, Stuart, FL 34995. Recording, R/E & UCC phone-772-288-5554; fax-772-223-7920; 8AM-5PM (EST) http://clerk-web.martin.fl.us/ClerkWeb/

Direct phone for index search requests- 772-288-5552. Index: All in one. Records indexed on a public use terminal back to 1986. Office personnel or visitors may perform searches. General index search fee $1.00 per name per year. $1.50-UCCs; searches not guaranteed. Office will search real estate records. Copy fee $1.00 per page. Plat copy- $5.00 each. Cert fee- $1.50 per doc plus copy fee. Payee- Clerk of Circuit Court. For information on bulk data please call information management or archives at 772-288-5985. **Online access to Real Estate, Deed, Lien, Mortgage records:** Access to the clerk of the circuit court recordings database are free at http://216.255.240.38/wb_or1/or_sch_1.asp. Also, online access to the state recorders' metasearch site is free at www.myfloridacounty.com. Fees apply for images. **Other phones:** Treasurer- 772-288-5595; Elections- 772-288-5637; Vital Records- 772-288-4000. **Property tax/Assessing-** 1111 SE Federal Hwy, Stuart, FL 34994; 772-288-5608, assessor fax-772-221-1346. (Appraiser/Auditor- 772-288-5608) www.pa.martin.fl.us/ **Online access-** Records on the county property appraiser database are free at www.pa.martin.fl.us/. Choose "Real Property Searches." Personal property searches are also available, and more. County tax collector data files are free at https://taxcol.martin.fl.us/itm/. Also, search Property Appraiser/GIS free at www.emapsplus.com/FLmartin/maps/.

Monroe County

County Clerk of the Circuit Court, PO Box 1980, Key West, FL 33041-1980. 305-292-3540, R/E recording phone-305-292-3507; fax-305-295-3623; 8:30AM-5PM (EST) www.clerk-of-the-court.com/

Index: All in one. Records indexed on a public use terminal back to 1996. Office personnel or visitors may perform searches. General index search fee $1.50 per name per year. Office will not search real estate records. Copy fee $1.00 per page. Cert fee- $2.50 per doc plus copy fee; exemplificaion- $7.00. Payee- Monroe County Clerk of Circuit Court. **Online access**

to Real Estate, Deed, Lien, Mortgage records: Access to the clerk of circuit courts database is free at www.clerk-of-the-court.com. **Other phones:** Treasurer- 305-292-3420; Vital Records- 305-292-3507; Tax Collector- 305-245-5000. **Property tax/Assessing**- PO Box 1176, 500 Whitehead St, #401, Key West, FL 33041-1176; 305-292-3420, assessor fax- 305-292-3501. **Online access**- Access property appraiser data free on the GIS-mapping site at www.mcpafl.org/GISMaps.aspx. Also, search property tax, tax deed sales, and occ. licenses free at www.monroetaxcollector.com.

Nassau County

County Clerk of the Circuit Court, PO Box 456, Fernandina Beach, FL 32035. 904-548-4604; fax-904-548-4549; 8:30AM-5PM; recording- 9AM-4PM (EST) www.nassauclerk.com
Index: All in one. Records indexed on a public use terminal back to 1982. Office personnel or visitors may perform searches. Search fee $2.00 per name per year. Will search UCC records. Copy fee $1.00 per page. Cert fee- $2.00 per doc plus copy fee. Payee- Nassau County Clerk of Circuit Court. **Online access to Real Estate, Deed, Lien, Marriage, Will, records:** Access recorders database free at www.nassauclerk.com/clerk/publicrecords/oncoreweb/Search.aspx. Access an index of recorded documents at www.myfloridacounty.com. Fees involved to order copies; save $1.50 per record by becoming a subscriber. **Other phones:** Tax Collector- 904-491-7400. **Property tax/Assessing**- PO Box 870, 76347 Veterans Way, Fernandina Beach, FL 32035; 904-491-7300, assessor fax- 904-491-3629. (Appraiser - 904-491-7300) www.nassauflpa.com **Online access**- Access property data free at www.nassauflpa.com/. Search Property Assessor/GIS free at www.emapsplus.com/FLnassau/maps/.

Okaloosa County

County Clerk of the Circuit Court, PO Drawer 1359, Crestview, FL 32536. 850-689-5000 x3361, R/E recording phone-850-689-5041; fax-850-689-5886; 8AM-5PM (CST) www.clerkofcourts.cc
Access an index of recorded documents at www.myfloridacounty.com. Fees involved to order copies; save $1.50 per record by becoming a subscriber. Index: All in one. Records indexed on a public use terminal back to 1983. Only the public may search. Copy fee $1.00 per page. Cert fee- $1.50 per doc plus copy fee; Exemplificaion is $6.00 add'l. Payee- Okaloosa County Clerk of Circuit Court. **Online access to Real Estate, Deed, Lien, Vital Statistic, Mortgage records:** Several databases are available. Access to Okaloosa County online system requires a monthly usage fee of $100. No addresses listed. Lending agency, traffic and domestic records are free. For info, contact Don Howard at 850-689-5000 x3361. Access clerk's land and official records for free at http://officialrecords.clerkofcourts.cc/; includes marriage, civil, traffic records. Also, online access to the state recorders' meta-search site is free at www.myfloridacounty.com. **Other phones:** Treasurer- 850-689-5801; Elections- 850-651-7272. **Other Online Records-** Access property appraiser records - sales lists free at www.okaloosapa.com. Access tax collector data at https://www.okaloosa.county-taxes.com/tcb/app/pt/main. Access data on the GIS-mapping site free at http://webgis.co.okaloosa.fl.us/okaloosagis/viewer.htm.

Okeechobee County

County Clerk of the Circuit Court, 312 NW 3rd St, #155; Clerk of Circuit Court - Official Records Div, Okeechobee, FL 34972. Recording, R/E & UCC phone-863-763-2131, UCC recording phone-863-763-0239; fax-863-763-5831; 8:30AM-5PM (EST) www.clerk.co.okeechobee.fl.us
Index: All in one. Records indexed on a public use terminal back to 12/1/70. Office personnel or visitors may perform searches. No record searches by phone. General index search fee $2.00 per year per name. Copy fee $1.00 per page. Cert fee- $2.00 per doc plus copy fee. Payee- Okeechobee County Clerk of Circuit Court. Office does not sell bulk data. **Online access to Real Estate, Deed, Lien, Judgment, Mortgage, Tax Deed records:** Search the statewide recording database via www.myfloridacounty.com. There is a fee to order. Also, search the Clerk of Courts Tax Deed data free at http://204.215.37.218/wb_or1/or_sch_1.asp. **Other phones:** Treasurer- 863-763-3421; Elections- 863-763-4014; Vital Records- 863-462-5819. **Property tax/Assessing**- 307 NW 5th Ave, #A, Okeechobee, FL 34972; 863-763-4422, assessor fax- 863-763-4745. (Appraiser/Auditor- 863-763-4422) http://okeechobeepa.com **Online access**- Search assessor data on the GIS site free at okeechobeepa.com/GIS/Search_F.asp?GIS. Also, search property on the private GIS site at www.emapsplus.com/FLOkeechobee/maps/.

Orange County

County Comptroller, PO Box 38; Official Records Dept., Orlando, FL 32802-0038. Recording, R/E & UCC phone-407-836-5115; fax-407-836-5120; 7:30AM-4:30PM (EST) www.occompt.com
Involved with the index of recorded documents at www.myfloridacounty.com.; fees involved to order copies. Index: All in one. Records indexed on a public use terminal back to 8/11/55. Document images veiwable when not prohibited by law from 1/1/70 to present. Some data and images from 1843-8/55 are also available. Office personnel or visitors may perform searches. General index search fee $2.00 per name per year. Office will search real estate records. Will search UCC records. Copy fee $1.00 per page; free if printed from web or self-serve at office. Cert fee- $2.00 per doc plus copy fee. Payee- Orange County Comptroller. **Online access to Real Estate, Deed, Lien records:** Real Estate, Lien, and Marriage records on the county Comptroller database are free at https://officialrecords.occompt.com/recorder/. Lending Agency data available. **Other phones:** Treasurer- 407-836-5715; Elections- 407-836-2070; Vital Records- 407-836-7155. **Property tax/Assessing**- 200 S Orange Ave #1500, Orlando, FL 33801; 407-836-2700, assessor fax- 407-836-0084. (Appraiser/Auditor- 407-836-5000) hours- 8AM-5PM **Online access**- Access appraiser records free at www.ocpafl.org/disclaimer.html; click on Record Searches; includes personal property and residential sales records. Search tax collector site free www.octaxcol.com includes tax sales. Search Property on the GIS site at www.emapsplus.com/FLorange/maps/.

Osceola County

County Clerk of the Circuit Court, 2 Courthouse Sq, #2000, Kissimmee, FL 34741-5491. Recording, R/E & UCC phone-407-742-3517, UCC recording phone-407-343-3517; fax-407-742-3534; 8:30AM-5PM; 8:30AM-4PM recording hours. (EST) www.osceolaclerk.com
Index: All in one. Records indexed on a public use terminal back to 1986. Office personnel or visitors may perform searches. Search fee $2.00 per name per year. Office will search real estate records (simple search only with payment). Office will not search UCC records or provide lien searches. Copy fee $1.00 per page. Plat copies $5.00. Cert fee- $2.00 per doc plus copy fee. Payee- Osceola County Clerk of Circuit Court. **Online access to Real Estate, Deed, Lien records:** Search recorded docs at www.myfloridacounty.com. Fees involved to order copies; save $1.50 per record by becoming a subscriber. Also, recording/land records at www.osceolaclerk.com. Click on On-Line Records Search, then Recording Records. **Other phones:** Elections- 407-742-6000; Vital Records- 407-343-2000; Tax Deeds- 407-742-3526. **Property tax/Assessing**- 2501 E Irlo Bronson Memorial Hwy, Kissimmee, FL 34744; 407-742-4000. (Appraiser/Auditor- 407-742-5000) To purchase database call 407-343-3700. Data also available on CD-ROM; Fees vary; tax roll data is $75. **Online access**- Subscription required for property appraiser records at www.osceolataxcollector.com/. Also, with registration & password, access Occ. licenses and tax collector data at www.osceolataxcollector.com. Also, search Property Assessor/GIS data free at www.emapsplus.com/FLosceola/maps/.

Palm Beach County

County Clerk of the Circuit Court, PO Box 4177, West Palm Beach, FL 33402. 561-355-2991, R/E recording phone-561-355-2932; fax-561-355-2633; 8AM-5PM (EST) www.pbcountyclerk.com
Index: All in one. Records indexed on computer back to 1968. Office personnel or visitors may perform searches. General search fee $10.00 per 1st page, $8.50 next. Copy fee $1.00 per page. Cert fee- $1.50 per doc plus copy fee. Payee- Palm Beach County Clerk of Circuit Court. CD-roms of indexes are available. **Online access to Real Estate, Deed, Lien, Judgment, Vital Statistic records:** Access clerk's recording database free at www.pbcountyclerk.com/records_home.html. Records go back to 1968; images back to 1968; includes marriage records 1979 to present. Also, search property/GIS free at www.emapsplus.com/FLpalmbeach/maps/. Also, access an index of recorded documents at www.myfloridacounty.com with fees involved to order copies. **Other phones:** Elections- 561-355-2650; Vital Records- 561-653-2350. **Property tax/Assessing**- 301 N Olive Ave, West Palm Beach, Fl 33401; 561-355-2866. (Appraiser - 561-355-2866) http://pbcgov.com/papa/ **Online**- Access property appraiser records at www.co.palm-beach.fl.us/papa/aspx/GeneralSearch/GeneralSearch.aspx. Search real estate, property tax, personal property data at www.pbcgov.com/tax/i&p_property.shtml. Also, search property/GIS free at www.emapsplus.com/FLpalmbeach/maps/. Search tax deeds at www.pbcountyclerk.com/dt_web2/or_sch_1.asp.

Pasco County

County Clerk of the Circuit Court, 38053 Live Oak Ave, Rm 205, Dade City, FL 33523-3894. 352-521-4469 or 4408, R/E recording phone-352-521-4469; 8:30AM-5PM (EST) www.pascoclerk.com
Index: All in one. Records indexed on a public use terminal back to 1975. Office personnel or visitors may perform searches. Search fee $1.50 per name. Real estate owner, mortgage, and property transfer searches available. Copy fee $1.00 per page. Cert fee- $1.50 per doc plus copy fee. Payee- Pasco County Clerk of Circuit Court. Official records may be purchased by "book" at $37.50 per book, contact Cindy Flack (352-521-4255) if there is any interest. **Online access to Real Estate, Deed, Lien, Vital Statistic records:** Several sources available. Access to real estate, liens, marriage records requires $25 annual fee plus a $50 deposit. Billing rate is $.05 per minute, $.03 evenings. For info, call 352-521-4529. Also, free access to indexes and copies at www.pascoclerk.com. Click on "records." Access an index of recorded documents at www.myfloridacounty.com. Fees involved to order copies. **Property tax/Assessing**- 352-521-4433. (Appraiser/Auditor- 352-521-4433) **Online access**- Access property appraiser data and sales data and maps free at http://appraiser.pascogov.com. Search tax records, personal property, business taxes at www.pascotaxes.com/search/prclsearch.asp.

Pinellas County

County Clerk of the Circuit Court, 315 Court St, Rm 150, Clearwater, FL 33756. 727-464-4876; fax-727-464-4383; 8AM-5PM (EST) www.pinellasclerk.org/
Index: many indices. Records indexed on a public use terminal back to 1987. Office will perform a UCC search but public must search other records themselves. Search fee $1.50. Limited real estate owner, mortgage, and property transfer searches available; book and page number must be provided. Copy fee $1.00 per page. Cert fee- $1.50 per doc plus copy fee. Payee- Pinellas County Clerk of Circuit Court. **Online access to Real Estate, Deed, Lien,**

Judgment records: Access recorded document index at www.myfloridacounty.com. Fees involved to order copies. **Property tax/Assessing**- PO Box 1957, 315 Court St, Rm 150, Clearwater, FL 33757; 727-464-3207, assessor fax- 727-464-3448. (Appraiser/Auditor- 727-464-3207) www.pcpao.org **Online access**- Assessor property records are free at www.pcpao.org. Also, search tax collector data free at https://www.pinellas.county-taxes.com/tcb/app/pt/main/. Tax deed sales lists are at www.pinellasclerk.org/tributeweb2/.

Polk County

County Clerk of the Circuit Court, PO Box 9000, Drawer CC-8, Bartow, FL 33831-9000. Recording, R/E & UCC phone-863-534-4516; fax-863-534-4008; 8AM-5PM (EST) www.polkcountyclerk.net
Index: Separate indices to search. Records indexed on computer from 1957 forward. Office personnel or visitors may perform searches. Search fee $2.00 per name per year; name searches are from 1957 to present only. Office will search real estate records. Will search UCC records. Copy fee $1.00 per page. Cert fee- $2.00 per doc plus copy fee. Payee- Clerk of Circuit Court. Bulk data available for purchase. **Online access to Real Estate, Deed, Lien, Vital Statistic records:** Search the clerk database at www.polkcountyclerk.net/RecordsSearch/disclaimer.aspx for free court records, deeds, mortgages, plats, marriages, resolutions. For copies of documents, call 863-534-4524; fee is $1.00 per page. **Other phones:** Elections- 863-534-5888; Vital Records- 863-519-7900. **Property tax/Assessing**- 255 N Wilson Ave, Barton, FL 33830; 863-534-4777, assessor fax- 863-534-4753. (Appraiser/Auditor- 863-534-4777) hours-8:30AM-5PM www.polkpa.org/ **Online access**- Access appraiser property tax, personal property, and sales data free at www.polkpa.org/CamaDisplay.aspx.

Putnam County

County Clerk of the Circuit Court, PO Box 758, Palatka, FL 32178-0758. Recording, R/E & UCC phone-386-329-0256; fax-386-329-0889; 8:30AM-5PM http://www1.putnam-fl.com/live/clkmain.asp
Index: All in one. Records indexed on a public use terminal back to 10/1983. Office personnel or visitors may perform searches. Search fee $2.00 per name. Copy fee $1.00 per page. Cert fee- $2.00 per doc plus copy fee. Payee- Putnam County Clerk of Circuit Court. Bulk data available for purchase, contact Melanie Bryan-Recording Dept at 386-329-0256 for CD-by the book or IT Dept at 386-329-0353 for raw data-ftp. **Online access to Real Estate, Deed, Lien, Mortgage records:** Access to the county clerk database requires a $400 setup fee and monthly charge of $40 plus $.05 per minute over 20 hours. Includes civil court records and real property records back to 10/1983. For info, call 904-329-0353. Also, access an index of recorded documents at www.myfloridacounty.com. Fees involved to order copies; save $1.50 per record by becoming a subscriber. **Other phones:** Elections- 386-329-0455; Vital Records- 386-329-0420. **Property tax/Assessing**- PO Box 1920, 312 Oak St, Palatka, FL 32177; 800-826-1437, 386-329-0286, assessor fax- 386-329-0447. (Appraiser/Auditor- 386-329-0286) **Online access**- Search property assessor data free on GIS site at www.emapsplus.com/FLPutnam/maps/. Also, search the online tax rolls at www.putnam-fl.com/app/disclaimer.htm. No name searching. Also, search the treasurer's tax rolls and occ. licensing at www.putnam-fl.com/txc/onlineinquiry.htm.

Santa Rosa County

County Clerk of the Circuit Court, PO Box 472, Milton, FL 32572. Recording, R/E & UCC phone-850-983-1966; fax-850-983-1991; 8AM-4:30PM (CST) http://www2.myfloridacounty.com/wps/wcm/connect/santarosaclerk
Index: All in one. Records indexed on a public use terminal back to 1982. Office personnel or visitors may perform searches. Search fee $1.00 per year. Office will not search real estate records. UCC search includes tax liens if requested. UCC search per debtor name- $1.50 per year, 5 year maximum. Copy fee $1.00 per page. Cert fee- $2.00 per doc plus copy fee. Payee- Santa Rosa County Clerk of Circuit Court. Bulk data available for purchase, indexes, official records, plats, contact Barbara Glover at 850-983-1970. **Online access to Real Estate, Deed, Lien, Marriage, Death, Judgment records:** Access to Clerk's recorded index is at http://oncoreweb.srccol.com/oncoreweb/. Or, go to www.myflorida.com where you may search the index free; fees involved to order copies or view images. **Other phones:** Treasurer- 850-983-1950; Elections-850-983-1900; Clerk of Courts-Research Dept- 850-983-1970. **Property tax/Assessing**- 850-983-1880. (Appraiser/Auditor- 850-983-1880) **Online access**- Access the appraiser property records free at www.srcpa.org/property.html or at the main Property Appraiser page at www.srcpa.org click on "Record Search". Also, search the real estate tax collector data for free at http://santarosataxcollector.governmax.com/collectmax/collect30.asp; occ. licenses at http://santarosataxcollector.governmax.com/collectmax/search_collect.asp?l_nm=occlic_bus_name&sid.

Sarasota County

County Clerk of the Circuit Court, PO Box 3079, Sarasota, FL 34230. Recording, R/E & UCC phone-941-861-7400; hours- 8:30AM-5PM (EST) www.sarasotaclerk.com
Index: All in one. Records indexed on a public use terminal back to 1983. Office personnel or visitors may perform searches. Office will search real estate records. UCC search per debtor name- $1.50 per year. Copy fee $1.00 per page. Cert fee- $1.50 per doc plus copy fee. Payee- Sarasota County Clerk of Circuit Court. **Online access to Real Estate, Deed, Lien, Vital Statistic, Marriage, Probate records:** Access Clerk of Circuit Court recordings database free at www.sarasotaclerk.com. Includes civil, criminal, and traffic court indexes. Also search indexes at www.sarasotaclerk.com. Search marriage licenses; probate also. Also, access index of recorded documents at www.myfloridacounty.com. Fees involved to order copies. **Other phones:** Elections-941-861-8600; Vital Records- 941-316-1043. **Other Online Records**- Access property appraiser data free at www.sarasotaproperty.net/search_real_property.asp; includes subdivision/condominium sales. Also, search tax collector and occ licenses at http://sarasotataxcollector.governmax.com/collectmax/collect30.asp. Search property assessor/GIS data at www.emapsplus.com/FLsarasota/maps/.

Seminole County

County Clerk of the Circuit Court, PO Box 8099, Attn: Recording Dept, Sanford, FL 32772-8099. 407-665-4336, R/E recording phone-407-665-4409; fax-407-330-7193; hours- 8AM-4:30PM (EST) www.seminoleclerk.org
Index: All in one. Records indexed on computer back to 1983. Office will perform a UCC search but public must search other records themselves. Search fee $1.00 per name per year; no title searches. Copy fee $1.00 per page. Cert fee- $2.00 per doc plus copy fee. Payee- Seminole County Clerk of Circuit Court. Bulk data available on film $25.00 per roll; contact James Paulus at 407-665-4495. **Online access to Real Estate, Deed, Lien, Marriage records:** Access the county clerk of circuit court's recordings database free at http://officialrecords.seminoleclerk.org/. **Other phones:** Elections- 407-708-7700. **Property tax/Assessing**- 1101 E 1st St, PO Box 630 (32772), Sanford, FL 32771; 407-665-1000, assessor fax- 407-665-7603. (Appraiser/Auditor- 407-665-7502) hours-8:30AM-5PM www.seminoletax.org/ **Online access**- Property appraisal tax records free at www.scpafl.org/scpaweb05/index.jsp also a map search. Access property and real estate tax data free at http://seminoletax.org/Tax/TaxSearch.shtml. Also, GIS free at www.emapsplus.com/FLseminole/maps/. Search tax collector personal property and real estate records free at http://seminoletax.org.

St. Johns County

County Clerk of the Circuit Court, 4010 Lewis Speedway, St. Augustine, FL 32095. 904-819-3600, R/E recording phone-904-819-3632; fax-904-819-3662; 8AM-5PM (No recording after 4:15PM). (EST) www.co.st-johns.fl.us
Index: All in one. Records indexed on a public use terminal back to 1990. Office personnel or visitors may perform searches. Search fee $1.00 per name. Office will search real estate records. Will search UCC records. UCC search per debtor name- $1.50 per name per year; tax liens included if requested. Copy fee $1.00 per page. Cert fee- $2.00 per doc plus copy fee. Payee- St. Johns County Clerk of Circuit Court. **Online access to Real Estate, Deed, Lien, Probate, UCC, Judgment records:** Access to the county Clerk of Circuit Court recording database is free at www.clk.co.st-johns.fl.us/ and Click on Recording. Search by name, parcel ID, instrument type. Includes civil and probate records, UCCs. Access an index of recorded documents at www.myfloridacounty.com. Fees involved to order copies; save $1.50 per record by becoming a subscriber. **Other phones:** Elections-904-823-2238; Vital Records- 904-825-5055; Tax Collector- 904-209-2250. **Property tax/Assessing**-4030 Lewis Speedway, #203, St. Augustine, Florida 32084; 904-827-5500, assessor fax- 904-827-5580. (Appraiser/Auditor- 904-827-5560) www.sjcpa.us **Online access**- Access property appraiser data free at www.sjcpa.us/Disclaimer%20for%20as400.htm. Also, search Property/GIS site free at www.emapsplus.com/FLstjohns/maps/.

St. Lucie County

County Clerk of the Circuit Court, PO Box 700, Fort Pierce, FL 34954. Recording, R/E & UCC phone-772-462-6928, UCC recording phone-772-462-6927; fax-772-462-1283; hours - 8AM-5PM (EST) www.slcclerkofcourt.com/
Index: All in one. Records indexed on a public use terminal back to 1992. Office personnel or visitors may perform searches. General index search fee $1.00 per year. Copy fee $1.00 per page.Real estate copy-$1.50 per page. Cert fee- $1.50 per doc plus copy fee. Payee- St. Lucie County Clerk of Circuit Court. **Online access to Real Estate, Deed, Lien, Marriage, Mortgage, Fictitious Name records:** Access clerk of circuit courts database of recordings free at http://public.slcclerkofcourt.com. Business searching is also available for a small fee. Access an index of recorded documents at www.myfloridacounty.com. Fees involved to order copies. **Other phones:** Treasurer- 772-462-1476; Vital Records- 772-462-3800. **Property tax/Assessing**- 2300 Virginia Ave, Ft. Pierce, FL 34982; 772-462-1650. (Appraiser/Auditor- 772-462-1000) **Online access**- Access property appraiser records free at www.paslc.org. Click on "Real estate" or "Personal property" for search options. Also, search 3 tax rolls- Real Estate, Tangibles, business- for free at https://www.stlucie.county-taxes.com/tcb/app/main/home. Also, earch assessor property data free at www.emapsplus.com/FLStLucie/maps/.

Sumter County

County Clerk of the Circuit Court, 209 N Florida St, Rm 106, Bushnell, FL 33513. 352-793-0215; fax-352-793-0233; hours- 8:30AM-5PM (EST) www.sumterclerk.com
Index: All in one. Records indexed on a public use terminal back to 1979. Office will perform a UCC search but public must search other records themselves. Search fee $1.50 per name per year. Copy fee $1.00 per page. Cert fee- $1.50 per page plus copy fee. Payee- Sumter County Clerk of Circuit Court. Some records available on CD-roms, contact Brian Berry. **Online access to Real Estate, Deed, Lien, Mortgage records:** Access an index of recorded documents at www.myfloridacounty.com. Fees involved to order copies; save $1.50 per record by

becoming a subscriber. **Property tax/Assessing**- 209 N Florida St, Bushnell, FL 33513; 352-793-0210, assessor fax- 352-793-0248. (Appraiser/Auditor- 352-793-0210) hours- 8AM-5PM **Online access**- Access county property assessor data free at http://qpublic.net/sumter/search1.html. Also, search tax collector and occupational licenses for free at http://sumtertaxcollector.governmax.com/collectmax/collect30.asp. Also, tax deed, foreclosures and other sales lists are available in pdf format.

Suwannee County

County Clerk of the Circuit Court, 200 S Ohio Ave, Live Oak, FL 32064. 386-362-0554; fax-386-362-0532; 8AM-4:15PM (EST) www.suwclerk.org
Index: All in one. Records indexed on a public use terminal back to 1/1/1983. Office personnel or visitors may perform searches. General search fee $1.00 per year per name. Office will not search real estate records. Tax liens not included in UCC search. UCC search per debtor name- $1.50 per name per year. Copy fee $1.00 per page. Cert fee- $2.00 per doc plus copy fee. Payee- Suwannee County Clerk of Circuit Court. **Online access to Real Estate, Deed, Lien, UCC, Mortgage, Marriage, Death records:** Access of the county clerk of circuit database index is free at www.suwclerk.org. This directs you to the statewide database; search index free; subscription required for documents. Also, document index for variety of recordings free at http://151.213.249.227/oncoreweb/ which includes Official Records for the County. **Other phones:** Treasurer- 386-362-0545; Elections- 386-362-2616; Vital Records- 386-362-0534. **Property tax/Assessing**- Property Appraiser, 215 Pine Ave SW #B, Live Oak, FL 32064; 386-362-1385, assessor fax- 386-364-3531. (Appraiser/Auditor- 386-362-1385) hours- 8:30AM-5PM www.suwanneepa.com/ **Online access**- Search property assessor data free at http://suwanneepa.com/GIS/Search_F.asp. Also, search on the GIS-mapping site at www.emapsplus.com/FLSuwannee/maps/. Also, search the tax collector database free at www.suwanneecountytax.com/ also register to view tax deed sale records.

Taylor County

County Clerk of the Circuit Court, PO Box 620, Perry, FL 32348. Recording, R/E & UCC phone-850-838-3506; fax-850-223-1836; 8AM-5PM (EST) http://www2.myfloridacounty.com/wps/wcm/connect/taylorclerk
Index: All in one. Records indexed on a public use terminal back to 1989. Office personnel or visitors may perform searches. Search fee $1.50 per year per name. Office will search real estate records. Will search UCC records. Copy fee $1.00 per page. Cert fee- $1.50 per doc plus copy fee. Payee- Taylor County Clerk of Circuit Court. Bulk data available for purchase on CD (indexes and official records); contact Gary Knowles 800-838-3506x113. **Online access to Real Estate, Deed, Lien, Judgment, Voter Registration records:** Access an index of recorded documents at www.myfloridacounty.com. Fees involved to order copies; save $1.50 per record by becoming a subscriber. Also, check voter registration for names free at https://www.voterfocus.com/vfvoters.php?county=taylor. **Other phones:** Elections- 850-838-3515; Vital Records- 850-838-3506; Tax Collector- 850-838-3517. **Property tax/Assessing**- 108 N Jefferson St, Ste 2, Perry, FL 32347; 850-838-3511. (Appraiser/Auditor- 850-838-3511) **Online**- Access property/GIS search free athttp://gis.taylorcountygov.com/public/default.aspx. Tax collector tax roll data free at http://fl-taylor-taxcollector.governmax.com/collectmax/collect30.asp

Union County

County Clerk of the Circuit Court, State Rd 100, Rm 103; Courthouse, Lake Butler, FL 32054. 386-496-3711; fax-386-496-1718; 8AM-5PM (EST) www.myfloridacounty.com
Index: All in one. Records indexed on a public use terminal back to 1983. Office personnel or visitors may perform searches. Search fee $1.50 per name, per year. Real estate owner, mortgage, and property transfer searches available. UCC search includes tax liens. Copy fee $1.00 per page. Cert fee- $2.00 per doc plus copy fee. Payee- Union County Clerk of Circuit Court. **Online access to Real Estate, Deed, Lien, Mortgage records:** Access an index of recorded documents at www.myfloridacounty.com. Fees involved to order copies; save $1.50 per record by becoming a subscriber. **Other phones:** Treasurer- 386-496-0099; Elections- 386-496-2236. **Property tax/Assessing**- 55 W Main, Rm 108 386-496-3331, assessor fax- 386-496-1842. (Appraiser/Auditor- 386-496-3431) http://unioncountytaxcollector.com **Online access**- Access assessor's records free at www.qpublic.net/union/search.html. Check tax records free at http://unioncountytaxcollector.com; click on "Tax Record Search" to search by name, parcel number, or address. Search property sales free at http://union.floridapa.com/GIS/Search_F.asp?SalesReport. Also, search the GIS-mapping site for assessor property data free at http://union.floridapa.com/GIS/Search_F.asp?GIS or at www.emapsplus.com/FLUnion/maps/.

Volusia County

County Clerk of the Circuit Court, PO Box 6043, Deland, FL 32721. Recording, R/E & UCC phone-386-736-5912; fax-386-740-5197; 8AM-4:30PM (EST) www.clerk.org/index.html
A private site has previous 2 weeks real estate, marriage, divorce records at http://extra.orlandosentinel.com/publicrecords/search.asp. Index: All in one. Records indexed on a public use terminal back to 1990. Only the public may search. Copy fee $1.00 per page. Cert fee- $2.00 per doc plus copy fee. Payee- Volusia County Clerk of Circuit Court. **Online access to Real Estate, Deed, Lien, Vital Statistic, Mortgage records:** Recording data is free at www.clerk.org. Click on Search Public Records. Recorder indices go back to 1990. Arrest ledger, tax deed sales and citations also at this website. County also offers full real estate, lien, court and vital records on a commercial site; set up is $100 with $25 monthly. For info, contact clerk. Also, access index of recorded documents at www.myfloridacounty.com. Fees involved to order copies; save $1.50 per record by becoming a subscriber. **Other phones:** Elections- 386-736-5930; Vital Records- 386-274-0615. **Property tax/Assessing**- 123 W Indiana, Deland, FL 32724; 386-736-5901, assessor fax- 386-943-7047. (Appraiser/Auditor- 386-736-5901) **Online access**- Access property search free at http://webserver.vcgov.org/vc_search.html. Also search property assessor/GIS free at www.emapsplus.com/FLVolusia/maps/.

Wakulla County

County Clerk of the Circuit Court, 3056 Crawfordville Hwy; Wakulla County Court House, Crawfordville, FL 32327. 850-926-0905, R/E recording phone-850-926-0326; fax-850-926-0938; 8AM-5PM (EST) www.wakullaclerk.com/
Index: All in one. Records indexed on a public use terminal back to 1990. Only the public may search. Copy fee $1.00 per page. Cert fee- $2.00 per doc plus copy fee. Payee- Wakulla County Clerk of Circuit Court. **Online access to Real Estate, Lien, Deed, Death, Marriage, UCC, Judgment records:** Access an index of recorded docs at www.wakullaclerk.com/oncoreweb/. Also, the Clerk's office has plat images online free at www.wakullaclerk.com/plats.asp Also, access index of recorded documents at www.myfloridacounty.com. Fees involved to order copies; save $1.50 per record by becoming a subscriber. **Other phones:** Treasurer- 850-926-3371. **Property tax/Assessing**- PO Box 26, 3115-A Crawfordville Hwy, Crawfordville, FL 32326; 850-926-0500, assessor fax- 850-926-6367. (Appraiser/Auditor- 850-926-3271) **Online access**- Access assessor property data free at www.qpublic.net/wakulla/search1.html. Access clerk of court's foreclosure monthly lists and Tax Deed Sales free at www.wakullaclerk.com/index.asp. Click on Link in Quick Links Section. Search tax collector data free at www.wakullacountytaxcollector.com/SearchSelect.aspx.

Walton County

County Clerk of the Circuit Court, PO Box 1260, De Funiak Springs, FL 32433. Recording, R/E & UCC phone-850-892-8115; fax-850-892-8523; 8AM-4:30PM (CST) http://clerkofcourts.co.walton.fl.us
Index: All in one. Records indexed on a public use terminal back to 1976. Office personnel or visitors may perform searches. Search fee $1.50 per year + $1.00 per name. Office will search real estate and UCC records. Copy fee $1.00 per page. Cert fee- $1.50 per doc plus copy fee. Payee- Walton County Clerk of Circuit Court. Bulk data available on CD's for purchase, contact Kim Anderson. **Online access to Real Estate, Grantor/Grantee, Deed, Lien, Vital Statistic records:** Records back to 1/1976 on the County Clerk database are free at http://clerkofcourts.co.wa lton.fl.us/ORSearch/. **Other phones:** Treasurer- 850-892-8121; Elections- 850-892-8112; Vital Records- 850-892-8015. **Property tax/Assessing**- 850-892-8121. (Appraiser/Auditor- 850-892-8123) **Online access**- Property appraiser records are free at www.qpublic.net/walton/search1.html. Also, search tax collector data free at http://fl-walton-taxcollector.governmaxa.com/collectmax/collect30.asp.

Washington County

County Clerk of the Circuit Court, PO Box 647, Chipley, FL 32428. Recording, R/E & UCC phone-850-638-6285; fax-850-638-6059; 8AM-4PM (CST) http://www2.myfloridacounty.com/wps/wcm/connect/washingtonclerk/
Index: All in one. Records indexed on a public use terminal back to 1980. Office will perform a UCC search but public must search other records themselves. UCC Search fee $2.00 per year per name. Copy fee $1.00 per page. Cert fee- $2.00 per doc plus copy fee. Payee- Washington County Clerk of Circuit Court. **Online access to Real Estate, Deed, Lien, Judgment records:** Access the index of recorded docs at www.mywashingtoncounty.com, via MyFlorida County.com; fees involved to order copies; save $1.50 per record by becoming a subscriber. Also, tax deed and foreclosures lists in pdf format can be downloaded from the clerk's website. **Other phones:** Elections- 850-638-6230; Tax Collector- 850-638-6276. **Property tax/Assessing**- PO Box 695, Chipley, FL 32428; 850-638-6275. (Appraiser/Auditor- 850-638-6205) **Online access**- Search the property appraiser sales and tax records for free at www.qpublic.net/washington/index-pa-search.html. Also, search the tax collector records for free at www.qpublic.net/wctc/index-tc-search.html..

Florida County Locator

You will usually be able to find the city name in the City/County Cross Reference below. In that case, it is a simple matter to determine the county from the cross reference. However, only the official US Postal Service city names are included in this index. There are an additional 40,000 place names that people use in their addresses. Therefore, we have also included a ZIP/City Cross Reference immediately following the City/County Cross Reference.

If you know the ZIP Code but the city name does not appear in the City/County Cross Reference index, look up the ZIP Code in the ZIP/City Cross Reference, find the city name, then look up the city name in the City/County Cross Reference. For example, you want to know the county for an address of Menands, NY 12204. There is no "Menands" in the City/County Cross Reference. The ZIP/City Cross Reference shows that ZIP Codes 12201-12288 are for the city of Albany. Looking back in the City/County Cross Reference, Albany is in Albany County.

Florida City/County Cross Reference

ABMPS Dade
ALACHUA Alachua
ALFORD (32420) Jackson(95), Washington(4)
ALTAMONTE SPRINGS Seminole
ALTHA Calhoun
ALTOONA (32702) Lake(83), Marion(16)
ALTURAS Polk
ALVA (33920) Lee(85), Hendry(14)
ANNA MARIA Manatee
ANTHONY Marion
APALACHICOLA Franklin
APOLLO BEACH Hillsborough
APOPKA (32703) Orange(79), Seminole(20)
APOPKA Orange
ARCADIA De Soto
ARCHER (32618) Alachua(73), Levy(26)
ARGYLE Walton
ARIPEKA Pasco
ASTATULA Lake
ASTOR (32102) Lake(83), Volusia(16)
ATLANTIC BEACH Duval
AUBURNDALE Polk
AVON PARK (33825) Highlands(98), Polk(1)
AVON PARK Highlands
BABSON PARK Polk
BAGDAD Santa Rosa
BAKER (32531) Okaloosa(97), Santa Rosa(2)
BALM Hillsborough
BARBERVILLE Volusia
BARTOW Polk
BASCOM Jackson
BAY PINES Pinellas
BELL Gilchrist
BELLE GLADE Palm Beach
BELLEAIR BEACH Pinellas
BELLEAIR SHORES Pinellas
BELLEVIEW Marion
BEVERLY HILLS Citrus
BIG PINE KEY Monroe
BLOUNTSTOWN Calhoun
BOCA GRANDE Lee
BOCA RATON Palm Beach
BOKEELIA Lee
BONIFAY (32425) Holmes(90), Washington(9)
BONITA SPRINGS (34134) Lee(89), Collier(10)
BONITA SPRINGS Lee
BOSTWICK Putnam
BOWLING GREEN (33834) Hardee(75), Manatee(18), Polk(6)
BOYNTON BEACH Palm Beach
BRADENTON Manatee
BRADENTON BEACH Manatee
BRADLEY Polk
BRANDON Hillsborough
BRANFORD (32008) Suwannee(66), Gilchrist(25), Lafayette(6), Dixie(1)
BRISTOL Liberty
BRONSON Levy
BROOKER (32622) Bradford(82), Alachua(17)
BROOKSVILLE Hernando
BROOKSVILLE Pasco
BRYANT Palm Beach
BRYCEVILLE Nassau
BUNNELL Flagler
BUSHNELL Sumter
CALLAHAN Nassau
CAMPBELLTON Jackson
CANAL POINT (33438) Palm Beach(62), Martin(37)
CANAL POINT Palm Beach
CANDLER Marion
CANTONMENT Escambia
CAPE CANAVERAL Brevard
CAPE CORAL Lee
CAPTIVA Lee
CARRABELLE Franklin
CARYVILLE (32427) Washington(93), Holmes(6)
CASSADAGA Volusia
CASSELBERRY Seminole
CEDAR KEY Levy
CENTER HILL Sumter
CENTURY Escambia
CHATTAHOOCHEE Gadsden
CHIEFLAND Levy
CHIPLEY Washington
CHOKOLOSKEE Collier
CHRISTMAS Orange
CITRA Marion
CLARCONA Orange
CLARKSVILLE Calhoun
CLEARWATER Pinellas
CLEARWATER BEACH Pinellas
CLERMONT (34714) Lake(95), Polk(4)
CLERMONT Lake
CLEWISTON (33440) Hendry(98), Palm Beach(1)
COCOA Brevard
COCOA BEACH Brevard
COLEMAN Sumter
COPELAND Collier
CORTEZ Manatee
COTTONDALE (32431) Jackson(79), Washington(20)
CRAWFORDVILLE Wakulla
CRESCENT CITY Putnam
CRESTVIEW (32539) Okaloosa(89), Walton(10)
CRESTVIEW Okaloosa
CROSS CITY Dixie
CRYSTAL BEACH Pinellas
CRYSTAL RIVER Citrus
CRYSTAL SPRINGS Pasco
CYPRESS Jackson
DADE CITY (33523) Pasco(83), Hernando(16)
DADE CITY Pasco
DANIA Broward
DAVENPORT (33896) Polk(89), Osceola(10)
DAVENPORT Polk
DAY Lafayette
DAYTONA BEACH Volusia
DE LEON SPRINGS Volusia
DEBARY Volusia
DEERFIELD BEACH Broward
DEFUNIAK SPRINGS Walton
DELAND (32720) Volusia(86), Lake(13)
DELAND Volusia
DELRAY BEACH Palm Beach
DELTONA Volusia
DESTIN Okaloosa
DOCTORS INLET Clay
DOVER Hillsborough
DUNDEE Polk
DUNEDIN Pinellas
DUNNELLON (34431) Marion(81), Levy(18)
DUNNELLON Citrus
DUNNELLON Marion
DURANT Hillsborough
EAGLE LAKE Polk
EARLETON Alachua
EAST PALATKA Putnam
EASTLAKE WEIR Marion
EASTPOINT Franklin
EATON PARK Polk
EBRO (32437) Washington(88), Bay(11)
EDGEWATER Volusia
EGLIN AFB Okaloosa
ELFERS Pasco
ELKTON St. Johns
ELLENTON Manatee
ENGLEWOOD (34223) Sarasota(75), Charlotte(24)
ENGLEWOOD Charlotte
ENGLEWOOD Sarasota
ESTERO Lee
EUSTIS Lake
EVERGLADES CITY Collier
EVINSTON Alachua
FAIRFIELD Marion
FEDHAVEN Polk
FELDA Hendry
FELLSMERE Indian River
FERNANDINA BEACH Nassau
FERNDALE Lake
FLAGLER BEACH Flagler
FLEMING ISLAND Clay
FLORAHOME Putnam
FLORAL CITY Citrus
FORT LAUDERDALE Broward
FORT MC COY Marion
FORT MEADE Polk
FORT MYERS (33917) Lee(98), Charlotte(1)
FORT MYERS Lee
FORT MYERS BEACH Lee
FORT OGDEN De Soto
FORT PIERCE St. Lucie
FORT WALTON BEACH Okaloosa
FORT WHITE Columbia
FOUNTAIN Bay
FREEPORT Walton
FROSTPROOF Polk
FRUITLAND PARK Lake
GAINESVILLE Alachua
GENEVA Seminole
GEORGETOWN Putnam
GIBSONTON Hillsborough
GLEN SAINT MARY Baker
GLENWOOD Volusia
GOLDENROD Seminole
GONZALEZ Escambia
GOODLAND Collier
GOTHA Orange
GRACEVILLE (32440) Jackson(86), Holmes(13)
GRAHAM Bradford
GRAND ISLAND Lake
GRAND RIDGE (32442) Jackson(90), . Calhoun(9)
GRANDIN Putnam
GRANT Brevard
GREEN COVE SPRINGS (32043) Clay(98), Putnam(1)
GREENSBORO Gadsden
GREENVILLE (32331) Madison(58), Jefferson(22), Taylor(19)
GREENWOOD Jackson
GRETNA Gadsden
GROVELAND Lake
GULF BREEZE (32561) Santa Rosa(54), Escambia(45)
GULF BREEZE Santa Rosa
GULF HAMMOCK Levy
HAINES CITY Polk
HALLANDALE Broward
HAMPTON (32044) Bradford(93), Alachua(6)
HAROLD Santa Rosa
HASTINGS St. Johns
HAVANA Gadsden
HAWTHORNE (32640) Alachua(58), Putnam(41)
HERNANDO Citrus
HIALEAH Dade
HIGH SPRINGS (32643) Alachua(61), Gilchrist(27), Columbia(10)
HIGH SPRINGS Alachua
HIGHLAND CITY Polk
HILLIARD Nassau
HOBE SOUND Martin
HOLDER Citrus
HOLIDAY Pasco
HOLLISTER Putnam
HOLLYWOOD Broward
HOLMES BEACH Manatee
HOLT (32564) Santa Rosa(87), Okaloosa(12)
HOMELAND Polk
HOMESTEAD Dade
HOMOSASSA Citrus
HOMOSASSA SPRINGS Citrus
HORSESHOE BEACH Dixie
HOSFORD Liberty
HOWEY IN THE HILLS Lake
HUDSON Pasco
HURLBURT FIELD Okaloosa
IMMOKALEE (34142) Collier(96), Lee(1), Hendry(1)
IMMOKALEE Collier

INDIALANTIC Brevard
INDIAN LAKE ESTATES Polk
INDIAN ROCKS BEACH Pinellas
INDIANTOWN Martin
INGLIS (34449) Levy(92), Citrus(7)
INTERCESSION CITY Osceola
INTERLACHEN Putnam
INVERNESS Citrus
ISLAMORADA Monroe
ISLAND GROVE Alachua
ISTACHATTA Hernando
JACKSONVILLE (32234) Duval(72), Clay(23), Nassau(3)
JACKSONVILLE Duval
JACKSONVILLE St. Johns
JACKSONVILLE BEACH Duval
JASPER Hamilton
JAY Santa Rosa
JENNINGS Hamilton
JENSEN BEACH Martin
JUPITER (33478) Palm Beach(93), Martin(6)
JUPITER Palm Beach
KATHLEEN (33849) Polk(93), Pasco(6)
KENANSVILLE Osceola
KEY BISCAYNE Dade
KEY COLONY BEACH Monroe
KEY LARGO Monroe
KEY WEST Monroe
KEYSTONE HEIGHTS (32656) Clay(83), Bradford(16)
KILLARNEY Orange
KINARD Calhoun
KISSIMMEE (34747) Osceola(98), Orange(1)
KISSIMMEE (34759) Polk(81), Osceola(18)
KISSIMMEE Osceola
LA CROSSE Alachua
LABELLE (33935) Hendry(82), Glades(17)
LABELLE Hendry
LACOOCHEE Pasco
LADY LAKE (32159) Lake(73), Sumter(26)
LADY LAKE (32162) Sumter(66), Marion(33)
LADY LAKE Lake
LAKE ALFRED Polk
LAKE BUTLER (32054) Union(88), Bradford(11)
LAKE CITY (32055) Columbia(97), Suwannee(2)
LAKE CITY Columbia
LAKE COMO Putnam
LAKE GENEVA Clay
LAKE HAMILTON Polk
LAKE HARBOR Palm Beach
LAKE HELEN Volusia
LAKE MARY Seminole
LAKE MONROE Seminole
LAKE PANASOFFKEE Sumter
LAKE PLACID Highlands
LAKE WALES Polk
LAKE WORTH Palm Beach
LAKELAND (33810) Polk(98), Hillsborough(1)
LAKELAND Polk
LAMONT (32336) Jefferson(65), Madison(19), Taylor(15)
LANARK VILLAGE Franklin
LAND O LAKES Pasco
LARGO Pinellas
LAUREL Sarasota
LAUREL HILL (32567) Walton(66), Okaloosa(33)
LAWTEY (32058) Bradford(96), Union(3)
LECANTO Citrus
LEE Madison
LEESBURG Lake
LEHIGH ACRES Lee
LITHIA (33547) Hillsborough(97), Polk(2)
LIVE OAK Suwannee
LLOYD Jefferson
LOCHLOOSA Alachua
LONG KEY Monroe
LONGBOAT KEY (34228) Sarasota(62), Manatee(37)
LONGWOOD Seminole
LORIDA Highlands
LOUGHMAN Polk
LOWELL Marion
LOXAHATCHEE Palm Beach
LULU Columbia
LUTZ (33559) Hillsborough(57), Pasco(42)
LYNN HAVEN Bay
MACCLENNY Baker
MAITLAND (32751) Orange(78), Seminole(21)
MAITLAND Orange
MALABAR Brevard
MALONE Jackson
MANASOTA Manatee
MANGO Hillsborough
MARATHON Monroe
MARATHON SHORES Monroe
MARCO ISLAND Collier
MARIANNA Jackson
MARY ESTHER Okaloosa
MASCOTTE Lake
MAYO Lafayette
MC ALPIN Suwannee
MC DAVID Escambia
MC INTOSH Marion
MELBOURNE Brevard
MELBOURNE BEACH Brevard
MELROSE (32666) Putnam(52), Alachua(18), Bradford(16), Clay(12)
MERRITT ISLAND Brevard
MEXICO BEACH Bay
MIAMI Dade
MIAMI BEACH Dade
MICANOPY (32667) Alachua(65), Marion(34)
MICCOSUKEE CPO Leon
MID FLORIDA Seminole
MIDDLEBURG Clay
MIDWAY Gadsden
MILLIGAN Okaloosa
MILTON Santa Rosa
MIMS (32754) Brevard(91), Volusia(8)
MINNEOLA Lake
MIRAMAR BEACH Walton
MOLINO Escambia
MONTICELLO (32344) Jefferson(98), Leon(1)
MONTICELLO Jefferson
MONTVERDE Lake
MOORE HAVEN Glades
MORRISTON (32668) Levy(81), Marion(18)
MOSSY HEAD Walton
MOUNT DORA (32757) Lake(93), Orange(6)
MOUNT DORA Lake
MOUNT DORA Seminole
MOUNT PLEASANT Gadsden
MULBERRY Polk
MURDOCK Charlotte
MYAKKA CITY Manatee
NALCREST Polk
NAPLES (34119) Collier(98), Lee(1)
NAPLES Collier
NEPTUNE BEACH Duval
NEW PORT RICHEY Pasco
NEW SMYRNA BEACH Volusia
NEWBERRY (32669) Alachua(79), Gilchrist(18), Levy(2)
NICEVILLE (32578) Okaloosa(92), Walton(7)
NICEVILLE Okaloosa
NICHOLS Polk
NOBLETON Hernando
NOCATEE De Soto
NOKOMIS Sarasota
NOMA Holmes
NORTH FORT MYERS (33917) Lee(98), Charlotte(1)
NORTH FORT MYERS Lee
NORTH PALM BEACH Palm Beach
NORTH PORT Sarasota
O BRIEN Suwannee
OAK HILL Volusia
OAKLAND Orange
OCALA Marion
OCHOPEE (34141) Collier(65), Dade(28), Monroe(5)
OCKLAWAHA Marion
OCOEE Orange
ODESSA (33556) Hillsborough(74), Pasco(25)
OKAHUMPKA Lake
OKEECHOBEE (34972) Okeechobee(98), Osceola(1)
OKEECHOBEE (34974) Okeechobee(89), Martin(3), Glades(3), Highlands(3)
OKEECHOBEE Okeechobee
OLD TOWN Dixie
OLDSMAR Pinellas
OLUSTEE Baker
ONA (33865) Hardee(97), De Soto(2)
ONECO Manatee
OPA LOCKA Dade
ORANGE CITY Volusia
ORANGE LAKE Marion
ORANGE PARK (32073) Clay(98), Duval(1)
ORANGE PARK Clay
ORANGE SPRINGS Marion
ORLANDO Brevard
ORLANDO Orange
ORMOND BEACH (32174) Volusia(98), Flagler(1)
ORMOND BEACH Volusia
OSPREY Sarasota
OSTEEN Volusia
OTTER CREEK Levy
OVERSTREET Gulf
OVIEDO Seminole
OXFORD (34484) Sumter(98), Marion(1)
OZONA Pinellas
PAHOKEE Palm Beach
PAISLEY Lake
PALATKA Putnam
PALM BAY Brevard
PALM BEACH Palm Beach
PALM BEACH GARDENS Palm Beach
PALM CITY (34990) Martin(95), St. Lucie(4)
PALM CITY Martin
PALM COAST Flagler
PALM HARBOR Pinellas
PALMDALE Glades
PALMETTO Manatee
PANACEA (32346) Wakulla(87), Franklin(12)
PANAMA CITY (32413) Bay(88), Walton(11)
PANAMA CITY Bay
PANAMA CITY BEACH (32413) Bay(88), Walton(11)
PANAMA CITY BEACH Bay
PARRISH Manatee
PATRICK A F B Brevard
PAXTON Walton
PENNEY FARMS Clay
PENSACOLA Escambia
PERRY Taylor
PIERSON Volusia
PINELAND Lee
PINELLAS PARK Pinellas
PINETTA Madison
PLACIDA Charlotte
PLANT CITY Hillsborough
PLYMOUTH Orange
POINT WASHINGTON Walton
POLK CITY Polk
POMONA PARK Putnam
POMPANO BEACH Broward
PONCE DE LEON (32455) Holmes(83), Walton(16)
PONTE VEDRA BEACH St. Johns
PORT CHARLOTTE Charlotte
PORT ORANGE Volusia
PORT RICHEY Pasco
PORT SAINT JOE (32456) Gulf(88), Bay(11)
PORT SAINT JOE Gulf
PORT SAINT LUCIE St. Lucie
PORT SALERNO Martin
PUNTA GORDA (33955) Charlotte(82), Lee(17)
PUNTA GORDA Charlotte
PUTNAM HALL Putnam
QUINCY Gadsden
RAIFORD (32083) Union(77), Bradford(22)
RAIFORD Union
REDDICK Marion
RIVER RANCH Polk
RIVERVIEW Hillsborough
ROCKLEDGE Brevard
ROSELAND Indian River
ROSEMARY BEACH (32461) Bay(50), Walton(50)
ROTONDA WEST Charlotte
RUSKIN Hillsborough
SAFETY HARBOR Pinellas
SAINT AUGUSTINE St. Johns
SAINT CLOUD Osceola
SAINT JAMES CITY Lee
SAINT LEO Pasco
SAINT MARKS Wakulla
SAINT PETERSBURG Pinellas
SALEM Taylor
SAN ANTONIO Pasco
SAN MATEO Putnam
SANDERSON Baker
SANFORD Seminole
SANIBEL Lee
SANTA ROSA BEACH Walton
SARASOTA (34243) Manatee(85), Sarasota(14)
SARASOTA Sarasota
SATELLITE BEACH Brevard
SATSUMA Putnam
SCOTTSMOOR Brevard
SEBASTIAN Brevard
SEBASTIAN Indian River
SEBRING Highlands
SEFFNER Hillsborough
SEMINOLE Pinellas
SEVILLE Volusia
SHADY GROVE Taylor
SHALIMAR Okaloosa
SHARPES Brevard
SILVER SPRINGS Marion
SNEADS Jackson
SOPCHOPPY Wakulla
SORRENTO Lake
SOUTH BAY Palm Beach
SOUTH FLORIDA Broward
SPARR Marion
SPRING HILL Hernando
STARKE (32091) Bradford(89), Clay(10)
STEINHATCHEE (32359) Dixie(62), Taylor(37)
STUART Martin
SUGARLOAF SHORES Monroe
SUMATRA Liberty
SUMMERFIELD Marion
SUMMERLAND KEY Monroe
SUMTERVILLE Sumter
SUN CITY Hillsborough
SUN CITY CENTER Hillsborough
SUNNYSIDE (32461) Bay(50), Walton(50)
SUWANNEE Dixie
SYDNEY Hillsborough
TALLAHASSEE Leon
TALLEVAST Manatee
TAMPA Hillsborough
TANGERINE Orange

TARPON SPRINGS Pinellas
TAVARES Lake
TAVERNIER Monroe
TELOGIA Liberty
TERRA CEIA Manatee
THONOTOSASSA Hillsborough
TITUSVILLE Brevard
TRENTON (32693) Gilchrist(64), Levy(35)
TRILBY Pasco
UMATILLA (32784) Lake(68), Marion(31)
VALPARAISO Okaloosa
VALRICO Hillsborough
VENICE Sarasota
VENUS (33960) Highlands(86), Glades(13)
VERNON (32462) Washington(71), Bay(17), Walton(10)
VERO BEACH Indian River
WABASSO Indian River
WACISSA Jefferson
WAKULLA SPRINGS Leon
WALDO (32694) Alachua(96), Bradford(3)
WAUCHULA Hardee
WAUSAU Washington
WAVERLY Polk
WEBSTER (33597) Sumter(84), Hernando(15)
WEIRSDALE (32195) Marion(83), Lake(16)
WELAKA Putnam
WELLBORN (32094) Suwannee(94), Columbia(5)
WEST PALM BEACH Palm Beach
WESTON Broward
WESTVILLE (32464) Holmes(63), Walton(36)
WEWAHITCHKA Calhoun
WEWAHITCHKA Gulf
WHITE SPRINGS (32096) Hamilton(52), Columbia(41), Suwannee(6)
WILDWOOD Sumter
WILLISTON (32696) Levy(91), Marion(8)
WIMAUMA (33598) Hillsborough(96), Manatee(3)
WINDERMERE Orange
WINTER BEACH Indian River
WINTER GARDEN (34787) Orange(96), Lake(3)
WINTER GARDEN Orange
WINTER HAVEN Polk
WINTER PARK (32792) Orange(68), Seminole(31)
WINTER PARK Orange
WINTER SPRINGS Seminole
WOODVILLE Leon
WORTHINGTON SPRINGS Union
YALAHA Lake
YANKEETOWN Levy
YOUNGSTOWN (32466) Bay(95), Washington(3), Calhoun(1)
YULEE Nassau
ZELLWOOD Orange
ZEPHYRHILLS (33540) Pasco(98), Hillsborough(1)
ZEPHYRHILLS Pasco
ZOLFO SPRINGS Hardee

Florida ZIP/City Cross Reference

32003-32003 ORANGE PARK
32004-32004 PONTE VEDRA BEACH
32006-32006 FLEMING ISLAND
32007-32007 BOSTWICK
32008-32008 BRANFORD
32009-32009 BRYCEVILLE
32011-32011 CALLAHAN
32013-32013 DAY
32024-32025 LAKE CITY
32026-32026 RAIFORD
32030-32030 DOCTORS INLET
32033-32033 ELKTON
32034-32035 FERNANDINA BEACH
32038-32038 FORT WHITE
32040-32040 GLEN SAINT MARY
32041-32041 YULEE
32042-32042 GRAHAM
32043-32043 GREEN COVE SPRINGS
32044-32044 HAMPTON
32046-32046 HILLIARD
32050-32050 MIDDLEBURG
32052-32052 JASPER
32053-32053 JENNINGS
32054-32054 LAKE BUTLER
32055-32056 LAKE CITY
32058-32058 LAWTEY
32059-32059 LEE
32060-32060 LIVE OAK
32061-32061 LULU
32062-32062 MC ALPIN
32063-32063 MACCLENNY
32064-32064 LIVE OAK
32065-32065 ORANGE PARK
32066-32066 MAYO
32067-32067 ORANGE PARK
32068-32068 MIDDLEBURG
32071-32071 O BRIEN
32072-32072 OLUSTEE
32073-32073 ORANGE PARK
32079-32079 PENNEY FARMS
32080-32080 SAINT AUGUSTINE
32082-32082 PONTE VEDRA BEACH
32083-32083 RAIFORD
32084-32086 SAINT AUGUSTINE
32087-32087 SANDERSON
32091-32091 STARKE
32092-32092 SAINT AUGUSTINE
32094-32094 WELLBORN
32095-32095 SAINT AUGUSTINE
32096-32096 WHITE SPRINGS
32097-32097 YULEE
32099-32099 JACKSONVILLE
32100-32100 DAYTONA BEACH
32102-32102 ASTOR
32105-32105 BARBERVILLE
32110-32110 BUNNELL
32111-32111 CANDLER
32112-32112 CRESCENT CITY
32113-32113 CITRA
32114-32123 DAYTONA BEACH
32123-32123 PORT ORANGE
32124-32127 DAYTONA BEACH
32127-32127 PORT ORANGE
32128-32128 DAYTONA BEACH
32129-32129 PORT ORANGE
32130-32130 DE LEON SPRINGS
32131-32131 EAST PALATKA
32132-32132 EDGEWATER
32133-32133 EASTLAKE WEIR
32134-32134 FORT MC COY
32135-32135 PALM COAST
32136-32136 FLAGLER BEACH
32137-32137 PALM COAST
32138-32138 GRANDIN
32139-32139 GEORGETOWN
32140-32140 FLORAHOME
32141-32141 EDGEWATER
32142-32142 PALM COAST
32145-32145 HASTINGS
32147-32147 HOLLISTER
32148-32149 INTERLACHEN
32151-32151 FLAGLER BEACH
32157-32157 LAKE COMO
32158-32159 LADY LAKE
32160-32160 LAKE GENEVA
32162-32162 LADY LAKE
32164-32164 PALM COAST
32168-32170 NEW SMYRNA BEACH
32173-32176 ORMOND BEACH
32177-32178 PALATKA
32179-32179 OCKLAWAHA
32180-32180 PIERSON
32181-32181 POMONA PARK
32182-32182 ORANGE SPRINGS
32183-32183 OCKLAWAHA
32185-32185 PUTNAM HALL
32187-32187 SAN MATEO
32189-32189 SATSUMA
32190-32190 SEVILLE
32192-32192 SPARR
32193-32193 WELAKA
32195-32195 WEIRSDALE
32198-32198 DAYTONA BEACH
32200-32232 JACKSONVILLE
32233-32233 ATLANTIC BEACH
32234-32239 JACKSONVILLE
32240-32240 JACKSONVILLE BEACH
32241-32247 JACKSONVILLE
32250-32250 JACKSONVILLE BEACH
32254-32260 JACKSONVILLE
32266-32266 NEPTUNE BEACH
32267-32297 JACKSONVILLE
32301-32304 TALLAHASSEE
32305-32305 WAKULLA SPRINGS
32305-32308 TALLAHASSEE
32309-32309 MICCOSUKEE CPO
32309-32318 TALLAHASSEE
32320-32320 APALACHICOLA
32321-32321 BRISTOL
32322-32322 CARRABELLE
32323-32323 LANARK VILLAGE
32324-32324 CHATTAHOOCHEE
32326-32327 CRAWFORDVILLE
32328-32328 EASTPOINT
32329-32329 APALACHICOLA
32330-32330 GREENSBORO
32331-32331 GREENVILLE
32332-32332 GRETNA
32333-32333 HAVANA
32334-32334 HOSFORD
32335-32335 SUMATRA
32336-32336 LAMONT
32337-32337 LLOYD
32340-32341 MADISON
32343-32343 MIDWAY
32344-32345 MONTICELLO
32346-32346 PANACEA
32347-32348 PERRY
32350-32350 PINETTA
32351-32351 QUINCY
32352-32352 MOUNT PLEASANT
32352-32353 QUINCY
32355-32355 SAINT MARKS
32356-32356 SALEM
32357-32357 SHADY GROVE
32358-32358 SOPCHOPPY
32359-32359 STEINHATCHEE
32360-32360 TELOGIA
32361-32361 WACISSA
32362-32362 WOODVILLE
32395-32399 TALLAHASSEE
32400-32406 PANAMA CITY
32407-32407 PANAMA CITY BEACH
32408-32409 PANAMA CITY
32410-32410 MEXICO BEACH
32411-32413 PANAMA CITY
32413-32413 PANAMA CITY BEACH
32417-32417 PANAMA CITY
32420-32420 ALFORD
32421-32421 ALTHA
32422-32422 ARGYLE
32423-32423 BASCOM
32424-32424 BLOUNTSTOWN
32425-32425 BONIFAY
32426-32426 CAMPBELLTON
32427-32427 CARYVILLE
32428-32428 CHIPLEY
32430-32430 CLARKSVILLE
32431-32431 COTTONDALE
32432-32432 CYPRESS
32433-32433 DEFUNIAK SPRINGS
32434-32434 MOSSY HEAD
32435-32435 DEFUNIAK SPRINGS
32437-32437 EBRO
32438-32438 FOUNTAIN
32439-32439 FREEPORT
32440-32440 GRACEVILLE
32442-32442 GRAND RIDGE
32443-32443 GREENWOOD
32444-32444 LYNN HAVEN
32445-32445 MALONE
32446-32448 MARIANNA
32449-32449 KINARD
32449-32449 WEWAHITCHKA
32452-32452 NOMA
32453-32453 OVERSTREET
32454-32454 POINT WASHINGTON
32455-32455 PONCE DE LEON
32456-32457 PORT SAINT JOE
32459-32459 SANTA ROSA BEACH
32460-32460 SNEADS
32461-32461 SUNNYSIDE
32461-32461 ROSEMARY BEACH
32462-32462 VERNON
32463-32463 WAUSAU
32464-32464 WESTVILLE
32465-32465 WEWAHITCHKA
32466-32466 YOUNGSTOWN
32500-32526 PENSACOLA
32530-32530 BAGDAD
32531-32531 BAKER
32533-32533 CANTONMENT
32534-32534 PENSACOLA
32535-32535 CENTURY
32536-32536 CRESTVIEW
32537-32537 MILLIGAN
32538-32538 PAXTON
32539-32539 CRESTVIEW
32540-32541 DESTIN
32542-32542 EGLIN AFB
32544-32544 HURLBURT FIELD
32547-32549 FORT WALTON BEACH
32550-32550 MIRAMAR BEACH
32559-32559 PENSACOLA
32560-32560 GONZALEZ
32561-32562 GULF BREEZE
32563-32563 HAROLD
32563-32563 GULF BREEZE
32564-32564 HOLT
32565-32565 JAY
32566-32566 GULF BREEZE
32567-32567 LAUREL HILL
32568-32568 MC DAVID
32569-32569 MARY ESTHER
32570-32572 MILTON
32573-32576 PENSACOLA
32577-32577 MOLINO
32578-32578 NICEVILLE
32579-32579 SHALIMAR
32580-32580 VALPARAISO
32581-32582 PENSACOLA
32583-32583 MILTON
32588-32588 NICEVILLE
32589-32598 PENSACOLA
32600-32614 GAINESVILLE
32615-32616 ALACHUA
32617-32617 ANTHONY
32618-32618 ARCHER
32619-32619 BELL
32621-32621 BRONSON
32622-32622 BROOKER
32625-32625 CEDAR KEY
32626-32626 CHIEFLAND
32627-32627 GAINESVILLE
32628-32628 CROSS CITY
32631-32631 EARLETON
32633-32633 EVINSTON
32634-32634 FAIRFIELD

32635-32635 GAINESVILLE
32639-32639 GULF HAMMOCK
32640-32640 HAWTHORNE
32641-32641 GAINESVILLE
32643-32643 HIGH SPRINGS
32644-32644 CHIEFLAND
32648-32648 HORSESHOE BEACH
32653-32653 GAINESVILLE
32654-32654 ISLAND GROVE
32655-32655 HIGH SPRINGS
32656-32656 KEYSTONE HEIGHTS
32658-32658 LA CROSSE
32662-32662 LOCHLOOSA
32663-32663 LOWELL
32664-32664 MC INTOSH
32666-32666 MELROSE
32667-32667 MICANOPY
32668-32668 MORRISTON
32669-32669 NEWBERRY
32680-32680 OLD TOWN
32681-32681 ORANGE LAKE
32683-32683 OTTER CREEK
32686-32686 REDDICK
32692-32692 SUWANNEE
32693-32693 TRENTON
32694-32694 WALDO
32696-32696 WILLISTON
32697-32697 WORTHINGTON SPRINGS
32701-32701 ALTAMONTE SPRINGS
32702-32702 ALTOONA
32703-32704 APOPKA
32706-32706 CASSADAGA
32707-32707 CASSELBERRY
32708-32708 WINTER SPRINGS
32709-32709 CHRISTMAS
32710-32710 CLARCONA
32712-32712 APOPKA
32713-32713 DEBARY
32714-32717 ALTAMONTE SPRINGS
32718-32718 CASSELBERRY
32719-32719 WINTER SPRINGS
32720-32721 DELAND
32722-32722 GLENWOOD
32723-32724 DELAND
32725-32725 DELTONA
32726-32727 EUSTIS
32728-32728 DELTONA
32730-32730 CASSELBERRY
32732-32732 GENEVA
32733-32733 GOLDENROD
32735-32735 GRAND ISLAND
32736-32736 EUSTIS
32738-32739 DELTONA
32744-32744 LAKE HELEN
32745-32745 MOUNT DORA
32745-32745 MID FLORIDA
32746-32746 LAKE MARY
32747-32747 LAKE MONROE
32750-32750 LONGWOOD
32751-32751 MAITLAND
32752-32752 LONGWOOD
32753-32753 DEBARY
32754-32754 MIMS
32756-32757 MOUNT DORA
32759-32759 OAK HILL
32762-32762 OVIEDO
32763-32763 ORANGE CITY
32764-32764 OSTEEN
32765-32766 OVIEDO
32767-32767 PAISLEY
32768-32768 PLYMOUTH
32771-32773 SANFORD
32774-32774 ORANGE CITY
32775-32775 SCOTTSMOOR
32776-32776 SORRENTO
32777-32777 TANGERINE
32778-32778 TAVARES
32779-32779 LONGWOOD
32780-32783 TITUSVILLE
32784-32784 UMATILLA
32789-32790 WINTER PARK
32791-32791 LONGWOOD
32792-32793 WINTER PARK
32794-32794 MAITLAND
32795-32795 LAKE MARY
32796-32796 TITUSVILLE
32798-32798 ZELLWOOD
32799-32799 MID FLORIDA
32800-32899 ORLANDO
32901-32902 MELBOURNE
32903-32903 INDIALANTIC
32904-32904 MELBOURNE
32905-32911 PALM BAY
32912-32919 MELBOURNE
32920-32920 CAPE CANAVERAL
32922-32924 COCOA
32925-32925 PATRICK A F B
32926-32927 COCOA
32931-32932 COCOA BEACH
32934-32936 MELBOURNE
32937-32937 SATELLITE BEACH
32940-32941 MELBOURNE
32948-32948 FELLSMERE
32949-32949 GRANT
32950-32950 MALABAR
32951-32951 MELBOURNE BEACH
32952-32954 MERRITT ISLAND
32955-32956 ROCKLEDGE
32957-32957 ROSELAND
32958-32958 SEBASTIAN
32959-32959 SHARPES
32960-32969 VERO BEACH
32970-32970 WABASSO
32971-32971 WINTER BEACH
32976-32978 SEBASTIAN
33001-33001 LONG KEY
33002-33002 HIALEAH
33004-33004 DANIA
33008-33009 HALLANDALE
33010-33018 HIALEAH
33019-33029 HOLLYWOOD
33030-33035 HOMESTEAD
33036-33036 ISLAMORADA
33037-33037 KEY LARGO
33039-33039 HOMESTEAD
33040-33041 KEY WEST
33042-33042 SUMMERLAND KEY
33043-33043 BIG PINE KEY
33044-33044 SUGARLOAF SHORES
33045-33045 KEY WEST
33050-33050 MARATHON
33051-33051 KEY COLONY BEACH
33052-33052 MARATHON SHORES
33054-33056 OPA LOCKA
33060-33069 POMPANO BEACH
33070-33070 TAVERNIER
33071-33077 POMPANO BEACH
33081-33081 HOLLYWOOD
33082-33082 SOUTH FLORIDA
33083-33084 HOLLYWOOD
33090-33092 HOMESTEAD
33093-33097 POMPANO BEACH
33100-33102 MIAMI
33103-33104 ABMPS
33107-33148 MIAMI
33149-33149 KEY BISCAYNE
33150-33154 MIAMI
33154-33154 MIAMI BEACH
33155-33239 MIAMI
33239-33239 MIAMI BEACH
33242-33299 MIAMI
33300-33326 FORT LAUDERDALE
33327-33327 WESTON
33327-33394 FORT LAUDERDALE
33401-33407 WEST PALM BEACH
33408-33408 NORTH PALM BEACH
33409-33410 WEST PALM BEACH
33410-33410 PALM BEACH GARDENS
33411-33422 WEST PALM BEACH
33424-33426 BOYNTON BEACH
33427-33429 BOCA RATON
33430-33430 BELLE GLADE
33431-33434 BOCA RATON
33435-33437 BOYNTON BEACH
33438-33438 CANAL POINT
33439-33439 BRYANT
33440-33440 CLEWISTON
33441-33443 DEERFIELD BEACH
33444-33448 DELRAY BEACH
33454-33454 LAKE WORTH
33455-33455 HOBE SOUND
33458-33458 JUPITER
33459-33459 LAKE HARBOR
33460-33464 LAKE WORTH
33464-33464 BOCA RATON
33465-33467 LAKE WORTH
33468-33469 JUPITER
33470-33470 LOXAHATCHEE
33471-33471 MOORE HAVEN
33474-33474 BOYNTON BEACH
33475-33475 HOBE SOUND
33476-33476 PAHOKEE
33477-33478 JUPITER
33480-33480 PALM BEACH
33481-33481 BOCA RATON
33482-33484 DELRAY BEACH
33486-33488 BOCA RATON
33491-33491 CANAL POINT
33493-33493 SOUTH BAY
33496-33499 BOCA RATON
33503-33503 BALM
33504-33504 BAY PINES
33508-33511 BRANDON
33513-33513 BUSHNELL
33514-33514 CENTER HILL
33521-33521 COLEMAN
33523-33523 DADE CITY
33524-33524 CRYSTAL SPRINGS
33525-33526 DADE CITY
33527-33527 DOVER
33530-33530 DURANT
33534-33534 GIBSONTON
33537-33537 LACOOCHEE
33538-33538 LAKE PANASOFFKEE
33539-33544 ZEPHYRHILLS
33547-33547 LITHIA
33548-33549 LUTZ
33550-33550 MANGO
33556-33556 ODESSA
33558-33559 LUTZ
33563-33567 PLANT CITY
33568-33569 RIVERVIEW
33570-33570 RUSKIN
33571-33571 SUN CITY CENTER
33572-33572 APOLLO BEACH
33573-33573 SUN CITY CENTER
33574-33574 SAINT LEO
33575-33575 RUSKIN
33576-33576 SAN ANTONIO
33583-33584 SEFFNER
33585-33585 SUMTERVILLE
33586-33586 SUN CITY
33587-33587 SYDNEY
33592-33592 THONOTOSASSA
33593-33593 TRILBY
33594-33595 VALRICO
33597-33597 WEBSTER
33598-33598 WIMAUMA
33600-33697 TAMPA
33700-33743 SAINT PETERSBURG
33744-33744 BAY PINES
33747-33747 SAINT PETERSBURG
33755-33767 CLEARWATER
33767-33767 CLEARWATER BEACH
33769-33769 CLEARWATER
33770-33771 LARGO
33772-33772 SEMINOLE
33773-33774 LARGO
33775-33776 SEMINOLE
33777-33777 LARGO
33777-33777 SEMINOLE
33778-33779 LARGO
33780-33782 PINELLAS PARK
33784-33784 SAINT PETERSBURG
33785-33785 INDIAN ROCKS BEACH
33786-33786 BELLEAIR BEACH
33801-33815 LAKELAND
33820-33820 ALTURAS
33821-33821 ARCADIA
33823-33823 AUBURNDALE
33825-33826 AVON PARK
33827-33827 BABSON PARK
33830-33831 BARTOW
33834-33834 BOWLING GREEN
33835-33835 BRADLEY
33836-33837 DAVENPORT
33838-33838 DUNDEE
33839-33839 EAGLE LAKE
33840-33840 EATON PARK
33841-33841 FORT MEADE
33842-33842 FORT OGDEN
33843-33843 FROSTPROOF
33844-33845 HAINES CITY
33846-33846 HIGHLAND CITY
33847-33847 HOMELAND
33848-33848 INTERCESSION CITY
33849-33849 KATHLEEN
33850-33850 LAKE ALFRED
33851-33851 LAKE HAMILTON
33852-33852 LAKE PLACID
33853-33853 LAKE WALES
33854-33854 FEDHAVEN
33855-33855 INDIAN LAKE ESTATES
33856-33856 NALCREST
33857-33857 LORIDA
33858-33858 LOUGHMAN
33859-33859 LAKE WALES
33860-33860 MULBERRY
33862-33862 LAKE PLACID
33863-33863 NICHOLS
33864-33864 NOCATEE
33865-33865 ONA
33867-33867 RIVER RANCH
33868-33868 POLK CITY
33870-33872 SEBRING
33873-33873 WAUCHULA
33875-33876 SEBRING
33877-33877 WAVERLY
33880-33888 WINTER HAVEN
33890-33890 ZOLFO SPRINGS
33896-33897 DAVENPORT
33898-33898 LAKE WALES
33900-33903 FORT MYERS
33903-33903 NORTH FORT MYERS
33904-33904 CAPE CORAL
33905-33908 FORT MYERS
33909-33910 CAPE CORAL
33911-33913 FORT MYERS
33914-33915 CAPE CORAL
33916-33917 FORT MYERS
33917-33917 NORTH FORT MYERS
33918-33918 FORT MYERS
33918-33918 NORTH FORT MYERS
33919-33919 FORT MYERS
33920-33920 ALVA
33921-33921 BOCA GRANDE
33922-33922 BOKEELIA
33923-33923 BONITA SPRINGS
33924-33924 CAPTIVA
33925-33925 CHOKOLOSKEE
33926-33926 COPELAND
33927-33927 PUNTA GORDA
33928-33928 ESTERO
33929-33929 EVERGLADES CITY
33930-33930 FELDA
33931-33932 FORT MYERS BEACH
33933-33933 GOODLAND
33934-33934 IMMOKALEE
33935-33935 LABELLE
33936-33936 LEHIGH ACRES
33937-33937 MARCO ISLAND
33938-33938 MURDOCK
33939-33942 NAPLES
33943-33943 OCHOPEE
33944-33944 PALMDALE
33945-33945 PINELAND
33946-33946 PLACIDA
33947-33947 ROTONDA WEST

33948-33949 PORT CHARLOTTE
33950-33951 PUNTA GORDA
33952-33954 PORT CHARLOTTE
33955-33955 PUNTA GORDA
33956-33956 SAINT JAMES CITY
33957-33957 SANIBEL
33959-33959 BONITA SPRINGS
33960-33960 VENUS
33961-33964 NAPLES
33965-33965 FORT MYERS
33969-33969 MARCO ISLAND
33970-33972 LEHIGH ACRES
33975-33975 LABELLE
33980-33981 PORT CHARLOTTE
33982-33983 PUNTA GORDA
33990-33993 CAPE CORAL
33994-33994 FORT MYERS
33999-34120 NAPLES
34133-34136 BONITA SPRINGS
34137-34137 COPELAND
34138-34138 CHOKOLOSKEE
34139-34139 EVERGLADES CITY
34140-34140 GOODLAND
34141-34141 OCHOPEE
34142-34143 IMMOKALEE
34145-34146 MARCO ISLAND
34201-34212 BRADENTON
34215-34215 CORTEZ
34216-34216 ANNA MARIA
34217-34217 BRADENTON BEACH
34218-34218 HOLMES BEACH
34219-34219 PARRISH
34220-34221 PALMETTO
34222-34222 ELLENTON
34223-34224 ENGLEWOOD
34228-34228 LONGBOAT KEY
34229-34229 OSPREY
34230-34243 SARASOTA
34250-34250 TERRA CEIA
34251-34251 MYAKKA CITY
34260-34260 MANASOTA
34264-34264 ONECO
34265-34266 ARCADIA
34267-34267 FORT OGDEN
34268-34268 NOCATEE
34269-34269 ARCADIA
34270-34270 TALLEVAST
34272-34272 LAUREL
34274-34275 NOKOMIS
34276-34278 SARASOTA
34280-34282 BRADENTON
34284-34285 VENICE
34286-34289 NORTH PORT
34292-34293 VENICE
34295-34295 ENGLEWOOD
34420-34421 BELLEVIEW
34423-34429 CRYSTAL RIVER
34430-34434 DUNNELLON
34436-34436 FLORAL CITY
34442-34442 HERNANDO
34445-34445 HOLDER
34446-34446 HOMOSASSA
34447-34447 HOMOSASSA SPRINGS
34448-34448 HOMOSASSA
34449-34449 INGLIS
34450-34453 INVERNESS
34460-34461 LECANTO
34464-34465 BEVERLY HILLS
34470-34483 OCALA
34484-34484 OXFORD
34487-34487 HOMOSASSA
34488-34489 SILVER SPRINGS
34491-34492 SUMMERFIELD
34498-34498 YANKEETOWN
34601-34605 BROOKSVILLE
34606-34608 SPRING HILL
34609-34610 BROOKSVILLE
34611-34611 SPRING HILL
34613-34614 BROOKSVILLE
34615-34630 CLEARWATER
34634-34635 BELLEAIR SHORES
34635-34635 INDIAN ROCKS BEACH
34636-34636 ISTACHATTA
34637-34639 LAND O LAKES
34640-34649 LARGO
34652-34656 NEW PORT RICHEY
34660-34660 OZONA
34661-34661 NOBLETON
34664-34666 PINELLAS PARK
34667-34667 HUDSON
34668-34668 PORT RICHEY
34669-34669 HUDSON
34673-34673 PORT RICHEY
34674-34674 HUDSON
34677-34677 OLDSMAR
34679-34679 ARIPEKA
34680-34680 ELFERS
34681-34681 CRYSTAL BEACH
34682-34685 PALM HARBOR
34688-34689 TARPON SPRINGS
34690-34692 HOLIDAY
34692-34692 TARPON SPRINGS
34695-34695 SAFETY HARBOR
34697-34698 DUNEDIN
34705-34705 ASTATULA
34711-34715 CLERMONT
34729-34729 FERNDALE
34731-34731 FRUITLAND PARK
34734-34734 GOTHA
34736-34736 GROVELAND
34737-34737 HOWEY IN THE HILLS
34739-34739 KENANSVILLE
34740-34740 KILLARNEY
34741-34747 KISSIMMEE
34748-34749 LEESBURG
34753-34753 MASCOTTE
34755-34755 MINNEOLA
34756-34756 MONTVERDE
34758-34759 KISSIMMEE
34760-34760 OAKLAND
34761-34761 OCOEE
34762-34762 OKAHUMPKA
34769-34773 SAINT CLOUD
34777-34778 WINTER GARDEN
34785-34785 WILDWOOD
34786-34786 WINDERMERE
34787-34787 WINTER GARDEN
34788-34789 LEESBURG
34797-34797 YALAHA
34945-34951 FORT PIERCE
34952-34953 PORT SAINT LUCIE
34954-34954 FORT PIERCE
34956-34956 INDIANTOWN
34957-34958 JENSEN BEACH
34972-34974 OKEECHOBEE
34979-34982 FORT PIERCE
34983-34988 PORT SAINT LUCIE
34990-34991 PALM CITY
34992-34992 PORT SALERNO
34994-34997 STUART

Georgia

General Help Numbers:

Governor's Office

203 State Capitol
Atlanta, GA 30334
www.ganet.org/governor/

404-656-1776
Fax 404-657-7332
8AM-4:30PM

Attorney General's Office

40 Capitol Square SW
Atlanta, GA 30334-1300
www.law.state.ga.us

404-656-3300
Fax 404-651- 9325
8AM-5PM

Legislative Records

State Capitol
General Assembly of Georgia
Atlanta, GA 30334
www.legis.state.ga.us

404-656-5040
Fax 404-656-5043
8:30AM-4:30PM

State Archives

Archives & History Department
5800 Jonesboro Rd.
Atlanta, GA 30260
http://sos.georgia.gov/archives/

678-364-3700
Fax 678-364-3856
8AM-4:45PM

State Specifics:

Capital:	Atlanta Fulton County
Time Zone:	EST
Number of Counties:	159
Population:	9,685,744
Web Site:	www.georgia.gov

State Agencies

Criminal Records

Georgia Bureau of Investigation, Attn: GCIC, PO Box 370748, Decatur, GA 30037-0748 (Courier address- 3121 Panthersville Rd, Decatur, GA); 404-244-2639, Fax- 404-270-8529; 8AM-4PM.

www.ganet.org/gbi/

GCIC is the central criminal records repository for the State. (Note: anyone with a signed release may make a record request at any local law enforcement office and the statewide record will be provided. Fees for this may vary; the maximum fee is $20.00.)

Indexing & Storage: Records available from 1972 forward. New records available for inquiry in 1-3 days. 70% of all arrests in database have final dispositions recorded, 82% for those arrests within last 5 years.

Searching: Records are available here to employers, government agencies including licensing agencies, and adoption and foster care providers. 100% of arrest records are fingerprint supported. Include in request- name, set of fingerprints, date of birth, sex, race, SSN. Certain law enforcement agencies, who are online, and local agencies may access and retrieve records for investigative/background purposes. These agencies have the option of requesting a signed release from subject or including a set of fingerprints. This data not released- juvenile records, traffic ticket information or out-of-state or federal charges. Information released includes arrest, disposition, and custodial information for offenses designated as fingerprintable by the State AG. Records without dispositions are released.

Access by: mail, in person.

Fee & Payment: Fee is $15.00 per name. If statutes require a FBI fingerprint check, fee is $19.25 if electronic and $26.00 if manual. Agencies may establish an account. Fee payee- Georgia Bureau of Investigations. Prepayment required. Money orders are accepted. No credit cards accepted.

Mail search: Turnaround time- 7 to 10 days. SASE not required.

In person: In-person requests are returned by mail in about 14 days.

Statewide Court Records

Administrative Office of the Courts, 244 Washington St SW, #300, Atlanta, GA 30334-5900; 404-656-5171, Fax- 404-651-6449; 8:30AM-5PM.

www.georgiacourts.org/aoc/

Except for certain online research capabilities, all court record access must be done at the local level.

Online search: Search the dockets of the Court of Appeals at www.gaappeals.us/. Search Supreme Court dockets at www.gasupreme.us/computer_docket.php. There is no statewide online access available for trial courts, although statewide access is planned. Make online purchases of certificates of admission and good standing ($3.00), Supreme Court opinions ($5.00), and certified copies of Supreme Court opinions ($8.00) using PayPal. Go to www.gasupreme.us/purchase_online.php.

Sexual Offender Registry

Georgia Bureau of Investigations, GCIC - Sexual Offender Registry, PO Box 370808, Decatur, GA 30037 (Courier address- 3121 Panthersville Rd, Decatur, GA 30037); 404-244-2600 (24 Hour Line to GBI), Fax- 404-270-8452; 8AM-4PM.

http://services.georgia.gov/gbi/gbisor/disclaim.html

The website outlines which offenders are in the searchable database at the website.

Indexing & Storage: Records available from 07/01/96 for information pertaining to sex offenders who have been released from prison, placed on probation, parole, or supervised release after July 1, 1996. New records available for inquiry in 2 days.

Searching: This data not released- if offender is deceased.

Access by: mail, in person, online.

Fee & Payment: There is no fee.

Mail search: Turnaround time- 7 to 10 days.

In person: in person requests are returned by mail in about 14 days if lists are involved.

Online search: Records may be searched at http://services.georgia.gov/gbi/gbisor/SORSearch.jsp. Earliest records go back to 07/01/96. Close to 80% of registered offenders have photographs on the web site. Searches may be conducted for sex offenders, absconders, and predators.

Incarceration Records

Georgia Department of Corrections, Inmate Records Office - 6th Fl, East Tower, 2 Martin Luther King, Jr. Drive, S.E., Atlanta, GA 30334-4900; 404-656-4661, Fax- 404-463-6232; 8AM-4:30PM.

www.dcor.state.ga.us

Email questions to info@dcor.state.ga.us.

Indexing & Storage: Records available on current and former inmates. New records available for inquiry in 1-3 days.

Searching: Include in request- name; DOB, Inmate number or SSN are helpful. Location, physical identifiers, conviction information, release dates, and inmate number are released. This data not released- first offender info after released.

Access by: mail, phone, fax, in person, online.

Fee & Payment: There is no fee for a PEN PAK, but $10.00 to exemplify the record. Prepayment required.

Mail search: Turnaround time- 7 to 14 days. This is for PEN PAK only. Request is sent to Sec of State's office for certification. SASE not required. Requests in writing must be on letterhead.

Phone search: Only general "public" information is released over the phone.

Fax search: Records are available by fax.

In person: You may make your record request in person; use the agency form. Results are available in two days.

Online search: The website has an extensive array of search capabilities. You can view a specific offender's record by entering a numeric identifier

Corporation, LP, LLP, LLC, Not-for-Profits

Sec of State - Corporation Division, Record Searches, 315 W Tower, #2 ML King Drive, Atlanta, GA 30334-1530; 404-656-2817; 9AM-5PM.

http://sos.georgia.gov/corporations/

Trade Names, Fictitious Names, Assumed Names and DBAs are found at the county level.

Indexing & Storage: Records available from the 1960s, and earlier if the filer has moved records from the county level to the state level. Indexes are maintained on microfilm and document imaging systems. New records available for inquiry immediately.

Searching: Date of incorporation, officer names, current status and registered name and address available at website. Copies and/or certificates can be ordered by mail or from the web.

Access by: mail, in person, online.

Fee & Payment: $10.00 fee certification, for a Certificate of Existence or Certificate of Search (certified copies). This includes 50 pages, if more then $.25 per page. A Certificate of Entity History is $50.00, copies included. Fee payee- Secretary of State. Prepayment required. Personal checks accepted. Major credit cards accepted only for online orders

Mail search: Turnaround time- 1 week. SASE not required.

In person: Immediate records only if expedited service fees paid.

Online search: Records are available from the corporation database on the Internet site above. The corporate database can be searched for free by entity name or registered agent at https://corp.sos.state.ga.us/corp/soskb/login.asp. Document Image and certificates can be also ordered for the quoted fees at that URL. Other services include name reservation, filing procedures, downloading of forms/applications. Also, search securities companies registered with the state at www.sos.ga.gov/sbr_weblookup_prod/.

Expedited service: Expedited service is available for mail and in person searches. Turnaround time- 24 hours. Add $50.00 per entity.

Trademarks/Servicemarks

Secretary of State, Trademark Division, 2 Martin Luther King, Room 315, W Tower, Atlanta, GA 30334-1530; 404-656-2861, Fax- 404-657-6380; 8AM-5PM.

www.georgiatrademarks.org/

Applications and filing instructions can be obtained at the website.

Indexing & Storage: Records available from the beginning of the Division and are maintained on computer. New records available for inquiry in 24 hours.

Searching: Records are permanently retained. Include in request- registration number. Search by mark name or description or by owner name or by goods and services. Will not expedite requests. The agency will accept counter requests, but records will be returned by mail.

Access by: mail, online.

Fee & Payment: $10.00 per record. Fee payee- Secretary of State Prepayment required. Personal checks accepted, credit cards are not.

Mail search: Turnaround time- 2 to 3 days. SASE not required.

Online search: A record database is searchable from the web. Search by registration #, mark name, description, connection, owner, or classification.

Uniform Commercial Code

Superior Court Clerks' Cooperative Authority, 1875 Century Blvd, #100, Atlanta, GA 30345; 404-327-9058, Fax- 404-327-7877; 8:30AM-5PM.

www.gsccca.org/Projects/aboutucc.asp

High volume, ongoing requesters can open a "search account" and receive expedited service. Online is suggested.

Indexing & Storage: Records available from 1-1-95, indexed on computer. New records available for inquiry in 3-4 days.

Searching: All uniform commercial code filings are filed at the county level. Since January 1, 1995, UCC filings are indexed statewide (older filings are only available at the county). Submit a UCC-11 to the address above to search new filings. Include in request- debtor name only. All tax liens are filed at the county level only.

Access by: mail, online.

Fee & Payment: Uncertified copies made by searcher are $.25 each, $1.00 if made by this office. A Certified search is $10.00. Certified copies are also available at the county level for $2.50 for first page. Fee payee- GSCCCA. Prepayment required. Personal checks accepted. Credit cards not accepted.

Mail search: Turnaround time- 1 day. SASE not required.

Online search: Free name searching is available at the website. Also search by secured party, tax payer ID, date, or file number. In order to view images, ongoing requesters can open a subscription account. There is a monthly charge of $9.95 and a $.25 fee per image for unlimited access to images. Billing is monthly. Requests for certified searches are offered for $10.00 per name. The system is open 24 hours daily. The website also includes real estate indexes and images, lien index, and notary index. Visit www.gsccca.org/Account/default.asp.

Other access: The entire UCC Central Index System can be purchased on a daily, weekly, biweekly basis. For more information, contact the Director's office.

Expedited service: Expedited service is available online.

Federal & State Tax Liens

Records not maintained by a state level agency.

All tax liens are filed at the county level.

Sales Tax Registrations

Taxpayer Services Division, Registration and Licensing Section, PO 49512, Atlanta, GA 30359-1512 (Courier address- 1800 Century Blvd, NE, Atlanta, GA 30345); 404-417-4490 (Registration), 404-417-6601 (General Info), Fax- 404-417-4318; 8AM-4:30PM.

www.etax.dor.ga.gov/

Check unclaimed funds at https://www.etax.dor.ga.gov/unclaimedproperty/main.aspx. Direct questions to taxpayer.services@dor.ga.gov.

Indexing & Storage: Records available for all active accounts which are kept on computer. Inactive accounts are on microfilm. New records available for inquiry in 10 business days.

Searching: This agency will confirm that a business is registered and active, but will not provide further information without consent. Include in request- sales & tax use permit number or business name.

Access by: mail, phone, in person.

Fee & Payment: Fee is $1.00 per page, if copies needed. Fee payee- GA Dept of Revenue Prepayment required. Personal checks accepted

Mail search: Turnaround time- 2 weeks. Please give reason for request. Requests in writing will be honored if over two.

Phone search: No fee for telephone request.

In person: No fee for request. Generally, the information is returned by mail in two weeks.

Birth Certificates

Department of Human Resources, Vital Records Unit, 2600 Skyland Dr NE, Atlanta, GA 30319-3640; 404-679-4702 (Pre-order), 877-572-6343 (Credit Card Line), Fax- 404-679-4730; 8AM-4:45PM.

http://health.state.ga.us/programs/vitalrecords/index.asp

Request forms may be printed from the web page.

Indexing & Storage: Records available from 1919 to present. New records available for inquiry in 1 month.

Searching: For investigative purposes or distant relatives, a signed release from person of record is required. Include in request- full name, names of parents, mother's maiden name, date of birth, place of birth. Email questions to phvitalrecords@gdph.state.ga.us.

Access by: mail, phone, fax, in person.

Fee & Payment: The fee is $10.00 per record. Add $5.00 per name requested for second copies. Multi year searches are $10.00 per three years or portions thereof. Fee payee- Georgia Department of Human Resources. Prepayment required. Major credit cards accepted.

Mail search: Turnaround time- 10 weeks or more. SASE not required.

Phone search: One may "re-order" by phone if coming into the office.

Fax search: Same criteria as phone searching.

In person: You can use the "pre-order" telephone number to call first so when you come in you merely need to pickup the document. Turnaround time is usually 30 minutes.

Expedited service: Records may be ordered online through an approved vendor - www.vitalchek.com. Extra fees apply for use of credit card and if express delivery requested. Turnaround time- overnight delivery.

Death Records

Department of Human Resources, Vital Records Unit, 2600 Skyland Dr NE, Atlanta, GA 30319-3640; 404-679-4702, 877-572-6343 (Credit Card Line), Fax- 404-679-4730; 8AM-4:45PM.

http://health.state.ga.us/programs/vitalrecords/index.asp

A request form may be downloaded from the web page.

Indexing & Storage: Records available from 1919 to present. New records available for inquiry in 1 month.

Searching: Death certificates are available to the general public. Cause of death is released to next of kin only. Include in request- full name, date of death, place of death. Age at death, sex and race are helpful. Email questions to phvitalrecords@gdph.state.ga.us.

Access by: mail, phone, fax, in person, online.

Fee & Payment: The fee is $10.00 per name. Add $5.00 per name for second copies. Multi year searches are $10.00 per three years or portions thereof. Fee payee- Georgia Department of Human Resources. Prepayment required. Major credit cards accepted.

Mail search: Turnaround time- 3 to 4 weeks. SASE not required.

Phone search: See expedited services.

Fax search: Same criteria as phone searching.

In person: Turnaround time 30 minutes.

Online search: Records may be ordered online through an approved vendor - www.vitalchek.com. The credit card fee applies.

Other access: The death index is available for the years 1919-1998 on microfiche for $50.00.

Expedited service: Records may be ordered online through an approved vendor - www.vitalchek.com. Extra fees apply for use of credit card and if express delivery requested. Turnaround time- overnight delivery.

Marriage Certificates

Department of Human Resources, Vital Records Unit, 2600 Skyland Dr NE, Atlanta, GA 30319-3640; 404-679-4702, 877-572-6343 (Credit Card Line), Fax- 404-679-4730; 8AM-4:45PM.

http://health.state.ga.us/programs/vitalrecords/index.asp

This agency will do search to identify the county of record and issue a certificate, but cannot issue a copy of the original record. Otherwise records must be obtained from the county of record.

Indexing & Storage: Records available from 1952-1996. Certified copies are only available at the county level.. New records available for inquiry in 1 month.

Searching: Certified copies of marriage licenses are available to the general public; but copies of the marriage application are only issued to bride and groom. Records may not be ordered via e-mail. Include in request- full names of husband and wife, date of marriage, place or county of marriage. Email questions to phvitalrecords@gdph.state.ga.us.

Access by: mail, phone, fax, in person.

Fee & Payment: The fee is $10.00, $5.00 for a second copy. For every additional three years searched, there is another $10.00 fee. Fee payee- Georgia Department of Human Resources. Prepayment required. Major credit cards accepted.

Mail search: Turnaround time- 3 to 4 weeks. SASE not required.

Phone search: See expedited services.

Fax search: Same criteria as phone searches.

In person: Turnaround time 30 minutes.

Other access: The marriage index is available on microfiche for $50.00, the set includes the years 1964-1998.

Expedited service: Records may be ordered online through an approved vendor - www.vitalchek.com. Extra fees apply for use of credit card and if express delivery requested. Turnaround time- overnight delivery.

Divorce Records

Department of Human Resources, Vital Records Unit, 2600 Skyland Dr NE, Atlanta, GA 30319-3640; 404-679-4702, 877-572-6343 (Credit Card Line), Fax- 404-679-4730; 8AM-4:45PM.

http://health.state.ga.us/programs/vitalrecords/index.asp

This agency will do search to identify the county of record and issue a certificate, but cannot issue a copy of the original record. Certified copies are only available at the county level.

Indexing & Storage: Records available from 1952. This is an index only, records are at the county level.

Searching: Email questions to phvitalrecords@gdph.state.ga.us.

Access by: mail, phone, fax, in person.

Fee & Payment: The fee is $10.00, $5.00 for a second copy. For every additional three years searched, there is another $10.00 fee. Fee payee- GA Department of Human Resources. Personal checks and major credit cards accepted.

Mail search: Records are available by mail.

Phone search: See expedited services.

Fax search: Same criteria as phone searches.

In person: Search of index availability immediately.

Other access: Divorce microfiche indexes are available to the public, sold in complete set for the years 1919-1998 for $50.00.

Expedited service: Records may be ordered online through an approved vendor - www.vitalchek.com. Extra fees apply for use of credit card and if express delivery requested.

Workers' Compensation Records

State Board of Workers Compensation, 270 Peachtree St, NW, Atlanta, GA 30303-1299; 404-656-3818, 800-533-0682; 8AM-4:30PM.

www.sbwc.georgia.gov

Indexing & Storage: Records available for 10 years plus present year. New records available for inquiry in 10-14 days.

Searching: Records are not open to the public. You must be a party to the claim or have authority. Include in request- claimant name, SSN, date of injury if known. A downloadable form can be used - WC-12.

Access by: mail.

Fee & Payment: The agency will bill for required fees. Fee payee- State Board of Workers Compensation. Personal checks accepted, credit cards are not.

Mail search: Turnaround time- 2 to 3 weeks. The fee is $10.00 for the first 10 pages plus $.50 per page for over 10 pages. Certification for a document is $10.00. SASE not required. No fee for mail request.

Driver Records

Department of Driver Services, Driver's Services Section, MVR Unit, PO Box 80447, Conyers, GA 30013 (Courier address- 2206 East View Parkway, Conyers, GA 30013); 678-413-8400; 8AM-3:30PM.

www.dds.ga.gov

Copies of tickets are not available from a central depository. It is recommended you go directly to the issuing court.

Indexing & Storage: Records available for either a 3 year record or a 7 year record. Accident involvement is shown if the driver was cited. The driver's address is part of the record. New records available for inquiry in ten days or more.

Searching: Georgia has strict rules concerning driver record access. If an individual requests a driving record on another, the driver's signature is needed. Large requesters must have "bulk-user certificates" on file. The driver's full name, DOB and license number are required. Direct questions to mvr@dds.ga.gov.

Access by: mail, in person, online.

Fee & Payment: $6.00 for a 3 year period; $8.00 for a 7 year period. Fee payee- Department of Driver Services Prepayment required. Cashier checks and money orders preferred. No personal checks or credit cards accepted.

Mail search: Turnaround time- 2 weeks. SASE is required.

In person: Walk-in requesters may receive up to three records while waiting, additional requests are processed overnight. Walk-in requests are also available at all driver's license offices.

Online search: Through the coordinated efforts of the GA Department of Motor Vehicle Safety and the Georgia Technology Authority, driving records are now available via the Internet for "certified users, including insurance, employers, and car rental companies. Requesters must complete several applications and user agreement forms. The fees are $6.00 for a three-year record and $8.00 for a seven-year record. For further information, visit https://online.dds.ga.gov/onlineservices/MVRInfo.aspx.

Expedited service: Has no regular policy for expediting requests but indicates it may place request at top of list if sent express.

Vehicle Ownership & Registration

Department of Revenue, Motor Vehicle Division, PO Box 740381, Atlanta, GA 30374-0381; 404-362-6500, Fax- 404-362-2729; 8AM-4:30PM.

http://motor.etax.dor.ga.gov/

Indexing & Storage: Records available from 2002 forward. New records available for inquiry immediately.

Searching: Records are not open to the general public and are restricted to authorized (notarized) agents or individuals, judgment creditor, tax collector, law enforcement officials, license dealers, etc. There is an online access mode for only GA licensed dealers. Include in request-statement of reason for requests, fee; must be on letterhead. Records are only released to casual requesters with notarized consent of the subject This data not released- insurance information

Access by: mail, in person, online.

Fee & Payment: Fees: $5.00 per record for VIN and title histories; $1.00 for a title or tag search computer print-out. Certified tag or title record is $10.00. Lien information is considered part of the title history. There is a full charge for a "no record found." Fee payee- Department of Revenue Prepayment required. Personal checks and major credit cards accepted.

Mail search: Turnaround time- 2 weeks. A SASE is requested.

In person: Turnaround time is while you wait unless certified copies needed.

Online search: Online subscription access available to Georgia dealers only; registration is required.

Expedited service: Will expedite if you provide a court date that indicates that the request must be received in a timely manner.

Accident Reports

Department of Transportation, GDOT Crash Reporting Unit, 935 East Confederate Ave, Shackleford Bldg #24, Atlanta, GA 30316; 404-635-8109, Fax- 404-635-8175; 8AM-4:30PM.

www.dot.state.ga.us/statistics/CrashData/Pages/default.aspx

Indexing & Storage: Records available for 10 years to present. New records available for inquiry in 30 days or less.

Searching: Only persons involved in the accident or their legal representative may obtain a copy, unless the subject has given written permission. Include in request- full name, date of accident, location of accident. Request form is at www.dot.state.ga.us/statistics/Documents/crash/requestt_form.pdf.

Access by: mail, in person.

Fee & Payment: The fee for a report is $5.00. There is no charge for a "no record found." Fee payee- Department of Transportation Prepayment required. Cash, money orders, certified checks, and cashier's checks are all accepted. No personal checks or credit cards accepted.

Mail search: Turnaround time- 1 week to 10 days. SASE not required.

In person: Request must be in writing. Turnaround time is within the hour.

Expedited service: Does not offer expedited service.

Vessel Ownership & Registration

Georgia Dept of Natural Resources, Boat Registration Office, 2065 US Hwy. 278, SE, Social Circle, GA 30025; 800-366-2661; 8AM-4:30PM.

www.georgiawildlife.com/boating.aspx

Liens are at the county level and will not show on records at this location. Titles are not used, for transfer of registration a bill of sale or Affidavit of Ownership is required.

Indexing & Storage: Records available from 1986 to present. Records are indexed on microfiche from 1986 to 1993 and on computer from 1994 to present. Paper records held for three years. New records available for inquiry in 45-60 days.

Searching: All motorized boats, and all sailboats 12 ft or longer must be registered, except boats operated exclusively on private ponds or lakes. Either the name, registration # or hull # must be submitted. All vessels built after 1972 must have a complete Hull Identification Number before the registration application can be processed.

Access by: mail, phone, fax, in person, online.

Fee & Payment: There is no search fee.

Mail search: Turnaround time- 1 to 2 weeks. SASE not required.

Phone search: Verification only.

Fax search: Same criteria as mail searching.

In person: Simple requests may be processed while you wait.

Online search: A download of the boat registration information by county or statewide is available at www.georgiawildlife.com/boatregistration_boating.aspx. You must has MS Access or Excel.

Legislation Records

General Assembly of Georgia, State Capitol, Atlanta, GA 30334; 404-656-5040 (Senate), 404-656-5015 (House), 678-364-3700 (Archives), Fax-404-656-5043; 8:30AM-4:30PM.

www.legis.state.ga.us

Indexing & Storage: Records available from 1967 to present. Records are computerized since 1995. The older the document, the longer the turnaround time. New records available for inquiry in 1 day.

Searching: Include in request- bill number, year. Either Senate or House Clerk can look up bills, but to receive copies of documents before 1995, go to the State Archives for copies of all bills.

Access by: mail, phone, in person, online.

Fee & Payment: The fee is $.10 per printed page if total exceeds $5.00. Fee payee- General Assembly of Georgia. Personal checks accepted, credit cards are not.

Mail search: Turnaround time- variable. Address questions to Senate to Room 353, House questions to Room 309. SASE not required.

Phone search: You may request bills by phone.

In person: You may request bills in person.

Online search: The Internet site listed above has bill information. Visit www.lexis-nexis.com/hottopics/gacode/default.asp for the Georgia Code.

Voter Registration

Secretary of State - Elections Division, 1104 West Tower, 2 Martin Luther King Dr SE, Atlanta, GA 30334-1530; 404-656-2871, 888-265-1115, Fax-404-651-9531; 8AM-5PM.

http://sos.georgia.gov/elections/

Data entry to the database is done at the county level.

Indexing & Storage: Records available from 1995, on computer. Data is keyed in by county personnel onto the state computer. New records available for inquiry in minutes.

Searching: Records may be ordered as a flat file in ASCII format directly from the website. Include in request- full name, date of birth, phone number of requester. All requests must be in writing. Records may be requested at county level, also. This data not released- SSNs or bulk information or lists for commercial purposes.

Access by: mail, phone, fax, online.

Fee & Payment: There is no fee for individual requests. Copies are $.25 per page. There are fees to purchase the database, and these fees can be found at the website. Fee payee- Secretary of State Prepayment required. Personal checks accepted.

Mail search: Turnaround time- 3 to 5 business days. SASE not required.

Phone search: Interactive phone service via the toll-free number provides district and precinct information.

Fax search: Fax searching of statutes is available.

Online search: Name and DOB needed to search unofficial registration information at http://sos.georgia.gov/elections/polllocator/PollLocator.aspx. The results will provide address and district-precinct information; no SSNs released.

Other access: CDs, Internet files, disks, and paper lists are available for purchase for non-commercial purposes. For fees go to http://sos.georgia.gov/elections/voter_registration/voter_reg_lists.htm

GED Certificates

GED Testing Service, 1800 Century Pl #300B, Atlanta, GA 30345; 404-679-1645, Fax- 406-679-4911; 8:30AM-4:30PM M-F.

www.dtae.org

Indexing & Storage: New records available for inquiry in 4 to 6 weeks.

Searching: Include in request- a signed release, name, year and location of test, date of birth, and SSN.

Access by: mail, in person.

Fee & Payment: The fee for a verification or for a copy of a transcript is $5.00 per record. A duplicate diploma is $8.00. Fee payee- GED Testing Service. Prepayment required. Money orders are accepted. No personal checks or credit cards accepted.

Mail search: Turnaround time- 4 weeks. SASE not required.

In person: Records may be picked up between 9AM and 4PM M,T,TH,F and till 7PM on Wed.

Hunting & Fishing License Information

Access to Records is Restricted.

Department of Natural Resources, License & Boat Registration Unit, 2065 U.S. Highway 278 SE, Social Circle, GA 30025; 800-366-2661, Fax- 770-414-3344; 8AM-4:30PM.

www.georgiawildlife.com

The request must be in writing and cite that under the Georgia Open Records Act you request that a search be done. The database may not be current for non-resident licenses and license purchases made via the website.

Georgia State Licensing Agencies

For details about the agency responsible for licensing/certifying/registering an item below or in the Agency Quick Finder section, match an item's number with the number of the agency in the *Licensing Agency Information* section.

Georgia Licenses Searchable Online

Acupuncturist #23 .... http://services.georgia.gov/dch/mebs/jsp/index.jsp
Air Conditioning Contractor #9 .... https://secure.sos.state.ga.us/myverification/
Architect #15 .... https://secure.sos.state.ga.us/myverification/
Athletic Agent #13 .... https://secure.sos.state.ga.us/myverification/
Athletic Trainer #16 .... https://secure.sos.state.ga.us/myverification/
Attorney #30 .... www.gabar.org/directories/member_directory_search/
Auctioneer/Auction Dealer #13 .... https://secure.sos.state.ga.us/myverification/
Audiologist #16 .... https://secure.sos.state.ga.us/myverification/
Barber/Barber Shop #19 .... https://secure.sos.state.ga.us/myverification/
Cemetery #26 .... https://secure.sos.state.ga.us/SBR_Weblookup_Prod/Search.aspx
Charity #26 .... https://secure.sos.state.ga.us/SBR_Weblookup_Prod/Search.aspx
Chiropractor #18 .... https://secure.sos.state.ga.us/myverification/
Cosmetologist/Cosmetology Shop #19 .... https://secure.sos.state.ga.us/myverification/
Counselor #10 .... https://secure.sos.state.ga.us/myverification/
Credit Union #17 .... https://dbfweb.dbf.state.ga.us/WebCUData.html
Dentist/Dental Hygienist #20 .... https://secure.sos.state.ga.us/myverification/
Detox Specialist #23 .... http://services.georgia.gov/dch/mebs/jsp/index.jsp
Dietitian #2 .... https://secure.sos.state.ga.us/myverification/
Drug Whlse/Retail/Mfg (Hospital) #31 .... https://secure.sos.state.ga.us/myverification/
Electrical Contractor #9 .... https://secure.sos.state.ga.us/myverification/
Embalmer #13 .... https://secure.sos.state.ga.us/myverification/
Engineer #11 .... https://secure.sos.state.ga.us/myverification/
Esthetician #19 .... https://secure.sos.state.ga.us/myverification/
Family Therapist #10 .... https://secure.sos.state.ga.us/myverification/
Financial Statement (Ethics Dept.) #22 .... www.ethics.ga.gov/EthicsWeb/lobbyists/lobbyist.aspx
Forester #35 .... https://secure.sos.state.ga.us/myverification/
Funeral Director/Appren/Firm #13 .... https://secure.sos.state.ga.us/myverification/
Geologist #29 .... https://secure.sos.state.ga.us/myverification/
Hearing Aid Dealer/Dispenser #21 .... https://secure.sos.state.ga.us/myverification/
Interior Designer #15 .... https://secure.sos.state.ga.us/myverification/
Landscape Architect #25 .... https://secure.sos.state.ga.us/myverification/
Liquor Control/Liquor Retailer #6 .... www.etax.dor.ga.gov/AlcoholRetailer/
Lobbyist/Lobbyist Organization #22 .... www.ethics.ga.gov/EthicsWeb/lobbyists/lobbyist.aspx
Low Voltage Contractor #9 .... https://secure.sos.state.ga.us/myverification/
Manicurist #19 .... https://secure.sos.state.ga.us/myverification/
Marriage Counselor #10 .... https://secure.sos.state.ga.us/myverification/
Medical Doctor #23 .... http://services.georgia.gov/dch/mebs/jsp/index.jsp
Nail Care #19 .... https://secure.sos.state.ga.us/myverification/
Notary Public #3 .... www.gsccca.org/search/notary/search.asp
Nuclear Pharmacist #31 .... https://secure.sos.state.ga.us/myverification/
Nurse-LPN #2 .... https://secure.sos.state.ga.us/myverification/
Nurse-RN #28 .... https://secure.sos.state.ga.us/myverification/
Nursing Home Administrator #16 .... https://secure.sos.state.ga.us/myverification/
Occupational Therapist/Assistant #2 .... https://secure.sos.state.ga.us/myverification/
Optician, Dispensing #21 .... https://secure.sos.state.ga.us/myverification/
Optometrist #21 .... https://secure.sos.state.ga.us/myverification/
Osteopathic Physician #23 .... http://services.georgia.gov/dch/mebs/jsp/index.jsp
Perfusionist #23 .... http://services.georgia.gov/dch/mebs/jsp/index.jsp
Pesticide Applicator/Contract'r/Worker #4 .... www.kellysolutions.com/ga/Applicators/index.htm
Pharmacist #31 .... https://secure.sos.state.ga.us/myverification/
Pharmacy School, Clinic Researcher #31 .... https://secure.sos.state.ga.us/myverification/
Physical Therapist/Therapist Asst #2 .... https://secure.sos.state.ga.us/myverification/
Physician Assistant #23 .... http://services.georgia.gov/dch/mebs/jsp/index.jsp
Plumber Journeyman/Contractor #9 .... https://secure.sos.state.ga.us/myverification/
Podiatrist #33 .... https://secure.sos.state.ga.us/myverification/Search.aspx
Poison Pharmacist #31 .... https://secure.sos.state.ga.us/myverification/
Private Detective #13 .... https://secure.sos.state.ga.us/myverification/
Psychologist #16 .... https://secure.sos.state.ga.us/myverification/
Public Accountant-CPA #14 .... https://secure.sos.state.ga.us/myverification/
Real Estate Agent/Seller/Broker #27 .... www.grec.state.ga.us/clsweb/realestate.aspx

Real Estate Appraiser #27	www.grec.state.ga.us/clsweb/appraiser.aspx
Real Estate Community Assn. Mgr. #27	www.grec.state.ga.us
Real Estate Firm #27	www.grec.state.ga.us/clsweb/company.aspx
Rebuilder, Motor Vehicle #13	https://secure.sos.state.ga.us/myverification/
Respiratory Care Practitioner #23	http://services.georgia.gov/dch/mebs/jsp/index.jsp
Salvage Pool Operator #13	https://secure.sos.state.ga.us/myverification/
Salvage Yard Dealer #13	https://secure.sos.state.ga.us/myverification/
School Librarian #12	https://secure.sos.state.ga.us/myverification/
Security Guard/Agency #13	https://secure.sos.state.ga.us/myverification/
Social Worker #10	https://secure.sos.state.ga.us/myverification/
Speech-Language Pathologist #16	https://secure.sos.state.ga.us/myverification/
Surveyor, Land #11	https://secure.sos.state.ga.us/myverification/
Teacher #7	https://www.gapsc.com/certification/look_up.asp
Used Car Dealer #13	https://secure.sos.state.ga.us/myverification/
Used Car Parts Dist. #13	https://secure.sos.state.ga.us/myverification/
Utility Contractor #9	https://secure.sos.state.ga.us/myverification/
Veterinarian/Veterinary Technician #36	https://secure.sos.state.ga.us/myverification/
Waste Water Lab Analyst #24	https://secure.sos.state.ga.us/myverification/
Water Lab/Distribution Operator #24	https://secure.sos.state.ga.us/myverification/
Water Operator Class 1-4 #24	https://secure.sos.state.ga.us/myverification/

Georgia Licensing Quick Finder

Acupuncturist #23	404-657-6490
Air Conditioning Contractor #9	478-207-2440
Amusement Ride Inspector #32	404-679-0687
Animal Technician, Veterinary #36	478-207-2440
Architect #15	478-207-2401
Asbestos Contractor #5	404.363.7026
Athletic Agent #13	478-207-1460
Athletic Trainer #16	478-207-1670
Attorney #30	404-527-8700
Auctioneer/Auction Dealer #13	478-207-1460
Audiologist #16	478-207-1670
Bank #17	770-986-1633
Barber/Barber Shop #19	478-207-1430
Boiler & Pressure Vessel #32	404-679-0687
Cemetery #26	404-656-3920
Charity #26	404-656-3920
Check Casher/Seller #17	770-986-1633
Chiropractor #18	478-207-2440
Coin-operated Machine #6	404-417-4490
Cosmetologist/Cosmetology Shop #19	478-207-1430
Counselor #10	478-207-1670
Court Reporter #1	404-656-6422
Credit Union #17	770-986-1637
Dental Hygienist #20	478-207-2440
Dentist #20	478-207-2440
Detox Specialist #23	404-656-3913
Dietitian #2	478-207-1620
Drug Whlse/Retail/Mfg (Hospital) #31	478-207-2440
EDP - Electronic Data Processor #17	770-986-1633
Electrical Contractor #9	478-207-2440
Elevator, Escalator #32	404-679-0687
Embalmer #13	478-207-1460
Emergency Medical Technician #34	404-248-8995
Engineer #11	478-207-2440
Esthetician #19	478-207-1430
Family Therapist #10	478-207-1670
Financial Statement (Ethics Dept.) #22	404-463-1980
Forester #35	478-207-1401
Funeral Director/Apprentice/Firm #13	478-207-1460
Geologist #29	478-207-1401
Hearing Aid Dealer/Dispenser #21	478-207-2440
Holding Company/Repres. Ofc #17	770-986-1633
Insurance Adjuster/Counselor #8	404-656-2101
Insurance Agent/Firm #8	404-656-2101
Interior Designer #15	478-207-2401
Investment Advisor Firm #26	404-656-3920
Landfill Inspector/Operator #5	404-362-2696
Landscape Architect #25	478-207-1401
Lead-based Paint Abatement #5	404.363.7026
Liquor Control #6	404-417-4490
Liquor Retailer #6	404-417-4490
Lobbyist #22	404-463-1980
Lobbyist Organization #22	404-463-1980
Low Voltage Contractor #9	478-207-2440
Manicurist #19	478-207-1430
Marriage Counselor #10	478-207-1670
Medical Doctor #23	404-657-6489
Mortgage Institution #17	770-986-1269
Nail Care #19	478-207-1430
Notary Public #3	404-327-6023
Nuclear Pharmacist #31	478-207-2440
Nurse-LPN #2	478-207-1620
Nurse-RN #28	478-207-1640
Nursing Home Administrator #16	478-207-1670
Occupational Therapist/Assistant #2	478-207-1620
Optician, Dispensing #21	478-207-2440
Optometrist #21	478-207-2440
Osteopathic Physician #23	404-657-6489
Perfusionist #23	404-463-2292
Pesticide Applicator #4	404-656-4958
Pesticide Contractor/Employee #4	404-656-4958
Pharmacist #31	478-207-2440
Pharmacy Sch'l, Clinic Research'r #31	478-207-2440
Physical Therapist/Therapist Asst #2	478-207-1620
Physician Assistant #23	404-657-4688
Plumber Journeyman/Contractor #9	478-207-2440
Podiatrist #33	478-207-2440
Poison Pharmacist #31	478-207-2440
Private Detective #13	478-207-1460
Psychologist #16	478-207-1670
Public Accountant-CPA #14	478-207-1401
Public Adjuster #8	404-656-2101
Real Estate Agent/Seller/Broker #27	404-656-3916
Real Estate Appraiser #27	404-656-3916
Real Estate Community Assn Mgr #27	404-656-3916
Real Estate Firm #27	404-656-3916
Rebuilder (Motor Vehicle) #13	478-207-1460
Respiratory Care Practitioner #23	404-656-3914
Salvage Pool Operator #13	478-207-1460
Salvage Yard Dealer #13	478-207-1460
School Administrator/Supervisor #7	404-657-9000
School Counselor/Social Worker #7	404-657-9000
School Librarian #12	478-207-2401
School Media Specialist #7	404-657-9000
Securities Salesperson/Dealer #26	404-656-3920
Security Guard/Agency #13	478-207-1460
Shorth'd Court Reporter/Stenomask #1	404-656-6422
Social Worker #10	478-207-1670
Speech-Language Pathologist #16	478-207-1670
Surplus Line Broker #8	404-656-2101
Surveyor, Land #11	478-207-2440
Teacher #7	404-657-9000
Timber Dealer/Processor #4	404-656-4958
Tobacco Seller #6	404-417-4490
Used Car Dealer #13	478-207-1460
Used Car Parts Dist. #13	478-207-1460
Utility Contractor #9	478-207-2440
Veterinarian/Veterinary Technic'n #36	478-207-2440
Veterinary Faculty #36	478-207-2440
Waste Water Lab Analyst #24	912-207-1460
Waste Water System Operator #24	912-207-1460
Water Lab/Distribution Operator #24	912-207-1460
Water Operator Class 1-4 #24	912-207-1460

Georgia Licensing Agency Information

#1 Clerk, Board of Court Reporting, 244 Washington St SW, #300, Atlanta, GA 30334; 404-656-6422, Fax- 404-651-6449. www.georgiacourts.org/agencies/bcr/

#2 Examining Boards Division, Board of Examiners of Licensed Practical Nurses, 237 Coliseum Dr, Macon, GA 31217; 478-207-2440, Fax- 478-207-1354. http://sos.georgia.gov/plb/lpn/ Search data at- https://secure.sos.state.ga.us/myverification/

#3 Clerks Authority, Notary Public Division, 1875 Century Blvd #100, Atlanta, GA 30345; 404-327-6023, Fax- 404-327-7887. 8:30AM-5PM. www.gsccca.org/Projects/aboutnp.asp Search data at- www.gsccca.org/search/notary/search.asp

#4 Department of Agriculture, Pesticide Division, 19 MLK Jr Dr SW, Rm 550, Atlanta, GA 30334; 404-656-4958, Fax- 404-657-8378. http://agr.georgia.gov/02/doa/home/0,2473,38902732,00.html;jsessionid=EA8077429BB0398266DF6B5A14A3DC8E Search at- www.kellysolutions.com/ga/Applicators/index.htm

#5 Department of Natural Resources, Environmental Protection Division, 2 Martin Luther King Jr Dr, Ste 1152, E Twr, Atlanta, GA 30334; 404.657.5947, Fax- 404-362-2693. www.gaepd.org/index.html

#6 Department of Revenue, Centralized Taxpayer Registration, 1800 Century Center Blvd. NE, Rm 4235, Atlanta, GA 30359-1512; 404-417-4490, 404-417-4900, Fax- 404-417-4901. www.etax.dor.ga.gov/AlcoholRetailer/ Search data at- www.etax.dor.ga.gov/AlcoholRetailer/free

#7 Professional Standards Commission, Teacher Certification, 2 Peachtree St, #6000, Atlanta, GA 30303; 404-657-9000. www.gapsc.com/Certification/index.asp To check teacher status, the SSN is required.

#8 Licensing Division, Insurance Commissioner's Office, 2 Martin Luther King Jr Dr, W Twr, #704, Atlanta, GA 30334; 404-656-2070, Fax- 404-657-8542. http://oci.georgia.gov/01/home/0,2197,858938,00.html

#9 State Construction Industry Licensing Board, 237 Coliseum Dr, Macon, GA 31217; 478-207-2440, Fax- 478-207-1425. 8AM-5PM. http://sos.georgia.gov/plb/construct/ Search data at- https://secure.sos.state.ga.us/myverification/ Will sell rosters. $25.00 fee for letter of verification or completion of form submitted from another state. Requests must be in writing.

#10 Examining Boards Division, Board of Counselors, Social Workers, Marriage/Family Therapists, 237 Coliseum Dr, Macon, GA 31217; 478-207-1670, Fax- 478-207-1676. http://sos.georgia.gov/plb/counselors/ Search at- https://secure.sos.state.ga.us/myverification/

#11 Examining Boards Division, Professional Engineers & Land Surveyors Board, 237 Coliseum Dr, Macon, GA 31217-3858; 478-207-2440, Fax- 478-207-1425. 8AM-5PM. http://sos.georgia.gov/plb/pels/ Search data at- https://secure.sos.state.ga.us/myverification/ Will sell rosters. $25.00 fee for letter of verification or completion of form submitted from another state. Requests must be in writing.

#12 Examining Boards Division, Board for the Certification of Librarians, 237 Coliseum Dr, Macon, GA 31217-3858; 478-207-2400, Fax- 478-207-1354. http://sos.georgia.gov/plb/librarians/ Search data at- https://secure.sos.state.ga.us/myverification/

#13 Professional Licensing, Licensing Boards, 237 Coliseum Dr, Macon, GA 31217; 478-207-2440, Fax- 478-207-1354. http://sos.georgia.gov/plb/ Search data at- https://secure.sos.state.ga.us/myverification/

#14 Examining Boards Division, Board of Accountancy, 237 Coliseum Dr, Macon, GA 31217-3858; 478-207-1400, Fax- 478-207-1410. http://sos.georgia.gov/plb/accountancy/ Search data at- https://secure.sos.state.ga.us/myverification/

#15 Examining Boards Division, Board of Architects and Interior Designers, 237 Coliseum Dr, Macon, GA 31217; 478-207-2400, Fax- 478-207-1410. http://sos.georgia.gov/plb/architects/ Search data at- https://secure.sos.state.ga.us/myverification/

#16 Examining Boards Division, State Examining Board-Medical, 237 Coliseum Dr, Macon, GA 31217; 478-207-1670, Fax- 478-207-1676. https://secure.sos.state.ga.us/myverification/ Search data at- https://secure.sos.state.ga.us/myverification/

#17 Department of Banking and Finance, Regulated Institutions, 2990 Brandywine Rd #200, Atlanta, GA 30341; 770-986-1633, Fax- 770-986-1654. Hours- 8AM-4:30PM. http://dbf.georgia.gov/02/dbf/home/0,2477,43414745,00.html

#18 Examining Boards Division, Board of Chiropractic Examiners, 237 Coliseum Dr, Macon, GA 31217; 478-207-2440, Fax- 478-207-1699. http://sos.georgia.gov/plb/chiro/ Search data at- https://secure.sos.state.ga.us/myverification/

#19 Examining Boards Division, Board of Cosmetology, 237 Coliseum Dr, Macon, GA 31217; 478-207-1430, Fax- 478-207-1442. http://sos.georgia.gov/plb/ Search data at- https://secure.sos.state.ga.us/myverification/

#20 Examining Boards Division, Board of Dentistry, 237 Coliseum Dr, Macon, GA 31217-3858; 478-207-2440, Fax- 478-207-1354. http://sos.georgia.gov/plb/dentistry/ Search data at- https://secure.sos.state.ga.us/myverification/

#21 Examining Boards Division, Board of Hearing Aid Dispensers, Board of Dispensing Opticians, Examiners in Optometry, 237 Coliseum Dr, Macon, GA 31217; 478-207-1686, Fax- 478-207-1699. http://sos.georgia.gov/plb/opticians/ Search at- https://secure.sos.state.ga.us/myverification/

#22 State Ethics Commission, 200 Piedmont Ave #1416 - W Twr, Atlanta, GA 30334; 404-463-1980, Fax- 404-463-1988. Hours- 8AM-5PM. http://ethics.georgia.gov Search data at- www.ethics.ga.gov/EthicsWeb/lobbyists/lobbyist.aspx At the website, choose the type of Lobbyist lists to examine.

#23 Examining Boards Division, Composite Board of Medical Examiners, 2 Peachtree St, NW, 36th Fl, Atlanta, GA 30303; 404-656-3913, Fax- 404-656-9723. www.medicalboard.georgia.gov Search data at- http://services.georgia.gov/dch/mebs/jsp/index.jsp Will sell lists or other means of verification.

#24 Examining Boards Division, Water & Wastewater Treatment Plant Operators & Laboratory Analysts, 237 Coliseum Dr, Macon, GA 31217; 404-207-1460, Fax- 404-207-1468. http://sos.georgia.gov/plb/water/ Search data at- https://secure.sos.state.ga.us/myverification/ Verification Letter from Board- $25.00 fee; "Roster Request Form" at website.

#25 Examining Boards Division, Board of Landscape Architects, 237 Coliseum Dr, Macon, GA 31217-3858; 478-207-2400, Fax- 478-207-1354. http://sos.georgia.gov/plb/landscape/ Search data at- https://secure.sos.state.ga.us/myverification/

#26 Securities & Business Regulation, Office of Secretary of State, 2 ML King Jr Dr SE, W Twr, #802, Atlanta, GA 30334-1530; 404-656-3920, Fax- 404-657-8410. http://sos.georgia.gov/securities/

#27 Real Estate Commission/Appraiser Board, 229 Peachtree St NE, International Tower, #1000, Atlanta, GA 30303-1605; 404-656-3916, Fax- 404-656-6650. Hours- 8AM-4:30PM. www.grec.state.ga.us Also search appraisers at www.asc.gov/content/category3/StateSites/displayStateSites.aspx?id=49.

#28 Examining Boards Division, Board of Nursing, 237 Coliseum Dr, Macon, GA 30217-3858; 478-207-1640, Fax- 478-207-1660. http://sos.georgia.gov/plb/rn/ Search data at- https://secure.sos.state.ga.us/myverification/

#29 Examining Boards Division, Board of Registration for Professional Geologists, 237 Coliseum Dr, Macon, GA 31217-3858; 478-207-1300, Fax- 478-207-1354. http://sos.georgia.gov/plb/geologists/ Search data at- https://secure.sos.state.ga.us/myverification/

#30 State Bar of Georgia, 104 Marietta St NW, #100, Atlanta, GA 30303; 404-527-8700, Fax- 404-527-8717. www.gabar.org Search data at- www.gabar.org/directories/member_directory_search/

#31 Examining Boards Division, Board of Pharmacy, 237 Coliseum Dr, Macon, GA 31217; 478-207-2440, Fax- 478-207-1354. http://sos.georgia.gov/plb/pharmacy/ Search data at- https://secure.sos.state.ga.us/myverification/

#32 Department of Labor, Safety Engineering Division, 1700 Century Cir NE, Atlanta, GA 30345; 404-679-0687, Fax- 404-679-5818. www.dol.state.ga.us

#33 Examining Boards Division, Board of Podiatry Examiners, 237 Coliseum Dr, Macon, GA 31217; 478-207-2440, Fax- 478-207-1354. http://sos.georgia.gov/plb/podiatry/ Search data at- https://secure.sos.state.ga.us/myverification/Search.aspx

#34 Emergency Medical Svcs, 2600 Skyland Dr, Upper Level, Atlanta, GA 30319; 404-248-8995, Fax- 404-248-8948. www.health.state.ga.us/programs/ems/index.asp

#35 Examining Boards Division, Board of Registration for Foresters, 237 Coliseum Dr, Macon, GA 31217; 478-207-2440, Fax- 478-207-1354. http://sos.georgia.gov/plb/foresters/ Search data at- https://secure.sos.state.ga.us/myverification/

#36 Examining Boards Division, Board of Veterinary Medicine, 237 Coliseum Dr, Macon, GA 31217; 478-207-2440, Fax- 478-207-1699. http://sos.georgia.gov/plb/veterinary/ Search data at- https://secure.sos.state.ga.us/myverification/

Georgia Federal Courts

The following list indicates the district and division name for each county in the state. If the bankruptcy court location is different from the district court, then the location of the bankruptcy court appears in parentheses.

County/Court Cross Reference

County	District	Division
Appling	Southern	Brunswick (Savannah)
Atkinson	Southern	Waycross (Savannah)
Bacon	Southern	Waycross (Savannah)
Baker	Middle	Albany/Americus (Macon)
Baldwin	Middle	Macon
Banks	Northern	Gainesville
Barrow	Northern	Gainesville
Bartow	Northern	Rome
Ben Hill	Middle	Albany/Americus (Macon)
Berrien	Middle	Valdosta (Columbus)
Bibb	Middle	Macon
Bleckley	Middle	Macon
Brantley	Southern	Waycross (Savannah)
Brooks	Middle	Thomasville (Columbus)
Bryan	Southern	Savannah
Bulloch	Southern	Statesboro (Augusta)
Burke	Southern	Augusta
Butts	Middle	Macon
Calhoun	Middle	Albany/Americus (Macon)
Camden	Southern	Brunswick (Savannah)
Candler	Southern	Statesboro (Augusta)
Carroll	Northern	Newnan
Catoosa	Northern	Rome
Charlton	Southern	Waycross (Savannah)
Chatham	Southern	Savannah
Chattahoochee	Middle	Columbus
Chattooga	Northern	Rome
Cherokee	Northern	Atlanta
Clarke	Middle	Athens (Macon)
Clay	Middle	Columbus
Clayton	Northern	Atlanta
Clinch	Middle	Valdosta (Columbus)
Cobb	Northern	Atlanta
Coffee	Southern	Waycross (Savannah)
Colquitt	Middle	Thomasville (Columbus)
Columbia	Southern	Augusta
Cook	Middle	Valdosta (Columbus)
Coweta	Northern	Newnan
Crawford	Middle	Macon
Crisp	Middle	Albany/Americus (Macon)
Dade	Northern	Rome
Dawson	Northern	Gainesville
De Kalb	Northern	Atlanta
Decatur	Middle	Thomasville (Columbus)
Dodge	Southern	Dublin (Augusta)
Dooly	Middle	Macon
Dougherty	Middle	Albany/Americus (Macon)
Douglas	Northern	Atlanta
Early	Middle	Albany/Americus (Macon)
Echols	Middle	Valdosta (Columbus)
Effingham	Southern	Savannah
Elbert	Middle	Athens (Macon)
Emanuel	Southern	Statesboro (Augusta)
Evans	Southern	Statesboro (Augusta)
Fannin	Northern	Gainesville
Fayette	Northern	Newnan
Floyd	Northern	Rome
Forsyth	Northern	Gainesville
Franklin	Middle	Athens (Macon)
Fulton	Northern	Atlanta
Gilmer	Northern	Gainesville
Glascock	Southern	Augusta
Glynn	Southern	Brunswick (Savannah)
Gordon	Northern	Rome
Grady	Middle	Thomasville (Columbus)
Greene	Middle	Athens (Macon)
Gwinnett	Northern	Atlanta
Habersham	Northern	Gainesville
Hall	Northern	Gainesville
Hancock	Middle	Macon
Haralson	Northern	Newnan
Harris	Middle	Columbus
Hart	Middle	Athens (Macon)
Heard	Northern	Newnan
Henry	Northern	Atlanta
Houston	Middle	Macon
Irwin	Middle	Valdosta (Columbus)
Jackson	Northern	Gainesville
Jasper	Middle	Macon
Jeff Davis	Southern	Brunswick (Savannah)
Jefferson	Southern	Augusta
Jenkins	Southern	Statesboro (Augusta)
Johnson	Southern	Dublin (Augusta)
Jones	Middle	Macon
Lamar	Middle	Macon
Lanier	Middle	Valdosta (Columbus)
Laurens	Southern	Dublin (Augusta)
Lee	Middle	Albany/Americus (Macon)
Liberty	Southern	Savannah
Lincoln	Southern	Augusta
Long	Southern	Brunswick (Savannah)
Lowndes	Middle	Valdosta (Columbus)
Lumpkin	Northern	Gainesville
Macon	Middle	Macon
Madison	Middle	Athens (Macon)
Marion	Middle	Columbus
McDuffie	Southern	Augusta
McIntosh	Southern	Brunswick (Savannah)
Meriwether	Northern	Newnan
Miller	Middle	Albany/Americus (Macon)
Mitchell	Middle	Albany/Americus (Macon)
Monroe	Middle	Macon
Montgomery	Southern	Dublin (Augusta)
Morgan	Middle	Athens (Macon)

County	District	Division
Murray	Northern	Rome
Muscogee	Middle	Columbus
Newton	Northern	Atlanta
Oconee	Middle	Athens (Macon)
Oglethorpe	Middle	Athens (Macon)
Paulding	Northern	Rome
Peach	Middle	Macon
Pickens	Northern	Gainesville
Pierce	Southern	Waycross (Savannah)
Pike	Northern	Newnan
Polk	Northern	Rome
Pulaski	Middle	Macon
Putnam	Middle	Macon
Quitman	Middle	Columbus
Rabun	Northern	Gainesville
Randolph	Middle	Columbus
Richmond	Southern	Augusta
Rockdale	Northern	Atlanta
Schley	Middle	Albany/Americus (Macon)
Screven	Southern	Statesboro (Augusta)
Seminole	Middle	Thomasville (Columbus)
Spalding	Northern	Newnan
Stephens	Northern	Gainesville
Stewart	Middle	Columbus
Sumter	Middle	Albany/Americus (Macon)
Talbot	Middle	Columbus
Taliaferro	Southern	Augusta
Tattnall	Southern	Statesboro (Augusta)
Taylor	Middle	Columbus
Telfair	Southern	Dublin (Augusta)
Terrell	Middle	Albany/Americus (Macon)
Thomas	Middle	Thomasville (Columbus)
Tift	Middle	Valdosta (Columbus)
Toombs	Southern	Statesboro (Augusta)
Towns	Northern	Gainesville
Treutlen	Southern	Dublin (Augusta)
Troup	Northern	Newnan
Turner	Middle	Albany/Americus (Macon)
Twiggs	Middle	Macon
Union	Northern	Gainesville
Upson	Middle	Macon
Walker	Northern	Rome
Walton	Middle	Athens (Macon)
Ware	Southern	Waycross (Savannah)
Warren	Southern	Augusta
Washington	Middle	Macon
Wayne	Southern	Brunswick (Savannah)
Webster	Middle	Albany/Americus (Macon)
Wheeler	Southern	Dublin (Augusta)
White	Northern	Gainesville
Whitfield	Northern	Rome
Wilcox	Middle	Macon
Wilkes	Southern	Augusta
Wilkinson	Middle	Macon
Worth	Middle	Albany/Americus (Macon)

Standards for Federal Courts: Fees are standard unless noted in profile. Search fee is $26.00 per item (one party name or case number). Copy fee is $.50 per page. Certification fee is $9.00 per document, double for exemplification, if available. Most courts require prepayment. Mail requests should enclose a SASE unless otherwise noted. Before releasing records, all courts require prepayment, unless noted.

District courts index by defendant and plaintiff and by case number. Bankruptcy courts usually index by debtor and case number. While most courts now have their indexes on computer, many may still maintain index card files as well. Courts will archive closed case files at different times.

There are numerous public access programs available to online subscribers. Search the U.S. Party/Case Index to find party names and case numbers among all courts. Individual case data is provided on PACER. A search of CM/ECF provides copies of cases filed electronically. For details about PACER, the US Party/Case Index, and CM/ECF see the Appendix or go to http://pacer.psc.uscourts.gov or call 800-676-6856.

US District Court Georgia Middle District

Albany/Americus Div. Court Clerk, CB King US Courthouse, 201 W Broad Ave, Albany, GA 31701, 229-430-8432; Fax- 229-430-8538. Hours-8:30AM-5PM. www.gamd.uscourts.gov

Counties/Note: Baker, Ben Hill, Calhoun, Crisp, Dougherty, Early, Lee, Miller, Mitchell, Schley, Sumter, Terrell, Turner, Webster, Worth. Ben Hill and Crisp were transferred from the Macon Division as of 10/1997.

Searches/Indexing: Include full name only in search request. Results do not include SSN or DOB. Will not fax back documents. New cases are in the index immediately after filing date. Both computer and card indexes maintained; computer back to 1991. District-wide searches available for files after 1/1991. Case files sent to archives 2 years after closed.

Search Access: Only docket info available by phone. **Mail:** Search usually completed- 24 hours. Include SASE for return. **Fax:** Written fax requests accepted. **In person:** 1 public terminal available. No self-serve copier.

Payment: Pay by major credit cards, money order, cashier's check, in-state business check. No personal checks. Payee: Clerk, USDC.

E-Services: PACER records go back to 1/1991. New records online after 1 day. ECF at https://ecf.gamd.uscourts.gov. Records, opinions, calendars available.

Athens Division Court Clerk, PO Box 1106, Athens, GA 30603 (In person: US Post Office and Courthouse, 115 E Hancock Ave, Athens, GA 30601), 706-227-1094; Fax- 706-546-2190. Hours-8:30AM-5PM. www.gamd.uscourts.gov

Counties/Note: Clarke, Elbert, Franklin, Greene, Hart, Madison, Morgan, Oconee, Oglethorpe, Walton. Closed cases before 4/1997 are located in the Macon Division.

Searches/Indexing: Include full name only in search request. Results do not include SSN or DOB. Will not fax back documents. New cases are in the index immediately after filing date. Both computer and card indexes maintained; computer back to 1991. District-wide searches available for files after 1/1991. Case files sent to archives 2 years after closed.

Search Access: Only docket info available by phone. **Mail:** Search usually completed- 1 day. Include SASE for return. **In person:** 1 public terminal available. No self-serve copier.

Payment: Pay by major credit cards, money order, cashier's check, business check. No personal checks. Payee: Clerk, USDC.

E-Services: PACER records go back to 1/1991. New records online after 1 day. ECF at https://ecf.gamd.uscourts.gov. Records, opinions, calendars available.

Columbus Division Court Clerk, PO Box 124, Columbus, GA 31902 (In person: US Post Office and Court House, 120 12th St, Rm 103, Columbus, GA 31901), 706-649-7816. Hours-8:30AM-5PM. www.gamd.uscourts.gov

Counties/Note: Chattahoochee, Clay, Harris, Marion, Muscogee, Quitman, Randolph, Stewart, Talbot, Taylor.

Searches/Indexing: Include full name only in search request. Results do not include SSN or DOB. Will not fax back documents. New cases are in the index immediately after filing date. All records now maintained on computer. District-wide searches available for files after 1/1991. Case files sent to archives 2 years after closed.

Search Access: Only docket info available by phone. **Mail:** Search usually completed- ASAP. Include SASE for return. **In person:** 1 public terminal available. No self-serve copier.

Payment: Pay by major credit cards, money order, cashier's check, business check. No personal checks. Payee: Clerk, US Courts.

E-Services: PACER records go back to 1/1991. New records online after 1 day. ECF at https://ecf.gamd.uscourts.gov. Records, opinions, calendars available.

Macon Division Court Clerk, PO Box 128, Macon, GA 31202-0128 (In person: Federal Bldg and US Courthouse, 475 Mulberry, #216, Macon, GA 31201), 478-752-3497; Fax- 478-752-3496. Hours-8:30AM-5PM. www.gamd.uscourts.gov

Counties/Note: Baldwin, Ben Hill, Bibb, Bleckley, Butts, Crawford, Crisp, Dooly, Hancock, Houston, Jasper, Jones, Lamar, Macon, Monroe, Peach, Pulaski, Putnam, Twiggs, Upson, Washington, Wilcox, Wilkinson. Athens Division cases closed before 4/1997 are also located at Macon.

Searches/Indexing: Include full name only in search request. Results do not include full SSN or full DOB. New cases are in the index immediately after filing date. Both computer and card indexes maintained. District-wide searches available for files after 1/1991. Case files sent to archives 2 years after closed.

Search Access: Only docket info available by phone. **Mail:** Search usually completed- 2 days. Include SASE for return. **In person:** 1 public terminal available. No self-serve copier.

Payment: Pay by major credit cards, money order, cashier's check, business check. No personal checks. Payee: Clerk, USDC.

E-Services: PACER records go back to 1/1991. New records online after 1 day. ECF at https://ecf.gamd.uscourts.gov. Records, opinions, calendars available.

Thomasville Division c/o Valdosta Division, PO Box 68, Valdosta, GA 31603 (In person: US Courthouse and Post Office, 401 N Patterson, Rm 212, Valdosta, GA 31601), 229-226-3651; 229-242-3616 Valdosta; Fax- 229-244-9547. Hours-8:30AM-5PM. www.gamd.uscourts.gov

Counties/Note: Brooks, Colquitt, Decatur, Grady, Seminole, Thomas. No criminal cases can be searched at Thomasville court, but trials held at Valdosta; see Macon Division for records.

Searches/Indexing: Include full name only in search request. Results do not include SSN or DOB. Will not fax back documents. New cases are in the index immediately after filing date. Both computer and card indexes maintained; computer back to 1991. District-wide searches available for files after 1/1991. Case files sent to archives 2 years after closed.

Search Access: Only docket info available by phone. **Mail:** Search usually completed- 48 hours. Include SASE for return. **Fax:** Written fax search requests accepted. **In person:** 1 public terminal available. No self-serve copier.

Payment: Pay by major credit cards, money order, cashier's check, business check. No personal checks. Payee: Clerk, USDC.

E-Services: PACER records go back to 1/1991. New records online after 1 day. ECF at https://ecf.gamd.uscourts.gov. Records, opinions, calendars available.

Valdosta Division Court Clerk, PO Box 68, Valdosta, GA 31603 (In person: US Courthouse and Post Office, 401 N Patterson, Rm 212, Valdosta), 229-242-3616; Fax- 229-244-9547. Hours-8:30AM-5PM. www.gamd.uscourts.gov

Counties/Note: Berrien, Clinch, Cook, Echols, Irwin, Lanier, Lowndes, Tift. No criminal cases can be searched at this court, but trials held at Valdosta; see Macon Division for records.

Searches/Indexing: Include full name only in search request. Results do not include SSN or DOB. Will not fax back documents. New cases are in the index immediately after filing date. Both computer and card indexes maintained; computer back to 1991. District-wide searches available for files after 1/1991. Case files sent to archives 2 years after closed.

Search Access: Only docket info available by phone. **Mail:** Search usually completed- 24 hours. Include SASE for return. **Fax:** Written fax search requests accepted. **In person:** 1 public terminal available. Self-serve copier available.

Payment: Pay by major credit cards, money order, cashier's check, business check. No personal checks. Payee: Clerk, USDC.

E-Services: PACER records go back to 1/1991. New records online after 1 day. ECF at https://ecf.gamd.uscourts.gov. Records, opinions, calendars available.

US Bankruptcy Court Georgia Middle District

Columbus (West) Division Court Clerk, PO Box 2147, Columbus, GA 31902 (In person: 901 Front Ave, 1 Arsenal Pl, Columbus, GA 31902), 706-649-7837; Fax- 706-649-7845. Hours-8:30AM-5PM. www.gamb.uscourts.gov

Counties/Note: Berrien, Brooks, Chattahoochee, Clay, Clinch, Colquitt, Cook, Decatur, Echols, Grady, Harris, Irwin, Lanier, Lowndes, Marion, Muscogee, Quitman, Randolph, Seminole, Stewart, Talbot, Taylor, Thomas, Tift. This court has records for the Thomasville and Valdosta Divisions, also Chapter 11 & 12 records for the Albany branch.

Searches/Indexing: Include SSN and any alias names for debtor in search request. Results do not include SSN or DOB. Will not fax back documents. New cases are in the index immediately after filing date.

Search Access: Docket info available by phone. Voice Case Information Service available, call VCIS at 800-211-3015 or 912-752-8183. **Mail:** Search usually completed- 2-3 days. Include SASE for return. **Fax:** Fax search requests accepted. **In person:** 1 public terminal available. No self-serve copier.

Payment: Pay by money order, cashier's check, business check. No personal checks. Credit cards accepted online at pay.gov - transaction fee applies. Payee: Clerk, US Bankruptcy Court.

E-Services: PACER integrated with ECF. PACER records go back to 3/1990, some back to 1985. New records online after 1 day. ECF at https://ecf.gamb.uscourts.gov. **Opinions Online:** www.gamb.uscourts.gov/opinions.htm. **Online Note:** Court calendars up to 2 weeks ahead free at https://ecf.gamb.uscourts.gov/cgi-bin/PublicCalendar.pl.

Macon (East) Division Court Clerk, PO Box 1957, Macon, GA 31201 (In person: 433 Cherry St, Macon, GA 31202), 478-752-3506; Fax- 478-752-8157. 8:30AM-5PM. www.gamb.uscourts.gov

Counties/Note: Baldwin, Baker, Ben Hill, Bibb, Bleckley, Butts, Calhoun, Clarke, Crawford, Crisp, Dooly, Dougherty, Early, Elbert, Franklin, Greene, Hancock, Hart, Houston, Jasper, Jones, Lamar, Lee, Macon, Madison, Miller, Mitchell, Monroe, Morgan, Oconee, Oglethorpe, Peach, Pulaski, Putnam, Schley, Sumter, Terrell, Turner, Twiggs, Upson, Walton, Washington, Webster, Wilcox, Wilkinson, Worth. This court has records for the Athens and Albany Divisions. This Macon branch does not have criminal records for Valdosta and Thomasville Divisions.

Searches/Indexing: Include SSN and any alias names for debtor in search request. Results include last 4 SSN digits. Will not fax back documents. New cases in the index immediately after filing.

Search Access: Court will only search for docket info by phone; limit is 3 searches per phone call. Voice Case Information Service available, call VCIS at 800-211-3015 or 478-752-8183. **Mail:** Search usually completed- 5 days. Include SASE for return. **In person:** 2 public terminals available. No self-serve copier.

Payment: Pay by money order, cashier's check, business check. No personal checks. Credit cards accepted online at pay.gov - transaction fee applies. Payee: Clerk, US Bankruptcy Court.

E-Services: PACER integrated with ECF. PACER records go back to 3/1990, some back to 1985. New records online after 1 day. ECF at https://ecf.gamb.uscourts.gov. **Opinions Online:** www.gamb.uscourts.gov/opinions.htm. Calendars up to 2 weeks ahead at https://ecf.gamb.uscourts.gov/cgi-bin/PublicCalendar.pl.

US District Court Georgia Northern District

Atlanta Division Court Clerk, 2211 US Courthouse, 75 Spring St SW, Atlanta, GA 30303-3361, 404-215-1600; Gen Info- 404-215-1660; records- 404-215-1655. Hours-8AM-4:45PM. www.gand.uscourts.gov

Counties/Note: Cherokee, Clayton, Cobb, De Kalb, Douglas, Fulton, Gwinnett, Henry, Newton, Rockdale.

Searches/Indexing: Search request requires name only. Results include last 4 SSN digits. Will not fax back documents. New cases are in the index 1 day after filing date.

Search Access: Only docket info is available by phone. **Mail:** Search usually completed- 5-10 working days. SASE not required. **In person:** 5 public terminals available. No self-serve copier.

Payment: Pay by major credit cards, no business or personal checks accepted. Payee: Clerk, US District Court.

E-Services: Document images available. PACER records go back to 8/1992. New records online after 1 day. ECF at https://ecf.gand.uscourts.gov. Opinions available through ECF website.

Gainesville Division Court Clerk, Federal Bldg Rm 201, 121 Spring St SE, Gainesville, GA 30501, 678-450-2760; Hours- 8AM-4:45PM. www.gand.uscourts.gov

Counties/Note: Banks, Barrow, Dawson, Fannin, Forsyth, Gilmer, Habersham, Hall, Jackson, Lumpkin, Pickens, Rabun, Stephens, Towns, Union, White.

Searches/Indexing: Search request requires name only. Results do not include SSN or DOB. Will not fax back documents. New cases are in the index 24 hours after filing date. Case files sent to archives 3 years after closed.

Search Access: Mail: Search usually completed- 24 hours. Include SASE for return. **In person:** 1 public terminal available. No self-serve copier.

Payment: Pay by no business or personal checks. Law firm checks/credit cards accepted. Payee: Clerk, US District Court.

E-Services: Document images available. PACER records go back to 8/1992. New records online after 1 day. ECF at https://ecf.gand.uscourts.gov. Opinions available through ECF website.

Newnan Division Court Clerk, 18 Greenville St, #352, Newnan, GA 30263, 678-423-3060. Hours-8AM-4:30PM. www.gand.uscourts.gov

Counties: Carroll, Coweta, Fayette, Haralson, Heard, Meriwether, Pike, Spalding, Troup.

Searches/Indexing: Search request requires name only. Results include last 4 SSN digits. Will not fax back documents. New cases are in the index immediately after filing date.

Search Access: Only docket info is available by phone. **Mail:** Search usually completed- 2 days. SASE not required. **In person:** 1 public terminal available. No self-serve copier.

Payment: Pay by no business or personal checks. Law firm checks accepted. Payee: Clerk, US District Court.

E-Services: Document images available. PACER records go back to 8/1992. New records online after 1 day. ECF at https://ecf.gand.uscourts.gov. Opinions available through ECF website.

Rome Division Court Clerk, 600 E 1st St, Rm 304, Rome, GA 30161, 706-378-4060. Hours- 8:30AM-5PM. www.gand.uscourts.gov

Counties/Note: Bartow, Catoosa, Chattooga, Dade, Floyd, Gordon, Murray, Paulding, Polk, Walker, Whitfield.

Searches/Indexing: Search request requires name only. Results include last 4 SSN digits. Will not fax back documents. New cases are in the index immediately after filing date. Computer, microfiche and card indexes maintained. Index prior to 1978 on index cards. Case files sent to archives 2-3 years after closed.

Search Access: Via phone, only docket info showing if a suit has been filed, date of filing, and if case is pending or closed is released. **Mail:** Search usually completed- 24 hours. Include SASE for return. **In person:** 1 public terminal available. No self-serve copier.

Payment: Pay by no business or personal checks. Law firm checks accepted. Payee: Clerk, US District Court.

E-Services: Document images available. PACER records go back to 8/1992. New records online after 1 day. ECF at https://ecf.gand.uscourts.gov. Opinions available through ECF website.

US Bankruptcy Court Georgia Northern District

Atlanta Div. Court Clerk, 1340 US Courthouse, 75 Spring St SW, Atlanta, GA 30303-3361, 404-215-1000; records- 404-215-1169; Fax-404-215-1221. Hours-8AM-4PM. www.ganb.uscourts.gov

Counties/Note: Cherokee, Clayton, Cobb, DeKalb, Douglas, Fulton, Gwinnett, Henry, Newton, Rockdale.

Searches/Indexing: Include SSN and full name in search request. Results include last 4 SSN digits. Will not fax back documents. New cases are in the index 1 day after filing date. Computer, microfiche and card indexes maintained. Paper case files archived 6 months after closing; electronic files maintained indefinitely.

Search Access: Docket info available by phone. Voice Case Information Service available, call VCIS at 800-510-8284 or 404-730-2866. **Mail:** Search usually completed- 1-2 days. Include SASE for return. **In person:** 6 public terminals available. Copies printed from public terminals- $.10 each. No self-serve copier.

Payment: Pay by money order, cashier's check, business check. No credit cards (except attorneys') accepted. Payee: Clerk, US Bankruptcy Court.

E-Services: PACER records go back to 8/1986. New records online after 1 day. ECF at https://ecf.ganb.uscourts.gov. **Opinions Online:** www.ganb.uscourts.gov/judges/opn/opn_index.php. **Note:** Opinions and calendars also on PACER.

Gainesville Div. Court Clerk, 121 Spring St SE, Rm 120, Gainesville, GA 30501, 678-450-2700. Hours-8AM-4PM. www.ganb.uscourts.gov

Counties/Note: Banks, Barrow, Dawson, Fannin, Forsyth, Gilmer, Habersham, Hall, Jackson, Lumpkin, Pickens, Rabun, Stephens, Towns, Union, White.

Searches/Indexing: Include full SSN and full name in search request. Results include last 4 SSN digits. Will not fax back documents. New cases are in the index immediately after filing date. Both computer and card indexes maintained; court maintains index cards on older cases. Paper case files archived 6 months after closing; electronic files maintained indefinitely.

Search Access: Docket info available via phone. Voice Case Information Service available, call VCIS at 800-510-8284 or 404-730-2866. **Mail:** Search usually completed- 1-2 days. Include SASE for return. **In person:** 6 public terminals available. No self-serve copier.

Payment: Pay by money order, cashier's or personal check. No credit cards (except attorneys') accepted. Payee: Clerk, US Bankruptcy Court.

E-Services: PACER records go back to 8/1986. New records online after 1 day. ECF at https://ecf.ganb.uscourts.gov. **Opinions Online:** www.ganb.uscourts.gov/judges/opn/opn_index.php. Opinions and calendars also on PACER.

Newnan Division Clerk of Court, PO Box 2328, Newnan, GA 30264 (In person: 18 Greenville St, Rm 220, Newnan), 678-423-3000. 8AM-4PM. www.ganb.uscourts.gov

Counties: Carroll, Coweta, Fayette, Haralson, Heard, Meriwether, Pike, Spalding, Troup.

Searches/Indexing: Include SSN and full name in search request. Results include last 4 SSN digits. Will not fax back documents. New cases are in the index 1 day after filing date. Card and microfiche indexes also available. Paper case files archived 6 months after closing; electronic files maintained indefinitely.

Search Access: Only docket info available by phone, no charge if case number is provided. Debtor's address and social security number not released. Voice Case Information Service available, call VCIS at 800-510-8284 or 404-730-2866. **Mail:** Search usually completed- 1-2 days. Include SASE for return. **In person:** 6 public terminals available. No self-serve copier.

Payment: Pay by money order, cashier's or personal check. No credit cards (except attorneys') accepted. Payee: Clerk, US Bankruptcy Court.

E-Services: PACER records go back to 8/1986. New records online after 1 day. ECF at https://ecf.ganb.uscourts.gov. **Opinions Online:** www.ganb.uscourts.gov/judges/opn/opn_index.php. **Online Note:** Opinions and calendars are available on PACER.

Rome Division Clerk of Court, 600 E 1st St, Rm 339, Rome, GA 30161-3187, 706-378-4000. Hours-8AM-4PM. www.ganb.uscourts.gov

Counties/Note: Bartow, Catoosa, Chattooga, Dade, Floyd, Gordon, Murray, Paulding, Polk, Walker, Whitfield.

Searches/Indexing: Include SSN and full name in search request. Results include last 4 SSN digits. Will not fax back documents. New cases are in the index immediately after filing date. Computer and card indexes maintained. Paper case files archived 6 months after closing; electronic files maintained indefinitely.

Search Access: Docket info available by phone. Voice Case Information Service available, call VCIS at 800-510-8284 or 404-730-2866. **Mail:** Search usually completed- 1-2 days. Include SASE for return. **In person:** 6 public terminals available. No self-serve copier.

Payment: Pay by money order, cashier's or personal check. No credit cards (except attorneys') accepted. Payee: Clerk, US Bankruptcy Court.

E-Services: PACER records go back to 8/1986. New records online after 1 day. ECF at https://ecf.ganb.uscourts.gov. **Opinions Online:** www.ganb.uscourts.gov/judges/opn/opn_index.php. **Online Note:** Opinions and calendars are available on PACER.

US District Court Georgia Southern District

Augusta Division Court Clerk, 600 James Brown Blvd, Federal Justice Ctr, Augusta, GA 30901, 706-849-4400. Hours- 8:30AM - 5PM. www.gasd.uscourts.gov

Counties/Note: Burke, Columbia, Dodge*, Glascock, Jefferson, Johnson*, Laurens*, Lincoln, McDuffie, Montgomery*, Richmond, Taliaferro, Telfair*, Treutlen*, Warren, Wheeler*, Wilkes. This division holds records for the unstaffed Dublin Division. Counties with asterisk (*) are part of the Dublin Division.

Searches/Indexing: Only party names required for a search. Results do not include SSN or DOB.

Will not fax back documents. New cases are in the index immediately after filing date. Records alphabetically indexed. Records stored by chronological case number order.

Search Access: Limited docket info available via phone. **Mail:** Search usually completed- 1-2 weeks. Include SASE for return. **In person:** 1 public terminal. No self-serve copier.

Payment: Pay by money order, cashier's or personal check. No credit cards. Payee: US Courts.

E-Services: Document images available. PACER records go back to 6/1995. New records online after 1 day. ECF at https://ecf.gasd.uscourts.gov. **Online Note:** Opinions and calendars on PACER.

Brunswick Division Court Clerk, 801 Gloucester St, Rm 220, Brunswick, GA 31520, 912-280-1330; Fax- 912-280-1331. Hours- 8:30AM-5PM. www.gasd.uscourts.gov

Counties/Note: Appling, Camden, Glynn, Jeff Davis, Long, McIntosh, Wayne.

Searches/Indexing: Only party names required for a search. Results do not include SSN or DOB. Will not fax back documents. New cases are in the index immediately after filing date. Computer index maintained; prior records indexed on microfiche. Records stored by chronological case number order.

Search Access: Limited docket info available via phone. **Mail:** Search usually completed- 1-2 days. Include SASE for return. **In person:** 1 public terminal. No self-serve copier.

Payment: Pay by money order, cashier's or personal check. No credit cards accepted. Payee: Clerk, US District Court.

E-Services: Document images available. PACER records go back to 6/1995. New records online after 1 day. ECF at https://ecf.gasd.uscourts.gov. **Online Note:** Opinions and calendars on PACER.

Savannah Division Court Clerk, 125 Bull St, Rm 304, Savannah, GA 31401, 912-650-4020; Fax- 912-650-4030. Hours - 8:30AM - 5PM. www.gasd.uscourts.gov

Counties/Note: Atkinson, Bacon, Bulloch, Brantley, Bryan, Candler, Charlton, Chatham, Coffee, Effingham, Emanuel, Evans, Jenkins, Liberty, Pierce, Screven, Tattnall, Toombs, Ware. Holds records for unstaffed Statesboro and Waycross Divisions.

Searches/Indexing: Only party names required for a search. Results do not include SSN or DOB. Will not fax back documents. New cases are in the index immediately after filing date. Computer index back to 1992 maintained; prior records on microfiche. Records stored by chronological case number order.

Search Access: Limited docket info available via phone. **Mail:** Search usually completed- 1-2 days. Include SASE for return. **In person:** 2 public terminals available. No self-serve copier.

Payment: Pay by money order, cashier's or personal check. No credit cards accepted. Payee: Clerk, US District Court.

E-Services: Document images available. PACER records go back to 6/1995. New records online after 1 day. ECF at https://ecf.gasd.uscourts.gov. **Online Note:** Opinions and calendars on PACER.

US Bankruptcy Court Georgia Southern District

Augusta Division Court Clerk, 600 James Brown Blvd, Plaza Bldg, Augusta, GA 30901, 706-724-2421. Hours- 8:30AM - 5PM. www.gas.uscourts.gov

Counties/Note: Bulloch, Burke, Candler, Columbia, Dodge, Emanuel, Evans, Glascock, Jefferson, Jenkins, Johnson, Laurens, Lincoln, McDuffie, Montgomery, Richmond, Screven, Taliaferro, Tattnall, Telfair, Toombs, Treutlen, Warren, Wheeler, Wilkes. Office of the Clerk is now imaging pleadings for posting to WebPACER/RACER, through the court's website. Court handles files for Statesboro, Dublin, and Augusta divisions.

Searches/Indexing: To search, include full name; SSN and DOB helpful. Results include last 4 SSN digits. Will not fax back documents. New cases are in the index immediately after filing date. District-wide searches available here back to 8/1985.

Search Access: If case number is provided via phone, docket info released. **Mail:** Search usually completed- 7 days. SASE not required. **In person:** 3 public terminals available. No self-serve copier.

Payment: Pay by money order, cashier's check, business check. No personal checks or credit cards. Payee: Clerk, US Bankruptcy Court.

E-Services: ECF replaces PACER and RACER. Document images available. PACER records go back to 8/1986. New records online immediately. ECF at https://ecf.gasb.uscourts.gov. **Opinion:** http://207.41.17.136/bkcyorders/dtSearch.html. **Online Note:** Search calendars at www.gas.uscourts.gov/publicwebcal/.

Savannah Division Court Clerk, PO Box 8347, Savannah, GA 31412 (In person: 125 Bull St, Rm 304, Savannah), 912-650-4020, 912-650-4100; records- 912-650-4107. Hours-8:30AM-5PM. www.gas.uscourts.gov

Counties/Note: Appling, Atkinson, Bacon, Brantley, Bryan, Camden, Charlton, Chatham, Coffee, Effingham, Glynn, Jeff Davis, Liberty, Long, McIntosh, Pierce, Ware, Wayne. Office of the Clerk is now imaging pleadings for posting to WebPACER/RACER, through the court's website. Court handles files for Waycross, Savannah, Statesboro, and Brunswick (912-280-1330, 801 Gloucester St #220) divisions.

Searches/Indexing: To search, include full name; SSN and DOB helpful. Results include last 4 SSN digits. Will not fax back documents. New cases are in the index immediately after filing date. District-wide searches available here back to 8/1985.

Search Access: Phone search is limited to info on computer. **Mail:** Search usually completed- 3 days. SASE not required. **In person:** 4 public terminals available. No self-serve copier.

Payment: Pay by money order, cashier's check, business check. No personal checks or credit cards. Payee: Clerk, US Bankruptcy Court.

E-Services: ECF replaces PACER and RACER. Document images available. PACER records go back to 1988. New records online after 1 day. ECF at https://ecf.gasb.uscourts.gov. **Opinions Online:** http://207.41.17.136/bkcyorders/dtSearch.html. **Online Note:** Search calendars at www.gas.uscourts.gov/publicwebcal/.

Georgia County Courts

Court	Jurisdiction	No. of Courts	How Organized
Superior Courts*	General	159	49 Circuits
State Courts*	Limited	71	71 Counties
Combined Superior/State Courts*		43	
Magistrate Courts*	Limited	159	By County
Civil Courts*	Limited	2	Bibb, Richmond
County Recorder's Courts	Limited	4	Chatham, DeKalb, Gwinnett, Muscogee
Municipal Courts	Municipal	350	City Court of Atlanta
Probate Courts*	Probate	159	By County
Juvenile Courts	Special	159	By County

* Profiled in this Sourcebook.

Court	CIVIL Tort	Contract	Real Estate	Min. Claim	Max. Claim	Small Claims	Estate	Eviction	Domestic Relations
Superior Courts*	X	X	X	$0	No Max			X	X
State Courts*	X	X		$0	No Max			X	
Combined Superior/ State Courts*	X	X	X	$0	No Max			X	
Magistrate Courts*	X	X		$0	$15,000	$15,000		X	
Combined Superior/ Magistrate Court*	X	X	X		varies	$15,000		X	
Civil Courts*	X	X		$0	varies				
Recorder's Courts									
Municipal Courts									
Probate Courts*							X		

Court	CRIMINAL Felony	Misdemeanor	DWI/DUI	Preliminary Hearing	Juvenile
Superior Courts*	X	X	X	X	
State Courts*		X	X	X	
Combined Superior/ State Courts*	X	X	X	X	
Magistrate Courts*		X		X	
Combined Superior/ Magistrate Court*	X	X	X	X	
Civil Courts*				X	
Recorder's Courts		X	X	X	
Municipal Courts		X	X	X	
Juvenile Courts					X

Administration

Court Administrator, 244 Washington St SW, Ste. 300, Atlanta, GA, 30334; 404-656-5171, Fax: 404-651-6449. (EST) www.georgiacourts.org

Court Structure

The Georgia court system has five classes of trial-level courts: the Magistrate, Probate, Juvenile, State, and Superior courts. In addition, there are approximately 350 municipal courts operating locally. The Superior Court, arranged in 49 circuits, is the court of general jurisdiction. The Superior Court will also assume the role of a State Court if the county does not have one. State courts exercise limited jurisdiction within one county. These judges hear misdemeanors including traffic violations, issue search and arrest warrants, hold preliminary hearings in criminal cases and try civil matters not reserved exclusively for the Superior Courts.

Magistrate Courts also issue arrest warrants and set bond on all felonies. Magistrate Courts also have jurisdiction for bad checks, arrest warrants, preliminary hearings, and county ordinance violations. The Magistrate Court has jurisdiction over civil actions under $15,000, also one type of misdemeanor related to passing bad checks. Two counties (Bibb and Richmond) have Civil/Magistrate courts with varied civil limits. Probate Courts can, in certain cases, issue search and arrest warrants, and hear miscellaneous misdemeanors.

Online Access

Search the dockets of the Court of Appeals at www.gaappeals.us/. Search dockets of the Supreme Court at www.gasupreme.us/computer_docket.php. Make online purchases of certificates of admission and good standing ($3.00), Supreme Court opinions ($5.00), and certified copies of Supreme Court opinions ($8.00) using Paypal. Go to www.gasupreme.us/purchase_online.php.

A limited number of county courts offer online access to court records, but there is no statewide online access available statewide.

Searching Tips, Fees, and Other Guidelines

Many Georgia county courts will not perform criminal record searches and, in many cases, will not do civil record searches. Hiring a local record retriever is advised. Many Georgia counties are small and no retriever may be available; if so, it is best to engage a retriever in a neighboring county or take the advice of most court clerks by asking a local law firm for assistance.

Appling County

Superior & State Court PO Box 269, 69 Tippins St #103, Baxley, GA 31513; 912-367-8126; fax: 912-367-8180; 8AM-5PM. ***Felony, Misdemeanor, Civil.***

Civil Records: Access: In person only. Visitors must perform in person searches themselves. Required to search: name, years to search. Civil cases indexed by defendant, plaintiff; index on docket books back to 1800s. Civil PAT goes back to 2004.

Criminal Records: Access: In person only. Visitors must perform in person searches themselves. Required to search: name, years to search, DOB; SSN helpful. Criminal docket on books back to 1800s. Criminal PAT available.

General Information: No juvenile, adoption, sealed, sexual, mental health or expunged records released. Will fax back documents. Court makes copy: $.25 first page, $.10 each add'l, self serve same. Certification fee: $2.50 plus $.50 per page after first. Payee: Court Clerk. Personal checks accepted; credit cards are not.

Magistrate Court PO Box 366, 72 Tippins St, Baxley, GA 31515; 912-367-8116, 367-8117; fax: 912-367-8182; 8:30AM-5PM. ***Misdemeanor, Civil Actions under $15,000, Eviction, Small Claims.***

Court also has jurisdiction for bad checks, arrest warrants, preliminary hearings, and county ordinance violations.

Probate Court 36 S Main St, Baxley, GA 31513; 912-367-8114; fax: 912-367-8166; 8:30AM-5PM. ***Probate.***

Atkinson County

Superior Court PO Box 6, South Main, Courthouse Square, Pearson, GA 31642; 912-422-3343; fax: 912-422-7025; 8AM-5PM. ***Felony, Misdemeanor, Civil.***

Civil Records: Access: In person only. Visitors must perform in person searches themselves. Required to search: name, years to search. Civil cases indexed by defendant. Civil records in docket books back to 1919. Public use terminal has civil records back to 1/2005.

Criminal Records: Access: In person only. Visitors must perform in person searches themselves. Required to search: name, years to search. Criminal records in docket books back to 1919.

General Information: No juvenile, adoption, sealed, sexual, mental health or expunged records released. Will fax documents $1.00 per page. Court makes copy: $.50 per page. Self serve: $.25 per page. Certification fee: $2.50 plus $.50 per page after first. Payee: Clerk of Superior Court. Personal checks accepted. Prepayment required.

Magistrate Court PO Box 674, 19 Roberts Ave W, Pearson, GA 31642; 912-422-7158; fax: 912-422-7989; 8AM-5PM. ***Civil Actions under $15,000, Eviction, Small Claims.***

Court also has jurisdiction for bad checks, arrest warrants, preliminary hearings, and county ordinance violations.

Probate Court PO Box 855, 19 Roberts Ave W, Pearson, GA 31642; 912-422-3552; fax: 912-422-7842; 8AM-5PM. ***Probate.***

Bacon County

Superior Court PO Box 376, Alma, GA 31510; 912-632-4915; probate phone: 912-632-7661; fax: 912-632-6545; 9AM-5PM. ***Felony, Misdemeanor, Civil.***

Civil Records: Access: Mail, in person. Both court and visitors may perform in person searches. No search fee. Required to search: name, years to search. Civil cases indexed by defendant, plaintiff, on index from 1970, archived to 1918, computerized since 2000. Mail turnaround time 1 week. Civil PAT goes back to 2000. PAT results show name only.

Criminal Records: Access: in person only. Both court and visitors may perform in person searches. No search fee. Required to search: name, years to search, DOB; also helpful: SSN, race, sex. Criminal records indexed from 1970, archived to 1918, computerized since 2000. Criminal PAT goes back to same as civil. PAT results show middle initial, DOB.

General Information: No juvenile, adoption, sealed, sexual, mental health, expunged or first offender records released. Will fax documents. Court makes copy: $1.00 per page. Self serve: $.25 per page. Certification fee: $2.50 plus $.50 per page after first. Payee: Clerk of Superior Court. Personal checks accepted; credit cards are not. Prepayment required. Mail requests: SASE required.

Magistrate Court Box 389, 502 W 12th St, Rm 100, Alma, GA 31510; 912-632-5961; civil phone: 912-632-7661; probate phone: 912-632-7661; fax: 912-632-7662; 9AM-5PM. ***Civil Actions under $15,000, Eviction, Small Claims.***

Court also has jurisdiction for bad checks, arrest warrants and preliminary hearings.

Probate Court PO Box 389, 502 W 12th St, Rm 100, Alma, GA 31510; 912-632-7661; fax: 912-632-7662; 9AM-5PM. ***Probate.***

Baker County

Superior Court PO Box 10, 167 Baker Pl, Courthouse, Newton, GA 39870; 229-734-3004; fax: 229-734-3004; 9AM-5PM. ***Felony, Misdemeanor, Civil.***

Civil Records: Access: In person only. Visitors must perform in person searches themselves. Required to search: name, years to search. Civil cases indexed by defendant. Civil records on index from 1850. Public use terminal has civil records back to 1998. Results include name and case number.

Criminal Records: Access: In person only. Visitors must perform in person searches themselves. Required to search: name, years to search, DOB; SSN helpful. Criminal records indexed from 1850.

General Information: No juvenile, adoption, sealed, sexual or expunged records released. Will not fax documents. Court makes copy: $.25 per page. Certification fee: $2.50 plus $.50 per page after first. Payee: Court Clerk. Personal checks accepted; credit cards are not. Prepayment required.

Magistrate Court PO Box 548, 167 Baker Pl, Newton, GA 39870; 229-734-3009; probate phone: same; fax: 229-734-8822; 9AM-5PM. ***Civil Actions under $15,000, Eviction, Small Claims.***

Court also has jurisdiction for bad checks, arrest warrants, preliminary hearings, and county ordinance violations. Probate fax is same as main fax number.

Probate Court PO Box 548, 167 Baker Pl, Newton, GA 39870; 229-734-3007; fax: 229-734-8822; 9AM-5PM M-W & F; 9AM-N TH. ***Probate.***

Baldwin County

Superior & State Court PO Drawer 987, Milledgeville, GA 31059-0987; 478-445-4007; criminal phone: 478-445-6949; civil phone: 478-445-6328; fax: 478-445-6039; 8:30AM-5PM. ***Felony, Misdemeanor, Civil.***

Numbers above are for Superior Court. State Court criminal is 445-1799, civil is 445-4698.

Civil Records: Access: In person only. Visitors must perform in person searches themselves. Required to search: name, years to search. Civil cases indexed by defendant, plaintiff, on docket from 1861; on computer back to 1996. Civil PAT goes back to 1998. PAT results show name only.

Criminal Records: Access: In person only. Visitors must perform in person searches themselves. Required to search: name, years to search. Criminal records on docket from 1861; on computer back to 1996. Criminal PAT goes back to same as civil. PAT results show name only.

General Information: No juvenile, adoption, sealed, sexual, mental health or expunged records released. Court makes copy: $.25 per page. Certification fee: $2.50 plus $.50 per page after first. Payee: Clerk of Courts. Personal checks accepted; credit cards are not. Prepayment required.

Magistrate Court 121 N Wilkinson St, #107, Milledgeville, GA 31061; 478-445-4446; fax: 478-445-5918; 8:30AM-5PM. ***Civil Actions under $15,000, Eviction, Small Claims.***

Court also has jurisdiction for bad checks, arrest warrants, preliminary hearings, and county ordinance violations.

Probate Court 121 N Wilkinson St, #109, Milledgeville, GA 31061; 478-445-4807; fax: 478-445-5178; 8:30AM-5PM. ***Probate.***

Banks County

Superior Court PO Box 337, 144 Yonah Homer Rd #8, Homer, GA 30547; 706-677-6243; fax: 706-677-6294; 8AM-5PM. ***Felony, Misdemeanor, Civil.***

Civil Records: Access: In person only. Visitors must perform in person searches themselves. Required to search: name, years to search. Civil cases indexed by defendant, plaintiff, on docket from 1960. Civil PAT goes back to 2000.
Criminal Records: Access: In person only. Visitors must perform in person searches themselves. Required to search: name, years to search, DOB. Criminal records on docket from 1960. Criminal PAT goes back to same as civil.
General Information: No juvenile, adoption, sealed, sexual, mental health or expunged records released. Will fax documents for $1.00 per page. Court makes copy: $.25 per page. Certification fee: $3.75 per doc. Payee: Clerk of Superior Court. Personal checks accepted. Visa/MC and debit cards accepted. Prepayment required.

Magistrate Court 144 Yonah Homer Rd #10, Homer, GA 30547-2614; 706-677-6270; criminal fax: 706-677-6215; civil fax: same; 8:30AM-5PM. ***Civil Actions under $15,000, Eviction, Small Claims.*** Court also has jurisdiction for bad checks, arrest warrants, preliminary hearings, and county ordinance violations.

Probate Court 144 Yonah Homer Rd,#7, Homer, GA 30547; 706-677-6250; fax: 706-677-2337; 8AM-5PM. ***Probate, Misdemeanor Traffic.***

Barrow County

Superior Court PO Box 1280, 40 N Broad St, Winder, GA 30680; 770-307-3035; fax: 770-867-4800; 8AM-5PM. ***Felony, Misdemeanor, Civil.***
Civil Records: Access: In person only. Visitors must perform in person searches themselves. Required to search: name, years to search. Civil cases indexed by defendant, plaintiff, on computer from 1990, docket from 1915. Civil PAT goes back to 1990.
Criminal Records: Access: In person only. Visitors must perform in person searches themselves. Required to search: name, years to search, DOB. Criminal records computerized from 1990, docket from 1915. Criminal PAT goes back to 1992.
General Information: No juvenile, adoption, sealed, sexual, mental health or expunged records released. Will fax documents $2.50 1st page, $1.00 each add'l page. Court makes copy: $1.00 per page. Self serve: $.25 per page. Certification fee: $2.50 1st page plus $.50 each add'l. Payee: Clerk of Superior Court. Business checks accepted. No credit cards accepted. Prepayment required.

Magistrate Court 30 N Broad St, #227, Winder, GA 30680; 770-307-3050; fax: 770-868-1440; 8AM-5PM. ***Civil Actions under $15,000, Eviction, Small Claims.*** www.barrowga.org/magistrate/ Court also has jurisdiction for bad checks, arrest warrants, preliminary hearings, and county ordinance violations.

Probate Court 30 N Broad St, #329, Barrow County Courthouse, Winder, GA 30680; 770-307-3045; fax: 770-307-4470; 8AM-4:30PM. ***Probate, Misdemeanor.***

Bartow County

Superior Court 135 W Cherokee Ave, #233, Cartersville, GA 30120; 770-387-5025; fax: 770-387-5611; 8AM-5PM. ***Felony, Misdemeanor, Civil.***
Civil Records: Access: In person only. Visitors must perform in person searches themselves. Required to search: name, years to search. Civil cases indexed by defendant, plaintiff, on computer from 9/92, on books from 1900s.
Criminal Records: Access: In person only. Visitors must perform in person searches themselves. Required to search: name, years to search, DOB, SSN, signed release. Criminal records on computer for 10 years, prior on books. Public use terminal has crim records back to 1992.
General Information: No juvenile, adoptions or sealed records released. Will not fax documents. Court makes copy: $.25 per page. Certification fee: $2.50 1st page plus $.25 each add'l page. Payee: Clerk of Superior Court. Personal checks accepted; credit cards are not. Prepayment required.

Magistrate Court 112 W Cherokee Ave, #101, Cartersville, GA 30120; 770-387-5070; fax: 770-387-5073; 7AM-5:30PM. ***Civil Actions under $15,000, Eviction, Small Claims, Misdemeanors.*** www.bartowcourt.com Court also has jurisdiction for bad checks, arrest warrants, preliminary hearings, and county ordinance violations.

Probate Court 135 W Cherokee, #243A, Cartersville, GA 30120; 770-387-5075; fax: 770-387-5074; 8AM-5PM. ***Probate, Traffic.*** www.bartowga.org/probate

Ben Hill County

Superior Court PO Box 1104, 115 S Sheridan, Fitzgerald, GA 31750; 229-426-5135; fax: 229-426-5487; 8AM-4:30PM. ***Felony, Misdemeanor, Civil.***
Civil Records: Access: In person only. Visitors must perform in person searches themselves. Required to search: name, years to search. Civil cases indexed by defendant. Civil records computerized since 1994, archived from 1907, docket 1907.
Criminal Records: Access: In person only. Visitors must perform in person searches themselves. Required to search: name, years to search, signed release; also helpful: DOB, SSN. Criminal records computerized since 1994, archived from 1907, docket 1907.
General Information: No juvenile, adoption, sealed, sexual, mental health or expunged records released. Will fax documents for $2.50 each. Court makes copy: $1.00 per page. Self serve: $.25 per page. Certification fee: $2.00 plus $.50 per page. Payee: Clerk. Personal checks accepted; credit cards are not. Prepayment required.

Magistrate Court Box 1163, 255 Appomattox Rd, Fitzgerald, GA 31750; 229-426-5141; fax: 229-426-5123; 8AM-5PM. ***Misdemeanor, Civil Actions under $15,000, Eviction, Small Claims.*** Court also has jurisdiction for bad checks, arrest warrants, preliminary hearings, and county ordinance violations.

Probate Court 111 S Sheridan St, Fitzgerald, GA 31750; 229-426-5137/229-426-5126; fax: 229-426-5486; 8:30AM-4:30PM. ***Probate, Misdemeanor.***

Berrien County

Superior Court PO Box 504, 210 N Davis St, 2nd Fl, Nashville, GA 31639; 229-686-5506; fax: 229-543-1032; 8AM-4:30PM. ***Felony, Misdemeanor, Civil.***
Civil Records: Access: In person only. Both court and visitors may perform in person searches. No search fee. Required to search: name, years to search. Civil cases indexed by defendant, plaintiff, on docket back to 1800.
Criminal Records: Access: In person only. Both court and visitors may perform in person searches. No search fee. Required to search: name, years to search, DOB; also helpful: SSN, race, sex. Criminal records on docket back to 1800.
General Information: No juvenile, adoption, sealed, sexual, mental health or expunged records released. Court makes copy: $.25 per page, self serve same. Certification fee: $2.50. Payee: Court Clerk. Personal checks accepted; credit cards are not. Prepayment required.

Magistrate Court PO Box 267, 201 N Davis St, 2nd Fl, #250, Nashville, GA 31639; 229-686-7019; fax: 229-686-6328; 8:30AM-4:30PM. ***Civil Actions under $15,000, Eviction, Small Claims.*** Court also has jurisdiction for bad checks, arrest warrants, preliminary hearings, and county ordinance violations.

Probate Court 205 N Jefferson St, Nashville, GA 31639; 229-686-5213; fax: 229-686-9495; 8AM-4:30PM. ***Probate.***

Bibb County

Superior Court PO Box 1015, 275 2nd St, Rm 216, Macon, GA 31202; 478-621-6527; fax: 478-621-6033; 8:30AM-5PM. ***Felony, Civil.*** www.co.bibb.ga.us/ Court suggests use of a retriever for record searches.
Civil Records: Access: In person, online. Both court and visitors may perform in person searches. No search fee. Required to search: name, years to search. Civil cases indexed by defendant, plaintiff, on computer from 1993, on books from 1823. Civil PAT goes back to 1995. PAT results show name, DOB. Terminal results also show SSNs. Court calendars online at www.co.bibb.ga.us/CalendarDirectory/CalendarDirectory.asp.
Criminal Records: Access: In person, online. Both court and visitors may perform in person searches. No search fee. Required to search: name, years to search, DOB, signed release; also helpful: SSN. Criminal records on computer since 1989. Criminal PAT goes back to 1993.PAT results show name, DOB. Terminal results include SSN. Superior court calendars at www.co.bibb.ga.us/CalendarDirectory/CalendarDirectory.asp.
General Information: No adoption or sealed records released. Will not fax documents. Court makes copy: $1.00 per page. Self serve: $.25 per page. Certification fee: $2.50 plus $.50 per page after first. Payee: Superior Court Clerk. Only cashiers checks and money orders accepted. No credit cards accepted. Prepayment required.

State Court PO Box 5086, 601 Mulberry St Rm 500, Macon, GA 31213-7199; 478-621-6676; criminal fax: 478-621-6326; civil fax: same; 8AM-5PM. ***Misdemeanor, Civil.*** www.co.bibb.ga.us
Civil Records: Access: Mail, in person, online. Both court and visitors may perform in person searches. No search fee. Required to search: name, years to search. Civil cases indexed by defendant, plaintiff, on computer from 1989, docket from 1952. Mail turnaround time 1 day usually. Civil PAT goes back to 1990. Search civil court calendars online at www.co.bibb.ga.us/StateCourtClerk/Civil/Default.htm. Website will have access to full court record indexes in the future.
Criminal Records: Access: Mail, in person. Both court and visitors may perform in person searches. No search fee. Required to search: name, years to search, DOB; also helpful: SSN, race, sex. Criminal records computerized from 1989, docket from 1945. Mail turnaround time usually 1 day. Criminal PAT goes back to 1989.
General Information: No juvenile, adoption, sealed, sexual, mental health or expunged records released. Will fax to toll-free line if 5 pages or less, otherwise documents mailed. Court makes copy: $.50 per page, self serve same. Certification fee: $2.50 per page. Exemplification is an add'l $5.00 per page. Payee: Bibb State Court Clerk. Business checks accepted. No credit cards accepted. Prepayment required. Mail requests: SASE required.

Civil & Magistrate Court 601 Mulberry, #101, Bibb County Courthouse, Macon, GA 31201; 478-621-6495; criminal phone: 478-621-6505; civil: 478-621-6495; fax: 478-621-5861; 8AM-5PM. ***Civil Actions under $25,000, Eviction, Small Claims.*** www.bibbcourt.com Searchable database not yet available for this jurisdiction.

Probate Court PO Box 6518, 601 Mulberry St, 207 Courthouse, Macon, GA 31208; 478-621-6494; fax: 478-621-6686; 8AM-5PM. ***Probate.*** www.co.bibb.ga.us/ProbateCourt/ProbateCourt.asp

Bleckley County

Superior Court PO Box 272, 112 N 2nd St, Cochran, GA 31014; 478-934-3210; fax: 478-934-6671; 8:30AM-5PM. ***Felony, Misdemeanor, Civil.*** www.gsccca.org/clerks/displayclerk.asp
Civil Records: Access: In person only. Visitors must perform in person searches themselves. Required to search: name, years to search. Civil cases indexed by defendant, plaintiff, archived from 1913, docket from 1913. Public use terminal has civil records back to 1995.
Criminal Records: Access: In person only. Visitors must perform in person searches themselves. Required to search: name, years to search, DOB; SSN helpful. Criminal records archived from 1913, docket from 1913.
General Information: No juvenile, adoption, sealed, sexual, mental health or expunged records released.

Will not fax documents. Court makes copy: $.25 per page, self serve same. Certification fee: $2.50 plus $.50 per page after first. Payee: Clerk of the Superior Court. No personal checks or credit cards accepted. Prepayment required.

Magistrate Court 112 N 2nd St, Cochran, GA 31014; 478-934-3202; fax: 478-934-7826; 8:30AM-5PM. ***Civil Actions under $15,000, Eviction, Small Claims.*** Court also has jurisdiction for bad checks, arrest warrants, preliminary hearings, and county ordinance violations.

Probate Court 112 N 2nd St, Cochran, GA 31014; 478-934-3204; fax: 478-934-3205; 8:30AM-5PM. ***Probate, Misdemeanor.***

Brantley County

Superior Court PO Box 1067, 117 Brantley St, Nahunta, GA 31553; 912-462-6280; fax: 912-462-6247; 8AM-5PM. ***Felony, Misdemeanor, Civil.***
Civil Records: Access: In person only. Visitors must perform in person searches themselves. Required to search: name, years to search. Civil cases indexed by defendant, plaintiff, on dockets from 1920; computerized records go back 1998. Public use terminal available, records go back to 2004.
Criminal Records: Access: In person only. Visitors must perform in person searches themselves. Required to search: name, years to search, DOB, SSN, signed release. Criminal docket index from 1920. Public use terminal available, crim records go back to same.
General Information: No juvenile, adoption, sealed, 1st offenders, expunged or confidential records released. Will not fax documents. Court makes copy: $1.00 per page. Cert fee: $2.50 plus $.50 per page after first. Payee: Superior Court Clerk. Personal checks accepted; credit cards are not. Prepayment required.

Magistrate Court PO Box 1150, 117 Brantley St, Nahunta, GA 31553; 912-462-6780; criminal fax: 912-462-6897; civil fax: same; 8AM-4:30PM. ***Civil Actions under $15,000, Eviction, Small Claims.*** Court also has jurisdiction for bad checks, arrest warrants, preliminary hearings, and county ordinance violations.

Probate Court PO Box 207, 117 Brantley St, Nahunta, GA 31553; 912-462-5192; fax: 912-462-8360; 8AM-5PM. ***Probate.***

Brooks County

Superior Court PO Box 630, 100 Schevens, Quitman, GA 31643; 229-263-4747/5150; civil phone: 229-263-8054; fax: 229-263-5050; 8AM-5PM. ***Felony, Misdemeanor, Civil.***
http://southernjudicialcircuit.com
Fax in a search request and the clerk says she will post it on the bulletin board and someone may perform the search for you.
Civil Records: Access: In person only. Visitors must perform in person searches themselves. Required to search: name, years to search. Civil cases indexed by defendant, plaintiff, in books back to 1857. Will accept phone requests for specific documents. Public use terminal has civil records back to 1/1993.
Criminal Records: Access: In person only. Visitors must perform in person searches themselves. Required to search: name, years to search, DOB; SSN helpful. Criminal records in books back to 1857.
General Information: No juvenile, adoption, sealed, sexual, mental health or expunged records released. Will fax documents to local or toll free line. Court makes copy: $.25 per page, self serve same. Cert fee: $2.50 plus $.50 per page after first. Payee: Clerk Superior Court. Business checks accepted. No credit cards accepted. Prepayment required.

Magistrate Court PO Box 387, 400 E Courtland Ave, Quitman, GA 31643; 229-263-9989; criminal fax: 229-263-7847; civil fax: same; 8AM-5PM. ***Civil Actions under $15,000, Eviction, Small Claims, Ordinance.***
Court also has jurisdiction for bad checks, arrest warrants, preliminary hearings, garnishments.

Probate Court PO Box 665, 100 Screven St, Quitman, GA 31643; 229-263-5567; fax: 229-263-5058; 8AM-5PM. ***Probate.***

Bryan County

Superior & State Court PO Box 670, 151 S College St, Pembroke, GA 31321; 912-653-3872; criminal phone: 912-653-3872 x3; civil phone: 912-653-3874; criminal fax: 912-653-3870; civil fax: 912-653-5255; 8AM-5PM. ***Felony, Misdemeanor, Civil.***
Civil Records: Access: In person only. Visitors must perform in person searches themselves. Required to search: name, years to search. Civil cases indexed by defendant, plaintiff, on dockets from 1960, recent records are computerized since 9/93. Civil PAT goes back to 1993.
Criminal Records: Access: In person only. Visitors must perform in person searches themselves. Required to search: name, years to search, DOB; SSN helpful. Criminal docket index from 1960, recent records are computerized since 9/93. Criminal PAT goes back to same as civil.
General Information: No juvenile, adoption, sealed, sexual, mental health or expunged records released. Will fax specific case file $2.00 1st page, $1.00 each add'l, if prepaid. Court makes copy: $1.00 per page. Self serve: $.25 per page. Certification fee: $2.50 per page. Payee: Clerk of Superior & State Court. Personal checks accepted; credit cards are not. Prepayment required.

Magistrate Court Box 670, 151 S College St, Pembroke, GA 31321; 912-653-3860; fax: 912-653-5254; 8AM-5PM. ***Civil Actions under $15,000, Eviction, Small Claims.*** www.bryancountyga.org
Court also has jurisdiction for bad checks, arrest warrants, preliminary hearings, and county ordinance violations.

Probate Court PO Box 418, 151 S College, #106, Pembroke, GA 31321; 912-653-3856; fax: 912-653-3845; 8:30AM-N, 1-5PM. ***Probate.***
www.georgiacourts.org/courts/probate/bryan/

Bulloch County

Superior & State Court Judicial Annex Bldg, 20 Siebald St, Statesboro, GA 30458; 912-764-9009; fax: 912-764-5953; 8AM-5PM. ***Felony, Misdemeanor, Civil.***
Civil Records: Access: In person only. Both court and visitors may perform in person searches. No search fee. Required to search: name, years to search. Civil cases indexed by defendant. Civil records on computer from 1991, dockets back to 1796. Civil PAT goes back to 1991. PAT results show name only.
Criminal Records: Access: In person only. Both court and visitors may perform in person searches. No search fee. Required to search: name, years to search. Criminal records computerized from 1991, dockets back to 1796. Criminal PAT goes back to 1991. PAT results show name only.
General Information: No juvenile, adoption, sexual, mental health or expunged records released. Will not fax documents. Court makes copy: $.25 per page, self serve same. Certification fee: $2.50 plus cert. Payee: Court Clerk. Personal checks accepted; credit cards are not. Prepayment required.

Magistrate Court Box 1004, 101 Oak St, 30458, Statesboro, GA 30459-1004; 912-764-6458, 912-764-5050; fax: 912-489-6731; 8AM-5PM. ***Civil Actions under $15,000, Eviction, Small Claims.***
Court also has jurisdiction for bad checks, arrest warrants, preliminary hearings, and county ordinance violations.

Probate Court PO Box 30458, 2 N Main St #103, Statesboro, GA 30459; 912-489-8749; fax: 912-764-8740; 8AM-5PM. ***Probate.***
Located in the Bulloch County Courthouse.

Burke County

Superior & State Court PO Box 803, 111 E 6th St, Rm 107, Waynesboro, GA 30830; 706-554-2279; fax: 706-554-7887; 9AM-5PM. ***Felony, Misdemeanor, Civil.***
Civil Records: Access: In person only. Visitors must perform in person searches themselves. Required to search: name, years to search. Civil cases indexed by defendant. Civil records on minute books back to 1856, indexed on computer since 1996. Public use terminal has civil records back to 1996. PAT results show middle initial, DOB.
Criminal Records: Access: In person only. Visitors must perform in person searches themselves. Required to search: name, years to search, DOB; SSN helpful. Criminal records on minute books back to 1856, indexed on computer since 1996. PAT results show middle initial, DOB.
General Information: No juvenile, adoption, sexual, mental health or expunged records released. Will not fax documents. Court makes copy: $1.50 per page. Self serve: $.25 per page. Certification fee: $2.50 plus $.50 per page after first. Payee: Clerk of Superior Court. Personal checks accepted; credit cards are not. Prepayment required.

Magistrate Court Box 401, 602 N Liberty St, Waynesboro, GA 30830; 706-554-4281; fax: 706-554-8772; 8AM-5PM. ***Civil Actions under $15,000, Eviction, Small Claims.***
Court also has jurisdiction for bad checks, arrest warrants, preliminary hearings, county ordinance violations.

Probate Court PO Box 322, 111 E 6th St, Waynesboro, GA 30830; 706-554-3000; fax: 706-554-6693; 9AM-5PM. ***Probate, Ordinance.***

Butts County

Superior Court PO Box 320, 26 3rd St, Jackson, GA 30233; 770-775-8215; fax: 770-504-1359; 8AM-5PM. ***Felony, Misdemeanor, Civil.***
Civil Records: Access: In person. Visitors must perform in person searches themselves. Required to search: name, years to search. Civil cases indexed by defendant, plaintiff, on dockets from 1966, computerized since 1998. Civil PAT goes back to 1998.
Criminal Records: Access: In person. Visitors must perform in person searches themselves. Required to search: name, years to search, signed release; also helpful: DOB, SSN, race, sex. Criminal docket index from 1966, computerized since 1998. Criminal PAT goes back to 1998.
General Information: No juvenile, adoption, sexual, mental health or expunged records released. Will not fax documents. Court makes copy: n/a. Self serve: $.25 per page. Certification fee: $2.50 plus $.50 per page. Payee: Clerk of Superior Court. Personal checks accepted; credit cards are not. Prepayment required.

Magistrate Court Box 457, 835 Ernest Biles Dr, Jackson, GA 30233; 770-775-8220; fax: 770-775-1954; 8:30AM-4:30PM. ***Civil Actions under $15,000, Eviction, Small Claims, Misdemeanor Fraud, Ordinance.***
Court also has jurisdiction for bad checks, arrest warrants, preliminary hearings, and county ordinance violations.

Probate Court 25 3rd St, #7, Jackson, GA 30233; 770-775-8204; fax: 770-775-8004; 8AM-5PM. ***Misdemeanor, Traffic, Probate.***

Calhoun County

Superior Court PO Box 69, Morgan, GA 39866; 229-849-2715; fax: 229-849-0072; 8AM-5PM. ***Felony, Misdemeanor, Civil.***
www.calhouncourtclerk.com/
Civil Records: Access: Fax, in person. Both court and visitors may perform in person searches. Search fee: $5.00 per name. Required to search: name, years to search, proof of payment, i.e. copy of check. Civil cases indexed by defendant, plaintiff, on dockets back to 1854. Civil PAT available. Only dockets available.
Criminal Records: Access: Mail, fax, in person. Both court and visitors may perform in person searches. Search fee: $5.00 per name. Required to search: name, years to search, DOB, proof of payment, i.e. copy of check. Criminal records on dockets back to 1854. Clerk will not do "lists of names" searches but if you have one or two names

they will search if you give them a toll-free fax number to return the results to. Criminal PAT available. Only dockets available.
General Information: No juvenile, adoption, sexual, mental health or expunged records released. Will fax $2.00 per page; no charge to toll-free numbers. Court makes copy: $1.00 per page. Self serve: $.25 per page. Certification fee: $3.00. Payee: Superior Court Clerk. Personal checks accepted; credit cards are not. Mail requests: SASE required.

Magistrate & Probate Court PO Box 87, 31 Court St #C, Morgan, GA 39866; 229-849-2115, 849-2116; fax: 229-849-2117; 8AM-5PM. ***Civil Actions under $15,000, Eviction, Small Claims, Probate.*** Court also has jurisdiction for bad checks, arrest warrants, preliminary hearings, and county ordinance violations.

Camden County

Superior Court PO Box 550, 210 E 4th St, Woodbine, GA 31569; 912-576-5631; fax: 912-576-5648; 9AM-5PM. ***Felony, Misdemeanor, Civil.***
Civil Records: Access: In person only. Visitors must perform in person searches themselves. Required to search: name, years to search. Civil cases indexed by defendant, plaintiff, on computer from 1989, on dockets from 1776. Civil PAT goes back to 1991.
Criminal Records: Access: In person only. Visitors must perform in person searches themselves. Required to search: name, years to search, signed release; also helpful: DOB, SSN. Criminal records computerized from 1989, on dockets from 1776. Criminal PAT goes back to 1989.
General Information: No juvenile, adoption, sexual or expunged records released. Will not fax out case files. Court makes copy: $1.00 per page. Self serve: $.25 per page. Certification fee: $2.50 plus $.50 per page. Payee: Clerk of Superior Court. Personal checks accepted; credit cards are not. Prepayment required.

Magistrate Court PO Box 386, 210 E 4th Street, Woodbine, GA 31569; 912-576-5658; fax: 912-576-7955; 9AM-5PM. ***Civil Actions under $15,000, Eviction, Small Claims.*** http://camdenmagcourt.com
Court also has jurisdiction for bad checks, arrest warrants, preliminary hearings, and county ordinance violations.

Probate Court PO Box 818, 210 E 4th St, Woodbine, GA 31569; 912-576-3785; fax: 912-576-5484; 9AM-5PM. ***Probate, Misdemeanor Drug, Traffic.*** Probate fax- 912-576-7145

Candler County

Superior & State Court PO Drawer 830, 355 Broad St, Metter, GA 30439; 912-685-5257; probate phone: 912-685-2357; fax: 912-685-2946; 8:30AM-5PM. ***Felony, Misdemeanor, Civil.***
Civil Records: Access: In person. Visitors must perform in person searches themselves. Required to search: name, years to search. Civil cases indexed by defendant, plaintiff, on dockets from 1914. Civil PAT goes back to 1995.
Criminal Records: Access: In person. Visitors must perform in person searches themselves. Required to search: name, years to search. Criminal docket index from 1914. Criminal PAT goes back to same as civil. PAT results show middle initial, DOB. Online results show middle initial, DOB.
General Information: No juvenile, adoption, mental health, expunged or sealed records released. Will fax documents to local or toll free line. Court makes copy: $.25 per page. Self serve: $.25 per page. Certification fee: $2.00 plus $.50 per page. Payee: Clerk of Superior & State Court. Personal checks accepted; credit cards are not. Prepayment required.

Magistrate Court 5 Courthouse Square, Metter, GA 30439; 912-685-2888; fax: 912-685-3995; 8:30AM-N, 1-5PM. ***Civil Actions under $15,000, Eviction, Small Claims.*** Court also has jurisdiction for bad checks, arrest warrants, preliminary hearings, and county ordinance violations.

Probate Court 35 Southwest Broad St, Ste B, Metter, GA 30439; 912-685-2357; fax: 912-685-5130; 8:30AM-5PM. ***Probate.***

Carroll County

Superior & State Court PO Box 1620, Carrollton, GA 30112; 770-214-3125; criminal phone: 770-830-5835 x2247/2239; civil phone: 770-830-5835 x2245/2246; probate phone: 770-830-5840; criminal fax: 770-214-3125; civil fax: same; 8AM-5PM. ***Felony, Misdemeanor, Civil.***
Civil Records: Access: Mail, in person. Both court and visitors may perform in person searches. Search fee: $5.00 per name. Required to search: name, years to search. Civil cases indexed by defendant, plaintiff, on computer from 1993, docket. Mail turnaround time 2 weeks. Civil PAT goes back to 9/00.
Criminal Records: Access: Mail, in person. Both court and visitors may perform in person searches. Search fee: $5.00 per name. Required to search: name, years to search, DOB; also helpful: SSN, race, sex. Criminal records computerized from 1986 for State Court, Superior Court records are computerized from 9/00 to present. Mail turnaround time 2 weeks. Criminal PAT goes back to same as civil.
General Information: No juvenile, adoption, sexual, mental health or expunged records released. Court makes copy: $.25 per page, self serve same. Certification fee: $2.50 plus $.50 per page after first. Payee: Clerk of Superior & State Court. Personal checks accepted; credit cards are not. Prepayment required. Mail requests: SASE required.

Magistrate Court 108 Courtyard Sq, Carrollton, GA 30117; 770-830-5874; criminal fax: 770-830-5851; civil fax: same; 8AM-5PM. ***Misdemeanors, Civil Actions under $15,000, Eviction, Small Claims.*** www.carrollcountyga.com/home/magistrate/
Court also has jurisdiction for bad checks, arrest warrants, preliminary hearings, and county ordinance violations.

Probate Court PO Box 338, 311 Newnan St, Rm 204, Carrollton, GA 30112; 770-830-5840; fax: 770-830-5995; 8AM-5PM. ***Probate.***

Catoosa County

Superior Court 875 Lafayette St, Ringgold, GA 30736; 706-935-4231; fax: 706-965-7431; 8:30AM-5PM. ***Felony, Misdemeanor, Civil.***
Civil Records: Access: In person only. Visitors must perform in person searches themselves. Required to search: name, years to search. Civil cases indexed by defendant, plaintiff, on dockets from 1800. Public use terminal available, records go back to 1996. PAT civil results show middle initial.
Criminal Records: Access: In person only. Visitors must perform in person searches themselves. Required to search: name, years to search, DOB. Criminal docket index from 1800. Public use terminal available, crim records go back to 1997.PAT results show name, DOB.
General Information: No juvenile, adoption, sexual, mental health or expunged records released. Will not fax documents. Court makes copy: $1.00 per page. Self serve: $.25 per page. Certification fee: $2.50 plus $.50 per page after first. Payee: Superior Court Clerk. Personal checks accepted; credit cards are not. Prepayment required.

Magistrate Court 877 Lafayette St, Ringgold, GA 30736; 706-935-3114; fax: 706-965-9036; 9AM-N, 1-5PM. ***Misdemeanor, Civil Actions under $15,00, Eviction, Small Claims, Ordinance.***

Probate Court 875 Lafayette St, Justice Bldg, Ringgold, GA 30736; 706-935-3511; fax: 706-935-3519; 8:30AM-5PM. ***Probate.***
This court will not perform mail searches.

Charlton County

Superior Court PO Box 760, Courthouse, 100 S Third St, Folkston, GA 31537; 912-496-2354; fax: 912-496-3882; 8:30AM-5PM. ***Felony, Misdemeanor, Civil.***
Civil Records: Access: In person only. Visitors must perform in person searches themselves. Required to search: name, years to search. Civil cases indexed by defendant. Civil records on index from 1954.
Criminal Records: Access: In person. Visitors must perform in person searches themselves. Required to search: name, years to search, DOB, SSN. Criminal records indexed from 1954.
General Information: No juvenile, adoption, sexual, mental health or expunged records released. Will not fax documents. Court makes copy: $.25 per page. Certification fee: $2.50 plus $.50 per page after first. Payee: Court Clerk. Personal checks accepted; credit cards are not. Prepayment required.

Magistrate Court 100 B County St, Folkston, GA 31537; 912-496-2617; fax: 912-496-2560; 9AM-4:30PM. ***Civil Actions under $15,000, Eviction, Small Claims.***
Court also has jurisdiction for bad checks, arrest warrants, preliminary hearings, and county ordinance violations.

Probate Court 100 S 3rd St, Folkston, GA 31537; 912-496-2230; fax: 912-496-7045; 8AM-5PM. ***Probate.***

Chatham County

Superior Court PO Box 10227, 133 Montgomery, Savannah, GA 31412-0427; 912-652-7197; criminal phone: 912-652-7209; civil phone: 912-652-7200; criminal fax: 912-652-7380; civil fax: same; 8AM-5PM. ***Felony, Civil.***
www.chathamcourts.org/chatcourts.html
Civil Records: Access: Mail, in person, online. Both court and visitors may perform in person searches. No search fee. Required to search: name, years to search. Civil cases indexed by defendant, plaintiff, on computer from 1984, archived back to 1900, dockets back to 1900s. Mail turnaround time 1 week. Civil PAT goes back to 1984. PAT civil results show middle initial. Search county court civil records at www.chathamcounty.org/jims/.
Criminal Records: Access: Mail, in person, online. Both court and visitors may perform in person searches. No search fee. Required to search: name, years to search, signed release; also helpful: DOB, SSN. Criminal records computerized from 1984, archived back to 1900, dockets back to 1900s. Mail turnaround time 1 week. Criminal PAT goes back to same as civil. PAT results show middle initial, DOB. Search county court criminal records at www.chathamcounty.org/jims/. Online results show middle initial, DOB.
General Information: Online identifiers in results same as on public terminal. No adoption records released. Will not fax documents. Court makes copy: $.25 per page. Certification fee: $2.00 plus $.50 per page. Payee: Court Clerk. Personal checks accepted; credit cards are not. Prepayment required. Mail requests: SASE requested.

State Court 133 Montgomery St, #308, County Courthouse, Savannah, GA 31401; 912-652-7224; fax: 912-652-7229; 8AM-5PM. ***Misdemeanor, Civil.*** www.statecourt.org
Search fines, tickets, and restitution records free at www.chathamcounty.org/jims/fines/default.asp.
Civil Records: Access: Mail, fax, in person, online. Both court and visitors may perform in person searches. Search fee: $3.00 per name. Required to search: name, years to search, address. Civil cases indexed by defendant, plaintiff, on computer from 1983, prior on books. Mail turnaround time 2 days. Civil PAT goes back to 1983. PAT results show name, DOB. Search county civil dockets and records free at www.chathamcounty.org/jims/. Search by name or case number.
Criminal Records: Access: Mail, fax, in person, online. Both court and visitors may perform in person searches. Search fee: $3.00 per name. Required to search: name, years to search. Criminal records computerized from 1983, prior on books. Results include name and address. Mail turnaround time 2 days. Criminal PAT goes back to 1983. Search county criminal dockets and records free at www.chathamcounty.org/jims/. Online results show name, DOB.
General Information: No first time criminal offender or sealed civil records released. Will fax documents $1.00 per page. Court makes copy: $1.00 per page. Self serve: $.25 per page. Certification fee: $2.50 plus $.50 per page. Payee: Clerk of State Court.

Only cashiers checks and money orders accepted. Visa/MC accepted. Prepayment required. Mail requests: SASE required.

Magistrate Court 133 Montgomery St, Rm 303, 3rd Fl, Savannah, GA 31401; 912-652-7181; fax: 912-652-7550; 8AM-5PM. ***Civil Actions under $15,000, Eviction, Small Claims.***
www.chathamcourts.org/chatcourts.html
Court also has jurisdiction for bad checks, arrest warrants, preliminary hearings, county ordinances. Search dockets at www.chathamcounty.org/jims/.

Probate Court 133 Montgomery St, Rm 509, Savannah, GA 31401; 912-652-7265; fax: 912-652-7262; 8AM-5PM. ***Probate.***
www.chathamcounty.org/probatecourt.html

Chattahoochee County

Superior & Magistrate Court PO Box 120, Cusseta, GA 31805; 706-989-3424; fax: 706-989-1508; 8AM-5PM. ***Felony, Misdemeanor, Civil, Eviction, Small Claims.***
Magistrate Court is 706-989-3643.
Civil Records: Access: In person only. Visitors must perform in person searches themselves. Required to search: name, years to search. Civil cases indexed by defendant, plaintiff, on dockets from 1854; on computer back to 1990. Civil PAT goes back to 1998 Magistrate. PAT results show name only.
Criminal Records: Access: In person only. Visitors must perform in person searches themselves. Required to search: name, years to search, DOB; SSN helpful. Criminal docket index from 1854. Criminal PAT goes back to 1854. PAT results show name only.
General Information: No juvenile, adoption, sexual, mental health or expunged records released. Will not fax documents. Court makes copy: $1.00 per page. Self serve: $.25 per page. Certification fee: $2.50 plus $.50 per page after first. Payee: Court Clerk. Business checks accepted. No credit cards accepted. Prepayment required.

Probate Court PO Box 119, 379 Broad Street, Cusseta, GA 31805; 706-989-3603; fax: 706-989-2015; 8AM-N, 1-5PM. ***Probate.***

Chattooga County

Superior & State Court PO Box 159, Summerville, GA 30747; 706-857-0706; fax: 706-857-0686; 8:30AM-5PM. ***Felony, Misdemeanor, Civil, Eviction, Small Claims.***
Civil Records: Access: In person only. Both court and visitors may perform in person searches. No search fee. Required to search: name, years to search. Civil cases indexed by defendant, plaintiff, on dockets from 1960. Civil PAT goes back to 2000.
Criminal Records: Access: In person only. Both court and visitors may perform in person searches. No search fee. Required to search: name, years to search, DOB; SSN helpful. Criminal docket index from 1960. Criminal PAT available.
General Information: No juvenile, adoption, sexual, mental health or expunged records released. Will not fax documents. Court makes copy: $.25 per page, self serve same. Certification fee: $2.50 plus $.50 per page after first. Payee: Clerk of Court. Personal checks accepted; credit cards are not. Prepayment required.

Magistrate Court 12 Cox St, Summerville, GA 30747; 706-857-0711; fax: 706-857-0675; 9AM-5PM. ***Civil Actions under $15,000, Eviction, Small Claims, Ordinance.*** Court also has jurisdiction for bad checks, arrest warrants, preliminary hearings, and county ordinance violations.

Probate Court PO Box 467, 10035 Commerce St, Summerville, GA 30747; 706-857-0709; fax: 706-857-0877; 8:30AM-N, 1-5PM. ***Probate.***

Cherokee County

Superior & State Court 90 North St, #G170, Canton, GA 30114; 678-493-6501; civil phone: 678-493-6511; fax: 770-479-0467; 8:30AM-5PM. ***Felony, Misdemeanor, Civil.***
www.cherokeega.com/ccweb/departments/clerkofcourts/
This court location also handles juvenile records.
Civil Records: Access: In person only. Visitors must perform in person searches themselves. Required to search: name. Civil cases indexed by defendant, plaintiff, on computer from 1970s, archived 1900-1991, on dockets back to 1900. Civil PAT goes back to 1970's.
Criminal Records: Access: Phone, mail, In person. Both court and visitors may perform in person searches. No search fee. Required to search: name, years to search. Criminal records computerized from 1970s, archived 1900-1990, on dockets back to 1900. There is a Criminal history Request Form available from the web. Criminal PAT goes back to same as civil.
General Information: No juvenile, adoption, sexual, mental health, expunged or confidential records released. Will not fax documents. Court makes copy: $1.00 per page. Self serve: $.25 per page. Certification fee: $2.50 plus $.50 per add'l page. Payee: Clerk of Court. Only cashiers checks, cash and money orders accepted. No credit cards accepted. Prepayment required. Mail requests: SASE required for criminal.

Magistrate Court 90 North St, #150, Canton, GA 30114; 678-493-6431; fax: 678-493-6440; 8:30AM-5PM. ***Civil Actions under $15,000, Eviction, Small Claims.*** www.cccourt.com
Court also has jurisdiction for bad checks, arrest warrants, preliminary hearings, and county ordinance violations.

Probate Court 90 North St, Rm 340, Canton, GA 30114; 678-493-6160; fax: 678-493-6170; 8AM-5PM. ***Probate.***

Clarke County

Superior & State Court PO Box 1805, 325 E Washington, Rm 450, Athens, GA 30603; 706-613-3190; fax: 706-613-3189; 8AM-5PM. ***Felony, Misdemeanor, Civil.***
http://athensclarke.allclerks.us
This court will perform no searches for the public.
Civil Records: Access: In person only. Visitors must perform in person searches themselves. Required to search: name, years to search. Civil cases indexed by defendant, plaintiff, on computer from 1993, docket books from 1801. Civil PAT goes back to 1993. PAT results show name only.
Criminal Records: Access: In person only. Visitors must perform in person searches themselves. Required to search: name, years to search, DOB. Criminal records computerized from 1993, docket books from 1801. Criminal PAT goes back to same as civil. PAT criminal results show middle initial.
General Information: No juvenile, adoptions, sealed, sexual, mental health or expunged records released. Will fax out documents $1.00 per page. Court makes copy: $.25 each; by mail copy fee is $1.00 per page. Self serve: $.25 per page. Certification fee: $2.50 plus $.50 per page after 1st. Payee: County Clerk. Local personal checks accepted. Visa/MC accepted. Prepayment required.

Magistrate Court PO Box 1868, 325 E Washington St, #230, Athens, GA 30603; 706-613-3310; fax: 706-613-3314; 8AM-5PM. ***Civil Actions under $15,000, Eviction, Small Claims.***
Court also has jurisdiction for bad checks, arrest warrants, and preliminary hearings, also foreclosures, garnishments, abandoned vehicles.

Probate Court 325 E Washington St, #215, Athens, GA 30601; 706-613-3320; fax: 706-613-3323; 8AM-5PM. ***Probate.***
www.athensclarkecounty.com/probatecourt/

Clay County

Superior Court PO Box 550, Ft Gaines, GA 39851; 229-768-2631; fax: 229-768-3047; 8AM-4:30PM. ***Felony, Misdemeanor, Civil, Eviction.***
Civil Records: Access: In person only. Visitors must perform in person searches themselves. Required to search: name, years to search. Civil cases indexed by defendant, plaintiff, on computer from 1990, on dockets from 1854. Civil PAT goes back to 1990. PAT results show name only.
Criminal Records: Access: In person only. Visitors must perform in person searches themselves. Required to search: name, years to search. Criminal records computerized from 1990, on dockets from 1854. Criminal PAT goes back to same as civil. PAT results show name only.
General Information: No juvenile, adoption, sexual, mental health or expunged records released. Court makes copy: $1.00 per page. Self serve: $.25 per page. Certification fee: $3.00. Payee: Superior Court Clerk. Personal checks accepted; credit cards are not. Prepayment required.

Magistrate Court PO Box 73, 210 S Washington St, Ft Gaines, GA 39851; 229-768-2841; fax: 229-768-3047; 8AM-4:30PM. ***Civil Actions under $15,000, Eviction, Small Claims.*** Court also has jurisdiction for bad checks, arrest warrants, preliminary hearings, and county ordinance violations.

Probate Court PO Box 448, 210 S Washington, Ft Gaines, GA 39851; 229-768-2445; fax: 229-768-3028; 8AM-4:30PM. ***Probate, Misdemeanor.***

Clayton County

Superior Court 9151 Tara Blvd, #ICL19, Jonesboro, GA 30236-4912; 770-477-3405; 8AM-5PM. ***Felony, Civil.***
www.co.clayton.ga.us/superior_court/clerk_of_courts/
Civil Records: Access: Mail, in person, online. Visitors must perform in person searches themselves. No search fee. Required to search: name, years to search. Civil cases indexed by defendant. Civil index on docket books for all records, on computer from 1996, on microfilm from 1990, archived from 1858-1982, dockets to 1858. Civil PAT goes back to 1996. PAT results show name only. Address not shown. Online access is the same as criminal, see below.
Criminal Records: Access: Mail, in person, online. Visitors must perform in person searches themselves. No search fee. Required to search: name, years to search, DOB; also helpful: race, sex. Criminal record keeping same as civil. Mail turnaround time 1 week. Criminal PAT goes back to 1985. PAT results show name only. Search records free at http://weba.co.clayton.ga.us:8006/index.shtml. Court calendars at www.co.clayton.ga.us/courtcalendars/index.htm. Searches and records also available on the statewide system.
General Information: No adoption, sexual, mental health or expunged records released. Will not fax documents. Court makes copy: $1.00 per page by mail; $.25 per page walk-in. Self serve: $.25 per page. Certification fee: $2.50 plus $.50 per page. Payee: Clerk of Superior Court. Only cashiers checks, money orders and attorney checks accepted. Major credit cards accepted. Prepayment required.

Magistrate Court 9151 Tara Blvd, #2TC08, Jonesboro, GA 30236-4912; 770-477-3444; fax: 770-473-5750; 8AM-5PM. ***Civil Actions under $15,000, Eviction, Small Claims. Ordinance.***
www.co.clayton.ga.us/courts.htm
Online access free at http://weba.co.clayton.ga.us:8006/index.shtml. Court also has jurisdiction for felony prelims, bad checks, arrest warrants, and county ordinance violations.

State Court 9151 Tara Blvd, #1CL181, Jonesboro, GA 30236; 770-477-3388; fax: 770-472-8159; 8AM-5PM. ***Misdemeanor.***
www.co.clayton.ga.us/state_court/clerk_of_courts/
Criminal Records: Access: In person, online. Visitors must perform in person searches themselves. Required to search: name, years to search. Criminal records computerized from 1984. Public use terminal has crim records back to 1990. Results include full name and birth year. Can search criminal database by name or case at http://weba.co.clayton.ga.us:8006/index.shtml
Online results show middle initial. Birth year included in online search results.
General Information: No juvenile, adoption, sexual, mental health or expunged records released. Will not fax documents. Court makes copy: $.25 per page. Certification fee: $2.50 plus $.50 per page after first. Payee: State Court Clerk. Business checks accepted.

No credit cards accepted. Prepayment required. Mail requests: SASE required for mail return of any copies.

Probate Court 121 S McDonough St, Annex 3, Jonesboro, GA 30236-3694; 770-477-3299; fax: 770-477-3306; 8AM-4:30PM. ***Probate.*** www.co.clayton.ga.us/probate_court/index.htm

Clinch County

Superior & State Court PO Box 433, Homerville, GA 31634; 912-487-5854; fax: 912-489-3083; 8AM-5PM. ***Felony, Misdemeanor, Civil.***
Civil Records: Access: Mail, in person. Both court and visitors may perform in person searches. No search fee. Required to search: name, years to search. Civil cases indexed by defendant, plaintiff, on dockets from 1900. Mail turnaround time 1-3 days. Civil PAT goes back to 1998.
Criminal Records: Access: Mail, in person. Both court and visitors may perform in person searches. No search fee. Required to search: name, years to search, DOB; also helpful: SSN, race, sex. Criminal docket index from 1900. Mail turnaround time 1-2 days. Criminal PAT goes back to same as civil.
General Information: No juvenile, adoption, sexual, mental health or expunged records released. Will fax documents $3.00 per page. Court makes copy: $.25 per page, self serve same. Certification fee: $3.00. Payee: Court Clerk. Personal checks accepted; credit cards are not. Prepayment required. Mail requests: SASE requested.

Magistrate Court 22 Court Square, Ste A, Homerville, GA 31634; 912-487-2514; fax: 912-487-5507; 9AM-N, 1-5PM. ***Civil Actions under $15,000, Eviction, Small Claims.*** Court also has jurisdiction for bad checks, arrest warrants, preliminary hearings, and county ordinance violations.

Probate Court PO Box 364, 25 Court Sq, #F, Homerville, GA 31634; 912-487-5523; fax: 912-487-3083; 9AM-N, 1-5PM. ***Probate.***

Cobb County

Superior Court PO Box 3370, 32 Wadell St, Murietta Sq, 5th Fl, Marietta, GA 30061; 770-528-1300, 770-528-1344; 8AM-5PM. ***Felony, Misdemeanor, Civil.*** www.cobbsuperiorcourtclerk.com
Court calendars available at www.cobbsuperiorcourtclerk.org/courts/Calendars.htm.
Civil Records: Access: Online, in person. Visitors must perform in person searches themselves. Required to search: name, years to search. Civil cases indexed by defendant, plaintiff, on computer from 1982, records on dockets from 1958. Civil PAT goes back to 1982. PAT results show middle initial, DOB, SSN. Civil indexes and images of Clerk from Superior Court are free at www.cobbsuperiorcourtclerk.org/courts/Civil.htm. Search by name, type or case number. Data updated Fridays. Images go back thru 2004.
Criminal Records: Access: Mail, online, in person. Both court and visitors may perform in person searches. No search fee. Required to search: name, years to search. Criminal records computerized from 1982, Records on dockets from 1958. Mail turnaround time 1-3 days. Criminal PAT goes back to same as civil. PAT results show middle initial, DOB, SSN. Criminal indexes and images from Clerk of Superior Court are free at www.cobbsuperiorcourtclerk.org/courts/Criminal.htm. Search by name, type or case number. Data updated Fridays but indexing can be nearly a month behind.
General Information: No juvenile, adoption, sexual, mental health or expunged records released. Will not fax out documents. Court makes copy: $.25 per page, self serve same. Certification fee: $2.00 plus $.50 per page. Payee: Clerk of Superior Court. Personal checks accepted; credit cards are not. Prepayment required. Mail requests: SASE required for criminal.

State Court - Civil & Criminal Divisions 12 E Park Sq, Marietta, GA 30090-9630; criminal phone: 770-528-1262; civil phone: 770-528-1203; criminal fax: 770-528-1268; civil fax: 770-528-1205; 8AM-5PM. ***Misdemeanor, Civil, Eviction, Traffic.*** www.cobbstatecourtclerk.com
Civil Records: Access: Phone, in person. Both court and visitors may perform in person searches. No search fee unless record is offsite (pre-2000 and also in the archives), then $7.00 per case retrieval fee. Required to search: name, years to search. Civil cases indexed by defendant, plaintiff, on computer since 3/10/97, docket books from 1965, and microfilm up to 1998. Court will do a simple lookup over the phone to determine if a name exists in the index. Civil PAT goes back to 3/10/97.
Criminal Records: Access: In person only. Visitors must perform in person searches themselves. Required to search: name, years to search, offense; also helpful: DOB. Criminal records on computer since 1981, docket books from 1965. Criminal PAT goes back to 1981. PAT results show middle initial, DOB.
General Information: No sealed records released. Will not fax documents. Court makes copy: $.25 per page. Certification fee: $3.00 plus copy costs. Payee: State Court Clerk. No personal checks accepted. Money orders accepted. Major credit cards accepted in person only. Prepayment required.

Magistrate Court 32 Waddell St, 3rd Fl, Marietta, GA 30090-9656; 770-528-8900; 8AM-5PM. ***Civil Actions under $15,000, Small Claims.*** www.cobbcountyga.gov/judicial/#magistrate
Court also has jurisdiction for bad checks, arrest warrants, preliminary hearings, and county ordinance violations.

Probate Court 32 Waddell St, Marietta, GA 30060; 770-528-1990; fax: 770-528-1996; 8AM-4:30PM. ***Probate.*** www.cobbcountyga.gov/judicial/#probate

Coffee County

Superior & State Court 101 S Peterson Ave #218B, Douglas, GA 31533; 912-384-2865; fax: 912-393-3252; 8:30AM-5PM. ***Felony, Misdemeanor, Civil.***
Civil Records: Access: In person only. Visitors must perform in person searches themselves. Required to search: name. Civil cases indexed by defendant, plaintiff, on dockets.
Criminal Records: Access: In person only. Visitors must perform in person searches themselves. Required to search: name, years to search. Criminal records on dockets.
General Information: No juvenile, adoption, sexual, mental health or expunged records released. Will not fax documents. Court makes copy: $.25 per page. Certification fee: $3.00 per cert. Payee: Clerk Superior Court. Business checks accepted. No credit cards.

Magistrate Court 101 S Peterson Ave, Douglas, GA 31533; criminal phone: 912-384-1381; civil phone: 912-384-2983; fax: 912-383-0800; 8:30AM-5PM. ***Civil Actions under $15,000, Eviction, Small Claims.*** www.coffeemagcourt.com
Court also has jurisdiction for bad checks, arrest warrants, preliminary hearings, and county ordinance violations.

Probate Court 101 S Peterson Ave, Douglas, GA 31533; 912-384-5213; fax: 912-383-8116; 8:30AM-5PM. ***Probate, Civil.*** www.qpublic.net/ga/coffee/index-pc.html

Colquitt County

Superior & State Court PO Box 2827, Moultrie, GA 31776; 229-616-7420; criminal phone: 229-616-7423 Sup; 616-7064 state; civil phone: 229-616-7066 Sup; 616-7420 state; fax: 229-616-7029; 8AM-5PM. ***Felony, Misdemeanor, Civil.*** http://southernjudicialcircuit.com
The court may be able to do a name search for no fee under certain circumstances, and they may honor mail search requests if SASE is provided, time permitting.
Civil Records: Access: In person only. Visitors must perform in person searches themselves. Required to search: name, years to search. Civil cases indexed by defendant, plaintiff, go back to 1800s, civil records on dockets books, computerized records go back to 1999. Civil PAT goes back to 1999.
Criminal Records: Access: In person only. Visitors must perform in person searches themselves. Required to search: name, years to search. Criminal docket on books; computerized records go back to 1999. Criminal PAT goes back to same as civil.
General Information: No juvenile, adoption, sexual, mental health or expunged records released. Will not fax documents. Court makes copy: $1.00 per page. Self serve: $.25 per page. Certification fee: $2.50. Payee: Court Clerk. Personal checks accepted; credit cards are not. Prepayment required.

Magistrate Court PO Box 70, 101 E Central Ave, Rm 175, Moultrie, GA 31768; 229-616-7450; fax: 229-616-7494; 8AM-5PM. ***Civil Actions under $15,000, Eviction, Small Claims.***
Court also has jurisdiction for bad checks, arrest warrants, preliminary hearings, and county ordinance violations.

Probate Court PO Box 264, County Courthouse, 9 S Main St, Rm 108, Moultrie, GA 31776-0264; 229-616-7415; fax: 229-616-7489; 8AM-5PM. ***Probate.***

Columbia County

Superior Court PO Box 2930, 640 Ronald Reagan Dr, Evans, GA 30809; 706-312-7139; fax: 706-312-7152; 8AM-5PM. ***Felony, Misdemeanor, Civil.***
Civil Records: Access: In person only. Visitors must perform in person searches themselves. Required to search: name, years to search. Civil cases indexed by plaintiff. Civil records on computer from 1987, prior on docket books. Civil PAT goes back to 1987. PAT results show middle initial, DOB. Terminal results also show SSNs.
Criminal Records: Access: In person only. Visitors must perform in person searches themselves. Required to search: name, years to search, DOB; SSN helpful. Criminal records computerized from 1987, prior on docket books. Criminal PAT goes back to 1987. PAT results show middle initial, DOB, SSN. Terminal results include SSN.
General Information: No juvenile, adoption, sexual, mental health or expunged records released. Will fax documents $1.00 per page. Court makes copy: $.25 per page. Certification fee: $2.00 plus $.50 per page. Payee: Clerk of Superior Court. No personal checks or credit cards accepted. Prepayment required.

Magistrate Court PO Box 777, 640 Ronald Reagan Dr, Evans, GA 30809; 706-868-3316; fax: 706-868-3314; 8AM-5PM. ***Civil Actions under $15,000, Eviction, Small Claims.*** www.columbiacountyga.gov/Index.aspx?page=2861
Court also has jurisdiction for bad checks, arrest warrants, preliminary hearings, and county ordinance violations.

Probate Court PO Box 525, 1956 Appling Harlem Hwy, Appling, GA 30802; 706-541-1254; fax: 706-541-4001; 8AM-4:30PM. ***Probate.***

Cook County

Superior Court 212 N Hutchinson Ave, Adel, GA 31620; 229-896-7717; fax: 229-896-7589; 8AM-5PM. ***Felony, Misdemeanor, Civil.*** www.gsccca.org/
Civil Records: Access: Phone, mail, in person. Both court and visitors may perform in person searches. Search fee: $10.00 per name, per 7 year period. Required to search: name, years to search. Civil cases indexed by defendant. Civil records on dockets books, microfilm. Mail turnaround time same day. Public use terminal has civil records back to 1992.
Criminal Records: Access: Mail, in person. Both court and visitors may perform in person searches. Search fee: $10.00 per name per 7 year period. Required to search: name, years to search, DOB, signed release; also helpful: SSN, race, sex. Criminal docket on books, microfilm. Mail turnaround time same day.
General Information: No juvenile, adoption, sexual, 1st offenders, mental health or expunged records

released. Will not fax documents. Court makes copy: $1.00 per page. Self serve: $.25 per page. Certification fee: $2.50 plus $.50 per page after first. Payee: Supreme Court Clerk. Business checks accepted. No credit cards accepted. Prepayment required. SASE not required.

Magistrate Court 1000 County Farm Rd, Adel, GA 31620; 229-896-3151; fax: 229-896-5186; 8AM-4:30PM. ***Civil Actions under $15,000, Eviction, Small Claims.***
Court also has jurisdiction for bad checks, arrest warrants, preliminary hearings, and county ordinance violations.

Probate Court 212 N Hutchinson Ave, Adel, GA 31620; 229-896-3941; fax: 229-896-6083; 8:30AM-5PM. ***Probate, Misdemeanor Traffic.***

Coweta County

Superior Court PO Box 943, 72 Greenville St, Newnan, GA 30264; 770-254-2693/2695; fax: 770-254-3700; 8AM-5PM. ***Felony, Civil.***
Civil Records: Access: Mail, in person, online. Visitors must perform in person searches themselves. Search fee: $5.00 per name. Required to search: name, years to search. Civil cases indexed by defendant, plaintiff, on computer from 1990, dockets books to 1970. Civil PAT goes back to 1990. Access court records free online at http://sccweb.coweta.ga.us/cmwebsearchppp/.
Criminal Records: Access: In person, online. Both court and visitors may perform in person searches. Search fee: $5.00 per name. Required to search: name, years to search, DOB. Criminal docket on books back to 1919. Court can only conduct felony searches from 1990 to present. Court says they will not do crim searches for private agencies. Criminal PAT goes back to same as civil. Access court records free online at http://sccweb.coweta.ga.us/cmwebsearchppp/.
General Information: No juvenile, adoption, sexual, mental health or expunged records released. Will fax documents $1.00 per page. Court makes copy: $1.00 per page. Self serve: $.25 per page. Certification fee: $2.50 plus $.50 per page after first. Payee: Clerk of Superior Court. Business checks accepted. No credit cards accepted. Prepayment required.

State Court PO Box 884, 72 Greenville St, Newnan, GA 30264-0884; 770-254-2699; fax: 770-252-6422; 8AM-5PM. ***Misdemeanor, Civil, Traffic.***
www.coweta.ga.us/Resources/stateclk.html
Civil Records: Access: In person, online. Both court and visitors may perform in person searches. No search fee, but a $5.00 fee applies to an older record found not onsite. Required to search: name, years to search. Civil cases indexed by defendant, plaintiff, on computer from 1990, dockets books to 1970. Civil PAT goes back to 1990. PAT results show middle initial, DOB. Current court calendar is available at the website; make court record searches free at www.courtinnovations.net/webcasemanagement/ and login as CowetaView and password coweta.
Criminal Records: Access: In person, online. Both court and visitors may perform in person searches. No search fee, but a $5.00 fee applies to an older record found not onsite. Required to search: name, years to search, DOB. Criminal docket on books back to 1919; on computer from 1990. Court can only retrieve records if given a case number. Criminal PAT goes back to 1990. PAT results show middle initial, DOB. Current court calendar is available at the website.
General Information: No juvenile, adoption, sexual, mental health or expunged records released. Will fax documents $2.00 per page. Court makes copy: $.25 per page. Certification fee: $2.50 plus $.50 per page after first. Payee: Clerk of State Court. Only cashiers checks and money orders accepted. Visa/MC accepted for fine payments only. Prepayment required.

Magistrate Court 72 Greenville St #1200, Newnan, GA 30263; 770-254-2610; fax: 770-254-2614; 8AM-5PM. ***Civil Actions under $15,000, Eviction, Small Claims.***
Court also has jurisdiction for bad checks, arrest warrants, preliminary hearings, and county ordinance violations.

Probate Court 22 E Broad St, Newnan, GA 30263; 770-254-2640; fax: 770-254-2648; 8AM-4:30PM. ***Probate.***
http://209.247.187.193/index.aspx?page=184

Crawford County

Superior Court PO Box 1037, 100 Hwy 42 South, Roberta, GA 31058; 478-836-3328; probate phone: 478-836-3313; fax: 478-836-9170; 8AM-5PM. ***Felony, Misdemeanor, Civil.***
Civil Records: Access: In person only. Visitors must perform in person searches themselves. Required to search: name, years to search. Civil cases indexed by defendant, plaintiff, on dockets books to 1830, records computerized since 1998. Civil PAT goes back to 1998.
Criminal Records: Access: In person only. Visitors must perform in person searches themselves. Required to search: name, years to search, DOB; also helpful: SSN, race, sex. Criminal docket on books to 1830, records computerized since 1998. Criminal PAT goes back to same as civil.
General Information: No juvenile, adoption, sexual, mental health or expunged records released. Will fax documents $2.50 1st page, $1.00 each add'l page, prepaid. Court makes copy: $1.00 per page. Self serve: $.25 per page. Certification fee: $2.50 first page, $.50 ea add'l. Payee: Clerk of Superior Court. Local personal checks accepted. No credit cards accepted. Prepayment required.

Probate Court PO Box 1028, GA Hwy 42 South, Knoxville, Roberta, GA 31078; 478-836-3313; fax: 478-836-4111; 8AM-5PM. ***Probate, Misdemeanor, Ordinance.*** Traffic records here also.

Magistrate Court PO Box 568, 100 US Hwy 42, Roberta, GA 31078; 478-836-5804; fax: 478-836-4340; 9AM-5PM. ***Misdemeanor, Eviction, Small Claims.*** Court also has jurisdiction for bad checks, arrest warrants, preliminary hearings, and county ordinance violations.

Crisp County

Superior & Juvenile Court PO Box 747, Cordele, GA 31010-0747; 229-276-2616; fax: 229-273-5750; 8:30AM-5PM. ***Felony, Misdemeanor, Civil Actions over $15,000.***
Civil Records: Access: Mail, in person. Visitors must perform in person searches themselves. No search fee. Required to search: name, years to search. Civil cases indexed by defendant. Civil index on docket books to 1905, computerized since 1994. Civil PAT goes back to 1994.
Criminal Records: Access: Mail, in person. Visitors must perform in person searches themselves. No search fee. Required to search: name, years to search; also helpful: SSN. Criminal docket on books to 1905, computerized since 1994. Mail turnaround time 1-2 days. Criminal PAT goes back to same as civil.
General Information: No juvenile, adoption, sexual, mental health or expunged records released. Fee to fax out file $2.50 1st page, $1.00 each add'l. Court makes copy: $1.00 per page. Self serve: $.25 per page. Certification fee: $2.00 plus $.50 per page. Cert fee includes copies. Payee: Clerk of Superior Court. Personal checks accepted. Prepayment required. Mail requests: SASE required.

Magistrate Court 210 S 7th St, Rm 102, Cordese, GA 31015; 229-276-2618; fax: 229-276-2634; 8:30AM-5PM. ***Civil Actions under $15,000, Eviction, Small Claims.***
Court also has jurisdiction for bad checks, arrest warrants, preliminary hearings, and county ordinance violations.

Probate Court 210 S 7th St, #103, Cordele, GA 31015; 229-276-2621; fax: 229-273-9184; 9AM-5PM. ***Probate, Misdemeanor, Traffic.***
Mailing address is PO Box 26, Cordele GA 31010-0026

Dade County

Superior Court PO Box 417, 12371 Main St, Trenton, GA 30752; 706-657-4778; Sm Claims 706-657-4113; probate phone: 706-657-4414; fax: 706-657-8284; 8:30AM-5PM. ***Felony, Misdemeanor, Civil, Eviction, Small Claims.***
www.dadeclerkofcourt.org
This office will not perform civil or criminal record searches.
Civil Records: Access: In person only. Only the court performs in person searches; visitors may not. No search fee. Required to search: name, years to search. Civil cases indexed by defendant, plaintiff, on computer back to 1/1999; prior on docket books. Civil PAT goes back to 1999. Calendars and attorney access is available at www.dadeclerkofcourt.org.
Criminal Records: Access: In person only. Only the court performs in person searches; visitors may not. No search fee. Required to search: name, years to search, DOB. Criminal records computerized from 1/1999; prior on docket books to 1900's. Criminal PAT available. Calendars and attorney access is available at www.dadeclerkofcourt.org.
General Information: No juvenile, adoption, sexual, mental health or expunged records released. Fee to fax out file $1.00 per page. Court makes copy: $1.00 per page. Self serve: $.25 per page. Certification fee: $2.00 plus $.50 per page after first. Payee: Superior Court. Personal checks accepted. Prepayment required.

Magistrate Court PO Box 1263, 75 Case Ave, Trenton, GA 30752; 706-657-4113; fax: 706-657-8618; 8AM-5PM. ***Civil Actions under $15,000, Eviction, Small Claims.***
Court also has jurisdiction for bad checks, arrest warrants, preliminary hearings, and county ordinance violations.

Probate Court PO Box 605, 75 Case Ave, Trenton, GA 30752; 706-657-4414; fax: 706-657-4305; 8:30AM-N,1-5PM. ***Probate, Misdemeanor Traffic.***

Dawson County

Superior Court 25 Tucker Ave, #106, Dawsonville, GA 30534; 706-344-3510; criminal phone: x262; civil phone: x261; criminal fax: 706-344-3511; civil fax: same; 8AM-5PM. ***Felony, Misdemeanor, Civil.***
Civil Records: Access: Phone, mail, fax, in person. Visitors must perform in person searches themselves. No search fee. Required to search: name, years to search. Civil cases indexed by plaintiff. Civil records on computer back to 1994, prior in dockets books. The court search only searches the computer index. Civil PAT goes back to 1994. PAT results show name only.
Criminal Records: Access: mail, fax, in person. Visitors must perform in person searches themselves. No search fee. Required to search: name, years to search, DOB; also helpful: SSN, race, sex. Criminal records computerized from 1994, prior in dockets books. The court search only searches the computer index. Mail turnaround time 1 week. Criminal PAT goes back to same as civil. PAT results show middle initial, DOB.
General Information: No juvenile, adoption, sexual, mental health or expunged records released. Will fax documents $1.00 per page. Court makes copy: $.25 per page, self serve same. Certification fee: $2.50. Payee: Superior Court. Personal checks accepted; credit cards are not. Prepayment required.

Magistrate Court 32 Jack Heard Rd #110, Dawsonville, GA 30534; 706-344-3730; fax: 706-265-8480; 8AM-8PM. ***Civil Actions under $15,000, Eviction, Small Claims.***
Court also has jurisdiction for bad checks, arrest warrants, preliminary hearings, and county ordinance violations.

Probate Court 25 Tucker Ave, #102, Dawsonville, GA 30534; 706-344-3580; fax: 706-265-6155; 8AM-5PM. ***Probate, Traffic.***

De Kalb County

Superior Court 556 N McDonough St, Decatur, GA 30030; 404-371-2836; criminal phone: 404-687-3875; civil phone: 404-687-3854; fax: 404-371-2635; 7:30AM-6PM. ***Felony, Misdemeanor, Civil.***
www.co.dekalb.ga.us/superior/index.htm
Civil Records: Access: In person, online. Visitors must perform in person searches themselves. Required to search: name, years to search. Civil cases indexed by defendant, plaintiff, on computer back 10 years, prior archived. Public use terminal available. Results include case number. Online access is free at www.ojs.dekalbga.org.
Criminal Records: Access: In person, online. Visitors must perform in person searches themselves. Required to search: name, years to search, DOB; also helpful: SSN, race, sex. Criminal records on computer back 10 years, on microfilm from 1947. Public use terminal available. Results include case number. Online access is free at www.ojs.dekalbga.org. Jail and inmate records are also available.
General Information: No juvenile, adoption, sexual, mental health or expunged records released. Will not fax documents. Court makes copy: $1.00 per page. Self serve: $.25 per page. Certification fee: $2.50 plus $.50 per page after first. Payee: Clerk of Superior Court. No personal checks or credit cards accepted. Prepayment required.

State Court 556 N McDonough St, Decatur, GA 30030; 404-371-2261; fax: 404-371-3064; 8:30AM-5PM. ***Misdemeanor, Civil.***
www.dekalbstatecourt.net
Civil located 4th Fl of the new addition. Misdemeanors located on 6th Fl #607.
Civil Records: Access: Mail, in person, online. Visitors must perform in person searches themselves. No search fee. Required to search: name, years to search. Civil cases indexed by defendant, plaintiff, on computer from 1988, back records on docket books. The court will perform limited searches. Public use terminal available. PAT results show name only. Online access is free at www.ojs.dekalbga.org. Also, current court calendars free at www.dekalbstatecourt.net.
Criminal Records: Access: In person, online, mail. Both court and visitors may perform in person searches. No search fee. Required to search: name. Criminal records computerized from 1988, back records on docket books. Mail turnaround time 7 days. Public use terminal available, crim records go back to 20 years.PAT results show name, DOB. Online access is free at www.ojs.dekalbga.org. Jail and inmate records also available. Also, current court calendars free at www.dekalbstatecourt.net. Online results show name, DOB.
General Information: Online identifiers in results same as on public terminal. Will not fax documents. Court makes copy: $.50 per page for civil; court will copy 'just a few for free' for criminal. Certification fee: $5.00 per doc. Payee: Court Clerk. Only attorney checks, cashiers checks and money orders accepted. Prepayment required. Mail requests: SASE requested.

Magistrate Court 556 N McDonough St, Rm 103, Decatur, GA 30030; 404-371-4766; 8:30AM-5PM. ***Civil Actions under $15,000, Eviction, Small Claims.*** http://dekalbstatecourt.net
Online access is available free at www.ojs.dekalbga.org. Court also has jurisdiction for bad checks, arrest warrants, preliminary hearings, and county ordinance violations.

Probate Court Courthouse, 556 N McDonough St, Rm 1100, Decatur, GA 30030; 404-371-2718; fax: 404-371-7055; 8:30AM-4:00PM. ***Probate.***
https://dklbweb.dekalbga.org/courts/probate/index.htm

Decatur County

Superior & State Court PO Box 336, 112 W Water St, Bainbridge, GA 39818; 229-248-3025; fax: 229-248-3029; 8AM-5PM. ***Felony, Misdemeanor, Civil.***
Civil Records: Access: In person only. Visitors must perform in person searches themselves. Required to search: name, years to search. Civil cases indexed by defendant, plaintiff; index in docket books from 1823; computerized from 1996. Civil PAT goes back to 1997. PAT results show name only.
Criminal Records: Access: In person only. Visitors must perform in person searches themselves. Required to search: name, years to search, DOB; SSN helpful. Criminal docket on books from 1823; computerized from 1996. Criminal PAT goes back to 1996.PAT results show name, DOB.
General Information: No juvenile, adoption, sexual, mental health or expunged records released. Will not fax documents. Court makes copy: $.25 per page. Certification fee: $2.50 plus $.50 per page. Payee: Court Clerk. No personal checks or credit cards accepted. Prepayment required.

Magistrate Court 912 Spring Creek Rd, Box #3, Bainbridge, GA 39817; 229-248-3014; fax: 229-248-3863; 9AM-5PM. ***Civil Actions under $15,000, Eviction, Small Claims.*** Court also has jurisdiction for bad checks, arrest warrants, preliminary hearings, and county ordinance violations.

Probate Court PO Box 234, 112 W Water St, Bainbridge, GA 39818; 229-248-3016; fax: 229-248-3858; 9AM-5PM. ***Probate.***

Dodge County

Superior Court PO Drawer 4276, 5401 Anson Ave, Eastman, GA 31023; 478-374-2871; fax: 478-374-3035; 9AM-5PM. ***Felony, Misdemeanor, Civil.***
Civil Records: Access: In person only. Visitors must perform in person searches themselves. Required to search: name, years to search. Civil cases indexed by defendant. Civil index on docket books.
Criminal Records: Access: In person only. Visitors must perform in person searches themselves. Required to search: name, years to search, DOB, signed release; SSN helpful. Criminal docket on books and computer.
General Information: No juvenile, adoption, sexual, mental health or expunged records released. Will fax documents $2.00 1st page, $1.00 each add'l page. Court makes copy: $.25 per page. Self serve: $.25 per page. Certification fee: $2.00 plus $.50 per page after first. Payee: Court Clerk. Personal checks accepted; credit cards are not. Prepayment required.

Magistrate Court 5018 Courthouse Cir, #202, Eastman, GA 31023; 478-374-7243/8144; fax: 478-374-5716; 8:30AM-N; 1-4:30PM. ***Civil Actions under $15,000, Eviction, Small Claims.***
Court also has jurisdiction for bad checks, arrest warrants, preliminary hearings, and county ordinance violations.

Probate Court PO Box 514, 5401 Anson Ave, Eastman, GA 31023; 478-374-3775/478-374-8152; fax: 478-374-9197; 9AM-5PM. ***Probate.***

Dooly County

Superior Court PO Box 326, 104 Second St, Vienna, GA 31092-0326; 229-268-4234; fax: 229-268-1427; 8:30AM-5PM. ***Felony, Misdemeanor, Civil.***
Civil Records: Access: In person only. Visitors must perform in person searches themselves. Required to search: name, years to search. Civil cases indexed by defendant, plaintiff, on computer since 1995. Court prefers to have public perform searches. Public use terminal has civil records back to 1995. PAT results show name, DOB, SSN.
Criminal Records: Access: In person only. Visitors must perform in person searches themselves. Required to search: name, years to search, DOB; also helpful: SSN, race, sex. Criminal records on computer since 1995, docket books prior to 1857. Prefer to have public to perform searches.
General Information: No juvenile, adoption, sexual, mental health or expunged records released. Will fax documents $2.50 per fax. Court makes copy: $1.00 per page. Self serve: $.25 per page. Certification fee: $2.50. Payee: Dooly County Superior Court Clerk. Personal checks accepted; credit cards are not. Prepayment required.

Magistrate Court PO Box 336, 209 D W Union St, Vienna, GA 31092; 229-268-4324; fax: 229-268-3585; 8AM-N, 1-5PM. ***Civil Actions under $15,000, Eviction, Small Claims.***
www.doolycourt.com Court also has jurisdiction for bad checks, arrest warrants, preliminary hearings, and ordinance violations.

Probate Court 104 2nd St South, Vienna, GA 31092; 229-268-4217 x1; fax: 229-268-6142; 8AM-5PM; Sat or by appointment. ***Probate, Misdemeanor, Traffic.***
www.doolycountyprobate.com
Misdemeanor records phone number is ext. 4.

Dougherty County

Superior & State Court PO Box 1827, 225 Pine Ave, #126, Albany, GA 31702; 229-431-2198; criminal fax: 229-878-3155; civil fax: 229-878-3165; 8:30AM-5PM. ***Felony, Misdemeanor, Civil.***
www.albany.ga.us/court_system/court_system.htm
Civil Records: Access: Online, in person. Visitors must perform in person searches themselves. Required to search: name, years to search. Civil cases indexed by defendant, plaintiff, on computer from 1992, overall records go back to 1854. Civil PAT goes back to 1992. Access pre-2003 civil and criminal court docket data free at www.albany.ga.us/court_system/court_clerk.htm The same system permits access to probate, tax, deeds, death certificate records, and older civil/criminal records.
Criminal Records: Access: Online, in person. Visitors must perform in person searches themselves. Required to search: name, years to search SSN. Criminal records computerized from 1992, overall records go back to 1854. Criminal PAT goes back to same as civil. PAT results show middle initial, DOB. Online access to criminal records is the same as civil.
General Information: Online identifiers in results same as on public terminal. No juvenile, adoption, sexual, mental health or expunged records released. Will fax documents $3.00 each. Court makes copy: $1.00 per page. Self serve: $.25 per page. Certification fee: $3.00 for 1st page. Copy fee for add'l pages. Payee: Court Clerk. Personal checks accepted; credit cards are not. Prepayment required.

Magistrate Court PO Box 1827, 225 Pine Ave, Rm 308, Albany, GA 31702; 229-431-3216; fax: 229-434-2692; 8:30AM-5PM. ***Civil Actions under $15,000, Eviction, Small Claims.***
www.doughertycourt.com Court also has jurisdiction for bad checks, arrest warrants, preliminary hearings, and county ordinance violations.

Probate Court PO Box 1827, 225 Pine Ave, #123, Albany, GA 31702; 229-431-2102; fax: 229-434-2694; 8:30AM-5PM. ***Probate.***
Search the probate court index free at www.albany.ga.us/court_system/court_clerk.htm.

Douglas County

Superior Court Douglas County Courthouse, 8700 Hospital Dr, Douglasville, GA 30134; 770-920-7252; 8AM-5PM. ***Felony, Misdemeanor, Civil.***
www.celebratedouglascounty.com/cgi-bin/MySQLdb?VIEW=/departments/view_dept.txt&cdept=33&department=Clerk%20of%20Superior%20Court
Civil Records: Access: In person only. Visitors must perform in person searches themselves. Required to search: name, years to search. Civil cases indexed by defendant, plaintiff, on computer from 1994, prior on docket books to 1871. Civil PAT goes back to 1994.
Criminal Records: Access: In person only. Visitors must perform in person searches themselves. Required to search: name, years to search, DOB, signed release; SSN helpful. Criminal records computerized from 1994, prior on docket books to 1871. Criminal PAT goes back to same as civil.PAT results show name, DOB.
General Information: No juvenile, adoption, sexual, mental health or expunged records released. Will not fax documents. Court makes copy: $1.00 per page. Self serve: $.25 per page. Certification fee: $2.50 plus $.50 per page. Payee: Clerk of Superior Court. Personal checks accepted from local bank only. No credit cards accepted. Prepayment required.

Magistrate Court 8700 Hospital Dr, Douglasville, GA 30134; 770-920-7215; 8AM-5PM. ***Civil Actions under $15,000, Eviction, Small Claims.*** www.celebratedouglascounty.com
Court also has jurisdiction for bad checks, arrest warrants, preliminary hearings, and county ordinance violations.

Probate Court 8700 Hospital Dr, Douglasville, GA 30134; 770-920-7249; fax: 770-920-7381; 8AM-5PM. ***Probate.***

Early County

Superior & State Court PO Box 849, Blakely, GA 39823; 229-723-3033; fax: 229-723-4411; 8AM-5PM. ***Felony, Misdemeanor, Civil.***
http://earlycounty.georgia.gov
Civil Records: Access: In person only. Visitors must perform in person searches themselves. Required to search: name, years to search. Civil cases indexed by defendant, plaintiff, on dockets.
Criminal Records: Access: In person only. Visitors must perform in person searches themselves. Required to search: name, years to search, DOB; SSN helpful. Criminal records on dockets.
General Information: No juvenile, adoption, sexual, mental health or expunged records released. Will fax documents $2.50 1st page, $1.00 each add'l page. Court makes copy: $1.00 per page. Self serve: $.25 per page. Certification fee: $2.50 plus $.50 per page after first. Payee: Court Clerk. Personal checks accepted; credit cards are not. Prepayment required.

Magistrate Court Early County Courthouse, Rm D, 111 Court Sq, Blakely, GA 39823; 229-723-3454 and 229-723-5492; fax: 229-723-5246; 8AM-5PM. ***Civil Actions under $15,000, Eviction, Small Claims, Probate, Ordinance.*** Court also has jurisdiction for bad checks, arrest warrants, preliminary hearings, and county ordinance violations.

Echols County

Superior Court PO Box 213, Statenville, GA 31648; 229-559-5642; fax: 229-559-5792; 8AM-N, 1-4:30PM. ***Felony, Misdemeanor, Civil.***
http://southernjudicialcircuit.com
Civil Records: Access: In person only. Visitors must perform in person searches themselves. Required to search: name, years to search. Civil cases indexed by defendant, plaintiff, on dockets books, computerized since 1995. Civil PAT goes back to 1995. PAT results show name only.
Criminal Records: Access: In person only. Visitors must perform in person searches themselves. Required to search: name, years to search. Criminal docket on books, computerized since 1995. Criminal PAT goes back to 1995. PAT results show name only.
General Information: No juvenile, adoption, sexual, mental health or expunged records released. Will fax out documents $2.50 1st page, $.50 each add'l. Court makes copy: $1.00 per page, self serve same. Certification fee: $2.00 1st page, $.50 each add'l page. Payee: Court Clerk. Personal checks accepted; credit cards are not. Prepayment required.

Magistrate & Probate Court PO Box 118, 110 Hwy 94 East, Statenville, GA 31648; 229-559-7526; fax: 229-559-8128; 8AM-4:30PM. ***Civil Actions under $15,000, Eviction, Small Claims, Probate.***
Court also has jurisdiction for bad checks, arrest warrants, preliminary hearings, and county ordinance violations. Name search for citations free at https://www.ncourt.com/courtpayment/Lookup.aspx?Juris=GAEchols.

Effingham County

Superior Court 700 N Pine St #100, Springfield, GA 31329-5079; 912-754-2146; civil phone: x3104; probate phone: 912-754-2112; 8:30AM-5PM. ***Felony, Misdemeanor, Civil.***
Civil Records: Access: Mail, in person. Both court and visitors may perform in person searches. Search fee: $20.00 per name. Required to search: name, years to search. Civil cases indexed by defendant, plaintiff, on computer from 1991, dockets books. Mail turnaround time 3-5 days. Civil PAT goes back to 1991.
Criminal Records: Access: Mail, in person. Both court and visitors may perform in person searches. Search fee: $20.00 per name. Required to search: name, years to search, DOB; also helpful: SSN, race, sex. Criminal records computerized from 1991, dockets books. Mail turnaround time 3-5 days. Criminal PAT goes back to same as civil. PAT results show name only.
General Information: No juvenile, adoption, sexual, mental health or expunged records released. Will not fax documents. Court makes copy: $.25 per page, self serve same. Certification fee: $2.50 plus $.50 per add'l page,. Payee: Court Clerk. Business checks accepted. No credit cards accepted. Prepayment required. Mail requests: SASE required.

Magistrate Court PO Box 819, 700 N Pine St, Springfield, GA 31329; 912-754-2124; fax: 912-754-4893; 8AM-5PM. ***Civil Actions under $15,000, Eviction, Small Claims, Ordinance.***
Court also has jurisdiction for bad checks, arrest warrants, preliminary hearings, and county ordinance violations.

Probate Court 700 N Pine St, #146, Springfield, GA 31329; 912-754-2112; fax: 912-754-3894; 8:30AM-5PM. ***Probate.***
www.effinghamcounty.org/pages/departments/probate_court/

Elbert County

Superior & State Court PO Box 619, 12 S Olive St, Elberton, GA 30635; 706-283-2005; criminal fax: 706-213-7286; civil fax: same; 8AM-5PM. ***Felony, Misdemeanor, Civil.***
Civil Records: Access: Mail, in person. Visitors must perform in person searches themselves. No search fee. Required to search: name, years to search. Civil cases indexed by defendant, plaintiff, on computer from 1996 excluding felonies; docket books prior. Civil PAT goes back to 1996. PAT results show name only.
Criminal Records: Access: Mail, in person. Visitors must perform in person searches themselves. No search fee. Required to search: name, years to search. Criminal records computerized from 1996 excluding felonies; docket books prior. Mail turnaround time 1 week. Criminal PAT goes back to same as civil. PAT criminal results show middle initial.
General Information: No juvenile, adoption, sexual, mental health or expunged records released. Will fax documents $2.50 1st page, $1.00 each add'l. Court makes copy: $.25 per page, self serve same. Certification fee: $2.00 per cert plus $.50 per page. Payee: Clerk of Court. No personal checks or credit cards accepted. Prepayment required.

Magistrate Court 12 S Oliver St, Elberton, GA 30635; 706-283-2027; fax: 706-283-2004; 8AM-5PM. ***Civil Actions under $15,000, Eviction, Small Claims.*** Court also has jurisdiction for bad checks, arrest warrants, preliminary hearings, and county ordinance violations.

Probate Court 45 Forest Ave, Suite 41, Elberton, GA 30635; 706-283-2016; fax: 706-283-9668; 8AM-5PM. ***Probate.***

Emanuel County

Superior & State Court PO Box 627, 125 S Main, Swainsboro, GA 30401; 478-237-8911; fax: 478-237-1220; 8AM-5PM. ***Felony, Misdemeanor, Civil.***
Civil Records: Access: In person only. Visitors must perform in person searches themselves. Required to search: name, years to search. Civil cases indexed by defendant, plaintiff, computerized since 1999, earlier on dockets books. Civil PAT available.
Criminal Records: Access: In person only. Visitors must perform in person searches themselves. Required to search: name, years to search, DOB; SSN helpful. Criminal records computerized since 1999, earlier on dockets books. Because there is no court record retrievers in this county, this office will accept a fax request but it must be on official company letterhead. They will review the request and are likely to perform the search. Criminal PAT available.
General Information: No juvenile, adoption, sexual, mental health or expunged records released. Will not fax documents. Court makes copy: $1.00 per page. Self serve: $.25 per page. Certification fee: $3.50 per doc. Payee: Court Clerk. Personal checks accepted; credit cards are not. Prepayment required.

Magistrate Court 107 N Main St, Swainsboro, GA 30401; 478-237-7278; fax: 478-237-9154; 8AM-5PM F-7:30-4:30. ***Civil Actions under $15,000, Eviction, Small Claims.***
Court also has jurisdiction for bad checks, arrest warrants, preliminary hearings, and county ordinance violations.

Probate Court PO Box 70, 125 S Main St, Swainsboro, GA 30401; 478-237-7091; fax: 478-237-2633; 8AM-5PM. ***Probate.***

Evans County

Superior & State Court PO Box 845, Claxton, GA 30417; 912-739-3868; fax: 912-739-2504; 8AM-5PM. ***Felony, Misdemeanor, Civil.***
Civil Records: Access: Mail, in person. Visitors must perform in person searches themselves. No search fee. Required to search: name, years to search. Civil cases indexed by defendant, plaintiff, on computer from 1989, dockets bookstore 1915. Mail requests must include case number. Civil PAT goes back to 1989.
Criminal Records: Access: Mail, in person. Visitors must perform in person searches themselves. No search fee. Required to search: name, years to search, DOB; SSN helpful. Criminal records computerized from 1989, dockets books to 1915. Mail requests must include case number. Criminal PAT goes back to same as civil.
General Information: No juvenile, adoption, sexual, mental health or expunged records released. Will not fax documents. Court makes copy: $1.00 per page. Self serve: $.25 per page. Certification fee: $2.50 plus $.50 per page after first. Payee: Court Clerk. Personal checks accepted; credit cards are not. Prepayment required. Mail requests: SASE required.

Magistrate Court Courthouse Annex, 7 Freeman St, Claxton, GA 30417; 912-739-3745; fax: 912-739-8856; 8AM-5PM. ***Civil Actions under $15,000, Eviction, Small Claims.*** Court also has jurisdiction for bad checks, arrest warrants, preliminary hearings, and county ordinance violations.

Probate Court PO Box 852, 201 Freeman St, Ste 9, Claxton, GA 30417; 912-739-4080; fax: 912-739-4077; 8AM-N, 1-5PM. ***Probate.***

Fannin County

Superior Court PO Box 1300, 420 W Main St, Blue Ridge, GA 30513; 706-632-2039; probate: 706-632-3011; 9AM-5PM. ***Felony, Misdemeanor, Civil.***
http://9thjudicialdistrict-ga.org/dca9apphp.shtml
Civil Records: Access: In person only. Visitors must perform in person searches themselves. Required to search: name, years to search. Civil cases indexed by defendant, plaintiff; index on docket books back to the early 1900's.
Criminal Records: Access: In person only. Visitors must perform in person searches themselves. Required to search: name, years to search, DOB, signed release; SSN helpful. Criminal docket on books back to the early 1900's.
General Information: No juvenile, adoption, or DD214 records released. Will not fax documents. Court makes copy: $1.00 per page. Self serve: $.25 per page. Certification fee: $2.50 plus $.50 per page after first. Payee: Fannin County Court Clerk. Personal checks accepted; credit cards are not. Prepayment required.

Magistrate Court 400 W Main St #202, Blue Ridge, GA 30513; 706-632-5558; fax: 706-632-8236; 9AM-5PM. ***Civil Actions under $15,000, Eviction, Small Claims, Misdemeanor.***
www.fannincountyga.org
Court also has jurisdiction for bad checks, arrest warrants, preliminary hearings, and county ordinance violations.

Probate Court 400 W Main St #204, Blue Ridge, GA 30513; 706-632-3011; fax: 706-632-7167; 8AM-5PM. ***Probate, Misdemeanor.***

Fayette County

Superior Court PO Box 130, 1 Center Dr (in the Justice Center), Fayetteville, GA 30214; 770-716-4290; criminal phone: 770-716-4293; civil phone: 770-716-4294; 8AM-5PM. ***Felony, Misdemeanor, Civil.*** www.admin.co.fayette.ga.us
The court will copy and mail specific documents for $1.00 per page.
Civil Records: Access: In person only. Visitors must perform in person searches themselves. Required to search: name, years to search. Civil cases indexed by defendant, plaintiff, on computer since 1989; prior records on dockets books (found at the vault). Civil PAT goes back to 1989. PAT results show name only. Index by last name, alpha.
Criminal Records: Access: In person only. Visitors must perform in person searches themselves. Required to search: name, years to search, DOB; SSN helpful. Criminal records on computer since 1991; prior records on dockets books. Criminal PAT goes back to 1991.
General Information: No juvenile, adoption, sexual, mental health or expunged records released. Will not fax documents. Court makes copy: $.25 per page, self serve same. Certification fee: $2.00 plus $.50 per page. Payee: Court Clerk. Only cashiers checks and money orders accepted. No credit cards accepted. Prepayment required.

Magistrate Court 1 Center Dr, Fayetteville, GA 30214-8401; 770-716-4230; fax: 770-716-4855; 8AM-5PM. ***Civil Actions under $15,000, Eviction, Small Claims.*** Court also has jurisdiction for bad checks, arrest warrants, and preliminary hearings.

Probate Court 1 Center Dr., Fayetteville, GA 30214; 770-716-4224; fax: 770-716-4854; 8AM-5PM. ***Probate.***

Floyd County

Superior Court PO Box 1110, #3 Government Plaza, #101, Rome, GA 30163; 706-291-5190; probate phone: 706-291-5136; fax: 706-233-0035; 8AM-5PM. ***Felony, Misdemeanor, Civil.*** www.floydcountyga.org/Courts/superior.htm
Civil Records: Access: Phone, in person. Visitors must perform in person searches themselves. No search fee. Required to search: name, years to search. Civil cases indexed by defendant, plaintiff, on computer since 11/95; prior on docket books to 1833. The court will only do a name search to determine if a case exists, then provides a case number. Civil PAT goes back to 11/1995.
Criminal Records: Access: In person only. Both court and visitors may perform in person searches. No search fee. Required to search: name, years to search, signed release. Criminal records on computer since 1/96; prior on docket books back to 1833. Court will only do a name search to determine if a case exists, then provides a case number. Criminal PAT goes back to 1/1996.PAT results show name, DOB.
General Information: No juvenile, adoption, sexual, mental health or expunged records released. Will fax out file for $1.00 per page. Court makes copy: $.50 per page, self serve same. Certification fee: $2.00. Payee: Court Clerk. No personal checks or credit cards accepted. Prepayment required.

Magistrate Court 3 Government Plaza, Rm 227, Rome, GA 30161; 706-291-5250; fax: 706-291-5269; 8:45AM-4:45PM. ***Misdemeanor, Civil Actions under $15,000, Eviction, Small Claims.*** http://georgiacourts.org/courts/magistrate/floyd/
Copy fee is $.25 a page; certification is $2.50; will fax results. Court also has jurisdiction for bad checks, arrest warrants, preliminary hearings, county ordinance violations, civil actions up to $15,000, dispossessories and garnishments.

Probate Court 3 Government Plaza, #201, County Administrative Offices, Rome, GA 30161; 706-291-5136/8; fax: 706-291-5189; 8AM-5:00PM. ***Probate, Traffic.***

Forsyth County

Superior & State Court 100 Courthouse Square, Rm 010, Cumming, GA 30040; 770-781-2120; fax: 770-886-2858; 8:30AM-5PM. ***Felony, Misdemeanor, Civil, Eviction.*** www.forsythco.com
Civil Records: Access: Mail, fax, in person. Both court and visitors may perform in person searches. No search fee. Required to search: name, years to search. Civil cases indexed by defendant. Civil records on computer since 1996; prior records on docket books back to 1832. Will search computer index back to 1999 only. Civil PAT goes back to 1980. PAT results show name only.
Criminal Records: Access: Mail, fax, in person. Both court and visitors may perform in person searches. No search fee. Required to search: name, years to search; SSN helpful. Criminal records on computer since late 1989. Court will search computer index back to 1999 only. Searches of older records must be performed in person. Criminal PAT goes back to 1999. PAT results show name only.
General Information: No juvenile, adoption, sexual, mental health or expunged records released. Will fax documents $3.00 per page. Court makes copy: $.25 per page, self serve same. Certification fee: $2.50 plus $.50 per page after first. Payee: Court Clerk. Personal checks accepted; credit cards are not. Prepayment required. SASE not required.

Magistrate Court 1090 Tribble Gap Rd, Cumming, GA 30040; 770-781-2211; fax: 770-844-7581; 8AM-4:30PM. ***Misdemeanor, Civil Actions under $15,000, Eviction, Small Claims.*** www.forsythco.com/department.asp?DeptID=12
Court also has jurisdiction for bad checks, arrest warrants, preliminary hearings, and county ordinance violations.

Probate Court 112 W Maple St, Cumming, GA 30040; 770-781-2140; fax: 770-886-2839; 8:30AM-5PM. ***Probate.*** www.forsythco.com/department.asp?DeptID=16

Franklin County

Superior Court PO Box 70, 9592 Lavonia Rd, Carnesville, GA 30521; 706-384-2514; 8AM-5PM. ***Felony, Misdemeanor, Civil.***
Civil Records: Access: In person only. Visitors must perform in person searches themselves. Required to search: name, years to search. Civil cases indexed by defendant, plaintiff, on computer since 2002; prior records on docket books. Civil PAT goes back to 2002.
Criminal Records: Access: In person only. Visitors must perform in person searches themselves. Required to search: name, years to search, DOB; SSN helpful. Criminal records on computer since 2002; prior records on docket books. Criminal PAT goes back to same as civil.
General Information: No juvenile, adoption, sexual, mental health or expunged records released. Will not fax documents. Court makes copy: $1.00 per page. Self serve: $.25 per page. Certification fee: $2.50 for 1st page, $.50 each add'l. Payee: Court Clerk. Personal checks accepted; credit cards are not. Prepayment required.

Magistrate Court 7085 Hwy 145, Ste B, Carnesville, GA 30521; 706-384-7473; fax: 706-384-4346; 8AM-5PM. ***Civil Actions under $15,000, Eviction, Small Claims.***
Court also has jurisdiction for bad checks, arrest warrants, preliminary hearings, and county ordinance violations.

Probate Court 7085 Highway 145, #A, Carnesville, GA 30521; 706-384-2403; fax: 706-384-2636; 8AM-5PM. ***Probate, Misdemeanor.***
This location also holds traffic misdemeanors and vital records.

Fulton County

Superior Court - Civil 136 Pryor St SW, Rm C-155, Superior Court Clerk, Atlanta, GA 30303; 404-730-5344, 730-5375; 8:30AM-5PM. ***Civil.*** www.fcclk.org
Phone for the Closed File Rm- 404-730-6872.
Civil Records: Access: Mail, in person, online. Both court and visitors may perform in person searches. Search fee: $15.00 per name. Required to search: name, years to search. Civil cases indexed by defendant, plaintiff, on computer since 1972. Mail turnaround time 2-5 days. Public use terminal has civil records back to 1972. PAT results show name only. Access Clerk of Superior Court Judicial civil records free at www.fcclkjudicialsearch.org/CivilSearch/civfrmd.htm. Search by either party name, case number, date range. Search includes status, attorney. Also Hearing Search free at www.fcclkjudicialsearch.org/CVHearSearch/cvhearfrmd.htm.
General Information: No juvenile, adoption, sexual, mental health, sealed or expunged records released. Will not fax documents. Court makes copy: $.25 per page. Certification fee: $2.50 for 1st page; $.50 each add'l. Includes copy fee. Payee: Clerk of Fulton Superior Court. In-state personal checks accepted. No credit cards accepted. Prepayment required. Mail requests: SASE requested.

Superior Court - Criminal 136 Pryor St SW, Rm 106, Atlanta, GA 30303; 404-730-5770 Admin; criminal phone: 404-730-5248; 8:30AM-5PM. ***Felony, Misdemeanor, Eviction.*** www.fcclk.org
File room phone- 404-730-5375.
Criminal Records: Access: In person only. Visitors must perform in person searches themselves. Required to search: name, years to search, DOB; charges helpful. Criminal records computerized from 1973. Criminal record room, who process criminal record requests, will accept requests for specific cases only, but will not do name searches per se. Public use terminal has crim records back to 1974.
General Information: No sealed or expunged records released. Will not fax out case files. Court makes copy: $1.00 per page. Certification fee: $2.50 for 1st page; $.50 each add'l, includes copies. Cert Dept. phone- 404-730-6872. Payee: Clerk of Superior Court. Personal checks accepted; credit cards are not. Prepayment required.

State Court TG100 Justice Center Twr, 185 Central Ave SW, Atlanta, GA 30303; 404-730-5000; criminal fax: 404-893-6602; civil fax: 404-730-8141; 8:30AM-5PM. ***Misdemeanor, Civil.***
Civil Records: Access: In person only. Both court and visitors may perform in person searches. Search fee: $15.00 if court performs search. Required to search: name, years to search. Civil cases indexed by defendant, plaintiff, on computer from 1984, books back to 1982. Civil PAT goes back to 1984.
Criminal Records: Access: In person only. Both court and visitors may perform in person searches. Search fee: $15.00 if court performs search. Required to search: name, years to search, DOB; also helpful, race, aliases, date of offense, sex, approximate arrest date. Criminal records computerized from 1984, books back to 1982. Criminal PAT goes back to same as civil.
General Information: No juvenile, adoption, sexual, mental health or expunged records released. Will not fax documents. Court makes copy: $.25 per page. Certification fee: $2.50 per page. Includes copy fee. Payee: Court Clerk. Business checks accepted. Visa/MC accepted. Prepayment required.

Magistrate Court 185 Central Ave SW, TG-700, Justice Ctr Tower, Atlanta, GA 30303; 404-730-5045; criminal phone: 404-730-4752; criminal fax: 404-893-6600; civil fax: 404-332-0352; 8:30AM-5PM. ***Civil Actions under $15,000, Eviction, Small Claims, Criminal Preliminaries.***
Court also has jurisdiction for bad checks, arrest warrants, and county ordinance violations. The criminal division (does no record checks) is located at 160 Prior St SW, J-135, phone and fax above.

Probate Court 136 Pryor St, # 230, Atlanta, GA 30303; 404-730-4640; fax404-730-8283; 8:30-5PM

Gilmer County

Superior Court #1 Westside Square, Ellijay, GA 30540; 706-635-4462; fax: 706-635-1462; 8:30AM-5PM. ***Felony, Misdemeanor, Civil.*** http://9thjudicialdistrict-ga.org/dca9apphp.shtml

Civil Records: Access: In person only. Visitors must perform in person searches themselves. Required to search: name, years to search. Civil cases indexed by defendant, plaintiff; index on docket books computerized records since 1994. Civil PAT goes back to 1994.

Criminal Records: Access: In person only. Visitors must perform in person searches themselves. Required to search: name, years to search, signed release; also helpful: DOB, SSN. Criminal docket on books; computerized since 1994. Criminal PAT goes back to same as civil.

General Information: No juvenile, adoption, sealed, sexual, mental health, expunged or sealed records released. Will not fax documents. Court makes copy: $1.00 per page. Self serve: $.25 per page. Certification fee: $2.50 plus $.50 per page after first. Payee: Superior Court Clerk. Personal checks accepted; credit cards are not. Prepayment required.

Magistrate Court 1 Broad St, Ste 001, Ellijay, GA 30540; 706-635-2515; fax: 706-635-7756; 8:30AM-5PM. ***Civil Actions under $15,000, Eviction, Small Claims.*** www.gilmercounty-ga.gov Court also has jurisdiction for bad checks, arrest warrants, preliminary hearings, and county ordinance violations.

Probate Court 51 Sand St., Ellijay, GA 30540; 706-635-4763; fax: 706-635-4761; 8:30AM-5PM. ***Probate.***

Glascock County

Superior Court PO Box 231, 62 E Main St, Gibson, GA 30810; 706-598-2084; criminal fax: 706-598-2577; civil fax: same; 8AM-5PM M,Tu,TH,F; Wed 8AM-N. ***Felony, Misdemeanor, Civil.***

Civil Records: Access: In person only. Visitors must perform in person searches themselves. Required to search: name, years to search. Civil cases indexed by defendant, plaintiff, on computer from 1991, records go back to 1990. Civil PAT goes back to 1991. Public access terminal has county cases only.

Criminal Records: Access: In person only. Visitors must perform in person searches themselves. Required to search: name, years to search, DOB; SSN helpful. Criminal records computerized from 1991 records go back to 1990. Criminal PAT goes back to same as civil. Public access terminal has county cases only.

General Information: No juvenile, adoption, sexual, mental health or expunged records released. Will fax specific case file $1.00 per page. Court makes copy: $1.00 per page. Self serve: $.25 per page. Certification fee: $2.50 plus $.50 per page copy fee after first. Payee: Court Clerk. Personal checks accepted; credit cards are not. Prepayment required.

Magistrate Court PO Box 201, 62 E Main St, Gibson, GA 30810; 706-598-2013; fax: 706-598-3577; 8AM-5PM, M,T,TH,F, 8AM-N, W. ***Misdemeanor, Civil Actions under $15,000, Eviction, Small Claims.*** Court also has jurisdiction for bad checks, arrest warrants, preliminary hearings, and county ordinance violations.

Probate Court 62 E Main St, 370 W Main St, Gibson, GA 30810; 706-598-3241; fax: 706-598-2471; 8AM-N, 1-5PM-M,T,TH,F; 8AM-Noon W. ***Probate.***

Glynn County

Superior Court PO Box 1355, Brunswick, GA 31521; 912-554-7272; criminal fax: 912-267-5625; civil fax: same; 8AM-5PM. ***Felony, Civil.***

Civil Records: Access: Phone, fax, mail, in person. Both court and visitors may perform in person searches. No search fee. Required to search: name, years to search. Civil cases indexed by defendant, plaintiff, on computer back to 1987, archived and in docket books from 1800s. Mail turnaround time 1-3 days. Civil PAT goes back to 1987.

Criminal Records: Access: Phone, fax, mail, in person. Both court and visitors may perform in person searches. No search fee. Required to search: name, years to search, DOB, signed release; also helpful: SSN, race, sex. Criminal records computerized from 1987, index back to 1800s. Mail turnaround time 1-3 days. Criminal PAT goes back to same as civil.

General Information: No juvenile, adoption, sexual, mental health or expunged records released. Fee to fax out file $5.00 each. Court makes copy: $.25 per page. Self serve: $.25 per page. Certification fee: $2.50 plus $.50 per copy. Payee: Court Clerk. Personal checks accepted; credit cards are not. Prepayment required. Will bill copy and cert fees. Mail requests: SASE requested.

State Court 701 "H" St, #104, Brunswick, GA 31520; 912-554-7325; fax: 912-261-3849; 9AM-5PM. ***Misdemeanor, Civil.***

Civil Records: Access: In person only. Visitors must perform in person searches themselves. Required to search: name, years to search. Civil cases indexed by defendant. Civil records on dockets books to 1980; on computer back to 1994. Civil PAT goes back to 1994. Results include name and case number.

Criminal Records: Access: In person only. Visitors must perform in person searches themselves. Required to search: name, years to search. Criminal docket on books to 1979; on computer back to 1994. Criminal PAT goes back to same as civil. Results include name and case number.

General Information: No juvenile, adoption, sexual, mental health or expunged records released. Will not fax documents. Court makes copy: $.25 per page. Certification fee: $2.50 plus $.50 per page. Payee: Clerk of State Court. Only cashiers checks and money orders accepted. No credit cards accepted. Prepayment required.

Magistrate Court PO Box 1355, 701 H St, Brunswick, GA 31521; 912-554-7250; fax: 912-267-5677; 8AM-5PM. ***Civil Actions under $15,000, Eviction, Small Claims.*** Court also has jurisdiction for bad checks, arrest warrants, preliminary hearings, and county ordinance violations.

Probate Court 11 Judicial Ln, #11, Brunswick, GA 31520; 912-554-7231; fax: 912-466-8001; 8AM-5PM. ***Civil, Small Claims, Probate.*** www.glynncounty.org/index.asp?nid=138

Gordon County

Superior Court 100 Wall St, #102, Calhoun, GA 30701; 706-629-9533; fax: 706-629-2139; 8:30AM-5PM. ***Felony, Misdemeanor, Civil.***

Civil Records: Access: Mail, fax, in person. Both court and visitors may perform in person searches. No search fee. Required to search: name, years to search. Civil cases indexed by defendant, plaintiff, on computer since 3/97; prior records on docket books. Mail turnaround time 1-2 days. Civil PAT goes back to 1997.

Criminal Records: Access: Mail, fax, in person. Both court and visitors may perform in person searches. No search fee. Required to search: name, years to search. Criminal records on computer since 3/97; prior records on docket books. Mail turnaround time 1-2 days. Criminal PAT goes back to same as civil.

General Information: No sealed records released. Will fax back documents. Court makes copy: $1.00 per page. Self serve: $.25 per page. Certification fee: $2.50. Payee: Superior Court Clerk. Personal checks accepted; credit cards are not. Prepayment required. Mail requests: SASE required.

Magistrate Court PO Box 1025, 100 S Wall St, Calhoun, GA 30701; 706-629-6818 x2270, x2271; criminal phone: 706-879-2272; civil phone: 706-879-2271; fax: 706-602-1751; 8:30AM-5PM. ***Misdemeanors, Civil Actions under $15,000, Eviction, Small Claims.*** www.gordoncourt.com Court also has jurisdiction for bad checks, arrest warrants, preliminary hearings, and county ordinance violations.

Probate Court PO Box 669, 30703, 100 S Wall St, Calhoun, GA 30701; 706-629-7314; fax: 706-629-4698; 8:30AM-5PM. ***Probate, Misdemeanor.***

Grady County

Superior Court 250 N Broad St, Box 8, Cairo, GA 39828; 229-377-2912; criminal fax: 229-377-7078; civil fax: same; 8AM-5PM. ***Felony, Misdemeanor, Civil.***

Civil Records: Access: In person only. Both court and visitors may perform in person searches. No search fee. Required to search: name, years to search. Civil cases indexed by defendant, plaintiff on computer. Civil records on computer since 1993; prior records on docket books from 1906 (interdependent only. Court will assist visitors with searches. Civil PAT goes back to 1993. PAT results show name only.

Criminal Records: Access: In person only. Visitors must perform in person searches themselves. Required to search: name, years to search. Criminal records on computer since 1993; prior records on docket books from 1906. Court will assist visitors with searches. Criminal PAT goes back to 1993. PAT results show name only.

General Information: No juvenile or adoption records released. Will not fax documents. Court makes copy: n/a. Self serve: $.25 per page. Certification fee: $2.00 per cert plus $.50 per page. Payee: Superior Court Clerk. Personal checks accepted; credit cards are not. Prepayment required.

Magistrate Court 250 N Broad St, Box 2, Cairo, GA 39828; 229-377-4132; fax: 229-377-4127; 8AM-5PM. ***Civil Actions under $15,000, Eviction, Small Claims.*** Court also has jurisdiction for bad checks, arrest warrants, preliminary hearings, alcohol and county ordinance violations.

Probate Court 250 N Broad St, Box #1, Courthouse, Cairo, GA 39828; 229-377-4621; fax: 229-378-8052; 8AM-5PM. ***Probate.*** www.georgiacourts.org/courts/probate/grady/index.html

Greene County

Superior & Juvenile Court 113 N Main St, #109, Greensboro, GA 30642; 706-453-3340; fax: 706-453-9179; 8AM-5PM. ***Felony, Misdemeanor, Civil, Eviction, Small Claims.***

Civil Records: Access: In person only. Visitors must perform in person searches themselves. Required to search: name, years to search. Civil cases indexed by defendant, plaintiff. Overall records go back to 1700. Computerized records go back to 2000. Civil PAT goes back to 2000.

Criminal Records: Access: In person only. Visitors must perform in person searches themselves. Required to search: name, years to search; SSN helpful. Overall records go back to 1700. Computerized records go back to 2000. Criminal PAT goes back to 2000.

General Information: No juvenile or adoption records released. Will not fax out documents. Court makes copy: $.25 per page. Cert fee: $2.50 per document. Payee: Superior Court Clerk. Personal checks okay; credit cards not. Prepayment required.

Magistrate & Probate Court 113 N Main St, #113, Greensboro, GA 30642; 706-453-3346; fax: 706-453-7649; 8AM-5PM. ***Civil Actions under $15,000, Eviction, Small Claims, Probate.*** https://www.gaprobate.org/find_court.asp Court also has jurisdiction for bad checks, arrest warrants, preliminary hearings, and county ordinance violations.

Gwinnett County

Superior & State Court PO Box 880, 75 Langley Dr, Lawrenceville, GA 30046; 770-822-8100; 8AM-5PM. ***Felony, Misdemeanor, Civil, Eviction, Small Claims.*** www.gwinnettcourts.com/home

Civil Records: Access: Online, in person. Visitors must perform in person searches themselves. Required to search: name, years to search. Civil cases indexed by defendant, plaintiff, on computer from 1990, prior records on card index. Civil PAT goes

back to 1990. Public terminal has Superior court records back to 1980. Online access to court case party index is free at www.gwinnettcourts.com/home.asp#partycasesearch/. Search by name or case number.
Criminal Records: Access: Online, in person. Visitors must perform in person searches themselves. Required to search: name, years to search. Criminal records computerized from 1990, prior records on card index. Criminal PAT goes back to same as civil. Public terminal 90% of info available to public, other 10% can only be searched by staff. Online access to criminal records is the same as civil.
General Information: No sealed records released. Will not fax out documents. Court makes copy: $.25 per page. Certification fee: $2.50 plus $.50 per page includes copy fee. Payee: Superior Court Clerk. Personal checks accepted; credit cards are not. Prepayment required.

Magistrate Court 75 Langley Dr, Justice & Admin. Ctr, Lawrenceville, GA 30045-6900; 770-822-8080; fax: 770-822-8075; 8AM-5PM. ***Civil Actions under $15,000, Eviction, Small Claims.*** www.gwinnettcourts.com/home
Court also has jurisdiction for bad checks, arrest warrants, preliminary hearings, and county ordinance violations. Search cases and calendars countywide free at www.gwinnettcourts.com/#home/

Probate Court Justice & Admin Ctr, 75 Langley Dr, Lawrenceville, GA 30045; 770-822-8250; fax: 770-822-8217; 8AM-4:30PM. ***Probate.***
Probate records may be available online free at www.gwinnettcourts.com/#home.

Habersham County

Superior & State Court 555 Monroe St, Unit 35, Clarkesville, GA 30523; 706-754-2923; probate phone: 706-754-2013; fax: 706-839-6351; 8AM-5PM. ***Felony, Misdemeanor, Civil.***
www.co.habersham.ga.us
Civil Records: Access: Mail, in person. Visitors must perform in person searches themselves. No search fee. Required to search: name, years to search. Civil cases indexed by defendant, plaintiff; index on docket books from 1819. Civil PAT goes back to 1992. PAT civil results show middle initial.
Criminal Records: Access: Mail, in person. Visitors must perform in person searches themselves. No search fee. Required to search: name, years to search. Criminal records indexed in books from 1819. Mail turnaround time 1-2 days. Criminal PAT goes back to same as civil.PAT results show name, DOB. Pre-200 cases may not show SSN or DOB.
General Information: No juvenile, sexual, mental health or expunged records released. Will fax documents to local or toll free line. Court makes copy: n/a. Self serve: $.25 per page. Certification fee: $3.00 per document. Payee: Court Clerk. No personal checks or credit cards accepted. Prepayment required. SASE not required.

Magistrate Court PO Box 580, 226 Grant St, Clarkesville, GA 30523; 706-754-4871; criminal phone: 706-754-0126; civil phone: 706-754-4871; fax: 706-839-7093; 8:30AM-5PM. ***Misdemeanor, Civil Actions under $15,000, Ordinance.***
www.co.habersham.ga.us Court also has jurisdiction for bad checks, arrest warrants, preliminary hearings, and county ordinance violations.

Probate Court PO Box 876, 555 Monroe St, County Courthouse, Clarkesville, GA 30523; 706-754-2013; fax: 706-754-5093; 8AM-5PM. ***Probate.***

Hall County

Superior & State Court PO Box 1336, 225 Green St, SE, Gainesville, GA 30503; 770-531-7025; criminal phone: 770-531-7025; fax: 770-531-7070; 8AM-5PM. ***Felony, Misdemeanor, Civil.***
www.hallcountycourts.com
Clerk and records located in the basement.
Civil Records: Access: In person only. Visitors must perform in person searches themselves. Required to search: name, years to search. Civil cases indexed by defendant, plaintiff, on computer back to 1989, dockets books from early 1900s in storage. Civil PAT goes back to 7/1989. PAT results show name only and include plaintiff/defendant.
Criminal Records: Access: In person only. Visitors must perform in person searches themselves. Required to search: name, years to search. Criminal records computerized from 1989, dockets books from early 1900s in storage. Criminal PAT goes back to same as civil; results show middle initial, DOB.
General Information: No juvenile, adoption, sexual, mental health or expunged records released. Will fax documents $1.00 per page. Court makes copy: $.25 per page. Certification fee: $2.00 plus $.50 per page. Payee: Court Clerk. Personal checks accepted. Prepayment required.

Magistrate Court PO Box 1435, 225 Green St, 2nd Fl, Gainesville, GA 30503; 770-531-6912; fax: 770-531-6917; 8AM-5PM. ***Civil Actions under $15,000, Eviction, Small Claims, Misdemeanors.***
www.hallcounty.org/judicial/#majistrate Court also has jurisdiction for bad checks, arrest warrants, preliminary hearings, and county ordinance violations.

Probate Court Hall County Courthouse, Rm 1000, 225 Green St, Gainesville, GA 30501; 770-531-6923; fax: 770-531-4946; 8:30AM-4:30PM. ***Probate.*** www.hallcounty.org/judicial/#probate
The search fee is $4.00 per record

Hancock County

Superior Court PO Box 451, Courthouse Sq, Sparta, GA 31087; 706-444-6644; fax: 706-444-5685; 9AM-5PM. ***Felony, Misdemeanor, Civil.***
Civil Records: Access: Mail, in person. Visitors must perform in person searches themselves. Search fee: $5.00 per name. Required to search: name, years to search. Civil cases indexed by defendant, plaintiff; index in docket books from 1991. Mail turnaround time 1 week.
Criminal Records: Access: Mail, in person. Visitors must perform in person searches themselves. Search fee: $5.00 per name. Required to search: name, years to search, DOB, signed release; also helpful: SSN, race, sex. Criminal docket on books since 1991. Mail turnaround time 1 week.
General Information: No juvenile, adoptions, sealed, sexual, mental health or expunged records released. Will not fax documents. Court makes copy: $.25 per page, self serve same. Certification fee: $2.50 1st page, $.50 each add'l page. Payee: Clerk of Superior Court. Personal checks accepted; credit cards are not. Prepayment required. Mail requests: SASE required.

Magistrate Court 40 Courthouse Square, Sparta, GA 31087; 706-444-6234; fax: 706-444-6178; 9AM-5PM. ***Civil Actions under $15,000, Eviction, Small Claims.*** Court also has jurisdiction for bad checks, arrest warrants, preliminary hearings, and county ordinance violations.

Probate Court 12630 Broad St, Sparta, GA 31087; 706-444-5343; fax: 706-444-8024; 8AM-5PM. ***Probate.*** www.hancockprobatecourtga.com/

Haralson County

Superior Court Drawer 849, 4485 Georgia Hwy 120, Buchanan, GA 30113; 770-646-2005; probate phone: 770-646-2008; fax: 770-646-8827; 8:30AM-5PM. ***Felony, Misdemeanor, Civil.***
Civil Records: Access: Mail, in person. Both court and visitors may perform in person searches. No search fee. Required to search: name, years to search. Civil cases indexed by defendant, plaintiff; index in docket books from the 1864. Mail turnaround time 1 week. Civil PAT goes back to 2005. PAT results show name, DOB.
Criminal Records: Access: Mail, in person. Both court and visitors may perform in person searches. No search fee. Required to search: name, years to search, signed release. Criminal docket on books from the 1864. Mail turnaround time 1 week. Criminal PAT goes back to 2005; results show name, DOB.
General Information: No juvenile, adoption, sexual, mental health or expunged records released. Will not fax documents. Court makes copy: $.50 per page criminal; civil- $.25 per page. Self serve: $.25 per page. Certification fee: $2.50 plus $.50 per page after first. Payee: Clerk of Superior Court. Personal checks accepted; credit cards are not. Prepayment required. Mail requests: SASE required.

Magistrate Court PO Box 1040, 4485 Hwy 120, Buchanan, GA 30113; 770-646-2015; fax: 770-646-6627; 8:30AM-5PM. ***Civil Actions under $15,000, Eviction, Small Claims.*** Court also has jurisdiction for bad checks, arrest warrants, preliminary hearings, and county ordinance violations.

Probate Court PO Box 620, 4485 Georgia Hwy 120, Buchanan, GA 30113; 770-646-2008; fax: 770-646-3419; 8:30AM-5PM. ***Probate.***

Harris County

Superior Court PO Box 528, 102 N College, Hamilton, GA 31811; 706-628-4944; fax: 706-628-7039; 8AM-5PM. ***Felony, Misdemeanor, Civil.***
Civil Records: Access: In person, online. Visitors must perform in person searches themselves. Required to search: name, years to search. Civil cases indexed by defendant, plaintiff; index in docket books from 1900; on computer back to 1999. Civil PAT goes back to 1999. PAT civil results show middle initial. Access court records by subscription; for information and signup contact Lisa Culpeper at 706-628-4944.
Criminal Records: Access: In person, online. Visitors must perform in person searches themselves. Required to search: name, years to search, DOB; also helpful: race, sex. Criminal docket on books from 1900; on computer back to 1999. Criminal PAT goes back to same as civil. PAT criminal results show middle initial. Access court records by subscription; for information and signup contact Lisa Culpeper at 706-628-4944.
General Information: Juvenile, adoption, sexual, mental health or expunged records are only released with a signed release. Will not fax documents. Court makes copy: $1.00 per page. Self serve: $.25 per page. Certification fee: $2.50 plus $.50 per page after first. Payee: Court Clerk. No personal checks or credit cards accepted. Prepayment required.

Magistrate Court PO Box 347, 102 N College St, Hamilton, GA 31811; 706-628-4977; fax: 706-628-5416; 8AM-5PM. ***Civil Actions under $15,000, Eviction, Small Claims.***
www.harrismagcourt.com Court also has jurisdiction for bad checks, arrest warrants, preliminary hearings, and county ordinance violations. Website may soon have court records available.

Probate PO Box 569, 102 N College St #116, Hamilton, GA 31811; 706-628-5038; fax: 706-628-7322; 8-5PM. ***Probate, Misdemeanor Traffic.***

Hart County

Superior Court PO Box 386, Hartwell, GA 30643; 706-376-7189; fax: 706-376-1277; 8:30AM-5PM. ***Felony, Misdemeanor, Civil.***
Civil Records: Access: In person only. Visitors must perform in person searches themselves. Required to search: name, years to search. Civil cases indexed by defendant, plaintiff, on computer back to 1997, dockets books from 1853. Civil PAT goes back to 1997.
Criminal Records: Access: In person only. Visitors must perform in person searches themselves. Required to search: name, years to search, DOB. Criminal records computerized from 1997, dockets books from 1853. Criminal PAT goes back to same as civil. PAT results show middle initial, DOB.
General Information: No juvenile, adoption, sexual, mental health or expunged records released. Will not fax documents. Court makes copy: $1.00 per page. Self serve: $.25 per page. Certification fee: $2.50 plus $.50 per page after first. Payee: Clerk of Court. Personal checks accepted; credit cards are not. Prepayment required.

Magistrate Court PO Box 698, 165 W Franklin, Hartwell, GA 30643; 706-376-6817; fax: 706-376-6821; 8:30AM-5PM. ***Civil Actions under $15,000, Eviction, Small Claims.*** www.hartmagcourt.com
Court also has jurisdiction for bad checks, arrest warrants, preliminary hearings, county ordinances.

Probate Court PO Box 1159, 185 W Franklin St, Hartwell, GA 30643; 706-376-2565; fax: 706-376-9032; 8:30AM-5PM. ***Probate, Misdemeanor Traffic.*** Also handles births, deaths, marriages, firearm permits, passports, elections

Heard County

Superior Court PO Box 249, 215 Court St, Franklin, GA 30217; 706-675-3301; fax: 706-675-0819; 8:30AM-5PM. ***Felony, Misdemeanor, Civil.***
Civil Records: Access: In person only. Visitors must perform in person searches themselves. Required to search: name, years to search. Civil cases indexed by defendant, plaintiff; index in docket books from 1894. Civil PAT goes back to 1996.
Criminal Records: Access: In person only. Visitors must perform in person searches themselves. Required to search: name, years to search, DOB, signed release; SSN helpful. Criminal docket on books from 1894. Criminal PAT goes back to same as civil.
General Information: No juvenile, adoptions, sealed, sexual, mental health or expunged records released. Will fax specific case file $1.00 per page. Court makes copy: $.25 per page. Certification fee: $2.50 plus $.50 per page after first. Payee: Court Clerk. No personal checks or credit cards accepted. Prepayment required.

Magistrate Court PO Box 395, 215 E Court Square, Rm 11, Franklin, GA 30217; 706-675-3002; fax: 706-675-0819; 8:30AM-5PM. ***Misdemeanor, Civil Actions under $15,000, Eviction, Small Claims.*** Court also has jurisdiction for bad checks, arrest warrants, preliminary hearings, county ordinances.

Probate Court PO Box 478, 215 E Court Sq, Rm 3, Franklin, GA 30217; 706-675-3353; fax: 706-675-0819; 8:30AM-5PM. ***Probate, Misdemeanor.***

Henry County

Superior Court One Courthouse Square, McDonough, GA 30253; 770-288-8022; fax: 770-898-7573; 8AM-5PM. ***Felony, Misdemeanor, Civil.***
Civil Records: Access: Phone, mail, in person. Visitors must perform in person searches themselves. No search fee. Required to search: name, years to search. Civil cases indexed by defendant, plaintiff; index in docket books from 1800s. Civil PAT goes back to 1993.
Criminal Records: Access: In person only. Visitors must perform in person searches themselves. Required to search: name, years to search, DOB, signed release; SSN helpful. Criminal docket on books from 1800s. Criminal PAT available.
General Information: No juvenile, adoption, sexual, mental health or expunged records released. No fee to fax documents. Court makes copy: $.25 per page, self serve same. Certification fee: $2.50 plus $.50 per add'l page. Payee: Clerk of Superior Court. Personal checks accepted; credit cards are not. Prepayment required.

Magistrate Court 44 John Frank Ward Blvd, One Judicial Ctr, ste. 260, McDonough, GA 30253; 770-288-7700; fax: 770-288-7142; 8AM-5PM. ***Misdemeanor, Civil Actions under $15,000, Eviction, Small Claims.***
www.co.henry.ga.us/MagistrateCourt/MagistrateCourtMain.htm Court also has jurisdiction for bad checks, arrest warrants, preliminary hearings, and county ordinance violations.

Probate Court 99 Sims St., McDonough, GA 30253; 770-288-7600; fax: 770-288-7616; 8AM-4:30PM. ***Probate.***
www.co.henry.ga.us/Probate/ProbateCourt.htm

Houston County

Superior Court 201 Perry Pky, Perry, GA 31069; 478-218-4720; criminal phone: 478-218-4730; civil phone: 478-218-4740; fax: 478-218-4745; 8:30AM-5PM. ***Felony, Misdemeanor, Civil.***
www.houstoncountyga.org/index.htm
Civil Records: Access: Phone, fax, mail, in person. Only the court performs in person searches; visitors may not. No search fee. Required to search: name, years to search. Civil cases indexed by defendant, plaintiff, on computer from 1984, dockets books back to 1823. Mail turnaround time 1-2 days. Civil PAT goes back to 1984. PAT results show name only.
Criminal Records: Access: Fax, mail, in person. Visitors must perform in person searches themselves. No search fee. Required to search: name, years to search, DOB; also helpful: SSN, race, sex. Criminal records computerized from 1984, dockets books back to 1823. Mail turnaround time 1-2 days. Criminal PAT goes back to same as civil. PAT results show name only.
General Information: No juvenile, adoption, mental health or expunged records released. Will fax documents. Court makes copy: $.25 per page, self serve same. Certification fee: $2.50 plus $.50 per page after first. Payee: Court Clerk. No personal checks or credit cards accepted. Prepayment required. Mail requests: SASE required.

State Court 202 Carl Vinson Pky, Warner Robins, GA 31088; 478-542-2105; fax: 478-542-2077; 8AM-5PM. ***Misdemeanor, Civil.***
www.houstoncountyga.org/index.htm
Civil Records: Access: Mail, fax, in person. Both court and visitors may perform in person searches. Search fee: $10.00 per name. Required to search: name, years to search. Civil cases indexed by defendant. Civil records on computer from 1987, dockets books from 1965. Mail turnaround time 3 days. Civil PAT goes back to 1987. PAT results show name only.
Criminal Records: Access: In person only. Visitors must perform in person searches themselves. Required to search: name, years to search, DOB; SSN helpful. Criminal records computerized from 1987, dockets books from 1965. Criminal PAT goes back to same as civil. PAT results show middle initial, DOB. Terminal results include SSN.
General Information: No juvenile, adoption, sexual, mental health or expunged records released. Court makes copy: $.25 per page, self serve same. Certification fee: $2.50 plus $.50 per page after first. Payee: Court Clerk. Only cashiers checks and money orders accepted. No credit cards accepted. Prepayment required. Mail requests: SASE required.

Magistrate Court 89 Cohen Walker Dr, Warner Robins, GA 31088; 478-987-4695; fax: 478-987-5249; 8AM-5PM. ***Civil Actions under $15,000, Eviction, Small Claims.***
http://georgiacourts.org/courts/magistrate/houston
Court also has jurisdiction for bad checks, arrest warrants, preliminary hearings, county ordinances.

Probate Court PO Box 1801, 201 N Perry Pky, Perry, GA 31069; 478-218-4710; fax: 478-218-4715; 8:30AM-4:30PM. ***Probate.***
www.houstoncountyga.org/government/probate%2Dcourt/

Irwin County

Superior Court 301 S Irwin Ave #103, Ocilla, GA 31774; 229-468-5356; fax: 229-468-9753; 8AM-5PM. ***Felony, Misdemeanor, Civil.***
Civil Records: Access: Phone, mail, in person. Visitors must perform in person searches themselves. No search fee. Required to search: name, years to search. Civil cases indexed by defendant, plaintiff; index in docket books from 1870s, records are not computerized. Court will not do general record searches; the specific case file must be given. Civil PAT goes back to 2003.
Criminal Records: Access: Phone, mail, in person. Visitors must perform in person searches themselves. No search fee. Required to search: name, years to search, DOB, signed release; also helpful: SSN, race, sex. Criminal docket on books from 1900, records are not computerized. Court will not do general record searches, the specific case file must be given. Mail turnaround time 2 days. Criminal PAT goes back to same as civil.
General Information: No juvenile, adoption, sexual, mental health or expunged records released. Will fax documents $2.50 1st page, $1.00 each add'l page. Court makes copy: $1.00 per page. Self serve: $.25 per page. Certification fee: $2.50 plus $.50 per page after first. Payee: Court Clerk. Personal checks accepted; credit cards are not. Prepayment required.

Magistrate Court 301 S Irwin Ave, #102, Ocilla, GA 31774; 229-468-7671; fax: 229-468-8444; 8AM-5PM, M-TH, 8AM-N, F. ***Civil Actions under $15,000, Eviction, Small Claims.*** Court also has jurisdiction for bad checks, arrest warrants, preliminary hearings, and county ordinance violations.

Probate Court 301 S Irwin Ave., Ocilla, GA 31774; 229-468-5138; fax: 229-468-5702; 8AM-N,1-5PM. ***Probate.***

Jackson County

Superior & State Court PO Box 7, 5000 Jackson Pkwy, #150, Jefferson, GA 30549; 706-387-6255; criminal phone: 707-387-6254; civil phone: 707-387-6248; fax: 706-387-6273; 8AM-5PM. ***Felony, Misdemeanor, Civil.***
http://jacksoncountygov.com/Index.aspx?page=81
Civil Records: Access: In person only. Visitors must perform in person searches themselves. Required to search: name, years to search. Civil cases indexed by defendant, plaintiff, on computer from 1992, on dockets books from 1800s. Civil PAT goes back to 1992.
Criminal Records: Access: Mail, in person. Visitors must perform in person searches themselves. Search fee: $25.00 per name. Required to search: name, years to search, DOB; SSN helpful. Criminal records computerized from 1992, on dockets books from 1800s. Criminal PAT goes back to same as civil.
General Information: No juvenile, adoption, sexual, mental health or expunged records released. Will not fax out documents. Court makes copy: $.25 per page. Self serve: $.25 per page. Certification fee: $2.50 plus $.50 per page after first. Payee: Court Clerk. No personal checks accepted. Prepayment required.

Magistrate Court 5000 Jackson Parkway #230, Jefferson, GA 30549; 706-335-6356; criminal fax: 706-387-6369; civil fax: same; 8AM-5PM. ***Civil Actions under $15,000, Eviction, Small Claims.*** Court also has jurisdiction for bad checks, arrest warrants, preliminary hearings, and county ordinance violations.

Probate Court 5000 Jackson Pky #140, Jefferson, GA 30549; 706-387-6275; fax: 706-387-6285; 8AM-5PM. ***Probate.***
www.jacksoncountygov.com/index.aspx?page=103
Jackson County Probate does not handle civil and criminal records.

Jasper County

Superior Court 126 W Green St, #110, Monticello, GA 31064; 706-468-4901; fax: 706-468-4946; 8AM-5PM. ***Felony, Misdemeanor, Civil.***
Civil Records: Access: In person only. Visitors must perform in person searches themselves. Required to search: name, years to search. Civil cases indexed by defendant, plaintiff, on computer from 1990, dockets books from 1807. Civil PAT goes back to 1990. PAT civil results show middle initial.
Criminal Records: Access: In person only. Visitors must perform in person searches themselves. Required to search: name, years to search, DOB; SSN helpful. Criminal records computerized from 1990, dockets books from 1807. Criminal PAT goes back to 1992. PAT results show middle initial, DOB.
General Information: No juvenile, adoption, sexual, mental health or expunged records released. Will not fax out documents. Court makes copy: $1.00 per page. Self serve: $.25 per page. Certification fee: $2.50 plus $.50 per page after first. Payee: Court Clerk. Personal checks accepted; credit cards are not. Prepayment required.

Magistrate Court 126 W Green St, #110, Monticello, GA 31064; 706-468-4909; fax: 706-468-4946; 8AM-5PM. ***Civil Actions under $15,000, Eviction, Small Claims.***
www.jaspercourt.com Access records online via the state system at www.gsccca.org. Court also has jurisdiction for bad checks, arrest warrants, preliminary hearings, and county ordinance violations.

Probate Court Jasper County Courthouse, 126 W Green St, #111, Monticello, GA 31064; 706-468-4903; fax: 706-468-4926; 8AM-4:30PM. ***Probate.***

Jeff Davis County

Superior & State Court PO Box 429, 14 Jeff Davis St, #105, Hazlehurst, GA 31539; 912-375-6615; fax: 912-375-6637; 8AM-5PM. ***Felony, Misdemeanor, Civil.***

Civil Records: Access: Mail, in person. Both court and visitors may perform in person searches. Search fee: $3.00 per name. Required to search: name, years to search. Civil cases indexed by defendant. Civil records on dockets books. Mail turnaround time 1 week.

Criminal Records: Access: Mail, in person. Both court and visitors may perform in person searches. Search fee: $3.00 per name. Required to search: name, years to search; also helpful- offense. Criminal docket on books. Mail turnaround time 1 week.

General Information: No juvenile, confidential, adoption or sealed records released. Fee to fax out file $2.00 1st page, $1.00 each add'l. Court makes copy: $.50 per page. Self serve: $.25 per page. Certification fee: $2.50 plus $.50 per page after first. Payee: Court Clerk. No personal checks accepted. Money orders only. No credit cards accepted. Prepayment required. Mail requests: SASE helpful.

Magistrate Court PO Box 568, 14 Jeff Davis St, Hazlehurst, GA 31539; 912-375-6630; fax: 912-375-6629; 8AM-5PM. ***Civil Actions under $15,000, Eviction, Small Claims.*** www.jeffdaviscourt.com Court also has jurisdiction for bad checks, arrest warrants, preliminary hearings, county ordinances.

Probate Court PO Box 446, 14 Jeff Davis St, Hazlehurst, GA 31539; 912-375-6626; fax: 912-375-0502; 9AM-5PM. ***Probate.***

Jefferson County

Superior & State Court PO Box 151, 202 E Broad St, Louisville, GA 30434; 478-625-7922; fax: 478-625-4037; 9AM-5PM. ***Felony, Misdemeanor, Civil.***

Civil Records: Access: In person only. Both court and visitors may perform in person searches. No search fee. Required to search: name, years to search. Civil cases indexed by defendant, plaintiff; index in docket books from 1865; on computer back to 1995. Civil PAT goes back to 1995. PAT results show name, DOB. Results include drivers license number and SSN.

Criminal Records: Access: In person only. Both court and visitors may perform in person searches. No search fee. Required to search: name, years to search, DOB or SSN. Criminal docket on books from 1865; on computer back to 1995. Criminal PAT goes back to same as civil.PAT results show name, DOB. Results include name, SSN, drivers license.

General Information: No juvenile, adoption, sexual, mental health or expunged records released. Will fax documents to local or toll-free number. Court makes copy: $.25 per page, self serve same. Certification fee: $2.50 plus $.50 per add'l page. Payee: Court Clerk. Personal checks accepted; credit cards are not. Prepayment required.

Magistrate Court PO Box 749, 911 Clarks Mill Rd, Louisville, GA 30434; 478-625-8834; fax: 478-625-4039; 8AM-5PM. ***Civil Actions under $15,000, Eviction, Small Claims.*** www.jeffersoncourt.com Court also has jurisdiction for bad checks, arrest warrants, preliminary hearings, county ordinances.

Probate Court PO Box 307, 202 E Broad St, Louisville, GA 30434; 478-625-3258; fax: 478-625-0245; 8AM-N, 1-5PM. ***Probate.***

Jenkins County

Superior & State Court PO Box 659, 611 Winthrop Ave, Millen, GA 30442; 478-982-4683; fax: 478-982-1274; 8:30AM-5PM. ***Felony, Misdemeanor, Civil.***

Civil Records: Access: In person only. Visitors must perform in person searches themselves. Required to search: name, years to search. Civil cases indexed by defendant. Civil records on dockets books. Civil PAT goes back to 1990.

Criminal Records: Access: In person only. Visitors must perform in person searches themselves. Required to search: name, years to search, DOB; SSN helpful. Criminal docket on books. Criminal PAT goes back to same as civil.

General Information: No juvenile, adoption, sexual, mental health or expunged records released. Will fax documents $.25 per page. Court makes copy: $.25 per page, self serve same. Certification fee: $2.50 plus $.25 per page after first. Payee: Clerk of Court. Personal checks accepted; credit cards are not. Prepayment required.

Magistrate Court PO Box 892, 611 Winthrop Ave, Courthouse Sq, Millen, GA 30442; 478-982-5580; fax: 478-982-4911; 8:30AM-5PM. ***Civil Actions under $15,000, Eviction, Small Claims, Misdemeanor, Ordinance.*** www.jenkinscourt.com Court also has jurisdiction for bad checks, arrest warrants, preliminary hearings, county ordinances.

Probate Court PO Box 904, 611 E Winthrope Ave, Millen, GA 30442; 478-982-5581; fax: 478-982-2829; 8:30AM-5PM. ***Probate.***

Johnson County

Superior & Magistrate Court PO Box 321, Wrightsville, GA 31096; 478-864-3484; fax: 478-864-1343; 9AM-5PM. ***Felony, Misdemeanor, Civil, Eviction, Small Claims.***

Civil Records: Access: In person only. Visitors must perform in person searches themselves. Required to search: name, years to search. Civil cases indexed by defendant, plaintiff, on computer from 1991, dockets books from 1859. **Criminal Records:** Access: In person only. Visitors must perform in person searches themselves. Required to search: name, years to search, DOB; SSN helpful. Criminal records computerized from 1991, dockets books from 1859.

General Information: No juvenile, adoption, sexual, mental health or expunged records released. Will fax documents $2.00 per fax. Court makes copy: $.25 per page, self serve same. Certification fee: $3.00 per cert. Payee: Court Clerk. Personal checks accepted. Prepayment required.

Probate Court PO Box 264, 101 Elm St, Wrightsville, GA 31096; 478-864-3316; fax: 478-864-0528; 9AM-5PM. ***Probate.***

Jones County

Superior Court PO Box 39, 110 S Jefferson St, Gray, GA 31032; 478-986-6671/6674````; 8:30AM-4:30PM. ***Felony, Misdemeanor, Civil over $15,000.***

Civil Records: Access: In person only. Visitors must perform in person searches themselves. Required to search: name, years to search. Civil cases indexed by defendant, plaintiff, on computer since 1989, dockets books from 1800s. The court will fax records not requiring a search, $5.00 minimum. Civil PAT goes back to 1995.

Criminal Records: Access: In person only. Visitors must perform in person searches themselves. Required to search: name, years to search, signed release. Criminal docket on books, computerized since 1995. Criminal PAT goes back same as civil.

General Information: No juvenile, adoption, sexual, mental health or expunged records released. Will fax out results $.50 per page, $5.00 minimum prepaid. Court makes copy: $.50 per page. Self serve: $.25 per page. Certification fee: $2.50 plus $.50 per page after first. Payee: Superior Court. Personal checks accepted; credit cards are not. Prepayment required.

Magistrate Court PO Box 88, 110 S Jefferson St, Gray, GA 31032; 478-986-5113; fax: 478-986-6536; 8:30AM-4:30PM. ***Civil under $15,000, Small Claims, Eviction.***

Probate Court PO Box 1359, 110 S Jefferson St, Gray, GA 31032; 478-986-6668; fax: 478-986-1715; 8AM-5PM. ***Probate, Traffic, Vital Records.*** Search for tickets free at https://www.ncourt.com/courtpayment/Lookup.aspx?Juris=GAJones.

Lamar County

Superior Court 326 Thomaston St, Box 7, Barnesville, GA 30204; 770-358-5145; criminal fax: 770-358-5814; civil fax: same; 8AM-5PM. ***Felony, Misdemeanor, Civil.***

Civil Records: Access: In person only. Visitors must perform in person searches themselves. Required to search: name, years to search. Civil cases indexed by defendant. Civil index in docket books from 1921; on computer back to 9/2000. Civil PAT goes back to 2000.

Criminal Records: Access: In person only. Visitors must perform in person searches themselves. Required to search: name, years to search, DOB, offense, date of offense; SSN helpful. Criminal docket on books from 1921; on computer back to 9/2000. Criminal PAT goes back to 2000.

General Information: No juvenile, adoption, sexual, mental health or expunged records released. Will not fax out case files. Court makes copy: $1.00 first page, $.50 each add'l. Self serve: $.25 per page. Cert fee: $2.50 for 1st page, $.50 each add'l page. Payee: Court Clerk. Personal checks accepted; credit cards are not. Prepayment required. Will bill copy fees.

Magistrate Court 121 Roberta Dr, #B, Barnesville, GA 30204; 770-358-5154; fax: 770-358-5214; 8AM-N, 1-5PM. ***Civil Actions under $15,000, Eviction, Small Claims.*** Court also has jurisdiction for bad checks, arrest warrants, preliminary hearings, and county ordinance violations.

Probate Court 326 Thomaston St, Barnesville, GA 30204; 770-358-5155; fax: 770-358-5348; 8AM-5PM. ***Probate, Misdemeanor, Traffic.***

Lanier County

Superior Court County Courthouse, 100 Main St, Ste 5, Lakeland, GA 31635; 229-482-3594; fax: 229-482-8333; 8AM-N, 1-5PM. ***Felony, Misdemeanor, Civil.***

Civil Records: Access: In person only. Visitors must perform in person searches themselves. Required to search: name, years to search. Civil cases indexed by defendant, plaintiff; index in docket books from 1921; on computer back to 1995.

Criminal Records: Access: In person only. Visitors must perform in person searches themselves. Required to search: name, years to search, DOB, signed release. Criminal docket on books from 1921; on computer back to 1995.

General Information: No juvenile, adoption, sexual, mental health or expunged records released. Will not fax documents. Court makes copy: $.25 per page. Self serve: $.25 per page. Certification fee: $3.00. Payee: Court Clerk. Personal checks accepted; credit cards are not. Prepayment required.

Magistrate Court 100 Main St, #3, County Courthouse, Lakeland, GA 31635; 229-482-2207; fax: 229-482-8358; 8AM-N; 1PM-5PM. ***Civil Actions under $15,000, Eviction, Small Claims.*** www.laniercourt.com Court also has jurisdiction for bad checks, arrest warrants, preliminary hearings, and county ordinance violations.

Probate Court County Courthouse, 100 Main St, #10, Lakeland, GA 31635; 229-482-3668; fax: 229-482-3680; 8AM-N, 1-5PM. ***Probate.***

Laurens County

Superior & Magistrate Court PO Box 2028, 101 N Jefferson, Dublin, GA 31021; 478-272-3210; fax: 478-275-2595; 8:30AM-5:30PM. ***Felony, Misdemeanor, Civil, Eviction, Small Claims.*** www.laurenscoga.org/

Civil Records: Access: In person only. Visitors must perform in person searches themselves. Civil cases indexed by defendant, plaintiff, on computer from 1992, dockets books from 1800s. Civil PAT goes back to 1992. **Criminal Records:** Access: In person only. Visitors must perform in person searches themselves. Criminal records computerized from 1992, dockets books from 1800s. Criminal PAT goes back to same as civil. PAT results show name, DOB, SSN. Results include name and address - docket sheets show DOB.

General Information: No juvenile, adoption, sexual, mental health or expunged records released. Will fax documents $2.50 flat fee. Court makes copy: $.25 per page, self serve same. Certification fee: $2.50 plus $.50 per page after first. Payee: Court Clerk. Personal checks accepted; credit cards are not. Prepayment required.

Probate Court PO Box 2098, 101 N Jefferson St, Courthouse, Dublin, GA 31040; 478-272-2566; fax: 478-277-2932; 8:30AM-5:30PM. ***Probate.***

Lee County

Superior Court PO Box 49, 100 Leslie Hwy, Leesburg, GA 31763; 229-759-6018; fax: 229-759-6049; 8AM-5PM. ***Felony, Misdemeanor, Civil.***

Civil Records: Access: In person. Only the court performs in person searches; visitors may not. Required to search: name, years to search. Civil cases indexed by defendant, plaintiff; index in docket books from 1850.

Criminal Records: Access: Mail, in person. Both court and visitors may perform in person searches. Search fee: $5.00. Required to search: name, years to search, DOB; also helpful: SSN, race, sex. Criminal docket on books from 1850, computerized since 1996. Mail turnaround time 1 week.

General Information: No juvenile, adoption, sexual, mental health or expunged records released. Will fax documents to local or toll free line. Court makes copy: $.25 per page. Self serve: $.25 per page. Certification fee: $2.00 per cert. Payee: Court Clerk. Personal checks accepted; credit cards are not. Prepayment required. Mail requests: SASE required.

Magistrate Court PO Box 522, 100 Leslie Hwy, Leesburg, GA 31763; 229-759-6016; fax: 229-759-3303; 8AM-5PM. ***Civil Actions under $15,000, Eviction, Small Claims.***

Court also has jurisdiction for bad checks, arrest warrants, preliminary hearings, and county ordinance violations.

Probate Court PO Box 592, 100 Leslie Hwy, Leesburg, GA 31763; 229-759-6005; fax: 229-759-3345; 8AM-5PM. ***Probate, Misdemeanor Traffic.***

Liberty County

Superior & State Court PO Box 50, 100 Main St, Courthouse, Hinesville, GA 31313-0050; 912-876-3625; criminal phone: 912-876-7340; civil phone: 912-876-7365; fax: 912-876-7394; 8AM-5PM. ***Felony, Misdemeanor, Civil.***
www.libertyco.com

Civil Records: Access: Fax, mail, in person. Both court and visitors may perform in person searches. Search fee: $12.81 per hour if over 15 minutes. Required to search: name, years to search, signed release. Civil cases indexed by defendant, plaintiff, on computer from 1986, dockets books from 1700s. Mail turnaround time 1-3 days. Civil PAT goes back to 1986. PAT results show middle initial, DOB. Terminal results also show SSNs.

Criminal Records: Access: In person only. Both court and visitors may perform in person searches. Required to search: name, years to search, DOB, signed release; also helpful: SSN, race, sex. Criminal records computerized from 1986, dockets books from 1700s. Criminal PAT goes back to same as civil. PAT results show middle initial, DOB. Terminal results include SSN.

General Information: No juvenile, adoption, sexual, mental health or expunged records released. Will fax documents $5.00 1st 5 pages, $1.00 each add'l pg. Court makes copy: $1.00 per page. Self serve: $.25 per page. Certification fee: $2.50 plus $.50 per page after first. Payee: Court Clerk. Business checks accepted. Visa/MC accepted; smallusage charge is added. Prepayment required. SASE not required.

Magistrate Court PO Box 912, 112 N Main St #103, Courthouse Annex, Hinesville, GA 31310; 912-368-2063; fax: 912-876-2474; 8AM-Noon,1-5PM. ***Civil Actions under $15,000, Eviction, Small Claims.*** www.libertyco.com

Court also has jurisdiction for bad checks, arrest warrants, preliminary hearings, Foreclosures, Garnishments, and county ordinance violations. Has a 2nd location at 110 N Main St in the main courthouse.

Probate Court PO Box 28, 112 N Main St, Rm 100, Hinesville, GA 31310; 912-876-3635; fax: 912-876-3589; 8AM-5PM. ***Probate.***

Lincoln County

Superior Court PO Box 340, Lincolnton, GA 30817; 706-359-5505; fax: 706-359-5027; 9AM-5PM. ***Felony, Misdemeanor, Civil.***
www.lincolncountyga.com/SuperiorCourts.asp

Civil Records: Access: In person only. Visitors must perform in person searches themselves. Required to search: name, years to search. Civil cases indexed by defendant, plaintiff; index on docket books from 1796, computerized since 1992. Civil PAT goes back to 1990. PAT civil results show middle initial. Daily calendars online at the website.

Criminal Records: Access: In person only. Visitors must perform in person searches themselves. Required to search: name, years to search. Criminal records indexed in books from 1796, records are not computerized. Criminal PAT goes back to same as civil. PAT results show name only. Daily calendars online at the website.

General Information: No adoption or juvenile records released. Will not fax documents. Court makes copy: $1.00 per page. Self serve: $.25 per page. Certification fee: $2.50. Payee: Superior Court Clerk. Personal checks accepted; credit cards are not.

Magistrate & Probate Court PO Box 205, 210 Humphrey St, Lincolnton, GA 30817; 706-359-5519; probate phone: 706-359-5528; fax: 706-359-5520; 8AM-5PM. ***Civil Actions under $15,000, Eviction, Small Claims, Probate.*** Court also has jurisdiction for bad checks, arrest warrants, preliminary hearings, and county ordinance violations.

Long County

Superior & State Court PO Box 458, Ludowici, GA 31316; 912-545-2123; fax: 912-545-2020; 8:30AM-5PM. ***Felony, Misdemeanor, Civil.***

Civil Records: Access: Mail, fax, in person. Both court and visitors may perform in person searches. Search fee: $5.00 per name. Required to search: name, years to search. Civil cases indexed by defendant, plaintiff; index on docket books, archived from 1921. Mail turnaround time 1 week. Civil PAT goes back to 1993.

Criminal Records: Access: Mail, fax, in person. Both court and visitors may perform in person searches. Search fee: $5.00 per name. Required to search: name, years to search, DOB; also helpful: SSN, race, sex. Criminal docket on books, archived from 1921. Mail turnaround time 1 week. Criminal PAT goes back to same as civil.

General Information: No juvenile, adoption, sealed, sexual, mental health, expunged or confidential records released. Will not fax documents. Court makes copy: $1.00 per page. Self serve: $.25 per page. Certification fee: $2.50 for 1st page, $.50 each add'l. Cert fee includes copies. Payee: Court Clerk. Business checks accepted. No credit cards accepted. Prepayment required. Mail requests: SASE required.

Magistrate & Probate Court PO Box 87, 49 McDonald St, Ludowici, GA 31316; 912-545-2315; probate phone: 912-545-2131; fax: 912-545-2029; 8:30AM-4:30PM. ***Civil Actions under $15,000, Eviction, Small Claims, Probate.***

Court also has jurisdiction for bad checks, arrest warrants, preliminary hearings, and county ordinance violations. Use PO Box 426 for probate Court.

Lowndes County

Superior & State Court PO Box 1349, 108 E Central Ave, Valdosta, GA 31603; 229-333-5127; fax: 229-333-7637; 8AM-5PM. ***Felony, Misdemeanor, Civil*** .http://georgiainfo.galileo.usg.edu/courthouses/lowndesCH.htm

Civil Records: Access: Mail, in person. Visitors must perform in person searches themselves. Search fee: $3.00 per name for mail requests. Required to search: name, years to search. Civil cases indexed by defendant, plaintiff, on computer from 1990, prior on dockets books. Civil PAT goes back to 1990. PAT results show name only.

Criminal Records: Access: In person only. Visitors must perform in person searches themselves. Required to search: name, years to search, DOB; SSN helpful. Criminal records computerized from 1984; prior records on docket books. Criminal PAT goes to 1984. PAT results show middle initial, DOB.

General Information: No juvenile, adoption, sexual, mental health or expunged records released. Fee to fax document $.25 per page. Court makes copy: $.25 per page, self serve same. Certification fee: $2.50 plus $.50 per page after 1st; $5.00 minimum. Payee: Court Clerk. Cashiers checks and money orders accepted. No credit cards accepted. Prepayment required.

Magistrate Court PO Box 1349, 108 E Central Ave, Valdosta, GA 31603; 229-671-2610; fax: 229-671-3442; 8AM-5PM. ***Civil Actions under $15,000, Eviction, Small Claims.***
www.lowndescounty.com/courts.asp?id=32

Court also has jurisdiction for bad checks, arrest warrants, preliminary hearings, county ordinances.

Probate Court 100 E Central Ave, Rm 105, Valdosta, GA 31601; 229-671-2650; fax: 229-333-7646; 8AM-5PM. ***Probate.***
www.lowndescounty.com/courts.asp?id=33

Lumpkin County

Superior, Juvenile & Magistrate Court 99 Courthouse Hill, #D, Dahlonega, GA 30533-0541; 706-864-3736; fax: 706-864-5298; 8AM-5PM. ***Felony, Misdemeanor, Civil, Eviction, Small Claims.*** For Magistrate Court criminal records info, call 706-864-7760.

Civil Records: Access: In person only. Visitors must perform in person searches themselves. Required to search: name, years to search; also helpful: address. Civil cases indexed by defendant, plaintiff, on computer from 1988, prior on dockets books to 1833. Civil PAT goes back to 1998.

Criminal Records: Access: In person only. Visitors must perform in person searches themselves. Required to search: name, years to search, DOB; SSN helpful. Criminal records computerized from 1988, prior on dockets books to 1833. Criminal PAT goes back to 1998. PAT results show middle initial, DOB, SSN. SSNs may appear on terminal results.

General Information: No juvenile, adoption, sealed records released. Will fax specific case file if copies prepaid. Court makes copy: $1.00 per page. Self serve: $.25 per page. Cert fee: $2.50 plus $.50 per page after first. Payee: Court Clerk. Personal checks accepted; credit cards are not. Prepayment required.

Probate Court 99 Courthouse Hill, #C, Dahlonega, GA 30533; 706-864-3847; fax: 706-864-9271; 8-5PM. ***Probate, Traffic, Vital Records.***

Macon County

Superior Court PO Box 337, Oglethorpe, GA 31068; 478-472-7661; fax: 478-472-4775; 8AM-5PM. ***Felony, Misdemeanor, Civil.***

This court no longer does any searches. Public access terminal has only real estate records available, everything else is in docket books.

Civil Records: Access: In person. Visitors must perform in person searches themselves. Civil cases indexed by defendant, plaintiff; index in docket books from 1800s. Civil PAT goes back to 2002. PAT results show name only.

Criminal Records: Access: In person only. Visitors must perform in person searches themselves. Criminal docket on books from 1800s. Criminal PAT goes back to 2002. PAT results show name only.

General Information: No juvenile, adoption, sexual, mental health or expunged records released. Will fax documents $2.00. Court makes copy: $1.00 per page. Self serve: $.25 per page. Certification fee: $2.50 1st page; $.50 each add'l. Payee: Court Clerk. Business checks accepted. No credit cards accepted.

Magistrate Court PO Box 605, Oglethorpe, GA 31068; 478-472-8509; fax: 478-472-8510; 8AM-N, 1-5PM. ***Civil Actions under $15,000, Eviction, Small Claims.*** www.maconmagcourt.com

Physical Address: 103 S Sumter St, Oglethorpe, GA 31069. Court also has jurisdiction for bad checks, arrest warrants, preliminary hearings, and county ordinance violations.

Probate Court PO Box 216, 121 S. Sumter St, Oglethorpe, GA 31068; 478-472-7685; fax: 478-472-5643; 8AM-N, 1-5PM. ***Probate.***

Madison County

Superior Court PO Box 247, Danielsville, GA 30633; 706-795-6310; fax: 706-795-2209; 8AM-5PM. ***Felony, Misdemeanor, Civil.***

Civil Records: Access: In person only. Visitors must perform in person searches themselves. Required to search: name, years to search. Civil cases indexed by defendant. Civil records on computer since 7/96, archived since 1811. Civil PAT goes back to 7/1997. PAT results show name only.

Criminal Records: Access: In person only. Visitors must perform in person searches themselves. Required to search: name, years to search, DOB; SSN helpful. Criminal records on computer since 7/96, archived since 1811. Criminal PAT goes back to 7/1996. PAT results show name only.

General Information: No juvenile, adoption, sexual, mental health or expunged records released. Will fax documents $2.50 1st page, $1.00 each add'l page. Court makes copy: $.25 per page, self serve same. Certification fee: $2.50 plus $.50 per page after first. Payee: Court Clerk. No personal checks or credit cards accepted. Prepayment required.

Magistrate Court PO Box 6, 91 Albany Ave, Danielsville, GA 30633; 706-795-6375; fax: 706-795-2222; 8AM-5PM. ***Civil Actions under $15,000, Eviction, Small Claims.*** Court also has jurisdiction for bad checks, arrest warrants, preliminary hearings, and county ordinance violations.

Probate Court PO Box 207, 91 Albany Ave, Danielsville, GA 30633; 706-795-6365; fax: 706-795-5933; 8AM-5PM. ***Probate.***

Marion County

Superior Court PO Box 41, 100 N Broad St, Buena Vista, GA 31803; 229-649-7321; fax: 229-649-7931; 8AM-5PM. ***Felony, Misdemeanor, Civil.***

Civil Records: Access: In person only. Visitors must perform in person searches themselves. Required to search: name, years to search. Civil cases indexed by defendant, plaintiff, on books.

Criminal Records: Access: In person only. Visitors must perform in person searches themselves. Required to search: name, years to search; SSN helpful. Criminal docket on books.

General Information: No juvenile, adoption, sexual, mental health or expunged records released. Will fax documents $1.00 per page. Court makes copy: $.25 per page, self serve same. Certification fee: $2.50 plus $.50 per page after first. Payee: Court Clerk. Personal checks accepted; credit cards are not. Prepayment required.

Magistrate & Probate Court PO Box 196, 100 N Broad St, Buena Vista, GA 31803; 229-649-5542; fax: 229-649-2059; 8:30AM-5PM. ***Civil under $15,000, Eviction, Small Claims, Probate.*** Court also has jurisdiction for bad checks, arrest warrants, preliminary hearings, and county ordinance violations.

McDuffie County

Superior Court PO Box 158, 337 Main St, Rm 101, Thomson, GA 30824; 706-595-2134; criminal phone: 706-595-2139; civil phone: 706-595-2138; probate phone: 706-595-2124; fax: 706-595-9150; 8AM-5PM. ***Felony, Misdemeanor, Civil.***

Civil Records: Access: In person only. Visitors must perform in person searches themselves. Required to search: name, years to search. Civil cases indexed by defendant, plaintiff, on computer from 1991, dockets books from 1871. Civil PAT goes back to 1991. PAT civil results show middle initial.

Criminal Records: Access: In person only. Visitors must perform in person searches themselves. Required to search: name, years to search, signed release; also helpful: DOB. Criminal records computerized from 1991, dockets books from 1800s. Criminal PAT goes back to same as civil. PAT results show middle initial, DOB.

General Information: No juvenile or adoption records released. Will not fax out documents. Court makes copy: $1.00 per page. Self serve: $.25 per page. Certification fee: $2.50 plus $.50 per page after first. Payee: Clerk Superior Court. Personal checks accepted; credit cards are not. Prepayment required.

Magistrate Court PO Box 252, 337 Main St, Thomson, GA 30824; 706-597-2618; criminal fax: 706-595-2041; civil fax: same; 8AM-5PM. ***Civil Actions under $15,000, Eviction, Small Claims.*** www.thomson-mcduffie.com Court also has jurisdiction for bad checks, arrest warrants, preliminary hearings, and county ordinance violations.

Probate Court PO Box 2028, 337 Main St, Rm 108, Thomson, GA 30824; 706-595-2124; fax: 706-597-2644; 8AM-5PM. ***Probate.*** www.thomson-mcduffie.com/artman/publish/mc-probate.shtml

McIntosh County

Superior & State Court PO Box 1661, 310 North Way, Darien, GA 31305; 912-437-6641; fax: 912-437-6673; 8AM-5PM. ***Felony, Misdemeanor, Civil.***

Civil Records: Access: In person only. Visitors must perform in person searches themselves. Required to search: name, years to search. Civil cases indexed by defendant, plaintiff, on computer from 1991. Civil PAT goes back to 1990. PAT civil results show middle initial.

Criminal Records: Access: In person only. Visitors must perform in person searches themselves. Required to search: name, years to search, DOB; SSN helpful. Criminal records computerized from 1991. Criminal PAT goes back to same as civil. PAT results show middle initial, DOB.

General Information: No juvenile, adoption, sexual, or expunged records released. Court makes copy: $.50 per page if court assists. Self serve: $.25 per page. Certification fee: $2.50. Payee: Court Clerk. Personal checks accepted; credit cards are not. Prepayment required.

Magistrate Court PO Box 459, 100 Madison, Darien, GA 31305; 912-437-4888; fax: 912-437-2768; 8AM-4:30PM. ***Civil Actions under $15,000, Eviction, Small Claims.*** Court also has jurisdiction for bad checks, arrest warrants, preliminary hearings, and county ordinance violations.

Probate Court PO Box 453, 310 Northway Hwy 17, Darien, GA 31305; 912-437-6636; fax: 912-437-6635; 8AM-5PM. ***Probate.*** www.darientel.net/~pcourt

Meriwether County

Superior Court PO Box 160, Greenville, GA 30222; 706-672-4416; fax: 706-672-9465; 8:30AM-5PM. ***Felony, Misdemeanor, Civil.*** This court will not do name searches.

Civil Records: Access: In person only. Visitors must perform in person searches themselves. Required to search: name, years to search. Civil cases indexed by defendant, plaintiff, on microfilm and computer from 1990, prior on writ and minute books to 1827. Civil PAT goes back to 1990.

Criminal Records: Access: In person only. Visitors must perform in person searches themselves. Required to search: name, years to search, DOB, SSN. Criminal records go back to 1827; on computer back to 1991. Criminal PAT goes back to 1991.

General Information: No juvenile, adoption, sexual, mental health or expunged records released. Will fax documents $2.50 1st page, $1.00 each add'l page. Court makes copy: $1.00 per page. Self serve: $.25 per page. Certification fee: $2.50 plus $.50 per page after first. Payee: Court Clerk. Business checks accepted. No credit cards accepted. Prepayment required.

Magistrate Court PO Box 702, 124 N Court Sq, Greenville, GA 30222; 706-672-1247; fax: 706-672-1172; 8:30AM-4:30PM. ***Civil Actions under $15,000, Eviction, Small Claims.*** Court also has jurisdiction for bad checks, arrest warrants, preliminary hearings, and county ordinance violations.

Probate Court PO Box 608, 100 N Court Sq, Greenville, GA 30222; 706-672-4952; probate phone: 706-672-1817; fax: 706-672-6660; 8:30AM-5PM. ***Probate.***

Miller County

Superior & State Court PO Box 66, Colquitt, GA 39837; 229-758-4102; fax: 229-758-6585; 9AM-5PM. ***Felony, Misdemeanor, Civil.***

Civil Records: Access: In person only. Visitors must perform in person searches themselves. Required to search: name, years to search. Civil cases indexed by defendant, plaintiff; index in docket books from 1800s, computerized from 1995. Civil PAT goes back to 1995. PAT results show name only.

Criminal Records: Access: In person only. Visitors must perform in person searches themselves. Required to search: name, years to search. Criminal docket on books from 1800s, computerized from 1995. Criminal PAT goes back to same as civil. PAT results show name only.

General Information: No juvenile or adoption records released. Will not fax documents. Court makes copy: $1.00 per page. Self serve: $.25 per page. Certification fee: $2.50 plus $1.00 per page after first. Payee: Court Clerk. Business checks accepted. No credit cards accepted. Prepayment required.

Magistrate & Probate Court 155 S 1st St, Box 1, Rm 110, Colquitt, GA 39837; 229-758-4110; fax: 229-758-8133; 9AM-5PM. ***Civil Actions under $15,000, Small Claims, Probate.*** Court also has jurisdiction for bad checks, arrest warrants, preliminary hearings, and county ordinance violations.

Mitchell County

Superior & State Court PO Box 427, 11 W Broad St, Camilla, GA 31730; 229-336-2022; fax: 229-336-9866; 8:30AM-5PM. ***Felony, Misdemeanor, Civil.***

Civil Records: Access: In person only. Visitors must perform in person searches themselves. Required to search: name, years to search. Civil cases indexed by defendant. Civil index in docket books from 1800s. Civil PAT goes back to 1997. PAT results show name only.

Criminal Records: Access: In person only. Visitors must perform in person searches themselves. Required to search: name, years to search, DOB; SSN helpful. Criminal docket on books from 1800s. Criminal PAT goes back to 2006. PAT results show name only.

General Information: No juvenile, adoption, sexual, mental health or expunged records released. Will fax documents $1.00 per page. Court makes copy: $.25 per page, self serve same. Certification fee: $2.50 per doc. Payee: Court Clerk. Personal checks accepted; credit cards are not. Prepayment required.

Magistrate Court PO Box 626, 22 N Court St, Camilla, GA 31730-0626; 229-336-2076/7; fax: 229-336-2039; 8:30AM-5PM. ***Civil Actions under $15,000, Eviction, Small Claims.*** Court also has jurisdiction for bad checks, arrest warrants, preliminary hearings, and county ordinance violations.

Probate Court PO Box 229, 11 W Broad St #102, Camilla, GA 31730; 229-336-2016; fax: 229-336-2354; 8:30AM-5PM. ***Probate.***

Monroe County

Superior Court PO Box 450, 15 W Main St, #1 Courthouse Sq, Forsyth, GA 31029; 478-994-7022; fax: 478-994-7053; 8AM-5PM. ***Felony, Misdemeanor, Civil.***

Civil Records: Access: Mail, in person. Visitors must perform in person searches themselves. No search fee. Required to search: name, years to search. Civil cases indexed by defendant, plaintiff, on name index 1986 forward. Civil PAT goes back to 1986.

Criminal Records: Access: Mail, in person. Both court and visitors may perform in person searches. No search fee. Required to search: name, years to search. Criminal records on name index from 1989. Mail request must have signed release. Mail turnaround time 3 days. Criminal PAT goes back to 1989.

General Information: No juvenile, adoption, sexual, mental health or expunged records released. Will not fax documents. Court makes copy: $1.00 per page.

Self serve: $.25 per page. Certification fee: $2.50 plus $.50 per page after first. Payee: Court Clerk. Personal checks accepted; credit cards are not. Prepayment required. Mail requests: SASE required.

Magistrate Court PO Box 974, 145 L Cary Bittick Dr, Justice Center, Forsyth, GA 31029; 478-994-7018; fax: 478-994-7284; 9:00AM-5:00PM. ***Civil Actions under $15,000, Eviction, Small Claims.*** www.monroemagcourt.com
Court also has jurisdiction for bad checks, arrest warrants, preliminary hearings, and county ordinance violations.

Probate Court PO Box 187, Courthouse, Rm 2, Forsyth, GA 31029; 478-994-7036; fax: 478-994-7054; 8AM-4:30PM. ***Probate, Misdemeanor Traffic.***

Montgomery County

Superior Court PO Box 311, Mt Vernon, GA 30445; 912-583-4401; fax: 912-583-4343; 8AM-5PM. ***Felony, Misdemeanor, Civil.***
Civil Records: Access: In person only. Visitors must perform in person searches themselves. Required to search: name, years to search. Civil cases indexed by defendant, plaintiff, on computer from 1993, on dockets from 1793. Civil PAT goes back to 1993.
Criminal Records: Access: In person only. Visitors must perform in person searches themselves. Required to search: name, years to search, DOB; SSN helpful. Criminal records computerized from 1993, on dockets from 1793. Criminal PAT goes back to same as civil. PAT results show middle initial, DOB. Terminal results include SSN.
General Information: No juvenile or adoption records released. Will fax documents $1.50 per page. Court makes copy: $1.00 per page. Self serve: $.25 per page. Certification fee: $2.50 per page. Payee: Superior Court Clerk. Personal checks accepted; credit cards are not. Prepayment required.

Magistrate Court PO Box 174, 400 Railroad Ave, Mt Vernon, GA 30445; 912-583-2170; fax: 912-583-4343; 8:30AM-4:30PM. ***Civil Actions under $15,000, Eviction, Small Claims.***
Court also has jurisdiction for bad checks, arrest warrants, preliminary hearings, and county ordinance violations.

Probate Court PO Box 444, 400 Railroad Ave, Mt Vernon, GA 30445; 912-583-2681; fax: 912-583-4343; 8-5PM. ***Probate, Misdemeanor-Traffic.***

Morgan County

Superior Court PO Drawer 551, 384 Hancock St, Madison, GA 30650; 706-342-3605; fax: 706-343-6462; 9AM-5PM. ***Felony, Misdemeanor, Civil.*** www.morganga.org/
Civil Records: Access: In person only. Visitors must perform in person searches themselves. Required to search: name, years to search. Civil cases indexed by defendant, plaintiff, on computer from 1986, on dockets from 1900s. Public use terminal available, records go back to 1986. PAT results show middle initial, DOB.
Criminal Records: Access: In person only. Visitors must perform in person searches themselves. Required to search: name, years to search, signed release. Criminal records computerized from 1986, on dockets from 1900s. Public use terminal available, crim records go back to 1986. PAT results show name only.
General Information: No juvenile, adoption, sexual, mental health or expunged records released. Will fax documents $2.50 1st page, $1.00 each add'l page. Court makes copy: $.25 per page, self serve same. Certification fee: $2.50 plus $.50 per page after first. Payee: Superior Court Clerk. Personal checks accepted; credit cards are not. Prepayment required.

Magistrate Court PO Box 589, 149 E Jefferson St, Madison, GA 30650; 706-342-3088; fax: 706-343-6364; 9AM-5PM. ***Civil Actions under $15,000, Eviction, Small Claims.*** www.morganga.org
Court also has jurisdiction for certain misdemeanors including bad checks, arrest warrants, preliminary hearings, and county ordinance violations.

Probate Court PO Box 857, 149 E Jefferson St, Madison, GA 30650; 706-343-6500; fax: 706-343-6465; 9AM-5PM. ***Probate.***
www.morganga.org/Courts/tabid/171/Default.aspx
This court also has Misdemeanor and Traffic cases.

Murray County

Superior Court PO Box 1000, 121 N Third Ave, Chatsworth, GA 30705; 706-695-2932; fax: 706-517-9672; 8:30AM-5PM. ***Felony, Misdemeanor, Civil.***
Civil Records: Access: In person only. Visitors must perform in person searches themselves. Required to search: name, years to search. Civil cases indexed by defendant, plaintiff, on dockets from 1940, prior to 1940 archived; computerized records since 2000. Civil PAT goes back to 2000.
Criminal Records: Access: In person only. Visitors must perform in person searches themselves. Required to search: name, years to search, signed release. Criminal docket index from 1940, prior to 1940 archived; computerized records since 2000. Criminal PAT goes back to same as civil.
General Information: No juvenile, adoption, sexual, mental health or expunged records released. Will not fax out documents. Court makes copy: $.25 per page, self serve same. Certification fee: $2.50 plus $.25 per page after first. Payee: Superior Court Clerk. Personal checks accepted; credit cards are not. Prepayment required.

Magistrate Court 121 N 4th Ave, Chatsworth, GA 30705; 706-517-1400 x210; fax: 706-695-7525; 8AM-5PM. ***Civil Actions under $15,000, Eviction, Small Claims.***
Court also has jurisdiction for bad checks, arrest warrants, preliminary hearings, and county ordinance violations.

Probate Court 115 Fort St, Chatsworth, GA 30705; 706-695-3812; fax: 706-517-1340; 8:30AM-5PM. ***Misdemeanor, Probate.***

Muscogee County

Superior & State Court PO Box 2145, 100 10th St, Columbus, GA 31902; 706-653-4351; fax: 706-653-4359; 8:30AM-5PM. ***Felony, Misdemeanor, Civil.*** www.muscogeecourts.com
Civil Records: Access: Mail, in person, online. Both court and visitors may perform in person searches. Search fee: $5.00 per name. Required to search: name, years to search. Civil cases indexed by defendant, plaintiff, on computer from 1989, on dockets from 1919 to 1989. Mail turnaround time 1 week. Civil PAT goes back to 1989. Dockets in pdf format are free at www.muscogeecourts.com. Also, a court case management system is available by subscription; username and password required.
Criminal Records: Access: Mail, in person, online. Both court and visitors may perform in person searches. Search fee: $5.00 per name. Required to search: name, years to search, DOB; also helpful: SSN. Criminal records on computer since 1989, on dockets from 1989 to 1957. Mail turnaround time 1 week. Criminal PAT goes back to same as civil. Online access to criminal is the same as civil; see above.
General Information: No adoption, sealed or first offender records released. Will fax documents $5.00 per fax. Court makes copy: $.25 per page, self serve same. Certification fee: $2.50 per cert plus $.50 per page after 1sst. Payee: Superior Court Clerk. Business checks accepted. No credit cards accepted. Prepayment required. Mail requests: SASE requested.

Magistrate Court PO Box 1340, 100 Tenth St, Columbus, GA 31902; 706-653-4390 ext1; fax: 706-653-4559; 9AM-N, 1-5PM. ***Civil Actions under $15,000, Eviction, Small Claims.***
www.columbusga.org/depts/ccg_depts.htm
Court also has jurisdiction for bad checks, arrest warrants, preliminary hearings, and county ordinance violations.

Probate Court PO Box 1340, 100 Tenth St, Columbus, GA 31902; 706-653-4333; 8:30AM-4PM. ***Probate.***

Newton County

Superior Court 1132 Usher St, Rm 338, Covington, GA 30014; 770-784-2035; probate phone: 770-784-2045; fax: 770-385-8930; 8AM-5PM. ***Felony, Misdemeanor, Civil.***
Civil Records: Access: In person only. Visitors must perform in person searches themselves. Required to search: name, years to search. Civil cases indexed by defendant, plaintiff, on computer from 1991, on dockets from 1900s. Civil PAT goes back to 1991.
Criminal Records: Access: In person only. Visitors must perform in person searches themselves. Required to search: name, years to search, signed release. Criminal records computerized from 1991, on dockets from 1900s. Criminal PAT goes back to same as civil. PAT results show middle initial, DOB, SSN.
General Information: No adoption, sexual, mental health or expunged records released. Will not fax documents. Court makes copy: $1.00 per page. Self serve: $.25 per page. Certification fee: $2.50 plus $.50 per page after first. Payee: Superior Court Clerk. No personal checks or credit cards accepted. Prepayment required.

Magistrate & Probate Court 1132 Usher St, Rm 148, Covington, GA 30014; 770-784-2045 or 770-784-2050; fax: 770-784-2145; 8AM-5PM. ***Civil Actions under $15,000, Eviction, Small Claims, Probate.*** Court also has jurisdiction for bad checks, arrest warrants, preliminary hearings, and county ordinance violations.

Oconee County

Superior & Magistrate Courts PO Box 1099, 23 N Main, Rm 208, Watkinsville, GA 30677; 706-769-3940; probate phone: 706-769-3936; fax: 706-769-3948; 8AM-5PM. ***Felony, Misdemeanor, Civil, Eviction, Small Claims.***
www.oconeecounty.com/Government/Judiciary/index.htm
Probate Ct in Rm 304, mail- PO Box 54.
Civil Records: Access: In person only. Visitors must perform in person searches themselves. Required to search: name, years to search. Civil cases indexed by defendant, plaintiff, on computer from 1989, on dockets from 1875. Civil PAT goes back to 1989.
Criminal Records: Access: In person only. Visitors must perform in person searches themselves. Required to search: name, years to search; also helpful: DOB, SSN. Criminal records computerized from 1989, on dockets from 1875. Criminal PAT goes back to same as civil.
General Information: No juvenile, adoption, sexual, mental health or expunged records released. Will fax documents $2.50 1st page, $1.00 each add'l page. Court makes copy: $.25 per page, self serve same. Certification fee: $2.50 plus $.50 per page after first. Payee: Superior Court Clerk. Personal checks accepted; credit cards are not. Prepayment required.

Probate Court PO Box 54, 23 N Main St, #304, Watkinsville, GA 30677; 706-769-3936; fax: 706-769-3934; 8AM-5PM. ***Probate.***
www.oconeecounty.com/Government/Judiciary/index.htm#probate

Oglethorpe County

Superior Court PO Box 68, Lexington, GA 30648; 706-743-5731; criminal fax: 706-743-5335; civil fax: same; 8AM-5PM. ***Felony, Misdemeanor, Civil.*** www.gsccca.org/Clerks/default.asp
Civil Records: Access: Mail, in person. Visitors must perform in person searches themselves. Search fee: $25.00. Required to search: name, years to search. Civil cases indexed by defendant. Civil records on computer from 1992, on dockets from 1900s. Mail turnaround time 1 day. Civil PAT goes back to 1992.
Criminal Records: Access: In person only. Visitors must perform in person searches themselves. Required to search: name, years to search, DOB; SSN helpful. Criminal records computerized from 1992, on dockets from 1900s. Criminal PAT goes back to same as civil.
General Information: No juvenile or adoption records released. Will fax documents $2.50 per page.

Court makes copy: $1.00 per page. Self serve: $.25 per page. Certification fee: $2.00 per cert plus $.50 per page copy fee. Payee: Superior Court Clerk. Personal checks accepted; credit cards are not. Prepayment required. Mail requests: SASE required for mail return of any copies.

Magistrate Court PO Box 356, 339 W Main St, Lexington, GA 30648; 706-743-8321; fax: 706-743-3177; 8AM-N, 1-5PM. ***Civil Actions under $15,000, Eviction, Small Claims.*** www.onlineoglethorpe.com
Court also has jurisdiction for bad checks, arrest warrants, preliminary hearings, and county ordinance violations.

Probate Court PO Box 70, 111 W Main St, Lexington, GA 30648; 706-743-5350; fax: 706-743-3514; 7:30AM-5PM, closed N-1PM F. ***Probate.*** www.onlineoglethorpe.com

Paulding County

Superior Court 11 Courthouse Square, Rm G3, Dallas, GA 30132; 770-443-7527; criminal phone: 770-505-6582; civil phone: 770-443-7529; fax: 770-505-3863; 8AM-5PM. ***Felony, Misdemeanor, Civil.*** www.paulding.gov/gov/clerksofcourt.asp
Civil Records: Access: In person only. Visitors must perform in person searches themselves. Required to search: name, years to search. Civil cases indexed by defendant, plaintiff, on computer from 1990, archived from 1850. Civil PAT goes back to 2001.
Criminal Records: Access: In person only. Visitors must perform in person searches themselves. Required to search: name, years to search, DOB; SSN helpful. Criminal docket on books. Criminal PAT goes back to 2001.
General Information: No juvenile, adoption, sexual, mental health or expunged records released. Will not fax documents. Court makes copy: $1.00 per page. Self serve: $.25 per page. Certification fee: $2.50 plus $.50 per page after first. Payee: Court Clerk. Personal checks accepted; credit cards are not. Prepayment required.

Magistrate Court 25 Courthouse Square, Rm 402, Dallas, GA 30132; 770-443-7533; probate phone: 770-443-7541; fax: 770-443-8980; 8AM-N, 1-5PM. ***Civil Actions under $15,000, Eviction, Small Claims.*** www.pauldingcourt.com
Court also has jurisdiction for bad checks, arrest warrants, preliminary hearings, and county ordinance violations.

Probate Court 25 Courthouse Sq. Annex, Rm 102, Dallas, GA 30132; 770-443-7541; fax: 770-443-7631; 8AM-N, 1-5PM. ***Probate.*** www.paulding.gov/living/probatecourt.asp

Peach County

Superior Court PO Box 389, Ft Valley, GA 31030; 478-825-5331; fax: 478-825-8662; 8:30AM-5PM. ***Felony, Misdemeanor, Civil.***
Civil Records: Access: Mail, in person. Both court and visitors may perform in person searches. No search fee. Required to search: name, years to search. Civil cases indexed by defendant, plaintiff, on computer back to 1997; on dockets from 1925. Mail turnaround time 1 week.
Criminal Records: Access: Mail, in person. Both court and visitors may perform in person searches. No search fee. Required to search: name, years to search, DOB; also helpful: SSN, race, sex. Criminal records computerized from 1997; on dockets from 1925. Mail turnaround time 1 week.
General Information: No juvenile, adoption, sexual, mental health or expunged records released. Will not fax documents. Court makes copy: $.25 per page, self serve same. Certification fee: $3.00. Payee: Court Clerk. Personal checks accepted; credit cards are not. Prepayment required. Mail requests: SASE required.

Magistrate Court 700 Spruce St, Wing A, Ft Valley, GA 31030; 478-825-2060; fax: 478-825-1893; 8AM-5PM. ***Civil Actions under $15,000, Eviction, Small Claims.***
Court also has jurisdiction for bad checks, arrest warrants, preliminary hearings, and county ordinance violations.

Probate Court PO Box 327, 205 W Church St, Ft Valley, GA 31030; 478-825-2313; fax: 478-825-2678; 8AM-5PM. ***Probate.***

Pickens County

Superior Court 52 N Main St, #102, Jasper, GA 30143; criminal phone: 706-253-8764; civil phone: 706-253-8763; fax: 706-253-8825; 8AM-5PM. ***Felony, Misdemeanor, Civil.*** http://9thjudicialdistrict-ga.org/dca9apphp.shtml
Civil Records: Access: In person only. Visitors must perform in person searches themselves. Required to search: name, years to search. Civil cases indexed by defendant, plaintiff, on computer from 1988, dockets from 1854. Civil PAT goes back to 1999.
Criminal Records: Access: In person only. Visitors must perform in person searches themselves. Required to search: name, years to search, DOB, signed release; SSN helpful. Criminal records computerized from 1988, dockets from 1854. Criminal PAT goes back to same as civil.
General Information: No juvenile, adoption, sexual, mental health or expunged records released. Court makes copy: $1.00 per page. Self serve: $.25 per page. Certification fee: $2.50 plus $.50 per page after first. Cert fee includes copies. Payee: Pickens Court Clerk. Personal checks accepted; credit cards are not. Prepayment required.

Magistrate Court 50 N Main St, #105, Jasper, GA 30143; 706-253-8747; fax: 706-253-8750; 8AM-5PM. ***Civil Actions under $15,000, Eviction, Small Claims.*** Court also has jurisdiction for bad checks, arrest warrants, preliminary hearings, and county ordinance violations.

Probate Court 50 N Main St, #203, Jasper, GA 30143; 706-253-8756; criminal phone: 706-253-8755; probate phone: 706-253-8757; fax: 706-253-8760; 8AM-N, 1-5PM. ***Probate, Misdemeanor, Traffic.*** Misdemeanors are limited to traffic and DNRs. Probate fax is same as main fax number.

Pierce County

Superior & State Court PO Box 588, 3550 Hwy 84, Blackshear, GA 31516; 912-449-2020; fax: 912-449-2106; 9AM-5PM. ***Felony, Misdemeanor, Civil.***
Court will provide assistance with your search, but will not name search for you.
Civil Records: Access: In person only. Visitors must perform in person searches themselves. Required to search: name, years to search. Civil cases indexed by defendant. Civil records on computer from 1991, on index from 1800s. Civil PAT goes back to 1991. PAT results show name only.
Criminal Records: Access: In person only. Visitors must perform in person searches themselves. Required to search: name, years to search. Criminal records computerized from 1991, on index from 1800s. Criminal PAT goes back to same as civil. PAT results show name only.
General Information: Will fax documents $1.00 per page. Court makes copy: $.25 per page, self serve same. Certification fee: $2.50 for 1st page, $.50 each add'l. Payee: Superior Court Clerk. Personal checks accepted; credit cards are not. Prepayment required.

Magistrate Court 3550 US Hwy 84, Blackshear, GA 31516-1926; 912-449-2027, 449-2007; fax: 912-449-2103; 9AM-5PM. ***Civil Actions under $15,000, Eviction, Small Claims.*** Court also has jurisdiction for bad checks, arrest warrants, preliminary hearings, and county ordinance violations.

Probate Court PO Box 406, 3330 W Highway 84, Blackshear, GA 31516; 912-449-2029; fax: 912-449-1417; 9AM-5PM. ***Probate.***

Pike County

Superior Court PO Box 10, 16001 Barnesville St, Zebulon, GA 30295; 770-567-2000; 8AM-5PM. ***Felony, Misdemeanor, Civil.***
Civil Records: Access: In person only. Visitors must perform in person searches themselves. Required to search: name, years to search. Civil cases indexed by defendant, plaintiff; index in docket books from 1823. Civil PAT goes back to 2001. PAT results show name, DOB. Terminal results may sometimes show SSN.
Criminal Records: Access: In person only. Visitors must perform in person searches themselves. Required to search: name, years to search. Criminal docket on books from 1823. Criminal PAT goes back to 2001.PAT results show name, DOB.
General Information: No juvenile, adoption, sexual, mental health or expunged records released. Will not fax documents. Court makes copy: $1.00 per page. Self serve: $.25 per page. Certification fee: $2.50 plus $.50 per page after first. Payee: Court Clerk. Personal checks accepted; credit cards are not. Prepayment required.

Magistrate Court PO Box 466, 331 Thomaston St, Zebulon, GA 30295; 770-567-2004; fax: 770-567-2023; 8AM-N, 1:30-5PM. ***Civil Actions under $15,000, Eviction, Small Claims.***
Court also has jurisdiction for bad checks, arrest warrants, preliminary hearings, and county ordinance violations.

Probate Court PO Box 324, 16001 Barnesville St, Zebulon, GA 30295; 770-567-8734; fax: 770-567-2019; 8:30AM-N; 1PM-5PM. ***Probate, Traffic.***

Polk County

Superior Court PO Box 948, 100 Proir St, Rm 106, Cedartown, GA 30125; 770-749-2114; fax: 770-749-2148; 9AM-5PM. ***Felony, Misdemeanor, Civil.***
Civil Records: Access: Mail, in person. Visitors must perform in person searches themselves. Search fee: $5.00 per name. Required to search: name, years to search. Civil cases indexed by defendant, plaintiff, on computer from 1991 to present, alpha indexes from 1930. Public use terminal available, records go back to 1991. PAT civil results show middle initial.
Criminal Records: Access: Mail, in person. Visitors must perform in person searches themselves. Search fee: $5.00 per name. Required to search: name, years to search, DOB, signed release; also helpful: race, sex. Criminal records computerized from 1991, alpha indexes from 1930. Public use terminal available, crim records go back to same. PAT criminal results show middle initial. Results include charges.
General Information: No adoption, sexual, mental health or expunged records released. Fee to fax out file $1.00 per page. Court makes copy: $.25 per page, self serve same. Certification fee: $2.50 plus $.50 per page after first. Payee: Court Clerk. Personal checks accepted. Make sure phone number is on check. No credit cards accepted. Prepayment required. Mail requests: SASE required.

Magistrate Court 100 Prior St, Rm 203, Cedartown, GA 30125; 770-749-2187; civil phone: 770-749-2130; criminal fax: 770-749-2186; civil fax: 770-749-2189; 9AM-5PM. ***Misdemeanor, Civil Actions under $15,000, Eviction, Small Claims, Ordinance.***
Rockmart, GA office: 200 S Marble St, Rockmart, GA 30153; 770-684-4718. Court also has jurisdiction for bad checks, arrest warrants, preliminary hearings, and county ordinance violations.

Probate Court County Courthouse, 100 Prior St, Rm 102, Cedartown, GA 30125; 770-749-2128/2129; fax: 770-749-2150; 9AM-4:45PM. ***Probate.*** www.polkcountygeorgia.us/courts.php
This location also holds traffic and vital records.

Pulaski County

Superior Court PO Box 60, Hawkinsville, GA 31036; 478-783-1911; fax: 478-892-3308; 8AM-5PM. ***Felony, Misdemeanor, Civil.***
Civil Records: Access: In person only. Visitors must perform in person searches themselves. Required to search: name, years to search. Civil cases indexed by defendant, plaintiff, on computer from 1986, alpha index from early 1800s. Civil PAT goes back to 1989. PAT results show name only.
Criminal Records: Access: In person only. Visitors must perform in person searches themselves. Required to search: name, years to search, signed

release; also helpful: DOB, SSN. Criminal records computerized from 1986, alpha index from early 1800s. Criminal PAT goes back to 1986. PAT results show name only.
General Information: No juvenile or adoption records released. Will not fax documents. Court makes copy: $1.00 per page. Self serve: $.25 per page. Certification fee: $2.00 plus $.50 per page. Payee: Court Clerk. Personal checks accepted; credit cards are not. Prepayment required.

Magistrate Court PO Box 667, #105 Courthouse Annex, Lumpkin St, Hawkinsville, GA 31036; 478-783-1357; fax: 478-783-9209; 8AM-5PM. ***Civil Actions under $15,000, Eviction, Small Claims.***
Court also has jurisdiction for bad checks, arrest warrants, preliminary hearings, county ordinances.

Probate Court PO Box 156, 350 Commerce St, Hawkinsville, GA 31036; 478-783-2061; fax: 478-783-9219; 8AM-5PM. ***Probate, Traffic.***

Putnam County

Superior & State Court County Courthouse, 100 Jefferson Ave #236, Eatonton, GA 31024; 706-485-4501 superior ct; 706-485-4056 state ct; criminal phone: x146; civil phone: x142; fax: 706-485-2875; 8AM-5PM. ***Felony, Misdemeanor, Civil.***
Civil Records: Access: In person only. Visitors must perform in person searches themselves. Required to search: name, years to search. Civil cases indexed by defendant, plaintiff, on computer since 1997; prior records on dockets to early 1900s. Civil PAT goes back to 1997. PAT results show name only.
Criminal Records: Access: In person only. Visitors must perform in person searches themselves. Required to search: name, years to search, DOB. Criminal records on computer since 1997; prior records on dockets to early 1930s. Criminal PAT goes back to same as civil. PAT results show name only.
General Information: No juvenile, adoption, sexual, mental health or expunged records released. Will not fax out case files. Court makes copy: $1.00 per page. Self serve: $.25 per page. Certification fee: $2.50 plus $.50 per add'l page. Payee: Court Clerk. Personal checks accepted. Prepayment required.

Magistrate Court 108 S Madison Ave, #101, 100 S Jefferson Ave, Rm 306, Eatonton, GA 31024; 706-485-4306; fax: 706-484-1814; 8AM-5PM. ***Civil Actions under $15,000, Eviction, Small Claims.*** http://putnamcountymagistrate.com/
Court also has jurisdiction for bad checks, arrest warrants, preliminary hearings, county ordinances.

Probate Court County Courthouse, 100 S Jefferson Ave #318, Eatonton, GA 31024; 706-485-5476/9761; fax: 706-485-2515; 8AM-5PM. ***Probate, Estate.*** www.putnamprobate.com/

Quitman County

Superior Court PO Box 307, Georgetown, GA 39854; 229-334-2578; fax: 229-334-3991; 8AM-N, 1-5PM. ***Felony, Misdemeanor, Civil.***
Civil Records: Access: In person only. Visitors must perform in person searches themselves. Required to search: name, years to search. Records indexed by plaintiff and defendant. Civil records go back to 1920s. Civil PAT goes back to 2002.
Criminal Records: Access: In person only. Visitors must perform in person searches themselves. Required to search: name, years to search, DOB; SSN helpful. Records go back to 1930s. Criminal PAT goes back to 2002.
General Information: No juvenile, adoption, sexual, mental health or expunged records released. Will fax documents $3.00 1st page, $1.00 each add'l page. Court makes copy: $1.00 per page. Self serve: $.25 per page. Certification fee: $2.50 for 1st page, $.50 each add'l. Payee: Clerk of Superior Court. No credit cards accepted. Prepayment required.

Magistrate & Probate Court PO Box 7, 115 Main St, Georgetown, GA 39854; 229-334-2224; fax: 229-334-6826; 8AM-5PM. ***Civil Actions under $15,000, Small Claims, Probate.*** Court also has jurisdiction for bad checks, arrest warrants, preliminary hearings, and county ordinance violations.

Rabun County

Superior Court 25 Courthouse Sq, #105, Clayton, GA 30525; 706-782-3615; fax: 706-782-1391; 8:30AM-5PM. ***Felony, Misdemeanor, Civil.***
Civil Records: Access: Mail, in person. Visitors must perform in person searches themselves. No search fee. Required to search: name, years to search. Civil cases indexed by defendant, plaintiff, on dockets from 1949; on computer since. Civil PAT goes back to 1993.
Criminal Records: Access: Mail, in person. Visitors must perform in person searches themselves. No search fee. Required to search: name, years to search, DOB, signed release; also helpful: SSN, race, sex. Criminal docket index from 1949; on computer since. Mail turnaround time is 1 week. Criminal PAT goes back to 1991.
General Information: No juvenile, adoption, sexual, mental health or expunged records released. Will fax documents $.25 per copy, prepaid. Court makes copy: $.25 per page, self serve same. Certification fee: $2.50 for 1st page, $.50 each add'l. Payee: Court Clerk. Personal checks and major credit cards accepted. Prepayment required.

Magistrate Court 25 Courthouse Sq, #105, Clayton, GA 30525; 706-782-3615; fax: 706-782-1391; 8:30AM-5PM. ***Civil Actions under $15,000, Eviction, Small Claims.*** Court also has jurisdiction for bad checks, arrest warrants, preliminary hearings, and county ordinance violations.

Probate Court 25 Courthouse Square, #215, Clayton, GA 30525; 706-782-3614; fax: 706-782-9278; 8:30AM-5PM. ***Probate.*** www.rabuncountygov.com/contactus.htm

Randolph County

Superior Court PO Box 98, Cuthbert, GA 39840; 229-732-2216; fax: 229-732-5881; 8AM-5PM. ***Felony, Misdemeanor, Civil.***
Civil Records: Access: In person only. Visitors must perform in person searches themselves. Required to search: name, years to search. Civil cases indexed by defendant. Civil records on index from 1835. Civil PAT goes back to 2005.
Criminal Records: Access: In person only. Visitors must perform in person searches themselves. Required to search: name, years to search, DOB; SSN helpful. Criminal records indexed from 1835. Criminal PAT goes back to same as civil.
General Information: No juvenile, adoption, sexual, mental health or expunged records released. Will fax documents for fee. Court makes copy: $1.00 per page. Self serve: $.25 per page. Certification fee: $2.00 plus $.50 per page after first. Payee: Court Clerk. Personal checks accepted; credit cards are not. Prepayment required.

Magistrate Court PO Box 6, 113 W Pearl St, Cuthbert, GA 39840; 229-732-6182; fax: 229-732-5635; 8AM-5PM; W 8AM-N. ***Civil Actions under $15,000, Eviction, Small Claims.***
Court also has jurisdiction for bad checks, arrest warrants, preliminary hearings, county ordinances.

Probate Court PO Box 424, 2005 S Wester St, Cuthbert, GA 39840; 229-732-2671; fax: 229-732-5781; 8AM-5PM. ***Probate.***

Richmond County

Superior Court 530 Greene St, Rm 503, Augusta, GA 30911; 706-821-2460; fax: 706-821-2448; 8:30AM-5PM. ***Felony, Misdemeanor, Civil.*** www.augustaga.gov/departments/clerk%5Fsup/
Civil Records: Access: Mail, in person, online. Visitors must perform in person searches themselves. No search fee. Required to search: name, years to search. Civil cases indexed by defendant, plaintiff; index on docket books and microfilm from 1940s; 1986 forward on computer. Civil PAT goes back to 1999. Access court index free at www.augustaga.gov/departments/clerk_sup/disclaimer.asp for records 2001 forward.
Criminal Records: Access: Mail, in person, online. Visitors must perform in person searches themselves. No search fee. Required to search: name, years to search. Civil records on docket books and microfilm from 1940s; 1986 forward on computer. Mail turnaround time 1 week. Criminal PAT available. Access court index free at www.augustaga.gov/departments/clerk_sup/disclaimer.asp for records 2001 forward. Search Marshal's complaints free at www.augustaga.gov/departments/marshals_office/litter_search.asp. Marshal's service tracking search free at www.augustaga.gov/departments/marshals_office/complaint_search.asp
General Information: No juvenile, adoption, sexual, mental health or expunged records released. Will not fax documents. Court makes copy: $.25 per page. Self serve: $.25 per page. Certification fee: $2.50 plus $.50 per page after first. Payee: Superior Court Clerk. No personal or business checks accepted. No credit cards accepted. Prepayment required. Mail requests: SASE requested.

State Court 401 Walton Way, #218A, Augusta, GA 30911; 706-821-1233; fax: 706-821-1218; 8:30AM-5PM. ***Misdemeanor, Civil.*** www.augustaga.gov
Civil Records: Access: In person, online. Visitors must perform in person searches themselves. Required to search: name, years to search. Civil cases indexed by defendant, plaintiff; index on docket books and microfilm from 1940s, prior archived; computerized records since 2001. Civil PAT goes back to 1999. PAT results show middle initial, DOB. Name search civil dockets free at www.augustaga.gov/departments/clerk_sup/disclaimer.asp.
Criminal Records: Access: In person only. Visitors must perform in person searches themselves. Required to search: name, years to search, DOB. Criminal docket on books and microfilm from 1940s, prior archived; computerized records since 2001. Criminal PAT goes back to 1/2001. PAT results show middle initial, DOB. Search state warrants free at www.augustaga.gov/departments/clerk_sup/disclaimer.asp. Search Marshal's complaints free at www.augustaga.gov/departments/marshals_office/litter_search.asp. Marshal's service tracking search free at www.augustaga.gov/departments/marshals_office/complaint_search.asp.
General Information: No juvenile, adoption, sexual, mental health or expunged records released. Court makes copy: $.25 per page. Certification fee: $2.50 plus $.50 per page after first. Payee: Court Clerk. Only cashiers checks and money orders accepted. No credit cards accepted. Prepayment required.

Civil & Magistrate Court 530 Greene St, Rm 705, Augusta, GA 30911; 706-821-2370; fax: 706-821-2381; 8:30AM-5PM. ***Civil Actions under $45,000, Eviction, Small Claims.*** www.augustaga.gov/departments/civil_magistrate/home.asp
Court does have some misdemeanor records that are city ordinance violations.
Civil Records: Access: Phone, mail, in person. Both court and visitors may perform in person searches. No search fee. Required to search: name, years to search. Civil cases indexed by defendant, plaintiff, on dockets back to 1982. Mail turnaround time 1 day.
General Information: Will fax documents to local or toll-free number. Court makes copy: $.25 per page. Certification fee: $5.00. Payee: Magistrate Court. Business checks accepted. No credit cards accepted. Prepayment required. Mail requests: SASE requested for civil.

Probate Court 530 Greene St, Rm 401, Augusta, GA 30911; 706-821-2434; fax: 706-821-2442; 8:30AM-5PM. ***Probate.***

Rockdale County

Superior Court PO Box 937, 922 Court St, Conyers, GA 30012; 770-929-4021; 8AM-4:45PM. ***Felony, Civil.*** www.rockdalecounty.org/
Civil Records: Access: In person only. Visitors must perform in person searches themselves. Required to search: name, years to search. Civil cases indexed by defendant, plaintiff, on computer back to 1993, in books from 1900. Civil PAT goes back to 1993.
Criminal Records: Access: In person only. Visitors must perform in person searches themselves.

Required to search: name, case number. Criminal records computerized from 1990, in books from 1900. Criminal PAT goes back to 1990.PAT results show name, DOB.
General Information: No juvenile, adoption, sexual, mental health or expunged records released. Will not fax documents. Court makes copy: $1.00 per page. Self serve: $.25 per page. Certification fee: $2.50 plus $.50 per page after first. Payee: Clerk Superior Court. Personal checks accepted; credit cards are not. Prepayment required.

State Court PO Box 938, Conyers, GA 30012; 770-929-4019; 8AM-4:45PM. ***Misdemeanor, Civil.***
Civil Records: Access: In person only. Visitors must perform in person searches themselves. Required to search: name, years to search. Civil cases indexed by defendant, plaintiff, on computer from 1994, on dockets to 1994. Civil PAT goes back to 1990.
Criminal Records: Access: In person only. Visitors must perform in person searches themselves. Required to search: name, years to search. Criminal records computerized from 1990, on dockets to 1990. Criminal PAT goes back to same as civil.
General Information: No juvenile, adoption, sexual, mental health or expunged records released. Will not fax documents. Court makes copy: $.25 per page. Certification fee: $2.50 plus $.50 per page after first. Payee: Rockdale State Court. Business checks accepted. Prepayment required.

Magistrate Court PO Box 289, 945 Court St, Conyers, GA 30012; 770-929-4075; fax: 770-785-2496; 8:30AM-4:30PM. ***Civil Actions under $15,000, Eviction, Small Claims.***
www.rockdalecounty.org/main.cfm?id=2259
Court also has jurisdiction for bad checks, arrest warrants, preliminary hearings, county ordinances.

Probate Court 922 Court St NE, Rm 107, Conyers, GA 30012; 770-929-4058; fax: 770-918-6502; 8:30AM-4:30PM. ***Probate.***
www.rockdalecounty.org/main.cfm?id=2131

Schley County

Superior Court PO Box 7, 14 S Broad St., Ellaville, GA 31806; 229-937-5581; criminal fax: 229-937-5588; civil fax: same; 8AM-N,1-5PM. ***Felony, Misdemeanor, Civil.***
Civil Records: Access: In person only. Visitors must perform in person searches themselves. Required to search: name, years to search. Civil cases indexed by defendant. Civil records in books from 1885.
Criminal Records: Access: In person only. Visitors must perform in person searches themselves. Required to search: name, years to search, DOB, signed release; SSN helpful. Criminal records in books from 1934.
General Information: No adoption records released. Will not fax out case files. Court makes copy: $.25 per page, self serve same. Certification fee: $5.00 per document includes copies. Payee: Clerk Superior Court. Personal checks accepted; credit cards are not. Prepayment required.

Magistrate Court PO Box 372, 14 Broad St, Ellaville, GA 31806; 229-937-5110; fax: 229-937-5010; 9AM-5PM (closed at noon). ***Misdemeanor, Civil Actions under $15,000, Eviction, Small Claims.***
Court also has jurisdiction for bad checks, arrest warrants, preliminary hearings, county ordinances.

Probate Court PO Box 385, 14 S Broad St, Ellaville, GA 31806; 229-937-2905; fax: 229-937-5588; 8:30AM-N, 1-5PM. ***Probate, Misdemeanor, Traffic.***

Screven County

Superior Court PO Box 156, 216 Mims Rd, Sylvania, GA 30467; 912-564-2614; fax: 912-564-2622; 8AM-5PM. ***Felony, Misdemeanor, Civil.***
Civil Records: Access: In person only. Visitors must perform in person searches themselves. Required to search: name, years to search. Civil cases indexed by defendant, plaintiff, on dockets. Civil PAT goes back to 1991.
Criminal Records: Access: In person only. Visitors must perform in person searches themselves. Required to search: name, years to search, DOB; SSN helpful. Criminal records on dockets. Criminal PAT goes back to same as civil.
General Information: No juvenile or adoption records released. Will fax documents $1.00 per page. Court makes copy: $1.00 per page. Self serve: $.25 per page. Certification fee: $3.00 first page, $1.50 ea add'l. Payee: Court Clerk. Personal checks accepted; credit cards are not. Prepayment required.

State Court PO Box 156, 216 Mims Rd, Sylvania, GA 30467; 912-564-2614; fax: 912-564-2622; 8AM-5PM. ***Misdemeanor, Civil.***
Civil Records: Access: In person only. Visitors must perform in person searches themselves. Required to search: name, years to search. Civil cases indexed by defendant, plaintiff, on dockets from 1793; computerized records since 1991. Civil PAT goes back to 1991.
Criminal Records: Access: In person only. Visitors must perform in person searches themselves. Required to search: name, years to search, DOB; SSN helpful. Criminal docket index from 1793; computerized records since 1991. Criminal PAT goes back to same as civil.
General Information: No juvenile, adoption, sexual, mental health or expunged records released. Will fax documents $1.00 per page. Court makes copy: $1.00 per page. Self serve: $.25 per page. Certification fee: $3.00 per cert. Payee: Court Clerk. Personal checks accepted; credit cards are not. Prepayment required.

Magistrate Court PO Box 64, 216 Mims Rd, Sylvania, GA 30467; 912-564-7375; fax: 912-564-5618; 8AM-5PM. ***Civil Actions under $15,000, Eviction, Small Claims.*** Court also has jurisdiction for bad checks, arrest warrants, preliminary hearings, and county ordinance violations.

Probate Court 216 Mims Rd, #107, Sylvania, GA 30467; 912-564-2783; fax: 912-564-9139; 8AM-5PM. ***Probate.***

Seminole County

Superior Court PO Box 672, 200 S Knox Ave, Donalsonville, GA 39845; 229-524-2525; fax: 229-524-8883; 8:30-5PM. ***Felony, Misdemeanor, Civil.***
Civil Records: Access: Fax, in person. Both court and visitors may perform in person searches. Search fee: $1.00 per name per year. Required to search: name, years to search. Civil cases indexed by defendant, plaintiff, on computer from 1994, on dockets from 1921.
Criminal Records: Access: Fax, mail, in person. Both court and visitors may perform in person searches. Search fee: $1.00 per name per year. Required to search: name, years to search, DOB, signed release; also helpful: SSN, race, sex. Criminal records computerized from 1994, on dockets from 1921. Mail turnaround time 1 day.
General Information: No juvenile, adoption, sexual, mental health or expunged records released. Will fax documents $1.00 per page. Court makes copy: $1.00 per page. Certification fee: $2.50 per page. Payee: Court Clerk. Personal checks accepted; credit cards are not. Prepayment required. Mail requests: SASE required.

Magistrate & Probate Court Seminole County Courthouse, 200 S Knox Ave, Donallsonville, GA 39845; 229-524-5256; fax: 229-524-8644; 8:30AM-5PM. ***Civil Actions under $15,000, Eviction, Small Claims.***
https://www.gaprobate.org/find_court.asp
Court also has jurisdiction for bad checks, arrest warrants, preliminary hearings, and county ordinance violations.

Spalding County

Superior Court PO Box 1046, Griffin, GA 30224; criminal phone: 770-467-4745; civil phone: 770-467-4746; 8AM-5PM. ***Felony, Misdemeanor, Civil.*** www.spaldingcounty.com/officials.htm
Civil Records: Access: In person. Visitors must perform in person searches themselves. Required to search: name, years to search. Civil cases indexed by defendant, plaintiff, on computer from 1995; on dockets from 1852. Mail for specific case info only, the court will not do name searches. Civil PAT goes back to 1995.
Criminal Records: Access: In person. Visitors must perform in person searches themselves. Required to search: name, years to search; also helpful: DOB, SSN, race, sex. Criminal records computerized from 1995; dockets from 1852. Court will not do name searches; will only process specific case files. Criminal PAT goes back to 1995.
General Information: No juvenile, adoption, sexual, mental health or expunged records released. Will not fax documents. Court makes copy: $.25 per page, self serve same. Certification fee: $2.50 per document; $.50 per page. Payee: Court Clerk. Business checks accepted. No personal checks accepted. Prepayment required.

State Court PO Box 1046, Griffin, GA 30224; 770-467-4356; criminal phone: 770-467-4745; civil phone: 770-467-4746; 8-5PM. ***Misdemeanor, Civil.***
Civil Records: Access: Mail, in person. Visitors must perform in person searches themselves. No search fee. Required to search: name, years to search. Civil cases indexed by defendant, plaintiff, on computer back to 1995; prior records on dockets from 1852. All search requests must be in writing. Mail access only for specific cases; no name searching by the court. Civil PAT goes back to 1995.
Criminal Records: Access: Mail, in person. Visitors must perform in person searches themselves. No search fee. Required to search: name, years to search, DOB; also helpful: SSN, race, sex. Criminal records computerized from 1995; prior records on dockets from 1852. Mail access for specific case information only; no name searching by the court. Mail turnaround time 2 days. Criminal PAT goes back to 1995.
General Information: No juvenile, adoption, sexual, mental health or expunged records released. Will not fax documents. Court makes copy: $.25 per page, self serve same. Certification fee: $2.50 per cert plus $.50 each add'l page. Payee: Court Clerk. Business checks accepted. No personal checks accepted. Prepayment required. Mail requests: SASE required.

Magistrate Court 132 E Solomon St, Griffin, GA 30223; 770-467-4320; fax: 770-467-0081; 8AM-5PM. ***Civil Actions under $15,000, Eviction, Small Claims.*** Court also has jurisdiction for bad checks, arrest warrants, preliminary hearings, and county ordinance violations.

Probate Court 132 E Solomon St, Griffin, GA 30223; 770-467-4340; fax: 770-467-4243; 8AM-N, 1-5PM. ***Probate.***

Stephens County

Superior Court 205 Alexander St N, #202, Toccoa, GA 30577; 706-886-9496; fax: 706-886-5710; 8AM-5PM. ***Felony, Misdemeanor, Civil.***
No name searches performed by court personnel; case number needed.
Civil Records: Access: In person only. Visitors must perform in person searches themselves. Required to search: name, years to search. Civil cases indexed by defendant, plaintiff, on computer back to 1988, on dockets from 1906. Civil PAT goes back to 1988.
Criminal Records: Access: In person only. Visitors must perform in person searches themselves. Required to search: name, years to search, DOB, signed release; SSN helpful. Criminal records computerized from 1988, on dockets from 1906. Criminal PAT goes back to 1990.
General Information: No juvenile, adoption, sexual, mental health or expunged records released. Fee to fax out documents prepaid: $2.00 1st page, $1.00 each add'l. Court makes copy: $1.00 per page. Self serve: $.25 per page. Certification fee: $2.50 plus $.50 per page after first. Payee: Court Clerk. Personal checks accepted; credit cards are not. Prepayment required.

State Court 205 N Alexander St, Rm 202, County Government Bldg, Toccoa, GA 30577; 706-886-3598/9496; fax: 706-886-5710; 8AM-5PM. ***Misdemeanor, Civil.***
This agency will not perform name searches.
Civil Records: Access: In person only. Visitors must perform in person searches themselves. Required to search: name, years to search. Civil cases indexed by

defendant, plaintiff, on computer back to 1991, on dockets from 1906. Civil PAT goes back to 1991. Personal identifiers on terminal results vary case to case.
Criminal Records: Access: In person only. Visitors must perform in person searches themselves. Required to search: name, years to search, DOB. Criminal records computerized from 1990, on dockets from 1906. Criminal PAT goes back to 1990. Personal identifiers on terminal results vary case to case.
General Information: No juvenile, adoption, sexual, mental health or expunged records released. Will not fax out case files. Court makes copy: $1.00 per page. Self serve: $.25 per page. Certification fee: $2.50 plus $.50 per page after first. Payee: Court Clerk. Personal checks accepted; credit cards are not. Prepayment required.

Magistrate Court 70 N Alexander St, Rm 107, Toccoa, GA 30577; 706-886-6205; fax: 706-886-5569; 8:30AM-5PM. ***Civil Actions under $15,000, Eviction, Small Claims.*** Court also has jurisdiction for bad checks, arrest warrants, preliminary hearings, and county ordinance violations.

Probate Court 70 N Alexander, Rm 108, Toccoa, GA 30577; 706-886-2828; fax: 706-886-2631; 8AM-5PM, closed for lunch hour. ***Probate.***

Stewart County

Superior Court PO Box 910, Main St, Lumpkin, GA 31815; 229-838-6220; fax: 229-838-4505; 8AM-4:30PM. ***Felony, Misdemeanor, Civil.***
Civil Records: Access: In person only. Visitors must perform in person searches themselves. Required to search: name, years to search; also helpful: address. Civil cases indexed by defendant. Civil index in books.
Criminal Records: Access: In person only. Visitors must perform in person searches themselves. Required to search: name, years to search; also helpful: address, DOB, SSN. Criminal docket on booksto 1840s.
General Information: No juvenile, adoption, sexual, mental health or sealed records are released. Will not fax documents. Court makes copy: $.50 per page. Self serve: $.25 per page. Certification fee: $2.50 plus $.50 per page after first. Payee: Clerk of Superior Court. Personal checks accepted; credit cards are not. Prepayment required.

Magistrate Court PO Box 712, 712 Broad St, Lumpkin, GA 31815; 229-838-0505; fax: 229-838-0015; 8AM-5PM. ***Civil Actions under $15,000, Eviction, Small Claims.*** Court also has jurisdiction for bad checks, arrest warrants, preliminary hearings, and county ordinance violations.

Probate Court PO Box 876, 1765 Main St, Lumpkin, GA 31815; 229-838-4394; fax: 229-838-9084; 8AM-N, 1-4:30PM. ***Probate, Traffic.***

Sumter County

State Court PO Box 333, Americus, GA 31709; 229-928-4537; 9-5PM. ***Felony, Misdemeanor, Civil.***
Civil Records: Access: In person only. Visitors must perform in person searches themselves. Required to search: name, years to search. Civil cases indexed by defendant, plaintiff, on dockets from late 1800s.
Criminal Records: Access: In person only. Visitors must perform in person searches themselves. Required to search: name, years to search, DOB. Criminal docket index from late 1800s.
General Information: No juvenile, adoption, sealed, sexual, mental health or expunged records released. Will not fax documents. Court makes copy: $.25 per page, self serve same. Certification fee: $2.50 plus $.50 per page. Certification only done if court performs makes the copy. Payee: Court Clerk. No out-of-county personal checks accepted. No credit cards accepted. Prepayment required.

Magistrate Court PO Box 563, 500 W Lamar St, Americus, GA 31709; 229-928-4524; fax: 229-928-4527; 9AM-5PM. ***Civil Actions under $15,000, Eviction, Small Claims.***
Court also has jurisdiction for bad checks, arrest warrants, preliminary hearings, county ordinances.

Probate Court PO Box 246, 500 W Lamar St, Americus, GA 31709; 229-928-4551; fax: 229-928-4622; 8AM-5PM. ***Probate.*** http://ga-sumtercounty.civicplus.com/index.asp?NID=102

Talbot County

Superior Court PO Box 325, Talbotton, GA 31827; 706-665-3239; fax: 706-665-8637; 8:30AM-5PM. ***Felony, Misdemeanor, Civil.***
Civil Records: Access: In person only. Visitors must perform in person searches themselves. Required to search: name, years to search. Civil cases indexed by defendant, plaintiff, on dockets from 1827. Civil PAT available.
Criminal Records: Access: In person only. Visitors must perform in person searches themselves. Required to search: name, years to search. Criminal records are computerized. Historical documents are indexed in docket books. Criminal PAT available.
General Information: No juvenile, adoption, sexual, mental health or expunged records released. Will fax documents $2.00 per page. Court makes copy: $.25 per page. Self serve: $.25 per page. Certification fee: $2.00 plus $.50 per page after first. Payee: Superior Court. Business checks accepted. No credit cards accepted. Prepayment required.

Magistrate & Probate Court PO Box 157, 26 S Washington St, Talbotton, GA 31827; 706-665-8866; fax: 706-665-8240; 8AM-5PM. ***Civil Actions under $15,000, Eviction, Small Claims, Probate.*** https://www.gaprobate.org/find_court.asp
Court also has jurisdiction for bad checks, arrest warrants, preliminary hearings, and county ordinance violations.

Taliaferro County

Superior Court PO Box 182, Crawfordville, GA 30631; 706-456-2123; fax: 706-456-2749; 9AM-5PM. ***Felony, Misdemeanor, Civil.***
Civil Records: Access: In person only. Visitors must perform in person searches themselves. Required to search: name, years to search. Civil cases indexed by defendant, plaintiff, on dockets from 1825.
Criminal Records: Access: In person only. Visitors must perform in person searches themselves. Required to search: name, years to search, DOB; SSN helpful. Criminal docket index from 1825.
General Information: No juvenile, adoption, sexual, mental health or expunged records released. Court makes copy: $1.00 per page. Self serve: $.25 per page. Certification fee: $2.00. Payee: Court Clerk. Personal checks accepted; credit cards are not. Prepayment required.

Magistrate & Probate Court PO Box 264, 113 Monument St, Courthouse, Crawfordville, GA 30631; 706-456-2253; fax: 706-456-3550; 9AM-5PM. ***Civil Actions under $15,000, Eviction, Small Claims, Probate, Misdemeanor Traffic.***
Court also has jurisdiction for bad checks, arrest warrants, preliminary hearings, and county ordinance violations.

Tattnall County

Superior & State Court PO Box 39, 111 N Main St, Reidsville, GA 30453; 912-557-6716; fax: 912-557-4861; 8AM-5PM. ***Felony, Misdemeanor, Civil.***
Civil Records: Access: In person only. Visitors must perform in person searches themselves. Required to search: name, years to search; also helpful: address. Civil cases indexed by defendant, plaintiff, on computer back to 1990; on dockets from 1800s. Civil PAT goes back to 1990.
Criminal Records: Access: In person only. Visitors must perform in person searches themselves. Required to search: name, years to search, DOB; SSN helpful. Criminal records computerized from 1990; on dockets from 1800s. Criminal PAT goes back to same as civil.
General Information: No juvenile, adoption, sexual, mental health or expunged records released. Will fax documents $2.50 per page. Court makes copy: $1.00 per page. Self serve: $.25 per page. Certification fee: $3.00 1st page plus $.50 each add'l. Payee: Court Clerk. Business checks accepted. No credit cards accepted. Prepayment required.

Magistrate Court PO Box 513, 101 S Main St, Courthouse Sq, Reidsville, GA 30453; 912-557-4372; fax: 912-557-3136; 8AM-5PM. ***Civil Actions under $15,000, Eviction, Small Claims.***
Court also has jurisdiction for bad checks, arrest warrants, preliminary hearings, and county ordinance violations, dispossery, writ of possessions, civil claims.

Probate Court PO Box 699, 111 N Main St, Reidsville, GA 30453; 912-557-6719; fax: 912-557-3976; 8:30AM-5PM. ***Probate.***

Taylor County

Superior Court PO Box 248, Courthouse Sq, Butler, GA 31006; 478-862-5594; criminal fax: 478-862-5334; civil fax: same; 8AM-5PM. ***Felony, Misdemeanor, Civil.***
Civil Records: Access: In person only. Visitors must perform in person searches themselves. Required to search: name, years to search. Civil cases indexed by defendant, plaintiff, on computer from 1991, dockets from 1852. Public use terminal has civil records back to 1995.
Criminal Records: Access: In person only. Visitors must perform in person searches themselves. Required to search: name, years to search, DOB; SSN helpful. Criminal records computerized from 1991, dockets from 1852.
General Information: No juvenile, adoption, sexual, mental health or expunged records released. Will fax specific case file $2.50 per page. Court makes copy: $1.00 per page. Self serve: $.25 per page. Certification fee: $2.50. Payee: Court Clerk. Personal checks accepted; credit cards are not. Prepayment required.

Magistrate & Probate Court PO Box 536, 2 N Broad St, Butler, GA 31006; 478-862-3357; fax: 478-862-9447; 8AM-5PM. ***Civil Actions under $15,000, Eviction, Small Claims, Probate, Traffic.*** https://www.gaprobate.org/find_court.asp
Court also has jurisdiction for bad checks, arrest warrants, preliminary hearings, and county ordinance violations.

Telfair County

Superior Court Courthouse, 128 Oak St, #2 (mailing), 5D Parsonage St (Physical), McRae, GA 31055; 229-868-6525; fax: 229-868-7956; 8:30AM-4:30PM. ***Felony, Misdemeanor, Civil.***
Civil Records: Access: In person only. Visitors must perform in person searches themselves. Required to search: name, years to search. Civil cases indexed by defendant. Civil records on dockets from early 1900s. Civil PAT goes back to 2001.
Criminal Records: Access: In person only. Visitors must perform in person searches themselves. Required to search: name, years to search, DOB, signed release; also helpful: SSN, race, sex. Criminal docket index from early 1900s. Criminal PAT goes back to 2001.
General Information: No juvenile, adoption, sexual, mental health or expunged records released. Will fax documents $2.00 per page. Court makes copy: $.25 per page, self serve same. Certification fee: $3.00. Payee: Court Clerk. Personal checks accepted; credit cards are not. Prepayment required.

Magistrate Court 128 E Oak St, #5, McRae, GA 31055; 229-868-6772; fax: 229-868-6902; 8AM-4:30PM. ***Civil Actions under $15,000, Eviction, Small Claims.***
Court also has jurisdiction for bad checks, arrest warrants, preliminary hearings, and county ordinance violations.

Probate Court 128 E Oak St, Suite 1, McRae, GA 31055; 229-868-6038; probate phone: 229-868-7987; fax: 229-868-7620; 8:30AM-N, 1-4:30PM. ***Probate, Misdemeanor, Traffic.*** http://telfaircounty.georgia.gov
Search the courts citations database free at https://www.ncourt.com/courtpayment/Lookup.aspx?Juris=GATelfair.

Terrell County

Superior Court PO Box 189, 513 S Main St, Dawson, GA 39842; 229-995-2631; 8:30AM-5PM. ***Felony, Misdemeanor, Civil.***

Civil Records: Access: In person only. Visitors must perform in person searches themselves. Required to search: name, years to search. Civil cases indexed by defendant. Civil records on computer from 1988, dockets books from 1900s. Civil PAT goes back to 1989.

Criminal Records: Access: In person only. Visitors must perform in person searches themselves. Required to search: name, years to search, DOB, signed release; SSN helpful. Criminal records computerized from 1988, dockets books from 1900s. Criminal PAT goes back to same as civil.

General Information: No juvenile, adoption, sexual, mental health or expunged records released. Will not fax documents. Court makes copy: $1.00 per page. Self serve: $.25 per page. Certification fee: $3.00 plus $.50 per page after first. Payee: Court Clerk. Business checks accepted. No credit cards accepted. Prepayment required.

Magistrate Court PO Box 793, 513 S Main St, Dawson, GA 39842; 229-995-3757; fax: 229-995-4496; 8AM-5PM. ***Civil Actions under $15,000, Eviction, Small Claims, Misdemeanors.***
Court also has jurisdiction for bad checks, arrest warrants, preliminary hearings, county ordinances.

Probate Court PO Box 67, 513 S Main St, Dawson, GA 39842; 229-995-5515; fax: 229-995-5574; 8AM-N, 1-5PM. ***Probate, Traffic.***

Thomas County

Superior & State Court PO Box 1995, 225 N Broad St, Thomasville, GA 31799; 229-225-4108; criminal fax: 229-225-4110; civil fax: same; 8AM-5PM. ***Felony, Misdemeanor, Civil.***
www.thomascoclerkofcourt.org

Civil Records: Access: In person only. Visitors must perform in person searches themselves. Required to search: name, years to search. Civil cases indexed by defendant, plaintiff, on computer from 1989, archived from 1826. Civil PAT goes back to 1989.

Criminal Records: Access: In person only. Visitors must perform in person searches themselves. Required to search: name, years to search, DOB; SSN helpful. Criminal records computerized since 1989. Criminal PAT goes back to same as civil. PAT results show middle initial, DOB, SSN.

General Information: No juvenile, adoption, sexual, mental health or expunged records released. Will fax specific case file $2.50 per fax, plus $1.00 per copy. Court makes copy: $1.00 per page. Self serve: $.50 per page. Certification fee: $2.00. Payee: Court Clerk. Personal checks accepted; credit cards are not. Prepayment required.

Magistrate Court PO Box 879, 921 Smith Ave, Bobby Hines Jail/Justice Center, Thomasville, GA 31799; 229-225-3330; fax: 229-225-3342; 8AM-5PM. ***Civil Actions under $15,000, Eviction, Small Claims.*** Court also has jurisdiction for bad checks, arrest warrants, preliminary hearings, and county ordinance violations.

Probate Court PO Box 1582, Thomasville, GA 31799; 229-225-4116; fax: 229-227-1698; 8AM-5PM. ***Probate.***
www.georgiacourts.org/courts/probate/thomas/
Physical Address: 225 N Broad St, Thomasville.

Tift County

Superior & State Court PO Box 354, 237 E 2nd St, Tifton, GA 31793; 229-386-7810; fax: 229-386-7813; 8AM-5PM. ***Felony, Misdemeanor, Civil.***
Call 229-786-7815 to reach the Superior Court.

Civil Records: Access: In person only. Visitors must perform in person searches themselves. Required to search: name, years to search. Civil cases indexed by defendant. Civil index in docket books from 1905. Civil PAT goes back to 2002. PAT results show name, DOB. Some results may show SSN.

Criminal Records: Access: In person only. Visitors must perform in person searches themselves. Required to search: name, years to search. Criminal docket on books from 1905. Criminal PAT goes back to same as civil.PAT results show name, DOB.

General Information: No juvenile, adoption, sexual, mental health or expunged records released. Will fax documents to local or toll-free number. Court makes copy: $.25 per page, self serve same. Certification fee: $2.50 plus $.50 per page after first. Payee: Court Clerk. Personal checks accepted; credit cards are not. Prepayment required.

Magistrate Court PO Box 214, 225 N Tift Ave, Tifton, GA 31793; 229-386-7907; fax: 229-386-7978; 8AM-5PM. ***Civil Actions under $15,000, Eviction, Small Claims.***
Court also has jurisdiction for bad checks, arrest warrants, preliminary hearings, county ordinances.

Probate Court PO Box 792, Tifton, GA 31793; 229-386-7914; fax: 229-386-7926; 8AM-5PM. ***Probate.*** www.tiftcounty.org Physical Address: 225 Tift Ave, Rm 117, Tifton, GA 31794

Toombs County

Superior & State Court PO Drawer 530, Lyons, GA 30436; 912-526-3501; fax: 912-526-1004; 8:30AM-5PM. ***Felony, Misdemeanor, Civil.***

Civil Records: Access: In person only. Visitors must perform in person searches themselves. Required to search: name, years to search. Civil cases indexed by defendant, plaintiff; index in docket books from 1908, on computer since 1995. Civil PAT goes back to 1995. PAT results show middle initial, DOB.

Criminal Records: Access: In person only. Visitors must perform in person searches themselves. Required to search: name, years to search, DOB; SSN helpful. Criminal docket on books from 1908, on computer since 1995. Criminal PAT goes back to same as civil. PAT results show middle initial, DOB.

General Information: No juvenile, adoption, sexual, mental health records released. Will not fax documents. Court makes copy: $1.00 per page. Self serve: $.25 per page. Certification fee: $2.50 plus $1.00 per page after first. Payee: Court Clerk. No personal checks or credit cards accepted. Prepayment required.

Magistrate Court PO Box 1460, 100 Courthouse Sq, Lyons, GA 30436; 912-526-8984; fax: 912-526-8985; 8:30AM-5PM. ***Civil Actions under $15,000, Eviction, Small Claims.*** Court also has jurisdiction for bad checks, arrest warrants, preliminary hearings, county ordinance violations.

Probate Court 100 Courthouse Sq, County Courthouse, PO Box 1370, Lyons, GA 30436; 912-526-8696; fax: 912-526-1008; 8:30-5PM. ***Probate.***

Towns County

Superior Court 48 River St, #E, Hiawassee, GA 30546; 706-896-2130; fax: 706-896-1772; 8:30AM-4:30PM. ***Felony, Misdemeanor, Civil.***

Civil Records: Access: In person only. Visitors must perform in person searches themselves. Required to search: name, years to search. Civil cases indexed by plaintiff. Civil index in docket books from 1923, records computerized 2002 forward. Public use terminal has civil records.

Criminal Records: Access: In person only. Visitors must perform in person searches themselves. Required to search: name, years to search, DOB, signed release; SSN helpful. Criminal docket on books to 1945, indexed by defendant; records computerized 2002 forward.

General Information: No juvenile, adoption, sexual, mental health or expunged records released. Will not fax documents. Court makes copy: $1.00 per page. Self serve: $.25 per page. Certification fee: $2.50 per page. Payee: Court Clerk. Personal checks accepted; credit cards are not. Prepayment required.

Magistrate & Probate Court 48 River St, #C, Hiawassee, GA 30546; 706-896-3467; fax: 706-896-1772; 8:30AM-4:30PM. ***Civil Actions under $15,000, Eviction, Small Claims, Probate.***
Court also has jurisdiction for arrest warrants, preliminary hearings, garnishments, traffic, and county ordinance violations.

Treutlen County

Superior & State Court 203 2nd St South, #301, Soperton, GA 30457; 912-529-4215; probate phone: 912-529-3342; fax: 912-529-6737; 8AM-5PM. ***Felony, Misdemeanor, Civil.***

Civil Records: Access: Mail, in person. Both court and visitors may perform in person searches. No search fee. Required to search: name, years to search. Civil cases indexed by defendant, plaintiff, on computer from 1991, dockets books from 1919. Mail turnaround 1-2 days. Civil PAT goes back to 1990.

Criminal Records: Access: Mail, in person. Both court and visitors may perform in person searches. No search fee. Required to search: name, years to search, DOB; also helpful: SSN, race, sex. Criminal records computerized from 1991, dockets books from 1919. Mail turnaround time 1-2 days. Criminal PAT goes back to same as civil.

General Information: No juvenile, adoption, sexual, mental health or expunged records released. Will not fax documents. Court makes copy: $1.00 per page. Self serve: $.25 per page. Certification fee: $2.50 plus $.50 per page after first. Payee: Court Clerk. Personal checks accepted; credit cards are not. Prepayment required. Mail requests: SASE required.

Magistrate & Probate Court 650 2nd St South, #101, Soperton, GA 30457; 912-529-3342; probate phone: 912-529-4320; criminal fax: 912-529-6838; civil fax: same; 8AM-5PM. ***Civil Actions under $15,000, Eviction, Small Claims, Probate.***
Court also has jurisdiction for bad checks, arrest warrants, preliminary hearings, county ordinances.

Troup County

Superior & State Court 900 Dallas St., LaGrange, GA 30240; 706-883-1740; criminal phone: x4; civil phone: x2; fax: 706-883-1724; 8AM-5PM. ***Felony, Misdemeanor, Civil.***
www.troupclerkofcourt.com

Civil Records: Access: In person only. Visitors must perform in person searches themselves. Required to search: name, years to search. Civil cases indexed by defendant, plaintiff, on computer from 1996, on docket books from 1940s. Civil PAT goes back to 1996.

Criminal Records: Access: In person only. Visitors must perform in person searches themselves. Required to search: name, years to search, DOB; SSN helpful. Criminal records computerized from 1996, on docket books from 1940s. Criminal PAT goes back to same as civil.

General Information: No juvenile, adoption, sexual, mental health or expunged records released. Will not fax documents. Court makes copy: $.25 per page. Certification fee: $2.50 plus $.50 per page. Cert fee includes copies. Payee: Court Clerk. Personal checks accepted if local. Prepayment required.

Magistrate Court 100 Ridley Ave, LaGrange, GA 30240; 706-883-1695; fax: 706-883-1632; 8AM-5PM. ***Civil Actions under $15,000, Eviction, Small Claims.*** Court also has jurisdiction for bad checks, arrest warrants, preliminary hearings, and county ordinance violations.

Probate Court 100 Ridley, Troup County Government Center, LaGrange, GA 30240; 706-883-1690; fax: 706-812-7933; 8AM-5PM (closed 1 hr at lunch). ***Probate.***
www.georgiacourts.org/courts/counties/troup/
Includes guardianship, administrations, custodial accounts, marriages, pistol licenses, passports, elections, and mental or substance abuse affidavits.

Turner County

Superior Court PO Box 106, 219 E College Ave, Ashburn, GA 31714; 229-567-2011; fax: 229-567-0450; 8AM-5PM. ***Felony, Misdemeanor, Civil.***

Civil Records: Access: In person only. Visitors must perform in person searches themselves. Required to search: name, years to search. Civil cases indexed by defendant, plaintiff; index on docket books, archived from 1905.

Criminal Records: Access: In person only. Visitors must perform in person searches themselves. Required to search: name, years to search, DOB,

signed release; SSN helpful. Criminal docket on books, archived from 1905.
General Information: No juvenile, adoption, sexual, mental health or expunged records released. Will fax documents $2.50. Court makes copy: $1.00 per page. Self serve: $.25 per page. Certification fee: $2.50 plus $1.00 per page after first. Payee: Court Clerk. No personal checks. Prepayment required.

Magistrate Court 219 E College, #2, Ashburn, GA 31714; 229-567-3155; 9AM-4:30PM. ***Civil Actions under $15,000, Eviction, Small Claims.***
Court also has jurisdiction for bad checks, arrest warrants, preliminary hearings, county ordinances.

Probate Court PO Box 2506, 219 E College Ave, Rm 4, Ashburn, GA 31714-2506; 229-567-2151; fax: 229-567-0358; 8AM-5PM, closed for lunch. ***Probate, Misdemeanor.***
Misdemeanors prior to 7/1/2002 only. Currently no new misdemeanor cases.

Twiggs County

Superior Court PO Box 234, 425 Railroad St North, Jeffersonville, GA 31044; 478-945-3350; fax: 478-945-6751; 8AM-5PM. ***Felony, Misdemeanor, Civil.***
Civil Records: Access: In person only. Visitors must perform in person searches themselves. Required to search: name, years to search. Civil cases indexed by defendant, plaintiff, on computer from 1991, dockets books to 1901. Civil PAT goes back to 1991.
Criminal Records: Access: In person only. Visitors must perform in person searches themselves. Required to search: name, years to search, DOB, signed release; SSN helpful. Criminal records computerized from 1991, dockets books to 1901. Criminal PAT goes back to same as civil.
General Information: No juvenile, adoption, sexual, mental health or expunged records released. Will fax documents to local or toll-free number. Court makes copy: $.25 per page, self serve same. Certification fee: $2.50 plus $.50 per page after first. Payee: Court Clerk. Personal checks accepted; credit cards are not. Prepayment required.

Magistrate Court PO Box 146, 425 N Railroad St #212, Jeffersonville, GA 31044; 478-945-3428; fax: 478-945-2083; 9AM-5PM. ***Civil Actions under $15,000, Eviction, Small Claims.***
Court also has jurisdiction for bad checks, arrest warrants, preliminary hearings, county ordinances.

Probate Court PO Box 186, 425 Railroad St N, Jeffersonville, GA 31044; 478-945-3390/3252; fax: 478-945-6070; 9AM-5PM. ***Probate, Misdemeanor Traffic.***

Union County

Superior Court 114 Courthouse St, #5, Blairsville, GA 30512; 706-439-6022; fax: 706-439-6026; 8AM-5PM. ***Felony, Misdemeanor, Civil.***
Civil Records: Access: In person only. Both court and visitors may perform in person searches. No search fee. Required to search: name, years to search. Civil cases indexed by defendant, plaintiff, on computer from 1993, on dockets from 1936. Civil PAT goes back to 1993.
Criminal Records: Access: In person only. Both court and visitors may perform in person searches. No search fee. Required to search: name, years to search, DOB, signed release; SSN helpful. Criminal docket on books from 1930; computerized back to 1997. Criminal PAT goes back to 1997. PAT results show name, DOB, SSN.
General Information: No juvenile, adoption, sexual, mental health or expunged records released. Will not fax documents. Court makes copy: $.25 per page, self serve same. Certification fee: $2.50 plus $.25 per page after first. Payee: Court Clerk. Personal checks accepted; credit cards are not. Prepayment required.

Magistrate Court 114 Courthouse St, #10, Blairsville, GA 30512; 706-439-6008; fax: 706-439-6104; 8AM-4:30PM. ***Civil Actions under $15,000, Eviction, Small Claims.***
Court also has jurisdiction for bad checks, arrest warrants, preliminary hearings, county ordinance violations, civil suits, foreclosures, abandonments and dispossessions.

Probate Court 114 Courthouse St, #8, Blairsville, GA 30512; 706-439-6006; fax: 706-439-6009; 8AM-4:30PM. ***Probate.***

Upson County

Superior Court PO Box 469, Thomaston, GA 30286; 706-647-7835; probate phone: 706-647-7015; fax: 706-647-8999; 8AM-5PM. ***Felony, Misdemeanor, Civil.***
Civil Records: Access: Mail, in person. Visitors must perform in person searches themselves. Search fee: $5.00. Required to search: name, years to search. Civil cases indexed by defendant, plaintiff; index in docket books from 1927; on computer back to 1990. Mail turnaround time 15 days.
Criminal Records: Access: Mail, in person. Visitors must perform in person searches themselves. Search fee: $1.00. Required to search: name, years to search, DOB; also helpful: SSN, race, sex. Criminal docket on books from 1937; on computer back to 1990. Mail turnaround time 15 days.
General Information: No juvenile, adoption, sexual, mental health or expunged records released. Will fax documents to local or toll-free number. Court makes copy: $1.00 per page. Self serve: $.25 per page. Certification fee: $2.50 plus $.50 per page after first. Payee: Court Clerk. No personal checks or credit cards accepted. Prepayment required.

Magistrate Court PO Box 890, 305 S Hightower, Thomaston, GA 30286; 706-647-6891; fax: 706-647-1248; 8AM-4:45PM. ***Civil Actions under $15,000, Eviction, Small Claims.***
Court also has jurisdiction for bad checks, arrest warrants, preliminary hearings, county ordinances.

Probate Court PO Box 906, 106 E Lee St, Thomaston, GA 30286; 706-647-7015; fax: 706-646-3341; 8-5PM. ***Probate, Misdemeanor Traffic.***

Walker County

Superior & State Court PO Box 448, 301 S Duke St, LaFayette, GA 30728; 706-638-1742; fax: 706-638-1779; 8AM-5PM. ***Felony, Misdemeanor, Civil.***
Civil Records: Access: In person only. Visitors must perform in person searches themselves. Required to search: name, years to search. Civil cases indexed by defendant, plaintiff; index in docket books from 1883; computerized since 2000.
Criminal Records: Access: In person only. Visitors must perform in person searches themselves. Required to search: name, years to search, DOB; SSN helpful. Criminal docket on books from 1883.
General Information: No juvenile, adoption, sexual, mental health or expunged records released. Will fax documents for $2.50 fee. Court makes copy: $1.00 per page. Self serve: $.25 per page. Certification fee: $2.00. Payee: Court Clerk. Personal checks accepted; credit cards are not. Prepayment required.

Magistrate Court 102 Napier St, LaFayette, GA 30728; 706-638-1217; fax: 706-638-1218; 8AM-5PM. ***Civil Actions under $15,000, Eviction, Small Claims.*** Court also has jurisdiction for bad checks, arrest warrants, search warrants, preliminary hearings (15K Civil), and county ordinance violations.

Probate Court PO Box 436, 103 S Duke St, Rm 101, LaFayette, GA 30728; 706-638-2852; fax: 706-638-2869; 8AM-5PM. ***Probate.***
www.co.walker.ga.us/Probate.htm

Walton County

Superior Court 303 S Hammond Dr, Ste 335, Monroe, GA 30655; 770-267-1307; fax: 770-267-1441; 8:30AM-5PM. ***Felony, Misdemeanor, Civil.***
Civil Records: Access: In person only. Visitors must perform in person searches themselves. Required to search: name, years to search. Civil cases indexed by defendant, plaintiff, on computer from 1990, dockets books from 1900s. PAT results show name only.
Criminal Records: Access: In person only. Visitors must perform in person searches themselves. Required to search: name, years to search; also helpful: DOB, race, sex. Criminal records computerized from 1990, dockets books from 1900s. PAT results show name only.
General Information: No juvenile, adoption, sexual, mental health or expunged records released. Will not fax documents. Court makes copy: $.25 per page, self serve same. Certification fee: $2.50 plus $.50 per page after first. Payee: Court Clerk. Personal checks accepted; credit cards are not. Prepayment required.

Magistrate Court 303 S Hammond Dr #116, Monroe, GA 30655; 770-267-1349; criminal fax: 770-266-1512; civil fax: same; 8:30AM-5PM. ***Civil Actions under $15,000, Eviction, Small Claims, Criminal warrants, Ordinance.***
www.waltonmagcourt.com Court also has jurisdiction for bad checks, arrest warrants, preliminary hearings, and county ordinance violations.

Probate Court 303 S Hammond Dr, Suite 118, Monroe, GA 30655; 770-267-1345, 266-1751; fax: 770-267-1417; 8:30AM-5PM. ***Probate, Misdemeanor.***
This location also has traffic records.

Ware County

Superior & State Court PO Box 776, 800 Church St #124, Waycross, GA 31502; 912-287-4340; fax: 912-287-2498; 9AM-5PM. ***Felony, Misdemeanor, Civil.***
Civil Records: Access: In person only. Visitors must perform in person searches themselves. Required to search: name, years to search. Civil cases indexed by defendant. Civil records on computer since 1995; prior records on dockets books from 1874.
Criminal Records: Access: In person only. Visitors must perform in person searches themselves. Required to search: name, years to search, DOB; SSN helpful. Criminal records on computer since 1995; prior records on dockets books from 1874.
General Information: No juvenile, adoption, sexual, mental health or expunged records released. Will not fax documents. Court makes copy: $1.00 per page. Self serve: $.25 per page. Certification fee: $2.50 plus $.50 per page after first. Payee: Court Clerk. Personal checks accepted; credit cards are not. Prepayment required.

Magistrate Court PO Box 17, 201 State St, Rm 102, Waycross, GA 31501; criminal phone: 912-287-4373; civil phone: 912-287-4375; criminal fax: 912-287-4377; civil fax: 912-287-4464; 9AM-5PM. ***Civil Actions under $15,000, Eviction, Small Claims, Foreclosure, Garnishment.***
www.waremagcourt.com/ Court also has jurisdiction for bad checks, arrest warrants, preliminary hearings, county ordinance and good behavior violations.

Probate Court Ware County Courthouse, 800 Church St, #123, Waycross, GA 31501; 912-287-4315/6; probate phone: 912-287-4316; fax: 912-287-4317; 9AM-5PM. ***Probate.***
www.georgiacourts.org/courts/probate/ware/index.shtm Probate fax is same as main fax number.

Warren County

Superior Court PO Box 227, 100 Main St, Warrenton, GA 30828; 706-465-2262; fax: 706-465-0232; 8AM-5PM. ***Felony, Misdemeanor, Civil.***
Civil Records: Access: Mail, in person. Visitors must perform in person searches themselves. No search fee. Required to search: name, years to search. Civil cases indexed by defendant, plaintiff; index on docket books to 1950. Civil PAT goes back to 1994.
Criminal Records: Access: Mail, in person. Visitors must perform in person searches themselves. No search fee. Required to search: name, years to search, DOB, signed release; also helpful: SSN, race, sex. Criminal docket on books to 1950, computerized since 2000. Criminal PAT goes back to 1994.
General Information: No juvenile, adoption, sexual, mental health or expunged records released. Will fax documents $2.50 1st page, $1.00 each add'l. Court makes copy: $1.00 per page. Self serve: $.25 per page. Certification fee: $2.50 for 1st page, $.50 each add'l. Payee: Court Clerk. No credit cards accepted. Prepayment required.

Magistrate Court PO Box 203, 521 Main St, Warrenton, GA 30828; 706-465-3123; fax: 706-

465-1300; 8AM-N, 1-5PM. ***Civil Actions under $15,000, Eviction, Small Claims.***
Court also has jurisdiction for bad checks, arrest warrants, preliminary hearings, county ordinances.

Probate Court PO Box 364, 100 Main St, Warrenton, GA 30828; 706-465-2227; fax: 706-465-1347; 8AM-4:30PM. ***Probate.***

Washington County

Superior & State Court PO Box 231, 132 W Haynes St, Sandersville, GA 31082; 478-552-3186; fax: 478-553-9969; 9AM-5PM. ***Felony, Misdemeanor, Civil.***
The court mentions that a record retriever named Janet Carrington, 478-552-5427 does perform record searches here.
Civil Records: Access: In person only. Visitors must perform in person searches themselves. Required to search: name, years to search. Civil cases indexed by defendant, plaintiff, on dockets books to 1869. Civil PAT goes back to 1995.
Criminal Records: Access: In person only. Visitors must perform in person searches themselves. Required to search: name, years to search. Criminal docket on books to 1869. Criminal PAT goes back to same as civil. PAT results show name, DOB, SSN.
General Information: No juvenile, adoption, sexual, mental health or expunged records released. Will fax documents to local or toll free line, if copy prepaid. Court makes copy: $1.00 per page. Self serve: $.25 per page. Certification fee: $3.00 plus $.50 per page. Payee: Court Clerk. No personal checks or credit cards accepted. Prepayment required.

Magistrate Court PO Box 1053, 132 W Haynes St, Ste 110, Sandersville, GA 31082; 478-552-3591; fax: 478-552-4010; 9AM-5PM. ***Civil Actions under $15,000, Eviction, Small Claims.***
Court also has jurisdiction for bad checks, arrest warrants, preliminary hearings, and county ordinance violations.

Probate Court PO Box 669, 132 W Haynes ST #106, Sandersville, GA 31082; 478-552-3304; fax: 478-552-3304; 9AM-N, 1-5PM. ***Probate.***

Wayne County

Superior & State Court PO Box 920, Jesup, GA 31598; 912-427-5930; fax: 912-427-5939; 8:30AM-5PM. ***Felony, Misdemeanor, Civil.***
Civil Records: Access: In person only. Visitors must perform in person searches themselves. Required to search: name, years to search. Civil cases indexed by defendant, plaintiff, on computer, on docket books from 1810. Civil PAT goes back to 1994. PAT civil results show middle initial. Terminal results also show SSNs.
Criminal Records: Access: In person only. Visitors must perform in person searches themselves. Required to search: name, years to search, DOB. Criminal records on computer, on docket books from 1810. Criminal PAT goes back to same as civil. PAT results show middle initial, DOB. Terminal results include SSN.
General Information: No juvenile, adoption, sexual, mental health or expunged records released. Will fax documents $.50 per page. Court makes copy: $.25 per page, self serve same. Certification fee: $2.50 plus $.50 per page after first. Payee: Superior Court Clerk. Personal checks accepted; credit cards are not. Prepayment required.

Magistrate Court PO Box 27, 174 N Brunswick St, Jesup, GA 31598; 912-427-5960; fax: 912-427-5962; 8:30AM-N; 1-5PM. ***Civil Actions under $15,000, Eviction, Small Claims.***
Court also has jurisdiction for bad checks, arrest warrants, preliminary hearings, bond hearings and county ordinance violations.

Probate Court 174 N Brunswick St, Jesup, GA 31546; 912-427-5940; fax: 912-427-5944; 8:30AM-5PM. ***Probate.***

Webster County

Superior Court PO Box 117, 6330 Hamilton St, Preston, GA 31824; 229-828-3525; fax: 229-828-6961; 9AM-5PM. ***Felony, Misdemeanor, Civil.***
Civil Records: Access: In person only. Visitors must perform in person searches themselves. Required to search: name, years to search. Civil cases indexed by defendant, plaintiff; index in docket books from 1860; computerized records since 2000. Civil PAT goes back to 2000.
Criminal Records: Access: In person only. Visitors must perform in person searches themselves. Required to search: name, years to search, signed release. Criminal docket on books from 1860; computerized records since 2000. Criminal PAT goes back to same as civil. PAT results show name, DOB, SSN.
General Information: No juvenile, adoption, sexual, mental health or expunged records released. Will fax documents $2.50 first page, $1.00 each add'l page. Court makes copy: $.25 per page, Legal size $2.00 per page, self serve same. Certification fee: $2.50 plus $.50 per page after 1st page. Payee: Clerk Superior Court. Personal checks accepted; credit cards are not. Prepayment required.

Magistrate & Probate Court PO Box 135, 6330 Hamilton St, Rm101, Preston, GA 31824; 229-828-3615; fax: 229-828-3616; 8AM-4:30PM. ***Civil Actions under $15,000, Eviction, Small Claims, Probate.***
This court will not give out SSNs. Court also has jurisdiction for bad checks, arrest warrants, preliminary hearings, and county ordinance violations

Wheeler County

Superior Court PO Box 38, Alamo, GA 30411; 912-568-7137; fax: 912-568-7453; 8AM-4PM. ***Felony, Misdemeanor, Civil.***
Civil Records: Access: In person only. Visitors must perform in person searches themselves. Required to search: name, years to search. Civil cases indexed by defendant. Civil index in docket books from 1913. Public use terminal has civil records.
Criminal Records: Access: In person only. Visitors must perform in person searches themselves. Required to search: name, years to search. Criminal docket on books from 1913.
General Information: No juvenile or adoption records released. Will not fax documents. Court makes copy: $.25 per page, self serve same. Certification fee: $2.50 plus $.50 per add'l page. Payee: Superior Court Clerk. Personal checks accepted; credit cards are not. Prepayment required.

Magistrate & Probate Court PO Box 477, 119 W Pearl St, Alamo, GA 30411; 912-568-7133; civil phone: same; probate phone: same; criminal fax: 912-568-1743; civil fax: same; 8AM-4PM. ***Civil Actions under $15,000, Eviction, Small Claims, Probate.***
Court also has jurisdiction for bad checks, arrest warrants, preliminary hearings, and county ordinance violations. Probate fax is same as main fax number.

White County

Superior Court 59 S Main St, #B, Cleveland, GA 30528; 706-865-2613; fax: 706-865-2613; 8:30AM-5PM. ***Felony, Misdemeanor, Civil.***
Civil Records: Access: Mail, in person. Visitors must perform in person searches themselves. No search fee. Required to search: name, years to search. Civil cases indexed by defendant, plaintiff, on computer from 1996, on docket books from 1857. Will accept mail requests if prepaid. Civil PAT goes back to 1996.
Criminal Records: Access: Mail, In person. Visitors must perform in person searches themselves. No search fee. Required to search: name, years to search. Criminal records computerized from 1996, on docket books from 1857. Will accept mail requests if prepaid. Mail turnaround time 10 days; search performed as time permits. Criminal PAT goes back to same as civil. PAT results show middle initial, DOB, SSN.
General Information: No juvenile, adoption, sexual, mental health or expunged records released. Will fax specific case file $1.00 per page fee, prepaid. Court makes copy: $1.00 per page. Self serve: $.25 per page. Certification fee: $2.50 plus $.50 per page after first. Payee: Superior Court Clerk. Business checks accepted. No credit cards accepted. Prepayment required. Mail requests: SASE required.

Magistrate Court 59 S Main St, #D, Cleveland, GA 30528; 706-865-6636; criminal phone: 706-865-2613; civil phone: same; criminal fax: 706-865-7738; civil fax: same; 8:30AM-5PM. ***Civil Actions under $15,000, Misdemeanor, Eviction, Small Claims.*** Court also has jurisdiction for bad checks, arrest warrants, preliminary hearings, and county ordinance violations.

Probate Court 59 S Main St, #H, Cleveland, GA 30528; 706-865-4141; fax: 706-865-1324; 8:30AM-5PM. ***Probate, Misdemeanor.***

Whitfield County

Superior Court PO Box 868, Dalton, GA 30722; 706-275-7450; criminal phone: 706-275-7483; civil phone: 706-275-7480; fax: 706-275-7456; 8AM-5PM. ***Felony, Misdemeanor, Civil.***
Street address is 205 N Selvidge St.
Civil Records: Access: In person only. Visitors must perform in person searches themselves. Required to search: name, years to search. Civil cases indexed by defendant, plaintiff, on computer from 1988, on docket books from 1852. Civil PAT goes back to 8/1988.
Criminal Records: Access: In person only. Visitors must perform in person searches themselves. Required to search: name, years to search, offense, date of offense. Criminal records computerized from 1988, on docket books from 1852. Criminal PAT goes back to same as civil.
General Information: No juvenile, adoption, sexual, mental health or expunged records released. Will not fax documents. Court makes copy: $.25 per page. Self serve: $.25 per page. Certification fee: $3.00 per cert. Payee: Superior Court Clerk. Business checks accepted. No credit cards. Prepayment required.

Magistrate Court PO Box 386, 205 N Selvidge St, Ground Fl, Dalton, GA 30722-0386; 706-278-5052; fax: 706-278-8810; 8AM-5PM. ***Civil Actions under $15,000, Eviction, Small Claims, Misdemeanor, Ordinance.***
www.whitfieldcountyga.com/Magistrate%20Court/magistrate_court.htm Court also has jurisdiction for bad checks, arrest warrants, preliminary hearings, and county ordinance violations.

Probate Court 205 N Selvidge St, Ste G, Dalton, GA 30720; 706-275-7400; fax: 706-281-1735; 8AM-4:45PM. ***Probate.***

Wilcox County

Superior & Magistrate Courts 103 N Broad St, Abbeville, GA 31001; 229-467-2442; probate phone: 229-467-2220; fax: 229-467-2886; 9AM-5PM. ***Felony, Misdemeanor, Civil, Eviction, Small Claims.*** Magistrate: 229-467-2458
Civil Records: Access: Mail, in person. Both court and visitors may perform in person searches. No search fee. Required to search: name, years to search. Civil cases indexed by defendant, plaintiff, on computer since 1995; prior records on docket books from 1950s. Mail turnaround time 1 week. Civil PAT available. PAT results show name only.
Criminal Records: Access: Mail, in person. Both court and visitors may perform in person searches. No search fee. Required to search: name, years to search, DOB; also helpful: SSN. Criminal records on computer since 1995; prior records on docket books from 1950s. Mail turnaround time 1 week. Criminal PAT available.PAT results show name, DOB.
General Information: No juvenile, adoption, sexual, mental health or expunged records released. Will not fax out documents. Court makes copy: $1.00 per page. Self serve: $.25 per page. Cert fee: $2.50 per page. Payee: Superior Court Clerk. Personal checks accepted; credit cards are not. Prepayment required.

Probate Court 103 N Broad St, Abbeville, GA 31001; 229-467-2220; fax: 229-467-2000; 9AM-5PM. ***Probate.***

Wilkes County

Superior Court 23 E Court St, Rm 205, Washington, GA 30673; 706-678-2423; fax: 706-678-2115; 9AM-5PM. ***Felony, Misdemeanor, Civil.***

Civil Records: Access: In person only. Visitors must perform in person searches themselves. Required to search: name, years to search. Civil cases indexed by defendant, plaintiff; index in docket books from 1700s, computerized from 1998. Civil PAT goes back to 1998.

Criminal Records: Access: In person only. Visitors must perform in person searches themselves. Required to search: name, years to search. Criminal docket on books from 1700s, computerized from 1998. Criminal PAT goes back to same as civil. PAT results show middle initial, DOB.

General Information: No juvenile or adoption records released. Will fax specific documents $2.50 1st page, $1.00 ea add'l. Court makes copy: $.25 per page. Self serve: $.25 per page. Certification fee: $2.50 plus $.50 per page after 1st. Payee: Superior Court Clerk. Personal checks accepted; credit cards are not. Prepayment required.

Magistrate Court 23 E Court St, Rm 427, Washington, GA 30673; 706-678-1881; fax: 706-678-1865; 8:30AM-5PM. ***Civil Actions under $15,000, Eviction, Small Claims.***

www.washingtonwilkes.org/Government.php

Court also has jurisdiction for bad checks, arrest warrants, preliminary hearings, and county ordinance violations.

Probate Court 23 E Court St, Rm 422, Washington, GA 30673; 706-678-2523; fax: 706-678-4854; 8:30AM-5PM. ***Probate.***

Wilkinson County

Superior Court PO Box 250, Irwinton, GA 31042; 478-946-2221; fax: 478-946-1497; 8AM-5PM. ***Felony, Misdemeanor, Civil.***

www.gsccca.org/clerks/

Civil Records: Access: In person only. Visitors must perform in person searches themselves. Required to search: name, years to search. Civil cases indexed by defendant, plaintiff, on computer from 1991, on docket books from 1900s. Civil PAT goes back to 1991.

Criminal Records: Access: In person only. Visitors must perform in person searches themselves. Required to search: name, years to search, DOB. Criminal records computerized from 1991, on docket books from 1900s. Criminal PAT goes back to 1991.

General Information: No juvenile, adoption, sexual, mental health or expunged records released. Will fax documents $5.00 plus $1.00 per page. Court makes copy: $1.00 per page. Self serve: $.25 per page. Certification fee: $2.50 per doc plus $.50 per page after 1st. Payee: Superior Court Clerk. Personal checks accepted; credit cards are not. Prepayment required.

Magistrate & Probate Court PO Box 201, 100 Bacon St, Irwinton, GA 31042; 478-946-2222/2439; fax: 478-946-3810; 8AM-5PM. ***Civil Actions under $15,000, Eviction, Small Claims, Probate.***

www.wilkinsoncourt.com

Court also has jurisdiction for bad checks, arrest warrants, preliminary hearings, and county ordinance violations.

Worth County

Superior & State Court 201 N Main St, Rm 13, Sylvester, GA 31791; 229-776-8205; criminal fax: 229-776-8237; civil fax: same; 8AM-5PM. ***Felony, Misdemeanor, Civil.***

Small Claims is in Magistrate Court.

Civil Records: Access: In person only. Visitors must perform in person searches themselves. Required to search: name, years to search. Civil cases indexed by defendant, plaintiff, computerized since 1995, on books since 1880, real estate records from 9/93. Civil PAT goes back to 1995.

Criminal Records: Access: In person only. Visitors must perform in person searches themselves. Required to search: name, years to search; SSN helpful. Criminal records computerized since 1995. Criminal PAT goes back to same as civil.

General Information: No juvenile, adoption, sexual, mental health or expunged records released. Will not fax out case files. Court makes copy: $1.00 per page. Self serve: $.25 per page. Certification fee: $2.50 1st page, $.50 each add'l. Payee: Superior Court Clerk. No personal checks or credit cards accepted. Prepayment required.

Magistrate Court PO Box 64, 201 N Main St, Rm 21, Sylvester, GA 31791; 229-776-8210; fax: 229-776-8245; 9AM-5PM except TH 9AM-N. ***Civil Actions under $15,000, Eviction, Small Claims.***

Probate Court 201 N Main St, Rm 12, Courthouse, Sylvester, GA 31791; 229-776-8207; fax: 229-776-1540; 8AM-5PM. ***Probate, Marriage.***

Georgia Recording Offices

ORGANIZATION: 159 counties, 159 recording offices. The recording officer is the Clerk of Superior Court. All transactions are recorded in a "General Execution Docket." Georgia is in the Eastern Time Zone (EST).

REAL ESTATE RECORDS: Most counties will not perform real estate searches. Copy fees are usually $.25 per page if you make it and $1.00 per page if the office makes it. Certification fees are usually $2.00-$2.50 per document - $1.00 for seal and $1.00 for stamp - plus $.50 per page.

UCC RECORDS: Only a few counties will perform local UCC searches. Use search request form UCC-11 for local searches. UCC copy fee is same as Real Estate Records.

TAX LIEN RECORDS: All tax liens on personal property are filed with the county Clerk of Superior Court in a "General Execution Docket" (grantor/grantee) or "Lien Index." Counties will not perform tax lien searches.

OTHER LIENS: Judgments, divorce-related judgments, hospital, materialman, county tax, lis pendens, child support, labor, mechanics.

ONLINE ACCESS: The Georgia Superior Court Clerk's Cooperative Authority (GSCCCA) at www.gsccca.org/search offers free access to a number of state indices. The Real Estate Index contains property transactions from all counties since January 1, 1999. The Lien Index includes liens filed on real and personal property. Throughput varies, but is generally from January 10, 2002. The UCC Index contains financing statement data from all counties since January, 1995 and can be searched by name, taxpayer ID, file date and file number. Additionally, the actual image of the corresponding UCC statement can be downloaded for a fee. Visit the GSCCCA website for details.

Appling County

County Superior Court Clerk, PO Box 269, Baxley, GA 31513. 912-367-8126; fax-912-367-8180; 8AM-5PM (EST)
Index: All in one. Records indexed on public terminal from 2004. Only the public may search. Copy fee $.25; real estate $.50 per page. Cert fee- $2.50 per cert plus copy fee. Payee- Appling County Clerk of Superior Court. **Online access to RE Deed, UCC, Lien, Notary, Plat records:** See www.gsccca.org for free access to Deeds back to 1999, Liens back to 2004, and UCCs back to 1995, plats back to 2004. **Other phones:** Treasurer- 912-367-8100. **Property tax/Assessing**- 69 Tippin St, #101, Baxley, GA 31513; 912-367-8109, Fax: 912-367-8183. Public use computer in office for index and records searches.

Atkinson County

County Superior Court Clerk, PO Box 6, Pearson, GA 31642. 912-422-3343; fax-912-422-7025; 8AM-5PM
Index: All in one. Records indexed on public terminal from 1998. Only the public may search. Copy fee $.25 per page. Cert fee- $2.50 per cert includes copy fee. Payee- Atkinson County Clerk of Superior Court. **Online access to RE Deed, UCC, Lien, Notary, Plat records:** See www.gsccca.org for free access to Deeds back to 1999, Liens back to 2004, and UCCs back to 1995, plats back to 2004. **Other phones:** Elections- 912-422-3552; Vital Records- 912-422-3552. **Property tax/Assessing**- PO Box 795, 19 Roberts Ave W, Pierson, GA 31642; 912-422-7382, Fax: 912-422-6555.

Bacon County

County Superior Court Clerk, PO Box 376, Alma, GA 31510. Recording, R/E & UCC phone-912-632-4915; fax-912-632-6545; 9AM-5PM (EST)
Index: Separate indices to search include real estate and liens. Records indexed on public terminal from 1995. Only the public may search. Will not search UCC records. Copy fee $1.00 per page.Real estate or tax lien copy- $.25 per page. Cert fee- $2.00 per doc, $.50 per page includes copy fee. Payee- Bacon County Clerk of Superior Court. Office does not sell bulk data. **Online access to RE Deed, UCC, Lien, Notary, Plat records:** See www.gsccca.org for free access to Deeds back to 1999, Liens back to 2004, and UCCs back to 1995, plats back to 2004. **Other phones:** Treasurer- 912-632-5214; Elections- 912-632-5551; Vital Records- 912-632-7661. **Property tax/Assessing**- PO Box 461, 502 W 12th S, Alma, GA 31510; 912-632-5215, Fax: 912-632-7251. **Online access**- Access assessor property and sales data free at http://qpublic.net/ga/bacon/.

Baker County

County Superior Court Clerk, PO Box 10, Newton, GA 39870. 229-734-3004; fax-229-734-7770; 9AM-5PM (EST)
Index: All in one. Records indexed on public terminal from 1998. Only the public may search. Copy fee $1.00 per page; self serve- $.25 each. Will fax back $1.00 per page (prepaid). Cert fee- $2.00 per cert plus copy fee. Payee- Baker County Clerk of Superior Court. **Online access to RE Deed, UCC, Lien, Notary, Plat records:** See www.gsccca.org for free access to Deeds back to 1999, Liens back to 2004, and UCCs back to 1995, plats back to 2004. **Property tax/Assessing**- PO Box 52, 167 Baker Pl, Newton, GA 39870; 229-734-3012, Fax: 229-734-3021. hours-8AM-5PM Public access computer available.

Baldwin County

County Superior Court Clerk, PO Drawer 987, Milledgeville, GA 31059. 478-445-4007, R/E recording phone-478-445-4008, UCC recording phone-478-445-5391; fax-478-445-6039; 8:30AM-5PM (EST) www.baldwincountyga.com
Index: Separate indices to search include deeds to 1986 on computer; liens to 2004 on computer. Records indexed on public terminal from 1986. Only the public may search. Will not search UCC records. Copy fee $.25 per page. Fax back- $1.00 per page. Cert fee- $2.50 per cert plus $.50 per page. Payee-Baldwin County Clerk of Superior Court. Office does not sell bulk data. **Online access to RE Deed, UCC, Lien, Notary, Plat records:** See www.gsccca.org for free access to Deeds back to 1999, Liens back to 2004, and UCCs back to 1995, plats back to 2004. **Other phones:** Treasurer- 478-434-4791; Elections-478-445-4526; Vital Records- 478-445-4807; Sheriff-478-445-4893. **Property tax/Assessing**- 121 N Wilkinson St, #114, Milledgeville, GA 31061; 478-453-5300, Fax: 478-445-5019. (Appraiser/Auditor-478-445-5300) **Online access**- Property searching available free at http://baldwinta.com/

Banks County

County Superior Court Clerk, 144 Yonah Homer Rd, #8, Homer, GA 30547-2614. Recording, R/E & UCC phone-706-677-6243, UCC recording phone-706-677-6248; fax-706-677-6294; 8AM-5PM (EST)
Index: Separate indices to search. Records indexed on public terminal from 1993. Only the public may search. Copy fee $1.00 per page. Cert fee- $3.75 per doc, $.50 per page. Payee- Banks County Clerk of Superior Court. Bulk data available for purchase, contact Tim Harper. **Online access to RE Deed, UCC, Lien, Notary, Plat records:** See www.gsccca.org for free access to Deeds back to 1999, Liens back to 2004, and UCCs back to 1995, plats back to 2004. **Other phones:** Treasurer- 706-677-6200; Elections- 706-677-6250; Vital Records-706-677-6258. **Property tax/Assessing**- 144 Yonah Homer Rd, #6, Homer, GA 30547; 706-677-6223, Fax: 706-677-6218. **Online access**- Access assessor property data free on the GIS-mapping site search page at www.bankscountymaps.com/reports/searchmenu.cfm.

Barrow County

County Superior Court Clerk, PO Box 1280, Winder, GA 30680. Recording, R/E & UCC phone-770-307-3035; fax-770-867-4800; 8AM-5PM (EST)
Index: Separate indices to search include grantor/grantee, liens. Records indexed on public terminal from 1992. Only the public may search. Copy fee $1.00 per page. Cert fee- $2.50 per doc, $.50 per page. Payee- Barrow County Clerk of Superior Court. **Online access to RE Deed, UCC, Lien, Notary, Plat records:** See www.gsccca.org for free access to Deeds back to 1999, Liens back to 2004, and UCCs back to 1995, plats back to 2004. **Other phones:** Treasurer- 770-307-3106; Elections- 770-307-3110; Vital Records- 770-307-3035. **Property tax/Assessing**- 233 E Broad St, Winder, GA 30680; 770-307-3108. **Online access**- Property searching for Barrow County available free at http://qpublic.net/ga/barrow/

Bartow County

County Superior Court Clerk, 135 W Cherokee Ave, #233, Cartersville, GA 30120. 770-387-5025; fax-770-387-5611; 8AM-5PM (EST)
Alternate fax number- 770-606-2389. Index: Separate indices to search include liens, deeds, civil and criminal, plats; indexed by year and division. Records indexed on public terminal from 1992. Only the public may search. Copy fee $.25 per page. Cert fee-$2.50 1st pg., $.25 each add'l pg plus copy fee. Payee-Bartow County Clerk of Superior Court. **Online**

access to RE Deed, UCC, Lien, Notary, Plat records: See www.gsccca.org for free access to Deeds back to 1999, Liens back to 2004, and UCCs back to 1995, plats back to 2004. **Property tax/Assessing-** 135 W Cherokee Ave, #243B, Cartersville, GA 30120; 770-387-5090, Fax: 770-606-2390. Help number- 770-886-4645. www.bartowga.org/bctaxa/

Ben Hill County

County Superior Court Clerk, PO Box 1104, Fitzgerald, GA 31750-1104. Recording, R/E & UCC phone-229-426-5135; fax-229-426-5487; 8:30AM-4:30PM (EST)
Index: Separate indices to search include recordings, courts. Records indexed on public terminal from 1995. Only the public may search. Copy fee $.25 per page; $1.00 per page if mailed. Cert fee- $1.00 per doc plus copy fee. Payee- Ben Hill County Clerk of Superior Court. **Online access to RE Deed, UCC, Lien, Notary, Plat records:** See www.gsccca.org for free access to Deeds back to 1999, Liens back to 2004, and UCCs back to 1995, plats back to 2004. **Other phones:** Elections- 229-426-5151. **Property tax/Assessing-** 113 S Sheridan St, Fitzgerald, GA 31750; 229-426-5147, Fax: 229-426-5103. hours- 8AM-5PM **Online access-** Free property records search at http://qpublic.net/ga/benhill/

Berrien County

County Superior Court Clerk, 101 E Marion Ave, #3, Nashville, GA 31639. Recording, R/E & UCC phone-229-686-5506; fax-229-543-1032; 8AM-4:30PM
Records indexed on public terminal from 1999. Only the public may search. Copy fee $1.00 per page. Cert fee- $2.50 per doc, $.50 per page includes copy fee. Payee- Berrien County Clerk of Superior Court. **Online access to RE Deed, UCC, Lien, Notary, Plat records:** See www.gsccca.org for free access to Deeds back to 1999, Liens back to 2004, and UCCs back to 1995, plats back to 2004. **Other phones:** Treasurer- 229-686-7461 (Tax Commissioner); Elections- 229-686-5215; Vital Records- 229-686-5213. **Property tax/Assessing-** PO Box 446, Nashville, GA 31639; 229-686-2149, Fax: 229-686-2243. hours- 8AM-5PM Public access computer available. **Online access-** Search property records free at http://qpublic.net/ga/berrien/search.html

Bibb County

County Superior Court Clerk, PO Box 1015, Macon, GA 31202-1015. 478-621-6527; fax-478-621-6033; 8:30AM-5PM (EST) www.co.bibb.ga.us/
Index: All in one. Records indexed on public terminal from 1996. Only the public may search. Copy fee $.25 per page. Cert fee- $2.50 per doc, $.50 per page. Payee- Bibb County Clerk of Superior Court. **Online access to RE Deed, UCC, Lien, Notary, Plat records:** See www.gsccca.org for Deed, Lien and UCC indexes. Also, search land, financing statements and liens on the Superior Court clerk search page for free at http://68.109.200.17/resolution/. **Other phones:** Treasurer- 478-621-6310. **Property tax/Assessing-** 653 2nd St, #1, Macon, GA 31201; 478-742-2254, Fax: 478-742-2839. **Online access-** Free property records search at www.co.bibb.ga.us/TaxA ssessors/index1.html. Also, search for property ownership for free at www.co.bibb.ga.us/engine ering/property/search.htm. Also, search property info at www.co.bibb.ga.us/gisonline/advancedsearch.asp and Ad Valorem tax statements at www.co.bibb.ga.us/TaxBills/Searchpage.asp.

Bleckley County

County Superior Court Clerk, 112 N 2nd, Cochran, GA 31014. 478-934-3210; fax-478-934-6671; 8:30AM-5PM (EST) Index: All in one. Records indexed on public terminal from 1995. Only the public may search. Copy fee $.25 per page. Cert fee- $2.50 1st pg., $.50 add'l page. Payee- Bleckley County Clerk of Superior Court. **Online access to RE Deed, UCC, Lien, Notary, Plat records:** See www.gsccca.org for free access to Deeds back to 1999, Liens back to 2004, and UCCs back to 1995, plats back to 2004. **Other phones:** Treasurer- 478-934-3200. **Property tax/Assessing-** 112 N 2nd St, Cochran, GA 31014; 478-934-3203, Fax: 478-934-3062.

Brantley County

County Superior Court Clerk, PO Box 1067, Nahunta, GA 31553. 912-462-5635, R/E recording phone-912-462-7682; fax-912-462-6247; 8AM-5PM (EST)
Index: Separate indices to search include grantee/grantor, Lien, Plat, Lis Pendens. Records indexed on public terminal from 1993. Only the public may search. Copy fee $1.00 per page. Cert fee- $2.00 per doc, $.50 per page. Payee- Brantley County Clerk of Superior Court. Office does not sell bulk data. **Online access to RE Deed, UCC, Lien, Notary, Plat records:** See www.gsccca.org for free access to Deeds back to 1999, Liens back to 2004, and UCCs back to 1995, plats back to 2004. **Other phones:** Treasurer- 912-462-5256; Elections- 912-462-6159; Vital Records- 912-462-5192. **Property tax/Assessing-** Po Box 22, 117 Brantley, Nahunta, GA 31553; 912-462-5251, Fax: 912-462-5453. hours- 8AM-4:30PM **Online access-** Access county property records free at www.qpublic.net/ga/brantley/.

Brooks County

County Superior Court Clerk, PO Box 630, Quitman, GA 31643. Recording, R/E & UCC phone-229-263-4747; fax-229-263-5050; 8AM-5PM (EST)
Index: Separate indices to search include grantor/grantee real estate, tax liens, GED, hospital liens, federal tax liens. Records indexed on public terminal from 1988. Only the public may search. Copy fee $1.00 per page; self serve- $.25 each. Will fax back $1.00 per page. Cert fee- $2.50 per doc, $.50 add'l page. Payee- Brooks County Clerk of Superior Court. Office does not sell bulk data. **Online access to RE Deed, UCC, Lien, Notary, Plat records:** See www.gsccca.org for free access to Deeds back to 1999, Liens back to 2004, and UCCs back to 1995, plats back to 2004. **Other phones:** Elections- 229-2635567; Vital Records- 229-263-7585. **Property tax/Assessing-** Old Amory Bldg, 610 S Highland Rd, Quitman, GA 31643; 229-263-7920, Fax: 229-263-5125. **Online access-** Property records searching available free at http://qpublic.net/ga/brooks/.

Bryan County

County Superior Court Clerk, PO Box 670, Pembroke, GA 31321. 912-653-3872, R/E recording phone-912-653-3872 option #4; fax-912-653-3805; 8AM-5PM (EST) www.bryancountyga.org
County does NOT do any searches; see the online service. Index: All in one. Records indexed on public terminal from 9/93. Only the public may search. Copy fee $1.00 per page. Cert fee- $2.50 per cert plus copy fee. Payee- Bryan County Clerk of Superior Court. **Online access to RE Deed, UCC, Lien, Notary, Plat records:** See www.gsccca.org for free access to Deeds back to 1999, Liens back to 2004, and UCCs back to 1995, plats back to 2004. **Other phones:** Treasurer- 912-653-3839; Elections- 912-653-3859; Vital Records- 912-653-3856; Tax Commissioner- 912-653-3880. **Property tax/ Assessing-** PO Box 1000, Pembroke, GA 31321; 912-653-3889, Fax: 912-653-3890. (Appraiser - 912-653-3889) **Online access-** Search property tax records free at http://qpublic.net/bryan/search1.html.

Bulloch County

County Superior Court Clerk, 20 Siebald St; Judicial Annex, Statesboro, GA 30458. 912-764-9009; fax-912-764-5953; 8-5 www.bullochtaxassessors.org
Index: All in one. Records indexed on public terminal from 1991. Office personnel or visitors may perform searches. Office will only do limited real estate searches. Copy fee $.25 per page; $.10 each after first 10. Cert fee- $2.50 per cert includes copy fee. Payee- Bulloch County Clerk of Superior Court. Contact county commissioner's office regarding the set-up of bulk data sales. **Online access to RE Deed, UCC, Lien, Notary, Plat records:** See www.gsccca.org for free access to Deeds back to 1999, Liens back to 2004, and UCCs back to 1995, plats back to 2004. **Other phones:** Treasurer- 912-764-6285. **Property tax/Assessing-** 115 N Main St, PO Box 1421, Statesboro, GA 30459-1421; 912-764-2181, Fax: 912-764-3142. **Online access-** Property records searches available at www.qpublic.net/bulloch/. Search by owner name, parcel number, location address, map, or sales.

Burke County

County Superior Court Clerk, PO Box 803, Waynesboro, GA 30830-0803. Recording, R/E & UCC phone-706-554-2279; fax-706-554-7887; 9AM-5PM (EST) www.burkechamber.org/
Index: Separate indices to search include real estate, lien, UCC, plats. Records indexed on public terminal from 1996. Only the public may search. Copy fee $1.00 per page.Real estate or tax lien copy- $.25 per page. Cert fee- $2.50 per doc, $.50 per page plus copy fee. Payee- Burke County Clerk of Superior Court. Office does not sell bulk data. **Online access to RE Deed, UCC, Lien, Notary, Plat records:** See www.gsccca.org for free access to Deeds back to 1999, Liens back to 2004, and UCCs back to 1995, plats back to 2004. **Other phones:** Treasurer- 706-554-2324; Elections- 706-554-7457; Vital Records- 706-554-3000; Tax Commissioner- 706-554-3223. **Property tax/Assessing-** PO Box 46, Waynesboro, Ga 30830; 706-554-2607, Fax: 706-554-1548. (Appraiser/Auditor- 706-554-2607) hours- 8:30AM-5PM **Online access-** Free property records search at http://qpublic.net/ga/burke/.

Butts County

County Superior Court Clerk, PO Box 320, Jackson, GA 30233. 770-775-8215; fax-770-504-1359; 8AM-5PM (EST)
Index: Separate indices to search. Records indexed on public terminal from 1998. Only the public may search. Copy fee $.25 per page. Cert fee- $2.50 per cert plus copy fee. Payee- Butts County Clerk of Superior Court. **Online access to RE Deed, UCC, Lien, Notary, Plat records:** See www.gsccca.org for free access to Deeds back to 1999, Liens back to 2004, and UCCs back to 1995, plats back to 2004. **Other phones:** Treasurer- 770-775-8200; Elections- 770-775-8202; Vital Records- 770-775-8204. **Property tax/Assessing-** 25 W 3rd St, #21, Jackson, GA 30233; 770-775-8207, Fax: 770-775-8249. hours- 8:30AM-4PM Public access computer in office. **Online access-** Free property records search at http://qpublic.net/ga/butts/.

Calhoun County

County Superior Court Clerk, PO Box 69, Morgan, GA 39866. 229-849-2715; fax-229-849-0072; 8AM-5PM (EST) www.calhouncourtclerk.com/
Index: All in one. Records indexed on public terminal from 1996. Office personnel or visitors may perform searches. Search fee $5.00 per name. Office will search real estate records. Will search UCC records. Copy fee $.25 per page. Cert fee- $3.00 per doc plus copy fee. Payee- Calhoun County Clerk of Superior Court. **Online access to RE Deed, UCC, Lien, Notary, Plat records:** See www.gsccca.org for access to Deeds back to 1999, Liens back to 2004, and UCCs back to 1995, plats back to 2004. **Other phones:** Treasurer- 229-849-2970; Elections- 229-849-2972; Vital Records- 229-849-2115; Tax Assessor- 229-849-4685. **Property tax/Assessing-** Courthouse Sq, Morgan, GA 39866; 229-849-4685, Fax: 229-849-0072. hours- 8AM-N; 1-5PM **Online access-** Property records for free at www.qpublic.net/ga/calhoun/.

Camden County

County Superior Court Clerk, PO Box 550, Woodbine, GA 31569-0550. 912-576-5631; fax-912-576-5648; 9AM-5PM (EST)

Index: All in one. Records indexed on public terminal from 1989. Only the public may search. Copy fee $.25 per page. Cert fee- $2.50 1st pg, $.50 each add'l. Payee- Camden County Clerk of Superior Court. **Online access to RE Deed, UCC, Lien, Notary, Plat records:** See www.gsccca.org for free access to Deeds back to 1999, Liens back to 2004, and UCCs back to 1995, plats back to 2004. **Other phones:** Treasurer- 912-576-5601. **Property tax/Assessing**- PO Box 939, 207 E 2nd St, Woodbine, GA 31569; 912-576-3241, Fax: 912-576-3014. Public access terminal available. **Online access**- Search property data free at www.camdencountymaps.com/.

Candler County

County Superior Court Clerk, PO Drawer 830, Metter, GA 30439. 912-685-5257; fax-912-685-2946; 8:30AM-5PM (EST)
Index: All in one. Records indexed on public terminal from 1997. Only the public may search. Copy fee $.25; tax lien or real estate $1.00 per page. Cert fee- $2.50 per doc, $.50 per page. Payee- Candler County Clerk of Superior Court. **Online access to RE Deed, UCC, Lien, Notary, Plat records:** See www.gsccca.org for free access to Deeds back to 1999, Liens back to 2004, and UCCs back to 1995, plats back to 2004. **Other phones:** Elections- 912-685-6687; Clerk of Court- 912-685-5257. **Property tax/Assessing**- Board of Tax Assessors, 35 SW Broad St, Courthouse Sq, Metter, GA 30439; 912-685-6346, Fax: 912-685-3818. (Appraiser/Auditor- 912-685-6346) No public access terminal. www.candlertax.org/ **Online access**- Access property records free at www.candlertax.org/.

Carroll County

County Superior Court Clerk, PO Box 1620, Carrollton, GA 30112. Recording, R/E & UCC phone-770-830-5830; fax-770-214-3584; 8AM-5PM (EST) www.carrollcountyga.com/
Index: Separate indices to search. Records indexed on public terminal from 1965 for deeds, 1994 for liens/plats. Office will perform a UCC search but public must search other records themselves. Copy fee $1.00 per page; plats- $2.00. Cert fee- $2.50 per cert plus copy fee. Payee- Carroll County Clerk of Superior Court. Office does not sell bulk data. **Online access to RE Deed, UCC, Lien, Notary, Plat records:** See www.gsccca.org for free access to Deeds back to 1999, Liens back to 2004, and UCCs back to 1995, plats back to 2004. **Other phones:** Treasurer- 770-830-5801; Elections- 770-830-5823; Vital Records- 770-836-6667. **Property tax/Assessing**- 423 College St, PO Box 338, Carrollton, GA 30112; 770-830-5812, Fax: 770-830-5810. (Appraiser/Auditor- 770-830-5812) **Online access**- Free property records search at http://qpublic.net/ga/carroll/

Catoosa County

County Superior Court Clerk, 875 Lafayette St; Courthouse, Ringgold, GA 30736. 706-935-4231; fax-none; 8:30AM-5PM (EST)
Index: All in one. Records indexed on a public use terminal back ten years. Only the public may search. Will not search UCC records. Copy fee $1.00 per page. Cert fee- $2.50 per doc, $.50 per page, includes copy fee. Payee- Catoosa County Clerk of Superior Court. **Online access to RE Deed, UCC, Lien, Notary, Plat records:** See www.gsccca.org for free access to Deeds back to 1999, Liens back to 2004, and UCCs back to 1995, plats back to 2004. **Other phones:** Treasurer- 706-935-2500. **Property tax/Assessing**- 798 Lafayette St, Ringgold, GA 30736; 706-965-3772.

Charlton County

County Superior Court Clerk, PO Box 760, Folkston, GA 31537. 912-496-2354; fax-912-496-3882; 8AM-5PM (EST) www.charltoncoc.com
Index: All in one. Records indexed on a public use terminal. Only the public may search. Copy fee $.25 per page. Cert fee- $2.50 per doc, plus $.25 per page, plus copy fee. Payee- Charlton County Clerk of Superior Court. **Online access to RE Deed, UCC, Lien, Notary, Plat records:** See www.gsccca.org for free access to Deeds back to 1999, Liens back to 2004, and UCCs back to 1995, plats back to 2004. **Property tax/Assessing**- 100 N 3rd St, Folskton, GA 31537; 912-496-7437.

Chatham County

County Superior Court Clerk, PO Box 10227, Savannah, GA 31412. Recording, R/E & UCC phone-912-652-7214; UCC recording phone-912-652-7219; fax-912-652-7380; 8AM-5PM (EST) www.chathamcourts.org
Index: Separate indices to search include civil, criminal, real estate, liens. Records indexed on public terminal from 1990. Only the public may search. Copy fee $.25 per page. Cert fee- $2.00 per doc + $.50 per page. Payee- Chatham County Clerk of Superior Court. Office does not sell bulk data. **Online access to RE Deed, UCC, Lien, Notary, Plat records:** See www.gsccca.org for free access to Deeds back to 1999, Liens back to 2004, and UCCs back to 1995, plats back to 2004. **Other phones:** Elections- 912-652-7494; Vital Records- 912-356-2108. **Property tax/Assessing**- 912-652-7127. **Online access**- Search the assessor database free at www.chathamcounty.org/prc.html.

Chattahoochee County

County Superior Court Clerk, PO Box 120, Cusseta, GA 31805-0120. Recording, R/E & UCC phone-706-989-3424; fax-706-989-1508; 8AM-5PM (EST)
Index: All in one. Records indexed on computer back to 1993. Only the public may search. Copy fee $.25 per page. Cert fee- $2.50 per cert plus $.50 each add'l page. Exemplified copies $5.00. Payee- Chattahoochee County Clerk of Superior Court. Office does not sell bulk data. **Online access to RE Deed, UCC, Lien, Notary, Plat records:** See www.gsccca.org for free access to Deeds back to 1999, Liens back to 2004, and UCCs back to 1995, plats back to 2004. **Other phones:** Elections- 706-989-3602; Vital Records- 706-989-3603. **Property tax/Assessing**- PO Box 192, 377 Broad St, Cusseta, GA 31805; 706-989-3249, Fax: 706-989-2013. **Online access**- Access county property data on the GIS-mapping site free at http://webmap.jws.com/chattahoochee/.

Chattooga County

County Superior Court Clerk, PO Box 159, Summerville, GA 30747. 706-857-0706; fax-706-857-0686; 8:30AM-5PM (EST)
Index: All in one. Records indexed on public terminal from 1990. Only the public may search. Copy fee $.25 per page. Cert fee- $2.00 per doc, $.50 per page. Payee- Chattooga County Clerk of Superior Court. Office does not sell bulk data. **Online access to RE Deed, UCC, Lien, Notary, Plat records:** See www.gsccca.org for free access to Deeds back to 1999, Liens back to 2004, and UCCs back to 1995, plats back to 2004. **Other phones:** Treasurer- 706-857-0703. **Property tax/Assessing**- 120 Cox St, PO Box 517, Summerville, GA 30747; 706-857-0737, Fax: 706-857-0748. **Online access**- Free county property records search at http://qpublic.net/ga/chattooga/.

Cherokee County

County Superior Court Clerk, 90 North St, #G-170, Canton, GA 30114. 678-493-6511, R/E recording phone-678-493-6536, UCC recording phone-678-493-6524; fax-770-479-0467; 8AM-5PM (EST) www.cherokeega.com
Index: Separate indices to search include real estate, liens, plats, hospital liens. Records indexed on public terminal from 1988. Only the public may search. Copy fee $1.00 per page. Cert fee- $2.50 per doc, $.50 per page, plus copy fee. Payee- Cherokee County Clerk of Superior Court. Office does not sell bulk data. **Online access to Real Estate, Grantor/Grantee, Deed, Lien, UCC, Plat records:** See www.gsccca.org for Deed, Lien and UCC indexes. Also, access recording records free at http://deeds.cherokeega.com/Search.aspx. **Other phones:** Elections- 770-479-0407; Vital Records- 678-493-6160; Tax Assessor- 678-493-6120. **Property tax/Assessing**- 100 North St, Ste G-20, Canton, GA 30114; 678-493-6120, Fax: 678-493-6125. (Appraiser/Auditor- 678-493-6140) www.cherokeega.com/ccweb/departments/assessor/ **Online access**- Free property records search from the county Tax Assessor's Database at www.cherokeega.com/ccweb/departments/assessor/

Clarke County

County Superior Court Clerk, PO Box 1805, Athens, GA 30603. 706-613-3190; fax-706-613-3189; 8AM-5PM (EST) http://athensclarke.allclerks.us
Is unified with Athens City to form Athens-Clarke County. Index: Separate indices to search include deeds, liens, plats, civil and criminal. Records indexed on public terminal from 1993. Only the public may search. Copy fee $1.00 per page, $.25 self serve. Cert fee- $2.50 1st page plus $.50 each add'l page includes copy fee. Payee- Clerk of Superior Court. **Online access to RE Deed, UCC, Lien, Notary, Plat records:** See www.gsccca.org for free access to Deeds back to 1999, Liens back to 2004, and UCCs back to 1995, plats back to 2004. **Other phones:** Treasurer- 706-613-3040. **Property tax/Assessing**- 325 E Washington, Rm 280, Athens, GA 30601; 706-613-3140, Fax: 706-613-3143. **Online access**- View property data for free at https://athens-clarke.ga.ezgov.com/ezproperty/revie w_search.jsp but no name searching.

Clay County

County Superior Court Clerk, PO Box 550, Fort Gaines, GA 39851-0550. 229-768-2631; fax-229-768-3047; 8AM-4:30PM www.claycountyga.org/
Index: All in one. Records indexed on computer back to 1990. Only the public may search. Copy fee $1.00 per page. Cert fee- $3.00 1st pg, $.50 each add'l, includes copy fee. Payee- Clay County Clerk of Superior Court. Office does not sell bulk data. **Online access to RE Deed, UCC, Lien, Notary, Plat records:** See www.gsccca.org for free access to Deeds back to 1999, Liens back to 2004, and UCCs back to 1995, plats back to 2004. **Other phones:** Treasurer- 229-768-3238; Elections- 229-768-2445; Vital Records- 229-768-2445; Tax Commissioner- 229-768-2915. **Property tax/Assessing**- PO Box 218, Fort Gaines, GA 39851; 229-768-2000, Fax: 229-768-2710. **Online access**- Free property records search at http://qpublic.net/ga/clay/

Clayton County

County Superior Court Clerk, 9151 Tara Blvd, Rm 202, Jonesboro, GA 30236. Recording, R/E & UCC phone-770-477-3395; fax-770-477-3490; 8AM-5PM www.co.clayton.ga.us/superior_court/clerk_of_courts
Index: Separate indices to search include GED, Real Estate and hospital. Records indexed on public terminal from 1993. Only the public may search. Office will search UCC records if customer has file number, records from 1992 to present. Copy fee $1.00 per page, $.25 self serve.Real estate or tax lien copy- $.25 per page. Cert fee- $2.00 per doc, $.50 per page includes copy fee. Payee- Clayton County Clerk of Superior Court. **Online access to RE Deed, UCC, Lien, Notary, Plat records:** See www.gsccca.org for free access to Deeds back to 1999, Liens back to 2004, and UCCs back to 1995, plats back to 2004. **Other phones:** Tax Commissioner- 770-477-3311; Probate Court -770-477-3301;. **Property tax/Assessing**- 121 S. McDonough St, 2nd Fl, PK Dixon Annex 2, Jonesboro, GA 30236; 770-477-3285; 447-3395, Fax: 770-477-4566. www.co.clayton.ga.us/tax_assessor/index.htm **Online access**- Search tax assessor records for free at www.qpublic.net/clayton/search.html. Also, search property card index free at http://weba.co.clayton.ga.us:8003/indextax.shtml.

Clinch County

County Superior Court Clerk, PO Box 433, Homerville, GA 31634. 912-487-5854; fax-912-487-3083; 8AM-5PM (EST)
Index: All in one. Records indexed on a public use terminal. Only the public may search. Copy fee $.25 per page. Cert fee- $2.50 per doc includes copy fee. Payee- Clinch County Clerk of Superior Court. **Online access to RE Deed, UCC, Lien, Notary, Plat records:** See www.gsccca.org for free access to Deeds back to 1999, Liens back to 2004, and UCCs back to 1995, plats back to 2004. **Other phones:** Elections- 912-487-3656. **Property tax/Assessing-** Appraiser, 25 Court Sq, #D, Homeville, GA 31634; 912-487-2561, Fax: 912-487-3083. (Appraiser/Auditor- 912-487-2561) **Online access-** Access to property data is free on the property records site at www.qpublic.net/ga/clinch/.

Cobb County

County Superior Court Clerk, PO Box 3490, Marietta, GA 30061. 770-528-1363; fax-770-528-1325; 8AM-5PM www.cobbsuperiorcourtclerk.org/index.htm
Index: All in one. Records indexed on public terminal from 1991. Only the public may search. Copy fee $1.00 per page; Self serve- $.25 per page. A computer printout is $2.50. Cert fee- $2.00 plus $.50 per pagel. Payee- Cobb County Clerk of Superior Court. Maps, title data, monuments data available from GIS-mapping dept. **Online access to Real Estate, Grantor/Grantee, Deed, Lien UCC records:** Property records on the County Superior Court Clerk website are free at www.cobbsuperiorcourtclerk.org/home.asp. Search by name, address, land description, instrument type, or book & page; includes court records. Also, see www.gsccca.org for online access to Deed, Plat and UCC indexes. **Other phones:** Treasurer- 770-528-8600. **Property tax/Assessing-** 736 Whitlock Ave, #200, PO Box 649, Marietta, GA 30061; 770-528-3100, Fax: 770-528-3100. **Online access-** Free property tax records search at www.cobbtax.org/Forms/HtmlFrame.aspx?mode=content/mainpage_taxes.htm. Also, search for parcel data on the GIS-mapping site free at http://gis.cobbcountyga.gov/. Click on Launch Online Mapping; no name searching. Also, search Tax Commissioner property tax records for free at www.cobbtax.org/Search/GenericSearch.aspx.

Coffee County

County Superior Court Clerk, 101 S Peterson Ave; Courthouse, Douglas, GA 31533. 912-384-2865, R/E recording phone-912-384-2865 x239; fax-912-393-3252; 8:30AM-5PM (EST)
Index: All in one. Records indexed on public terminal from 1993. Only the public may search. Copy fee $1.00 per page; self serve- $.25 each. Cert fee- $3.00 per cert plus copy fee. Payee- Coffee County Clerk of Superior Court. **Online access to RE Deed, UCC, Lien, Notary, Plat records:** See www.gsccca.org for free access to Deeds back to 1999, Liens back to 2004, and UCCs back to 1995, plats back to 2004. **Other phones:** Treasurer- 912-384-4799; Elections- 912-384-7018; Vital Records- 912-389-4458 (Clerk of Court). **Property tax/Assessing-** 101 S Peterson Ave, Courthouse Annex, #21, Douglas, GA 31533; 912-384-2136, Fax: 912-383-7369. (Appraiser- 912-384-2136) 8AM-5PM http://qpublic.net/ga/coffee/index-boa.html **Online access-** Access assessor data free at http://qpublic.net/ga/coffee/search1.html.

Colquitt County

County Superior Court Clerk, PO Box 2827, Moultrie, GA 31776-2827. 229-616-7420, R/E recording phone-229-616-7063, UCC recording phone-229-616-7420; fax-229-616-7029; 8AM-5PM
Index: All in one. Records indexed on public terminal from 1998. Only the public may search. Copy fee $1.00 per page; self serve- $.25 each. Cert fee- $2.00 per doc, $.50 per page plus copy fee. Payee- Colquitt County Clerk of Superior Court. Office does not sell bulk data. **Online access to RE Deed, UCC, Lien, Notary, Plat records:** See www.gsccca.org for free access to Deeds back to 1999, Liens back to 2004, and UCCs back to 1995, plats back to 2004. **Other phones:** Elections- 229-616-7056. **Property tax/Assessing-** 101 E Central Ave, PO Box 880, Moultrie, GA 31776; 229-616-7425, Fax: 229-616-7428. **Online access-** Free property records search at http://qpublic.net/ga/colquitt/

Columbia County

County Superior Court Clerk, PO Box 2930, Evans, GA 30809. 706-312-7139; fax-706-312-7152; 8AM-5PM (EST) http://columbiacountyga.gov
Index: All in one. Records indexed on public terminal from 1996. Only the public may search. Copy fee $1.00 per page; self serve- $.25 each. Cert fee- $2.00 per doc, $.50 per page plus copy fee. Payee- Columbia County Clerk of Superior Court. Office does not sell bulk data. **Online access to RE Deed, UCC, Lien, Notary, Plat records:** See www.gsccca.org for free access to Deeds back to 1999, Liens back to 2004, and UCCs back to 1995, plats back to 2004. **Property tax/Assessing-** 630 Ronald Reagan Dr, PO Box 498, Evans, GA 30809; 706-312-7474, Fax: 706-312-7476. Tax Commissioner in a separate office- fax is 706-312-1357. http://columbiacountyga.gov **Online access-** GIS Map information and parcel searching available online at www.columbiacountyga.gov. Also, search parcel data free on the mapping site at http://68.216.79.105/columbia/default.htm and click on parcel search.

Cook County

County Superior Court Clerk, 212 N Hutchinson Ave, Adel, GA 31620-2497. Recording, R/E & UCC phone-229-896-7717; 8AM-5PM (EST)
Office only records real estate transactions, not UCC.
Index: Separate indices to search. Records indexed on public terminal from 1993. Only the public may search. Copy fee $1.00 per page; self serve- $.25 each. No faxing. Cert fee- $2.50 per doc, $.50 per page includes copy fee. Payee- Cook County Clerk of Superior Court. **Online access to RE Deed, UCC, Lien, Notary, Plat records:** See www.gsccca.org for free access to Deeds back to 1999, Liens back to 2004, and UCCs back to 1995, plats back to 2004. **Other phones:** Elections- 229-896-3941. **Property tax/Assessing-** 209 N Parrish Ave, Adel, GA 31620; 229-896-3665, Fax: 229-896-3977. hours- 8:30AM-4:30PM **Online access-** Free property records search at http://qpublic.net/ga/cook/

Coweta County

County Superior Court Clerk, 72 Greenville St, Newnan, GA 30263. Recording, R/E & UCC phone-770-254-2690, UCC recording phone-770-254-2696; 8AM-5PM (EST)
Records indexed on public terminal from 1990. Only the public may search. Copy fee $1.00 per page; self serve- $.25 each. Will fax back $1.00 per page. Cert fee- $2.50 1st page, $.50 each add'l. Payee- Coweta County Clerk of Superior Court. **Online access to RE Deed, UCC, Lien, Notary, Plat records:** See www.gsccca.org for free access to Deeds back to 1999, Liens back to 2004, and UCCs back to 1995, plats back to 2004. **Property tax/Assessing-** 37 Perry St, Newnan, GA 30263; 770-254-2680, Fax: 770-254-2649. www.cowetatax.com/ **Online access-** Access to property records at www.cowetatax.com/.

Crawford County

County Superior Court Clerk, PO Box 1037, Roberta, GA 31078-1037. Recording, R/E & UCC phone-478-836-3328; 9AM-5PM (EST)
Index: Separate indices to search include grantor/grantee, liens. Records indexed on public terminal from 1999. Only the public may search. Copy fee $1.00 per page; $.25 self serve. Cert fee- $2.50 per doc plus $1.00 per page includes copy fee. Payee- Crawford County Clerk of Superior Court. **Online access to RE Deed, UCC, Lien, Notary, Plat records:** See www.gsccca.org for free access to Deeds back to 1999, Liens back to 2004, and UCCs back to 1995, plats back to 2004. **Other phones:** Treasurer- 478-836-3575; Elections- 478-836-1877; Vital Records- 478-836-3313. **Property tax/Assessing-** PO Box 1054, Roberta, GA 31078; 478-836-2800, Fax: 478-836-2229. (Appraiser/Auditor- 478-836-2800) **Online access-** Access GIS-mapping system free at www.crawfordcountymaps.com.

Crisp County

County Superior Court Clerk, PO Box 747, Cordele, GA 31010-0747. Recording, R/E & UCC phone-229-276-2616; fax-229-273-5750; 8:30AM-5PM (EST)
Index: All in one. Records indexed on public terminal from 1979 for criminal and 1981 for civil. Only the public may search. Copy fee $1.00 per page; $.25 self serve. Cert fee- $2.50 1st pg, $.50 each add'l includes copy fee. Payee- Crisp County Clerk of Superior Court. **Online access to RE Deed, UCC, Lien, Notary, Plat records:** See www.gsccca.org for free access to Deeds back to 1999, Liens back to 2004, and UCCs back to 1995, plats back to 2004. **Other phones:** Treasurer- 229-276-2672; Elections- 229-276-2611; Tax Commissioner- 229-276-2630. **Property tax/Assessing-** 210 S 7th St, Rm 301, Cordele, GA 31015; 229-276-2635, Fax: 229-276-2637. (Appraiser/Auditor- 229-276-2635) **Online access-** Access assessor data free at http://qpublic.net/ga/crisp/.

Dade County

County Superior Court Clerk, PO Box 417, Trenton, GA 30752. Recording, R/E & UCC phone-706-657-4778; fax-706-657-8284; 8:30AM-5PM (EST) www.dadegaclerkofcourt.com
Index: Separate indices to search include deeds, liens, courts. Records indexed on public terminal from 1992. Only the public may search. Copy fee $1.00 per page. Cert fee- $2.00 per doc, $.50 per page, plus copy fee. Payee- Dade County Clerk of Superior Court. Office does not sell bulk data. **Online access to RE Deed, UCC, Lien, Notary, Plat records:** See www.gsccca.org for Deed, Lien and UCC indexes. Attorney access to clerk records is available at www.dadeclerkofcourt.com. Calendars are also available. **Other phones:** Treasurer- 706-657-4625; Elections- 706-657-4414; Vital Records- 706-657-4414; Tax Commission- 706-657-7563. **Property tax/Assessing-** PO Box 421, 71 Case Ave, Trenton, GA 30752; 706-657-6341, Fax: 706-657-5109. (Appraiser/Auditor- 706-657-6341)

Dawson County

County Superior Court Clerk, 25 Tucker Ave, #106, Dawsonville, GA 30534-0222. 706-344-3510, R/E recording phone-706-344-3510 x229, UCC recording phone-706-344-3510 x225; fax-706-344-3511; 8AM-5PM (EST) www.dawsoncounty.org
Index: Separate indices to search. Records indexed on public terminal from 1987. Office will perform a UCC search but public must search other records themselves. Office will search real estate records (computer search only). Office will search UCC records on computer only. Copy fee $.25 per page. Cert fee- $2.50 per doc, $.25 per page, plus copy fee. Payee- Dawson County Clerk of Superior Court. **Online access to RE Deed, UCC, Lien, Notary, Plat records:** See www.gsccca.org for free access to Deeds back to 1999, Liens back to 2004, and UCCs back to 1995, plats back to 2004. **Other phones:** Elections- 706-344-3640; Civil Phone- x261; Criminal Phone -X228;. **Property tax/Assessing-** 78 E Howard Ave, #120, Dawsonville, GA 30534; 706-344-3590 x236, Fax: 706-344-1342. www.dawsontaxassessors.org **Online access-** Search the assessor property data and sales for free at www.qpublic.net/ga/dawson/search1.html. Also, access county property data for free at www.dawsontaxassessors.org/.

De Kalb County

Clerk of Superior Court, 556 N McDonough St; Courthouse, Ground Fl, Judicial Annex, Decatur, GA 30030. 404-371-2836, R/E recording phone-404-371-2836 x3741, UCC recording phone-404-371-2836 x3735; fax-404-371-2111; 7:30AM-6PM (EST) www.co.dekalb.ga.us/

Index: Index for each year; separate indices to search include deed, lien, UCC, suits. Records indexed on public terminal from 1978. Only the public may search. Self serve copies- $.25 per page. Cert fee- $2.50 per doc, $.50 per page includes copy fee. Payee- De Kalb County Clerk of Superior Court. Office does not sell bulk data. **Online access to Real Estate, Deed, UCC records:** See www.gsccca.org for Deed and UCC indexes. **Property tax/Assessing**- Property Appraisal Dept, 120 W Trinity Pl, #208, Decatur, GA 30030; 404-371-2781, Fax: 404-371-2791. https://dklbweb.dekalbga.org/TaxAssessor/ **Online access**- Search real estate data for free at https://dklbweb.dekalbga.org/TaxAssessor/realSearch.asp. No name searching. Search tax commissioner property tax data for free at https://dklbweb.dekalbga.org/taxcommissioner/search.asp. No name searching.

Decatur County

County Superior Court Clerk, PO Box 336, Bainbridge, GA 39818. Recording, R/E & UCC phone-229-248-3025; fax-229-248-3029; 8AM-5PM

Index: Separate indices to search include liens, UCCs, real estate. Records indexed on public terminal from 1995 (UCC). Only the public may search. Copy fee $.25 per page. Cert fee- $2.50 per doc, $.50 per page includes copy fee. Payee- Decatur County Clerk of Superior Court. Office does not sell bulk data. **Online access to RE Deed, UCC, Lien, Notary, Plat records:** See www.gsccca.org for free access to Deeds back to 1999, Liens back to 2004, and UCCs back to 1995, plats back to 2004. **Other phones:** Treasurer- 229-248-3030; Elections- 229-248-2087; Vital Records- 229-248-3055; Tax Commissioner- 229-248-3021. **Property tax/Assessing**- PO Box 1106, Bainbridge, GA 39818; 229-248-3008, Fax: 229-248-3053. (Appraiser/Auditor- 229-248-3008) **Online access**- Search the assessor property data and sales for free at www.qpublic.net/ga/decatur/.

Dodge County

County Superior Court Clerk, PO Box 4276, Eastman, GA 31023-4276. 478-374-2871; fax-478-374-3035; 9AM-5PM (EST)

Index: All in one. Records indexed on public terminal from 1992. Office will perform a UCC search but public must search other records themselves. Copy fee $1.00 per page; self serve- $.25 each. Will fax back $2.00 1st page, $1.00 each add'l. Cert fee- $2.50 per doc, plus $.50 per page. Payee- Dodge County Clerk of Superior Court. **Online access to RE Deed, UCC, Lien, Notary, Plat records:** See www.gsccca.org for free access to Deeds back to 1999, Liens back to 2004, and UCCs back to 1995, plats back to 2004. **Other phones:** Treasurer- 478-374-3775; Elections- 478-378-8123; Vital Records- 478-374-3775. **Property tax/Assessing**- 5018 Courthouse Circle, #201, Eastman, GA 31023; 478-374-8122, Fax: 478-374-4791. **Online access**- Search the assessor property data and sales for free at www.qpublic.net/ga/dodge/.

Dooly County

County Superior Court Clerk, PO Box 326, Vienna, GA 31092-0326. Recording, R/E & UCC phone-229-268-4234; fax-229-268-1427; 8:30AM-5PM (EST)

Index: All in one. Records indexed on public terminal from 1995. Only the public may search. Copy fee $1.00 per page; self serve- $.25 each. Cert fee- $2.50 per doc, $1.00 per page plus copy fee. Payee- Dooly County Clerk of Superior Court. **Online access to RE Deed, UCC, Lien, Notary, Plat records:** See www.gsccca.org for free access to Deeds back to 1999, Liens back to 2004, and UCCs back to 1995, plats back to 2004. **Other phones:** Treasurer- 229-268-4228. **Property tax/Assessing**- 105 W Cotton St, Rm 2, Vienna, GA 31092; 229-268-4719, Fax: 229-268-6849. **Online access**- Search the assessor property data and sales for free at www.qpublic.net/ga/dooly/.

Dougherty County

County Superior Court Clerk, PO Box 1827, Albany, GA 31701. Recording, R/E & UCC phone-229-431-2198; fax-229-878-3165; 8:30AM-5PM (EST) www.albany.ga.us/court_system/court_clerk.htm

Index: All in one. Records indexed on public terminal from 06/1984. Only the public may search. Copy fee $1.00 per page. Cert fee- $2.00 per doc, $1.00 per page. Payee- Dougherty County Clerk of Superior Court. **Online access to Real Estate, Tax, Court, Deed, Mortgage, UCC, Death, Trade Name records:** Access to the clerk of courts Dept. of Deeds public menu is at www.albany.ga.us/court_system/court_clerk.htm. Click on "Real Estate." Also, see www.gsccca.org for online access to Deed and UCC indexes. **Other phones:** Treasurer- 229-431-2130; Elections- 229-431-3247; Vital Records- 229-431-2102. **Property tax/Assessing**- 240 Pine Ave, PO Box 1827, Albany, GA 31701; 229-431-2130, Fax: 229-438-3997. **Online access**- Search the tax records system and sales lists free at www.qpublic.net/ga/dougherty/.

Douglas County

County Superior Court Clerk, 8700 Hospital Dr; Douglas County Courthouse, Douglasville, GA 30134. 770-920-7252, R/E recording phone-770-920-7257, UCC phone-770-920-7449; 8AM-5PM (EST)

Index: Separate indices to search include real estate, liens, plats, UCCs. Records indexed on public terminal from 1982. Only the public may search. Copy fee $1.00 per page; self serve- $.25 each.Real estate or tax lien copy- $.50 per page. Cert fee- $2.50 1st 2 pages, $.50 each add'l. Payee- Douglas County Clerk of Superior Court. Office does not sell bulk data. **Online access to RE Deed, UCC, Lien, Notary, Plat records:** See www.gsccca.org for free access to Deeds, Liens back to 2004, and UCCs back to 1995, plats back to 2004. **Other phones:** Elections- 770-920-7326; Vital Records- 770-920-7249. **Property tax/Assessing**- 8700 Hospital Dr, Douglas County Courthouse, Douglasville, GA 30134; 770-920-7228, Fax: 770-920-7521. (Appraiser/Auditor- 770-920-7228) www.celebratedouglascounty.com/ **Online access**- Access property data and gis-mapping free at http://douglas.binarybus.com/.

Early County

County Superior Court Clerk, PO Box 849, Blakely, GA 39823. Recording, R/E & UCC phone-229-723-3033; fax-229-723-4411; 8AM-5PM (EST)

Index: All in one. Records indexed on public terminal from 1994. Only the public may search. Copy fee $1.00 per page; self serve- $.25 per page. Cert fee- $2.50 per doc, $.50 per page. Payee- Early County Clerk of Superior Court. Office does not sell bulk data. **Online access to RE Deed, UCC, Lien, Notary, Plat records:** See www.gsccca.org for free access to Deeds back to 1999, Liens back to 2004, and UCCs back to 1995, plats back to 2004. **Other phones:** Treasurer- 229-723-4024. **Property tax/Assessing**- 15157 River St, Blakely, GA 39823; 229-723-3088, Fax: 229-723-8477. **Online access**- Search the assessor property data and sales for free at www.qpublic.net/ga/early/.

Echols County

County Superior Court Clerk, PO Box 213, Statenville, GA 31648. Recording, R/E & UCC phone-229-559-5642; fax-229-559-5792; 8AM-N, 1-4:30PM (EST)

Index: Separate indices to search include Platt, Lien, Deeds. Records indexed on public terminal from 5/24/93. Only the public may search. Copy fee $1.00 per page. $.25 per page if client does copy. Cert fee- $2.50 1st page, $.50 each add'l page includes copy. Payee- Echols County Clerk of Superior Court. **Online access to RE Deed, UCC, Lien, Notary, Plat records:** See www.gsccca.org for free access to Deeds back to 1999, Liens back to 2004, and UCCs back to 1995, plats back to 2004. **Other phones:** Treasurer- 229-559-6538; Elections- 229-559-7526; Vital Records- 229-559-5103; Tax Commissioner- 229-559-5253. **Property tax/Assessing**- PO Box 326, Statenville, GA 31648; 229-559-7370, Fax: 229-559-3842. hours- 8AM-4:30PM closed for lunch **Online access**- Search the assessor property data and sales for free at www.qpublic.net/ga/echols/.

Effingham County

County Superior Court Clerk, 700 N Pine St, #110, Springfield, GA 31329. 912-754-2118 x4, R/E recording phone-912-754-2145, UCC recording phone-912-754-2118; fax-n/a; 8:30AM-5PM (EST) www.effinghamcounty.org/

Index: All in one. Records indexed on public terminal from 1991. Only the public may search. Will not search UCC records. Copy fee $.25 per page. Cert fee- $2.00 per doc, $.50 per page, copies included. Payee- Effingham County Clerk of Superior Court. Office does not sell bulk data. **Online access to RE Deed, UCC, Lien, Notary, Plat records:** See www.gsccca.org for free access to Deeds back to 1999, Liens back to 2004, and UCCs back to 1995, plats back to 2004. **Other phones:** Elections- 912-754-2115; Vital Records- 912-754-2112; Tax Commissioner- 912-754-2121. **Property tax/Assessing**- PO Box 239, Springfield, GA 31329; 912-754-2125, Fax: 912-754-9506. **Online access**- Access assessor and parcel records free at www.qpublic.net/ga/effingham/search.html. Also, search assessment and property records free at www.qpublic.net/ga/effingham/search.html. Access to GIS/mapping free at www.effinghamcounty.org/Departments/GIS/CountyMaps/tabid/1573/Default.aspx.

Elbert County

County Superior Court Clerk, PO Box 619, Elberton, GA 30635. Recording, R/E & UCC phone-706-283-2005; fax-706-213-7286; 8AM-5PM (EST)

Index: Separate indices to search include grantor/grantee. Records indexed on public terminal from 1993. Only the public may search. Copy fee $1.00 per page. Cert fee- $2.00 per doc, $.50 per page plus copy fee. Payee- Elbert County Clerk of Superior Court. Office does not sell bulk data. **Online access to RE Deed, UCC, Lien, Notary, Plat records:** See www.gsccca.org for free access to Deeds back to 1999, Liens back to 2004, and UCCs back to 1995, plats back to 2004. **Other phones:** Treasurer- 706-283-2018; Elections- 706-283-2016; Vital Records- 706-283-2016. **Property tax/Assessing**- 45 Forest Ave, PO Box 602, Elberton, GA 30635; 706-283-2008, Fax: 706-283-2009. www.elbertassessors.com **Online access**- Search property data and sales records free at www.qpublic.net/elbert/search1.html.

Emanuel County

County Superior Court Clerk, PO Box 627, Swainsboro, GA 30401. Recording, R/E & UCC phone-478-237-8911; fax-478-237-1220; 8AM-5PM

Index: All in one. Records indexed on public terminal from 7/94. Only the public may search. Copy fee $.25 per page. Cert fee- $2.50 per doc, $.50 per page includes copy fee. Payee- Emanuel County Clerk of Superior Court. **Online access to RE Deed, UCC, Lien, Notary, Plat records:** See www.gsccca.org for free access to Deeds back to 1999, Liens back to 2004, and UCCs back to 1995, plats back to 2004. **Other phones:** Treasurer- 478-237-3881; Elections- 478-237-3471; Vital Records- 478-237-8918. **Property tax/Assessing**- 101 S Main St, 3rd Fl, Swainsboro, GA 30401; 478-237-1222, Fax: 478-237-9152. **Online access**- Access assessor property/sales data free at http://qpublic.net/ga/emanuel/search1.html

Evans County

County Superior Court Clerk, PO Box 845, Claxton, GA 30417. Recording, R/E & UCC phone-912-739-3868; fax-912-739-2504; 8AM-5PM (EST)

Index: Separate indices to search include UCC, real estate, liens. Records indexed on computer back to 1989. Only the public may search. Copy fee $1.00 per page. Self serve- $.25 per page. Cert fee- $2.00 per doc, $.50 per page; includes copy fee. Payee- Evans County Clerk of Superior Court. **Online access to RE Deed, UCC, Lien, Notary, Plat records:** See www.gsccca.org for free access to Deeds back to 1999, Liens back to 2004, and UCCs back to 1995, plats back to 2004. **Other phones:** Treasurer- 912-739-1147; Elections- 912-739-0708. **Property tax/Assessing**- 2 Freeman St, Claxton, GA 30417; 912-739-3424, Fax: 912-739-3424. **Online access**- Search the assessor property data and sales for free at www.qpublic.net/ga/evans/.

Fannin County

County Superior Court Clerk, PO Box 1300, Blue Ridge, GA 30513. Recording, R/E & UCC phone-706-632-2039; 9AM-5PM www.fannincountyga.org

Index: Separate indices to search include civil, criminal, real estate. Records indexed on public terminal from 1998 for real estate only. Only the public may search. Copy fee $1.00 per page, $.25 self serve. Cert fee- $2.50 per doc, $.50 per page plus copy fee. Payee- Fannin County Clerk of Superior Court. **Online access to RE Deed, UCC, Lien, Notary, Plat records:** See www.gsccca.org for free access to Deeds back to 1999, Liens back to 2004, and UCCs back to 1995, plats back to 2004. **Other phones:** Elections- 706-632-7740; Vital Records- 706-623-3011; Tax Commissioner- 706-632 2645. **Property tax/Assessing**- 400 W Main St, #102, Blue Ridge, GA 30513; 706-632-5954, Fax: 706-632-8753. (Appraiser/Auditor- 706-632-5954) hours- 8AM-5PM **Online access**- Search basic property records free at www.qpublic.net/ga/fannin/. Subscription is required for advanced data.

Fayette County

County Superior Court Clerk, PO Box 130, Fayetteville, GA 30214. 770-716-4290, R/E recording phone-770-716-4291; fax-770-716-4868; 8AM-4:30PM (EST) www.fayetteclerk.com

Index: All in one. Records indexed on public terminal from 1998. Only the public may search. Copy fee $1.00 per page; self serve- $.25 per page. Cert fee- $2.00 per doc, $.50 per page, plus copy fee. Payee- Fayette County Clerk of Superior Court. **Online access to RE Deed, UCC, Lien, Notary, Plat records:** See www.gsccca.org for free access to Deeds back to 1999, Liens back to 2004, and UCCs back to 1995, plats back to 2004. **Other phones:** Tax Commissioner- 770-461-3652. **Property tax/Assessing**- 140 W Stonewall Ave, #108, Fayetteville, GA 30214; 770-305-5402, Fax: 770-719-9230. 8AM-5PM www.fayettecountyga.gov/assessors_office/index.asp **Online access**- Records on the County Assessor database are free on the GIS-mapping site at www.fayettecountymaps.com.

Floyd County

County Superior Court Clerk, PO Box 1110, Rome, GA 30162-1110. Recording, R/E & UCC phone-706-291-5158, UCC recording phone-706-291-5206; fax-706-235-0035; 8AM-5PM (EST)

Index: Separate indices to search include liens, UCCs. Records indexed on public terminal from 10/1984. Only the public may search. Copy fee $1.00 per page.Real estate or tax lien copy- $.50 per page. Cert fee- $2.00 per doc, $.50 per page, plus copy fee. Payee- Floyd County Clerk of Superior Court. **Online access to RE Deed, UCC, Lien, Notary, Plat records:** See www.gsccca.org for free access to Deeds back to 1999, Liens back to 2004, and UCCs back to 1995, plats back to 2004. **Other phones:** Treasurer- 706-291-5148; Elections- 706-291-5168; Tax Office- 706-291-5147. **Property tax/Assessing**- 4 Government Plaza, #10, Rome, GA 30162; 706-291-5143, Fax: 706-291-5284. **Online access**- Access property data via the GIS-mapping site free at http://gis.romega.us/app/. Now has name searching. Access property, taxpayer, and vehicle records free at www.floydcountytax.com/search.aspx.

Forsyth County

County Superior Court Clerk, 100 Courthouse Sq, Rm 010, Cumming, GA 30040. Recording, R/E & UCC phone-770-781-2120, UCC recording phone-770-781-2120 x 2690; fax-770-886-2858; 8:30AM-5PM www.forsythco.com

Index: Separate indices to search include books back to 1832 and computer. Records indexed on a public use terminal; real estate index back to 1980, GED index back to 1991, plats index back to 1961, hospital lien index back to 12/30/03. Only the public may search. Copy fee $.25 per page; UCC page copy- $1.00. Cert fee- $2.50 per doc plus $.50 per page includes copy fee. Payee- Forsyth County Clerk of Superior Court. **Online access to RE Deed, Lien, UCC, Notary, Hospital Lien, Plat, Old Land, Trade Name records:** See www.gsccca.org for free access to Deeds back to 1999, Liens back to 2004, and UCCs back to 1995, plats back to 2004. Also, search land records, liens, plats, and trade names free at http://resolution.forsythco.com/. **Other phones:** Treasurer- 770-781-2110; Elections- 770-781-2118; Vital Records- 770-781-2140. **Property tax/Assessing**- 110 E Main St, #260, Cumming, GA 30040; 770-781-2106, Fax: 678-455-8493. (Appraiser/Auditor- 770-781-2106) www.forsythco.com/department.asp?DeptID=25 **Online access**- Search the county assessor data free at www.qpublic.net/ga/forsyth/search1.html.

Franklin County

County Superior Court Clerk, PO Box 70, Carnesville, GA 30521. Recording, R/E & UCC phone-706-384-2514, UCC recording phone-706-384-4858; fax-706-384-4384; 8AM-5PM (EST) www.franklincountyga.com/modules/news/

Records indexed on public terminal from 1994, Deeds. Only the public may search. Copy fee $1.00 per page.Real estate copy- $.25 per page. Cert fee- $2.50 1st page, $.50 each add'l page. Payee- Franklin County Clerk of Superior Court. **Online access to RE Deed, UCC, Lien, Notary, Plat records:** See www.gsccca.org for free access to Deeds back to 1999, Liens back to 2004, and UCCs back to 1995, plats back to 2004. **Other phones:** Treasurer- 706-384-2483; Elections- 706-384-2403; Vital Records- 706-384-2403. **Property tax/Assessing**- PO Box 10, Carnesville, GA 30521; 706-384-4896, Fax: 706-384-4333. **Online access**- Access assessor property and sales data free at http://qpublic.net/ga/franklin/search1.html. Also, access properrty tax data free at https://franklincounty.paytaxes.net/customer/enhanced_property_tax_search.php.

Fulton County

County Superior Court Clerk, 136 Pryor St, SW, Atlanta, GA 30303. 404-730-5371, R/E recording phone-404-730-5286, UCC recording phone-404-730-5553; 8:30AM-5PM (EST) www.fcclk.org

Index: Separate indices to search include deed, lien, GED, business, notice of commencement, federal tax liens, plats. Records indexed on public terminal from 1980. Only the public may search. Copy fee $1.00 per page; self serve- $.25 each. Cert fee- $2.00 per doc and $.50 per page. Payee- Fulton County Clerk of Superior Court. **Online access to RE Deed, UCC, Lien, Notary, Plat records:** See www.gsccca.org for free access to Deeds back to 1999, Liens back to 2004, and UCCs back to 1995, plats back to 2004. **Other phones:** Tax Lien Records- 404-730-5286; Copy requests -404-730-5286;. **Property tax/Assessing**- 141 Pryor St, #2052, Atlanta, GA 30303; 404-730-6440, Fax: 404-730-6881. **Online access**- Search property data free at www.fultonassessor.org/Main/home.aspx. Click on Property Search, but no name searching. Search tax commissioner delinquent property district lists at https://www.fultoncountytaxes.org/fultoniwr/Delinquent_Properties.htm. Also, search property tax bills at https://www.fultoncountytaxes.org/fultoniwr/11_dept_s_property_taxes.asp but no name searching.

Gilmer County

County Superior Court Clerk, 1 W Side Sq; Courthouse, Ellijay, GA 30540. Recording, R/E & UCC phone-706-635-4462; fax-706-635-1462; 8:30AM-5PM (EST)

Index: All in one. Records indexed on public terminal from 1991. Only the public may search. Copy fee $.25 per page. Cert fee- $2.50 per doc, $.50 per page. Payee- Gilmer County Clerk of Superior Court. **Online access to RE Deed, UCC, Lien, Notary, Plat records:** See www.gsccca.org for free access to Deeds back to 1999, Liens back to 2004, and UCCs back to 1995, plats back to 2004. **Other phones:** Treasurer- 706-635-4361. **Property tax/Assessing**- 163 Dalton St, Ellijay, GA 30540; 706-635-2703, 276-2742, Fax: 706-635-2721. www.gilmerassessors.com/ **Online access**- Access assessor property and sales data free at www.qpublic.net/ga/gilmer/search1.html.

Glascock County

County Superior Court Clerk, PO Box 231, Gibson, GA 30810. Recording, R/E & UCC phone-706-598-2084; fax-706-598-2577; 8AM-5PM M,T,TH, F; 8AM-Noon W. (EST)

Index: Separate indices to search include deeds, criminal. Records indexed on public terminal from 1924. Only the public may search. Copy fee $.25 per page. Cert fee- $2.50 per doc, $.50 per page, includes copy fee. Payee- Glascock County Clerk of Superior Court. **Online access to RE Deed, UCC, Lien, Notary, Plat records:** See www.gsccca.org for free access to Deeds back to 1999, Liens back to 2004, and UCCs back to 1995, plats back to 2004. **Other phones:** Treasurer- 706-598-2671; Elections- 706-598-3241. **Property tax/Assessing**- PO Box 221, 75 E Main St, Gibson, GA 30810; 706-598-2863, Fax: 706-598-2793. **Online access**- Access assessor parcel data free on the Central Savannah River Area GIS site at www.csrardc.org/. Click on Search and choose Glascock. Access to property data free go to www.qpublic.net/ga/glascock/.

Glynn County

County Superior Court Clerk, PO Box 1355, Brunswick, GA 31521-1355. 912-554-7288, R/E recording phone-912-554-7313; fax-912-267-5625; 8:30AM-5PM (EST)

Index: Separate indices to search include Property records, Liens, and Plats. Records indexed on public terminal from 1/1995. Office personnel or visitors may perform searches. Copy fee $.25 per page. Cert fee- $2.50 per doc, $.50 per page, plus copy fee. Payee- Glynn County Clerk of Superior Court. **Online access to RE Deed, UCC, Lien, Notary, Plat records:** See www.gsccca.org for free access to Deeds back to 1999, Liens back to 2004, and UCCs back to 1995, plats back to 2004. **Other phones:** Treasurer- 912-554-7120; Elections- 912-554-7060. **Property tax/Assessing**- 1725 Reynolds St #200, Brunswick, GA 31520; 912-554-7093, Fax: 912-267-5723. hours- 8AM-5PM www.glynncounty.org/index.asp?NID=207 **Online access**- Access the county assessor property tax records free on the GIS mapping site at http://glynn.binarybus.com. Click on Launch Free Standard Viewer. A subscription service also available with deeper data. Search appraisal office tax data free at http://glynn.binarybus.com/tapc/.

Gordon County

County Superior Court Clerk, 100 Wall St, #102; Courthouse, Calhoun, GA 30701. Recording, R/E & UCC phone-706-629-9533; fax-706-629-2139; 8:30AM-5PM (EST) www.gordoncounty.org/

Index: All in one. Records indexed on public terminal from 1997. Only the public may search. Copy fee

$1.00 per page; self serve- $.25 per page.Real estate or tax lien copy- $.50 per page. Cert fee- $2.50 per doc, $.50 per page, plus copy fee. Payee- Gordon County Clerk of Superior Court. **Online access to RE Deed, UCC, Lien, Notary, Plat records:** See www.gsccca.org for free access to Deeds back to 1999, Liens back to 2004, and UCCs back to 1995, plats back to 2004. **Other phones:** Elections- 706-629-7781; Vital Records- 706-629-7314. **Property tax/Assessing**- PO Box 533, 100 Wall St, Calhoun, GA 30701; 706-629-6812, Fax: 706-624-6494. **Online access**- Access property data free at http://gordon.binarybus.com/lookup/. Also, search property tax payment database free at https://gordon.paytaxes.net//customer/enhanced_property_tax_search.php

Grady County

County Superior Court Clerk, 250 N Broad St, Box 8, Cairo, GA 39828. Recording, R/E & UCC phone-229-377-2912; fax-229-377-7078; 8AM-5PM (EST)
Index: All in one. Deed Records indexed on public terminal from 1985. Only the public may search. Will not search UCC records. Copy fee $.25 per page. Cert fee- $2.50 per doc, $.50 per page. Payee- Grady County Clerk of Superior Court. **Online access to RE Deed, UCC, Lien, Notary, Plat records:** See www.gsccca.org for free access to Deeds back to 1999, Liens back to 2004, and UCCs back to 1995, plats back to 2004. **Other phones:** Registrar- 229-377-1897. **Property tax/Assessing**- PO Box 4, 250 N Broad St, Cairo, GA 39828; 229-377-3325, Fax: 229-337-4127.

Greene County

County Superior Court Clerk, 113 N Main St, #109; Courthouse, Greensboro, GA 30642-1107. 706-453-3340; fax-706-453-9179; 8AM-5PM (EST)
Index: All in one. Records indexed on public terminal from 1986. Only the public may search. Copy fee $.25 per page. Cert fee- $2.50 1st page, $.25 each add'l, plus copy fee. Payee- Greene County Clerk of Superior Court. **Online access to RE Deed, UCC, Lien, Notary, Plat records:** See www.gsccca.org for free access to Deeds back to 1999, Liens back to 2004, and UCCs back to 1995, plats back to 2004. **Property tax/Assessing**- 1034 Silver Dr, #102, Greensboro, GA 30642; 706-453-3355, Fax: 706-453-3355.

Gwinnett County

County Superior Court Clerk, PO Box 880, Lawrenceville, GA 30046. Recording, R/E & UCC phone-770-822-8100; 8AM-5PM (EST) www.gwinnettcourts.com/#deeds%7Clandrecords/
Index: Separate indices to search include real property index, court record index. Records indexed on public terminal from 1980. Only the public may search. Will not search UCC records. Copy fee $.25 per page. Cert fee- $2.50 1st page, $.50 per add'l page includes copy fee. Payee- Gwinnett County Clerk of Superior Court. Office does not sell bulk data. **Online access to RE Deed, UCC, Lien, Notary, Plat records:** See www.gsccca.org for free access to Deeds back to 1999, Liens back to 2004, and UCCs back to 1995, plats back to 2004. Also, search for civil court judgments at www.gwinnettcourts.com/home.asp#home/. **Other phones:** Treasurer-770-822-8000; Elections- 770-822-8787; Vital Records- 770-822-8250. **Property tax/Assessing**-75 Langley Dr, Lawrenceville, GA 30045; 770-822-7233, Fax: 770-822-7204. https://ssl.gwinnetttaxcommissioner.com/ **Online access**- Access property, property tax, GIS-mapping, treasurer, assessor data and more free at https://ssl.gwinnetttaxcommissioner.com/Property/Property.aspx. Also search property data and online payments free at https://ssl.gwinnetttaxcommissioner.com/Property/Search.aspx.

Habersham County

County Superior Court Clerk, PO Box 2320, Clarkesville, GA 30523-0039. Recording, R/E & UCC phone-706-754-2923; fax-706-839-6351; 8AM-5PM (EST) www.co.habersham.ga.us
Index: Separate indices to search include deeds, mortgages, liens, misc. Records indexed on public terminal from 1972. Only the public may search. Copy fee $.25 per page. Cert fee- $2.50 1st page, $.50 add'l includes copy fee. Payee- Habersham County Clerk of Superior Court. Office does not sell bulk data. **Online access to RE Deed, UCC, Lien, Notary, Plat records:** See www.gsccca.org for free access to Deeds back to 1999, Liens back to 2004, and UCCs back to 1995, plats back to 2004. **Other phones:** Treasurer- 706-754-6264; Elections- 706-754-2013; Vital Records- 706-754-2013. **Property tax/Assessing**- 555 Monroe St, Unit 26, Clarkesville, GA 30523; 706-754-2557, Fax: 706-754-8079. (Appraiser/Auditor- 706-754-2557) Appraiser at 115 Beaver Dam Rd. **Online** - Search property/GIS data free at www.emapsplus.com/GAHabers ham/maps/. Click on Owner to name search.

Hall County

County Superior Court Clerk, PO Box 1275; Real Estate Office, Gainesville, GA 30503-1336. Recording, R/E & UCC phone-770-531-7058; fax-770-536-0702; 8AM-5PM www.hallcounty.org
Index: Multiple indexes to search. Records indexed on computer back to 1993 for real estate; plats go back to 11/2003; UCC back to 1995; General index back to 1/03. Only the public may search. Copy fee $1.00 per page. Plat copy- $2.00 per page. Cert fee- $2.50 per doc, $.50 per page, plus copy fee. Payee- Hall County Clerk of Superior Court. Office does not sell bulk data. **Online access to RE Deed, UCC, Lien, Notary, Plat records:** See www.gsccca.org for free access to Deeds back to 1999, Liens back to 2004, and UCCs back to 1995, plats back to 2004. **Property tax/Assessing**- PO Box 2895, Gainesville, GA 30503; 770-531-6720, Fax: 770-531-3968. www.hallcounty.org/ **Online access**- Access property data free at http://gispublic.hallcounty.org. Click on quick search, then select name search.

Hancock County

County Superior Court Clerk, PO Box 451, Sparta, GA 31087. Recording, R/E & UCC phone-706-444-6644; fax-706-444-5685; 9AM-5PM (EST)
Index: Separate indices to search include real estate, liens, UCC, civil, criminal. Records indexed on public terminal from 2004. Only the public may search. Copy fee $.25 per page. Cert fee- $2.50 1st page, $.50 each add'l includes copy fee. Payee- Hancock County Clerk of Superior Court. **Online access to RE Deed, UCC, Lien, Notary, Plat records:** See www.gsccca.org for free access to Deeds back to 1999, Liens back to 2004, and UCCs back to 1995, plats back to 2004. **Other phones:** Treasurer- 706-444-5746; Elections- 706-444-5343; Vital Records-706-444-5343. **Property tax/ Assessing**- 64 Courthouse Sq, #B, Sparta, GA 31087; 706-444-5721, Fax: 706-444-7711. hours- 8AM-5PM **Online access**- Basic property data free at http://qpublic.net/ga/hancock/. Advanced features, multiple search types and full data also available by subscription.

Haralson County

County Superior Court Clerk, PO Drawer 849, Buchanan, GA 30113. Recording, R/E & UCC phone-770-646-2005; fax-770-646-8827; 8:30-5PM
Index: Separate indices to search. Records indexed on public terminal from 05/05. Only the public may perform title searches. Copy fee $1.00 per page. Cert fee- $2.50 per doc, $.50 per page plus copy fee. Payee- Haralson County Clerk of Superior Court. **Online access to RE Deed, UCC, Lien, Notary, Plat records:** See www.gsccca.org for free access to Deeds back to 1999, Liens back to 2004, and UCCs back to 1995, plats back to 2004. **Other phones:** Treasurer- 770-646-2022; Elections- 770-646-2010; Vital Records- 770-646-2008. **Property tax/Assessing**- PO Box 548, 4266 GA Hwy 120, Buchanan, GA 30113; 770-646-2022, Fax: 770-646-2050. (Appraiser/Auditor- 770-646-2022) **Online access**- Access assessor property records free at http://qpublic.net/ga/haralson/.

Harris County

County Superior Court Clerk, PO Box 528, Hamilton, GA 31811. 706-628-4944, R/E recording phone-706-628-5570; fax-706-628-7039; 8AM-5PM (EST)
Index: Separate indices to search include several indices by year. Records indexed on public terminal from 1993. Office will perform a UCC search but public must search other records themselves. Copy fee $1.00 per page; self serve- $.25 each. Cert fee- $2.50 per doc, $.50 per page includes copy fee. Payee-Harris County Clerk of Superior Court. **Online access to RE Deed, UCC, Lien, Notary, Plat records:** See www.gsccca.org for free access to Deeds back to 1999, Liens back to 2004, and UCCs back to 1995, plats back to 2004. **Other phones:** Treasurer- 706-628-4958; Elections- 706-628-5210; Tax Commissioner- 706-628-4843. **Property tax/Assessing**- PO Box 445, Hamilton, GA 31811; 706-628-5171, Fax: 706-628-4127. **Online access**-Access assessor property records free at http://qpublic.net/ga/harris/.

Hart County

County Superior Court Clerk, PO Box 386, Hartwell, GA 30643. Recording, R/E & UCC phone-706-376-7189; fax-706-376-1277; 8:30AM-5PM (EST)
Index: Separate indices to search. Records indexed on computer, but not all indices. Only the public may search. Copy fee $1.00 per page, $.25 self serve. Cert fee- $2.50 per doc plus $.50 per page. Payee- Hart County Clerk of Superior Court. Office does not sell bulk data. **Online access to RE Deed, UCC, Lien, Notary, Plat records:** See www.gsccca.org for free access to Deeds back to 1999, Liens back to 2004, and UCCs back to 1995, plats back to 2004. **Other phones:** Treasurer- 706-376-2024; Elections- 706-376-2565; Vital Records- 706-376-2565. **Property tax/Assessing**- PO Box 426, 165 W Franklin St, Hartwell, GA 30643; 706-376-3997, Fax: 706-376-0097. (Appraiser/Auditor- 706-376-3997) **Online access**- Access assessor property records free at http://qpublic.net/ga/hart/

Heard County

County Superior Court Clerk, PO Box 249, Franklin, GA 30217. 706-675-3301; fax-706-675-0819; 8:30AM-5PM (EST)
Index: All in one. Records indexed on public terminal from 1996. Only the public may search. Copy fee $1.00 per page; deeds- $10.00 1st page, $2.00 each add'l page. Cert fee- $2.50 per doc plus copy fee. Payee- Heard County Clerk of Superior Court. **Online access to RE Deed, UCC, Lien, Notary, Plat records:** See www.gsccca.org for free access to Deeds back to 1999, Liens back to 2004, and UCCs back to 1995, plats back to 2004. **Property tax/Assessing**- PO Box 476, 215 E Court Sq, #19, Franklin, GA 30217; 706-675-3786, Fax: 706-675-1123. **Online access**- Access appraiser property data free at http://qpublic.net/ga/heard/.

Henry County

County Superior Court Clerk, #1 Courthouse Sq, McDonough, GA 30253. 770-288-8022, R/E recording phone-770-954-2121; fax-770-898-7573; 8AM-5PM (EST) www.co.henry.ga.us
Index: All in one. Records indexed on public terminal from 1986. Only the public may search. Copy fee $.25 per page. Cert fee- $2.50 1st page, $.50 each add'l. Payee- Henry County Clerk of Superior Court. **Online access to RE Deed, UCC, Lien, Notary, Plat records:** See www.gsccca.org for free access to Deeds back to 1999, Liens back to 2004, and UCCs back to 1995, plats back to 2004. **Other phones:** Treasurer- 770-954-2470; Elections- 770-954-2069; Vital Records- 770-954-2303. **Property tax/Assessing**- 140 Henry Pky, McDonough, Ga 30253; 770-288-7999, Fax: 770-288-7961. www.co.henry.ga.us/ **Online access**- Search property

tax data free at www.co.henry.ga.us/MapsZonesDistricts/index_2.htm.

Houston County

County Superior Court Clerk, 201 N Perry Pky, Perry, GA 31069. Recording, R/E & UCC phone-478-218-4720; fax-478-218-4745; 8:30AM-5PM (EST) www.houstoncountyga.com
Index: All in one. Records indexed on computer. Only the public may search. Copy fee $.25 per page. Cert fee- $2.50 per doc, $.50 per page includes copy fee. Payee- Houston County Clerk of Superior Court. **Online access to RE Deed, UCC, Lien, Notary, Plat records:** See www.gsccca.org for free access to Deeds back to 1999, Liens back to 2004, and UCCs back to 1995, plats back to 2004. Also, the clerks recording indices of plats, land records, liens is free at http://68.227.93.141/resolution/. Pre-1998 real estate and pre-1994 financing statements are also available. **Other phones:** Elections- 478-987-1973; Vital Records- 478-218-4710; Marriage/Death/Births- 478-218-4710; Divorces -478-218-4740;. **Property tax/Assessing-** PO Box 1199, 201 Perry Pkwy, Perry, GA 31069; 478-218-4750, Fax: 478-218-4755. (Appraiser - 478-218-4750) hours- 8AM-5PM www.houstoncountyga.com/residents/houston-county-tax-assessor.aspx **Online access-** Access to assessor database free www.qpublic.net/ga/houston/.

Irwin County

County Superior Court Clerk, 301 S Irwin Ave, #103, Ocilla, GA 31774. 229-468-5356; fax-229-468-9753; 8AM-5PM (EST)
Index: Separate indices to search include GE Dkt, minute book. Records indexed on computer back to 2004. Only the public may search. Copy fee $1.00 per page. Cert fee- $2.50 per doc and $.50 per page, includes copy fee. Payee- Irwin County Clerk of Superior Court. **Online access to RE Deed, UCC, Lien, Notary, Plat records:** See www.gsccca.org for free access to Deeds back to 1999, Liens back to 2004, and UCCs back to 1995, plats back to 2004. **Other phones:** Treasurer- 229-468-5505; Elections- 229-468-5894; Vital Records- 229-468-5138. **Property tax/Assessing-** 202 S Irwin Ave, Ocilla, GA 31774; 229-468-5514, Fax: 229-468-5681.

Jackson County

County Superior Court Clerk, PO Box 7, Jefferson, GA 30549. 706-387-6255, R/E recording phone-706-387-6258; fax-706-387-6273; 8AM-5PM (EST) www.jacksoncountygov.com
Index: All in one. Records indexed on public terminal from 1988. Only the public may search. Copy fee $1.00 per page. Cert fee- $2.00 per doc, $.50 per page includes copy fee. Payee- Jackson County Clerk of Superior Court. **Online access to RE Deed, UCC, Lien, Notary, Plat records:** See www.gsccca.org for free access to Deeds back to 1999, Liens back to 2004, and UCCs back to 1995, plats back to 2004. **Other phones:** Elections- 706-367-6377; Vital Records- 706-387-6276. **Property tax/Assessing-** 67 Athens St, Jefferson, GA 30549; 706-367-6330, Fax: 706-367-5349. (Appraiser/Auditor- 706-367-6330) **Online access-** Access assessor property records free at http://qpublic.net/ga/jackson/.

Jasper County

County Superior Court Clerk, Courthouse, Monticello, GA 31064. 706-468-4901, R/E recording phone-706-468-4901 x226; fax-706-468-4946; 8AM-5PM (EST)
Index: Separate indices to search include lien, real estate. Records indexed on public terminal from 1993. Only the public may search. Copy fee $1.00 per page. Cert fee- $2.50 per doc, plus $.50 per page, includes copy fee. Payee- Jasper County Clerk of Superior Court. **Online access to RE Deed, UCC, Lien, Notary, Plat records:** See www.gsccca.org for free access to Deeds back to 1999, Liens back to 2004, and UCCs back to 1995, plats back to 2004. **Other phones:** Treasurer- 706-468-4900; Elections- 706-468-4903; Vital Records- 706-468-4903. **Property tax/Assessing-** 126 W Greene St, #124, Monticello, GA 31064; 706-468-4904, Fax: 706-468-4922. (Appraiser/Auditor- 706-468-4904) www.jaspercountyboa.org/ **Online access-** Access Property Records free at www.jaspercountyboa.org/ click on Search Records.

Jeff Davis County

County Superior Court Clerk, PO Box 429, Hazlehurst, GA 31539. Recording, R/E & UCC phone-912-375-6615; fax-912-375-6637; 8AM-5PM
Index: Separate indices to search include grantor/grantee indexes, criminal & civil docket indexes. Records indexed on computer back to 1/1/95. Office will perform a UCC search but public must search other records themselves. Will search UCC records. Copy fee $.50 per page. Cert fee- $2.00 per doc, $.50 per page. Payee- Jeff Davis County Clerk of Superior Court. Office does not sell bulk data. **Online access to RE Deed, UCC, Lien, Notary, Plat records:** See www.gsccca.org for free access to Deeds back to 1999, Liens back to 2004, and UCCs back to 1995, plats back to 2004. **Other phones:** Treasurer- 912-375-6611; Elections- 912-375-6635; Vital Records- 912375-6626. **Property tax/Assessing-** PO Box 590, 14 Jeff Davis St, Hazlehurst, GA 31539; 912-375-6624, Fax: 912-206-2021. (Appraiser/Auditor- 912-375-6624) **Online access-** Access assessor property and sales data free at http://qpublic.net/ga/jeffdavis/.

Jefferson County

County Superior Court Clerk, PO Box 151, Louisville, GA 30434. 478-625-7922; fax-478-625-4037; 9AM-5PM (EST)
Index: Separate indices to search. Record index not computerized. Only the public may search. Copy fee $.25 per page. Cert fee- $2.50 per doc, plus $.50 each add'l includes copies. Payee- Jefferson County Clerk of Superior Court. **Online access to RE Deed, UCC, Lien, Notary, Plat records:** See www.gsccca.org for free access to Deeds back to 1999, Liens back to 2004, and UCCs back to 1995, plats back to 2004. **Other phones:** Treasurer- 478-625-7736. **Property tax/Assessing-** PO Box 555, 202 E Broad St, Louisville, GA 30434; 478-625-8209, Fax: 478-625-4008. **Online access-** Access assessor property and sales data free at http://qpublic.net/ga/jefferson/search1.html. Also, access assessor parcel data may be on the Central Savannah River Area GIS site at www.csrardc.org/viewer.htm.

Jenkins County

County Superior Court Clerk, PO Box 659, Millen, GA 30442. Recording, R/E & UCC phone-478-982-4683; fax-478-982-1274; 8:30AM-5PM (EST)
Index: Separate indices to search include deeds, liens, plats. Records indexed on public terminal from 1999 for deeds, 2003 for liens. Only the public may search. Will not search UCC records. Copy fee $.25 per page. Cert fee- $2.50 per doc plus copy fee. Payee- Jenkins County Clerk of Superior Court. Office does not sell bulk data. **Online access to RE Deed, UCC, Lien, Notary, Plat records:** See www.gsccca.org for free access to Deeds back to 1999, Liens back to 2004, and UCCs back to 1995, plats back to 2004. **Other phones:** Elections- 478-982-3985; Vital Records- 478-982-2811 (Health Dept); Tax Commissioner- 478-982-4925; Probate Court -478-982-5581;. **Property tax/Assessing-** PO Box 935, 212 Harvey St, Millen, GA 30442; 478-982-4939, fax- 478-982-3706.

Johnson County

County Superior Court Clerk, PO Box 321, Wrightsville, GA 31096. 478-864-3484; fax-478-864-1343; 9AM-5PM (EST)
Index: All in one. Records indexed on public terminal from 1991. Only the public may search. Copy fee $.25 per page. Cert fee- $3.00 per doc plus copy fee. Payee- Johnson County Clerk of Superior Court. **Online access to RE Deed, UCC, Lien, Notary, Plat records:** See www.gsccca.org for free access to Deeds back to 1999, Liens back to 2004, and UCCs back to 1995, plats back to 2004. **Other phones:** Treasurer- 478-864-2565. **Property tax/Assessing-** PO Box 269, Wrightsville, GA 31096; 478-864-3325, Fax: 478-864-3325. www.georgiagis.com/Johnson/ **Online access-** Access property data on the GIS-mapping site free at www.georgiagis.com/Johnson/disclaimer.cfm.

Jones County

County Superior Court Clerk, PO Box 39, Gray, GA 31032. 478-986-6671; fax-478-986-2030; 8:30AM-4:30PM (EST)
Index: Separate indices to search include grantors/grantee, liens. Records indexed on computer back to 1990 for deeds, back to July, 1991 for liens. Only the public may search. Office will perform searches under very limited circumstances. Copy fee $.50 per page. Cert fee- $2.50 per doc plus copy fee. Payee- Jones County Clerk of Superior Court. Office does not sell bulk data. **Online access to RE Deed, UCC, Lien, Notary, Plat records:** See www.gsccca.org for free access to Deeds back to 1999, Liens back to 2004, and UCCs back to 1995, plats back to 2004. **Other phones:** Treasurer- 478-986-6538; Elections- 478-986-3222; Vital Records- 478-986-6668; Tax Commissioner- 478-986-6538. **Property tax/Assessing-** PO Box 1359, 166 Industrial Blvd, Gray, GA 31032; 478-986-6300, Fax: 478-986-6504. hours- 8AM-5PM **Online access-** Access assessor property records free at http://qpublic.net/ga/jones/.

Lamar County

County Superior Court Clerk, 326 Thomaston St, Box 7; Courthouse, Barnesville, GA 30204-1669. 770-358-5145; fax-770-358-5814; 8AM-5PM (EST)
Index: All in one. Records indexed on public terminal from 1990. Only the public may search; office can assist. Copy fee $.25 per page. Cert fee- $2.50 per doc, $.50 per page. Payee- Lamar County Clerk of Superior Court. **Online access to RE Deed, UCC, Lien, Notary, Plat records:** See www.gsccca.org for free access to Deeds back to 1999, Liens back to 2004, and UCCs back to 1995, plats back to 2004. **Other phones:** Treasurer- 770-358-5162. **Property tax/Assessing-** 408 Thomaston St, #8, Barnesville, GA 30204; 770-358-5161, Fax: 770-358-5149. **Online access-** Access assessor property records free at http://qpublic.net/ga/lamar/.

Lanier County

County Superior Court Clerk, 100 Main St; County Courthouse, Lakeland, GA 31635. 229-482-3594; fax-229-482-8333; 8AM-N,1PM-5PM (EST)
Index: All in one. Records indexed on public terminal from 1998. Only the public may search. Copy fee $.25 per page. Cert fee- $3.00 per cert plus copy fee. Payee- Lanier County Clerk of Superior Court. **Online access to RE Deed, UCC, Lien, Notary, Plat records:** See www.gsccca.org for free access to Deeds back to 1999, Liens back to 2004, and UCCs back to 1995, plats back to 2004. **Other phones:** Treasurer- 229-482-3795; Elections- 229-482-3665; Vital Records- 229-482-3668. **Property tax/Assessing-** 100 W Main St, #2, Courthouse, Lakeland, GA 31635; 229-482-2090, Fax: 229-482-2105. **Online access-** Access assessor property records free at http://qpublic.net/ga/lanier/.

Laurens County

County Superior Court Clerk, PO Box 2028, Dublin, GA 31040. Recording, R/E & UCC phone-478-272-3210; fax-478-275-2595; 8:30AM-5:30PM (EST)
Index: Separate indices to search include deed, UCC, courts. Records indexed on public terminal from 1992. Only the public may search. Copy fee $.25 per page. Cert fee- $2.50 per doc, $.50 per page. Payee- Laurens County Clerk of Superior Court. **Online access to RE Deed, UCC, Lien, Notary, Plat records:** See www.gsccca.org for free access to Deeds back to 1999, Liens back to 2004, and UCCs

back to 1995, plats back to 2004. **Other phones:** Treasurer- 478-272-6994; Elections- 478-272-2566; Vital Records- 478-272-2051. **Property tax/Assessing**- PO Box 2085, 101 N Jefferson St, Dublin, GA 31040; 478-272-6443, Fax: 478-272-8607. **Online access**- Access assessor property records free at http://qpublic.net/ga/laurens/.

Lee County

County Superior Court Clerk, PO Box 49, Leesburg, GA 31763. Recording, R/E & UCC phone-229-759-6018; fax-229-438-6049; 8AM-5PM (EST)
Index: Separate indices to search. Records indexed on public terminal from 1994. Only the public may search. Copy fee $.25 per page. Cert fee- $2.00 per doc, $1.00 per page plus copy fee. Payee- Lee County Clerk of Superior Court. **Online access to RE Deed, UCC, Lien, Notary, Plat records:** See www.gsccca.org for free access to Deeds back to 1999, Liens back to 2004, and UCCs back to 1995, plats back to 2004. **Other phones:** Treasurer- 229-759-6000; Elections- 229-759-6002; Vital Records- 229-759-6005. **Property tax/Assessing**- PO Box 424, 109 Leslie Hwy, Leesburg, GA 31763; 229-759-6010, Fax: 229-759-6382. **Online access**- Access assessor property and sales data free at http://qpublic.net/ga/lee/search1.html.

Liberty County

County Superior Court Clerk, PO Box 50, Hinesville, GA 31310. Recording, R/E phone-912-876-3625; fax-912-369-5463; 8AM-5PM www.libertyco.com
Index: All in one. Records indexed on public terminal from 1986. Only the public may search. Office will search only if you provide the year. Copy fee $1.00 per page. Cert fee- $2.50 per doc, $.50 per page. Payee- Liberty County Clerk of Superior Court. **Online access to RE Deed, UCC, Lien, Notary, Plat records:** See www.gsccca.org for free access to Deeds back to 1999, Liens back to 2004, and UCCs back to 1995, plats back to 2004. **Other phones:** Treasurer- 912-876-3389; Vital Records- 912-876-3625. **Property tax/Assessing**- PO Box 829, 112 N Main, #104, Hinesville, GA 31310; 912-876-2823, Fax: 912-876-2870. **Online access**- Search the assessor data free at http://ww2.libertycountyga.com:8088/EGSV2Liberty/RPSearch.do

Lincoln County

County Superior Court Clerk, PO Box 340, Lincolnton, GA 30817. Recording, R/E & UCC phone-706-359-5505; fax-706-359-5027; 9AM-5PM (EST) www.lincolncountyga.com/SuperiorCourts.asp
Index: All in one. Records indexed on public terminal from 1999. Only the public may search. General copy fee- $.25 per page. Cert fee- $2.50 per doc, $1.00 per page. Payee- Lincoln County Clerk of Superior Court. **Online access to RE Deed, UCC, Lien, Notary, Plat records:** See www.gsccca.org for free access to Deeds back to 1999, Liens back to 2004, and UCCs back to 1995, plats back to 2004. **Other phones:** Elections- 706-359-6126; Vital Records- 706-359-5528. **Property tax/Assessing**- 210 Humphrey St, PO Box 340, Lincolnton, GA 30817; 706-359-5502, Fax: 706-359-5503. (Appraiser/Auditor- 706-359-5502) hours- 8AM-5PM www.lincolncountyga.com/TaxAssessors.asp **Online access**- Search assessor property records and sales free at http://qpublic.net/ga/lincoln/. Also, access assessor parcel data free on the Central Savannah River Area GIS site at www.csrardc.org/. Click on Search and choose Lincoln.

Long County

County Superior Court Clerk, PO Box 458, Ludowici, GA 31316. Recording, R/E & UCC phone-912-545-2123; fax-912-545-2020; 8:30AM-5PM (EST)
Index: Separate indices to search include deeds, liens, plats, UCCs, hospital liens, GED. Records indexed on public terminal from 1993 (deeds). Only the public may search. Copy fee $1.50 per page; self serve $.25. Cert fee- $2.50 1st page; $.50 each add'l includes copy fee. Payee- Long County Clerk of Superior Court. Office does not sell bulk data. **Online access to RE Deed, UCC, Lien, Notary, Plat records:** See www.gsccca.org for free access to Deeds back to 1999, Liens back to 2004, and UCCs back to 1995, plats back to 2004. **Other phones:** Elections- 912-545-2234; Vital Records- 912-545-2131; Sheriffs Dept.- 912-545-2118; Tax Commis.- 912-545-2127. **Property tax/Assessing**- PO Box 642, Ludowici, GA 31316; 912-545-9111, Fax: 912-545-0096. hours- 8:30AM-4PM

Lowndes County

County Superior Court Clerk, PO Box 1349, Valdosta, GA 31601-1349. Recording, R/E & UCC phone-229-333-5125, UCC recording phone-229-333-5183; fax-229-333-7637; 8AM-5PM (EST)
Index: Separate indices to search include deeds, liens, hospital liens. Records indexed on public terminal from 1987. Only the public may search. Copy fee $.25 per page. Cert fee- $2.50 per doc plus $.50 per page. Payee- Lowndes County Clerk of Superior Court. **Online access to RE Deed, UCC, Lien, Notary, Plat records:** See www.gsccca.org for free access to Deeds back to 1999, Liens back to 2004, and UCCs back to 1995, plats back to 2004. **Other phones:** Treasurer- 229-671-2570. **Property tax/Assessing**- PO Box 1126, 300 N Patterson, Valdosta, 31603; 229-671-2540, fax- 229-333-7606. www.lowndescounty.com/boards.asp?id=15 **Online access**- Search site at http://qpublic.net/ga/lowndes/ converted to a fee-based service but free public search is still available. Other search abilities, data, maps available to subscribers; 1 user - $20/mo or $200/yr, fees increase for multiple users. Credit card required.

Lumpkin County

County Superior Court Clerk, 99 Courthouse Hill, #D, Dahlonega, GA 30533-0541. Recording, R/E & UCC phone-706-864-3736; fax-706-864-5298; 8AM-5PM
Index: Separate indices to search include real estate management and case management. Records indexed on computer back to 1986. Only the public may search. Will not search UCC records. Copy fee $1.00 per page if assistance provided, all public records computer generated copies $2.50 per page, $.25 self serve. Cert fee- $2.50 per doc, $.50 per each add'l page includes copy fee. Payee- Lumpkin County Clerk of Superior Court. **Online access to RE Deed, UCC, Lien, Notary, Plat records:** See www.gsccca.org for free access to Deeds back to 1999, Liens back to 2004, and UCCs back to 1995, plats back to 2004. **Other phones:** Treasurer- 706-864-3742; Elections- 706-864-6279; Vital Records- 706-864-3847. **Property tax/Assessing**- 25 Short St, #B, Dahlonega, GA 30533; 706-864-2433, Fax: 706-864-9806. (Appraiser/Auditor- 706-864-2433) **Online access**- Access appraiser property data free at http://qpublic.net/ga/lumpkin/search1.html.

Macon County

County Superior Court Clerk, PO Box 337, Oglethorpe, GA 31068. Recording, R/E & UCC phone-478-472-7661; fax-478-472-4775; 8AM-5PM
Index: All in one. Records indexed on a public use terminal; RE back to 1993, UCCs to 1995, plats to 2004; liens back to 2004. Only the public may search. Copy fee $1.00 per page if assisted: $.25 per page self serve. Cert fee- $2.50 per cert plus $.50 per page copy fee. Payee- Macon County Clerk of Superior Court. **Online access to RE Deed, UCC, Lien, Notary, Plat records:** See www.gsccca.org for free access to Deeds back to 1993, Liens back to 2004, and UCCs back to 1995, plats back to 2004. **Other phones:** Treasurer- 478-472-7031; Elections- 478-472-8520; Vital Records- 478-472-7685. **Property tax/Assessing**- PO Box 297, 122 Chatham St, Oglethorpe, GA 31068; 478-472-6560, Fax: 478-472-9463. (Appraiser/Auditor- 478-472-6560) **Online access**- Search assessor's information free at http://qpublic.net/ga/macon/search.html.

Madison County

County Superior Court Clerk, PO Box 247, Danielsville, GA 30633. Recording, R/E & UCC phone-706-795-6310; fax-706-795-2209; 8AM-5PM www.madisoncountyga.us/Dir/Departments/Clerk-of-Courts/5/
Index: Separate indices to search include liens, plats. Records indexed on computer back to 0101/93. Only the public may search. Copy fee $1.00 per page. Cert fee- $2.50 per cert includes copy fee. Payee- Madison County Clerk of Superior Court. **Online access to RE Deed, UCC, Lien, Notary, Plat records:** See www.gsccca.org for free access to Deeds back to 1999, Liens back to 2004, and UCCs back to 1995, plats back to 2004. **Property tax/Assessing**- PO Box 85, 91 Albany Ave, Danielsville, GA 30633; 706-795-6357, Fax: 706-795-5715. **Online access**- Access assessor property data free at www.qpublic.net/ga/madison/search1.html. Search tax bill data free at https://madison.paytaxes.net/customer/enhanced_property_tax_search.php.

Marion County

County Superior Court Clerk, PO Box 41, Buena Vista, GA 31803. Recording, R/E & UCC phone-229-649-7321; fax-229-649-7931; 9AM-5PM (EST)
Index: Separate indices to search include deeds, liens, plat, criminal, civil. Records indexed on public terminal from 1990. Only the public may search. Copy fee $1.00 per page. Cert fee- $2.50 per doc, $.50 per page. Payee- Marion County Clerk of Superior Court. **Online access to RE Deed, UCC, Lien, Notary, Plat records:** See www.gsccca.org for free access to Deeds back to 1999, Liens back to 2004, and UCCs back to 1995, plats back to 2004. **Other phones:** Treasurer- 229-649-2603; Elections- 229-649-2603; Vital Records- 229-649-5542. **Property tax/Assessing**- PO Box 721, 117 Baker St, Buena Vista, GA 31803; 229-649-5504, Fax: 229-649-3702. (Appraiser/Auditor- 229-649-5504) **Online access**- Access assessor property data free at http://qpublic.net/ga/marion/.

McDuffie County

County Superior Court Clerk, PO Box 158, Thomson, GA 30824-0150. Recording, R/E & UCC phone-706-595-2134; fax-706-595-9150; 8AM-5PM (EST) www.thomson-mcduffie.com
Unified with Thomson City to form Thomson-McDuffie County. Index: Separate indices to search include lien, plat & real estate in hard copy; UCC in separate online index, other electronic indexes can be searched in one index. Deed Records indexed on public terminal from 1991. Only the public may search. Copy fee $1.00 per page; self serve $.25. Cert fee- $2.00 per doc, $.50 per page includes copy fee. Payee- McDuffie County Clerk of Superior Court. **Online access to RE Deed, UCC, Lien, Notary, Plat records:** See www.gsccca.org for free access to Deeds back to 1999, Liens back to 2004, and UCCs back to 1995, plats back to 2004. **Other phones:** Elections- 706-595-2105; Vital Records- 706-595-2124; Commissioners- 706-595-2100. **Property tax/Assessing**- PO Box 697, 406 Main St, Thompson, GA 30824; 706-595-2128, Fax: 706-595-2129. (Appraiser/Auditor- 706-595-2128) **Online access**- Access to property records for free go to http://qpublic.net/ga/mcduffie/search.html

McIntosh County

County Superior Court Clerk, PO Box 1661, Darien, GA 31305. Recording, R/E & UCC phone-912-437-6641; fax-912-437-6673; 8AM-4:30PM (EST)
Index: Separate indices to search include deeds, liens, plats in separate paper indexes. Records indexed on public terminal from 1991. Only the public may search. General copy fee $1.00 per page. Cert fee- $2.50 per doc. Payee- McIntosh County Clerk of Superior Court. Office does not sell bulk data. **Online access to Real Estate, Deed, UCC, Lien records:** Call 800-304-5175 to subscribe to UCCs and Deed indexes online service. Deeds go back to 2000. See www.gsccca.org for online access to Deed, Lien and

UCC indexes. **Other phones:** Treasurer- 912-437-6641; Elections- 912-437-6605; Vital Records- 912-437-6636. **Property tax/Assessing-** PO Box 801, 404 Northway, Darien, GA 31305; 912-437-6663, Fax: 912-437-5264. (Appraiser/Auditor- 912-437-6663) www.mcintoshtaxassessor.com **Online access-** property assessor data free at www.mcintoshtaxassessor.com and click on Search Records.

Meriwether County

County Superior Court Clerk, PO Box 160, Greenville, GA 30222-0160. Recording, R/E & UCC phone-706-672-4416; fax-706-672-9465; 8:30AM-5PM (EST) http://gsccca.org/clerks/
Index: Separate indices to search include deed, lien, UCC, plat. Records indexed on public terminal from 1998. Only the public may search. Copy fee $1.00 per page. Cert fee- $2.50 per doc, $.50 per page, copies included. Payee- Meriwether County Clerk of Superior Court. **Online access to RE Deed, UCC, Lien, Notary, Plat records:** See www.gsccca.org for free access to Deeds back to 1999, Liens back to 2004, and UCCs back to 1995, plats back to 2004. **Other phones:** Treasurer- 706-672-4219; Elections- 706-672-4952; Vital Records- 706-672-4974. **Property tax/Assessing-** PO Box 187, Courthouse, Greenville, GA 30222; 706-672-4222, Fax: 706-672-6637. (Appraiser/Auditor- 706-672-4222) **Online access-** Access assessor property data free at http://qpublic.net/ga/meriwether/search.html.

Miller County

County Superior Court Clerk, PO Box 66, Colquitt, GA 39837. Recording, R/E & UCC phone-229-758-4102; fax-229-758-6585; 9AM-5PM (EST)
Index: Separate indices to search include deed, lien, hospital lien, civil and criminal. Deed and UCC records indexed on a public use terminal. Only the public may search. Copy fee $1.00 per page. Cert fee- $2.50 per cert plus copy fee. Payee- Miller County Clerk of Superior Court. **Online access to RE Deed, UCC, Lien, Notary, Plat records:** See www.gsccca.org for free access to Deeds back to 1999, Liens back to 2004, and UCCs back to 1995, plats back to 2004. **Other phones:** Treasurer- 229-758-4101; Elections- 229-758-4118; Vital Records- 229-758-4110. **Property tax/Assessing-** 155 S 1st St #6, Colquitt, GA 39837; 229-758-4100, Fax: 229-758-3946. (Appraiser/Auditor- 229-758-4100) hours- 8AM-5PM **Online access-** Free property records search on Assessor's Office website at www.qpublic.net/ga/miller/.

Mitchell County

County Superior Court Clerk, PO Box 427, Camilla, GA 31730. Recording, R/E & UCC phone-229-336-2022; fax-229-336-2003; 8:30AM-5PM (EST)
Records indexed on public terminal from 1996. Only the public may search. Copy fee $.25 per page. Cert fee- $2.50 1st page, $.50 each add'l, includes copy fee. Payee- Clerk of Superior Court. **Online access to RE Deed, UCC, Lien, Notary, Plat records:** See www.gsccca.org for free access to Deeds back to 1999, Liens back to 2004, UCCs back to 1995, plats back to 2004. **Other phones:** Treasurer- 229-336-2010; Elections- 229-336-2016; Vital Records- 229-336-2016. **Property tax/Assessing-** PO Box 6, 11W Broad St #101, Camilla, GA 31730; 229-336-2005, Fax: 229-336-2004. (Appraiser/Auditor- 229-336-2005) **Online access-** Access assessor records free at http://qpublic.net/ga/mitchell/search1.html.

Monroe County

County Superior Court Clerk, PO Box 450, Forsyth, GA 31029-0450. 478-994-7022; fax-478-994-7053; 8AM-5PM (EST)
Index: All in one. Records indexed on public terminal from 1990. Only the public may search. Copy fee $.25 per page. Cert fee- $2.50 per doc, $.50 per page. Payee- Monroe County Clerk of Superior Court. Office does not sell bulk data. **Online access to RE Deed, UCC, Lien, Notary, Plat records:** See www.gsccca.org for free access to Deeds back to 1999, Liens back to 2004, and UCCs back to 1995, plats back to 2004. **Other phones:** Elections- 478-994-7036; Vital Records- 478-994-7036. **Property tax/Assessing-** 38 W Main St, PO Box 869, Forsyth, GA 31029; 478-994-7038, Fax: 478-993-3080. (Appraiser/Auditor- 478-994-7038) **Online-** Search assessor's records at www.qpublic.net/ga/monroe/.

Montgomery County

County Superior Court Clerk, PO Box 311, Mount Vernon, GA 30445. 912-583-4401; fax-912-583-4343; 8:30AM-5PM (EST)
Index: All in one. Records indexed on public terminal from 1993. Only the public may search. Copy fee $1.00 per page. Cert fee- $2.00 per doc, $.50 per page. Payee- Clerk of Court. **Online access to RE Deed, UCC, Lien, Notary, Plat records:** See www.gsccca.org for free access to Deeds back to 1999, Liens back to 2004, and UCCs back to 1995, plats back to 2004. **Other phones:** Elections- 912-583-2681; Vital Records- 912-583-2681. **Property tax/Assessing-** PO Box 156, 411 S Railroad Ave, Mt Vernon, GA 30445; 912-583-4131, Fax: 912-583-4131. **Online access-** Access assessor records free at http://qpublic.net/ga/montgomery/. A subscription service with fuller data is also available.

Morgan County

County Superior Court Clerk, PO Drawer 551, Madison, GA 30650. 706-342-3605; fax-706-343-6462; 9AM-5PM (EST) www.morganga.org/
Index: Separate indices to search include real estate, liens, case management, UCCs. Records indexed on public terminal from 1993. Only the public may search. Will not search UCC records. Copy fee $1.00 per page; $.25 self serve. Cert fee- $2.50 per doc, $.50 per page plus copy fee. Payee- Morgan County Clerk of Superior Court. **Online access to RE Deed, UCC, Lien, Notary, Plat records:** See www.gsccca.org for free access to Deeds back to 1999, Liens back to 2004, and UCCs back to 1995, plats back to 2004. **Property tax/Assessing-** 158 E Washinton St, Madison, GA 30650; 706-342-0551, Fax: 706-342-6333. www.morganga.org **Online access-** Search assessor's records free at www.qpublic.net/ga/morgan/.

Murray County

County Superior Court Clerk, PO Box 1000, Chatsworth, GA 30705. 706-695-2932; fax-706-517-9672; 8:30AM-5PM (EST)
Index: Separate indices to search include deeds, liens. Records indexed on computer back to 898 for deeds, 1996 for liens. Only the public may search. Copy fee $.25 per page. Cert fee- $2.50 1st page; $.25 each add'l, includes copy fee. Payee- Murray County Clerk of Superior Court. **Online access to RE Deed, UCC, Lien, Notary, Plat records:** See www.gsccca.org for free access to Deeds back to 1999, Liens back to 2004, and UCCs back to 1995, plats back to 2004. **Other phones:** Treasurer- 706-695-3423; Elections- 706-517-1400 x232. **Property tax/Assessing-** 121 N 4th Ave, Chatsworth, GA 30705; 706-695-2521, Fax: 706-695-2125. (Appraiser/Auditor- 706-517-1400 x230) hours- 8AM-5PM **Online access-** Access assessor property data free at http://qpublic.net/ga/murray/search1.html.

Muscogee County

County Superior Court Clerk, PO Box 2145, Columbus, GA 31902-2145. 706-653-4358, R/E recording phone-706-653-4356; fax-706-653-4359; 8:30AM-5PM (EST) www.columbusga.org/
Index: All in one. Records indexed on computer back to 8/00 for deeds, 1/3/85 for liens. Only the public may search. Copy fee $.25 per page. Cert fee- $2.50 per cert plus $.50 per page. Payee- Muscogee County Clerk of Superior Court. **Online access to RE Deed, UCC, Lien, Notary, Plat records:** See www.gsccca.org for Deed, Lien and UCC indexes. Also, search the clerk's index free at http://clerkweb.columbusga.org/oncoreweb/default.aspx. **Other phones:** Treasurer- 706-653-4100. **Property tax/Assessing-** PO Box 1340, 110 9th st, Columbus, GA 31902; 706-653-4398, Fax: 706-653-4397. www.columbusga.org/Tax%20Assessors/ **Online access-** assessor property records free at http://ccga1.columbusga.org/PropertyInformation.nsf/

Newton County

County Superior Court Clerk, 1132 Usher St, 3rd Fl; Newton County Judicial Ctr, Covington, GA 30014. 770-784-2035, R/E recording phone-770-784-2040; fax-770-788-3717; 8AM-5PM (EST)
Index: All in one. Records indexed on public terminal from 1988. Only the public may search; office can assist. Office will not name search real estate records. Copy fee $.25 per page. Cert fee- $2.50 1st page, $.50 each add'l, plus copy fee. Payee- Newton County Clerk of Superior Court. **Online access to RE Deed, UCC, Lien, Notary, Plat records:** See www.gsccca.org for free access to Deeds back to 1999, Liens back to 2004, and UCCs back to 1995, plats back to 2004. **Other phones:** Elections- 770-784-2055; Vital Records- 770-784-2045. **Property tax/Assessing-** 1111 Usher St, 3rd Fl, Judicial Center, Covington, GA 30014; 770-784-2030, Fax: 770-784-2162. **Online access-** Search assessor and property data free at http://newton.binarybus.com/lookup/.

Oconee County

County Superior Court Clerk, PO Box 1099, Watkinsville, GA 30677. 706-769-3940; fax-706-769-3948; 8AM-5PM (EST)
Index: All in one. Records indexed on public terminal from 1989. Office will perform a UCC search but public must search other records themselves. Search fee-$10.00 per name. Office will not search real estate records. Copy fee $.25 per page. Cert fee- $2.50 per doc, $.50 per page. Payee- Oconee County Clerk of Superior Court. **Online access to RE Deed, UCC, Lien, Notary, Plat records:** See www.gsccca.org for free access to Deeds back to 1999, Liens back to 2004, and UCCs back to 1995, plats back to 2004. **Property tax/Assessing-** 23 N Main St, PO Box 145, Watkinsville, GA 30677; 706-769-3921, Fax: 706-769-3964. **Online access-** Search assessor's data online at http://qpublic.net/ga/oconee/index.html, also access GIS land data at www.oconeecounty.com

Oglethorpe County

County Superior Court Clerk, PO Box 68, Lexington, GA 30648-0068. Recording, R/E & UCC phone-706-743-5731; fax-706-743-5335; 8AM-5PM (EST)
Index: Separate indices to search include lien, court, real estate. Records indexed on a public use terminal back 10 years. Only the public may search. Copy fee $1.00 per page; $.25 self serve. Cert fee- $2.00 per doc, $.50 per page, includes copy fee. Payee- County Clerk of Superior Court. **Online access to RE Deed, UCC, Lien, Notary, Plat records:** See www.gsccca.org for free access to Deeds back to 1999, Liens back to 2004, and UCCs back to 1995, plats back to 2004. **Other phones:** Treasurer- 706-743-5270; Elections- 706-743-5350; Vital Records- 706-743-5350. **Property tax/Assessing-** PO Box 136, Lexington, GA 30648; 706-743-5166, Fax: 706-743-8219. **Online access-** Search assessor's information online at www.qpublic.net/ga/oglethorpe/.

Paulding County

County Superior Court Clerk, 11 Courthouse Sq, Rm G-2, Dallas, GA 30132. 770-443-7527 x259, R/E recording phone-770-443-7528, UCC recording phone-770-443-7527; fax-770-505-3863; 8AM-5PM
Index: All in one. Records indexed on public terminal from 1993. Office will perform a UCC online search but public must search other records themselves. Copy fee $.25 per page. Cert fee- $2.50 per doc plus $1.50 per add'l page. Payee- Paulding County Clerk of Superior Court. **Online access to RE Deed, UCC, Lien, Notary, Plat records:** See www.gsccca.org for free access to Deeds back to 1999, Liens back to 2004, and UCCs back to 1995, plats back to 2004. **Property tax/Assessing-** 25 Courthouse Sq, Rm 301,

Annex Bldg, Dallas, GA 30132; 770-443-7606, Fax: 770-443-7539.

Peach County

County Superior Court Clerk, PO Box 389, Fort Valley, GA 31030. 478-825-5331; fax-478-825-8662; 8:30-5PM www.peachcounty.net/clerkofcourt.cfm

Index: Separate indices to search include deeds, liens. Records indexed on computer back to 1997. Only the public may search. Copy fee $.25 per page. Cert fee- $2.50 per doc, $.50 per page, includes copy fee. Payee- Peach County Clerk of Superior Court. **Online access to RE Deed, UCC, Lien, Notary, Plat records:** See www.gsccca.org for free access to Deeds back to 1999, Liens back to 2004, and UCCs back to 1995, plats back to 2004. **Other phones:** Treasurer- 478-825-2535. **Property tax/Assessing-** 205 W Church St #205, Fort Valley, GA 31030; 478-825-5924, Fax: 478-825-2678. www.peachcounty.net/assessors.cfm **Online access-** Subscribe to the GIS-mapping site for property data at www.peachcountymaps.com. For registration and password, contact the Tax Office at 478-825-5924.

Pickens County

County Superior Court Clerk, PO Box 130, Jasper, GA 30143. 706-253-8763, R/E recording phone-706-253-8766, UCC recording phone-706-253-8773; 8AM-5PM (EST)

Index: Separate indices to search include lis pendens book, hospital lien book, consolidated lien book, deed books. Records indexed on public terminal from 1987. Only the public may search. Copy fee $1.00 per page.Real estate copy- $.25 per page. Cert fee- $2.50 1st page, $.50 each add'l page, includes copy fee. Payee- Pickens County Clerk of Superior Court. **Online access to RE Deed, UCC, Lien, Notary, Plat records:** See www.gsccca.org for free access to Deeds back to 1999, Liens back to 2004, and UCCs back to 1995, plats back to 2004. **Other phones:** Treasurer- 706-253-8810; Elections- 706-253-8781; Vital Records- 706-253-8755. **Property tax/Assessing-** 1266 E Church St #121, Jasper, GA 30143; 706-253-8700, Fax: 706-253-8703. **Online access-** Access assessor property records free at http://qpublic.net/ga/pickens/search1.html. Also, access records on the mapping site free at www.tscmaps.com/mg/ga/pickens/index.asp.

Pierce County

County Superior Court Clerk, PO Box 588, Blackshear, GA 31516. Recording, R/E & UCC phone-912-449-2020; fax-912-449-2106; 9AM-5PM (EST) www.piercecountyga.org/

Index: Separate indices to search include real estate, plat index, lien index. Records indexed on public terminal from 2003. Only the public may search. Copy fee $1.00 per page.Real estate or tax lien copy- $.50 per page. Cert fee- $2.50 per doc plus copy fee. Payee- Pierce County Clerk of Superior Court. **Online access to RE Deed, UCC, Lien, Notary, Plat records:** See www.gsccca.org for free access to Deeds back to 1999, Liens back to 2004, and UCCs back to 1995, plats back to 2004. **Other phones:** Elections- 912-449-2028. **Property tax/Assessing-** 312 Nichols St, Blackshear, GA 31516; 912-449-2025, Fax: 912-449-8071. (Appraiser - 912-449-2025) www.piercecountyga.org/ **Online access-** Search assessor's information online at www.qpublic.net/ga/pierce/.

Pike County

County Superior Court Clerk, PO Box 10, Zebulon, GA 30295. 770-567-2000; fax-770-567-2017; 8-5PM

Index: Separate indices to search include lien, plat, deeds. Record index not computerized. Only the public may search. Copy fee $1.00 per page; self serve- $.25 per page. Cert fee- $2.50 per doc, $.50 per page includes copy fee. Payee- Pike County Clerk of Superior Court. **Online access to RE Deed, UCC, Lien, Notary, Plat records:** See www.gsccca.org for free access to Deeds back to 1999, Liens back to 2004, and UCCs back to 1995, plats back to 2004. **Property tax/Assessing-** 73 Jackson St, PO Box 377, Zebulon, GA 30295; 770-567-2002, Fax: 770-567-2006. http://pikeassessor.com/ **Online access-** Access assessor data free at www.qpublic.net/ga/pike/search1.html.

Polk County

County Superior Court Clerk, PO Box 948, Cedartown, GA 30125. 770-749-2114; fax-770-749-2148; 9AM-5PM (EST)

Index: Separate indices to search. Records indexed on public terminal from 1991. Only the public may search. Copy fee $.25 per page. Cert fee- $2.50 per page. Payee- Polk County Clerk of Superior Court. Office does not sell bulk data. **Online access to RE Deed, UCC, Lien, Notary, Plat records:** See www.gsccca.org for free access to Deeds back to 1999, Liens back to 2004, and UCCs back to 1995, plats back to 2004. **Other phones:** Treasurer- 770-749-2108. **Property tax/Assessing-** 144 West Ave, #F, Cedartown, GA 30125; 770-749-2108, Fax: 770-749-8674. **Online access-** Access assessor property records free at http://qpublic.net/ga/polk/search1.html.

Pulaski County

County Superior Court Clerk, PO Box 60, Hawkinsville, GA 31036. Recording, R/E & UCC phone-478-783-1911; fax-478-892-3308; 8AM-5PM

Index: Separate indices must be searched. Records indexed on public terminal from 1992. Only the public may search. Copy fee $1.00 per page. Cert fee- $2.00 per doc, $.50 per page, includes copies. Payee- Pulaski County Clerk of Superior Court. Office does not sell bulk data. **Online access to RE Deed, UCC, Lien, Notary, Plat records:** See www.gsccca.org for free access to Deeds back to 1999, Liens back to 2004, and UCCs back to 1995, plats back to 2004. **Other phones:** Treasurer- 478-783-2811; Elections- 478-783-2061; Vital Records- 478-783-2061. **Property tax/Assessing-** PO Box 741, 105 Lumpkin St, Hawkinsville, GA 31036; 478-892-3564, Fax: 478-783-9209. **Online access-** Free property records search on Assessor's Office webpage at www.qpublic.net/ga/pulaski/.

Putnam County

County Superior Court Clerk, 100 S Jefferson St, #236; Courthouse, Eatonton, GA 31024-1087. Recording, R/E & UCC phone-706-485-4501; fax-706-485-2875; 8AM-5PM (EST)

Index: All in one. Records indexed on public terminal from 1992. Only the public may search. Copy fee $1.00 per page; $.25 self serve. Cert fee- $2.50 per doc plus $.50 per page. Payee- Putnam County Clerk of Superior Court. **Online access to RE Deed, UCC, Lien, Notary, Plat records:** See www.gsccca.org for free access to Deeds back to 1999, Liens back to 2004, and UCCs back to 1995, plats back to 2004. **Other phones:** Elections- 706-485-8683; Vital Records- 706-485-5476; Tax Commissioner- 706-485-5441. **Property tax/Assessing-** 100 S Jefferson St, Ste 109, Eatonton, GA 31024; 706-485-6376, Fax: 706-485-3151. **Online access-** Search assessor's information online at www.qpublic.net/ga/putnam/. Search by owner name, parcel #, location, legal info, real key, sales search and sales list.

Quitman County

County Superior Court Clerk, PO Box 307, Georgetown, GA 39854. Recording, R/E & UCC phone-229-334-2578; fax-229-334-3991; 8AM-N, 1-5PM (EST)

Index: Separate indices to search include deeds, liens, fed tax lien, etc. Records indexed on public terminal from 7/1/97. Only the public may search. Copy fee $1.00 per page. Real estate or tax lien copy- $.25 per page self serve. Cert fee- $2.50 1st pg., $.50 each add'l pg, includes copy fee. Payee- Quitman County Clerk of Superior Court. Office does not sell bulk data. **Online access to RE Deed, UCC, Lien, Notary, Plat records:** See www.gsccca.org for free access to Deeds back to 1999, Liens back to 2004, and UCCs back to 1995, plats back to 2004. **Other phones:** Treasurer- 229-334-0903; Elections- 229-334-2224; Vital Records- 229-334-2224. **Property tax/Assessing-** PO Box 582, Georgetown, GA 39854; 229-334-2159, Fax: 229-334-2158. (Appraiser/Auditor- 229-334-2159) hours- 8AM-5PM **Online access-** Free property records search on Tax Assessor's Office site at www.qpublic.net/ga/quitman/

Rabun County

County Superior Court Clerk, 25 Courthouse Sq, #105, Clayton, GA 30525. Recording, R/E phone-706-782-3615; fax-706-782-1391; 8:30AM-5PM www.rabuncountygov.com/clerkofsuperiorcourt.html

Index: Separate indices to search. Records indexed on public terminal from 1993. Only the public may search. Copy fee $.25 per page. Cert fee- $2.50 1st page, $.25 each add'l, plus copy fee. Payee- Rabun County Clerk of Superior Court. Office does not sell bulk data. **Online access to RE Deed, UCC, Lien, Notary, Plat records:** See www.gsccca.org for free access to Deeds back to 1999, Liens back to 2004, and UCCs back to 1995, plats back to 2004. **Other phones:** Treasurer- 706-782-3813; Elections- 706-782-2657; Vital Records- 706-782-3614. **Property tax/Assessing-** 25 Courthouse Sq, #145, Clayton, GA 30525; 706-782-5068, Fax: 706-782-7588. **Online access-** Rabun County property records found at www.qpublic.net/ga/rabun/search.html. Search by owner name, address, or parcel number.

Randolph County

County Superior Court Clerk, PO Box 98, Cuthbert, GA 39840. 229-732-2216; fax-229-732-5881; 8-5PM

Index: All in one. Records indexed on computer back to 2002. Only the public may search. Copy fee $.25 per page. Cert fee- $2.50 per doc plus copy fee. Payee- Randolph County Clerk of Superior Court. Office does not sell bulk data. **Online access to RE Deed, UCC, Lien, Notary, Plat records:** See www.gsccca.org for free access to Deeds back to 1999, Liens back to 2004, and UCCs back to 1995, plats back to 2004. **Other phones:** Treasurer- 229-732-6440. **Property tax/Assessing-** 2005 S Webster St, PO Box 344, Cuthbert, GA 39840; 229-732-2522, Fax: 229-732-5781. hours- 8AM-N, 1PM-5PM **Online access-** Free property records search on Tax Assessor's site at www.qpublic.net/ga/randolph/

Richmond County

County Superior Court Clerk, PO Box 2046, Augusta, GA 30901. 706-821-2460, R/E recording phone-706-821-2467, UCC recording phone-706-821-1297; fax-706-821-2448; hours - 8:30AM-5PM (EST) www.augustaga.gov/departments/clerk_sup/home.asp

Index: All in one. Records indexed on computer back to 1990. Only the public may search. Copy fee $1.00 per page; self serve- $.25 per page. Cert fee- $2.50 per doc, plus $50 per page. Payee- Richmond County Clerk of Superior Court. **Online access to RE Deed, UCC, Lien, Notary, Plat records:** See www.gsccca.org for free access to Deeds back to 1999, Liens back to 2004, and UCCs back to 1995, plats back to 2004. **Other phones:** Treasurer- 706-821-2391. **Property tax/Assessing-** 530 Green St, 1st Fl, Rm 104, Augusta, GA 30911; 706-821-2310, Fax: 706-821-2325. **Online-** Access GIS at http://augustaga.gov/departments/gis/home.asp. Access Real Estate Property Search System at http://mapweb.augustaga.gov/augusta/. Search parcels by owner name, address, subdivision, parcel number.

Rockdale County

County Superior Court Clerk, PO Box 937, Conyers, GA 30012. Recording, R/E phone-770-929-4068, UCC recording phone-770-929-4069; fax-770-761-3046; 8:15AM-4:45PM www.rockdalecounty.org

Index: Separate indices to search include deeds, liens. Records indexed on public terminal from 1993 for deeds, to 2004 for liens. Office will perform a UCC search but public must search other records themselves. Copy fee $1.00 per page; $.25 self serve. Cert fee- $2.50 per doc, $.50 per page, includes copy fee. Payee- Rockdale County Clerk of Superior Court.

Online access to RE Deed, UCC, Lien, Notary, Plat records: See www.gsccca.org for free access to Deeds back to 1999, Liens back to 2004, and UCCs back to 1995, plats back to 2004. **Other phones:** Treasurer- 770-929-4009. **Property tax/Assessing-** PO Box 562, 981 Milstead Ave, Conyerrs, GA 30012; 770-929-4024, Fax: 770-918-6433. www.rockdalecounty.org/main.cfm?id=2351 **Online access-** Access assessor property records free at http://qpublic.net/ga/rockdale/search1.html.

Schley County

County Superior Court Clerk, PO Box 7, Ellaville, GA 31806-0007. Recording, R/E & UCC phone-229-937-5581; 8AM-N,1-5PM (EST)
Index: Separate indices to search include deeds, UCCs. Deed records indexed on computer back to 1990; UCCs on pubic access terminal. Only the public may search. Copy fee $.25 per page. Cert fee- $5.00 per doc plus copy fee. Payee- Schley County Clerk of Superior Court. Office does not sell bulk data. **Online access to RE Deed, UCC, Lien, Notary, Plat records:** See www.gsccca.org for free access to Deeds back to 1999, Liens back to 2004, and UCCs back to 1995, plats back to 2004. **Other phones:** Elections- 229-937-2905; Vital Records- 229-937-2905; Tax Commissioner- 229-937-2689. **Property tax/Assessing-** PO Box 1141, Ellaville, GA 31806; 229-937-9169, Fax: 229-937-5588. (Appraiser/Auditor- 229-937-9169) **Online access-** Free property records search on Tax Assessor's Office site at www.qpublic.net/ga/schley/

Screven County

County Superior Court Clerk, PO Box 156, Sylvania, GA 30467. 912-564-2614; fax-912-564-2622; 8-5
Index: All in one. Records indexed on public terminal from 1988. Only the public may search. Copy fee $.25 per page. Cert fee- $3.00 1st page; $1.50 each add'l page. Payee- Screven County Clerk of Superior Court. **Online access to RE Deed, UCC, Lien, Notary, Plat records:** See www.gsccca.org for free access to Deeds back to 1999, Liens back to 2004, and UCCs back to 1995, plats back to 2004. **Property tax/Assessing-** 216 Mims Rd, PO Box 180, Sylvania, GA 30467; 912-564-7918, Fax: 912-564-5617. **Online access-** Search property records at www.qpublic.net/ga/screven/. Search by owner name, parcel number, address, legal info, real key, sales search and sales list.

Seminole County

County Superior Court Clerk, PO Box 672, Donalsonville, GA 39845. Recording, R/E & UCC phone-229-524-2525; fax-229-524-8883; 9AM-5PM
Index: All in one. Records indexed on public terminal from 1992. Only the public may search. Copy fee $1.00 per page. Cert fee- $2.00 per doc, $.50 per page plus copy fee. Payee- Seminole County Clerk of Superior Court. Office does not sell bulk data. **Online access to RE Deed, UCC, Lien, Notary, Plat records:** See www.gsccca.org for free access to Deeds back to 1992, Liens and UCCs back to 1995, plats back to 2004. **Other phones:** Treasurer- 229-524-2238; Elections- 229-524-5256; Vital Records- 229-524-5256. **Property tax/Assessing-** Courthouse, 200 S Knox St, Donalsonville, GA 39845; 229-524-5831, Fax: 229-524-8984.

Spalding County

County Superior Court Clerk, PO Box 1046, Griffin, GA 30224. 770-467-4356; 8AM-5PM (EST) http://spaldingcounty.com/
Index: All in one. Records indexed on public terminal from 1984. Only the public may search; office will assist. Copy fee $.25 per page. Cert fee- $2.50 per doc, $.50 per page, plus copy fee. Payee- Spalding County Clerk of Superior Court. **Online access to RE Deed, UCC, Lien, Notary, Plat records:** See www.gsccca.org for free access to Deeds back to 1999, Liens back to 2004, and UCCs back to 1995, plats back to 2004. Plats will soon be available. **Property tax/Assessing-** 119 E Solomon St, Griffin, GA 30223; 770-228-9900 x350, Fax: 770-467-4247. **Online access-** Tax assessors search site at www.qpublic.net/ga/spalding/. Search by owner name, parcel number, address, legal info, real key, sales search and sales list.

Stephens County

County Superior Court Clerk, 70 N Alexander St, Rm 202; Stephens County Government Bldg, Toccoa, GA 30577-2310. Recording, R/E & UCC phone-706-886-9496; fax-706-886-5710; 8AM-5PM (EST)
Index: Separate indices to search include criminal & civil cases, real estate documents, plats, liens. Records indexed on public terminal from 1978 for deeds. Only the public may search. Copy fee $1.00 per page. Cert fee- $2.50 1st page, $.50 each add'l includes copy fee. Payee- Stephens County Clerk of Superior Court. **Online access to RE Deed, UCC, Lien, Notary, Plat records:** See www.gsccca.org for free access to Deeds back to 1999, Liens back to 2004, and UCCs back to 1995, plats back to 2004. **Other phones:** Elections- 706-886-8954; Vital Records- 706-886-2828; Commissioners- 706-886-9491. **Property tax/Assessing-** 70 N Alexander St, Rm 101, PO Box 187, Toccoa, GA 30577; 706-886-4753, Fax: 706-886-0643. **Online access-** Tax Assessor records at www.qpublic.net/ga/stephens/ search by owner name; parcel number; location; map; sales list; sales search; legal info; PPN; and account number.

Stewart County

County Superior Court Clerk, PO Box 910, Lumpkin, GA 31815-0910. 229-838-6220; fax-229-838-4505; 8AM-4:30PM (EST)
Index: Separate indices to search include liens and deeds. Records indexed on public terminal from 1993. Only the public may search. Copy fee $.25 per page. Cert fee- $2.50 per doc, $.50 per page includes copy fee. Payee- County Clerk of Superior Court. **Online access to RE Deed, UCC, Lien, Notary, Plat records:** See www.gsccca.org for free access to Deeds back to 1999, Liens back to 2004, and UCCs back to 1995, plats back to 2004. **Other phones:** Elections- 229-838-4261; Tax Commissionor- 229-838-4267. **Property tax/ Assessing-** PO Box 844, 552 Dr MLK Dr, Lumpkin, GA 31815; 229-838-6058, Fax: 229-838-9856. hours- 8AM-N 1PM-4:30PM **Online access-** Access to property records for free go to www.qpublic.net/ga/stewart/

Sumter County

County Superior Court Clerk, PO Box 333, Americus, GA 31709. Recording, R/E & UCC phone-229-928-4537; fax-229-928-4539; 9AM-5PM (EST) www.sumtercountyga.us
Index: All in one. Records indexed on public terminal from 2005. Only the public may search. Copy fee $.25 per page. Mail copies $1.00 1st page, $.25 each add'l page. No out of town personal checks accepted. Cert fee- $2.50 per doc, $.50 per page. Payee- Sumter County Clerk of Superior Court. **Online access to RE Deed, UCC, Lien, Notary, Plat records:** See www.gsccca.org for free access to Deeds back to 1999, Liens back to 2004, and UCCs back to 1995, plats back to 2004. **Other phones:** Elections- 229-928-4580; Vital Records- 229-924-3637 (Health Dept). **Property tax/Assessing-** 500 W Lamar St, PO Box 1152, Americus, GA 31709; 229-928-4514, Fax: 229-928-4512. (Appraiser/Auditor- 229-928-4513) hours- 8AM-5PM http://sumtertax.com **Online access-** Tax assessor information at www.qpublic.net/ga/sumter/. Search records by owner name; parcel number; location; legal info; real key; sales search; sales list.

Talbot County

County Superior Court Clerk, PO Box 325, Talbotton, GA 31827-0325. 706-665-3239; fax-706-665-8637; 8:30AM-5PM (EST)
Index: All in one. Records indexed on public terminal from 1995. Only the public may search. Copy fee $.25 per page. Cert fee- $2.50 per doc, $.50 per page. Payee- Talbot County Clerk of Superior Court. **Online access to RE Deed, UCC, Lien, Notary, Plat records:** See www.gsccca.org for free access to Deeds back to 1999, Liens back to 2004, and UCCs back to 1995, plats back to 2004. **Other phones:** Treasurer- 706-665-3240. **Property tax/Assessing-** 38 S Jefferson Ave, Talbotton, GA 31827; 706-665-3377, Fax: 706-665-9158. 8AM-4:30PM http://qpublic.net/ga/talbot/body.html

Taliaferro County

County Superior Court Clerk, PO Box 182, Crawfordville, GA 30631. Recording, R/E & UCC phone-706-456-2123; fax-706-456-2749; 9-N, 1-5PM
Index: Separate indices to search include deeds, liens, plats. Records indexed. Office will perform a UCC search but public must search other records themselves. Copy fee $.25 per page. Cert fee- $2.00 per doc plus copy fee. Payee- Taliaferro County Clerk of Superior Court. Office does not sell bulk data. **Online access to RE Deed, UCC, Lien, Notary, Plat records:** See www.gsccca.org for free access to Deeds back to 1999, Liens back to 2004, and UCCs back to 1995, plats back to 2004. **Other phones:** Treasurer- 706-456-2229; Elections- 706-456-2253; Vital Records- 706-456-2316. **Property tax/Assessing-** PO Box 58, Crawfordville, GA 30631; 706-456-2717, Fax: 706-456-2904. hours- 9AM-5PM T & TH **Online access-** Access Property Records at http://qpublic.net/ga/taliaferro/. Access assessor parcel data free on the Central Savannah River Area GIS site at www.csrardc.org. Click on Search and choose Taliaferro.

Tattnall County

County Superior Court Clerk, PO Box 39, Reidsville, GA 30453. Recording, R/E & UCC phone-912-557-6716; fax-912-557-4861; 8AM-5PM (EST)
Index: Separate indices to search include real estate, federal tax liens, GED for liens. Records indexed on public terminal from 1989. Only the public may search. Copy fee $.25 per page. Cert fee- $3.00 per cert plus copy fee. Payee- Tattnall County Clerk of Superior Court. **Online access to RE Deed, UCC, Lien, Notary, Plat records:** See www.gsccca.org for free access to Deeds back to 1999, Liens back to 2004, and UCCs back to 1995, plats back to 2004. **Other phones:** Probate Court- 912-557-6917. **Property tax/Assessing-** PO Box 1010, 108 D W Brazell, Reidsville, GA 30453; 912-557-4010, Fax: 912-557-4024. (Appraiser/Auditor- 912-557-4010) **Online access-** Access Assessor property records free at http://qpublic.net/ga/tattnall/.

Taylor County

County Superior Court Clerk, PO Box 248, Butler, GA 31006. Recording, R/E & UCC phone-478-862-5594; fax-478-862-5334; 8AM-5PM (EST)
Index: Separate indices to search include grantor/grantee, hosp lien, GED. Records indexed on public terminal from 1995. Only the public may search. Copy fee $1.00 per page. Self serve copy fee- $.25 per page. Cert fee- $2.50 per doc, $.50 per page plus copy fee. Payee- Taylor County Clerk of Superior Court. Office does not sell bulk data. **Online access to RE Deed, UCC, Lien, Notary, Plat records:** See www.gsccca.org for free access to Deeds back to 1999, Liens back to 2004, and UCCs back to 1995, plats back to 2004. **Other phones:** Treasurer- 478-862-3336; Elections- 478-862-3997; Vital Records- 478-862-5574. **Property tax/Assessing-** PO Box 68, 2 N Broad St, Butler, GA 31006; 478-862-3802, Fax: 478-862-3633. **Online-** Access appraiser property records free at http://qpublic.net/ga/taylor/.

Telfair County

County Superior Court Clerk, 128 E Oak St, #2; Courthouse, McRae, GA 31055-1604. Recording, R/E & UCC phone-229-868-6525; fax-229-868-7956; 8:30AM-4:30PM (EST)
Index: All in one. Records indexed on public terminal from 1992. Only the public may search. Copy fee

$1.00 per page; self serve- $.25 per page. Will fax back $1.00 per page. Cert fee- $3.00 per doc plus $.25 per page plus copy fee. Payee- Telfair County Clerk of Superior Court. Office does not sell bulk data. **Online access to RE Deed, UCC, Lien, Notary, Plat records:** See www.gsccca.org for free access to Deeds back to 1999, Liens back to 2004, and UCCs back to 1995, plats back to 2004. **Other phones:** Elections- 229-868-6038; Vital Records- 229-868-6404. **Property tax/Assessing**- 128 E Oak St, McRae, GA 31055; 229-868-2896. (Appraiser/Auditor- 229-868-2896)

Terrell County

County Superior Court Clerk, PO Box 189, Dawson, GA 39842. 229-995-2631; fax-229-995-6453; 8:30AM-5PM (EST)
Index: All in one. Records indexed on public terminal from 1995. Only the public may search. Copy fee $1.00 per page. Cert fee- $3.00 1st page, $.50 each add'l, includes copy fee. Payee- Terrell County Clerk of Superior Court. **Online access to RE Deed, UCC, Lien, Notary, Plat records:** See www.gsccca.org for free access to Deeds back to 1999, Liens back to 2004, and UCCs back to 1995, plats back to 2004. **Other phones:** Treasurer- 229-995-5151. **Property tax/Assessing**- PO Box 382, Dawson, GA 39842; 229-995-5210, Fax: 229-995-3096. hours- 8AM- N 1PM-5PM **Online** - Access property appraiser records free at http://qpublic.net/ga/terrell/search1.html.

Thomas County

County Superior Court Clerk, PO Box 1995, Thomasville, GA 31799. 229-225-4108; fax-229-225-4110; 8AM-5PM www.thomascoclerkofcourt.org
Index: Separate indices to search include UCC, GED, deed, hospital lien, plat. Records indexed on public terminal from 1989. Only the public may search but the office may be willing to fulfill a faxed search request. Copy fee $1.00 per page. Cert fee- $2.00 per cert plus copy fee. Payee- Thomas County Clerk of Superior Court. **Online access to RE Deed, UCC, Lien, Notary, Plat records:** See www.gsccca.org for free access to Deeds back to 1999, Liens back to 2004, and UCCs back to 1995, plats back to 2004. **Other phones:** Treasurer- 229-225-4133; Elections- 229-225-4101; Vital Records- 229-226-4241. **Property tax/Assessing**- 101 S Broad St, Thomasville, GA 31792; 229-225-4133, Fax: 229-225-4123. (Appraiser/Auditor- 229-225-4133) **Online** - Access appraiser property records free at http://qpublic.net/ga/thomas/search1.html.

Tift County

County Superior Court Clerk, PO Box 354, Tifton, GA 31793. 229-386-7810; fax-229-386-7813; 8-5
Index: All in one. Records indexed on public terminal from 2004. Only the public may search. Copy fee $.25 per page. Cert fee- $2.50 per cert plus copy fee. Payee- Tift County Clerk of Superior Court. **Online access to RE Deed, UCC, Lien, Notary, Plat records:** See www.gsccca.org for free access to Deeds back to 1999, Liens back to 2004, and UCCs back to 1995, plats back to 2004. **Property tax/Assessing**- 237 E 2nd St, PO Box 134, Tifton, GA 31793; 229-386-7840, fax- 229-386-7844. www.tiftcounty.org/Departments/tax_assessor/tax_assessor.htm **Online access**- Access property data on the MapGuide viewer at www.tiftcountymaps.com/.

Toombs County

County Superior Court Clerk, PO Drawer 530, Lyons, GA 30436. Recording, R/E & UCC phone-912-526-3501; fax-912-526-1015; 8:30AM-5PM (EST)
Index: All in one. Records indexed on public terminal from 1985. Only the public may search. Copy fee $.25 per page. Cert fee- $2.50 1st page, $1.00 each add'l include copy fee. Payee- Toombs County Clerk of Superior Court. **Online access to RE Deed, UCC, Lien, Notary, Plat records:** See www.gsccca.org for free access to Deeds back to 1999, Liens back to 2004, and UCCs back to 1995, plats back to 2004. **Other phones:** Treasurer- 912-526-8575; Elections- 912-526-8696. **Property tax/Assessing**- 100 Courthouse Sq, Lyons, GA 30436; 912-526-6291, Fax: 912-526-1010. (Appraiser/Auditor- 912-526-6291) hours- 8AM-5PM

Towns County

County Superior Court Clerk, 48 River St, #E; Courthouse, Hiawassee, GA 30546. Recording, R/E & UCC phone-706-896-2130; fax-706-896-1772; 8:30AM-4:30PM (EST)
Index: All in one. Records indexed on public terminal from 1992. Only the public may search. Copy fee $1.00 per page. Cert fee- $2.50 per doc, $.50 per add'l page includes copy fee. Payee- Towns County Clerk of Superior Court. Office does not sell bulk data. **Online access to RE Deed, UCC, Lien, Notary, Plat records:** See www.gsccca.org for free access to Deeds back to 1992, Liens back to 2004, and UCCs back to 1995, plats back to 2004. **Other phones:** Treasurer- 706-896-2276; Elections- 706-896-4353; Vital Records- 706-896-3467. **Property tax/Assessing**- 48 River St, Ste G, Hiawassee, GA 30546; 706-896-3984, Fax: 706-896-6980. (Appraiser/Auditor- 706-896-3984) **Online access**- Free property records search on Tax Assessor's Office site at www.qpublic.net/ga/towns/

Treutlen County

County Superior Court Clerk, 203 2nd St S, #301, Soperton, GA 30457. Recording, R/E & UCC phone-912-529-4215; fax-912-529-6737; 8AM-5PM (EST)
Index: All in one. Records indexed on public terminal from 1993. Only the public may search. Copy fee $.25 per page. Cert fee- $2.00 per doc, $.50 per page. Payee- Treutlen County Clerk of Superior Court. Office does not sell bulk data. **Online access to RE Deed, UCC, Lien, Notary, Plat records:** See www.gsccca.org for free access to Deeds back to 1999, Liens back to 2004, and UCCs back to 1995, plats back to 2004. **Other phones:** Elections- 912-529-3098. **Property tax/Assessing**- 114 2nd St, Soperton, GA 30457; 912-529-4343, Fax: 912-529-6838.

Troup County

County Superior Court Clerk, PO Box 866, LaGrange, GA 30241-0866. Recording, R/E & UCC phone-706-883-1740; fax-706-883-1724; 8AM-5PM
Records indexed on public terminal from 1994. Only the public may search. Copy fee $1.00 per page. Cert fee- $2.50 per doc, $1.00 per page. Payee- Troup County Clerk of Superior Court. **Online access to RE Deed, UCC, Lien, Notary, Plat records:** See www.gsccca.org for free access to Deeds back to 1999, Liens back to 2004, and UCCs back to 1995, plats back to 2004. **Other phones:** Treasurer- 706-883-1620. **Property tax/Assessing**- 100 Ridley Ave, 2nd Fl, PO Box 1525, LaGrange, GA 30240; 706-883-1625, Fax: 706-883-1734. **Online access**- Troup County property records at http://hosted.3xatlanta.com/sites/troup/TCPropertyRecords.nsf. Search property records by parcel number, PPIN, property address, or owner name.

Turner County

County Superior Court Clerk, PO Box 106, Ashburn, GA 31714. Recording, R/E & UCC phone-229-567-2011; fax-229-567-0450; 8AM-5PM (EST)
Index: All in one. Records indexed on public terminal from 1995. Only the public may search. Copy fee $.25 per page. Cert fee- $2.50 1st page, $.50 each add'l, plus copy fee. Payee- Turner County Clerk of Superior Court. **Online access to RE Deed, UCC, Lien, Notary, Plat records:** See www.gsccca.org for free access to Deeds back to 1999, Liens back to 2004, and UCCs back to 1995, plats back to 2004. **Other phones:** Treasurer- 229-567-4313. **Property tax/Assessing**- 208 E College Ave, PO Box 191, Ashburn, GA 31714; 229-567-2334, Fax: 229-567-4794. (Appraiser/Auditor- 229-567-2334) **Online access**- Tax assessors website http://qpublic.net/ga/turner/. Search records by owner name, address, parcel number, legal info, real key, sales search, or sales list.

Twiggs County

County Superior Court Clerk, PO Box 234, Jeffersonville, GA 31044-0228. phone-478-945-3350; fax-478-945-6751; 8AM-5PM (EST)
Index: All in one. Records indexed on public terminal from 1990. Only the public may search. Copy fee $.25 per page. Cert fee- $2.50 1st page, $.50 each add'l plus copy fee. Payee- Twiggs County Clerk of Superior Court. Office does not sell bulk data. **Online access to RE Deed, UCC, Lien, Notary, Plat records:** See www.gsccca.org for free access to Deeds back to 1999, Liens back to 2004, and UCCs back to 1995, plats back to 2004. **Other phones:** Treasurer- 478-945-3629; Elections- 478-945-3639; Vital Records- 478-945-3390. **Property tax/Assessing**- 425 Railroad St, PO Box 111, Jeffersonville, GA 31044; 478-945-3663, Fax: 478-945-6008. (Appraiser/Auditor- 478-945-3663) hours- 8:30AM-5PM **Online access**- Map site at www.twiggscountymaps.com/ site requires the use of Autodesk's Mapguide Viewer, must download the installation program (MGControl6.5sp1.exe).

Union County

County Superior Court Clerk, 114 Courthouse St, #5, Blairsville, GA 30512. 706-439-6022; fax-706-439-6026; 8AM-5PM (EST)
Index: Separate indices to search include real estate, liens, UCCs. Records indexed on public terminal from 1987. Only the public may search. Copy fee $.25 per page. Cert fee- $2.50 per cert plus copy fee. Payee- Union County Clerk of Superior Court. **Online access to RE Deed, UCC, Lien, Notary, Plat records:** See www.gsccca.org for free access to Deeds back to 1999, Liens back to 2004, and UCCs back to 1995, plats back to 2004. **Other phones:** Treasurer- 706-439-6000. **Property tax/Assessing**- 114 Courthouse St, #4, Blairsville, GA 30512; 706-439-6011, Fax: 706-439-6012. **Online access**- Tax Assessors webpage at http://qpublic.net/ga/union/. Search property records by owner name, parcel number, address, legal info, real key, sales search, or sales list.

Upson County

County Superior Court Clerk, PO Box 469, Thomaston, GA 30286. Recording, R/E & UCC phone-706-647-7835; fax-706-647-8999; 8AM-5PM
Index: Separate indices to search include land records, liens, plats. Records indexed on computer back to 1998. Only the public may search. Copy fee $1.00 per page. Cert fee- $2.50 per doc, $.50 per page, plus copy fee. Payee- County Clerk of Superior Court. Office does not sell bulk data. **Online access to RE Deed, UCC, Lien, Notary, Plat records:** See www.gsccca.org for free access to Deeds back to 1999, Liens back to 2004, and UCCs back to 1995, plats back to 2004. **Other phones:** Elections- 706-647-6259. **Property tax/Assessing**- PO Box 508, Thomaston GA, 30286; 706-647-8176, Fax: 706-647-7818. **Online access**- Access assessor's data free at www.qpublic.net/ga/upson/search1.html.

Walker County

County Superior Court Clerk, PO Box 448, La Fayette, GA 30728. Recording, R/E & UCC phone-706-638-1742; fax-706-638-1779; 8AM-5PM (EST)
Index: Separate indices to search. Records indexed on computer back to 1993. Office will perform a UCC search but public must search other records themselves. Copy fee $1.00 per page. Cert fee- $10.00 per doc plus copy fee. Payee- Walker County Clerk of Superior Court. Office does not sell bulk data. **Online access to RE Deed, UCC, Lien, Notary, Plat records:** See www.gsccca.org for free access to Deeds back to 1999, Liens back to 2004, and UCCs back to 1995, plats back to 2004. **Other phones:** Treasurer- 706-638-2929; Elections- 706-638-4349. **Property tax/Assessing**- PO Box 1604, LaFayette, GA 30728; 706-638-4823, Fax: 706-638-8363. **Online access**- Access property data on the GIS-

mapping site free at www.georgiagis.com/walker/activexframeset.cfm.

Walton County

County Superior Court Clerk, 303 S Hammond Dr, #335, Monroe, GA 30655. Recording, R/E & UCC phone-770-267-1307; fax-770-267-1441; hours-8:30AM-5PM (EST)
Index: Separate indices to search include real estate, grantor/grantee, plats, liens. Records indexed on public terminal from 1991. Only the public may search. Copy fee $.25 per page. Cert fee- $2.50 1st page, $.50 each add'l page includes copy fee. Payee- Walton County Clerk of Superior Court. **Online access to RE Deed, UCC, Lien, Notary, Plat records:** See www.gsccca.org for free access to Deeds back to 1999, Liens back to 2004, and UCCs back to 1995, plats back to 2004. **Property tax/Assessing**- 303 S Hammond Dr, #109, Monroe, GA 30655; 770-267-1352, Fax: 770-267-1007. hours-8AM-5PM

Ware County

County Superior Court Clerk, PO Box 776, Waycross, GA 31502-0776. 912-287-4340; fax-912-287-2498; 9AM-5PM (EST) http://warecounty.com
Index: All in one. Records indexed on public terminal from 1985. Only the public may search. Copy fee $.25 per page. Cert fee- $2.50 per cert plus copy fee. Payee- Ware County Clerk of Superior Court. **Online access to RE Deed, UCC, Lien, Notary, Plat records:** See www.gsccca.org for free access to Deeds back to 1999, Liens back to 2004, and UCCs back to 1995, plats back to 2004. **Other phones:** Treasurer- 912-287-4305. **Property tax/Assessing**- 215 Oak St, Waycross, GA 31501; 912-287-4383, Fax: 912-287-4386. http://warecounty.com **Online access**- Free searching on Assessor office at http://qpublic.net/ga/ware/.

Warren County

County Superior Court Clerk, PO Box 227, Warrenton, GA 30828. Recording, R/E & UCC phone-706-465-2262; fax-706-465-0232; 8AM-N, 1-5PM (EST)
Index: Separate indices to search include books, deeds, plat, UCCs indices. Records indexed on computer and public use terminal back to 1/1/93. Only the public may search. Copy fee $1.00 per page.Real estate or tax lien copy- $.25 per page. Cert fee- $2.50 per doc, $.50 add'l. Payee- Warren County Clerk of Superior Court. **Online access to RE Deed, UCC, Lien, Notary, Plat records:** See www.gsccca.org for free access to Deeds back to 1999, Liens back to 2004, and UCCs back to 1995, plats back to 2004. **Other phones:** Treasurer- 706-465-2171. **Property tax/Assessing**- PO Box 723, 521 Main St #105, Warrenton, GA 30828; 706-465-3321, Fax: 706-465-1300. hours- 8AM-5PM **Online access**- Access assessor property records free at http://qpublic.net/ga/warren/search1.html. Also, access assessor parcel data free on the Central Savannah River Area GIS site at www.csrardc.org. Click on Search then County then choose Warren.

Washington County

County Superior Court Clerk, PO Box 231, Sandersville, GA 31082-0231. Recording, R/E & UCC phone-478-552-3186; fax-478-553-9969; hours-9AM-5PM (EST)
Index: Separate indices to search. Records indexed on public terminal from 1995. Only the public may search. Copy fee $1.00; if real estate $.25 per page. Cert fee- $2.50 per doc, $.50 per page. Payee- Washington County Clerk of Superior Court. Office does not sell bulk data. **Online access to RE Deed, UCC, Lien, Notary, Plat records:** See www.gsccca.org for free access to Deeds back to 1999, Liens back to 2004, and UCCs back to 1995, plats back to 2004. **Other phones:** Treasurer- 478-552-2144; Elections- 478-552-5239. **Property tax/Assessing**- PO Box 308, 121 Jones St, Sandersville, GA 31082; 478-552-2937. **Online access**- Free records search on Assessor's Office website at www.qpublic.net/ga/washington/.

Wayne County

County Superior Court Clerk, PO Box 920, Jesup, GA 31598-0920. Recording, R/E & UCC phone-912-427-5930; fax-912-427-5939; 8:30AM-5PM (EST)
Index: Separate indices to search include deed, plat, mortgage. Records indexed on public terminal from 1994. Only the public may search. Copy fee $.25 per page. Cert fee- $2.00 per doc, $.50 per page. Payee- Wayne County Clerk of Superior Court. **Online access to RE Deed, UCC, Lien, Notary, Plat records:** See www.gsccca.org for free access to Deeds back to 1999, Liens back to 2004, and UCCs back to 1995, plats back to 2004. **Other phones:** Treasurer- 912-427-5900; Elections- 912-427-5940. **Property tax/Assessing**- PO Box 174, 341 W Walnut St, Jessup, GA 31598; 912-427-5920, Fax: 912-427-5912. **Online access**- Access property records free at http://qpublic.net/ga/wayne/.

Webster County

County Superior Court Clerk, PO Box 117, Preston, GA 31824. 229-828-3525; fax-229-828-6961; 8AM-N, 12:30-4:30PM (EST)
Index: All in one. Records indexed on public terminal from 2002. Only the public may search. Copy fee $.25 per page. Cert fee- $2.50 1st page, $.50 each add'l. Payee- Webster County Clerk of Superior Court. **Online access to RE Deed, UCC, Lien, Notary, Plat records:** See www.gsccca.org for free access to Deeds back to 1999, Liens back to 2004, and UCCs back to 1995, plats back to 2004. **Property tax/Assessing**- 6330 Hamilton St Rm 104, County Courthouse, Preston, GA 31824; 229-828-6462, Fax: 229-828-3616. (Appraiser/Auditor- 229-828-6462) hours- 8AM-N **Online access**- Access to assessment/property tax and parcel searches for free go to http://qpublic.net/ga/webster/.

Wheeler County

County Superior Court Clerk, PO Box 38, Alamo, GA 30411-0038. Recording, R/E & UCC phone-912-568-7137; fax-912-568-7453; 8AM-4PM (EST)
Index: Separate indices to search include deeds, liens, plats. Records indexed on computer back to 1998. Only the public may search; may search paper index only. Copy fee $1.00 per page; self serve $.25. Cert fee- $2.50 per doc, $.50 per page plus copy fee. Payee- Wheeler County Clerk of Superior Court. Office does not sell bulk data. **Online access to RE Deed, UCC, Lien, Notary, Plat records:** See www.gsccca.org for free access to Deeds back to 1999, Liens back to 2004, UCCs back to 1995, plats back to 2004. **Other phones:** Treasurer- 912-568-7131; Elections- 912-568-7133; Vital Records- 912-568-7161. **Property tax/Assessing**- PO Box 149, Alamo, GA 30411; 912-568-7924, Fax: 912-568-7924. **Online access**- Access property and assessor data free at http://qpublic.net/ga/wheeler/.

White County

County Superior Court Clerk, 59 S Main St, #B; Courthouse, Cleveland, GA 30528. Recording, R/E & UCC phone-706-865-2613; fax-706-865-2613; 8:30AM-5PM (EST)
Index: Indices searchable by year. Records indexed on public terminal from 1998. Only the public may search. Copy fee $1.00 per page. Cert fee- $2.50 per doc, $.50 per add'l page, includes copy fee. Payee- White County Clerk of Superior Court. **Online access to RE Deed, UCC, Lien, Notary, Plat records:** See www.gsccca.org for free access to Deeds back to 1999, Liens back to 2004, and UCCs back to 1995, plats back to 2004. **Other phones:** Elections- 706-865-4141; Vital Records- 706-865-4141; County Commissioner- 706-865-2235. **Property tax/Assessing**- 59 S Main St, #E, Cleveland, GA 30528; 706-865-5328, Fax: 706-219-7679. (Appraiser/Auditor- 706-865-5328) hours- 8AM-5PM http://whitecounty.net **Online access**- Search assessor's webpage free at www.whitecounty.net/assessors_office/assessor.htm. Search of property records by parcel number, map number, owner first or last name, address.

Whitfield County

County Superior Court Clerk, PO Box 868, Dalton, GA 30722. 706-275-7450 (Crim) 7480 (Civil), R/E recording phone-706-275-7450; fax-706-275-7456; 8AM-5PM (EST) www.whitfieldcountyga.com/
Index: Separate indices to search include alpha by month. Records indexed on public terminal from 1971. Only the public may search. Copy fee $.25 per page. Cert fee- $3.00 per cert includes copy fee. Payee- Whitfield County Clerk of Superior Court. **Online access to RE Deed, UCC, Lien, Notary, Plat records:** See www.gsccca.org for free access to Deeds back to 1999, Liens back to 2004, and UCCs back to 1995, plats back to 2004. Also, access to deeds, plats, etc for free go to http://whitfieldmst.whitfieldcountyga.com:8085/searchext/ . **Other phones:** Treasurer- 706-275-7510. **Property tax/Assessing**- 205 N Selvidge St, Ste B, Dalton, GA 30720; 706-275-7410, Fax: 706-275-7544. www.whitfieldcountyga.com/TaxAssessor/tax_assessor.htm **Online access**- Access to property tax data is available free at www.whitfieldcountyga.com/GIS/Public/searchassessor.asp. A subscription service is also available for professions requiring full property data.

Wilcox County

County Superior Court Clerk, 103 N Broad St; Courthouse, Abbeville, GA 31001-1000. Recording, R/E & UCC phone-229-467-2442; fax-229-467-2886; 9AM-5PM (EST)
Index: Separate indices to search include deed, lien, UCC, plat. Records indexed on public terminal from 1993. Only the public may search. Copy fee $1.00 per page.Real estate or tax lien record copy- $.25 per page. Cert fee- $2.50 per doc, $.50 per add'l page, includes copy fee. Payee- County Clerk of Superior Court. **Online access to RE Deed, UCC, Lien, Notary, Plat records:** See www.gsccca.org for free access to Deeds back to 1999, Liens back to 2004, and UCCs back to 1995, plats back to 2004. **Other phones:** Treasurer- 229-467-2010; Elections- 229-467-2300; Vital Records- 229-467-2220. **Property tax/Assessing**- 103 N Broad St, Abbeville, GA 31001; 229-467-2428, Fax: 229-467-2028. (Appraiser/Auditor- 229-467-2028) hours- 8AM-5PM **Online access**- Access to property records on Assessor webpage at www.qpublic.net/ga/wilcox/. Basic search is free; sales and sketches require subscription.

Wilkes County

County Superior Court Clerk, 23 E Court St, Rm 205, Washington, GA 30673. Recording, R/E & UCC phone-706-678-2423; fax-706-678-2115; 9AM-5PM
Index: Separate indices to search include deed, lien, plat. Records indexed on computer back to 1998. Only the public may search. Copy fee $.25 per page. Cert fee- $2.00 per doc and $.50 per page. Payee- Wilkes County Superior Court Clerk. Office does not sell bulk data. **Online access to RE Deed, UCC, Lien, Notary, Plat records:** See www.gsccca.org for free access to Deeds back to 1999, Liens back to 2004, and UCCs back to 1995, plats back to 2004. **Other phones:** Elections- 706-678-2523; Births, Deaths- 706-678-2523; **Property tax/Assessing**- 23 E Court St, Rm 202, Washington, GA 30673; 706-678-7732. hours- 8AM-5PM A public access terminal is available. **Online access**- Free property records searching on Assessor's webpage at www.qpublic.net/ga/wilkes/

Wilkinson County

County Superior Court Clerk & Juvenile Court, PO Box 250, Irwinton, GA 31042-0250. Recording, R/E & UCC phone-478-946-2221; fax-478-946-1497; 8AM-5PM (EST)
Index: Separate indices to search include liens, real estate, divorces. Records indexed on public terminal

from 1993. Only the public may search. Will not search UCC records. Copy fee $1.00 per page; self serve $.25. Cert fee- $2.00 per doc, $.50 per page includes copy fee. Payee- Wilkinson County Clerk of Superior Court. Office does not sell bulk data. **Online access to RE Deed, UCC, Lien, Notary, Plat records:** See www.gsccca.org for free access to Deeds back to 1999, Liens back to 2004, and UCCs back to 1995, plats back to 2004. **Other phones:** Treasurer- 478-946-2236 (County Commissioner); Elections- 478-946-2188; Vital Records- 478-946-2222; Tax Commissioner- 478-946-2232. **Property tax/Assessing**- PO Box 189, Irwinton, GA 31042; 478-946-2076, Fax: 478-946-3767. **Online access**- Free property records search at www.qpublic.net/ga/wilkinson/

Worth County

County Superior Court Clerk, 201 N Main St, Rm 13; Courthouse, Sylvester, GA 31791. Recording, R/E & UCC phone-229-776-8205; fax-229-776-8237; 8AM-5PM (EST)

Index: Separate indices to search include books 1988-1993, books 1917-1988, liens, computer. Records indexed on computer back to 1992. Only the public may search. Copy fee $1.00 per page; self serve $.25. Cert fee- $2.50 per doc, $.50 per page, plus copy fee. Payee- Worth County Clerk of Superior Court. **Online access to RE Deed, UCC, Lien, Notary, Plat records:** See www.gsccca.org for free access to Deeds back to 1992, Liens back to 2004, and UCCs back to 1995, plats back to 2004. **Other phones:** Elections- 229-776-8208; Vital Records- 229-776-8207; Tax Office- 229-776-8204. **Property tax/Assessing**- 201 N Main St, Rm 16, Sylvester, GA 31791; 229-776-8203, Fax: 229-776-8244..

Georgia County Locator

You will usually be able to find the city name in the City/County Cross Reference below. In that case, it is a simple matter to determine the county from the cross reference. However, only the official US Postal Service city names are included in this index. There are an additional 40,000 place names that people use in their addresses. Therefore, we have also included a ZIP/City Cross Reference immediately following the City/County Cross Reference.

If you know the ZIP Code but the city name does not appear in the City/County Cross Reference index, look up the ZIP Code in the ZIP/City Cross Reference, find the city name, then look up the city name in the City/County Cross Reference. For example, you want to know the county for an address of Menands, NY 12204. There is no "Menands" in the City/County Cross Reference. The ZIP/City Cross Reference shows that ZIP Codes 12201-12288 are for the city of Albany. Looking back in the City/County Cross Reference, Albany is in Albany County.

Georgia City/County Cross Reference

ABBEVILLE Wilcox
ACWORTH (30102) Cherokee(53), Bartow(25), Cobb(21)
ACWORTH (30101) Cobb(71), Paulding(23), Bartow(4)
ADAIRSVILLE (30103) Bartow(66), Gordon(25), Floyd(8)
ADEL Cook
ADRIAN (31002) Emanuel(54), Johnson(25), Laurens(14), Treutlen(6)
AILEY Montgomery
ALAMO (30411) Wheeler(69), Laurens(30)
ALAPAHA (31622) Berrien(95), Irwin(4)
ALBANY (31701) Dougherty(96), Lee(3)
ALBANY (31705) Dougherty(89), Worth(5), Mitchell(4)
ALBANY (31721) Dougherty(87), Lee(8), Baker(2), Terrell(1)
ALBANY Dougherty
ALLENHURST (31301) Liberty(76), Long(23)
ALLENTOWN Wilkinson
ALMA (31510) Bacon(95), Pierce(4)
ALPHARETTA (30005) Fulton(81), Forsyth(18)
ALPHARETTA Fulton
ALSTON Montgomery
ALTO (30510) Habersham(62), Banks(30), Hall(6)
ALTO Habersham
AMBROSE Coffee
AMERICUS (31719) Sumter(91), Schley(8)
AMERICUS Sumter
ANDERSONVILLE (31711) Macon(80), Sumter(16), Schley(2)
APPLING Columbia
ARABI (31712) Crisp(82), Turner(11), Worth(6)
ARAGON (30104) Polk(72), Floyd(24), Bartow(3)
ARGYLE Clinch
ARLINGTON (39813) Calhoun(58), Early(40)
ARMUCHEE (30105) Floyd(67), Chattooga(32)
ARNOLDSVILLE (30619) Oglethorpe(91), Oconee(8)
ASHBURN (31714) Turner(96), Worth(2)
ATHENS (30601) Clarke(95), Madison(3), Jackson(1)
ATHENS (30606) Clarke(88), Oconee(11)
ATHENS (30607) Jackson(59), Clarke(40)
ATHENS Clarke
ATLANTA (30339) Cobb(96), Fulton(3)
ATLANTA (30338) De Kalb(98), Fulton(1)
ATLANTA (30360) De Kalb(79), Gwinnett(20)
ATLANTA (30324) Fulton(83), De Kalb(16)
ATLANTA (30349) Fulton(65), Clayton(34)
ATLANTA (30350) Fulton(97), De Kalb(2)
ATLANTA (30354) Fulton(91), Clayton(8)
ATLANTA De Kalb
ATLANTA Fulton
ATTAPULGUS Decatur
AUBURN (30011) Barrow(78), Gwinnett(21)
AUBURN Barrow
AUGUSTA (30907) Columbia(73), Richmond(26)
AUGUSTA (30909) Richmond(98), Columbia(1)
AUGUSTA Columbia
AUGUSTA Richmond
AUSTELL (30168) Cobb(90), Douglas(9)
AVERA (30803) Jefferson(92), Glascock(7)
AVONDALE ESTATES De Kalb
AXSON (31624) Atkinson(68), Coffee(23), Ware(8)
BACONTON Mitchell
BAINBRIDGE Decatur
BALDWIN Banks
BALL GROUND (30107) Cherokee(80), Pickens(14), Forsyth(4)
BARNESVILLE (30204) Lamar(95), Upson(3)
BARNEY Brooks
BARTOW (30413) Jefferson(71), Washington(27), Johnson(1)
BARWICK Brooks
BAXLEY Appling
BELLVILLE Evans
BERLIN Colquitt
BETHLEHEM (30620) Barrow(73), Gwinnett(19), Walton(6)
BISHOP (30621) Oconee(73), Morgan(26)
BLACKSHEAR Pierce
BLAIRSVILLE (30512) Union(98), Fannin(1)
BLAIRSVILLE Union
BLAKELY (39823) Early(97), Miller(2)
BLOOMINGDALE (31302) Chatham(55), Effingham(44)
BLUE RIDGE (30513) Fannin(89), Gilmer(10)
BLUFFTON (31724) Clay(89), Early(10)
BLUFFTON (39824) Early(54), Clay(45)
BLYTHE (30805) Burke(54), Richmond(45)
BOGART (30622) Oconee(61), Clarke(30), Jackson(8)
BOLINGBROKE Monroe
BONAIRE Houston
BONEVILLE McDuffie
BOSTON (31626) Thomas(82), Brooks(17)
BOSTWICK Morgan
BOWDON (30108) Carroll(95), Heard(4)
BOWDON JUNCTION Carroll
BOWERSVILLE Hart
BOWMAN (30624) Elbert(74), Hart(14), Madison(10)
BOX SPRINGS (31801) Talbot(58), Marion(39), Muscogee(1)
BRASELTON (30517) Jackson(63), Gwinnett(14), Hall(13), Barrow(8)
BREMEN (30110) Haralson(92), Carroll(7)
BRINSON (39825) Decatur(90), Seminole(9)
BRINSON Decatur
BRISTOL (31518) Appling(56), Pierce(26), Wayne(14), Bacon(2)
BRONWOOD Terrell
BROOKFIELD Tift
BROOKLET Bulloch
BROOKS (30205) Spalding(52), Fayette(47)
BROXTON (31519) Coffee(97), Jeff Davis(2)
BRUNSWICK Glynn
BUCHANAN (30113) Haralson(87), Polk(12)
BUCKHEAD (30625) Morgan(95), Putnam(4)
BUENA VISTA (31803) Marion(94), Schley(4)
BUFORD (30519) Gwinnett(93), Hall(6)
BUFORD Gwinnett
BUTLER Taylor
BYROMVILLE Dooly
BYRON (31008) Peach(67), Crawford(23), Houston(9)
CADWELL Laurens
CAIRO Grady
CALHOUN (30701) Gordon(98), Floyd(1)
CALHOUN Gordon
CALVARY Grady
CAMAK Warren
CAMILLA (31730) Mitchell(98), Decatur(1)
CANON (30520) Hart(60), Franklin(39)
CANTON Cherokee
CARLTON (30627) Madison(71), Oglethorpe(28)
CARNESVILLE (30521) Franklin(96), Banks(3)
CARROLLTON Carroll
CARTERSVILLE Bartow
CASSVILLE Bartow
CATAULA Harris
CAVE SPRING Floyd
CECIL Cook
CEDAR SPRINGS Early
CEDARTOWN (30125) Polk(98), Floyd(1)
CENTERVILLE Houston
CHATSWORTH Murray
CHAUNCEY (31011) Dodge(98), Laurens(1)
CHERRYLOG (30522) Gilmer(57), Fannin(42)
CHESTER (31012) Dodge(89), Bleckley(9), Laurens(1)
CHESTNUT MOUNTAIN Hall
CHICKAMAUGA (30707) Walker(97), Catoosa(2)
CHULA (31733) Tift(54), Irwin(44)
CISCO Murray
CLARKDALE Cobb
CLARKESVILLE (30523) Habersham(89), Rabun(10)
CLARKSTON De Kalb
CLAXTON (30417) Evans(89), Tattnall(10)
CLAYTON (30525) Rabun(98), Towns(1)
CLERMONT (30527) Hall(89), White(10)
CLEVELAND (30528) White(96), Lumpkin(3)
CLIMAX Decatur
CLINCHFIELD Houston
CLYO Effingham
COBB Sumter
COBBTOWN (30420) Tattnall(92), Candler(6)
COCHRAN (31014) Bleckley(85), Twiggs(11), Dodge(2)
COCHRAN Putnam
COHUTTA Whitfield
COLBERT (30628) Madison(93), Oglethorpe(6)
COLEMAN (39836) Clay(68), Randolph(31)
COLEMAN (31736) Randolph(80), Clay(19)
COLLINS Tattnall
COLQUITT (31737) Miller(96), Baker(2)
COLQUITT (39837) Miller(80), Early(13), Decatur(3), Baker(2)
COLUMBUS Muscogee
COMER (30629) Madison(91), Oglethorpe(8)
COMMERCE (30530) Jackson(41), Banks(26), Madison(22), Franklin(9)
COMMERCE Jackson
CONCORD Pike
CONLEY (30288) De Kalb(52), Clayton(47)
CONLEY Clayton
CONYERS (30012) Rockdale(97), De Kalb(1)
CONYERS (30013) Rockdale(93), Newton(6)
CONYERS Rockdale
COOLIDGE (31738) Thomas(88), Colquitt(11)
COOSA Floyd
CORDELE Crisp
CORNELIA Habersham
COTTON Mitchell
COVINGTON (30014) Newton(89), Walton(9)
COVINGTON Newton
CRANDALL Murray
CRAWFORD Oglethorpe
CRAWFORDVILLE (30631) Taliaferro(91), Wilkes(7), Greene(1)
CRESCENT McIntosh
CULLODEN (31016) Monroe(52), Upson(28), Crawford(14), Lamar(4)
CUMMING (30040) Forsyth(95), Cherokee(4)
CUMMING Forsyth
CUSSETA (31805) Chattahoochee(98), Stewart(1)
CUTHBERT (39840) Randolph(89), Calhoun(10)
CUTHBERT Randolph
DACULA (30019) Gwinnett(98), Walton(1)
DACULA Gwinnett
DAHLONEGA Lumpkin
DAISY Evans
DALLAS (30157) Paulding(98), Cobb(1)
DALLAS Paulding
DALTON Whitfield
DAMASCUS (31741) Early(73), Baker(19), Miller(6)
DAMASCUS (39841) Early(95), Miller(2), Baker(1)

DANIELSVILLE (30633) Madison(98), Franklin(1)
DANVILLE (31017) Twiggs(76), Wilkinson(19), Bleckley(4)
DARIEN McIntosh
DAVISBORO Washington
DAWSON (39842) Terrell(93), Calhoun(6)
DAWSON Terrell
DAWSONVILLE (30534) Dawson(86), Lumpkin(10), Forsyth(2)
DE SOTO (31743) Sumter(65), Lee(34)
DEARING (30808) McDuffie(97), Warren(2)
DECATUR De Kalb
DEMOREST Habersham
DENTON (31532) Jeff Davis(97), Coffee(2)
DEWY ROSE (30634) Elbert(55), Hart(44)
DEXTER Laurens
DILLARD Rabun
DIXIE Brooks
DOERUN (31744) Colquitt(66), Worth(29), Mitchell(4)
DONALSONVILLE Seminole
DOUGLAS Coffee
DOUGLASVILLE (30134) Douglas(62), Paulding(37)
DOUGLASVILLE Douglas
DOVER Screven
DRY BRANCH (31020) Twiggs(95), Bibb(4)
DU PONT (31630) Clinch(74), Echols(25)
DUBLIN Laurens
DUDLEY (31022) Laurens(97), Bleckley(1), Dodge(1)
DULUTH (30097) Gwinnett(48), Fulton(45), Forsyth(5)
DULUTH Fulton
DULUTH Gwinnett
EAST ELLIJAY Gilmer
EASTANOLLEE (30538) Stephens(72), Franklin(27)
EASTMAN Dodge
EATONTON Putnam
EDEN Effingham
EDISON (39846) Calhoun(95), Clay(4)
ELBERTON (30635) Elbert(98), Hart(1)
ELKO Houston
ELLABELL (31308) Bryan(77), Bulloch(22)
ELLAVILLE (31806) Schley(90), Macon(8)
ELLENTON Colquitt
ELLENWOOD (30294) De Kalb(42), Clayton(34), Henry(23)
ELLENWOOD Gwinnett
ELLERSLIE Harris
ELLIJAY (30536) Gilmer(98), Dawson(1)
ELLIJAY Gilmer
EMERSON Bartow
ENIGMA (31749) Berrien(65), Tift(32), Irwin(1)
EPWORTH Fannin
ESOM HILL Polk
ETON Murray
EVANS Columbia
EXPERIMENT Spalding
FAIRBURN (30213) Fulton(86), Fayette(13)
FAIRMOUNT (30139) Gordon(60), Pickens(33), Bartow(5)
FARGO (31631) Clinch(78), Charlton(13), Echols(8)
FARMINGTON Oconee
FAYETTEVILLE (30215) Fayette(92), Clayton(7)
FAYETTEVILLE Fayette
FELTON Haralson
FITZGERALD (31750) Ben Hill(86), Irwin(13)
FLEMING Liberty
FLINTSTONE Walker
FLOVILLA Butts
FLOWERY BRANCH Hall
FOLKSTON (31537) Charlton(93), Camden(6)
FOREST PARK Clayton
FORSYTH Monroe
FORT BENNING (31905) Chattahoochee(59), Muscogee(40)
FORT BENNING Muscogee
FORT GAINES Clay
FORT OGLETHORPE Catoosa
FORT STEWART (31314) Liberty(97), Bryan(1)
FORT STEWART Liberty
FORT VALLEY (31030) Peach(76), Crawford(20), Macon(2), Houston(1)
FORTSON (31808) Harris(65), Muscogee(34)
FOWLSTOWN Decatur
FRANKLIN Heard
FRANKLIN SPRINGS Franklin
FUNSTON Colquitt
GAINESVILLE (30506) Hall(95), Forsyth(4)
GAINESVILLE Hall
GARFIELD (30425) Emanuel(38), Bulloch(38), Jenkins(23)
GAY Meriwether
GENEVA Talbot
GEORGETOWN (39854) Clay(51), Quitman(48)
GEORGETOWN (31754) Quitman(89), Clay(11)
GIBSON (30810) Glascock(86), Warren(11), Jefferson(1)
GILLSVILLE (30543) Hall(59), Banks(24), Jackson(15)
GIRARD (30426) Burke(81), Screven(18)
GLENN Heard
GLENNVILLE (30427) Tattnall(98), Long(1)
GLENWOOD (30428) Wheeler(73), Laurens(26)
GOOD HOPE (30641) Walton(82), Morgan(16)
GORDON (31031) Wilkinson(65), Twiggs(21), Baldwin(7), Jones(5)
GOUGH Burke
GRACEWOOD Richmond
GRANTVILLE (30220) Meriwether(54), Coweta(45)
GRAY Jones
GRAYSON Gwinnett
GRAYSVILLE Catoosa
GREENSBORO Greene
GREENVILLE (30222) Meriwether(98), Troup(1)
GRIFFIN (30224) Spalding(91), Pike(6), Lamar(2)
GRIFFIN Spalding
GROVETOWN (30813) Columbia(95), Richmond(4)
GUYTON Effingham
HADDOCK (31033) Jones(86), Baldwin(13)
HAGAN Evans
HAHIRA (31632) Lowndes(58), Cook(41)
HAMILTON Harris
HAMPTON (30228) Henry(60), Clayton(34), Spalding(4)
HARALSON Coweta
HARDWICK Baldwin
HARLEM (30814) Columbia(98), McDuffie(1)
HARRISON Washington
HARTSFIELD Colquitt
HARTWELL Hart
HAWKINSVILLE (31036) Pulaski(86), Houston(13)
HAZLEHURST (31539) Jeff Davis(94), Appling(4)
HELEN White
HELENA (31037) Telfair(88), Wheeler(9), Dodge(1)
HEPHZIBAH (30815) Richmond(79), Burke(20)
HIAWASSEE Towns
HIGH SHOALS Morgan
HILLSBORO (31038) Jasper(74), Jones(23), Putnam(2)
HINESVILLE (31313) Liberty(98), Long(1)
HINESVILLE Liberty
HIRAM (30141) Paulding(96), Cobb(3)
HOBOKEN Brantley
HOGANSVILLE (30230) Troup(64), Heard(17), Meriwether(17), Coweta(1)
HOLLY SPRINGS Cherokee
HOMER Banks
HOMERVILLE Clinch
HORTENSE (31543) Wayne(50), Brantley(43), Glynn(5)
HOSCHTON (30548) Jackson(78), Gwinnett(10), Barrow(8), Hall(2)
HOWARD Taylor
HULL (30646) Madison(97), Jackson(1), Clarke(1)
IDEAL Macon
ILA Madison
INMAN Fayette
IRON CITY (39859) Seminole(96), Miller(3)
IRWINTON Wilkinson
IRWINVILLE Irwin
JACKSON (30233) Butts(82), Monroe(10), Henry(3), Lamar(2)
JACKSONVILLE Telfair
JAKIN Early
JASPER (30143) Pickens(98), Cherokee(1)
JEFFERSON Jackson
JEFFERSONVILLE (31044) Twiggs(98), Wilkinson(1)
JEKYLL ISLAND Glynn
JEKYLL ISLAND BRANCH Glynn
JENKINSBURG (30234) Butts(84), Henry(14)
JERSEY Walton
JESUP Wayne
JEWELL (31045) Warren(96), Hancock(3)
JONESBORO (30236) Clayton(94), Henry(5)
JONESBORO (30238) Clayton(94), Fayette(5)
JONESBORO Clayton
JULIETTE (31046) Monroe(88), Jones(11)
JUNCTION CITY Talbot
KATHLEEN Houston
KENNESAW Cobb
KEYSVILLE (30816) Burke(73), Jefferson(26)
KINGS BAY Camden
KINGSLAND Camden
KINGSTON (30145) Bartow(56), Floyd(43)
KITE (31049) Johnson(60), Emanuel(39)
KNOXVILLE Crawford
LA FAYETTE Walker
LAGRANGE (30240) Troup(98), Heard(1)
LAGRANGE Troup
LAKE PARK (31636) Lowndes(60), Echols(39)
LAKELAND Lanier
LAKEMONT Rabun
LAVONIA (30553) Franklin(63), Hart(36)
LAWRENCEVILLE Gwinnett
LEARY (31762) Baker(50), Calhoun(50)
LEARY (39862) Calhoun(96), Baker(3)
LEBANON Cherokee
LEESBURG Lee
LENOX (31637) Cook(88), Colquitt(5), Berrien(3), Tift(1)
LESLIE (31764) Sumter(92), Lee(7)
LEXINGTON Oglethorpe
LILBURN Gwinnett
LILLY Dooly
LINCOLNTON (30817) Lincoln(96), McDuffie(1), Wilkes(1)
LINDALE (30147) Floyd(94), Polk(5)
LITHIA SPRINGS Douglas
LITHONIA De Kalb
LIZELLA (31052) Bibb(55), Crawford(44)
LOCUST GROVE (30248) Henry(93), Spalding(4), Butts(1)
LOGANVILLE (30052) Walton(57), Gwinnett(40), Rockdale(1)
LOGANVILLE Gwinnett
LOOKOUT MOUNTAIN (30750) Walker(66), Dade(33)
LOUISVILLE (30434) Jefferson(96), Burke(3)
LOUVALE Stewart
LOVEJOY Clayton
LUDOWICI (31316) Long(98), Liberty(1)
LULA (30554) Hall(59), Banks(40)
LUMBER CITY (31549) Telfair(82), Wheeler(17)
LUMPKIN Stewart
LUTHERSVILLE Meriwether
LYERLY Chattooga
LYONS (30436) Toombs(89), Emanuel(5), Tattnall(5)
MABLETON Cobb
MACON (31210) Bibb(90), Monroe(9)
MACON (31211) Bibb(58), Jones(41)
MACON (31217) Bibb(51), Twiggs(37), Jones(10)
MACON (31220) Bibb(80), Monroe(19)
MACON Bibb
MADISON (30650) Morgan(93), Greene(5), Walton(1)
MANASSAS Tattnall
MANCHESTER (31816) Meriwether(90), Talbot(9)
MANOR Ware
MANSFIELD (30055) Jasper(49), Newton(44), Morgan(5)
MANSFIELD Jasper
MARBLE HILL (30148) Pickens(70), Dawson(29)
MARIETTA Cobb
MARSHALLVILLE Macon
MARTIN (30557) Franklin(55), Stephens(44)
MATTHEWS Jefferson
MAUK (31058) Taylor(47), Marion(45), Schley(6)
MAXEYS Oglethorpe
MAYSVILLE (30558) Jackson(53), Banks(46)
MC CAYSVILLE Fannin
MC INTYRE Wilkinson
MC RAE Telfair
MCDONOUGH (30252) Henry(98), Rockdale(1)
MCDONOUGH Henry
MEANSVILLE (30256) Pike(57), Upson(40), Lamar(2)
MEIGS (31765) Mitchell(42), Thomas(33), Colquitt(24)
MELDRIM Effingham
MENLO (30731) Chattooga(60), Walker(25), Dade(14)
MERIDIAN McIntosh
MERSHON (31551) Pierce(58), Bacon(41)
MESENA Warren
METTER Candler
MIDLAND (31820) Muscogee(65), Harris(34)
MIDVILLE (30441) Burke(49), Emanuel(49), Jenkins(1)
MIDWAY Liberty
MILAN (31060) Dodge(76), Telfair(23)
MILLEDGEVILLE (31061) Baldwin(94), Putnam(3), Wilkinson(1), Hancock(1)
MILLEDGEVILLE Baldwin
MILLEN (30442) Jenkins(93), Burke(4), Screven(1)
MILLWOOD (31552) Ware(67), Atkinson(28), Coffee(4)
MILNER (30257) Lamar(87), Pike(12)
MINERAL BLUFF Fannin
MITCHELL (30820) Glascock(47), Warren(45), Washington(6)
MOLENA (30258) Pike(72), Upson(27)
MONROE Walton
MONTEZUMA (31063) Dooly(67), Macon(32)
MONTICELLO Jasper

MONTROSE (31065) Laurens(87), Bleckley(8), Wilkinson(3)
MOODY A F B Lowndes
MORELAND Coweta
MORGAN Calhoun
MORGANTON (30560) Fannin(83), Union(16)
MORRIS (39867) Clay(83), Randolph(8), Quitman(5), Stewart(2)
MORRIS (31767) Quitman(60), Clay(29), Randolph(4), Stewart(4)
MORROW Clayton
MORVEN Brooks
MOULTRIE Colquitt
MOUNT AIRY Habersham
MOUNT BERRY Floyd
MOUNT VERNON Montgomery
MOUNT ZION Carroll
MOUNTAIN CITY Rabun
MURRAYVILLE (30564) Lumpkin(61), Hall(33), White(5)
MUSELLA (31066) Crawford(94), Monroe(3), Bibb(2)
MYSTIC Irwin
NAHUNTA (31553) Brantley(97), Charlton(2)
NASHVILLE Berrien
NAYLOR (31641) Lowndes(78), Lanier(21)
NELSON Cherokee
NEWBORN (30056) Jasper(56), Newton(22), Morgan(20)
NEWBORN Newton
NEWINGTON (30446) Screven(67), Effingham(32)
NEWNAN Coweta
NEWTON Baker
NICHOLLS (31554) Coffee(67), Bacon(22), Ware(9)
NICHOLSON (30565) Jackson(85), Madison(14)
NORCROSS (30092) Gwinnett(97), Fulton(2)
NORCROSS Gwinnett
NORMAN PARK (31771) Colquitt(97), Worth(2)
NORRISTOWN Emanuel
NORTH METRO Gwinnett
NORWOOD Warren
NUNEZ Emanuel
OAKFIELD Worth
OAKMAN Gordon
OAKWOOD Hall
OCHLOCKNEE (31773) Thomas(79), Grady(18), Colquitt(1)
OCILLA Irwin
OCONEE Washington
ODUM (31555) Wayne(85), Appling(14)
OFFERMAN Pierce
OGLETHORPE Macon
OLIVER Screven
OMAHA Stewart
OMEGA (31775) Colquitt(58), Tift(24), Worth(17)
ORCHARD HILL Spalding
OXFORD (30054) Newton(84), Walton(15)
OXFORD Newton
PALMETTO (30268) Fulton(81), Coweta(18)
PARROTT (31777) Terrell(81), Webster(18)
PARROTT (39877) Webster(81), Terrell(18)
PATTERSON (31557) Pierce(95), Appling(3)
PAVO (31778) Brooks(69), Thomas(28), Colquitt(1)
PEACHTREE CITY Fayette
PEARSON (31642) Atkinson(91), Coffee(5), Clinch(2)
PELHAM (31779) Mitchell(82), Grady(16)
PEMBROKE (31321) Bryan(54), Bulloch(45)
PENDERGRASS (30567) Jackson(74), Hall(25)
PERKINS (30822) Jenkins(96), Burke(3)
PERRY (31069) Houston(97), Peach(2)
PINE LAKE De Kalb
PINE MOUNTAIN (31822) Harris(67), Troup(24), Meriwether(8)
PINE MOUNTAIN VALLEY Harris
PINEHURST Dooly
PINEVIEW (31071) Wilcox(94), Pulaski(5)
PITTS (31072) Crisp(52), Wilcox(47)
PLAINFIELD Dodge
PLAINS (31780) Sumter(74), Webster(25)
PLAINVILLE (30733) Gordon(93), Floyd(6)
POOLER Chatham
PORTAL (30450) Bulloch(98), Emanuel(1)
PORTERDALE Fayette
PORTERDALE Newton
POULAN Worth
POWDER SPRINGS (30127) Cobb(80), Paulding(19)
POWDER SPRINGS Cobb
PRESTON Webster
PULASKI Candler
PUTNEY Dougherty
QUITMAN Brooks
RABUN GAP Rabun
RANGER (30734) Gordon(76), Pickens(23)
RAY CITY (31645) Berrien(51), Lowndes(26), Lanier(22)
RAYLE (30660) Wilkes(80), Oglethorpe(16), Taliaferro(3)
REBECCA (31783) Turner(60), Irwin(30), Ben Hill(9)
RED OAK Fulton
REDAN De Kalb
REGISTER (30452) Bulloch(97), Evans(1)
REIDSVILLE Tattnall
RENTZ Laurens
RESACA (30735) Gordon(63), Murray(22), Whitfield(14)
REX (30273) Clayton(92), Henry(7)
REYNOLDS (31076) Macon(69), Taylor(30)
RHINE (31077) Dodge(94), Telfair(5)
RICEBORO (31323) Liberty(94), McIntosh(5)
RICHLAND (31825) Webster(74), Stewart(24)
RICHMOND HILL Bryan
RINCON Effingham
RINGGOLD (30736) Catoosa(97), Walker(2)
RISING FAWN (30738) Dade(69), Walker(30)
RIVERDALE (30296) Clayton(81), Fulton(11), Fayette(6)
RIVERDALE Clayton
ROBERTA Crawford
ROCHELLE Wilcox
ROCK SPRING (30739) Walker(82), Catoosa(17)
ROCKLEDGE Laurens
ROCKMART (30153) Polk(65), Paulding(30), Haralson(4)
ROCKY FACE (30740) Whitfield(87), Walker(12)
ROCKY FORD (30455) Screven(98), Jenkins(1)
ROME Floyd
ROOPVILLE (30170) Heard(62), Carroll(37)
ROSSVILLE (30741) Walker(66), Catoosa(33)
ROSWELL (30075) Fulton(82), Cobb(15), Cherokee(1)
ROSWELL Fulton
ROYSTON (30662) Franklin(56), Hart(27), Madison(14), Elbert(1)
RUPERT (31081) Taylor(96), Macon(1), Schley(1)
RUTLEDGE Morgan
RYDAL (30171) Bartow(79), Gordon(20)
SAINT GEORGE Charlton
SAINT MARYS Camden
SAINT SIMONS ISLAND Glynn
SALE CITY (31784) Mitchell(95), Colquitt(4)
SANDERSVILLE Washington
SAPELO ISLAND McIntosh
SARDIS Burke
SARGENT Coweta
SASSER Terrell
SAUTEE NACOOCHEE (30571) White(97), Habersham(2)
SAVANNAH Chatham
SCOTLAND Telfair
SCOTTDALE De Kalb
SCREVEN Wayne
SEA ISLAND Glynn
SEA ISLAND BRANCH Glynn
SENOIA (30276) Coweta(82), Meriwether(12), Fayette(5)
SEVILLE Wilcox
SHADY DALE Jasper
SHANNON Floyd
SHARON Taliaferro
SHARPSBURG Coweta
SHELLMAN (31786) Randolph(95), Terrell(2), Calhoun(1)
SHELLMAN (39886) Randolph(63), Calhoun(34), Terrell(1)
SHILOH (31826) Talbot(63), Harris(36)
SILOAM Greene
SILVER CREEK (30173) Floyd(92), Polk(7)
SMARR Monroe
SMITHVILLE (31787) Lee(60), Sumter(39)
SMYRNA Cobb
SNELLVILLE (30039) Gwinnett(95), De Kalb(2), Rockdale(1)
SNELLVILLE Gwinnett
SOCIAL CIRCLE (30025) Walton(74), Newton(25)
SOCIAL CIRCLE Walton
SOPERTON (30457) Treutlen(94), Montgomery(3), Emanuel(1)
SPARKS Cook
SPARTA (31087) Hancock(95), Baldwin(3), Washington(1)
SPRINGFIELD Effingham
STAPLETON (30823) Warren(50), Jefferson(48)
STATENVILLE Echols
STATESBORO Bulloch
STATHAM (30666) Barrow(66), Oconee(25), Jackson(7)
STEPHENS Oglethorpe
STILLMORE Emanuel
STOCKBRIDGE (30281) Henry(88), Rockdale(5), Clayton(5)
STOCKTON (31649) Lanier(77), Echols(17), Clinch(5)
STONE MOUNTAIN (30087) De Kalb(57), Gwinnett(42)
STONE MOUNTAIN De Kalb
SUCHES (30572) Union(75), Fannin(24)
SUGAR VALLEY (30746) Gordon(96), Walker(3)
SUMMERTOWN Emanuel
SUMMERVILLE (30747) Chattooga(96), Walker(3)
SUMNER Worth
SUNNY SIDE Spalding
SURRENCY Appling
SUWANEE (30024) Gwinnett(72), Forsyth(25), Fulton(2)
SUWANEE Gwinnett
SWAINSBORO Emanuel
SYCAMORE (31790) Turner(98), Irwin(1)
SYLVANIA Screven
SYLVESTER (31791) Worth(98), Dougherty(1)
TALBOTTON Talbot
TALKING ROCK (30175) Pickens(62), Gilmer(37)
TALLAPOOSA Haralson
TALLULAH FALLS Rabun
TALMO (30575) Jackson(74), Hall(25)
TARRYTOWN (30470) Montgomery(83), Treutlen(16)
TATE Pickens
TAYLORSVILLE (30178) Bartow(81), Polk(17), Paulding(1)
TEMPLE (30179) Carroll(50), Paulding(32), Haralson(17)
TENNGA Murray
TENNILLE (31089) Washington(98), Johnson(1)
THE ROCK (30285) Upson(61), Pike(20), Lamar(18)
THOMASTON Upson
THOMASVILLE (31792) Thomas(97), Grady(2)
THOMASVILLE Thomas
THOMSON (30824) McDuffie(96), Warren(1), Columbia(1)
TIFTON Tift
TIGER Rabun
TIGNALL (30668) Wilkes(82), Lincoln(17)
TOCCOA (30577) Stephens(69), Franklin(22), Habersham(6), Banks(1)
TOCCOA Stephens
TOOMSBORO Wilkinson
TOWNSEND McIntosh
TRENTON Dade
TRION (30753) Chattooga(77), Walker(22)
TUCKER (30084) De Kalb(78), Gwinnett(21)
TUCKER De Kalb
TUNNEL HILL (30755) Whitfield(53), Catoosa(46)
TURIN Coweta
TURNERVILLE Habersham
TWIN CITY (30471) Emanuel(85), Bulloch(13), Candler(1)
TY TY (31795) Worth(56), Tift(43)
TYBEE ISLAND Chatham
TYRONE Fayette
UNADILLA (31091) Dooly(98), Houston(1)
UNION CITY Fulton
UNION POINT (30669) Greene(88), Oglethorpe(10)
UPATOI (31829) Muscogee(71), Harris(28)
UVALDA (30473) Toombs(61), Montgomery(38)
VALDOSTA (31605) Lowndes(97), Brooks(2)
VALDOSTA Lowndes
VALONA McIntosh
VARNELL Whitfield
VIDALIA (30474) Toombs(87), Montgomery(11), Emanuel(1)
VIDALIA Toombs
VIENNA (31092) Dooly(96), Crisp(3)
VILLA RICA (30180) Carroll(70), Douglas(20), Paulding(8)
WACO (30182) Carroll(62), Haralson(37)
WADLEY Jefferson
WALESKA Cherokee
WALTHOURVILLE Liberty
WARESBORO Ware
WARM SPRINGS (31830) Meriwether(96), Harris(3)
WARNER ROBINS Houston
WARRENTON Warren
WARTHEN Washington
WARWICK (31796) Worth(98), Crisp(1)
WASHINGTON Wilkes
WATKINSVILLE (30677) Oconee(96), Greene(3)
WAVERLY Camden
WAVERLY HALL (31831) Talbot(55), Harris(44)
WAYCROSS (31503) Ware(94), Brantley(4), Pierce(1)
WAYCROSS Ware
WAYNESBORO Burke

WAYNESVILLE (31566) Brantley(56), Camden(38), Glynn(4)
WEST GREEN (31567) Jeff Davis(58), Coffee(41)
WEST POINT (31833) Troup(70), Harris(29)
WESTON Webster
WHIGHAM Grady
WHITE (30184) Bartow(70), Cherokee(29)
WHITE OAK Camden
WHITE PLAINS (30678) Greene(96), Hancock(1), Taliaferro(1)
WHITESBURG (30185) Carroll(95), Douglas(4)
WILDWOOD Dade
WILEY Rabun
WILLACOOCHEE (31650) Coffee(70), Atkinson(28)
WILLIAMSON (30292) Pike(68), Spalding(31)
WINDER (30680) Barrow(98), Oconee(1)
WINSTON Douglas
WINTERVILLE (30683) Clarke(60), Oglethorpe(37), Madison(2)
WOODBINE Camden
WOODBURY Meriwether
WOODLAND Talbot
WOODSTOCK (30188) Cherokee(97), Cobb(2)
WOODSTOCK Cherokee
WRAY (31798) Irwin(50), Coffee(41), Ben Hill(7)
WRENS Jefferson
WRIGHTSVILLE (31096) Johnson(84), Washington(10), Laurens(5)
YATESVILLE (31097) Upson(89), Lamar(7), Monroe(3)
YOUNG HARRIS (30582) Towns(78), Union(21)
ZEBULON (30295) Pike(97), Lamar(2))

Georgia ZIP/City Cross Reference

In 2003, a number of Georgia Zip Codes were changed. This change affected 31 Zip Codes (listed below) beginning with 317. These 31 Zip Codes now begin with 398. The locations (and county in parenthesis) are: ARLINGTON (Calhoun), ATTAPULGUS (Decatur), BAINBRIDGE (Decatur), BLAKELY (Early), BLUFFTON (Clay), BRINSON (Decatur), BRONWOOD (Terrell), CAIRO (Grady), CALVARY (Grady), CEDAR SPRINGS (Early), CLIMAX (Decatur), COLEMAN (Randolph), COLQUITT (Miller), CUTHBERT (Randolph), DAMASCUS (Early), DAWSON (Terrell), DONALSONVILLE (Seminole), EDISON (Calhoun), FORT GAINES (Clay), FOWLSTOWN (Decatur), GEORGETOWN (Quitman), IRON CITY (Seminole), JAKIN (Early), LEARY (Calhoun), MORGAN (Calhoun), MORRIS (Quitman), NEWTON (Baker), PARROTT (Terrell), SASSER (Terrell), SHELLMAN (Randolph), WHIGHAM (Grady). There is one new Zip Code for Atlanta - 39901.

30001-30001 AUSTELL
30002-30002 AVONDALE ESTATES
30003-30003 NORCROSS
30004-30005 ALPHARETTA
30006-30008 MARIETTA
30009-30009 ALPHARETTA
30010-30010 NORCROSS
30011-30011 AUBURN
30012-30013 CONYERS
30014-30016 COVINGTON
30017-30017 GRAYSON
30018-30018 JERSEY
30019-30019 DACULA
30020-30020 CLARKDALE
30021-30021 CLARKSTON
30022-30023 ALPHARETTA
30024-30024 SUWANEE
30025-30025 SOCIAL CIRCLE
30026-30026 DULUTH
30026-30026 NORTH METRO
30027-30027 CONLEY
30028-30028 CUMMING
30029-30029 DULUTH
30029-30029 NORTH METRO
30030-30037 DECATUR
30038-30038 LITHONIA
30039-30039 SNELLVILLE
30040-30041 CUMMING
30042-30046 LAWRENCEVILLE
30047-30048 LILBURN
30049-30049 ELLENWOOD
30049-30049 LAWRENCEVILLE
30050-30051 FOREST PARK
30052-30052 LOGANVILLE
30054-30054 OXFORD
30055-30055 MANSFIELD
30056-30056 NEWBORN
30057-30057 LITHIA SPRINGS
30058-30058 LITHONIA
30059-30059 MABLETON
30060-30069 MARIETTA
30070-30070 PORTERDALE
30071-30071 NORCROSS
30072-30072 PINE LAKE
30073-30073 POWDER SPRINGS
30074-30074 REDAN
30075-30077 ROSWELL
30078-30078 SNELLVILLE
30079-30079 SCOTTDALE
30080-30082 SMYRNA
30083-30083 STONE MOUNTAIN
30084-30085 TUCKER
30086-30088 STONE MOUNTAIN
30089-30089 DECATUR
30090-30090 MARIETTA
30091-30093 NORCROSS
30094-30094 CONYERS
30095-30099 DULUTH
30101-30102 ACWORTH
30103-30103 ADAIRSVILLE
30104-30104 ARAGON
30105-30105 ARMUCHEE
30106-30106 AUSTELL
30107-30107 BALL GROUND
30108-30108 BOWDON
30109-30109 BOWDON JUNCTION
30110-30110 BREMEN
30111-30111 CLARKDALE
30112-30112 CARROLLTON
30113-30113 BUCHANAN
30114-30115 CANTON
30116-30119 CARROLLTON
30120-30121 CARTERSVILLE
30122-30122 LITHIA SPRINGS
30123-30123 CASSVILLE
30124-30124 CAVE SPRING
30125-30125 CEDARTOWN
30126-30126 MABLETON
30127-30127 POWDER SPRINGS
30128-30128 CUMMING
30129-30129 COOSA
30130-30131 CUMMING
30132-30132 DALLAS
30133-30135 DOUGLASVILLE
30136-30136 DULUTH
30137-30137 EMERSON
30138-30138 ESOM HILL
30139-30139 FAIRMOUNT
30140-30140 FELTON
30141-30141 HIRAM
30142-30142 HOLLY SPRINGS
30143-30143 JASPER
30144-30144 KENNESAW
30145-30145 KINGSTON
30146-30146 LEBANON
30147-30147 LINDALE
30148-30148 MARBLE HILL
30149-30149 MOUNT BERRY
30150-30150 MOUNT ZION
30151-30151 NELSON
30152-30152 KENNESAW
30153-30153 ROCKMART
30154-30154 DOUGLASVILLE
30155-30155 DULUTH
30156-30156 KENNESAW
30157-30157 DALLAS
30158-30159 NORTH METRO
30160-30160 KENNESAW
30161-30165 ROME
30168-30168 AUSTELL
30169-30169 CANTON
30170-30170 ROOPVILLE
30171-30171 RYDAL
30172-30172 SHANNON
30173-30173 SILVER CREEK
30174-30174 SUWANEE
30175-30175 TALKING ROCK
30176-30176 TALLAPOOSA
30177-30177 TATE
30178-30178 TAYLORSVILLE
30179-30179 TEMPLE
30180-30180 VILLA RICA
30182-30182 WACO
30183-30183 WALESKA
30184-30184 WHITE
30185-30185 WHITESBURG
30187-30187 WINSTON
30188-30189 WOODSTOCK
30195-30199 DULUTH
30201-30202 ALPHARETTA
30203-30203 AUBURN
30204-30204 BARNESVILLE
30205-30205 BROOKS
30206-30206 CONCORD
30207-30208 CONYERS
30209-30210 COVINGTON
30211-30211 DACULA
30212-30212 EXPERIMENT
30213-30213 FAIRBURN
30214-30215 FAYETTEVILLE
30216-30216 FLOVILLA
30217-30217 FRANKLIN
30218-30218 GAY
30219-30219 GLENN
30220-30220 GRANTVILLE
30221-30221 GRAYSON
30222-30222 GREENVILLE
30223-30224 GRIFFIN
30226-30226 LILBURN
30227-30227 LAWRENCEVILLE
30228-30228 HAMPTON
30229-30229 HARALSON
30230-30230 HOGANSVILLE
30232-30232 INMAN
30233-30233 JACKSON
30234-30234 JENKINSBURG
30235-30235 JERSEY
30236-30238 JONESBORO
30239-30239 ALPHARETTA
30240-30241 LAGRANGE
30243-30246 LAWRENCEVILLE
30247-30247 LILBURN
30248-30248 LOCUST GROVE
30249-30249 LOGANVILLE
30250-30250 LOVEJOY
30251-30251 LUTHERSVILLE
30252-30253 MCDONOUGH
30254-30254 NEWNAN
30255-30255 MANSFIELD
30256-30256 MEANSVILLE
30257-30257 MILNER
30258-30258 MOLENA
30259-30259 MORELAND
30260-30260 MORROW
30261-30261 LAGRANGE
30262-30262 NEWBORN
30263-30265 NEWNAN
30266-30266 ORCHARD HILL
30267-30267 OXFORD
30268-30268 PALMETTO
30269-30269 PEACHTREE CITY
30270-30270 PORTERDALE
30270-30270 PEACHTREE CITY
30271-30271 NEWNAN
30272-30272 RED OAK
30273-30273 REX
30274-30274 RIVERDALE
30275-30275 SARGENT
30276-30276 SENOIA
30277-30277 SHARPSBURG
30278-30278 SNELLVILLE
30279-30279 SOCIAL CIRCLE
30281-30281 STOCKBRIDGE
30284-30284 SUNNY SIDE
30285-30285 THE ROCK
30286-30286 THOMASTON
30287-30287 MORROW
30288-30288 CONLEY
30289-30289 TURIN
30290-30290 TYRONE
30291-30291 UNION CITY
30292-30292 WILLIAMSON
30293-30293 WOODBURY
30294-30294 ELLENWOOD
30295-30295 ZEBULON
30296-30296 RIVERDALE
30297-30298 FOREST PARK
30301-30399 ATLANTA
30401-30401 SWAINSBORO
30410-30410 AILEY
30411-30411 ALAMO
30412-30412 ALSTON
30413-30413 BARTOW
30414-30414 BELLVILLE
30415-30415 BROOKLET
30417-30417 CLAXTON

ZIP Range	City
30420-30420	COBBTOWN
30421-30421	COLLINS
30423-30423	DAISY
30424-30424	DOVER
30425-30425	GARFIELD
30426-30426	GIRARD
30427-30427	GLENNVILLE
30428-30428	GLENWOOD
30429-30429	HAGAN
30434-30434	LOUISVILLE
30436-30436	LYONS
30438-30438	MANASSAS
30439-30439	METTER
30441-30441	MIDVILLE
30442-30442	MILLEN
30445-30445	MOUNT VERNON
30446-30446	NEWINGTON
30447-30447	NORRISTOWN
30448-30448	NUNEZ
30449-30449	OLIVER
30450-30450	PORTAL
30451-30451	PULASKI
30452-30452	REGISTER
30453-30453	REIDSVILLE
30454-30454	ROCKLEDGE
30455-30455	ROCKY FORD
30456-30456	SARDIS
30457-30457	SOPERTON
30458-30461	STATESBORO
30464-30464	STILLMORE
30466-30466	SUMMERTOWN
30467-30467	SYLVANIA
30470-30470	TARRYTOWN
30471-30471	TWIN CITY
30473-30473	UVALDA
30474-30475	VIDALIA
30477-30477	WADLEY
30499-30499	REIDSVILLE
30501-30501	GAINESVILLE
30502-30502	CHESTNUT MOUNTAIN
30503-30507	GAINESVILLE
30510-30510	ALTO
30511-30511	BALDWIN
30512-30512	BLAIRSVILLE
30513-30513	BLUE RIDGE
30514-30514	BLAIRSVILLE
30515-30515	BUFORD
30516-30516	BOWERSVILLE
30517-30517	BRASELTON
30518-30519	BUFORD
30520-30520	CANON
30521-30521	CARNESVILLE
30522-30522	CHERRYLOG
30523-30523	CLARKESVILLE
30525-30525	CLAYTON
30527-30527	CLERMONT
30528-30528	CLEVELAND
30529-30530	COMMERCE
30531-30531	CORNELIA
30533-30533	DAHLONEGA
30534-30534	DAWSONVILLE
30535-30535	DEMOREST
30536-30536	ELLIJAY
30537-30537	DILLARD
30538-30538	EASTANOLLEE
30539-30539	EAST ELLIJAY
30540-30540	ELLIJAY
30541-30541	EPWORTH
30542-30542	FLOWERY BRANCH
30543-30543	GILLSVILLE
30544-30544	DEMOREST
30545-30545	HELEN
30546-30546	HIAWASSEE
30547-30547	HOMER
30548-30548	HOSCHTON
30549-30549	JEFFERSON
30552-30552	LAKEMONT
30553-30553	LAVONIA
30554-30554	LULA
30555-30555	MC CAYSVILLE
30557-30557	MARTIN
30558-30558	MAYSVILLE
30559-30559	MINERAL BLUFF
30560-30560	MORGANTON
30562-30562	MOUNTAIN CITY
30563-30563	MOUNT AIRY
30564-30564	MURRAYVILLE
30565-30565	NICHOLSON
30566-30566	OAKWOOD
30567-30567	PENDERGRASS
30568-30568	RABUN GAP
30571-30571	SAUTEE NACOOCHEE
30572-30572	SUCHES
30573-30573	TALLULAH FALLS
30575-30575	TALMO
30576-30576	TIGER
30577-30577	TOCCOA
30580-30580	TURNERVILLE
30581-30581	WILEY
30582-30582	YOUNG HARRIS
30596-30596	ALTO
30597-30597	DAHLONEGA
30598-30598	TOCCOA
30599-30599	COMMERCE
30601-30613	ATHENS
30619-30619	ARNOLDSVILLE
30620-30620	BETHLEHEM
30621-30621	BISHOP
30622-30622	BOGART
30623-30623	BOSTWICK
30624-30624	BOWMAN
30625-30625	BUCKHEAD
30627-30627	CARLTON
30628-30628	COLBERT
30629-30629	COMER
30630-30630	CRAWFORD
30631-30631	CRAWFORDVILLE
30633-30633	DANIELSVILLE
30634-30634	DEWY ROSE
30635-30635	ELBERTON
30638-30638	FARMINGTON
30639-30639	FRANKLIN SPRINGS
30641-30641	GOOD HOPE
30642-30642	GREENSBORO
30643-30643	HARTWELL
30645-30645	HIGH SHOALS
30646-30646	HULL
30647-30647	ILA
30648-30648	LEXINGTON
30650-30650	MADISON
30655-30656	MONROE
30660-30660	RAYLE
30662-30662	ROYSTON
30663-30663	RUTLEDGE
30664-30664	SHARON
30665-30665	SILOAM
30666-30666	STATHAM
30667-30667	STEPHENS
30668-30668	TIGNALL
30669-30669	UNION POINT
30671-30671	MAXEYS
30673-30673	WASHINGTON
30677-30677	WATKINSVILLE
30678-30678	WHITE PLAINS
30680-30680	WINDER
30683-30683	WINTERVILLE
30701-30703	CALHOUN
30705-30705	CHATSWORTH
30707-30707	CHICKAMAUGA
30708-30708	CISCO
30710-30710	COHUTTA
30711-30711	CRANDALL
30719-30722	DALTON
30724-30724	ETON
30725-30725	FLINTSTONE
30726-30726	GRAYSVILLE
30728-30728	LA FAYETTE
30730-30730	LYERLY
30731-30731	MENLO
30732-30732	OAKMAN
30733-30733	PLAINVILLE
30734-30734	RANGER
30735-30735	RESACA
30736-30736	RINGGOLD
30738-30738	RISING FAWN
30739-30739	ROCK SPRING
30740-30740	ROCKY FACE
30741-30741	ROSSVILLE
30742-30742	FORT OGLETHORPE
30746-30746	SUGAR VALLEY
30747-30747	SUMMERVILLE
30750-30750	LOOKOUT MOUNTAIN
30751-30751	TENNGA
30752-30752	TRENTON
30753-30753	TRION
30755-30755	TUNNEL HILL
30756-30756	VARNELL
30757-30757	WILDWOOD
30802-30802	APPLING
30803-30803	AVERA
30805-30805	BLYTHE
30806-30806	BONEVILLE
30807-30807	CAMAK
30808-30808	DEARING
30809-30809	EVANS
30810-30810	GIBSON
30811-30811	GOUGH
30812-30812	GRACEWOOD
30813-30813	GROVETOWN
30814-30814	HARLEM
30815-30815	HEPHZIBAH
30816-30816	KEYSVILLE
30817-30817	LINCOLNTON
30818-30818	MATTHEWS
30819-30819	MESENA
30820-30820	MITCHELL
30821-30821	NORWOOD
30822-30822	PERKINS
30823-30823	STAPLETON
30824-30824	THOMSON
30828-30828	WARRENTON
30830-30830	WAYNESBORO
30833-30833	WRENS
30900-30999	AUGUSTA
31001-31001	ABBEVILLE
31002-31002	ADRIAN
31003-31003	ALLENTOWN
31004-31004	BOLINGBROKE
31005-31005	BONAIRE
31006-31006	BUTLER
31007-31007	BYROMVILLE
31008-31008	BYRON
31009-31009	CADWELL
31010-31010	CORDELE
31011-31011	CHAUNCEY
31012-31012	CHESTER
31013-31013	CLINCHFIELD
31014-31014	COCHRAN
31015-31015	CORDELE
31016-31016	CULLODEN
31017-31017	DANVILLE
31018-31018	DAVISBORO
31019-31019	DEXTER
31020-31020	DRY BRANCH
31021-31021	DUBLIN
31022-31022	DUDLEY
31023-31023	EASTMAN
31024-31024	EATONTON
31025-31025	ELKO
31026-31026	COCHRAN
31026-31026	EATONTON
31027-31027	DUBLIN
31028-31028	CENTERVILLE
31029-31029	FORSYTH
31030-31030	FORT VALLEY
31031-31031	GORDON
31032-31032	GRAY
31033-31033	HADDOCK
31034-31034	HARDWICK
31035-31035	HARRISON
31036-31036	HAWKINSVILLE
31037-31037	HELENA
31038-31038	HILLSBORO
31039-31039	HOWARD
31040-31040	DUBLIN
31041-31041	IDEAL
31042-31042	IRWINTON
31044-31044	JEFFERSONVILLE
31045-31045	JEWELL
31046-31046	JULIETTE
31047-31047	KATHLEEN
31049-31049	KITE
31050-31050	KNOXVILLE
31051-31051	LILLY
31052-31052	LIZELLA
31054-31054	MC INTYRE
31055-31055	MC RAE
31057-31057	MARSHALLVILLE
31058-31058	MAUK
31059-31059	MILLEDGEVILLE
31060-31060	MILAN
31061-31062	MILLEDGEVILLE
31063-31063	MONTEZUMA
31064-31064	MONTICELLO
31065-31065	MONTROSE
31066-31066	MUSELLA
31067-31067	OCONEE
31068-31068	OGLETHORPE
31069-31069	PERRY
31070-31070	PINEHURST
31071-31071	PINEVIEW
31072-31072	PITTS
31073-31073	PLAINFIELD
31075-31075	RENTZ
31076-31076	REYNOLDS
31077-31077	RHINE
31078-31078	ROBERTA
31079-31079	ROCHELLE
31081-31081	RUPERT
31082-31082	SANDERSVILLE
31083-31083	SCOTLAND
31084-31084	SEVILLE
31085-31085	SHADY DALE
31086-31086	SMARR
31087-31087	SPARTA
31088-31088	WARNER ROBINS
31089-31089	TENNILLE
31090-31090	TOOMSBORO
31091-31091	UNADILLA
31092-31092	VIENNA
31093-31093	WARNER ROBINS
31094-31094	WARTHEN
31095-31095	WARNER ROBINS
31096-31096	WRIGHTSVILLE
31097-31097	YATESVILLE
31098-31099	WARNER ROBINS
31106-31199	ATLANTA
31200-31299	MACON
31301-31301	ALLENHURST
31302-31302	BLOOMINGDALE
31303-31303	CLYO
31304-31304	CRESCENT
31305-31305	DARIEN
31307-31307	EDEN
31308-31308	ELLABELL
31309-31309	FLEMING
31310-31310	HINESVILLE
31312-31312	GUYTON
31313-31313	HINESVILLE
31314-31315	FORT STEWART
31316-31316	LUDOWICI
31318-31318	MELDRIM
31319-31319	MERIDIAN
31320-31320	MIDWAY
31321-31321	PEMBROKE
31322-31322	POOLER
31323-31323	RICEBORO
31324-31324	RICHMOND HILL
31326-31326	RINCON
31327-31327	SAPELO ISLAND
31328-31328	TYBEE ISLAND
31329-31329	SPRINGFIELD
31331-31331	TOWNSEND
31332-31332	VALONA
31333-31333	WALTHOURVILLE
31400-31499	SAVANNAH
31501-31503	WAYCROSS
31510-31510	ALMA

ZIP Range	City
31512-31512	AMBROSE
31513-31515	BAXLEY
31516-31516	BLACKSHEAR
31518-31518	BRISTOL
31519-31519	BROXTON
31520-31521	BRUNSWICK
31522-31522	SAINT SIMONS ISLAND
31523-31525	BRUNSWICK
31527-31527	JEKYLL ISLAND
31527-31527	JEKYLL ISLAND BRANCH
31532-31532	DENTON
31533-31535	DOUGLAS
31537-31537	FOLKSTON
31539-31539	HAZLEHURST
31542-31542	HOBOKEN
31543-31543	HORTENSE
31544-31544	JACKSONVILLE
31545-31546	JESUP
31547-31547	KINGS BAY
31548-31548	KINGSLAND
31549-31549	LUMBER CITY
31550-31550	MANOR
31551-31551	MERSHON
31552-31552	MILLWOOD
31553-31553	NAHUNTA
31554-31554	NICHOLLS
31555-31555	ODUM
31556-31556	OFFERMAN
31557-31557	PATTERSON
31558-31558	SAINT MARYS
31560-31560	SCREVEN
31561-31561	SEA ISLAND
31561-31561	SEA ISLAND BRANCH
31562-31562	SAINT GEORGE
31563-31563	SURRENCY
31564-31564	WARESBORO
31565-31565	WAVERLY
31566-31566	WAYNESVILLE
31567-31567	WEST GREEN
31568-31568	WHITE OAK
31569-31569	WOODBINE
31598-31599	JESUP
31601-31606	VALDOSTA
31620-31620	ADEL
31622-31622	ALAPAHA
31623-31623	ARGYLE
31624-31624	AXSON
31625-31625	BARNEY
31626-31626	BOSTON
31627-31627	CECIL
31629-31629	DIXIE
31630-31630	DU PONT
31631-31631	FARGO
31632-31632	HAHIRA
31634-31634	HOMERVILLE
31635-31635	LAKELAND
31636-31636	LAKE PARK
31637-31637	LENOX
31638-31638	MORVEN
31639-31639	NASHVILLE
31641-31641	NAYLOR
31642-31642	PEARSON
31643-31643	QUITMAN
31645-31645	RAY CITY
31646-31646	SAINT GEORGE
31647-31647	SPARKS
31648-31648	STATENVILLE
31649-31649	STOCKTON
31650-31650	WILLACOOCHEE
31698-31699	VALDOSTA
31699-31699	MOODY A F B
31700-31708	ALBANY
31709-31710	AMERICUS
31711-31711	ANDERSONVILLE
31712-31712	ARABI
31713-31713	ARLINGTON
31714-31714	ASHBURN
31715-31715	ATTAPULGUS
31716-31716	BACONTON
31717-31718	BAINBRIDGE
31719-31719	AMERICUS
31720-31720	BARWICK
31721-31721	ALBANY
31722-31722	BERLIN
31723-31723	BLAKELY
31724-31724	BLUFFTON
31725-31725	BRINSON
31726-31726	BRONWOOD
31727-31727	BROOKFIELD
31728-31728	CAIRO
31729-31729	CALVARY
31730-31730	CAMILLA
31732-31732	CEDAR SPRINGS
31733-31733	CHULA
31734-31734	CLIMAX
31735-31735	COBB
31736-31736	COLEMAN
31737-31737	COLQUITT
31738-31738	COOLIDGE
31739-31739	COTTON
31740-31740	CUTHBERT
31741-31741	DAMASCUS
31742-31742	DAWSON
31743-31743	DE SOTO
31744-31744	DOERUN
31745-31745	DONALSONVILLE
31746-31746	EDISON
31747-31747	ELLENTON
31749-31749	ENIGMA
31750-31750	FITZGERALD
31751-31751	FORT GAINES
31752-31752	FOWLSTOWN
31753-31753	FUNSTON
31754-31754	GEORGETOWN
31756-31756	HARTSFIELD
31757-31758	THOMASVILLE
31759-31759	IRON CITY
31760-31760	IRWINVILLE
31761-31761	JAKIN
31762-31762	LEARY
31763-31763	LEESBURG
31764-31764	LESLIE
31765-31765	MEIGS
31766-31766	MORGAN
31767-31767	MORRIS
31768-31768	MOULTRIE
31769-31769	MYSTIC
31770-31770	NEWTON
31771-31771	NORMAN PARK
31772-31772	OAKFIELD
31773-31773	OCHLOCKNEE
31774-31774	OCILLA
31775-31775	OMEGA
31776-31776	MOULTRIE
31777-31777	PARROTT
31778-31778	PAVO
31779-31779	PELHAM
31780-31780	PLAINS
31781-31781	POULAN
31782-31782	PUTNEY
31783-31783	REBECCA
31784-31784	SALE CITY
31785-31785	SASSER
31786-31786	SHELLMAN
31787-31787	SMITHVILLE
31788-31788	MOULTRIE
31789-31789	SUMNER
31790-31790	SYCAMORE
31791-31791	SYLVESTER
31792-31792	THOMASVILLE
31793-31794	TIFTON
31795-31795	TY TY
31796-31796	WARWICK
31797-31797	WHIGHAM
31798-31798	WRAY
31799-31799	THOMASVILLE
31801-31801	BOX SPRINGS
31803-31803	BUENA VISTA
31804-31804	CATAULA
31805-31805	CUSSETA
31806-31806	ELLAVILLE
31807-31807	ELLERSLIE
31808-31808	FORTSON
31810-31810	GENEVA
31811-31811	HAMILTON
31812-31812	JUNCTION CITY
31814-31814	LOUVALE
31815-31815	LUMPKIN
31816-31816	MANCHESTER
31820-31820	MIDLAND
31821-31821	OMAHA
31822-31822	PINE MOUNTAIN
31823-31823	PINE MOUNTAIN VALLEY
31824-31824	PRESTON
31825-31825	RICHLAND
31826-31826	SHILOH
31827-31827	TALBOTTON
31829-31829	UPATOI
31830-31830	WARM SPRINGS
31831-31831	WAVERLY HALL
31832-31832	WESTON
31833-31833	WEST POINT
31836-31836	WOODLAND
31900-31904	COLUMBUS
31905-31905	FORT BENNING
31906-31994	COLUMBUS
31995-31995	FORT BENNING
31997-31999	COLUMBUS
39813-39813	ARLINGTON
39815-39815	ATTAPULGUS
39817-39819	BAINBRIDGE
39823-39823	BLAKELY
39824-39824	BLUFFTON
39825-39825	BRINSON
39826-39826	BRONWOOD
39827-39828	CAIRO
39829-39829	CALVARY
39832-39832	CEDAR SPRINGS
39834-39834	CLIMAX
39836-39836	COLEMAN
39837-39837	COLQUITT
39840-39840	CUTHBERT
39841-39841	DAMASCUS
39842-39842	DAWSON
39845-39845	DONALSONVILLE
39846-39846	EDISON
39851-39851	FORT GAINES
39852-39852	FOWLSTOWN
39854-39854	GEORGETOWN
39859-39859	IRON CITY
39861-39861	JAKIN
39862-39862	LEARY
39866-39866	MORGAN
39867-39867	MORRIS
39870-39870	NEWTON
39877-39877	PARROTT
39885-39885	SASSER
39886-39886	SHELLMAN
39897-39897	WHIGHAM
39901-39901	ATLANTA

Hawaii

General Help Numbers:

Governor's Office
State Capitol
415 S Beretania St
Honolulu, HI 96813
http://hawaii.gov/gov/
808-586-0034
Fax 808-586-0006
7:45AM-5PM

Attorney General's Office
425 Queen St
Honolulu, HI 96813
www.hawaii.gov/ag/
808-586-1500
Fax 808-586-1239
7:45AM-4:30PM

Legislative Records
Hawaii Legislature
415 S Beretania St
Honolulu, HI 96813
www.capitol.hawaii.gov
808-587-0700
Fax 808-586-3584
9AM-5PM

State Archives
Iolani Palace Grounds
Honolulu, HI 96813
http://hawaii.gov/dags/archives/
808-586-0329
Fax 808-586-0330
9AM-4PM

State Specifics:

Capital:	Honolulu Honolulu County
Time Zone:	HT (Hawaii Standard Time)
Number of Counties:	4
Population:	1,288,198
Web Site:	www.ehawaii.gov

State Agencies

Criminal Records

Hawaii Criminal Justice Data Center, Criminal Record Request, 465 S King St, Room 101, Honolulu, HI 96813; 808-587-3279; 8AM-4PM.

http://hawaii.gov/ag/hcjdc/

Indexing & Storage: Records available from the 1930's. New records available for inquiry in 1 to 20 days. Per a US DOJ Study in 2003, 90% of all arrests in database have final dispositions recorded, 91% for those arrests within last 5 years.

Searching: Include in request- any aliases. Also helpful are gender, date of birth, SSN. Submission of fingerprints is an option. Per a US DOJ Study in 2003, 99% of the records are fingerprint-supported. This data not released- non-conviction or pending data. Only records with convictions are released to the public. Records without dispositions are not released.

Access by: mail, in person, online.

Fee & Payment: The search fee for a name-based criminal record search or a fingerprint-based search is $20.00. A public access printout, available only in-person at this office or at main police stations, is $10.00. Certification fee: $10.00. Fee payee- Director of Finance, State of Hawaii. Prepayment required. Money orders and cashiers' checks are the only acceptable methods of payment. Credit cards accepted only for online searches.

Mail search: Turnaround time- 3 to 5 days. A SASE is not requested.

In person: The public may access conviction information at public access locations at the HCJDC. There is no fee to view a record, but $10.00 is charged for a computer printout.

Online search: Online access is available at eCrim at http://ecrim.ehawaii.gov/ahewa/. There is no fee to view the results of your search; the option is available to purchase a certified copy of the record for $13.00. Registration is required. Questions are directed to 808-587-4220.

Statewide Court Records

Administrative Director of Courts, 417 S. King St, Honolulu, HI 96813; 808-539-4900, 808-539-4909 (Public Affairs Office), Fax- 808-539-4801; 7:45AM-4:30PM.

www.courts.state.hi.us/

The web page offers public access to the state's court systems.

Online search: Free online access to Circuit Court and Family Court records is available from the home page. Search by name or case number. These records are not considered "official" for FCRA compliant searches. The system is open daily. Also, opinions from the appellate court are available from the home web page site.

Sexual Offender Registry

Hawaii Criminal Justice Data Center, Sexual Offender Registry, 465 S King St, Room 101, Honolulu, HI 96813; 808-587-3100, Fax- 808-857-3024; 8AM-4PM.

http://sexoffenders.ehawaii.gov/sexoffender/welcome.html

Information regarding covered offenders is permitted pursuant to Chapter 846E. Public access to this information is based solely on the fact of each offender's criminal conviction and is not based on an estimate of the offender's level of dangerousness.

Indexing & Storage: Records available from 1997. New records available for inquiry in 1-2 weeks.

Searching: The following information about offenders is available to the public: name, prior names, aliases, photograph, residence address, personal vehicles(s) driven, street name of employment, college/university affiliation, and crime for which convicted. Include in request- name or street and Zip Code.

Access by: in person, online.

In person: Information is available at Public Access locations at the HCJDC and main county police stations, including the Kona police station.

Online search: Search at http://sexoffenders.ehawaii.gov/sexoffender/search.html. Search by name, street or ZIP Code.

Incarceration Records

Hawaii Department of Public Safety, Inmate Classification, 919 Ala Moana Blvd #401, Honolulu, HI 96814; 808-587-2567, Fax- 808-587-2568; 7:45AM-4:30PM.

www.hawaii.gov/ag/hcjdc/

Indexing & Storage: Records available on current and former inmates. Some older records were lost when a new computer system was installed. New records available for inquiry in 1 to 20 days.

Searching: Include in request- name; DOB and SSN helpful. There is no fee. Records are considered public information.

Access by: mail, phone.

Mail search: Turnaround time- 1-2 days. A SASE is helpful.

Phone search: Limited information available by telephone.

Corporation, LP, LLC, LLP, Trade Name, Assumed Name, Trademarks, Servicemarks

Business Registration Division, PO Box 40, Honolulu, HI 96810 (Courier address- 335 Merchant St, 2nd Fl, Honolulu, HI 96813); 808-586-2727, 808-587-4220 (eHawaiiGov), Fax- 808-586-2733; 7:45AM-4:30PM.

http://hawaii.gov/dcca/areas/breg

Indexing & Storage: Records available from 1859 to present for active entities, 1900 to present for inactive entities. New records available for inquiry immediately.

Searching: There are no access restrictions. Records are open to the public. Include in request- full name of business. In addition to the articles of organization, business entity records available include: Annual Reports, Officers, Directors, DBAs, Prior (merged) names, Inactive and Reserved names.

Access by: mail, phone, fax, in person, online.

Fee & Payment: There is no search fee. The copy fee is $.25 per page. Fee payee- Business Registration Division. Prepayment required. Personal checks accepted. Credit cards accepted ($1.00 minimum charge).

Mail search: Turnaround time- 2 weeks. A SASE is requested.

Phone search: They will confirm data over the phone or let you know how many copies to prepay.

Fax search: Same criteria as mail searches.

In person: Turnaround time is while you wait.

Online search: access to business names available at http://hawaii.gov/dcca/areas/breg/online/. There are no fees, the system is open 24 hours. For assistance during business hours, call 808-586-2727. Tax license searching is available free at http://pahoehoe.ehawaii.gov/tls/app. Search by name, ID number of DBA name.

Other access: Bulk data can be purchased online through ehawaiigov.com. Visit the website or call 808-587-4220 for more information.

Uniform Commercial Code, Federal & State Tax Liens, Real Estate Recordings

UCC Division, Bureau of Conveyances, PO Box 2867, Honolulu, HI 96803 (Courier address- Dept. of Land & Natural Resources, 1151 Punchbowl St, Honolulu, HI 96813); 808-587-0154, Fax- 808-587-4380; 7:45AM-4:30PM.

http://hawaii.gov/dlnr.boc

The Bureau records, indexes, and microfilms over 344,000 Regular System and Land Court documents and maps annually; issues Land Court Certificates of Title; certifies copies of matters of record; and researches UCC requests.

Indexing & Storage: Records available from 1845. Records are online from 1976. Records are not destroyed.

Searching: Use search request form UCC-11. Include in request- debtor name. A UCC record does not include tax liens; a separate search is required.

Access by: mail, in person, online.

Fee & Payment: Fees are $25.00 per debtor name plus $5.00 for each financing statement and statement of assignment reported. Copies cost $1.00 per page. Fee payee- Bureau of Conveyances. Prepayment required. An initial fee of $25.00 must be paid in advance, additional fees will be invoiced. Personal checks accepted, credit cards are not.

Mail search: Turnaround time- 1 week. A SASE is requested.

In person: There is self-service in the public reference room.

Online search: Search the indices from 1976 forward at home page or from http://bocweb.dlnrbc.hawaii.gov/boc/. Search by grantor, grantee, business name. Includes real estate recordings.

Sales Tax Registrations

State does not impose sales tax.

Birth Certificates

State Department of Health, Vital Records Section, PO Box 3378, Honolulu, HI 96801 (Courier address- 1250 Punchbowl St, Room 103, Honolulu, HI 96813); 808-586-4533; 7:45AM-2:30PM (walk-in hours).

http://hawaii.gov/health/vital-records/

Upon request, a letter of verification attesting to the existence of a requested record on file with the Department of Health may be issued.

Indexing & Storage: Records available from mid 1800's to present. New records available for inquiry in 10-20 days.

Searching: Access to vital records is restricted by statute (HRS §338-18). After 75 years, records are considered genealogy records, but processing requests is not a priority. Direct questions to vr-info@doh.hawaii.gov. Include in request- full name, names of parents, mother's maiden name, DOB, place of birth, relationship to person of record, reason for information request, signed release. For a certified record, requestor must provide the information needed to 1) establish his/her direct and tangible interest in the record and 2) locate the desired record. Record request forms are available from the webpage.

Access by: mail, in person, online.

Fee & Payment: Fees are $10.00 for first copy and $4.00 for each subsequent copy of same record. Fee payee- State Department of Health. Prepayment required. Money orders, certified checks, and cashier's checks are accepted. No credit cards accepted.

Mail search: Turnaround time- 4 to 6 weeks. SASE not required.

In person: Unless proof of urgency established for same day service, results are mailed within 10 days. In person requests can be made 7:40AM to 2:30PM daily.

Online search: Requests may be placed for birth and marriage certificates on a limited basis at https://www.ehawaii.gov/doh/vitrec/exe/vitrec.cgi. There is an additional $1.50 fee for requests made via the Internet, use of a credit card is required.

Expedited service: Expedited service is available for mail searches. Turnaround time- 5 to 7 days. You must enclose a return pre-paid, self-addressed envelope.

Death Records

State Department of Health, Vital Records Section, PO Box 3378, Honolulu, HI 96801 (Courier address- 1250 Punchbowl St, Room 103, Honolulu, HI 96813); 808-586-4533; 7:45AM-2:30PM (walk-in hours).

http://hawaii.gov/health/vital-records/

Upon request, a letter of verification attesting to the existence of a requested record on file with the Department of Health may be issued.

Indexing & Storage: Records available from mid 1800's on, but early records are not complete. New records available for inquiry in 10-20 days.

Searching: Access to vital records is restricted by statute (HRS §338-18). After 75 years, records are considered genealogy records, but processing requests is not a priority. Direct questions to vr-info@doh.hawaii.gov. Include in request- full name, date of death, place of death, names of parents, relationship to person of record, reason for information request. An applicant/requestor must provide the information needed to 1) establish his/her direct and tangible interest in the record and 2) locate the desired record. Record request forms are available from the webpage.

Access by: mail, in person.

Fee & Payment: The fee is $10.00 per record and $4.00 for each subsequent copy of same record. Fee payee- State Department of Health. Prepayment required. Cashier's checks and money orders accepted. No credit cards accepted except online.

Mail search: Turnaround time- 4 to 6 weeks.

In person: Unless proof of urgency established for same day service, results are mailed within 10 days. In person requests can be made 7:40AM to 2:30PM daily.

Expedited service: Expedited service is available for mail searches. Turnaround time- 5 to 7 days. You must enclose a return pre-paid, self-addressed envelope.

Marriage Certificates

State Department of Health, Vital Records Section, PO Box 3378, Honolulu, HI 96801 (Courier address- 1250 Punchbowl St, Room 103, Honolulu, HI 96813); 808-586-4533; 7:45AM-2:30PM (walk-in hours).

http://hawaii.gov/health/vital-records/

Upon request, a letter of verification attesting to the existence of a requested record on file with the Department of Health may be issued.

Indexing & Storage: Records available from mid 1800's to present. New records available for inquiry in 3-5 days.

Searching: Access to vital records is restricted by statute (HRS §338-18). After 75 years, records are considered genealogy records, but processing requests is not a priority. Direct questions to vr-info@doh.hawaii.gov. Include in request- names of husband and wife, wife's maiden name, date of marriage, place or county of marriage, names of parents, relationship to person of record, reason for information request. An applicant/requestor must provide the information needed to 1) establish his/her direct and tangible interest in the record and 2) locate the desired record. Record request forms are available from the webpage.

Access by: mail, in person, online.

Fee & Payment: Fee is $10.00 per record and $4.00 for subsequent copy of same record. Fee payee- State Department of Health. Prepayment required. Cashier's check and money orders accepted. No credit cards accepted except online.

Mail search: Turnaround time- 4 to 6 weeks. SASE not required.

In person: Unless proof of urgency established for same day service, results are mailed within 10 days. In person requests can be made 7:40AM to 2:30PM daily.

Online search: Requests may also be placed for birth and marriage certificates on a limited basis through the Internet at https://www.ehawaii.gov/doh/vitrec/exe/vitrec.cgi. Results are mailed. There is an additional $1.50 fee for requests made through the Internet, use of a credit card is required.

Expedited service: Expedited service is available for mail searches. Turnaround time- 5 to 7 days. You must enclose a return pre-paid, self-addressed envelope.

Divorce Records

State Department of Health, Vital Records Section, PO Box 3378, Honolulu, HI 96801 (Courier address- 1250 Punchbowl St, Room 103, Honolulu, HI 96813); 808-586-4533; 7:45AM-2:30PM (walk-in hours).

http://hawaii.gov/health/vital-records/

Upon request, a letter of verification attesting to the existence of a requested record on file with the Department of Health may be issued.

Indexing & Storage: Records available from July 1951 to Dec 2002. Prior records and those from Jan. 2003 forward are held by the clerk of the court granting the decree. New records available for inquiry in 10-20 days.

Searching: Access to vital records is restricted by statute (HRS §338-18). After 75 years, records are considered genealogy records, but processing requests is not a priority. Direct questions to vr-info@doh.hawaii.gov. Include in request- names of husband and wife, date of divorce, place of divorce, relationship to person of record, reason for information request. An applicant/requestor must provide the information needed to 1) establish his/her direct and tangible interest in the record and 2) locate the desired record. Record request forms are available from the webpage.

Access by: mail, in person.

Fee & Payment: The fee is $10.00 per record and $4.00 each additional copy of same record. Fee payee- State Department of Health. Prepayment required. Cashier's check and money orders accepted. No credit cards accepted.

Mail search: Turnaround time- 4 to 6 weeks.

In person: Unless proof of urgency established for same day service, results are mailed within 10 days. In person requests can be made 7:40AM to 2:30PM daily. Turnaround time is 10 days or more.

Expedited service: Expedited service is available for mail searches. Turnaround time- 5 to 7 days. You must enclose a return pre-paid, self-addressed envelope.

Workers' Compensation Records

Labor & Industrial Relations, Disability Compensation Division, 830 Punchbowl St, Room 209, Honolulu, HI 96813; 808-586-9174, Fax-808-586-9219; 7:45AM-4:30PM.

http://hawaii.gov/labor/dcd/aboutwc.shtml

Indexing & Storage: Records available for the past 8 years. Prior records are in the State Archives but still must be requested through the Disability Compensation Division. New records available for inquiry in 2 to 7 days from receipt.

Searching: Must have a signed release from injured party or HI circuit court order signed by a judge. Include in request- signed released from claimant, SSN.

Access by: mail, fax, in person.

Fee & Payment: There is no search fee, copy fee is $.05 per page. Fee payee- Director of Finance. Prepayment required. Personal checks accepted, credit cards are not.

Mail search: Turnaround time- 6 to 12 weeks. A SASE is requested.

Fax search: Same criteria as mail searches.

In person: in person requests only saves mail time; results are mailed.

Driver Records

Traffic Violations Bureau, Driving Records, 1111 Alakea St, 2nd Fl, Honolulu, HI 96813; 808-538-5500 (Honolulu Courts), 808-961-7470 (Hawaii Courts), 808-244-2800 (Maui Courts), 808-482-2355 (Kauai Courts), Fax- 808-538-5520; 7:45AM-4:30PM (Till 9PM on Wed).

www.courts.state.hi.us/index.jsp

The TVB issues two documents. The Traffic Abstract (sometimes called public or abbreviated) shows moving violation convictions, but not juvenile records unless signed for. The Traffic Court Report shows all action, whether convicted or dismissed.

Indexing & Storage: Records available from 1995 on paper. New records available for inquiry immediately.

Searching: The Public Abstract is given to insurers and employers. Casual requesters can obtain records; however, personal information is not released. Include in request- full name, DOB and either license number or SSN. Note that records are maintained by the courts. The state DOT is not involved in record keeping at this time, see http://hawaii.gov/dot/highways/. This data not released- address and other personal information

Access by: mail, in person, online.

Fee & Payment: The fee is $7.00 per Abstract, $10.00 if online from HIC. The fee for a Report is $1.00 for first page, $.50 each add'l. There is a full charge even if no record is found. Copies of tickets are only available from the court where ticket was issued. Fee payee- District Court Prepayment required. The state requires a money order or cashier's check for mail-in requests; in-person requesters may use cash, credit cards, or business checks. Personal checks not accepted. Major credit cards are accepted for walk-in requesters.

Mail search: Turnaround time- 2 - 5 days. SASE is not required.

In person: Walk-in requests can be processed in five to twenty minutes at any county district traffic court or at the Traffic Violations Bureau Office in Honolulu.

Online search: Online ordering by DPPA complaint requesters is available from the state-designated entity - Hawaii Information

Consortium (HIC). The record fee is $10.00 per record plus a $75.00 annual subscription fee is required. Record requests are accepted via FTP. Results, if clear, are returned via FTP. Results with hits on convictions on the record are returned on paper. Visit their website at www.ehawaii.gov/dakine/docs/subscription.html or call HIC at 808-695-4620 for more information. Name checks of traffic court records may be ordered from the court.

Other access: HIC offers other means to obtain records. Please call the number listed above for more information.

Expedited service: Will expedite delivery if a pre-paid envelope is provided.

Vehicle Ownership & Registration

Access to Records is Restricted andat Local Level.

With the exception of the City and County of Honolulu, Hawaii does not offer access to vehicle registration or ownership records. Honolulu provides online inquiry at http://www4.honolulu.gov/mvrtitleinq. Must provide last four digits of VIN or plate. Vehicle identification numbers (VIN) and registration and title history information are not available to the public per Section 286-172, HI revised statutes.

County of Hawaii
East:Aupuni Center, 101 Pauahi Street, Suite 5, Hilo, HI 96720
West:75-5706 Kuakini Hwy, Suite 107, Kailua-Kona, HI 96740
www.co.hawaii.hi.us/info/mvr/fees.htm
Phone: (East) 808-961-8351
Phone: (West) 327-3543

City & County of Honolulu
Division of Motor Vehicles and Licensing
PO Box 30320
Honolulu, Hawaii 96820-0320
www.co.honolulu.hi.us/csd/vehicle/mvehicle.htm
Phone: 808-532-7700

County of Kauai
www.kauaigov.org/treasury.htm
Phone: 808-241-6577

County of Maui
Department of Finance, Division of Motor Vehicles & Licensing
Maui Mall Shopping Center
70 E. Kaahumanu Avenue, Suite A-17
Kahului, HI 96732-2176
www.mauicounty.gov/index.asp?nid=554
Phone:808-270-7363 Fax: 808-270-7858

Accident Reports

Records not maintained by a state level agency.

Accident reports are not available from the state. Records are maintained at the county level at the police departments and are only available to those involved.

Vessel Ownership & Registration

Land & Natural Resources, Division of Boating & Recreation, 333 Queen St Rm 300, Honolulu, HI 96813; 808-587-1970, Fax- 808-587-1977; 7:45AM-4:30PM.

http://hawaii.gov/dlnr/dbor/dbor.html

Vessels must be registered except a manually propelled recreational vessel; a recreational vessel eight feet or less in length propelled solely by sail; or motorboats used exclusively for racing.

Indexing & Storage: Records available from 1950s, computerized since 1994, and on microfiche from 1987 to 1994. New records available for inquiry in 30 days or less.

Searching: Requests must be made in writing and must include a statement revealing the purpose for which the information will be used. Name or hull ID number or registration number is required for search. Lien information is available here, name searches are permitted, but lien documents are filed at the Bureau of Conveyances (see UCC). This data not released- addresses or phone numbers.

Access by: mail, fax, in person, online.

Fee & Payment: There is no search fee.

Mail search: Turnaround time- 1 to 2 days. SASE not required.

Fax search: Same criteria as mail searching.

In person: Turnaround time is usually the same day.

Online search: Go to www.vessel.ehawaii.gov and click on the Public Search tab to view registration data. Search by vessel name, hull number or vessel number. A name search is not offered.

Legislation Records

Hawaii Legislature, 415 S Beretania St, Honolulu, HI 96813; 808-587-0700 (Reference Library (LRB)), 808-587-0478, Fax- 808-586-3584; 9AM-5PM.

www.capitol.hawaii.gov

Email questions to par@Capitol.hawaii.gov.

Indexing & Storage: Records available from 2000 to present. New records available for inquiry in 1 week.

Searching: Records computerized since 2000 on current computer system. Hard copies of bills 1996 to present are available at LRB library. Include in request- bill number, year. Contact the State Archives at 808-586-0329 for paper records prior to 1996. Any bills that have become Acts can also be found at the library.

Access by: mail, phone, in person, online.

Fee & Payment: There is no search fee nor a copy fee, unless extensive request is made. Self-serve copies from the LRB are $.10 per page.

Mail search: Turnaround time- 1 week. SASE is not requested.

Phone search: General information is available over the phone, copies can be requested for documents 1996 to present.

In person: Simple requests may be processed while you wait.

Online search: Access information through the Internet site including revised statutes, bill status, and documents. There is no fee, the system is up 24 hours.

Voter Registration

Access to Records is Restricted.

Office of Elections, Voter Registration, 802 Lehua Ave, Honolulu, HI 96782; 808-453-8683, Fax- 808-453-6006; 7:45AM-4:30PM.

http://hawaii.gov/elections/

Voter information is only available from the county clerks. Here are contact numbers. City and County of Honolulu 808-768-3800; County of Hawaii 808-961-8277; County of Maui 808-270-7749; County of Kauai 808-241-6350. Although this agency has a centralized database, it will not provide statewide lists and refers all requesters to the County Clerk in Honolulu.

GED Certificates (Diplomas)

Community Education, HI State Dept of Education, 475 22nd Ave, Bldg 302, Rm 124, Honolulu, HI 96816; 808-735-8371, Fax- 808-735-8375; 8AM-4PM.

GED verifications are issued to qualified individuals. This agency has a statewide database, but does not issue the certificate. Transcript copies are not available from this office and must be obtained from the testing facility.

Indexing & Storage: New records available for inquiry in 1 week.

Searching: If this agency does not have the record, they will assist the requester in locating the school that issued the GED. Include in request- signed release, date of birth, SSN, year of test, location.

Access by: mail, fax, in person.

Fee & Payment: There is no fee for a verification from this agency.

Mail search: Turnaround time- 1 to 2 weeks. A SASE is helpful.

Fax search: Same criteria as mail search.

In person: Same criteria as mail search.

Hunting & Fishing License Information

Access to Records is Restricted.

Department of Land & Natural Resources, Kalanimoku Bldg, 1151 Punchbowl St, Honolulu, HI 96813; 808-587-0100 (Fishing), 808-587-0166 (Hunting), Fax- 808-587-0160; 7:45AM-4:30PM.

http://hawaii.gov/dlnr

Fishing information is kept by the Aquatic Resources Division; Hunting information by the Division of Forestry & Wildlife (http://dofaw.net/). 808-587-0115 is fax for Fishing; 808-587-0160 is fax for Hunting. Limited record information is released to the public. Generally, this department's information is only released to law enforcement agencies. There is no "search engine" here. After 1 year, the records go the Archived Record Center.

Hawaii State Licensing Agencies

For details about the agency responsible for licensing/certifying/registering an item below or in the Agency Quick Finder section, match an item's number with the number of the agency in the *Licensing Agency Information* section.

Hawaii Licenses Searchable Online

Acupuncturist #4 .... http://pvl.ehawaii.gov/pvlsearch/app
Architect #19 .... http://pvl.ehawaii.gov/pvlsearch/app
Attorney #38 .... www.hsba.org/lawyerstatus.aspx
Auction #42 .... http://pvl.ehawaii.gov/pvlsearch/app
Bank/Bank Agency/Office #28 .... http://hawaii.gov/dcca/areas/dfi/regulate/regulate/
Barber Shop/Barber/Barber Appren. #5 http://pvl.ehawaii.gov/pvlsearch/app
Beauty Instructor #5 .... http://pvl.ehawaii.gov/pvlsearch/app
Beauty Operator/School/Shop #5 .... http://pvl.ehawaii.gov/pvlsearch/app
Boxer #24 .... http://pvl.ehawaii.gov/pvlsearch/app
Cemetery #42 .... http://pvl.ehawaii.gov/pvlsearch/app
Certified Public Accountant-CPA #21 .... http://pvl.ehawaii.gov/pvlsearch/app
Chiropractor #6 .... http://pvl.ehawaii.gov/pvlsearch/app
Collection Agency #42 .... http://pvl.ehawaii.gov/pvlsearch/app
Condominium Hotel Operator #34 .... http://pahoehoe.ehawaii.gov/ils/app
Condominium Managing Agent #34 ...... http://pahoehoe.ehawaii.gov/ils/app
Contractor #27 .... http://pvl.ehawaii.gov/pvlsearch/app
Credit Union #28 .... http://hawaii.gov/dcca/areas/dfi/regulate/regulate/
Dental Hygienist #7 .... http://pvl.ehawaii.gov/pvlsearch/app
Dentist #7 .... http://pvl.ehawaii.gov/pvlsearch/app
Elected Officials Fin'nc'l Disclosure #41 http://hawaii.gov/ethics/findisc
Electrician #29 .... http://pvl.ehawaii.gov/pvlsearch/app
Electrologist #42 .... http://pvl.ehawaii.gov/pvlsearch/app
Emergency Medical Personnel #13 .... http://pvl.ehawaii.gov/pvlsearch/app
Employment Agency #42 .... http://pvl.ehawaii.gov/pvlsearch/app
Engineer #19 .... http://pvl.ehawaii.gov/pvlsearch/app
Escrow Company #28 .... http://hawaii.gov/dcca/areas/dfi/regulate/regulate/
Financial Services Loan Company #28 . http://hawaii.gov/dcca/areas/dfi/regulate/regulate/
Guard/Agency #18 .... http://pvl.ehawaii.gov/pvlsearch/app
Hearing Aid Dealer/Fitter #30 .... http://pvl.ehawaii.gov/pvlsearch/app
Insurance Adjuster #31 .... http://pahoehoe.ehawaii.gov/ils/app
Insurance Agent /Producer/Solic't #31 .. http://pahoehoe.ehawaii.gov/ils/app
Lobbyist #41 .... http://hawaii.gov/ethics/lobby
Marriage & Family Therapist #42 .... http://pvl.ehawaii.gov/pvlsearch/app
Massage Therapist/Establishment #42 . http://pvl.ehawaii.gov/pvlsearch/app
Mechanic #42 .... http://pvl.ehawaii.gov/pvlsearch/app
Medical Doctor #13 .... http://pvl.ehawaii.gov/pvlsearch/app
Mortgage Broker/Solicitor #42 .... http://pvl.ehawaii.gov/pvlsearch/app
Motor Vehicle Dealer/Broker/Seller #42 http://pvl.ehawaii.gov/pvlsearch/app
Motor Vehicle Repair Dealer #42 .... http://pvl.ehawaii.gov/pvlsearch/app
Naturopathic Physician #10 .... http://pvl.ehawaii.gov/pvlsearch/app
Nurse #14 .... http://pvl.ehawaii.gov/pvlsearch/app
Nursing Home Administrator #12 .... http://pvl.ehawaii.gov/pvlsearch/app
Occupational Therapist #17 .... http://pvl.ehawaii.gov/pvlsearch/app
Optician, Dispensing #8 .... http://pvl.ehawaii.gov/pvlsearch/app
Optometrist #11 .... http://pvl.ehawaii.gov/pvlsearch/app
Osteopathic Physician #13 .... http://pvl.ehawaii.gov/pvlsearch/app
Pest Control Field Rep./Operator #32 ... http://pvl.ehawaii.gov/pvlsearch/app
Pesticide Dealer #2 .... http://hawaii.gov/hdoa/pi/pest/RUPD2008LIST.pdf
Pesticide Product #2 .... http://hawaii.gov/hdoa/pi/pest/liclist_alpha.pdf
Pharmacist/Pharmacy #16 .... http://pvl.ehawaii.gov/pvlsearch/app
Physical Therapist #17 .... http://pvl.ehawaii.gov/pvlsearch/app
Physician Assistant #13 .... http://pvl.ehawaii.gov/pvlsearch/app
Pilot, Port #42 .... http://pvl.ehawaii.gov/pvlsearch/app
Plumber #29 .... http://pvl.ehawaii.gov/pvlsearch/app
Podiatrist #13 .... http://pvl.ehawaii.gov/pvlsearch/app
PI / Investigation Agnecy #18 .... http://pvl.ehawaii.gov/pvlsearch/app
Psychologist #20 .... http://pvl.ehawaii.gov/pvlsearch/app

Public Accountant - PA #21 .... http://pvl.ehawaii.gov/pvlsearch/app
Real Estate Agent/Broker/Sales #34 ..... http://pahoehoe.ehawaii.gov/ils/app
Real Estate Appraiser #9 .... http://pvl.ehawaii.gov/pvlsearch/app
Savings & Loan Assoc./Bank #28 .... http://hawaii.gov/dcca/areas/dfi/regulate/regulate/
Social Worker #42 .... http://pvl.ehawaii.gov/pvlsearch/app
Speech Pathologist/Audiologist #22 ...... http://pvl.ehawaii.gov/pvlsearch/app
Tattoo Artist #15 .... http://hawaii.gov/health/environmental/sanitation/tattoo.html
Timeshare #42 .... http://pvl.ehawaii.gov/pvlsearch/app
Travel Agency #42 .... http://pvl.ehawaii.gov/pvlsearch/app
Trust Company #28 .... http://hawaii.gov/dcca/areas/dfi/regulate/regulate/
Veterinarian #23 .... http://pvl.ehawaii.gov/pvlsearch/app

Hawaii Licensing Quick Finder

Acupuncturist #4 808-586-2696
Airport Vendor #37 808-836-8533
Architect #19 808-586-3000
Attorney #38 808-537-1868
Auction #42 808-587-3222
Bank/Bank Agency/Office #28 808-586-2820
Barber Shop/Barber/Barber Appren #5 . 808-586-3000
Beauty Instructor #5 808-586-3000
Beauty Operator/School/Shop #5 808-586-3000
Boxer #24 808-586-2701
Boxing Manager #24 808-586-2701
Boxing Matchmaker #24 808-586-2701
Boxing Physician #24 808-586-2701
Boxing Professional/Promoter #24 808-586-2701
Boxing Second #24 808-586-2701
Boxing Timekeep'r/Judge/Referee #24 808-586-2701
Cable Franchise #26 808-586-2620
Cemetery #42 808-587-3222
Certified Public Accountant-CPA #21... 808-586-3000
Certified Shorthand Reporter (CSR) #1 808-539-4226
Chiropractor #6 808-586-3000
Clinical Lab Technic'n/Direct'r #40 808-453-6653
Clinical Lab Cytotechnologist #40 808-453-6653
Clinical Lab Technologist/Special't #40. 808-453-6653
Collection Agency #42 808-587-3222
Condominium Hotel Operator #34 808-587-3222
Condominium Managing Agent #34 808-587-3222
Contractor #27 808-586-3000
Credit Union #28 808-586-2820
Dental Hygienist #7 808-586-3000
Dentist #7 808-586-3000
Drivers License-CDL #39 808-487-5534
Drivers License-Regular #39 808-532-7730
Drug (Prescription) Dist./Whlse. #16 808-586-2694
Educational Administrator #35 808-586-3349
Elected Officials Fin'c'l Disclosure #41 808-587-0460
Electrician #29 808-586-3000
Electrologist #42 808-587-3222
Embalmer #15 808-586-8000
Emergency Medical Personnel #13 808-586-3000
Employment Agency #42 808-587-3222
Engineer #19 808-586-3000
Escrow Company #28 808-586-2820
Financial Services Loan Firm #28 808-586-2820
Guard/Agency #18 808-586-3000
Hearing Aid Dealer/Fitter #30 808-586-3000
Insurance Adjuster #31 808-586-2788
Insurance Agent/Producer/Solic't #31 .. 808-586-2788
Investment Advisor/Represent't've #25. 808-586-2730
Landscape Architect #19 808-586-3000
Lobbyist #41 808-587-0460
Marine License, Commercial #36 808-587-0100
Marriage & Family Therapist #42 808-587-3222
Massage Therapist/Establishment #42 808-587-3222
Mechanic #42 808-587-3222
Medical Doctor #13 808-586-3000
Mortgage Broker/Solicitor #42 808-587-3222
Motor Vehicle Dealer/Broker/Seller #42 808-587-3222
Motor Vehicle Repair Dealer #42 808-587-3222
Naturopathic Physician #10 808-586-3000
Notary Public #3 808-586-1218
Nuclear Medicine Technologist #33 808-586-4700
Nurse / Nurses' Aide #14 808-586-3000
Nursing Home Administrator #12 808-586-3000
Occupational Therapist #17 808-586-2698
Optician, Dispensing #8 808-586-2704
Optometrist #11 808-586-2694
Osteopathic Physician #13 808-586-3000
Pest Control Field Rep./Operator #32 .. 808-586-3000
Pesticide Applicator #2 808-973-9409
Pesticide Applicator, Private #2 808-973-9424
Pesticide Dealer #2 808-973-9413
Pesticide Product #2 808-973-9414
Pharmacist/Pharmacy #16 808-586-2694
Physical Therapist #17 808-586-2694
Physician Assistant #13 808-586-3000
Pilot, Port #42 808-587-3222
Plumber #29 808-586-3000
Podiatrist #13 808-586-2708
Private Detective #18 808-586-3000
Private Detective/Investigat'n Agcy #18 808-586-3000
Psychologist #20 808-587-3222
Public Accountant - PA #21 808-586-3000
Radiation Therapist #33 808-586-4700
Radiographer #33 808-586-4700
Real Estate Agent/Broker/Sales #34 ... 808-587-3222
Real Estate Appraiser #9 808-586-3000
Sanitarian #15 808-586-4576
Savings & Loan Association #28 808-586-2820
Savings Bank #28 808-586-2820
Securities Salesperson #25 808-586-2730
Social Worker #42 808-587-3222
Speech Pathologist/Audiologist #22 808-586-3000
Surveyor, Land #19 808-586-3000
Tattoo Artist #15 808-586-8000
Taxi Certifications #39 808-532-7730
Teacher #35 808-586-3349
Timeshare #42 808-587-3222
Travel Agency #42 808-587-3222
Trust Company #28 808-586-2820
Veterinarian #23 808-586-3000

Hawaii Licensing Agency Information

#1 Board of Certified Shorthand Reporters, 777 Punchbowl St, Honolulu, HI 96813; 808-539-4226, Fax- 808-539-4149. 7:45AM-4:30PM.

#2 Department of Agriculture, 1428 S King St, Honolulu, HI 96814; 808-973-9560, Fax- 808-973-9418. http://hawaii.gov/hdoa/pi/pest

#3 Department of Attorney General, Notary Public Office, 425 Queen St, Honolulu, HI 96813; 808-586-1218, Fax- 808-586-1205. Hours- 7:45AM-N. http://hawaii.gov/ag/notary/

#4 Department of Commerce & Consumer Affairs, Board of Acupuncture, PO Box 3469 (335 Merchant St), Honolulu, HI 96801; 808-586-2698, Fax- 808-586-2689. http://hawaii.gov/dcca/areas/pvl/boards/acupuncture/ Search data at- http://pvl.ehawaii.gov/pvlsearch/app

#5 Department of Commerce & Consumer Affairs, Board of Barbering & Cosmetology, PO Box 3469 (Attn BAR/COS, 335 Merchant St), Honolulu, HI 96801; 808-586-2696. 7:45AM-4:30PM. http://hawaii.gov/dcca/areas/pvl/boards/barber Search data at- http://pvl.ehawaii.gov/pvlsearch/app Rosters are available for sale but do not include personal info or addresses.

#6 Dept. of Commerce & Consumer Affairs, Board of Chiropractic Examiners, PO Box 3469, CHIRO (335 Merchant St), Honolulu, HI 96801; 808-586-2699, Fax- 808-586-2689. http://hawaii.gov/dcca/areas/pvl/boards/chiropractor/ Search data at- http://pvl.ehawaii.gov/pvlsearch/app

#7 Department of Commerce & Consumer Affairs, Board of Dental Examiners, PO Box 3469, DENTAL (335 Merchant St), Honolulu, HI 96801; 808-586-2702. 7:45AM-4:30PM. http://hawaii.gov/dcca/areas/pvl/boards/dentist/ Search at- http://pvl.ehawaii.gov/pvlsearch/app

#8 Department of Commerce & Consumer Affairs, Dispensing Optician Program, PO Box 3469, DOP (1010 Richards St), Honolulu, HI 96801; 808-586-2704, Fax- 808-586-3031. http://hawaii.gov/dcca/areas/pvl/programs/dispensingoptician/ Search data at- http://pvl.ehawaii.gov/pvlsearch/app

#9 Department of Commerce & Consumer Affairs, Professional & Vocational Licensing, Attn:REA, PO Box 3469 (335 Merchant St), Honolulu, HI 96801; 808-586-2701. Hours- 7:45AM-4:30PM. http://hawaii.gov/dcca/areas/pvl/programs/realestateappraiser/ Search data at- http://pvl.ehawaii.gov/pvlsearch/app

#10 Department of Commerce & Consumer Affairs, Board of Examiners in Naturopathy, PO Box 3469, NAT (1010 Richards St), Honolulu, HI 96801; 808-586-2704, Fax- 808-586-3031. Hours- 7:45AM-4:30PM. http://hawaii.gov/dcca/areas/pvl/boards/naturopathy/ Search data at- http://pvl.ehawaii.gov/pvlsearch/app

#11 Department of Commerce & Consumer Affairs, Board of Examiners in Optometry, PO Box 3469, OPT (335 Merchant St, 3rd Fl), Honolulu, HI 96801; 808-586-2694. http://hawaii.gov/dcca/areas/pvl/boards/optometry/

#12 Department of Commerce & Consumer Affairs, Nursing Home Administrators Program, PO Box 3469, NHA (335 Merchant St), Honolulu, HI 96801; 808-586-2695, Fax- 808-586-3031. Hours- 7:45AM-4:30PM. http://hawaii.gov/dcca/areas/pvl/programs/nursinghome/ Search data at- http://pvl.ehawaii.gov/pvlsearch/app

#13 Department of Commerce & Consumer Affairs, Board of Medical Examiners, PO Box 3469, BME (335 Merchant), Honolulu, HI 96801; 808-586-2708, Fax- 808-586-3031. 7:45AM-4:30PM. http://hawaii.gov/dcca/areas/pvl/boards/medical/ Search data at- http://pvl.ehawaii.gov/pvlsearch/app

#14 Department of Commerce & Consumer Affairs, Board of Nursing, PO Box 3469, BON (335 Merchant St), Honolulu, HI 96801; 808-586-2695, Fax-808-586-3031. 7:45AM-4:30PM http://hawaii.gov/dcca/areas/pvl/boards/nursing/ Search at- http://pvl.ehawaii.gov/pvlsearch/app

#15 Dept. of Health, Sanitation Branch, 591 Ala Moana Blvd, Honolulu, HI 96813; 808-586-8000, Fax- 808-586-8040. http://hawaii.gov/health/environmental/sanitation/index.html

#16 Department of Commerce & Consumer Affairs, Board of Pharmacy, PO Box 3469, PHAR (335 Merchant St, 3rd Fl), Honolulu, HI 96801; 808-586-2694. http://hawaii.gov/dcca/areas/pvl/boards/pharmacy/ Search data at- http://pvl.ehawaii.gov/pvlsearch/app

#17 Department of Commerce & Consumer Affairs, Board of Physical Therapy, PO Box 3469, PT (335 Merchant St, 3rd Fl), Honolulu, HI 96801; 808-586-2694. http://hawaii.gov/dcca/areas/pvl/boards/physicaltherapy/ Search data at- http://pvl.ehawaii.gov/pvlsearch/app

#18 Department of Commerce & Consumer Affairs, Board of Private Detectives & Guards, PO Box 3469, PDG (335 Merchant St), Honolulu, HI 96801; 808-586-2705, Fax- 808-586-2689. http://hawaii.gov/dcca/areas/pvl/boards/private/ Search at- http://pvl.ehawaii.gov/pvlsearch/app

#19 Department of Commerce & Consumer Affairs, Architects & Surveyors, Board of Prof. Engineers, PO Box 3469, EASLA (335 Merchant St), Honolulu, HI 96801; 808-586-2702. Hours- 7:45AM-4:30PM. http://hawaii.gov/dcca/areas/pvl/boards/engineer/

#20 Dept. of Commerce & Consumer Affairs, Board of Psychology, PO Box 3469, PSY (335 Merchant St, Rm 301), Honolulu, HI 96801; 808-586-2699. 7:45AM-4:30PM. http://hawaii.gov/dcca/areas/pvl/boards/psychology/

#21 Department of Commerce & Consumer Affairs, Board of Public Accountancy, PO Box 3469, Acct (335 Merchant St), Honolulu, HI 96801; 808-586-2696, Fax- 808-586-2874. Hours- 7:45AM-4:30PM. http://hawaii.gov/dcca/areas/pvl/boards/accountancy/ Search data at- http://pvl.ehawaii.gov/pvlsearch/app

#22 Dept. of Commerce & Consumer Affairs, Board of Speech Pathology & Audiology, PO Box 3469, SPAU (335 Merchant St, 3rd Fl), Honolulu, HI 96801; 808-586-2704. http://hawaii.gov/dcca/areas/pvl/boards/speech/ Search at- http://pvl.ehawaii.gov/pvlsearch/app

#23 Department of Commerce & Consumer Affairs, Board of Veterinary Examiners, PO Box 3469, VET (335 Merchant St), Honolulu, HI 96801; 808-586-2696, Fax- 808-586-2874. Hours- 7:45AM-4:30PM. http://hawaii.gov/dcca/areas/pvl/boards/veterinary/ Search data at- http://pvl.ehawaii.gov/pvlsearch/app

#24 Department of Commerce & Consumer Affairs, Boxing Commission, PO Box 3469, Boxing (1010 Richards St), Honolulu, HI 96801; 808-586-2701, Fax- 808-586-2689. http://hawaii.gov/dcca/areas/pvl/boards/boxing/

#25 Department of Commerce & Consumer Affairs, Business Registration Division, Securities Compliance Branch, PO Box 40 (335 Merchant St, Rm 205), Honolulu, HI 96810; 808-586-2744, Fax- 808-586-3977. http://hawaii.gov/dcca/areas/sec/

#26 Department of Commerce & Consumer Affairs, Cable TV Division, PO Box 541 (335 Merchant St, Rm 101), Honolulu, HI 96809; 808-586-2620, Fax- 808-586-2625. http://hawaii.gov/dcca/areas/catv

#27 Dept of Commerce & Consumer Affairs, Contractors License Board, PO Box 3469, CLB (335 Merchant St), Honolulu, HI 96801; 808-586-2700, Fax- 808-586-3031. http://hawaii.gov/dcca/areas/pvl/boards/contractor/ Search data at- http://pvl.ehawaii.gov/pvlsearch/app

#28 Department of Commerce & Consumer Affairs, Division of Financial Institutions, PO Box 2054 (335 Merchant St, Rm 221), Honolulu, HI 96805; 808-586-2820, Fax- 808-586-2818. 7:45AM-4:30PM. http://hawaii.gov/dcca/areas/dfi Search data at- www.hawaii.gov/dcca/areas/dfi/regulate/regulate/

#29 Department of Commerce & Consumer Affairs, Board of Electricians and Plumbers, PO Box 3469, EP (335 Merchant St), Honolulu, HI 96801; 808-586-2705. http://hawaii.gov/dcca/areas/pvl/boards/electrician/ Search data at- http://pvl.ehawaii.gov/pvlsearch/app

#30 Department of Commerce & Consumer Affairs, Hearing Aid Dealers & Fitters Program, PO Box 3469, HADF (335 Merchant St), Honolulu, HI 96801; 808-586-2698, Fax- 808-586-2689. http://hawaii.gov/dcca/areas/pvl/programs/hearing/ Search data at- http://pvl.ehawaii.gov/pvlsearch/app

#31 Department of Commerce & Consumer Affairs, Insurance Division, Licensing Branch, 335 Merchant St, #213, Honolulu, HI 96813; 808-586-2790, Fax- 808-587-6714. http://hawaii.gov/dcca/areas/ins/ Search data at- http://pahoehoe.ehawaii.gov/ils/app

#32 Department of Commerce & Consumer Affairs, Pest Control Board, PO Box 3469, PC (335 Merchant St), Honolulu, HI 96801; 808-586-2705, Fax- 808-586-2689. http://hawaii.gov/dcca/areas/pvl/boards/pestcontrol/ Search data at- http://pvl.ehawaii.gov/pvlsearch/app

#33 Dept of Health-NRIAQ Br., Radiologic Technology Board, 591 Ala Moana Blvd, Rm 133, Honolulu, HI 96813-4921; 808-586-4700, Fax- 808-586-5838. 7:45AM-4:30PM.

#34 Department of Commerce & Consumer Affairs, Real Estate Commission, 335 Merchant St, Rm 333, Honolulu, HI 96813; 808-586-2643. Hours- 7:45AM-4:30PM. http://hawaii.gov/hirec Search data at- http://pahoehoe.ehawaii.gov/ils/app

#35 Department of Education, Board of Education, PO Box 2360 (1390 Miller St), Honolulu, HI 96804; 808-586-3349, Fax- 808-586-3433. http://doe.k12.hi.us

#36 Department of Land & Natural Resources, Division of Aquatic Resources, 1151 Punchbowl St, Rm 330, Honolulu, HI 96813; 808-587-0100, Fax- 808-587-0115. www.state.hi.us/dlnr/dar/

#37 Department of Transportation, Airports Division, Airport District Manager, 400 Rodgers Blvd, 7th Fl, Honolulu, HI 96819-1897; 808-836-8533, Fax- 808-836-6682. www.state.hi.us/dot/airports/

#38 Hawaii State Bar Association, 1132 Bishop St, #906, Honolulu, HI 96813-2814; 808-537-1868, Fax- 808-521-7936. www.hsba.org

#39 Motor Vehicle Licensing Division, City Square Driver License, 1199 Dillingham St Rm A101, Honolulu, HI 96817; 808-532-7730, Fax- 808-832-2904. Hours- 7:45AM-4:30PM. School Bus and Regular Bus Drivers are part of the general "commercial drivers' license."

#40 Dept. of Health, Laboratory Licensing, 2725 Waimano Home Rd, Pearl City, HI 96782; 808-453-6653, Fax- 808-453-6662. http://hawaii.gov/health/laboratories/licensing/index.html

#41 State Ethics Commission, 1001 Bishop St, ASB Tower, #970, Honolulu, HI 96813; 808-587-0460, Fax- 808-587-0470. http://hawaii.gov/ethics Search data at- http://hawaii.gov/ethics

#42 Department of Commerce & Consumer Affairs, Professional & Vocational Licensing Div-Programs, 335 Merchant St, Rm 301, Honolulu, HI 96813; 808-587-3295 or 3222. Hours- 7:45AM-4:30PM. http://hawaii.gov/dcca/areas/pvl/ Search data at- http://pvl.ehawaii.gov/pvlsearch/app
For a PVL List Builder go to www.ehawaii.gov/dcca/pvllist/html/. There is a cost for this list.

Hawaii Federal Courts

The following list indicates the district and division name for each county in the state.

County/Court Cross Reference

County	Court
Hawaii	Honolulu
Honolulu	Honolulu
Kalawao	Honolulu
Kauai	Honolulu
Maui	Honolulu

US District Court District of Hawaii

Hawaii Division Court Clerk, 300 Ala Moana Blvd, Rm C-338, Honolulu, HI 96850, 808-541-1300 x8; records- 808-541-1890; Fax- 808-541-1303. Hours-8:30AM-4PM. www.hid.uscourts.gov

Counties/Note: All counties.

Searches/Indexing: Include full name in search request. Results do not include SSN or DOB. Will fax back documents for $.50 per page. New cases are in the index 24-48 hrs after filing date. Computer, microfiche and card indexes maintained. Case files sent to archives 1 year after closed.

Search Access: Mail: Search usually completed-1 week. Include SASE for return. **Fax:** Will accept fax request with case file number. **In person:** 3 public terminals available. No self-serve copier.

Payment: Pay by money order, cashier's or personal checks. No credit cards accepted. Payee: Clerk, US District Court.

E-Services: PACER now on ECF. PACER records go back to 10/1991. New records online after 1 day. ECF at https://ecf.hid.uscourts.gov. Opinions available on the ECF/PACER site. **Online Note:** Daily calendar at www.hid.uscourts.gov/.

US Bankruptcy Court District of Hawaii

Hawaii Division Court Clerk, 1132 Bishop St, Suite 250-L, Honolulu, HI 96813, 808-522-8100; Fax- 800-522-8120. Hours- 8:30AM - 4PM. www.hib.uscourts.gov

Counties/Note: All counties.

Searches/Indexing: Include full name and SSN in search request. Results include last 4 SSN digits. Will not fax back documents. New cases are in the index 24 hours after filing date. All records now maintained on computer.

Search Access: Only docket info is available by phone. Voice Case Information Service available, call VCIS at 808-522-8122. **Mail:** Search usually completed- 2 weeks. Include SASE for return. **In person:** 3 public terminals available. Computer generated copies- $.10 each.

Payment: Pay by money order, cashier's check. No debtor checks/credit cards accepted. Attorney checks accepted in person only. Payee: US Bankruptcy Court.

Standards for Federal Courts: Fees are standard unless noted in profile. Search fee is $26.00 per item (one party name or case number). Copy fee is $.50 per page. Certification fee is $9.00 per document, double for exemplification, if available. Most courts require prepayment. Mail requests should enclose a SASE unless otherwise noted. Before releasing records, all courts require prepayment, unless noted.

District courts index by defendant and plaintiff and by case number. Bankruptcy courts usually index by debtor and case number. While most courts now have their indexes on computer, many may still maintain index card files as well. Courts will archive closed case files at different times.

There are numerous public access programs available to online subscribers. Search the U.S. Party/Case Index to find party names and case numbers among all courts. Individual case data is provided on PACER. A search of CM/ECF provides copies of cases filed electronically. For details about PACER, the US Party/Case Index, and CM/ECF see the Appendix or go to http://pacer.psc.uscourts.gov or call 800-676-6856.

Hawaii County Courts

Court	Jurisdiction	No. of Courts	How Organized
Circuit Courts*	General	4	4 Circuits
District Courts*	Limited	7	4 Circuits

* Profiled in this Sourcebook.

Court	CIVIL Tort	Contract	Real Estate	Min. Claim	Max. Claim	Small Claims	Estate	Eviction	Domestic Relations
Circuit Courts*	X	X	X	$10,000	No Max		X		X
District Courts*	X	X	X	$0	$25,000	$3,500		X	

Court	CRIMINAL Felony	Misdemeanor	DWI/DUI	Preliminary Hearing	Juvenile
Circuit Courts*	X	X	X		X
District Courts*		X	X	X	

Administration

Administrative Director of Courts, Judicial Branch, 417 S King St, Honolulu, HI, 96813; 808-539-4900, Fax: 808-539-4855. Entire state is in the Hawaiian Time Zone. www.courts.state.hi.us/

Court Structure

Hawaii's trial level is comprised of Circuit Courts (includes Family Courts) and District Courts. These trial courts function in four judicial circuits: First (Oahu), Second (Maui-Molokai-Lanai), Third (Hawaii County), and Fifth (Kauai-Niihau). The Fourth Circuit was merged with the Third in 1943.

Circuit Courts are general jurisdiction and handle all jury trials, felony cases, and civil cases over $20,000, also probate and guardianship. There is con-current jurisdiction with District Courts in civil non-jury cases that specify amounts between $10,000-$25,000.The District Court handles criminal cases punishable by a fine and/or less than one year imprisonment and some civil cases up to $25,000, also landlord/tenant, traffic and DUI cases. The Family Court Division rules in all legal matters involving children, such as delinquency, waiver, status offenses, abuse and neglect, termination of parental rights, adoption, guardianships and detention. Also hears traditional domestic-relations cases, including divorce, nonsupport, paternity, uniform child custody jurisdiction cases and miscellaneous custody matters.

Online Access

Free online access to all Circuit Court and Family Court records, and civil records from the District Courts is available at www.courts.state.hi.us, click on the "Search Court Records" tab. Also, search the traffic case index here. Search by name or case number. These records are not considered "official" for FCRA compliant searches. Most courts offer access back to the mid 1980s. Opinions from the Appellate Court are available at the home page. Click on "Opinions."

Searching Tips, Fees, and Other Guidelines

Most Hawaii state courts offer a public access terminal to search records at the courthouse. Most courts charge $5.00 per name for a name search and $1.00 for the first copy and $.50 each add'l.

Hawaii County

3rd Circuit Court Legal Document Section PO Box 1007, 75 Apuni St, Hilo, HI 96721-1007; 808-961-7404; fax: 808-961-7416; 7:45AM-4:30PM. ***Felony, Misdemeanor, Civil Actions over $5,000, Probate.***
www.courts.state.hi.us/

Records are indexed for this county as 3 = Big Island.

Civil Records: Access: Mail, fax, in person, online. Both court and visitors may perform in person searches. Search fee: $5.00 per name. Required to search: name, years to search. Civil cases indexed by defendant, plaintiff, on computer from 1988, index card system prior to 1988. Mail turnaround time 2 days depending on staff coverage. Civil PAT goes back to 1987. PAT civil results show middle initial. Free record searching at http://hoohiki2.courts.state.hi.us/jud/Hoohiki/main.htm or click on "Search Court Records" at www.courts.state.hi.us/. Search back to 1983 by name, case number, or circuit.

Criminal Records: Access: Mail, fax, in person, online. Both court and visitors may perform in person searches. Search fee: $5.00 per name. Required to search: name, years to search. Criminal records computerized from 1988, index card system prior to 1988. Mail turnaround time 2 days depending upon staff coverage. Criminal PAT goes back to 1987. PAT criminal results show middle initial. Results may sometimes include other identifiers. Online access to criminal records is same as civil. Online results show middle initial.

General Information: Online identifiers in results same as on public terminal. No adoption, juvenile, dependencies, confidential records released without court's approval. Will fax documents to local or toll free line. Court makes copy: $1.00 first page, $.50 each add'l. Microfilm copy is $1.00 per page. Certification fee: $2.00; $4.00 for exemplification and certification together. Payee: Clerk, 3rd Circuit Court. Personal checks accepted; credit cards are not. Prepayment required. Mail requests: SASE required.

District Court PO Box 4879, Hilo, HI 96720; 808-961-7470; criminal fax: 808-961-7447; civil fax: same; 7:45AM-4:30PM. ***Misdemeanor, Civil Actions under $25,000, Eviction, Small Claims.***
www.courts.state.hi.us/

Civil Records: Access: Phone, fax, mail, in person, online. Only the court performs in person searches; visitors may not. Search fee: $5.00 per name. Required to search: name, years to search, case number; also helpful: address. Civil cases indexed by defendant. Civil records on ledgers from statehood. Mail turnaround time 1 week. Free record searching at http://hoohiki2.courts.state.hi.us/jud/Hoohiki/main.htm or click on "Search Court Records" at www.courts.state.hi.us/. Search by name or case number. Online results show middle initial.

Criminal Records: Access: Phone, fax, mail. Only the court performs in person searches; visitors may not. Search fee: $5.00 per name. Required to search: name, years to search, case number; also helpful:

address, DOB, SSN. Criminal records on computer since 3/1996. Mail turnaround time 1 week.
General Information: Online identifiers in results same as on public terminal. No family court records released. Will fax documents $2.00 1st page, $1.00 each add'l. Extra fee for out of state faxing. Court makes copy: $1.00 first page, $.50 each add'l. Off-site storage- usual copy fees plus $5.00. Certification fee: $2.00. Payee: Clerk of the District Court. Personal checks accepted. Credit cards accepted. Prepayment required. Mail requests: SASE requested.

Honolulu County

1st Circuit Court Legal Documents Branch, 777 Punchbowl St, 1st Fl, Honolulu, HI 96813; 808-539-4300; fax: 808-539-4314; 7:45AM-4:30PM (9AM-4PM files). ***Felony, Civil Actions over $5,000, Probate, Family.***
www.courts.state.hi.us/
Records are indexed for this county as 1 = Honolulu.
Civil Records: Access: Mail, in person, online. Both court and visitors may perform in person searches. Search fee: $5.00 per name. Required to search: name, years to search. Civil cases indexed by defendant, plaintiff, on computer back to 1984, on microfiche and archived from 1900. Mail turnaround time same day. Civil PAT available. PAT civil results show middle initial. Free record searching at http://hoohiki2.courts.state.hi.us/jud/Hoohiki/main.htm or click on "Search Court Records" at www.courts.state.hi.us/. Search back to 1983 by name, case number, or circuit.
Criminal Records: Access: Mail, in person, online. Both court and visitors may perform in person searches. Search fee: $5.00 per name. Required to search: name, years to search, DOB; also helpful: SSN. Criminal records computerized from 1984, on microfiche and archived from 1900. Mail turnaround time same day. Criminal PAT available. PAT criminal results show middle initial. Online access to criminal is the same as civil. Online results show middle initial.
General Information: Online identifiers in results same as on public terminal. No adoption, paternity or sealed records released. Will fax documents within US for $5.00 1st page, $2 each add'l; Foreign- $10.00 1st page and $5.00 each add'l. Court makes copy: $1.00 first page, $.50 each add'l. Microfilm service fee $5.00; cost of copies $1.00 per page. Self serve: $.15 per page. Certification fee: $2.00 per cert. Payee: 1st Circuit Court. Business checks accepted. No credit cards accepted. Prepayment required. Mail requests: SASE required.

District Court - Civil Division 1111 Alakea St, 3rd Fl, Honolulu, HI 96813; 808-538-5151; fax: 808-538-5444; 8AM-4:15PM. ***Civil Actions under $20,000, Eviction, Small Claims.***
www.courts.state.hi.us/
Civil Records: Access: Mail, in person, online. Both court and visitors may perform in person searches. Search fee: $5.00 per name. Required to search: name, years to search. Civil cases indexed by defendant. Civil records on computer from 1990; plaintiff index only on computer records. Mail turnaround time 1 week. Public use terminal has civil records back to 1990. PAT civil results show middle initial. Free record searching at http://hoohiki2.courts.state.hi.us/jud/Hoohiki/main.htm or click on "Search Court Records" at www.courts.state.hi.us/. Search by name or case number. Online results show middle initial.
General Information: Online identifiers in results same as on public terminal. No sealed records released. Will not fax documents. Court makes copy: $1.00 1st page; $.50 each add'l. Self serve: $.15 per page. Certification fee: $2.00 per cert. Payee: District Court of the 1st Circuit. Personal checks accepted. Visa/MC accepted. Prepayment required. Mail requests: SASE required.

District Court - Criminal Division 1111 Alakea St, 3rd Fl, Judicial Services, Honolulu, HI 96813; 808-538-5100; fax: 808-538-5111; 8AM-4:15PM. ***Misdemeanor, Traffic.***
www.courts.state.hi.us/
Criminal Records: Access: Fax, mail, in person. Only the court performs in person searches; visitors may not. Required to search: name, years to search, SSN, signed release, aliases; also helpful: address, DOB. Criminal records on computer go back to 1999. Mail turnaround time 1 week. Free traffic record searching at www.courts.state.hi.us. Click on "Search Court Records." Choose JIMS CourtConnect. Online results show middle initial.
General Information: Online identifiers in results same as on public terminal. No sealed records released. Will not fax documents. Court makes copy: $1.00 per page. Certification fee: $5.00 per cert. Payee: District Court of the 1st Judicial Circuit. Business checks accepted. Visa/MC accepted for traffic only. Prepayment required. Mail requests: SASE required.

Kauai County

5th Circuit Court 3970 Kaana St #207, Lihue, HI 96766; 808)-482-2300- info; Docs- 808-482-2330; fax: 808-482-2510; 7:45AM-4:30PM. ***Felony, Misdemeanor, Civil Actions over $20,000, Probate.***
www.courts.state.hi.us/
Records are indexed for this county as 4 = Kauai.
Civil Records: Access: Mail, in person, online. Both court and visitors may perform in person searches. Search fee: $5.00 per name. Required to search: name, years to search. Civil cases indexed by plaintiff & defendant. Civil records on computer from 1987, microfiche from 1960. Mail turnaround time approx. 1 week. Free record searching at http://hoohiki2.courts.state.hi.us/jud/Hoohiki/main.htm or click on "Search Court Records" at www.courts.state.hi.us/p. Search back to 1983 by name, case number, or circuit.
Criminal Records: Access: Mail, in person, online. Both court and visitors may perform in person searches. Search fee: $5.00 per name. Required to search: name, years to search, DOB; also helpful: SSN. Criminal records computerized from 1987, microfiche from 1960. Mail turnaround time approx. 1 week. Online access to criminal records is same as civil. Online results show middle initial.
General Information: Online identifiers in results same as on public terminal. No juvenile, dependencies records released. Will fax out documents, $2.00 1st page, $1.00 add'l within Hawaii; $5.00 1st page, $2.00 add'l in U.S.; $10.00 1st page, $5.00 add'l outside the U.S. Court makes copy: $1.00 first page, $.50 each add'l. Self serve: $.15 per page. Certification fee: $2.00. Payee: 5th Circuit Court. Only cashiers checks, money orders or cash accepted. No credit cards accepted. Prepayment required. Mail requests: SASE required.

District Court of the 5th Circuit - Civil 3970 Kaana St #207, Lihue, HI 96766; 808-482-2303; fax: 808-482-2553; 7:45AM-4:30PM. ***Civil Actions under $20,000, Eviction, Small Claims.***
www.courts.state.hi.us/
Civil Records: Access: Phone, fax, mail, in person, online. Both court and visitors may perform in person searches. Search fee: $5.00 per case. Required to search: name, years to search. Civil cases indexed by defendant, plaintiff; index on cards. Mail turnaround time 1-7 days. Public use terminal has civil records back to 2003. Free record searching at http://hoohiki2.courts.state.hi.us/jud/Hoohiki/main.htm or click on "Search Court Records" at www.courts.state.hi.us/. Search back to 1983 by name, case number, or circuit. Online results show middle initial.
General Information: Online identifiers in results same as on public terminal. No juvenile records released. Will fax out documents, $2.00 1st page, $1.00 add'l within Hawaii; $5.00 1st page, $2.00 add'l in U.S.; $10.00 1st page, $5.00 add'l outside the U.S. Court makes copy: $1.00 first page, $.50 each add'l. Self serve: $.15 per page. Certification fee: $2.00. Payee: District Court of the Fifth Judicial Circuit. Personal in-state checks accepted; no third party checks. No credit cards accepted. Prepayment required. Mail requests: SASE required for civil.

District Court of the 5th Circuit - Criminal 3970 Kaana St #207, Lihue, HI 96766; 808-482-2645; fax: 808-482-2693; 7:45AM-4:30PM. ***Misdemeanor, Traffic.***
www.courts.state.hi.us/
Criminal Records: Access: Phone, fax, mail, in person. Only the court performs in person searches; visitors may not. Search fee: $10.00. Required to search: name, years to search, DOB; also helpful: SSN. Mail turnaround time within 1 week. Online results show middle initial.
General Information: Will fax documents $2.00 1st page, $1.00 each add'l page. Court makes copy: $1.00 for first page, $.50 each add'l. Self serve: $.15 per page. Certification fee: $2.00 per cert. Payee: District Court. Personal checks accepted. Visa/MC accepted for traffic.

Maui County

2nd Circuit Court 2145 Main St, #106, Wailuku, HI 96793; 808-244-2969; fax: 808-244-2932; 7:45AM-4:30PM. ***Felony, Misdemeanor, Civil Actions over $5,000, Probate.***
www.courts.state.hi.us/
This court also covers Lanai and Molokai. Records are indexed for this county as 2 = Maui. Provide your toll-free number and they'll give you court costs.
Civil Records: Access: Mail, fax, in person, online. Both court and visitors may perform in person searches. Search fee: $5.00 per name. Required to search: name, years to search. Civil cases indexed by defendant, plaintiff, on computer from 10/85, some prior on microfiche; claims and small claims on computer back to 10/23/2003. Mail turnaround time 1 week. Civil PAT goes back to 1985. Terminal results may include address. Free record searching at http://hoohiki2.courts.state.hi.us/jud/Hoohiki/main.htm or click on "Search Court Records" at www.courts.state.hi.us/. Search back to 1983 by name, case number, or circuit.
Criminal Records: Access: Mail, fax, in person, online. Both court and visitors may perform in person searches. Search fee: $5.00 per name. Required to search: name, years to search; also helpful: DOB, SSN. Criminal records computerized from 10/85, some prior on microfiche. Mail turnaround time 1 week. Criminal PAT goes back to 1985. PAT criminal results show middle initial. Online access to criminal records is same as civil. Online results show middle initial.
General Information: Online identifiers in results same as on public terminal. No juvenile or paternity records released. Fee to fax out file $5.00 1st page, $2.00 each add'l in USA; $2.00 for first and $1.00 each add'l in Hawaii. Court makes copy: Microfilm, file marked copy- $1.00 per page; non-file marked- $1.00 1st page, $.50 each add'l. Certification fee: $2.00 per doc. Payee: Clerk, 2nd Circuit Court. Personal checks accepted; credit cards are not. Prepayment required. Mail requests: SASE required.

Lanai District Court PO Box 631376, Lanai City, HI 96763; 808-565-6447; fax: 808-565-7543; 7:45AM-4:30PM; counter hours- 8AM-4PM. ***Misdemeanor, Civil Actions under $20,000, Eviction, Small Claims.***
www.courts.state.hi.us/
Civil Records: Access: Mail, in person, online. Only the court performs in person searches; visitors may not. Search fee: $5.00 per search. Required to search: name, years to search. Civil cases indexed by defendant, plaintiff, on index and docket books back to statehood. Mail turnaround time 2-3 weeks. Free record searching at http://hoohiki2.courts.state.hi.us/jud/Hoohiki/main.htm or click on "Search Court Records" at www.courts.state.hi.us/. Search by name or case number. Records go back to 12/03. Online results show middle initial.
Criminal Records: Access: Mail, in person. Only the court performs in person searches; visitors may not. Search fee: $5.00 per search. Required to search: name, years to search; also helpful: DOB, SSN. Criminal records on computer since 1997. Mail turnaround time 2-3 weeks.
General Information: Online identifiers in results same as on public terminal. Court makes copy: $1.00 first page, $.50 each add'l. Certification fee: $1.00. Payee: Lanai District Court. Personal checks accepted. Credit cards accepted if paid through Wailuku Dist. Court. Prepayment required. Mail requests: SASE required.

Molokai District Court PO Box 284, Kaunakakai, HI 96748; 808-553-1100; fax: 808-553-3374; 8AM-4PM. ***Misdemeanor, Civil Actions under $20,000, Eviction, Small Claims.***
www.courts.state.hi.us/

Civil Records: Access: Mail, in person, online. Only the court performs in person searches; visitors may not. Search fee: $5.00 per name. Required to search: name, years to search, DOB, SSN. Civil cases indexed by defendant, plaintiff, on index and docket books back to statehood. Mail turnaround time 3 days Free record searching at http://hoohiki2.courts.state.hi.us/jud/Hoohiki/main.htm or click on "Search Court Records" at www.courts.state.hi.us/. Search by name or case number. Online results show middle initial.

Criminal Records: Access: Mail, in person. Only the court performs in person searches; visitors may not. Search fee: $5.00 per name. Required to search: name, years to search, DOB, SSN. Criminal records on computer since 1980. Mail turnaround time is 3 days.

General Information: Online identifiers in results same as on public terminal. No juvenile or paternity records released. Will fax documents to the mainland for $5.00 1st page, $2.00 each add'l; in Hawaii for $2.00 1st page, $1.00 each add'l. Court makes copy: $1.00 first page, $.50 each add'l. Certification fee: $2.00 per cert. Payee: Molokai District Court. Business checks accepted. No credit cards accepted. Prepayment required.

Wailuku District Court 2145 Main St, #137, Wailuku, HI 96793; 808-244-2969; fax: 808-244-2849; 7:45AM-4:30PM. ***Misdemeanor, Civil Actions under $20,000, Eviction, Small Claims, Traffic.***
www.courts.state.hi.us/

Provide your toll-free number and they'll give you court costs. Traffic phone- 808-244-2800.

Civil Records: Access: Mail, fax, in person, online. Only the court performs in person searches; visitors may not. Search fee: $5.00 per name per court. Required to search: name, years to search; also helpful: address. Civil cases indexed by defendant, plaintiff, on index and docket books. Mail turnaround time 2-3 weeks. Civil PAT available. Free record searching at http://hoohiki2.courts.state.hi.us/jud/Hoohiki/main.htm or click on "Search Court Records" at www.courts.state.hi.us/. Search by name or case number. Online results show middle initial.

Criminal Records: Access: Mail, fax, in person. Only the court performs in person searches; visitors may not. Search fee: $5.00 per name per court. Required to search: name, years to search, DOB, SSN. Criminal records on computer since 1980. Mail turnaround time 2-3 weeks. Criminal PAT available. PAT criminal results show middle initial.

General Information: Online identifiers in results same as on public terminal. Will fax documents $5.00 1st page, $2.00 each add'l. Within HI; $2.00 1st page, $1.00 each add'l. Court makes copy: $1.00 first page, $.50 each add'l. Certification fee: $2.00 per doc. Payee: District Court 2nd Circuit. Personal checks accepted, but no out-of-town checks. No credit cards accepted. Prepayment required. Mail requests: SASE required.

Hawaii Recording Office

ORGANIZATION: All UCC financing statements, tax liens, and real estate documents are filed centrally with the Bureau of Conveyances located in Honolulu. The entire state is in the Hawaii Time Zone (HT).

Bureau of Conveyances

Bureau of Conveyances, PO Box 2867, Honolulu, HI 96803. 808-587-0147; fax-808-587-4380; 8AM-3:30PM. (HT) www.hawaii.gov/dlnr/bc

Index: All in one. Records indexed on a public use terminal back to 1976. Office will perform a UCC search but public must search other records themselves. Office will not search real estate records. UCC search per debtor name- $25.00 minimum; Add'l charges for found records. Copy fee $1.00 per page. Cert fee- $1.00 per page includes copy fee. Payee- Bureau of Conveyances. **Online access to Real Estate, Recorder, Grantor-Grantee, Deed, Lien, Conveyances records:** Indices to all documents recorded in the Bureau of Conveyances from 1976 to current are online at http://bocweb.dlnrbc.hawaii.gov/boc/. Certified copies of documents may also be ordered. **Other phones:** Land Court- 808-587-0138; Regular System Records -808-587-0134.

Property tax/Assessor- 842 Bethel St, Honolulu, HI 96813; 808-527-5541/5511, assessor fax- 808-527-5540. **Online Assessor**- Property records from the Hawaii County property assessor database are free at www.hawaiipropertytax.com. Also, search Honolulu real estate records at www.honolulupropertytax.com. No name searching. Maui Assessor Property records are free at www.mauipropertytax.com.

Hawaii County Locator

You will usually be able to find the city name in the City/County Cross Reference below. In that case, it is a simple matter to determine the county from the cross reference. However, only the official US Postal Service city names are included in this index. There are an additional 40,000 place names that people use in their addresses. Therefore, we have also included a ZIP/City Cross Reference immediately following the City/County Cross Reference.

If you know the ZIP Code but the city name does not appear in the City/County Cross Reference index, look up the ZIP Code in the ZIP/City Cross Reference, find the city name, then look up the city name in the City/County Cross Reference. For example, you want to know the county for an address of Menands, NY 12204. There is no "Menands" in the City/County Cross Reference. The ZIP/City Cross Reference shows that ZIP Codes 12201-12288 are for the city of Albany. Looking back in the City/County Cross Reference, Albany is in Albany County.

Hawaii City/County Cross Reference

City	County
AIEA	Honolulu
ANAHOLA	Kauai
BARBERS POINT	Honolulu
BARBERS POINT N A S	Honolulu
CAMP H M SMITH	Honolulu
CAPTAIN COOK	Hawaii
ELEELE	Kauai
EWA BEACH	Honolulu
FORT SHAFTER	Honolulu
HAIKU	Maui
HAKALAU	Hawaii
HALEIWA	Honolulu
HANA	Maui
HANALEI	Kauai
HANAMAULU	Kauai
HANAPEPE	Kauai
HAUULA	Honolulu
HAWAII NATIONAL PARK	Hawaii
HAWI	Hawaii
HICKAM AFB	Honolulu
HILO	Hawaii
HOLUALOA	Hawaii
HONAUNAU	Hawaii
HONOKAA	Hawaii
HONOLULU	Honolulu
HONOMU	Hawaii
HOOLEHUA	Maui
KAAAWA	Honolulu
KAHUKU	Honolulu
KAHULUI	Maui
KAILUA	Honolulu
KAILUA KONA	Hawaii
KALAHEO	Kauai
KALAUPAPA	Maui
KAMUELA	Hawaii
KANEOHE	Honolulu
KAPAA	Kauai
KAPAAU	Hawaii
KAPOLEI	Honolulu
KAUMAKANI	Kauai
KAUNAKAKAI	Maui
KEAAU	Hawaii
KEALAKEKUA	Hawaii
KEALIA	Kauai
KEAUHOU	Hawaii
KEKAHA	Kauai
KIHEI	Maui
KILAUEA	Kauai
KOLOA	Kauai
KUALAPUU	Maui
KULA	Maui
KUNIA	Honolulu
KURTISTOWN	Hawaii
LAHAINA	Maui
LAIE	Honolulu
LANAI CITY	Maui
LAUPAHOEHOE	Hawaii
LAWAI	Kauai
LIHUE	Kauai
M C B H KANEOHE BAY	Honolulu
MAKAWAO	Maui
MAKAWELI	Kauai
MAUNALOA	Maui
MILILANI	Honolulu
MOUNTAIN VIEW	Hawaii
NAALEHU	Hawaii
NINOLE	Hawaii
OCEAN VIEW	Hawaii
OOKALA	Hawaii
PAAUHAU	Hawaii
PAAUILO	Hawaii
PAHALA	Hawaii
PAHOA	Hawaii
PAIA	Maui
PAPAALOA	Hawaii
PAPAIKOU	Hawaii
PEARL CITY	Honolulu
PEARL HARBOR	Honolulu
PEPEEKEO	Hawaii
PRINCEVILLE	Kauai
PUKALANI	Maui
PUUNENE	Maui
SCHOFIELD BARRACKS	Honolulu
TAMC	Honolulu
TRIPLER ARMY MEDICAL CTR	Honolulu
VOLCANO	Hawaii
WAHIAWA	Honolulu
WAIALUA	Honolulu
WAIANAE	Honolulu
WAIKOLOA	Hawaii
WAILUKU	Maui
WAIMANALO	Honolulu
WAIMEA	Kauai
WAIPAHU	Honolulu
WAKE ISLAND	Honolulu
WHEELER ARMY AIRFIELD	Honolulu

ZIP/City Cross Reference

ZIP	City
96701-96701	AIEA
96703-96703	ANAHOLA
96704-96704	CAPTAIN COOK
96705-96705	ELEELE
96706-96706	EWA BEACH
96707-96707	KAPOLEI
96708-96708	HAIKU
96709-96709	KAPOLEI
96710-96710	HAKALAU
96712-96712	HALEIWA
96713-96713	HANA
96714-96714	HANALEI
96715-96715	HANAMAULU
96716-96716	HANAPEPE
96717-96717	HAUULA
96718-96718	HAWAII NATIONAL PARK
96719-96719	HAWI
96720-96721	HILO
96722-96722	PRINCEVILLE
96725-96725	HOLUALOA
96726-96726	HONAUNAU
96727-96727	HONOKAA
96728-96728	HONOMU
96729-96729	HOOLEHUA
96730-96730	KAAAWA
96731-96731	KAHUKU
96732-96733	KAHULUI
96734-96734	KAILUA
96737-96737	OCEAN VIEW
96738-96738	WAIKOLOA
96739-96739	KEAUHOU
96740-96740	KAILUA KONA
96741-96741	KALAHEO
96742-96742	KALAUPAPA
96743-96743	KAMUELA
96744-96744	KANEOHE
96745-96745	KAILUA KONA
96746-96746	KAPAA
96747-96747	KAUMAKANI
96748-96748	KAUNAKAKAI
96749-96749	KEAAU
96750-96750	KEALAKEKUA
96751-96751	KEALIA
96752-96752	KEKAHA
96753-96753	KIHEI
96754-96754	KILAUEA
96755-96755	KAPAAU
96756-96756	KOLOA
96757-96757	KUALAPUU
96759-96759	KUNIA
96760-96760	KURTISTOWN
96761-96761	LAHAINA
96762-96762	LAIE
96763-96763	LANAI CITY
96764-96764	LAUPAHOEHOE
96765-96765	LAWAI
96766-96766	LIHUE
96767-96767	LAHAINA
96768-96768	MAKAWAO
96769-96769	MAKAWELI
96770-96770	MAUNALOA
96771-96771	MOUNTAIN VIEW
96772-96772	NAALEHU
96773-96773	NINOLE
96774-96774	OOKALA
96775-96775	PAAUHAU
96776-96776	PAAUILO
96777-96777	PAHALA
96778-96778	PAHOA
96779-96779	PAIA
96780-96780	PAPAALOA
96781-96781	PAPAIKOU
96782-96782	PEARL CITY
96783-96783	PEPEEKEO
96784-96784	PUUNENE
96785-96785	VOLCANO
96786-96786	WAHIAWA
96788-96788	PUKALANI
96789-96789	MILILANI
96790-96790	KULA
96791-96791	WAIALUA
96792-96792	WAIANAE
96793-96793	WAILUKU
96795-96795	WAIMANALO
96796-96796	WAIMEA
96797-96797	WAIPAHU
96800-96850	HONOLULU
96853-96853	HICKAM AFB
96854-96854	WHEELER ARMY AIRFIELD
96857-96857	SCHOFIELD BARRACKS
96858-96858	FORT SHAFTER
96859-96859	TRIPLER ARMY MED CTR
96859-96859	TAMC
96860-96860	PEARL HARBOR
96861-96861	CAMP H M SMITH
96862-96862	BARBERS POINT N A S
96862-96862	BARBERS POINT
96863-96863	M C B H KANEOHE BAY
96898-96898	WAKE ISLAND

Idaho

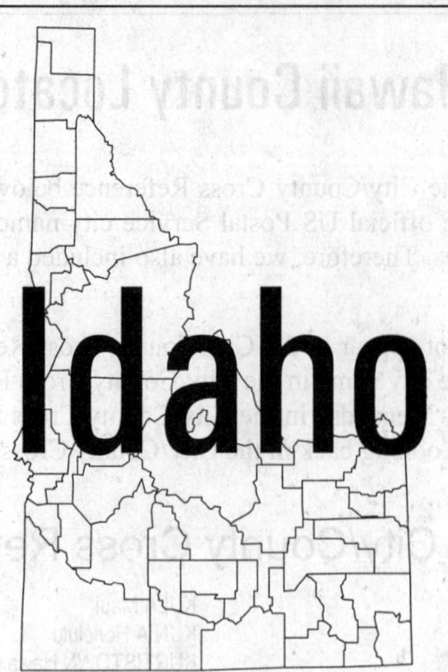

General Help Numbers:

Governor's Office
PO Box 83720 — 208-334-2100
Boise, ID 83720-0034 — Fax 208-334-2175
http://gov.idaho.gov/ — 8AM-6PM

Attorney General's Office
PO Box 83720 — 208-334-2400
Boise, ID 83720-0010 — Fax 208-334-2530
http://www2.state.id.us/ag — 8AM-5PM

Legislative Records
PO Box 83720 — 208-334-2475
Boise, ID 83720-0054 — Fax 208-334-2125
www.legislature.idaho.gov/ — 8AM-5PM

State Archives
Historical Library & Archives — 208-334-3356
2205 Old Penitentiary Rd — Fax 208-334-3198
Boise, ID 83712 — 9AM-5PM
http://idahohistory.net

State Specifics:

Capital: Boise, Ada County

Time Zone: MST*

* Idaho's ten northwestern-most counties are PST: They are: Benewah, Bonner, Boundary, Clearwater, Idaho, Kootenai, Latah, Lewis, Nez Perce, Shoshone.

Number of Counties: 44

Population: 1,523,816

Web Site: www.idaho.gov

State Agencies

Criminal Records

State Repository, Bureau of Criminal Identification, PO Box 700, Meridian, ID 83680-0700 (Courier address- 700 S Stratford Dr, Meridian, ID 83642); 208-884-7130, Fax- 208-884-7193; 8AM-4PM.

www.isp.state.id.us

A signed release is not required, but suggested; see below.

Indexing & Storage: Records available from 1960 or until person reaches 99. New records available for inquiry in about 1 day. 66% of all arrests in database have final dispositions recorded, and at least 67% for those arrests within last 5 years.

Searching: Include in request- name, DOB. SSN and alias will aid in identification. Fingerprints are optional but may be required to establish positive identification. Fingerprint searches take 1-3 days. 100% of records are fingerprint-supported. This data not released- juvenile records unless charged as an adult. A record of an arrest without disposition after 12 months from date of arrest will only be given if signed release presented. Requests without the release will receive only records with dispositions.

Access by: mail, in person.

Fee & Payment: The $10.00 fee per person is applicable for either a name search or a fingerprint search. Fee payee- Idaho State Police Prepayment required. Cashier check or money order is preferred form of payment. Personal checks accepted, credit cards are not.

Mail search: Turnaround time- 3 to 7 days. An SASE is not required.

In person: You may request information in person, but results are still mailed.

Statewide Court Records

Administrative Director of the Courts, Clerk of the Courts, PO Box 83720, Boise, ID 83720-0101 (Courier address- 451 W State St, Boise, ID 83720); 208-334-2246, 208-334-2210 (Clerk of Court Office), Fax- 208-334-2616; 9AM-5PM.

www.isc.idaho.gov/

For tribal court information, visit www.isc.idaho.gov/tribalmn.htm.

Online search: Free access to Idaho trial court records index at www.idcourts.us is searchable by name statewide or by county; Results date back to 1995 or further depending on the county. Online results include identifiers year of birth and middle initial. The following personal information is not released: DL, address, and first 6 characters of the SSN. Also, appellate and supreme court opinions are available at www.isc.idaho.gov/opinions/.

Sexual Offender Registry

State Repository, Central Sexual Offender Registry, PO Box 700, Meridian, ID 83680-0700 (Courier - 700 S Stratford Dr, Meridian, 83642); 208-884-7305, Fax- 208-884-7193; 8AM-5PM.

www.isp.state.id.us

Questions may be directed to idsor@isp.idaho.gov.

Indexing & Storage: Records available from 07/01/93. New records available for inquiry in about 3 days.

Searching: Requests may be made on a named individual or a list of registered sex offenders by ZIP Code or county.

Online search: Access from the web page is available to the public. Inquires can be made by name, address, or by county or ZIP Code. Mapping is also available.

Incarceration Records

Idaho Department of Corrections, Records Bureau, 1299 N. Orchard Street, Suite 110, Boise, ID 83706; 208-658-2000, Fax- 208-327-7444; 8AM-5PM. www.idoc.idaho.gov/

Indexing & Storage: Records available on current and former inmates. New records available for inquiry in about 3 days.

Searching: Include in request- first and last name. DOB, SSN, DOC number are helpful.

Access by: mail, phone, fax, in person, online.

Fee & Payment: Cost is $3.00 for pulling from state storage, if required. Copies are $.10 per page after 5 pages. Prepayment required if over $5.00. Personal checks not accepted.

Mail search: Turnaround time- 5 to 7 days. Requests in writing must be specific about information requested. Use SASE or you will be charged for postage. SASE not required.

Phone search: Limited searching by phone, "is subject there or not." **Fax search:** Only if just needing an inmate location.

In person: The public has right to view records in person upon making a written request to schedule an appointment with records custodian.

Online search: This database search at https://www.accessidaho.org/public/corr/offender/search.html provides information about offenders currently under Idaho Department of Correction jurisdiction: those incarcerated, on probation, or on parole. Names of individuals who have served time and satisfied their sentence will appear - their convictions will not.

Corporation, LP, LLP, LLC, Trademarks/Servicemarks, Assumed Name

Secretary of State, Corporation Division, PO Box 83720, Boise, ID 83720-0080 (Courier address- 450 N 4th St, Boise, ID 83720); 208-334-2301, Fax- 208-334-2080; 8AM-5PM.

www.sos.idaho.gov/corp/corindex.htm

Since 1/1/97, fictitious or assumed names are filed at this office. (Previously they were recorded at the county level.) Not-for-profits records here, also.

Indexing & Storage: Records available for all entities back to 1880's. New records available for inquiry in 24 hours.

Searching: Ongoing requesters should establish a pre-paid account. Include in request- full name of business, specific records that you need copies of. In addition to the articles of organization, business entity records available include: Annual Reports, Officers, Directors, Prior names, filing status and Reserved names, and Filing History. Cross reference of owners/officers is not avail.

Access by: mail, phone, fax, in person, online.

Fee & Payment: There is no search fee. The fee for copies is $.25 per page. Certification is $10.00 as is a Certification of Existence. Add $1.00 if a credit card is used. Fee payee- Secretary of State. Prepayment required. Personal checks and major credit cards accepted.

Mail search: Turnaround time- 1 to 2 days. SASE not required.

Phone search: There is a limit of 3 entities per call. **Fax search:** Copies cost an additional $.50 each if returned by fax.

In person: Agency suggests to call first with request info so that they can pull file.

Online search: Business Entity Searches at www.accessidaho.org/public/sos/corp/search.html?SearchFormstep=crit. This is a free Internet service open 24 hours daily. Includes not-for-profit entities. Trademarks may be searched at www.accessidaho.org/public/sos/trademark/search.html.

Other access: There are a variety of formats and media available for bulk purchase requesters. Requesters can subscriber to a monthly CD update.

Expedited service: is available. Turnaround time- 1 day. Add $20.00 per document.

Uniform Commercial Code, Federal & State Tax Liens

UCC Division, Secretary of State, PO Box 83720, Boise, ID 83720-0080 (Courier address- 700 W Jefferson, Boise, ID 83720); 208-334-3191, Fax- 208-334-2847; 8AM-5PM.

www.sos.idaho.gov/ucc/uccindex.htm

Indexing & Storage: Records available from 1967. If purged or lapsed, kept until 1997. New records available for inquiry in 1 to 2 days.

Searching: The search includes federal tax liens, farm filings, UCC1 financial statements, and seed and labor filings. There is also an agricultural commodity lien search. Federal tax liens on individuals are filed at the county level. Include in request- debtor name. For state tax liens that closed prior to 01/07/98, one must search at the county. On that date, the state took over the filing and database of state tax liens. This data not released- SSNs.

Access by: mail, phone, fax, in person, online.

Fee & Payment: UCC 1 searches are $12.00 per name; otherwise $6.00 for one "type" and $12.00 for two or more "types." Copies are $1.00 per page if no file number given and $.25 per page if file name given. Other fees involved for other filings. Fee payee- Secretary of State. Prepayment required. Personal checks & credit cards accepted.

Mail search: Turnaround time- 1 to 2 days. SASE not required.

Phone search: They will tell whether a filing exists. **Fax search:** There is an additional fee of $.50 per page to fax out.

In person: You may request information in person, time permitting.

Online search: There is a free limited search at https://www.accessidaho.org/secure/sos/liens/search.html. We recommend professional searchers to subscribe to the extensive commercial service at this site. The fee is $3.00 per name searched with a $95.00 annual subscription fee.

Other access: A summary data file on current filing is available on CD.

Expedited service: An expedited search is available for an additional $10.00.

Sales Tax Registrations

Revenue Operations Division, Records Management, PO Box 36, Boise, ID 83722 (Courier address- 800 Park, Boise, ID 83722); 208-334-7793, 208-334-7792 (Records Management), Fax- 208-334-7650; 8AM-5:00PM.

www.tax.idaho.gov/

Indexing & Storage: Records available from 2002. The agency maintains records on computer since 2002 and on microfiche from 2001 to present. New records available in 90 days.

Searching: This agency will only confirm that a business is registered if a tax permit number is provided. They will provide no other information. The only information released is that within public domain. Include in request- full name and address of entity. They will also search if provided with a tax permit number, a DBA or an EIN.

Access by: mail, phone, fax, in person, online.

Fee & Payment: There is no search fee, but there is a fee for postage for mail requests or for faxing. Fee payee- ISTC, PO Box 36, Boise, ID 83732. Prepayment required. Personal checks accepted, credit cards are not.

Mail search: Turnaround time- 1 to 10 days. The copy fee is $.10 per page, after 20 pages. SASE not required.

Phone search: No fee for telephone request. Only general information is released. **Fax search:** The fee is $1.00 per page. Turnaround time 24 hours.

In person: Copy fees apply.

Online search: Email requests are accepted at rmcmichael@tax.id.gov.

Birth Certificates

Vital Records, PO Box 83720, Boise, ID 83720-0036 (Courier address- 450 W State St, 1st Floor, Boise, ID 83702); 208-334-5980, Fax- 866-599-4629; 8AM-5PM. www.healthandwelfare.idaho.gov/site/3335/default.aspx

Indexing & Storage: Records available on computer from July 1911 to present. Prior records at the county. New records available in 2 weeks.

Searching: Records are confidential for 100 years. Only immediate family or legal representative may receive records as well as those who have a notarized release from persons of record or an immediate family member. Include in request- full name, names of parents, mother's maiden name, date of birth, city of birth, relationship to person of record, reason for information request. Also include a copy of a photo ID and sign the request. This data not released- adoption or sealed records.

Access by: mail, fax.

Fee & Payment: The fee is $13.00 per name or additional copy. Add $5.00 for photo certification copy. Add $5.00 for rush orders. Fee payee- Vital

Records. Prepayment required. Credit cards accepted for fax requests only. Personal checks accepted. Major credit cards accepted.

Mail search: Turnaround time- 2 to 3 weeks. SASE not required. Send an additional $5.00 to cut turnaround time to 2-3 days.

Fax search: See Expedited Service.

Expedited service: Expedited service is available for fax and online requests. The fee is $23.50 plus cost of return by FedEx or mail. Service is performed by a vendor - www.vitalchek.com. Requests received by noon (MT) will be processed within 2 working days if requesting express delivery; otherwise 1 week turnaround.

Death Records

Vital Records, PO Box 83720, Boise, ID 83720-0036 (Courier address- 450 W State St, 1st Floor, Boise, ID 83702); 208-334-5980, Fax- 866-599-4629; 8AM-5PM.

www.healthandwelfare.idaho.gov/site/3335/default.aspx

Indexing & Storage: Records available from July 1911 to present. From 1911 to 1807, records at county. New records available in 2 weeks.

Searching: Records are confidential for 50 years and are available only to immediate family members or legal representatives or a person who has a notarized release from persons of record or an immediate family member. Include in request- full name, date of death, city of death, relationship to person of record, reason for information request, copy of photo ID or DL of requester.

Access by: mail, fax, online.

Fee & Payment: The fee is $13.00 per name or additional copy. Add $5.00 for certification. Add $5.00 for rush orders. Fee payee- Vital Records. Prepayment required. Credit cards are accepted with fax requests only. Personal checks accepted. Major credit cards accepted.

Mail search: Turnaround time- 2 to 3 weeks. SASE not required.

Fax search: See Expedited Services.

Online search: The agency has made the death index of records from 1911 - 1956 available at http://abish.byui.edu/specialCollections/fhc/Death/searchForm.cfm. There is no fee. No online access available for newer records, but requests can be made online via a vendor www.vitalchek.com.

Expedited service: Expedited service is available for fax and online requests. The fee is $23.50 plus cost of return by express delivery. Service is performed by a vendor - www.vitalchek.com.

Marriage Certificates

Vital Records, PO Box 83720, Boise, ID 83720-0036 (Courier address- 450 W State St, 1st Floor, Boise, ID 83702); 208-334-5980, Fax- 866-599-4629; 8AM-5PM. www.healthandwelfare.idaho.gov/site/3335/default.aspx

Indexing & Storage: Records available from May 1947 to present. Prior records at the county. New records available for inquiry in 4 to 6 weeks.

Searching: Records are confidential for 50 years. Only immediate family members and legal representatives may obtain recent records, others may obtain records with a notarized release from a family member or person of record. Include in request- names of husband and wife, date of marriage, city of marriage, relationship, copy of photo ID or DL of requester.

Access by: mail, fax.

Fee & Payment: The fee is $13.00 per name or additional copy. Add $5.00 for certification. Add $5.00 for rush orders. Fee payee- Vital Records. Prepayment required. Credit cards accepted with fax requests only. Personal checks accepted. Major credit cards accepted.

Mail search: Turnaround time- 2 to 3 weeks. SASE not required. **Fax search:** See Expedited Services.

Expedited service: Expedited service is available for fax and online requests. The fee is $23.50 plus cost of return by express delivery. Service is performed by a vendor - www.vitalchek.com.

Divorce Records

Vital Records, PO Box 83720, Boise, ID 83720-0036 (Courier address- 450 W State St, 1st Floor, Boise, ID 83702); 208-334-5980, Fax- 866-599-4629; 8AM-5PM.

www.healthandwelfare.idaho.gov/site/3335/default.aspx

This agency only maintains certificates of divorce; copies of decrees available via the court system.

Indexing & Storage: Records available from May 1947 to present. New records available for inquiry immediately.

Searching: Records are confidential for 50 years and are available only to immediate family members, legal representatives, and a person with a notarized signed release from persons of record or immediate family. Include in request- names of husband and wife, date of divorce, city of divorce, relationship, copy of photo ID or DL of requester.

Access by: mail, fax.

Fee & Payment: The fee is $13.00 per name or additional copy. Add $5.00 for certification. Add $5.00 for rush orders. Fee payee- Vital Records. Prepayment required. Credit cards are accepted with fax requests only. Personal checks accepted. Major credit cards accepted.

Mail search: Turnaround time- 2 to 3 weeks. SASE not required. **Fax search:** See Expedited Services.

Expedited service: Expedited service is available for fax and online requests. The fee is $23.50 plus cost of return by express delivery. Service is performed by a vendor - www.vitalchek.com.

Workers' Compensation Records

Industrial Commission of Idaho, Attn: Records Management, PO Box 83720, Boise, ID 83720-0041; 208-334-6000, 800-950-2110, Fax- 208-334-2321; 8AM-5PM. www.iic.idaho.gov/

Indexing & Storage: Records available from 1917 on. New records available for inquiry immediately.

Searching: RMR-1 is used by parties to an open claim or closed claim or the Ind. Spec. Indemnity Fund. RMR-2 is used by an employers subject to ADA and who has made offer of employment. RMR-3 is used by employers and prospective employers not subject to ADA. Include in request- claimant name, SSN, date of accident and claim number. RMR-4 is for subject to get own record. RMR-2 forms require notarized signature. Form RMR-3 requires non-notarized signature. This data not released- psychiatric information.

Access by: mail, phone, fax, in person.

Fee & Payment: No copy fee for paper copy requests under 100 pages or microfilm copies under 50 pages. If more, hard copy costs are charged $.05 per paper page, $.15 per microfilm page PLUS labor cost. Fee payee- Industrial Commission. Charges that total under $5.00 are waived. Prepayment required if over $50 and for individual. Personal checks accepted, credit cards are not.

Mail search: Turnaround time- 3 days. If copies fees are charged, then there will be a charge for postage unless SASE provided.

Phone search: Limited data is given over the phone.

Fax search: Fax searching available, except if the RMR-2 Form is used.

In person: One may request information in person; however, not all files are available the same day because some files are not on site and must be ordered from storage.

Driver Records

Idaho Transportation Department, Driver's Services, PO Box 34, Boise, ID 83731-0034 (Courier address- 3311 W State, Boise, ID 83703); 208-334-8736, Fax- 208-334-8739; 8:30AM-5PM.

www.itd.idaho.gov/dmv/

Indexing & Storage: Records available for at least 3 years for moving violations, DUIs and suspensions. Accidents are not shown on the record. New records available for inquiry in 1 day from receipt.

Searching: Personal information is not released to casual requesters unless the requestor claims a valid authorization. A request form is available at the web page. Include in request- driver's license number and DOB are used for the primary search. If no record is found, a secondary search is performed using the name and DOB, or name and license number. This data not released- SSNs, medical information, signature, address.

Access by: mail, fax, online.

Fee & Payment: The fee is $4.00 per record. Convenience fees are added for online and batch searches. Fee payee- Idaho Transportation Department. Prepayment required. Ongoing requesters can set up an account. Personal checks, Visa, and MasterCard accepted.

Mail search: Turnaround time- 3 to 5 days. Mail-in requesters are asked to use the state form. SASE not required.

Fax search: Fax requests for records are accepted, if paid by a credit card or by account. Call 208-334-8761 to set up an account.

Online search: Idaho offers online access (CICS) to the driver license files through its portal provider, Access Idaho. Fee is $6.00. Idaho drivers can also order their own record from this site, fee is $6.24. For more information about a subscriber account, call 208-332-0102 or visit www.accessidaho.org. There is a free DL status check at https://www.accessidaho.org/secure/itd/reinstatement/index.html. Be aware that Access Idaho refers to driving records as 'Driver License Records' and refers to records related to vehicle title or registration as MVRs.

Other access: Idaho offers bulk retrieval of basic drivers license information with a signed contract. For information, call 208-334-8602.

Vehicle Ownership & Registration, Vessel Ownership

Idaho Transportation Department, Vehicle Services, PO Box 34, Boise, ID 83731-0034 (Courier address- 3311 W State St, Boise, ID 83707); 208-334-8649, 208-334-8663, Fax- 208-334-8542; 8:30AM-5PM.

www.itd.idaho.gov/dmv/vehicleservices/vs.htm

Model year vessels 2000 or newer that have either a motor or permanently attached sail or are longer than 12 feet must be titled. If a lien is placed on a model year older than 2000, then that vessel must be titled.

Indexing & Storage: Records available from 1981. New records available for inquiry in 1 day.

Searching: Personal information is not released to casual requesters unless the requestor claims a valid authorization. Use of the request form is suggested (found at www.itd.idaho.gov/dmv/vehicleservices/documents/3374.pdf). Include in request- name, VIN, license plate number for search, current address is also helpful. Include requester's name, address and authorization claimed. This data not released- SSNs or medical records.

Access by: mail, fax, online.

Fee & Payment: The fee is $4.00 for current title with lien information or for a registration search. A complete title history (using the microfilm) is $8.00. Convenience fees are added for online and batch searches. Fee payee- Idaho Transportation Department. Prepayment required. Motor vehicle record accounts may be established by calling 208-334-8761. Personal checks, Visa/MC accepted.

Mail search: Turnaround time- 5 to 10 days. Information request forms are available. SASE not required.

Fax search: You may fax a request with a major credit card. Results, except for title history records, can be returned by fax to local or toll-fee number for no additional fee. Turnaround time three days.

In person: This office does not provide counter service, but information is provided in person at any County Assessor auto licensing location statewide.

Online search: Idaho offers online and batch access to registration and title files through its portal provider Access Idaho. Records are $6.00 each or $3.50 for a lien search for subscribers. For more information, call 208-332-0102 or visit www.accessidaho.org. There is a $95 annual subscription fee. Interestingly, be aware that Access Idaho refers to these as records MVRs; they do not mean driving records.

Other access: Idaho offers bulk retrieval of registration, ownership, and vehicle information with a signed contract. For more information, call 208-334-8601.

Accident Reports

Idaho Transportation Department, Traffic and Highway Safety-Accident Records, PO Box 7129, Boise, ID 83707-1129 (Courier address- 3311 W State St, Boise, ID 83707); 208-334-8100, Fax-208-334-4430; 8AM-12:00PM; 1PM-5PM.

Indexing & Storage: Records available from 1970's (on microfilm) to present. New records available for inquiry in 1 day for electronic reports, 3 months if paper.

Searching: Include in request- full name, date of accident, location of accident, driver's license number.

Access by: mail, phone, fax, in person.

Fee & Payment: The fee is $4.00 per report plus handling. Fee payee- Idaho Transportation Department, Financial Control. Prepayment required. Personal checks and credit cards accepted.

Mail search: Turnaround time- 2 weeks. A SASE is requested.

Phone search: No fee for telephone request. Fee charged if copies sent. Turnaround time is 2 weeks.

Fax search: Turnaround time 2 weeks.

In person: It is suggested that walk-in requesters call first before going to department should the state have to locate the records on microfilm.

Other access: Computer files may be purchased with prepaid deposit plus computer charges. However, the file will not contain addresses, citation information, or drivers' license numbers and other personal information. Annual databases may be purchased.

Vessel Registration

Idaho Parks & Recreation, Vessel Registration Records, PO Box 83720, Boise, ID 83720-0065 (Courier address- 5657 Warm Springs, Boise, ID 83712); 208-514-2480, Fax- 208-334-2639; 8AM-5PM.

http://parksandrecreation.idaho.gov/recreation/boating.aspx

Registration issued here, titles by the Vehicle Service at DOT. Any vessel 2000 or newer must be titled if with a permanently attached mode of propulsion or if longer than 12 feet or if a lien exists.

Indexing & Storage: Records available from 1987 to present. Older records are available, but to search them, you must know the registration #. Records are indexed on computer. All boats with motors and/or sails must be registered. New records available for inquiry in minutes.

Searching: Registration records are open to the public. Record information can be verified or provide; however state statutes forbid the release of commercial lists. Include in request- owner's name or hull # or registration #.

Access by: mail, in person.

Fee & Payment: There is no search fee for a simple request, but fees are charged for custom data searches. Call for estimate.

Mail search: Turnaround time- 10 working days. SASE not required.

In person: Counter service available.

Legislation Records

Legislative Services Office, Research and Legislation, PO Box 83720, Boise, ID 83720-0054 (Courier address- 514 W Jefferson, Boise, ID 83720); 208-334-2475, Fax- 208-334-2125; 8AM-5PM. www.legislature.idaho.gov

Sessions are from January to the end of March.

Indexing & Storage: Records available from 1960 to present. Legislative information from 1998 to present is available at the Internet. New records available for inquiry in 1 day.

Voter Registration

Access to Records is Restricted.

State Elections Office, Sec of State, PO Box 83720, Boise, ID 83720-0080 (Courier address- 304 N 8th St, Rm 149, Boise, ID 83720); 208-334-2852, Fax- 208-334-2282; 8AM-5PM.

www.idahovotes.gov

Access to the state's centralized database is only available for political purposes. A CD may be purchased for $20. Individual name look-ups must be done by the county clerks.

GED Certificates

Department of Education, GED Testing, PO Box 83720, Boise, ID 83720-0027; 208-332-6928, Fax-208-334-6205; 8AM-Noon, closed Wed.

www.sde.idaho.gov/AdultEducation/default.asp

Indexing & Storage: New records available for inquiry in 1 week.

Searching: Include in request- SSN, date of birth, name at time of test. Date and location of test is helpful. A signed release is necessary for copies of transcripts or for scores. Will not expedite requests, but will fax back unofficial transcripts only if the request was for an official transcript.

Access by: mail, phone, fax, in person.

Fee & Payment: There is a $5.00 fee for a copy of a transcript or a verification.

Mail search: Turnaround time- up to 3 weeks. The agency holds the request until the check or money order clears. A money order will clear up to 2 weeks quicker. SASE not required.

Phone search: No fee for telephone request. Verification only over the phone.

Fax search: Turnaround time is 1 day, but only for a verification, not for a transcript.

In person: Information is released immediately. Requester must have picture ID.

Hunting & Fishing License Information

Access to Records is Restricted.

ID Department of Fish & Game, Licenses Division, PO Box 25, Boise, ID 83707-0025 (Courier address- 1075 Park Blvd, Boise, 83707); 208-334-2592, 208-334-3736 (Enforcement Office), Fax- 208-334-2148; 8AM-5PM. http://fishandgame.idaho.gov

This office will not release individual records with personal information including addresses, they will only confirm is there is a license issued. Name searches are not done.

Idaho State Licensing Agencies

For details about the agency responsible for licensing/certifying/registering an item below or in the Agency Quick Finder section, match an item's number with the number of the agency in the *Licensing Agency Information* section.

Idaho Licenses Searchable Online

Acupuncturist #19 .... https://secure.ibol.idaho.gov/eIBOLPublic/LPRBrowser.aspx
Applicator, Pesticide, Private/Com #20 . www.agri.state.id.us/Categories/Pesticides/licensing/licenseLookUp.php
Appraiser, General/Resid'l/Trainee #19.. https://secure.ibol.idaho.gov/eIBOLPublic/LPRBrowser.aspx
Architect #19 .... https://secure.ibol.idaho.gov/eIBOLPublic/LPRBrowser.aspx
Assignee (Lender) #21 .... http://finance.idaho.gov/LicenseeSearch.aspx
Athlete Agent #19 .... https://secure.ibol.idaho.gov/eIBOLPublic/LPRBrowser.aspx
Athletic Trainer #30........ www.accessidaho.org/public/bomed/license/search.html
Attorney #29 .... http://www2.state.id.us/isb/gen/menu.htm#Mem
Audiologist #19 .... https://secure.ibol.idaho.gov/eIBOLPublic/LPRBrowser.aspx
Backflow Assembly Tester #19........ https://secure.ibol.idaho.gov/eIBOLPublic/LPRBrowser.aspx
Bank #21........ http://finance.idaho.gov/LicenseeSearch.aspx
Barber School/Instructor #19 .... https://secure.ibol.idaho.gov/eIBOLPublic/LPRBrowser.aspx
Barber/Barber Shop/School #19........ https://secure.ibol.idaho.gov/eIBOLPublic/LPRBrowser.aspx
Chemigator #20 .... www.agri.state.id.us/Categories/Pesticides/licensing/licenseLookUp.php
Chiropractor #19 .... https://secure.ibol.idaho.gov/eIBOLPublic/LPRBrowser.aspx
Clinical Nurse Specialist #14 .... http://www2.state.id.us/ibn/licenseesearch.htm
Collection Agency/Collector #21........ http://finance.idaho.gov/LicenseeSearch.aspx
Construction Mgr, Public Works #31 ..... https://www.dbs.idaho.gov/edbspublic/lprbrowser.aspx
Consumer Loan Co. & Credit Seller #21 http://finance.idaho.gov/LicenseeSearch.aspx
Contracting Business #19........ https://secure.ibol.idaho.gov/eIBOLPublic/LPRBrowser.aspx
Contractor, Public Works #31 .... https://www.dbs.idaho.gov/edbspublic/lprbrowser.aspx
Contractor, Registered #19........ https://secure.ibol.idaho.gov/eIBOLPublic/LPRBrowser.aspx
Cosmetics Dealer, Retail #19 .... https://secure.ibol.idaho.gov/eIBOLPublic/LPRBrowser.aspx
Cosmetologist/Cosmetology Salon #19.. https://secure.ibol.idaho.gov/eIBOLPublic/LPRBrowser.aspx
Cosmetology School/Instructor #19........ https://secure.ibol.idaho.gov/eIBOLPublic/LPRBrowser.aspx
Counselor, Clinical #19........ https://secure.ibol.idaho.gov/eIBOLPublic/LPRBrowser.aspx
Counselor, Professional #19........ https://secure.ibol.idaho.gov/eIBOLPublic/LPRBrowser.aspx
Credit Seller #21 .... http://finance.idaho.gov/LicenseeSearch.aspx
Credit Union #21 .... http://finance.idaho.gov/LicenseeSearch.aspx
Crematory #3........ https://secure.ibol.idaho.gov/eIBOLPublic/LPRBrowser.aspx
Dental Assistant/Hygienist/Spec'l't #13 . http://www2.state.id.us/isbd/search.cfm
Dentist #13........ http://www2.state.id.us/isbd/search.cfm
Denturist #19 .... https://secure.ibol.idaho.gov/eIBOLPublic/LPRBrowser.aspx
Denturist Intern/Establishment #19........ https://secure.ibol.idaho.gov/eIBOLPublic/LPRBrowser.aspx
Dietitian #30........ www.accessidaho.org/public/bomed/license/search.html
Drinking Water Professionals #19 .... https://secure.ibol.idaho.gov/eIBOLPublic/LPRBrowser.aspx
Elections & Campaign Disclosure #28 .. www.idsos.state.id.us/notary/npindex.htm
Electrical Apprentice/Journeyman #10 .. https://www.dbs.idaho.gov/edbspublic/lprbrowser.aspx
Electrical Inspector/Contractor #10........ https://www.dbs.idaho.gov/edbspublic/lprbrowser.aspx
Electrolysis, Electrolysis Instructor #19 . https://secure.ibol.idaho.gov/eIBOLPublic/LPRBrowser.aspx
Engineer #17 .... www.ipels.idaho.gov/rostdown.htm
Escrow Licensee #21........ http://finance.idaho.gov/LicenseeSearch.aspx
Esthetician, Esthetician Instructor #19 .. https://secure.ibol.idaho.gov/eIBOLPublic/LPRBrowser.aspx
Finance Company #21........ http://finance.idaho.gov/LicenseeSearch.aspx
Fire Sprinkler System Contractor #23 ... www.doi.idaho.gov/sfm/SprinklerContractorList.aspx
Fireworks License #23........ www.doi.idaho.gov/sfm/FireworksVendorList.aspx
Funeral Director/Dir. Trainee #3 .... https://secure.ibol.idaho.gov/eIBOLPublic/LPRBrowser.aspx
Funeral Establishment #3........ https://secure.ibol.idaho.gov/eIBOLPublic/LPRBrowser.aspx
Geologist #18........ http://ibol.idaho.gov/IBOL/Procedures/bol%20search.htm
Glamour Photography Studio #19 .... https://secure.ibol.idaho.gov/eIBOLPublic/LPRBrowser.aspx
Guide #15 .... www.oglb.idaho.gov/ofdirectory.htm
Hearing Aid Fitter/Dealer #19 .... https://secure.ibol.idaho.gov/eIBOLPublic/LPRBrowser.aspx
HVAC Contractor/Journeyman #10 .... https://www.dbs.idaho.gov/edbspublic/lprbrowser.aspx
Insurance Producer #24 .... www.doi.idaho.gov/Insurance/search.aspx
Insurance Surplus Lines Broker #24...... www.doi.idaho.gov/Insurance/search.aspx
Insurer, Domestic/Mutual/Foreign #24... www.doi.idaho.gov/Insurance/search.aspx
Landscape Architect #19 .... https://secure.ibol.idaho.gov/eIBOLPublic/LPRBrowser.aspx

Lobbyist #28 .... www.idsos.state.id.us/elect/lobbyist/lobinfo.htm
LPG Dealer/Facility #19 .... https://secure.ibol.idaho.gov/eIBOLPublic/LPRBrowser.aspx
Manufact'd Homes-Housing Related #10 https://www.dbs.idaho.gov/edbspublic/lprbrowser.aspx
Manufact'd Housing Dealer/Mfg. #10 .... https://www.dbs.idaho.gov/edbspublic/lprbrowser.aspx
Manufactured Commercial Building #10. https://www.dbs.idaho.gov/edbspublic/lprbrowser.aspx
Marriage & Family Counselor #19 .... https://secure.ibol.idaho.gov/eIBOLPublic/LPRBrowser.aspx
Medical Doctor #30 .... www.accessidaho.org/public/bomed/license/search.html
Medical Resident #30 .... www.accessidaho.org/public/bomed/license/search.html
Medical, Temporary #30 .... www.accessidaho.org/public/bomed/license/search.html
Midwife Nurse #14 .... http://www2.state.id.us/ibn/licenseesearch.htm
Money Transmitter #21 .... http://finance.idaho.gov/LicenseeSearch.aspx
Mortgage Broker/Banker #21 .... http://finance.idaho.gov/LicenseeSearch.aspx
Mortgage Company #21 .... http://finance.idaho.gov/LicenseeSearch.aspx
Mortgage Loan Originator #21 .... http://finance.idaho.gov/LicenseeSearch.aspx
Mortician/Mortician Resi.Trainee #3 ...... https://secure.ibol.idaho.gov/eIBOLPublic/LPRBrowser.aspx
Nail Technician/Instructor #19 .... https://secure.ibol.idaho.gov/eIBOLPublic/LPRBrowser.aspx
Naturopath #19 .... https://secure.ibol.idaho.gov/eIBOLPublic/LPRBrowser.aspx
Notary Public #28 .... www.idsos.state.id.us/notary/npindex.htm
Nurse #14 .... http://www2.state.id.us/ibn/licenseesearch.htm
Nurse Anesthetist #14 .... http://www2.state.id.us/ibn/licenseesearch.htm
Nurse-LPN/RN #14 .... http://www2.state.id.us/ibn/licenseesearch.htm
Nursing Care (Skilled) Facility #8 .... https://secure.ibol.idaho.gov/eIBOLPublic/LPRBrowser.aspx
Nursing Home Administrator #19 .... https://secure.ibol.idaho.gov/eIBOLPublic/LPRBrowser.aspx
Occupational Therapist/Assistant #30 ... www.accessidaho.org/public/bomed/license/search.html
Optometrist #19 .... https://secure.ibol.idaho.gov/eIBOLPublic/LPRBrowser.aspx
Osteopathic Physician #30 .... www.accessidaho.org/public/bomed/license/search.html
Outfitter #15 .... www.oglb.idaho.gov/ofdirectory.htm
Payday Lender #21 .... http://finance.idaho.gov/LicenseeSearch.aspx
Pest Control Consultant #6 .... www.agri.state.id.us/Categories/Pesticides/licensing/licenseLookUp.php
Pesticide Appl'c't'r/Oper'r/Dealer/Mfg #6 www.agri.state.id.us/Categories/Pesticides/licensing/licenseLookUp.php
Pharmacist/Pharm't Intern/Preceptor#16 https://www2.state.id.us/secure/bop/bop_Licensee_Search_Form.cfm
Physical Therapist/Assistant #30 .... www.accessidaho.org/public/bomed/license/search.html
Physician Assistant #30 .... www.accessidaho.org/public/bomed/license/search.html
Plumbing Apprentice/Journeyman #10 .. https://www.dbs.idaho.gov/edbspublic/lprbrowser.aspx
Plumbing Inspector/Contractor #10 .... https://www.dbs.idaho.gov/edbspublic/lprbrowser.aspx
Podiatrist #19 .... https://secure.ibol.idaho.gov/eIBOLPublic/LPRBrowser.aspx
Polysomnography Tech/Trainee #30 ..... www.accessidaho.org/public/bomed/license/search.html
Polysomnography Technologist #30 ...... www.accessidaho.org/public/bomed/license/search.html
Psychologist #19 .... https://secure.ibol.idaho.gov/eIBOLPublic/LPRBrowser.aspx
Psychology Service Extender #19 .... https://secure.ibol.idaho.gov/eIBOLPublic/LPRBrowser.aspx
Public Accountant Firm #12 .... www.isba.idaho.gov/htm/accountantsearch.htm
Public Accountant-CPA #12 .... www.isba.idaho.gov/htm/accountantsearch.htm
Public Accountant-LPA #12 .... www.isba.idaho.gov/htm/accountantsearch.htm
Real Estate Agent/Broker/Firm #34 .... www.irec.idaho.gov/licensee-search.html
Real Estate Appraiser #19 .... https://secure.ibol.idaho.gov/eIBOLPublic/LPRBrowser.aspx
Residential Care Administrator #19 .... https://secure.ibol.idaho.gov/eIBOLPublic/LPRBrowser.aspx
Residential Care Facility #8 .... https://secure.ibol.idaho.gov/eIBOLPublic/LPRBrowser.aspx
Respiratory Therapist #30 .... www.accessidaho.org/public/bomed/license/search.html
Securities Broker/Seller/Issuer #21 .... http://finance.idaho.gov/LicenseeSearch.aspx
Shorthand Reporter #4 .... http://ibol.idaho.gov/IBOL/Procedures/bol%20search.htm
Social Worker #19 .... https://secure.ibol.idaho.gov/eIBOLPublic/LPRBrowser.aspx
Speech/Language Pathologist #19 .... https://secure.ibol.idaho.gov/eIBOLPublic/LPRBrowser.aspx
Surveyor, Land #17 .... www.ipels.idaho.gov/rostdown.htm
Temporary Medical #30 .... www.accessidaho.org/public/bomed/license/search.html
Title Loan Lender #21 .... http://finance.idaho.gov/LicenseeSearch.aspx
Trust Company #21 .... http://finance.idaho.gov/LicenseeSearch.aspx
Utility Regulator #27 .... www.puc.idaho.gov
Veterinarian/Veterinary Technician #1 .. www.bovm.state.id.us/searches/bovm_license_search_form.cfm
Waste Water Professionals #19 .... https://secure.ibol.idaho.gov/eIBOLPublic/LPRBrowser.aspx
Waste Water Treatment Operator #19 .. https://secure.ibol.idaho.gov/eIBOLPublic/LPRBrowser.aspx
Water Collection Operator #19 .... https://secure.ibol.idaho.gov/eIBOLPublic/LPRBrowser.aspx
Water Distribution Operator #19 .... https://secure.ibol.idaho.gov/eIBOLPublic/LPRBrowser.aspx
Water Rights Examiner #26 .... www.idwr.idaho.gov/water/rights/examiners.htm
Water Treatment Operator #19 .... https://secure.ibol.idaho.gov/eIBOLPublic/LPRBrowser.aspx

Idaho Licensing Quick Finder

Acupuncturist #19 208-334-3233
Applicator, Pesticide, Private/Com #20 208-332-8500
Appraiser, General/Resid'l/Trainee #19 208-334-3233
Aquaculture Operation #20 208-332-8500
Architect #19 208-334-3233
Artificial Inseminator #20 208-332-8500
Asbestos Worker #10 208-334-2129
Assignee (Lender) #21 208-332-8002
Athlete Agent #19 208-334-3233
Athletic Trainer #30 208-327-7000
Attorney #29 208-344-4500
Audiologist #19 208-334-3233
Backflow Assembly Tester #19 208-334-3233
Bakery #11 208-327-7499
Bank #21 208-332-8005
Barber School/Instructor #19 208-334-3233
Barber/Barber Shop/School #19 208-334-3233
Bed and Breakfast #11 208-327-7499
Beekeeper #20 208-332-8500
Beer/Wine License, Whlse/Retail #25 .. 208-884-7060
Boiler Inspector #10 208-334-2129
Boiler Safety Code Approval #10 208-334-2129
Bottling Plant #11 208-327-7499
Boxer #32 208-221-6534
Boxing/Wrestling Event #32 208-221-6534
Boxing/Wrestling Professional #32 208-221-6534
Brewery #25 208-884-7060
Brokerage Dealer #12 208-334-2490
Building Inspector #10 208-334-3896
Care Facility for Retarded, Intermedi. #8208-334-6626
Care Facility, Nursing #8 208-334-6626
Chemigator #20 208-332-8500
Child Care Institution/Agency #7 208-334-5700
Child Care Licensee #7 208-334-5700
Chiropractor #19 208-334-3233
Clinical Laboratory Registration #2 208-334-2235
Clinical Nurse Specialist #14 .... 208-334-3110 x21
Collection Agency/Collector #21 208-332-8002
Commission Merchant #20 208-332-8500
Commodity Dealer #20 208-332-8500
Communication Disorders Specialist #5
.... 208-332-6887, 208-332-6881
Construction Mgr, Public Works #31 208-334-4057
Consumer Loan Co. & Credit Seller #21208-332-8002
Contracting Business #19 208-334-3233
Contractor, Public Works #31 208-334-4057
Contractor, Registered #19 208-334-3233
Controlled Substance Registrant #16 208-334-2356
Cosmetics Dealer, Retail #19 208-334-3233
Cosmetologist/Cosmetol'gy Salon #19 .. 208-334-3233
Cosmetology School/Instructor #19 208-334-3233
Counselor, Clinical #19 208-334-3233
Counselor, Debt/Credit #21 208-332-8002
Counselor, Professional #19 208-334-3233
Credit Seller #21 208-332-8002
Credit Union #21 208-332-8003
Crematory #3 208-334-3233
Dairy Farm/Dairy Prod't Processor #20 . 208-332-8500
Day Care Center Inspector #11 208-327-7499
Day Care Center/Home #7 208-334-5700
Dental Assistant #13 208-334-2369
Dental Hygienist #13 208-334-2369
Dental Specialists #13 208-334-2369
Dentist #13 208-334-2369
Denturist #19 208-334-3233
Denturist Intern/Establishment #19 208-334-3233
Dietitian #30 208-327-7000
Driller, Rotary #26 208-287-4800
Drinking Water Professionals #19 208-334-3233
Drug Mfg./Repackager/Whlse. #16 208-334-2356
Drug Outlet, ie. Nursing Home #16 208-334-2356
Drug Seller, Non-Pharm., ie. Grocery #16
.... 208-334-2356
Egg Distributor/Grader #20 208-332-8500
Elections & Campaign Disclosure #28 . 208-334-2852

Electrical Apprentice/Journeyman #10 . 208-334-2183
Electrical Inspector/Contractor #10 208-334-2183
Electrolysis, Electrolysis Instructor #19 . 208-334-3233
Elevator Installation/Repairmen #10 208-334-2129
Emergency Medical Technician #9 208-334-4000
Engineer #17 208-334-3860
Escrow Licensee #21 208-332-8002
Esthetician, Esthetician Instructor #19 . 208-334-3233
Euthanasia Agency #1 208-332-8588
Euthanasia Technician #1 208-332-8588
Exceptional Child Sch'l Pgrm Advisor #5
.... 208-332-6887, 208-332-6881
Farm Produce Dealer/Broker #20 208-332-8500
Feed Manufacturer, Commercial #20 208-332-8500
Fertilizer Manufact'r, Commercial #20 . 208-332-8500
Finance Company #21 208-332-8002
Fire Inspector #23 208-334-4370
Fire Sprinkler Fitter #23 208-334-4370
Fire Sprinkler System Contractor #23 .. 208-334-4370
Fireworks License #23 208-334-4370
Fishing, Commercial #22 208-334-3700
Florist/Nurseryman #20 208-332-8620
Food Establishment Studied #11 208-327-7499
Food Processing/Mfg. Plant #11 208-327-7499
Food Warehouse, Cold Storage #11 208-327-7499
Foster Home #7 208-334-5700
Funeral Director/Dir. Trainee #3 208-334-3233
Funeral Establishment #3 208-334-3233
Fur Buyer #22 208-334-3700
Game Farm (Commercial Wildlife) #22 . 208-334-3700
Geologist #18 208-334-2268
Glamour Photography Studio #19 208-334-3233
Grocery Store #11 208-327-7499
Guide #15 208-327-7380
Hearing Aid Fitter/Dealer #19 208-334-3233
Horse Racing Event/Occupation #33 208-884-7080
Hospital (Child or Elderly) #8 208-334-6626
HVAC Contractor/Journeyman #10 208-334-3950
Insurance Producer #24 208-334-4250
Insurance Surplus Lines Broker #24 208-334-4250
Insurer, Domestic/Mutual/Foreign #24 . 208-334-4250
Investment Advisor #21 208-332-8004
Landscape Architect #19 208-334-3233
Liquor License, Retail #25 208-884-7060
Livestock Auction Market #20 208-332-8500
Livestock Brand #25 208-884-7070
Loan Agent / Collection Officer #12 208-334-2490
Lobbyist #28 208-334-2852
Logging #10 208-334-3950
LPG Dealer/Facility #19 208-334-3233
Mammography #2 208-334-2235
Manufact'd Homes- Housing Related #10
.... 208-334-3896
Marriage & Family Counselor #19 208-334-3233
Medical Doctor #30 208-327-7000
Medical Resident #30 208-327-7000
Medical, Temporary #30 208-327-7000
Midwife Nurse #14 .... 208-334-3110 x21
Milk/Dairy Product Stor./Haul/Handler #20
.... 208-332-8500
Mine Safety Training #10 208-334-2129
Mixer-Loader #20 208-332-8500
Money Transmitter #21 208-332-8002
Mortgage Broker/Banker #21 208-332-8002
Mortgage Company #21 208-332-8002
Mortgage Loan Originator #21 208-332-8002
Mortician/Mortician Resi.Trainee #3 208-334-3233
Nail Technician/Instructor #19 208-334-3233
Naturopath #19 208-334-3233
Notary Public #28 208-334-2300
Nurse #14 .... 208-334-3110 X21
Nurse Anesthetist #14 .... 208-334-3110 x21
Nurse-LPN/RN #14 .... 208-334-3110 X21
Nursing Assistant #14 800-748-2480
Nursing Care (Skilled) Facility #8 208-334-6626

Nursing Home Administrator #19 208-334-3233
Occupational Therapist/Assistant #30 . 208-327-7000
Optometrist #19 208-334-3233
Organic Certification #20 208-332-8620
Osteopathic Physician #30 208-327-7000
Outfitter #15 208-327-7380
Paramedic (EMT) #9 208-334-4000
Payday Lender #21 208-332-8002
Pest Control Consultant #6 208-332-8600
Pesticide Appl't'r/Oper'r/Dealer/Mfg #6 208-332-8600
Pharmacist/Pharmac't Intern/Preceptor #16
.... 208-334-2356
Pharmacy/Drug Store/Mailer #16 208-334-2356
Physical Therapist/Assistant #30 208-327-7000
Physician Assistant #30 208-327-7000
Plumbing Apprentice/Journeyman #10 208-334-3442
Plumbing Inspector/Contractor #10 208-334-3442
Podiatrist #19 208-334-3233
Police (Peace) Officer #25 208-884-7250
Polysomnography Tech./Trainee #30 .. 208-327-7000
Psychologist #19 208-334-3233
Psychology Service Extender #19 208-334-3233
Public Accountant Firm/CPA/LPA #12 .. 208-334-2490
Public Commodity Warehouse #20 208-332-8500
Real Estate Agent/Broker/Firm #34 208-334-3285
Real Estate Appraiser #19 208-334-3233
Recreational Vehicle Manufact'r #10 208-334-3896
Rehabilitation Facility #8 208-334-6626
Residential Care Administrator #19 208-334-3233
Residential Care Facility #8 208-334-6626
Residential School #7 208-334-5700
Respiratory Therapist #30 208-327-7000
Restaurant Sanitation Standard #11 208-327-7499
Savings & Loan Association #21 208-332-8005
School Counselor #5 .... 208-332-6887, 208-332-6881
School Nurse #5 .... 208-332-6887, 208-332-6881
School Principal/Superintendent #5
.... 208-332-6887, 208-332-6881
Securities Broker/Seller/Issuer #21 208-332-8004
Seed Company #20 208-332-8620
Septic System Permit #11 208-327-7499
Septic Tank Pumper #11 208-327-7499
Shooting Preserve #22 208-334-3700
Shorthand Reporter #4 208-334-2517
Social Worker #19 208-334-3233
Soil & Plant Amendment Mfg. #20 208-332-8620
Solicitor (Financial) #21 208-332-8002
Special Education Director #5
.... 208-332-6887, 208-332-6881
Speech/Language Pathologist #19 208-334-3233
Subdivision Approval #11 208-327-7499
Substance Abuse Treatment Ctr #7 208-334-5700
Subsurface Sewage License #11 208-327-7499
Surveyor, Land #17 208-334-3860
Swimming Pool Operator #11 208-327-7499
Taxidermist #22 208-334-3700
Teacher #5 .... 208-332-6887, 208-332-6881
Temporary Medical #30 208-327-7000
Title Loan Lender #21 208-332-8002
Trapper/Junior Trapper #22 208-334-3700
Trust Company #21 208-332-8005
Utility Regulator Gas/Water/Power/Phone #27
.... 208-334-0300
Veterinarian/Veterinary Technician #1 . 208-332-8588
Veterinary Drug Outlet/Technician #16 208-334-2356
Waste Water Professionals #19 208-334-3233
Water Collection/Dist. Operator #19 208-334-3233
Water Laboratory #2 .... 208-334-2235 x233
Water Rights Examiner #26 208-287-4800
Water Treatment Operator #19 208-334-3233
Water Well Driller #26 208-287-4800
Weighmaster #20 208-332-8500
Winery #25 208-884-7060
Wrestler #32 208-221-6534
X-ray Equipment #2 .... 208-334-2235 x245

Idaho Licensing Agency Information

#1 Board of Veterinary Medicine, PO Box 7249 (2270 Old Penitentiary Rd-83712), Boise, ID 83707; 208-332-8588, Fax- 208-334-2170. Hours- 8AM-5PM. www.bovm.state.id.us

#2 Bureau of Laboratories, 2220 Old Penitentiary Rd, Boise, ID 83712; 208-334-2235, Fax- 208-334-2382. www.healthandwelfare.idaho.gov/site/3384/default.aspx

#3 Bureau of Occupational Licenses, Mortician Board of Examiners, 1109 Main St, #220, Boise, ID 83702-5642; 208-334-3233, Fax- 208-334-3945. www.ibol.idaho.gov/mor.htm Search data at- https://secure.ibol.idaho.gov/eIBOLPublic/LPRBrowser.aspx

#4 Certified Shorthand Reporters Board, 1109 Main St #220, Boise, ID 83702; 208-334-2517, Fax- 208-334-5211. http://ibol.idaho.gov/sre.htm

#5 Department of Education, Teacher Certification, PO Box 83720 (650 W State St), Boise, ID 83720-0027; 208-332-6800, Fax- 208-334-2228. Hours- 8AM-5PM. www.sde.idaho.gov/site/teacher_certification/

#6 Department of Agriculture, Pesticides Division - Licensing, 2270 Old Penitentiary Rd, Boise, ID 83712; 208-332-8600, Fax- 208-334-3547. Hours- 8AM-5PM. www.agri.state.id.us/Categories/Pesticides/indexPesticides.php Search data at- www.agri.state.id.us/Categories/Pesticides/licensing/licenseLookUp.php

#7 Department of Health & Welfare, Division of Family and Community Services, 450 W State St, 5th Fl, Boise, ID 83720; 208-334-5700, Fax- 208-332-7331. www.healthandwelfare.idaho.gov/site/3327/default.aspx

#8 Department of Health & Welfare, Bureau of Facility Standards, 3380 Americana Terr #260, Boise, ID 83720-0036; 208-334-6626, Fax- 208-364-1888.

#9 Department of Health & Welfare, Bureau of Emergency Medical Services, 590 W Washington, Boise, ID 83702; 208-334-4000, Fax- 208-334-4015. www.healthandwelfare.idaho.gov/site/3344/default.aspx

#10 Division of Building Safety, 1090 E Watertower St, Meridian, ID 83642; 208-334-3950, Fax- 208-334-2683. Hours- 8AM-5PM. http://dbs.idaho.gov Fax number for Electrical-208-855-2165; Plumbing-208-855-9339.

#11 Environmental Health Department, Bakery & Related Licensing, 707 N Armstrong Place, Boise, ID 83704; 208-375-5211, Fax- 208-327-8550. http://cdhd.idaho.gov/EH/food/forms.htm

#12 Board of Accountancy, PO Box 83720 (3101 W Main St #210--83702), Boise, ID 83720; 208-334-2490, Fax- 208-334-2615. www.isba.idaho.gov Search data at- www.isba.idaho.gov/htm/accountantsearch.htm

#13 Board of Dentistry, P.O. Box 83720 (350 N 9th St #M-100), Boise, ID 83720; 208-334-2369, Fax- 208-334-3247. http://www2.state.id.us/isbd/ Search data at- http://www2.state.id.us/isbd/search.cfm

#14 Board of Nursing, PO Box 83720 (280 N 8th St, #210), Boise, ID 83720-0061; 208-334-3110, Fax- 208-334-3262. Hours- 8AM-5PM. http://www2.state.id.us/ibn/ Search data at- http://www2.state.id.us/ibn/licenseesearch.htm Will sell/provide lists or offer other means of verification.

#15 Board of Outfitters & Guides, 1365 N Orchard St, Rm 172, Boise, ID 83706; 208-327-7380, Fax- 208-327-7382. www.oglb.idaho.gov Search data at- www.oglb.idaho.gov/ofdirectory.htm Scroll to the bottom of the page to find the appropriate links for searching.

#16 Board of Pharmacy, Box 83720 (3380 Americana Terr, #320), Boise, ID 83720-0067; 208-334-2356, Fax- 208-334-3536. http://bop.accessidaho.org/ List available for $53.00 each; written request and prepayment required. Applications are available online.

#17 Board of Professional Engineers & Surveyors, 5535 W Overland Rd, Boise, ID 83705; 208-373-7210, Fax- 208-373-7213. www.ipels.idaho.gov Search data at- www.ipels.idaho.gov/rostdown.htm

#18 Board of Professional Geologists, 1109 Main St #220, Boise, ID 83702-5642; 208-334-2268. http://ibol.idaho.gov/geo.htm Search at- http://ibol.idaho.gov/IBOL/Procedures/bol%20search.htm

#19 Bureau of Occupational Licenses, 1109 Main St #220, Boise, ID 83702; 208-334-3233, Fax- 208-334-3945. Hours- 8AM-5PM. www.ibol.idaho.gov Search data at- https://secure.ibol.idaho.gov/eIBOLPublic/LPRBrowser.aspx

#20 Dept. of Agriculture, Inspections/ Registrations, 2270 Old Penitentiary Rd, Boise, ID 83712; 208-332-8500, Fax- 208-334-2170. www.agri.state.id.us/Categories/InspectionsExams/indexInspectExams.php

#21 Department of Finance, Financial Bureau, PO Box 83720 (800 Park Blvd #200), Boise, ID 83720-0031; 208-332-8000, Fax- 208-332-8098. http://finance.idaho.gov

#22 Department of Fish & Game, PO Box 25 (600 S Walnut), Boise, ID 83707; 208-334-3700, Fax- 208-334-2114. http://fishandgame.idaho.gov

#23 Department of Insurance, State Fire Marshall, 700 W State St, 3rd Fl, Boise, ID 83720-0043; 208-334-4370, Fax- 208-334-4375. Hours- 8AM-5PM. www.doi.idaho.gov/sfm/firemars.aspx Provides lists of names, addresses and phone numbers. These can be mailed, emailed or faxed. You may also call the office at any time.

#24 Department of Insurance, PO Box 83720, 700 W State St, 3rd Fl, Boise, ID 83720-0043; 208-334-4250, Fax- 208-334-4398. Hours- 8AM-5PM. www.doi.idaho.gov Search data at- www.doi.idaho.gov/Insurance/search.aspx

#25 State Police, 700 S Stratford Dr, Meridian, ID 83642; 208-884-7000, Fax- 208-884-7090. Hours- 8AM-5PM. www.isp.state.id.us

#26 Department of Water Resources, PO Box 83720, 322 E Front St, Boise, ID 83720-0098; 208-287-4800, Fax- 208-287-6700. www.idwr.idaho.gov/

#27 Public Utilities Commission, PO Box 83720 (472 W Washington St), Boise, ID 83720; 208-334-0300, Fax- 208-334-3762. Hours- 8AM-5PM. www.puc.idaho.gov

#28 Secretary of State, PO Box 83720 (450 N 4th St), Boise, ID 83720-0800; 208-334-2300, Fax- 208-334-2282. www.idsos.state.id.us

#29 State Bar, PO Box 895, Boise, ID 83701; 208-334-4500, Fax- 208-334-4515. http://www2.state.id.us/isb/ Search data at- http://www2.state.id.us/isb/gen/menu.htm#m

#30 Board of Medicine, PO Box 83720 (1755 Westgate Dr), Boise, ID 83720-0058; 208-327-7000, Fax- 208-327-7005. www.bom.state.id.us Search data at- www.accessidaho.org/public/bomed/license/search.html

#31 Division of Building Safety, Public Works Contractors Board, 1090 E Watertower St, Meridian, ID 83642; 208-334-4057, Fax- 208-855-9666. http://dbs.idaho.gov/publicworks/ Search data at- https://www.dbs.idaho.gov/edbspublic/lprbrowser.aspx

#32 State Athletic Department, 800 Park Blvd Plaza 4, PO Box 36, Boise, ID 83722-0410; 208-221-6534, Fax- 208-334-7844. http://accessidaho.org/info/athletic_commission.html

#33 Horse Racing Commission, PO Box 700 (700 Stratford Dr), Meridian, ID 83680-0700; 208-884-7080, Fax- 208-884-7098. www.isp.state.id.us/race/

#34 Real Estate Commission, 633 N 4th St, Boise, ID 83720-0077; 208-334-3285, Fax- 208-334-2050. www.idahorealestatecommission.com Search data at- www.irec.idaho.gov/licensee-search.html

Idaho Federal Courts

The following list indicates the district and division name for each county in the state. If the bankruptcy court location is different from the district court, then the location of the bankruptcy court appears in parentheses.

County/Court Cross Reference

County	Court	County	Court
Ada	Boise	Gem	Boise
Adams	Boise	Gooding	Boise
Bannock	Pocatello	Idaho	Pocatello (Moscow)
Bear Lake	Pocatello	Jefferson	Pocatello
Benewah	Coeur d' Alene	Jerome	Boise
Bingham	Pocatello	Kootenai	Coeur d' Alene
Blaine	Boise	Latah	Moscow
Boise	Boise	Lemhi	Pocatello
Bonner	Coeur d' Alene	Lewis	Moscow
Bonneville	Pocatello	Lincoln	Boise
Boundary	Coeur d' Alene	Madison	Pocatello
Butte	Pocatello	Minidoka	Boise
Camas	Boise	Nez Perce	Moscow
Canyon	Boise	Oneida	Pocatello
Caribou	Pocatello	Owyhee	Boise
Cassia	Boise	Payette	Boise
Clark	Pocatello	Power	Pocatello
Clearwater	Moscow	Shoshone	Coeur d' Alene
Custer	Pocatello	Teton	Pocatello
Elmore	Boise	Twin Falls	Boise
Franklin	Pocatello	Valley	Boise
Fremont	Pocatello	Washington	Boise

Standards for Federal Courts: Fees are standard unless noted in profile. Search fee is $26.00 per item (one party name or case number). Copy fee is $.50 per page. Certification fee is $9.00 per document, double for exemplification, if available. Most courts require prepayment. Mail requests should enclose a SASE unless otherwise noted. Before releasing records, all courts require prepayment, unless noted.

District courts index by defendant and plaintiff and by case number. Bankruptcy courts usually index by debtor and case number. While most courts now have their indexes on computer, many may still maintain index card files as well. Courts will archive closed case files at different times.

There are numerous public access programs available to online subscribers. Search the U.S. Party/Case Index to find party names and case numbers among all courts. Individual case data is provided on PACER. A search of CM/ECF provides copies of cases filed electronically. For details about PACER, the US Party/Case Index, and CM/ECF see the Appendix or go to http://pacer.psc.uscourts.gov or call 800-676-6856.

US District Court District of Idaho

Boise Division Court Clerk, Federal Bldg, 550 W Fort St, Rm 400, Boise, ID 83724, 866-496-1250, 208-334-1361; Fax- 208-334-9362. Hours-8AM-5PM. www.id.uscourts.gov

Counties/Note: Ada, Adams, Blaine, Boise, Camas, Canyon, Cassia, Elmore, Gem, Gooding, Jerome, Lincoln, Minidoka, Owyhee, Payette, Twin Falls, Valley, Washington.

Searches/Indexing: Search computer statewide from any terminal at any of the 4 courts. Results do not include SSN or DOB but may include address. Will not fax back documents. New cases are in the index immediately after filing date. Both computer and card indexes maintained; computer back to 1990; images back to 1999.

Search Access: With case number, all public index info released via phone. **Mail:** Search usually completed- 2-7 days. Include SASE for return. **In person:** 2 public terminals available. No self-serve copier available. Court can recommend an outside vendor to make copies.

Payment: Pay by money order, cashier's or personal check. No credit cards. Payee: US District Court Clerk. Prepayment required for large requests.

E-Services: This court is new to PACER so civil records only go back a few years, and criminal records may not be available. New records online after 2 days. ECF at https://ecf.idd.uscourts.gov. View recent Written Decisions free at main website, click on Attorney Resources then Written decisions. **Online Note:** To view calendars, click on Calendars at main website, choose type.

Coeur d' Alene Division Court Clerk, 205 N 4th, Rm 202, Coeur d'Alene, ID 83814, 866-299-5515, 208-664-4925; Fax- 208-765-0270. Hours-8AM-5PM. www.id.uscourts.gov

Counties/Note: Benewah, Bonner, Boundary, Kootenai, Shoshone.

Searches/Indexing: Search computer statewide from any terminal at any of the 4 courts. Results do not include SSN or DOB but may include address. Will not fax back documents. New cases are in the index immediately after filing date. Both computer and card indexes maintained; computer back to 1990; images back to 1999.

Search Access: With case number, all public index info released via phone. **Mail:** Search usually completed- 2-7 days. Include SASE for return. **In person:** Public terminals available. No self-serve copier.

Payment: Pay by money order, cashier's or personal check. No credit cards. Payee: Court Clerk. Prepayment required for large requests.

E-Services: This court is new to PACER so civil records only go back a few years, and criminal records may not be available. New records online after 2 days. ECF at https://ecf.idd.uscourts.gov. View recent Written Decisions free at main website, click on Attorney Resources then Written decisions. **Online Note:** To view calendars, click on Calendars at main website, choose type.

Moscow Division Court Clerk, 220 E 5th St, Rm 304, Moscow, ID 83843, 208-882-7612; Fax- 208-883-1576. Hours- 8AM - 5PM. www.id.uscourts.gov

Counties: Clearwater, Latah, Lewis, Nez Perce.

Searches/Indexing: Search computer statewide from any terminal at any of the 4 courts. Results do not include SSN or DOB but may include address. Will not fax back documents. New cases are in the index immediately after filing date. Both computer and card indexes maintained; computer back to 1990; images back to 1999.

Search Access: With case number, all public index info released via phone. **Mail:** Search usually completed- 2-7 days. Include SASE for return. **In person:** Public terminals available. Self-serve copies from computer- $.10 each.

Payment: Pay by money order, cashier's or personal check. No credit cards. Payee: Court Clerk. Prepayment required for large requests.

E-Services: This court is new to PACER so civil records only go back a few years, and criminal records may not be available. New records online after 2 days. ECF at https://ecf.idd.uscourts.gov. View recent Written Decisions free at main website, click on Attorney Resources then Written decisions. **Online Note:** To view calendars, click on Calendars at main website, choose type.

Pocatello Division Court Clerk, 801 E Sherman, Rm 119, Pocatello, ID 83201, 866-444-6086, 208-478-4123; Fax- 208-478-4106. Hours- 8AM-5PM. www.id.uscourts.gov

Counties/Note: Bannock, Bear Lake, Bingham, Bonneville, Butte, Caribou, Clark, Custer, Franklin, Fremont, Idaho, Jefferson, Lemhi, Madison, Oneida, Power, Teton.

Searches/Indexing: Search computer statewide from any terminal at any of the 4 courts. Results do not include SSN or DOB but may include address. Will not fax back documents. New cases are in the index immediately after filing date. Both computer and card indexes maintained; computer back to 1990; images back to 1999.

Search Access: With case number, all public index info released via phone. **Mail:** Search usually completed- 2-7 days. Include SASE for return. **In person:** Public terminals available. No self-serve copier.

Payment: Pay by money order, cashier's or personal check. No credit cards. Payee: Court Clerk. Prepayment required for large requests.

E-Services: This court is new to PACER so civil records only go back a few years, and criminal records may not be available. New records online after 2 days. ECF at https://ecf.idd.uscourts.gov. View recent Written Decisions free at main website, click on Attorney Resources then Written decisions. **Online Note:** To view calendars, click on Calendars at main website, choose type.

US Bankruptcy Court District of Idaho

Boise Division Court Clerk, US Courthouse - Bankruptcy Div, 550 W Fort St, Rm 400, Boise, ID 83724, 866-496-1250, 208-334-1074; Fax-208-334-9362. 8AM-5PM. www.id.uscourts.gov

Counties/Note: Ada, Adams, Blaine, Boise, Camas, Canyon, Cassia, Elmore, Gem, Gooding, Jerome, Lincoln, Minidoka, Owyhee, Payette, Twin Falls, Valley, Washington.

Searches/Indexing: Include full name and SSN in search request. Results include last 4 SSN digits, address; DOB may also appear. Will fax back documents for fee. New cases are in the index immediately after filing date. Computer and paper indexes maintained.

Search Access: Only docket info is available by phone. Voice Case Information Service available, call VCIS at 208-334-9386. **Mail:** Search usually completed- 24 hours. SASE not required. **Fax:** Fax search requests accepted. **In person:** 2 public terminals available back to 1993. No self-serve copier. Court can recommend an outside vendor to search and make copies.

Payment: Pay by money order, cashier's check. No personal checks or credit cards.

E-Services: PACER records go back to 9/1990. New records online after 1 day. ECF at https://ecf.idd.uscourts.gov. **Opinions:** www.id.uscourts.gov/cfCourt/decisions/bk_decisionlist.cfm. **Online Note:** Search archived bankruptcy cases free at www.id.uscourts.gov/cfCourt/CourtArchives/Archive_SearchForm.cfm. To view calendars, click on Calendars at main website, choose type.

Coeur d' Alene Division Court Clerk, 205 N 4th St, Rm202, Coeur d'Alene, ID 83814, 866-299-5515, 208-664-4925; Fax- 208-765-0270. Hours-8AM-5PM. www.id.uscourts.gov

Counties/Note: Benewah, Bonner, Boundary, Kootenai, Shoshone.

Searches/Indexing: Include full name and SSN in search request. Results include last 4 SSN digits, address; DOB may also appear. Will fax back documents for fee. New cases are in the index immediately after filing date. Computer and paper indexes maintained. Case files sent to archives 6 months after closed.

Search Access: Only docket info is available by phone. Voice Case Information Service available, call VCIS at 208-334-9386. **Mail:** Search usually completed- 24 hours. Include SASE for return. **Fax:** Fax search requests accepted. **In person:** 1 public terminal available back to 1989. No self-serve copier.

Payment: Pay by money order, cashier's check. No personal checks or credit cards. Payee: US Bankruptcy Court.

E-Services: PACER records go back to 9/1990. New records online after 1 day. ECF at https://ecf.idd.uscourts.gov. **Opinions:** www.id.uscourts.gov/cfCourt/decisions/bk_decisionlist.cfm. **Online Note:** Search archived bankruptcy cases free at www.id.uscourts.gov/cfCourt/CourtArchives/Archive_SearchForm.cfm. To view calendars, click on Calendars at main website, choose type.

Moscow - Northern Division Court Clerk, 220 E 5th St, Rm 304, Moscow, ID 83843, 208-882-7612; Fax- 208-883-1576. 8AM-5PM. www.id.uscourts.gov

Counties/Note: Clearwater, Idaho, Latah, Lewis, Nez Perce.

Searches/Indexing: Include full name and SSN in search request. Results include last 4 SSN digits, address; DOB may also appear. Will fax back documents for fee. New cases are in the index immediately after filing date. Computer and paper indexes maintained.

Search Access: Only docket info is available by phone. Voice Case Information Service available, call VCIS at 208-334-9386. **Mail:** Search usually completed- 1 week. Include SASE for return. **Fax:** Fax search requests accepted. **In person:** 1 public terminal available; index back to 1991. No self-serve copier.

Payment: Pay by money order, cashier's check. No personal checks or credit cards. Payee: US Bankruptcy Court.

E-Services: PACER records go back to 9/1990. New records online after 1 day. ECF at https://ecf.idd.uscourts.gov. **Opinions:** www.id.uscourts.gov/cfCourt/decisions/bk_decisionlist.cfm. **Online Note:** Search archived bankruptcy cases free at www.id.uscourts.gov/cfCourt/CourtArchives/Archive_SearchForm.cfm. To view calendars, click on Calendars at main website, choose type.

Pocatello Div. Court Clerk, 801 E Sherman, Rm 119, Pocatello, ID 83201, 866-444-6086, 208-478-4123; Fax- 208-478-4106. 8AM-5PM. www.id.uscourts.gov

Counties/Note: Bannock, Bear Lake, Bingham, Bonneville, Butte, Caribou, Clark, Custer, Franklin, Fremont, Jefferson, Lemhi, Madison, Oneida, Power, Teton.

Searches/Indexing: Include full name and SSN in search request. Results include last 4 SSN digits, address; DOB may also appear. Will fax back documents for fee. New cases are in the index immediately after filing date. Computer and paper indexes maintained.

Search Access: Only docket info is available by phone. Voice Case Information Service available, call VCIS at 208-334-9386. **Mail:** Search usually completed- 24 hours. Include SASE for return. **Fax:** Fax search requests accepted if you have a deposit account. **In person:** No self-serve copier.

Payment: Pay by money order, cashier's check, business check. No personal checks or credit cards. Payee: US Bankruptcy Court.

E-Services: PACER records go back to 9/1990. New records online after 1 day. ECF at https://ecf.idd.uscourts.gov. **Opinions:** www.id.uscourts.gov/cfCourt/decisions/bk_decisionlist.cfm. **Online Note:** Search archived bankruptcy cases free at www.id.uscourts.gov/cfCourt/CourtArchives/Archive_SearchForm.cfm. To view calendars, click on Calendars at main website, choose type.

Idaho County Courts

Court	Jurisdiction	No. of Courts	How Organized
District Courts*	General	46	7 Districts
Magistrates Division*	Limited	46	7 Districts
Combined Courts*		44	

* Profiled in this Sourcebook.

Court	CIVIL								
	Tort	Contract	Real Estate	Min. Claim	Max. Claim	Small Claims	Estate	Eviction	Domestic Relations
District Courts*	X	X	X	$0	No Max				
Magistrates Division*	X	X	X	$0	$10,000	$4,000	X	X	X

Court	CRIMINAL				
	Felony	Misdemeanor	DWI/DUI	Preliminary Hearing	Juvenile
District Courts*	X	X	X	X	
Magistrates Division*			X	X	X

Administration

Administrative Director of Courts, Supreme Court Building, PO Box 83720, Boise, ID, 83720-0101; 208-334-2246, Fax: 208-334-2146 or 2616. www.isc.idaho.gov

Court Structure

District judges hear felony criminal cases and civil actions if the amount involved is more than $10,000, and appeals of decisions of the Magistrate Division. District judges may also hear domestic relation cases, such as divorces and child custody matters, but in most counties, such cases are handled by Magistrate judges.The Magistrate Division hears probate matters, divorce proceedings, juvenile proceedings, initial felony proceedings through the preliminary hearing, criminal misdemeanors, infractions, civil cases when the amount in dispute does not exceed $10,000. Magistrates also hear Small Claims cases, established for disputes of $4,000 or less.

Online Access

Free access to Idaho trial court records index at www.idcourts.us is searchable by name statewide or by county. Results date back to 1995 or further depending on the county. Online results include identifiers year of birth and middle initial. The following personal information is not released: DL, address, and first 6 characters of the SSN. All courts provide public access terminals onsite. Also, appellate and supreme court opinions are available at www.isc.idaho.gov/opinions/.

Searching Tips, Fees, and Other Guidelines

A statewide court administrative rule states that record custodians do not have a duty to "compile or summarize information contained in a record, nor ... to create new records for the requesting party." Under this rule, some courts will not perform searches. A detailed description of the court rules regarding access to records may be found in Idaho Court Administrative Rule 32.

Many courts require a signed release for employment record searches. The following fees are mandated statewide but not always followed: search fee- none (but 11 courts charge $4.00 or $5.00 per name search); certification fee- $1.00 (can be $1.50) per document plus copy fee; copy fee- $1.00 per page. Prepayment required unless otherwise noted.

Ada County

Ada County Criminal Court 200 W Front St, Rm 1190, Boise, ID 83702-5931; 208-287-6900; criminal phone: x2; fax: 208-287-6919; 8AM-5PM (MST). ***Felony, Misdemeanor, Traffic.***
http://www2.state.id.us/fourthjudicial

Criminal Records: Access: Mail, in person, online. Both court and visitors may perform in person searches. No search fee. Required to search: name, years to search; also helpful: address, DOB, SSN. Criminal records computerized from 1985, microfiche from 1983, docket books back to statehood. Mail turnaround time up to 1-7 days. Public use terminal has crim records back to 1980. PAT results show middle initial, DOB. Search trial court index back to 1995 and calendars free at https://www.idcourts.us. Online results show middle initial, DOB. **General Information:** No alcohol level or confidential evaluation records released. Will fax documents to local or toll free line. Court makes copy: $1.00 per page. Cert fee: $1.50. Payee: Ada County. Personal checks accepted; credit cards are not. Mail requests: SASE required.

County District & Magistrate Cts - Civil 200 W Front, Rm 1155, Boise, ID 83702-5931; 208-287-6900; fax: 208-287-6919; 8AM-5PM (MST). ***Civil, Eviction, Small Claims, Probate.***
http://www2.state.id.us/fourthjudicial

Civil Records: Access: Mail, in person, online. Both court and visitors may perform in person searches. No search fee. Required to search: name, years to search; also helpful: address. Civil cases indexed by defendant, plaintiff, on computer since 1985, microfiche and docket books from 1860s. Mail turnaround time 1-7 days. Civil PAT goes back to 1994. PAT civil results show middle initial. Search trial court records back to 1995 and calendars free at https://www.idcourts.us. Online results show middle initial, DOB.
General Information: No juvenile, adoption, child protection records released. Will fax documents to local or toll free line. Court makes copy: $1.00 per page. Cert fee: $1.00 per page. Payee: Ada County. No personal checks accepted. Credit cards accepted in person only. Mail requests: SASE required.

Adams County

District & Magistrate Courts PO Box 48, Council, ID 83612; 208-253-4561/4233; criminal fax: 208-253-4880; civil fax: same; 8AM-5PM (MST). ***Felony, Misdemeanor, Civil, Eviction, Small Claims, Probate.*** www.co.adams.id.us
Probate fax is same as main fax number.

Civil Records: Access: Fax, mail, in person, online. Both court and visitors may perform in person searches. No search fee. Required to search: name, years to search. Civil cases indexed by defendant, plaintiff, on computer back to 1993, docket books from 1911. Mail turnaround time 2 days. Civil PAT goes back to 1993. PAT civil results show middle initial. Search trial court records back to 1995 and calendars free at https://www.idcourts.us.

Criminal Records: Access: Fax, mail, in person, online. Both court and visitors may perform in person searches. No search fee. Required to search: name, years to search, signed release, DOB or SSN. Criminal records computerized from 1993, docket books from 1911. Mail turnaround time 2 days. Criminal PAT goes back to same as civil. PAT results show middle initial, DOB. Search trial court index back to 1995 and calendars free at https://www.idcourts.us. Online results show middle initial, DOB.
General Information: No juvenile, sealed cases records released. Will fax documents $2.00 per page. Court makes copy: $1.00 per page, self serve same. Certification fee: $1.00. Payee: Adams County. Personal checks and major credit cards accepted. Mail requests: SASE requested.

Bannock County

District & Magistrate Courts 624 E Center, Rm 220, Pocatello, ID 83201; 208-236-7351; criminal phone: 208-236-7273; civil phone: 208-236-7350; probate phone: 208-236-7351; criminal fax: 208-236-7293; civil fax: 208-236-7013; 8AM-5PM (MST). ***Felony, Misdemeanor, Civil, Eviction, Small Claims, Probate, Infractions.***
www.co.bannock.id.us/clkcrt1.htm
Phone number for Misdemeanors- 208-236-7272.
Civil Records: Access: Fax, mail, in person, online. Both court and visitors may perform in person searches. No search fee, unless extensive research involved. Required to search: name, years to search. Civil cases indexed by defendant, plaintiff, on computer from 1986, on docket books from 1970s. Mail turnaround time 1 day to 2 weeks. Civil PAT goes back to 1995. PAT results show middle initial, DOB. Search trial court records back to 1995 and calendars at https://www.idcourts.us.
Criminal Records: Access: Fax, mail, in person, online. Both court and visitors may perform in person searches. No search fee, unless extensive research involved. Required to search: name, years to search; also helpful: DOB, SSN. Criminal records computerized from 1986, on docket books from 1970s. Mail turnaround time 1 day to 2 weeks. Criminal PAT goes back to same as civil. PAT results show middle initial, DOB. Search trial court index back to 1995 and calendars free at https://www.idcourts.us. Online results show middle initial, DOB.
General Information: No adoption, mental, juvenile, termination, domestic violence records released. Will fax documents $1.00 per page. Court makes copy: $1.00 per page. Certification fee: $1.50 per page. Payee: Bannock District Court. Personal checks accepted; credit cards are not. SASE required.

Bear Lake County

District & Magistrate Courts PO Box 190, Paris, ID 83261; 208-945-2208 x5; criminal fax: 208-945-2780; civil fax: same; 8:30AM-5PM (MST). ***Felony, Misdemeanor, Civil, Eviction, Small Claims, Probate.***
Civil Records: Access: Fax, mail, online. Only the court performs in person searches; visitors may not. No search fee. Required to search: name, years to search. Civil cases indexed by defendant, plaintiff, on computer back to 1991, docket books from early 1900s. Mail turnaround time 2-3 days. Public use terminal available, records go back to 1991. PAT civil results show middle initial. Search trial court records back to 1995 and calendars free at https://www.idcourts.us.
Criminal Records: Access: Fax, mail, online. Only the court performs in person searches; visitors may not. No search fee. Required to search: name, years to search, DOB; also helpful: SSN, signed release. Criminal records computerized from 1991, docket books from early 1900s. Mail turnaround time 2-3 days. Public use terminal available. PAT results show middle initial, DOB. Search trial court index back to 1995 and calendars free at https://www.idcourts.us. Online results show middle initial, DOB.
General Information: No juvenile, CPA, divorce records released. Will fax documents $1.00 per page. Court makes copy: $1.00 per page, self serve same. Certification fee: $1.50 per document. Payee: Clerk of Court. Business checks accepted. Credit cards accepted. Mail requests: SASE required.

Benewah County

District & Magistrate Courts Courthouse, 701 College Ave, St Maries, ID 83861; 208-245-3241; criminal fax: 208-245-3046; civil fax: same; 9AM-5PM (PST). ***Felony, Misdemeanor, Civil, Eviction, Small Claims, Probate.***
Civil Records: Access: Fax, mail, in person, online. Only the court performs in person searches; visitors may not. Search fee: $5.00 per name. Required to search: name, years to search. Civil cases indexed by defendant, plaintiff, on computer from 1991, index cards and docket books from early 1900s. Note: Fax requests must include copy of fees check. Mail turnaround time 3 days. Civil PAT goes back to 1991. PAT civil results show middle initial. Search trial court records back to 1995 and calendars free at https://www.idcourts.us.
Criminal Records: Access: Mail, fax, in person, online. Only the court performs in person searches; visitors may not. Search fee: $5.00 per name. If printout required $.15 per page. Required to search: name, years to search. Criminal records computerized from 1991, index cards and docket books from early 1900s. Note: Fax requests must include copy of fees check. Mail turnaround time 3-5 days. Criminal PAT goes back to 1991. PAT results show middle initial, DOB. Search trial court index back to 1995 and calendars free at https://www.idcourts.us. Online results show middle initial, DOB.
General Information: No juvenile, adoptions, mental commitments or sealed records released. No fee to fax documents if search fee paid. Court makes copy: $1.00 per page. Certification fee: $1.00 per seal. Payee: Clerk of Court. Personal checks accepted. Mail requests: SASE required.

Bingham County

District & Magistrate Courts 501 N Maple St, #402, Blackfoot, ID 83221-1700; 208-785-8040 X3154-Dist, X3121-Magis; criminal phone: X3118, X3117 or X3122; civil phone: X3123 or X3124; probate phone: X3123 or X3124; criminal fax: 208-785-3167; civil fax: same; 8AM-N, 1-5PM (MST). ***Felony, Misdemeanor, Civil, Eviction, Small Claims, Probate, Traffic.***
Direct phone for District Ct is 208-782-3145. Small Claims phone X3120. Probate fax is same as main fax number.
Civil Records: Access: Phone, fax, mail, in person, online. Both court and visitors may perform in person searches. No search fee. Required to search: name, years to search; also helpful: address. Civil cases indexed by defendant, plaintiff, on computer from 1989, from microfiche from 1865. Mail turnaround time 1-2 weeks. Civil PAT goes back to 1989. PAT civil results show middle initial. Search trial court records back to 1995 and calendars free at https://www.idcourts.us.
Criminal Records: Access: Phone, fax, mail, in person, online. Visitors must perform in person searches themselves. No search fee. Required to search: name, years to search, signed release; also helpful: address, DOB, SSN. Criminal records computerized from 1989, from microfiche from 1865. Mail turnaround time 1-2 weeks. Criminal PAT goes back to same as civil. PAT results show middle initial, DOB. Search trial court index back to 1995 and calendars free at https://www.idcourts.us. Online results show middle initial, DOB.
General Information: No juvenile, adoption, mental records released. Will not fax documents. Court makes copy: $1.00 per page. Cert fee: $1.00 per page. Payee: Clerk of Court. Personal checks accepted. Visa/MC accepted. Mail requests: SASE required.

Blaine County

District & Magistrate Courts 201 2nd Ave S, #106, Hailey, ID 83333; 208-788-5521; fax: 208-788-5527; 9-5PM (MST). ***Felony, Misdemeanor, Civil, Eviction, Small Claims, Probate.***
The Magistrate Court (Misdemeanor, Small Claims, Eviction, Probate) are also in #106; Magistrate Court phone is 208-788-5525; fax 208-788-5527.
Civil Records: Access: In person, online. Visitors must perform in person searches themselves. Required to search: name, years to search. Civil cases indexed by defendant, plaintiff, on computer from 11/1992. Civil PAT goes back to 11/1992. PAT results show middle initial, DOB. Search trial court records back to 1995 and calendars free at https://www.idcourts.us.
Criminal Records: Access: In person, online. Visitors must perform in person searches themselves. Required to search: name, years to search, DOB, SSN. Criminal records on computer since 1988. Criminal PAT goes back to same as civil. PAT results show middle initial, DOB. Search trial court index back to 1995 and calendars free at https://www.idcourts.us. Online results show middle initial, DOB.
General Information: No sealed juvenile records released; unsealed juvenile records are on court's database. Will fax documents $1.00 per page. Court makes copy: $1.00 per page. Certification fee: $1.00 per document. Payee: Clerk of Court. Personal checks accepted. Visa/MC accepted. Mail requests: SASE required for mail return of any copies.

Boise County

District & Magistrate Courts PO Box 126, Idaho City, ID 83631; 208-392-4452; fax: 208-392-6712; 8AM-5PM (MST). ***Felony, Misdemeanor, Civil, Eviction, Small Claims, Probate.***
Court recommends document retriever Heidi at 208-392-6709.
Civil Records: Access: In person, online. Visitors must perform in person searches themselves. Required to search: name, years to search. Civil cases indexed by defendant, plaintiff, on computer from 6/90, on docket books from 1863. Civil PAT goes back to 1989. PAT civil results show middle initial. Search trial court records back to 1995 and calendars free at https://www.idcourts.us.
Criminal Records: Access: In person, online. Visitors must perform in person searches themselves. Required to search: name, years to search, SSN; also helpful: DOB. Criminal records computerized from 6/90, on docket books from 1863. Criminal PAT goes back to same as civil. PAT results show middle initial, DOB. Search trial court index back to 1995 and calendars free at https://www.idcourts.us. Online results show middle initial, DOB.
General Information: No juvenile, adoption records released. Will fax documents $5.00 1st page, $1.00 each add'l page. Court makes copy: $1.25 per page. Certification fee: $1.50 per page. Payee: Boise County. Personal checks accepted. Visa/MC and debit cards accepted.

Bonner County

District & Magistrate Courts 215 S 1st Ave, Sandpoint, ID 83864; 208-265-1432; fax: 208-265-1447; 9AM-5PM (PST). ***Felony, Misdemeanor, Civil, Eviction, Small Claims, Probate.***
Civil Records: Access: In person, online. Visitors must perform in person searches themselves. Required to search: name, years to search; also helpful: address. Civil cases indexed by defendant, plaintiff, on computer from 1990, index and docket books from 1907. Civil PAT goes back to 1990. PAT results show middle initial, DOB. Search trial court records back to 1995 and calendars free at https://www.idcourts.us.
Criminal Records: Access: In person, online. Visitors must perform in person searches themselves. Required to search: name, years to search; also helpful: address, DOB, SSN. Criminal records computerized from 1990, index and docket books from 1907. Criminal PAT goes back to same as civil. PAT results show middle initial, DOB. Search trial court index back to 1995 and calendars free at https://www.idcourts.us. Online results show middle initial, DOB.
General Information: No juvenile records released. Will not fax documents. Court makes copy: $1.00 per page, self serve same. Certification fee: $1.00 per cert.

Payee: Bonner County Clerk. Personal checks accepted. Visa/MC accepted.

Bonneville County

District & Magistrate Courts 605 N Capital, Idaho Falls, ID 83402; 208-529-1350 x1379; fax: 208-529-1300; 8AM-5PM (MST). ***Felony, Misdemeanor, Civil, Eviction, Small Claims, Probate.*** www.co.bonneville.id.us

Civil Records: Access: Mail, in person, online. Visitors must perform in person searches themselves. No search fee. Required to search: name, years to search, case type. Civil cases indexed by defendant, plaintiff, on computer from civil from 1991. Docket books by case number ongoing. Actual case records are archived before 10/91. Civil PAT goes back to 1991. PAT results show middle initial, DOB. Search trial court records back to 1995 and calendars at https://www.idcourts.us.

Criminal Records: Access: Mail, in person, online. Visitors must perform in person searches themselves. No search fee. Required to search: name, years to search, DOB, signed release; also helpful: SSN, offense. Criminal misdemeanor records on computer from 1983, felony on computer from 1991. Criminal on microfiche from 1977. Docket books by case number ongoing. Criminal PAT goes back to same as civil. PAT results show middle initial, DOB. Search trial court index back to 1995 and calendars free at https://www.idcourts.us. Online results show middle initial, DOB. Court PATs are very similar to online results- online shows year of birth only, if available.

General Information: No child protective, protection orders, juvenile, sanity, adoption or termination records released. Will fax documents $2.00 per page. Court makes copy: $1.00 per page. Cert fee: $1.00 per page. Payee: Bonneville County. No personal checks accepted. Visa/MC and debit cards accepted.

Boundary County

District & Magistrate Courts Boundary County Courthouse, PO Box 419, Bonners Ferry, ID 83805; 208-267-5504; fax: 208-267-7814; 9AM-5PM (PST). ***Felony, Misdemeanor, Civil, Eviction, Small Claims, Probate.*** www.boundarycountyid.org/court/index.htm

Civil Records: Access: In person, online. Visitors must perform in person searches themselves. Required to search: name, years to search; also helpful: address. Civil cases indexed by defendant, plaintiff, on computer from 1989; by case number, index books, cards or microfiche by name from early 1900s. Civil PAT goes back to 1989. PAT civil results show middle initial. Results include name and DOB. Search trial court records back to 1995 and calendars free at https://www.idcourts.us.

Criminal Records: Access: In person, online. Visitors must perform in person searches themselves. Required to search: name, years to search, SSN; also helpful: DOB. Criminal records computerized from 1989; by case number, index books, cards or microfiche by name from early 1900s. Criminal PAT goes back to same as civil. PAT results show middle initial, DOB. Results include name and DOB. Search trial court index back to 1995 and calendars at https://www.idcourts.us. Online results show middle initial, DOB.

General Information: No sealed records released. Will fax documents for fee; long distance- $3.00 1st page, $1.00 each add'l; local fax- $2.00 1st page, $.50 each add'l. Court makes copy: $1.00 per page. Cert fee: $1.00 per page. Payee: Clerk of Court. Personal checks and major credit cards accepted.

Butte County

District & Magistrate Courts 326 W Grand Ave, Arco, ID 83213; 208-527-8259; fax: 208-527-3448; 9AM-N; 1PM-5PM (MST). ***Felony, Misdemeanor, Civil, Eviction, Small Claims, Probate.***

Civil Records: Access: Phone, fax, mail, in person, online. Both court and visitors may perform in person searches. No search fee. Required to search: name, years to search; also helpful: address. Civil cases indexed by defendant, plaintiff, on computer from 1993, archives prior. Docket books by case number from early 1910s. Mail turnaround time 1 week. Civil PAT goes back to 1993. PAT results show middle initial, DOB. Search trial court records back to 1995 and calendars free at https://www.idcourts.us.

Criminal Records: Access: Phone, fax, mail, in person, online. Both court and visitors may perform in person searches. No search fee. Required to search: name, years to search; also helpful: address, DOB, SSN. Criminal records computerized from 1993 archives prior. Docket books by case number from early 1910s. Mail turnaround time 1 week. Criminal PAT goes back to 1993. PAT results show middle initial, DOB. Search trial court index back to 1995 and calendars free at https://www.idcourts.us. Online results show middle initial, DOB.

General Information: No juvenile records released. Fee to fax out file $1.00 per page. Court makes copy: $1.00 per page. Self serve: $.10 per page. Certification fee: $1.00 per page. Payee: Butte County Magistrate Court. Personal checks accepted; credit cards are not. Mail requests: SASE required.

Camas County

District & Magistrate Courts PO Box 430, Fairfield, ID 83327; 208-764-2238; criminal fax: 208-764-2349; civil fax: same; 8:30AM-N, 1-5PM (MST). ***Felony, Misdemeanor, Civil, Eviction, Small Claims, Probate.***

Probate fax is same as main fax number.

Civil Records: Access: Mail, in person, online. Both court and visitors may perform in person searches. No search fee. Required to search: name, years to search; also helpful: address. Civil cases indexed by defendant, plaintiff, from archives from 1917. Register of actions by case number. Mail turnaround time same day. Civil PAT goes back to 1994. PAT civil results show middle initial. Search trial court records back to 1995 and calendars free at https://www.idcourts.us.

Criminal Records: Access: Mail, in person, online. Both court and visitors may perform in person searches. No search fee. Required to search: name, years to search; also helpful: address, DOB, SSN. Criminal records from archives from 1917. Register of actions by case number. Mail turnaround time 1 day. Criminal PAT goes back to 1994. PAT results show middle initial, DOB. Search trial court index back to 1995 and calendars free at https://www.idcourts.us. Online results show middle initial, DOB.

General Information: No juvenile or domestic violence records released. Will fax documents to local or toll free line. Court makes copy: $1.00 per page, self serve same. Certification fee: $1.00. Payee: Camas County Courthouse. Personal checks accepted; credit cards are not. Mail requests: SASE required.

Canyon County

District & Magistrate Courts 1115 Albany, Caldwell, ID 83605; 208-454-6894; criminal phone: 208-454-7571; civil phone: 208-454-7570; fax: 208-454-7525; 8:30AM-5PM (MST). ***Felony, Misdemeanor, Civil, Eviction, Small Claims, Probate.*** www.the3rdjudicialdistrict.com

Small claims phone is 208-454-7577

Civil Records: Access: In person, online. Visitors must perform in person searches themselves. Required to search: name, years to search, or case number. Civil cases indexed by defendant, plaintiff, on computer from 1989, microfiche from 1800s, and docket books. Public use terminal has civil records back to 1989. PAT results show middle initial, DOB. Search trial court records back to 1995 and calendars free at https://www.idcourts.us. Access the daily court calendar free at www.the3rdjudicialdistrict.com.

Criminal Records: Access: In person, online. Visitors must perform in person searches themselves. Required to search: name, years to search; also helpful: DOB, case number. Criminal records computerized from 1989, microfiche from 1800s, and docket books. PAT results show middle initial, DOB. Search trial court index back to 1995 and calendars free at https://www.idcourts.us. Access daily court calendar at www.the3rdjudicialdistrict.com. Online results show middle initial, DOB.

General Information: No adoption, mental, domestic violence records not released. Will not fax documents. Court makes copy: $1.00 per page. Self serve: $.25 per page, coin-operated machine and court will not provide change. Certification fee: $1.00 per page. Payee: Clerk of Court. Only cashiers checks and money orders accepted. Visa/MC accepted plus $3.00 technology fee. Mail requests: SASE required for mail return of any copies.

Caribou County

District & Magistrate Courts 159 S Main, Soda Springs, ID 83276; 208-547-4342; fax: 208-547-4759; 9AM-5PM (MST). ***Felony, Misdemeanor, Civil, Eviction, Small Claims, Probate.***

Civil Records: Access: Phone, fax, mail, in person, online. Both court and visitors may perform in person searches. No search fee. Required to search: name, years to search. Civil cases indexed by defendant, plaintiff, on computer from 1989, from 1930 archived in vault. Mail turnaround time up to 1 week. Civil PAT goes back to 1989. PAT results show middle initial, DOB. Search trial court records back to 1995 and calendars free at https://www.idcourts.us.

Criminal Records: Access: Phone, fax, mail, in person, online. Both court and visitors may perform in person searches. No search fee. Required to search: name, years to search, DOB, SSN; also helpful: address. Criminal records computerized from 1989, from 1930 archived in vault. Mail turnaround time up to 1 week. Criminal PAT goes back to same as civil. PAT results show middle initial, DOB. Search trial court index back to 1995 and calendars free at https://www.idcourts.us. Online results show middle initial, DOB.

General Information: No adoption, guardianship records released. Will fax documents $2.00 1st page, $1.00 each add'l. Court makes copy: $1.00 per page, self serve same. Certification fee: $1.50. Payee: Clerk of Court. Business checks accepted. Out of state checks not accepted. No credit cards accepted. Mail requests: SASE required.

Cassia County

District & Magistrate Courts 1459 Overland, Burley, ID 83318; 208-878-7351; probate phone: 208-878-7351; criminal fax: 208-878-1003; civil fax: same; 8:30AM-5PM (MST). ***Felony, Misdemeanor, Civil, Eviction, Small Claims, Probate.*** http://cassiacounty.org/judicial/index.htm

Probate is a separate index at this same address. Probate fax is same as main fax number.

Civil Records: Access: Phone, fax, mail, in person, online. Both court and visitors may perform in person searches. No search fee. Required to search: name, years to search; also helpful: address. Civil cases indexed by defendant, plaintiff, on computer from 1990, archives from 1900s. Mail turnaround time 1-2 days. Civil PAT goes back to 1990. PAT civil results show middle initial. Search trial court records back to 1995 and calendars free at https://www.idcourts.us.

Criminal Records: Access: Fax, mail, in person, online. Both court and visitors may perform in person searches. No search fee. Required to search: name, years to search; also helpful: address, DOB, SSN. Criminal records computerized from 1990, archives from 1900s. Mail turnaround time 1-2 days. Criminal PAT goes back to same as civil. PAT results show middle initial, DOB. Search trial court index back to 1995 and calendars free at https://www.idcourts.us. Online results show middle initial, DOB.

General Information: No juvenile, adoption, mental commitment, child protection records released. Will fax documents $2.50 per page. Court makes copy: $1.00 per page. Self serve: $1.00 per page if court's document; $.15 in not. Cert fee: $1.50 per page. Payee: Clerk of Court. Personal checks and major credit cards accepted. Mail requests: SASE required.

Clark County

District & Magistrate Courts PO Box 205, Dubois, ID 83423; 208-374-5402; fax: 208-374-5609; 9AM-5PM (MST). ***Felony, Misdemeanor, Civil, Eviction, Small Claims, Probate.***

This court does not normally perform record searches, however they also say that there is no one locally who will perform them either; the court may perform record searches under these limiting circumstances.

Civil Records: Access: Mail, fax, in person, online. Both court and visitors may perform in person searches. No search fee. Required to search: name, years to search; also helpful: address. Civil cases indexed by defendant, plaintiff, on computer from 1985, on microfiche for civil judgments and from archives from 1919. Civil PAT goes back to 10 years. PAT results show middle initial, DOB. Search trial court records back to 1995 and calendars free at https://www.idcourts.us.

Criminal Records: Access: Mail, fax, in person, online. Visitors must perform in person searches themselves. No search fee. Required to search: name, years to search; also helpful: address, DOB, SSN. Criminal records computerized from 1985. Criminal PAT goes back to same as civil. PAT results show middle initial, DOB. Search trial court index back to 1995 and calendars at https://www.idcourts.us. Online results show middle initial, DOB.

General Information: No juvenile, adoption records released. Will not fax documents. Court makes copy: n/a. Self serve: $1.00 per page. Certification fee: $1.00 per page. Payee: Clerk of Court. Personal checks accepted; credit cards are not. Mail requests: SASE required.

Clearwater County

District & Magistrate Courts PO Box 586, 150 Michigan Ave, Orofino, ID 83544; 208-476-5596; 8:30AM-5PM (PST). ***Felony, Misdemeanor, Civil, Eviction, Small Claims, Probate.***

Civil Records: Access: Phone, fax, mail, in person, online. Only the court performs in person searches; visitors may not. No search fee. Required to search: name, years to search. Civil cases indexed by defendant, plaintiff, on computer from 8/91, in docket books prior to 1911. Mail turnaround time 7 days. PAT civil results show middle initial. Search trial court records back to 1995 and calendars free at https://www.idcourts.us.

Criminal Records: Access: Phone, fax, mail, in person, online. Only the court performs in person searches; visitors may not. No search fee. Required to search: name or case number, years to search. Criminal records computerized from 8/91, in docket books prior to 1911. Mail turnaround time 7 days. PAT results show middle initial, DOB. Search trial court index back to 1995 and calendars free at https://www.idcourts.us. Online results show middle initial, DOB.

General Information: No juvenile, domestic violence, adoption, social records released. Will fax documents $1.00 per page. Court makes copy: $1.00 per page. Certification fee: $1.00. Payee: Clerk of Court. Business checks accepted. Visa/MC accepted. Mail requests: SASE requested.

Custer County

District & Magistrate Courts PO Box 385, Challis, ID 83226; 208-879-2359; criminal fax: 208-879-6412; civil fax: same; 8AM-5PM (MST). ***Felony, Misdemeanor, Civil, Eviction, Small Claims, Probate.*** www.co.custer.id.us

Probate fax is same as main fax number.

Civil Records: Access: Phone, mail, in person, online. Both court and visitors may perform in person searches. Search fee: $5.00 per name. Required to search: name, years to search. Civil cases indexed by defendant. Civil records on computer from 1989, archived from early 1900s. Mail turnaround time 1 week. Civil PAT goes back to 1989. PAT civil results show middle initial. Search trial court records back to 1995 and calendars free at https://www.idcourts.us.

Criminal Records: Access: Phone, mail, in person, online. Both court and visitors may perform in person searches. Search fee: $5.00 per name. Required to search: name, years to search, DOB, signed release; also helpful: SSN. Criminal records computerized from 1989, archived from early 1900s. Mail turnaround time 1 week. Criminal PAT goes back to same as civil. PAT results show middle initial, DOB. Search trial court index back to 1995 and calendars free at https://www.idcourts.us. Online results show middle initial, DOB.

General Information: No juvenile, adoption records released. Will fax out documents for $1.00 per page. Court makes copy: $1.00 per page. Certification fee: $1.00 per page. Payee: Custer County. Personal checks and major credit cards accepted.

Elmore County

District & Magistrate Courts 150 S 4th E, #5, Mountain Home, ID 83647; 208-587-2133 x208; fax: 208-587-2134; 9AM-5PM (MST). ***Felony, Misdemeanor, Civil, Eviction, Small Claims, Probate.***

Civil Records: Access: In person, online. Visitors must perform in person searches themselves. Required to search: name; also helpful: years to search. Civil cases indexed by defendant, plaintiff, on computer from 1992, on microfiche from 1972, archived from early 1900s. Civil PAT goes back to 1992. PAT civil results show middle initial. Search trial court records back to 1995 and calendars free at https://www.idcourts.us.

Criminal Records: Access: In person, online. Visitors must perform in person searches themselves. Required to search: name, DOB, signed release; also helpful: years to search, SSN. Criminal records computerized from 1992, on microfiche from 1972, archived from early 1900s. Criminal PAT goes back to same as civil. PAT results show middle initial, DOB. Search trial court index back to 1995 and calendars free at https://www.idcourts.us. Online results show middle initial, DOB.

General Information: No juvenile, adoption, domestic violence, mental commitment records released. Will fax specific case file $1.00 per page. Court makes copy: $1.00 per page. Certification fee: $1.00 per page. Payee: Elmore County. Personal checks accepted; credit cards are not.

Franklin County

District & Magistrate Courts 39 W Oneida, Preston, ID 83263; 208-852-0877; fax: 208-852-2926; 9AM-5PM (MST). ***Felony, Misdemeanor, Civil, Eviction, Small Claims, Probate.***

Civil Records: Access: Phone, fax, mail, in person, online. Both court and visitors may perform in person searches. Search fee: $5.00 per name. Required to search: name, years to search. Civil cases indexed by defendant, plaintiff, on computer from 1987, microfiche from 1983, archived from 1920. Mail turnaround time 2-3 days. Civil PAT goes back to 1984. PAT results show middle initial, DOB, SSN. Search trial court records back to 1995 and calendars free at https://www.idcourts.us.

Criminal Records: Access: Phone, fax, mail, in person, online. Both court and visitors may perform in person searches. Search fee: $5.00 per name for a report history. Required to search: name, years to search; also helpful: DOB, SSN. Criminal records computerized from 1987, microfiche from 1977, archived from 1920. Mail turnaround time 2-3 days. Criminal PAT goes back to same as civil. PAT results show middle initial, DOB, SSN. Terminal results include driver license number. Search trial court index back to 1995 and calendars free at https://www.idcourts.us. Online results show middle initial, DOB.

General Information: No adoption records released. No fee to fax documents locally only. Court makes copy: $1.00 per page. Certification fee: $1.00 per cert. Payee: Clerk of Court. Personal checks and major credit cards accepted. Mail requests: SASE required.

Fremont County

District & Magistrate Courts 151 W 1st N, Rm 15, St Anthony, ID 83445; 208-624-7401; criminal fax: 208-624-4607; civil fax: same; 9AM-5PM (MST). ***Felony, Misdemeanor, Civil, Eviction, Small Claims, Probate.***

Address search requests to attention of Tawna. Thursday is the best day for in person searches. Probate fax is same as main fax number.

Civil Records: Access: Phone, fax, mail, in person, online. Both court and visitors may perform in person searches. No search fee; add $4.00 if search request is mailed or faxed in. Required to search: name, years to search; also helpful: address. Civil cases indexed by defendant, plaintiff, on computer back to 1990, microfiche for last 20 years, prior archives. Mail turnaround time 1 week. Civil PAT goes back to 1990. PAT results show middle initial, DOB. Search trial court records back to 1995 and calendars at https://www.idcourts.us.

Criminal Records: Access: Fax, mail, in person, online. Both court and visitors may perform in person searches. No search fee; add $4.00 if search request is mailed or faxed in. Required to search: name, years to search, DOB; also helpful: SSN. Criminal records computerized from 1990, microfiche for last 20 years, prior archives. Mail turnaround time 1 week. Criminal PAT goes back to same as civil. PAT results show middle initial, DOB. Search trial court index back to 1995 and calendars free at https://www.idcourts.us. Online results show middle initial, DOB.

General Information: No adoption or juvenile records released. Fee to fax out file $2.00 per page or free to toll-free line. Court makes copy: $1.00 per page, self serve same. Certification fee: $1.00 per page. Payee: Clerk of Court. Personal checks accepted. Visa/MC accepted but with a $3.00 Tech Fee added. Mail requests: SASE required.

Gem County

District & Magistrate Courts 415 E Main St, Emmett, ID 83617; 208-365-5621-District Court 208-365-4221-Magistrate Court; fax: 208-365-6172; 8AM-5PM (MST). ***Felony, Misdemeanor, Civil, Eviction, Small Claims, Probate.*** www.co.gem.id.us/judicial/default.htm

Civil Records: Access: Mail, in person, online. Both court and visitors may perform in person searches. Search fee: $5.00 per name. Required to search: name, years to search; also helpful: address. Civil cases indexed by defendant, plaintiff, on computer from 1990, on microfiche and archived from 1916. Mail turnaround time 5 days. Civil PAT goes back to 1990. PAT results show middle initial, DOB. Search trial court records back to 1995 and calendars free at https://www.idcourts.us.

Criminal Records: Access: Mail, in person, online. Both court and visitors may perform in person searches. Search fee: $5.00 per name per court. Required to search: name, years to search, DOB, SSN; also helpful: address. Criminal records computerized from 1990, on microfiche and archived from 1972. Mail turnaround time 5 days. Criminal PAT goes back to same as civil. PAT results show middle initial, DOB. Search trial court index back to 1995 and calendars at https://www.idcourts.us. Online results show middle initial, DOB.

General Information: No juvenile, adoption records or domestic violence released. Will fax documents to local or toll free line. Court makes copy: $1.00 per page. Certification fee: $1.00. Payee: Gem County. Personal checks and major credit cards accepted. Mail requests: SASE required.

Gooding County

District & Magistrate Courts PO Box 27, Gooding, ID 83330; criminal phone: 208-934-4861; civil phone: 208-934-4261; fax: 208-934-4408; 9AM-5PM (MST). ***Felony, Misdemeanor, Civil, Eviction, Small Claims, Probate.***

Magistrate Court can be reached at 208-934-4261. Magistrate Court address is PO Box 477. Only felony records are available at District Court.

Civil Records: Access: In person, online. Visitors must perform in person searches themselves. Required to search: name, years to search. Civil cases indexed by defendant, plaintiff, on computer from 1994, on microfiche, docket books from 1860s. Public use terminal available, records go back to 8/94. PAT civil results show middle initial. Search trial court records back to 1995 and calendars free at https://www.idcourts.us.

Criminal Records: Access: In person, online. Visitors must perform in person searches themselves. Required to search: name, years to search, DOB, SSN. Criminal records computerized from 1994, on microfiche, docket books from 1860s. Public use terminal available, crim records go back to same. PAT results show middle initial, DOB. Search trial court index back to 1995 and calendars free at https://www.idcourts.us. Online results show middle initial, DOB.
General Information: No juvenile, adoption, domestic violence records released. Fee to fax out file $1.00 per page. Court makes copy: $1.00 per page. Certification fee: $1.00. Payee: Gooding County Clerk. Personal checks accepted.

Idaho County

District & Magistrate Courts 320 W Main, Grangeville, ID 83530; 208-983-2776; criminal fax: 208-983-2376; civil fax: same; 8:30AM-5PM (PST). ***Felony, Misdemeanor, Civil, Eviction, Small Claims, Probate.***
Probate fax is same as main fax number.
Civil Records: Access: Phone, fax, mail, in person, online. Only the court performs in person searches; visitors may not. No search fee. Required to search: name, years to search. Civil cases indexed by defendant, plaintiff, on computer from 1989, on microfiche and archived from late 1800s. Mail turnaround time same week. Civil PAT available. Search trial court records back to 1995 and calendars free at https://www.idcourts.us.
Criminal Records: Access: Phone, fax, mail, in person, online. Only the court performs in person searches; visitors may not. No search fee. Required to search: name, years to search. Criminal records computerized from 1989, on microfiche and archived from late 1800s. Mail turnaround time same week. Criminal PAT available. PAT results show middle initial, DOB, SSN. Search trial court index back to 1995 and calendars at https://www.idcourts.us. Online results show middle initial, DOB.
General Information: No domestic violence, juvenile, hospitalization, adoption, termination records released. Will fax documents $1.00 per page. Court makes copy: $1.00 per page. Certification fee: $1.00 per cert. Payee: Idaho County. Personal checks accepted; credit cards are not. SASE not required.

Jefferson County

District & Magistrate Courts 210 Courthouse Way #120, Rigby, ID 83442; 208-745-7736; probate phone: same; fax: 208-745-6636; 9AM-5PM (MST). ***Felony, Misdemeanor, Civil, Eviction, Small Claims, Probate.***
Information is on the public access computer; please use this before requesting the clerks' assistance.
Civil Records: Access: In person, online. Both court and visitors may perform in person searches. No search fee. Required to search: name, years to search. Civil cases indexed by defendant, plaintiff, archived from early 1900s; on computer back to 8/1992. Civil PAT goes back to 8/1992. PAT civil results show middle initial. Search trial court records back to 1995 and calendars at https://www.idcourts.us.
Criminal Records: Access: In person, online. Both court and visitors may perform in person searches. No search fee. Required to search: name, years to search, DOB. Criminal records archived from early 1900s; on computer back to 8/1992. Criminal PAT goes back to same as civil. PAT results show middle initial, DOB. Search trial court index back to 1995 and calendars free at https://www.idcourts.us. Online results show middle initial, DOB.
General Information: No juvenile, adoption, some domestic records released. Will fax back $1.00 per page. Court makes copy: $1.00 per page. Certification fee: $1.00 per page. Payee: Clerk of Court. Personal checks accepted; credit cards are not.

Jerome County

District & Magistrate Courts 233 W Main St, Jerome, ID 83338; 208-644-2600; fax: 208-644-2609; 8:30AM-5PM (MST). ***Felony, Misdemeanor, Civil, Eviction, Small Claims, Probate.***

Civil Records: Access: Fax, mail, in person, online. Visitors must perform in person searches themselves. No search fee. Required to search: name, years to search. Civil cases indexed by defendant, plaintiff, on computer back to 1991, prior on microfiche back to 1919. Note: Court will perform civil search only for requests with dates prior to 1991. Civil PAT goes back to 1991. PAT results show middle initial, DOB. Search trial court records back to 1995 and calendars free at https://www.idcourts.us.
Criminal Records: Access: Fax, mail, in person, online. Visitors must perform in person searches themselves. No search fee. Required to search: name, years to search, address, DOB, SSN. Criminal records computerized from 1991, prior on microfiche back to 1919. Note: Will not do background searches. Mail turnaround time 7-10 business days. Criminal PAT goes back to 1991. PAT results show middle initial, DOB. Search trial court index back to 1995 and calendars free at https://www.idcourts.us. Online results show middle initial, DOB.
General Information: No juvenile records released without court approval. Will fax documents $3.00 1st page, $2.50 each add'l. Court makes copy: $1.00 per page. Certification fee: $1.50 per page. Payee: Clerk of Court. Personal checks accepted; credit cards are not. Mail requests: SASE required.

Kootenai County

District & Magistrate Court PO Box 9000, 324 W Garden Ave, Coeur d'Alene, ID 83816-9000; 208-446-1180; criminal phone: 208-446-1170; civil: 208-446-1160; probate: 208-446-1160; fax: 208-446-1188; 9AM-5PM (PST). ***Felony, Misdemeanor, Civil, Eviction, Small Claims, Probate.***
www.co.kootenai.id.us/departments/districtcourt
Civil Records: Access: Mail, in person, online. Visitors must perform in person searches themselves. Search fee: $.10 a page found. Required to search: name, years to search. Civil cases indexed by defendant, plaintiff, on computer from 1989, on microfiche from 1881, archived from 1819. Mail turnaround time 2 days. Civil PAT goes back to 1989. PAT civil results show middle initial. Search trial court records back to 1995 and calendars free at https://www.idcourts.us.
Criminal Records: Access: Mail, in person, online. Visitors must perform in person searches themselves. Search fee: $.10 a page found. Required to search: name, years to search; also helpful: DOB, SSN. Criminal records computerized from 1989, on microfiche from 1881, archived from 1819. Mail turnaround time in 2 days. Criminal PAT goes back to same as civil. PAT results show middle initial, DOB. Search trial court index back to 1995 and calendars free at https://www.idcourts.us. Online results show middle initial, DOB.
General Information: No sealed, adoption, parental termination, mentally incapacitated records released. Will fax documents to local or toll free line. Court makes copy: $1.00 per page. Certification fee: $1.00; exemplification: $4.00; pluss copy fee. Payee: Clerk of Court. Personal checks accepted. Credit cards accepted through Official Payments 800-533-0743. Mail requests: SASE required.

Latah County

District & Magistrate Courts PO Box 8068, Moscow, ID 83843; 208-883-2255; fax: 208-883-2259; 8:30AM-5PM M,W; 8AM-5PM T,TH,F (PST). ***Felony, Misdemeanor, Civil, Eviction, Small Claims, Probate.*** www.latah.id.us
Civil Records: Access: Phone, fax, mail, in person, online. Both court and visitors may perform in person searches. Search fee: $4.00 per name. Required to search: name, years to search; also helpful: address. Civil cases indexed by defendant, plaintiff, on computer from 1986, archived from 5/1888. Mail turnaround time 1-2 days. Civil PAT goes back to 1992. PAT civil results show middle initial. Search trial court records back to 1995 and calendars free at https://www.idcourts.us.
Criminal Records: Access: Phone, fax, mail, in person, online. Both court and visitors may perform in person searches. Search fee: $4.00 per name. Required to search: name, years to search; also helpful: address, DOB, SSN. Criminal records computerized from 1986, archived from 5/1888. Mail turnaround time 1-2 days. Criminal PAT goes back to same as civil. PAT results show middle initial, DOB. Search trial court index back to 1995 and calendars free at https://www.idcourts.us. Online results show middle initial, DOB.
General Information: No adoption, sealed juvenile, or hospitalization records released. Will fax documents to local or toll free line. Court makes copy: $1.00 per page. Certification fee: $1.00 per page plus copy fee if the court makes copy. If copy is provided to be certified, $.50 per page plus $1.00. Payee: District Court Clerk of Court. Personal checks accepted; credit cards are not. SASE not required.

Lemhi County

District & Magistrate Courts 206 Courthouse Dr, Salmon, ID 83467; 208-756-2815; criminal phone: x225; civil phone: x225; probate phone: x242; criminal fax: 208-756-8424; civil fax: 208-756-8424; 8AM-5PM (MST). ***Felony, Misdemeanor, Civil, Eviction, Small Claims, Probate.***
Probate fax- 208-756-4673
Civil Records: Access: Phone, fax, mail, in person, online. Both court and visitors may perform in person searches. Search fee: $5.00 per name. Required to search: name, years to search; also helpful: address. Civil cases indexed by defendant, plaintiff, on computer from 1991, on microfiche from 1964, archives from 1869. Mail turnaround time 1-3 days. Civil PAT goes back to 1991. PAT civil results show middle initial. Search trial court records back to 1995 and calendars free at https://www.idcourts.us.
Criminal Records: Access: Phone, fax, mail, in person, online. Both court and visitors may perform in person searches. Search fee: $5.00 per name. Required to search: name, years to search; also helpful: address, DOB, SSN. Criminal records computerized from 1991, on microfiche from 1964, archives from 1869. Mail turnaround time 1 day. Criminal PAT goes back to same as civil. PAT results show middle initial, DOB. Search trial court index back to 1995 and calendars free at https://www.idcourts.us. Online results show middle initial, DOB.
General Information: No PSI, sealed records released. Fee to fax out file $1.00 per page. Court makes copy: $1.00 per page, self serve same. Certification fee: $1.00 per document and $.50 per page. Payee: Lemhi County Clerk. Personal checks accepted; credit cards are not. Mail requests: SASE requested.

Lewis County

District & Magistrate Courts 510 Oak St, Rm #1, Nezperce, ID 83543-5065; 208-937-2251; fax: 208-937-9233; 9AM-5PM (PST). ***Felony, Misdemeanor, Civil, Eviction, Small Claims, Probate.***
Civil Records: Access: Phone, fax, mail, in person, online. Only the court performs in person searches; visitors may not. No search fee. Required to search: name, years to search. Civil cases indexed by defendant, plaintiff, on computer from 1991, archived from late 1911. Mail turnaround time 1 week. PAT civil results show middle initial. Search trial court records back to 1995 and calendars free at https://www.idcourts.us.
Criminal Records: Access: Phone, fax, mail, in person, online. Only the court performs in person searches; visitors may not. No search fee. Required to search: name, years to search; also helpful: DOB, SSN. Criminal records computerized from 1991, archived from late 1911. Mail turnaround time 1 week. PAT results show middle initial, DOB. Search trial court index back to 1995 and calendars free at https://www.idcourts.us. Online results show middle initial, DOB.
General Information: No juvenile, adoption records released. Will fax documents $1.00 per page. Court makes copy: $1.00 per page. Certification fee: $1.00. Payee: Clerk of Court. Two-party checks not accepted. Major credit cards accepted. Mail requests: SASE required.

Lincoln County

District & Magistrate Courts 111 W B St, Shoshone, ID 83352; 208-886-2173; fax: 208-886-2458; 8:30AM-5PM (MST). ***Felony, Misdemeanor, Civil, Eviction, Small Claims, Probate.***

Civil Records: Access: In person, mail, fax, online. Both court and visitors may perform in person searches. No search fee. Required to search: name, years to search. Civil cases indexed by defendant, plaintiff, on computer from 1992, archives from 1800s. Mail turnaround time 5 days. Civil PAT goes back to 1995. PAT civil results show middle initial. Search trial court records back to 1995 and calendars free at https://www.idcourts.us.

Criminal Records: Access: In person, mail, fax, online. Both court and visitors may perform in person searches. No search fee. Required to search: name, years to search; also helpful: DOB, SSN. Criminal records computerized from 1992, archives from 1800s. Mail turnaround time 5 days. Criminal PAT goes back to same as civil. PAT results show middle initial, DOB. Search trial court index back to 1995 and calendars free at https://www.idcourts.us. Online results show middle initial, DOB.

General Information: No juvenile, domestic violence, sealed records released. Will not fax documents. Court makes copy: $1.00 per page. Certification fee: $1.50. Payee: Lincoln County Courts. Personal checks accepted; credit cards are not. Mail requests: SASE required.

Madison County

District & Magistrate Courts PO Box 389, Rexburg, ID 83440; 208-356-9383; fax: 208-356-5425; 9AM-5PM (MST). ***Felony, Misdemeanor, Civil, Eviction, Small Claims, Probate.***

Civil Records: Access: In person, online. Both court and visitors may perform in person searches. No search fee. Required to search: name, years to search; also helpful: address. Civil cases indexed by defendant, plaintiff, on computer from 1991, microfilm and archives from early 1900s. Civil PAT goes back to 1991. PAT civil results show middle initial. Search trial court records back to 1995 and calendars free at https://www.idcourts.us.

Criminal Records: Access: In person, online. Visitors must perform in person searches themselves. Required to search: name, years to search; also helpful: address, DOB, SSN. Criminal records computerized from 1991, microfilm and archives from early 1900s. Criminal PAT goes back to same as civil. PAT results show middle initial, DOB. Search trial court index back to 1995 and calendars free at https://www.idcourts.us. Online results show middle initial, DOB.

General Information: No juvenile records released. Will not fax documents. Court makes copy: $1.00 per page. Certification fee: $1.00. Payee: Clerk of Court. Personal checks accepted.

Minidoka County

District & Magistrate Courts PO Box 368, Rupert, ID 83350; 208-436-9041 (Dist) 436-7186 (Magis); criminal fax: 208-436-5857; civil fax: same; 8:30AM-5PM (MST). ***Felony, Misdemeanor, Civil, Eviction, Small Claims, Probate.*** www.minidoka.id.us/judicial/default.htm

Probate fax is same as main fax number. District Ct direct fax number is 208-436-5272.

Civil Records: Access: In person, online. Visitors must perform in person searches themselves. Required to search: name, years to search. Civil cases indexed by defendant, plaintiff, on computer from 1989, archives from early 1900s. Civil PAT goes back to 1989. PAT results show middle initial, DOB. Search trial court records back to 1995 and calendars free at https://www.idcourts.us.

Criminal Records: Access: In person, online. Visitors must perform in person searches themselves. Required to search: name, years to search, DOB, SSN, signed release. Criminal records computerized from 1989, archives from early 1900s. Criminal PAT goes back to same as civil. PAT results show middle initial, DOB. Terminal may also be searched by address and DR number. Search trial court index back to 1995 and calendars free at https://www.idcourts.us. Online results show middle initial, DOB.

General Information: Juvenile records released with a signed release. Will fax documents $.50 per page. Court makes copy: $1.00 per page. Certification fee: $1.00 per document. Payee: Clerk of Court. Personal checks accepted; credit cards are not. Mail requests: SASE required for mail return of any copies.

Nez Perce County

District & Magistrate Court PO Box 896, 1230 Main St, Lewiston, ID 83501; 208-799-3040; fax: 208-799-3058; 8AM-5PM (PST). ***Felony, Misdemeanor, Civil, Eviction, Small Claims, Probate.***

www.co.nezperce.id.us/clerk/clerk.htm

Civil Records: Access: Phone, fax, mail, in person, online. Both court and visitors may perform in person searches. No search fee. Required to search: name; also helpful: years to search. Civil cases indexed by defendant, plaintiff, on computer from 1990, microfiche from 1970 and archives from late 1800s. Mail turnaround time- 10 day waiting period. Civil PAT goes back to 1983. PAT civil results show middle initial. Search trial court records back to 1995 and calendars free at https://www.idcourts.us.

Criminal Records: Access: Phone, fax, mail, in person, online. Both court and visitors may perform in person searches. No search fee. Required to search: name, DOB; also helpful: years to search, aliases, SSN. Criminal records computerized from 1990, microfiche from 1970 and archives from late 1800s. Mail turnaround time 10 day waiting period. Criminal PAT goes back to same as civil. PAT results show middle initial, DOB. Search trial court index back to 1995 and calendars free at https://www.idcourts.us. Online results show middle initial, DOB.

General Information: Will fax documents $1.00 per doc, $1.00 1st page, If long-distance, add $.50 each add'l minute. Court makes copy: $1.00 per page. Certification fee: $1.00 per doc. Payee: Clerk of Court. Personal checks accepted. Visa/MC accepted. Mail requests: SASE required.

Oneida County

District & Magistrate Courts 10 Court St, Malad City, ID 83252; 208-766-4116; criminal fax: 208-766-2990; civil fax: same; 9AM-5PM (MST). ***Felony, Misdemeanor, Civil, Eviction, Small Claims, Probate.***

Probate is a separate index at the same address. Probate fax is same as main fax number.

Civil Records: Access: Phone, fax, mail, in person, online. Both court and visitors may perform in person searches. No search fee. Required to search: name, years to search; also helpful: address. Civil cases indexed by case number, defendant, plaintiff. Civil records on computer from 7/90, archives from 1886. Mail turnaround time 1-2 days. Public use terminal has civil records back to 1990. PAT civil results show middle initial. Search trial court records back to 1995 and calendars free at https://www.idcourts.us.

Criminal Records: Access: Phone, fax, mail, in person, online. Both court and visitors may perform in person searches. No search fee. Required to search: name, years to search; also helpful: address, DOB, SSN. Criminal records computerized from 7/90, archives from 1886. Mail turnaround time 1-2 days. PAT results show middle initial, DOB. Search trial court index back to 1995 and calendars free at https://www.idcourts.us. Online results show middle initial, DOB.

General Information: No juvenile, adoption records released. Will fax documents $1.00 per page. Court makes copy: $1.00 per page, self serve same. Certification fee: $1.00 per page. Payee: Clerk of Court. Personal checks accepted. Mail requests: SASE requested.

Owyhee County

District & Magistrate Courts-I PO Box 128, 20381 State Hwy 78, Courthouse, Murphy, ID 83650; 208-495-2806; fax: 208-495-1226; 8:30AM-5PM (MST). ***Felony, Misdemeanor, Civil, Eviction, Small Claims, Probate.***

www.owyheecounty.net/index1.php?court

Civil Records: Access: Mail, fax, in person, online. Only the court performs in person searches; visitors may not. Search fee: $5.00 per name found. Required to search: name, years to search. Civil cases indexed by defendant, plaintiff, on computer from 1992, archives from 1800s. Mail turnaround time 5-10 days; archived records require longer. PAT civil results show middle initial. Search trial court records back to 1995 and calendars free at https://www.idcourts.us.

Criminal Records: Access: Fax, mail, in person, online. Only the court performs in person searches; visitors may not. Search fee: $5.00 per name found. Required to search: name, years to search; also helpful: DOB. Criminal records computerized from 1992, archives from 1800s. Note: Signed release required for search of juvenile records. Mail turnaround time 5-10 days, longer if records archived. PAT results show middle initial, DOB. Search trial court index back to 1995 and calendars free at https://www.idcourts.us. Online results show middle initial, DOB.

General Information: No adoption, juvenile (except for some that are open), domestic violence records released. Fee to fax out file $5.00 each. Court makes copy: $1.00 per page. Certification fee: $1.00 per page. Payee: Owyhee County. Only cashiers checks and money orders accepted. No credit cards accepted. Mail requests: Include $.43 for return postage, or SASE.

Homedale Magistrate Court 31 W Wyoming, Homedale, ID 83628-3402; 208-337-4540; criminal fax: 208-337-3035; civil fax: same; 8:30AM-5PM (MST). ***Misdemeanor, Civil Actions under $10,000, Eviction, Small Claims.***

www.owyheecounty.net/index1.php?court

Civil Records: Access: Mail, in person, online. Only the court performs in person searches; visitors may not. No search fee. Required to search: name, years to search; also helpful: address. Civil cases indexed by defendant. Civil records on computer from 1992, archives from 1975. Mail turnaround time 2 days. PAT civil results show middle initial. Search trial court records back to 1995 and calendars free at https://www.idcourts.us.

Criminal Records: Access: Mail, in person, online. Only the court performs in person searches; visitors may not. No search fee. Required to search: name, years to search; also helpful: address, DOB, SSN. Criminal records computerized from 1992, archives from 1975. Mail turnaround time 2 days. PAT results show middle initial, DOB. Search trial court index back to 1995 and calendars free at https://www.idcourts.us. Online results show middle initial, DOB.

General Information: No juvenile or mental records released. Will fax documents $5.00 each 1st 2 pages, $2.00 pages 3-10; $.75 each add'l. Court makes copy: $1.00 per page. Certification fee: $1.00 per page. Payee: Clerk of Court. Personal checks accepted; credit cards are not. Mail requests: SASE required.

Payette County

District & Magistrate Courts 1130 3rd Ave N, #104, Payette, ID 83661; 208-642-6000 (Dist) 642-6010(Magis); criminal fax: 208-642-6011; civil fax: same; 9AM-5PM (MST). ***Felony, Misdemeanor, Civil, Eviction, Small Claims, Probate.*** www.payettecounty.org/

District Court is Rm 104; Magistrate Court is Rm 106. Probate fax is same as main fax number.

Civil Records: Access: Fax, mail, in person, online. Both court and visitors may perform in person searches. Search fee: $5.00 per name. Required to search: name, years to search; also helpful: address. Civil cases indexed by defendant, plaintiff, on computer back to 1992, prior on microfiche or archived from 1917. Mail turnaround time 1 day. Civil PAT goes back to 1992. PAT civil results

show middle initial. Search trial court records back to 1995 and calendars at https://www.idcourts.us.
Criminal Records: Access: Fax, mail, in person, online. Both court and visitors may perform in person searches. Search fee: $5.00 per name. Required to search: name, years to search, signed release; also helpful: address, DOB, SSN. Criminal records computerized from 1992, prior microfiche or archived from 1917. Mail turnaround time 1 day. Criminal PAT goes back to same as civil. PAT results show middle initial, DOB. Search trial court index back to 1995 and calendars free at https://www.idcourts.us. Online results show middle initial, DOB.
General Information: No juvenile, adoption records released. Will fax documents after payment. Court makes copy: $1.00 per page, self serve same. Certification fee: $1.00 per doc. Payee: Clerk of Court. Personal checks accepted. Major credit cards accepted for fine payments only. Mail requests: SASE required.

Power County

District & Magistrate Courts 543 Bannock Ave, American Falls, ID 83211; 208-226-7611 (Dist) 226-7618(Magistrate); fax: 208-226-7612; 9AM-5PM (MST). ***Felony, Misdemeanor, Civil, Eviction, Small Claims, Probate.***
www.co.power.id.us/
Civil Records: Access: Phone, fax, mail, in person, online. Both court and visitors may perform in person searches. Search fee: $5.00 per name found. Required to search: name, years to search. Civil cases indexed by defendant, plaintiff, on computer from 1994, prior archived from 1913. Mail turnaround time 3-10 days. Civil PAT goes back to 1994. PAT civil results show middle initial. Search trial court records back to 1995 and calendars free at https://www.idcourts.us.
Criminal Records: Access: Phone, fax, mail, in person, online. Both court and visitors may perform in person searches. Search fee: $5.00 per name found. Required to search: name, years to search, DOB, SSN, signed release. Criminal records computerized from 1988, prior archived from 1913. Mail turnaround time 10 days. Criminal PAT goes back to 1988. PAT results show middle initial, DOB. Search trial court index back to 1995 and calendars free at https://www.idcourts.us. Online results show middle initial, DOB.
General Information: No juvenile, mental commitment records released. Fee to fax out file $1.00 per page. Court makes copy: $1.00 per page, self serve same. Certification fee: $1.50 per cert. Payee: Power County Magistrate Court. Cashiers check or money order accepted. Visa/MC accepted. Mail requests: SASE required.

Shoshone County

District & Magistrate Courts 700 Bank St, Wallace, ID 83873; 208-752-1266; criminal fax: 208-753-0921; civil fax: same; 9AM-5PM (PST). ***Felony, Misdemeanor, Civil, Eviction, Small Claims, Probate.***
Probate fax is same as main fax number.
Civil Records: Access: Phone, fax, mail, in person, online. Both court and visitors may perform in person searches. No search fee. Required to search: name, years to search; also helpful: address. Civil cases indexed by defendant, plaintiff, on computer from 1988, archived from late 1880s. Note: Juvenile case information not available by fax. Mail turnaround time 1-2 days. Civil PAT goes back to 6/1995. PAT results show middle initial, DOB. Search trial court records back to 1995 and calendars free at https://www.idcourts.us.
Criminal Records: Access: Phone, mail, in person, online. Both court and visitors may perform in person searches. No search fee. Required to search: name, years to search; also helpful: address, DOB, SSN. Criminal records computerized from 1988, archived from late 1880s. Mail turnaround time 1-2 days. Criminal PAT goes back to same as civil. PAT results show middle initial, DOB. Search trial court index back to 1995 and calendars free at https://www.idcourts.us. Online results show middle initial, DOB.
General Information: No special proceeding, juvenile records released. Will fax documents $2.00 1st page, $1.00 each add'l. Add $1.00 1st page if long distance. Court makes copy: $1.00 per page. Certification fee: $1.00. Payee: Clerk of Court. Personal checks accepted. Will accept debit cards in person only; Credit cards in person and over phone. Mail requests: SASE required.

Teton County

District & Magistrate Courts 89 N Main, #5, Driggs, ID 83422; 208-354-2239; probate phone: same; 9AM-5PM (MST). ***Felony, Misdemeanor, Civil, Eviction, Small Claims, Probate.***
Address and telephone given above are for District Court. If you wish to access only the Magistrate Court and call 208-354-2239.
Civil Records: Access: Phone, fax, mail, in person, online. Both court and visitors may perform in person searches. Search fee: $5.00 per name. Required to search: name, years to search; also helpful: address. Civil cases indexed by defendant, plaintiff, on computer from 1992, archives from 1974, I-Star since 1992. Mail turnaround time 3 days. Civil PAT goes back to 1992. PAT civil results show middle initial. Search trial court records back to 1995 and calendars at https://www.idcourts.us.
Criminal Records: Access: Phone, fax, mail, in person, online. Both court and visitors may perform in person searches. Search fee: $5.00 per name. Required to search: name, years to search; also helpful: address, DOB, SSN. Criminal records computerized from 1992, archives from 1974, I-Star since 1993. Note: The court only performs research on Fridays. Mail turnaround time 1-7 days. Criminal PAT goes back to same as civil. PAT results show middle initial, DOB. Search trial court index back to 1995 and calendars free at https://www.idcourts.us. Online results show middle initial, DOB.
General Information: No juvenile, DV records released. Will fax documents $2.00 per page. Court makes copy: $1.00 per page, self serve same. Certification fee: $1.00. Payee: Clerk of Court. Personal checks accepted; credit cards are not. Mail requests: SASE required.

Twin Falls County

District & Magistrate Courts PO Box 126, Twin Falls, ID 83303-0126; 208-736-4013; fax: 208-736-4155; 8AM-5PM (MST). ***Felony, Misdemeanor, Civil, Eviction, Small Claims, Probate.***
Civil Records: Access: In person, online. Visitors must perform in person searches themselves. Required to search: name, years to search; also helpful: address. Civil cases indexed by defendant, plaintiff, on computer from 12/1989, archives from early 1900s. Civil PAT goes back to 12/1989. PAT civil results show middle initial. Search trial court records back to 1995 and calendars free at https://www.idcourts.us.
Criminal Records: Access: In person, online. Visitors must perform in person searches themselves. Required to search: name, years to search; also helpful: address, DOB, SSN. Criminal records computerized from 12/1989, archives from 1951 felonies, 1970 for misdemeanors. Criminal PAT goes back to same as civil. PAT results show middle initial, DOB. Search trial court index back to 1995 and calendars at https://www.idcourts.us. Online results show middle initial, DOB.
General Information: No adoption, termination, juvenile records released. Will fax out document $2.50 each. Court makes copy: $1.00 per page. Certification fee: $1.00 per doc. Payee: Court Services. Personal checks accepted. Visa/MC accepted; add $3.00 technology cost.

Valley County

District & Magistrate Courts-I PO Box 1350, Cascade, ID 83611; 208-382-7178; fax: 208-382-7184; 8AM-5PM (MST). ***Felony, Misdemeanor, Civil, Eviction, Small Claims, Probate.***
A Courthouse Annex in McCall handles Juvenile. However, the McCall Court does not do background checks nor does the court in Cascade.
Civil Records: Access: In person, online. Both court and visitors may perform in person searches. No search fee. Required to search: name, case number, years to search; also helpful: address. Civil cases indexed by defendant, plaintiff, on computer from 1990, microfiche and archives from early 1900s. Civil PAT goes back to 1990. PAT civil results show middle initial. Search trial court records back to 1995 and calendars at https://www.idcourts.us.
Criminal Records: Access: In person, online. Both court and visitors may perform in person searches. No search fee. Required to search: name, case number, years to search; also helpful: address, DOB, SSN. Criminal records computerized from 1990, microfiche and archives from early 1900s. Criminal PAT goes back to same as civil. PAT results show middle initial, DOB. Search trial court index back to 1995 and calendars at https://www.idcourts.us. Online results show middle initial, DOB.
General Information: No juvenile records released. Will fax documents $1.00 per page. Court makes copy: $1.00 per page. Self serve: is available. Certification fee: $1.00 per page. Payee: Valley County. Two-party or out-of-country (w/o printed-stamped US Funds) checks not accepted. No credit cards accepted. Mail requests: SASE required for mail return of any copies.

Washington County

District & Magistrate Courts PO Box 670, Weiser, ID 83672; 208-414-2092; fax: 208-414-3925; 8:30AM-5PM (MST). ***Felony, Misdemeanor, Civil, Eviction, Small Claims, Probate.***
www.the3rdjudicialdistrict.com
This court will only perform searches for probate records; these requests must be in writing. Turnaround time on probate records is 3-10 days.
Civil Records: Access: In person, online. Visitors must perform in person searches themselves. Required to search: name. Civil cases indexed by defendant, plaintiff, on computer from 2/90, archives from late 1800s. Civil PAT goes back to 2/1990. PAT civil results show middle initial. Search trial court records back to 1995 and calendars free at https://www.idcourts.us.
Criminal Records: Access: In person, online. Visitors must perform in person searches themselves. Required to search: name. Criminal records computerized from 2/90, archives from late 1800s. Criminal PAT goes back to same as civil. PAT results show middle initial, DOB. Search trial court index back to 1995 and calendars free at https://www.idcourts.us. Online results show middle initial, DOB.
General Information: No juvenile, adoption, hospitalization, child protection-termination of parental rights records released. Will not fax documents. Court makes copy: $1.00 per page, self serve same. Certification fee: $1.00. Payee: Washington County. Business checks accepted if local. No credit cards accepted.

Idaho Recording Offices

ORGANIZATION: 44 counties, 44 recording offices. The recording officer is the County Recorder. Many counties utilize a grantor/grantee index containing all transactions recorded with them. 34 counties are in the Mountain Time Zone, and the uppermost 10 are in the Pacific Time Zone.

REAL ESTATE: Most counties will not perform real estate name searches. Copy fee is $1.00 per page, with a few exceptions for less. Certification fee is usually $1.00.

UCC RECORDS: Financing statements are filed at the state level except for real estate related filings. All counties will perform UCC searches. UCC search fee is usually $6.00 per debtor name for a listing of filings and $12.00 per debtor name for a listing plus copies. Separately ordered copies are $1.00 per page.

TAX LIEN RECORDS: Until July 1, 1998, state tax liens were filed at the local county recorder. Now they are filed with the Secretary of State who has all active case files. Federal tax liens on personal property of businesses are filed with the Secretary of State. Other federal tax liens are filed with the county recorder. Some counties will perform a combined state and federal tax lien search for $5.00 while others counties will not perform tax lien searches.

OTHER LIENS: Judgments, hospital, labor, mechanics, divorce-related judgments.

ONLINE ACCESS: Few counties offer web access. Many counties property data is found at www.etitlesearch.com; fees and registration required. The Secretary of State's office offers online access to UCCs.

Ada County

County Clerk & Recorder, 200 W Front St, Rm 1207, Boise, ID 83702. 208-287-6840; fax-208-287-6849; 8AM-5PM (MST)

Marriage license applications searchable here - other vital records are not. Index: Separate indices to search include microfilm, computer. Records indexed on a public use terminal back to 1982. Office personnel assists visitors to perform searches. Search fee-$6.00 UCC informly; $12.00 UCC info and copies; $22.00 full lien search. Office will not search real estate records. UCC each includes federal tax liens if requested. Copy fee $1.00 per page. Cert fee- $1.00 per doc plus copy fee. Payee- Ada County Clerk & Recorder. Bulk data available for purchase, contact Gail Garrett-Supervisor. **Other phones:** Treasurer-208-287-6800; Elections- 208-287-6860; Vital Records- 208-334-5980. **Property tax/Assessing-** 200 W Front St, Rm 2210, Boise, ID 83702; 208-287-7200, assessor fax- 208-287-7209. Public access terminal available. www.adacountyassessor.org **Online access-** Search the property assessor database for property data for free at www.adacountyassessor.org. Click on "Online Property Information System". No name searching.

Adams County

County Clerk & Recorder, PO Box 48, Council, ID 83612. 208-253-4561; fax-208-253-4880; 8AM-5PM (MST) www.co.adams.id.us

Index: All in one. Records indexed on a public use terminal back to 1980. Only the public may search. Copy fee $1.00 per recorded docs per page; $4.00 per page for surveys & flats. Cert fee- $1.00 per cert plus copy fee. Payee- Adams County Clerk and Recorder. **Other phones:** Treasurer- 208-253-4263; Elections-208-253-4561; Vital Records- 208-253-4561. **Property tax/Assessing-** PO Box 46, 201 Industrial Ave, Council, ID 83612; 208-253-4271, assessor fax-208-253-4361.

Bannock County

County Clerk & Recorder, 624 E Center, Rm 211; Courthouse, Pocatello, ID 83201. Recording, R/E & UCC phone-208-236-7340; fax-208-236-7345; 8AM-5PM www.co.bannock.id.us/recorder/index.htm

Index: All in one. Records indexed on a public use terminal back to 1989. Office personnel or visitors may perform searches. Search fee $6.00 per name. Office will search real estate records. Office will not search UCC records. Copy fee $1.00 per page. Cert fee- $1.00 per page. Payee- Bannock County Clerk and Recorder. Office does not sell bulk data. **Property tax/Assessing-** PO Box 4969, 624 E Center St, Pocatello, ID 83205; 208-236-7260, assessor fax-208-236-7074.

Bear Lake County

County Clerk & Recorder, PO Box 190, Paris, ID 83261. Recording, R/E & UCC phone-208-945-2212 x5; fax-208-945-2780; 8:30AM-5PM (MST) www.bearlakecounty.info

Index: Separate indices to search include mortgage, assignments, deed books. Records indexed on computer back to 1990. Office will perform a UCC search but public must search other records themselves. Copy fee $1.00 per page, survey copy-$4.00 per page. Cert fee- $1.00 per doc plus copy fee. Payee- Bear Lake County Clerk and Recorder. Office does not sell bulk data. **Other phones:** Treasurer-208-945-2130 x7; Elections- 208-945-2212 x5; Vital Records- 208-945-2212 x5. **Property tax/Assessing-** PO Box 190, 7 E Center, Paris, ID 83261; 208-945-2155 x4, assessor fax- 208-945-2887. Public access terminal available.

Benewah County

County Clerk & Recorder, 701 College, St. Maries, ID 83861. Recording, R/E & UCC phone-208-245-3212; fax-208-245-9152; 9AM-5PM (PST)

Index: Separate indices to search. Records indexed on computer back to 1986. Office will perform a UCC search but public must search other records themselves. Copy fee $1.00 per page. Cert fee- $1.00 per cert plus copy fee. Payee- Benewah County Clerk and Recorder. Office does not sell bulk data. **Online access to Real Estate, Deed records:** Recording office land data to be available to the public soon at www.etitlesearch.com; registration and fees required. **Other phones:** Treasurer- 208-245-2421; Elections-208-245-3212. **Property tax/Assessing-** 701 College Ave, St. Maries, ID 83861; 208-245-2821, assessor fax- 208-245-2317.

Bingham County

County Clerk & Recorder, 501 N Maple, #205, Blackfoot, ID 83221. Recording, R/E & UCC phone-208-782-3163; fax-208-785-4131; 8AM-5PM (MST) www.co.bingham.id.us

Index: All in one. Records indexed on a public use terminal back to 00. Only the public may search. Will not search UCC records. Copy fee $1.00 per page. Cert fee- $1.00 per page plus copy fee. Payee-Bingham County Clerk and Recorder. Office does not sell bulk data. **Other phones:** Treasurer- 208-782-3090; Elections- 208-782-3164; Vital Records- 208-334-5980. **Property tax/Assessing-** 501 N Maple, #305, Blackfoot, ID 83221; 208-782-3016, assessor fax- 208-785-4131. (Appraiser/Auditor- 208-782-3024) hours- 9AM-5PM

Blaine County

County Clerk & Recorder, 206 1st Ave S, #200, Hailey, ID 83333. Recording, R/E & UCC phone-208-788-5505; fax-208-788-5501; 9AM-5PM (MST) www.co.blaine.id.us

Index: All in one by name. Records indexed on a public use terminal back to 100. Office personnel or visitors may perform searches. Office will search real estate records. Will search UCC records. UCC info request only per debtor name- $6.00. UCC search & copy request per debtor name- $12.00. Copy fee $1.00 per page. Cert fee- $1.00 per cert plus copy fee. Payee- Blaine County Recorder. **Other phones:** Treasurer- 208-788-5530; Elections- 208-788-5510; Court Records- 208-788-5521. **Property tax/Assessing-** 219 1st Ave S, #101, Hailey, ID 83333; 208-788-5535, fax- 208-788-5542. (Appraiser/Auditor- 208-788-5535) www.co.blaine.id.us

Boise County

County Clerk & Recorder, PO Box 1300, Idaho City, ID 83631. Recording, R/E & UCC phone-208-392-4431; fax-208-392-4473; 8AM-5PM (MST) www.boisecounty.us/Clerk_Auditor_Recorder.aspx

Index: All recorded documents indexed by type - over 50 types. Records indexed on a public use terminal back to 1986. Office will perform a UCC search (request must be in writing) and real estate search, but public must search other records themselves. No fee for search. Copy fee $1.00 per page for recorded document, $.25 per page for all other copies. Cert fee-$1.50 per doc plus copy fee. Payee- Boise County Clerk and Recorder. **Other phones:** Treasurer- 208-392-4441; Elections- 208-392-4431; 208-392-6636. **Property tax/Assessing-** PO Box 1300, Idaho City, ID 83631; 208-392-4415, fax- 208-392-4473. (Appraiser- 208-392-4415) www.boisecounty.us/Assessor.aspx

Bonner County

County Clerk & Recorder, 215 S 1st, Sandpoint, ID 83864. 208-265-1432, R/E recording phone-208-265-1490; fax-208-265-1447; 9AM-5PM (PST)

Index: Separate indices to search. Records indexed on a public use terminal back to 1992. Only the public may search. Copy fee $1.00 per page. Cert fee- $1.00 per cert plus copy fee. Payee- Bonner County Clerk and Recorder. **Other phones:** Treasurer- 208-265-1433; Elections- 208-265-1490. **Property tax/**

Assessing- 127 S 1st Ave, #2, Sandpoint, ID 83864; 208-265-1440, assessor fax- 208-265-1451. Public access computer in office for index and records searching. www.co.bonner.id.us/assessor/index.html **Online access**- Maps and downloadable GIS data are available free at www.co.bonner.id.us/gis/index.html.

Bonneville County

County Clerk & Recorder, 605 N Capital Ave, Idaho Falls, ID 83402-3582. 208-529-1120, R/E recording phone-208-529-1350 x1350; fax-208-529-1311; 8AM-5PM (MST) www.co.bonneville.id.us
Index: All in one. Records indexed on a public use terminal back to 1994. Office personnel or visitors may perform searches. Office will not search real estate records. Copy fee $1.00 per page. Cert fee- $1.00 per cert plus copy fee. Payee- Bonneville County. **Other phones:** Treasurer- 208-529-1350 x1380; Elections- 208-529-1350 x1363; Vital Records- 208-529-1350 x1350. **Property tax/Assessing**- 605 N Capital Ave, Idaho Falls, ID 83402-3582; 208-529-1350 x1320, assessor fax- 208-528-5509. Appraiser/Auditor- 208-529-1350 x1361 Limited info available on a public access computer terminal in office.

Boundary County

County Clerk & Recorder, PO Box 419, Bonners Ferry, ID 83805. Recording, R/E & UCC phone-208-267-2242; fax-208-267-7814; 9AM-5PM (PST) www.boundarycountyid.org
Index: All in one. Records indexed on a public use terminal back to 1986. Office will perform a UCC search but public must search other records themselves. UCC info request only per debtor name- $6.00. UCC search & copy request per debtor name- $12.00. Copy fee $1.00 per page. Cert fee- $1.00 per cert plus copy fee. Payee- Boundary County Clerk and Recorder. Surveys available for purchase on CD from Recording Department, $700.00. **Other phones:** Treasurer- 208-267-3291; Elections- 208-267-2242; Vital Records- 208-267-2242. **Property tax/Assessing**- PO Box 57, Bonners Ferry, ID 83805; 208-267-3301, assessor fax- 208-267-6291. (Appraiser/Auditor- 208-267-3301) Public access computer in office for index and records searching.

Butte County

County Clerk & Recorder, PO Box 737, Arco, ID 83213. Recording, R/E & UCC phone-208-527-3021; fax-208-527-3295; 9AM-5PM (MST)
Index: Separate indices to search include books, scanner, microfilm. Records indexed on a by-appointment public use terminal back to 1983. Only the public may search. Will not search UCC records. Copy fee $1.00 per page. Cert fee- $2.50 per page plus copy fee. Payee- Butte County Clerk and Recorder. **Other phones:** Treasurer- 208-527-3047; Elections- 208-527-3021. **Property tax/Assessing**- PO Box 157, 248 W Grand, Arco, ID 83213; 208-527-8288, assessor fax- 208-527-3916. hours- 9AM-N 1PM-5PM

Camas County

County Clerk & Recorder, PO Box 430, Fairfield, ID 83327-0430. Recording, R/E & UCC phone-208-764-2242; fax-208-764-2349; 8:30AM-N, 1-5PM (MST)
Index: Separate indices to search include books. Records indexed on computer back to 7/18/07. Office personnel or visitors may perform searches. General search fee $5.00 per name. Office will not search real estate records. UCC search per debtor name- $10.00. Copy fee $1.00 per page. Cert fee- $1.00 per cert plus copy fee. Payee- Camas County Clerk and Recorder. Office does not sell bulk data. **Other phones:** Treasurer- 208-764-2126; Elections- 208-764-2242; Vital Records- 208-764-2242. **Property tax/Assessing**- PO Box 430, 505 Soldier Rd, Fairfield, ID 83327; 208-764-2370, assessor fax- 208-764-2349. (Appraiser/Auditor- 208-764-2370)

Canyon County

County Recorder, 1115 Albany St, Caldwell, ID 83605. 208-454-7556, R/E recording phone-208-453-4830, UCC recording phone-208-454-7556; fax-208-454-6689; 8AM-5PM (MST) www.canyonco.org/clerk.aspx?id=70
Index: All in one. Records indexed on a public use terminal back to 1983. Office personnel or visitors may perform searches. General index search fee $5.00 per name. Only 2 real estate searches per customer. Tax liens not included in UCC search. UCC search per debtor name- $6.00. UCC search & copy request per search name- $12.00. General copy fee- $1.00 per page. Copies included in UCC search fee. Cert fee- $1.00 per doc plus copy fee. Payee- Canyon County Recorder. Bulk data available for purchase, contact Jean, or Joe Cox at 208-454-7437. **Other phones:** Treasurer- 208-454-7354; Elections- 208-454-7562; Vital Records- 208-334-5980. **Property tax/Assessing**- 1115 Albany St, Rm 343, Caldwell, ID 83605; 208-454-7431, assessor fax- 208-454-7349. www.canyonco.org/assessor.aspx?id=96 **Online access**- Access to the Assessor and Treasurer's databases requires $35 registration/setup fee and $150 yearly fee. For subscription info, email clane@canyoncounty.org or call 208-454-7401 or visit the website.

Caribou County

County Clerk & Recorder, PO Box 775, Soda Springs, ID 83276-0775. Recording, R/E & UCC phone-208-547-4324; fax-208-547-4759; 9AM-5PM (MST)
Index: All in one. Records indexed on a public use terminal back to 1998. Only the public may search. Copy fee $1.00 per page. Cert fee- $1.00 per doc plus copy fee. Payee- Caribou County Clerk and Recorder. **Other phones:** Treasurer- 208-547-3726. **Property tax/Assessing**- PO Box 775, 159 S Main St, Soda Springs, ID 83276; 208-547-4749. Public access computer in office for index and records searching.

Cassia County

County Clerk & Recorder, 1459 Overland Ave, Rm 105, Burley, ID 83318. Recording, R/E & UCC phone-208-878-5240; fax-208-878-8825; 8:30AM-5PM (MST) www.cassiacounty.org/clerk-auditor-recorder/index.htm
Index: Separate indices to search include 3 systems, depending upon doc year. Records indexed on a public use terminal back to 11/1991. Only the public may search. Copy fee $1.00 per page. Fax back- $2.50 per doc, payment in advance. Cert fee- $1.00 per doc plus copy fee. Payee- Cassia County Recorder. **Other phones:** Treasurer- 208-878-7202; Elections- 208-878-5240; Vital Records- 208-878-5240; Property- 208-878-3540. **Property tax/Assessing**- 203 E 15th St, Burley, ID 83318; 208-878-3540, assessor fax- 208-878-1014. (Appraiser/Auditor- 208-878-1004) Public access computer in office for index and records searching. www.cassiacounty.org/assessor/index.htm

Clark County

County Clerk & Recorder, PO Box 205, Dubois, ID 83423. 208-374-5304; fax-208-374-5609; 9AM-5PM (MST)
Index: All in one. Records indexed on a public use terminal back 10 years. Office will perform a UCC search but public must search other records themselves. Copy fee $.25 per page. Cert fee- $1.00 per page plus copy fee. Payee- Clark County Clerk and Recorder. **Other phones:** Treasurer- 208-374-5455; Elections- 208-374-5304. **Property tax/Assessing**- PO Box 224, 320 W Main St, Dubois, ID 83423; 208-374-5404, fax- 208-374-5609.

Clearwater County

County Clerk & Recorder, PO Box 586, Orofino, ID 83544-0586. Recording, R/E & UCC phone-208-476-5615; fax-208-476-9315; 8AM-5PM (PST) www.clearwatercounty.org
Index: All in one. All current records available. Office will perform a UCC search but public must search other records themselves. UCC information or copy request (per debtor name)- $12.00. Info request only- $6.00. Copy fee $1.00 per page. Cert fee- $1.00 per cert plus copy fee. Payee- Clearwater County Clerk and Recorder. **Other phones:** Treasurer- 208-476-5213; Elections- 208-476-5615; Vital Records- 208-476-5615. **Property tax/Assessing**- PO Box 626, Orofino, ID 83544; 208-476-7042, assessor fax- 208-476-4842. (Appraiser/Auditor- 208-476-7042) http://clearwatercounty.org

Custer County

County Clerk & Recorder, PO Box 385, Challis, ID 83226. 208-879-2360; fax-208-879-5246; 8AM-5PM (MST) www.co.custer.id.us
Index: All in one. Records indexed on computer back to 11/98. Only the public may search. Copy fee $1.00 per page. Cert fee- $1.00 per doc includes copy fee. Payee- Custer County Clerk and Recorder. Office does not sell bulk data. **Other phones:** Treasurer- 208-879-2330; Elections- 208-879-2360; Vital Records- 208-879-2360. **Property tax/Assessing**- PO Box 597, Challis, ID 83226; 208-879-2325, assessor fax- 208-879-6690. A parcel viewer is available for public use in office.

Elmore County

County Clerk & Recorder, 150 S 4th E, #3, Mountain Home, ID 83647-3097. 208-587-2130 x500, R/E recording phone-208-587-2130; fax-208-587-2159; 9AM-5PM (MST) http://elmorecounty.org/
Index: All in one. Records indexed on a public use terminal back to 4/98. Only the public may search. General copy fee $1.00 per page. UCC copy- $6.00 per doc. Cert fee- $1.00 per cert plus copy fee. Payee- Elmore County. **Other phones:** Treasurer- 208-587-2138; Elections- 208-587-2130; Vital Records- 208-587-2130. **Property tax/Assessing**- 150 S 4th St #2, Mountain Home, ID 83647-3097; 208-587-2130 x507, assessor fax- 208-587-1883. (Appraiser/Auditor- 208-587-2130 x507) hours- 9AM-4:30PM A public use computer terminal is available in office for index and records searching. http://elmorecounty.org

Franklin County

County Clerk & Recorder, 39 W Oneida, Preston, ID 83263. Recording, R/E & UCC phone-208-852-1090; fax-208-852-1094; 9AM-5PM (MST)
Index: All in one. Records indexed on a public use terminal back to 1913. Office personnel or visitors may perform searches. Search fee $12.00 per name. Office will search real estate records. Copy fee $1.00 per page. Cert fee- $1.00 per doc. Payee- Franklin County Clerk and Recorder. Office does not sell bulk data. **Other phones:** Treasurer- 208-852-1095; Elections- 208-852-1090; Vital Records- 208-852-1090. **Property tax/Assessing**- 51 W Oneida, Presto, ID 83263; 208-852-1091, assessor fax- 208-852-1096. (Appraiser/Auditor- 208-852-1091) Public access computer in office for index/records searching.

Fremont County

County Clerk & Recorder, 151 W 1st N, Rm12, St. Anthony, ID 83445. Recording, R/E & UCC phone-208-624-3148; fax-208-624-7335; 8AM-5PM (MST) www.co.fremont.id.us/departments/index.htm
Index: All in one. Records indexed on a public use terminal back to 00. Only the public may search. Copy fee $1.00 per page. Cert fee- $1.00 per page plus copy fee. Payee- Fremont County Clerk and Recorder. Office does sell bulk data, contact Barbara Millward at 208-589-9075. **Other phones:** Treasurer- 208-624-3361; Elections- 208-624-7332; Vital Records- 208-624-3148; Commissioners- 208-624-4271. **Property tax/Assessing**- 151 W 1st N, St. Anthony, ID 83445; 208-624-7984, assessor fax- 208-624-7477. (Appraiser/Auditor- 208-624-7984) hours- 9AM-5PM www.co.fremont.id.us/departments/assessor/index.htm **Online access**- Access to property records for free go to www.co.fremont.id.us/map_frame.htm

Gem County

County Clerk & Recorder, 415 E Main, Emmett, ID 83617. Recording, R/E & UCC phone-208-365-4561; fax-208-365-7795; 8AM-5PM (MST) www.co.gem.id.us
Index: Indices by name. Records indexed on computer back to 1986. Only the public may search. Copy fee $1.00 per page. Cert fee- $1.00 per instrument plus copy fee. Payee- Gem County Clerk and Recorder. Contact Shelly Ganners, County Clerk. **Other phones:** Treasurer- 208-365-3272; Elections- 208-365-4561; Vital Records- 208-334-5980. **Property tax/Assessing**- 415 E Main, Emmett, ID 83617; 208-365-2982, assessor fax- 208-365-2163. (Appraiser - 208-365-2982)

Gooding County

County Clerk & Recorder, PO Box 417, Gooding, ID 83330. Recording, R/E & UCC phone-208-934-4841; fax-208-934-5085; 9AM-5PM (MST)
Index: All records prior to 1997 are in books or on microfilm. Records indexed on a public use terminal back to 1997. Office personnel or visitors may perform searches. Office will not search real estate records. Tax liens not included in $12.00 UCC search. Copy fee $1.00 per page. Cert fee- $1.00 per page plus copy fee. Payee- Gooding County Clerk and Recorder. **Other phones:** Treasurer- 208-935-5673; Elections- 208-934-4841. **Property tax/Assessing**- PO Box 417, 624 Main St, Gooding, ID 83330; 208-934-5666, assessor fax- 208-934-5667.

Idaho County

County Clerk & Recorder, 320 W Main, Rm 5, Grangeville, ID 83530. 208-983-2751; fax-208-983-1428; 8:30AM-5PM (PST) www.idahocounty.org
Index: All in one. Public may search; office will search index only if time allows. No fee for search. Copy fee $1.00 per page. Cert fee- $1.00 per doc plus copy fee. Payee- Idaho County Recorder. **Other phones:** Treasurer- 208-983-2801. **Property tax/Assessing**- 320 W Main, Rm 1, Grangeville, ID 83530; 208-983-2742, assessor fax- 208-983-0667. www.idahocounty.org/idaho/assessor/index.htm

Jefferson County

County Clerk & Recorder, 210 Courthouse Way, #100, Rigby, ID 83442. Recording, R/E & UCC phone-208-745-7756; fax-208-745-6636; 9AM-5PM (MST) www.co.jefferson.id.us/clerk/index.asp
Index: All in one. Records indexed on a public use terminal back to 1986. Only the public may search. General copy fee $1.00 per page. Cert fee- $1.00 per page plus copy fee. Payee- Jefferson County Clerk and Recorder. **Other phones:** Treasurer- 208-745-9219; Elections- 208-745-7756. **Property tax/Assessing**- PO Box 538, Rigby, ID 83442; 208-745-9215, assessor fax- 208-745-5240. Public access computer for records and index searching. www.co.jefferson.id.us/assessor/index.asp

Jerome County

County Clerk & Recorder, 300 N Lincoln, Rm 301; Courthouse, Jerome, ID 83338. Recording, R/E & UCC phone-208-644-2700; fax-208-644-2709; 8:30AM-5:00PM (MST) https://co.jerome.id.us/
Index: Separate indices to search in computer or on microfiche. Records indexed on a public use terminal back to 1/1/1990. Office personnel or visitors may perform searches. Search fee $5.00 per name. Copy fee $1.00 per page. Cert fee- $1.00 per cert plus copy fee. Payee- Jerome County Clerk and Recorder. **Other phones:** Treasurer- 208-644-2720; Elections- 208-644-2700; Courts- 208-644-2600. **Property tax/Assessing**- 300 N Lincoln, Courthouse, Rm 205, Jerome, ID 83338; 208-644-2740, assessor fax- 208-644-2749. (Appraiser/Auditor- 208-644-2740) Public access computer for records and index searching.

Kootenai County

County Recorder, PO Box 9000, Coeur d'Alene, ID 83816-9000. 208-446-1480; fax-n/a; 9AM-5PM (PST) www.co.kootenai.id.us/departments/recorder/
Index: All in one. Records indexed on a public use terminal back to 1990. Office will perform a UCC search but public must search other records themselves. UCC search per debtor name- $6.00; with copies- $12.00. Office will not search real estate records. Copy fee $1.00 per page. Cert fee- $1.00 per cert plus copy fee. Payee- Kootenai County Recorder's Office. Office does not sell bulk data. **Other phones:** Treasurer- 208-446-1005 x1005; Elections- 208-446-1030. **Property tax/Assessing**- PO Box 9000, 451 Government Way, Coeur d'Alene, ID 83816-9000; 208-446-1500 x1500, assessor fax- 208-446-1501. www.kcgov.us/departments/assessor/ **Online access**- Access assessor data free on the mapping site at www.kcgov.us/departments/mapping/mapSearch/. Login as Guest to search without registration.

Latah County

County Clerk & Recorder, PO Box 8068, Moscow, ID 83843-0568. Recording, R/E & UCC phone-208-883-2249; fax-208-883-7203; 8AM-5PM (PST) www.latah.id.us
Index: All in one. Records indexed on a public use terminal back to 1986. Office will perform a UCC search but public must search other records themselves. Copy fee $1.00 per page. Cert fee- $1.00 per doc plus copy fee. Payee- Latah County Recorder. **Other phones:** Treasurer- 208-883-2296; Elections- 208-883-2278; Vital Records- 208-334-5980 (Boise); Auditor- 208-883-2249. **Property tax/Assessing**- 522 S Adams, Rm 109, PO Box 8068, Moscow, ID 83843-0568; 208-883-5710, assessor fax- 208-883-2298. (Appraiser - 208-883-5710)

Lemhi County

County Clerk & Recorder, 206 Courthouse Dr, Salmon, ID 83467. Recording, R/E & UCC phone-208-756-2815 x224; fax-208-756-8424; 8AM-5PM (MST) www.lemhicountyidaho.org
Index: Separate indices to search include deeds, mortgages, assignments, agreements, marriages, releases, mining claims, leases. Records indexed on a public use terminal back to 1984. Office personnel or visitors may perform searches. General search fee $20.00 per name. RE searches by office are not guaranteed. Will search UCC records. Copy fee $1.00 per page. Cert fee- $1.00 per cert plus copy fee. Payee- Lemhi County Clerk and Recorder. Bulk data available for purchase on disc or Laserfiche. **Other phones:** Treasurer- 208-756-2816 x227; Elections- 208-756-2815 x221; Vital Records- 208-756-2815 x224. **Property tax/Assessing**- 206 Courthouse Dr, Salmon, ID 83467; 208-756-3116 x232, assessor fax- 208-756-3173. Public access computer for records and index searching. www.lemhicountyidaho.org/asMotorVeh.htm

Lewis County

County Clerk & Recorder, 510 Oak St, Rm 1, Nezperce, ID 83543. 208-937-2661; fax-208-937-9234; 9AM-5PM (PST) www.lewiscountyid.us
Index: All in one. Records indexed on a public use terminal back to 1988. Office will perform a UCC search but public must search other records themselves. Search fee $6.00 per name, $12.00 includes copies-for UCC's. Copy fee $1.00 per page. Cert fee- $1.00 per cert plus copy fee. Payee- Lewis County Clerk and Recorder. **Other phones:** Treasurer- 208-937-2341; Elections- 208-937-2661; Vital Records- 208-937-2661. **Property tax/Assessing**- 510 Oak St, Rm 3, Nezperce, ID 83543; 208-937-2261, assessor fax- 208-937-9234. https://fortress.wa.gov/lewisco/home/lc/Assessor/Default.aspx?lcID=75 **Online access**- Access property and assessor data on the PATS system free at https://fortress.wa.gov/lewisco/home/PATS/ but no name searching.

Lincoln County

County Clerk & Recorder, 111 W B St, Shoshone, ID 83352-5364. Recording, R/E & UCC phone-208-886-7641; fax-208-886-2798; 8:30AM-5PM (MST)
Index: Separate indices to search include books, disks and computer. Records indexed on computer back to 1989. Only the public may search. Copy fee $1.00 per page. Cert fee- $1.00 per cert includes copy fee. Payee- Lincoln County Clerk and Recorder. **Other phones:** Treasurer- 208-886-7681; Elections- 208-886-7641; Vital Records- 208-886-7641. **Property tax/Assessing**- 111 W "B" St, Courthouse, Shoshone, ID 83352-5364; 208-886-2161, assessor fax- n/a. (Appraiser - 208-886-2161);

Madison County

County Clerk & Recorder, PO Box 389, Rexburg, ID 83440. 208-359-6200 x1, R/E recording phone-208-356-3662; fax-208-356-8396; 9AM-5PM (MST) www.co.madison.id.us
Index: Separate indices to search. Records indexed on a public use terminal back to 1987. Only the public may search. Copy fee $1.00 per page. Cert fee- $1.00 per cert plus copy fee. Payee- Madison County Clerk and Recorder. Plat sales only, inquire at assessor's office. **Other phones:** Treasurer- 208-356-6871; Elections- 208-356-3662. **Property tax/Assessing**- PO Box 389, 134 E Main Admin Bldg, Rexburg, ID; 208-356-3071, assessor fax- 208-359-0856. **Online access**- Limited assessor information available at www.co.madison.id.us/modules/smartsection/category.php?categoryid=1

Minidoka County

County Clerk & Recorder, PO Box 368, Rupert, ID 83350-0368. Recording, R/E & UCC phone-208-436-9511; fax-208-436-0737; 8:30AM-5PM (MST) www.minidoka.id.us
Treasurer located at 715 G St. Index: Separate indices to search include books, card, computer, microfiche. Records indexed on a public use terminal back to 1992. Only the public may search. Copy fee $1.00 per page. Cert fee- $1.00 per cert plus copy fee. Payee- Minidoka County Recorder. Office does not sell bulk data. **Other phones:** Treasurer- 208-436-7188; Elections- 208-436-9511; Vital Records- 208-436-9511. **Property tax/Assessing**- 702 G St, PO Box 368, Rupert, ID 83350; 208-436-7181, fax- 208-436-1176. (Appraiser/Auditor- 208-436-7181) www.minidoka.id.us/assessor/default.htm

Nez Perce County

County Clerk & Recorder, PO Box 896, Lewiston, ID 83501-0896. Recording, R/E & UCC phone-208-799-3020; fax-208-799-3070; 8AM-5PM (PST) www.co.nezperce.id.us
Index: Books and computer. Records indexed on a public use terminal back to 1984. Only the public may search. Copy fee $1.00 per page. Cert fee- $1.00 per cert plus copy fee. Payee- Nez Perce County Auditor and Recorder. **Other phones:** Treasurer- 208-799-3030; Elections- 208-799-3023; Vital Records- 208-799-3020. **Property tax/Assessing**- PO Box 896, 1230 Main St, Rm 100, Lewiston, ID 83501-0896; 208-799-3010, assessor fax- 208-799-3037. www.co.nezperce.id.us/assessors/Assessor/tabid/160/Default.aspx

Oneida County

County Clerk & Recorder, 10 Court St, Malad, ID 83252. 208-766-4116 x100, R/E recording phone-208-76-4116 x100/101/102; fax-208-766-2448; 9AM-5PM (MST)
Index: Separate indices to search include deeds, mortgages, judgments, liens and contracts. Record index not computerized. Only the public may search. Copy fee $1.00 per page. Cert fee- $1.00 per cert plus copy fee. Payee- Oneida County Clerk and Recorder. **Other phones:** Treasurer- 208-766-2962; Elections- 208-76-4116 x100 or 102. **Property tax/Assessing**- 10 Court St, Malad, ID 83252; 208-766-2954 X4, assessor fax- 208-766-2998. (Appraiser/Auditor- 208-766-4116 x109, 106 or 116);

Owyhee County

County Clerk & Recorder, PO Box 128, Murphy, ID 83650. Recording, R/E & UCC phone-208-495-2421; fax-208-495-1173; 8:30AM-N, 1-5PM (MST) www.owyheecounty.net

Index: All in one. Records indexed on a public use terminal back to 1989. Only the public may search. Will not search UCC records. Copy fee $1.00 per page. Cert fee- $1.00 per page plus copy fee. Payee- Owyhee County Clerk and Recorder. Contact Charlotte Sherburn, Clerk, for information on bulk data sale. **Other phones:** Treasurer- 208-495-1158; Elections- 208-495-2421; Vital Records- 208-495-2421. **Property tax/Assessing**- PO Box 128, Murphy, ID 83650; 208-495-2817, assessor fax- 208-495-1483. (Appraiser/Auditor- 208-495-2817) A public access terminal available in clerk's office.

Payette County

County Clerk & Recorder, 1130 3rd Ave N, #104, Payette, ID 83661. Recording, R/E & UCC phone-208-642-6000; fax-208-642-6011; 9AM-5PM (MST) www.payettecounty.org

Index: All in one. Records indexed on a public use terminal back to 1992. Only the public may search. Copy fee $1.00 per page. Surveys/plats- $4.00 per page. Cert fee- $1.00 per cert plus copy fee. Payee- Payette County Clerk and Recorder. Office does not sell bulk data. **Online access to Real Estate, Deed, Grantor/Grantee, Deed records:** Access to recorded documents is free at www.payettecounty.org/clerk/imagesilo.html. Username is "public" and password is "look." . **Other phones:** Treasurer- 208-642-6005; Elections- 208-642-6000. **Property tax/Assessing**- 1130 3rd Ave N, #102, Payette, ID 83661; 208-642-6012, assessor fax- 208-642-6040. www.payettecounty.org/assessor/assessor.html

Power County

County Clerk & Recorder, 543 Bannock, American Falls, ID 83211. Recording, R/E & UCC phone-208-226-7611; fax-208-226-7612; 9AM-5PM (MST) www.co.power.id.us

Index: All in one. Records indexed on a public use terminal back to 1986. Office will perform a UCC search but public must search other records themselves. Search fee $6.00. Copy fee $.50 per page. Cert fee- $1.00 per cert plus copy fee. Payee- Power County Clerk and Recorder. Office does not sell bulk data. **Other phones:** Treasurer- 208-226-7614; Elections- 208-226-7611; Vital Records- 208-226-7611. **Property tax/Assessing**- 543 Bannock, American Falls, ID 83211; 208-226-7616, assessor fax- 208-226-7612. Public access terminal available. www.co.power.id.us/assessor/default.htm

Shoshone County

County Clerk & Recorder, 700 Bank St, #120; Courthouse, Wallace, ID 83873-2348. Recording, R/E & UCC phone-208-752-1264; fax-208-753-2711; 9AM-5PM (PST)

Index: All in one. Records indexed on a public use terminal back to 12/1984. Office will perform a UCC search (current) but public must search other records themselves. Copy fee $1.00 per page. Survey records- $2.50 per page. Cert fee- $1.00 per doc plus copy fee. Payee- Shoshone County Clerk and Recorder. Office does not sell bulk data. **Other phones:** Treasurer- 208-752-1261; Elections- 208-752-1264; Vital Records- 208-752-1264; Auditor- 208-752-1264. **Property tax/Assessing**- 700 Bank St, #100, Wallace, ID 83873; 208-752-1202, assessor fax- 208-753-2711. (Appraiser/Auditor- 208-752-1202) hours- 8AM-5PM

Teton County

County Clerk & Recorder, 89 N Main, #1, Driggs, ID 83422. Recording, R/E & UCC phone-208-354-2905; fax-208-354-8410; 9AM-5PM (MST) http://tetoncountyidaho.gov/dept_clerk.php

Index: All in one. Records indexed on a public use terminal back to 1998. Office personnel or visitors may perform searches. Search fee $5.00 per name. Office will search real estate records. UCC search includes tax liens. Separate state or fed tax lien search- $6.00 per debtor. Copy fee $1.00 per page. Cert fee- $1.50 per cert plus copy fee. Payee- Teton County Clerk and Recorder. **Other phones:** Treasurer- 208-354-2254; Elections- 208-354-2905. **Property tax/Assessing**- 89 N Main St, #3, Driggs, ID 83422; 208-354-3507, assessor fax- 208-354-8410. (Appraiser/Auditor- 208-354-3507);

Twin Falls County

County Clerk & Recorder, PO Box 126, Twin Falls, ID 83303-0126. Recording, R/E & UCC phone-208-736-4004; fax-208-736-4182; 8AM-5PM (MST) www.twinfallscounty.org

Index: Pre-1991 indices on microfilm or binders. Began scanning images on computer in 1991. Only the public may search. Copy fee $1.00 per page. Cert fee- $1.00 per cert plus copy fee. Payee- Twin Falls County Clerk and Recorder. Office does not sell bulk data. **Other phones:** Treasurer- 208-736-4008; Elections- 208-736-4004; Vital Records- 208-334-5980. **Property tax/Assessing**- PO Box 265, 425 Shoshone St N, 3rd Fl, Twin Falls, ID 83303; 208-736-4010, fax- 208-736-4181. Public access computer available. www.twinfallscounty.org/dir/assessor.htm

Valley County

County Clerk & Recorder, PO Box 1350, Cascade, ID 83611-1350. 208-382-7100; fax-208-382-7107; 9AM-5PM (MST) www.co.valley.id.us

Index: All in one. Records indexed on a public use terminal back to 1985. Only the public may search. Copy fee $1.00 per page. Cert fee- $1.00 per cert plus copy fee. Payee- Valley County Clerk and Recorder. **Other phones:** Treasurer- 208-382-7110; Elections- 208-382-7100. **Property tax/Assessing**- PO Box 1350, Cascade, ID 83611; 208-382-7126, assessor fax- 208-382-7187. hours- 8AM-5PM www.co.valley.id.us/assessor.htm

Washington County

County Clerk & Recorder, PO Box 670, Weiser, ID 83672-0670. Recording, R/E & UCC phone-208-414-2092; fax-208-414-3925; 8:30AM-5PM (MST) http://co.washington.id.us

They record at www.ruralnetwork.net, must use full email and password to log in. Index: Separate indexes to search include deeds back to 1879. Deeds indexed on computer back to 1956. Office will perform a UCC search (with fee) but public must search other records themselves. UCC search per debtor name $6.00; $12.00 for search & copies. Copy fee $1.00 per page. Cert fee- $1.00 per doc plus copy fee. Payee- Washington County Clerk and Recorder. Contact county recorder for purchase of bulk data. **Other phones:** Treasurer- 208-414-0324; Elections- 208-414-2092; Vital Records- 208-414-2092 (1907-1911 only); Vital Statistics (Boise, ID) -288-334-5988;. **Property tax/Assessing**- 256 E Court St, Weiser, ID 83672-0670; 208-414-2000, fax- 208-414-1928. (Appraiser -208-414-2000) Public access computer available. www.co.washington.id.us/assessor/index.htm.

Idaho County Locator

You will usually be able to find the city name in the City/County Cross Reference below. In that case, it is a simple matter to determine the county from the cross reference. However, only the official US Postal Service city names are included here. We have also included a ZIP/City Cross Reference immediately following the City/County Cross Reference. If you know the ZIP Code but the city name does not appear in the City/County Cross Reference, look up the ZIP Code in the ZIP/City Cross Reference, find the city name, then look up the city name in the City/County Cross Reference.

Idaho City/County Cross Reference

ABERDEEN Bingham
AHSAHKA Clearwater
ALBION Cassia
ALMO Cassia
AMERICAN FALLS Power
ARBON Power
ARCO Butte
ARIMO Bannock
ASHTON Fremont
ATHOL (83801) Kootenai(87), Bonner(12)
ATLANTA Elmore
ATOMIC CITY Bingham
AVERY Shoshone
BANCROFT Caribou
BANKS Boise
BASALT Bingham
BAYVIEW (83803) Kootenai(93), Bonner(6)
BELLEVUE Blaine
BERN Bear Lake
BLACKFOOT Bingham
BLANCHARD Bonner
BLISS Gooding
BLOOMINGTON Bear Lake
BOISE (83716) Ada(69), Boise(28), Elmore(2)
BOISE Ada
BONNERS FERRY Boundary
BOVILL Latah
BRUNEAU Owyhee
BUHL Twin Falls
BURLEY Cassia
CALDER Shoshone
CALDWELL (83607) Canyon(94), Payette(4), Gem(1)
CALDWELL Canyon
CAMBRIDGE Washington
CAREY Blaine
CAREYWOOD Bonner
CARMEN Lemhi
CASCADE Valley
CASTLEFORD Twin Falls
CATALDO (83810) Kootenai(97), Shoshone(2)
CHALLIS (83226) Custer(98), Lemhi(1)
CHESTER Fremont
CLARK FORK Bonner
CLARKIA Shoshone
CLAYTON Custer
CLIFTON Franklin
COBALT Lemhi
COCOLALLA Bonner
COEUR D ALENE Kootenai
COLBURN Bonner
CONDA Caribou
COOLIN Bonner
CORRAL Camas
COTTONWOOD Idaho
COUNCIL Adams
CRAIGMONT Lewis
CULDESAC (83524) Nez Perce(96), Lewis(3)
DAYTON Franklin
DEARY Latah
DECLO Cassia
DESMET Benewah
DIETRICH Lincoln
DINGLE Bear Lake
DONNELLY Valley
DOVER Bonner
DOWNEY Bannock
DRIGGS Teton
DUBOIS Clark
EAGLE Ada
EASTPORT Boundary
EDEN Jerome
ELBA Cassia
ELK CITY Idaho
ELK RIVER Clearwater
ELLIS (83235) Custer(82), Lemhi(17)
EMMETT Gem
FAIRFIELD Camas
FELT Teton
FENN Idaho
FERDINAND Idaho
FERNWOOD (83830) Benewah(94), Shoshone(5)
FILER Twin Falls
FIRTH Bingham
FISH HAVEN Bear Lake
FORT HALL Bingham
FRANKLIN Franklin
FRUITLAND Payette
FRUITVALE Adams
GARDEN VALLEY Boise
GENESEE (83832) Latah(67), Nez Perce(32)
GENEVA Bear Lake
GEORGETOWN Bear Lake
GIBBONSVILLE Lemhi
GLENNS FERRY Elmore
GOODING Gooding
GRACE Caribou
GRAND VIEW Owyhee
GRANGEVILLE Idaho
GREENCREEK Idaho
GREENLEAF Canyon
HAGERMAN (83332) Gooding(82), Twin Falls(17)
HAILEY Blaine
HAMER Jefferson
HAMMETT (83627) Elmore(98), Owyhee(1)
HANSEN Twin Falls
HARRISON Kootenai
HARVARD Latah
HAYDEN Kootenai
HAZELTON Jerome
HEADQUARTERS Clearwater
HEYBURN (83336) Minidoka(72), Cassia(27)
HILL CITY Camas
HOLBROOK Oneida
HOMEDALE Owyhee
HOPE Bonner
HORSESHOE BEND (83629) Boise(91), Gem(8)
HOWE Butte
HUSTON Canyon
IDAHO CITY Boise
IDAHO FALLS Bonneville
INDIAN VALLEY (83632) Adams(90), Washington(9)
INKOM Bannock
IONA Bonneville
IRWIN Bonneville
ISLAND PARK Fremont
JEROME (83338) Jerome(98), Gooding(1)
JULIAETTA (83535) Latah(92), Nez Perce(7)
KAMIAH (83536) Idaho(68), Lewis(31)
KELLOGG Shoshone
KENDRICK (83537) Nez Perce(76), Latah(23)
KETCHUM (83340) Blaine(98), Custer(1)
KIMBERLY Twin Falls
KING HILL Elmore
KINGSTON Shoshone
KOOSKIA Idaho
KOOTENAI Bonner
KUNA (83634) Ada(95), Canyon(4)
LACLEDE Bonner
LAKE FORK Valley
LAPWAI Nez Perce
LAVA HOT SPRINGS Bannock
LEADORE (83464) Lemhi(98), Clark(1)
LEMHI Lemhi
LENORE (83541) Nez Perce(52), Clearwater(47)
LETHA Gem
LEWISTON Nez Perce
LEWISVILLE Jefferson
LOWMAN Boise
LUCILE Idaho
MACKAY Custer
MACKS INN Fremont
MALAD CITY Oneida
MALTA Cassia
MARSING Owyhee
MAY (83253) Lemhi(86), Custer(13)
MC CALL (83638) Valley(96), Adams(2)
MC CAMMON Bannock
MCCALL (83638) Valley(96), Adams(2)
MEDIMONT Kootenai
MELBA (83641) Canyon(50), Owyhee(41), Ada(8)
MENAN (83434) Jefferson(91), Madison(8)
MERIDIAN Ada
MESA Adams
MIDDLETON Canyon
MIDVALE Washington
MINIDOKA Minidoka
MONTEVIEW Jefferson
MONTPELIER Bear Lake
MOORE Butte
MORELAND Bingham
MOSCOW Latah
MOUNTAIN HOME Elmore
MOUNTAIN HOME A F B Elmore
MOYIE SPRINGS Boundary
MULLAN Shoshone
MURPHY Owyhee
MURRAY Shoshone
MURTAUGH (83344) Twin Falls(78), Cassia(21)
NAMPA (83687) Canyon(98), Ada(1)
NAMPA Canyon
NAPLES Boundary
NEW MEADOWS (83654) Adams(98), Idaho(1)
NEW PLYMOUTH Payette
NEWDALE (83436) Madison(57), Teton(28), Fremont(13)
NEZPERCE Lewis
NORDMAN Bonner
NORTH FORK Lemhi
NOTUS Canyon
OAKLEY Cassia
OLA Gem
OLDTOWN Bonner
OROFINO Clearwater
OSBURN Shoshone
OVID Bear Lake
PALISADES Bonneville
PARIS Bear Lake
PARKER Fremont
PARMA (83660) Canyon(89), Payette(10)
PAUL (83347) Lincoln(73), Jerome(18), Minidoka(8)
PAYETTE Payette
PECK Nez Perce
PICABO Blaine
PIERCE Clearwater
PINEHURST Shoshone
PINGREE Bingham
PLACERVILLE Boise
PLUMMER Benewah
POCATELLO (83202) Bannock(96), Bingham(3)
POCATELLO (83204) Bannock(94), Power(5)
POCATELLO Bannock
POLLOCK (83547) Idaho(80), Adams(20)
PONDERAY Bonner
PORTHILL Boundary
POST FALLS Kootenai
POTLATCH Latah
PRESTON Franklin
PRIEST RIVER Bonner
PRINCETON Latah
RATHDRUM Kootenai
REUBENS (83548) Nez Perce(65), Lewis(34)
REXBURG Madison
RICHFIELD Lincoln
RIGBY Jefferson
RIGGINS Idaho
RIRIE (83443) Bonneville(54), Jefferson(45)
ROBERTS Jefferson
ROCKLAND Power
ROGERSON Twin Falls
RUPERT Minidoka
SAGLE Bonner
SAINT ANTHONY Fremont
SAINT CHARLES Bear Lake
SAINT MARIES (83861) Benewah(88), Kootenai(11)
SALMON Lemhi
SAMUELS Bonner
SANDPOINT Bonner
SANTA Benewah
SHELLEY (83274) Bingham(98), Bonneville(1)
SHOSHONE Lincoln
SHOUP Lemhi
SILVERTON Shoshone
SMELTERVILLE Shoshone
SODA SPRINGS (83276) Caribou(91), Bear Lake(8)
SPALDING Nez Perce
SPENCER Clark
SPIRIT LAKE (83869) Kootenai(73), Bonner(26)
SPRINGFIELD Bingham
SQUIRREL Fremont
STANLEY Custer
STAR (83669) Ada(90), Canyon(9)
STITES Idaho
STONE Oneida
SUGAR CITY (83448) Madison(76), Fremont(23)
SUN VALLEY Blaine
SWAN VALLEY Bonneville
SWANLAKE Bannock
SWEET (83670) Gem(92), Boise(7)

TENDOY Lemhi
TENSED Benewah
TERRETON Jefferson
TETON (83451) Fremont(64), Madison(35)
TETONIA Teton
THATCHER Franklin
TROY Latah
TWIN FALLS Twin Falls
UCON Bonneville
VICTOR Teton
VIOLA Latah
WALLACE Shoshone
WARREN Idaho
WAYAN (83285) Caribou(50), Bonneville(49)
WEIPPE Clearwater
WEISER Washington
WENDELL Gooding
WESTON Franklin
WHITE BIRD Idaho
WILDER Canyon
WINCHESTER Lewis
WORLEY Kootenai
YELLOW PINE Valley

Idaho ZIP/City Cross Reference

83201-83202 POCATELLO
83203-83203 FORT HALL
83204-83209 POCATELLO
83210-83210 ABERDEEN
83211-83211 AMERICAN FALLS
83212-83212 ARBON
83213-83213 ARCO
83214-83214 ARIMO
83215-83215 ATOMIC CITY
83217-83217 BANCROFT
83218-83218 BASALT
83220-83220 BERN
83221-83221 BLACKFOOT
83223-83223 BLOOMINGTON
83226-83226 CHALLIS
83227-83227 CLAYTON
83228-83228 CLIFTON
83229-83229 COBALT
83230-83230 CONDA
83231-83231 MOORE
83232-83232 DAYTON
83233-83233 DINGLE
83234-83234 DOWNEY
83235-83235 ELLIS
83236-83236 FIRTH
83237-83237 FRANKLIN
83238-83238 GENEVA
83239-83239 GEORGETOWN
83241-83241 GRACE
83243-83243 HOLBROOK
83244-83244 HOWE
83245-83245 INKOM
83246-83246 LAVA HOT SPRINGS
83250-83250 MC CAMMON
83251-83251 MACKAY
83252-83252 MALAD CITY
83253-83253 MAY
83254-83254 MONTPELIER
83255-83255 MOORE
83256-83256 MORELAND
83260-83260 OVID
83261-83261 PARIS
83262-83262 PINGREE
83263-83263 PRESTON
83271-83271 ROCKLAND
83272-83272 SAINT CHARLES
83274-83274 SHELLEY
83276-83276 SODA SPRINGS
83277-83277 SPRINGFIELD
83278-83278 STANLEY
83280-83280 STONE
83281-83281 SWANLAKE
83283-83283 THATCHER
83285-83285 WAYAN
83286-83286 WESTON
83287-83287 FISH HAVEN
83301-83301 TWIN FALLS
83302-83302 ROGERSON
83303-83303 TWIN FALLS
83311-83311 ALBION
83312-83312 ALMO
83313-83313 BELLEVUE
83314-83314 BLISS
83316-83316 BUHL
83318-83318 BURLEY
83320-83320 CAREY
83321-83321 CASTLEFORD
83322-83322 CORRAL
83323-83323 DECLO
83324-83324 DIETRICH
83325-83325 EDEN
83326-83326 ELBA
83327-83327 FAIRFIELD
83328-83328 FILER
83330-83330 GOODING
83332-83332 HAGERMAN
83333-83333 HAILEY
83334-83334 HANSEN
83335-83335 HAZELTON
83336-83336 HEYBURN
83337-83337 HILL CITY
83338-83338 JEROME
83340-83340 KETCHUM
83341-83341 KIMBERLY
83342-83342 MALTA
83343-83343 MINIDOKA
83344-83344 MURTAUGH
83346-83346 OAKLEY
83347-83347 PAUL
83348-83348 PICABO
83349-83349 RICHFIELD
83350-83350 RUPERT
83352-83352 SHOSHONE
83353-83354 SUN VALLEY
83355-83355 WENDELL
83401-83406 IDAHO FALLS
83415-83415 IDAHO FALLS
83420-83420 ASHTON
83421-83421 CHESTER
83422-83422 DRIGGS
83423-83423 DUBOIS
83424-83424 FELT
83425-83425 HAMER
83427-83427 IONA
83428-83428 IRWIN
83429-83429 ISLAND PARK
83431-83431 LEWISVILLE
83433-83433 MACKS INN
83434-83434 MENAN
83435-83435 MONTEVIEW
83436-83436 NEWDALE
83437-83437 PALISADES
83438-83438 PARKER
83440-83441 REXBURG
83442-83442 RIGBY
83443-83443 RIRIE
83444-83444 ROBERTS
83445-83445 SAINT ANTHONY
83446-83446 SPENCER
83447-83447 SQUIRREL
83448-83448 SUGAR CITY
83449-83449 SWAN VALLEY
83450-83450 TERRETON
83451-83451 TETON
83452-83452 TETONIA
83454-83454 UCON
83455-83455 VICTOR
83460-83460 REXBURG
83462-83462 CARMEN
83463-83463 GIBBONSVILLE
83464-83464 LEADORE
83465-83465 LEMHI
83466-83466 NORTH FORK
83467-83467 SALMON
83468-83468 TENDOY
83469-83469 SHOUP
83501-83501 LEWISTON
83520-83520 AHSAHKA
83522-83522 COTTONWOOD
83523-83523 CRAIGMONT
83524-83524 CULDESAC
83525-83525 ELK CITY
83526-83526 FERDINAND
83530-83530 GRANGEVILLE
83531-83531 FENN
83533-83533 GREENCREEK
83534-83534 HEADQUARTERS
83535-83535 JULIAETTA
83536-83536 KAMIAH
83537-83537 KENDRICK
83538-83538 COTTONWOOD
83539-83539 KOOSKIA
83540-83540 LAPWAI
83541-83541 LENORE
83542-83542 LUCILE
83543-83543 NEZPERCE
83544-83544 OROFINO
83545-83545 PECK
83546-83546 PIERCE
83547-83547 POLLOCK
83548-83548 REUBENS
83549-83549 RIGGINS
83551-83551 SPALDING
83552-83552 STITES
83553-83553 WEIPPE
83554-83554 WHITE BIRD
83555-83555 WINCHESTER
83601-83601 ATLANTA
83602-83602 BANKS
83604-83604 BRUNEAU
83605-83607 CALDWELL
83610-83610 CAMBRIDGE
83611-83611 CASCADE
83612-83612 COUNCIL
83615-83615 DONNELLY
83616-83616 EAGLE
83617-83617 EMMETT
83619-83619 FRUITLAND
83620-83620 FRUITVALE
83622-83622 GARDEN VALLEY
83623-83623 GLENNS FERRY
83624-83624 GRAND VIEW
83626-83626 GREENLEAF
83627-83627 HAMMETT
83628-83628 HOMEDALE
83629-83629 HORSESHOE BEND
83630-83630 HUSTON
83631-83631 IDAHO CITY
83632-83632 INDIAN VALLEY
83633-83633 KING HILL
83634-83634 KUNA
83635-83635 LAKE FORK
83636-83636 LETHA
83637-83637 LOWMAN
83638-83638 MC CALL
83638-83638 MCCALL
83639-83639 MARSING
83641-83641 MELBA
83642-83642 MERIDIAN
83643-83643 MESA
83644-83644 MIDDLETON
83645-83645 MIDVALE
83647-83647 MOUNTAIN HOME
83648-83648 MOUNTAIN HOME A F B
83650-83650 MURPHY
83651-83653 NAMPA
83654-83654 NEW MEADOWS
83655-83655 NEW PLYMOUTH
83656-83656 NOTUS
83657-83657 OLA
83660-83660 PARMA
83661-83661 PAYETTE
83666-83666 PLACERVILLE
83669-83669 STAR
83670-83670 SWEET
83671-83671 WARREN
83672-83672 WEISER
83676-83676 WILDER
83677-83677 YELLOW PINE
83680-83680 MERIDIAN
83686-83687 NAMPA
83700-83799 BOISE
83801-83801 ATHOL
83802-83802 AVERY
83803-83803 BAYVIEW
83804-83804 BLANCHARD
83805-83805 BONNERS FERRY
83806-83806 BOVILL
83808-83808 CALDER
83809-83809 CAREYWOOD
83810-83810 CATALDO
83811-83811 CLARK FORK
83812-83812 CLARKIA
83813-83813 COCOLALLA
83814-83816 COEUR D ALENE
83821-83821 COOLIN
83822-83822 OLDTOWN
83823-83823 DEARY
83824-83824 DESMET
83825-83825 DOVER
83826-83826 EASTPORT
83827-83827 ELK RIVER
83830-83830 FERNWOOD
83832-83832 GENESEE
83833-83833 HARRISON
83834-83834 HARVARD
83835-83835 HAYDEN
83836-83836 HOPE
83837-83837 KELLOGG
83839-83839 KINGSTON
83840-83840 KOOTENAI
83841-83841 LACLEDE
83842-83842 MEDIMONT
83843-83844 MOSCOW
83845-83845 MOYIE SPRINGS
83846-83846 MULLAN
83847-83847 NAPLES
83848-83848 NORDMAN
83849-83849 OSBURN
83850-83850 PINEHURST
83851-83851 PLUMMER
83852-83852 PONDERAY
83853-83853 PORTHILL
83854-83854 POST FALLS
83855-83855 POTLATCH
83856-83856 PRIEST RIVER
83857-83857 PRINCETON
83858-83858 RATHDRUM
83860-83860 SAGLE
83861-83861 SAINT MARIES
83862-83862 SAMUELS
83864-83864 SANDPOINT
83865-83865 COLBURN
83866-83866 SANTA
83867-83867 SILVERTON
83868-83868 SMELTERVILLE
83869-83869 SPIRIT LAKE
83870-83870 TENSED
83871-83871 TROY
83872-83872 VIOLA
83873-83873 WALLACE
83874-83874 MURRAY
83876-83876 WORLEY
83877-83877 POST FALLS
83888-83888 SANDPOINT

Illinois

General Help Numbers:

Governor's Office

207 State House	217-782-6830
Springfield, IL 62706	Fax 217-524-0897
www.illinois.gov/gov/	8:30AM-5PM

Attorney General's Office

500 S 2nd St	217-782-1090
Springfield, IL 62706	Fax 217-524-4701
www.ag.state.il.us	8:45AM-4:45PM

Legislative Records

Illinois General Assembly	217-782-3944
House (or Senate) Bills Division	217-782-7017
Springfield, IL 62706	Fax 217-524-6059
www.ilga.gov/	8AM-4:30PM

State Archives

Archives Division	217-782-4682
Norton Bldg, Capitol Complex	Fax 217-524-3930
Springfield, IL 62756	8AM-4:30PM M-F,
www.sos.state.il.us/departments/archives/archives.html	8AM-3:30PM SAT

State Specifics:

Capital:	Springfield Sangamon County
Time Zone:	CST
Number of Counties:	102
Population:	12,091,563
Web Site:	www.illinois.gov

State Agencies

Criminal Records

IL State Police Bureau of Identification, Civil Processing Unit, 260 N Chicago St, Joliet, IL 60432-4075; 815-740-5160, 815-740-5216 (Forms); 8AM-4PM; phone inquiries- 7AM-5PM.

www.isp.state.il.us/crimhistory/crimhistoryhome.cfm

Indexing & Storage: Records available from 1932 forward. New records available for inquiry in 1 to 5 days. 52% of all arrests in database have final dispositions recorded, 52% for those arrests within last 5 years.

Searching: Requester must use the Uniform Conviction Information Form ISP6-405B. Personal requests are honored per Illinois statute. 100% of arrest records are fingerprint supported. Include in request- name, date of birth, sex, race. Fingerprint cards are an option; a fingerprint search using Form ISP6-404B is recommended in order to assure proper identification. All forms can be ordered (but not downloaded) at the website. Maiden names must be submitted as a separate request, fee. This data not released- records with warrants only, juvenile records unless juvenile convicted by an adult court of law. No records are released without a disposition of conviction.

Access by: mail, in person, online.

Fee & Payment: The search fee is $16.00 per form, $30 if paying with a check from a non-US bank. A fingerprint search is $20.00 ($50.00 if check is not from a US bank). Electronic access is less (see below). Fee payee- Illinois State Police. Prepayment required. Electronic and ongoing UCIA requesters must prepay for records in groups of 35 at a time. Personal checks accepted, credit cards are not.

Mail search: Turnaround time- 3 to 4 weeks. SASE not required.

In person: An in person search saves mailing time only.

Online search: Online access costs $10.00 per name or $16.00 if fingerprints submitted electronically ($20 if fingerprints submitted manually); discounts for quantities. Upon signing an interagency agreement with ISP and establishing an escrow account, users can submit inquiries by email. Responses are sent back in 24 to 48 hours by either email or fax. Visit www.isp.state.il.us/services/convictioninquiries.cfm to enroll.

Statewide Court Records

Administrative Office of Courts, 3101 Old Jacksonville Road, Springfield, IL 62704; 217-558-4490, Fax- 217-785-3905; 8AM-5PM.

www.state.il.us/court/

Except for certain online research capabilities, all trial court record access must be done at the local level. There is a support and enforcement office located at 222 N. LaSalle - 13th Floor, Chicago, IL 60601, 312-793-3250.

Access by: online.

Online search: The web page offers access to supreme and appellate opinions. There is no statewide public online system for local court records. A few Circuit Courts offer online access. A vendor, Judici.com, offers free searching for a few counties with a fee service for multi-county searching.

Sexual Offender Registry

Illinois State Police, SOR Unit, 801 S 7th Street #200 South, Springfield, IL 62794; 217-785-0653; Fax- 217-7 82-4996; 8:30AM-5PM M-F.

www.isp.state.il.us/sor/

Persons required to register as Sex Offenders are persons who have been charged of an offense listed in Illinois Compiled Statutes 730 ILCS 150/2. This office address is temporary due to storm. Will change in April 14, 2008.

Indexing & Storage: New records available for inquiry in 1 to 5 days.

Searching: Illinois Compiled Statutes (730 ILCS 152/115 (a) and (b)) mandate that the Illinois State Police ("ISP") establish and maintain a statewide Sex Offender Database, accessible on the Internet. A status field indicates if offender listed as "COMPLIANT" are in good standing with the Sex Offender Registration Laws. Offenders listed as "NON-COMPLIANT" have failed to maintain accurate registration information.

Access by: online.

Online search: The website provides an online listing of sex offenders required to register in the State of Illinois. The database is updated daily and allows searching by name, city, county, and ZIP Code.

Incarceration Records

Illinois Department of Corrections, PO Box 19277, Springfield, IL 62794-9277 (Courier address- 1301 Concordia Court, Springfield, IL 62794); 217-522-2666 x2008, 217-558-2200 (Inmate Search), Fax-217-524-6856; 8:30AM-5PM M-F.

www.idoc.state.il.us

Offender information is available to the general public and private organizations.

Indexing & Storage: Records available on current and former inmates, except online is inmates and parolees. New records available for inquiry in 1 to 5 days.

Searching: Records are never destroyed, but are archived. Include in request- full name and DOB, IBOC #, gender, race helpful. For a online search, you can provide name or DOB or IDOC #. Location, conviction information, physical identifiers, and release dates are reported. This data not released- medical records

Access by: mail, online.

Mail search: Turnaround time- 1 to 2 weeks. SASE not required.

Online search: Click on Inmate Search at the website or at www.idoc.state.il.us/subsections/search/default.asp.

Other access: A CD of data since 1982 may be purchased for $45. Send request to FOIA Officer at address above.

Corporation, LLC, LP, LLP, LLLP, RLLP, Trade Names, Assumed Name

Department of Business Services, Corporate Department, 330 Howlett Bldg, 3rd Floor, Copy Section, Springfield, IL 62756 (Courier address- 501 S 2nd St, Springfield, IL 62756); 217-782-6875 (Corps), 217-524-8008 (LLCs), Fax- 217-558-0076; 8AM-4:30PM.

www.ilsos.net

Indexing & Storage: Records available from mid-1800's on. Closed records are stored at the State Archives. Only limited information is available for corporations dissolved before 1986. New records available for inquiry immediately.

Searching: Records are on micro-film from 1984. In-house computer has name of agent, state and date of incorporation, etc. Include in request- full name of business, corporation file number. In addition to the articles of organization, business entity records available include: Annual Reports, Officers, Directors, Prior (merged) names, Assumed names, and Inactive names. This data not released- financial records

Access by: mail, phone, fax, in person, online.

Fee & Payment: For corps, LLCs, etc., $25.00 for a copy of a document (certified or not), or Good Standing or status certificate. For not-for-profit $5.00 for copy of any document plus are $.50 per page after initial 10 pages. Certification is $5.00. Fee payee- Secretary of State. Prepayment required. There is an additional $2.50 charge to use a credit card. Personal checks accepted. Visa/MC/Discover accepted.

Mail search: Turnaround time- 5 to 7 days. A SASE is requested.

Phone search: Expedited copy service is available using a credit card.

Fax search: Limited information can be requested by fax.

In person: Turnaround time is variable.

Online search: The website gives free access to corporate and LLC records at www.ilsos.gov/corporatellc/. A commercial access program is also available. Fees vary. Potential users must submit in writing the purpose of the request. Submit your request to become involved in this program to the Director's Office. Search the database for registrations of LP, LLP, LLLP, and RLLP at www.ilsos.gov/lprpsearch.

Other access: List or bulk file purchases are available. Contact the Director's office for details.

Expedited service: Expedited service is available for phone and fax searches. Turnaround time- 24 hours. Add $50.00 per business name for a certified copy and $20.00 for a Good Standing or abstract of corporate record. Add $2.00 to use credit card.

Uniform Commercial Code, Federal Tax Liens

Secretary of State, UCC Division, 2nd & Edwards St, Howlett Bldg, Room 350 West, Springfield, IL 62756; 217-782-7518; 8AM-4:30PM.

www.cyberdriveillinois.com

Indexing & Storage: Records available from 1962 on microfilm. Records are computerized since 1972, as digital images since 2000. New records available for inquiry in 48 hours.

Searching: Use search request form UCC-11. Request searches for federal tax liens on businesses since 1988 separately with a fee of $5.00. Federal tax liens on individuals and all state tax liens are filed at the county level. Include in request- debtor name and address. Records are not reported on searches one year after lapsing, per RA-9.

Access by: mail, in person, online.

Fee & Payment: A UCC search is $10.00 per debtor name. A federal tax lien search only is available for $5.00 plus $.50 per page of copies. UCC copies are $1.00 per page. Fee payee-Secretary of State. Prepayment required. Personal checks accepted. Visa/MC/Discover accepted.

Mail search: Turnaround time- 48 hours. A SASE is requested.

In person: Documents can be viewed at no charge.

Online search: Searching is offered at www.ilsos.gov/UCC/.

Other access: The entire database can be purchased and for $2500 with weekly updates at $200 per week. A CD update service is available for $250 per month.

State Tax Liens

Records not maintained by a state level agency.

All state tax liens are filed at the county.

Sales Tax Registrations

Revenue Department, Sales & Use Tax Services, PO Box 19041, Springfield, IL 62794-9041 (Courier address- 101 W Jefferson, Springfield, IL 62702); 800-732-8866, 217-782-3336, Fax- 217-782-4217; 8AM-5PM.

www.tax.illinois.gov/

Indexing & Storage: Records available for all active businesses with the state, records can go back to the 1930s.

Searching: This agency will only confirm that a business is registered and if registered as a retailer or reseller. They provide no other information. Since the report contains the SSN of the owner, the report is only returned to the owner. Include in request- tax number or business name. The state tax permit or federal tax ID is also helpful.

Access by: mail, phone, in person.

Fee & Payment: The fee is $5.00 per return.

Mail search: Turnaround time- 7 to 10 days. A SASE is requested.

Phone search: Will do up to 5 confirmations at a time.

In person: Turnaround time is variable.

Birth Certificates

IL Department of Public Health, Division of Vital Records, 605 W Jefferson St, Springfield, IL 62702-5097; 217-782-6554, 217-782-6553 (Instructions), Fax- 217-523-2648; 8:30AM-4PM

www.idph.state.il.us/vitalrecords/index.htm

Indexing & Storage: Records available from 1916 to present. New records available for inquiry in 1 to 2 months.

Searching: Birth records are not considered public records. Copies are available to subject if 18 years old, parents, or legal guardian (with court order). Include in request- full name, date of birth, place of birth, relationship to person of record, names of parents, mother's maiden name, signature of requester and photo ID with daytime phone. Place of birth can be city or county. Include name of hospital, if known. This data not released- sealed records.

Access by: mail, fax, in person, online.

Fee & Payment: Fees are $10.00 per name for a computer abstract and $15.00 per name for a certified copy of original. Add $2.00 for each additional copy. Fee payee- Illinois Department of Public Health. Prepayment required. Personal checks and major credit cards accepted.

Mail search: Turnaround time- 6 weeks. SASE not required.

Fax search: See expedited service below.

In person: Usually records can be picked up same day or are mailed within a day or two.

Online search: Records may requested from www.vitalchek.com, a state-endorsed vendor. Also, detailed instructions are at the website. Requests are processed within 3-5 days.

Expedited service: Expedited service is available for online and fax searches. Turnaround time- 3- 5 days. Use of credit card required, add $8.50; add $17.00 for express delivery.

Death Records

IL Department of Public Health, Division of Vital Records, 605 W Jefferson St, Springfield, IL 62702-5097; 217-782-6554, 217-782-6553 (Instructions), Fax- 217-523-2648; 8:30AM-4PM.

www.idph.state.il.us/vitalrecords/index.htm

Indexing & Storage: Records available from 1916 to present. New records available for inquiry in the next month.

Searching: Death records are not considered public documents. Copies are available to person with property rights and or an interest in the record. Once records are 20 years old, they are open for genealogical searches. Include in request- full name, date of death, place of death, relationship to person of record, parents' names, reason for request, photo ID and signature of requester.

Access by: mail, fax, in person, online.

Fee & Payment: Fees are $17.00 for a certified Death Certificate, or $10.00 if for genealogy (archived) records. Fee payee- Illinois Department of Public Health. Prepayment required. Personal checks and major credit cards accepted.

Mail search: Turnaround time- 10 to 12 weeks. SASE not required.

Fax search: See expedited service.

In person: Usually records can be picked up same day or are mailed within a day or two.

Online search: Records may be requested from www.vitalchek.com, a state-endorsed vendor. Detailed instructions are at the website. Also, the state archives database of Illinois Death Certificates 1916-1950 is available free at www.cyberdriveillinois.com/departments/archives/genealogy/forms/idphdeathsrch.html.

Expedited service: Expedited service is available for online and fax searches. Turnaround time- 3- 5 days. Use of credit card required, add $8.50; add $17.00 for express delivery.

Marriage Certificates, Divorce Records

Department of Public Health, Division of Vital Records, 605 W Jefferson St, Springfield, IL 62702-5097; 217-782-6554.

www.idph.state.il.us/vitalrecords/index.htm

State will verify marriage or divorce from 1962-present, but will not issue certificate. Records of marriage and divorce are found at the county of issue.

Searching: Verification requests must be in writing.

Access by: mail, in person, online.

Fee & Payment: There is a fee of $5.00 per event requested. Fee payee- Illinois Department of Public Health.

Mail search: Turnaround time- up to 6 weeks. Verification requests accepted.

In person: Verification requests accepted.

Online search: There is a free online search of a statewide Marriage Index for 1763-1900 found at the Illinois State Archives website at www.cyberdriveillinois.com/departments/archives/marriage.html.

Workers' Compensation Records

IL Workers' Compensation Commission, 100 W Randolph, 8th Floor, Chicago, IL 60601; 312-814-6611, 866-352-3033; 8:30AM-5PM.

www.iwcc.il.gov

The website lists current status on a case.

Indexing & Storage: Records available on computer from 1982 to present, on microfiche from 1927 to 1981. Settled file copies are stored in Springfield, but must be requested from Chicago. Data is indexed by name and file number. New records available for inquiry in 1 week.

Searching: Include in request- claimant name, the SSN and date of accident are very helpful. Include case number and company name.

Access by: mail, phone, in person, online.

Fee & Payment: There is no charge for a small file. For "large files," the office will contact you and suggest you use a record retrieval service. If your request is large enough to warrant the use of a copy service, the service will have its own fees that must be paid by you. Personal checks are accepted.

Mail search: Turnaround time- 2 weeks. A SASE is not requested.

Phone search: Information about a case is accessed by the file number. The staff will do a name search if you have enough information for them to do so.

In person: There are several public access terminals available in the office.

Online search: Case information for any case is available at the webpage. Click on the IIC box on the right side of the screen.

Driver Records

Abstract Information Unit, Drivers Services Department, 2701 S Dirksen Parkway, Springfield, IL 62723; 217-782-2720; 8AM-4:30PM.

www.sos.state.il.us

No personal identifiable information is provided on record unless requester is exempt. Exempt requesters include business representatives with a legitimate business need (e.g. insurance, financial institutions, employers, etc.).

Indexing & Storage: Records available for 4 years for moving violations; 7 years for suspension; lifetime for DWI. Commercial Driver records can go back 10 years for serious violations. New records available for inquiry in 2 weeks.

Searching: Non-exempt requesters, with no consent, may receive records without personal information, but there is a 10 day waiting period while the state notifies the subject. Include in request- full name, date of birth, sex. Exempt requesters qualify per DPPA guidelines and receive full record information. This data not released- SSN.

Access by: mail, phone, in person, online.

Fee & Payment: The fee is $12.00 per record, which includes certification. There is a full charge for a "no record found." Fee payee- Secretary of State. Prepayment required. Personal checks accepted, credit cards are not.

Mail search: Turnaround time- 10 days. SASE not required.

Phone search: A status is provided by phone, records are not.

In person: Up to five requests will be processed immediately if requester meets the access requirement (see above). Requests are available from any full-time Driver Services Facility statewide.

Online search: A program for high volume, approved users may be available. Records are $12.00 each. Call 217-785-3094 for further information.

Other access: Overnight cartridge batch processing may be available to high volume users (there is a 200 request minimum per day). Call 217-785-3094 for more information.

Vehicle Ownership & Registration

Vehicle Services Department, Vehicle Record Inquiry, 501 S 2nd Street #408, Springfield, IL 62756; 217-782-6992, 217-785-3000, Fax- 217-524-0122; 8AM-4:30PM.

www.sos.state.il.us

Indexing & Storage: Records available for 10 years to present. New records available for inquiry in 1 to 2 weeks.

Searching: Personal information is not released for non-business purposes. Bulk sales are not permitted for solicitation purposes. Include in request- name, reason for search. Records are open to "Exempt" requesters include courts, law enforcement, legal representatives (including licensed IL PIs) the insurance industry and others designated per DPPA. A non-exempt requester receives data without personal information.

Access by: mail, fax, in person.

Fee & Payment: The fee is $5.00 per record search, $10.00 for a certified document. Fee payee- Secretary of State. Prepayment required. Personal checks accepted. MasterCard, Visa, Discover accepted.

Mail search: Turnaround time- 4 to 7 days. One may search by mail, but there is a 10 day delay if the requester is not "exempt." A SASE is not requested.

Fax search: Fax requests are accepted for approved accounts.

In person: Walk-in requesters may retrieve data immediately; however, if requester is not exempt there is a 10 day delay.

Other access: This agency will sell customized, bulk requests upon approval of purpose and with a signed contract. Contact the Data Processing Division in Room 400.

Accident Reports (Crash Reports)

Illinois State Police, Patrol Records Unit, PO Box 19461, Springfield, IL 62794; 217-785-0612, Fax-217-785-2325; 8AM-5PM.

www.isp.state.il.us

To request report if crash occurred on IL Tollway System, send check or money order payable to: IL Toll Highway Authority, Attn: State Police District 15, One Authority Drive, Downers Grove, IL 60515.

Indexing & Storage: Records available from 1976 to present. New records available for inquiry in 2-4 weeks.

Searching: If the accident was not investigated by the State Police, then the requestors must contact the local law enforcement authority that did the investigation. Include in request- date, location, at least one driver's name, and report # if known. Crash reports are considered public record and are available without restriction. Items needed by the requester include date, names of drivers involved, report number, and an exact location.

Access by: mail, phone, online.

Fee & Payment: The fee is $5.00 per report or $20.00 for a reconstruction report. Add $1.00 if ordered online. Fee payee- Illinois State Police. Prepayment required. Personal checks accepted. Credit cards accepted for online requesting only.

Mail search: Turnaround time- 7 to 10 days. If requester provides prepaid express envelope & label, the request will be returned quicker. A SASE is requested.

Phone search: You may call to get verify certain information, but copies of records are only released with written requests or online.

Online search: Records can be requested and paid for online via E-Pay at the webpage. Visit www.isp.state.il.us/traffic/crashreports.cfm. The fee is $6.00 per report.

Vessel Ownership & Registration

Department of Natural Resources, One Natural Resources Way, Springfield, IL 62702; 800-382-1696, 217-557-0180, Fax- 217-782-5016; 8:30AM-5PM.

www.dnr.state.il.us/admin/boats.htm

Lien information will show on the history report.

Indexing & Storage: Records available from 1982 to the present. Snow mobile records are also available. Records are indexed on computer. All boats must be titled and registered unless if only used non-motorized on own property. New records available for inquiry in 8 weeks.

Searching: Include in request- name or hull ID or registration #. Include reason for request.

Access by: mail, phone.

Fee & Payment: There is a $5.00 fee for any search, including a title history search. Fee payee- IL Dept of Natural Resources. Prepayment required. Personal checks accepted, credit cards are not.

Mail search: Turnaround time- 4 to 6 weeks. SASE not required.

Phone search: They will give very limited name search and verification information, time permitting.

Other access: Bulk data may be released via a FOIA request. Write for details.

Legislation Records

Illinois General Assembly, Legislative Information System, 705 Stratton Building, Springfield, IL 62706; 217-782-3944 (Bill Status Only), 217-782-7017 (Index Div-Older Bills), 217-782-5799 (House Bills), 217-782-9778 (Senate Bills), Fax-217-524-6059; 8AM-4:30PM.

www.ilga.gov

Previous session bills must be obtained from: Senate 217-792-6970; House 217-782-5799. Cost is $.10 per page. Senate Clerk Fax 217-524-6059, House Clerk Fax 217-524-3885.

Indexing & Storage: Records available from 1971 to present.

Searching: Include in request- bill number. For statutes, it is suggested to go to a local law library or visit the Internet site. Complete statutes are not available from this office.

Access by: mail, phone, in person, online.

Fee & Payment: All copies of documents are considered as certified. There is no search fee, copies are free if from the last two sessions, otherwise $0.10 each. Fee payee- Illinois General Assembly. Personal checks accepted, credit cards are not.

Mail search: Turnaround time- 4 days. SASE not required.

Phone search: Records are available by phone.

In person: Simple requests may be processed while you wait.

Online search: The Internet site offers free access but the state has a disclaimer which says the site should not be relied upon as an official record of action. A number of record content types are offered. Also, there is a legislator lookup at the main website. The Illinois Complied Statutes are found at www.ilga.gov/legislation/ilcs/ilcs.asp.

Other access: A prepayment of $500.00 is required to obtain a printed copy of all bills.

Voter Registration

Access to Records is Restricted.

IL State Board of Elections, Voter Registration Services, 1020 S Spring, Springfield, IL 62704; 217-782-4141, Fax- 217-782-5959; 8AM-4:30PM.

www.elections.state.il.us

The data is not considered public record at the state level and is only available in bulk format to political committees and government agencies. County Clerks and Board of Election Commissioners control the information at the local level.

GED Certificates

Access to Records is Restricted.

Illinois Community College Board, GED Testing, 401 East Capitol, Springfield, IL 62701; 217-558-5668, Fax- 217-558-6700; 8AM-5PM.

www.iccb.state.il.us/gedtesting.html

This agency does not offer a verification or copy service for GED records. All GED information requests must be made at the Regional Office of Education in the county where the testing took place.

Hunting & Fishing License Information

Access to Records is Restricted.

IL Dept of Natural Resources, License Section, PO Box 19459, Springfield, IL 62794; 217-782-2965, Fax- 217-782-5016; 8:30AM-5PM.

http://dnr.state.il.us

The agency is created a central database effective 01/06. There are many vendors who sell licenses. A vendor list can be searched at http://dnr.state.il.us/admin/systems/licensing/Vendors.htm. FOIA requests processed by the legal Division. Direct questions to dnr.license@illinois.gov.

Illinois State Licensing Agencies

For details about the agency responsible for licensing/certifying/registering an item below or in the Agency Quick Finder section, match an item's number with the number of the agency in the *Licensing Agency Information* section.

Illinois Licenses Searchable Online

Acupuncturist #11 .... https://www.idfpr.com/dpr/licenselookup/default.asp
Alarm Contractor #11 .... https://www.idfpr.com/dpr/licenselookup/default.asp
Alcohol Abuse Counselor #21 .... www.iaodapca.org
Amusement Attraction/Ride #5 .... www.state.il.us/agency/idol/Listings/Carnlist.htm
Architect #11 .... https://www.idfpr.com/dpr/licenselookup/default.asp
Armed Security Agency/Agent #11 .... https://www.idfpr.com/dpr/licenselookup/default.asp
Asbestos Contractor #17 .... www.idph.state.il.us/
Athletic Trainer #11 .... https://www.idfpr.com/dpr/licenselookup/default.asp
Attorney #1 .... www.iardc.org/lawyersearch.asp
Auctioneer #29 .... https://www.idfpr.com/DPR/licenselookup/default.asp
Audiologist #11 .... https://www.idfpr.com/dpr/licenselookup/default.asp
Bank #29 .... www.obrelookupclear.state.il.us/default.asp
Barber #11 .... https://www.idfpr.com/dpr/licenselookup/default.asp
Bilingual Teacher, Transitional #28 .... https://secqa1.isbe.net/otis/
Bull Ride #5 .... www.state.il.us/agency/idol/Listings/Carnlist.htm
Bungee Jump #5 .... www.state.il.us/agency/idol/Listings/Carnlist.htm
Carnival #5 .... www.state.il.us/agency/idol/Listings/Carnlist.htm
Check Seller/Distributor #29 .... www.obrelookupclear.state.il.us/default.asp
Chiropractor #11 .... https://www.idfpr.com/dpr/licenselookup/default.asp
Classr'm Training Course, Basic #11 .... https://www.idfpr.com/dpr/licenselookup/default.asp
Collection Agency #11 .... https://www.idfpr.com/dpr/licenselookup/default.asp
Controlled Substance Registrant #11 .... https://www.idfpr.com/dpr/licenselookup/default.asp
Cosmetologist #11 .... https://www.idfpr.com/dpr/licenselookup/default.asp
Counselor/Clinical Prof Counselor #11 .... https://www.idfpr.com/dpr/licenselookup/default.asp
CPA- Public Accountant #11 .... https://www.idfpr.com/dpr/licenselookup/default.asp
Dentist/Dental Hygienist #11 .... https://www.idfpr.com/dpr/licenselookup/default.asp
Design Firm #11 .... https://www.idfpr.com/dpr/licenselookup/default.asp
Dietitian/Nutrition Counselor #11 .... https://www.idfpr.com/dpr/licenselookup/default.asp
Doctor/Physician #11 .... https://www.idfpr.com/dpr/licenselookup/default.asp
Drug Distributor, Wholesale #11 .... https://www.idfpr.com/dpr/licenselookup/default.asp
Early Childhood Teacher #28 .... https://secqa1.isbe.net/otis/
Engineer, Structural #11 .... https://www.idfpr.com/dpr/licenselookup/default.asp
Engineer/Engineer Intern #11 .... https://www.idfpr.com/dpr/licenselookup/default.asp
Environmental Health Practitioner #11 .... https://www.idfpr.com/dpr/licenselookup/default.asp
Esthetician #11 .... https://www.idfpr.com/dpr/licenselookup/default.asp
Euthanasia Tech #11 .... https://www.idfpr.com/dpr/licenselookup/default.asp
Firearms Trainer #11 .... https://www.idfpr.com/dpr/licenselookup/default.asp
Funeral Director/Embalmer #11 .... https://www.idfpr.com/dpr/licenselookup/default.asp
Gambling Addiction Counselor #21 .... www.iaodapca.org
Gaming/Gambling Supplier #20 .... www.igb.state.il.us/Pending/ILSUPPUBweb.pdf
Geologist #11 .... https://www.idfpr.com/dpr/licenselookup/default.asp
Go-kart track #5 .... www.state.il.us/agency/idol/Listings/Carnlist.htm
Home Health Aide (CNAs-ASHHA) #13 .... www.idph.state.il.us/nar/home.htm
Home Inspector #29 .... www.obrelookupclear.state.il.us/defaultRE.asp
Home Medical Equip Provider #11 .... https://www.idfpr.com/dpr/licenselookup/default.asp
Insurance Producer #4 .... http://neonwebh.cmcf.state.il.us:8080/ins/imsfor
Interior Designer #11 .... https://www.idfpr.com/dpr/licenselookup/default.asp
Landscape Architect #11 .... https://www.idfpr.com/dpr/licenselookup/default.asp
Lead Contractor #17 .... http://app.idph.state.il.us/Envhealth/Lead/LeadProfessionalListing.asp
Lead Risk Assessor/Insp./Supr. #17 .... http://app.idph.state.il.us/Envhealth/Lead/LeadProfessionalListing.asp
Lead Training Provider #17 .... http://app.idph.state.il.us/Envhealth/lead/LeadProfessionalListing.asp
Liquor License, Retail/Dist./Mfg. #25 .... http://www2.state.il.us/lcc/license_search.asp
Lobbyist #14 .... www.cyberdriveillinois.com/departments/index/lobbyist/home.html
Locksmith #11 .... https://www.idfpr.com/dpr/licenselookup/default.asp
Long Term Care Insurance Firm #4 .... http://neonwebh.cmcf.state.il.us:8080/ins/imsfor
Marriage & Family Therapist #11 .... https://www.idfpr.com/dpr/licenselookup/default.asp
Massage Therapist #11 .... https://www.idfpr.com/dpr/licenselookup/default.asp

Medical Corporation #11 .... https://www.idfpr.com/dpr/licenselookup/default.asp
Medical Doctor #11 .... https://www.idfpr.com/dpr/licenselookup/default.asp
Mental Health Counselor #21 .... www.iaodapca.org
Mortgage Banker/Broker #29 .... www.obrelookupclear.state.il.us/default.asp
Nail Technician #11 .... https://www.idfpr.com/dpr/licenselookup/default.asp
Naprapath #11 .... https://www.idfpr.com/dpr/licenselookup/default.asp
Notary Public #14 .... www.cyberdriveillinois.com/departments/index/notary/home.html
Nuclear Medicine Technologist #9 .... https://www.state.il.us/iema/dns.asp
Nurse, LPN, RN, APN #11 .... https://www.idfpr.com/dpr/licenselookup/default.asp
Nurses' Aide #13 .... www.idph.state.il.us/nar/home.htm
Nursing Home #12 .... https://www.idfpr.com/dpr/licenselookup/default.asp
Nursing Home Administrator #17 .... https://www.idfpr.com/DPR/licenselookup/default.asp
Occupational Aide #12 .... https://www.idfpr.com/dpr/licenselookup/default.asp
Occupational Therapist #11 .... https://www.idfpr.com/dpr/licenselookup/default.asp
Optometrist #11 .... https://www.idfpr.com/dpr/licenselookup/default.asp
Orthotist #11 .... https://www.idfpr.com/dpr/licenselookup/default.asp
Osteopathic Physician #11 .... https://www.idfpr.com/dpr/licenselookup/default.asp
Pawnbroker #29 .... www.obrelookupclear.state.il.us/default.asp
Pedorthist #11 .... https://www.idfpr.com/dpr/licenselookup/default.asp
Perfusionist #11 .... https://www.idfpr.com/dpr/licenselookup/default.asp
Pest Control Technician/Business #17 .... www.idph.state.il.us/
Pesticide Applicator #17 .... www.idph.state.il.us/
Pharmacist/Pharmacy #11 .... https://www.idfpr.com/dpr/licenselookup/default.asp
Physical Aide #12 .... https://www.idfpr.com/dpr/licenselookup/default.asp
Physical Therapist #11 .... https://www.idfpr.com/DPR/licenselookup/default.asp
Physician Assistant #11 .... https://www.idfpr.com/dpr/licenselookup/default.asp
Podiatrist #11 .... https://www.idfpr.com/dpr/licenselookup/default.asp
Police Trainer/Training Facility #19 .... www.ptb.state.il.us/allfacilities.asp
Polygraph/Deception Detect.Examin'r #11 https://www.idfpr.com/dpr/licenselookup/default.asp
Private Detective #11 .... https://www.idfpr.com/dpr/licenselookup/default.asp
Private Security Contractor #11 .... https://www.idfpr.com/dpr/licenselookup/default.asp
Psychologist #11 .... https://www.idfpr.com/dpr/licenselookup/default.asp
Psychology Business #11 .... https://www.idfpr.com/dpr/licenselookup/default.asp
Public Accountant-CPA #11 .... https://www.idfpr.com/dpr/licenselookup/default.asp
Radiation Therapist #9 .... https://www.state.il.us/iema/dns.asp
Radon Measurement Specialist #9 .... https://www.state.il.us/iema/radon/RadonCounty_Frames.asp
Real Estate Agent/Broker/Seller #29 .... www.obrelookupclear.state.il.us/defaultRE.asp
Real Estate Appraiser #29 .... www.obrelookupclear.state.il.us/defaultRE.asp
Rehabilitation Aide #12 .... https://www.idfpr.com/dpr/licenselookup/default.asp
Respiratory Care Practitioner #11 .... https://www.idfpr.com/dpr/licenselookup/default.asp
Roofer #11 .... https://www.idfpr.com/dpr/licenselookup/default.asp
Roofing Contractor #11 .... https://www.idfpr.com/dpr/licenselookup/default.asp
Savings & Loan Association #29 .... www.obrelookupclear.state.il.us/default.asp
Savings Bank #29 .... www.obrelookupclear.state.il.us/default.asp
Securities Salesperson/Dealer #16 .... www.finra.org/Investors/ToolsCalculators/BrokerCheck/index.htm
Security Force #11 .... https://www.idfpr.com/dpr/licenselookup/default.asp
Security Guard Firm/Agency #11 .... https://www.idfpr.com/dpr/licenselookup/default.asp
Sewage System Contractor #17 .... www.idph.state.il.us/
Shorthand Reporter #11 .... https://www.idfpr.com/dpr/licenselookup/default.asp
Ski Lift, Tram #5 .... www.state.il.us/agency/idol/Listings/Carnlist.htm
Social Worker #11 .... https://www.idfpr.com/dpr/licenselookup/default.asp
Special Teacher #28 .... https://secqa1.isbe.net/otis/
Speech-Language Pathologist #11 .... https://www.idfpr.com/dpr/licenselookup/default.asp
Stock Broker #16 .... www.finra.org/Investors/ToolsCalculators/BrokerCheck/index.htm
Substance Abuse Counselor #21 .... www.iaodapca.org
Substitute Teacher #28 .... https://secqa1.isbe.net/otis/
Surgical Technician #11 .... https://www.idfpr.com/dpr/licenselookup/default.asp
Surveyor, Land #11 .... https://www.idfpr.com/dpr/licenselookup/default.asp
Teacher #28 .... https://secqa1.isbe.net/otis/
Timber Buyer #3 .... www.dnr.state.il.us/law3/timber.htm
Timeshare #11 .... https://www.idfpr.com/dpr/licenselookup/default.asp
Timeshare/Land Sales #29 .... www.obrelookupclear.state.il.us/defaultRE.asp
Veterinarian #11 .... https://www.idfpr.com/dpr/licenselookup/default.asp
Water Well & Pump Install Contr. #17 .... www.idph.state.il.us/
Water Well Contractor/IDPH #17 .... www.idph.state.il.us/

Illinois Licensing Quick Finder

Accident Reconstructer #19 217-782-4540
Acupuncturist #11 217-785-0800
Alarm Contractor #11 217-785-0800
Alcohol Abuse Counselor #21 217-698-8110
Ambulance Service #13 217-785-2080
Amusement Attraction/Ride #5 217-782-9347
Animal Breeder #6 217-785-3423
Animal Health Tech, Racing #26 312-814-2600
Aquaculturist #6 217-785-3423
Architect #11 217-785-0800
Armed Security Agency/Agent #11 217-785-0800
Asbestos Contractor #17 217-782-3517
Athletic Trainer #11 217-785-0800
ATM Privately Owned #29 312-793-3000
Attorney #1 217-522-6838
Auctioneer #29 312-793-8704
Auctioneer, Vehicle #30 217-782-7817
Audiologist #11 217-785-0800
Automotive Parts Recycler #30 217-782-7817
Bank #29 312-793-3000
Barber #11 217-785-0800
Bilingual Teacher, Transitional #28 800-845-8749
Bingo Operation #18 217-785-5864
Blacksmith/Farrier/Horseshoer #26 312-814-2600
Blaster #7 217-782-4970
Boiler Inspector #10 217-782-2696
Boxing/Wrestling Event/Profess'n'l #11 217-785-0800
Breath Analyzer Operator #13 217-782-1571
Bull Ride #5 217-782-9347
Bungee Jump #5 217-782-9347
Business Broker #16 217-785-4932
Business Opportunity Offering #16 217-785-7371
Carnival #5 217-782-9347
Charitable Game #18 217-785-5864
Check Seller/Distributor #29 312-793-3000
Child Care Facility #2 217-785-2688
Chiropractor #11 217-785-0800
Classr'm Training Course, Basic #11 217-785-0800
Coal Mine Worker #8 217-782-6791
Collection Agency #11 217-785-0800
Controlled Substance Registrant #11 217-785-0800
Coroner (County) #19 217-782-4540
Corporate Fiduciary #29 312-793-3000
Correction Officer (County) #19 217-782-4540
Cosmetologist #11 217-785-0800
Counselor/Clinical Prof Counselor #11 217-785-0800
CPA- Public Accountant #11 217-785-0800
Criminal Electronic Surve'l Officer #19 217-782-4540
Cross-connect Control Device Insp.#24 217-782-1020
Day Care #2 217-785-2688
Dentist/Dental Hygienist #11 217-785-0800
Design Firm #11 217-785-0800
Dietitian/Nutrition Counselor #11 217-785-0800
Distrib. System Operator, Public #24 217-782-9720
Doctor/Physician #11 217-785-0800
Driving Instructor #7 847-437-3953
Drug Distributor, Wholesale #11 217-785-0800
Early Childhood Teacher #28 800-845-8749
Emergency Medical Technician #13 217-785-2080
Employee Leasing Company #4 217-782-6366
Employment Agency #23 312-793-2810
Engineer, Structural #11 217-785-0800
Engineer/Engineer Intern #11 217-785-0800
Environmental Health Practitioner #11 217-785-0800
Esthetician #11 217-785-0800
Euthanasia Tech #11 217-785-0800
Explosive Magazine Storage #8 217-782-9976
Explosive, General Use #8 217-782-9976
Firearms Regulation (Firearm Owner) #27 217-782-7980
Firearms Trainer #11 217-785-0800
Fish Dealer #6 217-785-3423
Fisherman, Commercial #6 217-785-3423
Food Process'ng Plant/Warehouse #13 217-785-2439
Food Service Sanitation Manager #13 217-785-2439
Funeral Director/Embalmer #11 217-785-0800
Fur Buyer/Tanner/Dyer #6 217-785-3423
Gambling Addiction Counselor #21 217-698-8110
Gambling Employee #20 312-814-4702
Gaming/Gambling Supplier #20 312-814-4702
Geologist #11 217-785-0800
Go-kart track #5 217-782-9347
Hearing Instrument Dispenser #15 217-782-4733
Hearing Screening Technician #15 217-782-4733
HMO/PPA #4 217-782-6366
Home Health Aide-CNAs-ASHHA #13 2170785-5133
Home Health Care Agency #13 217-782-7412
Home Inspector #29 217-782-3000
Home Medical Equip Provider #11 217-785-0800
Hospital #13 217-782-7412
Hunting Area Operator #6 217-785-3423
Industrial Radiographer #9 217-785-9913
Insurance Producer #4 217-782-6366
Interior Designer #11 217-785-0800
Intertrack Employee/Totalizator Oper. #26 312-814-2600
Investment Adviser #16 217-785-4938
Investment Adviser Repr's't #16 217-557-4609
Jockey/Apprentice/Jockey Agent #26 312-814-2600
Laboratory Analysis Technician #13 217-785-8820
Land Sale #11 217-785-0800
Landfill Chief Operator #24 217-782-9877
Landscape Architect #11 217-785-0800
Law Enforcement Officer #19 217-782-4540
Lead Contractor #17 217-782-3517
Lead Risk Assessor/Insp./Supr. #17 217-782-3517
Lead Training Provider #17 217-782-3517
Liquor License, Retail/Dist./Mfg. #25 312-814-3930
Loan Broker #16 217-785-4932
Lobbyist #14 217-782-7017
Locksmith #11 217-785-0800
Long Term Care Insurance Firm #4 217-782-6366
Marriage & Family Therapist #11 217-785-0800
Massage Therapist #11 217-785-0800
Medical Corporation #11 217-785-0800
Medical Doctor #11 217-785-0800
Mental Health Counselor #21 217-698-8110
Mine Engineer/Foreman #8 217-782-6791
Mine Rescue Supvr/Assist #8 217-782-6791
Mine Supervisor #8 217-782-6791
Mortgage Banker/Broker #29 217-793-1409
Motor Vehicle Dealer, New #30 217-782-7817
Nail Technician #11 217-785-0800
Naprapath #11 217-785-0800
Notary Public #14 217-782-0705
Nuclear Medicine Technologist #9 217-785-9913
Nurse, LPN, RN, APN #11 217-785-0800
Nurses' Aide #13 217-785-5133
Nursing Agency #23 312-793-1817
Nursing Home #12 217-782-1200
Nursing Home Administrator #17 217-782-0514
Occupational Aide #12 217-782-1200
Occupational Therapist #11 217-785-0800
Optometrist #11 217-785-0800
Orthotist #11 217-785-0800
Osteopathic Physician #11 217-785-0800
Pari-Mutuel Employee #26 312-814-2600
Pawnbroker #29 312-793-3000
Pedorthist #11 217-785-0800
Perfusionist #11 217-785-0800
Pest Control Technician/Business #17 217-782-4674
Pesticide Applicator #17 217-782-5830
Pharmacist/Pharmacy #11 217-785-0800
Physical Aide #12 217-782-1200
Physical Therapist #11 217-785-0800
Physician Assistant #11 217-785-0800
Plumber #17 217-782-4977
Plumber Apprentice #13 217-785-1153
Podiatrist #11 217-785-0800
Police Trainer/Training Facility #19 217-782-4540
Polygraph/Deception Detection Examiner #11 217-785-0800
Pony Person/Exercise Person/Groom #26 312-814-2600
Private Detective #11 217-785-0800
Private Security Contractor #11 217-785-0800
Psychologist #11 217-785-0800
Psychology Business #11 217-785-0800
Public Accountant-CPA #11 217-785-0800
Pull Tab Operator #18 217-785-5864
Racetrack #26 312-814-2600
Racetrack Authorized Agent #26 312-814-2600
Racetrack Driver #26 312-814-2600
Racetrack Owner #26 312-814-2600
Racetrack Trainer/Driver #26 312-814-2600
Racetrack Vendor/Vendor Helper #26 312-814-2600
Racing Stabling Facility, Off Track #26 312-814-2600
Radiation Therapist #9 217-785-9913
Radon Measurement Specialist #9 217-782-1325
Real Estate Agent/Broker/Seller #29 312-793-8704
Real Estate Appraiser #29 312-793-8704
Rehabilitation Aide #12 217-782-1200
Respiratory Care Practitioner #11 217-785-0800
Restaurant & Retail Food Store #17 217-785-2439
Riverboat Employee #20 312-814-4702
Roofer #11 217-785-0800
Roofing Contractor #11 217-785-0800
Salvage Firm #13 217-785-2439
Savings & Loan Association #29 217-782-9043
Savings Bank #29 217-782-9043
School Business Official #28 800-845-8749
School Guidance Counselor #28 800-845-8749
School Media Specialist/Librarian #28 800-845-8749
School Nurse #28 800-845-8749
School Principal/Super./Admin. #28 800-845-8749
School Psychologist #28 800-845-8749
Scrap Processor #30 217-782-7817
Securities Salesperson/Dealer #16 217-785-4933
Security Force #11 217-785-0800
Security Guard Firm/Agency #11 217-785-0800
Sewage System Contractor #17 217-782-5830
Sheriff Law Enforcement Officer #19 217-782-4540
Shorthand Reporter #11 217-785-0800
Ski Lift, Tram #5 217-782-9347
Social Worker #11 217-785-0800
Special Teacher #28 800-845-8749
Speech-Language Pathologist #11 217-785-0800
Stock Broker #16 217-785-4950
Substance Abuse Counselor #21 217-698-8110
Substitute Teacher #28 800-845-8749
Surgical Technician #11 217-785-0800
Surveyor, Land #11 217-785-0800
Tanning Facility #17 217-785-2439
Taxidermist #6 217-785-3423
Teacher #28 800-845-8749
Timber Buyer #3 217-782-6431
Timeshare #11 217-785-0800
Timeshare/Land Sales #29 312-793-8704
Totalizator Oper./Intertrack Employee #26 312-814-2600
Trust Company #29 312-793-3000
Underground Shot Firer #8 217-782-6791
Used Vehicle Dealer #30 217-782-7817
Vehicle Rebuilder/Repair #30 217-782-7817
Veterinarian #11 217-785-0800
Veterinarian/Vet Assistant, Racing #26 312-814-2600
Vision Screening Technician #15 217-782-4733
Waste Water Plant Operator #24 217-782-9720
Water Supply Operator #24 217-782-9720
Water Well & Pump Install Contr. #17 217-782-5830
Water Well Contractor/IDPH #17 217-782-5830
Weighing/Measure Serviceman #22 217-785-8301

Illinois Licensing Agency Information

#1 Attorney Registration & Disciplinary Commission of Supreme Court of IL, 1 N Old Capitol Plaza, #333, Springfield, IL 62701; 217-522-6838, Fax- 217-522-2417. www.iardc.org Search data at- www.iardc.org/lawyersearch.asp

#2 Department of Children & Family Services, 406 E Monroe St, Springfield, IL 62701; 217-785-2509, Fax- 217-785-1052. www.state.il.us/dcfs/index.shtml

#3 Department of Natural Resources, Division of Forest Services, 1 Natural Resources Way, Springfield, IL 62702; 217-782-6431, Fax- 217-785-8405. www.dnr.state.il.us/law3/timber.htm

#4 Department of Insurance, 320 W Washington St, Springfield, IL 62767-0001; 217-782-4515, Fax- 217-782-5020. www.ins.state.il.us

#5 Department of Labor, Carnival & Amusement Ride Safety Division, 1 West Old State Capitol Plaza, #300, Springfield, IL 62701; 217-782-9347, Fax- 217-782-0596. www.state.il.us/agency/idol/ Search data at- www.state.il.us/agency/idol/Listings/Carnlist.htm

#6 Department of Natural Resources, Commercial Permits, One Natural Resources Way, Springfield, IL 62702-1271; 217-785-3423, Fax- 217-782-5016. Hours- 8:30AM-4:30PM. http://dnr.state.il.us

#7 Secretary of State, Commercial Driver Training, 650 Roppolo Dr, Elk Grove, IL 60007; 847-437-3953, Fax- 847-437-3911. www.cyberdriveillinois.com

#8 Department of Natural Resources, Office of Mine & Minerals, One Natural Resources Way, Springfield, IL 62702-1271; 217-782-6791, Fax- 217-524-4819. Hours- 8AM-4:30PM. http://dnr.state.il.us/mines/

#9 Emergency Management Agency, 2200 S Dirksen Pky, Springfield, IL 62703; 217-782-2700, Fax- 217-785-9962. www.state.il.us/iema/

#10 State Fire Marshall, 1035 Stevenson Dr, Springfield, IL 62703; 217-782-2696, Fax- 217-782-1062. www.state.il.us/osfm/

#11 Department of Professional Regulation, Professions/Occupations/Entities, 320 W Washington, 3rd Fl, Springfield, IL 62786; 217-785-0800, Fax- 217-782-7645. www.idfpr.com Search data at- https://www.idfpr.com/dpr/licenselookup/default.asp

#12 Healthcare and Family Services, Bureau of Long-Term Care, 201 S Grand Ave E, Springfield, IL 62763-0001; 217-782-1200, Fax- 217-524-7114. www.dpaillinois.com Search data at- https://www.idfpr.com/dpr/licenselookup/default.asp

#13 Department of Public Health, Education & Training Section, 525 W Jefferson St, 4th Fl, Springfield, IL 62761; 217-782-4977, Fax- 217-782-3987. www.idph.state.il.us

#14 Secretary of State, Index Dept., 111 E Monroe St, Springfield, IL 62756; 217-782-7017, Fax- 217-524-0930. www.cyberdriveillinois.com/departments/index/

#15 Department of Public Health, Division of Health Assessment & Screening, 500 E Monroe, 1st Fl, Springfield, IL 62701; 217-782-4733, Fax- 217-557-5324. www.idph.state.il.us

#16 Secretary of State, Securities Department, 300 W Jefferson St, Suite 300A, Springfield, IL 62702; 217-782-2256, Fax- 217-782-8876. Hours- 8AM-4:30PM. www.cyberdriveillinois.com/departments/securities/ Search data at- www.finra.org/Investors/ToolsCalculators/BrokerCheck/index.htm

#17 Department of Public Health, Environmental Health, 535 W Jefferson St, 3rd Fl, Springfield, IL 62761; 217-782-5830, Fax- 217-785-0253. www.idph.state.il.us/envhealth/ehhome.htm

#18 Department of Revenue, Bingo Division, 101 W Jefferson St, Springfield, IL 62702; 217-524-4164, Fax- 217-557-4398. 8AM-5PM. www.iltax.com/CharityGaming/index.htm

#19 Law Enforcement & Standards Training Board, 600 S 2nd St, #300, Springfield, IL 62704; 217-782-4540, Fax- 217-524-5350. Hours- 8:30AM-5PM. www.ptb.state.il.us

#20 Gaming Board, 160 N LaSalle #300, Chicago, IL 60601; 312-814-4700, Fax- 312-814-4602. www.igb.state.il.us

#21 Counselor Certification Department, IAODAPCA, 401 E Sangamon Ave, Springfield, IL 62702; 217-698-8110, Fax- 217-698-8234. www.iaodapca.org

#22 Department of Agriculture, State Fairgrounds, PO Box 19281, Springfield, IL 62794-9281; 217-785-8301, Fax- 217-524-7801. www.agr.state.il.us

#23 Department of Labor, State of Illinois Bldg, 160 N LaSalle, #C1300, Chicago, IL 60601; 312-793-2810, Fax- 312-793-5257. Hours- 8:30AM-5PM. www.state.il.us/agency/idol/index.htm

#24 Environmental Protection Agency, PO Box 19276 (1021 N Grand Ave E), Springfield, IL 62794-9276; 217-782-3397, Fax- 217-782-0075. www.epa.state.il.us/water/

#25 Freedom of Information Compliance Officer, Liquor Control Commission, 100 W Randolph, #7-801, Chicago, IL 60601; 312-814-2206, Fax- 312-814-2241. www.state.il.us/lcc/ Search data at- http://www2.state.il.us/lcc/license_search.asp

#26 Racing Board, 100 W Randolph, #11-100, Chicago, IL 60601; 312-814-2600, Fax- 312-814-5062. Hours- 8:30AM-5PM. www.state.il.us/agency/irb/ Racetracks: Arlington Park (847-255-4300); Balmoral Park (708-672-7544); Fairmount Park (618-345-4300); Hawthorne RaceCourse (708-780-3700) & Maywood Park (708-343-4800).

#27 State Police, FOID, 100 Iles Park Pl, Springfield, IL 62708; 217-782-7980, Fax- 217-782-9139. www.isp.state.il.us/foid/firearms.cfm

#28 Division of Professional Certification, Board of Education, 100 N 1st St, Springfield, IL 62777; 866-262-6663, 217 782-4321, Fax- 217-524-4928. www.isbe.net/certification/ Search data at- https://secqa1.isbe.net/otis/

#29 Office of Banks & Real Estate, Bureaus of Res. Finance; Banks & Trusts; Real Estate Professions, 500 E Monroe, Springfield, IL 62701-1509; 217-782-3000, Fax- 217-558-4297. www.obre.state.il.us/AGENCY/licenseinfo.htm Search data at- www.obrelookupclear.state.il.us/default.asp

#30 Secretary of State, Vehicle Services, Dealers/Remitters, 501 S 2nd St, Rm 069, Springfield, IL 62756; 217-782-7817, Fax- 217-524-0120. www.sos.state.il.us

Illinois Federal Courts

The following list indicates the district and division name for each county in the state. If the bankruptcy court location is different from the district court, then the location of the bankruptcy court appears in parentheses.

County/Court Cross Reference

County	District	Division
Adams	Central	Springfield
Alexander	Southern	Benton
Bond	Southern	East St Louis
Boone	Northern	Rockford
Brown	Central	Springfield
Bureau	Central	Peoria
Calhoun	Southern	East St Louis
Carroll	Northern	Rockford
Cass	Central	Springfield
Champaign	Central	Danville/Urbana (Danville)
Christian	Central	Springfield
Clark	Southern	Benton (East St Louis)
Clay	Southern	Benton (East St Louis)
Clinton	Southern	East St Louis
Coles	Central	Danville/Urbana (Danville)
Cook	Northern	Chicago (Eastern)
Crawford	Southern	Benton (East St Louis)
Cumberland	Southern	Benton
De Kalb	Northern	Rockford
De Witt	Central	Springfield
Douglas	Central	Danville/Urbana (Danville)
Du Page	Northern	Chicago (Eastern)
Edgar	Central	Danville/Urbana (Danville)
Edwards	Southern	Benton
Effingham	Southern	Benton (East St Louis)
Fayette	Southern	East St Louis
Ford	Central	Danville/Urbana (Danville)
Franklin	Southern	Benton
Fulton	Central	Peoria
Gallatin	Southern	Benton
Greene	Central	Springfield
Grundy	Northern	Chicago (Eastern)
Hamilton	Southern	Benton
Hancock	Central	Peoria
Hardin	Southern	Benton
Henderson	Central	Rock Island (Peoria)
Henry	Central	Rock Island (Peoria)
Iroquois	Central	Danville/Urbana (Danville)
Jackson	Southern	Benton
Jasper	Southern	Benton (East St Louis)
Jefferson	Southern	Benton
Jersey	Southern	East St Louis
Jo Daviess	Northern	Rockford
Johnson	Southern	Benton
Kane	Northern	Chicago (Eastern)
Kankakee	Central	Danville/Urbana (Danville)
Kendall	Northern	Chicago (Eastern)
Knox	Central	Peoria
La Salle	Northern	Chicago (Eastern)
Lake	Northern	Chicago (Eastern)
Lawrence	Southern	Benton (East St Louis)
Lee	Northern	Rockford
Livingston	Central	Peoria (Danville)
Logan	Central	Springfield
Macon	Central	Danville/Urbana (Sprngfld)
Macoupin	Central	Springfield
Madison	Southern	East St Louis
Marion	Southern	East St Louis
Marshall	Central	Peoria
Mason	Central	Springfield
Massac	Southern	Benton
McDonough	Central	Peoria
McHenry	Northern	Rockford
McLean	Central	Peoria (Springfield)
Menard	Central	Springfield
Mercer	Central	Rock Island (Peoria)
Monroe	Southern	East St Louis
Montgomery	Central	Springfield
Morgan	Central	Springfield
Moultrie	Central	Danville/Urbana (Danville)
Ogle	Northern	Rockford
Peoria	Central	Peoria
Perry	Southern	Benton
Piatt	Central	Danville/Urbana (Danville)
Pike	Central	Springfield
Pope	Southern	Benton
Pulaski	Southern	Benton
Putnam	Central	Peoria
Randolph	Southern	East St Louis
Richland	Southern	Benton (East St Louis)
Rock Island	Central	Rock Island (Peoria)
Saline	Southern	Benton
Sangamon	Central	Springfield
Schuyler	Central	Springfield
Scott	Central	Springfield
Shelby	Central	Springfield
St. Clair	Southern	East St Louis
Stark	Central	Peoria
Stephenson	Northern	Rockford
Tazewell	Central	Peoria
Union	Southern	Benton
Vermilion	Central	Danville/Urbana (Danville)
Wabash	Southern	Benton
Warren	Central	Rock Island (Peoria)
Washington	Southern	East St Louis (Benton)
Wayne	Southern	Benton
White	Southern	Benton
Whiteside	Northern	Rockford
Will	Northern	Chicago (Eastern)
Williamson	Southern	Benton
Winnebago	Northern	Rockford
Woodford	Central	Peoria

Standards for Federal Courts: Fees are standard unless noted in profile. Search fee is $26.00 per item (one party name or case number). Copy fee is $.50 per page. Certification fee is $9.00 per document, double for exemplification, if available. Most courts require prepayment. Mail requests should enclose a SASE unless otherwise noted. Before releasing records, all courts require prepayment, unless noted.

District courts index by defendant and plaintiff and by case number. Bankruptcy courts usually index by debtor and case number. While most courts now have their indexes on computer, many may still maintain index card files as well. Courts will archive closed case files at different times.

There are numerous public access programs available to online subscribers. Search the U.S. Party/Case Index to find party names and case numbers among all courts. Individual case data is provided on PACER. A search of CM/ECF provides copies of cases filed electronically. For details about PACER, the US Party/Case Index, and CM/ECF see the Appendix or go to http://pacer.psc.uscourts.gov or call 800-676-6856.

US District Court Illinois Central District

Peoria Division US District Clerk Office, 309 Federal Bldg, 100 NE Monroe St, Peoria, IL 61602, 309-671-7117; Fax- 309-671-7120. Hours-8AM-5PM. www.ilcd.uscourts.gov

Counties/Note: Bureau, Fulton, Hancock, Knox, Livingston, McDonough, McLean, Marshall, Peoria, Putnam, Stark, Tazewell, Woodford.

Searches/Indexing: Search request requires name only. Results do not include SSN or DOB. Will not fax back documents. New cases are in the index immediately after filing date. Both computer and card indexes maintained; computer back to 1992. District-wide searches available for civil cases from 11/1989; criminal from 4/1992. Case files sent to archives 5-7 years after closed.

Search Access: Only docket info available by phone. **Mail:** Search usually completed- 1 week. Include SASE for return. **In person:** 1 public terminal available. No self-serve copier.

Payment: Pay by Visa/MC, money order, cashier's check, law firm check. No personal checks. Payee: Clerk, US District Court.

E-Services: PACER records go back to 1995. New records online after 1 day. ECF at https://ecf.ilcd.uscourts.gov. **Opinions Online:** www.ilcd.uscourts.gov/orders&opinions.htm.

Rock Island Division US District Clerk Office, 40 US Court House, 211 19th St, Rock Island, IL 61201, 309-793-5778; Fax- 309-793-5878. Hours-8AM-5PM. www.ilcd.uscourts.gov

Counties/Note: Henderson, Henry, Mercer, Rock Island, Warren.

Searches/Indexing: Search request requires name only. Results do not include SSN or DOB. Will not fax back documents. New cases are in the index immediately after filing date. Both computer and card indexes maintained; civil computer index goes back to 1989, criminal to 1992. District-wide searches available for civil cases from 11/1989; criminal from 4/1992. Case files sent to archives 5 years after closed.

Search Access: All info not sealed is available via phone. **Mail:** Search usually completed- 1-2 days. Include SASE for return. **In person:** 1 public terminal available. No self-serve copier.

Payment: Pay by Visa/MC, money order, cashier's check, business check. No personal checks. Payee: Clerk of US District Court.

E-Services: PACER records go back to 1995. New records online after 1 day. ECF at https://ecf.ilcd.uscourts.gov. **Opinions Online:** www.ilcd.uscourts.gov/orders&opinions.htm.

Springfield Division Clerk of Court, 151 US Courthouse, 600 E Monroe, Springfield, IL 62701, 217-492-4020; Fax- 217-492-4028. 8AM-5PM. www.ilcd.uscourts.gov

Counties/Note: Adams, Brown, Cass, Christian, De Witt, Greene, Logan, Macoupin, Mason, Menard, Montgomery, Morgan, Pike, Sangamon, Schuyler, Scott, Shelby.

Searches/Indexing: Search request requires name only. Results do not include SSN or DOB. Will not fax back documents. New cases are in the index immediately after filing date. Both computer and card indexes maintained; civil on computer back to 1988; criminal to 1992. District-wide searches available for civil cases from 11/1989; criminal from 4/1992. Case files sent to archives 5-7 years after closed.

Search Access: Only docket info available by phone. **Mail:** Search usually completed- 1 week. Include SASE for return. **In person:** 1 public terminal available. Self-serve copier available.

Payment: Pay by Visa/MC, money order, cashier's check, business check. No personal checks. Payee: US District Court Clerk.

E-Services: PACER records go back to 1995. ECF at https://ecf.ilcd.uscourts.gov. **Opinions Online:** www.ilcd.uscourts.gov/orders&opinions.htm.

Urbana Division Court Clerk, 218 US Courthouse, 201 S Vine St, Urbana, IL 61802, 217-373-5830; Fax- 217-373-5834. 8AM-5PM. www.ilcd.uscourts.gov

Counties/Note: Champaign, Coles, Douglas, Edgar, Ford, Iroquois, Kankakee, Macon, Moultrie, Piatt, Vermilion.

Searches/Indexing: Search request requires name only. Results do not include SSN or DOB. Will not fax back documents. New cases are in the index immediately after filing date. Both computer and card indexes maintained; computer index goes back to 1989. District-wide searches available for civil cases from 11/1989; criminal from 4/1992. Case files sent to archives 5-7 years after closed.

Search Access: Only docket info available by phone. **Mail:** Search usually completed- 1 week. Include SASE for return. **In person:** 1 public terminal available. No self-serve copier.

Payment: Pay by Visa/MC/AmEx, money order, cashier's check. No personal checks. Payee: Clerk, US District Court. Copy fee is $.50 per page if case is prior to 9/2004.

E-Services: PACER records go back to 1995. New records online after 1 day. ECF at https://ecf.ilcd.uscourts.gov. **Opinions Online:** www.ilcd.uscourts.gov/orders&opinions.htm.

US Bankruptcy Court Illinois Central District

Danville Division Court Clerk, 201 N Vermilion #130, Danville, IL 61832-4733, 217-431-4820; Fax- 217-431-2694. 7:30AM-4:30PM. www.ilcb.uscourts.gov

Counties/Note: Champaign, Coles, Douglas, Edgar, Ford, Iroquois, Kankakee, Livingston, Moultrie, Piatt, Vermilion.

Searches/Indexing: Include address and last 4 SSN digits in search request. Results do not include SSN or DOB. Rarely will fax back docs; fee applies. New cases are in the index 24 hours after filing date. After 4/12/04 all records on computer only. No paper files available.

Search Access: Docket info available via phone. Voice Case Information Service available, call VCIS at 800-827-9005 or 217-492-4550. **Mail:** Search usually completed- 1-2 days. Include SASE for return. **In person:** 2 public terminals available. Computer generated copies $.10 each.

Payment: Pay by money order, cashier's check, business check. No personal checks or credit cards. Payee: US Bankruptcy Court.

E-Services: PACER-http://pacer.ilcb.uscourts.gov for pre-2004 cases. PACER records go back to 1989-90. New records online after 1 day. ECF at www.ilcb.uscourts.gov/CMECF/cmecf.htm.

Opinions: www.ilcb.uscourts.gov/Opinions/opinions.asp. **Note:** Hearing calendars on ECF system.

Peoria Div. Court Clerk, 100 NE Monroe, Rm 216, Peoria, IL 61602, 309-671-7035; Fax- 309-671-7076. 8AM-5PM. www.ilcb.uscourts.gov

Counties/Note: Bureau, Fulton, Hancock, Henderson, Henry, Knox, Marshall, McDonough, Mercer, Peoria, Putnam, Rock Island, Stark, Tazewell, Warren, Woodford.

Searches/Indexing: Include address and last 4 SSN digits in search request. Results do not include SSN or DOB. Will not fax back documents. New cases are in the index 24 hours after filing date. After 4/12/04 all records on computer only. All cases available electronically.

Search Access: Docket info available via phone. Voice Case Information Service available, call VCIS at 800-827-9005 or 217-492-4550. **Mail:** Search usually completed- 1-2 days. Include SASE for return. **In person:** 2 public terminals available. No self-serve copier.

Payment: Pay by money order, cashier's check, business check. No personal checks or credit cards. Payee: US Bankruptcy Court. Will invoice for copy fees only.

E-Services: PACER-http://pacer.ilcb.uscourts.gov for pre-2004 cases. PACER records go back to 1989-90. New records online after 1 day. ECF at www.ilcb.uscourts.gov/CMECF/cmecf.htm.

Opinions Online: www.ilcb.uscourts.gov/Opinions/opinions.asp. **Online Note:** Hearing calendars on ECF system.

Springfield Division Court Clerk, 226 US Courthouse, 600 E Monroe St, 2nd Fl, Springfield, IL 62701, 217-492-4551; Fax- 217-492-4556. Hours-8AM-5PM. www.ilcb.uscourts.gov

Counties/Note: Adams, Brown, Cass, Christian, De Witt, Greene, Logan, Macon, Macoupin, Mason, McLean, Menard, Montgomery, Morgan, Pike, Sangamon, Schuyler, Scott, Shelby.

Searches/Indexing: Include address and last 4 SSN digits in search request. Results do not include SSN or DOB. Will not fax back documents. New cases are in the index 24 hours after filing date. After 4/12/04 all records on computer only. All cases available electronically.

Search Access: Docket info available via phone. Voice Case Information Service available, call VCIS at 800-827-9005 or 217-492-4550. **Mail:** Search usually completed- 2-3 days. Include SASE for return. **In person:** 3 public terminals available. No self-serve copier.

Payment: Pay by money order, cashier's check, business check. No personal checks or credit cards. Payee: US Bankruptcy Court. Will invoice for copy fees only.

E-Services: PACER-http://pacer.ilcb.uscourts.gov for pre-2004 cases. PACER records go back to 1989-90. New records online after 1 day. ECF at www.ilcb.uscourts.gov/CMECF/cmecf.htm. **Opinions Online:** www.ilcb.uscourts.gov/Opinions/opinions.asp. **Online Note:** Hearing calendars on ECF system.

US District Court Illinois Northern District

Chicago (Eastern) Division Court Clerk, 20th Fl, 219 S Dearborn St, Chicago, IL 60604, 312-435-5670/5691/5698; records- 312-435-5863; Fax- 312-554-8675. 8:30AM-4:30PM; phone inquires 8:30AM-5PM. www.ilnd.uscourts.gov

Counties/Note: Cook, Du Page, Grundy, Kane, Kendall, Lake, La Salle, Will. District wide searches available from this location.

Searches/Indexing: Search request requires name only. Results do not include SSN or DOB. May fax back docs $.50 per page and will fax invoices for search and fees, which are later mailed after payment. New cases are in the index 2 days after filing date. Computer index back to mid-1980s maintained. Most documents filed after 1/15/2005 are maintained electronically only. Case files sent to archives 1-5 years after closed.

Search Access: Only docket info available by phone. Phone inquiries should be made from 8:15AM-5PM. **Mail:** Search usually completed- 2 days. Include SASE for return. **Fax:** Fax search requests accepted. **In person:** 15-20 public terminals available. Self-serve copier- $.25 per pg.

Payment: Pay by Visa/MC (in person only), money order, cashier's or personal check. Payee: Clerk, US District Court.

E-Services: PACER records go back to 1988. New records online after 1 day. ECF at https://ecf.ilnd.uscourts.gov. **Opinions Online:** www.ilnd.uscourts.gov/RACER2/index.html. **Note:** Online ruling data at www.nysd.uscourts.gov/courtweb/public.htm. Daily calendar at www.ilnd.uscourts.gov/DAILYCAL/eventskd.htm.

Rockford (Western) Division Court Clerk, 211 S Court St, Rm 211, Rockford, IL 61101, 815-987-4354/4355; Fax- 815-987-4291. Hours- 8:30AM-4:30PM; phone inquires 8:15AM-5PM. www.ilnd.uscourts.gov

Counties/Note: Boone, Carroll, De Kalb, Jo Daviess, Lee, McHenry, Ogle, Stephenson, Whiteside, Winnebago. District wide searches available from this location.

Searches/Indexing: Search request requires name only. Results do not include SSN or DOB. Will fax back documents for $.50 per page. New cases are in the index 2 days after filing date. Computer index back to mid-1980s maintained. Most documents filed after 1/15/2005 are maintained electronically only. Case files sent to archives 1-5 years after closed.

Search Access: Only docket info available by phone. Phone inquiries should be made from 8:15AM-5PM. **Mail:** Search usually completed- 1-2 days. SASE not required. **Fax:** Fax search requests accepted. **In person:** 1 public terminal available. No self-serve copier.

Payment: Pay by money order, cashier's or personal check. Payee: Clerk, US District Court.

E-Services: PACER records go back to 1988. New records online after 1 day. ECF at https://ecf.ilnd.uscourts.gov. **Opinions Online:** www.ilnd.uscourts.gov/RACER2/index.html. **Note:** Online ruling data at www.nysd.uscourts.gov/courtweb/public.htm. Daily calendar at www.ilnd.uscourts.gov/DAILYCAL/eventskd.htm

US Bankruptcy Court Illinois Northern District

Chicago (Eastern) Division Court Clerk, 219 S Dearborn St, Chicago, IL 60604-1802, 312-435-5694; records- 312-435-5862; Fax- 312-408-7750. 9AM-4:30PM. www.ilnb.uscourts.gov

Counties/Note: Cook, Du Page, Grundy, Kane, Kendall, La Salle, Lake, Will. Chicago Division also has branch courts in Geneva, Joliet, Park City, and Wheaton.

Searches/Indexing: Include name and address or SSN in search request. Results include last 4 SSN digits. Will not fax back documents. New cases are in the index immediately after filing date. Computer index back to 1994 maintained.

Search Access: Limited search; if case number is provided by phone, any docket sheet data is released via phone Voice Case Information Service available, call VCIS at 888-232-6814 or 312-408-5089. **Mail:** Search usually completed- 1 week. Include SASE for return. **In person:** 6 public terminals available. Self-serve copier available. Court can recommend an outside vendor to make copies.

Payment: Pay by credit cards, money order, cashier's check, attorney/business check. No debtor checks/credit cards accepted. Payee: Clerk, US Bankruptcy Court.

E-Services: Access to PACER/RACER is available at the website. Document images available. PACER records go back to 7/1993. New records online after 1 day. ECF at https://ecf.ilnb.uscourts.gov. Case Image Viewing available; access fee $.08 per page. MegaCase info link at main website. **Online Note:** Judges calendars at www.ilnb.uscourts.gov/Judgess.htm.

Rockford (Western) Division Court Clerk, Rm 110, 211 S Court St, Rockford, IL 61101, 815-987-4350; Fax- 815-987-4205. 9AM-4:30PM. www.ilnb.uscourts.gov

Counties/Note: Boone, Carroll, De Kalb, Jo Daviess, Lee, McHenry, Ogle, Stephenson, Whiteside, Winnebago. Rockford Division also has a branch court in Sterling.

Searches/Indexing: Include name and address or SSN in search request. Results include last 4 SSN digits. Will not fax back documents. New cases are in the index immediately after filing date. Computer index back to 1994 maintained.

Search Access: Only docket info is available by phone. Voice Case Information Service available, call VCIS at 888-232-6814 or 312-408-5089. **Mail:** Search usually completed- 10 days. Include SASE for return. **In person:** 2 public access terminals available. No self-serve copier.

Payment: Pay by credit cards, money order, cashier's check, attorney/business check. No debtor checks/credit cards accepted. Payee: Clerk, US Bankruptcy Court.

E-Services: Access to PACER/RACER is available at the website. Document images available. PACER records go back to 1992. New records online after 1 day. ECF at https://ecf.ilnb.uscourts.gov. Case Image Viewing available; access fee $.08 per page. MegaCase info link at main website. **Online Note:** Judges calendars at www.ilnb.uscourts.gov/Judgess.htm.

US District Court Illinois Southern District

Benton Division Court Clerk, 301 W Main St, Benton, IL 62812, 618-439-7760. 9AM-4:30PM. www.ilsd.uscourts.gov

Counties/Note: Alexander, Clark, Clay, Crawford, Cumberland, Edwards, Effingham, Franklin, Gallatin, Hamilton, Hardin, Jackson, Jasper, Jefferson, Johnson, Lawrence, Massac, Perry, Pope, Pulaski, Richland, Saline, Union, Wabash, Wayne, White, Williamson. Cases may also be allocated to the East St Louis Division.

Searches/Indexing: Name and date required to search for records. Results do not include SSN or DOB. New cases are in the index immediately after filing date. Computer, microfiche and card indexes maintained, full computer records back to 2003; incomplete back to 1990. Case files sent to archives as deemed necessary.

Search Access: Docket info available via phone. **Mail:** Search usually completed- 2 days. Include SASE for return. **In person:** 1 public terminal available. Self-serve copies $.50 each.

Payment: Pay by Visa/MC, money order, cashier's or personal check. Payee: Clerk, US District Court. Except in an emergency, prepayment required. **E-Services:** PACER records go back to 1985. New records online after 1 day. ECF at https://ecf.ilsd.uscourts.gov. **Opinions Online:** www.ilsd.uscourts.gov/opinions.cfm.

East St Louis Division Court Clerk, 750 Missouri Ave, East St Louis, IL 62201, 618-482-9371. 9AM-4:30PM. www.ilsd.uscourts.gov

Counties/Note: Bond, Calhoun, Clinton, Fayette, Jersey, Madison, Marion, Monroe, Randolph, St. Clair, Washington. Cases for these counties may also be allocated to the Benton Division.

Searches/Indexing: Name and date required to search for records. Results do not include SSN or DOB. New cases are in the index immediately after filing date. Computer, microfiche and card indexes maintained, full computer records back to 2003; incomplete back to 1990. Case files sent to archives as deemed necessary.

Search Access: Docket info available via phone. **Mail:** Search usually completed- 2 days. Include SASE for return. **In person:** 1 public terminal available. No self-serve copier.

Payment: Pay by Visa/MC, money order, cashier's or personal check. Payee: Clerk, US District Court. Except in an emergency,

E-Services: PACER records go back to 1985. New records online after 1 day. ECF at https://ecf.ilsd.uscourts.gov. **Opinions Online:** www.ilsd.uscourts.gov/opinions.cfm.

US Bankruptcy Court Illinois Southern District

Benton Div. Court Clerk, Federal Courthouse, 301 W Main, Benton, IL 62812, 618-435-2200. Hours-8AM-4:30PM. www.ilsb.uscourts.gov

Counties/Note: Alexander, Edwards, Franklin, Gallatin, Hamilton, Hardin, Jackson, Jefferson, Johnson, Massac, Perry, Pope, Pulaski, Randolph, Saline, Union, Wabash, Washington, Wayne, White, Williamson.

Searches/Indexing: Include full name plus SSN or EIN in search request. Results do not include SSN or DOB. Will not fax back documents. New cases are in the index immediately after filing date. Case files are kept electronically only. District-wide searches available here.

Search Access: Voice Case Information Service available, call VCIS at 800-726-5622 (within IL) or 618-482-9365. **Mail:** Search usually completed-within 1-2 days. Include SASE for return. **In person:** Computer generated copies- $.10 each.

Payment: Pay by Visa/MC, money order, cashier's check, business check. No debtor checks accepted. Payee: Clerk, US Bankruptcy Court.

E-Services: PACER records go back to 1/1989. New records online immediately. ECF at https://ecf.ilsb.uscourts.gov. Calendars on ECF system. **Opinions Online:** www.ilsb.uscourts.gov/search_main/opinionsearch.asp.

East St Louis Division Court Clerk, Federal Courthouse, 750 Missouri Ave, East St Louis, IL 62201, 618-482-9400. Hours-8AM-4:30PM. www.ilsb.uscourts.gov

Counties/Note: Bond, Calhoun, Clark, Clay, Clinton, Crawford, Cumberland, Effingham, Fayette, Jasper, Jersey, Lawrence, Madison, Marion, Monroe, Richland, St. Clair.

Searches/Indexing: Include full name plus SSN or EIN in search request. Results do not include SSN or DOB. Will not fax back documents. New cases are in the index immediately after filing date. All records now maintained on computer only. District-wide searches available here.

Search Access: Voice Case Information Service available, call VCIS at 800-726-5622 (within IL) or 618-482-9365. **Mail:** Search usually completed-within 1-2 days. SASE required. **In person:** 3 public terminals available. Computer generated copies- $.10 each.

Payment: Pay by Visa/MC, money order, cashier's or business check. No debtor checks accepted. Payee: Clerk, US Bankruptcy Court.

E-Services: PACER records go back to 1/1989. New records online after immeidately. ECF at https://ecf.ilsb.uscourts.gov. Calendars on ECF system. **Opinions Online:** www.ilsb.uscourts.gov/search_main/opinionsearch.asp.

Illinois County Courts

Court	Jurisdiction	No. of Courts	How Organized
Circuit Courts*	General	106	23 Circuits

* Profiled in this Sourcebook.

Court	CIVIL								
	Tort	Contract	Real Estate	Min. Claim	Max. Claim	Small Claims	Estate	Eviction	Domestic Relations
Circuit Courts*	X	X	X	$0	No Max	$10000	X	X	X

Court	CRIMINAL				
	Felony	Misdemeanor	DWI/DUI	Preliminary Hearing	Juvenile
Circuit Courts*	X	X	X	X	X

Administration

Administrative Office of Courts, 3101 Old Jacksonville Road, Springfield, IL 62704; 217-558-4490, Fax 217-785-3905. (CST) www.state.il.us/court/

Court Structure

The Circuit Court has jurisdiction for all matters properly brought before it and shares jurisdiction with the Supreme Court to hear cases relating to revenue, mandamus, prohibition, and habeas corpus. Illinois is divided into twenty-three circuits. Five are single county circuits (Cook, Will, DuPage, Lake, and McHenry) and the remaining eighteen circuits comprise as few as two and as many as twelve counties each. There are two types of judges in the circuit court: circuit judges and associate judges. Circuit judges, elected for six years, can hear any kind of case. An associate judge can hear any case, except criminal cases punishable by a prison term of one year or more (felonies). Probate is handled by the Circuit Court in all counties. The Circuit Court of Cook County is the largest unified court system in the world. Its 2,300-person staff handles approximately 2.4 million cases each year.

Online Access

While there is no statewide public online system available, other than Appellate Court and Supreme Court opinions from the website. A number of Illinois Circuit Courts offer online access, many through a vendor at www.judici.com.

Searching Tips, Fees, and Other Guidelines

The search fee is set by the Clerk of Courts Act (705 ILCS 105). The statute sets different pricing court filings and services based on county population tiers (under 500,000, between 500,000 and 3,000,000, and over 3,000,000) . The higher the population, the higher the fee. For record searching fees, the statute also gives a minimum and maximim that that can be charged with rules how to reach the maximim. Searching is supposed to be calculated at a per year searched basis. In general, search fees range from $4.00 to $9.00 per name per year. Copy fees are generally $1.00 or $2.00 for the first page then $.50 per page for the next 19, then $.25 per page. Usually. The bottom line is you will find pricing all over the board. Prepayment is required unless otherwise noted.

In most courts, both civil and criminal data is on computer from the same starting date. At least 90% of the courts offer public access terminals to look-up docket data.

Adams County

Circuit Court 521 Vermont St, Quincy, IL 62301; 217-277-2100; criminal phone: 217-277-2113; civil phone: 217-277-2106; probate phone: 217-277-2100; fax: 217-277-2116; 8:15AM-4:30PM. ***Felony, Misdemeanor, Civil, Eviction, Small Claims, Probate.*** www.co.adams.il.us

Civil Records: Access: Phone, mail, fax, in person, online, email. Both court and visitors may perform in person searches. Search fee: $6.00 per name. Fee is $10.00 for years prior to 1987. Required to search: name, years to search. Civil cases indexed by defendant, plaintiff, on computer from 1987, books and index cards from 1920. Mail turnaround time 2-3 days. Civil PAT goes back to 1987. Results include name and case number. Online access to 8th Circuit Clerk of Court records is free at www.judici.com/courts/cases/case_search.jsp?court=IL001025J. Search by name, case or docket number back to 1987. Direct email search requests to rfrese@co.adams.il.us.

Criminal Records: Access: Phone, mail, fax, in person, online, email. Both court and visitors may perform in person searches. Search fee: $6.00 per name. Fee is $10.00 for years prior to 1987. Required to search: name, years to search, DOB. Criminal records computerized from 1987, books and index cards from 1920. Mail turnaround time 2-3 days. Criminal PAT goes back to same as civil. PAT results show middle initial, DOB. Online access to criminal records is the same as civil. The county inmate list and warrant list is at the home page. Direct email requests to rfrese@co.adams.il.us.

General Information: Online identifiers in results same as on public terminal. No juvenile or adoption records released. Will not fax documents. Court makes copy: $.50 per page. Cert fee: $6.00. Payee: Clerk of Circuit Court. Personal checks accepted; credit cards are not. Mail requests: SASE required.

Alexander County

Circuit Court 2000 Washington Ave, Cairo, IL 62914; 618-734-0107; fax: 618-734-7003; 8AM-N-1-4PM. ***Felony, Misdemeanor, Civil, Eviction, Small Claims, Probate.***

Civil Records: Access: Fax, mail, in person. Only the court performs in person searches; visitors may not. Search fee: $6.00 per name per year. Required to search: name, years to search. Civil cases indexed by defendant, plaintiff, on computer from 1987, books and index cards from 1800s. Mail turnaround 1 day.

Criminal Records: Access: Fax, mail, in person. Only the court performs in person searches; visitors may not. Search fee: $6.00 per name per year. Required to search: name. Criminal records computerized from 1987, books and index cards from 1800s. Mail turnaround time 1 day.

General Information: No juvenile or adoption records released. Will fax documents to local or toll free line. Court makes copy: $2.00 1st page; $.50 each for 2-19 pages; then $.25 each add'l. Certification fee: $6.00 per cert. Payee: Clerk of Circuit Court. Business checks accepted; no personal checks. No credit cards accepted. Mail requests: SASE required.

Bond County

Circuit Court 200 W College Ave, Greenville, IL 62246; 618-664-3208; criminal fax: 618-664-2257; civil fax: same; 8AM-4:30PM. ***Felony, Misdemeanor, Civil, Small Claims, Probate.*** www.bondcountyil.com/circuitclerk

Probate fax is same as main fax number.

Civil Records: Access: Mail, in person, online. Both court and visitors may perform in person searches. Search fee: $5.00 per name per year. Required to search: name, years to search. Civil cases indexed by defendant, plaintiff, on computer back to 1/87 (and are limited); in index books from 1900s. Mail turnaround time 1-2 weeks. Civil PAT goes back to 1987. PAT results show name only. Online access is same as criminal, see below.

Criminal Records: Access: Mail, in person, online. Both court and visitors may perform in person searches. Search fee: $5.00 per name per year. Required to search: name, years to search, DOB. Criminal records computerized from 1964; index books from 1900s. Mail turnaround time 1-2 weeks. Criminal PAT goes back to 1964. PAT results show middle initial, DOB. Online access is free at www.judici.com/courts/cases/index.jsp?court=IL003015J. Premium/fee service is also available. Online results show middle initial, DOB.
General Information: No juvenile or adoption records released. Will fax documents to local or toll-free number. Court makes copy: $.50 per page, self serve same. Cert fee: $4.00. Payee: Clerk of Circuit Court. Personal checks accepted; credit cards are not. Mail requests: SASE required.

Boone County

Circuit Court 601 N Main, #303, Belvidere, IL 61008; 815-544-0371; criminal phone: x2; civil phone: x1; probate phone: x6924; fax: 815-547-9213; 8:30AM-5PM. ***Felony, Misdemeanor, Civil, Eviction, Small Claims, Probate.***
www.boonecountyil.org
Search fee includes both civil and criminal index. Fax search requests must be on letterhead.
Civil Records: Access: Mail, fax, in person, online. Both court and visitors may perform in person searches. Search fee: $6.00 per name per year. Required to search: name, years to search. Civil cases indexed by defendant, plaintiff, on computer since 8/1993, on index books from 1800s. Mail turnaround time 1-2 days. Civil PAT goes back to 9/1993. Search cases free online at www.judici.com/courts/cases/case_search.jsp?court=IL004015J. Also, a premium fee service is available.
Criminal Records: Access: Mail, fax, in person, online. Both court and visitors may perform in person searches. Search fee: $6.00 per name per year. Required to search: name, years to search, DOB. Records on computer since 8/1993, on index books from 1800s. Mail turnaround time 1-2 days. Criminal PAT goes back to 9/1993. PAT results show middle initial, DOB, SSN. Online access is same as civil. Online results show middle initial.
General Information: No juvenile or adoption records released. Will not fax documents. Court makes copy: $2.00 1st page, $.50 each add'l. Certification fee: $6.00 per document. Payee: Clerk of Circuit Court. Personal checks accepted. Major credit cards accepted via phone or on the internet. Mail requests: SASE required.

Brown County

Circuit Court Courthouse, 200 Court St, Rm 5, Mt Sterling, IL 62353; 217-773-2713 X2; fax: 217-773-3648; 8:30AM-4:30PM. ***Felony, Misdemeanor, Civil, Eviction, Small Claims, Probate.***
Civil Records: Access: Phone, fax, mail, in person. Both court and visitors may perform in person searches. Search fee: $4.00 per name per year. Required to search: name, years to search. Civil cases indexed by defendant, plaintiff, on computer since 1994, on index books from 1830s. Mail turnaround time 1 week. Civil PAT goes back to 1994.
Criminal Records: Access: Phone, fax, mail, in person. Both court and visitors may perform in person searches. Search fee: $4.00 per name per year. Required to search: name, years to search, DOB, signed release. Criminal records on computer since 1994, on index books from 1830s. Mail turnaround time 1 week. Criminal PAT goes back to 1994.
General Information: No juvenile or adoption records released. Will fax documents $3.00 per page. Court makes copy: $.35 per page. Certification fee: $2.00. Payee: Clerk of Circuit Court. Only cashiers checks and money orders accepted. No credit cards accepted. Mail requests: SASE required.

Bureau County

Circuit Court 702 S Main, Princeton, IL 61356; 815-872-2001; fax: 815-872-0027; 8AM-4PM. ***Felony, Misdemeanor, Civil, Eviction, Small Claims, Probate.*** www.bccirclk.gov
Civil Records: Access: In person, online. Both court and visitors may perform in person searches. Search fee: No charge for public access searches, but no papers printed. Required to search: name, years to search. Civil cases indexed by defendant, plaintiff, on computer from 8/1988, prior on index books. Civil PAT goes back to 8/1988. Online access to Judicial Circuit records is free at http://75.149.91.99/bureau/caseinfo.htm. Index includes dates, defendants, record sheets and dispositions and goes back to 8/1988.
Criminal Records: Access: Mail, in person, online. Both court and visitors may perform in person searches. Search fee: No charge if defendant searches, but no papers printed. Required to search: name, years to search, DOB. Criminal records computerized from 8/1988, prior on index books. Mail turnaround time 1 week. Criminal PAT goes back to same as civil. Online access to criminal records is the same as civil.
General Information: No juvenile or adoption records released. Fee to fax out file $2.00 1st pg; $1.00 each add'l. Court makes copy: $.50 for pages 1-19, $.25 for page 20 and over, self serve same. Certification fee: $6.00. Payee: Bureau County Circuit Clerk. No personal checks accepted. Money orders accepted. No credit cards accepted. Mail requests: SASE required for criminal.

Calhoun County

Circuit Court PO Box 486 (101 N County Rd, Hardin, IL 62047; 618-576-2451; fax: 618-576-9541; 8:30AM-4:30PM. ***Felony, Misdemeanor, Civil, Eviction, Small Claims, Probate.***
Probate is a separate index at this same address. Probate fax is same as main fax number.
Civil Records: Access: Phone, fax, mail, in person. Both court and visitors may perform in person searches. Search fee: $6.00 per name. Required to search: name, years to search. Civil cases indexed by defendant, plaintiff; index on docket books from 1800s, computerized since 7/98. Mail turnaround time 1 day.
Criminal Records: Access: Phone, fax, mail, in person. Both court and visitors may perform in person searches. Search fee: $6.00 per name. Required to search: name, years to search, DOB. Criminal records indexed in books from 1800s, computerized since 7/98. Mail turnaround 1 day.
General Information: No juvenile or adoption records released. No fee to fax documents. Court makes copy: $2.00 first page; $.50 each for 2-19 pages; then $.25 each add'l, self serve same. Certification fee: $2.00. Payee: Clerk of Circuit Court. Only cashiers checks and money orders accepted. No credit cards accepted. Mail requests: SASE required or include postage.

Carroll County

Circuit Court 301 N Main St, PO Box 32, Mt Carroll, IL 61053; 815-244-0230; fax: 815-244-3869; 8:30AM-4:30PM. ***Felony, Misdemeanor, Civil, Eviction, Small Claims, Probate.***
www.15thjudicialcircuit.com
Civil Records: Access: Mail, in person, online. Both court and visitors may perform in person searches. Search fee: $6.00 per name per year. Required to search: name, years to search. Civil cases indexed by defendant. Civil records on computer from 1988, prior on index books. Mail turnaround time 2-3 days. Civil PAT goes back to 1988. Access is free to civil, small claims, probate and traffic records at www.judici.com/courts/index.jsp?court=IL008015J. Records go back to 1988. A premium fee service is also available.
Criminal Records: Access: Mail, in person, online. Both court and visitors may perform in person searches. Search fee: $6.00 per name per year. Required to search: name, years to search, DOB. Criminal records computerized from 1988, prior on index books. Mail turnaround time 2-3 days. Criminal PAT goes back to same as civil. Criminal records access is free at www.judici.com/courts/index.jsp?court=IL008015J. Records go back to 1988.
General Information: No juvenile, mental health or adoption records released. Will not fax documents. Court makes copy: $2.00 1st page, $.50 each add'l. Certification fee: $10.00 per doc. Payee: Clerk of Circuit Court. Local personal checks accepted. No credit cards accepted. Mail requests: SASE required.

Cass County

Circuit Court PO Box 203, Virginia, IL 62691; 217-452-7225; 8:30-4:30PM. ***Felony, Misdemeanor, Civil, Eviction, Small Claims, Probate.***
Civil Records: Access: Mail, in person. Visitors must perform in person searches themselves. Search fee: $6.00 per name per year, for search conducted by staff. Required to search: name, years to search. Civil cases indexed by defendant, plaintiff; index on docket books from 1800s. Mail turnaround time 1-2 weeks. Civil PAT goes back to 8/8/1998.
Criminal Records: Access: Mail, in person. Visitors must perform in person searches themselves. Search fee: $6.00 per name per year, for search performed by staff. Required to search: name, years to search, DOB; also helpful: SSN. Criminal records indexed in books from 1800s, on computer back 1998 to present. Mail turnaround time 1-2 weeks. Criminal PAT goes back to same as civil.
General Information: No juvenile or adoption records released. Will not fax documents. Court makes copy: $1.00 1st page, $.50 each add'l. Certification fee: $5.00 per document. Payee: Cass County Circuit Clerk. Personal checks accepted; credit cards are not. Mail requests: SASE required.

Champaign County

Circuit Court 101 E Main, Urbana, IL 61801; criminal phone: 217-384-3727; civil phone: 217-384-3725; fax: 217-384-3879; 8AM-4:30PM. ***Felony, Misdemeanor, Civil, Eviction, Small Claims, Probate.*** www.cccircuitclerk.com
Civil Records: Access: Mail, in person, online. Both court and visitors may perform in person searches. Search fee: $6.00 per name per year. Required to search: name, years to search. Civil cases indexed by defendant, plaintiff, on computer from 1986, index books from 1800s. Mail turnaround time 1-2 weeks. Civil PAT goes back to 1992. Access to the circuit clerk's case query online system called PASS is now free at https://secure.jtsmith.com/clerk/clerk.asp. Online case records go back to '92.
Criminal Records: Access: Mail, online, in person. Both court and visitors may perform in person searches. Search fee: $6.00 per name per year. Required to search: name, years to search; also helpful: DOB, SSN. Criminal records computerized from 1988, index books from 1800s. Mail turnaround time 1-2 weeks. Criminal PAT goes back to 1992.PAT results show name, DOB. Online access to criminal records is the same as civil. Online results show name, DOB.
General Information: Online identifiers in results same as on public terminal. No juvenile or adoption records released. Will fax documents $1.50 1st page, $.50 ea add'l. Court makes copy: $1.00 1st page, $.50 add'l page. Certification fee: $2.00. Payee: Clerk of Circuit Court. Personal checks accepted. Visa/MC accepted; usage fee $5.00 per transaction. Mail requests: SASE required.

Christian County

Circuit Court PO Box 617, Taylorville, IL 62568; 217-824-4966; fax: 217-824-5030; 8AM-4PM. ***Felony, Misdemeanor, Civil, Eviction, Small Claims, Probate.***
Civil Records: Access: Phone, mail, in person. Both court and visitors may perform in person searches. Search fee: $5.00 per name per year. Required to search: name; also helpful: years to search. Civil cases indexed by defendant, plaintiff, on computer from 1988, index books from 1840. Mail turnaround time 1-2 days. Civil PAT goes back to 1988. PAT results show middle initial, DOB.
Criminal Records: Access: Phone, mail, in person. Both court and visitors may perform in person searches. Search fee: $5.00 per name per year. Required to search: name; also helpful: years to search, DOB. Criminal records computerized from 1988, index books from 1840. Mail turnaround time 1-2 days. Criminal PAT goes back to same as civil. PAT results show middle initial, DOB.
General Information: No juvenile or adoption records released. Will fax documents to toll free or

local number. Court makes copy: $1.00 1st page, $.50 each add'l. Certification fee: $6.00. Payee: Clerk of Circuit Court. Business checks accepted. No credit cards accepted. Mail requests: SASE required.

Clark County

Circuit Court PO Box 187, 501 Archer Ave, Marshall, IL 62441; 217-826-2811; criminal phone: 217-826-2811; fax: 217-826-1391; 8AM-4PM. ***Felony, Misdemeanor, Civil, Eviction, Small Claims, Probate.***

Civil Records: Access: Mail, in person, online. Both court and visitors may perform in person searches. Search fee: $6.00 per name per year. Required to search: name, years to search; also helpful: address. Civil cases indexed by defendant, plaintiff, on computer from 1989, index books from 1800s. Mail turnaround time 1 week. Civil PAT goes back to 8/1989. Results include name and case number. Court index and records free at www.judici.com/courts/cases/case_search.jsp?court=IL012015J.

Criminal Records: Access: Mail, in person, online. Both court and visitors may perform in person searches. Search fee: $6.00 per name per year. Required to search: name, years to search, DOB, signed release; also helpful: address, SSN. Criminal records computerized from 1989, index books from 1800s. Mail turnaround time 1 week. Criminal PAT goes back to same as civil. Results include name and DOB. Access to criminal records online is same as civil, see above.

General Information: No juvenile, maternity, or adoption records released. Will not fax documents. Court makes copy: $2.00 1st page, $.50 each add'l. $.25 per page after 19. Certification fee: $6.00. Payee: Clerk of Circuit Court. Only cashiers checks and money orders accepted. No credit cards accepted. Mail requests: SASE required.

Clay County

Circuit Court PO Box 100, 111 Chestnut St, Louisville, IL 62858; 618-665-3523; fax: 618-665-3543; 8AM-4PM. ***Felony, Misdemeanor, Civil, Eviction, Small Claims, Probate.***

www.claycountyillinois.org/index.aspx?page=14

Probate fax is same as main fax number.

Civil Records: Access: Fax, mail, in person, online. Both court and visitors may perform in person searches. Search fee: $5.00 per name. Fee is $5.00 per year prior to 1988. Required to search: name, years to search. Civil cases indexed by defendant. Civil records on computer from 1988, index books from 1850s. Mail turnaround time 2-3 days. Civil PAT goes back to 1988. Search cases free online at www.judici.com/courts/cases/case_search.jsp?court=IL013015J. A premium fee service is available.

Criminal Records: Access: Fax, mail, in person, online. Both court and visitors may perform in person searches. Search fee: $5.00 per name. Fee is $5.00 per year prior to 1988. Required to search: name, years to search; also helpful: DOB. Criminal records computerized from 1988, index books from 1850s. Mail turnaround time 2-3 days. Criminal PAT goes back to same as civil. Online access to criminal same as civil, see above.

General Information: No juvenile or adoption records released. Will fax documents $1.00 1st page, $.50 each add'l. Court makes copy: $1.00 1st page, $.50 each add'l; After 20 pages $.25 each. Certification fee: $6.00. Payee: Clerk of Circuit Court. No personal checks accepted. Credit card accepted through Government Payment Service at 888-604-7888. Mail requests: SASE required.

Clinton County

Circuit Court County Courthouse, PO Box 407, Carlyle, IL 62231; 618-594-2464; 8AM-4PM. ***Felony, Misdemeanor, Civil, Eviction, Small Claims, Probate.***

Civil Records: Access: Mail, in person, online. Both court and visitors may perform in person searches. Search fee: $10.00 per name. Fee is for 10 year search. Required to search: name, years to search. Civil cases indexed by defendant, plaintiff, on computer from 1988, index books from 1825. Mail turnaround time 2-4 days. Civil PAT goes back to 1988. Search cases free online at www.judici.com/courts/cases/index.jsp?court=IL014015J. Also, a premium fee service is available.

Criminal Records: Access: Mail, in person, online. Both court and visitors may perform in person searches. Search fee: $10.00 per name. Flat fee for 10 year search. Required to search: name, years to search, DOB. Criminal records computerized from 1988, index books from 1825. Mail turnaround time 2-4 days. Criminal PAT goes back to same as civil. Online access to criminal same as civil, see above.

General Information: No juvenile or adoption records released. Will not fax documents. Court makes copy: $.50 per page. Certification fee: $6.00 per document. Payee: Clerk of Circuit Court. Personal checks accepted; credit cards are not. Mail requests: SASE required.

Coles County

Circuit Court PO Box 48, 651 Jackson, Charleston, IL 61920; 217-348-0516; fax: 217-348-7324; 8:30AM-4:30PM. ***Felony, Misdemeanor, Civil, Eviction, Small Claims, Probate.***

www.judici.com/courts/index.jsp?court=IL015025J

Civil Records: Access: Fax, mail, in person, online. Both court and visitors may perform in person searches. Search fee: $6.00 per year. Required to search: name, years to search. Civil cases indexed by defendant, plaintiff, on computer from 1989, index books from 1800s. Mail turnaround time 1 day or same day. Civil PAT goes back to 1989. Results include name and case number. Access civil, small claims, probate and traffic records for free at www.judici.com/courts/index.jsp?court=IL015025J, to 1989. A premium fee service is also available.

Criminal Records: Access: Fax, mail, in person, online. Both court and visitors may perform in person searches. Search fee: $6.00 per name per year. Required to search: name, years to search, DOB; also helpful: SSN. Criminal records computerized from 1989, index books from 1800s. Note: Results include name, address and case number. Mail turnaround time 1-2 days. Criminal PAT goes back to 1989. PAT results show middle initial, DOB. Criminal records access is free at www.judici.com/courts/index.jsp?court=IL015025J Online results show name, DOB.

General Information: No juvenile or adoption records released. Will fax documents to local or toll free line. Court makes copy: $2.00 1st page; $.50 each add'l. Certification fee: $10.00. Payee: Clerk of Circuit Court. Personal checks accepted if Illinois, with driver license number. No credit cards accepted. Mail requests: SASE required.

Cook County

Circuit Court - Criminal Division 2650 S California Ave, #526, Chicago, IL 60608; 773-869-2965 records; 773-869-3140 Admin; criminal phone: 773-869-3677 Admin only; fax: 773-869-4511; 8:30AM-4:30PM. ***Felony.***

www.cookcountyclerkofcourt.org

Records Dept on 5th Fl. Cases are heard in six district courts within the county and each court also has a central index. This location houses felony records only, but both felony and misdemeanor are on this division's computer system.

Criminal Records: Access: Mail, in person. Both court and visitors may perform in person searches. Search fee: $9.00 per name per year per division. Required to search: name, years to search, DOB. Criminal records on computer since 1964; prior records on microfiche from 1800s. Note: No hard copies of misdemeanors here; you must get them from the branch where they were heard. Mail turnaround time 7-10 days. Pre-2003 archived records may take add'l 2-3 processing days. Public use terminal has crim records back to 1985. PAT results show middle initial, DOB. Multiple public terminals in the lobby - includes felony and all misdemeanors from branches. A search or record request form is at http://198.173.15.31/forms/pdf_files/CriminalForm.pdf.

General Information: No juvenile or adoption records released. Will not fax documents. Court makes copy: $2.00 1st page, $.50 each add'l. $.25 per page after 20. Certification fee: $9.00 per doc. Payee: Clerk of Circuit Court. Personal checks accepted with drivers license number. No credit cards accepted. Mail requests: SASE required.

Circuit Court - Chicago District 1 50 W Washington, Rm 601, Chicago, IL 60602; 312-603-5030; criminal phone: 312-603-4641; civil phone: 312-603-5145; probate phone: 312-603-6441; 8:30AM-4:30PM. ***Misdemeanor, Civil Action under $100,000, Eviction, Small Claims, Probate.***

www.cookcountyclerkofcourt.org

Cases heard in 6 district courts within the county. Each court has a central index, but all case files wind up here. Probate is a separate division in Rm 1202.

Civil Records: Access: Phone, mail, online, in person. Both court and visitors may perform in person searches. Search fee: $9.00 per name per year and district or division. Required to search: name, years to search. Civil cases indexed by defendant, plaintiff, on computer from 1983, index books from 1800s. Note: An online search request form is at http://198.173.15.31/forms/pdf_files/CivilForm.pdf. Mail turnaround time 1 week. Civil PAT goes back to 1985. Search full case dockets free at www.cookcountyclerkofcourt.org and click on Online Case Info. Limited "case snapshots" and probate are also at www.cookcountyclerkofcourt.org and click on Online Case Info. Search by name, number, or date. Data includes up to 3 parties, attorneys, case type, filing date, the amount of damages sought, division/district, and most current court date. Online results show middle initial. Also, new county dockets DB at http://198.173.15.31/V2/COUNTY/.

Criminal Records: Access: Phone, mail, in person. Visitors must perform in person searches themselves. Search fee: $9.00 per name per year per district. Required to search: name, years to search, DOB. Note: Search misdemeanors in person in Rm 1006. Phone inquiries are to check case status only. Download criminal records search request form at http://198.173.15.31/forms/pdf_files/CriminalForm.pdf. Mail turnaround time 1 week. Criminal PAT goes back to same as civil.

General Information: No juvenile or adoption records released. Will not fax documents. Court makes copy: $2.00 1st page, $.50 each add'l. Self serve: $.50 per page. Certification fee: $9.00 per doc. Payee: Clerk of Circuit Court. On personal checks write your SSN and driver's license numbers. No credit cards accepted. Mail requests: SASE required.

Bridgeview District 5 10220 S 76th Ave, Rm 121, Bridgeview Court Bldg, Bridgeview, IL 60453; 708-974-6500; criminal phone: 708-974-6387; civil phone: 708-974-6599; fax: 708-974-6384; 8:30AM-4:30PM. ***Felony, Misdemeanor, Civil Action under $100,000, Eviction, Small Claims.***

www.cookcountyclerkofcourt.org

Alsip, Bedford Pk, Bridgeview, Burbank, Countryside, Evergreen Pk, Forest View, Hickory Hills, Hinsdale, Hodgkins, Hometown, Justice, Lagrange, Lemont, Lyons, McCook, Oak Lawn, Orland Hills, Palos Park, Stickney, Summit, West Haven, Willow Springs, Worth.

Civil Records: Access: Mail, in person, online. Visitors must perform in person searches themselves. Search fee: $9.00 per name per year and district or division. Required to search: name, years to search. Civil cases indexed by defendant, plaintiff, computerized since 1985, microfiche to early 1970s. Mail turnaround time 1-2 days. Civil PAT goes back to 1985. PAT results show name only. Online case information is available; see Circuit Court - Chicago Division for details. Online results show middle initial.

Criminal Records: Access: Mail, in person. Visitors must perform in person searches themselves. Search fee: $9.00 per name per year per district. Required to search: name. Criminal records computerized since 1985, prior on microfiche to early 1970s. Note: Misdemeanor records (countywide) are also located at Circuit Court - Chicago Dist 1, Richard J. Daley Ctr, 50 W. Washington Ave, Rm 1006, Chicago, IL 60602. Mail turnaround time varies. Criminal PAT goes back to same as civil. PAT results show name only. Felony mail requests- download criminal search request form at http://198.173.15.31/forms/pdf_files/CriminalForm.pdf; mail to Clerk of Circuit Court, Criminal

Div - Records, 2650 S California, Chicago, IL 60608, 773-869-3147.
General Information: Will not fax documents. Court makes copy: $2.00 1st page, $.50 each add'l. Certification fee: $9.00 per doc. Payee: Clerk of Circuit Court. On personal checks write your SSN and driver's license numbers. Major credit cards accepted for traffic court only. Mail requests: SASE required.

Markham District 6 16501 S Kedzie Pkwy, Rm 119, Markham, IL 60426-5509; 708-210-4551, 210-4553, 210-4455; criminal phone: 708-210-4588; civil phone: 708-210-4227; fax: 708-210-4682; 8:30AM-4:30PM. ***Felony, Misdemeanor, Civil Action under $30,000, Eviction, Small Claims, Traffic.***
www.cookcountyclerkofcourt.org
Blue Is, Burnham, Calumet, Chicago Hgts, Crestwood, Crete, Dixmoor, Dolton, Flossmoor, Glenwood, Harvey, Hazelcrest, Homewood, Lansing, Lynwood, Markham, Matteson, Midlothian, Oak Forest, Posen, Riverdale, Robbins, Sauk Village, Tinley Pk.
Civil Records: Access: Mail, in person, online. Visitors must perform in person searches themselves. Search fee: $9.00 per name per year and district or division. Required to search: name. Civil cases indexed by defendant, plaintiff, computerized since 1989. Mail turnaround time 2 weeks. Civil PAT goes back to 1985. Results include name and case number. Online case information is available; see Circuit Court - Chicago Division for details. Online results show middle initial.
Criminal Records: Access: Mail, in person. Visitors must perform in person searches themselves. Search fee: $9.00 per name per year this division. Required to search: name, years to search. Misdemeanor records go back 10 years. Note: Misdemeanor records (county-wide) are also located at Circuit Court - Chicago Dist 1, Richard J. Daley Ctr, 50 W. Washington Ave, Rm 1006, Chicago, IL 60602. Mail turnaround time 2 weeks. Criminal PAT goes back to 1985. PAT results show middle initial, DOB. Felony mail requests- download criminal search request form at http://198.173.15.31/forms/pdf_files/CriminalForm.pdf; mail to Clerk of Circuit Court, Criminal Div - Records, 2650 S California, Chicago, IL 60608, 773-869-3147.
General Information: Will not fax documents. Court makes copy: $2.00 1st page, $.50 each add'l. Self serve: $.25 per page. Certification fee: $9.00 per doc. Payee: Clerk of Circuit Court. On personal checks write your SSN and driver's license numbers. No credit cards accepted. Mail requests: SASE required.

Maywood District 4 1500 S Maybrook Dr, Rm 236, Maywood, IL 60153-2410; 708-865-6040; criminal phone: 708-865-5517; civil phone: 708-865-5187; fax: 708-865-4881; 8:30AM-4:30PM. ***Felony, Misdemeanor, Civil Action under $100,000, Eviction, Small Claims.***
www.cookcountyclerkofcourt.org
Bellwood, Berkeley, Berwyn, Broadview, Brookfield, Cicero, Elmwood Park, Forest Park, Franklin Park, Hillside, La Grange Park, Maywood, Melrose Park, Northlake, North Riverside, Oak Park, River Forest, River Grove, Riverside, Stone Park, Westchester.
Civil Records: Access: Mail, in person, online. Both court and visitors may perform in person searches. Search fee: $9.00 per name per year and district or division. Required to search: name; also helpful: years to search. Civil cases indexed by defendant, plaintiff, computerized since 1982, docket books to 1970s, prior archived. Mail turnaround time 1-2 days. Civil PAT goes back to 1988. PAT civil results show middle initial. Online case info is available; see Circuit Court Chicago Div. for details. Online results show middle initial.
Criminal Records: Access: Mail, in person. Both court and visitors may perform in person searches. Search fee: $9.00 per name per year per district. Required to search: name, years to search, DOB. Note: Misdemeanor records (countywide) are also located at Circuit Court - Chicago Dist 1, Richard J. Daley Ctr, 50 W. Washington Ave, Rm 1006, Chicago, IL 60602. Mail turnaround time varies. Criminal PAT goes back to 1989. PAT criminal results show middle initial. Felony mail requests- download criminal search request form at http://198.173.15.31/forms/pdf_files/CriminalForm.pdf; mail to Clerk of Circuit Court, Criminal Div - Records, 2650 S California, Chicago, IL 60608, 773-869-3147.
General Information: Will not fax documents. Court makes copy: $2.00 1st page, $.50 each add'l. Certification fee: $9.00 per doc. Payee: Clerk of Circuit Court. On personal checks write your driver's license number. Major credit cards accepted for traffic and criminal fines. Mail requests: SASE required.

Rolling Meadows District 3 2121 Euclid Ave, Rm 121, Rolling Meadows, IL 60008-1566; 847-818-2850/818-3000; criminal phone: 847-818-2928; civil phone: 847-818-2300; fax: 847-818-2706; 8:30AM-4:30PM. ***Felony, Misdemeanor, Civil Action under $100,000, Eviction, Small Claims.***
www.cookcountyclerkofcourt.org
Arlington Hgts, Barrington, Bartlett, Bensonville, Buffalo Grove, Elgin, Elk Grove Village, Hanover Pk, Harwood Hgts, Inverness, Mt. Prospect, Norridge, Palatine, Prospect Hgts, Rolling Meadows, Roselle, Rosemont, Schaumburg, Schiller Pk, Wheeling.
Civil Records: Access: Mail, in person, online. Visitors must perform in person searches themselves. Search fee: $9.00 per name per year and district or division. Required to search: name; also helpful: years to search. Civil cases indexed by defendant, plaintiff, are computerized since 1986. Mail turnaround time 1-2 days. Civil PAT goes back to 1985. PAT civil results show middle initial. Online case information is available; see Circuit Court - Chicago Division for details. Online results show middle initial.
Criminal Records: Access: Mail, in person. Visitors must perform in person searches themselves. Search fee: $9.00 per name per year per district. Required to search: name, years to search; also helpful: DOB, SSN. Criminal records on computer, also plaintiff/defendant index on microfilm back to 1871. Note: Misdemeanor records (countywide) are also located at Circuit Court - Chicago Dist 1, Richard J. Daley Ctr, 50 W. Washington Ave, Rm 1006, Chicago, IL 60602. Mail turnaround time varies. Criminal PAT goes back to same as civil. PAT criminal results show middle initial. Felony mail requests- download criminal search request form at http://198.173.15.31/forms/pdf_files/CriminalForm.pdf; mail to Clerk of Circuit Court, Crim Div - Records, 2650 S California, Chicago, 773-869-3147.
General Information: Will not fax documents. Court makes copy: $2.00 1st page, $.50 each add'l. Certification fee: $9.00 per doc. Payee: Clerk of Circuit Court. On personal checks write your SSN and driver's license numbers. Visa/MC accepted for traffic court only. Mail requests: SASE required.

Skokie District 2 Skokie Court Bldg, Rm 136, 5600 Old Orchard Rd, Skokie, IL 60076-1023; 847-470-7250; fax: 847-470-5090; 8:30AM-4:30PM. ***Felony, Misdemeanor, Civil Action under $100,000, Eviction, Small Claims.***
www.cookcountyclerkofcourt.org
Deerfield, Des Plaines, Evanston, Glencoe, Glenview, Golf, Kenilworth, Lincolnwood, Morton Grove, Niles, Northbrook, Northfield, Park Ridge, Prospect Heights, Skokie, Wilmette, Winnetka.
Civil Records: Access: Phone, mail, online, in person. Visitors must perform in person searches themselves. Search fee: $9.00 per name per year and district or division. Required to search: name, years to search. Civil cases indexed by defendant, plaintiff, computerized since 1983. Mail turnaround time 1-3 weeks. Civil PAT goes back to 1988. 2 public access terminals are in the Info booth and 2 in Rm 136. Results include some addresses. Online case information is available; see Circuit Court - Chicago Division for details. Online results show middle initial.
Criminal Records: Access: Mail, in person. Both court and visitors may perform in person searches. Search fee: $9.00 per name per year per district; will only do 1 or 2 names per request. Required to search: name, years to search; also helpful: DOB, SSN. Note: Misdemeanor records (countywide) are also located at Circuit Court - Chicago Dist 1, Richard J. Daley Ctr, 50 W. Washington Ave, Rm 1006, Chicago, IL 60602. Mail turnaround time 1 week to 1 month. Criminal PAT goes back to same as civil. PAT results show middle initial, DOB. 2 public access terminals are in the Info booth and 2 in Rm 136. Felony mail requests- download criminal search request form at http://198.173.15.31/forms/pdf_files/CriminalForm.pdf; mail to Clerk of Circuit Court, Criminal Div - Records, 2650 S California, Chicago, IL 60608, 773-869-3147.
General Information: All records are public. Will not fax documents. Court makes copy: $2.00 1st page, $.50 each add'l. Self serve: $.50 per page. Certification fee: $9.00 per doc. Payee: Clerk of Circuit Court. On personal checks write your SSN and driver's license numbers. Visa/MC accepted for traffic court only. SASE not required.

Crawford County

Circuit Court PO Box 655, Robinson, IL 62454-0655; 618-544-3512; fax: 618-546-5628; 8AM-4PM. ***Felony, Misdemeanor, Civil, Eviction, Small Claims, Probate.***
www.crawfordcountycentral.com/circuitclerk/index.htm
Civil Records: Access: Fax, mail, in person, online. Both court and visitors may perform in person searches. Search fee: $4.00 per name per year. Required to search: name, years to search. Civil cases indexed by defendant, plaintiff, on computer from 1989, index books from 1800s. Mail turnaround time 2-4 days. Civil PAT goes back to 1992. PAT results show middle initial, DOB. Access is free to civil, small claims, probate and traffic records at www.judici.com/courts/cases/index.jsp?court=IL017015J. Premium fee service also available.
Criminal Records: Access: Fax, mail, in person, online. Both court and visitors may perform in person searches. Search fee: $4.00 per name per year. Required to search: name, years to search, DOB. Criminal records computerized from 1989, index books from 1800s. Mail turnaround time up to 1 week. Criminal PAT goes back to same as civil. PAT results show middle initial, DOB. Criminal records access is free at www.judici.com/courts/cases/index.jsp?court=IL017015J. Online results show middle initial, DOB.
General Information: No juvenile or adoption records released. Will fax documents $2.00 1st page, $.25 each add'l. Court makes copy: $1.00 1st page, $.50 each add'l, self serve same. Certification fee: $5.00. Payee: Circuit Clerk. Personal checks accepted; credit cards are not. Mail requests: SASE required.

Cumberland County

Circuit Court PO Box 145, Toledo, IL 62468; 217-849-3601; fax: 217-849-2655; 8AM-4PM. ***Felony, Misdemeanor, Civil, Eviction, Small Claims, Probate.***
Civil Records: Access: Fax, mail, in person. Both court and visitors may perform in person searches. Search fee: $6.00 per name per year. Required to search: name, years to search. Civil cases indexed by defendant, plaintiff, on computer from 1990, index books from 1885. Mail turnaround time up to 1 week. Civil PAT goes back to 1990. PAT results show middle initial, DOB.
Criminal Records: Access: Fax, mail, in person. Both court and visitors may perform in person searches. Search fee: $6.00 per name per year. Required to search: name, years to search; also helpful: DOB, SSN. Criminal records computerized from 1990, index books from 1885. Mail turnaround time up to 1 week. Criminal PAT goes back to same as civil; results show middle initial, DOB.
General Information: No juvenile or adoption records released. Will fax out documents. Court makes copy: $2.00 1st page, $.50 each next 19, then $.25 per add'l. Certification fee: $10.00. Payee: Clerk of Circuit Court. Only cashiers checks and money orders accepted. No credit cards accepted. Mail requests: SASE required.

De Kalb County

Circuit Court 133 W State St, Sycamore, IL 60178; criminal phone: 815-895-7138; civil phone: 815-895-7131; fax: 815-895-7140; 8:30AM-4:30PM. ***Felony, Misdemeanor, Civil, Eviction, Small Claims, Probate.*** www.circuitclerk.org/

Civil Records: Access: Mail, in person, online. Both court and visitors may perform in person searches. Search fee: $4.00 per name per year. Required to search: name, years to search; also helpful: address. Civil cases indexed by defendant, plaintiff, on computer since 1987, records go back to 1858. Mail turnaround time 2 weeks. Civil PAT goes back to 1987. PAT results show middle initial, DOB. Online access to civil court records is the same as criminal, see below.

Criminal Records: Access: Mail, in person, online. Both court and visitors may perform in person searches. Search fee: $4.00 per name per year. Required to search: name, years to search, signed release; also helpful: address, DOB. Criminal records on computer since 9/91, on index books back 60 years. Mail turnaround time 2 weeks. Criminal PAT goes back to 1991. PAT results show middle initial, DOB. Online access to court records is via a internet subscription system. Fee is $20 per month or $240 per year for this county or $300 for Will, Madison, Sangamon, Winnebago, Kane, Kendall, DeKalb courts. Visit www.clericusmagnus.com or call 866-511-2892. Online results show middle initial, DOB.

General Information: Online identifiers in results same as on public terminal. No juvenile or adoption records released. Will not fax documents. Court makes copy: $1.00 1st page, $.50 each add'l. After 20 pages $.25 each. Certification fee: $5.00. Payee: DeKalb County Circuit Clerk. Personal checks accepted. Visa/MC accepted via phone only. Mail requests: SASE required.

De Witt County

Circuit Court 201 Washington St, Clinton, IL 61727; 217-935-2195; fax: 217-935-3310; 8:30AM-4:30PM. ***Felony, Misdemeanor, Civil, Eviction, Small Claims, Probate.***

Civil Records: Access: Mail, fax, in person, online. Both court and visitors may perform in person searches. Search fee: $4.00 per name per year. Required to search: name, years to search. Civil cases indexed by defendant. Civil records on computer from 1989, index books from 1839. Mail turnaround time 1-2 weeks. Civil PAT goes back to 1989. Access court index and records free at www.judici.com/courts/cases/case_search.jsp?court=IL020015J.

Criminal Records: Access: Mail, fax, online, in person. Both court and visitors may perform in person searches. Search fee: $4.00 per name per year. Required to search: name, years to search, DOB. Criminal records computerized from 1989, index books from 1839. Mail turnaround time 1-2 weeks. Criminal PAT goes back to same as civil. Access to criminal court records online is same as civil, see above.

General Information: No juvenile or adoption records released. Will fax documents to local or toll free line. Court makes copy: $2.00 1st page, $.50 each add'l, after 20 $.25 each, self serve same. Certification fee: $10.00 per document. Payee: Clerk of Circuit Court. Only cashiers checks and money orders accepted. No credit or debit cards accepted. To make payments 24/7, go to www.GovPayNOW.com or call 888-604-7888. Mail requests: SASE required.

Douglas County

Circuit Court PO Box 50, Tuscola, IL 61953; 217-253-2352; criminal phone: 217-253-2353 - Traffic; 8:30AM-4:30PM. ***Felony, Misdemeanor, Civil, Eviction, Small Claims, Probate.***

Civil Records: Access: Phone, mail, in person. Both court and visitors may perform in person searches. Search fee: $5.00 per name per year. Required to search: name, years to search. Civil cases indexed by defendant, plaintiff, on computer from 1989, index books from 1859. Mail turnaround time 1 week. Civil PAT goes back to 1989.

Criminal Records: Access: Mail, in person. Both court and visitors may perform in person searches. Search fee: $5.00 per name per year. Required to search: name, years to search; also helpful: DOB, SSN. Criminal records computerized from 1989, index books from 1859. Mail turnaround time 1 week. Criminal PAT goes back to same as civil.

General Information: No juvenile or adoption records released. Will fax documents $5.00 for 1st 4 pages; $1.00 each add'l. Court makes copy: $1.00 1st page, $.50 each add'l. After 20 pages $.25 each. Certification fee: $2.00. Payee: Douglas County Circuit Clerk. Personal checks accepted; credit cards are not. Mail requests: SASE required.

Du Page County

Circuit Court 505 N County Farm Rd, Wheaton, IL 60187; 630-407-8700; fax: 630-407-8575; 8:30AM-4:30PM. ***Felony, Misdemeanor, Civil, Eviction, Small Claims, Probate.*** www.co.dupage.il.us/courtclerk

Civil Records: Access: Mail, in person. Both court and visitors may perform in person searches. Search fee: $6.00 per name per year. Required to search: name, years to search. Civil cases indexed by defendant, plaintiff, online from 1976, microfilm records back to 1939, index records back to 1839. All document files after 1/92 are on optical disk. Mail turnaround time 1 week. Civil PAT goes back to 1976. PAT civil results show middle initial.

Criminal Records: Access: Mail, in person. Both court and visitors may perform in person searches. Search fee: $6.00 per name per year. Required to search: name, years to search, DOB. Criminal records online from 1976, microfilm records back to 1939, index records back to 1839. All document files after 1/01/92 are on optical disk. Mail turnaround time 1 week. Criminal PAT goes back to same as civil. PAT results show middle initial, DOB.

General Information: No juvenile or adoption records released. Will not fax documents. Court makes copy: $2.00 1st page, $.50 each add'l. Certification fee: $6.00 per doc. Payee: Clerk of Circuit Court. Personal checks accepted. Visa/MC accepted. Mail requests: SASE required.

Edgar County

Circuit Court County Courthouse, 115 W Court, Paris, IL 61944; 217-466-7447; fax: 217-466-7443; 8AM-4PM. ***Felony, Misdemeanor, Civil, Eviction, Small Claims, Probate.***

Civil Records: Access: Phone, mail, in person, online. Both court and visitors may perform in person searches. Search fee: $4.00 per name per year. Required to search: Name, years to search. Civil cases indexed by defendant, plaintiff, on computer from 1992, index books from 1823. Mail turnaround time 2-3 days. Civil PAT goes back to 1992-3. PAT results show middle initial, DOB. Terminal results also show SSNs. Access civil, small claims, probate, traffic records free at www.judici.com/courts/cases/case_search.jsp?court=IL023015J. A premium fee service also available.

Criminal Records: Access: In person only. Both court and visitors may perform in person searches. Search fee: $4.00 per name per year. Required to search: Name, years to search, DOB. Criminal records computerized from 1992, index books from 1880. Criminal PAT goes back to same as civil. PAT results show middle initial, DOB. Terminal results include SSN. Online access to criminal is the same as civil, above.

General Information: No juvenile or adoption records released. Will not fax documents. Court makes copy: $2.00 1st page; $1.00 each add'l. Self serve: $1.00 per page. Cert fee: $10.00 per cert. Payee: Circuit Clerk. Personal checks accepted; credit cards are not. Mail requests: SASE required for civil.

Edwards County

Circuit Court County Courthouse, Albion, IL 62806; 618-445-2016; fax: 618-445-4943; 8AM-4PM. ***Felony, Misdemeanor, Civil, Eviction, Small Claims, Probate.***

Civil Records: Access: Mail, in person, online. Both court and visitors may perform in person searches. Search fee: $4.00 per name per year. Required to search: name, years to search. Civil cases indexed by defendant. Civil records on computer from 1988, books and index cards from 1815. Mail turnaround time 1 week. Civil PAT goes back to 1988. Access free to civil, small claims, probate, traffic records at www.judici.com/courts/cases/index.jsp?court=IL024015J. Premium fee service also available.

Criminal Records: Access: Mail, in person, online. Both court and visitors may perform in person searches. Search fee: $4.00 per name per year. Required to search: name, years to search, DOB. Criminal records computerized from 1988, index books from 1815. Mail turnaround time 1 week. Criminal PAT goes back to same as civil. Criminal records access is free at www.judici.com/courts/cases/index.jsp?court=IL024015J.

General Information: No juvenile or adoption records released. Will fax documents to local or toll-free number $2.00 per page. Court makes copy: $.50 per page, self serve same. Certification fee: $5.00. Payee: Clerk of Circuit Court. Only cashiers checks and money orders accepted. No credit cards accepted. Mail requests: SASE required.

Effingham County

Circuit Court PO Box 586, 100 E Jefferson, Effingham, IL 62401; 217-342-4065; criminal fax: 217-342-6183; civil fax: same; 8AM-4PM. ***Felony, Misdemeanor, Civil, Small Claims, Probate.*** Probate fax is same as main fax number.

Civil Records: Access: Mail, in person, online. Both court and visitors may perform in person searches. Search fee: $5.00 per name; also $5.00 per year if prior to 1988; $5.00 per page for computer generated info. Required to search: name, years to search; also helpful: address. Civil cases indexed by defendant, plaintiff, on computer from 1988, index books from 1800s. Mail turnaround time 1 week. Civil PAT goes back to 1988. Access is free to civil, small claims, probate and traffic records at www.judici.com/courts/cases/index.jsp?court=IL025015J. A premium fee service also available.

Criminal Records: Access: Mail, in person, online. Both court and visitors may perform in person searches. Search fee: $5.00 per name; also $5.00 per year if prior to 1988; $5.00 per page for computer generated info. Required to search: name, years to search, DOB; also helpful: address. Criminal records computerized from 1988, index books from 1800s. Mail turnaround time 1 week. Criminal PAT goes back to same as civil.PAT results show name, DOB. Criminal records access free at www.judici.com/courts/cases/index.jsp?court=IL025015J.

General Information: Online identifiers in results same as on public terminal. No juvenile or adoption records released. Will not fax documents. Court makes copy: $1.00 1st page, $.50 each add'l. $.25 per page after 20. Certification fee: $6.00 per document. Payee: Effingham County Circuit Clerk. Pre-approved business checks accepted; no personal checks. Major credit cards accepted. Mail requests: SASE required.

Fayette County

Circuit Court 221 S 7th St, Vandalia, IL 62471; 618-283-5009; fax: 618-283-4490; 8AM-4PM. ***Felony, Misdemeanor, Civil, Eviction, Small Claims, Probate.***

Civil Records: Access: Phone, mail, fax, in person, online. Both court and visitors may perform in person searches. Search fee: $5.00 per name per year. Required to search: name, years to search. Civil cases indexed by defendant. Civil records on computer from 1988, index books from 1800s. Mail turnaround time 1 month. Civil PAT goes back to 1989. PAT results show name, DOB. Access court index and records free at www.judici.com/courts/cases/case_search.jsp?court=IL026015J.

Criminal Records: Access: Phone, mail, fax, in person, online. Both court and visitors may perform in person searches. Search fee: $5.00 per name per year. Required to search: name, years to search, DOB. Criminal records computerized from 1988, index books from 1800s. Mail turnaround time 1 month. Criminal PAT goes back to 1989.PAT results show name, DOB. Access to criminal records is same as civil, see above.

General Information: No juvenile, impounded or adoption records released. Will fax documents. Court makes copy: $1.00 1st page, $.50 each add'l. Self serve: $.25 per page. Certification fee: $2.00. Payee: Clerk of Circuit Court. Business checks accepted. No credit cards accepted. Mail requests: SASE required.

Ford County

Circuit Court 200 W State St, Paxton, IL 60957; 217-379-2641; criminal fax: 217-379-3445; civil fax: same; 8:30AM-4:30PM. ***Felony, Misdemeanor, Civil, Eviction, Small Claims, Probate.***
Probate fax is same as main fax number.

Civil Records: Access: Mail, fax, in person, online. Both court and visitors may perform in person searches. Search fee: $4.00 per name per year. Required to search: name, years to search. Civil cases indexed by defendant. Civil index on docket books from 1800s; on computer back to 3/2000. Mail turnaround time 2 days. Civil PAT goes back to 3/2000. PAT results show middle initial, DOB. Records back to 1980s may be available. Search cases free online at www.judici.com/courts/cases/index.jsp?court=IL027015J. Also, a premium fee service is available.

Criminal Records: Access: Mail, fax, in person, online. Both court and visitors may perform in person searches. Search fee: $4.00 per name per year. Required to search: name, years to search, DOB (signed release if for juvenile). Criminal records indexed in books from 1800s; on computer back to 3/2000. Mail turnaround time 2 days. Criminal PAT goes back to same as civil. PAT results show middle initial, DOB. Some records back to 1980s may be available. Online access to criminal is same as civil, see above.

General Information: No juvenile or adoption records released. Will fax documents to local or toll free line. Court makes copy: $1.00 1st page, $.50 each add'l; after 20- $.25 each add'l, self serve same. Certification fee: $5.00 per certification. Payee: Clerk of Circuit Court. Personal checks accepted; credit cards are not. Mail requests: SASE required.

Franklin County

Circuit Court County Courthouse, PO Box 485, Benton, IL 62812; 618-439-2011; civil phone: same; fax: 618-439-4119; 8AM-4PM. ***Felony, Misdemeanor, Civil, Small Claims, Probate, Eviction, Traffic.***
Traffic 618-438-6731.

Civil Records: Access: Fax, mail, in person, online. Both court and visitors may perform in person searches. Search fee: $4.00 per name per year. Required to search: name, years to search. Civil cases indexed by defendant, plaintiff, on computer from 1987, index books from 1843. Civil PAT goes back to 1987. PAT results show middle initial, DOB, SSN. Access is free to civil, small claims, probate and traffic records at www.judici.com/courts/cases/index.jsp?court=IL028015J. A premium fee service also available.

Criminal Records: Access: Fax, mail, in person, online. Both court and visitors may perform in person searches. Search fee: $4.00 per name per year. Required to search: name, years to search, DOB. Criminal records computerized from 1987, index books from 1843. Note: Results also include address. Criminal PAT goes back to same as civil. PAT results show middle initial, DOB, SSN. Criminal records access is free at www.judici.com/courts/cases/index.jsp?court=IL028015J. Online results show middle initial, DOB.

General Information: Online identifiers in results same as on public terminal. No juvenile or adoption records released. Will not fax documents. Court makes copy: $1.00 1st page, $.50 each add'l, self serve same. Certification fee: $5.00 per cert. Payee: Franklin County Circuit Clerk. Only cashiers checks and money orders accepted. No credit cards accepted. Mail requests: SASE required.

Fulton County

Circuit Court PO Box 152, Lewistown, IL 61542; 309-547-3041; criminal fax: 309-547-3674; civil fax: same; 8AM-4PM. ***Felony, Misdemeanor, Civil, Eviction, Small Claims, Probate.***
www.9thjudicial.org/Fulton/indexFulton.htm
Probate fax is same as main fax number.

Civil Records: Access: Phone, mail, fax, in person. Both court and visitors may perform in person searches. Search fee: $5.00 per name per year. Required to search: name, years to search. Civil cases indexed by defendant, plaintiff, on computer back to 1990, index books from 1900. Mail turnaround time 2-3 days. Civil PAT goes back to 1992. PAT results show name only.

Criminal Records: Access: Mail, in person. Both court and visitors may perform in person searches. Search fee: $5.00 per name per year. Required to search: name, years to search; also helpful: DOB. Criminal records computerized from 1990, index books from 1879. Mail turnaround time 1-2 days; older, archived records require add'l 2-3 days. Criminal PAT goes back to 1992. PAT results show name only.

General Information: No juvenile, impounded or adoption records released. Court makes copy: $2.00 1st page, $.50 each add'l; $.25 each after 19 pgs. Certification fee: $3.00. Payee: Fulton County Circuit Clerk. Business checks accepted. Visa/MC accepted. Mail requests: SASE required.

Gallatin County

Circuit Court County Courthouse, PO Box 249, Shawneetown, IL 62984; 618-269-3140; fax: 618-269-4324; 8AM-N, 1-4PM. ***Felony, Misdemeanor, Civil, Eviction, Small Claims, Probate.***

Civil Records: Access: Fax, mail, in person. Both court and visitors may perform in person searches. Search fee: $6.00 per name, per year. Required to search: name, years to search. Civil cases indexed by defendant, plaintiff; index on docket books from 1800s; computerized records since 10/1999. Mail turnaround time 1 week. Civil PAT goes back to 10/1999. PAT results show name only.

Criminal Records: Access: Fax, mail, in person. Both court and visitors may perform in person searches. Search fee: $6.00 per name, per year. Required to search: name, years to search, DOB, signed release. Criminal records indexed in books from 1800s; computerized records since 10/1999. Mail turnaround time 1 week. Criminal PAT goes back to same as civil; results show name only.

General Information: No juvenile or adoption records released. Will fax documents $2.00 1st page, $1.00 ea. add'l page. Court makes copy: $.25 per page, self serve same. Certification fee: $3.00 per cert. Payee: Clerk of Circuit Court. Business checks accepted. No credit cards accepted. Mail requests: SASE required.

Greene County

Circuit Court 519 N Main, County Courthouse, Carrollton, IL 62016; 217-942-3421; fax: 217-942-5431; 8AM-4PM. ***Felony, Misdemeanor, Civil, Eviction, Small Claims, Probate.***

Civil Records: Access: Phone, mail, in person. Both court and visitors may perform in person searches. Search fee: $5.00 per name. Required to search: name, years to search. Civil cases indexed by defendant, plaintiff; index on docket books from 1830s; computerized since 2000. Mail turnaround time 1-2 days. Civil PAT goes back to 2000.

Criminal Records: Access: Phone, fax, mail, in person. Both court and visitors may perform in person searches. Search fee: $5.00 per name. Required to search: name, years to search, DOB. Criminal records indexed in books from 1875; computerized since 2000. Note: No felony searches by phone. Include signed release with felony search requests. Mail turnaround time 1-2 days. Criminal PAT goes back to same as civil.

General Information: No juvenile or adoption records released. Will fax documents $.25 per page. Court makes copy: $.25 per page. Self serve: $.10 per page. Certification fee: $5.00. Payee: Clerk of Circuit Court. Personal checks accepted; credit cards are not. Mail requests: SASE required.

Grundy County

Circuit Court PO Box 707, Morris, IL 60450; 815-941-3256; criminal fax: 815-941-3265; civil fax: same; 8AM-4:30PM. ***Felony, Misdemeanor, Civil, Eviction, Small Claims, Probate.***
Probate fax is same as main fax number.

Civil Records: Access: Mail, in person. Both court and visitors may perform in person searches. Search fee: $5.00 per name per year. Required to search: name, years to search. Civil cases indexed by defendant, plaintiff, on computer back to 1988. Mail turnaround time 1-2 days. Civil PAT goes back to 1988. PAT civil results show middle initial.

Criminal Records: Access: Mail, in person. Both court and visitors may perform in person searches. Search fee: $5.00 per name per year. Required to search: name, years to search, DOB, signed release. Criminal records computerized from 1988. Mail turnaround time 1-2 days. Criminal PAT goes back to 1988. PAT criminal results show middle initial.

General Information: No juvenile or adoption records released. Will not fax documents. Court makes copy: $2.00 1st page; $.50 each add'l. Certification fee: $4.00 per document. Payee: Clerk of Circuit Court. Personal checks accepted. Major credit cards accepted; add $5.00 transaction fee. Mail requests: SASE required.

Hamilton County

Circuit Court 100 S Jackson, Courthouse, McLeansboro, IL 62859; 618-643-3224; criminal fax: 618-643-3455; civil fax: same; 8AM-4:30PM. ***Felony, Misdemeanor, Civil, Eviction, Small Claims, Probate.*** Probate is a separate index at this address. Probate fax is same as main fax number.

Civil Records: Access: Mail, in person, online. Both court and visitors may perform in person searches. Search fee: $4.00 per name per year. Required to search: name, years to search. Civil cases indexed by defendant, plaintiff; index on docket books from 1800s; computer records go back to 1990. Mail turnaround time 1-2 days. Civil PAT goes back to 1//2002. PAT civil results show middle initial. Access is free to civil, small claims, probate and traffic records at www.judici.com/courts/cases/index.jsp?court=IL033025J. Premium fee service also available.

Criminal Records: Access: Mail, in person, online. Both court and visitors may perform in person searches. Search fee: $4.00 per name per year. Required to search: name, years to search, DOB. Criminal records indexed in books from 1800s; computer records go back to 1990. Mail turnaround time 1-2 days. Criminal PAT goes back to same as civil. PAT results show middle initial, DOB. Criminal records access is free at www.judici.com/courts/cases/index.jsp?court=IL033025J. Online results show middle initial, DOB.

General Information: Online identifiers in results same as on public terminal. No juvenile or adoption records released. Will fax documents. Court makes copy: $.50 per page, self serve same. Certification fee: $5.00. Payee: Clerk of Circuit Court. No personal checks accepted. Credit cards accepted, additional fees involved. Mail requests: SASE required.

Hancock County

Circuit Court PO Box 189, 500 Main St, #8, Carthage, IL 62321; 217-357-2616; fax: 217-357-2231; 8AM-4PM. ***Felony, Misdemeanor, Civil, Eviction, Small Claims, Probate.***

Civil Records: Access: Fax, mail, in person. Both court and visitors may perform in person searches. Search fee: $5.00 per name per year. Required to search: name, years to search. Civil cases indexed by defendant, plaintiff, on computer from 1992, index books from 1800s. Note: For fax searches, they will only search to determine if a record exists. Mail turnaround time 1 week.

Criminal Records: Access: Fax, mail, in person. Both court and visitors may perform in person searches. Search fee: $5.00 per name. Required to search: name, years to search, DOB. Criminal records computerized from 1992, index books from 1970, archived to 1800s. Note: For phone and fax searches, they will only search to determine if a record exists. Mail turnaround time 1 week.

General Information: No juvenile or adoption records released. Will fax documents no fee. Court makes copy: $2.00 1st page, $.50 each add'l. Certification fee: $3.00. Payee: Clerk of Circuit Court. Personal checks accepted, if local bank. Mail requests: SASE required.

Hardin County

Circuit Court PO Box 308, Main & Market Sts, County Courthouse, Elizabethtown, IL 62931; 618-287-2735; criminal fax: 618-287-2713; civil fax: same; 8AM-4PM. ***Felony, Misdemeanor, Civil, Eviction, Small Claims, Probate.***
Probate fax is same as main fax number.
Civil Records: Access: Mail, fax, in person. Both court and visitors may perform in person searches. Search fee: $6.00 per name per year. Required to search: name, years to search. Civil cases indexed by defendant, plaintiff, on computer back to 2000/2002; on index books from 1800s. Mail turnaround time 1 week.
Criminal Records: Access: Mail, fax, in person. Both court and visitors may perform in person searches. Search fee: $6.00 per name per year. Required to search: name, years to search, DOB. Criminal records computerized from 2000/2002; on index books from 1800s. Mail turnaround 1 week.
General Information: No juvenile or adoption records released. Fee to fax out file $2.00 for 1st 2 pages; $.50 each add'l page. Court makes copy: $1.00 1st page; $.50 each add'l. Certification fee: $6.00 per document plus copy fee; certified judgment is $10.00. Payee: Circuit Clerk. Business check, cashiers check or money order accepted. No credit cards accepted. Mail requests: SASE required.

Henderson County

Circuit Court County Courthouse, PO Box 546, Oquawka, IL 61469; 309-867-3121; fax: 309-867-3207; 8AM-4PM. ***Felony, Misdemeanor, Civil, Eviction, Small Claims, Probate.***
Civil Records: Access: Phone, mail, in person. Both court and visitors may perform in person searches. Search fee: $5.00 per name per year. Required to search: name, years to search. Civil cases indexed by defendant, plaintiff, on computer from 1991, index books from 1800s. Mail turnaround time 1 day to 1 week. Civil PAT goes back to 1991.
Criminal Records: Access: Phone, mail, in person. Both court and visitors may perform in person searches. Search fee: $5.00 per name per year. Required to search: name, years to search, DOB; also helpful: SSN. Criminal records computerized from 1991, index books from 1800s. Mail turnaround 1 day - 1 wk. Criminal PAT goes back same as civil.
General Information: No juvenile or adoption records released. Will not fax documents. Court makes copy: $2.00 1st page; $.50 each for 2-19 pages; then $.25 per page. Certification fee: $3.00 1st page plus $.50 each add'l. Payee: Clerk of Circuit Court. Personal checks accepted; credit cards are not. Mail requests: SASE required.

Henry County

Circuit Court 307 W Center St, County Courthouse, Cambridge, IL 61238; 309-937-3572; criminal fax: 309-937-3990; civil fax: same; 8AM-4:30PM. ***Felony, Misdemeanor, Civil, Eviction, Small Claims, Probate.***
www.henrycty.com/codepartments/CircuitClerk/index.html
Probate is a separate index at this same address. Probate fax is same as main fax number.
Civil Records: Access: Mail, in person, online. Both court and visitors may perform in person searches. Search fee: $6.00 per name per year. Required to search: name, years to search. Civil cases indexed by defendant. Civil records on computer from 1989, index books from 1800s. Mail turnaround time 2 weeks. Civil PAT goes back to 1989. Terminal results may include address. Access is free to civil, small claims, probate and traffic records at www.judici.com/courts/index.jsp?court=IL037015J. A premium fee service also available.
Criminal Records: Access: Mail, in person, online. Both court and visitors may perform in person searches. Search fee: $6.00 per name per year. Required to search: name, middle initial, years to search, DOB; also helpful-last known address. Criminal records computerized from 1989, index books from 1800s. Mail turnaround time 2 weeks. Criminal PAT goes back to same as civil. Criminal records access is free at www.judici.com/courts/index.jsp?court=IL037015J.
General Information: Online identifiers in results same as on public terminal. No juvenile or adoption records released. Will fax documents to local or toll free line. Court makes copy: $2.00 1st page, $.50 each add'l. Document hard copy from automated system-$6.00. Certification fee: $6.00 per page plus copy fee; Exemplifications are $6.00. Payee: Clerk of Circuit Court. Only cashiers checks and money orders accepted. No credit cards accepted. Mail requests: SASE required.

Iroquois County

Circuit Court 550 S 10th St, Watseka, IL 60970; 815-432-6950 (-6952 Traf); fax: 815-432-6953; 8:30AM-4:30PM. ***Felony, Misdemeanor, Civil, Eviction, Small Claims, Probate.***
www.judici.com/courts/index.jsp?court=IL038025J
Civil Records: Access: Fax, mail, in person, online. Both court and visitors may perform in person searches. Search fee: $6.00 per name per year. Required to search: name, years to search. Civil cases indexed by defendant. Civil index on docket books from 1900, computerized since 1993. Mail turnaround time 1-2 days. Civil PAT goes back to 1993. PAT results show name, DOB. Search cases free online at www.judici.com/courts/cases/index.jsp?court=IL038025J. A premium fee service is also available.
Criminal Records: Access: Fax, mail, in person, online. Both court and visitors may perform in person searches. Search fee: $6.00 per name per year. Required to search: name, years to search, DOB. Criminal records indexed in books from 1820, computerized since 1993. Mail turnaround time 1-2 days. Criminal PAT goes back to 1988.PAT results show name, DOB. Results includes disposition if available. Access criminal records free at www.judici.com/courts/cases/index.jsp?court=IL038025J. Online results show name, DOB. Results include dispositions if available.
General Information: No juvenile or adoption records released. Fee to fax out file $6.00 per document. Court makes copy: $.50 per page. Certification fee: $2.00. Payee: Clerk of Circuit Court. Local personal checks accepted. Visa/MC, Discover, debit cards accepted; add $5.00 usage surcharge. Mail requests: SASE required.

Jackson County

Circuit Court PO Drawer 730, 1001 Walnut, County Courthouse, Murphysboro, IL 62966; 618-687-7300; 8AM-4PM. ***Felony, Misdemeanor, Civil, Eviction, Small Claims, Probate.***
www.circuitclerk.co.jackson.il.us/index-2.html
Civil Records: Access: Mail, in person, online. Both court and visitors may perform in person searches. Search fee: $4.00 per name per year. Required to search: name, years to search. Civil cases indexed by defendant, plaintiff, on computer from 1986, index books from 1860. Mail turnaround time 1-2 weeks. Civil PAT goes back to 1970. PAT results show middle initial, DOB. Access civil, small claims, and traffic records free at the home page or at www.judici.com/search/search.html?court=IL039015J. Also, premium service with full info is available $77 per 6-months.
Criminal Records: Access: Mail, in person, online. Both court and visitors may perform in person searches. Search fee: $4.00 per name per year. Required to search: name, years to search. Criminal records computerized from 1986, index books from 1860. Mail turnaround time 1-2 weeks. Criminal PAT goes back to same as civil. PAT results show middle initial, DOB. Criminal records access is free from home page. Click on "Case information." Also, premiums service subscription with full info is available $77 per 6-months, see www.judici.com/search/search.html?court=IL039015J. Online results show middle initial, DOB.
General Information: Online identifiers in results same as on public terminal. No juvenile or adoption records released. May fax documents if not busy. Court makes copy: $1.00 1st page, $.50 each add'l. Certification fee: $10.00 per doc. Payee: Circuit Clerk. Personal checks accepted; credit cards are not. Mail requests: SASE required.

Jasper County

Circuit Court 100 W Jourdan St, Newton, IL 62448; 618-783-2524; criminal fax: 618-783-8626; civil fax: same; 8AM-4PM. ***Felony, Misdemeanor, Civil, Eviction, Small Claims, Probate.***
Probate is a separate index at this same address. Probate fax is same as main fax number.
Civil Records: Access: Mail, in person. Both court and visitors may perform in person searches. Search fee: $5.00 per name. Required to search: name, years to search; also helpful: address. Civil cases indexed by defendant, plaintiff, on computer from 1988, index books from 1835. Mail turnaround time 1 week.
Criminal Records: Access: Mail, in person. Both court and visitors may perform in person searches. Search fee: $5.00 per name. Required to search: name, years to search, DOB, sex, signed release. Criminal records computerized from 1988, index books from 1835. Mail turnaround time 1 week.
General Information: No juvenile or adoption records released. Fee to fax out file $2.00 each. Court makes copy: $1.00 1st page; $.50 each add'l. Certification fee: $6.00 per cert. Payee: Clerk of Circuit Court. Personal checks accepted; credit cards are not. Mail requests: SASE required.

Jefferson County

Circuit Court PO Box 1266, 100 10th St, Mt Vernon, IL 62864; 618-244-8008; fax: 618-244-8029; 8AM-4PM. ***Felony, Misdemeanor, Civil, Eviction, Small Claims, Probate.***
Civil Records: Access: Phone, fax, mail, in person, online. Both court and visitors may perform in person searches. Search fee: $8.00. Required to search: name, years to search. Civil cases indexed by defendant. Civil records on computer back to 1988, index books from 1800s. Note: Fax requests must be followed by original by mail before being processed. Mail turnaround time 1-2 weeks. Civil PAT goes back to 1988. Online access to 2nd Circuit Clerk of Court records is free at www.judici.com/courts/index.jsp?court=IL041025J. A premium fee service also available.
Criminal Records: Access: Phone, fax, mail, in person, online. Both court and visitors may perform in person searches. Search fee: $8.00. Required to search: name, years to search, DOB, SSN. Criminal records computerized from 1988, index books from 1800s. Mail turnaround time 1-2 weeks. Criminal PAT goes back to same as civil. Online access to criminal is the same as civil.
General Information: Sealed records not released. Will fax documents $.25 per page plus phone charge. Court makes copy: $.50 per page, up to 100, then $.25 per page over 100. No certification fee. Payee: Clerk of Circuit Court. Only cashiers checks and money orders accepted. No credit cards accepted. Mail requests: SASE required.

Jersey County

Circuit Court 201 W Pearl St, Jerseyville, IL 62052; 618-498-5571; fax: 618-498-6128; 8:30AM-4:30PM. ***Felony, Misdemeanor, Civil, Eviction, Small Claims, Probate.***
www.jerseycounty-il.us
Civil Records: Access: Fax, mail, in person, online. Both court and visitors may perform in person searches. Search fee: $5.00 per name. Required to search: name, years to search. Civil cases indexed by defendant. Civil records on computer from 1991, index books from 1800s. Mail turnaround time 1 week. Public use terminal available, records go back to 1990. PAT civil results show middle initial. Court records may be accessed free at www.jerseycounty-il.us by clicking on Court Record Search.
Criminal Records: Access: Fax, mail, in person, online. Both court and visitors may perform in person searches. Search fee: $5.00 per name. Required to search: name, years to search, DOB. Criminal records computerized from 1991, index books from 1800s. Mail turnaround time 1 week. Public use terminal available, crim records go back

to same. PAT criminal results show middle initial. Online access to criminal is the same as civil. Online results show middle initial.

General Information: No juvenile or adoption records released. Will fax out docs. Court makes copy: $.50 per page. Self serve: $.25 per page. Certification fee: $2 for 1st 2 pages; $.50 each add'l. Payee: Clerk of Circuit Court. Personal checks accepted; credit cards are not. Mail requests: SASE required.

Jo Daviess County

Circuit Court 330 N Bench St, Galena, IL 61036; 815-777-2295/0037; criminal phone: 815-777-2295; civil phone: 815-777-0037; probate phone: 815-777-0037; fax: 815-776-9146; 8AM-4PM. ***Felony, Misdemeanor, Civil, Eviction, Small Claims, Probate.*** www.jodaviess.org/index.asp

Civil Records: Access: Mail, in person, online. Visitors must perform in person searches themselves. No search fee. Required to search: name, years to search. Civil cases indexed by defendant, plaintiff, on computer since 1992, on index books from 1960; will and probate back to 1850. Note: Clerk accepts mail requests to perform a probate search for $6.00, paid in advance. Civil PAT goes back to 1992. PAT civil results show middle initial. Access is free to civil, small claims, probate and traffic records at www.judici.com/courts/index.jsp?court=IL043015J. A premium fee service also available.

Criminal Records: Access: Mail, in person, online. Both court and visitors may perform in person searches. Search fee: $6.00 per name. Fee is for 1992 to present. Prior to 1992 $6.00 per name per year. Required to search: name, years to search, DOB. Criminal records on computer since 1992, on index books from 1960. Mail turnaround time 1 week. Criminal PAT goes back to same as civil. PAT criminal results show middle initial. Online access to criminal records is free at www.judici.com/courts/index.jsp?court=IL043015J. Online results show middle initial.

General Information: Online identifiers in results same as on public terminal. No juvenile or adoption records released. Will fax documents; fee is same as copy fee; to toll- free number only. Court makes copy: $.50 per page, self serve same. Certification fee: $10.00 per cert includes copies. Payee: Circuit Clerk. Business checks accepted. Major credit cards accepted. Mail requests: SASE required.

Johnson County

Circuit Court PO Box 517, Vienna, IL 62995; 618-658-4751; criminal fax: 618-658-2908; civil fax: same; 8AM-4PM. ***Felony, Misdemeanor, Civil, Eviction, Small Claims, Probate.***
Probate fax is same as main fax number.

Civil Records: Access: Mail, in person. Both court and visitors may perform in person searches. Search fee: $6.00 per name per year. Required to search: name, years to search. Civil cases indexed by defendant, plaintiff, on computer from 1987, index books from 1930s. Mail turnaround time 1 week. Civil PAT goes back to 1987. PAT results show name only.

Criminal Records: Access: Mail, in person. Both court and visitors may perform in person searches. Search fee: $6.00 per case per year. Required to search: name, years to search, DOB. Criminal records computerized from 1987, index books from 1930s. Mail turnaround time 1 week. Criminal PAT goes back to same as civil; results show name only.

General Information: No juvenile or adoption records released. Will fax documents if prepaid. Court makes copy: $.50 per page, self serve same. Certification fee: $10.00 per certification. Payee: Circuit Clerk. Business checks accepted. No credit cards accepted. Mail requests: SASE required.

Kane County

Circuit Court PO Box 112, Geneva, IL 60134; 630-232-3413; fax: 630-208-2172; 8:30AM-4:30PM M,T,TH,F; open til 7PM W. ***Felony, Misdemeanor, Civil, Eviction, Small Claims, Probate.*** www.cic.co.kane.il.us

Civil Records: Access: Phone, fax, mail, in person, online. Both court and visitors may perform in person searches. Search fee: $6.00 per name per year. Required to search: name, years to search. Civil cases indexed by defendant, plaintiff, on computer from 1986, index books from 1800s. Mail turnaround time 2 days. Civil PAT goes back to 1986. PAT civil results show middle initial. Multiple public access terminals are available. Online access to civil court records is the same as criminal, see below.

Criminal Records: Access: Phone, fax, mail, in person, online. Both court and visitors may perform in person searches. Search fee: $6.00 per name per year. Required to search: name, years to search, DOB. Criminal records computerized from 1986, index books from 1800s. Mail turnaround time 2 days. Criminal PAT goes back to same as civil. PAT results show middle initial, DOB. Multiple public access terminals are available. Results may include DL number. Also search online free at www.cic.co.kane.il.us/OnlineCourtInformation.asp. Also, online access to court records is also via subscription system. $59 setup fee plus $20 per month or $240 per year for this county or $300 for Will, Madison, Sangamon, Winnebago, Kane, Kendall, DeKalb courts. Visit www.clericusmagnus.com or call 866-511-2892. Online results show middle initial, DOB. Electronic results may include DL number.

General Information: No juvenile, mental health or adoption records released. Will fax documents $2.00 1st page, $.50 each add'l. Court makes copy: $2.00 1st page, $.50 each next 19, then $.25 per add'l. Certification fee: $4.00. Judgment orders certification fee $10.00. Payee: Clerk of Circuit Court. Personal checks accepted. Credit cards accepted. Mail requests: SASE required.

Kankakee County

Circuit Court 450 E Court St, County Courthouse, Kankakee, IL 60901; 815-937-2905; fax: 815-939-8830; 8:30AM-4:30PM. ***Felony, Misdemeanor, Civil, Eviction, Small Claims, Probate.***

Civil Records: Access: Mail, in person. Both court and visitors may perform in person searches. Search fee: $5.00 per name per year. Required to search: name, years to search. Civil cases indexed by defendant, plaintiff, on computer from 1990, index books from 1800s. Mail turnaround time 1-2 weeks. Civil PAT goes back to 1990. PAT results show name only. Results include case number.

Criminal Records: Access: Mail, in person. Both court and visitors may perform in person searches. Search fee: $5.00 per name per year. Required to search: name, years to search, DOB. Criminal records computerized from 1990, index books from 1800s. Mail turnaround 1-2 weeks. Criminal PAT goes back same as civil. PAT results show name only.

General Information: No juvenile, impounded, mental health, expunged or adoption records released. Will not fax documents. Court makes copy: $2.00 1st page, $.50 each add'l. Certification fee: $5.00 per certification. Payee: Clerk of Circuit Court. Personal checks accepted; credit cards are not. Mail requests: SASE required.

Kendall County

Circuit Court Kendall County Courthouse, 807 W John St, Yorkville, IL 60560; 630-553-4183; criminal phone: 630-553-4184; civil phone: 630-553-4183; fax: 630-553-4964; 8AM-4:30PM. ***Felony, Misdemeanor, Civil, Eviction, Small Claims, Probate.*** Traffic/DUI at 630-553-4185.

Civil Records: Access: Mail, in person, online. Both court and visitors may perform in person searches. Search fee: $4.00 per name per year. Required to search: name, years to search. Civil cases indexed by defendant, plaintiff, on computer since 1992, on index books from 1800s. Mail turnaround time 2-3 days. Civil PAT goes back to 1992. Results include name and case number. Online access to civil court records is the same as criminal, see below

Criminal Records: Access: Mail, in person, online. Both court and visitors may perform in person searches. Search fee: $4.00 per name per year. Required to search: name, years to search, DOB. Criminal records on computer since 1992, on index books from 1800s. Mail turnaround time 2-3 days. Criminal PAT goes back to same as civil. PAT results show name, DOB, SSN. Online access to court records is via subscription system. $59 setup fee plus $20 per month or $240 per year for this county or $300 for Will, Madison, Sangamon, Winnebago, Kane, Kendall, DeKalb courts. Visit www.clericusmagnus.com or call 866-511-2892.

General Information: No juvenile or adoption records released. Will not fax out documents. Court makes copy: $2.00 1st page, $.50 each add'l. $4.00 per page when hard copy printouts are maintained on an automated medium. Cert fee: $4.00 per doc. Payee: Clerk of Circuit Court. Personal checks accepted; credit cards are not. Mail requests: SASE required.

Knox County

Circuit Court 200 S Cherry St, Galesburg, IL 61401; 309-343-3121, 345-3817-Clerk; fax: 309-345-0098; 8:30AM-4:30PM. ***Felony, Misdemeanor, Civil, Eviction, Small Claims, Probate.***
Search fee includes civil and criminal indexes.

Civil Records: Access: Fax, mail, in person. Both court and visitors may perform in person searches. Search fee: $5.00 per year per name. Required to search: name, years to search. Civil cases indexed by defendant, plaintiff; index on docket books from 1800s. Mail turnaround time 1 week. Civil PAT goes back to 2000. PAT results show name only.

Criminal Records: Access: Fax, mail, in person. Both court and visitors may perform in person searches. Search fee: $5.00 per year per name. Required to search: name, years to search, DOB, sex. Criminal records indexed in books from 1800s. Mail turnaround time 1 week. Criminal PAT goes back to same as civil. Address does not appear on all terminal results.

General Information: No juvenile or adoption records released. Will fax back documents no add'l fee. Court makes copy: $2.00 1st page, $.50 each add'l.A self-serve copier is located in the basement. Certification fee: $3.00 per page. Payee: Clerk of Circuit Court. Personal checks accepted; credit cards are not. SASE not required.

La Salle County

Circuit Court - Civil Division 119 W Madison St, Ottawa, IL 61350-0617; 815-434-8671; fax: 815-433-9198; 8AM-4:30PM. ***Civil, Eviction, Small Claims, Probate.***
www.lasallecounty.com

Civil Records: Access: Online, in person. Both court and visitors may perform in person searches. No search fee. Required to search: name, years to search. Civil cases indexed by defendant, plaintiff. Some records on computer since late 1980s; prior records on index books from 1800s. Public use terminal has civil records back to 1989. Results include name and case number. Online access to Judicial Circuit records requires a $200 setup fee (waived for not-for-profits) and $.10 per minute usage fee. Call Clerk's office at 815-434-8671 for details.

General Information: Online identifiers in results same as on public terminal. No juvenile or adoption records released. Will not fax documents. Court makes copy: $2.00 1st page, $.50 each add'l. Cert fee: $6.00 per doc. Payee: Clerk of Circuit Court. Personal checks accepted. Visa/MC accepted.

Circuit Court - Criminal Division 707 Etna Rd, #141, Ottawa, IL 61360; 815-434-8271; fax: 815-434-8299; 8AM-4:30PM. ***Felony, Misdemeanor.*** www.lasallecounty.com

Criminal Records: Access: In person, online. Visitors must perform in person searches themselves. Required to search: name, years to search; also helpful: DOB. Criminal records go back to 1985. Note: Results include address. Public use terminal has crim records back to 1984. PAT results show name only. Online access to Judicial Circuit records requires a $200 setup fee (waived

for not-for-profits) and $.10 per minute usage fee. Call the Clerk's office at 815-434-8671 for details. Online results show middle initial, DOB.
General Information: Online identifiers in results same as on public terminal. No juvenile or adoption records released. Will fax documents to local or toll-free number. Court makes copy: $2.00 1st page, $.50 each add'l. Certification fee: $6.00 per doc. Payee: Clerk of Circuit Court. Personal checks accepted. Credit cards accepted; $3.00 usage fee added per transaction. Mail requests: SASE required.

Lake County

Circuit Court 18 N County St, Waukegan, IL 60085; 847-377-3380; criminal phone: 847-377-3278; civil phone: 847-377-3209; 8:30AM-5PM. ***Felony, Misdemeanor, Civil, Eviction, Small Claims, Probate.*** www.co.lake.il.us/circlk/
Civil Records: Access: Mail, in person. Both court and visitors may perform in person searches. Search fee: $6.00 per name per year. Required to search: name, years to search. Civil cases indexed by defendant, plaintiff, on computer or microfiche from 1968, index books from 1800s. Mail turnaround time 1-2 days. Civil PAT goes back to 1985.
Criminal Records: Access: Mail, in person. Both court and visitors may perform in person searches. Search fee: $6.00 per name per year. Required to search: name, years to search, DOB. Criminal records on computer or microfiche from 1968, index books from 1800s. Mail turnaround time 1-2 days. Criminal PAT goes back to same as civil.
General Information: No juvenile or adoption records released. Will not fax documents. Court makes copy: $2.00 1st pg, $.50 each add'l to 19, then $.25 ea, self serve same. Certification fee: $6.00 per doc. Payee: Clerk of the Circuit Court. No personal checks accepted. Discover cards accepted in person only. Mail requests: SASE required.

Lawrence County

Circuit Court County Courthouse, 1100 State St, Lawrenceville, IL 62439; 618-943-2815; fax: 618-943-5205; 8AM-4PM. ***Felony, Misdemeanor, Civil, Eviction, Small Claims, Probate.***
Probate is a separate index at this same address.
Civil Records: Access: Mail, in person, online. Both court and visitors may perform in person searches. Search fee: $4.00 per name per year. Required to search: name, years to search, address. Civil cases indexed by defendant, plaintiff, on computer from 10/99, index books from 1800s. Mail turnaround time 2-3 days. Access is free to civil, small claims, probate and traffic records at www.judici.com/courts/cases/index.jsp?court=IL051015J. Premium fee service also available.
Criminal Records: Access: Mail, in person, online. Both court and visitors may perform in person searches. Search fee: $4.00 per name per year. Required to search: name, years to search, address, DOB, SSN, signed release. Criminal records computerized from 10/99, index books from 1800s. Mail turnaround time 2-3 days. Criminal records access is free at www.judici.com/courts/cases/index.jsp?court=IL051015J.
General Information: No juvenile or adoption records released. Will fax documents $1.00 1st page, $.50 each add'l; after 20 pages, will copy for $.25 per page. Court makes copy: $1.00 1st page, $.50 each add'l; after 20- $.25 each add'l. Certification fee: $5.00. Payee: Clerk of Circuit Court. Only cashiers checks and money orders accepted. No credit cards accepted. Mail requests: SASE required.

Lee County

Circuit Court 309 S Galena, #320, Dixon, IL 61021; 815-284-5234; fax: 815-288-5615; 8:30AM-4:30PM. ***Felony, Misdemeanor, Civil, Eviction, Small Claims, Probate.***
Civil Records: Access: Mail, in person, online. Both court and visitors may perform in person searches. Search fee: $6.00 per name per year. Required to search: name, years to search. Civil cases indexed by defendant, plaintiff, on computer from 1989, index books from 1800s. Mail turnaround time 1 week. Civil PAT goes back to 8/1989. PAT civil results show middle initial. Access is free to civil, small claims, probate and traffic records at www.judici.com/courts/index.jsp?court=IL052025J. A premium fee service also available.
Criminal Records: Access: Mail, in person, online. Both court and visitors may perform in person searches. Search fee: $6.00 per name per year. Required to search: name, years to search, DOB; also helpful: SSN. Criminal records computerized from 1989, index books from 1800s. Mail turnaround time 1 week. Criminal PAT goes back to same as civil. PAT criminal results show middle initial. Criminal records access is free at www.judici.com/courts/index.jsp?court=IL052025J. Online results show middle initial.
General Information: Online identifiers in results same as on public terminal. No juvenile, impounded or adoption records released. Will not fax documents. Court makes copy: $.50 per page. Certification fee: $2.00 per cert. Payee: Clerk of Circuit Court. Personal checks accepted. Mail requests: SASE required.

Livingston County

Circuit Court 112 W Madison St, Pontiac, IL 61764; 815-844-2602; criminal phone: x1; civil phone: x2; probate phone: x3 (also Juvenile); criminal fax: 815-844-2322; civil fax: same; 8AM-4:30PM. ***Felony, Misdemeanor, Civil, Eviction, Small Claims, Probate.***
Small claims phone is x4, and tax deeds phone is x5. Probate fax is same as main fax number.
Civil Records: Access: Mail, in person, online. Both court and visitors may perform in person searches. Search fee: $4.00 per name per year. Required to search: name, years to search; also helpful: address. Civil cases indexed by defendant, plaintiff, on computer from 1989 (child support since 1988), index books from 1837. Mail turnaround time 3-5 days. Civil PAT goes back to 1989. PAT results show middle initial, DOB. Probate along with divorce, traffic, miscellaneous remedy cases, law, all in separate indexes at this same address. Search probate index 1837-1958 at www.cyberdriveillinois.com/departments/archives/pontiac.html.
Criminal Records: Access: Mail, in person. Both court and visitors may perform in person searches. Search fee: $4.00 per name per year. Required to search: name, years to search, DOB, SSN; also helpful: address. Criminal records computerized from 1989, index books from 1837. Note: Signed release by juvenile required for juvenile cases. Mail turnaround time 3-5 days. Criminal PAT goes back to same as civil. PAT results show middle initial, DOB.
General Information: No juvenile, impound or adoption records released. Fee to fax out file $3.00 per fax. Court makes copy: $1.00 1st page; $.50 each add'l; after 19 pages $.25 each. Self serve: $.25 per page. Certification fee: $2.00 per document. Payee: Livingston County Circuit Clerk. Checks or cash only accepted in civil division. Major credit cards accepted in traffic division only. Mail requests: SASE required.

Logan County

Circuit Court County Courthouse, PO Box 158, Lincoln, IL 62656; 217-735-2376; criminal phone: 217-735-2376/2377; civil phone: 217-732-1163; criminal fax: 217-732-1231; civil fax: 217-732-1232; 8:30AM-4:30PM. ***Felony, Misdemeanor, Civil, Eviction, Small Claims, Probate.***
www.co.logan.il.us/circuit_clerk/
Civil Records: Access: Mail, fax, in person, online. Both court and visitors may perform in person searches. Search fee: $5.00 per name per year. Required to search: name, years to search. Civil cases indexed by defendant, plaintiff, on computer back to 1990, index books from 1857. Mail turnaround time 1 week. Civil PAT goes back to 1989. PAT results show middle initial, DOB. Online access to civil, small claims, probate and traffic records is free at www.judici.com/courts/cases/index.jsp?court=IL054025J. A premium fee service is also available.
Criminal Records: Access: Mail, fax, in person, online. Both court and visitors may perform in person searches. Search fee: $5.00 per name per year. Required to search: name, years to search, DOB; also helpful: sex. Criminal records computerized from 1990, index books from 1857. Mail turnaround time 1 week. Criminal PAT goes back to same as civil. PAT results show middle initial, DOB. Criminal records access is free at www.judici.com/courts/cases/index.jsp?court=IL054025J. Online results show middle initial, DOB.
General Information: Online identifiers in results same as on public terminal. No juvenile or adoption records released. Will not fax documents. Court makes copy: $2.00 1st page, $.50 each add'l. $.25 per page after 19. Certification fee: $5.00 per doc. Payee: Carla Bender, Circuit Clerk. Business or personal checks accepted. Visa/MC accepted. SASE not required.

Macon County

Circuit Court 253 E Wood St, Decatur, IL 62523; criminal phone: 217-421-0272; civil phone: 217-424-1454; probate phone: 217-424-1455; fax: 217-424-1350; 8AM-4:30PM. ***Felony, Misdemeanor, Civil, Eviction, Small Claims, Probate.***
www.court.co.macon.il.us
Civil Records: Access: Phone, fax, mail, online, in person. Both court and visitors may perform in person searches. Search fee: $6.00 per name per year. Required to search: name, years to search. Civil cases indexed by defendant, plaintiff, on computer from 1989, index books from 1800s. Mail turnaround time 1 week. Civil PAT goes back to 1989. Access to court records is free at www.court.co.macon.il.us/Templates/SearchCaseInfo.htm. Search docket information back to 04/96. Includes traffic, probate, family, small claims.
Criminal Records: Access: Fax, mail, online, in person. Both court and visitors may perform in person searches. Search fee: $6.00 per name per year. Required to search: name, years to search; also helpful: DOB. Criminal records computerized from 1989, index books from 1800s. Mail turnaround time 1 week. Criminal PAT goes back to same as civil. Access to court records is free online at www.court.co.macon.il.us/Templates/SearchCaseInfo.htm. Search docket information back to 04/96.
General Information: No juvenile or adoption records released. Will fax documents to local or toll free line, if not certified copy. Court makes copy: $2.00 1st page, $.50 each add'l. Certification fee: $2.00 per cert. Payee: Macon County Circuit Clerk. No personal checks accepted. Money orders, certified checks, or cash only. No credit cards accepted. Mail requests: SASE required.

Macoupin County

Circuit Court PO Box 197, Carlinville, IL 62626; 217-854-3211; fax: 217-854-7361; 8:30AM-4:30PM. ***Felony, Misdemeanor, Civil, Eviction, Small Claims, Probate.***
Civil Records: Access: Mail, in person, online. Both court and visitors may perform in person searches. Search fee: $6.00 per name per year. Required to search: name, years to search. Civil cases indexed by defendant, plaintiff, on computer from 1994, index books from 1837. Mail turnaround time 1 month to 6 weeks. Civil PAT goes back to 1994. PAT results show middle initial, DOB. Access court index and records free at www.judici.com/courts/cases/case_search.jsp?court=IL059015J.
Criminal Records: Access: Mail, in person, online. Both court and visitors may perform in person searches. Search fee: $6.00 per name per year. Required to search: name, years to search; also helpful: DOB. Criminal records computerized from 1994, index books from 1837. Mail turnaround time 1 month to 6 weeks. Criminal PAT goes back to same as civil. PAT results show middle initial, DOB. Access to criminal records online is same as civil, see above.
General Information: No juvenile or adoption records released. Will fax documents; fee is same as copy fees. Court makes copy: $2.00 1st page, $.50 each add'l. $.25 per page after 19. Certification fee: $6.00. Payee: Mike Mathis Circuit Clerk. Personal checks accepted; credit cards are not. Mail requests: SASE required.

Madison County

Circuit Court - Civil/Misdemeanor Div.

155 N Main St, Edwardsville, IL 62025; 618-692-6240 x5; fax: 618-692-0676; 8:30AM-4:30PM. ***Misdemeanor, Civil, Eviction, Small Claims, Probate.*** www.co.madison.il.us

Civil Records: Access: Mail, in person, online. Both court and visitors may perform in person searches. Search fee: $6.00 per name per year. Required to search: name, years to search. Civil cases indexed by defendant, plaintiff, on computer from 1990, index books from 1800s. Mail turnaround time 10-15 days. Civil PAT goes back to 1995. PAT results show name and some may include middle initial. Online access to court records is via subscription system. $59 setup fee plus $20 per month or $240 per year for this county or $300 for Will, Madison, Sangamon, Winnebago, Kane, Kendall, DeKalb courts. Visit www.clericusmagnus.com or call 866-511-2892.

Criminal Records: Access: Mail, in person, online. Both court and visitors may perform in person searches. Search fee: $6.00 per name per year. Required to search: name, years to search, DOB. Criminal records computerized from 1990, index books from 1800s. Mail turnaround time 10-15 days. Criminal PAT goes back to same as civil.PAT results show name, DOB. Results may include middle initial. Online access to misdemeanor records is the same as civil, see above. Online results show name, DOB.

General Information: No juvenile, mental health, adoption records released. Will fax documents to local or toll free line. Court makes copy: $2.00 1st page; $.50 each for pgs 2-19; $.25 ea add'l pg. Certification fee: $6.00. Payee: Clerk of Circuit Court. Personal checks accepted. Mail requests: SASE required.

Circuit Court - Felony Division

155 N Main St, Edwardsville, IL 62025; 618-696-3800; fax: 618-655-2006; 8:30AM-4:30PM. ***Felony.*** www.co.madison.il.us

Criminal Records: Access: Mail, in person, online. Both court and visitors may perform in person searches. Search fee: $6.00 per name per year. Required to search: name, years to search, DOB. Criminal records computerized from 1995, index books from 1958. Mail turnaround time 10-15 days. Public use terminal has crim records back to 1995.PAT results show name, DOB. Online access to court records is via subscription system. $59 setup fee plus $20 per month or $240 per year for this county or $300 for Will, Madison, Sangamon, Winnebago, Kane, Kendall, DeKalb courts. Visit www.clericusmagnus.com or call 866-511-2892. Online results show name, DOB.

General Information: Online identifiers in results same as on public terminal. No juvenile, mental health, adoption records released. Will fax documents to local or toll free line. Court makes copy: $2.00 1st page; $.50 each for pgs 2-19; $.25 ea add'l pg. Certification fee: $6.00. Payee: Clerk of Circuit Court. Personal checks accepted; credit cards are not. Mail requests: SASE required.

Marion County

Circuit Court

PO Box 130, 100 E Main, Salem, IL 62881; 618-548-3856; fax: 618-740-0118; 8AM-4PM. ***Felony, Misdemeanor, Civil, Eviction, Small Claims, Probate.***

Civil Records: Access: Mail, in person, online. Visitors must perform in person searches themselves. Search fee: $5.00 per name. Required to search: name, years to search. Civil cases indexed by defendant, plaintiff, on computer from 1988, index books from 1800s. Mail turnaround time 2-3 days. Civil PAT goes back to 1988. PAT results show name only. Results include case number. Online access to civil, small claims, probate and traffic records is free at www.judici.com/courts/cases/index.jsp?court=IL061015J. A premium fee service is also available.

Criminal Records: Access: Mail, in person, online. Visitors must perform in person searches themselves. Search fee: $5.00 per name. Required to search: name, years to search; also helpful: DOB, SSN. Criminal records computerized from 1988, index books from 1800s. Note: Results include address, driver license number and case number. Mail turnaround time 2-3 days. Criminal PAT goes back to same as civil. PAT results show middle initial, DOB, SSN. Results include driver license number and case number. Criminal records access is free at www.judici.com/courts/cases/index.jsp?court=IL061015J. Online results show middle initial, DOB.

General Information: Online identifiers in results same as on public terminal. No juvenile or adoption records released. Will not fax documents. Court makes copy: $1.00 1st page, $.50 each add'l. Certification fee: $6.00 per doc. Payee: Clerk of Circuit Court. Only cashiers checks and money orders accepted. No credit cards accepted.

Marshall County

Circuit Court

PO Box 328, Lacon, IL 61540-0328; 309-246-6435; probate phone: same; fax: 309-246-2173; 8:30AM-N, 1-4:30PM. ***Felony, Misdemeanor, Civil, Eviction, Small Claims, Probate.***

Civil Records: Access: Mail, in person. Both court and visitors may perform in person searches. Search fee: $6.00 per name per year. Required to search: name, years to search. Civil cases indexed by defendant, plaintiff, on computer from 1988, microfiche since 1964, index books from 1800s. Mail turnaround 1 week. Civil PAT goes back to 1988.

Criminal Records: Access: Mail, in person. Both court and visitors may perform in person searches. Search fee: $6.00 per name per year. Required to search: name, years to search, DOB. Criminal records computerized from 1988, microfiche since 1964, index books from 1800s. Mail turnaround time 1 week. Criminal PAT goes back to same as civil. PAT results show middle initial, DOB, SSN.

General Information: No juvenile or adoption records released. Will fax documents to local or toll free line. Court makes copy: $.50 per page. Certification fee: $4.00. Payee: Clerk of Circuit Court. Personal checks and major credit cards accepted. Mail requests: SASE required.

Mason County

Circuit Court

125 N Plum, Havana, IL 62644; 309-543-6619; criminal fax: 309-543-4214; civil fax: same; 8AM-4PM. ***Felony, Misdemeanor, Civil, Eviction, Small Claims, Probate.*** www.masoncountyil.org

Probate fax is same as main fax number.

Civil Records: Access: Mail, in person. Both court and visitors may perform in person searches. Search fee: $5.00 per name per year. Required to search: name, years to search. Civil cases indexed by defendant, plaintiff, on computer from 1989, index books from 1800s. Mail turnaround time 1-2 weeks. Civil PAT goes back to 1989. PAT civil results show middle initial.

Criminal Records: Access: Mail, in person. Both court and visitors may perform in person searches. Search fee: $5.00 per name per year. Required to search: name, years to search, DOB. Criminal records computerized from 1989, index books from 1800s. Mail turnaround time 1-2 weeks. Criminal PAT goes back to same as civil. PAT results show middle initial, DOB.

General Information: No juvenile or adoption records released. Will fax documents $5.00 per fax. Court makes copy: $1.00 1st page, $.50 each add'l. Self serve: $.25 per page. Certification fee: $2.50 per cert. Payee: Clerk of Circuit Court. Only cashiers checks and money orders accepted. No credit cards accepted. Mail requests: SASE required.

Massac County

Circuit Court

PO Box 152, Courthouse Sq, Metropolis, IL 62960; 618-524-9359; fax: 618-524-4850; 8AM-N, 1-4PM. ***Felony, Misdemeanor, Civil, Eviction, Small Claims, Probate.***

Civil Records: Access: Mail, in person. Both court and visitors may perform in person searches. Search fee: $6.00 per name. Required to search: name, years to search. Civil cases indexed by defendant. Civil records on computer from 1986, index books from 1800s. Mail turnaround time 5 business days. Civil PAT goes back to 1986. PAT results show middle initial, DOB.

Criminal Records: Access: Mail, in person. Both court and visitors may perform in person searches. Search fee: $6.00 per name. Required to search: name, years to search, DOB, signed release. Criminal records computerized from 1986, index books from 1800s. Mail turnaround time 5 business days. Criminal PAT goes back to same as civil. PAT results show middle initial, DOB.

General Information: No juvenile or adoption records released. Will not fax documents. Court makes copy: $.10 per page. Certification fee: $3.00. Payee: Clerk of Circuit Court. Only cashiers checks and money orders accepted. No credit cards accepted. Mail requests: SASE required.

McDonough County

Circuit Court

County Courthouse, #1 Courthouse Sq, Macomb, IL 61455; 309-837-4889; probate phone: same; fax: 309-833-4493; 8AM-4PM. ***Felony, Misdemeanor, Civil, Eviction, Small Claims, Probate.*** www.9thjudicial.org/

Traffic cases can be reached at 309-836-2777.

Civil Records: Access: Phone, fax, mail, in person. Both court and visitors may perform in person searches. Search fee: $5.00 per name per year. Required to search: name, years to search. Civil cases indexed by defendant, plaintiff, on computer from 1991, index books from 1800s. Mail turnaround time 1 week. Civil PAT goes back to 1990. PAT civil results show middle initial.

Criminal Records: Access: Phone, fax, mail, in person. Both court and visitors may perform in person searches. Search fee: $5.00 per name per year. Required to search: name, years to search; also helpful: SSN. Criminal records computerized from 1991, index books from 1800s. Mail turnaround time 1 week. Criminal PAT goes back to 1985. PAT criminal results show middle initial.

General Information: No juvenile or adoption records released. Fee to fax out file $2.00 per page. Court makes copy: $2.00 1st page; $.50 each add'l 19 pages; $.25 each add'l. Certification fee: $3.00. Payee: Clerk of Circuit Court. Personal checks accepted for civil; not for criminal. Mail requests: SASE required.

McHenry County

Circuit Court

2200 N Seminary Ave, Rte 47, Woodstock, IL 60098; 815-334-4310; criminal phone: 815-334-4190 misd./traf; fax: 815-338-8583; 8AM-4:30PM. ***Felony, Misdemeanor, Civil, Eviction, Small Claims, Probate, Traffic.*** www.mchenrycircuitclerk.org

Felony Dept is Rm 353. There is also a Branch Court at 333 S Green St, McHenry.

Civil Records: Access: Phone, fax, mail, online, in person. Both court and visitors may perform in person searches. Search fee: $6.00 per name per year. Required to search: name, years to search. Civil cases indexed by defendant, plaintiff, on computer from 1991, index books from 1800s. Mail turnaround time 1 week. Civil PAT goes back to 1991. PAT civil results show middle initial. Access to civil, traffic and domestic records is the same as criminal, see below.

Criminal Records: Access: Phone, fax, mail, online, in person. Both court and visitors may perform in person searches. Search fee: $6.00 per name per year. Required to search: name, years to search, DOB. Criminal records computerized from 1990, index books from 1800s. Note: Phone searches are limited to one only. Mail turnaround time 1 week; criminal requests processed same day. Criminal PAT goes back to 1991. PAT results show middle initial, DOB. Access to records on the remote online system requires $750 license fee and $53.50 password card fee, plus $50 per month. Records date back to 1990 with civil, criminal, probate, traffic, and domestic records. For more info, call 815-334-4193. Online results show middle initial, DOB.

General Information: Online identifiers in results same as on public terminal. No juvenile or adoption records released. Will not fax documents. Court makes copy: $2.00 1st page, $.50 each pages 2-19; after 19 pages $.25 each. Cert fee: $6.00 per doc.

Payee: Clerk of Circuit Court. Personal checks and credit cards accepted. Mail requests: SASE required.

McLean County

Circuit Court Circuit Clerk, PO Box 2420, Bloomington, IL 61702-2420; 309-888-5301; criminal phone: 309-888-5321; civil phone: 309-888-5341; 8:30AM-4:30PM. ***Felony, Misdemeanor, Civil, Eviction, Small Claims, Probate.***
www.mcleancountyil.gov
Civil Records: Access: Mail, in person. Both court and visitors may perform in person searches. Search fee: $6.00 per name per year. Required to search: name, years to search. Civil cases indexed by defendant, plaintiff, on computer from 1991, index books from 1800s. Mail turnaround time 10 days.
Criminal Records: Access: Mail, in person, online. Both court and visitors may perform in person searches. Search fee: $6.00 per name per year. Required to search: name, years to search, DOB; also helpful: address, SSN. Criminal records computerized from 1991, index books from 1800s. Mail turnaround time 10 days. Public use terminal has crim records back to 1991. PAT results show middle initial, DOB. Free public access at www.mcleancountyil.gov/circuitclerk/PA_main.htm. System has traffic as well as criminal index.
General Information: No juvenile or adoption records released. Will not fax documents. Court makes copy: $2.00 1st page, $.50 each add'l. Certification fee: $6.00. Payee: McLean County Circuit Clerk. Personal checks accepted; credit cards are not. Mail requests: SASE required.

Menard County

Circuit Court PO Box 466, Petersburg, IL 62675; 217-632-2615; fax: 217-632-4124; 8:30AM-4:30PM. ***Felony, Misdemeanor, Civil, Eviction, Small Claims, Probate.***
Civil Records: Access: Mail, in person. Both court and visitors may perform in person searches. Search fee: $6.00 per name per year. Required to search: name, years to search. Civil cases indexed by defendant. Civil records on computer from 3/1994, on index books from 1839. Mail turnaround 2 days.
Criminal Records: Access: Mail, in person. Both court and visitors may perform in person searches. Search fee: $6.00 per name per year. Required to search: name, years to search, DOB. Criminal records computerized from 3/1994, on index books from 1839. Mail turnaround time 2 days.
General Information: No juvenile or adoption records released. Will not fax documents. Court makes copy: $1.00 1st page, $.50 each add'l. Certification fee: $2.00. Payee: Clerk of Circuit Court. Only cashiers checks and money orders accepted. No credit cards accepted. Mail requests: SASE required.

Mercer County

Circuit Court PO Box 175, 100 SE 3rd St, Aledo, IL 61231; 309-582-7122; criminal fax: 309-582-7121; civil fax: same; 8AM-4PM. ***Felony, Misdemeanor, Civil, Eviction, Small Claims, Probate.*** www.mercercountyil.org
Probate fax is same as main fax number.
Civil Records: Access: Fax, mail, in person, online. Both court and visitors may perform in person searches. No search fee. Required to search: name, years to search. Civil cases indexed by defendant, plaintiff, on computer from 1989, index books from 1800s. Mail turnaround time 2-3 days. Civil PAT goes back to 1988. Access is free to civil, small claims, probate and traffic records at www.judici.com/courts/index.jsp?court=IL066015J. Premium fee service also available.
Criminal Records: Access: Phone, fax, mail, in person, online. Both court and visitors may perform in person searches. Search fee: $5.00 per name per year. Required to search: name, years to search, DOB. Criminal records computerized from 1989, index books from 1800s. Mail turnaround time 2-3 days. Criminal PAT goes back to same as civil. PAT results show name, DOB, SSN. Criminal records access is free at www.judici.com/courts/index.jsp?court=IL066015J.
General Information: Online identifiers in results same as on public terminal. No juvenile or adoption records released. Fee to fax out file $1.00 per page. Court makes copy: $.50 per page, self serve same. Certification fee: $5.00 per cert, includes copies. Payee: Clerk of Circuit Court. Business checks accepted. No credit cards accepted. Mail requests: SASE required.

Monroe County

Circuit Court 100 S Main St, Waterloo, IL 62298; 618-939-8681; criminal phone: x273; civil phone: x274; probate phone: x274; criminal fax: 618-939-1929; civil fax: same; 8AM-4:30PM. ***Felony, Misdemeanor, Civil, Eviction, Small Claims, Probate.*** Probate fax is same as main fax number.
Civil Records: Access: Mail, fax, in person. Both court and visitors may perform in person searches. Search fee: $6.00 per name per year. Required to search: name, years to search, DOB. Civil cases indexed by defendant, plaintiff, on computer from 1992, index books from 1818. Mail turnaround time 1 week. Civil PAT goes back to 1992.
Criminal Records: Access: Mail, fax, in person. Both court and visitors may perform in person searches. Search fee: $6.00 per name per year. Required to search: name, years to search, DOB. Criminal records computerized from 1992, index books from 1818. Mail turnaround time 1 week. Criminal PAT goes back to same as civil.
General Information: No juvenile or adoption records released. No fee to fax documents. Court makes copy: $1.00 1st page, $.50 each add'l. After 20 pages $.25 each. Self serve: $.20 per page. Certification fee: $5.00 per cert. Payee: Circuit Clerk. Business checks accepted. No credit cards accepted. Mail requests: SASE required.

Montgomery County

Circuit Court 120 N Main, PO Box C, Hillsboro, IL 62049; 217-532-9546; criminal phone: 217-532-9547; civil phone: 217-532-9546; probate phone: 217-532-9545; fax: 217-532-9614; 8AM-4PM. ***Felony, Misdemeanor, Civil, Eviction, Small Claims, Probate.***
www.montgomeryco.com/circlerk.htm
Civil Records: Access: Mail, in person, online. Both court and visitors may perform in person searches. Search fee: $5.00 per name per year. Required to search: name, years to search. Civil cases indexed by defendant, plaintiff, on computer from 1988, index books from 1821, microfiche (probate only) since 1939. Mail turnaround time 1 week. Civil PAT goes back to 1988. PAT results show name, DOB. Search cases free online at www.judici.com/courts/cases/case_search.jsp?court=IL068015J. Also, a premium fee service is available.
Criminal Records: Access: Mail, online, in person. Both court and visitors may perform in person searches. Search fee: $5.00 per name per year. Required to search: name, years to search, DOB. Criminal records computerized from 1988, index books from 1821, microfiche (probate only) since 1939. Mail turnaround time 1 week. Criminal PAT goes back to same as civil. Online access to criminal same as civil, see above.
General Information: No juvenile or adoption records released. Will not fax documents. Court makes copy: $.50 per page. Self serve: $.25 per page. Certification fee: $10.00 per doc. Payee: Clerk of Circuit Court. Only cashiers checks and money orders accepted. Credit cards accepted, service fees through outside venders (e-pay & GPS). They do not swipe cards at counter. Mail requests: SASE required.

Morgan County

Circuit Court PO Box 1120, 300 W State St, Jacksonville, IL 62651; 217-243-5419; criminal fax: 217-243-2009; civil fax: same; 8:30AM-4:30PM. ***Felony, Misdemeanor, Civil, Eviction, Small Claims, Probate.*** www.morgancounty-il.com
Probate is a separate index at this same address. Probate fax is same as main fax number. For payment of fines, fees and costs go to www.governmentpaymentservice.com.
Civil Records: Access: Mail, in person, online. Both court and visitors may perform in person searches. Search fee: $5.00 per name per year. Required to search: name, years to search. Civil cases indexed by defendant, plaintiff, on computer from 1990, index books from mid 1800s. Mail turnaround time 1 week. Civil PAT goes back to 1990. PAT civil results show middle initial. Access court index and records free at www.judici.com/courts/cases/case_search.jsp?court=IL069015J.
Criminal Records: Access: Mail, in person, online. Both court and visitors may perform in person searches. Search fee: $5.00 per name per year. Required to search: name, years to search, DOB. Criminal records computerized from 1990, index books from mid 1800s. Mail turnaround time 1 week. Criminal PAT goes back to 1990.PAT results show name, DOB. Access to criminal court records online is same as civil, see above. Online results show middle initial, DOB.
General Information: No juvenile or adoption records released. Will fax documents $1.50 1st page, $.50 ea add'l. Court makes copy: $1.50 1st page, $.50 each add'l, self serve same. Certification fee: $4.00 per document. Payee: Clerk of Circuit Court. Only cashiers checks and money orders accepted. No credit cards accepted. Mail requests: SASE required.

Moultrie County

Circuit Court 10 S Main, #7, Moultrie County Courthouse, Sullivan, IL 61951; 217-728-4622; criminal fax: 217-728-7833; civil fax: same; 8:30AM-4:30PM. ***Felony, Misdemeanor, Civil, Eviction, Small Claims, Probate.***
www.circuit-clerk.moultrie.il.us
Probate fax is same as main fax number.
Civil Records: Access: Mail, in person, online. Both court and visitors may perform in person searches. Search fee: $4.00 per name per year. Required to search: name, years to search. Civil cases indexed by defendant. Civil records on computer from 1990, index books from 1850. Mail turnaround time 1 week. Access court index and records free at www.judici.com/courts/cases/case_search.jsp?court=IL070015J.
Criminal Records: Access: Mail, in person, online. Both court and visitors may perform in person searches. Search fee: $4.00 per name per year. Required to search: name, years to search, DOB. Criminal records computerized from 1990, index books from 1850. Mail turnaround time 1 week. Access to criminal court records online is same as civil, see above. Online results show middle initial, DOB.
General Information: No juvenile or adoption records released. If necessary, Will fax documents $2.00 per page fax fee, up to 10 pages. Court makes copy: $.50 per page. Certification fee: $2.00 per cert. Payee: Clerk of Circuit Court. Business checks accepted. No credit cards accepted. Mail requests: SASE required.

Ogle County

Circuit Court 106 S Fifth St #300, Oregon, IL 61061; 815-732-1130; criminal phone: 815-732-1140; civil phone: 815-732-1130; fax: 815-732-9093; 8:30AM-4:30PM. ***Felony, Misdemeanor, Civil, Eviction, Small Claims, Probate.***
www.oglecounty.org/marty/circuitclerk.html
Civil Records: Access: Mail, in person, online. Both court and visitors may perform in person searches. Search fee: $6.00 per name per year. Required to search: name, years to search. Civil cases indexed by defendant, plaintiff, on computer back to 1994; prior records on microfiche last 10 years, index books from 1836. Mail turnaround time 2-3 weeks. Civil PAT goes back to 1994. Access is free to civil, small claims, probate and traffic records at www.judici.com/courts/cases/index.jsp?court=IL071015J. Premium fee service also available.
Criminal Records: Access: Mail, online, in person. Only the court performs in person searches; visitors may not. Search fee: $6.00 per name per year. Required to search: name, years to search, DOB. Criminal records computerized from 1989; prior records on microfiche last 10 years, index books from 1836. Mail turnaround time 2-3 weeks. Criminal PAT goes back to 1989. Criminal records access is free at www.judici.com/courts/cases/index.jsp?court=IL071015J.

General Information: No juvenile or adoption records released. Will not fax documents. Court makes copy: $2.00 1st page, $.50 each add'l. $.25 per page after 19. Certification fee: $10.00 per document. Payee: Clerk of Circuit Court. Only cashiers checks and money orders accepted. No credit cards accepted. Mail requests: SASE required.

Peoria County

Circuit Court 324 Main St, Rm G22, Peoria, IL 61602; 309-672-6953; fax: 309-677-6228; 8:30AM-5PM. ***Felony, Misdemeanor, Civil, Eviction, Small Claims, Probate.***

Civil Records: Access: Phone, mail, in person. Both court and visitors may perform in person searches. Search fee: $6.00 per name per year. Required to search: name, years to search. Civil cases indexed by defendant, plaintiff, on computer from 1986 (traffic), from 1987 (civil), archived from 1800s. Mail turnaround time 1 week. Civil PAT goes back to 1979. PAT results show name, DOB. Results include name and case number.

Criminal Records: Access: Phone, mail, in person. Both court and visitors may perform in person searches. Search fee: $6.00 per name per year, Add'l $10.00 to mail. Required to search: name, years to search, DOB; also helpful: SSN. Criminal records computerized from 1978, archived from 1800s. Mail turnaround time 1 week. Criminal PAT goes back same as civil. Results include name, case number.

General Information: No juvenile or adoption records released. Will not fax documents. Court makes copy: $2.00 1st page, $.50 each add'l. Certification fee: $6.00 per doc. Payee: Clerk of Circuit Court. Personal checks accepted. Credit cards accepted. Mail requests: SASE required.

Perry County

Circuit Court PO Box 219, Pinckneyville, IL 62274; 618-357-6726; fax: 618-357-8336; 8AM-4PM. ***Felony, Misdemeanor, Civil, Eviction, Small Claims, Probate.***

Probate is a separate index at this same address.

Civil Records: Access: Mail, in person. Both court and visitors may perform in person searches. Search fee: $5.00 per name per year. Required to search: name, years to search. Civil cases indexed by defendant, plaintiff, on computer from 1990, index books from 1800s. Mail turnaround time up to 1 week. Civil PAT goes back to 1990. PAT civil results show middle initial.

Criminal Records: Access: Mail, in person. Both court and visitors may perform in person searches. Search fee: $5.00 per name per year. Required to search: name, years to search; also helpful: DOB. Criminal records computerized from 1990, index books from 1800s. Mail turnaround time up to 1 week. Criminal PAT goes back to same as civil. PAT results show middle initial, DOB.

General Information: No juvenile or adoption records released. Will not fax documents. Court makes copy: $1.00 1st page; $.50 each add'l; after 19 pages $.25 each. Certification fee: $2.00. Payee: Clerk of Circuit Court. Only cashiers checks and money orders accepted. No credit cards accepted. Mail requests: SASE required.

Piatt County

Circuit Court PO Box 288, 101 W Washington, Monticello, IL 61856; 217-762-4966; probate phone: same; fax: 217-762-5906; 8:30AM-4:30PM. ***Felony, Misdemeanor, Civil, Eviction, Small Claims, Probate.*** www.piattcounty.org/

Probate fax is same as main fax number.

Civil Records: Access: Phone, fax, mail, in person. Both court and visitors may perform in person searches. No search fee. Required to search: name, years to search. Civil cases indexed by defendant, plaintiff, on computer since 1988, index books from 1800s. Mail turnaround time 2-3 days. Civil PAT available.

Criminal Records: Access: Phone, fax, mail, in person. Both court and visitors may perform in person searches. No search fee. Required to search: name, years to search, DOB; also helpful: SSN. Criminal records on computer since 1988, index books from 1800s. Mail turnaround time 2-3 days. Criminal PAT available.

General Information: No juvenile or adoption records released. Will fax documents $2.00 1st page, $1.00 each add'l. Court makes copy: $1.00 1st page, $.50 each add'l. No certification fee. Payee: Clerk of Circuit Court. Business checks accepted. No Visa credit cards accepted. SASE not required.

Pike County

Circuit Court Pike County Courthouse, 100 E Washington St, Pittsfield, IL 62363; 217-285-6612; criminal fax: 217-285-4726; civil fax: same; 8:30AM-4:30PM. ***Felony, Misdemeanor, Civil, Eviction, Small Claims, Probate.***

Civil Records: Access: Mail, in person, online. Both court and visitors may perform in person searches. Search fee: $6.00 per name per year. Required to search: name, years to search. Civil cases indexed by defendant, plaintiff, on computer since 1992, index books from 1800s. Mail turnaround time ASAP. Public use terminal has civil records back to 1992. Access is free to civil, small claims, probate and traffic records at www.judici.com/courts/index.jsp?court=IL075015J. Premium fee service also available.

Criminal Records: Access: Mail, in person, online. Both court and visitors may perform in person searches. Search fee: $6.00 per name per year. Required to search: name, years to search; also helpful: SSN. Criminal records on computer since 1992, index books from 1800s. Mail turnaround time ASAP. Criminal records access is free at www.judici.com/courts/index.jsp?court=IL075015J.

General Information: No juvenile or adoption records released. Will fax out civil documents only. Court makes copy: $2.00 1st page, $.50 each add'l. $.25 per page after 19. Self serve: $.25 per page. Certification fee: $6.00 per document includes copies; $10.00 for judgment. Payee: Circuit Clerk. No personal checks accepted; money order or cash only. No credit cards accepted. SASE required.

Pope County

Circuit Court PO Box 438, Golconda, IL 62938; 618-683-3941; fax: 618-683-3018; 8AM-4PM. ***Felony, Misdemeanor, Civil, Eviction, Small Claims, Probate.***

Civil Records: Access: Phone, fax, mail, in person. Both court and visitors may perform in person searches. Search fee: $6.00 per name per year. Required to search: name, years to search. Civil cases indexed by defendant. Civil records on computer from 1989, index books from 1800s. Mail turnaround time 2-3 days. Civil PAT goes back to 1989.

Criminal Records: Access: Phone, fax, mail, in person. Both court and visitors may perform in person searches. Search fee: $6.00 per name per year. Required to search: name, years to search, DOB. Criminal records computerized from 1989, index books from 1800s. Mail turnaround time 2-3 days. Criminal PAT goes back to same as civil.

General Information: No juvenile or adoption records released. Will fax documents $.50 per page. Court makes copy: $.25 per page, self serve same. Certification fee: $6.00. Payee: Circuit Clerk. Business checks accepted. No credit cards accepted. Mail requests: SASE required.

Pulaski County

Circuit Court 500 Illinois Ave, Rm C, Mound City, IL 62963; 618-748-9300; fax: 618-748-9329; 8AM-N, 1-4PM. ***Felony, Misdemeanor, Civil, Eviction, Small Claims, Probate.***

Civil Records: Access: Mail, in person. Both court and visitors may perform in person searches. Search fee: $6.00 per name. Required to search: name, years to search. Civil cases indexed by defendant, plaintiff, on computer since 1989, on books prior. Mail turnaround time 1 week.

Criminal Records: Access: Mail, in person. Both court and visitors may perform in person searches. Search fee: $6.00 per name per year. Required to search: name, years to search, signed release; also helpful: DOB, SSN. Criminal records on computer since 1989, on books prior. Mail turnaround 1 week.

General Information: No juvenile, adoption records released. Will fax documents to local or toll-free number. Court makes copy: $1.00 1st page, $.50 each add'l. After 20 pages $.25 each. Certification fee: $6.00 per doc. Payee: Clerk of Circuit Court. Only cashiers checks and money orders accepted. No credit cards accepted. Mail requests: SASE required.

Putnam County

Circuit Court 120 N 4th St, Hennepin, IL 61327; 815-925-7016; probate phone: same; fax: 815-925-7492; 9AM-4PM. ***Felony, Misdemeanor, Civil, Eviction, Small Claims, Probate.***

Civil Records: Access: Mail, in person. Both court and visitors may perform in person searches. Search fee: $5.00 per name. Fee is per 5 years searched. Required to search: name, years to search. Civil cases indexed by defendant. Civil records on computer from 1991, index books from 1836. Mail turnaround time 3 days. Civil PAT goes back to 1991. PAT results show name, DOB.

Criminal Records: Access: Mail, in person. Both court and visitors may perform in person searches. Search fee: $5.00 per name. Fee is per 5 years searched. Required to search: name, years to search, DOB. Criminal records computerized from 1991, index books from 1836. Note: No criminal searches performed on Thursdays. Mail turnaround time 3 days. Criminal PAT goes back to same as civil.PAT results show name, DOB.

General Information: No juvenile or adoption records released. Will fax documents $.50 per page. Court makes copy: $.50 per page. $.25 per page after 20. Certification fee: $2.00. Payee: Clerk of Circuit Court. Only cashiers checks and money orders accepted. No credit cards accepted. Mail requests: SASE required.

Randolph County

Circuit Court County Courthouse, Rm 302, #1 Taylor St, Chester, IL 62233; 618-826-5000 X194; fax: 618-826-3761; 8-4PM. ***Felony, Misdemeanor, Civil, Eviction, Small Claims, Probate.***

Civil Records: Access: Mail, in person. Both court and visitors may perform in person searches. Search fee: $4.00 per name per year. Required to search: name, years to search. Civil cases indexed by defendant, plaintiff, on computer from 1992, index books from 1800s. Visitors can search both. Mail turnaround time 1-2 days. Civil PAT goes back to 1992. PAT results show name only.

Criminal Records: Access: Mail, in person. Both court and visitors may perform in person searches. Search fee: $4.00 per name per year. Required to search: name, years to search, DOB. Criminal records computerized from 1992, index books from 1800s. Visitors can search both. Mail turnaround time 1-2 days. Criminal PAT goes back to same as civil. PAT results show name only.

General Information: No juvenile or adoption records released. Will fax documents to local or toll-free number. Court makes copy: $.50 per page. Certification fee: $4.00 for seal and $1.00 1st page and $.50 each add'l page. Payee: Clerk of Circuit Court. Business checks accepted. No credit cards accepted. Mail requests: SASE required.

Richland County

Circuit Court 103 W Main, #21, Olney, IL 62450; 618-392-2151; criminal fax: 618-392-5041; civil fax: same; 8AM-4PM. ***Felony, Misdemeanor, Civil, Eviction, Small Claims, Probate.***

Probate fax is same as main fax number.

Civil Records: Access: Phone, mail, fax, in person, online. Both court and visitors may perform in person searches. Search fee: $4.00 per name per year. $25.00 maxiumum. Required to search: name, years to search. Civil cases indexed by defendant. Civil index on docket books from 1867; on computer back to 1999. Mail turnaround time 1-2 weeks. Civil PAT goes back to 1999. PAT results show middle initial, DOB. Access is free to civil, small claims, probate and traffic records at www.judici.com/courts/cases/index.jsp?court=IL080015J. Premium fee service also available.

Criminal Records: Access: Mail, in person, online. Both court and visitors may perform in person

searches. Search fee: $4.00 per name per year. $25.00 maxiumum. Required to search: name, years to search, DOB. Criminal records indexed in books from 1867; on computer back to 1986. Mail turnaround time 1-2 weeks. Criminal PAT goes back to same as civil. PAT results show middle initial, DOB. Criminal records access is free at www.judici.com/courts/cases/index.jsp?court=IL080015J. Online results show middle initial, DOB.
General Information: No juvenile or adoption records released. Will fax documents $.25 per page. Court makes copy: $.50 per page; add'l page after 19-$.25. Certification fee: $5.00 per certification. Payee: Clerk of Circuit Court. Only cashiers checks and money orders accepted. No credit cards accepted. Mail requests: SASE required.

Rock Island County

Circuit Court PO Box 5230, 210 15th St, Rock Island, IL 61204-5230; 309-786-4451; fax: 309-786-3029; 8AM-4:30PM. ***Felony, Misdemeanor, Civil, Eviction, Small Claims, Probate.***
www.co.rock-island.il.us/CoClk.aspx?id=547
Search fee includes both the civil and criminal indexes.
Civil Records: Access: Mail, in person, online. Both court and visitors may perform in person searches. Search fee: $6.00 per name per year. Required to search: name, years to search. Civil cases indexed by defendant, plaintiff, on computer from 1989, index books from 1950s. Mail turnaround time 1 week. Civil PAT goes back to 5/1989. PAT results show name only. Full access to court records on the remote online system requires contract and $12.75 per month. Civil, criminal, probate, traffic, and domestic records can be accessed by name or case number. Also, access to civil, small claims, probate and traffic records is free at www.judici.com/courts/cases/index.jsp?court=IL081025J.
Criminal Records: Access: Mail, in person, online. Both court and visitors may perform in person searches. Search fee: $6.00 per name per year. Required to search: name, years to search, DOB. Criminal records computerized from 1989, index books from 1950s. Mail turnaround time 1 week. Criminal PAT goes back to 5/1989. PAT results show middle initial, but not all records include DOBs. Online access to criminal records is the same as civil - there are two methods.
General Information: No juvenile or adoption records released. Will not fax documents. Court makes copy: $2.00 1st page, $.50 each next 19, then $.25 per add'l. Certification fee: $6.00 per doc. Payee: Circuit Clerks Office. Money orders accepted. Visa/MC accepted; there is a $4.75 usage fee and $5.00 minimum. Mail requests: SASE required.

Saline County

Circuit Court County Courthouse, Harrisburg, IL 62946; 618-253-5096; probate phone: same; fax: 618-253-3904; 8-4PM. ***Felony, Misdemeanor, Civil, Eviction, Small Claims, Probate.***
Civil Records: Access: Fax, mail, in person, phone. Both court and visitors may perform in person searches. Search fee: $5.00 per name per year. Required to search: name, years to search. Civil cases indexed by defendant, plaintiff, on computer back to 1986, index books archived from 1886. Mail turnaround time 1 week. Civil PAT goes back to 1986. PAT results show middle initial, DOB.
Criminal Records: Access: Fax, mail, in person, phone. Both court and visitors may perform in person searches. Search fee: $5.00 per name per year. Required to search: name, years to search, DOB. Criminal records computerized from 1986, index books archived from 1800s. Mail turnaround time 1-2 weeks. Criminal PAT goes back to same as civil. PAT results show middle initial, DOB.
General Information: No juvenile or adoption records released. Fee to fax out file $2.00 1st page, $1.00 each add'l. Court makes copy: $1.00 1st page, $.50 each add'l. Self serve: $.10 per page. Certification fee: $5.00. Payee: Clerk of Circuit Court. Business checks accepted. Credit cards accepted in person, $5.00 fee extra. SASE required.

Sangamon County

Circuit Court 200 S 9th St, Rm 405, Springfield, IL 62701; 217-753-6674; fax: 217-753-6665; 8:30AM-4:30PM. ***Felony, Misdemeanor, Civil, Eviction, Small Claims, Probate.***
www.sangamoncountycircuitclerk.org
Civil Records: Access: Fax, mail, in person, online. Both court and visitors may perform in person searches. Search fee: $4.00 per name per year. Required to search: name, years to search. Civil cases indexed by defendant, plaintiff, on computer from 1990, index books from 1800s. Mail turnaround time 1-2 weeks. Civil PAT goes back to 1990. PAT results show middle initial, DOB. Online access to civil records is the same as criminal, see below.
Criminal Records: Access: Fax, mail, in person, online. Both court and visitors may perform in person searches. Search fee: $4.00 per name per year. Required to search: name, years to search, DOB. Criminal records computerized from 1993, index books from 1800s. Mail turnaround time 1-2 weeks. Criminal PAT goes back to 1993. PAT results show middle initial, DOB. Online access to court records is via subscription system. $20 per month or $240 per year for this county or $300 for Will, Madison, Sangamon, Winnebago, Kane, Kendall, DeKalb courts. Visit www.clericusmagnus.com or call 866-511-2892. Online results show middle initial, DOB.
General Information: No juvenile, mental health, adoption records released. No fee to fax documents. Court makes copy: $2.00 1st page, $.50 each add'l. $.25 per page after 19. Certification fee: $4.00. Payee: Circuit Clerk. Personal checks and major credit cards accepted. Mail requests: SASE required.

Schuyler County

Circuit Court PO Box 80, Rushville, IL 62681; 217-322-4633; fax: 217-322-6164; 8AM-4PM. ***Felony, Misdemeanor, Civil, Eviction, Small Claims, Probate.***
Civil Records: Access: Mail, in person. Both court and visitors may perform in person searches. Search fee: $6.00 per name per year. Required to search: name, years to search. Civil cases indexed by defendant. Civil records on computer from 1988, index books from 1800s. Mail turnaround 1 week.
Criminal Records: Access: Mail, in person. Both court and visitors may perform in person searches. Search fee: $6.00 per name per year. Required to search: name, years to search, DOB. Criminal records computerized from 1988, index books from 1800s. Mail turnaround time 1 week.
General Information: No juvenile or adoption records released. Fee to fax out file $1.00 per page. Court makes copy: $2.00 1st page, $.50 each add'l. $.25 per page after 19. Certification fee: $10.00. Payee: Clerk of Circuit Court. Only cashiers checks and money orders accepted. No credit cards accepted. Mail requests: SASE required.

Scott County

Circuit Court 35 E Market St, Winchester, IL 62694; 217-742-5217; fax: 217-742-5853; 8AM-N, 1-4PM. ***Felony, Misdemeanor, Civil, Eviction, Small Claims, Probate.***
Civil Records: Access: Mail, in person. Both court and visitors may perform in person searches. Search fee: $6.00 per name per year. Required to search: name, years to search. Civil cases indexed by defendant, plaintiff; index on docket books from 1800s. Mail turnaround time 1 week.
Criminal Records: Access: Mail, in person. Both court and visitors may perform in person searches. Search fee: $6.00 per name per year. Required to search: name, years to search, DOB. Criminal records indexed in books from 1800s. Mail turnaround time 1 week.
General Information: No juvenile or adoption records released. Will not fax documents. Court makes copy: $1.00 1st page, $.50 each add'l. After 20 pages $.25 each, self serve same. Certification fee: $2.00. Payee: Clerk of Circuit Court. Only cashiers checks and money orders accepted. Call 888-604-7888 to use credit card. SASE required.

Shelby County

Circuit Court County Courthouse, PO Box 469, Shelbyville, IL 62565; 217-774-4212; criminal fax: 217-774-4109; civil fax: same; 8AM-4PM. ***Felony, Misdemeanor, Civil, Eviction, Small Claims, Probate.***
Probate fax is same as main fax number.
Civil Records: Access: Fax, mail, in person, online. Both court and visitors may perform in person searches. Search fee: $5.00 per name per year. Required to search: name, years to search. Civil cases indexed by defendant, plaintiff, on computer from 1988, index books from 1848. Mail turnaround time 1-2 weeks. Civil PAT goes back to 1988. Access is free to civil, small claims, probate, traffic records at www.judici.com/courts/cases/index.jsp?court=IL087025J. Premium fee service also available.
Criminal Records: Access: Fax, mail, in person, online. Both court and visitors may perform in person searches. Search fee: $5.00 per name per year. Required to search: name, years to search, DOB. Criminal records computerized from 1988, index books from 1848. Mail turnaround time 1-2 weeks. Criminal PAT goes back to same as civil. PAT results show middle initial, DOB. Criminal records access is free at www.judici.com/courts/cases/index.jsp?court=IL087025J. Online results show name, DOB.
General Information: Online identifiers in results same as on public terminal. No juvenile or adoption records released. Will fax documents $5.00 per name. Court makes copy: $1.00 1st page, $.50 each add'l. Self serve: $.25 per page. Certification fee: $10.00 per document plus copy fee for add'l pages. Payee: Circuit Clerk. Personal checks accepted; credit cards are not. Mail requests: SASE required.

St. Clair County

Circuit Court 10 Public Square, Belleville, IL 62220-1623; 618-277-6832; criminal phone: x4 for felony; probate phone: x2307; fax: 618-825-2742; 8AM-4PM. ***Felony, Misdemeanor, Civil, Eviction, Small Claims, Probate.***
Civil Records: Access: Mail, in person. Both court and visitors may perform in person searches. Search fee: $6.00 per name per year. Required to search: name, years to search; also helpful: address. Civil cases indexed by defendant, plaintiff, on computer from 1990, microfiche from 1800s. Mail turnaround time 1-2 days. Civil PAT goes back to 1990. Results include case number.
Criminal Records: Access: Mail, in person. Both court and visitors may perform in person searches. Search fee: $6.00 per name per year. Required to search: name, years to search, DOB. Criminal records computerized from 1990 (with some info available back to 1980) microfiche from 1800s. Cases prior to 1995 archived in basement. Mail turnaround time 1-2 days. Criminal PAT goes back to same as civil. PAT results show middle initial, DOB. Results also give charges, disposition, key dates.
General Information: No juvenile or adoption records released. Will not fax documents. Court makes copy: $2.00 1st page, $.50 each add'l. $.25 per page after 19. Certification fee: $6.00. Payee: Clerk of Circuit Court. Personal checks not excepted. No credit cards accepted. Mail requests: SASE required.

Stark County

Circuit Court 130 W Main St, Toulon, IL 61483; 309-286-5941; probate phone: same; fax: 309-286-4039; 8:30AM-4:30PM. ***Felony, Misdemeanor, Civil, Eviction, Small Claims, Probate.***
Civil Records: Access: Mail, in person. Both court and visitors may perform in person searches. Search fee: $6.00 per name per year. Required to search: name, years to search. Civil cases indexed by defendant. Civil index on docket books from 1800s. Mail turnaround time 2-3 days. Civil PAT goes back to 2001.
Criminal Records: Access: Mail, in person. Both court and visitors may perform in person searches. Search fee: $6.00 per name per year. Required to search: name, years to search, DOB. Criminal records indexed in books from 1800s. Mail turnaround time 2-3 days. Criminal PAT goes back to same as civil.

General Information: No juvenile or adoption records released. Will not fax documents. Court makes copy: $1.00 1st page, $.50 each add'l, self serve same. Certification fee: $4.00. Payee: Clerk of Circuit Court. Personal checks accepted; credit cards are not. Mail requests: SASE required.

Stephenson County

Circuit Court 15 N Galena Ave, 2nd Fl, Freeport, IL 61032; 815-235-8266; criminal fax: 815-233-1576; civil fax: 815-235-8262; 8:30AM-4:30PM. ***Felony, Misdemeanor, Civil, Eviction, Small Claims, Probate.***
www.co.stephenson.il.us/circuitclerk/

Civil Records: Access: Mail, in person, online. Only the court performs in person searches; visitors may not. Search fee: $6.00 per name per year. Required to search: name, years to search. Civil cases indexed by defendant, plaintiff, on computer from 8/1989, index books from 1875. Mail turnaround time 5-15 days. Civil PAT goes back to 1989. PAT results show name only. Access is free to civil, small claims, probate and traffic records at www.judici.com/courts/index.jsp?court=IL089015J. Premium fee service also available.

Criminal Records: Access: Mail, in person, online. Only the court performs in person searches; visitors may not. Search fee: $6.00 per name per year. Required to search: name, years to search, DOB. Criminal records computerized from 8/1989, index books from 1875. Mail turnaround time 5-15 days. Criminal PAT available. PAT results show name only. Criminal records access is free at www.judici.com/courts/index.jsp?court=IL089015J. Online results show name only.

General Information: Online identifiers in results same as on public terminal. No juvenile or adoption records released. Will not fax documents. Court makes copy: $2.00 1st page, $.50 each add'l, self serve same. Certification fee: $10.00. Payee: Clerk of Circuit Court. Business checks accepted. Credit cards accepted. Mail requests: SASE required.

Tazewell County

Circuit Court Courthouse, 243 Court St, Pekin, IL 61554; 309-477-2214; criminal phone: 309-477-2775; civil phone: 309-477-2775; probate phone: same; fax: 309-353-7801; 8:30AM-5PM. ***Felony, Misdemeanor, Civil, Small Claims, Probate.***

Civil Records: Access: Mail, in person. Both court and visitors may perform in person searches. Search fee: $6.00 per name per year. Required to search: name, years to search. Civil cases indexed by defendant, plaintiff, on computer from 2/89 index books from 1800s. Mail turnaround time 3-4 days. Civil PAT goes back to 2/1989.

Criminal Records: Access: Mail, in person. Both court and visitors may perform in person searches. Search fee: $6.00 per name per year. Required to search: name, years to search, DOB, signed release. Criminal records computerized from 2/89 index books from 1800s. Mail turnaround time 3-4 days. Criminal PAT goes back to same as civil.

General Information: No juvenile or adoption records released. Court makes copy: $2.00 1st page, $.50 each add'l. $.25 per page after 19, self serve same. Certification fee: $6.00. Payee: Clerk of Circuit Court. Cashiers checks and money orders accepted; personal checks accepted for add'l $2.00 fee. Credit cards accepted in person only. A convenience fee of $5.00 added on charge up to $100.00; add $5.00 more if over $100.00. Online payments can be made at www.illinoisepay.com. Mail request: SASE required.

Union County

Circuit Court Union County Courthouse, 309 W Market, Rm 101, Jonesboro, IL 62952; 618-833-5913; fax: 618-833-5223; 8AM-N,1-4PM. ***Felony, Misdemeanor, Civil, Eviction, Small Claims, Probate.***

Civil Records: Access: Fax, mail, in person, online. Both court and visitors may perform in person searches. Search fee: $6.00 per name per year. Required to search: name, years to search. Civil cases indexed by defendant, plaintiff, on computer from 1986, index books from 1800s. Note: Public can only search paper records up to 1986. Only court personnel have access to computer records. Mail turnaround time 1 week. Access is free to civil, small claims, probate and traffic records at www.judici.com/courts/index.jsp?court=IL091015J. Premium fee service also available.

Criminal Records: Access: Fax, mail, in person, online. Both court and visitors may perform in person searches. Search fee: $6.00 per name per year. Required to search: name, years to search; also helpful: DOB. Criminal records computerized from 1986, index books from 1800s. Note: In person criminal record search procedures are the same as civil. Mail turnaround time 1 week. Criminal records access is free at www.judici.com/courts/index.jsp?court=IL091015J.

General Information: No juvenile or adoption records released. Fee to fax out file $5.00. Court makes copy: $2.00 1st page, $.50 each add'l 19 pages; $.25 each add'l. Certification fee: $6.00 per doc. Payee: Lorraine Moreland, Circuit Clerk. Business checks accepted. No personal checks or credit cards accepted. Mail requests: SASE required.

Vermilion County

Circuit Court 7 N Vermilion, Danville, IL 61832; 217-554-7700; probate phone: 217-554-7734; fax: 217-554-7728; 8:30AM-4:30PM. ***Felony, Misdemeanor, Civil, Eviction, Small Claims, Probate.*** www.co.vermilion.il.us

Civil Records: Access: Phone, mail, in person, online. Only the court performs in person searches; visitors may not. Search fee: $6.00 per name per year. Required to search: name, years to search. Civil cases indexed by defendant, plaintiff, on computer from 1989; microfilm from 3/1949 to 5/1989; index books from 1800s. Mail turnaround time 2-3 days. Civil PAT goes back to 1989. PAT results show middle initial, DOB, SSN. Search the index at www.judici.com/courts/cases/case_search.jsp?court=IL092015J. Records are current to 1989. Premium fee service also available.

Criminal Records: Access: Phone, mail, in person, online. Only the court performs in person searches; visitors may not. Search fee: $6.00 per name per year. Required to search: name, years to search, DOB; also helpful: SSN. Criminal records computerized from 1989; microfilm from 3/1949 to 5/1989; index books from 1800s. Mail turnaround time 1 week. Criminal PAT goes back to 1989. PAT results show middle initial, DOB, SSN. Search index at www.judici.com/courts/cases/case_search.jsp?court=IL092015J. Records are current to 1989.

General Information: No juvenile, impounded, mental health or adoption records released. Will not fax documents. Court makes copy: $2.00 1st page, $.50 each add'l. Self serve: $.10 per page. Certification fee: $5.00 per doc. Payee: Clerk of Circuit Court. Business checks accepted. No credit cards accepted. Mail requests: SASE required.

Wabash County

Circuit Court PO Drawer 997, 401 Market St, Mt Carmel, IL 62863; 618-262-5362; criminal fax: 618-263-4441; civil fax: same; 8AM-5PM. ***Felony, Misdemeanor, Civil, Eviction, Small Claims, Probate.*** Probate fax is same as main fax number.

Civil Records: Access: Mail, in person, online. Both court and visitors may perform in person searches. Search fee: $4.00 per name per year. Required to search: name, years to search. Civil cases indexed by defendant, plaintiff, on computer from 1988, index books from 1800s. Mail turnaround time 5 days. Civil PAT goes back to 1988. PAT results show name, DOB. Results include name and case number. Access is free to civil, small claims, probate and traffic records at www.judici.com/courts/cases/index.jsp?court=IL093015J. Premium fee service also available.

Criminal Records: Access: Mail, in person, online. Both court and visitors may perform in person searches. Search fee: $4.00 per name per year. Required to search: name, years to search, DOB. Criminal records computerized from 1988, index books from 1800s. Note: Results include name and case number. Mail turnaround time 5 days. Criminal PAT goes back to same as civil.PAT results show name, DOB. Results include name and case number. Criminal records access is free at www.judici.com/courts/cases/index.jsp?court=IL093015J. Online results show name, DOB.

General Information: Online identifiers in results same as on public terminal. No juvenile or adoption records released. Will fax out docs if all fees prepaid. Court makes copy: $.50 each 1st 20 pages; $.25 each add'l. Self serve: $.25 per page. Certification fee: $5.00 per seal. Payee: Clerk of Circuit Court. Only cashiers checks and money orders accepted. No credit cards accepted. Mail requests: SASE required.

Warren County

Circuit Court 100 W Broadway, Monmouth, IL 61462; 309-734-5179; criminal phone: x302; civil phone: x304; probate phone: x306; fax: 309-734-4151; 8AM-4:30PM. ***Felony, Misdemeanor, Civil, Eviction, Small Claims, Probate.***

Civil Records: Access: Mail, in person. Both court and visitors may perform in person searches. Search fee: $5.00 per name per year. Required to search: name, years to search. Civil cases indexed by defendant. Civil records on computer from 2000, index books from 1800s. Mail turnaround time 7-10 days. Civil PAT goes back to 1999. PAT civil results show middle initial.

Criminal Records: Access: Mail, in person. Both court and visitors may perform in person searches. Search fee: $5.00 per name per year. Required to search: name, years to search, DOB. Criminal records computerized from 2000, index books from 1800s. Mail turnaround time 7-10 days. Criminal PAT goes back to same as civil. PAT results show middle initial, DOB.

General Information: No juvenile or adoption records released. Will fax documents uncertified. Court makes copy: $2.00 1st page; $.50 each add'l. Certification fee: $3.00. Payee: Clerk of Circuit Court. Only cashiers checks and money orders accepted. No credit cards accepted. Mail requests: SASE required.

Washington County

Circuit Court 101 E St Louis St, Nashville, IL 62263; 618-327-4800 X305; criminal fax: 618-327-3583; civil fax: same; 8AM-4PM. ***Felony, Misdemeanor, Civil, Eviction, Small Claims, Probate.*** Probate fax is same as main fax number.

Civil Records: Access: Mail, in person, online. Both court and visitors may perform in person searches. Search fee: $5.00 per name per year. Required to search: name, years to search. Civil cases indexed by defendant, plaintiff, on computer since 1998; 1988 for child support; prior records on index books from 1800s. Mail turnaround time 3-5 days. Civil PAT goes back to 1997. PAT results show middle initial, DOB. Access is free to civil, small claims, probate and traffic records at www.judici.com/courts/index.jsp?court=IL095015J. Premium fee service also available.

Criminal Records: Access: Mail, in person, online. Both court and visitors may perform in person searches. Search fee: $5.00 per name per year. Required to search: name, years to search; also helpful: DOB. Criminal records on computer since 1998; 1988 for child support; prior records on index books from 1800s. Mail turnaround time 3-5 days. Criminal PAT goes back to same as civil. PAT results show middle initial, DOB. Criminal records access is free at www.judici.com/courts/index.jsp?court=IL095015J. Online results show middle initial, DOB.

General Information: No juvenile or adoption records released. Will fax documents to local or toll free line. Court makes copy: $1.00 per page. Self serve: $.50 per page. Certification fee: $3.00 per document. Payee: Washington County Circuit Clerk. No personal checks accepted. Will bill to attorneys. Mail requests: SASE required.

Wayne County

Circuit Court County Courthouse, 307 E Main St, Fairfield, IL 62837; 618-842-7684; criminal fax: 618-842-2556; civil fax: same; 8AM-4:30PM. ***Felony, Misdemeanor, Civil, Small Claims, Probate.***
www.illinoissecondcircuit.info/county_wayne.html
Probate fax is same as main fax number.

Civil Records: Access: Mail, fax, in person, online. Both court and visitors may perform in person searches. Search fee: $4.00 per name per year. Required to search: name, years to search. Civil cases indexed by defendant, plaintiff, on computer back to 11/88, index books from 1800s. Mail turnaround time 1 week. Civil PAT goes back to 1988. PAT civil results show middle initial. Access is free to civil, small claims, probate and traffic records at www.judici.com/courts/cases/index.jsp?court=IL093015J. Premium fee service also available.

Criminal Records: Access: Mail, fax, in person, online. Both court and visitors may perform in person searches. Search fee: $4.00 per name per year. Required to search: name, years to search, DOB. Criminal records computerized back 1/1990. Mail turnaround time 1 week. Criminal PAT goes back to same as civil. PAT criminal results show middle initial. Criminal records access is free at www.judici.com/courts/cases/index.jsp?court=IL093015J. Online results show middle initial.

General Information: Online identifiers in results same as on public terminal. No juvenile or adoption records released. Will fax documents. Court makes copy: $1.00 1st page, $.50 each add'l, self serve same. Certification fee: $5.00 per certification. Payee: Clerk of Circuit Court. Only cashiers checks and money orders accepted. Visa/MC/AmEx cards accepted through Illinoispay.com. SASE required.

White County

Circuit Court PO Box 310, 301 E Main, County Courthouse, Carmi, IL 62821; 618-382-2321 x4; criminal fax: 618-382-2322; civil fax: same; 8AM-4PM. ***Felony, Misdemeanor, Civil, Small Claims, Probate.*** Probate fax is same as main fax number.

Civil Records: Access: Fax, mail, in person, online. Both court and visitors may perform in person searches. Search fee: $4.00 per name per year. Required to search: name, years to search. Civil cases indexed by defendant, plaintiff, on computer from 1992, index books from 1800s. Mail turnaround time 1-2 weeks. Civil PAT goes back to 1992. Results include name and case number. Access is free to civil, small claims, probate and traffic records at www.judici.com/courts/cases/index.jsp?court=IL097015J. Premium fee service also available.

Criminal Records: Access: Fax, mail, in person, online. Both court and visitors may perform in person searches. Search fee: $4.00 per name per year. Required to search: name, years to search; also helpful: DOB. Criminal records computerized from 1992, index books from 1800s. Mail turnaround time 1-2 weeks. Criminal PAT goes back to same as civil. Results include name and DOB. Criminal records access is free at www.judici.com/courts/cases/index.jsp?court=IL097015J.

General Information: Online identifiers in results same as on public terminal. No juvenile or adoption records released. Will fax documents $2.00 per page. Court makes copy: $.50 per page, self serve same. Certification fee: $5.00 1st page. Payee: Clerk of Circuit Court. Only cashier's checks or money orders accepted. No credit cards accepted. Mail requests: SASE required.

Whiteside County

Circuit Court 200 E Knox St, Morrison, IL 61270-2698; 815-772-5188; fax: 815-772-5187; 8:30AM-4:30PM. ***Felony, Misdemeanor, Civil, Eviction, Small Claims, Probate.***

Civil Records: Access: Phone, fax, mail, in person, online. Both court and visitors may perform in person searches. Search fee: $6.00 per name. Required to search: name, years to search. Civil cases indexed by defendant. Civil records on computer from 1989, index books from 1800s. Mail turnaround time 1 month. Civil PAT goes back to 1989. PAT civil results show middle initial. Access is free to civil, small claims, probate and traffic records at www.judici.com/courts/cases/case_search.jsp?court=IL098015J. Premium fee service also available.

Criminal Records: Access: Phone, fax, mail, in person, online. Both court and visitors may perform in person searches. Search fee: $6.00 per name. Required to search: name, years to search, DOB. Criminal records computerized from 1988, index books from 1800s. Mail turnaround time 1 month. Criminal PAT goes back to same as civil. PAT results show middle initial, DOB. Access to criminal records is the same as civil. Online results show middle initial, DOB. Middle initial shows if results if middle initial provided to court record.

General Information: Online identifiers in results same as on public terminal. No juvenile or adoption records released. No fee to fax documents locally only. Court makes copy: $1.50 1st page, $.50 each add'l up to 20, $.25 each add'l. Certification fee: $4.00. Payee: Clerk of Circuit Court. Personal checks accepted for search/copy-related fees. No credit cards accepted. Mail requests: SASE required.

Will County

Circuit Court 14 W Jefferson St, #212, Joliet, IL 60432; 815-727-8592; probate phone: 815-730-7155; fax: 815-727-8896; 8:30AM-4:30PM. ***Felony, Misdemeanor, Civil, Eviction, Small Claims, Probate.*** www.willcountycircuitcourt.com Probate fax- 815-730-7160

Civil Records: Access: Fax, mail, in person, online. Both court and visitors may perform in person searches. Search fee: $6.00 per name per year. Required to search: name, years to search. Civil cases indexed by defendant, plaintiff, on computer from 1989, index books from 1800s. Mail turnaround time 48 hours. Civil PAT goes back to 10 years. PAT civil results show middle initial. Online access to civil court records is the same as criminal, see below.

Criminal Records: Access: Fax, mail, in person, online. Both court and visitors may perform in person searches. Search fee: $6.00 per name per year. Required to search: name, years to search, DOB. Criminal records computerized from 1989, index books from 1800s. Mail turnaround time 2 weeks. Criminal PAT goes back to same as civil. PAT results show middle initial, DOB. Online access to court records is via subscription system. $59 setup fee plus $20 per month or $240 per year for this county or $300 for Will, Madison, Sangamon, Winnebago, Kane, Kendall, DeKalb courts. Visit www.clericusmagnus.com or call 866-511-2892. Online results show middle initial, DOB.

General Information: No juvenile, adoption, mental health records released. Will not fax documents. Court makes copy: $2.00 1st page; $.50 each for 2-19 pages; then $.25 each add'l per case. Certification fee: $6.00. Payee: Pamela J McGuire Clerk of Circuit Court. Cash, cashiers checks and money orders accepted. No personal checks. Major credit cards accepted. Mail requests: SASE required.

Williamson County

Circuit Court 200 W Jefferson St, Marion, IL 62959; 618-997-1301 X153; 8AM-4PM. ***Felony, Misdemeanor, Civil, Eviction, Small Claims, Probate.***
www.state.il.us/court/CircuitCourt/default.asp

Civil Records: Access: Mail, in person, online. Both court and visitors may perform in person searches. Search fee: $4.00 per name per year. Required to search: name, years to search. Civil cases indexed by defendant, plaintiff, on computer from 7/86, index books from 1800s. Mail turnaround time 1 week. Civil PAT goes back to 7/1986. Search cases free online at www.judici.com/courts/cases/case_search.jsp?court=IL100025J. Also, a premium fee service is available. Also, court calendars free at http://williamsoncountycourthouse.com/p/calendars.php.

Criminal Records: Access: Mail, in person, online. Both court and visitors may perform in person searches. Search fee: $4.00 per name per year. Required to search: name, years to search, DOB. Criminal records computerized from 7/86, index books from 1800s. Mail turnaround time 1 week. Criminal PAT goes back to same as civil.PAT results show name, DOB. Online access to criminal same as civil, see above. Online results show name, DOB.

General Information: Online identifiers in results same as on public terminal. No juvenile or adoption records released. Will not fax documents. Court makes copy: $1.00 1st page, $.50 each add'l. Certification fee: $2.00. Payee: Clerk of Circuit Court. Business checks accepted. No credit cards accepted. Mail requests: SASE required.

Winnebago County

Circuit Court 400 W State St, Rockford, IL 61101; 815-319-4500; fax: 815-319-4571; 8AM-5PM. ***Felony, Misdemeanor, Civil, Eviction, Small Claims, Probate.***
www.cc.co.winnebago.il.us
Criminal records is in Rm 108. Civil is Rm 104.

Civil Records: Access: Phone, mail, in person, online. Both court and visitors may perform in person searches. Search fee: $6.00 per name per year. Required to search: name, years to search. Civil cases indexed by defendant, plaintiff, on computer back to 1983; prior records on index books from 1800s. Mail turnaround time 1 week. Civil PAT goes back to 1980. Online access to civil court records is the same as criminal, see below.

Criminal Records: Access: Phone, mail, in person, online. Both court and visitors may perform in person searches. Search fee: $6.00 per name per year. Required to search: name, years to search, DOB. Criminal records computerized from 1983; prior records on index books from 1800s. Mail turnaround time 1 week. Criminal PAT goes back to 1985. Online access to court records is via subscription system. Visit www.clericusmagnus.com or call 866-319-4303.

General Information: No juvenile, mental or adoption records released. Will fax documents to local or toll-free number. Court makes copy: $2.00 1st page, $.50 each add'l. $.25 per page after 19. Certification fee: $6.00 per doc. Payee: Clerk of Circuit Court. Personal checks accepted. Mail requests: SASE required.

Woodford County

Circuit Court PO Box 284, 115 N Main, County Courthouse #201, Eureka, IL 61530; 309-467-3312; 8AM-5PM. ***Felony, Misdemeanor, Civil, Eviction, Small Claims, Probate.***

Civil Records: Access: Mail, in person, online. Both court and visitors may perform in person searches. Search fee: $5.00 per name per year. Required to search: name, years to search. Civil cases indexed by defendant, plaintiff, on computer from 1990, index books from 1800s. Mail turnaround time 2-3 days. Civil PAT goes back to 1990. Online access to civil cases same as criminal, see below.

Criminal Records: Access: Mail, in person, online. Both court and visitors may perform in person searches. Search fee: $5.00 per name per year. Required to search: name, years to search, DOB. Criminal records computerized from 1990, index books from 1800s. Mail turnaround time 2-3 days. Criminal PAT goes back to same as civil. Online access to criminal cases free at www.judici.com/courts/cases/case_search.jsp?court=IL102015J. Premium fee subscription services also available.

General Information: No juvenile or adoption records released. Will not fax documents. Court makes copy: $.50 per page. Certification fee: $4.00. Cert fee includes copies. Payee: Woodford County Circuit Clerk. Personal checks accepted; credit cards are not. Mail requests: SASE required.

Illinois Recording Offices

ORGANIZATION: 102 counties, 102 recording offices. The recording officer is the County Recorder, but some counties prefer the name Recorder of Deeds. Many counties utilize a grantor/grantee index containing all transactions. Cook County had separate offices for real estate recording and UCC filing until they combined offices June 30, 2001. Since that date only UCC extension, amendments or terminations can be filed on exisiting UCCs, with exception of UCCs on real estate related collateral which are still filed here. Illinois is in the Central Time Zone (CST).

REAL ESTATE RECORDS: Most counties will not perform real estate searches. Cost of certified copies varies widely but many counties charge the same as the cost of recording the document. Tax records are usually located at the Treasurer's Office.

UCC RECORDS: Financing statements are filed at the state level except for real estate related filings which are filed with the County Recorder. Most counties will perform UCC searches. Use search request form UCC-11. UCC search fee is usually $10.00 per debtor name/address combination. UCC copy fee is usually $1.00 per page.

TAX LIEN RECORDS: Federal tax liens on personal property of businesses are filed with the Secretary of State. Other federal and all state tax liens on personal property are filed with the County Recorder. Some counties will perform tax lien searches for $5.00-$10.00 per name (state and federal are separate searches in many of these counties) and $1.00 per page of copy.

OTHER LIENS: Judgments, mechanics, contractor, medical, lis pendens, oil & gas, mobile home.

ONLINE ACCESS: A number of counties offer online access. Search statewide UCCs at www.ilsos.gov/UCC/.

Adams County

County Recorder, 507 Vermont St, #110, Quincy, IL 62301. Recording, R/E & UCC phone-217-277-2125; 8:30AM-4:30PM (CST) www.co.adams.il.us

Index: All in one. Records indexed on a public use terminal back to 2/95. Only the public may search. Will not search UCC records. Copy fee $1.00 per page. Cert fee- $12.00 per cert + $1.00 per page for copies after 4 pages. Payee- Adams County Clerk/Recorder. Office does not sell bulk data. **Other phones:** Treasurer- 217-277-2248; Elections- 217-277-2157; Vital Records- 217-277-2158. **Property tax/Assessing-** 507 Vermont St, Quincy, IL 62301; 217-277-2136, assessor fax- 217-277-2152. **Online access-** Access property data free at www.emapsplus.com/ILAdams/maps/ including name searching.

Alexander County

County Recorder, 2000 Washington Ave, Cairo, IL 62914. Recording, R/E & UCC phone-618-734-7000; fax-618-734-7002; 8AM-N, 1-4PM (CST)

Index: Separate indices to search include mortgages, deeds, deaths, births, marriages, releases, misc, liens. Records indexed on computer back to 1990. Only the public may search. Copy fee $1.00 per page. Cert fee- $5.00 per cert plus copy fee. Payee- Alexander County Recorder. **Other phones:** Treasurer- 618-734-7009; Elections- 618-734-7000; Vital Records- 618-734-7000. **Property tax/Assessing-** Same address as recording office. 618-734-7011, assessor fax- 618-734-7012.

Bond County

County Recorder, 203 W College Ave, Greenville, IL 62246. 618-664-0449; fax-618-664-9414; 8AM-4PM

Index: Separate indices to search include grantor/grantee. Records indexed on a public use terminal back to 4/15/05. Only the public may search. Copy fee $1.00 per page. Cert fee- $25.00 1st 4 pages, $1.00 each add'l page. Payee- Bond County Recorder. Office does not sell bulk data. **Other phones:** Treasurer- 618-664-0618; Elections- 618-664-0449; Vital Records- 618-664-0449. **Property tax/Assessing-** 203 W College Ave, Greenville, IL 62246; 618-664-2848, assessor fax- 618-664-9414. A public access terminal is available.

Boone County

County Recorder, 601 N Main St, #202, Belvidere, IL 61008. 815-544-3103; fax-815-547-8701; 8:30AM-5PM (CST) www.boonecountyil.org

Index: All in one. Records indexed on a public use terminal back to 1990. Only the public may search. Copy fee $1.00 per page. Cert fee- Same as original recording fee, includes copy fee. Payee- Boone County Recorder. **Other phones:** Treasurer- 815-544-2666; Elections- 815-544-3103; Vital Records- 815-544-3103. **Property tax/Assessing-** 601 N Main St, #104, Belvidere, IL 61008; 815-544-2958, assessor fax- 815-544-2958. www.boonecountyil.org/assessor/assessor.htm **Online access-** Property assessments and tax info is free at www.boonecountyil.org/assessor/assessor.htm. Also, access to property data is free at www.helpillinois.net/boone/public.htm but no name searching. Access land data on commercial site - PropertyMax - at http://booneilpropertymax.governmaxa.com/propertymax/rover30.asp. Subscription packages from $20.00 per month.

Brown County

County Recorder, 200 Court St, Rm 4; Courthouse, Mount Sterling, IL 62353-1285. Recording, R/E & UCC phone-217-773-3421; fax-217-773-2233; 8:30AM-4:30PM (CST)

Index: All in one. Record index not computerized. Office will perform a UCC search but public must search other records themselves. Search fee $13.00. Office will not search real estate records. Copy fee $.35 for 8 1/2 x 11 and 8 1/2 x 14, $.75 for 11 x 17. per page. Cert fee- $48.00 per cert, plus $1.00 per add'l page. Payee- Brown County Recorder. **Other phones:** Treasurer- 217-773-3133; Elections- 217-773-3421; Vital Records- 217-773-3421. **Property tax/Assessing-** 200 Court St, #3, Mount Sterling, IL 62353; 217-773-3415, assessor fax- 217-773-2233.

Bureau County

County Recorder, 700 S Main St; Courthouse, Princeton, IL 61356. Recording, R/E & UCC phone-815-875-3239; fax-815-879-4803; 8AM-4PM (CST)

Index: Separate indices to search include grantor/grantee, tract, federal tax liens, state tax liens, unemployment tax, retailers tax, public aid liens, child support liens. Records indexed on a public use terminal back to 00. Only the public may search. Copy fee $.50 per page. Cert fee- $15.00 for 1st 4 pages; $1.00 each add'l, includes copy fee. Payee- Bureau County Recorder. Office does not sell bulk data. **Online access to Real Estate, Deed, Lien records:** Recorder's office has a subscription service with web access to land records and lien documents; Monthly $50.00 fee; Images go back to 10/1992, index to 8/1986. call recorder for details. Also, access recording office data by subscription on either the Laredo system using subscription and fees or the Tapestry System using credit card, http://tapestry.fidlar.com/. $3.99 search; $.50 per image. **Other phones:** Treasurer- 815-875-3241; Elections- 815-875-2014; Vital Records- 815-875-3239. **Property tax/Assessing-** Same address as recording office. 815-875-6478, assessor fax- 815-879-0504. A public access terminal is available for record searches.

Calhoun County

County Clerk & Recorder, PO Box 187, Hardin, IL 62047. 618-576-2351; fax-618-576-2895; 8:30AM-4:30PM (CST)

Index: Separate indices to search include grantor/grantee, Tract index. Records indexed on computer back to 1992. Office will perform a UCC search but public must search other records themselves. Search fee $10.00 per name. Copy fee $1.00 per page. Cert fee- $5.00 per cert includes copy fee. Payee- Calhoun County Clerk and Recorder. **Other phones:** Treasurer- 618-576-2421; Elections- 618-576-2351; Vital Records- 618-576-2351. **Property tax/Assessing-** PO Box 307, 1 Country Rd, Hardin, Ill 62047; 618-576-8041 x1, assessor fax- 618-576-2895.

Carroll County

County Recorder, PO Box 152, Mount Carroll, IL 61053. 815-244-0223; fax-815-244-3709; 8:30AM-4:30AM (CST) www.carroll-county.net/

Index: All in one. Records indexed on a public use terminal back to 1993. Only the public may search. Copy fee $2.00 per page. Cert fee- same as original recording fee. Payee- Carroll County Recorder. **Other phones:** Treasurer- 815-244-0243. **Property tax/Assessing-** PO Box 227, 301 N Main St, Mount Carroll, IL 61053; 815-244-0238, assessor fax- 815-244-1046. www.carroll-county.net/

Cass County

County Recorder, 100 E Springfield St, Virginia, IL 62691. 217-452-2277 x4; fax-217-452-7219; 8:30AM-4:30PM (CST)

Index: Separate indices to search. Record index not computerized. Only the public may search. Copy fee $1.25 per page if agency makes the copy. If public makes copy, fee is $.25. Cert fee- $15.00 plus copy fee. Payee- Cass County Recorder. Office does not sell bulk data. **Other phones:** Treasurer- 217-452-2277 x1; Elections- 217-452-2277 x4. **Property tax/Assessing**- 100 E Springfield St, Virginia, IL 62691; 217-452-2277 x5, assessor fax- 217-452-7219. **Online access**- Search assessor property data for a fee on the GIS system at http://beacon.schneidercorp.com/.

Champaign County

County Recorder, 1776 E Washington, Urbana, IL 61802. 217-384-3774; fax-217-344-1663; 8AM-4:30 www.co.champaign.il.us/recorder/recorder.htm

Index: All in one. Records indexed on a public use terminal back to 1975. Only the public may search. General copy fee $1.50 per page. Cert fee- $12.00 per cert + $1.00 per page after 4 pages. Payee- Champaign County Recorder. **Online access to Real Estate, Deed, Lien records:** Recorder land data by subscription on either the Laredo system using subscription and fees or the Tapestry System using credit card, http://tapestry.fidlar.com; $3.99 search; $.50 per image. Index goes back to 5/1975; images to 1/1987. **Other phones:** Treasurer- 217-384-3743. **Property tax/Assessing**- 1776 E Washington, Urbana, IL 61802; 217-384-3760, assessor fax- 217-384-3762. www.co.champaign.il.us/ccao **Online access**- Search property tax records free at www.co.champaign.il.us/ccao/Assessors.htm. Also, search the treasurer's real estate property tax database free at www.co.champaign.il.us/taxlookup but no name searching.

Christian County

County Recorder, PO Box 647, Taylorville, IL 62568. Recording, R/E & UCC phone-217-824-4960; fax-217-824-5105; 8AM-4PM (CST)

Index: All in one. Records indexed on a public use terminal back to 1990. Only the public may search. Copy fee $1.00 per page. Cert fee- $50.00 per cert includes copy fee, first 4 pgs. $1.00 each there after. Payee- Christian County Recorder. Office does sell bulk data. **Online access to Real Estate, Deed, Lien, UCC records:** Recorder land data by subscription on either the Laredo system using subscription and fees or the Tapestry System using credit card, http://tapestry.fidlar.com; $3.99 search; $.50 per image. Index and images go back to 1/1990. **Other phones:** Treasurer- 217-824-4889; Elections- 217-824-4969; Vital Records- 217-824-4969. **Property tax/Assessing**- PO Box 647, 101 S Main St, Taylorville, IL 62568; 217-824-5900, assessor fax- 217-824-5105.

Clark County

County Recorder, Courthouse, Marshall, IL 62441. Recording, R/E & UCC phone-217-826-8311; fax-217-826-2519; 8AM-4PM www.clarkcountyil.org

Index: Separate indices to search include grantor/grantee, mortgagor/mortgagee, financing statements, misc, liens, O&G lease, O&G assign, memo of judgments. Record index not computerized. Office will not search real estate records. Will not search UCC records. Copy fee $.50 per page. Fax copies $1.00 per page. Cert fee- $14.00 per cert includes copy fee. Payee- Clark County Recorder. Office does not sell bulk data. **Other phones:** Treasurer- 217-826-5721; Elections- 217-826-8311; Vital Records- 217-826-8311. **Property tax/Assessing**- 501 Archer Ave, Marshall, IL 62441; 217-826-5815, assessor fax- 217-826-5674. A public access terminal is available.

Clay County

County Recorder, PO Box 160, Louisville, IL 62858-0160. Recording, R/E & UCC phone-618-665-3626; fax-618-665-3607; 8AM-4PM (CST)

Index: All in one but segregated by mortgage, judgment, state lien, federal lien. Records indexed on a public use terminal back to 100. Office personnel or visitors may perform searches. Search fee $5.00 per name per 5 years per index. Real estate owner, mortgage, and property transfer searches available. Will search UCC records. Copy fee $1.00 per page; if from book, $1.50 for 1st page, $.50 each add'l. Cert fee- $20.00 per doc includes copy fee. Payee- Clay County Recorder. Office does not sell bulk data. **Other phones:** Treasurer- 618-665-3727; Elections- 618-665-3626; Vital Records- 618-665-3626. **Property tax/Assessing**- PO Box 178, Louisville, IL 62858; 618-665-3370, assessor fax- 618-665-3158.

Clinton County

County Recorder, PO Box 308, Carlyle, IL 62231. Recording, R/E & UCC phone-618-594-2464, UCC recording phone-618-594-0142; fax-618-594-0195; 8AM-4PM (CST) www.clintonco.org

Index: All in one. Records indexed on a public use terminal back to 8/1/88. Office will perform a UCC search but public must search other records themselves. Tax lien search fee $10.00 per debtor. Copy fee $1.00 per page. Cert fee- $1.00 per cert plus copy fee. Payee- Clinton County Recorder. **Online access to Real Estate, Deed, Lien records:** Recorder land data by subscription on either the Laredo system using subscription and fees or the Tapestry System using credit card, http://tapestry.fidlar.com; $3.99 search; $.50 per image. Index back to 1988; images to 1992. **Other phones:** Treasurer- 618-594-2464; Elections- 618-594-2464; Vital Records- 618-594-2464. **Property tax/Assessing**- 850 Fairplex, Rm 640, Carlyle, IL 62231; 618-594-2464, assessor fax- 618-594-0198. A public access terminal is available for record searches.

Coles County

County Recorder, 651 Jackson Ave, Rm 122, Charleston, IL 61920. 217-348-7325, R/E recording phone-217-348-0525; fax-217-348-7337; 8:30AM-4:30PM www.co.coles.il.us/CoClerk/index.htm

Index: Separate indices to search include grantor/grantee, mortgagor/mortgagee. Records indexed on a public use terminal back to 12/1/78. Only the public may search. Copy fee $5.00 per instrument up to 10 pages, $1.00 each add'l page. Cert fee- $5.00 1st 4 pages, then $1.00 per page; does not include copy fee. cert plus copy fee. Payee- Coles County Recorder. Office does not sell bulk data. **Online access to Real Estate, Deed, Lien, UCC records:** Record index from the recorder's database back to 1978 is free at https://www.illandrecords.com/illr/il029/index.jsp. Fees apply to see images and make copies. **Other phones:** Treasurer- 217-348-0511; Elections- 217-348-0524; Vital Records- 217-348-0501. **Property tax/Assessing**- PO Box 453, 651 Jackson Ave, #133, Charleston, IL 61920; 217-348-0508, assessor fax- 217-348-7363. www.co.coles.il.us/sofa/index.htm **Online** - Access property tax data free at www.fikeandfike.com/propertytax/Home/Home.aspx?c=15.

Cook County Recorder

Recorder of Deeds, 118 N Clark St, #120, Chicago, IL 60602. 312-603-5050, R/E recording phone-312-603-5066, UCC recording phone-312-603-5050; fax-312-603-5107; 8AM-4:55PM (CST) www.ccrd.info

Except for real estate related UCCs, no UCC filings recorded here after June 30, 2001. Only UCC records prior to this date can be searched. Index: All in one. Records indexed on a public use terminal back to 1985. Office will perform a UCC and Tax lien search but public must search other records themselves. Search fee $10.00 per name. Office will not search real estate records. Copy fee $1.00 per page. Cert fee- $20.00 1st page, $2.00 each add'l page plus copy fee. Payee- Cook County Recorder. Office sells bulk data on CD's, contact Khesi Pillows, 312-603-5070. **Online access to Real Estate, Grantor/Grantee, Deed, Mortgage records:** Search Grantor/Grantee index and locate property data at www.ccrd.info. Fee for documents. Search DIMS database of recordings since 10/1985; registration and fees apply. Includes Treasurer's Current Year Tax System APIN and DuPage recorder. Sign-up info is at www.ccrd.info/CCRD/il031/index.jsp. Also, you may purchase the real estate transfer list; $100 per year on disk or $50 if you pick-up at agency. **Other phones:** Treasurer- 312-443-4436; Elections- 312-603-0906; Vital Records- 312-603-7790. **Property tax/Assessing**- 118 N Clark St, Chicago, IL 60602; 312-443-7550. hours- 8:30AM-5PM www.cookcountyassessor.com/ **Online access**- Online search and retrieval of parcel data with GIS pictures of residential and nonresidential properties as well as prior and current assessment values are available. Also, search assessor data at www.cookcountyassessor.com - no name searching.

Crawford County

County Recorder, PO Box 616, Robinson, IL 62454-0602. Recording, R/E & UCC phone-618-546-1212; fax-618-546-0140; 8AM-4PM (CST) http://crawfordcountycentral.com/coclerk/

Index: Separate indices to search include grantor/grantee. Records indexed on a public use terminal back to 1980. Office will perform a UCC search but public must search other records themselves. Search fee $10.00 per name. Real estate search not guaranteed. Copy fee $1.00 per page. Cert fee- $13.00 per cert includes copy fee. Payee- Crawford County Recorder. For bulk data sales please contact Patty Lycan, County Clerk. **Other phones:** Treasurer- 618-544-2614; Elections- 618-546-2590; Vital Records- 618-546-1212. **Property tax/Assessing**- 100 Douglas St, Courthouse Annex, Robinson, IL 62454; 618-544-8221, assessor fax- 618-544-5943. A public access terminal is available.

Cumberland County

County Recorder, PO Box 146, Toledo, IL 62468. Recording, R/E & UCC phone-217-849-2631; fax-217-849-2968; 8AM-4PM www.cumberlandco.org

Index: All in one. Records indexed on a public use terminal back to 1990. Only the public may search. Copy fee $.50 per page. Cert fee- $12.00 per cert includes copy fee. Payee- Cumberland County Recorder. Office does not sell bulk data. **Other phones:** Treasurer- 217-849-2321; Elections- 217-849-2631; Vital Records- 217-849-2631. **Property tax/Assessing**- PO Box 217, 140 Courthouse Sq, Toledo, IL 62468; 217-849-3831, assessor fax- 217-849-2183. www.cumberlandco.org/

De Kalb County

County Recorder, 110 E Sycamore St, Sycamore, IL 60178. 815-895-7156; fax-815-895-7148; 8:30AM-4:30PM (CST) www.dekalbcounty.org

Index: All in one. Records indexed on a public use terminal back to 1987. Office will perform a UCC search but public must search other records themselves. Search fee $10.00 per name. Copy fee $1.00 per page. Cert fee- $39.00 1st 4 pages, $1.00 each add'l page. Payee- De Kalb County Recorder. Bulk data available for purchase, daily documents bought weekly, monthly or yearly - contact Judy Butler. **Online access to Real Estate, Deed, Lien records:** The County online system requires a $350 subscription fee, with a per minute charge of $.25, $.50 if printing. Records date back to 1980. Lending agency data is available. For further info, contact recorder office. **Other phones:** Treasurer- 815-895-7112; Elections- 815-895-7150; Vital Records- 815-895-7111. **Property tax/Assessing**- 110 E Sycamore St, Sycamore, IL 60178; 815-895-7120, assessor fax- 815-895-1684. **Online** - Search property assessor data free at www.dekalbcounty.org/GIS/TASDisclaimer.html. Also, GIS mapping search page available through the county website. Also, you may subscribe, fees involved, to the Treasurer's PIN - Parcel Info Network - at http://dcggisweb.co.de-kalb.il.us/taxquery/welcome.asp.

De Witt County

County Recorder, PO Box 439, Clinton, IL 61727-0439. Recording, R/E & UCC phone-217-935-2119; fax-217-935-4596; 8:30AM-4:30PM (CST)
Index: Separate indices to search include grantor/grantee, Lot and section. Records indexed on a public use terminal back to 2005. Only the public may search. Will not search UCC records. Copy fee $1.00 per page.Real estate record copy- $.50 per page. Cert fee- $2.50 per doc plus copy fee. Payee- De Witt County Recorder. **Other phones:** Treasurer- 217-935-2359; Elections- 217-935-2119; Vital Records-217-935-2119. **Property tax/Assessing**- 201 W Washington St, Clinton, IL 61727; 217-935-2242. (Appraiser/Auditor- 217-935-2242) **Online access**- Access parcel data free at http://helpillinois.net/dewitt/treasurer.htm. Click on Real Estate Tax Inquiry.

Douglas County

County Recorder, PO Box 467, Tuscola, IL 61953-0467. Recording, R/E & UCC phone-217-253-4410; fax-217-253-2233; 8:30AM-4:30PM (CST)
Index: All in one. Records indexed on a public use terminal back to 1992. Office will perform a UCC search but public must search other records themselves. Search fee $10.00. General copy fee $1.00 per document.Real estate copy- $2.00 per document if mailed. Cert fee- $8.00 per cert includes copy fee. Payee- Douglas County Recorder. **Other phones:** Treasurer- 217-253-4011; Elections- 217-253-2411; Vital Records- 217-253-2411. **Property tax/Assessing**- 401 S Center St, #103, Tuscola, IL 61953; 217-253-3031, assessor fax- 217-253-9301.

Du Page County

County Recorder, PO Box 936, Wheaton, IL 60189. Recording, R/E & UCC phone-630-407-5400; fax-630-407-5300; hours- 8AM-4:30PM (CST) www.dupageco.org/recorder/
Index: All in one. Records indexed on computer back to 1976. Office personnel or visitors may perform searches. UCC search per debtor name/address is $10.00. Copy fee $.50 per page. Cert fee- $5.00 per cert plus copy fee. Payee- Du Page County Recorder. **Online access to Real Estate, Deed, Lien records:** For access to Du Page County database one must lease a live interface telephone line from a carrier to establish a connection. There is a fee of $.05 per transaction. Records date back to 1977. For info, contact Fred Kieltcka at 630-682-7030. Internet access is available via the recorder website; click on Online Documents. Fees per document, username and password required. **Other phones:** Treasurer- 630-407-5900; Elections- 630-407-5600; Vital Records-630-407-5500. **Property tax/Assessing**- 421 N County Farm Rd, Wheaton, IL 60187; 630-407-5858, assessor fax- 630-407-5860. www.dupageco.org/soa/ **Online** - Search Wayne Township property records at www.waynetownshipassessor.com/disclaimer.html. Search Bloomingdale Township property records at www.bloomingdaletownshipassessor.com/Assessor/Search.asp. Search Wheatland Township at www.wheatlandtownship.com/sd/wlt/AssessorDB/Search.aspx. Search Addison Township records at www.addisontownship.com/SD/addison/assessordb/search.aspx?ID=2. No name searching in any of these.

Edgar County

County Clerk & Recorder, 115 W Court St, Rm J, Paris, IL 61944-1785. Recording, R/E & UCC phone-217-466-7433; fax-217-466-7430; 8AM-4PM (CST) www.edgarcounty-il.gov
Index: All in one since 1/01/94. Records indexed on computer since 1/1/94. Office personnel or visitors may perform searches. Search fee $10.00. Limited real estate owner, mortgage, and property transfer searches available. Tax liens not included in UCC search. Copy fee $1.00 per page. Cert fee- $12.00 1st 4 pages; $1.00 each add'l, copies included. Payee- Edgar County Recorder. Office does not sell bulk data. **Other phones:** Treasurer- 217-466-7446; Elections- 217-466-7433; Vital Records- 217-466-7433. **Property tax/Assessing**- 111 N Central, Paris, IL 61944; 217-466-7418, assessor fax- 217-466-7495.

Edwards County

County Recorder, 50 E Main St; Courthouse, Albion, IL 62806-1294. Recording, R/E & UCC phone-618-445-2115; fax-618-445-4941; 8AM-4PM (CST)
Index: Separate indices to search include grantor/grantee, tract, entry book. Record index not computerized. Only the public may search. Copy fee $1.00 per copy. Self-serve copy- $.50 each. Cert fee- $10.00 per cert includes copy fee. Payee- Edwards County Recorder. Office does not sell bulk data. **Other phones:** Treasurer- 618-445-3581; Elections-618-445-2115; Vital Records- 618-445-2115. **Property tax/ Assessing**- 50 E Main St, Courthouse, Albion, IL 62806; 618-445-3591, assessor fax- 618-445-3693.

Effingham County

County Clerk & Recorder, PO Box 628, Effingham, IL 62401-0628. Recording, R/E & UCC phone-217-342-6535; fax-217-342-3577; 8AM-4PM (CST) www.co.effingham.il.us/clerkrecorder.html
Index: All in one. Records indexed on a public use terminal back to 1987. Office will perform a UCC search but public must search other records themselves. Search fee $10.00 per debtor. Copy fee $1.00 per duc up to 4 pages. Cert fee- $12.00 per cert includes copy fee. Payee- Effingham County Clerk and Recorder. Office does not sell bulk data. **Other phones:** Treasurer- 217-342-6844; Elections- 217-342-6535; Vital Records- 217-342-6535. **Property tax/Assessing**- 101 N 4th St, #302, Effingham, IL 62401; 217-324-6711, assessor fax- 217-342-6124. **Online access**- Access to tax parcel data is free or by subscription to the GIS site at www.co.effingham.il.us/GIS.html.

Fayette County

County Recorder, PO Box 401, Vandalia, IL 62471-0401. Recording, R/E & UCC phone-618-283-5000; fax-618-283-5004; 8AM-4PM (CST)
Index: Separate indices to search include grantor/grantee by date. Records indexed on a public use terminal back to 2000. Only the public may search. Will not search UCC records. Copy fee $1.00 per page. Cert fee- $12.00 for 1st 4 pages includes 1st 4 copy pages. Payee- Fayette County Recorder. Bulk data available for purchase, contact Terri Braun. **Other phones:** Treasurer- 618-283-5022; Elections-618-283-5000; Vital Records- 618-283-5000. **Property tax/Assessing**- 221 S 7th St #8, Vandalia, IL 62471; 618-283-5020, assessor fax- 618-283-8784.

Ford County

County Recorder, 200 W State St, Rm 101, Paxton, IL 60957. 217-379-9400; fax-217-379-9409; 8:30AM-4:30PM (CST) www.prairienet.org
Index: All in one. Record index not computerized. Office personnel or visitors may perform searches. All requests must be requested in writing. Search fee-$10.00 per search. Copy fee $1.00 per page. Cert fee-$12.00 for 1st 4 pages, $1.00 each add'l page. Payee-Ford County Recorder. **Other phones:** Treasurer-217-379-9467; Elections- 217-379-9400; Vital Records- 217-379-9400. **Property tax/Assessing**-200 W State St, Rm 104, Paxton, IL 60957-1183; 217-379-9433, assessor fax- 217-379-9435.

Franklin County

County Clerk & Recorder, PO Box 607, Benton, IL 62812. Recording, R/E & UCC phone-618-438-3221; fax-618-435-3405; 8AM-4PM (CST)
Index: Separate indices to search include grantor/grantee, mortgagors/ mortgagees, misc., federal lien tax notice, retailer's occupation tax lien, judgment, military, state income tax lien, mechanic lien, corporation, oil & gas leases. Records indexed on a public use terminal back to 1990. Only the public may search. Copy fee $1.00 per page. Must have a written request for copies, prepaid.Real estate record copy- $.50 per page. Cert fee- $1.00 per cert plus copy fee. Payee- Franklin County Clerk & Recorder. Office will sell entry book printouts and other data in bulk; contact Karen. **Other phones:** Treasurer- 618-438-7311; Elections- 618-438-3403; Vital Records- 618-438-3221. **Property tax/Assessing**- 202 W Main, Benton, IL 62812; 618-438-4331, assessor fax- 618-439-3029. A public access terminal is available.

Fulton County

County Recorder, PO Box 226, Lewistown, IL 61542. 309-547-3041, R/E recording phone-309-547-3041 x43; 8AM-4PM (CST) www.fultonco.org
Index: All in one. Records indexed on a public use terminal back to 1984. Office will perform a UCC search but public must search other records themselves. Search fee $10.00 per name/address. Copy fee $1.00 per page. Cert fee- $5.00 per doc plus copy fee. Payee- Fulton County Recorder. **Online access to Real Estate, Deed, Lien records:** Recorder land data by subscription on either the Laredo system using subscription and fees or the Tapestry System using credit card, http://tapestry.fidlar.com; $3.99 search; $.50 per image. Index goes back to 6/1985; images to 6/1999. **Other phones:** Treasurer- 309-547-3041 x25; Elections- 309-547-3041 x704; Vital Records- 309-547-3041 x 42. **Property tax/Assessing**- PO Box 283, 100 N Main, Courthouse, Lewistown, IL 61542; 309-547-3041 x58. A public access terminal is available.

Gallatin County

County Recorder, PO Box 550, Shawneetown, IL 62984. Recording, R/E & UCC phone-618-269-3025; fax-618-269-3343; 8AM-4PM (CST)
Index: Separate indices to search include grantor/grantee. Records indexed on computer 3/91. Office personnel or visitors may perform searches. Search fee $10.00 per name. Office will search real estate records. Will not search UCC records. Copy fee $1.00 per page.Real estate record copy- $.50 per page. Cert fee- $10.00 per cert plus copy fee. Payee-Gallatin County Recorder. Office does not sell bulk data. **Other phones:** Treasurer- 618-269-3022; Elections- 618-269-3025; Vital Records- 618-269-3025. **Property tax/Assessing**- PO Box 640, Shawneetown, IL 62984; 618-269-3791, assessor fax-618-269-3585. (Appraiser/Auditor- 618-269-3791) A public access terminal is available.

Greene County

County Recorder, 519 N Main St; Courthouse, Carrollton, IL 62016-1033. Recording, R/E & UCC phone-217-942-5443; fax-217-942-9323; 8AM-4PM
Index: All in one. Records indexed on a public use terminal back to 1997. Office will perform a UCC search (5 yrs previous) but public must search other records themselves. Search fee $10.00 per name. Copy fee $.25 per page. $2.00 minimum mailing fee. Cert fee- $50.00 per cert includes copy fee. Payee-Greene County Recorder. Office does not sell bulk data. **Other phones:** Treasurer- 217-942-5124; Elections- 217-942-5443; Vital Records- 217-942-5443. **Property tax/Assessing**- 519 N Main St, Courthouse, Carrollton, IL 62016; 217-942-6412, assessor fax- 217-942-9323. A public access terminal for record searches in the Treasurer's office.

Grundy County

County Recorder, PO Box 675, Morris, IL 60450-0675. 815-941-3224; fax-815-942-2222; 8AM-4:30PM (CST) www.grundyco.org
Index: Separate indices to search. Records indexed on a public use terminal back to 1989 (names). Office will perform a tax lien search but public must search other records themselves. Search fee $10.00 per name. Copy fee $1.00 per page. Cert fee- $2.00 per page includes copy fee. Payee- Grundy County Recorder. **Other phones:** Treasurer- 815-941-3215; Elections-815-941-3221; Vital Records- 815-941-3222. **Property tax/Assessing**- 111 E Washington St,

Morris, IL 60450; 815-941-3269, assessor fax- 815-941-2126. www.grundyco.org/assessor/assessor.shtml

Hamilton County

County Recorder, 100 S Jackson St, Rm 2; Courthouse, McLeansboro, IL 62859-1489. phone-618-643-2721; fax-n/a; 8AM-4:30PM (CST)
Index: Separate indices to search include grantor/grantee, mortgage/mortgagee. Records indexed on a public use terminal back to 100; deeds back to 1980; mortgages to 1995. Office will perform a UCC search but public must search other records themselves. Search fee $10.00 per name per index. Copy fee $1.00 per page. Cert fee- $5.00 1st 4 pages; $1.00 each add'l, copies included. Payee- Hamilton County Recorder. Office does not sell bulk data. **Other phones:** Treasurer- 618-643-3313; Elections-618-643-2721; Vital Records- 618-643-2721. **Property tax/Assessing**- 100 S Jackson, 3rd Fl, Courthouse, McLeansboro, IL 62859; 618-643-3971, assessor fax- 618-643-3821. hours- 8AM-N, 1PM-4:30PM A public access terminal is available for record searches.

Hancock County

County Recorder, PO Box 39, Carthage, IL 62321-0039. Recording, R/E & UCC phone-217-357-3911; 8AM-4PM (CST) www.hancockcountyclerk.org
Index: All in one. Records indexed on a public use terminal back to 1995. Office will perform a UCC search but public must search other records themselves. Search fee-$10.00. Copy fee $.50 per copy if off computer; $1.00 per page if off microfiche. Cert fee- $15.00 per doc plus copy fee. Payee-Hancock County Recorder. **Other phones:** Treasurer-217-357-3986; Elections- 217-357-3911; Vital Records- 217-357-3911. **Property tax/Assessing**- PO Box 444, Carthage, Il 62321; 217-357-2615, assessor fax- 217-357-6607. (Appraiser/Auditor- 217-357-3519) A public access terminal is available.

Hardin County

County Recorder, PO Box 187, Elizabethtown, IL 62931. Recording, R/E & UCC phone-618-287-2251; fax-618-287-2661; 8AM-4PM (CST)
Index: All in one. Records indexed on computer back to 1985. Index in books back to 1884. Office personnel or visitors may perform searches. Search fee $10.00 per name. Office will search real estate records. Copy fee $1.00 per page. Cert fee- $5.00 per cert plus copy fee. Payee- Hardin County Recorder. Hard copies of bulk data available for purchase. Fees are 12.00 per month for tax forms and real estate records. **Other phones:** Treasurer- 618-287-2053; Elections- 618-287-2251; Vital Records- 618-287-2251; Circuit Clerk- 618-287-2735; Other Fax -618-287-2661;. **Property tax/Assessing**- PO Box 119, Elizabethtown, IL 62931; 618-287-3551, assessor fax-618-287-7833.

Henderson County

County Recorder, PO Box 308, Oquawka, IL 61469-0308. Recording, R/E & UCC phone-309-867-2911; fax-309-867-2033; 8AM-4PM (CST)
Index: More than one index. Record index not computerized. Only the public may search. Copy fee $.50 per page. Cert fee- $12.00 per cert plus copy fee. Payee- Henderson County Recorder. Office does not sell bulk data. **Other phones:** Treasurer- 309-867-4141; Elections- 309-867-2911; Vital Records- 309-867-2911. **Property tax/Assessing**- PO Box 342, Oquawka, IL 61469; 309-867-3291, assessor fax-309-867-2033.

Henry County

County Recorder, 307 W Center St; County Courthouse, Cambridge, IL 61238. 309-937-3486; fax-309-937-2796; 8AM-4:30PM (CST) www.henryc ty.com/codepartments/recorder/index.html
Index: All in one. Records indexed on a public use terminal back to 1990. Only the public may search. Copy fee $.50 per page. Cert fee- $41.00 1st 4 pages includes copy fee. Payee- Henry County Recorder. **Other phones:** Treasurer- 309-937-3576; Elections-309-937-3492; Vital Records- 309-937-3575. **Property tax/Assessing**- Same address as recording office. 309-937-3570, assessor fax- 309-937-3949. **Online** - Access to the assessor property database is free at www.henrycty.com/assessor/initialsearch.asp. Access the treasurer's tax payment data free at www.henrycty.com/treasurer/search.asp. Search county foreclosure list free at www.foreclosur e.com/search.html?rsp=6252&st=IL&cno=073.

Iroquois County

County Recorder, 1001 E Grant St, Rm 104, Watseka, IL 60970. 815-432-6962; fax-815-432-3894; 8:30AM-4:30PM (CST) www.co.iroquois.il.us/
Index: All in one. Records indexed on a public use terminal back to 7/01. Only the public may search. Copy fee $3.00 1st 4 pages, $1.00 each add'l. Cert fee-$5.00 per cert plus copy fee. Payee- Iroquois County Recorder. **Other phones:** Treasurer- 815-432-6985; Elections- 815-432-6960; Vital Records- 815-432-6960. **Property tax/Assessing**- 1001 E Grant St, Rm 106, Watseka, IL 60970; 815-432-6978, assessor fax-815-432-6999. A public access terminal is available. www.co.iroquois.il.us/?page_id=15#

Jackson County

County Recorder, 1001 Walnut, The Courthouse, Murphysboro, IL 62966. 618-687-7360; fax-618-687-7359; 8AM-4PM (CST) www.jacksoncounty-il.gov/
Index: All in one. Records indexed on a public use terminal back to 1989. Only the public may search. Copy fee $.50 per page. Cert fee- $31.50 first 4 pgs. $1.00 each there after. Payee- Jackson County Recorder. **Online access to Grantor/Grantee, Real Estate. Judgments, Assumed Name records:** Access to records at http://tapestry.fidlar.com/ for a fee - $5.95 per search and $.50 per page for copy. **Other phones:** Treasurer- 618-687-3555; Elections-618-687-7366; Vital Records- 618-687-7361. **Property tax/Assessing**- 20 S 10th St, Murphysboro, IL 62966; 618-687-7220, assessor fax- 618-687-7243. A public access terminal is available.

Jasper County

County Recorder, 204 W Washington St, #2, Newton, IL 62448. Recording, R/E & UCC phone-618-783-3124; fax-618-783-4137; 8AM-4PM (CST)
Index: Separate indices to search include books. Record index not computerized. Office will perform a UCC search but public must search other records themselves. Search fee $10.00 per name prepaid. Office will not search real estate records. Copy fee $.50 per page. Cert fee- $5.00 cert includes copy fee for 1st 2 pages; add $1.00 each for add'l pages. Payee-Jasper County Recorder. Office does not sell bulk data. **Other phones:** Treasurer- 618-783-3211; Elections- 618-783-3124; Vital Records- 618-783-3124. **Property tax/Assessing**- 204 W Washington St, Newton, IL 62448; 618-783-8042, assessor fax-618-783-2627.

Jefferson County

County Recorder, 100 S 10th St, Rm 105; Courthouse, Mount Vernon, IL 62864. 618-244-8020; 8AM-5PM (CST)
Include SASE if requesting specific documents. Index: All in one. Records indexed on a public use terminal back to 08/1987. Only the public may search. Copy fee $1.00 per page. Cert fee- $5.00 per cert plus copy fee. Payee- Jefferson County Recorder. Office will sell copy of monthly Entry Book for $50.00 plus postage; fees subject to increase. **Other phones:** Treasurer- 618-244-8010. **Property tax/Assessing**-100 S 10th St, Courthouse, Mount Vernon, IL 62064; 618-244-8016, assessor fax- 618-244-1499.

Jersey County

County Recorder, 200 N Lafayette, #2, Jerseyville, IL 62052. Recording, R/E & UCC phone-618-498-5571 x117/8; fax-618-498-7823; 8:30AM-4:30PM (CST) www.jerseycounty-il.us
Index: All in one. Records indexed on computer back to October 1965. Office will perform a UCC search (on computer only) but public must search other records themselves. Search fee $10.00 per name. Copy fee $2.00 per document. $2.00 per UCC. Cert fee- $10.00 per cert includes copy fee. Payee- Jersey County Recorder. **Other phones:** Treasurer- 618-498-5571 x110; Elections- 618-498-5571 x112; Vital Records- 618-498-5571 x113. **Property tax/Assessing**- 200 N Lafayette, #4, Jerseyville, IL 62052; 618-498-5571 x126.

Jo Daviess County

County Recorder, 330 N Bench St, Rm 104, Galena, IL 61036. 815-777-0161, R/E recording phone-815-777-9694; fax-815-777-3688; 8AM-4PM (CST) www.jodaviess.org
Index: All in one. Records indexed on a public use terminal back to 1989. Office will perform a UCC search but public must search other records themselves. Search fee $10.00. Copy fee $.50 per page, $1.00 per copy if mailed. Cert fee- Same as original recording fee, includes copies. Payee- Jo Daviess County Recorder. **Other phones:** Treasurer-815-777-0355; Elections- 815-777-0161; Vital Records- 815-777-0161. **Property tax/Assessing**-330 N Bench St, Rm 105, Galena, IL 61036; 815-777-1016, assessor fax- 815-777-9422. Public access terminal in City Clerk office. www.jodaviess.org

Johnson County

County Recorder, PO Box 96, Vienna, IL 62995. Recording, R/E & UCC phone-618-658-3611; fax-618-658-9665; 8AM-N,1-4PM (CST)
Index: All in one. Records indexed on a public use terminal back to 08/2003. Office personnel or visitors may perform searches. General index search fee $10.00 per book/name. Office will search real estate records. Will search UCC records. Separate state tax lien search- $10.00 per debtor. Separate federal tax lien search- $10.00 per debtor. Copy fee $1.00 per document. Cert fee- $7.00 per cert includes copy fee. Payee- Johnson County Recorder. Office does not sell bulk data. **Other phones:** Treasurer- 618-658-8042; Elections- 618-658-3611; Vital Records- 618-658-3611. **Property tax/Assessing**- PO Box 337, Courthouse Sq, Vienna, IL 62995; 618-658-8010, assessor fax- 618-658-4209.

Kane County

County Recorder, PO Box 71, Geneva, IL 60134. Recording, R/E & UCC phone-630-232-5935; fax-630-232-5945; 8:30AM-4:30PM (CST) www.countyofkane.org/Pages/default.aspx
Index: Separate indices to search. Records indexed on a public use terminal from 1987 to present, previous in track books, grantor/grantee indexes, etc. Office will perform a UCC search but public must search other records themselves. Search fee $10.00 per search. Copy fee $1.00 per page. Cert fee- Same as recording fee minus RHSP charge. Payee- Kane County Recorder. **Online access to Real Estate, Deed, Lien, Tract, Plat records:** Access recorders real estate records free at www.kanecountyrecorder.net/lrs/Source/Home.aspx. **Other phones:** Treasurer- 630-232-3565; Elections-630-232-5990; Vital Records- 630-232-5950. **Property tax/Assessing**- 719 S Batavia Ave, Bldg C, Geneva, IL 60134; 630-232-3818, assessor fax- 630-208-3824. www.co.kane.il.us/soa/ **Online access**-Search the treasurer's property tax info free at www.co.kane.il.us/treasurer/. Search by parcel number only; no name searching.

Kankakee County

County Recorder, 189 E Court St, Kankakee, IL 60901. Recording, R/E & UCC phone-815-937-2980; fax-815-937-3657; 8:30AM-4:30PM (CST)
Index: All in one. Records indexed on a public use terminal back to 1992. Office will perform a UCC search but public must search other records themselves. No fee for search. General copy fee $1.00 per page, $10.00 for plat copy.Real estate record

copy- $.25 per page. Cert fee- Same as original recording fee plus copy fee. Payee- Kankakee County Recorder. Bulk data available for purchase in CD form of all documents, contact Mark Regel at 312-914-6051. **Other phones:** Treasurer- 815-937-2960; Elections- 815-937-2990; Vital Records- 815-937-2990. **Property tax/Assessing**- 189 E Court St, Kankakee, IL 60901; 815-937-2945, assessor fax-815-937-2946. Public access terminal available.

Kendall County

County Recorder, 111 W Fox St, Yorkville, IL 60560. Recording, R/E & UCC phone-630-553-4112; fax-630-553-5283; 8AM-4:30PM (CST)
Index: All in one. Records indexed in books and microfilm from 1986 and before. Only the public may search. Copy fee $.50 per page, map copies $5.00 each. Cert fee- $27.00 for 1st 4 pages; $1.00 each add'l page includes copy fee. Payee- Kendall County Recorder. Bulk data available for purchase from ACS at 888-363-6720. **Other phones:** Treasurer- 630-553-4124; Elections- 630-553-4105; Vital Records- 630-553-4104. **Property tax/Assessing**- 111 W Fox St, Yorkville, IL 60560; 630-553-4146, assessor fax-630-553-4157. (Appraiser/Auditor- 630-553-4146) Public access terminal available. **Online access**- Search property data free at www.co.kendall.il.us/propertyservices.htm. Search tax data by name or parcel number.

Knox County

County Recorder, 200 S Cherry; County Courthouse, Galesburg, IL 61401. 309-345-3818; fax-309-345-3842; 8:30AM-4:30PM (CST)
Index: All in one. Records indexed on a public use terminal back to 1989. Only the public may search. Copy fee $.25 per page. Cert fee- $12.00 per 4 pages includes copy fee. Payee- Knox County Recorder. Bulk data available for purchase in CD's, contact Carol Hallam. **Online access to Real Estate, Deed, Lien, Mortgage, Judgment records:** Recording office data by subscription on either the Laredo system using subscription and fees or the Tapestry System using credit card, http://tapestry.fidlar.com/; $3.99 search; $.50 per image. Index goes back to 1989; images from 12/01 to current. **Other phones:** Treasurer- 309-345-3863; Elections- 309-345-3815. **Property tax/Assessing**- 121 S Prairie St, #1, Galesburg, IL 61401; 309-345-3806, assessor fax-309-343-0063.

La Salle County

County Recorder, PO Box 189, Ottawa, IL 61350. Recording, R/E & UCC phone-815-434-8226; fax-815-434-8260; 8AM-4:30PM www.lasallecounty.org
Index: All in one. Records indexed on a public use terminal back to 7/82. Office will perform a UCC search but public must search other records themselves. Search fee $10.00 per address. Copy fee $1.00 per page. Cert fee- $10.00 per doc plus copy fee. $3.00 per doc online. Payee- La Salle County Recorder. Bulk data can be purchased in PDF files available on monthly basis, or microfilm available weekly. **Online access to Real Estate, Grantor/Grantee, Deed, Lien, Judgment, UCC, Mortgage, Birth, Death, Marriage records:** Search the recorded data back to 1992 free at www.lasallecounty.org/np/recorder/index.htm and click on Online Document Search. Registration is suggested. Fees for images, plats, and deeper info. **Other phones:** Treasurer- 815-434-8220; Elections-815-434-8202; Vital Records- 815-434-8202. **Property tax/Assessing**- 707 Etna Rd, Government Ctr, Ottawa, IL 61350; 815-434-8280, assessor fax-815-434-8327. **Online access**- Last 2 years assessment data (Parcel number required) and treasurer parcel data (name search okay) can be accessed free at www.lasallecounty.org/contents3.htm. Also, 1999-2000 Assessor/property records at www.lasallecounty.org/cidnet/asrpfull.htm. Registration and password required; $200.00 per year fee, plus per minute charges. For info, 815-434-8233.

Lake County

County Recorder, 18 N County St, 2nd Fl; Courthouse, Waukegan, IL 60085-4358. phone-847-377-2575; fax-847-625-7200; 8:30AM-5PM (CST) www.lakecountyil.gov/recorder/default.htm
Index: All in one. Records indexed on a public use terminal back to 1980. Only the public may search. Copy fee $1.00 per page. Cert fee- $1.00 per page plus copy fee. Payee- Lake County Recorder. **Online access to Real Estate, Grantor/Grantee, Deed, Lien, Mortgage, Judgment, Lis Penden records:** Access to county recorded documents is by subscription; fee is $50 per month, per user. Index and images go back to 1980; older records being added. for info and signup, call 847-377-2069. **Other phones:** Treasurer- 847-377-2323; Elections- 847-377-3610; Vital Records- 847-377-3610. **Property tax/Assessing**- 18 N County St, 7th Fl, Waukegan, IL 60085-4351; 847-377-2050, fax- 847-625-7410. www.lakecountyil.gov/Assessments/Default.htm
Online access- Search the tax assessor's database at www.lakecountyil.gov/Assessments/AssessmentInformation/PropertyTaxAssessmentInfo/Default.htm. No name searching. Also, search property by address or legal description for free on the GIS-mapping site at http://gis2.co.lake.il.us/maps/.

Lawrence County

County Clerk, 1100 State St, Courthouse, Lawrenceville, IL 62439. Recording, R/E & UCC phone-618-943-5126; fax-618-943-5205; 9AM-5PM
Index: All in one. Records indexed on computer back to 1987. Office will perform a UCC search but public must search other records themselves. Search fee $10.00 per name. Copy fee $1.00 1st page; $.50 each add'l. Cert fee- $12.00 per doc or same as recording fee, includes copies. Payee- Lawrence County Recorder. **Other phones:** Treasurer- 618-943-2016; Elections- 618-943-3786; Vital Records- 618-943-2346. **Property tax/Assessing**- 1106 Jefferson, Lawrenceville, IL 62439; 618-943-2719, assessor fax-618-943-6688.

Lee County

County Recorder, PO Box 329, Dixon, IL 61021-0329. 815-288-3309; fax-815-288-6492; 8:30AM-4:30PM (CST)
Index: All in one. Records indexed on a public use terminal back to 1000. Office will perform a UCC search but public must search other records themselves. Search fee $16.00 per name for UCC's. Copy fee $1.00 per page. Cert fee- Same as original recording fee includes copy fee. Payee- Lee County Recorder. **Other phones:** Treasurer- 815-288-4477; Elections- 815-288-3309; Vital Records- 815-288-3309. **Property tax/Assessing**- 112 E 2nd St, Dixon, IL 61021; 815-288-4483, assessor fax- 815-288-7153.

Livingston County

County Recorder, 112 W Madison; Courthouse, Pontiac, IL 61764-1871. Recording, R/E & UCC phone-815-844-2006; fax-815-842-1844; 8AM-4:30PM (CST) www.livingstoncounty-il.org
Index: Separate indices to search include land tract books, as well as computer scanned documents. Records indexed on a public use terminal back to 2002. Only the public may search. Office will show public how to look up. Office will search real estate records if time allows; search fee $5.00. Office will search UCC records if time allows, search fee $10.00. Copy fee $1.00 per page. Cert fee- $5.00 up to 6 pages than $1.00 per page plus copy fee. Payee- Livingston County Recorder. Office does not sell bulk data. **Other phones:** Treasurer- 815-844-2306; Elections- 815-842-9318; Vital Records- 815-844-2006. **Property tax/Assessing**- 110 W Water, #2, Pontiac, IL 61764; 815-844-7214, assessor fax- 815-844-2324. www.livingston.illinoisassessors.com
Online access- Free parcel search at www.livingston.illinoisa ssessors.com/basic-search.php?nz=a2, no name searching. Advanced property searches available at www.livingston.illinoisassessors.com/search.php?mode=search but registration required. Call assessor's office for subscription information.

Logan County

County Recorder, PO Box 278, Lincoln, IL 62656. Recording, R/E & UCC phone-217-732-4148; fax-217-732-6064; 8:30AM-4:30PM (CST) www.co.logan.il.us/county_clerk/
Index: Separate indices to search include grantor/grantee. Records indexed on a public use terminal back to 1984. Office will perform a UCC search but public must search other records themselves. Search fee $10.00. Copy fee $1.00 per page.Real estate or tax lien copy- $.25 per page. Cert fee- $46.00 per doc plus copy fee. Payee- Logan County Recorder. **Other phones:** Treasurer- 217-732-3761; Elections- 217-732-4148; Vital Records-217-732-4148. **Property tax/Assessing**- 122 N Mclean St, Lincoln, IL 62656; 217-732-9635, assessor fax- 217-732-9515. www.co.logan.il.us
Online access- Search the tax assessor database at http://loganilpropertymax.governmaxa.com/propertymax/rover30.asp. Also, access property data free at www.co.logan.il.us/treasurer/.

Macon County

County Recorder, 141 S Main St, Rm 201, Decatur, IL 62523-1293. Recording, R/E & UCC phone-217-424-1359; fax-217-428-2908; 8:30AM-4:30PM (CST) www.maconcounty-il.gov
Index: Computer and tract index. Records indexed on a public use terminal back to 00. Office will perform a UCC search for a fee, but public must search other records themselves. Copy fee varies depending on how many pages, can range from $3.00 and up. Cert fee- $10.00. Payee- Macon County Recorder. Data from previous month available in bulk on CD for $60.00. **Online access to Real Estate, Deed, Lien, Judgment, UCC records:** Searching recorded data free at http://64.107.106.116/. **Other phones:** Treasurer- 217-424-1426; Elections- 217-424-1309; Vital Records- 217-424-1305. **Property tax/Assessing**- 141 S Main St, Room 401, Decatur, IL 62523-1293; 217-424-1364, assessor fax- 217-424-1374. hours- 8:30AM-4PM Public access terminals in treasurer's office and recorder's office.

Macoupin County

County Recorder, PO Box 107, Carlinville, IL 62626. Recording, R/E & UCC phone-217-854-3214; fax-217-854-7347; 8:30AM-4:30PM (CST) www.macoupincountyil.gov/county_clerk.htm
Index: All in one. Records indexed on computer back to 0101/01. Only the public may search. Copy fee $1.00 per 4 pages. Cert fee- $10.00 per cert plus copy fee. Payee- Macoupin County Recorder. **Other phones:** Treasurer- 217-854-4014; Elections- 217-854-3214; Vital Records- 217-854-3214; Circuit Clerk- 217-854-3211. **Property tax/Assessing**- 201 E Main St, Po Box 15, Carlinville, IL 62626; 217-854-8281 x3, fax- 217-854-4505. Public access terminal available.

Madison County

County Recorder, PO Box 308, Edwardsville, IL 62025-0308. Recording, R/E & UCC phone-618-296-4475, UCC recording phone-618-296-4777; fax-618-692-9843; 8:30AM-4:30PM www.co.madison.il.us
Index: All in one. Records indexed on a public use terminal back to 6/85. Office will perform a UCC search but public must search other records themselves. Search fee $10.00 per name. Copy fee $1.00 per page. Cert fee- $12.00 per doc + $1 per page beyond 4, plus copy fee. Payee- Madison County Recorder. **Online access to Real Estate, Deed, Lien records:** Recorder land data by subscription on either the Laredo system using subscription and fees or the Tapestry System using credit card, http://tapestry.fidlar.com; $3.99 search; $.50 per image. Index goes back to 1/1985; images to 1/1996. Also, access is at www.co.madison.il.us/Recorder/laredo_info.shtml. **Other phones:** Treasurer- 618-692-6260; Elections-

618-296-4682; Vital Records- 618-296-4685; Assessors Office- (618) 692-7040 x4586. **Property tax/Assessing**- 157 N Main St, #229, Edwardsville, IL 62025; 618-692-6270, assessor fax- 618-692-8298. (Appraiser - 618-296-4586) www.co.madison.il.us/CCAO/CCAO.shtml **Online** - Free parcel data at http://reweb1.co.madison.il.us/Forms/Search.aspx. Search by name, address or parcel number.

Marion County

County Recorder, PO Box 637, Salem, IL 62881. 618-548-3400, R/E recording phone-618-548-3852; fax-618-548-2226; 8AM-4PM (CST)
Index: All in one. Records indexed on a public use terminal back to 1000. Only the public may search. Copy fee $1.00 1st page; $.50 each add'l; self-serve-$.25 each. Cert fee- $12.00 per cert (1st 4 pages); $1.00 per page plus copy fee. Payee- Marion County Recorder. **Other phones:** Treasurer- 618-548-3858; Elections- 618-548-3400; Vital Records- 618-548-3850. **Property tax/Assessing**- 100 E Main St, Rm 101, Salem, IL 62881; 618-548-3853, assessor fax-618-548-6509. Public access terminal in office.

Marshall County

County Recorder, PO Box 328, Lacon, IL 61540-0328. Recording, R/E & UCC phone-309-246-6325; fax-309-246-3667; 8:30AM-4:30PM (CST) http://co.marshall.il.us
Index: All in one. Records indexed on a public use terminal back to 1988. Only the public may search. Copy fee $1.00 per page by mail; $.50 per page in person. Cert fee- $25.00-1st 4 pages, $1.00 per add'l page. Payee- Marshall County Recorder. Office does not sell bulk data. **Other phones:** Treasurer- 309-246-6085; Elections- 309-246-6325; Vital Records- 309-246-6325. **Property tax/Assessing**- PO Box 328, Lacon, IL 61540; 309-246-2350, assessor fax- 309-246-3667. www.co.marshall.il.us **Online access**- Access to assessor property records is by subscription; $20 per month, minimum of 3 months. Contact the Assessor office for signup- 309-246-2350.

Mason County

County Recorder, PO Box 77, Havana, IL 62644. Recording, R/E & UCC phone-309-543-6661; fax-309-543-2085; 8AM-4PM (CST)
Index: All in one. Records indexed on a public use terminal back to 1992. Only the public may search. Copy fee $.50 per page. Cert fee- $5.00 per doc includes copy fee. Death records $7.00. Payee- Mason County Recorder. Office does not sell bulk data. **Other phones:** Treasurer- 309-543-3359; Elections-309-543-6661; Vital Records- 309-543-6661. **Property tax/Assessing**- 125 N Plum, Havana, IL 62644; 309-543-4775. hours- 8:30AM-4:30PM

Massac County

County Recorder, PO Box 429, Metropolis, IL 62960. Recording, R/E & UCC phone-618-524-5213; fax-618-524-8514; 8AM-4PM (CST)
Index: All in one; liens separate before 1986. Records indexed on a public use terminal back to 1991. Only the public may search. Copy fee $.25 per page. If copies are requested to be faxed-up to 10 pages, $1.00 per copy. Cert fee- $5.00 per cert includes copy fee. Payee- Massac County Recorder. Office does not sell bulk data. **Other phones:** Treasurer- 618-524-5121; Elections- 618-524-5213; Vital Records- 618-524-5213. **Property tax/Assessing**- 618-524-9632.

McDonough County

County Recorder, 1 Courthouse Sq, Macomb, IL 61455. Recording, R/E & UCC phone-309-833-2474; fax-309-837-1154; 8AM-4PM (CST)
Index: Separate indices to search include tracts. Records indexed on a public use terminal back to 2000. Only the public may search. Copy fee $.50 per page. Cert fee- Land Records- $42.00 1st 4 pages, $1.00 each add'l page. Payee- McDonough County Recorder. Office does not sell bulk data. **Other phones:** Treasurer- 309-833-2032; Elections- 309-833-4649; Vital Records- 309-833-2474. **Property tax/Assessing**- 1 Courthouse Sq, Macomb, IL 61455; 309-833-5305, assessor fax- 309-836-3013. Public access terminal in office.

McHenry County

County Recorder, 2200 N Seminary Ave, Rm 109, Woodstock, IL 60098. 815-334-4110; fax-815-338-9612; 8AM-4:30PM (CST) www.co.mchenry.il.us/Common/CountyDpt/Recorder/default.asp
Must come in, no phone searches. Index: Separate indices to search. Records indexed on a public use terminal back to 9/1/70. Office personnel or visitors may perform searches. Search fee $10.00 per name. Office will not search real estate records. Copy fee $1.50 1st page, $.50 each add'l. Cert fee- $12.00 for 1st 4 pages, $1.00 each add'l page plus copy fee. Payee- McHenry County Recorder. **Online access to Real Estate, Deed, Lien records:** Access recorder land data by subscription on either the Laredo system using subscription and fees or the Tapestry System using credit card, http://tapestry.fidlar.com; $3.99 search; $.50 per image. Index and images go back to 9/1972 . **Property tax/Assessing**- 2200 N Seminary Ave (mailing), 667 Ware Rd, Rm 106 (physical), Woodstock, IL 60098; 815-334-4290, assessor fax-815-338-8522. www.co.mchenry.il.us/Common/CountyDpt/Assess/default.asp **Online access**- Records on the County Treasurer Inquiry site are free at www.co.mchenry.il.us/common/countyDpt/treas/default.asp. Sheriff's foreclosure list is free at www.co.mchenry.il.us.

McLean County

County Recorder, PO Box 2400, Bloomington, IL 61702-2400. Recording, R/E & UCC phone-309-888-5170; fax-309-888-5927; 8AM-4:30PM (CST) www.mcleancountyil.gov/recorder/
Index: Separate indices to search include birth certificate, land records. Records indexed on a public use terminal back to 1970. Only the public may search. Copy fee $1.00 1st page; $.25 each add'l page. Cert fee- $12.00 1st 4 pgs, then $1.00. Payee- McLean County Recorder. Office does sell bulk data, contact Lee Newcom for information about subscription. **Online access to Real Estate, Deed, UCC, Lien, Assumed Name, Elected Official records:** Access to recorder official records and UCCs is free at www.mcleancountyil.gov/resolution/. Also, access county parcel and mobile home lots free at www.mcleancountyil.gov/tax/; no name searching. Also, search the assumed named list at www.mcleancountyil.gov/CountyClerk/CountyClerkAssumedNamesMain.asp. Search election officials by precinct at the website. **Other phones:** Treasurer-309-888-5180; Elections- 309-888-5190. **Property tax/Assessing**- 115 E Washington St, PO Box 2400, Bloomington, IL 61702-2400; 309-888-5130, fax-309-888-5208. http://mcleancountyil.gov/Assessor/ **Online access**- Access Township of Normal assessor database free at www.normaltownship.org/assessor/parcelsearch.php. No name searching; parcel number or address required. Access City of Bloomington assessor database free at www.assessor-blm.com/prop ertydatabase.htm. No name searching; parcel number or address required.

Menard County

County Recorder, PO Box 465, Petersburg, IL 62675. 217-632-2415, R/E recording phone-217-632-3201; fax-217-632-4301; 8:30AM-4:30PM (CST)
Index: All in one. Records indexed on a public use terminal back to 1987. Office will perform a UCC search but public must search other records themselves. Search fee-$3.00 per name. Copy fee $1.00 per page. Cert fee- $9.00 per doc includes copy fee. Payee- Menard County Recorder. Office does not sell bulk data. **Other phones:** Treasurer- 217-632-2333; Elections- 217-632-3201; Vital Records- 217-632-3201. **Property tax/Assessing**- PO Box 436, Petersburg, IL 62675; 217-632-4461, assessor fax-217-632-3978. (Appraiser/Auditor- 217-632-4461) Public access terminal in office.

Mercer County

County Recorder, PO Box 66, Aledo, IL 61231. Recording, R/E & UCC phone-309-582-7021; fax-309-582-7022; 8AM-4PM (CST)
Index: All in one. Records indexed on a public use terminal back to 9/97. Office will perform a UCC search but public must search other records themselves. Search fee-$10.00 per name. Copy fee $1.00 per page from computer; $.50 per page from old books. Cert fee- fee to cert same as recording fee. Payee- Mercer County Recorder. Office does not sell bulk data. **Other phones:** Treasurer- 309-582-2524; Elections- 309-582-7021; Vital Records- 309-582-7021. **Property tax/Assessing**- 100 SE 3rd St, PO Box 86, Aledo, IL 61231; 309-582-7814.

Monroe County

County Recorder, 100 S Main; Courthouse, Waterloo, IL 62298-1399. 618-939-8681; 8AM-4:30PM (CST)
Index: All in one. Records indexed on a public use terminal back to 1984. Only the public may search. Copy fee $1.00 per page. Cert fee- $12.50 per doc plus copy fee. Payee- Monroe County Recorder. Office does not sell bulk data. **Online access to Real Estate, Deed, Lien records:** Recorder land data by subscription on either the Laredo system using subscription and fees or Tapestry System using credit card, http://tapestry.fidlar.com; $3.99 search; $.50 per image. Index goes back to 1/1984; images to 6/1/2002. **Other phones:** Treasurer- 618-939-8681 x213. **Property tax/Assessing**- 100 S Main, Courthouse, Waterloo, IL 62298-1399; 618-939-8681 x211, assessor fax- 618-939-9141. Public access terminal available.

Montgomery County

County Recorder, 1 Courthouse Sq; PO Box 595, Hillsboro, IL 62049-0595. Recording, R/E & UCC phone-217-532-9535; fax-217-532-9581; 8AM-4PM (CST) www.montgomeryco.com
Index: Separate indices to search include Tract-1822-1990, Grantor/Grantee, Computer-ACS land records back to 1991. Records indexed on computer back to 1991. Office will perform a UCC search but public must search other records themselves. Copy fee $1.00 per page.Payee- Montgomery County Recorder. Office does not sell bulk data. **Other phones:** Treasurer- 217-532-9521; Elections- 217-532-9538; Vital Records- 217-532-9537. **Property tax/ Assessing**- 1 Courthouse Ln, 3rd FL, Hillsboro, IL 62049-0595; 217-532-9595, assessor fax- 217-532-9599. Public access terminal available.

Morgan County

County Recorder, PO Box 1387, Jacksonville, IL 62651. Recording, R/E & UCC phone-217-243-8581; fax-217-243-8368; 8:30AM-4:30PM (CST)
Index: All in one. Records indexed on a public use terminal back to 4/87. Office will perform a UCC and Tax lien search but public must search other records themselves. Search fee $10.00. Copy fee $1.00 per page. Cert fee- $5.00 per doc plus copy fee. Payee-Morgan County Recorder. **Online access to Real Estate, Deed records:** Access recording office land data at www.etitlesearch.com; registration required, fee based on usage. **Other phones:** Treasurer- 217-243-4311; Elections- 217-243-8581; Vital Records-217-243-8581. **Property tax/Assessing**- 300 W State St, Jacksonville, IL 62650; 217-243-8557, assessor fax- 217-243-7510. **Online access**- Access to property records for free go to http://beacon.schneidercorp.com/

Moultrie County

County Recorder, 10 S Main, #6; Courthouse, Sullivan, IL 61951. Recording, R/E & UCC phone-217-728-4389; fax-217-728-8178; 8:30AM-4:30PM
Index: All in one. Records indexed on a public use terminal back to 1/1/92. Office will perform a UCC search but public must search other records themselves. Search fee $10.00 per name. Copy fee $.25 per page. Cert fee- $14.00 per cert plus copy fee. Payee- Moultrie County Recorder. Office does not

sell bulk data. **Other phones:** Treasurer- 217-728-4032; Elections- 217-728-4389; Vital Records- 217-728-4389; Circuit Clerk- 217-728-4622. **Property tax/Assessing**- 10 S Main, #8, Sullivan, IL 61951; 217-728-4951, assessor fax- 217-728-9311. Computer access terminal available in office.

Ogle County

County Recorder, PO Box 357, Oregon, IL 61061. 815-732-1115 x269/1, R/E recording phone-815-732-1115 x269/270/271; 8:30AM-4:30PM (CST)
Index: Separate indices to search include grantor/grantee. Records indexed on a public use terminal back to 10/1/1984. Office will perform a UCC and Tax lien search but public must search other records themselves. Search fee $10.00. Copy fee $1.00 per page. Cert fee- $25.50 per doc plus copy fee. Payee- Ogle County Recorder. **Online access to Real Estate, Deed, UCC records:** Access to recorder data is available for subscription at https://www.illandrecords.com/illr/il141/index.jsp. Also, the index of recorded documents may be accessed from https://www.landaccess.com. **Other phones:** Treasurer- 815-732-1100 x202/201/310 & 286; Elections- 815-732-1110 x012/213/281/214 & 215; Vital Records- 815-732-1110 x012/213/281/214 & 215. **Property tax/Assessing**- PO Box 40, Oregon, IL 61061; 815-732-1150 x239, 256, 257, 258, 305, fax- 815-732-6273. www.oglecounty.org/soa.html **Online access**- Search assessor property data for a fee on the GIS and land records system at http://beacon.schneidercorp.com/ but registration and username required for a name search.

Peoria County

County Recorder, 324 Main St, Rm G04; County Courthouse, Peoria, IL 61602. Recording, R/E & UCC phone-309-672-6090; fax-309-677-6202; 9AM-5PM (CST) www.co.peoria.il.us
Index: Separate indices to search. Records indexed on a public use terminal back to 1988. Office will perform a UCC search but public must search other records themselves. UCC search per debtor name/address- $10.00. Copy fee $.50 per page. Cert fee- Same as current recording fee. Payee- Peoria County Recorder. **Online access to Real Estate, Deed records:** Recorder's office has a subscription service with web access to land records and other official documents; call Recorder for details. **Other phones:** Treasurer- 309-672-6065. **Property tax/Assessing**- 324 Main St, Courthouse, Rm 301, Peoria, IL 61602; 309-672-6910, assessor fax- 309-672-6075. 8:30AM-5PM www.peoriacounty.org

Perry County

County Recorder, PO Box 438, Pinckneyville, IL 62274. Recording, R/E & UCC phone-618-357-5116; fax-618-357-3194; hours - 8AM-4PM (CST) www.perrycountyil.org
Index: All in one. Records indexed on a public use terminal back to 04/15/1987. Office personnel or visitors may perform searches. Search fee $10.00 per name. Office will not search real estate records. Will search UCC records. Copy fee $3.00 per document. Cert fee- $5.00 per doc includes copy fee. Payee- Perry County Recorder. Bulk data available for purchase, contact Kevin Kern, County Clerk. **Online access to Real Estate, Deed records:** Searching is planned at www.perrycountyil.org. **Other phones:** Treasurer- 618-357-5002; Elections- 618-357-5116; Vital Records- 618-357-5116. **Property tax/Assessing**- PO Box 177, Pinchneyville, IL 62274; 618-357-2209, assessor fax- 618-357-2269. Public access terminal available.

Piatt County

County Recorder, PO Box 558, Monticello, IL 61856-0558. Recording, R/E & UCC phone-217-762-9487; fax-217-762-7563; 8:30AM-4:30PM (CST) www.piattcounty.org
Index: All in one. Records indexed on a public use terminal back to 1/1/1988. Office will perform a UCC search but public must search other records themselves. Search fee $10.00 per name. General copy fee $.50 per page. $1.00 per page for mailed copies. Cert fee- $8.00 per file plus $.50 per page after 8 pages. Payee- Piatt County Recorder. **Other phones:** Treasurer- 217-762-4866; Elections- 217-762-9487; Vital Records- 217-762-9487. **Property tax/Assessing**- 101 W Washington, #102, Monticello, IL 61856; 217-762-4266, assessor fax- 217-762-9716. Public access computer in treasurer's office only.

Pike County

County Recorder, 100 E Washington St; Courthouse, Pittsfield, IL 62363. Recording, R/E & UCC phone-217-285-6812; fax-217-285-5820; 8:30AM-4PM
Index: All in one. Records indexed on a public use terminal back to 1990. Office will perform a UCC search but public must search other records themselves. Search fee $10.00. Office will not search real estate records. Copy fee $1.00 per page. Cert fee-$10.00 per doc includes copy fee. Payee- Pike County Recorder. **Other phones:** Treasurer- 217-285-4218; Elections- 217-285-6812; Vital Records- 217-285-6812. **Property tax/Assessing**- 100 E Washington St, Courthouse, Pittsfield, IL 62363; 217-285-2382, assessor fax- 217-285-1227. Public access terminal in Clerk and Recorder's office.

Pope County

County Recorder, PO Box 216, Golconda, IL 62938. 618-683-4466; fax-618-683-4466; 8AM-N, 1-4PM
Index: Separate indices to search. Record index not computerized. Office personnel or visitors may perform searches. Search fee $10.00 per name. Office will search real estate records. Will search UCC records. Copy fee $.25 per page. Cert fee- $5.00 per cert includes copy fee. Payee- Pope County Recorder. **Other phones:** Treasurer- 618-683-5501. **Property tax/Assessing**- PO Box 579, Golconda, IL 62938; 618-683-6231, assessor fax- 618-683-6231. Public access terminal in Treasurer's office.

Pulaski County

County Recorder, PO Box 118, Mound City, IL 62963. 618-748-9360; fax-618-748-9305; 8AM-N, 1PM-4PM (CST)
Index: Separate indices to search. Records indexed on computer back to 1990. Office personnel or visitors may perform searches. Search fee $10.00 per name. Will not do a federal or state tax lien search. Copy fee $.50 per page. Cert fee- $7.00 per doc plus copy fee. Payee- Pulaski County Recorder. Office does not sell bulk data. **Other phones:** Treasurer- 618-748-9322; Elections- 618-748-9360; Vital Records- 618-748-9360. **Property tax/Assessing**- 500 Illinois Ave, Rm F, Mound City, IL 62963; 618-748-9321, assessor fax- 618-748-9046. No public terminal available.

Putnam County

County Recorder, PO Box 236, Hennepin, IL 61327. Recording, R/E & UCC phone-815-925-7129; fax-815-925-7549; 9-4PM www.countyofputnam.com
Index: Separate indices; Entry Book, Grantor/Grantee, Tract index, Fed & State tax lien, Lis Pendens, Judgment Memo. Record index not computerized. Office personnel or visitors may perform searches. Search fee $10.00. Office will not search real estate records. Will not search UCC records. Copy fee $.50 per page. Cert fee- $37.00 per doc; includes 4 pages, $1.00 each add'l page. Payee- Putnam County Recorder. Office does not sell bulk data. **Other phones:** Treasurer- 815-925-7226; Elections- 815-925-7129; Vital Records- 815-925-7129. **Property tax/Assessing**- PO Box 242, County Courthouse, Hennepin, IL 61327; 815-925-7238, assessor fax-815-925-7549. (Appraiser/Auditor- 815-925-7238);

Randolph County

County Recorder, 1 Taylor St, Rm 202, Chester, IL 62233. 618-826-5000 x191, R/E recording phone-x191; fax-618-826-3750; 8AM-4PM (CST) www.randolphco.org
Index: Separate indices to search include deeds, mtgs, judgments, UCCs. Records indexed on a public use terminal back to 1989. Office personnel or visitors may perform searches. Search fee $10.00 per name; $5.00 per document. Copy fee $.50 per page. Mailing fee is $.75. Cert fee- $26.00 for 4 pages, $1.00 each add'l page. Payee- Randolph County Recorder. **Online access to Real Estate, Deed, Lien records:** Recorder land data by subscription on either the Laredo system using subscription and fees or the Tapestry System using credit card, http://tapestry.fidlar.com; $3.99 search; $.50 per image. Images back to 5/3/1993; index to 1989. **Other phones:** Treasurer- x191; Elections- x191; Vital Records- x191. **Property tax/Assessing**- 1 Taylor St, Room 203, Chester Il 62233-0309; 618-826-5000 x192, assessor fax- 618-826-3750.

Richland County

County Recorder, 103 W Main; Olney, IL 62450. 618-392-3111; fax-618-393-4005; 8AM-4PM (CST)
Index: Separate indices to search include grantor/grantee. Record index not computerized. Office will perform a UCC search but public must search other records themselves. UCC search per debtor name/address- $10.00. UCC copy fee $2.00 per page.Real estate or tax lien record copy- $6.00 per document. Cert fee- please ask for verification. Payee-Richland County Recorder. Office does not sell bulk data. **Other phones:** Treasurer- 618-392-8341; Elections- 618-392-3111; Vital Records- 618-392-3111. **Property tax/Assessing**- 103 W Main, Courthouse, Olney, IL 62450; 618-395-4387, assessor fax- 618-395-4387.

Rock Island County

County Recorder, PO Box 3067, Rock Island, IL 61204. 309-558-3360; fax-309-558-3642; 8AM-4:30PM www.rockislandcounty.org/Rec.aspx?id=123
Index: All in one. Records indexed on a public use terminal back to 1982. Office personnel or visitors may perform searches. Search fee $10.00 per name. Office will do basic search for real estate records (not extensive searches). Will search UCC records if UCC #11 form is filled out with $10.00 fee. Real estate or tax lien copy- $.25 per page; $2.00 each if mailed. Xerox or printer aperture card avail for $1.00. Cert fee- Certified copies $49.00. Payee- Rock Island County Recorder. Office does not sell bulk data. **Online access to Real Estate, Deed, Lien, Subdivision records:** Recorder land data by subscription on either the Laredo system using subscription and fees or the Tapestry System using credit card, http://tapestry.fidlar.com; $3.99 search; $.50 per image. Index goes back to 1982, images 1992; subdivisions back to 8/21/1995. Also, for the application for certified copy of vital records go to http://ricoclerk.revealed.net/. **Other phones:** Switch Board for County- 309-786-4451. **Property tax/Assessing**- 1504 3rd Ave, 2nd Fl, Rock Island, IL 61201-8624; 309-558-3660, assessor fax- 309-558-3658. **Online access**- Access to property tax searches at www.rockislandcounty.org/Index.aspx?id=6374. Moline Town assessor records are free at www.molinetownship.com/OnlineSearch/Search.asp. No name searching.

Saline County

County Recorder, 10 E Poplar, #17, Harrisburg, IL 62946. 618-253-8197, R/E recording phone-618-253-3073; fax-618-252-3073; 8AM-4PM (CST)
Index: Separate indices to search include grantor/grantee. Records indexed on computer back to 1991. Only the public may search. General copy fee $1.00; tax lien $.50 per page.Real estate records other than deeds- $.50 per page. Cert fee- $12.00 per doc includes copy fee. Payee- Saline County Recorder. Office does not sell bulk data. **Other phones:** Treasurer- 618-253-6915; Elections- 618-253-3028; Vital Records- 618-253-8197. **Property tax/Assessing**- 10 E Poplar St #23, Harrisburg, IL 62946; 618-252-0691, assessor fax- 618-252-2339. Public access terminal in Treasurer's office.

Sangamon County

County Recorder, PO Box 669, Springfield, IL 62705-0669. 217-535-3150; fax-217-535-3159; 8:30AM-5PM (CST) www.co.sangamon.il.us
Index: All in one. Records indexed on a public use terminal back to 1990. Only the public may search. Copy fee $2.00 1st 2 pages, $.25 each add'l page. Cert fee- $26.00 per cert includes copy fee. Payee- Sangamon County Recorder. Office does sell bulk data, contact Mary Ann Lamm. **Online access to Real Estate, Deed, Lien records:** Recorder land data by subscription on either the Laredo system using subscription and fees or the Tapestry System using credit card, http://tapestry.fidlar.com; $3.99 search; $.50 per image. Images goes back to 1992; index to 1970. **Other phones:** Treasurer- 217-753-6800. **Property tax/Assessing**- 200 S 9th St, Rm 210, Springfield, IL 62705; 217-753-6805, assessor fax-217-535-3143. www.co.sangamon.il.us/ **Online access**- View the status of property tax payments or property assessments at http://tax.co.sangamon.il.us/SangamonCountyWeb/index.jsp

Schuyler County

County Recorder, PO Box 200, Rushville, IL 62681. Recording, R/E & UCC phone-217-322-4734; fax-217-322-6164; hours- 8AM-4PM (CST) www.schuylercountyillinois.com
Index: Separate indices to search include entry book, grantor/grantee, tract, state and federal lien books. Records indexed on a public use terminal back to 1001/2005. Office will perform a UCC search but public must search other records themselves. Search fee $10.00 per name or $30.00 an hour. Copy fee $.50 per page. Cert fee- $7.00 per cert 1st 4 pages includes copy fee. Payee- Schuyler County Recorder. **Other phones:** Treasurer- 217-322-3830; Elections- 217-322-4734; Vital Records- 217-322-4734. **Property tax/Assessing**- Schuyler County Chief Assessor, PO Box 285, Rushville, IL 62681; 217-322-4432, assessor fax- 217-322-6164.

Scott County

County Recorder, 35 E Market St; Courthouse, Winchester, IL 62694. Recording, R/E & UCC phone-217-742-3178; fax-217-742-5853; 8AM-4PM
Index: All in one. Record index not computerized. Office personnel or visitors may perform searches. Search fee $10.00. Real estate owner, mortgage, and property transfer searches available. Office will not search UCC records. Copy fee $1.00 per page. Cert fee- $24.00 per cert includes copy fee. Payee- Scott County Recorder. Office does not sell bulk data. **Other phones:** Treasurer- 217-742-3368; Elections-217-742-3178; Vital Records- 217-742-3178. **Property tax/Assessing**- 35 E Market St, Courthouse, Winchester, IL 62694; 217-742-5751, assessor fax-217-742-5751.

Shelby County

County Recorder, PO Box 230, Shelbyville, IL 62565. 217-774-4421; fax-217-774-5291; 8AM-4PM
Index: All in one. Records indexed on a public use terminal back to 9/90. Only the public may search. Copy fee $1.00 per page. Cert fee- $36.00 per cert plus copy fee. Payee- Shelby County Recorder. Office does not sell bulk data. **Other phones:** Treasurer-217-774-3841; Elections- 217-774-4421; Vital Records- 217-774-4421. **Property tax/Assessing**- PO Box 416, Shelbyville, IL 62565; 217-774-5579, assessor fax- 217-774-5291.

St. Clair County

County Recorder, PO Box 543, Belleville, IL 62222. 618-277-6600; 8:30AM-5PM (CST) https://www.stclaircountyrecorder.com/app/static
Index: Separate indices to search include prior to 1986 grantor/grantee in books and film. Records indexed on a public use terminal back to 1986. Prior to 1986 maintained in grantor/grantee books and film in office. Office will perform a UCC search but public must search other records themselves. Search fee $13.00 per name/address, Attn- Debra J. Office will not search real estate records. Copy fee $1.00 per page for UCC, all others $2.00 per page. Plats from $2.00 - $10.00. Cert fee- Same fee as original recording fee minus state surcharge. Payee- St. Clair County Recorder of Deeds. Bulk data available for purchase, contact Glenda Johnson for weekly CD of recorded data minus DD214's. $50.00 per week fee + 1 time set up fee. **Online access to Real Estate, Grantor/Grantee, Deed, Lien, Judgment records:** Access to the recorder records is free at https://www.stclaircountyrecorder.com/app/static. Three search methods are available. Copy fee online is $3.50 per page. **Other phones:** Treasurer- 618-277-6600 x2448; Elections- 770-531-6600 x2363. **Property tax/Assessing**- 10 Public Sq, Belleville, IL 62220; 618-277-6600 x2509, assessor fax- 618-233-4072. **Access**- parcel data free at www.co.st-clair.il.us/Departments/Assessor+Department/parcel.htm.

Stark County

County Recorder, PO Box 97, Toulon, IL 61483. Recording, R/E & UCC phone-309-286-5911; fax-309-286-4039; 8:30AM-4:30PM www.starkcourt.org
Index: All in one. Record index not computerized. Office will perform a UCC search but public must search other records themselves. Search fee $10.00. Copy fee $.50 per page. Cert fee- $5.00 per copy includes copy fee. Payee- Stark County Recorder. **Other phones:** Treasurer- 309-286-5901; Elections-309-286-5911; Vital Records- 309-286-5911. **Property tax/Assessing**- PO Box 386, Toulon, IL 61483; 309-286-7172, assessor fax- 309-286-4441. No public terminal available.

Stephenson County

County Recorder, 15 N Galena Ave, #1, Freeport, IL 61032. 815-235-8385; fax-none; 8:30AM-4:30PM
Index: Separate indices to search. Records indexed on a public use terminal back to 1985. Office personnel or visitors may perform searches. Search fee $10.00 per name. Office will search real estate records by letter request only. Copy fee $1.00 per page. Cert fee- $12.00 per cert plus copy fee after 4 pages. Payee- Stephenson County Recorder. Office does not sell bulk data. **Other phones:** Treasurer- 815-235-8264. **Property tax/Assessing**- 15 N Galena Ave, Freeport, IL 61032; 815-235-8260, assessor fax- 815-235-8366. Public access terminal available.

Tazewell County

County Recorder, PO Box 36, Pekin, IL 61555-0036. Recording, R/E & UCC phone-309-477-2210; fax-309-477-2321; 8:30AM-5PM (CST) www.tazewellcounty.org/cor.html
Index: All in one. Records indexed on a public use terminal back to 0101/1991. Office will perform a UCC search but public must search other records themselves. Search fee $15.00 for UCC search. Copy fee $.50 per page. $1.00 per page to fax. Cert fee- $12.00 1st 4 pages; $1.00 each add'l page, includes copy fee. Payee- Tazewell County Recorder. **Other phones:** Treasurer- 309-477-2284. **Property tax/Assessing**- 11 S 4th St, Rm 401, Pekin, IL 61554; 309-477-2275, assessor fax- 309-477-2204.

Union County

County Recorder, 309 W Market St, Jonesboro, IL 62952. 618-833-5711; fax-618-833-8712; 8AM-N, 1-4PM (CST)
Index: Separate indices to search include liens and mortgages, real estate, births & deaths. Record index not computerized. Only the public may search. Copy fee $.50 per page. Cert fee- $5.00 per cert plus copy fee. Payee- Union County Recorder. Office does not sell bulk data. **Other phones:** Treasurer- 618-833-5621. **Property tax/Assessing**- 302 W Market St, Jonesboro, IL 62952; 618-833-8051, assessor fax-618-833-7099.

Vermilion County

County Recorder, 6 N Vermilion St, Danville, IL 61832-5877. 217-554-6041; fax-217-554-6047; 8AM-4:30PM www.vercounty.org/recorder.htm
Index: Separate indices to search include books, microfilm, tract cards, computer. Records indexed on computer back to 7/87. Only the public may search. Copy fee $1.00 1st page; $.50 each add'l. Cert fee- $12.00 per cert up to 4 pages, $1.00 for add'l pages, includes copy fee. Payee- Vermilion County Recorder. Office does not sell bulk data. **Online access to Real Estate, Deed. Lien, UCC records:** Access real estate records at https://www.illandrecords.com/illr/il183/index.jsp. There is a $5.00 fee per doc found and $5.00 fee to view it, or you may subscribe for $1000 per month. Also, recorder land data by subscription on either the Laredo system (subscription & fees) or the Tapestry System (use credit card) at http://tapestry.fidlar.com; $3.99 search; $.50 per image. Index and images go back to 7/1/1987. **Other phones:** Treasurer- 217-554-6081. **Property tax/Assessing**- 6 N Vermillion St, Courthouse Annex, 4th Fl, Danville, Il 61832-5877; 217-554-1940, assessor fax- 217-554-1955. www.vercounty.org/SupAssm.htm **Online access**- Access property data free on the gis-mapping site at www.vcgis.org/. Find information on subscribing to the county's property tax database at www.vercounty.org/TechServ/taxinquiry.pdf.

Wabash County

County Recorder, PO Box 277, Mount Carmel, IL 62863. Recording, R/E & UCC phone-618-262-4561; 8AM-5PM (CST)
Index: All in one. Records indexed on computer, no images. Back to 1857. Only the public may search. Office will not search real estate records. Will not search UCC records. Copy fee $1.00 per page.Real estate or tax lien copy- $.50 per page. Cert fee- $12.00 1st 4 pg, then $1.00 each add'l. Payee- Wabash County Recorder. **Other phones:** Treasurer- 618-262-5262; Elections- 618-262-4561; Vital Records-618-262-4561. **Property tax/Assessing**- 401 Market St, Mount Carmel, IL 62863; 618-262-4463. hours-8AM-4:30PM Public terminal in Treasurer's office.

Warren County

County Recorder, 100 W Broadway; Courthouse, Monmouth, IL 61462-1797. Recording, R/E & UCC phone-309-734-8592; fax-309-734-7406; 8AM-4:30PM (CST)
Index: Separate indices to search include tracts, computer. Records indexed on a public use terminal back to 1986. Only the public may search. Copy fee $.50 per page. Cert fee- same as recording fee. Payee- Warren County Recorder. Office does not sell bulk data. **Other phones:** Treasurer- 309-734-8536; Elections- 309-734-4612; Vital Records- 309-734-8592. **Property tax/Assessing**- 100 W Broadway, Monmouth, IL 61462-1797; 309-734-8561.

Washington County

County Recorder, 101 E St. Louis St; County Courthouse, Nashville, IL 62263-1105. Recording, R/E & UCC phone-618-327-4800 x300; fax-618-327-3582; 8AM-4PM (CST)
Index: Separate indices to search. Records indexed on a public use terminal back to 10/2001. Office will perform a UCC search but public must search other records themselves. Search fee $10.00 plus copy fee. Copy fee $1.00 per page. Cert fee- $5.00 per cert plus $1.00 per page includes copy fee. Payee- Washington County Recorder. **Other phones:** Treasurer- 618-327-4800 x315; Elections- 618-327-4800 x300; Vital Records- 618-327-4800 x300. **Property tax/Assessing**- 101 E St Louis St, Courthouse, Nashville, IL 62263; 618-327-4800 x325.

Wayne County

County Recorder, PO Box 187, Fairfield, IL 62837. Recording, R/E & UCC phone-618-842-5182; fax-618-842-6427; 8AM-4:30PM (CST)
Records indexed between 1886 and May, 1988 are book indexes, from June, 1988 to present on computer. Office personnel or visitors may perform searches. Search fee $10.00 per name with request of specific years searched, anything over 10 years is

$1.00 per year. Copy fee $1.00 per page. Cert fee- $5.00 per cert plus copy fee. Payee- Wayne County Recorder. Office does not sell bulk data. **Other phones:** Treasurer- 618-842-5087; Elections- 618-842-5182; Vital Records- 618-842-5182. **Property tax/Assessing**- PO Box 384, Fairfield, IL 62837; 618-842-2582, assessor fax- 618-847-5713. Public access terminal available.

White County

County Clerk/Recorder, PO Box 339, Carmi, IL 62821. Recording, R/E & UCC phone-618-382-7211; 8AM-4PM (CST) www.whitecounty-il.gov/departments/countyclerk.asp

Index: All in one. Records indexed on computer back to 3/15/07. Office will perform a UCC search but public must search other records themselves. Search fee $10.00. Copy fee $2.00 per page. Cert fee- $28.00 1st 4 pg, then $1.00 each add'l, includes copies. Payee- White County Recorder. **Other phones:** Treasurer- 618-382-8122; Elections- 618-382-7211; Vital Records- 618-382-7211. **Property tax/Assessing**- PO Box 44, 314 E Cherry St, Carmi, IL 62821; 618-382-2332.

Whiteside County

County Recorder, 200 E Knox St, Morrison, IL 61270. Recording, R/E & UCC phone-815-772-5192; fax-815-772-5241; 8:30AM-4:30PM (CST) www.whiteside.org

Index: Separate indices to search include entry book, grantor/grantee, tract index. Records indexed on a public use terminal back to 1989. Office will perform a UCC search but public must search other records themselves. Copy fee $.50 per page.Payee- Whiteside County Recorder. Office does not sell bulk data. **Other phones:** Treasurer- 815-772-5196; Vital Records- 815-772-5189. **Property tax/Assessing**- 200 E Knox St, Morrison, IL 61270; 815-772-5195, assessor fax- 815-772-7673. www.whiteside.org/assessor/2.html **Online access**- Search assessor property data for a fee on the GIS system at http://beacon.schneidercorp.com/?site=WhitesideCountyIL.

Will County

County Recorder, 58 E Clinton, #100, Joliet, IL 60432. 815-740-4637; fax-815-740-4697; 8:30AM-4:30PM (CST) www.willcountyrecorder.com

Satellite Office: 241 Canterbury Ln, Bolingbrook, IL 60440 (630-759-5780). Index: All in one. Record index is computerized. Office will perform a UCC search but public must search other records themselves. Search fee-$10.00 per name. Office will not search real estate records. Copy fee $1.00 per page. Website copy rates differ. Cert fee- Same as original recording fee. Payee- Will County Recorder. **Online access to Real Estate, Deed, Lien, Mortgage, Voter Registration, Corporation, UCC, Judgment records:** Access to the Recorder's real estate and lien records back to 1965 free at www.willcountyrecorder.com; fees apply for full data and to print copies. Access voter registration data free at https://www.willcountydata.com/voterstatus/Voter_lookup_input.htm. **Other phones:** Treasurer- 815-740-4675; Elections- 815-740-4615. **Property tax/Assessing**- Supervisor of Assessments, 302 N Chicago St, Joliet, IL 60432; 815-740-4648, assessor fax- 815-740-4696. www.willcountysoa.com **Online access**- Access to property/parcel number for free go to www.willcountysoa.com/disclaimer.aspx.

Williamson County

County Recorder, PO Box 1108, Marion, IL 62959-1108. Recording, R/E & UCC phone-618-997-1301 X121; fax-618-993-2071; 8AM-4PM (CST)

Index: Separate indices to search include mortgage, deed, miscellaneous. Records indexed on computer back to 1992. Office personnel or visitors may perform searches. Search fee $10.00 per name. Copy fee $1.00 per page. Cert fee- $5.00 per cert plus copy fee. Payee- Williamson County Recorder. Office does not sell bulk data. **Other phones:** Treasurer- 618-997-1301 x129; Elections- 618-997-1301 x102; Vital Records- 618-997-1301 x102. **Property tax/Assessing**- 200 W Jefferson, Marion, IL 62959; 618-997-1301 x164, assessor fax- 618-997-5541.

Winnebago County

County Recorder, 404 Elm St, Rm 405, Rockford, IL 61101. 815-987-3100, R/E recording phone-815-987-3010; fax-815-961-3261; 8AM-4PM (CST) www.co.winnebago.il.us

Index: Separate indices to search include computer, books to 1993. Records indexed on a public use terminal back to 1980. Office personnel or visitors may perform searches. General search fee $5.00. UCC and real estate search fee - $13.75. Copy fee $.25 per page. Cert fee- $25.00 add'l $1.00 per page, includes copies. Payee- Winnebago County Recorder. Office does not sell bulk data. **Online access to Real Estate, Deed records:** Access county property and court data by subscription at www.co.winnebago.il.us; registration and $10.00 per month fee required. Also, access county land and UCC records at https://www.illandrecords.com/illr/il201/index.jsp but must pay per use or subscribe. **Other phones:** Treasurer- 815-987-3010; Elections- 815-987-3086; Vital Records- 815-987-3050. **Property tax/Assessing**- 404 Elm St, Rockford, IL 61101; 815-987-3025, assessor fax- 815-319-4461. hours- 8AM-5PM **Online**- Access parcel and assessment data free at http://cis.co.winnebago.il.us/property/sofa/c-sofa_inqIndex.asp. Registration and password required to access fuller data. Search property data at http://cis.co.winnebago.il.us/property/treas/Treas_inqLOGIN.asp. Get userID and password from treasurer office. Also, access property data via the GIS- site free at http://ims.wingis.org/ParcelSearch.asp. Also, search Rockford Township assessment data free at www.rockfordtownshipassessor.net/propertysearch.asp.

Woodford County

County Recorder, 115 N Main, Rm 202; Courthouse, Eureka, IL 61530-1273. Recording, R/E & UCC phone-309-467-2822; fax-309-467-7391; 8AM-5PM www.woodford-county.org/index.php?section=73

Index: Separate indices to search include books and computer. Records indexed on a public use terminal back to 1986. Only the public may search. Copy fee $.25 per page. Cert fee- $38.00 1st 4 pages; $1.00 each add'l page. Payee- Woodford County Recorder. **Other phones:** Treasurer- 309-467-4621; Elections- 309-467-2822; Vital Records- 309-467-2822. **Property tax/Assessing**- 115 N Main, Rm 101, Eureka, IL 61530-1273; 309-467-3708, assessor fax- 309-467-7329.

Illinois County Locator

You will usually be able to find the city name in the City/County Cross Reference below. In that case, it is a simple matter to determine the county from the cross reference. However, only the official US Postal Service city names are included in this index. There are an additional 40,000 place names that people use in their addresses. Therefore, we have also included a ZIP/City Cross Reference immediately following the City/County Cross Reference.

If you know the ZIP Code but the city name does not appear in the City/County Cross Reference index, look up the ZIP Code in the ZIP/City Cross Reference, find the city name, then look up the city name in the City/County Cross Reference. For example, you want to know the county for an address of Menands, NY 12204. There is no "Menands" in the City/County Cross Reference. The ZIP/City Cross Reference shows that ZIP Codes 12201-12288 are for the city of Albany. Looking back in the City/County Cross Reference, Albany is in Albany County.

Illinois City/County Cross Reference

ABINGDON (61410) Knox(97), Warren(2)
ADAIR McDonough
ADDIEVILLE Washington
ADDISON Du Page
ADRIAN Hancock
AKIN Franklin
ALBANY Whiteside
ALBERS Clinton
ALBION Edwards
ALDEN McHenry
ALEDO Mercer
ALEXANDER (62601) Morgan(93), Sangamon(6)
ALEXIS (61412) Mercer(83), Warren(16)
ALGONQUIN (60102) McHenry(82), Kane(17)
ALHAMBRA Madison
ALLENDALE Wabash
ALLERTON (61810) Vermilion(71), Douglas(14), Edgar(12), Champaign(1)
ALMA Marion
ALPHA Henry
ALSEY Scott
ALSIP Cook
ALTAMONT (62411) Effingham(98), Fayette(1)
ALTO PASS (62905) Union(79), Jackson(20)
ALTON (62002) Madison(98), Macoupin(1)
ALTONA (61414) Knox(68), Henry(31)
ALVIN Vermilion
AMBOY Lee
AMF OHARE Cook
ANCHOR (61720) McLean(91), Ford(8)
ANCONA Livingston
ANDALUSIA Rock Island
ANDOVER Henry
ANNA Union
ANNAPOLIS (62413) Crawford(93), Clark(6)
ANNAWAN Henry
ANTIOCH Lake
APPLE RIVER Jo Daviess
ARCOLA (61910) Douglas(86), Coles(13)
ARENZVILLE (62611) Cass(83), Morgan(16)
ARGENTA Macon
ARLINGTON Bureau
ARLINGTON HEIGHTS Cook
ARMINGTON (61721) Tazewell(92), Logan(7)
ARMSTRONG Vermilion
AROMA PARK Kankakee
ARROWSMITH McLean
ARTHUR (61911) Douglas(54), Moultrie(41), Coles(4)
ASHKUM Iroquois
ASHLAND (62612) Cass(76), Morgan(22)
ASHLEY (62808) Washington(81), Jefferson(18)
ASHMORE Coles
ASHTON (61006) Lee(78), Ogle(21)
ASSUMPTION (62510) Christian(86), Shelby(13)
ASTORIA Fulton
ATHENS (62613) Menard(95), Logan(3)
ATKINSON Henry
ATLANTA (61723) Logan(98), McLean(1)
ATWATER Macoupin
ATWOOD (61913) Douglas(64), Piatt(34), Moultrie(1)
AUBURN Sangamon
AUGUSTA (62311) Hancock(90), Schuyler(5), Adams(3)
AURORA (60504) Du Page(76), Kane(12), Will(9), Kendall(2)
AURORA Du Page
AURORA Kane
AVA Jackson
AVISTON (62216) Clinton(97), Madison(2)
AVON (61415) Fulton(80), Warren(19)
BAILEYVILLE (61007) Ogle(69), Stephenson(30)
BALDWIN Randolph
BARDOLPH McDonough
BARNHILL Wayne
BARRINGTON (60010) Lake(57), Cook(36), McHenry(4)
BARRINGTON Lake
BARRY (62312) Pike(85), Adams(14)
BARSTOW Rock Island
BARTELSO Clinton
BARTLETT (60103) Du Page(50), Cook(49)
BASCO Hancock
BATAVIA Kane
BATCHTOWN Calhoun
BATH Mason
BAYLIS (62314) Pike(76), Adams(22)
BEARDSTOWN Cass
BEASON (62512) Logan(93), De Witt(6)
BEAVERVILLE (60912) Kankakee(56), Iroquois(43)
BECKEMEYER Clinton
BEDFORD PARK Cook
BEECHER (60401) Will(97), Kankakee(2)
BEECHER CITY (62414) Effingham(63), Fayette(27), Shelby(9)
BELKNAP (62908) Massac(53), Johnson(46)
BELLE RIVE (62810) Jefferson(95), Hamilton(2), Wayne(1)
BELLEVILLE St. Clair
BELLFLOWER McLean
BELLMONT Wabash
BELLWOOD Cook
BELVIDERE Boone
BEMENT Piatt
BENLD Macoupin
BENSENVILLE Du Page
BENSON Woodford
BENTON Franklin
BERKELEY Cook
BERWICK Warren
BERWYN Cook
BETHALTO Madison
BETHANY (61914) Moultrie(97), Macon(2)
BIG ROCK (60511) Kane(94), De Kalb(5)
BIGGSVILLE Henderson
BINGHAM Fayette
BIRDS Lawrence
BISHOP HILL Henry
BISMARCK Vermilion
BLACKSTONE Livingston
BLANDINSVILLE (61420) McDonough(91), Hancock(8)
BLOOMINGDALE Du Page
BLOOMINGTON McLean
BLUE ISLAND Cook
BLUE MOUND (62513) Macon(76), Christian(23)
BLUFF SPRINGS Cass
BLUFFS (62621) Scott(94), Morgan(5)
BLUFORD (62814) Jefferson(98), Wayne(1)
BOLES Johnson
BOLINGBROOK (60440) Will(97), Du Page(2)
BOLINGBROOK Will
BONDVILLE Champaign
BONE GAP Edwards
BONFIELD Kankakee
BONNIE Jefferson
BOODY Macon
BOURBONNAIS Kankakee
BOWEN (62316) Hancock(97), Adams(2)
BRACEVILLE (60407) Grundy(51), Will(47)
BRADFORD (61421) Stark(58), Bureau(34), Marshall(6)
BRADLEY Kankakee
BRAIDWOOD Will
BREESE Clinton
BRIDGEPORT Lawrence
BRIDGEVIEW Cook
BRIGHTON (62012) Jersey(46), Macoupin(45), Madison(7)
BRIMFIELD Peoria
BRISTOL Kendall
BROADLANDS (61816) Champaign(97), Douglas(2)
BROADVIEW Cook
BROCTON (61917) Edgar(95), Douglas(4)
BROOKFIELD Cook
BROOKPORT (62910) Massac(96), Pope(3)
BROUGHTON Hamilton
BROWNING (62624) Schuyler(97), Fulton(2)
BROWNS (62818) Wabash(61), Edwards(38)
BROWNSTOWN Fayette
BRUSSELS Calhoun
BRYANT Fulton
BUCKINGHAM (60917) Kankakee(90), Livingston(8)
BUCKLEY Iroquois
BUCKNER Franklin
BUDA Bureau
BUFFALO Sangamon
BUFFALO GROVE (60089) Lake(57), Cook(42)
BUFFALO PRAIRIE Rock Island
BULPITT Christian
BUNCOMBE (62912) Johnson(55), Union(44)
BUNKER HILL Macoupin
BURBANK Cook
BUREAU Bureau
BURLINGTON Kane
BURNSIDE Hancock
BURNT PRAIRIE (62820) White(86), Wayne(13)
BUSHNELL McDonough
BUTLER Montgomery
BYRON Ogle
CABERY (60919) Kankakee(43), Ford(31), Livingston(25)
CACHE Alexander
CAIRO Alexander
CALEDONIA (61011) Boone(70), Winnebago(29)
CALHOUN Richland
CALUMET CITY Cook
CAMARGO Douglas
CAMBRIA Williamson
CAMBRIDGE Henry
CAMDEN Schuyler
CAMERON Warren
CAMP GROVE Marshall
CAMP POINT Adams
CAMPBELL HILL (62916) Jackson(77), Randolph(12), Perry(10)
CAMPUS Livingston
CANTON Fulton
CANTRALL Sangamon
CAPRON Boone
CARBON CLIFF Rock Island
CARBONDALE (62902) Jackson(70), Williamson(27)
CARBONDALE Jackson
CARLINVILLE Macoupin
CARLOCK (61725) McLean(70), Woodford(29)
CARLYLE Clinton
CARMAN Henderson
CARMI White
CAROL STREAM Cook
CAROL STREAM Du Page
CARPENTERSVILLE Kane
CARRIER MILLS (62917) Saline(88), Williamson(11)
CARROLLTON Greene
CARTERVILLE Williamson
CARTHAGE Hancock
CARY (60013) McHenry(94), Lake(5)
CASEY (62420) Clark(85), Cumberland(11), Coles(1)
CASEYVILLE St. Clair
CASTLETON Stark
CATLIN Vermilion
CAVE IN ROCK Hardin
CEDAR POINT La Salle
CEDARVILLE Stephenson
CENTRALIA (62801) Marion(67), Clinton(22), Washington(6), Jefferson(4)
CERRO GORDO (61818) Piatt(77), Macon(22)
CHADWICK (61014) Carroll(82), Whiteside(17)

CHAMBERSBURG (62323) Pike(91), Brown(8)
CHAMPAIGN Champaign
CHANA Ogle
CHANDLERVILLE (62627) Cass(71), Mason(28)
CHANNAHON (60410) Will(94), Grundy(5)
CHAPIN (62628) Morgan(87), Scott(12)
CHARLESTON Coles
CHATHAM Sangamon
CHATSWORTH Livingston
CHEBANSE (60922) Kankakee(62), Iroquois(37)
CHENOA (61726) McLean(94), Livingston(5)
CHERRY Bureau
CHERRY VALLEY (61016) Winnebago(88), Boone(11)
CHESTER Randolph
CHESTERFIELD (62630) Macoupin(97), Greene(1)
CHESTNUT Logan
CHICAGO Cook
CHICAGO HEIGHTS Cook
CHICAGO RIDGE Cook
CHILLICOTHE (61523) Peoria(97), Marshall(2)
CHRISMAN Edgar
CHRISTOPHER Franklin
CICERO Cook
CISCO (61830) Piatt(70), Macon(29)
CISNE Wayne
CISSNA PARK Iroquois
CLARE De Kalb
CLAREMONT (62421) Richland(97), Crawford(1), Lawrence(1)
CLARENDON HILLS Du Page
CLAY CITY (62824) Clay(95), Wayne(4)
CLAYTON (62324) Adams(97), Brown(2)
CLAYTONVILLE Iroquois
CLIFTON Iroquois
CLINTON De Witt
COAL CITY Grundy
COAL VALLEY (61240) Rock Island(75), Henry(24)
COATSBURG Adams
COBDEN Union
COELLO Franklin
COFFEEN Montgomery
COLCHESTER (62326) McDonough(97), Hancock(2)
COLETA Whiteside
COLFAX McLean
COLLINSVILLE (62234) Madison(90), St. Clair(9)
COLLISON Vermilion
COLMAR McDonough
COLONA Henry
COLP Williamson
COLUMBIA (62236) Monroe(94), St. Clair(5)
COLUSA Hancock
COMPTON Lee
CONCORD Morgan
CONGERVILLE (61729) Woodford(96), McLean(3)
COOKSVILLE McLean
CORDOVA Rock Island
CORNELL Livingston
CORNLAND Logan
CORTLAND De Kalb
COTTAGE HILLS Madison
COULTERVILLE (62237) Randolph(46), Washington(27), Perry(26)
COUNTRY CLUB HILLS Cook
COWDEN (62422) Shelby(74), Fayette(25)
CREAL SPRINGS (62922) Williamson(71), Johnson(28)
CRESCENT CITY Iroquois
CRESTON Ogle
CRETE Will
CREVE COEUR Tazewell
CROPSEY (61731) McLean(67), Ford(31), Livingston(1)
CROSSVILLE White
CRYSTAL LAKE McHenry
CUBA Fulton
CULLOM (60929) Livingston(89), Ford(10)
CUTLER (62238) Perry(95), Randolph(4)
CYPRESS (62923) Johnson(85), Pulaski(8), Union(5)
DAHINDA Knox
DAHLGREN (62828) Hamilton(97), Wayne(2)
DAKOTA Stephenson
DALE Hamilton
DALLAS CITY (62330) Hancock(93), Henderson(6)
DALTON CITY (61925) Macon(57), Moultrie(42)
DALZELL Bureau
DANA (61321) La Salle(87), Livingston(4), Woodford(4), Marshall(3)
DANFORTH Iroquois
DANVERS (61732) McLean(63), Tazewell(36)
DANVILLE Vermilion
DARIEN Du Page
DAVIS (61019) Stephenson(65), Winnebago(34)
DAVIS JUNCTION (61020) Ogle(94), Winnebago(5)
DAWSON Sangamon
DE KALB De Kalb
DE LAND Piatt
DE SOTO (62924) Jackson(80), Williamson(19)
DECATUR Macon
DEER CREEK Tazewell
DEER GROVE (61243) Whiteside(89), Bureau(5), Lee(5)
DEERE CO GROUP CLAIMS Rock Island
DEERFIELD (60015) Lake(95), Cook(4)
DEERFIELD Cook
DEKALB De Kalb
DELAVAN Tazewell
DENNISON (62423) Clark(90), Edgar(9)
DEPUE Bureau
DES PLAINES Cook
DEWEY (61840) Champaign(97), Ford(2)
DEWITT De Witt
DIETERICH (62424) Effingham(90), Jasper(9)
DIVERNON Sangamon
DIX (62830) Jefferson(95), Marion(4)
DIXON (61021) Lee(91), Ogle(8)
DOLTON Cook
DONGOLA (62926) Union(90), Pulaski(9)
DONNELLSON (62019) Montgomery(52), Bond(47)
DONOVAN Iroquois
DORSEY (62021) Madison(93), Macoupin(6)
DOVER Bureau
DOW Jersey
DOWELL Jackson
DOWNERS GROVE Du Page
DOWNS McLean
DU BOIS (62831) Washington(91), Perry(8)
DU QUOIN (62832) Perry(96), Jackson(3)
DUNDAS (62425) Richland(86), Jasper(13)
DUNDEE Kane
DUNFERMLINE Fulton
DUNLAP Peoria
DUPO St. Clair
DURAND Winnebago
DWIGHT (60420) Livingston(93), Grundy(6)
EAGARVILLE Macoupin
EARLVILLE (60518) La Salle(72), De Kalb(22), Lee(4)
EAST ALTON Madison
EAST CARONDELET (62240) St. Clair(97), Monroe(2)
EAST DUBUQUE Jo Daviess
EAST GALESBURG Knox
EAST LYNN Vermilion
EAST MOLINE Rock Island
EAST PEORIA (61611) Tazewell(86), Woodford(13)
EAST SAINT LOUIS St. Clair
EASTON Mason
EDDYVILLE Pope
EDELSTEIN (61526) Peoria(90), Marshall(8), Stark(1)
EDGEWOOD (62426) Effingham(58), Clay(37), Fayette(4)
EDINBURG Christian
EDWARDS Peoria
EDWARDSVILLE Madison
EFFINGHAM Effingham
EL PASO (61738) Woodford(96), McLean(2)
ELBURN Kane
ELCO Alexander
ELDENA Lee
ELDORADO (62930) Saline(98), Gallatin(1)
ELDRED Greene
ELEROY Stephenson
ELGIN (60120) Kane(56), Cook(43)
ELGIN Du Page
ELGIN Kane
ELIZABETH (61028) Jo Daviess(98), Carroll(1)
ELIZABETHTOWN (62931) Hardin(82), Gallatin(17)
ELK GROVE VILLAGE (60007) Cook(96), Du Page(3)
ELK GROVE VILLAGE Cook
ELKHART Logan
ELKVILLE Jackson
ELLERY (62833) Edwards(56), Wayne(43)
ELLIOTT Ford
ELLIS GROVE Randolph
ELLISVILLE Fulton
ELLSWORTH McLean
ELMHURST Du Page
ELMWOOD Peoria
ELMWOOD PARK Cook
ELSAH Jersey
ELVASTON Hancock
ELWIN Macon
ELWOOD Will
EMDEN (62635) Tazewell(94), Logan(5)
EMINGTON Livingston
EMMA White
ENERGY Williamson
ENFIELD (62835) White(94), Hamilton(5)
EOLA Du Page
EQUALITY (62934) Gallatin(68), Saline(31)
ERIE (61250) Whiteside(94), Henry(5)
ESMOND (60129) Ogle(53), De Kalb(46)
ESSEX (60935) Kankakee(98), Will(1)
EUREKA Woodford
EVANSTON Cook
EVANSVILLE Randolph
EVERGREEN PARK Cook
EWING (62836) Franklin(98), Jefferson(1)
FAIRBURY (61739) Livingston(97), McLean(2)
FAIRFIELD Wayne
FAIRMOUNT Vermilion
FAIRVIEW Fulton
FAIRVIEW HEIGHTS St. Clair
FARINA (62838) Fayette(55), Clay(29), Marion(13), Effingham(1)
FARMER CITY (61842) De Witt(89), McLean(9), Piatt(1)
FARMERSVILLE Montgomery
FARMINGTON (61531) Fulton(92), Peoria(5), Knox(1)
FENTON (61251) Whiteside(95), Rock Island(5)
FERRIS Hancock
FIATT Fulton
FIDELITY Jersey
FIELDON (62031) Jersey(97), Greene(2)
FILLMORE Montgomery
FINDLAY Shelby
FISHER (61843) Champaign(94), McLean(5)
FITHIAN Vermilion
FLANAGAN Livingston
FLAT ROCK (62427) Crawford(93), Lawrence(6)
FLORA Clay
FLOSSMOOR Cook
FOOSLAND (61845) Champaign(76), Ford(14), McLean(9)
FOREST CITY Mason
FOREST PARK Cook
FORREST Livingston
FORRESTON Ogle
FORSYTH Macon
FORT SHERIDAN Lake
FOWLER Adams
FOX LAKE Lake
FOX RIVER GROVE (60021) McHenry(96), Lake(3)
FOX VALLEY Du Page
FRANKFORT Will
FRANKFORT HEIGHTS Franklin
FRANKLIN (62638) Morgan(98), Macoupin(1)
FRANKLIN GROVE (61031) Lee(96), Ogle(3)
FRANKLIN PARK Cook
FRANKLIN PARK Du Page
FREDERICK Schuyler
FREEBURG St. Clair
FREEMAN SPUR Williamson
FREEPORT Stephenson
FULTON Whiteside
FULTS Monroe
GALATIA (62935) Saline(97), Hamilton(1)
GALATIA Saline
GALENA Jo Daviess
GALESBURG Knox
GALT Whiteside
GALVA (61434) Henry(97), Knox(1)
GARDEN PRAIRIE (61038) Boone(89), McHenry(10)
GARDNER Grundy
GAYS (61928) Moultrie(75), Coles(16), Shelby(7)
GEFF Wayne
GENESEO Henry
GENEVA Kane
GENOA De Kalb
GEORGETOWN Vermilion
GERLAW Warren
GERMAN VALLEY (61039) Stephenson(69), Ogle(30)
GERMANTOWN Clinton
GIBSON CITY (60936) Ford(98), Champaign(1)
GIFFORD Champaign
GILBERTS Kane
GILLESPIE Macoupin
GILMAN Iroquois
GILSON Knox
GIRARD (62640) Macoupin(89), Montgomery(10)
GLADSTONE Henderson
GLASFORD (61533) Peoria(82), Fulton(17)
GLEN CARBON Madison
GLEN ELLYN Du Page
GLENARM Sangamon
GLENCOE Cook
GLENDALE HEIGHTS Du Page
GLENVIEW Cook
GLENVIEW NAS Cook
GLENWOOD Cook
GODFREY (62035) Madison(87), Jersey(12)
GOLCONDA (62938) Pope(90), Hardin(5), Massac(4)
GOLDEN Adams
GOLDEN EAGLE Calhoun

GOLDEN GATE Wayne
GOLF Cook
GOOD HOPE McDonough
GOODFIELD Woodford
GOODWINE Iroquois
GOREVILLE (62939) Johnson(92), Williamson(4), Union(3)
GORHAM Jackson
GRAFTON Jersey
GRAND CHAIN (62941) Pulaski(61), Massac(38)
GRAND RIDGE La Salle
GRAND TOWER Jackson
GRANITE CITY Madison
GRANT PARK (60940) Kankakee(95), Will(4)
GRANTSBURG (62943) Johnson(76), Massac(19), Pope(4)
GRANVILLE Putnam
GRAYMONT Livingston
GRAYSLAKE Lake
GRAYVILLE (62844) White(57), Edwards(42)
GREAT LAKES Lake
GREEN VALLEY Tazewell
GREENFIELD (62044) Greene(87), Macoupin(12)
GREENUP Cumberland
GREENVIEW Menard
GREENVILLE Bond
GRIDLEY (61744) McLean(91), Livingston(8)
GRIGGSVILLE Pike
GROVELAND Tazewell
GURNEE Lake
HAGARSTOWN Fayette
HAMBURG Calhoun
HAMEL Madison
HAMILTON Hancock
HAMLETSBURG Pope
HAMMOND (61929) Piatt(97), Moultrie(2)
HAMPSHIRE (60140) Kane(98), De Kalb(1)
HAMPTON Rock Island
HANNA CITY Peoria
HANOVER Jo Daviess
HANOVER PARK (60133) Cook(57), Du Page(42)
HARDIN Calhoun
HARMON (61042) Lee(98), Whiteside(1)
HARRISBURG Saline
HARRISTOWN Macon
HARTFORD Madison
HARTSBURG (62643) Montgomery(60), Logan(40)
HARVARD McHenry
HARVEL (62538) Montgomery(83), Christian(16)
HARVEY Cook
HARWOOD HEIGHTS Cook
HAVANA (62644) Mason(94), Fulton(5)
HAZEL CREST Cook
HEBRON McHenry
HECKER Monroe
HENDERSON Knox
HENNEPIN Putnam
HENNING Vermilion
HENRY Marshall
HERALD White
HEROD (62947) Saline(43), Hardin(31), Pope(25)
HERRICK (62431) Shelby(53), Fayette(46)
HERRIN Williamson
HERSCHER (60941) Kankakee(96), Iroquois(2), Ford(1)
HETTICK Macoupin
HEYWORTH (61745) McLean(96), De Witt(3)
HICKORY HILLS Cook
HIDALGO Jasper
HIGHLAND (62249) Madison(94), Clinton(4)
HIGHLAND PARK Lake
HIGHWOOD Lake
HILLSBORO Montgomery
HILLSDALE Rock Island
HILLSIDE Cook
HILLVIEW Greene
HINCKLEY De Kalb
HINDSBORO (61930) Douglas(81), Coles(18)
HINES Cook
HINSDALE (60527) Du Page(91), Cook(8)
HINSDALE Du Page
HOFFMAN Clinton
HOFFMAN ESTATES Cook
HOLCOMB Ogle
HOMER (61849) Champaign(84), Vermilion(15)
HOMETOWN Cook
HOMEWOOD Cook
HOOPESTON (60942) Vermilion(91), Iroquois(8)
HOOPPOLE Henry
HOPEDALE Tazewell
HOPKINS PARK Kankakee
HOYLETON Washington
HUDSON (61748) McLean(98), Woodford(1)
HUEY Clinton
HULL (62343) Pike(89), Adams(10)
HUMBOLDT Coles
HUME Edgar
HUNTLEY (60142) McHenry(76), Kane(23)
HUNTSVILLE Schuyler
HURST Williamson
HUTSONVILLE Crawford
ILLINOIS CITY (61259) Rock Island(98), Mercer(1)
ILLIOPOLIS (62539) Sangamon(94), Macon(5)
INA (62846) Jefferson(98), Franklin(1)
INDIANOLA (61850) Vermilion(98), Edgar(1)
INDUSTRY (61440) McDonough(97), Schuyler(2)
INGLESIDE Lake
INGRAHAM (62434) Jasper(84), Clay(15)
IOLA Clay
IPAVA Fulton
IROQUOIS Iroquois
IRVING Montgomery
IRVINGTON Washington
ISLAND LAKE (60042) Lake(51), McHenry(48)
ITASCA Du Page
IUKA Marion
IVESDALE (61851) Champaign(89), Piatt(8), Douglas(2)
JACKSONVILLE Morgan
JACOB Jackson
JANESVILLE Cumberland
JEFFERSON BANK Peoria
JERSEYVILLE Jersey
JEWETT (62436) Jasper(59), Cumberland(40)
JOHNSONVILLE Wayne
JOHNSTON CITY Williamson
JOLIET Will
JONESBORO Union
JOPPA Massac
JOY (61260) Mercer(94), Rock Island(5)
JUNCTION Gallatin
JUSTICE Cook
KAMPSVILLE (62053) Calhoun(97), Pike(2)
KANE (62054) Greene(58), Jersey(41)
KANEVILLE Kane
KANKAKEE Kankakee
KANSAS (61933) Edgar(85), Clark(12), Coles(2)
KARBERS RIDGE Hardin
KARNAK (62956) Pulaski(50), Massac(48)
KASBEER Bureau
KEENES (62851) Wayne(65), Jefferson(27), Marion(7)
KEENSBURG Wabash
KEITHSBURG (61442) Mercer(95), Henderson(4)
KELL (62853) Marion(98), Jefferson(1)
KEMPTON (60946) Ford(81), Livingston(18)
KENILWORTH Cook
KENNEY (61749) De Witt(72), Logan(15), Macon(12)
KENT (61044) Stephenson(65), Jo Daviess(35)
KEWANEE Henry
KEYESPORT (62253) Bond(59), Clinton(37), Fayette(3)
KILBOURNE Mason
KINCAID Christian
KINDERHOOK Pike
KINGS Ogle
KINGSTON (60145) De Kalb(93), Boone(6)
KINGSTON MINES Peoria
KINMUNDY (62854) Marion(97), Clay(1), Fayette(1)
KINSMAN (60437) Grundy(97), La Salle(2)
KIRKLAND (60146) De Kalb(89), Boone(8), Ogle(1), Winnebago(1)
KIRKWOOD (61447) Warren(92), Henderson(7)
KNOXVILLE Knox
LA FAYETTE (61449) Knox(53), Stark(46)
LA GRANGE Cook
LA GRANGE PARK Cook
LA HARPE (61450) Hancock(56), McDonough(41), Henderson(1)
LA MOILLE (61330) Bureau(52), Lee(47)
LA PLACE Piatt
LA PRAIRIE (62346) Adams(63), Schuyler(22), Hancock(14)
LA ROSE Marshall
LA SALLE La Salle
LACON Marshall
LADD Bureau
LAFOX Kane
LAKE BLUFF Lake
LAKE FOREST Lake
LAKE FORK Logan
LAKE IN THE HILLS McHenry
LAKE VILLA Lake
LAKE ZURICH Lake
LAKEWOOD Shelby
LANARK Carroll
LANCASTER Wabash
LANE De Witt
LANSING Cook
LATHAM (62543) Logan(82), Macon(17)
LAURA (61451) Peoria(92), Stark(7)
LAWNDALE Logan
LAWRENCEVILLE Lawrence
LE ROY McLean
LEAF RIVER (61047) Ogle(96), Winnebago(2), Stephenson(1)
LEBANON St. Clair
LEE (60530) Lee(56), De Kalb(43)
LEE CENTER Lee
LELAND (60531) La Salle(64), De Kalb(35)
LEMONT (60439) Cook(51), Du Page(44), Will(4)
LENA (61048) Stephenson(96), Jo Daviess(3)
LENZBURG (62255) St. Clair(92), Washington(7)
LEONORE La Salle
LERNA (62440) Coles(72), Cumberland(27)
LEWISTOWN Fulton
LEXINGTON McLean
LIBERTY Adams
LIBERTYVILLE Lake
LIMA Adams
LINCOLN Logan
LINCOLN'S NEW SALEM Menard
LINCOLNSHIRE Lake
LINCOLNWOOD Cook
LINDENWOOD Ogle
LISLE Du Page
LITCHFIELD (62056) Montgomery(93), Macoupin(6)
LITERBERRY Morgan
LITTLE YORK (61453) Warren(87), Henderson(12)
LITTLETON (61452) Schuyler(83), McDonough(16)
LIVERPOOL Fulton
LIVINGSTON Madison
LOAMI Sangamon
LOCKPORT Will
LODA (60948) Iroquois(95), Ford(4)
LOGAN Franklin
LOMAX Henderson
LOMBARD Du Page
LONDON MILLS (61544) Fulton(86), Knox(13)
LONG GROVE Lake
LONG POINT Livingston
LONGVIEW (61852) Champaign(82), Douglas(17)
LOOGOOTEE Fayette
LORAINE (62349) Adams(94), Hancock(5)
LOSTANT (61334) La Salle(89), Putnam(9)
LOUISVILLE Clay
LOVEJOY St. Clair
LOVES PARK (61111) Winnebago(97), Boone(2)
LOVES PARK Winnebago
LOVINGTON (61937) Moultrie(94), Macon(3), Piatt(1)
LOWDER Sangamon
LOWPOINT Woodford
LUDLOW (60949) Champaign(90), Ford(9)
LYNDON Whiteside
LYNN CENTER (61262) Henry(92), Mercer(7)
LYONS Cook
MACEDONIA (62860) Franklin(88), Hamilton(11)
MACHESNEY PARK Winnebago
MACKINAW Tazewell
MACOMB McDonough
MACON Macon
MAEYSTOWN Monroe
MAGNOLIA (61336) Putnam(96), Marshall(3)
MAHOMET Champaign
MAKANDA (62958) Jackson(69), Williamson(15), Union(14)
MALDEN Bureau
MALTA De Kalb
MANCHESTER Scott
MANHATTAN Will
MANITO (61546) Mason(83), Tazewell(16)
MANLIUS Bureau
MANSFIELD (61854) Piatt(95), McLean(4)
MANTENO (60950) Kankakee(98), Will(1)
MAPLE PARK (60151) Kane(81), De Kalb(18)
MAPLETON Peoria
MAQUON Knox
MARENGO McHenry
MARIETTA (61459) Fulton(60), McDonough(39)
MARINE Madison
MARION Williamson
MARISSA (62257) St. Clair(70), Washington(27), Randolph(1)
MARK Putnam
MARKHAM Cook
MAROA Macon
MARSEILLES La Salle
MARSHALL (62441) Clark(98), Edgar(1)
MARTINSVILLE (62442) Clark(98), Crawford(1)
MARTINTON Iroquois
MARYVILLE Madison

MASCOUTAH St. Clair
MASON (62443) Effingham(90), Clay(9)
MASON CITY Mason
MATHERVILLE Mercer
MATTESON Cook
MATTOON Coles
MAUNIE White
MAYWOOD Cook
MAZON Grundy
MC CLURE (62957) Alexander(65), Union(34)
MC CONNELL Stephenson
MC HENRY McHenry
MC LEAN (61754) McLean(96), Logan(3)
MC LEANSBORO Hamilton
MC NABB Putnam
MCHENRY (60051) McHenry(89), Lake(10)
MCHENRY Cook
MCHENRY McHenry
MECHANICSBURG (62545) Sangamon(63), Christian(36)
MEDIA (61460) Henderson(95), Warren(4)
MEDINAH Du Page
MEDORA (62063) Jersey(58), Macoupin(41)
MELROSE PARK Cook
MELVIN (60952) Ford(95), Livingston(4)
MENARD Randolph
MENDON (62351) Adams(85), Hancock(14)
MENDOTA (61342) La Salle(97), Bureau(1), Lee(1)
MEREDOSIA (62665) Morgan(95), Scott(2), Cass(2)
MERNA McLean
METAMORA Woodford
METCALF Edgar
METROPOLIS Massac
MICHAEL Calhoun
MIDDLETOWN (62666) Logan(85), Menard(14)
MIDLOTHIAN Cook
MILAN Rock Island
MILFORD Iroquois
MILL SHOALS White
MILLBROOK Kendall
MILLCREEK Union
MILLEDGEVILLE (61051) Carroll(94), Ogle(3), Whiteside(2)
MILLER CITY Alexander
MILLINGTON Kendall
MILLSTADT St. Clair
MILMINE Piatt
MILTON Pike
MINERAL Bureau
MINIER Tazewell
MINONK (61760) Woodford(93), Marshall(6)
MINOOKA (60447) Grundy(48), Kendall(26), Will(24)
MOBIL OIL CREDIT CORP Du Page
MODE Shelby
MODESTO (62667) Macoupin(98), Morgan(1)
MODOC Randolph
MOKENA Will
MOLINE Rock Island
MOMENCE Kankakee
MONEE Will
MONMOUTH Warren
MONROE CENTER (61052) Ogle(94), Winnebago(2), De Kalb(2)
MONTGOMERY (60538) Kendall(61), Kane(38)
MONTGOMERY WARD Du Page
MONTICELLO Piatt
MONTROSE (62445) Jasper(55), Cumberland(33), Effingham(11)
MOOSEHEART Kane
MORO Madison
MORRIS Grundy
MORRISON Whiteside
MORRISONVILLE (62546) Christian(90), Montgomery(9)
MORTON Tazewell
MORTON GROVE Cook
MOSSVILLE Peoria
MOUND CITY Pulaski
MOUNDS Pulaski
MOUNT AUBURN (62547) Christian(97), Macon(2)
MOUNT CARMEL Wabash
MOUNT CARROLL (61053) Carroll(92), Jo Daviess(7)
MOUNT ERIE Wayne
MOUNT MORRIS Ogle
MOUNT OLIVE (62069) Macoupin(97), Montgomery(2)
MOUNT PROSPECT Cook
MOUNT PULASKI Logan
MOUNT STERLING Brown
MOUNT VERNON Jefferson
MOWEAQUA (62550) Shelby(63), Christian(36)
MOZIER Calhoun
MT ZION Macon
MUDDY Saline
MULBERRY GROVE (62262) Bond(87), Fayette(11), Montgomery(1)
MULKEYTOWN Franklin
MUNCIE Vermilion
MUNDELEIN Lake
MURDOCK Douglas
MURPHYSBORO Jackson
MURRAYVILLE Morgan
NACHUSA Lee
NAPERVILLE (60565) Du Page(65), Will(34)
NAPERVILLE (60564) Will(81), Du Page(18)
NAPERVILLE Du Page
NASHVILLE Washington
NASON Jefferson
NATIONAL STOCK YARDS St. Clair
NAUVOO Hancock
NEBO (62355) Pike(62), Calhoun(37)
NELSON Lee
NEOGA (62447) Cumberland(87), Shelby(11), Coles(1)
NEPONSET (61345) Bureau(97), Stark(2)
NEW ATHENS (62264) St. Clair(97), Monroe(2)
NEW BADEN (62265) Clinton(91), St. Clair(8)
NEW BEDFORD Bureau
NEW BERLIN Sangamon
NEW BOSTON Mercer
NEW BURNSIDE (62967) Johnson(88), Williamson(11)
NEW CANTON Pike
NEW DOUGLAS (62074) Madison(90), Bond(4), Macoupin(3), Montgomery(1)
NEW HAVEN (62867) Gallatin(59), White(40)
NEW HOLLAND (62671) Logan(95), Mason(4)
NEW LENOX Will
NEW MEMPHIS Clinton
NEW SALEM Pike
NEW WINDSOR (61465) Mercer(88), Henry(11)
NEWARK (60541) Kendall(91), Grundy(6), La Salle(2)
NEWMAN (61942) Douglas(91), Edgar(8)
NEWTON (62448) Jasper(97), Richland(2)
NIANTIC Macon
NILES Cook
NILWOOD Macoupin
NIOTA Hancock
NOBLE (62868) Richland(94), Clay(4), Wayne(1)
NOKOMIS (62075) Montgomery(95), Christian(4)
NORA Jo Daviess
NORMAL McLean
NORRIS Fulton
NORRIS CITY (62869) White(94), Gallatin(3), Hamilton(1)
NORTH AURORA Kane
NORTH CHICAGO Lake
NORTH HENDERSON (61466) Mercer(96), Warren(2)
NORTHBROOK Cook
O FALLON St. Clair
OAK FOREST Cook
OAK LAWN Cook
OAK PARK Cook
OAKDALE (62268) Washington(94), Perry(5)
OAKFORD (62673) Cass(51), Menard(48)
OAKLAND (61943) Coles(78), Douglas(14), Edgar(6)
OAKLEY Macon
OAKWOOD Vermilion
OBLONG (62449) Crawford(90), Jasper(8)
OCONEE (62553) Shelby(50), Christian(29), Montgomery(20)
ODELL Livingston
ODIN Marion
OGDEN (61859) Champaign(88), Vermilion(11)
OGLESBY La Salle
OHIO (61349) Bureau(77), Lee(21), Cass(1)
OHLMAN Montgomery
OKAWVILLE Washington
OLIVE BRANCH Alexander
OLMSTED Pulaski
OLNEY Richland
OLYMPIA FIELDS Cook
OMAHA Gallatin
ONARGA Iroquois
ONEIDA Knox
OPDYKE Jefferson
OPHEIM Henry
OPHIEM Henry
OQUAWKA Henderson
ORANGEVILLE Stephenson
ORAVILLE Jackson
OREANA Macon
OREGON Ogle
ORIENT Franklin
ORION (61273) Henry(83), Rock Island(16)
ORLAND PARK Cook
OSCO Henry
OSWEGO Kendall
OTTAWA La Salle
OWANECO (62555) Christian(91), Macon(8)
OZARK Johnson
PALATINE (60074) Cook(98), Lake(1)
PALATINE Cook
PALESTINE Crawford
PALMER Christian
PALMYRA Macoupin
PALOMA Adams
PALOS HEIGHTS Cook
PALOS HILLS Cook
PALOS PARK Cook
PANA (62557) Christian(92), Shelby(5), Montgomery(1)
PANAMA Montgomery
PAPINEAU Iroquois
PARIS Edgar
PARK FOREST (60466) Cook(54), Will(45)
PARK RIDGE Cook
PARKERSBURG Richland
PATOKA (62875) Marion(94), Fayette(5)
PATTERSON Greene
PAW PAW Lee
PAWNEE (62558) Sangamon(88), Christian(8), Montgomery(2)
PAXTON (60957) Ford(96), Champaign(2)
PAYSON Adams
PEARL (62361) Pike(97), Calhoun(2)
PEARL CITY (61062) Stephenson(96), Jo Daviess(2)
PECATONICA (61063) Winnebago(91), Stephenson(8)
PEKIN Tazewell
PENFIELD (61862) Champaign(79), Vermilion(20)
PEORIA Peoria
PEORIA HEIGHTS Peoria
PEOTONE (60468) Will(97), Kankakee(2)
PERCY (62272) Randolph(80), Perry(19)
PERKS Pulaski
PERRY Pike
PERU (61354) La Salle(98), Bureau(1)
PESOTUM Champaign
PETERSBURG Menard
PHILO Champaign
PIASA (62079) Macoupin(66), Jersey(33)
PIERRON Bond
PINCKNEYVILLE Perry
PIPER CITY (60959) Ford(93), Livingston(5)
PITTSBURG Williamson
PITTSFIELD Pike
PLAINFIELD (60544) Will(98), Kendall(1)
PLAINVIEW Macoupin
PLAINVILLE Adams
PLANO Kendall
PLATO CENTER Kane
PLEASANT HILL (62366) Pike(98), Calhoun(1)
PLEASANT PLAINS Sangamon
PLYMOUTH (62367) Hancock(50), McDonough(41), Schuyler(7)
POCAHONTAS (62275) Bond(68), Madison(22), Clinton(8)
POLO Ogle
POMONA Jackson
PONTIAC Livingston
POPLAR GROVE Boone
PORT BYRON Rock Island
POSEN Cook
POTOMAC Vermilion
PRAIRIE CITY McDonough
PRAIRIE DU ROCHER (62277) Randolph(57), Monroe(42)
PREEMPTION Mercer
PRINCETON Bureau
PRINCEVILLE (61559) Peoria(97), Stark(2)
PROPHETSTOWN (61277) Whiteside(80), Henry(19)
PROSPECT HEIGHTS Cook
PULASKI Pulaski
PUTNAM (61560) Putnam(93), Bureau(4), Marshall(2)
QUINCY Adams
RADOM Washington
RALEIGH Saline
RAMSEY (62080) Fayette(92), Montgomery(6), Shelby(1)
RANKIN (60960) Vermilion(72), Ford(21), Iroquois(3), Champaign(2)
RANSOM (60470) La Salle(90), Grundy(6), Livingston(2)
RANTOUL Champaign
RAPIDS CITY Rock Island
RARITAN Henderson
RAYMOND (62560) Montgomery(90), Macoupin(9)
RED BUD (62278) Randolph(68), Monroe(31)
REDDICK (60961) Kankakee(83), Livingston(13), Grundy(2)
REDMON Edgar
RENAULT Monroe
REYNOLDS (61279) Rock Island(73), Mercer(26)
RICHMOND McHenry
RICHTON PARK Cook
RICHVIEW (62877) Washington(97), Jefferson(2)

RIDGE FARM (61870) Vermilion(95), Edgar(4)
RIDGWAY Gallatin
RIDOTT Stephenson
RINARD Wayne
RINGWOOD McHenry
RIO (61472) Knox(98), Mercer(1)
RIVER FOREST Cook
RIVER GROVE Cook
RIVERDALE Cook
RIVERSIDE Cook
RIVERTON Sangamon
ROANOKE Woodford
ROBBINS Cook
ROBERTS (60962) Ford(97), Livingston(2)
ROBINSON Crawford
ROCHELLE (61068) Ogle(97), Lee(1)
ROCHESTER (62563) Sangamon(96), Christian(3)
ROCK CITY Stephenson
ROCK FALLS Whiteside
ROCK ISLAND Rock Island
ROCKBRIDGE (62081) Greene(98), Jersey(2)
ROCKFORD (61102) Winnebago(98), Ogle(1)
ROCKFORD (61114) Winnebago(96), Boone(3)
ROCKFORD Winnebago
ROCKPORT Pike
ROCKTON Winnebago
ROCKWOOD (62280) Jackson(58), Randolph(41)
ROLLING MEADOWS Cook
ROME Peoria
ROMEOVILLE Will
ROODHOUSE (62082) Greene(88), Scott(9), Morgan(1)
ROSAMOND (62083) Christian(61), Montgomery(38)
ROSCOE (61073) Winnebago(98), Boone(1)
ROSELLE (60172) Du Page(81), Cook(18)
ROSEVILLE (61473) McDonough(69), Warren(30)
ROSICLARE Hardin
ROSSVILLE Vermilion
ROUND LAKE Lake
ROXANA Madison
ROYAL Champaign
ROYALTON Franklin
RUSHVILLE Schuyler
RUSSELL Lake
RUTLAND (61358) La Salle(75), Marshall(24)
SADORUS (61872) Champaign(90), Douglas(9)
SAILOR SPRINGS Clay
SAINT ANNE (60964) Kankakee(93), Iroquois(6)
SAINT AUGUSTINE (61474) Knox(93), Warren(5), Fulton(1)
SAINT CHARLES Kane
SAINT DAVID Fulton
SAINT ELMO (62458) Fayette(91), Effingham(8)
SAINT FRANCISVILLE (62460) Lawrence(89), Wabash(10)
SAINT JACOB Madison
SAINT JOSEPH Champaign
SAINT LIBORY St. Clair
SAINT PETER Fayette
SAINTE MARIE Jasper
SALEM Marion
SAN JOSE (62682) Mason(82), Tazewell(9), Logan(8)
SANDOVAL (62882) Marion(92), Clinton(7)
SANDWICH (60548) De Kalb(77), La Salle(19), Kendall(3)
SAUNEMIN Livingston
SAVANNA Carroll
SAVOY Champaign
SAWYERVILLE Macoupin
SAYBROOK McLean
SCALES MOUND Jo Daviess
SCHAUMBURG Cook
SCHELLER (62883) Jefferson(62), Franklin(29), Perry(7)
SCHILLER PARK Cook
SCIOTA (61475) McDonough(87), Warren(11)
SCIOTO MILLS Stephenson
SCIOTO MILLSX Stephenson
SCOTT AIR FORCE BASE St. Clair
SCOTTVILLE Macoupin
SEATON (61476) Mercer(88), Henderson(10), Warren(1)
SEATONVILLE Bureau
SECOR Woodford
SENECA (61360) La Salle(83), Grundy(16)
SERENA La Salle
SESSER Franklin
SEWARD Winnebago
SEYMOUR Champaign
SHABBONA De Kalb
SHANNON (61078) Carroll(84), Stephenson(8), Ogle(7)
SHATTUC Clinton
SHAWNEETOWN Gallatin
SHEFFIELD Bureau
SHELBYVILLE Shelby
SHELDON Iroquois
SHERIDAN La Salle
SHERMAN Sangamon
SHERRARD Mercer
SHIPMAN Macoupin
SHIRLAND Winnebago
SHIRLEY McLean
SHOBONIER (62885) Fayette(95), Marion(4)
SHUMWAY (62461) Effingham(93), Shelby(6)
SIBLEY Ford
SIDELL (61876) Vermilion(84), Edgar(15)
SIDNEY Champaign
SIGEL (62462) Cumberland(59), Shelby(39), Effingham(1)
SILVIS Rock Island
SIMPSON (62985) Johnson(86), Pope(13)
SIMS Wayne
SKOKIE Cook
SMITHBORO Bond
SMITHFIELD Fulton
SMITHSHIRE (61478) Warren(94), Henderson(5)
SMITHTON St. Clair
SOLON MILLS McHenry
SOMONAUK (60552) De Kalb(58), La Salle(41)
SORENTO (62086) Bond(81), Montgomery(16), Madison(1)
SOUTH BELOIT (61080) Winnebago(96), Boone(3)
SOUTH ELGIN Kane
SOUTH HOLLAND Cook
SOUTH PEKIN Tazewell
SOUTH ROXANA Madison
SOUTH WILMINGTON Grundy
SPARLAND (61565) Marshall(95), Peoria(4)
SPARTA Randolph
SPEER Stark
SPRING GROVE (60081) McHenry(79), Lake(20)
SPRING VALLEY Bureau
SPRINGERTON (62887) White(78), Hamilton(21)
SPRINGFIELD Sangamon
STANDARD Putnam
STANDARD CITY Macoupin
STANFORD McLean
STAUNTON (62088) Macoupin(85), Madison(14)
STEELEVILLE Randolph
STEGER (60475) Will(56), Cook(43)
STERLING (61081) Whiteside(98), Lee(1)
STEWARD (60553) Lee(98), De Kalb(1)
STEWARDSON Shelby
STILLMAN VALLEY (61084) Ogle(95), Winnebago(4)
STOCKLAND Iroquois
STOCKTON Jo Daviess
STONE PARK Cook
STONEFORT (62987) Saline(57), Williamson(34), Pope(7)
STONINGTON Christian
STOY Crawford
STRASBURG Shelby
STRAWN (61775) Livingston(90), Ford(9)
STREAMWOOD Cook
STREATOR (61364) La Salle(91), Livingston(8)
STRONGHURST Henderson
SUBLETTE Lee
SUGAR GROVE Kane
SULLIVAN Moultrie
SUMMER HILL Pike
SUMMERFIELD St. Clair
SUMMIT ARGO Cook
SUMNER (62466) Lawrence(88), Crawford(6), Richland(5)
SUTTER (62373) Hancock(94), Adams(5)
SYCAMORE (60178) De Kalb(97), Kane(2)
TABLE GROVE (61482) Fulton(52), Knox(25), McDonough(21)
TALLULA Menard
TAMAROA Perry
TAMMS Alexander
TAMPICO (61283) Whiteside(49), Bureau(48), Henry(2)
TAYLOR RIDGE Rock Island
TAYLOR SPRINGS Montgomery
TAYLORVILLE Christian
TECHNY Cook
TENNESSEE (62374) McDonough(58), Hancock(41)
TEUTOPOLIS (62467) Effingham(86), Jasper(8), Cumberland(5)
TEXICO (62889) Jefferson(69), Marion(30)
THAWVILLE (60968) Iroquois(56), Ford(41), Livingston(1)
THAYER Sangamon
THEBES Alexander
THOMASBORO Champaign
THOMPSONVILLE (62890) Franklin(67), Williamson(24), Saline(6), Hamilton(1)
THOMSON Carroll
THORNTON Cook
TILDEN Randolph
TILTON Vermilion
TIMEWELL (62375) Brown(97), Adams(2)
TINLEY PARK (60477) Cook(95), Will(4)
TISKILWA Bureau
TOLEDO Cumberland
TOLONO Champaign
TOLUCA Marshall
TONICA (61370) La Salle(98), Putnam(1)
TOPEKA Mason
TOULON (61483) Stark(61), Henry(38)
TOVEY Christian
TOWANDA McLean
TOWER HILL Shelby
TREMONT Tazewell
TRENTON (62293) Clinton(73), St. Clair(16), Madison(9)
TRILLA (62469) Cumberland(76), Coles(23)
TRIUMPH La Salle
TRIVOLI (61569) Peoria(97), Fulton(2)
TROY Madison
TROY GROVE La Salle
TUNNEL HILL Johnson
TUSCOLA Douglas
ULLIN (62992) Pulaski(97), Alexander(2)
UNION McHenry
UNION HILL Kankakee
UNITY Alexander
URBANA Champaign
URSA Adams
UTICA La Salle
VALIER Franklin
VALMEYER Monroe
VAN ORIN Bureau
VANDALIA Fayette
VARNA Marshall
VENEDY Washington
VENICE (62090) Madison(97), St. Clair(2)
VERGENNES Jackson
VERMILION Edgar
VERMONT (61484) McDonough(64), Fulton(34), Schuyler(1)
VERNON (62892) Marion(90), Fayette(9)
VERNON HILLS Lake
VERONA Grundy
VERSAILLES Brown
VICTORIA Knox
VIENNA Johnson
VILLA GROVE (61956) Douglas(95), Champaign(4)
VILLA PARK Du Page
VILLA RIDGE Pulaski
VIOLA Mercer
VIRDEN (62690) Macoupin(89), Montgomery(5), Sangamon(4)
VIRGIL Kane
VIRGINIA Cass
WADSWORTH Lake
WAGGONER (62572) Macoupin(58), Montgomery(41)
WALNUT (61376) Bureau(92), Lee(7)
WALNUT HILL (62893) Marion(57), Jefferson(42)
WALSH Randolph
WALSHVILLE Montgomery
WALTONVILLE Jefferson
WAPELLA De Witt
WARREN (61087) Jo Daviess(98), Stephenson(1)
WARRENSBURG Macon
WARRENVILLE Du Page
WARSAW (62379) Hancock(95), Adams(4)
WASCO Kane
WASHBURN (61570) Woodford(77), Marshall(22)
WASHINGTON Tazewell
WATAGA Knox
WATERLOO (62298) Monroe(92), St. Clair(7)
WATERMAN De Kalb
WATSEKA Iroquois
WATSON Effingham
WAUCONDA Lake
WAUKEGAN Lake
WAVERLY (62692) Morgan(76), Sangamon(23)
WAYNE (60184) Du Page(59), Kane(40)
WAYNE CITY (62895) Wayne(95), Hamilton(4)
WAYNESVILLE De Witt
WEDRON La Salle
WELDON (61882) De Witt(91), Macon(7)
WELLINGTON Iroquois
WENONA (61377) Marshall(88), La Salle(11)
WEST BROOKLYN Lee
WEST CHICAGO (60185) Du Page(98), Kane(1)
WEST CHICAGO Du Page
WEST FRANKFORT (62896) Franklin(94), Williamson(5)
WEST LIBERTY Jasper
WEST POINT Hancock
WEST SALEM (62476) Edwards(77), Wabash(19), Lawrence(1), Richland(1)
WEST UNION Clark
WEST YORK (62478) Clark(55), Crawford(44)
WESTCHESTER Cook

WESTERN SPRINGS Cook
WESTERVELT Shelby
WESTFIELD (62474) Clark(90), Coles(9)
WESTMONT Du Page
WESTVILLE Vermilion
WHEATON Du Page
WHEELER (62479) Jasper(97), Effingham(2)
WHEELING (60090) Cook(98), Lake(1)
WHITE HALL Greene
WHITE HEATH (61884) Piatt(77), Champaign(22)
WHITTINGTON Franklin
WILLIAMSFIELD (61489) Knox(89), Peoria(10)
WILLIAMSVILLE (62693) Sangamon(88), Logan(11)
WILLISVILLE Perry
WILLOW HILL Jasper
WILLOW SPRINGS Cook
WILLOWBROOK (60527) Du Page(91), Cook(8)
WILMETTE Cook
WILMINGTON (60481) Will(98), Grundy(1)
WILSONVILLE Macoupin
WINCHESTER (62694) Scott(86), Morgan(13)
WINDSOR (61957) Shelby(93), Moultrie(6)
WINFIELD Du Page
WINNEBAGO Winnebago
WINNETKA Cook
WINSLOW Stephenson
WINTHROP HARBOR Lake
WITT Montgomery
WOLF LAKE Union
WONDER LAKE McHenry
WOOD DALE Du Page
WOOD RIVER Madison
WOODHULL (61490) McDonough(47), Henry(47), Knox(4)
WOODLAND Iroquois
WOODLAWN Jefferson
WOODRIDGE Du Page
WOODSON Morgan
WOODSTOCK McHenry
WOOSUNG Ogle
WORDEN Madison
WORTH Cook
WRIGHTS Greene
WYANET Bureau
WYOMING (61491) Stark(96), Marshall(3)
XENIA (62899) Clay(96), Marion(3)
YALE (62481) Jasper(97), Cumberland(2)
YATES CITY Knox
YORKVILLE Kendall
ZEIGLER Franklin
ZION Lake

Illinois ZIP/City Cross Reference

60000-60000 PALATINE
60001-60001 ALDEN
60002-60002 ANTIOCH
60004-60006 ARLINGTON HEIGHTS
60007-60007 ELK GROVE VILLAGE
60008-60008 ROLLING MEADOWS
60009-60009 ELK GROVE VILLAGE
60010-60011 BARRINGTON
60012-60012 CRYSTAL LAKE
60013-60013 CARY
60014-60014 CRYSTAL LAKE
60015-60015 DEERFIELD
60016-60019 DES PLAINES
60020-60020 FOX LAKE
60021-60021 FOX RIVER GROVE
60022-60022 GLENCOE
60025-60025 GLENVIEW
60026-60026 GLENVIEW NAS
60029-60029 GOLF
60030-60030 GRAYSLAKE
60031-60031 GURNEE
60033-60033 HARVARD
60034-60034 HEBRON
60035-60035 HIGHLAND PARK
60037-60037 FORT SHERIDAN
60038-60038 PALATINE
60039-60039 CRYSTAL LAKE
60040-60040 HIGHWOOD
60041-60041 INGLESIDE
60042-60042 ISLAND LAKE
60043-60043 KENILWORTH
60044-60044 LAKE BLUFF
60045-60045 LAKE FOREST
60046-60046 LAKE VILLA
60047-60047 LAKE ZURICH
60048-60048 LIBERTYVILLE
60049-60049 LONG GROVE
60050-60050 MC HENRY
60050-60050 MCHENRY
60051-60051 MC HENRY
60051-60051 MCHENRY
60053-60053 MORTON GROVE
60055-60055 PALATINE
60056-60056 MOUNT PROSPECT
60060-60060 MUNDELEIN
60061-60061 VERNON HILLS
60062-60062 NORTHBROOK
60063-60063 DEERFIELD
60064-60064 NORTH CHICAGO
60065-60065 NORTHBROOK
60067-60067 PALATINE
60068-60068 PARK RIDGE
60069-60069 LINCOLNSHIRE
60070-60070 PROSPECT HEIGHTS
60071-60071 RICHMOND
60072-60072 RINGWOOD
60073-60073 ROUND LAKE
60074-60074 PALATINE
60075-60075 RUSSELL
60076-60077 SKOKIE
60078-60078 PALATINE
60079-60079 WAUKEGAN
60080-60080 SOLON MILLS
60081-60081 SPRING GROVE
60082-60082 TECHNY
60083-60083 WADSWORTH
60084-60084 WAUCONDA
60085-60085 WAUKEGAN
60086-60086 NORTH CHICAGO
60087-60087 WAUKEGAN
60088-60088 GREAT LAKES
60089-60089 BUFFALO GROVE
60090-60090 WHEELING
60091-60091 WILMETTE
60092-60092 LIBERTYVILLE
60093-60093 WINNETKA
60094-60095 PALATINE
60096-60096 WINTHROP HARBOR
60097-60097 WONDER LAKE
60098-60098 WOODSTOCK
60099-60099 ZION
60100-60100 CAROL STREAM
60101-60101 ADDISON
60102-60102 ALGONQUIN
60103-60103 BARTLETT
60104-60104 BELLWOOD
60105-60106 BENSENVILLE
60107-60107 STREAMWOOD
60108-60108 BLOOMINGDALE
60109-60109 BURLINGTON
60110-60110 CARPENTERSVILLE
60111-60111 CLARE
60112-60112 CORTLAND
60113-60113 CRESTON
60114-60114 ADDISON
60115-60115 DE KALB
60115-60115 DEKALB
60116-60116 CAROL STREAM
60117-60117 BLOOMINGDALE
60118-60118 DUNDEE
60119-60119 ELBURN
60120-60122 ELGIN
60122-60122 CAROL STREAM
60123-60123 ELGIN
60125-60125 CAROL STREAM
60126-60126 ELMHURST
60128-60128 CAROL STREAM
60129-60129 ESMOND
60130-60130 FOREST PARK
60131-60131 FRANKLIN PARK
60132-60132 CAROL STREAM
60133-60133 HANOVER PARK
60134-60134 GENEVA
60135-60135 GENOA
60136-60136 GILBERTS
60137-60138 GLEN ELLYN
60139-60139 GLENDALE HEIGHTS
60140-60140 HAMPSHIRE
60141-60141 HINES
60142-60142 HUNTLEY
60143-60143 ITASCA
60144-60144 KANEVILLE
60145-60145 KINGSTON
60146-60146 KIRKLAND
60147-60147 LAFOX
60148-60148 LOMBARD
60149-60149 MONTGOMERY WARD
60150-60150 MALTA
60151-60151 MAPLE PARK
60152-60152 MARENGO
60153-60153 MAYWOOD
60154-60154 WESTCHESTER
60155-60155 CAROL STREAM
60155-60155 BROADVIEW
60156-60156 LAKE IN THE HILLS
60157-60157 MEDINAH
60158-60158 CAROL STREAM
60159-60159 SCHAUMBURG
60160-60161 MELROSE PARK
60162-60162 HILLSIDE
60163-60163 BERKELEY
60164-60164 MELROSE PARK
60165-60165 STONE PARK
60168-60168 SCHAUMBURG
60170-60170 PLATO CENTER
60171-60171 RIVER GROVE
60172-60172 ROSELLE
60173-60173 SCHAUMBURG
60174-60175 SAINT CHARLES
60176-60176 SCHILLER PARK
60177-60177 SOUTH ELGIN
60178-60178 SYCAMORE
60179-60179 HOFFMAN ESTATES
60180-60180 UNION
60181-60181 VILLA PARK
60182-60182 VIRGIL
60183-60183 WASCO
60184-60184 WAYNE
60185-60186 WEST CHICAGO
60187-60187 WHEATON
60188-60188 CAROL STREAM
60189-60189 WHEATON
60190-60190 WINFIELD
60191-60191 WOOD DALE
60192-60196 SCHAUMBURG
60197-60199 CAROL STREAM
60201-60209 EVANSTON
60251-60251 PALATINE
60296-60297 MCHENRY
60301-60304 OAK PARK
60305-60305 RIVER FOREST
60351-60351 CAROL STREAM
60352-60352 MOBIL OIL CREDIT CORP
60353-60353 CAROL STREAM
60398-60398 FRANKLIN PARK
60399-60399 BENSENVILLE
60401-60401 BEECHER
60402-60402 BERWYN
60406-60406 BLUE ISLAND
60407-60407 BRACEVILLE
60408-60408 BRAIDWOOD
60409-60409 CALUMET CITY
60410-60410 CHANNAHON
60411-60412 CHICAGO HEIGHTS
60415-60415 CHICAGO RIDGE
60416-60416 COAL CITY
60417-60417 CRETE
60419-60419 DOLTON
60420-60420 DWIGHT
60421-60421 ELWOOD
60422-60422 FLOSSMOOR
60423-60423 FRANKFORT
60424-60424 GARDNER
60425-60425 GLENWOOD
60426-60426 HARVEY
60428-60428 MARKHAM
60429-60429 HAZEL CREST
60430-60430 HOMEWOOD
60431-60436 JOLIET
60437-60437 KINSMAN
60438-60438 LANSING
60439-60439 LEMONT
60440-60440 BOLINGBROOK
60441-60441 LOCKPORT
60442-60442 MANHATTAN
60443-60443 MATTESON
60444-60444 MAZON
60445-60445 MIDLOTHIAN
60446-60446 ROMEOVILLE
60447-60447 MINOOKA
60448-60448 MOKENA
60449-60449 MONEE
60450-60450 MORRIS
60451-60451 NEW LENOX
60452-60452 OAK FOREST
60453-60454 OAK LAWN
60455-60455 BRIDGEVIEW
60456-60456 HOMETOWN
60457-60457 HICKORY HILLS
60458-60458 JUSTICE
60459-60459 BURBANK
60460-60460 ODELL
60461-60461 OLYMPIA FIELDS
60462-60462 ORLAND PARK
60463-60463 PALOS HEIGHTS
60464-60464 PALOS PARK
60465-60465 PALOS HILLS
60466-60466 PARK FOREST
60467-60467 ORLAND PARK
60468-60468 PEOTONE
60469-60469 POSEN
60470-60470 RANSOM
60471-60471 RICHTON PARK
60472-60472 ROBBINS
60473-60473 SOUTH HOLLAND
60474-60474 SOUTH WILMINGTON
60475-60475 STEGER
60476-60476 THORNTON
60477-60477 TINLEY PARK
60478-60478 COUNTRY CLUB HILLS
60479-60479 VERONA
60480-60480 WILLOW SPRINGS
60481-60481 WILMINGTON
60482-60482 WORTH
60490-60490 BOLINGBROOK
60491-60491 LOCKPORT
60499-60499 BEDFORD PARK
60501-60501 SUMMIT ARGO

ZIP Range	City
60502-60507	AURORA
60510-60510	BATAVIA
60511-60511	BIG ROCK
60512-60512	BRISTOL
60513-60513	BROOKFIELD
60514-60514	CLARENDON HILLS
60515-60516	DOWNERS GROVE
60517-60517	WOODRIDGE
60518-60518	EARLVILLE
60519-60519	EOLA
60520-60520	HINCKLEY
60521-60523	HINSDALE
60525-60525	LA GRANGE
60526-60526	LA GRANGE PARK
60527-60527	HINSDALE
60527-60527	WILLOWBROOK
60530-60530	LEE
60531-60531	LELAND
60532-60532	LISLE
60534-60534	LYONS
60536-60536	MILLBROOK
60537-60537	MILLINGTON
60538-60538	MONTGOMERY
60539-60539	MOOSEHEART
60540-60540	NAPERVILLE
60541-60541	NEWARK
60542-60542	NORTH AURORA
60543-60543	OSWEGO
60544-60544	PLAINFIELD
60545-60545	PLANO
60546-60546	RIVERSIDE
60548-60548	SANDWICH
60549-60549	SERENA
60550-60550	SHABBONA
60551-60551	SHERIDAN
60552-60552	SOMONAUK
60553-60553	STEWARD
60554-60554	SUGAR GROVE
60555-60555	WARRENVILLE
60556-60556	WATERMAN
60557-60557	WEDRON
60558-60558	WESTERN SPRINGS
60559-60559	WESTMONT
60560-60560	YORKVILLE
60561-60561	DARIEN
60563-60567	NAPERVILLE
60568-60568	AURORA
60570-60570	HINSDALE
60572-60572	AURORA
50585-60586	AURORA
60597-60597	FOX VALLEY
60598-60598	AURORA
60599-60599	FOX VALLEY
60600-60626	CHICAGO
60627-60627	RIVERDALE
60628-60634	CHICAGO
60635-60635	ELMWOOD PARK
60636-60649	CHICAGO
60650-60650	CICERO
60651-60665	CHICAGO
60666-60666	AMF OHARE
60667-60701	CHICAGO
60706-60706	HARWOOD HEIGHTS
60707-60707	ELMWOOD PARK
60712-60712	LINCOLNWOOD
60714-60714	NILES
60799-60799	CHICAGO
60803-60803	ALSIP
60804-60804	CICERO
60805-60805	EVERGREEN PARK
60827-60827	RIVERDALE
60901-60902	KANKAKEE
60910-60910	AROMA PARK
60911-60911	ASHKUM
60912-60912	BEAVERVILLE
60913-60913	BONFIELD
60914-60914	BOURBONNAIS
60915-60915	BRADLEY
60917-60917	BUCKINGHAM
60918-60918	BUCKLEY
60919-60919	CABERY
60920-60920	CAMPUS
60921-60921	CHATSWORTH
60922-60922	CHEBANSE
60924-60924	CISSNA PARK
60926-60926	CLAYTONVILLE
60927-60927	CLIFTON
60928-60928	CRESCENT CITY
60929-60929	CULLOM
60930-60930	DANFORTH
60931-60931	DONOVAN
60932-60932	EAST LYNN
60933-60933	ELLIOTT
60934-60934	EMINGTON
60935-60935	ESSEX
60936-60936	GIBSON CITY
60938-60938	GILMAN
60939-60939	GOODWINE
60940-60940	GRANT PARK
60941-60941	HERSCHER
60942-60942	HOOPESTON
60944-60944	HOPKINS PARK
60945-60945	IROQUOIS
60946-60946	KEMPTON
60948-60948	LODA
60949-60949	LUDLOW
60950-60950	MANTENO
60951-60951	MARTINTON
60952-60952	MELVIN
60953-60953	MILFORD
60954-60954	MOMENCE
60955-60955	ONARGA
60956-60956	PAPINEAU
60957-60957	PAXTON
60959-60959	PIPER CITY
60960-60960	RANKIN
60961-60961	REDDICK
60962-60962	ROBERTS
60963-60963	ROSSVILLE
60964-60964	SAINT ANNE
60966-60966	SHELDON
60967-60967	STOCKLAND
60968-60968	THAWVILLE
60969-60969	UNION HILL
60970-60970	WATSEKA
60973-60973	WELLINGTON
60974-60974	WOODLAND
61001-61001	APPLE RIVER
61006-61006	ASHTON
61007-61007	BAILEYVILLE
61008-61008	BELVIDERE
61010-61010	BYRON
61011-61011	CALEDONIA
61012-61012	CAPRON
61013-61013	CEDARVILLE
61014-61014	CHADWICK
61015-61015	CHANA
61016-61016	CHERRY VALLEY
61017-61017	COLETA
61018-61018	DAKOTA
61019-61019	DAVIS
61020-61020	DAVIS JUNCTION
61021-61021	DIXON
61024-61024	DURAND
61025-61025	EAST DUBUQUE
61027-61027	ELEROY
61028-61028	ELIZABETH
61030-61030	FORRESTON
61031-61031	FRANKLIN GROVE
61032-61032	FREEPORT
61036-61036	GALENA
61037-61037	GALT
61038-61038	GARDEN PRAIRIE
61039-61039	GERMAN VALLEY
61041-61041	HANOVER
61042-61042	HARMON
61043-61043	HOLCOMB
61044-61044	KENT
61045-61045	KINGS
61046-61046	LANARK
61047-61047	LEAF RIVER
61048-61048	LENA
61049-61049	LINDENWOOD
61050-61050	MC CONNELL
61051-61051	MILLEDGEVILLE
61052-61052	MONROE CENTER
61053-61053	MOUNT CARROLL
61054-61054	MOUNT MORRIS
61057-61057	NACHUSA
61058-61058	NELSON
61059-61059	NORA
61060-61060	ORANGEVILLE
61061-61061	OREGON
61062-61062	PEARL CITY
61063-61063	PECATONICA
61064-61064	POLO
61065-61065	POPLAR GROVE
61067-61067	RIDOTT
61068-61068	ROCHELLE
61070-61070	ROCK CITY
61071-61071	ROCK FALLS
61072-61072	ROCKTON
61073-61073	ROSCOE
61074-61074	SAVANNA
61075-61075	SCALES MOUND
61076-61076	SCIOTO MILLS
61076-61076	SCIOTO MILLSX
61077-61077	SEWARD
61078-61078	SHANNON
61079-61079	SHIRLAND
61080-61080	SOUTH BELOIT
61081-61081	STERLING
61084-61084	STILLMAN VALLEY
61085-61085	STOCKTON
61087-61087	WARREN
61088-61088	WINNEBAGO
61089-61089	WINSLOW
61091-61091	WOOSUNG
61100-61110	ROCKFORD
61111-61111	LOVES PARK
61112-61114	ROCKFORD
61115-61115	MACHESNEY PARK
61125-61126	ROCKFORD
61130-61132	LOVES PARK
61201-61206	ROCK ISLAND
61230-61230	ALBANY
61231-61231	ALEDO
61232-61232	ANDALUSIA
61233-61233	ANDOVER
61234-61234	ANNAWAN
61235-61235	ATKINSON
61236-61236	BARSTOW
61237-61237	BUFFALO PRAIRIE
61238-61238	CAMBRIDGE
61239-61239	CARBON CLIFF
61240-61240	COAL VALLEY
61241-61241	COLONA
61242-61242	CORDOVA
61243-61243	DEER GROVE
61244-61244	EAST MOLINE
61249-61249	DEERE CO GROUP CLAIMS
61250-61250	ERIE
61251-61251	FENTON
61252-61252	FULTON
61254-61254	GENESEO
61256-61256	HAMPTON
61257-61257	HILLSDALE
61258-61258	HOOPPOLE
61259-61259	ILLINOIS CITY
61260-61260	JOY
61261-61261	LYNDON
61262-61262	LYNN CENTER
61263-61263	MATHERVILLE
61264-61264	MILAN
61265-61266	MOLINE
61270-61270	MORRISON
61272-61272	NEW BOSTON
61273-61273	ORION
61274-61274	OSCO
61275-61275	PORT BYRON
61276-61276	PREEMPTION
61277-61277	PROPHETSTOWN
61278-61278	RAPIDS CITY
61279-61279	REYNOLDS
61281-61281	SHERRARD
61282-61282	SILVIS
61283-61283	TAMPICO
61284-61284	TAYLOR RIDGE
61285-61285	THOMSON
61299-61299	ROCK ISLAND
61301-61301	LA SALLE
61310-61310	AMBOY
61311-61311	ANCONA
61312-61312	ARLINGTON
61313-61313	BLACKSTONE
61314-61314	BUDA
61315-61315	BUREAU
61316-61316	CEDAR POINT
61317-61317	CHERRY
61318-61318	COMPTON
61319-61319	CORNELL
61320-61320	DALZELL
61321-61321	DANA
61322-61322	DEPUE
61323-61323	DOVER
61324-61324	ELDENA
61325-61325	GRAND RIDGE
61326-61326	GRANVILLE
61327-61327	HENNEPIN
61328-61328	KASBEER
61329-61329	LADD
61330-61330	LA MOILLE
61331-61331	LEE CENTER
61332-61332	LEONORE
61333-61333	LONG POINT
61334-61334	LOSTANT
61335-61335	MC NABB
61336-61336	MAGNOLIA
61337-61337	MALDEN
61338-61338	MANLIUS
61340-61340	MARK
61341-61341	MARSEILLES
61342-61342	MENDOTA
61344-61344	MINERAL
61345-61345	NEPONSET
61346-61346	NEW BEDFORD
61348-61348	OGLESBY
61349-61349	OHIO
61350-61350	OTTAWA
61353-61353	PAW PAW
61354-61354	PERU
61356-61356	PRINCETON
61358-61358	RUTLAND
61359-61359	SEATONVILLE
61360-61360	SENECA
61361-61361	SHEFFIELD
61362-61362	SPRING VALLEY
61363-61363	STANDARD
61364-61364	STREATOR
61367-61367	SUBLETTE
61368-61368	TISKILWA
61369-61369	TOLUCA
61370-61370	TONICA
61371-61371	TRIUMPH
61372-61372	TROY GROVE
61373-61373	UTICA
61374-61374	VAN ORIN
61375-61375	VARNA
61376-61376	WALNUT
61377-61377	WENONA
61378-61378	WEST BROOKLYN
61379-61379	WYANET
61401-61402	GALESBURG
61410-61410	ABINGDON
61411-61411	ADAIR
61412-61412	ALEXIS
61413-61413	ALPHA
61414-61414	ALTONA
61415-61415	AVON
61416-61416	BARDOLPH
61417-61417	BERWICK
61418-61418	BIGGSVILLE
61419-61419	BISHOP HILL
61420-61420	BLANDINSVILLE
61421-61421	BRADFORD
61422-61422	BUSHNELL
61423-61423	CAMERON
61424-61424	CAMP GROVE

ZIP Range	City
61425-61425	CARMAN
61426-61426	CASTLETON
61427-61427	CUBA
61428-61428	DAHINDA
61430-61430	EAST GALESBURG
61431-61431	ELLISVILLE
61432-61432	FAIRVIEW
61433-61433	FIATT
61434-61434	GALVA
61435-61435	GERLAW
61436-61436	GILSON
61437-61437	GLADSTONE
61438-61438	GOOD HOPE
61439-61439	HENDERSON
61440-61440	INDUSTRY
61441-61441	IPAVA
61442-61442	KEITHSBURG
61443-61443	KEWANEE
61447-61447	KIRKWOOD
61448-61448	KNOXVILLE
61449-61449	LA FAYETTE
61450-61450	LA HARPE
61451-61451	LAURA
61452-61452	LITTLETON
61453-61453	LITTLE YORK
61454-61454	LOMAX
61455-61455	MACOMB
61458-61458	MAQUON
61459-61459	MARIETTA
61460-61460	MEDIA
61462-61462	MONMOUTH
61465-61465	NEW WINDSOR
61466-61466	NORTH HENDERSON
61467-61467	ONEIDA
61468-61468	OPHEIM
61468-61468	OPHIEM
61469-61469	OQUAWKA
61470-61470	PRAIRIE CITY
61471-61471	RARITAN
61472-61472	RIO
61473-61473	ROSEVILLE
61474-61474	SAINT AUGUSTINE
61475-61475	SCIOTA
61476-61476	SEATON
61477-61477	SMITHFIELD
61478-61478	SMITHSHIRE
61479-61479	SPEER
61480-61480	STRONGHURST
61482-61482	TABLE GROVE
61483-61483	TOULON
61484-61484	VERMONT
61485-61485	VICTORIA
61486-61486	VIOLA
61488-61488	WATAGA
61489-61489	WILLIAMSFIELD
61490-61490	WOODHULL
61491-61491	WYOMING
61501-61501	ASTORIA
61516-61516	BENSON
61517-61518	BRIMFIELD
61519-61519	BRYANT
61520-61520	CANTON
61523-61523	CHILLICOTHE
61524-61524	DUNFERMLINE
61525-61525	DUNLAP
61526-61526	EDELSTEIN
61528-61528	EDWARDS
61529-61529	ELMWOOD
61530-61530	EUREKA
61531-61531	FARMINGTON
61532-61532	FOREST CITY
61533-61533	GLASFORD
61534-61534	GREEN VALLEY
61535-61535	GROVELAND
61536-61536	HANNA CITY
61537-61537	HENRY
61539-61539	KINGSTON MINES
61540-61540	LACON
61541-61541	LA ROSE
61542-61542	LEWISTOWN
61543-61543	LIVERPOOL
61544-61544	LONDON MILLS
61545-61545	LOWPOINT
61546-61546	MANITO
61547-61547	MAPLETON
61548-61548	METAMORA
61550-61550	MORTON
61552-61552	MOSSVILLE
61553-61553	NORRIS
61554-61558	PEKIN
61559-61559	PRINCEVILLE
61560-61560	PUTNAM
61561-61561	ROANOKE
61562-61562	ROME
61563-61563	SAINT DAVID
61564-61564	SOUTH PEKIN
61565-61565	SPARLAND
61567-61567	TOPEKA
61568-61568	TREMONT
61569-61569	TRIVOLI
61570-61570	WASHBURN
61571-61571	WASHINGTON
61572-61572	YATES CITY
61600-61607	PEORIA
61610-61610	CREVE COEUR
61611-61611	EAST PEORIA
61612-61615	PEORIA
61616-61616	PEORIA HEIGHTS
61625-61644	PEORIA
61649-61649	JEFFERSON BANK
61650-61656	PEORIA
61701-61710	BLOOMINGTON
61720-61720	ANCHOR
61721-61721	ARMINGTON
61722-61722	ARROWSMITH
61723-61723	ATLANTA
61724-61724	BELLFLOWER
61725-61725	CARLOCK
61726-61726	CHENOA
61727-61727	CLINTON
61728-61728	COLFAX
61729-61729	CONGERVILLE
61730-61730	COOKSVILLE
61731-61731	CROPSEY
61732-61732	DANVERS
61733-61733	DEER CREEK
61734-61734	DELAVAN
61735-61735	DEWITT
61736-61736	DOWNS
61737-61737	ELLSWORTH
61738-61738	EL PASO
61739-61739	FAIRBURY
61740-61740	FLANAGAN
61741-61741	FORREST
61742-61742	GOODFIELD
61743-61743	GRAYMONT
61744-61744	GRIDLEY
61745-61745	HEYWORTH
61747-61747	HOPEDALE
61748-61748	HUDSON
61749-61749	KENNEY
61750-61750	LANE
61751-61751	LAWNDALE
61752-61752	LE ROY
61753-61753	LEXINGTON
61754-61754	MC LEAN
61755-61755	MACKINAW
61756-61756	MAROA
61758-61758	MERNA
61759-61759	MINIER
61760-61760	MINONK
61761-61761	NORMAL
61764-61764	PONTIAC
61769-61769	SAUNEMIN
61770-61770	SAYBROOK
61771-61771	SECOR
61772-61772	SHIRLEY
61773-61773	SIBLEY
61774-61774	STANFORD
61775-61775	STRAWN
61776-61776	TOWANDA
61777-61777	WAPELLA
61778-61778	WAYNESVILLE
61790-61790	NORMAL
61791-61799	BLOOMINGTON
61801-61803	URBANA
61810-61810	ALLERTON
61811-61811	ALVIN
61812-61812	ARMSTRONG
61813-61813	BEMENT
61814-61814	BISMARCK
61815-61815	BONDVILLE
61816-61816	BROADLANDS
61817-61817	CATLIN
61818-61818	CERRO GORDO
61820-61826	CHAMPAIGN
61830-61830	CISCO
61831-61831	COLLISON
61832-61832	DANVILLE
61833-61833	TILTON
61834-61834	DANVILLE
61839-61839	DE LAND
61840-61840	DEWEY
61841-61841	FAIRMOUNT
61842-61842	FARMER CITY
61843-61843	FISHER
61844-61844	FITHIAN
61845-61845	FOOSLAND
61846-61846	GEORGETOWN
61847-61847	GIFFORD
61848-61848	HENNING
61849-61849	HOMER
61850-61850	INDIANOLA
61851-61851	IVESDALE
61852-61852	LONGVIEW
61853-61853	MAHOMET
61854-61854	MANSFIELD
61855-61855	MILMINE
61856-61856	MONTICELLO
61857-61857	MUNCIE
61858-61858	OAKWOOD
61859-61859	OGDEN
61862-61862	PENFIELD
61863-61863	PESOTUM
61864-61864	PHILO
61865-61865	POTOMAC
61866-61868	RANTOUL
61870-61870	RIDGE FARM
61871-61871	ROYAL
61872-61872	SADORUS
61873-61873	SAINT JOSEPH
61874-61874	SAVOY
61875-61875	SEYMOUR
61876-61876	SIDELL
61877-61877	SIDNEY
61878-61878	THOMASBORO
61880-61880	TOLONO
61882-61882	WELDON
61883-61883	WESTVILLE
61884-61884	WHITE HEATH
61910-61910	ARCOLA
61911-61911	ARTHUR
61912-61912	ASHMORE
61913-61913	ATWOOD
61914-61914	BETHANY
61917-61917	BROCTON
61919-61919	CAMARGO
61920-61920	CHARLESTON
61924-61924	CHRISMAN
61925-61925	DALTON CITY
61928-61928	GAYS
61929-61929	HAMMOND
61930-61930	HINDSBORO
61931-61931	HUMBOLDT
61932-61932	HUME
61933-61933	KANSAS
61936-61936	LA PLACE
61937-61937	LOVINGTON
61938-61938	MATTOON
61940-61940	METCALF
61941-61941	MURDOCK
61942-61942	NEWMAN
61943-61943	OAKLAND
61944-61944	PARIS
61949-61949	REDMON
61951-61951	SULLIVAN
61953-61953	TUSCOLA
61955-61955	VERMILION
61956-61956	VILLA GROVE
61957-61957	WINDSOR
62001-62001	ALHAMBRA
62002-62002	ALTON
62006-62006	BATCHTOWN
62009-62009	BENLD
62010-62010	BETHALTO
62011-62011	BINGHAM
62012-62012	BRIGHTON
62013-62013	BRUSSELS
62014-62014	BUNKER HILL
62015-62015	BUTLER
62016-62016	CARROLLTON
62017-62017	COFFEEN
62018-62018	COTTAGE HILLS
62019-62019	DONNELLSON
62021-62021	DORSEY
62022-62022	DOW
62023-62023	EAGARVILLE
62024-62024	EAST ALTON
62025-62026	EDWARDSVILLE
62027-62027	ELDRED
62028-62028	ELSAH
62030-62030	FIDELITY
62031-62031	FIELDON
62032-62032	FILLMORE
62033-62033	GILLESPIE
62034-62034	GLEN CARBON
62035-62035	GODFREY
62036-62036	GOLDEN EAGLE
62037-62037	GRAFTON
62040-62040	GRANITE CITY
62044-62044	GREENFIELD
62045-62045	HAMBURG
62046-62046	HAMEL
62047-62047	HARDIN
62048-62048	HARTFORD
62049-62049	HILLSBORO
62050-62050	HILLVIEW
62051-62051	IRVING
62052-62052	JERSEYVILLE
62053-62053	KAMPSVILLE
62054-62054	KANE
62056-62056	LITCHFIELD
62058-62058	LIVINGSTON
62059-62059	LOVEJOY
62060-62060	MADISON
62061-62061	MARINE
62062-62062	MARYVILLE
62063-62063	MEDORA
62065-62065	MICHAEL
62067-62067	MORO
62069-62069	MOUNT OLIVE
62070-62070	MOZIER
62071-62071	NATIONAL STOCK YARDS
62074-62074	NEW DOUGLAS
62075-62075	NOKOMIS
62076-62076	OHLMAN
62077-62077	PANAMA
62078-62078	PATTERSON
62079-62079	PIASA
62080-62080	RAMSEY
62081-62081	ROCKBRIDGE
62082-62082	ROODHOUSE
62083-62083	ROSAMOND
62084-62084	ROXANA
62085-62085	SAWYERVILLE
62086-62086	SORENTO
62087-62087	SOUTH ROXANA
62088-62088	STAUNTON
62089-62089	TAYLOR SPRINGS
62090-62090	VENICE
62091-62091	WALSHVILLE
62092-62092	WHITE HALL
62093-62093	WILSONVILLE
62094-62094	WITT
62095-62095	WOOD RIVER
62097-62097	WORDEN
62098-62098	WRIGHTS
62201-62207	EAST SAINT LOUIS

Zip	City
62208-62208	FAIRVIEW HEIGHTS
62214-62214	ADDIEVILLE
62215-62215	ALBERS
62216-62216	AVISTON
62217-62217	BALDWIN
62218-62218	BARTELSO
62219-62219	BECKEMEYER
62220-62223	BELLEVILLE
62224-62224	MASCOUTAH
62225-62225	SCOTT AIR FORCE BASE
62226-62226	BELLEVILLE
62230-62230	BREESE
62231-62231	CARLYLE
62232-62232	CASEYVILLE
62233-62233	CHESTER
62234-62234	COLLINSVILLE
62236-62236	COLUMBIA
62237-62237	COULTERVILLE
62238-62238	CUTLER
62239-62239	DUPO
62240-62240	EAST CARONDELET
62241-62241	ELLIS GROVE
62242-62242	EVANSVILLE
62243-62243	FREEBURG
62244-62244	FULTS
62245-62245	GERMANTOWN
62246-62246	GREENVILLE
62247-62247	HAGARSTOWN
62248-62248	HECKER
62249-62249	HIGHLAND
62250-62250	HOFFMAN
62252-62252	HUEY
62253-62253	KEYESPORT
62254-62254	LEBANON
62255-62255	LENZBURG
62256-62256	MAEYSTOWN
62257-62257	MARISSA
62258-62258	MASCOUTAH
62259-62259	MENARD
62260-62260	MILLSTADT
62261-62261	MODOC
62262-62262	MULBERRY GROVE
62263-62263	NASHVILLE
62264-62264	NEW ATHENS
62265-62265	NEW BADEN
62266-62266	NEW MEMPHIS
62268-62268	OAKDALE
62269-62269	O FALLON
62271-62271	OKAWVILLE
62272-62272	PERCY
62273-62273	PIERRON
62274-62274	PINCKNEYVILLE
62275-62275	POCAHONTAS
62277-62277	PRAIRIE DU ROCHER
62278-62278	RED BUD
62279-62279	RENAULT
62280-62280	ROCKWOOD
62281-62281	SAINT JACOB
62282-62282	SAINT LIBORY
62283-62283	SHATTUC
62284-62284	SMITHBORO
62285-62285	SMITHTON
62286-62286	SPARTA
62288-62288	STEELEVILLE
62289-62289	SUMMERFIELD
62292-62292	TILDEN
62293-62293	TRENTON
62294-62294	TROY
62295-62295	VALMEYER
62296-62296	VENEDY
62297-62297	WALSH
62298-62298	WATERLOO
62301-62306	QUINCY
62310-62310	ADRIAN
62311-62311	AUGUSTA
62312-62312	BARRY
62313-62313	BASCO
62314-62314	BAYLIS
62316-62316	BOWEN
62318-62318	BURNSIDE
62319-62319	CAMDEN
62320-62320	CAMP POINT
62321-62321	CARTHAGE
62323-62323	CHAMBERSBURG
62324-62324	CLAYTON
62325-62325	COATSBURG
62326-62326	COLCHESTER
62327-62327	COLMAR
62328-62328	QUINCY
62329-62329	COLUSA
62330-62330	DALLAS CITY
62332-62332	PITTSFIELD
62334-62334	ELVASTON
62336-62336	FERRIS
62338-62338	FOWLER
62339-62339	GOLDEN
62340-62340	GRIGGSVILLE
62341-62341	HAMILTON
62343-62343	HULL
62344-62344	HUNTSVILLE
62345-62345	KINDERHOOK
62346-62346	LA PRAIRIE
62347-62347	LIBERTY
62348-62348	LIMA
62349-62349	LORAINE
62351-62351	MENDON
62352-62352	MILTON
62353-62353	MOUNT STERLING
62354-62354	NAUVOO
62355-62355	NEBO
62356-62356	NEW CANTON
62357-62357	NEW SALEM
62358-62358	NIOTA
62359-62359	PALOMA
62360-62360	PAYSON
62361-62361	PEARL
62362-62362	PERRY
62363-62363	PITTSFIELD
62365-62365	PLAINVILLE
62366-62366	PLEASANT HILL
62367-62367	PLYMOUTH
62370-62370	ROCKPORT
62372-62372	SUMMER HILL
62373-62373	SUTTER
62374-62374	TENNESSEE
62375-62375	TIMEWELL
62376-62376	URSA
62378-62378	VERSAILLES
62379-62379	WARSAW
62380-62380	WEST POINT
62401-62401	EFFINGHAM
62410-62410	ALLENDALE
62411-62411	ALTAMONT
62413-62413	ANNAPOLIS
62414-62414	BEECHER CITY
62415-62415	BIRDS
62417-62417	BRIDGEPORT
62418-62418	BROWNSTOWN
62419-62419	CALHOUN
62420-62420	CASEY
62421-62421	CLAREMONT
62422-62422	COWDEN
62423-62423	DENNISON
62424-62424	DIETERICH
62425-62425	DUNDAS
62426-62426	EDGEWOOD
62427-62427	FLAT ROCK
62428-62428	GREENUP
62431-62431	HERRICK
62432-62432	HIDALGO
62433-62433	HUTSONVILLE
62434-62434	INGRAHAM
62435-62435	JANESVILLE
62436-62436	JEWETT
62438-62438	LAKEWOOD
62439-62439	LAWRENCEVILLE
62440-62440	LERNA
62441-62441	MARSHALL
62442-62442	MARTINSVILLE
62443-62443	MASON
62444-62444	MODE
62445-62445	MONTROSE
62446-62446	MOUNT ERIE
62447-62447	NEOGA
62448-62448	NEWTON
62449-62449	OBLONG
62450-62450	OLNEY
62451-62451	PALESTINE
62452-62452	PARKERSBURG
62454-62454	ROBINSON
62458-62458	SAINT ELMO
62459-62459	SAINTE MARIE
62460-62460	SAINT FRANCISVILLE
62461-62461	SHUMWAY
62462-62462	SIGEL
62463-62463	STEWARDSON
62464-62464	STOY
62465-62465	STRASBURG
62466-62466	SUMNER
62467-62467	TEUTOPOLIS
62468-62468	TOLEDO
62469-62469	TRILLA
62471-62471	VANDALIA
62473-62473	WATSON
62474-62474	WESTFIELD
62475-62475	WEST LIBERTY
62476-62476	WEST SALEM
62477-62477	WEST UNION
62478-62478	WEST YORK
62479-62479	WHEELER
62480-62480	WILLOW HILL
62481-62481	YALE
62501-62501	ARGENTA
62510-62510	ASSUMPTION
62511-62511	ATWATER
62512-62512	BEASON
62513-62513	BLUE MOUND
62514-62514	BOODY
62515-62515	BUFFALO
62517-62517	BULPITT
62518-62518	CHESTNUT
62519-62519	CORNLAND
62520-62520	DAWSON
62521-62527	DECATUR
62530-62530	DIVERNON
62531-62531	EDINBURG
62532-62532	ELWIN
62533-62533	FARMERSVILLE
62534-62534	FINDLAY
62535-62535	FORSYTH
62536-62536	GLENARM
62537-62537	HARRISTOWN
62538-62538	HARVEL
62539-62539	ILLIOPOLIS
62540-62540	KINCAID
62541-62541	LAKE FORK
62543-62543	LATHAM
62544-62544	MACON
62545-62545	MECHANICSBURG
62546-62546	MORRISONVILLE
62547-62547	MOUNT AUBURN
62548-62548	MOUNT PULASKI
62549-62549	MT ZION
62550-62550	MOWEAQUA
62551-62551	NIANTIC
62552-62552	OAKLEY
62553-62553	OCONEE
62554-62554	OREANA
62555-62555	OWANECO
62556-62556	PALMER
62557-62557	PANA
62558-62558	PAWNEE
62560-62560	RAYMOND
62561-62561	RIVERTON
62563-62563	ROCHESTER
62565-62565	SHELBYVILLE
62567-62567	STONINGTON
62568-62568	TAYLORVILLE
62570-62570	TOVEY
62571-62571	TOWER HILL
62572-62572	WAGGONER
62573-62573	WARRENSBURG
62574-62574	WESTERVELT
62601-62601	ALEXANDER
62610-62610	ALSEY
62611-62611	ARENZVILLE
62612-62612	ASHLAND
62613-62613	ATHENS
62615-62615	AUBURN
62617-62617	BATH
62618-62618	BEARDSTOWN
62621-62621	BLUFFS
62622-62622	BLUFF SPRINGS
62624-62624	BROWNING
62625-62625	CANTRALL
62626-62626	CARLINVILLE
62627-62627	CHANDLERVILLE
62628-62628	CHAPIN
62629-62629	CHATHAM
62630-62630	CHESTERFIELD
62631-62631	CONCORD
62633-62633	EASTON
62634-62634	ELKHART
62635-62635	EMDEN
62638-62638	FRANKLIN
62639-62639	FREDERICK
62640-62640	GIRARD
62642-62642	GREENVIEW
62643-62643	HARTSBURG
62644-62644	HAVANA
62649-62649	HETTICK
62650-62651	JACKSONVILLE
62655-62655	KILBOURNE
62656-62656	LINCOLN
62659-62659	LINCOLN'S NEW SALEM
62660-62660	LITERBERRY
62661-62661	LOAMI
62662-62662	LOWDER
62663-62663	MANCHESTER
62664-62664	MASON CITY
62665-62665	MEREDOSIA
62666-62666	MIDDLETOWN
62667-62667	MODESTO
62668-62668	MURRAYVILLE
62670-62670	NEW BERLIN
62671-62671	NEW HOLLAND
62672-62672	NILWOOD
62673-62673	OAKFORD
62674-62674	PALMYRA
62675-62675	PETERSBURG
62676-62676	PLAINVIEW
62677-62677	PLEASANT PLAINS
62681-62681	RUSHVILLE
62682-62682	SAN JOSE
62683-62683	SCOTTVILLE
62684-62684	SHERMAN
62685-62685	SHIPMAN
62686-62686	STANDARD CITY
62688-62688	TALLULA
62689-62689	THAYER
62690-62690	VIRDEN
62691-62691	VIRGINIA
62692-62692	WAVERLY
62693-62693	WILLIAMSVILLE
62694-62694	WINCHESTER
62695-62695	WOODSON
62700-62796	SPRINGFIELD
62801-62801	CENTRALIA
62803-62803	HOYLETON
62805-62805	AKIN
62806-62806	ALBION
62807-62807	ALMA
62808-62808	ASHLEY
62809-62809	BARNHILL
62810-62810	BELLE RIVE
62811-62811	BELLMONT
62812-62812	BENTON
62814-62814	BLUFORD
62815-62815	BONE GAP
62816-62816	BONNIE
62817-62817	BROUGHTON
62818-62818	BROWNS
62819-62819	BUCKNER
62820-62820	BURNT PRAIRIE
62821-62821	CARMI
62822-62822	CHRISTOPHER
62823-62823	CISNE
62824-62824	CLAY CITY

ZIP	City
62825-62825	COELLO
62827-62827	CROSSVILLE
62828-62828	DAHLGREN
62829-62829	DALE
62830-62830	DIX
62831-62831	DU BOIS
62832-62832	DU QUOIN
62833-62833	ELLERY
62834-62834	EMMA
62835-62835	ENFIELD
62836-62836	EWING
62837-62837	FAIRFIELD
62838-62838	FARINA
62839-62839	FLORA
62840-62840	FRANKFORT HEIGHTS
62841-62841	FREEMAN SPUR
62842-62842	GEFF
62843-62843	GOLDEN GATE
62844-62844	GRAYVILLE
62845-62845	HERALD
62846-62846	INA
62847-62847	IOLA
62848-62848	IRVINGTON
62849-62849	IUKA
62850-62850	JOHNSONVILLE
62851-62851	KEENES
62852-62852	KEENSBURG
62853-62853	KELL
62854-62854	KINMUNDY
62855-62855	LANCASTER
62856-62856	LOGAN
62857-62857	LOOGOOTEE
62858-62858	LOUISVILLE
62859-62859	MC LEANSBORO
62860-62860	MACEDONIA
62861-62861	MAUNIE
62862-62862	MILL SHOALS
62863-62863	MOUNT CARMEL
62864-62864	MOUNT VERNON
62865-62865	MULKEYTOWN
62866-62866	NASON
62867-62867	NEW HAVEN
62868-62868	NOBLE
62869-62869	NORRIS CITY
62870-62870	ODIN
62871-62871	OMAHA
62872-62872	OPDYKE
62874-62874	ORIENT
62875-62875	PATOKA
62876-62876	RADOM
62877-62877	RICHVIEW
62878-62878	RINARD
62879-62879	SAILOR SPRINGS
62880-62880	SAINT PETER
62881-62881	SALEM
62882-62882	SANDOVAL
62883-62883	SCHELLER
62884-62884	SESSER
62885-62885	SHOBONIER
62886-62886	SIMS
62887-62887	SPRINGERTON
62888-62888	TAMAROA
62889-62889	TEXICO
62890-62890	THOMPSONVILLE
62891-62891	VALIER
62892-62892	VERNON
62893-62893	WALNUT HILL
62894-62894	WALTONVILLE
62895-62895	WAYNE CITY
62896-62896	WEST FRANKFORT
62897-62897	WHITTINGTON
62898-62898	WOODLAWN
62899-62899	XENIA
62901-62903	CARBONDALE
62905-62905	ALTO PASS
62906-62906	ANNA
62907-62907	AVA
62908-62908	BELKNAP
62909-62909	BOLES
62910-62910	BROOKPORT
62912-62912	BUNCOMBE
62913-62913	CACHE
62914-62914	CAIRO
62915-62915	CAMBRIA
62916-62916	CAMPBELL HILL
62917-62917	CARRIER MILLS
62918-62918	CARTERVILLE
62919-62919	CAVE IN ROCK
62920-62920	COBDEN
62921-62921	COLP
62922-62922	CREAL SPRINGS
62923-62923	CYPRESS
62924-62924	DE SOTO
62926-62926	DONGOLA
62927-62927	DOWELL
62928-62928	EDDYVILLE
62929-62929	ELCO
62930-62930	ELDORADO
62931-62931	ELIZABETHTOWN
62932-62932	ELKVILLE
62933-62933	ENERGY
62934-62934	EQUALITY
62935-62935	GALATIA
62938-62938	GOLCONDA
62939-62939	GOREVILLE
62940-62940	GORHAM
62941-62941	GRAND CHAIN
62942-62942	GRAND TOWER
62943-62943	GRANTSBURG
62944-62944	HAMLETSBURG
62945-62945	GALATIA
62946-62946	HARRISBURG
62947-62947	HEROD
62948-62948	HERRIN
62949-62949	HURST
62950-62950	JACOB
62951-62951	JOHNSTON CITY
62952-62952	JONESBORO
62953-62953	JOPPA
62954-62954	JUNCTION
62955-62955	KARBERS RIDGE
62956-62956	KARNAK
62957-62957	MC CLURE
62958-62958	MAKANDA
62959-62959	MARION
62960-62960	METROPOLIS
62961-62961	MILLCREEK
62962-62962	MILLER CITY
62963-62963	MOUND CITY
62964-62964	MOUNDS
62965-62965	MUDDY
62966-62966	MURPHYSBORO
62967-62967	NEW BURNSIDE
62969-62969	OLIVE BRANCH
62970-62970	OLMSTED
62971-62971	ORAVILLE
62972-62972	OZARK
62973-62973	PERKS
62974-62974	PITTSBURG
62975-62975	POMONA
62976-62976	PULASKI
62977-62977	RALEIGH
62979-62979	RIDGWAY
62982-62982	ROSICLARE
62983-62983	ROYALTON
62984-62984	SHAWNEETOWN
62985-62985	SIMPSON
62987-62987	STONEFORT
62988-62988	TAMMS
62990-62990	THEBES
62991-62991	TUNNEL HILL
62992-62992	ULLIN
62993-62993	UNITY
62994-62994	VERGENNES
62995-62995	VIENNA
62996-62996	VILLA RIDGE
62997-62997	WILLISVILLE
62998-62998	WOLF LAKE
62999-62999	ZEIGLER

Indiana

General Help Numbers:

Governor's Office

200 W. Washington St.
Indianapolis, IN 46204-2797
www.in.gov/gov

317-232-4567
Fax 317-232-3443
8AM-5PM

Attorney General's Office

302 W Washington
Indianapolis, IN 46204
www.in.gov/attorneygeneral

317-232-6201
Fax 317-232-7979
8:30AM-5PM

Legislative Records

Legislative Services Agency
200 W Washington, Room 301
Indianapolis, IN 46204-2789
www.in.gov/legislative

317-232-9856
8:15AM-4:45PM

State Archives

Commission on Public Records
6440 E 30th St
Indianapolis, IN 46219
www.in.gov/icpr

317-591-5222
Fax 317-591-5324
8AM-4:30PM

State Specifics:

Capital: Indianapolis
Marion County

Time Zone: EST*

* 11 western Indiana counties are CST and observe DST. They are: Gibson, Jasper, Laporte, Lake, Newton, Porter, Posey, Spencer, Vanderburgh, Warrick. The remainder are EST and do not observe DST except for Clark, Dearborn, Floyd, Harrison, Ohio.

Number of Counties: 92

Population: 6,376,792

Web Site: www.in.gov

State Agencies

Criminal Records

Indiana State Police, Criminal History Records, PO Box 6188, Indianapolis, IN 46206-6188; 317-232-5424, Fax- 317-233-8813; 8AM-4PM.

www.IN.gov/isp/

Indexing & Storage: Records available from 1935. New records available for inquiry in 10 days. Approximately 45% of all arrests in database have final dispositions recorded, over 50% for those arrests within last 5 years. This agency now is notified when charges are made after fingerprints are submitted.

Searching: The release of records is governed by IC 10-13-3-27. A "Limited Criminal History" is available to designated entities including employers, licensing agencies, schools, and certain other designates. Include in request- full name, date of birth, sex, race. Use State Form 8053 is required for mail or in-person requests. Go to www.in.gov/ai/appfiles/isp-lch/ for the link. Submitting fingerprints is an option, but if requesting record on oneself. 100% of the records are fingerprint-supported. This data not released- ISP case reports and arrests over 1 year with no disposition. Record will show all activity, including arrests, dismissals, and convictions. But, if a charge is over a year old with no disposition, then the record will not be released.

Access by: mail, in person, online.

Fee & Payment: For mail or in-person requests, the fee for employers is $7.00 per name for a limited criminal history if no fingerprints used. The fee for a fingerprint search is $10.00. If subject requests own record, fee is $10.00, and this is for a FULL record. Fee payee- State of Indiana. Prepayment required. Ongoing requesters (20 records per months for 3 months) may open a monthly billing account. Cash, money orders, and certified checks are accepted. No bills over $10.00

accepted in person. Credit cards accepted only online.

Mail search: Turnaround time- Two weeks. Use State Form 8053, which can be downloaded from the web site at www.in.gov/ai/appfiles/isp-lch//LCHrequest.pdf.

In person: Requester must have picture ID, turnaround time is 15-20 minutes, but the full record is mailed out 4 days later.

Online search: A Limited Criminal History with only felonies and class A misdemeanor arrests is available at www.in.gov/ai/appfiles/isp-lch//. Using a credit card, the search fee is $16.32. Subscribers to accessIndiana can obtain records for $15.00 per search or for no charge if statutorily exempt, or $7.00 with a government exemption. Response of No Records Found is an official search result. The state's Attorney General's Office has a searchable web page of companies that have violated consumer laws. Visit http://atgindsha01.atg.in.gov/cpd/enforcement/search.aspx.

Statewide Court Records

State Court Administrator, Indiana Supreme Court, 30 South Meridian Street, Suite 500, Indianapolis, IN 46204; 317-232-2542, Fax- 317-233-6586; 8:30AM-4:30PM.

www.in.gov/judiciary/

Except for the online research capabilities described below, all court record access must be done at the local level.

Indexing & Storage: Records available from 1982.

Access by: online.

Online search: There is no statewide trial court records service available, but many counties offer an online subscription service at https://www.doxpop.com/prod/. The website above gives free access to an index of docket information for Supreme, Appeals, and Tax Court cases.

Sexual Offender Registry

Sex and Violent Offender Directory Manager, Indiana Government Center South, E334, 302 W. Washington Street, Indianapolis, IN 46204; 317-232-1232, Fax- 317-233-1474.

www.insor.org/insasoweb/

Indiana law requires the state to maintain a directory of individuals who have been convicted of one or more of the sex and violent offenses requiring registration with local sheriff departments.

Indexing & Storage: Records available from 04/01/89.

Searching: Email questions to svor@cji.in.gov. While this state agency will help requesters to a point, most searchers are directed to the local sheriffs' offices or to the web page.

Access by: mail, phone, in person, online.

Mail search: Turnaround time- 3 - 5 days.

Phone search: Limited phone searching is available.

In person: No searching in person at this agency, but you may search at any of the local sheriff's offices in the state.

Online search: The website has a searching capabilities by name and city or county at www.insor.org/insasoweb/.

Incarceration Records

Indiana Department of Correction, IGCS, Supervisor of Records, Room E-334, 302 W. Washington Street, Indianapolis, IN 46204; 317-232-5765, Fax- 317-232-5728; 8AM-4:30PM.

www.in.gov/idoc/

Indexing & Storage: Records available on current and former inmates. New records available for inquiry in 10 days.

Searching: Computerized records go back to 1989. Include in request- first and last name; the DOB and SSN helpful. Location, DOC number, physical identifiers, sentencing and conviction information, and release dates are released.

Access by: mail, phone, fax, online.

Fee & Payment: Fee is $.10 per page. Fee payee- Department of Corrections Prepayment required. Personal checks not accepted.

Mail search: Turnaround time- 5 to 10 working days.

Phone search: Limited searching available by phone.

Fax search: Fax requests are accepted.

Online search: At the website, click on Offender Locator or visit www.in.gov/apps/indcorrection/ofs/. To search online provide either full name or inmate number.

Corporation, LP, LLC, LLP, Fictitious/Assumed Name

Corporation Division, Secretary of State, 302 W Washington St, Room E018, Indianapolis, IN 46204; 317-232-6576, Fax- 317-233-3387; 8AM-5:30PM M-F.

www.in.gov/sos/

This agency also holds Agricultural Cooperative and Business Trust records.

Indexing & Storage: Records available for all active entities and most inactives. Inactive packets can be archived after 2 years, but are not destroyed. New records available for inquiry in 1-3 days after receipt.

Searching: There are no restrictions, all information is public record. Include in request- full name of business, specific records that you need copies of. Other records available include: Annual or Bi-annual Reports, Officers (when applicable), Prior (merged) names, Inactive and Reserved names, Assumed Business names, and Registered Agent and address. This data not released- SSNs

Access by: mail, phone, fax, in person, online.

Fee & Payment: There is no search fee. Copies cost $1.00 per page plus $15.00 for document certification. Due & Diligent Searches may be ordered for information that cannot be found initially. Fee payee- Secretary of State. Will invoice. The state has pre-paid accounts for filing only. Personal checks accepted. Credit cards accepted online.

Mail search: Turnaround time- 3 to 5 days. No pre-payments accepted for mail requests. Due & Diligent searches take 10 business days. A SASE is welcomed.

Phone search: Limited verification information is available.

Fax search: Records may be requested by fax, but are not returned by fax.

In person: Requests submitted by noon are ready by noon the next day. Requests after 12 noon are ready within 2 business days.

Online search: You can conduct Business Entity Name Searches, Name Availability Checks and acquire official Certificates of Existence or Authorization at www.in.gov/sos/business/corporations.html. The site also gives access to UCC records. Frequent users of Business Services Online should subscribe to accessIndiana at www.ai.org/ai/business/. Also, search securities companies registered with the state at www.in.gov/apps/sos/securities/sos_securities.

Other access: Monthly lists of all new businesses are available online, as are bulk data and specialized searches. Look for Special Business Entity Search Orders at the website.

Trademarks/Servicemarks

Secretary of State, Trademark Division, 302 W Washington St, IGC-South, Room E018, Indianapolis, IN 46204; 317-232-6540, Fax- 317-233-1915; 8:AM-5:30PM.

www.in.gov/sos/business/trademarks.html

These records are considered public and are available with no restrictions.

Indexing & Storage: Records available for active trademarks. New records available for inquiry in 2 to 3 days.

Searching: Include in request- either name, description, or owner name. Search requires trademark/servicemark name or file ID number. It generally takes 2 to 3 days to search for logo/designs, but name of mark searches can be done immediately. If you have the file ID number, it will help.

Access by: mail, phone, fax, in person, online.

Mail search: Turnaround time- 2 to 3 days. A SASE is requested.

Phone search: Limited searching by telephone; will do 2 or 3 names only.

Fax search: Limited searching by fax; will do 2 or 3 names only.

In person: You may request information in person, however, the search clerk is not available full-time.

Online search: Visit www.in.gov/apps/sos/trademarks/. This database contains information regarding the status of all trademarks on file with the state of Indiana. Access is free. Results allow one to view application, certificate or the mark.

Other access: One may purchase the database, see the website for details and fees.

Uniform Commercial Code

UCC Division, Secretary of State, 302 West Washington St, Room E-018, Indianapolis, IN 46204; 317-233-3984, Fax- 317-233-3387; 8AM-5:30PM.

www.in.gov/sos/business/ucc.html

Indexing & Storage: Records available from 1964 or one year after lapse. New records available for inquiry in up to 3 days.

Searching: Use the state request form. All tax liens are filed at the county level. Include in request- debtor name or initial financing statement number.

Access by: mail, in person, online.

Fee & Payment: The search fee of $5.00 per debtor name, which includes all copies. Fee payee- Secretary of State. Prepayment required. Personal checks and credit cards accepted.

Mail search: Turnaround time- 2 days. An SASE is requested.

In person: Turnaround time is 2 days

Online search: You may browse lien records at https://secure.in.gov/sos/bus_service/online_ucc/browse/default.asp. There is no charge. An official search may be performed for $4.08. If requester is subscriber to AccessIndiana then fee to obtain record is $3.00. Filing services are also available to subscribers. Bulk downloads and special orders are available online.

Federal & State Tax Liens

Records not maintained by a state level agency.

All tax liens are found at the county level.

Sales Tax Registrations

IN Dept of Revenue, Sales Tax Registrations, PO Box 7218, Indianapolis, IN 46207 (Courier address- 100 N Senate Ave, Rm N105, Indianapolis, IN 46204); 317-233-4015, Fax- 317-232-2103; 8AM-4:30PM.

www.in.gov/dor/

Searching: This agency will only confirm whether a company is registered. No other information will be given about the company. The database is not available for purchase. Include in request- legal name and address or Indiana Tax ID or Federal Tax ID.

Access by: mail, phone.

Mail search: Turnaround time- 4 to 6 weeks. No fee for mail request.

Phone search: No fee for telephone request. This is very limited, only one search permitted.

Birth Certificates

State Department of Health, Vital Records Office, PO Box 7125, Indianapolis, IN 46206-7125 (Courier address- 2 N. Meridian, Indianapolis, IN 46204); 317-233-2700, Fax- 317-233-7210; 8:15AM-4:45PM.

www.in.gov/isdh/20243.htm

The information is also available at each local county health department of the birth.

Indexing & Storage: Records available from October 1907 on and are computerized since 1978. New records available for inquiry in 12 weeks.

Searching: Must have a signed release from person of record or be immediate family member or show direct need. Include in request- full name, names of parents, mother's maiden name, date of birth, place of birth, relationship to person of record, reason for information request. This data not released- court orders and certain adoption records.

Access by: mail, phone, in person, online.

Fee & Payment: Search is $10.00 per name. If exact date of birth is not known there is an additional fee of $10.00 for each 5 years searched. Add $4.00 per name requested for each additional copy of same record. Fee payee- Indiana State Department of Health. Prepayment required. Personal checks accepted. Major credit cards accepted by VitalChek.

Mail search: Turnaround time- 3 to 4 weeks. Must include a copy of a signature ID with your request. SASE not required.

Phone search: Record requests (except for genealogy records) are available by phone with use of credit card. Available from VitalChek at 866-601-0891 (approved third party vendor), see expedited service.

In person: Only available between 10AM-2PM, it takes about 45 minutes to process the request.

Online search: Records may be ordered online via the website, but the requester must still fax a photo copy of an ID before the record request is processed. Also, records may requested from www.vitalchek.com, a state-endorsed vendor.

Expedited service: Available from the vendor mentioned above, requesters must pay vendor fee of $12.95 and also express delivery if desired. Turnaround time- 2-3 days.

Death Records

State Department of Health, Vital Records Office, PO Box 7125, Indianapolis, IN 46206-7125 (Courier address- 2 N. Meridian, Indianapolis, IN 46204); 317-233-2700, Fax- 317-233-7210; 8:15AM-4:45PM.

www.in.gov/isdh/20243.htm

Indexing & Storage: Records available from 1900 on. New records available for inquiry in 12 weeks.

Searching: This index is not for public review. You must have a signed release from immediate family member. Include a copy of your photo ID with your request. Include in request- full name, date of death, place of death, relationship to person of record, reason for information request.

Access by: mail, phone, fax, in person, online.

Fee & Payment: Fee is $8.00 per name. If exact date of death is not known, there is a $8.00 fee for each 5 years searched. Add $4.00 per name requested for each additional copy of same record. Fee payee- Indiana State Department of Health. Prepayment required. Personal checks accepted. Major credit cards accepted by VitalChek.

Mail search: Turnaround time- 1 month. SASE not required.

Phone search: Searching by telephone. Available from VitalChek at 866-601-0891 (approved third party vendor).

Fax search: This is via the vender at 866-559-9631. See expedited service for fees.

In person: Available from 10AM-2PM.

Online search: Records may requested from www.vitalchek.com, a state-endorsed vendor.

Expedited service: Available from the vendor mentioned above, requesters must pay vendor fee of $12.95 and also express delivery if desired. Turnaround time- 2-3 days.

Marriage Certificates, Divorce Records

Records not maintained by a state level agency.

Marriage and divorce records are found at county of issue. The index of marriages can also be found at the Indiana State Library, the throughput varies however.

Workers' Compensation Records

Workers Compensation Board, 402 W Washington St, Room W196, Indianapolis, IN 46204-2753; 317-232-3808, Fax- 317-233-5493; 8AM-4:30PM.

www.in.gov/wcb/

Claims information for disputes that require a hearing are available online, those are the only online records available.

Indexing & Storage: Records available for past 9 years. New records available for inquiry in up to 2 weeks.

Searching: Must have a notarized authorization release from claimant or a subpoena to obtain records from this agency. Requests are reviewed by the Executive Secretary who decides whether to release the information. Include in request- claimant name, SSN, date of accident, reason for information request.

Access by: mail, online.

Fee & Payment: Copies are $.10 per page, there is no search fee. Fee payee- Workers Compensation Board. Personal checks accepted, credit cards are not.

Mail search: Turnaround time- variable. A SASE is required.

Online search: Search disputed claims at http://wcbnec03.wcb.state.in.us/search.asp.

Driver Records

BMV-Driving Records, 100 N Senate Ave, Indiana Government Center North, Room N405, Indianapolis, IN 46204; 317-233-6000; 8:15AM-4:30PM.

www.IN.gov/bmv/

Copies of tickets are available at the address listed above for a fee of $8.00.

Indexing & Storage: Records available for 7 years (10 years if requested) for moving violations, DWIs and suspensions. Accidents reported to the state police appear on the record. New records available for inquiry in 1-3 weeks.

Searching: Personal information is not disclosed to casual requesters. Further, a driver's SSN, driver's license number or Federal ID number is not disclosed to all non-governmental requesters. Include in request- ID number, name, DOB. Use State Form 48430 which requires signature and copy of ID of requester. Form is found on web.

Access by: mail, in person, online.

Fee & Payment: The fee is $4.00 per record (except for online requests), $8.00 for a complete history. Add $4.00 for certification. Turnaround time is 4 to 6 weeks for histories. Fee payee- Bureau of Motor Vehicles. Prepayment required. Personal checks accepted, credit cards are not.

Mail search: Turnaround time- 5 to 7 days. SASE not required.

In person: Up to ten requests are processed at one time for a walk-in requester at the Customer Service Center located at 531 Virginia Ave, Indianapolis or at any of the Regional Service Centers.

Online search: IN.gov is the state owned interactive information and communication system which provides batch and interactive access to driving records. There is an annual $50.00 fee. Online access costs $7.50 per record. For more information, call 317-233-2010 or go to www.in.gov/subscriber_center.htm.

Vehicle, Vessel Ownership & Registration

Bureau of Motor Vehicles, Records, 100 N Senate Ave, Room N404, Indianapolis, IN 46204; 317-233-2513 (Titles), 317-233-6000 (Registration); 8:15AM-4:45PM.

www.in.gov/bmv/

Bulk record requests are not available from this agency.

Indexing & Storage: Records available for 3 years on computer and up to ten years on microfilm. All motor boats that were valued over $3,000 when new must be titled and registered. New records available for inquiry in minutes.

Searching: Casual requesters can obtain records, but no personal information is released on subjects without consent. Vehicle owner's SSN, driver's license number, and Federal ID number cannot be disclosed to all non-governmental requesters. Include in request- state form 46449. There are five types of records available for search; title inquiry, title history, registration inquiry, registration history, and registration copy. The title history will show liens on paper. The title inquiry will show current listed lien holder.

Access by: mail, in person, online.

Fee & Payment: For vehicles, the fee is $4.00 per "inquiry" and $8.00 per "history." For watercraft, the fee is $4.00 for all title and registration searches. Certification is an additional $4.00. Fee payee- Bureau of Motor Vehicles. Prepayment required. Personal checks accepted, credit cards are not.

Mail search: Turnaround time- within 2 weeks. SASE not required.

In person: The walk-in address for the Customer Service Center is 531 Virginia Ave, Indianapolis. There are several other locations in the state that will process requests Turnaround time depends on availability of personnel. Title histories are not provided on an immediate basis, they must be returned by mail.

Online search: AccessIndiana at 317-233-2010 is the state appointed vendor. Visit www.in.gov for more information. Search the Indiana Bureau of Motor Vehicles database for title and lien information by VIN number, title number, or SSN; Salvage titles included. The fee is $5.00 per record plus an annual fee of $50.00.

Accident Reports

Holt, Sheets - Crash Records Section, 100 N Senate, Room N301, Indiana Government Center, Indianapolis, IN 46204; 317-215-8300, Fax- 317-234-2041; 8AM-4PM.

www.buycrash.com/Public/CommunitySearch.aspx

The keeper of the records is privatized, but located within the state agency as listed above.

Indexing & Storage: Records available from 20 years to present. Older records are archived on microfiche. New records available for inquiry in 2 hours to 2 weeks.

Searching: The only reports released are those of the officers. Indiana operator report forms are not released. Include in request- full name, date of accident, location of accident.

Access by: mail, in person, online.

Fee & Payment: The fee is $12.00 per report if 2003 or newer. Older reports must be researched on microfiche and incur a $25.00 per hour fee. Fee payee- Indiana State Police. Prepayment required. Personal and business checks accepted. major credit cards accepted.

Mail search: Turnaround time- 2-8 days. SASE is required.

In person: Normal turnaround time is while you wait. If you are requesting all accidents on a "name," this request should be in writing and will take longer.

Online search: Records may be downloaded online as a PDF file, after fee payment.

Other access: For information about bulk file purchasing, contact the Data Section at 317-233-5133.

Legislation Records

Legislative Services Agency, State House, 200 W Washington, Room 302, Indianapolis, IN 46204-2789; 317-232-9856, Fax- 317-232-7257; 8:15AM-4:45PM.

www.in.gov/legislative/

Sessions start in January. Long sessions (61 days) are in the odd years; short sessions (30 days) are in the even years. Bills prior to 1990 are stored in the State Law Library.

Indexing & Storage: Records available from 1980 to present.

Searching: Include in request- bill number. Can search on code citation also.

Access by: mail, phone, in person, online.

Fee & Payment: Fees are $.15 per copy plus postage. Fee payee- Legislative Services Agency. Prepayment required. Personal checks accepted, credit cards are not.

Mail search: Turnaround time- 1 to 4 days. SASE not required.

Phone search: You may request the cost of sending documents, but all requests must be prepaid.

In person: Simple requests may be processed while you wait.

Online search: All legislative information is available over the Internet. The Indiana Code is also available.

Voter Registration

Access to Records is Restricted.

Election Division, 302 Washington, Room E-204, Indianapolis, IN 46204-2767; 317-232-3939, Fax- 317-233-6793; 8:30AM-4:30PM.

www.IN.gov/sos/elections/

This agency will not sell records for commercial or investigative reasons, but will sell data in bulk format for political purposes for $5,000. In general, the Circuit Court has records locally. Campaign finance reports are searchable at the website, which is full of good information about elections in IN.

GED Certificates

Office of Adult Education, GED Records, 151 W Ohio St, Indianapolis, IN 46204-2798; 317-232-0522, Fax- 317-233-0859; 8AM-4:30PM.

www.doe.state.in.us/adulted/

The suggested Release Form is available online at the website. This agency also releases diplomas and transcripts of scores.

Indexing & Storage: Records available from 1974 (microfiche). New records available for inquiry in six weeks.

Searching: Include in request- signed release, name, year of test, date of birth, city of test, and a phone number where you can be reached.

Access by: mail, fax.

Fee & Payment: There is no fee. Email requests are accepted, but, like all requests, a signed release is required.

Mail search: Turnaround time- 5 to 7 days. An SASE is not required.

Fax search: Records are available by fax.

Hunting & Fishing License Information

Access to Records is Restricted.

Natural Resources Department, Customer Service Center, 402 W Washington, W-160, Indianapolis, IN 46204; 317-232-4080, Fax- 317-232-8150; 8:15AM-4:45PM.

www.in.gov/dnr/fishwild/

The records are not released to the public. Attorneys may obtain records only if hunting or fishing laws have been broken. This agency and accessindiana will not do look-ups on the system and will not make lists available.

Indiana State Licensing Agencies

For details about the agency responsible for licensing/certifying/registering an item below or in the Agency Quick Finder section, match an item's number with the number of the agency in the *Licensing Agency Information* section.

Indiana Licenses Searchable Online

Acupuncturist #9 .... https://extranet.in.gov/WebLookup/Search.aspx
Alcohol Bev. Dist./Retail'r/Employee #1 . www.in.gov/ai/appfiles/atc-license-lookup/
Alcoholic Beverage Dealer/Mfg #1 .... www.in.gov/ai/appfiles/atc-license-lookup/
Appraiser, Residential/General #18....... https://extranet.in.gov/WebLookup/Search.aspx
Appraiser, Trainee/Temp #18 .... https://extranet.in.gov/WebLookup/Search.aspx
Architect #18 .... https://extranet.in.gov/WebLookup/Search.aspx
Athletic Trainer #9 .... https://extranet.in.gov/WebLookup/Search.aspx
Attorney #15 .... http://hats.courts.state.in.us/rollatty/roa1_inp.jsp
Auctioneer #18 .... https://extranet.in.gov/WebLookup/Search.aspx
Audiologist #9 .... https://extranet.in.gov/WebLookup/Search.aspx
Bank & Trust Company #6 .... http://extranet.dfi.in.gov/dfidb/deplist.aspx
Barber/Barber Instructor #18 .... https://extranet.in.gov/WebLookup/Search.aspx
Boxer #18 .... https://extranet.in.gov/WebLookup/Search.aspx
Boxing Occupation #18 .... https://extranet.in.gov/WebLookup/Search.aspx
Check Casher #6 .... http://extranet.dfi.in.gov/dfidb/nondeplist.aspx
Child Care Ctr/Home/Provider #10 .... https://secure.in.gov/apps/fssa/carefinder/index.html
Chiropractor #9 .... https://extranet.in.gov/WebLookup/Search.aspx
Clinical Nurse Specialist #9 .... https://extranet.in.gov/WebLookup/Search.aspx
Collection Agency #19 .... www.in.gov/apps/sos/securities/sos_securities
Cosmetologist #18 .... https://extranet.in.gov/WebLookup/Search.aspx
CPA-Public Accountant #18 .... https://extranet.in.gov/WebLookup/Search.aspx
Credit Union #6 .... http://extranet.dfi.in.gov/dfidb/deplist.aspx
Dental Anesthetist/Dental Hygienist #9 . https://extranet.in.gov/WebLookup/Search.aspx
Dentist #9 .... https://extranet.in.gov/WebLookup/Search.aspx
Dietitian #9 .... https://extranet.in.gov/WebLookup/Search.aspx
Electrologist #18 .... https://extranet.in.gov/WebLookup/Search.aspx
Embalmer #18 .... https://extranet.in.gov/WebLookup/Search.aspx
EMS Providers #11 .... www.in.gov/dhs/files/prov_name.pdf
Engineer #18 .... https://extranet.in.gov/WebLookup/Search.aspx
Engineering Intern #18 .... https://extranet.in.gov/WebLookup/Search.aspx
Environmental Health Specialist #9 .... https://extranet.in.gov/WebLookup/Search.aspx
Esthetician #18 .... https://extranet.in.gov/WebLookup/Search.aspx
Funeral/Cemetery Director #18 .... https://extranet.in.gov/WebLookup/Search.aspx
Hazardous Waste Facility/Handler #5 ... https://extranet.in.gov/mylicense/
Health Services Administrator #9 .... https://extranet.in.gov/WebLookup/Search.aspx
Hearing Aid Dealer #9 .... https://extranet.in.gov/WebLookup/Search.aspx
Hypnotist #9 .... https://extranet.in.gov/WebLookup/Search.aspx
Industrial Authority, State #6 .... http://extranet.dfi.in.gov/dfidb/deplist.aspx
Insurance Agent/Consultant #7 .... https://www.sircon.com/ComplianceExpress/Inquiry/consumerInquiry.do?nonSscrb=Y
Investment Advisor #19 .... www.in.gov/apps/sos/securities/sos_securities
Landscape Architect #18 .... https://extranet.in.gov/WebLookup/Search.aspx
Lender, Small #6 .... http://extranet.dfi.in.gov/dfidb/nondeplist.aspx
Loan Broker #19 .... www.in.gov/apps/sos/securities/sos_securities
Lobbyist, Executive Branch #22 .... https://secure.in.gov/apps/idoa/regfile/search.aspx
Lobbyist, Legislative #23 .... www.in.gov/ilrc/data/index.html
Lottery Retailer #16 .... www.in.gov/hoosierlottery/games/retailerlocator.asp
Manicurist #18 .... https://extranet.in.gov/WebLookup/Search.aspx
Marriage & Family Therapist #9 .... https://extranet.in.gov/WebLookup/Search.aspx
Medical Doctor #9 .... https://extranet.in.gov/WebLookup/Search.aspx
Medical Residency Permit #9 .... https://extranet.in.gov/WebLookup/Search.aspx
Mental Health Counselor #9 .... https://extranet.in.gov/WebLookup/Search.aspx
Midwife Nurse #9 .... https://extranet.in.gov/WebLookup/Search.aspx
Money Transmitter #6 .... http://extranet.dfi.in.gov/dfidb/nondeplist.aspx
Notary Public #17 .... www.in.gov/apps/sos/notary/sos_notary
Nurse Midwife #9 .... https://extranet.in.gov/WebLookup/Search.aspx
Nurse-RN/LPN #9 .... https://extranet.in.gov/WebLookup/Search.aspx
Nursing Home Administrator #9 .... https://extranet.in.gov/WebLookup/Search.aspx

Occupational Therapist #9	https://extranet.in.gov/WebLookup/Search.aspx
Occupational Therapy Assistant #9	https://extranet.in.gov/WebLookup/Search.aspx
Optometrist #9	https://extranet.in.gov/WebLookup/Search.aspx
Optometrist Drug Certification #9	https://extranet.in.gov/WebLookup/Search.aspx
Osteopathic Physician #9	https://extranet.in.gov/WebLookup/Search.aspx
Pawnbroker #6	http://extranet.dfi.in.gov/dfidb/nondeplist.aspx
Pesticide Ap/Technician/Consultant #3	www.isco.purdue.edu/pesticide/index_pest1.html
Pharmacist/Intern/Technician #9	https://extranet.in.gov/WebLookup/Search.aspx
Physical Therapist/Therapist Asst #9	https://extranet.in.gov/WebLookup/Search.aspx
Physician #9	https://extranet.in.gov/WebLookup/Search.aspx
Physician Assistant #9	https://extranet.in.gov/WebLookup/Search.aspx
PI Company Employee #18	https://extranet.in.gov/WebLookup/Search.aspx
Placement Officer, School #14	http://mustang.doe.state.in.us/TEACH/teach_inq.cfm
Plumber #18	https://extranet.in.gov/WebLookup/Search.aspx
Plumbing Contractor #18	https://extranet.in.gov/WebLookup/Search.aspx
Podiatrist #9	https://extranet.in.gov/WebLookup/Search.aspx
Polygraph Examiner #21	www.indianapolygraphassociation.com/members.asp
Private Detective #18	https://extranet.in.gov/WebLookup/Search.aspx
Psychologist #9	https://extranet.in.gov/WebLookup/Search.aspx
Public Accountant #18	https://extranet.in.gov/WebLookup/Search.aspx
Real Estate Agent/Broker/Seller #18	https://extranet.in.gov/WebLookup/Search.aspx
Real Estate Appraiser #18	https://extranet.in.gov/WebLookup/Search.aspx
Rental Purchase Lender #6	http://extranet.dfi.in.gov/dfidb/nondeplist.aspx
Respiratory Care Practitioner #9	https://extranet.in.gov/WebLookup/Search.aspx
Savings & Loan #6	http://extranet.dfi.in.gov/dfidb/deplist.aspx
School Administr'r/Principal/Dir'ct'r #14	http://mustang.doe.state.in.us/TEACH/teach_inq.cfm
School Counselor #14	http://mustang.doe.state.in.us/TEACH/teach_inq.cfm
School Nurse #14	http://mustang.doe.state.in.us/TEACH/teach_inq.cfm
Securities Broker/Dealer #19	www.in.gov/apps/sos/securities/sos_securities
Shampoo Operator #18	https://extranet.in.gov/WebLookup/Search.aspx
Social Worker #9	https://extranet.in.gov/WebLookup/Search.aspx
Solid Waste Facility #5	https://extranet.in.gov/mylicense/
Speech Pathologist #9	https://extranet.in.gov/WebLookup/Search.aspx
Surveyor, Land #18	https://extranet.in.gov/WebLookup/Search.aspx
Teacher #14	http://mustang.doe.state.in.us/TEACH/teach_inq.cfm
Trust Company #6	http://extranet.dfi.in.gov/dfidb/deplist.aspx
Veterinarian #9	https://extranet.in.gov/WebLookup/Search.aspx
Veterinary Tech #9	https://extranet.in.gov/WebLookup/Search.aspx
Waste Tire Processor/Transporter #5	https://extranet.in.gov/mylicense/
Waste Water Treatm't Plant Operat'r #5	https://extranet.in.gov/mylicense/
Yard Waste Composting Facility #5	https://extranet.in.gov/mylicense/

Indiana Licensing Quick Finder

Acupuncturist #9	888-333-7515
Alcoholic Bev. Dist./Retail'r/Employee #1	317-232-2430
Alcoholic Beverage Dealer/Mfg #1	317-232-2430
Animal (Dead) Renderer #2	317-227-0300
Appraiser, Residential/General #18	888-333-7515
Appraiser, Trainee/Temp #18	888-333-7515
Architect #18	888-333-7515
Asbestos Contractor #4	317-232-4861
Asbestos Disposal Mgr/Worker #4	317-232-8232
Asbestos Inspec./Supvr./Designer #4	317-232-8232
Asbestos Mgmt Planner #4	317-232-8232
Asbestos Training Provider #4	317-232-8219
Athletic Trainer #9	888-333-7515
Attorney #15	317-232-5861
Auctioneer #18	888-333-7515
Audiologist #9	888-333-7515
Bail Bondsman/Agent #7	317-232-5249
Bank & Trust Company #6	317-232-5846
Barber/Barber Instructor #18	888-333-7515
Boiler & Pressure Vessel Inspec #8	317-232-1921
Boxer #18	888-333-7515
Boxing Occupation #18	888-333-7515
Brand, Livestock #2	317-227-0300
Check Casher #6	317-232-3955
Child Care Center #10	317-232-4469
Child Care Home/Provider #10	317-232-4521
Chiropractor #9	888-333-7515
Clinical Nurse Specialist #9	888-333-7515
Collection Agency #19	317-232-6681
Consumer Credit Grantor #6	317-232-5849
Cosmetologist #18	888-333-7515
CPA-Public Accountant #18	888-333-7515
Credit Union #6	317-232-5851
Dairy-related Occupation #2	317-227-0300
Dental Anesthetist #9	888-333-7515
Dental Hygienist #9	888-333-7515
Dentist #9	888-333-7515
Dietitian #9	888-333-7515
Electrologist #18	888-333-7515
Elevator Safety Contractor #8	317-232-2670
Embalmer #18	888-333-7515
Emergency Medical Technician #11	317-233-0208
EMS Providers #11	317-233-0208
Engineer #18	888-333-7515
Engineering Intern #18	888-333-7515
Environmental Health Specialist #9	888-333-7515
Esthetician #18	888-333-7515
Funeral/Cemetery Director #18	888-333-7515
Grain Bank/Warehouse #12	317-232-1358
Grain Buyer #12	317-232-1358
Hazardous Waste Facility/Handler #5	317-232-8603
Health Services Administrator #9	888-333-7515
Hearing Aid Dealer #9	888-333-7515
Horse Racing Occupation #13	317-233-3119
Hypnotist #9	888-333-7515
Industrial Authority, State #6	317-232-5851
Insurance Adjuster #7	317-232-2414
Insurance Agent/Consultant #7	317-232-2414
Investment Advisor #19	317-232-0111
Landscape Architect #18	888-333-7515
Lead Contractor #4	317-232-4861
Lead Inspector #4	317-233-6514
Lead Project Designer #4	317-233-6514
Lead Project Supervisor #4	317-233-6514
Lead Risk Assessor #4	317-233-6514
Lead Training Course Provider #4	317-232-8219
Lead Worker #4	317-233-6514
Lender, Small #6	317-232-3955
Livestock Dealer/market #2	317-227-0300
Livestock Transportation #2	317-227-0300
Loan Broker #19	317-232-6681
Lobbyist, Executive Branch #22	317-234-4431
Lobbyist, Legislative #23	317-232-9860
Lottery Retailer #16	317-264-4800
Manicurist #18	888-333-7515

Manufactured Home Builder #8............317-232-1408
Marriage & Family Therapist #9..........888-333-7515
Meat & Poultry #2..............................317-227-0300
Medical Doctor #9..............................888-333-7515
Medical Residency Permit #9.............888-333-7515
Mental Health Counselor #9...............888-333-7515
Midwife Nurse #9...............................888-333-7515
Money Transmitter #6.........................317-232-3955
Notary Public #17...............................317-232-6542
Nurse Midwife #9................................888-333-7515
Nurse-RN/LPN #9...............................888-333-7515
Nursing Home Administrator #9..........888-333-7515
Occupational Therapist #9..................888-333-7515
Occupational Therapy Assistant #9......888-333-7515
Optometrist #9....................................888-333-7515
Optometrist Drug Certification #9........888-333-7515
Osteopathic Physician #9....................888-333-7515
Pawnbroker #6.....................................317-232-3955
Pesticide Applicator #3.......................765-494-1594
Pesticide Technician/Consultant #3.....765-494-1594
Pharmacist/Pharmacist Intern #9........888-333-7515
Pharmacy Technician #9......................888-333-7515
Physical Therapist/Therapist Asst #9...888-333-7515
Physician #9..888-333-7515
Physician Assistant #9........................888-333-7515
PI Company Employee #18..................888-333-7515
Placement Officer, School #14............317-232-9010
Plumber #18...888-333-7515
Plumbing Contractor #18......................888-333-7515
Podiatrist #9...888-333-7515
Polygraph Examiner #21......................317-232-8263
Private Detective #18..........................888-333-7515
Psychologist #9...................................888-333-7515
Public Accountant #18..........................888-333-7515
Radiologic Technologist #20...............317-233-7565
Real Estate Agent/Broker/Seller #18...888-333-7515
Real Estate Appraiser #18..................888-333-7515
Recovery Agent #7..............................317-232-5249
Rental Purchase Lender #6.................317-232-3955
Respiratory Care Practitioner #9.........888-333-7515
Savings & Loan #6...............................317-232-5851
School Administr'r/Principal/Director #14317-232-9010
School Counselor #14..........................317-232-9010
School Nurse #14.................................317-232-9010
Securities Broker/Dealer #19...............317-232-0093
Securities Sales Agent #19..................317-232-0093
Shampoo Operator #18.........................888-333-7515
Social Worker #9..................................888-333-7515
Solid Waste Facility #5.........................317-232-8603
Speech Pathologist #9.........................888-333-7515
Surveyor, Land #18..............................888-333-7515
Teacher #14..317-232-9010
Trust Company #6.................................317-232-5851
Underground Storage Tank #8.............317-233-3560
Veterinarian #9.....................................888-333-7515
Veterinary Tech #9................................888-333-7515
Warehouse, Agricultural, etc. #12........317-232-1358
Waste Tire Processor/Transporter #5..317-232-8603
Waste Water Treatm't Plant Oper'r #5.317-232-8666
Yard Waste Composting Facility #5.....317-232-8603

Indiana Licensing Agency Information

#1 Alcohol and Tobacco Commission, 302 W Washington St, Rm E114, Indianapolis, IN 46204; 317-232-2430, Fax- 317-234-1520. www.in.gov/atc/ Search data at- www.in.gov/ai/appfiles/atc-license-lookup/

#2 Licensing & Compliance, Board of Animal Health, 805 Beachway Dr, #50, Indianapolis, IN 46224; 317-227-0300, Fax- 317-227-0330. www.state.in.us/boah/

#3 Dept. of Biochemistry, Office of Indiana State Chemist, 175 S University St, Purdue University, West Lafayette, IN 47907-2063; 765-494-1492, Fax- 765-494-4331. 8AM-5PM. www.isco.purdue.edu Search at- www.isco.purdue.edu/pesticide/index_pest1.html

#4 Department of Environmental Management, Asbestos/Lead Program, 100 N Senate Ave, Indianapolis, IN 46204-6015; 317-232-8232, Fax- 317-232-3257. www.IN.gov/idem/

#5 Dept of Environmental Mgmt, Office of Land Quality, 100 N Senate Ave, Indianapolis, IN 46204-2251; 317-232-8603, Fax- 317-232-6647. www.in.gov/idem/5221.htm Search data at- https://extranet.in.gov/mylicense/

#6 Department of Financial Institutions, 30 S Meridian St, #300, Indianapolis, IN 46204-2759; 317-232-3955, Fax- 317-232-7655. www.in.gov/dfi/

#7 Department of Insurance, 311 W Washington St, Indianapolis, IN 46204-2787; 317-232-2411, Fax- 317-232-5251. www.in.gov/idoi/

#8 Fire & Building Services, Indiana Department of Homeland Security, 402 W Washington St, Rm E241, Indianapolis, IN 46204; 317-232-2222, Fax- 317-232-0146. www.in.gov/dhs/2394.htm

#9 Professional Licensing Agency, 402 W Washington St, Rm W072, Indianapolis, IN 46204-2758; 317-232-2960, Fax- 317-233-4236. Hours- 8AM-4:30PM. www.in.gov/pla/ Search data at- https://extranet.in.gov/WebLookup/Search.aspx To search online, subscribe to AIIN.

#10 Family and Social Services Administration, Bureau of Child Development, 402 W Washington St, Rm W386, Indianapolis, IN 46201; 317-232-1144 or 877-511-1144, Fax- 317-234-1513. Hours- 8AM-4:30PM. www.in.gov/fssa/2552.htm Search data at- https://secure.in.gov/apps/fssa/carefinder/index.html

#11 Homeland Security, EMS Certification, 302 W Washington St, #E239, Indianapolis, IN 46204; 317-233-0208, Fax- 317-233-8394. www.in.gov/dhs/2341.htm

#12 Grain Buyers & Warehouse Licensing Agency, 101 W Ohio St, #1200, Indianapolis, IN 46204-2810; 317-232-1356, Fax- 317-232-1362. www.in.gov/isda/2405.htm Confidentiality Clause in governing statute prevents giving listing of licensees.

#13 Horse Racing Licensing, 150 W Market St, ISTA Center, #530, Indianapolis, IN 46204; 317-233-3119, Fax- 317-233-4470. www.in.gov/hrc/

#14 Professional Standards Board, 101 W Ohio St, #300, Indianapolis, IN 46204; 317-232-9010, 1-866-542-3672, Fax- 317-232-9023. Hours- 8AM-4:30PM. www.doe.state.in.us/dps/ Search data at- http://mustang.doe.state.in.us/TEACH/teach_inq.cfm

#15 Clerk of the Indiana Supreme Court, Roll of Attorneys, 200 W Washington St, 217 State House, Indianapolis, IN 46204; 317-232-1930, Fax- 317-232-8365. www.IN.gov/judiciary/ Search data at- http://hats.courts.state.in.us/rollatty/roa1_inp.jsp

#16 Lottery Commission of Indiana, 201 S Capitol Ave, #1100, Indianapolis, IN 46225; 317-264-4800, Fax- 317-264-4908. 8AM-5PM. www.in.gov/hoosierlottery/index1024.asp

#17 Business Services Division - Notary, Office of Secretary of State, Statehouse, #201, Indianapolis, IN 46204; 317-232-6542, Fax- 317-233-3283. www.in.gov/sos/business/notary/ Search data at- www.in.gov/apps/sos/notary/sos_notary

#18 Professional Licensing Agency, Boards & Commissions, 402 W Washington St, Rm W072, Indianapolis, IN 46204; 317-232-2980, Fax- 317-232-2312. www.in.gov/pla/boards.htm Search data at- https://extranet.in.gov/WebLookup/Search.aspx

#19 Secretary of State, Securities Division, 302 W Washington, Rm E-111, Indianapolis, IN 46204; 317-232-6681, Fax- 317-233-3675. Hours- 8AM-5:30PM. www.in.gov/sos/securities/ Search data at- www.in.gov/apps/sos/securities/sos_securities

#20 Division of Indoor & Radiologic Health, Board of Health, 2 N Meridian St, 5F, Indianapolis, IN 46204-3010; 317-233-7150, Fax- 317-233-7154.

#21 Polygraph Certification Indiana State Police, Indiana Government Ctr, 100 N Senate Ave, Gov't Center North, #312, Indianapolis, IN 46204-2259; 317-232-8263. www.indianapolygraphassociation.com Search data at- www.indianapolygraphassociation.com/members.asp The online member list is provided by the IN Polygraph Association, not the state police agency given here.

#22 Executive Branch Lobbying, Department of Administration, 402 W Washington St., Rm 479, Indianapolis, IN 46204; 317-234-4431. www.in.gov/idoa/2885.htm Search data at- https://secure.in.gov/apps/idoa/regfile/search.aspx Do not confuse with Legislative Branch Lobbyists who are in separate listing.

#23 Lobby Registration Commission, 10 W Market St, #1760, Indianapolis, IN 46204; 317-232-9860, Fax- 317-233-0077. www.in.gov/ilrc/ilrc/index.html Search data at- www.in.gov/ilrc/data/index.html Do not confuse with Executive Branch Lobbyists who are in separate listing.

Indiana Federal Courts

The following list indicates the district and division name for each county in the state. If the bankruptcy court location is different from the district court, then the location of the bankruptcy court appears in parentheses.

County/Court Cross Reference

County	District	Division
Adams	Northern	Fort Wayne
Allen	Northern	Fort Wayne
Bartholomew	Southern	Indianapolis
Benton	Northern	Lafayette (Hammond at Lafayette)
Blackford	Northern	Fort Wayne
Boone	Southern	Indianapolis
Brown	Southern	Indianapolis
Carroll	Northern	Lafayette (Hammond at Lafayette)
Cass	Northern	South Bend
Clark	Southern	New Albany
Clay	Southern	Terre Haute
Clinton	Southern	Indianapolis
Crawford	Southern	New Albany
Daviess	Southern	Evansville
DeKalb	Northern	Fort Wayne
Dearborn	Southern	New Albany
Decatur	Southern	Indianapolis
Delaware	Southern	Indianapolis
Dubois	Southern	Evansville
Elkhart	Northern	South Bend
Fayette	Southern	Indianapolis
Floyd	Southern	New Albany
Fountain	Southern	Indianapolis
Franklin	Southern	Indianapolis
Fulton	Northern	South Bend
Gibson	Southern	Evansville
Grant	Northern	Fort Wayne
Greene	Southern	Terre Haute
Hamilton	Southern	Indianapolis
Hancock	Southern	Indianapolis
Harrison	Southern	New Albany
Hendricks	Southern	Indianapolis
Henry	Southern	Indianapolis
Howard	Southern	Indianapolis
Huntington	Northern	Fort Wayne
Jackson	Southern	New Albany
Jasper	Northern	Lafayette (Hammond at Lafayette)
Jay	Northern	Fort Wayne
Jefferson	Southern	New Albany
Jennings	Southern	New Albany
Johnson	Southern	Indianapolis
Knox	Southern	Terre Haute
Kosciusko	Northern	South Bend
La Porte	Northern	South Bend
LaGrange	Northern	Fort Wayne
Lake	Northern	Hammond (Hammond. at Gary)
Lawrence	Southern	New Albany
Madison	Southern	Indianapolis
Marion	Southern	Indianapolis
Marshall	Northern	South Bend
Martin	Southern	Evansville
Miami	Northern	South Bend
Monroe	Southern	Indianapolis
Montgomery	Southern	Indianapolis
Morgan	Southern	Indianapolis
Newton	Northern	Lafayette (Hammond at Lafayette)
Noble	Northern	Fort Wayne
Ohio	Southern	New Albany
Orange	Southern	New Albany
Owen	Southern	Terre Haute
Parke	Southern	Terre Haute
Perry	Southern	Evansville
Pike	Southern	Evansville
Porter	Northern	Hammond (Hammond. at Gary)
Posey	Southern	Evansville
Pulaski	Northern	South Bend
Putnam	Southern	Terre Haute
Randolph	Southern	Indianapolis
Ripley	Southern	New Albany
Rush	Southern	Indianapolis
Scott	Southern	New Albany
Shelby	Southern	Indianapolis
Spencer	Southern	Evansville
St. Joseph	Northern	South Bend
Starke	Northern	South Bend
Steuben	Northern	Fort Wayne
Sullivan	Southern	Terre Haute
Switzerland	Southern	New Albany
Tippecanoe	Northern	Lafayette (Hammond at Lafayette)
Tipton	Southern	Indianapolis
Union	Southern	Indianapolis
Vanderburgh	Southern	Evansville
Vermillion	Southern	Terre Haute
Vigo	Southern	Terre Haute
Wabash	Northern	South Bend
Warren	Northern	Lafayette (Hammond at Lafayette)
Warrick	Southern	Evansville
Washington	Southern	New Albany
Wayne	Southern	Indianapolis
Wells	Northern	Fort Wayne
White	Northern	Lafayette (Hammond at Lafayette)
Whitley	Northern	Fort Wayne

Standards for Federal Courts: Fees are standard unless noted in profile. Search fee is $26.00 per item (one party name or case number). Copy fee is $.50 per page. Certification fee is $9.00 per document, double for exemplification, if available. Most courts require prepayment. Mail requests should enclose a SASE unless otherwise noted. Before releasing records, all courts require prepayment, unless noted.

District courts index by defendant and plaintiff and by case number. Bankruptcy courts usually index by debtor and case number. While most courts now have their indexes on computer, many may still maintain index card files as well. Courts will archive closed case files at different times.

There are numerous public access programs available to online subscribers. Search the U.S. Party/Case Index to find party names and case numbers among all courts. Individual case data is provided on PACER. A search of CM/ECF provides copies of cases filed electronically. For details about PACER, the US Party/Case Index, and CM/ECF see the Appendix or go to http://pacer.psc.uscourts.gov or call 800-676-6856.

US District Court Indiana Northern District

Fort Wayne Division Court Clerk, Rm 1108, Federal Bldg, 1300 S Harrison St, Fort Wayne, IN 46802, 260-423-3000. Hours- 9AM-4PM. www.innd.uscourts.gov/fortwayne.shtml

Counties/Note: Adams, Allen, Blackford, DeKalb, Grant, Huntington, Jay, Lagrange, Noble, Steuben, Wells, Whitley.

Searches/Indexing: Include full name, SSN, or DOB in search request. Results do not include SSN or DOB. Will not fax back documents. New cases are in the index 1-5 days after filing date. Both computer and card indexes maintained; computer index goes back to 1991. Only the court may search the card index.

Search Access: Only case names and numbers is released via phone. **Mail:** Search usually completed- 3 days. Include SASE for return. **In person:** 1 public terminal available. No self-serve copier.

Payment: Pay by money order, cashier's or attorneys' check. No credit cards or personal checks accepted. Payee: Clerk, US District Court.

E-Services: PACER records go back to 1994. New records online immediately. ECF at https://ecf.innd.uscourts.gov. Opinions, calendars and case records are on the PACER ECF system.

Hammond Div. Court Clerk, 5400 Federal Plaza, Hammond, IN 46320, 219-852-6500. 9AM-4PM. www.innd.uscourts.gov/hammond.shtml

Counties/Note: Lake, Porter. Hammond Division is in Central Time Zone, same as Chicago.

Searches/Indexing: Include full name, SSN, or DOB in search request. Results do not include SSN or DOB. Will not fax back documents. New cases are in the index 1-2 days after filing date. Computer index back to 1992 maintained.

Search Access: Only docket info is available by phone. **Mail:** Search usually completed- 1 week. Include SASE for return. **In person:** 1 public terminal available. No self-serve copier.

Payment: Pay by money order, cashier's or attorney check. No credit cards or personal checks accepted. Payee: Clerk, US District Court.

E-Services: PACER records go back to 1994. New records online immediately. ECF at https://ecf.innd.uscourts.gov. Opinions, calendars and case records are on the PACER ECF system.

Lafayette Div. Court Clerk, 230 N 4th St, Lafayette, IN 47901, 765-420-6250; Fax- 765-420-6273. Hours- 9AM-N, 1-4PM. www.innd.uscourts.gov/lafayette.shtml

Counties/Note: Benton, Carroll, Jasper, Newton, Tippecanoe, Warren, White.

Newton and Jasper counties are on Central Daylight Savings Time. The rest of the Lafayette Division is on Eastern Daylight Savings Time.

Searches/Indexing: Include full name, SSN, or DOB in search request. Results do not include SSN or DOB. Will not fax back documents. New cases are in the index 24 hours after filing date. Computer index maintained; microfiche index available. Closed case files sent to archives at end of the year. Computerized case files sent to archives every 2-4 years.

Search Access: Only docket info is available by phone. **Mail:** Search usually completed- 3 days. Include SASE for return. **Fax:** Will accept fax requests for defendant or plaintiff names. **In person:** 1 public terminal available. No self-serve copier.

Payment: Pay by money order, cashier's or attorney check. No credit cards or personal checks accepted. Payee: Clerk, US District Court.

E-Services: PACER records go back to 1994. New records online immediately. ECF at https://ecf.innd.uscourts.gov. Opinions, calendars and case records are on the PACER ECF system.

South Bend Division Court Clerk, 204 S Main, Rm 102, South Bend, IN 46601, 574-246-8000; Fax- 574-246-8002. Hours-9AM-4PM. www.innd.uscourts.gov/southbend.shtml

Counties/Note: Cass, Elkhart, Fulton, Kosciusko, La Porte, Marshall, Miami, Pulaski, St. Joseph, Starke, Wabash. The South Bend Division is in Eastern Time Zone.

Searches/Indexing: Include full name, SSN, or DOB in search request. Results do not include SSN or DOB. Will not fax back documents. New cases are in the index 2 days after filing date.

Search Access: Only docket info is available by phone. **Mail:** Search usually completed- 3 days. Include SASE for return. **In person:** 1 public terminal available. No self-serve copier.

Payment: Pay by money order, cashier's or attorneys' check. No credit cards or personal checks accepted. Payee: Clerk, US District Court.

E-Services: PACER records go back to 1994. New records online immediately. ECF at https://ecf.innd.uscourts.gov. Opinions, calendars and case records are on the PACER ECF system.

US Bankruptcy Court Indiana Northern District

Fort Wayne Division Clerk of Court, 1188 Federal Bldg, 1300 S Harrison St, Fort Wayne, IN 46802-3435, 260-420-5100; Hours- 9AM-4PM. www.innb.uscourts.gov

Counties/Note: Adams, Allen, Blackford, DeKalb, Grant, Huntington, Jay, Lagrange, Noble, Steuben, Wells, Whitley.

Searches/Indexing: Search request requires name only. Results include last 4 SSN digits. Will not fax back documents. New cases are in the index 48 hours after filing. Computer index maintained. A card index used for cases prior to 1992. Paper files sent to archives 2 years after closed.

Search Access: Only docket info is available by phone. Voice Case Information Service available, call VCIS at 800-755-8393 or 574-968-2275. **Mail:** Include SASE for return. **In person:** 2 public terminals available. No self-serve copier.

Payment: Pay by Visa/MC, money order, cashier's or personal check. No debtor checks, business checks, or credit cards accepted. Payee: Clerk, US Bankruptcy Court.

E-Services: ECF and PACER records go back to 1992. New records online immediately. ECF at https://ecf.innb.uscourts.gov. **Opinions Online:** www.innb.uscourts.gov/opinions/. **Note:** Judges calendars at www.innb.uscourts.gov/courtcal.htm. Calendars also available on ECF system.

Hammond Division Clerk of Court, 5400 Federal Plaza, Hammond, IN 46320, 219-852-3480; Hours-9AM-4PM. www.innb.uscourts.gov

Counties/Note: Lake, Porter. Court located at corner of Hohman Ave and Douglas St, across from St. Margaret's Hospital.

Searches/Indexing: Search request requires name only. Results include last 4 SSN digits. Will not fax back documents. New cases are in the index 48 hours after filing. Computer index maintained. A card index used for cases prior to 1992. Paper files sent to archives 2 years after closed.

Search Access: Only docket info is available by phone. Voice Case Information Service available, call VCIS at 800-755-8393 or 574-968-2275. **Mail:** Include SASE for return. **In person:** 3 public terminals available. No self-serve copier.

Payment: Pay by Visa/MC, money order, cashier's or personal check. No debtor checks/credit cards or business checks accepted. Payee: Clerk, US Bankruptcy Court.

E-Services: ECF and PACER records go back to 1992. New records online immediately. ECF at https://ecf.innb.uscourts.gov. **Opinions Online:** www.innb.uscourts.gov/opinions/. **Note:** Judges calendars at www.innb.uscourts.gov/courtcal.htm. Calendars also available on ECF system.

Hammond at Lafayette Division Clerk of Court, PO Box 558, Lafayette, IN 47902-0558 (In person: Charles A. Halleck Federal Building, 230 N 4th St, Lafayette), 765-420-6300. Hours- 9AM-4PM. www.innb.uscourts.gov

Counties/Note: Benton, Carroll, Jasper, Newton, Tippecanoe, Warren, White.

Searches/Indexing: Search request requires name only. Results include last 4 SSN digits. Will not fax back documents. New cases are in the index 48 hours after filing date. Computer index maintained. A card index used for cases prior to

1992. Open records located at Ft. Wayne Division. Paper files sent to archives 2 years after closed.

Search Access: Voice Case Information Service available, call VCIS at 800-755-8393 or 574-968-2275. **Mail:** Include SASE for return. **In person:** 2 public terminals available. No self-serve copier.

Payment: Pay by Visa/MC, money order, cashier's or personal check. No debtor checks, business checks, or credit cards accepted. Payee: Clerk, US Bankruptcy Court.

E-Services: ECF and PACER records go back to 1992. New records online immediately. ECF at https://ecf.innb.uscourts.gov. **Opinions Online:** www.innb.uscourts.gov/opinions/. **Note:** Judges calendars at www.innb.uscourts.gov/courtcal.htm. Calendars also available on ECF system.

South Bend Division Clerk of Court, 401 S Michigan St, South Bend, IN 46601, 574-968-2100; Hours-9AM-4PM. www.innb.uscourts.gov

Counties/Note: Cass, Elkhart, Fulton, Kosciusko, La Porte, Marshall, Miami, Pulaski, St. Joseph, Starke, Wabash.

Searches/Indexing: Search request requires name only. Results include last 4 SSN digits. Will not fax back documents. New cases are in the index 48 hours after filing. Computer index maintained. A card index used for cases prior to 1992. Paper files sent to archives 2 years after closed.

Search Access: Only docket info is available by phone. Voice Case Information Service available, call VCIS at 800-755-8393 or 574-968-2275. **Mail:** Include SASE for return. **In person:** 2 public terminals available. No self-serve copier.

Payment: Pay by Visa/MC, money order, cashier's or personal check. No debtor checks/credit cards or business checks accepted. Payee: Clerk, US Bankruptcy Court.

E-Services: ECF and PACER records go back to 1992. New records online immediately. ECF at https://ecf.innb.uscourts.gov. **Opinions Online:** www.innb.uscourts.gov/opinions/. **Note:** Judges calendars at www.innb.uscourts.gov/courtcal.htm. Calendars also available on ECF system.

US District Court
Indiana Southern District

Evansville Div. Court Clerk, 304 Federal Bldg, 101 NW Martin Luther King Blvd, Evansville, IN 47708, 812-434-6410; Fax-812-434-6418. 8:30AM-5PM. www.insd.uscourts.gov

Counties: Daviess, Dubois, Gibson, Martin, Perry, Pike, Posey, Spencer, Vanderburgh, Warrick.

Searches/Indexing: Include SSN, address, gender in search request along with name. Results include last 4 SSN digits. Will not fax back documents. New cases are in the index immediately after filing. Cases prior to 1992 indexed by name only on index cards.

Search Access: Only docket info released by phone. **Mail:** Search usually completed- 1-2 days. SASE not required. **In person:** 1 public terminal available. No self-serve copier.

Payment: Pay by money order, cashier's or personal check. No credit cards accepted. Payee: Clerk, US District Court.

E-Services: New records online immediately. ECF at https://ecf.insd.uscourts.gov. At www.insd.uscourts.gov, click on Case Information then Search all Court Opinions. Search recent opinions at www.insd.uscourts.gov/News/recent_opinions.htm **Online Note:** Search case records free at www.insd.uscourts.gov/Search/case_search.htm; Crim cases before 2008 but civil 1991-2002 only.

Indianapolis Div. Court Clerk, Federal Bldg and US Courthouse, 46 E Ohio St, Rm 105, Indianapolis, IN 46204, 317-229-3700; Fax-317-229-3959. 8:30AM-5PM. www.insd.uscourts.gov

Counties/Note: Bartholomew, Boone, Brown, Clinton, Decatur, Delaware, Fayette, Fountain, Franklin, Hamilton, Hancock, Hendricks, Henry, Howard, Johnson, Madison, Marion, Monroe, Montgomery, Morgan, Randolph, Rush, Shelby, Tipton, Union, Wayne.

Searches/Indexing: Include SSN, address, gender in search request along with name. Results include last 4 SSN digits. Will not fax back documents. New cases are in the index immediately after filing date. District-wide searches available here.

Search Access: Only info on docket sheet face released via phone. **Mail:** Search usually completed- 1-2 days. SASE not required. **In person:** Public access terminal goes back to 7/2002. No self-serve copier.

Payment: Pay by Visa/MC, money order, cashier's, or business checks. No personal checks. Payee: Clerk, US District Court.

E-Services: New records online immediately. ECF at https://ecf.insd.uscourts.gov. At www.insd.uscourts.gov, click on Case Information then Search all Court Opinions. Search recent opinions at www.insd.uscourts.gov/News/recent_opinions.htm **Online Note:** Search case records free at www.insd.uscourts.gov/Search/case_search.htm; Crim cases before 2008 but civil 1991-2002 only.

New Albany Division Court Clerk, 210 Federal Bldg, 121 W Spring St, New Albany, IN 47150, 812-542-4510; Fax-812-542-4515. 8:30AM-5PM. www.insd.uscourts.gov

Counties: Clark, Crawford, Dearborn, Floyd, Harrison, Jackson, Jefferson, Jennings, Lawrence, Ohio, Orange, Ripley, Scott, Switzerland, Washington.

Searches/Indexing: Include SSN, address, gender in search request along with name. Results include last 4 SSN digits. Will not fax back documents. New cases are in the index immediately after filing date. Computer index back to 7/2002 maintained. A card index also maintained. Files may also be in Indianapolis or Evansville Divisions.

Search Access: Mail: Search usually completed- 1-2 days. Include SASE for return. **In person:** No public access terminals. No self-serve copier.

Payment: Pay by money order, cashier's or personal check. No credit cards accepted. Payee: Clerk, US District Court.

E-Services: New records online immediately. ECF at https://ecf.insd.uscourts.gov. At www.insd.uscourts.gov, click on Case Information then Search all Court Opinions. Search recent opinions at www.insd.uscourts.gov/News/recent_opinions.htm **Online Note:** Search case records free at www.insd.uscourts.gov/Search/case_search.htm; Crim cases before 2008 but civil 1991-2002 only.

Terre Haute Division Court Clerk, 210 Federal Bldg, 30 N 7th St, Terre Haute, IN 47808, 812-234-9484; Fax-812-238-1831. 8:30AM-5PM. www.insd.uscourts.gov

Counties/Note: Clay, Greene, Knox, Owen, Parke, Putnam, Sullivan, Vermillion, Vigo.

Searches/Indexing: Include SSN, address, gender in search request along with name. Results include last 4 SSN digits. Will not fax back documents. New cases are in the index immediately after filing date. Computer index maintained back to 1993.

Search Access: All info not sealed is available via phone. **Mail:** Search usually completed- 1 week. Include SASE for return. **In person:** No self-serve copier.

Payment: Pay by money order, cashier's or personal check. No credit cards accepted. Payee: Clerk, US District Court.

E-Services: New records online immediately. ECF at https://ecf.insd.uscourts.gov. At www.insd.uscourts.gov, click on Case Information then Search all Court Opinions. Search recent opinions at www.insd.uscourts.gov/News/recent_opinions.htm **Online Note:** Search case records free at www.insd.uscourts.gov/Search/case_search.htm; Crim cases before 2008 but civil 1991-2002 only.

US Bankruptcy Court
Indiana Southern District

Evansville Div. Court Clerk, 352 Federal Bldg, 101 NW Martin Luther King Blvd, Evansville, IN 47708, 812-434-6470; Fax-812-434-6471. 8AM-4:30PM. www.insb.uscourts.gov

Counties: Daviess, Dubois, Gibson, Martin, Perry, Pike, Posey, Spencer, Vanderburgh, Warrick.

Searches/Indexing: Include SSN or DOB and full name so court can identify. Results include last 4 SSN digits. Will not fax back documents. New cases are in the index 1-2 days after filing date. Computer index back to 10/12/04 maintained. Records stored electronically since 1986. Paper case files sent to archives as cases are closed. Electronic cases maintained indefinitely.

Search Access: Voice Case Information Service available, call VCIS at 800-335-8003 or 317-229-3888. **Mail:** Search usually completed- 1-7 days. Include SASE for return. **Fax:** Fax search requests accepted. **In person:** Self-serve copies $.50 each.

Payment: Pay by Visa/MC, money order, cashier's or personal check. No debtor checks accepted. Payee: Clerk, US Bankruptcy Court.

E-Services: PACER at www.insb.uscourts.gov. Click on "Case Search." Registration and fees required. Document images available. The free case lookup system is no longer found. PACER records go back to 1988. New records online after 1 day. ECF at https://ecf.insb.uscourts.gov. **Opinions Online:** http://pacer.insb.uscourts.gov/public/default.asp. Includes judge calendars.

Indianapolis Division Court Clerk, PO Box 44978, Indianapolis, IN 46244 (In person: US Courthouse, Rm 116, 46 E Ohio St, Indianapolis, IN 46244), 317-229-3800; records- 317-229-3842; Fax- 317-229-3801. Hours- 8AM - 4:30PM. www.insb.uscourts.gov

Counties/Note: Bartholomew, Boone, Brown, Clinton, Decatur, Delaware, Fayette, Fountain, Franklin, Hamilton, Hancock, Hendricks, Henry, Howard, Johnson, Madison, Marion, Monroe, Montgomery, Morgan, Randolph, Rush, Shelby, Tipton, Union, Wayne.

Searches/Indexing: Include SSN and full name so that court can identify. Results include last 4 SSN digits. Will not fax back documents. New cases are in the index 48 hours after filing date. Computer index back to 10/12/04 maintained. Records stored electronically since 1986. Paper case files sent to archives as cases are closed. Electronic cases maintained indefinitely.

Search Access: Voice Case Information Service available, call VCIS at 800-335-8003 or 317-229-3888. **Mail:** Search usually completed- 1 day. Include SASE for return. **In person:** 2 public terminals. Computer generated copies- $.10 each.

Payment: Pay by Visa/MC, money order, cashier's or personal check. No debtor checks accepted. Payee: Clerk, US Bankruptcy Court (SDIN).

E-Services: PACER at www.insb.uscourts.gov. Click on "Case Search." Registration and fees required. Document images available. The free case lookup system is no longer found. PACER records go back to 1988. New records online after 1 day. ECF at https://ecf.insb.uscourts.gov. **Opinions Online:** http://pacer.insb.uscourts.gov/public/default.asp. Includes judge calendars.

New Albany Div. Court Clerk, US Courthouse, Rm 110, 121 W Spring St, New Albany, IN 47150, 812-542-4540; Fax- 812-542-4541. 8AM-4:30PM. www.insb.uscourts.gov

Counties: Clark, Crawford, Dearborn, Floyd, Harrison, Jackson, Jefferson, Jennings, Lawrence, Ohio, Orange, Ripley, Scott, Switzerland, Washington.

Searches/Indexing: Include SSN and full name so that court can identify. Results include last 4 SSN digits. Will not fax back documents. New cases are in the index 48 hours after filing date. Computer index back to 10/12/04 maintained. Records stored electronically since 1986. Paper case files sent to archives as cases are closed. Electronic cases maintained indefinitely.

Search Access: Voice Case Information Service available, call VCIS at 800-335-8003 or 317-229-3888. **Mail:** Search usually completed- 1-7 days. Include SASE for return. **In person:** No self-serve copier.

Payment: Pay by Visa/MC, money order, cashier's or personal check. No debtor checks accepted. Payee: Clerk, US Bankruptcy Court (SDIN).

E-Services: PACER at www.insb.uscourts.gov. Click on "Case Search." Registration and fees required. Document images available. The free case lookup system is no longer found. PACER records go back to 1988. New records online after 1 day. ECF at https://ecf.insb.uscourts.gov. **Opinions Online:** http://pacer.insb.uscourts.gov/public/default.asp. Includes judge calendars.

Terre Haute Div. Court Clerk, Federal Bldg Rm 207, 30 N 7th St, Terre Haute, IN 47808, 812-238-1550; Fax- 812-238-1831. Hours-8:30AM-4:30PM. www.insb.uscourts.gov

Counties/Note: Clay, Greene, Knox, Owen, Parke, Putnam, Sullivan, Vermillion, Vigo.

Searches/Indexing: Include SSN or DOB and full name so court can identify. Results include last 4 SSN digits. Will not fax back documents. New cases are in the index 48 hours after filing date. Computer index back to 10/12/04 maintained. Records stored electronically since 1986. Paper case files sent to archives as cases are closed. Electronic cases maintained indefinitely.

Search Access: Voice Case Information Service available, call VCIS at 800-335-8003 or 317-229-3888. **Mail:** Search usually completed- 1 day. Include SASE for return. **In person:** No self-serve copier.

Payment: Pay by Visa/MC, money order, cashier's or personal check. No debtor checks accepted. Payee: Clerk, US Bankruptcy Court. Search fee charged if a detailed search is required.

E-Services: PACER at www.insb.uscourts.gov. Click on "Case Search." Registration and fees required. Document images available. The free case lookup system is no longer found. PACER records go back to 1988. New records online after 1 day. ECF at https://ecf.insb.uscourts.gov. **Opinions Online:** http://pacer.insb.uscourts.gov/public/default.asp. Includes judge calendars.

Indiana County Courts

Court	Jurisdiction	No. of Courts	How Organized
Circuit Courts*	General	24	91 Circuits
Superior Courts*	General	4	
Combined Courts*		68	
County Courts*	Limited	Comb	
Combined Circuit/County*		4	
City Courts	Limited	48	
Small Claims - Marion County	Special	9	
Town Courts	Municipal	27	
Probate Court	Special	1	St. Joseph County

* Profiled in this Sourcebook.

Court	CIVIL Tort	Contract	Real Estate	Min. Claim	Max. Claim	Small Claims	Estate	Eviction	Domestic Relations
Circuit Courts*	X	X		$0	No Max	$6000	X		X
Superior Courts*	X	X	X	$0	No Max	$6000	X		X
County Courts*	X	X	X	$0	$10,000	$6000		X	X
City Courts	X	X		$0	$2500			X	X
Town Courts									X
Probate Court							X		

Court	CRIMINAL Felony	Misdemeanor	DWI/DUI	Preliminary Hearing	Juvenile
Circuit Courts*	X	X	X	X	X
Superior Courts*	X	X	X	X	X
County Courts*	X	X	X	X	
City Courts		X	X	X	
Town Courts		X	X	X	
Probate Court					X

Administration

State Court Administrator, 30 South Meridian Street, Suite 500, Indianapolis, IN, 46204; 317-232-2542, Fax 317-233-6586. www.in.gov/judiciary

Court Structure

Indiana has 92 counties, and 90 of these counties comprise their own circuit, with their own Circuit Court. The remaining two small counties (Ohio and Dearborn counties) have combined to form one circuit. Trial courts include Circuit Courts, Superior Courts, and local City or Town Courts. Circuit Courts have unlimited trial jurisdiction in all cases, except when exclusive or concurrent jurisdiction is conferred upon other courts. In counties without Superior Courts, the Circuit Courts in addition to all other cases, also handle small claims cases for civil disputes involving less than $6,000 and minor offenses, such as misdemeanors, ordinance violations, and Class D felonies. County Courts are a thing of the past and have been restructured into divisions of the Superior Courts. Note that Small Claims cases in Marion County are heard at the township and records are maintained at that level.

Online Access

Implementation of an online record search system available for the public, called Odyssey, has five counties on the system, with plans for more to be added. Visit http://mycase.in.gov/default.aspx.

Also, a vendor is working closely with many counties to provide electroinc access. An expanding limited free search of open case index is available at www.doxpop.com/prod/welcome.jsp. Full access to case records requires registration and subscription, $25.00 per month minimum. Although not statewide, this is an expanding service that is also adding recording office data.

The home page gives free access to an index of docket information for Supreme, Appeals, and Tax Court cases.

Searching Tips, Fees, and Other Guidelines

The Circuit Court Clerk/County Clerk in a county is the same individual and is responsible for keeping all county judicial records. However, we recommend that, when requesting a record, the request indicate which court heard the case (Circuit or Superior). Many courts do not perform searches, especially criminal searches, based on a 7/8/96 statement by the State Board of Accounts. State statute sets the certification fee as $1.00 per document plus copy fee and $1.00 per page for copies, but many courts do not follow these prices.

Adams County

Circuit & Superior Court PO Box 189, 112 S 2nd St, Decatur, IN 46733; 260-724-5309; fax: 260-724-5313; 8AM-4:30PM (EST). ***Felony, Misdemeanor, Civil, Eviction, Small Claims, Probate.***

Civil Records: Access: In person only. Visitors must perform in person searches themselves. Required to search: name, years to search. Civil cases indexed by defendant, plaintiff, on computer from 1992, archived from 1876. Some records on index cards. Civil PAT goes back to 1979. Public terminal has limited data available.

Criminal Records: Access: In person only. Visitors must perform in person searches themselves. Required to search: name, years to search, DOB; SSN helpful. Criminal records computerized from 1992, archived from 1876. Some records on index cards. Criminal PAT goes back to same as civil. Public terminal has limited data available.

General Information: No juvenile, adoption, mental health or sealed records released. Will fax specific case file $1.00 per page. Court makes copy: $1.00 per page. Certification fee: $1.00 per page. Payee: Adams County Clerk. Only cashiers checks and money orders accepted. No credit cards accepted. Prepayment required.

Allen County

Circuit & Superior Court 715 S Calhoun St, Rm 201, Courthouse, Attn; Records Mgmt Rm 203, Ft Wayne, IN 46802; 260-449-7890; fax: 260-449-7929; 8AM-4:30PM (EST). ***Felony, Misdemeanor, Civil, Eviction, Small Claims, Probate.*** www.co.allen.in.us

Main number is 260-449-7245; misdemeanor & traffic 260-449-7175; small claims 260-449-7130; Court Admin.- Circuit 449-7602, Superior 449-7681.

Civil Records: Access: In person, online. Visitors must perform in person searches themselves. Required to search: name, years to search. Civil cases indexed by defendant, plaintiff. Recent civil cases on computer back to 10/1995; some prior records on microfiche, archived and index from 1824. Civil PAT goes back to 10/1995. PAT civil results show middle initial. Access civil records by subscription to doxpop at https://www.doxpop.com/prod/court/. Free index search.

Criminal Records: Access: In person, online. Visitors must perform in person searches themselves. Required to search: name, years to search. Felony cases on computer back to 2/1994; some prior records on microfiche, archived and index from 1824. Criminal PAT goes back to 2/1994. PAT results show middle initial, DOB. Results include next hearing date if any. Access to criminal data online is same as civil, see above.

General Information: No juvenile, adoption or sealed records released. Will not fax out case files. Court makes copy: $1.00 per page. Certification fee: $1.00 per doc. Payee: Clerk of Allen Circuit Court. Business checks accepted. No credit cards accepted. Prepayment required.

Bartholomew County

Circuit & Superior Court PO Box 924, Columbus, IN 47202-0924; 812-379-1600; criminal fax: 812-379-1675; civil fax: same; 8AM-5PM (EST). ***Felony, Misdemeanor, Civil, Eviction, Small Claims, Probate.*** www.bartholomewco.com

This court will only search felony and misdemeanor cases. Probate fax is same as main fax number.

Civil Records: Access: In person, online. Visitors must perform in person searches themselves. Required to search: name, DOB, SSN. Civil cases indexed by plaintiff. Civil records on computer from 1985. Civil PAT goes back to 1985. Online subscription service at https://www.doxpop.com/prod/. Fees involved. Records date from 5/85.

Criminal Records: Access: Fax, mail, in person, online. Visitors must perform in person searches themselves. No search fee. Required to search: name, years to search, DOB. Criminal records computerized from 1985. Criminal PAT goes back to same as civil. Online access to criminal is same as civil.

General Information: Online identifiers in results same as on public terminal. No juvenile, mental health, adoption or sealed released. All searches 1985 to present. Will fax out specific case files $5.00 per name; no fee to toll-free number. Court makes copy: $.25 per page, self serve same. Certification fee: $1.00 per page. Payee: Bartholomew County Clerk. Personal checks accepted; credit cards are not. Mail requests: SASE required.

Benton County

Circuit Court 706 E 5th St, #37, Fowler, IN 47944-1556; 765-884-0930; fax: 765-884-0322; 8:30AM-4PM (EST). ***Felony, Misdemeanor, Civil, Eviction, Small Claims, Probate.***

Civil Records: Access: In person only. Visitors must perform in person searches themselves. Required to search: name, years to search. Civil cases indexed by defendant, plaintiff, on computer from 1992, on index books from 1860. Civil PAT goes back to 1992. PAT results show middle initial, DOB.

Criminal Records: Access: Mail, in person, fax. Both court and visitors may perform in person searches. Search fee: $8.00 per name; send search requests to attention of Natalie Kidd in clerk's office. Required to search: name, years to search, DOB. Criminal records computerized from 1992, on index books from 1860. Mail turnaround time 2-3 days. Criminal PAT goes back to same as civil. PAT results show middle initial, DOB.

General Information: No juvenile, mental, adoption or sealed released. Will fax documents to local or toll free line, fax copy of check for searching. Court makes copy: $1.00 per page, self serve same. Certification fee: $1.00. Payee: Benton County Clerk. Only cashiers checks, business checks and money orders accepted. No credit cards. Prepayment required. Mail requests: SASE required for criminal.

Blackford County

Circuit & Superior Court 110 W Washington St, Hartford City, IN 47348; 765-348-1130; fax: 765-348-7234; 8AM-4PM (EST). ***Felony, Misdemeanor, Civil, Eviction, Small Claims, Probate.***

Civil Records: Access: Fax, mail, in person. Visitors must perform in person searches themselves. No search fee. Required to search: name. Civil cases indexed by defendant, plaintiff, on computer from 1991, on index from 1800. Civil PAT goes back to 1991. PAT results show middle initial, DOB.

Criminal Records: Access: Fax, mail, in person. Visitors must perform in person searches themselves. No search fee. Required to search: name; also helpful: SSN, DOB, years to search. court records on computer from 1991, on index from 1800. Mail turnaround time 1 week. Criminal PAT goes back to same as civil. PAT results show middle initial, DOB.

General Information: No juvenile, mental, adoption or sealed released. Fee to fax out file $1.00 per page. Court makes copy: $1.00 per page. Certification fee: $2.00 per cert. Payee: Clerk of Blackford County. Business and personal checks accepted. No credit cards accepted. Prepayment required. Mail requests: SASE required.

Boone County

Circuit & Superior Court I & II Rm 212, Courthouse Sq, Lebanon, IN 46052; 765-482-3510; fax: 765-485-0150; 7AM-4PM (EST). ***Felony, Misdemeanor, Civil, Eviction, Small Claims, Probate.*** http://boonecounty.in.gov/Default.aspx?tabid=103

Civil Records: Access: Mail, in person. Both court and visitors may perform in person searches. No search fee. Required to search: name, years to search. Civil cases indexed by defendant, plaintiff, on index from 1900. Mail turnaround time 1 week. Civil PAT goes back to 2002.

Criminal Records: Access: Mail, in person. Both court and visitors may perform in person searches. No search fee. Required to search: name, years to search; also helpful: SSN. Criminal records indexed from 1900. Mail turnaround time 1 week. Criminal PAT goes back to 1994.

General Information: No juvenile, mental, adoption or sealed released. Will fax documents to local or toll free line. Court makes copy: $1.00 per page. Certification fee: $2.00 per cert. Payee: Boone County Clerk. Business checks accepted, no personal checks. Prepayment required. Mail requests: SASE required.

Brown County

Circuit Court Box 85, 20 E Main, Nashville, IN 47448; 812-988-5510; fax: 812-988-5562; 8AM-4PM (EST). ***Felony, Misdemeanor, Civil, Eviction, Small Claims, Probate.***

Civil Records: Access: In person, online. Visitors must perform in person searches themselves. Required to search: name, years to search. Civil cases indexed by defendant, plaintiff, open cases on computer from 1993, in entry books from early 1800s. Pre-2005 records not indexed by SSN, but SSNs can be viewed. Civil PAT goes back to 1993. PAT results show name, DOB, SSN. Results include last 4 digits of SSN. Fee access to civil records back to 1993 is by subscription at https://www.doxpop.com/prod/; free access limited to only current open cases.

Criminal Records: Access: In person, online. Visitors must perform in person searches themselves. Required to search: name, years to search, DOB; also helpful: SSN. Criminal records open cases on computer from 1993, in entry books from early 1800s. Pre-2005 records not indexed by SSN, but SSNs can be viewed. Criminal PAT goes back to same as civil. Fee access to civil records back to 1993 by subscription at www.doxpop.com; free access limited to only current open cases.

General Information: No juvenile, mental, adoption or sealed records released. Will not fax documents. Court makes copy: $1.00 per page, self serve same. Certification fee: $1.00. Payee: County Clerk. Local personal checks accepted. No credit cards accepted. Prepayment required.

Carroll County

Circuit & Superior Court Courthouse, 101 W Main, Delphi, IN 46923; 765-564-4485; fax: 765-564-1835; 8AM-5PM M,T,Th,F; 8AM-N W (EST). ***Felony, Misdemeanor, Civil, Eviction, Small Claims, Probate.***

Civil Records: Access: In person only. Visitors must perform in person searches themselves. Required to search: name, years to search. Civil cases indexed by defendant, plaintiff, archived from 1981, on index from 1828.

Criminal Records: Access: In person only. Visitors must perform in person searches themselves. Required to search: name, years to search. Criminal records archived from 1981, on index from 1828.

General Information: No juvenile, mental, adoption or sealed released. Will not fax documents. Court makes copy: $1.00 per page. Certification fee: $1.00.

Payee: Carroll County Clerk. No personal checks or credit cards accepted. Prepayment required.

Cass County

Circuit & Superior Court 200 Court Park, Logansport, IN 46947; 574-753-7730; fax: 574-753-3596; 8AM-4PM (EST). ***Felony, Misdemeanor, Civil, Eviction, Small Claims, Probate.***
www.co.cass.in.us/dav/courts/circuit.html

Civil Records: Access: Mail, in person. Both court and visitors may perform in person searches. No search fee. Required to search: name, years to search. Civil cases indexed by defendant, plaintiff, on computer from 1989, on index from 1830s. Mail turnaround time 2 weeks. Civil PAT goes back to 1989. PAT results show name only.

Criminal Records: Access: Mail, in person. Both court and visitors may perform in person searches. No search fee. Required to search: name, years to search, DOB; also helpful: SSN, signed release. Criminal records computerized from 1989, on index from 1830s. Mail turnaround time 2 weeks. Criminal PAT goes back to same as civil. PAT results show middle initial, DOB.

General Information: No juvenile, mental, adoption or sealed released. Will not fax documents. Court makes copy: $.10 per page. Certification fee: $3.00. Payee: Cass County Clerk. No personal checks; use money order. Prepayment required. Mail requests: SASE requested.

Clark County

Circuit & Superior Court 501 E Court, Rm 137, Jeffersonville, IN 47130; 812-285-6244; 8:30AM-4:30PM; 8:30-N Sat (EST). ***Felony, Misdemeanor, Civil, Eviction, Small Claims, Probate.***
www.clarkprosecutor.org/html/courts/courts.htm

The County Court converted to a Superior Court on 01/01/2009.

Civil Records: Access: In person only. Visitors must perform in person searches themselves. Required to search: name, years to search; also helpful: address. Civil cases indexed by defendant, plaintiff, on computer since 8/92, on books from 1900. Civil PAT goes back to 1993. PAT civil results show middle initial. Results sometimes last 4 digits on SSN.

Criminal Records: Access: In person only. Visitors must perform in person searches themselves. Required to search: name, years to search; also helpful: DOB, SSN. Criminal records on computer since 8/92, on books from 1900. Criminal PAT goes back to 1992. PAT results show middle initial, DOB, SSN. Physical traits appear in terminal results.

General Information: No juvenile, mental, adoption or sealed released. Court makes copy: $.10 per page. Certification fee: $1.00 per cert. Payee: County Clerk. Business checks accepted. No credit cards accepted. Prepayment required.

Clay County

Circuit & Superior Court 609 E National Ave, #213, Brazil, IN 47834; 812-448-9024; fax: 812-446-9602; 8AM-4PM (EST). ***Felony, Misdemeanor, Civil, Eviction, Small Claims, Probate.***
www.claycountyin.gov/metadot/index.pl

Civil Records: Access: Phone, In person, online. Visitors must perform in person searches themselves. No search fee. Required to search: name, years to search; also helpful: address. Civil cases indexed by defendant, plaintiff, on index from 1850; on computer back to 1995. Note: Clerk will only phone search the computer for current cases only. Civil PAT goes back to 1996 but not complete. PAT results show middle initial, DOB. Online subscription service at https://www.doxpop.com. Fees involved. A limited free search of open cases is available. Online index goes back to 9/1994; images to 8/2000.

Criminal Records: Access: Phone, In person, online. Visitors must perform in person searches themselves. No search fee. Required to search: name, years to search, address, DOB; also helpful-SSN, signed release. Criminal records indexed from 1850; on computer back to 1995. Note: Clerk will only phone search the computer for current cases only. Criminal PAT goes back to 1996 but not complete. PAT results show middle initial, DOB. Online access to criminal records is the same as civil.

General Information: No juvenile, mental, adoption or sealed released. Court makes copy: $1.00 per page, self serve same. Certification fee: $1.00. Payee: County Clerk. Business checks accepted. No credit cards accepted. Prepayment required.

Clinton County

Circuit & Superior Court 265 Courthouse Square, Frankfort, IN 46041; 765-659-6335; fax: 765-659-6347; 8AM-4PM; 8:AM-N TH (EST). ***Felony, Misdemeanor, Civil, Eviction, Small Claims, Probate.***

Civil Records: Access: In person, online. Visitors must perform in person searches themselves. Required to search: name, years to search. Civil cases indexed by defendant, plaintiff, on computer from 1991, on microfiche and index from 1900s. Civil PAT goes back to 1991. Online subscription service at https://www.doxpop.com. Fees involved. Records date from 01/91. A limited free search of open cases is available.

Criminal Records: Access: In person, online. Visitors must perform in person searches themselves. Required to search: name, years to search, signed release; also helpful: DOB. Criminal records computerized from 1991, on microfiche and index from 1900s. Criminal PAT goes back to same as civil. Online access to criminal records is the same as civil.

General Information: No juvenile, mental, adoption or sealed released. Will not fax documents. Court makes copy: $1.00 per page. Certification fee: $1.00 per page. Payee: County Clerk. Business checks accepted. Major credit cards accepted. Prepayment required.

Crawford County

Circuit Court Box 375, English, IN 47118; 812-338-2565; criminal fax: 812-338-2507; civil fax: same; 8AM-4PM M,F; 8AM-6PM T-TH (EST). ***Felony, Misdemeanor, Civil, Eviction, Small Claims, Probate.***

Probate fax is same as main fax number.

Civil Records: Access: In person only. Visitors must perform in person searches themselves. Required to search: name, years to search. Civil cases indexed by defendant, plaintiff, on index from 1900s.

Criminal Records: Access: Fax, mail, in person. Only the court performs in person searches; visitors may not. Search fee: $5.00 per name. Required to search: name, years to search, DOB, SSN, signed release. Criminal records indexed from 1900s. Mail turnaround time 1 week.

General Information: No juvenile, mental, adoption or sealed released. No fee to fax documents. Court makes copy: $1.00 per page. Self serve: $.50 per page. Certification fee: $2.00 per document. Payee: County Clerk. Business checks accepted. No credit cards accepted. Prepayment required. SASE not required.

Daviess County

Circuit & Superior Court PO Box 739, Washington, IN 47501; 812-254-8664; criminal phone: 812-254-8669; civil phone: 812-254-8664; probate phone: 812-254-8664; fax: 812-254-8698; 8AM-4PM (EST). ***Felony, Misdemeanor, Civil, Eviction, Small Claims, Probate.***

Election phone number: 812-254-8679; Small Claims phone number: 812-254-8669.

Civil Records: Access: Mail, in person, online. Both court and visitors may perform in person searches. No search fee. Required to search: name, years to search. Civil cases indexed by defendant, plaintiff, on index from 1900s; recent on computer since 1993. Mail turnaround time varies. Civil PAT goes back to 1994. Online subscription service at https://www.doxpop.com. Fees involved. Records date from 02/94. A limited free search of open cases is available.

Criminal Records: Access: Mail, in person, online. Both court and visitors may perform in person searches. No search fee. Required to search: name, years to search. Criminal records indexed from 1900s; recent on computer since 1994. Mail turnaround time varies. Criminal PAT available. Online access to criminal records is the same as civil. Online results show name, DOB.

General Information: No juvenile, mental, adoption or sealed records released. Will not fax documents. Court makes copy: $1.00 per page, self serve same. Certification fee: $1.00 per cert. Payee: Daviess County Clerk. Business checks accepted. No credit cards accepted. Prepayment required. Mail requests: SASE required.

Dearborn County

Circuit & Superior Court 1 & 2 Courthouse, 215 W High St, Lawrenceburg, IN 47025; 812-537-8867; fax: 812-532-2021; 8:30AM-4:30PM (EST). ***Felony, Misdemeanor, Civil, Eviction, Small Claims, Probate.***
www.dearborncounty.org/datafiles/judges.html

Mail searches are ONLY done for marriage licenses and FBI searches.

Civil Records: Access: In person only. Visitors must perform in person searches themselves. Required to search: name, years to search. Civil cases indexed by defendant, plaintiff, on computer from 1992, on index from 1970s. Civil PAT goes back to 2000. PAT results show name only.

Criminal Records: Access: In person only. Visitors must perform in person searches themselves. Required to search: name, years to search, DOB; SSN helpful. Criminal records computerized from 1992, on index from 1970s, archived to 1930. Criminal PAT goes back to same as civil. PAT results show name only.

General Information: No juvenile, mental, adoption or sealed records released. Will not fax documents. Court makes copy: $1.00 per page. Certification fee: $1.00 per cert. Payee: Circuit Court Clerk. Only cashiers checks and money orders accepted. No credit cards accepted. Prepayment required.

Decatur County

Circuit & Superior Court 150 Courthouse Square, #244, Greensburg, IN 47240; 812-663-8223/8642; fax: 812-662-6627; 8AM-4PM M-TH; 8AM-5PM F (EST). ***Felony, Misdemeanor, Civil, Eviction, Small Claims, Probate.***
www.decaturcounty.in.gov

Civil Records: Access: In person, online. Visitors must perform in person searches themselves. Required to search: name, years to search. Civil cases indexed by defendant, plaintiff, on index from 1823; on computer back to 1998. Civil PAT goes back to 1998. Online subscription service at https://www.doxpop.com. Fees involved. A limited free search of open cases is available. Online records go back to 12/1998.

Criminal Records: Access: In person, online. Visitors must perform in person searches themselves. Required to search: name, years to search, DOB; SSN helpful. Criminal records indexed from 1823; on computer back to 1998. Criminal PAT goes back to same as civil. Online access to criminal records is the same as civil.

General Information: No juvenile, mental, adoption or sealed released. Will fax specific case file if situation warrants. Court makes copy: $.10 per page, self serve same. Certification fee: $2.00 per doc. Payee: Decatur County Clerk. No personal checks or credit cards accepted. Prepayment required.

DeKalb County

Circuit & Superior Court 1 & 2 PO Box 230, Auburn, IN 46706; 260-925-0912; fax: 260-925-5126; 8:30AM-4:30PM (EST). ***Felony, Misdemeanor, Civil, Eviction, Small Claims, Probate.***

There are three working courts here. Superior I has traffic and criminal. Superior II has small claims and evictions.

Civil Records: Access: In person, online. Both court and visitors may perform in person searches. No search fee. Required to search: name, years to search. Civil cases indexed by defendant, plaintiff, on computer back to 1987, on index from 1913. Civil PAT goes back to 1987. PAT results show name only. Search the docket by case number, party

name or attorney name at http://mycase.in.gov/default.aspx.
Criminal Records: Access: In person, online. Both court and visitors may perform in person searches. No search fee. Required to search: name, years to search, DOB. Criminal records computerized from 1987, on index from 1913. Note: Court will process case files if case number known. Criminal PAT goes back to same as civil. PAT results show middle initial, DOB. Access court record index free at http://mycase.in.gov/default.aspx.
General Information: No juvenile, mental, adoption or sealed released. Will fax documents $1.00 per page. Court makes copy: $1.00 per page, self serve same. Certification fee: $1.00. Payee: DeKalb County Clerk. Only cashiers checks and money orders accepted. Major credit cards accepted. Prepayment required. Mail requests: SASE required for mail return of any copies.

Delaware County

Circuit Court Box 1089, Muncie, IN 47308; 765-747-7726; fax: 765-747-7768; 8:30AM-4:30PM (EST). ***Felony, Misdemeanor, Civil, Small Claims, Probate.*** www.dcclerk.org
Civil Records: Access: Fax, mail, in person, online. Both court and visitors may perform in person searches. No search fee. Required to search: name, years to search. Civil cases indexed by defendant, plaintiff, on computer from 1989, on microfiche, archived and on index from 1800. Mail turnaround time varies. Civil PAT goes back to 1989. Online subscription service at https://www.doxpop.com. Fees involved. Records date from 1/89. A limited free search of open cases is available. Index from Muncie City court also available online.
Criminal Records: Access: In person, online. Visitors must perform in person searches themselves. Required to search: name, years to search, DOB, SSN. Criminal records computerized from 1989, on microfiche, archived and on index from 1800. Criminal PAT goes back to same as civil. Also, an online subscription service is at www.doxpop.com. Fees involved. Records date from 01/89. A limited free search of open cases is available. An index from the Muncie City court is also available online.
General Information: No juvenile, mental, adoption or sealed released. Fee to fax out file $2.00. Court makes copy: $.10 per page. Certification fee: $1.00. Payee: Delaware County Clerk. Business checks accepted. No credit cards accepted. Prepayment required. Mail requests: SASE required.

Dubois County

Circuit & Superior Court 1 Courthouse Square, Jasper, IN 47546; 812-481-7035; fax: 812-481-7044; 8AM-4PM (CST). ***Felony, Misdemeanor, Civil, Eviction, Small Claims, Probate.*** www.visitduboiscounty.com/
Civil Records: Access: In person, online. Visitors must perform in person searches themselves. Required to search: name; also helpful: years to search. Civil cases indexed by defendant, plaintiff, on computer from 8\93, on index books from 1930. Civil PAT goes back to 1993. Online subscription service at https://www.doxpop.com. Fees involved. Records date back to 10/1993. A limited free search of open cases is available.
Criminal Records: Access: In person, online. Visitors must perform in person searches themselves. Required to search: name; also helpful: years to search. Criminal records computerized from 8\93, on index books from 1930. Criminal PAT goes back to same as civil. Online access to criminal index same as civil.
General Information: No juvenile, mental, adoption or sealed records released. Will fax documents $3.00 1st page, $1.00 ea add'l page. Court makes copy: $.25 per page, self serve same. Certification fee: $1.00. Payee: Court Clerk. Personal checks accepted; credit cards are not. Prepayment required. Mail requests: SASE required for mail return of any copies.

Elkhart County

Elkhart Superior Courts 1, 2, 5, 6 315 S 2nd St, Elkhart, IN 46516; 574-523-2233 (1&2 clerk) /2305 (#5 clerk); fax: 574-523-2018; 8AM-4PM T-F; 8AM-5PM M (EST). ***Felony, Misdemeanor, Civil, Eviction, Small Claims, Probate.*** www.in.gov/judiciary/elkhart/
Civil Records: Access: In person, online. Visitors must perform in person searches themselves. Required to search: name, years to search. Civil cases indexed by defendant, plaintiff, archived from 1830; on computer since 1995. Civil PAT goes back to 1996. PAT results show middle initial, DOB. Results give last 4 digits of SSN only. Online subscription service at https://www.doxpop.com. Fees involved. Records date from 1/92. A limited free search of open cases is available.
Criminal Records: Access: In person, online. Visitors must perform in person searches themselves. Required to search: name, years to search, DOB; also helpful: SSN. Criminal records archived from 1830; on computer since 1995. Criminal PAT goes back to same as civil. PAT results show middle initial, DOB. Results give last 4 digits of SSN only. Identifiers are not always available. Online access to criminal records is the same as civil. Online results show middle initial, DOB. Terminal results include SSN.
General Information: Online identifiers in results same as on public terminal. No juvenile, mental, adoption or sealed records released. Will not fax documents. Court makes copy: $1.00 per page, self serve same. Certification fee: $2.00. Payee: Court Clerk. No personal checks or credit cards accepted.

Goshen Circuit & Superior Courts 3, 4 Courthouse, 101 N Main St, Goshen, IN 46526; 574-535-6429; fax: 574-535-6471; 8AM-5PM M, 8AM-4PM T-F (EST). ***Felony, Misdemeanor, Civil, Eviction, Small Claims, Probate.*** www.elkhartcountyindiana.com/administrative/clerk.html
Includes Circuit Court (Rm 204) and Superior Court 3 (Rm 205, 535-6438) and 4 (Rm 105, 535-6403).
Civil Records: Access: In person, online. Visitors must perform in person searches themselves. Required to search: name, years to search. Civil cases indexed by defendant, plaintiff, archived from 1830; on computer since 1996. Some records on index books. Civil PAT goes back to 1996. PAT results show name only. Online subscription service at https://www.doxpop.com. Fees involved; $39.00 per month. Records date from 01/92. A limited free search of open cases is available.
Criminal Records: Access: In person, online. Visitors must perform in person searches themselves. Required to search: name, years to search, DOB; also helpful: SSN. Criminal records archived from 1830; on computer since 1996. Some records on index books. Criminal PAT goes back to 1996. PAT results show middle initial, DOB. Online access to criminal records is the same as civil. Online results show middle initial, DOB.
General Information: No juvenile, mental, adoption or sealed records released. Will not fax documents. Court makes copy: $1.00 per page. Certification fee: $1.00 per cert. Payee: Court Clerk. No personal checks or credit cards. Prepayment required. Mail requests: SASE required for mail return of any copies.

Fayette County

Circuit & Superior Court 401 Central Ave, Connersville, IN 47331; 765-825-1813; fax: 765-827-4902; 8:30AM-4PM, till 5PM W (EST). ***Felony, Misdemeanor, Civil, Eviction, Small Claims, Probate.*** www.co.fayette.in.us
Civil Records: Access: In person, online. Visitors must perform in person searches themselves. Required to search: name, years to search. Civil cases indexed by defendant, plaintiff, on computer from 1988 (Circuit), 1992 (Superior). Civil PAT goes back to 1990. PAT results show name only. Online subscription service at https://www.doxpop.com. Fees involved; $39.00 per month. Records date from 01/96. A limited free search of open cases is available.
Criminal Records: Access: In person, online. Visitors must perform in person searches themselves. Required to search: name, years to search. Criminal records computerized from 1988 (Circuit), 1992 (Superior). Criminal PAT goes back to same as civil. PAT results show name only. Online access to criminal records is the same as civil. Online also includes tax warrants.
General Information: No juvenile, mental, adoption or sealed released. Will not fax documents. Court makes copy: $1.00 per page. Self serve: $1.00 per page. Certification fee: $1.00. Payee: Fayette County Clerk. Only cashiers checks and money orders accepted. No credit cards. Prepayment required.

Floyd County

Circuit & Superior Court Box 1056, City County Bldg, 311 1st St, New Albany, IN 47150; 812-948-5413/5411; fax: 812-948-4711; 8AM-4PM (EST). ***Felony, Misdemeanor, Civil, Eviction, Small Claims, Probate.***
Probate is a separate index at this same address. Probate fax is same as main fax number. The County Court converted to a Superior Court on 01/01/2009.
Civil Records: Access: Mail, in person. Visitors must perform in person searches themselves. No search fee. Required to search: name, years to search. Civil cases indexed by defendant, plaintiff, on computer from 1988, archived from 1978, on index from 1819. Civil PAT goes back to 1988.
Criminal Records: Access: Mail, in person. Visitors must perform in person searches themselves. Search fee: $5.00. Required to search: name, years to search; also helpful: SSN. Criminal records computerized from 1988, archived from 1978, on index from 1819. Mail turnaround time 1-2 days. Criminal PAT goes back to same as civil. Access to court records is no longer found online.
General Information: No juvenile, mental, adoption or sealed released. Will not fax documents. Court makes copy: $.10 per page, self serve same. Certification fee: $1.00 per page. Payee: Court Clerk. Personal checks and major credit cards accepted. Prepayment required. Mail requests: SASE required.

Fountain County

Circuit Court Box 183, Covington, IN 47932; 765-793-2192; fax: 765-793-5002; 8AM-4PM (EST). ***Felony, Misdemeanor, Civil, Eviction, Small Claims, Probate.*** www.co.fountain.in.us/clerk/
Civil Records: Access: Mail, in person, online. Both court and visitors may perform in person searches. No search fee. Required to search: name, years to search. Civil cases indexed by defendant, plaintiff, on computer from 1995. Mail turnaround time 1-2 days if records after 1989, 4-5 days if prior. Civil PAT goes back to mid-1995. Online subscription service at https://www.doxpop.com. Fees involved. Records date from 9/95. A limited free search of open cases is available.
Criminal Records: Access: Mail, in person, online. Both court and visitors may perform in person searches. No search fee. Required to search: name, years to search. Criminal records computerized from 1995. Mail turnaround time 1-2 days if records after 1989, 4-5 days if prior. Criminal PAT goes back to same as civil.PAT results show name, DOB. Online subscription service at https://www.doxpop.com. Fees involved. Records date from 9/95. A limited free search of open cases is available. Online results show name, DOB.
General Information: No juvenile, mental, adoption or sealed released. Will not fax documents. Court makes copy: $1.00 per page, self serve same. Certification fee: $1.00. Payee: Court Clerk. No personal checks or credit cards accepted. Prepayment required. Mail requests: SASE required.

Franklin County

Circuit Court 459 Main, Brookville, IN 47012; 765-647-5111; fax: 765-647-3224; 8:30AM-4PM (EST). ***Felony, Misdemeanor, Civil, Eviction, Small Claims, Probate.***
Civil Records: Access: In person only. Visitors must perform in person searches themselves. Required to search: name, years to search. Civil cases indexed by defendant, plaintiff, indexed. Public use terminal available, records go back to 04/00.

Criminal Records: Access: In person only. Visitors must perform in person searches themselves. Required to search: name, years to search. Criminal records on index. Public use terminal available, crim records go back to same.
General Information: No juvenile, mental, adoption or sealed released. Will fax documents $1.00 per page. Court makes copy: $1.00 per page. Certification fee: $1.00. Payee: Court Clerk. Personal checks accepted; credit cards are not. Prepayment required.

Fulton County

Circuit Court/Superior Court 815 Main St, PO Box 524, Rochester, IN 46975; 574-223-2911; criminal phone: 574-223-7712; civil: 574-223-7714; probate: 574-223-7715; criminal fax: 574-223-8304; civil fax: same; 8AM-4PM M-TH; 8AM-5PM F (EST). ***Felony, Misdemeanor, Civil, Eviction, Small Claims, Probate.*** www.co.fulton.in.us
Probate fax is same as main fax number.
Civil Records: Access: Mail, in person, online. Both court and visitors may perform in person searches. No search fee. Required to search: name, years to search. Civil cases indexed by defendant, plaintiff, on computer from 1989, on microfiche, archived and on index from 1845. Mail turnaround time 3-4 days. Civil PAT goes back to 1999. Online subscription service at https://www.doxpop.com. Fees involved. Records date back to 1/1999. A limited free search of open cases is available.
Criminal Records: Access: Mail, in person, online. Both court and visitors may perform in person searches. No search fee. Required to search: name, years to search. Criminal records computerized from 1989, on microfiche, archived and on index from 1845. Mail turnaround time 3-4 days. Criminal PAT goes back to same as civil. Online access to criminal is the same as civil.
General Information: No juvenile, mental, adoption or sealed released. Will fax documents $4.00 per page. Court makes copy: $1.00 per page. Certification fee: $1.00. Payee: Court Clerk. Business checks accepted. No credit cards accepted. Prepayment required. Mail requests: SASE Required.

Gibson County

Circuit & Superior Court Courthouse, PO Box 630, Princeton, IN 47670; 812-386-6474; fax: 812-385-5025; 8AM-4PM (CST). ***Felony, Misdemeanor, Civil, Eviction, Small Claims, Probate.***
Probate fax is same as main fax number.
Civil Records: Access: In person, online. Visitors must perform in person searches themselves. Required to search: name, years to search. Civil cases indexed by defendant, plaintiff, on computer 1/1996 for Superior; 1990 for Circuit. On microfiche from 1940, on index from 1813. Civil PAT goes back to 1/1996 for superior; 1990 for Circuit. PAT civil results show middle initial. Online subscription service at https://www.doxpop.com. Fees involved. Superior records date from 1/96.; circuit from 05/05. Has limited free search of open cases.
Criminal Records: Access: In person, online. Visitors must perform in person searches themselves. Required to search: name, years to search. Criminal records on computer 1/1996 for Superior; 1990 for Circuit. On microfiche from 1940, on index from 1813. Criminal PAT goes back to same as civil. PAT results show middle initial, DOB. Online access to criminal is same as civil.
General Information: No juvenile, mental, adoption or sealed records released. Will not fax out case files. Court makes copy: $.35 per page; $.25 for non-orders.Copy fee $1.00 per page with Judge's signature. Certification fee: $1.00 per doc. Payee: Court Clerk. Business checks accepted for copy payment. No personal checks or credit cards accepted. Prepayment required.

Grant County

Circuit & Superior Court Courthouse 101 E 4th St, Marion, IN 46952; 765-668-8121; criminal fax: 765-668-6541; civil fax: same; 8AM-4PM (EST). ***Felony, Misdemeanor, Civil, Eviction, Small Claims, Probate.*** www.grantcounty.net
Probate is in a separate index at this address. Probate fax is same as main fax number.
Civil Records: Access: In person, online. Visitors must perform in person searches themselves. Required to search: name, years to search; also helpful: address. Civil cases indexed by defendant, plaintiff, on computer from 1989, on index from 1881. Civil PAT goes back to 7/1989. Online subscription service at https://www.doxpop.com. Fees involved. Records date back to 8/1989. A limited free search of open cases is available. Index from Gas City Court also available online. Search Marion-Center Township and Marion-Washington Township court records free at http://mycase.in.gov/default.aspx.
Criminal Records: Access: In person, online. Visitors must perform in person searches themselves. Required to search: name, years to search; also helpful: DOB, SSN. Criminal records computerized from 1989, on index from 1881. Criminal PAT goes back to same as civil. Online access to criminal is the same as civil.
General Information: No juvenile, adoption, mental health or sealed records released. Will fax specific case file $1.00 per page fee. Court makes copy: $.10 per page, self serve same. Certification fee: $1.00 per certification. Payee: Court Clerk. No personal checks or credit cards accepted. Prepayment required.

Greene County

Circuit & Superior Court PO Box 229, 1 Main St, Bloomfield, IN 47424; 812-384-8532; fax: 812-384-8458; 8AM-4PM (EST). ***Felony, Misdemeanor, Civil, Eviction, Small Claims, Probate.***
Civil Records: Access: In person only. Both court and visitors may perform in person searches. No search fee. Required to search: name, years to search. Civil cases indexed by defendant, plaintiff. Records in books.
Criminal Records: Access: In person only. Both court and visitors may perform in person searches. No search fee. Required to search: name, years to search. Criminal records in books.
General Information: No juvenile, mental, adoption or sealed released. Court makes copy: $1.00 per page. Certification fee: $1.00. Payee: Court Clerk. Only cashiers checks and money orders accepted. Major credit cards accepted. Prepayment required.

Hamilton County

Circuit & Superior Court One Hamilton County Square, #106, Noblesville, IN 46060-2233; 317-776-9629; criminal fax: 317-776-9727; civil fax: same; 8AM-4:30PM (EST). ***Felony, Misdemeanor, Civil, Eviction, Small Claims, Probate.*** www.ai.org/hcc/
Probate fax is same as main fax number.
Civil Records: Access: In person, online. Visitors must perform in person searches themselves. Required to search: name, years to search. Civil cases indexed by defendant, plaintiff. Civil indices on computer from 1987, on index from 1920s. Civil PAT goes back to mid-1986. PAT civil results show middle initial. Online subscription service at https://www.doxpop.com. Fees involved. Records date from 01/1987. A limited free search of open cases is available.
Criminal Records: Access: In person, online. Visitors must perform in person searches themselves. Required to search: name, years to search. Criminal records computerized from 1987, on index from 5/1933. Criminal PAT goes back to same as civil. PAT results show middle initial, DOB. Online access to criminal same as civil.
General Information: No juvenile, mental, adoption or sealed released. Will not fax out case files. Court makes copy: $.50 per page, self serve same. Certification fee: $1.00 plus $.50 per page. Payee: Court Clerk. Business checks accepted. No credit cards accepted. Prepayment required.

Hancock County

Circuit & Superior Court 9 E Main St, Rm 201, Greenfield, IN 46140; 317-477-1109; fax: 317-477-1163; 8AM-4PM (EST). ***Felony, Misdemeanor, Civil, Eviction, Small Claims, Probate.***
Civil Records: Access: In person, online. Both court and visitors may perform in person searches. No search fee. Required to search: name, years to search. Civil cases indexed by defendant, plaintiff, on computer from 7/88, on index and archived from 1883. Public use terminal available. PAT results show middle initial, DOB. Online subscription service at https://www.doxpop.com. Fees involved. Records date from 7/98. A limited free search of open cases is available.
Criminal Records: Access: In person, online. Both court and visitors may perform in person searches. No search fee. Required to search: name, years to search, DOB; SSN helpful. Criminal records computerized from 7/88, on index and archived from 1883. Public use terminal available. PAT results show middle initial, DOB. Online access to criminal is same as civil.
General Information: No juvenile, mental, adoption or sealed released. Will not fax documents. Court makes copy: $1.00 per page for case history, otherwise $.25 per page. Self serve: $.25 per page. Certification fee: $1.00. Payee: Court Clerk. Only cashier checks or money orders accepted. No credit cards accepted; debit cards okay. Prepayment required.

Harrison County

Circuit Court 300 N Capitol, Corydon, IN 47112; 812-738-4289; criminal phone: 812-738-8149; civil phone: 812-738-4289; probate phone: 812-738-4289; criminal fax: 812-738-2459; civil fax: 812-738-3126; 8AM-4:30PM (EST). ***Civil, Eviction, Probate.***
Probate fax- 812-738-3126
Civil Records: Access: In person only. Visitors must perform in person searches themselves. Required to search: name, years to search. Civil cases indexed by defendant, plaintiff, on index from 1900. Note: Court personnel will only do record searching when they have time; strongly urge using a retriever. Public use terminal has civil records.
Criminal Records: Access: In person. Visitors must perform in person searches themselves. Required to search: name, years to search, DOB; also helpful-SSN. Criminal records indexed from 1900; on computer back to 1992. Note: Court personnel only do record searching when they have time; suggest to use a retriever.
General Information: No juvenile, mental, adoption or sealed released. Fee to fax out file $1.00 per page. Court makes copy: $1.00 per page, self serve same. Certification fee: $1.00 per document. Payee: Court Clerk. Cashiers checks and money orders accepted. No credit cards accepted. Prepayment required.

Superior Court 1445 Gardner Ln, #3126, Corydon, IN 47112; 812-738-8149; criminal fax: 812-738-2459; civil fax: same; 8AM-4:30PM (EST). ***Felony, Misdemeanor, Civil, Small Claims.***
Civil Records: Access: In person only. Visitors must perform in person searches themselves. Required to search: name, years to search. Civil cases indexed by defendant, plaintiff, on index from 1976; on computer back to 1992. Civil PAT goes back to 1992; indexes only. Public access terminal in lobby.
Criminal Records: Access: In person only. Visitors must perform in person searches themselves. Required to search: name, years to search, DOB; also helpful-SSN. Criminal records indexed from 1976; on computer back to 1992. Criminal PAT goes back to same as civil. Public access terminal in lobby.
General Information: No juvenile, mental, adoption or sealed released. Will not fax out case files. Court makes copy: $1.00 per page, self serve same. Certification fee: $1.00 per document. Payee: Court Clerk. Only cashiers checks and money orders accepted. Visa/MC accepted. Prepayment required.

Hendricks County

Circuit & Superior Court 51 W Main St, #104, Danville, IN 46122; 317-745-9231; fax: 317-745-9306; 8AM-4PM (EST). ***Felony, Misdemeanor, Civil, Eviction, Small Claims, Probate.***
www.co.hendricks.in.us/
Civil Records: Access: In person, mail, online. Visitors must perform in person searches themselves. No search fee. Required to search: name, years to search. Civil cases indexed by defendant, plaintiff, on computer since late 1992, on index from 1800s. Civil PAT goes back to 9/1992. PAT results

show name, DOB. Will only do mail request if out of state. Online docket found at http://hendricks.nasaview.com/terms.php. Records available to 1992.
Criminal Records: Access: In person, mail, online. Visitors must perform in person searches themselves. No search fee. Required to search: name, years to search; also helpful: DOB, SSN. Criminal records on computer since late 1992, on index from 1800s. Note: Court will only do mail request if out of state. Mail turnaround time is 72 hours. Criminal PAT goes back to same as civil.PAT results show name, DOB. Search docket online at http://hendricks.nasaview.com/terms.php. Records go back to 1992.
General Information: Online identifiers in results same as on public terminal. No juvenile, mental, adoption or sealed released. Will not fax documents. Court makes copy: $1.00 per page. Certification fee: $1.00. Payee: Hendricks County Clerk. Business checks accepted. No credit cards accepted. Prepayment required. Mail requests: SASE not required but add'l postage may be billed for over 10 pages.

Henry County

Circuit & Superior Courts I & II PO Box B, New Castle, IN 47362; 765-529-6401; criminal fax: 765-521-7046; civil fax: same; 8AM-4PM (EST). ***Felony, Misdemeanor, Civil, Eviction, Small Claims, Probate.***
www.henryco.net/
Probate fax is same as main fax number.
Civil Records: Access: In person, online. Visitors must perform in person searches themselves. Required to search: name, years to search. Civil cases indexed by plaintiff. Civil records on computer from 02/1991, manual records from 1822. Civil PAT goes back to 2/1991. PAT results show middle initial, DOB. Online subscription service at https://www.doxpop.com. Fees involved. Records date back to 1/1991. A limited free search of open cases is available.
Criminal Records: Access: In person, online. Visitors must perform in person searches themselves. Required to search: name, years to search. Records on computer from 02/1991, manual records from 1822. Criminal PAT goes back to same as civil. PAT results show middle initial, DOB. Online access to criminal is the same as civil. Online results show middle initial, DOB.
General Information: No juvenile, mental, protective orders, adoption or any other confidential records. Will not fax out case files. Court makes copy: $1.00 per page. Certification fee: $1.00 per document. Payee: Henry County Clerk. Only cashiers checks and money orders accepted. No credit cards accepted. Prepayment required.

Howard County

Circuit & Superior Court 104 N Buckeye, Rm 114, Kokomo, IN 46901; 765-456-2204; criminal phone: 765-456-2000; civil phone: 765-456-2000; criminal fax: 765-456-2267; civil fax: same; 8AM-4PM (EST). ***Felony, Misdemeanor, Civil, Eviction, Small Claims, Probate.***
http://co.howard.in.us/clerk1
Small claims phone-765-456-2204.
Civil Records: Access: In person, online. Visitors must perform in person searches themselves. Required to search: name, years to search. Civil cases indexed by defendant, plaintiff, on computer since 1994, on microfiche from early 1800s. Civil PAT goes back to 1994. PAT results show middle initial, DOB. Online subscription service at https://www.doxpop.com. Fees involved. Records date from 07/94. A limited free search of open cases is available.
Criminal Records: Access: In person, online. Visitors must perform in person searches themselves. Required to search: name, years to search; also helpful: DOB. Criminal records on computer since 1992, on microfiche from early 1800s. Criminal PAT goes back to same as civil. PAT results show middle initial, DOB. Online access to criminal records is the same as civil. Online results show middle initial, DOB.

General Information: Online identifiers in results same as on public terminal. No juvenile, mental, adoption or sealed records released. Will fax documents $.20 per page. Court makes copy: $.20 per page from printed records. Self serve: $.20 per page. Certification fee: $1.00. Payee: County Clerk. Only cashiers checks and money orders accepted. No credit cards accepted. Prepayment required. May pay through 3rd party "PayTrust".

Huntington County

Circuit & Superior Court PO Box 228, Huntington, IN 46750; 260-358-4817; fax: 260-358-4880; 8AM-4:30PM (EST). ***Felony, Misdemeanor, Civil, Eviction, Small Claims, Probate.***
Civil Records: Access: Fax, phone, mail, in person. Both court and visitors may perform in person searches. No search fee. Required to search: name, years to search. Civil cases indexed by defendant, plaintiff, on computer from 1990, on microfiche from 1970, on index and archived from 1800s. Civil PAT goes back to 1990.
Criminal Records: Access: In person only. Visitors must perform in person searches themselves. Required to search: name, years to search. Criminal records computerized from 1990, on microfiche from 1970, on index and archived from 1800s. Criminal PAT goes back to same as civil.
General Information: No juvenile, mental, adoption or sealed released. Will fax documents to local or toll free line. Court makes copy: $1.00 per page. Certification fee: $1.00 per cert. Payee: County Clerk. No personal checks or credit cards accepted. Prepayment required. SASE not required.

Jackson County

Circuit Court PO Box 318, Brownstown, IN 47220; 812-358-6117; criminal phone: 812-358-6116; civil phone: 812-358-6116; probate phone: 812-358-6133; fax: 812-358-6187; civil fax: same; 8AM-4:30PM (EST). ***Felony, Misdemeanor, Civil, Eviction, Small Claims, Probate.***
Court will not perform searches for private companies. Probate fax is same as main fax number.
Civil Records: Access: In person only. Visitors must perform in person searches themselves. Required to search: name, years to search. Civil cases indexed by defendant, plaintiff, on computer from 1989, on index from 1800s. Civil PAT goes back to 1989.
Criminal Records: Access: In person only. Visitors must perform in person searches themselves. Required to search: name, years to search; also helpful: DOB, SSN. Criminal records computerized from 1989, on index from 1800s. Note: Will recommend local document retrievers to do searches for you. Criminal PAT goes back to same as civil.
General Information: No juvenile, mental, adoption or sealed released. Will fax documents $5.00 per doc; no fee to toll-free number. Court makes copy: $1.00 per page, self serve same. Certification fee: $1.00 per document. Payee: Jackson County Clerk. No personal checks or credit cards accepted. Prepayment required.

Superior Court PO Box 788, Seymour, IN 47274; 812-522-9676; criminal fax: 812-523-6065; civil fax: same; 8AM-4:30PM (EST). ***Misdemeanor, Civil, Eviction, Small Claims.***
Civil Records: Access: Mail, in person. Visitors must perform in person searches themselves. No search fee. Required to search: name, years to search. Civil cases indexed by defendant, plaintiff, on computer from 1989, on index from 1800s.
Criminal Records: Access: In person only. Visitors must perform in person searches themselves. Required to search: name, years to search; also helpful: DOB, SSN. Criminal records computerized from 1989, on index from 1800s.
General Information: No juvenile, mental, adoption or sealed released. Will fax documents $5.00 per doc; no fee to toll-free number. Court makes copy: $1.00 per page, self serve same. Certification fee: $1.00 per page. Payee: Jackson County Clerk. Only cashiers checks and money orders accepted. No credit cards accepted. Prepayment required. SASE not required.

Jasper County

Circuit Court 115 W Washington, Rensselaer, IN 47978; 219-866-4941; criminal phone: 219-866-4926/4921; civil phone: 219-866-4926/4921; probate phone: 218-866-4929; fax: 219-866-9450; 8AM-4PM (CST). ***Felony, Misdemeanor, Civil, Eviction, Small Claims, Probate.***
www.jaspercountyin.gov/Default.aspx?tabid=58
This court also handles juvenile, paternity and adoption.
219-866-4909 Traffic; 219-866-4928 Child Support
Civil Records: Access: Mail, in person. Both court and visitors may perform in person searches. No search fee. Required to search: name, years to search. Civil cases indexed by defendant, plaintiff. County records on computer from 1976, circuit from 1989. Some records on index from 1900s. Mail turnaround time 1 day. Civil PAT goes back to 1989.
Criminal Records: Access: Mail, in person. Both court and visitors may perform in person searches. No search fee. Required to search: name, years to search; also helpful: DOB, SSN. County records on computer from 1976, circuit from 1989. Some records on index from 1900s. Mail turnaround time 1 day. Criminal PAT goes back to same as civil.
General Information: No juvenile, mental, adoption or sealed released. Will fax documents $5.00 per page. Court makes copy: $.50 per page. Certification fee: $1.00 per page. Payee: Jasper County Clerk. No personal or business checks accepted. No credit cards. Prepayment required. Mail requests: SASE required.

Superior Court 115 W Washington St, #103, Rensselaer, IN 47978; 219-866-4971; criminal phone: 21-866-4922/4912; civil phone: 21-866-4922/4912; probate phone: 219-866-4912; fax: 219-866-9450; 8AM-4PM (CST). ***Felony, Misdemeanor, Civil, Probate.***
www.jaspercountyin.gov/Default.aspx?tabid=58
Civil Records: Access: Mail, in person. Both court and visitors may perform in person searches. No search fee. Required to search: name, years to search. Civil cases indexed by defendant, plaintiff. County records on computer from 1976, circuit from 1989. Some records on index from 1800s. Mail turnaround 1 day to 1 week. Civil PAT goes back to 1989.
Criminal Records: Access: Mail, in person. Both court and visitors may perform in person searches. No search fee. Required to search: name, years to search. County records on computer from 1976, circuit from 1989. Some records on index from 1800s. Mail turnaround time 1 day to 1 week. Criminal PAT goes back to same as civil.
General Information: No juvenile, mental, adoption or sealed released. Will fax documents $5.00 per page. Court makes copy: $.50 per page. Non-case related copies are $.10 per page. Certification fee: $1.00 per page includes copy fee. Payee: County Clerk. Cashiers checks and money orders accepted. No credit cards accepted. Prepayment required. Mail requests: SASE required.

Jay County

Circuit & Superior Court 120 N Court St, Courthouse, Portland, IN 47371; 260-726-4951; fax: 260-726-6922; 8:30AM-4:30PM (EST). ***Felony, Misdemeanor, Civil, Eviction, Small Claims, Probate.*** www.co.jay.in.us
Civil Records: Access: In person, online. Visitors must perform in person searches themselves. Required to search: name, years to search; also helpful: address. Civil cases indexed by defendant, plaintiff, on computer from 8\94, prior on microfiche from 1979, on index books from 1900. Civil PAT goes back to 1994. Online subscription service at https://www.doxpop.com. Fees involved. Records date from 03/94. A limited free search of open cases is available.
Criminal Records: Access: Mail, in person, online. Visitors must perform in person searches themselves. No search fee. Required to search: name, years to search, DOB; also helpful: SSN, address. Criminal records computerized from 8\94, prior on microfiche from 1979, on index books from 1900. Criminal PAT goes back to same as civil. Online access to criminal records is the same as civil.

General Information: Online identifiers in results same as on public terminal. No juvenile, mental, adoption or sealed records released. Will fax documents $1.00 per page. Court makes copy: $1.00 per page. Certification fee: $1.00 per page. Payee: Court Clerk. Personal and business checks accepted. No credit cards accepted. Prepayment required. Mail requests: SASE required.

Jefferson County

Circuit & Superior Court Courthouse, 300 E Main St, Rm 203, Madison, IN 47250; 812-265-8923; probate phone: 812-265-8928; fax: 812-265-4980; 8AM-4PM (EST). ***Felony, Misdemeanor, Civil, Eviction, Small Claims, Probate.***

Civil Records: Access: In person only. Visitors must perform in person searches themselves. Required to search: name, years to search. Civil cases indexed by plaintiff, defendant. Civil records on index from 1975, computerized since 1995. Civil PAT goes back to 1995. PAT results show middle initial, DOB.

Criminal Records: Access: In person only. Visitors must perform in person searches themselves. Required to search: Name, years to search, address, DOB, SSN. Criminal records indexed from 1975, computerized since 1995. Criminal PAT goes back to same as civil. PAT results show middle initial, DOB.

General Information: No juvenile, mental, adoption or sealed released. Will fax documents $1.00 per page. Court makes copy: $1.00 per page, self serve same. Certification fee: $1.00 per page. Payee: County Clerk. Only cashiers checks and money orders accepted. No credit cards. Prepayment required.

Jennings County

Circuit Court Courthouse, PO Box 385, Vernon, IN 47282; 812-352-3070; fax: 812-352-3076; 8AM-4PM (EST). ***Felony, Misdemeanor, Civil, Eviction, Small Claims, Probate.***

Civil Records: Access: In person only. Visitors must perform in person searches themselves. Required to search: name, years to search. Civil cases indexed by defendant, plaintiff, on index from 1930; computerized since 2000. Civil PAT goes back to 10/2000.

Criminal Records: Access: In person only. Visitors must perform in person searches themselves. Required to search: name, years to search, DOB; SSN helpful. Criminal records indexed from 1930; computerized since 2000. Criminal PAT goes back to same as civil.

General Information: No juvenile, mental, adoption or sealed released. Will fax documents to local or toll-free number. Court makes copy: $.25 per page, self serve same. Certification fee: $1.00. Payee: County Clerk. Personal checks accepted; credit cards are not. Prepayment required.

Johnson County

Circuit & Superior Court Courthouse, PO Box 368, Franklin, IN 46131; 317-736-3708; criminal phone: 317-736-3951; civil phone: 317-736-3708; probate phone: 317-736-3913; criminal fax: 317-736-3749; civil fax: 317-736-4972; 8AM-4:30PM (EST). ***Felony, Misdemeanor, Civil, Eviction, Small Claims, Probate.*** www.co.johnson.in.us/

Civil Records: Access: Mail (as time allows), in person, online. Visitors must perform in person searches themselves. No search fee. Required to search: name, years to search. Civil cases indexed by defendant, plaintiff, on computer back 10 years. Mail turnaround time 1-2 days. Civil PAT goes back to 1989. Online subscription service at https://www.doxpop.com. Fees involved. Records date from 08/89. A limited free search of open cases is available.

Criminal Records: Access: In person, online. Visitors must perform in person searches themselves. Required to search: name, years to search; also helpful: DOB, SSN. Criminal records on computer back 15 years. Criminal PAT goes back to same as civil.PAT results show name, DOB. Online access is the same as civil. Online results show name, DOB.

General Information: Online identifiers in results same as on public terminal. No juvenile, mental, adoption or sealed released. Will fax documents to local number. Court makes copy: $1.00 per page. Self serve: $.50 per page. Certification fee: $1.00 per page. Payee: County Clerk. Business checks accepted. No credit cards accepted. Prepayment required. Mail requests: SASE required.

Knox County

Circuit & Superior Court 101 N 7th St, #28, Vincennes, IN 47591; 812-885-2521; criminal fax: 812-895-4929; civil fax: same; 8AM-4PM (EST). ***Felony, Misdemeanor, Civil, Eviction, Small Claims, Probate.***

Probate fax is same as main fax number.

Civil Records: Access: In person only. Visitors must perform in person searches themselves. Required to search: name, years to search. Civil cases indexed by defendant, plaintiff; index on docket books from 1800s.

Criminal Records: Access: In person only. Visitors must perform in person searches themselves. Required to search: name, years to search. Criminal records indexed in books from 1800s.

General Information: No juvenile, mental, adoption or sealed released. Will fax documents for no fee. Court makes copy: $1.00 per page, self serve same. Certification fee: $1.00 per page. Payee: Knox County Clerk. Personal checks accepted; credit cards are not. Prepayment required.

Kosciusko County

Circuit & Superior Court 121 N Lake, Warsaw, IN 46580; 574-372-2331; criminal phone: 574-372-2457 (1st), 372-2453 (2nd & 3rd); civil phone: 574-372-2331; probate phone: 574-372-2330; criminal fax: 574-372-2338; civil fax: same; 8AM-4:30PM (EST). ***Felony, Misdemeanor, Civil, Eviction, Small Claims, Probate.***

www.kcgov.com/ Probate records on same computer system, but actual index is separate. Probate fax is same as main fax number.

Civil Records: Access: Fax, in person, online. Both court and visitors may perform in person searches. No search fee. Required to search: name, years to search. Civil cases indexed by defendant, plaintiff, on computer from 10/1/93, general index from 1908. Civil PAT goes back to 1993. DOB, SSN, middle initial sometimes available. Online subscription service at https://www.doxpop.com. Fees involved. Data goes back to 10/1991. A limited free search of open cases is available. Also, access to be available through the court website soon.

Criminal Records: Access: Fax, in person, online. Both court and visitors may perform in person searches. No search fee. Required to search: name, years to search; also helpful-DOB, SSN. DL#. Criminal records computerized from 10/1/93, general index from 1908. Criminal PAT goes back to same as civil. PAT criminal results show middle initial. Online access to criminal is same as civil.

General Information: No juvenile, mental, adoption or sealed released. Will fax documents to toll free number only. Court makes copy: $.05 per page, $1.00 minimum. Self serve: $.05 per page. Certification fee: $1.00 per certification. Payee: County Clerk. Personal checks accepted; credit cards are not. Prepayment required. Mail requests: SASE required for mail return of any copies.

La Porte County

Circuit & Superior Court 813 Lincolnway, La Porte, IN 46350; 219-326-6808; criminal fax: 219-326-6626; civil fax: same; 8AM-4PM (CST). ***Felony, Misdemeanor, Civil, Eviction, Probate.***

Microfilm department- x2435/2276. Probate fax number same as main fax.

Civil Records: Access: In person, fax, online. Visitors must perform in person searches themselves. Search fee: $1.00 per page. Required to search: name, years to search. Civil cases indexed by defendant, plaintiff, on microfiche and index from 1900. Civil PAT goes back to 10 years. PAT results show middle initial, DOB. Online subscription service at https://www.doxpop.com. Fees involved. Records date from 03/98. A limited free search of open cases is available.

Criminal Records: Access: In person, fax, online. Visitors must perform in person searches themselves. Search fee: $1.00 per page. Required to search: name, years to search. Criminal records on microfiche and index from 1900. Criminal PAT goes back to same as civil. PAT results show middle initial, DOB. Online access is same as civil.

General Information: No juvenile, mental, adoption or sealed released. Will fax documents if all fees prepaid. Court makes copy: $1.00 per page, self serve same. Certification fee: $1.00 per page. Payee: Court Clerk. Business checks accepted. No credit cards accepted. Prepayment required.

LaGrange County

Circuit & Superior Court 105 N Detroit St, Courthouse, LaGrange, IN 46761; 260-499-6368; civil phone: 260-499-6375; fax: 260-499-6403; 8AM-4PM T-F, 8AM-5PM M (EST). ***Felony, Misdemeanor, Civil, Eviction, Small Claims, Probate.*** www.lagrangecounty.org/

Civil Records: Access: Phone, mail, in person, online. Visitors must perform in person searches themselves. No search fee. Required to search: name, years to search. Civil cases indexed by defendant, plaintiff, on computer from 1990, on books from 1900. Civil PAT goes back to 1991. PAT results show middle initial, DOB, SSN. Online subscription service at https://www.doxpop.com. Fees involved. Records date back to 1/1990. A limited free search of open cases is available.

Criminal Records: Access: Phone, mail, in person, online. Visitors must perform in person searches themselves. No search fee. Required to search: name, years to search; also helpful: DOB, SSN. Criminal records computerized from 1990, on books from 1900. Mail turnaround time 1-2 days from 1/1/90; 30 days if prior to 1/1/90. Criminal PAT goes back to 1991. PAT results show middle initial, DOB, SSN. Online access to criminal records is the same as civil, results show middle initial, DOB, SSN.

General Information: No juvenile, mental, adoption or sealed released. Will not fax documents. Court makes copy: $1.00 per page. Certification fee: $1.00 per cert. Payee: LaGrange County Clerk. Personal checks accepted; credit cards are not. Prepayment required. Mail requests: SASE requested.

Lake County

Circuit & Superior Court 2293 N Main St, Courthouse, Crown Point, IN 46307; 219-755-3460; criminal phone: 219-755-3477; civil phone: 219-755-3462; probate phone: 219-755-3468; criminal fax: 219-755-3781; civil fax: 219-755-3520; 8:30AM-4PM (CST). ***Felony, Misdemeanor, Civil, Eviction, Small Claims, Probate.***

www.lakecountyin.org/index.jsp

Telephone of traffic, D-felonies, and misdemeanors is 219-755-3620.

Civil Records: Access: Mail, fax, in person, online. Both court and visitors may perform in person searches. No search fee. Required to search: name, years to search; also helpful: address. Civil cases indexed by defendant, plaintiff, go back to 1920s; on microfiche back to 1983; on computer back to 1990s. Note: Fax requests must be on letterhead. Mail turnaround time 1 week. Civil PAT goes back to 1990. Online search for docket records available at https://www.lakecountyin.org/portal/media-type/html/user/anon/page/online-docket. Search free but $.25 per page copy fee with $1.00 minimum.

Criminal Records: Access: Mail, in person, online. Both court and visitors may perform in person searches. Search fee: $7.00. Required to search: name, years to search, DOB, SSN; also helpful: address. Criminal records go back to 1900s; on microfiche back to 1983; on computer back to 1990s. Note: Search requests for background checks are forwarded to the County Bureau of Identification, 219-755-3316. Authorization required. Mail turnaround time 1 week. Criminal PAT goes back to same as civil. Online search of docket records at https://www.lakecountyin.org/portal/media-type/html/user/anon/page/online-docket. Search free but $.25 per page copy fee with $1.00 minimum.

General Information: No juvenile, mental, adoption or sealed released. Will fax documents $1.00 per page fee. Court makes copy: $1.00 per page. Certification fee: $1.00 per page. Payee: Lake County Clerk. Business checks accepted. No credit cards accepted. Prepayment required. SASE not required.

Lawrence County

Circuit & Superior Court 31 Courthouse, 916 15th St, Bedford, IN 47421; 812-275-7543; fax: 812-277-2024; 8:30AM-4:30PM (EST). ***Felony, Misdemeanor, Civil, Eviction, Small Claims, Probate.***

Superior Court I is 812-275-3124; Superior Court II is 812-275-4161. All small claims are filed in Superior II. The County Court converted to a Superior Court on 01/01/2009.

Civil Records: Access: In person only. Visitors must perform in person searches themselves. Required to search: name, years to search. Civil cases indexed by plaintiff. Civil records on computer from 1987, on index from 1817. Civil PAT goes back to 1987. PAT results show name, DOB.

Criminal Records: Access: In person only. Visitors must perform in person searches themselves. Required to search: name, years to search, DOB. Criminal records computerized from 1987, on index from 1817. Criminal PAT goes back same as civil.

General Information: No juvenile, mental, adoption or sealed released. Court makes copy: $1.00 per page. Certification fee: $1.00 per cert. Payee: Lawrence County Clerk. Only cashiers checks and money orders accepted. No credit cards. Prepayment required.

Madison County

Circuit & Superior Court PO Box 1277, 16 E 9th St, Anderson, IN 46015-1277; 765-641-9443; probate phone: 765-641-9467; fax: 765-640-4203; 8AM-4PM (EST). ***Felony, Misdemeanor, Civil, Eviction, Small Claims, Probate.*** www.madisoncountyindiana.org/judicial.html

Civil Records: Access: In person, online. Visitors must perform in person searches themselves. Required to search: name, years to search. Civil cases indexed by defendant. Civil records on microfiche and archived from 1950, on index from 1900. Civil PAT goes back to 1986. Online subscription service at https://www.doxpop.com. Fees involved. Records date back to 8/1987. A limited free search of open cases is available. Searching also available for Anderson City back to 1989.

Criminal Records: Access: In person, online. Visitors must perform in person searches themselves. Required to search: name, years to search, signed release. Criminal records on microfiche and archived from 1950, on index from 1900. Criminal PAT goes back to 1900. Online access to criminal is the same as civil except there are no criminal case records from Circuit court available.

General Information: No juvenile, mental, adoption or sealed records released. Will not fax documents. Court makes copy: $1.00 per page. Certification fee: $2.00. Payee: County Clerk. Business checks accepted. No credit cards. Prepayment required.

Marion County

Circuit & Superior Court 200 E Washington St, Indianapolis, IN 46204; criminal phone: 317-327-4733; civil phone: 317-327-4740; probate phone: 317-327-4718; fax: 317-327-3893; 8AM-4:30PM (EST). ***Felony, Misdemeanor, Civil, Probate.*** www.indygov.org/eGov/County/Clerk/home.htm

The Municipal Court of Marion County, once separate, is now part of Superior Court. All records are merged.

Civil Records: Access: Mail, in person, online. Both court and visitors may perform in person searches. No search fee. In person searches are performed on the computer system. Required to search: name, years to search. Civil cases indexed by defendant, plaintiff, on computer back to 1981, on microfiche, archived and on index from 1912. Small claims records are held by the township in which they w. Note: Small Claims office is at 317-327-5060, www.centergov.org/court/. There are 9 different small claims courts. Mail turnaround time 1-2 days. Public use terminal available. Search names online for free at www.civicnet.net. There is a $7.50 charge assessed to view each Case Summary. Online records go back to 1991. Also, search Center, Franklin and Washington Township civil, family, and probate dockets free at http://mycase.in.gov/default.aspx.

Criminal Records: Access: Mail, online, in person. Both court and visitors may perform in person searches. No search fee. Required to search: name, years to search, DOB; also helpful: SSN. Criminal records computerized from 1981, on microfiche, archived and on index from 1912. Small claims records are held by the township in which the. Mail turnaround time 1-2 days. Public use terminal available. Access to online criminal records at https://www.civicnet.net/criminal/ requires a subscription or you may search at rate of $4.50 per name and pay with credit card. Criminal records go back to 1988. Also, search Washington Township criminal dockets and citations free at http://mycase.in.gov/default.aspx.

General Information: No juvenile, mental, adoption or sealed released. Will not fax documents. Court makes copy: $1.00 per page, self serve same, though visitors must first be issued a copy code. Certification fee: $1.00; Exemplification fee- $4.00. Payee: County Clerk. Personal checks accepted with mail requests. No credit cards accepted. Prepayment required. Mail requests: SASE required.

Marshall County

Circuit & Superior Court 1 & 2 211 W Madison St, Plymouth, IN 46563; 574-936-8922; fax: 574-936-8893; 8AM-4PM (EST). ***Felony, Misdemeanor, Civil, Eviction, Small Claims, Probate.*** www.co.marshall.in.us/

Civil Records: Access: In person, online. Visitors must perform in person searches themselves. Required to search: name, years to search; also helpful: address. Civil cases indexed by defendant, plaintiff, on computer from 1989, on microfiche, archived and on index from 1835. Civil PAT goes back to 1991. Online subscription service at https://www.doxpop.com. Fees involved. Records date from 09/88. A limited free search of open cases is available.

Criminal Records: Access: In person, online. Visitors must perform in person searches themselves. Required to search: name, years to search, signed release; also helpful: address, DOB, SSN. Criminal records computerized from 1989, on microfiche, archived and on index from 1835. Criminal PAT goes back to 1988. Online access to criminal records is the same as civil.

General Information: No juvenile, mental, adoption or sealed released. Will fax out specific case files for $5.00 1st page; $1.00 each add'l, not to exceed $10.00. Court makes copy: $1.00 per page, self serve same. Certification fee: $2.00. Payee: County Clerk. Business checks accepted. No credit cards accepted. Prepayment required.

Martin County

Circuit Court PO Box 120 (111 Main St), Shoals, IN 47581; 812-247-3651; criminal fax: 812-247-2791; civil fax: same; 8AM-4PM (EST). ***Felony, Misdemeanor, Civil, Eviction, Small Claims, Probate.*** Probate fax is same as main fax number.

Civil Records: Access: In person only. Visitors must perform in person searches themselves. Required to search: name, years to search. Civil cases indexed by defendant, plaintiff; index on docket books. Public use terminal available, records go back to 2003.

Criminal Records: Access: In person only. Visitors must perform in person searches themselves. Required to search: name, years to search, DOB or SSN. Criminal records indexed in books. Public use terminal available, crim records go back to same.

General Information: No juvenile, mental, adoption, or sealed records released. Will fax documents to local or toll free line. Court makes copy: $1.00 per page. Certification fee: $2.00 per certification. Payee: County Clerk. Business checks accepted. No credit cards accepted. Prepayment required.

Miami County

Circuit & Superior Court PO Box 184, Peru, IN 46970; 765-472-3901; fax: 765-472-1778; 8AM-4PM (EST). ***Felony, Misdemeanor, Civil, Eviction, Small Claims, Probate.*** www.miamicountyin.gov

Civil Records: Access: Fax, mail, in person, online. Both court and visitors may perform in person searches. No search fee. Required to search: name, years to search. Civil cases indexed by defendant, plaintiff, on computer back to 4/1998, archived from 1900s. Some records on docket books by case number and alpha. Mail turnaround time 1-2 days. Civil PAT goes back to 1/1998. PAT civil results show middle initial. The court is working on adding more older records to the public system. Online subscription service at https://www.doxpop.com. Fees involved. Records date from 03/98. A limited free search of open cases is available.

Criminal Records: Access: Fax, mail, in person, online. Both court and visitors may perform in person searches. No search fee. Required to search: name, years to search, DOB, SSN, signed release. Criminal records computerized from 4/1998; archived from 1900s. Some records on docket books by case number and alpha. Mail turnaround time 1-2 days. Criminal PAT goes back to same as civil. PAT criminal results show middle initial. The court is working on adding more older records to the public system. Online access to criminal records is the same as civil; results show middle initial.

General Information: Online identifiers in results same as on public terminal. No juvenile, mental, adoption, or sealed released. Will fax documents $1.00 per page; no fee for toll free or local call. Court makes copy: $1.00 per page, self serve same. Certification fee: $1.00. Payee: Miami County Clerk. Personal checks accepted; credit cards are not. Prepayment required. SASE not required.

Monroe County

Circuit Court PO Box 547, Bloomington, IN 47402; 812-349-2614; criminal fax: 812-349-2610; civil fax: same; 8AM-4PM (EST). ***Felony, Misdemeanor, Civil, Eviction, Small Claims, Probate.*** www.co.monroe.in.us

Probate fax is same as main fax number.

Civil Records: Access: Mail, fax, in person, online. Both court and visitors may perform in person searches. No search fee. Required to search: name, years to search. Civil cases indexed by defendant, plaintiff, on computer from 1993. Some records on docket books by case number and alpha. In the process of putting records on microfilm. Mail turnaround time 48 hours. Civil PAT goes back to 8/1993. Search the docket by case number, party name or attorney name at http://mycase.in.gov/default.aspx.

Criminal Records: Access: Mail, fax, in person, online. Both court and visitors may perform in person searches. No search fee. Required to search: name, years to search, DOB. Criminal records computerized from 1993. Some records on docket books by case number and alpha. In the process of putting records on microfilm. Mail turnaround time 48 hours. Criminal PAT goes back to same as civil. Online access free at http://mycase.in.gov/default.aspx. Includes criminal and citations.

General Information: No juvenile, mental, adoption or sealed released. Fee to fax out file $1.00 per page. Court makes copy: $1.00 per page, self serve same. Certification fee: $1.00 per page. Payee: Monroe County Clerk. No personal checks or credit cards accepted. Prepayment required.

Montgomery County

Circuit & Superior Court PO Box 768, Crawfordsville, IN 47933; 765-364-6430; criminal fax: 765-364-6355; civil fax: same; 8:30AM-4:30PM (EST). ***Felony, Misdemeanor, Civil, Eviction, Small Claims, Probate.*** www.montgomeryco.net

Probate is a separate index at this same address. Probate fax is same as main fax number. There is a Superior Court 1 and a Superior Court 2 which was formerly known as the County Court.

Civil Records: Access: Phone, fax, mail, in person, online. Both court and visitors may perform in person searches. No search fee. Required to search: name, years to search. Civil cases indexed by defendant, plaintiff, on computer from 1990, some on microfiche and docket books, and archived from 1800s. Note: Indicate types of cases sought in mail search request. Mail turnaround time 1 week. Civil PAT goes back to 1990. Online subscription service at https://www.doxpop.com. Fees involved. Records date from 01/90. A limited free search of open cases is available.
Criminal Records: Access: Mail, fax, in person, online. Both court and visitors may perform in person searches. No search fee. Required to search: name, years to search, DOB; also helpful: SSN. Criminal records computerized from 1990, some on microfiche and docket books, and archived from 1800s. Mail turnaround time 1 week. Criminal PAT goes back to same as civil. Online access to criminal records is the same as civil.
General Information: Online identifiers in results same as on public terminal. No juvenile, mental, adoption or sealed released. Will fax documents $1.00 per page plus $3.25 fax fee. Court makes copy: $1.00 per page, self serve same. Certification fee: $2.00 per page includes copy fee. Payee: Montgomery County Clerk. Business checks accepted. No credit cards accepted. Prepayment required. Mail requests: SASE required.

Morgan County

Circuit & Superior Court PO Box 1556, Martinsville, IN 46151; 765-342-1025; fax: 765-342-1111; 8AM-4PM M,T,TH; 8AM-5PM W; 8AM-4:30PM F (EST). ***Felony, Misdemeanor, Civil, Eviction, Small Claims, Probate.***
Civil Records: Access: In person, online. Visitors must perform in person searches themselves. Required to search: name, years to search. Civil cases indexed by defendant, plaintiff, archived from 1970; on computer back to 1993. Some records on index cards. Note: In some instances, limited information is given over the phone if the docket number is known. Civil PAT goes back to 1995. Online subscription service at https://www.doxpop.com. Fees involved. Records date from 01/1997. A limited free search of open cases is available.
Criminal Records: Access: In person, online. Visitors must perform in person searches themselves. Required to search: name, years to search, DOB; SSN helpful, signed release. Criminal records archived from 1970; on microfilm 1992-95, on computer back to 1993. Criminal PAT goes back to same as civil. Online access is same as civil.
General Information: No juvenile, mental, adoption or sealed released. Will fax documents to local or toll-free number. Court makes copy: $1.00 per page. Certification fee: $1.00 per page. Payee: Morgan County Clerk. Personal checks accepted. Debit or redit cards accepted for anything over $15.00. Prepayment required. Credit cards not okay over the internet except for CS and judgment payments. Mail requests: SASE required for mail return of any copies.

Newton County

Circuit & Superior Court PO Box 49, 201 N 3rd St, Kentland, IN 47951; 219-474-6081; fax: 219-474-5749; 8AM-4PM (CST). ***Felony, Misdemeanor, Civil, Eviction, Small Claims, Probate.*** Search fee includes both courts, civil and criminal indexes.
Civil Records: Access: Mail, in person. Both court and visitors may perform in person searches. Search fee: $3.00 per name. Required to search: name, years to search. Civil cases indexed by defendant, plaintiff, on index from 1937, partial on microfiche; on computer back to 1996. Mail turnaround time 1-2 weeks. Civil PAT goes back to 1995. PAT results show name only.
Criminal Records: Access: Mail, in person. Both court and visitors may perform in person searches. Search fee: $3.00 per name. Required to search: name, years to search, DOB, signed release; also helpful: SSN. Criminal records indexed from 1937, partial on microfiche; on computer back to 1996. Mail turnaround time 1-2 weeks. Criminal PAT goes back to same as civil. PAT results show name only. For identification purposes, find case numbers on public terminal, then clerk will pull files and match them based on personal identifiers.
General Information: No juvenile, mental, adoption or sealed records released. Will not fax out documents. Court makes copy: $.25 per page. Certification fee: $1.25 per doc. Payee: Clerk of Newton Circuit Court. Business checks accepted. No credit cards accepted. Prepayment required. Mail requests: SASE required.

Noble County

Circuit, Superior I & Superior II Court 101 N Orange St, Albion, IN 46701; 260-636-2736; civil phone: same; probate phone: same; criminal fax: 260-636-4000; civil fax: same; 8AM-4PM (EST). ***Felony, Misdemeanor, Civil, Eviction, Small Claims, Probate.*** www.nobleco.org/
Clerk's office manages records for all three courts. Circuit Court phone is 260-636-2128. Probate fax is same as main fax number.
Civil Records: Access: In person, online. Visitors must perform in person searches themselves. Required to search: name, years to search. Civil cases indexed by defendant, plaintiff; index on cards and docket books to 1856; on computer back to 1992. Note: Court will accept genealogy search requests by mail. Civil PAT goes back to 1992. Public access terminal- court will assist in instructing users for genealogy purposes. Access court records free at http://noble.nasaview.com/terms.php.
Criminal Records: Access: In person, online. Visitors must perform in person searches themselves. Required to search: name, years to search; also helpful: DOB. Criminal records indexed on cards and docket books to 1856; on computer back to 1992. Criminal PAT goes back to 1992. Public terminals located in Recorder's office. Online access to criminal same as civil, see above.
General Information: No juvenile, mental, adoption or sealed released. Will not fax documents. Court makes copy: $1.00 per page. Certification fee: $1.00 per certification. Payee: Noble County Clerk. No personal checks accepted. Major credit cards accepted; a usage fee applies. Prepayment required. SASE required for mail return of any copies.

Ohio County

Circuit & Superior Court PO Box 185, Rising Sun, IN 47040; 812-438-2610; fax: 812-438-1215; 9AM-4PM M,T,TH,F 9AM-N Sat (EST). ***Felony, Misdemeanor, Civil, Eviction, Small Claims, Probate.***
Civil Records: Access: In person only. Both court and visitors may perform in person searches. No search fee. Required to search: name, years to search. Civil cases indexed by defendant, plaintiff, archived from 1844; on computer back to 8/1999.
Criminal Records: Access: In person only. Visitors must perform in person searches themselves. Required to search: name, years to search. Criminal records computerized from 8/1999.
General Information: No juvenile, mental, adoption or sealed released. Fee to fax out file $3.00 1st page, $1.00 each add'l, prepaid. Court makes copy: $1.00 per page, self serve same. Certification fee: $2.00. Payee: Ohio County Clerk. No personal checks or credit cards accepted. Prepayment required.

Orange County

Circuit Court Courthouse, Court St, Paoli, IN 47454; 812-723-2649; criminal fax: 812-723-0239; civil fax: same; 8AM-4PM (EST). ***Felony, Civil, Eviction, Small Claims, Probate.***
Probate is a separate index at this same address. See County Superior Court for misdemeanors and Class D (minor) felonies. Probate fax same as main fax.
Civil Records: Access: Mail, fax, in person. Both court and visitors may perform in person searches. No search fee. Required to search: name, years to search. Civil cases indexed by defendant, plaintiff, archived from 1874. Some records on docket books. Mail turnaround time 2 weeks.
Criminal Records: Access: Mail, fax, in person. Both court and visitors may perform in person searches. No search fee. Required to search: name, years to search. Criminal records archived from 1874. Some records on docket books. Mail turnaround time 2 weeks.
General Information: No juvenile, mental, adoption or sealed released. Will fax documents. Court makes copy: $1.00 per page. Self serve: $.10 per page. Certification fee: $1.00 per document. Payee: Orange Circuit Clerk. Only cashiers checks and money orders accepted. No credit cards accepted. Prepayment required. Mail requests: SASE required.

Superior Court 205 E Main St, Paoli, IN 47454; 812-723-3322; criminal phone: 812-723-2403; civil phone: 812-723-2403; fax: 812-723-5839; 8AM-N, 1-4PM (EST). ***Felony, Misdemeanor, Civil, Eviction, Small Claims, Probate.***
Civil Records: Access: In person. Both court and visitors may perform in person searches. No search fee. Required to search: name, years to search. Civil cases indexed by defendant, plaintiff, go back to 1978. Note: Direct search requests to "the Circuit and Superior Court."
Criminal Records: Access: In person. Both court and visitors may perform in person searches. No search fee. Required to search: name, years to search. Criminal records archived from 1874. Some records on docket books. Note: Direct search requests to "the Circuit and County Court.".
General Information: No juvenile, mental, adoption or sealed released. Will fax documents to local or toll-free number. Court makes copy: $1.00 per page. Certification fee: $1.00 per doc. Payee: Orange Superior Court Clerk. Only cashiers checks and money orders accepted. No credit cards accepted. Prepayment required.

Owen County

Circuit Court PO Box 146, Courthouse, Spencer, IN 47460; 812-829-5015; fax: 812-829-5147; 8AM-4PM (EST). ***Felony, Misdemeanor, Civil, Eviction, Small Claims, Probate.***
Civil Records: Access: In person only. Visitors must perform in person searches themselves. Required to search: name, years to search. Civil cases indexed by defendant, plaintiff, archived from 1800s. Some records on docket books. Limited as of 04/18/07.
Criminal Records: Access: In person only. Visitors must perform in person searches themselves. Required to search: name, years to search. Criminal records archived from 1800s. Some records on docket books. Limited as of 04/18/07.
General Information: No juvenile, mental, adoption or sealed records released. Will fax documents $1.00 per page. Court makes copy: $1.00 per page, self serve same. Certification fee: $1.00 per page. Payee: Owen County Clerk. Business checks accepted. No credit cards accepted. Prepayment required.

Parke County

Circuit Court 116 W High St, Rm 204, Rockville, IN 47872; 765-569-5132; fax: 765-569-4222; 8AM-4PM (EST). ***Felony, Misdemeanor, Civil, Eviction, Small Claims, Probate.***
Civil Records: Access: In person only. Visitors must perform in person searches themselves. Required to search: name, years to search. Civil cases indexed by defendant, plaintiff, archived from 1880s. Some records on docket books.
Criminal Records: Access: In person only. Visitors must perform in person searches themselves. Required to search: name, years to search. Criminal records archived from 1880s. Some records on docket books.
General Information: No juvenile, mental, adoption or sealed released. Will fax out documents no fee. Court makes copy: n/a. Self serve: $1.00 per page. Cert fee: $2.00. Payee: Parke County Clerk. No personal checks or credit cards. Prepayment required.

Perry County

Circuit Court 2219 Payne St, #219, Courthouse, Circuit Clerk, Tell City, IN 47586; 812-547-3741; fax: 812-547-9782; 8AM-4PM (EST). ***Felony, Misdemeanor, Civil, Eviction, Small Claims, Probate.*** www.perrycountyin.org/
Civil Records: Access: In person, online. Both court and visitors may perform in person searches. No

search fee. Required to search: name, years to search. Civil cases indexed by defendant, plaintiff, archived from 1900s. Some records on dockets. Civil PAT goes back to 1997. Online subscription service at https://www.doxpop.com. Fees involved. Records date back to 7/1997.
Criminal Records: Access: In person, online. Both court and visitors may perform in person searches. No search fee. Required to search: name, years to search. Criminal records archived from 1900s. Some records on dockets. Criminal PAT goes back to same as civil. Online access same as civil.
General Information: No juvenile, mental, adoption or sealed released. Court makes copy: $.50 per page. Certification fee: $1.00 per cert. Payee: Perry County Clerk. Business checks accepted. No credit cards accepted. Prepayment required.

Pike County

Circuit Court PO Box 407, Petersburg, IN 47567; 812-354-6025/6026; probate phone: 812-354-6025; fax: 812-354-3552; 8AM-4PM (EST). ***Felony, Misdemeanor, Civil, Eviction, Small Claims, Probate.*** Probate fax- 812-354-6369
Civil Records: Access: In person, online. Both court and visitors may perform in person searches. No search fee. Required to search: name, years to search. Civil cases indexed by defendant, plaintiff, archived from 1817. Some records on docket books and index file; on computer since 7/99. Civil PAT goes back to 1999. PAT results show name only. Online subscription service at https://www.doxpop.com. Fees involved. A limited free search of open cases is available.
Criminal Records: Access: In person, online. Both court and visitors may perform in person searches. No search fee. Required to search: name, years to search, DOB. Criminal records archived from 1817. Some records on docket books and index file; on computer since 7/99. Criminal PAT goes back to same. PAT results show name only. Online access to criminal same as civil. Online results show name only.
General Information: No juvenile, mental, adoption or sealed released. Will fax documents $.25 per side, $10.00 minimum. Court makes copy: $1.00 per page, self serve same. Certification fee: $1.00 per cert. Payee: Pike County Clerk. Only cashiers checks and money orders accepted. No credit cards accepted. Prepayment required.

Porter County

Circuit Court Records Division, Courthouse, 16 E Lincolnway, Rm 217, Valparaiso, IN 46383-5659; 219-465-3453; 8:30AM-4:30PM (CST). ***Felony, Misdemeanor, Civil, Eviction, Small Claims, Probate.*** www.porterco.org
Eviction and small claims in Rm 211, 219-465-3413.
Civil Records: Access: Mail, in person. Both court and visitors may perform in person searches. No search fee. Required to search: name, years to search. Civil cases indexed by defendant, plaintiff, on computer index from 1990. Circuit Court records kept from 1844, Superior Court records from 1895. Probate records from Circuit Court. Mail turnaround time 1-2 weeks. Civil PAT goes back to 2000. PAT civil results show middle initial.
Criminal Records: Access: Mail, in person. Both court and visitors may perform in person searches. No search fee. Required to search: name, years to search. Criminal records on computer index since 1990. Circuit Court criminal records kept from 1877, Superior Court from 1895. Mail turnaround time 1-2 weeks. Criminal PAT goes back to same as civil. PAT criminal results show middle initial.
General Information: No juvenile, mental, adoption or sealed released. Will not fax documents. Court makes copy: $1.00 per page, self serve same. Certification fee: $1.00 per document. Payee: Porter County Clerk. Only cashiers checks and money orders accepted. Prepayment required. Mail requests: SASE required.

Superior Court 3560 Willow Creek Dr, Portage, IN 46368; 219-759-8217; 8:30AM-4:30PM (CST). ***Misdemeanor, Civil, Small Claims, Probate.*** www.porterco.org/
Online access may be available later this year.
Civil Records: Access: Mail, in person. Both court and visitors may perform in person searches. No search fee. Required to search: name, years to search. Civil cases indexed by defendant, plaintiff, on computer since 1991; prior records on manual index. Mail turnaround time 1 week. Civil PAT goes back to 1997. PAT results show name only.
Criminal Records: Access: Mail, in person. Both court and visitors may perform in person searches. No search fee. Required to search: name, years to search; also helpful: DOB, SSN. Criminal records on computer since 1991; prior records on manual index. Mail turnaround time 1 week. Criminal PAT goes back to 1997. PAT results show name only.
General Information: No juvenile, mental, adoption or sealed records released. Fee to fax document $.79 per page. Court makes copy: $2.00 per page. Certification fee: $1.00 per cert. Payee: Porter County Clerk. Only cashiers checks and money orders accepted. No credit cards. Prepayment required.

Posey County

Circuit & Superior Court PO Box 606, 300 Main St, Mount Vernon, IN 47620-0606; 812-838-1306; criminal phone: 812-838-8367; civil phone: 812-838-8368; probate phone: 812-838-1306; criminal fax: 812-838-1307; civil fax: same; 8AM-4PM (CST). ***Felony, Misdemeanor, Civil, Eviction, Small Claims, Probate.***
Probate fax is same as main fax number.
Civil Records: Access: In person only. Only the court performs in person searches; visitors may not. Search fee: $1.00 per page found by court. Required to search: name, years to search; also helpful: address. Civil cases indexed by defendant, plaintiff, on computer since 8/88, prior on docket books. Civil PAT available. PAT results show name only. Public terminal available in Superior Court.
Criminal Records: Access: In person only. Only the court performs in person searches; visitors may not. Search fee: $1.00 per page found by court. Required to search: name, years to search; also helpful: DOB, SSN. Criminal records on computer since 8/88, prior on docket books. Criminal PAT available. PAT results show name only.
General Information: No juvenile, mental, adoption or sealed released. Will fax documents $1.00 per page. Court makes copy: $1.00 per page. Self serve: $1.00 per page. Certification fee: $1.00. Payee: Posey County Clerk. Only cashiers checks and money orders accepted. Major credit cards. Prepayment required.

Pulaski County

Circuit Court 112 E Main, Rm 230, Winamac, IN 46996; 574-946-3313; criminal fax: 574-946-4953; civil fax: same; 8AM-4PM (EST). ***Felony, Civil, Probate.***
Civil suits, eviction and small claims are managed by the Superior Court. Probate fax is same as main fax number.
Civil Records: Access: In person only. Visitors must perform in person searches themselves. Required to search: name, years to search. Civil cases indexed by defendant. Civil records archived from 1850s. Some records on docket books. On computer back to 2000. Public use terminal available, records go back to 2000.
Criminal Records: Access: In person only. Visitors must perform in person searches themselves. Required to search: name, years to search; SSN helpful. Criminal records archived from 1850s. Some records on docket books. On computer back to 1998 (circuit court-2000). Public use terminal available, crim records go back to 2000.
General Information: No juvenile, mental, adoption or sealed records released. Will fax documents $3.00 fee. Court makes copy: $.10 per page, self serve same. Certification fee: $2.00 per cert. Payee: Pulaski County Clerk. Only cashiers checks and money orders accepted. No credit cards. Prepayment required.

Superior Court 112 E Main St, Winamac, IN 46996; 574-946-3371; criminal fax: 574-946-3573; civil fax: same; 8AM-4PM (EST). ***Misdemeanor, Civil, Eviction, Small Claims, Traffic.***
Add'l current civil records can be found at the Circuit Court. The advantage this court offers is that it will do limited phone index searches and the Circuit Court will not.
Civil Records: Access: Phone, in person. Visitors must perform in person searches themselves. No search fee. Required to search: name, years to search. Civil cases indexed by defendant. Most records go back a maximum of two years; older records found at Circuit Court Clerk office. Civil PAT goes back to 1996.
Criminal Records: Access: Phone, in person. Visitors must perform in person searches themselves. No search fee. Required to search: Name only. Misdemeanor records go back a maximum of two years; older records found at Circuit Court Clerk office. Note: Clerk will do short, usually single name searches for no fee over the phone. Criminal PAT goes back to same as civil.PAT results show name, DOB. Results include last 4 digits of SSN.
General Information: No juvenile, mental, adoption or sealed records released. Court makes copy: $.50 per page. Certification fee: $2.00. Payee: Pulaski County. Only cashiers checks and money orders accepted. No credit cards. Prepayment required.

Putnam County

Circuit & Superior Court PO Box 546, Greencastle, IN 46135; 765-653-2648; probate phone: 765-653-2649; fax: 765-653-8405; 8AM-4PM (EST). ***Felony, Misdemeanor, Civil, Eviction, Small Claims, Probate.***
Civil Records: Access: In person, online. Visitors must perform in person searches themselves. Required to search: name, years to search. Civil cases indexed by defendant, plaintiff; index on docket books from 1991, archived from 1800s. Some records on docket books. Civil PAT goes back to 1998 Circuit; 1993 Superior. PAT results show middle initial, DOB. Online subscription service at https://www.doxpop.com. Fees involved. Records date from 01/92. A limited free search of open cases is available.
Criminal Records: Access: In person, online. Visitors must perform in person searches themselves. Required to search: name, years to search; also helpful: DOB, SSN. Criminal records indexed in books from 1991, archived from 1800s. Some records on docket books. Criminal PAT goes back to same as civil. PAT results show middle initial, DOB. Online access to criminal same as civil. Online results show middle initial, DOB.
General Information: No juvenile, mental, adoption or sealed released. Will not fax documents. Court makes copy: $1.00 per page, self serve same. Certification fee: $1.00. Payee: Putnam County Clerk. Business checks accepted. No credit cards accepted. Prepayment required. Mail requests: SASE required for mail return of any copies.

Randolph County

Circuit & Superior Court PO Box 230 Courthouse, Winchester, IN 47394-0230; 765-584-7207; fax: 765-584-7186; 8AM-4PM (EST). ***Felony, Misdemeanor, Civil, Eviction, Small Claims, Probate.***
Civil Records: Access: Fax, mail, in person, online. Visitors must perform in person searches themselves. No search fee. Required to search: name, years to search. Civil cases indexed by defendant, plaintiff, archived from early 1800s, computerized from 1994. Records on docket books and microfiche. Civil PAT goes back to 6/1994. Online subscription service at https://www.doxpop.com. Fees involved. Records date from 06/94. A limited free search of open cases is available.
Criminal Records: Access: Fax, mail, in person, online. Visitors must perform in person searches themselves. No search fee. Required to search: name, years to search. Criminal records archived from early 1800s, computerized since 1994. Records on docket books and microfiche. Mail turnaround time 3 days. Criminal PAT goes back to same as civil. Online access to criminal records is the same as civil.
General Information: No juvenile, mental, adoption or sealed released. Will fax documents $4.00 1st page, $.75 each add'l. Court makes copy: $1.00 per page,

self serve same. Certification fee: $1.00. Payee: Randolph County Clerk. Checks and money orders accepted. No credit cards accepted. Prepayment required. Mail requests: SASE required.

Ripley County

Circuit Court PO Box 177, Versailles, IN 47042; 812-689-6115; fax: 812-689-6000; 8AM-4PM (EST). ***Felony, Misdemeanor, Civil, Eviction, Small Claims, Probate.*** www.ripleycounty.com

Civil Records: Access: Phone, mail, in person, online. Both court and visitors may perform in person searches. No search fee. Required to search: name, years to search. Civil cases indexed by defendant, plaintiff, on computer since 1993, archived from 1800s. Some records on docket books. Mail turnaround time 1 week. Public use terminal available, records go back to 1993. Online subscription service at https://www.doxpop.com. Fees involved. Records date from 07/1993. A limited free search of open cases is available.

Criminal Records: Access: Mail, in person, online. Both court and visitors may perform in person searches. No search fee. Required to search: name, years to search, DOB, signed release; also helpful: SSN. Criminal records on computer since 1993, archived from 1800s. Some records on docket books. Mail turnaround time 1 week. Public use terminal available, crim records go back to same. Online access to criminal is same as civil.

General Information: No juvenile, mental, adoption or sealed records released. Will fax documents $1.00 per page, prepaid. Court makes copy: $1.00 per page, self serve same. Certification fee: $3.00. Payee: Clerk of Ripley Circuit Court. Personal checks accepted; credit cards are not. Prepayment required. Mail requests: SASE required.

Rush County

Circuit & Superior Court PO Box 429, Rushville, IN 46173; 765-932-2086; fax: 765-932-4165; 8AM-4PM (EST). ***Felony, Misdemeanor, Civil, Eviction, Small Claims, Probate.***

This office will not conduct general searches, but will pull files if the specific case number is given.

Civil Records: Access: In person only. Visitors must perform in person searches themselves. Required to search: name, years to search. Civil cases indexed by defendant, plaintiff, archived from 1822. Some records on docket books.

Criminal Records: Access: In person only. Visitors must perform in person searches themselves. Required to search: name, years to search, DOB; SSN, cause number helpful. Criminal records archived from 1822. Some records on docket books. Note: Court will only search the status of an open case, and you need to provide case number of it.

General Information: No juvenile, mental, adoption or sealed records released. Will fax documents $1.00 per page. Court makes copy: $1.00 per page, self serve same. Certification fee: $1.00 per unit. Payee: Rush County Clerk. Business checks accepted. No credit cards accepted. Prepayment required.

Scott County

Circuit & Superior Court 1 E McClain Ave, #120, Scottsburg, IN 47170; 812-752-8420; fax: 812-752-5459; 8:30AM-4:30PM (EST). ***Felony, Misdemeanor, Civil, Eviction, Small Claims, Probate.***

Civil Records: Access: In person only. Visitors must perform in person searches themselves. Required to search: name, years to search; also helpful: address. Civil cases indexed by defendant, plaintiff, on computer from 2/90, on docket books from 1970. Note: Court will only search if provided a case number. Civil PAT goes back to 1990. PAT results show middle initial, DOB.

Criminal Records: Access: In person only. Visitors must perform in person searches themselves. Required to search: name, years to search; also helpful: DOB, SSN. Criminal records computerized from 2/90, on docket books from 1970. Note: Court will only search if provided a case number. Criminal PAT goes back to 1990. PAT results show middle initial, DOB.

General Information: No juvenile, mental, adoption or sealed released. Court makes copy: $1.00 per page. Certification fee: $2.00 per cert. Payee: Scott County Clerk. Business checks accepted. Major credit cards accepted (beginning after 11/2008). Prepayment required.

Shelby County

Circuit & Superior Court 407 S Harrison St, Shelbyville, IN 46176; 317-392-6350; fax: 317-392-6339; 8AM-4PM (EST). ***Felony, Misdemeanor, Civil, Eviction, Small Claims, Probate.***

Civil Records: Access: Phone, in person. Visitors must perform in person searches themselves. No search fee. Required to search: name, years to search. Civil cases indexed by defendant, plaintiff, on computer since 7/95. Note: If you call, the clerk can search the docket on computer; they will only pull and copy files on Thursdays. Civil PAT goes back to 1995. PAT results show middle initial, but terminal results do not always show the DOB.

Criminal Records: Access: Phone, in person. Visitors must perform in person searches themselves. No search fee. Required to search: name, years to search. Criminal records on computer since 7/95. Note: If you call, the clerk can search the docket on computer; they will only pull and copy files on Thursdays. Criminal PAT goes back to same as civil. PAT results show middle initial, DOB.

General Information: No juvenile, mental, adoption or sealed released. Will not fax documents. Court makes copy: $.10 per page. Certification fee: $1.00 per doc. Payee: Clerk of Court. No personal checks or credit cards accepted. Prepayment required.

Spencer County

Circuit Court PO Box 12, Rockport, IN 47635; 812-649-6027; criminal fax: 812-649-6030; civil fax: same; 8AM-4PM (CST). ***Felony, Misdemeanor, Civil, Eviction, Small Claims, Probate.***

Probate is a separate index at this same address. Probate fax is same as main fax number.

Civil Records: Access: In person, online. Visitors must perform in person searches themselves. Required to search: name, years to search. Civil cases indexed by defendant, plaintiff, archived from early 1900s. Some records on docket books. Child support cases on computer. Starting 2/02 all new cases are computerized. Civil PAT goes back to 2002. PAT results show name only. Online subscription service at https://www.doxpop.com. Fees involved. Records date from 1/02.

Criminal Records: Access: In person, online. Visitors must perform in person searches themselves. Required to search: name, years to search. Criminal records archived from early 1900s. Some records on docket books. Starting 2/02 all new cases are computerized. Criminal PAT goes back to same as civil. PAT criminal results show middle initial. Online access to criminal is same as civil. Online results show name only.

General Information: No juvenile, mental, adoption or sealed released. Will fax out specific case files for no fee once all other fees are paid. Court makes copy: $1.00 per page, self serve same. Certification fee: $1.00 per document. Payee: Spencer Circuit Court. Only cashiers checks and money orders accepted. No credit cards accepted. Prepayment required. Mail requests: SASE required for mail return of any copies.

St. Joseph County

Circuit & Superior Court 101 S Main St, South Bend, IN 46601; 574-235-9635; fax: 574-235-9838; 8-4:30PM (EST). ***Felony, Misdemeanor, Civil, Eviction, Small Claims, Probate.***

Civil Records: Access: Mail, in person. Visitors must perform in person searches themselves. No search fee. Required to search: name, years to search. Civil cases indexed by defendant, plaintiff, on general index from 1962, computerized since 1992. Civil PAT goes back to 1992. PAT results show name only.

Criminal Records: Access: In person only. Visitors must perform in person searches themselves. Required to search: name, years to search; also helpful: address, DOB, SSN. Criminal records on general index from 1962, computerized since 1984. Criminal PAT goes back to 1986 (Misd), 1992 (Felony). PAT results show name only.

General Information: No juvenile, mental, adoption or sealed released. Will fax documents to local or toll-free number; will not fax certified documents. Court makes copy: $.05 per page.Copy fee may increase in 2008. Certification fee: $1.00. Payee: St Joseph County Clerk. Business checks accepted. No credit cards accepted. Prepayment required. Mail requests: SASE required for civil.

Starke County

Circuit Court PO Box 395, Courthouse, Knox, IN 46534; 574-772-9128; probate phone: 574-772-9162; fax: 574-772-9169; 8:30AM-4PM (CST). ***Felony, Misdemeanor, Civil, Eviction, Small Claims, Probate.*** www.in-map.net/counties/STARKE/government/index.htm

Civil Records: Access: In person, online. Both court and visitors may perform in person searches. No search fee. Required to search: name, years to search. Civil cases indexed by defendant, plaintiff, archived from 1850s. Some records on docket books. Civil PAT goes back to 2006. PAT results show middle initial, DOB. Online subscription service at https://www.doxpop.com. Fees involved. Records date back to 9/2005 A limited free search of open cases is available.

Criminal Records: Access: In person, online. Both court and visitors may perform in person searches. No search fee. Required to search: name, years to search, DOB. Criminal records archived from 1850s. Some records on docket books. Criminal PAT goes back to 2006. PAT results show middle initial, but DOB does not always appear in results. Online access to criminal records is the same as civil. Online results show middle initial, but DOB does not always appear on criminal online results.

General Information: No juvenile, mental, adoption or sealed released. Will fax documents $1.00 per page. Court makes copy: $1.00 per page. Certification fee: $2.00. Payee: Clerk of Stark Circuit Court. No business checks accepted. No credit cards accepted. Prepayment required.

Steuben County

Circuit & Superior Court 55 S Public Square, Courthouse, Angola, IN 46703; 260-668-1000; criminal phone: x2270; civil phone: x2240; 8AM-4:30PM (EST). ***Felony, Misdemeanor, Civil, Eviction, Small Claims, Probate.*** www.steubencounty.com/departments/court/court.aspx

Civil Records: Access: In person only. Visitors must perform in person searches themselves. Required to search: name, years to search. Civil cases indexed by defendant, plaintiff, archived from 1800s. Some records on docket books. Civil PAT goes back to 1995.

Criminal Records: Access: In person only. Visitors must perform in person searches themselves. Required to search: name, years to search. Criminal records archived from 1800s, computerized since 6/94. Some records on docket books. Criminal PAT goes back to same as civil.

General Information: No juvenile, mental, adoption, some probate, or sealed released. Will not fax documents. Court makes copy: $1.00 per page. Certification fee: $2.00. Payee: Steuben County Clerk. Only cashiers checks and money orders accepted. No credit cards accepted. Prepayment required.

Sullivan County

Circuit & Superior Court PO Box 370, 100 Courthouse Sq, Rm 304, Sullivan, IN 47882-0370; 812-268-4657; probate phone: 812-268-4411; fax: 812-268-7027; 8AM-4PM (EST). ***Felony, Misdemeanor, Civil, Eviction, Small Claims, Probate.***

Civil Records: Access: In person, online. Visitors must perform in person searches themselves. Required to search: name, years to search; also helpful: address. Civil cases indexed by defendant, plaintiff; index on docket books or general index from late 1850's; computerized from 1999. Civil PAT goes back to 1991. PAT results show name only. Online subscription service at https://www.doxpop.com.

Fees involved. Records date from 04/1999. A limited free search of open cases is available.
Criminal Records: Access: In person, online. Visitors must perform in person searches themselves. Required to search: name, years to search, DOB, signed release; also helpful: address, SSN. Criminal docket on books or general index from late 1850's; computerized from 1999. Criminal PAT goes back to 1993. PAT results show name only. Online access to criminal records is the same as civil. Online results show name only.
General Information: No juvenile, mental, adoption or sealed released. Will not fax documents. Court makes copy: $1.00 per page, self serve same. Certification fee: $1.00 per page. Payee: Sullivan County. No personal checks accepted; business check okay. Major credit cards accepted at 888-604-7888; mention pay location 5208. Prepayment required.

Switzerland County

Circuit & Superior Court Courthouse, 212 W Main St, Vevay, IN 47043; 812-427-3175; criminal fax: 812-427-2017; civil fax: same; 8AM-3:30PM M-W,F; 8AM-N TH (EST). ***Felony, Misdemeanor, Civil, Eviction, Small Claims, Probate.***
Probate fax is same as main fax number.
Civil Records: Access: In person only. Visitors must perform in person searches themselves. Required to search: name, years to search, DOB. Civil cases indexed by defendant, plaintiff, archived from 1900s. All records on docket books or general index. Civil PAT goes back to 2/2001. PAT results show middle initial, DOB.
Criminal Records: Access: In person only. Visitors must perform in person searches themselves. Required to search: name, years to search, DOB. Criminal records archived from 1900s. All records on docket books or general index. Criminal PAT goes back to same as civil. PAT results show middle initial, DOB.
General Information: No juvenile, mental, adoption or sealed records released. Will not fax documents. Court makes copy: first 4 pages free, $1.00 for 5th page, then $.25 each add'l, self serve same. Certification fee: $1.00 per page. Payee: Switzerland County Clerk. No personal checks or credit cards accepted. Prepayment required.

Tippecanoe County

Circuit & Superior Court PO Box 1665, Lafayette, IN 47902; 765-423-9326; probate phone: 765-423-9343; fax: 765-423-9194; 8AM-4:30PM (EST). ***Felony, Misdemeanor, Civil, Eviction, Small Claims, Probate.*** www.tippecanoe.in.gov
Civil Records: Access: In person, mail, online. Visitors must perform in person searches themselves. No search fee. Required to search: name, years to search. Civil cases indexed by defendant, plaintiff, on computer from 1987, on microfiche from 1900. Some records on index and docket books. Civil PAT goes back to mid 1980s. Online access to court records through CourtView are free at www.county.tippecanoe.in.us/court/pa.urd/pamw6500-display.
Criminal Records: Access: In person, mail, online. Visitors must perform in person searches themselves. No search fee. Required to search: name, years to search; also helpful: DOB, SSN, sex, signed release. Criminal records computerized from 1987, on microfiche from 1900. Some records on index and docket books. Criminal PAT goes back to same as civil. Online access to criminal records is the same as civil.
General Information: No juvenile, mental, adoption or sealed released. Will fax documents $2.00 per page. Court makes copy: $1.00 per page. Self serve: $.05 per page. Certification fee: $1.00. Payee: Tippecanoe County Clerk. Business checks accepted. No credit cards accepted. Prepayment required. SASE not required.

Tipton County

Circuit Court 101 E Jefferson, 3rd Fl, County Courthouse, Tipton, IN 46072; 765-675-2795; fax: 765-675-4103; 8AM-4PM M-TH; 8AM-5PM F (EST). ***Felony, Misdemeanor, Civil, Eviction, Small Claims, Probate.***
Civil Records: Access: In person, online. Visitors must perform in person searches themselves. Required to search: name, years to search. Civil cases indexed by defendant, plaintiff, on card file and archived from 1930s. Search the docket by case number, party name or attorney name at http://mycase.in.gov/default.aspx.
Criminal Records: Access: In person, online. Visitors must perform in person searches themselves. Required to search: name, years to search. Criminal records on card file and archived from 1930s. Online access free at http://mycase.in.gov/default.aspx. Includes criminal and citations.
General Information: No juvenile, mental, adoption or sealed released. Will fax documents $1.00 per page. Court makes copy: $1.00 per page, self serve same. Certification fee: $1.00. Payee: Tipton County Clerk. Personal checks accepted; credit cards are not. Prepayment required.

Union County

Circuit Court 26 W Union St, Liberty, IN 47353; 765-458-6121; fax: 765-458-5263; 8AM-4PM (EST). ***Felony, Misdemeanor, Civil, Eviction, Small Claims, Probate.***
Civil Records: Access: In person only. Visitors must perform in person searches themselves. Required to search: name, years to search. Civil cases indexed by defendant, plaintiff, archived from 1821. Some records on docket books or entry books.
Criminal Records: Access: In person only. Visitors must perform in person searches themselves. Required to search: name, years to search, DOB. Criminal records archived from 1821. Some records on docket books or entry books.
General Information: No juvenile, mental, adoption or sealed records released. Will not fax documents. Court makes copy: $1.00 per page. Certification fee: $2.00 per cert. Payee: Union County Clerk. Only cashiers checks and money orders accepted. No credit cards accepted. Prepayment required.

Vanderburgh County

Circuit & Superior Court PO Box 3356, Civic Ctr Courts Bldg - Rm 216, Evansville, IN 47732-3356; 812-435-5160; criminal phone: 812-435-5169; civil phone: 812-435-5722; probate phone: 812-435-5377; fax: 812-435-5849; 7:30AM-4:30PM (CST). ***Felony, Misdemeanor, Civil, Eviction, Small Claims, Probate.***
www.vanderburghgov.org/home/index.asp?page=66
Civil Records: Access: In person only. Visitors must perform in person searches themselves. Required to search: name, years to search. Civil cases indexed by defendant, plaintiff, on computer back to 1991, archived from 1900s. Some records on index books. Civil PAT goes back to 1991. PAT results show middle initial, DOB. Public terminal closes 4PM.
Criminal Records: Access: In person only. Visitors must perform in person searches themselves. Required to search: name, years to search, DOB, SSN. Criminal records computerized from 1991, archived from 1900s. Some records on index books. Criminal PAT goes back to same as civil. PAT results show middle initial, DOB. Public terminal closes at 4PM.
General Information: No juvenile, mental, adoption or sealed released. Will not fax documents. Court makes copy: $1.00 per page. Self serve: $1.00 per page. Certification fee: $1.00. Payee: Vanderburgh County Clerk. Business checks accepted. No credit cards accepted. Prepayment required.

Vermillion County

Circuit Court PO Box 10, Newport, IN 47966-0010; 765-492-3500; fax: 765-492-5001; 8AM-4PM (EST). ***Felony, Misdemeanor, Civil, Eviction, Small Claims, Probate.***
Civil Records: Access: In person only. Visitors must perform in person searches themselves. Required to search: name. Civil cases indexed by defendant, plaintiff. Records on computer go back to 1994; archived from 1824. Some records on docket books.
Criminal Records: Access: In person only. Visitors must perform in person searches themselves. Required to search: name. Records on computer go back to 1994; archived from 1825. Some records on docket books.
General Information: No juvenile, mental, adoption or sealed released. Will not fax documents. Court makes copy: $1.00 per page, self serve same. Certification fee: $2.00. Payee: Vermillion County Clerk. Business checks accepted. No credit cards accepted. Prepayment required.

Vigo County

Circuit Court PO Box 8449, Courthouse, 2nd Fl, Terre Haute, IN 47807-8449; 812-462-3211; fax: 812-232-2921; 8AM-4PM (EST). ***Felony, Misdemeanor, Civil, Eviction, Small Claims, Probate.*** www.vigocounty.org/courts/
Civil Records: Access: Mail, in person, online. Visitors must perform in person searches themselves. No search fee. Required to search: name, years to search. Civil cases indexed by defendant, plaintiff; index on docket books; on computer back to 8/1996. Civil PAT goes back to 1996. PAT results show name only. Online subscription service at https://www.doxpop.com. Fees involved. Records date from 04/96. A limited free search of open cases is available.
Criminal Records: Access: In person, online. Visitors must perform in person searches themselves. Required to search: name, years to search; also helpful: DOB. Criminal records indexed in books; on computer back to 8/1996. Criminal PAT goes back to same as civil. Online access to criminal records is the same as civil.
General Information: No juvenile, mental, adoption or sealed released. Will not fax documents. Court makes copy: $1.00 per page. Certification fee: $1.00 per cert. Payee: Vigo County Clerk. Only cashiers checks and money orders accepted. No credit cards. Prepayment required. Mail requests: SASE required.

Wabash County

Circuit & Superior Court 69 W Hill St, Wabash, IN 46992; 260-563-0661 X230; fax: 260-569-1352; 8AM-4PM (EST). ***Felony, Misdemeanor, Civil, Eviction, Small Claims, Probate.***
Civil Records: Access: In person, online. Visitors must perform in person searches themselves. Required to search: name, years to search. Civil cases indexed by defendant, plaintiff, archived from 1800s; on computer since 1989. Some judgments on fee books. Civil PAT goes back to 1989. PAT results show name only. Online subscription service at https://www.doxpop.com. Fees involved. Records date from 08/89. A limited free search of open cases is available.
Criminal Records: Access: In person, online. Visitors must perform in person searches themselves. Required to search: name, years to search, DOB; also helpful: SSN. Criminal records archived from 1800s; on computer since 1989. Some judgments on fee books. Criminal PAT goes back to same as civil. PAT results show name only. Online access to criminal records is the same as civil. Online results show name only.
General Information: Online identifiers in results same as on public terminal. No juvenile, mental, adoption or sealed records released. Will fax documents $2.00 1st page, $1.00 each add'l page. Court makes copy: $1.00 per page. Certification fee: $1.00. Payee: Wabash County Clerk. Business checks accepted. No credit cards. Prepayment required.

Warren County

Circuit Court 125 N Monroe, #11, Williamsport, IN 47993; 765-762-3510; fax: 765-762-7251; 8AM-4PM (EST). ***Felony, Misdemeanor, Civil, Eviction, Small Claims, Probate.***
Civil Records: Access: In person, online. Both court and visitors may perform in person searches. No search fee. Required to search: name, years to search. Civil cases indexed by defendant, plaintiff, archived from 1828. Some records on docket books. Search the docket by case number, party name or attorney name at http://mycase.in.gov/default.aspx.
Criminal Records: Access: In person, online. Both court and visitors may perform in person searches. No search fee. Required to search: name, years to search, DOB; SSN helpful. Criminal records archived

from 1828. Some records on docket books. Online access free at http://mycase.in.gov/default.aspx. Includes criminal and citations.
General Information: No juvenile, mental, adoption or sealed released. Fee to fax out is $1.00 per page. Court makes copy: $1.00 per page. Certification fee: $1.00 per cert. Payee: Warren County Clerk. Personal checks accepted; credit cards are not. Prepayment required.

Warrick County

Circuit & Superior Court One County Square, #200, Boonville, IN 47601; 812-897-6160; fax: 812-897-6400; 8AM-4PM (CST). ***Felony, Misdemeanor, Civil, Eviction, Small Claims, Probate.***
www.warrickcounty.gov/
Civil Records: Access: In person, online. Both court and visitors may perform in person searches. No search fee. Required to search: name, years to search. Civil cases indexed by defendant, plaintiff, on computer from 1987, archived from 1900s. Some records on index books. Civil PAT goes back to 1987. Online subscription service at https://www.doxpop.com. Fees involved. Records date from 06/87. A limited free search of open cases is available.
Criminal Records: Access: In person, online. Both court and visitors may perform in person searches. No search fee. Required to search: name, years to search; also helpful: DOB, SSN. Criminal records computerized from 1987, archived from 1900s. Some records on index books. Criminal PAT goes back to same as civil.PAT results show name, DOB. Online subscription service at https://www.doxpop.com. Fees involved. Records date from 08/89. A limited free search of open cases is available.
General Information: No juvenile, mental, adoption or sealed released. Will not fax out case file copies. Court makes copy: $1.00 per page. Certification fee: $1.00 per cert. Payee: Warrick County Clerk. Business checks accepted; no personal checks. No credit cards accepted. Prepayment required. Mail requests: SASE required for mail return of any copies.

Washington County

Circuit & Superior Court Courthouse, 99 Public Sq, #102, Salem, IN 47167; criminal phone: 812-883-1634; civil phone: 812-883-5748; probate phone: 812-883-5748; fax: 812-883-8108; 8:30AM-4PM M-TH, 8:30AM-6PM F (EST). ***Felony, Misdemeanor, Civil, Small Claims, Probate.***
www.washingtoncountyindiana.com/circuit.html
Will only return calls to toll-free numbers. Traffic phone number same as criminal.
Civil Records: Access: In person only. Visitors must perform in person searches themselves. Required to search: name, years to search; also helpful: address. Civil cases indexed by defendant, plaintiff, on books, archived from 1820. Some records on docket books.
Criminal Records: Access: In person only. Both court and visitors may perform in person searches. No search fee. Required to search: name, years to search, DOB; also helpful: address, SSN. Criminal index on computer from 1980, docket books and archived from 1820.
General Information: No juvenile, mental, adoption or sealed released; no information given out via telephone. Will not fax out case files. Court makes copy: $1.00 per page, self serve same. Certification fee: $1.00. Payee: Washington County Clerk. Only cashiers checks and money orders accepted. No credit cards accepted. Prepayment required.

Wayne County

Circuit & Superior Court Courthouse, 301 E Main St, Richmond, IN 47374; 765-973-9220; criminal phone: 765-973-9218 Circ Ct; civil phone: 765-973-9220 Circ Ct; criminal fax: 765-973-9490; civil fax: same; 8:30AM-5PM M; 8:30AM-4:30PM T-F (EST). ***Felony, Misdemeanor, Civil, Eviction, Small Claims, Probate.***
www.co.wayne.in.us/courts
Circuit clerk- 765-973-9266; Superior Ct #1 - 765-973-9259; Superior Ct #2- 765-973-9260; Small claims- 765-973-9202.
Civil Records: Access: Mail, fax, in person, online. Visitors must perform in person searches themselves. No search fee. Required to search: name, years to search. Civil cases indexed by defendant, plaintiff, on computer from 4/90, circuit on microfiche from 1957, superior on microfiche from 1960 to 1971, all archived from 1800s. Some records. Note: Fax request must be on letterhead. Civil PAT goes back to 1990. Access records via subscription service at https://www.doxpop.com. Fees involved. Records date from 3/90; a limited free search of open cases is available.
Criminal Records: Access: Mail, fax, in person, online. Both court and visitors may perform in person searches. No search fee. Required to search: name, years to search, fax request on letterhead. Criminal records computerized from 4/90, circuit on microfiche from 1957, superior on microfiche 1960-1971, all archived from 1800s. Note: Fax request must be on letterhead. Mail turnaround time 1 week. Criminal PAT goes back to same as civil. Online access to criminal records is same as civil.
General Information: No juvenile, mental, adoption or sealed released. Will not fax documents. Court makes copy: $1.00 per page. Certification fee: $1.00 per cert. Payee: Wayne County Clerk. Personal checks accepted. Prepayment required. Mail requests: SASE required.

Wells County

Circuit & Superior Court 102 W Market, Rm 201, Bluffton, IN 46714; 260-824-6479; probate phone: 260-824-6480; fax: 260-824-6559; 8AM-4:30PM (EST). ***Civil, Probate.***
www.wellscounty.org/superiorcourt.htm
There is also a Bluffton City Court, which is online and mentioned here. Probate fax is same as main fax.
Civil Records: Access: In person, online. Visitors must perform in person searches themselves. Required to search: name, years to search. Civil cases indexed by defendant, plaintiff, archived from 1837. Some records on docket books. Civil PAT goes back to 2/2002. Online subscription service to Bluffton city courts at https://www.doxpop.com. Fees involved. A limited free search of open cases is available. Online index goes back to 1/2000.
Criminal Records: Access: In person, online. Visitors must perform in person searches themselves. Required to search: name, years to search, DOB; SSN helpful. Criminal records archived from 1837. Some records on docket books. Criminal PAT available. Online access to Blufton city criminal records is the same as civil.
General Information: No juvenile, mental, adoption or sealed released. Will not fax out case files. Court makes copy: $1.00 per page, self serve same. Certification fee: $1.00. Payee: Wells County Clerk. Personal checks accepted; credit cards are not. Prepayment required.

White County

Circuit Court PO Box 350, 110 N Main, Monticello, IN 47960; 574-583-7032; fax: 574-583-1532; 8AM-4PM (EST). ***Civil, Probate.***
Civil Records: Access: In person, online. Visitors must perform in person searches themselves. Required to search: name, years to search. Civil cases indexed by defendant, plaintiff, on indexes and files, some records on docket books back to 1950s. Public use terminal has civil records back to 1/2006. PAT results show middle initial, DOB, SSN. Online subscription service at https://www.doxpop.com. Fees involved. Index goes back to 1/2006. A limited free search of open cases is available. Online results show middle initial, DOB, SSN.
General Information: No juvenile, mental, adoption or sealed released. Will not fax documents. Court makes copy: $1.00 per page, self serve same. Certification fee: $1.00. Payee: White County Clerk. Personal checks accepted; credit cards are not. Prepayment required.

Superior Court PO Box 1005, 110 N Main, Monticello, IN 47960; 574-583-9520; criminal fax: 574-583-2437; civil fax: 574-583-1532; 8AM-4PM (EST). ***Felony, Misdemeanor, Eviction, Small Claims.***
Civil Records: Access: In person, online. Both court and visitors may perform in person searches. No search fee. Required to search: name, years to search. Civil cases indexed by defendant, plaintiff, on indexes and files, some records on docket books. Note: Court will perform search only if a date is provided Public use terminal available, records go back to 2006. Online subscription service at https://www.doxpop.com. Fees involved. Index goes back to 1/2006. A limited free search of open cases is available.
Criminal Records: Access: In person, online. Visitors must perform in person searches themselves. Required to search: name, years to search. Criminal records on indexes and files, some records on docket books. Note: Court will criminal search only if a date is provided. Public use terminal available, crim records go back to same as civil. Online access to criminal is same as civil.
General Information: No juvenile, mental, adoption or sealed released. Will fax specific case file. Court makes copy: $1.00 per page. Certification fee: $1.00 per page. Payee: White County Clerk. No out-of-state checks accepted. No credit cards accepted. Prepayment required.

Whitley County

Circuit & Superior Court 101 W Van Buren, Rm 10, Columbia City, IN 46725; 260-248-3102; fax: 260-248-3137; 8AM-4:30PM (EST). ***Felony, Misdemeanor, Civil, Eviction, Small Claims, Probate.***
Civil Records: Access: In person, online. Visitors must perform in person searches themselves. Required to search: name, years to search. Civil cases indexed by defendant, plaintiff, on computer from 1999. Some records on docket books. Civil PAT goes back to 1993 (Circuit); 1988 (Superior). PAT results show middle initial, DOB. Online subscription service at https://www.doxpop.com. Fees involved. Records date from 01/1999. A limited free search of open cases is available.
Criminal Records: Access: In person, online. Visitors must perform in person searches themselves. Required to search: name, years to search; also helpful: DOB. Criminal records computerized from 1999. Some records on docket books back to 1900. Criminal PAT goes back to same as civil. PAT results show middle initial, DOB. Online access same as civil. Online results show middle initial, DOB.
General Information: No juvenile, mental, adoption or sealed released. Will not fax documents. Court makes copy: $1.00 per page. Certification fee: $1.00. Payee: Whitley County Clerk. Only cashiers checks and money orders accepted. No credit cards accepted. Prepayment required. Mail requests: SASE required for mail return of any copies.

Indiana Recording Offices

ORGANIZATION: 92 counties, 92 recording offices. The recording officer is the County Recorder; see the office of the Circuit Clerk for state tax liens on personal property. Many counties utilize a "Miscellaneous Index" for tax and other liens. 82 Indiana counties are in the Eastern Time Zone (EST) and 10 others in the extreme northwest (Jasper, Lake, LaPorte, Newton, Porter) and southwest (Gibson, Posey, Spencer, Vanderburgh, Warrick) are in the Central Time Zone (CST - and observe DST as well). Most among the 82 EST counties do not observe daylight savings time, though there are usually a few exceptions who do observe it including Clark, Dearborn, Floyd, Harrison, and Ohio counties. This may vary from year to year.

REAL ESTATE RECORDS: Most counties will not perform real estate name searches. Real estate record copy fee is $1.00 per page and certification fee is $5.00 per document.

UCC RECORDS: Financing statements are filed at the state level except for real estate related collateral which are filed with the County Recorder. However, prior to July, 2001, consumer goods collateral were also filed at the County Recorder and these older records can be searched there. Since July, 2002, farm collateral changed from local to state centralized filing. Most counties will perform UCC searches. Use search request form UCC-11. UCC search fee is usually $10.00 per debtor name and $5.00 for each add'l name. Many counties also charge $.50 for a financing statement reported on a search.

TAX LIEN RECORDS: All federal tax liens on personal property are filed with the County Recorder. State tax liens on personal property are filed with the Circuit Clerk in a different office than the Recorder. Refer to the County Court section for information on Indiana Circuit Courts. Most counties will not perform tax lien searches.

OTHER LIENS: Judgments, mechanics, hospital, sewer, utility, innkeeper.

ONLINE ACCESS: A growing number of agencies offer online access. Notable is the subscription service offered by Marion County at www.civicnet.net. Also, browse statewide UCC lien records at https://secure.in.gov/sos/bus_service/online_ucc/browse/default.asp

Adams County

County Recorder, 313 W Jefferson, Rm 240; Adams County Service Complex, Decatur, IN 46733. Recording, R/E & UCC phone-260-724-5343; fax-260-724-5344; 8AM-4:30PM (EST)

Index: All in one. Records indexed on a public use terminal back to 1990. Only the public may search. Copy fee $1.00 per page. UCC copy fee- none. Cert fee- $5.00 per doc plus copy fee. Payee- Adams County Recorder. Office does sell bulk data on CD's, contact Connie Moser. **Other phones:** Treasurer- 260-724-5353; Auditor- 260-724-5300. **Property tax/Assessing**- 313 W Jefferson, Rm 230, Adams County Service Complex, Decatur, IN 46733; 260-724-5301, assessor fax- 260-724-5302. www.adams-county.com/assessor.html **Online access**- Access to property tax and GIS-mapping site free at www.adams-county.com/gis.html

Allen County

County Recorder, 1 E Main St, Rm 206; City County Bldg, Fort Wayne, IN 46802-1890. Recording, R/E & UCC phone-260-449-7165; fax-260-449-3261; 8AM-4:30PM (EST) www.allencountyrecorder.us/

Index: 1972 and prior on film and books; later computerized. Records indexed on a public use terminal back to 1973. Office personnel will help you search, but not search for you. Search fee-$10.00; $5.00 each add'l name. Copy fee $1.00 per page. $5.00 for oversized bond, $6.00 for oversized mylar. Cert fee- $5.00 per doc plus copy fee. Payee- Allen County Recorder. Bulk data available for purchase; contact Anita Mather, Chief Clerk. **Online access to Real Estate, Deed, Lien records:** Access real estate recording data back to 1/1979 free at http://inallen.fidlar.com/websearch/. Also, access recording office data by subscription on either the Laredo system using subscription and fees or the Tapestry System using credit card, http://tapestry.fidlar.com. **Other phones:** Treasurer- 260-428-7693; Elections- 260-449-7329; Vital Records- 260-449-7147. **Property tax/Assessing**- 1 E Main St, #104, City-County Bldg, Fort Wayne, IN 46802; 260-449-7123, assessor fax- 260-449-4621. www.allencountyassessor.org **Online access**- Access property database card data free at www.co.allen.in.us/CustomApps/PropCard/address_search.php.

Bartholomew County

County Recorder, PO Box 1121, Columbus, IN 47202-1121. 812-379-1520, R/E recording phone-812-379-1510; fax-812-375-5440; 8AM-5PM (EST) www.bartholomewco.com

Index: Separate indices to search include deeds, mortgages, releases, miscellaneous. Records indexed on a public use terminal back to 1985. Office will perform a UCC search but public must search other records themselves. Search fee-$10.00; $5.00 each add'l name. Office will not search real estate records. Office will search active UCC records with written UCC search request. Copy fee $1.00 per page. Cert fee- $5.00 per doc plus copy fee. Payee- Bartholomew County Recorder. Office does not sell bulk data. **Other phones:** Treasurer- 812-379-1530; Elections- 812-379-1604; Vital Records- 812-379-1550. **Property tax/Assessing**- 440 3rd St #201 (county), #202 (city), Columbus, IN 47201; 812-379-1505, assessor fax- 812-379-1613. Public access terminal available. www.bartholomewco.com **Online access**- Access to county Public Access Geographic Information System is free at http://gis.bartholomewco.com/ and you must have an email for free registration and login.

Benton County

County Recorder, 706 E 5th St, #24, Fowler, IN 47944-1556. Recording, R/E & UCC phone-765-884-1630; fax-765-884-2013; 8:30AM-4PM (EST)

Index: Separate indices to search include Mtg, Deed, Computer, Misc. Records indexed on a public use terminal back to 0701/2002. Office will perform a UCC search but public must search other records themselves. Search fee-$10.00 per name. Copy fee $1.00 per page. UCC copy fee- none. Cert fee- $5.00 per doc plus copy fee. Payee- Benton County Recorder. Office does not sell bulk data. **Other phones:** Treasurer- 765-884-1070; Elections- 765-884-0930; Vital Records- 765-884-1728. **Property tax/Assessing**- 706 E 5th St, Fowler, IN 47944; 765-884-1205, assessor fax- 765-884-2074. A public access terminal is available.

Blackford County

County Recorder, 110 W Washington St; Courthouse, Hartford City, IN 47348. Recording, R/E & UCC phone-765-348-2207; fax-765-348-7222; 8AM-4PM (EST) www.blackfordcounty.com/

Index: Separate indices to search include computer, books. Records indexed on computer back to 1992. Only the public may search. Will not search UCC records (after 6 years UCC's are shredded). Copy fee $1.00 per page. Cert fee- $5.00 per doc includes copy fee. Payee- Blackford County Recorder. Office does not sell bulk data. **Other phones:** Treasurer- 765-348-2504; Elections- 765-348-7217; Vital Records- 765-348-2207. **Property tax/Assessing**- 110 W Washington St, Courthouse, Hartford City, IN 47348; 765-348-1707, assessor fax- 765-348-7222. **Online**- property data at http://beacon.schneidercorp.com/. Registration, username and password required.

Boone County

County Recorder, 202 Courthouse Sq, Lebanon, IN 46052. 765-482-3070, R/E recording phone-765-482-2940, UCC recording phone-765-482-3070; 8AM-4PM (EST) www.boonecounty.in.gov

Index: All in one. Records indexed on a public use terminal back to 1996. Office will perform a UCC search but public must search other records themselves. Search fee-$10.00; $5.00 each add'l name. Copy fee $1.00 per page. Cert fee- $5.00 per doc plus copy fee. Payee- Boone County Recorder. Office does not sell bulk data. **Other phones:** Treasurer- 765-482-2880; Elections- 765-482-3510. **Property tax/Assessing**- 115 Courthouse Sq,

Lebanon, IN 46052; 765-482-0140, assessor fax- 765-483-5239. 7AM-4PM www.boonecounty.in.gov **Online**- Search property data free on GIS site at http://boonecounty.in.gov/Default.aspx?tabid=57. At map, click on 'Search for' at bottom left and choose 'parcels' to search by name.

Brown County

County Recorder, PO Box 86, Nashville, IN 47448. Recording, R/E & UCC phone-812-988-5462; fax-812-988-5520; 8AM-4PM (EST)
Index: All in one. Records indexed on a public use terminal back to 1988. Office will perform a UCC search but public must search other records themselves. Copy fee $1.00 per page. UCC copy fee-none. Cert fee- $5.00 per doc plus copy fee. Payee- Brown County Recorder. Office does not sell bulk data. **Other phones:** Treasurer- 812-988-5458; Elections- 812-988-5510; Vital Records- 812-988-2255. **Property tax/Assessing**- PO Box 351, 201 Locust St, Nashville, IN 47448; 812-988-5466, assessor fax- 812-988-5520.

Carroll County

County Recorder, 101 W Main St; Courthouse, Delphi, IN 46923-1522. Recording, R/E & UCC phone-765-564-2124; fax-765-564-2576; 8AM-5PM M,T,TH,F; 8AM-N W. (EST)
Index: All in one. Records indexed on a public use terminal back to 1994. Office will perform a UCC search but public must search other records themselves. Copy fee $1.00 per page. Cert fee- $7.00 per doc plus copy fee. Payee- Carroll County Recorder. Office does not sell bulk data. **Other phones:** Treasurer- 765-564-3446; Elections- 765-564-4485; Vital Records- 765-564-3420. **Property tax/Assessing**- 101 W Main St, Delphi, IN 46923; 765-564-3444, assessor fax- 765-564-6202.

Cass County

County Recorder, 200 Court Park, Logansport, IN 46947. 574-753-7810; fax-574-735-0712; 8AM-4PM (EST) www.in-map.net/counties/CASS/recorder/
Index: All in one. Records indexed on a public use terminal back to 1996. Office will perform a UCC search but public must search other records themselves. Search fee-$10.00 per name, plus $5.00 each add'l name. Copy fee $1.00 per page. UCC copy fee- none. Cert fee- $5.00 per doc plus copy fee. Payee- Cass County Recorder. Office does not sell bulk data. **Other phones:** Treasurer- 574-753-7720. **Property tax/Assessing**- 200 Court Park, #305, Logansport, IL 46947; 574-753-7720.

Clark County

County Recorder, 501 E Court Ave, Rm 105, Jeffersonville, IN 47130. 812-285-6236; 8:30AM-4:30PM (EST)
Index: Separate indices to search include various books, computer. Records indexed on a public use terminal back to 1999. Office will perform a UCC search but public must search other records themselves. Search fee-$9.00 per name. Copy fee $1.00 per page. Cert fee- $5.00 per doc plus copy fee. Payee- Clark County Recorder. Office does not sell bulk data. **Other phones:** Treasurer- 812-285-6205. **Property tax/Assessing**- 501 E Court Ave, Rm 111, Jeffersonville, IN 47130; 812-285-6224, assessor fax- 812-280-5627. A public access terminal is available for record searches in the office. **Online access**- Online access to property records is available at http://in10.plexisgroup.com/ecama/index.cfm.

Clay County

County Recorder, 609 E National Ave, Rm 111; Courthouse, Brazil, IN 47834. Recording, R/E & UCC phone-812-448-9005; fax-812-446-5095; 8AM-4PM (EST) www.claycountyin.gov
Index: Separate indices to search include deed, mortgage, misc, UCC, tax lien, old age, veteran. Records indexed on a public use terminal back to 1991; deeds back to 1947. Office will perform a UCC search but public must search other records themselves. UCC search on UCC 11 form per debtor name- $10.00; $5.00 each add'l name. Copy fee $1.00 per page; $2.00 per oversized page. Cert fee- $5.00 per doc plus copy fee. Payee- Clay County Recorder. **Other phones:** Treasurer- 812-448-9009; Elections- 812-448-9023; Vital Records- 812-448-9018. **Property tax/Assessing**- 609 E National Ave, 1st Fl, Rm 118, Brazil, IN 47834; 812-448-9013, assessor fax- 812-442-9600. A public access terminal is available.

Clinton County

Recorder, 270 Courthouse Sq, Frankfort, IN 46041-1957. Recording, R/E phone-765-659-6320; fax-765-659-6391; 8AM-4PM M,W; 8AM-N Th. (EST)
Index: Separate indices to search include searches by date. Records indexed on a public use terminal back to 8/95. Office will perform a UCC search but public must search other records themselves. Search fee-$10.00; $5.00 each add'l name. Office will not search real estate records. Copy fee $1.00 per page. Copy larger that 9 X 14 1/2-$2.00 per page. UCC copy fee-none. Cert fee- $5.00 per doc plus copy fee. Payee- Clinton County Recorder. **Other phones:** Treasurer- 765-659-6325; Elections- 765-659-6335; Vital Records- 765-659-6385. **Property tax/Assessing**- 430 Courthouse Sq, Frankfort, IN 46041; 765-659-6315, assessor fax- 765-659-0609. **Online access**- Search assessor property data for a fee on the GIS system at http://beacon.schneidercorp.com/. Registration and username required.

Crawford County

County Recorder, PO Box 214, English, IN 47118-0214. Recording, R/E & UCC phone-812-338-2615; fax-812-338-2507; 8AM-4PM M & F; 8AM-6PM T & Th; Closed W. (EST)
Index: Separate indices to search include deed, mortgage, misc, survey, UCCs. Records indexed on a public use terminal back to 1998. Office will perform a UCC search but public must search other records themselves. Copy fee $1.00 per page. Cert fee- $5.00 per doc plus copy fee. Payee- Crawford County Recorder. Bulk data available for purchase, contact Dawn. **Other phones:** Treasurer- 812-338-2651; Elections- 812-338-2565. **Property tax/Assessing**- PO Box 376, County Courthouse, English, IN 47118-0316; 812-338-2402, assessor fax- 812-338-2507.

Daviess County

Recorder, PO Box 793, Washington, IN 47501. 812-254-8675; fax-812-254-8697; 8AM-4PM (EST)
Index: Separate indices to search include mortgages, deeds, miscellaneous. Records indexed on a public use terminal back to 1997. Only the public may search. Copy fee $1.00 per page. UCC copy fee-none. Cert fee- $5.00 per doc plus copy fee. Payee- Daviess County Recorder. **Other phones:** Treasurer- 812-254-8677. **Property tax/Assessing**- 200 E Walnut St, Washington, IN 47501; 812-254-8660, assessor fax- 812-254-8647. A public access terminal is available for record searches in the Treasurers office. **Online** - Online access to property records is at http://in14.plexisgroup.com/ecama/index.cfm.

Dearborn County

County Recorder, 215-B W High St, Lawrenceburg, IN 47025. Recording, R/E & UCC phone-812-537-8837; fax-none; 8:30AM-4:30PM (EST)
Index: All in one. Records indexed on a public use terminal back to 2000. Office will perform a UCC search but public must search other records themselves. Search fee-$10.00 per search. Office will not search real estate records. Will search UCC records. Copy fee $1.00 per page if legal size or smaller, $2.00 per page if larger than legal. Cert fee- $8.00 per doc plus copy fee. Payee- County Recorder. Office does not sell bulk data. **Other phones:** Treasurer- 812-537-8811; Elections- 812-537-8867; Vitals- 812-537-8826. **Property tax/Assessing**- 215-B W High St, Rm 203, Admin Bldg, Lawrenceburg, IN 47025; 812-537-8809, assessor fax- 812-532-3214. www.dearborncountyassessor.com **Online**- free property search at http://in-dearborn-assessor.governmaxa.com/propertymax/rover30.asp.

Decatur County

County Recorder, 150 Courthouse Sq, #121, Greensburg, IN 47240. Recording, R/E & UCC phone-812-663-4681; fax-812-663-2407; 8AM-4PM; till 5PM Fri. (EST)
Index: All in one. Records indexed on computer back to 2003. Only the public may search. Copy fee $1.00 per page. Cert fee- $5.00 per doc plus copy fee. Payee- Decatur County Recorder. Office does not sell bulk data. **Other phones:** Treasurer- 812-663-4190; Elections- 812-663-8223; Vital Records- 812-663-8301. **Property tax/Assessing**- 150 Courthouse Sq, #105, Greensburg, IN 47240; 812-663-4868, assessor fax- 812-662-6392. (Appraiser/Auditor- 812-663-2570) hours- 8AM-4PM M-TH; 8AM-5PM F www.decaturcounty.in.gov/assessor/assessor.htm
Online access- Access county property data for free at http://beacon.schneidercorp.com/

DeKalb County

County Recorder, PO Box 810, Auburn, IN 46706. Recording, R/E & UCC phone-260-925-2112; fax-260-925-5126; 8:30AM-4:30PM (EST)
Index: All in one. Records indexed on a public use terminal back to 12/5/1995. Office will perform a UCC search but public must search other records themselves. Search fee $10.00. Copy fee $1.00 per page. UCC copy fee- none. Cert fee- $5.00 per doc plus copy fee. Payee- DeKalb County Recorder. Office does not sell bulk data. **Other phones:** Treasurer- 260-925-2712; Elections- 260-925-0912; Vital - 260-925-2220. **Property tax/Assessing**- 100 S Main St, County Courthouse, Auburn, IN 46706; 260-925-1824, assessor fax- 260-927-4795.

Delaware County

County Recorder, 100 W Main St, Rm 209, Muncie, IN 47305. 765-747-7804; fax-765-747-7756; 8:30AM-4:30PM (EST)
Index: Separate indices to search- pre-2005 doc type and books, 2005-forward by Doc ID. Records indexed on a public use terminal back to 1988. Office will perform a UCC search but public must search other records themselves. Search fee-$10.00; $5.00 each add'l name. Copy fee $1.00 per page. Cert fee- $5.00 per doc plus copy fees; no fee to certify UCCs. Payee- Delaware County Recorder. Office does not sell bulk data. **Other phones:** Treasurer- 765-747-7808; Elections- 765-747-7726; Vital Records- 765-747-7721. **Property tax/Assessing**- 100 W Main St, #100, Muncie, IN 47305; 765-747-7715, assessor fax- 765-747-7762. (Appraiser/Auditor- 765-747-7717)

Dubois County

County Recorder, 1 Courthouse Sq, Rm 101, Jasper, IN 47546. Recording, R/E & UCC phone-812-481-7067; fax-812-481-7044; 8AM-4PM (EST)
Index: Books and computers. Records indexed on a public use terminal back to 1994. Only the public may search. Copy fee $1.00 per page. Cert fee- $5.00 per page plus copy fee. Payee- Dubois County Recorder. Bulk data available on CD; contact recorder. **Online access to Real Estate, Deed, Lien, Judgment records:** Online access to recorded records available via Doxpop.com subscription service. Index goes back to 4/1994, images to 12/1999. **Other phones:** Treasurer- 812-481-7080; Elections- 812-481-7035; Vitals- 812-481-7050. **Property tax/Assessing**- One Courthouse Sq, Jasper, IN 47546; 812-481-7010, fax-812-481-7014. www.duboiscountyassessor.com
Online access- Access property data free at www.duboiscountyassessor.com/propertymax/rover30.asp.

Elkhart County

County Recorder, PO Box 837, Goshen, IN 46527. 574-535-6754, R/E recording phone-574-535-6756, UCC recording phone-574-535-6754; fax-574-535-6747; 8AM-5PM M, 8AM-4PM T- F. (EST) www.elkhartcountyindiana.com/departments/recorder

Index: All in one. Records indexed on a public use terminal back to 1987. Office will perform a UCC search (only those that have not lasped) with information request but public must search other records themselves. Search fee-$10.00; $5.00 each add'l name. Copy fee $1.00 per page. Cert fee- $5.00 per doc plus copy fee. Payee- Elkhart County Recorder. Bulk images available at $.07 per image, $1.00 for special documents. **Online access to Real Estate, Deed, Lien, GIS/mapping records:** Access to simple guest browse at www.elkhartcountyindiana.com/departments/recorder/. For subscription information, contact the Elkhart County Recorder's Office. **Other phones:** Treasurer- 574-535-6759; Elections- 574-535-6469; Vital Records- 574-523-2107; Voter Registration- 574-535-6775. **Property tax/Assessing**- 117 N 2nd St, Goshen, IN 46526; 574-535-6702, assessor fax- 574-535-6646. www.elkhartcountyindiana.com **Online access**- Search parcel data for free at www.macoggis.com and includes Michiana area which is St Joseph and Elkhart Counties.

Fayette County

County Recorder, 401 N Central Ave, Connersville, IN 47331. 765-825-3051, R/E recording phone-765-825-4931; 8:30AM-4PM (EST) www.co.fayette.in.us

Index: Pre-1994 records indices include UCC, deed, mortgage, misc. Records indexed on a public use terminal back to 1994. Office will perform a UCC search but public must search other records themselves. Office will not search real estate records. UCC search on UCC 11 form per debtor name- $10.00; $5.00 each add'l name. Copy fee $1.00 per page. Cert fee- $5.00 per doc plus copy fee. Payee- Fayette County Recorder. Bulk data available for purchase on microfilm, contact Melinda Sudhoff, Fayette County Recorder. **Other phones:** Treasurer- 765-825-1013; Elections- 765-825-1813; Recorder- 765-825-3051; Health Dept -765-825-4013;. **Property tax/Assessing**- 401 N Central Ave, Connersville, IN 47331; 765-825-4931, assessor fax- 765-827-1211. hours- 8AM-4PM http://in-fayette-assessor.governmaxa.com **Online access**- Access assessor property record cards and tax records free at www.co.fayette.in.us/auditor.htm. Also access property data free at http://in-fayette-assessor.governmaxa.com/propertymax/rover30.asp.

Floyd County

County Recorder, PO Box 878, New Albany, IN 47151-0878. Recording, R/E & UCC phone-812-948-5430; fax-812-949-7727; 8AM-4PM (EST) www.floydcounty.in.gov

Index: All in one. Records indexed on a public use terminal back to 1987. Office will perform a UCC search but public must search other records themselves. Search fee-$10.00 per name. State tax liens at county clerk's office. Copy fee $1.00 per page. Cert fee- $5.00 per doc plus copy fee. Payee- Floyd County Recorder. Office does not sell bulk data. **Online access to Real Estate, Deed, Mortgage, Plat, UCC, Miscellaneous records:** Access recording records free at http://in-floyd-recorder.governmaxa.com/recordmax/record40.asp. **Other phones:** Treasurer- 812-948-5477; Elections- 812-948-5419; Vital Records- 812-948-4726. **Property tax/Assessing**- 311 W 1st St, Rm 110, New Albany, IN 47150; 812-948-5420, assessor fax- 812-941-4570. A public access terminal available.

Fountain County

County Recorder, PO Box 55, Covington, IN 47932. Recording, R/E & UCC phone-765-793-2431; fax-765-793-6211; 8AM-4PM (EST)

Index: All in one. Records indexed on a public use terminal back to 6/92. Only the public may search. Copy fee $.10 per page for 8 1/2 x 11, $.15 per page for 8 1/2 x 14, $.25 per page for 11x17. Cert fee- $5.00 per doc plus copy fee. Payee- Fountain County Recorder. Bulk data available for purchase, contact Brenda K Holzer. **Other phones:** Treasurer- 765-793-3691; Elections- 765-793-2192; Vital Records- 765-793-3035. **Property tax/Assessing**- 301 4th St, Covington, IN 47932; 765-793-3481, assessor fax- 765-793-6217. **Online access**- assessor property tax and property sales data free at http://in-fayette-assessor.governmaxa.com/propertymax/rover30.asp.

Franklin County

County Recorder, 1010 Franklin Ave, Rm 110, Brookville, IN 47012-1486. Recording, R/E & UCC phone-765-647-5131; 8:30AM-4PM (EST) www.franklincounty.in.gov

Index: Separate indices to search. Records indexed on a public use terminal back to 2002. Office will perform a UCC search but public must search other records themselves. Copy fee $1.00 per page. Cert fee- $5.00 per doc plus copy fee. Payee- Franklin County Recorder. Office does not sell bulk data. **Online access to Real Estate, Deed, Lien, Judgment records:** Online access to recorded records available via Doxpop.com subscription service. Index and images go back to 2002. **Other phones:** Treasurer- 765-647-5121; Elections- 765-647-5111; Vital Records- 765-647-4322. **Property tax/Assessing**- 1010 Franklin Ave, Brookville, IN 47012-1486; 765-647-4921. **Online**- Free search at http://in-franklin-assessor.governmaxa.com/propertymax/rover30.asp. Search by name, address, parcel number. Also, access GIS web map free at http://thinkopengis.franklin.in.wthengineering.com/. To name search, click on Parcel.

Fulton County

County Recorder, 125 E 9th St, Rochester, IN 46975. Recording, R/E & UCC phone-574-223-2914; fax-574-223-4734; 8AM-4PM; till 5PM Fri. (EST)

Index: Separate indices to search by instrument number and by book & page number. Records indexed on a public use terminal back to 5/13/96. Office will perform a UCC search but public must search other records themselves. Search fee-$10.00 per name. Copy fee $1.00 per page. UCC copy fee- none. Cert fee- $5.00 per doc plus copy fee. Payee- Fulton County Recorder. CDs of instrument numbers available for purchase. **Other phones:** Treasurer- 574-223-7705; Vital Records- 574-223-2881. **Property tax/Assessing**- 125 E 9th St, #26, Rochester, IN 46975; 574-223-2801, assessor fax- 574-224-2801.

Gibson County

County Recorder, PO Box 1078, Princeton, IN 47670. Recording, R/E & UCC phone-812-385-3332; fax-812-386-9502; 8AM-4PM (CST)

Index: Pre-7/1987 records on microfilm; pre 10/1968 records on books. Records indexed on computer back to 7/87. Only the public may search. Copy fee $1.00 per page. Cert fee- $5.00 per doc plus copy fee. Payee- Gibson County Recorder. **Other phones:** Treasurer- 812-385-2540; Elections- 812-385-8401; Vital Records- 812-385-3831. **Property tax/Assessing**- 101 N Main, Courthouse, Princeton, IN 47670; 812-385-5286, assessor fax- 812-386-6757. (Appraiser/Auditor- 812-385-4927) **Online access**- Access assessor property data free at http://in-gibson-assessor.governmaxa.com. Click on "Start your search." Also, search for property assessor parcel data at http://beacon.schneidercorp.com/ but registration and password required.

Grant County

Recorder, 401 S Adams St, Marion, IN 46953. 765-668-6559; 8AM-4PM (EST) www.grantcounty.net

Index: Separate indices to search. Records indexed on a public use terminal back to 1990. Office personnel or visitors may perform searches. Search fee- $9.00 per name; $5.00 each add'l name. Office can search real estate records if not busy. Will help search UCC records, not insured. Copy fee $1.00 per page of recorded documents. Cert fee- $5.00 per doc plus copy fee; no fee to certify UCCs. Payee- Grant County Recorder. Bulk data available for purchase, contact the county commissioner (must sign a contract). **Online access to Real Estate, Deed, UCC, Mortgage, Voter Registration records:** Access to recorder data at http://recorder.grant.in.uinquire.us/. Click on "Recorder Information." Also, voter registration is free at http://voters.grant.in.uinquire.us/nxweb.exe; registration, login, and password required. **Other phones:** Treasurer- 765-668-6556; Elections- 765-668-8121; Vital Records- 765-651-2401. **Property tax/Assessing**- 401 S Adams St, #528, Marion, IN 46953; 765-668-4773, assessor fax- 765-664-5555. www.grantcounty.net **Online access**- Access to assessor property data is free at www.xsoftin.com/grant/parcelsearch.aspx. Tax data is free at http://auditor.grant.in.uinquire.us/. Click on "Tax Information."

Greene County

County Recorder, PO Box 309, Bloomfield, IN 47424. 812-384-2020, R/E recording phone-812-384-2020 & 812-384-2023, UCC recording phone-812-384-2021 & 812-384-2023; fax-812-384-2044; 8AM-4PM (EST) www.co.greene.in.us

Index: All in one back to 11/2002, prior is in books with indexes. Records indexed books prior to 11/18/2002, after 11/18/2002 maintained in one index. Office will perform a UCC search but public must search other records themselves. Search fee for UCC search. Copy fee $1.00 per page. Cert fee- $5.00 per doc plus copy fee. Payee- Greene Co. Recorder. **Other phones:** Treasurer- 812-384-4378; Elections- 812-384-2015; Vital Records- 812-384-2016. **Property tax/Assessing**- Greene County Assessor's Office, Greene County Courthouse, Bloomfield, IN 47424; 812-384-2003, assessor fax- 812-384-9785.

Hamilton County

County Recorder, 33 N 9th St, Ste 309; Courthouse, Noblesville, IN 46060. Recording, R/E & UCC phone-317-776-9618, UCC recording phone-317-776-9688; fax-317-776-8200; 8AM-4:30PM (EST) www.co.hamilton.in.us/departments.asp?id=2320

Index: Separate indices to search include computer, also books, microfilm back to late 1800s. Records indexed on a public use terminal back to 1987. Only the public may search. Copy fee $1.00 per page. Cert fee- $5.00 per doc plus copy fee. Payee- Hamilton County Recorder. Office does not sell bulk data. **Online access to Real Estate, Deed, Tax Lien, Judgment records:** Index of recorded documents is available from 01/87 -- and scanned images from 02/96 available for subscribers -- at https://www.doxpop.com/prod/recorder/. **Other phones:** Treasurer- 317-776-9620. **Property tax/Assessing**- 33 N 9th St, #214, Noblesville, IN 46060; 317-776-9617, assessor fax- 317-776-9665. www.co.hamilton.in.us/departments.asp?id=4179 **Online access**- Access property and tax information at www.co.hamilton.in.us/apps/reports/defaulttax2.asp but no name searching. View county maps at www.co.hamilton.in.us/gis/start.html. Search auditor data at. www.hamiltoncountyauditor.org/realestate/.

Hancock County

County Recorder, 111 American Legion Pl, #202, Greenfield, IN 46140. 317-477-1142; 8AM-4PM (EST) www.hancockcoingov.org/recorder/

Index: Separate indices to search include computer, microfilm back to 1969, books. Records indexed on a public use terminal back to 1990. Office will perform a UCC search but public must search other records themselves. Copy fee $1.00 per page, copies larger than 8 1/2 x 14 are $20.00 per page. Cert fee- $5.00 per doc plus copy fee. Payee- Hancock County Recorder. CDs of bulk information available for purchase; contact Vickie Holden. **Other phones:** Treasurer- 317-477-1152; Elections- 317-477-1171; Vital Records- 317-477-1125. **Property tax/Assessing**- 111 American Legion Pl, #204, Greenfield, IN 46140; 317-477-1102, assessor fax- 317-477-1104. **Online**- Access to assessor property data is free on the gis-mapping site at http://beacon.schneidercorp.com/?site=HancockCountyIN. Click on Search to search by name. Also, sales disclosure data is free at www.hancoc

kcoingov.org/assessor/sales_disclosure_search.asp. Also, search City of Greenfield property data free at http://beacon.schneidercorp.com/.

Harrison County

County Recorder, 300 N Capitol Ave, Rm 204; Courthouse, Corydon, IN 47112. Recording, R/E & UCC phone-812-738-3788; fax-812-738-1153; 8AM-4:30PM (EST)
Index: Separate indices to search. Records indexed on a public use terminal back to 11/1992. Office will perform a UCC search but public must search other records themselves. Search fee-$10.00; $5.00 each add'l name. Copy fee $.50 per page. Cert fee- $5.00 per doc plus copy fee. Payee- Harrison County Recorder. Office does not sell bulk data. **Other phones:** Treasurer- 812-738-2348; Elections- 812-738-3126; Vital Records- 812-738-3237. **Property tax/Assessing**- 300 N Capitol Ave, #303, Corydon, IN 47112; 812-738-4280, assessor fax- 812-738-0805. www.harrisoncounty.in.gov/assessor.htm **Online access**- Access property and assessor data free on the GIS-mapping search site at www.harrisoncounty.in.gov/GIS.htm.

Hendricks County

County Recorder, 355 S Washington, Danville, IN 46122. Recording, R/E & UCC phone-317-745-9224; fax-none; 8AM-4PM (EST) www.co.hendricks.in.us
Index: All in one. Records indexed on a public use terminal back to 1990. Office will perform a UCC search but public must search other records themselves. UCC search on UCC 11 form per debtor name- $10.00; $5.00 each add'l name. Copy fee $1.00 per page. UCC copy fee- none. Cert fee- $5.00 per doc plus copy fee. Payee- Hendricks County Recorder. **Other phones:** Treasurer- 317-745-9220; Elections- 317-745-9249; Vital Records- 317-745-9249. **Property tax/Assessing**- 355 S Washington Dr, #201, Danville, IN 46122; 317-745-9207, assessor fax- 317-718-6622. (Appraiser/Auditor- 317-745-9206) www.co.hendricks.in.us/ **Online access**- Search the assessor's property data free at www.co.hendricks.in.us/DWLookup/Disclaimer.asp. Access county property data on the GIS mapping site is free at http://in32.plexisgroup.com/map/index.html. Click on "Query" to select query by owner name. Also, search the GIS mapping for Town of Plainfield data free at http://beacon.schneidercorp.com.

Henry County

County Recorder, PO Box K, New Castle, IN 47362. Recording, R/E & UCC phone-765-529-4304; fax-765-521-7017; hours- 8AM-4PM (EST) www.henryco.net/cm/node/35
Index: Separate indices to search include deed, mortgage, misc, RE, FTR. Records indexed on a public use terminal back to 1991. Office will perform a UCC search but public must search other records themselves. Search fee-$10.00; $5.00 each add'l name. Copy fee $1.00 per page, plats- $2.00. Cert fee- $5.00 per doc plus copy fee. Payee- Henry County Recorder. **Other phones:** Treasurer- 765-529-4404; Elections- 765-529-6401; Vital Records- 765-521-7058; Auditor- 765-529-2800. **Property tax/Assessing**- 101 S Main St, 3rd Fl, New Castle, IN 47362; 765-529-2104, assessor fax- 765-521-7083. www.henryco.net/cm/node/7 **Online access**- Access property assessment lookup free at www.henryco.net/cm/node/8. Also, search the property tax payment site free at https://www.paytrustsolutions.com/paytrust/SelectTransactionType.do?action=view&transactionTypeId=168.

Howard County

County Recorder, PO Box 733, Kokomo, IN 46903-0733. 765-456-2210; fax-765-456-2056; 8AM-4PM (EST)
Index: All in one. Records indexed on a public use terminal back to 5/98. Only the public may search. Copy fee $1.00 per page. Cert fee- $5.00 per doc plus copy fee. Payee- Howard County Recorder. Office does not sell bulk data. **Other phones:** Treasurer- 317-456-2213. **Property tax/Assessing**- 236 N Main St, Rm 336, Kokomo, IN 46901 765-456-2211, assessor fax- 765-456-2053. http://co.howard.in.us/Center_Township_Assessor/index.htm **Online access**- Search assessor property data free on the GIS system at http://beacon.schneidercorp.com/ with registration and username required.

Huntington County

County Recorder, 201 N Jefferson St, Rm 101, Huntington, IN 46750-2841. Recording, R/E & UCC phone-260-358-4848; 8AM-4:30PM (EST) www.huntington.in.us
Index: Separate indices to search include books, computer. Records indexed on a public use terminal back to 1990. Records maintained back 188 years. Office personnel or visitors may perform searches. Office will not search real estate records. UCC search on UCC 11 form per debtor name- $10.00; $5.00 each add'l name. Will not do federal tax lien search. Copy fee $1.00 per page, $2.00 per page for copies larger that 8.5" x 14". per page. Cert fee- $5.00 per doc plus copy fee. Payee- Huntington County Recorder. **Other phones:** Treasurer- 260-358-4860. **Property tax/Assessing**- 201 N Jefferson St, #206, Huntington, IN 46750; 260-358-4802, assessor fax- 260-358-4823. www.huntington.in.us **Online access**- Access to the assessor property data is free on the gis-mapping site at http://gis.huntington.in.us/.

Jackson County

County Recorder, PO Box 75, Brownstown, IN 47220. 812-358-6113; 8AM-4:30PM (EST)
Index: Separate indices to search. Records indexed on a public use terminal back to 11/1992. Office will perform a UCC search but public must search other records themselves. UCC search on UCC 11 form per debtor name- $10.00; $7.00 each add'l name. Copy fee $1.00 per page. Cert fee- $5.00 per doc plus copy fee. Payee- Jackson County Recorder. **Other phones:** Treasurer- 812-358-6125; Elections- 812-358-6159. **Property tax/Assessing**- 111 S Main, #116, Brownstown, IN 47220; 812-358-6111, assessor fax- 812-358-3704. hours- 8AM-4PM **Online access**- Access to property tax, GIS/mapping and assessment info for free at http://thinkopengis.jackson.in.wthengineering.com/. This is a private website.

Jasper County

Recorder, 115 W Washington St, Rensselaer, IN 47978. 219-866-4923, R/E recording phone-219-866-4930 (Auditor), fax-219-866-4940; 8AM-4PM (CST) www.jaspercountyin.gov/Default.aspx?tabid=70
Index: Separate indices to search include deeds, mtgs, misc, psf, UCCs. Records indexed on a public use terminal back to 10/1995. Only the public may search. Copy fee $1.00 per page. UCC copy fee- none. Cert fee- $5.00 per doc plus copy fee. Payee- Jasper County Recorder. Office does not sell bulk data. **Other phones:** Treasurer- 219-866-4938; Elections- 219-866-4926. **Property tax/Assessing**- 115 W Washington, Rm 104, Rensselaer, IN 47978; 219-866-4915, assessor fax- 219-866-4940. www.jaspercountyin.gov/Default.aspx?tabid=55

Jay County

County Recorder, 120 W Main St, Portland, IN 47371. Recording, R/E & UCC phone-260-726-6940; fax-n/a; 8:30AM-4:30PM (EST) www.co.jay.in.us
Index: All in one. Records indexed on a public use terminal back to 1/97. Office will perform a UCC search but public must search other records themselves. Search fee $10.00 for 1st, $5.00 each add'l. Office will not search real estate records. Will search UCC records. Copy fee $1.00 per page. UCC copy fee- none. Cert fee- $5.00 per doc plus copy fee. Payee- Jay County Recorder. **Other phones:** Treasurer- 260-726-6925. **Property tax/Assessing**- 120 W Main St, Portland IN 47371; 260-726-4456, assessor fax- 260-726-6944. **Online access**- Access to GIS-mapping property data is free at http://in38.plexisgroup.com/map/index.cfm and click on Query to name search.

Jefferson County

County Recorder, 300 E Main St, Rm 104; Courthouse, Madison, IN 47250. Recording, R/E & UCC phone-812-265-8902; 8AM-4PM (EST)
Index: Separate indices to search include pre 1999, deeds, mortgages, misc. May be searched at Room 104. Records indexed on a public use terminal back to 1993 for index, 9/1698 for image. Office will perform a UCC search but public must search other records themselves. Copy fee $1.00 per page. Cert fee- $5.00 per doc plus copy fee. Payee- Jefferson County Recorder. Office does not sell bulk data. **Other phones:** Treasurer- 812-265-8910; Elections- 812-265-8926; Health Dept -812-273-1942;. **Property tax/Assessing**- 300 E Main St, Courthouse, Rm 105, Madison, IN 47250; 812-265-8905, assessor fax- 812-273-2625. A public access terminal available.

Jennings County

County Recorder, PO Box 397, Vernon, IN 47282-0397. Recording, R/E & UCC phone-812-352-3053; fax-812-352-3000; hours- 8AM-4PM (EST) www.jenningscounty-in.gov
Index: Separate indices to search include UCCs. Records indexed on a public use terminal back to 10/07, previous records use book and page. Only the public may search. Copy fee $1.00 per page. Cert fee- $5.00 per doc plus copy fee. Payee- Jennings County Recorder. Office does not sell bulk data. **Other phones:** Treasurer- 812-352-3060; Elections- 812-352-3080; Vital Records- 812-352-3024; Auditors Phone- 812-352-3016; Clerks Phone -812-352-3070;. **Property tax/Assessing**- 200 E Brown St, PO Box 384, Vernon, IN 47282; 812-352-3013, assessor fax- 812-352-3000. (Appraiser/Auditor- 812-352-3016) www.jenningscounty-in.gov **Online** - Access assessor property data free on the gis-mapping site at http://thinkopengis.jennings.in.wthtechnology.com/.

Johnson County

County Recorder, PO Box 489, Franklin, IN 46131. Recording, R/E & UCC phone-317-736-3718; fax-317-736-4776; 8AM-4:30PM (EST)
Index: All in one. Records indexed on a public use terminal back to 09/1994. Office will perform a UCC search but public must search other records themselves. Search fee-$10.00 per name. Copy fee $1.00 per page. UCC copy fee- none. Cert fee- $5.00 per doc plus copy fee. Payee- Johnson County Recorder. Office does not sell bulk data. **Other phones:** Treasurer- 317-736-3711; Elections- 317-736-3789; Vital Records- 317-736-3775; Assessor County- 317-736-3715. **Property tax/Assessing**- 86 W Court St, Franklin IN 46131; 317-736-3030. A public access terminal is available. **Online access**- Access to the assessor GIS database of property and sales data is free at http://beacon.schneidercorp.com/.

Knox County

County Recorder, 111 N 7th St; Courthouse, Vincennes, IN 47591. 812-885-2508; fax-812-885-2509; 8AM-4PM (EST)
Index: Separate indexes to search. Records indexed on a public use terminal back to 2002. Only the public may search. Copy fee $1.00 per page. UCC copy fee- none. To copy & fax to toll-free number- $2.00; $3.00 to non-toll-free number. Cert fee- $5.00 per doc plus copy fee. Payee- Knox County Recorder. Office does not sell bulk data. **Other phones:** Treasurer- 812-885-2506; Elections- 812-895-4928; Vital Records- 812-882-8080. **Property tax/Assessing**- 111 N 7th St, Vincennes, IN 47591; 812-885-2513, assessor fax- 812-886-3414. www.knoxcountyassessor.com

Kosciusko County

Recorder, 100 W Center St, Rm 14; Courthouse, Warsaw, IN 46580. Recording, R/E & UCC phone-574-372-2360; fax-574-372-2469; 8AM-4:30PM (EST) http://kcgov.com/countyOfficeSelect.asp

Index: All in one. Records indexed on a public use terminal back to 1991. Office personnel or visitors may perform searches. Search fee $10.00 per name. Office will not search real estate or tax lien records. Will search UCC records. General copy fee- $1.00 per copy. Plats- $2.00 each. Cert fee- $5.00 per cert plus copy fee. Payee- Kosciusko County Recorder. CDs of bulk information available for $.07 per image. **Other phones:** Treasurer- 574-372-2370; Elections- 574-372-2329; Vital Records- 574-372-2329. **Property tax/Assessing**- 100 W Center, #209, Warsaw, IN 46580; 574-372-2310, assessor fax- 574-372-2469. **Online** - Access to property records on GIS mapping site at http://beacon.schneidercorp.com/?site=KosciuskoCountyIn.

La Porte County

County Recorder, 555 Michigan Ave #201, La Porte, IN 46350-3488. 219-326-6808, R/E recording phone-219-326-6808 x2257; fax-219-326-0828; 8AM-4PM (recording hours 8AM-3PM). (CST) www.laportecounty.org/

Index: All in one. Records indexed on a public use terminal back to 1974. Office will perform a UCC search but public must search other records themselves. UCC search on UCC 11 form per debtor name- $10.00; $5.00 each add'l name. Copy fee $1.00 per page. UCC copy fee- none. Cert fee- $5.00 per doc plus copy fee. Payee- La Porte County Recorder. CD ans E-mail Recording information available; Contact Emmy LeDonne with request. **Online access to Real Estate, Deed, Lien records:** Recorder land data by subscription on either the Laredo system using subscription and fees or the Tapestry System using credit card, http://tapestry.fidlar.com; $3.99 search; $1.00 per image. Index back to 1974; images to 1974. **Other phones:** Treasurer- 219-326-6808 x2490; Elections- 219-326-6808 x2242; Vital Records- 219-326-6808 x2200. **Property tax/Assessing**- 555 Michigan Ave #204, La Porte IN 46350; 219-326-6808 x2233, assessor fax- 219-326-7084. hours-8AM-4PM www.xsoftin.com/laporte/ **Online access**- Access to parcel searches for free go to www.xsoftin.com/laporte/

LaGrange County

County Recorder, PO Box 214, LaGrange, IN 46761. 260-499-6320, R/E recording phone-260-499-6394, UCC recording phone-260-499-6320; 8AM-5PM M; 8AM-4PM T-F. (EST) www.lagrangecounty.org

Index: All in onc. Records indexed on a public use terminal back to 1997. Office will perform a UCC search but public must search other records themselves. Search fee-$10.00. Office will not search real estate records. Copy fee $1.00 per page. UCC copy fee- none. Cert fee- $5.00 per doc plus copy fee. Payee- LaGrange County Recorder. **Other phones:** Treasurer- 260-499-6316; Elections- 260-499-6368; Vital Records- 260-499-4182. **Property tax/Assessing**- 114 W Michigan St, #3, LaGrange, IN 46761; 260-499-6319. **Online access**- Access assessor's data and search free at http://in-lagrange-assessor.governmax.com/propertymax/rover30.asp.

Lake County

County Recorder, 2293 N Main St, Bldg A, 2nd Fl, Crown Point, IN 46307. 219-755-3730, R/E recording phone-219-755-3157; fax-219-755-3257; 8:30AM-4:30PM (CST) www.lakecountyin.org/index.jsp

Index: All in one. Records indexed on computer back to1995. Office personnel or visitors may perform searches. Search fee $10.00; $5.00 each add'l. Office will search real estate records. Office will not search UCC records. Copy fee $1.00 per page. UCC copy fee- none. Cert fee- $5.00 per doc plus copy fee. Payee- Lake County Recorder. Office does not sell bulk data. **Other phones:** Treasurer- 219-755-3760; Elections- 219-755-3795; Vital Records- 219-755-3655; General- 219-755-3000. **Property tax/Assessing**- 2293 N Main St, Bldg A, 2nd Fl, Crown Point, IN 46307; 219-755-3100, assessor fax-219-755-3022. www.lakecountyin.org/index.jsp **Online access**- Access property tax data online at http://in-lake-assessor.governmaxa.com/propertymax/rover30.asp. Search free as Guest, but no name searching. Subscription service allows name searching; sub fee is $19.95 per month.

Lawrence County

County Recorder, 916 15th St, Rm 21, Bedford, IN 47421. Recording, R/E & UCC phone-812-275-3245; fax-812-275-4138; 8:30AM-4:30PM (EST)

Index: All in one. Records indexed on computer back to 12/94. Only office personnel may search. Office will not search real estate records. Will search UCC records. UCC search on UCC 11 form per debtor name- $10.00; $5.00 each add'l name. Copy fee $1.00 per page. UCC copy fee- none. Cert fee- $5.00 per doc plus copy fee. Payee- Lawrence County Recorder. Office does not sell bulk data. **Other phones:** Treasurer- 812-275-2431; Elections- 812-275-2036. **Property tax/Assessing**- 916 15th St, Bedford IN 47421; 812-275-5405, assessor fax- 812-275-4164. (Appraiser/Auditor- 812-275-3111) No public assess terminal available.

Madison County

County Recorder, 16 E 9th St, Rm 205, Anderson, IN 46016. 765-641-9613, R/E recording phone-765-641-9615, UCC recording phone-765-608-7828; fax-765-641-9617; 8AM-4PM (EST)

Index: All in one. Records indexed on a public use terminal back to 11/1989. Office personnel or visitors may perform searches. Search fee $8.00 per name. Office will search real estate records. Will search UCC records. Copy fee $1.00 per page. Cert fee- $5.00 per doc plus copy fee. Payee- Madison County Recorder. **Other phones:** Treasurer- 765-641-9645; Elections- 765-641-9459; Vital Records- 765-641-9433. **Property tax/Assessing**- 16 E 9th St, Anderson, IN 46016; 765-641-9401, assessor fax-765-608-9707. Public access terminal available.

Marion County

County Recorder, 200 E Washington, #721; City-County Bldg, Indianapolis, IN 46204. 317-327-4020, R/E recording phone-317-327-4018, UCC phone-317-327-4015; fax-317-327-3942; 8-4:30PM (EST) www.indy.gov/EGOV/COUNTY/RECORDER/

Index: All in one. Records indexed on a public use terminal back to 1964. Only the public may search. Copy fee $1.00 per page. UCC copy fee- none. Cert fee- $5.00 per doc plus copy fee. Payee- Marion County Recorder. Acquire recording data on customized CD-rom and in specialized online reports. **Online access to Real Estate, Lien, Deed, UCC, Property Tax records:** Access to Marion County online records requires a $200 set up fee, plus an escrow balance of at least $100 must be maintained. add'l charges are $.25 per minute, $.05 display charge for 1st page; $.05 each add'l page. Records date back to 1964; images from 1964. Federal tax liens and UCC data available. For info, contact Mike Kerner at 317-327-4587 or visit www.civicnet.net. Also, access recording office land data at www.etitlesearch.com. Registration required, fee based on usage. **Other phones:** Treasurer- 317-327-4040; Auditor- 317-327-4646. **Property tax/Assessing**- 200 E Washington St, #1121, Indianapolis, IN 46204; 317-327-4907, assessor fax- 317-327-5190. **Online**- Property tax data free http://cms.indygov.org/MyAssessedValue/. Also, search City of Beech Grove property data at http://beacon.schneidercorp.com/ with registration required.

Marshall County

County Recorder, 112 W Jefferson St, Rm 201, Plymouth, IN 46563. Recording, R/E & UCC phone-574-935-8515; fax-574-935-5099; 8AM-4PM (EST) www.co.marshall.in.us

Index: All in one. Records indexed on a public use terminal back to 7/96. Only the public may search. Copy fee $1.00 per page; $2.00 per page over-sized. Cert fee- $5.00 per doc plus copy fee. Payee- Marshall County Recorder. Bulk data available for purchase with signed contract that records will not be re-sold to anyone. **Other phones:** Treasurer- 574-935-8518; Elections- 574-936-8922. **Property tax/Assessing**- 112 W Jefferson St, Rm 207, Plymouth, IN 46563; 574-935-8525, assessor fax- 574-936-4863. www.co.marshall.in.us/Departments/Assessor/assessor.htm **Online access**- Search property data at http://beacon.schneidercorp.com/.

Martin County

County Recorder, PO Box 147, Shoals, IN 47581. Recording, R/E & UCC phone-812-247-2420; fax-812-247-2756; 8AM-4PM (EST)

Index: All in one. Records indexed on a public use terminal back to 2003. Only the public may search. Copy fee $1.00 per page. Cert fee- $5.00 per doc plus copy fee. Payee- Martin County Recorder. **Other phones:** Treasurer- 812-247-3701. **Property tax/Assessing**- PO Box 38, 111 Main St, Shoals, IN 47581; 812-247-2070, assessor fax- 812-247-2756. Public access terminal in auditors office.

Miami County

County Recorder, 25 N Broadway, #205, Peru, IN 46970. 765-472-3901; fax-765-472-8585; 8AM-4PM (EST) www.miamicountyin.gov/

Index: Separate indices to search include deeds, mortgages, misc. Records indexed on a public use terminal back to 1995 except mortgage (exception 01/97 to 8/21/97). Office personnel or visitors may perform searches. Search fee $10.00 per name. Will search UCC records. Copy fee $1.00 per page. UCC copy fee- $8.00 per name. Cert fee- $5.00 per doc plus copy fee. Payee- Miami County Recorder. Bulk data available for purchase for $.07 per image (cannot be resold). **Online access to Assessment, Property Tax, GIS/Mapping, Voter Registration records:** Access to records for free at www.miamicountyin.gov/ . **Property tax/Assessing**- 25 N Broadway, Peru, IN 46970; 765-472-3901 x263, fax- 765-472-5948.

Monroe County

County Recorder, PO Box 1634, Bloomington, IN 47402. Recording, R/E phone-812-349-2520; 8AM-4PM (EST) www.co.monroe.in.us/recorder/index.htm

Two assessors here; one county and one township. Index: Separate indices to search deeds, mortgages, misc. All indices computerized since 05/91; images available on computer since 010199. Office will perform a UCC search but public must search other records themselves. Office will not search real estate records. UCC search on UCC 11 form per debtor name- $10.00; $5.00 each add'l name. Copy fee $1.00 per page. Cert fee- $5.00 per cert plus copy fee. Payee- Monroe County Recorder. Bulk data available for purchase, contact Mike Szakaly. **Other phones:** Treasurer- 812-349-2530; Elections- 812-349-2615; Vital Records- 812-349-2543. **Property tax/Assessing**- 100 W Kirkwood, Bloomington, IN 47404; 812-349-2502, assessor fax- 812-349-2898. www.co.monroe.in.us/countyassessor/index.htm **Online access**- Access to GIS/Maps information for free go to http://in53.plexisgroup.com/

Montgomery County

County Recorder, 100 E Main St, #104, Crawfordsville, IN 47933. 765-364-6415; fax-765-364-6404; 8AM-4PM (EST)

Fax machine is in Auditor's office, so include fax cover letters. Index: Separate indices to search. Records indexed on a public use terminal back to 6/95. Office will perform a UCC search but public must search other records themselves. Search fee- $10.00 for UCC. Copy fee $1.00 per page. UCC copy fee- none. Cert fee- $5.00 per doc plus copy fee. Payee- Montgomery County Recorder. Bulk data available for purchase on a monthly basis, contact Michelle Cash. **Other phones:** Treasurer- 765-364-6410; Elections- 765-364-6437. **Property tax/Assessing**- 100 E Main St, Crawfordsville, IN 47933; 765-364-6420, assessor fax- 765-364-6369.

Morgan County

County Recorder, PO Box 1653, Martinsville, IN 46151. Recording, R/E & UCC phone-765-342-1077; 8AM-4PM M-Th, 8AM-5PM F. (EST)
Index: All in one. Records indexed on a public use terminal back to 4/94. Only the public may search. Copy fee $1.00 per page. Cert fee- $5.00 per doc plus copy fee. Payee- Morgan County Recorder. Bulk Data available for purchase on CD, contact Recorder's office. **Other phones:** Treasurer- 765-342-1048; Elections- 765-342-1029; Vital Records- 765-342-6621. **Property tax/Assessing**- 180 S Main St, #218, Martinsville, IN 46151; 765-342-1065, assessor fax-765-342-1097. hours- 8AM-4PM Public access terminal available.

Newton County

Recorder, 201 N 3rd St, Box 49, Kentland, IN 47951. 219-474-6081; fax-219-474-5749; 8AM-4PM (CST)
Records indexed on a public use terminal back to 1995. Office personnel or visitors may perform searches. UCC search on UCC 11 form per debtor name- $10.00; $5.00 each add'l name. Will not do federal tax lien search. Copy fee $1.00 per page. UCC copy fee- none. Cert fee- $5.00 per doc plus copy fee. Payee- Newton County Recorder. Office does not sell bulk data. **Other phones:** Treasurer- 219-474-6081. **Property tax/Assessing**- 1 Courthouse Sq, Kentland, IN 47951; 219-474-6081, assessor fax- 219-474-3540. **Online**- Access assessor's property data free at http://in56.plexisgroup.com/ecama/propsearch.cfm.

Noble County

County Recorder, 101 N Orange St, Rm 210, Albion, IN 46701. Recording, R/E phone-260-636-2672; fax-260-636-3264; 8AM-4PM (EST) www.nobleco.org
Index: Separate indices to search include deeds, mortgages, miscellaneous, bonds, discharges. Records indexed on a public use terminal back to 6/93. Only the public may search. Copy fee $1.00 per page. UCC copy fee- none. Cert fee- $5.00 per doc plus copy fee. Payee- Noble County Recorder. Office does not sell bulk data. **Other phones:** Treasurer- 260-636-2644. **Property tax/Assessing**- 101 N Orange St, Albion, IN 46701; 260-636-2297, assessor fax- 260-636-3538. **Online access**- Access the property ownership roster in pdf format for free at www.nobleco.org/GIS/Land_Ownership_Roster.pdf.

Ohio County

County Recorder, 413 Main St; Courthouse, Rising Sun, IN 47040. Recording, R/E & UCC phone-812-438-3369; fax-812-438-3369; 9AM-4PM M,T,TH,F; 9AM-12 Sat; Closed Wed. (EST)
Index: All in one. Records indexed on a public use terminal back to 2000. Office will perform a UCC search but public must search other records themselves. Search fee-$10.00; $5.00 each add'l name. Copy fee $1.00 per page. UCC copy fee- none. Cert fee- $5.00 per doc plus copy fee. Payee- Ohio County Recorder. Office does not sell bulk data. **Other phones:** Treasurer- 812-438-2724; Elections-812-438-2610; Vital Records- 812-438-2551. **Property tax/Assessing**- 413 Main St, Rising Sun, IN 47040; 812-438-3264. www.ohiocountyassessor.com **Online** - Access property data free at http://in-ohio-assessor.governmaxa.com/propertymax/rover30.asp. Click on property search, then search by owner, address or parcel number.

Orange County

County Recorder, 205 E Main St, #8, Paoli, IN 47454. 812-723-7114; fax-none; 8AM-4PM (EST)
Index: Separate indices to search. Records indexed on a public use terminal back to 1993, deeds only back to 1955. Office personnel or visitors may perform searches. UCC search on UCC 11 form per debtor name- $10.00; $5.00 each add'l name. Copy fee $1.00 per page. UCC copy fee- none. Cert fee- $5.00 per doc for deeds plus copy fee; $15.00 per doc for everything else. Payee- Orange County Recorder. Bulk data available for purchase, contact Stacie Owen. **Property tax/Assessing**- 205 E Main St, #7, Paoli, IN 47454; 812-723-3600x8. www.inorangeassessor.com

Owen County

County Recorder, Courthouse, Spencer, IN 47460. 812-829-5013; fax-812-829-5014; 8AM-4PM (EST)
Index: Separate indices to search include deeds, mortgages, miscellaneous, UCC files. Records indexed on a public use terminal back to 1991; 1978 for deeds. Office will perform a UCC search but public must search other records themselves. Copy fee $1.00 per page. Cert fee- $5.00 per doc plus copy fee. Payee- Owen County Recorder. Contact Pat Figg for information on paper copies of bulk information. **Other phones:** Treasurer- 812-829-5011; Elections-812-829-5015; Vital Records- 812-829-5017. **Property tax/Assessing**- 60 S Main St, Courthouse, Spencer, IN 47460; 812-829-5018.

Parke County

County Recorder, 116 W High St, Rm 102, Rockville, IN 47872-1787. Recording, R/E & UCC phone-765-569-3419; fax-765-569-4037; 8AM-4PM (EST)
Fax to- Attention Recorder. Index: Separate indices to search include computer, also general books, deeds. Records indexed on a public use terminal back to 3/96. Only the public may search. Copy fee $1.00 per page. UCC copy fee- none. Cert fee- $5.00 per doc plus copy fee. Payee- Parke County Recorder. Office does not sell bulk data. **Other phones:** Treasurer-765-569-3437. **Property tax/Assessing**- 116 W High St, Rockville, IN 47872; 765-569-3490, assessor fax-765-569-4037. A public access terminal is available.

Perry County

County Recorder, 2219 Payne St, Rm W2, Tell City, IN 47586-2830. Recording, R/E & UCC phone-812-547-4261; fax-812-547-9788; 8AM-4PM (CST)
Index: All in one. Records indexed on a public use terminal back to 1999. Only the public may search. Copy fee $1.00 per page. For UCC copy information request form must be sent in. Cert fee- $5.00 per doc plus copy fee. Payee- Perry County Recorder. **Other phones:** Treasurer- 812-547-4816; Elections- 812-547-3741; Vital Records- 812-547-2746. **Property tax/Assessing**- 2219 Payne St, Tell City, IN 47586; 812-547-5531, assessor fax- 812-547-9779.

Pike County

County Recorder, 801 E Main St; Courthouse, Petersburg, IN 47567-1298. 812-354-6747; fax-812-354-9431; 8AM-4PM (EST)
Index: Separate indices to search include deed, mortgage, misc. Records indexed on computer back to 1/94. Office will perform a UCC search but public must search other records themselves. Copy fee $1.00 per page. Cert fee- $5.00 per doc plus copy fee. Payee- Pike County Recorder. Office does not sell bulk data. **Other phones:** Treasurer- 812-354-6363; Elections- 812-354-6025; Vital Records- 812-354-8797. **Property tax/Assessing**- 801 E Main St, Courthouse, Petersburg, IN 47567; 812-354-6584, assessor fax- 812-354-3500.

Porter County

County Recorder, 155 Indiana Ave, #210, Valparaiso, IN 46383. Recording, R/E & UCC phone-219-465-3465, UCC recording phone-219-465-3374; 8:30AM-4:30PM (CST) www.porterco.org
Index: All in one. Records indexed on computer back to 1992. Only the public may search. Copy fee $1.00 per page. Plats- $2.50 per page. Cert fee- $5.00 per doc plus copy fee. Payee- Porter County Recorder. Office does not sell bulk data. **Online access to Real Estate, Deed, Lien records:** Recorder land data by subscription on either the Laredo system using subscription and fees or the Tapestry System using credit card, http://tapestry.fidlar.com; $3.99 search; $1.00 per image. Index goes back to 1991; images to 1975. The county offers an enhanced access subscription system for county property data and court information for $50.00 per month for 40 hours; contract and info available at www.porterco.org/enhanced_access.html. **Other phones:** Treasurer- 219-465-3470. **Property tax/Assessing**- 155 Indiana Ave, #211, Valparaiso, IN 46383; 219-465-3460. www.porterco.org **Online access**- Access to property assessment data and sales is free at http://in64.plexisgroup.com/ecama/. Also search property tax information for free at www.porterco.org/taxes.html.

Posey County

County Recorder, 126 E 3rd St, #215, Mount Vernon, IN 47620. Recording, R/E & UCC phone-812-838-1314; fax-812-838-8563; 8AM-4PM (CST)
Index: Separate indices to search include deeds, grantor/grantee, mortgages, etc. Records indexed on computer back to May, 1993. Office will perform a UCC search but public must search other records themselves. Search fee-$10.00 per name. Copy fee $1.00 per page. Cert fee- $5.00 per doc plus copy fee. Payee- Posey County Recorder. Bulk records are available to purchase on DVD, contact Martha Breeze. **Other phones:** Treasurer- 812-838-1316; Elections- 812-838-1339; Vital Records- 812-838-1328; Auditor- 812-838-1300. **Property tax/Assessing**- 126 E 3rd St, #132, Mount Vernon, IN 47620; 812-838-1309, assessor fax- 812-838-8270.

Pulaski County

Recorder, 112 E Main St, Rm 220; Courthouse, Winamac, IN 46996. Recording, R/E phone-574-946-3844; fax-574-946-6139; 8AM-4PM (EST)
Index: All in one. Records indexed on a public use terminal back to 3/94. Office will perform a UCC search but public must search other records themselves. Office will not search real estate records. UCC search on UCC 11 form per debtor name-$10.00; $5.00 each add'l name. Copy fee $1.00 per page. UCC copy fee- none. Cert fee- $5.00 per doc plus copy fee. Payee- Pulaski County Recorder. **Other phones:** Treasurer- 574-946-3632; Elections-574-946-3313; Vital Records- 574-946-6080. **Property tax/Assessing**- 112 E Main St, #120, Winamac, IN 46996; 574-946-3845, assessor fax-574-946-7648.

Putnam County

County Recorder, Courthouse Sq, Rm 25, Greencastle, IN 46135. Recording, R/E & UCC phone-765-653-5613; fax-765-653-2378; 8AM-4PM (EST) www.co.putnam.in.us
Index: All in one. Records indexed on computer back to 1998. Office will perform a UCC search but public must search other records themselves. Copy fee $1.00 per page. Cert fee- $5.00 per doc plus copy fee. Payee- Putnam County Recorder. Bulk data available for purchase, contact Jeanette Summitt, County Recorder. **Other phones:** Treasurer- 765-653-4510; Elections- 765-653-2648; Vital Records- 765-653-5210. **Property tax/Assessing**- 1 Courthouse Sq, #11, Greencastle, IN 46135; 765-653-4312, assessor fax-765-653-2842. www.putnamcounty.org/assessor/

Randolph County

Recorder, 100 S Main St, Rm 101; Courthouse, Winchester, IN 47394-1899. Recording, R/E & UCC phone-765-584-7300; fax-n/a; 8AM-4PM (EST)
Index: Indexed by deed, mortgage, misc. Records indexed on a public use terminal back to 1993. Office will perform a UCC search but public must search other records themselves. Office will not search real estate records. UCC search on UCC 11 form per debtor name- $10.00; $5.00 each add'l name. Will not do federal tax lien search. Copy fee $1.00 per page; $2.00 if oversized page. UCC copy fee- $1.00. Cert fee- $5.00 per doc plus copy fee. Payee- Randolph County Recorder. Images available for purchase, contact Jane Grove- Recorder. **Other phones:** Treasurer- 765-584-0704; Vital Records- 765-584-1155. **Property tax/Assessing**- 100 S Main St, Rm 103, Winchester, IN 47394; 765-584-2427, assessor fax- 765-584-2958. http://in-randolph-assessor.governmax.com/

Ripley County

County Recorder, PO Box 404, Versailles, IN 47042. Recording, R/E & UCC phone-812-689-5808; fax-812-689-0048; 8AM-4PM (EST)
Index: All in one. Records indexed on a public use terminal back to 1988. Office will perform a UCC search but public must search other records themselves. UCC search on UCC 11 form per debtor name- $10.00; $5.00 each add'l name. Copy fee $1.00 per page. UCC copy fee- none. Cert fee- $5.00 per doc plus copy fee. Payee- Ripley County Recorder. Office does not sell bulk data. **Other phones:** Treasurer- 812-689-6352. **Property tax/Assessing-** PO Box 382, Versailles, IN 47042; 812-689-5656, assessor fax- 812-689-4850.

Rush County

County Recorder, 101 E 2nd St, Rm 208; Courthouse, Rushville, IN 46173. 765-932-2388; 8-4PM (EST)
Index: Separate indices to search. Records indexed on a public use terminal back to 8/97. Office will perform a UCC search but public must search other records themselves. Search fee $10.00; $5.00 each add'l. Copy fee $1.00 per page. Cert fee- $5.00 per doc plus copy fee. Payee- Rush County Recorder. Bulk data available for purchase, contact Sally Niedenthal. **Other phones:** Treasurer- 765-932-2386; Elections- 765-932-2086; Vital Records- 765-932-3103. **Property tax/Assessing-** 101 E 2nd St, #210, Rushville, IN 46173; 765-932-3242.

Scott County

County Recorder, 1 E McClain St, #100, Scottsburg, IN 47170. 812-752-8442; fax-812-752-2678; 8:30AM-4:30PM (EST)
Records indexed on a public use terminal back to 1992. Office will perform a UCC search but public must search other records themselves. UCC search on UCC 11 form per debtor name- $10.00; $5.00 each add'l name. Copy fee $1.00 per page. UCC copy fee- none. Cert fee- $5.00 per doc plus copy fee. Payee- Scott County Recorder. Office does not sell bulk data. **Other phones:** Treasurer- 812-752-8414; Elections- 812-752-8420. **Property tax/Assessing-** 1 E McClain St, #150, Scottsburg, IN 47170; 812-752-8436, fax- 812-752-8437. A public access terminal available.

Shelby County

County Recorder, 25 W Polk, #101; Courthouse Annex, Shelbyville, IN 46176. Recording, R/E & UCC phone-317-392-6370; fax-317-392-6393; 7AM-5PM M-TH; Closed on Fri. (EST) www.co.shelby.in.us/
Index: All in one. Records indexed on a public use terminal back to 1999. Office will perform a UCC search but public must search other records themselves. Search fee-$10.00 plus $5.00 per name. Copy fee $1.00 per page. UCC copy fee- none. Cert fee- $5.00 per doc plus copy fee. Payee- Shelby County Recorder. **Online access to Real Estate, Deed, Tax Lien, Judgment records:** Online access to recorded records available via Doxpop.com subscription service. Index and images go back to 5/1998. **Other phones:** Treasurer- 317-392-6375; Elections- 317-392-6320. **Property tax/Assessing-** 25 W Polk, Courthouse Annex, Shelbyville, IN 46176; 317-392-6305. hours- 8AM-4PM

Spencer County

County Recorder, 200 Main; Courthouse, Rockport, IN 47635. 812-649-6013; fax-812-649-6015; 8AM-4PM (CST) www.spencercounty.in.gov
Index: All in one. Records indexed on computer back to 1998. Office will perform a UCC search but public must search other records themselves. UCC search on UCC 11 form per debtor name- $10.00; $5.00 each add'l name. Copy fee $1.00 per page. UCC copy fee- none. Cert fee- $5.00 per doc plus copy fee. Payee- Spencer County Recorder. Office does not sell bulk data. **Other phones:** Treasurer- 812-649-4556. **Property tax/Assessing-** 200 Main, Courthouse, Rockport, IN 47635; 812-649-6012, assessor fax- 812-649-6012.

St. Joseph County

County Recorder, 227 W Jefferson, Rm 321, South Bend, IN 46601. Recording, R/E & UCC phone-574-235-9525; fax-574-235-5170; 8AM-4:30PM (EST) www.stjosephcountyindiana.com
Records indexed on computer from 1991 to present, prior in index books. Office will perform a UCC search but public must search other records themselves. Will search UCC records only if search request filled out. Copy fee $1.00 per page; larger pages- $2.00 per page. Cert fee- $5.00 per doc plus copy fee. Payee- St. Joseph County Recorder. Bulk data available for purchase. **Online access to Real Estate, Deed, Lien records:** Recorder land data by subscription on either the Laredo system using subscription and fees or the Tapestry System using credit card, http://tapestry.fidlar.com; $5.95 search; $1.00 per image. Index back to 12/1992; images back to 1992. **Other phones:** Treasurer- 574-235-9531; Elections- 574-235-9635; Vital Records- 574-235-6719. **Property tax/Assessing-** 227 W Jefferson, 3rd Fl, South Bend, IN 46601; 574-235-9523, assessor fax- 574-235-5554. **Online access-** Search parcel data for free at www.macoggis.com and includes Michiana area which is St Joseph and Elkhart Counties.

Starke County

County Recorder, PO Box 1, Knox, IN 46534. 574-772-9110, R/E recording phone-574-772-9109; fax-574-772-9178; 8AM-4PM (CST)
Index: Separate indices to search. Records indexed on a public use terminal back to 2001. Office will perform a UCC search but public must search other records themselves. UCC search on UCC 11 form per debtor name- $10.00; $5.00 each add'l name. Copy fee $1.00 per page. UCC copy fee- none. Cert fee- $5.00 per doc plus copy fee. Payee- Starke County Recorder. Office does not sell bulk data. **Other phones:** Treasurer- 574-772-9113. **Property tax/Assessing-** 53 E Mound St, Knox, IN 46534; 574-772-9107, assessor fax- 574-772-9116.

Steuben County

County Recorder, 317 S Wayne St, #2F, Angola, IN 46703. Recording, R/E & UCC phone-260-668-1000 x1700; fax-260-665-8483; 8AM-4:30PM (EST) www.co.steuben.in.us/departments/recorder/recorder.aspx
Index: All in one. Records indexed on a public use terminal back to 1994. Only the public may search. Copy fee $1.00 per page. UCC copy fee- none. Cert fee- $5.00 per doc plus copy fee. Payee- Steuben County Recorder. Office does not sell bulk data. **Other phones:** Treasurer- 260-668-1000 x1900; Elections- 260-668-1000 x2220; Vital Records- 260-668-1000 x1500. **Property tax/Assessing-** 317 S Wayne St, #2G, Angola, IN 46703-1900; 260-668-1000 x1000, assessor fax- 260-665-8483. www.co.steuben.in.us/departments/assessors/assessors.aspx **Online access-** Access property data free on the GIS mapping site at www.co.steuben.in.us/. Also, access parcel and subdivision data free on the GIS mapping site at http://beacon.schneidercorp.com/?site=SteubenCountyIN.

Sullivan County

County Recorder, 100 Courthouse Sq, Rm 205, Sullivan, IN 47882-1565. 812-268-4844; fax-812-268-0521; 8AM-4PM (EST)
Index: All in one. Records indexed on a public use terminal back to 8/00. Office will perform a UCC search but public must search other records themselves. Search fee-$10.00 plus $5.00 for each add'l name. Copy fee $1.00 per page. Cert fee- $5.00 per doc plus copy fee. Payee- Sullivan County Recorder. **Other phones:** Treasurer- 812-268-6410; Elections- 812-268-4657; Vital Records- 812-268-4029. **Property tax/Assessing-** 100 Courthouse Sq, #227, Sullivan, IN 47882; 812-268-5110.

Switzerland County

County Recorder, 212 W Main; Courthouse, Vevay, IN 47043. 812-427-2544; fax- 812-427-3160; 8AM-3:30PM (EST)
Index: Separate indices to search include deeds, mortgages, liens, misc. Records indexed on a public use terminal back to 12/1988. Only the public may search. Copy fee $1.00 per copy. Cert fee- $5.00 per doc plus copy fee. Payee- Switzerland County Recorder. Office does not sell bulk data. **Other phones:** Treasurer- 812-427-3369; Elections- 812-427-3175; Auditor- 812-427-3302. **Property tax/Assessing-** 212 W Main, Vevay, IN 47043; 812-427-3379, assessor fax- 812-427-3160. A public access terminal is available.

Tippecanoe County

County Recorder, 20 N 3rd St, Lafayette, IN 47901. Recording, R/E & UCC phone-765-423-9352, UCC recording phone-765-423-9353; fax-765-420-8489; 8AM-4:30PM (EST) www.tippecanoe.in.gov/
Fax to- Attention Recorder. Index: All in one. Records indexed on a public use terminal back to 1986. Office will perform a UCC search (for a fee) but public must search other records themselves. Copy fee $1.00 per page. UCC copy fee- none. Cert fee- $5.00 per doc plus copy fee. Payee- Tippecanoe County Recorder. A CD listing all properties in Tippecanoe County is available. **Other phones:** Treasurer- 765042309273. **Property tax/Assessing-** 20 N 3rd St, Lafayette, IN 47901; 765-423-9255, assessor fax- 765-423-9790. Public access terminals are available during business hours that allow full access to both the tax database and the assessment database. www.tippecanoe.in.gov/assessor/ **Online access-** A subscription fee of $10 per month plus a one-time set-up fee of $50 allows full access to both the tax database and the assessment database. Click on Access Property Tax & Assessment Records. Also, access to the county GIS-mapping site free at http://gis.tippecanoe.in.gov/public/.

Tipton County

Recorder, 101 E Jefferson St, 2nd Fl; Courthouse, Tipton, IN 46072. 765-675-4614; fax-765-675-3893; 8AM-5PM (EST) www.tiptoncounty.in.gov/
Index: Separate indices to search include deed, mortgage, misc. Records indexed on computer back to 5/96. Office will perform a UCC search but public must search other records themselves. Search fee- $10.00 per name, each add'l $5.00. Copy fee $1.00 per page. Cert fee- $5.00 per doc plus copy fee. Payee- Tipton County Recorder. Office does not sell bulk data. **Other phones:** Treasurer- 765-675-2742; Vital Records- 765-675-8741; Clerk's Office- 765-675-2795. **Property tax/Assessing-** 101 E Jefferson St, Tipton, IN 46072; 765-675-2465, assessor fax- 765-675-3603. (Appraiser/Auditor- 765-675-2724) hours- 8AM-4PM www.tiptoncounty.in.gov/ **Online access-** Search assessor property data free on the GIS system at the Tipton county site or at http://beacon.schneidercorp.com/.

Union County

County Recorder, 26 W Union St, Liberty, IN 47353. Recording, R/E & UCC phone-765-458-5434; fax-765-458-1082; 8AM-N, 1-4PM (EST)
Index: Separate indices to search. Record index newly computerized in late 2006; available on public access terminal. Historic records being added. Only the public may search. Copy fee $1.00 per page. UCC copy fee- none. Cert fee- $5.00 per doc plus copy fee. Payee- Union County Recorder. Bulk data available for purchase, all recorded documents from 10/06 to present. Must sign agreement not to re-sale. Certified check. **Other phones:** Treasurer- 765-458-6491; Elections- 765-458-6121; Auditor- 765-458-5464. **Property tax/Assessing-** 26 W Union St, County Courthouse, Liberty, IN 47353; 765-458-5464, assessor fax- 765-458-5263. **Online access-** Assessor records not yet available online.

Vanderburgh County

County Recorder, PO Box 1037, Evansville, IN 47706. Recording, R/E & UCC phone-812-435-5215; fax-812-435-5580; 8AM-4:30PM (CST) www.vanderburghgov.org/Index.aspx?page=69

Index: Separate indices to search include books, computer. Records indexed on computer back to 1980. Office will perform a UCC search but public must search other records themselves. UCC search on UCC 11 form per debtor name- $10.00; $5.00 each add'l name. Copy fee $1.00 per page. UCC copy fee- none. Cert fee- $5.00 per doc plus copy fee. Payee- Vanderburgh County Recorder. **Other phones:** Treasurer- 812-435-5248; Elections- 812-435-5160; Vital Records- 812-435-5681. **Property tax/Assessing**- 1 NW Martin Luther King Jr Blvd, #227, Evansville IN 47708; 812-435-5267, assessor fax- 812-435-5530. **Online**- Access assessor property database free at www.vanderburghassessor.org/.

Vermillion County

County Recorder, PO Box 145, Newport, IN 47966-0145. 765-492-5003, R/E recording phone-765-492-3570, UCC recording phone-765-492-5003; fax-765-492-5000; hours- 8AM-4PM (EST) www.vermilliongov.us/home.html

765-492-5000 fax number is shared with the Auditor. Index: Separate indices to search include mortgages and misc. deeds, imaged by instrument number. Records indexed on computer back to 1994. Office will perform a UCC search but public must search other records themselves. UCC search fee $10.00 per debtor name. Copy fee $1.00 per page. Cert fee- $5.00 per doc plus copy fee. Payee- Vermillion County Recorder. Office does not sell bulk data. **Other phones:** Treasurer- 765-492-3460; Elections- 765-492-3500; Vital Records- 765-832-3622. **Property tax/Assessing**- PO Box 268, Newport, IN 47966; 765-492-5004.

Vigo County

Recorder, 199 Oak St, Terre Haute, IN 47807. Recording, R/E phone-812-462-3301; fax-812-232-2219; 8-4PM (EST) www.vigocounty.org/recorder/

Index: Separate indices to search include deeds, mortgages, misc. Records indexed on a public use terminal back to 11/1996. Office personnel will perform non-detail record searches, including RE and UCC records. Search fee $10.00. Copy fee $1.00 per page. For copies larger than 8 1/2 x 14- $2.00 per page. Will fax back $1.00 per page. Cert fee- $5.00 per doc plus copy fee. Payee- Vigo County Recorder. Record images can be bought on CD-rom for $.06 per image, contact LouAnn Miller. **Online access to Real Estate, Deed, Tax Lien, Judgment records:** Online access to recorded records available via Doxpop.com subscription service. Index goes back to 11/1996, images to 1/2001. Also images can be purchased at doxpop.com at $1.00 per image back to 2001. **Other phones:** Treasurer- 812-462-3251; Elections- 812-462-3211; Vital Records- 812-462-2442. **Property tax/Assessing**- 189 Oak St, Terre haute, IN 47807; 812-462-3358. (Appraiser/Auditor- 812-462-3358 x219) **Online** - Search Vigo County property data by parcel, name, address www.vigocounty.org/assessor/ by clicking on Search Vigo County Property information. Also, search property data for a fee at http://beacon.schneidercorp.com/ with registration and password; includes City of Terra Haute.

Wabash County

County Recorder, One W Hill St; Courthouse, Wabash, IN 46992. Recording, R/E & UCC phone-260-563-0661 x253; hours- 8AM-4PM (EST) www.wabashcounty.in.gov

Index: All in one. Records indexed on a public use terminal back to 4/1/03. Only the public may search. Copy fee $1.00 per page. UCC copy fee- none. Cert fee- $5.00 per doc plus copy fee. Payee- Wabash County Recorder. Disc of land record information is available to title companies. **Other phones:** Treasurer- 260-563-0661 x259; Elections- 260-563-0661 x238. **Property tax/Assessing**- One W Hill St, Courthouse, Wabash, IN 46992; 260-563-0661 x227, fax- 260-563-3451. www.wabashcounty.in.gov **Online**- Access property data free from the Property List at http://assessor.wabash.in.datapitstop.us. Click on Property Information.

Warren County

County Recorder, 125 N Monroe, #10; Courthouse, Williamsport, IN 47993-1162. 765-762-3174; fax-765-762-7244; 8AM-4PM (EST)

Index: Separate indices to search include computer & books. Records indexed on a public use terminal back to 1/1/1997. Office will perform a UCC search but public must search other records themselves. UCC search on UCC 11 form per debtor name- $10.00; $5.00 each add'l name. Copy fee $1.00 per page. Cert fee- $5.00 per doc plus copy fee. Payee- Warren County Recorder. Office does not sell bulk data. **Other phones:** Treasurer- 765-762-3562; Elections- 765-762-3510. **Property tax/Assessing**- 25 N Monroe, Courthouse #3, Williamsport, IN 47993; 765-764-4528, assessor fax- 765-762-7216.

Warrick County

County Recorder, PO Box 285, Boonville, IN 47601. Recording, R/E & UCC phone-812-897-6165; fax-812-897-6168; hours- 8AM-4PM (CST) www.warrickcounty.gov/depatments/recorder.htm

Index: Separate indices to search. Records indexed on computer, books and aperture cards. Office will perform a UCC search but public must search other records themselves. UCC search on UCC 11 form per debtor name- $10.00. Copy fee $1.00 per page. Cert fee- $5.00 per doc plus copy fee. Payee- Warrick County Recorder. Office does not sell bulk data. **Other phones:** Treasurer- 812-897-6166; Elections-812-897-6161. **Property tax/Assessing**- One County Sq, Rm 280, Boonville, IN 47601; 812-897-6125, assessor fax- 812-897-3560. Public access computer in office for index and records searching. www.warrickcounty.gov **Online**- Access property data free at www.emapsplus.com/ILAdams/maps/ including name searching. Assessor's property tax data free at www.warrickcounty.gov/warrickassessor/. GIS Map information available at http://thinkopengis.warrick.in.wthengineering.com/.

Washington County

County Recorder, 99 Public Sq, #100, Salem, IN 47167. 812-883-4001; fax-812-883-4020; 8:30AM-4PM M-Th; 8:30AM-6PM Fri. (EST)

Index: Separate indices to search include deed, mortgage, misc, UCCs, veteran discharge, cemetery all before 1997. Records indexed on computer back to October, 1996. Office will perform a UCC search but public must search other records themselves. Search fee-$10.00 per name. Copy fee $1.00 per page. Cert fee- $5.00 per doc plus copy fee. Payee- Washington County Recorder. Bulk data available for purchase, contact Cindy Zink. **Other phones:** Treasurer- 812-883-3307; Elections- 812-883-5748; Vital Records-812-883-5603. **Property tax/Assessing**- 99 Public Square, #105, Salem, IN 47167; 812-883-4000.

Wayne County

County Recorder, 401 E Main St; County Admin Bldg, Richmond, IN 47374. Recording, R/E & UCC phone-765-973-9235; fax-765-973-9341; 8:30AM-5PM M; 8:30AM-4:30 PM T-F. (EST) http://co.wayne.in.us/recorder/

Index: Separate indices to search include pre-1994 books, computer 1994 to present. Records indexed on a public use terminal back to 1994. Only the public may search. Copy fee $1.00 per page. Cert fee- $5.00 per doc plus copy fee. Payee- Wayne County Recorder. Bulk data available for purchase. **Online access to Real Estate, Deed, Lien, Mortgage, Assumed Name, Marriage records:** Access recorded document indexes through a private company at https://www.doxpop.com/prod/recorder/. Subscriptions start at $25.00 monthly; add'l $1.00 or less fee to purchase a full-size document. Index goes back to 1/1994; images to 4/2000. Also, marriage records being added irregularly to the website at www.co.wayne.in.us/marriage/retrieve.cgi. Records are from 1811 forward. **Other phones:** Treasurer-765-973-9238; Elections- 765-973-9226; Vital Records- 765-973-9245. **Property tax/Assessing**- 401 E Main St, Richmond, IN 47374; 765-973-9254, assessor fax- 765-973-9307. hours- 8AM-5PM Public access computer in office for index and records searching. www.co.wayne.in.us **Online access**- Access county property records free at http://prc.co.wayne.in.us but this site is dated 2004. Also, search current property tax records free at the gis-mapping site at www.gis.co.wayne.in.us/. Free registration required. Also, search plat records free at the gis-mapping site at www.gis.co.wayne.in.us/. Also, access sheriff tax sale list free at www.co.wayne.in.us/legals/sales.html.

Wells County

County Recorder, 102 W Market St, #203; Courthouse, Bluffton, IN 46714. Recording, R/E & UCC phone-260-824-6507; fax-260-824-1238; 8AM-4:30PM (EST) www.wellscounty.org

Index: All in one. Records indexed on a public use terminal back to 11/2001. Office will perform a UCC search but public must search other records themselves. Search fee-$10.00 for UCC search plus $5.00 each add'l name per search. Copy fee $1.00 per page. UCC copy fee- none. Cert fee- $5.00 per doc plus copy fee. Payee- Wells County Recorder. Bulk data available for purchase in microfilm form, contact Sandy or Rina. **Other phones:** Treasurer- 260-824-6514; Elections- 260-824-6482; Vital Records- 260-824-6489; Auditor- 260-824-6470. **Property tax/Assessing**- 102 W Market St, #202, Bluffton, IN 46714; 260-824-6476, assessor fax- 260-824-6518. (Appraiser/Auditor- 260-824-6476) Public access computer in office. www.wellscounty.org **Online**- Access assessor records free on GIS-mapping site at http://beacon.schneidercorp.com/?site=WellsCountyIN. At map page, click on Search to search by name.

White County

County Recorder, PO Box 127, Monticello, IN 47960. 574-583-5912; fax-574-583-1521; 8AM-4PM (EST)

Index: Separate indices to search include before 1982 in books & page, 1982 forward on computer. Records indexed on computer back to 1988. Only the public may search. Copy fee $1.00 per page. Cert fee- $5.00 per doc plus copy fee. Payee- White County Recorder. Office does not sell bulk data. **Online access to Real Estate, Deed, Lien records:** Recorder land data by subscription on either the Laredo system using subscription and fees or the Tapestry System using credit card, http://tapestry.fidlar.com; $3.99 search; $1.00 per image. Index and images go back to 1980. **Other phones:** Treasurer- 574-583-5771; Elections- 574-583-1531; Vital Records- 574-583-8254. **Property tax/Assessing**- 110 N Main, Monticello, IN 47960; 574-583-7755, assessor fax-574-583-0885. **Online access**- Property and tax data is available at www.wcgconline.net/

Whitley County

County Recorder, 220 W Van Buren St, #206; County Gov't Ctr, Columbia City, IN 46725. Recording, R/E & UCC phone-260-248-3106; fax-260-248-3163; 8AM-4:30PM (EST)

Index: Separate indices to search include mortgage, deed, UCC, misc. Records indexed on a public use terminal back to 9/1/01. Only the public may search. Copy fee $1.00 per page. UCC copy fee- none. Cert fee- $5.00 per doc plus copy fee. Payee- Whitley County Recorder. **Other phones:** Treasurer- 260-248-3105; Elections- 260-248-3102. **Property tax/Assessing**- 220 W Van Buren St, #202, Columbia City, IN 46725; 260-248-3109, assessor fax- 260-248-3163. **Online access**- Search assessor property data free on the GIS system at http://beacon.schneidercorp.com/.

Indiana County Locator

You will usually be able to find the city name in the City/County Cross Reference below. In that case, it is a simple matter to determine the county from the cross reference. However, only the official US Postal Service city names are included in this index. There are an additional 40,000 place names that people use in their addresses. Therefore, we have also included a ZIP/City Cross Reference immediately following the City/County Cross Reference.

If you know the ZIP Code but the city name does not appear in the City/County Cross Reference index, look up the ZIP Code in the ZIP/City Cross Reference, find the city name, then look up the city name in the City/County Cross Reference. For example, you want to know the county for an address of Menands, NY 12204. There is no "Menands" in the City/County Cross Reference. The ZIP/City Cross Reference shows that ZIP Codes 12201-12288 are for the city of Albany. Looking back in the City/County Cross Reference, Albany is in Albany County.

Indiana City/County Cross Reference

ADVANCE Boone
AKRON (46910) Fulton(58), Kosciusko(31), Miami(9)
ALAMO Montgomery
ALBANY (47320) Delaware(92), Randolph(7)
ALBION Noble
ALEXANDRIA (46001) Madison(97), Delaware(2)
AMBIA (47917) Warren(51), Benton(48)
AMBOY (46911) Miami(89), Wabash(10)
AMO Hendricks
ANDERSON (46017) Madison(96), Delaware(3)
ANDERSON Madison
ANDREWS (46702) Huntington(91), Wabash(8)
ANGOLA Steuben
ARCADIA Hamilton
ARCOLA Allen
ARGOS (46501) Marshall(96), Fulton(3)
ARLINGTON (46104) Rush(98), Shelby(1)
ASHLEY (46705) DeKalb(70), Steuben(29)
ATHENS Fulton
ATLANTA (46031) Hamilton(62), Tipton(37)
ATTICA (47918) Fountain(81), Warren(17), Tippecanoe(1)
ATWOOD Kosciusko
AUBURN (46706) DeKalb(98), Allen(1)
AURORA Dearborn
AUSTIN (47102) Scott(85), Jackson(14)
AVILLA (46710) Noble(96), DeKalb(3)
AVOCA Lawrence
AVON Hendricks
BAINBRIDGE Putnam
BARGERSVILLE (46106) Johnson(96), Morgan(3)
BATESVILLE (47006) Franklin(58), Ripley(40)
BATH (47010) Franklin(69), Union(30)
BATTLE GROUND (47920) Tippecanoe(79), White(14), Carroll(6)
BEDFORD Lawrence
BEECH GROVE Marion
BELLMORE Parke
BENNINGTON (47011) Switzerland(55), Ohio(44)
BENTONVILLE Fayette
BERNE Adams
BETHLEHEM Clark
BEVERLY SHORES Porter
BICKNELL Knox
BIPPUS Huntington
BIRDSEYE (47513) Dubois(78), Crawford(15), Perry(4), Orange(1)
BLANFORD Vermillion
BLOOMFIELD Greene
BLOOMINGDALE Parke
BLOOMINGTON (47404) Monroe(98), Owen(1)
BLOOMINGTON Monroe
BLUFFTON (46714) Wells(96), Adams(3)
BOGGSTOWN (46110) Shelby(94), Johnson(5)
BOONE GROVE Porter
BOONVILLE (47601) Warrick(98), Spencer(1)
BORDEN (47106) Clark(90), Washington(5), Floyd(4)
BOSTON Wayne
BOSWELL (47921) Benton(81), Warren(18)
BOURBON (46504) Marshall(96), Kosciusko(3)
BOWLING GREEN (47833) Owen(51), Clay(48)
BRADFORD Harrison
BRANCHVILLE Perry
BRAZIL (47834) Clay(89), Vigo(6), Parke(4)
BREMEN (46506) Marshall(88), St. Joseph(11)
BRIDGETON Parke
BRIMFIELD Noble
BRINGHURST Carroll
BRISTOL Elkhart
BRISTOW Perry
BROOK (47922) Newton(94), Jasper(5)
BROOKLYN Morgan
BROOKSTON (47923) White(87), Carroll(12)
BROOKVILLE Franklin
BROWNSBURG Hendricks
BROWNSTOWN Jackson
BROWNSVILLE (47325) Union(78), Fayette(19), Wayne(2)
BRUCEVILLE Knox
BRYANT (47326) Jay(96), Adams(2)
BUCK CREEK Tippecanoe
BUCKSKIN Gibson
BUFFALO White
BUNKER HILL Miami
BURKET Kosciusko
BURLINGTON Carroll
BURNETTSVILLE (47926) White(67), Carroll(29), Cass(2)
BURNEY Decatur
BURROWS Carroll
BUTLER DeKalb
BUTLERVILLE Jennings
CAMBRIDGE CITY (47327) Wayne(94), Henry(4)
CAMBY (46113) Morgan(55), Marion(29), Hendricks(15)
CAMDEN (46917) Carroll(98), Cass(1)
CAMPBELLSBURG (47108) Washington(91), Orange(8)
CANAAN (47224) Jefferson(98), Switzerland(1)
CANNELBURG Daviess
CANNELTON Perry
CARBON (47837) Parke(66), Clay(33)
CARLISLE Sullivan
CARMEL Hamilton
CARTERSBURG Hendricks
CARTHAGE (46115) Rush(94), Hancock(5)
CAYUGA Vermillion
CEDAR GROVE Franklin
CEDAR LAKE Lake
CELESTINE Dubois
CENTERPOINT (47840) Clay(95), Putnam(4)
CENTERVILLE Wayne
CENTRAL Harrison
CHALMERS White
CHANDLER Warrick
CHARLESTOWN Clark
CHARLOTTESVILLE (46117) Hancock(89), Henry(10)
CHESTERTON Porter
CHRISNEY Spencer
CHURUBUSCO (46723) Whitley(63), Allen(23), Noble(12)
CICERO Hamilton
CLARKS HILL (47930) Tippecanoe(73), Montgomery(14), Clinton(11)
CLARKSBURG Decatur
CLARKSVILLE Clark
CLAY CITY (47841) Clay(98), Owen(1)
CLAYPOOL Kosciusko
CLAYTON (46118) Hendricks(97), Morgan(2)
CLEAR CREEK Monroe
CLIFFORD Bartholomew
CLINTON Vermillion
CLOVERDALE (46120) Putnam(74), Owen(20), Morgan(4)
COAL CITY (47427) Owen(86), Clay(13)
COALMONT Clay
COATESVILLE (46121) Hendricks(56), Putnam(43)
COLBURN Tippecanoe
COLFAX (46035) Clinton(69), Boone(26), Montgomery(3)
COLUMBIA CITY (46725) Whitley(96), Noble(2)
COLUMBUS (47201) Bartholomew(95), Brown(4)
COLUMBUS Bartholomew
COMMISKEY (47227) Jennings(80), Jefferson(19)
CONNERSVILLE Fayette
CONVERSE (46919) Grant(53), Miami(37), Howard(8), Wabash(1)
CORTLAND Jackson
CORUNNA (46730) DeKalb(97), Noble(2)
CORY (47846) Clay(98), Vigo(1)
CORYDON Harrison
COVINGTON (47932) Fountain(89), Warren(5), Vermillion(4)
CRAIGVILLE (46731) Wells(90), Adams(9)
CRANDALL Harrison
CRANE Martin
CRAWFORDSVILLE Montgomery
CROMWELL (46732) Noble(57), Kosciusko(42)
CROSS PLAINS Ripley
CROTHERSVILLE (47229) Jackson(89), Jennings(10)
CROWN POINT (46307) Lake(98), Porter(1)
CROWN POINT Lake
CULVER (46511) Marshall(77), Starke(10), Fulton(10), Pulaski(1)
CUTLER (46920) Carroll(98), Clinton(1)
CYNTHIANA (47612) Posey(79), Gibson(20)
DALE (47523) Spencer(37), Dubois(33), Warrick(29)
DALEVILLE (47334) Delaware(98), Henry(1)
DANA Vermillion
DANVILLE Hendricks
DARLINGTON Montgomery
DAYTON Tippecanoe
DECATUR Adams
DECKER Knox
DEEDSVILLE Miami
DELONG Fulton
DELPHI Carroll
DEMOTTE (46310) Jasper(82), Newton(17)
DENHAM Pulaski
DENVER (46926) Miami(95), Cass(3)
DEPAUW Harrison
DEPUTY (47230) Jefferson(91), Jennings(8)
DERBY Perry
DILLSBORO (47018) Dearborn(97), Ohio(2)
DONALDSON Marshall
DUBLIN Wayne
DUBOIS (47527) Dubois(97), Orange(1)
DUGGER (47848) Sullivan(96), Greene(3)
DUNKIRK (47336) Jay(63), Blackford(20), Delaware(16)
DUNREITH Henry
DUPONT (47231) Jefferson(74), Jennings(25)
DYER Lake
EARL PARK (47942) Benton(96), Newton(3)
EARL PARK Benton
EAST CHICAGO Lake
EAST ENTERPRISE Switzerland
EATON (47338) Delaware(98), Blackford(1)
ECKERTY Crawford
ECONOMY Wayne
EDINBURGH (46124) Johnson(54), Bartholomew(26), Shelby(19)
EDWARDSPORT (47528) Knox(98), Sullivan(1)
ELBERFELD (47613) Warrick(91), Gibson(7)
ELIZABETH (47117) Harrison(97), Floyd(2)
ELIZABETHTOWN (47232) Bartholomew(69), Jennings(30)
ELKHART Elkhart
ELLETTSVILLE Monroe
ELNORA (47529) Daviess(96), Greene(3)
ELWOOD (46036) Madison(91), Tipton(7)
EMINENCE Morgan
EMISON Knox
ENGLISH (47118) Crawford(67), Orange(27), Perry(5)
ETNA GREEN (46524) Kosciusko(97), Marshall(2)

EVANSTON Spencer
EVANSVILLE (47712) Vanderburgh(86), Posey(13)
EVANSVILLE Vanderburgh
FAIR OAKS (47943) Jasper(55), Newton(45)
FAIRBANKS Sullivan
FAIRLAND Shelby
FAIRMOUNT (46928) Grant(97), Madison(2)
FALMOUTH (46127) Rush(75), Fayette(24)
FARMERSBURG (47850) Sullivan(76), Vigo(23)
FARMLAND Randolph
FERDINAND (47532) Dubois(69), Spencer(27), Perry(2)
FILLMORE Putnam
FINLY Hancock
FISHERS Hamilton
FLAT ROCK (47234) Shelby(92), Bartholomew(7)
FLORA (46929) Carroll(91), Howard(8)
FLORENCE Switzerland
FLOYDS KNOBS (47119) Floyd(95), Clark(4)
FOLSOMVILLE Warrick
FONTANET Vigo
FOREST Clinton
FORT BRANCH Gibson
FORT RITNER Lawrence
FORT WAYNE (46818) Allen(98), Whitley(1)
FORT WAYNE Allen
FORTVILLE (46040) Hancock(73), Hamilton(19), Madison(6)
FOUNTAIN CITY (47341) Wayne(97), Randolph(2)
FOUNTAINTOWN (46130) Shelby(72), Hancock(27)
FOWLER Benton
FOWLERTON Grant
FRANCESVILLE (47946) Pulaski(83), Jasper(15)
FRANCISCO Gibson
FRANKFORT (46041) Clinton(98), Carroll(1)
FRANKLIN Johnson
FRANKTON Madison
FREDERICKSBURG (47120) Washington(97), Harrison(2)
FREEDOM Owen
FREELANDVILLE Knox
FREETOWN (47235) Jackson(71), Brown(28)
FREMONT Steuben
FRENCH LICK (47432) Orange(87), Dubois(11), Martin(1)
FRIENDSHIP Ripley
FULDA Spencer
FULTON Fulton
GALVESTON (46932) Cass(90), Howard(5), Miami(4)
GARRETT DeKalb
GARY (46403) Lake(98), Porter(1)
GARY Lake
GAS CITY Grant
GASTON (47342) Delaware(97), Grant(1)
GENEVA (46740) Adams(93), Wells(4), Jay(2)
GENTRYVILLE (47537) Spencer(68), Warrick(31)
GEORGETOWN (47122) Floyd(62), Harrison(37)
GLENWOOD (46133) Fayette(57), Rush(42)
GOLDSMITH Tipton
GOODLAND (47948) Newton(72), Jasper(15), Benton(12)
GOSHEN Elkhart
GOSPORT (47433) Owen(72), Monroe(16), Morgan(10)
GRABILL Allen
GRAMMER Bartholomew
GRANDVIEW Spencer
GRANGER (46530) St. Joseph(95), Elkhart(4)
GRANTSBURG Crawford
GRASS CREEK Fulton
GRAYSVILLE Sullivan
GREENCASTLE (46135) Putnam(98), Parke(1)
GREENFIELD Hancock
GREENS FORK Wayne
GREENSBORO Henry
GREENSBURG Decatur
GREENTOWN Howard
GREENVILLE (47124) Floyd(74), Harrison(25)
GREENWOOD Johnson
GRIFFIN (47616) Posey(85), Gibson(14)
GRIFFITH Lake
GRISSOM AFB Miami
GRISSOM ARB Miami
GROVERTOWN (46531) Starke(97), Marshall(2)
GUILFORD Dearborn
GWYNNEVILLE Shelby
HAGERSTOWN (47346) Wayne(96), Henry(3)
HAMILTON (46742) Steuben(84), DeKalb(15)
HAMLET (46532) Starke(60), La Porte(39)
HAMMOND Lake
HANNA La Porte
HANOVER Jefferson
HARDINSBURG (47125) Orange(56), Washington(43)
HARLAN Allen
HARMONY Clay
HARRODSBURG Monroe
HARTFORD CITY Blackford
HARTSVILLE (47244) Bartholomew(74), Decatur(25)
HATFIELD Spencer
HAUBSTADT (47639) Gibson(76), Vanderburgh(21), Warrick(1)
HAYDEN Jennings
HAZLETON (47640) Gibson(70), Pike(29)
HEBRON (46341) Porter(79), Lake(17), Jasper(1)
HELMSBURG Brown
HELTONVILLE (47436) Lawrence(92), Monroe(7)
HEMLOCK Howard
HENRYVILLE (47126) Clark(95), Washington(3), Scott(1)
HIGHLAND Lake
HILLISBURG Clinton
HILLSBORO (47949) Fountain(97), Montgomery(2)
HILLSDALE Vermillion
HOAGLAND (46745) Allen(97), Adams(2)
HOBART (46342) Lake(98), Porter(1)
HOBBS Tipton
HOLLAND (47541) Dubois(74), Pike(18), Warrick(4), Spencer(2)
HOLTON Ripley
HOMER Rush
HOPE Bartholomew
HOWE LaGrange
HUDSON (46747) Steuben(77), LaGrange(13), DeKalb(8)
HUNTERTOWN (46748) Allen(96), DeKalb(2), Noble(1)
HUNTINGBURG (47542) Dubois(97), Pike(2)
HUNTINGTON Huntington
HURON Lawrence
HYMERA Sullivan
IDAVILLE (47950) White(91), Carroll(8)
INDIANAPOLIS (46229) Marion(92), Hancock(7)
INDIANAPOLIS (46234) Marion(67), Hendricks(32)
INDIANAPOLIS (46239) Marion(98), Hancock(1)
INDIANAPOLIS (46256) Marion(93), Hamilton(6)
INDIANAPOLIS (46259) Marion(91), Shelby(4), Johnson(3)
INDIANAPOLIS (46278) Marion(94), Hendricks(5)
INDIANAPOLIS Hamilton
INDIANAPOLIS Marion
INGALLS Madison
INGLEFIELD Vanderburgh
IRELAND Dubois
JAMESTOWN (46147) Boone(91), Hendricks(8)
JASONVILLE (47438) Greene(70), Clay(24), Sullivan(5)
JASPER Dubois
JEFFERSONVILLE Clark
JONESBORO Grant
JONESVILLE Bartholomew
JUDSON Parke
KEMPTON (46049) Tipton(91), Clinton(8)
KENDALLVILLE Noble
KENNARD Henry
KENTLAND Newton
KEWANNA (46939) Fulton(93), Pulaski(6)
KEYSTONE Wells
KIMMELL Noble
KINGMAN (47952) Fountain(84), Parke(15)
KINGSBURY La Porte
KINGSFORD HEIGHTS La Porte
KIRKLIN (46050) Clinton(73), Boone(22), Tipton(3)
KNIGHTSTOWN (46148) Henry(84), Rush(15)
KNIGHTSVILLE Clay
KNOX Starke
KOKOMO (46901) Howard(98), Miami(1)
KOKOMO Howard
KOLEEN Greene
KOUTS Porter
KURTZ Jackson
LA CROSSE (46348) La Porte(98), Porter(1)
LA FONTAINE (46940) Wabash(87), Huntington(8), Grant(3)
LA PORTE La Porte
LACONIA Harrison
LADOGA (47954) Montgomery(94), Putnam(4)
LAFAYETTE Tippecanoe
LAGRANGE (46761) LaGrange(95), Steuben(4)
LAGRO Wabash
LAKE CICOTT Cass
LAKE STATION Lake
LAKE VILLAGE Newton
LAKETON Wabash
LAKEVILLE (46536) St. Joseph(92), Marshall(7)
LAMAR Spencer
LANDESS Grant
LANESVILLE (47136) Harrison(81), Floyd(18)
LAOTTO (46763) Noble(85), DeKalb(14)
LAPAZ Marshall
LAPEL Madison
LAPORTE La Porte
LARWILL (46764) Whitley(92), Noble(7)
LAUREL Franklin
LAWRENCEBURG Dearborn
LEAVENWORTH (47137) Crawford(96), Perry(2)
LEBANON Boone
LEESBURG Kosciusko
LEITERS FORD Fulton
LEO Allen
LEOPOLD Perry
LEROY Lake
LEWIS (47858) Vigo(48), Clay(37), Sullivan(14)
LEWISVILLE (47352) Rush(52), Henry(46), Fayette(1)
LEXINGTON (47138) Jefferson(52), Scott(46)
LIBERTY (47353) Union(94), Franklin(5)
LIBERTY CENTER (46766) Wells(98), Huntington(1)
LIBERTY MILLS Wabash
LIGONIER (46767) Noble(96), Elkhart(1), LaGrange(1)
LINCOLN CITY Spencer
LINDEN (47955) Montgomery(97), Tippecanoe(2)
LINN GROVE Adams
LINTON Greene
LITTLE YORK Washington
LIZTON Hendricks
LOGANSPORT (46947) Cass(98), Carroll(1)
LOOGOOTEE (47553) Martin(79), Daviess(20)
LOSANTVILLE (47354) Randolph(72), Henry(16), Delaware(6), Wayne(4)
LOWELL Lake
LUCERNE (46950) Cass(96), Fulton(3)
LYNN Randolph
LYNNVILLE (47619) Warrick(92), Gibson(6)
LYONS Greene
MACKEY Gibson
MACY (46951) Miami(70), Fulton(29)
MADISON (47250) Jefferson(96), Ripley(2), Switzerland(1)
MAGNET Perry
MANILLA (46150) Rush(92), Shelby(7)
MARENGO (47140) Orange(53), Crawford(46)
MARIAH HILL Spencer
MARION Grant
MARKLE (46770) Wells(73), Huntington(26)
MARKLEVILLE (46056) Madison(82), Hancock(14), Henry(3)
MARSHALL Parke
MARTINSVILLE Morgan
MARYSVILLE (47141) Clark(92), Scott(7)
MATTHEWS Grant
MAUCKPORT Harrison
MAXWELL Hancock
MAYS Rush
MC CORDSVILLE (46055) Hancock(75), Hamilton(24)
MECCA Parke
MEDARYVILLE (47957) Pulaski(89), Jasper(10)
MEDORA (47260) Jackson(98), Lawrence(1)
MELLOTT Fountain
MEMPHIS Clark
MENTONE (46539) Kosciusko(91), Fulton(6), Marshall(2)
MEROM Sullivan
MERRILLVILLE Lake
METAMORA Franklin
MEXICO Miami
MIAMI Miami
MICHIGAN CITY (46360) La Porte(94), Porter(5)
MICHIGAN CITY La Porte
MICHIGANTOWN Clinton
MIDDLEBURY (46540) Elkhart(90), LaGrange(9)
MIDDLETOWN (47356) Henry(92), Madison(5), Delaware(2)
MIDLAND Greene
MILAN Ripley
MILFORD (46542) Kosciusko(95), Elkhart(4)
MILL CREEK La Porte
MILLERSBURG (46543) Elkhart(71), LaGrange(27), Noble(1)
MILLHOUSEN Decatur

MILLTOWN (47145) Crawford(96), Washington(3)
MILROY (46156) Rush(95), Decatur(4)
MILTON (47357) Wayne(71), Fayette(22), Madison(5)
MISHAWAKA St. Joseph
MITCHELL Lawrence
MODOC (47358) Randolph(98), Wayne(1)
MONGO LaGrange
MONON (47959) White(87), Jasper(9), Pulaski(2)
MONROE Adams
MONROE CITY Knox
MONROEVILLE (46773) Allen(89), Adams(10)
MONROVIA Morgan
MONTEREY (46960) Pulaski(62), Starke(30), Fulton(6)
MONTEZUMA Parke
MONTGOMERY Daviess
MONTICELLO (47960) White(88), Carroll(11)
MONTMORENCI Tippecanoe
MONTPELIER (47359) Blackford(87), Wells(11)
MOORELAND (47360) Henry(94), Wayne(3), Randolph(1)
MOORES HILL Dearborn
MOORESVILLE (46158) Morgan(90), Hendricks(9)
MORGANTOWN (46160) Brown(53), Morgan(29), Johnson(16)
MOROCCO Newton
MORRIS Ripley
MORRISTOWN (46161) Shelby(74), Hancock(17), Rush(7)
MOUNT AYR Newton
MOUNT PLEASANT Perry
MOUNT SAINT FRANCIS Floyd
MOUNT SUMMIT Henry
MOUNT VERNON Posey
MULBERRY (46058) Clinton(97), Tippecanoe(2)
MUNCIE Delaware
MUNSTER Lake
NABB (47147) Clark(42), Scott(31), Jefferson(25)
NAPOLEON Ripley
NAPPANEE (46550) Elkhart(84), Kosciusko(10), Marshall(4)
NASHVILLE (47448) Brown(98), Monroe(1)
NEBRASKA Jennings
NEEDHAM (46162) Johnson(57), Shelby(42)
NEW ALBANY Floyd
NEW CARLISLE (46552) La Porte(56), St. Joseph(43)
NEW CASTLE Henry
NEW GOSHEN Vigo
NEW HARMONY Posey
NEW HAVEN Allen
NEW LEBANON Sullivan
NEW LISBON Henry
NEW MARKET Montgomery
NEW MIDDLETOWN Harrison
NEW PALESTINE (46163) Hancock(94), Shelby(4)
NEW PARIS Elkhart
NEW POINT Decatur
NEW RICHMOND (47967) Montgomery(92), Tippecanoe(7)
NEW ROSS (47968) Montgomery(86), Boone(8), Hendricks(4)
NEW SALISBURY Harrison
NEW TRENTON Franklin
NEW WASHINGTON Clark
NEW WAVERLY Cass
NEWBERRY (47449) Greene(93), Daviess(5), Martin(1)
NEWBURGH Warrick
NEWPORT Vermillion
NEWTOWN Fountain
NINEVEH (46164) Brown(69), Johnson(30)
NOBLESVILLE Hamilton
NORMAN (47264) Jackson(72), Lawrence(24), Monroe(3)
NORTH JUDSON (46366) Starke(96), Pulaski(3)
NORTH LIBERTY (46554) St. Joseph(97), La Porte(2)
NORTH MANCHESTER (46962) Wabash(94), Kosciusko(5)
NORTH SALEM (46165) Hendricks(98), Putnam(1)
NORTH VERNON Jennings
NORTH WEBSTER Kosciusko
NOTRE DAME St. Joseph
OAKFORD Howard
OAKLAND CITY (47660) Gibson(85), Pike(13)
OAKTOWN (47561) Knox(93), Sullivan(6)
OAKVILLE Delaware
ODON Daviess
OLDENBURG Franklin
ONWARD Cass
OOLITIC Lawrence
ORA Starke
ORESTES Madison
ORLAND (46776) Steuben(76), LaGrange(23)
ORLEANS (47452) Orange(82), Lawrence(16)
OSCEOLA (46561) St. Joseph(87), Elkhart(12)
OSGOOD Ripley
OSSIAN (46777) Wells(93), Allen(3), Adams(2)
OSSIAN Steuben
OSSIAN Wells
OTISCO Clark
OTTERBEIN (47970) Benton(45), Warren(34), Tippecanoe(18)
OTWELL (47564) Pike(87), Dubois(12)
OWENSBURG Greene
OWENSVILLE Gibson
OXFORD Benton
PALMYRA (47164) Harrison(72), Washington(27)
PAOLI Orange
PARAGON (46166) Morgan(89), Owen(10)
PARIS CROSSING (47270) Jennings(93), Jefferson(6)
PARKER CITY (47368) Randolph(84), Delaware(15)
PATOKA Gibson
PATRICKSBURG Owen
PATRIOT Switzerland
PAXTON Sullivan
PEKIN (47165) Washington(96), Clark(1), Floyd(1)
PENCE Warren
PENDLETON (46064) Madison(94), Hancock(4)
PENNVILLE (47369) Jay(95), Blackford(4)
PERRYSVILLE Vermillion
PERSHING Wayne
PERU (46970) Miami(93), Cass(3), Wabash(2)
PETERSBURG Pike
PETROLEUM Wells
PIERCETON (46562) Kosciusko(85), Noble(8), Whitley(6)
PIERCEVILLE Ripley
PIMENTO (47866) Vigo(96), Sullivan(3)
PINE VILLAGE (47975) Warren(93), Benton(6)
PITTSBORO (46167) Hendricks(98), Boone(1)
PLAINFIELD Hendricks
PLAINVILLE Daviess
PLEASANT LAKE Steuben
PLEASANT MILLS Adams
PLYMOUTH Marshall
POLAND (47868) Owen(83), Clay(13), Putnam(2)
PONETO Wells
PORTAGE Porter
PORTLAND Jay
POSEYVILLE (47633) Posey(93), Gibson(4), Vanderburgh(1)
PRAIRIE CREEK Vigo
PRAIRIETON Vigo
PREBLE Adams
PRINCETON Gibson
PUTNAMVILLE Putnam
QUINCY (47456) Owen(60), Morgan(35), Putnam(4)
RAGSDALE Knox
RAMSEY Harrison
REDKEY (47373) Jay(82), Randolph(17)
REELSVILLE Putnam
REMINGTON (47977) Jasper(79), Benton(19), White(1)
RENSSELAER Jasper
REYNOLDS White
RICHLAND Spencer
RICHMOND Wayne
RIDGEVILLE (47380) Randolph(91), Jay(8)
RILEY Vigo
RISING SUN Ohio
ROACHDALE (46172) Putnam(97), Montgomery(2)
ROANN (46974) Wabash(61), Miami(38)
ROANOKE (46783) Huntington(50), Allen(39), Whitley(8), Wells(2)
ROCHESTER Fulton
ROCKFIELD Carroll
ROCKPORT Spencer
ROCKVILLE Parke
ROLLING PRAIRIE La Porte
ROME Perry
ROME CITY Noble
ROMNEY (47981) Tippecanoe(88), Montgomery(11)
ROSEDALE (47874) Parke(51), Vigo(33), Clay(14)
ROSELAWN Newton
ROSSVILLE (46065) Clinton(59), Carroll(40)
ROYAL CENTER (46978) Cass(93), Pulaski(3), White(3)
RUSHVILLE Rush
RUSSELLVILLE (46175) Putnam(89), Parke(7), Montgomery(3)
RUSSIAVILLE (46979) Howard(83), Clinton(10), Tipton(3), Carroll(1)
SAINT ANTHONY Dubois
SAINT BERNICE Vermillion
SAINT CROIX (47576) Perry(95), Crawford(4)
SAINT JOE DeKalb
SAINT JOHN Lake
SAINT MARY OF THE WOODS Vigo
SAINT MEINRAD (47577) Spencer(93), Perry(6)
SAINT PAUL (47272) Decatur(69), Shelby(28), Rush(2)
SALAMONIA Jay
SALEM Washington
SAN PIERRE (46374) Starke(95), Pulaski(3)
SANDBORN (47578) Knox(81), Greene(17)
SANDFORD Vigo
SANTA CLAUS Spencer
SARATOGA Randolph
SCHERERVILLE Lake
SCHNEIDER Lake
SCHNELLVILLE Dubois
SCIPIO Jennings
SCOTLAND Greene
SCOTTSBURG (47170) Scott(84), Washington(14)
SEDALIA Clinton
SEELYVILLE Vigo
SELLERSBURG (47172) Clark(92), Floyd(7)
SELMA Delaware
SERVIA Wabash
SEYMOUR (47274) Jackson(93), Bartholomew(3), Jennings(2)
SHARPSVILLE (46068) Tipton(90), Howard(9)
SHELBURN Sullivan
SHELBY Lake
SHEPARDSVILLE Vigo
SHERIDAN (46069) Hamilton(68), Boone(27), Clinton(4)
SHIPSHEWANA LaGrange
SHIRLEY (47384) Henry(72), Hancock(27)
SHOALS Martin
SIDNEY Kosciusko
SILVER LAKE (46982) Kosciusko(75), Wabash(20), Fulton(3)
SIMS Grant
SMITHVILLE Monroe
SOLSBERRY (47459) Greene(87), Owen(11)
SOMERSET Wabash
SOMERVILLE Gibson
SOUTH BEND St. Joseph
SOUTH MILFORD LaGrange
SOUTH WHITLEY (46787) Whitley(91), Kosciusko(7)
SPENCER Owen
SPENCERVILLE (46788) Allen(64), DeKalb(35)
SPICELAND Henry
SPRINGPORT (47386) Henry(97), Delaware(2)
SPRINGVILLE (47462) Lawrence(82), Greene(8), Monroe(8)
SPURGEON Pike
STANFORD Monroe
STAR CITY (46985) Pulaski(96), White(3)
STATE LINE Warren
STAUNTON Clay
STENDAL Pike
STILESVILLE (46180) Morgan(56), Hendricks(43)
STINESVILLE Monroe
STOCKWELL Tippecanoe
STRAUGHN (47387) Henry(98), Fayette(1)
STROH LaGrange
SULLIVAN Sullivan
SULPHUR Crawford
SULPHUR SPRINGS Henry
SUMAVA RESORTS Newton
SUMMITVILLE (46070) Madison(94), Delaware(3), Grant(2)
SUNMAN (47041) Ripley(61), Dearborn(38)
SWAYZEE (46986) Grant(98), Howard(1)
SWEETSER Grant
SWITZ CITY Greene
SYRACUSE (46567) Kosciusko(96), Elkhart(3)
TALBOT Benton
TANGIER Parke
TASWELL (47175) Crawford(92), Orange(7)
TAYLORSVILLE Bartholomew
TEFFT Jasper
TELL CITY Perry
TEMPLETON Benton
TENNYSON (47637) Warrick(87), Spencer(12)
TERRE HAUTE Vigo
THAYER Newton
THORNTOWN Boone
TIPPECANOE (46570) Marshall(88), Fulton(11)
TIPTON Tipton
TOBINSPORT Perry
TOPEKA (46571) LaGrange(98), Noble(1)
TRAFALGAR (46181) Johnson(84), Brown(15)
TROY (47588) Spencer(89), Perry(10)

TUNNELTON Lawrence
TWELVE MILE (46988) Cass(97), Fulton(2)
TYNER Marshall
UNDERWOOD (47177) Scott(57), Clark(42)
UNION CITY (47390) Randolph(95), Jay(4)
UNION MILLS (46382) La Porte(98), Lake(1)
UNIONDALE Wells
UNIONVILLE (47468) Monroe(59), Brown(40)
UNIVERSAL Vermillion
UPLAND (46989) Grant(96), Blackford(2), Delaware(1)
URBANA Wabash
VALLONIA (47281) Jackson(58), Washington(41)
VALPARAISO Porter
VAN BUREN (46991) Grant(85), Huntington(12), Wells(2)
VEEDERSBURG Fountain
VELPEN (47590) Pike(86), Dubois(13)
VERNON Jennings
VERSAILLES Ripley
VEVAY (47043) Switzerland(97), Jefferson(2)
VINCENNES Knox
WABASH Wabash
WADESVILLE Posey
WAKARUSA (46573) Elkhart(74), St. Joseph(25)
WALDRON (46182) Shelby(81), Rush(18)
WALKERTON (46574) St. Joseph(38), Marshall(22), Starke(21), La Porte(17)
WALLACE Fountain
WALTON Cass
WANATAH La Porte
WARREN (46792) Huntington(82), Wells(17)
WARSAW Kosciusko
WASHINGTON Daviess
WATERLOO (46793) DeKalb(98), Steuben(1)
WAVELAND (47989) Montgomery(81), Parke(15), Putnam(3)
WAWAKA Noble
WAYNETOWN (47990) Montgomery(86), Fountain(13)
WEBSTER Wayne
WEST BADEN SPRINGS Orange
WEST COLLEGE CORNER (47003) Franklin(86), Union(13)
WEST HARRISON (47060) Dearborn(72), Franklin(27)
WEST LAFAYETTE Tippecanoe
WEST LEBANON Warren
WEST MIDDLETON Howard
WEST NEWTON Marion
WEST TERRE HAUTE Vigo
WESTFIELD Hamilton
WESTPHALIA Knox
WESTPOINT Tippecanoe
WESTPORT (47283) Decatur(92), Bartholomew(4), Jennings(2)
WESTVILLE (46391) La Porte(76), Porter(23)
WHEATFIELD Jasper
WHEATLAND Knox
WHEELER Porter
WHITELAND Johnson
WHITESTOWN Boone
WHITING Lake
WILKINSON (46186) Hancock(96), Henry(3)
WILLIAMS (47470) Lawrence(97), Martin(2)
WILLIAMSBURG (47393) Wayne(71), Randolph(28)
WILLIAMSPORT Warren
WILLOW BRANCH Hancock
WINAMAC Pulaski
WINCHESTER Randolph
WINDFALL (46076) Tipton(94), Howard(5)
WINGATE (47994) Montgomery(77), Fountain(18), Tippecanoe(3)
WINONA LAKE Kosciusko
WINSLOW Pike
WOLCOTT (47995) White(96), Jasper(2)
WOLCOTTVILLE (46795) LaGrange(89), Noble(9)
WOLFLAKE Noble
WOODBURN Allen
WORTHINGTON (47471) Greene(81), Owen(18)
WYATT St. Joseph
YEOMAN Carroll
YODER (46798) Allen(92), Wells(7)
YORKTOWN Delaware
YOUNG AMERICA Cass
ZANESVILLE Allen
ZIONSVILLE (46077) Boone(91), Hamilton(7), Marion(1)

Indiana ZIP/City Cross Reference

46001-46001 ALEXANDRIA
46011-46018 ANDERSON
46030-46030 ARCADIA
46031-46031 ATLANTA
46032-46033 CARMEL
46034-46034 CICERO
46035-46035 COLFAX
46036-46036 ELWOOD
46037-46038 FISHERS
46039-46039 FOREST
46040-46040 FORTVILLE
46041-46041 FRANKFORT
46044-46044 FRANKTON
46045-46045 GOLDSMITH
46046-46046 HILLISBURG
46047-46047 HOBBS
46048-46048 INGALLS
46049-46049 KEMPTON
46050-46050 KIRKLIN
46051-46051 LAPEL
46052-46052 LEBANON
46055-46055 MC CORDSVILLE
46056-46056 MARKLEVILLE
46057-46057 MICHIGANTOWN
46058-46058 MULBERRY
46060-46062 NOBLESVILLE
46063-46063 ORESTES
46064-46064 PENDLETON
46065-46065 ROSSVILLE
46067-46067 SEDALIA
46068-46068 SHARPSVILLE
46069-46069 SHERIDAN
46070-46070 SUMMITVILLE
46071-46071 THORNTOWN
46072-46072 TIPTON
46074-46074 WESTFIELD
46075-46075 WHITESTOWN
46076-46076 WINDFALL
46077-46077 ZIONSVILLE
46082-46082 CARMEL
46102-46102 ADVANCE
46103-46103 AMO
46104-46104 ARLINGTON
46105-46105 BAINBRIDGE
46106-46106 BARGERSVILLE
46107-46107 BEECH GROVE
46110-46110 BOGGSTOWN
46111-46111 BROOKLYN
46112-46112 BROWNSBURG
46113-46113 CAMBY
46114-46114 CARTERSBURG
46115-46115 CARTHAGE
46117-46117 CHARLOTTESVILLE
46118-46118 CLAYTON
46120-46120 CLOVERDALE
46121-46121 COATESVILLE
46122-46122 DANVILLE
46123-46123 AVON
46124-46124 EDINBURGH
46125-46125 EMINENCE
46126-46126 FAIRLAND
46127-46127 FALMOUTH
46128-46128 FILLMORE
46129-46129 FINLY
46130-46130 FOUNTAINTOWN
46131-46131 FRANKLIN
46133-46133 GLENWOOD
46135-46135 GREENCASTLE
46140-46140 GREENFIELD
46142-46143 GREENWOOD
46144-46144 GWYNNEVILLE
46146-46146 HOMER
46147-46147 JAMESTOWN
46148-46148 KNIGHTSTOWN
46149-46149 LIZTON
46150-46150 MANILLA
46151-46151 MARTINSVILLE
46154-46154 MAXWELL
46155-46155 MAYS
46156-46156 MILROY
46157-46157 MONROVIA
46158-46158 MOORESVILLE
46160-46160 MORGANTOWN
46161-46161 MORRISTOWN
46162-46162 NEEDHAM
46163-46163 NEW PALESTINE
46164-46164 NINEVEH
46165-46165 NORTH SALEM
46166-46166 PARAGON
46167-46167 PITTSBORO
46168-46168 PLAINFIELD
46170-46170 PUTNAMVILLE
46171-46171 REELSVILLE
46172-46172 ROACHDALE
46173-46173 RUSHVILLE
46175-46175 RUSSELLVILLE
46176-46176 SHELBYVILLE
46180-46180 STILESVILLE
46181-46181 TRAFALGAR
46182-46182 WALDRON
46183-46183 WEST NEWTON
46184-46184 WHITELAND
46186-46186 WILKINSON
46187-46187 WILLOW BRANCH
46200-46298 INDIANAPOLIS
46301-46301 BEVERLY SHORES
46302-46302 BOONE GROVE
46303-46303 CEDAR LAKE
46304-46304 CHESTERTON
46307-46308 CROWN POINT
46310-46310 DEMOTTE
46311-46311 DYER
46312-46312 EAST CHICAGO
46319-46319 GRIFFITH
46320-46320 HAMMOND
46321-46321 MUNSTER
46322-46322 HIGHLAND
46323-46327 HAMMOND
46340-46340 HANNA
46341-46341 HEBRON
46342-46342 HOBART
46345-46345 KINGSBURY
46346-46346 KINGSFORD HEIGHTS
46347-46347 KOUTS
46348-46348 LA CROSSE
46349-46349 LAKE VILLAGE
46350-46350 LA PORTE
46350-46350 LAPORTE
46351-46352 LA PORTE
46352-46352 LAPORTE
46355-46355 LEROY
46356-46356 LOWELL
46360-46361 MICHIGAN CITY
46365-46365 MILL CREEK
46366-46366 NORTH JUDSON
46367-46367 LA PORTE
46368-46368 PORTAGE
46371-46371 ROLLING PRAIRIE
46372-46372 ROSELAWN
46373-46373 SAINT JOHN
46374-46374 SAN PIERRE
46375-46375 SCHERERVILLE
46376-46376 SCHNEIDER
46377-46377 SHELBY
46379-46379 SUMAVA RESORTS
46380-46380 TEFFT
46381-46381 THAYER
46382-46382 UNION MILLS
46383-46385 VALPARAISO
46390-46390 WANATAH
46391-46391 WESTVILLE
46392-46392 WHEATFIELD
46393-46393 WHEELER
46394-46394 WHITING
46399-46399 LOWELL
46400-46404 GARY
46405-46405 LAKE STATION
46406-46409 GARY
46410-46411 MERRILLVILLE
46501-46501 ARGOS
46502-46502 ATWOOD
46504-46504 BOURBON
46506-46506 BREMEN
46507-46507 BRISTOL
46508-46508 BURKET
46510-46510 CLAYPOOL
46511-46511 CULVER
46513-46513 DONALDSON
46514-46517 ELKHART
46524-46524 ETNA GREEN
46526-46528 GOSHEN
46530-46530 GRANGER
46531-46531 GROVERTOWN
46532-46532 HAMLET
46534-46534 KNOX
46536-46536 LAKEVILLE
46537-46537 LAPAZ
46538-46538 LEESBURG
46539-46539 MENTONE
46540-46540 MIDDLEBURY
46542-46542 MILFORD
46543-46543 MILLERSBURG
46544-46546 MISHAWAKA
46550-46550 NAPPANEE
46552-46552 NEW CARLISLE
46553-46553 NEW PARIS
46554-46554 NORTH LIBERTY
46555-46555 NORTH WEBSTER
46556-46556 NOTRE DAME
46561-46561 OSCEOLA
46562-46562 PIERCETON
46563-46563 PLYMOUTH
46565-46565 SHIPSHEWANA
46566-46566 SIDNEY
46567-46567 SYRACUSE
46570-46570 TIPPECANOE
46571-46571 TOPEKA
46572-46572 TYNER
46573-46573 WAKARUSA
46574-46574 WALKERTON
46580-46582 WARSAW
46590-46590 WINONA LAKE
46595-46595 WYATT
46600-46699 SOUTH BEND

46701-46701 ALBION
46702-46702 ANDREWS
46703-46703 ANGOLA
46704-46704 ARCOLA
46705-46705 ASHLEY
46706-46706 AUBURN
46710-46710 AVILLA
46711-46711 BERNE
46713-46713 BIPPUS
46714-46714 BLUFFTON
46720-46720 BRIMFIELD
46721-46721 BUTLER
46723-46723 CHURUBUSCO
46725-46725 COLUMBIA CITY
46730-46730 CORUNNA
46731-46731 CRAIGVILLE
46732-46732 CROMWELL
46733-46733 DECATUR
46737-46737 FREMONT
46738-46738 GARRETT
46740-46740 GENEVA
46741-46741 GRABILL
46742-46742 HAMILTON
46743-46743 HARLAN
46744-46744 OSSIAN
46745-46745 HOAGLAND
46746-46746 HOWE
46747-46747 HUDSON
46748-46748 HUNTERTOWN
46750-46750 HUNTINGTON
46755-46755 KENDALLVILLE
46759-46759 KEYSTONE
46760-46760 KIMMELL
46761-46761 LAGRANGE
46763-46763 LAOTTO
46764-46764 LARWILL
46765-46765 LEO
46766-46766 LIBERTY CENTER
46767-46767 LIGONIER
46769-46769 LINN GROVE
46770-46770 MARKLE
46771-46771 MONGO
46772-46772 MONROE
46773-46773 MONROEVILLE
46774-46774 NEW HAVEN
46776-46776 ORLAND
46777-46777 OSSIAN
46778-46778 PETROLEUM
46779-46779 PLEASANT LAKE
46780-46780 PLEASANT MILLS
46781-46781 PONETO
46782-46782 PREBLE
46783-46783 ROANOKE
46784-46784 ROME CITY
46785-46785 SAINT JOE
46786-46786 SOUTH MILFORD
46787-46787 SOUTH WHITLEY
46788-46788 SPENCERVILLE
46789-46789 STROH
46790-46790 OSSIAN
46791-46791 UNIONDALE
46792-46792 WARREN
46793-46793 WATERLOO
46794-46794 WAWAKA
46795-46795 WOLCOTTVILLE
46796-46796 WOLFLAKE
46797-46797 WOODBURN
46798-46798 YODER
46799-46799 ZANESVILLE
46800-46899 FORT WAYNE
46901-46904 KOKOMO
46910-46910 AKRON
46911-46911 AMBOY
46912-46912 ATHENS
46913-46913 BRINGHURST
46914-46914 BUNKER HILL
46915-46915 BURLINGTON
46916-46916 BURROWS
46917-46917 CAMDEN
46919-46919 CONVERSE
46920-46920 CUTLER
46921-46921 DEEDSVILLE
46922-46922 DELONG
46923-46923 DELPHI
46925-46925 DENHAM
46926-46926 DENVER
46928-46928 FAIRMOUNT
46929-46929 FLORA
46930-46930 FOWLERTON
46931-46931 FULTON
46932-46932 GALVESTON
46933-46933 GAS CITY
46935-46935 GRASS CREEK
46936-46936 GREENTOWN
46937-46937 HEMLOCK
46938-46938 JONESBORO
46939-46939 KEWANNA
46940-46940 LA FONTAINE
46941-46941 LAGRO
46942-46942 LAKE CICOTT
46943-46943 LAKETON
46944-46944 LANDESS
46945-46945 LEITERS FORD
46946-46946 LIBERTY MILLS
46947-46947 LOGANSPORT
46950-46950 LUCERNE
46951-46951 MACY
46952-46953 MARION
46957-46957 MATTHEWS
46958-46958 MEXICO
46959-46959 MIAMI
46960-46960 MONTEREY
46961-46961 NEW WAVERLY
46962-46962 NORTH MANCHESTER
46965-46965 OAKFORD
46967-46967 ONWARD
46968-46968 ORA
46970-46970 PERU
46971-46971 GRISSOM AFB
46971-46971 GRISSOM ARB
46974-46974 ROANN
46975-46975 ROCHESTER
46977-46977 ROCKFIELD
46978-46978 ROYAL CENTER
46979-46979 RUSSIAVILLE
46980-46980 SERVIA
46982-46982 SILVER LAKE
46983-46983 SIMS
46984-46984 SOMERSET
46985-46985 STAR CITY
46986-46986 SWAYZEE
46987-46987 SWEETSER
46988-46988 TWELVE MILE
46989-46989 UPLAND
46990-46990 URBANA
46991-46991 VAN BUREN
46992-46992 WABASH
46994-46994 WALTON
46995-46995 WEST MIDDLETON
46996-46996 WINAMAC
46998-46998 YOUNG AMERICA
47001-47001 AURORA
47003-47003 WEST COLLEGE CORNER
47006-47006 BATESVILLE
47010-47010 BATH
47011-47011 BENNINGTON
47012-47012 BROOKVILLE
47016-47016 CEDAR GROVE
47017-47017 CROSS PLAINS
47018-47018 DILLSBORO
47019-47019 EAST ENTERPRISE
47020-47020 FLORENCE
47021-47021 FRIENDSHIP
47022-47022 GUILFORD
47023-47023 HOLTON
47024-47024 LAUREL
47025-47025 LAWRENCEBURG
47030-47030 METAMORA
47031-47031 MILAN
47032-47032 MOORES HILL
47033-47033 MORRIS
47034-47034 NAPOLEON
47035-47035 NEW TRENTON
47036-47036 OLDENBURG
47037-47037 OSGOOD
47038-47038 PATRIOT
47039-47039 PIERCEVILLE
47040-47040 RISING SUN
47041-47041 SUNMAN
47042-47042 VERSAILLES
47043-47043 VEVAY
47060-47060 WEST HARRISON
47102-47102 AUSTIN
47104-47104 BETHLEHEM
47106-47106 BORDEN
47107-47107 BRADFORD
47108-47108 CAMPBELLSBURG
47110-47110 CENTRAL
47111-47111 CHARLESTOWN
47112-47112 CORYDON
47114-47114 CRANDALL
47115-47115 DEPAUW
47116-47116 ECKERTY
47117-47117 ELIZABETH
47118-47118 ENGLISH
47119-47119 FLOYDS KNOBS
47120-47120 FREDERICKSBURG
47122-47122 GEORGETOWN
47123-47123 GRANTSBURG
47124-47124 GREENVILLE
47125-47125 HARDINSBURG
47126-47126 HENRYVILLE
47129-47129 CLARKSVILLE
47130-47134 JEFFERSONVILLE
47135-47135 LACONIA
47136-47136 LANESVILLE
47137-47137 LEAVENWORTH
47138-47138 LEXINGTON
47139-47139 LITTLE YORK
47140-47140 MARENGO
47141-47141 MARYSVILLE
47142-47142 MAUCKPORT
47143-47143 MEMPHIS
47144-47144 JEFFERSONVILLE
47145-47145 MILLTOWN
47146-47146 MOUNT SAINT FRANCIS
47147-47147 NABB
47150-47151 NEW ALBANY
47160-47160 NEW MIDDLETOWN
47161-47161 NEW SALISBURY
47162-47162 NEW WASHINGTON
47163-47163 OTISCO
47164-47164 PALMYRA
47165-47165 PEKIN
47166-47166 RAMSEY
47167-47167 SALEM
47170-47170 SCOTTSBURG
47172-47172 SELLERSBURG
47174-47174 SULPHUR
47175-47175 TASWELL
47177-47177 UNDERWOOD
47199-47199 JEFFERSONVILLE
47201-47203 COLUMBUS
47220-47220 BROWNSTOWN
47222-47222 BURNEY
47223-47223 BUTLERVILLE
47224-47224 CANAAN
47225-47225 CLARKSBURG
47226-47226 CLIFFORD
47227-47227 COMMISKEY
47228-47228 CORTLAND
47229-47229 CROTHERSVILLE
47230-47230 DEPUTY
47231-47231 DUPONT
47232-47232 ELIZABETHTOWN
47234-47234 FLAT ROCK
47235-47235 FREETOWN
47236-47236 GRAMMER
47240-47240 GREENSBURG
47243-47243 HANOVER
47244-47244 HARTSVILLE
47245-47245 HAYDEN
47246-47246 HOPE
47247-47247 JONESVILLE
47249-47249 KURTZ
47250-47250 MADISON
47260-47260 MEDORA
47261-47261 MILLHOUSEN
47262-47262 NEBRASKA
47263-47263 NEW POINT
47264-47264 NORMAN
47265-47265 NORTH VERNON
47270-47270 PARIS CROSSING
47272-47272 SAINT PAUL
47273-47273 SCIPIO
47274-47274 SEYMOUR
47280-47280 TAYLORSVILLE
47281-47281 VALLONIA
47282-47282 VERNON
47283-47283 WESTPORT
47302-47308 MUNCIE
47320-47320 ALBANY
47322-47322 BENTONVILLE
47324-47324 BOSTON
47325-47325 BROWNSVILLE
47326-47326 BRYANT
47327-47327 CAMBRIDGE CITY
47330-47330 CENTERVILLE
47331-47331 CONNERSVILLE
47334-47334 DALEVILLE
47335-47335 DUBLIN
47336-47336 DUNKIRK
47337-47337 DUNREITH
47338-47338 EATON
47339-47339 ECONOMY
47340-47340 FARMLAND
47341-47341 FOUNTAIN CITY
47342-47342 GASTON
47344-47344 GREENSBORO
47345-47345 GREENS FORK
47346-47346 HAGERSTOWN
47348-47348 HARTFORD CITY
47351-47351 KENNARD
47352-47352 LEWISVILLE
47353-47353 LIBERTY
47354-47354 LOSANTVILLE
47355-47355 LYNN
47356-47356 MIDDLETOWN
47357-47357 MILTON
47358-47358 MODOC
47359-47359 MONTPELIER
47360-47360 MOORELAND
47361-47361 MOUNT SUMMIT
47362-47362 NEW CASTLE
47366-47366 NEW LISBON
47367-47367 OAKVILLE
47368-47368 PARKER CITY
47369-47369 PENNVILLE
47370-47370 PERSHING
47371-47371 PORTLAND
47373-47373 REDKEY
47374-47375 RICHMOND
47380-47380 RIDGEVILLE
47381-47381 SALAMONIA
47382-47382 SARATOGA
47383-47383 SELMA
47384-47384 SHIRLEY
47385-47385 SPICELAND
47386-47386 SPRINGPORT
47387-47387 STRAUGHN
47388-47388 SULPHUR SPRINGS
47390-47390 UNION CITY
47392-47392 WEBSTER
47393-47393 WILLIAMSBURG
47394-47394 WINCHESTER
47396-47396 YORKTOWN
47401-47408 BLOOMINGTON
47420-47420 AVOCA
47421-47421 BEDFORD
47424-47424 BLOOMFIELD
47426-47426 CLEAR CREEK
47427-47427 COAL CITY
47429-47429 ELLETTSVILLE
47430-47430 FORT RITNER
47431-47431 FREEDOM
47432-47432 FRENCH LICK
47433-47433 GOSPORT
47434-47434 HARRODSBURG

ZIP Range	City
47435-47435	HELMSBURG
47436-47436	HELTONVILLE
47437-47437	HURON
47438-47438	JASONVILLE
47439-47439	KOLEEN
47441-47441	LINTON
47443-47443	LYONS
47445-47445	MIDLAND
47446-47446	MITCHELL
47448-47448	NASHVILLE
47449-47449	NEWBERRY
47451-47451	OOLITIC
47452-47452	ORLEANS
47453-47453	OWENSBURG
47454-47454	PAOLI
47455-47455	PATRICKSBURG
47456-47456	QUINCY
47457-47457	SCOTLAND
47458-47458	SMITHVILLE
47459-47459	SOLSBERRY
47460-47460	SPENCER
47462-47462	SPRINGVILLE
47463-47463	STANFORD
47464-47464	STINESVILLE
47465-47465	SWITZ CITY
47467-47467	TUNNELTON
47468-47468	UNIONVILLE
47469-47469	WEST BADEN SPRINGS
47470-47470	WILLIAMS
47471-47471	WORTHINGTON
47490-47490	BLOOMINGTON
47501-47501	WASHINGTON
47512-47512	BICKNELL
47513-47513	BIRDSEYE
47514-47514	BRANCHVILLE
47515-47515	BRISTOW
47516-47516	BRUCEVILLE
47519-47519	CANNELBURG
47520-47520	CANNELTON
47521-47521	CELESTINE
47522-47522	CRANE
47523-47523	DALE
47524-47524	DECKER
47525-47525	DERBY
47527-47527	DUBOIS
47528-47528	EDWARDSPORT
47529-47529	ELNORA
47530-47530	EMISON
47531-47531	EVANSTON
47532-47532	FERDINAND
47535-47535	FREELANDVILLE
47536-47536	FULDA
47537-47537	GENTRYVILLE
47541-47541	HOLLAND
47542-47542	HUNTINGBURG
47545-47545	IRELAND
47546-47549	JASPER
47550-47550	LAMAR
47551-47551	LEOPOLD
47552-47552	LINCOLN CITY
47553-47553	LOOGOOTEE
47555-47555	MAGNET
47556-47556	MARIAH HILL
47557-47557	MONROE CITY
47558-47558	MONTGOMERY
47559-47559	MOUNT PLEASANT
47561-47561	OAKTOWN
47562-47562	ODON
47564-47564	OTWELL
47567-47567	PETERSBURG
47568-47568	PLAINVILLE
47573-47573	RAGSDALE
47574-47574	ROME
47575-47575	SAINT ANTHONY
47576-47576	SAINT CROIX
47577-47577	SAINT MEINRAD
47578-47578	SANDBORN
47579-47579	SANTA CLAUS
47580-47580	SCHNELLVILLE
47581-47581	SHOALS
47584-47584	SPURGEON
47585-47585	STENDAL
47586-47586	TELL CITY
47587-47587	TOBINSPORT
47588-47588	TROY
47590-47590	VELPEN
47591-47591	VINCENNES
47596-47596	WESTPHALIA
47597-47597	WHEATLAND
47598-47598	WINSLOW
47601-47601	BOONVILLE
47610-47610	CHANDLER
47611-47611	CHRISNEY
47612-47612	CYNTHIANA
47613-47613	ELBERFELD
47614-47614	FOLSOMVILLE
47615-47615	GRANDVIEW
47616-47616	GRIFFIN
47617-47617	HATFIELD
47618-47618	INGLEFIELD
47619-47619	LYNNVILLE
47620-47620	MOUNT VERNON
47629-47630	NEWBURGH
47631-47631	NEW HARMONY
47633-47633	POSEYVILLE
47634-47634	RICHLAND
47635-47635	ROCKPORT
47637-47637	TENNYSON
47638-47638	WADESVILLE
47639-47639	HAUBSTADT
47640-47640	HAZLETON
47647-47647	BUCKSKIN
47648-47648	FORT BRANCH
47649-47649	FRANCISCO
47654-47654	MACKEY
47660-47660	OAKLAND CITY
47665-47665	OWENSVILLE
47666-47666	PATOKA
47670-47671	PRINCETON
47683-47683	SOMERVILLE
47700-47750	EVANSVILLE
47801-47814	TERRE HAUTE
47830-47830	BELLMORE
47831-47831	BLANFORD
47832-47832	BLOOMINGDALE
47833-47833	BOWLING GREEN
47834-47834	BRAZIL
47836-47836	BRIDGETON
47837-47837	CARBON
47838-47838	CARLISLE
47840-47840	CENTERPOINT
47841-47841	CLAY CITY
47842-47842	CLINTON
47845-47845	COALMONT
47846-47846	CORY
47847-47847	DANA
47848-47848	DUGGER
47849-47849	FAIRBANKS
47850-47850	FARMERSBURG
47851-47851	FONTANET
47852-47852	GRAYSVILLE
47853-47853	HARMONY
47854-47854	HILLSDALE
47855-47855	HYMERA
47856-47856	JUDSON
47857-47857	KNIGHTSVILLE
47858-47858	LEWIS
47859-47859	MARSHALL
47860-47860	MECCA
47861-47861	MEROM
47862-47862	MONTEZUMA
47863-47863	NEW GOSHEN
47864-47864	NEW LEBANON
47865-47865	PAXTON
47866-47866	PIMENTO
47868-47868	POLAND
47869-47869	PRAIRIE CREEK
47870-47870	PRAIRIETON
47871-47871	RILEY
47872-47872	ROCKVILLE
47874-47874	ROSEDALE
47875-47875	SAINT BERNICE
47876-47876	SAINT MARY OF THE WOODS
47877-47877	SANDFORD
47878-47878	SEELYVILLE
47879-47879	SHELBURN
47880-47880	SHEPARDSVILLE
47881-47881	STAUNTON
47882-47882	SULLIVAN
47884-47884	UNIVERSAL
47885-47885	WEST TERRE HAUTE
47901-47905	LAFAYETTE
47906-47907	WEST LAFAYETTE
47909-47909	LAFAYETTE
47916-47916	ALAMO
47917-47917	AMBIA
47918-47918	ATTICA
47920-47920	BATTLE GROUND
47921-47921	BOSWELL
47922-47922	BROOK
47923-47923	BROOKSTON
47924-47924	BUCK CREEK
47925-47925	BUFFALO
47926-47926	BURNETTSVILLE
47928-47928	CAYUGA
47929-47929	CHALMERS
47930-47930	CLARKS HILL
47931-47931	COLBURN
47932-47932	COVINGTON
47933-47939	CRAWFORDSVILLE
47940-47940	DARLINGTON
47941-47941	DAYTON
47942-47942	EARL PARK
47943-47943	FAIR OAKS
47944-47944	FOWLER
47946-47946	FRANCESVILLE
47948-47948	GOODLAND
47949-47949	HILLSBORO
47950-47950	IDAVILLE
47951-47951	KENTLAND
47952-47952	KINGMAN
47954-47954	LADOGA
47955-47955	LINDEN
47957-47957	MEDARYVILLE
47958-47958	MELLOTT
47959-47959	MONON
47960-47960	MONTICELLO
47962-47962	MONTMORENCI
47963-47963	MOROCCO
47964-47964	MOUNT AYR
47965-47965	NEW MARKET
47966-47966	NEWPORT
47967-47967	NEW RICHMOND
47968-47968	NEW ROSS
47969-47969	NEWTOWN
47970-47970	OTTERBEIN
47971-47971	OXFORD
47973-47973	PENCE
47974-47974	PERRYSVILLE
47975-47975	PINE VILLAGE
47976-47976	EARL PARK
47977-47977	REMINGTON
47978-47978	RENSSELAER
47980-47980	REYNOLDS
47981-47981	ROMNEY
47982-47982	STATE LINE
47983-47983	STOCKWELL
47984-47984	TALBOT
47985-47985	TANGIER
47986-47986	TEMPLETON
47987-47987	VEEDERSBURG
47988-47988	WALLACE
47989-47989	WAVELAND
47990-47990	WAYNETOWN
47991-47991	WEST LEBANON
47992-47992	WESTPOINT
47993-47993	WILLIAMSPORT
47994-47994	WINGATE
47995-47995	WOLCOTT
47996-47996	WEST LAFAYETTE
47997-47997	YEOMAN

General Help Numbers:

Governor's Office

State Capitol Bldg — 515-281-5211
Des Moines, IA 50319 — Fax 515-281-6611
www.governor.iowa.gov/ — 8AM-4:30PM

Attorney General's Office

Hoover Bldg — 515-281-5164
1305 E Walnut St — Fax 515-281-4209
Des Moines, IA 50319 — 8AM-4:30PM
www.state.ia.us/government/ag/index.html

Legislative Records

Legislative Information Office
State Capitol — 515-281-5129
Des Moines, IA 50319 — Fax 515-281-8027
www.legis.state.ia.us — 8AM-4:30PM

State Archives

Library/Archives — 515-281-5111
600 E. Locust — Fax 515-282-0502
Des Moines, IA 50319-0290 — 9AM-4:30PM TU-SAT
www.iowahistory.org — Open Mondays June-Aug

State Specifics:

Capital:	Des Moines Polk County
Time Zone:	CST
Number of Counties:	99
Population:	3,002,555
Web Site:	www.iowa.gov/

State Agencies

Criminal Records

DPS - Division of Criminal Investigations, Records Unit, 215 E 7th St, Des Moines, IA 50319; 515-725-6066 (Records), Fax- 515-725-6073; 8AM-4:30PM.

www.dps.state.ia.us/DCI/index.shtml

Iowa law requires employers to pay the fee for potential employees record checks. (This is normal operating procedure when an employer uses a pre-employment screening company in compliance with FCRA.)

Indexing & Storage: Records available until the person is 80 years old or passes away. There is a computerized index going back to 1935. 100% of arrest records are fingerprint supported. New records available for inquiry in up to 10 days. Records normally destroyed after If DCI does not receive a fingerprint card and/or a disposition form, arrest information will be purged from DCI files. This is why DCI does not guarantee/certify a person has not been convicted in an IA court. 95% of all arrests in database have final dispositions recorded, 84% for those arrests within last 5 years.

Searching: A signed release or waiver is not required, nor are fingerprints. If a waiver is included, the report will show any arrest over 18 months old without a disposition, otherwise not. Email questions to cchinfo@dps.state.ia.us. Include in request- full name, date of birth, sex. The SSN and middle name are helpful. Be sure to give the full name. Request form is required for each surname. Form can be obtained from the web by fax, mail, or in person. A returned record is genuine if the DCI logo is imbedded, except if returned by fax. A signed release by subject entitles requester to all records including those without dispositions (up to 4 years old). If the subject's signed release is not presented, then no arrest records over 18 months old without dispositions are released.

Access by: mail, fax, in person.

Fee & Payment: The fee for a record search is $13.00 per surname for mail back, $15.00 for fax back (account required), and $10.00 for in person searches. Volunteers are $5 per surname. Fee payee- Iowa Division of Criminal Investigation. Payment is required unless account established. Personal checks, Visa, and MasterCard accepted.

Mail search: Turnaround time- 3 days to 4 weeks. SASE not required.

Fax search: Requester must have an account and either agree to fax back service or provide prepaid SASEs. The fee is $15.00 per record. Turnaround time is up to 4 days.

In person: Records may be ordered and received in person, but only the subject or their attorney qualifies for an immediate response.

Other access: Although this agency does not offer online access, there is online free access to the statewide Iowa Judicial System courts database at www.judicial.state.ia.us/.

Expedited service: Add $2.00 per record to receive back by fax.

Statewide Court Records

Clerk of Supreme Court, Judicial Branch Bldg, 111 East Court Ave, Des Moines, IA 50319; 515-281-5241 (AOC), 515-281-5911 (Supreme Ct Clerk), 515-242-6164 (Supreme Ct Clerk Fax), Fax- 515-242-0014; 8AM-4:30PM.

www.judicial.state.ia.us

Access docket information using the online system described below. Copies of case files must be obtained from the trial courts.

Access by: mail, fax, online.

Mail search: The search consists of the free webpage lookup. Written requests will be honored if search is not extensive.

Fax search: Fax requests for basic information are accepted.

Online search: Criminal, civil, probate, traffic and appellate information is available from all 99 counties from the web page. There is no fee for basic information including filings, criminal charges, dispositions, child support payments, and fine payments. For a $25 monthly registration fee you may access the "advanced search" section that for additional case information including case schedules, judgment index, lien index, exhibit lists, bonds, and service returns. Name searches are available statewide or on a specific county basis. Although records are updated daily, the historical records offered are not from the same starting date on a county-by-county basis. Also, from the home page one may access supreme and appellate court opinions.

Other access: The State Law Library (515-281-5124) has case information.

Sexual Offender Registry

Division of Criminal Investigations, SOR Unit -, 215 East 7th St, Des Moines, IA 50319-0041; 515-725-6050, Fax- 515-725-6040; 8AM-4:30PM.

www.iowasexoffender.com/

The Iowa Sex Offender Registry became law on July 1, 1995 and is found in Chapter 692A Code of Iowa.

Indexing & Storage: Records available from 07/01/95, if online back to 1999. New records available for inquiry in up to 2 days.

Searching: Include in request- date of birth, address if known, SSN helpful. This office will not permit walk-in requesters, it is suggested to visit the local police of sheriff office.

Access by: mail, online.

Mail search: Turnaround time- 1 to 2 days. SASE not required.

Online search: The website permits name searching, enables a requester to be notified on the movement of an offender, and provides a map of registrants.

Incarceration Records

Iowa Department of Corrections, 510 E 12th Street,, Des Moines, IA 50319; 515-725-5701, Fax- 515-725-5799; 8AM-4:30PM.

www.doc.state.ia.us

Indexing & Storage: Records available on current and former inmates. New records available for inquiry in up to 10 days.

Searching: Computer records go back to 1986. Include in request- full name and DOB or SSN. Location, physical identifiers, county of conviction, and conviction information details are released. Deeper records - sentencing information - are also available; please include details of reason for request. This data not released- medical or home address data.

Access by: mail, phone, fax, in person, online.

Fee & Payment: Search fee is $12.00 per hour plus postage fee. Copy fee is $.15 per page. Fee payee- Treasurer, State of Iowa, Dept. of Corrections. Prepayment required. Personal checks accepted, credit cards are not.

Mail search: Turnaround time- 1 to 10 days. Turnaround time on archived records is significantly longer. SASE not required.

Phone search: Name searching for basic information is available by phone.

Fax search: Requesters may fax to number above.

In person: Limited counter service is available.

Online search: At the agency website, click on Offender Information for an inmate search.

Other access: Bulk records are not available, but should be in the future.

Corporation, LLC, LP, Fictitious Name, Trademarks/Servicemarks

Secretary of State - Business Services Div, 321 E 12th Street, 1st Floor, Lucas Bldg, Des Moines, IA 50319; 515-281-5204, Fax- 515-242-5953; 8AM-4:30PM. www.sos.state.ia.us

Indexing & Storage: Records available from the late 1800s. New records available for inquiry immediately.

Searching: Include in request- full name of business or filing number, specific records that you need copies of. In addition to the articles of organization, business entity records available include: Annual/Biennial Reports, Officers, Directors, Fictitious names, Prior (merged) names, Inactive and Reserved names.

Access by: mail, phone, fax, in person, online.

Fee & Payment: A Certificate of Existence is $5.00. Copies are $1.00 each, certification is an additional $5.00 per document set. Fee payee- Secretary of State. Prepayment required. A charge account may be established for ongoing requesters. Call 515-281-5204 for more details. Personal checks, Visa, and MasterCard accepted.

Mail search: Turnaround time- 2 to 3 days. A SASE is requested. No fee for mail request.

Phone search: No fee for telephone request. You are restricted to 3 requests per call.

Fax search: Add $1.00 for each page that is faxed. Turnaround time is 2 days.

In person: No fee for request.

Online search: For free searching, go to www.sos.state.ia.us/corp/corp_search.asp.

Other access: This agency will sell the records in database format. Call the number listed above and ask for Karen Ubaldo.

Uniform Commercial Code, Federal Tax Liens

UCC Division - Sec of State, 321 E 12th Street, 1st Floor, Lucas Bldg, Des Moines, IA 50319; 515-281-5204, Fax- 515-242-5953; 8AM-4:30PM.

www.sos.state.ia.us

Indexing & Storage: Records available from 1966 and are computerized. All current records are on optical disk. New records available for inquiry in 1 to 3 days.

Searching: Use search request form UCC-11. Specify if you also want federal tax liens and include another search fee. Federal tax liens on individuals and all state tax liens are filed at the county level. Include in request- debtor name or filing number. Copies of filings may be requested at time of search, but do not ask for copies with your initial request unless you have a charge account.

Access by: mail, phone, fax, in person, online.

Fee & Payment: The fee is $5.00 per debtor name, $6.00 for federal liens. UCC copies are $1.00 per page, federal tax line copies are $5.00 per page. Fee payee- Secretary of State. Prepayment required. Personal checks, Visa, and MasterCard accepted.

Mail search: Turnaround time- 1 to 2 days. A SASE is requested.

Phone search: A telephone search is available with a prepaid or charge account, or with credit card. **Fax search:** Use of a credit card or charge account is required.

In person: Simple requests may be processed while you wait.

Online search: Visit www.sos.state.ia.us/Search/UCC/search.aspx?ucc. This search uses the filing office standard search logic for UCC or federal tax liens. It allows one to print a certified lien search report. By default the search reveals all liens that have not reached their lapse date. UCC searches have the option to include liens that have lapsed within the past year. Also, alternative search is at www.sos.state.ia.us/Search/UCCAlternative/search.aspx. This is helpful in finding names that are similar too but not exactly the same as the name searched.

State Tax Liens

Records not maintained by a state level agency.

Records are found at the county recorder's offices.

Sales Tax Registrations

Department of Revenue, Taxpayer Services, Hoover State Office Bldg, Des Moines, IA 50306-0465; 515-281-3114, Fax- 515-242-6487; 8AM-4PM. www.state.ia.us/tax/

Indexing & Storage: Records available for 3 years. New records available for inquiry in 1 to 6 months.

Searching: This agency will provide any information found on the face of the Tax Permit-business name, business address, and tax permit number. Information not released includes telephone numbers, tax liabilities, taxes collected, officers, federal Ides, etc. Include in request-business name. They will also search by tax permit number. Requests are accepted by email at idr@iowa.gov.

Access by: mail, phone, fax.

Fee & Payment: There is no search fee; however, there is a $5.00 copy fee per document. Fee payee-Treasurer State of Iowa. Prepayment required. Personal checks accepted, credit cards are not.

Mail search: Turnaround time- 14 to 21 days. SASE not required.

Phone search: Limited information is available by phone. **Fax search:** Records are available by fax.

Other access: The agency will provide the database on lists, fees vary from $20.00 to $45.00.

Birth Certificates

Iowa Department of Public Health, Bureau of Vital Records, 321 E 12th St, Lucas Bldg, Des Moines, IA 50319-0075; 515-281-4944, 515-281-5871 (Message Recording), Fax- 515-281-0479; 7AM-4:45PM.

www.idph.state.ia.us/apl/health_statistics.asp#vital

All vital records are open for inspection at the county level, usually for a $15.00 fee.

Indexing & Storage: Records available from 1880 to present. New records available for inquiry in 30 days to 6 weeks.

Searching: Adoption records are not released. Include in request- full name, names of parents, mother's maiden name, date of birth, place of birth, relationship to person of record, reason for information request. Must have copy of a photo ID (mail) or a photo ID (in person) to search. The requester's signature must be notarized. A request form is available from the web.

Access by: mail, phone, in person, online.

Fee & Payment: The search fee is $15.00 per index searched. There is an additional $9.00 fee to use a credit card (see below). For records 1880 to 1915, a $15.00 per year fee is charged. Fee payee-Iowa Department of Public Health. Prepayment required. Personal checks and major credit cards accepted.

Mail search: Turnaround time- 30-35 days.

Phone search: Record requests (except for genealogy records) are available by phone with use of credit card. The added fee is $9.00, the wait on the phone can be 20 minutes. If you wish to call a vendor's toll-free line for quicker service, the added fee is $13.00. Call 866-809-0290.

In person: Same day service is not available. Turnaround time is 48 hours.

Online search: The agency promotes a vendor - www.vitalchek.com - as the online means to order records. Additional fees ($13.00) involved and use of credit card required.

Expedited service: Available from the vendor mentioned above, requesters must also pay for express delivery.

Death Records

Iowa Department of Public Health, Bureau of Vital Records, 321 E 12th St, Lucas Bldg, Des Moines, IA 50319-0075; 515-281-4944, 515-281-5871 (Message Recording), Fax- 515-281-0479; 7AM-4:45PM.

www.idph.state.ia.us/apl/health_statistics.asp#vital

Indexing & Storage: Records available from 1880 to present. From 1880 to 1895 there is no index, the county of occurrence must be submitted with request. New records available for inquiry in up to 60 days.

Searching: Include in request- full name, date of death, place of death, relationship to person of record, reason for information request. Must have copy of a photo ID (mail) or a photo ID (in person) to search. The requester's signature must be notarized. A request form available from the web.

Access by: mail, phone, in person.

Fee & Payment: The search fee is $15.00 per index searched. There is an additional $5.50 fee when using a credit card. If searching 1880-1895, an additional $15.00 per year required. Fee payee-Iowa Department of Public Health. Prepayment required. Personal checks and major credit cards accepted.

Mail search: Turnaround time- 30-35 days.

Phone search: Record requests (except for genealogy records) are available by phone with use of credit card. The added fee is $9.00, the wait on the phone can be 20 minutes. If you wish to call a vendor's toll-free line for quicker service, the added fee is $13.00. Call 866-809-0290.

In person: Same day service in not available. Turnaround time is 48 hours.

Expedited service: Available from the vendor mentioned above, requesters must also pay for express delivery.

Marriage Certificates

Iowa Department of Public Health, Bureau of Vital Records, 321 E 12th St, Lucas Bldg, Des Moines, IA 50319-0075; 515-281-4944, 515-281-5871 (Message Recording), Fax- 515-281-0479; 7AM-4:45PM.

www.idph.state.ia.us/apl/health_statistics.asp#vital

Indexing & Storage: Records available from 1880. Records from 1880 to 1915 have to be searched by year. 1916 forward are indexed. New records available for inquiry in up to 4 weeks.

Searching: Include in request- names of husband and wife, date of marriage, place or county of marriage. Must have copy of a photo ID (mail) or a photo ID (in person) to search. The requester's signature must be notarized. A request form is available from the web.

Access by: mail, phone, in person.

Fee & Payment: The search fee is $15.00 per record. There is an additional $5.50 fee when using a credit card. If searching 1880-1915, an additional $15.00 per year required. Fee payee-Iowa Department of Public Health. Prepayment required. Personal checks and major credit cards accepted.

Mail search: Turnaround time- 30-35 days.

Phone search: Record requests (except for genealogy records) are available by phone with use of credit card. The added fee is $9.00, the wait on the phone can be 20 minutes. If you wish to call a vendor's toll-free line for quicker service, the added fee is $13.00. Call 866-809-0290.

In person: Same day service is not available. Turnaround time is 48 hours.

Expedited service: Available from the vendor mentioned above, requesters must also pay for express delivery.

Divorce Records

Records not maintained by a state level agency.

Divorce records are found at the county court issuing the decree. In general, records are available from 1880. Iowa Bureau of Vital Records does keep a divorce index, but no records.

Workers' Compensation Records

Iowa Workforce Development, Division of Workers' Compensation, 1000 E Grand Ave, Des Moines, IA 50319; 515-281-5387, Fax- 515-281-6501; 8AM-4:30PM.

www.iowaworkforce.org/wc/

Regular, ongoing requesters may apply for charge accounts.

Indexing & Storage: Records available from 1985 to present, 20 years on paper. New records available for inquiry in 2 weeks.

Searching: Include in request- claimant name, SSN, place of employment at time of accident. Waiver must be signed also. Older records may take as long as 6 weeks to research. This data not released- video tapes

Access by: mail, fax, in person.

Fee & Payment: The search fee is $24.00 per hour, with a $6.00 minimum. For individual claims histories fee is $6.00 per request up to 6 people, then $1.00 per person. Photo copies are $.10 per page, fax copies $.75 per page. Fee payee-Workers' Compensation. Prepayment required. Personal checks accepted, credit cards are not.

Mail search: Turnaround time- 3 to 5 days. A SASE is requested.

Fax search: Fax requests accepted.

In person: Files are available for personal viewing only if requested in advance, with signed waiver.

Other access: This agency sells its entire database or can sell data transmissions of pages ($.045 per page).

Driver Records

Department of Transportation, Driver Service Records Section, PO Box 9204, Des Moines, IA 50306-9204 (Courier address- 6310 SE Convenience Blvd, Ankeny IA 50021); 515-244-9124, 800-532-1121 (Iowa only), Fax- 515-237-3152; 8AM-4:30PM.

www.iowadot.gov/mvd/

Copies of tickets can be requested from this address for $.50 per copy.

Indexing & Storage: Records available for 5 to 7 years for moving violations; 12 years for DWIs; 3 to 7 years after closed for suspensions. The driver's address is shown on the record. Accidents are listed, but fault is not shown.

Searching: Non-permissible use requesters receive records without personal information, unless written consent of the subject is presented. Include in request- full name, driver's license number, date of birth. All convictions are listed on the record. "Countable Moving Violations" shown include all moving violations

Access by: mail, fax, in person, online.

Fee & Payment: The fee for a certified mail-in or walk-in request is $5.50 per record. Electronic records are $8.50 each. There is no charge for a no record found. Fee payee- Treasurer, State of Iowa. Prepayment required. Personal checks accepted, credit cards are not.

Mail search: Turnaround time- 5 to 10 days. An account can be established for on-going requesters. SASE not required.

Fax search: Pre-approved accounts may be able to fax to IowaAccess, but not to this agency.

In person: The public access terminal is no longer available. Records must be ordered from personnel.

Online search: The state requires that all ongoing requesters/users access records via IowaAccess. The fee is $8.50 per record, the service is interactive or batch. Requesters must be approved and open an account. The records contain personal information, so requesters must comply with DPPA. For more information, contact IowaAccess at 515-323-3468 or 866-492-3468.

Other access: Per DPPA provisions, the state will sell the header file on a per computer minute basis. Also, a driver license/suspension/revocation file is available via FTP. Call 512-244-1052 for details.

Vehicle Ownership & Registration

Department of Transportation, Office of Vehicle Services, PO Box 9278, Des Moines, IA 50306-9278; 515-237-3148, 515-237-3049, Fax- 515-237-3056; 8AM-4:30PM. www.iowadot.gov/mvd/

Vehicle lien information is not maintained by this department.

Indexing & Storage: Records available for 7 years for title; for 3 years for registration.

Searching: Vehicle registration information is released to casual requesters, but personal information is not given without written consent of the subject. The state is in compliance with DPPA. Records may be accessed by VIN, name, title no. and plate - subject to DPPA and Iowa Code 321.11.

Access by: mail, fax, in person, online.

Fee & Payment: Fees: $.50 per certified record. Computer printout is $1.00. Record search-$5.00 per quarter hour or fraction thereof. Fee payee- Iowa Department of Transportation. Prepayment required. Personal checks accepted, credit cards are not.

Mail search: Turnaround time- within 30 days. No SASE required.

Fax search: Fax searching is available for approved account holders.

In person: You may request information in person, but results may still be mailed, depending on workload.

Online search: Online access is available to those who qualify per DPPA including dealers, Iowa licensed investigators and security companies. There is no fee. All accounts must register and be pre-approved per DPPA. Write to the Office of Motor Vehicle, explaining purpose/use of records.

Other access: Iowa makes the entire vehicle file or selected data available for purchase. Weekly updates are also available for those purchasers. Requesters subject to DPPA requirements. For more information, call 515-237-3110.

Accident Reports

Department of Transportation, Office of Driver Services, PO Box 9204, Des Moines, IA 50306-9204 (Courier address- 6310 SE Convenience Blvd, Ankeny, IA 50021); 515-244-9124, 800-532-1121, Fax- 515-239-1837; 8AM-4:30PM. www.iowadot.gov/mvd/ods/index.htm

County sheriffs in Iowa are authorized to furnish copies of officer accident reports, but not all do.

Indexing & Storage: Records available for five years. New records available for inquiry in three days.

Searching: Accident reports are available only to the person involved in accident or the person's insurance company or attorney. However, the agency will provided limited information such as date, time, location, circumstances. Direct questions to ods@dot.iowa.gov. Include in request- full name, date of accident, location of accident. Will not expedite requests. This data not released- personal information of the other party.

Access by: mail, fax, in person.

Fee & Payment: The fee is $4.00 per officer report. Fee payee- Treasurer, State of Iowa. Prepayment required. The state allows regular, ongoing requesters to open a deposit account. Personal checks accepted, credit cards are not.

Mail search: Turnaround time- 2 to 3 weeks. SASE not required. **Fax search:** Same criteria as mail searches.

In person: Turnaround time for walk-in requesters is generally immediate.

Vessel Ownership & Registration

Records not maintained by a state level agency.

All titles, registrations, and liens are handled by the county recorder's office. However, this office does have a database of titles and registration information and does permit record searching, except for liens.

Legislation Records

Iowa General Assembly, Legislative Information Office G-16, State Capitol, Des Moines, IA 50319; 515-281-5129, Fax- 515-281-8027; 8AM-4:30PM.

www.legis.state.ia.us

For copies of bills before 1996, it is suggested to go to Iowa Law Library (515-281-5124).

Voter Registration

Secretary of State - Voter Registration, Lucas Building, 1st Floor, 321 E. 12th St, Des Moines, IA 50319; 515-281-0145, Fax- 515-281-7142; 8AM-4:30PM.

www.sos.state.ia.us/elections/index.html

Indexing & Storage: Records available for active records. New records available for inquiry immediately.

Searching: E-mail requests to sos@sos.state.ia.us. Include in request- name and telephone number. This data not released- SSNs, DLs, or bulk information or lists for commercial purposes.

Access by: mail, phone, fax, in person.

Fee & Payment: There is no fee to view a single record. Lists may be purchased, but only for political purposes. For pricing, visit www.sos.state.ia.us/pdfs/elections/VoterListRequest.pdf.

Mail search: Turnaround time- 3 to 4 days. SASE nor required. **Phone search:** Will only confirm. **Fax search:** Fax requests are accepted if verification request list is short.

In person: Records may be viewed.

Other access: Information is available on disk or paper for political purposes only. Data can be sorted by any field on the registration file. Fees are determined by media. Electronic records are $.50 per thousand.

GED Certificates

Department of Education, GED Records, Grimes State Office Building, Des Moines, IA 50319-0146; 515-281-7308, 515-281-3640, Fax- 515-281-6544; 8AM-4:30PM.

www.readiowa.org/

GED document request forms are available from the webpage. Also, the webpage has links for the GED Record Specialists and Chief Examiners of Iowa Community Colleges.

Indexing & Storage: Records available from 1966 forward on two databases and on microfiche. If record is not in the database, contact the community college which handled the test score. New records available for inquiry in 1 month.

Searching: Include in request- signed release, SSN, DOB. Note that a signed release is required for either a verification or a copy of a diploma or transcript. The year and city of test are also helpful. The GED Document Request Form is found at www.readiowa.org/forms.html. This data not released- addresses and personal information. Records are not released for solicitation of business or offers.

Access by: mail, phone, fax, in person.

Fee & Payment: There is a $5.00 fee for a copy of a transcript or a diploma, $3.00 for a second transcript. There is no fee for a verification. Fee payee- IA Department of Education. Prepayment required. Money orders are accepted. No personal checks or credit cards accepted.

Mail search: Turnaround time- 1 to 3 days. A SASE is requested.

Phone search: Limited information is available. **Fax search:** They will return verification data by fax to local or toll-free numbers. **In person:** Limited information given across-the-counter.

Other access: There are several different statewide GED databases available.

Hunting & Fishing License Information

Department of Natural Resources, Wallace Building, 502 E 9th Street, Des Moines, IA 50319-0034; 515-242-5918, Fax- 515-281-8895; 8AM-4:30PM. www.iowadnr.gov/wildlife/index.html

Indexing & Storage: Records available from 2001 on computer.

Online search: One may search, by name or partial SSN, the status of a turkey application online, name list with city given.

Other access: Bulk data is released on CD, call for details on pricing.

Iowa State Licensing Agencies

For details about the agency responsible for licensing/certifying/registering an item below or in the Agency Quick Finder section, match an item's number with the number of the agency in the *Licensing Agency Information* section.

Iowa Licenses Searchable Online

Acupuncturist #14 .... http://medicalboard.iowa.gov/FindADoc.html
Adoption Investigator #18 .... www.dhs.iowa.gov/Partners/Partners_Providers/FindAProvider/LicensingAdoptFC.html
Anesthesiologist #14 .... http://medicalboard.iowa.gov/FindADoc.html
Architect #10 .... www.state.ia.us/government/com/prof/home.html
Asbestos Contractor/Worker #27 .... http://www2.iwd.state.ia.us/LaborServices/LabrAsbs.nsf
Asbestos Project Designer/Planner #27 .... http://www2.iwd.state.ia.us/LaborServices/LabrAsbs.nsf
Athletic Trainer #22 .... https://eservices.iowa.gov/licensediniowa/index.php?pgname=pubsearch
Attorney #11 .... https://www.iacourtcommissions.org/icc/SearchLawyer.do
Audiologist #22 .... https://eservices.iowa.gov/licensediniowa/index.php?pgname=pubsearch
Bank #4 .... www.idob.state.ia.us
Barber #22 .... https://eservices.iowa.gov/licensediniowa/index.php?pgname=pubsearch
Chiropractor #22 .... https://eservices.iowa.gov/licensediniowa/index.php?pgname=pubsearch
Controlled Substance Registrant #16 .... www.state.ia.us/ibpe/verification.html
Cosmetologist #24 .... https://eservices.iowa.gov/licensediniowa/index.php?pgname=pubsearch
Cosmetol'y Salon/School/Instruct #24 .... https://eservices.iowa.gov/licensediniowa/index.php?pgname=pubsearch
Crematory #22 .... https://eservices.iowa.gov/licensediniowa/index.php?pgname=pubsearch
Debt Management Company #4 .... www.idob.state.ia.us/license/lic_default.htm
Delayed Deposit Service Business #4 .... www.idob.state.ia.us/license/lic_default.htm
Dietitian #22 .... https://eservices.iowa.gov/licensediniowa/index.php?pgname=pubsearch
Doctor #14 .... http://medicalboard.iowa.gov/FindADoc.html
Drug Distributor/Whlse./Mfg. #16 .... www.state.ia.us/ibpe/verification.html
Electrologist #24 .... https://eservices.iowa.gov/licensediniowa/index.php?pgname=pubsearch
Emergency Med. Tech. - Paramedic #29 .... www.idph.state.ia.us/ems/report_get_provider_list.asp
EMS Bureau Staff/Svc/Provider #29 .... www.idph.state.ia.us/ems/report_get_provider_list.asp
Engineer #10 .... www.state.ia.us/government/com/prof/home.html
Esthetician #24 .... https://eservices.iowa.gov/licensediniowa/index.php?pgname=pubsearch
Excursion Gambling Boat #19 .... www.iowa.gov/irgc/
Finance Company #4 .... www.idob.state.ia.us/license/lic_default.htm
First Response Paramedic #29 .... www.idph.state.ia.us/ems/report_get_provider_list.asp
Foster Care #17 .... www.dhs.iowa.gov/docs/LicFacs.xls
Funeral Director/Home #22 .... https://eservices.iowa.gov/licensediniowa/index.php?pgname=pubsearch
Group Foster Care #17 .... www.dhs.iowa.gov/docs/LicFacs.xls
Hearing Aid Dispenser/Dealer #22 .... https://eservices.iowa.gov/licensediniowa/index.php?pgname=pubsearch
Insurance Agency / Company #7 .... www.iid.state.ia.us/agent_company_search/find_insuranceco.asp
Landscape Architect #10 .... www.state.ia.us/government/com/prof/home.html
Lobbyist #8 .... http://coolice.legis.state.ia.us/Cool-ICE/default.asp?Category=Matt&Service=Lobby
Manicurist #24 .... https://eservices.iowa.gov/licensediniowa/index.php?pgname=pubsearch
Marriage & Family Therapist #22 .... https://eservices.iowa.gov/licensediniowa/index.php?pgname=pubsearch
Massage Therapist #22 .... https://eservices.iowa.gov/licensediniowa/index.php?pgname=pubsearch
Medical Doctor #14 .... http://medicalboard.iowa.gov/FindADoc.html
Mental Health Counselor #22 .... https://eservices.iowa.gov/licensediniowa/index.php?pgname=pubsearch
Money Transmitter #4 .... www.idob.state.ia.us/license/lic_default.htm
Mortgage Banker/Broker #4 .... www.idob.state.ia.us/license/lic_default.htm
Mortgage Loan Service #4 .... www.idob.state.ia.us/license/lic_default.htm
Mortuary Science #22 .... https://eservices.iowa.gov/licensediniowa/index.php?pgname=pubsearch
Nail Technologist #24 .... https://eservices.iowa.gov/licensediniowa/index.php?pgname=pubsearch
Notary Public #21 .... www.sos.state.ia.us/search/notary/
Nurse #15 .... www.state.ia.us/nursing/index.html
Nurse, Advance Registered Practice #15 .... www.state.ia.us/nursing/index.html
Nurse-LPN #15 .... www.state.ia.us/nursing/index.html
Nursing Home Administrator #22 .... https://eservices.iowa.gov/licensediniowa/index.php?pgname=pubsearch
Occupational Therapist/Assistant #22 .... https://eservices.iowa.gov/licensediniowa/index.php?pgname=pubsearch
Optometrist #22 .... https://eservices.iowa.gov/licensediniowa/index.php?pgname=pubsearch
Orthopedic Doctor #14 .... http://medicalboard.iowa.gov/FindADoc.html
Osteopathic Physician #14 .... http://medicalboard.iowa.gov/FindADoc.html
Pari-Mutuel Race Track Enclosure #19 .... www.iowa.gov/irgc/
Pediatrician #14 .... http://medicalboard.iowa.gov/FindADoc.html

Pesticide Commercial Applicator #3	www.kellysolutions.com/ia/Business/index.asp
Pesticide Commercial Certification #3	www.kellysolutions.com/ia/Applicators/index.asp
Pesticide Dealer #3	www.kellysolutions.com/ia/Dealers/index.asp
Pesticide Private Applicator #3	www.kellysolutions.com/ia/Applicators/index.asp
Pharmacist/Pharmacist Tech/Intern #16	www.state.ia.us/ibpe/verification.html
Pharmacy #16	www.state.ia.us/ibpe/verification.html
Physical Therapist/Assistant #22	https://eservices.iowa.gov/licensediniowa/index.php?pgname=pubsearch
Physician Assistant #22	https://eservices.iowa.gov/licensediniowa/index.php?pgname=pubsearch
Podiatrist #22	https://eservices.iowa.gov/licensediniowa/index.php?pgname=pubsearch
Psychiatrist #14	http://medicalboard.iowa.gov/FindADoc.html
Psychologist #22	https://eservices.iowa.gov/licensediniowa/index.php?pgname=pubsearch
Real Estate Agent/Broker/Sales #10	www.state.ia.us/government/com/prof/home.html
Real Estate Appraiser #23	https://eservices.iowa.gov/licensediniowa/index.php?pgname=pubsearch
Respiratory Therapist #22	https://eservices.iowa.gov/licensediniowa/index.php?pgname=pubsearch
School Principal/Superint'd'nt/Coach #12	www.boee.iowa.gov/search_warn.html
Shorthand Reporter #11	https://www.iacourtcommissions.org/icc/SearchCsr.do
Social Worker #22	https://eservices.iowa.gov/licensediniowa/index.php?pgname=pubsearch
Speech Pathologist/Audiologist #22	https://eservices.iowa.gov/licensediniowa/index.php?pgname=pubsearch
Surveyor, Land #10	www.state.ia.us/government/com/prof/home.html
Tattoo Artist #22	https://eservices.iowa.gov/licensediniowa/index.php?pgname=pubsearch
Teacher #12	www.boee.iowa.gov/search_warn.html

Iowa Licensing Quick Finder

Acupuncturist #14	515-281-5171
Adoption Investigator #18	515-281-6220
Alcoholic Bev. Retail/Whlse./Mfg. #5	515-281-7430
Amusement Ride Inspection #27	515-281-5415
Anesthesiologist #14	515-281-5171
Animal Entry Regulation #2	515-281-5304
Appraiser #10	515-281-7393
Architect #10	515-281-7393
Asbestos Contractor/Worker #27	515-281-6175
Asbestos Inspector #27	515-281-6175
Asbestos Project Designer/Planner #27	515-281-6175
Athletic Agent #21	515-281-5204
Athletic Trainer #22	515-281-4401
Attorney #11	515-281-5911
Audiologist #22	515-281-6959
Bail Enforcement #25	515-725-6230
Bank #4	515-281-4014
Barber #22	515-281-6959
Boarding Kennel #2	515-281-7583
Boiler Inspector #27	515-281-6533
Boxer/Boxing Event #27	515-281-3447
Bull Breeder #2	515-281-8285
Bus Driver #28	515-237-3079
Chiropractor #22	515-281-4287
Commercial Breeder/Kennel #2	515-281-7583
Contractor #27	515-242-5871
Controlled Substance Registrant #16	515-281-5944
Cosmetologist #24	515-281-4416
Cosmetol'y Salon/School/Instruct #24	515-281-4416
Credit Union #6	515-281-6514
Crematory #22	515-281-4287
Day Care #17	515-281-0390
Dealer #2	515-281-7583
Debt Management Company #4	515-281-4014
Delayed Deposit Service Business #4	515-281-4014
Dental Hygienist #13	515-281-5047
Dentist #13	515-281-5047
Dietitian #22	515-281-6959
Doctor #14	515-281-5171
Drug Distributor/Whlse./Mfg. #16	515-281-5944
Electrologist #24	515-281-4416
Elevator/Escalator Inspection #27	515-281-5415
Emergency Med. Tech/Paramedic #29	515-281-0620
EMS Bureau Staff/Svc/Prpvider #29	515-281-0620
Engineer #10	515-281-4126
Entry Permit #2	515-281-5547
Esthetician #24	515-281-4416
Excursion Gambling Boat #19	515-281-7352
Family Foster Care #17	515-281-6220
Finance Company #4	515-281-4014
First Response Paramedic #29	515-281-0620
Foster Care #17	515-281-6220
Funeral Director/Home #22	515-281-4287
Greyhound #2	515-281-7583
Group Foster Care #17	515-281-6220
Hatchery Dealer #2	515-281-8285
HazHat Registration/Storage #27	515- 281-5151
Hearing Aid Dispenser/Dealer #22	515-281-6959
Instructional School #21	515-281-5204
Insurance Agency/Producer #7	515-281-7757
Insurance Company #7	515-281-7367
Landfill Operator #20	515-281-6807
Landscape Architect #10	515-281-4126
Livestock Dealer/Agent/Market #2	515-281-8285
Lobbyist #8	515-281-5381
Lottery Retailer #26	515-281-7900
Manicurist #24	515-281-4416
Marriage & Family Therapist #22	515-281-4422
Massage Therapist #22	515-281-6959
Medical Doctor #14	515-281-5171
Mental Health Counselor #22	515-281-4422
Merchant, Transient #21	515-281-5204
Money Transmitter #4	515-281-4014
Mortgage Banker/Broker #4	515-281-4014
Mortgage Loan Service #4	515-281-4014
Mortuary Science #22	515-281-4287
Nail Technologist #24	515-281-4416
Notary Public #21	515-281-5204
Nuclear Medicine Technologist #9	515-281-0415
Nurse, Advance Regist'd Practice #15	515-281-3255
Nurse-LPN #15	515-281-3255
Nursing Home Administrator #22	515-281-4401
Occupational Therapist/Assistant #22	515-281-4401
Optometrist #22	515-281-4287
Orthopedic Doctor #14	515-281-5171
OSHA Training/Trainer #27	515-281-7629
Osteopathic Physician #14	515-281-5171
Pari-Mutuel Race Track Enclosure #19	515-281-7352
Pediatrician #14	515-281-5171
Pesticide Commercial Applicator #3	515-281-5601
Pesticide Commercial Certification #3	515-281-5601
Pesticide Dealer #3	515-281-5601
Pesticide Private Applicator #3	515-281-4339
Pet Shop #2	515-281-7583
Pharmacist/Pharmacist Tech/Intern #16	515-281-5944
Pharmacy #16	515-281-5944
Physical Therapist/Assistant #22	515-281-4401
Physician Assistant #22	515-281-4401
Pig Dealer/Agent #2	515-281-8285
Podiatrist #22	515-281-4287
Polygraph Examiner #30	515-281-7610
Post-Secondary School #21	515-281-5204
Poultry Buyer #2	515-281-8285
Pound/Animal Shelter/Priv. Pound #2	515-281-7583
Private Investigative Agency #25	515-725-6230
Private Security Agency #25	515-725-6230
Psychiatrist #14	515-281-5171
Psychologist #22	515-281-4401
Public Accountant-CPA #10	515-281-4126
Public Auctions #2	515-281-7583
Radiation Therapist #9	515-281-0415
Radioactive Material #9	515-281-0422
Radiographer, Medical #9	515-281-0415
Radon Specialist #9	515-281-4928
Real Estate Agent/Broker/Sales #10	515-281-7393
Real Estate Appraiser #23	515-281-7393
Registered Federal Dealer #2	515-281-7583
Rendering Plant #2	515-281-8285
Research Facility #2	515-281-7583
Respiratory Therapist #22	515-281-4287
School Counselor / Coach #12	515-281-3482
School Principal/Superintendent #12	515-281-3482
Securities Agent/Broker/Dealer #7	515-281-4441
Sheep Dealer #2	515-281-8285
Shootfighting Event #27	515-281-3447
Shorthand Reporter #11	515-725-8029
Social Worker #22	515-281-4422
Solid Waste Compost Oper'tor #20	515-281-5918
Solid Waste Incinerator Operator #20	515-281-6807
Speech Pathologist/Audiologist #22	515-281-6959
Surveyor, Land #10	515-281-4126
Tattoo Artist #22	515-281-8074
Taxi Driver #28	515-237-3079
Teacher #12	515-281-3482
Travel Agency #21	515-281-5204
Truck Driver #28	515-237-3079
Veterinarian #2	515-281-8617
Veterinary Technician #2	515-281-8617
Voting Booth/Equipment #1	515-281-0145
Waste Water Lagoon/Treatm't Oper'tor #20	515-725-0284
Water Distribution Operator #20	515-725-0284
Water Treatment Operator #20	515-725-0284
Well Driller #20	515-725-0284
Wrestler/Wrestling Event #27	515-281-3447
Youth Work Permitee #27	515-281-6574

Iowa Licensing Agency Information

#1 Attn: Sandy Steinbach, Secretary of State's Office, 321 E 12th St, 1st Fl, Lucas Bldg, Des Moines, IA 50319; 515-281-0145, Fax- 515-281-7142. Hours- 8AM-4:30PM. www.sos.state.ia.us

#2 Department of Agriculture, Animal Industry Bureau, CP & RA, 502 E 9th St, Wallace State Office Bldg, Des Moines, IA 50319; 515-281-8617, Fax- 515-281-4282. www.iowaagriculture.gov/animals.asp

#3 Department of Agriculture, Pesticide Division, Wallace State Office Bldg, 502 E 9th St, Des Moines, IA 50319; 515-281-8591, Fax- 515-242-6497. Hours- 8AM-4:30PM. www.iowaagriculture.gov/pesticides.asp

#4 Department of Commerce, Iowa Division of Banking, 200 E Grand Ave, Ste 300, Des Moines, IA 50309; 515-281-4014, Fax- 515-281-4862. www.idob.state.ia.us Search data at- www.idob.state.ia.us/license/lic_default.htm

#5 Department of Commerce, Alcoholic Beverage Division, 1918 SE Hulsizer Ave, Ankeny, IA 50021; 515-281-7432, Fax- 515-281-7375. www.iowaabd.com

#6 Department of Commerce, Credit Union Division, 200 E Grand Ave #370, Des Moines, IA 50309; 515-281-6514, Fax- 515-281-7595. www.iacudiv.state.ia.us

#7 Iowa Insurance Division, 330 Maple St, Des Moines, IA 50319-0065; 515-281-5705, Fax- 515-281-3059. www.iid.state.ia.us

#8 Lobbyist Registration, Chief Clerk of the House, Statehouse, Des Moines, IA 50319; 515-281-5381. Hours- 8AM-4:30PM. www.legis.state.ia.us Search data at- www.legis.state.ia.us/Lobbyist.html

#9 Department of Public Health, Bureau of Radiological Health, Lucas State Office Bldg 5th Fl, 321 E 12th St, Des Moines, IA 50319; 515-281-3478, Fax- 515-281-4529. www.idph.state.ia.us/eh/radiological_health.asp

#10 Dept of Commerce, Professional Licensing Division, 1920 SE Hulsizer Ave, Ankeny, IA 50021; 515-281-7447, Fax- 515-281-7411. www.state.ia.us/government/com/prof/home.html Search data at- www.state.ia.us/government/com/prof/home.html

#11 Supreme Court Clerk's Office, Legal Boards, 1111 E Court Ave, Des Moines, IA 50319; 515-281-5911, Fax- 515-242-6164. Hours- 8AM-4:30PM. www.judicial.state.ia.us Search data at- https://www.iacourtcommissions.org/icc/

#12 Board of Education Examiners, Grimes State Office Bldg, 400 E 14th St, Des Moines, IA 50319; 515-281-3482, Fax- 515-281-7669. Hours- 8AM-4:30PM. www.iowa.gov/educate/ Search- www.boee.iowa.gov/search_warn.html

#13 Board of Dental Examiners, 400 SW 8th St, #D, Des Moines, IA 50309-4687; 515-281-5157, Fax- 515-281-7969. Hours- 8AM-4:30PM. www.state.ia.us/dentalboard/ Phone verifications accepted- 515-281-5047.

#14 Board of Medical Examiners, 400 SW 8th #C, Des Moines, IA 50309-4686; 515-281-5171, Fax- 515-242-5908. 8AM-4:30PM. http://medicalboard.iowa.gov/ Search data at- http://medicalboard.iowa.gov/FindADoc.html Automated phone system verifications, call 515-281-5171.

#15 Board of Nursing, 400 SW 8th St, #B River Point Business Pk, Des Moines, IA 50309-4685; 515-281-3255, Fax- 515-281-4825. 8AM-4:30PM. www.state.ia.us/nursing/ Search data at- www.state.ia.us/nursing/index.html Rosters available. Forms available at www.state.ia.us/nursing/, select general info.

#16 Board of Pharmacy Examiners, 400 SW 8th St, #E, Des Moines, IA 50308; 515-281-5944, Fax- 515-281-4609. 8AM-4:30PM. www.state.ia.us/ibpe/index.htm Search data at- www.state.ia.us/ibpe/verification.html Licensing data available in Excel lists.

#17 Department of Human Services, Child & Family Services, 1305 E Walnut, Hoover State Office Bldg, 5th Fl, Des Moines, IA 50319-0114; 515-281-6220. www.dhs.iowa.gov/Consumers/Child_Care/ChildCareMenu.html Search data at- www.dhs.iowa.gov/docs/LicFacs.xls

#18 Department of Human Services, Division of Child & Family Services, 1305 E Walnut, Hoover Bldg., 5th Fl, Des Moines, IA 50319-0114; 515-281-6220, Fax- 515-242-6036. www.dhs.iowa.gov/Partners/Partners_Providers/FindAProvider/LicensingAdoptFC.html

#19 Department of Inspections & Appeals, Racing & Gaming Commission, 717 E Court, #B, Des Moines, IA 50309; 515-281-7352, Fax- 515-242-6560. Hours- 8AM-4:30PM. www.iowa.gov/irgc/

#20 Department of Natural Resources, 502 E 9th St, Wallace State Office Bldg, Des Moines, IA 50319-0034; 515-281-5918, Fax- 515-281-6794. Hours- 8AM-4:30PM. www.iowadnr.com/waste/index.html

#21 Secretary of State, 321 E 12th St, Lucas Bldg, 1st Fl, Des Moines, IA 50319; 515-281-5204, Fax- 515-242-5953. 8AM-4:30PM. www.sos.state.ia.us

#22 Department of Public Health, Division of Professional Licensure, 321 E 12th St, Des Moines, IA 50319; 515-281-0254, Fax- 515-281-3121. Hours- 8AM-4:30PM. www.idph.state.ia.us/licensure/

#23 Real Estate Appraiser Board, 1920 SE Hulsizer Ave, Ankeny, IA 50021-3941; 515-281-4126, Fax- 515-281-7411. www.state.ia.us/government/com/prof/appraiser/home.html Search data at- https://eservices.iowa.gov/licensediniowa/index.php?pgname=pubsearch

#24 Bureau of Professional Licensure, Board of Cosmetology Arts & Sciences Examiners, 321 E 12th St, Lucas State Office Bldg 5th Fl, Des Moines, IA 50319-0075; 515-281-4416, Fax- 515-281-3121. Hours- 8AM-4:30PM. www.idph.state.ia.us/licensure/board_home.asp?board=cos Search data at- https://eservices.iowa.gov/licensediniowa/index.php?pgname=pubsearch

#25 Program Services Bureau, Administrative Svcs Div, Department of Public Safety, 215 E 7th St, 4th Fl, Wallace State Office Bldg, Des Moines, IA 50319; 515-725-6230, Fax- 515-725-6264. Hours- 8AM-4:30PM. www.dps.state.ia.us/asd/pi_licensing.shtml

#26 Department of Revenue & Finance, Lottery Board, 2323 Grand Ave, Des Moines, IA 50312; 515-281-7900, Fax- 515-281-7882. www.ialottery.com

#27 Labor Services Division, Workforce Development, 1000 E Grand Ave, Des Moines, IA 50319-0209; 515-281-5387, Fax- 515-281-7995. Hours- 8AM-4:30PM. www.iowaworkforce.org/labor/

#28 Department of Transportation, Motor Vehicle Division, Office of Driver Svcs, PO Box 9204, Des Moines, IA 50306-9204; 515-244-9124, Fax- 515-239-1837. www.iowadot.gov/mvd/ods/

#29 Bureau of EMS, Department of Public Health, 321 E 12th St, Lucas State Office Bldg, Des Moines, IA 30319; 515-281-0620, 800-728-3367, Fax- 515-281-0488. 8AM-4:30PM. www.idph.state.ia.us/ems/ Search data at- www.idph.state.ia.us/ems/report_get_provider_list.asp List of EMS providers available at www.idph.state.ia.us/ems/report_get_provider_list.asp. Services list at www.idph.state.ia.us/ems/report_get_service_list.asp.

#30 Division of Administrative Svcs, Polygraph Section, Department of Public Safety, Wallace State Office Bldg, 3rd Fl, Des Moines, IA 50319; 515-281-7610. http://iwin.iwd.state.ia.us/iowa/OIC?action=license&licid=0000000385

Iowa Federal Courts

The following list indicates the district and division name for each county in the state. If the bankruptcy court location is different from the district court, then the location of the bankruptcy court appears in parentheses.

Iowa County/Court Cross Reference

County	District	Division
Adair	Southern	Council Bluffs (Des Moines)
Adams	Southern	Council Bluffs (Des Moines)
Allamakee	Northern	Cedar Rapids
Appanoose	Southern	Des Moines (Central)
Audubon	Southern	Council Bluffs (Des Moines)
Benton	Northern	Cedar Rapids
Black Hawk	Northern	Cedar Rapids
Boone	Southern	Des Moines (Central)
Bremer	Northern	Cedar Rapids
Buchanan	Northern	Cedar Rapids
Buena Vista	Northern	Sioux City (Cedar Rapids)
Butler	Northern	Sioux City (Cedar Rapids)
Calhoun	Northern	Sioux City (Cedar Rapids)
Carroll	Northern	Sioux City (Cedar Rapids)
Cass	Southern	Council Bluffs (Des Moines)
Cedar	Northern	Cedar Rapids
Cerro Gordo	Northern	Cedar Rapids
Cherokee	Northern	Sioux City (Cedar Rapids)
Chickasaw	Northern	Cedar Rapids
Clarke	Southern	Council Bluffs (Des Moines)
Clay	Northern	Sioux City (Cedar Rapids)
Clayton	Northern	Cedar Rapids
Clinton	Southern	Council Bluffs (Des Moines)
Crawford	Northern	Sioux City (Cedar Rapids)
Dallas	Southern	Des Moines (Central)
Davis	Southern	Des Moines (Central)
Decatur	Southern	Council Bluffs (Des Moines)
Delaware	Northern	Cedar Rapids
Des Moines	Southern	Des Moines (Central)
Dickinson	Northern	Sioux City (Cedar Rapids)
Dubuque	Northern	Cedar Rapids
Emmet	Northern	Sioux City (Cedar Rapids)
Fayette	Northern	Cedar Rapids
Floyd	Northern	Cedar Rapids
Franklin	Northern	Sioux City (Cedar Rapids)
Fremont	Southern	Council Bluffs (Des Moines)
Greene	Southern	Des Moines (Central)
Grundy	Northern	Cedar Rapids
Guthrie	Southern	Des Moines (Central)
Hamilton	Northern	Sioux City (Cedar Rapids)
Hancock	Northern	Sioux City (Cedar Rapids)
Hardin	Northern	Cedar Rapids
Harrison	Southern	Council Bluffs (Des Moines)
Henry	Southern	Davenport (Des Moines)
Howard	Northern	Cedar Rapids
Humboldt	Northern	Sioux City (Cedar Rapids)
Ida	Northern	Sioux City (Cedar Rapids)
Iowa	Northern	Cedar Rapids
Jackson	Northern	Cedar Rapids
Jasper	Southern	Des Moines (Central)
Jefferson	Southern	Des Moines (Central)
Johnson	Southern	Davenport (Des Moines)
Jones	Northern	Cedar Rapids
Keokuk	Southern	Des Moines (Central)
Kossuth	Northern	Sioux City (Cedar Rapids)
Lee	Southern	Davenport (Des Moines)
Linn	Northern	Cedar Rapids
Louisa	Southern	Davenport (Des Moines)
Lucas	Southern	Council Bluffs (Des Moines)
Lyon	Northern	Sioux City (Cedar Rapids)
Madison	Southern	Des Moines (Central)
Mahaska	Southern	Des Moines (Central)
Marion	Southern	Des Moines (Central)
Marshall	Southern	Des Moines (Central)
Mills	Southern	Council Bluffs (Des Moines)
Mitchell	Northern	Cedar Rapids
Monona	Northern	Sioux City (Cedar Rapids)
Monroe	Southern	Des Moines (Central)
Montgomery	Southern	Council Bluffs (Des Moines)
Muscatine	Southern	Davenport (Des Moines)
O'Brien	Northern	Sioux City (Cedar Rapids)
Osceola	Northern	Sioux City (Cedar Rapids)
Page	Southern	Council Bluffs (Des Moines)
Palo Alto	Northern	Sioux City (Cedar Rapids)
Plymouth	Northern	Sioux City (Cedar Rapids)
Pocahontas	Northern	Sioux City (Cedar Rapids)
Polk	Southern	Des Moines (Central)
Pottawattamie	Southern	Council Bluffs (Des Moines)
Poweshiek	Southern	Des Moines (Central)
Ringgold	Southern	Council Bluffs (Des Moines)
Sac	Northern	Sioux City (Cedar Rapids)
Scott	Southern	Davenport (Des Moines)
Shelby	Southern	Council Bluffs (Des Moines)
Sioux	Northern	Sioux City (Cedar Rapids)
Story	Southern	Des Moines (Central)
Tama	Northern	Cedar Rapids
Taylor	Southern	Council Bluffs (Des Moines)
Union	Southern	Council Bluffs (Des Moines)
Van Buren	Southern	Davenport (Des Moines)
Wapello	Southern	Des Moines (Central)
Warren	Southern	Des Moines (Central)
Washington	Southern	Davenport (Des Moines)
Wayne	Southern	Council Bluffs (Des Moines)
Webster	Northern	Sioux City (Cedar Rapids)
Winnebago	Northern	Sioux City (Cedar Rapids)
Winneshiek	Northern	Cedar Rapids
Woodbury	Northern	Sioux City (Cedar Rapids)
Worth	Northern	Sioux City (Cedar Rapids)
Wright	Northern	Sioux City (Cedar Rapids)

Standards for Federal Courts: Fees are standard unless noted in profile. Search fee is $26.00 per item (one party name or case number). Copy fee is $.50 per page. Certification fee is $9.00 per document, double for exemplification, if available. Most courts require prepayment. Mail requests should enclose a SASE unless otherwise noted. Before releasing records, all courts require prepayment, unless noted.

District courts index by defendant and plaintiff and by case number. Bankruptcy courts usually index by debtor and case number. While most courts now have their indexes on computer, many may still maintain index card files as well. Courts will archive closed case files at different times.

There are numerous public access programs available to online subscribers. Search the U.S. Party/Case Index to find party names and case numbers among all courts. Individual case data is provided on PACER. A search of CM/ECF provides copies of cases filed electronically. For details about PACER, the US Party/Case Index, and CM/ECF see the Appendix or go to http://pacer.psc.uscourts.gov or call 800-676-6856.

US District Court Iowa Northern District

Cedar Rapids (Eastern) Division Clerk of Court, 4200 C St SW, Cedar Rapids, IA 52404, 319-286-2300; Fax- 319-286-2301. Hours- 8AM-N, 12:30-4:30PM. www.iand.uscourts.gov

Counties/Note: Allamakee, Benton, Black Hawk, Bremer, Buchanan, Cedar, Chickasaw, Clayton, Delaware, Dubuque, Fayette, Floyd, Grundy, Hardin, Howard, Iowa, Jackson, Jones, Linn, Mitchell, Tama, Winneshiek.

Searches/Indexing: Include name only in search request. Results do not include SSN or DOB. Will not fax back documents. New cases are in the index immediately after filing date. Computer index back to 1995 maintained.

Search Access: Anything public record is released via phone, but only for one name per call. **Mail:** Search usually completed- 1-2 days. SASE required. **In person:** No self-serve copier.

Payment: Pay by money order, cashier's or attorney check. No personal checks. Attorney credit cards accepted. Payee: Clerk, US District Court. Copies printed of computer are $.10 each.

E-Services: PACER records go back to 11/1992. New records online after 1 day. ECF at https://ecf.iand.uscourts.gov. **Opinions Online:** www.iand.uscourts.gov. Click on Decisions/ Opinions and Jury Verdicts.

Sioux City (Western) Division Court Clerk, 320 6th St, Federal Bldg, Rm 301, Sioux City, IA 51101, 712-233-3900. Hours-8AM-4:30PM. www.iand.uscourts.gov

Counties/Note: Buena Vista, Butler, Calhoun, Carroll, Cerro Gordo, Cherokee, Clay, Crawford, Dickinson, Emmet, Franklin, Hamilton, Hancock, Humboldt, Ida, Kossuth, Lyon, Monona, O'Brien, Osceola, Palo Alto, Plymouth, Pocahontas, Sac, Sioux, Webster, Winnebago, Woodbury, Worth, Wright. This court also has records for the Ft. Dodge, Independence, and Mason City Divisions, but not Green, Boone or Marshall counties. Court is held occasionally held at Ft. Dodge, but records are at Sioux City.

Searches/Indexing: Include name only in search request. Results do not include SSN or DOB. Will not fax back documents. New cases are in the index immediately after filing date. Computer index back to 1995 maintained.

Search Access: Only docket info available by phone. **Mail:** Search usually completed- 2-3 days. Include SASE for return. **In person:** 1 public terminal available. No self-serve copier.

Payment: Pay by money order, cashier's or attorney check. No personal checks. Attorney credit cards accepted. Payee: Clerk, US District Court. Copies printed of computer are $.10 each.

E-Services: PACER records go back to 11/1992. New records online after 1 day. ECF at https://ecf.iand.uscourts.gov. **Opinions Online:** www.iand.uscourts.gov. Click on Decisions/ Opinions and Jury Verdicts.

US Bankruptcy Court Iowa Northern District

Cedar Rapids (Eastern) Division Court Clerk, PO Box 74890, Cedar Rapids, IA 52407-4890 (In person: 425 2nd St SE, 8th Fl, Cedar Rapids, IA 52401), 319-286-2200; Fax- 319-286-2280. 8AM-4:30PM. www.ianb.uscourts.gov

Counties/Note: Allamakee, Benton, Black Hawk, Bremer, Buchanan, Cedar, Chickasaw, Clayton, Delaware, Dubuque, Fayette, Floyd, Grundy, Howard, Iowa, Jackson, Jones, Linn, Mitchell, Tama, Winneshiek. Also holds records for Dubuque and Independence Divisions. You may also access electronic records of cases from the Western Division at Cedar Rapids.

Searches/Indexing: Include SSN in search request. Results include name and case number. Will fax back documents $.50 per page. New cases are in the index immediately after filing date. District-wide searches available here back to 1988.

Search Access: Minimal info released via phone; not all docket info is released. Voice Case Information Service available, call VCIS at 800-249-9859 or 319-286-2282. **Mail:** Search usually completed- 2 days. Include SASE for return. **Fax:** Fax search requests accepted. **In person:** Computer generated copies- $.10 each.

Payment: Pay by Visa/MC, money order, cashier's check, business check. No personal checks. Law firm checks accepted if in-state. Payee: Clerk, US Bankruptcy Court.

E-Services: Document images available. ECF electronic searching only, limited to electronically filed cases. ECF at https://ecf.ianb.uscourts.gov. **Opinions Online:** www.ianb.uscourts.gov/decframe.html. Also, search unclaimed funds database free at www.ianb.uscourts.gov/UnclaimedFunds/UnclaimedIndex.html. **Online Note:** Calendars free at www.ianb.uscourts.gov/. Access Judgment book at www.ianb.uscourts.gov/jbook/index.html.

Sioux City (Western) Division Court Clerk, PO Box 3857, Sioux City, IA 51102-3857 (In person: Federal Bldg, 320 6th St, Sioux City, IA 51101), 712-233-3939; Fax- 712-233-3942. Hours-8AM-4:30PM. www.ianb.uscourts.gov

Counties/Note: Buena Vista, Calhoun, Carroll, Cerro Gordo, Cherokee, Clay, Crawford, Dickinson, Emmet, Floyd, Franklin, Hamilton, Hancock, Hardin, Humboldt, Ida, Kossuth, Lyon, Mitchell, Monona, O'Brien, Osceola, Palo Alto, Plymouth, Pocahontas, Sac, Sioux, Webster, Winnebago, Woodbury, Worth, Wright. Also holds records for Mason City and Fort Dodge Divisions. Also, access electronic records of cases from the Eastern Div. at Sioux City.

Searches/Indexing: Include SSN in search request. Results include name and case number. Will fax back documents $.50 per page. New cases are in the index immediately after filing date. District-wide searches available here back to 1988.

Search Access: Minimal info released via phone; not all docket info is released. Voice Case Information Service available, call VCIS at 800-249-9859 or 319-362-9906. **Mail:** Search usually completed- 2 days. Include SASE for return. **Fax:** Fax search and case file requests accepted. **In person:** 2 public terminals available. Computer generated copies- $.10 each.

Payment: Pay by Visa/MC, money order, cashier's check, business check. No personal checks. Law firm checks accepted if in-state. Payee: Clerk, US Bankruptcy Court.

E-Services: Document images available. ECF electronic searching only, limited to electronically filed cases. ECF at https://ecf.ianb.uscourts.gov. **Opinions Online:** www.ianb.uscourts.gov/decframe.html. Also, search unclaimed funds database free at www.ianb.uscourts.gov/UnclaimedFunds/UnclaimedIndex.html. **Online Note:** Calendars free at www.ianb.uscourts.gov/. Access the Judgment book at www.ianb.uscourts.gov/jbook/index.html.

US District Court Iowa Southern District

Council Bluffs (Western) Division Court Clerk, PO Box 307, Council Bluffs, IA 51502 (In person: 8 S 6th St, Rm 313, Council Bluffs, IA 51502), 712-328-0283; Fax- 712-328-1241. Hours- 8AM-4:30PM M; 8AM-5PM T-F. www.iasd.uscourts.gov

Counties Audubon, Cass, Fremont, Harrison, Mills, Montgomery, Page, Pottawattamie, Shelby.

Searches/Indexing: Search request requires name only. Results do not include SSN or DOB. Will fax back documents for fee. New cases are in the index 1 day after filing date. Computer index back to 1990 maintained. Case files are all electronic; never purged.

Search Access: Docket info available via phone. **Mail:** Search usually completed- 2-3 days. SASE required. **Fax:** Fax search same as mail. **In person:** Self-serve copies $.50 each.

Payment: Pay by Visa/MC, money order, cashier's or personal check. Payee: Clerk, US District Court. Search fee is charged if the clerk's staff is required to spend more than 5 minutes searching.

E-Services: Document images available. PACER records go back to mid 1989. New records online after 1 day. ECF at https://ecf.iasd.uscourts.gov. **Opinions Online:** www.iasd.uscourts.gov/iasd/opinions.nsf/main/page. **Note:** Court calendars at www.iasd.uscourts.gov/iasd/judgecal.nsf/main/page.

Davenport (Eastern) Division Court Clerk, 131 E 4th St, Rm 150, Davenport, IA 52801, 563-884-7607; Fax- 563-884-7615. Hours- 8AM-5PM. www.iasd.uscourts.gov

Counties/Note: Henry, Johnson, Lee, Louisa, Muscatine, Scott, Van Buren, Washington.

Searches/Indexing: Search request requires name only. Results do not include SSN or DOB. Will fax back documents for fee. New cases are in the index 1 day after filing date. Both computer and card indexes maintained. Case files are all electronic; never purged.

Search Access: Docket info available via phone. **Mail:** Search usually completed- 5-10 days. SASE required. **Fax:** Fax search same as mail. **In person:** 2 public terminals available.

Payment: Pay by money order, cashier's or personal check. No credit cards accepted. Payee: Clerk, US District Court. Will bill fees.

E-Services: Document images available. PACER records go back to mid 1989. New records online after 1 day. ECF at https://ecf.iasd.uscourts.gov. **Opinions Online:** www.iasd.uscourts.gov/iasd/opinions.nsf/main/page. **Note:** Court calendars free at www.iasd.uscourts.gov/iasd/judgecal.nsf/main/page.

Des Moines (Central) Division Court Clerk, PO Box 9344, Des Moines, IA 50306-9344 (In person: 123 E. Walnut St, Rm 300, Des Moines, IA 50306), 515-284-6248; Fax- 515-284-6418. Hours-8AM-5PM. www.iasd.uscourts.gov

Counties/Note: Adair, Adams, Appanoose, Boone, Clarke, Clinton, Dallas, Davis, Decatur, Des Moines, Greene, Guthrie, Jasper, Jefferson, Keokuk, Lucas, Madison, Mahaska, Marion, Marshall, Monroe, Polk, Poweshiek, Ringgold, Story, Taylor, Union, Wapello, Warren, Wayne.

Searches/Indexing: Search request requires name only. Results do not include SSN or DOB. Will fax back documents for fee. New cases are in the index 1 day after filing date. Computer index back to 1990 maintained. Records stored by date filed and closed. Only the clerk can conduct criminal searches. Case files are all electronic; never purged.

Search Access: Docket info available via phone. **Mail:** Search usually completed- 1-2 days. SASE required. **Fax:** Fax search same as mail. **In person:** No self-serve copier.

Payment: Pay by Visa/MC, money order, cashier's or personal check, credit card. Payee: Clerk, US District Court. Court will bill.

E-Services: Document images available. PACER records go back to mid 1989. New records online after 1 day. ECF at https://ecf.iasd.uscourts.gov. **Opinions Online:** www.iasd.uscourts.gov/iasd/opinions.nsf/main/page. **Note:** Court calendars free at www.iasd.uscourts.gov/iasd/judgecal.nsf/main/page.

US Bankruptcy Court Iowa Southern District

Des Moines Div. Court Clerk, PO Box 9264, Des Moines, IA 50306-9264 (In person: 300 US Courthouse Annex, 110 E Court Ave, Des Moines, IA 50309), 515-284-6230; Fax- 515-284-6404. 8AM-5PM. www.iasb.uscourts.gov

Counties/Note: Adair, Adams, Appanoose, Audubon, Boone, Cass, Clarke, Clinton, Dallas, Davis, Decatur, Des Moines, Fremont, Greene, Guthrie, Harrison, Henry, Jasper, Jefferson, Johnson, Keokuk, Lee, Louisa, Lucas, Madison, Mahaska, Marion, Marshall, Mills, Monroe, Montgomery, Muscatine, Page, Polk, Pottawattamie, Poweshiek, Ringgold, Scott, Shelby, Story, Taylor, Union, Van Buren, Wapello, Warren, Washington, Wayne.

Searches/Indexing: Include SSN in search request. Results include dba, fka (alias) but no DOB or SSN. Will not fax back documents. New cases are in the index immediately after filing date.

Search Access: info released via phone is: name, case number, chapter date file, assets, attorney, attorney's telephone number, trustee, judge, status and discharge. info is available from June 1987. Voice Case Information Service available, call VCIS at 888-219-5534 or 515-284-6427. **Mail:** Search usually completed- 3-4 working days. Include SASE for return. **In person:** 2 public terminals available. No self-serve copier.

Payment: Pay by Visa/MC, money order, cashier's check, business check. No personal checks. Payee: US Bankruptcy Court.

E-Services: PACER-CM/ECF online system access only, $.08 per page. PACER records go back to 6/1987. New records online immediately. ECF at https://ecf.iasb.uscourts.gov. **Opinions:** www.iasb.uscourts.gov/homepage.asp?sPage=decisions. **Online Note:** Calendars available free at the homepage at www.iasb.uscourts.gov/.

Iowa County Courts

Court	Jurisdiction	No. of Courts	How Organized
District Courts*	General	100	8 Districts in 99 counties

* Profiled in this Sourcebook.

	CIVIL								
Court	Tort	Contract	Real Estate	Min. Claim	Max. Claim	Small Claims	Estate	Eviction	Domestic Relations
District Courts*	X	X	X	$0	No Max	$5000	X	X	X

	CRIMINAL				
Court	Felony	Misdemeanor	DWI/DUI	Preliminary Hearing	Juvenile
District Courts*	X	X	X	X	X

Administration

State Court Administrator, Judicial Branch Bldg, 1111 East Court Ave, Des Moines, IA, 50319; 515-281-5241 (Supreme Ct Clerk- 515-281-5911), Fax: 515-242-0014 (Supreme Ct Clerk Fax-515-242-6164). www.judicial.state.ia.us

Court Structure

The District Court is the court of general jurisdiction. Vital records (except divorces) were moved from the courts to the County Recorder's office in each county. Divorce records are still held by the County Clerk of Courts. Prepayment required unless noted.

Online Access

From the home page www.iowacourts.gov/ one may access Supreme Court and Appellate Court opinions. District criminal, civil (including divorce cases with financials/custody data), probate, and traffic information is available from all 99 Iowa counties at www.iowacourts.state.ia.us/ESAWebApp/SelectFrame. Name searches are available on either a statewide or specific county basis. Names of juveniles who are 10 to 17 will only appear for completed cases with a guilty verdict. There is no fee for basic information. A $25.00 per month pay system is offered for more detailed requests. While this is an excellent site with much information, there is one important consideration to keep in mind– although records are updated daily, the historical records offered are not from the same starting date.

Searching Tips, Fees, and Other Guidelines

In most courts, the copy fee is $.50 per page, the certification fee is $10.00 plus copy fee. Most courts do not do searches and recommend either in person searches or use of a record retriever. Most courts have a public access terminal for access to that court's records.

Adair County

5th District Court 400 Public Sq, #7, Greenfield, IA 50849; 641-743-2445; fax: 641-743-2974; 8AM-4:30PM. ***Felony, Misdemeanor, Civil, Eviction, Small Claims, Probate.***
www.iowacourts.gov/District_Courts/District_Five/

Civil Records: Access: In person, online. Both court and visitors may perform in person searches. No search fee. Required to search: name, years to search. Civil cases indexed by defendant, plaintiff; index in docket books from late 1800s, computerized since 11/1996. Civil PAT goes back to 1997. PAT results show middle initial, DOB. Search civil, probate, and appellate information at www.iowacourts.state.ia.us/ESAWebApp/SelectFrame. Basic Search is free. Advanced Search with more details and higher degree of currency is $25.00 per month.

Criminal Records: Access: In person, online. Visitors must perform in person searches themselves. Required to search: name, years to search, DOB, signed release; also helpful: SSN. Criminal docket on books from late 1800s, computerized since 11/1996. Criminal PAT goes back to same as civil. Online search of record index for criminal, traffic and appellate information same as described under Civil, including the free and subscription services. Online results show middle initial, DOB. Rarely the DOB or middle name may be missing from PAT or online results.

General Information: Online identifiers in results same as on public terminal. No juvenile, sealed, dissolution of marriage, mental health domestic abuse or deferred records released. Will fax documents $.50 per page. Court makes copy: $.50 per page, self serve same. Certification fee: $10.00. Payee: Clerk of Court. Personal checks and major credit cards accepted.

Adams County

5th District Court Courthouse, PO Box 484, Corning, IA 50841; 641-322-4711; fax: 641-322-4523; 8AM-4:30PM. ***Felony, Misdemeanor, Civil, Eviction, Small Claims, Probate.***
www.iowacourts.gov/District_Courts/District_Five/
Probate fax is same as main fax number.

Civil Records: Access: In person, online. Visitors must perform in person searches themselves. Required to search: name, years to search. Civil cases indexed by defendant, plaintiff; index in docket books from late 1800s, on computer back to 11/96. Public use terminal has civil records back to 1996. Search civil, probate, and appellate information at www.iowacourts.state.ia.us/ESAWebApp/SelectFrame. Basic Search is free. Advanced Search with more details and higher degree of currency is $25.00 per month.

Criminal Records: Access: In person, online. Visitors must perform in person searches themselves. Required to search: name, years to search, signed release. Criminal docket on books from late 1800s, on computer back to 11/96. Online search of record index for criminal, traffic and appellate information same as described under Civil, including the free and subscription services. Online results show middle initial, DOB. Rarely the DOB or middle name may be missing from PAT or online results.

General Information: Online identifiers in results same as on public terminal. No sealed, dissolution of marriage, mental health, sealed or expunged records released. Will fax documents $.50 per page. Court makes copy: $.50 per page. Certification fee: $10.00. Payee: Clerk of Court. Personal checks accepted. Visa/MC accepted.

Allamakee County

1st District Court Clerk of Court, PO Box 248, Waukon, IA 52172; 563-568-6351; fax: 563-568-6353; 8AM-4:30PM. ***Felony, Misdemeanor, Civil, Eviction, Small Claims, Probate.***
www.iowacourts.gov/District_Courts/District_One/

Civil Records: Access: In person, online. Visitors must perform in person searches themselves. Required to search: name, years to search. Civil cases indexed by defendant, plaintiff. All judgments on computer back to 4/1997; on index books back to 1880, probate back to 1852. Civil PAT goes back to 4/1997. PAT results show middle initial, DOB. Search civil, probate, and appellate information at www.iowacourts.state.ia.us/ESAWebApp/SelectFrame. Basic Search is free. Advanced Search with more details and higher degree of currency is $25.00 per month.

Criminal Records: Access: In person, online. Visitors must perform in person searches themselves. Required to search: name, years to search, signed release. Criminal docket on books from 1800s; on computer back to 4/1997. Criminal PAT goes back to same as civil. Online search of record index for criminal, traffic and appellate information same as described under Civil, including the free and subscription services. Online results show middle initial, DOB. Rarely the DOB or middle name may be missing from PAT or online results.

General Information: Online identifiers in results same as on public terminal. No juvenile, adoption, sealed, pending dissolution of marriage, mental health, domestic abuse or deferred records released. Will not fax documents. Court makes copy: $.50 per page, self serve same. Cert fee: $10.00. Payee: Clerk of Court. Personal checks accepted. Credit cards accepted for website fine payments only. Mail requests: SASE required for mail return of any copies.

Appanoose County

8th District Court PO Box 400, Centerville, IA 52544; 641-856-6101; fax: 641-856-2282; 8AM-4:30PM. ***Felony, Misdemeanor, Civil, Eviction, Small Claims, Probate.***
www.iowacourts.gov/District_Courts/District_Eight/

Civil Records: Access: In person, online. Visitors must perform in person searches themselves. Required to search: name, years to search. Civil cases indexed by defendant, plaintiff; index in docket books from 1847, on computer back to 2/96. Civil PAT goes back to 1996. Search civil, probate, and appellate information at www.iowacourts.state.ia.us/ESAWebApp/SelectFrame. Basic Search is free. Advanced Search with more details and higher degree of currency is $25.00 per month.

Criminal Records: Access: In person, online. Visitors must perform in person searches themselves. Required to search: name, years to search, signed release. Criminal docket on books from 1847, on computer back to 2/96. Criminal PAT goes back to same as civil. Online search of record index for criminal, traffic and appellate information same as described under Civil, including the free and subscription services. Online results show middle initial, DOB. Rarely the DOB or middle name may be missing from PAT or online results.

General Information: Online identifiers in results same as on public terminal. No juvenile, sealed, dissolution of marriage, mental health, domestic abuse or deferred records released. Will fax documents to local or toll-free number. Court makes copy: $.50 per page. Certification fee: $10.00. Payee: Clerk of Court. Personal checks accepted. Visa/MC accepted.

Audubon County

4th District Court 318 Leroy St, #6, Audubon, IA 50025; 712-563-4275; fax: 712-563-4276; 8AM-4:30PM. ***Felony, Misdemeanor, Civil, Eviction, Small Claims, Probate.***
www.iowacourts.gov/District_Courts/District_Four/

Civil Records: Access: In person, online. Visitors must perform in person searches themselves. Required to search: name, years to search; also helpful: address. Civil cases indexed by defendant, plaintiff; index in docket books from 1930s, computerized since 1996. Civil PAT goes back to 11/1996. PAT results show middle initial, DOB. Search civil, probate, and appellate information at www.iowacourts.state.ia.us/ESAWebApp/SelectFrame. Basic Search is free. Advanced Search with more details and higher degree of currency is $25.00 per month.

Criminal Records: Access: In person, online. Visitors must perform in person searches themselves. Required to search: name, years to search; also helpful: DOB, SSN, address. Criminal docket on books from late 1800s. Criminal PAT goes back to same as civil. Online search of record index for criminal, traffic and appellate information same as described under Civil, including the free and subscription services. Online results show middle initial, DOB. Rarely the DOB or middle name may be missing from PAT or online results.

General Information: Online identifiers in results same as on public terminal. No juvenile, sealed, dissolution of marriage, mental health, domestic abuse or deferred records released. Will fax documents $2.00 per fax. Court makes copy: $.50 per page. Certification fee: $10.00 per doc includes copies. Payee: Clerk of Court. Personal checks accepted; credit cards are not. Mail requests: SASE required for mail return of any copies.

Benton County

6th District Court PO Box 719, 111 E 4th St, 2nd Fl, Vinton, IA 52349; 319-472-2766; fax: 319-472-2747; 8AM-4:30PM. ***Felony, Misdemeanor, Civil, Eviction, Small Claims, Probate.***
www.iowacourts.gov/District_Courts/District_Six/

Civil Records: Access: In person, online. Visitors must perform in person searches themselves. Required to search: name, years to search. Civil cases indexed by defendant, plaintiff, on original record books from 1800s, index is on computer since 6/95. Civil PAT goes back to 1995. PAT civil results show middle initial. Identifiers do not appear on all records. Search civil, probate, and appellate information at www.iowacourts.state.ia.us/ESAWebApp/SelectFrame. Basic Search is free. Advanced Search with more details and higher degree of currency is $25.00 per month.

Criminal Records: Access: In person, online. Visitors must perform in person searches themselves. Required to search: name, years to search. Criminal records on original record books from 1800s, index is on computer since 6/95. Criminal PAT goes back to 1995. PAT results show middle initial, but DOBs appear on most records, not all. Online search of record index for criminal, traffic and appellate information same as described under Civil, including the free and subscription services. Online results show middle initial, DOB. Rarely the DOB or middle name may be missing from PAT or online results.

General Information: Online identifiers in results same as on public terminal. No juvenile, sealed, dissolution of marriage, mental health, domestic abuse or deferred records released. Will fax out documents for $1.00 per page. Court makes copy: $.50 per page. Certification fee: $10.00 per doc. Payee: Clerk of Court. Personal checks accepted. Visa/MC accepted.

Black Hawk County

1st District Court 316 E 5th St, Waterloo, IA 50703; 319-833-3331; probate: x 1856; fax: 319-833-3251; 8AM-4:30PM. ***Felony, Misdemeanor, Civil, Eviction, Small Claims, Probate.***
www.iowacourts.gov/District_Courts/District_One/

Civil Records: Access: In person, online. Visitors must perform in person searches themselves. Required to search: name, years to search. Civil cases indexed by defendant, plaintiff, on computer from 1992, docket books from early 1900s. Civil PAT goes back to 1992. Search civil, probate, and appellate information at www.iowacourts.state.ia.us/ESAWebApp/SelectFrame. Basic Search is free. Advanced Search with more details and higher degree of currency is $25.00 per month.

Criminal Records: Access: In person, online. Visitors must perform in person searches themselves. Required to search: name, years to search; also helpful: DOB, SSN. Criminal records computerized from 1992, docket books from early 1900s. Criminal PAT goes back to same as civil. Online search of record index for criminal, traffic and appellate information same as described under Civil, including the free and subscription services. Online results show middle initial, DOB. Rarely the DOB or middle name may be missing from PAT or online results.

General Information: Online identifiers in results same as on public terminal. No juvenile, sealed, dissolution of marriage, mental health, domestic abuse or deferred records released. Will not fax documents. Court makes copy: $.50 per page. Certification fee: $10.00. Payee: District Court. Personal checks and major credit cards accepted.

Boone County

2nd District Court 201 State St, Boone, IA 50036; 515-433-0561; fax: 515-433-0563; 8AM-4:30PM. ***Felony, Misdemeanor, Civil, Eviction, Small Claims, Probate.***
www.iowacourts.gov/District_Courts/District_Two/

Civil Records: Access: In person, online. Visitors must perform in person searches themselves. Required to search: name, years to search. Civil cases indexed by defendant, plaintiff; index in docket books from 1890s; computerized records go back to 1996. Civil PAT goes back to 1996. Search civil, probate, and appellate information at www.iowacourts.state.ia.us/ESAWebApp/SelectFrame. Basic Search is free. Advanced Search with more details and higher degree of currency is $25.00 per month.

Criminal Records: Access: In person, online. Visitors must perform in person searches themselves. Required to search: name, years to search, offense, date of offense. Criminal docket on books from 1890s; computerized records go back to 1996. Criminal PAT goes back to same as civil. Online search of record index for criminal, traffic and appellate information same as described under Civil, including the free and subscription services. Online results show middle initial, DOB. Rarely the DOB or middle name may be missing from PAT or online results.

General Information: Online identifiers in results same as on public terminal. No juvenile, sealed, dissolution of marriage, mental health, domestic abuse or deferred records released. Will fax documents $1.00 per page. Court makes copy: $.50 per page. Certification fee: $10.00. Payee: Clerk of Court. Personal checks accepted. Visa/MC accepted.

Bremer County

2nd District Court PO Box 328, Waverly, IA 50677; 319-352-5661; fax: 319-352-1054; 8AM-4:30PM. ***Felony, Misdemeanor, Civil, Eviction, Small Claims, Probate.***
www.iowacourts.gov/District_Courts/District_Two/

Civil Records: Access: In person, online. Visitors must perform in person searches themselves. Required to search: name, years to search. Civil cases indexed by defendant, plaintiff, on computer since 7/97; prior records on docket books from 1900's. Civil PAT goes back to 1998. PAT results show middle initial, DOB. Public Terminal also has add'l filings. Search civil, probate, and appellate information at www.iowacourts.state.ia.us/ESAWebApp/SelectFrame. Basic Search is free. Advanced Search with more details and higher degree of currency is $25.00 per month.

Criminal Records: Access: In person, online. Visitors must perform in person searches themselves. Required to search: name, years to search. Criminal records go back to 1900's; computerized records go back to 1996. Criminal PAT goes back to 1998. PAT results show middle initial, DOB. Public Terminal also has add'l filings. Online search of record index for criminal, traffic and appellate information same as described under Civil, including the free and subscription services. Online results show middle initial, DOB. Rarely the DOB or middle name may be missing from PAT or online results.

General Information: Online identifiers in results same as on public terminal. No juvenile, sealed, dissolution of marriage, mental health, domestic abuse or deferred records released. Will fax specific file for $1.00 per page. Court makes copy: $.50 per page, self serve same. Certification fee: $10.00. Payee: Clerk of Court. Personal checks and credit cards accepted. Mail requests: SASE required for mail return of any copies.

Buchanan County

1st District Court PO Box 259, Independence, IA 50644; 319-334-2196; fax: 319-334-7455; 8AM-4:30PM. ***Felony, Misdemeanor, Civil, Eviction, Small Claims, Probate.***
www.iowacourts.gov/District_Courts/District_One/
Probate is in a separate index at this address.

Civil Records: Access: In person, online. Both court and visitors may perform in person searches. No search fee. Required to search: name, years to search. Civil cases indexed by defendant, plaintiff; index in docket books from 1800s; computerized since 1996. Civil PAT goes back to 1985. PAT results show middle initial, DOB. Search civil, probate, and appellate information at www.iowacourts.state.ia.us/ESAWebApp/SelectFrame. Basic Search is free. Advanced Search with more details and higher degree of currency is $25.00 per month.

Criminal Records: Access: Mail, in person, online. Both court and visitors may perform in person searches. No search fee. Required to search: name, years to search. Criminal docket on books from 1800s; computerized since 1996. Mail turnaround time 2 days. Criminal PAT goes back to same as civil. Online search of record index for criminal, traffic and appellate information same as described under Civil, including the free and subscription

services. Online results show middle initial, DOB. Rarely the DOB or middle name may be missing from PAT or online results.
General Information: Online identifiers in results same as on public terminal. No juvenile, sealed, dissolution of marriage, mental health, domestic abuse or deferred records released. Will not fax documents. Court makes copy: $.50 per page. Self serve: none. Certification fee: $10.00 per document. Payee: Clerk of Court. Personal checks and credit cards accepted. Mail requests: SASE required.

Buena Vista County

3rd District Court PO Box 1186, Storm Lake, IA 50588; 712-749-2546; fax: 712-749-2700; 8AM-4:30PM. ***Felony, Misdemeanor, Civil, Eviction, Small Claims, Probate.***
www.iowacourts.gov/District_Courts/District_Three/
Civil Records: Access: In person, online. Visitors must perform in person searches themselves. Required to search: name, years to search. Civil cases indexed by defendant, plaintiff; index on cards from early 1900s; on computer back to 1996. Civil PAT goes back to 1995. PAT results show middle initial, DOB. Search civil, probate, and appellate information at www.iowacourts.state.ia.us/ESAWebApp/SelectFrame. Basic Search is free. Advanced Search with more details and higher degree of currency is $25.00 per month.
Criminal Records: Access: In person, online. Visitors must perform in person searches themselves. Required to search: name, years to search. Criminal records indexed on cards from early 1900s; on computer back to 1994. Criminal PAT goes back to same as civil. Online search of record index for criminal, traffic and appellate information same as described under Civil, including the free and subscription services. Online results show middle initial, DOB. Rarely the DOB or middle name may be missing from PAT or online results.
General Information: Online identifiers in results same as on public terminal. No juvenile, sealed, dissolution of marriage, mental health, domestic abuse or deferred records released. Will fax out documents no fee. Court makes copy: $.50 per page. Certification fee: $10.00 per document. Payee: Clerk of Court. Personal checks and credit cards accepted. Mail requests: SASE required for mail return of any copies.

Butler County

2nd District Court PO Box 307, Allison, IA 50602; 319-267-2487; fax: 319-267-2488; 8AM-4:30PM. ***Felony, Misdemeanor, Civil, Eviction, Small Claims, Probate.***
www.iowacourts.gov/District_Courts/District_Two/
Civil Records: Access: In person, online. Visitors must perform in person searches themselves. Required to search: name, years to search. Civil cases indexed by defendant, plaintiff; index in docket books from 1800s, on computer back to 4/97. Civil PAT goes back to 4/1997. PAT results show middle initial, DOB. Search civil, probate, and appellate information at www.iowacourts.state.ia.us/ESAWebApp/SelectFrame. Basic Search is free. Advanced Search with more details and higher degree of currency is $25.00 per month.
Criminal Records: Access: In person, online. Visitors must perform in person searches themselves. Required to search: name, years to search. Criminal docket on books from 1800s, on computer back to 4/97. Criminal PAT goes back to same as civil. Online search of record index for criminal, traffic and appellate information same as Civil, including the free and subscription services. Online results show middle initial, DOB. Rarely the DOB or middle name may be missing from PAT or online results.
General Information: Online identifiers in results same as on public terminal. No juvenile, sealed, dissolution of marriage, mental health, domestic abuse or deferred records released. Will fax documents $1.00 per page. Court makes copy: $.50 per page, self serve same. Certification fee: $10.00. Payee: Clerk of Court. Personal checks accepted. Visa/MC accepted.
Mail requests: SASE required for mail return of any copies.

Calhoun County

2nd District Court 416 Fourth St #5, Rockwell City, IA 50579; 712-297-8122; fax: 712-297-5082; 8AM-4:30PM. ***Felony, Misdemeanor, Civil, Eviction, Small Claims, Probate.***
www.iowacourts.gov/District_Courts/District_Two/
Civil Records: Access: In person, online. Visitors must perform in person searches themselves. Required to search: name, years to search. Civil cases indexed by defendant, plaintiff; index in docket books from 1880s, computerized since 7/97. Civil PAT goes back to 7/1997. PAT results show middle initial, DOB. Search civil, probate, and appellate information at www.iowacourts.state.ia.us/ESAWebApp/SelectFrame. Basic Search is free. Advanced Search with more details and higher degree of currency is $25.00 per month.
Criminal Records: Access: In person, online. Visitors must perform in person searches themselves. Required to search: name, years to search, DOB, signed release; also helpful: SSN. Criminal docket on books from 1880s, computerized since 7/97. Criminal PAT goes back to 7/1997. PAT results show middle initial, DOB. Online search of record index for criminal, traffic and appellate information same as described under Civil, including the free and subscription services. Online results show middle initial, DOB. Rarely the DOB or middle name may be missing from PAT or online results.
General Information: Online identifiers in results same as on public terminal. No juvenile, sealed, pending dissolution of marriage, mental health, domestic abuse or deferred records released. Will fax out specific case files for $1.00 per page. Court makes copy: $.50 per page. Certification fee: $10.00 per document. Payee: Clerk of the Court. Personal checks and credit cards accepted.

Carroll County

2nd District Court PO Box 867, Carroll, IA 51401; 712-792-4327; criminal fax: 712-792-4328; civil fax: same; 8AM-4:30PM. ***Felony, Misdemeanor, Civil, Eviction, Small Claims, Probate.***
www.iowacourts.gov/District_Courts/District_Two/
Probate fax is same as main fax number.
Civil Records: Access: In person, online. Visitors must perform in person searches themselves. Required to search: name, years to search. Civil cases indexed by defendant, plaintiff; index on docket books from 1800s; computerized records go back to 1993 on a limited basis. Everything from 9/1997 to present. Civil PAT goes back to 1997. Search civil, probate, and appellate information at www.iowacourts.state.ia.us/ESAWebApp/SelectFrame. Basic Search is free. Advanced Search with more details and higher degree of currency is $25.00 per month.
Criminal Records: Access: In person, online. Visitors must perform in person searches themselves. Required to search: name, years to search. Criminal records computerized from 6/1993, index books from 1800s. Criminal PAT goes back to same as civil. Online search of record index for criminal, traffic and appellate information same as described under Civil, including the free and subscription services. Online results show middle initial, DOB. Rarely the DOB or middle name may be missing from PAT or online results.
General Information: Online identifiers in results same as on public terminal. No juvenile, sealed, dissolution of marriage, mental health, domestic abuse or deferred records released. Will fax out specific case files for $1.00 per page. Court makes copy: $.50 per page. Self serve: $.25 per page. Certification fee: $10.00. Payee: Clerk of Court. Personal checks and major credit cards accepted. Mail requests: SASE required for mail return of any copies.

Cass County

4th District Court 5 W 7th St, Courthouse, Atlantic, IA 50022; 712-243-2105; fax: 712-243-4661; 8AM-4:30PM. ***Felony, Misdemeanor, Civil, Eviction, Small Claims, Probate.***
www.iowacourts.gov/District_Courts/District_Four/
Civil Records: Access: In person, online. Visitors must perform in person searches themselves. Required to search: name, years to search. Civil cases indexed by defendant, plaintiff; index in docket books from early 1900s; on computer back to 11/1996. Civil PAT goes back to 11/1996. Search civil, probate, and appellate information at www.iowacourts.state.ia.us/ESAWebApp/SelectFrame. Basic Search is free. Advanced Search with more details and higher degree of currency is $25.00 per month.
Criminal Records: Access: In person, online. Visitors must perform in person searches themselves. Required to search: name, years to search, signed release; also helpful: DOB, SSN. Criminal docket on books from 1880s; on computer back to 11/1996. Criminal PAT goes back to same as civil. Online search of record index for criminal, traffic and appellate information same as described under Civil, including the free and subscription services. Online results show middle initial, DOB. Rarely the DOB or middle name may be missing from PAT or online results.
General Information: Online identifiers in results same as on public terminal. No juvenile, sealed, dissolution of marriage, mental health, domestic abuse or deferred records released. Will fax documents to local or toll-free number. Court makes copy: $.50 per page. Certification fee: $10.00. Payee: Clerk of Court. Personal checks accepted. Visa/MC accepted.

Cedar County

7th District Court 400 Cedar St, Attn: Cedar County Clerk of Court, Tipton, IA 52772; 563-886-2101; fax: 563-886-3594; 8AM-4:30PM. ***Felony, Misdemeanor, Civil, Eviction, Small Claims, Probate.*** www.iowacourts.gov/District_Courts/District_Seven/index.asp
Magistrate Office phone number 563-886-6981.
Civil Records: Access: In person, online. Visitors must perform in person searches themselves. Required to search: name, years to search. Civil cases indexed by defendant, plaintiff, on computer since 10/1996; on microfiche and docket books from 1839. Civil PAT goes back to 10/1996. Search civil, probate, and appellate information at www.iowacourts.state.ia.us/ESAWebApp/SelectFrame. Basic Search is free. Advanced Search with more details and higher degree of currency is $25.00 per month.
Criminal Records: Access: In person, online. Visitors must perform in person searches themselves. Required to search: name, years to search; also helpful: DOB, SSN, signed release. Criminal records on computer since 7/1992; on microfiche and docket books from 1839. Criminal PAT goes back to 7/1992. Online search of record index for criminal, traffic and appellate information same as described under Civil, including the free and subscription services. Online results show middle initial, DOB. Rarely the DOB or middle name may be missing from PAT or online results.
General Information: Online identifiers in results same as on public terminal. No juvenile, sealed, dissolution of marriage, mental health, domestic abuse or deferred records released. Will not fax documents. Court makes copy: $.50 per page, self serve same. Certification fee: $10.00 per doc. Payee: Clerk of Court. Only cashiers checks and money orders accepted. No credit cards accepted.

Cerro Gordo County

2nd District Court 220 N Washington, Mason City, IA 50401; 641-424-6431; criminal phone: x3; civil phone: x4; probate phone: x7; fax: 641-424-6726; 8AM-4:30PM. ***Felony, Misdemeanor, Civil, Eviction, Small Claims, Probate.***
www.iowacourts.gov/District_Courts/District_Two/

Civil Records: Access: In person, online. Visitors must perform in person searches themselves. Required to search: name, years to search. Civil cases indexed by defendant, plaintiff, on computer since 1996: prior records on docket books from early 1900s. Civil PAT goes back to 1996. PAT results show name only. Search civil, probate, and appellate information at www.iowacourts.state.ia.us/ESAWebApp/SelectFrame. Basic Search is free. Advanced Search with more details and higher degree of currency is $25.00 per month.

Criminal Records: Access: In person, online. Visitors must perform in person searches themselves. Required to search: name, years to search; also helpful: DOB, SSN. Criminal records on computer since 4/95; prior records on index cards from 1977; prior to 1977 on docket books. Criminal PAT goes back to 1995. PAT results show name only. Online search of record index for criminal, traffic and appellate information same as described under Civil, including the free and subscription services. Online results show middle initial, DOB. Rarely the DOB or middle name may be missing from PAT or online results.

General Information: Online identifiers in results same as on public terminal. No Sealed, mental health, domestic abuse or deferred records that have been expunged released. Will fax documents $1.00 per page. Court makes copy: $.50 per page. Cert fee: $10.00 per doc. Payee: Clerk of Court. Personal checks and credit cards accepted.

Cherokee County

3rd District Court 520 W Main St, Cherokee, IA 51012; 712-225-6744; probate phone: 712-225-6744; fax: 712-225-6749; 8AM-4:30PM. ***Felony, Misdemeanor, Civil, Eviction, Small Claims, Probate.***

www.iowacourts.gov/District_Courts/District_Three/

Civil Records: Access: In person, online. Visitors must perform in person searches themselves. Required to search: name, years to search. Civil cases indexed by defendant, plaintiff; index in docket books from 1800s, indexed on computer since 1997. Civil PAT goes back to 1997. PAT results show middle initial, DOB. Search civil, probate, and appellate information at www.iowacourts.state.ia.us/ESAWebApp/SelectFrame. Basic Search is free. Advanced Search with more details and higher degree of currency is $25.00 per month.

Criminal Records: Access: In person, online. Visitors must perform in person searches themselves. Required to search: name, years to search. Criminal records index is computerized since 1997. Criminal PAT goes back to same as civil. Online search of record index for criminal, traffic and appellate information same as described under Civil, including the free and subscription services. Online results show middle initial, DOB. Rarely the DOB or middle name may be missing from PAT or online results.

General Information: Online identifiers in results same as on public terminal. No juvenile, sealed, dissolution of marriage, mental health, domestic abuse or deferred records released. Will fax documents to local or toll-free number. Court makes copy: $.50 per page. Certification fee: $10.00. Payee: Clerk of Court. Personal checks accepted. Visa/MC accepted.

Chickasaw County

1st District Court County Courthouse, 8 E Prospect, New Hampton, IA 50659; 641-394-2106; fax: 641-394-5106; 8AM-4:30PM. ***Felony, Misdemeanor, Civil, Eviction, Small Claims, Probate.***

www.iowacourts.gov/District_Courts/District_One/

Civil Records: Access: In person, online. Visitors must perform in person searches themselves. Required to search: name, years to search. Civil cases indexed by defendant, plaintiff; index in docket books from late 1800s; on computer back to 1996. Civil PAT goes back to 1996. Search civil, probate, and appellate information at www.iowacourts.state.ia.us/ESAWebApp/SelectFrame. Basic Search is free. Advanced Search with more details and higher degree of currency is $25.00 per month.

Criminal Records: Access: In person, online. Visitors must perform in person searches themselves. Required to search: name, years to search, signed release. Criminal docket on books from late 1800s; on computer back to 1996. Criminal PAT goes back to same as civil. Online search of record index for criminal, traffic and appellate information same as described under Civil, including the free and subscription services. Online results show middle initial, DOB. Rarely the DOB or middle name may be missing from PAT or online results.

General Information: Online identifiers in results same as on public terminal. No juvenile, sealed, dissolution of marriage, adoption, mental health, domestic abuse or deferred records released. Will fax documents for no fee. Court makes copy: $.50 per page, $.25 per page after 1st 10. Certification fee: $10.00 per doc. Payee: Clerk of District Court. Personal checks and credit cards accepted. Mail requests: SASE required for mail return of any copies.

Clarke County

5th District Court 100 S Main St, Clarke County Courthouse, Osceola, IA 50213; 641-342-6096; fax: 641-342-2463; 8AM-4:30PM. ***Felony, Misdemeanor, Civil, Eviction, Small Claims, Probate.***

www.iowacourts.gov/District_Courts/District_Five/

Civil Records: Access: In person, online. Both court and visitors may perform in person searches. No search fee. Required to search: name, years to search. Civil cases indexed by defendant, plaintiff; index in docket books from early 1900s, on computer back to 7/96. Civil PAT goes back to 1996. Search civil, probate, and appellate information at www.iowacourts.state.ia.us/ESAWebApp/SelectFrame. Basic Search is free. Advanced Search with more details and higher degree of currency is $25.00 per month.

Criminal Records: Access: In person, online. Both court and visitors may perform in person searches. No search fee. Required to search: name, years to search; also helpful: SSN. Criminal docket on books from early 1900s, on computer back to 7/96. Criminal PAT goes back to 1996. Online search of record index for criminal, traffic and appellate information same as described under Civil, including the free and subscription services. Online results show middle initial, DOB. Rarely the DOB or middle name may be missing from PAT or online results.

General Information: Online identifiers in results same as on public terminal. No juvenile, sealed, dissolution of marriage, mental health, domestic abuse or deferred records released. Will fax documents to local or toll-free number. Court makes copy: $.50 per page. Certification fee: $10.00. Payee: Clerk of Court. Personal checks accepted. Visa/MC accepted. Mail requests: SASE required for mail return of any copies.

Clay County

3rd District Court 215 W 4th St, Courthouse, Spencer, IA 51301; 712-262-4335; fax: 712-262-6042; 8AM-4:30PM. ***Felony, Misdemeanor, Civil, Eviction, Small Claims, Probate.***

www.iowacourts.gov/District_Courts/District_Three/

Civil Records: Access: In person, online. Visitors must perform in person searches themselves. Required to search: name, years to search. Civil cases indexed by defendant, plaintiff, on microfilm from to 1972 to 1995, docket books from 1800s, on computer back to 8/18/97. Civil PAT goes back to 8/18/97. PAT results show middle initial, DOB. Search civil, probate, and appellate information at www.iowacourts.state.ia.us/ESAWebApp/SelectFrame. Basic Search is free. Advanced Search with more details and higher degree of currency is $25.00 per month.

Criminal Records: Access: In person, online. Visitors must perform in person searches themselves. Required to search: name, years to search. Criminal records on microfilm from to 1972 to 1995, docket books from 1800s, on computer back to 1/7/97. Criminal PAT goes back to 1/7/1997. PAT results show middle initial, DOB. Online search of record index for criminal, traffic and appellate information same as described under Civil, including the free and subscription services. Online results show middle initial, DOB. Rarely the DOB or middle name may be missing from PAT or online results.

General Information: Online identifiers in results same as on public terminal. No juvenile, sealed, pending dissolution of marriage, mental health, sealed domestic abuse or deferred records released. Will fax documents. Court makes copy: $.50 per page, self serve same. Certification fee: $10.00. Payee: Clerk of Court. Personal checks accepted. Visa/MC accepted.

Clayton County

1st District Court PO Box 418, Clayton County Courthouse, Elkader, IA 52043; 563-245-2204; fax: 563-245-1175; 8AM-4:30PM. ***Felony, Misdemeanor, Civil, Eviction, Small Claims, Probate.***

www.iowacourts.gov/District_Courts/District_One/

Civil Records: Access: In person, online. Visitors must perform in person searches themselves. Required to search: name, years to search. Civil cases indexed by defendant, plaintiff; index in docket books from late 1880s, on computer back to 4/97. Civil PAT goes back to 1997. PAT results show middle initial, DOB. Search civil, probate, and appellate information at www.iowacourts.state.ia.us/ESAWebApp/SelectFrame. Basic Search is free. Advanced Search with more details and higher degree of currency is $25.00 per month.

Criminal Records: Access: In person, online. Visitors must perform in person searches themselves. Required to search: name, years to search. Criminal docket on books from late 1880s, on computer back to 4/97. Criminal PAT goes back to same as civil. Online search of record index for criminal, traffic and appellate information same as described under Civil, including the free and subscription services. Online results show middle initial, DOB. Rarely the DOB or middle name may be missing from PAT or online results.

General Information: Online identifiers in results same as on public terminal. No juvenile unless child is age 10 or older and offense is considered a public offense, sealed, dissolution of marriage, mental health, or deferred records released. Court makes copy: $.50 per page, self serve same. Certification fee: $10.00. Payee: Clerk of Court. Personal checks and credit cards accepted.

Clinton County

7th District Court PO Box 2957, 612 N 2nd St, Courthouse, Clinton, IA 52733; 563-243-6213; criminal phone: x4140; civil phone: x4236; probate phone: x4234; criminal fax: 563-243-3655; civil fax: n/a; 8AM-4:30PM. ***Felony, Misdemeanor, Civil, Eviction, Small Claims, Probate.***

www.iowacourts.gov/District_Courts/District_Seven/index.asp

Civil Records: Access: In person, online. Visitors must perform in person searches themselves. Required to search: name, years to search. Civil cases indexed by defendant. Civil records on computer since 1993, on docket books prior. Civil PAT goes back to 1993. PAT results show middle initial, DOB. Search civil, probate, and appellate information at www.iowacourts.state.ia.us/ESAWebApp/SelectFrame. Basic Search is free. Advanced Search with more details and higher degree of currency is $25.00 per month.

Criminal Records: Access: In person, online. Visitors must perform in person searches themselves. Required to search: name, years to search, DOB, signed release. Criminal records on computer since 1980, on docket books prior. Criminal PAT goes back to same as civil. Online search of record index for criminal, traffic and appellate information same as described under Civil, including the free and subscription services. Online results show middle initial, DOB. Rarely the DOB or middle name may be missing from PAT or online results.

General Information: Online identifiers in results same as on public terminal. No juvenile, adoption, sealed, dissolution of marriage before decree, mental health, domestic abuse or deferred records released.

Will not fax documents. Court makes copy: $.50 per page. Cert fee: $10.00 per document. Payee: Clerk of Court. Personal checks accepted. Visa/MC accepted.

Crawford County

3rd District Court 1202 Broadway, Ste 1P, Denison, IA 51442; 712-263-2242; fax: 712-263-5753; 8AM-4:30PM. ***Felony, Misdemeanor, Civil, Eviction, Small Claims, Probate.***

www.iowacourts.gov/District_Courts/District_Three/

Civil Records: Access: In person, online. Visitors must perform in person searches themselves. Required to search: name, years to search. Civil cases indexed by defendant, plaintiff, available since 1937, on docket books from 1869, on computer back to 9/2/97, Small Claims to 3/6/97, Probate to 5/8/97. Public use terminal available. PAT results show middle initial, DOB. Search civil, probate, and appellate information at www.iowacourts.state.ia.us/ESAWebApp/SelectFrame. Basic Search is free. Advanced Search with more details and higher degree of currency is $25.00 per month.

Criminal Records: Access: In person, online. Visitors must perform in person searches themselves. Required to search: name, years to search. Criminal records available since 1937, on docket books from 1869, on computer back to 10/96, Traffic to 1/16/96. Public use terminal available. PAT results show middle initial, DOB. Online search of record index for criminal, traffic and appellate information same as described under Civil, including the free and subscription services. Online results show middle initial, DOB. Rarely the DOB or middle name may be missing from PAT or online results.

General Information: Online identifiers in results same as on public terminal. Dissolution of marriage decrees, domestic abuse records, if not sealed, are released. Will fax documents if not to lengthy. Court makes copy: $.50 per page, self serve same. Certification fee: $10.00 per doc. Exemplification fee $20.00. Payee: Clerk of Court. Personal checks accepted. Visa/MC accepted.

Dallas County

5th District Court 801 Court St, Attn Court Clerk, Adel, IA 50003; criminal phone: 515-993-5816; civil phone: 515-993-6856; probate: 515-993-6856; criminal fax: 515-993-6991; civil fax: 515-993-4752; 8AM-4:30PM. ***Felony, Misdemeanor, Civil, Eviction, Small Claims, Probate.***

www.iowacourts.gov/District_Courts/District_Five/

Probate records are in a separate index. Probate fax-515-993-4752

Civil Records: Access: In person, online. Visitors must perform in person searches themselves. Required to search: name, years to search. Civil cases indexed by defendant, plaintiff; index in docket books from 1800s; computerized records since 1996. Civil PAT goes back to 1996. PAT results show middle initial, DOB. Search civil, probate, and appellate information at www.iowacourts.state.ia.us/ESAWebApp/SelectFrame. Basic Search is free. Advanced Search with more details and higher degree of currency is $25.00 per month.

Criminal Records: Access: In person, online. Visitors must perform in person searches themselves. Required to search: name, years to search. Criminal docket on books from 1800s; computerized records since 1996. Criminal PAT goes back to same as civil. Online search of record index for criminal, traffic and appellate information same as described under Civil, including free and subscription services. Online results show middle initial, DOB. Rarely the DOB or middle name may be missing from PAT or online results.

General Information: Online identifiers in results same as on public terminal. No juvenile, sealed, dissolution of marriage, mental health, domestic abuse or deferred records released. Will fax documents, no fee. Court makes copy: $.50 per page. Cert fee: $10.00. Payee: Clerk of Court. Personal checks and major credit cards accepted.

Davis County

8th District Court Davis County Courthouse, Bloomfield, IA 52537; 641-664-2011; fax: 641-664-2041; 8AM-4:30PM. ***Felony, Misdemeanor, Civil, Eviction, Small Claims, Probate.***

www.iowacourts.gov/District_Courts/District_Eight/

Civil Records: Access: In person, online. Visitors must perform in person searches themselves. Required to search: name, years to search. Civil cases indexed by defendant, plaintiff; index in docket books from late 1800s; computerized since 1997. Civil PAT goes back to 1997. PAT results show middle initial, DOB. Search civil, probate, and appellate information at www.iowacourts.state.ia.us/ESAWebApp/SelectFrame. Basic Search is free. Advanced Search with more details and higher degree of currency is $25.00 per month.

Criminal Records: Access: In person, online. Visitors must perform in person searches themselves. Required to search: name, years to search, DOB. Criminal docket on books from late 1800s; computerized since 1997. Criminal PAT goes back to same as civil. Online search of record index for criminal, traffic and appellate information same as described under Civil, including the free and subscription services. Online results show middle initial, DOB. Rarely the DOB or middle name may be missing from PAT or online results.

General Information: Online identifiers in results same as on public terminal. No juvenile, sealed, dissolution of marriage, mental health, domestic abuse or deferred records released. Will fax documents $5.00 minimum. Court makes copy: $.50 per page. Cert fee: $10.00 per document. Payee: Clerk of Court. Personal checks accepted. Visa/MC accepted.

Decatur County

5th District Court 207 N Main St, Leon, IA 50144; 641-446-4331; fax: 641-446-3759; 8AM-4:30PM. ***Felony, Misdemeanor, Civil, Eviction, Small Claims, Probate.***

www.iowacourts.gov/District_Courts/District_Five/

Probate fax is same as main fax number.

Civil Records: Access: In person, online. Visitors must perform in person searches themselves. Required to search: name, years to search. Civil cases indexed by defendant, plaintiff; index on docket books since 1880; on computer back to 1996. Note: Probate is a separate index at this same address. Civil PAT goes back to 1996. Search civil, probate, and appellate information at www.iowacourts.state.ia.us/ESAWebApp/SelectFrame. Basic Search is free. Advanced Search with more details and higher degree of currency is $25.00 per month.

Criminal Records: Access: In person, online. Visitors must perform in person searches themselves. Required to search: name, years to search, DOB or SSN. Criminal docket on books since 1880; on computer back to 1996. Criminal PAT goes back to same as civil. Online search of record index for criminal, traffic and appellate information same as described under Civil, including the free and subscription services. Online results show middle initial, DOB. Rarely the DOB or middle name may be missing from PAT or online results.

General Information: Online identifiers in results same as on public terminal. No juvenile, sealed, dissolution of marriage, mental health, domestic abuse or deferred records released. Will not fax documents. Court makes copy: $.50 per page. Certification fee: $10.00 per document. Payee: Clerk of Court. Personal checks and major credit cards accepted.

Delaware County

District Court Delaware County Courthouse, 301 E. Main St, PO Box 527, Manchester, IA 52057; 563-927-4942; fax: 563-927-3074; 8AM-4:30PM. ***Felony, Misdemeanor, Civil, Eviction, Small Claims, Probate.***

www.iowacourts.gov/District_Courts/District_One/

Civil Records: Access: In person, online. Visitors must perform in person searches themselves. Required to search: name, years to search. Civil cases indexed by defendant, plaintiff; index in docket books from late 1800s; on computer back to 1996. Civil PAT goes back to 1996. PAT results show middle initial, DOB. Search civil, probate, and appellate information at www.iowacourts.state.ia.us/ESAWebApp/SelectFrame. Basic Search is free. Advanced Search with more details and higher degree of currency is $25.00 per month.

Criminal Records: Access: In person, online. Visitors must perform in person searches themselves. Required to search: name, years to search. Criminal docket on books from late 1800s; on computer back to 1996. Criminal PAT goes back to same as civil. Online search of record index for criminal, traffic and appellate information same as described under Civil, including the free and subscription services. Online results show middle initial, DOB. Rarely the DOB or middle name may be missing from PAT or online results.

General Information: Online identifiers in results same as on public terminal. No juvenile, sealed, dissolution of marriage, mental health, domestic abuse or deferred records released. Will fax documents to local or toll-free number. Court makes copy: $.50 per page. Cert fee: $10.00 per doc. Payee: Clerk of Court. Personal checks accepted. Visa/MC accepted.

Des Moines County

8th District Court 513 Main St, PO Box 158, Burlington, IA 52601; 319-753-8262/8262; fax: 319-753-8253; 8AM-4:30PM. ***Felony, Misdemeanor, Civil, Eviction, Small Claims, Probate.***

www.iowacourts.gov/District_Courts/District_Eight/

City of Des Moines is not located here; see Polk county.

Civil Records: Access: In person, online. Visitors must perform in person searches themselves. Required to search: name, years to search; also helpful: address. Civil cases indexed by defendant, plaintiff, on computer from 7/1992, docket books prior. Civil PAT goes back to 1992. PAT results show middle initial, DOB. Search civil, probate, and appellate information at www.iowacourts.state.ia.us/ESAWebApp/SelectFrame. Basic Search is free. Advanced Search with more details and higher degree of currency is $25.00 per month.

Criminal Records: Access: In person, online. Visitors must perform in person searches themselves. Required to search: name, years to search, aliases; also helpful: DOB, SSN. Criminal records computerized from 7/1992, docket books prior. Criminal PAT goes back to same as civil. Online search of record index for criminal, traffic and appellate information same as described under Civil, including the free and subscription services. Online results show middle initial, DOB. Rarely the DOB or middle name may be missing from PAT or online results.

General Information: Online identifiers in results same as on public terminal. No juvenile, sealed, dissolution of marriage, mental health, domestic abuse or deferred records released. Will fax documents $1.00 per page, $5.00 minimum. Court makes copy: $.50 per page, self serve same. Certification fee: $10.00. Payee: Clerk of Court. Personal checks and credit cards accepted.

Dickinson County

3rd District Court 1802 Hill Ave, Ste 2506, Spirit Lake, IA 51360; 712-336-1138; fax: 712-336-4005; 8AM-4:30PM. ***Felony, Misdemeanor, Civil, Eviction, Small Claims, Probate.***

www.iowacourts.gov/District_Courts/District_Three/

Civil Records: Access: In person, online. Visitors must perform in person searches themselves. Required to search: name, years to search. Civil cases indexed by defendant, plaintiff. Early information on microfiche, docket books from 1800s; computerized back to 1992. Civil PAT goes back to 1995. PAT results show middle initial, DOB. Search civil, probate, appellate info at www.iowacourts.state.ia.us/ESAWebApp/SelectFrame. Basic Search is free. Advanced Search with more details and higher degree of currency is $25.00 per month.

Criminal Records: Access: In person, online. Visitors must perform in person searches

themselves. Required to search: name, years to search. Criminal records early information on microfiche, docket books from 1800s; computerized back to 1992. Criminal PAT goes back to 1993. PAT results show middle initial, DOB. Online search of record index for criminal, traffic and appellate information same as described under Civil, including the free and subscription services. Online results show middle initial, DOB. Rarely the DOB or middle name may be missing from PAT or online results.
General Information: Online identifiers in results same as on public terminal. No juvenile, sealed, dissolution of marriage, mental health, domestic abuse or deferred records released. Will fax documents $1.00 per page. Court makes copy: $.50 per page, self serve same. Certification fee: $10.00. Payee: Clerk of Court. Personal checks accepted. Visa/MC accepted for traffic and criminal only.

Dubuque County

1st District Court PO Box 1220, Dubuque, IA 52004-1220; 563-589-4418; 8AM-4:30PM. ***Felony, Misdemeanor, Civil, Eviction, Small Claims, Probate.***
www.iowacourts.gov/District_Courts/District_One/
Civil Records: Access: In person, online. Visitors must perform in person searches themselves. Required to search: name, years to search. Civil cases indexed by defendant, plaintiff, on computer since 7/1994, on docket books from 1900s. Civil PAT goes back to 1994. PAT results show middle initial, DOB. Search civil, probate, and appellate information at www.iowacourts.state.ia.us/ESAWebApp/SelectFrame. Basic Search is free. Advanced Search with more details is $25.00 per month.
Criminal Records: Access: In person, online. Visitors must perform in person searches themselves. Required to search: name, years to search; also helpful: DOB, SSN. Criminal records on computer since 7/1994, on docket books from 1900s. Criminal PAT goes back to same as civil. Online search of record index for criminal, traffic and appellate information same as described under Civil, including the free and subscription services. Online results show middle initial, DOB. Rarely the DOB or middle name may be missing from PAT or online results.
General Information: Online identifiers in results same as on public terminal. No juvenile, sealed, dissolution of marriage, mental health, domestic abuse or expunged records released. Will not fax documents. Court makes copy: $.50 per page, self serve same. Certification fee: $10.00 per document. Payee: Clerk of District Court. Local checks accepted. Visa/MC accepted.

Emmet County

3rd District Court Emmet County, 609 1st Ave N, Estherville, IA 51334; 712-362-3325; fax: 712-362-5329; 8AM-4:30PM. ***Felony, Misdemeanor, Civil, Eviction, Small Claims, Probate.***
www.iowacourts.gov/District_Courts/District_Three/
Civil Records: Access: In person, online. Visitors must perform in person searches themselves. Required to search: name, years to search. Civil cases indexed by defendant, plaintiff; index in docket books from 1900s, on computer back to 2/96. Civil PAT goes back to 1997. PAT results show name only. Search civil, probate, and appellate information at www.iowacourts.state.ia.us/ESAWebApp/SelectFrame. Basic Search is free. Advanced Search with more details and higher degree of currency is $25.00 per month.
Criminal Records: Access: In person, online. Visitors must perform in person searches themselves. Required to search: name, years to search. Criminal docket on books from 1900s, on computer back to 2/96. Criminal PAT goes back to same as civil. PAT results show name, but terminal results do not always include the DOB. Online search of record index for criminal, traffic and appellate information same as described under Civil, including the free and subscription services. Online results show middle initial, DOB. Rarely the DOB or middle name may be missing from PAT or online results.
General Information: Online identifiers in results same as on public terminal. No juvenile, sealed, dissolution of marriage, mental health, domestic abuse or deferred records released. Will fax documents to local or toll-free number. Court makes copy: $.50 per page, self serve same. Certification fee: $10.00 per doc. Payee: Clerk of Court. Personal checks and credit cards accepted.

Fayette County

Fayette County District Court PO Box 458, West Union, IA 52175; 563-422-5694; fax: 563-422-3137; 8AM-4:30PM. ***Felony, Misdemeanor, Civil, Eviction, Small Claims, Probate, Traffic.***
www.iowacourts.gov/District_Courts/District_One/
Civil Records: Access: In person, online. Visitors must perform in person searches themselves. Required to search: name, years to search. Civil cases indexed by defendant, plaintiff; index in docket books from 1900s, on computer back to 8/96. Civil PAT goes back to 1996. PAT results show middle initial, DOB. Search civil, probate, and appellate information at www.iowacourts.state.ia.us/ESAWebApp/SelectFrame. Basic Search is free. Advanced Search with more details and higher degree of currency is $25.00 per month.
Criminal Records: Access: In person, online. Visitors must perform in person searches themselves. Required to search: name, years to search. Criminal docket on books from 1900s; 1940-1960 on CD-ROM, on computer back to 8/96. Criminal PAT goes back to same as civil. Online search of record index for criminal, traffic and appellate information same as described under Civil, including the free and subscription services. Online results show middle initial, DOB. Rarely the DOB or middle name may be missing from PAT or online results.
General Information: Online identifiers in results same as on public terminal. No juvenile, sealed, dissolution of marriage, mental health, domestic abuse or deferred records released. Will not fax documents. Court makes copy: $.50 per page. Certification fee: $10.00 per doc. Payee: Clerk of Court. Personal checks accepted; credit cards are not.

Floyd County

2nd District Court 101 S Main St #306, Charles City, IA 50616; 641-228-7777; fax: 641-228-7772; 8AM-4:30PM. ***Felony, Misdemeanor, Civil, Eviction, Small Claims, Probate.***
www.iowacourts.gov/District_Courts/District_Two/
Civil Records: Access: In person, online. Visitors must perform in person searches themselves. Required to search: name, years to search. Civil cases indexed by defendant, plaintiff, in docket books, are computerized since 1996. Civil PAT goes back to 5/1996. PAT results show middle initial, DOB, SSN. Search civil, probate, and appellate information at www.iowacourts.state.ia.us/ESAWebApp/SelectFrame. Basic Search is free. Advanced Search with more details and higher degree of currency is $25.00 per month.
Criminal Records: Access: In person, online. Visitors must perform in person searches themselves. Required to search: name, years to search, DOB, signed release; also helpful: SSN. Criminal records in docket books, are computerized since 1996. Criminal PAT goes back to same as civil. PAT results show middle initial, DOB, SSN. Online search of record index for criminal, traffic and appellate information same as described under Civil, including the free and subscription services. Online results show middle initial, DOB. Rarely the DOB or middle name may be missing from PAT or online results.
General Information: Online identifiers in results same as on public terminal. No juvenile, sealed, dissolution of marriage, mental health, domestic abuse or deferred records released. Will not fax documents. Court makes copy: $.50 per page, self serve same. Certification fee: $10.00. Payee: Clerk of Court. Personal checks accepted. Visa/MC accepted. Mail requests: SASE required for mail return of any copies.

Franklin County

2nd Judicial District Court 12 1st Ave NW, PO Box 28, Hampton, IA 50441; 641-456-5626; fax: 641-456-5628; 8-4PM. ***Felony, Misdemeanor, Civil, Eviction, Small Claims, Probate.***
www.iowacourts.gov/District_Courts/District_Two/
Civil Records: Access: In person, online. Visitors must perform in person searches themselves. Required to search: name, years to search. Civil cases indexed by defendant, plaintiff, on microfiche and/or microfilm from 1860 to 1984, on docket books from 1984 to present. Note: The court will retrieve records if you have a case file number; get that number off the web search or PAT results. Civil PAT goes back to 4/1997. PAT results show middle initial, DOB. Search civil, probate, and appellate information back to 4/1997 at www.iowacourts.state.ia.us/ESAWebApp/SelectFrame. Basic Search is free. Advanced Search with more details and higher degree of currency is $25.00 per month.
Criminal Records: Access: In person, online. Visitors must perform in person searches themselves. Required to search: name, years to search. Criminal records on microfiche and/or microfilm from 1860 to 1984, on docket books from 1984 to present. Criminal PAT goes back to same as civil. Online search of record index for criminal, traffic and appellate information same as described under Civil, including the free and subscription services. The court will retrieve records if you have a case file number; get that number off the web search or PAT results. Online results show middle initial, DOB. Rarely the DOB or middle name may be missing from PAT or online results.
General Information: Online identifiers in results same as on public terminal. No juvenile, sealed, dissolution of marriage, mental health, domestic abuse or deferred records released. Will fax out specific case files for $1.00 per page. Court makes copy: $.50 per page. Cert fee: $10.00 per doc. Payee: Clerk of District Court. Personal checks, Visa/MC accepted.

Fremont County

4th District Court PO Box 549, Sidney, IA 51652; 712-374-2232; fax: 712-374-3330; 8AM-4:30PM. ***Felony, Misdemeanor, Civil, Eviction, Small Claims, Probate.***
www.iowacourts.gov/District_Courts/District_Four/
Civil Records: Access: In person, online. Visitors must perform in person searches themselves. Required to search: name. Civil cases indexed by defendant, plaintiff. Computerized from 11/96, civil records in docket books and microfiche from the 1930's. Civil PAT goes back to 11/1996. PAT results show middle initial, DOB. Search civil, probate, and appellate information at www.iowacourts.state.ia.us/ESAWebApp/SelectFrame. Basic Search is free. Advanced Search with more details and higher degree of currency is $25.00 per month.
Criminal Records: Access: In person, online. Visitors must perform in person searches themselves. Required to search: name. Computerized from 11/96, criminal records in docket books and microfiche from the 1930's. Criminal PAT goes back to same as civil. Online search of record index for criminal, traffic and appellate information same as described under Civil, including the free and subscription services. Online results show middle initial, DOB. Rarely the DOB or middle name may be missing from PAT or online results.
General Information: Online identifiers in results same as on public terminal. No juvenile, sealed, pending, dissolution of marriage, mental health, domestic abuse or expunged records released. Will not fax documents. Court makes copy: $.50 per page, self serve same. Cert fee: $10.00 per document. Payee: Clerk of Court. Personal checks accepted; credit cards are not. Mail requests: SASE required for mail return of any copies.

Greene County

2nd District Court Greene County Courthouse, 114 N Chestnut, Jefferson, IA 50129; 515-386-2516;

fax: 515-386-2321; 8-4:30. ***Felony, Misdemeanor, Civil, Eviction, Small Claims, Probate.***
www.iowacourts.gov/District_Courts/District_Two/
Probate fax is same as main fax number.
Civil Records: Access: In person, online. Visitors must perform in person searches themselves. Required to search: name, years to search. Civil cases indexed by defendant, plaintiff, on microfiche from 1981 back to establishment of court, docket books from 1800s, on computer back to 7/97. Civil PAT goes back to 7/1997. Search civil, probate, and appellate information at www.iowacourts.state.ia.us/ESAWebApp/SelectFrame. Basic Search is free. Advanced Search with more details and higher degree of currency is $25.00 per month.
Criminal Records: Access: In person, online. Visitors must perform in person searches themselves. Required to search: name, years to search. Criminal records on microfiche from 1981 back to establishment of court, docket books from 1800s, on computer back to 7/97. Criminal PAT goes back to same as civil. Online search of record index for criminal, traffic and appellate information same as described under Civil, including the free and subscription services. Online results show middle initial, DOB. Rarely the DOB or middle name may be missing from PAT or online results.
General Information: Online identifiers in results same as on public terminal. No juvenile, sealed, dissolution of marriage, mental health, domestic abuse or deferred records released. Will fax $1.00 per page. Court makes copy: $.50 per page, self serve same. Certification fee: $10.00. Payee: Clerk of Court. Personal checks accepted. Visa/MC accepted.

Grundy County

1st District Court Grundy County Courthouse, 706 G Ave, Grundy Center, IA 50638; 319-824-5229; fax: 319-824-3447; 8AM-4:30PM. ***Felony, Misdemeanor, Civil, Eviction, Small Claims, Probate.***
www.grundycounty.org/clerkofcourt/index.asp
Civil Records: Access: In person, online. Visitors must perform in person searches themselves. Required to search: name, years to search. Civil cases indexed by defendant, plaintiff; index in docket books from 1881, on computer back to 4/97. Civil PAT goes back to 1997. PAT results show middle initial, DOB. Search civil, probate, and appellate information at www.iowacourts.state.ia.us/ESAWebApp/SelectFrame. Records complete back to 4/97 Basic Search is free. Advanced Search with more details and higher degree of currency is $25.00 per month.
Criminal Records: Access: In person, online. Visitors must perform in person searches themselves. Required to search: name, years to search. Criminal docket on books from 1881, on computer back to 4/97. Criminal PAT goes back to same as civil. Online search of record index for criminal, traffic and appellate information same as described under Civil, including the free and subscription services. Online results show middle initial, DOB. Rarely the DOB or middle name may be missing from PAT or online results.
General Information: Online identifiers in results same as on public terminal. No pending, confidential, juvenile, sealed, dissolution of marriage, mental health, or expunged records released. Will not fax documents. Court makes copy: $.50 per page. Cert fee: $10.00. Payee: Clerk of Court. Personal checks and credit cards accepted. Mail requests: SASE required for mail return of any copies.

Guthrie County

5th District Court Courthouse, 200 N 5th St, Guthrie Center, IA 50115; 641-747-3415; fax: 641-747-2420; 8AM-4:30PM. ***Felony, Misdemeanor, Civil, Eviction, Small Claims, Probate.***
www.iowacourts.gov/District_Courts/District_Five/
Civil Records: Access: In person, online. Visitors must perform in person searches themselves. Required to search: name, case number, years to search. Civil cases indexed by defendant, plaintiff, on computer since 11/96; prior records on docket books from 1880s. Civil PAT goes back to 1996. Search civil, probate, and appellate information at www.iowacourts.state.ia.us/ESAWebApp/SelectFrame. Basic Search is free. Advanced Search with more details and higher degree of currency is $25.00 per month.
Criminal Records: Access: In person, online. Visitors must perform in person searches themselves. Required to search: name, case number, years to search. Criminal records on computer since 11/96; prior records on docket books from 1880s. Criminal PAT goes back to same as civil. Online search of record index for criminal, traffic and appellate information same as described under Civil, including the free and subscription services. Online results show middle initial, DOB. Rarely the DOB or middle name may be missing from PAT or online results.
General Information: Online identifiers in results same as on public terminal. No juvenile, sealed, dissolution of marriage, mental health, domestic abuse or deferred records released. Will fax documents with $.50 per page prepayment. Court makes copy: $.50 per page. Certification fee: $10.00. Payee: Clerk of Court. Personal checks accepted.

Hamilton County

2nd District Court Courthouse, PO Box 845, Webster City, IA 50595; 515-832-9600; fax: 515-832-9519; 8AM-4:30PM. ***Felony, Misdemeanor, Civil, Eviction, Small Claims, Probate.***
www.iowacourts.gov/District_Courts/District_Two/
Probate fax is same as main fax number.
Civil Records: Access: In person, online. Visitors must perform in person searches themselves. Required to search: name, years to search. Civil cases indexed by defendant, plaintiff, on microfiche from 1939, docket books from 1880s. Civil PAT goes back to 1996. PAT results show middle initial, DOB. Search civil, probate, and appellate information at www.iowacourts.state.ia.us/ESAWebApp/SelectFrame. Basic Search is free. Advanced Search with more details and higher degree of currency is $25.00 per month.
Criminal Records: Access: In person, online. Visitors must perform in person searches themselves. Required to search: name, years to search. Criminal records go back to 1996. Criminal PAT goes back to 1996. PAT results show middle initial, DOB. Online search of record index for criminal, traffic and appellate information same as described under Civil, including the free and subscription services. Online results show middle initial, DOB. Rarely the DOB or middle name may be missing from PAT or online results.
General Information: Online identifiers in results same as on public terminal. No juvenile, sealed, dissolution of marriage, mental health, domestic abuse records released. Will fax out specific case files for $1.00 per page. Court makes copy: $.50 per page. Certification fee: $10.00. Payee: Clerk of Court. Personal checks accepted. Visa/MC accepted.

Hancock County

2nd District Court 855 State St, Garner, IA 50438; 641-923-2532; fax: 641-923-3521; 9AM-3:30PM. ***Felony, Misdemeanor, Civil, Eviction, Small Claims, Probate.***
www.iowacourts.gov/District_Courts/District_Two/
Court will only retrieve cases where you provide case number info.
Civil Records: Access: In person, online. Visitors must perform in person searches themselves. Required to search: name, years to search. Civil cases indexed by defendant, plaintiff; index in docket books from 1880s; on computer since 1997. Civil PAT goes back to 1997. Search civil, probate, and appellate information at www.iowacourts.state.ia.us/ESAWebApp/SelectFrame. Basic Search is free. Advanced Search with more details and higher degree of currency is $25.00 per month.
Criminal Records: Access: In person, online. Visitors must perform in person searches themselves. Required to search: name, years to search. Criminal docket on books from 1880s; on computer since 1997. Criminal PAT goes back to same as civil. Online search of record index for criminal, traffic and appellate information same as described under Civil, including the free and subscription services. Online results show middle initial, DOB. Rarely the DOB or middle name may be missing from PAT or online results.
General Information: Online identifiers in results same as on public terminal. No juvenile, sealed, dissolution of marriage, mental health, domestic abuse or deferred records released. Will fax documents $1.00 per page. Court makes copy: $.50 per page. Cert fee: $10.00. Payee: Clerk of Court. Personal checks and credit cards accepted. Mail requests: SASE required for mail return of any copies.

Hardin County

2nd District Court PO Box 495, Courthouse, Eldora, IA 50627; 641-858-2328; fax: 641-858-2320; 8AM-4:30PM. ***Felony, Misdemeanor, Civil, Eviction, Small Claims, Probate.***
www.iowacourts.gov/District_Courts/District_Two/
Civil Records: Access: In person, online. Visitors must perform in person searches themselves. Required to search: name, years to search. Civil cases indexed by defendant, plaintiff; index in docket books from 1880s, on computer back to 2/96. Civil PAT goes back to 1996. PAT results show middle initial, DOB. Search civil, probate, and appellate information at www.iowacourts.state.ia.us/ESAWebApp/SelectFrame. Basic Search is free. Advanced Search with more details and higher degree of currency is $25.00 per month.
Criminal Records: Access: In person, online. Visitors must perform in person searches themselves. Required to search: name, years to search. Criminal docket on books from 1880s, on computer back to 2/96. Criminal PAT goes back to same as civil. Online search of record index for criminal, traffic and appellate information same as described under Civil, including the free and subscription services. Online results show middle initial, DOB. Rarely the DOB or middle name may be missing from PAT or online results.
General Information: Online identifiers in results same as on public terminal. No juvenile, sealed, dissolution of marriage, mental health, domestic abuse or deferred records released. Will fax documents to local or toll-free number. Court makes copy: $.50 per page. Cert fee: $10.00 per doc. Payee: Clerk of Court. Personal checks accepted; credit cards are not.

Harrison County

District Court Court House, Logan, IA 51546; 712-644-2665; fax: 712-644-2615; 8:30AM-4:30PM. ***Felony, Misdemeanor, Civil, Eviction, Small Claims, Probate.***
www.iowacourts.gov/District_Courts/District_Four/
Civil Records: Access: In person, online. Visitors must perform in person searches themselves. Required to search: name, years to search. Civil cases indexed by defendant, plaintiff, on computer since 11/96; prior on docket books since 1840s in Clerk's office. Civil PAT goes back to 11/1996. PAT results show middle initial, DOB. Search civil, probate, and appellate information at www.iowacourts.state.ia.us/ESAWebApp/SelectFrame. Basic Search is free. Advanced Search with more details and higher degree of currency is $25.00 per month.
Criminal Records: Access: In person, online. Visitors must perform in person searches themselves. Required to search: name, years to search. Criminal records on computer since 11/96, prior on docket books from 1840s in Clerk's office. Criminal PAT goes back to same as civil. Online search of record index for criminal, traffic and appellate information same as described under Civil, including the free and subscription services. Online results show middle initial, DOB. Rarely the DOB or middle name may be missing from PAT or online results.
General Information: Online identifiers in results same as on public terminal. No juvenile, sealed, confidential, dissolution of marriage, mental health, or deferred records released. Will fax documents $2.00 fee plus copy fees. Court makes copy: $.50 per page. Certification fee: $10.00 per document. Payee: Clerk of Court. Personal checks and credit cards accepted.

Henry County

8th District Court Clerk of Court, PO Box 176, Mount Pleasant, IA 52641; criminal phone: 319-385-3150/319-385-4203; civil phone: 319-385-2632; probate phone: 319-385-2632; fax: 319-385-4144; 8AM-4:30PM. ***Felony, Misdemeanor, Civil, Eviction, Small Claims, Probate.***
www.iowacourts.gov/District_Courts/District_Eight/
Probate is a separate index at this same address. Probate fax- 319-385-4144

Civil Records: Access: In person, online. Visitors must perform in person searches themselves. Required to search: name, years to search. Civil cases indexed by defendant, plaintiff; index in docket books from 1880s, on computer back to 10/1986. Civil PAT goes back to 1996. PAT results show middle initial, DOB, SSN. Search civil, probate, and appellate information at www.iowacourts.state.ia.us/ESAWebApp/SelectFrame. Basic Search is free. Advanced Search with more details and higher degree of currency is $25.00 per month.

Criminal Records: Access: In person, online. Visitors must perform in person searches themselves. Required to search: name, years to search, DOB; also helpful: address, SSN. Criminal docket on books from early 1900s, on computer back to 2/96. Criminal PAT goes back to 1996. PAT results show middle initial, DOB, SSN. Online search of record index for criminal, traffic and appellate information same as described under Civil, including the free and subscription services. Online results show middle initial, DOB. Rarely the DOB or middle name may be missing from PAT or online results.

General Information: Online identifiers in results same as on public terminal. No juvenile, sealed, dissolution of marriage, mental health, domestic abuse or deferred records released. Will fax documents $1.00 per page, $5.00 minimum. Court makes copy: $.50 per page, self serve same. Certification fee: $10.00 per certification. Payee: Clerk of Court. Personal checks and major credit cards accepted.

Howard County

1st District Court Courthouse, 137 N Elm St, Cresco, IA 52136; 563-547-2661; fax: 563-547-3605; 8AM-4:30PM. ***Felony, Misdemeanor, Civil, Eviction, Small Claims, Probate.***
www.iowacourts.gov/District_Courts/District_One/

Civil Records: Access: In person, online. Visitors must perform in person searches themselves. Required to search: name, years to search. Civil cases indexed by defendant, plaintiff; index in docket books from 1900s, on computer back to 4/97. Civil PAT goes back to 1997. Search civil, probate, and appellate information at www.iowacourts.state.ia.us/ESAWebApp/SelectFrame. Basic Search is free. Advanced Search with more details and higher degree of currency is $25.00 per month.

Criminal Records: Access: In person, online. Visitors must perform in person searches themselves. Required to search: name, years to search, DOB. Criminal docket on books from 1900s, on computer back to 4/97. Criminal PAT goes back to same as civil. Online search of record index for criminal, traffic and appellate information same as described under Civil, including the free and subscription services. Online results show middle initial, DOB. Rarely the DOB or middle name may be missing from PAT or online results.

General Information: Online identifiers in results same as on public terminal. No juvenile, sealed, pending, dissolution of marriage, mental health, domestic abuse or deferred records released. Will fax documents to local or toll-free number. Court makes copy: $.50 per page. Certification fee: $10.00 per doc. Payee: Clerk of Court. Personal checks and major credit cards accepted.

Humboldt County

2nd District Court PO Box 100, 203 Main St, Dakota City, IA 50529; 515-332-1806; fax: 515-332-7100; 8AM-4:30PM. ***Felony, Misdemeanor, Civil, Eviction, Small Claims, Probate.***
www.iowacourts.gov/District_Courts/District_Two/

Civil Records: Access: In person, online. Visitors must perform in person searches themselves. Required to search: name, years to search. Civil cases indexed by defendant, plaintiff; index in docket books from early 1900s; computerized records since 7/97. Civil PAT goes back to 7/1997. Search civil, probate, and appellate information at www.iowacourts.state.ia.us/ESAWebApp/SelectFrame. Basic Search is free. Advanced Search with more details and higher degree of currency is $25.00 per month.

Criminal Records: Access: In person, online. Visitors must perform in person searches themselves. Required to search: name, years to search. Criminal docket on books from early 1900s; computerized records since 7/97. Criminal PAT goes back to same as civil. Online search of record index for criminal, traffic and appellate information same as described under Civil, including the free and subscription services. Online results show middle initial, DOB. Rarely the DOB or middle name may be missing from PAT or online results.

General Information: Online identifiers in results same as on public terminal. No juvenile, sealed, dissolution of marriage, mental health, domestic abuse or deferred records released. Will fax documents to local or toll-free number. Court makes copy: $.50 per page. Certification fee: $10.00 per doc. Payee: Clerk of Court. Personal checks accepted. Visa/MC accepted.

Ida County

3rd District Court Courthouse, 401 Moorehead St, Ida Grove, IA 51445; 712-364-2628; fax: 712-364-2699; 8AM-4:30PM. ***Felony, Misdemeanor, Civil, Eviction, Small Claims, Probate.***
www.iowacourts.gov/District_Courts/District_Three/

Civil Records: Access: In person, online. Visitors must perform in person searches themselves. Required to search: name, years to search. Civil cases indexed by defendant, plaintiff; index in docket books from early 1800s, computerized since 7/97. Civil PAT goes back to 7/1997. Search civil, probate, and appellate information at www.iowacourts.state.ia.us/ESAWebApp/SelectFrame. Basic Search is free. Advanced Search with more details and higher degree of currency is $25.00 per month.

Criminal Records: Access: In person, online. Visitors must perform in person searches themselves. Required to search: name, years to search. Criminal docket on books from early 1800s, computerized since 7/97. Criminal PAT goes back to same as civil. Online search of record index for criminal, traffic and appellate information same as described under Civil, including the free and subscription services. Online results show middle initial, DOB. Rarely the DOB or middle name may be missing from PAT or online results.

General Information: Online identifiers in results same as on public terminal. No juvenile, sealed, dissolution of marriage, mental health, domestic abuse or deferred records released. Will fax document for $1.00 per page. Court makes copy: $.50 per page. Certification fee: $10.00 per doc. Payee: Clerk of Court. Personal checks accepted. Visa/MC accepted.

Iowa County

6th District Court PO Box 266, Marengo, IA 52301; 319-642-3914; 8AM-4:30PM. ***Felony, Misdemeanor, Civil, Eviction, Small Claims, Probate.***
www.iowacourts.gov/District_Courts/District_Six/

Civil Records: Access: In person, online. Visitors must perform in person searches themselves. Required to search: name, years to search. Civil cases indexed by defendant, plaintiff; index in docket books from early 1800s; on computer back to 2/97. Civil PAT goes back to 2/1997. PAT results show middle initial, DOB. Search civil, probate, and appellate information at www.iowacourts.state.ia.us/ESAWebApp/SelectFrame. Basic Search is free. Advanced Search with more details and higher degree of currency is $25.00 per month.

Criminal Records: Access: Mail, in person, online. Visitors must perform in person searches themselves. No search fee. Required to search: name, years to search. Criminal docket on books from early 1800s; on computer back to 2/1997. Mail turnaround is as time permits. Criminal PAT goes back to same as civil.PAT results show name, DOB. Search record index for criminal, traffic and appellate information online same as Civil, including the free and subscription services. Online results show middle initial, DOB. Rarely the DOB or middle name may be missing from PAT or online results.

General Information: Online identifiers in results same as on public terminal. No juvenile, sealed, dissolution of marriage, mental health, domestic abuse or deferred records released. Will fax documents to local or toll-free number. Court makes copy: $.50 per page. Certification fee: $10.00 per doc. Payee: Clerk of Court. Personal checks accepted. Visa/MC accepted.

Jackson County

7th District Court 201 W Platt, Maquoketa, IA 52060; 563-652-4946; criminal fax: 563-652-2708; civil fax: same; 8AM-4:30PM. ***Felony, Misdemeanor, Civil, Eviction, Small Claims, Probate.***
www.iowacourts.gov/District_Courts/District_Seven/index.asp
Probate is a separate index at this same address. Probate fax is same as main fax number.

Civil Records: Access: In person, online. Visitors must perform in person searches themselves. Required to search: name, years to search. Civil cases indexed by defendant, plaintiff, on computer since 1994, on docket books from 1900s. Civil PAT goes back to 1997. Search civil, probate, and appellate information at www.iowacourts.state.ia.us/ESAWebApp/SelectFrame. Basic Search is free. Advanced Search with more details and higher degree of currency is $25.00 per month.

Criminal Records: Access: In person, online. Visitors must perform in person searches themselves. Required to search: name, years to search, DOB; also helpful: SSN. Criminal records on computer since 1994, on docket books from 1900s. Criminal PAT goes back to 1993. Online search of record index for criminal, traffic and appellate information same as described under Civil, including the free and subscription services. Online results show middle initial, DOB. Rarely the DOB or middle name may be missing from PAT or online results.

General Information: Online identifiers in results same as on public terminal. No juvenile, sealed, dissolution of marriage, mental health, domestic abuse or deferred records released. Court makes copy: $.50 per page. Certification fee: $10.00 per document. Payee: Clerk of Court. Personal checks accepted.

Jasper County

5th District Court 101 1st St N, Rm 104, Newton, IA 50208; 641-792-3255; criminal phone: 641-792-9161; civil phone: 641-792-3255; probate phone: 641-792-3255; fax: 641-792-2818; 8AM-4:30PM. ***Felony, Misdemeanor, Civil, Eviction, Small Claims, Probate.***
www.iowacourts.gov/District_Courts/District_Five/
Probate is a separate index at this same address.

Civil Records: Access: In person, online. Visitors must perform in person searches themselves. Required to search: name, years to search. Civil cases indexed by defendant, plaintiff, on computer since 1994, docket books from 1900s. Note: Court will pull file if given case number. Civil PAT goes back to 1994. PAT results show middle initial, DOB. Search civil, probate, and appellate information at www.iowacourts.state.ia.us/ESAWebApp/SelectFrame. Basic Search is free. Advanced Search with more details and higher degree of currency is $25.00 per month.

Criminal Records: Access: In person, online. Visitors must perform in person searches themselves. Required to search: name, years to search. Criminal records on computer since 1994, docket books from 1900s. Note: Court will pull file if given case number. Criminal PAT goes back to same as civil. Online search of record index for

criminal, traffic and appellate information same as described under Civil, including the free and subscription services. Online results show middle initial, DOB. Rarely the DOB or middle name may be missing from PAT or online results.
General Information: Online identifiers in results same as on public terminal. No juvenile, sealed, dissolution of marriage, mental health, or deferred records released. Juvenile delinquency is public record, not CINA< FINA termination of adoption. Will not fax documents. Court makes copy: $.50 per page, self serve same. Certification fee: $10.00 per document includes copies. Payee: Clerk of Court. Personal checks and major credit cards accepted.

Jefferson County

8th District Court PO Box 984, 51 W Briggs, #5, Fairfield, IA 52556; 641-472-3454; fax: 641-472-9472; 8AM-4:30PM. ***Felony, Misdemeanor, Civil, Eviction, Small Claims, Probate.***
www.iowacourts.gov/District_Courts/District_Eight/
Civil Records: Access: In person, online. Visitors must perform in person searches themselves. Required to search: name, years to search. Civil cases indexed by defendant, plaintiff; index in docket books from 1800s, on computer back to 2/96. Civil PAT goes back to 1/1996. PAT results show middle initial, DOB. Search civil, probate, and appellate information at www.iowacourts.state.ia.us/ESAWebApp/SelectFrame. Basic Search is free. Advanced Search with more details and higher degree of currency is $25.00 per month.
Criminal Records: Access: In person, online. Visitors must perform in person searches themselves. Required to search: name, years to search, DOB. Criminal docket on books from 1800s, on computer back to 2/96. Criminal PAT goes back to same as civil. Online search of record index for criminal, traffic and appellate information same as described under Civil, including the free and subscription services. Online results show middle initial, DOB. Rarely the DOB or middle name may be missing from PAT or online results.
General Information: Online identifiers in results same as on public terminal. No juvenile, sealed, dissolution of marriage, mental health, domestic abuse or deferred records released. Will fax documents $1.00 per page. Court makes copy: $.50 per page. Certification fee: $10.00 per doc; exemplification-$20.00. Payee: Clerk of Court. Personal checks accepted. Visa/MC accepted.

Johnson County

6th District Court PO Box 2510, Iowa City, IA 52244; 319-356-6060; 8AM-4:30PM. ***Felony, Misdemeanor, Civil, Eviction, Small Claims, Probate.***
www.iowacourts.gov/District_Courts/District_Six/
Civil Records: Access: In person, online. Visitors must perform in person searches themselves. Required to search: name, years to search. Civil cases indexed by defendant, plaintiff; index on docket books and microfilm from 1880s, on computer back to 4/93. Civil PAT goes back to 1994. Search civil, probate, and appellate information at www.iowacourts.state.ia.us/ESAWebApp/SelectFrame. Basic Search is free. Advanced Search with more details and higher degree of currency is $25.00 per month.
Criminal Records: Access: In person, online. Visitors must perform in person searches themselves. Required to search: name, years to search; also helpful: address, DOB, SSN. Criminal docket on books and microfilm from 1880s, on computer back to 4/93. Criminal PAT goes back to same as civil. Online search of record index for criminal, traffic and appellate information same as described under Civil, including the free and subscription services. Online results show middle initial, DOB. Rarely the DOB or middle name may be missing from PAT or online results.
General Information: Online identifiers in results same as on public terminal. No juvenile, sealed, dissolution of marriage, mental health, domestic abuse or deferred records released. Will fax documents $5.00 plus $.50 per page fee. Court makes copy: $.50 per page, self serve same. Certification fee: $10.00. Payee: Clerk of Court. Personal checks and major credit cards accepted.

Jones County

6th District Court Attn: Clerk of District Court, PO Box 19, 500 W Main St, Anamosa, IA 52205; 319-462-4341; fax: 319-462-5827; 8AM-4:30PM. ***Felony, Misdemeanor, Civil, Eviction, Small Claims, Probate.***
www.iowacourts.gov/District_Courts/District_Six/
Civil Records: Access: In person, online. Visitors must perform in person searches themselves. Required to search: name, years to search. Civil cases indexed by defendant, plaintiff; index in docket books from mid 1800s; dockets on computer back to 6/1997. Civil PAT goes back to 1997. PAT results show middle initial, DOB. Search civil, probate, and appellate information at www.iowacourts.state.ia.us/ESAWebApp/SelectFrame. Basic Search is free. Advanced Search with more details and higher degree of currency is $25.00 per month.
Criminal Records: Access: In person, online. Visitors must perform in person searches themselves. Required to search: name, years to search. Criminal docket on books from early 1900s; dockets on computer back to 11/1996. Criminal PAT goes back to 1996. PAT results show middle initial, DOB. Online search of record index for criminal, traffic and appellate information same as described under Civil, including the free and subscription services. Online results show middle initial, DOB. Rarely the DOB or middle name may be missing from PAT or online results.
General Information: Online identifiers in results same as on public terminal. No juvenile, sealed, dissolution of marriage (prior to decree), mental health or deferred records released. Will fax documents to local or toll-free number. Court makes copy: $.50 per page. Cert fee: $10.00. Payee: Clerk of Court. Personal checks accepted. Visa/MC accepted.

Keokuk County

8th District Court 101 S Main, Courthouse, Sigourney, IA 52591; 641-622-2210; fax: 641-622-2171; 8AM-4:30PM. ***Felony, Misdemeanor, Civil, Eviction, Small Claims, Probate.***
www.iowacourts.gov/District_Courts/District_Eight/
Civil Records: Access: In person, online. Visitors must perform in person searches themselves. Required to search: name, years to search. Civil cases indexed by defendant, plaintiff; index in docket books from 1888; on computer back to 2/1997. Civil PAT goes back to 2/1997. PAT results show middle initial, DOB. Search civil, probate, and appellate information at www.iowacourts.state.ia.us/ESAWebApp/SelectFrame. Basic Search is free. Advanced Search with more details and higher degree of currency is $25.00 per month.
Criminal Records: Access: In person, online. Visitors must perform in person searches themselves. Required to search: name, years to search. Criminal docket on books from 1888; on computer back to 2/1997. Criminal PAT goes back to same as civil. Online search of record index for criminal, traffic and appellate information same as described under Civil, including the free and subscription services. Online results show middle initial, DOB. Rarely the DOB or middle name may be missing from PAT or online results.
General Information: Online identifiers in results same as on public terminal. No juvenile, sealed, dissolution of marriage, mental health, domestic abuse or deferred records released. Will fax documents $1.00 per page. Court makes copy: $.50 per page. Certification fee: $10.00 per doc. Payee: Clerk of Court. Personal checks accepted; credit cards are not.

Kossuth County

3rd District Court Kossuth County Courthouse, 114 W State St, Algona, IA 50511; 515-295-3240; fax: 515-295-2820; 8AM-4:30PM. ***Felony, Misdemeanor, Civil, Eviction, Small Claims, Probate.***
www.iowacourts.gov/District_Courts/District_Three/
Civil Records: Access: In person, online. Visitors must perform in person searches themselves. Required to search: name, years to search. Civil cases indexed by defendant, plaintiff, on computer since 9/97; prior records on dockets. Civil PAT goes back to 9/1997. PAT results show middle initial, DOB. Search civil, probate, and appellate information at www.iowacourts.state.ia.us/ESAWebApp/SelectFrame. Basic Search is free. Advanced Search with more details and higher degree of currency is $25.00 per month.
Criminal Records: Access: In person, online. Visitors must perform in person searches themselves. Required to search: name, years to search. Criminal records on computer since 9/97; prior records on dockets. Criminal PAT goes back to same as civil. Online search of record index for criminal, traffic and appellate information same as described under Civil, including the free and subscription services. Online results show middle initial, DOB. Rarely the DOB or middle name may be missing from PAT or online results.
General Information: Online identifiers in results same as on public terminal. No juvenile, sealed, dissolution of marriage, mental health, domestic abuse or deferred records released. Will fax documents $1.00 per page prepaid. Court makes copy: $.50 per page. Cert fee: $10.00 per doc. Payee: Clerk of Court. Personal checks accepted; credit cards are not.

Lee County

8th District Court PO Box 1443, 701 Ave F, Ft Madison, IA 52627; criminal phone: 319-372-4553; civil phone: 319-372-3523; fax: 319-372-2557; 8AM-4:30PM. ***Felony, Misdemeanor, Civil, Eviction, Small Claims, Probate.***
www.iowacourts.gov/District_Courts/District_Eight/
Civil Records: Access: In person, online. Visitors must perform in person searches themselves. Required to search: name, years to search. Civil cases indexed by defendant, plaintiff; index in docket books from early 1800s; computerized from 1996. Civil PAT goes back to 1996. Search civil, probate, and appellate information at www.iowacourts.state.ia.us/ESAWebApp/SelectFrame. Basic Search is free. Advanced Search with more details and higher degree of currency is $25.00 per month.
Criminal Records: Access: In person, online. Visitors must perform in person searches themselves. Required to search: name, years to search. Criminal docket on books from early 1800s; computerized from 1996. Criminal PAT goes back to same as civil. Online search of record index for criminal, traffic and appellate information same as described under Civil, including the free and subscription services. Online results show middle initial, DOB. Rarely the DOB or middle name may be missing from PAT or online results.
General Information: Online identifiers in results same as on public terminal. No sealed, pending dissolution of marriage, mental health, domestic abuse or deferred records released. Will fax documents $1.00 per page, $5.00 minimum. Court makes copy: $.50 per page, self serve same. Cert fee: $10.00. Payee: Clerk of Court. Personal checks accepted.

Linn County

District Court Linn County Courthouse, PO Box 1468, Cedar Rapids, IA 52406-1468; 319-398-3411; criminal phone: x1132; civil phone: x1212; fax: 319-398-3449; 8AM-4:30PM. ***Felony, Misdemeanor, Civil, Eviction, Small Claims, Probate.***
www.iowacourts.gov/District_Courts/District_Six/
Civil Records: Access: In person, online. Visitors must perform in person searches themselves. Required to search: name, years to search. Civil cases indexed by defendant, plaintiff, on computer from 1995, docket books from early 1900s. Civil PAT goes back to 1995. PAT results show middle initial, DOB. Search civil, probate, and appellate information at www.iowacourts.state.ia.us/ESAWebApp/SelectFrame. Basic Search is free. Advanced Search with more details and higher degree of currency is $25.00 per month.
Criminal Records: Access: In person, online. Visitors must perform in person searches themselves. Required to search: name, years to search; also helpful: address, DOB. Criminal records on computer since 1993. Criminal PAT goes back to

1993. PAT results show middle initial, DOB. Online search of record index for criminal, traffic and appellate information same as described under Civil, including the free and subscription services. Online results show middle initial, DOB. Rarely the DOB or middle name may be missing from PAT or online results.
General Information: Online identifiers in results same as on public terminal. No juvenile, sealed, pending dissolution of marriage, mental health, or deferred records released. Will fax documents $.50 per page. Court makes copy: $.50 per page. Certification fee: $10.00. Payee: Clerk of Court. Personal checks accepted; credit cards are not. Mail requests: SASE required for mail return of any copies.

Louisa County

8th District Court PO Box 268, 117 S Main, Wapello, IA 52653; 319-523-4541; fax: 319-523-4542; 8AM-4:30PM. ***Felony, Misdemeanor, Civil, Eviction, Small Claims, Probate.***
www.iowacourts.gov/District_Courts/District_Eight/
Civil Records: Access: In person, online. Both court and visitors may perform in person searches. No search fee. Required to search: name, years to search. Civil cases indexed by defendant, plaintiff; index in docket books from 1920s, on computer since 2/97. Civil PAT goes back to 2/1997. Results include name and case number. Search civil, probate, and appellate information at www.iowacourts.state.ia.us/ESAWebApp/SelectFrame. Basic Search is free. Advanced Search with more details and higher degree of currency is $25.00 per month.
Criminal Records: Access: In person, online. Both court and visitors may perform in person searches. No search fee. Required to search: name, years to search, DOB, signed release; also helpful: SSN. Criminal docket on books from 1920s, on computer since 2/97. Note: Results include name, address and case number. Criminal PAT goes back to same as civil. PAT results show name only. Online search of record index for criminal, traffic and appellate information same as described under Civil, including the free and subscription services. Online results show middle initial, DOB. Rarely the DOB or middle name may be missing from PAT or online results.
General Information: Online identifiers in results same as on public terminal. No juvenile, sealed, dissolution of marriage, mental health, domestic abuse or deferred records released. Will fax documents $1.00 per page, minimum fee- $5.00. Court makes copy: $.50 per page. Certification fee: $10.00. Payee: Clerk of Court. Personal checks and credit cards accepted.

Lucas County

5th District Court Courthouse, 916 Braden, Chariton, IA 50049; 641-774-4421; fax: 641-774-8669; 8AM-4:30PM. ***Felony, Misdemeanor, Civil, Eviction, Small Claims, Probate.***
www.iowacourts.gov/District_Courts/District_Five/
Search the online docket record by using a case number, a party's name, or an attorney's name at www.iowacourts.state.ia.us/ESAWebApp/SelectFrame. Probate fax is same as main fax number.
Civil Records: Access: In person, online. Visitors must perform in person searches themselves. Required to search: name, years to search. Civil cases indexed by defendant, plaintiff; index in docket books from 1880s; on computer back to 1997. Civil PAT goes back to 2/1997. Search civil, probate, and appellate information at www.iowacourts.state.ia.us/ESAWebApp/SelectFrame. Basic Search is free. Advanced Search with more details and higher degree of currency is $25.00 per month.
Criminal Records: Access: In person, online. Visitors must perform in person searches themselves. Required to search: name, years to search, signed release; also helpful: SSN. Criminal docket on books from 1880s; on computer back to 1997. Criminal PAT goes back to same as civil. Online search of record index for criminal, traffic and appellate information same as described under Civil, including the free and subscription services. Online results show middle initial, DOB. Rarely the DOB or middle name may be missing from PAT or online results.
General Information: Online identifiers in results same as on public terminal. No juvenile, adoption, sealed, dissolution of marriage, mental health, domestic abuse or deferred records released. Will fax out specific case files for $1.00 per page. Court makes copy: $.50 per page, self serve same. Certification fee: $10.00 per certification. Payee: Clerk of District Court. Personal checks and credit cards accepted.

Lyon County

3rd District Court 206 S. 2nd Ave, Courthouse, Rock Rapids, IA 51246; 712-472-2623; fax: 712-472-2422; 8AM-4:30PM. ***Felony, Misdemeanor, Civil, Eviction, Small Claims, Probate.***
www.iowacourts.gov/District_Courts/District_Three/
Civil Records: Access: In person, online. Visitors must perform in person searches themselves. Required to search: name, years to search. Civil cases indexed by defendant, plaintiff; index in docket books from 1880s, on computer back to 9/97. Civil PAT goes back to 1997. Search civil, probate, and appellate information at www.iowacourts.state.ia.us/ESAWebApp/SelectFrame. Basic Search is free. Advanced Search with more details and higher degree of currency is $25.00 per month.
Criminal Records: Access: In person, online. Visitors must perform in person searches themselves. Required to search: name, years to search. Criminal docket on books from 1880s, on computer back to 9/97. Criminal PAT goes back to same as civil. Online search of record index for criminal, traffic and appellate information same as described under Civil, including the free and subscription services. Online results show middle initial, DOB. Rarely the DOB or middle name may be missing from PAT or online results.
General Information: Online identifiers in results same as on public terminal. No juvenile, sealed, dissolution of marriage, mental health, domestic abuse or deferred records released. Will fax documents to local or toll-free number. Court makes copy: $.50 per page. Cert fee: $10.00 per doc. Payee: Clerk of Court. Personal checks and credit cards accepted.

Madison County

5th District Court PO Box 152, 112 N John Wayne Dr, Winterset, IA 50273; 515-462-4451; fax: 515-462-9825; 8AM-4:30PM. ***Felony, Misdemeanor, Civil, Eviction, Small Claims, Probate.***
www.iowacourts.gov/District_Courts/District_Five/
Civil Records: Access: In person, online. Visitors must perform in person searches themselves. Required to search: name, years to search. Civil cases indexed by plaintiff. Civil index in docket books from 1880s; computerized records since 1996. Civil PAT goes back to 1996. Results include name and case number. Search civil, probate, and appellate information at www.iowacourts.state.ia.us/ESAWebApp/SelectFrame. Basic Search is free. Advanced Search with more details and higher degree of currency is $25.00 per month.
Criminal Records: Access: In person, online. Visitors must perform in person searches themselves. Required to search: name, years to search; also helpful: DOB. Criminal docket on books from 1880s; computerized records since 1996. Misdemeanors from 1974 to present. Criminal PAT goes back to same as civil. Online search of record index for criminal, traffic and appellate information same as described under Civil, including the free and subscription services. Online results show middle initial, DOB. Rarely the DOB or middle name may be missing from PAT or online results.
General Information: Online identifiers in results same as on public terminal. No juvenile, sealed, dissolution of marriage, mental health, domestic abuse of deferred records released. Will not fax documents. Court makes copy: $.50 per page. Certification fee: $10.00 per doc. Payee: Clerk of Court. Personal checks accepted; credit cards are not.

Mahaska County

8th District Court Courthouse, 106 S 1st St, Oskaloosa, IA 52577; 641-673-7786; fax: 641-672-1256; 8AM-4:30PM. ***Felony, Misdemeanor, Civil, Eviction, Small Claims, Probate.***
www.iowacourts.gov/District_Courts/District_Eight/
Civil Records: Access: In person, online. Visitors must perform in person searches themselves. Required to search: name, years to search. Civil cases indexed by defendant, plaintiff; index in docket books from 1880s; computerized records since 1995. Civil PAT goes back to 1996. PAT results show middle initial, DOB. Results include case number. Search civil, probate, and appellate information at www.iowacourts.state.ia.us/ESAWebApp/SelectFrame. Basic Search is free. Advanced Search with more details and higher degree of currency is $25.00 per month.
Criminal Records: Access: In person, online. Visitors must perform in person searches themselves. Required to search: name, years to search. Criminal docket on books from 1880s; computerized records since 1995. Note: Results include case number. Criminal PAT goes back to 1995. PAT results show middle initial, DOB. Online search of record index for criminal, traffic and appellate information same as described under Civil, including the free and subscription services. Online results show middle initial, DOB. Rarely the DOB or middle name may be missing from PAT or online results.
General Information: Online identifiers in results same as on public terminal. No juvenile, sealed, dissolution of marriage, mental health, domestic abuse or deferred records released. Will fax documents $1.00 per page, $5.00 minimum. Court makes copy: $.50 per page. Docket copy $1.00 per page. Cert fee: $10.00. Payee: Clerk of Court. Personal checks accepted. Visa/MC accepted online only.

Marion County

5th District Court PO Box 497, Knoxville, IA 50138; 641-828-2207; fax: 641-828-7580; 8AM-4:30PM. ***Felony, Misdemeanor, Civil, Eviction, Small Claims, Probate.***
www.iowacourts.gov/District_Courts/District_Five/
Civil Records: Access: In person, online. Visitors must perform in person searches themselves. Required to search: name, years to search. Civil cases indexed by defendant, plaintiff, on computer since 1992, docket books from 1896. Civil PAT goes back to 1994. PAT results show middle initial, DOB. Search civil, probate, and appellate information at www.iowacourts.state.ia.us/ESAWebApp/SelectFrame. Basic Search is free. Advanced Search with more details and higher degree of currency is $25.00 per month.
Criminal Records: Access: In person, online. Visitors must perform in person searches themselves. Required to search: name, years to search. Criminal records on computer since 1992, docket books from 1896. Criminal PAT goes back to 1993. PAT results show middle initial, DOB. Online search of record index for criminal, traffic and appellate information same as described under Civil, including the free and subscription services. Online results show middle initial, DOB. Rarely the DOB or middle name may be missing from PAT or online results.
General Information: Online identifiers in results same as on public terminal. Delinquencies are public, not CINA, FINA, Termination or adoptions. No juvenile, sealed, dissolution of marriage, or mental health records released. Will not fax documents. Court makes copy: $.50 per page, self serve same. Certification fee: $10.00. Payee: Clerk of Court. Personal checks accepted. Visa/MC accepted. Mail requests: SASE required for mail return of any copies.

Marshall County

2nd District Court Courthouse, 17 E Main St, Marshalltown, IA 50158; 641-754-1603; fax: 641-754-1600; 8AM-4:30PM. ***Felony, Misdemeanor, Civil, Eviction, Small Claims, Probate.***
www.iowacourts.gov/District_Courts/District_Two/

Civil Records: Access: In person, online. Visitors must perform in person searches themselves. Required to search: name, years to search. Civil cases indexed by defendant, plaintiff, on computer since 6/1994, docket books from late 1800s. Civil PAT goes back to 1994. Search civil, probate, and appellate information at www.iowacourts.state.ia.us/ESAWebApp/SelectFrame. Basic Search is free. Advanced Search with more details and higher degree of currency is $25.00 per month.
Criminal Records: Access: In person, online. Visitors must perform in person searches themselves. Required to search: name, years to search; also helpful: DOB, SSN. Criminal records on computer since 8/1992, docket books from late 1800s. Criminal PAT goes back to 8/1992. Online search of record index for criminal, traffic and appellate information same as described under Civil, including the free and subscription services. Online results show middle initial, DOB. Rarely the DOB or middle name may be missing from PAT or online results.
General Information: Online identifiers in results same as on public terminal. No juvenile, sealed, pending dissolution of marriage, mental health, sealed domestic abuse and deferred records released. Will fax documents $1.00 per page. Court makes copy: $.50 per page, self serve same. Certification fee: $10.00 per document. Payee: Clerk of Court. Personal checks and major credit cards accepted.

Mills County

4th District Court 418 Sharp St, Courthouse, Glenwood, IA 51534; 712-527-4880; fax: 712-527-4936; 8AM-4:30PM. ***Felony, Misdemeanor, Civil, Eviction, Small Claims, Probate.***
www.iowacourts.gov/District_Courts/District_Four/
Civil Records: Access: In person, online. Visitors must perform in person searches themselves. Required to search: name, years to search. Civil cases indexed by defendant, plaintiff; index on docket books since 1880s; computerized records since 02/96. Civil PAT goes back to 2/1996. PAT results show middle initial, DOB. Search civil, probate, and appellate information at www.iowacourts.state.ia.us/ESAWebApp/SelectFrame. Basic Search is free. Advanced Search with more details and higher degree of currency is $25.00 per month.
Criminal Records: Access: In person, online. Visitors must perform in person searches themselves. Required to search: name, years to search. Criminal docket on books since 1880s; computerized records since 2/96. Criminal PAT goes back to same as civil. Online search of record index for criminal, traffic and appellate information same as described under Civil, including the free and subscription services. Online results show middle initial, DOB. Rarely the DOB or middle name may be missing from PAT or online results.
General Information: Online identifiers in results same as on public terminal. No juvenile, sealed, dissolution of marriage, mental health, domestic abuse or deferred records released. Will fax documents $2.00 per fax plus copy fees if necessary. Court makes copy: $.50 per page, self serve same. Certification fee: $10.00. Payee: Clerk of Court. Personal checks accepted; credit cards are not. Mail requests: SASE required for mail return of any copies.

Mitchell County

2nd District Court 508 State St, Osage, IA 50461; 641-732-3726; fax: 641-732-3728; 9AM-3:30PM. ***Felony, Misdemeanor, Civil, Eviction, Small Claims, Probate.***
www.iowacourts.gov/District_Courts/District_Two/
Probate fax is same as main fax number.
Civil Records: Access: In person, online. Visitors must perform in person searches themselves. Required to search: name, years to search. Civil cases indexed by defendant, plaintiff; index in docket books from 1880s, computerized since 1997. Civil PAT goes back to 4/1997. PAT results show middle initial, DOB. Search civil, probate, and appellate information at www.iowacourts.state.ia.us/ESAWebApp/SelectFrame. Basic Search is free. Advanced Search with more details and higher degree of currency is $25.00 per month.
Criminal Records: Access: In person, online. Visitors must perform in person searches themselves. Required to search: name, years to search, signed release. Criminal docket on books from 1880s, computerized since 1997. Criminal PAT goes back to same as civil. Online search of record index for criminal, traffic and appellate information same as described under Civil, including the free and subscription services. Online results show middle initial, DOB. Rarely the DOB or middle name may be missing from PAT or online results.
General Information: Online identifiers in results same as on public terminal. No juvenile, sealed, dissolution of marriage, mental health, domestic abuse or deferred records released. Will fax documents $1.00 per page. Court makes copy: $.50 per page, self serve same. Certification fee: $10.00 per document. Payee: Clerk of Court. Personal checks and major credit cards accepted. Mail requests: SASE required for mail return of any copies.

Monona County

3rd District Court 610 Iowa Ave, Attn: Clerk of Court, Onawa, IA 51040; 712-423-2491; fax: 712-423-2744; 8AM-4:30PM. ***Felony, Misdemeanor, Civil, Eviction, Small Claims, Probate.***
www.iowacourts.gov/District_Courts/District_Three/
Civil Records: Access: In person, online. Visitors must perform in person searches themselves. Required to search: name, years to search. Civil cases indexed by defendant, plaintiff, on computer since 7/97; prior records on microfiche and docket books from 1880s. Civil PAT goes back to 1997. Results include name and case number. Search civil, probate, and appellate information at www.iowacourts.state.ia.us/ESAWebApp/SelectFrame. Basic Search is free. Advanced Search with more details and higher degree of currency is $25.00 per month.
Criminal Records: Access: In person, online. Visitors must perform in person searches themselves. Required to search: name, years to search. Criminal records on computer since 7/97; prior records on microfiche and docket books from 1880s. Criminal PAT goes back to same as civil. PAT results show middle initial, DOB, SSN. Online search of record index for criminal, traffic and appellate information same as described under Civil, including the free and subscription services. Online results show middle initial, DOB. Rarely the DOB or middle name may be missing from PAT or online results.
General Information: Online identifiers in results same as on public terminal. No juvenile, sealed, dissolution of marriage, mental health, or deferred records released. Will not fax out documents. Court makes copy: $.50 per page. Certification fee: $10.00. Payee: Clerk of Court. Personal checks accepted. Visa/MC accepted.

Monroe County

8th District Court Courthouse, 10 Benton Ave E, Albia, IA 52531; 641-932-5212; fax: 641-932-3245; 8AM-4:30PM. ***Felony, Misdemeanor, Civil, Eviction, Small Claims, Probate.***
www.iowacourts.gov/District_Courts/District_Eight/
Civil Records: Access: In person, online. Visitors must perform in person searches themselves. Required to search: name, years to search. Civil cases indexed by defendant, plaintiff; index in docket books from late 1800s, on computer back to 2/97. Civil PAT goes back to 1997. Results include name and case number. Search civil, probate, and appellate information at www.iowacourts.state.ia.us/ESAWebApp/SelectFrame. Basic Search is free. Advanced Search with more details and higher degree of currency is $25.00 per month.
Criminal Records: Access: In person, online. Visitors must perform in person searches themselves. Required to search: name, years to search, DOB, signed release; also helpful: SSN. Criminal docket on books from late 1800s, on computer back to 2/97. Criminal PAT goes back to same as civil. Online search of record index for criminal, traffic and appellate information same as described under Civil, including the free and subscription services. Online results show middle initial, DOB. Rarely the DOB or middle name may be missing from PAT or online results.
General Information: Online identifiers in results same as on public terminal. No juvenile, sealed, dissolution of marriage, mental health, domestic abuse or deferred records released. Will fax documents $5.00 per page. Court makes copy: $.50 per page. Certification fee: $10.00 per doc. Payee: Clerk of Court. Personal checks accepted. Visa/MC accepted.

Montgomery County

4th District Court PO Box 469, Red Oak, IA 51566; 712-623-4986; fax: 712-623-4987; 8:30AM-4:30PM. ***Felony, Misdemeanor, Civil, Eviction, Small Claims, Probate.***
www.iowacourts.gov/District_Courts/District_Four/
Civil Records: Access: In person, online. Visitors must perform in person searches themselves. Required to search: name, years to search. Civil cases indexed by defendant, plaintiff; index in docket books from 1940, microfiche prior, on computer back to 6/96. Civil PAT goes back to 6/1996. Search civil, probate, and appellate information at www.iowacourts.state.ia.us/ESAWebApp/SelectFrame. Basic Search is free. Advanced Search with more details and higher degree of currency is $25.00 per month.
Criminal Records: Access: In person, online. Visitors must perform in person searches themselves. Required to search: name, years to search. Criminal docket on books from 1940, microfiche prior, on computer back to 6/96. Criminal PAT goes back to same as civil. Online search of record index for criminal, traffic and appellate information same as described under Civil, including the free and subscription services. Online results show middle initial, DOB. Rarely the DOB or middle name may be missing from PAT or online results.
General Information: Online identifiers in results same as on public terminal. No juvenile, sealed, dissolution of marriage, mental health or deferred records released. Will fax documents $2.00 fax fee plus $.50 per page. Court makes copy: $.50 per page. Certification fee: $10.00. Payee: Clerk of Court. Personal checks accepted; credit cards are not. Mail requests: SASE required for mail return of any copies.

Muscatine County

7th District Court 401 E Third St, Courthouse, Muscatine, IA 52761; 563-263-6511; criminal phone: 563-263-2447; fax: 563-264-3622; 8AM-4:30PM. ***Felony, Misdemeanor, Civil, Eviction, Small Claims, Probate.***
www.iowacourts.gov/District_Courts/District_Seven/index.asp
Civil Records: Access: In person, online. Visitors must perform in person searches themselves. Required to search: name, years to search. Civil cases indexed by defendant, plaintiff; index on docket books, on computer since 10/95. Civil PAT goes back to 10/1995. PAT results show middle initial, DOB. Search civil, probate, and appellate information at www.iowacourts.state.ia.us/ESAWebApp/SelectFrame. Basic Search is free. Advanced Search with more details and higher degree of currency is $25.00 per month.
Criminal Records: Access: In person, online. Visitors must perform in person searches themselves. Required to search: name, years to search. Criminal Records are computerized since 4/94. Criminal PAT goes back to 4/1994. PAT results show middle initial, DOB. Online search of record index for criminal, traffic and appellate information same as described under Civil, including the free and subscription services. Online results show middle initial, DOB. Rarely the DOB or middle name may be missing from PAT or online results.
General Information: Online identifiers in results same as on public terminal. No juvenile, sealed, dissolutions of marriage, mental health, domestic abuse or deferred records released. Will fax out documents for $.50 per page. Court makes copy: $.50

per page. Cert fee: $10.00. Payee: Clerk of Court. Personal checks accepted; credit cards are not. Mail requests: SASE required for mail return of any copies.

O'Brien County

3rd District Court Courthouse, Criminal Records, Primghar, IA 51245; 712-957-3255 or 5860; fax: 712-957-2965; 8AM-4:30PM. ***Felony, Misdemeanor, Civil, Eviction, Small Claims, Probate.***
www.iowacourts.gov/District_Courts/District_Three/

Civil Records: Access: In person, online. Both court and visitors may perform in person searches. Search fee: $10.00 per name. Required to search: name, years to search. Civil cases indexed by defendant, plaintiff; index in docket books from late 1800s; computerized since 1997. Civil PAT goes back to 9/1997. PAT results show middle initial, DOB. Search civil, probate, and appellate information at www.iowacourts.state.ia.us/ESAWebApp/SelectFrame. Basic Search is free. Advanced Search with more details and higher degree of currency is $25.00 per month.

Criminal Records: Access: In person, online. Both court and visitors may perform in person searches. Search fee: $10.00 per name. Required to search: name, years to search; also helpful: DOB, SSN. Criminal docket on books from late 1800s; computerized since 1997. Criminal PAT goes back to same as civil. Online search of record index for criminal, traffic and appellate information same as described under Civil, including the free and subscription services. Online results show middle initial, DOB. Rarely the DOB or middle name may be missing from PAT or online results.

General Information: Online identifiers in results same as on public terminal. No juvenile, sealed, dissolution of marriage, mental health records released. Will fax documents $1.00 1st page and $.50 per add'l page. Court makes copy: $.50 per page, self serve same. Certification fee: $10.00. Payee: Clerk of Court. Personal checks accepted. No credit cards accepted for copies.

Osceola County

3rd District Court Courthouse, Criminal Records, Sibley, IA 51249; 712-754-3595; fax: 712-754-2480; 8AM-4:30PM (may be closed Monday & Wednesday). ***Felony, Misdemeanor, Civil, Eviction, Small Claims, Probate.***
www.iowacourts.gov/District_Courts/District_Three/
Probate fax is same as main fax number.

Civil Records: Access: In person, online. Visitors must perform in person searches themselves. Required to search: name, years to search. Civil cases indexed by defendant, plaintiff; index in docket books from 1883; on computer back to 1997. Civil PAT goes back to 9/1997. Search civil, probate, and appellate information at www.iowacourts.state.ia.us/ESAWebApp/SelectFrame. Basic Search is free. Advanced Search with more details and higher degree of currency is $25.00 per month.

Criminal Records: Access: In person, online. Visitors must perform in person searches themselves. Required to search: name, years to search. Criminal docket on books from 1883; on computer back to 1997. Criminal PAT goes back to same as civil. Online search of record index for criminal, traffic and appellate information same as described under Civil, including the free and subscription services. Online results show middle initial, DOB. Rarely the DOB or middle name may be missing from PAT or online results.

General Information: Online identifiers in results same as on public terminal. No juvenile, sealed, dissolution of marriage, mental health, or deferred records released. Will fax documents $.50 per page. Court makes copy: $.50 per page, self serve same. Certification fee: $10.00. Payee: Clerk of Court. Personal checks and credit cards accepted.

Page County

4th District Court 112 E Main, Box 263, Clarinda, IA 51632; 712-542-3214; criminal fax: 712-542-5460; civil fax: same; 8AM-4:30PM. ***Felony, Misdemeanor, Civil, Eviction, Small Claims, Probate.***
www.iowacourts.gov/District_Courts/District_Four/
Probate records are a separate index at this address. Probate fax is same as main fax number.

Civil Records: Access: In person, online. Visitors must perform in person searches themselves. Required to search: name, years to search. Civil cases indexed by defendant, plaintiff; index on docket books; on computer back to 1995. Civil PAT goes back to 1995. Results include name and DOB. Search civil, probate, and appellate information at www.iowacourts.state.ia.us/ESAWebApp/SelectFrame. Basic Search is free. Advanced Search with more details and higher degree of currency is $25.00 per month.

Criminal Records: Access: In person, online. Visitors must perform in person searches themselves. Required to search: name, years to search, DOB, SSN, signed release. Criminal docket on books; on computer back to 1995. Criminal PAT goes back to same as civil. Results include name and DOB. Online search of record index for criminal, traffic and appellate information same as described under Civil, including the free and subscription services. Online results show middle initial, DOB. Rarely the DOB or middle name may be missing from PAT or online results.

General Information: Online identifiers in results same as on public terminal. No juvenile, sealed dissolution of marriage, mental health or deferred records released. Will fax out specific case files for $2.00. Court makes copy: $.50 per page, self serve same. Cert fee: $10.00. Payee: Clerk of District Court. Personal checks and credit cards accepted.

Palo Alto County

3rd District Court PO Box 387, Emmetsburg, IA 50536; 712-852-3603; fax: 712-852-2274; 8AM-4:30PM. ***Felony, Misdemeanor, Civil, Eviction, Small Claims, Probate.***
www.iowacourts.gov/District_Courts/District_Three/

Civil Records: Access: In person, online. Visitors must perform in person searches themselves. Required to search: name, years to search. Civil cases indexed by defendant, plaintiff; index in docket books from 1800s; computerized from 1997. Civil PAT goes back to 1997. Search civil, probate, and appellate information at www.iowacourts.state.ia.us/ESAWebApp/SelectFrame. Basic Search is free. Advanced Search with more details and higher degree of currency is $25.00 per month.

Criminal Records: Access: In person, online. Visitors must perform in person searches themselves. Required to search: name, years to search, DOB, SSN. Criminal docket on books from 1800s; computerized from 1997. Criminal PAT goes back to same as civil. Online search of record index for criminal, traffic and appellate information same as described under Civil, including the free and subscription services. Online results show middle initial, DOB. Rarely the DOB or middle name may be missing from PAT or online results.

General Information: Online identifiers in results same as on public terminal. No juvenile, sealed, dissolution of marriage, mental health, domestic abuse or deferred records released. Will not fax documents. Court makes copy: $.50 per page. Certification fee: $10.00 per doc. Payee: Clerk of Court. Personal checks accepted; credit cards are not. Mail requests: SASE required for mail return of any copies.

Plymouth County

3rd Judicial District Plymouth County Clerk of District Court, 215 Fourth Ave SE, Courthouse, Le Mars, IA 51031; 712-546-4215; fax: 712-546-8430; 8AM-4:30PM. ***Felony, Misdemeanor, Civil, Eviction, Small Claims, Probate.***
www.iowacourts.gov/District_Courts/District_Three/

Civil Records: Access: In person, online. Visitors must perform in person searches themselves. Required to search: name, years to search. Civil cases indexed by defendant, plaintiff; index in docket books from 1895 to 11/92, docket cards from 11/92 to 7/97, on computer back to 7/97. Civil PAT goes back to 1997. Search civil, probate, and appellate information at www.iowacourts.state.ia.us/ESAWebApp/SelectFrame. Basic Search is free. Advanced Search with more details and higher degree of currency is $25.00 per month.

Criminal Records: Access: In person, online. Visitors must perform in person searches themselves. Required to search: name, years to search. Criminal docket on books from 1895 to 11/92, docket cards from 11/92 to 7/97, on computer back to 7/97. Criminal PAT goes back to same as civil. Online search of record index for criminal, traffic and appellate information same as described under Civil, including the free and subscription services. Online results show middle initial, DOB. Rarely the DOB or middle name may be missing from PAT or online results.

General Information: Online identifiers in results same as on public terminal. No juvenile, (sealed, dissolution of marriage), mental health, domestic abuse or deferred records released. Will fax out specific case files for $.50 per page. Court makes copy: $.50 per page. Certification fee: $10.00. Payee: Clerk of Court. Personal checks and credit cards accepted. Mail requests: SASE required for mail return of any copies.

Pocahontas County

2nd District Court Courthouse, 99 Court Square, #6, Pocahontas, IA 50574; 712-335-4208; fax: 712-335-5045; 9AM-3:30PM (public hours). ***Felony, Misdemeanor, Civil, Eviction, Small Claims, Probate.***
www.iowacourts.gov/District_Courts/District_Two/

Civil Records: Access: In person, online. Visitors must perform in person searches themselves. Required to search: name, years to search. Civil cases indexed by defendant, plaintiff; index in docket books from 1880s, on computer back to 7/97. Civil PAT goes back to 7/1997. Results include financial information. Search civil, probate, and appellate information at www.iowacourts.state.ia.us/ESAWebApp/SelectFrame. Basic Search is free. Advanced Search with more details and higher degree of currency is $25.00 per month.

Criminal Records: Access: In person, online. Visitors must perform in person searches themselves. Required to search: name, years to search, DOB. Criminal docket on books from 1880s, on computer back to 7/97. Criminal PAT goes back to same as civil. Results include financial information. Online search of record index for criminal, traffic and appellate information same as described under Civil, including the free and subscription services. Online results show middle initial, DOB. Rarely the DOB or middle name may be missing from PAT or online results.

General Information: Online identifiers in results same as on public terminal. No juvenile, sealed, dissolution of marriage, mental health, domestic abuse or deferred records released. Will fax documents $1.00 per page. Court makes copy: $.50 per page. Certification fee: $10.00; exemplification fee $20.00. Payee: Clerk of Court. Personal checks accepted; credit cards are not.

Polk County

District Court 500 Mulberry St, #212, Des Moines, IA 50309; 515-286-3772; criminal fax: 515-323-5250; civil fax: 515-286-3172; 8AM-4:30PM. ***Felony, Misdemeanor, Civil, Eviction, Small Claims, Probate.***
www.iowacourts.gov/District_Courts/District_Five/

Civil Records: Access: In person, online. Visitors must perform in person searches themselves. Required to search: name, years to search; also helpful: address. Civil cases indexed by defendant, plaintiff, on computer back to 1990; docket books and index cards from 1880s and microfilm prior to 1970. Note: Mail search requests are not recommended. Civil PAT goes back to 1991. Results include name and case number. Search civil, probate, and appellate information at www.iowacourts.state.ia.us/ESAWebApp/SelectFrame. Basic Search is free. Advanced Search with more details and higher degree of currency is $25.00 per month.

Criminal Records: Access: In person, online. Visitors must perform in person searches themselves. Required to search: name, years to search, address, DOB; also helpful: SSN. Criminal

records computerized from 1990; docket books and index cards from 1880s and microfilm prior to 1970. Note: Mail search requests are not recommended. Criminal PAT goes back to same as civil. Online search of record index for criminal, traffic and appellate information same as described under Civil, including the free and subscription services. Online results show middle initial, DOB. Rarely the DOB or middle name may be missing from PAT or online results.
General Information: Online identifiers in results same as on public terminal. No juvenile, child, sealed, pending dissolution of marriage, mental health, expunged, domestic abuse or deferred records released. Will fax documents $1.00 per page. Court makes copy: $.50 per page. Certification fee: $10.00 per seal. Payee: Clerk of Court. Personal checks and major credit cards accepted.

Pottawattamie County

4th District Court 227 S 6th St, Council Bluffs, IA 51501; 712-328-5604; fax: 712-328-4810; 8AM-4:30PM. ***Felony, Misdemeanor, Civil, Eviction, Small Claims, Probate.***
www.iowacourts.gov/District_Courts/District_Four/
Civil Records: Access: In person, mail, online. Visitors must perform in person searches themselves. No search fee. Required to search: name, years to search. Civil cases indexed by defendant, plaintiff, on computer from 1978, index books prior. Records are being microfilmed as load permits. Public use terminal available, records go back to 1995. Search civil, probate, and appellate information at www.iowacourts.state.ia.us/ESAWebApp/SelectFrame. Basic Search is free. Advanced Search with more details and higher degree of currency is $25.00 per month.
Criminal Records: Access: In person, online. Visitors must perform in person searches themselves. Required to search: name, years to search. Criminal records computerized from 1978, index books prior. Records are being microfilmed as load permits. Public use terminal available, crim records go back to 1992. Online search of record index for criminal, traffic and appellate information same as described under Civil, including the free and subscription services. Online results show middle initial, DOB. Rarely the DOB or middle name may be missing from PAT or online results.
General Information: Online identifiers in results same as on public terminal. No juvenile, sealed, pending dissolution of marriage, mental health, domestic abuse or deferred records released. Will fax documents $2.00. Court makes copy: $.50 per page. Certification fee: $10.00. Payee: Clerk of Court. Personal checks accepted; credit cards are not. Mail requests: SASE required for mail return of any copies.

Poweshiek County

8th District Court PO Box 218, Montezuma, IA 50171; 641-623-5644; fax: 641-623-5320; 8AM-4:30PM. ***Felony, Misdemeanor, Civil, Eviction, Small Claims, Probate.***
www.iowacourts.gov/District_Courts/District_Eight/
Civil Records: Access: In person, online. Visitors must perform in person searches themselves. Required to search: name, years to search. Civil cases indexed by defendant, plaintiff; index on cards from 1980, docket books from early 1900s, computer since 7/95. Civil PAT goes back to 7/1995. PAT results show middle initial, DOB. Search civil, probate, and appellate information at www.iowacourts.state.ia.us/ESAWebApp/SelectFrame. Basic Search is free. Advanced Search with more details and higher degree of currency is $25.00 per month.
Criminal Records: Access: In person, online. Visitors must perform in person searches themselves. Required to search: name, years to search. Criminal records on computer since 1995, index cards since 1980, docket books from early 1900s. Criminal PAT goes back to same as civil. Online search of record index for criminal, traffic and appellate information same as described under Civil, including the free and subscription services. Rarely the DOB or middle name may be missing from PAT or online results.
General Information: Online identifiers in results same as on public terminal. No juvenile, sealed, pending, dissolution of marriage, mental health, domestic abuse or deferred records released. Will fax documents $1.00 per page if prepaid. Court makes copy: $.50 per page. Certification fee: $10.00. Payee: Clerk of Court. Personal checks accepted; credit cards are not.

Ringgold County

5th District Court PO Box 523, 109 W Madison, Mount Ayr, IA 50854; 641-464-3234; fax: 641-464-2478; 8AM-4:30PM. ***Felony, Misdemeanor, Civil, Small Claims, Probate, Traffic.***
www.iowacourts.gov/District_Courts/District_Five/
Civil Records: Access: In person, online. Visitors must perform in person searches themselves. Required to search: name, years to search. Civil cases indexed by defendant, plaintiff; index on docket books; on computer back to 11/1996. Civil PAT goes back to 11/1996. Search civil, probate, and appellate information at www.iowacourts.state.ia.us/ESAWebApp/SelectFrame. Basic Search is free. Advanced Search with more details and higher degree of currency is $25.00 per month.
Criminal Records: Access: In person, online. Visitors must perform in person searches themselves. Required to search: name, years to search. Criminal docket on books; on computer back to 11/1996. Criminal PAT goes back to same as civil. Online search of record index for criminal, traffic and appellate information same as described under Civil, including the free and subscription services. Online results show middle initial, DOB. Rarely the DOB or middle name may be missing from PAT or online results.
General Information: Online identifiers in results same as on public terminal. No CINA, juvenile, sealed, pending dissolution of marriage, mental health or expunged records released. Will fax out documents $.50 per page. Court makes copy: $.50 per page. Certification fee: $10.00. Payee: Clerk of Court. Personal checks accepted. Visa/MC accepted.

Sac County

2nd District Court PO Box 368, Sac City, IA 50583; 712-662-7791; fax: 712-662-7978; 8AM-4:30PM. ***Felony, Misdemeanor, Civil, Eviction, Small Claims, Probate.***
www.iowacourts.gov/District_Courts/District_Two/
Civil Records: Access: In person, online. Visitors must perform in person searches themselves. Required to search: name. Civil cases indexed by defendant, plaintiff, go back to 1888; on computer back to 7/1997. Civil PAT goes back to 7/1997. PAT results show middle initial, DOB. Search civil, probate, and appellate information at www.iowacourts.state.ia.us/ESAWebApp/SelectFrame. Basic Search is free. Advanced Search with more details and higher degree of currency is $25.00 per month.
Criminal Records: Access: In person, online. Visitors must perform in person searches themselves. Required to search: name, approximate date. Criminal records go back to 1888; on computer back to 7/1997. Note: Court may assist in search, if necessary. Criminal PAT goes back to same as civil. Online search of record index for criminal, traffic and appellate information same as described under Civil, including the free and subscription services. Online results show middle initial, DOB. Rarely the DOB or middle name may be missing from PAT or online results.
General Information: Online identifiers in results same as on public terminal. No juvenile, sealed, pending dissolution of marriage, mental health, domestic abuse or deferred records released. Will fax documents for $1.00 per page fee. Court makes copy: $.50 per page. Cert fee: $10.00. Payee: Clerk of Court. Personal checks accepted. Visa/MC accepted.

Scott County

7th District Court 416 W 4th St, Davenport, IA 52801; criminal phone: 563-326-8786; civil phone: 563-326-8647; probate phone: 563-326-8648; fax: 563-326-8298; 8AM-4:30PM. ***Felony, Misdemeanor, Civil, Eviction, Small Claims, Probate.***
www.iowacourts.gov/District_Courts/District_Seven/index.asp
Civil Records: Access: In person, online. Visitors must perform in person searches themselves. Required to search: name, years to search. Civil cases indexed by defendant, plaintiff, on computer back to 11/1993, docket books prior. Civil PAT goes back to 1992. PAT results show middle initial, DOB. Search civil, probate, and appellate information at www.iowacourts.state.ia.us/ESAWebApp/SelectFrame. Basic Search is free. Advanced Search with more details and higher degree of currency is $25.00 per month.
Criminal Records: Access: In person, online. Visitors must perform in person searches themselves. Required to search: name, years to search, DOB; also helpful: SSN. Criminal records computerized from 1992, printouts and docket books prior. Criminal PAT goes back to same as civil. Online search of record index for criminal, traffic and appellate information same as described under Civil, including the free and subscription services. Online results show middle initial, DOB. Rarely the DOB or middle name may be missing from PAT or online results.
General Information: Online identifiers in results same as on public terminal. No juvenile, sealed, dissolution of marriage, mental health, domestic abuse or deferred records released. Court makes copy: $.50 per page. Certification fee: $10.00 per doc. Payee: Clerk of Court. Personal checks and credit cards accepted. Mail requests: SASE required for mail return of any copies.

Shelby County

4th District Court PO Box 431, 6th & Court St, Harlan, IA 51537; 712-755-5543; fax: 712-755-2667; 8AM-4:30PM. ***Felony, Misdemeanor, Civil, Eviction, Small Claims, Probate.***
www.iowacourts.gov/District_Courts/District_Four/
The court will not perform name searches.
Civil Records: Access: In person, online. Visitors must perform in person searches themselves. Required to search: name, years to search. Civil cases indexed by defendant, plaintiff, on original files back to 1969, microfilm prior, on computer back to 10/95. Public use terminal available. PAT results show middle initial, DOB. Results include case number. Search civil, probate, and appellate information at www.iowacourts.state.ia.us/ESAWebApp/SelectFrame. Basic Search is free. Advanced Search with more details and higher degree of currency is $25.00 per month.
Criminal Records: Access: In person, online. Visitors must perform in person searches themselves. Required to search: name, years to search; also helpful: DOB. Criminal records on original files back to 1980, microfilm prior, on computer back to 10/95. Public use terminal available. PAT results show middle initial, DOB. Online search of record index for criminal, traffic and appellate information same as described under Civil, including the free and subscription services. Online results show middle initial, DOB. Rarely the DOB or middle name may be missing from PAT or online results.
General Information: Online identifiers in results same as on public terminal. No juvenile, sealed, dissolution of marriage, mental health, domestic abuse or deferred records released. Will fax out specific case files for $2.00 plus $.50 per page. Court makes copy: $.50 per page. Cert fee: $10.00. Payee: Clerk of Court. Personal checks accepted; credit cards are not.

Sioux County

3rd District Court PO Box 47, 210 Central Ave SW, Courthouse, Orange City, IA 51041; 712-737-2286; fax: 712-737-8908; 8AM-4:30PM. ***Felony, Misdemeanor, Civil, Eviction, Small Claims, Probate.***
www.iowacourts.gov/District_Courts/District_Three/
Civil Records: Access: In person, online. Visitors must perform in person searches themselves. Required to search: name, years to search. Civil cases indexed by defendant, plaintiff; index in docket books

from 1800s; computerized records since 9/97. Civil PAT goes back to 1997. PAT results show middle initial, DOB. Results include case number. Search civil, probate, and appellate information at www.iowacourts.state.ia.us/ESAWebApp/SelectFrame. Basic Search is free. Advanced Search with more details and higher degree of currency is $25.00 per month.
Criminal Records: Access: In person, online. Visitors must perform in person searches themselves. Required to search: name, years to search, signed release. Criminal docket on books from 1800s; computerized records since 9/97. Criminal PAT goes back to same as civil. Online search of record index for criminal, traffic and appellate information same as described under Civil, including the free and subscription services. Online results show middle initial, DOB. Rarely the DOB or middle name may be missing from PAT or online results.
General Information: Online identifiers in results same as on public terminal. No juvenile, sealed, dissolution of marriage, mental health, domestic abuse or deferred records released. Will fax documents $1.00 per page. Court makes copy: $.50 per page. Certification fee: $10.00 per doc. Payee: Clerk of Court. Personal checks accepted. Visa/MC accepted.

Story County

2nd District Court PO Box 408, 1315 S B Ave, Nevada, IA 50201; 515-382-7410; 8AM-4:30PM. ***Felony, Misdemeanor, Civil, Probate.***
www.iowacourts.gov/District_Courts/District_Two/
Also has a branch in Ames that handles minor misdemeanors, traffic, and small claims at 515-239-5140.
Civil Records: Access: In person, online. Visitors must perform in person searches themselves. Required to search: name, years to search. Civil cases indexed by defendant, plaintiff; index in docket books from 1900s; on computer back to 1995. Civil PAT goes back to 1995. PAT results show name only. Search civil, probate, and appellate information at www.iowacourts.state.ia.us/ESAWebApp/SelectFrame. Basic Search is free. Advanced Search with more details and higher degree of currency is $25.00 per month.
Criminal Records: Access: In person, online. Visitors must perform in person searches themselves. Required to search: name, years to search. Criminal records on computer since 1992, prior on docket books. Criminal PAT goes back to 1992. PAT results show middle initial, DOB. Online search of record index for criminal, traffic and appellate information same as described under Civil, including the free and subscription services. Online results show middle initial, DOB. Rarely the DOB or middle name may be missing from PAT or online results.
General Information: Online identifiers in results same as on public terminal. No sealed, pending dissolution of marriage, mental health, or expunged records released. Will not fax documents. Court makes copy: $.50 per page. Certification fee: $10.00 per cert. Payee: Clerk of Court. Personal checks accepted. Visa/MC accepted.

Ames Associate District Court PO Box 748, 515 Clark St, Ames, IA 50010; 515-239-5140; fax: 515-239-5141; 8AM-4:30PM. ***Misdemeanor (Minor), Small Claims, Eviction.***
www.iowacourts.gov/District_Courts/District_Two/
A branch of the District Court in Nevada.
Civil Records: Access: In person, online. Visitors must perform in person searches themselves. Required to search: name, years to search. Civil cases indexed by defendant, plaintiff, on computer back to 1995. Civil PAT goes back to 7/1995. Search civil, probate, and appellate information at www.iowacourts.state.ia.us/ESAWebApp/SelectFrame. Basic Search is free. Advanced Search with more details and higher degree of currency is $25.00 per month.
Criminal Records: Access: In person, online. Visitors must perform in person searches themselves. Required to search: name, approx date of offense. Criminal records on computer since 1992, prior on docket books. Criminal PAT goes back to 3/1995. Online search of record index for criminal, traffic and appellate information same as described under Civil, including the free and subscription services. Online results show middle initial, DOB. Rarely the DOB or middle name may be missing from PAT or online results.
General Information: Online identifiers in results same as on public terminal. No sealed or expunged records released. Will not fax documents. Court makes copy: $.50 per page, self serve same. Certification fee: $10.00. Payee: Clerk of Court. Personal checks accepted; credit cards are not.

Tama County

6th Judicial District Court PO Box 306, 100 W High St, Toledo, IA 52342; 641-484-3721; criminal fax: 641-484-6403; civil fax: same; 8AM-4:30PM. ***Felony, Misdemeanor, Civil, Eviction, Small Claims, Probate.***
www.iowacourts.gov/District_Courts/District_Six/
Probate fax is same as main fax number.
Civil Records: Access: In person, online. Visitors must perform in person searches themselves. Required to search: name, years to search. Civil cases indexed by defendant, plaintiff; index in docket books from 1880s; computerized records since 1997. Magistrate dockets to 1972, prior to 1972, Justice of the Peace. Public use terminal has civil records back to 1997. PAT results show middle initial, DOB. Results include name and case number. Search civil, probate, and appellate information at www.iowacourts.state.ia.us/ESAWebApp/SelectFrame. Basic Search is free. Advanced Search with more details and higher degree of currency is $25.00 per month.
Criminal Records: Access: In person, online. Visitors must perform in person searches themselves. Required to search: name, years to search. Criminal docket on books from 1880s; computerized records since 1995. Magistrate dockets to 1972, prior to 1972, Justice of the Peace. Note: Results include name, DOB and case number. Online search of record index for criminal, traffic and appellate information same as described under Civil, including the free and subscription services. Online results show middle initial, DOB. Rarely the DOB or middle name may be missing from PAT or online results.
General Information: Online identifiers in results same as on public terminal. No juvenile, sealed, dissolution of marriage, mental health, domestic abuse or deferred records released. Will fax documents for no fee. Court makes copy: $.50 per page, self serve same. Certification fee: $10.00. Payee: Clerk of Court. Personal checks accepted. Visa/MC accepted.

Taylor County

5th District Court 405 Jefferson, #4, County Courthouse, Bedford, IA 50833; 712-523-2095; fax: 712-523-2936; 8AM-4:30PM. ***Felony, Misdemeanor, Civil, Eviction, Small Claims, Probate.***
www.iowacourts.gov/District_Courts/District_Five/
Civil Records: Access: In person, online. Visitors must perform in person searches themselves. Required to search: name, years to search. Civil cases indexed by defendant, plaintiff, on computer since 11/01/96; prior to 1880s. Public use terminal available, records go back to 10 years. PAT results show middle initial, but DOB not always available. Search civil, probate, and appellate information at www.iowacourts.state.ia.us/ESAWebApp/SelectFrame. Basic Search is free. Advanced Search with more details and higher degree of currency is $25.00 per month.
Criminal Records: Access: In person, online. Visitors must perform in person searches themselves. Required to search: name, years to search. Criminal records on computer since 11/01/96; prior to 1880s. Public use terminal available, crim records go back to 10 years. PAT results show middle initial, but DOB not always available. Online search of record index for criminal, traffic and appellate information same as described under Civil, including the free and subscription services. Online results show middle initial, DOB. Rarely the DOB or middle name may be missing from PAT or online results.
General Information: Online identifiers in results same as on public terminal. No juvenile, sealed, dissolution of marriage, mental health, domestic abuse or deferred records released. Will fax out specific case files to local or toll free line. Court makes copy: $.50 per page, self serve same. Certification fee: $10.00. Payee: Clerk of Court. Personal checks accepted; credit cards are not.

Union County

5th District Court Courthouse, Creston, IA 50801; 641-782-7315; criminal fax: 641-782-8241; civil fax: same; 8AM-4:30PM. ***Felony, Misdemeanor, Civil, Eviction, Small Claims, Probate.***
www.iowacourts.gov/District_Courts/District_Five/
Probate fax is same as main fax number.
Civil Records: Access: In person, online. Visitors must perform in person searches themselves. Required to search: name, years to search. Civil cases indexed by defendant, plaintiff; index in docket books from 1900s; computerized back to 10/1996. Civil PAT goes back to 10/1996. Search civil, probate, and appellate information at www.iowacourts.state.ia.us/ESAWebApp/SelectFrame. Basic Search is free. Advanced Search with more details and higher degree of currency is $25.00 per month.
Criminal Records: Access: In person, online. Visitors must perform in person searches themselves. Required to search: name, years to search. Criminal docket on books from 1900s; computerized back to 10/1996. Criminal PAT goes back to same as civil. Online search of record index for criminal, traffic and appellate information same as described under Civil, including the free and subscription services. Online results show middle initial, DOB. Rarely the DOB or middle name may be missing from PAT or online results.
General Information: Online identifiers in results same as on public terminal. No juvenile cases less than 10 years, sealed, pending dissolution of marriage, mental health, or deferred records released. No fee to fax documents. Court makes copy: $.50 per page, self serve same. Certification fee: $10.00. Payee: Clerk of Court. Personal checks and major credit cards accepted.

Van Buren County

8th District Court PO Box 495, Courthouse, Keosauqua, IA 52565; 319-293-3108; fax: 319-293-3811; 8AM-4:30PM. ***Felony, Misdemeanor, Civil, Eviction, Small Claims, Probate.***
www.iowacourts.gov/District_Courts/District_Eight/
Civil Records: Access: In person, online. Visitors must perform in person searches themselves. Required to search: name, years to search. Civil cases indexed by defendant, plaintiff; index in docket books from 1837, computerized since 1997. Civil PAT goes back to 1997. PAT results show middle initial, DOB. Probate is also on public terminal from 1997 to present, in dockets (if available) prior to 1997. Search civil, probate, and appellate information at www.iowacourts.state.ia.us/ESAWebApp/SelectFrame. Basic Search is free. Advanced Search with more details and higher degree of currency is $25.00 per month.
Criminal Records: Access: In person, online. Visitors must perform in person searches themselves. Required to search: name, years to search, DOB. Criminal docket on books from 1837, computerized since 1997. Criminal PAT goes back to 1997. PAT results show middle initial, DOB. Online search of record index for criminal, traffic and appellate information same as described under Civil, including the free and subscription services. Online results show middle initial, DOB. Rarely the DOB or middle name may be missing from PAT or online results.
General Information: Online identifiers in results same as on public terminal. No sealed, mental health, or sealed records released; will release unsealed juvenile, marriage dissolution or DA records if after July, 2000. Will fax documents $1.00 per page.

$5.00 minimum. Court makes copy: $.50 per page, self serve same. Certification fee: $10.00. Payee: Clerk of Court. Personal checks accepted. Visa/MC accepted.

Wapello County

8th District Court 101 W 4th, Ottumwa, IA 52501; 641-683-0060; fax: 641-683-0064; 8AM-4:30PM. ***Felony, Misdemeanor, Civil, Eviction, Small Claims, Probate.***
www.iowacourts.gov/District_Courts/District_Eight/
SSNs are only maintained on a confidential sheet not available to the public.
Civil Records: Access: In person, online. Visitors must perform in person searches themselves. Required to search: name, years to search. Civil cases indexed by defendant, plaintiff, on computer back to 5/1994; docket books prior. Civil PAT goes back to 1995. PAT results show middle initial, DOB. Search civil, probate, and appellate information at www.iowacourts.state.ia.us/ESAWebApp/SelectFrame. Basic Search is free. Advanced Search with more details and higher degree of currency is $25.00 per month.
Criminal Records: Access: In person, online. Visitors must perform in person searches themselves. Required to search: name, years to search, DOB; also helpful: SSN. Criminal records computerized from 5/1994; docket books prior. Criminal PAT goes back to same as civil. Online search of record index for criminal, traffic and appellate information same as described under Civil, including the free and subscription services. Online results show middle initial, DOB. Rarely the DOB or middle name may be missing from PAT or online results.
General Information: Online identifiers in results same as on public terminal. No juvenile, sealed, dissolution of marriage, mental health, domestic abuse or deferred records released. Will fax documents $5.00 minimum, plus $.50 per page. Court makes copy: $.50 per page. Certification fee: $10.00 per doc. Payee: Clerk of Court. Personal checks and credit cards accepted.

Warren County

5th District Court PO Box 379, 115 N Howard, Indianola, IA 50125; 515-961-1033; criminal phone: 515-961-1033; civil phone: 515-961-1027; probate phone: 515-961-1037; fax: 515-961-1071; 8AM-4:30PM. ***Felony, Misdemeanor, Civil, Eviction, Small Claims, Probate.***
www.iowacourts.gov/District_Courts/District_Five/
Civil Records: Access: In person, online. Visitors must perform in person searches themselves. Required to search: name, years to search. Civil cases indexed by defendant, plaintiff, on computer back to 10/1995; prior on docket books to 1925. Civil PAT goes back to 1995. Results include name and case number. Search civil, probate, and appellate information at www.iowacourts.state.ia.us/ESAWebApp/SelectFrame. Basic Search is free. Advanced Search with more details and higher degree of currency is $25.00 per month.
Criminal Records: Access: In person, online. Visitors must perform in person searches themselves. Required to search: name, years to search. Criminal records computerized from 10/1995; prior on docket books to 1945. Criminal PAT goes back to same as civil. Results include name and case number. Online search of record index for criminal, traffic and appellate information same as described under Civil, including the free and subscription services. Online results show middle initial, DOB. Rarely the DOB or middle name may be missing from PAT or online results.
General Information: Online identifiers in results same as on public terminal. No juvenile, sealed, dissolution of marriage, mental health, domestic abuse or deferred records released. Will not fax documents. Court makes copy: $.50 per page, self serve same. Certification fee: $10.00. Payee: Clerk of Court. Personal checks and major credit cards accepted.

Washington County

8th District Court PO Box 391, 224 W Main, Washington, IA 52353; 319-653-7741; fax: 319-653-7787; 8AM-4:30PM. ***Felony, Misdemeanor, Civil, Eviction, Small Claims, Probate.***
www.iowacourts.gov/District_Courts/District_Eight/
Civil Records: Access: In person, online. Visitors must perform in person searches themselves. Required to search: name, years to search. Civil cases indexed by defendant, plaintiff, on computer back to 1997, microfilm from 1940, docket books since court inception. Civil PAT goes back to 1997. Search civil, probate, and appellate information at www.iowacourts.state.ia.us/ESAWebApp/SelectFrame. Basic Search is free. Advanced Search with more details and higher degree of currency is $25.00 per month.
Criminal Records: Access: In person, online. Visitors must perform in person searches themselves. Required to search: name, years to search. Criminal records computerized from 1997, microfilm from 1940, docket books since court inception. Criminal PAT goes back to same as civil. Online search of record index for criminal, traffic and appellate information same as described under Civil, including the free and subscription services. Online results show middle initial, DOB. Rarely the DOB or middle name may be missing from PAT or online results.
General Information: Online identifiers in results same as on public terminal. No juvenile, sealed, dissolution of marriage, mental health, domestic abuse or deferred records released. Will fax documents $1.00 per page, $5.00 minimum. Court makes copy: $.50 per page. Certification fee: $10.00 per doc. Payee: Clerk of Court. Personal checks accepted. Visa/MC accepted.

Wayne County

5th District Court PO Box 424, Corydon, IA 50060; 641-872-2264; civil phone: same; criminal fax: 641-872-2431; civil fax: same; 8AM-4:30PM. ***Felony, Misdemeanor, Civil, Eviction, Small Claims, Probate.***
www.iowacourts.gov/District_Courts/District_Five/
Probate fax is same as main fax number.
Civil Records: Access: In person, online. Visitors must perform in person searches themselves. Required to search: name, years to search. Civil cases indexed by defendant, plaintiff, on dockets from 1890, on computer back to 2/97. Civil PAT goes back to 2/1997. Search civil, probate, and appellate information at www.iowacourts.state.ia.us/ESAWebApp/SelectFrame. Basic Search is free. Advanced Search with more details and higher degree of currency is $25.00 per month.
Criminal Records: Access: In person, online. Visitors must perform in person searches themselves. Required to search: name, years to search, DOB. Criminal docket index from 1890, on computer back to 2/97. Criminal PAT goes back to same as civil. Online search of record index for criminal, traffic and appellate information same as described under Civil, including the free and subscription services. Online results show middle initial, DOB. Rarely the DOB or middle name may be missing from PAT or online results.
General Information: Online identifiers in results same as on public terminal. No juvenile, sealed, dissolution of marriage, mental health, domestic abuse or deferred records released. Will not fax documents. Court makes copy: $.50 per page. Certification fee: $10.00. Payee: Clerk of Court. Personal checks accepted. Visa/MC accepted. Mail requests: SASE required for mail return of any copies.

Webster County

2nd District Court 701 Central Ave, Courthouse, Ft Dodge, IA 50501; 515-576-7115; fax: 515-576-0555; 8-4:30. ***Felony, Misdemeanor, Civil, Eviction, Small Claims, Probate.***
www.iowacourts.gov/District_Courts/District_Two/
Probate fax is same as main fax number.
Civil Records: Access: In person, online. Visitors must perform in person searches themselves. Required to search: name, years to search. Civil cases indexed by defendant, plaintiff; index in docket books from 1800s, on computer since 1995. Civil PAT goes back to 1995. Results include name and case number. Search civil, probate, and appellate information at www.iowacourts.state.ia.us/ESAWebApp/SelectFrame. Basic Search is free. Advanced Search with more details and higher degree of currency is $25.00 per month.
Criminal Records: Access: In person, online. Visitors must perform in person searches themselves. Required to search: name, years to search, signed release. Criminal docket on books from 1800s, on computer since 1995. Criminal PAT goes back to 1995. PAT results show middle initial, DOB. Results include case number. Online search of record index for criminal, traffic and appellate information same as described under Civil, including the free and subscription services. Online results show middle initial, DOB. Rarely the DOB or middle name may be missing from PAT or online results.
General Information: Online identifiers in results same as on public terminal. No juvenile, sealed, dissolution of marriage, mental health, domestic abuse or deferred records released. Will fax documents $1.00 per page. Court makes copy: $.50 per page. Certification fee: $10.00. Payee: Clerk of Court. Personal checks and credit cards accepted.

Winnebago County

2nd District Court 126 S Clark, Ste 6, Forest City, IA 50436; 641-585-4520; fax: 641-585-2615; 9AM-3:30PM. ***Felony, Misdemeanor, Civil, Eviction, Small Claims, Probate.***
www.iowacourts.gov/District_Courts/District_Two/
Probate fax is same as main fax number.
Civil Records: Access: In person, online. Visitors must perform in person searches themselves. Required to search: name, years to search; also helpful: address. Civil cases indexed by defendant, plaintiff, on dockets from 1880s; on computer since 9/1997. Civil PAT goes back to 9/1997. Results include name and case number. Search civil, probate, and appellate information at www.iowacourts.state.ia.us/ESAWebApp/SelectFrame. Basic Search is free. Advanced Search with more details and higher degree of currency is $25.00 per month.
Criminal Records: Access: In person, online. Visitors must perform in person searches themselves. Required to search: name, years to search; also helpful: address, DOB, aliases, offense, date of offense. Criminal docket index from 1940s; on computer since 9/1997. Criminal PAT goes back to same as civil. Online search of record index for criminal, traffic and appellate information same as described under Civil, including the free and subscription services. Online results show middle initial, DOB. Rarely the DOB or middle name may be missing from PAT or online results.
General Information: Online identifiers in results same as on public terminal. No juvenile, pending or dismissed dissolution of marriage, mental health, criminal expunged or substance abuse records released. Domestic abuse law change states that parts of the file may be public, depending on Judge's order. Will not fax documents. Court makes copy: $.50 per page. Certification fee: $10.00 per document. Payee: Clerk of Court. Personal checks and credit cards accepted.

Winneshiek County

1st District Court 201 W Main St, Decorah, IA 52101; 563-382-2469; fax: 563-382-0603; 8AM-4:30PM. ***Felony, Misdemeanor, Civil, Eviction, Small Claims, Probate.***
www.iowacourts.gov/District_Courts/District_One/
Civil Records: Access: In person, online. Visitors must perform in person searches themselves. Required to search: name, years to search. Civil cases indexed by defendant, plaintiff, on computer since 1992, docket books since 1860s. Civil PAT goes back to 1992. PAT results show middle initial, DOB. Search civil, probate, and appellate information at www.iowacourts.state.ia.us/ESAWebApp/SelectFrame. Basic Search is free.

Advanced Search with more details and higher degree of currency is $25.00 per month.
Criminal Records: Access: In person, online. Visitors must perform in person searches themselves. Required to search: name, years to search, signed release. Criminal records on computer since 1991, docket books since 1860s. Criminal PAT goes back to 1991. Online search of record index for criminal, traffic and appellate information same as described under Civil, including the free and subscription services. Online results show middle initial, DOB. Rarely the DOB or middle name may be missing from PAT or online results.
General Information: Online identifiers in results same as on public terminal. No juvenile, sealed, dissolution of marriage, mental health, domestic abuse or deferred records released. Will fax documents to local or toll-free number. Court makes copy: $.50 per page. Self serve: $.25 per page. Certification fee: $10.00 per document. Payee: Clerk of Court. Personal checks accepted; credit cards are not. Mail requests: SASE required for mail return of any copies.

Woodbury County

3rd District Court Woodbury County Courthouse, 620 Douglas, Rm 101, Sioux City, IA 51101-1248; criminal phone: 712-279-6611; civil phone: 712-279-6612; probate phone: 712-279-6614; fax: 712-279-6021; 8AM-4:30PM. ***Felony, Civil, Probate.***
www.iowacourts.gov/District_Courts/District_Three/
Civil Records: Access: In person, online. Visitors must perform in person searches themselves. Required to search: name, years to search. Civil cases indexed by defendant, plaintiff; index on docket books from early 1900; on computer from 7/95. Civil PAT goes back to 7/1995. PAT results show middle initial, DOB. Public terminal has probate record index back to 7/1995. Results include first and last name, case number. Search civil, probate, and appellate information at www.iowacourts.state.ia.us/ESAWebApp/SelectFrame. Records also found at www.judicial.state.ia.us/ Basic Search is free. Advanced Search with more details and higher degree of currency is $25.00 per month.
Criminal Records: Access: In person, online. Visitors must perform in person searches themselves. Required to search: name, years to search. Criminal records indexed in books from early 1900; on computer from 10/95. Note: Results include first and last name, case number. Criminal PAT goes back to 10/1995. PAT results show middle initial, DOB. Results include first and last name, case number. Online search of record index for criminal, traffic and appellate information same as described under Civil, including the free and subscription services. Online results show middle initial, DOB. Rarely the DOB or middle name may be missing from PAT or online results.
General Information: Online identifiers in results same as on public terminal. No sealed, adoption, substance abuse, pending dissolution of marriage, or mental health records released. Will fax documents to local or toll-free number. Court makes copy: $.50 per page. Certification fee: $10.00; Exemplification fee-$20.00. Payee: Clerk of Court. Personal checks accepted. Visa/MC accepted. Mail requests: SASE required for mail return of any copies.

Associate District Court 407 7th St, County Clerk at Law Enforcement Ctr, Sioux City, IA 51101; 712-279-6624; fax: 712-279-9564; 8AM-4:30PM. ***Misdemeanor, Civil, Eviction, Small Claims.***
www.iowacourts.gov/District_Courts/District_Three/
Civil Records: Access: In person, online. Visitors must perform in person searches themselves. Required to search: name, years to search. Civil cases indexed by defendant, plaintiff; index in docket books from early 1900; on computer from 7/95. Civil PAT goes back to 1992. PAT results show middle initial, DOB. Results include plaintiff and defendant. Search civil, probate, and appellate information at www.iowacourts.state.ia.us/ESAWebApp/SelectFrame. Basic Search is free. Advanced Search with more details and higher degree of currency is $25.00 per month.
Criminal Records: Access: In person, online. Visitors must perform in person searches themselves. Required to search: name, years to search. Criminal Records indexed on computer since 1992; on computer from 7/92. Criminal PAT goes back to same as civil. PAT results show middle initial, DOB. Results include the charge. Online search of record index for criminal, traffic and appellate information same as described under Civil, including the free and subscription services. Online results show middle initial, DOB. Rarely the DOB or middle name may be missing from PAT or online results.
General Information: Online identifiers in results same as on public terminal. No juvenile records released. Court makes copy: $.50 per page, self serve same. Certification fee: $10.00. Payee: Clerk of Court. Personal checks accepted. Visa/MC accepted.

Worth County

2nd District Court 1000 Central Ave, Northwood, IA 50459; 641-324-2840; fax: 641-324-2360; 9AM-3:30PM. ***Felony, Misdemeanor, Civil, Eviction, Small Claims, Probate.***
www.iowacourts.gov/District_Courts/District_Two/
Case number required for documents.
Civil Records: Access: In person, online. Visitors must perform in person searches themselves. Required to search: name, years to search. Civil cases indexed by defendant, plaintiff, on computer and docket books, on computer back to 4/97. Civil PAT goes back to 4/1997. Search civil, probate, and appellate information at www.iowacourts.state.ia.us/ESAWebApp/SelectFrame. Basic Search is free. Advanced Search with more details and higher degree of currency is $25.00 per month.
Criminal Records: Access: In person, online. Visitors must perform in person searches themselves. Required to search: name, years to search. Criminal records on computer and docket books, on computer back to 4/97. Criminal PAT goes back to same as civil. Online search of record index for criminal, traffic and appellate information same as described under Civil, including the free and subscription services. Online results show middle initial, DOB. Rarely the DOB or middle name may be missing from PAT or online results.
General Information: Online identifiers in results same as on public terminal. No juvenile, sealed, dissolution of marriage, mental health, domestic abuse, dismissed, or deferred records released. Will fax out specific case files. Court makes copy: $.50 per page. Certification fee: $10.00 per doc. Payee: Clerk of Court. Personal checks and credit cards accepted.

Wright County

2nd District Court PO Box 306, Clarion, IA 50525; 515-532-3113; fax: 515-532-2343; 8AM-4:30PM. ***Felony, Misdemeanor, Civil, Eviction, Small Claims, Probate.***
www.iowacourts.gov/District_Courts/District_Two/
Probate is separate index at this same address. Probate fax is same as main fax number.
Civil Records: Access: In person, online. Visitors must perform in person searches themselves. Required to search: name, years to search. Civil cases indexed by defendant, plaintiff; index in docket books from 1880; on computer since 1997. Civil PAT goes back to 1997. Search civil, probate, and appellate information at www.iowacourts.state.ia.us/ESAWebApp/SelectFrame. Basic Search is free. Advanced Search with more details and higher degree of currency is $25.00 per month.
Criminal Records: Access: In person, online. Visitors must perform in person searches themselves. Required to search: name, years to search; also helpful: DOB, SSN. Criminal docket on books from 1880s; on computer since 1997. Criminal PAT goes back to same as civil. Online search of record index for criminal, traffic and appellate information same as described under Civil, including the free and subscription services. Online results show middle initial, DOB. Rarely the DOB or middle name may be missing from PAT or online results.
General Information: Online identifiers in results same as on public terminal. No juvenile, sealed, dissolution of marriage, mental health, domestic abuse or deferred records released. Will fax out specific case files for $2.00. Court makes copy: $.50 per page, self serve same. Certification fee: $10.00 per document. Payee: Clerk of Court. Personal checks accepted. Visa/MC accepted.

Iowa Recording Offices

ORGANIZATION: 99 counties, 100 recording offices. Lee County has two recording offices. The recording officer is the County Recorder. Many counties utilize a grantor/grantee index containing all transactions recorded with them. Iowa is in the Central Time Zone (CST).

REAL ESTATE RECORDS: Most Iowa counties are hesitant to perform real estate searches but about half will provide a listing from the grantor/grantee index with the understanding that it is not certified in the sense that a title search is. Certification of copies costs $5.00 per document. Copy fees vary.

UCC RECORDS: Financing statements are filed at the state level except for real estate related collateral filed with the County Recorder. Prior to July, 2001, UCC on consumer goods were also filed at the County Recorder and these older records can be searched here. Half of Iowa's counties will do UCC searches. UCC search fee is usually $5.00 per debtor name ($6.00 if the standard UCC-11 Form is not used). UCC copy fee is usually $1.00 per page.

TAX LIEN RECORDS: Federal tax liens on personal property of businesses are filed with the Secretary of State. Other federal and all state tax liens on personal property are filed with the County Recorder. County search practices vary widely; about half provide some sort of tax lien search.

OTHER LIENS: Home improvement, job service.

ONLINE ACCESS: Recorded land document index is available on the state system at http://iowalandrecords.org for free, but images require registration - but images may not be available until redaction is completed. The fee to be implemented for images is $5.00 per doc plus $1.00 per page plus $3.50 for shipping, handling and online service. The free index search results include name, doc type, county, book&page number, and rec date.

A links list for assessor records for 66 counties plus cities of Ames, Cedar Rapids, Davenport, Dubuque, Iowa City, and Souix City is at www.iowaassessors.com, but note that many of the links are routed to http://beacon.schneidercorp.com. A statewide Property Tax lookup and payment page is at www.iowatreasurers.org/iscta/access/home.do. First, select county then follow prompts to the search page where you can first lookup the name, then parcel information.

Search UCCs free on the statewide site at www.sos.state.ia.us/Search/UCC/search.aspx?ucc.

Adair County

County Recorder, 400 Public Sq, #1; Courthouse, Ste 6, Greenfield, IA 50849. 641-743-2411; fax-641-743-2565; 8AM-4:30PM (CST)

Index: All in one. Records indexed on a public use terminal back to 1991. Only the public may search. Will not search UCC records. Copy fee $1.00 per page. Cert fee- $5.00 per doc plus copy fee. Payee- Adair County Recorder. Assessment or recorded data available in bulk, made custom to your specifications. **Online access to Real Estate, Deed, Lien, Mortgage records:** At http://iowalandrecords.org/portal/clris/CountiesTab, an index of recorded land records is available from 1/1/1991. **Other phones:** Treasurer- 641-743-2312; Elections- 641-743-2546; Vital Records- 641-743-2411. **Property tax/Assessing-** 400 Public Sq #1, Courthouse, Greenfield, IA 50849; 641-743-2531, assessor fax- 641-743-2565. (Appraiser/Auditor- 641-743-2546) Public access terminal available. **Online access-** the assessor database of property and sales data is free at www.adair.iowaassessors.com. At http://iowalandrecords.org/portal/clris/SwitchToCountiesTab, an index of recorded land records is available from 1/1991; images from 7/2002.

Adams County

County Recorder, PO Box 28, Corning, IA 50841. Recording, R/E phone-641-322-3744; fax-641-322-3744; 8:30AM-4:30PM www.adamscountyia.com/

Index: Pre-1990 indices are deeds, mortgages, misc. Records indexed on computer back to 4/88. Only the public may search. Copy fee $.50 per page. For fax, fee is $2.00 1st page, $1.00 each add'l page. Cert fee- $5.00 per doc plus copy fee. Payee- Adams County Recorder. Office does not sell bulk data. **Online access to Real Estate, Deed, Lien, UCC, Judgment records:** At http://iowalandrecords.org/portal/clris/CountiesTab, an index of recorded land records is available from 1/1995; images from 1/2005. **Other phones:** Treasurer- 641-322-3210; Elections- 641-322-3340; Vital Records- 641-322-3744; Clerk of Court- 641-322-4711. **Property tax/Assessing-** PO Box 28, 500 9th St, Corning, IA 50841; 641-322-4312, assessor fax- 641-322-3071.

Allamakee County

County Recorder, 110 Allamakee St; Courthouse, Waukon, IA 52172-1794. Recording, R/E & UCC phone-563-568-2364; fax-563-568-6419; 8AM-4PM (CST) www.co.allamakee.ia.us

Index: All in one. Records indexed on computer back to 1983. Only the public may search. Copy fee $.50 per page; vital record copy- $5.00. Cert fee- $5.00 per doc plus copy fee. Payee- Allamakee County Recorder. Office does not sell bulk data. **Online access to Real Estate, Deed, Lien, Judgment records:** At http://iowalandrecords.org/portal/clris/CountiesTab an index and images of recorded land records available from 1994. **Other phones:** Treasurer- 563-568-3793; Elections- 563-568-3522; Vital Records- 563-568-2364. **Property tax/Assessing-** 110 Allamakee St, Waukon, IA 52172-; 563-568-3145, assessor fax- 563-568-0096. www.co.allamakee.ia.us/assessor.htm **Online access-** Search assessor property data free on the GIS system at http://beacon.schneidercorp.com/.

Appanoose County

County Recorder, 201 N 12th St; Courthouse, Centerville, IA 52544. Recording, R/E phone-641-856-6103; fax-641-856-8023; 8:30AM-4:30PM

Index: All in one. Records indexed on a public use terminal back to 7/1/01. Office personnel or visitors may perform searches. Search fee $5.00. Copy fee $3.00, if real estate $.25 per page. Cert fee- $5 per doc plus copy fee. Will not certify UCCs. Payee- Appanoose County Recorder. **Online access to Real Estate, Deed, Lien, UCC, Judgment records:** At http://iowalandrecords.org/portal/clris/CountiesTab, an index of recorded land records and images are available from 06/2001. **Other phones:** Treasurer- 641-856-3097; Elections- 641-856-6191; Vital Records- 641-856-6103. **Property tax/Assessing-** 201 N 12th St, Centerville, IA 52544; 641-437-4529, assessor fax- 641-856-3062. hours- 8AM-4PM www.appanoosecounty.net/assessor/assessor.php **Online** - Access to property/parcels for free go to www.appanoosecounty.net/assessor/assessor.php

Audubon County

County Recorder, 318 Leroy St, #7, Audubon, IA 50025-1255. Recording, R/E & UCC phone-712-563-2119; fax-712-563-4677; 8AM-4:30PM (CST)

Index: All in one. Records indexed on a public use terminal back to 1992. Only the public may search. Copy fee $1.00 per page. Cert fee- $5.00 per doc plus copy fee. Payee- County Recorder of Deeds. **Online access to Real Estate, Deed, Lien, Mortgage records:** At http://iowalandrecords.org/portal/clris/CountiesTab, an index and images of recorded land records available back to 5/11/2006 . **Other phones:** Treasurer- 712-563-2293; Vital Records- 712-563-2119. **Property tax/Assessing-** 318 Leroy St, Ste 2, Audubon, IA 50025; 712-563-3418, assessor fax- 712-563-2003. **Online access-** Search assessor property data for a fee on the GIS system at http://beacon.schneidercorp.com/. Registration and username required.

Benton County

County Recorder, 111 E 4th St, 1st Fl; Courthouse, Vinton, IA 52349. 319-472-3309; fax-319-472-3647; 8AM-4:30PM (CST) www.cobentoniaus.com/

Index: All in one. Records indexed on a public use terminal back to 7/1/01. Only the public may search. Copy fee $.50 per page. Cert fee- $5.00 per doc plus copy fee. Payee- Benton County Recorder. **Online access to Real Estate, Deed, Lien, UCC, Judgment**

records: At http://iowalandrecords.org/portal/clris/CountiesTab, an index of recorded land records and images are available from 2/26/2004. **Other phones:** Treasurer- 319-472-2450; Elections- 319-472-2365; Vital Records- 319-472-3309. **Property tax/Assessing**- 111 E 4th St, 2nd Fl, PO Box 549, Vinton, IA 52349; 319-472-5211, assessor fax- 319-472-5212. www.cobentoniaus.com/ **Online access**- Search assessor property data free on the GIS system at http://beacon.schneidercorp.com/.

Black Hawk County

County Recorder, 316 E 5th St, Rm 208; Courthouse, Waterloo, IA 50703-4774. 319-833-3171, R/E phone-319-833-3012; fax-319-833-3170; 8AM-4:30PM www.co.black-hawk.ia.us/depts/recorder.html

Index: Separate indices to search. Records indexed on a public use terminal back to 1989. Office personnel or visitors may perform searches. Search fee-$5.00 per name. Office will search real estate records. Will not search UCC records. Copy fee $1.00 per page. Cert fee- $5.00 per doc plus copy fee. Payee- Black Hawk County Recorder. Office does not sell bulk data. **Online access to Real Estate, Deed, Lien, Mortgage records:** At http://iowalandrecords.org/portal/clris/CountiesTab, an index of recorded land records are available from 1/1/2002; images from 5/1/2002. **Other phones:** Treasurer- 319-833-3013; Elections- 319-833-3007; Vital Records- 319-833-3012. **Property tax/Assessing**- 316 E 5th St, Rm 209, Waterloo, IA 50703; 319-833-3006, fax- 319-833-3100. www.co.black-hawk.ia.us/depts/assessor.html **Online access**- Access to the assessor database of property and sales data is free at www.co.black-hawk.ia.us/depts/bhentry.htm but no name searching. Also, search the tax delinquencies list free, manually at www.co.black-hawk.ia.us/depts/treasurer.html.

Boone County

County Recorder, 201 State St, Boone, IA 50036-3987. Recording, R/E & UCC phone-515-433-0514; fax-515-433-4972; 8-4:30PM www.co.boone.ia.us

Index: All in one. Records indexed on a public use terminal back to 1995. Office will perform a tax lien search but public must search other records themselves. No fee for search. Time permitting, office will search real estate records back a few years only. Will not search UCC records. Copy fee $.50 per page. Cert fee- $5.00 per doc plus copy fee. Payee- Boone County Recorder. Reports are available for purchase; reports can be by dates or names. **Online access to Real Estate, Deed, Lien, UCC, Judgment records:** At http://iowalandrecords.org/portal/clris/CountiesTab, an index of recorded land records and their images are available back to 5/1996. **Other phones:** Treasurer- 515-433-0510; Elections- 515-433-0502; Vital Records- 515-433-0514. **Property tax/Assessing**- 201 State St, Boone, IA 50036; 515-433-0508, assessor fax- 515-433-0509. **Online**- Access to the assessor GIS database of property and sales data is free at http://beacon.schneidercorp.com/.

Bremer County

County Recorder, 415 E Bremer Ave, Waverly, IA 50677. Recording, R/E phone-319-352-0401; fax-319-352-0518; 8AM-4:30PM www.co.bremer.ia.us

Index: All in one. Records indexed on a public use terminal back to 1983. Office personnel or visitors may perform searches. General index search performed by phone is free; otherwise search fee is $5.00. Copy fee $.50 per page. Cert fee- $5.00 per cert plus copy fee. Payee- Bremer County Recorder. Office does not sell bulk data. **Online access to Real Estate, Deed records:** At http://iowalandrecords.org/portal/clris/CountiesTab, an index of recorded land records and their images are available from 05/2002. **Other phones:** Treasurer- 319-352-0242; Elections- 319-352-0340; Vital Records- 319-352-0401. **Property tax/Assessing**- 415 E Bremer Ave, Courthouse, Waverly, IA 50677; 319-352-0145, assessor fax- 319-352-0150. hours- 8AM-4PM **Online access**- Search assessor property records at http://bremer.iowaassessors.com - no name searching.

Buchanan County

County Recorder, PO Box 298, Independence, IA 50644-0298. Recording, R/E & UCC phone-319-334-4259; fax-319-334-7453; 8AM-4:30PM (CST) www.growbuchanan.com/

Index: All in one. Records indexed on computer back to 1994. Office will perform a search but public must search other records themselves. Search fee $5.00 per name, prepaid. Office will not search real estate records. Copy fee $1.00 per page.Real estate record copy- $.50 per page. Cert fee- $5.00 per cert plus copy fee. Payee- Buchanan County Recorder. Office does not sell bulk data. **Online access to Real Estate, Grantor/Grantee, Deed, Lien, Mortgage, Judgment, UCC records:** Access recorders land index back to 1/2004 free at http://iowalandrecords.org/portal/clris/CountiesTab. **Other phones:** Treasurer- 319-334-4340; Elections-319-334-4109; Vital Records- 319-334-4259. **Property tax/Assessing**- PO Box 388, 210th Ave NE, Independence, IA 50644; 319-334-2706, assessor fax- 319-334-7451. hours- 8AM-4PM **Online access**- Access county property data free at http://buchanan.iowaassessors.com/ but no name searching. Includes property sales.

Buena Vista County

County Recorder, PO Box 454, Storm Lake, IA 50588. 712-749-2539; fax-712-749-2539; 8AM-4:30PM (CST) www.co.buena-vista.ia.us

Index: Separate indices to search. Records indexed on computer back to 1983. Office personnel or visitors may perform searches. Search fee $5.00 per name. Office will not search UCC records. Copy fee $1.00 per page.Real estate record copy- $.50 per page. Cert fee- $5.00 1st page, $.50 each add'l, includes copy fee. Payee- Buena Vista County Recorder. Minimum charge of $60.00 for this service. **Online access to Real Estate, Deed, Lien, UCC, Judgment records:** http://iowalandrecords.org/portal/clris/CountiesTab, an index of recorded land records and their images are available from 1/1999. **Other phones:** Treasurer-712-749-5533. **Property tax/Assessing**- PO Box 148, Storm Lake, IA 50588; 712-749-2543, assessor fax-712-749-2544. **Online access**- Search the property assessor and Ag sales databases for free at www.co.buena-vista.ia.us/assessors/ no name search.

Butler County

County Recorder, PO Box 346, Allison, IA 50602. 319-267-2735; fax-319-267-2675; 8AM-4PM (CST) www.butlercoiowa.org/recordercontact.htm

Index: All in one. Records indexed on a public use terminal back to 2000. Office will perform a UCC search (current only) but public must search other records themselves. Copy fee $1.00 per page. Faxed copies $2.50 1st page $1.00 each add'l page.Real estate record copy- $.50 per page. Cert fee- $5.00 per doc plus copy fee. Payee- Butler County Recorder. Office does not sell bulk data. **Online access to Real Estate, Deed records:** At http://iowalandrecords.org/portal/clris/CountiesTab, an index of recorded land records and their images are available from 1/2004. **Property tax/Assessing**- PO Box 346, 428 6th St, Allison, IA 50602; 319-267-2264, assessor fax- 319-267-2625. hours- 7:30AM-4:30PM www.butlercoiowa.org/assessorcontact.htm **Online access**- Search county property data free at http://butler.iowaassessors.com/ - no name searching.

Calhoun County

County Recorder, 416 4th St, #3; County Courthouse, Rockwell City, IA 50579. Recording, R/E & UCC phone-712-297-8121; fax-712-297-5000; 8:30AM-4:30PM (CST) www.calhouncountyiowa.com

Index: All in one. Records indexed on a public use terminal back to 1989. Only the public may search. Copy fee $.25 per page, $1.00 minimum. Cert fee-$5.00 per doc plus copy fee. Payee- Calhoun County Recorder. Office does not sell bulk data. **Online access to Real Estate, Deed records:** At http://iowalandrecords.org/portal/clris/CountiesTab, an index of recorded land records and their images are available from 1989. **Other phones:** Treasurer- 712-297-7111; Vital Records- 712-297-8121. **Property tax/Assessing**- 416 4th St, #6, Rockwell City, IA 50579; 712-297-7500, assessor fax- 712-297-5607. **Online access**- Access to the assessor database of property and sales data is free at www.calhoun.iowaassessors.com. Access to the treasurers property database is free; see Online Access note at beginning of section.

Carroll County

County Recorder, PO Box 782, Carroll, IA 51401-0782. Recording, R/E phone-712-792-3328; fax-712-792-9493; 8AM-4:30PM (CST) www.co.carroll.ia.us

Index: All in one. Records indexed on a public use terminal back to 1992. Office personnel or visitors may perform searches. Search fee $6.00 per name. Copy fee $1.00 per page. Include SASE for return of document.Real estate record copy- $.50 per page. Cert fee- $5.00 per doc plus copy fee. Payee- Carroll County Recorder of Deeds. **Online access to Real Estate, Deed records:** At http://iowalandrecords.org/portal/clris/CountiesTab, an index of recorded land records is available from 1/2000. **Other phones:** Treasurer- 712-792-1200; Vital Records- 712-792-3328. **Property tax/Assessing**- 114 E 6th St, Carroll, IA 51401; 712-792-9973, assessor fax- 712-775-2148. **Online access**- Access to the assessor database of property and sales data is free at www.co.carroll.ia.us/Assessor/property_records.htm.

Cass County

County Recorder, 5 W 7th, Atlantic, IA 50022-1492. 712-243-1692; fax-712-243-6660; 8AM-4:30PM (CST) www.casscountyiowa.org

Only the public may search. Copy fee $1.00 per page. Cert fee- $5.00 per doc plus copy fee. Payee- Cass County Recorder. **Online access to Real Estate, Deed, Lien, UCC records:** At http://iowalandrecords.org/portal/clris/CountiesTab, an index of recorded land records and their images are available from 1/1991. **Other phones:** Treasurer- 712-243-5503; Elections- 712-243-4570; Vital Records- 712-243-1692. **Property tax/Assessing**- 5 W 7th St, Atlantic, 50022; 712-243-2005, fax- 712-243-6660.

Cedar County

County Recorder, 400 Cedar St; Courthouse, Tipton, IA 52772-1752. Recording, R/E & UCC phone-563-886-2230; fax-563-886-2120; 8AM-4PM (CST) www.cedarcounty.org

DO NOT fax or e-mail requests. Index: Separate indices to search include indexes from 1984 forward. Images not available at this site. Records indexed on computer. Only the public may search. General copy fee $1.00; real estate record $.25 per page, $1.00 minimum. Cert fee- $5.00 per doc plus copy fee. Payee- Cedar County Recorder. Office does not sell bulk data. **Online access to Real Estate, Deed, Lien, UCC records:** At http://iowalandrecords.org/portal/clris/CountiesTab, an index of recorded land records is available from 1/1998, their images are available from 1/2004. **Other phones:** Treasurer- 563-886-2557; Elections- 563-886-3168; Vital Records- 563-886-2230. **Property tax/Assessing**- 400 Cedar St, Tipton, IA 52772; 563-886-6413, assessor fax- 563-886-2144. **Online access**- Search county property and sales data free at http://cedar.iowaassessors.com/ but no name searching.

Cerro Gordo County

County Recorder, 220 N Washington, Mason City, IA 50401. Recording, R/E & UCC phone-641-421-3056; fax-641-421-3154; hours- 8AM-4:30PM (CST) www.co.cerro-gordo.ia.us

Index: All in one. Records indexed on a public use terminal back to 1987. Only the public may search. Copy fee $.50 per page. Cert fee- $5.00 per doc plus copy fee. Payee- Cerro Gordo County Recorder of Deeds. Office does not sell bulk data. **Online access to Real Estate, Deed, Lien records:** Access to recorded documents at www.co.cerro-gordo.ia.us/document_search/docindex_search.cfm.

Also, with registration you search county land records on the statewide site at http://iowalandrecords.org/portal/clris/CountiesTab. **Other phones:** Treasurer- 641-421-3037; Elections- 641-421-3027; Vital Records- 641-421-3062. **Property tax/Assessing**- 220 N Washington St, Mason City, IA 50401; 641-421-3065 (county); -3061 (city), assessor fax- 641-421-3078. www.co.cerro-gordo.ia.us/Cnty_Asr/CntyAsr_Overview.cfm **Online access**- Access to the County and Mason City property records is free at www.co.cerro-gordo.ia.us/property_search/property_search.cfm.

Cherokee County

County Recorder, Drawer G, Cherokee, IA 51012. Recording, R/E & UCC phone-712-225-6735; fax-712-225-6754; hours - 8AM-4:30PM (CST) http://cherokeecountyiowa.com
Index: All in one. Records indexed on a public use terminal back to 1988. Only the public may search. Office will not search real estate records. Office will not search UCC records. Copy fee $.50 per page. Cert fee- $5.00 per doc plus copy fee. Payee- Cherokee County Recorder of Deeds. Office does not sell bulk data. **Online access to Real Estate, Deed, Lien, UCC, Judgment records:** At http://iowalandrecords.org/portal/clris/CountiesTab, an index of recorded land records is available from 1/2000, images available from 03/2002. Also, access to real estate and tax information for free go to http://lti.gmdsolutions.com/cherokee/index.html . **Other phones:** Treasurer- 712-225-6740; Elections-712-225-6704; Vital Records- 712-225-6735. **Property tax/Assessing**- Courthouse, Cherokee, IA 51012; 712-225-6701, assessor fax- 712-225-6484. (Appraiser/Auditor- 712-225-6701);

Chickasaw County

County Recorder, PO Box 14, New Hampton, IA 50659. Recording, R/E & UCC phone-641-394-2336; fax-641-394-2816; hours - 8:30AM-4:30PM (CST) www.chickasawcoia.org/Recorder/
Index: All in one. Records indexed on a public use terminal back to 1999. Office personnel or visitors may perform searches. Search fee $6.00 per debtor for federal tax liens. Office will search real estate records on the computer index only. Office will not search UCC records. Copy fee $.50 per page; self-serve $.25 per page. Cert fee- $5.00 per doc plus copy fee. Payee- Chickasaw County Recorder. Grantor/Grantee index available in paper format. **Online access to Real Estate, Deed, Lien, UCC, Judgment records:** At http://iowalandrecords.org/portal/clris/CountiesTab, an index of recorded land records and their images are available from 1/2002. **Other phones:** Treasurer-641-394-2107; Elections- 641-394-2100; Vital Records- 641-394-2336. **Property tax/Assessing**- PO Box 94, 8 E Prospect St, New Hampton, IA 50659; 641-394-2813, assessor fax- 641-394-3840. hours-8AM-4PM **Online access**- Search assessor property data free on the GIS system at http://beacon.schneidercorp.com/ but name searching requires you to have an account.

Clarke County

County Recorder, 100 S Main, Courthouse, Osceola, IA 50213. 641-342-3313; fax-641-342-3313; 8:30AM-4:30PM www.clarkecountyiowa.org/ClarkeCounty/mainhome.do
Index: All in one. Records indexed on a public use terminal back to 1999. Only the public may search. Copy fee $.50 per page; $5.00 for genealogy records; $1.00 per page for plats. Cert fee- $5.00 per doc plus copy fee. Payee- Clarke County Recorder. Bulk data available for purchase, contact Pennie Gonseth, Recorder. **Online access to Real Estate, Deed records:** At http://iowalandrecords.org/portal/clris/CountiesTab, an index of recorded land records and their images are available from 1/2004. **Other phones:** Treasurer- 641-342-3311; Elections- 641-342-3315; Vital Records- 641-342-3313. **Property tax/Assessing**- 100 S Main, Osceola, IA 50213; 641-342-3817, assessor fax- 641-342-3817. **Online access**- Search parcels free on the GIS-mapping site at www.clarkecoiagis.com/clarke/

Clay County

County Recorder, 300 W 4th St, #3; Admin Bldg, Spencer, IA 51301-3806. Recording, R/E & UCC phone-712-262-1081; fax-712-264-3983; 8AM-4:30PM (CST) www.co.clay.ia.us
Index: All in one. Records indexed on a public use terminal back to 1984. Only the public may search. Copy fee $1.00 per page. Copy fee for Federal Tax Lien is $5.00. Cert fee- $5.00 per doc plus copy fee. Payee- Clay County Recorder. **Online access to Real Estate, Deed, Mortgage records:** Access recorded doc index free at http://lti.gmdsolutions.com/clay/rindex.html. At http://iowalandrecords.org/portal/clris/SwitchToCountiesTab, an index of recorded land records and their images are available back to 1/2004. **Other phones:** Treasurer- 712-262-2179; Elections-712-262-1569; Vital Records- 712-262-1081. **Property tax/Assessing**- PO Box 452, 300 W 4th St, Spencer, IA 51301-0452; 712-262-1986, assessor fax-712-262-5257. (Appraiser/Auditor- 712-262-1986) **Online** - Search assessments, parcels, and sales free at http://clay.iowaassessors.com. Also, search tax sale certificates free at http://lti.gmdsolutions.com/clay/tindex.html. Also, search land and tax database free at http://lti.gmdsolutions.com/clay/index.html.

Clayton County

County Recorder, PO Box 278, Elkader, IA 52043. Recording, R/E phone-563-245-2710; fax-563-245-2353; 8AM-4:30PM www.claytoncountyiowa.net
Index: All in one. Records indexed on a public use terminal back to 6/92. Only the public may search. Copy fee $1.00 per page. Cert fee- $5.00 per doc plus copy fee. Payee- Clayton County Recorder. **Online access to Real Estate, Deed, Lien records:** Access land records free at http://iowalandrecords.org/portal/clris/CountiesTab, index and images available after required registration and login. **Other phones:** Treasurer- 563-245-1807; Elections- 563-245-1106; Vital Records- 563-245-2710; Clerk of Court- 563-245-2204. **Property tax/Assessing**- PO Box 416, 111 High St, Elkader, IA 52043; 563-245-2533, assessor fax- 563-245-1823. (Appraiser/Auditor- 563-245-2533) www.clayton.iowaassessors.com **Online access**- Search county property records free at http://clayton.iowaassessors.com/.

Clinton County

County Recorder, PO Box 2957, Clinton, IA 52733-2957. 563-244-0565 x0544, R/E recording phone-563-244-0565; fax-563-242-8412; 8AM-4:30PM www.clintoncountyiowa.com/recorder/default.asp
Index: All in one. Records indexed on a public use terminal back to 1988. Only the public may search. Copy fee $1.00 per page. Cert fee- $5.00 per doc plus copy fee. Payee- Clinton County Recorder of Deeds. **Online access to Real Estate, Deed records:** At http://iowalandrecords.org/portal/clris/CountiesTab, an index of recorded land records. **Other phones:** Treasurer- 563-242-0573; Elections- 563-244-0568; Vital Records- 563-244-0565 /0544. **Property tax/Assessing**- PO Box 2957, Clinton, IA 52733-2957; 563-242-0568. **Online access**- Access to the assessor database of property and sales data is free at www.qpublic.net/clinton/search1.html.

Crawford County

County Recorder, 1202 Broadway, Denison, IA 51442. Recording, R/E & UCC phone-712-263-3643; fax-712-263-3413; hours - 8AM-4:30PM (CST) http://crawfordcounty.org
Index: All in one. Records indexed on computer from 1989 to present, prior indexes are all separate: land deed, land mortgages, town deeds, town mortgages, misc. Only the public may search. Copy fee $.25 per page. Cert fee- $5.00 per doc plus $1.00 per page copy fee. Payee- Crawford County Recorder. Bulk data (land record index & images) available for purchase, contact Denise Meeves, County Recorder. **Online access to Real Estate, Deed, Lien, UCC records:** At http://iowalandrecords.org/portal/clris/CountiesTab, view an index of recorded land records from 1/1993, images from 1/2004. **Other phones:** Treasurer- 712-263-2648; Elections- 712-263-3045; Vital Records- 712-263-3643; no info given over the phone. **Property tax/Assessing**- 1202 Broadway, PO Box 444, Denison, IA 51442; 712-263-3447, assessor fax- 712-263-8668. hours- 8AM-4PM **Online access**- Search county property records free at http://crawford.iowaassessors.com but no name searching or sales info until you subscribe.

Dallas County

County Recorder, PO Box 38, Adel, IA 50003-0038. Recording, R/E & UCC phone-515-993-5804; 8AM-4:30PM (CST)
Records indexed on computer back to 1987, books back to 1880. Office personnel or visitors may perform searches. Search fee $6.00 per name. Copy fee $.50 per page. Cert fee- $5.00 per doc plus copy fee. Payee- Dallas County Recorder. **Online access to Real Estate, Deed records:** At http://iowalandrecords.org/portal/clris/CountiesTab, an index of recorded land records and their image. **Other phones:** Treasurer- 515-993-5808; Vital Records- 515-993-5804. **Property tax/Assessing**- 801 Court St, Adel, IA 50003; 515-993-5802, assessor fax- 515-589-7807. **Online access**- Access to the assessor database of property and sales data is free at www.dallas.iowaassessors.com. At http://iowalandrecords.org/portal/clris/SwitchToCountiesTab, view an index of recorded land records from 1/2004.

Davis County

County Recorder, 100 Courthouse Sq, #7, Bloomfield, IA 52537. Recording, R/E & UCC phone-641-664-2321; fax-641-664-3082; 7:30AM-4:30PM (CST) www.daviscountyrecorder.org
Index: All in one. Records indexed on a public use terminal back to 1950. Office will perform a UCC search but public must search other records themselves. Search fee $5.00. Copy fee $1.00 per page.Real estate record copy- $.30 per page. Cert fee- $5.00 per doc plus copy fee. Payee- Davis County Recorder. **Online access to Real Estate, Deed, Lien, UCC, Judgment records:** At http://iowalandrecords.org/portal/clris/CountiesTab, view an index of recorded land records from 1/1980, images from 3/15/2002. **Other phones:** Treasurer- 641-664-2155; Elections- 641-664-2101; Vital Records- 641-664-2321. **Property tax/Assessing**- Davis County Courthouse, Bloomfield, IA 52537; 641-664-3101. **Online access**- Access to the assessor GIS database of property and sales data is free at http://beacon.schneidercorp.com/.

Decatur County

County Recorder, 207 N Main St, Leon, IA 50144. 641-446-4322; fax-641-446-7159; 8AM-4:30PM
Records indexed on computer back to 1999. Office personnel or visitors may perform searches. Search fee $5.00 per name. Office will not search real estate records. Copy fee $1.00, if real estate $.25 per page. Cert fee- $4.00 per cert plus copy fee. Payee- Decatur County Recorder. **Online access to Real Estate, Deed records:** At http://iowalandrecords.org/portal/clris/CountiesTab view an index of recorded land records from 1/2004, images from 1/2004. **Property tax/Assessing**- 207 N Main St, Leon, IA 50144; 641-446-4314, assessor fax- 641-446-8643. hours- 8AM-4PM

Delaware County

County Recorder, 301 E Main; Courthouse, Manchester, IA 52057. 563-927-4665; fax-563-927-3641; 8AM-4:30PM (CST)
Index: All in one. Records indexed on computer back to1980. Office personnel or visitors may perform searches. Search fee $7.00 per name. Office will not search UCC or real estate records. Copy fee $1.00 per page.Real estate record copy- $.50 per page. Cert fee- $5.00 per doc plus copy fee. Payee- Delaware County

Recorder. **Online access to Real Estate, Deed records:** At http://iowalandrecords.org/portal/clris/CountiesTab, view an index of recorded land records from 1/2004, images from 1/2004. **Other phones:** Treasurer- 563-927-2845. **Property tax/Assessing-** 301 E Main St, Manchester, IA 52057; 563-927-2526, assessor fax- 563-927-6462. hours- 8AM-4PM. Public access terminal available. **Online access-** Search assessor property data for a fee on the GIS system at http://beacon.schneidercorp.com/. Registration and username required.

Des Moines County

County Recorder, PO Box 277, Burlington, IA 52601-0277. Recording, R/E & UCC phone-319-753-8221; fax-319-753-8721; 8AM-4:30PM (CST) www.co.des-moines.ia.us
Index: Separate indices to search include computer and legal books. Records indexed on a public use terminal back to 1992. Only the public may search. Will not search UCC records. General copy fee $1.00 per page. Real estate copy- $1.00 per page if on microfilm; $2.00 if faxed. Cert fee- $5.00 per doc plus copy fee. Payee- Des Moines County Recorder. Office does not sell bulk data. **Online access to Real Estate, Deed, Mortgage records:** At http://iowalandrecords.org/portal/clris/CountiesTab, view an index of recorded land records from 1/2000, images from 9/2003. **Other phones:** Treasurer- 319-753-8252; Elections- 319-753-8266; Vital Records-319-753-8221; Motor Vehicle- 319-753-8273; GIS Mapping Dept. -319-753-8759;. **Property tax/Assessing-** PO Box 277, 513 N Main St, Burlington, IA 52601-0277; 319-753-8224, assessor fax- 319-753-8721. (Appraiser/Auditor- 319-753-8255) Public access computer available. http://co.des-moines.ia.us **Online access-** Access to the assessor database of property and sales data is free at www.dmcgis.com/.

Dickinson County

County Recorder, PO Box OE, Spirit Lake, IA 51360. Recording, R/E phone-712-336-1495; fax-712-336-6310; 8AM-4:30PM www.co.dickinson.ia.us/
Index: All in one. Records indexed on computer back to 1993. Only the public may search. Copy fee $.50 per page. Cert fee- $5.00 per doc plus copy fee. Payee- Dickinson County Recorder. Office does not sell bulk data. **Online access to Real Estate, Grantor/Grantee, Deed records:** Access to recorder's records for a fee go to http://iowalandrecords.org/portal/clris/CountiesTab. **Other phones:** Treasurer- 712-336-1205; Vital Records- 712-336-1495. **Property tax/Assessing-** 1802 Hill Ave, Spirit Lake, IA 51360; 712-336-2687. **Online access-** Access to the assessor database of property and sales data is free at http://dickinson.iowaassessors.com. Also, search parcels and sales free at www.co.dickinson.ia.us/Department/Assessor.asp.

Dubuque County

County Recorder, 720 Central, #9; Courthouse, Dubuque, IA 52001. Recording, R/E & UCC phone-563-589-4434; fax-563-589-4484; 8AM-4:30PM (CST) www.dubuquecounty.org
Index: All in one. Records indexed on a public use terminal back to 1988. Office will perform a UCC search but public must search other records themselves. Search fee $5.00. Copy fee $1.00 per page. Cert fee- $2.00 per doc plus copy fee. Payee- Dubuque County Recorder. **Online access to Real Estate, Deed, Lien, Judgment, Corporation records:** Access recorder general, tax lien, and corporations indexes at www.dbqco.org/resolution/. General index goes back to 1988; tax liens to 10/19/2005, corporations to 1/1972. Also, at http://iowalandrecords.org/portal/clris/SwitchToCountiesTab, view index and images of recorded land records from 1/1987. **Other phones:** Treasurer- 563-589-4436; Elections- 563-589-4458; Vital Records-563-589-4434. **Property tax/Assessing-** 720 Central Ave, Dubuque, IA 52001; 563-589-4416, assessor fax- 563-589-7807. **Online access-** Access the assessor database of property and sales data free at http://beacon.schneidercorp.com -no name searching.

Emmet County

County Recorder, 609 1st Ave N, Estherville, IA 51334. Recording, R/E phone-712-362-4115; fax-712-362-7454; hours- 8AM-4:30PM (CST) www.emmetcountyia.com/recorder.htm
Index: All in one. Records indexed on a public use terminal back to 1987. Only the public may search. Copy fee $.50 per page (real estate). Cert fee- $5.00 per doc plus copy fee. Payee- Emmet County Recorder. **Online access to Real Estate, Deed records:** At http://iowalandrecords.org/portal/clris/CountiesTab, view an index of recorded land records from 1/2003, images from 1/2004. **Other phones:** Treasurer- 712-362-3824; Elections- 712-362-4261; Vital Records- 712-362-4115; Clerk of Court- 712-362-3325. **Property tax/Assessing-** 609 1st Ave N, Estherville, IA 51334; 712-362-2609, assessor fax-712-362-7454. (Appraiser/Auditor- 712-362-2609) www.emmetcountyia.com/serv01.htm **Online access-** Access the assessor GIS database of property and sales data free at http://beacon.schneidercorp.com/.

Fayette County

Recorder, PO Box 226, West Union, IA 52175-0226. 563-422-3687; fax-563-422-3739; 8AM-4PM www.fayettecountyiowa.org/RECORDER.html
Index: All in one. Records indexed on a public use terminal back to 1985. Office personnel or visitors may perform searches. Search fee $5.00 per name. Office will not search real estate records. Copy fee $1.00 per page.Real estate record copy- $.50 per page. Cert fee- $5.00 per cert plus $.50 per page copy fee. Payee- Fayette County Recorder. Call to arrange. **Online access to Real Estate, Deed records:** At http://iowalandrecords.org/portal/clris/CountiesTab, view an index of recorded land records from 1/2004, images from 1/2004. **Other phones:** Treasurer- 563-422-3787; Elections- 563-422-3497; Vital Records-563-422-3680. **Property tax/Assessing-** PO Box 167, 114 Bine St, West Union, 52175; 563-422-3397. No public terminal available. www.fayettecountyiowa.org/ASSESSOR.html **Online access-** Access to the assessor GIS database of property and sales data is free at http://beacon.schneidercorp.com/.

Floyd County

County Recorder, 101 S Main; Courthouse, Charles City, IA 50616. Recording, R/E & UCC phone-641-257-6154; fax-641-228-6458; 8AM-4:30PM (CST) www.floydcoia.org
Index: All in one. Records indexed on a public use terminal back to 1987. Only the public may search. Copy fee $.50 per page. $1.00 per page to fax back. Cert fee- $5.00 per doc plus copy fee. Payee- Floyd County Recorder. Office does not sell bulk data. **Online access to Real Estate, Deed, Lien, UCC, Judgment records:** At http://iowalandrecords.org/portal/clris/CountiesTab view an index of recorded land records from 3/1995, images from 8/22/1996. **Other phones:** Treasurer- 641-257-6118; Elections- 641-257-6131; Vital Records- 641-257-6154. **Property tax/Assessing-** 101 S Main, Courthouse, Charles City, IA 50616; 641-257-6152. No public terminal available. www.floydcoia.org **Online access-** Search assessor property data free on the GIS system at http://beacon.schneidercorp.com/ but name searching requires registration and password. Also, access property and sales data is free at www.floydcoia.org/features/gis.asp.

Franklin County

County Recorder, PO Box 26, Hampton, IA 50441. 641-456-5675; fax-641-456-6009; 8AM-4PM (CST)
Index: All in one after 1985. Records indexed on a public use terminal back to 10/1/2001. Only the public may search. Real estate copy $.50 per page with $1.00 minimum if mailed out. Cert fee- $5.00 per doc plus copy fee. Payee- Franklin County Recorder. **Online access to Real Estate, Deed, Lien records:** At http://iowalandrecords.org/portal/clris/CountiesTab sign up for free access to index of recorded land records from 10/2001, images from 10/2001. **Other phones:** Treasurer- 641-456-5678; Elections- 641-456-5622. **Property tax/Assessing-** PO Box 575, Hampton, IA 50441; 641-456-5118, assessor fax-641-456-6005.

Fremont County

County Recorder, PO Box 295, Sidney, IA 51652. Recording, R/E & UCC phone-712-374-2315; fax-712-374-2826; hours- 8AM-4:30PM (CST) www.co.fremont.ia.us/fremcorecd.htm
Index: All in one. Records indexed on a public use terminal back to 1984. Only the public may search. Copy fee $.50 per page. Cert fee- $5.00 per doc plus copy fee. Payee- Fremont County Recorder. Office does not sell bulk data. **Online access to Real Estate, Deed, Lien, UCC records:** At http://iowalandrecords.org/portal/clris/CountiesTab, view an index of recorded land records from 1/1983, images from 1/1983. **Other phones:** Treasurer- 712-374-2122; Elections- 712-374-2031; Vital Records-712-374-2315; County Clerk- 712-374-2232. **Property tax/Assessing-** PO Box 760, 506 Filmore St, Sidney, IA 51652; 712-374-2631, assessor fax-712-374-3202. hours- 8:30AM-4:30PM No public terminal. www.co.fremont.ia.us/fremcoassr.htm

Greene County

County Recorder, 114 N Chestnut St; Courthouse, Jefferson, IA 50129. Recording, R/E & UCC phone-515-386-5670; fax-515-386-5274; 8AM-4:30PM (CST) www.co.greene.ia.us/recorder/recorder.htm
Index: All in one alpha. Records indexed on a public use terminal back to 1988. Office will perform a tax lien search but public must search other records themselves. UCC search per debtor name- $5.00. Separate federal/state combined tax lien search- $6.00 per debtor. Copy fee $1.00, if real estate $.25 per page. $1.25 per page if mailed. Cert fee- $5.00 per doc plus copy fee. Payee- Greene County Recorder. **Online access to Real Estate, Deed, Lien, UCC, Judgment records:** At http://iowalandrecords.org/portal/clris/CountiesTab view an index of recorded land records from 1/1988, images from 1/1988. **Other phones:** Treasurer- 515-386-5675; Elections- 515-386-5680; Vital Records- 515-386-5670. **Property tax/Assessing-** 114 N Chestnut St, 1st Fl, Courthouse, Jefferson, IA 50129; 515-386-5660, assessor fax- 515-386-1216. (Appraiser/Auditor- 515-386-5680) www.co.greene.ia.us/assessor/assessor.htm **Online access-** Access to the assessor database of property and sales data is free at http://greene.iowaassessors.com.

Grundy County

County Recorder, 706 G Ave, Grundy Center, IA 50638-1440. Recording, R/E & UCC phone-319-824-3234; fax-319-824-3017; 8AM-4:30PM (CST)
Index: All in one. Records indexed on a public use terminal. Records back to 1984. Only the public may search. Copy fee $1.00 per page. Cert fee- $5.00 per doc plus copy fee. Payee- Grundy County Recorder. **Online access to Real Estate, Deed records:** At http://iowalandrecords.org/portal/clris/CountiesTab, view an index of recorded land records from 1/2004, images from 1/2004. **Other phones:** Treasurer- 319-824-3412; Elections- 319-824-3122; Vital Records-319-824-3234. **Property tax/Assessing-** 706 G Ave, Grundy Center, IA 50638; 319-824-6216, assessor fax- 319-824-6009. **Online access-** Access to the assessor GIS database of property and sales data is free at http://beacon.schneidercorp.com/ but registration and fee required to name search.

Guthrie County

County Recorder, 200 N 5th; Courthouse, Guthrie Center, IA 50115. Recording, R/E & UCC phone-641-747-3412; fax-641-747-3081; 8AM-4:30PM (CST) www.guthriecounty.org/recorder/index.html
Index: All in one. Records indexed on computer back to 1987. Office will perform a UCC search but public

must search other records themselves. General copy fee $.25 per page. Vital records- $5.00 each. Cert fee- $5.00 per doc plus copy fee. Payee- Guthrie County Recorder. Office does not sell bulk data. **Online access to Real Estate, Deed records:** At http://iowalandrecords.org/portal/clris/CountiesTab, view an index of recorded land records from 1/2004, images from 1/2004. **Other phones:** Treasurer- 641-747-3414; Elections- 641-747-3619; Vital Records- 641-747-3412. **Property tax/Assessing**- 200 N 5th, Courthouse, Guthrie Center, IA 50115; 641-747-3319, assessor fax- 641-747-8206. (Appraiser/Auditor- 641-747-3319) No public terminal. www.guthriecounty.org/assessor/index.html **Online access**- Access to the assessor database of property and sales data is free at www.guthrie.iowaassessors.com.

Hamilton County

County Recorder, PO Box 126, Webster City, IA 50595-0126. 515-832-9535; fax-515-832-8620; 8AM-4:30PM (CST) www.hamiltoncounty.org
Index: All in one. Records indexed on a public use terminal back to 1985. Only the public may search. Copy fee $.50 per page; UCC copy fee- $1.00. Cert fee- $5.00 1st page plus copy fee. Payee- Hamilton County Recorder. **Online access to Real Estate, Deed, Lien, UCC, Judgment records:** At http://iowalandrecords.org/portal/clris/CountiesTab, view an index of recorded land records from 7/02. **Other phones:** Treasurer- 515-832-9542; Elections- 515-832-9510; Vital Records- 515-832-9535. **Property tax/Assessing**- 2300 Superior St, Webster City, IA 50595; 515-832-9505, assessor fax- 515-832-9506. **Online access**- Search assessor property records and residential and commercial sales free at http://hamilton.iowaassessors.com.

Hancock County

County Recorder, 855 State St, Garner, IA 50438. Recording, R/E & UCC phone-641-923-2464, UCC recording phone-641-923-2404; fax-641-923-3912; 8AM-4PM (CST) www.hancockcountyia.org
Index: All in one 1991-present. Records indexed on a public use terminal back to 1991. Only the public may search. Copy fee $1.00 per page.Real estate or tax lien copy- $.50 per page. Cert fee- $5.00 per doc plus copy fee. Payee- Hancock County Recorder. Office does not sell bulk data. **Online access to Real Estate, Deed records:** At http://iowalandrecords.org/portal/clris/CountiesTab, view an index of recorded land records from 1/2004, images from 1997-2008. **Other phones:** Treasurer- 641-923-3122; Elections- 641-923-3163; Vital Records- 641-923-2464. **Property tax/Assessing**- PO Box70, 855 State St, Garner, IA 50438; 641-923-2269, assessor fax- 641-923-2269. (Appraiser/Auditor- 641-923-2269);

Hardin County

County Recorder, PO Box 443, Eldora, IA 50627. 641-939-8178; fax-641-939-8245; 8AM-4:30PM
Index: All in one. Records indexed on a public use terminal back to 1984. Only the public may search. Will not search UCC records. Copy fee $1.00; if real estate $.50 per page. Cert fee- $5.00 per cert plus copy fee. Payee- Hardin County Recorder. **Online access to Real Estate, Deed records:** At http://iowalandrecords.org/portal/clris/CountiesTab, view an index of recorded land records from 2000 to current. **Other phones:** Treasurer- 641-939-8226; Drivers License- 641-939-8328. **Property tax/Assessing**- 1215 Edington Ave, Eldora, IA 50627; 641-939-8100, assessor fax- 641-939-8245. (Appraiser/Auditor- 641-939-8230) **Online access**- Search City of Iowa Falls assessor property data for a fee on GIS at http://beacon.schneidercorp.com/. Registration and username required.

Harrison County

County Recorder, Courthouse, Logan, IA 51546. Recording, R/E & UCC phone-712-644-2545; fax-712-644-3157; 8AM-4:30PM (CST)
Index: All in one. Records indexed on a public use terminal as far back as 1983. Office personnel or visitors may perform searches. Search fee $5.00 per name. Office will not search real estate records. Copy fee $1.00 per page.Real estate record copy- $.50 per page. Will fax back- $2.00 1st page, $1.00 each add'l. Cert fee- $5.00 per doc plus copy fee. Payee- Harrison County Recorder. Office does not sell bulk data. **Online access to Real Estate, Deed records:** At http://iowalandrecords.org/portal/clris/CountiesTab, view an index of recorded land records from 1/2004. **Other phones:** Treasurer- 712-644-2750; Elections- 712-644-2401; Vital Records- 712-644-2545. **Property tax/Assessing**- Harrison County Courthouse, Harrison County Auditor's Office, Logan, IA 51546; 712-644-3101, assessor fax- 712-644-2643. **Online access**- Access to the assessor database of property and sales data and maps is free at http://maps.harrisoncountyia.org. Also, search assessor property data free on the GIS system at http://beacon.schneidercorp.com/.

Henry County

County Recorder, PO Box 106, Mount Pleasant, IA 52641. 319-385-0765; fax-319-385-3601; 8AM-4:30PM (CST) www.henrycountyiowa.us
Index: All in one. Records indexed on a public use terminal back to 1984. Only the public may search. Copy fee $.50 per page. Cert fee- $5.00 per page plus copy fee. Payee- Henry County Recorder. Bulk data available for purchase. **Online access to Real Estate, Deed records:** At http://iowalandrecords.org/portal/clris/CountiesTab, view an index of recorded land records from 1/2002, images from 1/2002. **Other phones:** Treasurer- 319-385-0763; Elections- 319-385-0756; Vital Records- 319-385-0765. **Property tax/Assessing**- 100 E Washington St, #102, Mt. Pleasant, 52641; 319-385-0750, fax- 319-385-0751. www.henrycountyiowa.us/offices/assessor/index.htm **Online** - Assessor records for free on GIS system at http://beacon.schneidercorp.com/?site=HenryCountyIA.

Howard County

County Recorder, 137 N Elm; Court House, Cresco, IA 52136. 563-547-3621, R/E recording phone-563-547-5038, UCC recording phone-563-547-3621; fax-563-547-1103; 8AM-4:30PM (CST)
Index: All in one. Records indexed on computer back to 2001. Only the public may search. Copy fee $.50 per page in person, $2.50 minimum for fax back or email. Cert fee- $5.00 per doc plus copy fee. Payee- Howard County Recorder. Office does not sell bulk data. **Online access to Real Estate, Deed, Lien records:** At http://iowalandrecords.org/portal/clris/CountiesTab, view an index of recorded land records from 1/2004. **Other phones:** Treasurer- 563-547-3860; Vital Records- 563-547-3621; Auditor- 563-547-2880. **Property tax/Assessing**- 137 N Elm St, Cresco, IA 52136; 563-547-3409, assessor fax- 563-547-2802.

Humboldt County

County Recorder, PO Box 100, Dakota City, IA 50529-0100. 515-332-3693; fax-515-332-1738; 8AM-4:30PM (CST)
Index: Separate indices to search. Records indexed on a public use terminal back to 7/1/97. Only the public may search. General copy fee $1.00 per page.Real estate or tax lien record copy- $.25 per page. Cert fee- $5.00 1st page, $1.00 each add'l, plus copy fee. Payee- Humboldt County Recorder. Office does not sell bulk data. **Online access to Real Estate, Deed, Property Sales records:** At http://iowalandrecords.org/portal/clris/CountiesTab, view an index of recorded land records from 1/2004, images from 1/2004. **Other phones:** Treasurer- 515-332-1681; Elections- 515-332-1571; Vital Records- 515-332-3693. **Property tax/Assessing**- PO Box 100, 203 Main St, Dakota City, IA 50529-0100; 515-332-1463. **Online access**- Assessor property records and sales free at www.humboldt.iowaassessors.com.

Ida County

County Recorder, 401 Moorehead; Courthouse, Ida Grove, IA 51445. Recording, R/E & UCC phone-712-364-2220; fax-712-364-3929; 8AM-4:30PM
Index: Separate indices to search include birth, death, marriage, mortgage, deeds, tax liens, change of title, plats, misc. Records indexed on a public use terminal go back to 2002. Only the public may search. Copy fee $.25 per page. Cert fee- $5.00 per doc plus copy fee. Payee- Ida County Recorder. Office does not sell bulk data. **Online access to Real Estate, Deed records:** At http://iowalandrecords.org/portal/clris/CountiesTab, view an index of recorded land records from 1/2003. **Other phones:** Treasurer- 712-364-2287; Elections- 712-364-2620; Vital Records- 712-364-2220. **Property tax/Assessing**- 401 Moorehead, Ida Grove, IA 51445; 712-364-3622, assessor fax-712-364-3929.

Iowa County

County Recorder, PO Box 185, Marengo, IA 52301. Recording, R/E & UCC phone-319-642-3622; fax-319-642-5562; 7:30AM-4:30PM www.co.iowa.ia.us
Index: All in one. Records indexed on a public use terminal back to 1992. Office will perform a UCC search but public must search other records themselves. UCC search fee $10.00 per name. Copy fee $1.00 per page. Cert fee- $5.00 per doc plus $2.00 per page. Payee- Iowa County Recorder. Contact Sue Peterson, Recorder. **Online access to Real Estate, Grantor/Grantee, Deed records:** Access real estate indexing free at http://lti.gmdsolutions.com/iowa/rindex.html. Also, at http://iowalandrecords.org/portal/clris/CountiesTab, view an index of recorded land records back to 1/2004. **Other phones:** Treasurer- 319-642-3672; Elections- 319-642-3923; Vital Records- 319-642-3622. **Property tax/Assessing**- PO Box 347, 901 Court Ave, Marengo, IA 52301; 319-642-3851. hours- 8AM-4:30PM **Online access**- Access to the assessor database of property and sales data is free at http://iowa.iowaassessors.com. Also search free at http://lti.gmdsolutions.com/iowa/index.html. Search county Tax Sale Certificates free at http://lti.gmdsolutions.com/iowa/tindex.html.

Jackson County

County Recorder, 201 W Platt; Courthouse, Maquoketa, IA 52060. Recording, R/E & UCC phone-563-652-2504; fax-563-652-6460; 8:30AM-4:30PM (CST) www.jacksoncountyiowa.com
Index: All in one. Records indexed on computer back to 1987. Only the public may search. General copy fee-$.50 per page. Cert fee- $5.00 plus $.50 per page for real estate filings, includes copy fee; vital records cert- $15.00 each. Payee- Jackson County Recorder. Individual requests for bulk data should be directed to Arlene Schauf, Registrar. **Online access to Real Estate, Deed, Lien, UCC, Judgment records:** At http://iowalandrecords.org/portal/clris/CountiesTab, view an index of recorded land records from 1/1998, images from 1/1998. **Other phones:** Treasurer- 563-652-5649; Elections- 563-652-3144; Vital Records- 563-652-2504. **Property tax/Assessing**- Real Property Assessor, 201 W Platt, Courthouse, Maquoketa, IA 52060; 563-652-4935, assessor fax- 563-652-7195. **Online access**- Search assessor property data for a fee on the GIS system at http://beacon.schneidercorp.com/. Registration and username required.

Jasper County

County Recorder, PO Box 665, Newton, IA 50208. 641-792-5442, R/E recording phone-647-792-5442; fax-641-791-3680; 8AM-5PM (CST)
Index: All in one. Records indexed on a public use terminal back to 1988. Only the public may search. Copy fee $1.00 per page. Vital record copy or federal tax lien- $5.00 per doc. Fee to fax back- $2.00 per

page. Cert fee- $5.00 per doc, up to 10 pages, $.25 each add'l page plus copy fee. Payee- Jasper County Recorder. **Online Real Estate, Deed records:** At http://iowalandrecords.org/portal/clris/CountiesTab, view an index of recorded land records from 1/2004, images from 1/2004. **Other phones:** Treasurer- 641-792-6115; Elections- 641-792-7350; Vital Records- 647-792-5442. **Property tax/Assessing**- PO Box 665, 101 1st St N, Newton, IA 50208; 641-792-6195, assessor fax- 641-791-1602. hours- 8AM-4:30PM **Online access**- Access to the assessor database of property and sales data is free at http://jasper.iowaassessors.com/

Jefferson County

County Recorder, 51 W Briggs, Fairfield, IA 52556-2820. Recording, R/E & UCC phone-641-472-4331; fax-641-472-2597; 8AM-4:30PM (CST)

Index: All in one. Records indexed on a public use terminal back to 1985. Office will perform a UCC search (with proper forms) but public must search other records themselves. Office will not search real estate records. UCC search includes tax liens if requested. UCC search per debtor name- $5.00. UCC search request using non-standard form (per name)- $6.00. State tax lien searches are uncertified and performed at no charge. Separate federal tax lien search- $6.00 per debtor. Copy fee $.50 per page; UCC copy- $1.00 per page. Cert fee- $2.00 per doc plus copy fee. Payee- Jefferson County Recorder. Office does not sell bulk data. **Online access to Real Estate, Grantor/Grantee, Deed, Lien records:** With registration and username, access land records free on private site at http://iowalandrecords.org/portal/clris/CountiesTab. Online records from 1/1/2004 to present only. **Other phones:** Treasurer- 641-472-2349; Elections- 641-472-2840; Vital Records- 641-472-4331. **Property tax/Assessing**- PO Box 308, 51 E Briggs St, Fairfield, IA 52556-0308; 641-472-2849, assessor fax- 641-472-6695. (Appraiser/Auditor- 641-472-2840) Public access terminal available. **Online**- Access to the assessor database of property and sales data is free at http://jefferson.iowaassessors.com but no name searching.

Johnson County

County Recorder, 913 S Dubuque St, Iowa City, IA 52240-4273. 319-356-6093; fax-319-339-6181; 8AM-5PM www.johnson-county.com/recorder/

Index: Separate indices to search include books by years, computer. Records indexed on a public use terminal back to 11/1983. Office will perform a UCC search (must have request on correct request form only) but public must search other records themselves. Search fee $5.00 per name. Copy fee $.25 per page. Vital records $1.00 per page. Will fax back for $1.00 per page. Cert fee- $2.00 per doc includes up to 8 pages of copies. Payee- Johnson County Recorder. **Online access to Real Estate, Deed, Lien, Mortgage, Corporation records:** Access the recorders data free at http://www2.johnson-county.com/resolution/. Images and indexes go back to 11/1983, Book 670. At www.iowalandrecords.org, view index of recorded land records from 2004, images from 2/27/2004. **Other phones:** Treasurer- 319-356-6087; Elections- 319-356-6004; Vital Records- 319-356-6093. **Property tax/Assessing**- 913 S Dubuque, #205, Iowa City, IA 52240; 319-356-6078, assessor fax- 319-339-6160. **Online access**- Access to the assessor database of property and sales data is free at http://beacon.schneidercorp.com/?site=JohnsonCountyIA but no name searching. Access Iowa City assessor and property data free at http://iowacity.iowaassessors.com.

Jones County

County Recorder, 500 W Main, Rm 116; Courthouse, Anamosa, IA 52205-1632. Recording, R/E & UCC phone-319-462-2477; fax-319-462-5802; 8AM-4:30PM http://jonescountyiowa.org/recorder.aspx

Index: Pre-1990 records in a number of indices. Records indexed on computer back to 7/1/93. Office will perform a UCC search but public must search other records themselves. Search fee-$5.00 per name. Copy fee $1.00 per page.Real estate or tax lien record copy- $.50 per page. Cert fee- $5.00 per doc plus copy fee. Payee- Jones County Recorder. Property-related bulk data available for purchase upon request. **Online access to Real Estate, Deed records:** At http://iowalandrecords.org/portal/clris/CountiesTab, view an index of recorded land records from 1993, images from 1993. **Other phones:** Treasurer- 319-462-3550; Elections- 319-462-2282; Vital Records- 319-462-2477. **Property tax/Assessing**- 500 W Main St, Rm 123, Anamosa, IA 52205; 319-462-2671, assessor fax- 319-462-5320. http://jonescountyiowa.org/assessor.aspx **Online access**- For access to parcels/land data for free go to http://beacon.schneidercorp.com/.

Keokuk County

County Recorder, 101 S Main St; Courthouse, Sigourney, IA 52591. Recording, R/E & UCC phone-641-622-2540; fax-641-622-3789; 8AM-4:30PM (CST) www.keokukcountyia.com

Index: All in one. Records indexed on a public use terminal back to 1989. Office personnel or visitors may perform searches. Search fee $5.00. Office will not search real estate records. Office will not search UCC records. Copy fee $1.00 per page. Cert fee- $5.00 1st page includes copy fee. Payee- Keokuk County Recorder. For bulk data information contact Melissa R. Bird, Keokuk County Recorder. **Online Real Estate, Deed, Lien, UCC, Judgment records:** at http://iowalandrecords.org/portal/clris/CountiesTab, view an index of recorded land records from 1/1989. **Other phones:** Treasurer- 641-622-2421; Elections- 641-622-2320; Vital Records- 641-622-2540. **Property tax/Assessing**- 101 S Main St, Sigourney, IA 52591; 641-622-2560, assessor fax- 641-622-2760. **Online access**- Access to the assessor GIS database of property and sales data is free at http://beacon.schneidercorp.com/.

Kossuth County

County Recorder, 114 W State, Algona, IA 50511. 515-295-5660; fax-515-295-3071; 8AM-4PM (CST)

Index: All in one. Records indexed on a public use terminal back to 1993. Only the public may search. Copy fee $1.00 per page.Real estate record copy- $.50 per page. Cert fee- $5.00 1st page, $2.50 each add'l. Payee- Kossuth County Recorder. Office does not sell bulk data. **Online Real Estate, Deed, Lien, UCC, Judgment records:** At http://iowalandrecords.org/portal/clris/CountiesTab, view an index of recorded land records from 1/2004, images from 1/2004. **Other phones:** Treasurer- 515-295- 3404. **Property tax/Assessing**- 114 W State, Algona, IA 50511; 515-295-3857, assessor fax- 515-295-3071. **Online access**- Access to the assessor database of property and county sales data is free at www.co.kossuth.ia.us/assessor/assessor.htm.

Lee County (Northern District)

County Recorder, PO Box 322, Fort Madison, IA 52627-0322. Recording, R/E & UCC phone-319-372-4662; fax-319-372-7033; 8:30AM-4:30PM (CST) www.leecounty.org

Index: All in one. Records indexed on a public use terminal back to 1984. Office personnel or visitors may perform searches. Search fee-$5.00 UCC's. Office will not search real estate records. Tax liens not included in UCC search. This agency will not do a state tax lien search. Separate federal tax lien search- $6.00 per debtor. Copy fee $1.00 per UCC or tax lien page. Real estate record copy- $.35 per page. Cert fee- $5.00 per cert plus copy fee. Payee- Lee County Recorder. Bulk data is available for purchase, contact Recorder Larry Holtkamp for info. **Online Real Estate, Deed, Lien, UCC, Judgment, Sales records:** at http://iowalandrecords.org/portal/clris/CountiesTab, view an index of recorded land records from 1/2003, images from 1/2003. **Other phones:** Treasurer- 319-372-3405; Elections- 319-372-3705; Vital Records- 319-372-4662. **Property tax/Assessing**- 933 Ave H, Fort Madison, IA 52627; 319-372-6302, assessor fax- 319-372-7033. **Online access**- Access to the assessor database of property and sales data is free at http://lee.iowaassessors.com.

Lee County (Southern District)

County Recorder, PO Box 160, Keokuk, IA 52632. Recording, R/E & UCC phone-319-524-1126; fax-319-524-1544; 8:30AM-4:30PM www.leecounty.org

Index: All in one. Records indexed on a public use terminal back to 1984. Office will perform a UCC or tax lien search but public must search other records themselves. UCC search request must be on correct form. Copy fee $1.00 per page.Real estate record copy- $.35 per page. Cert fee- $5.00 per doc plus copy fee. Payee- Lee County Recorder. Bulk data is available for purchase, contact Recorder Larry Holtkamp for info. **Online access to Real Estate, Deed, Lien, UCC, Judgment, Sales records:** At http://iowalandrecords.org/portal/clris/CountiesTab, view an index of recorded land records from 11/2002, images from 1/2004. **Other phones:** Treasurer- 319-524-1550; Elections- 319-524-2482; Vital Records- 319-524-1126. **Property tax/Assessing**- 25 N 7th, Keokuk, IA 52632; 319-524-1375, assessor fax- 319-524-1544. (Appraiser/Auditor- 319-524-2482) **Online access**- Access to the assessor database of property and sales data is free at http://lee.iowaassessors.com.

Linn County

County Recorder, PO Box 1406, Cedar Rapids, IA 52406-1406. Recording, R/E & UCC phone-319-892-5420; fax-319-892-5459; 8AM-5PM (CST) www.linncountyrecorder.com

Index: All in one. Records indexed on a public use terminal back to 1975. Office personnel or visitors may perform searches. No fee for search. Office will only do simple computer name search of real estate records. Will not search UCC records. Copy fee $1.00 per page. Cert fee- $5.00 per doc plus copy fee. Payee- Linn County Recorder. **Online access to Real Estate, Deed, Lien, UCC records:** At http://iowalandrecords.org/portal/clris/CountiesTab, view an index of recorded land records from 1/1990, images from 1/1990. **Other phones:** Treasurer- 319-892-5550; Elections- 319-892-5400; Vital Records- 319-892-5445. **Property tax/Assessing**- 2600 Edgewood Rd SW #726, Cedar Rapids, IA 52404; 319-892-5220, assessor fax- 319-892-5239. **Online access**- Access to the assessor property data is free at www.linn.iowaassessors.com/search.php. Also, access to City of Cedar Rapids property data is free at www.cedar-rapids.org/assessor/pmc/ no name search.

Louisa County

County Recorder, PO Box 264, Wapello, IA 52653-0264. 319-523-5361, R/E recording phone-319-523-3371; fax-319-523-5364; 8AM-4:30PM (CST) www.louisacountyiowa.org/

Index: All in one. Records indexed on a public use terminal back to 1980. Only the public may search. Copy fee $5.00 per page for Vitals, $.50 per page for all other copies. Cert fee- $5.00 per cert plus copy fee. Payee- Louisa County Recorder. Bulk data sale can be arranged by email or purchased on CD. Contact Leanne Black. **Online Real Estate, Deed records:** At http://iowalandrecords.org/portal/clris/CountiesTab, view an index of recorded land records from 1/1980, images from 11/1992. **Other phones:** Treasurer- 319-523-4451; Elections- 319-523-3371; Vital Records- 319-523-5361. **Property tax/Assessing**- PO Box 284, 117 S Main St, Wapello, IA 52653; 319-523-6111, assessor fax- 319-523-8175. **Online**- Access the assessor database of property and sales data is free at http://beacon.schneidercorp.com/?site=LouisaCountyIA.

Lucas County

Recorder, 916 Braden, Courthouse, Chariton, IA 50049. 641-774-2413; fax-641-774-1619; 8AM-4PM Records indexed on a public use terminal back to 1985. Only the public may search. Copy fee $1.00 per page.Real estate or tax lien copy- $.25 per page. Cert fee- $5.00 per doc plus copy fee. Payee- Lucas

County Recorder. **Online access to Real Estate, Deed records:** At http://iowalandrecords.org/portal/clris/CountiesTab, view an index of recorded land records from 1/2004, images from 1/2004. **Other phones:** Treasurer- 641-774-5213; Elections- 641-774-4512; Vital Records- 641-774-2413. **Property tax/Assessing**- 916 Braden, Chariton, IA 50049; 641-774-4411, assessor fax- 641-774-8827.

Lyon County

County Recorder, 206 S 2nd Ave; Courthouse, Rock Rapids, IA 51246. Recording, R/E & UCC phone-712-472-2381; fax-same; 8AM-4:30PM (CST)
Index: All in one. Records indexed on a public use terminal back to 1/1995. Office personnel or visitors may perform searches. Search fee $6.00 per name. Office will not search real estate records. Copy fee $1.00 per page. Fax $2.00 per page. Cert fee- $5.00 per doc plus copy fee. Payee- Lyon County Recorder. Office does not sell bulk data. **Online access to Real Estate, Deed, Property Sale records:** At http://iowalandrecords.org/portal/clris/CountiesTab, view an index of recorded land records from 1/2004, images from 1/2004. **Other phones:** Treasurer- 712-472-3703; Elections- 712-472-3713; Vital Records- 712-472-2381. **Property tax/Assessing**- 206 2nd Ave, Rock Rapids, IA 51246; 712-472-3592, assessor fax- 712-472-3598. **Online access**- Access to the assessor database of property and sales data is free at http://lyon.iowaassessors.com/.

Madison County

County Recorder, PO Box 152, Winterset, IA 50273-0152. Recording, R/E phone-515-462-3771; fax-515-462-5006; 8AM-4:30PM www.madisoncoia.us
Index: All in one. Records indexed on a public use terminal back to 1987. Office personnel or visitors may perform searches. Search fee-$5.00 per name. Office will not search real estate records. Copy fee $.50 per page. Marriage Certificate copy- $5.00; $15.00 is certified. Cert fee- $5.00 per doc plus copy fee. Payee- Madison County Recorder. **Online access to Real Estate, Grantor/Grantee, Deed, Mortgage, Lien records:** At http://iowalandrecords.org/portal/clris/CountiesTab, view an index of recorded land records from 1/1999. Also, search free at http://lti.gmdsolutions.com/madison/rindex.html. **Other phones:** Treasurer- 515-462-1542; Elections- 515-462-3914; Vital Records- 515-462-3771. **Property tax/Assessing**- PO Box 152, 112 N John Wayne Dr, Courthouse, Winterset, IA 50273; 515-462-4303, assessor fax- 515-462-5888. www.madisoncoia.us/offices/assessor/index.htm **Online access**- Access the assessor database of property data free at http://lti.gmdsolutions.com/madison/index.html. Also search free at http://madison.iowaassessors.com/. Search tax sales certificates free at http://lti.gmdsolutions.com/madison/tindex.html.

Mahaska County

County Recorder, 106 S 1st St; Courthouse, Oskaloosa, IA 52577. 641-673-8187; fax-641-673-8979; 8AM-4:30PM (CST) http://mahaskacounty.org Courthouse- 641-673-8979. Index: All in one. Records indexed on a public use terminal back to 2002. Office will perform a UCC search but public must search other records themselves. Copy fee $1.00 per page. Cert fee- $10.00 per doc plus copy fee. Payee- Mahaska County Recorder. Office does not sell bulk data. **Online Real Estate, Deed, Lien records:** At http://iowalandrecords.org/portal/clris/CountiesTab, view an index of recorded land records from 1/2004. **Other phones:** Treasurer- 641-673-5482; Vital Records- 641-673-8187. **Property tax/Assessing**- 106 S 1st St, Courthouse, 1st Fl, SE Corner, Oskaloosa, IA 52577; 641-673-5805, assessor fax- 641-673-2564. http://mahaskacounty.org **Online access**- Access to the assessor GIS database of property and sales data is free at http://beacon.schneidercorp.com/.

Marion County

County Recorder, 214 E Main St, Knoxville, IA 50138. Recording, R/E & UCC phone-641-828-2211; fax-641-828-3538; 8AM-4:30PM (CST) www.co.marion.ia.us/offices/recorder/index.htm
Index: All in one. Records indexed on a public use terminal back to 1986. Office personnel or visitors may perform searches. Office will not search real estate records. UCC search includes tax liens if requested. UCC search per debtor name- $5.00. UCC search request using non-standard form (per name)- $6.00. Copy fee $.50 per page. Cert fee- $5.00 per doc plus copy fee. Payee- Marion County Recorder. Office does not sell bulk data. **Online access to Real Estate, Deed, Lien records:** At http://iowalandrecords.org/portal/clris/CountiesTab, view an index of recorded land records from 06/2003, images from 06/2003. **Other phones:** Treasurer- 641-828-2202; Elections- 641-828-2217; Vital Records- 641-828-2211. **Property tax/Assessing**- 214 E Main St, #10, Courthouse, Knoxville, IA 50138; 641-828-2215, assessor fax- 641-842-3593. A public access terminal available. www.co.marion.ia.us/offices/assessor/index.htm **Online access**- Access to the assessor GIS database of property and sales data is free at http://beacon.schneidercorp.com/.

Marshall County

County Recorder, PO Box 573, Marshalltown, IA 50158-0573. 641-754-6355; fax-641-754-6349; 8AM-4:30PM www.marshallcountyrecorder.com
Index: All in one. Records indexed on a public use terminal back to 1/1983. Office will perform a UCC search but public must search other records themselves. Search fee $6.00 per UCC. Copy fee $1.00 per page. Cert fee- $5.00 fee plus $1.00 per page copy fee. Payee- Marshall County Recorder. **Online access to Real Estate, Deed, Lien, UCC records:** Access the recorders land & UCC indexes free at http://ntcott.co.marshall.ia.us/ResolutionPublic/. Records go back to 1983, images only 1980-82. Also, search on statewide land records site- http://iowalandrecords.org/portal/clris/CountiesTab. **Other phones:** Treasurer- 641-754-6366; Elections- 641-754-6302; Vital Records- 641-754-6355; Auditor- 641-754-6323; Clerk of Court -641-754-1603;. **Property tax/Assessing**- 1 E Main St, Marshalltown, IA 50158; 641-754-6305. **Online access**- Access to the assessor property record card system and sales data free at www.co.marshall.ia.us/departments/assessor/disclaimer_html.

Mills County

County Recorder, 418 Sharp St; Courthouse, Glenwood, IA 51534. 712-527-9315; fax-712-527-1507; 8AM-4:30PM (CST) www.millscoia.us/offices/recorder/index.htm
Index: All in one. Records indexed on a public use terminal back to 1995. Only the public may search. Copy fee $1.00 per page. Cert fee- $5.00 per doc plus copy fee. Payee- Mills County Recorder. Office does not sell bulk data. **Online access to Real Estate, Deed, Lien, UCC, Judgment records:** At http://iowalandrecords.org/portal/clris/CountiesTab, view an index of recorded land records from 2/1995, images from 1/2004. Also, search free at http://lti.gmdsolutions.com/mills/rindex.html. **Other phones:** Treasurer- 712-527-4419. **Property tax/Assessing**- 418 Sharp St, Glenwood, IA 51534; 712-527-4883, assessor fax- 712-527-4884. A public terminal available. www.millscoia.us/offices/assessor/index.htm **Online access**- Access to the assessor database of property and tax sales data is free at http://lti.gmdsolutions.com/mills/index.html. also, search tax sale certificates free at http://lti.gmdsolutions.com/mills/tindex.html.

Mitchell County

County Recorder, 508 State St, Osage, IA 50461-1250. 641-732-5861, R/E recording phone-641-732-5861 x7; fax-641-732-5218; 8AM-4:30PM (CST)
Index: All in one. Records indexed on computer from July, 2000 to present, prior to July, 2000 indexed in books. Only the public may search. Copy fee $.50 per page. Cert fee- $5.00 per doc plus copy fee. Payee- Mitchell County Recorder. Office does not sell bulk data. **Online access to Real Estate, Deed, Lien, UCC records:** At http://iowalandrecords.org/portal/clris/CountiesTab, view an index of recorded land records from 1/2000, images from 03/09/2004. **Other phones:** Treasurer- 641-732-5861 x8; Elections- 641-732-5861 x3; Vital Records- 641-732-5861 x7. **Property tax/Assessing**- 508 State St, Osage, IA 50461-1250; 641-732-5861 x2, assessor fax- 641-732-5218. hours- 9AM-3:30PM

Monona County

County Recorder, PO Box 53, Onawa, IA 51040. Recording, R/E & UCC phone-712-433-2575; fax-712-433-3034; 8AM-4:30PM (CST)
Index: All in one. Records indexed on a public use terminal back to 1991. Only the public may search. Copy fee $.40 per page. Vital records- $15.00 certified copy. Cert fee- $5.00 per page includes copy fee. Payee- Monona County Recorder. Office does not sell bulk data. **Online access to Real Estate, Deed, Lien records:** At http://iowalandrecords.org/portal/clris/CountiesTab, view an index of recorded land records from 3/2004, images from 3/2004. **Other phones:** Treasurer- 712-433-2347; Elections- 712-433-2191; Vital Records- 712-433-2575. **Property tax/Assessing**- 610 Iowa Ave, Onawa, IA 51040; 712-433-2271, assessor fax- 712-433-9578. www.iowa-assessors.org/htdocs/Assessors_of_Iowa/Monona/default.htm **Online access**- Access to the assessor GIS database of property and sales data is free at http://beacon.schneidercorp.com/.

Monroe County

County Recorder, 10 Benton Ave E; Courthouse, Albia, IA 52531. 641-932-5164; fax-641-932-2863; 8AM-4PM (CST)
Index: All in one. Records indexed on a public use terminal back to 1992. Office personnel or visitors may perform searches. Real estate owner, mortgage, and property transfer searches available. Copy fee $1.00 per page, $.25 self serve. Cert fee- $5.00 per doc plus $.25 per page. Payee- Monroe County Recorder. **Online access to Real Estate, Deed records:** At http://iowalandrecords.org/portal/clris/CountiesTab, view an index of recorded land records from 1/2004, images from 1/2004. **Other phones:** Treasurer- 641-932-5011. **Property tax/Assessing**- 10 Benton Ave E, Albia, IA 52531; 641-932-2180.

Montgomery County

County Recorder, PO Box 469, Red Oak, IA 51566. Recording, R/E & UCC phone-712-623-4363; fax-712-623-8915; 8AM-4:30PM (CST)
Index: All in one. Records indexed on a public use terminal back to 1987. Only the public may search. Will not search UCC records. Copy fee $.50 per page in person; mailed $1.00 1st page, $.50 each add'l page, Faxed- $2.00 1st page, $1.00 each add'l page. Cert fee- $5.00 per cert plus copy fee for add'l pages. Payee- Montgomery County Recorder. Office does not sell bulk data. **Online access to Real Estate, Deed, Lien, UCC, Judgment records:** At http://iowalandrecords.org/portal/clris/CountiesTab, view an index of recorded land records from 7/1987. **Other phones:** Treasurer- 712-623-3292; Elections- 712-623-5127; Vital Records- 712-623-4363. **Property tax/Assessing**- PO Box 469, 105 E Coolbaugh St, Red Oak, IA 51566; 712-623-4171, assessor fax- 712-623-6540. **Online** - Access to the assessor GIS database of property and sales data is free at http://beacon.schneidercorp.com/ but no name searching.

Muscatine County

County Recorder, 414 E 3rd St, #103; Courthouse, Muscatine, IA 52761-4166. Recording, R/E & UCC phone-563-263-7741; fax-563-263-7248; 8AM-4:30PM (CST) www.co.muscatine.ia.us
Index: All in one. Records indexed on a public use terminal back to 1989. Only the public may search.

Copy fee $1.00 per page; fee to fax back- $1.50 per page. Cert fee- $5.00 per doc plus copy fee. Payee- Muscatine County Recorder. **Online access to Real Estate, Deed records:** At http://iowalandrecords.org/portal/clris/CountiesTab, view an index of recorded land records from 1/1989, images from 1/1989. **Other phones:** Treasurer- 563-263-7113; Elections- 563-263-5821; Vital Records- 563-263-7741. **Property tax/Assessing-** 414 E 3rd St, #202, Muscatine, IA 52761; 563-263-7061, assessor fax- 563-262-4169. **Online access-** Search area property and sales data free at http://beacon.schneidercorp.com/, registration required to name search.

O'Brien County

County Recorder, PO Box 340, Primghar, IA 51245-0340. Recording, R/E & UCC phone-712-957-3045; fax-712-957-3046; hours - 8AM-4:30PM (CST) www.obriencounty.com/government/recorder.htm

Office will do verbal record searches on computer back to 1988, but will not guarantee results. Index: All in one. Records indexed on a public use terminal back to 1988. Office personnel or visitors may perform searches. Office will not search real estate records. Office will not search UCC records. Federal/state combined tax lien search fee- $5.00 per page. Copy fee $1.00 per page.Real estate record copy- $.50 per page or $1.00 per page in older books. Cert fee- $5.00 per doc plus copy fee. Payee- O'Brien County Recorder. Bulk data available for purchase, contact Kurt, Susan or Julie for details. **Online access to Real Estate, Deed, Lien, UCC records:** At http://iowalandrecords.org/portal/clris/CountiesTab, view an index of recorded land records from 1/1988, images from 1/2004. **Other phones:** Treasurer- 712-957-3210 or 4185; Elections- 712-957-3225; Vital Records- 712-957-3045; Clerk of Court- 712-957-3255. **Property tax/Assessing-** PO Box 446, 155 S Hayes Ave, Primghar, IA 51245; 712-957-3205, assessor fax- 712-957-8014.

Osceola County

County Recorder, 300 7th St; Courthouse, Sibley, IA 51249-1695. Recording, R/E & UCC phone-712-754-3345; fax-712-754-3743; 8AM-4:30PM (CST)

Index: All in one. Records indexed on a public use terminal back to 1985. Office will perform a UCC search but public must search other records themselves. Search fee $6.00 per name. Copy fee $1.00 per page. Cert fee- $5.00 per cert plus copy fee. Payee- Osceola County Recorder. Office does not sell bulk data. **Online access to Real Estate, Deed, Lien, UCC, Judgment records:** At http://iowalandrecords.org/portal/clris/CountiesTab, view an index of recorded land records from 1/2004, images back to 2000 being added during 2006. **Other phones:** Treasurer- 712-754-3217; Elections- 712-754-2241; Vital Records- 712-754-3345; Assessor- 712-754-3438. **Property tax/Assessing-** 300 7th St, Sibley, IA 51249-1695; 712-754-3438, fax- 712-754-3743.

Page County

County Recorder, 112 E Main St; Courthouse, Clarinda, IA 51632. 712-542-3130; fax-712-542-3636; 8AM-4:30PM (CST)

Index: All in one. Records indexed on a public use terminal back to 1986. Office personnel or visitors may perform searches. Search fee $11.00 per name. Office will not search real estate records. Office will not search UCC records. Copy fee $1.00 per page. Fax fee is $1.75 per page.Real estate record copy- $.50 per page. Cert fee- $5.00 per doc plus copy fee. Payee- Page County Recorder. Bulk data available for purchase; contact Darla. **Online access to Real Estate, Deed, Lien, UCC, Judgment records:** At http://iowalandrecords.org/portal/clris/CountiesTab, view an index of recorded land records from 1/2004, images from 1/2004. **Other phones:** Treasurer- 712-542-5322. **Property tax/Assessing-** PO Box 332, 112 E Main St, Clarinda, IA 51632; 712-542-2516, assessor fax- 712-542-6005.

Palo Alto County

County Recorder, PO Box 248, Emmetsburg, IA 50536. Recording, R/E & UCC phone-712-852-3701; fax-712-852-3704; 8AM-4PM (CST)

Index: All in one. Records indexed on a public use terminal back to 1984. Only the public may search. Copy fee $.50 per page. Cert fee- $5.00 per cert plus copy fee. Payee- Palo Alto County Recorder. **Online access to Real Estate, Deed, Lien, UCC, Judgment records:** At http://iowalandrecords.org/portal/clris/CountiesTab, view an index of recorded land records from 1/2004, images are being added weekly. **Other phones:** Treasurer- 712-852-3844; Elections- 712-852-2924; Vital Records- 712-852-3701. **Property tax/Assessing-** 1010 Broadway Ave, Emmetsburg, IA 50536; 712-852-3823, assessor fax- 712-852-3825.

Plymouth County

County Recorder, 215 4th Ave SE; Courthouse, Le Mars, IA 51031. Recording, R/E & UCC phone-712-546-4020; fax-712-546-7304; 8AM-5PM (CST) www.co.plymouth.ia.us

Index: All in one. Records indexed on a public use terminal back to 1991. Office personnel or visitors may perform searches. Tax lien search or UCC search fee- $5.00 per debtor. Office will not search real estate records. Tax liens not included in UCC search. Copy fee $.50 per page. Cert fee- $5.00 per certification plus $.50 per page. Payee- Plymouth County Recorder. **Online access to Real Estate, Deed, Lien, UCC, Judgment records:** At http://iowalandrecords.org/portal/clris/CountiesTab, view an index of recorded land records from 01/1998, images from 01/1998 (might be currently unavailable). **Other phones:** Treasurer- 712-546-7078; Elections- 712-546-6100; Treasurer Phone (Alt.)- 712-546-7056. **Property tax/Assessing-** 215 4th Ave SE, Le Mars, IA 51031; 712-546-4705, assessor fax- 712-548-5255. **Online access-** Access the assessor database of property and sales data free at http://plymouth.iowaassessors.com.

Pocahontas County

County Recorder, 99 Court Sq, #5, Pocahontas, IA 50574-1621. Recording, R/E & UCC phone-712-335-4404; fax-712-335-4502; 8AM-4PM (CST)

Index: Separate indices to search include deeds, mortgage, miscellaneous. Records indexed on computer back to 1991. Visitors may perform searches; office will perform very limited searches; may search for a name for free. Copy fee $1.00, if real estate $.50 per page. Cert fee- $5.00 per cert plus copy fee. Payee- Pocahontas County Recorder. **Online Real Estate, Deed, Lien, UCC, Judgment records:** at http://iowalandrecords.org/portal/clris/CountiesTab, view an index of recorded land records from 07/1991. **Other phones:** Treasurer- 712-335-4334; Elections- 712-335-3361; Vital Records- 712-335-4404. **Property tax/Assessing-** 99 Courthouse Sq, #5, Pocahontas, IA 50574-1621; 712-335-5016.

Polk County

County Recorder, 111 Court Ave, Rm 250; County Admin Bldg, Des Moines, IA 50309. Recording, R/E & UCC phone-515-286-3160, UCC recording phone-515-286-2241; fax-515-323-5393; 7:30AM-5:00PM (CST) http://recorder.co.polk.ia.us

Index: All in one. Records indexed on a public use terminal back to 1992. Only the public may search. Copy fee $.50 per page. Cert fee- $5.00 per doc plus copy fee. Payee- Polk County Recorder. **Online access to Real Estate, Deed, Lien, UCC, Plat records:** Access to the Recorder's Index Search is free at http://landrecords.polkcountyiowa.gov/resolution/. Also includes trade names, financing statements, and plats. **Other phones:** Treasurer- 515-286-3060; Elections- 515-286-3247; Vital Records- 515-286-3781. **Property tax/Assessing-** 111 Court Ave, Rm 195, Des Moines, IA 50309; 515-286-3014, assessor fax- 515-286-3386. hours- 7AM-5PM www.assess.co.polk.ia.us **Online access-** Access to the Polk County assessor database is free at www.assess.co.polk.ia.us/web/basic/search.html. Search by property or by sales. Also, download residential, commercial, or agricultural data free at www.assess.co.polk.ia.us/web/basic/exports.html.

Pottawattamie County

County Recorder, 227 S 6th St, Council Bluffs, IA 51501. Recording, R/E & UCC phone-712-328-5612; fax-712-328-4738; 8AM-4PM www.pottcounty.com

Index: All in one. Records indexed on computer back to 1989. Images available back to 11/02. Office will perform a UCC search but public must search other records themselves. Copy fee $1.00 per page. Cert fee- $5.00 per doc plus $.75 copy fee. Payee- Pottawattamie County Recorder. **Online access to Real Estate, Deed, Lien, Mortgage records:** Access to real estate parcel information for free go to www.pottcounty.com/html/Parcel_Info.asp. **Other phones:** Treasurer- 712-328-5627; Elections- 712-328-5700 (Auditor); Vital Records- 712-328-5612; Recorder's Office Info Line- 712-328-5725. **Property tax/Assessing-** PO Box 1076, 227 S 6th St, Council Bluffs, IA 51502; 712-328-5617, assessor fax- 712-328-4841. www.pottco.org **Online access-** Records on the County Courthouse/Council Bluffs property database and sales are free at www.pottco.org and click on real estate. Search by owner name, address, or parcel number. Records since 7/1/89, images since 10/20/2002. Also, search the sheriff foreclosure sale at http://pottcounty.com/html/Sheriff_Foreclosure.php.

Poweshiek County

County Recorder, PO Box 656, Montezuma, IA 50171-0656. Recording, R/E & UCC phone-641-623-5434; fax-641-623-2928; 8AM-4PM (CST) www.poweshiekcounty.org/recorder1.htm

Index: All in one. Records indexed on a public use terminal back to 1984. Only the public may search. Copy fee $.50 per page, $2.00 if mailed. Cert fee- $5.00 per doc plus copy fee. Payee- Poweshiek County Recorder. **Online access to Real Estate, Deed, Lien, Mortgage records:** At http://iowalandrecords.org/portal/clris/CountiesTab, view an index of recorded land records from 7/3/1989. **Other phones:** Treasurer- 641-623-5128; Elections- 641-623-5443; Vital Records- 641-623-5434. **Property tax/Assessing-** PO Box 516, 302 E Main St, Montezuma, IA 50171; 641-623-5445, assessor fax- 641-623-2576. www.poweshiekcounty.org/assessor1.htm **Online access-** Access to the assessor database of property and sales data is free at http://poweshiek.iowaassessors.com.

Ringgold County

County Recorder, 109 W Madison, #204, Mount Ayr, IA 50854. Recording, R/E & UCC phone-641-464-3231; fax-641-464-2568; 8AM-4PM (CST)

Index: All in one. Records indexed on a public use terminal back to 1990. Office personnel or visitors may perform searches. Search fee $7.00 per UCC search. Office will search real estate records. Will search UCC records. Fax fee $2.00 1st page, $1.00 each add'l. Real estate record copy- $.50 per page. Cert fee- $5.00 per doc plus copy fee. Payee- Ringgold County Recorder. **Online Real Estate, Deed, Lien records:** access land records free at http://iowalandrecords.org/portal/clris/CountiesTab. Access is free after required sign-up, but there is a fee per document. **Other phones:** Treasurer- 641-464-3230; Elections- 641-464-3239; Vital Records- 641-464-3231. **Property tax/Assessing-** 109 W Madison, Mount Ayr, IA 50854; 641-464-3233, assessor fax- 641-464-0663. www.ringgoldcounty.us **Online-** Property sales data cards available free at www.iowa-assessors.org:8080/cgi/wiki.pl?Sales_Property_Cards.

Sac County

County Recorder, 100 NW State St, Sac City, IA 50583. Recording, R/E phone-712-662-7789; fax-712-662-6298; 8AM-4:30PM www.saccounty.org

Index: Separate indices to search include computer, index books. Records indexed on computer back to 1990. Only the public may search. Office will search UCC records if customer is present. Copy fee $.50 per page. Add add'l $.50 per page for large docs. Cert fee-

$5.00 per cert plus copy fee. Payee- Sac County Recorder. **Online Real Estate, Deed, Lien, UCC, Judgment records:** At http://iowalandrecords.org/portal/clris/CountiesTab, view an index of recorded land records from 1/2002, images from 1/2003. **Other phones:** Treasurer- 712-662-7411; Elections- 712-662-7310; Vital Records- 712-662-7789. **Property tax/Assessing**- PO Box 326, 100 NW State St, Sac City, IA 50583; 712-662-4492, assessor fax- 712-662-7358. www.saccounty.org/assessor/index.asp **Online access**- Assessor's property records online for a small fee; contact the Auditors Office at 712-662-7310 or visit www.saccounty.org/features/gis.asp. Also, search property data after registration on the GIS system at http://beacon.schneidercorp.com/. and registration and a fee applies.

Scott County

County Recorder, 600 W 4th St, Davenport, IA 52801-1003. Recording, R/E & UCC phone-563-326-8621; fax-563-328-3225; 8AM-4:30PM (CST) www.scottcountyiowa.com

Index: Separate indices to search include affidavits, articles of corp, liens, lands, trade names, plats. Records indexed on a public use terminal back to 1989. Only the public may search. Will not search UCC records. Copy fee $1.00 per page. Cert fee- $5.00 per doc plus copy fee. Payee- Scott County Recorder. **Online access to Real Estate, Deed, Lien, UCC, Trade Name records:** At http://iowalandrecords.org/portal/clris/CountiesTab, view an index of recorded land records back to 1/1989 Also see www.scottcountyiowa.com/recorder/records.php for recorder records; includes land, lien, plats, incorporations, trade names, and UCCs back to 1/1989. **Other phones:** Treasurer- 563-326-8664; Elections- 563-326-8631; Vital Records- 563-326-8650. **Property tax/Assessing**- 600 W 4th St, Davenport, IA 52801; 563-326-8635, assessor fax- 563-328-3218. www.scottcountyiowa.com/assessor/ **Online access**- Access to assessor property records is free at www.scottcountyiowa.com/query.php. Also, sheriff sales lists free at www.scottcountyiowa.com/sheriff/sales.php.

Shelby County

County Recorder, PO Box 67, Harlan, IA 51537-0067. 712-755-5640; fax-712-755-7556; 8AM-4:30PM (CST) www.shco.org/recorder.htm

Index: All in one. Records indexed on a public use terminal back to 1/1988. Only the public may search. Office will not search real estate records. Copy fee $1.00 per page. Vital stat- $5.00 per page. Cert fee- $5.00 per doc plus copy fee. Payee- Shelby County Recorder. **Online access to Real Estate, Deed, Lien, UCC, Judgment records:** At http://iowalandrecords.org/portal/clris/CountiesTab, view an index of recorded land records from 1/2000, images from 1/2000. Also, access recording office land data at www.etitlesearch.com; registration required, fee based on usage. **Other phones:** Treasurer- 712-755-5847; Elections- 712-755-3831; Vital Records- 712-755-5640; County Auditor- 712-755-3831. **Property tax/Assessing**- 612 Court St, Harlan, IA 51537; 712-755-5718, assessor fax- 712-755-7556. www.shco.org/assessor.htm **Online access**- Access to the assessor GIS database of property and sales data is free at http://beacon.schneidercorp.com/ but no name searching.

Sioux County

County Recorder, PO Box 48, Orange City, IA 51041. Recording, R/E & UCC phone-712-737-2229; fax-712-737-2230; 8AM-4:30PM (CST) www.siouxcounty.org

Index: All in one. Records indexed on a public use terminal back to 1986. Office personnel or visitors may perform searches. Office will not search real estate records. Tax liens not included in UCC search. UCC search per debtor name- $5.00. UCC search request using non-standard form (per name)- $6.00. Tax lien search fee- $6.00 per debtor. Copy fee $1.00 per page; if real estate $.50 per page. Cert fee- $2.00 per page includes copy fee. Payee- Sioux County Recorder. Office does not sell bulk data. **Online access to Real Estate, Deed records:** At http://iowalandrecords.org/portal/clris/CountiesTab, view an index of recorded land records from 1/2004. **Other phones:** Treasurer- 712-737-3505; Elections- 712-737-2216; Vital Records- 712-737-2229. **Property tax/Assessing**- PO Box 18, 210 Central SW, Orange City, IA 51041; 712-737-4274, assessor fax- 712-737-6482. (Appraiser/Auditor- 712-737-4274) www.siouxcounty.org/assessor.htm **Online access**- Access property data information free at http://gis.siouxcounty.org/gisweb/assessmenthome.asp. Also, search the treasurer's property tax records online by subscription; for info please contact Micah at 712-737-6818, http://siouxcounty.org/treasurer.htm.

Story County

County Recorder, PO Box 55, Nevada, IA 50201-0055. 515-382-7230, R/E recording phone-515-382-7214, UCC recording phone-515-382-7230; fax-515-382-7239; 8AM-5PM (No recording after 3:30PM). (CST) www.storycounty.com/

Index: All in one. Records indexed on a public use terminal back to 1976. Office personnel or visitors may perform searches. If the office searches fee is $5.00 per name. Will not search UCC records. Copy fee $1.00 per page. Cert fee- $5.00 per doc plus copy fee. Payee- Story County Recorder. Bulk data available for purchase on CD, contact Stacie 515-382-7233. **Online Real Estate, Grantor/Grantee, Deed, Mortgage, UCC records:** At http://iowalandrecords.org/portal/clris/CountiesTab, view an index of recorded land records from 1979-2000, images from 1979-2000. **Other phones:** Treasurer- 515-382-7330; Elections- 515-382-7217; Vital Records- 515-382-7237; Deputy Assessor- 515-382-7322. **Property tax/Assessing**- 900 6th St, Nevada, IA 50201; 515-382-7322, fax- 515-382-7326. (Appraiser/Auditor- 515-382-7322) www.storycounty.com/index.aspx?DN=8,6,1,Documents **Online access**- Records on the county assessor database are free at http://beacon.schneidercorp.com/?site=StoryCountyIA. Also, City of Ames property assessor data and sales is free at http://beacon.schneidercorp.com/?site=StoryCountyIA but no name searching.

Tama County

County Recorder, PO Box 82, Toledo, IA 52342. 641-484-3320, R/E recording phone-641-484-2740, UCC recording phone-641-484-3320; fax-641-484-8246; 8AM-4:30PM (CST) www.tamacounty.org

Index: Separate indices to search include Mortgages (land & town), Deeds (land & town), Miscellaneous. Records indexed on a public use terminal back to 1996. Only the public may search. Will not search UCC records. Copy fee $.50 per page; fax fee $1.00 per page. Cert fee- $5.00 per doc plus $.50 per page. Payee- Tama County Recorder. Office does not sell bulk data. **Online Real Estate, Deed records:** At http://iowalandrecords.org/portal/clris/CountiesTab, view an index of recorded land records from 1/1/97, images from 6/16/2004. **Other phones:** Treasurer- 641-484-3141; Elections- 641-484-2740; Vital Records- 641-484-3320. **Property tax/Assessing**- 104 W State St, PO Box 91, Toledo, IA 52342; 641-484-3545, assessor fax- 641-484-6093. **Online access**- Access to the assessor database of property and sales data is free at http://tama.iowaassessors.com.

Taylor County

County Recorder, 405 Jefferson St; Courthouse, Bedford, IA 50833. 712-523-2275; fax-712-523-2895; 8AM-4:30PM (CST)

Index: All in one. Records indexed on a public use terminal back to 1994. Only the public may search. Copy fee $.50 per page. Cert fee- $2.00 per page plus copy fee. Payee- Taylor County Recorder. Office does not sell bulk data. **Online Real Estate, Deed records:** at http://iowalandrecords.org/portal/clris/CountiesTab, view an index of recorded land records from 1/2004. **Other phones:** Treasurer- 712-523-2080. **Property tax/Assessing**- 405 Jefferson St, Courthouse Ste 5, Bedford, IA 50833; 712-523-2444, assessor fax- 712-523-3262. Office does not have public access computer.

Union County

County Recorder, 300 N Pine St, Creston, IA 50801. 641-782-1725; fax-641-782-1709; 8:30AM-4:30PM (CST) www.unioncountyiowa.org/

Index: All in one. Records indexed on a public use terminal back to 1978. Office personnel or visitors may perform searches. Search fee $5.00 per name. Office will not search real estate records. Office will not search tax liens. General copy fee $.50 per page; UCC copy- $1.00 per page. Cert fee- $5.00 per doc plus copy fee. Payee- Union County Recorder. **Online access to Real Estate, Deed records:** At http://iowalandrecords.org/portal/clris/CountiesTab, view an index of recorded land records from 1/2005, images from 1/2005. **Other phones:** Treasurer- 641-782-1710; Elections- 641-782-1701. **Property tax/Assessing**- 300 N Pine St, #108, Creston, IA 50801; 641-782-1735, assessor fax- 641-782-8030.

Van Buren County

County Recorder, PO Box 455, Keosauqua, IA 52565. Recording, R/E & UCC phone-319-293-3240; fax-319-293-6327; 8AM-4:30PM (CST)

Index: All in one. Records indexed on a public use terminal back to 7/1/88. Office will perform a UCC search but public must search other records themselves. Real estate copy $.25 per page. Uncertified vital record- $3.00. Cert fee- $2.50 per doc plus copy fee. Payee- Van Buren County Recorder. **Online access to Real Estate, Deed, Lien, UCC, Judgment records:** At http://iowalandrecords.org/po rtal/clris/CountiesTab, view an index of recorded land records from 1/2004 (images start 7/1/06). **Other phones:** Treasurer- 319-293-3110; Elections- 319-293-3129; Vital Records- 319-293-3240. **Property tax/Assessing**- PO Box 493, Keosauqua, IA 52565; 319-293-3001, assessor fax- 319-293-6404. http://vanburen.iowaassessors.com/ **Online access**- Search parcel data information free at http://vanburen.iowaassessors.com/search.php?mode=search&showdis=true. Advanced search by document type available at http://vanburen.iowaassessors.com/search.php?mode=advsearch&showdis=true.

Wapello County

County Recorder, 101 W 4th St, Ottumwa, IA 52501. 641-683-0046, R/E recording phone-641-683-0045; fax-641-683-0019; 8AM-4:30PM (CST)

Index: All in one. Records indexed on a public use terminal back to 1989. Office will perform a UCC search but public must search other records themselves. Office will not search real estate records. Copy fee $.25 per page. Fax, $3.00 first page, $1.00 per page after. Cert fee- $5.00 per doc plus copy fee. Payee- Wapello County Recorder. **Online access to Real Estate, Deed records:** At http://iowalandrecords.org/portal/clris/CountiesTab, view an index of recorded land records from 1/2003, images from 1/2003. **Other phones:** Treasurer- 641-683-0040; Elections- 641-683-0020; Vital Records- 641-683-0047. **Property tax/Assessing**- 101 W 4th, Ottumwa, IA 52501; 641-683-0088, assessor fax- 641-683-0083. **Online access**- Search assessor property and sales data free at http://wapello.iowaassessors.com/.

Warren County

Recorder, 301 N Buxton, #109, Indianola, IA 50125. 515-961-1089; 8AM-4:30PM www.co.warren.ia.us

Index: All in one. Records indexed on a public use terminal back to 1991. Office personnel or visitors may perform searches. Office will search real estate records. Will not search UCC records. Mail requests must include a SASE. UCC search per debtor name- $5.00. Copy fee $1.00 per page. Cert fee- $5.00 per doc plus copy fee. Payee- Warren County Recorder. **Online access to Real Estate, Deed, Lien records:** at http://iowalandrecords.org/portal/clris/CountiesTab, view an index of recorded land records from 1/1994, images from 1/1995. **Other phones:** Treasurer- 515-961-1110; Elections- 515-961-1020. **Property tax/Assessing**- 301 Buxton, #108, Indianola, IA 50125; 515-961-1010, assessor fax- 515-961-1079. **Online access**- Access to property sales data is free at http://beacon.schneidercorp.com/.

Washington County

County Recorder, PO Box 889, Washington, IA 52353-0889. Recording, R/E & UCC phone-319-653-7727; fax-319-653-7754; 8AM-4:30PM (CST) http://iowalandrecords.org/portal/

Index: All in one. Records indexed on a public use terminal back to 11/1992. Office personnel (limited) or visitors may perform searches. Office can perform mortgage searches - uncertified scan of computer index. Office will not search UCC records; will search tax liens. Tax lien search fee- $6.00 per debtor. General copy fee $1.00 if mailing. Real estate copy-minimum $1.00 + $.40 per page. Cert fee- $5.00 per doc plus copy fee. Payee- Washington County Recorder. **Online Real Estate, Deed records:** At http://iowalandrecords.org/portal/clris/CountiesTab, view an index of recorded land records from 1/1992, images from 1/1992. **Other phones:** Treasurer- 319-653-7726; Elections- 319-653-7777; Vital Records-319-653-7727. **Property tax/Assessing**- 210 W Main St, McCreedy Bldg, 1st Fl, Washington, IA 52353; 319-653-7738, assessor fax- 319-653-7783. http://co.washington.ia.us/departments/assessor/index.html **Online access**- Access to the assessor database of property and sales data is free at http://washington.iowaassessors.com.

Wayne County

County Recorder, PO Box 435, Corydon, IA 50060. Recording, R/E & UCC phone-641-872-1676; fax-641-872-2843; 8AM-4PM (CST)

Index: Separate indices to search include deeds, mortgages, mortgage release, contracts, miscellaneous. Records indexed on a public use terminal back to 1988. Office personnel or visitors may perform searches. Search fee-$16.00 per hour/minimum of one-quarter of an hour. General copy fee $.25 per page ($.50 for two sided-regular size), $.50 per page ($1.00 for two sided legal size). Fax fee- $3.00 1st page, $2.00 each add'l. Vital record copy- $15.00. Cert fee- $5.00 1st page; $1.00 each add'l page, plus copy fee. Payee- Wayne County Recorder. Office does not sell bulk data. **Online Real Estate, Deed, Lien, UCC, Judgment records:** At http://iowalandrecords.org/portal/clris/CountiesTab, view an index of recorded land records from 1/1998, images from 1/1998. **Other phones:** Treasurer- 641-872-2515; Elections- 641-872-2242; Vital Records-641-872-1676. **Property tax/Assessing**- PO Box 435, Corydon, IA 50060; 641-872-2663, assessor fax- 641-872-2884. A public access terminal available. www.wayne.iowaassessors.com/ **Online access**- For parcel searches for free go to www.wayne.iowaassessors.com/.

Webster County

County Recorder, PO Box 1253, Fort Dodge, IA 50501. Recording, R/E & UCC phone-515-576-2401; fax-515-574-3723; 8AM-4:30PM (CST) www.webstercountyia.org

Index: All in one. Records indexed on a public use terminal back to 1994. Only the public may search. Copy fee $1.00 per page. Cert fee- $6.00 per doc plus copy fee. Payee- Webster County Recorder. **Online Real Estate, Deed, Lien, UCC, Judgment records:** at http://iowalandrecords.org/portal/clris/CountiesTab, view an index of recorded land records from 1/2002, images from 1/2002. **Other phones:** Treasurer- 515-576-2731; Elections- 515-573-7175; Vital Records-515-576-2401. **Property tax/Assessing**- 701 Central Ave, Fort Dodge, IA 50501; 515-576-4721, assessor fax- 515-573-5871. hours- 8AM-1-4:30PM www.webstercountyia.org **Online access**- Access to the assessor database of property and sales data is free at http://webster.iowaassessors.com but no name searching. Also, property data is free at www.webstercountyia.org

Winnebago County

County Recorder, 126 S Clark St, #1; Courthouse, Forest City, IA 50436-1706. Recording, R/E phone-641-585-2094; fax-641-585-1094; 8AM-4:30PM

Index: All in one. Records indexed on a public use terminal back to 2/95. Only the public may search. Copy fee $.50 per page. Cert fee- $5.00 per doc includes copy fee. Payee- Winnebago County Recorder. **Online Real Estate, Deed, Lien records:** at http://iowalandrecords.org/portal/clris/CountiesTab, view an index of recorded land records from 1/2003, images from 1/2003. **Other phones:** Treasurer- 641-585-2322; Elections- 641-585-3412; Vital Records-641-585-2094. **Property tax/Assessing**- 126 S Clark St, #1, Forest City, IA 50436-1706; 641-585-2163, assessor fax- 641-585-2891. (Appraiser/Auditor- 641-585-3412) **Online access**- Property data may be searched free at the GIS map site http://beacon.schneidercorp.com/?site=WinnebagoCountyIA. Also, access to the assessor GIS database of property and sales data is free at http://beacon.schneidercorp.com/. Also, access to records for free go to http://iowalandrecords.org/portal/clris/SwitchToSearchSimpleTab#firstLevelTabs.

Winneshiek County

County Recorder, 201 W Main St, Decorah, IA 52101. 563-382-3486; fax-563-387-4083; 8AM-4PM

Index: All in one. Records indexed on a public use terminal back to 1990. Only the public may search. Office will not search real estate records. Copy fee $1.00 per page. Cert fee- $5.00 per doc plus copy fee. Payee- Winneshiek County Recorder. **Online access to Real Estate, Deed records:** At http://iowalandrecords.org/portal/clris/CountiesTab, view an index of recorded land records from 1/2004. **Other phones:** Treasurer- 563-382-3753; Elections-563-382-5085; Vital Records- 563-382-3486. **Property tax/Assessing**- 201 W Main St, Decorah, IA 52101; 563-382-5356, assessor fax- 563-387-4082. **Online access**- Access to the assessor database of property and sales data free at http://beacon.schneidercorp.com/?site=WinneshiekCountyIA.

Woodbury County

County Auditor & Recorder, 620 Douglas St, Rm 106, Sioux City, IA 51101. Recording, R/E & UCC phone-712-279-6528; fax-712-233-8946; 8AM-4:30PM (CST) www.woodburyiowa.com

Index: All in one. Records indexed on computer from 6/94 to present, prior to 6/94 is in books. Only the public may search. Copy fee $.50 per page. Cert fee- $5.00 per doc plus copy fee. Payee- Woodbury County Auditor & Recorder. Office does not sell bulk data. **Online access to Real Estate, Deed, Lien, UCC, Judgment records:** At http://iowalandrecords.org/portal/clris/CountiesTab, view index of recorded land records from 6/1994, images from 3/2002. **Other phones:** Treasurer- 712-279-6495; Elections- 712-279-6465; Vital Records- 712-279-6266. **Property tax/Assessing**- 620 Douglas St, Courthouse 701, Sioux City, IA 51101; 712-279-6535, assessor fax- 712-279-6896. www.woodburyiowa.com/departments/AssessorCity/ **Online access**- Access to the assessor GIS database of property and sales data is free at http://beacon.schneidercorp.com/ but no name searching. Name search county property free at www.woodburyiowa.com/treasurertaxdata/. Also, search tax sale properties free at www.woodburyiowa.com/departments/treasurer/taxsale.asp. Also, search property free at http://sidwellmaps.com/website/siouxcity/php/index.php but no name searching.

Worth County

County Recorder, 1000 Central Ave, Northwood, IA 50459. Recording, R/E & UCC phone-641-324-2734; fax-641-324-3682; 8AM-4PM www.worthcounty.org

Index: All in one. Records indexed on a public use terminal back to 1994. Office personnel or visitors may perform searches but office will not guarantee anything. Office will search real estate records. Will not search UCC records. General copy fee $1.00 per page.Real estate record copy- $.50 per page in person, $1.00 per page if mailed, $1.50 per page if faxed. Cert fee- $5.00 per doc plus copy fee. Payee- Worth County Recorder. **Online access to Real Estate, Deed, Lien, UCC, Judgment records:** At http://iowalandrecords.org/portal/clris/CountiesTab, view an index of recorded land records from 11/2003, images from 11/2003. **Other phones:** Treasurer- 641-324-2942; Elections- 641-324-2316; Vital Records-641-324-2734. **Property tax/Assessing**- 1000 Central Ave, Northwood, IA 50459; 641-324-1198, assessor fax- 641-324-3685.

Wright County

County Recorder, PO Box 187, Clarion, IA 50525. Recording, R/E & UCC phone-515-532-3204; fax-515-532-2669; hours- 8AM-4PM (CST) www.wrightcounty.org/county_offices.htm

Index: All in one. Records indexed on a public use terminal back to 1992. Only the public may search. Copy fee $1.00 per page.Real estate record copy- $.50 per page. Cert fee- $5.00 per doc plus copy fee. Payee- Wright County Recorder. **Online Real Estate, Deed, Lien, UCC, Judgment, Sales records:** At http://iowalandrecords.org/portal/clris/CountiesTab, view an index of recorded land records from 1/2004, images from 1/2004. **Other phones:** Treasurer- 515-532-2691. **Property tax/Assessing**- PO Box 428, Clarion, IA 50525; 515-532-3737, assessor fax- 515-532-3501. **Online access**- Search assessor property and sales data free at www.wright.iowaassessors.com.

Iowa County Locator

You will usually be able to find the city name in the City/County Cross Reference below. In that case, it is a simple matter to determine the county from the cross reference. However, only the official US Postal Service city names are included in this index. We have also included a ZIP/City Cross Reference immediately following the City/County Cross Reference.

Iowa City/County Cross Reference

A C NIELSEN CO Clinton
ACKLEY (50601) Hardin(71), Franklin(11), Butler(9), Grundy(7)
ACKWORTH Warren
ADAIR (50002) Adair(68), Guthrie(30), Audubon(1)
ADEL Dallas
AFTON Union
AGENCY Wapello
AINSWORTH Washington
AKRON Plymouth
ALBERT CITY (50510) Buena Vista(84), Pocahontas(15)
ALBIA Monroe
ALBION Marshall
ALBURNETT Linn
ALDEN (50006) Hardin(84), Franklin(14)
ALEXANDER (50420) Franklin(84), Wright(10), Story(4)
ALGONA Kossuth
ALLEMAN Polk
ALLENDORF Osceola
ALLERTON Wayne
ALLISON Butler
ALPHA Fayette
ALTA Buena Vista
ALTA VISTA (50603) Chickasaw(85), Howard(13)
ALTON (51003) Sioux(98), Plymouth(1)
ALTOONA Polk
ALVORD Lyon
AMANA (52203) Iowa(84), Johnson(14)
AMANA Iowa
AMES (50014) Story(96), Boone(3)
AMES Story
ANAMOSA Jones
ANDOVER Clinton
ANDREW Jackson
ANITA (50020) Cass(87), Adair(6), Audubon(5)
ANKENY Polk
ANTHON Woodbury
APLINGTON (50604) Butler(85), Grundy(14)
ARCADIA Carroll
ARCHER O'Brien
AREDALE (50605) Butler(69), Franklin(30)
ARGYLE Lee
ARION Crawford
ARISPE Union
ARLINGTON (50606) Fayette(94), Clayton(5)
ARMSTRONG (50514) Emmet(79), Kossuth(20)
ARNOLDS PARK Dickinson
ARTHUR (51431) Ida(87), Sac(12)
ASHTON (51232) Osceola(76), Lyon(19), O'Brien(2)
ASPINWALL Crawford
AT AND T Pottawattamie
ATALISSA (52720) Muscatine(78), Cedar(21)
ATKINS Benton
ATLANTIC (50022) Cass(98), Audubon(1)
AUBURN (51433) Sac(59), Calhoun(39), Carroll(1)
AUDUBON Audubon
AURELIA (51005) Cherokee(87), Buena Vista(12)
AURORA (50607) Buchanan(60), Fayette(39)
AUSTINVILLE Butler
AVOCA (51521) Pottawattamie(91), Shelby(8)
AYRSHIRE (50515) Palo Alto(81), Clay(18)
BADGER (50516) Webster(88), Humboldt(11)
BAGLEY (50026) Guthrie(71), Greene(28)
BALDWIN (52207) Jackson(90), Clinton(9)
BANCROFT Kossuth
BARNES CITY (50027) Mahaska(97), Poweshiek(2)
BARNUM Webster
BARTLETT Fremont
BATAVIA (52533) Jefferson(71), Wapello(28)
BATTLE CREEK (51006) Ida(90), Woodbury(9)
BAXTER Jasper
BAYARD (50029) Guthrie(96), Greene(3)
BEACON Mahaska
BEACONSFIELD Ringgold
BEAMAN (50609) Grundy(73), Marshall(20), Tama(5)
BEAVER Boone
BEDFORD Taylor
BELLE PLAINE (52208) Benton(93), Iowa(3), Tama(1)
BELLEVUE Jackson
BELMOND Wright
BENNETT Cedar
BENTON Ringgold
BERNARD (52032) Dubuque(59), Jackson(36), Jones(4)
BERWICK Polk
BETTENDORF Scott
BEVINGTON Madison
BIG ROCK Scott
BIRMINGHAM (52535) Van Buren(96), Jefferson(3)
BLAIRSBURG (50034) Hamilton(85), Wright(14)
BLAIRSTOWN (52209) Benton(96), Iowa(3)
BLAKESBURG (52536) Wapello(88), Monroe(9), Davis(2)
BLANCHARD Page
BLENCOE (51523) Monona(95), Harrison(4)
BLOCKTON (50836) Taylor(90), Ringgold(9)
BLOOMFIELD (52537) Davis(95), Wapello(4)
BLUE GRASS (52726) Scott(91), Muscatine(8)
BODE (50519) Humboldt(71), Kossuth(28)
BONAPARTE Van Buren
BONDURANT Polk
BOONE Boone
BOONEVILLE Dallas
BOUTON (50039) Dallas(96), Boone(3)
BOXHOLM Boone
BOYDEN (51234) Sioux(97), Lyon(2)
BRADDYVILLE Page
BRADFORD Franklin
BRADGATE (50520) Humboldt(95), Pocahontas(4)
BRANDON Buchanan
BRAYTON (50042) Audubon(92), Cass(7)
BREDA (51436) Carroll(75), Sac(13), Crawford(10)
BRIDGEWATER (50837) Adair(74), Cass(18), Adams(6)
BRIGHTON (52540) Jefferson(50), Washington(49)
BRISTOW Butler
BRITT Hancock
BRONSON Woodbury
BROOKLYN Poweshiek
BRUNSVILLE Plymouth
BRYANT Clinton
BUCKEYE Hardin
BUCKINGHAM Tama
BUFFALO Scott
BUFFALO CENTER (50424) Winnebago(88), Kossuth(11)
BURLINGTON Des Moines
BURNSIDE Webster
BURR OAK Winneshiek
BURT Kossuth
BUSSEY (50044) Marion(73), Mahaska(19), Monroe(7)
CALAMUS Clinton
CALLENDER Webster
CALMAR (52132) Winneshiek(86), Howard(13)
CALUMET O'Brien
CAMANCHE Clinton
CAMBRIDGE (50046) Story(81), Polk(18)
CANTRIL Van Buren
CARBON Adams
CARLISLE (50047) Warren(87), Polk(12)
CARNARVON Sac
CARPENTER Mitchell
CARROLL Carroll
CARSON Pottawattamie
CARTER LAKE Pottawattamie
CASCADE (52033) Dubuque(70), Jones(30)
CASEY (50048) Guthrie(73), Adair(26)
CASTALIA (52133) Winneshiek(72), Fayette(27)
CASTANA Monona
CEDAR Mahaska
CEDAR FALLS (50613) Black Hawk(97), Grundy(1)
CEDAR FALLS Black Hawk
CEDAR RAPIDS Linn
CENTER JUNCTION Jones
CENTER POINT (52213) Linn(90), Benton(7), Scott(1)
CENTERVILLE Appanoose
CENTRAL CITY Linn
CHAPIN Franklin
CHARITON Lucas
CHARLES CITY Floyd
CHARLOTTE (52731) Clinton(91), Jackson(8)
CHARTER OAK Crawford
CHATSWORTH Sioux
CHELSEA (52215) Tama(83), Poweshiek(17)
CHEROKEE Cherokee
CHESTER Howard
CHILLICOTHE Wapello
CHURDAN (50050) Greene(95), Calhoun(3), Carroll(1)
CHURDAN Greene
CINCINNATI Appanoose
CLARE (50524) Webster(94), Pocahontas(2), Humboldt(1)
CLARENCE (52216) Cedar(86), Jones(13)
CLARINDA Page
CLARION Wright
CLARKSVILLE Butler
CLEAR LAKE Cerro Gordo
CLEARFIELD (50840) Taylor(80), Ringgold(19)
CLEGHORN (51014) Cherokee(98), O'Brien(1)
CLEMONS Marshall
CLERMONT (52135) Fayette(97), Clayton(2)
CLIMBING HILL Woodbury
CLINTON Clinton
CLIO Wayne
CLIVE (50325) Polk(87), Dallas(12)
CLUTIER Tama
COGGON (52218) Linn(86), Delaware(13)
COIN Page
COLESBURG (52035) Clayton(71), Delaware(18), Dubuque(10)
COLFAX Jasper
COLLEGE SPRINGS Page
COLLINS (50055) Story(69), Jasper(28), Marshall(2)
COLO Story
COLUMBIA Marion
COLUMBUS CITY Louisa
COLUMBUS JUNCTION (52738) Louisa(95), Washington(4)
COLWELL Floyd
CONESVILLE (52739) Louisa(65), Muscatine(34)
CONRAD (50621) Grundy(92), Marshall(7)
CONROY Iowa
COON RAPIDS (50058) Carroll(80), Guthrie(11), Audubon(5), Greene(3)
COOPER Greene
CORALVILLE Johnson
CORNING (50841) Adams(94), Taylor(5)
CORRECTIONVILLE (51016) Woodbury(93), Ida(6)
CORWITH (50430) Hancock(64), Kossuth(29), Humboldt(2), Wright(2)
CORYDON Wayne
COULTER Franklin
COUNCIL BLUFFS (51503) Pottawattamie(98), Mills(1)
COUNCIL BLUFFS Pottawattamie
CRAIG Plymouth
CRAWFORDSVILLE (52621) Washington(69), Louisa(29), Henry(1)
CRESCENT Pottawattamie
CRESCO (52136) Howard(92), Winneshiek(7)
CRESTON (50801) Union(96), Adair(1), Adams(1)
CROMWELL Union
CRYSTAL LAKE Hancock
CUMBERLAND (50843) Cass(96), Adams(3)
CUMMING (50061) Warren(60), Madison(15), Dallas(11), Polk(11)
CURLEW Palo Alto
CUSHING (51018) Woodbury(60), Ida(39)
CYLINDER Palo Alto
DAKOTA CITY Humboldt
DALLAS Marion
DALLAS CENTER Dallas
DANA (50064) Greene(94), Boone(6)
DANBURY (51019) Woodbury(79), Ida(8), Monona(6), Crawford(5)
DANVILLE (52623) Des Moines(91), Henry(8)
DAVENPORT Scott
DAVIS CITY Decatur
DAWSON Dallas

DAYTON (50530) Webster(96), Boone(3)
DE SOTO Dallas
DE WITT Clinton
DECATUR Decatur
DECORAH Winneshiek
DEDHAM (51440) Carroll(97), Audubon(2)
DEEP RIVER (52222) Poweshiek(73), Iowa(26)
DEFIANCE (51527) Shelby(84), Crawford(16)
DELAWARE Delaware
DELHI Delaware
DELMAR (52037) Clinton(93), Jackson(6)
DELOIT Crawford
DELPHOS Ringgold
DELTA (52550) Keokuk(98), Mahaska(1)
DENISON Crawford
DENMARK Lee
DENVER Bremer
DERBY (50068) Wayne(64), Lucas(35)
DES MOINES (50320) Polk(89), Warren(10)
DES MOINES Polk
DEWAR Black Hawk
DEXTER (50070) Dallas(34), Guthrie(25), Madison(23), Adair(17)
DIAGONAL (50845) Ringgold(97), Union(2)
DICKENS (51333) Clay(97), Dickinson(2)
DIKE Grundy
DIXON Scott
DOLLIVER Emmet
DONAHUE Scott
DONNELLSON Lee
DOON (51235) Lyon(96), Sioux(3)
DORCHESTER (52140) Allamakee(94), Winneshiek(5)
DOUDS (52551) Van Buren(96), Davis(3)
DOUGHERTY (50433) Cerro Gordo(53), Floyd(18), Franklin(18), Butler(9)
DOW CITY Crawford
DOWS (50071) Wright(53), Franklin(46)
DRAKESVILLE (52552) Davis(94), Wapello(5)
DUBUQUE Dubuque
DUMONT (50625) Butler(92), Franklin(7)
DUNCOMBE (50532) Webster(94), Hamilton(4)
DUNDEE Delaware
DUNKERTON Black Hawk
DUNLAP (51529) Harrison(81), Crawford(8), Monona(6), Shelby(2)
DURANGO Dubuque
DURANT (52747) Cedar(63), Scott(24), Muscatine(12)
DYERSVILLE (52040) Dubuque(94), Delaware(5)
DYSART (52224) Tama(71), Benton(27)
EAGLE GROVE (50533) Wright(96), Humboldt(2), Webster(1)
EARLHAM (50072) Madison(77), Dallas(22)
EARLING Shelby
EARLVILLE Delaware
EARLY Sac
EDDYVILLE (52553) Wapello(47), Mahaska(41), Monroe(11)
EDGEWOOD (52042) Clayton(75), Delaware(24)
ELBERON (52225) Tama(82), Benton(17)
ELDON (52554) Wapello(88), Davis(4), Jefferson(3), Van Buren(2)
ELDORA (50627) Hardin(95), Grundy(4)
ELDRIDGE Scott
ELGIN (52141) Fayette(71), Clayton(28)
ELK HORN (51531) Shelby(86), Audubon(13)
ELKADER Clayton
ELKHART Polk
ELKPORT Clayton
ELLIOTT (51532) Montgomery(55), Pottawattamie(38), Cass(6)
ELLSTON (50074) Ringgold(97), Union(2)
ELLSWORTH (50075) Hamilton(88), Pocahontas(11)
ELMA (50628) Howard(97), Mitchell(2)
ELWOOD Clinton
ELY (52227) Linn(97), Johnson(2)
EMERSON (51533) Mills(68), Montgomery(31)
EMMETSBURG Palo Alto
EPWORTH Dubuque
ESSEX (51638) Page(97), Montgomery(2)
ESTHERVILLE (51334) Emmet(98), Dickinson(1)
EVANSDALE Black Hawk
EVERLY (51338) Clay(82), Dickinson(17)
EXIRA (50076) Audubon(98), Guthrie(1)
EXLINE Appanoose
FAIRBANK (50629) Buchanan(44), Fayette(28), Black Hawk(15), Bremer(10)
FAIRFAX (52228) Linn(80), Benton(11), Johnson(7)
FARLEY Dubuque
FARMERSBURG Clayton
FARMINGTON (52626) Van Buren(75), Lee(24)
FARNHAMVILLE (50538) Calhoun(91), Webster(8)
FARRAGUT Fremont
FAYETTE Fayette
FENTON (50539) Kossuth(81), Palo Alto(18)
FERGUSON Marshall
FERTILE (50434) Cerro Gordo(87), Worth(11)
FESTINA Winneshiek
FLORIS Davis
FLOYD Floyd
FONDA (50540) Pocahontas(82), Calhoun(14), Buena Vista(1), Sac(1)
FONDA Pocahontas
FONTANELLE Adair
FOREST CITY (50436) Winnebago(91), Hancock(8)
FORT ATKINSON (52144) Winneshiek(78), Fayette(12), Chickasaw(8)
FORT DODGE Webster
FORT MADISON Lee
FOSTORIA Clay
FREDERICKSBURG (50630) Chickasaw(92), Bremer(7)
FREDERIKA Bremer
FREMONT (52561) Mahaska(73), Keokuk(15), Benton(11)
FRUITLAND Muscatine
GALT Wright
GALVA (51020) Ida(66), Sac(17), Cherokee(15)
GARBER Clayton
GARDEN CITY Hardin
GARDEN GROVE Decatur
GARNAVILLO Clayton
GARNER Hancock
GARRISON Benton
GARWIN (50632) Tama(83), Marshall(16)
GENEVA Franklin
GEORGE Lyon
GIBSON (50104) Keokuk(82), Poweshiek(12), Mahaska(5)
GIFFORD Hardin
GILBERT Story
GILBERTVILLE Black Hawk
GILLETT GROVE Clay
GILMAN (50106) Marshall(71), Jasper(15), Tama(9), Poweshiek(3)
GILMORE CITY (50541) Pocahontas(50), Humboldt(49)
GLADBROOK (50635) Tama(94), Marshall(5)
GLENWOOD Mills
GLIDDEN (51443) Carroll(98), Greene(1)
GOLDFIELD (50542) Wright(80), Humboldt(19)
GOODELL Hancock
GOOSE LAKE Clinton
GOWRIE (50543) Webster(94), Greene(5)
GRAETTINGER (51342) Palo Alto(81), Emmet(18)
GRAFTON (50440) Worth(98), Mitchell(1)
GRAND JUNCTION (50107) Greene(95), Boone(3)
GRAND MOUND Clinton
GRAND RIVER (50108) Decatur(90), Clarke(8)
GRANDVIEW Louisa
GRANGER (50109) Polk(61), Dallas(38)
GRANT Montgomery
GRANVILLE (51022) Sioux(59), O'Brien(39)
GRAVITY Taylor
GRAY Audubon
GREELEY (52050) Delaware(87), Clayton(12)
GREEN MOUNTAIN Marshall
GREENE (50636) Butler(83), Floyd(16)
GREENFIELD Adair
GREENVILLE Clay
GRIMES (50111) Polk(95), Dallas(4)
GRINNELL (50112) Poweshiek(89), Jasper(10)
GRINNELL Poweshiek
GRISWOLD (51535) Cass(52), Pottawattamie(47)
GRUNDY CENTER Grundy
GRUVER Emmet
GUERNSEY (52221) Poweshiek(88), Iowa(11)
GUTHRIE CENTER Guthrie
GUTTENBERG (52052) Clayton(93), Dubuque(6)
HALBUR Carroll
HALE Jones
HAMBURG Fremont
HAMLIN (50117) Audubon(98), Guthrie(1)
HAMPTON Franklin
HANCOCK Pottawattamie
HANLONTOWN (50444) Worth(80), Cerro Gordo(18), Winnebago(1)
HANSELL Franklin
HARCOURT (50544) Webster(98), Greene(1)
HARDY Humboldt
HARLAN Shelby
HARPER Keokuk
HARPERS FERRY Allamakee
HARRIS (51345) Osceola(94), Dickinson(5)
HARTFORD Warren
HARTLEY (51346) O'Brien(89), Osceola(6), Clay(4)
HARTWICK (52232) Poweshiek(85), Iowa(14)
HARVEY Marion
HASTINGS Mills
HAVELOCK (50546) Pocahontas(97), Palo Alto(2)
HAVERHILL Marshall
HAWARDEN Sioux
HAWKEYE Fayette
HAYESVILLE Keokuk
HAZLETON Buchanan
HEDRICK (52563) Keokuk(67), Wapello(31), Jefferson(1)
HENDERSON (51541) Mills(71), Pottawattamie(19), Montgomery(9)
HIAWATHA Linn
HIGHLANDVILLE Winneshiek
HILLS Johnson
HILLSBORO (52630) Van Buren(55), Henry(26), Lee(17)
HINTON Plymouth
HOLLAND Grundy
HOLSTEIN (51025) Ida(86), Cherokee(7), Woodbury(5)
HOLY CROSS (52053) Dubuque(83), Clayton(16)
HOMESTEAD (52236) Iowa(98), Johnson(2)
HONEY CREEK Pottawattamie
HOPKINTON (52237) Delaware(94), Dubuque(3), Jones(1)
HORNICK (51026) Woodbury(75), Monona(24)
HOSPERS (51238) Sioux(64), O'Brien(35)
HOUGHTON Lee
HUBBARD (50122) Hardin(98), Story(1)
HUDSON (50643) Black Hawk(93), Grundy(6)
HULL Sioux
HUMBOLDT (50548) Humboldt(98), Webster(1)
HUMESTON (50123) Wayne(78), Lucas(10), Decatur(8), Clarke(1)
HUXLEY (50124) Story(93), Polk(6)
IDA GROVE Ida
IMOGENE (51645) Fremont(53), Mills(36), Page(6), Montgomery(2)
INDEPENDENCE Buchanan
INDIANOLA Warren
INWOOD (51240) Lyon(90), Sioux(9)
IONIA (50645) Chickasaw(97), Floyd(2)
IOWA CITY Johnson
IOWA FALLS (50126) Hardin(97), Franklin(2)
IRA Jasper
IRETON (51027) Sioux(81), Plymouth(18)
IRWIN Shelby
JACKSON JUNCTION Winneshiek
JAMAICA (50128) Guthrie(63), Greene(24), Dallas(12)
JANESVILLE (50647) Bremer(54), Black Hawk(45)
JEFFERSON Greene
JESUP (50648) Buchanan(90), Black Hawk(9)
JEWELL Hamilton
JOHNSTON Polk
JOICE (50446) Worth(81), Winnebago(19)
JOLLEY Calhoun
KALONA (52247) Washington(66), Johnson(33)
KAMRAR Hamilton
KANAWHA (50447) Hancock(76), Wright(23)
KELLERTON (50133) Ringgold(97), Decatur(2)
KELLEY (50134) Story(78), Boone(21)
KELLOGG Jasper
KENSETT Worth
KENT (50850) Adams(50), Union(49)
KEOKUK Lee
KEOSAUQUA Van Buren
KEOTA (52248) Keokuk(72), Washington(27)
KESLEY Butler
KESWICK (50136) Keokuk(95), Iowa(3)
KEYSTONE Benton
KILLDUFF Jasper
KIMBALLTON (51543) Audubon(84), Shelby(15)
KINGSLEY (51028) Plymouth(82), Woodbury(17)
KINROSS Keokuk
KIRKMAN Shelby
KIRKVILLE Wapello
KIRON (51448) Crawford(65), Sac(18), Ida(15)
KLEMME (50449) Cerro Gordo(65), Hancock(34)
KNIERIM Calhoun
KNOXVILLE Marion
LA MOTTE (52054) Jackson(97), Dubuque(2)
LA PORTE CITY (50651) Black Hawk(93), Benton(6)
LACONA (50139) Warren(69), Lucas(20), Marion(9)
LADORA Iowa
LAKE CITY (51449) Calhoun(96), Carroll(3)
LAKE MILLS (50450) Winnebago(94), Worth(5)
LAKE PARK Dickinson

LAKE VIEW Sac
LAKOTA Kossuth
LAMONI (50140) Decatur(91), Ringgold(8)
LAMONT (50650) Buchanan(71), Fayette(26), Delaware(2)
LANESBORO Carroll
LANGWORTHY Jones
LANSING Allamakee
LARCHWOOD Lyon
LARRABEE (51029) Cherokee(95), O'Brien(4)
LATIMER Franklin
LAUREL (50141) Marshall(53), Jasper(46)
LAURENS (50554) Pocahontas(96), Palo Alto(2), Buena Vista(1)
LAWLER (52154) Chickasaw(94), Howard(5)
LAWTON Woodbury
LE CLAIRE Scott
LE GRAND Marshall
LE MARS Plymouth
LEDYARD Kossuth
LEHIGH Webster
LEIGHTON (50143) Mahaska(97), Marion(2)
LELAND Winnebago
LENOX (50851) Taylor(77), Adams(11), Union(8), Ringgold(2)
LEON Decatur
LESTER Lyon
LETTS (52754) Louisa(77), Muscatine(22)
LEWIS (51544) Cass(77), Pottawattamie(22)
LIBERTY CENTER Warren
LIBERTYVILLE (52567) Jefferson(83), Van Buren(16)
LIDDERDALE Carroll
LIME SPRINGS Howard
LINCOLN Tama
LINDEN (50146) Dallas(88), Guthrie(11)
LINEVILLE (50147) Wayne(85), Marion(14)
LINN GROVE (51033) Buena Vista(60), Clay(39)
LISBON (52253) Linn(71), Cedar(13), Jones(10), Johnson(4)
LISCOMB (50148) Marshall(88), Grundy(11)
LITTLE CEDAR Mitchell
LITTLE ROCK (51243) Lyon(91), Osceola(8)
LITTLE SIOUX (51545) Harrison(89), Monona(10)
LITTLEPORT Clayton
LIVERMORE (50558) Humboldt(54), Kossuth(45)
LOCKRIDGE (52635) Jefferson(74), Henry(25)
LOGAN Harrison
LOHRVILLE (51453) Calhoun(91), Carroll(7), Greene(1)
LONE ROCK Kossuth
LONE TREE (52755) Johnson(87), Louisa(10), Muscatine(1)
LONG GROVE (52756) Scott(98), Clinton(1)
LORIMOR (50149) Union(68), Madison(31)
LOST NATION Clinton
LOVILIA (50150) Monroe(98), Marion(1)
LOW MOOR Clinton
LOWDEN (52255) Cedar(97), Clinton(2)
LU VERNE (50560) Kossuth(81), Humboldt(18)
LUANA (52156) Clayton(83), Allamakee(16)
LUCAS (50151) Lucas(55), Warren(43), Clarke(1)
LUTHER Boone
LUXEMBURG Dubuque
LUZERNE (52257) Benton(98), Iowa(1)
LYNNVILLE (50153) Jasper(91), Mahaska(5), Poweshiek(2)
LYTTON (50561) Calhoun(58), Sac(41)
MACEDONIA Pottawattamie
MACKSBURG (50155) Madison(94), Adair(4), Union(1)
MADRID (50156) Boone(96), Polk(2), Dallas(1)
MAGNOLIA Harrison
MALCOM Poweshiek
MALLARD (50562) Palo Alto(88), Pocahontas(11)
MALOY Ringgold
MALVERN Mills
MANCHESTER Delaware
MANILLA (51454) Crawford(70), Shelby(29)
MANLY (50456) Worth(96), Cerro Gordo(3)
MANNING (51455) Carroll(85), Crawford(7), Audubon(5), Shelby(1)
MANSON (50563) Calhoun(81), Pocahontas(15), Webster(2)
MAPLETON (51034) Monona(92), Woodbury(5), Crawford(1)
MAQUOKETA (52060) Jackson(98), Clinton(1)
MARATHON Buena Vista
MARBLE ROCK Floyd
MARCUS (51035) Cherokee(93), Plymouth(5)
MARENGO (52301) Iowa(98), Benton(1)
MARION Linn
MARNE (51552) Cass(78), Shelby(20), Pottawattamie(1)
MARQUETTE Clayton
MARSHALLTOWN Marshall
MARTELLE (52305) Jones(86), Linn(13)
MARTENSDALE Warren
MARTINSBURG Keokuk
MASON CITY Cerro Gordo
MASONVILLE (50654) Delaware(64), Buchanan(35)
MASSENA (50853) Cass(96), Adams(3)
MATLOCK Sioux
MAURICE Sioux
MAXWELL (50161) Story(58), Polk(40), Jasper(1)
MAY CITY Osceola
MAYNARD Fayette
MC CALLSBURG (50154) Story(90), Hardin(9)
MC CAUSLAND Scott
MC CLELLAND Pottawattamie
MC GREGOR Clayton
MC INTIRE Mitchell
MECHANICSVILLE (52306) Cedar(78), Jones(21)
MEDIAPOLIS Des Moines
MELBOURNE (50162) Marshall(97), Jasper(2)
MELCHER Marion
MELROSE (52569) Monroe(68), Appanoose(17), Wayne(9), Lucas(3)
MELVIN (51350) Osceola(96), O'Brien(3)
MENLO (50164) Guthrie(70), Adair(29)
MERIDEN Cherokee
MERRILL Plymouth
MESERVEY (50457) Cerro Gordo(51), Hancock(22), Franklin(18), Wright(8)
MIDDLE AMANA Iowa
MIDDLETOWN Des Moines
MILES (52064) Jackson(93), Clinton(6)
MILFORD Dickinson
MILLERSBURG Iowa
MILLERTON Wayne
MILO Warren
MILTON (52570) Van Buren(84), Davis(15)
MINBURN Dallas
MINDEN Pottawattamie
MINEOLA Mills
MINGO (50168) Jasper(95), Polk(4)
MISSOURI VALLEY (51555) Harrison(80), Pottawattamie(19)
MITCHELLVILLE (50169) Polk(81), Jasper(18)
MODALE Harrison
MONDAMIN Harrison
MONMOUTH (52309) Jackson(74), Jones(25)
MONONA (52159) Clayton(75), Allamakee(24)
MONROE (50170) Jasper(87), Marion(12)
MONTEZUMA (50171) Poweshiek(98), Mahaska(1)
MONTEZUMA Poweshiek
MONTICELLO Jones
MONTOUR Tama
MONTPELIER Muscatine
MONTROSE Lee
MOORHEAD (51558) Monona(92), Harrison(7)
MOORLAND (50566) Webster(98), Calhoun(1)
MORAVIA (52571) Appanoose(90), Monroe(9)
MORLEY Jones
MORNING SUN (52640) Louisa(74), Des Moines(25)
MORRISON Grundy
MOSCOW (52760) Muscatine(62), Cedar(37)
MOULTON (52572) Appanoose(92), Davis(7)
MOUNT AUBURN Benton
MOUNT AYR Ringgold
MOUNT PLEASANT (52641) Henry(96), Washington(2)
MOUNT STERLING Van Buren
MOUNT UNION (52644) Henry(70), Des Moines(29)
MOUNT VERNON Linn
MOVILLE Woodbury
MURRAY (50174) Clarke(97), Union(2)
MUSCATINE (52761) Muscatine(96), Louisa(2)
MYSTIC Appanoose
NASHUA (50658) Chickasaw(85), Floyd(12), Bremer(2)
NEMAHA Sac
NEOLA (51559) Pottawattamie(96), Harrison(3)
NEVADA Story
NEW ALBIN Allamakee
NEW HAMPTON Chickasaw
NEW HARTFORD (50660) Butler(84), Grundy(15)
NEW LIBERTY (52765) Scott(87), Cedar(12)
NEW LONDON (52645) Henry(86), Des Moines(13)
NEW MARKET (51646) Taylor(97), Page(2)
NEW PROVIDENCE (50206) Hardin(88), Marshall(7), Story(4)
NEW SHARON (50207) Mahaska(98), Poweshiek(1)
NEW VIENNA (52065) Dubuque(89), Delaware(10)
NEW VIRGINIA (50210) Warren(91), Clarke(8)
NEWELL (50568) Buena Vista(90), Sac(8)
NEWHALL Benton
NEWTON Jasper
NICHOLS (52766) Muscatine(93), Johnson(6)
NODAWAY (50857) Adams(76), Taylor(19), Montgomery(3)
NORA SPRINGS (50458) Floyd(64), Cerro Gordo(31), Mitchell(4)
NORTH BUENA VISTA Clayton
NORTH ENGLISH (52316) Iowa(88), Keokuk(11)
NORTH LIBERTY Johnson
NORTH WASHINGTON Chickasaw
NORTHBORO (51647) Page(80), Fremont(19)
NORTHWOOD Worth
NORWALK Warren
NORWAY (52318) Benton(75), Iowa(24)
NUMA Appanoose
OAKDALE Johnson
OAKLAND Pottawattamie
OAKVILLE (52646) Louisa(53), Des Moines(46)
OCHEYEDAN Osceola
ODEBOLT Sac
OELWEIN Fayette
OGDEN Boone
OKOBOJI Dickinson
OLDS Henry
OLIN (52320) Jones(93), Cedar(6)
OLLIE (52576) Keokuk(98), Jefferson(1)
ONAWA Monona
ONSLOW Jones
ORAN Fayette
ORANGE CITY Sioux
ORCHARD (50460) Mitchell(75), Floyd(24)
ORIENT Adair
OSAGE Mitchell
OSCEOLA Clarke
OSKALOOSA Mahaska
OSSIAN (52161) Winneshiek(84), Fayette(15)
OTHO Webster
OTLEY (50214) Marion(98), Jasper(1)
OTO Woodbury
OTTOSEN (50570) Humboldt(60), Kossuth(37), Pocahontas(1)
OTTUMWA Wapello
OXFORD (52322) Johnson(97), Iowa(2)
OXFORD JUNCTION (52323) Jones(83), Clinton(7), Linn(4), Cedar(4)
OYENS Plymouth
PACIFIC JUNCTION Mills
PACKWOOD (52580) Jefferson(95), Keokuk(4)
PALMER Pocahontas
PALO (52324) Linn(85), Benton(14)
PANAMA (51562) Shelby(97), Harrison(2)
PANORA Guthrie
PARKERSBURG (50665) Butler(76), Grundy(23)
PARNELL (52325) Iowa(85), Johnson(14)
PATON (50217) Greene(79), Boone(14), Webster(5)
PATTERSON Madison
PAULLINA (51046) O'Brien(96), Cherokee(3)
PELLA (50219) Marion(94), Mahaska(5)
PEOSTA Dubuque
PERCIVAL Fremont
PERRY (50220) Dallas(93), Boone(5)
PERSHING Marion
PERSIA (51563) Harrison(97), Shelby(2)
PERU (50222) Madison(98), Clarke(1)
PETERSON (51047) Clay(70), Buena Vista(16), Cherokee(9), O'Brien(4)
PIERSON (51048) Woodbury(71), Cherokee(28)
PILOT GROVE Lee
PILOT MOUND Boone
PISGAH Harrison
PLAINFIELD (50666) Bremer(73), Butler(26)
PLANO (52581) Appanoose(95), Wayne(4)
PLEASANT VALLEY Scott
PLEASANTVILLE (50225) Marion(71), Warren(28)
PLOVER Pocahontas
PLYMOUTH (50464) Cerro Gordo(77), Worth(20), Mitchell(2)
POCAHONTAS Pocahontas
POLK CITY (50226) Polk(97), Boone(2)
POMEROY (50575) Calhoun(66), Pocahontas(33)
POPEJOY Franklin
PORTSMOUTH (51565) Shelby(79), Harrison(20)
POSTVILLE (52162) Allamakee(55), Clayton(32), Winneshiek(8), Fayette(3)
PRAIRIE CITY (50228) Jasper(96), Polk(1), Marion(1)
PRAIRIEBURG Linn

PRESCOTT (50859) Adams(97), Adair(2)
PRESTON (52069) Jackson(94), Clinton(5)
PRIMGHAR O'Brien
PRINCETON Scott
PROLE (50229) Warren(89), Madison(10)
PROMISE CITY Wayne
PROTIVIN Howard
PULASKI Davis
QUASQUETON Buchanan
QUIMBY Cherokee
RADCLIFFE (50230) Hardin(70), Hamilton(27), Story(1)
RAKE Winnebago
RALSTON Carroll
RANDALIA Fayette
RANDALL Hamilton
RANDOLPH (51649) Fremont(98), Mills(1)
RAYMOND Black Hawk
READLYN Bremer
REASNOR Jasper
RED OAK Montgomery
REDDING Ringgold
REDFIELD (50233) Dallas(88), Guthrie(11)
REINBECK (50669) Grundy(90), Tama(7), Black Hawk(1)
REMBRANDT Buena Vista
REMSEN (51050) Plymouth(98), Cherokee(1)
RENWICK (50577) Humboldt(69), Wright(30)
RHODES (50234) Marshall(77), Jasper(22)
RICEVILLE (50466) Howard(51), Mitchell(48)
RICHLAND (52585) Keokuk(59), Washington(30), Jefferson(9)
RICKETTS Crawford
RIDGEWAY Winneshiek
RINARD Calhoun
RINGSTED (50578) Emmet(93), Palo Alto(3), Kossuth(3)
RIPPEY (50235) Greene(91), Boone(5), Dallas(2)
RIVERSIDE (52327) Washington(68), Johnson(28), Louisa(2)
RIVERTON Fremont
ROBINS Linn
ROCK FALLS Cerro Gordo
ROCK RAPIDS Lyon
ROCK VALLEY (51247) Sioux(98), Lyon(1)
ROCKFORD (50468) Floyd(86), Cerro Gordo(13)
ROCKWELL Cerro Gordo
ROCKWELL CITY Calhoun
RODMAN Palo Alto
RODNEY (51051) Monona(92), Woodbury(7)
ROLAND (50236) Story(97), Hamilton(2)
ROLFE (50581) Pocahontas(98), Palo Alto(1)
ROME Henry
ROSE HILL (52586) Mahaska(92), Keokuk(7)
ROWAN (50470) Wright(96), Franklin(3)
ROWLEY Buchanan
ROYAL Clay
RUDD (50471) Floyd(94), Mitchell(5)
RUNNELLS (50237) Polk(92), Jasper(4), Marion(2)
RUSSELL (50238) Lucas(92), Wayne(7)
RUTHVEN (51358) Palo Alto(80), Clay(19)
RUTLAND Humboldt
RYAN Delaware
SABULA (52070) Jackson(89), Clinton(10)
SAC CITY Sac
SAINT ANSGAR (50472) Mitchell(95), Worth(4)
SAINT ANTHONY (50239) Marshall(87), Story(12)
SAINT CHARLES (50240) Warren(60), Madison(39)
SAINT DONATUS Jackson
SAINT LUCAS Fayette
SAINT MARYS Warren
SAINT OLAF Clayton
SAINT PAUL Lee
SALEM (52649) Henry(86), Lee(13)
SALIX Woodbury
SANBORN O'Brien
SCARVILLE Winnebago
SCHALLER (51053) Sac(91), Ida(6), Buena Vista(2)
SCHLESWIG (51461) Crawford(94), Ida(5)
SCOTCH GROVE Jones
SCRANTON (51462) Greene(97), Carroll(2)
SEARSBORO (50242) Poweshiek(94), Jasper(5)
SELMA (52588) Van Buren(73), Davis(25), Jefferson(1)
SERGEANT BLUFF Woodbury
SEYMOUR (52590) Wayne(90), Appanoose(9)
SHAMBAUGH Page
SHANNON CITY (50861) Union(76), Ringgold(23)
SHARPSBURG Taylor
SHEFFIELD (50475) Franklin(76), Cerro Gordo(23)
SHELBY (51570) Shelby(56), Pottawattamie(36), Harrison(6)
SHELDAHL Polk
SHELDON (51201) O'Brien(89), Sioux(9)
SHELL ROCK Butler
SHELLSBURG Benton
SHENANDOAH (51603) Page(85), Fremont(14)
SHENANDOAH Page
SHERRILL (52073) Dubuque(97), Clayton(2)
SIBLEY Osceola
SIDNEY Fremont
SIGOURNEY Keokuk
SILVER CITY (51571) Mills(53), Pottawattamie(46)
SIOUX CENTER Sioux
SIOUX CITY (51109) Woodbury(87), Plymouth(12)
SIOUX CITY Woodbury
SIOUX RAPIDS (50585) Buena Vista(71), Clay(28)
SLATER (50244) Story(72), Polk(25), Boone(2)
SLOAN (51055) Woodbury(66), Monona(33)
SMITHLAND (51056) Woodbury(92), Monona(7)
SOLDIER Monona
SOLON Johnson
SOMERS (50586) Calhoun(89), Webster(10)
SOUTH AMANA Iowa
SOUTH ENGLISH Keokuk
SPENCER Clay
SPERRY Des Moines
SPILLVILLE Winneshiek
SPIRIT LAKE Dickinson
SPRAGUEVILLE Jackson
SPRINGBROOK Jackson
SPRINGVILLE Linn
STACYVILLE Mitchell
STANHOPE Hamilton
STANLEY (50671) Fayette(72), Buchanan(27)
STANTON Montgomery
STANWOOD Cedar
STATE CENTER (50247) Marshall(94), Story(5)
STEAMBOAT ROCK (50672) Hardin(91), Grundy(8)
STOCKPORT (52651) Van Buren(93), Jefferson(6)
STOCKTON (52769) Scott(66), Muscatine(31), Henry(1)
STORM LAKE Buena Vista
STORY CITY (50248) Story(87), Hamilton(10), Boone(2)
STOUT Grundy
STRATFORD (50249) Hamilton(77), Webster(14), Boone(7)
STRAWBERRY POINT (52076) Clayton(95), Delaware(3), Fayette(1)
STRUBLE Plymouth
STUART (50250) Guthrie(74), Adair(25)
SULLY Jasper
SUMNER (50674) Bremer(72), Fayette(21), Chickasaw(6)
SUPERIOR Dickinson
SUTHERLAND (51058) O'Brien(95), Clay(2), Cherokee(1)
SWALEDALE Cerro Gordo
SWAN (50252) Warren(68), Marion(31)
SWEA CITY Kossuth
SWEDESBURG Henry
SWISHER (52338) Johnson(94), Linn(5)
TABOR (51653) Fremont(64), Mills(35)
TAINTOR Mahaska
TAMA Tama
TEEDS GROVE Clinton
TEMPLETON (51463) Carroll(98), Audubon(1)
TENNANT Shelby
TERRIL (51364) Dickinson(75), Clay(16), Emmet(8)
THAYER (50254) Union(97), Clarke(3)
THOMPSON Winnebago
THOR (50591) Humboldt(84), Webster(15)
THORNBURG Keokuk
THORNTON (50479) Cerro Gordo(89), Franklin(10)
THURMAN Fremont
TIFFIN Johnson
TINGLEY Ringgold
TIPTON Cedar
TITONKA (50480) Kossuth(94), Hancock(3), Winnebago(1)
TODDVILLE Linn
TOETERVILLE Mitchell
TOLEDO Tama
TORONTO Clinton
TRACY (50256) Marion(75), Mahaska(24)
TRAER Tama
TREYNOR Pottawattamie
TRIPOLI Bremer
TROY MILLS Linn
TRUESDALE Buena Vista
TRURO (50257) Madison(69), Warren(16), Clarke(14)
TURIN Monona
UDELL Appanoose
UNDERWOOD Pottawattamie
UNION (50258) Hardin(78), Marshall(20), Grundy(1)
UNIONVILLE (52594) Appanoose(68), Davis(31)
UNIVERSITY PARK Mahaska
URBANA Benton
URBANDALE (50323) Polk(59), Dallas(40)
URBANDALE Polk
UTE (51060) Monona(85), Crawford(14)
VAIL Crawford
VAN HORNE Benton
VAN METER (50261) Dallas(55), Madison(44)
VAN WERT Decatur
VARINA Pocahontas
VENTURA (50482) Cerro Gordo(87), Hancock(12)
VICTOR (52347) Iowa(79), Poweshiek(20)
VILLISCA (50864) Montgomery(85), Page(9), Taylor(2), Cass(1)
VINCENT Webster
VINING Tama
VINTON Benton
VIOLA Linn
VOLGA Clayton
WADENA (52169) Fayette(95), Clayton(4)
WALCOTT (52773) Scott(98), Muscatine(1)
WALFORD Benton
WALKER (52352) Linn(98), Buchanan(1)
WALL LAKE (51466) Sac(93), Carroll(3), Crawford(3)
WALLINGFORD Emmet
WALNUT (51577) Pottawattamie(74), Shelby(24)
WAPELLO Louisa
WASHINGTON Washington
WASHTA (51061) Cherokee(79), Ida(19)
WATERLOO Black Hawk
WATERVILLE Allamakee
WATKINS Benton
WAUCOMA (52171) Fayette(70), Chickasaw(15), Winneshiek(13)
WAUKEE Dallas
WAUKON (52172) Allamakee(98), Winneshiek(1)
WAVERLY Bremer
WAYLAND (52654) Henry(84), Washington(14)
WEBB (51366) Clay(92), Buena Vista(7)
WEBSTER (52355) Keokuk(94), Iowa(5)
WEBSTER CITY Hamilton
WELDON (50264) Decatur(66), Clarke(33)
WELLMAN (52356) Washington(78), Johnson(11), Iowa(8)
WELLSBURG (50680) Grundy(98), Hardin(1)
WELTON Clinton
WESLEY (50483) Kossuth(78), Hancock(21)
WEST AMANA Iowa
WEST BEND (50597) Kossuth(55), Palo Alto(41), Humboldt(1)
WEST BRANCH (52358) Cedar(84), Johnson(15)
WEST BURLINGTON Des Moines
WEST CHESTER Washington
WEST DES MOINES (50266) Polk(75), Dallas(25)
WEST DES MOINES Polk
WEST GROVE Davis
WEST LIBERTY Muscatine
WEST POINT (52656) Lee(98), Henry(1)
WEST UNION Fayette
WESTFIELD Plymouth
WESTGATE Fayette
WESTPHALIA Shelby
WESTSIDE (51467) Crawford(72), Carroll(27)
WEVER (52658) Lee(87), Des Moines(12)
WHAT CHEER (50268) Keokuk(93), Mahaska(6)
WHEATLAND (52777) Clinton(94), Cedar(5)
WHITING Monona
WHITTEMORE (50598) Kossuth(76), Palo Alto(23)
WHITTEN Hardin
WILLIAMS (50271) Hamilton(91), Wright(8)
WILLIAMSBURG Iowa
WILLIAMSON Lucas
WILTON (52778) Muscatine(56), Cedar(43)
WINFIELD (52659) Henry(84), Louisa(15)
WINTERSET Madison
WINTHROP Buchanan
WIOTA Cass
WODEN (50484) Winnebago(49), Hancock(47), Kossuth(3)
WOODBINE Harrison
WOODBURN (50275) Clarke(86), Lucas(13)
WOODWARD (50276) Dallas(72), Boone(27)
WOOLSTOCK (50599) Wright(80), Hamilton(19)
WORTHINGTON (52078) Dubuque(79), Delaware(20)
WYOMING Jones
YALE (50277) Guthrie(84), Dallas(15)
YARMOUTH Des Moines
YORKTOWN Page
ZEARING Story
ZWINGLE (52079) Dubuque(50), Jackson(50)

Iowa ZIP/City Cross Reference

ZIP	City
50001-50001	ACKWORTH
50002-50002	ADAIR
50003-50003	ADEL
50005-50005	ALBION
50006-50006	ALDEN
50007-50007	ALLEMAN
50008-50008	ALLERTON
50009-50009	ALTOONA
50010-50014	AMES
50015-50015	ANKENY
50020-50020	ANITA
50021-50021	ANKENY
50022-50022	ATLANTIC
50023-50023	ANKENY
50025-50025	AUDUBON
50026-50026	BAGLEY
50027-50027	BARNES CITY
50028-50028	BAXTER
50029-50029	BAYARD
50030-50030	BEACONSFIELD
50031-50031	BEAVER
50032-50032	BERWICK
50033-50033	BEVINGTON
50034-50034	BLAIRSBURG
50035-50035	BONDURANT
50036-50037	BOONE
50038-50038	BOONEVILLE
50039-50039	BOUTON
50040-50040	BOXHOLM
50041-50041	BRADFORD
50042-50042	BRAYTON
50043-50043	BUCKEYE
50044-50044	BUSSEY
50046-50046	CAMBRIDGE
50047-50047	CARLISLE
50048-50048	CASEY
50049-50049	CHARITON
50050-50050	CHURDAN
50051-50051	CLEMONS
50052-50052	CLIO
50054-50054	COLFAX
50055-50055	COLLINS
50056-50056	COLO
50057-50057	COLUMBIA
50058-50058	COON RAPIDS
50059-50059	COOPER
50060-50060	CORYDON
50061-50061	CUMMING
50062-50062	DALLAS
50063-50063	DALLAS CENTER
50064-50064	DANA
50065-50065	DAVIS CITY
50066-50066	DAWSON
50067-50067	DECATUR
50068-50068	DERBY
50069-50069	DE SOTO
50070-50070	DEXTER
50071-50071	DOWS
50072-50072	EARLHAM
50073-50073	ELKHART
50074-50074	ELLSTON
50075-50075	ELLSWORTH
50076-50076	EXIRA
50077-50077	CHURDAN
50078-50078	FERGUSON
50101-50101	GALT
50102-50102	GARDEN CITY
50103-50103	GARDEN GROVE
50104-50104	GIBSON
50105-50105	GILBERT
50106-50106	GILMAN
50107-50107	GRAND JUNCTION
50108-50108	GRAND RIVER
50109-50109	GRANGER
50110-50110	GRAY
50111-50111	GRIMES
50112-50112	GRINNELL
50115-50115	GUTHRIE CENTER
50116-50116	HAMILTON
50117-50117	HAMLIN
50118-50118	HARTFORD
50119-50119	HARVEY
50120-50120	HAVERHILL
50122-50122	HUBBARD
50123-50123	HUMESTON
50124-50124	HUXLEY
50125-50125	INDIANOLA
50126-50126	IOWA FALLS
50127-50127	IRA
50128-50128	JAMAICA
50129-50129	JEFFERSON
50130-50130	JEWELL
50131-50131	JOHNSTON
50132-50132	KAMRAR
50133-50133	KELLERTON
50134-50134	KELLEY
50135-50135	KELLOGG
50136-50136	KESWICK
50137-50137	KILLDUFF
50138-50138	KNOXVILLE
50139-50139	LACONA
50140-50140	LAMONI
50141-50141	LAUREL
50142-50142	LE GRAND
50143-50143	LEIGHTON
50144-50144	LEON
50145-50145	LIBERTY CENTER
50146-50146	LINDEN
50147-50147	LINEVILLE
50148-50148	LISCOMB
50149-50149	LORIMOR
50150-50150	LOVILIA
50151-50151	LUCAS
50152-50152	LUTHER
50153-50153	LYNNVILLE
50154-50154	MC CALLSBURG
50155-50155	MACKSBURG
50156-50156	MADRID
50157-50157	MALCOM
50158-50158	MARSHALLTOWN
50160-50160	MARTENSDALE
50161-50161	MAXWELL
50162-50162	MELBOURNE
50163-50163	MELCHER
50164-50164	MENLO
50165-50165	MILLERTON
50166-50166	MILO
50167-50167	MINBURN
50168-50168	MINGO
50169-50169	MITCHELLVILLE
50170-50170	MONROE
50171-50172	MONTEZUMA
50173-50173	MONTOUR
50174-50174	MURRAY
50177-50177	GRINNELL
50197-50198	KNOXVILLE
50201-50201	NEVADA
50206-50206	NEW PROVIDENCE
50207-50207	NEW SHARON
50208-50208	NEWTON
50210-50210	NEW VIRGINIA
50211-50211	NORWALK
50212-50212	OGDEN
50213-50213	OSCEOLA
50214-50214	OTLEY
50216-50216	PANORA
50217-50217	PATON
50218-50218	PATTERSON
50219-50219	PELLA
50220-50220	PERRY
50221-50221	PERSHING
50222-50222	PERU
50223-50223	PILOT MOUND
50225-50225	PLEASANTVILLE
50226-50226	POLK CITY
50227-50227	POPEJOY
50228-50228	PRAIRIE CITY
50229-50229	PROLE
50230-50230	RADCLIFFE
50231-50231	RANDALL
50232-50232	REASNOR
50233-50233	REDFIELD
50234-50234	RHODES
50235-50235	RIPPEY
50236-50236	ROLAND
50237-50237	RUNNELLS
50238-50238	RUSSELL
50239-50239	SAINT ANTHONY
50240-50240	SAINT CHARLES
50241-50241	SAINT MARYS
50242-50242	SEARSBORO
50243-50243	SHELDAHL
50244-50244	SLATER
50246-50246	STANHOPE
50247-50247	STATE CENTER
50248-50248	STORY CITY
50249-50249	STRATFORD
50250-50250	STUART
50251-50251	SULLY
50252-50252	SWAN
50253-50253	TAINTOR
50254-50254	THAYER
50255-50255	THORNBURG
50256-50256	TRACY
50257-50257	TRURO
50258-50258	UNION
50259-50259	GIFFORD
50261-50261	VAN METER
50262-50262	VAN WERT
50263-50263	WAUKEE
50264-50264	WELDON
50265-50266	WEST DES MOINES
50268-50268	WHAT CHEER
50269-50269	WHITTEN
50271-50271	WILLIAMS
50272-50272	WILLIAMSON
50273-50273	WINTERSET
50274-50274	WIOTA
50275-50275	WOODBURN
50276-50276	WOODWARD
50277-50277	YALE
50278-50278	ZEARING
50300-50321	DES MOINES
50322-50323	URBANDALE
50325-50325	CLIVE
50327-50397	DES MOINES
50398-50398	WEST DES MOINES
50401-50402	MASON CITY
50420-50420	ALEXANDER
50421-50421	BELMOND
50423-50423	BRITT
50424-50424	BUFFALO CENTER
50426-50426	CARPENTER
50427-50427	CHAPIN
50428-50428	CLEAR LAKE
50430-50430	CORWITH
50431-50431	COULTER
50432-50432	CRYSTAL LAKE
50433-50433	DOUGHERTY
50434-50434	FERTILE
50435-50435	FLOYD
50436-50436	FOREST CITY
50438-50438	GARNER
50439-50439	GOODELL
50440-50440	GRAFTON
50441-50441	HAMPTON
50444-50444	HANLONTOWN
50446-50446	JOICE
50447-50447	KANAWHA
50448-50448	KENSETT
50449-50449	KLEMME
50450-50450	LAKE MILLS
50451-50451	LAKOTA
50452-50452	LATIMER
50453-50453	LELAND
50454-50454	LITTLE CEDAR
50455-50455	MC INTIRE
50456-50456	MANLY
50457-50457	MESERVEY
50458-50458	NORA SPRINGS
50459-50459	NORTHWOOD
50460-50460	ORCHARD
50461-50461	OSAGE
50464-50464	PLYMOUTH
50465-50465	RAKE
50466-50466	RICEVILLE
50467-50467	ROCK FALLS
50468-50468	ROCKFORD
50469-50469	ROCKWELL
50470-50470	ROWAN
50471-50471	RUDD
50472-50472	SAINT ANSGAR
50473-50473	SCARVILLE
50475-50475	SHEFFIELD
50476-50476	STACYVILLE
50477-50477	SWALEDALE
50478-50478	THOMPSON
50479-50479	THORNTON
50480-50480	TITONKA
50481-50481	TOETERVILLE
50482-50482	VENTURA
50483-50483	WESLEY
50484-50484	WODEN
50501-50501	FORT DODGE
50510-50510	ALBERT CITY
50511-50511	ALGONA
50514-50514	ARMSTRONG
50515-50515	AYRSHIRE
50516-50516	BADGER
50517-50517	BANCROFT
50518-50518	BARNUM
50519-50519	BODE
50520-50520	BRADGATE
50521-50521	BURNSIDE
50522-50522	BURT
50523-50523	CALLENDER
50524-50524	CLARE
50525-50526	CLARION
50527-50527	CURLEW
50528-50528	CYLINDER
50529-50529	DAKOTA CITY
50530-50530	DAYTON
50531-50531	DOLLIVER
50532-50532	DUNCOMBE
50533-50533	EAGLE GROVE
50535-50535	EARLY
50536-50536	EMMETSBURG
50538-50538	FARNHAMVILLE
50539-50539	FENTON
50540-50540	FONDA
50541-50541	GILMORE CITY
50542-50542	GOLDFIELD
50543-50543	GOWRIE
50544-50544	HARCOURT
50545-50545	HARDY
50546-50546	HAVELOCK
50548-50548	HUMBOLDT
50551-50551	JOLLEY
50552-50552	KNIERIM
50553-50553	FONDA
50554-50554	LAURENS
50556-50556	LEDYARD
50557-50557	LEHIGH
50558-50558	LIVERMORE
50559-50559	LONE ROCK
50560-50560	LU VERNE
50561-50561	LYTTON
50562-50562	MALLARD
50563-50563	MANSON
50565-50565	MARATHON
50566-50566	MOORLAND
50567-50567	NEMAHA
50568-50568	NEWELL
50569-50569	OTHO
50570-50570	OTTOSEN
50571-50571	PALMER
50573-50573	PLOVER
50574-50574	POCAHONTAS
50575-50575	POMEROY
50576-50576	REMBRANDT
50577-50577	RENWICK
50578-50578	RINGSTED
50579-50579	ROCKWELL CITY
50580-50580	RODMAN

ZIP	City
50581-50581	ROLFE
50582-50582	RUTLAND
50583-50583	SAC CITY
50585-50585	SIOUX RAPIDS
50586-50586	SOMERS
50587-50587	RINARD
50588-50588	STORM LAKE
50590-50590	SWEA CITY
50591-50591	THOR
50592-50592	TRUESDALE
50593-50593	VARINA
50594-50594	VINCENT
50595-50595	WEBSTER CITY
50597-50597	WEST BEND
50598-50598	WHITTEMORE
50599-50599	WOOLSTOCK
50601-50601	ACKLEY
50602-50602	ALLISON
50603-50603	ALTA VISTA
50604-50604	APLINGTON
50605-50605	AREDALE
50606-50606	ARLINGTON
50607-50607	AURORA
50608-50608	AUSTINVILLE
50609-50609	BEAMAN
50611-50611	BRISTOW
50612-50612	BUCKINGHAM
50613-50614	CEDAR FALLS
50616-50616	CHARLES CITY
50619-50619	CLARKSVILLE
50620-50620	COLWELL
50621-50621	CONRAD
50622-50622	DENVER
50623-50623	DEWAR
50624-50624	DIKE
50625-50625	DUMONT
50626-50626	DUNKERTON
50627-50627	ELDORA
50628-50628	ELMA
50629-50629	FAIRBANK
50630-50630	FREDERICKSBURG
50631-50631	FREDERIKA
50632-50632	GARWIN
50633-50633	GENEVA
50634-50634	GILBERTVILLE
50635-50635	GLADBROOK
50636-50636	GREENE
50637-50637	GREEN MOUNTAIN
50638-50638	GRUNDY CENTER
50640-50640	HANSELL
50641-50641	HAZLETON
50642-50642	HOLLAND
50643-50643	HUDSON
50644-50644	INDEPENDENCE
50645-50645	IONIA
50647-50647	JANESVILLE
50648-50648	JESUP
50649-50649	KESLEY
50650-50650	LAMONT
50651-50651	LA PORTE CITY
50652-50652	LINCOLN
50653-50653	MARBLE ROCK
50654-50654	MASONVILLE
50655-50655	MAYNARD
50657-50657	MORRISON
50658-50658	NASHUA
50659-50659	NEW HAMPTON
50660-50660	NEW HARTFORD
50661-50661	NORTH WASHINGTON
50662-50662	OELWEIN
50664-50664	ORAN
50665-50665	PARKERSBURG
50666-50666	PLAINFIELD
50667-50667	RAYMOND
50668-50668	READLYN
50669-50669	REINBECK
50670-50670	SHELL ROCK
50671-50671	STANLEY
50672-50672	STEAMBOAT ROCK
50673-50673	STOUT
50674-50674	SUMNER
50675-50675	TRAER
50676-50676	TRIPOLI

ZIP	City
50677-50677	WAVERLY
50680-50680	WELLSBURG
50681-50681	WESTGATE
50682-50682	WINTHROP
50700-50706	WATERLOO
50707-50707	EVANSDALE
50799-50799	WATERLOO
50801-50801	CRESTON
50830-50830	AFTON
50831-50831	ARISPE
50833-50833	BEDFORD
50835-50835	BENTON
50836-50836	BLOCKTON
50837-50837	BRIDGEWATER
50839-50839	CARBON
50840-50840	CLEARFIELD
50841-50841	CORNING
50842-50842	CROMWELL
50843-50843	CUMBERLAND
50844-50844	DELPHOS
50845-50845	DIAGONAL
50846-50846	FONTANELLE
50847-50847	GRANT
50848-50848	GRAVITY
50849-50849	GREENFIELD
50850-50850	KENT
50851-50851	LENOX
50852-50852	MALOY
50853-50853	MASSENA
50854-50854	MOUNT AYR
50857-50857	NODAWAY
50858-50858	ORIENT
50859-50859	PRESCOTT
50860-50860	REDDING
50861-50861	SHANNON CITY
50862-50862	SHARPSBURG
50863-50863	TINGLEY
50864-50864	VILLISCA
50936-50981	DES MOINES
51001-51001	AKRON
51002-51002	ALTA
51003-51003	ALTON
51004-51004	ANTHON
51005-51005	AURELIA
51006-51006	BATTLE CREEK
51007-51007	BRONSON
51008-51008	BRUNSVILLE
51009-51009	CALUMET
51010-51010	CASTANA
51011-51011	CHATSWORTH
51012-51012	CHEROKEE
51014-51014	CLEGHORN
51015-51015	CLIMBING HILL
51016-51016	CORRECTIONVILLE
51017-51017	CRAIG
51018-51018	CUSHING
51019-51019	DANBURY
51020-51020	GALVA
51022-51022	GRANVILLE
51023-51023	HAWARDEN
51024-51024	HINTON
51025-51025	HOLSTEIN
51026-51026	HORNICK
51027-51027	IRETON
51028-51028	KINGSLEY
51029-51029	LARRABEE
51030-51030	LAWTON
51031-51031	LE MARS
51033-51033	LINN GROVE
51034-51034	MAPLETON
51035-51035	MARCUS
51036-51036	MAURICE
51037-51037	MERIDEN
51038-51038	MERRILL
51039-51039	MOVILLE
51040-51040	ONAWA
51041-51041	ORANGE CITY
51044-51044	OTO
51045-51045	OYENS
51046-51046	PAULLINA
51047-51047	PETERSON
51048-51048	PIERSON
51049-51049	QUIMBY

ZIP	City
51050-51050	REMSEN
51051-51051	RODNEY
51052-51052	SALIX
51053-51053	SCHALLER
51054-51054	SERGEANT BLUFF
51055-51055	SLOAN
51056-51056	SMITHLAND
51057-51057	STRUBLE
51058-51058	SUTHERLAND
51059-51059	TURIN
51060-51060	UTE
51061-51061	WASHTA
51062-51062	WESTFIELD
51063-51063	WHITING
51100-51111	SIOUX CITY
51201-51201	SHELDON
51230-51230	ALVORD
51231-51231	ARCHER
51232-51232	ASHTON
51234-51234	BOYDEN
51235-51235	DOON
51237-51237	GEORGE
51238-51238	HOSPERS
51239-51239	HULL
51240-51240	INWOOD
51241-51241	LARCHWOOD
51242-51242	LESTER
51243-51243	LITTLE ROCK
51244-51244	MATLOCK
51245-51245	PRIMGHAR
51246-51246	ROCK RAPIDS
51247-51247	ROCK VALLEY
51248-51248	SANBORN
51249-51249	SIBLEY
51250-51250	SIOUX CENTER
51301-51301	SPENCER
51330-51330	ALLENDORF
51331-51331	ARNOLDS PARK
51333-51333	DICKENS
51334-51334	ESTHERVILLE
51338-51338	EVERLY
51340-51340	FOSTORIA
51341-51341	GILLETT GROVE
51342-51342	GRAETTINGER
51343-51343	GREENVILLE
51344-51344	GRUVER
51345-51345	HARRIS
51346-51346	HARTLEY
51347-51347	LAKE PARK
51349-51349	MAY CITY
51350-51350	MELVIN
51351-51351	MILFORD
51354-51354	OCHEYEDAN
51355-51355	OKOBOJI
51357-51357	ROYAL
51358-51358	RUTHVEN
51360-51360	SPIRIT LAKE
51363-51363	SUPERIOR
51364-51364	TERRIL
51365-51365	WALLINGFORD
51366-51366	WEBB
51401-51401	CARROLL
51430-51430	ARCADIA
51431-51431	ARTHUR
51432-51432	ASPINWALL
51433-51433	AUBURN
51436-51436	BREDA
51437-51437	CARNARVON
51439-51439	CHARTER OAK
51440-51440	DEDHAM
51441-51441	DELOIT
51442-51442	DENISON
51443-51443	GLIDDEN
51444-51444	HALBUR
51445-51445	IDA GROVE
51446-51446	IRWIN
51447-51447	KIRKMAN
51448-51448	KIRON
51449-51449	LAKE CITY
51450-51450	LAKE VIEW
51451-51451	LANESBORO
51452-51452	LIDDERDALE
51453-51453	LOHRVILLE

ZIP	City
51454-51454	MANILLA
51455-51455	MANNING
51458-51458	ODEBOLT
51459-51459	RALSTON
51460-51460	RICKETTS
51461-51461	SCHLESWIG
51462-51462	SCRANTON
51463-51463	TEMPLETON
51465-51465	VAIL
51466-51466	WALL LAKE
51467-51467	WESTSIDE
51501-51503	COUNCIL BLUFFS
51510-51510	CARTER LAKE
51519-51519	AT AND T
51520-51520	ARION
51521-51521	AVOCA
51523-51523	BLENCOE
51525-51525	CARSON
51526-51526	CRESCENT
51527-51527	DEFIANCE
51528-51528	DOW CITY
51529-51529	DUNLAP
51530-51530	EARLING
51531-51531	ELK HORN
51532-51532	ELLIOTT
51533-51533	EMERSON
51534-51534	GLENWOOD
51535-51535	GRISWOLD
51536-51536	HANCOCK
51537-51537	HARLAN
51540-51540	HASTINGS
51541-51541	HENDERSON
51542-51542	HONEY CREEK
51543-51543	KIMBALLTON
51544-51544	LEWIS
51545-51545	LITTLE SIOUX
51546-51546	LOGAN
51548-51548	MC CLELLAND
51549-51549	MACEDONIA
51550-51550	MAGNOLIA
51551-51551	MALVERN
51552-51552	MARNE
51553-51553	MINDEN
51554-51554	MINEOLA
51555-51555	MISSOURI VALLEY
51556-51556	MODALE
51557-51557	MONDAMIN
51558-51558	MOORHEAD
51559-51559	NEOLA
51560-51560	OAKLAND
51561-51561	PACIFIC JUNCTION
51562-51562	PANAMA
51563-51563	PERSIA
51564-51564	PISGAH
51565-51565	PORTSMOUTH
51566-51566	RED OAK
51570-51570	SHELBY
51571-51571	SILVER CITY
51572-51572	SOLDIER
51573-51573	STANTON
51574-51574	TENNANT
51575-51575	TREYNOR
51576-51576	UNDERWOOD
51577-51577	WALNUT
51578-51578	WESTPHALIA
51579-51579	WOODBINE
51591-51591	RED OAK
51593-51593	HARLAN
51601-51603	SHENANDOAH
51630-51630	BLANCHARD
51631-51631	BRADDYVILLE
51632-51632	CLARINDA
51636-51636	COIN
51637-51637	COLLEGE SPRINGS
51638-51638	ESSEX
51639-51639	FARRAGUT
51640-51640	HAMBURG
51645-51645	IMOGENE
51646-51646	NEW MARKET
51647-51647	NORTHBORO
51648-51648	PERCIVAL
51649-51649	RANDOLPH
51650-51650	RIVERTON

51651-51651 SHAMBAUGH
51652-51652 SIDNEY
51653-51653 TABOR
51654-51654 THURMAN
51655-51655 BARTLETT
51656-51656 YORKTOWN
51693-51693 SHENANDOAH
52001-52004 DUBUQUE
52030-52030 ANDREW
52031-52031 BELLEVUE
52032-52032 BERNARD
52033-52033 CASCADE
52035-52035 COLESBURG
52036-52036 DELAWARE
52037-52037 DELMAR
52038-52038 DUNDEE
52039-52039 DURANGO
52040-52040 DYERSVILLE
52041-52041 EARLVILLE
52042-52042 EDGEWOOD
52043-52043 ELKADER
52044-52044 ELKPORT
52045-52045 EPWORTH
52046-52046 FARLEY
52047-52047 FARMERSBURG
52048-52048 GARBER
52049-52049 GARNAVILLO
52050-52050 GREELEY
52052-52052 GUTTENBERG
52053-52053 HOLY CROSS
52054-52054 LA MOTTE
52055-52055 LITTLEPORT
52056-52056 LUXEMBURG
52057-52057 MANCHESTER
52060-52060 MAQUOKETA
52064-52064 MILES
52065-52065 NEW VIENNA
52066-52066 NORTH BUENA VISTA
52068-52068 PEOSTA
52069-52069 PRESTON
52070-52070 SABULA
52071-52071 SAINT DONATUS
52072-52072 SAINT OLAF
52073-52073 SHERRILL
52074-52074 SPRAGUEVILLE
52075-52075 SPRINGBROOK
52076-52076 STRAWBERRY POINT
52077-52077 VOLGA
52078-52078 WORTHINGTON
52079-52079 ZWINGLE
52099-52099 DUBUQUE
52101-52101 DECORAH
52130-52130 ALPHA
52131-52131 BURR OAK
52132-52132 CALMAR
52133-52133 CASTALIA
52134-52134 CHESTER
52135-52135 CLERMONT
52136-52136 CRESCO
52140-52140 DORCHESTER
52141-52141 ELGIN
52142-52142 FAYETTE
52143-52143 FESTINA
52144-52144 FORT ATKINSON
52146-52146 HARPERS FERRY
52147-52147 HAWKEYE
52149-52149 HIGHLANDVILLE
52150-52150 JACKSON JUNCTION
52151-52151 LANSING
52154-52154 LAWLER
52155-52155 LIME SPRINGS
52156-52156 LUANA
52157-52157 MC GREGOR
52158-52158 MARQUETTE
52159-52159 MONONA
52160-52160 NEW ALBIN
52161-52161 OSSIAN
52162-52162 POSTVILLE
52163-52163 PROTIVIN
52164-52164 RANDALIA
52165-52165 RIDGEWAY
52166-52166 SAINT LUCAS
52168-52168 SPILLVILLE
52169-52169 WADENA
52170-52170 WATERVILLE
52171-52171 WAUCOMA
52172-52172 WAUKON
52175-52175 WEST UNION
52201-52201 AINSWORTH
52202-52202 ALBURNETT
52203-52204 AMANA
52205-52205 ANAMOSA
52206-52206 ATKINS
52207-52207 BALDWIN
52208-52208 BELLE PLAINE
52209-52209 BLAIRSTOWN
52210-52210 BRANDON
52211-52211 BROOKLYN
52212-52212 CENTER JUNCTION
52213-52213 CENTER POINT
52214-52214 CENTRAL CITY
52215-52215 CHELSEA
52216-52216 CLARENCE
52217-52217 CLUTIER
52218-52218 COGGON
52219-52219 PRAIRIEBURG
52220-52220 CONROY
52221-52221 GUERNSEY
52222-52222 DEEP RIVER
52223-52223 DELHI
52224-52224 DYSART
52225-52225 ELBERON
52226-52226 ELWOOD
52227-52227 ELY
52228-52228 FAIRFAX
52229-52229 GARRISON
52230-52230 HALE
52231-52231 HARPER
52232-52232 HARTWICK
52233-52233 HIAWATHA
52235-52235 HILLS
52236-52236 HOMESTEAD
52237-52237 HOPKINTON
52240-52240 IOWA CITY
52241-52241 CORALVILLE
52242-52246 IOWA CITY
52247-52247 KALONA
52248-52248 KEOTA
52249-52249 KEYSTONE
52250-52250 KINROSS
52251-52251 LADORA
52252-52252 LANGWORTHY
52253-52253 LISBON
52254-52254 LOST NATION
52255-52255 LOWDEN
52257-52257 LUZERNE
52301-52301 MARENGO
52302-52302 MARION
52305-52305 MARTELLE
52306-52306 MECHANICSVILLE
52307-52307 MIDDLE AMANA
52308-52308 MILLERSBURG
52309-52309 MONMOUTH
52310-52310 MONTICELLO
52312-52312 MORLEY
52313-52313 MOUNT AUBURN
52314-52314 MOUNT VERNON
52315-52315 NEWHALL
52316-52316 NORTH ENGLISH
52317-52317 NORTH LIBERTY
52318-52318 NORWAY
52319-52319 OAKDALE
52320-52320 OLIN
52321-52321 ONSLOW
52322-52322 OXFORD
52323-52323 OXFORD JUNCTION
52324-52324 PALO
52325-52325 PARNELL
52326-52326 QUASQUETON
52327-52327 RIVERSIDE
52328-52328 ROBINS
52329-52329 ROWLEY
52330-52330 RYAN
52331-52331 SCOTCH GROVE
52332-52332 SHELLSBURG
52333-52333 SOLON
52334-52334 SOUTH AMANA
52335-52335 SOUTH ENGLISH
52336-52336 SPRINGVILLE
52337-52337 STANWOOD
52338-52338 SWISHER
52339-52339 TAMA
52340-52340 TIFFIN
52341-52341 TODDVILLE
52342-52342 TOLEDO
52343-52343 TORONTO
52344-52344 TROY MILLS
52345-52345 URBANA
52346-52346 VAN HORNE
52347-52347 VICTOR
52348-52348 VINING
52349-52349 VINTON
52350-52350 VIOLA
52351-52351 WALFORD
52352-52352 WALKER
52353-52353 WASHINGTON
52354-52354 WATKINS
52355-52355 WEBSTER
52356-52356 WELLMAN
52357-52357 WEST AMANA
52358-52358 WEST BRANCH
52359-52359 WEST CHESTER
52361-52361 WILLIAMSBURG
52362-52362 WYOMING
52400-52499 CEDAR RAPIDS
52501-52501 OTTUMWA
52530-52530 AGENCY
52531-52531 ALBIA
52533-52533 BATAVIA
52534-52534 BEACON
52535-52535 BIRMINGHAM
52536-52536 BLAKESBURG
52537-52537 BLOOMFIELD
52538-52538 WEST GROVE
52540-52540 BRIGHTON
52542-52542 CANTRIL
52543-52543 CEDAR
52544-52544 CENTERVILLE
52548-52548 CHILLICOTHE
52549-52549 CINCINNATI
52550-52550 DELTA
52551-52551 DOUDS
52552-52552 DRAKESVILLE
52553-52553 EDDYVILLE
52554-52554 ELDON
52555-52555 EXLINE
52556-52557 FAIRFIELD
52560-52560 FLORIS
52561-52561 FREMONT
52562-52562 HAYESVILLE
52563-52563 HEDRICK
52565-52565 KEOSAUQUA
52566-52566 KIRKVILLE
52567-52567 LIBERTYVILLE
52568-52568 MARTINSBURG
52569-52569 MELROSE
52570-52570 MILTON
52571-52571 MORAVIA
52572-52572 MOULTON
52573-52573 MOUNT STERLING
52574-52574 MYSTIC
52575-52575 NUMA
52576-52576 OLLIE
52577-52577 OSKALOOSA
52580-52580 PACKWOOD
52581-52581 PLANO
52583-52583 PROMISE CITY
52584-52584 PULASKI
52585-52585 RICHLAND
52586-52586 ROSE HILL
52588-52588 SELMA
52590-52590 SEYMOUR
52591-52591 SIGOURNEY
52593-52593 UDELL
52594-52594 UNIONVILLE
52595-52595 UNIVERSITY PARK
52601-52601 BURLINGTON
52619-52619 ARGYLE
52620-52620 BONAPARTE
52621-52621 CRAWFORDSVILLE
52623-52623 DANVILLE
52624-52624 DENMARK
52625-52625 DONNELLSON
52626-52626 FARMINGTON
52627-52627 FORT MADISON
52630-52630 HILLSBORO
52631-52631 HOUGHTON
52632-52632 KEOKUK
52635-52635 LOCKRIDGE
52637-52637 MEDIAPOLIS
52638-52638 MIDDLETOWN
52639-52639 MONTROSE
52640-52640 MORNING SUN
52641-52641 MOUNT PLEASANT
52642-52642 ROME
52644-52644 MOUNT UNION
52645-52645 NEW LONDON
52646-52646 OAKVILLE
52647-52647 OLDS
52648-52648 PILOT GROVE
52649-52649 SALEM
52650-52650 SPERRY
52651-52651 STOCKPORT
52652-52652 SWEDESBURG
52653-52653 WAPELLO
52654-52654 WAYLAND
52655-52655 WEST BURLINGTON
52656-52656 WEST POINT
52657-52657 SAINT PAUL
52658-52658 WEVER
52659-52659 WINFIELD
52660-52660 YARMOUTH
52701-52701 ANDOVER
52720-52720 ATALISSA
52721-52721 BENNETT
52722-52722 BETTENDORF
52725-52725 BIG ROCK
52726-52726 BLUE GRASS
52727-52727 BRYANT
52728-52728 BUFFALO
52729-52729 CALAMUS
52730-52730 CAMANCHE
52731-52731 CHARLOTTE
52732-52733 CLINTON
52734-52734 A C NIELSEN CO
52736-52736 CLINTON
52737-52737 COLUMBUS CITY
52739-52739 CONESVILLE
52742-52742 DE WITT
52745-52745 DIXON
52746-52746 DONAHUE
52747-52747 DURANT
52748-52748 ELDRIDGE
52749-52749 FRUITLAND
52750-52750 GOOSE LAKE
52751-52751 GRAND MOUND
52752-52752 GRANDVIEW
52753-52753 LE CLAIRE
52754-52754 LETTS
52755-52755 LONE TREE
52756-52756 LONG GROVE
52757-52757 LOW MOOR
52758-52758 MC CAUSLAND
52759-52759 MONTPELIER
52760-52760 MOSCOW
52761-52761 MUSCATINE
52765-52765 NEW LIBERTY
52766-52766 NICHOLS
52767-52767 PLEASANT VALLEY
52768-52768 PRINCETON
52769-52769 STOCKTON
52771-52771 TEEDS GROVE
52772-52772 TIPTON
52773-52773 WALCOTT
52774-52774 WELTON
52776-52776 WEST LIBERTY
52777-52777 WHEATLAND
52778-52778 WILTON
52800-52809 DAVENPORT

General Help Numbers:

Governor's Office

State Capitol Bldg, Room 212S — 785-296-3232
Topeka, KS 66612-1590 — Fax 785-296-7973
www.governor.ks.gov/ — 8AM-5PM

Attorney General's Office

Memorial Hall — 785-296-2215
120 SW 10th Ave — Fax 785-296-6296
Topeka, KS 66612-1597 — 8AM-5PM
www.ksag.org/home/

Legislative Records

Kansas State Library, Capitol Bldg — 785-296-2149
300 SW 10th Ave — Fax 785-296-6650
Topeka, KS 66612 — 8AM-5PM
www.kslegislature.org/legsrv-legisportal/index.do

State Archives

Library and Archives Division — 785-272-8681
6425 SW 6th Ave — Fax 785-272-8682
Topeka, KS 66615-1099 — 9AM-4:30PM M-SAT
www.kshs.org/research/collections/documents/

State Specifics:

Capital: Topeka
Shawnee County

Time Zone: CST*

* Kansas' five western-most counties are MST: They are: Greeley, Hamilton, Kearny, Sherman, Wallace,

Number of Counties: 105

Population: 2,802,134

Website: www.kansas.gov

State Agencies

Criminal Records

Kansas Bureau of Investigation, Criminal Records Division, 1620 SW Tyler, Crim. History Record Sec., Topeka, KS 66612-1837; 785-296-8200, Fax- 785-368-7162; 8AM-5PM.

www.accesskansas.org/kbi/

Agencies dealing with children, the elderly or disabled clientele may qualify for reduced fees for record checks. These accounts are known as Caretaker accounts.

Indexing & Storage: Records available from 1939 to present. New records available for inquiry in up to 4 days. 50% of all arrests in database have final dispositions recorded, 65% for those arrests within last 5 years.

Searching: The criminal history information maintained by the KBI includes felony and misdemeanor arrests, prosecution data, court dispositions and information of incarceration in state-operated confinement facilities. Include in request- full name, sex, race, date of birth, SSN. Each request must be on a separate "Records Check Request Form.". Fingerprints are optional. Approximately 85% of records are fingerprint supported; approximately 50% of records are automated. This data not released- expunged records, non-convictions or juvenile records except to Criminal justice agencies and agencies required by law. Records of arrests within the past 12 months are also released when the records of disposition have not yet been received. Records released include court convictions for violations of law that are felonies or class A or class B misdemeanors as well as municipal ordinances or county resolutions that are equivalent to class A or class B misdemeanors under state statute. Class C misdemeanor assaults are also part of the database.

Access by: mail, fax, online.

Fee & Payment: Fees: $17.50 for a name check online; $20.00 by mail; $29.75 for fingerprint search. Add $10.00 for certification. If a "caregiver" fee is $12.50 for online name check and fingerprint check is $19.75. Fee payee- KBI Records Fees Fund. Prepayment required. Personal checks and credit cards are accepted.

Mail search: Turnaround time- 7-10 days. A SASE is not requested.

Fax search: Prior arrangement is required, same criteria as mail.

Online search: Anyone may obtain non-certified criminal records online at www.accesskansas.org/kbi/criminalhistory/. The system is also available for premium subscribers of accessKansas. The fee is $17.50 per record; credit cards accepted online. The system is unavailable between the hours of midnight and 4 AM daily. A Kansas "Most Wanted" list is available at www.accesskansas.org/kbi/mw.htm.

Statewide Court Records

Court Administration, Office of Judicial Administration, 301 SW 10th St, Rm 337, Topeka, KS 66612-1507; 785-296-2556, Fax- 785-296-7076; 8AM-5PM. www.kscourts.org

This agency will do searches on Appellate cases for $12.00 per hour. Copies are $.25 per page, add $1.00 if certified.

Access by: phone, online.

Phone search: For information on appellate cases, call the Clerk of the Appellate Court.

Online search: Commercial online access for civil and criminal records is available for District Court Records for 73 of 105 counties. Access is web-based at www.kansas.gov/subscribers/. An initial $95.00 subscription is required, access fees are involved. The system also provides state criminal records and motor vehicle records among other records. For additional information or a registration packet, telephone 800-4-KANSAS (800-452-6727) or visit the web page. The court homepage above offers free online access to published opinions of the Supreme and Appellate courts, as well as case information for the Appellate courts.

Sexual Offender Registry

Kansas Bureau of Investigation, Offender Registration, 1620 SW Tyler, Topeka, KS 66612-1837; 785-296-2841, Fax- 785-296-6781; 8AM-5PM. www.kansas.gov/kbi/ro.shtml

There are over 4,370 offenders registered in the state.

Indexing & Storage: Records available from 4/14/1994 forward. New records available for inquiry in 24 hours.

Searching: Further information on any registered offender in the file can be obtained from the sheriff's office in the registrant's county of residence. Include in request- name, DOB. SSN is helpful. This data not released- SSNs.

Access by: mail, fax, in person, online.

Mail search: Turnaround time- 1 to 2 days. A SASE is requested.

Fax search: Prior arrangement is required, same criteria as mail.

In person: Search in person at this office or at local sheriff offices in the state.

Online search: Searching is available at the website. All open registrants are searchable. The information contained in a registration entry was provided by the registrant. Neither the Kansas Bureau of Investigation (KBI) nor the sheriff's office can guarantee the accuracy of this information.

Incarceration Records

Kansas Department of Corrections, Public Information Officer, 900 SW Jackson, 4th floor, Topeka, KS 66612-1284; 785-296-3310, 785-296-5873, Fax- 785-296-0014; 8AM-5PM.

www.dc.state.ks.us/

General questions can be sent to kdocpub@kdoc.dc.state.ks.us.

Indexing & Storage: Records available on current and former inmates. New records available for inquiry in up to 4 days.

Searching: Include in request- full name. The date of birth and SSN are helpful. Location, KDOC number, physical identifiers, sentencing and conviction information, disciplinary record, and custody or supervision level are available. This data not released- medical, mental health, substance abuse

Access by: mail, phone, fax, online.

Fee & Payment: Copy fee is $.25 per page. Bulk data requests incur fees. Prepayment not required. Personal checks accepted.

Mail search: Turnaround time- 2 to 4 weeks. SASE is required.

Phone search: Name searching permitted by phone.

Fax search: Same criteria as mail.

Online search: Web access to the database known as KASPER gives information on offenders who are: currently incarcerated; under post-incarceration supervision; and, who have been discharged from a sentence. The database does not have information available about inmates sent to Kansas under the provisions of the interstate compact agreement. Go to www.dc.state.ks.us/kasper. Also, view the escapee list at www.dc.state.ks.us/kasper/index.htm.

Other access: Bulk lists are available on CD for $.01 per record.

Corporation, LP, LLC

Secretary of State, Memorial Hall, 1st Floor, 120 SW 10th Ave, Topeka, KS 66612-1594; 785-296-4564, Fax- 785-296-4570; 8AM-5PM.

www.kssos.org/business/business.html

Kansas does not have statutes requiring or permitting the registration or filing of DBAs or fictitious names.

Indexing & Storage: Records available since the applicable laws have been in effect. All Annual Reports are on microfilm at the Historical Society. New records available for inquiry immediately.

Searching: Items not released include confidential annual report balance sheets and copies of extensions. Include in request- full name of business, specific records that you need copies of. Records include articles of incorporation, all amendments and Annual Reports.

Access by: mail, phone, fax, in person, online.

Fee & Payment: There is no search fee. Plain copies are $1.00 per page. A certificate of good standing is $15.00, $12.50 if electronic. A letter of good standing is $10.00, $8.50 if electronic. Fee payee- Secretary of State. Prepayment required. Prepaid accounts are available. Personal checks accepted. Major credit cards accepted.

Mail search: Turnaround time- 2 to 3 days. SASE not required.

Phone search: Records may be ordered using a credit card.

Fax search: Items can be returned by fax for an additional $2.00 for the first page and $1.00 each additional page.

In person: No fee for request.

Online search: Free entity searching available at www.accesskansas.org/srv-corporations/index.do. Search by company name or organizational number. There is no fee to search records, but must be a subscriber to order copies of letters or certificates of good standings.

Trademarks/Servicemarks

Secretary of State, Trademarks/Servicemarks Division, 120 SW 10th Ave, Rm 100, Topeka, KS 66612-1240; 785-296-4564, Fax- 785-296-4570; 8AM-5PM. www.kssos.org

Indexing & Storage: Records available from the 1950s, all on computer. New records available for inquiry in 2 to 3 days.

Searching: All information recorded is available to the public. However, Kansas law prohibits the use of names and/or addresses derived from public record for solicitation purposes. Include in request- trademark/servicemark name, name of owner. The search provides the names and addresses of owners, date of filing, and class code of filing.

Access by: mail, phone, fax, in person, online.

Fee & Payment: There is no search fee. Copies are $1.00 per page. Certification is $15.00 plus the copy fees. Fee payee- Secretary of State. Prepayment required. The Secretary of State's office offers prepaid accounts for all regular, ongoing requesters. Personal checks, Visa, and MasterCard accepted.

Mail search: Turnaround time- 1 to 2 days. A mail request must include the name of trademark/servicemark and/or the owner's name. SASE not required. No fee for mail request.

Phone search: No fee for telephone request. They will give you limited information from the computer index.

Fax search: Turnaround time 24 hours.

In person: No fee for request.

Online search: Free searching by a variety of ways (keyword, owner, trademark, etc.) at www.kssos.org/business/trademark/trademark_search.aspx.

Other access: For bulk file purchase call Ann at 785-296-6271.

Uniform Commercial Code, Federal & State Tax Liens

Secretary of State - UCC Searches, Memorial Hall, 1st Fl, 120 SW 10th Ave, Topeka, KS 66612; 785-296-4564, Fax- 785-296-4570; 8AM-5PM.

www.kssos.org/business/business_ucc.html

Name searches are performed with the exact spelling of the name given. Each name variation will involve a separate search.

Indexing & Storage: Records available from 1966 on computer, from 1966 to present on microfiche with exception of electronic filings. These images available from July 30, 2001. New records available for inquiry in 2-3 business days.

Searching: Use search request form UCC-II. The search includes federal tax liens. All state tax liens are filed at the county level. Include in request-debtor name. One must order copies to receive collateral information. No collateral data is given over the phone. This data not released- SSN, FEIN

Access by: mail, fax, in person, online.

Fee & Payment: The search fee is $20.00 per name, $10.00 if searched online, and copies are $1.00 per page. Fee payee- Secretary of State. Prepayment required. Personal checks, Visa, and MasterCard accepted.

Mail search: Turnaround time- 3 days. The search is done on the name exactly as presented. If there is a possibility of a variation, each variation must be submitted. A SASE is not requested.

Fax search: Same criteria as mail searching. You can have information returned by fax for an additional $2.00 for the first page and $1.00 each additional page. Use of credit card required.

In person: Unless extensive list given, data available while you wait.

Online search: Online service is provided by accessKansas at www.kansas.gov/subscribers/services.html. The system is open 24 hours daily. A subscription is required with a modest annual fee. UCC records are $10.00 per record. This is the same online system used for corporation records. For more information, call at 800-4-KANSAS or go to www.kansas.gov and review Subscription Center services.

Other access: Records in a bulk or database format is available from accessKansas.com.

Sales Tax Registrations

Access to Records is Restricted.

Kansas Department of Revenue, Record Requests, Docking State Office Bldg, 915 SW Harrison, Topeka, KS 66625-3570; 785-296-3081, Fax- 785-296-7928; 8AM-5PM.

www.ksrevenue.org

Sales tax registration information is considered confidential and not public record. For complete contact data see www.ksrevenue.org/taxbuscontact.htm.

Birth Certificates

Kansas Department of Health & Environment, Office of Vital Statistics, 1000 SW Jackson, #120, Topeka, KS 66612-2221; 785-296-1400, 785-296-3253 (Order via vendor), Fax- 785-296-8075; 8AM-5PM.

www.kdheks.gov/vital/

Vital records are not considered public records in Kansas. Uncertified copies or verifications are not provided to the public. Birth certificates began being filed with the Office July 1, 1911.

Indexing & Storage: Records available from July 1911 to present. Delayed birth registrations from the late-1800s are available. New records available for inquiry in approximately 2 weeks.

Searching: Must have a signed release from person of record or have direct interest for personal or property right. You must also include photocopy of your government-issued photo ID (DL, for instance). Include in request- full name, names of parents, mother's maiden name, date of birth, place of birth, relationship to person of record, reason for information request, daytime phone. Pre-1940 records may be requested by an individual related as at least a cousin. Post 1940 records must be requested by an immediate family member.

Access by: mail, phone, fax, in person, online.

Fee & Payment: The fee is $12.00 for first certified copy, includes search of 5 years. Additional fee required for additional years searched. Add $7.00 for each additional copy of same record. Fee payee- Vital Statistics. Prepayment required. There is an additional $9.00 VitalChek fee with the use of a credit card. Personal checks accepted. Major credit cards accepted.

Mail search: Turnaround time- 5-10 business days. Include copy of your government-issued photo ID. A SASE is requested.

Phone search: You must use a credit card for an additional $9.00 fee. Turnaround time is within 3 business days. Phone service hours are from 8am to 4pm.

Fax search: Same criteria as phone searches, but must use designated vendor VitalChek at 785-357-4332.

In person: Available 9AM to 4PM. You must complete an application and provide your photo ID. Turnaround time: 20 to 30 minutes.

Online search: Records may be ordered online via a state designated vendor VitalChek at www.vitalchek.com.

Expedited service: Expedited service is available for credit card searches through VitalChek. Turnaround time- 3 to 5 days. Overnight mail services for return of documents is available for $22.50 plus credit card fee and record fee. Requests may require up to 24 business hours to process.

Death Records

Kansas State Department of Health & Environment, Office of Vital Statistics, 1000 SW Jackson, #120, Topeka, KS 66612-2221; 785-296-1400, 785-296-3253 (Order via vendor), Fax- 785-296-8075; 8AM-5PM.

www.kdheks.gov/vital/

Vital records are not considered public records in Kansas. Uncertified copies or verifications are not provided to the public.

Indexing & Storage: Records available from July 1, 1911 to present. New records available for inquiry immediately.

Searching: Must have a signed release from immediate family member or show direct interest for personal or property right. You must also include photocopy of your government-issued photo ID (DL, for instance). Include in request- full name, date of death, place of death, relationship to person of record, reason for information request. Please include a daytime phone number.

Access by: mail, phone, fax, in person, online.

Fee & Payment: The fee is $13.00 for first certified copy, includes search of 5 years. Additional fee required for additional years searched. Add $8.00 for each additional copy of same record. Fee payee- Vital Statistics. Prepayment required. Money orders are accepted. There is a $9.00 VitalChek fee for the use of a credit card. Personal checks accepted. Major credit cards accepted.

Mail search: Turnaround time- 5-10 business days. Must include a personal ID. A SASE is requested.

Phone search: Use a credit card required for an additional $9.00 fee. Turnaround time is within 3 business days.

Fax search: Same criteria as phone searches, but must use designated vendor VitalChek at 785-357-4332.

In person: Available 9AM to 4PM. Must complete an application and provide your personal photo ID. Turnaround time 20 to 30 minutes.

Online search: Records may be ordered online via a state designated vendor VitalChek at www.vitalchek.com.

Expedited service: Expedited service is available for credit card searches through VitalChek. Turnaround time- 3 to 5 days. Overnight mail services for return of documents is available for $22.50 plus credit card fee and record fee. Requests may require up to 24 business hours to process.

Marriage Certificates

Kansas State Department of Health & Environment, Office of Vital Statistics, 1000 SW Jackson, #120, Topeka, KS 66612-2221; 785-296-1400, 785-296-3253 (Order via vendor), Fax- 785-296-8075; 8AM-5PM.

www.kdheks.gov/vital/

Vital records are not considered public records in Kansas. Uncertified copies or verifications are not provided to the public. However, marriage information is available to the public at the county level where event took place.

Indexing & Storage: Records available from May 1, 1913 to present. Records prior to 1913 are found at county of issue. Records are computerized from 1993. New records available for inquiry in 2 months.

Searching: Must have a signed release from person of record or have direct interest in personal or property right. You must also include photocopy of your government-issued photo ID (DL, for instance). Include in request- names of husband and wife, date of marriage, place or county of marriage, relationship to person of record, reason for information request, wife's maiden name. Include a daytime phone number.

Access by: mail, phone, fax, in person, online.

Fee & Payment: The fee is $12.00 for first certified copy, includes search of 5 years. Additional fee required for additional years searched. Add $7.00 for each additional copy of same record. Fee payee- Vital Statistics. Prepayment required. Money orders are accepted. Personal checks accepted. Major credit cards accepted.

Mail search: Turnaround time- 5-10 business days. Must include a personal ID number. A SASE is requested.

Phone search: You must use a credit card for an additional $9.00 fee. Turnaround time is within 3 business days.

Fax search: Same criteria as phone searches, but must use designated vendor VitalChek at 785-357-4332.

In person: You must complete an application and provide your photo ID. Available 9AM to 4PM. Turnaround time 20 to 30 minutes.

Online search: Records may be ordered online via a state designated vendor VitalChek at www.vitalchek.com.

Expedited service: Expedited service is available for credit card searches through VitalChek. Turnaround time- 3 to 5 days. Overnight mail services for return of documents is available for $22.50 plus credit card fee and record fee. Requests may require up to 24 business hours to process.

Divorce Records

Kansas State Department of Health & Environment, Office of Vital Statistics, 1000 SW Jackson, #120, Topeka, KS 66612-2221; 785-296-1400, 785-296-3253 (Order via vendor), Fax- 785-296-8075; 8AM-5PM.

www.kdheks.gov/vital/

The agency will issue a divorce certificate, but a copy of the decree must be ordered from the county of issue. Divorce records are not open to the public here, but are at county. Uncertified copies or verifications are not provided to the public.

Indexing & Storage: Records available from July 1, 1951 to present. Records prior to July 1, 1951 are found at county of issue. New records available for inquiry in the second month after the divorce is filed.

Searching: Must have a signed release from person of record or show direct interest in personal or property right. You must also include photocopy of your government-issued photo ID (DL, for instance). Include in request- names of husband and wife, date of divorce, county of divorce, relationship to person of record, reason for information request. Include your daytime telephone number. Pre-1940 records may be requested by an individual related as at least a cousin. Post 1940 records must be requested by an immediate family member.

Access by: mail, phone, fax, in person, online.

Fee & Payment: The fee is $12.00 for first certified copy, includes search of 5 years. Additional fee required for additional years searched. Add $7.00 for each additional copy of same record. Fee payee- Vital Statistics. Prepayment required. Money orders are accepted. Personal checks accepted. Major credit cards accepted.

Mail search: Turnaround time- 5-10 business days. A SASE is requested.

Phone search: Must use a credit card for an additional $9.00 fee. Turnaround time is within 3 business days.

Fax search: Same criteria as phone searches, but must use designated vendor VitalChek at 785-357-4332.

In person: You must complete an application and provide your photo ID. Available 9AM to 4PM. Turnaround time is 20-30 minutes.

Online search: Records may be ordered online via a state designated vendor VitalChek at www.vitalchek.com.

Expedited service: Expedited service is available for credit card searches through VitalChek. Turnaround time- 3 to 5 days. Overnight mail services for return of documents is available for $22.50 plus credit card fee and record fee. Requests may require up to 24 business hours to process.

Workers' Compensation Records

Department of Labor, Workers Compensation Division, 800 SW Jackson, Suite 600, Topeka, KS 66612-1227; 785-296-6762, Fax- 785-291-3430; 8AM-5PM.

www.dol.ks.gov/index.html

Indexing & Storage: Records available from the mid-1970's on. New records available for inquiry immediately.

Searching: Information not released includes financial information submitted by employer, peer review records, and records related to safety inspections. Medical records are only released to those authorized by law, and are not open to the general public. Include in request- claimant name, SSN, signed release. All requests must be on Division Forms. The forms are available from the web or can be faxed. Employers may receive medical records if a job has been conditionally offered and there is a signed release by the subject.

Access by: mail, phone, fax, in person.

Fee & Payment: There is no search fee unless extensive searching is involved, then is based on staff's time. Prepayment required. Fee payee- Department of Labor

Mail search: Turnaround time- 1 week to 10 days. SASE not required.

Phone search: Some records are available for verification by phone.

Fax search: Fax searching available.

In person: Requests maintained off premises will take 2 days to obtain.

Driver Records, Accident Reports

Department of Revenue, Driver Control Bureau, PO Box 12021, Topeka, KS 66612-2021 (Courier address- Docking State Office Building, 915 Harrison, Rm 100, Topeka, KS 66612); 785-296-3671, Fax- 785-296-6851; 8AM-4:45PM.

www.ksrevenue.org/vehicle.htm

The state does not record speeding violations of 10 mph or less over in a 55 to 75 speed zone or 6 mph or less in a 30 to 54 speed zone.

Indexing & Storage: Records available for 5-10 years for most violations and lifetime for DWIs. New records available for inquiry in 2 to 21 days.

Searching: Permissible use requesters should use Form TR/DL 302. Casual requesters must secure written consent from subject before any records are released and use Form TR/DL 301. Forms available on the web. Include in request- full name, DOB. License #. The driver license number and either full name or DOB are required when ordering a driving record. The driver's address will show on the record. For an accident report, include the full name, DOB and/or VIN number, and date of accident. This data not released- medical information.

Access by: mail, in person, online.

Fee & Payment: The fee is $6.00 for a walk-in or mail-in request for a driving record. An accident report is available for $6.00 per page and copies of tickets $6.00 each. Fee payee- Department of Revenue. Prepayment required. Personal checks accepted, credit cards are not.

Mail search: Turnaround time- 2 to 5 days. A SASE is requested.

In person: Walk-in requests are usually processed within 30 minutes. Local law enforcement agencies may also honor driving record requests at a higher cost.

Online search: Kansas has contracted with the Kansas.gov (800-452-6727) to service all electronic media requests of driver license histories at www.kansas.gov/subscribers/. The fee per record is $6.00 for batch requests or $6.50 for immediate inquiry. There is an initial $75 subscription fee and an annual $60 fee. Billing is monthly. I not paid via EFT, a 3% surcharge is added. The system is open 24 hours a day, 7 days a week. Batch requests are available at 7:30 am (if ordered by 10 pm the previous day).

Vehicle Ownership & Registration

Division of Vehicles, Title and Registration Bureau, 915 Harrison, Rm 155, Topeka, KS 66626-0001; 785-296-3621, 785-271-3127 (Motor Carrier Svcs), Fax- 785-296-3852; 8AM-4:45PM.

www.ksrevenue.org/vehicle.htm

Indexing & Storage: Records available from approximately 1940. Older records are on microfiche, on microfilm from 1970-1987, and computerized since 1988. New records available for inquiry in 8 weeks from application date.

Searching: Casual requesters can only obtain records with consent of subject. Records are restricted from purchase for the purpose of obtaining address mail lists for selling property or services. Include in request- Form TR/DL302 for permissible requests. Casual requesters must secure written consent from subject before any records are released and use Form TR/DL 301.

Access by: mail, in person, online.

Fee & Payment: The fee for a title/registration verification depends on the request mode, noted as below. Fee payee- Kansas Department of Revenue. Prepayment required. Personal checks accepted, credit cards are not.

Mail search: Turnaround time- 2 weeks. The fee for a title or registration verification is $6.00. The fee for a title application copy of a vehicle title history is $10.00. A SASE is requested.

In person: Inquires are processed while you wait; however, requests must include form mentioned above. Same fees as by mail.

Online search: Online batch inquires are $6.00 per record; online interactive requests are $6.50 per record. Visit www.kansas.gov for a complete description of accessKansas (800-452-6727), the state authorized vendor. There is an initial $75 subscription fee and an annual $60 fee to access records from Kansas.Gov.

Vessel Ownership & Registration

Kansas Department of Wildlife & Parks, Boat Registration, 512 SE 25th Ave, Pratt, KS 67124-8174; 620-672-5911, Fax- 620-672-3013; 8AM-5PM M-F.

www.kdwp.state.ks.us/news/boating

All boats powered by gasoline, diesel, electric, or sail, must be registered and numbered. Sailboards and personal watercraft are considered boats. Boats are not titled.

Indexing & Storage: Records available from 1967 to present. Records are indexed on computer.

Titles are not required. All motorized or sailboats must be registered. New records available for inquiry in 2-3 weeks.

Searching: All requests must be submitted in writing with specific reason given for the request. No information is released for solicitation purposes. Include in request- name, either KA# or hull #, and name of person making request. Liens must be searched at the county level.

Access by: mail, fax, in person.

Fee & Payment: There is no search fee, unless extensive searching is requested.

Mail search: Turnaround time- 3-5 days. SASE not required.

Fax search: Same criteria as mail searching.

In person: Inquires are processed while you wait; however, requests must be in writing.

Legislation Records

Kansas State Library, Capitol Bldg, 300 SW 10th Ave, Topeka, KS 66612; 785-296-2149, Fax- 785-296-6650; 8AM-5PM.

www.kslegislature.org/legsrv-legisportal/index.do

Indexing & Storage: Records available from 1908 to present. Records are on computer since 1981. New records available for inquiry in 1 Day.

Searching: Include in request- bill number or bill topic and year.

Access by: mail, phone, fax, in person, online.

Fee & Payment: First 20 pages are free for all searches. Copies are $.10 a page. Fee payee- Kansas State Library. Personal checks accepted, credit cards are not.

Mail search: Turnaround time- 1 to 2 days. SASE not required. No fee for mail request.

Phone search: No fee for telephone request.

Fax search: Fax searching available. Include phone number or fax number.

In person: No fee for request.

Online search: The website has bill information for the last 10 sessions. The site also contains access to the state statutes.

Voter Registration

Access to Records is Restricted.

Secretary of State - Elections Division, Memorial Hall, 1st Floor, 120 SW 10th Ave, Topeka, KS 66612-1594; 785-296-4561, Fax- 785-291-3051; 8AM-5PM.

www.kssos.org

Individual records must be searched at the county level. This agency will sell the database on disk or CD for $200.00 only for political purposes; request form at www.kssos.org/forms/elections/CVR.pdf.

GED Certificates

Kansas Board of Regents, GED Records, 1000 SW Jackson St #520, Topeka, KS 66612-1368; 785-296-3191, Fax- 785-296-4526; 8AM-5PM.

www.kansasregents.org

Indexing & Storage: Records available from the 1940s. New records available for inquiry in 3 weeks.

Searching: Include in request- name at time of test, DOB, SSN, signed release and requester phone number. Also include the date of the test.

Access by: mail, in person.

Fee & Payment: There is a $10.00 fee for a verification, transcript, or a duplicate diploma. Fee payee- Kansas Board of Regents. Prepayment required. Cash and money orders are accepted. No personal checks or credit cards accepted.

Mail search: Turnaround time- 1 week. SASE not required.

In person: Walk-in requests are accepted.

Hunting & Fishing License Information

Dept of Wildlife & Parks, Licensing and Permits, 512 SE 25th Ave, Pratt, KS 67124-8174; 620-672-5911, Fax- 620-672-3014; 8AM-5PM.

www.kdwp.state.ks.us

Indexing & Storage: Records available for 2 years. New records available for inquiry in 1 month.

Searching: For hunting and fishing license information, requester must indicate what information is required and its intended use. Requests for information to be used for the sale of products or services will not be answered. Include in request- full name, date of birth and an Open Records Certification to be completed. Suggest to call first.

Access by: mail, fax, in person.

Fee & Payment: One must have Department approval. The agency reserves the right to recover costs for voluminous requests at $.10 per copy plus labor. Prepayment required. Personal checks accepted.

Mail search: Turnaround time- 1 to 3 days. SASE not required.

Fax search: Fax lists are accepted if prior arrangements made.

In person: Counter service available.

Other access: The database may be purchased on CD.

Kansas State Licensing Searchable Online

For details about the agency responsible for licensing/certifying/registering an item below or in the Agency Quick Finder section, match an item's number with the number of the agency in the *Licensing Agency Information* section.

Adult Care Home Administrator #16...... https://www.kdhehealthlicense.org/
Alcohol/Drug Counselor #3.................. www.ksbsrb.org/verification.html
Ambulance Attendant #8..................... www.ksbems.org/attendants.pdf
Ambulance Service #8........................ www.ksbems.org/ambser2005.pdf
Architect #14.................................... www.accesskansas.org/roster-search/index.html
Athletic Trainer #10........................... www.docboard.org/ks/df/kssearch.htm
Audiologist #16.................................. https://www.kdhehealthlicense.org/
Body Piercer #6.................................. www.accesskansas.org/kboc/LicenseeDatabase.htm
Certified Public Accountant-CPA #4...... www.da.ks.gov/boa/searchforindividual.aspx
Charity Organization #27.................... www.kscharitycheck.org
Chiropractor #10................................ www.docboard.org/ks/df/kssearch.htm
Clinical Psychotherapist #3................ www.ksbsrb.org/verification.html
Cosmetic Facility #6.......................... www.accesskansas.org/kboc/LicenseeDatabase.htm
Cosmetologist/Technician/Instruct'r #6... www.accesskansas.org/kboc/LicenseeDatabase.htm
Cosmetology-related School #6............ www.accesskansas.org/kboc/SchoolListing.htm
Counselor, Professional #3................. www.ksbsrb.org/verification.html
CPA Firm #4...................................... www.da.ks.gov/boa/SearchforFirms.aspx
Crematory #11.................................. www.kansas.gov/ksbma/listings.html
Dental Hygienist #19.......................... www.accesskansas.org/srv-dental-verification/start.do
Dentist #19....................................... www.accesskansas.org/srv-dental-verification/start.do
Dietitian #16..................................... https://www.kdhehealthlicense.org/
Electrologist #6................................. www.accesskansas.org/kboc/LicenseeDatabase.htm
Embalmer #11................................... www.kansas.gov/ksbma/listings.html
Engineer #14..................................... www.accesskansas.org/roster-search/index.html
Esthetician #6................................... www.accesskansas.org/kboc/LicenseeDatabase.htm
Funeral Director/Establishment #11...... www.kansas.gov/ksbma/listings.html
Geologist #14.................................... www.accesskansas.org/roster-search/index.html
Home Health Aide #16........................ www.ksnurseaidregistry.org
Insurance Agent #22.......................... http://towerii.ksinsurance.org/agent/agent.jsp?pagnam=agentsearch
Insurance Company #22...................... http://towerii.ksinsurance.org/agent/agency.jsp?pagnam=agencysearch
Landscape Architect #14.................... www.accesskansas.org/roster-search/index.html
Lobbyist #27..................................... www.kssos.org/elections/elections_lobbyists.html
Marriage & Family Therapist #3........... www.ksbsrb.org/verification.html
Medical Doctor/Medical Sch'/ #10........ www.docboard.org/ks/df/kssearch.htm
Medication Aide #16........................... www.ksnurseaidregistry.org
Nail Technician #6............................. www.accesskansas.org/kboc/LicenseeDatabase.htm
Nurse #12... https://www.accesskansas.org/app/nursing/verification/
Nurses' Aide #16............................... www.ksnurseaidregistry.org
Occupational Therapist/Assistant #10.... www.docboard.org/ks/df/kssearch.htm
Optometrist #26................................. www.kssbeo.com/license.htm
Osteopathic Physician #10.................. www.docboard.org/ks/df/kssearch.htm
Permanent Cosmetic Technician #6...... www.accesskansas.org/kboc/LicenseeDatabase.htm
Pharmacist #13.................................. https://www.accesskansas.org/pharmacy_verification/index.html
Physical Therapist/Assistant #10.......... www.docboard.org/ks/df/kssearch.htm
Physician Assistant #10...................... www.docboard.org/ks/df/kssearch.htm
Podiatrist #10................................... www.docboard.org/ks/df/kssearch.htm
Private Investigator #23..................... https://www.accesskansas.org/ssrv-kbi-pi-verify/index.do
Psychologist #3................................. www.ksbsrb.org/verification.html
Radiologic Technologist #10................ www.docboard.org/ks/df/kssearch.htm
Real Estate Agent/Seller/Broker #31..... https://www.accesskansas.org/ssrv-krec-verification/index.do
Real Estate Appraiser #28.................. www.accesskansas.org/srv-appraiser/index.do
Respiratory Therapist/Student #10........ www.docboard.org/ks/df/kssearch.htm
Social Worker #3............................... www.ksbsrb.org/verification.html
Speech/Language Pathologist #16........ https://www.kdhehealthlicense.org/
Surveyor, Land #14............................ www.accesskansas.org/roster-search/index.html
Tanning Facility #6............................ www.accesskansas.org/kboc/LicenseeDatabase.htm
Tattoo Artist #6................................. www.accesskansas.org/kboc/LicenseeDatabase.htm
Teacher #7....................................... https://online.ksde.org/teal/cert_search.aspx
Veterinarian #15............................... www.accesskansas.org/veterinary/listing.html

Kansas Licensing Quick Finder

Abstractor #1 620-544-2311
Adult Care Home Administrator #16 785-296-0061
Alcohol License #20 785-368-8222
Alcohol/Drug Counselor #3 785-296-3240
Ambulance Attendant #8 785-296-7296
Ambulance Service #8 785-296-7296
Animal Facility Inspector #2 785-296-2326
Architect #14 785-296-3054
Athletic Trainer #10 785-296-7413
Attorney #17 785-296-8409
Audiologist #16 785-296-0061
Barber #5 785-296-2211
Barber College #5 785-296-2211
Barber Shop #5 785-296-2211
Body Piercer #6 785-296-3155
Brand #2 785-296-2326
Certified Court Reporter #17 785-296-2852
Certified Public Accountant-CPA #4 785-296-2162
Charity Organization #27 785-296-4565
Child Care Attendant #30 785-296-1270
Chiropractor #10 785-296-7413
Clinical Psychotherapist #3 785-296-3240
Cosmetic Facility #6 785-296-3155
Cosmetologist/Technician #6 785-296-3155
Cosmetology School Instructor #6 785-296-3155
Cosmetology-related School #6 785-296-3155
Counselor, Professional #3 785-296-3240
CPA Firm #4 785-296-2162
Crematories #11 785-296-3980
Dental Hygienist #19 785-296-6400
Dentist #19 785-296-6400
Dietitian #16 785-296-0061
Drug Tax Stamp #20 785-368-8222
Electrologist #6 785-296-3155
Embalmer #11 785-296-3980
Emergency Medical Technician #8 785-296-7296
Engineer #14 785-296-3054
Esthetician #6 785-296-3155
Fundraiser/Professional Solicitor #27 785-296-4565
Funeral Director/Assis't Financ'l Dir #11 785-296-3980
Funeral Establishments #11 785-296-3980
Geologist #14 785-296-3054
Hearing Aid Dispenser #9 316-263-0774
Home Health Aide #16 785-296-6877
Insurance Agent/Company #22 785-296-3071
Investment Advisor #29 785-296-3307
Landscape Architect #14 785-296-3054
Livestock Inspector #2 785-296-2326
Lobbyist #27 785-296-3488
Marriage & Family Therapist #3 785-296-3240
Medical Doctor #10 785-296-7413
Medical School #10 785-296-7413
Medication Aide #16 785-296-6877
Nail Technician #6 785-296-3155
Notary Public #27 785-296-2239
Nurse #12 785-296-4929
Nurses' Aide #16 785-296-6877
Occupational Therapist/Assistant #10 785-296-7413
Optometrist #26 785-832-9986
Osteopathic Physician #10 785-296-7413
Permanent Cosmetic Technician #6 785-296-3155
Pesticide Applicator #24 785-296-4702
Pesticide Dealer #24 785-296-4702
Pharmacist #13 785-296-8420
Physical Therapist/Assistant #10 785-296-7413
Physician Assistant #10 785-296-7413
Podiatrist #10 785-296-7413
Private Investigator #23 785-296-4436
Psychologist #3 785-296-3240
Psychologist, Masters Level #3 785-296-3240
Racing & Wagering Equipment/Svc #25 785-296-5800
Racing Concessionaire #25 785-296-5800
Racing Facility Owner/Manager #25 785-296-5800
Racing Occupation #25 785-296-5800
Racing Organization #25 785-296-5800
Radiologic Technologist #10 785-296-7413
Real Estate Agent/Seller #31 785-296-3411
Real Estate Appraiser #28 785-271-3373
Real Estate Broker #31 785-296-3411
Respiratory Therapist/Student #10 785-296-7413
Salon #5 785-296-2211
School Administrator #7 785-296-2288
School Counselor #7 785-296-2288
School Library Media Specialist #7 785-296-2288
School Nurse #7 785-296-2288
Securities Agent #29 785-296-3307
Securities Broker/Dealer #29 785-296-3307
Social Worker #3 785-296-3240
Special Investigator Agriculture #2 785-296-2326
Speech/Language Pathologist #16 785-296-0061
Surveyor, Land #14 785-296-3054
Tanning Facility #6 785-296-3155
Tattoo Artist #6 785-296-3155
Teacher #7 785-296-2288
Tobacco Registration/License #20 785-368-8222
Veterinarian #15 785-456-8781

Kansas Licensing Agency Information

#1 Abstracters Board of Examiners, PO Box 549 (521 S Main), Hugoton, KS 67951-0549; 620-544-2311, Fax- 620-544-8029. Hours- 9AM-N, 1PM-5PM. www.kansasgreenteams.org/abstracters-board-examiners

#2 Animal Health Department, 708 SW Jackson, Topeka, KS 66603-3714; 785-296-2326, Fax- 785-296-1765. www.accesskansas.org/kahd/

#3 Behavioral Sciences Regulatory Board, 712 S Kansas Ave, Topeka, KS 66603-3817; 785-296-3240, Fax- 785-296-3112. Hours- 8AM-4:30PM. www.ksbsrb.org Search data at- www.ksbsrb.org/verification.html

#4 Board of Accountancy, 900 SW Jackson St, #556, Topeka, KS 66612-1239; 785-296-2162, Fax- 785-291-3501. Hours- 8AM-4:30PM. www.ksboa.org Search data at- www.da.ks.gov/boa/searchforindividual.aspx

#5 Board of Barbering, 700 SW Jackson, #1002, Topeka, KS 66603; 785-296-2211, Fax- 785-368-7071. Hours- 8:30AM-5PM. www.manta.com/coms2/dnbcompany_fxh1ml

#6 Board of Cosmetology, 714 SW Jackson #100, Topeka, KS 66603; 785-296-3155, Fax- 785-296-3002. www.accesskansas.org/kboc/ Search data at- www.accesskansas.org/kboc/LicenseeDatabase.htm

#7 Board of Education, 120 SE 10th Ave, Topeka, KS 66612-1182; 785-296-3201, Fax- 785-296-7933. http://www3.ksde.org/Welcome.html Search at- https://online.ksde.org/teal/cert_search.aspx Check status and verify at 785-296-2288.

#8 Board of Emergency Medical Services, 900 SW Jackson #1031, Landon State Office Bldg, Topeka, KS 66612-1228; 785-296-7296, Fax- 785-296-6212. www.ksbems.org

#9 Board of Examiners for Hearing Aid Dispensers, PO Box 252 (216 E 1st St N), Wichita, KS 67201-0252; 316-263-0774, Fax- 316-264-2681. Hours- 10AM-3PM T W TH.

#10 Board of Healing Arts, 235 S Topeka Blvd, Topeka, KS 66603-3068; 785-296-7413, Fax- 785-296-0852. Hours- 8AM-4:30PM. www.ksbha.org Search data at- www.docboard.org/ks/df/kssearch.htm

#11 Board of Mortuary Arts, 700 SW Jackson, #904, Topeka, KS 66603-3733; 785-296-3980, Fax- 785-296-0891. www.kansas.gov/ksbma/ Search at- www.kansas.gov/ksbma/listings.html

#12 Board of Nursing, 900 SW Jackson, Rm 1051, Landon State Office Bldg, Topeka, KS 66612-1230; 785-296-4929, Fax- 785-296-3929. Hours- 8AM-4:30PM. www.ksbn.org Search data at- https://www.accesskansas.org/app/nursing/verification/ Registered users of INK (Information Network of Kansas) can subscribe and get license verifications for $.25; Non-subscribers fee is $1.00 each.

#13 Board of Pharmacy, 900 Jackson, Landon State Office Bldg, Rm 560, Topeka, KS 66612-1231; 785-296-4056, Fax- 785-296-8420. www.accesskansas.org/pharmacy/ Search at- https://www.accesskansas.org/pharmacy_verification/index.html

#14 Board of Technical Professions, 900 SW Jackson, Rm 507, Topeka, KS 66120-1257; 765-296-3053. www.accesskansas.org/ksbtp/ Search data at- www.accesskansas.org/roster-search/index.html

#15 Board of Veterinary Examiners, PO Box 242 (1003 Lincoln Ave), Wamego, KS 66547-0242; 785-456-8781, Fax- 785-456-8782. 8AM-5PM. www.accesskansas.org/veterinary/ Search data at- www.accesskansas.org/veterinary/listing.html

#16 Department of Health & Environment, Bureau of Health Facilities, 1000 SW Jackson #200, Topeka, KS 66612-1290; 785-296-1240, Fax- 785-296-3075. www.kdheks.gov/hoc/

#17 Clerk of Appellate Courts, 301 SW 10th Avenue Rm 374, Topeka, KS 66612-1507; 785-296-3229, Fax- 785-296-1028. Hours- 8AM-5PM. www.kscourts.org

#19 Dental Board, 900 SW Jackson St Rm 564-S, Topeka, KS 66612-1220; 785-296-6400, Fax- 785-296-3116. Hours- 8AM-4:30PM. www.accesskansas.org/kdb/ Search at- www.acc esskansas.org/srv-dental-verification/start.do Another license verification site www.accesskansas.org/kdb/verification.html.

#20 Department of Revenue, Alcoholic Beverage Control, 915 SW Harrison St, Rm 214, Topeka, KS 66625-3512; 785-296-7015,

Fax- 785-296-7185. Hours- 8AM-5PM. www.ksrevenue.org/abc.htm

#22 Insurance Department, 420 SW 9th St, Topeka, KS 66612-1678; 785-296-3071, Fax- 785-296-2283. www.ksinsurance.org Search data at- http://towerii.ksinsurance.org/agent/index.jsp

#23 Bureau of Investigation, Private Detective Licensing Unit, 1620 SW Tyler St, Topeka, KS 66612-1837; 785-296-8200, Fax- 785-296-6781. Hours- 8:30AM-4:30PM. www.accesskansas.org/kbi/ Search data at- https://www.accesskansas.org/ssrv-kbi-pi-verify/index.do

#24 Department of Agriculture, Records Center, 109 SW 9th St, Topeka, KS 66612; 785-296-2263, Fax- 785-296-0673. www.ksda.gov

#25 Racing Commission, 700 SW Harrison, #420, Topeka, KS 66603-3754; 785-296-5800, Fax- 785-296-0900. Hours- 7:30AM-4:30PM. www.ksracing.org/

#26 Board of Examiners in Optometry, 3109 W. 6th St. #B, Lawrence, KS 66049; 785-832-9986, Fax- 785-832-9986. www.kssbeo.com Search data at- www.kssbeo.com/license.htm National Directory of Optometrist at www.arbo.org/index.php?action=findanoptometrist.

#27 Office of Secretary of State, Memorial Hall, 1st Floor, 120 SW 10th Av, Topeka, KS 66612-1594; 785-296-4564. Hours- 8AM-5PM. www.kssos.org/main.html

#28 Office of the Commissioner of Banks, Real Estate Appraisal Board, 700 SW Jackson #1102, Jayhawk Twr, Roof Garden Level, Topeka, KS 66603; 785-296-6736, Fax- 785-271-3370. Hours- 8AM-4:30PM. www.kansas.gov/kreab/

#29 Securities Commissioner, 618 S Kansas Ave 2nd Fl, Topeka, KS 66603-3804; 785-296-3307, Fax- 785-296-6872. www.securities.state.ks.us

#30 Child Care Licensing & Registration, 1000 SW Jackson #200, Topeka, KS 66612; 785-296-1270, Fax- 785-296-0803. www.kdheks.gov/bcclr/

#31 Real Estate Commission, Licensing Board, 120 SE 6th, 3 Townsite Plaza #200, Topeka, KS 66603-3511; 785-296-3411, Fax- 785-296-1771. www.accesskansas.org/krec/ Search data at- https://www.accesskansas.org/ssrv-krec-verification/index.do Search results are limited to 15 results at one time if a general name or city search is requested.

Kansas Federal Courts

The following list indicates the district and division name for each county in the state. If the bankruptcy court location is different from the district court, then the location of the bankruptcy court appears in parentheses.

County/Court Cross Reference

County	Court
Allen	Topeka
Anderson	Topeka
Atchison	Kansas City
Barber	Wichita
Barton	Wichita
Bourbon	Kansas City
Brown	Kansas City
Butler	Wichita
Chase	Topeka
Chautauqua	Wichita
Cherokee	Kansas City
Cheyenne	Wichita
Clark	Wichita
Clay	Topeka
Cloud	Topeka
Coffey	Topeka
Comanche	Kansas City (Wichita)
Cowley	Wichita
Crawford	Kansas City
Decatur	Wichita
Dickinson	Topeka
Doniphan	Kansas City
Douglas	Topeka
Edwards	Wichita
Elk	Wichita
Ellis	Wichita
Ellsworth	Wichita
Finney	Wichita
Ford	Wichita
Franklin	Topeka
Geary	Topeka
Gove	Wichita
Graham	Wichita
Grant	Wichita
Gray	Wichita
Greeley	Wichita
Greenwood	Wichita
Hamilton	Wichita
Harper	Wichita
Harvey	Wichita
Haskell	Wichita
Hodgeman	Wichita
Jackson	Topeka
Jefferson	Wichita
Jewell	Topeka
Johnson	Kansas City
Kearny	Wichita
Kingman	Wichita
Kiowa	Wichita
Labette	Kansas City
Lane	Wichita
Leavenworth	Kansas City
Lincoln	Topeka
Linn	Kansas City
Logan	Wichita
Lyon	Topeka
Marion	Topeka
Marshall	Kansas City
McPherson	Wichita
Meade	Wichita
Miami	Kansas City
Mitchell	Topeka
Montgomery	Wichita
Morris	Topeka
Morton	Wichita
Nemaha	Kansas City
Neosho	Topeka
Ness	Wichita
Norton	Wichita
Osage	Topeka
Osborne	Wichita
Ottawa	Topeka
Pawnee	Wichita
Phillips	Wichita
Pottawatomie	Topeka
Pratt	Wichita
Rawlins	Wichita
Reno	Wichita
Republic	Topeka
Rice	Wichita
Riley	Topeka
Rooks	Wichita
Rush	Wichita
Russell	Wichita
Saline	Topeka
Scott	Wichita
Sedgwick	Wichita
Seward	Wichita
Shawnee	Topeka
Sheridan	Wichita
Sherman	Wichita
Smith	Wichita
Stafford	Wichita
Stanton	Wichita
Stevens	Wichita
Sumner	Wichita
Thomas	Wichita
Trego	Wichita
Wabaunsee	Topeka
Wallace	Wichita
Washington	Topeka
Wichita	Wichita
Wilson	Topeka
Woodson	Topeka
Wyandotte	Kansas City

Standards for Federal Courts: Fees are standard unless noted in profile. Search fee is $26.00 per item (one party name or case number). Copy fee is $.50 per page. Certification fee is $9.00 per document, double for exemplification, if available. Most courts require prepayment. Mail requests should enclose a SASE unless otherwise noted. Before releasing records, all courts require prepayment, unless noted.

District courts index by defendant and plaintiff and by case number. Bankruptcy courts usually index by debtor and case number. While most courts now have their indexes on computer, many may still maintain index card files as well. Courts will archive closed case files at different times.

There are numerous public access programs available to online subscribers. Search the U.S. Party/Case Index to find party names and case numbers among all courts. Individual case data is provided on PACER. A search of CM/ECF provides copies of cases filed electronically. For details about PACER, the US Party/Case Index, and CM/ECF see the Appendix or go to http://pacer.psc.uscourts.gov or call 800-676-6856.

US District Court District of Kansas

Kansas City Division Clerk, US District Court, 500 State Ave, Rm 259 US Courthouse, Kansas City, KS 66101, 913-551-6719; Fax- 913-551-6942. 9AM-4:30PM. www.ksd.uscourts.gov

Counties/Note: Atchison, Bourbon, Brown, Cherokee, Crawford, Doniphan, Johnson, Labette, Leavenworth, Linn, Marshall, Miami, Nemaha, Wyandotte.

Searches/Indexing: In a search, include a full name and a date. Results do not include SSN or DOB. Will fax back documents for $.10 per page fee. New cases are in the index immediately after filing date. Computer, microfiche and card indexes maintained, computer back to 1995. Case files sent to archives 1 year after closed.

Search Access: Limited search; only docket info is released via phone if you have a case number. **Mail:** Search usually completed- 5-7 days. Include SASE for return. **Fax:** Fax search requests accepted. **In person:** 2 public terminals available. No self-serve copier.

Payment: Pay by Visa/MC/AmEx/Discover, money order, cashier's, business or personal check. Payee: Clerk, US District Court. No search fee is charged unless certification is required. All searches requiring certification conducted by the Wichita office.

E-Services: PACER records go back to 1991. New records online after 1 day. ECF at https://ecf.ksd.uscourts.gov. Opinions available via ECF website.

Topeka Division Clerk, US District Court, 444 SE Quincy, Rm 490 US Courthouse, Topeka, KS 66683, 785-295-2610. Hours-9AM-4:30PM. www.ksd.uscourts.gov

Counties/Note: Allen, Anderson, Chase, Clay, Cloud, Coffey, Dickinson, Douglas, Franklin, Geary, Jackson, Jewell, Lincoln, Lyon, Marion, Mitchell, Morris, Neosho, Osage, Ottawa, Pottawatomie, Republic, Riley, Saline, Shawnee, Wabaunsee, Washington, Wilson, Woodson.

Searches/Indexing: In a search, include a full name and a date. Results do not include SSN or DOB. Will fax back documents for fee. New cases are in the index 24 hours after filing date. Both computer and card indexes maintained. Case files sent to archives 1 year after closed.

Search Access: Docket info available via phone. **Mail:** Search usually completed- 2 days. Include SASE for return. **In person:** 2 public terminals available. No self-serve copier. Copies of electronic documents- $.10 per page.

Payment: Pay by Visa/MC/AmEx/Discover, money order, cashier's or personal check. Payee: Clerk, US District Court.

E-Services: PACER records go back to 1991. New records online after 1 day. ECF at https://ecf.ksd.uscourts.gov. Opinions available via ECF website.

Wichita Division Clerk, US District Court, 401 N Market, Rm 204 US Courthouse, Wichita, KS 67202-2096, 316-269-6491. 9AM-4:30PM. www.ksd.uscourts.gov

Counties/Note: All counties in Kansas; cases may be heard from counties in the other divisions.

Searches/Indexing: Include full name only in search request; add DOB or SSN if case before 3/2003. Results do not include SSN or DOB if after 3/2003. Court recommends verification through Probation Office of US Attorney office. Will fax back documents for fee. New cases are in the index immediately after filing date. Criminal records indexed on computer back to 1994; civil to 1990. Earlier indexes on microfiche, index cards. District-wide searches available here. Case files sent to archives 1 year after closed.

Search Access: Docket info available via phone. **Mail:** Search usually completed- 5-7 days. Include SASE for return. **In person:** 2 public terminals available. No self-serve copier.

Payment: Pay by Visa/MC/AmEx/Discover, credit cards, personal or business checks. Payee: Clerk, US District Court.

E-Services: PACER records go back to 1991. New records online after 1 day. ECF at https://ecf.ksd.uscourts.gov. Opinions available via ECF website.

US Bankruptcy Court District of Kansas

Kansas City Division Court Clerk, 500 State Ave, #161 US Courthouse, Kansas City, KS 66101, 913-551-6732; Fax- 913-551-6715. Hours-9AM-4PM. www.ksb.uscourts.gov

Counties/Note: Atchison, Bourbon, Brown, Cherokee, Comanche, Crawford, Doniphan, Johnson, Labette, Leavenworth, Linn, Marshall, Miami, Nemaha, Wyandotte. May have cases from other counties, and cases from counties listed here may be assigned elsewhere. Case numbers beginning with 1 assigned to Wichita; 2s assigned to Kansas City; 4s assigned to Topeka.

Searches/Indexing: Include SSN in search request; also- approximate year of filing. Results include last 4 SSN digits. New cases are in the index 1 day after filing date. Computer and microfiche indexes maintained. District-wide searches from 1989 forward available here. Master listing for pre-1989 cases available from Topeka Office. Case files archived every 6 months.

Search Access: Only docket info is available by phone. Voice Case Information Service available, call VCIS at 800-827-9028. **Mail:** Search usually completed- 1-2 days. Include SASE for return. **In person:** 2 public terminals, back to 1980s. Self-serve copies $.25 each.

Payment: Pay by credit cards (atty only, paying online), money order, cashier's check only. No debtor checks accepted. Payee: Clerk of US Bankruptcy Court.

E-Services: Document images available. PACER records go back to 1988. New records online after 1 day. ECF at https://ecf.ksb.uscourts.gov. Access opinions via main website. **Online Note:** Motion dockets and calendars free at www.ksb.uscourts.gov/motion.html.

Topeka Division Court Clerk, 240 US Courthouse, 444 SE Quincy, Topeka, KS 66683, 785-295-2750. 9AM-4PM. www.ksb.uscourts.gov

Counties/Note: Allen, Anderson, Chase, Clay, Cloud, Coffey, Dickinson, Douglas, Franklin, Geary, Jackson, Jewell, Lincoln, Lyon, Marion, Mitchell, Morris, Neosho, Osage, Ottawa, Pottawatomie, Republic, Riley, Saline, Shawnee, Wabaunsee, Washington, Wilson, Woodson. May have cases from other counties, and cases from counties listed here may be assigned elsewhere. Case numbers beginning with 1 assigned to Wichita; 2s assigned to Kansas City; 4s assigned to Topeka.

Searches/Indexing: Include SSN in search request. Results include last 4 SSN digits. New cases are in the index 1 day after filing date. Computer and microfiche indexes maintained. Case files archived every 6 months.

Search Access: Only docket info is available by phone. Voice Case Information Service available, call VCIS at 800-827-9028. **Mail:** Search usually completed- 1 week. SASE not required. **In person:** 2 public terminals; back to 1980s. Self-serve copies $.25 each.

Payment: Pay by credit cards (atty only, paying online), money order, cashier's or personal check. No debtor checks accepted. Payee: Clerk, US Bankruptcy Court.

E-Services: Document images available. PACER records go back to 1988. New records online after 1 day. ECF at https://ecf.ksb.uscourts.gov. Access opinions via main website. **Online Note:** Motion dockets and calendars free at www.ksb.uscourts.gov/motion.html.

Wichita Division Court Clerk, #167 US Courthouse, 401 N Market, Wichita, KS 67202, 316-269-6486; Fax- 316-269-6181. 9AM-4PM. www.ksb.uscourts.gov

Counties/Note: Barber, Barton, Butler, Chautauqua, Cheyenne, Clark, Comanche, Cowley, Decatur, Edwards, Elk, Ellis, Ellsworth, Finney, Ford, Gove, Graham, Grant, Gray, Greeley, Greenwood, Hamilton, Harper, Harvey, Haskell, Hodgeman, Jefferson, Kearny, Kingman, Kiowa, Lane, Logan, McPherson, Meade, Montgomery, Morton, Ness, Norton, Osborne, Pawnee, Phillips, Pratt, Rawlins, Reno, Rice, Rooks, Rush, Russell, Scott, Sedgwick, Seward, Sheridan, Smith, Stafford, Stanton, Stevens, Sumner, Thomas, Trego, Wallace, Wichita. May have cases from other counties, and cases from counties listed may be assigned elsewhere. Case numbers beginning with 1 assigned to Wichita; 2s assigned to Kansas City; 4s assigned to Topeka.

Searches/Indexing: Include SSN in search request. Results include last 4 SSN digits. New cases are in the index 1 day after filing date. Computer and microfiche indexes maintained. District-wide searches from 1989 forward available here. Case files archived every 6 months.

Search Access: Only attorneys, trustees, hearing and file dates released via phone. Voice Case Information Service available, call VCIS at 800-827-9028. **Mail:** Search usually completed- 3-4 working days. SASE not required. **In person:** 3 public terminals; back to 1980s. Self-serve copies $.25 each.

Payment: Pay by credit cards (atty only, paying online), money order, cashier's check. No debtor checks accepted. Payee: Clerk, Bankruptcy Court.

E-Services: Document images available. PACER records go back to 1988. New records online after 1 day. ECF at https://ecf.ksb.uscourts.gov. Access opinions via main website. **Online Note:** Motion dockets and calendars free at www.ksb.uscourts.gov/motion.html.

Kansas County Courts

Court	Jurisdiction	No. of Courts	How Organized
District Courts*	General	110	31 Districts
Municipal Courts	Municipal	350	

* Profiled in this Sourcebook.

Court	CIVIL								
	Tort	Contract	Real Estate	Min. Claim	Max. Claim	Small Claims	Estate	Eviction	Domestic Relations
District Courts*	X	X	X	$0	No Max	$4000	X	X	
Municipal Courts									

Court	CRIMINAL				
	Felony	Misdemeanor	DWI/DUI	Preliminary Hearing	Juvenile
District Courts*	X	X	X	X	X
Municipal Courts			X		

Administration

Office of Judicial Administration, 301 SW 10th Street, Rm 337, Topeka, KS, 66612; 785-296-2556, Fax: 785-296-7076. www.kscourts.org

Court Structure

The District Court is the court of general jurisdiction. There are 110 courts in 31 districts in 105 counties. If an individual in Municipal Court wants a jury trial, the request must be filed de novo in a District Court. Marriage and divorce records are with the Clerk of the District Court where they occurred as well as at the state vital records agency.

Online Access

Commercial online access for civil and criminal records is available for District Court Records in 73 counties. Access at www.kansas.gov/subscribers/. An initial $95.00 subscription is required, access fees are involved. The system also provides state criminal records and motor vehicle records among other records. For additional information or a registration packet, telephone 800-4-KANSAS (800-452-6727) or visit the web page.

The Kansas Appellate Courts offer free online access to case information at www.kscourts.org. Published opinions from the Appellate Courts and Supreme Court are also available.

Searching Tips, Fees, and Other Guidelines

Five counties - Cowley, Crawford, Labette, Montgomery, and Neosho - have two hearing locations but only one record center, which is the location shown herein. Many Kansas courts do not do criminal record searches and refer all criminal name searches to the Kansas Bureau of Investigation. The Kansas Legislature's Administrative Order 156 (Fall, 2000) allows courts to charge up to $12.00 per hour for search services, though courts may set their own search fees, if any. Prepayment is required unless otherwise noted.

Allen County

District Court PO Box 630, 1 N Washington St, Iola, KS 66749; 620-365-1425; fax: 620-365-1429; 8AM-5PM (CST). ***Felony, Misdemeanor, Civil, Eviction, Small Claims, Probate.*** www.31stjudicialdistrict.org

Civil Records: Access: Fax, mail, in person, online. Both court and visitors may perform in person searches. Search fee: $12.00 per hour. Required to search: name, years to search. Civil cases indexed by defendant, plaintiff, on computer from 1993, manual index from 1800s. Mail turnaround time 3-4 days Public use terminal has civil records back to 1993. PAT results show name, DOB. Access back to 11/1/02 is at www.kansas.gov/subscribers/. A $95.00 annual subscription required plus usage fee as low as $1.00 per search. Also, court calendars, limited action hearing results, and service results appear on the court's main website.

Criminal Records: Access: Online. No criminal searching at this court. Search fee: $12.00 per hour. Criminal records computerized from 1993, manual index from 1800s. All criminal searches are referred to the KBI, unless a case number is provided. The fees described here for criminal records only pertain if a case # is given. PAT results show name, DOB. Access back to 11/1/02 at www.kansas.gov/subscribers/. A $95.00 annual subscription required plus usage fee as low as $1.00 per search. Also, court calendars, limited action hearing results, and service results appear on the court's main website.

General Information: No juvenile (under the age of 15), mental health, sealed or expunged records released. Accepts requests via email, but cannot return results by email. Fee to fax out file $1.00 per page. Court makes copy: $.50 per page. Cert fee: $1.00. Payee: Clerk of Court. Personal checks accepted; credit cards are not. Mail requests: SASE required.

Anderson County

District Court PO Box 305, Garnett, KS 66032; 785-448-6886; criminal fax: 785-448-3230; civil fax: same; 8AM-N, 1PM-4PM (CST). ***Felony, Misdemeanor, Civil, Eviction, Small Claims, Probate.*** www.kscourts.org/dstcts/4anco.htm

Probate fax is same as main fax number.

Civil Records: Access: Fax, mail, in person, online. Both court and visitors may perform in person searches. Search fee: $12.00 per hour. Required to search: name, years to search. Civil cases indexed by defendant, plaintiff, on computer from 1977, index books from 1800s. Mail turnaround time 3 days. Civil PAT goes back to 1977. PAT results show name only. Public terminal includes probate, marriage, etc. This court is not on statewide system. Access back to 11/1/02 at www.kansas.gov/subscribers/. A $95.00 annual subscription required plus usage fee as low as $1.00 per search. Also, current court calendars are free at www.franklincoks.org/4thdistrict.htm. Access old probate court records up to 2/15/2001 free at www.kscourts.org/dstcts/4anprrec.htm as well as on the subscription service. Access marriage records by alpha search up to 8/29/2001 for free at www.kscourts.org/dstcts/4anmrsqy.htm.

Criminal Records: Access: Fax, mail, in person, online. Visitors must perform in person searches themselves. Search fee: $12.00 per hour. Required to search: name, years to search. Criminal records computerized from 1977, index books from 1800s. For criminal record searches, the court urges requesters to contact the KS Bureau of Investigations. Mail turnaround time within 3 days. Criminal PAT goes back to same as civil. PAT results show name only. Access back to 11/1/02 at www.kansas.gov/subscribers/. A $95.00 annual subscription required plus usage fee as low as $1.00 per search. Also, local court website access to criminal index and calendars is the same as civil.

General Information: Online identifiers in results same as on public terminal. No juvenile, mental health, sealed or expunged records released. Will fax documents $2.00 1st page, $.50 each add'l. Court makes copy: $.25 per page, self serve same.

Certification fee: $1.00 per document. Payee: District Court. Personal checks and major credit cards accepted. Mail requests: SASE required.

Atchison County

District Court PO Box 408, Atchison, KS 66002; 913-367-7400; criminal fax: 913-367-1171; civil fax: same; 8AM-5PM (CST). ***Felony, Misdemeanor, Civil, Eviction, Small Claims, Probate.***

Civil Records: Access: Fax, mail, in person. Both court and visitors may perform in person searches. Search fee: $12.00 per hour. Required to search: name, years to search. Civil cases indexed by defendant, plaintiff, on computer from 1991, index books from 1900s, archives from 1860s. Mail turnaround time 1-5 days. Civil PAT goes back to 1990. PAT civil results show middle initial.

Criminal Records: Access: In person only. Visitors must perform in person searches themselves. Required to search: name, years to search. Criminal records computerized from 1991, index books from 1900s, archives from 1860s. Criminal PAT goes back to same as civil. PAT criminal results show middle initial.

General Information: No juvenile, mental health, sealed or expunged records released. Will fax documents $1.25 per page. Court makes copy: $.25 per page. Certification fee: $1.00. Payee: District Court. Personal checks accepted; credit cards are not. Mail requests: SASE required for civil.

Barber County

District Court 118 E Washington, Medicine Lodge, KS 67104; 620-886-5639; fax: 620-886-5854; 8AM-N,1-5PM (CST). ***Felony, Misdemeanor, Civil, Eviction, Small Claims, Probate.*** www.kscourts.org/Districts/

Civil Records: Access: In person, online. Visitors must perform in person searches themselves. Required to search: name, years to search. Civil cases indexed by defendant, plaintiff, on computer from 1990, microfiche from 1900-1976, index cards from 1800s. Civil PAT goes back to 1990. PAT results show name only. Access back to 11/1/02 at www.kansas.gov/subscribers/. A $95.00 annual subscription required plus usage fee as low as $1.00 per search.

Criminal Records: Access: In person, online. Visitors must perform in person searches themselves. Required to search: name, years to search. Criminal records computerized from 1990, microfiche from 1900-1976, index cards from 1800s. Criminal PAT goes back to same as civil. Access at www.kansas.gov/subscribers/. A $95.00 annual subscription is required plus usage fee as little as $1.00 per search.

General Information: No juvenile, mental health, sealed or expunged records released. Will fax documents $1.00 per page, with a $10.00 page limit. Court makes copy: $.25 per page. Certification fee: $1.00 per cert. Payee: District Court. Personal checks accepted; credit cards are not.

Barton County

District Court 1400 Main, Rm 306, Great Bend, KS 67530; 620-793-1856; criminal fax: 620-793-1860; civil fax: same; 8AM-5PM (CST). ***Felony, Misdemeanor, Civil, Eviction, Small Claims, Probate.*** Probate fax is same as main fax number.

Civil Records: Access: Fax, mail, in person, online. Both court and visitors may perform in person searches. Search fee: $12.00 per hour. Minimum of $12.00 in advance. Required to search: name, years to search. Civil cases indexed by defendant, plaintiff, on computer 1990, microfiche and archives from 1800s, index from 1987. Mail turnaround time 3 days. Civil PAT goes back to 1990. PAT civil results show middle initial. Access back to 11/1/02 at www.kansas.gov/subscribers/. A $95.00 annual subscription required plus usage fee as low as $1.00 per search.

Criminal Records: Access: Fax, mail, in person, online. Both court and visitors may perform in person searches. Search fee: $12.00 per hour. Minimum of $12.00 in advance. Required to search: name, years to search. Criminal records on computer 1990, microfiche and archives from 1800s, index from 1987. Screening firm and employment-related searches and bulk requests will be referred to the state criminal record agency. Mail turnaround time 3 days. Criminal PAT goes back to same as civil. PAT criminal results show middle initial. Online access to criminal records is the same as civil.

General Information: No juvenile, mental health, sealed or expunged records released. Will fax documents $.50 per page. Court makes copy: $.35 per page; $.1.00 for microfilm copies. No certification fee. Payee: Clerk of Court. Personal checks accepted; credit cards are not. Mail requests: SASE required.

Bourbon County

District Court PO Box 868, Fort Scott, KS 66701; 620-223-0780; criminal phone: 620-223-1838; civil phone: 620-223-0780; probate phone: 620-223-1380; criminal fax: 620-223-5303; civil fax: same; 8:30AM-4:30PM (CST). ***Felony, Misdemeanor, Civil, Eviction, Small Claims, Probate.*** Probate fax is same as main fax number.

Civil Records: Access: In person, online. Visitors must perform in person searches themselves. Required to search: name, years to search. Civil cases indexed by defendant, plaintiff, on computer since 1990, index on computer since 1985. Civil PAT goes back to 20 years. Access back to 11/1/02 at www.kansas.gov/subscribers/. A $95.00 annual subscription required plus usage fee as low as $1.00 per search.

Criminal Records: Access: In person, online. Visitors must perform in person searches themselves. Required to search: name, years to search; SSN helpful. Criminal records on computer since 1990, index on computer since 1985. Criminal PAT goes back to same as civil. Online access to criminal records is the same as civil.

General Information: No juvenile, mental health, sealed or expunged records released. Will not fax out case files. Court makes copy: $.25 per page. Self serve: $.10 per page. Certification fee: $1.00 per document. Payee: Clerk of Court. Personal checks accepted; credit cards are not.

Brown County

District Court PO Box 417, Hiawatha, KS 66434; 785-742-7481; criminal fax: 785-742-3506; civil fax: same; 8AM-5PM (CST). ***Felony, Misdemeanor, Civil, Eviction, Small Claims, Probate.*** Probate fax is same as main fax number.

Civil Records: Access: Phone, fax, mail, in person, online. Both court and visitors may perform in person searches. Search fee: $12.00 per hour. Required to search: name, years to search. Civil cases indexed by defendant, plaintiff, on computer from 1982, microfiche from 1900s, index books from 1900s. Mail turnaround time 1-2 days. Civil PAT goes back to 1982. Access back to 11/1/02 at www.kansas.gov/subscribers/. A $95.00 annual subscription required plus usage fee as low as $1.00 per search.

Criminal Records: Access: Phone, fax, mail, in person, online. Both court and visitors may perform in person searches. Search fee: $12.00 per hour. Required to search: name, years to search; also helpful: SSN. Criminal records computerized from 1982, microfiche and index books from 1900s. Mail turnaround time 1-2 days. Criminal PAT goes back to same as civil. Online access to criminal records is the same as civil.

General Information: No juvenile, mental health, sealed or expunged records released. Fee to fax out file $1.00 per page. Court makes copy: $.50 first page, $.25 each add'l. Certification fee: $1.00 per document. Payee: District Court. Personal checks accepted; credit cards are not. Mail requests: SASE required.

Butler County

District Court 201 W Pine, #101, El Dorado, KS 67042; 316-322-4370; fax: 316-321-9486; 8AM-5PM (CST). ***Felony, Misdemeanor, Civil, Eviction, Small Claims, Probate.***

Civil Records: Access: In person, online. Visitors must perform in person searches themselves. Required to search: name, years to search. Civil cases indexed by defendant, plaintiff, on computer from 1992, index cards from 1800s. Civil PAT goes back to 1992. PAT civil results show middle initial. Access back to 11/1/02 at www.kansas.gov/subscribers/. A $95.00 annual subscription required plus usage fee as low as $1.00 per search.

Criminal Records: Access: Fax, in person, online. Visitors must perform in person searches themselves. Search fee: $12.00 per hour. Required to search: name, years to search, SSN. Criminal records computerized from 1992, index cards from 1800s. The court will not perform a name search and sends requesters to the state Bureau of Investigations. Search fees below involved records from a specific case only. Criminal PAT goes back to same as civil. PAT criminal results show middle initial. Online access to criminal records is the same as civil.

General Information: No juvenile, mental health, sealed or expunged records released. Will fax documents if prepaid. Court makes copy: $.50 per page; $1.00 if from microfilm, self serve same. Cert fee: $1.00 per page. Payee: Clerk of District Court. Personal checks accepted; credit cards are not.

Chase County

District Court PO Box 529, Cottonwood Falls, KS 66845; 620-273-6319; fax: 620-273-6890; 8AM-5PM (CST). ***Felony, Misdemeanor, Civil, Eviction, Small Claims, Probate.***

Civil Records: Access: In person only. Visitors must perform in person searches themselves. Required to search: name, years to search. Civil cases indexed by defendant, plaintiff, on computer from late 1990, microfiche from 1860, index books from 1860; visitors may search the printed index desk copy. Civil PAT goes back to 1991.

Criminal Records: Access: In person only. Visitors must perform in person searches themselves. Required to search: name, years to search. Criminal records computerized from late 1990, microfiche from 1860, index books from 1860; visitors may search the printed index desk copy. Criminal PAT goes back to same as civil.

General Information: No juvenile, mental health, sealed or expunged records released. Will not fax documents. Court makes copy: $.50 per page. Certification fee: $2.00 per cert. Payee: District Court. Personal checks accepted; credit cards are not.

Chautauqua County

District Court PO Box 306, 215 N Chautauqua, Sedan, KS 67361; 620-725-5870; criminal fax: 620-725-3027; civil fax: same; 8AM-4PM (CST). ***Felony, Misdemeanor, Civil, Eviction, Small Claims, Probate.*** www.14thjudicialdistrict-ks.org

Probate fax is same as main fax number.

Civil Records: Access: Mail, in person. Both court and visitors may perform in person searches. Search fee: $12.00 per hour. Required to search: name, years to search. Civil cases indexed by defendant, plaintiff, on computer from 1990, archives from 1950, index cards from 1870. Mail turnaround time 1-2 weeks. Civil PAT goes back to 1990. PAT results show middle initial, DOB. Terminal results also show SSNs.

Criminal Records: Access: Mail, in person. Both court and visitors may perform in person searches. Search fee: $12.00 per hour. Required to search: name, years to search; also helpful: DOB. Criminal records computerized from 1990, archives from 1950, index cards from 1870. Mail turnaround time 1-2 weeks. Criminal PAT goes back to same as civil. PAT results show middle initial, DOB. Terminal results include SSN.

General Information: No juvenile, mental health, sealed or expunged records released. Will fax documents. Court makes copy: $.25 per page, self serve same. Certification fee: $1.00 per certification. Payee: District Court. Personal checks accepted; credit cards are not. Mail requests: SASE required.

Cherokee County

District Court PO Box 189, Columbus, KS 66725; 620-429-3880; fax: 620-429-1130; 8AM-5PM (CST). ***Felony, Misdemeanor, Civil, Eviction, Small Claims, Probate.***

Civil Records: Access: Mail, fax, in person. Visitors must perform in person searches themselves. Search fee: $12.00 per hour. Required to search: name, years to search. Civil cases indexed by defendant, plaintiff, on computer back 16 years, index books from 1867. Mail turnaround time 3 days. Civil PAT goes back to 1990.
Criminal Records: Access: Mail, fax, in person. Visitors must perform in person searches themselves. Search fee: $12.00 per hour. Required to search: name, years to search; also helpful: SSN. Criminal records on computer back 16 years, index books from 1867. Mail turnaround time 3 days. Criminal PAT goes back to same as civil.
General Information: No juvenile, mental health, sealed or expunged records released. Will not fax documents. Court makes copy: $.25 per page. Certification fee: $1.25 per page includes copy. Payee: District Court. Personal checks have 14-day hold. No credit cards. Mail requests: SASE required.

Cheyenne County

District Court PO Box 646, St Francis, KS 67756; 785-332-8850; fax: 785-332-8851; civil 8AM-N,1-5PM (CST). ***Felony, Misdemeanor, Civil, Eviction, Small Claims, Probate.***
Probate records on a separate index. Court personnel will NOT do any record searching for the public. Probate fax is same as main fax number.
Civil Records: Access: In person only. Visitors must perform in person searches themselves. Required to search: name, years to search. Civil cases indexed by defendant, plaintiff, on strip index from 1989, index cards from 1870.
Criminal Records: Access: In person only. Visitors must perform in person searches. Required to search: name, years to search. Criminal records on strip index from 1989, index cards from 1870.
General Information: No juvenile, adoptions, mental health, sealed or expunged records released. Will fax documents $1.00 per page; free if toll free line used. Court makes copy: $.25 per page, self serve same. Certification fee: $1.00 per cert. Payee: Clerk of Court. Personal checks accepted; credit cards are not.

Clark County

District Court PO Box 790, Ashland, KS 67831; 620-635-2753; criminal fax: 620-635-2155; civil fax: same; 8AM-5PM (CST). ***Felony, Misdemeanor, Civil, Eviction, Small Claims, Probate.***
www.kscourts.org/dstcts/16dstct.htm
Probate fax is same as main fax number.
Civil Records: Access: Mail, fax, in person, online. Both court and visitors may perform in person searches. Search fee: $12.00 per search. Required to search: name, years to search. Civil cases indexed by defendant, plaintiff, on computer from 1992, microfiche and archives from 1800s, index cards from 1800s. Mail turnaround time 2 days. Civil PAT goes back to 2004. PAT results show name only. Access back to 11/1/02 at www.kansas.gov/subscribers/. A $95.00 annual subscription required plus usage fee as low as $1.00 per search.
Criminal Records: Access: Mail, fax, in person, online. Both court and visitors may perform in person searches. Search fee: $12.00 per search. Required to search: name, years to search; also helpful: SSN. Criminal records indexed on cards. Mail turnaround time 2 days. Criminal PAT goes back to 2004. PAT results show middle initial, DOB. Online access to criminal records is the same as civil.
General Information: No juvenile, mental health, sealed or expunged records released. Will fax documents. Court makes copy: $.25 per page, self serve same. Certification fee: $1.00. Payee: District Court. Personal checks accepted; credit cards are not. Mail requests: SASE required.

Clay County

District Court PO Box 203, Clay Center, KS 67432; 785-632-3443; fax: 785-632-2651; 8AM-5PM, closed N-1PM (CST). ***Felony, Misdemeanor, Civil, Eviction, Small Claims, Probate.***
Civil Records: Access: Mail, in person, online. Visitors must perform in person searches themselves. Search fee: $12.00 per name. Required to search: name, years to search. Civil cases indexed by defendant, plaintiff, on computer from 7/1994, index books from late 1800s. Mail turnaround time 3 days. Civil PAT goes back to 7/1994. Access back to 11/1/02 at www.kansas.gov/subscribers/. A $95.00 annual subscription required plus usage fee as low as $1.00 per search.
Criminal Records: Access: Mail, in person, online. Visitors must perform in person searches themselves. Search fee: $12.00 per name. Required to search: name. Criminal records computerized from 7/1994, index books from late 1800s. Mail turnaround time 3 days. Criminal PAT goes back to same as civil. Online access to criminal records is the same as civil.
General Information: No juvenile, adoption, mental health, sealed or expunged records released. Will fax out documents $2.00 1st page, $.50 each add'l. Court makes copy: $.25 per page. Self serve: $.25 per page. Certification fee: $1.00. Payee: Clerk of District Court. Personal checks accepted; credit cards are not. Mail requests: SASE required.

Cloud County

District Court 811 Washington #310, Concordia, KS 66901; 785-243-8124; fax: 785-243-8188; 8AM-5PM (CST). ***Felony, Misdemeanor, Civil, Eviction, Small Claims, Probate.***
www.kscourts.org/dstcts/12dstct.htm
Civil Records: Access: Phone, fax, mail, in person, online. Visitors must perform in person searches themselves. Search fee: $12.00 per hour. Required to search: name, years to search. Civil cases indexed by defendant, plaintiff, in print indexes from 1992, index books prior to 1992. Mail turnaround time 3-4 days. Civil PAT goes back to 1994. Access back to 11/1/02 at www.kansas.gov/subscribers/. A $95.00 annual subscription required plus usage fee as low as $1.00 per search.
Criminal Records: Access: Fax, mail, in person, online. Both court and visitors may perform in person searches. Search fee: $12.00 per hour. Required to search: name, years to search; also helpful: SSN, DOB. Criminal records in print indexes from 1992, index books prior to 1992. Mail turnaround time 3-4 days. Criminal PAT goes back to same as civil. Online access to criminal records is the same as civil.
General Information: No juvenile, mental health, sealed or expunged records released. Will fax documents $2.00 per page. Court makes copy: $.25 per page.If SASE not sent will charge the cost of postage. Certification fee: $1.00 per page. Payee: Clerk of Court. Personal checks accepted; credit cards are not. Mail requests: SASE requested.

Coffey County

District Court PO Box 330, Burlington, KS 66839; 620-364-8628; fax: 620-364-8535; 8AM-4PM (CST). ***Felony, Misdemeanor, Civil, Eviction, Small Claims, Probate.***
www.kscourts.org/dstcts/4coco.htm
Direct email record requests to debbiecoffeyco@hotmail.com.
Civil Records: Access: Mail, fax, in person, email, online. Both court and visitors may perform in person searches. Search fee: $12.00 per hour. Required to search: name, years to search. Civil cases indexed by defendant, plaintiff, on computer back to 1800s. Mail turnaround time 3 days. Public use terminal available, records go back to 1800's. PAT results show name only. Current court calendars are free online at www.franklincoks.org/4thdistrict/coffeybydate.html. Probate and marriage records are accessible at this website, marriages at www.kscourts.org/dstcts/4comarec.htm to 1/18/2001. Also, access courts back to 11/1/02 at www.kansas.gov/subscribers/. A $95.00 annual subscription required plus usage fee as low as $1.00 per search.
Criminal Records: Access: Mail, fax, in person, email, online. Both court and visitors may perform in person searches. Search fee: $12.00 per hour. Required to search: name, years to search, DOB. Criminal records computerized from 1800s. The court will not do name searches for employment purposes and refers requesters to the state agency - KBI. Mail turnaround time 3 days. Public use terminal available, crim records go back to same. PAT results show name only. Online access to subscription service and the court calendar is the same as civil. Online results show name only.
General Information: No juvenile, mental health, sealed or expunged records released. Fee to fax out file $2.00 1st page; $.50 each add'l. Court makes copy: $.25 per page, self serve same. Certification fee: $1.00. Payee: Clerk of District Court. Personal checks accepted; credit cards are not. Mail requests: SASE required.

Comanche County

District Court PO Box 722, Coldwater, KS 67029; 620-582-2182; criminal fax: 620-582-2603; civil fax: same; 8AM-5PM (CST). ***Felony, Misdemeanor, Civil, Eviction, Small Claims, Probate.*** www.kscourts.org/dstcts/16dstct.htm
Probate fax is same as main fax number.
Civil Records: Access: In person, online. Both court and visitors may perform in person searches. No search fee. Required to search: name, years to search. Civil cases indexed by defendant, plaintiff, on computer back to 2004 (child support only), index cards from 1886. Civil PAT goes back to 2004. PAT results show middle initial, DOB. Access back to 11/1/02 at www.kansas.gov/subscribers/. A $95.00 annual subscription required plus usage fee as low as $1.00 per search.
Criminal Records: Access: In person, online. Both court and visitors may perform in person searches. No search fee. Required to search: name, years to search; SSN helpful. Criminal records indexed on cards from 1886. Criminal PAT goes back to same as civil. Online access to criminal records is the same as civil.
General Information: No juvenile, mental health, sealed or expunged records released. Will fax specific case file $1.00 per page. Court makes copy: $.25 per page, self serve same. Certification fee: $1.00 per page. Payee: District Court. Personal checks accepted; credit cards are not.

Cowley County

Arkansas City District Court PO Box 1152, Arkansas City, KS 67005; 620-441-4520; criminal fax: 620-442-7213; civil fax: same; 8AM-N,1-4PM (CST). ***Felony, Misdemeanor, Civil, Eviction, Small Claims, Probate.***
This court covers the southern part of the county. Many felony records are kept at Winfield. Probate fax is same as main fax number.
Civil Records: Access: Fax, mail, in person. Both court and visitors may perform in person searches. Search fee: $12.00 per name. Required to search: name, years to search. Civil cases indexed by defendant, plaintiff, from 1977. This Court facility in existence since 1977, so no records prior to that date. Computer records commencing 1994. Mail turnaround time 1 week. Civil PAT goes back to 1994. PAT civil results show middle initial. Results include docket notes.
Criminal Records: Access: Fax, mail, in person. Both court and visitors may perform in person searches. Search fee: $12.00 per name. Required to search: name, years to search, SSN. Criminal records from 1977. Court facility in existence since 1977, so no records prior to that date. Computer records commencing 1994. Mail turnaround time 1 week. Criminal PAT goes back to same as civil. PAT criminal results show middle initial. Results include docket notes.
General Information: No juvenile, mental health, sealed or expunged records released. Will fax documents $1.00 per page. Court makes copy: $.50 per page. Certification fee: $1.00 per doc. Payee: Clerk of Court. Personal checks accepted; credit cards are not. Mail requests: SASE helpful.

Winfield District Court PO Box 472, Winfield, KS 67156; 620-221-5470; fax: 620-221-1097; 8AM-N,1-4PM (CST). ***Felony, Misdemeanor, Civil, Eviction, Small Claims, Probate.***
This court covers northern part of county.
Civil Records: Access: Fax, mail, in person. Both court and visitors may perform in person searches.

Search fee: $12.00 per name. Required to search: name, years to search. Civil cases indexed by defendant, plaintiff, on computer since 1994, index cards from 1874. Mail turnaround time 1 week. Civil PAT goes back to 1994. PAT civil results show middle initial.
Criminal Records: Access: Fax, mail, in person. Both court and visitors may perform in person searches. Search fee: $12.00 per name. Required to search: name, years to search. Criminal records on computer since 1994, index cards from 1874. Mail turnaround time 1 week. Criminal PAT goes back to same as civil; crim results show middle initial.
General Information: No juvenile, mental health, sealed or expunged records released. Court makes copy: $.50 per page. Certification fee: $1.00 per cert. Payee: Clerk of Court. Personal checks accepted; credit cards are not. Mail requests: SASE required.

Crawford County

Girard District Court PO Box 69, Girard, KS 66743; 620-724-6211; fax: 620-724-4987; 8AM-5PM (CST). ***Felony, Misdemeanor, Civil, Probate.***
Records on computer are maintained here for the Pittsburg District Court as well since 8/92. For prior cases, search both courts separately.
Civil Records: Access: Fax, mail, in person. Both court and visitors may perform in person searches. Search fee: $12.00 per hour. Required to search: name, years to search. Civil cases indexed by defendant, plaintiff, on computer since 8/1992, microfiche from 1977, index cards from 1977. Mail turnaround 3 days. Civil PAT goes back to 1977.
Criminal Records: Access: Phone, fax, in person. Both court and visitors may perform in person searches. Search fee: $12.00 per hour. Required to search: name, years to search. Criminal records on computer since 8/1992, microfiche from 1977, index cards from 1977. Employment/work-related/credit mail inquires are referred to the Kansas Bureau of Investigation. Criminal PAT goes back to same as civil.
General Information: No confidential juvenile, mental health, sealed or expunged records released. Will fax documents $2.50 per page. Court makes copy: $.25 per page. Certification fee: $1.00. Payee: Clerk of Court. Personal checks accepted; credit cards are not. Mail requests: SASE required.

Pittsburg District Court 602 N Locust, Pittsburg, KS 66762; 620-231-0391; fax: 620-231-0316; 8AM-5PM (CST). ***Misdemeanor, Civil, Eviction, Small Claims, Probate.***
www.kscourts.org (then access 11th Judicial District
Records back to 8/92 can be searched at Girard District Court as well; Girard and Pittsburg share a computer system. For cases prior to 8/92, search both courts separately. Probate fax is same as main fax.
Civil Records: Access: Fax, mail, in person. Both court and visitors may perform in person searches. Search fee: $12.00 per hour. Required to search: name, years to search. Civil cases indexed by defendant, plaintiff, on computer since 8/1992, microfiche from 1977, index cards from 1977. Mail turnaround time 3 days. Civil PAT goes back to 8/1992. PAT civil results show middle initial.
Criminal Records: Access: Mail, in person. Both court and visitors may perform in person searches. Search fee: $12.00 per hour. Required to search: name, years to search. Criminal records on computer since 8/1992, microfiche from 1977, index cards from 1977. Employment/work-related mail inquires are referred to the Kansas Bureau of Investigation. Mail requests must be on courts form, call court for form and they will fax it to you. Mail turnaround time 3 days. Criminal PAT goes back to same as civil. PAT criminal results show middle initial.
General Information: No juvenile, mental health, sealed or expunged records released. Will fax documents $2.50 per page. Court makes copy: $.25 per page, self serve same. Certification fee: $1.00. Payee: Clerk of Court. Personal checks accepted; credit cards are not. Mail requests: SASE required.

Decatur County

District Court PO Box 89, Oberlin, KS 67749; 785-475-8107; fax: 785-475-8170; 8AM-5PM (CST). ***Felony, Misdemeanor, Civil, Eviction, Small Claims, Probate.***
Civil Records: Access: In person, online. Both court and visitors may perform in person searches. Search fee: $4.00 per name. Required to search: name, years to search. Civil cases indexed by defendant, plaintiff; index on docket books from 1870. Civil PAT goes back to 2004. PAT civil results show middle initial. Access back to 11/1/02 at www.kansas.gov/subscribers/. A $95.00 annual subscription required plus usage fee as low as $1.00 per search.
Criminal Records: Access: In person, online. Both court and visitors may perform in person searches. Search fee: $4.00 per name. Required to search: name, years to search. Criminal records indexed in books from 1870. Criminal PAT goes back to same as civil. PAT criminal results show middle initial. Online access to criminal records is same as civil.
General Information: No adoption, juvenile, mental health, sealed or expunged records released. Will fax documents $1.00 1st page, $.25 each add'l page. Court makes copy: $.25 per page. Certification fee: $1.00. Payee: Clerk of District Court. Personal checks accepted; credit cards are not.

Dickinson County

District Court PO Box 127, Abilene, KS 67410; 785-263-3142; criminal phone: x305; civil phone: x301; probate phone: x304; fax: 785-263-4407; 8AM-5PM (CST). ***Felony, Misdemeanor, Civil, Eviction, Small Claims, Probate.*** www.8thjd.com
Probate fax is same as main fax number.
Civil Records: Access: Mail, fax, in person, email, online. Both court and visitors may perform in person searches. Search fee: $12.00 per hour. Required to search: name, years to search. Civil cases indexed by defendant, plaintiff, on computer since 7/92, on index books prior. Direct email civil record requests to dkcdc@8thjd.com Mail turnaround time 3 days. Civil PAT goes back to 7/1992. PAT civil results show middle initial. Access back to 11/1/02 at www.kansas.gov/subscri bers/. A $95.00 annual subscription required plus usage fee as low as $1.00 per search.
Criminal Records: Access: Mail, in person, online. Visitors must perform in person searches themselves. Search fee: $12.00 per hour. Required to search: name, years to search, DOB; also helpful: SSN. Criminal records on computer since 7/92, on index books prior. Will search only if case number is provided. Court directs search requests to KBI. Criminal PAT goes back to same as civil. PAT criminal results show middle initial. Online access to criminal records is the same as civil.
General Information: No juvenile, mental health, sealed or expunged records released. Will fax documents $2.00 per page. Court makes copy: $1.00 for first 4 pages; $.25 each add'l, self serve same. Certification fee: $1.00 per document. Payee: Clerk of District Court. Personal checks accepted; credit cards are not. Mail requests: SASE required.

Doniphan County

District Court PO Box 295, Troy, KS 66087; 785-985-3582; criminal fax: 785-985-2402; civil fax: same; 8AM-5PM (CST). ***Felony, Misdemeanor, Civil, Eviction, Small Claims, Probate.***
Probate fax is same as main fax number.
Civil Records: Access: Phone, fax, mail, in person, online. Both court and visitors may perform in person searches. Search fee: $12.00 per hour. Required to search: name, years to search. Civil cases indexed by defendant, plaintiff, on computer since 1992; index cards from 1856. Mail turnaround time 1-2 days. Civil PAT goes back to 1992. Access back to 11/1/02 at www.kansas.gov/subscribers/. A $95.00 annual subscription required plus usage fee as low as $1.00 per search.
Criminal Records: Access: Phone, fax, mail, in person, online. Both court and visitors may perform in person searches. Search fee: $12.00 per hour. Required to search: name, years to search; also helpful: address, DOB. Criminal records on computer since 1992; index cards from 1852. Mail turnaround 1-2 days. Criminal PAT goes back to same as civil. Online access to criminal records is same as civil.
General Information: No juvenile, mental health, sealed or expunged records released. Fee to fax out file $2.00 1st page, $1.00 ea add'l. Court makes copy: $.50 first page, $.25 each add'l. Self serve: $.25 per page. Certification fee: $1.00 per document. Payee: Clerk of Court. Personal checks accepted; credit cards are not. Mail requests: SASE required.

Douglas County

District Court 111 E 11th St, Lawrence, KS 66044-2966; 785-832-5356; fax: 785-832-5174; 8AM-5PM (CST). ***Felony, Misdemeanor, Civil, Eviction, Small Claims, Probate.***
www.douglas-county.com/District_Court/dc.asp
Civil Records: Access: Phone, fax, mail, in person, online. Both court and visitors may perform in person searches. Search fee: $14.00 per hour. Required to search: name, years to search. Civil cases indexed by defendant, plaintiff; index on cards from 1863, archived from 1865 on film, indexed on computer since 1989. All written requests must include a phone number. Mail turnaround time 3 days. Civil PAT goes back to 1995. PAT civil results show middle initial. Access back to 11/1/02 at www.kansas.gov/subscribers/. A $95.00 annual subscription required plus usage fee as low as $1.00 per search.
Criminal Records: Access: Phone, fax, mail, in person, online. Both court and visitors may perform in person searches. Search fee: $14.00 per hour. Required to search: name, years to search; also helpful: DOB, SSN. Criminal records computerized from 1989, index cards 1860, archived from 1865. All other background check requests must be in writing. Mail turnaround time 3 days. Criminal PAT goes back to same as civil. PAT criminal results show middle initial. Online access to criminal records is the same as civil.
General Information: No juvenile, mental health, sealed or expunged records released. Will fax documents $2.00 each. Court makes copy: $.25 per page. Cert fee: $1.00 per cert. Authentications- $2.00 each. Payee: Clerk of Court. Personal checks accepted; credit cards are not. SASE not required.

Edwards County

District Court PO Box 232, Kinsley, KS 67547; 620-659-2442; fax: 620-659-2998; 8AM-5PM (CST). ***Felony, Misdemeanor, Civil, Eviction, Small Claims, Probate.***
www.kscourts.org/dstcts/24dstct.htm
Civil Records: Access: Mail, in person, online. Both court and visitors may perform in person searches. Search fee: $12.00 per name. Required to search: name, years to search. Civil cases indexed by defendant, plaintiff; index on docket books from 1800s. Mail turnaround time 2 days Civil PAT goes back to 10/2002. PAT civil results show middle initial. Access back to 11/1/02 at www.kansas.gov/subscribers/. A $95.00 annual subscription required plus usage fee as low as $1.00 per search.
Criminal Records: Access: Mail, in person, online. Both court and visitors may perform in person searches. Search fee: $12.00 per name. Required to search: name, years to search. Criminal records indexed in books from 1800s. Mail turnaround time is 2 days. Criminal PAT goes back to same as civil. PAT criminal results show middle initial. Online access to criminal records is same as civil.
General Information: No juvenile, adoption, mental health, sealed or expunged records released. Will fax documents to local or toll free line. Court makes copy: $.25 per page. Certification fee: $1.00. Payee: Clerk District Court. Personal checks accepted; credit cards are not. Mail requests: SASE required.

Elk County

District Court PO Box 306, Howard, KS 67349; 620-374-2370; fax: 620-374-3531; 8AM-4:30PM (CST). ***Felony, Misdemeanor, Civil, Eviction, Small Claims, Probate.***
Probate fax is same as main fax number.

Civil Records: Access: Mail, in person. Both court and visitors may perform in person searches. Search fee: Depending on difficulty, clerk may charge $12 per hr search fee. Required to search: name, years to search. Civil cases indexed by defendant, plaintiff; index on docket books from 1907. Mail turnaround time 1-2 days. Civil PAT goes back to 1984.
Criminal Records: Access: Mail, in person. Both court and visitors may perform in person searches. Search fee: Depending on difficulty, clerk may charge $12 per hr search fee. Required to search: name, years to search. Criminal records indexed in books from 1956; on computer back to 1984. Record searchers are encouraged to contact the state criminal record agency. Mail turnaround time 1-2 days. Criminal PAT goes back to same as civil.
General Information: No juvenile, mental health, sealed or expunged records released. Fee to fax out doc $2 plus $.50 per page. Court makes copy: $.50 per page, self serve same. Certification fee: $1.00 per document. Payee: Clerk of District Court. Personal checks accepted; credit cards are not. Mail requests: SASE required.

Ellis County

District Court PO Box 8, 1204 Fort St, 3rd Fl, Hays, KS 67601; 785-628-9415; criminal fax: 785-628-8415; civil fax: same; 8AM-5PM (CST). ***Felony, Misdemeanor, Civil, Eviction, Small Claims, Probate.*** www.23rdjudicial.org/ellis.htm
Probate fax is same as main fax number.
Civil Records: Access: Mail, in person, online. Both court and visitors may perform in person searches. Search fee: $12.00 per hour. Required to search: name, years to search. Civil cases indexed by defendant, plaintiff, on computer from 1991, microfiche from 1900s, index cards from 1800s, archives from 1800s. Mail turnaround time 3-5 days. Civil PAT goes back to 1991. Access back to 11/1/02 at www.kansas.gov/subscribers/. A $95.00 annual subscription required plus usage fee as low as $1.00 per search.
Criminal Records: Access: In person, online. Visitors must perform in person searches themselves. Required to search: name, years to search. Criminal records computerized from 1991, microfiche from 1900s, index cards from 1800s, archives from 1800s. Criminal PAT goes back to same as civil. Online access to criminal records is same as civil. Case filings previous week online.
General Information: No juvenile, mental health, sealed or expunged records released. Will fax documents $.50 1st page, $.25 each add'l page. Court makes copy: $.25 per page. Certification fee: $1.00 per cert. Payee: Clerk of Court. Personal checks accepted. Credit cards only accepted through INK. Mail requests: SASE required for civil.

Ellsworth County

District Court 210 N Kansas, Ellsworth, KS 67439-3118; 785-472-3832; fax: 785-472-5712; 8AM-5PM (CST). ***Felony, Misdemeanor, Civil, Eviction, Small Claims, Probate.***
Civil Records: Access: Phone, fax, mail, in person, online. Both court and visitors may perform in person searches. No search fee. Required to search: name, years to search. Civil cases indexed by defendant, plaintiff, on computer from 1994, microfiche from 1900s, books from late 1800s. Mail turnaround time 1-2 days. Access back to 11/1/02 at www.kansas.gov/subscribers/. A $95.00 annual subscription required plus usage fee as low as $1.00 per search.
Criminal Records: Access: Phone, fax, mail, in person, online. Both court and visitors may perform in person searches. No search fee. Required to search: name, years to search; also helpful: SSN. Criminal records computerized from 1994, microfiche from 1900s, books from late 1800s. Mail turnaround time 1-2 days. Online access to criminal records is the same as civil.
General Information: No juvenile, mental health, sealed or expunged records released. Will fax documents $.50 per page. Court makes copy: $.35 per page. No certification fee. Payee: District Court. Personal checks accepted; credit cards are not. Mail requests: SASE required.

Finney County

District Court PO Box 798, Garden City, KS 67846; criminal: 620-271-6132; civil: 620-271-6121; fax: 620-271-6140; 8AM-4PM (CST). ***Felony, Civil, Eviction, Small Claims, Probate., Misdemeanor***
Civil Records: Access: In person, online. Visitors must perform in person searches themselves. Required to search: name, years to search. Civil cases indexed by defendant, plaintiff, on computer from 1991, microfiche from 1900s, index books from 1900s. Civil PAT goes back to 1991. Access back to 11/1/02 at www.kansas.gov/subscribers/. A $95.00 annual subscription required plus usage fee as low as $1.00 per search.
Criminal Records: Access: In person, online. Visitors must perform in person searches themselves. Required to search: name, years to search. Criminal records computerized from 1991, microfiche from 1900s, index books from 1900s. Criminal PAT goes back to same as civil. Online access to criminal records is the same as civil.
General Information: No juvenile, Mental health, sealed or expunged records released. Court makes copy: $.25 per page, $1.00 minimum. Cert fee: $1.00 per doc,. Payee: District Ct. Personal checks accepted.

Ford County

District Court 101 W Spruce, Dodge City, KS 67801; 620-227-4609; criminal phone: 620-227-4608; civil phone: 620-227-4610; probate phone: 620-277-4606; criminal fax: 620-227-6799; civil fax: same; 8AM-5PM (CST). ***Felony, Misdemeanor, Civil, Eviction, Small Claims, Probate.***
www.kscourts.org/dstcts/16dstct.htm
Probate fax is same as main fax number.
Civil Records: Access: Mail, in person, online. Both court and visitors may perform in person searches. Search fee: $12.00 per hour. Required to search: name, case number. Civil cases indexed by defendant, plaintiff, on computer back to 10/1991, microfiche/film from 1900s, index books from 1900s. Mail turnaround time 3 days. Civil PAT goes back to 10/1991. Access back to 11/1/02 at www.kansas.gov/subscribers/. A $95.00 annual subscription required plus usage fee as low as $1.00 per search.
Criminal Records: Access: In person, online. Both court and visitors may perform in person searches. Search fee: $12.00 per hour. Required to search: name, case number. Criminal records computerized from 10/1991, microfiche/film from 1900s, index books from 1900s. Criminal record searches for military employment are referred to KBI or Division of Motor Vehicles. Criminal PAT goes back to same as civil. Online access to criminal records is the same as civil.
General Information: No juvenile, mental health, sealed or expunged records released. Fee to fax specific case file $1.00 per page. Court makes copy: $.25 per page, self serve same. Certification fee: $1.00 per document. Payee: Clerk of District Court. Personal checks accepted; credit cards are not.

Franklin County

District Court PO Box 637 (301 S Main), Ottawa, KS 66067; 785-242-6000; criminal fax: 785-242-5970; civil fax: same; 8AM-N, 1PM-4PM (CST). ***Felony, Misdemeanor, Civil, Eviction, Small Claims, Probate.*** www.kscourts.org/dstcts/4frco.htm
Probate fax is same as main fax number.
Civil Records: Access: Mail, fax, in person, online. Both court and visitors may perform in person searches. Search fee: $12.00 per hour. Required to search: name, years to search. Civil cases indexed by defendant, plaintiff, on computer back to 1979, index books from 1800s. Mail turnaround time 1-3 days. Civil PAT goes back to 1979. Access back to 11/1/02 at www.kansas.gov/subscribers/. A $95.00 annual subscription required plus usage fee as low as $1.00 per search. Current court calendars free at www.franklincoks.org/4thdistrict/franklinbydate.html. Also, access to probate court records is free at www.kscourts.org/dstcts/4frprrec.htm. Access to county marriage records is by alpha search for free at www.kscourts.org/dstcts/4frmarec.htm.
Criminal Records: Access: In person, online. Visitors must perform in person searches themselves. Required to search: name, years to search, SSN. Criminal records computerized from 1980, index books from 1800s. Criminal PAT goes back to 1980. Online access to criminal docket and calendars is the same as civil.
General Information: No juvenile, mental health, sealed or expunged records released. Will fax documents to local or toll free line. Court makes copy: $.25 per page. Certification fee: $1.00. Payee: Clerk of District Court. Personal checks and credit cards accepted. Mail requests: SASE required for civil.

Geary County

District Court PO Box 1147, Junction City, KS 66441; 785-762-5221; fax: 785-762-4420; 8AM-5PM (CST). ***Felony, Misdemeanor, Civil, Eviction, Small Claims, Probate.*** www.8thjd.com
Civil Records: Access: Mail, in person, email. Visitors must perform in person searches themselves. Search fee: $12.00 per hour. Required to search: name, years to search. Civil cases indexed by defendant, plaintiff, on computer from 1992, microfiche, index books and archives from 1894. Direct email record requests to gecdc@oz-online.net. Mail turnaround time 3 days. Civil PAT goes back to 1992.
Criminal Records: Access: Mail, in person, email. Both court and visitors may perform in person searches. Search fee: $12.00 per hour. Required to search: name, charges, date of offense. Criminal records computerized from 1992, microfiche, index books and archives from 1894. Direct email record requests to gecdc@oz-online.net. Mail turnaround time 3 days. Criminal PAT goes back to same as civil.
General Information: No juvenile, adoption, mental health, sealed or expunged records released. Fee to fax out file $2.00 per page. Court makes copy: $.25 per page, $1.00 minimum. Certification fee: $1.00. Exeplification fee- $2.00. Payee: Clerk of Court. Personal checks accepted; credit cards are not. Mail requests: SASE required.

Gove County

District Court PO Box 97, Gove, KS 67736; 785-938-2310; probate phone: same; fax: 785-938-2312; 8AM-N, 1-5PM (CST). ***Felony, Misdemeanor, Civil, Eviction, Small Claims, Probate.***
www.23rdjudicial.org
Civil Records: Access: Fax, mail, in person, online. Both court and visitors may perform in person searches. Search fee: $12.00 per hour. Required to search: name, years to search. Civil cases indexed by defendant, plaintiff, on computer from 1992, index books from 1890 through present. Mail turnaround time 1-2 days. Civil PAT goes back to 1992. PAT civil results show middle initial. Access back to 11/1/02 at www.kansas.gov/subscribers/. A $95.00 annual subscription required plus usage fee as low as $1.00 per search. Case filings from previous week available online at the county site.
Criminal Records: Access: Fax, mail, in person, online. Both court and visitors may perform in person searches. Search fee: $12.00 per hour. Required to search: name, years to search. Criminal records computerized from 1992, index books from 1890 through present. Mail turnaround time 1-2 days. Criminal PAT goes back to 1992. PAT criminal results show middle initial. Online access to criminal records is the same as civil. Case filings from previous week available online. Criminal records available for a fee at www.accesskansas.org/kbi/criminalhistory/.
General Information: No juvenile, mental health, sealed or expunged records released. Fee to fax out file $1.00 per page. Court makes copy: $.25 per page, self serve same. Certification fee: $1.00. Payee: Clerk of District Court. Personal checks accepted; credit cards are not. Mail requests: SASE required.

Graham County

District Court 410 N Pomeroy, Hill City, KS 67642; 785-421-3458; fax: 785-421-5463; 8AM-5PM (CST). ***Felony, Misdemeanor, Civil, Eviction, Small Claims, Probate.***

Probate is a separate index at this same address. Probate fax- 785-421-5463

Civil Records: Access: In person, online. Visitors must perform in person searches themselves. Civil cases indexed by defendant, plaintiff; index on docket books from 1880s; computerized records go back to 2004. Access back to 11/1/02 at www.kansas.gov/subscribers/. A $95.00 annual subscription required plus usage fee as low as $1.00 per search.

Criminal Records: Access: Mail, in person, online. Visitors must perform in person searches themselves. Search fee: $12.00 per hour. Required to search: name, years to search, DOB; also helpful: SSN, signed release. Criminal records indexed in books from 1880s; computerized records go back to 2004. Mail turnaround time 2 days. Online access to criminal records is the same as civil.

General Information: No juvenile, mental health, sealed or expunged records released. Will fax documents to local or toll free line. Court makes copy: $.25 per page. Cert fee: $1.00 per instrument. Payee: Clerk of District Court. Personal checks accepted; credit cards are not. Mail requests: SASE required.

Grant County

District Court 108 S Glenn St, Ulysses, KS 67880; 620-356-1526; fax: 620-353-2131; 8AM-N, 1-5PM (CST). ***Felony, Misdemeanor, Civil, Eviction, Small Claims, Probate.***

Search includes both civil and criminal indexes. Court will perform searches as time permits.

Civil Records: Access: Mail, fax, in person. Visitors must perform in person searches themselves. Search fee: $12.80 per hour. Required to search: name, years to search. Civil cases indexed by defendant, plaintiff, on computer from 1977, microfiche index from 1880s. Mail turnaround time 2-7 days. Civil PAT goes back to 1977.

Criminal Records: Access: In person only. Visitors must perform in person searches themselves. Search fee: $12.80 per hour. Required to search: name, years to search. Criminal records computerized from 1977, microfiche index from 1880s. This court often refers searchers to the state Bureau of investigations, including in-person searchers. Mail turnaround time 2-7 days. Criminal PAT goes back to 1977.

General Information: No juvenile, mental health, sealed or expunged records released. Will not fax documents. Court makes copy: $.50 per page. Certification fee: $1.00 per seal. Payee: District Court. Personal checks accepted; credit cards are not.

Gray County

District Court PO Box 487, 300 S Main, Cimarron, KS 67835; 620-855-3812; fax: 620-855-7037; 8AM-5PM (CST). ***Felony, Misdemeanor, Civil, Eviction, Small Claims, Probate.***
www.kscourts.org/dstcts/16dstct.htm

To access public records send a fax or written request to Gray County District Court, PO Box 487, Cimarron, KS 67835.

Civil Records: Access: Fax, mail, in person, online. Visitors must perform in person searches themselves. Search fee: $12.00 per hour. Required to search: name; also helpful: years to search. Civil cases indexed by defendant, plaintiff, on computer from 1990, index books from 1800s. To access public records send a written request to: Gray County District Court, PO Box 487, Cimarron, KS 67835. Fax requests must be pre-paid. Civil PAT goes back to 1990. Access back to 11/1/02 at www.kansas.gov/subscribers/. A $95.00 annual subscription required plus usage fee as low as $1.00 per search.

Criminal Records: Access: Fax, mail, in person, online. Visitors must perform in person searches themselves. Search fee: $12.00 per hour. Required to search: name, years to search; also helpful: address, DOB. Criminal records computerized from 1990, index books from 1800s. Fax requests must be pre-paid. Criminal records search for employment, credit, and the like shall be referred to KS Bureau of Investigation or the Division of Vehicles. Mail turnaround time 1 day. Criminal PAT goes back to same as civil. PAT results show middle initial, DOB. Online access to criminal records is the same as civil.

General Information: No juvenile, mental health, sealed or expunged records released. Will fax documents $1.00 per page. Court makes copy: $.50 per page. Self serve: $.25 per page. Certification fee: $1.00. Payee: Clerk of District Court. Personal checks accepted; credit cards are not. Mail requests: SASE required.

Greeley County

District Court PO Box 516, Tribune, KS 67879; 620-376-4292; 8AM-N, 1-5PM (MST). ***Felony, Misdemeanor, Civil, Eviction, Small Claims, Probate.***

Civil Records: Access: In person, online. Visitors must perform in person searches themselves. Required to search: name. Civil cases indexed by defendant, plaintiff, on hardcopy index from beginning. Civil PAT goes back to 1986. Access back to 11/1/02 at www.kansas.gov/subscribers/. A $95.00 annual subscription required plus usage fee as low as $1.00 per search.

Criminal Records: Access: In person, online. Visitors must perform in person searches themselves. Required to search: name, DOB. Criminal records on hardcopy index from beginning. Criminal PAT goes back to 1986. Online access to criminal records is the same as civil.

General Information: No juvenile, mental health, sealed or expunged records released. Will fax documents $1.00 per page. Court makes copy: $.50 per page. Certification fee: $1.00 per doc. Payee: Clerk of the District Court. Personal checks accepted; credit cards are not.

Greenwood County

District Court 311 N Main, Eureka, KS 67045; 620-583-8153; fax: 620-583-6818; 8AM-5PM (CST). ***Felony, Misdemeanor, Civil, Eviction, Small Claims, Probate.***

Civil Records: Access: Mail, in person, online. Both court and visitors may perform in person searches. Search fee: $12.00 per hour if search conducted by court personnel. Required to search: name, case number. Civil cases indexed by defendant, plaintiff, on computer from 1993, index cards from 1800s. Mail turnaround time 1-3 days. Civil PAT goes back to 1993. Identifiers in results varies. Access back to 11/1/02 at www.kansas.gov/subscribers/. A $95.00 annual subscription required plus usage fee as low as $1.00 per search.

Criminal Records: Access: Mail, in person, online. Both court and visitors may perform in person searches. Search fee: $12.00 per hour if search performed by court personnel. Required to search: name, case number. Criminal records computerized from 1993, index cards from 1800s. Mail turnaround time 1-3 days. Criminal PAT goes back to 1993. Identifiers in results varies. Online access to criminal records is the same as civil.

General Information: No juvenile, mental health, sealed or expunged records released. Will fax documents to local or toll free line. Court makes copy: $.50 per page. Self serve: $.50 per page. Cert fee: $1.00. Payee: Clerk of Court. Personal checks okay; credit cards are not. Mail request: SASE required.

Hamilton County

District Court PO Box 745, Syracuse, KS 67878; 620-384-5159; fax: 620-384-7806; 8AM-5PM (MST). ***Felony, Misdemeanor, Civil, Eviction, Small Claims, Probate.*** Probate fax is same as main fax.

Civil Records: Access: In person, online. Visitors must perform in person searches themselves. Required to search: name, years to search. Civil cases indexed by defendant, plaintiff, on computer from 1985, microfiche, archives and index cards from 1880s. Civil PAT goes back to 1985. PAT civil results show middle initial. Access back to 11/1/02 at www.kansas.gov/subscribers/. A $95.00 annual subscription required plus usage fee as low as $1.00 per search.

Criminal Records: Access: In person, online. Visitors must perform in person searches themselves. Required to search: name, years to search. Criminal records computerized from 1985, microfiche, archives and index cards from 1880s. Criminal PAT goes back to same as civil. PAT criminal results show middle initial. Online access to criminal records is the same as civil.

General Information: No juvenile, mental health, sealed or expunged records released. Will fax specific case file $1.00 per page. Court makes copy: $.25 per page, self serve same. Certification fee: $1.00. Payee: Clerk of District Court. Personal checks accepted; credit cards are not.

Harper County

District Court PO Box 467, 201 N Jennings, Anthony, KS 67003; 620-842-3721; fax: 620-842-6025; 8AM-N, 1-5PM (CST). ***Felony, Misdemeanor, Civil, Eviction, Small Claims, Probate.***

Civil Records: Access: In person, online. Visitors must perform in person searches themselves. Required to search: name, years to search. Civil cases indexed by defendant, plaintiff, on computer from 1976, microfiche, index books and archives from 1887. Civil PAT goes back to 1970's. PAT results show name and include driver license info (height, weight, color of eyes). Access back to 11/1/02 at www.kansas.gov/subscribers/. A $95.00 annual subscription required plus usage fee as low as $1.00 per search.

Criminal Records: Access: In person, online. Visitors must perform in person searches themselves. Required to search: name, years to search, SSN. Criminal records computerized from 1976, index books and archives from 1887. Criminal PAT goes back to same as civil. PAT results show middle initial, DOB. Results include driver license information (height, weight, color of eyes). Online access to criminal records is the same as civil.

General Information: No juvenile, mental health, sealed or expunged records released. Will fax documents $1.00 per page. Court makes copy: $.25 per page. Certification fee: $1.00 per cert. Payee: Clerk of District Court. Personal checks accepted; credit cards are not.

Harvey County

District Court PO Box 665, Newton, KS 67114-0665; 316-284-6890; criminal: 316-284-6896; civil: 316-284-6894; probate: 316-284-6824; fax: 316-283-4601; 9AM-5PM (CST). ***Felony, Misdemeanor, Civil, Eviction, Small Claims, Probate.***

Civil Records: Access: Mail, fax, in person, email. Both court and visitors may perform in person searches. Search fee: $12.00 per hour. Required to search: name, years to search. Civil cases indexed by defendant, plaintiff; index on docket books from 1800s; on computer back to mid 1970s. Direct email civil record requests to robinb@kscourt.net. Mail turnaround time 3-5 days. Public use terminal available, records go back to 1960's. PAT civil results show middle initial.

Criminal Records: Access: Mail, fax, in person. Both court and visitors may perform in person searches. Search fee: $12.00 per name. Required to search: name, years to search, DOB; also helpful-SSN, signed release. Criminal records computerized since 1960s, archived from 1800s. Call KBI for thorough statewide search. Mail turnaround time 3-5 days. Public use terminal available, crim records go back to same. PAT criminal results show middle initial.

General Information: No juvenile, mental health, sealed or expunged records released. Will fax documents $1.00 per page. Court makes copy: $.50 per page, self serve same. Cert fee: $1.00. Payee: Clerk of District Court. Personal checks accepted; credit cards are not. Mail requests: SASE helpful.

Haskell County

District Court PO Box 146, Sublette, KS 67877; 620-675-2671; fax: 620-675-8599; 8AM-5PM (CST). ***Felony, Misdemeanor, Civil, Eviction, Small Claims, Probate.***

Civil Records: Access: Phone, mail, fax, in person. Both court and visitors may perform in person searches. Search fee: $12.00 per hour. Required to search: name, years to search. Civil cases indexed by defendant, plaintiff, on computer from 1990, index books from 1874. Civil PAT goes back to 1990.

Criminal Records: Access: In person only. Visitors must perform in person searches themselves. Required to search: name, years to search. Criminal records computerized from 1990, index books from 1874. Criminal PAT goes back to 1990.
General Information: No juvenile, mental health, sealed or expunged records released. Will fax documents $3.00 plus $.25 per page. Court makes copy: $.25 per page, self serve same. Certification fee: $1.00. Payee: Clerk of District Court. Personal checks accepted; credit cards are not. Mail requests: SASE requested for civil.

Hodgeman County

District Court PO Box 187, Jetmore, KS 67854; 620-357-6522; criminal fax: 620-357-6216; civil fax: same; 8AM-5PM (CST). ***Felony, Misdemeanor, Civil, Eviction, Small Claims, Probate.***
www.kscourts.org/dstcts/24dstct.htm
Probate is a separate index at this same address. Probate fax is same as main fax number.
Civil Records: Access: Phone, fax, mail, in person, online. Both court and visitors may perform in person searches. Search fee: $12.00 per hour. Required to search: name, years to search. Civil cases indexed by defendant, plaintiff; index on cards and books from 1800s. Mail turnaround time 1-2 days. Access back to 11/1/02 at www.kansas.gov/subscribers/. A $95.00 annual subscription required plus usage fee as low as $1.00 per search.
Criminal Records: Access: In person, online. Visitors must perform in person searches themselves. Required to search: name, years to search; SSN helpful. Criminal records indexed on cards and books from 1800s. Online access to criminal records is the same as civil.
General Information: No juvenile, mental health, sealed or expunged records released. Will fax documents $.50 per page. Court makes copy: $.25 per page. Certification fee: $1.00 per page. Payee: Clerk of Court. Personal checks accepted; credit cards are not. Must prepay for mail and fax. Mail requests: SASE required for civil.

Jackson County

District Court 400 New York Ave, #311, Holton, KS 66436; 785-364-2191; fax: 785-364-3804; 8AM-4:30PM (CST). ***Felony, Misdemeanor, Civil, Eviction, Small Claims, Probate.***
Civil Records: Access: In person only. Visitors must perform in person searches themselves. Required to search: name, years to search. Civil cases indexed by defendant, plaintiff; index on cards from 1800s, recent records computerized. Civil PAT goes back to 1850s. PAT civil results show middle initial. Results include height, weight, race of known.
Criminal Records: Access: In person only. Visitors must perform in person searches themselves. Required to search: name, years to search. Criminal records indexed on cards from 1800s, recent records computerized. Criminal PAT goes back to same as civil. PAT criminal results show middle initial. Results include height, weight, race of known.
General Information: No juvenile, mental health, sealed or expunged records released. Will fax documents $2.00 per 10 pages. Court makes copy: $.25 per page, self serve same. Certification fee: $1.00. Payee: Clerk of District Court. Personal checks accepted; credit cards are not.

Jefferson County

District Court PO Box 327, Oskaloosa, KS 66066; 785-863-2461; fax: 785-863-2369; 8AM-4PM (CST). ***Felony, Misdemeanor, Civil, Eviction, Small Claims, Probate.*** www.jfcountyks.com/
Civil Records: Access: In person only. Visitors must perform in person searches themselves. Required to search: name, years to search. Civil cases indexed by defendant, plaintiff, on computer since 1/77, on index books from 1855. Civil PAT goes back to 1977.
Criminal Records: Access: In person only. Visitors must perform in person searches themselves. Required to search: name, years to search; SSN helpful. Criminal records indexed in books from 1855, computerized since 1/77. Criminal PAT goes back to same as civil.
General Information: No juvenile, mental health, sealed or expunged records released. Will fax documents to local or toll-free number. Court makes copy: $.25 per page, self serve same. Certification fee: $1.00. Payee: District Court. Personal checks accepted; credit cards are not.

Jewell County

District Court 307 N Commercial, Mankato, KS 66956; 785-378-4030; fax: 785-378-4035; 8AM-5PM (CST). ***Felony, Misdemeanor, Civil, Eviction, Small Claims, Probate.***
www.kscourts.org/dstcts/12dstct.htm
Civil Records: Access: In person, online. Both court and visitors may perform in person searches. No search fee. Required to search: name, years to search. Civil cases indexed by defendant, plaintiff; index on docket books from 1871. Civil PAT goes back to 1995. Access back to 11/1/02 at www.kansas.gov/subscribers/. A $95.00 annual subscription required plus usage fee as low as $1.00 per search.
Criminal Records: Access: In person, online. Both court and visitors may perform in person searches. No search fee. Required to search: name, years to search. Criminal records indexed in books from 1871. Criminal PAT goes back to same as civil. Online access to criminal records is the same as civil.
General Information: No juvenile, mental health, adoption, sealed or expunged records released. Will fax documents $3.00 per page. Court makes copy: $.25 per page. Cert fee: $1.25. Payee: District Court. Personal checks accepted; credit cards are not. Mail requests: SASE required for mail return of any copies.

Johnson County

District Court 100 N Kansas, Olathe, KS 66061; 913-715-3480; criminal phone: 913-715-3460; civil phone: 913-715-3400, or 3500; criminal fax: 913-715-3481; civil fax: 913-715-3401; 8AM-5PM (CST). ***Felony, Misdemeanor, Civil, Eviction, Small Claims, Probate.*** www.jococourts.org/
Search requests should be made to the Records Center, phone 913-715-3480. Court says that non-online requests for criminal record "searches" for employment, credit, or the like will be referred to Records Dept at Kansas Bureau of Investigation, 785-296-8200.
Civil Records: Access: Phone, Mail, In person, online. Both court and visitors may perform in person searches. Search fee: $12.00 per hour. Required to search: name, years to search. Civil cases indexed by defendant, plaintiff, on computer from 1980, microfiche, archives and index prior. Criminal/Civil Division is on the 2nd Fl Civil PAT goes back to 1968. PAT results show name only. Search Johnson County District Court records available free at www.jococourts.org with index back to 1980. Also, access back to 11/1/02 at www.kansas.gov/subscribers/. A $95.00 annual subscription required plus usage fee as low as $1.00 per search.
Criminal Records: Access: In person, online. Both court and visitors may perform in person searches. Search fee: $12.00 per hour. Required to search: name, years to search. Criminal records computerized from 1980, microfiche, archives and index prior. Criminal PAT goes back to same as civil. PAT results show name only. Online access to criminal records is the same as civil.
General Information: Online identifiers in results same as on public terminal. No juvenile, mental health, sealed or expunged records released. No employment searches. Will fax documents $2.50 per page. Court makes copy: $.50 per page; records prior to 1997 $10.00 flat fee. Self serve: $.50 per page. Certification fee: $1.00 per cert, Authentication fee $2.00 per authentication. Payee: Clerk of the District Court. Cashiers checks and money orders accepted. Major credit cards accepted.

Kearny County

District Court PO Box 64, 304 N Main Rd, Lakin, KS 67860; 620-355-6481; fax: 620-355-7462; 8AM-N,1-5PM (CST). ***Felony, Misdemeanor, Civil, Eviction, Small Claims, Probate.***
Civil Records: Access: Mail, in person, online. Visitors must perform in person searches themselves. Search fee: $12.00 per hour; but court will only search if you provide a case number. Required to search: name, years to search. Civil cases indexed by defendant, plaintiff, on computer from 1991, index books from 1900s. A case number must be provided with mail search requests. Mail turnaround time 3 days. Civil PAT goes back to 6/1991. PAT civil results show middle initial. Access back to 11/1/02 at www.kansas.gov/subscribers/. A $95.00 annual subscription required plus usage fee as low as $1.00 per search.
Criminal Records: Access: Mail, in person, online. Visitors must perform in person searches themselves. Search fee: $12.00 per hour, but court will only search if you provide a case number. Required to search: name, years to search. Criminal records computerized from 1991, index books from 1900s. A case number must be provided with mail search requests. Mail turnaround time 3 days. Criminal PAT goes back to same as civil. PAT results show name only. Online access to criminal records is the same as civil.
General Information: No juvenile, mental health, adoption, sealed or expunged records released. Will fax documents $1.00 per page prepaid. Court makes copy: $.25 per page, self serve same. Certification fee: $1.00. Payee: District Court. Personal checks accepted; credit cards are not. Mail requests: SASE required.

Kingman County

District Court PO Box 495 (130 N Spruce St), Kingman, KS 67068; 620-532-5151; criminal fax: 620-532-2952; civil fax: same; 8AM-N, 1-5PM (CST). ***Felony, Misdemeanor, Civil, Eviction, Small Claims, Probate.***
www.kscourts.org/dstcts/30dstct.htm
Probate fax is same as main fax number.
Civil Records: Access: Mail, fax, in person. Both court and visitors may perform in person searches. Search fee: $12.00 per hour. Required to search: name, years to search. Civil cases indexed by defendant, plaintiff, on computer from 1990, microfiche, archives and index cards from 1800s. Mail turnaround time 1-2 days. Civil PAT goes back to 1980s.
Criminal Records: Access: Mail, fax, in person. Both court and visitors may perform in person searches. Search fee: $12.00 per hour. Required to search: name, years to search; also helpful: case type. Criminal records computerized from 1990, microfiche, archives and index cards from 1800s. Mail turnaround time 1-2 days. Criminal PAT goes back to same as civil.
General Information: No juvenile, mental health, sealed or expunged records released. Fee to fax out file $1.00 per page. Court makes copy: $.25 per page, self serve same. Certification fee: $1.00 per pleading. Payee: Clerk of Court. Personal checks accepted; credit cards are not. Mail requests: SASE required.

Kiowa County

District Court 211 E Florida, Greensburg, KS 67054; 620-723-3317; probate phone: same; fax: 620-723-2970; 8AM-5PM (CST). ***Felony, Misdemeanor, Civil, Eviction, Small Claims, Probate.*** www.kscourts.org/dstcts/16dstct.htm
Probate fax is same as main fax number.
Civil Records: Access: Fax, mail, in person, online. Both court and visitors may perform in person searches. Search fee: $12.00 per hour. Required to search: name, years to search. Civil cases indexed by defendant, plaintiff, archived and on index books from 1800s; computerized back to 1980. Mail turnaround time 7 days. Civil PAT goes back to 1900's. Access back to 11/1/02 at www.kansas.gov/subscribers/. A $95.00 annual subscription required plus usage fee as low as $1.00 per search.
Criminal Records: Access: Fax, mail, in person, online. Both court and visitors may perform in person searches. Search fee: $12.00 per hour. Required to search: name, years to search, signed release; also helpful: DOB. Criminal records archived and on index books from 1800s; computerized back to 1940. Mail turnaround time 7 days. Criminal PAT goes back to same as civil. Online access to criminal records is the same as civil.

General Information: No juvenile, mental health, sealed or expunged records released. Fee to fax out file $1.00 per page. Court makes copy: $.25 per page. Self serve: $.10 per page. Certification fee: $1.00. Payee: Clerk of District Court. Personal checks accepted. Mail requests: SASE required.

Labette County

District Court - Oswego Courthouse, 501 Merchant, 3rd Fl, Oswego, KS 67356; 620-795-4533 x245; criminal fax: 620-795-3056; civil fax: same; 8AM-5PM (CST). ***Felony, Misdemeanor, Civil, Eviction, Small Claims, Probate.***
Probate fax is same as main fax number.
Civil Records: Access: In person, mail, fax. Visitors must perform in person searches themselves. Search fee: $12.00 per hr; $6.00 min. Required to search: name, years to search. Civil cases indexed by defendant, plaintiff, on computer since 1992. Civil PAT goes back to 1994.
Criminal Records: Access: In person, mail, fax. Visitors must perform in person searches themselves. Search fee: $12.00 per hr; $6.00 min. Required to search: name, years to search; also helpful: DOB, SSN. Criminal records on computer since 1992. Criminal PAT goes back to same as civil. Results include year of birth.
General Information: no juvenile, adoption, mental health, sealed or expunged records released. Will fax documents, fee is $2.50 per page. Court makes copy: $.25 per page, self serve same. Certification fee: $1.00 per certification. Payee: Clerk of District Court. Personal checks accepted; credit cards are not. Mail requests: SASE required.

District Court - Parsons 201 S Central, Parsons, KS 67357; 620-421-4120; fax: 620-421-3633; 8AM-5PM (CST). ***Felony, Misdemeanor, Civil, Eviction, Small Claims, Probate.***
Civil Records: Access: Mail, fax, in person. Both court and visitors may perform in person searches. Search fee: $12.00 per hr; $6.00 min. Required to search: name, years to search. Civil cases indexed by defendant, plaintiff, on computer from 1992, index books from 1874. Mail turnaround time 1-2 days. Civil PAT goes back to 1992.
Criminal Records: Access: Mail, fax, in person. Both court and visitors may perform in person searches. Search fee: $12.00 per hr; $6.00 min. Required to search: name, years to search. Criminal records computerized from 1992, index books from 1874. Mail turnaround time 1-2 days. Criminal PAT goes back to same as civil.
General Information: No juvenile, adoption, mental health, sealed or expunged records released. Will fax documents $2.50 per page fee. Court makes copy: $.25 per page. Certification fee: $1.00 per cert. Payee: Clerk of District Court. Personal checks accepted. Visa/MC accepted. Mail requests: SASE required.

Lane County

District Court PO Box 188, 144 S Lane, Dighton, KS 67839; 620-397-2805; fax: 620-397-5526; 8AM-5PM (CST). ***Felony, Misdemeanor, Civil, Eviction, Small Claims, Probate.***
www.kscourts.org/dstcts/24dstct.htm
Civil Records: Access: Mail, in person, online. Both court and visitors may perform in person searches. Search fee: $12.00 per name. Required to search: name, years to search. Civil cases indexed by defendant, plaintiff, on computer since 1993; prior records from 1800s. Mail turnaround time 1 week. Civil PAT goes back to 2000. Access back to 11/1/02 at www.kansas.gov/subscribers/. A $95.00 annual subscription required plus usage fee as low as $1.00 per search.
Criminal Records: Access: Mail, in person, online. Visitors must perform in person searches themselves. Search fee: $12.00 per name. Required to search: name, years to search; also helpful: SSN. Criminal records on computer since 1993; prior records from 1800s. Mail turnaround time 1 week. Criminal PAT goes back to 2000. Online access to criminal records is the same as civil.
General Information: No juvenile, mental health, sealed or expunged records released. Will not fax documents. Court makes copy: $.25 per page. Certification fee: $1.00 per page. Payee: Clerk of Court. Personal checks accepted. Money order and cash accepted. No credit cards accepted. Mail requests: SASE required.

Leavenworth County

District Court Leavenworth Justice Center, 601 S 3rd St, #3051, Leavenworth, KS 66048; 913-684-0700; criminal phone: 913-684-0704; civil phone: 913-684-0701; fax: 913-684-0492; 8AM-5PM (CST). ***Felony, Misdemeanor, Civil, Eviction, Small Claims, Probate.***
Civil Records: Access: Mail, in person. Both court and visitors may perform in person searches. Search fee: $12.00 per hour, if extensive. Required to search: name, years to search. Civil cases indexed by defendant, plaintiff, on computer from 1990, microfiche to 1952 and index books from 1901. Mail turnaround time 3-4 days. Civil PAT goes back to 1990. PAT results show name, DOB.
Criminal Records: Access: Mail, in person. Visitors must perform in person searches themselves. Search fee: $12.00 per hour, if extensive. Required to search: name, years to search; also helpful: SSN. Criminal records computerized from 1990, microfiche and index books from 1960. Mail turnaround time 3-4 days. Criminal PAT goes back to same as civil.PAT results show name, DOB.
General Information: No juvenile, mental health, sealed or expunged records released. Will fax documents $1.00 per page, prepaid. Court makes copy: $.25 per page, self serve same. Certification fee: $1.00 per page. Payee: Clerk of District Court. Personal checks accepted; credit cards are not. Mail requests: SASE required.

Lincoln County

District Court 216 E Lincoln Ave, Lincoln, KS 67455; 785-524-4057; criminal fax: 785-524-3204; civil fax: same; 8AM-N, 1-5PM (CST). ***Felony, Misdemeanor, Civil, Eviction, Small Claims, Probate.*** www.kscourts.org/dstcts/12dstct.htm
Probate fax is same as main fax number.
Civil Records: Access: Fax, mail, in person, online. Only the court performs in person searches; visitors may not. No search fee. Required to search: name; also helpful: years to search. Civil cases indexed by defendant, plaintiff. All records on computer. Access back to 11/1/02 at www.kansas.gov/subscribers/. A $95.00 annual subscription required plus usage fee as low as $1.00 per search.
Criminal Records: Access: In person, phone, online. Only the court performs in person searches; visitors may not. No search fee. Required to search: name; also helpful: years to search, DOB, SSN. Criminal records on computer since 1980, on index cards from 1880. Will search 1 name by phone only, maybe. Public use terminal has crim records back to 2007. Online access to criminal records is the same as civil.
General Information: No juvenile, mental health, sealed or expunged records released. Will fax documents $3.00 per page. Court makes copy: $.25 per page. Certification fee: $1.00. Payee: Clerk of Court. Personal checks accepted; credit cards are not.

Linn County

District Court PO Box 350, 318 Chestnut St., Mound City, KS 66056-0350; 913-795-2660; fax: 913-795-2004; 8AM-4:30PM (CST). ***Felony, Misdemeanor, Civil, Eviction, Small Claims, Probate.*** www.kscourts.org/dstcts/6dstct.htm
Probate fax is same as main fax number.
Civil Records: Access: In person only. Visitors must perform in person searches themselves. Required to search: name, years to search. Cases indexed by defendant, plaintiff, on computer from 1990, archives & index books from 1854. PAT goes back to 1800s.
Criminal Records: Access: In person only. Visitors must perform in person searches themselves. Required to search: name, years to search. Criminal records computerized from 1990, archives and index books from 1886. Criminal PAT goes back to 1975.
General Information: No juvenile, mental health, sealed or expunged records released. Will not fax out case files. Court makes copy: $.25 per page. Certification fee: $1.25. Payee: Clerk of District Court. Personal checks accepted; credit cards are not.

Logan County

District Court 710 W 2nd St, Oakley, KS 67748-1233; 785-672-3654; 8:30AM-N, 1-5PM (CST). ***Felony, Misdemeanor, Civil, Eviction, Small Claims, Probate.***
Civil Records: Access: In person only. Visitors must perform in person searches themselves. Required to search: name; also helpful: years to search. Civil cases indexed by defendant, plaintiff, on computer back to 1887. Civil PAT goes back to 1887. PAT results show name only.
Criminal Records: Access: In person only. Visitors must perform in person searches themselves. Required to search: name; SSN helpful, years to search. Criminal records computerized from 1887. Criminal PAT goes back to same as civil. PAT results show name only.
General Information: No juvenile, mental health, sealed or expunged records released. Will fax documents $1.00 per page. Court makes copy: $.25 per page. Certification fee: $1.00; authentication-$2.00. Payee: Clerk of District Court. Personal checks accepted; credit cards are not.

Lyon County

District Court 430 Commercial St, Emporia, KS 66801; 620-341-3281; fax: 620-341-3497; 8AM-4PM (CST). ***Felony, Misdemeanor, Civil, Eviction, Small Claims, Probate.***
www.lyoncounty.org/FifthJudicialDistrict.htm
Probate fax is same as main fax number.
Civil Records: Access: Fax, mail, in person, online. Both court and visitors may perform in person searches. Search fee: $12.00 per hour. Required to search: name, years to search. Civil cases indexed by defendant, plaintiff. Records maintained since 1859. Mail turnaround time 3 days maximum. Civil PAT goes back to 1998. Access back to 11/1/02 at www.kansas.gov/subscribers/. A $95.00 annual subscription required plus usage fee as low as $1.00 per search.
Criminal Records: Access: Fax, mail, in person, online. Both court and visitors may perform in person searches. Required to search: name, years to search. Records maintained since 1859. All requests for criminal searches referred to Kansas Bureau of Investigations (KBI). Criminal PAT goes back to same as civil. Online access to criminal records is the same as civil.
General Information: No mental health, sealed or expunged records released. Will fax documents $1.00 per page. Court makes copy: $.50 per page, self serve same. Certification fee: $2.00 per document. Payee: Clerk of District Court. Personal checks accepted; credit cards are not. SASE not required.

Marion County

District Court PO Box 298, Marion, KS 66861; 620-382-2104; criminal fax: 620-382-2259; civil fax: same; 8AM-5PM (CST). ***Felony, Misdemeanor, Civil, Eviction, Small Claims, Probate.***
www.8thjd.com Probate fax is same as main fax.
Civil Records: Access: In person, online. Visitors must perform in person searches themselves. Required to search: name, years to search. Civil cases indexed by defendant, plaintiff, on computer from 7/1992, on index cards from 1800s. Civil PAT goes back to 1992. Access back to 11/1/02 at www.kansas.gov/subscribers/. A $95.00 annual subscription required plus usage fee as low as $1.00 per search.
Criminal Records: Access: In person only. Visitors must perform in person searches themselves. Required to search: name, years to search. Criminal records computerized from 7/1992, on index cards from 1800s. Criminal PAT goes back to same as civil. Online access to criminal records is the same as civil.
General Information: No juvenile, mental health, sealed or expunged records released. Will not fax out case files. Court makes copy: $1.00 per page; $.25 each after 1st 4. Certification fee: $1.00 per cert. Payee: District Court. Personal checks accepted; credit cards are not.

Marshall County

District Court PO Box 149, 1201 Broadway, Office #5, Marysville, KS 66508; 785-562-5301; fax: 785-562-2458; 8AM-5PM; Search hours: 8:30AM-4:30PM (CST). ***Felony, Misdemeanor, Civil, Eviction, Small Claims, Probate.***
www.kansas.gov/index.php

Civil Records: Access: Fax, mail, in person, online. Both court and visitors may perform in person searches. Search fee: $12.00 per hour. Required to search: name, years to search. Civil cases indexed by defendant, plaintiff, on computer from 1980, microfiche from 1977 (earlier records on roll-marriage licenses on computer index 1860s, forward/naturalizations. Mail turnaround time 1-2 days. Civil PAT goes back to 1980. PAT results show name only. Access back to 11/1/02 at www.kansas.gov/subscribers/. A $95.00 annual subscription required plus usage fee as low as $1.00 per search.

Criminal Records: Access: Fax, mail, in person, online. Both court and visitors may perform in person searches. Search fee: $12.00 per hour. Required to search: name, years to search. Criminal records computerized from 1986, microfiche from 1977. Mail turnaround time 1-2 days. Criminal PAT goes back to 1982. PAT results show name only. Online access to criminal records is the same as civil.

General Information: No juvenile, offender under 14 years of age, no child in need of care, mental health, sealed or expunged records released. Will fax documents $2.00 1st page, $1.00 each add'l. Court makes copy: $.50 first page, $.25 each add'l. Certification fee: $1.00. Payee: Clerk of Court. Personal checks accepted; credit cards are not. Mail requests: SASE required.

McPherson County

District Court PO Box 1106, McPherson, KS 67460; 620-241-3422; fax: 620-241-1372; 8AM-5PM (CST). ***Felony, Misdemeanor, Civil, Eviction, Small Claims, Probate.***

Civil Records: Access: Mail, in person. Both court and visitors may perform in person searches. Search fee: $12.00 per hour. Required to search: name, years to search. Civil cases indexed by defendant, plaintiff, on microfilm from 1953, index cards from 1900s. Mail turnaround time 1-3 days. Civil PAT goes back to 1980s. PAT civil results show middle initial.

Criminal Records: Access: Mail, in person. Both court and visitors may perform in person searches. Search fee: $12.00 per hour. Required to search: name, years to search; also helpful: SSN. Criminal records on microfilm from 1953, index cards from 1900s. Mail turnaround time 1-3 days. Criminal PAT goes back to same as civil. PAT criminal results show middle initial.

General Information: No juvenile, mental health, sealed or expunged records released. Will fax documents $1.00 per page. Court makes copy: $.50 per page. Certification fee: $1.00. Payee: District Court. Personal checks accepted. Mail requests: SASE required.

Meade County

District Court PO Box 623, Meade, KS 67864; 620-873-8750; fax: 620-873-8759; 8AM-5PM (CST). ***Felony, Misdemeanor, Civil, Eviction, Small Claims, Probate.***
www.kscourts.org/dstcts/16dstct.htm

All employment background checks requested by mail, phone, or fax are referred to the KBI (state agency for criminal records).

Civil Records: Access: Fax, mail, in person, online. Both court and visitors may perform in person searches. Search fee: $12.00 per hour. Required to search: name, years to search. Civil cases indexed by defendant, plaintiff, on computer from 1990, index cards from 1896. Mail turnaround time 2-3 days Civil PAT goes back to 1992. PAT results show middle initial, DOB. Access back to 11/1/02 at www.kansas.gov/subscribers/. A $95.00 annual subscription required plus usage fee as low as $1.00 per search.

Criminal Records: Access: Fax, mail, in person, online. Both court and visitors may perform in person searches. Search fee: $12.00 per hour. Required to search: name, years to search. Criminal records computerized from 1990, index cards from 1896. Mail turnaround time is 2-3 days. Criminal PAT goes back to 1992. PAT results show middle initial, DOB. Online access to criminal records is the same as civil.

General Information: No juvenile, mental health, sealed or expunged records released. Will fax documents $2.00 1st page, $.50 each add'l. Court makes copy: $.25 per page. Certification fee: $1.00 per page. Payee: Clerk of Court. Personal checks accepted; credit cards are not. Mail requests: SASE required.

Miami County

District Court PO Box 187, 120 S Pearl St, Paola, KS 66071; 913-294-3326; fax: 913-294-2535; 8AM-4:30PM, W closed Noon hour (CST). ***Felony, Misdemeanor, Civil, Eviction, Small Claims, Probate.***

Civil Records: Access: In person only. Visitors must perform in person searches themselves. Required to search: name, years to search. Civil cases indexed by defendant, plaintiff, on computer from 1984, index cards from 1890s. Civil PAT goes back to 1987.

Criminal Records: Access: In person only. Both court and visitors may perform in person searches. No search fee. Required to search: name, years to search; SSN helpful. Criminal records computerized from 1984, index cards from 1890s. Criminal PAT goes back to same as civil.

General Information: No juvenile, mental health, sealed or expunged records released. Will fax specific document for $.50 per page. Court makes copy: $.50 per page. Self serve: $.25 per page. Certification fee: $1.50 per page. Payee: District Court. Personal checks accepted; credit cards are not.

Mitchell County

District Court 115 S Hersey, Beloit, KS 67420; 785-738-2151; criminal fax: 785-738-4101; civil fax: same; 8AM-5PM (CST). ***Felony, Misdemeanor, Civil, Eviction, Small Claims, Probate.***
www.kscourts.org/dstcts/12dstct.htm

Probate is a separate index at this same address. Probate fax is same as main fax number.

Civil Records: Access: Mail, in person, online. Both court and visitors may perform in person searches. Search fee: $12.00 per hour. Required to search: name, years to search. Civil cases indexed by defendant, plaintiff; index on cards from 1876. Mail turnaround time 1-2 days. Civil PAT goes back to 2003. PAT civil results show middle initial. Access back to 11/1/02 at www.kansas.gov/subscribers/. A $95.00 annual subscription required plus usage fee as low as $1.00 per search.

Criminal Records: Access: Mail, in person, online. Both court and visitors may perform in person searches. Search fee: $12.00 per hour. Required to search: name, years to search. Criminal records indexed on cards from 1977, archived to 1870. Mail turnaround time 1-2 days. Criminal PAT goes back to 2003. PAT criminal results show middle initial. Online access to criminal records is same as civil.

General Information: No juvenile, mental health, sealed or expunged records released. Will fax documents. Court makes copy: $.25 per page, self serve same. Certification fee: $1.00 per page. Payee: Clerk of Court. Personal checks accepted; credit cards are not. Mail requests: SASE required.

Montgomery County

Independence District Court 300 E Main St, #201, Independence, KS 67301; 620-330-1070; fax: 620-331-6120; 8AM-5PM (CST). ***Felony, Misdemeanor, Civil, Eviction, Small Claims, Probate.*** www.14thjudicialdistrict-ks.org

Civil Records: Access: Fax, mail, in person. Both court and visitors may perform in person searches. Search fee: $12.00 per hour. $6.00 minimum. Required to search: name, years to search. Civil cases indexed by defendant, plaintiff, on computer since 1992, on microfiche from 1870-1930, archives 1930-1992, index cards from 1870. This court covers civil cases for the northern part of the county. It is suggested to search both courts. Mail turnaround time 72 hours. Civil PAT goes back to 1993. PAT civil results show middle initial.

Criminal Records: Access: Fax, mail, in person. Both court and visitors may perform in person searches. Search fee: $12.00 per hour. $6.00 minimum. Required to search: name, years to search; also helpful: SSN. Criminal records on computer since 1992, on microfiche from 1870-1930, archives 1930-1992, index cards from 1870. Mail turnaround time 72 hours. Criminal PAT goes back to same as civil. PAT criminal results show middle initial.

General Information: No juvenile, adoptions, mental health, sealed or expunged records released. Will fax documents $5.00 1st page, $1.00 each add'l. Court makes copy: $.25 per page. Certification fee: $1.00. Payee: Clerk of Court. Personal checks accepted; credit cards are not. SASE not required.

Coffeyville District Court 102 W 7th St, #A, Coffeyville, KS 67337; 620-251-1060; fax: 620-251-2734; 8:30AM-N, 1-4:30PM (CST). ***Civil, Eviction, Small Claims, Probate.***

This court covers civil cases for the southern part of the county, although cases can be filed in either court. It is recommended to search both courts

Civil Records: Access: Fax, mail, in person. Both court and visitors may perform in person searches. Search fee: $12.80 per hour; $6.00 minimum. Required to search: name, years to search. Civil cases indexed by defendant, plaintiff, on computer back to 1992, on paper, fiche, etc. since 1924. Mail turnaround time 72 hours. Public use terminal has civil records. PAT civil results show middle initial.

General Information: No juvenile, mental health, sealed, adoption, or expunged records released. Fee to fax out file $1.00 per page. Court makes copy: $.25 per page. Certification fee: $1.00 per page. Payee: Clerk of Court. Personal checks accepted; credit cards are not. Mail requests: SASE requested.

Morris County

District Court County Courthouse, 501 W Main St, Council Grove, KS 66846; 620-767-6838; fax: 620-767-6488; 8AM-5PM (CST). ***Felony, Misdemeanor, Civil, Eviction, Small Claims, Probate.*** www.8thjd.com

Civil Records: Access: Fax, mail, in person, online. Both court and visitors may perform in person searches. Search fee: $12.00 per hour. Required to search: name, years to search. Civil cases indexed by defendant, plaintiff, on computer since 1992, on microfiche, archives and index cards from 1860. Mail turnaround time 1-2 days. Civil PAT goes back to 1992. PAT results show name only. Access back to 11/1/02 at www.kansas.gov/subscribers/. A $95.00 annual subscription required plus usage fee as low as $1.00 per search.

Criminal Records: Access: Fax, mail, in person, online. Both court and visitors may perform in person searches. Search fee: $12.00 per hour. Required to search: name, years to search. Criminal records on computer since 1992, on microfiche, archives and index cards from 1860. Mail turnaround time 1-2 days. Criminal PAT goes back to same as civil. PAT results show name only. Online access to criminal records is the same as civil.

General Info: Will fax documents $1.00 per page. Court makes copy: $.25 per page. Cert fee: $1.00. Payee: Clerk of Court. Personal checks accepted; credit cards are not. Mail requests: SASE required.

Morton County

District Court PO Box 825, 1025 Morton St, Elkhart, KS 67950; 620-697-2563; criminal fax: 620-697-4289; civil fax: same; 8AM-N, 1-5PM (CST). ***Felony, Misdemeanor, Civil, Eviction, Small Claims, Probate.*** Probate fax same as main fax.

Civil Records: Access: Mail, fax, in person, online. Both court and visitors may perform in person searches. Search fee: $12.80 per hour. Required to search: name, years to search. Civil cases indexed by defendant, plaintiff, on computer from 1800s. Mail turnaround time same day. Civil PAT goes back to 1992. Access back to 11/1/02 at www.kansas.gov/subscribers/. A $95.00 annual subscription required plus usage fee as low as $1.00 per search.

Criminal Records: Access: In person, online. Visitors must perform in person searches themselves. Required to search: name, years to search. Criminal records computerized from 1800s. Criminal PAT goes back to 1977. Online access to criminal records is the same as civil.
General Information: No juvenile, mental health, sealed or expunged records released. Fee to fax out file: $3.00 1st pg.; $.50 each add'l. Court makes copy: $.25 per page. Self serve: $.25 per page. Certification fee: $1.00 per certification. Payee: Clerk of Court. Two party checks or credit cards not accepted.

Nemaha County

District Court PO Box 213, Seneca, KS 66538; 785-336-2146; probate phone: same; fax: 785-336-6450; 8AM-5PM (CST). ***Felony, Misdemeanor, Civil, Eviction, Small Claims, Probate.***
Civil Records: Access: Phone, mail, in person, online. Both court and visitors may perform in person searches. Search fee: $12.00 per hour. Required to search: name, years to search. Civil cases indexed by defendant, plaintiff, on computer from 1977, index cards from 1870. Mail turnaround time 1-2 days. Civil PAT goes back to 1977. PAT results show name and sex of the defendant. Access back to 11/1/02 at www.kansas.gov/subscribers/. A $95.00 annual subscription required plus usage fee as low as $1.00 per search.
Criminal Records: Access: In person, online. Visitors must perform in person searches themselves. Required to search: name, years to search, SSN. Criminal records computerized from 1977, index cards from 1870. Criminal PAT goes back to 1977. PAT results show name only. The sex of the defendant is also on search results. Online access to criminal records is same as civil.
General Information: No juvenile, mental health, sealed or expunged records released. Will fax documents $2.00 1st page, $1.00 each add'l. Court makes copy: $.25 per page. Certification fee: $1.00. Payee: Clerk of District Court. Business checks accepted. No credit cards accepted. Mail requests: SASE required.

Neosho County

Erie District Court Neosho County Courthouse, PO Box 19, Erie, KS 66733; 620-244-3831; criminal phone: 620-431-5700; fax: 620-244-3830; 8AM-N, 1-4:30PM (CST). ***Felony, Misdemeanor, Civil, Eviction, Small Claims, Probate.***
www.31stjudicialdistrict.org/
This is the main court for the county. The web page gives hearing results and information concerning service of process in Chapter 61 cases and includes information covering the previous month.
Civil Records: Access: Fax, mail, in person, online. Both court and visitors may perform in person searches. Search fee: $12.00 per name. Required to search: name, years to search. Civil cases indexed by defendant, plaintiff; index on cards from 1900s; on computer back to 1993. Mail turnaround time 1-3 days. Civil PAT goes back to 1993. PAT civil results show middle initial. Access back to 11/1/02 at www.kansas.gov/subscribers/. A $95.00 annual subscription required plus usage fee as low as $1.00 per search. Also, court calendars, limited action hearing results, and service results appear online on the court website.
Criminal Records: Access: Mail, in person, online. Visitors must perform in person searches themselves. Search fee: $12.00 per name. Required to search: name, years to search, DOB. Criminal records indexed on cards from 1900s; on computer back to 1993. Limited mail searches are okay, lists should be sent to the central state agency. Searches for employment, credit or the like are referred to KBI. Mail turnaround time 1-3 days. Criminal PAT goes back to same as civil. PAT criminal results show middle initial. Court calendars, limited action hearing results, and service results appear on the court website. Also, access back to 11/1/02 at www.kansas.gov/subscribers/. A $95.00 annual subscription required plus usage fee as low as $1.00 per search.
General Information: No juvenile, mental health, sealed or expunged records released. Fee to fax out file $1.00 per page. Court makes copy: $.50 per page. Certification fee: $1.00. Payee: Clerk of Court. Personal checks accepted; credit cards are not. Mail requests: SASE required.

Chanute District Court 102 S Lincoln, PO Box 889, Chanute, KS 66720; 620-431-5700; criminal phone: Option 2; civil phone: same; criminal fax: 620-431-5710; civil fax: same; 8AM-5PM (CST). ***Felony, Misdemeanor, Civil, Eviction, Small Claims.*** www.31stjudicialdistrict.org
This is a branch court of Erie.
Civil Records: Access: Mail, in person, online. Both court and visitors may perform in person searches. Search fee: $12.00 per hour. Required to search: name, years to search. Civil cases indexed by defendant, plaintiff, on computer since 1993; prior back to 1955. Civil PAT goes back to 1993. PAT civil results show middle initial. Access back to 11/1/02 at www.kansas.gov/subscribers/. A $95.00 annual subscription required plus usage fee as low as $1.00 per search. Also, court calendars, limited action hearing results, and service results appear on the court website.
Criminal Records: Access: In person, online. Both court and visitors may perform in person searches. Search fee: $12.00 per hour per name. Required to search: name, years to search. Criminal records on computer since 1993; prior back to 1955. Criminal PAT goes back to same as civil. PAT criminal results show middle initial. Court calendars, limited action hearing results, and service results appear on the court website. Also, access back to 11/1/02 at www.kansas.gov/subscribers/. A $95.00 annual subscription required plus usage fee as low as $1.00 per search.
General Information: No juvenile, mental health, sealed or expunged records released. Fee to fax out file $1.00 per page. Court makes copy: $.50 per page. Certification fee: $1.00 per cert. Payee: Clerk of District Court. Personal checks accepted; credit cards are not. SASE not required.

Ness County

District Court PO Box 445, 100 S Kansas, Courthouse, Ness City, KS 67560; 785-798-3693; fax: 785-798-3348; 8AM-5PM (CST). ***Felony, Misdemeanor, Civil, Eviction, Small Claims, Probate.*** Probate is a separate index at this same address. Probate fax is same as main fax number.
Civil Records: Access: Fax, mail, in person, online. Both court and visitors may perform in person searches. Search fee: $12.00 per name. Required to search: name, years to search. Civil cases indexed by defendant, plaintiff; index on docket books from 1885. Mail turnaround time 1 week. Civil PAT goes back to 2003. PAT results show name only. Access back to 11/1/02 at www.kansas.gov/subscribers/. A $95.00 annual subscription required plus usage fee as low as $1.00 per search.
Criminal Records: Access: Fax, mail, in person, online. Visitors must perform in person searches themselves. Search fee: $12.00 per name. Required to search: name, years to search. Criminal records indexed in books from 1885. Court prefers that you use a local retriever to do searches; the court rarely performs them for the public. Mail turnaround time 1 week. Criminal PAT goes back to same as civil. Terminal results sometimes shows DOB. Online access to criminal records is same as civil.
General Information: No juvenile, mental health, sealed or expunged records released. Fee to fax out file $1.00 per page. Court makes copy: $.25 per page, self serve same. Certification fee: $1.00 per page. Payee: Clerk of Court. Personal checks accepted; credit cards are not. SASE not required.

Norton County

District Court PO Box 70, Norton, KS 67654; 785-877-5720; probate phone: same; fax: 785-877-5722; 8AM-5PM (CST). ***Felony, Misdemeanor, Civil, Eviction, Small Claims, Probate.***
Civil Records: Access: Mail, in person, online. Both court and visitors may perform in person searches. Search fee: $12.00 per hour. Required to search: name, years to search. Civil cases indexed by defendant, plaintiff, on index from 1900s. Mail turnaround time 1 week. Civil PAT goes back to 2004. PAT civil results show middle initial. Access back to 11/1/02 at www.kansas.gov/subscribers/. A $95.00 annual subscription required plus usage fee as low as $1.00 per search.
Criminal Records: Access: Mail, in person, online. Visitors must perform in person searches themselves. Search fee: $12.00 per hour. Required to search: name, years to search. Criminal records indexed from 1900s. Mail turnaround time 1 week. Criminal PAT goes back to same as civil. PAT criminal results show middle initial. Online access to criminal records is the same as civil.
General Information: No juvenile, mental health, sealed or expunged records released. Will fax documents to local or toll free line. Court makes copy: $.25 per page, self serve same. Certification fee: $1.00. Payee: Clerk of District Court. Personal checks accepted; credit cards are not. Mail requests: SASE required.

Osage County

District Court PO Box 549, Lyndon, KS 66451; 785-828-4514; fax: 785-828-4704; 8AM-N,1-4PM (CST). ***Felony, Misdemeanor, Civil, Eviction, Small Claims, Probate.***
www.kscourts.org/dstcts/4osco.htm
Civil Records: Access: In person, online. Visitors must perform in person searches themselves. Required to search: name, years to search. Civil cases indexed by defendant, plaintiff, on computer from 1980. Civil PAT goes back to 1980. PAT civil results show middle initial. Current court calendars are free online at www.franklincoks.org/4thdistrict/osagebydate.html. Also, access to old probate court and marriage records is free at www.kscourts.org/dstcts/4osco.htm Also, access back to 11/1/02 at www.kansas.gov/subscribers/. A $95.00 annual subscription required plus usage fee as low as $1.00 per search.
Criminal Records: Access: In person, online. Visitors must perform in person searches themselves. Required to search: name, years to search. Criminal records computerized from 1980. This agency will NOT do name searches. Contact the KBI state agency. Criminal PAT goes back to 1980. PAT criminal results show middle initial. Online access to criminal records is the same as civil. Online results show middle initial.
General Information: Online identifiers in results same as on public terminal. No juvenile, mental health, sealed or expunged records released. Will not fax documents. Court makes copy: $.25 per page. Certification fee: $1.00. Payee: Clerk of Court. Business checks accepted.

Osborne County

District Court PO Box 160, 423 W Main, Osborne, KS 67473; 785-346-5911; fax: 785-346-5992; 8AM-N, 1-5PM (CST). ***Felony, Misdemeanor, Civil, Eviction, Small Claims, Probate.***
Civil Records: Access: Mail, fax, in person, online. Visitors must perform in person searches themselves. Search fee: $12.00 per hour. Required to search: name, years to search. Civil cases indexed by defendant, plaintiff, on microfiche from 1872-1980, index books from 1981, index cards from 1872. Mail turnaround time 3 days. Access back to 11/1/02 at www.kansas.gov/subscribers/. A $95.00 annual subscription required plus usage fee as low as $1.00 per search.
Criminal Records: Access: Mail, fax, in person, online. Both court and visitors may perform in person searches. Search fee: $12.00 per hour. Required to search: name, years to search; also helpful: SSN. Criminal records on microfiche from 1872-1980, index books from 1981, index cards from 1872. Mail turnaround time 3 days. Online access to criminal records is the same as civil.
General Information: No juvenile, mental health, sealed or expunged records released. Will fax documents $.50 per page. Court makes copy: $.25 per page. Self serve: $.10 per page. Certification fee: $1.00 per doc. Payee: Clerk of District Court. Personal checks accepted. Money order and cash accepted. No credit cards accepted.

Ottawa County

District Court 307 N Concord, Minneapolis, KS 67467; 785-392-2917; fax: 785-392-3626; 8AM-N;1-5PM (CST). ***Felony, Misdemeanor, Civil, Eviction, Small Claims, Probate.***
www.ottawacounty.org/index.asp?DocumentID=319
Archival searches done as spare time permits. Probate fax is same as main fax number.

Civil Records: Access: Mail, fax, in person, online. Both court and visitors may perform in person searches. Search fee: $9.00 per hour. Required to search: name, years to search. Civil cases indexed by defendant, plaintiff, on index from 1800s; computerized records since 1990. Mail turnaround time 3 days. Civil PAT goes back to 2000. PAT civil results show middle initial. Access back to 11/1/02 at www.kansas.gov/subscribers/. A $95.00 annual subscription required plus usage fee as low as $1.00 per search.

Criminal Records: Access: In person, online. Both court and visitors may perform in person searches. No search fee. Required to search: name, years to search; SSN helpful. Criminal records indexed from 1800s; computerized records since 1990. Criminal PAT goes back to 1999. PAT results show name only. Criminal records on terminal may not be complete. Online access to criminal records is the same as civil.

General Information: No juvenile, mental health, sealed or expunged records released. Will fax documents to local or toll-free number. Court makes copy: $.25 per page, self serve same. Certification fee: $2.00 per doc. Payee: Clerk of District Court. Personal checks accepted; credit cards are not.

Pawnee County

District Court PO Box 270, Larned, KS 67550; 620-285-6937; fax: 620-285-3665; 8AM-5PM (CST). ***Felony, Misdemeanor, Civil, Eviction, Small Claims, Probate.***
www.kscourts.org/dstcts/24dstct.htm

Civil Records: Access: Fax, mail, in person, online. Both court and visitors may perform in person searches. Search fee: $12.00 an hour. Required to search: name, years to search. Civil cases indexed by defendant, plaintiff, on computer from 2002, index cards from 1900s. Mail turnaround time 1 day. Civil PAT goes back to 2002. PAT results show name only. Access back to 11/1/02 at www.kansas.gov/subscribers/. A $95.00 annual subscription required plus usage fee as low as $1.00 per search.

Criminal Records: Access: Fax, mail, in person, online. Visitors must perform in person searches themselves. Search fee: $12.00 an hour. Required to search: name, years to search; also helpful: SSN. Criminal records computerized from 2002, index cards from 1900s. Mail turnaround time 1-2 days. Criminal PAT goes back to 2002. PAT results show name only. Online access to criminal records is the same as civil.

General Information: No juvenile, mental health, sealed or expunged records released. Will fax documents $.50 per page. Court makes copy: $.25 per page, self serve same. Certification fee: $1.00 per page. Payee: Clerk of District Court. Personal checks accepted; credit cards are not. Mail requests: SASE required.

Phillips County

District Court PO Box 564, 301 State St, Phillipsburg, KS 67661; 785-543-6830; fax: 785-543-6832; 8AM-5PM (CST). ***Felony, Misdemeanor, Civil, Eviction, Small Claims, Probate.***

Civil Records: Access: Mail, fax, in person, online. Visitors must perform in person searches themselves. No search fee. Required to search: name, years to search. Civil cases indexed by defendant, plaintiff, on index from 1900s; on computer back to 1994. Civil PAT goes back to 2/2004. PAT civil results show middle initial. Access back to 11/1/02 at www.kansas.gov/subscribers/. A $95.00 annual subscription required plus usage fee as low as $1.00 per search.

Criminal Records: Access: Mail, fax, in person, online. Both court and visitors may perform in person searches. No search fee. Required to search: name, years to search; also helpful: DOB, SSN. Criminal records indexed from 1900s; on computer back to 1994. Mail turnaround time 2 days. Criminal PAT goes back to same as civil. PAT criminal results show middle initial. Online access to criminal records is the same as civil.

General Information: No juvenile, mental health, sealed or expunged records released. Will fax documents $.50 per page. Court makes copy: $.25 per page. Self serve: $.10 per page. Certification fee: $1.00 per cert. Payee: Clerk of District Court. Personal checks accepted; credit cards are not. Mail requests: SASE required for criminal.

Pottawatomie County

District Court PO Box 129, Westmoreland, KS 66549; 785-457-3392; fax: 785-457-2107; 8AM-4PM (CST). ***Felony, Misdemeanor, Civil, Eviction, Small Claims, Probate.***

Civil Records: Access: In person only. Visitors must perform in person searches themselves. Required to search: name, years to search. Civil cases indexed by defendant, plaintiff, computerized since 1998, on microfiche from 1800s, index from 1800s. Civil PAT goes back to 1997. Results include case number.

Criminal Records: Access: In person only. Visitors must perform in person searches themselves. Required to search: name, years to search; SSN helpful. Criminal records computerized since 1998, on microfiche from 1800s, index from 1800s. Criminal PAT goes back to same as civil.

General Information: No juvenile, mental health, sealed or expunged records released. Will only fax results to attorneys involved in cases for $2.00 plus $.25 per page after the 1st 3 pages. Court makes copy: $.25 per page. Self serve: $.15 per page. Certification fee: $2.00 per doc. Payee: Clerk of District Court. Personal checks accepted; credit cards are not.

Pratt County

District Court PO Box 984, Pratt, KS 67124; 620-672-4100; criminal fax: 620-672-2902; civil fax: same; 8AM-N, 1-5PM (CST). ***Felony, Misdemeanor, Civil, Eviction, Small Claims, Probate.*** www.prattcounty.org
Probate fax is same as main fax number.

Civil Records: Access: Mail, fax, in person, online. Both court and visitors may perform in person searches. Search fee: $12.00 per hour, 15 minute minimum. Required to search: name, years to search. Civil cases indexed by defendant, plaintiff, on computer back to 1988, microfiche, archives, index from 1878. Mail turnaround time 48 hours. Civil PAT goes back to 1988. Access back to 11/1/02 at www.kansas.gov/subscribers/. A $95.00 annual subscription required plus usage fee as low as $1.00 per search.

Criminal Records: Access: In person, online. Both court and visitors may perform in person searches. Search fee: $12.00 per hour. Required to search: name, years to search, DOB; also helpful: SSN, signed release. Criminal records computerized from 1988, microfiche, archives, index from 1878. Criminal PAT goes back to same as civil. Online access to criminal records is the same as civil.

General Information: No juvenile, mental health, sealed or expunged records released. Fee to fax out file $1.00 per page. Court makes copy: $.25 per page. Certification fee: $1.00 per item. Payee: Clerk of District Court. Personal checks accepted; credit cards are not. Mail requests: SASE required.

Rawlins County

District Court 607 Main, #F, Atwood, KS 67730; 785-626-3465; fax: 785-626-3350; 9AM-5PM (CST). ***Felony, Misdemeanor, Civil, Eviction, Small Claims, Probate.***

Civil Records: Access: In person, online. Visitors must perform in person searches themselves. Required to search: name, years to search. Civil cases indexed by defendant, plaintiff, on index from 1900s. Civil PAT goes back to 3/2004. Access back to 3/2004 at www.kansas.gov/subscribers/. A $95.00 annual subscription required plus usage fee as low as $1.00 per search.

Criminal Records: Access: In person only. Visitors must perform in person searches themselves. Required to search: name, years to search. Criminal records indexed from 1900s. This agency refers requesters to the Kansas Bureau of Investigations. Criminal PAT goes back to same as civil.

General Information: No juvenile, mental health, sealed or expunged records released. Court makes copy: $.25 per page. Certification fee: $1.00. Payee: Clerk of District Court. Only in-state checks accepted. No credit cards accepted.

Reno County

District Court 206 W 1st, Hutchinson, KS 67501; 620-694-2956; fax: 620-694-2958; 8AM-N, 1-5PM (CST). ***Felony, Misdemeanor, Civil, Eviction, Small Claims, Probate.***

Civil Records: Access: Mail, in person, online. Visitors must perform in person searches themselves. Search fee: $1.00 per 5 minutes. Required to search: name, years to search. Civil cases indexed by defendant, plaintiff, on computer from 1/1992, index cards from 1900s. Court personnel will only search pre-1/1992 records. Mail turnaround time 3-5 days in-state; 3-10 days out-of-state. Civil PAT goes back to 1/1992. PAT civil results show middle initial. Access back to 11/1/02 at www.kansas.gov/subscribers/. A $95.00 annual subscription required plus usage fee as low as $1.00 per search.

Criminal Records: Access: Mail, In person, online. Visitors must perform in person searches themselves. No search fee. Required to search: name, years to search, DOB, signed release; also helpful: address, SSN. Criminal records computerized from 1992, index cards from 1900s. Court personnel here will only search pre-1/1992 records at a rate of $1.00 per 5 minutes. Mail turnaround time 3-5 days (requestor in-state); 3-10 days (out-of-state). Criminal PAT goes back to same as civil. PAT criminal results show middle initial. Online access to criminal records is the same as civil. Court recommends statewide crim history check system at www.accesskansas.org/kbi/criminalhistory/ for cases after 4/1/2003.

General Information: No mental health, juvenile (some), sealed or expunged records released. Will not fax documents. Court makes copy: $.25 per page. Certification fee: $1.00. Payee: Clerk of District Court. Personal checks accepted; credit cards are not. Mail requests: SASE required.

Republic County

District Court PO Box 8, Belleville, KS 66935; 785-527-7234; criminal fax: 785-527-5029; civil fax: same; 8AM-5PM (CST). ***Felony, Misdemeanor, Civil, Eviction, Small Claims, Probate.***
www.kscourts.org/dstcts/12dstct.htm
Probate is a separate index at the same address. Probate fax is same as main fax number.

Civil Records: Access: Mail, in person, online. Both court and visitors may perform in person searches. Search fee: $12.00 per hour. Required to search: name, years to search. Civil cases indexed by defendant, plaintiff, on index cards from 1869. Mail turnaround time 1-3 days. Civil PAT goes back to 2004. PAT results show name only. Access back to 11/1/02 at www.kansas.gov/subscribers/. A $95.00 annual subscription required plus usage fee as low as $1.00 per search.

Criminal Records: Access: In person, online. Visitors must perform in person searches themselves. Required to search: name, years to search. Criminal records indexed on cards from 1869. Criminal PAT goes back to 1/2004. PAT results show name only. Online access to criminal records is the same as civil.

General Information: No juvenile, mental health, sealed or expunged records released. Will fax documents $3.00 per page. Court makes copy: $.25 per page. Certification fee: $1.00 per document. Payee: Clerk of Court. Personal checks accepted; credit cards are not. Mail requests: SASE required for civil.

Rice County

District Court 101 W Commercial, Lyons, KS 67554; 620-257-2383; criminal fax: 620-257-3826; civil fax: same; 8AM-5PM (CST). ***Felony, Misdemeanor, Civil, Eviction, Small Claims, Probate.*** www.ricecounty.us

Probate fax is same as main fax number.

Civil Records: Access: Fax, mail, in person. Both court and visitors may perform in person searches. Search fee: $12.00 per hour. Required to search: name, years to search. Civil cases indexed by defendant, plaintiff, on computer from 1880. Mail turnaround time 3 days. Civil PAT goes back to 1880s.

Criminal Records: Access: Fax, mail, in person. Visitors must perform in person searches themselves. No search fee. Required to search: name, years to search; also helpful: SSN. Criminal records index on computer from 1880. All criminal searches are referred to the KBI. Mail turnaround time 1-3 days. Criminal PAT goes back to same as civil.

General Information: No juvenile unless designated by judge, mental health, sealed or expunged records released. Fee to fax document $.50 per page. Court makes copy: $1.00 first page, $.25 each add'l, self serve same. No certification fee. Payee: Clerk of Court. Personal checks accepted; credit cards are not. Mail requests: SASE required.

Riley County

District Court PO Box 158, Manhattan, KS 66505-0158; 785-537-6364; fax: 785-537-6382; 8:30AM-5PM (CST). ***Felony, Misdemeanor, Civil, Eviction, Small Claims, Probate.***

Civil Records: Access: In person, online. Visitors must perform in person searches themselves. Required to search: name, years to search. Civil cases indexed by defendant, plaintiff, on computer back to 10/93; prior records in index journals. The court or visitors may perform the in person search for dates after 7/2003. Civil PAT goes back to 1993. Access back to 11/1/02 at www.kansas.gov/subscribers/. A $95.00 annual subscription required plus usage fee as low as $1.00 per search.

Criminal Records: Access: In person, online. Visitors must perform in person searches themselves. Required to search: name, years to search; also helpful: DOB, SSN. Criminal records computerized from 1986, microfiche, archives and index cards from 1900s. The court or visitors may perform the in person search for dates after 7/2003. Criminal PAT goes back to 1986. Online access to criminal records is the same as civil.

General Information: No mental health, sealed or expunged records released. Will not fax documents. Court makes copy: $.25 per page. Certification fee: $1.00. Payee: Clerk of Court. Personal checks accepted; credit cards are not.

Rooks County

District Court 115 N Walnut, PO Box 532, Stockton, KS 67669; 785-425-6718; fax: 785-425-6568; 8AM-5PM (CST). ***Felony, Misdemeanor, Civil, Eviction, Small Claims, Probate.*** www.23rdjudicial.org/rooks.htm

Civil Records: Access: Mail, in person, online. Both court and visitors may perform in person searches. Search fee: $12.80 per hour. Required to search: name, years to search. Civil cases indexed by defendant, plaintiff; index on cards from 1888; on computer since 1995. Mail turnaround time 1-3 days. Civil PAT goes back to 1995. PAT civil results show middle initial. Case filings from previous week available on the court website. Also, access back to 11/1/02 at www.kansas.gov/subscribers/. A $95.00 annual subscription required plus usage fee as low as $1.00 per search.

Criminal Records: Access: In person, online. Both court and visitors may perform in person searches. No search fee. Required to search: name, years to search; also helpful: DOB, SSN. Criminal records indexed on cards from 1888; on computer since. The court personnel will not do criminal record searches for the public. Criminal PAT goes back to 1996. Online access to criminal records is the same as civil. Case filings from previous week available on the court website.

General Information: No juvenile, adoption, mental health, sealed or expunged records released. Fee to fax out file $2.50 1st page and $1.50 ea add'l. Court makes copy: $.25 per page, self serve same. Certification fee: $2.00. Payee: Clerk of Court. Personal checks accepted; credit cards are not. Mail requests: SASE required for civil.

Rush County

District Court PO Box 387, La Crosse, KS 67548; 785-222-2718; criminal fax: 785-222-2748; civil fax: same; 8AM-5PM (CST). ***Felony, Misdemeanor, Civil, Eviction, Small Claims, Probate.*** www.kscourts.org/dstcts/24dstct.htm

Probate is separate index at this same address. Probate fax is same as main fax number.

Civil Records: Access: Phone, fax, mail, in person, online. Both court and visitors may perform in person searches. Search fee: $12.00 per hour. Required to search: name, years to search. Civil cases indexed by defendant, plaintiff, on computer from 4/2003, on index from 1800s. Mail turnaround time 3 days. Civil PAT goes back to 2003. PAT results show name only. Access back to 11/1/02 at www.kansas.gov/subscribers/. A $95.00 annual subscription required plus usage fee as low as $1.00 per search.

Criminal Records: Access: In person, online. Visitors must perform in person searches themselves. Required to search: name, years to search; SSN helpful. Criminal records computerized from 4/1994, on index from 1800s. Criminal PAT goes back to same as civil.PAT results show name, DOB. Online access to criminal records is the same as civil.

General Information: No juvenile, mental health, sealed or expunged records released. Will fax documents $.50 per page. Court makes copy: $.25 per page, self serve same. Certification fee: $1.00 per page. Payee: Clerk of District Court. Personal checks accepted; credit cards are not. Mail requests: SASE required for civil.

Russell County

District Court PO Box 876, Russell, KS 67665; 785-483-5641; fax: 785-483-2448; 8AM-5PM (CST). ***Felony, Misdemeanor, Civil, Eviction, Small Claims, Probate.***

Civil Records: Access: Fax, mail, in person, online. Both court and visitors may perform in person searches. Search fee: $12.00 per hour. Required to search: name, years to search. Civil cases indexed by defendant, plaintiff, on computer from 1990, index cards from 1900s. Mail turnaround time 3 days. Civil PAT goes back to 1990. Access back to 11/1/02 at www.kansas.gov/subscribers/. A $95.00 annual subscription required plus usage fee as low as $1.00 per search.

Criminal Records: Access: Fax, mail, in person, online. Both court and visitors may perform in person searches. Search fee: $12.00 per hour. Required to search: name, years to search, DOB. Criminal records computerized from 1990, index cards from 1900s. Mail turnaround time 3 days. Criminal PAT goes back to same as civil. Online access to criminal records is the same as civil.

General Information: No juvenile, mental health, sealed or expunged records released. Fee to fax document $.50 per page. Court makes copy: $.50 per page. Self serve: $.50 per page. No certification fee. Payee: Clerk of Court. Personal checks accepted; credit cards are not. Mail requests: SASE required.

Saline County

District Court PO Box 1760, 300 S Ash St, Salina, KS 67402-1760; 785-309-5831; civil phone: 785-309-5836; fax: 785-309-5845; 8AM-4PM (CST). ***Felony, Misdemeanor, Civil, Eviction, Small Claims, Probate.***

Can fax requests and call following day to follow up. Clerk recommends following up on mailed requests also via phone.

Civil Records: Access: Mail, in person, online. Both court and visitors may perform in person searches. Search fee: $12.00 per hour. Required to search: name, years to search, address. Civil cases indexed by defendant, plaintiff, on computer from 1990, index from early 1900s. Mail turnaround time 1 week. Civil PAT goes back to 2003. PAT results show name only. Access back to 11/1/02 at www.kansas.gov/subscribers/. A $95.00 annual subscription required plus usage fee as low as $1.00 per search.

Criminal Records: Access: Mail, in person, online. Both court and visitors may perform in person searches. Search fee: $12.00 per hour. Required to search: name, years to search, address, DOB, SSN, signed release. Criminal records computerized from 1990, index from early 1900s. Mail turnaround time 1 week. Criminal PAT goes back to 2003. PAT results show name only. Online access to criminal records is the same as civil.

General Information: No juvenile, mental health, sealed or expunged records released. Will not fax documents. Court makes copy: $.25 per page. Certification fee: $1.00. Payee: Clerk of District Court. Personal checks accepted; credit cards are not. SASE not required.

Scott County

District Court 303 Court St, Scott City, KS 67871; 620-872-7208; fax: 620-872-3683; 8AM-N, 1-5PM (CST). ***Felony, Misdemeanor, Civil, Eviction, Small Claims, Probate.***

Civil Records: Access: Mail, fax, in person, online. Both court and visitors may perform in person searches. Search fee: $12.00 per hour per custodian of records' estimate. Required to search: name, years to search. Civil cases indexed by defendant, plaintiff, on computer back to 1992, index cards from 1980s. Mail turnaround time 2-3 days. Civil PAT goes back to 1992. Results may include DOB or address, but not always. Access back to 11/1/02 at www.kansas.gov/subscribers/. A $95.00 annual subscription required plus usage fee as low as $1.00 per search.

Criminal Records: Access: In person, online, mail. Visitors must perform in person searches themselves. Search fee: $12.00 per hour per custodian of records' estimate. Required to search: name, years to search, DOB. Criminal records computerized from 1992, index cards from 1980s. Court will perform short searches only; usually directs searchers to state KBI. Mail turnaround time 2-3 days. Criminal PAT goes back to same as civil. Results may include DOB or address, but not always. Online access to criminal records is the same as civil.

General Information: No juvenile, mental health, sealed or expunged records released. Fee to fax out file $1.00 per page. Court makes copy: $.25 per page. Certification fee: $1.00 per cert. Payee: Clerk of Court. Personal checks accepted; credit cards are not. Mail requests: SASE required.

Sedgwick County

District Court 525 N Main, Wichita, KS 67203; 316-660-5800; criminal phone: 316-660-5719; civil phone: 316-660-5803; probate phone: 316-660-5721; fax: 316-660-5784; 8AM-4PM (CST). ***Felony, Misdemeanor, Civil, Eviction, Small Claims, Probate.*** www.dc18.org

Civil Records: Access: Fax, mail, online, in person. Both court and visitors may perform in person searches. Search fee: $12.00 per hour. Fee charged if more than 15 minutes. Required to search: name, years to search; case number helpful. Civil cases indexed by defendant, plaintiff, on computer from 1983, microfiche from 1982, archives from 1977 and index cards from 1900s. Email record requests to micro@dc18.org Mail turnaround time 7-10 days. Civil PAT goes back to 1984. PAT civil results show middle initial. Access at www.kansas.gov/subscribers/. A $95.00 annual subscription required plus usage fee as low as $1.00 per search. Search pre-2003 cases are on a separate system. System also includes probate, traffic, domestic, and criminal cases. For more information, call 316-383-7563 or visit website.

Criminal Records: Access: In person, online. Both court and visitors may perform in person searches. Search fee: $12.00 per hour. Fee charged if more than

15 minutes. Required to search: name, years to search; case number helpful. Criminal records computerized from 1983, microfiche from 1982, archives from 1977 and index cards from 1900s. Criminal PAT goes back to 1983. PAT criminal results show middle initial. Online access to criminal records is the same as civil. Online results show middle initial.
General Information: No juvenile, adoption, mental health, sealed or expunged records released. Will fax documents $2.00 1st page, $1.00 each add'l, maximum of 10 pages. Court makes copy: $.25 per page, self serve same. Cert fee: $1.00 per cert. Payee: Clerk of Court. Personal checks accepted; credit cards are not. Mail requests: SASE required for civil.

Seward County

District Court 415 N Washington, #103, Liberal, KS 67901; 620-626-3375; criminal phone: 620-626-3234; civil phone: 620-626-3391; probate phone: 620-626-3232; fax: 620-626-3302; 8:30AM-5PM (CST). ***Felony, Misdemeanor, Civil, Eviction, Small Claims, Probate.***
Court will do searches on occasion, fee is $12.00 per hour. The Small Claims Court can be reached at 620-626-3232.
Civil Records: Access: Mail, in person, online. Visitors must perform in person searches themselves. Search fee: $12.00 per name. Required to search: name, years to search. Civil cases indexed by defendant, plaintiff, on computer back to 1977, index from 1900s. Civil PAT goes back to 1977. Access back to 11/1/02 at www.kansas.gov/subscribers/. A $95.00 annual subscription required plus usage fee as low as $1.00 per search.
Criminal Records: Access: Mail, in person, online. Visitors must perform in person searches themselves. Search fee: $12.00 per name. Required to search: name, years to search; SSN helpful. Criminal records computerized from 1977, index from 1900s. Criminal PAT goes back to same as civil. Online access to criminal records is the same as civil.
General Information: No juvenile, mental health, sealed or expunged records released. Will fax specific case file $2.00 1st page; $.50 each add'l page. Court makes copy: $.25 per page, self serve same. Certification fee: $1.00 per seal. Payee: Clerk of District Court. Personal checks accepted; credit cards are not.

Shawnee County

District Court 200 E 7th Rm 209, Topeka, KS 66603; 785-233-8200 X4327; criminal phone: x5157; civil phone: x5158; probate phone: x4358; criminal fax: 785-291-4908; civil fax: 785-291-4911; 8AM-5PM (CST). ***Felony, Misdemeanor, Civil, Eviction, Small Claims, Probate, Traffic.***
www.shawneecourt.org
Civil Records: Access: Fax, mail, in person, online. Both court and visitors may perform in person searches. Search fee: $12.00 per hour. Required to search: name, years to search. Civil cases indexed by defendant, plaintiff, on computer from 1980, microfiche from 1950, archives and index from 1800s. Mail turnaround time 3-4 days. Civil PAT goes back to 1988. See www.shawneecourt.org/doe/index.html. Also, online access to court record images is free at www.shawneecourt.org/img_temp.htm. Also find "viewing restricted" domestic documents here. Also, daily dockets lists free at www.shawneecourt.org/docket/.
Criminal Records: Access: Fax, mail, in person, online. Both court and visitors may perform in person searches. Search fee: $12.00 per hour. Required to search: name, years to search, DOB. Criminal records computerized from 1980, microfiche from 1950, archives and index from 1800s. Mail turnaround time 3-4 days. Criminal PAT goes back to 1984. Online access to criminal records and dockets is the same as civil.
General Information: No juvenile, mental health, sealed or expunged records released. Will fax documents to local or toll free line. Court makes copy: $.50 per page. Certification fee: $2.25 for Authentication; $1.25 for certification. Payee: Clerk of District Court. Personal checks and credit cards accepted. SASE not required.

Sheridan County

District Court PO Box 753, Hoxie, KS 67740; 785-675-3451; criminal fax: 785-675-2256; civil fax: same; 8AM-N, 1PM-5PM (CST). ***Felony, Misdemeanor, Civil, Eviction, Small Claims, Probate.***
Probate records prior to 2004 are on a separate index. Probate fax is same as main fax number.
Civil Records: Access: Phone, fax, mail, in person. Both court and visitors may perform in person searches. Search fee: $12.00 per hour. Required to search: name, years to search. Civil cases indexed by defendant, plaintiff, on strip index from 1885. Mail requests require use of a special form. Mail turnaround 1-2 days. Civil PAT goes back to 2004.
Criminal Records: Access: Phone, fax, mail, in person. Both court and visitors may perform in person searches. Search fee: $12.00 per hour. Required to search: name, years to search, signed release. Criminal records computerized from 2004; partial computer records back to 1995; on strip index from 1885. Mail turnaround time 1-2 days. Criminal PAT goes back to same as civil. PAT results show name only.
General Information: No juvenile, mental health, sealed or expunged records released. Will fax documents to local or toll free line. Court makes copy: $.25 per page, self serve same. Certification fee: $1.00 per page includes copies. Payee: Clerk of Court. Personal checks accepted; credit cards are not. Mail requests: SASE required.

Sherman County

District Court 813 Broadway, Rm 201, Goodland, KS 67735; 785-890-4850; criminal phone: 785-890-4854; civil phone: 785-890-4853; probate phone: same; fax: 785-890-4858; 8AM-N, 1-5PM (MST). ***Felony, Misdemeanor, Civil, Eviction, Small Claims, Probate.***
Civil Records: Access: In person only. Visitors must perform in person searches themselves. Required to search: name, years to search. Civil cases indexed by defendant, plaintiff; index in docket books from 1900s. Civil PAT goes back to 2004. PAT civil results show middle initial.
Criminal Records: Access: In person only. Visitors must perform in person searches themselves. Required to search: name, years to search; SSN helpful. Criminal docket on books from 1900s. Criminal PAT available. PAT criminal results show middle initial.
General Information: No juvenile before 1997, mental health, sealed or expunged records released. Will fax documents $1.00 per page. Court makes copy: $.25 per page. Certification fee: $1.00. Payee: Clerk of District Court. Personal checks accepted; credit cards are not.

Smith County

District Court PO Box 273, 18 S Branch, Smith Center, KS 66967; 785-282-5140/41; fax: 785-282-5145; 8AM-Noon, 1PM-5PM (CST). ***Felony, Misdemeanor, Civil, Eviction, Small Claims, Probate.***
Civil Records: Access: In person, fax, online. Visitors must perform in person searches themselves. Search fee: $5.00 with results, $3.00 without results. Required to search: name, years to search. Civil cases indexed by defendant, plaintiff; index on cards from 1873. Civil PAT goes back to 2004. PAT results show name and can contain DOB. Access back to 11/1/02 at www.kansas.gov/subscribers/. A $95.00 annual subscription required plus usage fee as low as $1.00 per search.
Criminal Records: Access: In person, fax, online. Visitors must perform in person searches themselves. Search fee: $5.00 with results, $3.00 without results. Required to search: name, years to search; SSN helpful. Criminal records indexed on cards from 1873. Criminal PAT goes back to 2004.PAT results show name, DOB. Online access to criminal records is the same as civil.
General Information: No juvenile, mental health, sealed or expunged records released. Will fax documents $.75 per page. Court makes copy: $.25 per page, self serve same. Certification fee: $1.00 per page. Payee: Clerk of Court. Personal checks accepted; credit cards are not.

Stafford County

District Court PO Box 365, St John, KS 67576; 620-549-3295; criminal fax: 620-549-3298; civil fax: same; 8AM-5PM (CST). ***Felony, Misdemeanor, Civil, Eviction, Small Claims, Probate.***
www.staffordcounty.org
Probate fax is same as main fax number.
Civil Records: Access: Phone, mail, fax, in person, email, online. Both court and visitors may perform in person searches. Search fee: $12.00 per hour, 15 minutes minimum. Required to search: name, years to search. Civil cases indexed by defendant, plaintiff, on computer from 1988, microfiche and index from 1900s. Direct email civil record requests to mgatton@embacqmail.com. Mail turnaround time 3 days. Civil PAT goes back to 1988. Access back to 11/1/02 at www.kansas.gov/subscribers/. A $95.00 annual subscription required plus usage fee as low as $1.00 per search.
Criminal Records: Access: In person, online. Visitors must perform in person searches themselves. Required to search: name, years to search. Criminal records computerized from 1988, microfiche and index from 1900s. All other requests must go to the Kansas Bureau of Investigations. Criminal PAT goes back to same as civil. Online access to criminal records is the same as civil.
General Information: No juvenile, mental health, sealed or expunged records released. Will not fax documents. Court makes copy: $.50 per page. No certification fee. Payee: Clerk of District Court. Personal checks accepted; credit cards are not. Mail requests: SASE required for civil.

Stanton County

District Court PO Box 913, Johnson, KS 67855; 620-492-2180; fax: 620-492-6410; 8AM-5PM (CST). ***Felony, Misdemeanor, Civil, Eviction, Small Claims, Probate.***
Civil Records: Access: Phone, fax, mail, in person, online. Both court and visitors may perform in person searches. Search fee: $12.00 per hour. Required to search: name, years to search. Civil cases indexed by defendant, plaintiff, on computer from 1977, index from 1887. Mail turnaround time 1-3 days. Civil PAT goes back to 1977. Access back to 11/1/02 at www.kansas.gov/subscribers/. A $95.00 annual subscription required plus usage fee as low as $1.00 per search.
Criminal Records: Access: Phone, fax, mail, in person, online. Both court and visitors may perform in person searches. Search fee: $12.00 per hour. Required to search: name, years to search, DOB, SSN. Criminal records computerized from 1977, index from 1887. Mail turnaround time 1-3 days. Criminal PAT goes back to 1977. Online access to criminal records is the same as civil.
General Information: No juvenile, mental health, sealed or expunged records released. Will fax documents $2.50 1st page, $.50 each add'l. Court makes copy: $.25 per page, self serve same. Certification fee: $1.00 per cert. Payee: Clerk of District Court. Personal checks accepted; credit cards are not. Mail requests: SASE required.

Stevens County

District Court 200 E 6th, Hugoton, KS 67951; 620-544-2484; criminal fax: 620-544-2528; civil fax: same; 8AM-5PM Closed noon-1PM (CST). ***Felony, Misdemeanor, Civil, Eviction, Small Claims, Probate.*** Probate fax is same as main fax.
Civil Records: Access: Mail, fax, in person, online. Both court and visitors may perform in person searches. Search fee: $12.50 per hour. Required to search: name, years to search. Civil cases indexed by defendant, plaintiff, on computer, microfiche, archives and index from 1887. Mail turnaround time 3 days. Civil PAT goes back to 1887. PAT results show name only. Access back to 11/1/02 at www.kansas.gov/subscribers/. A $95.00 annual

subscription required plus usage fee as low as $1.00 per search.
Criminal Records: Access: Online only. Visitors must perform in person searches themselves. Required to search: name, years to search; also helpful: SSN. Criminal records computerized from 1991, microfiche, archives and index from 1887. Criminal PAT goes back to 1991 approximately. PAT results show name only. Online access to criminal records is the same as civil.
General Information: No juvenile, mental health, sealed or expunged records released. Fee to fax out file $3.00 plus $.25 per page. Court makes copy: $.25 per page, self serve same. Certification fee: $1.25 per page. Payee: Clerk of District Court. Personal checks accepted; credit cards are not. Must prepay for fax and mail. Mail requests: SASE required.

Sumner County

District Court PO Box 399, County Courthouse, Wellington, KS 67152; 620-326-5936; probate phone: 620-399-1042; criminal fax: 620-326-5365; civil fax: same; 8AM-N, 1-5PM (CST). ***Felony, Misdemeanor, Civil, Eviction, Small Claims, Probate.*** www.accesskansas.org
Court will not perform searches for "employment purposes" nor do they perform lien searches. Court prefers that you summit requests on their request form. Probate fax is same as main fax number.
Civil Records: Access: Mail, fax, in person. Both court and visitors may perform in person searches. Search fee: $12.00 per hour. Required to search: name, years to search. Civil cases indexed by defendant, plaintiff, on computer back to 1991, index cards from 1800s for probate. Will not do any lien searches, no name searches over the phone, specific case number needed. Mail turnaround time 1-3 days. Civil PAT goes back to 1991.
Criminal Records: Access: Mail, fax, in person. Both court and visitors may perform in person searches. Search fee: $12.00 per hour. Required to search: name, years to search; also helpful: case number. Criminal records computerized from 1991, index cards from 1800s for probate. Will not search any name over phone unless specific case number is given. Don't do searches for employment purposes. Mail turnaround time 1-3 days. Criminal PAT goes back to same as civil.
General Information: No juvenile, mental health, sealed or expunged records released. Will fax documents $1.00 per page up to 10 pages only. Court makes copy: $.25 per page. Certification fee: $2.00. Payee: Clerk of Court. Personal checks accepted; credit cards are not. SASE not required.

Thomas County

District Court PO Box 805, 300 N Court Ave, Colby, KS 67701; 785-460-4540; criminal fax: 785-460-2291; civil fax: same; 8:30AM-5PM (CST). ***Felony, Misdemeanor, Civil, Eviction, Small Claims, Probate.***
Civil Records: Access: Fax, mail, in person. Both court and visitors may perform in person searches. Search fee: $12.00 per hour. Required to search: name, years to search. Civil cases indexed by defendant, plaintiff, on index from 1887. Civil PAT goes back to 1996.
Criminal Records: Access: Fax, mail, in person. Both court and visitors may perform in person searches. Search fee: $12.00 per hour. Required to search: name, years to search, DOB, sex; also helpful: SSN. Criminal records indexed from 1887. Criminal PAT goes back to same as civil.
General Information: No juvenile, mental health, sealed or expunged records released. Will fax documents $1.00 per page. Court makes copy: $.25 per page. Certification fee: $1.00 per page. Payee: Clerk. Personal checks accepted. Mail requests: SASE required.

Trego County

District Court 216 N Main, WaKeeney, KS 67672; 785-743-2148; criminal fax: 785-743-2726; civil fax: same; 8AM-N, 1-5PM (CST). ***Felony, Misdemeanor, Civil, Eviction, Small Claims, Probate.*** www.23rdjudicial.org
Probate fax is same as main fax number.
Civil Records: Access: Phone, mail, fax, in person, online. Both court and visitors may perform in person searches. Search fee: $12.00 per hour. Required to search: name, years to search. Civil cases indexed by defendant, plaintiff, on computer since 1996; prior records on card index. Mail turnaround time 1-2 days. Civil PAT goes back to 1996. PAT civil results show middle initial. 2002 to present includes DOB and SSN. Case filings from previous week available on the court website. Also, access back to 11/1/02 at www.kansas.gov/subscribers/. A $95.00 annual subscription required plus usage fee as low as $1.00 per search.
Criminal Records: Access: Mail, in person, online. Only the court performs in person searches; visitors may not. Search fee: $12.00 per hour. Required to search: name, years to search; also helpful: DOB, SSN, sex. Criminal records on computer since 1996; prior records on card index. Mail turnaround time 1-2 days. Criminal PAT available. PAT criminal results show middle initial. 2002 to present includes DOB and SSN. Online access to criminal records is same as civil.
General Information: No juvenile, mental health, sealed or expunged records released. Fee to fax out file $2.00 1st page; $.50 each add'l. Court makes copy: $.25 per page, self serve same. Certification fee: $1.00 per page. Payee: Clerk of Court. Personal checks accepted; credit cards are not. Mail requests: SASE required.

Wabaunsee County

District Court Courthouse, PO Box 278, Alma, KS 66401; 785-765-2406; fax: 785-765-2487; 8AM-4:30PM (CST). ***Felony, Misdemeanor, Civil, Eviction, Small Claims, Probate.***
Civil Records: Access: In person only. Visitors must perform in person searches themselves. Required to search: name, years to search. Civil cases indexed by defendant, plaintiff, on book index from 1800s; on computer back to 1996. Civil PAT goes back to 1996. PAT results show middle initial, DOB, SSN. Terminal results also show SSNs.
Criminal Records: Access: In person only. Visitors must perform in person searches themselves. Required to search: name, years to search; SSN helpful. Criminal docket on books index from 1800s; on computer back to 1996. Criminal PAT goes back to 1996. PAT results show middle initial, DOB, SSN. Terminal results also show SSN.
General Information: No juvenile, mental health, sealed or expunged records released. Will not fax documents. Court makes copy: $.50 per page. Certification fee: $1.25. Payee: Clerk of District Court. Personal checks accepted; credit cards are not.

Wallace County

District Court PO Box 8, Sharon Springs, KS 67758; 785-852-4289; criminal fax: 785-852-4271; civil fax: same; 8AM-N,1-5PM (MST). ***Felony, Misdemeanor, Civil, Eviction, Small Claims, Probate.*** Probate fax is same as main fax.
Civil Records: Access: Mail, in person, fax. Both court and visitors may perform in person searches. Search fee: $12.00 per hour. Required to search: name; also helpful: years to search. Civil cases indexed by defendant, plaintiff, on index from 1887. A case number must be provided; court will not do name searches. Mail turnaround time 2 days. Civil PAT available.
Criminal Records: Access: In person only. Visitors must perform in person searches themselves. Required to search: name; also helpful: years to search. Criminal records indexed from 1887. Criminal PAT available.
General Information: No juvenile offender (under 14 years old), juvenile in need of care, adoption, mental health, sealed or expunged records released. Will fax documents to local or toll free line. Court makes copy: $.25 per page, self serve same. Certification fee: $1.00 per page. Payee: Clerk of Court. Personal checks accepted; credit cards are not. Mail requests: SASE helpful.

Washington County

District Court Courthouse, 214 C St, Washington, KS 66968; 785-325-2381; criminal fax: 785-325-2557; civil fax: same; 8AM-N,1-5PM (CST). ***Felony, Misdemeanor, Civil, Eviction, Small Claims, Probate.*** www.kscourts.org/dstcts/12dstct.htm
Probate fax is same as main fax number.
Civil Records: Access: In person, online. Visitors must perform in person searches themselves. Required to search: name, years to search. Civil cases indexed by defendant, plaintiff, on card index from 1887; on computer back to 1995. Civil PAT goes back to 6/2003. PAT civil results show middle initial. Access back to 11/1/02 at www.kansas.gov/subscribers/. A $95.00 annual subscription required plus usage fee as low as $1.00 per search.
Criminal Records: Access: In person, online. Visitors must perform in person searches themselves. Required to search: name, years to search. Criminal records on card index from 1887; on computer back to 1995. Criminal PAT goes back to 6/2003. PAT criminal results show middle initial. Online access to criminal records is same as civil.
General Information: No juvenile, mental health, sealed or expunged records released. Fee to fax out file $3.00 per page. Court makes copy: $.25 per page, self serve same. Certification fee: $1.00 per document. Payee: Washington County District Court. Personal checks accepted; credit cards are not.

Wichita County

District Court PO Box 968, 206 S 4th St, Leoti, KS 67861; 620-375-4454; fax: 620-375-2999; 8AM-5PM (CST). ***Felony, Misdemeanor, Civil, Eviction, Small Claims, Probate.***
This court is not in City of Wichita, KS. City of Wichita, KS is in Sedgwick County.
Civil Records: Access: Mail, in person, online. Both court and visitors may perform in person searches. Search fee: $12.00 per hour. Required to search: name, years to search. Civil cases indexed by defendant, plaintiff, on computer back to 1986, on index from 1900. Civil PAT goes back to 1986. Access back to 11/1/02 at www.kansas.gov/subscribers/. A $95.00 annual subscription required plus usage fee as low as $1.00 per search.
Criminal Records: Access: In person, online. Visitors must perform in person searches themselves. Required to search: name. Criminal records computerized from 1986, on index from 1900. Criminal records are through the KBI. Criminal PAT goes back to same as civil. Online access to criminal records is the same as civil.
General Information: No juvenile, mental health, sealed or expunged records released. Will fax documents $1.00 per page. Court makes copy: $.20 per page, self serve same. Certification fee: $1.00. Payee: Clerk of District Court. Personal checks accepted; credit cards are not. Mail requests: SASE required for civil.

Wilson County

District Court PO Box 300, Fredonia, KS 66736; 620-378-4533; criminal fax: 620-378-4531; civil fax: same; 8AM-5PM (CST). ***Felony, Misdemeanor, Civil, Eviction, Small Claims, Probate.*** www.31stjudicialdistrict.org
Probate fax is same as main fax number.
Civil Records: Access: Fax, mail, in person, online. Both court and visitors may perform in person searches. Search fee: $12.00 per hour. Required to search: name, years to search, request in writing. Civil cases indexed by defendant, plaintiff, on computer since 1993, index cards from 1864. Mail turnaround time 1-3 weeks. Civil PAT goes back to 1993. PAT civil results show middle initial. Court calendars, limited action hearing results, and service results appear on the court website. Also, access back to 11/1/02 at www.kansas.gov/subscribers/. A $95.00 annual subscription required plus usage fee as low as $1.00 per search.
Criminal Records: Access: In person, online. Visitors must perform in person searches themselves. Required to search: name, years to search; also helpful: SSN. Criminal records on

computer since 1993, manual index from 1864. Criminal PAT goes back to same as civil. PAT criminal results show middle initial. Court calendars, limited action hearing results, and service results appear on the court website. Access back to 11/1/02 at www.kansas.gov/subscribers/. A $95.00 annual subscription required plus usage fee as low as $1.00 per search.

General Information: No juvenile, mental health, sealed or expunged records released. Will fax documents $1.00 per page. Court makes copy: $.50 per page. Certification fee: $1.00 per page. Payee: Clerk of Court. Personal checks accepted; credit cards are not. Mail requests: SASE required.

Woodson County

District Court PO Box 228, Yates Center, KS 66783; 620-625-8610; criminal fax: 620-625-8674; civil fax: same; 8AM-N; 1-5PM (CST). ***Felony, Misdemeanor, Civil, Eviction, Small Claims, Probate, Traffic.*** www.31stjudicialdistrict.org

Court calendar is on website above. Probate fax is same as main fax number.

Civil Records: Access: Mail, in person, online. Both court and visitors may perform in person searches. Search fee: $12.00 per hour. Required to search: name, years to search. Civil cases indexed by defendant, plaintiff, on index from 1880s, on computer since 1993. Mail turnaround time 1 day. Civil PAT goes back to 1993. PAT results show name only. Court calendars, limited action hearing results, and service results appear on the website. Access back to 11/1/02 at www.kansas.gov/subscribers/. A $95.00 annual subscription required plus usage fee as low as $1.00 per search.

Criminal Records: Access: In person, online. Visitors must perform in person searches themselves. Required to search: name, years to search. Criminal records indexed from 1880s, on computer since 1993. Phone inquiries referred to KBI at 785-296-8200. Criminal PAT goes back to same as civil. PAT results show name only. Court calendars, limited action hearing results, and service results appear on the website. Access back to 11/1/02 at www.kansas.gov/subscribers/. A $95.00 annual subscription required plus usage fee as low as $1.00 per search.

General Information: No juvenile (under age 14 years), mental health, sealed or expunged records released. Fee to fax out file $1.00 per page. Court makes copy: $.50 per page, self serve same. Certification fee: $1.00 per cert. Payee: District Court. Business checks accepted. No credit cards accepted. Mail requests: SASE required for civil.

Wyandotte County

District Court 710 N 7th St, Kansas City, KS 66101; criminal phone: 913-573-2905; civil phone: 913-573-2901; probate phone: 913-573-2834; criminal fax: 913-573-8177; civil fax: 913-573-4134; 8AM-5PM (CST). ***Felony, Misdemeanor, Civil, Eviction, Small Claims, Probate.***

Fax number for the Limited Civil Division is 913-573-4135.

Civil Records: Access: In person, online. Both court and visitors may perform in person searches. No search fee. Required to search: name, years to search. Civil cases indexed by defendant, plaintiff, on computer from 1975, microfiche, archives and index from 1900s. Civil PAT goes back to 1975. PAT results show name only. Access at www.kansas.gov/subscribers/. A $95.00 annual subscription required plus usage fee as low as $1.00 per search. Search pre-7/2004 cases on a separate system.

Criminal Records: Access: In person, online. Visitors must perform in person searches themselves. Required to search: name, years to search, DOB, SSN. Criminal records computerized from 1972, microfiche, archives and index from early 1900s. Refer phone inquires to KBI at 785-296-8200. Criminal PAT goes back to 1972. PAT results show name only. Online access to criminal records is the same as civil.

General Information: No juvenile, mental health, sealed or expunged records released. Court makes copy: $.25 per page. Certification fee: $1.00. Payee: Clerk of District Court. Personal checks accepted; credit cards are not. Prepayment required.

Kansas Recording Offices

ORGANIZATION: 105 counties, 105 recording offices. The recording officer is the Register of Deeds. Many counties utilize a "Miscellaneous Index" for tax and other liens, separate from real estate records. 101 Kansas counties are in the Central Time Zone (CST) and 4 counties – Greeley, Hamilton, Sherman, Wallace – are in the Mountain Time Zone (MST).

REAL ESTATE RECORDS: Most counties will not perform real estate searches although some will do as an accommodation with the understanding that they are not "certified searches." Some counties will also do a search to determine owner based upon legal description. Copy fees vary; usually $1.00 in half the counties, less in others. Certification fee usually $1.00 per document. Tax records located at the Appraiser's Office.

UCC RECORDS: Financing statements are filed at the state level except for real estate related collateral which are filed with the Register of Deeds. However, prior to July, 2001, consumer goods collateral were also filed at the Register of Deeds and these older records can be searched here. Most counties will perform UCC searches. UCC search fee is usually $15.00 per debtor name. UCC copy fee is usually $1.00 per page.

TAX LIEN RECORDS: Federal tax liens on personal property of businesses are filed with the Secretary of State. Other federal tax liens and all state tax liens on personal property are filed with the county Register of Deeds. Most counties automatically include tax liens on personal property with a UCC search. Tax liens on personal property may usually be searched separately for $8.00 per name.

OTHER LIENS: Mechanics, harvesters, lis pendens, threshers.

ONLINE ACCESS: A number of counties have online access to recorder records; Statewide online UCC service is provided by accessKansas www.kansas.gov/subscribers/services.html. UCC subscriptions are modest annual fee.

Allen County

County Register of Deeds, 1 N Washington Ave, Iola, KS 66749. Recording, R/E & UCC phone-620-365-1412; fax-620-365-1414; 8AM-5PM (CST) www.ksrods.org

Index: Separate indices to search include mortgages, surveys, deeds & misc in books. Records indexed on computer from 1995 to present, all records are also indexed to books also. Office personnel or visitors may perform searches. Search fee $15.00 per hour. Office will search real estate records. Will not search UCC records. Copy fee $1.00 per page if faxed, $.50 per page if mailed plus postage. Bound books add'l $1.00 per page. Cert fee- $1.00 per doc plus copy fee. Payee- Allen County Register of Deeds. Bulk data available for purchase on CD-Register of Deeds office must sign open records form first. **Online access to Deeds records:** Access to count land records go to www.fidlartechnologies.com/. Subscription fees charged per month. **Other phones:** Treasurer- 620-365-1409; Elections- 620-365-1407; Vital Records- 785-296-1400 (Topeka); Clerk of District Court (Marriage, etc.)- 620-365-1425; City of Iola Clerk (Birth & Death before 1911) -620-365-4910;. **Property tax/Assessing-** 1 N Washington Ave, Iola, KS 66749; 620-365-1415, assessor fax- 620-365-1417. (Appraiser/Auditor- 620-365-1415) No computer access terminal available, office will do searches. www.allencounty.org/apprais/index.htm

Anderson County

County Register of Deeds, 100 E 4th St; Courthouse, Garnett, KS 66032-1503. Recording, R/E & UCC phone-785-448-3715; fax-785-448-3275; 8AM-5PM

Index: Separate indices to search include deed, mortgage, oil & gas books, misc. Records indexed on a public use terminal back to 1997. Office personnel or visitors may perform searches. Search fee-$15.00 per name. Office will not search real estate records. Will search UCC records. Copy fee $1.00 per page. Cert fee- $1.00 per page plus copy fee. Payee- Anderson County Register of Deeds. Bulk data available for purchase; contact office. **Other phones:** Treasurer- 785-448-5824; Elections- 785-448-6841. **Property tax/Assessing-** 100 E 4th Ave, Courthouse, Garnett, KS 66032-1503; 785-448-6844, assessor fax- 785-448-5621. (Appraiser/Auditor- 785-448-6844) http://skyways.lib.ks.us/counties/AN/

Atchison County

County Register of Deeds, 423 N 5th St; Courthouse, Atchison, KS 66002-1861. Recording, R/E phone-913-367-2568; fax-913-367-8441; 8:30AM-5PM

Index: Separate indices to search. Records indexed on a public use terminal back to 1996. Office personnel or visitors may perform searches; office personnel will not perform title searches. Search fee $15.00. Copy fee $.50 per page. UCCs- $1.00 per page. Cert fee- $1.00 per doc plus copy fee. Payee- Atchison County Register of Deeds. **Other phones:** Treasurer- 913-367-5332; Elections- 913-367-1653; Vital Records- 913-367-1653. **Property tax/Assessing-** 423 N 5th St, Courthouse, Atchison, KS 66002-1861; 913-367-4400, assessor fax- 913-367-0227. (Appraiser/Auditor- 913-367-4400) Office will perform searches. **Online** - Search property and tax data free at www.atchisoncountyks.org/Appraisal.asp. Not regularly updated.

Barber County

County Register of Deeds, 120 E Washington St; Courthouse, Medicine Lodge, KS 67104. 620-886-3981; fax-620-886-5045; 8:30AM-5PM (CST)

Index: Separate indices to search include deeds, mortgages, tract indexes, misc. Records indexed on a public use terminal back to 1990. Office personnel or visitors may perform searches. Search fee $15.00 per name. Office will search real estate records on a limited basis. Copy fee $1.00 per page.Real estate record copy- $.25 per page standard; bond books and index books add'l fees. Cert fee- $1.00 per cert plus copy fee. Payee- Barber County Register of Deeds. Office does not sell bulk data. **Other phones:** Treasurer- 620-886-3775; Elections- 620-886-3961. **Property tax/Assessing-** 120 E Washington, Medicine Lodge, KS 67104; 620-886-3795, assessor fax- 620-886-3845. (appraiser/auditor- 620-886-3723)

Barton County

County Register of Deeds, 1400 Main St, #205; Courthouse, Great Bend, KS 67530-4037. Recording, R/E & UCC phone-620-793-1849; fax-620-793-1981; 8AM-5PM (CST) www.bartoncounty.org

Index: Separate indices to search include deeds, general, mortgage, lien, military. Records indexed on a public use terminal back to 1998. Office personnel or visitors may perform searches. Search fee $15.00. Office searches of real estate records are very limited. Use national search form for UCC requests. Copy fee $1.00 per page. Cert fee- $1.00 per cert plus copy fee. Payee- Barton County Register of Deeds. Office does not sell bulk data. **Other phones:** Treasurer- 620-793-1827; Elections- 620-793-1835; Vital Records- 620-793-1870. **Property tax/Assessing-** 1400 Main St, Courthouse, #206, Great Bend, KS 67530-4037; 620-793-1821, assessor fax- 620-793-1820. (Appraiser/Auditor- 620-793-1821) No public terminal available in office. Office will search RE records but not UCC. www.bartoncounty.org/ **Online**- Access County Property value list by address and name at www.bartoncounty.org/propvals.pdf.

Bourbon County

County Register of Deeds, 210 S National, Fort Scott, KS 66701. 620-223-3800 x17, R/E recording phone-x17; fax-620-223-5241; 8:30AM-4:30PM (CST) http://bourboncountyks.org

Index: All in one. Records indexed on computer back to 1993. Office personnel or visitors may perform searches. Search fee $15.00. Office will not search real estate records. Will search UCC records. Copy fee $.25 per page; $.35 each for legal size; $5.0 each for 11x17. Cert fee- $1.00 per cert plus copy fee. Payee- Bourbon County Register of Deeds. Office does not sell bulk data. **Online access to Real Estate, Deed, Lien records:** Access recordings on the Deeds Management System subscription service at http://bourboncountyks.org/dms_online_search.htm. User name and password required; contact Register of Deeds to register. **Other phones:** Treasurer- x15; Elections- x14; Vital Records- x14. **Property tax/Assessing-** 210 S National, Fort Scott, KS 66701; 620-223-3800 x16, assessor fax- 620-223-3418. (Appraiser/Auditor- 620-223-3418 x34) **Online-** Access property data index free at www.bourbon.kansasgov.c om/parcel/. Subscription is required for full data. These is also a separate subscription level for appraisers. Contact Appraiser's office at 620-223-3800 x34. Also, search property tax data at www.bourboncountyks.org/tax_search.htm. Also, search county property tax data at www.bourbon.kansasgov.com/tax/ or subscribe for full data; contact the Treasurer's office.

Brown County

County Register of Deeds, 601 Oregon; Courthouse, Hiawatha, KS 66434. Recording, R/E & UCC phone-785-742-3741; fax-785-742-7705; 8AM-5PM (CST) www.brown.kansasgov.com/MV2Base.asp?VarCN=2
Index: Separate indices to search include UCCs, tax liens. Record index not computerized. Only the public may search. Copy fee $1.00 per page.Real estate record copy- $.30 per page. Cert fee- $1.00 per cert plus copy fee. Payee- Brown County Register of Deeds. **Online access to Real Estate, Deed, Other County Data records:** Access to recorded docs and tax records and CAMA online is currently under development; see www.brown.kansasgov.com/MV2Base.asp?VarCN=513. Contact office at 785-742-3741 8AM-5PM; subscription for $250.00 per yr. **Other phones:** Treasurer- 785-742-2051; Elections- 785-742-2581. **Property tax/Assessing-** 601 Oregon St, Hiawatha, KS 66434; 785-742-7232, assessor fax-785-742-7661. (Appraiser/Auditor- 785-742-7232) **Online access-** Search assessment data free or by subscription at www.brown.kansasgov.com/parcel/.

Butler County

County Register of Deeds, 205 W Central, #104; Courthouse, El Dorado, KS 67042. Recording, R/E & UCC phone-316-322-4113, UCC recording phone-316-322-4112; fax-316-322-4118; 8AM-5PM (CST) www.bucoks.com/depts/regdeeds/register_of_deeds.htm
Index: Separate indices to search include land books, Grantee/Grantor book, computer. Land book index back to 1961. Records indexed on a public use terminal back to 1993; grantor/grantee index back to 1868. Office will perform a UCC search back to 1993 but public must search other records themselves. Search fee $15.00 per name. Office will not do title searches. UCC requests must be in writing on Information Request form. Copy fee $1.00 per page. Cert fee- $1.00 per cert plus copy fee. Payee- Butler County Register of Deeds. Office does not sell bulk data. **Online access to Real Estate, Grantor/Grantee, Deed, Lien records:** An index of recorded real estate records from 1993 forward at www.bucoks.com/depts/regdeeds/disclaimer.htm. **Other phones:** Treasurer- 316-322-4210; Elections-316-322-4233; Vital Records- 785-296-1400 (State of Kansas). **Property tax/Assessing-** 205 W Central, Courthouse, #104, El Dorado, KS 67042; 316-321-4220, assessor fax- 316-321-1011. (Appraiser/Auditor- 316-322-4220) **Online-** Access the appraiser's Real Estate Market Values data free at www.bucoks.com/depts/appr/values/values.htm. No name searching. Also search tax and property data at www.bucoks.com/depts/regdeeds/disclaimer.htm.

Chase County

County Register of Deeds, PO Box 253, Cottonwood Falls, KS 66845-0529. Recording, R/E & UCC phone-620-273-6398; fax-620-273-6617; 8AM-5PM
Index: Separate indices to search include UCC, numerical land. Records indexed on computer back to 1996. Office personnel or visitors may perform searches. General search fee $5.00 per name. UCC or tax lien search per debtor name- $15.00. Copy fee $1.00 per page. Cert fee- $1.00 per cert plus $.50 per page copy fee. Payee- Chase County Register of Deeds. **Other phones:** Treasurer- 620-273-6493; Elections- 620-273-6423; Vital Records- 620-273-6398. **Property tax/Assessing-** PO Box 529, 220 Broadway St, Cottonwood Falls, KS 66845-0529; 620-273-6423, assessor fax- 620-273-6617. (Appraiser/Auditor- 620-273-6306) Public access terminal at district court ofc.

Chautauqua County

County Register of Deeds, 215 N Chautauqua; Courthouse, Sedan, KS 67361. 620-725-5830; fax-620-725-5831; 8AM-N,1-4PM (CST)
Index: All in one. Record index not computerized. Office personnel or visitors may perform searches. Search fee $15.00 per name. Office will not search real estate records. Copy fee $1.00 per page. Cert fee- $1.00 per cert plus copy fee. Payee- Chautauqua County Register of Deeds. **Other phones:** Treasurer-620-725-5800. **Property tax/Assessing-** 215 N Chautauqua, Sedan, KS 67361; 620-725-5820, fax-620-725-5823.

Cherokee County

County Register of Deeds, PO Box 228, Columbus, KS 66725. Recording, R/E & UCC phone-620-429-3777; fax-620-429-1362; 9AM-5PM (CST)
Index: All in one. Records indexed on a public use terminal back to 4/1/05. Only the public may search. Copy fee $1.00 per page. Cert fee- $1.00 per cert plus copy fee. Payee- Cherokee County Register of Deeds. **Other phones:** Treasurer- 620-429-2418; Elections-620-429-8043; Vital Records- 620-429-3880. **Property tax/Assessing-** 110 W Maple, Columbus, KS 66725; 620-429-3984, assessor fax- 620-429-1985. (Appraiser/Auditor- 620-429-3984)

Cheyenne County

County Register of Deeds, PO Box 907, St. Francis, KS 67756-0907. Recording, R/E & UCC phone-785-332-8820; fax-785-332-8825; 8AM-N,1-5PM (CST) www.cheyennecounty.org
Index: Separate indices to search include books. Record index not computerized. Only the public may search. Copy fee $1.00 per page if clerk does it, $.50 per page self serve. Real estate record copy- $.35 per page. Cert fee- $1.00 per cert plus copy fee. Payee- Cheyenne County Register of Deeds. **Other phones:** Treasurer- 785-332-8810; Elections- 785-332-8800; Vital Records- 785-332-8850. **Property tax/Assessing-** PO Box 782, 212 E Washington St, St. Francis, KS 67756-0907; 785-332-8830, assessor fax- 878-332-8825. (Appraiser/Auditor- 785-332-8830) hours- 8AM-5PM www.cheyennecounty.org/appraiser.htm

Clark County

County Register of Deeds, PO Box 222, Ashland, KS 67831-0222. Recording, R/E & UCC phone-620-635-2812; fax-620-635-2393; 8:30AM-4:30PM (CST) www.clarkcountyks.com/page.php?8
Index: Separate indices to search include books. Records indexed on computer. Office will perform a UCC search (only by written request) but public must search other records themselves. Copy fee $.25 per page. Cert fee- $1.00 per cert plus copy fee. Payee-Clark County Register of Deeds. **Other phones:** Treasurer- 620-635-2745; Elections- 620-635-2813; Vital Records- 795-296-1400. **Property tax/Assessing-** 813 Highland, Courthouse, Ashland, KS 67831; 620-635-2142, assessor fax- 620-635-2393. (auditor- 620-635-2142);

Clay County

County Register of Deeds, PO Box 63, Clay Center, KS 67432. Recording, R/E & UCC phone-785-632-3811; fax-785-632-2736; 8AM-5PM (CST)
Index: All in one. Records indexed on a public use terminal back to 1997. Only the public may search. Copy fee $1.00 per page.Real estate or tax lien copy-$.50 per page. Cert fee- $1.00 per cert plus copy fee. Payee- Clay County Register of Deeds. **Other phones:** Treasurer- 785-632-3282; Elections- 785-632-2552; Vital Records- 795-296-1400. **Property tax/Assessing-** PO Box 806, 712 5th St, Clay Center, KS 67432; 785-632-2800, fax- 785-632-5264.

Cloud County

County Register of Deeds, PO Box 96, Concordia, KS 66901-0096. Recording, R/E & UCC phone-785-243-8121; fax-785-243-8123; 8AM-4:30PM (CST) www.cloudcountyks.org/MV2Base.asp?VarCN=57
Index: All in one. Records indexed on a public use terminal back to 1997. Office personnel or visitors may perform searches. Search fee $15.00 per name. Office will not search real estate records. UCC search includes tax liens. Copy fee $1.00 per page. Cert fee-$3.00 per cert includes copy fee. Payee- Cloud County Register of Deeds. **Other phones:** Treasurer-785-243-8115; Elections- 785-243-8110; Vital Records- 785-243-8123; State Office- 785-296-1401. **Property tax/Assessing-** 811 Washington St, Concordia, KS 66901; 785-243-8100, assessor fax-785-243-8105. (Appraiser/Auditor- 785-243-8100) Bulk data available for purchase; inquire at office. www.cloudcountyks.org **Online access-** Search property tax information free at www.cloud.kansasgov.com/Tax/. Parcel searches free at www.cloudcountyks.org/Parcel/

Coffey County

County Register of Deeds, 110 S 6th St, Rm 205; Courthouse, Burlington, KS 66839. 620-364-2423; fax-620-364-8975; 8AM-5PM (CST) www.coffeycountyks.org
Index: Separate indices to search include deed, mortgage, misc or oil & gas books. All documents indexed by legal description or in misc books. Records indexed on a public use terminal back to 1998. Office personnel or visitors may perform searches. Search fee $15.00. Office will not search real estate records. UCC search includes tax liens. Copy fee $1.00 per page.Real estate record copy- $.50 per page. Fee to fax results $2.00 per page. Cert fee-$1.00 per cert plus copy fee. Payee- Coffey County Register of Deeds. **Online access to Marriage records:** Access to marriage records is by alpha search up to 1/18/2001 for free at www.kscourts.org/dstcts/4osmarec.htm. **Other phones:** Treasurer- 620-364-5532; Elections- 620-364-2191. **Property tax/Assessing-** County Appraiser, 110 S 6th St Rm 206, Burlington, KS 66839; 620-364-8426, assessor fax- 620-364-8428. No public access computer. www.coffeycountyks.org/service3.html

Comanche County

County Register of Deeds, PO Box 576, Coldwater, KS 67029-0576. Recording, R/E & UCC phone-620-582-2152; fax-620-582-2390; 9AM-N,1-5PM (CST)
Index: Separate indices to search include tract, grantor/grantee. Records indexed on a public use terminal back to 1/2/2005. Office will perform a UCC or tax lien search but public must search other records themselves. Search fee $15.00 per name. Copy fee $.50 per page. Cert fee- $1.00 per cert plus copy fee. Payee- Comanche County Register of Deeds. **Other phones:** Treasurer- 620-582-2964; Elections- 620-582-2361. **Property tax/Assessing-** 201 S New York, Courthouse, Coldwater, KS 67029; 620-582-2544, assessor fax- 620-582-2544. (Appraiser/Auditor- 620-582-2544)

Cowley County

County Register of Deeds, PO Box 741, Winfield, KS 67156-0471. 620-221-5461; fax-620-221-5463; 8AM-N,1-5PM (CST)
Index: All in one. Records indexed on a public use terminal back to 1989. Only the public may search. Copy fee $1.00 per page. Cert fee- $1.00 per cert plus copy fee. Payee- Cowley County Register of Deeds. Maps, etc. available for purchase in print form. **Other phones:** Treasurer- 620-221-5412; Vital Records-795-296-1400. **Property tax/Assessing-** PO Box 641, 311 E 9th St, Courthouse, Winfield, KS 67156; 620-221-5430, assessor fax- 620-221-5442. (Appraiser/Auditor- 620-221-5431) hours- 8AM-5PM Public access terminal available. www.cowleycounty.org/appraiser.asp **Online** - Search property data free at www.cowleycounty.org/parcel/V2RunLev2.asp?submit1=OK.

Crawford County

County Register of Deeds, PO Box 44, Girard, KS 66743. Recording, R/E & UCC phone-620-724-8218; fax-620-724-8823; 8:30AM-4:30PM (CST)
Index: All in one. Record index not computerized. Office will perform a UCC search but public must search other records themselves. Search fee $8.00 per name. Office will search real estate records. Copy fee $1.00 per page.Real estate record copy- $.50 per page. Cert fee- $1.00 per cert plus copy fee. Payee-Crawford County Register of Deeds. **Online access to Real Estate, Deed, Lien records:** Recorder land data

by subscription on either the Laredo system using subscription and fees or the Tapestry System using credit card, http://tapestry.fidlar.com; $3.99 search; $1.00 per image. Index goes back to 1991; images to 8/1/99. **Other phones:** Treasurer- 620-724-8222; Elections- 620-724-6115; Vital Records- 620-724-6211. **Property tax/Assessing**- PO Box 217, 111 E Forest, Girard, KS 66743; 620-724-6431, assessor fax- 620-724-8171.

Decatur County

County Register of Deeds, PO Box 167, Oberlin, KS 67749-0167. Recording, R/E & UCC phone-785-475-8105; fax-785-475-8150; 8AM-N, 1PM-5PM (CST)
Index: Separate indexs to search include numeric, real estate descriptions, UCC and misc. Record index not computerized. Office personnel or visitors may perform searches. No fee for search. Office will search real estate records phone request by legal description; last deed, last mortgage of record only. Office will search UCC records with a written request and $15.00 per name. Copy fee $.25 per page. Cert fee- $1.00 per cert includes plus copy fee. Payee- Decatur County Register of Deeds. **Other phones:** Treasurer- 785-475-8103; Elections- 785-475-8102; Vital Records- 785-475-8105; County Clerk- 785-475-8102. **Property tax/Assessing**- PO Box 28, 120 E Hall, Oberlin, KS 67749-0028; 785-475-8109, assessor fax- 785-475-8130. (Appraiser/Auditor- 785-475-8109).

Dickinson County

County Register of Deeds, PO Box 517, Abilene, KS 67410. Recording, R/E & UCC phone-785-263-3073; fax-785-263-0428; hours- 8AM-5PM (CST) http://dkcoks.org/index.asp?nid=69
Index: Separate indices to search include deed, mortgage, misc. Records indexed on a public use terminal back to 2000. Office will perform a UCC search but public must search other records themselves. Copy fee $.50 per page. UCC copy $1.00 per page. Cert fee- $1.00 per cert plus copy fee. Payee- Dickinson County Register of Deeds. **Other phones:** Treasurer- 785-263-3231; Elections- 785-263-3774; Vital Records- 785-263-3073. **Property tax/Assessing**- 1st & Buckeye Sts, Courthouse, Abilene, KS 67410; 785-263-4418, assessor fax- 785-263-0061. www.dkcoks.org/inde x.asp?nid=56 **Online access**- Access property tax data free at www.dickinson.kansasgov.com/parcel/

Doniphan County

County Register of Deeds, PO Box 73, Troy, KS 66087. Recording, R/E & UCC phone-785-985-3932; fax-785-985-3723; 8AM-5PM www.dpcountyks.com
Index: All in one. Record index not computerized. Office personnel or visitors may perform searches. Search fee $15.00 per search. Copy fee $.50 per page. UCC's $1.00 per page. Cert fee- $1.00 per cert plus copy fee. Payee- Doniphan County Register of Deeds. **Other phones:** Treasurer- 785-985-3831; Elections-785-985-3513. **Property tax/Assessing**- 120 E Chestnut St,, Troy, KS 66087; 785-985-3977, assessor fax- 785-985-3723. (Appraiser/Auditor- 785-985-3977).

Douglas County

County Register of Deeds, 1100 Massachusetts; Courthouse, Lawrence, KS 66044-3097. 785-832-5282/5283, R/E recording phone-785-832-5282, UCC recording phone-785-832-5283; fax-785-330-2807; 8AM-5PM (CST) www.douglas-county.com
Index: All in one. Records indexed on a public use terminal back to 1990. Also, written land indexes. Office will perform a UCC search (with request form plus payment) but public must search other records themselves. Search fee $15.00 per name. Office will not search real estate records. Copy fee $.50 per page. UCC copy $1.00 per page. Plat copy $5.00 each (25 X 36). Cert fee- $1.00 per document plus copy fee. Payee- Douglas County Register of Deeds. Electronic/CD/DVD bulk data available for purchase, contact office with inquiry. Must be accompanied by written request. **Online access to Real Estate, Deed, Lien, Court, Voter Registration records:** Register of Deeds data by subscription; for info and signup call IT Dept at 785-832-5183/5299. Yearly sub is $360 plus $60 setup fee and may include courts. Check voter registration names at www.douglas-county.com/clerk/regvoters.asp. **Other phones:** Treasurer- 785-841-5105; Elections- 785-832-5267. **Property tax/Assessing**- 1100 Massachusetts, Courthouse, Lawrence, KS 66044-3097; 785-832-5133, assessor fax- 785-841-0021. (Appraiser/Auditor- 785-832-5290) Public access terminal for in-office searches. **Online access**- Two sites provide free access to assessor records. Find County Property Appraiser records at www.douglas-county.com/value/disclaimer.asp. Property valuations also free at http://old.hometown.lawrence.com/valuation/valuation.cgi. Also, view parcel property on GIS mapping site free at www.douglas-county.com/egovt/mapviewer.asp - no name search.

Edwards County

County Register of Deeds, PO Box 264, Kinsley, KS 67547-0264. Recording, R/E & UCC phone-620-659-3131, UCC recording phone-620-657-3131; fax-620-659-2583; 8AM-5PM (CST)
Index: Separate indices to search include deeds, mortgages, misc. Record index not computerized. Office will perform a UCC search but public must search other records themselves. Copy fee $1.00 per page. Cert fee- $1.00 per cert plus copy fee. Payee- Edwards County Register of Deeds. **Other phones:** Treasurer- 620-659-3132; Elections- 620-659-3000; Vital Records- 795-296-1400. **Property tax/Assessing**- 312 Massachusetts, Kinsley, KS 67547; 620-659-3001, fax- 620-659-2583. (Appraiser - 620-659-3001);

Elk County

County Register of Deeds, PO Box 476, Howard, KS 67349-0476. Recording, R/E & UCC phone-620-374-2472; fax-620-374-2771; 7AM-5:30PM M-TH (Closed Fri). (CST)
Index: Separate indices to search include mortgages, affidavits. Record index not computerized. Office personnel or visitors may perform searches. Search fee $5.00 per name for real estate and geneology. Office will search real estate records. Will search UCC records for a charge of $15.00 per written request. Copy fee $1.00 per page.Real estate record copy- $.25 per page. Cert fee- $1.00 per cert plus copy fee. Payee- Elk County Register of Deeds. **Other phones:** Treasurer- 620-374-2256; Elections- 620-374-2490; Vital Records- 620-374-2370. **Property tax/Assessing**- 127 N Pine, Howard, KS 67349; 620-374-2832, assessor fax- 620-374-3510. (Appraiser/Auditor- 620-374-2832);

Ellis County

County Register of Deeds, PO Box 654, Hays, KS 67601. 785-628-9450, R/E recording phone-785-628-9452, UCC recording phone-785-628-9450; fax-785-628-9451; 8AM-5PM (CST) www.ksrods.org
Index: All in one. Records indexed on a public use terminal back to 1987. Office personnel or visitors may perform searches. Search fee $15.00 per debtor. Office will search real estate records. UCC search includes tax liens if requested. Copy fee $1.00 per page.Real estate record copy- $.25 per page. Cert fee- $1.00 per cert plus copy fee. Payee- Ellis County Register of Deeds. Bulk data available for purchase of real estate (buyer history) and geneolgy searches, contact office. **Other phones:** Treasurer- 785-628-9466; Elections- 785-628-9410; Vital Records- 785-628-9450; Second Phone- 785-628-9452; District Court -785-628-9417;. **Property tax/Assessing**- 1204 Fort St, PO Box 309, Hays, KS 67601; 785-628-9400, assessor fax- 785-628-9403. (Appraiser - 785-628-9400) www.ellisco.net/index.asp?DocumentID=220 **Online** - Access to assessor property data is available free at www.ellisco.net/index.asp?page=app_search.

Ellsworth County

County Register of Deeds, 210 N Kansas #7; Courthouse, Ellsworth, KS 67439-3110. 785-472-3022; fax-785-472-4912; 8AM-5PM (CST) www.ellsworthcounty.org
Index: All in one. Records indexed on computer back to 1995. Office will perform a UCC search (for a fee) but public must search other records themselves. Copy fee $1.00 per page. Cert fee- $1.00 per cert plus $.25 copy fee. Payee- Ellsworth County Register of Deeds. **Other phones:** Treasurer- 785-472-4152; Elections- 785-472-4161. **Property tax/Assessing**- 210 N Kansas, #7, Courthouse, Ellsworth, KS 67439-3110; 785-472-3165, assessor fax- 785-472-3110.

Finney County

County Register of Deeds, PO Box M, Garden City, KS 67846. Recording, R/E & UCC phone-620-272-3520; fax-620-272-3624; 8AM-5PM (CST) www.finneycounty.org
Index: All in one. Records indexed on a public use terminal back to 1988. Office personnel or visitors may perform searches. Search fee $15.00 per name. Office will search real estate records. Will search UCC records. Copy fee $.25 per sheet, $1.00 minimum charge. Cert fee- $1.00 per cert plus copy fee. Payee- Finney County Register of Deeds. **Online access to Real Estate, Liens, Parcel records:** Access to records for free go to www.efinneycounty.net/parcel/. **Other phones:** Treasurer- 620-373-3526; Elections- 620-272-3523. **Property tax/Assessing**- PO Box 873, Garden City, KS 67846; 620-272-3517, assessor fax- 620-272-3851. (Appraiser/Auditor- 620-272-3585) **Online access**- GIS-Map searching available free at www.finneycounty.net/publicaccess.htm.

Ford County

County Register of Deeds, PO Box 1352, Dodge City, KS 67801-1352. Recording, R/E & UCC phone-620-227-4565, UCC recording phone-620-227-4568; fax-620-227-4566; 9AM-5PM (CST)
Index: Separate indices to search include deeds, mortgage, mortgage release, oil & gas, oil & gas assign and release, and miscellaneous. Records indexed on a public use terminal back to 4/01. Only the public may search. Copy fee $.50 per page. UCC copy fee- $1.00 per page. Fax back- $1.00 plus $.50 per page. Cert fee- $1.00 per cert plus copy fee. Payee- Ford County Register of Deeds. **Other phones:** Treasurer- 620-227-4535; Elections- 620-227-4553. **Property tax/Assessing**- 100 Gunsmoke, 3rd Fl, Dodge City, KS 67801; 620-227-4516. (Appraiser/Auditor- 620-227-4570) **Online access**- Property information including parcels and taxes are available at www.fordcounty.net/

Franklin County

County Register of Deeds, 315 S Main, Rm 103; Courthouse, Ottawa, KS 66067-2335. 785-229-3440; fax-785-229-3441; 8-4:30PM www.franklincoks.org
Index: All in one. Records indexed on a public use terminal back to 1993. Office will perform a UCC and Tax lien search but public must search other records themselves. Search fee $15.00. Office will look up current owner for real estate only. Copy fee $.25 per page. Cert fee- $1.00 per cert plus copy fee. Payee- Franklin County Register of Deeds. **Other phones:** Treasurer- 785-229-3450; Elections- 785-229-3410; Vitals- 785-229-6000. **Property tax/Assessing**- 315 Main St, Courthouse, Ottawa, KS 66067-2335; 785-229-3420, assessor fax- 785-229-3430.

Geary County

County Register of Deeds, PO Box 927, Junction City, KS 66441-2591. 785-238-5531; fax-785-762-2642; 8:30AM-5PM (CST) www.geary.kansasgov.com/MV2Base.asp?VarCN=171
Index: Separate indices to search include land records/deeds. Records indexed on a public use terminal. Only the public may search. Copy fee $1.00 per page. Cert fee- $1.00 per cert plus copy fee. Payee- Geary County Register of Deeds. **Online**

access to Real Estate, Deed records: County offers a fee system to access recorded document index and images. Index goes back to 1992, images back to 1/2001, using the DMS On-line Access Module. Webpage has limited info about registering; call the office for an information packet. **Other phones:** Treasurer- 785-238-3912; Elections- 785-238-5531; Vital Records- 795-296-1400. **Property tax/Assessing**- 200 E 8th St, County Office Bldg, Junction City, KS 66441; 785-238-4407, fax- 785-762-4670. www.geary.kansasgov.com/MV2Base.asp?VarCN=192 **Online access**- With registration or without, search the parcel search database free at www.geary.kansasgov.com/parcel/v2loginreg.asp.

Gove County

County Register of Deeds, PO Box 116, Gove, KS 67736. Recording, R/E & UCC phone-785-938-4465; fax-785-938-4486; 8AM-N, 12:30-4:30PM (CST)
Index: All in one. Records indexed on a public use terminal back 2 years. Office personnel or visitors may perform searches. Search fee $15.00 per name. Copy fee $.50 per page; UCC copy $1.00 per page. Cert fee- $1.00 per cert plus copy fee. Payee- Gove County Register of Deeds. **Other phones:** Treasurer- 785-938-2275; Elections- 785-938-2300; Vital Records- 785-938-4465. **Property tax/Assessing**- PO Box 128, 520 Washington St, Gove, KS 67736; 785-938-2301, assessor- 785-938-4486. (Appraiser/Auditor- 785-938-2301) hours- 8AM-4:30PM

Graham County

County Register of Deeds, 410 N Pomeroy, Hill City, KS 67642. Recording, R/E & UCC phone-785-421-2551; fax-785-421-2784; 8AM-5PM (CST) www.grahamcountyks.com/page.php?4
Index: Separate indices to search include 5 tract indexes and 1 misc. Records indexed on a public use terminal. Office personnel or visitors may perform searches. Search fee $15.00 per name. Office will perform limited real estate record searches. Copy fee $1.00 per page. Cert fee- $1.00 per cert plus copy fee. Payee- Graham County Register of Deeds. **Other phones:** Treasurer- 785-674-2331; Elections- 785-421-2551; Vital Records- 795-296-1400. **Property tax/Assessing**- Appraiser, 401 N Pomeroy, Hill City, KS 67642; 785-674-2196, assessor fax- 785-421-2199. www.grahamcountyks.com/page.php?28

Grant County

County Register of Deeds, 108 S Glenn, Lower Level, Ulysses, KS 67880. Recording, R/E & UCC phone-620-356-1538; fax-620-356-5379; 9AM-5PM (CST)
Index: All in one. Record index not computerized. Only the public may search. Copy fee $1.00 per page. Cert fee- $1.00 per cert plus copy fee. Payee- Grant County Register of Deeds. **Other phones:** Treasurer-620-356-1551; Elections- 620-356-1335. **Property tax/Assessing**- 108 S Glenn, Ulysses, KS 67880; 620-356-3362, assessor fax- 620-424-1852. (Appraiser/Auditor- 620-356-3362)

Gray County

County Register of Deeds, PO Box 487, Cimarron, KS 67835-0487. 620-855-3835; fax-620-855-3107; 8AM-5PM (CST)
Index: Separate indices to search include range index and city index. Records indexed on a public use terminal back to 1999. Office personnel or visitors may perform searches. Search fee $15.00 per name. Office will search limited real estate records. Copy fee $.50 per page. Fax fee $1.00 per page. Cert fee- $1.00 per cert plus copy fee. Payee- Gray County Register of Deeds. **Other phones:** Treasurer- 620-855-3861; Elections- 620-855-3618. **Property tax/Assessing**- Gray County Appraiser's Office, Rm 102, PO Box 487, 300 S Main St, Cimarron, KS 67835-0487; 620-855-3858, assessor fax- 620-855-3107. (Appraiser/Auditor- 620-855-3858) fax number is for Register of Deeds office. Public access terminal available.

Greeley County

County Register of Deeds, PO Box 12, Tribune, KS 67879. 620-376-4275; fax-620-376-2294; 9AM-5PM (MST) www.greeleycountygovernment.org
Index: All in one. Records indexed on computer back to 1995. Office personnel or visitors may perform searches. Office will not search real estate records. UCC search includes tax liens. UCC search per debtor name- $15.00. Separate federal/state combined tax lien search- $8.00 per debtor. Copy fee $1.00 per page. Cert fee- $1.00 per doc plus copy fee. Payee- Greeley County Register of Deeds. **Other phones:** Treasurer- 620-376-4413. **Property tax/Assessing**- PO Box 140, 208 Harper, Tribune, KS 67879; 620-376-4057, assessor fax- 620-376-4359.

Greenwood County

County Register of Deeds, 311 N Main; Courthouse, Eureka, KS 67045-1311. 620-583-8162; fax-620-583-8178; 8AM-5PM (CST) www.greenwoodcounty.org/
Index: Separate indices to search include books. Records indexed on a public use terminal back to current owner. Office personnel or visitors may perform searches. Search fee $15.00 per name. Office will not search real estate records. Will search UCC records. Copy fee $1.00 per page, $.75 for mail copy. Cert fee- $1.00 per cert plus copy fee. Payee- Greenwood County Register of Deeds. **Other phones:** Treasurer- 620-583-8146; Vital Records-795-296-1400. **Property tax/Assessing**- 311 N Main, Courthouse, Eureka, KS 67045; 620-583-7431, assessor fax- 620-583-6013.

Hamilton County

County Register of Deeds, PO Box 1167, Syracuse, KS 67878. Recording, R/E & UCC phone-620-384-6925; fax-620-384-5853; 8AM-N, 1-4:30PM (MST)
Index: All in one. Record index not computerized. Office personnel or visitors may perform searches. Search fee $15.00. Real estate search is for last recorded deed only. Office does not perform UCC searches. Copy fee $.25 per page, UCC copies $1.00 per page. Cert fee- $1.00 per doc plus copy fee. Payee- Hamilton County Register of Deeds. **Other phones:** Treasurer- 620-384-5522. **Property tax/Assessing**- 219 N Main, Syracuse, KS 67878; 620-384-5451, assessor fax- 620-384-5853. (Auditor- 620-384-5451)

Harper County

County Register of Deeds, 201 N Jennings; Courthouse, Anthony, KS 67003. Recording, R/E & UCC phone-620-842-5336; fax-620-842-3455; 8AM-5PM (CST) www.harpercountyks.gov
Index: Separate indices to search include deeds, mortgages, oil & gas, misc. Records indexed on a public use terminal back to 10/17/2005. Office will perform a UCC search but public must search other records themselves. Search fee-$15.00 for UCC. Copy fee $1.00 per page. Cert fee- $1.00 per cert plus copy fee. Payee- Harper County Register of Deeds. **Other phones:** Treasurer- 620-842-5191; Elections- 620-842-5555. **Property tax/Assessing**- 201 N Jennings, Anthony, KS 67003; 620-842-3718, assessor fax- 620-842-3455. Public access terminal available.

Harvey County

County Register of Deeds, PO Box 687, Newton, KS 67114-0687. Recording, R/E & UCC phone-316-284-6950; fax-316-284-6951; 8AM-5PM (CST) www.harveycounty.com
Index: Separate indices to search include tract books. Records indexed back to 1872. Office personnel (acting on an information request) or visitors may perform searches. Search fee $15.00 per name. Office will search real estate records for last deed only. Office will search UCC records with correct filing request. Copy fee $1.00 per page. Cert fee- $1.00 per cert plus copy fee. Payee- Harvey County Register of Deeds. **Other phones:** Treasurer- 316-284-6976; Elections- 316-284-6842. **Property tax/Assessing**- 800 N Main St, Newton, KS 67114; 316-284-6815. (Appraiser/Auditor- 316-284-6815) **Online access**- Access property tax records from the appraiser and treasurer free at www.harvey.kansasgov.com/parcel/DisclaimerLev2.asp. Also, with registration and password you may access deeper property data at www.harvey.kansasgov.com/parcel/v2loginreg.asp.

Haskell County

County Register of Deeds, PO Box 656, Sublette, KS 67877. 620-675-8343; fax-620-675-8329; 9AM-N,1PM-5PM www.haskellcounty.org/register.html
Index: Separate indices to search include deeds, mortgages, misc. Records indexed on a public use terminal. They are working on going all the way back to the beginning. Office personnel or visitors may perform searches. Search fee $15.00 per name. Office will search real estate records for $10.00 per hour. Copy fee $.25 per page. Fax fee $2.00 plus copy fee. Cert fee- $1.00 per cert plus copy fee. Payee- Haskell County Register of Deeds. **Other phones:** Treasurer-620-675-2265; Elections- 620-675-2263. **Property tax/Assessing**- 300 S Inmann, Sublette, KS 67877; 620-675-8269, assessor fax- 620-675-2681.

Hodgeman County

County Register of Deeds, PO Box 505, Jetmore, KS 67854-0505. Recording, R/E & UCC phone-620-357-8536; 9AM-N, 1PM-5PM (CST)
Index: Separate indices to search include city and rural in two different books. Record index not computerized. Office personnel will perform small searches or visitors may perform searches. Search fee $15.00 per name. Office will not search real estate records. UCC search request must be on proper form. Copy fee $1.00 per page' plats/maps- $5.00. Cert fee- $1.00 per cert plus copy fee. Payee- Hodgeman County Register of Deeds. **Other phones:** Treasurer-620-357-6236; Elections- 620-330-1200 (County Clerk); Vital Records- 795-296-1400. **Property tax/Assessing**- PO Box 247, 500 Main St, Courthouse, Jetmore, KS 67854; 620-357-8366, assessor fax- 620-357-8300.

Jackson County

County Register of Deeds, 415 New York, Rm 203; Courthouse, Holton, KS 66436. 785-364-3591; fax-785-364-3420; 8AM-4:30PM (CST)
Index: Separate indices to search include land tract index and computer. Records indexed on a public use terminal back to 1988. Office will perform a UCC search but public must search other records themselves. Search fee $15.00 for UCC search. Office will not search real estate records. Copy fee $1.00 per page.Real estate record copy- $.25 per page after the first. Cert fee- $1.00 per cert plus copy fee. Payee- Jackson County Register of Deeds. **Other phones:** Treasurer- 785-364-3791; Elections- 785-364-5200. **Property tax/Assessing**- 400 New York Ave, Holton, KS 66436; 785-364-2358, assessor fax- 785-364-5257. (Appraiser/Auditor- 785-364-5256)

Jefferson County

County Register of Deeds, PO Box 352, Oskaloosa, KS 66066-0352. Recording, R/E & UCC phone-785-863-2243; fax-785-863-2602; 8AM-6:30PM M; 8AM-4PM T-F. (CST) www.jfcountyks.com
Index: All in one. Records indexed on computer back to 1997. Office will perform a UCC search but public must search other records themselves. General index search fee $15.00 per hour. Office will not search real estate records. Copy fee $1.00 per page. Cert fee- $1.00 per cert plus copy fee. Payee- Jefferson County Register of Deeds. Treasurer- 785-863-2691; Elections- 785-863-2272; Vitals- 785-296-1400. **Property tax/Assessing**- PO Box 331, Oskaloosa, KS 66066; 785-863-2080, assessor fax- 785-863-2069. (Appraiser - 785-863-2552) http://appraiser.jfcountyks.com/ **Online access**- Access parcel data free at http://appraiser.jfcountyks.com/parcel/disclaimerlev2.asp. Registration and login required for full data.

Jewell County

County Register of Deeds, 307 N Commercial St; Courthouse, Mankato, KS 66956-2093. Recording, R/E & UCC phone-785-378-4070; fax-785-378-4075; 8:30AM-N, 1-4:30PM (CST)
Index: Separate indices to search. Record index not computerized. Office personnel or visitors may perform searches. Limit on amount done by office personnel. Index search fee $5.00 per hour. Office will search limited real estate records. Will search limited UCC records and fee charged. Copy fee $1.00 per page. Cert fee- $1.00 per cert plus copy fee. Payee- Jewell County Register of Deeds. **Other phones:** Treasurer- 785-378-4090; Elections- 785-378-4020. **Property tax/Assessing-** 307 N Commercial, Mankato, KS 66956; 785-378-4000, assessor fax- 785-378-4075. (Appraiser/Auditor- 785-378-4000);

Johnson County

County Register of Deeds, PO Box 700, Olathe, KS 66051. 913-715-0775, R/E recording phone-913-715-2600, UCC recording phone-913-715-2300; fax-913-715-0800; 8AM-5PM (CST) http://rta.jocogov.org/
Index: All in one. Records indexed on a public use terminal back to 1987. Office personnel or visitors may perform searches. General search fee $8.00 per name. Office will not search real estate records. UCC search per debtor name- $20.00. Copy fee $1.00 per page. Cert fee- $1.00 per cert plus copy fee. Payee- Department of Records & Tax Administration, or RTA. **Other phones:** Treasurer- 913-715-2600; Elections- 913-782-3441; Vital Records- 795-296-1400. **Property tax/Assessing-** 11811 S Sunset Dr, #2100, Olathe, KS 66061; 913-715-9000, assessor fax- 913-715-0010. http://appraiser.jocogov.org/ **Online access-** Search records on the Land Records database free at http://land.jocogov.org/default.aspx - no name search.

Kearny County

County Register of Deeds, PO Box 42, Lakin, KS 67860. Recording, R/E & UCC phone-620-355-6241; fax-620-355-7382; 8AM-5PM (CST)
Index: All in one. Records indexed on a public use terminal back to 1991. Office will perform a UCC search (with proper forms and fees) but public must search other records themselves. Search fee $15.00 per name. Office will not search real estate records. Copy fee $1.00 per page for UCC.Real estate record copy- $.25 per page. Cert fee- $1.00 per cert plus copy fee. Payee- Kearny County Register of Deeds. **Other phones:** Treasurer- 620-355-6372; Elections- 620-355-6422; Vital Records- 795-785-1400. **Property tax/Assessing-** 304 N Main St, PO Box 1250, Lakin, KS 67860; 620-355-6427, assessor fax- 620-355-6404. (Appraiser/Auditor- 620-355-6427) No public terminal available in office, office personnel will perform searches. Terminal available in Register of Deeds office.

Kingman County

County Register of Deeds, 130 N Spruce, Kingman, KS 67068. Recording, R/E & UCC phone-620-532-3211; fax-620-532-5079; 8AM--5PM (CST)
Index: All in one. Record index not computerized. Office personnel or visitors may perform searches. Office will not search real estate records. UCC search per debtor name- $15.00. Copy fee $1.00 per page. Cert fee- $1.00 per cert plus copy fee. Payee- Kingman County Register of Deeds. **Other phones:** Treasurer- 620-532-3461; Elections- 620-532-2521. **Property tax/Assessing-** 130 N Spruce, Kingman, KS 67068; 620-532-3356, assessor fax- 620-532-3732. (Appraiser/Auditor- 620-532-2256)

Kiowa County

County Register of Deeds, 211 E Florida, Greensburg, KS 67054. 620-723-2441; fax-620-723-3302; 8AM-5PM www.kiowacounty.us/registerofdeeds.htm
Index: All in one. Record index not computerized. Office personnel or visitors may perform searches. Search fee $15.00. Office will search real estate records. Copy fee $1.00 per page. Cert fee- $1.00 per cert plus copy fee. Payee- Kiowa County Register of Deeds. **Other phones:** Treasurer- 620-723-2681. **Property tax/Assessing-** 211 E Florida, Greensburg, KS 67054; 620-723-3366. (Appraiser 620-723-3301)

Labette County

Register of Deeds, 521 Merchant; Courthouse, Oswego, KS 67356. Recording, R/E & UCC phone-620-795-4931; fax-620-795-2212; 8AM-5PM (CST)
Index: Separate indices to search include legal. Records (deeds only) indexed on computer back to 1999. Office will perform a UCC search up to 5 years, on UCC search form only, but public must search other records themselves. Search fee-$15.00 UCC. Office will search real estate records (last deed only). UCC search per debtor name- $15.00. Copy fee $.25 per page. Cert fee- $1.50 per cert plus copy fee. Payee- Labette County Register of Deeds. **Other phones:** Treasurer- 620-795-2918; Elections- 620-795-2138. **Property tax/Assessing-** PO Box 387, 501 Merchant, Oswego, KS 67356; 620-795-2548x239. (Appraiser/Auditor- 620-795-2548);

Lane County

County Register of Deeds, PO Box 805, Dighton, KS 67839-0805. Recording, R/E & UCC phone-620-397-2803; fax-620-397-5937; 8AM-N,1-5PM (CST)
Index: Separate indices to search include mortgage, deed, assign, misc indexes. Record index not computerized. Office personnel or visitors may perform searches. Search fee $15.00 per debtor. Real estate owner, mortgage, and property transfer searches available. Will search UCC records. Copy fee $1.00 per document. Cert fee- $1.00 per cert plus copy fee. Payee- Lane County Register of Deeds. **Other phones:** Treasurer- 620-397-2802; Elections- 620-397-5356. **Property tax/Assessing-** PO Box 250, Dighton, KS 67839; 620-397-2804, assessor fax- 620-397-2781. (Appraiser/Auditor- 620-397-2804) hours- 8AM-5PM

Leavenworth County

County Register of Deeds, 300 Walnut, Rm 103; Courthouse, Leavenworth, KS 66048. Recording, R/E & UCC phone-913-684-0424; fax-913-684-0406; 8AM-5PM (CST) www.leavenworthcounty.org
Index: All in one. Records indexed on a public use terminal back to 1995. Office will perform a UCC search but public must search other records themselves. General search fee $8.00 per name. Office will not search real estate records. UCC search per debtor name- $15.00. Copy fee $1.00 for 1st page; $.50 each add'l. Cert fee- $1.00 per cert plus copy fee. Payee- Leavenworth County Register of Deeds. Bulk data available for purchase in subscription form. **Online access to Real Estate, Deed, Lien records:** Recorder land data by subscription on either the Laredo system using subscription and fees or the Tapestry System using credit card, http://tapestry.fidlar.com; $3.99 search; $1.00 per image. **Other phones:** Treasurer- 913-684-0430; Elections- 913-684-0421; Vital Records- 795-296-1400. **Property tax/Assessing-** 300 Walnut, Rm 103, Courthouse, Leavenworth, KS 66048; 913-684-0440, assessor fax- 913-684-2547. (Appraiser/Auditor- 913-684-0440) Public access terminal available. www.leavenworthcounty.org/appr/appr.asp **Online-** Free search of county parcel data at www.leavenworthcounty.org/cama/disclaimerlev1.asp.

Lincoln County

County Register of Deeds, 216 E Lincoln, Lincoln, KS 67455-2056. 785-524-4657; fax-785-524-5003; 8AM-N,12:30PM-4:30PM (CST) www.lincolncoks.com/MV2Base.asp?VarCN=4
Index: Separate indices to search include mtgs, deeds, misc. Records indexed on computer back to 1975. Only the public may search. Copy fee $.35 per page. Cert fee- $1.00 per cert plus copy fee. Payee- Lincoln County Register of Deeds. **Other phones:** Treasurer- 785-524-4190; Elections- 785-524-4757. **Property tax/Assessing-** 216 E Lincoln, Lincoln, KS 67455; 785-524-4657. (Appraiser/Auditor- 785-524-4958) hours- 8AM-4:15PM

Linn County

County Register of Deeds, PO Box 350, Mound City, KS 66056-0350. Recording, R/E & UCC phone-913-795-2226; fax-913-795-2889; 8AM-N, 12:30-4:30PM (CST) www.linncountyks.com
Index: Separate indices to search include range land, subdivisions, cemeteries, UCCs & liens. Records indexed on a public use terminal back 10 + years. Office will perform a UCC search but public must search other records themselves. Search fee $15.00 per name. Office will not search real estate records. Copy fee $1.00 per page for UCC copies. Cert fee- $1.00 per cert plus copy fee. Payee- Linn County Register of Deeds. **Other phones:** Treasurer- 913-795-2227; Elections- 913-795-2668; Vital Records- 913-795-2660. **Property tax/Assessing-** PO Box 350, Mound City, KS 66056-0350; 913-795-2536, assessor fax- 913-795-2889. hours- 8AM-4:30PM www.linncountyks.com/html/appraiser.html **Online access-** Request treasurer's Tax foreclosure sale information at www.linncountyks.com/html/taxsalehome.html. County Maps available at www.linncountyks.com/html/maps.htm.

Logan County

County Register of Deeds, 710 W 2nd St; Courthouse, Oakley, KS 67748. Recording, R/E & UCC phone-785-672-4224; fax-785-672-3517; 8AM-5PM (CST)
Index: All in one. Record index not computerized. Office personnel or visitors may perform searches. Search fee $15.00 per name. Office will not search real estate records. Copy fee $1.00 per page.Real estate or tax lien copy- $.25 per page, $1.00 per page mailed or faxed. Cert fee- $1.00 per cert plus copy fee. Payee- Logan County Register of Deeds. **Other phones:** Treasurer- 785-672-3216; Elections- 785-672-4244; County Clerk- 785-672-4244. **Property tax/Assessing-** 710 W 2nd St, Oakley, KS 67748; 785-672-4821, assessor fax- 785-672-3347. (Appraiser/Auditor- 785-672-4821)

Lyon County

County Register of Deeds, 430 Commercial St, Emporia, KS 66801. Recording, R/E & UCC phone-620-341-3241; fax-620-341-3438; 8AM-5PM (CST) www.lyoncounty.org/Register_of_Deeds.htm
Index: All in one. Record index not computerized. Office personnel or visitors may perform searches. Search fee $15.00 per name. Copy fee $1.00 per page. Cert fee- $1.00 per cert plus copy fee. Payee- Lyon County Register of Deeds. **Property tax/Assessing-** 430 Commercial St, County Courthouse, Emporia, KS 66801; 620-341-3302, assessor fax- 620-341-3249. www.lyoncounty.org/Appraiser.htm **Online-** free parcel data at www.lyoncounty.org/parcel/ or register for full data with the Appraiser's office. Also, check tax sale notices free at www.lyoncounty.org/Tax_Sale_Notices.htm.

Marion County

Register of Deeds, PO Box 158, Marion, KS 66861. 620-382-2151; fax-620-382-3420; 8:30AM-5PM www.marioncoks.net/MV2Base.asp?VarCN=2
Index: Separate indices to search- numerical. Records indexed on a public use terminal back to 2004. Office will perform a UCC search but public must search other records themselves. UCC search per debtor name- $15.00. UCC search includes tax liens if requested. Copy fee $.50 per page. Cert fee- $1.00 per cert plus copy fee. Payee- Marion County Register of Deeds. **Other phones:** Treasurer- 620-382-2180; Elections- 620-382-2185. **Property tax/Assessing-** 200 S 3rd St, #2, Marion, KS 66861; 620-382-3715, assessor fax- 620-382-8400. (Appraiser/Auditor- 620-382-3778) www.marioncoks.net/MV2Base.asp?VarCN=51 **Online access-** Access property tax records at www.marion.kansasgov.com/Tax/TaxSearch.asp.

Marshall County

County Register of Deeds, PO Box 391; Courthouse, Marysville, KS 66508. Recording, R/E & UCC phone-785-562-3226; fax-785-562-5685; 8:30AM-5PM (CST)
Actual marriage licenses from 1860 to 6/18/1942 may be viewed and copied from 1-4PM. Records located in old historical courthouse next door at 1207 Broadway, phone 785-562-5012. Index: Separate indices to search include Range 6,7,8,9,10. All city indexes separate. Records indexed on a public use terminal back to 1987. Office will perform a UCC search but public must search other records themselves. UCC search fee $15.00 per debtor name. Limited searches only on real estate of last deed of record, need legal description, not address to do search. Copy fee $1.00 per page. Cert fee- $2.00 per cert includes copy fee. Payee- Marshall County Register of Deeds. **Other phones:** Treasurer- 785-562-5363; Elections- 785-562-5361. **Property tax/Assessing**- PO Box 391, Courthouse, 1201 Broadway, #B6, Marysville, KS 66508; 785-562-3301, assessor fax- 785-562-3320. (Appraiser/Auditor- 785-562-3301) www.marshall.kansasgov.com/MV2Base.asp?VarCN=3 **Online access**- Access property values free at www.marshall.kansasgov.com/Parcel/.

McPherson County

County Register of Deeds, PO Box 86, McPherson, KS 67460. Recording, R/E & UCC phone-620-241-5050; fax-620-245-0749; 8AM-5PM (CST) www.mcphersoncountyks.us
Index: Searchable by document type. Records indexed on a public use terminal back to 1997. Office will perform a UCC search (with correct requet form) but public must search other records themselves. Search fee $15.00. Copy fee $1.00 1st page, $.50 each add'l page. Cert fee- $1.00 per cert includes copy fee. Payee- McPherson County Register of Deeds. **Online access to Real Estate, Deed records:** Access recording office land data at www.etitlesearch.com; registration required, fee based on usage. **Other phones:** Treasurer- 620-241-3664; Elections- 620-241-3656. **Property tax/Assessing**- PO Box 530, 117 N Maple St, McPherson, KS 67460; 620-241-5870, fax- 620-245-0085. (Appraiser/Auditor - 620-241-5870) www.mcphersoncountyks.us/index.asp?NID=4 **Online access**- property data free at www.mcphersoncountyks.us/Appraisal.asp.

Meade County

County Register of Deeds, PO Box 399, Meade, KS 67864-0399. 620-873-8705, R/E recording phone-602-873-8705, UCC recording phone-620-873-8705; fax-620-873-8707; hours - 8AM-5PM (CST) www.meadeco.org/MV2Base.asp?VarCN=12
Index: All in one. Records indexed on computer back to 04/94. Office personnel or visitors may perform searches. Search fee $15.00 per name. Office will not do "detailed" real estate record searches. Office will search UCC records with the correct UCC search form. Copy fee $1.00 per page if mailed out.Real estate record copy- $.50 per page. Fax $3.00 1st page, $1.00 per add'l page. Cert fee- $1.00 per cert plus copy fee. Payee- Meade County Register of Deeds. **Other phones:** Treasurer- 620-873-8741; Elections-620-873-8701; Vital Records- 620-873-8750. **Property tax/Assessing**- PO Box 278, 200 N Fowler, Meade, KS 67864-0278; 620-873-8710, assessor fax-620-873-8713. (Appraiser/Auditor- 620-873-8714) www.meadeco.org/MV2Base.asp?VarCN=2

Miami County

County Register of Deeds, 201 S Pearl St, #101, Paola, KS 66071. 913-294-3716, R/E recording phone-913-294-9311; fax-913-294-9515; 8AM-4:30PM (CST) www.miamicountyks.org
Index: All in one. Records indexed on a public use terminal back to 1995. Only the public may search. Copy fee $1.00 per page. Cert fee- $1.00 per cert plus copy fee. Payee- Miami County Register of Deeds. **Online access to Real Estate, Deed, Lien records:** Recorder land data by subscription on either the Laredo system using subscription and fees or the Tapestry System using credit card, http://tapestry.fidlar.com; $3.99 search; $1.00 per image. Index goes back to 1994; some deed images go back to 10/1932, mortgages to 11/1993. **Other phones:** Treasurer- 913-294-2353; Elections- 913-294-3976; Vital Records- 795-296-1400. **Property tax/Assessing**- 201 S Pearl St, #101, Paola, KS 66071; 913-294-9311, assessor fax- 913-294-9584. **Online**- Access property data and cemetery data free at http://beacon.schneidercorp.com/?site=MiamiCountyKS. Registration, username and password required.

Mitchell County

Register of Deeds, PO Box 6, Beloit, KS 67420. 785-738-3854; fax-785-738-5844; 8:30AM-5PM (CST)
Index: Separate indices to search include deeds, mortgages, misc. Record index not computerized. Office personnel or visitors may perform searches. Search fee $8.00 per name. Office will not search real estate records. Will search UCC records. Copy fee $1.00 per page. Cert fee- $1.00 per cert plus copy fee. Payee- Mitchell County Register of Deeds. **Other phones:** Treasurer- 785-738-3411; Elections- 785-738-3652. **Property tax/Assessing**- PO Box 5, Beloit, KS 67420; 785-738-5061, assessor fax- 785-738-3787.

Montgomery County

Register of Deeds, PO Box 647, Independence, KS 67301. 620-330-1140; fax-620-330-1144; 8:30AM-5PM (CST) www.mgcountyks.org/reg_of_deeds.htm
Index: All in one. Records indexed on a public use terminal back to 1991. Office personnel or visitors may perform searches. Search fee $15.00 per name. Office will not search real estate records. Office will not search UCC records. Copy fee $1.00 per page. Cert fee- $1.00 per cert plus copy fee. Payee- Montgomery County Register of Deeds. **Other phones:** Treasurer- 620-331-3040; Elections- 620-330-1200 (County Clerk); Vital Records- 795-296-1400; Taxes- 620-330-1100. **Property tax/Assessing**- PO Box 507, 217 E Mrytle St, Independence, KS 67301; 620-330-1050, assessor fax- 620-330-1177. (Appraiser - 620-330-1050);

Morris County

County Register of Deeds, Courthouse, Council Grove, KS 66846. 620-767-5614; fax-620-767-6712; 8AM-5PM (CST)
Index: All in one. Records indexed on a public use terminal back to 1994. Office will perform a UCC search (request must be in writing) but public must search other records themselves. Search fee $8.00 per name. Copy fee $1.00 per page. Cert fee- $1.00 per page includes copy. Payee- Morris County Register of Deeds. Treasurer- 620-767-5617; Elections- 620-767-5518. **Property tax/Assessing**- 501 W Main St, Council Grove, KS 66846; 620-767-5617, assessor fax- 620-767-7717. (Appraiser/Auditor- 620-767-5533) 8AM-4:30PM

Morton County

County Register of Deeds, PO Box 756, Elkhart, KS 67950-0756. Recording, R/E & UCC phone-620-697-2561; fax-620-697-4386; 9AM-5PM (CST)
Index: Separate indices to search include platted, unplatted, misc. Records indexed on a public use terminal back to 1991. Office personnel or visitors may perform searches. General search fee $8.00 per name. Office will not search real estate records. Office will not search UCC records. Copy fee $1.00 first page (can be emailed), $.25 each add'l page per doc, $2.00 per page for faxed copy fee. Cert fee- $1.00 per doc $.25 per page. Payee- Morton County Register of Deeds. **Other phones:** Treasurer- 620-697-2560; Elections- 620-697-2157. **Property tax/Assessing**-1025 Morton, Elkhart, KS 67950; 620-697-2106, assessor fax- 620-697-2899. (Appraiser/Auditor- 620-697-2106) www.mtcoks.com/appraiser/appraiser.html

Nemaha County

County Register of Deeds, PO Box 186, Seneca, KS 66538. Recording, R/E & UCC phone-785-336-2120; fax-785-336-3373; 8AM-4:30PM (CST) www.nemaha.kansasgov.com/MV2Base.asp?VarCN=8
Index: All in one. Record index not computerized. Only the public may search. Copy fee $.25 per page; $.35 for legal size. Cert fee- $1.00 per cert plus copy fee. Payee- Nemaha County Register of Deeds. **Other phones:** Treasurer- 785-336-2106; Elections- 620-330-1200; Vital Records- 795-296-1400; Clerk- 785-336-2170. **Property tax/Assessing**- 607 Nemaha, Courthouse, Seneca, KS 66538; 785-336-2179, assessor fax- 785-336-3373. **Online**- Access property data free or by registering for full subscription access at www.nemaha.kansasgov.com/parcel/. Click on 'Parcel Search Level One' for free access and name search. Subscription for full data is $200 per year.

Neosho County

County Register of Deeds, PO Box 138, Erie, KS 66733-0138. 620-244-3858; fax-620-244-3860; 8AM-4:30 www.neoshocountyks.org/regofdeeds.asp
Records indexed on a public use terminal back to 1995. Only the public may search. Copy fee $.25 per page; $1.00 per page for UCC and fax back service. Cert fee- $1.00 per cert plus copy fee. Payee- Neosho County Register of Deeds. **Other phones:** Treasurer-620-244-3800; Elections- 620-244-3811. **Property tax/Assessing**- PO Box 184, 100 S Main, Rm 104, Erie, KS 66733-0184; 620-244-3821, assessor fax-620-244-3867.

Ness County

County Register of Deeds, PO Box 127, Ness City, KS 67560. 785-798-3127; fax-785-798-2166; 8AM-N, 1PM-5PM (CST)
Index: Separate indices to search include books. Record index not computerized. Only the public may search. Copy fee $1.00 per page. Cert fee- $2.00 for 1st 2 pages, $1.00 each add'l page. Payee- Ness County Register of Deeds. **Property tax/Assessing**-202 W Sycamore, Ness City, KS 67560; 785-798-2777, fax- 785-798-3829. Public terminal available.

Norton County

County Register of Deeds, PO Box 70, Norton, KS 67654. Recording, R/E & UCC phone-785-877-5765; fax-785-877-5703; 8AM-N, 1PM-5PM (CST) www.nortoncounty.net/deeds.htm
Index: Separate indices to search include numerical books (5), grantor/grantee, miscellaneous index books, city books. Records indexed on computer back to 1999. Office personnel or visitors may perform searches. Search fee $15.00 per name. Must be sent on information request form. Office will not search real estate records. Will not search UCC records. Copy fee $1.00 per page. Cert fee- $1.00 per cert plus copy fee. Payee- Norton County Register of Deeds. Treasurer- 785-877-5795; Elections- 785-877-5710. **Property tax/Assessing**- 105 S Kansas, Courthouse, Norton, KS 67654; 785-877-5700, assessor fax- 785-877-5703. (Appraiser/Auditor- 785-877-5700).

Osage County

County Register of Deeds, PO Box 265, Lyndon, KS 66451-0265. 785-828-4523, R/E recording phone-913-828-4923; fax-785-828-3648; 8AM-5PM (CST) www.osageco.org/MV2Base.asp?VarCN=120
Index: Separate indices to search include numerical land, UCCs, power of attorneys, military discharges. Records indexed on a public use terminal back to 1985. Office personnel (time permitting) or visitors may perform searches. Office will not search real estate records. UCC search includes tax liens if requested. UCC search per debtor name- $15.00; includes 1st 10 copy pages free. Copy fee $1.00 per page.Real estate copy- $1.00 for 1st page & $.25 per add'l page. Cert fee- $1.00 per page plus copy fee. Payee- Osage County Register of Deeds. **Other phones:** Treasurer- 913-828-4923; Elections- 785-828-4812; Vital Records- 795-296-1400. **Property tax/Assessing**- 717 Topeka Ave, P.O. Box 292,

Lyndon, KS 66451; 785-828-3124, assessor fax- 785-828-4749. (Appraiser/Auditor - 913-828-3124) www.osageco.org/MV2Base.asp?VarCN=21 **Online access-** Online access to property appraiser is free at www.osageco.org/MV2Base.asp?VarCN=34. There are two levels- public and registered user. The latter can see sales as well as property data.

Osborne County

County Register of Deeds, PO Box 160, Osborne, KS 67473-0160. 785-346-2452; fax-785-346-5252; 8:30AM-N, 1-5PM (CST) www.osbornecounty.org
Index: Separate indices to search include city and township. Records indexed on computer back to 1996. Office personnel or visitors may perform searches. General index search fee $7.00 per hour. UCC search on UCC form per debtor name $15.00. Office will not search real estate records. UCC copy fee $1.00 per page.Real estate record copy- $.25 per page plus postage. Cert fee- $1.00 per cert plus copy fee. Payee- Osborne County Register of Deeds. **Other phones:** Treasurer- 785-346-2251; Elections- 785-346-2431. **Property tax/Assessing-** PO Box 160, 423 W Main, Osborne, KS 67473; 785-346-2310. (Appraiser/Auditor- 785-346-2310) **Online access-** Access to property appraisal land data is free at www.osbornecounty.org. Search field is at bottom right of page. CAMA Records found at www.osbornecounty.org also Tax Sale data.

Ottawa County

County Register of Deeds, 307 N Concord, #107; Courthouse, Minneapolis, KS 67467-2140. Recording, R/E phone-785-392-2078; fax-785-392-3605; 8AM-N,1-5PM www.ottawacounty.org
Index: Separate indices to search include numeric by legal desc., general by name. Record index not computerized. Office personnel or visitors may perform searches. Search fee $15.00 per name. Office will not search real estate records. Will search UCC records if proper UCC Information Request form is sent with proper fee. Copy fee $.25 per page. Cert fee- $1.00 per cert plus copy fee. Payee- Ottawa County Register of Deeds. **Other phones:** Treasurer- 785-392-3129; Elections- 785-392-2279; District Court Clerk- 785-392-2917. **Property tax/Assessing-** 307 N Concord, #105, Courthouse, Minneapolis, KS 67467-2140; 785-392-3037, assessor fax- 785-392-2605. (Appraiser/Auditor- 785-392-3037) hours- 8AM-5PM **Online access-** Search property data at www.ottawacounty.org on lower right hand of page.

Pawnee County

County Register of Deeds, 715 Broadway St, 2nd Fl, Rm 1; Courthouse, Larned, KS 67550-3097. Recording, R/E & UCC phone-620-285-3276; fax-620-285-2908; hours - 8:30AM-5PM (CST) www.pawneecountykansas.com
Index: Separate indices to search include land index and reception index. Records being indexed on computer. Office personnel or visitors may perform searches. No search fee for general index. Office will look up last deed of record and do a simple name search. Office will search UCC records if correct form is used. UCC search includes tax liens if requested. UCC search per debtor name- $15.00. Copy fee $1.00 per page for mailed or faxed, $.30 for copies at office. Cert fee- $1.00 per cert plus copy fees. Payee- Pawnee County. **Other phones:** Treasurer- 620-285-3746; Elections- 620-285-3721; Vitals- 620-285-6937. **Property tax/Assessing-** 715 Broadway, 2nd Fl, Larned, KS 67550; 620-285-2915, assessor fax- 620-285-3802. (Appraiser/Auditor- 620-285-2915) **Online-** Access public parcel search site at www.pawneecountykansas.com/MV2Base.asp?VarCN=2. A Level One search is free; deeper searching requires username and password.

Phillips County

County Register of Deeds, 310 State St; Courthouse, Phillipsburg, KS 67661. 785-543-6875, R/E recording phone-620-330-1200; hours - 8AM-5PM (CST) www.phillipscounty.org/registerdeeds.html
Index: All in one. Record index not computerized. Only the public may search. General copy fee $1.00 per page.Real estate record copy- $.25 per page. Cert fee- $1.00 per cert plus copy fee. Payee- Phillips County Register of Deeds. **Other phones:** Treasurer- 785-543-6895; Elections- 785-543-6825; Vital Records- 795-296-1400. **Property tax/Assessing-** 310 State St, Courthouse, Phillipsburg, KS 67661; 785-543-6810, fax- 785-543-6827. (Appraiser - 785-543-6810);

Pottawatomie County

County Register of Deeds, PO Box 186, Westmoreland, KS 66549. 785-457-3471; fax-785-457-3577; 8AM-4:30PM (CST) www.pottcounty.org
Index: All in one. Records indexed. Office will perform a UCC search with request form; public may search other records themselves. Search fee $15.00 per name. Office will not search real estate records. Copy fee $.50 per page. Cert fee- $1.00 per cert plus copy fee. Payee- Pottawatomie County Register of Deeds. **Other phones:** Treasurer- 785-457-3681. **Property tax/Assessing-** PO Box 288, Westmoreland, KS 66549; 785-457-3500, assessor fax- 785-457-2855. **Online access-** Access county parcel search free at www.pottawatomie.kansasgov.com/parcel/V2RunLev1.asp?submit1=OK. For fuller data, obtain username and password from Appraiser. Also, search GIS maps free at www.pottcounty.org/Website/PottCoMaps/viewer.htm.

Pratt County

County Register of Deeds, PO Box 873, Pratt, KS 67124. Recording, R/E phone-620-672-4140; fax-620-672-9541; 8AM-N,1-5PM www.prattcounty.org
Index: Separate indices to search include tract indexes by legal description, cross grantor/grantee indexes by name. Records indexed on computer back to 1995. Only the public may search. Office will search UCC records with an information request form. Copy fee $1.00 minimum charge. Real estate record copy- $.50 per page. Cert fee- $1.00 per cert plus copy fee. Payee- Pratt County Register of Deeds. **Other phones:** Treasurer- 620-672-4116; Elections- 620-672-4110; District Court (probates & state tax liens)- 620-672-4100. **Property tax/Assessing-** PO Box 966, Pratt, KS 67124; 620-672-4112, assessor fax- 620-672-4108. (Appraiser/Auditor- 620-672-4112) hours- 8AM-5PM Public access terminal available.

Rawlins County

County Register of Deeds, PO Box 201, Atwood, KS 67730. Recording, R/E & UCC phone-785-626-3172; fax-785-626-9481; 9AM-N,1-5PM (CST)
Index: All in one. Record index not computerized. Only the public may search. Copy fee $1.00 per page. Cert fee- $1.00 per page. Payee- Rawlins County Register of Deeds. **Other phones:** Treasurer- 785-626-3331; Elections- 785-626-3251; Vital Records- 795-296-1400. **Property tax/Assessing-** 607 Main St, Courthouse, Atwood, KS 67730; 785-626-3101.

Reno County

County Register of Deeds, 206 W 1st Ave, Hutchinson, KS 67501. 620-694-2942; fax-620-694-2944; 8AM-5PM (CST) www.renogov.org
Index: Separate indices to search include books. Records indexed on a public use terminal. Only the public may search. Copy fee $1.00 per page. Cert fee- $1.00 per cert plus copy fee. Payee- Reno County Register of Deeds. **Other phones:** Treasurer- 620-694-2938; Vital Records- 795-296-1400. **Property tax/Assessing-** 206 W 1st Ave, Hutchinson, KS 67501; 620-694-2915, assessor fax- 620-694-2987. Public access terminal available. www.renogov.org **Online access-** Parcel Information, Election Results, Tax Information, free at www.renogov.org/.

Republic County

County Register of Deeds, 1815 M St, #3, Belleville, KS 66935. 785-527-7238; fax-785-527-2659; 7:30AM-4:30PM (CST) www.republiccounty.org
Index: Separate indices to search are according to township and range. Record index not computerized. Only the public may search. Copy fee $.25 per page. Cert fee- $1.00 per cert plus copy fee. Payee- Republic County Register of Deeds. **Other phones:** Treasurer- 785-527-7236; Elections- 785-527-7231. **Property tax/Assessing-** 1815 M St, Belleville, KS 66935; 785-527-7229, assessor fax- 785-527-2839. www.republiccounty.org **Online access-** Access to parcel/property records for free go to www.republiccounty.org/parcel/

Rice County

County Register of Deeds, 101 W Commercial, 2nd Fl, Lyons, KS 67554. Recording, R/E & UCC phone-620-257-2931; fax-same; 8AM-5PM (CST) www.ricecounty.us/registerofdeeds.htm
Index: Separate indices to search include deeds, mortgage, O&G records, misc and numerical indexes. Records indexed on a public use terminal back to 1998. Only the public may search. Copy fee $1.00 per page, $.25 each add'l page. Cert fee- $1.00 per cert plus copy fee. Payee- Rice County Register of Deeds. **Other phones:** Treasurer- 620-257-2852; Elections- 620-257-2232; Vital Records- 795-296-1400. **Property tax/Assessing-** County Appraiser, 101 W Commercial, Lyons, 67554; 620-257-3611, assessor fax- 620-257-0073. www.ricecounty.us/appraiser.htm

Riley County

County Register of Deeds, 5th & Humboldt Sts; 110 Courthouse Plaza, Manhattan, KS 66502-6018. Recording, R/E & UCC phone-785-537-6340; fax-785-537-6343; 8AM-5PM www.rileycountyks.gov
Index: All in one. Records indexed on a public use terminal back to 1850. Office personnel or visitors may perform searches. Search fee $15.00 for UCC. Office will not search real estate records, unless minor in nature. UCC search includes tax liens. Copy fee $1.00 per page. Cert fee- $1.00 per cert plus copy fee. Payee- Riley County Register of Deeds. **Online access to Real Estate, Deed, Lien, UCC records:** Access to recorder office land data is by subscription; Fee is $100 per year plus $.50 per page printed. Records go back to 1850. Registration through the Recorder's Office. **Other phones:** Treasurer- 785-537-6320; Elections- 785-537-6300. **Property tax/Assessing-** 110 Courthouse Plaza, 5th & Humboldt Sts, Manhattan, KS 66502-6018; 785-537-6310, assessor fax- 785-537-6312. (Appraiser/Auditor- 785-537-6310) **Online** - Access appraisal data for free at www.rileycountyks.gov/index.asp?NID=84

Rooks County

County Register of Deeds, 115 N Walnut St, Stockton, KS 67669. 785-425-6291; fax-785-425-6497; 8AM-N,1-5PM (CST)
Index: All in one. Records indexed on a public use terminal. Office personnel or visitors may perform searches. UCC search per debtor name- $15.00. Office will not search real estate records. Tax liens not included in UCC search. Requests must be submitted on the state approved form. Copy fee $1.00 per page. Cert fee- $1.00 per cert plus copy fee. Submit separate checks for cert fees and copy fees. Payee- Rooks County Register of Deeds. **Other phones:** Treasurer- 785-425-6161. **Property tax/Assessing-** 115 N Walnut, Stockton, KS 67669; 785-425-6262, assessor fax- 785-425-7001. hours- 8AM-5PM

Rush County

County Register of Deeds, PO Box 117, La Crosse, KS 67548. 785-222-3312; fax-785-222-3559; 8:30AM-N, 1-5PM (CST)
Index: Separate indices to search include general index and numerical index. Records indexed on a public use terminal back to 4/03. Only the public may search. Copy fee $1.00 per instrument, if clerk has to research records and $.25 per page over 4 pages. Otherwise, copy fee is $.25 per page. Cert fee- $2.00 per cert includes copy fee. Payee- Rush County Register of Deeds. **Other phones:** Treasurer- 785-222-3416. **Property tax/Assessing-** 785-222-2659.

Russell County

County Register of Deeds, PO Box 191, Russell, KS 67665. Recording, R/E & UCC phone-785-483-4612; fax-785-483-5725; 8AM-5PM (CST) www.russell.kansasgov.com/MV2Base.asp?VarCN=13
Index: All in one. Records indexed on a public use terminal back to 1995. Books back to 1966. Office personnel or visitors may perform searches. Search fee $15.00 per name. Office will not search real estate records. Copy fee $1.00 per page.Real estate or tax lien copy- $.50 per page. Cert fee- $1.00 per cert plus copy fee. Payee- Russell County Register of Deeds. **Other phones:** Treasurer- 785-483-2251; Elections-785-483-4641. **Property tax/Assessing**- 401 N Main St, Courthouse, Russell, KS 67665; 785-483-5551, assessor fax- 785-483-5725. (Appraiser/Auditor- 785-483-5551) A public access terminal is available. www.russell.kansasgov.com/MV2Base.asp?VarCN=9 **Online access**- Access assessor property data free at www.russell.kansasgov.com/parcel/.

Saline County

County Register of Deeds, PO Box 5040, Salina, KS 67402-5040. 785-309-5855; fax-785-309-5856; 8am-5pm. www.saline.org/MV2Base.asp?VarCN=80
Index: All in one. Records indexed on a public use terminal back to 1995. Office will perform a UCC search but public must search other records themselves. UCC search fee $15.00 per name. General copy fee $1.00 per page. Cert fee- $1.00 per cert plus copy fee. Payee- Saline County Register of Deeds. **Other phones:** Treasurer- 785-309-5860. **Property tax/Assessing**- PO Box 5040, 300 W Ash, Rm 108, Salina, KS 67402-5040; 785-309-5800, assessor fax- 785-309-5802. (Appraiser/Auditor- 785-309-5800) A public access terminal is available. www.saline.org/MV2Base.asp?VarCN=88 **Online**- Access property data free at www.saline.org/parcel/ and click on Parcel Search Public.

Scott County

County Register of Deeds, 303 Court St; Courthouse, Scott City, KS 67871. Recording, R/E & UCC phone-620-872-3155; fax-620-872-7145; 8AM-5PM (CST) www.scott.kansasgov.com/MV2Base.asp?VarCN=29
Index: All in one. Records indexed on a public use terminal back to 1989. Office personnel or visitors may perform searches. Search fee $15.00 per name. Real estate searches are subject to limitations. UCC search request must be on national request form and be prepaid. Copy fee $.25, $.50 for color copy per page. Cert fee- $1.00 per cert plus copy fee. Payee- Scott County Register of Deeds. Treasurer- 620-872-2640; Elections- 620-872-2420. **Property tax/Assessing**- 303 Court St, Courthouse 620-872-5446, fax- 620-872-7145. (Appraiser - 620-872-5446) www.scott.kansasgov.com/MV2Contacts.asp?VarCN=1 **Online access**- Access parcel data free at www.scott.kansasgov.com/parcel/v2loginreg.asp. Registration and password required for full data.

Sedgwick County

County Register of Deeds, PO Box 3326, Wichita, KS 67201-3326. Recording, R/E & UCC phone-316-660-9400; fax-316-383-8066; 8AM-5PM (CST) www.sedgwickcounty.org/deeds/
Index: All in one. Records indexed on a public use terminal back to 4/1/88. Office personnel or visitors may perform searches. Search fee $20.00 per name, $15.00 per name for UCC's. Office will search real estate records. Will search UCC records. Copy fee $1.00 per page. Cert fee- $1.00 per cert plus copy fee. Payee- Sedgwick County Register of Deeds. **Online access to Real Estate, Deed, Lien, Property Sale, Probate records:** Access to the exhaustive County online system (all departments) require a $225 set up fee, $49 monthly fee and a per transaction fee of $.09. For info on this and county record access generally, call 316-660-9860. Also, access recorder deeds free at https://rod.sedgwickcounty.org. Also, access marriage, courts, probate records with subscription at www.kansas.gov/index.php. **Other phones:** Treasurer- 316-660-9100; Elections- 316-660-7100; Vital Records- 795-296-1400; County Clerk- 316-660-9200. **Property tax/Assessing**- 525 N Main, #227, Wichita, KS 67201; 316-660-9110, assessor fax- 316-660-5479. (Appraiser/Auditor- 316-660-9110) **Online access**- Search property appraisal/tax at www.sedgwickcounty.org/realpropertyinfo/realproperty.html. Also, access property appraisal and tax data free at https://ssc.sedgwickcounty.org/taxwebasp/searchlinks.aspx but no name searching.

Seward County

County Register of Deeds, 415 N Washington, #105; Courthouse, Liberal, KS 67901. Recording, R/E & UCC phone-620-626-3220, UCC recording phone-620-626-3223; fax-620-626-3362; 8AM-5PM (CST) www.sewardcountyks.org
Index: Separate numerical indices to search include city, township. Records indexed on a public use terminal back to 1887. Office personnel or visitors may perform searches. Tax lien or UCC search (request in writing) per debtor name-$15.00. This office will do limited real estate searches. Will search UCC records gpt $15.00 per name and search request on approved form. Copy fee $1.00 per page. $2.00 per page for copies of indexes. Fee for mailing is $1.00, $2.00 for faxing. Cert fee- $1.00 per cert plus copy fee. Payee- Seward County Register of Deeds. **Other phones:** Treasurer- 620-626-3219; Elections- 620-626-3201; Vital Records- 913-296-1400. **Property tax/Assessing**- 415 N Washington St, Liberal, KS 67901; 620-626-3252, assessor fax- 620-626-3259. (Appraiser/Auditor- 620-626-3252)

Shawnee County

County Register of Deeds, 200 E 7th St, #108, Topeka, KS 66603-3932. Recording, R/E & UCC phone-785-233-8200 x4020, UCC recording phone-785-233-8200 x4021; fax-785-291-4950; 8AM-4:30PM (CST) www.co.shawnee.ks.us/rd/
Index: Separate indices to search include grantee/grantor, numerical, computer & books (depending on age of document). Records indexed on a public use terminal back to 1988. Office personnel or visitors may perform searches. Search fee for UCC- $15.00 per name. Office will do a last deed only search or other very limited search. Office will not search UCC records. Copy fee $1.50 per page. Cert fee- $1.00 per doc plus copy fee. Payee- Shawnee County Register of Deeds. Bulk data available for purchase; contact county information officer- county clerk, x4155. **Other phones:** Treasurer- 785-233-8200 x5161; Elections- 785-266-0285; Vital Records- 795-296-1400; County Clerk- 785-233-8200. **Property tax/Assessing**- 200 E 7th St, Topeka, KS 66603; 785-233-8200 x5151. (Appraiser/Auditor- 785-233-2882 x6000) **Online access**- Access the residential property list free at www.co.shawnee.ks.us/AP/R_prop/Disclaimer.shtm; commercial at www.co.shawnee.ks.us/ap/C_prop/Disclaimer.shtm. Also search the county mapping site for parcel owner and map data at. http://maps.kansasgis.org/sn_co/ims.cfm.

Sheridan County

County Register of Deeds, PO Box 899, Hoxie, KS 67740-0899. 785-675-3741; fax-785-675-3050; 8AM-N,1-5PM (CST)
Index: Separate indices to search. Record index not computerized. Office personnel or visitors may perform searches. Search fee $15.00 per name. Office will not search real estate records. Copy fee $1.00 per page. Cert fee- $1.00 per cert plus copy fee. Payee- Sheridan County Register of Deeds. **Other phones:** Treasurer- 785-675-3622; Elections- 913-782-3441; Vital Records- 795-296-1400. **Property tax/Assessing**- PO Box 899, 925 9th St, Courthouse, Hoxie, KS 67740; 785-675-3932, assessor fax- 785-675-3050.

Sherman County

Register of Deeds, 813 Broadway, Rm 104, Goodland, KS 67735. Recording, R/E phone-785-890-4845; fax-785-890-4848; 8-5 (MST) www.sherman.kansasgov.com/MV2Base.asp?VarCN=171
Index: Separate indices to search include numeric, grantor/grantee, misc., mortgagor/mortgagee. Record index not computerized. Records on books back to 1886. Only the public may search. Copy fee $.25 per page. Cert fee- $1.00 per cert includes copy fee. Payee- Sherman County Register of Deeds. **Other phones:** Treasurer- 785-890-4810; Elections- 785-890-4800; Vital Records- 795-296-1400. **Property tax/Assessing**- 813 Broadway, Rm 302, Goodland, 67735; 785-890-4825, fax- 785-890-4830. (Appraiser/785-890-4825);

Smith County

County Register of Deeds, 218 S Grant, Smith Center, KS 66967. Recording, R/E & UCC phone-785-282-5160; fax-785-282-6257; 8AM-N, 1PM-5PM (CST) www.smithcoks.com
Index: All in one. Record index not computerized. Office personnel or visitors may perform searches. General index search fee $8.00 per name. Office will search real estate records. Office will not search UCC records. UCC copy fee $2.00 per page.Real estate record copy- $1.00 per page. Cert fee- $1.00 per page includes copy fee. Payee- Smith County Register of Deeds. **Other phones:** Treasurer- 785-282-5170; Elections- 785-282-5110. **Property tax/Assessing**- 218 S Grant, Smith Center, KS 66967; 785-282-5100, assessor fax- 785-686-4014. (Appraiser/Auditor- 785-282-5100) **Online**- Search parcel data free at www.smithcoks.com/parcel/.

Stafford County

County Register of Deeds, 209 N Broadway, 2nd Fl; County Courthouse, St. John, KS 67576. 620-549-3505; fax-620-549-3503; 8AM-5PM (CST) www.staffordcounty.org/regofdeeds.html
Records indexed on a public use terminal back to 2003. Office will perform a UCC search but public must search other records themselves. Office will not search real estate records. UCC search per debtor name- $15.00. Copy fee $.50 per page, faxed copies billed at $1.00 per page, copies of records from 2000 to present can be emailed for $1.00 for 1st page, $.25 each add'l page. Cert fee- $.50 per cert plus copy fee. Payee- Stafford County Register of Deeds. **Other phones:** Treasurer- 620-549-3508; Elections- 620-549-3509. **Property tax/Assessing**- 209 N Broadway, St. John, KS 67576; 620-549-3540, fax-620-549-6335. (Appraiser-620-549-3540)

Stanton County

Register of Deeds, PO Box 716, Johnson, KS 67855. 620-492-2190; fax-620-492-2688; 8:30AM-N, 1-5,
Index: All in one. Records indexed on a public use terminal back to 1991. Office will perform a UCC search but public must search other records themselves. Search fee $15.00 per name. Office will not search real estate records. Copy fee $1.00 per page. Cert fee- $1.00 per cert plus copy fee. Payee- Stanton County Register of Deeds. **Other phones:** Treasurer- 620-492-2160; Vital Records- 795-296-1400. **Property tax/Assessing**- PO Box 389, Johnson, 67855; 620-492-6896, fax- 620-492-2688.

Stevens County

County Register of Deeds, 200 E 6th St, Hugoton, KS 67951. Recording, R/E & UCC phone-620-544-2630; fax-620-544-4081; 9AM-5PM (CST)
Index: Separate indices. Record index not computerized. Only the public may search. Copy fee $1.00 per page.Real estate record copy- $.25 per page. Cert fee- $1.00 per cert plus copy fee. Payee- Stevens County Register of Deeds. **Other phones:** Treasurer-620-544-2542; Elections- 620-544-2541; Vital Records- 795-296-1400. **Property tax/Assessing**- 200 E 6th St, Hugoton, KS 67951; 620-544-2993, assessor fax- 620-544-8596. (Appraiser/Auditor- 620-544-2693);

Sumner County

County Register of Deeds, PO Box 469, Wellington, KS 67152. Recording, R/E & UCC phone-620-326-2041; fax-620-399-1087; 8AM-5PM (CST) www.co.sumner.ks.us/MV2Contacts.asp?VarCN=20

Index: Separate indices to search include grantor/grantee, mortgage, oil & gas, misc. books. Records indexed on a public use terminal back to 1998. Office personnel or visitors may perform searches. Search fee $15.00 per name. Office will not search UCC records. Copy fee $1.00 per page. Cert fee- $1.00 per cert plus copy fee. Payee- Sumner County Register of Deeds. **Other phones:** Treasurer- 620-326-3371; Elections- 620-326-3395; Vital Records- 795-296-1400. **Property tax/Assessing-** 501 N Washington, Wellington, KS 67152; 620-326-8986, fax- 620-326-6103. (Appraiser - 620-326-8986) www.co.sumner.ks.us/MV2Base.asp?VarCN=27

Online - Access to the Parcel Search is free or by registration for username and password from appraiser, at www.co.sumner.ks.us/parcel%20lookup/V2LoginReg.asp. Perform a level one tax search free at www.co.sumner.ks.us/tax/. To search with registering, click on Tax Search Level 1. Register with treasurer to access more data.

Thomas County

Register of Deeds, 300 N Court, Colby, KS 67701. Recording, R/E & UCC phone-785-460-4535; fax-785-460-4512; 8AM-N, 1PM-5PM (CST) http://thomascountyks.com/page.php?9

Index: All in one. Records indexed on a public use terminal and books back to 0400. Office personnel or visitors may perform searches. Search fee $15.00 per name. Office will not search real estate records. Office will search UCC records if in writing and on proper form. Copy fee $.25 per page; UCCs $1.00 per page. Cert fee- $1.00 per cert plus copy fee. Payee- Thomas County Register of Deeds. Treasurer- 785-460-4520; Elections- 785-460-4500. **Property tax/Assessing-** 300 N Court, Colby, KS 67701; 785-460-4525, fax-785-460-4527. (Appraiser - 785-460-4525) hours- 8AM-5PM www.thomascountyks.com/page.php?2

Online- Access parcel search database with subscription, login and password at www.thomas.kansasgov.com/parcel/ or click on Disclaimer for free search.

Trego County

County Register of Deeds, 216 Main, WaKeeney, KS 67672-2189. Recording, R/E & UCC phone-785-743-6622; fax-785-743-2461; 8:30AM-5PM (CST)

Index: Separate indices to search are by range, city and city subdivisions. Records indexed on a public use terminal back to 7/15/92. Office personnel or visitors may perform searches. Search fee $15.00. Office will search real estate records if it is not too extensive. Copy fee $1.00 per page. Cert fee- $1.00 per cert plus copy fee. Payee- Trego County Register of Deeds. **Other phones:** Treasurer- 785-743-2001; Elections- 785-743-5773. **Property tax/Assessing-** 216 Main, Wa Keeney, KS 67672-2189; 785-743-5758, assessor fax- 785-743-6463. (Appraiser - 785-743-5758) Public access terminal available.

Wabaunsee County

County Register of Deeds, PO Box 278, Alma, KS 66401-0278. Recording, R/E phone-785-765-3822; fax-785-765-3824; 8AM-4:30PM (CST) www.wabaunsee.kansasgov.com/MV2Base.asp?VarCN=5

Index: Separate indices to search include numerical, misc, and UCC. Record index not computerized. Office will perform a UCC search but public must search other records themselves. UCC search per debtor name- $15.00 but must be on their UCC request form. Copy fee $1.00 per page.Real estate record copy- $.50 per page. Cert fee- $1.00 per cert plus $.50 per page. Payee- Wabaunsee County Register of Deeds. **Other phones:** Treasurer- 785-765-3812; Elections- 785-765-2421; Vital Records- 785-765-3822. **Property tax/Assessing-** 215 Kansas Ave, Alma, KS 6640; 785-765-3508, assessor fax- 785-765-3482. (Appraiser/Auditor- 785-765-3508)

Online - Access to the assessor parcel search data is at www.wabaunsee.kansasgov.com/Parcel/V2RunLev1.asp?submit1=OK; registration is asked for full data, but you may search basic data for free. To subscribe, phone 785-765-3508. Also, access the treasurer's property tax data free at www.wabaunsee.kansasgov.com/MV2Base.asp?VarCN=22.

Wallace County

Register of Deeds, PO Box 10, Sharon Springs, KS 67758-9998. Recording, R/E phone-785-852-4283; fax-785-852-4783; 8AM-N, 1-5PM (MST)

Index: UCCs indexed separately. Record index not computerized. Only the public may search. Will search UCC records if you have the correct UCC request form and $15.00 fee. Copy fee $.25 per page.UCC copies are $1.00 per page. Cert fee- $1.00 per cert plus copy fee. Payee- Wallace County Register of Deeds. **Other phones:** Treasurer- 785-852-4281; Elections- 785-852-4282; Vital Records- 795-296-1400. **Property tax/Assessing-** PO Box 607, 313 N Main, Courthouse, Sharon Springs, KS 67758; 785-852-4206, fax- 785-852-4783. (Appraiser - 785-852-4206)

Washington County

County Register of Deeds, 214 C St; Courthouse, Washington, KS 66968-1928. Recording, R/E & UCC phone-785-325-2286; fax-785-325-2830; 8AM-5PM (CST) www.washingtonks.net

Index: All in one. Records indexed on a public use terminal back to 1998. Office personnel or visitors may perform searches. Search fee $15.00 for UCC search. Office will give real estate information at no charge. UCC search includes tax liens. Copy fee $1.00 per page.Real estate record copy- $.25 per page; from old bound books- $.50 per page. Cert fee- $1.00 per cert includes copy fee. Payee- Washington County Register of Deeds. **Other phones:** Treasurer- 785-325-2461; Elections- 785-325-2974; Vital Records- 785-296-1400 (Topeka, KS). **Property tax/Assessing-** 214 C St, Washington, KS 66968; 785-325-2236, assessor fax- 785-325-2895. (Appraiser/Auditor- 785-325-2236);

Wichita County

County Register of Deeds, PO Box 472, Leoti, KS 67861-0472. Recording, R/E & UCC phone-620-375-2733; fax-316-375-4350; 8AM-N,1-5PM (CST)

Index: Separate indices to search include Platt or City Platt. Record index not computerized. Only the public may search. If office does search, fee $15.00 per name. Copy fee $1.00 per page. Cert fee- $1.00 per page plus copy fee. Payee- Wichita County Register of Deeds. **Other phones:** Treasurer- 620-375-2713; Elections- 620-375-2731. **Property tax/Assessing-** PO Box 968, 206 S 4th, Leoti, KS 67861; 620-375-4242, assessor fax- 620-375-4350. (Appraiser/Auditor- 620-375-4242);

Wilson County

Register of Deeds, 615 Madison St, Rm 106; Fredonia, KS 66736-1396. Recording, R/E phone-620-378-3662; fax-620-378-4762; 8AM-5PM (CST)

Index: All in one. Records indexed on a public use terminal back to 2002. Office will perform a UCC search but public must search other records themselves. Copy fee $1.00 per page. Cert fee- $1.00 per cert plus copy fee. Payee- Wilson County Register of Deeds. **Other phones:** Treasurer- 620-378-2775; Elections- 620-378-2186; Vital Records- 795-296-1400. **Property tax/Assessing-** 615 Madison St, Rm 102, 615 Madison St, Courthouse, Fredonia, KS 66736; 620-378-2187, assessor fax- 620-378-3021. (Appraiser/Auditor- 620-378-2507) **Online access-** Access to property records for free go to http://beacon.scheidercorp.com.

Woodson County

Register of Deeds, 105 W Rutledge, Rm 101, Yates Center, KS 66783-1499. 620-625-8635; fax-620-625-2522; 8AM-N,1-5PM www.woodsoncounty.net

Index: Separate indices to search. Records indexed on computer back to 1997. Office personnel or visitors may perform searches. Search fee-$15.00 per name. Office will search real estate records. Will search UCC records. General copy fee-$1.50 per page.Real estate or tax lien copy- $.50 per page. Cert fee- $1.00 per cert plus copy fee. Payee- Woodson County Register of Deeds. **Other phones:** Treasurer- 620-625-8650; Elections- 620-625-8605. **Property tax/Assessing-** 105 W Rutledge, #102, Yates Center, KS 66783; 620-625-8600, assessor fax- 620-625-8602. **Online access-** Access property data free or by registering for full subscription access at www.woodson.kansasgov.com/parcel/. Click on 'Parcel Search Level One' for free access and name search. Sub service for full data is $200 per year.

Wyandotte County

County Register of Deeds, 710 N 7th St; Courthouse, Kansas City, KS 66101-3084. Recording, R/E & UCC phone-913-573-2841; fax-913-321-3075; 8AM-5PM (CST) www.wycokck.org

Index: All in one. Records indexed on a public use terminal back to 1991. Office will perform a UCC search but public must search other records themselves. Copy fee $1.00 per page. Cert fee- $1.00 per cert plus copy fee. Payee- Wyandotte County Register of Deeds. **Online access to Real Estate, Deed, Lien, Judgment records:** Register has online subscription services named Laredo and Tapestry; index goes back to 1975 (1983 missing), images to 1991. Tapestry accepts credit card searches $3.99 a search, $.50 per image. Also, Judgments and Liens are by subscription at www.kansas.gov/index.php. **Other phones:** Treasurer- 913-573-2823; Elections- 913-334-1414; Vital Records- 795-296-1400. **Property tax/Assessing-** 8200 State Ave, Kansas City, KS 66112; 913-287-2641, assessor fax- 913-334-0418. (Appraiser/Auditor- 913-573-2889) Public access terminal available. A private company sells county tax claim data, view list free at www.xspand.com/investors/realestate_sale/index.aspx. www.wycokck.org **Online access-** The property dial-up services requires a $20 set up fee, $5 monthly minimum and $.05 each transaction. Lending agency info also available. Contact Louise Sachen 913-573-2885 for signup. Also, records from the County Treasurer Tax database are free at https://www.accesskansas.org/wyandotte-propertytax/index.html. Name search for personal property only; property searches require street number/name.

Kansas County Locator

You will usually be able to find the city name in the City/County Cross Reference below. In that case, it is a simple matter to determine the county from the cross reference. However, only the official US Postal Service city names are included in this index. There are an additional 40,000 place names that people use in their addresses. Therefore, we have also included a ZIP/City Cross Reference immediately following the City/County Cross Reference.

If you know the ZIP Code but the city name does not appear in the City/County Cross Reference index, look up the ZIP Code in the ZIP/City Cross Reference, find the city name, then look up the city name in the City/County Cross Reference. For example, you want to know the county for an address of Menands, NY 12204. There is no "Menands" in the City/County Cross Reference. The ZIP/City Cross Reference shows that ZIP Codes 12201-12288 are for the city of Albany. Looking back in the City/County Cross Reference, Albany is in Albany County.

City/County Cross Reference

ABBYVILLE Reno
ABILENE Dickinson
ADA (67414) Ottawa(94), Lincoln(5)
ADMIRE Lyon
AGENDA Republic
AGRA Phillips
ALBERT (67511) Barton(56), Rush(43)
ALDEN (67512) Rice(90), Reno(9)
ALEXANDER (67513) Rush(90), Pawnee(9)
ALLEN Lyon
ALMA Wabaunsee
ALMENA (67622) Norton(98), Phillips(1)
ALTA VISTA (66834) Wabaunsee(52), Morris(19), Jackson(17), Geary(10)
ALTAMONT Labette
ALTON (67623) Osborne(96), Smith(3)
ALTOONA Wilson
AMERICUS Lyon
AMES Cloud
ANDALE Sedgwick
ANDOVER Butler
ANTHONY Harper
ARCADIA (66711) Crawford(96), Bourbon(3)
ARCADIA Bourbon
ARGONIA (67004) Sumner(86), Harper(12)
ARKANSAS CITY Cowley
ARLINGTON Reno
ARMA Crawford
ARNOLD (67515) Ness(75), Trego(24)
ASHLAND Clark
ASSARIA (67416) Saline(97), McPherson(2)
ATCHISON (66002) Atchison(93), Leavenworth(5), Jefferson(1)
ATHOL Smith
ATLANTA (67008) Cowley(69), Butler(30)
ATTICA (67009) Harper(97), Barber(2)
ATWOOD Rawlins
AUBURN (66402) Shawnee(98), Osage(1)
AUGUSTA Butler
AURORA Cloud
AXTELL (66403) Marshall(93), Nemaha(6)
BAILEYVILLE (66404) Nemaha(94), Marshall(5)
BALDWIN CITY (66006) Douglas(95), Franklin(4)
BARNARD (67418) Lincoln(91), Mitchell(8)
BARNES (66933) Washington(93), Riley(6)
BARTLETT Labette
BASEHOR Leavenworth
BAXTER SPRINGS Cherokee
BAZINE Ness
BEATTIE Marshall
BEAUMONT Butler
BEAVER Barton
BEELER (67518) Ness(74), Lane(25)
BELLE PLAINE Sumner
BELLEVILLE Republic
BELOIT (67420) Mitchell(97), Cloud(1)
BELPRE (67519) Edwards(90), Pawnee(10)
BELVIDERE Kiowa
BELVUE (66407) Wabaunsee(70), Pottawatomie(29)
BENDENA Doniphan
BENEDICT Wilson
BENNINGTON Ottawa
BENTLEY Sedgwick
BENTON (67017) Butler(89), Sedgwick(10)
BERN Nemaha
BERRYTON (66409) Shawnee(91), Douglas(6), Osage(2)
BEVERLY (67423) Lincoln(98), Ellsworth(1)
BIRD CITY Cheyenne
BISON Rush
BLUE MOUND (66010) Linn(96), Bourbon(2)
BLUE RAPIDS (66411) Marshall(97), Riley(2)
BLUFF CITY (67018) Harper(91), Sumner(8)
BOGUE Graham
BONNER SPRINGS (66012) Wyandotte(65), Leavenworth(34)
BREMEN (66412) Marshall(93), Washington(6)
BREWSTER (67732) Thomas(59), Sherman(32), Rawlins(7)
BRONSON (66716) Bourbon(94), Allen(5)
BROOKVILLE (67425) Saline(58), Ellsworth(40), Lincoln(1)
BROWNELL (67521) Ness(89), Trego(10)
BUCKLIN (67834) Ford(92), Clark(6)
BUCYRUS (66013) Johnson(52), Miami(47)
BUFFALO (66717) Wilson(96), Woodson(3)
BUHLER (67522) Reno(91), Harvey(8)
BUNKER HILL Russell
BURDEN Cowley
BURDETT (67523) Pawnee(92), Hodgeman(7)
BURDICK (66838) Morris(93), Marion(4), Chase(1)
BURLINGAME (66413) Osage(95), Lyon(3), Wabaunsee(1)
BURLINGTON Coffey
BURNS (66840) Butler(58), Marion(36), Chase(5)
BURR OAK Jewell
BURRTON (67020) Harvey(58), Reno(37), Sedgwick(3)
BUSHTON (67427) Rice(81), Ellsworth(16), Barton(2)
BYERS (67021) Pratt(94), Stafford(5)
CALDWELL Sumner
CAMBRIDGE Cowley
CANEY Montgomery
CANTON (67428) McPherson(93), Marion(6)
CARBONDALE Osage
CARLTON Dickinson
CASSODAY Butler
CATHARINE Ellis
CAWKER CITY (67430) Mitchell(75), Jewell(17), Osborne(4), Smith(2)
CEDAR Smith
CEDAR POINT (66843) Chase(97), Marion(2)
CEDAR VALE (67024) Chautauqua(77), Cowley(22)
CENTERVILLE (66014) Anderson(52), Linn(47)
CENTRALIA Nemaha
CHANUTE (66720) Neosho(96), Wilson(3)
CHAPMAN Dickinson
CHASE Rice
CHAUTAUQUA Chautauqua
CHENEY (67025) Sedgwick(72), Kingman(26)
CHEROKEE Crawford
CHERRYVALE (67335) Montgomery(87), Labette(12)
CHETOPA (67336) Labette(75), Cherokee(24)
CIMARRON (67835) Gray(73), Finney(22), Hodgeman(3)
CIRCLEVILLE Jackson
CLAFLIN (67525) Barton(96), Rice(3)
CLAY CENTER (67432) Clay(98), Ottawa(1)
CLAYTON (67629) Norton(81), Decatur(18)
CLEARVIEW CITY Johnson
CLEARWATER (67026) Sedgwick(96), Sumner(3)
CLIFTON (66937) Washington(83), Clay(16)
CLYDE (66938) Cloud(80), Washington(11), Republic(4), Clay(3)
COATS (67028) Pratt(60), Kiowa(25), Barber(13)
CODELL Rooks
COFFEYVILLE (67337) Montgomery(95), Labette(4)
COLBY Thomas
COLDWATER (67029) Comanche(97), Kiowa(2)
COLLYER (67631) Trego(73), Graham(22), Gove(3), Sheridan(1)
COLONY (66015) Anderson(79), Coffey(20)
COLUMBUS Cherokee
COLWICH Sedgwick
CONCORDIA (66901) Cloud(97), Republic(2)
CONWAY SPRINGS (67031) Sumner(96), Sedgwick(3)
COOLIDGE Hamilton
COPELAND (67837) Haskell(55), Gray(39), Meade(5)
CORNING Nemaha
COTTONWOOD FALLS Chase
COUNCIL GROVE (66846) Morris(94), Lyon(4)
COURTLAND (66939) Republic(92), Jewell(7)
COYVILLE Wilson
CRESTLINE Cherokee
CUBA (66940) Republic(98), Washington(1)
CUMMINGS Atchison
CUNNINGHAM (67035) Kingman(71), Pratt(18), Reno(9)
DAMAR (67632) Rooks(73), Graham(26)
DANVILLE Harper
DE SOTO Johnson
DEARING Montgomery
DEERFIELD (67838) Kearny(62), Finney(37)
DELIA Jackson
DELPHOS (67436) Ottawa(84), Cloud(15)
DENISON (66419) Jackson(87), Jefferson(12)
DENNIS Labette
DENNIS THE MENACE Sedgwick
DENTON Doniphan
DERBY Sedgwick
DEXTER Cowley
DIGHTON (67839) Lane(92), Gove(6)
DODGE CITY Ford
DORRANCE (67634) Russell(98), Barton(1)
DOUGLASS (67039) Butler(97), Cowley(1)
DOVER Shawnee
DOWNS (67437) Osborne(95), Smith(4)
DRESDEN (67635) Decatur(70), Sheridan(29)
DURHAM Marion
DWIGHT (66849) Morris(63), Geary(36)
EASTON Leavenworth
EDGERTON (66021) Johnson(71), Miami(26), Douglas(2)
EDMOND (67636) Norton(82), Graham(17)
EDNA Labette
EDSON Sherman
EDWARDSVILLE Wyandotte
EFFINGHAM Atchison
EL DORADO Butler
ELBING Butler
ELK CITY (67344) Montgomery(65), Chautauqua(21), Elk(13)
ELK FALLS Elk
ELKHART Morton
ELLINWOOD (67526) Barton(94), Rice(4), Stafford(1)
ELLIS (67637) Ellis(87), Trego(12)
ELLSWORTH Ellsworth
ELMDALE Chase
ELSMORE Allen
ELWOOD Doniphan
EMMETT (66422) Pottawatomie(54), Jackson(45)
EMPORIA Lyon
ENGLEWOOD Clark
ENSIGN (67841) Gray(80), Ford(19)
ENTERPRISE Dickinson
ERIE Neosho
ESBON Jewell
ESKRIDGE Wabaunsee
EUDORA (66025) Douglas(76), Johnson(22)
EUREKA Greenwood
EVEREST (66424) Brown(89), Atchison(10)
FAIRVIEW Brown

FALL RIVER (67047) Greenwood(67), Elk(20), Wilson(11)
FALUN (67442) Saline(97), McPherson(2)
FARLINGTON Crawford
FLORENCE Marion
FONTANA Miami
FORD Ford
FORMOSO (66942) Jewell(98), Republic(1)
FORT DODGE Ford
FORT LEAVENWORTH Leavenworth
FORT RILEY Geary
FORT SCOTT Bourbon
FOSTORIA Pottawatomie
FOWLER (67844) Meade(80), Ford(13), Gray(5)
FRANKFORT (66427) Marshall(97), Pottawatomie(2)
FRANKLIN Crawford
FREDONIA Wilson
FREEPORT (67049) Harper(90), Sumner(10)
FRONTENAC Crawford
FULTON (66738) Bourbon(97), Linn(2)
GALENA Cherokee
GALESBURG Neosho
GALVA McPherson
GARDEN CITY Finney
GARDEN PLAIN Sedgwick
GARDNER Johnson
GARFIELD Pawnee
GARLAND Bourbon
GARNETT Anderson
GAS Allen
GAYLORD (67638) Smith(98), Osborne(1)
GEM (67734) Thomas(52), Rawlins(47)
GENESEO (67444) Rice(65), Ellsworth(34)
GEUDA SPRINGS (67051) Sumner(83), Cowley(16)
GIRARD Crawford
GLADE (67639) Phillips(96), Rooks(3)
GLASCO (67445) Cloud(92), Ottawa(7)
GLEN ELDER (67446) Mitchell(91), Jewell(8)
GODDARD Sedgwick
GOESSEL Marion
GOFF Nemaha
GOODLAND Sherman
GORHAM (67640) Russell(73), Ellis(26)
GOVE Gove
GRAINFIELD (67737) Gove(75), Sheridan(25)
GRANTVILLE Jefferson
GREAT BEND (67530) Barton(98), Stafford(1)
GREELEY (66033) Anderson(62), Franklin(35), Linn(2)
GREEN (67447) Clay(61), Riley(38)
GREENLEAF Washington
GREENSBURG Kiowa
GREENWICH Sedgwick
GRENOLA (67346) Elk(75), Chautauqua(25)
GRIDLEY (66852) Coffey(82), Greenwood(10), Woodson(6)
GRINNELL (67738) Gove(73), Sheridan(26)
GYPSUM (67448) Saline(47), McPherson(26), Dickinson(22), Marion(3)
HADDAM (66944) Washington(96), Republic(3)
HALSTEAD Harvey
HAMILTON Greenwood
HANOVER Washington
HANSTON (67849) Hodgeman(97), Ness(2)
HARDTNER Barber
HARLAN Smith
HARPER (67058) Harper(97), Kingman(2)
HARTFORD (66854) Lyon(78), Coffey(21)
HARVEYVILLE (66431) Wabaunsee(91), Shawnee(8)
HAVANA (67347) Montgomery(67), Chautauqua(32)
HAVEN Reno
HAVENSVILLE (66432) Pottawatomie(78), Jackson(20), Nemaha(1)
HAVILAND (67059) Kiowa(75), Edwards(16), Pratt(7)
HAYS Ellis
HAYSVILLE Sedgwick
HAZELTON (67061) Barber(68), Harper(31)
HEALY (67850) Lane(84), Scott(10), Gove(4)
HEPLER (66746) Crawford(91), Bourbon(8)
HERINGTON (67449) Dickinson(81), Morris(17)
HERNDON (67739) Rawlins(95), Decatur(4)
HESSTON Harvey
HIAWATHA Brown
HIGHLAND Doniphan
HILL CITY Graham
HILLSBORO Marion
HILLSDALE Miami
HOISINGTON Barton
HOLCOMB (67851) Finney(95), Kearny(2), Scott(1)
HOLLENBERG Washington
HOLTON (66436) Jackson(97), Atchison(2)
HOLYROOD (67450) Ellsworth(84), Barton(14), Russell(1)
HOME Marshall
HOPE (67451) Dickinson(98), Marion(1)
HORTON (66439) Brown(84), Jackson(10), Atchison(5)
HOWARD Elk
HOXIE (67740) Sheridan(97), Graham(2)
HOYT (66440) Jackson(98), Shawnee(1)
HUDSON Stafford
HUGOTON Stevens
HUMBOLDT Allen
HUNTER (67452) Lincoln(54), Mitchell(45)
HUTCHINSON Reno
INDEPENDENCE Montgomery
INGALLS (67853) Gray(90), Finney(9)
INMAN (67546) McPherson(86), Rice(6), Reno(5)
IOLA Allen
ISABEL (67065) Barber(59), Pratt(38), Kingman(1)
IUKA Pratt
JAMESTOWN (66948) Cloud(81), Republic(18)
JENNINGS (67643) Decatur(94), Sheridan(5)
JETMORE Hodgeman
JEWELL Jewell
JOHNSON (67855) Stanton(96), Grant(2), Morton(1)
JUNCTION CITY Geary
KALVESTA Finney
KANOPOLIS Ellsworth
KANORADO (67741) Sherman(95), Cheyenne(2), Wallace(1)
KANSAS CITY (66109) Wyandotte(97), Leavenworth(2)
KANSAS CITY Wyandotte
KECHI Sedgwick
KENDALL (67857) Hamilton(55), Kearny(44)
KENSINGTON (66951) Smith(75), Phillips(24)
KINCAID (66039) Anderson(89), Allen(10)
KINGMAN (67068) Kingman(98), Reno(1)
KINGSDOWN (67858) Ford(90), Clark(9)
KINSLEY (67547) Edwards(97), Hodgeman(1)
KIOWA Barber
KIRWIN (67644) Phillips(91), Smith(5), Rooks(3)
KISMET Seward
LA CROSSE Rush
LA CYGNE Linn
LA HARPE Allen
LAKE CITY Barber
LAKIN Kearny
LAMONT Greenwood
LANCASTER Atchison
LANE Franklin
LANSING Leavenworth
LARNED (67550) Pawnee(97), Stafford(1)
LATHAM (67072) Butler(87), Cowley(12)
LAWRENCE (66044) Douglas(92), Jefferson(4), Leavenworth(3)
LAWRENCE Douglas
LE ROY Coffey
LEAVENWORTH Leavenworth
LEBANON (66952) Smith(98), Jewell(1)
LEBO (66856) Coffey(70), Osage(29)
LECOMPTON Douglas
LEHIGH Marion
LENEXA Johnson
LENORA (67645) Norton(73), Graham(26)
LEON Butler
LEONARDVILLE Riley
LEOTI (67861) Wichita(96), Logan(3)
LEVANT Thomas
LEWIS Edwards
LIBERAL Seward
LIBERTY (67351) Montgomery(85), Labette(14)
LIEBENTHAL Rush
LINCOLN Lincoln
LINCOLNVILLE (66858) Marion(97), Chase(2)
LINDSBORG (67456) McPherson(89), Saline(10)
LINN Washington
LINWOOD Leavenworth
LITTLE RIVER Rice
LOGAN (67646) Phillips(78), Rooks(9), Graham(7), Norton(4)
LONG ISLAND Phillips
LONGFORD (67458) Clay(83), Ottawa(15)
LONGTON (67352) Elk(96), Chautauqua(3)
LORRAINE Ellsworth
LOST SPRINGS (66859) Marion(86), Morris(13)
LOUISBURG Miami
LOUISVILLE Pottawatomie
LUCAS (67648) Russell(75), Osborne(18), Lincoln(6)
LUDELL Rawlins
LURAY (67649) Russell(65), Osborne(34)
LYNDON Osage
LYONS Rice
MACKSVILLE (67557) Stafford(59), Pratt(19), Pawnee(14), Edwards(6)
MADISON (66860) Greenwood(58), Lyon(41)
MAHASKA (66955) Washington(98), Republic(1)
MAIZE Sedgwick
MANCHESTER Dickinson
MANHATTAN (66503) Riley(98), Pottawatomie(1)
MANHATTAN Riley
MANKATO Jewell
MANTER (67862) Stanton(75), Morton(24)
MAPLE CITY Cowley
MAPLE HILL Wabaunsee
MAPLETON (66754) Bourbon(96), Linn(3)
MARIENTHAL Wichita
MARION Marion
MARQUETTE (67464) McPherson(75), Ellsworth(24)
MARYSVILLE Marshall
MATFIELD GREEN Chase
MAYETTA Jackson
MAYFIELD Sumner
MC CONNELL A F B Sedgwick
MC CRACKEN (67556) Rush(67), Ellis(16), Ness(15)
MC CUNE (66753) Crawford(96), Labette(4)
MC DONALD (67745) Rawlins(75), Cheyenne(25)
MC FARLAND Wabaunsee
MC LOUTH (66054) Jefferson(69), Leavenworth(30)
MCCONNELL AFB Sedgwick
MCPHERSON McPherson
MEADE Meade
MEDICINE LODGE Barber
MELVERN Osage
MENTOR Saline
MERIDEN (66512) Jefferson(90), Jackson(6), Shawnee(3)
MILAN Sumner
MILFORD Geary
MILTON (67106) Sumner(62), Sedgwick(35), Kingman(2)
MILTONVALE (67466) Cloud(60), Ottawa(25), Clay(14)
MINNEAPOLIS Ottawa
MINNEOLA (67865) Ford(65), Clark(34)
MISSION Johnson
MOLINE (67353) Elk(75), Chautauqua(24)
MONTEZUMA (67867) Gray(96), Meade(3)
MONUMENT (67747) Logan(90), Thomas(9)
MORAN (66755) Allen(98), Bourbon(1)
MORGANVILLE Clay
MORLAND Graham
MORRILL Brown
MORROWVILLE Washington
MOSCOW Stevens
MOUND CITY Linn
MOUND VALLEY Labette
MOUNDRIDGE (67107) McPherson(68), Harvey(31)
MOUNT HOPE (67108) Sedgwick(59), Reno(40)
MULBERRY Crawford
MULLINVILLE Kiowa
MULVANE (67110) Sedgwick(68), Sumner(30), Cowley(1)
MUNDEN Republic
MURDOCK Kingman
MUSCOTAH (66058) Jackson(66), Atchison(33)
NARKA (66960) Republic(97), Washington(2)
NASHVILLE (67112) Kingman(86), Barber(13)
NATOMA (67651) Osborne(66), Rooks(26), Ellis(5), Russell(1)
NEAL Greenwood
NEKOMA (67559) Rush(84), Pawnee(15)
NEODESHA (66757) Wilson(92), Montgomery(7)
NEOSHO FALLS (66758) Coffey(54), Woodson(40), Anderson(2), Allen(1)
NEOSHO RAPIDS (66864) Lyon(90), Coffey(9)
NESS CITY Ness
NETAWAKA (66516) Jackson(78), Brown(21)
NEW ALBANY Wilson
NEW ALMELO Norton
NEW CAMBRIA (67470) Saline(89), Ottawa(10)
NEW CENTURY Johnson
NEWTON (67114) Harvey(95), Butler(2), Marion(1)
NICKERSON Reno
NIOTAZE Chautauqua
NORCATUR (67653) Decatur(70), Norton(29)
NORTH NEWTON Harvey
NORTON Norton
NORTONVILLE (66060) Jefferson(51), Atchison(48)
NORWAY Republic

NORWICH (67118) Kingman(94), Sedgwick(2), Harper(1), Sumner(1)
OAKHILL (67472) Clay(70), Ottawa(29)
OAKLEY (67748) Logan(83), Thomas(11), Gove(4)
OBERLIN (67749) Decatur(98), Rawlins(1)
ODIN Barton
OFFERLE (67563) Edwards(56), Ford(38), Hodgeman(4)
OGALLAH (67656) Trego(92), Graham(7)
OGDEN Riley
OKETO Marshall
OLATHE Johnson
OLMITZ Barton
OLPE Lyon
OLSBURG Pottawatomie
ONAGA (66521) Pottawatomie(94), Nemaha(5)
ONEIDA Nemaha
OPOLIS Crawford
OSAGE CITY Osage
OSAWATOMIE (66064) Miami(96), Franklin(3)
OSBORNE Osborne
OSKALOOSA Jefferson
OSWEGO (67356) Labette(98), Cherokee(1)
OTIS (67565) Rush(87), Barton(10), Russell(1)
OTTAWA Franklin
OVERBROOK (66524) Osage(58), Douglas(28), Shawnee(9), Franklin(2)
OVERLAND PARK Johnson
OXFORD (67119) Sumner(67), Cowley(32)
OZAWKIE Jefferson
PALCO (67657) Rooks(60), Graham(37), Trego(2)
PALMER (66962) Washington(88), Clay(11)
PAOLA Miami
PARADISE (67658) Russell(67), Osborne(32)
PARK (67751) Gove(69), Sheridan(30)
PARKER (66072) Linn(94), Miami(4)
PARSONS (67357) Labette(93), Neosho(6)
PARTRIDGE Reno
PAWNEE ROCK (67567) Barton(61), Pawnee(24), Stafford(9), Rush(5)
PAXICO Wabaunsee
PEABODY (66866) Marion(93), Harvey(5)
PECK (67120) Sedgwick(70), Sumner(29)
PENOKEE Graham
PERRY Jefferson
PERU Chautauqua
PFEIFER Ellis
PHILLIPSBURG Phillips
PIEDMONT (67122) Greenwood(65), Elk(34)
PIERCEVILLE Finney
PIQUA Woodson
PITTSBURG (66762) Crawford(97), Cherokee(2)
PLAINS (67869) Meade(86), Seward(13)
PLAINVILLE Rooks
PLEASANTON Linn
PLEVNA Reno
POMONA Franklin
PORTIS (67474) Osborne(72), Smith(27)
POTTER Atchison
POTWIN Butler
POWHATTAN Brown
PRAIRIE VIEW (67664) Phillips(92), Norton(7)
PRATT Pratt
PRESCOTT Linn
PRETTY PRAIRIE (67570) Reno(90), Kingman(9)
PRINCETON Franklin
PROTECTION (67127) Comanche(88), Clark(11)
QUENEMO Osage
QUINTER (67752) Gove(91), Sheridan(8)
RAGO Kingman
RAMONA (67475) Marion(63), Dickinson(36)
RANDALL Jewell
RANDOLPH Riley
RANSOM (67572) Ness(81), Trego(18)
RANTOUL (66079) Franklin(94), Miami(5)
RAYMOND Rice
READING (66868) Lyon(88), Osage(10)
REDFIELD Bourbon
REPUBLIC Republic
REXFORD (67753) Thomas(63), Sheridan(30), Rawlins(5)
RICHFIELD Morton
RICHMOND (66080) Franklin(77), Anderson(22)
RILEY Riley
RIVERTON Cherokee
ROBINSON (66532) Brown(72), Doniphan(27)
ROCK (67131) Cowley(98), Butler(1)
ROLLA (67954) Morton(74), Stevens(25)
ROSALIA Butler
ROSE HILL (67133) Butler(98), Sedgwick(1)
ROSSVILLE (66533) Shawnee(97), Jackson(3)
ROXBURY McPherson
ROZEL Pawnee
RUSH CENTER (67575) Rush(96), Pawnee(3)
RUSSELL (67665) Russell(98), Barton(1)
RUSSELL SPRINGS Logan
SABETHA (66534) Nemaha(92), Brown(7)
SAINT FRANCIS Cheyenne
SAINT GEORGE Pottawatomie
SAINT JOHN (67576) Stafford(96), Pratt(3)
SAINT MARYS (66536) Pottawatomie(94), Wabaunsee(2), Shawnee(2)
SAINT PAUL Neosho
SALINA Saline
SATANTA (67870) Haskell(78), Grant(16), Seward(5)
SAVONBURG (66772) Allen(97), Bourbon(2)
SAWYER (67134) Pratt(89), Barber(10)
SCAMMON Cherokee
SCANDIA Republic
SCHOENCHEN Ellis
SCOTT CITY (67871) Scott(97), Finney(1)
SCRANTON Osage
SEDAN Chautauqua
SEDGWICK (67135) Harvey(60), Sedgwick(39)
SELDEN (67757) Sheridan(57), Decatur(38), Thomas(4)
SENECA Nemaha
SEVERY (67137) Greenwood(88), Elk(11)
SEWARD Stafford
SHARON (67138) Barber(97), Harper(2)
SHARON SPRINGS Wallace
SHAWNEE Johnson
SHAWNEE MISSION Johnson
SHIELDS (67874) Lane(86), Gove(13)
SILVER LAKE (66539) Shawnee(97), Jackson(2)
SIMPSON Mitchell
SMITH CENTER Smith
SMOLAN Saline
SOLDIER (66540) Jackson(96), Nemaha(3)
SOLOMON (67480) Dickinson(59), Saline(20), Ottawa(19)
SOUTH HAVEN Sumner
SOUTH HUTCHINSON Reno
SPEARVILLE (67876) Ford(91), Hodgeman(8)
SPIVEY Kingman
SPRING HILL (66083) Johnson(62), Miami(37)
STAFFORD Stafford
STARK (66775) Neosho(98), Bourbon(1)
STERLING (67579) Rice(81), Reno(18)
STILWELL Johnson
STOCKTON Rooks
STRONG CITY Chase
STUDLEY (67759) Sheridan(89), Graham(10)
STUTTGART Phillips
SUBLETTE (67877) Haskell(93), Seward(6)
SUMMERFIELD Marshall
SUN CITY Barber
SYCAMORE Montgomery
SYLVAN GROVE (67481) Lincoln(96), Russell(3)
SYLVIA Reno
SYRACUSE (67878) Hamilton(85), Stanton(14)
TALMAGE Dickinson
TAMPA Marion
TECUMSEH Shawnee
TESCOTT (67484) Ottawa(80), Saline(15), Lincoln(3)
THAYER (66776) Neosho(82), Wilson(15)
TIMKEN (67582) Rush(98), Pawnee(1)
TIPTON (67485) Osborne(53), Mitchell(46)
TONGANOXIE Leavenworth
TOPEKA (66615) Shawnee(87), Wabaunsee(12)
TOPEKA (66617) Shawnee(90), Jefferson(8)
TOPEKA Shawnee
TORONTO (66777) Woodson(87), Greenwood(11), Wilson(1)
TOWANDA Butler
TREECE Cherokee
TRIBUNE Greeley
TROY Doniphan
TURON (67583) Reno(49), Pratt(41), Stafford(9)
TURON Pratt
TYRO Montgomery
UDALL (67146) Cowley(93), Sumner(6)
ULYSSES (67880) Grant(98), Kearny(1)
UNIONTOWN Bourbon
UTICA (67584) Ness(56), Gove(23), Lane(10), Trego(9)
VALLEY CENTER (67147) Sedgwick(97), Harvey(2)
VALLEY FALLS (66088) Jefferson(97), Atchison(2)
VASSAR Osage
VERMILLION (66544) Marshall(95), Nemaha(4)
VICTORIA Ellis
VIOLA Sedgwick
VIRGIL (66870) Greenwood(97), Woodson(2)
VLIETS Marshall
WA KEENEY (67672) Trego(96), Graham(3)
WAKARUSA (66546) Shawnee(86), Osage(13)
WAKEFIELD (67487) Clay(90), Dickinson(7), Geary(2)
WALDO (67673) Russell(82), Osborne(17)
WALDRON Harper
WALKER Ellis
WALLACE (67761) Wallace(70), Logan(26), Wichita(2)
WALNUT (66780) Bourbon(78), Crawford(20), Neosho(1)
WALTON (67151) Harvey(89), Marion(10)
WAMEGO (66547) Pottawatomie(88), Wabaunsee(11)
WATERVILLE (66548) Marshall(95), Washington(2), Riley(1)
WATHENA Doniphan
WAVERLY (66871) Coffey(96), Osage(3)
WEBBER Jewell
WEIR Cherokee
WELDA (66091) Anderson(97), Franklin(2)
WELLINGTON Sumner
WELLS Ottawa
WELLSVILLE (66092) Franklin(66), Miami(25), Douglas(7)
WESKAN (67762) Wallace(98), Greeley(1)
WEST MINERAL Cherokee
WESTMORELAND Pottawatomie
WESTPHALIA (66093) Anderson(56), Coffey(43)
WETMORE (66550) Nemaha(80), Jackson(10), Brown(8)
WHEATON (66551) Pottawatomie(98), Marshall(1)
WHITE CITY (66872) Morris(96), Geary(3)
WHITE CLOUD (66094) Doniphan(98), Brown(1)
WHITEWATER (67154) Butler(94), Harvey(5)
WHITING Jackson
WICHITA (67230) Sedgwick(96), Butler(3)
WICHITA Sedgwick
WILLIAMSBURG (66095) Franklin(88), Anderson(10)
WILMORE (67155) Comanche(84), Kiowa(15)
WILSEY Morris
WILSON (67490) Ellsworth(82), Russell(10), Lincoln(6)
WINCHESTER (66097) Jefferson(98), Leavenworth(1)
WINDOM (67491) McPherson(77), Rice(22)
WINFIELD Cowley
WINONA (67764) Logan(88), Thomas(11)
WOODBINE Dickinson
WOODSTON Rooks
WRIGHT Ford
YATES CENTER Woodson
YODER Reno
ZENDA (67159) Kingman(83), Harper(16)
ZURICH (67676) Rooks(90), Ellis(9)

Kansas ZIP/City Cross Reference

ZIP Range	City
66002-66002	ATCHISON
66006-66006	BALDWIN CITY
66007-66007	BASEHOR
66008-66008	BENDENA
66010-66010	BLUE MOUND
66012-66012	BONNER SPRINGS
66013-66013	BUCYRUS
66014-66014	CENTERVILLE
66015-66015	COLONY
66016-66016	CUMMINGS
66017-66017	DENTON
66018-66018	DE SOTO
66019-66019	CLEARVIEW CITY
66020-66020	EASTON
66021-66021	EDGERTON
66023-66023	EFFINGHAM
66024-66024	ELWOOD
66025-66025	EUDORA
66026-66026	FONTANA
66027-66027	FORT LEAVENWORTH
66030-66030	GARDNER
66031-66031	NEW CENTURY
66032-66032	GARNETT
66033-66033	GREELEY
66035-66035	HIGHLAND
66036-66036	HILLSDALE
66039-66039	KINCAID
66040-66040	LA CYGNE
66041-66041	LANCASTER
66042-66042	LANE
66043-66043	LANSING
66044-66047	LAWRENCE
66048-66048	LEAVENWORTH
66049-66049	LAWRENCE
66050-66050	LECOMPTON
66051-66051	OLATHE
66052-66052	LINWOOD
66053-66053	LOUISBURG
66054-66054	MC LOUTH
66056-66056	MOUND CITY
66058-66058	MUSCOTAH
66060-66060	NORTONVILLE
66061-66063	OLATHE
66064-66064	OSAWATOMIE
66066-66066	OSKALOOSA
66067-66067	OTTAWA
66070-66070	OZAWKIE
66071-66071	PAOLA
66072-66072	PARKER
66073-66073	PERRY
66075-66075	PLEASANTON
66076-66076	POMONA
66077-66077	POTTER
66078-66078	PRINCETON
66079-66079	RANTOUL
66080-66080	RICHMOND
66083-66083	SPRING HILL
66085-66085	STILWELL
66086-66086	TONGANOXIE
66087-66087	TROY
66088-66088	VALLEY FALLS
66090-66090	WATHENA
66091-66091	WELDA
66092-66092	WELLSVILLE
66093-66093	WESTPHALIA
66094-66094	WHITE CLOUD
66095-66095	WILLIAMSBURG
66097-66097	WINCHESTER
66100-66112	KANSAS CITY
66113-66113	EDWARDSVILLE
66115-66160	KANSAS CITY
66200-66201	SHAWNEE MISSION
66201-66201	MISSION
66202-66222	SHAWNEE MISSION
66222-66222	MISSION
66223-66251	SHAWNEE MISSION
66251-66251	OVERLAND PARK
66262-66283	SHAWNEE MISSION
66283-66283	OVERLAND PARK
66285-66285	SHAWNEE MISSION
66285-66285	LENEXA
66286-66286	SHAWNEE MISSION
66286-66286	SHAWNEE
66401-66401	ALMA
66402-66402	AUBURN
66403-66403	AXTELL
66404-66404	BAILEYVILLE
66406-66406	BEATTIE
66407-66407	BELVUE
66408-66408	BERN
66409-66409	BERRYTON
66411-66411	BLUE RAPIDS
66412-66412	BREMEN
66413-66413	BURLINGAME
66414-66414	CARBONDALE
66415-66415	CENTRALIA
66416-66416	CIRCLEVILLE
66417-66417	CORNING
66418-66418	DELIA
66419-66419	DENISON
66420-66420	DOVER
66422-66422	EMMETT
66423-66423	ESKRIDGE
66424-66424	EVEREST
66425-66425	FAIRVIEW
66426-66426	FOSTORIA
66427-66427	FRANKFORT
66428-66428	GOFF
66429-66429	GRANTVILLE
66431-66431	HARVEYVILLE
66432-66432	HAVENSVILLE
66433-66433	MARYSVILLE
66434-66435	HIAWATHA
66436-66436	HOLTON
66438-66438	HOME
66439-66439	HORTON
66440-66440	HOYT
66441-66441	JUNCTION CITY
66442-66442	FORT RILEY
66449-66449	LEONARDVILLE
66450-66450	LOUISVILLE
66451-66451	LYNDON
66501-66501	MC FARLAND
66502-66506	MANHATTAN
66507-66507	MAPLE HILL
66508-66508	MARYSVILLE
66509-66509	MAYETTA
66510-66510	MELVERN
66512-66512	MERIDEN
66514-66514	MILFORD
66515-66515	MORRILL
66516-66516	NETAWAKA
66517-66517	OGDEN
66518-66518	OKETO
66520-66520	OLSBURG
66521-66521	ONAGA
66522-66522	ONEIDA
66523-66523	OSAGE CITY
66524-66524	OVERBROOK
66526-66526	PAXICO
66527-66527	POWHATTAN
66528-66528	QUENEMO
66531-66531	RILEY
66532-66532	ROBINSON
66533-66533	ROSSVILLE
66534-66534	SABETHA
66535-66535	SAINT GEORGE
66536-66536	SAINT MARYS
66537-66537	SCRANTON
66538-66538	SENECA
66539-66539	SILVER LAKE
66540-66540	SOLDIER
66541-66541	SUMMERFIELD
66542-66542	TECUMSEH
66543-66543	VASSAR
66544-66544	VERMILLION
66545-66545	VLIETS
66546-66546	WAKARUSA
66547-66547	WAMEGO
66548-66548	WATERVILLE
66549-66549	WESTMORELAND
66550-66550	WETMORE
66551-66551	WHEATON
66552-66552	WHITING
66554-66554	RANDOLPH
66555-66555	MARYSVILLE
66600-66699	TOPEKA
66701-66701	FORT SCOTT
66710-66710	ALTOONA
66711-66711	ARCADIA
66712-66712	ARMA
66713-66713	BAXTER SPRINGS
66714-66714	BENEDICT
66716-66716	BRONSON
66717-66717	BUFFALO
66720-66720	CHANUTE
66724-66724	CHEROKEE
66725-66725	COLUMBUS
66727-66727	COYVILLE
66728-66728	CRESTLINE
66732-66732	ELSMORE
66733-66733	ERIE
66734-66734	FARLINGTON
66735-66735	FRANKLIN
66736-66736	FREDONIA
66738-66738	FULTON
66739-66739	GALENA
66740-66740	GALESBURG
66741-66741	GARLAND
66741-66741	ARCADIA
66742-66742	GAS
66743-66743	GIRARD
66746-66746	HEPLER
66748-66748	HUMBOLDT
66749-66749	IOLA
66751-66751	LA HARPE
66753-66753	MC CUNE
66754-66754	MAPLETON
66755-66755	MORAN
66756-66756	MULBERRY
66757-66757	NEODESHA
66758-66758	NEOSHO FALLS
66759-66759	NEW ALBANY
66760-66760	OPOLIS
66761-66761	PIQUA
66762-66762	PITTSBURG
66763-66763	FRONTENAC
66767-66767	PRESCOTT
66769-66769	REDFIELD
66770-66770	RIVERTON
66771-66771	SAINT PAUL
66772-66772	SAVONBURG
66773-66773	SCAMMON
66775-66775	STARK
66776-66776	THAYER
66777-66777	TORONTO
66778-66778	TREECE
66779-66779	UNIONTOWN
66780-66780	WALNUT
66781-66781	WEIR
66782-66782	WEST MINERAL
66783-66783	YATES CENTER
66801-66801	EMPORIA
66830-66830	ADMIRE
66833-66833	ALLEN
66834-66834	ALTA VISTA
66835-66835	AMERICUS
66838-66838	BURDICK
66839-66839	BURLINGTON
66840-66840	BURNS
66842-66842	CASSODAY
66843-66843	CEDAR POINT
66845-66845	COTTONWOOD FALLS
66846-66846	COUNCIL GROVE
66849-66849	DWIGHT
66850-66850	ELMDALE
66851-66851	FLORENCE
66852-66852	GRIDLEY
66853-66853	HAMILTON
66854-66854	HARTFORD
66855-66855	LAMONT
66856-66856	LEBO
66857-66857	LE ROY
66858-66858	LINCOLNVILLE
66859-66859	LOST SPRINGS
66860-66860	MADISON
66861-66861	MARION
66862-66862	MATFIELD GREEN
66863-66863	NEAL
66864-66864	NEOSHO RAPIDS
66865-66865	OLPE
66866-66866	PEABODY
66868-66868	READING
66869-66869	STRONG CITY
66870-66870	VIRGIL
66871-66871	WAVERLY
66872-66872	WHITE CITY
66873-66873	WILSEY
66901-66901	CONCORDIA
66930-66930	AGENDA
66931-66931	AMES
66932-66932	ATHOL
66933-66933	BARNES
66935-66935	BELLEVILLE
66936-66936	BURR OAK
66937-66937	CLIFTON
66938-66938	CLYDE
66939-66939	COURTLAND
66940-66940	CUBA
66941-66941	ESBON
66942-66942	FORMOSO
66943-66943	GREENLEAF
66944-66944	HADDAM
66945-66945	HANOVER
66946-66946	HOLLENBERG
66948-66948	JAMESTOWN
66949-66949	JEWELL
66951-66951	KENSINGTON
66952-66952	LEBANON
66953-66953	LINN
66955-66955	MAHASKA
66956-66956	MANKATO
66958-66958	MORROWVILLE
66959-66959	MUNDEN
66960-66960	NARKA
66961-66961	NORWAY
66962-66962	PALMER
66963-66963	RANDALL
66964-66964	REPUBLIC
66966-66966	SCANDIA
66967-66967	SMITH CENTER
66968-66968	WASHINGTON
66970-66970	WEBBER
67001-67001	ANDALE
67002-67002	ANDOVER
67003-67003	ANTHONY
67004-67004	ARGONIA
67005-67005	ARKANSAS CITY
67008-67008	ATLANTA
67009-67009	ATTICA
67010-67010	AUGUSTA
67012-67012	BEAUMONT
67013-67013	BELLE PLAINE
67015-67015	BELVIDERE
67016-67016	BENTLEY
67017-67017	BENTON
67018-67018	BLUFF CITY
67019-67019	BURDEN
67020-67020	BURRTON
67021-67021	BYERS
67022-67022	CALDWELL
67023-67023	CAMBRIDGE
67024-67024	CEDAR VALE
67025-67025	CHENEY
67026-67026	CLEARWATER
67028-67028	COATS
67029-67029	COLDWATER
67030-67030	COLWICH
67031-67031	CONWAY SPRINGS
67032-67032	CALDWELL
67035-67035	CUNNINGHAM
67036-67036	DANVILLE
67037-67037	DERBY
67038-67038	DEXTER
67039-67039	DOUGLASS
67041-67041	ELBING
67042-67042	EL DORADO
67045-67045	EUREKA
67047-67047	FALL RIVER
67049-67049	FREEPORT
67050-67050	GARDEN PLAIN
67051-67051	GEUDA SPRINGS
67052-67052	GODDARD
67053-67053	GOESSEL
67054-67054	GREENSBURG
67055-67055	GREENWICH
67056-67056	HALSTEAD
67057-67057	HARDTNER
67058-67058	HARPER
67059-67059	HAVILAND

67060-67060 HAYSVILLE
67061-67061 HAZELTON
67062-67062 HESSTON
67063-67063 HILLSBORO
67065-67065 ISABEL
67066-67066 IUKA
67067-67067 KECHI
67068-67068 KINGMAN
67070-67070 KIOWA
67071-67071 LAKE CITY
67072-67072 LATHAM
67073-67073 LEHIGH
67074-67074 LEON
67101-67101 MAIZE
67102-67102 MAPLE CITY
67103-67103 MAYFIELD
67104-67104 MEDICINE LODGE
67105-67105 MILAN
67106-67106 MILTON
67107-67107 MOUNDRIDGE
67108-67108 MOUNT HOPE
67109-67109 MULLINVILLE
67110-67110 MULVANE
67111-67111 MURDOCK
67112-67112 NASHVILLE
67114-67114 NEWTON
67117-67117 NORTH NEWTON
67118-67118 NORWICH
67119-67119 OXFORD
67120-67120 PECK
67122-67122 PIEDMONT
67123-67123 POTWIN
67124-67124 PRATT
67127-67127 PROTECTION
67128-67128 RAGO
67131-67131 ROCK
67132-67132 ROSALIA
67133-67133 ROSE HILL
67134-67134 SAWYER
67135-67135 SEDGWICK
67137-67137 SEVERY
67138-67138 SHARON
67140-67140 SOUTH HAVEN
67142-67142 SPIVEY
67143-67143 SUN CITY
67144-67144 TOWANDA
67146-67146 UDALL
67147-67147 VALLEY CENTER
67149-67149 VIOLA
67150-67150 WALDRON
67151-67151 WALTON
67152-67152 WELLINGTON
67154-67154 WHITEWATER
67155-67155 WILMORE
67156-67156 WINFIELD
67159-67159 ZENDA
67200-67220 WICHITA
67221-67221 MC CONNELL A F B
67221-67221 MCCONNELL AFB
67223-67236 WICHITA
67240-67240 DENNIS THE MENACE
67251-67278 WICHITA
67301-67301 INDEPENDENCE
67330-67330 ALTAMONT
67332-67332 BARTLETT
67333-67333 CANEY
67334-67334 CHAUTAUQUA
67335-67335 CHERRYVALE
67336-67336 CHETOPA
67337-67337 COFFEYVILLE
67340-67340 DEARING
67341-67341 DENNIS
67342-67342 EDNA
67344-67344 ELK CITY
67345-67345 ELK FALLS
67346-67346 GRENOLA
67347-67347 HAVANA
67349-67349 HOWARD
67351-67351 LIBERTY
67352-67352 LONGTON
67353-67353 MOLINE
67354-67354 MOUND VALLEY
67355-67355 NIOTAZE
67356-67356 OSWEGO
67357-67357 PARSONS
67360-67360 PERU
67361-67361 SEDAN
67363-67363 SYCAMORE
67364-67364 TYRO
67401-67402 SALINA
67410-67410 ABILENE
67414-67414 ADA
67416-67416 ASSARIA
67417-67417 AURORA
67418-67418 BARNARD
67420-67420 BELOIT
67422-67422 BENNINGTON
67423-67423 BEVERLY
67425-67425 BROOKVILLE
67427-67427 BUSHTON
67428-67428 CANTON
67429-67429 CARLTON
67430-67430 CAWKER CITY
67431-67431 CHAPMAN
67432-67432 CLAY CENTER
67436-67436 DELPHOS
67437-67437 DOWNS
67438-67438 DURHAM
67439-67439 ELLSWORTH
67441-67441 ENTERPRISE
67442-67442 FALUN
67443-67443 GALVA
67444-67444 GENESEO
67445-67445 GLASCO
67446-67446 GLEN ELDER
67447-67447 GREEN
67448-67448 GYPSUM
67449-67449 HERINGTON
67450-67450 HOLYROOD
67451-67451 HOPE
67452-67452 HUNTER
67454-67454 KANOPOLIS
67455-67455 LINCOLN
67456-67456 LINDSBORG
67457-67457 LITTLE RIVER
67458-67458 LONGFORD
67459-67459 LORRAINE
67460-67460 MCPHERSON
67463-67463 MANCHESTER
67464-67464 MARQUETTE
67465-67465 MENTOR
67466-67466 MILTONVALE
67467-67467 MINNEAPOLIS
67468-67468 MORGANVILLE
67469-67469 ENTERPRISE
67470-67470 NEW CAMBRIA
67472-67472 OAKHILL
67473-67473 OSBORNE
67474-67474 PORTIS
67475-67475 RAMONA
67476-67476 ROXBURY
67478-67478 SIMPSON
67479-67479 SMOLAN
67480-67480 SOLOMON
67481-67481 SYLVAN GROVE
67482-67482 TALMAGE
67483-67483 TAMPA
67484-67484 TESCOTT
67485-67485 TIPTON
67487-67487 WAKEFIELD
67488-67488 WELLS
67490-67490 WILSON
67491-67491 WINDOM
67492-67492 WOODBINE
67501-67504 HUTCHINSON
67505-67505 SOUTH HUTCHINSON
67510-67510 ABBYVILLE
67511-67511 ALBERT
67512-67512 ALDEN
67513-67513 ALEXANDER
67514-67514 ARLINGTON
67515-67515 ARNOLD
67516-67516 BAZINE
67517-67517 BEAVER
67518-67518 BEELER
67519-67519 BELPRE
67520-67520 BISON
67521-67521 BROWNELL
67522-67522 BUHLER
67523-67523 BURDETT
67524-67524 CHASE
67525-67525 CLAFLIN
67526-67526 ELLINWOOD
67529-67529 GARFIELD
67530-67530 GREAT BEND
67543-67543 HAVEN
67544-67544 HOISINGTON
67545-67545 HUDSON
67546-67546 INMAN
67547-67547 KINSLEY
67548-67548 LA CROSSE
67550-67550 LARNED
67552-67552 LEWIS
67553-67553 LIEBENTHAL
67554-67554 LYONS
67556-67556 MC CRACKEN
67557-67557 MACKSVILLE
67559-67559 NEKOMA
67560-67560 NESS CITY
67561-67561 NICKERSON
67562-67562 ODIN
67563-67563 OFFERLE
67564-67564 OLMITZ
67565-67565 OTIS
67566-67566 PARTRIDGE
67567-67567 PAWNEE ROCK
67568-67568 PLEVNA
67569-67569 TURON
67570-67570 PRETTY PRAIRIE
67572-67572 RANSOM
67573-67573 RAYMOND
67574-67574 ROZEL
67575-67575 RUSH CENTER
67576-67576 SAINT JOHN
67577-67577 SEWARD
67578-67578 STAFFORD
67579-67579 STERLING
67581-67581 SYLVIA
67582-67582 TIMKEN
67583-67583 TURON
67584-67584 UTICA
67585-67585 YODER
67601-67601 HAYS
67621-67621 AGRA
67622-67622 ALMENA
67623-67623 ALTON
67625-67625 BOGUE
67626-67626 BUNKER HILL
67627-67627 CATHARINE
67628-67628 CEDAR
67629-67629 CLAYTON
67630-67630 CODELL
67631-67631 COLLYER
67632-67632 DAMAR
67634-67634 DORRANCE
67635-67635 DRESDEN
67636-67636 EDMOND
67637-67637 ELLIS
67638-67638 GAYLORD
67639-67639 GLADE
67640-67640 GORHAM
67641-67641 HARLAN
67642-67642 HILL CITY
67643-67643 JENNINGS
67644-67644 KIRWIN
67645-67645 LENORA
67646-67646 LOGAN
67647-67647 LONG ISLAND
67648-67648 LUCAS
67649-67649 LURAY
67650-67650 MORLAND
67651-67651 NATOMA
67652-67652 NEW ALMELO
67653-67653 NORCATUR
67654-67654 NORTON
67656-67656 OGALLAH
67657-67657 PALCO
67658-67658 PARADISE
67659-67659 PENOKEE
67660-67660 PFEIFER
67661-67661 PHILLIPSBURG
67663-67663 PLAINVILLE
67664-67664 PRAIRIE VIEW
67665-67665 RUSSELL
67667-67667 SCHOENCHEN
67669-67669 STOCKTON
67670-67670 STUTTGART
67671-67671 VICTORIA
67672-67672 WA KEENEY
67673-67673 WALDO
67674-67674 WALKER
67675-67675 WOODSTON
67676-67676 ZURICH
67701-67701 COLBY
67730-67730 ATWOOD
67731-67731 BIRD CITY
67732-67732 BREWSTER
67733-67733 EDSON
67734-67734 GEM
67735-67735 GOODLAND
67736-67736 GOVE
67737-67737 GRAINFIELD
67738-67738 GRINNELL
67739-67739 HERNDON
67740-67740 HOXIE
67741-67741 KANORADO
67743-67743 LEVANT
67744-67744 LUDELL
67745-67745 MC DONALD
67747-67747 MONUMENT
67748-67748 OAKLEY
67749-67749 OBERLIN
67751-67751 PARK
67752-67752 QUINTER
67753-67753 REXFORD
67755-67755 RUSSELL SPRINGS
67756-67756 SAINT FRANCIS
67757-67757 SELDEN
67758-67758 SHARON SPRINGS
67759-67759 STUDLEY
67761-67761 WALLACE
67762-67762 WESKAN
67764-67764 WINONA
67801-67801 DODGE CITY
67831-67831 ASHLAND
67834-67834 BUCKLIN
67835-67835 CIMARRON
67836-67836 COOLIDGE
67837-67837 COPELAND
67838-67838 DEERFIELD
67839-67839 DIGHTON
67840-67840 ENGLEWOOD
67841-67841 ENSIGN
67842-67842 FORD
67843-67843 FORT DODGE
67844-67844 FOWLER
67846-67846 GARDEN CITY
67849-67849 HANSTON
67850-67850 HEALY
67851-67851 HOLCOMB
67853-67853 INGALLS
67854-67854 JETMORE
67855-67855 JOHNSON
67856-67856 KALVESTA
67857-67857 KENDALL
67858-67858 KINGSDOWN
67859-67859 KISMET
67860-67860 LAKIN
67861-67861 LEOTI
67862-67862 MANTER
67863-67863 MARIENTHAL
67864-67864 MEADE
67865-67865 MINNEOLA
67867-67867 MONTEZUMA
67868-67868 PIERCEVILLE
67869-67869 PLAINS
67870-67870 SATANTA
67871-67871 SCOTT CITY
67874-67874 SHIELDS
67876-67876 SPEARVILLE
67877-67877 SUBLETTE
67878-67878 SYRACUSE
67879-67879 TRIBUNE
67880-67880 ULYSSES
67882-67882 WRIGHT
67901-67905 LIBERAL
67950-67950 ELKHART
67951-67951 HUGOTON
67952-67952 MOSCOW
67953-67953 RICHFIELD
67954-67954 ROLLA

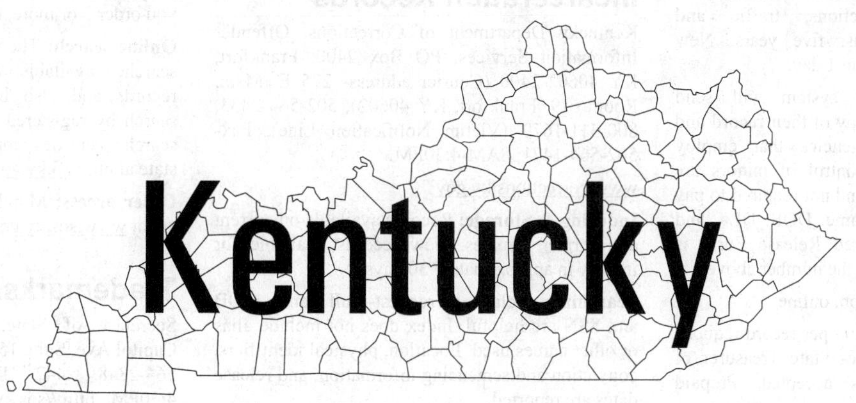

General Help Numbers:

Governor's Office
700 Capitol Ave, Room 100
Frankfort, KY 40601
http://governor.ky.gov/
502-564-2611
Fax 502-564-2517
7:30AM-5PM

Attorney General's Office
700 Capitol Ave, Ste. 118
Frankfort, KY 40601
http://ag.ky.gov/
502-696-5300
Fax 502-564-2894
8AM-5PM

Legislative Records
Kentucky General Assembly, Research Commission
700 Capitol Ave, Room 300
Frankfort, KY 40601
http://www.lrc.ky.gov/
502-564-8100
Fax 502-564-6543
8AM-4:30PM

State Archives
300 Coffee Tree Rd
Frankfort, KY 40601
www.kdla.ky.gov/index.htm
502-564-8300
Fax 502-564-5773
8AM-4PM

State Specifics:

Capital: Frankfort, Franklin County

Time Zone: EST*

* Kentucky's forty western-most counties are CST: They are: Adair, Allen, Ballard, Barren, Breckinridge, Butler, Caldwell, Calloway, Carlisle, Christian, Clinton, Crittenden, Cumberland, Daviess, Edmonson, Fulton, Graves, Grayson, Hancock, Hart, Henderson, Hickman, Hopkins, Livingstone, Logan, Marshall, McCracken, McLean, Metcalfe, Monroe, Muhlenberg, Ohio,Russell, Simpson, Todd, Trigg, Union, Warren, Wayne, and Webster.

Number of Counties: 120

Population: 4,269,245

Web Site: www.kentucky.gov/

State Agencies

Criminal Records

Kentucky State Police, Criminal Identification & Records Branch, 1250 Louisville Rd, Frankfort, KY 40601; 502-227-8713, Fax- 502-226-7422; 8AM-4:30PM. www.kentuckystatepolice.org

Interestingly, local Kentucky courts will not do criminal searches. They refer all requesters to the Administrative Office of Courts in Frankfort, KY; phone 502-573-2350. This office will also suggest to check the court system.

Indexing & Storage: Records available from 1952 on for criminal records. Nearly 95% of records are automated. 75% of arrest records are fingerprint supported. New records available for inquiry in no more than 3 minutes. 69% of all arrests in database have final dispositions recorded, 59% for those arrests within last 5 years.

Searching: Records are available to all requesters as long as a signed release is submitted. Special forms are suggested for certain employment purposes such as nursing, schools, lottery, EMT, YMCA, daycare, and adoptive/foster parent background searches. Include in request- signed release from subject with witness signature, full name, date of birth, SSN, reason for information request. Certain authorized searches require fingerprints to be submitted. Request forms may be downloaded from the webpage. Statistical information about criminal offenses and accidents is available from 1971 on. This data not released- when individual tried as a juvenile. Also, the agency states it will not sell bulk data. Records without dispositions, including pending and dismissed cases, are not released.

Access by: mail, in person.

Fee & Payment: The fee is $10.00 per name. Fee payee- Kentucky State Treasurer. Personal checks accepted, credit cards are not.

Mail search: Turnaround time- 2 to 3 weeks. A SASE is requested.

In person: Turnaround time is while you wait. There is a limit of 5 searches.

Statewide Court Records

Administrative Office of the Courts, Records Unit, 100 Millcreek Park, Frankfort, KY 40601; 502-573-1682, 800-928-6381 (Records Unit), Fax- 502-573-1669; 7:30AM-5PM.

http://courts.ky.gov/aoc/

Administrative Office of the Courts offers a service of providing statewide criminal background checks.

Indexing & Storage: Records available back to 1978 for felony convictions, traffic and misdemeanors back at least five years. New records available for inquiry in 1 day.

Searching: The CourtNet system will send individuals being check a copy of their record and the requester's names. Agencies that employ persons with supervisory control of minors are considered Youth Requests and not required to pay a fee. Include in request- name, DOB, DL#, and SSN if known. The required Release Form is available from the AOC, call the number above.

Access by: mail, fax, in person, online.

Fee & Payment: Fee is $10.00 per record request, $15.00 if by fax. Fee payee- State Treasurer of Kentucky Personal checks accepted. Prepaid accounts are offered.

Mail search: Turnaround time- 2 days. A SASE is required. Search results may be returned by email upon request.

Fax search: Pre-paid search request is permitted. Requests are accepted through 10:30 PM on weekdays. Response is by either email or fax.

In person: Walk-in hours are above; drive-through until 10:30PM.

Online search: Search District Court criminal records at http://apps.kycourts.net/CourtRecords/. The disclaimer states this data should not be used for employment purposes. You may search six days of daily court calendars by county for free at http://apps.kycourts.net/dockets/. KY Bar attorneys may register to use the KCOJ court records data at http://apps.kycourts.net/courtrecordsKBA/, this is a commercial system. From the home page above search Supreme Court docket info and Appellate opinions.

Sexual Offender Registry

Kentucky State Police, Criminal Identification and Records Branch, 1250 Louisville Rd, Frankfort, KY 40601; 502-227-8700, 866-564-5652 (Alert Line), Fax- 502-226-7419; 8AM-4:30PM.

http://kspsor.state.ky.us

The Alert Line is open 24 hours daily. Sex offenders must register their location for a minimum of ten years or a maximum of their lifetime, depending on crime.

Indexing & Storage: Records available from 7/15/94 forward (convictions) or incarcerated or sentenced if after July 15, 1998. New records available for inquiry in 1 hour.

Searching: Only offenders convicted of statutorily covered crimes who are convicted after July 15, 1994 or incarcerated or sentenced after July 15, 1998 are listed. This data not released- information that identifies a victim, fingerprints, SSNs, vehicle registration data.

Access by: phone, online.

Phone search: Open 24-hours daily, the Alert Line provides up-to-date information. Provide your telephone number and up to three ZIP Codes to monitor. You will be notified if registered sex offender is moving into one of the ZIP Code areas that you entered, and directed to the website for more information.

Online search: Access is available via the website; all registrants are listed. Online searches must provide one of the following fields: Last Name, City, ZIP, or County.

Other access: None

Incarceration Records

Kentucky Department of Corrections, Offender Information Services, PO Box 2400, Frankfort, KY 40602-2400 (Courier address- 275 E. Main, Room 619, Frankfort, KY 40602); 502-564-2433, 800-511-1670 (Victim Notification Line), Fax-502-564-1471; 8AM-4:30PM.

www.corrections.ky.gov

Indexing & Storage: Records available on current and former inmates. New records available for inquiry in approximately 30 days.

Searching: Include in request- full name. DOB and SSN are helpful. Index does not include alias or other names used. Location, physical identifiers, conviction and sentencing information, and release dates are reported.

Access by: mail, fax, online.

Fee & Payment: Copy fee is $.10 per page. There is no search fee. Fee payee- Kentucky Treasurer Prepayment required Personal checks and credit cards accepted.

Mail search: Turnaround time- 1 to 2 weeks. Older, archived records require a longer turnaround time. A SASE or postage is requested.

Fax search: Can request via fax.

Online search: The website http://apps.corrections.ky.gov/KOOL/ioffsrch.asp provides current inmate information on the Kentucky Online Offender Lookup (KOOL) system as a service to the public. It can take as long as 120 days for the data to be current.

Other access: The IT Department has the database on CD available for $50.00; call 502-564-4360.

Expedited service: Will expedite processing if reason is given for delivering the record in a timely manner.

Corporation, LP, Assumed Name, LLC Records

Secretary of State, Corporate Records - Records, PO Box 718, Frankfort, KY 40602-0718 (Courier address- 700 Capitol Ave, Room 156, Frankfort, KY 40601); 502-564-7330, Fax- 502-564-4075; 8AM-4:30PM. http://sos.ky.gov/business/

Indexing & Storage: Records available from the 1977 forward on computer index. Hard copies are on microfilm. Records inactive by 1976 are archived and it takes 2 weeks to research. New records available for inquiry immediately.

Searching: Computer records contain name, dates, current registered agent and initial incorporators and initial directors. They do contain current lists of officers and directors when available. Include in request- full name of business. A request form for copies or documents may be downloaded from the web.

Access by: mail, phone, fax, in person, online.

Fee & Payment: There is no search fee. Copies are $5.00 for the first 5 pages and $.50 ea add'l. Certification is an additional $5.00 order. A Certificate of Good Standing is $10.00. Fee payee-Secretary of State. Prepayment required. If certified copies are needed, call first. Personal checks and credit cards accepted.

Mail search: Turnaround time- 2 to 3 days. SASE not required.

Phone search: Only information on the computer system is released over the phone. **Fax search:** Fax requests accepted with a credit card.

In person: Turnaround time while you wait. If you order 5 or more, they will mail records to you.

Online search: The web page has several distinct searches available. Search business filings and records and also business organizations. Also search by registered agent or officer name. Also, search securities companies registered with the state at http://fi.ky.gov/scr/ifs/old/sec/default.asp.

Other access: Monthly lists of new corporations are at www.sos.ky.gov/business/bulkdata/.

Trademarks/Servicemarks

Secretary of State, Trademarks Section, 700 Capitol Ave, Suite 152, Frankfort, KY 40601; 502-564-2848 x442, Fax- 502-564-4075; 8AM-4:30PM. http://sos.ky.gov/business/trademarks/

Indexing & Storage: Records available from 1967. Original documents kept 3 years. New records available for inquiry in minutes.

Searching: Include the trademark/servicemark name or applicant name or certification number. Also, wordmark and description helps.

Access by: mail, phone, fax, in person, online.

Fee & Payment: There is no fee.

Mail search: Turnaround time- 1 week. A SASE is requested.

Phone search: Ask for Johnna Ballinger.

Fax search: Fax requests accepted.

In person: Turnaround time is while you wait.

Online search: Free, searchable database at http://apps.sos.ky.gov/business/trademarks/.

Uniform Commercial Code

UCC Branch, Secretary of State, PO Box 1470, Frankfort, KY 40601; 502-564-2848, Fax- 502-564-7411; 8AM-4:30PM.

http://sos.ky.gov/business/ucc/

Indexing & Storage: Records available up to one year after a lapse date. New records available for inquiry in 24 hours.

Searching: The Secretary of State maintains a searchable index for all active UCC records that provides for the retrieval of a record by the name of the debtor and by the file number of the initial financing statement to which the record relates. Include in request- full debtor name on Form UCC-11. The name will be searched exactly as provided on form. This data not released- personal information (has been redacted).

Access by: mail, in person, online.

Fee & Payment: $5.00 for a certified search. $.10 per page for copies of UCC records. $10 for all written financing statements and amendments, $20.00 if over 2 pages. Ongoing requesters may open a pre-paid account with a $250 deposit. Fee payee- KY State Treasurer. Prepayment no required. Overpayments will be returned. Personal checks accepted. Major credit cards accepted.

Mail search: Turnaround time- 1-3 business days. Full names are required.

In person: The physical address is Room 153 of the Capitol. Turnaround time is while you wait. If you order extensive records, they will mail the results to you.

Online search: UCC record searching is offered free of charge at the website or see http://sos.ky.gov/business/ucc/online/. Search by debtor name or file number. SSNs are withheld from the online system.

Other access: Monthly or weekly lists of new UCC filing at www.sos.ky.gov/business/bulkdata/.

Federal & State Tax Liens

Records not maintained by a state level agency.

All tax liens are at the county level.

Sales Tax Registrations

Dept of Revenue, Tax Compliance Bureau, Sales Tax Division, Station 53, PO Box 181, Frankfort, KY 40602-0181 (Courier address- 200 Fair Oaks, Bldg 2, Frankfort, KY 40602); 502-564-5170, Fax- 502-564-2041; 8AM-4:30PM.

http://revenue.ky.gov

This agency will only confirm if a tax permit exists. The agency will NOT confirm if a business is registered. They will provide no other information.

Indexing & Storage: Records available from the 1970's, from 1998 on paper. Records are indexed on computer from 1996 to present, and on microfilm from 1985 to 1995. New records available for inquiry in up to 3 months.

Searching: Include in request- tax permit number. This data not released- personal, confidential data.

Access by: mail, in person.

Mail search: Turnaround time- 2 to 3 months. A SASE is requested. No fee for mail request.

In person: No fee for request.

Birth Certificates

Department for Public Health, Vital Statistics, 275 E Main St - IE-A, Frankfort, KY 40621-0001; 502-564-4212, 877- 817-7362 (Order), Fax- 502-227-0032; 8AM-4:30PM.

http://chfs.ky.gov/dph/vital/

The state's Birth Certificate Request Form is at http://chfs.ky.gov/forms/default.htm and click on Birth Certificate Application.

Indexing & Storage: Records available from 1911 to present. New records available for inquiry in 1 month.

Searching: Include in request- full name, names of parents, mother's maiden name, date of birth, place of birth. Provide a daytime phone number.

Access by: mail, phone, fax, in person, online.

Fee & Payment: Searches are $10.00 per name. Add $10.50 if using a credit card. Fee payee- Kentucky State Treasurer. Prepayment required. Personal checks, money orders accepted. Major credit cards accepted.

Mail search: Turnaround time- 30 working days. SASE not required.

Phone search: Must use a credit card (add $10.50 fee) for a phone request. Turnaround time is up to 30 days.

Fax search: Order by fax from fax 877-435-5584. Use of credit card required.

In person: Turnaround time 1 1/2 hour.

Online search: Records may be ordered online via a state designated vendor at www.vitalchek.com.

Expedited service: Expedited service is available for mail, phone, online and fax orders. Turnaround time- overnight delivery. Additional fees involved for use of credit card ($10.95) and shipping.

Death Records

Department for Public Health, Vital Statistics, 275 E Main St - IE-A, Frankfort, KY 40621-0001; 502-564-4212, 877- 817-7362 (Order), Fax- 502-227-0032; 8AM-4:30PM.

http://chfs.ky.gov/dph/vital/

Indexing & Storage: Records from 1911 on. New records available for inquiry in 1 month.

Searching: Include in request- full name, date of death, county of death. Provide a daytime phone number.

Access by: mail, phone, fax, in person, online.

Fee & Payment: The fee is $6.00 per name. Fee payee- Kentucky State Treasurer. Prepayment required. Personal checks, money orders accepted. Major credit cards accepted.

Mail search: Turnaround time- 30 working days. SASE not required.

Phone search: Must use a credit card (add $10.50 fee) to make phone request. Turnaround time is up to 30 days. **Fax search:** Order by fax from fax 877-435-5584. Use of credit card required.

In person: Turnaround time 1 1/2 hour.

Online search: In cooperation with the University of Kentucky, there is a searchable death index at http://ukcc.uky.edu/vitalrec/. This is for non-commercial use only. Records are from 1911 through 1992. Also, a free genealogy site at http://vitals.rootsweb.ancestry.com/ky/death/search.cgi. Death Indexes from 1911-2000 is available. Search by surname, given name, place of death, residence, or year. Records may be ordered online via state designated vendor at www.vitalchek.com.

Expedited service: Expedited service is available for mail, phone, online and fax orders. Turnaround time- overnight delivery. Additional fees involved for use of credit card and shipping.

Marriage Certificates

Department for Public Health, Vital Statistics, 275 E Main St - IE-A, Frankfort, KY 40621-0001; 502-564-4212, 877- 817-7362 (Order), Fax- 502-227-0032; 8AM-4:30PM.

http://chfs.ky.gov/dph/vital/

Indexing & Storage: Records available from June 1958 to present. New records available for inquiry in 1 to 2 months.

Searching: Copies of marriage certificates prior to June 1958 may be obtained from the County Clerk in the county where the license was issued. Include in request- names of husband and wife, date of marriage, place or county of marriage. Must also include where marriage license was obtained and a daytime phone number.

Access by: mail, phone, fax, in person, online.

Fee & Payment: The fee is $6.00 per name. Fee payee- Kentucky State Treasurer. Prepayment required. Personal checks, money orders accepted. Major credit cards accepted.

Mail search: Turnaround time- 30 working days. SASE not required.

Phone search: Must use a credit card (add $10.50 fee) for a phone request. Turnaround time 5 days.

Fax search: Order by fax from fax 877-435-5584. Use of credit card required.

In person: Turnaround time 1 1/2 hour.

Online search: In cooperation with the University of Kentucky, a searchable index is available on the Internet at http://ukcc.uky.edu/vitalrec/. The index runs from 1973 through 1993. This is for non-commercial use only. Records may be ordered online via a state designated vendor at www.vitalchek.com.

Other access: Contact Libraries and Archives.

Expedited service: Expedited service is available for mail, phone, online and fax orders. Turnaround time- overnight delivery. Additional fees involved for use of credit card and shipping.

Divorce Records

Department for Public Health, Vital Statistics, 275 E Main St - IE-A, Frankfort, KY 40621-0001; 502-564-4212, 877- 817-7362 (Order), Fax- 502-227-0032; 8AM-4:30PM.

http://chfs.ky.gov/dph/vital/

Indexing & Storage: Records available from June, 1958 to present. New records available for inquiry in 1 to 2 months.

Searching: Records of divorce proceedings are available from the Clerk of the Circuit Court that granted the decree. Include in request- names of husband and wife, date of divorce, place of divorce. Provide a daytime phone number.

Access by: mail, phone, fax, in person, online.

Fee & Payment: The fee is $6.00 per name. Fee payee- Kentucky State Treasurer. Prepayment required. Personal checks, money orders accepted. Major credit cards accepted.

Mail search: Turnaround time- 30 working days. SASE not required.

Phone search: Must use a credit card (add $10.50 fee) for a phone request. Turnaround time 5 days.

Fax search: Order by fax from fax 877-435-5584. Use of credit card required.

In person: Turnaround time 1 1/2 hour.

Online search: In cooperation with the University of Kentucky, there is a searchable index on the Internet at http://ukcc.uky.edu/vitalrec/. This is for non-commercial use only. The index is for 1973-1993. Records may be ordered online via a state designated vendor at www.vitalchek.com.

Other access: Contact Libraries and Archives.

Expedited service: Expedited service is available for mail, phone, online and fax orders. Turnaround time- overnight delivery. Additional fees involved for use of credit card and shipping.

Workers' Compensation Records

Kentucky Office of Workers' Claims, Prevention Park, 657 Chamberlin Avenue, Frankfort, KY 40601; 502-564-5550 x4532, Fax- 502-564-9533; 8AM-4:30PM.

www.labor.ky.gov/workersclaims/

The Case Files Section has been administratively moved to be under the Claims Assignment section

Indexing & Storage: Records available from 1982 to present on computer. New records available for inquiry immediately.

Searching: Must have a signed release from claimant only for copies of first report. Otherwise, information is open to the public per KRS 61.870 through 61.884. Include in request- claimant name, SSN, date of accident, place of employment at time of accident. This data not released- SSNs, addresses or personal information (height, weight, sex, eye color, etc.).

Access by: mail, phone, fax, in person.

Fee & Payment: Fees are $.50 per page from microfilm and photocopies are $.10 per page. Fee payee- Kentucky State Treasurer. Payment may be submitted at the time records are picked up. Otherwise, an invoice will be mailed at the end of the month. Personal checks accepted, credit cards are not.

Mail search: Turnaround time- 2 to 4 weeks. Requests are processed in order by the date received. A SASE is requested.

Phone search: Some data available via phone.

Fax search: Fax requests are processed by date of receipt same as requests that are mailed.

In person: The office will have the records ready for you if you call ahead first and make an appointment.

Other access: A listing of file contents may be requested. Call for details.

Expedited service: If requesting agency provides account number for FedEx, then documents will be expedited.

Driver Records

Division of Driver Licensing, KY Transportation Cabinet, 200 Mero Street, Frankfort, KY 40622; 502-564-6800 x2250, Fax- 502-564-5787; 8AM-4:30PM. http://drlic.kytc.ky.gov/

Requests for copies of tickets must be submitted in writing to Cabinets Record Custodian, Department of Administrative Services, at the address listed above. There is a $.10 fee per document.

Indexing & Storage: Records available for 3 years for moving violations, DWIs and suspensions. Accidents are not reported on 3 years records. New records available for inquiry in 5 to 10 days.

Searching: Casual requesters can obtain record information, but personal information is "cloaked" unless written consent by subject is provided. Request forms are found at http://transportation.ky.gov/kytci-forms/formslibrary.htm. The SSN or DL, the full name and DOB are needed when ordering. The driver's address is not included as part of the search report without a release from the driver.

Access by: mail, in person, online.

Fee & Payment: The fee is $3.00 per record, $5.00 if online. Fee payee- Kentucky State Treasurer. Business checks accepted. Credit cards accepted.

Mail search: Turnaround time- 3 to 5 days.

In person: Walk-in requesters may receive records immediately at the address listed above or at any one of 13 field offices in the state.

Online search: There are 2 systems, both accessible from Kentucky.gov. Permissible use requesters who are permitted to obtain personal information can order by batch. Fee is $5.00 per record, billing is monthly. Accounts must be approved by the Commissioner's office. For more details, call Kentucky.gov at 502-875-3733. Records without personal information can be obtained on an interactive basis at http://dhr.ky.gov/DHRWeb/. The $5.00 fee applies and use of a credit card is required.

Vehicle, Vessel Ownership & Registration

Department of Motor Vehicles, Division of Motor Vehicle Licensing, 200 Mero St, 2nd Fl, Frankfort, KY 40622; 502-564-5301 (Registration), 502-564-2737 (Title), 502-564-3298 (Other), Fax- 502-564-1686; 8AM-4:30PM. www.kytc.state.ky.us

The state adopted all 14 permissible uses per DPPA guidelines.

Indexing & Storage: Records available from 1992 to present for title histories and registration records. Prior vessel records are kept by Circuit Clerks. Only motorized vessels must be titled and registered. New records available for inquiry in 1-4 weeks.

Searching: Vehicle and ownership records are not open to the public without consent of subject. Vendors must submit either TC96-16 or TC96-325 when requesting data. Include in request- name, DOB, and DL. Will not to a name and DOB only search, also will not search by SSN. The state reports current lien information. This data not released- SSNs.

Access by: mail, in person, online.

Fee & Payment: The fee is $2.00 per record request. Certification is an additional $2.00. There is a full charge for a "no record found." Fee payee- Kentucky State Treasurer Prepayment required. Cash and money orders are accepted. Personal checks accepted, credit cards are not.

Mail search: Turnaround time- 5 to 10 days. A SASE is requested.

In person: Turnaround time is while you wait (typically, 15 minutes to 1 hour).

Online search: Electronic access is available to approved, ongoing requesters with a permissible use. The system, run by Kentucky.gov, is open 24/7 and provides immediate results after requests are sent. The fee is $0.44 per record. Requesters must be approved by the Commissioner's office and have an account with Kentucky.gov. There is a $75.00 annual subscription fee. For more information, call Kentucky.gov at 502-875-3733 or email support@kentucky.gov.

Other access: Kentucky has the ability to supply customized bulk delivery of vehicle registration information. The request must be in writing with the intended use outlined. For more information, call 502-564-5301.

Expedited service: Expedited service is available for walk-ins only. You must set up an account.

Accident Reports

State Police, Criminal Ident. & Records Branch, 1250 Louisville Rd, Frankfort, KY 40601; 502-226-2169, Fax- 502-226-7418; 8AM-4:30PM.

www.kentuckystatepolice.org

Pursuant to KRS 189.635, complete collision reports are not public record.

Indexing & Storage: Records available for past 10 years. New records available for inquiry in less than 1 day.

Searching: Requests must be made through "open records." Statistical detailed listing of accidents at specific locations without personal identifying information is available for a fee with a written request. For more information phone 502-226-2169 for details. Search requirements include the date, driver's name and location.

Access by: mail, fax, in person.

Fee & Payment: The charge is $5.00 per report. Fee payee- KY State Treasurer. Prepayment required. Personal checks and money orders accepted. No credit cards accepted.

Mail search: Turnaround time- 1 to 2 weeks. A SASE is requested.

Fax search: Fax requests accepted.

In person: Counter service is available.

Other access: Specific accident statistics may be obtained by phoning the statistics coordinator.

Legislation Records

Kentucky General Assembly, Legislative Research Commission, 700 Capitol Ave, Rm 85, Frankfort, KY 40601; 502-564-8100 x342 (Bill Room), 502-564-8100 x340 (LRC Library), Fax- 502-564-6543; 8AM-4:30PM. www.lrc.ky.gov

Indexing & Storage: Records available from 1986 on computer, and from 1950 in hard copy. Kentucky Acts from 1820 to present are available in hard copy.

Searching: Include in request- bill number, session year or subject matter.

Access by: mail, phone, fax, in person, online.

Fee & Payment: Minimum fee $1.00. Fees over $1.00 are invoiced. You pay postage/UPS charges over 8 ounces. Copies are $.15 each. Fee payee- LRC. Personal checks accepted, credit cards not.

Mail search: Turnaround time- variable.

Phone search: Records are available by phone.

Fax search: The fee is $.65 per page.

In person: Simple requests may be processed while you wait. Hours are 8AM to 4:30PM.

Online search: The website has an extensive searching mechanism for bills, actions, summaries, and statutes. Search for bills free at www.lrc.ky.gov/legislation.htm. The text of all bills is in Word Windows format.

Expedited service: Expedited service is available for regular accounts. Fax service offered for an additional fee.

Voter Registration

State Board of Elections, 140 Walnut, Frankfort, KY 40601; 502-573-7100, Fax- 502-573-4369; 8AM-4:30PM.

http://elect.ky.gov/registrationinfo/

Call or fax to request a copy of the agency's data request form. Bulk data is available for political purposes or specific research purposes only. For individual searches, it is best to go to the county level.

Indexing & Storage: New records available for inquiry in 2 months.

Searching: The agency will provide verification of records and voting histories upon receipt of a written request (using their form). Requests are accepted by email as long as requester's signature is apparent, use PDF. For questions, contact sheilar.bryant@ky.gov. Include in request- name and SSN or DOB. Address is helpful. This data not released- SSNs, bulk information or information to ineligible persons, pursuant to state statutes.

Access by: mail, fax, in person, online.

Fee & Payment: There is no search fee. There is a $.10 per page copy fee. Fee payee- Kentucky State Treasurer.

Mail search: Turnaround time- 3 business days. Turnaround time is longer for information exempted by statute.

Fax search: Records are available by fax. Suggest to call to confirm receipt of fax.

In person: Records may be ordered (with written request) and picked up in person. Law allows for 3 business day turnaround.

Online search: The agency offers a voter information status search at https://cdcbp.ky.gov/VICWeb/index.jsp. First name, last name and DOB are required.

Other access: Data is available on CD-Rom, labels or lists for eligible persons, pursuant to state statutes.

GED Certificates

Kentucky Adult Education, GED Program, 1024 Capital Center Drive #250, Frankfort, KY 40601; 502-573-5114 x309, Fax- 502-573-5436; 8AM-4:30PM. http://kyae.ky.gov/students/ged.htm

Only government agencies may request by fax.

Indexing & Storage: Records available from 1940's. New records available for inquiry in 7 business days after test.

Searching: There is no fee distinction between requesting a verification or copy of a transcript. A request form for a transcript is available at the web page. Include in request- (if written request) name at time test taken, date/year of test, date of birth, SSN, and location of test. Agencies requesting via online must submit signed release. The signed release is required unless coming from a not-for-profit educational entity requesting group information.

Access by: mail, in person, online.

Fee & Payment: The fee for verification is $5.00. A copy of transcript is $5.00 each. Fee payee- KY State Treasurer. Prepayment required. Money orders are accepted. Personal checks not accepted. Major credit and debit cards accepted.

Mail search: Turnaround time- 1 week or less. SASE is preferred, but not required.

In person: in person searchers must bring a photo ID. Turnaround time is same day. Office is closed 11:30 AM thru 1:30 PM.

Online search: Requests for transcripts ($5.00) may be submitted online at https://ged.ky.gov. Requests are accepted from agency, but a signed released must be submitted.

Hunting & Fishing License Information

Fish & Wildlife Resources Department, Division of Administrative Services, 1 Sportsman Lane, Arnold Mitchell Bldg, Frankfort, KY 40601; 502-564-3400, Fax- 502-564-0506; 8AM-4:30PM.

www.fw.ky.gov

A database has been created, starting in 1996. Records are not released without written request and for good reason. Records are not available for commercial mail lists. Older records are archived in boxes. Record retrieval extremely difficult.

Indexing & Storage: Records available for the past two years (actual copies). Prior records are archived and not readily available. New records available for inquiry in 16 days.

Searching: Requests must be in writing and addressed to the Records Custodian's Office. The general public cannot receive records, beyond the type of license issued. Include in request- full name; include SSN if possible. By law, the agency will respond to all search requests within three days. This data not released- SSN, address, DOB

Access by: mail, fax, in person.

Fee & Payment: Fees are $.10 per page plus cost of postage. Will invoice, personal checks accepted.

Mail search: Turnaround time- 3 days. Records are available by mail.

Fax search: Records may be requested by fax.

In person: Limited information available in person, extensive lists will be mailed.

Kentucky State Licensing Agencies

For details about the agency responsible for licensing/certifying/registering an item below or in the Agency Quick Finder section, match an item's number with the number of the agency in the *Licensing Agency Information* section.

Kentucky Licenses Searchable Online

Addiction Psychiatrist MD #41	http://web1.ky.gov/gensearch/
Alcohol/Drug Counselor #15	https://web1.ky.gov/OnPPub/Verification.aspx
Anesthesiologist #41	http://web1.ky.gov/gensearch/
Architect #7	http://kybera.com/roster.shtml
Art Therapist #15	https://web1.ky.gov/OnPPub/Verification.aspx
Athlete Agent #15	https://web1.ky.gov/OnPPub/Verification.aspx
Athletic Trainer, Medical #41	http://web1.ky.gov/gensearch/
Attorney #2	www.kybar.org/Default.aspx?tabid=26
Auctioneer, Livestock, Ltd. #4	http://web1.ky.gov/gensearch/LicenseSearch.aspx?AGY=3
Auctioneer, Tobacco, Ltd. #4	http://web1.ky.gov/gensearch/LicenseSearch.aspx?AGY=3
Auctioneer/Auctioneer Apprentice #4	http://web1.ky.gov/gensearch/LicenseSearch.aspx?AGY=3
Audiologist #15	https://web1.ky.gov/OnPPub/Verification.aspx
Bank #18	www.kfi.ky.gov/search.htm
Broker/Dealer Agent, Securities #18	www.kfi.ky.gov/search.htm
Check Casher #18	www.kfi.ky.gov/search.htm
Check Seller #18	www.kfi.ky.gov/search.htm
Chiropractor #35	http://web1.ky.gov/gensearch/LicenseSearch.aspx?AGY=22
Cosmetologist #37	www.hnslicense.net
Counselor, Pastoral #15	https://web1.ky.gov/OnPPub/Verification.aspx
Counselor, Professional #15	https://web1.ky.gov/OnPPub/Verification.aspx
CPA #3	http://web1.ky.gov/GenSearch/LicenseSearch.aspx?AGY=7
CPA Company #3	http://web1.ky.gov/GenSearch/LicenseSearch.aspx?AGY=6
Credit Union #18	www.kfi.ky.gov/search.htm
Dental Hygienist #6	http://web1.ky.gov/gensearch/LicenseSearch.aspx?AGY=11
Dental Laboratory #6	http://web1.ky.gov/gensearch/LicenseSearch.aspx?AGY=13
Dentist #6	http://web1.ky.gov/gensearch/LicenseSearch.aspx?AGY=9
Dialysis Technician #9	https://secure.kentucky.gov/kbn/bulkvalidation/basic.aspx
Dietitian/Nutritionist #15	https://web1.ky.gov/OnPPub/Verification.aspx
Driver Training Instructor, Public/Priv. #42	www.kde.state.ky.us/KDE/Administrative+Resources/Transportation/Driver+Training+Program.htm
EDP Servicer #18	www.kfi.ky.gov/search.htm
Electrical Contractor #26	https://hbc.ky.gov/licensing/electrical/license_lookup.asp
Electrical Inspector #26	https://hbc.ky.gov/licensing/electrical/license_lookup.asp
Engineer #39	http://apps.kyboels.ky.gov/SearchableRoster.aspx
Engineer/Land Surveyor Firm #39	http://apps.kyboels.ky.gov/SearchableRoster.aspx
Esthetician #37	www.hnslicense.net
Geologist #15	https://web1.ky.gov/OnPPub/Verification.aspx
Hearing Instrument Specialist #15	https://web1.ky.gov/OnPPub/Verification.aspx
Home Health Aid #9	https://secure.kentucky.gov/kbn/bulkvalidation/basic.aspx
Insurance Agent #21	www.doi.state.ky.us/kentucky/ALSearch/Agent/Default.aspx
Insurance CE Provider #21	www.doi.state.ky.us/kentucky/search/provider/
Insurance Company/Insurer #21	http://doi.ppr.ky.gov/kentucky/ALSearch/Company/Default.aspx
Interior Designer #7	www.kybera.com/idlist.shtml
Investment Advisor/Representative #18	www.kfi.ky.gov/search.htm
Investment Company #18	www.kfi.ky.gov/search.htm
Legislative Employer of Lobbyists #40	http://klec.ky.gov/reports/employersagents.htm
Liquor License #1	http://migration.kentucky.gov/abc/licenseLookup/
Loan Company, Comm./Industrial #18	www.kfi.ky.gov/search.htm
Lobbyist #40	http://klec.ky.gov/reports/employersagents.htm
Malt Beverage Distributor #1	http://migration.kentucky.gov/abc/licenseLookup/
Marriage & Family Therapist #15	https://web1.ky.gov/OnPPub/Verification.aspx
Medical Doctor/Surgeon #41	http://web1.ky.gov/gensearch/
Medical Specialist MD #41	http://web1.ky.gov/gensearch/
Midwife Nurse #9	https://secure.kentucky.gov/kbn/bulkvalidation/basic.aspx
Mortgage Broker #18	www.kfi.ky.gov/search.htm
Mortgage Loan Company #18	www.kfi.ky.gov/search.htm
Nail Technician #37	www.hnslicense.net
Notary Public #30	http://apps.sos.ky.gov/adminservices/notaries/

Nurse Anesthetist #9	https://secure.kentucky.gov/kbn/bulkvalidation/basic.aspx
Nurse Clinical Specialist #9	https://secure.kentucky.gov/kbn/bulkvalidation/basic.aspx
Nurse Work Permit #9	https://secure.kentucky.gov/kbn/bulkvalidation/basic.aspx
Nurse-RN/LPN #9	https://secure.kentucky.gov/kbn/bulkvalidation/basic.aspx
Nurses Aide #9	https://secure.kentucky.gov/kbn/bulkvalidation/basic.aspx
Nursing Home Administrator #15	https://web1.ky.gov/OnPPub/Verification.aspx
Occupational Therapist/Assistant #15	https://web1.ky.gov/OnPPub/Verification.aspx
Ophthalmic Dispenser #10	https://web1.ky.gov/OnPPub/Verification.aspx
Optician/Apprentice #10	https://web1.ky.gov/OnPPub/Verification.aspx
Optometrist #11	http://web1.ky.gov/gensearch/LicenseSearch.aspx?AGY=8
Osteopathic Physician #41	http://web1.ky.gov/gensearch/
Physical Therapist #38	http://web1.ky.gov/gensearch/
Physical Therapist Assistant #38	http://web1.ky.gov/gensearch/
Physician Assistant #41	http://web1.ky.gov/gensearch/
Plumber #26	https://hbc.ky.gov/licensing/electrical/license_lookup.asp
Podiatrist #27	http://web1.ky.gov/gensearch/LicenseSearch.aspx?AGY=24
Private Investigator #15	https://web1.ky.gov/OnPPub/Verification.aspx
Property Valuation Administrator #34 ...	http://revenue.ky.gov/NR/rdonlyres/A49D334B-21F9-43E5-9D64-9EBF57681D4F/0/pvadirectoryJan06.pdf
Proprietary Education School #15	https://web1.ky.gov/OnPPub/Verification.aspx
Psychiatrist MD #41	http://web1.ky.gov/gensearch/
Psychologist #15	https://web1.ky.gov/OnPPub/Verification.aspx
Public Accountant Company #3	http://web1.ky.gov/GenSearch/LicenseSearch.aspx?AGY=6
Public Accountant-CPA #3	http://web1.ky.gov/GenSearch/LicenseSearch.aspx?AGY=7
Real Estate Agent/Broker/Sales #33	http://weba.state.ky.us/realestate/
Real Estate Appraiser #32	www.kreab.ky.gov/appraiserstatus/
Real Estate Brokerage/Firm #33	http://weba.state.ky.us/realestate/
Retired LPN #9	http://kbn.ky.gov/onlinesrvs/retired.htm
Savings & Loan #18	www.kfi.ky.gov/search.htm
School Administrator #25	www.kyepsb.net
School Guidance Counselor #25	www.kyepsb.net
School Media Librarian #25	www.kyepsb.net
School Nurse #25	www.kyepsb.net
School Social Worker/Psychologist #25	www.kyepsb.net
Securities Agent #18	www.kfi.ky.gov/search.htm
Securities Broker/Dealer #18	www.kfi.ky.gov/search.htm
Securities, Agent of Issuer #18	www.kfi.ky.gov/search.htm
Sexual Assault Nurse Examiner #9	https://secure.kentucky.gov/kbn/bulkvalidation/basic.aspx
Social Worker #15	https://web1.ky.gov/OnPPub/Verification.aspx
Speech-Language Pathologist #15	https://web1.ky.gov/OnPPub/Verification.aspx
Surveyor, Land #39	http://apps.kyboels.ky.gov/SearchableRoster.aspx
Teacher #25	www.kyepsb.net
Trust Company #18	www.kfi.ky.gov/search.htm
Veterinarian #15	https://web1.ky.gov/OnPPub/Verification.aspx

Kentucky Licensing Quick Finder

Addiction Psychiatrist MD #41	502-429-7150
Alcohol/Drug Counselor #15	502-564-3296 x226
Ambulance Provider #14	859-256-3565
Anesthesiologist #41	502-429-7150
Animal Technician #15	502-564-3296
Architect #7	859-246-2069
Art Therapist #15	502-564-3296 x230
Athlete Agent #15	502-564-3296 x222
Athletic Trainer, Medical #41	502-429-7150
Attorney #2	502-564-3795
Auctioneer, Livestock, Ltd. #4	502-429-7145
Auctioneer, Tobacco, Ltd. #4	502-429-7145
Auctioneer/Auctioneer Apprentice #4	502-429-7145
Audiologist #15	502-564-3296 x240
Bank #18	502-573-3390
Barber #5	502-429-7148
Blacksmith #31	859-246-2040
Boiler Contractor/Insp./Installer #26	502-573-0373
Broker/Dealer Agent, Securities #18	502-573-3390
Building Inspector #26	502-564-8090
Check Casher #18	502-573-3390
Check Seller #18	502-573-3390•
Child Care Facility #13	502-564-7962
Chiropractor #35	270-651-2522
Compost Operator #24	502-565-6716
Coroner #17	859-622-1328
Cosmetologist #37	502-564-4262
Counselor, Pastoral #15	502-564-3296 x226
Counselor, Professional #15	502-564-3296 x226
CPA #3	502-595-3037
CPA Company #3	502-595-3037
Credit Union #18	502-573-3390
Dental Hygienist #6	502-429-7280
Dental Laboratory #6	502-429-7280
Dental Laboratory Technician #6	502-429-7280
Dentist #6	502-429-7280
Dialysis Technician #9	502-429-3300 x290
Dietitian/Nutritionist #15	502-564-3296 x227
Driver Training Instructor, Public/Priv. #42	502-226-7404
Drug Manufacturer/Wholesaler #12	[859] 246-2820
EDP Servicer #18	502-573-3390
Electrical Contractor #26	502-573-0382
Electrical Inspector #26	502-573-0382
Elevator Inspector #26	502-573-0382
Embalmer #36	502-241-3918
EMS Instructor #14	859-256-3565
EMT, Basic #14	859-256-3565
EMT, First Response #14	859-256-3565
Engineer #39	502-573-2680
Engineer/Land Surveyor Firm #39	502-573-2680
Esthetician #37	502-564-4262
Exterminator #16	502-573-0282
Fire Alarm System Inspector #26	502-573-0382
Fire Protection Sprinkler Installer #26	502-564-3626
Fire Suppression System Inspect'r #26	502-564-8090
Fishing, Commercial #20	800-858-1549
Funeral Director/Apprentice #36	502-241-3918
Funeral Establishment #36	502-241-3918
Fur Buyer/Processor #20	800-858-1549

Geologist #15 .... 502-564-3296 x227
Guide, Hunting & Fishing #20 800-858-1549
Health Care Facility #13 502-564-7963
Hearing Instrument Specialist #15 502-564-3296 x240
Home Health Aid #9 502-429-3300
Horse Claimer #31 859-246-2040
Horse Farm Manager/Agent #31 859-246-2040
Horse Owner/Trainer/Asst. Trainer #31 829-246-2040
Horse Racing Occupation #31 859-246-2040
Horse Racing Official/Auth'r'zed Agent #31 859-246-2040
Horse Veterinarian/Veterin'y Assist. #31 859-246-2040
Horse Veterinary Dental Technic'n #31. 859-246-2040
HVAC Contractor #26 502-564-1436
HVAC Journeyman/Master/Mech'c #26 502-564-1436
Insurance Adjuster #21 502-564-6004
Insurance Agent #21 502-564-6004
Insurance CE Provider #21 502-564-6004
Insurance Company/Insurer #21 502-564-6004
Insurance Consultant/Solicitor #21 502-564-6004
Interior Designer #7 859-246-2069
Interpreters for the Deaf #15 .... 502-564-3296 x239
Investment Advisor/Representat've #18. 502-573-3390
Investment Company #18 502-573-3390
Jockey Agent #31 859-246-2040
Jockey/Jockey Apprentice #31 859-246-2040
Lake Operator #20 800-858-1549
Landfarm Operator #24 502-564-6716
Landfill Operator/Manager #24 502-564-6716
Law Enforcem'nt Training Instruc'r #17. 859-622-1328
Legislative Employer of Lobbyists #40. 502-573-2863
Liquor License #1 502-564-4850
Loan Company, Comm./Industrial #18. 502-573-3390
Lobbyist #40 502-573-2863
Malt Beverage Distributor #1 502-564-4850
Marriage & Family Therapist #15. 502-564-3296 x239
Medical Doctor/Surgeon #41 502-429-7150
Medical Specialist MD #41 502-429-7150
Midwife Nurse #9 502-429-3300
Milk Sampler/Weigher/Tester #43 859-257-2785
Mine Safety Instructor #22 502-573-0140
Miner #22 502-573-0140
Mining Blaster #22 502-573-0140
Mining Fire Boss #22 502-573-0140
Mining Inspector/Foreman #22 502-573-0140
Mortgage Broker #18 502-573-3390
Mortgage Loan Company #18 502-573-3390
Nail Technician #37 502-564-4262
Notary Public #30 502-564-3490
Nurse Anesthetist #9 502-429-3300
Nurse Clinical Specialist #9 502-429-3300
Nurse Work Permit #9 502-429-3300
Nurse-RN/LPN #9 502-429-3300
Nurses Aide #9 502-429-3300
Nursing Home Administrator #15. 502-564-3296 x222
Occupational Therapist/Assistant #15.. 502-564-3296
Ophthalmic Dispenser #10 .... 502-564-3296 x227
Optician/Apprentice #10 .... 502-564-3296 x227
Optometrist #11 859-246-2744
Osteopathic Physician #41 502-429-7150
Paramedic #14 859-256-3565
Pari-Mutuel Employee #31 859-246-2040
Pesticide Applicator #16 502-573-0282
Pesticide Dealer #16 502-573-0282
Pharmacist #12 859-246-2820
Pharmacy #12 859-246-2820
Physical Therapist #38 502-429-7140
Physical Therapist Assistant #38 502-429-7140
Physician Assistant #41 502-429-7150
Plans & Specifications Inspector #26 502-564-8090
Plumber #26 502-573-0397
Podiatrist #27 270-834-8932
Police Officer #17 859-622-1328
Polygraph Examiner/Examiner Trainee #28 502-564-5230
Private Investigator #15 502-564-3296
Property Valuation Administrator #34 502-564-8334
Proprietary Education School #15 502-564-4233
Psychiatrist MD #41 502-429-7150
Psychologist #15 .... 502-564-3296 x225
Public Accountant Company #3 502-595-3037
Public Accountant-CPA #3 502-595-3037
Racetrack Occupation (vendors, etc.) #31 859-246-2040
Racing Association Employee #31 859-246-2040
Racing Vendor/Vendor Employee #31. 859-246-2040
Radiation Operator #44 502-564-3700
Radiation Producing Machine #44 502-564-3700
Radioactive Material Licensee #44 502-564-3700
Real Estate Agent/Broker/Sales #33 502-429-7250
Real Estate Appraiser #32 859-543-8943
Real Estate Brokerage/Firm #33 502-429-7250
Rehabilitation Counselor #23 502-564-4440
Retired LPN #9 502-429-3300
Sanitarian #8 502-564-7398
Savings & Loan #18 502-573-3390
School Administrator #25 502-564-4606
School Bus Driver #19 502-564-5279
School Guidance Counselor #25 502-564-4606
School Media Librarian #25 502-564-4606
School Nurse #25 502-564-4606
School Social Worker/Psycholog't #25. 502-564-4606
Securities Agent #18 502-573-3390
Securities Broker/Dealer #18 502-573-3390
Securities, Agent of Issuer #18 502-573-3390
Septic System Installer, Onsite #8 502-564-4856
Sexual Assault Nurse Examiner #9 502-429-3300
Social Worker #15 .... 502-564-3296 x230
Speech-Language Pathol'g't #15. 502-564-3296 x240
Stable Employee #31 859-246-2040
Surveyor, Land #39 502-573-2680
Taxidermist #20 800-858-1549
Teacher #25 502-564-4606
Trust Company #18 502-573-3390
Veterinarian #15 .... 502-564-3296 x223
Waste Water System Operator #29 502-564-0323
Water Treat'mt/Dist. System Operator #29 502-564-0323

Kentucky Licensing Agency Information

#1 Alcoholic Beverage Control Department, 1003 Twilight Trail, #A2, Frankfort, KY 40601; 502-564-4850, Fax- 502-564-1442. http://abc.ky.gov/ Search data at- http://migration.kentucky.gov/abc/licenseLookup/

#2 Bar Association, 514 W Main St, Frankfort, KY 40601-1883; 502-564-3795, Fax- 502-564-3225. Hours- 8AM-4:30PM. www.kybar.org Search data at- www.kybar.org/Default.aspx?tabid=26

#3 Board of Accountancy, 332 W Broadway, #310, Louisville, KY 40202; 502-595-3037, Fax- 502-595-4500. Hours- 8:30AM-4:30PM. http://cpa.ky.gov

#4 Board of Auctioneers, 9112 Leesgate Rd, #5, Louisville, KY 40222-5089; 502-429-7145, Fax- 502-429-7147. http://auctioneers.ky.gov Search data at- http://web1.ky.gov/gensearch/LicenseSearch.aspx?AGY=3

#5 Board of Barbering, 9114 Leesgate Rd, #6, Louisville, KY 40222-5055; 502-429-7148, Fax- 502-429-7149. Hours- 8AM-4:30PM. http://barbering.ky.gov

#6 Board of Dentistry, 312 Whittington Pky, #101, Louisville, KY 40222; 502-429-7280, Fax- 502-429-7282. Hours- 8AM-N, 1-4:30PM. http://dentistry.ky.gov

#7 Board of Architects, 2624 Research Park Dr, #101, Lexington, KY 40511; 859-246-2069, Fax- 859-246-2431. http://kybera.com Search data at- http://kybera.com/roster.shtml

#8 Department for Public Health, Registered Sanitarian Examining Committee, 275 E Main, HS1EB, Frankfort, KY 40621; 502-564-7398, Fax- 502-564-6533. http://chfs.ky.gov/dph/

#9 Board of Nursing, 312 Whittington Pky, #300, Louisville, KY 40222-5172; 502-429-3300, Fax- 502-429-3311. Hours- 8:30AM-4:30PM. http://kbn.ky.gov Search data at- https://secure.kentucky.gov/kbn/bulkvalidation/basic.aspx SSN required to search; $1.00 fee per name. Bulk data downloads also available, https://secure.kentucky.gov/portal/registration.aspx.

#10 Division of Occupations and Professions, Board of Ophthalmic Dispensers, PO Box 1360 (700 Capitol Ave, #118), Frankfort, KY 40602; 502-564-3296 x226, Fax- 502-564-4818. 8AM-5PM. http://finance.ky.gov/ourcabinet/caboff/OAS/op/ophdis/ Search data at- https://web1.ky.gov/OnPPub/Verification.aspx

#11 Board of Optometric Examiners, 2624 Research Pk Dr #305, Lexington, KY 40511; 859-246-2744, Fax- 859-246-2746. http://optometry.ky.gov Search data at- http://web1.ky.gov/gensearch/LicenseSearch.aspx?AGY=8

#12 Board of Pharmacy, 2624 Research Park Dr, #302, Lexington, KY 40511; 859-246-2820, Fax- 859-246-2823. http://pharmacy.ky.gov Oral verification is limited to status and expiration date. Requests for add'l information must be in writing accompanied by a $5.00 fee. Copies of disciplinary orders/detailed searches may be more costly.

#13 Division of Licensing & Regulations, Cabinet for Health & Family Services, 275 E Main St, Frankfort, KY 40621-0001; 502-564-7962 or 7963, Fax- 502-564-6546. http://chfs.ky.gov/Lic/

#14 Board of Emergency Medical Services, 300 N Main St, Versailles, KY 40383; 859-256-3565, Fax- 859-256-3128. http://kbems.kctcs.edu/

#15 Department of Administration, Division of Occupations & Professions, PO Box 1360, Frankfort, KY 40602; 502-564-3296, Fax- 502-564-4818. http://finance.ky.gov/ourcabinet/caboff/OAS/op/ Search data at- https://web1.ky.gov/OnPPub/Verification.aspx

#16 Department of Agriculture, Division of Pesticide Regulation, 107 Corporate Dr, Frankfort, KY 40601; 502-573-0282, Fax- 502-573-0303. www.kyagr.com

#17 Department of Criminal Justice Training, 521 Lancaster Ave, Richmond, KY 40475; 859-622-1328, Fax- 859-622-2740. http://docjt.jus.state.ky.us

#18 Department of Financial Institutions, Division of Law & Regulatory Compliance, 1025 Capitol Center Dr, #200, Frankfort, KY 40601; 502-573-3390, Fax- 502-573-0086. www.kfi.ky.gov Search data at- www.kfi.ky.gov/search.htm

#19 Department of Education, Pupil Transportation, 500 Mero St, 15th Fl, Frankfort, KY 40601; 502-564-5279, Fax- 502-564-9574. www.kde.state.ky.us/KDE/Administrative+Resources/Transportation/

#20 Department of Fish & Wildlife, #1 Sportsman's Lane, Frankfort, KY 40601; 800-858-1549, Fax- 502-564-9136. http://fw.ky.gov

#21 Department of Insurance, Licensing Division, PO Box 517 (215 W Main St), Frankfort, KY 40602-0517; 502-564-6004; 800-595-6053, Fax- 502-564-6030. Hours- 8AM-4:30PM. www.doi.state.ky.us/kentucky/

#22 Department of Mines & Minerals, 1025 Capital Center Drive, Frankfort, KY 40602-2244; 502-573-0140, Fax- 502-573-0152. www.omsl.ky.gov

#23 Department of Vocational Rehabilitation, 209 St Clair St, Frankfort, KY 40601; 502-564-4440, Fax- 502-564-6745. http://kydvr.state.ky.us/

#24 Division of Waste Management, 14 Reilly Rd, Frankfort, KY 40601; 502-564-6716, Fax-502-564-4049. www.waste.ky.gov

#25 Education Professional Standards Board, 100 Airport Rd, 3rd Fl, Frankfort, KY 40601; 502-564-4606, Fax- 502-564-7080. www.kyepsb.net Search data at- https://wd.kyepsb.net/EPSB.WebApps/KECI/

#26 Department of Housing, Buildings, and Construction, 101 Sea Hero Rd, #100, Frankfort, KY 40601; 502-573-0365 x125, Fax- 502-573-1057. http://dhbc.ky.gov/

#27 Board of Podiatry, PO Box 174, Glasgow, KY 42142-0174; 270-834-8932, Fax- 270-834-1437. www.podiatry.ky.gov Search data at- http://web1.ky.gov/gensearch/LicenseSearch.aspx?AGY=24

#28 State Police, Central Laboratory Branch, Polygraph Unit, 100 Sower Blvd, #102, Frankfort, KY 40601; 502-564-5230; 800-326-4879, Fax- 502-573-2101. www.kentuckystatepolice.org

#29 Division of Compliance Assistance, Environmental and Public Protection Cabinet-Operator Certification Program, 300 Fair Oaks Lane, Frankfort, KY 40601; 502-564-0323, Fax- 502-564-9720. Hours- 7:30AM-4:30PM. www.dca.ky.gov/certification

#30 Office of Secretary of State, Notary Branch, PO Box 821 (700 Capital Ave, #86), Frankfort, KY 40602-0821; 502-564-2848, Fax- 502-564-1484. Hours- 8AM-4:30PM. http://sos.ky.gov/adminservices/notaries/ Search data at- http://apps.sos.ky.gov/adminservices/notaries/

#31 Horse Racing Authority, 4063 Iron Works Pky, Bldg B, Lexington, KY 40511; 859-246-2040, Fax- 859-246-2039. Hours- 8AM-4:30PM. http://krc.ppr.ky.gov/

#32 Real Estate Appraisers Board, 2624 Research Park Dr, #204, Lexington, KY 40511; 859-543-8943, Fax- 859-543-0028. Hours- 8AM-4:30PM. www.kreab.ky.gov

#33 Real Estate Commission, 10200 Linn Station Rd, #201, Louisville, KY 40223; 502-429-7250, Fax- 502-429-7246. http://krec.ky.gov

#34 Office of Property Valuation, Department of Revenue, 501 High St, Station 33, Frankfort, KY 40620; 502-564-8334, Fax- 502-564-8368. http://revenue.ky.gov/default.htm

#35 Board of Chiropractic Examiners, 209 S Green St (PO Box 183), Glasgow, KY 42142-0183; 270-651-2522, Fax- 270-651-8784. 8AM-4PM. http://kbce.ky.gov Search data at- http://web1.ky.gov/gensearch/LicenseSearch.aspx?AGY=22

#36 Board of Embalmers & Funeral Directors, PO Box 324, Crestwood, KY 40014; 502-241-3918, Fax- 502-241-4297. 8AM-4:30PM.

#37 Board of Hairdressers & Cosmetologists, 111 St James Court, #A, Frankfort, KY 40601; 502-564-4262, Fax- 502-564-0481. Hours- 8AM-4:30PM. www.kbhc.ky.gov Search data at- www.hnslicense.net

#38 Board of Physical Therapy, 312 Whittington Pky, #102, Louisville, KY 40222; 502-429-7140, Fax- (502) 429-7142. Hours- 8:30AM-4:30PM. http://pt.ky.gov Search data at- http://web1.ky.gov/gensearch/

#39 Professional Engineers & Land Surveyors, Board of Licensure, 160 Democrat Dr, Frankfort, KY 40601; 502-573-2680, Fax- 502-573-6687. http://kyboels.ky.gov Search data at- http://apps.kyboels.ky.gov/SearchableRoster.aspx

#40 Legislative Ethics Commission, 22 Mill Creek Park, Frankfort, KY 40601; 502-573-2863, Fax- 502-573-2929. http://klec.ky.gov/reports/ Search data at- http://klec.ky.gov/reports/employersagents.htm

#41 Board of Medical Licensure, 310 Whittington Pky, #1B, Louisville, KY 40222; 502-429-7150, Fax- 502-429-7158. Hours- 8AM-4:30PM. http://kbml.ky.gov/ Search data at- http://web1.ky.gov/gensearch/ Use the fee dialup service only if you have a license or certification number.

#42 State Police Driver Testing Section, 1240 Airport Rd, Frankfort, KY 40601; 502-226-7404, Fax- 502-226-7412.

#43 Division of Regulatory Services, 103 Regulatory Service Bldg, Lexington, KY 40546-0275; 859-257-2785, Fax- 859-323-9931. Hours- 8AM-5PM. www.rs.uky.edu

#44 Radiation Health & Toxic Agents Branch, Department of Public Health, 275 E Main St, Frankfort, KY 40621; 502-564-3700, Fax- 502-564-1492. http://chfs.ky.gov/dph/radiation.htm

Kentucky Federal Courts

The following list indicates the district and division name for each county in the state. If the bankruptcy court location is different from the district court, then the location of the bankruptcy court appears in parentheses.

County/Court Cross Reference

County	District	Division
Adair	Western	Bowling Green (Louisville)
Allen	Western	Bowling Green (Louisville)
Anderson	Eastern	Frankfort (Lexington)
Ballard	Western	Paducah (Louisville)
Barren	Western	Bowling Green (Louisville)
Bath	Eastern	Lexington
Bell	Eastern	London (Lexington)
Boone	Eastern	Covington (Lexington)
Bourbon	Eastern	Lexington
Boyd	Eastern	Ashland (Lexington)
Boyle	Eastern	Lexington
Bracken	Eastern	Covington (Lexington)
Breathitt	Eastern	Lexington
Breckinridge	Western	Louisville
Bullitt	Western	Louisville
Butler	Western	Bowling Green (Louisville)
Caldwell	Western	Paducah (Louisville)
Calloway	Western	Paducah (Louisville)
Campbell	Eastern	Covington (Lexington)
Carlisle	Western	Paducah (Louisville)
Carroll	Eastern	Frankfort (Lexington)
Carter	Eastern	Ashland (Lexington)
Casey	Western	Bowling Green (Louisville)
Christian	Western	Paducah (Louisville)
Clark	Eastern	Lexington
Clay	Eastern	London (Lexington)
Clinton	Western	Bowling Green (Louisville)
Crittenden	Western	Paducah (Louisville)
Cumberland	Western	Bowling Green (Louisville)
Daviess	Western	Owensboro (Louisville)
Edmonson	Western	Bowling Green (Louisville)
Elliott	Eastern	Ashland (Lexington)
Estill	Eastern	Lexington
Fayette	Eastern	Lexington
Fleming	Eastern	Lexington
Floyd	Eastern	Pikeville (Lexington)
Franklin	Eastern	Frankfort (Lexington)
Fulton	Western	Paducah (Louisville)
Gallatin	Eastern	Covington (Lexington)
Garrard	Eastern	Lexington
Grant	Eastern	Covington (Lexington)
Graves	Western	Paducah (Louisville)
Grayson	Western	Owensboro (Louisville)
Green	Western	Bowling Green (Louisville)
Greenup	Eastern	Ashland (Lexington)
Hancock	Western	Owensboro (Louisville)
Hardin	Western	Louisville
Harlan	Eastern	London (Lexington)
Harrison	Eastern	Lexington
Hart	Western	Bowling Green (Louisville)
Henderson	Western	Owensboro (Louisville)
Henry	Eastern	Frankfort (Lexington)
Hickman	Western	Paducah (Louisville)
Hopkins	Western	Owensboro (Louisville)
Jackson	Eastern	London (Lexington)
Jefferson	Western	Louisville
Jessamine	Eastern	Lexington
Johnson	Eastern	Pikeville (Lexington)
Kenton	Eastern	Covington (Lexington)
Knott	Eastern	Pikeville (Lexington)
Knox	Eastern	London (Lexington)
Larue	Western	Louisville
Laurel	Eastern	London (Lexington)
Lawrence	Eastern	Ashland (Lexington)
Lee	Eastern	Lexington
Leslie	Eastern	London (Lexington)
Letcher	Eastern	Pikeville (Lexington)
Lewis	Eastern	Ashland (Lexington)
Lincoln	Eastern	Lexington
Livingston	Western	Paducah (Louisville)
Logan	Western	Bowling Green (Louisville)
Lyon	Western	Paducah (Louisville)
Madison	Eastern	Lexington
Magoffin	Eastern	Pikeville (Lexington)
Marion	Western	Louisville
Marshall	Western	Paducah (Louisville)
Martin	Eastern	Pikeville (Lexington)
Mason	Eastern	Covington (Lexington)
McCracken	Western	Paducah (Louisville)
McCreary	Eastern	London (Lexington)
McLean	Western	Owensboro (Louisville)
Meade	Western	Louisville
Menifee	Eastern	Lexington
Mercer	Eastern	Lexington
Metcalfe	Western	Bowling Green (Louisville)
Monroe	Western	Bowling Green (Louisville)
Montgomery	Eastern	Lexington
Morgan	Eastern	Ashland (Lexington)
Muhlenberg	Western	Owensboro (Louisville)
Nelson	Western	Louisville
Nicholas	Eastern	Lexington
Ohio	Western	Owensboro (Louisville)
Oldham	Western	Louisville
Owen	Eastern	Frankfort (Lexington)
Owsley	Eastern	London (Lexington)
Pendleton	Eastern	Covington (Lexington)
Perry	Eastern	Lexington
Pike	Eastern	Pikeville (Lexington)
Powell	Eastern	Lexington
Pulaski	Eastern	London (Lexington)
Robertson	Eastern	Covington (Lexington)
Rockcastle	Eastern	London (Lexington)
Rowan	Eastern	Ashland (Lexington)
Russell	Western	Bowling Green (Louisville)
Scott	Eastern	Lexington
Shelby	Eastern	Frankfort (Lexington)
Simpson	Western	Bowling Green (Louisville)
Spencer	Western	Louisville
Taylor	Western	Bowling Green (Louisville)
Todd	Western	Bowling Green (Louisville)
Trigg	Western	Paducah (Louisville)
Trimble	Eastern	Frankfort (Lexington)
Union	Western	Owensboro (Louisville)
Warren	Western	Bowling Green (Louisville)
Washington	Western	Louisville
Wayne	Eastern	London (Lexington)
Webster	Western	Owensboro (Louisville)
Whitley	Eastern	London (Lexington)
Wolfe	Eastern	Lexington
Woodford	Eastern	Lexington

Standards for Federal Courts: Fees are standard unless noted in profile. Search fee is $26.00 per item (one party name or case number). Copy fee is $.50 per page. Certification fee is $9.00 per document, double for exemplification, if available. Most courts require prepayment. Mail requests should enclose a SASE unless otherwise noted. Before releasing records, all courts require prepayment, unless noted.

District courts index by defendant and plaintiff and by case number. Bankruptcy courts usually index by debtor and case number. While most courts now have their indexes on computer, many may still maintain index card files as well. Courts will archive closed case files at different times.

There are numerous public access programs available to online subscribers. Search the U.S. Party/Case Index to find party names and case numbers among all courts. Individual case data is provided on PACER. A search of CM/ECF provides copies of cases filed electronically. For details about PACER, the US Party/Case Index, and CM/ECF see the Appendix or go to http://pacer.psc.uscourts.gov or call 800-676-6856.

US District Court Kentucky Eastern District

Ashland Division Court Clerk, 336 Carl Perkins Federal Bldg, 1405 Greenup Ave, Ashland, KY 41101, 606-329-8652. Hours-8:30AM-5PM. www.kyed.uscourts.gov

Counties/Note: Boyd, Carter, Elliott, Greenup, Lawrence, Lewis, Morgan, Rowan. Lexington Division has district master index.

Searches/Indexing: Search request requires name only. Results do not include SSN or DOB. Will not fax back documents. New cases are in the index immediately after filing date. Both computer and card indexes maintained; computer index back to 1992. Case files sent to archives 5 years after closed.

Search Access: Only docket info from active cases is released via phone. **Mail:** Search usually completed- 1-2 days. SASE not required. **In person:** 1 public terminal available. No self-serve copier.

Payment: Pay by Visa/MC, money order, cashier's or personal check. Payee: Clerk, USDC.

E-Services: PACER records go back to 9/1991. New records online after 1 day. ECF at https://ecf.kyed.uscourts.gov. Opinions on cases back to 3/17/2003 in pdf format on ECF system. **Note:** For calendars, click on "Court/Hearing Schedule" at www.kyed.uscourts.gov.

Covington Division Court Clerk, PO Box 1073, Covington, KY 41012 (In person: US Courthouse, Rm 289, 35 W 5th St, Covington, KY 41011), 859-392-7925. Hours- 8:30AM - 5PM. www.kyed.uscourts.gov

Counties: Boone, Bracken, Campbell, Gallatin, Grant, Kenton, Mason, Pendleton, Robertson.

Searches/Indexing: Search request requires name only. Results do not include SSN or DOB. Will not fax back documents. New cases are in the index immediately after filing date. Both computer and card indexes maintained. Case files sent to archives 5 years after closed.

Search Access: Only docket info available by phone. **Mail:** Search usually completed- 48 hours. Turnaround time for written requests varies. Include SASE for return. **In person:** 1 public terminal available. No self-serve copier. Copies from computer are $.10 per page.

Payment: Pay by Visa/MC, money order, cashier's or personal check. Payee: Clerk, US District Court.

E-Services: PACER records go back to 9/1991. New records online after 1 day. ECF at https://ecf.kyed.uscourts.gov. Opinions on cases back to 3/17/2003 in pdf format on ECF system. **Note:** For calendars, click on "Court/Hearing Schedule" at www.kyed.uscourts.gov.

Frankfort Division Court Clerk, 313 John Watts Federal Bldg, 330 W Broadway, Frankfort, KY 40601, 502-223-5225. Hours-8:30AM-5PM. www.kyed.uscourts.gov

Counties/Note: Anderson, Carroll, Franklin, Henry, Owen, Shelby, Trimble.

Searches/Indexing: Search request requires name only. Results do not include SSN or DOB. Will not fax back documents. New cases are in the index immediately after filing date. Both computer and card indexes maintained; on computer back to 1/1993. Files sent to archives 5 years after closed.

Search Access: Only docket info available by phone. **Mail:** Search usually completed- 1-2 days. SASE not required. **In person:** 1 public terminal available. No self-serve copier.

Payment: Pay by Visa/MC, money order, cashier's or personal check. Payee: Clerk, US District Court.

E-Services: PACER records go back to 9/1991. New records online after 1 day. ECF at https://ecf.kyed.uscourts.gov. Opinions on cases back to 3/17/2003 in pdf format on ECF system. **Note:** For calendars, click on "Court/Hearing Schedule" at www.kyed.uscourts.gov.

Lexington Division Court Clerk, PO Box 3074, Lexington, KY 40588-3074 (In person: 101 Barr St, Rm 206, Lexington), 859-233-2503. Hours-8:30AM-5PM. www.kyed.uscourts.gov

Counties/Note: Bath, Bourbon, Boyle, Breathitt, Clark, Estill, Fayette, Fleming, Garrard, Harrison, Jessamine, Lee, Lincoln, Madison, Menifee, Mercer, Montgomery, Nicholas, Perry, Powell, Scott, Wolfe, Woodford.

Searches/Indexing: Search request requires name only. Results do not include SSN or DOB. Office cannot guarantee identity match. Will not fax back documents. New cases are in the index 24 hours after filing date. Computer and card indexes maintained; computer back to 10/1992. Case files sent to archives 5 years after closed.

Search Access: Only docket info from active cases is released via phone. **Mail:** Search usually completed- 2-3 weeks. SASE not required. **In person:** 1 public terminal available. No self-serve copier.

Payment: Pay by Visa/MC, money order, cashier's or personal check. Payee: Clerk, USDC.

E-Services: PACER records go back to 10/1992. New records online after 1 day. ECF at https://ecf.kyed.uscourts.gov. Opinions on cases back to 3/17/2003 in pdf format on ECF system. **Note:** For calendars, click on "Court/Hearing Schedule" at www.kyed.uscourts.gov.

London Division Court Clerk, PO Box 5121, London, KY 40745-5121 (In person: 124 US Courthouse, 310 S Main St, London, KY 40741), 606-877-7910. Hours - 8:30AM - 5PM. www.kyed.uscourts.gov

Counties/Note: Bell, Clay, Harlan, Jackson, Knox, Laurel, Leslie, McCreary, Owsley, Pulaski, Rockcastle, Wayne, Whitley.

Searches/Indexing: Search request requires name only. Results do not include SSN or DOB. Will not fax back documents. New cases are in the index immediately after filing date. Computer index back to 3/2003 maintained. Case files sent to archives 5 years after closed.

Search Access: Only docket info available by phone. **Mail:** Search usually completed- 1 day. Include SASE for return. **In person:** 1 public terminal available. No self-serve copier.

Payment: Visa/MC, money order, cashier's, business or personal check. Payee: Clerk, USDC.

E-Services: PACER records go back to 9/1991. New records online after 1 day. ECF at https://ecf.kyed.uscourts.gov. Opinions on cases back to 3/17/2003 in pdf format on ECF system. **Note:** For calendars, click on "Court/Hearing Schedule" at www.kyed.uscourts.gov.

Pikeville Division Office of the Clerk, 203 Federal Bldg, 110 Main St, Pikeville, KY 41501, 606-437-6160. Hours - 8:30AM - 5PM. www.kyed.uscourts.gov

Counties/Note: Floyd, Johnson, Knott, Letcher, Magoffin, Martin, Pike.

Searches/Indexing: Search request requires name only. Results do not include SSN or DOB. Will not fax back documents. New cases are in the index immediately after filing date. Both computer and card indexes maintained; on computer back to 1/1993. Files sent to archives 5 years after closed.

Search Access: Only date of filing and case status is released via phone. **Mail:** Search usually completed- 24 hours. SASE not required. **In person:** 1 public terminal available. Self-serve copies from computer- $.10 each.

Payment: Pay by Visa/MC, money order, cashier's or personal check. Payee: Clerk, US District Court. Prepayment required except for KY attorneys.

E-Services: PACER records go back to 9/1991. New records online after 1 day. ECF at https://ecf.kyed.uscourts.gov. Opinions on cases back to 3/17/2003 in pdf format on ECF system. **Note:** For calendars, click on "Court/Hearing Schedule" at www.kyed.uscourts.gov.

US Bankruptcy Court Kentucky Eastern District

Lexington Division Court Clerk, PO Box 1111, Lexington, KY 40589-1111 (In person: Community Trust Bldg, Suite 202, 100 E Vine St, Lexington, KY 40507), 859-233-2608. Hours-8:30AM-4PM. www.kyeb.uscourts.gov

Counties/Note: Anderson, Bath, Bell, Boone, Bourbon, Boyd, Boyle, Bracken, Breathitt, Campbell, Carroll, Carter, Clark, Clay, Elliott, Estill, Fayette, Fleming, Floyd, Franklin, Gallatin, Garrard, Grant, Greenup, Harlan, Harrison, Henry, Jackson, Jessamine, Johnson, Kenton, Knott, Knox, Laurel, Lawrence, Lee, Leslie, Letcher,

Lewis, Lincoln, Madison, Magoffin, Martin, Mason, McCreary, Menifee, Mercer, Montgomery, Morgan, Nicholas, Owen, Owsley, Pendleton, Perry, Pike, Powell, Pulaski, Robertson, Rockcastle, Rowan, Scott, Shelby, Trimble, Wayne, Whitley, Wolfe, Woodford.

Searches/Indexing: Include name and/or SSN in search request. Results include last 4 SSN digits only. Will not fax back documents. New cases are in the index 3 days after filing date.

Search Access: Only docket info is available by phone. Voice Case Information Service available, call VCIS at 800-998-2650 or 859-233-2650. **Mail:** Search usually completed- 5 days. Include SASE for return. **In person:** 4 public terminals available. Computer generated copies- $.10 each.

Payment: Pay by credit cards, money order, cashier's check, business check. No personal checks. Visa/MC accepted from attorneys only. Payee: Clerk, US Bankruptcy Court. Prepayment required except for pauper filings.

E-Services: Search closed cases index free at www.kyeb.uscourts.gov/frc/frc_search.htm. These are closed, non-electronic cases only, pre-8/1/2002. PACER records go back to 7/1992. New records online immediately. ECF at https://ecf.kyeb.uscourts.gov. **Opinions Online:** www.kyeb.uscourts.gov/searchsite.htm. **Online Note:** Access calendars free at www.kyeb.uscourts.gov/calendar.htm.

US District Court Kentucky Western District

Bowling Green Div. Court Clerk, US District Court, 241 E Main St, Rm 120, Bowling Green, KY 42101-2175, 270-393-2500; Fax- 270-393-2519. 8:30AM-5PM. www.kywd.uscourts.gov

Counties/Note: Adair, Allen, Barren, Butler, Casey, Clinton, Cumberland, Edmonson, Green, Hart, Logan, Metcalfe, Monroe, Russell, Simpson, Taylor, Todd, Warren.

Searches/Indexing: Include full name in search request. Results do not include SSN or DOB. Will not fax back documents. New cases are in the index immediately after filing date. Both computer and card indexes maintained.

Search Access: Only docket info is available by phone. **Mail:** Search usually completed- 1-2 days. Include SASE for return. **Fax:** Written fax search requests accepted with prepayment. **In person:** 1 public terminal available. Self-serve copies $.50.

Payment: Pay by money order, cashier's or personal check. No credit cards accepted. Payee: Clerk, US District Court.

E-Services: PACER/ECF records go back to 1992. New records online immediately. ECF at https://ecf.kywd.uscourts.gov. **Opinions Online:** www.kywd.uscourts.gov/judicialOpinionsSearch.php. **Online Note:** Calendars available at www.kywd.uscourts.gov/CourtCalendars.php.

Louisville Division Clerk, US District Court, 601 W Broadway, Rm 106, Louisville, KY 40202, 502-625-3500; Fax- 502-625-3880. 8:30AM-4:30PM. www.kywd.uscourts.gov

Counties/Note: Breckinridge, Bullitt, Hardin, Jefferson, Larue, Marion, Meade, Nelson, Oldham, Spencer, Washington.

Searches/Indexing: Include full name in search request. Results do not include SSN or DOB. Will not fax back documents. New cases are in the index immediately after filing date. Computer, microfiche and card indexes maintained. Records on index cards 1938-1979. Records indexed on microfiche 1979 to 4/92. Records after 4/92 are on the automated system. District-wide searches available here for cases back to 1938.

Search Access: Only docket info is available by phone. **Mail:** Search usually completed- 5-10 working days. Include SASE for return. **Fax:** Written fax search and case file requests accepted with credit card. **In person:** 2 public terminals available. No self-serve copier.

Payment: Pay by Visa/MC, money order, cashier's or personal check. Payee: Clerk, US District Court.

E-Services: PACER/ECF records go back to 1992. New records online immediately. ECF at https://ecf.kywd.uscourts.gov. **Opinions Online:** www.kywd.uscourts.gov/judicialOpinionsSearch.php. **Online Note:** Calendars available at www.kywd.uscourts.gov/CourtCalendars.php.

Owensboro Division Court Clerk, Federal Bldg, Rm 126, 423 Frederica St, Owensboro, KY 42301, 270-689-4400; Fax- 207-689-4419. Hours- 8AM-4:30PM. www.kywd.uscourts.gov

Counties/Note: Daviess, Grayson, Hancock, Henderson, Hopkins, McLean, Muhlenberg, Ohio, Union, Webster.

Searches/Indexing: Court needs the correct name, date, or criminal or civil case number to search. Results do not include SSN or DOB. Will only fax back documents in extreme emergencies. New cases are in the index immediately after filing date. Computer index maintained back to 1990.

Search Access: Only docket info is available by phone. **Mail:** Search usually completed- 2-3 days. SASE not required. **Fax:** Written fax search requests accepted with prepayment. **In person:** 1 public terminal available. Self-serve copies- $.50 per page. Copies printed from court's CM/ECT system are $.10 each.

Payment: Pay by money order, cashier's, business or personal check. Credit cards accepted at the Louisville office only. Payee: Clerk, US District Court. Court will bill to in-state searchers only.

E-Services: Court has converted its online WebPACER/PACER service over to ECF. PACER/ECF records go back to 1990. New records online immediately. ECF at https://ecf.kywd.uscourts.gov. **Opinions Online:** www.kywd.uscourts.gov/judicialOpinionsSearch.php. **Online Note:** Calendars available at www.kywd.uscourts.gov/CourtCalendars.php.

Paducah Division Court Clerk, 501 Broadway, Ste 127, Paducah, KY 42001, 270-415-6400; Fax- 270-415-6419. Hours-8:30AM-5PM. www.kywd.uscourts.gov

Counties: Ballard, Caldwell, Calloway, Carlisle, Christian, Crittenden, Fulton, Graves, Hickman, Livingston, Lyon, McCracken, Marshall, Trigg.

Searches/Indexing: Include full name in search request. Results do not include SSN or DOB. Will not fax back documents. New cases are in the index immediately after filing date. Both computer and card indexes maintained; computer index back to 1992.

Search Access: Only docket info is available by phone. **Mail:** Search usually completed- 3-4 working days. Include SASE for return. **Fax:** Written fax search requests accepted with prepayment. **In person:** 1 public terminal available. Self-serve copies $.50 each.

Payment: Pay by Visa/MC, money order, cashier's or personal check. Payee: Clerk, US District Court.

E-Services: PACER/ECF records go back to 1992. New records online immediately. ECF at https://ecf.kywd.uscourts.gov. **Opinions Online:** www.kywd.uscourts.gov/judicialOpinionsSearch.php. **Online Note:** Calendars available at www.kywd.uscourts.gov/CourtCalendars.php.

US Bankruptcy Court Kentucky Western District

Louisville Division Court Clerk, 601 W Broadway, Ste. 450, US Courthouse, Louisville, KY 40202, 502-627-5700. 8:30AM-4:30PM. www.kywb.uscourts.gov

Counties/Note: Adair, Allen, Ballard, Barren, Breckinridge, Bullitt, Butler, Caldwell, Calloway, Carlisle, Casey, Christian, Clinton, Crittenden, Cumberland, Daviess, Edmonson, Fulton, Graves, Grayson, Green, Hancock, Hardin, Hart, Henderson, Hickman, Hopkins, Jefferson, Larue, Livingston, Logan, Lyon, Marion, Marshall, McCracken, McLean, Meade, Metcalfe, Monroe, Muhlenberg, Nelson, Ohio, Oldham, Russell, Simpson, Spencer, Taylor, Todd, Trigg, Union, Warren, Washington, Webster.

Searches/Indexing: Search request requires name, also SSN or DOB and detailed info on the nature of the request. Results include last 4 SSN digits. Will fax back in emergency, $.50 per page. New cases are in the index immediately after filing date. Maintains records for all district divisions. District-wide searches available here.

Search Access: Only basic case info is available by phone. Voice Case Information Service available, call VCIS at 800-263-9385 or 502-627-5660. **Mail:** Search usually completed- 2 days. Include SASE for return. **In person:** 2 public terminals available. Self-serve copies $.15 each.

Payment: Pay by money order, cashier's check, business check. No personal checks. Attorneys Visa/MC okay. Payee: Clerk, Bankruptcy Court.

E-Services: PACER records go back to 7/1992. New records online immediately. ECF at https://ecf.kywb.uscourts.gov. **Opinions Online:** www.kywb.uscourts.gov/opinions/main.php.

Kentucky County Courts

Court	Jurisdiction	No. of Courts	How Organized
Circuit Courts*	General	19	57 Judicial Circuits
District Courts*	Limited	19	60 Judicial Districts
Combined*		102	

* Profiled in this Sourcebook.

Court	CIVIL								
	Tort	Contract	Real Estate	Min. Claim	Max. Claim	Small Claims	Estate	Eviction	Domestic Relations
Circuit Courts*	X	X	X	$4000	No Max				X
District Courts*	X	X	X	$0	$4000	$1500	X	X	X

Court	CRIMINAL				
	Felony	Misdemeanor	DWI/DUI	Preliminary Hearing	Juvenile
Circuit Courts*	X				
District Courts*		X	X	X	X

Administration

Administrative Office of Courts, Records Unit, 100 Mill Creek Park, Frankfort, KY, 40601; 502-573-1682, Fax: 502-573-1669. http://courts.ky.gov/

Court Structure

The Circuit Court is the court of general jurisdiction and the District Court is the limited jurisdiction court. Most of Kentucky's counties combined the courts into one location and records are co-mingled. Circuit Courts have jurisdiction over cases involving capital offenses and felonies, divorces, adoptions, terminations of parental rights, land dispute title problems, and contested probates of will. Juvenile matters, city and county ordinances, misdemeanors, traffic offenses, uncontested probate of wills, felony preliminary hearings, and civil cases involving $4,000 or less are heard in District Court. 90% of all Kentuckians involved in court proceedings appear in District Court.

Online Access

There is a free access to limited criminal record info at http://apps.kycourts.net/CourtRecords/. Results produce a list with case numbers and names. Also, you may search daily court calendars by county for free at http://apps.kycourts.net/dockets. KY Bar attorneys may register to use the KCOJ court records data at http://apps.kycourts.net/courtrecordsKBA/, this is a commerial system. No courts offer direct online access to record images.

Search opinons and case information from the Supreme Court and Court of Appeals at http://courts.ky.gov/research/.

Searching Tips, Fees, and Other Guidelines

Until 1978, county judges handled all cases. Therefore, most District Court and Circuit Court records go back only to 1978. Records prior to that time are archived. Prepayment of fees is always required unless noted.

The Administrative Office of the Courts offers a service of providing statewide criminal background checks. They provide the record via fax, standard mail, walk-in, or drive-thru service. Their CourtNet Criminal History database contains records of all misdemeanor and traffic cases for at least the last five years, and for felonies dating back to 1978, from all 120 counties. The required Release Form is available from the AOC at the number above. A check or money order for the search fee of $10.00 per requested individual, $15.00 if requested by fax. All accounts must set up a prepaid bank. A SASE must accompany the request.

Adair County

Circuit & District Court 500 Public Square, #6, Columbia, KY 42728; 270-384-2626; fax: 270-384-4299; 8AM-4PM (CST). ***Felony, Misdemeanor, Civil, Eviction, Small Claims, Probate.***

Civil Records: Access: In person, online. Visitors must perform in person searches themselves. Required to search: name, years to search. Civil records on computer since 6/1993, prior records on docket books since 1978. Civil PAT goes back to 6/1993. Free index search by name at http://apps.kycourts.net/CourtRecords/.

Criminal Records: Access: Mail, in person, online. Visitors must perform in person searches themselves. No search fee. Required to search: name, years to search, SSN. Criminal records on computer since 6/1993, prior records on docket books since 1978. Mail requests must be made to Pretrial Services, 100 Millcreek Pk, Frankfort KY 40601, 800-928-6381. Mail turnaround time same day. Criminal PAT goes back to same as civil. Online access same as civil; results show middle initial.

General Information: No adoption, mental, juvenile, or sealed records released. Court makes copy: $.25 per page, self serve same. No cert fee. Payee: Circuit Clerk. No personal checks or credit cards accepted.

Allen County

Circuit & District Court PO Box 477, Scottsville, KY 42164; 270-237-3561; fax: 270-237-9120; 8-4:30PM (CST). ***Felony, Misdemeanor, Civil, Eviction, Small Claims, Probate.***

Civil Records: Access: In person, online. Visitors must perform in person searches themselves. Required to search: name, years to search. Civil cases indexed by defendant, plaintiff, on computer since 1992, records on index cards from 1980 to 1992, prior records on books. Civil PAT goes back to 9/1992. PAT results show middle initial, DOB. Results on a public terminal sometimes shows last 4 digits of SSN. Free index search by name at http://apps.kycourts.net/CourtRecords/.

Criminal Records: Access: In person, online. Visitors must perform in person searches themselves. Required to search: name, years to search; SSN helpful. Criminal records computerized from 1992, records on index cards from 1978 to 1992, prior records on books. Court recommends that criminal search requests be directed to the State of Kentucky AOC, 502-573-2350. Criminal PAT goes back to same as civil. PAT results show middle initial, DOB. Results on a public terminal sometimes shows last 4 digits of SSN. Online access same as civil; results show middle initial.

General Information: No adoption, mental, juvenile, or sealed records released. Will fax documents for no fee. Court makes copy: $.25 per page. Certification fee: $5.00 per doc. Payee: Circuit Clerk. Local personal checks accepted. No credit cards accepted.

Anderson County

Circuit Court 151 S Main St, Courthouse, Lawrenceburg, KY 40342; 502-839-3508; fax: 502-839-4995; 8:30AM-5PM (EST). ***Felony, Civil Actions over $4,000.***

Civil Records: Access: Mail, In person, online. Only the court performs in person searches; visitors may not. No search fee. Required to search: name, years to search. Civil cases indexed by defendant, plaintiff, on computer since 8/1994, prior records on docket books since 1978. Free index search by name at http://apps.kycourts.net/CourtRecords/.

Criminal Records: Access: In person, online. Only the court performs in person searches; visitors may not. Required to search: name, years to search; also helpful: DOB, SSN. Criminal records may be on computer back to 1994. All record requests are referred to the state agency at 800-928-6381. Online access same as civil; results show middle initial.

General Information: No adoption, mental, juvenile, or sealed records released. Court makes copy: $.25 per page. Certification fee: $5.00 per doc. Payee: Clerk of Circuit Court. Personal checks accepted; credit cards are not.

District Court 151 S Main, Lawrenceburg, KY 40342; 502-839-3508; fax: 502-839-4995; 8:30AM-N, 1-5PM M-TH; 8:30AM-6PM F (EST). ***Misdemeanor, Civil Actions under $4,000, Eviction, Small Claims, Probate.*** District Court has combined with the Circuit court, so fees and access may now be the same as the Circuit court.

Civil Records: Access: In person, online. Both court and visitors may perform in person searches. No search fee. Required to search: name, years to search. Civil cases indexed by defendant, plaintiff, on computer since 8/1994, prior records on index cards back to 1978. Free index search by name at http://apps.kycourts.net/CourtRecords/.

Criminal Records: Access: Online. Both court and visitors may perform in person searches. Required to search: name, years to search; also helpful: DOB, SSN. Criminal records computerized from 1994; prior records on index cards back to 1978. All requests are referred to Pre-trial Services at 800-928-6381. Court will not do searches and offers no means to look up a name in an index; there is no way to get the case number. Must go to Frankfort for criminal records for name and county to retrieve. Online access same as civil. results show middle initial.

General Information: No adoption, mental, juvenile, or sealed records released. Will not fax documents. Court makes copy: $1.00 per page criminal; civil-$.25 per page. Certification fee: $5.00 per doc. Payee: Anderson County District Court. Business checks accepted. No credit cards accepted.

Ballard County

Circuit & District Court Box 265, Wickliffe, KY 42087; 270-335-5123; fax: 270-335-3849; 8AM-4PM (CST). ***Felony, Misdemeanor, Civil, Eviction, Small Claims, Probate.***

Civil Records: Access: In person, online. Both court and visitors may perform in person searches. No search fee. Required to search: name, years to search. Civil cases indexed by defendant, plaintiff, on computer since 1992, prior records on books to 1978. Civil PAT goes back to 1992. Free index search by name at http://apps.kycourts.net/CourtRecords/.

Criminal Records: Access: In person, online. Visitors must perform in person searches themselves. Required to search: name, years to search, DOB. Criminal records on computer since 1992, prior records on books to 1978. Criminal PAT goes back to same as civil. Online access same as civil; results show middle initial.

General Information: No adoption, mental, juvenile, or sealed records released. Fee to fax out file $2.00 1st page, $1.00 each addl. Court makes copy: $.25 per page, self serve same. Certification fee: $5.00 per doc. Payee: Circuit Clerk. Only cashiers checks and money orders accepted. No credit cards accepted.

Barren County

Circuit & District Court PO Box 1359, 100 Courthouse Sq, Glasgow, KY 42142-1359; 270-651-3763; fax: 270-651-6203; 8AM-4:30PM (CST). ***Felony, Misdemeanor, Civil, Eviction, Small Claims, Probate.*** www.courts.ky.gov

Civil Records: Access: In person, online. Visitors must perform in person searches themselves. Required to search: name, years to search. Civil cases indexed by defendant, plaintiff, on computer back to 10/1991, prior records on index books since 1800s are kept in Frankfurt, KY. Civil PAT goes back to 10/1991. Results include DOB in some cases. Free index search by name at http://apps.kycourts.net/CourtRecords/.

Criminal Records: Access: In person, online. Visitors must perform in person searches themselves. Required to search: name, years to search, DOB; SSN helpful. Criminal records computerized from 10/1991, prior records on index books since 1800s are kept in Frankfort, KY. Criminal record search requests should be directed to AOC Pre-Trial Services in Frankfort, 800-928-6381. Criminal PAT goes back to same as civil. PAT results show middle initial; terminal results may include DOB and SSN. Online access same as civil; results show middle initial.

General Information: No adoption, mental, juvenile, or sealed records released. Will not fax out case files. Court makes copy: $.25 per page, self serve same. Certification fee: $5.00 per doc. Payee: Circuit Clerk. Personal checks accepted except for restitution payments. Major credit cards accepted.

Bath County

Circuit & District Court PO Box 558, 19 E Main, Owingsville, KY 40360; 606-674-2186 X6821; fax: 606-674-3996; 8AM-4PM (EST). ***Felony, Misdemeanor, Civil, Eviction, Small Claims, Probate.***

Civil Records: Access: In person, online. Visitors must perform in person searches themselves. Required to search: name, years to search. Civil cases indexed by defendant, plaintiff, computerized since 1994, on docket books since 1978, prior records archived. Civil PAT goes back to 1994. Free index search at http://apps.kycourts.net/CourtRecords/.

Criminal Records: Access: In person, online. Visitors must perform in person searches themselves. Required to search: name, years to search, DOB, SSN. Criminal records computerized since 1994, on docket books since 1978, prior records archived. Criminal PAT goes back to same as civil. Online access same as civil; results show middle initial.

General Information: No adoption, mental, juvenile, or sealed records released. Will fax documents $2.00 per page fee. Court makes copy: $.25 per page, self serve same. Certification fee: $5.00 per doc. Payee: Circuit Clerk. No personal checks or credit cards accepted.

Bell County

Circuit & District Court Box 307, Pineville, KY 40977; 606-337-2942; probate phone: 606-337-9900; criminal fax: 606-337-8850; civil fax: same; 8AM-4PM (EST). ***Felony, Misdemeanor, Civil, Eviction, Small Claims, Probate.*** http://courts.ky.gov/Counties/Bell/default.htm Probate fax is same as main fax number.

Civil Records: Access: Phone, mail, in person, online. Both court and visitors may perform in person searches. No search fee. Required to search: name, years to search. Civil cases indexed by defendant, plaintiff, on computer since 8/91, prior records on docket books since 1978. Civil PAT goes back to 8/1991. PAT results show middle initial, DOB. Free index search by name at http://apps.kycourts.net/CourtRecords/.

Criminal Records: Access: In person, online. Visitors must perform in person searches themselves. Search fee: Court will do a index search for the name and tell you how many records they find, for no fee. Required to search: name, years to search. Criminal records on computer since 8/91, prior records on docket books since 1978. Criminal PAT goes back to same as civil. PAT results show middle initial, DOB. Online access same as civil; results show middle initial.

General Information: No adoption, mental, juvenile, or sealed records released. will fax documents, $2.00 1st page, $1.00 each add'l. Court makes copy: $.25 per page, self serve same. Certification fee: $5.00. Payee: Circuit Clerk. Personal checks accepted. Mail requests: SASE required for civil.

Boone County

Circuit & District Court 6025 Rogers Ln, #141, Burlington, KY 41005; 859-334-2286; criminal phone: 859-334-3536 District; civil phone: 859-334-2287 District; fax: 859-334-3650; 8:30AM-4:30PM (EST). ***Felony, Misdemeanor, Civil, Eviction, Small Claims, Probate.***

Civil Records: Access: In person, online. Both court and visitors may perform in person searches. No search fee. Required to search: name, years to search. Civil cases indexed by defendant, plaintiff, on computer since 7/1990, on index card file since 1978, prior records on books. Civil PAT goes back to 7/1990. PAT civil results show middle initial. Free index search by name at http://apps.kycourts.net/CourtRecords/.

Criminal Records: Access: In person, online. Visitors must perform in person searches themselves. Required to search: name, years to search, DOB; SSN helpful. Criminal records on computer since 7/1990, on index card file since 1978, prior records on books. Criminal PAT goes back to same as civil. PAT criminal results show middle initial. Online access same as civil; results show middle initial.

General Information: No adoption, mental, juvenile, or sealed records released. Fee to fax out file $3.00 per page. Court makes copy: $.25 per page, self serve same. Certification fee: $5.00 per doc. Payee: Circuit Clerk. Only cashiers checks and money orders accepted. Visa/MC accepted.

Bourbon County

Circuit & District Court Box 740, 310 Main St, Courthouse Annex, Paris, KY 40361; 859-987-2624; fax: 859-987-6049; 8:30AM-4:30PM (EST). ***Felony, Misdemeanor, Civil, Eviction, Small Claims, Probate.***

Civil Records: Access: In person, online. Visitors must perform in person searches themselves. Required to search: name, years to search. Civil cases indexed by defendant, plaintiff, on computer since 11/1991, prior records on books. Civil PAT goes back to 1991. PAT results show middle initial, DOB. Free index search by name at http://apps.kycourts.net/CourtRecords/.

Criminal Records: Access: In person, online. Visitors must perform in person searches themselves. Required to search: name, years to search; SSN helpful. Criminal records on computer since 11/1991, prior records on books. Criminal PAT goes back to same as civil. PAT results show middle initial, DOB. Online access same as civil; results show middle initial.

General Information: No adoption, mental, juvenile, or sealed records released. Will not fax documents. Court makes copy: $.25 per page, self serve same. Certification fee: $5.00. Payee: Circuit Clerk. Local personal checks accepted. No credit cards accepted.

Boyd County

Circuit & District Court Box 694, Catlettsburg, KY 41129-0694; 606-739-4131, 4132, 4133; fax: 606-739-6330; 8:30AM-4PM (EST). ***Felony, Misdemeanor, Civil, Eviction, Small Claims, Probate.*** Alternative fax- 606-739-5793.

Civil Records: Access: In person, online. Visitors must perform in person searches themselves. Required to search: name, years to search. Civil cases indexed by defendant, plaintiff, on computer since 1991, prior records on index cards since 1978. Civil PAT goes back to 1991. PAT civil results show middle initial. Free index search by name at http://apps.kycourts.net/CourtRecords/.

Criminal Records: Access: In person, online. Visitors must perform in person searches themselves. Required to search: name, years to

search; also helpful: DOB, SSN. Criminal records on computer since 1991, on index cards since 1978; misdemeanor & traffic from 1995. Criminal PAT goes back to same as civil. PAT criminal results show middle initial. Online access same as civil; results show middle initial.
General Information: No adoption, mental, juvenile, or sealed records released. Court makes copy: $.25 per page. Cert fee: $5.00 per doc. Payee: Circuit Clerk. Personal checks accepted; credit cards are not.

Boyle County

Circuit Court 321 Main St, Danville, KY 40422; 859-239-7442; criminal fax: 859-239-7000; civil fax: same; 8AM-4:30PM (EST). ***Felony, Civil Actions over $4,000.***
Civil Records: Access: In person, online. Both court and visitors may perform in person searches. No search fee. Required to search: name, years to search. Civil cases indexed by defendant, plaintiff, on computer since 8/91, prior records on index cards. Civil PAT goes back to 8/1991. Results include year of birth and last 4 numbers of social security. Free index search by name at http://apps.kycourts.net/CourtRecords/.
Criminal Records: Access: In person, online. Visitors must perform in person searches themselves. Required to search: name, years to search, and DOB, SSN if available. Criminal records on computer since 8/91, prior records on index cards. This office will not perform criminal name checks; will refer you to the state Pre-Trial Services, 900-928-6381 which has a $10 per name fee. Criminal PAT goes back to same as civil. Results include year of birth and last 4 numbers of social security. Search parties and case number index only free at http://apps.kycourts.net/CourtRecords/. Online results show middle initial.
General Information: No adoption, mental, juvenile, or sealed records released. Will fax documents $1.00 per page; cannot fax certified pages. Court makes copy: $.25 per page, self serve same. Certification fee: $5.00. Payee: Circuit Clerk. No personal checks or credit cards accepted. Mail requests: SASE required for mail return of any copies.

District Court Courthouse, 3rd Fl, Danville, KY 40422; 859-239-7362; fax: 859-239-7807; 8AM-4:30PM (EST). ***Misdemeanor, Civil Actions under $4,000, Eviction, Small Claims, Probate.***
Public access terminals in the Circuit Clerk's office
Civil Records: Access: In person, online. Visitors must perform in person searches themselves. Required to search: name, years to search. Civil cases indexed by defendant, plaintiff, on computer since 8/91, prior records on index cards since 1977. Civil PAT goes back to 8/1991. PAT results show middle initial but only year of DOB and last 4 digits of SSN appear. Free index search by name at http://apps.kycourts.net/CourtRecords/.
Criminal Records: Access: In person, online. Visitors must perform in person searches themselves. Required to search: name, DOB, SSN. Criminal records on computer since 8/91; prior records on card index. Office can retrieve specified documents but will not perform criminal name checks. Criminal PAT goes back to same as civil. PAT results show middle initial, but only year of DOB and last 4 digits of SSN appear. Online access same as civil; results show middle initial.
General Information: No adoption, mental, juvenile, or sealed records released. Will fax out documents $1.00 per page, uncertified. Court makes copy: $.25 per page. Self serve: $.25 per page. Certification fee: $5.00 per doc. Payee: District Clerk. Personal checks accepted; credit cards are not.

Bracken County

Circuit & District Court PO Box 205, 116 W. Miami St, Brooksville, KY 41004-0205; 606-735-3328; criminal fax: 606-735-3900; civil fax: same; 8AM-4:30PM M,T,TH,F; 8:30AM-N W,Sat (EST). ***Felony, Misdemeanor, Civil, Eviction, Small Claims, Probate.*** http://courts.ky.gov/Counties/Bracken/
Probate fax is same as main fax number.
Civil Records: Access: Mail, in person, online. Both court and visitors may perform in person searches. No search fee. Required to search: name, years to search. Civil cases indexed by defendant, plaintiff, on computer since 1993, prior records on docket books since 1797. Mail turnaround time 3-5 days. Civil PAT goes back to 8/1992. PAT civil results show middle initial. Free index search by name at http://apps.kycourts.net/CourtRecords/.
Criminal Records: Access: In person, online. Visitors must perform in person searches themselves. Required to search: name, years to search. Criminal records on computer since 1993, prior records on docket books since 1797. Criminal PAT goes back to same as civil. PAT results show middle initial, DOB. Online access same as civil; results show middle initial.
General Information: No adoption, mental, juvenile, or sealed records released. Will not fax documents. Court makes copy: $.25 per page, self serve same. Certification fee: $5.00 per doc. Payee: Circuit Clerk. Mail requests: SASE required for civil.

Breathitt County

Circuit & District Court 1131 Main St, Jackson, KY 41339; 606-666-5768; fax: 606-666-4893; 8AM-4PM M,T,TH,F; 8AM-N W; 9AM-N Sat (EST). ***Felony, Misdemeanor, Civil, Eviction, Small Claims, Probate.***
Civil Records: Access: Phone, fax, mail, in person, online. Both court and visitors may perform in person searches. No search fee. Required to search: name, years to search. Civil cases indexed by defendant, plaintiff, in files since 1987. Mail turnaround time 2-3 days. Civil PAT goes back to 1995. PAT results show name, DOB. Free index search at http://apps.kycourts.net/CourtRecords/.
Criminal Records: Access: Phone, fax, mail, in person, online. Both court and visitors may perform in person searches. No search fee. Required to search: name, years to search, DOB, SSN, signed release. Criminal records in files since 1987. Mail turnaround time 2-3 days. Criminal PAT goes back to same as civil.PAT results show name, DOB. Online access same as civil; results show middle initial.
General Information: No adoption, mental, juvenile, or sealed records released. Will not fax documents. Court makes copy: $.25 per page. Certification fee: $5.00 per cert. Payee: Circuit Clerk. Personal checks okay; no credit cards. Mail requests: SASE required.

Breckinridge County

Circuit & District Court PO Box 111, Hardinsburg, KY 40143; 270-756-2239; fax: 270-756-1129; 8AM-4PM (CST). ***Felony, Misdemeanor, Civil, Eviction, Small Claims, Probate.***
Civil Records: Access: In person, online. Visitors must perform in person searches themselves. Required to search: name, years to search. Civil cases indexed by defendant, plaintiff, on computer back to 8/1994, on index cards since 1978, prior records in office 1992-present, all others in Frankfort on docket books sin. Public use terminal available. Free index search at http://apps.kycourts.net/CourtRecords/.
Criminal Records: Access: In person, online. Visitors must perform in person searches themselves. Required to search: name, years to search, DOB, SSN. Criminal records computerized from 8/1994, on index cards since 1978, prior records on docket books since the 1800s. Public use terminal available. Online access same as civil; results show middle initial.
General Information: No adoption, mental, juvenile, or sealed records released. Will fax documents $2.00 1st page, $1.00 ea add'l, prepaid. Court makes copy: $.25 per page, self serve same. Certification fee: $5.00. Payee: Circuit Clerk. Personal checks accepted; credit cards are not. Mail requests: SASE required for mail return of any copies.

Bullitt County

Circuit & District Court Box 746, Shephardsville, KY 40165; 502-543-7104; fax: 502-543-7158; 8AM-4PM (EST). ***Felony, Misdemeanor, Civil, Eviction, Small Claims, Probate.***
www.courts.ky.gov/counties/bullitt/
The District Court can be reached at 502-543-2244.
Civil Records: Access: In person, online. Visitors must perform in person searches themselves. Required to search: name. Civil cases indexed by defendant, plaintiff, on computer since 11/91, prior records on index cards since the 1800s. Civil PAT goes back to 11/1991. Free index search by name at http://apps.kycourts.net/CourtRecords/.
Criminal Records: Access: In person, online. Visitors must perform in person searches themselves. Required to search: name, years to search, DOB, SSN. Criminal records on computer since 11/91, prior records on index cards since the 1800s. Criminal PAT goes back to same as civil. Online access same as civil; results show middle initial.
General Information: No adoption, mental, juvenile, or sealed records released. Fee to fax out case file is $2.00 per page. Court makes copy: $.25 per page, self serve same. Certification fee: $5.00. Payee: Circuit Clerk. Personal checks accepted; credit cards are not.

Butler County

Circuit & District Court Box 625, 110 N Main St, Morgantown, KY 42261; 270-526-5631; probate phone: same; fax: 270-526-6763; 8AM-4PM M-F; 9AM-N Sat (CST). ***Felony, Misdemeanor, Civil, Eviction, Small Claims, Probate.***
Civil Records: Access: Mail, in person, online. Both court and visitors may perform in person searches. No search fee. Required to search: name, years to search. Civil cases indexed by defendant, plaintiff, on computer since 1993, prior records on index cards since the 1800s. Mail turnaround time 1 week. Civil PAT goes back to 1993. PAT results show middle initial, DOB, SSN. Free index search by name at http://apps.kycourts.net/CourtRecords/.
Criminal Records: Access: Mail, in person, online. Both court and visitors may perform in person searches. No search fee. Required to search: name, years to search, DOB; also helpful: SSN. Criminal records on computer since 1993, prior records on index cards since the 1800s, easily accessible from 1978. Mail turnaround time 1 week. Criminal PAT goes back to same as civil. Online access same as civil; results show middle initial.
General Information: No adoption, mental, juvenile, or sealed records released. Will not fax documents. Court makes copy: $.25 per page. No certification fee. Payee: Circuit Clerk. Personal checks accepted; credit cards are not. Mail requests: SASE required.

Caldwell County

Circuit & District Court 105 W Court Sq, Princeton, KY 42445; 270-365-6884; criminal fax: 270-365-9171; civil fax: same; 8AM-4PM (CST). ***Felony, Misdemeanor, Civil, Eviction, Small Claims, Probate.*** Probate fax is same as main fax.
www.sangamoncountycircuitclerk.org
Civil Records: Access: In person, online. Visitors must perform in person searches themselves. Required to search: name, years to search. Civil cases indexed by defendant, plaintiff; index on cards; on computer back to 9/94. Civil PAT goes back to 9/1994. Free index search by name at http://apps.kycourts.net/CourtRecords/. Also, online access by subscription available at www.janojustice.com/products/magnus_dot_com/cm.htm. Email salcs@janojustice.com for information, fees and set-up.
Criminal Records: Access: In person, online. Visitors must perform in person searches themselves. Required to search: name, years to search, DOB; also helpful: SSN. Criminal records indexed on cards; on computer back to 9/94. Criminal PAT goes back to same as civil. Online access same as civil; results show middle initial.
General Information: No adoption, mental, juvenile, or sealed records released. Fee to fax out file $2.00 1st page, $1.00 each add'l. Court makes copy: $.25 per page; copy request must include postage, self serve same. Certification fee: $5.00 per doc. Payee: Circuit Clerk. Personal checks accepted; credit cards are not.

Calloway County

Circuit & District Court 312 N 4th St, Murray, KY 42071; 270-753-2714; fax: 270-759-9822; 8AM-5:30PM M-TH; 8AM-4:30PM F (CST). ***Felony, Misdemeanor, Civil, Eviction, Small Claims,***

Probate. Circuit court civil and criminal phone number is 270-753-2773.
Civil Records: Access: Mail, in person, online. Both court and visitors may perform in person searches. No search fee. Required to search: name, years to search. Civil cases indexed by defendant, plaintiff, on computer since 6/92, on index cards since 1978. Prior to 1978 records are archived in Frankfurt. Civil PAT goes back to 1978. PAT results show name, DOB. Free index search by name at http://apps.kycourts.net/CourtRecords/.
Criminal Records: Access: In person, online. Visitors must perform in person searches themselves. Required to search: name, years to search, DOB; SSN helpful. Criminal records on computer since 6/92, on index cards since 1978. Prior to 1978 records are archived in Frankfurt. This agency sends criminal case search requesters to Pre-trial Services at 502-928-6381, fee involved. Criminal PAT goes back to same as civil. PAT results show middle initial, DOB. Terminal results include SSN. Online access same as civil; results show middle initial.
General Information: No adoption, mental, juvenile, or sealed records released. Will fax documents $3.00 1st page, $1.00 ea add'l. Court makes copy: $.25 per page, self serve same. Certification fee: $5.00. Payee: Circuit Clerk. Personal checks and major credit cards accepted. Mail requests: SASE required for civil.

Campbell County

Circuit Court 330 York St, Rm 8, Newport, KY 41071; 859-292-6314; probate phone: 859-292-6305; fax: 859-431-0116; 8:30AM-4PM (EST). ***Felony, Civil Actions over $4,000.***
http://courts.ky.gov/Counties/Campbell/default.htm
Probate address is 600 Columbia St.
Civil Records: Access: Mail, in person, online. Visitors must perform in person searches themselves. Search fee: Fee based on number of copy pages. Required to search: name, years to search. Civil cases indexed by defendant, plaintiff, on computer since 1992, prior records on index cards since 1978. Civil PAT goes back to 1992. PAT results show name, DOB. Public terminal results may also show SSN. Free index search by name at http://apps.kycourts.net/CourtRecords/.
Criminal Records: Access: Mail, in person, online. Visitors must perform in person searches themselves. Search fee: Fee based on number of copy pages. Required to search: name, years to search; SSN helpful. Criminal records on computer since 1992, prior records on index cards since 1978. Criminal PAT goes back to same as civil.PAT results show name, DOB. Public terminal results may also show SSN. Online access same as civil; results show middle initial.
General Information: No adoption, mental, juvenile, or sealed records released. Will not fax out case files. Court makes copy: $.25 per page, self serve same. Certification fee: $5.00 per doc. Payee: Campbell Circuit Court. Personal checks accepted; credit cards are not.

District Court 600 Columbia St, Newport, KY 41071-1816; 859-292-6305; fax: 859-292-6593; 8AM-4PM (EST). ***Misdemeanor, Civil Actions under $4,000, Eviction, Small Claims, Probate.***
http://courts.ky.gov/Counties/Campbell/default.htm
Probate fax is same as main fax number.
Civil Records: Access: Mail, in person, online. Both court and visitors may perform in person searches. Search fee: $10.00 (probate searches only). Required to search: name, years to search. Civil cases indexed by defendant, plaintiff, on computer back to 1992, prior records on index cards to 1978. Civil PAT goes back to 1992. PAT civil results show middle initial. Search parties, court dates and case index free at http://apps.kycourts.net/CourtRecords/.
Criminal Records: Access: In person, online. Visitors must perform in person searches themselves. Required to search: name, years to search. Criminal records computerized from 1992, prior records on index cards to 1978. Criminal PAT goes back to same as civil. PAT criminal results show middle initial. Online access same as civil; results show middle initial.

General Information: No adoption, mental, juvenile, or sealed records released. Will not fax documents. Court makes copy: $.25 per page, self serve same. Certification fee: $5.00 per doc. Payee: Campbell Circuit Clerk. Business checks accepted. No credit cards accepted.. Mail requests: SASE required for civil.

Carlisle County

Circuit & District Court Box 337, Bardwell, KY 42023; 270-628-5425; fax: 270-628-5456; 8AM-4PM (CST). ***Felony, Misdemeanor, Civil, Eviction, Small Claims, Probate.***
Civil Records: Access: Phone, fax, mail, in person, online. Both court and visitors may perform in person searches. No search fee. Required to search: name, years to search. Civil cases indexed by defendant, plaintiff, on computer since 5/1993, records on docket books since 1978, prior records archived. Mail turnaround time 1-5 days. Civil PAT goes back to 1993. Free index search by name at http://apps.kycourts.net/CourtRecords/.
Criminal Records: Access: Phone, fax, mail, in person, online. Both court and visitors may perform in person searches. No search fee. Required to search: name, years to search. Criminal records on computer since 5/1993, records on docket books since 1978, prior records archived. Mail turnaround time 1-5 days. Criminal PAT goes back to same as civil. PAT results show middle initial, DOB. Terminal results include SSN. Online access same as civil; results show middle initial.
General Information: No adoption, mental, juvenile, or sealed records released. Will fax documents $2.00 per page. Court makes copy: $.25 per page, self serve same. Certification fee: $5.00. Payee: Circuit Clerk. Personal checks accepted; credit cards are not. Mail requests: SASE required.

Carroll County

Circuit & District Court 802 Clay St, Carrollton, KY 41008; 502-732-4305; fax: 502-732-8138; 8AM-4:30PM (EST). ***Felony, Misdemeanor, Civil, Eviction, Small Claims, Probate.***
Civil Records: Access: In person, online. Visitors must perform in person searches themselves. Required to search: name, years to search. Civil cases indexed by defendant, plaintiff, on computer since 1994, on docket books since 1988. Records before 1988 archived in Frankfurt. Civil PAT goes back to 1994. Free index search by name at http://apps.kycourts.net/CourtRecords/.
Criminal Records: Access: In person, online. Visitors must perform in person searches themselves. Required to search: name, years to search, DOB; SSN helpful. Criminal records on computer since 1994, on docket books since 1988. Records before 1988 archived in Frankfurt. Criminal PAT goes back to same as civil. Online access same as civil; results show middle initial.
General Information: No adoption, mental, juvenile, or sealed records released. Will not fax out case files. Court makes copy: $.25 per page. Certification fee: $5.00 per cert. Payee: Circuit Clerk. Personal checks accepted; credit cards are not. Mail requests: SASE required for mail return of any copies.

Carter County

Circuit Court 100 E Main St, Carter County Justice Center, Grayson, KY 41143; 606-474-5191; fax: 606-474-8826; 8:30AM-4PM; 9AM-N Sat (EST). ***Felony, Civil Actions over $4,000.***
Civil Records: Access: In person, online. Visitors must perform in person searches themselves. Required to search: name, years to search. Civil cases indexed by defendant, plaintiff, on computer since 1994, records archived since 1978, prior records are archived. Civil PAT goes back to 1994. Free index search at http://apps.kycourts.net/CourtRecords/.
Criminal Records: Access: In person, online. Visitors must perform in person searches themselves. Required to search: name, years to search, DOB, SSN. Criminal records on computer since 1994, records archived since 1978, prior records are archived. Criminal PAT goes back to 1994. Online access same as civil; results show middle initial.

General Information: No adoption, mental, juvenile, or sealed records released. Will not fax documents. Court makes copy: $.25 per page. Certification fee: $5.00 per doc. Payee: Carter County Circuit Clerk. Personal checks accepted; credit cards are not.

District Court Carter County Justice Center, 100 E Main, Grayson, KY 41143; 606-474-6572; fax: 606-474-8584; 8:30AM-4PM (EST). ***Misdemeanor, Civil Actions under $4,000, Eviction, Small Claims, Probate.***
Civil Records: Access: Mail, in person, online. Both court and visitors may perform in person searches. No search fee. Required to search: name, years to search. Civil cases indexed by defendant, plaintiff, on computer since 1994, prior records on index cards. Civil PAT goes back to 4/1994. Free index search by name at http://apps.kycourts.net/CourtRecords/.
Criminal Records: Access: In person, online. Visitors must perform in person searches themselves. Required to search: name, years to search, DOB; SSN helpful. Criminal records on computer since 1994, prior records on index cards. Criminal PAT goes back to same as civil. Results include last 4 digits of SSN, DOB year only. Online access same as civil; results show middle initial.
General Information: No adoption, mental, juvenile, or sealed records released. Will fax documents $3.00 1st page, $1.00 each add'l page. Court makes copy: $.25 per page. Certification fee: $5.00. Payee: District Clerk. Personal checks accepted; credit cards are not. Mail requests: SASE required for civil.

Casey County

Circuit & District Court PO Box 147, Liberty, KY 42539; 606-787-6510/606-787-6761; fax: 606-787-2497; 7AM-5PM (EST). ***Felony, Misdemeanor, Civil, Eviction, Small Claims, Probate.***
This court asks all pre-trial record requests go to the Administrative office of the Courts in Frankfort.
Civil Records: Access: In person, online. Visitors must perform in person searches themselves. Required to search: name, years to search. Civil cases indexed by defendant, plaintiff; index on cards since 1978, prior records archived, computerized from 1995. Civil PAT goes back to 1995. PAT civil results show middle initial. Free index search by name at http://apps.kycourts.net/CourtRecords/.
Criminal Records: Access: In person, online. Visitors must perform in person searches themselves. Required to search: name, years to search, DOB, SSN. Criminal records indexed on cards since 1978, prior records archived, computerized from 1995. Criminal PAT goes back to same as civil. PAT criminal results show middle initial. Online access same as civil; results show middle initial.
General Information: No adoption, mental, juvenile, or sealed records released. Will fax documents $1.00 per page fee. Court makes copy: $.25 per page, self serve same. Certification fee: $5.00. Payee: Circuit Clerk. Personal checks accepted; credit cards are not.

Christian County

Circuit & District Court Christian County Justice Ctr, 100 Justice Way, Hopkinsville, KY 42240; 270-889-6539; fax: 270-889-6564; 8AM-4:30PM (CST). ***Felony, Misdemeanor, Civil, Eviction, Small Claims, Probate.***
Fax number above is for District Court.
Civil Records: Access: In person, online. Visitors must perform in person searches themselves. Required to search: name, years to search. Civil cases indexed by defendant, plaintiff, on computer since 1991, prior records on index cards since 1978. Civil PAT goes back to 1991. Free index search by name at http://apps.kycourts.net/CourtRecords/.
Criminal Records: Access: In person, online. Visitors must perform in person searches themselves. Required to search: name, years to search; also helpful: DOB, SSN. Criminal records on computer since 1991, prior records on index cards since 1978. Searchers must fill out request form, state reason why copies are needed, and provide copy of ID or drivers license. Direct written criminal records checks to Pretrial Services Records Division, 502-573-1682 or 800-928-6381.

Criminal PAT goes back to same as civil. Online access same as civil; results show middle initial.
General Information: No adoption, mental, juvenile, or sealed records released. Will not fax documents. Court makes copy: $.25 per page. Certification fee: $5.00 per doc. Payee: Circuit Clerk. No personal checks accepted. Visa/MC accepted.

Clark County

Circuit Court Box 687, Winchester, KY 40392; 859-737-7264; fax: 859-737-7005; 8AM-4PM (EST). ***Felony, Civil Actions over $4,000.***
Civil Records: Access: In person, online. Visitors must perform in person searches themselves. Required to search: name, years to search; also helpful: address. Civil cases indexed by defendant, plaintiff, on computer since 1989, on index cards since 1950, prior records archived since the 1700s. Civil PAT goes back to 1989. Free index search by name at http://apps.kycourts.net/CourtRecords/.
Criminal Records: Access: In person, online. Visitors must perform in person searches themselves. Required to search: name, years to search; also helpful: address, DOB, SSN. Criminal records on computer since 1989, on index cards since 1950, prior records archived since the 1700s. Criminal PAT goes back to same as civil. Online access same as civil; results show middle initial.
General Information: No adoption, mental, juvenile, or sealed records released. Will not fax documents. Court makes copy: $.25 per page. Certification fee: $5.00 per doc. Payee: Circuit Clerk. Personal checks accepted; credit cards are not.

District Court PO Box 687, 17 Cleveland Ave, Courthouse Annex, Winchester, KY 40392-0687; 859-737-7264; fax: 859-737-7005; 8AM-4PM (EST). ***Misdemeanor, Civil under $4,000, Eviction, Small Claims, Probate.*** Probate fax same as main fax.
Civil Records: Access: In person, online. Both court and visitors may perform in person searches. No search fee. Required to search: name, years to search. Civil cases indexed by defendant, plaintiff, on computer since 1989, on docket books since 1978, prior records on archived. Civil PAT goes back to 1989. Free index search by name at http://apps.kycourts.net/CourtRecords/.
Criminal Records: Access: In person, online. Both court and visitors may perform in person searches. No search fee. Required to search: name, years to search; also helpful: DOB, SSN. Criminal records on computer since 1989, on docket books since 1978, prior records on archived. Criminal PAT goes back to same as civil. Online access same as civil; results show middle initial.
General Information: No adoption, mental, juvenile, or sealed records released. Will not fax documents. Court makes copy: $.25 per page, self serve same. Certification fee: $5.00. Payee: District Clerk. Personal checks accepted; credit cards are not.

Clay County

Circuit & District Court 316 Main St #108, Manchester, KY 40962; 606-598-3663; fax: 606-598-4047; 7:30AM-4:30PM (EST). ***Felony, Civil, Misdemeanor, Eviction, Small Claims, Probate.***
Civil Records: Access: In person, online. Visitors must perform in person searches themselves. Required to search: name, years to search. Civil cases indexed by defendant, plaintiff, on computer back to 1992, on index cards since 1978, records through 1991 in archives. Civil PAT goes back to 1992. Free index search by name at http://apps.kycourts.net/CourtRecords/.
Criminal Records: Access: In person, online. Visitors must perform in person searches themselves. Required to search: name, years to search, DOB; SSN helpful. Criminal records computerized from 1992, on index cards since 1978, records through 1991 in archives. Criminal PAT goes back to same as civil. Online access same as civil; results show middle initial.
General Information: No adoption, mental, juvenile, or sealed records released. Will not fax documents. Court makes copy: $.25 per page, self serve same. Certification fee: $5.00 per doc. Payee: Circuit Clerk. Personal checks accepted. Visa/MC accepted.

Clinton County

Circuit & District Court Courthouse 2nd Fl, 100 S Cross St, Albany, KY 42602; 606-387-6424; fax: 606-387-8154; 8AM-4:30PM M-F; 8AM-N Sat (CST). ***Felony, Misdemeanor, Civil, Eviction, Small Claims, Probate.***
www.courts.ky.gov/Counties/Clinton/default.htm
Civil Records: Access: Phone, mail, in person, online. Both court and visitors may perform in person searches. No search fee. Required to search: name, years to search. Civil cases indexed by defendant, plaintiff, on computer since 8/92, on docket books since 1978, prior records archived to 1865. Mail turnaround time 5 days. Civil PAT goes back to 8/1992. Free index search by name at http://apps.kycourts.net/CourtRecords/.
Criminal Records: Access: In person, online. Visitors must perform in person searches themselves. Required to search: name, years to search, SSN; also helpful: DOB. Criminal records on computer since 8/92, on docket books since 1978, prior records archive to 1865. This court refers criminal requests to state Pre-Trial Services. Criminal PAT goes back to same as civil. Online access same as civil; results show middle initial.
General Information: No adoption, mental, juvenile, or sealed records released. Will not fax documents. Court makes copy: $.25 per page. Cert fee: $5.00 per doc. Payee: Circuit Clerk. Personal checks accepted; credit cards are not. Mail requests: SASE required.

Crittenden County

Circuit & District Court 107 S Main, Marion, KY 42064; 270-965-4200 (and) 270-965-4046; fax: 270-965-4572; 8AM-4:30PM (CST). ***Felony, Misdemeanor, Civil, Eviction, Small Claims, Probate, Traffic.***
Civil Records: Access: In person, online. Visitors must perform in person searches themselves. Required to search: name, years to search. Civil cases indexed by defendant, plaintiff; index on cards since 1978; on computer back to 9/94. Civil PAT back to 9/1994. PAT results show name only. Free index search at http://apps.kycourts.net/CourtRecords/
Criminal Records: Access: In person, online. Visitors must perform in person searches themselves. Required to search: name, years to search. Circuit criminal records on index cards since 1978; on computer back to 9/94; District Criminal 9/94 to present. Criminal PAT goes back to same as civil. Online access same as civil; results show middle initial.
General Information: No adoption, mental, juvenile, or sealed records released. Fee to fax out file $2.00 1st page; $1.00 each add'l. Court makes copy: $.25 per page. Certification fee: $5.00. Payee: Circuit Clerk. No personal checks or credit cards accepted.

Cumberland County

Circuit & District Court PO Box 395, Burkesville, KY 42717-0395; 270-864-2611; fax: 270-864-1227; 8AM-4PM (CST). ***Felony, Misdemeanor, Civil, Eviction, Small Claims, Probate.***
Civil Records: Access: In person, online. Visitors must perform in person searches themselves. Required to search: name, years to search. Civil cases indexed by defendant, plaintiff, on computer back to 6/93, on docket cards from 1978, prior records archived. Civil PAT goes back to 6/1993. PAT results show name only. Free index search by name at http://apps.kycourts.net/CourtRecords/.
Criminal Records: Access: In person, online. Visitors must perform in person searches themselves. Required to search: name, years to search, DOB; SSN helpful. Criminal records computerized from 6/93, on docket cards from 1978, prior records archived. Criminal PAT goes back to same as civil. PAT results show name only. Online access same as civil; results show middle initial.
General Information: No adoption, mental, juvenile, or sealed records released. Fee to fax out file $2.00 plus $1.00 per page. Court makes copy: $.25 per page. Self serve: $.25 per page. Certification fee: $5.00 per doc. Payee: Circuit Clerk. Personal checks accepted; credit cards are not.

Daviess County

Circuit & District Court PO Box 277, 100 E Second St, Owensboro, KY 42302; 270-687-7330-Circuit Crim; criminal phone: 270-687-7329-Circuit Crim; 270-687-7200-District Crim; civil phone: 270-687-7220-Circuit Civil; 270-687-7205-District Civil; probate phone: 270-687-7207; 8AM-4PM (CST). ***Felony, Misdemeanor, Civil, Eviction, Small Claims, Probate.***
These courts function as a combined court, that is, a criminal search includes Circuit and District courts, ditto for Civil.
Civil Records: Access: In person, online. Visitors must perform in person searches themselves. Required to search: name, years to search. Civil cases indexed by defendant, plaintiff, on computer since 4/91, on index cards since 1978, prior records on docket books since 1809. Civil PAT goes back to 4/1991. PAT civil results show middle initial. Public terminals located on 2nd Fl and there is a person to assist you. Free index search by name at http://apps.kycourts.net/CourtRecords/.
Criminal Records: Access: In person, online. Visitors must perform in person searches themselves. Required to search: name, years to search, DOB, SSN. Criminal records on computer since 4/91, on index cards since 1978, prior records on docket books since 1809. Criminal PAT goes back to 4/1991. PAT criminal results show middle initial. Public terminals located on 2nd Fl and there is a person to assist you. Online access same as civil; results show middle initial.
General Information: No adoption, mental, juvenile, or sealed records released. Will not fax documents. Court makes copy: $.25 per page. Certification fee: $5.00 per cert. Payee: Circuit Clerk. Local business checks accepted; no personal checks. No credit cards accepted.

Edmonson County

Circuit & District Court Box 739, 110 Cross Main St., Brownsville, KY 42210; 270-597-2584; probate phone: 270-597-3918; fax: 270-597-2884; 8AM-4:30PM M-W,F; 8AM-N TH,S (CST). ***Felony, Misdemeanor, Civil, Eviction, Small Claims, Probate.***
Civil Records: Access: In person, online. Visitors must perform in person searches themselves. Required to search: name, years to search, address. Civil cases indexed by defendant, plaintiff, computerized since 1995, on index cards and docket books from 1800s. Civil PAT goes back to 1995. PAT results show middle initial, DOB, SSN. SSN also appears on terminal search results. Free index search at http://apps.kycourts.net/CourtRecords/.
Criminal Records: Access: In person, online. Visitors must perform in person searches themselves. Required to search: name, years to search, DOB, SSN. Criminal records computerized since 1995, on index cards and docket books from 1800s. Criminal PAT goes back to same as civil. PAT results show middle initial, DOB, SSN. Terminal results include SSN. Online access same as civil; results show middle initial.
General Information: No adoption, mental, juvenile, or sealed records released. Will not fax documents. Court makes copy: $.25 per page, self serve same. Certification fee: $5.00. Payee: Circuit Clerk. Personal checks accepted; credit cards are not.

Elliott County

Circuit & District Court PO Box 788, Corner of Main and Jane Caudill St, Sandy Hook, KY 41171; 606-738-5238; fax: 606-738-6962; 8AM-4PM M-F; 9AM-N Sat (EST). ***Felony, Misdemeanor, Civil, Eviction, Small Claims, Probate.***
Civil Records: Access: In person, online. Both court and visitors may perform in person searches. No search fee. Required to search: name, years to search. Civil cases indexed by defendant, plaintiff, on computer since 10/1992, prior records on index cards since 1978. Civil PAT goes back to 10/1992. PAT results show middle initial, DOB. Terminal results also show SSNs. Free index search by name at http://apps.kycourts.net/CourtRecords/.

Criminal Records: Access: In person, online. Both court and visitors may perform in person searches. No search fee. Required to search: name, years to search; SSN helpful. Criminal records on computer since 10/1992, prior records on index cards since 1978. Mail requests for criminal searches may be made to state Pre-Trial Svcs, 502-573-1682. Criminal PAT goes back to same as civil. PAT results show middle initial, DOB. Online access same as civil; results show middle initial.

General Information: No adoption, mental, juvenile, or sealed records released. Will fax specific case file $2.00 1st page; $1.00 each add'l. Court makes copy: $.25 per page, self serve same. Certification fee: $5.00 per doc. Payee: Circuit Clerk. Personal checks accepted; credit cards are not.

Estill County

Circuit & District Court 130 Main St, Rm 207, Irvine, KY 40336; 606-723-3970; fax: 606-723-1158; 8AM-4PM M-TH; 8AM-6:30PM F (EST). ***Felony, Misdemeanor, Civil, Eviction, Small Claims, Probate.***
Probate index is separate at this same address.

Civil Records: Access: Phone, fax, mail, in person, online. Both court and visitors may perform in person searches. No search fee. Required to search: name, years to search. Civil cases indexed by defendant, plaintiff; index on cards and computer back to 1994; older at archives. Mail turnaround time 2-4 days. Civil PAT goes back to 1994. Free index search by name at http://apps.kycourts.net/CourtRecords/.

Criminal Records: Access: In person, online. Both court and visitors may perform in person searches. No search fee. Required to search: name, years to search, DOB. Criminal records go back to 1994. Court generally directs search requesters to the state AOC Pretrial Services. Criminal PAT goes back to same as civil. Online access same as civil; results show middle initial.

General Information: No adoption, mental, juvenile, or sealed records released. Fee to fax out file $1.00 per page. Court makes copy: $.25 per page, self serve same. Certification fee: $5.00 per doc includes copy fee. Payee: Circuit Clerk. Personal checks accepted; credit cards are not. Mail requests: SASE required.

Fayette County

Circuit Court - Criminal & Civil Divisions 120 N Limestone, Lexington, KY 40507; criminal phone: 859-246-2224; civil phone: 859-246-2141; fax: 859-246-2530; 8:30AM-4:30PM (EST). ***Felony, Civil Actions over $4,000.***
http://courts.ky.gov/Counties/Fayette/default.htm
Fax for appeals- 859-246-2146.

Civil Records: Access: In person, online. Both court and visitors may perform in person searches. Search fee: $5.00 per name. Required to search: name, years to search. Civil cases indexed by defendant, plaintiff, on computer since 4/1993, on index cards since 1978, prior records on books and archived. Civil PAT goes back to 1988. Free index search at http://apps.kycourts.net/CourtRecords/.

Criminal Records: Access: In person, online. Both court and visitors may perform in person searches. Search fee: $5.00 per name. Required to search: name, years to search; also helpful: DOB, SSN. Criminal records on computer since 4/1993, on index cards since 1978, prior records on books and archived. Criminal PAT goes back to 1993.PAT results show name, DOB. Terminal results include SSN. Online access same as civil; results show middle initial.

General Information: No adoption, juvenile, mental, or sealed records released. Court makes copy: $.25 per page. Certification fee: $5.00 per doc. Payee: Fayette County Circuit Clerk. No Personal checks and major credit cards accepted.

District Court Criminal & Civil 150 N Limestone, Lexington, KY 40507; 859-246-2141; criminal phone: 859-246-2228; civil: 859-246-2240; probate: 859-246-2242; fax: 859-246-2146; 8AM-4PM (EST). ***Misdemeanor, Civil Actions under $4,000, Eviction, Small Claims, Probate.***
http://courts.ky.gov/Counties/Fayette/default.htm
Probate and civil is in Rm D101; criminal and traffic in D157.

Civil Records: Access: Mail, in person, online. Both court and visitors may perform in person searches. Search fee: $5.00 per name. Required to search: name, years to search. Civil cases indexed by defendant, plaintiff, on computer since 1992, prior records on index cards since 1977. Mail turnaround time 1 week Civil PAT goes back to 1992. PAT civil results show middle initial. Free index search by name at http://apps.kycourts.net/CourtRecords/.

Criminal Records: Access: In person, online. Visitors must perform in person searches themselves. Required to search: name, years to search, DOB; SSN helpful. Criminal records on computer since 1977. Criminal PAT goes back to same as civil. PAT results show middle initial, DOB. Online access same as civil; results show middle initial.

General Information: No adoption, mental, juvenile, or sealed records released. Will not fax documents. Court makes copy: $.25 per page. Certification fee: $5.00 per cert, $.75 for an attested copy. Payee: District Clerk. Personal checks accepted; credit cards are not. Mail requests: SASE required for civil.

Fleming County

Circuit & District Court Courthouse 100 Court Square, Flemingsburg, KY 41041; 606-845-7011; fax: 606-849-2400; 8AM-4:30PM (EST). ***Felony, Misdemeanor, Civil, Eviction, Small Claims, Probate, Traffic.***

Civil Records: Access: Phone, mail, in person, online. Both court and visitors may perform in person searches. No search fee. Required to search: name, years to search. Civil cases indexed by defendant, plaintiff, on computer since 5/1994, prior records on index cards back to 1992. Mail turnaround time 1-3 days. Civil PAT goes back to 4/1994. Free index search by name at http://apps.kycourts.net/CourtRecords/.

Criminal Records: Access: In person, online. Both court and visitors may perform in person searches. No search fee. Required to search: name, years to search, DOB; SSN helpful. Criminal records on computer since 5/1994, prior records on index cards since 1978. Criminal PAT goes back to same as civil. Online access same as civil; results show middle initial.

General Information: No adoption, mental, juvenile, or sealed records released. Fee to fax out file $1.00 per page. Court makes copy: $.25 per page, self serve same. Certification fee: $5.00. Payee: Circuit Clerk. Personal checks accepted; credit cards are not. Mail requests: SASE required.

Floyd County

Circuit Court 127 S Lake Dr, Prestonsburg, KY 41653-3368; 606-889-1658; civil phone: 606-889-1650; fax: 606-889-1666; 8AM-4PM (EST). ***Felony, Civil Actions over $4,000.***

Civil Records: Access: Mail, in person, online. Both court and visitors may perform in person searches. No search fee. Required to search: name, years to search. Civil cases indexed by defendant, plaintiff, on computer since 9/1991, prior records on index cards since 1978. Mail turnaround time 2-4 days. Civil PAT goes back to 1991. PAT civil results show middle initial. Free index search by name at http://apps.kycourts.net/CourtRecords/.

Criminal Records: Access: Mail, in person, online. Both court and visitors may perform in person searches. No search fee. Required to search: name, years to search, DOB, SSN. Criminal records on computer since 9/1991, prior records on index cards since 1978. Mail turnaround time 2-4 days. Criminal PAT goes back to same as civil. PAT results show middle initial, DOB. Terminal results include SSN. Online access same as civil; results show middle initial.

General Information: No adoption, mental, juvenile, or sealed records released. Will fax documents $2.00 1st page; $1.00 ea add'l page. Court makes copy: $.25 per page. Self serve: no charge if paper provided. Certification fee: $5.00. Payee: Clerk of Circuit Court. Personal checks accepted; credit cards are not. Mail requests: SASE required.

District Court 127 S Lake Dr, Prestonsburg, KY 41653; 606-889-1658; criminal: 606-889-1672; probate: 606-889-1650; fax: 606-889-1652; 8AM-4PM (EST). ***Misdemeanor, Small Claims, Probate.***
Small claims- 606-889-1650.

Civil Records: Access: Mail, in person, online. No search fee. Required to search: name, years to search. Civil records on computer since 1991, prior records on index cards since 1978. Records are only kept for five years in this office. Free index search by name at http://apps.kycourts.net/CourtRecords/.

Criminal Records: Access: Mail, in person, online. Only the court performs in person searches; visitors may not. No search fee. Required to search: name, years to search; also helpful: SSN. Criminal records on computer since 1991, prior records in index cards since 1989. Records are only kept for five years in this office. Mail turnaround time 2-4 days. Public use terminal has crim records back to 1991.PAT results show name, DOB. Search parties and case number index only free at http://apps.kycourts.net/CourtRecords/. Online results show middle initial.

General Information: No adoption, mental, juvenile, or sealed records released. Will not fax documents. Court makes copy: $.25 per page. Certification fee: $5.00. Payee: Floyd District Court. Personal checks accepted; credit cards are not. Mail requests: SASE required.

Franklin County

Circuit Court Box 678, 214 St Clair St, Frankfort, KY 40602; 502-564-8380; criminal phone: 502-573-2350/Adm; fax: 502-564-8188; 7:30AM-5PM (EST). ***Felony, Civil Actions over $4,000.***
http://courts.ky.gov/Counties/Franklin/default.htm
Criminal records located at; AOC, 100 Mill Creek Park, Frankfort KY 40601- walk-in 7AM-3PM or drive thru 7AM -10PM

Civil Records: Access: In person, online. Visitors must perform in person searches themselves. Required to search: name, years to search. Civil cases indexed by defendant, plaintiff, on computer since 1990, prior records on index cards since 1978. Civil PAT goes back to 1990. Free index search by name at http://apps.kycourts.net/CourtRecords/.

Criminal Records: Access: In person, online. Visitors must perform in person searches themselves. Required to search: name, years to search, DOB, SSN. Criminal records on computer since 1990, prior records on index cards since 1978. All requests are referred to the state Administrative Office of Courts, which is located here in Frankfort. Criminal PAT goes back to 1990. Online access same as civil; results show middle initial.

General Information: No adoption, mental, juvenile, or sealed records released. Will fax documents $2.00 1st page, $1.00 each add'l, limit 10 pages. Court makes copy: $.25 per page, self serve same. Certification fee: $5.00 per doc. Payee: Circuit Clerk. Personal checks accepted; credit cards are not.

District Court Box 678, Frankfort, KY 40602; 502-564-7013; fax: 502-564-8188; 8AM-4:30PM (EST). ***Misdemeanor, Civil Actions under $4,000, Eviction, Small Claims, Probate.***
http://courts.ky.gov/counties/franklin

Civil Records: Access: In person, online. Visitors must perform in person searches themselves. Required to search: name, years to search. Civil cases indexed by defendant, plaintiff, on computer since 1990, records on index cards since 1978, prior records archived. Civil PAT goes back to 1990. PAT civil results show middle initial. Free index search by name at http://apps.kycourts.net/CourtRecords/.

Criminal Records: Access: In person, online. Visitors must perform in person searches themselves. Required to search: name, years to search, DOB. Criminal records on computer since 1990, records on index cards since 1978, prior records archived. Criminal PAT goes back to same as civil. PAT results show middle initial, DOB. Terminal results also include race, gender, physicals, eyes. Online access same as civil; results show middle initial.

General Information: No adoption, mental, juvenile, or sealed records released. Will fax documents $2.00

1st page, $1.00 each add'l page, limit 10 pages. Court makes copy: $.25 per page, self serve same. Certification fee: $5.00 per doc. Payee: Franklin Circuit Clerk. Personal checks accepted; credit cards are not.

Fulton County

Circuit & District Court Box 198, Hickman, KY 42050; 270-236-3944; fax: 270-236-3729; 8AM-4PM (CST). ***Felony, Misdemeanor, Civil, Eviction, Small Claims, Probate.***

Six days of the court docket information can be found at www.kycourts.com.

Civil Records: Access: Mail, in person, online. Both court and visitors may perform in person searches. No search fee. Required to search: name, years to search. Civil cases indexed by defendant, plaintiff, on index from 1980, computerized from 1995, and archived since 1843. Civil PAT goes back to 1978. Free index search by name at http://apps.kycourts.net/CourtRecords/.

Criminal Records: Access: In person, online. Visitors must perform in person searches themselves. Required to search: name, years to search. Criminal records indexed from 1980, computerized from 1995, and archived since 1843. Criminal PAT goes back to same as civil. Online access same as civil; results show middle initial.

General Information: No adoption, mental, juvenile, or sealed records released. Will not fax documents. Court makes copy: $.25 per page, self serve same. Certification fee: $5.00. Payee: Circuit Clerk. Personal checks accepted; credit cards are not. Mail requests: SASE required for civil.

Gallatin County

Circuit Court PO Box 256, 100 Main St, Warsaw, KY 41095; 859-567-5241; criminal fax: 859-567-7420; civil fax: same; 8AM-4:30PM M,T,TH,F; closed W (EST). ***Felony, Civil Actions over $4,000.***

Civil Records: Access: Mail, in person, online. Both court and visitors may perform in person searches. No search fee. Required to search: name, years to search. Civil cases indexed by defendant, plaintiff, go back to 1990. Computerized records go to 1993. Mail turnaround time 4 days. Civil PAT goes back to 1995. Free index search by name at http://apps.kycourts.net/CourtRecords/.

Criminal Records: Access: Mail, in person, online. Both court and visitors may perform in person searches. No search fee. Required to search: name, years to search; also helpful: SSN. Criminal records go back to 1990. Computerized records to 1993. Mail turnaround time 4 days. Criminal PAT goes back to same as civil. Online access same as civil; results show middle initial.

General Information: No adoption, mental, juvenile, or sealed records released. Will fax documents $2.00 per page, $3.00 per document. Court makes copy: $.25 per page, self serve same. Certification fee: $5.00 per cert. Payee: Circuit Clerk. Personal checks accepted. Mail requests: SASE required.

District Court Box 256, Warsaw, KY 41095; 859-567-2388; probate phone: 859-567-2388; fax: 859-567-1492; 8AM-4:30PM T-F; 8AM-6PM M (EST). ***Misdemeanor, Civil Actions under $4,000, Eviction, Small Claims, Probate.***

Probate fax- 859-567-1492

Civil Records: Access: Fax, mail, in person, online. Both court and visitors may perform in person searches. No search fee. Required to search: name, years to search. Civil cases indexed by defendant, plaintiff, on computer since 10/1994, prior records on index cards since 1978. Mail turnaround time 1-2 days. Civil PAT goes back to 10/1994. Free index search at http://apps.kycourts.net/CourtRecords/.

Criminal Records: Access: Fax, mail, in person, online. Both court and visitors may perform in person searches. No search fee. Required to search: name, years to search, DOB; also helpful: SSN. Criminal records on computer since 10/1994, prior records on index cards since 1978. Mail turnaround time 1-2 days. Criminal PAT goes back to same as civil. Online access same as civil; results show middle initial.

General Information: No adoption, mental, juvenile, or sealed records released. Fee to fax out file $2.00 per page plus $3.00 per document. Court makes copy: $.25 per page, self serve same. Certification fee: $5.00 per doc. Payee: District Clerk. Personal checks accepted; credit cards are not.

Garrard County

Circuit & District Court 7 Public Square, Courthouse Annex, Lancaster, KY 40444; 859-792-6032; fax: 859-792-6414; 8AM-4PM M,T,TH,F, 8AM-N W,Sat (EST). ***Felony, Misdemeanor, Civil, Eviction, Small Claims, Probate.***

Circuit Clerk can be reached at 859-792-2961.

Civil Records: Access: In person, online. Visitors must perform in person searches themselves. Required to search: name, years to search. Civil cases indexed by defendant, plaintiff, in index since 1978. Civil PAT available. PAT results show name, DOB. Free index search by name at http://apps.kycourts.net/CourtRecords/.

Criminal Records: Access: In person, online. Visitors must perform in person searches themselves. Required to search: name, years to search; also helpful: address, DOB, SSN. Criminal records in index since 1978. Criminal PAT available. Online access same as civil; results show middle initial.

General Information: No adoption, mental, juvenile, or sealed records released. Court makes copy: $.25 per page. Self serve: $.25 per page. Certification fee: $5.00 per doc. Payee: Circuit Clerk. Personal checks accepted; credit cards are not.

Grant County

Circuit & District Court Courthouse 101 N Main, Williamstown, KY 41097; 859-824-4467 (Circuit) 859-823-5251 (District); fax: 859-824-0183; 8AM-5PM M; 8AM-4PM T-F; 8:30AM-12 Sat (EST). ***Felony, Misdemeanor, Civil, Eviction, Small Claims, Probate.***

Current (1 week) of dockets available at http://courts.ky.gov/. District Court records destroyed before 2000.

Civil Records: Access: In person, online. Visitors must perform in person searches themselves. Required to search: name, years to search. Civil cases indexed by defendant, plaintiff, on computer back to 1992, prior records on index cards since 1977. Civil PAT goes back to 7/1992. Free index search by name at http://apps.kycourts.net/CourtRecords/.

Criminal Records: Access: In person, online. Visitors must perform in person searches themselves. Required to search: name, years to search, DOB; SSN helpful. Criminal records computerized from 1992, prior records on index cards since 1977. Criminal PAT goes back to same as civil. Online access same as civil; results show middle initial.

General Information: No adoption, mental, juvenile, or sealed records released. Will fax specific docket for $2.00 for 1st page; $1.00 each add'l page. Court makes copy: $.25 per page, self serve same. Certification fee: $5.00. Payee: Circuit Clerk. Personal checks accepted; credit cards are not.

Graves County

Circuit & District Court Courthouse 100 E Broadway, Mayfield, KY 42066; 270-247-1733; fax: 270-247-7358; 8AM-4:30PM (CST). ***Felony, Misdemeanor, Civil, Eviction, Small Claims, Probate.***

Civil Records: Access: In person, online. Visitors must perform in person searches themselves. Required to search: name, years to search. Civil cases indexed by defendant, plaintiff, on computer since 6/1994, prior records on index cards since 1978. Civil PAT goes back to 6/1994. PAT results show name, DOB. Free index search by name at http://apps.kycourts.net/CourtRecords/.

Criminal Records: Access: In person, online. Visitors must perform in person searches themselves. Required to search: name, years to search, DOB; SSN helpful. Criminal records on computer since 6/1994, prior records on index cards since 1978. Criminal PAT goes back to same as civil.PAT results show name, DOB. Online access same as civil; results show middle initial.

General Information: No adoption, mental, juvenile, or sealed records released. Will fax specific case file $3.00 plus $1.00 per page if specific case docket requested. Court makes copy: $.25 per page. Certification fee: $5.00 per doc. Payee: Circuit Clerk. Personal checks and major credit cards accepted.

Grayson County

Circuit & District Court Clerk's Office, 125 E White Oak, Leitchfield, KY 42754; 270-259-3040; fax: 270-259-9866; 8AM-4:30PM T,W,F; 8AM-5:30PM M,TH (CST). ***Felony, Misdemeanor, Civil, Eviction, Small Claims, Probate.***

Civil Records: Access: Mail, in person, online. Both court and visitors may perform in person searches. Search fee: $10.00 per name. Required to search: name, years to search. Civil cases indexed by defendant, plaintiff, on computer since 5/94, prior records on index cards since 1978. Mail turnaround time 5 days. Civil PAT goes back to 5/1994. PAT civil results show middle initial. Free index search by name at http://apps.kycourts.net/CourtRecords/.

Criminal Records: Access: Mail, in person, online. Both court and visitors may perform in person searches. Search fee: $10.00. Required to search: name, years to search; also helpful: DOB, SSN. Criminal records on computer since 5/94, prior records on index cards since 1978. Mail turnaround time 2 days. Criminal PAT goes back to same as civil. PAT criminal results show middle initial. Online access same as civil; results show middle initial.

General Information: No adoption, mental, juvenile, or sealed records released. Will fax documents $1.00 per page. Court makes copy: $.25 per page, self serve same. Certification fee: $5.00. Payee: Circuit Clerk. Personal checks accepted. Mail requests: SASE required.

Green County

Circuit & District Court 203 W Court St, Greensburg, KY 42743; 270-932-5631; fax: 270-932-6468; 8AM-4PM M-W & F; 8AM-N Sat; Closed on TH (EST). ***Felony, Misdemeanor, Civil, Eviction, Small Claims, Probate.***

Civil Records: Access: Fax, mail, in person, online. Both court and visitors may perform in person searches. No search fee. Required to search: name, years to search; also helpful: address. Civil cases indexed by defendant, plaintiff; index on cards and computer since 1978. Mail turnaround time 1-2 days. Civil PAT goes back to 1996. PAT results show name, DOB. Free index search by name at http://apps.kycourts.net/CourtRecords/.

Criminal Records: Access: Fax, mail, in person, online. Both court and visitors may perform in person searches. No search fee. Required to search: name, years to search; also helpful: address, DOB, SSN. Criminal records indexed on cards and computer since 1978. Mail turnaround time 1-2 days. Criminal PAT available. Online access same as civil; results show middle initial.

General Information: No adoption, mental, juvenile, or sealed records released. Will fax documents to local or toll-free number. Court makes copy: $.25 per page. Certification fee: $5.00 per doc. Payee: Circuit Clerk. Personal checks accepted; credit cards are not. Mail requests: SASE required.

Greenup County

Circuit & District Court Courthouse Annex, 101 Harrison St, Greenup, KY 41144; 606-473-9869; probate phone: same; fax: 606-473-7388; 9AM-4:30PM (EST). ***Felony, Misdemeanor, Civil, Eviction, Small Claims, Probate.***

http://courts.ky.gov/counties/Greenup/

Civil Records: Access: In person, online. Both court and visitors may perform in person searches. No search fee. Required to search: name, years to search. Civil cases indexed by defendant, plaintiff, on computer since 1990, prior records on index cards since 1978. Civil PAT goes back to 1990. PAT results show name, DOB. Results include first and last names, SSN. Free index search by name at http://apps.kycourts.net/CourtRecords/.

Criminal Records: Access: In person, online. Visitors must perform in person searches themselves. Required to search: name, years to search, DOB; SSN helpful. Criminal records on computer since 1990, prior records on index cards since 1978. Criminal PAT goes back to same as civil. Results include first and last names. Online access same as civil; results show middle initial.
General Information: No adoption, mental, juvenile, or sealed records released. Will fax documents $3.00 per fax. Court makes copy: $.35 per page, self serve same. Certification fee: $5.00. Payee: Circuit Clerk. Personal checks, money orders, cash and cashier checks accepted. All major credit cards accepted.

Hancock County

Circuit & District Court Courthouse, PO Box 250, Hawesville, KY 42348; 270-927-8144; fax: 270-927-8629; 8AM-4PM M,T,W,F; 8AM-5:30PM TH (CST). ***Felony, Misdemeanor, Civil, Eviction, Small Claims, Probate.***
Civil Records: Access: Mail, in person, online. Both court and visitors may perform in person searches. No search fee. Required to search: name, years to search. Civil cases indexed by defendant, plaintiff, on computer since 8/1994, prior records on index cards. Civil PAT goes back to 8/1994. PAT civil results show middle initial. Free index search by name at http://apps.kycourts.net/CourtRecords/.
Criminal Records: Access: Mail, in person, online. Both court and visitors may perform in person searches. No search fee. Required to search: name, years to search, DOB; SSN helpful. Criminal records on computer since 8/1994, prior records on index cards. Court recommends that you do searches through the state AOC in Frankfort. Criminal PAT goes back to 8/1994. PAT criminal results show middle initial. Online access same as civil; results show middle initial.
General Information: No adoption, mental, juvenile, or sealed records released. Fee to fax specific case file $2.00 for 1st page; $1.00 each add'l. Court makes copy: $.25 per page. Certification fee: $5.00 per doc. Payee: Circuit Clerk. Personal checks accepted; credit cards are not.

Hardin County

Circuit & District Court Hardin County Justice Ctr, 120 E Dixie Ave, Elizabethtown, KY 42701; 270-766-5000; fax: 270-766-5243; 8AM-4:30PM (EST). ***Felony, Misdemeanor, Civil, Eviction, Small Claims, Probate.***
Civil Records: Access: In person, online. Visitors must perform in person searches themselves. Required to search: name, years to search. Civil cases indexed by defendant, plaintiff, on computer since 3/28/94, prior records on index cards since 1978. Civil cases do not always have DOB or SSN. Civil PAT goes back to 1994. Free index search by name at http://apps.kycourts.net/CourtRecords/.
Criminal Records: Access: In person, online. Visitors must perform in person searches themselves. Required to search: name, years to search, DOB. Criminal records on computer since 3/28/94, prior records on index cards since 1978. Criminal PAT goes back to same as civil. Online access same as civil; results show middle initial.
General Information: No adoption, mental, juvenile, motor vehicle or sealed records released. Will fax specific document for $2.00 1st page, $1.00 each add'l page, payable in advance by money order only. Court makes copy: $.25 per page. Certification fee: $5.00 per doc. Payee: Circuit Clerk. Money orders only accepted. No credit cards accepted.

Radcliff District Court 220 Freedom Way, Radcliff, KY 40160; 270-351-1299/4799; fax: 270-351-1301; 8AM-N, 12:30-4PM (EST). ***Probate, Eviction, Civil under $4000.00, Small Claim.***

Harlan County

Circuit & District Court Box 190, Harlan, KY 40831; 606-573-2680; fax: 606-573-5895; 8AM-4:30PM (EST). ***Felony, Misdemeanor, Civil, Eviction, Small Claims, Probate.***
Civil Records: Access: In person, online. Visitors must perform in person searches themselves. Required to search: name, years to search. Civil cases indexed by defendant, plaintiff, on computer since 8/1991, on index cards since 1978, records prior to 1991 are archived in Frankfort. Civil PAT goes back to 7/1991. PAT results show name and sometimes the birth year shows. Free index search at http://apps.kycourts.net/CourtRecords/.
Criminal Records: Access: In person, online. Visitors must perform in person searches themselves. Required to search: name, years to search, DOB; SSN helpful. Criminal records on computer since 8/1991, on index cards since 1978, records prior to 1991 archived in Frankfort. Criminal PAT goes back to same as civil. PAT results show name only. Online access same as civil; results show middle initial.
General Information: No adoption, mental, juvenile, sealed or domestic violence records released. Will fax specific case file $2.00 1st page, $1.00 each add'l. Court makes copy: $.25 per page. Certification fee: $5.00 per doc. Payee: Circuit Clerk. Local personal checks accepted only. No credit cards accepted.

Harrison County

Circuit & District Court 115 Court St #1, Cynthiana, KY 41031; 859-234-1914; fax: 859-234-6787; 8:30AM-4:30PM, 9AM-N Sat (EST). ***Felony, Misdemeanor, Civil, Eviction, Small Claims, Probate.***
Civil Records: Access: Mail, in person, online. Both court and visitors may perform in person searches. No search fee. Required to search: name, years to search. Civil cases indexed by defendant, plaintiff; index on cards since 1978 (circuit only); on computer back to 1995; others back to 1953. Mail turnaround time 1 week. Civil PAT goes back to 1995. Free index search by name at http://apps.kycourts.net/CourtRecords/.
Criminal Records: Access: In person, online. Visitors must perform in person searches themselves. Required to search: name, years to search, DOB; SSN helpful. Criminal records indexed on cards since 1978 (circuit only); on computer back to 1995; others back to 1953. Criminal PAT goes back to same as civil. Online access same as civil; results show middle initial.
General Information: No adoption, mental, juvenile, or sealed records released. Will not fax documents. Court makes copy: $.25 per page, self serve same. Certification fee: $5.00. Payee: Circuit Clerk. Personal checks accepted; credit cards are not. Mail requests: SASE required for civil.

Hart County

Circuit & District Court PO Box 248, 117 E South St, Munfordville, KY 42765; 270-524-5181; fax: 270-524-7202; 8AM-4PM, till 5PM M (CST). ***Felony, Misdemeanor, Civil, Eviction, Small Claims, Probate.***
Civil Records: Access: In person, online. Visitors must perform in person searches themselves. Required to search: name, years to search; also helpful: address. Civil cases indexed by defendant, plaintiff; index on cards since 1978, computerized since 3/95. Civil PAT goes back to 3/1995. Free index search by name at http://apps.kycourts.net/CourtRecords/.
Criminal Records: Access: In person, online. Visitors must perform in person searches themselves. Required to search: name, years to search, DOB, SSN; also helpful: address. Criminal records indexed on cards since 1978, computerized since 3/95. Criminal PAT goes back to same as civil. Online access same as civil; results show middle initial.
General Information: No adoption, mental, juvenile, or sealed records released. Will not fax documents. Court makes copy: $.25 per page, self serve same. Certification fee: $5.00. Payee: Circuit Clerk. Business checks accepted. No credit cards accepted.

Henderson County

Circuit & District Court PO Box 675, 5 N Main, Judicial Ctr, Henderson, KY 42419; 270-826-2405/1566; fax: 270-831-2710; 8AM-4:30PM (CST). ***Felony, Civil Actions over $4,000.***
Fax number is for both District and Circuit Courts.
Civil Records: Access: In person, online. Visitors must perform in person searches themselves. Required to search: name, years to search. Civil cases indexed by defendant, plaintiff, on computer from 3/1991, records on index cards from 1978 to 3/1991. Civil PAT goes back to 1991. Free index search by name at http://apps.kycourts.net/CourtRecords/.
Criminal Records: Access: In person, online. Visitors must perform in person searches themselves. Required to search: name, years to search, DOB. Criminal records computerized from 3/1991, records on index cards from 1978 to 3/1991. Criminal PAT goes back to same as civil. Online access same as civil; results show middle initial.
General Information: No adoption, mental, juvenile, or sealed records released. Will fax documents $2.00 1st page, $1.00 ea. add'l, including coversheet. Court makes copy: $.25 per page, self serve same. Certification fee: $5.00 per doc. Payee: Circuit Clerk. Personal checks accepted; credit cards are not. Mail requests: SASE required for mail return of any copies.

Henry County

Circuit & District Court PO Box 359, 30 N Main St, New Castle, KY 40050; 502-845-7551 dist; 502-845-2868 Circ; fax: 502-845-2969; 7:30AM-=5:30PM (EST). ***Felony, Misdemeanor, Civil, Eviction, Small Claims, Probate.***
Civil Records: Access: In person, online. Visitors must perform in person searches themselves. Required to search: name, years to search. Civil cases indexed by defendant, plaintiff, on computer since 5/1994, records on docket books since 1800s. Civil PAT goes back to 5/1994. PAT results show middle initial, DOB. Free index search by name at http://apps.kycourts.net/CourtRecords/.
Criminal Records: Access: In person, online. Visitors must perform in person searches themselves. Required to search: name, years to search; SSN helpful. Criminal records on computer since 5/1994, records on docket books since 1800s. Criminal PAT goes back to same as civil. PAT results show middle initial, DOB. Online access same as civil; results show middle initial.
General Information: No adoption, mental, juvenile, or sealed records released. Will fax documents $2.00 1st page, $1.00 each add'l. Court makes copy: $.25 per page, self serve same. Certification fee: $5.00 per doc. Payee: Circuit Clerk. Personal checks accepted; credit cards are not.

Hickman County

Circuit & District Court 109 S Washington St, Clinton, KY 42031; 270-653-3901; criminal fax: 270-653-3989; civil fax: same; 8AM-4PM (CST). ***Felony, Misdemeanor, Civil, Eviction, Small Claims, Probate.***
Probate fax is same as main fax number.
Civil Records: Access: Mail, in person, online. Both court and visitors may perform in person searches. No search fee. Required to search: name, years to search. Civil cases indexed by defendant, plaintiff, on computer from 6/94 to present, on index from 1978 to 6/94. If court does search, request must be in writing. Mail turnaround time same day if possible. Civil PAT goes back to 6/1994. Free index search by name at http://apps.kycourts.net/CourtRecords/.
Criminal Records: Access: Mail, in person, online. Both court and visitors may perform in person searches. No search fee. Required to search: name, years to search, DOB; also helpful: SSN. Criminal records computerized from 6/94 to present, on index from 1978 to 6/94. Requests must be in writing. Mail turnaround time same day. Criminal PAT goes back to same as civil. Online access same as civil; results show middle initial.
General Information: No adoption, mental, juvenile, or sealed records released. Will fax out documents $2.00 1st page, $1.00 each add'l. Court makes copy: $.25 per page. Certification fee: $5.00 per cert. Payee: Circuit Clerk. Personal checks accepted; credit cards are not. Mail requests: SASE required.

Hopkins County

Circuit & District Court Courthouse 30 S Main St, Madisonville, KY 42431; criminal phone: 270-824-7501; civil phone: 270-824-7502; probate phone: 270-824-7509; fax: 270-824-7032; 7:30AM-4PM (CST). ***Felony, Misdemeanor, Civil, Eviction, Small Claims, Probate.***

Probate fax is same as main fax number.

Civil Records: Access: In person, online. Visitors must perform in person searches themselves. Required to search: name, years to search. Civil cases indexed by defendant, plaintiff, on computer back to 6/1991; on index cards from 1978 to 1991. For searches prior to 1990, fill out search requests form to search archives in Frankfort. Civil PAT goes back to 1992. PAT results show middle initial, DOB. Free index search by name at http://apps.kycourts.net/CourtRecords/.

Criminal Records: Access: In person, online. Visitors must perform in person searches themselves. Required to search: name, years to search, signed release; also helpful: DOB, SSN. Criminal records computerized from 6/1991, on index cards from 1978 to 1991, archived since 1800s. Criminal PAT goes back to same as civil. PAT results show middle initial, DOB. Online access same as civil; results show middle initial.

General Information: No adoption, mental, juvenile, or sealed records released. Will not fax out documents. Court makes copy: $.25 per page. Certification fee: $5.00. Payee: Circuit Clerk. Personal checks accepted. Visa/MC/AmEx accepted.

Jackson County

Circuit Court PO Box 84, McKee, KY 40447; 606-287-7783; criminal phone: 606-287-8651; civil phone: 606-287-7783; criminal fax: 606-287-3277; civil fax: same; 8AM-4PM M-F; 8AM-N Sat (EST). ***Felony, Civil Actions over $4,000.***

Civil Records: Access: Fax, mail, in person, online. Both court and visitors may perform in person searches. No search fee. Required to search: name, years to search; also helpful: address. Civil cases indexed by defendant, plaintiff, on computer from 5/1993 to present, on index cards from 1978 to 1993. Mail turnaround time 2 days. Civil PAT goes back to 1993. Free index search by name at http://apps.kycourts.net/CourtRecords/.

Criminal Records: Access: Fax, mail, in person, online. Both court and visitors may perform in person searches. No search fee. Required to search: name, years to search, DOB; also helpful: SSN. Criminal records computerized from 5/1993 to present, on index cards from 1990 to 1993. Mail turnaround time 2 days. Criminal PAT goes back to same as civil. PAT results show middle initial, DOB. Terminal results include SSN. Online access same as civil; results show middle initial.

General Information: No adoption, mental, juvenile, or sealed records released. Fee to fax out file $1.00 per page. Court makes copy: $.25 per page, self serve same. Certification fee: $5.00 per cert. Payee: Jackson County Circuit Clerk. Personal checks accepted; credit cards are not. Mail requests: SASE required.

District Court PO Box 84, McKee, KY 40447; 606-287-8651; probate phone: same; fax: 606-287-3277; 8AM-4PM M-F; 8AM-N Sat (EST). ***Misdemeanor, Civil Actions under $4,000, Eviction, Small Claims, Probate.***

Civil Records: Access: Fax, mail, in person, online. Both court and visitors may perform in person searches. No search fee. Required to search: name, years to search. Civil cases indexed by defendant, plaintiff, on computer back to 5/1993, on index cards from 1978. Mail turnaround time 1 week. Civil PAT goes back to 5/1993. PAT civil results show middle initial. Free index search by name at http://apps.kycourts.net/CourtRecords/.

Criminal Records: Access: Fax, mail, in person, online. Both court and visitors may perform in person searches. No search fee. Required to search: name, years to search, DOB; also helpful: SSN. Criminal records computerized from 5/1993; on index cards from 1990. Mail turnaround time 1 week. Criminal PAT goes back to same as civil. PAT results show middle initial, DOB. Terminal results include SSN. Online access same as civil; results show middle initial.

General Information: No adoption, mental, juvenile, or sealed records released. Will fax documents $2.00 1st page, $1.00 ea add'l. Court makes copy: $.25 per page, self serve same. Certification fee: $5.00. Payee: Jackson County District Clerk. Personal checks accepted; credit cards are not. Mail requests: SASE required.

Jefferson County

Circuit Court 600 W Jefferson St, Circuit Clerk, Louisville, KY 40202; 502-595-3055; fax: 502-595-4128; 8:30am-4:30PM. ***Felony, Civil Actions over $4,000.***

Contact the Records Division at 1-800-928-2350.

Civil Records: Access: In person, online. Visitors must perform in person searches themselves. Required to search: name, years to search. Civil cases indexed by defendant, plaintiff, on computer from 1991, prior in index cards. Civil PAT goes back to 1991. Free index search by name at http://apps.kycourts.net/CourtRecords/.

Criminal Records: Access: In person, online. Visitors must perform in person searches themselves. Required to search: name, years to search. Criminal records computerized from 1991, prior in index cards. Criminal PAT goes back to same as civil. Online access same as civil; results show middle initial.

General Information: No adoption or sealed records released. Court makes copy: $.25 per page. Certification fee: $5.00 per doc. Payee: Circuit Clerk. Personal checks accepted.

District Court 600 W Jefferson St, Hall of Justice, Louisville, KY 40202; 502-595-3055; criminal phone: 502-595-4320; civil phone: 502-595-3015; fax: 502-595-4629; 8:30AM-4:30PM (EST). ***Misdemeanor, Civil Actions under $4,000, Eviction, Small Claims, Probate.***

Civil Records: Access: In person, online. Visitors must perform in person searches themselves. Required to search: name, years to search. Civil cases indexed by defendant, plaintiff, on computer back to 3/93; index cards 1978 to 1988. Civil PAT goes back to 1988. PAT civil results show middle initial. Free index search by name at http://apps.kycourts.net/CourtRecords/.

Criminal Records: Access: In person, online. Visitors must perform in person searches themselves. Required to search: name, years to search. Criminal records computerized from 3/93; on index cards 1978 to 1988. Criminal PAT goes back to same as civil. PAT results show middle initial, DOB. Online access same as civil; results show middle initial.

General Information: No adoption, mental, juvenile, or sealed records released. Court makes copy: $.25 per page. Certification fee: $5.00 per doc. Payee: Circuit Clerk. Personal checks accepted. Credit cards accepted for District Criminal Traffic only.

Jessamine County

Circuit Court 107 N Main St, Nicholasville, KY 40356; 859-885-4531; 8AM-4:30PM M,T,W,F; 8AM-N Th (EST). ***Felony, Civil Actions over $4,000, Traffic.***

Civil Records: Access: In person, online. Visitors must perform in person searches themselves. Required to search: name, years to search. Civil cases indexed by defendant, plaintiff, on computer from 6/1992 to present, on index cards from 1978 to 1992. Civil PAT goes back to 6/1992. Free index search by name at http://apps.kycourts.net/CourtRecords/.

Criminal Records: Access: In person, online. Visitors must perform in person searches themselves. Required to search: name, years to search, DOB; also helpful: SSN. Criminal records computerized from 6/1992 to present, on index cards from 1978 to 1992. Criminal PAT goes back to same as civil. PAT criminal results show middle initial. Online access same as civil; results show middle initial.

General Information: No adoption, mental, juvenile, or sealed records released. Court makes copy: $.25 per page. Certification fee: $5.00 per doc. Payee: Jessamine Circuit Clerk. Personal checks accepted. Visa/MC accepted.

District Court 107 N Main St, Nicholasville, KY 40356; 859-887-1005; fax: 859-887-0425; 8AM-4:30PM M-W; 8AM-N TH; 8AM-4:30PM F (EST). ***Misdemeanor, Civil Actions under $4,000, Eviction, Small Claims, Probate.***

Civil Records: Access: Mail, in person, online. Both court and visitors may perform in person searches. No search fee. Required to search: name, years to search. Civil cases indexed by defendant, plaintiff, on computer since 1992, on file cards prior. Mail turnaround time 2-4 days. Civil PAT goes back to 1992. Free index search by name at http://apps.kycourts.net/CourtRecords/.

Criminal Records: Access: Mail, in person, online. Both court and visitors may perform in person searches. No search fee. Required to search: name, years to search; also helpful: DOB, SSN. Criminal records on computer since 1992, on file cards prior. Mail turnaround time 2-4 days. Criminal PAT goes back to same as civil. Online access same as civil; results show middle initial.

General Information: No adoption, mental, juvenile, or sealed records released. Court makes copy: $.25 per page. Self serve: $.25 per page. Certification fee: $5.00 per doc. Payee: District Clerk. Personal checks and major credit cards accepted. Mail requests: SASE required.

Johnson County

Circuit & District Court 908 Third St, #109, Paintsville, KY 41240; 606-297-9567; criminal fax: 606-297-9573; civil fax: same; 8AM-4PM (EST). ***Felony, Misdemeanor, Civil, Eviction, Small Claims, Probate.***

http://courts.ky.gov/counties/Johnson/

Probate fax is same as main fax number.

Civil Records: Access: Phone, mail, in person, online. Both court and visitors may perform in person searches. No search fee. Required to search: name, years to search. Civil cases indexed by defendant, plaintiff, on computer since 9/88, on index cards from 1978 to 1995, books from 1843 to 1978. From 1992 and prior files are at the archives in Fran. Mail turnaround time 3 days. Civil PAT goes back to 10/1988. PAT results show name only. Free index search by name at http://apps.kycourts.net/CourtRecords/.

Criminal Records: Access: In person, online. Visitors must perform in person searches themselves. Required to search: name, years to search, DOB, SSN. Criminal records on computer since 9/88, on index cards from 1978 to 1988, books from 1843 to 1978. From 1992 and prior files are at the archives in F. Court will not conduct searches. Contact AOC for statewide search by mail. Criminal PAT goes back to same as civil. PAT results show name only. Online access same as civil; results show middle initial.

General Information: No adoption, mental, juvenile, or sealed records released. Will not fax documents. Court makes copy: $.25 per page. Certification fee: $5.00. Add'l fee for copies. Payee: Circuit Clerk. Personal checks accepted; credit cards are not. Mail requests: SASE required for civil.

Kenton County

Circuit Court PO Box 669, 230 Madison Ave, Covington, KY 41011; 859-292-6521; fax: 859-292-6611; 8AM-4:30PM (EST). ***Felony, Civil Actions over $4,000.***

http://courts.ky.gov/Counties/Kenton/default.htm

Civil Records: Access: Mail, in person, online. Both court and visitors may perform in person searches. No search fee. Required to search: name, years to search. Civil cases indexed by defendant, plaintiff, on computer back to 6/12/89, on index cards from 1800s. Mail turnaround time 7 days. Civil PAT goes back to 6/12/89. PAT civil results show middle initial. Free index search by name at http://apps.kycourts.net/CourtRecords/.

Criminal Records: Access: In person, online. Visitors must perform in person searches themselves. Required to search: name, years to search, DOB or SSN. Criminal records computerized

from 4/27/90. Criminal PAT goes back to 4/27/90. PAT criminal results show middle initial. Online access same as civil; results show middle initial.
General Information: No adoption, mental, juvenile, or sealed records released. Will not fax documents. Court makes copy: $.25 per page.Video of hearings are $15.00, turnaround time 7-14 days. Certification fee: $5.00 per cert. Payee: Kenton Circuit Clerk. Personal checks and major credit cards accepted. Mail requests: SASE required for civil.

District Court 230 Madison Ave, 3rd Fl, Covington, KY 41011; 859-292-6523; fax: 859-292-6611; 7AM-5PM (EST). ***Misdemeanor, Civil Actions under $4,000, Eviction, Small Claims, Probate.***
http://courts.ky.gov/Counties/Kenton/default.htm
Civil Records: Access: Mail, in person, online. Only the court performs in person searches; visitors may not. No search fee. Required to search: name, years to search. Civil cases indexed by defendant, plaintiff, on computer from 6/9/89 to present, on index cards from 1985. Mail turnaround time 1 week. Civil PAT goes back to 1991. Free index search by name at http://apps.kycourts.net/CourtRecords/.
Criminal Records: Access: In person, online. Visitors must perform in person searches themselves. Required to search: name, years to search DOB; SSN helpful. Criminal records computerized from 5/20/91 to present, index cards held since 1996. Criminal PAT goes back to 1991. Online access same as civil; results show middle initial.
General Information: No adoption, mental, juvenile, or sealed records released. Fee to fax out file $3.00 each. Court makes copy: $.25 per page. Certification fee: $5.00 per doc. Payee: District Clerk. Cashiers checks, money orders, and local checks accepted. Major credit cards accepted. Mail requests: SASE required for civil.

Knott County

Circuit & District Court PO Box 1317, 53 W Main St, Hindman, KY 41822; 606-785-5021; fax: 606-785-3994; 8AM-4PM M-F; 8AM-N 1st & 4th Sats (EST). ***Felony, Misdemeanor, Civil, Eviction, Small Claims, Probate.***
Civil Records: Access: In person, online. Visitors must perform in person searches themselves. Required to search: name, years to search. Civil cases indexed by defendant, plaintiff, in index files, computerized since 11/94. Civil PAT goes back to 11/1994. PAT results show middle initial, DOB, SSN. Not all public terminal results show identifiers. Free index search by name at http://apps.kycourts.net/CourtRecords/.
Criminal Records: Access: In person, online. Visitors must perform in person searches themselves. Required to search: name, years to search, DOB; also helpful: SSN. Criminal records in index files; on computer back to 11/1994. Criminal PAT goes back to 11/1994. PAT results show middle initial, DOB, SSN. Online access same as civil; results show middle initial.
General Information: No adoption, mental, juvenile, or sealed records released. Will fax documents to local or toll free line. Court makes copy: $.25 per page. Certification fee: $5.00 per doc. Payee: Circuit Clerk. Personal checks accepted; credit cards are not.

Knox County

Circuit & District Court PO Box 760, 401 Court Sq #202, Barbourville, KY 40906; 606-546-3075 (Circ. Ct), 546-3232 (Dist); fax: 606-546-7949; 8AM-4:30PM M-F; 8:30AM-N Sat (EST). ***Felony, Misdemeanor, Civil, Eviction, Small Claims, Probate.***
Civil Records: Access: In person, online. Visitors must perform in person searches themselves. Required to search: name, years to search. Civil cases indexed by defendant, plaintiff, go back to 1978; on computer back to 7/92. Civil PAT goes back to 7/1994. Free index search by name at http://apps.kycourts.net/CourtRecords/.
Criminal Records: Access: In person, online. Visitors must perform in person searches themselves. Required to search: name, years to search, DOB; SSN helpful. Criminal records go back to 1978; on computer back to 7/92. Criminal PAT goes back to same as civil. Online access same as civil; results show middle initial.
General Information: No adoption, mental, juvenile, or sealed records released. Court makes copy: $.25 per page. Certification fee: $5.00 per doc. Payee: Circuit Clerk. No personal checks accepted. Visa/MC accepted.

Larue County

Circuit & District Court PO Box 191, 209 W High St, Courthouse Annex, Hodgenville, KY 42748; 270-358-3421; criminal fax: 270-358-3731; civil fax: same; 8AM-4PM M-F, 9AM-Noon Sat; closed N-1PM W (EST). ***Felony, Misdemeanor, Civil, Eviction, Small Claims, Probate.***
http://courts.ky.gov/counties/Larue/
Probate fax is same as main fax number.
Civil Records: Access: In person, online. Both court and visitors may perform in person searches. No search fee. Required to search: name, years to search. Civil cases indexed by defendant, plaintiff, on computer since 1995. Civil PAT goes back to 1995. Free index search by name at http://apps.kycourts.net/CourtRecords/.
Criminal Records: Access: In person, online. Both court and visitors may perform in person searches. No search fee. Required to search: name, years to search, DOB; SSN helpful. Criminal records on computer since 1995. Criminal PAT goes back to same as civil. Online access same as civil; results show middle initial.
General Information: No adoption, mental, juvenile, or sealed records released. No fee to fax specific case file. Court makes copy: $.25 per page, self serve same. No certification fee. Payee: Circuit Clerk. Personal checks accepted; credit cards are not.

Laurel County

Circuit & District Court PO Box 1798, 103 S Broad St, Courthouse Annex 2, London, KY 40743-1798; 606-330-2078; probate phone: 606-864-7445; fax: 606-330-2084; 8AM-4:30PM M-F; 9AM-N Sat (EST). ***Felony, Misdemeanor, Civil, Eviction, Small Claims, Probate.***
Civil Records: Access: In person, online. Visitors must perform in person searches themselves. Required to search: name, years to search. Civil cases indexed by defendant, plaintiff, on computer from 7/94, and index books from 1992. Civil PAT goes back to 1994. PAT results show middle initial, DOB. Free index search by name at http://apps.kycourts.net/CourtRecords/. Also, dockets free at http://apps.kycourts.net/dockets/.
Criminal Records: Access: In person, online. Visitors must perform in person searches themselves. Required to search: name, years to search, DOB, SSN. Criminal records computerized from 7/94, and index books from 1987. Criminal PAT goes back to same as civil. PAT results show middle initial, DOB. Online access same as civil; results show middle initial.
General Information: No adoption, mental, juvenile, or sealed records released. Will not fax documents. Court makes copy: $.25 per page. Certification fee: $5.00. Payee: Circuit Clerk. Personal checks accepted; credit cards are not.

Lawrence County

Circuit & District Court PO Box 847, Courthouse, Louisa, KY 41230; 606-638-4215; fax: 606-638-0264; 8:30AM-4PM, 8:30AM-N 1st & last Sat of month (EST). ***Felony, Misdemeanor, Civil, Eviction, Small Claims, Probate.***
Civil Records: Access: Mail, fax, in person, online. Both court and visitors may perform in person searches. No search fee. Required to search: name, years to search. Civil cases indexed by defendant, plaintiff, on computer from 11/94, index cards from 1978. Mail turnaround time within 1 week. Civil PAT goes back to 1995. PAT results show name only. Free index search by name at http://apps.kycourts.net/CourtRecords/.
Criminal Records: Access: In person, online. Visitors must perform in person searches themselves. Required to search: name, years to search; also helpful: DOB, SSN. Criminal records computerized from 11/94, index cards from 1978. Criminal PAT goes back to 1995. Online access same as civil; results show middle initial.
General Information: No adoption, mental, juvenile, or sealed records released. Fee to fax out file $2.00 per page. Court makes copy: $.25 per page. Certification fee: $5.00 per doc. Payee: Circuit Clerk. Personal checks accepted; credit cards are not. Mail requests: SASE required for civil.

Lee County

Circuit & District Court PO Box E, 256 Main St, Beattyville, KY 41311; 606-464-8400; fax: 606-464-0144; 8AM-4PM M-F; 8:30AM-11:30AM 1st Sat of month only (EST). ***Felony, Misdemeanor, Civil, Eviction, Small Claims, Probate.***
Civil Records: Access: In person, online. Visitors must perform in person searches themselves. Required to search: name, years to search. Civil cases indexed by defendant, plaintiff, on computer from 9/94 to present, on index cards from 1978. Civil PAT goes back to 9/1994. PAT results show name, DOB. Free index search by name at http://apps.kycourts.net/CourtRecords/.
Criminal Records: Access: In person, online. Visitors must perform in person searches themselves. Required to search: name, years to search, DOB; SSN helpful. Criminal records computerized from 9/94 to present, on index cards from 1978. Criminal PAT goes back to same as civil.PAT results show name, DOB. Online access same as civil; results show middle initial.
General Information: No adoption, mental, juvenile, or sealed records released. Will not fax documents. Court makes copy: $.25 per page. Certification fee: $5.00 per doc. Payee: Circuit Clerk. Only cashiers checks, money orders and attorney checks accepted. No credit cards accepted.

Leslie County

Circuit & District Court PO Box 1750, 22010 Main St, Hyden, KY 41749; 606-672-2505; probate phone: 606-672-2503; fax: 606-672-5128; 8AM-4PM M-F; 8AM-N Sat (EST). ***Felony, Misdemeanor, Civil, Eviction, Small Claims, Probate.***
Civil Records: Access: In person, online. Visitors must perform in person searches themselves. Required to search: name, years to search. Civil cases indexed by plaintiff. Civil records on computer and index books. Civil PAT goes back to 1993. Free index search by name at http://apps.kycourts.net/CourtRecords/.
Criminal Records: Access: In person, online. Visitors must perform in person searches themselves. Required to search: name, years to search; also helpful: address, DOB, SSN. Criminal records on computer and index books. Criminal PAT goes back to same as civil. Online access same as civil; results show middle initial.
General Information: No adoption, mental, juvenile, or sealed records released. Will not fax documents. Court makes copy: $.25 per page. Certification fee: $5.00. Payee: Circuit Clerk. Personal checks accepted; credit cards are not.

Letcher County

Circuit & District Court 156 W Main St, #201, Whitesburg, KY 41858; 606-633-7559/8810; fax: 606-633-5864; 8AM-4PM; 8:30AM-12PM 1st Sat monthly (EST). ***Felony, Misdemeanor, Civil, Eviction, Small Claims, Probate.***
Civil Records: Access: Fax, mail, in person, online. Both court and visitors may perform in person searches. No search fee. Required to search: name, years to search; also helpful: address. Civil cases indexed by defendant, plaintiff, on computer go back to 11/1991; on index books from 1986 to 1991. Files maintained in office. Records from 1985 to 1800s in archives in. Civil PAT goes back to 1991. Free index search by name at http://apps.kycourts.net/CourtRecords/.
Criminal Records: Access: In person, online. Visitors must perform in person searches themselves. Required to search: name, years to search, DOB, SSN; also helpful: address. Criminal records on computer go back to 11/1991; on index

cards from 1986 to 1991. Files maintained in office. Records from 1985 to 1800s in archives. Contact AOC 800-928-6381 for statewide search by mail. Criminal PAT goes back to same as civil. Online access same as civil; results show middle initial.
General Information: No adoption, mental, juvenile, or sealed records released. Fee to fax out file $2.00 1st page, $1.00 each add'l. Court makes copy: $.25 per page. Certification fee: $5.00. Payee: Circuit Clerk. Personal checks accepted; credit cards are not. Mail requests: SASE required for civil.

Lewis County

Circuit & District Court PO Box 70, Vanceburg, KY 41179; 606-796-3053; fax: 606-796-3030; 8AM-4:30PM M,T,TH,F 8:30-N W,Sat (EST). ***Felony, Misdemeanor, Civil, Eviction, Small Claims, Probate.***
Civil Records: Access: Phone, mail, in person, online. Both court and visitors may perform in person searches. No search fee. Required to search: name, years to search. Civil cases indexed by defendant, plaintiff. Computerized from 1994, civil records on index cards back to 1955. Mail turnaround time within 1 week. Civil PAT goes back to 1994. PAT civil results show middle initial. Free index search by name at http://apps.kycourts.net/CourtRecords/.
Criminal Records: Access: Mail, in person, online. Both court and visitors may perform in person searches. No search fee. Required to search: name, years to search, DOB; also helpful: SSN. Computerized from 1994, criminal records on index cards back to 1960s. Mail turnaround time within 1 week. Criminal PAT goes back to same as civil. PAT criminal results show middle initial. Online access same as civil; results show middle initial.
General Information: No adoption, mental, juvenile, or sealed records released. Will fax documents to local or toll-free number. Court makes copy: $.25 per page, self serve same. Certification fee: $5.00. Payee: Circuit Clerk. Personal checks accepted; credit cards are not. Mail requests: SASE required.

Lincoln County

Circuit & District Court 101 E Main, Stanford, KY 40484; 606-365-2535; fax: 606-365-3389; 8AM-4PM; 9AM-N Sat (EST). ***Felony, Misdemeanor, Civil, Eviction, Small Claims, Probate.***
Civil Records: Access: In person, online. Visitors must perform in person searches themselves. Required to search: name, years to search. Civil cases indexed by defendant, plaintiff, on computer from 5/94, index cards prior, archived from 1978 to 1900. Civil PAT goes back to 1994. Free index search by name at http://apps.kycourts.net/CourtRecords/.
Criminal Records: Access: In person, online. Visitors must perform in person searches themselves. Required to search: name, years to search; SSN helpful. Criminal records computerized from 5/94, index cards prior, archived from 1978 to 1900. Criminal PAT goes back to same as civil. Online access same as civil; results show middle initial.
General Information: No adoption, mental, juvenile, or sealed records released. Will not fax documents. Court makes copy: $.25 per page. No certification fee. Payee: Circuit Clerk. Personal checks accepted; credit cards are not.

Livingston County

Circuit & District Court PO Box 160, Smithland, KY 42081; 270-928-2172; probate phone: same; fax: 270-928-2976; 8AM-6PM M 8AM-4PM T-F (CST). ***Felony, Misdemeanor, Civil, Eviction, Small Claims, Probate.***
Civil Records: Access: In person, online. Visitors must perform in person searches themselves. Required to search: name, years to search. Civil cases indexed by defendant, plaintiff, on computer from 1993 to present, index cards prior, archived from 1799 to 1851. Civil PAT goes back to 1993. Free index search at http://apps.kycourts.net/CourtRecords/.
Criminal Records: Access: In person, online. Visitors must perform in person searches themselves. Required to search: name, years to search, DOB; SSN helpful. Criminal records computerized from 1993 to present, index cards prior, archived from 1799 to 1851. Criminal PAT goes back to same as civil. Online access same as civil; results show middle initial.
General Information: No adoption, mental, juvenile, or sealed records released. Will fax documents $2.00 1st page, $1.00 each add'l page. Court makes copy: $.25 per page. Certification fee: $5.00. Payee: Circuit Clerk. No out-of-state personal checks accepted. No credit cards accepted.

Logan County

Circuit Court Box 420, W 4th St, Russellville, KY 42276-0420; 270-726-2424; fax: 270-726-7893; 8AM-4:30PM M-TH (CST). ***Felony, Civil Actions over $4,000.***
Civil Records: Access: In person, online. Visitors must perform in person searches themselves. Required to search: name, years to search. Civil cases indexed by defendant, plaintiff, on computer from 4/1992 to present, on index card from 1978 to 1992. Civil PAT goes back to 1992. Free index search by name at http://apps.kycourts.net/CourtRecords/.
Criminal Records: Access: In person, online. Visitors must perform in person searches themselves. Required to search: name, years to search, DOB, SSN. Criminal records computerized from 4/1992 to present, on index card from 1978 to 1992. Criminal PAT goes back to same as civil. Online access same as civil; results show middle initial.
General Information: No adoption, mental, juvenile or sealed records released. Will not fax documents. Court makes copy: $.25 per page. Certification fee: $5.00. Payee: Circuit Clerk. Only cashiers checks and money orders accepted. No credit cards accepted. Mail requests: SASE required for mail return of any copies.

District Court Box 420, Russellville, KY 42276; 270-726-3107; probate phone: 270-726-3108; fax: 270-726-7893; 8AM-4:30PM (CST). ***Misdemeanor, Civil Actions under $4,000, Eviction, Small Claims, Probate.***
Civil Records: Access: In person, online. Visitors must perform in person searches themselves. Required to search: name, years to search. Civil cases indexed by defendant, plaintiff, on computer since 1992, index cards from 1978 to 1992. Civil PAT goes back to 1992. Free index search by name at http://apps.kycourts.net/CourtRecords/.
Criminal Records: Access: In person, online. Visitors must perform in person searches themselves. Required to search: name, years to search, DOB; SSN helpful. Criminal records on computer since 1992, index cards from 1978 to 1991. Criminal PAT goes back to same as civil. Online access same as civil; results show middle initial.
General Information: No adoption, mental, juvenile, or sealed records released. Will not fax documents. Court makes copy: $.25 per page, self serve same. Certification fee: $5.00. Payee: Logan District Clerk. Personal checks accepted; credit cards are not. Mail requests: SASE required for mail return of any copies.

Lyon County

Circuit & District Court Box 565, Eddyville, KY 42038; 270-388-7231 Circ Ct; 270-388-2727 Dist Ct; fax: 270-388-9135; 8AM-4PM (CST). ***Felony, Misdemeanor, Civil, Eviction, Small Claims, Probate.*** http://courts.ky.gov/counties/Lyon/
This court also handles domestic violence, traffic, and juvenile cases.
Civil Records: Access: In person, online. Visitors must perform in person searches themselves. Required to search: name, years to search. Civil cases indexed by defendant, plaintiff, on computer from 11/94 to present, on index cards from 1978 to 1994. Civil PAT goes back to 1995. Free index search by name at http://apps.kycourts.net/CourtRecords/.
Criminal Records: Access: In person, online. Visitors must perform in person searches themselves. Required to search: name, years to search, DOB; SSN helpful. Criminal records computerized from 11/94 to present. Circuit court records are on index cards from 1978 to 1994, but not District court records. Criminal PAT goes back to same as civil. Online access same as civil; results show middle initial.
General Information: No adoption, mental, juvenile, or sealed records released. Will fax documents $3.00 per page. Court makes copy: $.25 per page, self serve same. Certification fee: $5.00 per doc. Payee: Circuit Clerk. No personal checks or credit cards accepted.

Madison County

Circuit Court PO Box 813, 101 W Main St, County Courthouse, Richmond, KY 40476-0813; 859-624-4793; fax: 859-625-0598; 8AM-4PM (EST). ***Felony, Civil Actions over $4,000.*** http://courts.ky.gov/Counties/Madison/default.htm
Civil Records: Access: In person, online. Visitors must perform in person searches themselves. Required to search: name, years to search. Civil cases indexed by defendant, plaintiff, on computer back to 10/1990 to present, on index cards from 1978 to 1990. Civil PAT goes back to 10/1990. Free index search by name at http://apps.kycourts.net/CourtRecords/.
Criminal Records: Access: In person, online. Visitors must perform in person searches themselves. Required to search: name, years to search; also helpful: DOB, SSN. Criminal records computerized from 10/1990 to present, on index cards from 1978 to 1990. Contact AOC for statewide searches by mail. Criminal PAT goes back to same as civil. Online access same as civil; results show middle initial.
General Information: No adoption, mental, juvenile, or sealed records released. Will fax out documents for $3.50. Court makes copy: $.25 per page, self serve same. Certification fee: $5.00. Payee: Madison Circuit Clerk. Personal checks accepted. Visa/MC accepted.

District Court Madison Hall of Justice, 351 W Main St, Richmond, KY 40475; 859-624-4722; fax: 859-624-4746; 8AM-4PM (EST). ***Misdemeanor, Civil Actions under $4,000, Eviction, Small Claims, Probate.***
Civil Records: Access: In person, online. Visitors must perform in person searches themselves. Required to search: name, years to search. Civil cases indexed by defendant, plaintiff, go back to 11/90; computerized. Civil PAT goes back to 1991. Free index search by name at http://apps.kycourts.net/CourtRecords/.
Criminal Records: Access: In person, online. Visitors must perform in person searches themselves. Required to search: name, years to search, DOB; SSN helpful. Criminal records go back to 1999; computerized. Criminal PAT goes back to 1999. Online access same as civil; results show middle initial.
General Information: No adoption, mental, juvenile, or sealed records released. Fee to fax out file $2.00 per page. Court makes copy: $.25 per page. Self serve: $.25 per page. Certification fee: $5.00 per doc. Payee: District Court. Personal checks accepted. Visa/MC accepted.

Magoffin County

Circuit & District Court PO Box 147, 100 E Maple St, Salyersville, KY 41465; 606-349-2215; fax: 606-349-2209; 8AM-4PM (EST). ***Felony, Misdemeanor, Civil, Eviction, Small Claims, Probate.***
Civil Records: Access: In person, online. Both court and visitors may perform in person searches. No search fee. Required to search: name, years to search. Civil cases indexed by defendant, plaintiff, on computer from 3/1993 to present, on index cards from 1978 to 1993. Cases before 1990 are in archives. Civil PAT goes back to 1993. Free index search by name at http://apps.kycourts.net/CourtRecords/.
Criminal Records: Access: In person, online. Both court and visitors may perform in person searches. No search fee. Required to search: name, years to search, DOB; also helpful: SSN. Criminal records computerized from 3/1993 to present, on index cards from 1978 to 1993. Cases before 1990 are in archives. Results include addresses. Criminal PAT goes back to same as civil.PAT results show name, DOB. Terminal results include SSN. Online access same as civil; results show middle initial.

General Information: No adoption, mental, juvenile, or sealed records released. Fee to fax non-certified file is $2.00 1st page, $1.00 each add'l. Court makes copy: $.25 per page. Certification fee: $5.00; Seal $1.00 extra. Payee: Circuit Clerk. Personal checks accepted; credit cards are not.

Marion County

Circuit & District Court 120 W Main St, #6, Lebanon, KY 40033; 270-692-2681; fax: 270-692-3097; 8:30AM-4:30PM; 8:30AM-N Sat (EST). ***Felony, Misdemeanor, Civil, Eviction, Small Claims, Probate.***

Civil Records: Access: In person, online. Visitors must perform in person searches themselves. Required to search: name, years to search. Civil cases indexed by defendant, plaintiff, on computer from 5/1993 to present, on index cards from 1978 to 1993. Civil PAT goes back to 1993. PAT results show name, DOB. Terminal results may include SSN. Free index search by name at http://apps.kycourts.net/CourtRecords/.

Criminal Records: Access: In person, online. Visitors must perform in person searches themselves. Required to search: name, years to search; SSN helpful. Criminal records computerized from 5/1993 to present, on index cards from 1978 to 1993. Criminal PAT goes back to same as civil.PAT results show name, DOB. Online access same as civil; results show middle initial.

General Information: No adoption, mental, juvenile, or sealed records released. Will fax documents $2.00 1st page, $1.00 each add'l. Court makes copy: $.25 per page. Certification fee: $5.00. Payee: Circuit Clerk. Personal checks accepted; credit cards are not.

Marshall County

Circuit & District Court 80 Judicial Dr, Unit #101, Benton, KY 42025; 270-527-3883/1721; probate phone: 270-527-1721; criminal fax: 270-527-5865; civil fax: same; 8AM-4:30PM (CST). ***Felony, Misdemeanor, Civil, Eviction, Small Claims, Probate, Juvenile, Domestic Violence, Traffic.***
http://courts.ky.gov/Counties/Marshall/default.htm
Probate fax is same as main fax number.

Civil Records: Access: Fax, mail, in person, online. Both court and visitors may perform in person searches. No search fee. Required to search: name, years to search. Civil cases indexed by defendant, plaintiff, on computer since 8/1992 to present, on index books from 1978 to 1992. Mail turnaround time 3 days. Public use terminal has civil records back to 8/1992. PAT results show name, DOB. Terminal results also show SSNs. Free index search at http://apps.kycourts.net/CourtRecords/.

Criminal Records: Access: Phone, fax, mail, in person. Both court and visitors may perform in person searches. No search fee. Required to search: name, years to search, DOB; also helpful: SSN. Criminal records on computer since 8/1992 to present, on index books from 1978 to 1992. Mail turnaround time 3 days. Online access same as civil; results show middle initial.

General Information: No adoption, mental, juvenile, or sealed records released. Fee to fax out file $2.00 1st page, $1.00 each add'l. Court makes copy: $.25 per page, self serve same. Certification fee: $5.00 per cert. Payee: Circuit Clerk. Personal checks accepted. Visa/MC accepted. Mail requests: SASE required.

Martin County

Circuit & District Court Box 430, 98 Court St, Inez, KY 41224; 606-298-3508; fax: 606-298-4202; 8AM-4:30PM except 1st & 3rd Th 8AM-7PM (EST). ***Felony, Misdemeanor, Civil, Eviction, Small Claims, Probate.***

Civil Records: Access: Mail, in person, online. Both court and visitors may perform in person searches. No search fee. Required to search: name, years to search. Civil cases indexed by defendant, plaintiff, on computer since 4/1994, District on index books since 1987, Circuit on index books since 1978, prior records on docket books. Civil PAT goes back to 4/1994. Free index search by name at http://apps.kycourts.net/CourtRecords/.

Criminal Records: Access: In person, online. Visitors must perform in person searches themselves. Required to search: name, years to search; also helpful: DOB, SSN. Criminal records on computer since 4/1994, District on index books since 1987, Circuit on index books since 1978, prior records on docket books. Criminal PAT goes back to same as civil. Online access same as civil; results show middle initial.

General Information: No adoption, mental, juvenile, or sealed records released. Will not fax documents. Court makes copy: $.25 per page; return postage required. Certification fee: $5.00 per doc. Payee: Circuit Clerk. Personal checks accepted; credit cards are not. Mail requests: SASE required for civil.

Mason County

Circuit Court 100 W 3rd St, Maysville, KY 41056; 606-564-4340; civil phone: 606-564-4340; criminal fax: 606-564-0932; civil fax: same; 8:30AM-4:30PM (EST). ***Felony, Civil over $4,000.***
http://courts.ky.gov/Counties/Mason/default.htm

Civil Records: Access: In person, online. Visitors must perform in person searches themselves. Required to search: name, years to search. Civil cases indexed by defendant, plaintiff, on computer back to 4/1994, records on index books since 1929, prior records archived from 1798. Civil PAT goes back to 1994. Free index search by name at http://apps.kycourts.net/CourtRecords/.

Criminal Records: Access: In person, online. Visitors must perform in person searches themselves. Required to search: name, years to search, DOB. Criminal records computerized from 4/1994, records on index books since 1929, prior records archived from 1798. Criminal PAT goes back to same as civil. Online access same as civil; results show middle initial.

General Information: No adoption, mental, juvenile, or sealed records released. Will not fax out case files. Court makes copy: $.25 per page. Certification fee: $5.00 per cert includes copies. Payee: Kentucky State Treasurer. Personal checks or money order accepted. Major credit cards accepted.

District Court 100 W 3rd St, Maysville, KY 41056; 606-564-4011; criminal fax: 606-564-0932; civil fax: same; 8:30AM-4:30PM (EST). ***Misdemeanor, Civil Actions under $4000, Eviction, Small Claims, Probate.***
Probate fax is same as main fax number.

Civil Records: Access: In person, online. Visitors must perform in person searches themselves. Required to search: name, years to search. Civil cases indexed by defendant, plaintiff, on computer since 4/1994, prior records on index books from 1978. Civil PAT goes back to 1994. Free index search by name at http://apps.kycourts.net/CourtRecords/.

Criminal Records: Access: In person, online. Visitors must perform in person searches themselves. Required to search: name, years to search. Criminal records on computer since 4/1994, prior records on index books from 1983. Criminal PAT goes back to same as civil. Online access same as civil; results show middle initial.

General Information: No adoption, mental, juvenile, or sealed records released. Will not fax out case files. Court makes copy: $.25 per page. Certification fee: $5.00 per cert. Payee: Kentucky State Treasurer. Personal checks accepted. Credit cards accepted.

McCracken County

Circuit Court Box 1455, 301 S 6th St, Paducah, KY 42002-1455; 270-575-7280; 8:30AM-5PM M; 8:30AM-4:30PM T-F (CST). ***Felony, Civil Actions over $4,000.*** Visitors may only search from 2PM-4PM on Thursday.

Civil Records: Access: In person, online. Both court and visitors may perform in person searches. No search fee. Required to search: name, years to search. Civil cases indexed by defendant, plaintiff, on computer since 9/1991, prior records on index cards since 1978. Civil PAT goes back to 1991. Free index search by name at http://apps.kycourts.net/CourtRecords/.

Criminal Records: Access: In person, online. Both court and visitors may perform in person searches. No search fee. Required to search: name, years to search; also helpful: DOB. Criminal records on computer since 9/1991, prior records on index cards since 1978. Criminal PAT goes back to same as civil. Online access same as civil; results show middle initial.

General Information: No adoption, mental, juvenile, or sealed records released. Will not fax documents. Court makes copy: $.25 per page. Self serve: $.25 per page. Certification fee: $5.00. Payee: Circuit Clerk. Personal checks accepted; credit cards are not.

District Court Box 1436, Paducah, KY 42002; 270-575-7270; fax: 270-575-7029; 8:30AM-5PM; 8:30AM-4:30PM T-F (CST). ***Misdemeanor, Civil under $4,000, Eviction, Small Claims, Probate.***

Civil Records: Access: In person, online. Visitors must perform in person searches themselves. Required to search: name, years to search. Civil cases indexed by defendant, plaintiff, on computer since 9/91, on index books since 1978, prior records archived from the 1900s. Visitors may search only from 2PM to 4PM on Thursday. Civil PAT goes back to 1992. PAT results show name, DOB. Free index search by name at http://apps.kycourts.net/CourtRecords/.

Criminal Records: Access: In person, online. Visitors must perform in person searches themselves. Required to search: name, years to search; SSN helpful. Criminal records on computer since 9/91, on index books since 1982, prior records archived from the 1900s. Criminal PAT goes back to same as civil.PAT results show name, DOB. Online access same as civil; results show middle initial.

General Information: No adoption, mental, juvenile, or sealed records released. Will not fax documents. Court makes copy: $.25 per page. Certification fee: $5.00. Payee: District Clerk. Personal checks accepted; credit cards are not.

McCreary County

Circuit & District Court Box 40, Whitley City, KY 42653; 606-376-5041; criminal fax: 606-376-8844; civil fax: same; 8:30AM-4:30PM (EST). ***Felony, Misdemeanor, Civil, Eviction, Small Claims, Probate.***

Civil Records: Access: Mail, in person, online. Both court and visitors may perform in person searches. No search fee. Required to search: name, years to search; also helpful: address. Civil cases indexed by defendant, plaintiff, go back to 1992; on computer back to 1995. Civil PAT goes back to 1995. Free index search by name at http://apps.kycourts.net/CourtRecords/.

Criminal Records: Access: In person, online. Both court and visitors may perform in person searches. No search fee. Required to search: name, years to search, DOB, SSN; also helpful: address. Criminal records go back to 1992; on computer back to 1995. Court directs criminal search requests to Pretrial Svcs in Frankfort, 800-928-6381. Criminal PAT goes back to 1995. Online access same as civil; results show middle initial.

General Information: No adoption, mental, juvenile, or sealed records released. Will fax documents $2.00 per page. Court makes copy: $.25 per page, self serve same. Certification fee: $5.00 per doc. Payee: Circuit Clerk. Personal checks accepted; credit cards are not. Mail requests: SASE required.

McLean County

Circuit & District Court Box 145 (210 E Main St), Calhoun, KY 42327; 270-273-3966; criminal fax: 270-273-5918; civil fax: same; 8AM-4:30PM; till 6PM F (CST). ***Felony, Misdemeanor, Civil, Eviction, Small Claims, Probate.***
Probate fax is same as main fax number.

Civil Records: Access: Mail, in person, online. Both court and visitors may perform in person searches. No search fee. Required to search: name, years to search. Civil cases indexed by defendant, plaintiff, on computer since 1991, prior records on index cards since 1978. Civil PAT goes back to 1991. PAT results show name, DOB. Terminal results also show SSNs. Free index search by name at http://apps.kycourts.net/CourtRecords/.

Criminal Records: Access: In person, online. Both court and visitors may perform in person searches. No search fee. Required to search: name, years to

search, DOB; SSN helpful. Criminal records on computer since 1991, prior records on index cards since 1978. The court refers all written requests to the Administrative Office of Courts in Frankfort. Criminal PAT goes back to same as civil. PAT results show middle initial, DOB. Online access same as civil; results show middle initial.
General Information: No adoption, mental, juvenile, or sealed records released. Will fax documents to local or toll free line. Court makes copy: $.25 per page. Certification fee: $5.00 per doc includes copies. Payee: Circuit Clerk. Personal checks accepted; credit cards are not.

Meade County

Circuit & District Court 516 Hillcrest Dr #4, Courthouse, Brandenburg, KY 40108; 270-422-4961; fax: 270-422-2147; 8AM-4:30AM; til 6:30PM TH (EST). ***Felony, Misdemeanor, Civil, Eviction, Small Claims, Probate.***
Court asks all record requests go to the AOC office in Frankfort.
Civil Records: Access: In person, mail, fax, online. Visitors must perform in person searches themselves. No search fee. Required to search: name, years to search. Civil cases indexed by defendant, plaintiff, on computer since 2/95, prior on index cards. Civil PAT goes back to 2/1995. Free index search by name at http://apps.kycourts.net/CourtRecords/.
Criminal Records: Access: In person, online. Visitors must perform in person searches themselves. Required to search: name, years to search. Criminal records on computer since 2/95, prior on index cards. Criminal PAT goes back to same as civil. Online access same as civil; results show middle initial.
General Information: No adoption, mental, juvenile, or sealed records released. Will not fax documents. Court makes copy: $.25 per page, self serve same. Certification fee: $5.00. Payee: Circuit Clerk. Personal checks accepted; credit cards are not. Mail requests: SASE required.

Menifee County

Circuit & District Court Box 172, 12 Main St, Frenchburg, KY 40322; 606-768-2461; probate phone: same; fax: 606-768-2462; 8AM-4PM (EST). ***Felony, Misdemeanor, Civil, Eviction, Small Claims, Probate.***
Civil Records: Access: In person, online. Visitors must perform in person searches themselves. Required to search: name, years to search. Civil cases indexed by defendant, plaintiff; index on cards from 1978 to 1994. Civil PAT goes back to 1995. PAT results show name only. Free index search by name at http://apps.kycourts.net/CourtRecords/.
Criminal Records: Access: In person, online. Visitors must perform in person searches themselves. Required to search: name, years to search. Criminal records indexed on cards from 1978 to 1994. Criminal PAT goes back to same as civil. PAT results show name only. Online access same as civil; results show middle initial.
General Information: No adoption, mental, juvenile, or sealed records released. Will not fax documents. Court makes copy: $.25 per page. Certification fee: $5.00. Payee: Circuit Clerk. Personal checks accepted, must have local contact info. No credit cards accepted.

Mercer County

Circuit & District Court 224 Main St S, Courthouse, Harrodsburg, KY 40330-1696; 859-734-6306; criminal phone: 859-734-6307; civil phone: 859-734-6305; probate phone: 859-734-6305; fax: 859-734-9159; 8AM-4:30PM (EST). ***Felony, Misdemeanor, Civil, Eviction, Small Claims, Probate.***
Circuit Civil & Criminal 859-734-6306.
Civil Records: Access: In person, online. Visitors must perform in person searches themselves. Required to search: name, years to search. Civil cases indexed by defendant, plaintiff, on computer back to 1993; prior in index books. Civil PAT goes back to 1991. Free index search by name at http://apps.kycourts.net/CourtRecords/.
Criminal Records: Access: In person, online. Visitors must perform in person searches themselves. Required to search: name, years to search; also helpful: DOB, SSN. Criminal records computerized from 1993; prior in index books. Criminal PAT goes back to same as civil. Online access same as civil; results show middle initial.
General Information: No adoption, mental, juvenile, or sealed records released. Court makes copy: $.25 per page, self serve same. Certification fee: $5.00 per cert. Payee: Circuit Clerk. Personal checks accepted; credit cards are not.

Metcalfe County

Circuit & District Court Box 485, 201 E Stockton St, Edmonton, KY 42129; 270-432-3663; fax: 270-432-4437; 8AM-4PM (CST). ***Felony, Misdemeanor, Civil, Eviction, Small Claims, Probate.***
Civil Records: Access: Phone, fax, mail, in person, online. Both court and visitors may perform in person searches. No search fee. Required to search: name, years to search. Civil cases indexed by defendant, plaintiff, on computer back to 1992, prior records on index cards since 1978. Mail turnaround time 1-2 days. Civil PAT goes back to 1978. PAT results show name, DOB. Results include case number. Free index search by name at http://apps.kycourts.net/CourtRecords/.
Criminal Records: Access: Phone, fax, mail, in person, online. Both court and visitors may perform in person searches. No search fee. Required to search: name, years to search, DOB, SSN, signed release. Criminal records computerized from 1992, prior records on index cards since 1980. Mail turnaround time 1-2 days. Criminal PAT goes back to 1982.PAT results show name, DOB. Results include case number. Online access same as civil; results show middle initial.
General Information: No adoption, mental, juvenile, or sealed records released. Fee to fax out file $2.00 1st page; $1.00 each add'l. Court makes copy: $.25 per page, self serve same. Certification fee: $5.00 per doc. Payee: Circuit Clerk. Personal checks accepted; credit cards are not. Mail requests: SASE required.

Monroe County

Circuit & District Court 200 N Main St #B, Tompkinsville, KY 42167; 270-487-5480; probate phone: same; fax: 270-487-0068; 8AM-4PM (CST). ***Felony, Misdemeanor, Civil, Eviction, Small Claims, Probate.***
Civil Records: Access: In person, online. Both court and visitors may perform in person searches. No search fee. Required to search: name, years to search. Civil cases indexed by defendant, plaintiff, kept in files. Civil PAT goes back to 1995. PAT results show middle initial, DOB. Terminal results may include last four digits of SSN. Free index search by name at http://apps.kycourts.net/CourtRecords/.
Criminal Records: Access: In person, online. Both court and visitors may perform in person searches. No search fee. Required to search: name, years to search. Criminal records kept in files. Criminal PAT goes back to same as civil. PAT results show middle initial, DOB. Online access same as civil; results show middle initial.
General Information: No adoption, mental, juvenile, or sealed records released. Will fax back documents. Court makes copy: $.25 per page, self serve same. Certification fee: $5.00. Payee: Circuit Clerk. Personal checks accepted; credit cards are not.

Montgomery County

Circuit & District Court PO Box 327, 1 Court St, Courthouse, Mt Sterling, KY 40353; 859-498-5966; fax: 859-498-9341; 8:30AM-4PM (EST). ***Felony, Misdemeanor, Civil, Eviction, Small Claims, Probate.***
Civil Records: Access: In person, online. Both court and visitors may perform in person searches. No search fee. Required to search: name, years to search. Civil cases indexed by defendant, plaintiff, on computer since 8/1991, on index cards from 1978-1991, prior records on docket books (at archives). Civil PAT goes back to 8/1991. Free index search by name at http://apps.kycourts.net/CourtRecords/.
Criminal Records: Access: In person, online. Visitors must perform in person searches themselves. Required to search: name, years to search. Criminal records on computer since 8/1991, on index cards from 1978-1991, prior records on docket books (at archives). Criminal PAT goes back to same as civil. Online access same as civil; results show middle initial.
General Information: No adoption, mental, juvenile, or sealed records released. Will not fax documents. Court makes copy: $.25 per page. Certification fee: $5.00. Payee: Circuit Clerk. Personal checks accepted; credit cards are not.

Morgan County

Circuit & District Court Box 85, West Liberty, KY 41472; 606-743-3763; criminal fax: 606-743-2633; civil fax: same; 8AM-4PM (EST). ***Felony, Misdemeanor, Civil, Eviction, Small Claims, Probate.*** Probate fax is same as main fax.
Civil Records: Access: Mail, in person, online. Both court and visitors may perform in person searches. No search fee. Required to search: name, years to search. Civil cases indexed by defendant, plaintiff, on computer back to 9/1993. Mail turnaround time 1 day. Civil PAT goes back to 9/1992. Free index search at http://apps.kycourts.net/CourtRecords/.
Criminal Records: Access: Mail, in person, online. Both court and visitors may perform in person searches. No search fee. Required to search: name, years to search. Criminal records computerized from 9/1993. Mail turnaround time 1 day. Criminal PAT goes back to same as civil. Online access same as civil; results show middle initial.
General Information: No adoption, mental, juvenile, or sealed records released. Will fax documents if they have time; fee is $2.00 1st page, $1.00 each add'l. Court makes copy: $.25 per page, self serve same. Certification fee: $5.00 per doc. Payee: Circuit Clerk. Personal checks accepted; credit cards are not. Mail requests: SASE requested.

Muhlenberg County

Circuit Court PO Box 776, Greenville, KY 42345; 270-338-4850 (Felony); fax: 270-338-0177; 8AM-4PM (CST). ***Felony, Civil Actions over $4,000.***
Direct mail felony record requests to state AOC.
Civil Records: Access: In person, online. Visitors must perform in person searches themselves. Required to search: name, years to search. Civil cases indexed by defendant, plaintiff, on computer since 5/1992, records on index since 1978, records archived if before 1985. Civil PAT goes back to 1992. Free search at http://apps.kycourts.net/CourtRecords/.
Criminal Records: Access: In person, online. Visitors must perform in person searches themselves. Required to search: name, years to search, SSN; also helpful: DOB. Criminal records on computer since 5/1992, records on index since 1978, records archived if before 1985. Criminal PAT goes back to same as civil. Online access same as civil; results show middle initial.
General Information: No adoption, mental, juvenile, or sealed records released. Court makes copy: $.25 per page. Certification fee: $5.00. Payee: Circuit Clerk. Personal checks accepted; credit cards are not.

District Court Box 776, Greenville, KY 42345; 270-338-0995; fax: 270-338-0177; 8AM-4PM (CST). ***Misdemeanor, Civil Actions under $4,000, Eviction, Small Claims, Probate.***
Civil Records: Access: In person, online. Visitors must perform in person searches themselves. Required to search: name, years to search. Civil cases indexed by defendant, plaintiff, on computer since 1992, on index books from 1978, archived if before 1985. Civil PAT goes back to 1992. Free index search at http://apps.kycourts.net/CourtRecords/.
Criminal Records: Access: In person only. Visitors must perform in person searches themselves. Required to search: name, years to search. Criminal records on computer since 1992, on index books from 1978, archived if before 1985. The court recommends all requesters go to the State Administrative Office of the Courts. Criminal PAT goes back to same as civil. Online access same as civil; results show middle initial.
General Information: No adoption, mental, juvenile, or sealed records released. Court makes copy: $.25

per page. Self serve: none. Certification fee: $5.00 per doc. Payee: District Clerk. Personal checks accepted; credit cards are not.

Nelson County

Circuit & District Court 200 Nelson County Plaza, Bardstown, KY 40004; 502-348-3648; 8:30AM-4:30PM (EST). ***Felony, Misdemeanor, Civil, Eviction, Small Claims, Probate.***

Civil Records: Access: In person, online. Both court and visitors may perform in person searches. No search fee. Required to search: name, years to search. Civil cases indexed by defendant, plaintiff, on computer since 1990, on index since 1978, prior records archived from 1940. Civil PAT goes back to 1990. Free index search by name at http://apps.kycourts.net/CourtRecords/.

Criminal Records: Access: In person, online. Both court and visitors may perform in person searches. No search fee. Required to search: name, years to search, DOB; also helpful: SSN. Criminal records on computer since 1990, on index since 1978, prior records archived from 1940. Criminal PAT goes back to same as civil. Online access same as civil; results show middle initial.

General Information: No adoption, mental, juvenile, domestic violence or sealed records released. Will not fax documents. Court makes copy: $.25 per page.A drivers' license is required before they'll make copies for you. Certification fee: $5.00 per doc plus copy fees. Payee: Circuit Clerk. Personal checks accepted; credit cards are not.

Nicholas County

Circuit & District Court PO Box 109, 125 Main St, Carlisle, KY 40311; 859-289-2336; fax: 859-289-6141; 8:30AM-4:30PM (EST). ***Felony, Misdemeanor, Civil, Eviction, Small Claims, Probate.***

Civil Records: Access: In person, online. Both court and visitors may perform in person searches. No search fee. Required to search: name, years to search, written request. Civil cases indexed by defendant, plaintiff, on computer since 3/1993, prior records on index cards. Civil PAT goes back to 1993. PAT civil results show middle initial. Free index search by name at http://apps.kycourts.net/CourtRecords/.

Criminal Records: Access: In person, online. Both court and visitors may perform in person searches. No search fee. Required to search: name, years to search, written request. Criminal records on computer since 3/1993, prior records on index cards. Criminal PAT goes back to 1993. PAT criminal results show middle initial. Online access same as civil; results show middle initial.

General Information: No adoption, mental, juvenile, or sealed records released. Will fax documents $2.00 1st page, $1.00 each add'l page. Court makes copy: $.25 per page. Certification fee: $5.00. Payee: Circuit Clerk. Personal checks accepted; credit cards are not.

Ohio County

Circuit & District Court PO Box 67, 130 E Washington, #300, Hartford, KY 42347; 270-298-3671; fax: 270-298-9565; 8:30AM-4:30PM (CST). ***Felony, Misdemeanor, Civil, Eviction, Small Claims, Probate.***

Civil Records: Access: In person, online. Visitors must perform in person searches themselves. Required to search: name, years to search. Civil cases indexed by defendant, plaintiff, on computer since 10/91, Circuit court on index books since 1800s, District court on index books since 1987, prior records archived. Civil PAT goes back to 1992. Free index search at http://apps.kycourts.net/CourtRecords/.

Criminal Records: Access: In person, online. Visitors must perform in person searches themselves. Required to search: name, years to search. Criminal records on computer since 10/91, Circuit court on index books since 1800s, District court on index books since 1987, prior records archived. Criminal PAT goes back to same as civil.PAT results show name, DOB. Online access same as civil; results show middle initial.

General Information: No adoption, mental, juvenile, or sealed records released. Will not fax out documents. Court makes copy: $.25 per page. Self serve: $.25 per page. Certification fee: $5.00 per doc. Payee: Circuit Clerk. No personal checks or credit cards accepted.

Oldham County

Circuit & District Court 100 W Main St, La Grange, KY 40031; 502-222-9837; probate phone: 502-222-5621; fax: 502-222-3047; 8AM-4PM (EST). ***Felony, Misdemeanor, Civil, Eviction, Small Claims, Probate.***

http://courts.ky.gov/courts/circuit/familycourt/sites/henryoldhamtrimble.htm

Criminal record requests are referred to the AOC Pre-Trial Services in Frankfort, 800-928-6381. District Traffic phone number 222-0522.

Civil Records: Access: In person, online. Visitors must perform in person searches themselves. Required to search: name, years to search. Civil cases indexed by defendant, plaintiff, on computer since 1991, on index books since 1978, prior records archived since 1800s. Civil PAT goes back to 9/1991. Free index search by name at http://apps.kycourts.net/CourtRecords/.

Criminal Records: Access: In person, online. Visitors must perform in person searches themselves. Required to search: name, years to search; DOB helpful. Circuit criminal records on computer since 9/1991, on index books since 1978. District criminal on computer since 9/1991, indexed back to 1983. Criminal PAT goes back to 9/1991. PAT results show middle initial, SSN plus DOB year only. Online access same as civil. Online results show DOB year only, plus address and middle initial.

General Information: No adoption, mental, juvenile, or sealed records released. Will fax specific file data for $2.00 per doc plus $1.00 per page. Court makes copy: $.25 per page. Certification fee: $5.00. Payee: Circuit Clerk. Personal checks accepted; credit cards are not.

Owen County

Circuit & District Court PO Box 473, 100 N Thomas, Owenton, KY 40359; 502-484-2232; fax: 502-484-0625; 8AM-4:30PM (EST). ***Felony, Misdemeanor, Civil, Eviction, Small Claims, Probate.***

Civil Records: Access: In person, online. Both court and visitors may perform in person searches. No search fee. Required to search: name, years to search. Civil cases indexed by defendant, plaintiff, on computer since 1992, prior records on index books since 1946. Cases before 1978 transferred to state archives. Civil PAT goes back to 1978. PAT results show name, DOB. Free index search by name at http://apps.kycourts.net/CourtRecords/.

Criminal Records: Access: In person, online. Both court and visitors may perform in person searches. No search fee. Required to search: name, years to search, DOB, SSN. Criminal records on computer since 1992, prior records on index books since 1946. Cases before 1978 transferred to state archives. Court suggests statewide search through AOC. at 502-573-2350. Criminal PAT goes back to same as civil.PAT results show name, DOB. Online access same as civil; results show middle initial.

General Information: No adoption, mental, juvenile, or sealed records released. Will not fax documents. Court makes copy: $.25 per page, self serve same. Certification fee: $5.00. Payee: Circuit Clerk. Personal checks accepted. Money order and cash accepted. No credit cards accepted. Mail requests: SASE required for mail return of any copies.

Owsley County

Circuit & District Court PO Box 130, North Court St, Booneville, KY 41314; 606-593-6226; probate phone: 606-593-6529; fax: 606-593-6343; 8AM-4PM M-F, 8AM-N Sat (EST). ***Felony, Misdemeanor, Civil, Eviction, Small Claims, Probate.***

http://courts.ky.gov/counties/owsley/default.htm

Civil Records: Access: In person, online. Visitors must perform in person searches themselves. Required to search: name, years to search. Civil cases indexed by defendant, plaintiff, on computer since 10/1994, prior records on index cards since 1967. Civil PAT goes back to 1994. PAT results show middle initial, DOB. Free index search by name at http://apps.kycourts.net/CourtRecords/.

Criminal Records: Access: In person, online. Visitors must perform in person searches themselves. Required to search: name, years to search, DOB or SSN. Criminal records on computer since 10/1994, prior records on index cards since 1967. Criminal PAT goes back to same as civil. PAT results show middle initial, DOB. Online access same as civil; results show middle initial.

General Information: No adoption, mental, juvenile, or sealed records released. Will fax out files $2.00 1st page; $1.00 ea add'l. Court makes copy: $.25 per page. Certification fee: $5.00. Payee: Circuit Clerk. Personal checks accepted; credit cards are not.

Pendleton County

Circuit & District Court PO Box 69, 223 Main St, Falmouth, KY 41040; 859-654-3347; fax: 859-654-3405; 8AM-4PM (EST). ***Felony, Misdemeanor, Civil, Eviction, Small Claims, Probate.***

Civil Records: Access: Mail, in person, online. Both court and visitors may perform in person searches. No search fee. Required to search: name, years to search. Civil cases indexed by defendant, plaintiff, on computer since 1922, prior records on index books since 1978. Mail turnaround time 1 week Civil PAT goes back to 1999 for District; 1992 for Circuit. Free index search by name at http://apps.kycourts.net/CourtRecords/.

Criminal Records: Access: In person, online. Both court and visitors may perform in person searches. No search fee. Required to search: name, years to search. Criminal records on computer since 1999, prior records on index books since 1978. Criminal PAT available. Online access same as civil; results show middle initial.

General Information: No adoption, mental, juvenile, or sealed records released. Will not fax documents. Court makes copy: $.25 per page. Certification fee: $5.00. Payee: Circuit Clerk. Personal checks accepted; credit cards are not. SASE not required. SASE or postage included in payment.

Perry County

Circuit Court Box 7433, Hazard, KY 41701; 606-435-6000; fax: 606-435-6143; 8AM-4PM (EST). ***Felony, Civil Actions over $4,000.***

Civil Records: Access: In person, online. Visitors must perform in person searches themselves. Required to search: name, years to search. Civil cases indexed by defendant, plaintiff, on computer since 10/1991, prior records on index cards since 1978. Civil PAT goes back to 1992. Free index search by name at http://apps.kycourts.net/CourtRecords/.

Criminal Records: Access: In person, online. Visitors must perform in person searches themselves. Required to search: name, years to search. Criminal records on computer since 10/1991, prior records on index cards since 1978. Criminal PAT goes back to same as civil. Online access same as civil; results show middle initial.

General Information: No adoption, mental, juvenile, or sealed records released. Court makes copy: $.25 per page. Certification fee: $5.00 per doc. Payee: Circuit Clerk. Personal checks accepted; credit cards are not.

District Court PO Box 7433, 545 Main St, Hazard, KY 41702; 606-435-6002; probate phone: same; fax: 606-435-6143; 8AM-4PM (EST). ***Misdemeanor, Civil Actions under $4,000, Eviction, Small Claims, Probate.***

Civil Records: Access: In person, online. No search fee. Required to search: name, years to search. Civil cases indexed by defendant, plaintiff, on computer since 1991, records on index books since 1978, prior records archived since 1900s. Civil PAT goes back to 1991. Free index search by name at http://apps.kycourts.net/CourtRecords/.

Criminal Records: Access: In person, online. Visitors must perform in person searches themselves. Required to search: name, years to search. Criminal records on computer since 1991, records on index books since 1978, prior records archived since 1900s. Criminal PAT goes back to

same as civil. Online access same as civil; results show middle initial.
General Information: No adoption, mental, juvenile, or sealed records released. Will fax 1 page but not multiple pages. Court makes copy: $.25 per page. Certification fee: $5.00. Payee: District Clerk. Personal checks accepted; credit cards are not.

Pike County

Circuit & District Court PO Box 1002, 179 Division St #336, Pikeville, KY 41502; 606-433-7557; fax: 606-433-7044; 8AM-4:30PM (EST). ***Felony, Misdemeanor, Civil, Eviction, Small Claims, Probate.***
Civil Records: Access: In person, online. Both court and visitors may perform in person searches. No search fee. Required to search: name, years to search. Civil cases indexed by defendant, plaintiff, on computer since 3/1994, prior records on index cards from 1978. Civil PAT goes back to 3/1994. PAT civil results show middle initial. Free index search by name at http://apps.kycourts.net/CourtRecords/.
Criminal Records: Access: In person, online. Both court and visitors may perform in person searches. No search fee. Required to search: name, years to search. Criminal records on computer since 3/1994, prior records on index cards from 1978. Criminal PAT goes back to same as civil. PAT results show middle initial, DOB. Online access same as civil; results show middle initial.
General Information: No adoption, mental, juvenile, or sealed records released. Will not fax documents. Court makes copy: $.25 per page. Certification fee: $5.00 per doc. Payee: Circuit Clerk. Personal checks accepted; credit cards are not.

Powell County

Circuit & District Court Box 578, 525 Washington St, Stanton, KY 40380; 606-663-4141; criminal phone: 606-663-4142; civil phone: same; probate phone: same; criminal fax: 606-663-2710; civil fax: same; 8AM-6PM M,F; 8AM-4:30PM T,W,TH (EST). ***Felony, Misdemeanor, Civil, Eviction, Small Claims, Probate.***
Probate fax is same as main fax number.
Civil Records: Access: Mail, in person, online. Both court and visitors may perform in person searches. No search fee. Required to search: name, years to search. Civil cases indexed by defendant, plaintiff, on computer since 1993, prior records on index cards since 1978. Civil PAT goes back to 1993. Free index search by name at http://apps.kycourts.net/CourtRecords/.
Criminal Records: Access: In person, online. Visitors must perform in person searches themselves. Required to search: name, years to search, DOB; SSN helpful. Criminal records on computer since 1993, prior records on index cards since 1978. This office will not provide criminal record checks. Criminal PAT goes back to same as civil. Online access same as civil; results show middle initial.
General Information: No adoption, mental, juvenile, or sealed records released. Will not fax documents. Court makes copy: $.25 per page, self serve same. Certification fee: $5.00 per cert. Payee: Circuit Clerk. No personal checks; money orders preferred. No credit cards accepted. Mail requests: SASE required for civil.

Pulaski County

Circuit & District Court PO Box 664, 100 N Main, Courthouse Sq 3rd Fl, Somerset, KY 42502; 606-677-4029; probate phone: same; fax: 606-677-4002; 8AM-4:30PM M-F, 8AM-N Sat (EST). ***Felony, Misdemeanor, Civil, Eviction, Small Claims, Probate.***
Civil Records: Access: In person, online. Visitors must perform in person searches themselves. Required to search: name, years to search. Civil cases indexed by defendant, plaintiff, on computer since 1991, prior records on index books from 1978. Civil PAT goes back to 1991. Free index search by name at http://apps.kycourts.net/CourtRecords/.
Criminal Records: Access: Mail, in person, online. Visitors must perform in person searches themselves. Search fee: $10.00 per name but request must be on AOC Form PT-49 only. Required to search: name, years to search. Criminal records on computer since 1991, prior records on index books from 1978. Criminal PAT goes back to same as civil. Online access same as civil; results show middle initial.
General Information: No adoption, mental, juvenile, or sealed records released. Court makes copy: $.25 per page, self serve same. Certification fee: $5.00 per doc. Payee: Circuit Clerk. Personal checks accepted; credit cards are not.

Robertson County

Circuit & District Court PO Box 63, 211 Court St, Mt Olivet, KY 41064; 606-724-5993; fax: 606-724-5721; 8:30AM-4:30PM (EST). ***Felony, Misdemeanor, Civil, Eviction, Small Claims, Probate.***
Civil Records: Access: In person, online. Visitors must perform in person searches themselves. Required to search: name, years to search. Civil cases indexed by defendant, plaintiff, on computer to 1995, previous on index cards. Civil PAT goes back to 1995. Free index search by name at http://apps.kycourts.net/CourtRecords/.
Criminal Records: Access: In person, online. Visitors must perform in person searches themselves. Required to search: name, years to search; also helpful: DOB, SSN. Criminal records on computer to 1995, previous on index cards. Criminal PAT goes back to same as civil. Online access same as civil; results show middle initial.
General Information: No adoption, mental, juvenile, or sealed records released. Will not fax documents. Court makes copy: $.25 per page. Certification fee: $5.00 per doc. Payee: Circuit Clerk. Personal checks accepted; credit cards are not.

Rockcastle County

Circuit & District Court Courthouse Annex, 1st Fl, 205 E Main St., Rm 102, Mt Vernon, KY 40456; 606-256-2581; 8AM-4PM M-W & F; 8AM-6PM Th; 8:30AM-N Sat (EST). ***Felony, Misdemeanor, Civil, Eviction, Small Claims, Probate.***
Civil Records: Access: In person, online. Visitors must perform in person searches themselves. Required to search: name, years to search. Civil cases indexed by defendant, plaintiff, on computer since 1991, index cards from 1978 to 1990, prior are archived at Frankfort. Civil PAT goes back to 1991. PAT results show name only. Free index search by name at http://apps.kycourts.net/CourtRecords/.
Criminal Records: Access: In person, online. Visitors must perform in person searches themselves. Required to search: name, years to search, DOB; SSN helpful. Criminal Records from 1991 to present are available. A form is available to request a criminal history through AOC Retrieval Services. This court provides the form via mail if you provide them a SASE. Criminal PAT goes back to same as civil. PAT results show name only. Online access same as civil; results show middle initial.
General Information: No adoption, mental, juvenile, or sealed records released. Will not fax documents. Court makes copy: $.25 per page. Certification fee: $5.00 per doc. Payee: Circuit Clerk. Personal checks accepted; credit cards are not.

Rowan County

Circuit & District Court 627 E Main, Morehead, KY 40351-1398; 606-784-4210; fax: 606-783-8504; 8:30AM-4:30PM M-TH; 8:30AM-6PM F (EST). ***Felony, Misdemeanor, Civil, Eviction, Small Claims, Probate.***
http://courts.ky.gov/Counties/Rowan/default.htm
Civil Records: Access: In person, online. Visitors must perform in person searches themselves. Required to search: name, years to search. Civil cases indexed by defendant, plaintiff, on computer from 1991, index cards from 1989, archived from 1900. Civil PAT goes back to 1991. Free index search by name at http://apps.kycourts.net/CourtRecords/.
Criminal Records: Access: In person, online. Visitors must perform in person searches themselves. Required to search: name, years to search. Criminal records computerized from 1991, index cards from 1989, archived from 1900. Criminal PAT goes back to 1991. Online access same as civil; results show middle initial.
General Information: No adoption, mental, juvenile, or sealed records released. Will not fax out documents. Court makes copy: $.25 per page. Certification fee: $1.00 per page. Payee: Circuit Clerk. Only cashiers checks and money orders accepted. No credit cards accepted.

Russell County

Circuit & District Court 410 Monument Square, #203, Jamestown, KY 42629; 270-343-2185; probate phone: 270-343-2185; fax: 270-343-5808; 7:30AM-5PM (CST). ***Felony, Misdemeanor, Civil, Eviction, Small Claims, Probate.***
Probate fax is same as main fax number.
Civil Records: Access: In person, online. Visitors must perform in person searches themselves. Required to search: name, years to search. Civil cases indexed by defendant, plaintiff, on computer from 8/1994, index cards from 1978-1994, prior archived at Frankfort. Civil PAT goes back to 1994. Free index search at http://apps.kycourts.net/CourtRecords/.
Criminal Records: Access: In person, online. Visitors must perform in person searches themselves. Required to search: name, years to search. Criminal records computerized from 8/1994, index cards from 1978-1994, prior archived at Frankfort. Criminal PAT goes back to same as civil. Online access same as civil; results show middle initial.
General Information: No adoption, mental, juvenile, or sealed records released. Will not fax documents. Court makes copy: $.25 per page, self serve same. Certification fee: $5.00. Payee: Circuit Clerk. Personal checks accepted; credit cards are not.

Scott County

Circuit & District Court 119 N Hamilton, Georgetown, KY 40324; 502-863-0474; probate phone: same; fax: 502-863-9089; 8:30AM-4:30PM (EST). ***Felony, Misdemeanor, Civil, Eviction, Small Claims, Probate.***
http://courts.ky.gov/Counties/Scott/default.htm
Civil Records: Access: Mail, in person, online. Both court and visitors may perform in person searches. No search fee. Required to search: name, years to search. Civil cases indexed by defendant, plaintiff, on computer since 1992, index cards from 1978 to 1992, in books prior. Mail turnaround time varies. Civil PAT goes back to 1992. PAT results show name, DOB. Terminal results also show SSNs. Free index search by name at http://apps.kycourts.net/CourtRecords/.
Criminal Records: Access: Mail, in person, online. Both court and visitors may perform in person searches. No search fee. Required to search: name, years to search; also helpful: SSN. Criminal records on computer since 1992, index cards from 1978 to 1992, in books prior. Mail turnaround time varies. Criminal PAT goes back to same as civil.PAT results show name, DOB. Terminal results include SSN. Online access same as civil; results show middle initial.
General Information: No adoption, mental, juvenile, paternity and domestic violence records released. Will not fax documents. Court makes copy: $.25 per page, self serve same. Certification fee: $5.00. Payee: Circuit Clerk. Personal checks accepted; credit cards are not. Mail requests: SASE required.

Shelby County

Circuit & District Court 501 Main St, Shelbyville, KY 40065; 502-633-1287; civil phone: 502-633-4736 (Dist Ct); fax: 502-633-0146; 8:30AM-4:30PM (EST). ***Felony, Misdemeanor, Civil, Eviction, Small Claims, Probate.***
Fax for misdemeanor clerk is 502-633-6421.
Civil Records: Access: Mail, in person, online. Both court and visitors may perform in person searches. No search fee. Required to search: name, years to search. Civil cases indexed by defendant, plaintiff, on computer back to 9/91; index cards from 1978 to 1991. Civil PAT goes back to 1991. PAT results show name, DOB. Free index search by name at http://apps.kycourts.net/CourtRecords/.

Criminal Records: Access: In person, online. Visitors must perform in person searches themselves. Required to search: name, years to search, DOB. Criminal records computerized from 9/91; index cards from 1978 to 1991. Criminal PAT goes back to same as civil.PAT results show name, DOB. Online access same as civil; results show middle initial.
General Information: No adoption, mental, juvenile, or sealed records released. Will fax documents $2.00 per page. Court makes copy: $.25 per page. Certification fee: $5.00 per doc. Payee: Circuit Clerk. Personal checks accepted; credit cards are not. Mail requests: SASE required for civil.

Simpson County

Circuit & District Court Box 261, Franklin, KY 42135-0261; 270-586-8910/4241; fax: 270-586-0265; 8AM-4PM (CST). ***Felony, Misdemeanor, Civil, Eviction, Small Claims, Probate.***
http://courts.ky.gov/Counties/Simpson/default.htm
Civil Records: Access: In person, online. Both court and visitors may perform in person searches. No search fee. Required to search: name, years to search. Civil cases indexed by defendant, plaintiff, on computer since 11/92, manual prior to 1978. Civil PAT goes back to 11/1992. Free index search by name at http://apps.kycourts.net/CourtRecords/.
Criminal Records: Access: In person, online. Visitors must perform in person searches themselves. Required to search: name, years to search, DOB, SSN. Criminal records on computer since 11/92, card index back to 1978. Criminal PAT goes back to same as civil. Online access same as civil; results show middle initial.
General Information: No adoption, mental, juvenile, or sealed records released. Court makes copy: $.25 per page. Certification fee: $5.00. Payee: Circuit Clerk. Only cashiers checks and money orders accepted. No credit cards accepted.

Spencer County

Circuit & District Court Box 282, Taylorsville, KY 40071; 502-477-3220; probate phone: same; fax: 502-477-9368; 7AM-4PM; 8AM-11:30AM Sat (EST). ***Felony, Misdemeanor, Civil, Eviction, Small Claims, Probate.***
Civil Records: Access: Mail, in person, online. Visitors must perform in person searches themselves. No search fee. Required to search: name, years to search. Civil cases indexed by defendant, plaintiff, on computer from 8/94 to present, index cards from 1978 to 1994. Civil PAT goes back to 1997. Free index search by name at http://apps.kycourts.net/CourtRecords/.
Criminal Records: Access: Mail, in person, online. Visitors must perform in person searches themselves. No search fee. Required to search: name, years to search, DOB; also helpful: SSN. Criminal records computerized from 8/94 to present, index cards from 1978 to 1994. Mail turnaround time 1-4 days. Criminal PAT goes back to same as civil. Online access same as civil; results show middle initial.
General Information: No adoption, mental, juvenile, or sealed records released. Will not fax documents. Court makes copy: $.25 per page, self serve same. Certification fee: $5.00. Payee: Circuit Clerk. Personal checks accepted; credit cards are not. Mail requests: SASE required.

Taylor County

Circuit & District Court 203 N Court Courthouse, Campbellsville, KY 42718; 270-465-6686; fax: 270-789-4356; 8AM-4:30PM (EST). ***Felony, Misdemeanor, Civil, Eviction, Small Claims, Probate.***
Civil Records: Access: In person, online. Both court and visitors may perform in person searches. No search fee. Required to search: name, years to search. Civil cases indexed by defendant, plaintiff, on computer from 1993 to present, index cards from 1978 to 1993. Civil PAT goes back to mid-1993. PAT results show name only. Free index search by name at http://apps.kycourts.net/CourtRecords/.
Criminal Records: Access: In person, online. Visitors must perform in person searches themselves. Required to search: name, years to search, DOB, SSN. Criminal records computerized from 1993 to present, index cards from 1978 to 1993. Criminal PAT goes back to same as civil. PAT results show middle initial, DOB. Terminal results include SSN. Online access same as civil; results show middle initial.
General Information: No adoption, mental, juvenile, or sealed records released. Will fax documents $2.00 1st page, $1.00 ea add'l. Court makes copy: $.25 per page. Self serve: $.15 per page. Certification fee: $5.00 per doc. Payee: Circuit Clerk. Personal checks accepted; credit cards are not.

Todd County

Circuit & District Court Box 337, 202 E Washington St, Elkton, KY 42220; 270-265-2343 Circ Ct; 270-265-5631 Dist Ct; fax: 270-265-2122; 8AM-4:30PM (CST). ***Felony, Misdemeanor, Civil, Eviction, Small Claims, Probate.***
Civil Records: Access: In person, online. Visitors must perform in person searches themselves. Required to search: name, years to search. Civil cases indexed by defendant, plaintiff, on computer since 1/1993, index cards from 1978-1993, index books prior to 1978. Civil PAT goes back to 1993. PAT results show name only. Free index search by name at http://apps.kycourts.net/CourtRecords/.
Criminal Records: Access: In person, online. Visitors must perform in person searches themselves. Required to search: name, years to search. Criminal records on computer since 1/1993, index cards from 1978-1993, index books prior to 1978. Criminal PAT goes back to same as civil. PAT results show middle initial, DOB. Online access same as civil; results show middle initial.
General Information: No adoption, mental, juvenile, or sealed records released. Will fax back documents. Court makes copy: $.25 per page. Certification fee: $5.00 per doc. Payee: Circuit Clerk. Personal checks accepted; credit cards are not.

Trigg County

Circuit & District Court Box 673, Cadiz, KY 42211; 270-522-6270; probate phone: 270-522-7070; fax: 270-522-5828; 8AM-4PM (CST). ***Felony, Misdemeanor, Civil, Eviction, Small Claims, Probate.*** http://courts.ky.gov/counties/Trigg/
District Court can be reached at 270-522-7070. Probate is a separate index at this same address.
Civil Records: Access: In person, online. Visitors must perform in person searches themselves. Required to search: name, years to search. Civil cases indexed by defendant, plaintiff, on computer from 4/1993 to present, index cards from 1978 to 1993. Civil PAT goes back to 4/1993. PAT results show name only. Free index search by name at http://apps.kycourts.net/CourtRecords/.
Criminal Records: Access: In person, online. Visitors must perform in person searches themselves. Required to search: name, years to search, DOB; SSN helpful. Criminal records computerized from 4/1993 to present, index cards from 1978 to 1993. Criminal PAT goes back to same as civil. PAT results show name only. Online access same as civil; results show middle initial.
General Information: No adoption, mental, juvenile, or sealed records released. Will not fax out case files. Court makes copy: $.25 per page, self serve same. Certification fee: $5.00 per doc. Payee: Circuit Clerk. Only cashiers checks and money orders accepted. No credit cards accepted.

Trimble County

Circuit & District Court Box 248, Bedford, KY 40006; 502-255-3213, 502-255-3525 (District); criminal phone: 502-255-3213; civil phone: 502-255-3525; probate phone: 502-255-3525; criminal fax: 502-255-4953; civil fax: 502-255-3525; 8AM-4:30PM M,T,TH,F 8AM-N Sat (EST). ***Felony, Misdemeanor, Civil, Eviction, Small Claims, Probate.***
Probate records in separate index at this same address. Probate fax- 502-255-3525
Civil Records: Access: Mail, in person, online. Both court and visitors may perform in person searches. No search fee. Required to search: name, years to search. Civil cases indexed by defendant, plaintiff, on computer and in folders from 1993 to present, folders 1978 to 1992, archives prior to 1978. Mail turnaround time 2-4 days. Civil PAT goes back to 1993. Free index search by name at http://apps.kycourts.net/CourtRecords/.
Criminal Records: Access: In person, online. Visitors must perform in person searches themselves. Required to search: name, years to search, DOB; SSN helpful. Criminal records on computer and in folders from 1993 to present, folders 1978 to 1992, archives prior to 1978. Criminal PAT goes back to same as civil. Online access same as civil; results show middle initial.
General Information: No adoption, mental, juvenile, or sealed records released. Will not fax documents. Court makes copy: $.25 per page. Certification fee: $5.00 per doc includes copies. Payee: Circuit Clerk. Only cashiers checks and money orders accepted. No credit cards accepted. Mail requests: SASE required for civil.

Union County

Circuit & District Court PO Box 59, Morganfield, KY 42437; 270-389-0800/0804; criminal fax: 270-389-9887; civil fax: same; 8AM-4PM (CST). ***Felony, Misdemeanor, Civil, Eviction, Small Claims, Probate.***
No searches performed on Thursday. Circuit Court phone- 270-389-1811. Probate fax is same as main fax number.
Civil Records: Access: Mail, in person, online. Both court and visitors may perform in person searches. No search fee. Required to search: name, years to search. Civil cases indexed by defendant, plaintiff, on computer since 6/1994 (new records only); prior on index cards and archived. Mail turnaround time 1 week. Civil PAT goes back to 6/1994. Free index search at http://apps.kycourts.net/CourtRecords/.
Criminal Records: Access: In person, online. Visitors must perform in person searches themselves. Required to search: name, years to search, DOB, SSN. Criminal records on computer since 6/1994 (new records only); prior on index cards and archived. Contact AOC for statewide search by mail; criminal requests to be acquired through Pre-Trial Svcs in Frankfort. Criminal PAT goes back to same as civil. Online access same as civil; results show middle initial.
General Information: No adoption, mental, juvenile, or sealed records released. Will not fax documents. Court makes copy: $.25 per page. Certification fee: $5.00 per doc. Payee: Circuit Clerk. Business checks accepted. No credit cards accepted. Mail requests: SASE required for civil.

Warren County

Circuit & District Court 1001 Center St #102, Bowling Green, KY 42101-2184; 270-746-7400; probate phone: same; fax: 270-746-7501; 8AM-4:30PM (CST). ***Felony, Misdemeanor, Civil, Eviction, Small Claims, Probate.***
Civil Records: Access: In person, online. Visitors must perform in person searches themselves. Required to search: name, years to search. Civil cases indexed by defendant, plaintiff, on computer since 1989. Civil PAT goes back to 2001. PAT results show name aznd some may include an SSN. On the terminal, small claims court records only go back to 2001. Free index search by name at http://apps.kycourts.net/CourtRecords/.
Criminal Records: Access: In person, online. Visitors must perform in person searches themselves. Required to search: name, years to search; also helpful: DOB, SSN. Criminal records on computer since 1990. Criminal PAT goes back to 1990.PAT results show name, DOB. Misdemeanor court records only go back to 2001. Online access same as civil; results show middle initial.
General Information: No adoption, mental, juvenile, or sealed records released. Will fax documents $2.00 1st page, $1.00 ea add'l. Court makes copy: $.25 per page, self serve same. Certification fee: $5.00. Payee: Circuit Clerk. Personal checks accepted. All major credit cards accepted.

Washington County

Circuit & District Court PO Box 346, Springfield, KY 40069; 859-336-3761; probate phone: same; fax: 859-336-9824; 8AM-4:30PM; 8:30AM-N on Sat (EST). ***Felony, Misdemeanor, Civil, Eviction, Small Claims, Probate.***

Civil Records: Access: In person, online. Both court and visitors may perform in person searches. No search fee. Required to search: name, years to search. Civil cases indexed by defendant, plaintiff, on computer, index cards and archived. Civil PAT goes back to 1994. Free index search by name at http://apps.kycourts.net/CourtRecords/.

Criminal Records: Access: In person, online. Both court and visitors may perform in person searches. No search fee. Required to search: name, years to search, DOB. Criminal records on computer, index cards and archived. Mail requests must be made to Pretrial Services, 100 Millcreek Park, Frankfort, KY 40602, 800-928-6381. Criminal PAT goes back to same as civil. Online access same as civil; results show middle initial.

General Information: No adoption, mental, juvenile, or sealed records released. Will not fax documents. Court makes copy: $.25 per page, self serve same. Certification fee: $5.00. Payee: Circuit Clerk. Personal checks accepted; credit cards are not.

Wayne County

Circuit & District Court 125 W Columbia Ave, Monticello, KY 42633-1448; 606-348-5841; fax: 606-348-4225; 8AM-4:15PM; 8:30AM-N Sat (EST). ***Felony, Misdemeanor, Civil, Eviction, Small Claims, Probate.***

http://courts.ky.gov/counties/Wayne/

Civil Records: Access: Mail, in person, online. Visitors must perform in person searches themselves. Search fee: $5.00 per name. Required to search: name, years to search. Civil cases indexed by defendant, plaintiff, on computer from 10/92 to present, index cards from 1978 to 1992. Mail turnaround time 5 days. Civil PAT goes back to 1993. Free index search by name at http://apps.kycourts.net/CourtRecords/.

Criminal Records: Access: Mail, in person, online. Visitors must perform in person searches themselves. Search fee: $5.00 per name. Required to search: name, years to search; also helpful: DOB, SSN. Criminal records computerized from 10/92 to present, index cards from 1978 to 1992. Mail turnaround time 5 days. Criminal PAT goes back to same as civil. Online access same as civil; results show middle initial.

General Information: No adoption, mental, juvenile, or sealed records released. Will not fax documents. Court makes copy: $.25 per page. Certification fee: $5.00 per doc. Payee: Circuit Clerk. Personal checks accepted; credit cards are not. Mail requests: SASE required.

Webster County

Circuit & District Court PO Box 290, 25 US Hwy 41A South, Dixon, KY 42409; 270-639-9160; probate phone: 270-639-9300- district ct; fax: 270-639-6757; 8AM-4PM (CST). ***Felony, Misdemeanor, Civil, Eviction, Small Claims, Probate.***

http://courts.ky.gov/counties/webster/

Civil Records: Access: Fax, mail, in person, online. Both court and visitors may perform in person searches. No search fee. Required to search: name, years to search. Civil cases indexed by defendant, plaintiff, in office from 1987 to present, prior records are at Frankfort archives. Mail turnaround time 1 day. Civil PAT goes back to 6/1994. PAT civil results show middle initial. Free index search by name at http://apps.kycourts.net/CourtRecords/.

Criminal Records: Access: Fax, mail, in person, online. Both court and visitors may perform in person searches. No search fee. Required to search: name, years to search. Circuit criminal records in office from 1987 to present, prior records are at Frankfort archives; District Court to 1999. Mail turnaround time 1 day. Criminal PAT goes back to same as civil. PAT results show middle initial, DOB. Results include last 4 digits of SSN. Online access same as civil; results show middle initial.

General Information: No adoption, mental, juvenile, or sealed records released. Fee to fax out file $2.00 1st page, $1.00 each add'l. Court makes copy: $.25 per page, self serve same. Certification fee: $5.00. Payee: Circuit Clerk. Personal checks accepted; credit cards are not. Mail requests: SASE required.

Whitley County

Williamsburg Circuit & District Court Box 329, 200 Main St, Courthouse Sq, Williamsburg, KY 40769; 606-549-2973; fax: 606-549-3393; 8AM-4PM (EST). ***Felony, Misdemeanor, Civil, Eviction, Small Claims, Probate.***

Circuit court can be reached at 606-549-2973. District court can be reached at 606-549-5162.

Civil Records: Access: In person, online. Visitors must perform in person searches themselves. Required to search: name, years to search. Civil cases indexed by defendant, plaintiff, on computer from 1993 to present, index cards from 1978 to 1993. Civil PAT goes back to 1993. Free index search by name at http://apps.kycourts.net/CourtRecords/.

Criminal Records: Access: In person, online. Visitors must perform in person searches themselves. Required to search: name, years to search; also helpful: DOB, SSN. Criminal records computerized from 1993 to present, index cards from 1978 to 1993. Criminal PAT goes back to same as civil. Online access same as civil; results show middle initial.

General Information: No adoption, mental, juvenile, or sealed records released. Will not fax documents. Court makes copy: $.25 per page. Certification fee: $5.00 per doc. Payee: Whitley Circuit Clerk. Personal checks accepted. Visa/MC and debit cards accepted.

Corbin District Court 805 S Main St #10, Corbin, KY 40701; 606-523-1085; fax: 606-523-2049; 8AM-4PM (EST). ***Felony, Misdemeanor, Civil, Eviction, Small Claims, Probate.***

Civil Records: Access: In person, online. Visitors must perform in person searches themselves. Required to search: name, years to search. Civil cases indexed by defendant, plaintiff, on computer from 1993 to present, index books prior. Civil PAT goes back to 1993. PAT results show middle initial, DOB. Free index search by name at http://apps.kycourts.net/CourtRecords/.

Criminal Records: Access: In person, online. Visitors must perform in person searches themselves. Required to search: name, years to search. Criminal records computerized from 1993 to present, index books prior. Criminal PAT goes back to same as civil. PAT results show middle initial, DOB. Online access same as civil; results show middle initial.

General Information: No adoption, mental, juvenile or sealed records released. Will not fax documents. Court makes copy: $.25 per page. Certification fee: $5.00. Payee: Whitley District Court. Personal checks accepted. Visa/MC accepted.

Wolfe County

Circuit & District Court Box 296, Campton, KY 41301; 606-668-3736; fax: 606-668-3198; 8AM-4:30PM (EST). ***Felony, Misdemeanor, Civil, Eviction, Small Claims, Probate.***

http://courts.ky.gov/Counties/Wolfe/default.htm

Civil Records: Access: Mail, in person, online. Visitors must perform in person searches themselves. No search fee. Required to search: name, years to search. Civil cases indexed by defendant, plaintiff, on computer from 1992 to present, index books prior. Civil PAT goes back to 1992. Free index search by name at http://apps.kycourts.net/CourtRecords/.

Criminal Records: Access: Mail, in person, online. Visitors must perform in person searches themselves. No search fee. Required to search: name, years to search; also helpful: DOB, SSN. Criminal records computerized from 1992 to present, index books prior. Mail requests should be directed to Pretrial Services, 100 Millcreek Park, Frankfort, KY 40601, 502-573-2350. Mail turnaround time same day. Criminal PAT goes back to same as civil. Online access same as civil; results show middle initial.

General Information: No adoption, mental, juvenile, or sealed records released. Court makes copy: $.25 per page, self serve same. Certification fee: $5.00. Payee: Circuit Clerk. Personal checks accepted; credit cards are not. Mail requests: SASE required.

Woodford County

Circuit & District Court 130 Court St, Versailles, KY 40383; 859-873-3711; fax: 859-879-8531; 8AM-4PM M-TH; 8AM-5:30PM F (EST). ***Felony, Misdemeanor, Civil, Eviction, Small Claims, Probate.***

Civil Records: Access: In person, online. Visitors must perform in person searches themselves. Required to search: name, years to search. Civil cases indexed by defendant, plaintiff, on computer from 2/91 to present, index cards from 1978 to 1991. Civil PAT goes back to 1991. Free index search by name at http://apps.kycourts.net/CourtRecords/.

Criminal Records: Access: In person, online. Visitors must perform in person searches themselves. Required to search: name, years to search; SSN helpful. Criminal records computerized from 2/91 to present, index cards from 1978 to 1991. Criminal PAT goes back to same as civil. Online access same as civil; results show middle initial.

General Information: No adoption, mental, juvenile, or sealed records released. Will not fax documents. Court makes copy: $.25 per page, self serve same. Certification fee: $5.00. Payee: Circuit Clerk. Personal checks accepted; credit cards are not.

Kentucky Recording Offices

ORGANIZATION: 120 counties, 122 recording offices. The recording officer is the County Clerk. Kenton County has two recording offices. 80 Kentucky counties are in the Eastern Time Zone (EST) and 40 are in the Central Time Zone (CST). Many offices are open until Noon on Saturdays.

REAL ESTATE RECORDS: Only a few counties will perform real estate searches. Copy fees vary. Certification fee is usually $5.00 per document. Tax records are maintained by the Property Valuation Administrator, designated as the "Assessor" in this section.

UCC RECORDS: Under revised Article 9, Kentucky changed from a "local filing state" to a "central filing state" with filing at the Secretary of State, UCC Branch. Collateral on non-resident debtors were always filed at the state level. Real estate related UCCs are still found at the County Clerk's office. Many counties will not perform UCC searches. Use search request form UCC-11. UCC search fee is $5.00 per debtor name. Copy fees vary widely. Jefferson County has a separate office for UCC filing until June 30, 2001; that office now only handles extensions, terminations and amendments to exisiting filings and will searches for those filings.

TAX LIEN RECORDS: All federal and state tax liens on personal property are filed with the County Clerk, often in an "Encumbrance Book." Most counties will not perform tax lien searches.

OTHER LIENS: Judgments, motor vehicle, mechanics, lis pendens, bail bond

ONLINE ACCESS: A number of counties offer free access to assessor or real estate records. Several other counties offer commercial systems. Search the statewide UCC index free at http://sos.ky.gov/business/ucc/online/.

Adair County

County Clerk, 424 Public Sq, #2, Columbia, KY 42728. Recording, R/E & UCC phone-270-384-2801; fax-270-384-4805; 8AM-4PM (CST) www.adaircounty.ky.gov/cogov/departments/coclerk.htm
Index: All in one. Records indexed on a public use terminal back to 1960. Only the public may search. Copy fee $1.00 per page. Cert fee- $5.00 per cert plus copy fee. Payee- Adair County Clerk. **Other phones:** Elections- 270-384-2801; Vital Records- 270-384-2801. **Property tax/Assessing**- 424 Public Sq, Columbia, KY 42728; 270-384-2801, assessor fax-270-384-4805. hours- 8AM-4PM; 8:30AM-12N Sat Public access computer available.

Allen County

County Clerk, 201 W Main St, Rm 6, Scottsville, KY 42164. Recording, R/E & UCC phone-270-237-3706; fax-270-237-9206; 8AM-4:30PM, 8AM-N Sat. (CST)
Index: All in one. Records indexed on a public use terminal back to 1968; online records only verified back to 1968. Office will perform a UCC search but public must search other records themselves. Search fee $5.00. Copy fee $.25 per page. Cert fee- $5.00 for 1st 3 pages; $.50 each add'l page. Payee- Allen County Clerk. **Other phones:** Treasurer- 270-237-3631; Elections- 270-237-3706. **Property tax/Assessing**- 201 W Main St, Rm 1, PO Box 397, Scottsville, KY 42164; 270-237-3711, assessor fax-270-237-5074. hours- 8:30AM-4:30PM **Online access**- General property valuation information available at www.allenpva.ky.gov.

Anderson County

County Clerk, 151 S Main, Lawrenceburg, KY 40342. 502-839-3041; fax-502-839-3043; 8:30AM-5PM T-F; 8:30AM-6PM M (EST)
Index: All in one. Records indexed on computer back to 1/1/67. Only the public may search. Copy fee $.25 per page. Cert fee- $5.00 per doc includes copy fee. Payee- Anderson County Clerk. **Other phones:** Treasurer- 502-839-3471; Elections- 502-839-3041; Vital Records- 502-564-4212. **Property tax/Assessing**- 101 Ollie Bowen Dr, Lawrenceburg, KY 40342; 502-839-4061, assessor fax- 502-839-3648. (Appraiser/Auditor- 502-839-4061) hours-8:30AM-4:30PM www.andersonpva.com **Online access**- Access to property records for free go to www.pvdnetwork.com/PVDNet.asp?SiteID=100

Ballard County

County Clerk, PO Box 145, Wickliffe, KY 42087. phone-270-335-5168; fax-270-335-3081; 8AM-4PM; 8AM-5:30PM last Friday of month. (CST)
Index: All in one. Record index not computerized. Office personnel or visitors may perform searches. Search fee $5.00 per name. Office can perform mortgage searches. UCC each includes tax liens if requested. Copy fee $.50 per page. Cert fee- $5.00 per cert includes copy fee. Payee- Ballard County Clerk. **Other phones:** Treasurer- 270-335-5176; Elections- 270-335-5168; Vital Records- 270-335-5123. **Property tax/Assessing**- 132 N 4th St, Wickliffe, KY 42087; 270-335-3400, assessor fax- 270-335-3460. hours- 8AM-4PM Public access computer in office for index and records searches.

Barren County

County Clerk, 117 N Public Sq, #1A, Glasgow, KY 42141-2869. phone-270-651-5200; fax-270-651-1083; 8AM-4:30AM M-F; 8AM-N Sat. (CST)
Index: Indexed by years, alpha. Records indexed on a public use terminal back to 1991; delinquent taxes back to 1988. Only the public may search. Copy fee $1.00, if real estate $.25 per page. Marriage cert copy-$6.00. Cert fee- $6.00 per cert includes copy fee. Payee- Barren County Clerk. **Other phones:** Treasurer- 270-651-3338; Elections- 270-651-5200. **Property tax/Assessing**- PO Box 1836, 117 N Public Sq, Assessing Office, #2B, Glasgow, KY 42142-1836; 270-651-2026, assessor fax- 270-651-6895. hours- 8AM-4PM www.bradbaileypva.com/

Bath County

County Clerk, PO Box 609, Owingsville, KY 40360. 606-674-2613; fax-606-674-9526; 8AM-4PM (EST)
Index: All in one. Records indexed on a public use terminal back to 2004. Only the public may search. Copy fee $1.00 per page. Cert fee- $10.00 per doc plus copy fee. Payee- Bath County Clerk. **Other phones:** Treasurer- 606-674-6627. **Property tax/Assessing**- 17 Main St, Owingsville, KY 40360; 606-674-6382, assessor fax- 606-674-9526.

Bell County

County Clerk, PO Box 157, Pineville, KY 40977. Recording, R/E & UCC phone-606-337-6143; fax-606-337-5415; 8AM-4PM M-F; 8AM-N Sat. (EST)
Index: All in one. Records indexed on a public use terminal back to 1978. Office will perform a UCC search but public must search other records themselves. Search fee $5.00 per name. Copy fee $2.00 per page. Cert fee- $5.00 per cert plus copy fee. Payee- Bell County Clerk. **Other phones:** Treasurer- 606-337-2497; Elections- 606-337-6143. **Property tax/Assessing**- 101 Courthouse Sq, PO Box 255, Pineville, KY 40977; 606-337-2720, assessor fax-606-337-2566. hours- 8AM-4PM Public use computer in office for index and records searches.

Boone County

County Clerk, PO Box 874, Burlington, KY 41005. 859-334-2137, R/E recording phone-859-334-3624; fax-859-334-2193; 8:30AM-4:30PM M,Th,F; 8:30AM-6PM T,W. (EST) www.boonecountyky.org/
Index: Separate indices to search include books. Records indexed on a public use terminal back to 1999. Office will perform a UCC search but public must search other records themselves. UCC search fee $5.00. Copy fee $1.00 per page.Real estate record copy- $.50 per page. Cert fee- $5.00 per cert plus copy fee $.50 per page over 3. Payee- Boone County Clerk. Office does sell bulk data, contact Cindy Rich at above phone number. **Online access to Real Estate, Deed, Lien, UCC, Marriage records:** Access the county clerk database through eCCLIX, a fee-based service; $200.00 sign-up and $65.00 monthly. Records go back to 1989; images to 1998. For info, see the website or call 502-266-9445. **Other phones:** Treasurer- 859-334-2150; Elections- 859-334-2130. **Property tax/Assessing**- PO Box 388, Burlington, KY 41005; 859-334-2181, assessor fax- 359-334-2126. Public access terminals available. www.boonepva.org/ **Online access**- Assessor property data is available at www.boonepva.org/

Bourbon County

County Clerk, PO Box 312, Paris, KY 40362-0312. phone-859-987-2142; fax-859-987-5660; 8:30AM-4:30PM M-TH; 8:30AM-6PM F. (EST)
Index: Indexes are 1786-1982, 1982-1989, 1989-present. Records indexed on a public use terminal back to 12/1989. Only the public may search. Copy fee- $.25 per page self serve. UCC copy fee $2.00 per page.Real estate or tax lien record copy- $3.50 per doc. Cert fee- $5.00 per cert includes copy fee, but if over 3 pages add $.50 per page. Payee- Bourbon County Clerk. **Other phones:** Treasurer- 859-987-2139; Elections- 859-987-2142; Vital Records- 502-564-4212. **Property tax/Assessing**- 301 Main St, Courthouse, Ste 15, Paris, KY 40362; 859-987-2152. hours- 8:30AM-4:30PM Public use computer in office for index and records searches.

Boyd County

County Clerk, PO Box 523, Catlettsburg, KY 41129. 606-739-5116; fax-606-739-6357; 8:30AM-4PM Main Office; 10:30AM-6PM Branch. (EST)
Records indexed on computer back to 1979. Only the public may search. Copy fee $.50 per page. Cert fee- $5.00 per doc includes 3 copy pages; each add'l page- $.50. Payee- Boyd County Clerk. **Online access to Real Estate, Deed, Lien records:** Access to the County Clerk online records requires a $10 monthly usage fee but this is only available to local attorneys; records date back to 1/1979. Lending agency data is available. For info, contact Doris Stephen Hollan-Clerk or Kathy Fisher at 606-739-5116. **Other phones:** Treasurer- 606-739-4242. **Property tax/Assessing**- 2800 Louisa St, #302, Catlettsburg, KY 41129; 606-739-5173, assessor fax- 606-739-4188. 8AM-4PM www.boydpva.com/ **Online access**- Access to property tax index is free at www.pvdnetwork.com/PVDNet.asp?SiteID=102.

Boyle County

County Clerk, 321 W Main St, Rm 123, Danville, KY 40422-1837. phone-859-238-1112; fax-859-238-1114; 8:30AM-5PM M; 8:30AM-4PM T-F. (EST)
Index: All in one. Records indexed on a public use terminal back to 1991. Only the public may search. Search fee $1.00 for computer page. Copy fee $.50 per page. Cert fee- $5.00 per cert plus copy fee. Payee- Boyle County Clerk. **Other phones:** Treasurer- 859-238-1118; Vital Records- 502-564-4212 (Frankfort, KY). **Property tax/Assessing**- 321 N Main, #127, Danville, KY 40422; 859-238-1104, assessor fax- 859-238-1131. **Online**-Access property tax index free at www.pvdnetwork.com/PVDNet.asp?SiteID=106. A subscription required for full data; $100 for 120 documents, and up to 1200 docs for $750 per year.

Bracken County

County Clerk, PO Box 147, Brooksville, KY 41004-0147. Recording, R/E & UCC phone-606-735-2952; fax-606-735-2687; 8AM-4PM M,T,TH; 8AM-N W,Sat; Fri til 5PM (EST)
Has an Augusta office; hours- 9AM-4PM Fri. Index: All in one. Records indexed on a public use terminal back to 2001. Only the public may search. Copy fee $.25 per page. Cert fee- $5.00 per cert includes copy fee; add $.50 each page after 3 pgs. Payee- Bracken County Clerk. **Other phones:** Treasurer- 606-735-2125; Elections- 606-735-2952606-735-2952; Vital Records- 606-735-2952 (after 1900). **Property tax/Assessing**- 116 W Miami St, PO Box 310, Brooksville, KY 41004-0147; 606-735-2228, assessor fax- 606-735-2618. (Appraiser/Auditor- 606-735-2228) hours- 8AM-4PM M,T,TH,F; 8AM-N W, Sat Public use terminal available in office for record and index searches.

Breathitt County

County Clerk, 1137 Main St, Jackson, KY 41339. 606-666-3800; fax-606-666-3807; 8AM-4PM M,T,TH,F; 8AM-N W; 9AM-N Sat. (EST)
Index: Separate indices to search include index books, computer. Records indexed on a public use terminal back to 1949. Office will perform a UCC search but public must search other records themselves. Search fee $5.00 per name. Office will only search real estate records if deed book and page number provided. Real estate record copy- $.50 per page. UCC copy fee- $1.50 per page. Cert fee- $5.00 per doc includes copy fee. Payee- Breathitt County Clerk. Bulk data available for purchase, contact Tony Watts. **Other phones:** Treasurer- 606-666-3800; Elections- 606-666-3800. **Property tax/Assessing**- 1137 Main St, Jackson, KY 41339; 606-666-7906, assessor fax- 606-666-7325. hours- 8AM-4PM M,T,TH,F; 8AM-N W

Breckinridge County

County Clerk, PO Box 538, Hardinsburg, KY 40143. Recording, R/E & UCC phone-270-756-6166, UCC recording phone-270-756-2246; fax-270-756-1569; 8AM-4PM, 8AM-N Sat. (CST)
Index: Separate indices to search include deeds, mortgages, leases, misc. Records indexed on a public use terminal back to 09/1996. Only the public may search. Copy fee $1.00 per page. Cert fee- $5.00 per cert plus $.25 per page. Payee- Breckinridge County Clerk. **Online access to Real Estate, Deed, Lien, Mortgage records:** Access to land index back to 1996 and images to 8/20/2007 by subscription at www.titlesearcher.com/countyInfo.php?cnum=S99. **Other phones:** Treasurer- 270-756-2269; Elections- 270-756-2246. **Property tax/Assessing**- PO Box 516, Courthouse Sq, Hardinsburg, KY 40143; 270-756-5154, assessor fax- 270-580-4244.

Bullitt County

County Clerk, PO Box 6, Shepherdsville, KY 40165-0006. Recording, R/E & UCC phone-502-543-2513; fax-502-543-9121; 8AM-4PM M,T,W,F; 8AM-6PM Th. (EST) www.bullittcountyclerk.ky.gov
Index: All in one. Records indexed on a public use terminal back to 010100. Office will perform a UCC search but public must search other records themselves. UCC search per debtor name- $5.00. General copy fee $5.00 per doc.Real estate or tax lien copy- $.30 per page walk-in or $1.50 per page by mail. Cert fee- $5.00 per cert includes copy fee. Payee- Bullitt County Clerk. **Other phones:** Treasurer- 502-543-2262; Elections- 502-543-2513; Vital Records- 502-543-2415; Tax Collector- 502-543-2514. **Property tax/Assessing**- 149 N Walnut St, PO Box 6, Shepherdsville, KY 40165-0006; 502-543-7480, assessor fax- 502-543-8690. hours- 8AM-4PM, till 6PM Th. Public use computer in office for index and records searches.

Butler County

County Clerk, PO Box 449, Morgantown, KY 42261. 270-526-5676; fax-270-526-2658; 8AM-4PM (CST)
Index: Separate indices to search. Records indexed on computer back to 1993. Only the public may search. Copy fee $.25 per page. Cert fee- $5.00 per cert includes 3 copy pages; $.50 each add'l page. Payee- Butler County Clerk. **Other phones:** Treasurer- 270-526-3433; Elections- 270-526-5676. **Property tax/Assessing**- 110 N Main St, PO Box 538, Morgantown, KY 42261; 270-526-3455, assessor fax- 270-526-0692.

Caldwell County

County Clerk, 100 E Market St, Rm 23, Princeton, KY 42445. Recording, R/E & UCC phone-270-365-6754; fax-270-365-7447; 8AM-4PM (CST)
Index: Separate indices to search include deeds, mortgages, liens, leases, fixture filings, power of attorney, wills, marriages, misc. Records indexed on a public use terminal. Office personnel or visitors may perform searches. No RE search fee $5.00 per name. Office will not search real estate records. Copy fee $.50 per page. Cert fee- $5.00 per cert includes copy fee. Payee- Caldwell County Clerk. **Online access to Real Estate, Deed, Lien, Marriage, UCC records:** Register to receive free username and password to search recording indexes free at http://216.135.47.158/search/. **Other phones:** Treasurer- 270-365-9776; Elections- 270-365-6754. **Property tax/Assessing**- 100 E Market St, Princeton, KY 42445; 270-365-7227.

Calloway County

County Clerk, 101 S 5th St, Murray, KY 42071-2569. 270-753-3923, R/E recording phone-270-767-0429; fax-270-759-9611; 8AM-4:30PM (CST)
Index: All in one. Records indexed on a public use terminal back to 11/1987. Office will perform a UCC search but public must search other records themselves. Search fee $5.00 per name. Office will not search real estate records. Copy fee $.10 per page.Real estate or tax lien copy- $.50 per page. Cert fee- 5.00 per cert plus $.50 per page. Payee- Calloway County Clerk. Office does sell bulk data on CD's, contact Antonia at 270-767-0429. **Other phones:** Elections- 270-753-3937; Vital Records- 270-767-0429. **Property tax/Assessing**- 101 S 5th St, Murray, KY 42071; 270-753-3482, assessor fax- 270-759-9611. **Online access**- Access to property data is free at www.ccpva.org/searchdb/default.htm.

Campbell County

County Clerk, 4th & York Sts; Courthouse, Newport, KY 41071. 859-292-3850, R/E recording phone-859-292-3845, UCC recording phone-859-292-3850; fax-859-292-3887; 8:30AM-6PM M; 8:30AM-4PM T-F; 9AM-N Sat. (EST) www.campbellcounty.ky.gov/
Index: Separate indices to search include deeds, mortgages, misc, business org, articles of inc, state & federal tax liens, probate, mechanics liens, court orders, fiscal court. Records indexed on a public use terminal back to 1995. Office will perform a UCC search but public must search other records themselves. UCC search per debtor name- $5.00. Copy fee $1.00 per page.Real estate or tax lien copy- $.50 per page. Cert fee- $5.00 1st 3 pages; $.50 each add'l page plus copy fee. Payee- Campbell County Clerk. Office does sell bulk data. **Other phones:** Treasurer- 859-292-3838; Elections- 859-292-3885. **Property tax/Assessing**- 330 York St, Newport, KY 41071; 859-292-3871, assessor fax- 859-292-0353. (Appraiser/Auditor- 859-292-3871) hours- 8:30AM-4:15PM www.campbellcountyky.org **Online access**- Search county clerk and PVA records at www.campbellcountykyrecords.org. Login and password are required. Subscription fees vary from $5.00 hourly, $25 daily, $100 monthly, $1200 yearly; $200 setup fee applies to monthly or yearly. Also, access to the Property Valuation Administrator assessment search at www.campbellcountykypva.org/ Search by any or all: owner name, parcel ID, etc.

Carlisle County

County Clerk, PO Box 176, Bardwell, KY 42023. Recording, R/E & UCC phone-270-628-3233; fax-270-628-0191; 8:30AM-4PM (CST)
Index: All in one. Records indexed on a public use terminal back to 1974. Only the public may search. Copy fee $.10 per page. Cert fee- $5.00 per cert includes copy fee. Payee- Carlisle County Clerk. **Other phones:** Treasurer- 270-628-3922; Elections- 270-628-3233; Vital Records- 270-628-3233. **Property tax/Assessing**- 77 E Court St, Bardwell, KY 42023; 270-628-5498, assessor fax- 270-628-5498. hours- 8AM-4PM Public access terminal available.

Carroll County

County Clerk, 440 Main St; Courthouse, Carrollton, KY 41008. Recording, R/E & UCC phone-502-732-7005; fax-502-732-7007; 8:30AM-4:30PM (EST)
Index: Separate indices to search include marriage licenses, wills on computer; land records, mortgages, tax liens & UCCs on computer back to 1990. Other indexes prior to 1990. Records indexed on a public use terminal back to 1990. Office will perform a UCC search but public must search other records themselves. UCC search per debtor name- $5.00. Copy fee $.25 per page. Cert fee- $5.00 per cert up to 3 pgs; $.50 each add'l page. Payee- Carroll County Clerk. **Other phones:** Treasurer- 502-732-7000; Elections- 502-732-7005; Vital Records- 502-564-4212. **Property tax/Assessing**- 440 Main St, Courthouse Annex, Carrollton, KY 41008; 502-732-5448, fax- 502-732-6316. Public computer available.

Carter County

County Clerk, 300 W Main St, Rm 232, Grayson, KY 41143. phone-606-474-5188; fax-606-474-6883; 8:30AM-4PM; 8:30AM-N Sat. (EST)
Index: All in one. Records indexed on a public use terminal back to 1975. Office personnel or visitors may perform searches. Search fee $5.00. Office performs no title searches. Copy fee $.50 per page. Cert fee- $5.00 per doc includes copy fee. Payee- Carter County Clerk. **Other phones:** Treasurer- 606-474-9551; Elections- 606-474-5188; Vital Records- 606-474-5188. **Property tax/Assessing**- 300 W Main St, Rm 214, Grayson, KY 41143; 606-474-5663. www.pvdnetwork.com/122/splash.asp **Online access**-

Search property data free at www.pvdnetwork.com/pvdnet.asp?siteid=122. Tax roll and deeper property data also available by subscription.

Casey County

County Clerk, Box 310, Liberty, KY 42539. Recording, R/E & UCC phone-606-787-6471; fax-606-787-9155; 8AM-4:30PM M-F; 8AM-N Sat. (EST) www.kyhometown.com/liberty/
Index: Separate indices to search include multiple volumes back to 1807. Records indexed on a public use terminal back to 1807. Only the public may search. Copy fee $.25 per page. Cert fee- $5.00 per cert plus copy fee. Payee- Casey County Clerk. **Other phones:** Treasurer- 606-787-6154; Elections- 606-787-6471; Vital Records- 606-787-6471. **Property tax/Assessing**- PO Box 38, Liberty, KY 42539; 606-787-7621. (Appraiser/Auditor- 606-787-7621)

Christian County

County Clerk, 511 S Main, Hopkinsville, KY 42240. 270-887-4105, R/E recording phone-270-887-4109, UCC recording phone-270-887-4105; fax-270-887-4186; 8AM-4PM M-W; 8AM-6PM Th; 8AM-4:30PM Fri. (CST)
Index: Various separate indices to search. Records indexed on a public use terminal back to 1987 for Deeds/Mortgages. Only the public may search. Copy fee $.50 per page. Cert fee- $5.00 per cert plus copy fee. Payee- Christian County Clerk. **Online access to Real Estate, Deed, Marriage, Tax Lien, UCC, Will records:** Access recorded docs by subscription; username and password required. Contact Betty via county clerk's office, request must be in writing. $75 set-up and $50 monthly fee. Marriage index back to 1973, Wills back to 8/2002, mortgage index 1940-1984, mortgage and land recording index and images back to 1987. **Other phones:** Treasurer- 270-887-4103; Elections- 270-887-4105. **Property tax/Assessing**- 501 Main St, PO Box 96, Hopkinsville, KY 42240; 270-887-4115, assessor fax-270-887-4120. (Appraiser/Auditor- 270-887-4115) 8AM-4PM **Online**- Access property tax data by subscription at http://christianpva.com/wps-html/TaxRoll/; fees as low as $50 for 60 records.

Clark County

County Clerk, PO Box 4060, Winchester, KY 40392. 859-745-0280, R/E recording phone-859-745-0282, UCC recording phone-859-745-0280; fax-859-745-4251; 8AM-5PM M; 8AM-4PM T-F. (EST)
Index: Separate indices to search. Records indexed on computer back to 1/91. Only the public may search. Copy fee $.25 per page. Cert fee- $5.00 per cert includes copy fee. Payee- Clark County Clerk. **Other phones:** Treasurer- 859-745-0200; Elections- 859-745-0280; Vital Records- 859-745-0282. **Property tax/Assessing**- 34 S Main St, Winchester, KY 40391; 859-745-0250, assessor fax- 859-745-0203. hours- 8AM-4PM **Online access**- Online access by subscription, call office for info and signup.

Clay County

County Clerk, 102 Richmond Rd, #101, Manchester, KY 40962. 606-598-2544; fax-606-599-0603; 8AM-4:30PM M-F; 8AM-N Sat. (EST)
Index: Separate indices to search. Records indexed on computer back to 1990; deed and mortgage records go back 30 years. Only the public may search. Copy fee $.50 per page. Cert fee- $5.00 1st 3 pages, $.50 each add'l page. Payee- Clay County Clerk. **Other phones:** Treasurer- 606-598-2071; Elections- 606-598-2544. **Property tax/Assessing**- 102 Richmond Rd, #200, Manchester, KY 40962; 606-598-3832, assessor fax-606-598-4318. hours- 8AM-4:30PM Public use computer in office for index and records searches.

Clinton County

County Clerk, 212 Washington St; Courthouse, Albany, KY 42602. Recording, R/E & UCC phone-606-387-5943; fax-606-387-5258; 8AM-4PM; 8AM-N Sat. (CST) Index: All in one. Records indexed on a public use terminal back to 1930. Only the public may search. Copy fee $1.00 per page. Cert fee- $3.50 per cert plus copy fee. Payee- Clinton County Clerk. Bulk data available to purchase, contact Jim Elmore for details. **Other phones:** Treasurer- 606-387-5234; Elections- 606-387-5943; Vital Records- 606-387-5943. **Property tax/Assessing**- 100 S Cross St, Albany, KY 42602; 606-387-5938, assessor fax- 606-387-8190. 8AM-4PM Public terminal available.

Crittenden County

County Clerk, 107 S Main, #203; Courthouse, Marion, KY 42064. Recording, R/E & UCC phone-270-965-3403; fax-270-965-3447; 8AM-4:30PM M-F; 8AM-11:30AM Sat. (CST)
Index: All in one. Records indexed on a public use terminal back to 1843. Only the public may search. Office may search real estate records depending on type of search. Copy fee $.50 per page. Cert fee-$5.00 1st 3 pages, $.50 each add'l page. Payee-Crittenden County Clerk. **Other phones:** Treasurer-270-965-5251; Elections- 270-965-3403. **Property tax/Assessing**- 107 S Main, Courthouse, Marion, KY 42064; 270-965-4598, assessor fax- 270-965-9733. www.crittendenpva.com **Online access**- Access to data is available by subscription, fees start at 120 hits for $100. per 12 months; see www.crittendenpva.com/wps-html/TaxRoll/.

Cumberland County

County Clerk, PO Box 276, Burkesville, KY 42717. Recording, R/E & UCC phone-270-864-3726; fax-270-864-5884; 8AM-4:30PM; 8AM-N Sat. (CST)
Index: Separate indices to search include deed, mortgage, lis penden, lien, misc. Records indexed on a public use terminal back to 1969. Only the public may search. Copy fee $.25 per page. Cert fee- $5.00 per cert plus copy fee. Payee- Cumberland County Clerk. **Other phones:** Treasurer- 270-864-3444; Elections- 270-864-3726. **Property tax/Assessing**-PO Box 431, Burkesville, KY 42717; 270-864-5161, assessor fax- 270-864-1471. hours- 8AM-4:30PM Public use computer in office for searches.

Daviess County

County Clerk, PO Box 609, Owensboro, KY 42302. 270-685-8420, R/E recording phone-270-685-8434, UCC recording phone- 270-685-8420; fax-270-685-2431; hours - 8AM-4:30PM (CST) www.daviessky.org/index.asp?PageID=7923
Index: All in one. Records indexed on a public use terminal back to 1990. Only the public may search. Copy fee $.25 per page. Cert fee- $5.00 per cert up to 3 copy pages; $.50 each add'l page. Payee- Daviess County Clerk. **Other phones:** Treasurer- 270-685-8424; Elections- 270-685-8434. **Property tax/Assessing**- 212 St. Anne St, Rm 102, PO Box 609, Owensboro, KY 43202; 270-685-8474, assessor fax- 270-685-8493. www.daviesskypva.org **Online access**- Access to property records free go to www.daviesskypva.org/

Edmonson County

County Clerk, PO Box 830, Brownsville, KY 42210-0830. Recording, R/E & UCC phone-270-597-2624; fax-270-597-9714; 8AM-4:30PM M,T,W,F; 8AM-N Th; 8AM-N Sat. (CST)
Index: Separate indices to search. Records indexed on a public use terminal back to 9/05. Office personnel or visitors may perform searches. Office will search UCC records if time allows. Search fee $5.00 per name. Copy fee $.50 per page. Cert fee- $5.00 per cert includes copy fee. Payee- Edmonson County Clerk. **Other phones:** Treasurer- 270-597-2819; Elections-270-597-2624; Vital Records- 270-597-2624. **Property tax/Assessing**- 110 E Main, Brownsville, KY 42210; 270-597-2381, fax- 270-597-1602.

Elliott County

County Clerk, PO Box 225, Sandy Hook, KY 41171-0225. Recording, R/E & UCC phone-606-738-5421; fax-606-738-4462; 8AM-4PM; 9AM-N Sat. (EST)
Index: Separate indices to search include lis pendens, mortgage, wills, misc prior to 1997; thereafter in one. Record index not computerized. Only the public may search. Copy fee $.50 per page. Cert fee- $5.00 per page includes copy fee. Payee- Elliott County Clerk. **Other phones:** Treasurer- 606-738-5821; Elections-606-738-5421; Vital Records- 606-738-5421. **Property tax/Assessing**- Main & James Sts, PO Box 690, Sandy Hook, KY 41171; 606-738-5090, assessor fax- 606-738-4459. Public use computer in office.

Estill County

County Clerk, PO Box 59, Irvine, KY 40336. Recording, R/E & UCC phone-606-723-5156, UCC recording phone-606-723-5157; fax-606-723-5108; 8AM-4PM M,T,TH,F; 8AM-N W,Sat. (EST)
Index: All in one. Records indexed on a public use terminal back to 1808. Office will perform a UCC search (only verify if on record) but public must search other records themselves. Copy fee $.25 per page. Cert fee- $5.00 per cert includes copy fee. Payee- Estill County Clerk. **Other phones:** Treasurer-606-723-4822; Elections- 606-723-5156. **Property tax/Assessing**- 130 Main St, Rm 104, Irvine, KY 40336; 606-723-4569, assessor fax- 606-723-0073. hours- 8AM-4PM **Online access**- No public use computer terminal. Office will search.

Fayette County

County Clerk, 162 E Main St, Lexington, KY 40507-1334. Recording, R/E & UCC phone-859-253-3344; fax-859-225-5754; 8AM-4:30PM (EST) www.fayettecountyclerk.com/fccweb/
Index: All in one. Records indexed on a public use terminal back to 1970. Office will perform a UCC search but public must search other records themselves. Search fee-$5.00 per name. Copy fee $.50 per page. Cert fee- $5.00 per doc; $.50 per page after first 3 pages. Payee- Fayette County Clerk. **Other phones:** Treasurer- 859-258-3300; Elections- 859-253-3344. **Property tax/Assessing**- 101 E Vine St, 6th Fl, Lexington, KY 40507; 859-254-2722, assessor fax- 859-246-2729. **Online access**- Search property index free at www.fayettepva.com/Main/Home.aspx. No name searching. Subscription fees have been dropped, tax roll/property search info is now free.

Fleming County

County Clerk, 100 Court Sq, Rm 101, Flemingsburg, KY 41041. Recording, R/E & UCC phone-606-845-8461; fax-606-845-0212; 8:30AM-4:30PM M-F; 8:30AM-N Sat. (EST)
Index: All in one. Records indexed on a public use terminal back to 100. Only the public may search. Copy fee $.25 per page; UCC copy fee- $1.00 per page. Cert fee- $5.00 per cert includes copy fee. Payee- Fleming County Clerk. **Other phones:** Treasurer- 606-845-8801; Elections- 606-845-8461; Vital Records- 606-845-8461. **Property tax/Assessing**- 100 Court Sq, Flemingsburg, KY 41041; 606-845-1401, assessor fax- 606-845-1602.

Floyd County

County Clerk, PO Box 1089, Prestonsburg, KY 41653-5089. 606-886-3816; fax-606-886-8089; 8-4:30 M,T,W,Th; 8AM-6PM F; 9AM-N Sat. (EST)
Index: Separate indices to search include hard copy, computer. Records indexed on a public use terminal back to 1985. Only the public may search. Copy fee $.25 per page. Cert fee- $5.00 per doc plus copy fee. Payee- Floyd County Clerk. **Other phones:** Elections- 606-886-3816. **Property tax/Assessing**-149 S Central, Courthouse, Prestonsburg, KY 41653; 606-886-9622, fax- 606-889-0591. hours- 8AM-4PM

Franklin County

County Clerk, PO Box 338, Frankfort, KY 40602. 502-875-8703, R/E recording phone-502-875-8710, UCC recording phone-502-875-8703; fax-502-875-8718; 8-4:30PM (EST) www.franklincountyclerk.org
Index: All in one. Records indexed on a public use terminal back to 1980. Only the public may search. Copy fee $1.00 per page, if real estate $.25 per page. Cert fee- $5.00 per doc includes copy fee. Payee-Franklin County Clerk. **Other phones:** Treasurer-

502-875-8747; Elections- 502-875-8704; Vital Records- 502-564-4212. **Property tax/Assessing**- 315 W Main St, Courthouse Annex, Frankfort, KY 40601; 502-875-8780, assessor fax- 502-226-5495. **Online**- Access to property index is free at www.franklincountypva.com/. Subscription required for full data; $150 per 6 months or $250 per year.

Fulton County

County Clerk, PO Box 126, Hickman, KY 42050. 270-236-2727; fax-270-236-2522; 8AM-4PM (CST)
Record index not computerized. Only the public may search. Copy fee $1.00 per page. Cert fee- $5.00 per cert plus copy fee. Payee- Fulton County Clerk. **Other phones:** Treasurer- 270-236-2594. **Property tax/Assessing**- 2216 Myron Cory Dr #2, Hickman, KY 42050; 270-236-2548, assessor fax- 270-236-2598. www.fultonpva.com

Gallatin County

County Clerk, PO Box 1309, Warsaw, KY 41095. phone-859-567-5411; fax-859-567-5444; 8AM-5PM M; 8AM-4:30PM T-F; 8AM-N Sat. (EST)
Index: Separate indices to search. Records indexed on a public use terminal back to 11/98. Book indexes prior to 1998. Only the public may search. Copy fee $2.00, if real estate or tax lien $.25 per page. Cert fee- $5.00 per cert includes copy fee. Payee- Gallatin County Clerk. **Other phones:** Treasurer- 859-567-5691; Elections- 859-567-5411; Vital Records- 859-567-5411. **Property tax/Assessing**- 100 Washington St, PO Box 883, Warsaw, KY 41095; 859-567-5621, assessor fax- 859-567-7807. 8AM-4:30PM Public use computer in office for index and records searches.

Garrard County

County Clerk, 15 Public Sq, #5; Courthouse Bldg, Lancaster, KY 40444. Recording, R/E & UCC phone-859-792-3071; fax-859-792-6751; 8AM-4PM M,T,TH,F; 8AM-N W,Sat. (EST)
Berea, KY addresses may be in Madison County' parts of Crab Orchard are in Lincoln County. Index: All in one. Records indexed on a public use terminal back to 1990. Office personnel or visitors may perform searches. Search fee $5.00 per name. Office search of real estate records is limited. Office will not search UCC records. Copy fee $5.00 per document. Cert fee- $5.00 per cert plus copy fee. Payee- Garrard County Clerk. **Other phones:** Treasurer- 859-792-4178; Elections- 859-792-3071; Vital Records- 859-792-3071. **Property tax/Assessing**- 15 Public Sq, #5, Courthouse Bldg, Ste 1, Lancaster, KY 40444; 859-792-3291, assessor fax- 859-792-2210. (Appraiser/Auditor- 859-792-3291) **Online access**- Access county property assessment data index free at www.pvdnetwork.com/pvdnet.asp?siteid=121. For full data, a subscription is required; yearly fee or 120 documents for $100.00.

Grant County

County Clerk, 107 N Main St; Courthouse Annex, Williamstown, KY 41097. 859-824-3321; fax-859-824-3367; 8:30AM-4PM M-F; 8:30AM-N Sat. (EST)
Index: All in one. Records indexed on a public use terminal back to 00. Office will perform a UCC search but public must search other records themselves. Search fee $5.00 per name. Copy fee $.25 per record. Cert fee- $5.00 per cert, includes copies. Payee- Grant County Clerk. **Other phones:** Treasurer- 859-824-7561; Elections- 859-824-3321. **Property tax/Assessing**- 101 N Main St, Williamstown, KY 41097; 859-824-6511, assessor fax- 859-824-6502. hours- 8AM-4PM, 8:30AM-N Sat Public use computer terminal available in office. www.grantpva.com/Home/tabid/883/Default.aspx
Online access- Access property index free at www.grantpva.com/PublicSearch/tabid/920/Default.aspx. Subscription required for full data, 120 documents for $100 up to 500 for $250.

Graves County

County Clerk, Courthouse, Mayfield, KY 42066. 270-247-1676, R/E recording phone-270-247-1697, UCC recording phone-270-247-1676; fax-270-247-1274; 8AM-4:30PM M-Th; 8AM-6PM F. (CST)
Index: All in one. Records indexed on a public use terminal back to 7/74. Office will perform a UCC search but public must search other records themselves. Search fee $5.00 per name. General copy fee- $.50 per page; UCC copy fee $2.00. Cert fee- $5.00 per doc plus copy fee. Payee- Graves County Clerk. **Other phones:** Treasurer- 270-247-3626; Elections- 270-247-1676; Vital Records- 270-247-1697. **Property tax/ Assessing**- 101 E South St, #5, Mayfield, KY 42066; 270-247-3301, fax- 270-247-0205. hours- 8AM-4PM

Grayson County

County Clerk, 10 Public Sq, Leitchfield, KY 42754. phone-270-259-5295, UCC recording phone-270-259-3201; fax-270-230-0881; 8AM-4PM M,T,W; 8AM-N Th,Sat; 8AM-5PM F. (CST)
Index: Separate indices to search include UCC, Deed. Records indexed on computer back to 1986. Office will perform a UCC search but public must search other records themselves. Copy fee $.25 per side. Fax copy $6.00, Mail copy $5.00 payable in advance with letter of request. Cert fee- $5.00 per cert includes copy fee. Payee- Grayson County Clerk. **Other phones:** Treasurer- 270-259-5000; Elections- 270-259-3201; Vitals- 270-259-5295; deeds- 270-259-5295. **Property tax/Assessing**- 10 Public Sq, Leitchfield, KY 42754; 270-259-4838.

Green County

County Clerk, 203 W Court St, Greensburg, KY 42743. 270-932-5386; fax-270-932-6241; 8AM-4PM M-W,F; 8-11AM Th,Sat. (CST)
Index: All in one. Records indexed on a public use terminal back to 1983. Only the public may search. Copy fee $1.50 per instrument; $.50 per page generally. Cert fee- $5.00 per cert includes copies. Payee- Green County Clerk. **Other phones:** Treasurer- 270-932-4024. **Property tax/Assessing**- 103 S 1st St, Greensburg, KY 42743; 270-932-7518, assessor fax- 270-932-5412. hours- 8AM-4PM

Greenup County

County Clerk, PO Box 686, Greenup, KY 41144-0686. 606-473-7396 OR 606-473-7394, R/E recording phone-606-473-7396; fax-606-473-5354; 9AM-4:30PM (EST) www.greenupcountyclerk.com
Index: Pre-1993 records on separate indices by doc type. Records indexed on computer back to 1993. Deeds and Mortgages back to 1950's. Office will perform a UCC search but public must search other records themselves. Search fee-$5.00 per name. Copy fee $.50 per page. Cert fee- $5.00 per cert includes copy fee. Payee- Greenup County Clerk. Bulk data available in paper format only; contact Joan Burnett. **Other phones:** Treasurer- 606-473-5350; Elections-606-473-7396; Vital Records- 606-473-7396. **Property tax/Assessing**- 301 Main St, Courthouse, Rm 209, Greenup, KY 41144; 606-473-9984, assessor fax- 606-473-4203. hours- 8AM-4PM Public use computer in office for index and records searches.

Hancock County

County Clerk, PO Box 146, Hawesville, KY 42348. phone-270-927-6117; fax-270-927-8639; 8AM-4PM M-W,F; 8AM-5:30PM Th. (CST)
Index: All in one. Records indexed on a public use terminal back to 1990. Only the public may search. General copy fee $.25 per page. Cert fee- $5.00 per cert plus copy fee. Payee- Hancock County Clerk. **Other phones:** Treasurer- 270-927-8101; Elections-270-927-6117. **Property tax/Assessing**- PO Box 523, 225 Main Cross St, Hawesville, KY 42348; 270-927-6846, assessor fax- 270-927-9955. (Appraiser/Auditor- 270-927-6846) hours- 8AM-4PM **Online access**- View Delinquent tax list free at www.hancockky.us/Government/DelTaxBill.htm.

Hardin County

County Clerk, PO Box 1030, Elizabethtown, KY 42702. Recording, R/E & UCC phone-270-765-2171, UCC recording phone-270-765-4116; fax-270-765-6193; 8AM-4:30PM (EST) www.hccoky.org
Index: Separate indices to search include grantor/grantee. Records indexed on a public use terminal back to 1978 for deeds, 1974 for mortgages. Only the public may search. Copy fee $.25 per page. Cert fee- $5.00 per doc, $.50 after 3 pages for copy fee; $6.00 if to be returned by mail. Payee- Hardin County Clerk. **Online access to Real Estate, Deed, Mortgage, Marriage, Will, Assumed Name records:** Access the Clerk's permanent and temporary records search free at www.hccoky.org/search.asp. Deeds go back to 1978; mortgages to 1974; most other records all available. **Other phones:** Treasurer-270-765-2350; Elections- 270-765-6762; Vital Records- 270-765-2171. **Property tax/Assessing**- PO Box 70, #14 Public Sq, 2nd Fl, Ste 2, Elizabethtown, KY 42702; 270-765-2129, assessor fax- 270-737-5365. (Appraiser/Auditor- 270-765-2129) **Online**- Search County Parcels at www.hardincountypva.com/parcelsearch.asp. Property maps available at www.hardincountypva.com/propertymaps.asp. Form for requests for reproduction of public records found at www.hardincountypva.com/pdfs/repreq.pdf.

Harlan County

County Clerk, PO Box 670, Harlan, KY 40831-0670. Recording, R/E & UCC phone-606-573-3636; fax-606-573-0064; 8:30AM-4:30PM (EST)
Index: All in one. Records indexed on a public use terminal back to 1978. Office will perform a UCC search but public must search other records themselves. UCC search per debtor name- $5.00. Copy fee $1.00 per page.Real estate or tax lien copy-$.50 per page. Cert fee- $5.00 per cert plus copy fee. Payee- Harlan County Clerk. Treasurer- 606-573-4771; Elections- 606-573-3636. **Property tax/ Assessing**- PO Box 206, Harlan, KY 40831; 606-573-1990, assessor fax- 606-573-9141. 8AM-4:30PM

Harrison County

County Clerk, 313 Oddville Rd, Cynthiana, KY 41031. 859-234-7130, R/E recording phone-859-235-0513; fax-859-234-8049; 8:30AM-4:30PM M T W F; 8:30AM-6PM TH. (EST)
Deed room phone 859-235-0513. Index: Separate indices to search include records prior to 1985, after 1985 all documents are on computer. Records indexed on computer from 1985 to present, prior to 1985 they are in book indexes. Office will perform a UCC search but public must search other records themselves. Search fee $3.00 per name; must be written request. Copy fee $.25 per page. Cert fee-$5.00 per doc includes copy fee; add $.50 per page after 1st 3 pgs. Payee- Harrison County Clerk. **Other phones:** Treasurer- 859-234-7136; Elections- 859-234-7130. **Property tax/Assessing**- 313 Oddville Ave, Cynthiana, KY 41031; 859-234-7133, assessor fax- 859-234-7139. hours- 8AM-4:30PM

Hart County

County Clerk, PO Box 277, Munfordville, KY 42765. Recording, R/E & UCC phone-270-524-2751; fax-270-524-0458; 8AM-4PM; 9AM-N Sat. (CST)
Index: All in one. Records indexed on a public use terminal back to 1995. Only the public may search. Copy fee $.50 per page. Cert fee- $5.00 per cert plus copy fee. Payee- Hart County Clerk. **Other phones:** Treasurer- 270-524-9474. **Property tax/Assessing**-118 E Union St, Munfordville, KY 42765; 270-524-2321, assessor fax- 270-524-2322. hours- 8AM-4PM Public use computer in office. www.hartpva.com
Online access- Access to property tax/assessment records at www.hartpva.com/. Must register/pay fee for records.

Henderson County

County Clerk, PO Box 374, Henderson, KY 42419-0374. phone-270-826-3906; fax-270-826-9677; 8AM-4:30PM M-Th; 8AM-6PM F. (CST)
Index: All in one. Records indexed on a public use terminal back to 1992 to present. Office will perform a UCC search but public must search other records

themselves. UCC search per debtor name- $5.00 per name. Copy fee $.25 per file; $2.00 minimum purchase if mail return. Cert fee- $5.00 per cert includes copy fee. Payee- Henderson County Clerk. **Other phones:** Treasurer- 270-826-3233; Elections- 270-826-3906. **Property tax/Assessing**- PO Box 2003, 20 N Main S, Henderson, KY 42419; 270-827-6024, assessor fax- 270-827-6023. (Appraiser/Auditor- 270-826-6024) **Online**- Access county property assessment index free at www.pvdnetwork.com/pvdnet.asp?siteid=104. For full data, a subscription is required; yearly for $275 or $25 per month.

Henry County

County Clerk, PO Box 615, New Castle, KY 40050-0615. 502-845-5705; fax-502-845-5708; 8AM-5PM; M ; 8AM-4PM,T,W,Th F. (EST)
Index: All in one. All records indexed on computer since 801/1996. Only the public may search. Copy fee $.25 per page; $.25 self serve per page. Cert fee- $5.00 includes copy fee; add $.50 per pg copy fee if doc exceeds 3 pages. Payee- Henry County Clerk. **Other phones:** Treasurer- 502-845-5707; Elections- 502-845-5705. **Property tax/Assessing**- 23 S Property Rd, PO Box 11, New Castle, KY 40050; 502-845-5740, assessor fax- 502-845-5709. hours- 8AM-6PM M; 8-4:30 T-F **Online**- Access property assessment index at www.henrypva.com/Default.aspx?tabid=674. A subscription is required for full data; 120 docs for $120 yearly or unlimited docs for $250 yearly.

Hickman County

County Clerk, 110 E Clay; Courthouse, Clinton, KY 42031-1296. 270-653-2131; fax-270-653-2831; 8:30AM-4PM (CST)
Index: Separate indices to search include deeds, mortgages, liens, wills, orders. Records indexed on a public use terminal back to 1962. Office will perform a UCC search but public must search other records themselves. Search fee-$5.00 per name. Copy fee $.25 per page in person. Cert fee- $5.00 per cert includes copy fee. Payee- Hickman County Clerk. Treasurer- 270-653-6195; Elections- 270-653-2131; Vitals- 270-653-6110. **Property tax/Assessing**- 110 E Clay, Courthouse, Clinton, KY 42031; 270-653-5521, assessor fax- 270-653-4248. hours- 8AM-4PM

Hopkins County

County Clerk, 24 Union St, Madisonville, KY 42431. 270-821-7361 x502, R/E recording phone-270-821-7361, UCC recording phone-270-821-7361 x508; fax-270-821-7000; 8AM-4PM (CST)
Their address will change in 2007. Will be located across from the Courthouse on Union St. Index: Separate indices to search include deeds, mortgages, encumbrances, leases and POA, wills, articles of veterans discharge, plats, fixture filings, misc, marriages, county court orders. Land records indexed on computer back to 1976; federal tax liens to 1985. Only the public may search. Copy fee $.50 per page. Cert fee- $5.00 per cert plus copy fee. Payee- Hopkins County Clerk. **Other phones:** Treasurer- 270-825-2666; Elections- 270-821-7361 x201. **Property tax/Assessing**- 25 E Center St, Madisonville, KY 42431; 270-821-3092, fax- 270-825-5012. **Online** - Access property assessment index at www.pvdnetwork.com/PVDNet.asp?SiteID=119. A subscription is required for full data; 120 docs for $120 yearly or unlimited docs for $250 yearly.

Jackson County

County Clerk, PO Box 339, McKee, KY 40447. 606-287-7800; fax-606-287-4505; 8AM-4PM M-F; 8:30AM-N Sat. (EST)
Index: All in one. Records indexed on computer back to 1856. Only the public may search. Will not search UCC records. Copy fee $.25 per page. Cert fee- $5.00 per cert plus copy fee. Payee- Jackson County Clerk. Treasurer- 606-287-8562; Elections- 606-287-7800; Vital Records- 606-287-7800. **Property tax/Assessing**- 101 Main St, McKee, KY 40447; 606-287-7634, assessor fax- 606-287-7079. 8AM-4PM

Jefferson County

County Clerk, PO Box 35339, Louisville, KY 40232-5339. 502-574-5700, Lien/UCC- 502-574-6130, R/E recording phone-502-574-6220; fax-502-574-5909; 8:30-4:30PM (EST) www.jeffersoncountyclerk.org/
Deed Rm phone- 502-574-6220. Index: All in one. Records indexed on a public use terminal back to 1993 for UCCs,1993-2003 for title liens, 1984 for real estate. Only the public may search. Copy fee $2.00 up to 3 pages, $.50 each add'l page. Cert fee- $5.00 per cert includes up to 3 pages of copies. Payee- Jefferson County Clerk. **Online access to Real Estate, Grantor/Grantee, Deed, Lien, Will, Voter Registration records:** Access county land records free at www.landrecords.jcc.ky.gov; 8AM-midnight. Images go back to 6/1992. Check voter registration by name free at https://cdcbp.ky.gov/VICWeb/index.jsp. Also, access to land records for free go to www.landrecords.jcc.ky.gov/records/S0Search.html. **Other phones:** Indexing -502-574-8105. **Property tax/Assessing**- 531 Court Pl #504, Fiscal Court Bldg, Louisville, KY 40202-3393; 502-574-6380. www.pvalouky.org/ **Online access**- Access to the county property valuation administrator's assessment roll is free at www.pvalouky.org. Click on 'Assessment Roll.' No name searching. There is also a subscription service, 502-574-6380 for info/signup.

Jessamine County

County Clerk, 101 N Main St, Nicholasville, KY 40356-1270. Recording, R/E & UCC phone-859-885-4161; fax-859-885-5837; 8AM-5PM M; 8AM-4PM T,W,F; 8AM-N Th; 9AM-N Sat. (EST)
Index: Separate indices to search. Records indexed on a public use terminal back to 1991. Office will perform a UCC search but public must search other records themselves. Copy fee $.50 per page. Cert fee- $5.00 per doc plus copy fee. Payee- Jessamine County Clerk. **Other phones:** Treasurer- 859-885-4500; Elections- 859-885-4161. **Property tax/Assessing**- 101 N Main St, Nicholasville, KY 40356; 859-885-4931, assessor fax- 859-885-9964. hours- 8AM-4PM

Johnson County

County Clerk, 230 Court St, #124; Courthouse, Paintsville, KY 41240. 606-789-2557; fax-606-789-2559; 8AM-4:30PM, 8:30AM-N Sat. (EST)
Index: Indexed by years. Records indexed on a public use terminal back to 1984; deeds back to 1940. Only the public may search. Copy fee $.25 per page. Cert fee- $5.00 per cert plus copy fee. Payee- Johnson County Clerk. **Property tax/Assessing**- 230 Court St, 2nd Fl, #229, Paintsville, KY 41240; 606-789-2564, assessor fax- 606-789-2565. hours- 8AM-4PM

Kenton County (1st District)

County Clerk, PO Box 1109, Covington, KY 41012. 859-392-1600; 392-1653, records, R/E recording phone-859-392-1653, UCC recording phone-859-392-1650; fax-859-392-1639; 8:30AM-4PM M,T,Th,F; 8:30AM-6PM Wed. (EST) www.kcor.org
For records prior to 1991, each of the two Kenton City offices must be searched separately. Index: All in one. Records indexed on a public use terminal back to 1991. Only the public may search. Copy fee- real estate $.25 per page. Cert fee- $5.00 per page includes copy fee. Payee- Kenton County Clerk. Bulk data available for purchase, contact IT Dept at 859-392-1460. **Online access to Real Estate, Deed, Lien, Mortgage records:** Access the county clerks official data or the Property Valuation database at www.kcor.org. To search the summarized guest access, click "Property Data" and click "Guest Access" and "PVA Real Estate". Records go back to 4/15/1991. For full, professional property data you may subscribe; fee for clerk only- $75.00; PVA only $50.00; PVA plus clerk official records- $100 per month. $5.00 per hour and 12-hr for $25 accounts also available. **Other phones:** Treasurer- 859-392-1420; Elections- 859-392-1620; Vital Records- 859-392-1650 (Marriage License Only). **Property tax/Assessing**- 303 Court St, Covington, KY 41011; 859-392-1750, assessor fax- 859-392-1770.

Kenton County (2nd District)

County Clerk, PO Box 38, Independence, KY 41051. 859-392-1692, R/E recording phone-859-392-1691, UCC recording phone-859-392-1692; fax-859-392-1681; 8:30AM-4PM M,T,Th,F; 8:30AM-6PM W. (EST) www.kentonpva.com
For records prior to 1991, each of the two Kenton City offices must be searched separately. Index: All in one. Records indexed on a public use terminal back to 05/1991. Office will perform a UCC search but public must search other records themselves. General copy fee $1.00 per page. Real estate or tax lien copy- $.25 per page. Cert fee- $5.00 per cert includes copy fee. Payee- Kenton County Clerk. **Online Real Estate, Deed, Lien, Mortgage records:** Online access is the same as is it in the Kenton County office in Covington. **Other phones:** Treasurer- 859-392-1420; Elections- 859-392-1620; Vital Records- 502-564-4212 (Frankfort); Divorce Records- 859-292-6521. **Property tax/Assessing**- 303 Court St, Rm 210, Covington, KY 41011; 859-392-1750, assessor fax- 859-392-1770. hours- 8:30AM-4:30PM **Online access**- Access the county Property Valuation database at www.kcor.org. Search for free using "Guest Access." For full, professional property data you may subscribe; fee for username and password is $50. per month, or use hourly account. Also, access the property valuation site for a fee at www.kentonpva.com/ 859-392-1750.

Knott County

County Clerk, PO Box 446, Hindman, KY 41822. 606-785-5651; fax-606-785-0996; 8AM-4PM, 8AM-N Sat. (EST) _Index: Separate indices to search include 10-15 index books. Record index not computerized. Only the public may search. Copy fee $.50 per page. Cert fee- $5.00 per cert plus copy fee. Payee- Knott County Clerk. **Other phones:** Treasurer- 606-785-5592. **Property tax/Assessing**- PO Box 1021, 54 W Main, Hindman, 41822; 606-785-5569, fax- 606-785-5569.

Knox County

County Clerk, 401 Court Sq, #102, Barbourville, KY 40906. Recording, R/E & UCC phone-606-546-3568; fax-606-546-3589; 8:30AM-4PM (EST)
Index: Various indexes 1800-1995, later on computer. Records indexed on a public use terminal back to 1996. Only the public may search. Copy fee $.50 per page. Cert fee- $5.00 per cert includes copy fee. Payee- Knox County Clerk. Treasurer- 606-546-6192; Elections- 606-546-3568; Vitals- 502-564-4212. **Property tax/Assessing**- 401 Court Sq, Barbourville, KY 40906; 606-546-4113, fax- 606-672-5611.

Larue County

County Clerk, 209 W High St, Hodgenville, KY 42748. 270-358-3544; fax-270-358-4528; 8AM-4:30PM M,T,Th,F; 8AM-N W,Sat. (EST) Separate indices to search include grantor/grantee, Tract index. Records indexed on a public use terminal back to 1985. Only the public may search. Copy fee $1.00 per page. Cert fee- $5.00 per page includes copy fee. Payee- Larue County Clerk. **Other phones:** Treasurer- 270-358-4400. **Property tax/Assessing**- 209 W High St, #1, Hodgenville, KY 42748; 270-358-4202, assessor fax- 270-358-0552. hours- 8AM-4PM Public access terminal available.

Laurel County

County Clerk, 101 S Main, Rm 203; Courthouse, London, KY 40741. 606-864-5158; fax-606-864-7369; 8AM-4:30PM; 8:30AM-N Sat. (EST)
Index: All in one. Records indexed on a public use terminal back to 1983. Only the public may search. Copy fee $2.00, if tax lien or real estate $.50 per page. Cert fee- $5.00 for 1st 3 pages plus copy fee. Payee- Laurel County Clerk. **Property tax/Assessing**- 101 S Main, Rm 127, Courthouse, London, KY 40741; 606-

864-2889, assessor fax- 606-864-5387. hours- 8AM-4:30PM; 8:30AM-11:45AM Sat Public access terminals available. **Online access**- Access the property records free at www.pvdnetwork.com/107/splash.asp.

Lawrence County

County Clerk, 122 S Main Cross St, Louisa, KY 41230. Recording, R/E & UCC phone-606-638-4108, UCC recording phone-606-638-0504; fax-606-638-0638; 8:30AM-4PM; 8:30AM-N Sat. (EST)
Index: Separate indices to search. Records indexed on computer from 2000-2005, before 2000 in index books. Office will perform a UCC search for $5.00 per name but public must search other records themselves. Copy fee $.50 per page. Cert fee- $5.00 per cert includes copy fee. Payee- Lawrence County Clerk. **Other phones:** Treasurer- 606-638-4102; Elections- 606-638-4108; Vital Records- 606-638-4108. **Property tax/Assessing**- 122 S Main Cross St, Louisa, KY 41230; 606-638-4743, assessor fax- 606-638-9067. (Appraiser/Auditor- 606-638-4743) hours- 8AM-4PM Public access computer in office for index and records searching. **Online** - Access the property index free at www.pvdnetwork.com/PVDNet.asp?SiteID=108. A subscription is required for full data; 120 documents for $120 yearly up to 1200 docs for $750.

Lee County

County Clerk, PO Box 551, Beattyville, KY 41311. Recording, R/E & UCC phone-606-464-4115; fax-606-464-4102; 8-4 (EST) www.leecounty.ky.gov/
Index: Separate indices to search for most documents. Records indexed on a public use terminal back to 1968. Office will perform a UCC search but public must search other records themselves. Copy fee $.25 per page. Cert fee- $5.00 per cert includes copy fee. Payee- Lee County Clerk. **Other phones:** Treasurer- 606-464-4100; Elections- 606-464-4115; 2nd Main Number -606-464-4116. **Property tax/Assessing**- PO Box 1008, 256 Main, Rm 10, Beattyville, KY 41311; 606-464-4105, assessor fax- 606-464-4102. Public access terminal available.

Leslie County

County Clerk, PO Box 916, Hyden, KY 41749-0916. Recording, R/E & UCC phone-606-672-2193; fax-606-672-4264; 8AM-5PM; 8AM-N Sat. (EST)
Index: Separate indices to search include grantor/grantee, cross. Records indexed on a public use terminal; deeds go back to 1878. Office will perform a UCC search but public must search other records themselves. Copy fee $.50 per page. Cert fee- $5.00 per cert plus copy fee; add $.50 per page is exceeds 3 pages. Payee- Leslie County Clerk. **Other phones:** Treasurer- 606-672-3901; Elections- 606-672-2995; Vital Records- 606-672-2193. **Property tax/Assessing**- PO Box 1591, Courthouse, Hyden, KY 41749; 606-672-2456, assessor fax- 606-672-5611. hours- 8AM-4PM

Letcher County

County Clerk, 156 Main St, #102, Whitesburg, KY 41858. 606-633-2432; fax-606-632-9282; 8:30AM-4PM; 8:30AM-N Sat. (EST)
Index: All in one. Records indexed on a public use terminal back to 1849. Only the public may search. Copy fee $.50 per page. Cert fee- $5.00 per cert includes copy fee. Payee- Letcher County Clerk. **Property tax/Assessing**- 156 Main St, Whitesburg, KY 41858; 606-633-2182, fax- 606-725-9082.

Lewis County

County Clerk, PO Box 129, Vanceburg, KY 41179-0129. Recording, R/E & UCC phone-606-796-3062; fax-606-796-6511; 8:30AM-4:30PM M T Th F; 8:30AM-N Wed. (EST)
Index: Separate indices to search include deeds, mortgages, release, assignments and enc indexed grantor/grantee. Leases & right, misc fixture filings, delinquent tax have separate indexes on computer. Office will perform a UCC search but public must search other records themselves. Copy fee $.50 per page. Cert fee- $5.50 per cert plus copy fee. Payee- Shirley A. Hinton, Lewis County Clerk. **Other phones:** Treasurer- 606-796-2722; Elections- 606-796-2311; Vital Records- 606-796-3062. **Property tax/Assessing**- PO Box 490, 112 2nd St, 1st Fl, Vanceburg, KY 41179; 606-796-2622, assessor fax- 606-796-3950. 8AM-4:30PM except Wed til 2PM

Lincoln County

County Clerk, 102 E Main St #3; Courthouse, Stanford, KY 40484. Recording, R/E & UCC phone-606-365-4570; fax-606-365-4572; 8AM-4PM M-F; 9AM-N Sat. (EST)
Index: All in one. Records indexed on a public use terminal back to 1978. Office will perform a UCC search but public must search other records themselves. Search fee-$5.00 per name. Copy fee $.50 per page. Cert fee- $5.00 per cert plus copy fee. Payee- Lincoln County Clerk. **Other phones:** Treasurer- 606-365-4590; Elections- 606-365-4570. **Property tax/Assessing**- 201 E Main St, #2, Stanford, KY 40484; 606-365-4550, assessor fax- 606-365-2159. hours- 8AM-4PM Public access computer in office for index and records searching.

Livingston County

County Clerk, PO Box 400, Smithland, KY 42081-0400. Recording, R/E & UCC phone-270-928-2162; fax-270-928-2162; 8AM-4PM; til 6PM M (CST)
Index: All in one. Records indexed on a public use terminal back to 1799. Only the public may search. Copy fee $.50 per page, fax copy charges $1.00 per page. Cert fee- $5.00 per cert includes copy fee. Payee- Livingston County Clerk. **Other phones:** Vital Records- 270-928-2162 (old records only-current thru State). **Property tax/Assessing**- PO Box 77, Smithland, KY 42081; 270-928-2524.

Logan County

County Clerk, PO Box 358, Russellville, KY 42276-0358. 270-726-6061 x501, R/E recording phone-270-726-6061; fax-270-726-4355; 8:30-4:30PM (CST)
Index: Separate indices to search include older books, 1992-present on computer. Some records indexed on a public use terminal. Only the public may search. Copy fee $.25 per page. Cert fee- $5.00 per cert includes copy fee. Payee- Logan County Clerk. **Other phones:** Treasurer- 270-726-2167; Elections- 270-726-6061; Vital Records- 270-726-6061. **Property tax/Asscssing**- 229 W 3rd St, Russellville, KY 42276; 270-726-8334, assessor fax- 270-725-9082. hours- 8AM-4PM M-TH; 8AM-5PM Fri. A public access terminal is available. www.loganpva.com **Online access**- Access to property tax and property sale data for fee at www.loganpva.com/wps-html/TaxRoll/

Lyon County

County Clerk, PO Box 310, Eddyville, KY 42038. Recording, R/E & UCC phone-270-388-2331; fax-270-388-0634; 8:30AM-4PM (EST) www.lyoncounty.com/VoterRegistration.htm
Index: Separate indices to search include deeds, mortgages, liens. Records indexed on a public use terminal back to 1977. Only the public may search. Copy fee $1.00 per page. Cert fee- $3.50 per cert plus copy fee. Payee- Lyon County Clerk. **Online access to Deed, Mortgage, Deed, Lien, UCC, Marriage, Will, Plat, Delinquent Tax records:** Access county recorded dockets and images free at http://68.222.251.95/search/. Password and user ID is "public". **Other phones:** Treasurer- 270-388-7193; Elections- 270-388-2331. **Property tax/Assessing**- 500 B W Dale Ave, PO Box 148, Eddyville, KY 42038; 270-388-7271, assessor fax- 270-388-0715. www.lyonpva.com/index.php?p=pvatake

Madison County

County Clerk, 101 W Main St; County Courthouse, Richmond, KY 40475-1415. 859-624-4704; fax-859-624-8474; 8AM-4:30PM M-F; till 6:30PM Th. (EST)
Index: Separate indices to search include books. Records indexed on a public use terminal back to 1986. Office will perform a UCC search but public must search other records themselves. UCC search per debtor name- $5.00. Copy fee $1.00 per page. Cert fee- $10.00 per cert. Payee- Madison County Clerk. **Property tax/Assessing**- 101 W Main St, County Courthouse, Richmond, KY 40475-1415; 859-624-4704, assessor fax- 859-624-8474. hours- 8AM-4:30PM; 8AM-6:30PM Th. Public access computer in office.

Magoffin County

County Clerk, PO Box 1535, Salyersville, KY 41465-1535. Recording, R/E & UCC phone-606-349-2216; fax-606-349-2328; 8:30-4PM; 8:30AM-N Sat. (EST)
Index: Separate indices to search include books. Record index not computerized. Office will perform a UCC search but public must search other records themselves. No fee for search. Copy fee $.25 per page. Cert fee- $5.00 per page plus copy fee. Payee- Magoffin County Clerk. **Other phones:** Treasurer- 606-349-2313; Elections- 606-349-6194; Vital Records- 606-349-2216. **Property tax/Assessing**- PO Box 148, 457 Parkway Dr, Courthouse, Salyersville, KY 41465; 606-349-6198. hours- 8:30AM-4PM

Marion County

County Clerk, 223 N Spaulding; County Office Complex, Lebanon, KY 40033. 270-692-2651; fax-270-692-9811; 8:30-4:30PM; 8:30AM-N Sat. (EST) www.marioncounty.ky.gov/elected/coclerk.htm
Index: All in one. Records indexed on a public use terminal back to 1978 for mortgages, 1957 for deeds. Only the public may search. Copy fee $.25 per page. Cert fee- $5.00 flat fee. Payee- Marion County Clerk. **Other phones:** Treasurer- 270-692-3451. **Property tax/Assessing**- 223 N Spaulding, County Office Complex, #202 270-692-3401, assessor fax- 270-699-2918. hours- 8:30AM-4:30PM Public access terminal available.

Marshall County

County Clerk, 1101 Main St; Courthouse, Benton, KY 42025. 270-527-4740, R/E recording phone-270-527-4746; fax-270-527-4738; 8AM-4:30PM (CST)
Index: Separate indices to search include books, computer. Records indexed on a public use terminal back to 1982. Only the public may search. Copy fee $1.00 per page. Cert fee- $5.00 per cert plus copy fee. Payee- Marshall County Clerk. **Other phones:** Treasurer- 270-527-4725; Elections- 270-527-4740. **Property tax/Assessing**- 1101 Main St, Benton, KY 42025; 270-527-4728, assessor fax- 270-527-4736. **Online access**- Access to PVA property data requires registration, username and password at http://marshallpva.ky.gov/PVA/. Subscription fees apply. 270-527-4728, email marshallpva@ky.gov.

Martin County

County Clerk, PO Box 460, Inez, KY 41224-0485. Recording, R/E & UCC phone-606-298-2810; fax-606-298-0143; 8AM-5PM; 8AM-N Sat. (EST)
Index: All in one. Records indexed on a public use terminal back to 1988. Office personnel or visitors may perform searches. Copy fee $.50 per page. Cert fee- $5.00 per cert includes copy fee. Payee- Martin County Clerk. **Other phones:** Treasurer- 606-298-2800; Elections- 606-298-2810; Vital Records- 606-298-7752. **Property tax/Assessing**- PO Box 341, Inez, KY 41224; 606-298-2807, fax- 606-298-2808.

Mason County

County Clerk, PO Box 234, Maysville, KY 41056. Recording, R/E phone-606-564-3341; fax-606-564-8979; 9AM-5PM M-F; 9-11:30AM Sat. (EST)
Index: Separate indices to search include records prior to 1995 in books (mortgage, deed, encumbrance, etc), after 1994 all documents are indexed on the computer. Records indexed on a public use terminal back to 01/1995. Office will perform a UCC search but public must search other records themselves. UCC search per debtor name- $5.00. Copy fee $.25 per page. Cert fee- $5.00 per first 3 pages, $.25 each add'l page. Includes copy fee. Payee- Mason County Clerk.

Other phones: Treasurer- 606-564-6381; Elections- 606-564-3341. **Property tax/Assessing**- 220 Suton St, Maysville, KY 41056; 606-564-3700, assessor fax- 606-564-7958.

McCracken County

County Clerk, PO Box 609, Paducah, KY 42002-0609. 270-444-4700, R/E recording phone-270-444-4700 x2552; fax-270-444-4704; 8:30AM-4:30PM; M until 5:30PM (CST) http://paducahky.gov/county/elected_officials/county_clerk.php
Index: Separate indices to search include computer and books. Records indexed on a public use terminal back to 1990. Office will perform a UCC search but public must search other records themselves. Search fee-$5.00 per name. Copy fee $.50 per page. Cert fee-$5.00 per cert plus copy fee. Payee- McCracken County Clerk. **Other phones:** Treasurer- 270-444-4725; Elections- 270-444-4700 x2579. **Property tax/Assessing**- 621 Washington St, Paducah, KY 42002-0609; 270-444-4712, assessor fax- 270-444-4714. hours- 8AM-4:30PM Public access terminal available. www.pva.paducah.com/ **Online access**- Access to tax roll data with subscription, username at www.pva.paducah.com/taxroll/records.html.

McCreary County

County Clerk, PO Box 699, Whitley City, KY 42653. 606-376-2411; fax-606-376-3898; 8:30AM-4:30PM M-F; 9AM-N Sat. (EST)
Index: All in one. Records indexed on a public use terminal back to 1964. Office will perform a UCC search but public must search other records themselves. Office will not search real estate records. UCC search per debtor name- $5.00. Copy fee $1.00 per page. Cert fee- $3.50 per cert plus copy fee. Payee- McCreary County Clerk. **Property tax/Assessing**- PO Box 609, Courthouse, Whitley City, KY 42653; 606-376-2514, assessor fax- 606-376-4152. hours- 8:30AM-4:30PM

McLean County

County Clerk, PO Box 57, Calhoun, KY 42327-0057. Recording, R/E & UCC phone-270-273-3082; fax-270-273-5084; 8AM-4:30PM; 9AM-N Sat. (CST)
Index: Pre-1995 records indexed in separate books. Mechanic liens in front of each book. Records indexed on a public use terminal back to 1983 for most instruments; deeds back to 1937; lease/deliq. taxes back to 1995. Office personnel or visitors may perform searches. Search fee-$5.00 per name. Office will not search real estate records. Will not search UCC records. Copy fee $.50 per page. Cert fee- $5.00 per instrument plus copy fee. Payee- McLean County Clerk. **Other phones:** Treasurer- 270-273-9964; Elections- 270-273-3082; Vital Records- 270-273-3291; Sheriff- 270-273-3276; Judge Executive -270-273-03215. **Property tax/Assessing**- PO Box 246, 180 E 2nd St, Calhoun, KY 42327-0246; 270-273-3291, assessor fax- 270-273-9963. 8AM-4:30PM

Meade County

County Clerk, PO Box 614, Brandenburg, KY 40108. 270-422-2152; fax-270-422-2158; 8AM-4:30PM; 9AM-N Sat. (EST) www.countyclerk.meadecounty.ky.gov/
Index: Separate indices to search include grantor/grantee. Records indexed on computer back to 1967. Only the public may search. Copy fee $.10 per page. Cert fee- $5.00 per cert includes copy fee. Payee- Meade County Clerk. **Online access to Real Estate, Deed, Lien, Judgment, Marriage, Will records:** Access to recorder office records is by internet subscription; fee is $50 monthly; signup through recorder office, contact Katrina. Index back to 1828, images to late 1960's. No images of wills. **Other phones:** Treasurer- 270-422-2152; Elections- 270-422-2152. **Property tax/Assessing**- 516 Hillcrest Dr, #3, Brandenburg, KY 40108; 270-422-2178, assessor fax- 270-422-5199. Public terminal available.

Menifee County

County Clerk, PO Box 123, Frenchburg, KY 40322-0123. Recording, R/E & UCC phone-606-768-3512; fax-606-768-6738; 8:30AM-4PM M,T,W,F; 8:30-11:30AM Th,Sat. (EST)
Index: All in one. Records indexed on a public use terminal back to 9/12/97. Office will perform a UCC search but public must search other records themselves. Copy fee $.25 per page. Cert fee- $5.00 per doc plus copy fee. Payee- Menifee County Clerk. Treasurer- 606-768-2931; Elections- 606-768-3512; Vital Records- 606-768-3512. **Property tax/Assessing**- PO Box 36, 12 Main St, Frenchburg, KY 40322; 606-768-3514, fax- 606-768-6738. 7:30-4PM

Mercer County

County Clerk, PO Box 426, Harrodsburg, KY 40330. 859-734-6313, R/E recording phone-859-734-6312; fax-859-734-6309; 8AM-4:30PM (EST)
Index: All in one. Records indexed on a public use terminal back to 1980. Office will perform a UCC search but public must search other records themselves. Copy fee $.10 per page. Cert fee- $5.00 per cert plus copy fee. Payee- Mercer County Clerk. Treasurer- 859-734-6300; Elections- 859-734-6310; Vital Records- 859-734-6312. **Property tax/Assessing**- 113 E Office St, Harrodsburg, KY 40330; 859-734-6330, assessor fax- 859-734-6331.

Metcalfe County

County Clerk, PO Box 25, Edmonton, KY 42129. 270-432-4821; fax-270-432-5176; 8AM-4PM (CST)
Index: All in one. Records indexed on a public use terminal back to 1973. Only the public may search. Copy fee $.25 per page. Cert fee- $5.00 per cert includes copy fee. Payee- Metcalfe County Clerk. **Other phones:** Treasurer- 270-432-3181; Elections- 270-432-4821. **Property tax/Assessing**- PO Box 939, 100 E Stockton, Edmonton, KY 42129; 270-432-3162, assessor fax- 270-432-3163. hours- 8AM-4PM; 8AM-N Sat Public access terminal available.

Monroe County

200 N Main St, #D, Tompkinsville, KY 42167-1548. Recording, R/E & UCC phone-270-487-5471; fax-270-487-5976; 8AM-4PM M-F; 8AM-N Sat. (CST)
Index: Separate books arranged by year. Records indexed on a public use terminal back to 1950. Office will perform a UCC search but public must search other records themselves. Search fee $5.00 per name. Office will not search real estate records. Copy fee $.25 per page. Cert fee- $5.00 per cert includes copy fee. Payee- Monroe County Clerk. Contact Sheila Comer or Patsy Jernigan. **Other phones:** Treasurer- 270-487-5505; Elections- 270-487-5471; Vital Records- 270-487-8821. **Property tax/Assessing**- 200 N Main St, #A, Tompkinsville, KY 42167; 270-487-6401, assessor fax- 270-487-9212. hours- 8AM-4:30PM; 8AM-N last Sat of month. Public access terminal available.

Montgomery County

County Clerk, PO Box 414, Mount Sterling, KY 40353. phone-859-498-8700; fax-859-498-8729; 8:30AM-4PM M-Th; 8:30-5PM F. (EST)
Alternate fax number- 859-498-8738. Index: Separate indices to search include grantor/grantee. Records indexed on computer from 1990 to present and 1796-1899, books from 1900-1989. Office personnel or visitors may perform searches. Search fee-$5.00 per name. Office will not search real estate records. Copy fee $.25 per page. Fee is $.50 for records from 19th or 18th centuries. Cert fee- $5.00 1st 3 pages; $.50 each add'l page. Payee- Montgomery County Clerk. **Other phones:** Treasurer- 859-498-8703; Elections- 859-498-8700; Vital Records- 859-498-8700. **Property tax/Assessing**- 44 W Main St, Mt Sterling, KY 40353; 859-498-8710, assessor fax- 859-498-8719. hours- 8AM-4PM Public access terminal available. www.montgomerypva.com **Online access**- Access to PVA property data requires registration, username and password at www.montgomerypva.com/. Subscription fees apply.

Morgan County

County Clerk, PO Box 26, West Liberty, KY 41472. Recording, R/E & UCC phone-606-743-3949; fax-606-743-2111; 8AM-4PM; 8AM-N Sat. (EST)
Index: Separate indices to search include all records before 1978, marriage records are separate. Records indexed on a public use terminal back to 1/05. Office will perform a UCC search but public must search other records themselves. Copy fee $.50 per page. Cert fee- $5.00 per cert includes copy fee. Payee- Morgan County Clerk. **Other phones:** Treasurer- 606-743-3195; Elections- 606-743-3949; Vital Records- 606-743-3949. **Property tax/Assessing**- PO Box 57, 450 Prestonburg St, West Liberty, KY 41472; 606-743-3349, fax- 606-743-9395. (Appraiser - 606-743-3349) hours- 8AM-4PM. Public access terminal available.

Muhlenberg County

County Clerk, PO Box 525, Greenville, KY 42345. 270-338-1441; fax-270-338-1774; 8AM-4PM; til 6PM F. (CST)
$5.00 to fax back. $1.00 for research per book. Index: Separate indices to search. Records indexed on computer back to 1984. Only the public may search. Office will not search real estate records; no title searches. General copy fee- $.25 per page. Cert fee- $5.00 per cert includes copy fee. Payee- Muhlenberg County Clerk. Elections- 270-338-1441. **Property tax/Assessing**- 109 E Main Cross Rd, Greenville, KY 42345; 270-338-4664, assessor fax- 270-838-0674.

Nelson County

County Clerk, PO Box 312, Bardstown, KY 40004. Recording, R/E & UCC phone-502-348-1830, UCC recording phone-502-564-3490; fax-502-348-1822; 8:30AM-4:30PM M-F; 8AM-11:45AM Sat. (EST)
Index: All in one. Records indexed on a public use terminal back to 1/1/1984. Office will perform a UCC search but public must search other records themselves. Search fee $5.00. Copy fee $.50 per page after 1st three pages. Cert fee- $5.00 per cert plus copy fee. Payee- Nelson County Clerk. **Other phones:** Treasurer- 502-348-1800; Elections- 502-348-1829; Vital Records- 502-564-4212. **Property tax/Assessing**- 113 E Stephen Foster Ave, Bardstown, KY 40004; 502-348-1810, assessor fax-502-348-1812. (Appraiser/Auditor- 502-348-1810) 8:30AM-4:30PM Public terminal available.

Nicholas County

County Clerk, PO Box 227, Carlisle, KY 40311. Recording, R/E & UCC phone-859-289-3730; fax-859-289-3709; 8AM-4:30PM M,T,TH,F; 8AM-5:30PM W. (EST)
Index: All in one. Records indexed on a public use terminal back to 1916. Office personnel or visitors may perform searches. Search fee $5.00 per name. Office will not search real estate records. Will search UCC records. Copy fee $.25 per page. Cert fee- $5.00 per cert plus copy fee. Payee- Nicholas County Clerk. **Other phones:** Treasurer- 859-289-3725; Elections-859-289-3730. **Property tax/Assessing**- PO Box 2, 125 E Main St, Courthouse, Carlisle, KY 40311; 859-289-3735, assessor fax- 859-289-3735. hours-8:30AM-4:30PM Public access terminal available.

Ohio County

County Clerk, 301 S Main St, #201, Hartford, KY 42347. 270-298-4422; fax-270-298-4425; 8AM-4:30PM; 8AM-N Sat. (CST)
Index: All in one. Records indexed on a public use terminal back to 7/90. Only the public may search. Copy fee $.25 per page. Cert fee- $5.00 per cert includes copy fee. Payee- Ohio County Clerk. **Other phones:** Treasurer- 270-298-4403; Elections- 270-298-4423. **Property tax/Assessing**- PO Box 187, 301 S Main St, Hartford, KY 42347; 270-298-4433, assessor fax- 270-298-4435. 8AM-4:30PM Public terminal available. www.pvdnetwork.com/pvdnet.asp?siteid=103 **Online** - Access property index free at www.pvdnetwork.com/PVDNet.asp?SiteID=103. A

subscription is required for full data; 120 documents for $120 yearly up to 1200 docs for $750.

Oldham County

County Clerk, 100 W Jefferson St, LaGrange, KY 40031. Recording, R/E & UCC phone-502-222-9311; fax-502-222-3208; 8:30AM-4PM M-W,F; 8:30AM-6PM Th. (EST) http://oldhamcounty.state.ky.us
Index: Separate indices to search. Records indexed on a public use terminal back to 1980. Office will perform a UCC search but public must search other records themselves. UCC search per debtor name- $5.00. Copy fee $.10 per page. Cert fee- $5.00 per cert first 3 pages; $.50 per add'l page. Payee- Oldham County Clerk. **Online access to Real Estate, Lien, UCC, Marriage records:** Access to the database is through eCCLIX database, a fee-based service; $200.00 sign-up & $65.00 monthly. Real estate records and marriages go back to 1980. UCC images to 2/97. For info, see http://oldhamcounty.state.ky.us/ecclix.stm or call 502-266-9445. **Other phones:** Elections- 502-222-0047. **Property tax/Assessing**- 110 W Jefferson, LaGrange, KY 40031; 502-222-9320, assessor fax- 502-222-4516. 9AM-5PM **Online** - Access property index free at www.pvdnetwork.com/PVDNet.asp?SiteID=111. Subscription required for full data; 25 docs for $25; 50 docs for $50; 75 docs for $75; 150 docs for $150; 300 docs for $250 and 600 docs for $350.

Owen County

County Clerk, 136 W Bryan St, Owenton, KY 40359-0338. 502-484-2213; fax-502-484-1002; 8AM-4PM M,T,TH,F; 8AM-N Sat; Closed Wed. (EST) www.owencounty.ky.gov/clerk/
Index: All in one. Records indexed on a public use terminal back to 1986. Only the public may search. Copy fee $.10 per page. Cert fee- $5.00 per instrument includes copy fee. Payee- Owen County Clerk. Delinquent tax list available. **Online Real Estate, Deed, Lien, Mortgage records:** Access index back to 1986 and images to 4/8/2208 by subscription at www.titlesearcher.com/countyInfo.php?cnum=T66. **Other phones:** Treasurer- 502-484-3557; Elections- 502-484-2213; Vital Records- 502-484-2213. **Property tax/Assessing**- 100 N Thomas, Owenton, KY 40359; 502-484-5172, fax- 502-484-0664.

Owsley County

County Clerk, PO Box 500, Booneville, KY 41314. 606-593-5735; fax-606-593-5737; 8AM-4PM M-F; 8AM-12 Sat. (EST)
Index: All in one. Records indexed on a public use terminal back to 1929. Only the public may search. General copy fee $.25 per page. Cert fee- $5.00 per cert includes copy fee. Payee- Owsley County Clerk. **Other phones:** Treasurer- 606-593-6202; Elections- 606-593-5735. **Property tax/Assessing**- PO Box 337, Booneville, KY 41314; 606-593-6265. 8AM-4PM

Pendleton County

County Clerk, PO Box 112, Falmouth, KY 41040. phone-859-654-3380; fax-859-654-5600; 8:30AM-4PM M-F; 8:30AM-N Sat. (EST)
Index: Separate indices to search include wills, deeds, mortgages, articles in incorporation, mechanic liens, etc. Records indexed on computer back to 10/1/04. Only the public may search. Copy fee $.25 per page. Cert fee- $5.00 per cert for 1st 3 pages; add $.50 per add'l page. Payee- Pendleton County Clerk. This office will provide monthly CD-rom of deeds and mortgage records. **Other phones:** Treasurer- 859-654-4321; Elections- 859-654-3380. **Property tax/Assessing**- 233 Main St, Rm 4, Falmouth, KY 41040; 859-654-6055, assessor fax- 859-654-2999. (Appraiser/Auditor- 859-654-3380) hours- 8AM-4PM M-F; 8:30AM-N Sat. A public terminal is available. www.pvdnetwork.com/120/splash.asp **Online access**- Access property index free at www.pvdnetwork.com/PVDNet.asp?SiteID=120. Subscription and payment arrangement is required to view full data.

Perry County

County Clerk, PO Box 150, Hazard, KY 41702. Recording, R/E & UCC phone-606-436-4614; fax-606-439-0557; 8AM-4PM (EST)
Office will fax back for $1.00 per page. Index: Separate indices to search include grantor/grantee, cclix (computer). Records indexed on a public use terminal back to 99. Only the public may search. Office will check to see if name exists. Copy fee $.50 per page. Cert fee- $5.00 per cert includes copy fee. Payee- Perry County Clerk. Treasurer- 606-436-1816; Elections- 606-436-3090; Vital Records- 502-564-4212. **Property tax/Assessing**- 481 Main St, Courthouse, Hazard, KY 41701; 606-436-4914, assessor fax- 606-439-2214.

Pike County

County Clerk, PO Box 631, Pikeville, KY 41502-0631. 606-432-6240, R/E recording phone-606-432-6208, UCC recording phone-606-432-6240; fax-606-432-6222; 8:30AM-4:30 M,T,W,Th; 8:30-6PM F; 8:30AM-N Sat. (EST)
Index: Separate indices to search include deeds, mortgages, will, liens, art of inc. Records indexed on a public use terminal back to 2007,prior on books. Only the public may search. Copy fee $.50 per page. Cert fee- $5.00 per cert includes copy fee. Payee- Pike County Clerk. **Other phones:** Elections- 606-432-6205; Vital Records- 606-432-6211. **Property tax/Assessing**- 146 Main St, #303, Pikeville, KY 41502; 606-432-6201, assessor fax- 606-432-2296. hours- 8AM-4:30PM Public access terminal available.

Powell County

County Clerk, PO Box 548, Stanton, KY 40380. Recording, R/E & UCC phone-606-663-6444; fax-606-663-6406; 9AM-6PM M & F; 9AM-4:30PM T & W; 9AM-Noon Th. (EST)
Index: All in one. Records indexed on a public use terminal back to 9/91; mortgages and deeds back to 1864. Only the public may search. Copy fee $.50 per page. Cert fee- $5.00 per cert includes copy fee. Payee- Powell County Clerk. Bulk data available for purchase, printouts for dates requested at $.50 per page. **Other phones:** Treasurer- 606-663-2834; Elections- 606-663-6444; Vital Records- 502-564-4212. **Property tax/Assessing**- PO Box 277, Stanton, KY 40380; 606-663-4184, fax- 606-663-0947. (Appraiser-606-663-4184). No public terminal.

Pulaski County

County Clerk, PO Box 724, Somerset, KY 42502. Recording, R/E & UCC phone-606-679-2042; fax-606-678-0073; 8AM-4:30PM (EST)
Index: All in one. Records indexed on a public use terminal back to 1990. Only the public may search. Copy fee $.50 per page. Cert fee- $5.00 per cert plus copy fee. Payee- Pulaski County Clerk. **Other phones:** Treasurer- 606-679-1311; Elections- 606-679-2042; Vital Records- 877-817-7362. **Property tax/Assessing**- PO Box 110, Somerset, KY 42502; 606-679-1812, assessor fax- 606-678-5724. www.pulaskipva.com **Online access**- Access to property index is free at www.pulaskipva.com/. A subscription is required for full data; 100 records a month for $25 up to 5000 a year for $600.

Robertson County

County Clerk, PO Box 75, Mount Olivet, KY 41064. 606-724-5212; fax-606-724-5022; 9AM-N, 1-4PM M,T,Th,F; 9AM-N Wed, Sat. (EST)
Index: All in one. Records indexed on computer back to 1967. Only the public may search. Copy fee $.10 per page. Cert fee- $6.50 per cert, up to 3 pages. Payee- Robertson County Clerk. **Other phones:** Elections- 606-724-5212; Vital Records- 606-724-5212. **Property tax/Assessing**- 26 Court St, Courthouse Annex, Mount Olivet, KY 41064; 606-724-5213, assessor fax- 606-724-5022. hours- 7:30AM-N 1PM-4PM M,T,TH,F; 7:30AM-N W

Rockcastle County

County Clerk, 205 E Main St, #6, Mount Vernon, KY 40456. phone-606-256-2831; fax-606-256-4302; 8:30AM-4PM; 8:30AM-N Sat. (EST)
Index: Separate indices to search include deeds, mortgages; like documents in single indices. Record index not computerized. Office will perform a UCC search but public must search other records themselves. UCC search per debtor name- $5.00. Copy fee $.25 per page. Cert fee- $5.00 per doc plus copy fee. Payee- Rockcastle County Clerk. **Other phones:** Treasurer- 606-256-3623; Elections- 606-256-2831; Vital Records- 606-256-2831. **Property tax/Assessing**- 205 E Main St, Mount Vernon, KY 40456; 606-256-4194, assessor fax- 606-256-8624. hours- 8AM-4PM

Rowan County

County Clerk, 627 E Main St, 2nd Fl; Courthouse, Morehead, KY 40351. Recording, R/E & UCC phone-606-784-5212; fax-606-784-2923; 8AM-4PM M-TH; 8AM-6PM F. (EST)
Index: All in one. Records indexed on a public use terminal back to 1880. Only the public may search. Copy fee $.25 per page; Fax copy $1.00 per page. Cert fee- $5.00 per cert, copy fee included. Payee- Rowan County Clerk. **Other phones:** Treasurer- 606-784-4211; Elections- 606-784-5212; Vital Records- 502-564-4212. **Property tax/Assessing**- 627 E Main St, Courthouse, 2nd Fl, Morehead, KY 40351; 606-784-5512, assessor fax- 606-784-0030. hours- 8:30AM-4:30PM www.rowanpva.com **Online access**- Access to county tax rolls requires registration and password; fees apply, see www.rowanpva.com/wps-html/TaxRoll/. 120 records over 12 months is $100, up to 1200 records for $750.

Russell County

County Clerk, PO Box 579, Jamestown, KY 42629-0579. 270-343-2125; fax-270-343-4700; 8AM-4PM M-F; 8-11AM Sat. (CST)
Index: Separate indices to search include grantor/grantee. Record index not computerized. Office personnel or visitors may perform searches. Search fee $5.00 per name; must be written request. Copy fee $.25 per page. Cert fee- $5.00 per cert includes copy fee. Payee- Russell County Clerk. **Other phones:** Treasurer- 270-343-2112; Elections- 270-343-2125. **Property tax/Assessing**- 410 Monument Sq, Jamestown, KY 42629; 270-343-4395, assessor fax- 270-343-5198.

Scott County

County Clerk, 101 E Main St; Courthouse, Georgetown, KY 40324-1794. 502-863-7875; fax-502-863-7898; 8:30AM-6PM M-Th; 8:30AM-4:30PM F. (EST) www.scottcountyclerk.com
Index: All in one. Records indexed on a public use terminal back to 5/93. Office will perform a UCC search but public must search other records themselves. Search fee-$5.00 per name. Copy fee $.25 per page. Cert fee- $5.00 per cert includes copy fee. Payee- Scott County Clerk. **Other phones:** Treasurer- 502-863-7850. **Property tax/Assessing**- 101 E Main St, Courthouse, Georgetown, KY 40324; 502-863-7885, assessor fax- 502-863-7899. www.scpva.com **Online**- Access property data after registration, at http://scpva.com/resources.html

Shelby County

County Clerk, PO Box 819, Shelbyville, KY 40066-0819. Recording, R/E & UCC phone-502-633-4410, UCC recording phone-502-513-0265; fax-502-633-7887; 8:30AM-4:30PM M,T,W,F; 8:30AM-6PM Th. (EST) www.shelbycountyclerk.com
Index: All in one. Records indexed on a public use terminal back to 1960. Only the public may search. Copy fee $1.00 per page.Real estate record copy- $.10 per page. Cert fee- $5.00 per cert plus copy fee. Payee- Shelby County Clerk. **Online access to Real Estate, Deed records:** Access via the eCCLIX system at www.shelbycountyclerk.com/ecclix.stm. Images go back to 1998; index to 1995. Sign-up fee is

$100 plus $65 per month for unlimited access. For more info, phone 502-266-9445. **Other phones:** Treasurer- 502-633-1220; Elections- 502-633-4410; Vital Records- 502-564-4212. **Property tax/Assessing**- 501 Washington, Shelbyville, KY 40065; 502-633-4403, assessor fax- 502-633-4408. **Online access**- Access to property index is free at www.pvdnetwork.com/PVDNet.asp?SiteID=112. A subscription is required for full data; 120 records for $100 or unlimited access for $250 yearly.

Simpson County

County Clerk, PO Box 268, Franklin, KY 42135-0268. Recording, R/E & UCC phone-270-586-8161; fax-270-586-6464; 8AM-4PM (CST) www.simpsoncountyclerk.ky.gov
Index: All in one. Records indexed on a public use terminal back to 1997. Only the public may search. Copy fee $.50 per page. Cert fee- $6.00 per cert plus copy fee. Payee- Simpson County Clerk. **Other phones:** Treasurer- 270-586-7184; Elections- 270-586-8161; Vital Records- 270-586-8161. **Property tax/Assessing**- PO Box 424, 103 W Cedar St, County Annex Bldg, Franklin, KY 42135; 270-586-4261, assessor fax- 270-586-0278.

Spencer County

County Clerk, PO Box 544, Taylorsville, KY 40071. 502-477-3215; fax-502-477-3216; 8AM-4:30PM M-F; til 6PM Th; 8AM-11:30 Sat. (EST)
Index: Indices by instrument type. Records indexed on a public use terminal back to 1960. Office will perform a UCC search but public must search other records themselves. Search fee $5.00 per name or parcel. Will search delinquent taxes. Copy fee $.25 per page. Cert fee- $5.00 per cert includes copy fee. Payee- Spencer County Clerk. **Other phones:** Treasurer- 502-477-3211; Elections- 502-477-3215. **Property tax/Assessing**- Courthouse, Main St, Taylorsville, KY 40071; 502-477-3207, assessor fax- 502-477-3208. hours- 8AM-4PM

Taylor County

County Clerk, 203 N Court St, #5, Campbellsville, KY 42718-2298. Recording, R/E & UCC phone-270-465-6677; fax-270-789-1144; 8AM-4:30PM M-Th; 8AM-5PM F. (EST)
Index: All in one. Records indexed on a public use terminal back to 1848. Only the public may search. General copy fee $.25 per page. Cert fee- $5.00. Payee- Taylor County Clerk. **Other phones:** Treasurer- 270-789-1008. **Property tax/Assessing**- 203 N Court St, #8, Courthouse, Campbellsville, KY 42718; 270-465-5811, assessor fax- 270-789-0782. hours- 8AM-4:30PM Public access terminal available.

Todd County

County Clerk, PO Box 307, Elkton, KY 42220. 270-265-9966 x1; fax-270-265-2588; 8-4:30PM (CST)
Index: Separate indices to search include book and computer. Records indexed on a public use terminal back to 7/03. Only the public may search. Office will not search real estate records. Will not search UCC records. Copy fee $.25 per page. Cert fee- $5.00 per cert plus copy fee. Payee- Todd County Clerk. **Other phones:** Treasurer- 270-265-9966 x226; Elections- 270-265-9966 x226. **Property tax/Assessing**- PO Box 593, 200 Washington St, Elkton, KY 42220; 270-265-9966 x4, assessor fax- 270-265-5615. Public access terminal available.

Trigg County

County Clerk, PO Box 1310, Cadiz, KY 42211. Recording, R/E & UCC phone-270-522-6661; fax-270-522-6662; 8AM-4PM (CST)
Index: All in one. Records indexed on a public use terminal back to 1975. Office personnel or visitors may perform searches. Search fee $5.00 per name. Office will search limited real estate records. Copy fee $1.00 per page. Cert fee- $5.00 per cert includes copy fee. Payee- Trigg County Clerk. Bulk data available for purchase, contact Clerk's office at 270-522-6661. **Other phones:** Treasurer- 270-522-8459; Elections- 270-522-6661. **Property tax/Assessing**- PO Box 1776, Cadiz, KY 42211; 270-522-3271, assessor fax- 270-522-3272. Public access terminal available.

Trimble County

County Clerk, PO Box 262, Bedford, KY 40006-0262. Recording, R/E & UCC phone-502-255-7174; fax-502-255-7045; 8:30AM-4:30PM M,T,Th,F; 8:30AM-N Sat. (EST)
Index: All in one. Records indexed on computer. Only the public may search. Copy fee $.25 per page. Cert fee- $5.00 per cert includes copy fee. Payee- Trimble County Clerk. **Other phones:** Treasurer- 502-255-7196; Elections- 502-255-7174; Vital Records- 502-255-7174. **Property tax/Assessing**- Courthouse, Bedford, KY 40006; 502-255-3592, assessor fax- 502-255-0654.

Union County

County Clerk, PO Box 119, Morganfield, KY 42437-0119. 270-389-1334; fax-270-389-9135; 8AM-4PM (CST)
Index: All in one. Records indexed on a public use terminal back to 1980. Only the public may search. Copy fee $.50 per page. Cert fee- $5.00 per cert. Payee- Union County Clerk. **Property tax/Assessing**- PO Box 177, Morganfield, KY 42437; 270-389-1933, assessor fax- 270-389-2276. A public access terminal is available.

Warren County

County Clerk, PO Box 478, Bowling Green, KY 42102-0478. Recording, R/E & UCC phone-270-842-9416; fax-270-843-5319; 8:30AM-4:30PM (CST) http://warrencounty.state.ky.us
Index: All in one. Records indexed on a public use terminal back to 1981. Only the public may search. Copy fee $5.00 per doc. Cert fee- $5.00 per cert plus copy fee. Payee- Warren County Clerk. **Online access to Real Estate, Deed, Lien, UCC, Marriage, Mortgage, Plat, Will records:** Access the county clerk database through eCCLIX, a fee-based service; $200.00 sign-up and $65.00 monthly. Records go back to 1989; images to 1998. For info, see the website or call 502-266-9445. **Other phones:** Treasurer- 270-842-5805; Elections- 270-842-5306; Vital Records- 270-842-9416. **Property tax/Assessing**- PO Box 1269, Bowling Green, KY 42101-1269; 270-843-3268, assessor fax- 270-781-5767. www.kywarrenpva.com/ **Online** - Property data available at https://warrenpva.ky.gov/TelicPVWI/Inq.dll/SearchInput. Use 'guest' as username and 'password' for password for free access

Washington County

County Clerk, PO Box 446, Springfield, KY 40069. 859-336-5425; fax-859-336-5408; 9AM-4:30PM; 9AM-N Sat. (EST)
Index: All in one. Records indexed on a public use terminal back to 1960. Office will perform a UCC search but public must search other records themselves. Copy fee $.25 per page. Fee to fax back- $5.00 per doc. Cert fee- $5.00 per cert includes copy fee. Payee- Washington County Clerk. **Other phones:** Treasurer- 859-336-5430; Elections- 859-336-5425. **Property tax/Assessing**- 120 E Main St, Springfield, KY 40069; 859-336-5420, assessor fax- 859-336-5416. hours- 8AM-4:30PM

Wayne County

County Clerk, 109 N Main St, 1st Fl, #3, Monticello, KY 42633. Recording, R/E & UCC phone-606-348-6661; fax-606-348-8303; 8AM-4PM; 8AM-11:45PM Sat. (EST)
Index: Separate indices to search include computer, book, and print-out. Records indexed on a public use terminal back to 1996; deeds back to 7/16/74; mortgages 9/5/75. Only the public may search. Office will not search real estate records. Copy fee $.10 per page. Cert fee- $5.00 per cert includes copy fee. Payee- Wayne County Clerk. **Other phones:** Treasurer- 606-348-8411; Elections- 606-348-6661; Vital Records- 606-348-6661. **Property tax/Assessing**- 109 N Main St, #4, Monticello, KY 42633; 606-348-6621, assessor fax- 606-348-3673. www.waynepva.ky.gov **Online access**- Access to property tax information for free go to www.waynepva.ky.gov/

Webster County

County Clerk, PO Box 19, Dixon, KY 42409-0019. Recording, R/E & UCC phone-270-639-7006; fax-270-639-7029; 8AM-4PM M; 8AM-4PM T-F; 8-11AM S. (CST)
Index: Separate indices to search include a card system, deeds, mortgages, wills, leases, etc; castle system, title, lien/UCC; cats system, delinquent taxes. Records indexed on a public use terminal back to 10/1994. Office personnel or visitors may perform searches. Search fee $5.00 per name. Office will not search real estate records. Copy fee $.25; real estate or tax lien $.50 per page. Cert fee- $5.00 per cert includes copy fee. Payee- Webster County Clerk. Tax roll lists yearly or quarterly from the county PVA, 270-639-7016. Sales lists also for purchase. **Other phones:** Treasurer- 270-639-5042; Elections- 270-639-7006. **Property tax/Assessing**- PO Box 88, 25 US 41A, Dixon, KY 42409; 270-639-7016, assessor fax- 270-639-7009. (Appraiser/Auditor- 270-639-7016) hours- 8AM-4PM www.webstercountypva.com/ **Online access**- Access GIS-mapping and property data free at http://kygeonet.ky.gov/pva/webster/viewer.htm but no name searching; parcel number required.

Whitley County

County Clerk, PO Box 8, Williamsburg, KY 40769. Recording, R/E & UCC phone-606-549-6002; fax-606-549-2790; 7:30AM-6PM Mon; 7:30AM-4:30PM T-F. (EST)
Index: Separate indices to search include books by type. Records indexed on computer; back to dates vary. Office will perform a UCC search but public must search other records themselves. Search fee $5.00. Copy fee $.50 per page; fax back $2.50 per page. Cert fee- $5.00 per cert plus copy fee. Payee- Whitley County Clerk. **Other phones:** Treasurer- 606-549-6010; Elections- 606-549-6002. **Property tax/Assessing**- PO Box 462, Williamsburg, KY 40769; 606-549-6008, assessor fax- 606-5496042.

Wolfe County

County Clerk, PO Box 400, Campton, KY 41301. Recording, R/E & UCC phone-606-668-3515; fax-606-668-3367; 8AM-4PM M,T,Th,F,Sat; Closed Wed. (EST)
Index: All in one. Records indexed on a public use terminal back to 1980. Only the public may search. Copy fee $1.00 per page. Cert fee- $5.00 per page plus copy fee. Payee- Wolfe County Clerk. **Other phones:** Treasurer- 606-668-4060; Elections- 606-668-3515; Vital Records- 606-668-4212. **Property tax/Assessing**- PO Box 155, 100 Court St, Campton, KY 41301; 606-668-6923, assessor fax- 606-668-9957. (Appraiser/Auditor- 606-668-6925) No public terminal available.

Woodford County

County Clerk, 103 S Main St, Rm 120; Courthouse, Versailles, KY 40383. Recording, R/E & UCC phone-859-873-3421; fax-859-873-6985; 8AM-4PM M,T,W,Th; 8AM-5:30PM F. (EST)
Index: Separate indices to search include cott index, chattel mortgages, taxes, etc. Record index not computerized. Only the public may search. Copy fee $.25 per page. Cert fee- $5.00 per cert plus copy fee. Payee- Woodford County Clerk. **Other phones:** Treasurer- 859-873-6122; Elections- 859-873-3421; Vital Records- 859-873-4101. **Property tax/Assessing**- 103 S Main St, #108, Versailles, KY 40383; 859-873-4101, assessor fax- 859-873-7874. www.woodfordpva.com **Online access**- Access to property index is free at www.pvdnetwork.com/PVDNet.asp?SiteID=118. A subscription is required for full data; 120 records for $100 or unlimited access for $250 yearly.

Kentucky County Locator

You will usually be able to find the city name in the City/County Cross Reference below. In that case, it is a simple matter to determine the county from the cross reference. However, only the official US Postal Service city names are included in this index. There are an additional 40,000 place names that people use in their addresses. Therefore, we have also included a ZIP/City Cross Reference immediately following the City/County Cross Reference.

If you know the ZIP Code but the city name does not appear in the City/County Cross Reference index, look up the ZIP Code in the ZIP/City Cross Reference, find the city name, then look up the city name in the City/County Cross Reference.

Kentucky City/County Cross Reference

AARON (42601) Clinton(97), Russell(2)
ABERDEEN Butler
ACORN Pulaski
ADAIRVILLE (42202) Logan(98), Simpson(1)
ADAMS Lawrence
ADOLPHUS Allen
AGES BROOKSIDE Harlan
ALBANY Clinton
ALEXANDRIA Campbell
ALLEGRE Todd
ALLEN Floyd
ALLENSVILLE (42204) Todd(78), Logan(21)
ALLOCK Perry
ALMO Calloway
ALPHA (42603) Clinton(69), Wayne(30)
ALTRO Breathitt
ALVATON (42122) Warren(94), Allen(5)
AMBURGEY Knott
ANNVILLE (40402) Jackson(95), Clay(4)
ARGILLITE Greenup
ARJAY Bell
ARLINGTON (42021) Carlisle(92), Hickman(7)
ARTEMUS Knox
ARY Perry
ASHCAMP Pike
ASHER Leslie
ASHLAND (41102) Boyd(93), Greenup(6)
ASHLAND Boyd
ATHOL Breathitt
AUBURN (42206) Logan(92), Simpson(6), Warren(1)
AUGUSTA Bracken
AUSTIN Barren
AUXIER Floyd
AVAWAM Perry
AXTEL Breckinridge
BAGDAD (40003) Shelby(83), Franklin(16)
BAKERTON Cumberland
BANDANA Ballard
BANNER Floyd
BARBOURVILLE Knox
BARDSTOWN Nelson
BARDWELL Carlisle
BARLOW Ballard
BASKETT Henderson
BATTLETOWN Meade
BAXTER Harlan
BAYS Breathitt
BEAR BRANCH Leslie
BEATTYVILLE Lee
BEAUMONT Metcalfe
BEAUTY Martin
BEAVER Floyd
BEAVER DAM (42320) Ohio(98), Butler(1)
BEDFORD (40006) Trimble(97), Carroll(2)
BEE SPRING Edmonson
BEECH CREEK Muhlenberg
BEECH GROVE McLean
BEECHMONT Muhlenberg
BELCHER Pike
BELFRY Pike
BELLEVUE Campbell
BELTON Muhlenberg
BENHAM Harlan
BENTON (42025) Marshall(98), Calloway(1)
BEREA (40403) Madison(87), Garrard(10), Rockcastle(2)
BEREA Madison
BERRY (41003) Harrison(67), Grant(19), Pendleton(12)
BETHANY Wolfe
BETHEL Bath
BETHELRIDGE Casey
BETHLEHEM Henry
BETSY LAYNE (41605) Floyd(89), Pike(10)
BEULAH HEIGHTS McCreary
BEVERLY (40913) Bell(57), Clay(42)
BEVINSVILLE Floyd
BIG CLIFTY (42712) Grayson(60), Hardin(39)
BIG CREEK Clay
BIG LAUREL (40808) Harlan(50), Leslie(50)
BIG SPRING (40106) Breckinridge(80), Hardin(20)
BIGHILL Madison
BIMBLE Knox
BLACKEY Letcher
BLACKFORD Webster
BLAINE Lawrence
BLANDVILLE Ballard
BLEDSOE (40810) Harlan(87), Leslie(12)
BLOOMFIELD (40008) Nelson(89), Spencer(9)
BLUE RIVER Floyd
BLUEHOLE Clay
BOAZ (42027) Graves(80), McCracken(19)
BOND Jackson
BONNIEVILLE Hart
BONNYMAN Perry
BOONEVILLE (41314) Breathitt(56), Owsley(43)
BOONS CAMP Johnson
BOSTON Nelson
BOW (42714) Cumberland(92), Clinton(7)
BOWEN Powell
BOWLING GREEN (42101) Warren(96), Edmonson(2)
BOWLING GREEN Warren
BRADFORDSVILLE (40009) Marion(78), Taylor(16), Casey(5)
BRANDENBURG Meade
BREEDING (42715) Adair(94), Metcalfe(4), Cumberland(1)
BREMEN Muhlenberg
BRINKLEY Knott
BRODHEAD (40409) Rockcastle(90), Lincoln(9)
BRONSTON (42518) Pulaski(96), Wayne(3)
BROOKLYN Butler
BROOKS (40109) Bullitt(97), Jefferson(2)
BROOKSVILLE Bracken
BROWDER Muhlenberg
BROWNS FORK Perry
BROWNSVILLE Edmonson
BRUIN Elliott
BRYANTS STORE Knox
BRYANTSVILLE Garrard
BUCKHORN (41721) Perry(94), Breathitt(5)
BUCKNER Oldham
BUFFALO (42716) Larue(75), Green(20), Taylor(3)
BULAN (41722) Perry(65), Knott(34)
BURDINE Letcher
BURGIN Mercer
BURKESVILLE Cumberland
BURKHART Wolfe
BURLINGTON Boone
BURNA Livingston
BURNSIDE Pulaski
BURNWELL Pike
BUSH Laurel
BUSKIRK Morgan
BUSY (41723) Perry(76), Leslie(23)
BUTLER Pendleton
BYPRO Floyd
CADIZ Trigg
CALHOUN (42327) McLean(97), Daviess(2)
CALIFORNIA Campbell
CALVERT CITY Marshall
CALVIN Bell
CAMP DIX Lewis
CAMPBELLSBURG (40011) Henry(76), Trimble(18), Carroll(4)
CAMPBELLSVILLE (42718) Taylor(92), Marion(3), Green(2), Larue(1)
CAMPBELLSVILLE Taylor
CAMPTON (41301) Wolfe(93), Breathitt(3), Lee(2)
CANADA Pike
CANE VALLEY Adair
CANEY Morgan
CANEYVILLE (42721) Grayson(89), Butler(7), Edmonson(3)
CANMER Hart
CANNEL CITY Morgan
CANNON Knox
CANOE Breathitt
CANTON Trigg
CARLISLE (40311) Nicholas(90), Bourbon(8)
CARRIE Knott
CARTER Carter
CARVER Magoffin
CASEY CREEK (42723) Adair(61), Taylor(31), Casey(6)
CASEY CREEKG (42723) Adair(61), Taylor(31), Casey(6)
CATLETTSBURG (41129) Boyd(87), Lawrence(12)
CAVE CITY (42127) Barren(92), Hart(7)
CAWOOD Harlan
CECILIA Hardin
CENTER (42214) Metcalfe(70), Green(29)
CENTERTOWN Ohio
CENTRAL CITY Muhlenberg
CERULEAN (42215) Christian(52), Trigg(47)
CHAPLIN Nelson
CHAPPELL Leslie
CHAVIES Perry
CINDA Leslie
CISCO Magoffin
CLARKSON Grayson
CLAY (42404) Webster(90), Union(9)
CLAY CITY Powell
CLAYHOLE Breathitt
CLEARFIELD Rowan
CLEATON Muhlenberg
CLERMONT Bullitt
CLIFTY Todd
CLINTON Hickman
CLOSPLINT Harlan
CLOVERPORT Breckinridge
COALGOOD Harlan
COBHILL Estill
COLDIRON Harlan
COLUMBIA Adair
COLUMBUS Hickman
COMBS Perry
CONCORD Lewis
CONFLUENCE Leslie
CONLEY Magoffin
CONSTANCE Boone
CONSTANTINE Breckinridge
CONWAY Rockcastle
COOPERSVILLE Wayne
CORBIN (40701) Whitley(51), Knox(24), Laurel(24)
CORBIN Whitley
CORINTH (41010) Grant(59), Owen(30), Harrison(7), Scott(1)
CORNETTSVILLE (41731) Perry(68), Letcher(31)
CORYDON Henderson
COTTLE Morgan
COVINGTON Kenton
COXS CREEK (40013) Nelson(78), Spencer(13), Bullitt(7)
CRAB ORCHARD (40419) Lincoln(70), Garrard(17), Rockcastle(8), Pulaski(4)
CRANKS Harlan
CRAYNE Crittenden
CRAYNOR Floyd
CRESTWOOD Oldham
CRITTENDEN (41030) Grant(70), Boone(28), Kenton(1)
CROCKETT Morgan
CROFTON Christian
CROMONA Letcher
CROMWELL (42333) Ohio(87), Butler(12)
CROWN Letcher
CRYSTAL (40420) Lee(83), Estill(16)
CUB RUN (42729) Hart(70), Edmonson(29)
CULVER Elliott
CUMBERLAND (40823) Harlan(97), Letcher(2)
CUNDIFF Adair
CUNNINGHAM (42035) Carlisle(82), Graves(17)
CURDSVILLE Daviess
CUSTER Breckinridge
CUTSHIN Leslie
CYNTHIANA (41031) Harrison(97), Nicholas(1), Bourbon(1)
DABOLT Jackson
DAISY Perry
DANA Floyd
DANVILLE (40422) Boyle(98), Lincoln(1)
DANVILLE Boyle
DAVID Floyd

DAWSON SPRINGS (42408) Hopkins(86), Caldwell(10), Christian(3)
DAYHOIT Harlan
DAYTON Campbell
DE MOSSVILLE Pendleton
DEANE (41812) Letcher(81), Knott(18)
DEBORD Martin
DECOY (41321) Knott(80), Breathitt(20)
DEFOE Henry
DELPHIA Perry
DELTA Wayne
DEMA Knott
DENNISTON Menifee
DENTON (41132) Carter(75), Lawrence(22), Boyd(1)
DENVER Johnson
DEWITT Knox
DEXTER (42036) Calloway(98), Marshall(1)
DICE Perry
DINGUS Morgan
DIXON Webster
DIZNEY Harlan
DORTON Pike
DOVER (41034) Mason(97), Bracken(2)
DRAFFIN Pike
DRAKE Warren
DRAKESBORO Muhlenberg
DREYFUS Madison
DRIFT Floyd
DRY RIDGE Grant
DUBRE (42731) Cumberland(74), Metcalfe(25)
DUNBAR Butler
DUNDEE Ohio
DUNMOR (42339) Muhlenberg(92), Butler(7)
DUNNVILLE (42528) Casey(93), Russell(4), Adair(1)
DWALE Floyd
DWARF Perry
DYCUSBURG Crittenden
EARLINGTON Hopkins
EAST BERNSTADT Laurel
EAST POINT (41216) Floyd(52), Johnson(47)
EASTERN Floyd
EASTVIEW Hardin
EASTWOOD Jefferson
EDDYVILLE Lyon
EDMONTON (42129) Metcalfe(93), Adair(6)
EDNA Magoffin
EGYPT Jackson
EIGHTY EIGHT Barren
EKRON Meade
ELIZABETHTOWN Hardin
ELIZAVILLE Fleming
ELK HORN (42733) Taylor(79), Casey(17), Adair(3)
ELKFORK Morgan
ELKHORN CITY Pike
ELKTON (42220) Todd(97), Muhlenberg(1)
ELLIOTTVILLE Rowan
ELSIE Magoffin
EMERSON Lewis
EMINENCE (40019) Henry(97), Shelby(2)
EMLYN Whitley
EMMA Floyd
EMMALENA Knott
ENDICOTT Floyd
EOLIA Letcher
ERILINE Clay
ERLANGER Kenton
ERMINE Letcher
ESSIE Leslie
ESTILL Floyd
ETOILE Barren
EUBANK (42567) Pulaski(89), Lincoln(10)
EVARTS Harlan
EWING Fleming
EZEL Morgan
FAIRDALE Jefferson
FAIRFIELD Nelson
FAIRPLAY Adair
FAIRVIEW Christian
FALCON Magoffin
FALL ROCK Clay
FALLS OF ROUGH (40119) Grayson(61), Breckinridge(36), Ohio(2)
FALMOUTH Pendleton
FANCY FARM (42039) Graves(45), Carlisle(34), Hickman(20)
FARMERS Rowan
FARMINGTON (42040) Graves(76), Calloway(23)
FAUBUSH (42532) Pulaski(58), Russell(35), Wayne(6)
FEDSCREEK Pike
FERGUSON Pulaski
FILLMORE Lee
FINCHVILLE Shelby
FINLEY (42736) Taylor(56), Marion(43)
FIREBRICK Lewis
FISHERVILLE (40023) Spencer(51), Jefferson(47)
FISTY Knott
FLAT FORK Magoffin
FLAT LICK Knox
FLATGAP (41219) Johnson(98), Lawrence(1)
FLATWOODS Greenup
FLEMINGSBURG Fleming
FLORENCE Boone
FOGERTOWN Clay
FORD Clark
FORDS BRANCH Pike
FORDSVILLE (42343) Ohio(71), Hancock(28)
FOREST HILLS Pike
FORT CAMPBELL Christian
FORT KNOX (40121) Hardin(75), Meade(24)
FORT THOMAS Campbell
FOSTER Bracken
FOUNTAIN RUN (42133) Monroe(51), Barren(31), Allen(17)
FOURMILE (40939) Knox(71), Bell(28)
FRAKES (40940) Whitley(67), Bell(32)
FRANKFORT (40601) Franklin(96), Woodford(1), Shelby(1)
FRANKFORT Franklin
FRANKLIN (42134) Simpson(94), Allen(5)
FRANKLIN Simpson
FRAZER Wayne
FREDONIA (42411) Caldwell(60), Crittenden(34), Lyon(5)
FREDVILLE Magoffin
FREEBURN Pike
FRENCHBURG Menifee
FRITZ Magoffin
FT MITCHELL Kenton
FUGET Johnson
FULTON (42041) Fulton(71), Graves(16), Hickman(11)
GALVESTON Floyd
GAMALIEL Monroe
GAPVILLE Magoffin
GARFIELD (40140) Breckinridge(98), Hardin(1)
GARNER Knott
GARRARD Clay
GARRETT (41630) Floyd(52), Knott(47)
GARRISON (41141) Greenup(90), Lewis(5), Carter(3)
GAYS CREEK Perry
GEORGETOWN Scott
GERMANTOWN (41044) Mason(82), Bracken(17)
GHENT Carroll
GILBERTSVILLE Marshall
GILLMORE Wolfe
GIRDLER Knox
GLASGOW Barren
GLENCOE (41046) Grant(84), Gallatin(15)
GLENDALE Hardin
GLENS FORK (42741) Adair(94), Russell(5)
GLENVIEW Jefferson
GOODY Pike
GOOSE ROCK Clay
GORDON Letcher
GOSHEN Oldham
GRACEY (42232) Christian(71), Trigg(28)
GRADYVILLE Adair
GRAHAM Muhlenberg
GRAHN Carter
GRAND RIVERS Livingston
GRATZ Owen
GRAVEL SWITCH (40328) Boyle(40), Marion(38), Casey(19), Washington(1)
GRAY (40734) Knox(97), Laurel(2)
GRAY HAWK Jackson
GRAYS KNOB Harlan
GRAYSON (41143) Carter(90), Greenup(9)
GREEN HALL Owsley
GREEN ROAD Knox
GREENSBURG (42743) Green(98), Adair(1)
GREENUP Greenup
GREENVILLE Muhlenberg
GRETHEL Floyd
GULSTON Harlan
GUNLOCK Magoffin
GUSTON (40142) Meade(95), Breckinridge(4)
GUTHRIE Todd
GYPSY Magoffin
HADDIX Breathitt
HADLEY Warren
HAGERHILL Johnson
HALDEMAN Rowan
HALFWAY Allen
HALLIE Letcher
HALO Floyd
HAMLIN Calloway
HAMPTON Livingston
HANSON Hopkins
HAPPY Perry
HARDBURLY Perry
HARDIN (42048) Marshall(96), Calloway(3)
HARDINSBURG Breckinridge
HARDY Pike
HARDYVILLE (42746) Hart(78), Metcalfe(13), Green(7), Barren(1)
HARLAN Harlan
HARNED Breckinridge
HAROLD Floyd
HARRODS CREEK Jefferson
HARRODSBURG (40330) Mercer(95), Washington(4)
HARTFORD Ohio
HAWESVILLE (42348) Hancock(97), Daviess(2)
HAZARD (41701) Perry(90), Knott(9)
HAZARD Perry
HAZEL Calloway
HAZEL GREEN (41332) Morgan(62), Wolfe(37)
HEBRON Boone
HEIDELBERG Lee
HEIDRICK Knox
HELLIER Pike
HELTON (40840) Leslie(78), Harlan(21)
HENDERSON Henderson
HENDRICKS Magoffin
HERD Jackson
HERNDON (42236) Christian(87), Trigg(12)
HESTAND (42151) Monroe(91), Metcalfe(8)
HI HAT Floyd
HICKMAN Fulton
HICKORY Graves
HILLSBORO Fleming
HILLVIEW Bullitt
HIMA Clay
HINDMAN Knott
HINKLE Knox
HIPPO Floyd
HISEVILLE Barren
HITCHINS Carter
HODGENVILLE Larue
HOLLAND Allen
HOLLYBUSH Knott
HOLMES MILL Harlan
HONAKER Floyd
HOPE (40334) Bath(92), Montgomery(7)
HOPKINSVILLE Christian
HORSE BRANCH (42349) Ohio(82), Grayson(17)
HORSE CAVE (42749) Hart(90), Metcalfe(7), Barren(2)
HOSKINSTON Leslie
HOWARDSTOWN (40028) Nelson(84), Larue(16)
HUDDY Pike
HUDSON Breckinridge
HUEYSVILLE (41640) Knott(66), Floyd(33)
HUFF Edmonson
HULEN Bell
HUNTER Floyd
HUNTSVILLE Butler
HUSTONVILLE (40437) Lincoln(67), Casey(32)
HYDEN Leslie
INDEPENDENCE Kenton
INEZ Martin
INGLE Pulaski
INGRAM Bell
INSKO Morgan
IRVINE (40336) Estill(98), Lee(1)
IRVINGTON Breckinridge
ISLAND McLean
ISLAND CITY Owsley
ISOM Letcher
ISONVILLE Elliott
IVEL Floyd
IVYTON Magoffin
JACKHORN Letcher
JACKSON (41339) Breathitt(97), Knott(2)
JACOBS Carter
JAMBOREE Pike
JAMESTOWN Russell
JEFF Perry
JEFFERSONVILLE Montgomery
JENKINS (41537) Letcher(93), Pike(6)
JEREMIAH Letcher
JETSON Butler
JOB Martin
JOHNS RUN Carter
JONANCY Pike
JONESVILLE Grant
JUNCTION CITY (40440) Boyle(97), Lincoln(2)
KEATON Johnson
KEAVY Laurel
KEENE Jessamine
KEITH Harlan
KENTON Kenton
KENVIR Harlan
KERBY KNOB Jackson
KETTLE Cumberland
KETTLE ISLAND Bell
KEVIL (42053) McCracken(57), Ballard(42)
KIMPER Pike
KINGS MOUNTAIN (40442) Lincoln(50), Casey(49)
KIRKSEY (42054) Calloway(79), Marshall(14), Graves(5)
KITE Knott
KNIFLEY Adair
KNOB LICK (42154) Metcalfe(87), Barren(12)
KONA Letcher
KRYPTON (41754) Perry(97), Leslie(2)
KUTTAWA Lyon
LA CENTER Ballard
LA FAYETTE Christian

LA GRANGE (40031) Oldham(94), Henry(5)
LA GRANGE Oldham
LACKEY (41643) Knott(88), Floyd(11)
LAMB (42155) Barren(60), Monroe(39)
LAMBRIC Breathitt
LAMERO Rockcastle
LANCASTER (40444) Garrard(98), Lincoln(1)
LANCASTER Garrard
LANGLEY Floyd
LATONIA Kenton
LAWRENCEBURG Anderson
LEANDER Johnson
LEATHERWOOD Perry
LEBANON Marion
LEBANON JUNCTION (40150) Bullitt(97), Hardin(2)
LEBURN Knott
LEDBETTER Livingston
LEE CITY Wolfe
LEECO Lee
LEITCHFIELD (42754) Grayson(91), Breckinridge(8)
LEITCHFIELD Grayson
LEJUNIOR Harlan
LENOX Morgan
LEROSE Owsley
LETCHER Letcher
LEWISBURG (42256) Logan(74), Butler(13), Todd(11)
LEWISPORT (42351) Hancock(90), Daviess(9)
LEXINGTON (40509) Fayette(98), Clark(1)
LEXINGTON (40511) Fayette(97), Scott(1)
LEXINGTON (40515) Fayette(95), Jessamine(3)
LEXINGTON (40516) Fayette(89), Bourbon(10)
LEXINGTON Fayette
LIBERTY Casey
LICK CREEK Pike
LILY Laurel
LINDSEYVILLE Edmonson
LINEFORK Letcher
LITTCARR Knott
LITTLE Breathitt
LIVERMORE (42352) McLean(93), Ohio(6)
LIVINGSTON Rockcastle
LLOYD Greenup
LOCKPORT Henry
LOLA Livingston
LONDON Laurel
LONE Lee
LOOKOUT Pike
LORETTO (40037) Marion(75), Washington(13), Nelson(10)
LOST CREEK (41348) Breathitt(91), Perry(8)
LOUISA Lawrence
LOUISVILLE (40229) Jefferson(63), Bullitt(36)
LOUISVILLE (40241) Jefferson(98), Oldham(1)
LOUISVILLE (40245) Jefferson(90), Shelby(8)
LOUISVILLE (40299) Jefferson(98), Bullitt(1)
LOUISVILLE Jefferson
LOVELACEVILLE Ballard
LOVELY Martin
LOWES Graves
LOWMANSVILLE (41232) Lawrence(72), Johnson(27)
LOYALL Harlan
LUCAS Barren
LYNCH Harlan
LYNNVILLE Graves
MACEDONIA Breathitt
MACEO Daviess
MACKVILLE Washington
MADISONVILLE Hopkins
MAGNOLIA (42757) Larue(48), Hart(45), Green(6)
MAJESTIC Pike
MALLIE Knott
MALONE Morgan
MAMMOTH CAVE Edmonson
MANCHESTER Clay
MANITOU Hopkins
MANNSVILLE Taylor
MAPLE MOUNT Daviess
MARIBA Menifee
MARION (42064) Crittenden(98), Caldwell(1)
MARROWBONE Cumberland
MARSHALLVILLE Magoffin
MARSHES SIDING McCreary
MARTHA (41159) Lawrence(97), Johnson(2)
MARTIN Floyd
MARY ALICE Harlan
MARYDELL Laurel
MASON Grant
MASONIC HOME Jefferson
MAYFIELD Graves
MAYKING Letcher
MAYSLICK (41055) Mason(86), Fleming(13)
MAYSVILLE Mason
MAZIE Lawrence
MC ANDREWS Pike
MC CARR Pike
MC COMBS (41545) Pike(90), Floyd(10)
MC DANIELS Breckinridge
MC DOWELL Floyd
MC HENRY Ohio
MC KEE (40447) Jackson(96), Rockcastle(1), Estill(1)
MC KINNEY Lincoln
MC QUADY Breckinridge
MC ROBERTS Letcher
MC VEIGH Pike
MEALLY Johnson
MEANS (40346) Menifee(79), Bath(12), Montgomery(8)
MELBER (42069) Graves(80), McCracken(17), Carlisle(2)
MELBOURNE Campbell
MELVIN Floyd
MIDDLEBURG Casey
MIDDLESBORO Bell
MIDWAY (40347) Woodford(90), Franklin(5), Scott(3)
MIGRATE Fayette
MILBURN Carlisle
MILFORD Bracken
MILL SPRINGS Wayne
MILLERSBURG Bourbon
MILLS Knox
MILLSTONE Letcher
MILLTOWN Adair
MILLWOOD Grayson
MILTON (40045) Trimble(85), Carroll(14)
MIMA Morgan
MINERVA Mason
MINNIE Floyd
MIRACLE Bell
MISTLETOE Owsley
MITCHELLSBURG Boyle
MIZE Morgan
MONTICELLO Wayne
MONTPELIER Adair
MOON Morgan
MOOREFIELD Nicholas
MOORMAN Muhlenberg
MOREHEAD (40351) Rowan(98), Elliott(1)
MORGANFIELD (42437) Union(97), Webster(2)
MORGANTOWN Butler
MORNING VIEW Kenton
MORRILL Jackson
MORTONS GAP Hopkins
MOUNT EDEN (40046) Spencer(78), Anderson(14), Shelby(7)
MOUNT HERMON Monroe
MOUNT OLIVET Robertson
MOUNT SHERMAN (42764) Green(57), Larue(39), Hart(3)
MOUNT STERLING (40353) Montgomery(97), Clark(1)
MOUNT VERNON Rockcastle
MOUNT WASHINGTON Bullitt
MOUSIE Knott
MOUTHCARD Pike
MOZELLE Leslie
MULDRAUGH Meade
MUNFORDVILLE Hart
MURRAY Calloway
MUSES MILLS Fleming
MYRA Pike
NANCY (42544) Pulaski(75), Wayne(17), Russell(7)
NARROWS Ohio
NAZARETH Nelson
NEAFUS Grayson
NEBO (42441) Hopkins(96), Webster(3)
NELSE Pike
NEON Letcher
NERINX Marion
NEVISDALE Whitley
NEW CONCORD Calloway
NEW HAVEN (40051) Nelson(80), Larue(19)
NEW HOPE (40052) Nelson(77), Marion(17), Larue(5)
NEW LIBERTY Owen
NEWPORT Campbell
NICHOLASVILLE Jessamine
NOCTOR Breathitt
NORTH MIDDLETOWN Bourbon
NORTONVILLE (42442) Hopkins(96), Christian(3)
OAK GROVE Christian
OAKLAND Warren
OAKVILLE Logan
OFFUTT Johnson
OIL SPRINGS Johnson
OLATON (42361) Ohio(89), Grayson(10)
OLD LANDING Lee
OLDTOWN Greenup
OLIVE HILL (41164) Carter(97), Elliott(1)
OLLIE Edmonson
OLMSTEAD (42265) Logan(88), Todd(11)
OLYMPIA Bath
ONEIDA Clay
OPHIR Morgan
ORLANDO Rockcastle
OVEN FORK Letcher
OWENSBORO Daviess
OWENTON Owen
OWINGSVILLE (40360) Bath(93), Montgomery(6)
PADUCAH McCracken
PAINT LICK (40461) Garrard(61), Madison(38)
PAINTSVILLE Johnson
PARIS Bourbon
PARK CITY (42160) Barren(74), Edmonson(25)
PARKERS LAKE McCreary
PARKSVILLE (40464) Boyle(86), Casey(13)
PARROT Jackson
PARTRIDGE Letcher
PATHFORK Harlan
PAW PAW Pike
PAYNEVILLE Meade
PELLVILLE Hancock
PEMBROKE (42266) Christian(92), Todd(7)
PENDLETON (40055) Trimble(42), Henry(37), Oldham(20)
PENROD Muhlenberg
PEOPLES Jackson
PERRY PARK Owen
PERRYVILLE (40468) Boyle(88), Washington(6), Mercer(4)
PETERSBURG Boone
PEWEE VALLEY Oldham
PEYTONSBURG Cumberland
PHELPS Pike
PHILPOT (42366) Daviess(95), Hancock(3), Ohio(1)
PHYLLIS Pike
PIKEVILLE Pike
PILGRIM Martin
PINE KNOT McCreary
PINE RIDGE (41360) Wolfe(92), Powell(7)
PINE TOP Knott
PINEVILLE Bell
PINSONFORK Pike
PIPPA PASSES Knott
PITTSBURG Laurel
PLANK Clay
PLEASUREVILLE (40057) Henry(72), Shelby(27)
PLUMMERS LANDING Fleming
POMEROYTON Menifee
POOLE Webster
PORT ROYAL Henry
POWDERLY Muhlenberg
PREMIUM Letcher
PRESTON Bath
PRESTONSBURG Floyd
PRIMROSE Lee
PRINCETON (42445) Caldwell(93), Lyon(2), Hopkins(2), Trigg(1)
PRINTER Floyd
PROSPECT (40059) Jefferson(56), Oldham(43)
PROVIDENCE (42450) Webster(88), Hopkins(7), Crittenden(4)
PROVO Butler
PRYSE Estill
PUTNEY Harlan
QUALITY (42268) Butler(72), Logan(27)
QUICKSAND Breathitt
QUINCY Lewis
RACCOON Pike
RADCLIFF Hardin
RANSOM Pike
RAVEN Knott
RAVENNA Estill
RAYWICK Marion
REDFOX Knott
REED Henderson
REGINA Pike
RENFRO VALLEY Rockcastle
REVELO McCreary
REYNOLDS STATION (42368) Hancock(74), Ohio(25)
RHODELIA (40161) Meade(92), Breckinridge(8)
RICETOWN Owsley
RICHARDSON Lawrence
RICHARDSVILLE Warren
RICHMOND Madison
RINEYVILLE Hardin
RIVER (41254) Johnson(88), Lawrence(11)
ROARK (40979) Leslie(82), Clay(17)
ROBARDS (42452) Henderson(88), Webster(11)
ROBINSON CREEK Pike
ROCHESTER Butler
ROCKFIELD (42274) Warren(93), Logan(6)
ROCKHOLDS (40759) Whitley(85), Knox(14)
ROCKHOUSE Pike
ROCKPORT Ohio
ROCKY HILL Edmonson
ROCKYBRANCH Wayne
ROGERS Wolfe
ROSINE Ohio
ROUNDHILL (42275) Butler(66), Edmonson(33)
ROUSSEAU Breathitt

ROWDY Perry
ROWLETTS Hart
ROXANA Letcher
ROYALTON Magoffin
RUMSEY McLean
RUSH (41168) Boyd(64), Carter(34)
RUSSELL Greenup
RUSSELL SPRINGS (42642) Russell(93), Adair(5), Casey(1)
RUSSELLVILLE Logan
SACRAMENTO (42372) McLean(56), Muhlenberg(43)
SADIEVILLE (40370) Harrison(58), Scott(41)
SAINT CATHARINE Washington
SAINT CHARLES Hopkins
SAINT FRANCIS Marion
SAINT HELENS Lee
SAINT JOSEPH Daviess
SAINT MARY Marion
SAINT PAUL Lewis
SALDEE Breathitt
SALEM (42078) Livingston(64), Crittenden(35)
SALT LICK (40371) Bath(90), Menifee(9)
SALVISA (40372) Mercer(94), Anderson(5)
SALYERSVILLE Magoffin
SANDERS Carroll
SANDGAP Jackson
SANDY HOOK Elliott
SASSAFRAS Knott
SAUL Perry
SAWYER McCreary
SCALF Knox
SCIENCE HILL Pulaski
SCOTTSVILLE Allen
SCUDDY Perry
SE REE Breckinridge
SEBREE Webster
SECO Letcher
SEDALIA Graves
SEITZ Magoffin
SEXTONS CREEK (40983) Clay(91), Owsley(8)
SHARON GROVE Todd
SHARPSBURG (40374) Bath(86), Nicholas(11), Bourbon(2)
SHELBIANA Pike
SHELBY GAP Pike
SHEPHERDSVILLE Bullitt
SHOPVILLE Pulaski
SIDNEY Pike
SILER (40763) Whitley(84), Bell(15)
SILVER GROVE Campbell
SILVERHILL Morgan
SIMPSONVILLE Shelby
SITKA Johnson
SIZEROCK Leslie
SLADE Powell
SLAUGHTERS (42456) Webster(68), Hopkins(31)
SLEMP Perry
SLOANS VALLEY Pulaski
SMILAX Leslie
SMITH Harlan
SMITH MILLS Henderson
SMITHFIELD (40068) Henry(79), Shelby(10), Oldham(9)
SMITHLAND Livingston
SMITHS GROVE (42171) Warren(42), Edmonson(32), Barren(24)
SOLDIER Carter
SOMERSET Pulaski
SONORA (42776) Hardin(72), Larue(27)
SOUTH CARROLLTON Muhlenberg
SOUTH PORTSMOUTH (41174) Greenup(97), Lewis(2)
SOUTH SHORE Greenup
SOUTH UNION Logan
SOUTH WILLIAMSON Pike
SPARTA (41086) Owen(86), Gallatin(13)
SPEIGHT Pike
SPOTTSVILLE Henderson
SPRING LICK Grayson
SPRINGFIELD (40069) Washington(98), Marion(1)
STAB Pulaski
STAFFORDSVILLE Johnson
STAMBAUGH Johnson
STAMPING GROUND (40379) Scott(77), Owen(19), Franklin(3)
STANFORD (40484) Lincoln(94), Garrard(4)
STANLEY Daviess
STANTON (40380) Powell(95), Estill(4)
STANVILLE (41659) Floyd(93), Pike(6)
STEARNS McCreary
STEELE Pike
STEFF Grayson
STEPHENS Elliott
STEPHENSBURG Hardin
STEPHENSPORT Breckinridge
STEUBENVILLE Wayne
STINNETT Leslie
STONE Pike
STONEY FORK (40988) Harlan(53), Bell(46)
STOPOVER Pike
STRUNK McCreary
STURGIS (42459) Union(93), Crittenden(6)
SULLIVAN Union
SULPHUR Henry
SUMMER SHADE (42166) Metcalfe(67), Monroe(18), Barren(14)
SUMMERSVILLE (42782) Green(93), Hart(6)
SUMMIT Hardin
SUNFISH Edmonson
SWAMP BRANCH Johnson
SWEEDEN Edmonson
SYMSONIA (42082) Graves(72), Marshall(23), McCracken(4)
TALBERT Breathitt
TALCUM (41765) Knott(85), Perry(14)
TALLEGA Lee
TATEVILLE Pulaski
TAYLORSVILLE (40071) Spencer(90), Bullitt(8)
TEABERRY Floyd
THELMA Johnson
THORNTON Letcher
THOUSANDSTICKS Leslie
THREEFORKS Martin
TILINE Livingston
TOLER Pike
TOLLESBORO Lewis
TOLU Crittenden
TOMAHAWK Martin
TOMPKINSVILLE Monroe
TOPMOST Knott
TOTZ Harlan
TRAM Floyd
TRENTON (42286) Todd(96), Christian(3)
TROSPER Knox
TURKEY CREEK (41570) Pike(96), Martin(3)
TURNERS STATION (40075) Henry(77), Carroll(22)
TUTOR KEY Johnson
TYNER Jackson
TYPO Perry
ULYSSES Lawrence
UNION Boone
UNION STAR (40171) Meade(86), Breckinridge(13)
UNIONTOWN (42461) Union(95), Henderson(4)
UPTON (42784) Hardin(48), Larue(29), Hart(22)
UTICA (42376) Daviess(72), Ohio(20), McLean(7)
VAN LEAR Johnson
VANCEBURG (41179) Lewis(96), Carter(3)
VANCLEVE Breathitt
VARNEY Pike
VENTRESS Hardin
VERONA Boone
VERSAILLES (40383) Woodford(96), Jessamine(3)
VERSAILLES Woodford
VERTREES Hardin
VEST Knott
VICCO (41773) Perry(63), Knott(36)
VINCENT Owsley
VINE GROVE (40175) Hardin(53), Meade(45), Breckinridge(1)
VIPER Perry
VIRGIE Pike
VOLGA Johnson
WACO (40385) Madison(98), Estill(1)
WADDY (40076) Shelby(80), Franklin(12), Anderson(6)
WALKER Knox
WALLINGFORD (41093) Fleming(97), Lewis(2)
WALLINS CREEK Harlan
WALNUT GROVE Pulaski
WALTON Boone
WANETA Jackson
WARBRANCH (40874) Leslie(94), Clay(5)
WARFIELD Martin
WARSAW Gallatin
WASHINGTON Mason
WATER VALLEY (42085) Graves(68), Hickman(31)
WATERVIEW Cumberland
WAVERLY (42462) Union(90), Henderson(9)
WAX Grayson
WAYLAND Floyd
WAYNESBURG (40489) Lincoln(89), Casey(10)
WEBBVILLE (41180) Lawrence(90), Carter(9)
WEBSTER (40176) Breckinridge(95), Meade(4)
WEEKSBURY Floyd
WELCHS CREEK Butler
WELLINGTON (40387) Menifee(91), Morgan(7), Wolfe(1)
WENDOVER Leslie
WEST LIBERTY (41472) Morgan(98), Elliott(1)
WEST LOUISVILLE Daviess
WEST PADUCAH McCracken
WEST POINT (40177) Hardin(80), Bullitt(13), Jefferson(6)
WEST PRESTONSBURG Floyd
WEST SOMERSET Pulaski
WEST VAN LEAR Johnson
WESTPORT Oldham
WESTVIEW Breckinridge
WHEATCROFT Webster
WHEATLEY Owen
WHEELWRIGHT Floyd
WHICK Breathitt
WHITE MILLS Hardin
WHITE OAK Morgan
WHITE PLAINS (42464) Hopkins(72), Muhlenberg(15), Christian(11)
WHITEHOUSE Johnson
WHITESBURG Letcher
WHITESVILLE (42378) Daviess(55), Ohio(44)
WHITLEY CITY McCreary
WICKLIFFE Ballard
WIDECREEK Breathitt
WILDIE Rockcastle
WILLARD Carter
WILLIAMSBURG (40769) Whitley(98), McCreary(1)
WILLIAMSPORT Johnson
WILLIAMSTOWN Grant
WILLISBURG (40078) Washington(97), Mercer(1), Anderson(1)
WILLOW SHADE Metcalfe
WILMORE (40390) Jessamine(98), Woodford(1)
WINCHESTER Clark
WIND CAVE Jackson
WINDSOR Casey
WINDY Wayne
WINGO (42088) Graves(84), Hickman(15)
WINSTON Estill
WITTENSVILLE Johnson
WOODBINE (40771) Knox(86), Whitley(13)
WOODBURN (42170) Warren(62), Simpson(37)
WOODBURY Butler
WOODMAN Pike
WOOLLUM (40999) Knox(98), Clay(1)
WOOTON Leslie
WORTHINGTON Greenup
WORTHVILLE (41098) Owen(96), Carroll(3)
WRIGLEY Morgan
YEADDISS Leslie
YERKES Perry
YOSEMITE Casey
ZACHARIAH Lee
ZOE Lee

Kentucky ZIP/City Cross Reference

40003-40003 BAGDAD
40004-40004 BARDSTOWN
40006-40006 BEDFORD
40007-40007 BETHLEHEM
40008-40008 BLOOMFIELD
40009-40009 BRADFORDSVILLE
40010-40010 BUCKNER
40011-40011 CAMPBELLSBURG
40012-40012 CHAPLIN
40013-40013 COXS CREEK
40014-40014 CRESTWOOD
40017-40017 DEFOE
40018-40018 EASTWOOD
40019-40019 EMINENCE
40020-40020 FAIRFIELD
40022-40022 FINCHVILLE
40023-40023 FISHERVILLE
40025-40025 GLENVIEW
40026-40026 GOSHEN
40027-40027 HARRODS CREEK
40028-40028 HOWARDSTOWN
40031-40032 LA GRANGE
40033-40033 LEBANON
40036-40036 LOCKPORT
40037-40037 LORETTO
40040-40040 MACKVILLE
40041-40041 MASONIC HOME
40045-40045 MILTON
40046-40046 MOUNT EDEN
40047-40047 MOUNT WASHINGTON
40048-40048 NAZARETH
40049-40049 NERINX
40050-40050 NEW CASTLE
40051-40051 NEW HAVEN
40052-40052 NEW HOPE
40055-40055 PENDLETON
40056-40056 PEWEE VALLEY
40057-40057 PLEASUREVILLE
40058-40058 PORT ROYAL
40059-40059 PROSPECT

ZIP Range	City
40060-40060	RAYWICK
40061-40061	SAINT CATHARINE
40062-40062	SAINT FRANCIS
40063-40063	SAINT MARY
40065-40066	SHELBYVILLE
40067-40067	SIMPSONVILLE
40068-40068	SMITHFIELD
40069-40069	SPRINGFIELD
40070-40070	SULPHUR
40071-40071	TAYLORSVILLE
40075-40075	TURNERS STATION
40076-40076	WADDY
40077-40077	WESTPORT
40078-40078	WILLISBURG
40103-40103	AXTEL
40104-40104	BATTLETOWN
40106-40106	BIG SPRING
40107-40107	BOSTON
40108-40108	BRANDENBURG
40109-40109	BROOKS
40110-40110	CLERMONT
40111-40111	CLOVERPORT
40114-40114	CONSTANTINE
40115-40115	CUSTER
40117-40117	EKRON
40118-40118	FAIRDALE
40119-40119	FALLS OF ROUGH
40121-40121	FORT KNOX
40129-40129	HILLVIEW
40140-40140	GARFIELD
40142-40142	GUSTON
40143-40143	HARDINSBURG
40144-40144	HARNED
40145-40145	HUDSON
40146-40146	IRVINGTON
40150-40150	LEBANON JUNCTION
40152-40152	MC DANIELS
40153-40153	MC QUADY
40155-40155	MULDRAUGH
40157-40157	PAYNEVILLE
40159-40160	RADCLIFF
40161-40161	RHODELIA
40162-40162	RINEYVILLE
40164-40164	SE REE
40165-40165	SHEPHERDSVILLE
40170-40170	STEPHENSPORT
40171-40171	UNION STAR
40175-40175	VINE GROVE
40176-40176	WEBSTER
40177-40177	WEST POINT
40178-40178	WESTVIEW
40200-40299	LOUISVILLE
40306-40306	BETHEL
40309-40309	BOWEN
40310-40310	BURGIN
40311-40311	CARLISLE
40312-40312	CLAY CITY
40313-40313	CLEARFIELD
40316-40316	DENNISTON
40317-40317	ELLIOTTVILLE
40319-40319	FARMERS
40320-40320	FORD
40322-40322	FRENCHBURG
40324-40324	GEORGETOWN
40327-40327	GRATZ
40328-40328	GRAVEL SWITCH
40329-40329	HALDEMAN
40330-40330	HARRODSBURG
40334-40334	HOPE
40336-40336	IRVINE
40337-40337	JEFFERSONVILLE
40339-40339	KEENE
40340-40340	NICHOLASVILLE
40341-40341	LAMERO
40342-40342	LAWRENCEBURG
40345-40345	MARIBA
40346-40346	MEANS
40347-40347	MIDWAY
40348-40348	MILLERSBURG
40350-40350	MOOREFIELD
40351-40351	MOREHEAD
40353-40353	MOUNT STERLING
40355-40355	NEW LIBERTY
40356-40356	NICHOLASVILLE
40357-40357	NORTH MIDDLETOWN
40358-40358	OLYMPIA
40359-40359	OWENTON
40360-40360	OWINGSVILLE
40361-40362	PARIS
40363-40363	PERRY PARK
40365-40365	POMEROYTON
40366-40366	PRESTON
40370-40370	SADIEVILLE
40371-40371	SALT LICK
40372-40372	SALVISA
40374-40374	SHARPSBURG
40376-40376	SLADE
40379-40379	STAMPING GROUND
40380-40380	STANTON
40383-40384	VERSAILLES
40385-40385	WACO
40386-40386	VERSAILLES
40387-40387	WELLINGTON
40389-40389	WHEATLEY
40390-40390	WILMORE
40391-40392	WINCHESTER
40402-40402	ANNVILLE
40403-40404	BEREA
40405-40405	BIGHILL
40407-40407	BOND
40409-40409	BRODHEAD
40410-40410	BRYANTSVILLE
40415-40415	COBHILL
40417-40417	CONWAY
40419-40419	CRAB ORCHARD
40420-40420	CRYSTAL
40421-40421	DABOLT
40422-40423	DANVILLE
40426-40426	DREYFUS
40430-40430	EGYPT
40434-40434	GRAY HAWK
40435-40435	HERD
40437-40437	HUSTONVILLE
40440-40440	JUNCTION CITY
40441-40441	KERBY KNOB
40442-40442	KINGS MOUNTAIN
40444-40444	LANCASTER
40445-40445	LIVINGSTON
40446-40446	LANCASTER
40447-40447	MC KEE
40448-40448	MC KINNEY
40452-40452	MITCHELLSBURG
40455-40455	MORRILL
40456-40456	MOUNT VERNON
40460-40460	ORLANDO
40461-40461	PAINT LICK
40464-40464	PARKSVILLE
40465-40465	PARROT
40467-40467	PEOPLES
40468-40468	PERRYVILLE
40471-40471	PRYSE
40472-40472	RAVENNA
40473-40473	RENFRO VALLEY
40475-40476	RICHMOND
40481-40481	SANDGAP
40484-40484	STANFORD
40486-40486	TYNER
40488-40488	WANETA
40489-40489	WAYNESBURG
40492-40492	WILDIE
40494-40494	WIND CAVE
40495-40495	WINSTON
40500-40598	LEXINGTON
40601-40622	FRANKFORT
40701-40702	CORBIN
40724-40724	BUSH
40729-40729	EAST BERNSTADT
40730-40730	EMLYN
40734-40734	GRAY
40737-40737	KEAVY
40740-40740	LILY
40741-40748	LONDON
40751-40751	MARYDELL
40754-40754	NEVISDALE
40755-40755	PITTSBURG
40759-40759	ROCKHOLDS
40763-40763	SILER
40769-40769	WILLIAMSBURG
40771-40771	WOODBINE
40801-40801	AGES BROOKSIDE
40803-40803	ASHER
40806-40806	BAXTER
40807-40807	BENHAM
40808-40808	BIG LAUREL
40810-40810	BLEDSOE
40813-40813	CALVIN
40815-40815	CAWOOD
40816-40816	CHAPPELL
40818-40818	COALGOOD
40819-40819	COLDIRON
40820-40820	CRANKS
40823-40823	CUMBERLAND
40824-40824	DAYHOIT
40825-40825	DIZNEY
40826-40826	EOLIA
40827-40827	ESSIE
40828-40828	EVARTS
40829-40829	GRAYS KNOB
40830-40830	GULSTON
40831-40831	HARLAN
40840-40840	HELTON
40843-40843	HOLMES MILL
40844-40844	HOSKINSTON
40845-40845	HULEN
40846-40846	KEITH
40847-40847	KENVIR
40849-40849	LEJUNIOR
40854-40854	LOYALL
40855-40855	LYNCH
40856-40856	MIRACLE
40858-40858	MOZELLE
40861-40861	OVEN FORK
40862-40862	PARTRIDGE
40863-40863	PATHFORK
40865-40865	PUTNEY
40867-40867	SMITH
40868-40868	STINNETT
40870-40870	TOTZ
40873-40873	WALLINS CREEK
40874-40874	WARBRANCH
40902-40902	ARJAY
40903-40903	ARTEMUS
40906-40911	BARBOURVILLE
40913-40913	BEVERLY
40914-40914	BIG CREEK
40915-40915	BIMBLE
40917-40917	BLUEHOLE
40921-40921	BRYANTS STORE
40923-40923	CANNON
40927-40927	CLOSPLINT
40930-40930	DEWITT
40931-40931	ERILINE
40932-40932	FALL ROCK
40935-40935	FLAT LICK
40936-40936	FOGERTOWN
40939-40939	FOURMILE
40940-40940	FRAKES
40941-40941	GARRARD
40943-40943	GIRDLER
40944-40944	GOOSE ROCK
40946-40946	GREEN ROAD
40949-40949	HEIDRICK
40951-40951	HIMA
40953-40953	HINKLE
40955-40955	INGRAM
40958-40958	KETTLE ISLAND
40962-40962	MANCHESTER
40964-40964	MARY ALICE
40965-40965	MIDDLESBORO
40970-40970	MILLS
40972-40972	ONEIDA
40977-40977	PINEVILLE
40978-40978	PLANK
40979-40979	ROARK
40981-40981	SAUL
40982-40982	SCALF
40983-40983	SEXTONS CREEK
40988-40988	STONEY FORK
40995-40995	TROSPER
40997-40997	WALKER
40999-40999	WOOLLUM
41001-41001	ALEXANDRIA
41002-41002	AUGUSTA
41003-41003	BERRY
41004-41004	BROOKSVILLE
41005-41005	BURLINGTON
41006-41006	BUTLER
41007-41007	CALIFORNIA
41008-41008	CARROLLTON
41009-41009	CONSTANCE
41010-41010	CORINTH
41011-41014	COVINGTON
41015-41015	LATONIA
41016-41016	COVINGTON
41017-41017	FT MITCHELL
41018-41018	ERLANGER
41019-41019	COVINGTON
41022-41022	FLORENCE
41030-41030	CRITTENDEN
41031-41031	CYNTHIANA
41033-41033	DE MOSSVILLE
41034-41034	DOVER
41035-41035	DRY RIDGE
41037-41037	ELIZAVILLE
41039-41039	EWING
41040-41040	FALMOUTH
41041-41041	FLEMINGSBURG
41042-41042	FLORENCE
41043-41043	FOSTER
41044-41044	GERMANTOWN
41045-41045	GHENT
41046-41046	GLENCOE
41048-41048	HEBRON
41049-41049	HILLSBORO
41051-41051	INDEPENDENCE
41052-41052	JONESVILLE
41053-41053	KENTON
41054-41054	MASON
41055-41055	MAYSLICK
41056-41056	MAYSVILLE
41059-41059	MELBOURNE
41061-41061	MILFORD
41062-41062	MINERVA
41063-41063	MORNING VIEW
41064-41064	MOUNT OLIVET
41065-41065	MUSES MILLS
41071-41072	NEWPORT
41073-41073	BELLEVUE
41074-41074	DAYTON
41075-41075	FORT THOMAS
41076-41076	NEWPORT
41080-41080	PETERSBURG
41081-41081	PLUMMERS LANDING
41083-41083	SANDERS
41085-41085	SILVER GROVE
41086-41086	SPARTA
41091-41091	UNION
41092-41092	VERONA
41093-41093	WALLINGFORD
41094-41094	WALTON
41095-41095	WARSAW
41096-41096	WASHINGTON
41097-41097	WILLIAMSTOWN
41098-41098	WORTHVILLE
41099-41099	NEWPORT
41101-41114	ASHLAND
41121-41121	ARGILLITE
41124-41124	BLAINE
41125-41125	BRUIN
41127-41127	CAMP DIX
41128-41128	CARTER
41129-41129	CATLETTSBURG
41131-41131	CONCORD
41132-41132	DENTON
41135-41135	EMERSON
41137-41137	FIREBRICK
41139-41139	FLATWOODS
41141-41141	GARRISON

41142-41142 GRAHN
41143-41143 GRAYSON
41144-41144 GREENUP
41146-41146 HITCHINS
41149-41149 ISONVILLE
41150-41150 JACOBS
41152-41152 JOHNS RUN
41156-41156 LLOYD
41159-41159 MARTHA
41160-41160 MAZIE
41163-41163 OLDTOWN
41164-41164 OLIVE HILL
41166-41166 QUINCY
41168-41168 RUSH
41169-41169 RUSSELL
41170-41170 SAINT PAUL
41171-41171 SANDY HOOK
41173-41173 SOLDIER
41174-41174 SOUTH PORTSMOUTH
41175-41175 SOUTH SHORE
41177-41177 STEPHENS
41179-41179 VANCEBURG
41180-41180 WEBBVILLE
41181-41181 WILLARD
41183-41183 WORTHINGTON
41189-41189 TOLLESBORO
41201-41201 ADAMS
41203-41203 BEAUTY
41204-41204 BOONS CAMP
41211-41211 CULVER
41214-41214 DEBORD
41215-41215 DENVER
41216-41216 EAST POINT
41219-41219 FLATGAP
41220-41220 FUGET
41222-41222 HAGERHILL
41224-41224 INEZ
41225-41225 JOB
41226-41226 KEATON
41228-41228 LEANDER
41230-41230 LOUISA
41231-41231 LOVELY
41232-41232 LOWMANSVILLE
41234-41234 MEALLY
41237-41237 OFFUTT
41238-41238 OIL SPRINGS
41240-41240 PAINTSVILLE
41250-41250 PILGRIM
41253-41253 RICHARDSON
41254-41254 RIVER
41255-41255 SITKA
41256-41256 STAFFORDSVILLE
41257-41257 STAMBAUGH
41258-41258 SWAMP BRANCH
41260-41260 THELMA
41261-41261 THREEFORKS
41262-41262 TOMAHAWK
41263-41263 TUTOR KEY
41264-41264 ULYSSES
41265-41265 VAN LEAR
41266-41266 VOLGA
41267-41267 WARFIELD
41268-41268 WEST VAN LEAR
41269-41269 WHITEHOUSE
41271-41271 WILLIAMSPORT
41274-41274 WITTENSVILLE
41301-41301 CAMPTON
41306-41306 ALTRO
41307-41307 ATHOL
41310-41310 BAYS
41311-41311 BEATTYVILLE
41313-41313 BETHANY
41314-41314 BOONEVILLE
41315-41315 BURKHART
41316-41316 CANOE
41317-41317 CLAYHOLE
41321-41321 DECOY
41323-41323 FILLMORE
41327-41327 GILLMORE
41328-41328 GREEN HALL
41331-41331 HADDIX
41332-41332 HAZEL GREEN
41333-41333 HEIDELBERG
41338-41338 ISLAND CITY
41339-41339 JACKSON
41340-41340 LAMBRIC
41342-41342 LEE CITY
41343-41343 LEECO
41344-41344 LEROSE
41346-41346 LITTLE
41347-41347 LONE
41348-41348 LOST CREEK
41351-41351 MISTLETOE
41352-41352 MIZE
41357-41357 NOCTOR
41358-41358 OLD LANDING
41360-41360 PINE RIDGE
41362-41362 PRIMROSE
41363-41363 QUICKSAND
41364-41364 RICETOWN
41365-41365 ROGERS
41366-41366 ROUSSEAU
41367-41367 ROWDY
41368-41368 SAINT HELENS
41369-41369 SALDEE
41370-41370 MACEDONIA
41377-41377 TALBERT
41378-41378 TALLEGA
41385-41385 VANCLEVE
41386-41386 VINCENT
41390-41390 WHICK
41391-41391 WIDECREEK
41396-41396 ZACHARIAH
41397-41397 ZOE
41406-41406 BUSKIRK
41407-41407 CANEY
41408-41408 CANNEL CITY
41409-41409 CARVER
41410-41410 CISCO
41411-41411 CONLEY
41412-41412 COTTLE
41413-41413 CROCKETT
41417-41417 DINGUS
41419-41419 EDNA
41421-41421 ELKFORK
41422-41422 ELSIE
41425-41425 EZEL
41426-41426 FALCON
41427-41427 FLAT FORK
41430-41430 FREDVILLE
41431-41431 FRITZ
41433-41433 GAPVILLE
41438-41438 GYPSY
41441-41441 HENDRICKS
41443-41443 INSKO
41444-41444 IVYTON
41447-41447 LENOX
41451-41451 MALONE
41452-41452 MARSHALLVILLE
41456-41456 MIMA
41457-41457 MOON
41459-41459 OPHIR
41464-41464 ROYALTON
41465-41465 SALYERSVILLE
41466-41466 SEITZ
41467-41467 SILVERHILL
41472-41472 WEST LIBERTY
41474-41474 WHITE OAK
41477-41477 WRIGLEY
41501-41502 PIKEVILLE
41503-41503 SOUTH WILLIAMSON
41512-41512 ASHCAMP
41513-41513 BELCHER
41514-41514 BELFRY
41517-41517 BURDINE
41518-41518 BURNWELL
41519-41519 CANADA
41520-41520 DORTON
41521-41521 DRAFFIN
41522-41522 ELKHORN CITY
41524-41524 FEDSCREEK
41526-41526 FORDS BRANCH
41527-41527 FOREST HILLS
41528-41528 FREEBURN
41529-41529 GOODY
41531-41531 HARDY
41534-41534 HELLIER
41535-41535 HUDDY
41536-41536 JAMBOREE
41537-41537 JENKINS
41538-41538 JONANCY
41539-41539 KIMPER
41540-41540 LICK CREEK
41542-41542 LOOKOUT
41543-41543 MC ANDREWS
41544-41544 MC CARR
41545-41545 MC COMBS
41546-41546 MC VEIGH
41547-41547 MAJESTIC
41548-41548 MOUTHCARD
41549-41549 MYRA
41550-41550 NELSE
41551-41551 PAW PAW
41553-41553 PHELPS
41554-41554 PHYLLIS
41555-41555 PINSONFORK
41557-41557 RACCOON
41558-41558 RANSOM
41559-41559 REGINA
41560-41560 ROBINSON CREEK
41561-41561 ROCKHOUSE
41562-41562 SHELBIANA
41563-41563 SHELBY GAP
41564-41564 SIDNEY
41565-41565 SPEIGHT
41566-41566 STEELE
41567-41567 STONE
41568-41568 STOPOVER
41569-41569 TOLER
41570-41570 TURKEY CREEK
41571-41571 VARNEY
41572-41572 VIRGIE
41574-41574 WOODMAN
41601-41601 ALLEN
41602-41602 AUXIER
41603-41603 BANNER
41604-41604 BEAVER
41605-41605 BETSY LAYNE
41606-41606 BEVINSVILLE
41607-41607 BLUE RIVER
41612-41612 BYPRO
41614-41614 CRAYNOR
41615-41615 DANA
41616-41616 DAVID
41619-41619 DRIFT
41621-41621 DWALE
41622-41622 EASTERN
41625-41625 EMMA
41626-41626 ENDICOTT
41627-41627 ESTILL
41629-41629 GALVESTON
41630-41630 GARRETT
41631-41631 GRETHEL
41632-41632 GUNLOCK
41633-41633 HALO
41635-41635 HAROLD
41636-41636 HI HAT
41637-41637 HIPPO
41639-41639 HONAKER
41640-41640 HUEYSVILLE
41641-41641 HUNTER
41642-41642 IVEL
41643-41643 LACKEY
41645-41645 LANGLEY
41647-41647 MC DOWELL
41649-41649 MARTIN
41650-41650 MELVIN
41651-41651 MINNIE
41653-41653 PRESTONSBURG
41655-41655 PRINTER
41659-41659 STANVILLE
41660-41660 TEABERRY
41663-41663 TRAM
41666-41666 WAYLAND
41667-41667 WEEKSBURY
41668-41668 WEST PRESTONSBURG
41669-41669 WHEELWRIGHT
41701-41702 HAZARD
41710-41710 ALLOCK
41712-41712 ARY
41713-41713 AVAWAM
41714-41714 BEAR BRANCH
41719-41719 BONNYMAN
41720-41720 BROWNS FORK
41721-41721 BUCKHORN
41722-41722 BULAN
41723-41723 BUSY
41725-41725 CARRIE
41727-41727 CHAVIES
41728-41728 CINDA
41729-41729 COMBS
41730-41730 CONFLUENCE
41731-41731 CORNETTSVILLE
41732-41732 CUTSHIN
41733-41733 DAISY
41735-41735 DELPHIA
41736-41736 DICE
41739-41739 DWARF
41740-41740 EMMALENA
41743-41743 FISTY
41745-41745 GAYS CREEK
41746-41746 HAPPY
41747-41747 HARDBURLY
41749-41749 HYDEN
41751-41751 JEFF
41754-41754 KRYPTON
41756-41756 LEATHERWOOD
41759-41759 SASSAFRAS
41760-41760 SCUDDY
41762-41762 SIZEROCK
41763-41763 SLEMP
41764-41764 SMILAX
41765-41765 TALCUM
41766-41766 THOUSANDSTICKS
41771-41771 TYPO
41772-41772 VEST
41773-41773 VICCO
41774-41774 VIPER
41775-41775 WENDOVER
41776-41776 WOOTON
41777-41777 YEADDISS
41778-41778 YERKES
41801-41801 AMBURGEY
41804-41804 BLACKEY
41805-41805 BRINKLEY
41810-41810 CROMONA
41811-41811 CROWN
41812-41812 DEANE
41815-41815 ERMINE
41817-41817 GARNER
41819-41819 GORDON
41821-41821 HALLIE
41822-41822 HINDMAN
41823-41823 HOLLYBUSH
41824-41824 ISOM
41825-41825 JACKHORN
41826-41826 JEREMIAH
41828-41828 KITE
41829-41829 KONA
41831-41831 LEBURN
41832-41832 LETCHER
41833-41833 LINEFORK
41834-41834 LITTCARR
41835-41835 MC ROBERTS
41836-41836 MALLIE
41837-41837 MAYKING
41838-41838 MILLSTONE
41839-41839 MOUSIE
41840-41840 NEON
41843-41843 PINE TOP
41844-41844 PIPPA PASSES
41845-41845 PREMIUM
41847-41847 REDFOX
41848-41848 ROXANA
41849-41849 SECO
41855-41855 THORNTON
41858-41858 WHITESBURG
41859-41859 DEMA

ZIP Range	City
41861-41861	RAVEN
41862-41862	TOPMOST
41901-41906	MIGRATE
42001-42003	PADUCAH
42020-42020	ALMO
42021-42021	ARLINGTON
42022-42022	BANDANA
42023-42023	BARDWELL
42024-42024	BARLOW
42025-42025	BENTON
42026-42026	BLANDVILLE
42027-42027	BOAZ
42028-42028	BURNA
42029-42029	CALVERT CITY
42031-42031	CLINTON
42032-42032	COLUMBUS
42033-42033	CRAYNE
42035-42035	CUNNINGHAM
42036-42036	DEXTER
42037-42037	DYCUSBURG
42038-42038	EDDYVILLE
42039-42039	FANCY FARM
42040-42040	FARMINGTON
42041-42041	FULTON
42044-42044	GILBERTSVILLE
42045-42045	GRAND RIVERS
42046-42046	HAMLIN
42047-42047	HAMPTON
42048-42048	HARDIN
42049-42049	HAZEL
42050-42050	HICKMAN
42051-42051	HICKORY
42053-42053	KEVIL
42054-42054	KIRKSEY
42055-42055	KUTTAWA
42056-42056	LA CENTER
42058-42058	LEDBETTER
42059-42059	LOLA
42060-42060	LOVELACEVILLE
42061-42061	LOWES
42063-42063	LYNNVILLE
42064-42064	MARION
42066-42066	MAYFIELD
42069-42069	MELBER
42070-42070	MILBURN
42071-42071	MURRAY
42076-42076	NEW CONCORD
42078-42078	SALEM
42079-42079	SEDALIA
42081-42081	SMITHLAND
42082-42082	SYMSONIA
42083-42083	TILINE
42084-42084	TOLU
42085-42085	WATER VALLEY
42086-42086	WEST PADUCAH
42087-42087	WICKLIFFE
42088-42088	WINGO
42101-42104	BOWLING GREEN
42120-42120	ADOLPHUS
42122-42122	ALVATON
42123-42123	AUSTIN
42124-42124	BEAUMONT
42127-42127	CAVE CITY
42128-42128	DRAKE
42129-42129	EDMONTON
42130-42130	EIGHTY EIGHT
42131-42131	ETOILE
42133-42133	FOUNTAIN RUN
42134-42135	FRANKLIN
42140-42140	GAMALIEL
42141-42142	GLASGOW
42150-42150	HALFWAY
42151-42151	HESTAND
42152-42152	HISEVILLE
42153-42153	HOLLAND
42154-42154	KNOB LICK
42155-42155	LAMB
42156-42156	LUCAS
42157-42157	MOUNT HERMON
42159-42159	OAKLAND
42160-42160	PARK CITY
42163-42163	ROCKY HILL
42164-42164	SCOTTSVILLE
42166-42166	SUMMER SHADE
42167-42167	TOMPKINSVILLE
42169-42169	WILLOW SHADE
42170-42170	WOODBURN
42171-42171	SMITHS GROVE
42201-42201	ABERDEEN
42202-42202	ADAIRVILLE
42203-42203	ALLEGRE
42204-42204	ALLENSVILLE
42206-42206	AUBURN
42207-42207	BEE SPRING
42209-42209	BROOKLYN
42210-42210	BROWNSVILLE
42211-42211	CADIZ
42212-42212	CANTON
42214-42214	CENTER
42215-42215	CERULEAN
42216-42216	CLIFTY
42217-42217	CROFTON
42219-42219	DUNBAR
42220-42220	ELKTON
42221-42221	FAIRVIEW
42223-42223	FORT CAMPBELL
42232-42232	GRACEY
42234-42234	GUTHRIE
42235-42235	HADLEY
42236-42236	HERNDON
42240-42241	HOPKINSVILLE
42250-42250	HUFF
42251-42251	HUNTSVILLE
42252-42252	JETSON
42254-42254	LA FAYETTE
42256-42256	LEWISBURG
42257-42257	LINDSEYVILLE
42259-42259	MAMMOTH CAVE
42261-42261	MORGANTOWN
42262-42262	OAK GROVE
42263-42263	OAKVILLE
42264-42264	OLLIE
42265-42265	OLMSTEAD
42266-42266	PEMBROKE
42267-42267	PROVO
42268-42268	QUALITY
42270-42270	RICHARDSVILLE
42273-42273	ROCHESTER
42274-42274	ROCKFIELD
42275-42275	ROUNDHILL
42276-42276	RUSSELLVILLE
42280-42280	SHARON GROVE
42283-42283	SOUTH UNION
42284-42284	SUNFISH
42285-42285	SWEEDEN
42286-42286	TRENTON
42287-42287	WELCHS CREEK
42288-42288	WOODBURY
42301-42304	OWENSBORO
42320-42320	BEAVER DAM
42321-42321	BEECH CREEK
42322-42322	BEECH GROVE
42323-42323	BEECHMONT
42324-42324	BELTON
42325-42325	BREMEN
42326-42326	BROWDER
42327-42327	CALHOUN
42328-42328	CENTERTOWN
42330-42330	CENTRAL CITY
42332-42332	CLEATON
42333-42333	CROMWELL
42334-42334	CURDSVILLE
42337-42337	DRAKESBORO
42338-42338	DUNDEE
42339-42339	DUNMOR
42343-42343	FORDSVILLE
42344-42344	GRAHAM
42345-42345	GREENVILLE
42347-42347	HARTFORD
42348-42348	HAWESVILLE
42349-42349	HORSE BRANCH
42350-42350	ISLAND
42351-42351	LEWISPORT
42352-42352	LIVERMORE
42354-42354	MC HENRY
42355-42355	MACEO
42356-42356	MAPLE MOUNT
42357-42357	MOORMAN
42358-42358	NARROWS
42361-42361	OLATON
42364-42364	PELLVILLE
42365-42365	PENROD
42366-42366	PHILPOT
42367-42367	POWDERLY
42368-42368	REYNOLDS STATION
42369-42369	ROCKPORT
42370-42370	ROSINE
42371-42371	RUMSEY
42372-42372	SACRAMENTO
42373-42373	SAINT JOSEPH
42374-42374	SOUTH CARROLLTON
42375-42375	STANLEY
42376-42376	UTICA
42377-42377	WEST LOUISVILLE
42378-42378	WHITESVILLE
42402-42402	BASKETT
42403-42403	BLACKFORD
42404-42404	CLAY
42406-42406	CORYDON
42408-42408	DAWSON SPRINGS
42409-42409	DIXON
42410-42410	EARLINGTON
42411-42411	FREDONIA
42413-42413	HANSON
42419-42420	HENDERSON
42431-42431	MADISONVILLE
42436-42436	MANITOU
42437-42437	MORGANFIELD
42440-42440	MORTONS GAP
42441-42441	NEBO
42442-42442	NORTONVILLE
42444-42444	POOLE
42445-42445	PRINCETON
42450-42450	PROVIDENCE
42451-42451	REED
42452-42452	ROBARDS
42453-42453	SAINT CHARLES
42455-42455	SEBREE
42456-42456	SLAUGHTERS
42457-42457	SMITH MILLS
42458-42458	SPOTTSVILLE
42459-42459	STURGIS
42460-42460	SULLIVAN
42461-42461	UNIONTOWN
42462-42462	WAVERLY
42463-42463	WHEATCROFT
42464-42464	WHITE PLAINS
42501-42503	SOMERSET
42510-42510	ACORN
42516-42516	BETHELRIDGE
42518-42518	BRONSTON
42519-42519	BURNSIDE
42528-42528	DUNNVILLE
42532-42532	FAUBUSH
42533-42533	FERGUSON
42536-42536	INGLE
42539-42539	LIBERTY
42541-42541	MIDDLEBURG
42544-42544	NANCY
42553-42553	SCIENCE HILL
42554-42554	SHOPVILLE
42555-42555	SLOANS VALLEY
42557-42557	STAB
42558-42558	TATEVILLE
42563-42563	WALNUT GROVE
42564-42564	WEST SOMERSET
42565-42565	WINDSOR
42566-42566	YOSEMITE
42567-42567	EUBANK
42601-42601	AARON
42602-42602	ALBANY
42603-42603	ALPHA
42607-42607	BEULAH HEIGHTS
42611-42611	COOPERSVILLE
42613-42613	DELTA
42618-42618	FRAZER
42629-42629	JAMESTOWN
42631-42631	MARSHES SIDING
42632-42632	MILL SPRINGS
42633-42633	MONTICELLO
42634-42634	PARKERS LAKE
42635-42635	PINE KNOT
42638-42638	REVELO
42640-42640	ROCKYBRANCH
42642-42642	RUSSELL SPRINGS
42643-42643	SAWYER
42647-42647	STEARNS
42648-42648	STEUBENVILLE
42649-42649	STRUNK
42653-42653	WHITLEY CITY
42655-42655	WINDY
42701-42702	ELIZABETHTOWN
42711-42711	BAKERTON
42712-42712	BIG CLIFTY
42713-42713	BONNIEVILLE
42714-42714	BOW
42715-42715	BREEDING
42716-42716	BUFFALO
42717-42717	BURKESVILLE
42718-42719	CAMPBELLSVILLE
42720-42720	CANE VALLEY
42721-42721	CANEYVILLE
42722-42722	CANMER
42723-42723	CASEY CREEKG
42723-42723	CASEY CREEK
42724-42724	CECILIA
42726-42726	CLARKSON
42728-42728	COLUMBIA
42729-42729	CUB RUN
42730-42730	CUNDIFF
42731-42731	DUBRE
42732-42732	EASTVIEW
42733-42733	ELK HORN
42735-42735	FAIRPLAY
42736-42736	FINLEY
42740-42740	GLENDALE
42741-42741	GLENS FORK
42742-42742	GRADYVILLE
42743-42743	GREENSBURG
42746-42746	HARDYVILLE
42748-42748	HODGENVILLE
42749-42749	HORSE CAVE
42752-42752	KETTLE
42753-42753	KNIFLEY
42754-42755	LEITCHFIELD
42757-42757	MAGNOLIA
42758-42758	MANNSVILLE
42759-42759	MARROWBONE
42761-42761	MILLTOWN
42762-42762	MILLWOOD
42763-42763	MONTPELIER
42764-42764	MOUNT SHERMAN
42765-42765	MUNFORDVILLE
42766-42766	NEAFUS
42768-42768	PEYTONSBURG
42772-42772	ROWLETTS
42776-42776	SONORA
42779-42779	SPRING LICK
42780-42780	STEFF
42781-42781	STEPHENSBURG
42782-42782	SUMMERSVILLE
42783-42783	SUMMIT
42784-42784	UPTON
42785-42785	VENTRESS
42785-42785	VERTREES
42786-42786	WATERVIEW
42787-42787	WAX
42788-42788	WHITE MILLS

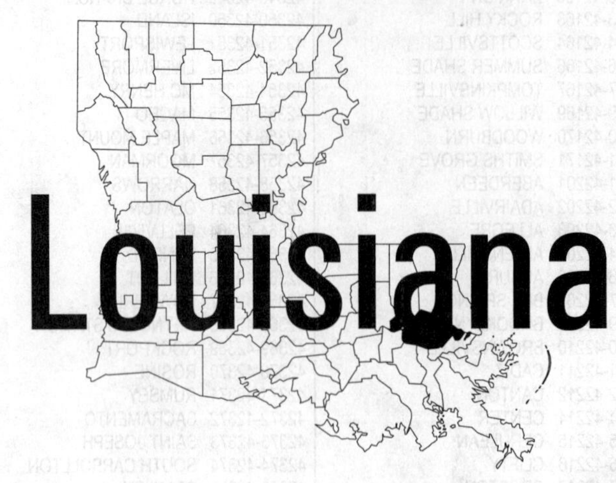

Louisiana

General Help Numbers:

Governor's Office
PO Box 94004 225-342-0991
Baton Rouge, LA 70804-9004 Fax 225-342-7099
www.gov.state.la.us 8AM-5PM

Attorney General's Office
LA Department of Justice 225-326-6705
PO Box 94005 Fax 225-326-6797
Baton Rouge, LA 70804-9005 8:30AM-5PM
www.ag.state.la.us

Legislative Records
State Capitol, 2nd Floor 225-342-2456
PO Box 44486
Baton Rouge, LA 70804 8AM-5PM
www.legis.state.la.us

State Archives
Records Mgt, & History 225-922-1000
3851 Essen Lane Fax 225-922-0433
Baton Rouge, LA 70809-2137 8AM-4:30PM,
9AM-5PM SAT; 1PM-5PM SU
www.sos.louisiana.gov/tabid/53/Default.aspx

State Specifics:

Capital:	Baton Rouge East Baton Rouge Parish
Time Zone:	CST
Number of Parishes:	64
Population:	4,410,796
Web Site:	www.louisiana.gov

State Agencies

Criminal Records

Access to Records is Restricted.

State Police, Bureau of Criminal Identification, 7919 Independence Blvd, Baton Rouge, LA 70806; 225-925-6095, Fax- 225-925-7005; 8AM-4:30PM. www.lsp.org/index.html

Records ARE RESTRICTED and are not available to the public in general. Records are available for employment or licensing purposes as state law dictates. Authorized forms are available from this department.

Statewide Court Records

Judicial Administrator, Judicial Council of the Supreme Court, 400 Royal Street, Suite 1190, New Orleans, LA 70130-8101; 504-310-2550, Fax-504-310-2587; 9AM-5PM. www.lasc.org

Trial court information must be obtained from the parish level courts.

Indexing & Storage: New records available for inquiry in 24 hours.

Access by: mail, online.

Fee & Payment: There is no search fee

Mail search: Turnaround time- 72 hours. Submit helpful-specific information such as DOB, years to search. Include your name and contact information. Appellate and Supreme Court records are available by mail.

Online search: Search current Supreme Courts dockets from the home page. Search opinions from the state Supreme Court at www.lasc.org/opinion_search.asp. Online records go back to 1995.

Sexual Offender Registry

State Police, Sex Offender and Child Predator Registry, PO Box 66614, Box A-6, Baton Rouge, LA 70896; 225-925-6100, 800-858-0551, Fax-225-925-7005; 8AM-4:30PM.

http://lasocpr1.lsp.org

The Sex Offender and Child Predator Registry program is statutorily provided through La. R. S. 15:542 & 15:542.1, et. seq., of the Louisiana Criminal Code.

Indexing & Storage: Records available from 6/18/92. New records available for inquiry in 1 to 3 days.

Searching: This agency does not answer search requests made directly from the public; to search, you must make your request via a local law enforcement agency, who must make the request on their official letterhead. Email add'l questions to SOCPR@dps.state.la.us. Include in request- name or ZIP Code or parish or park or school. This data not released- LACCH Rap sheets are not available via Fax or Email.

Access by: phone, online.

Phone search: You must supply name, race, sex, DOB in a phone request. Request can be delayed due to limited staff.

Online search: Search by name, ZIP Code, or view the entire list at the website. Also search by city, school area or parish. Also, email requests are accepted, use SOCPR@dps.state.la.us.

Expedited service: Will try to expedite request, if requested.

Incarceration Records

Department of Public Safety and Corrections, PO Box 94304, Attn: Office of Adult Services, Baton Rouge, LA 70804; 225-342-9711 (Inmate Locator), Fax- 225-342-3349; 8AM-4:30PM.

www.corrections.state.la.us

Indexing & Storage: Records available on current and former inmates. New records available for inquiry in 1 to 3 days.

Searching: Under state law, the complete records of offenders, past, present, or future, in the custody of the Department of Public Safety and Corrections, Corrections Services, is confidential and cannot be disclosed, directly or indirectly, to anyone. Include in request- full name; DOC number helpful. Only location is released. Records computerized since 1975.

Access by: mail, phone, fax, online.

Fee & Payment: There is no fee.

Mail search: Turnaround time- 30 days. SASE not required.

Phone search: Limited name searching available by phone.

Fax search: Location requests are available by fax.

Online search: Currently, the Department does not have inmate locator capabilities. However, the web page refers searchers to www.vinelink.com.

Corporation, LP, LLP, LLC, Trademarks/Servicemarks

Commercial Division, Corporation Department, PO Box 94125, Baton Rouge, LA 70804-9125 (Courier address- 8585 Archives Ave, Baton Rouge, LA 70809); 225-925-4704, Fax- 225-922-0435; 8AM-4:30PM. www.sos.louisiana.gov/

Fictitious Names and Assumed Names are found at the parish level.

Indexing & Storage: Records available from mid-1800s. New records available for inquiry immediately.

Searching: Include in request- full name of business. In addition to the articles of organization, business entity records available include: Annual Reports, Officers, Directors, Prior (merged) names, Inactive names, and Reserved names.

Access by: mail, phone, fax, in person, online.

Fee & Payment: Copies cost $15.00 without amendments and $25.00 with amendments and $10.00 plus a fee of $.25 per page after 40 pages for specific query searches on computer. Fee payee- Secretary of State. Prepayment required. Personal checks and major credit cards accepted.

Mail search: Turnaround time- 5 to 10 working days. SASE not required.

Phone search: You may call for information; however, only limited information is available.

Fax search: There is an additional $1.00 per page fee if returned by fax. Turnaround time is 5 to 10 working days.

In person: There is a free public access terminal.

Online search: Search by name or charter document number at the web page listed above. Instructions are given.

Other access: Bulk sale of corporation, LLC, partnership, and trademark information is available for approved entities. For more info, call 225-925-4704.

Expedited service: Expedited service is available for mail and phone searches. Turnaround time- 1 day. Add $30.00 per business name for next day, $50.00 for asap or priority.

Uniform Commercial Code

Secretary of State, UCC Records, PO Box 94125, Baton Rouge, LA 70804-9125; 225-922-1193, Fax- 225-922-0452; 8AM-4:30PM.

www.sos.louisiana.gov/tabid/99/Default.aspx

The statewide index of UCC filings is available in each parish office. All tax liens and financial statements are filed at the parish level. IRS liens show up on UCC records. Records CANNOT be obtained from this office, except via the online system.

Indexing & Storage: Records available for all active listings and one year after lapse date. Records are indexed on computer since 1990. New records available for inquiry in 2 days.

Searching: All filing information including debtor names, property descriptions, and subsequent filings are available. Mail-in requests are sent to any parish, as all searches reflect statewide information.

Access by: online.

Fee & Payment: Fees are only for the online service. Fee payee- Secretary of State. Prepayment required. Personal checks accepted. Credit cards not accepted.

Online search: An annual $400 fee gives unlimited access to UCC filing information at Direct Access. This dial-up service is open from 6:30 AM to 11 PM daily. Most any software communications program can be configured to work. For further information, visit www.sos.louisiana.gov/tabid/130/Default.aspx or call the number above or 225-925-4701.

Federal & State Tax Liens

Records not maintained by a state level agency.

Records are filed with the Clerk of Court at the parish level.

Sales Tax Registrations

Access to Records is Restricted.

Revenue Department, Taxpayer Services Division, PO Box 201, Baton Rouge, LA 70821-0201 (Courier address- 617 N 3rd St, Baton Rouge, LA 70802); 225-219-7356, Fax- 225-219-2210; 8AM-4:30PM. www.gov.louisiana.gov/

This agency will confirm if an entity has a sales tax permit. It will only provide registration information to the registrant itself.

Birth Certificates

Vital Records Registry, Office of Public Health, PO Box 60630, New Orleans, LA 70160 (Courier address- 325 Loyola Ave Room 102, New Orleans, LA 70112); 504-219-4500, 800-454-9570, 877-605-8562 (VitalChek), Fax- 866-761-1855; 8AM-4:30PM.

www.dhh.louisiana.gov/offices/?ID=252

Some certificates (all types of vital records) contain information at the bottom of the document that is confidential and not released to anyone. This information is used for statistical purposes and varies depending on legislative action.

Indexing & Storage: Records available from 1915 on. Birth records for only the City of New Orleans are available for 100 years. Records older than 100 years should be ordered from the State Archives. New records available for inquiry immediately.

Searching: Birth certificates are considered confidential for 100 years. Requesters must be related to the person of record or have a signed release. Include in request- full name, names of parents, mother's maiden name, date of birth, place of birth, relationship to person of record, reason for information request. Older records must be searched at the State Archives 225-922-1184.

Access by: mail, phone, fax, in person, online.

Fee & Payment: A "long form" birth certificate is $15.00, while a "birth card" is $9.00. Fee payee- Vital Records Registry. Prepayment required. Credit cards are not accepted for mail requests. Personal checks, Visa, and MasterCard accepted.

Mail search: Turnaround time- 4-6 weeks. SASE not required.

Phone search: Use the VitalChek number above.

Fax search: Fax requests accepted, use of credit card required.

In person: In person search requires a photo ID. Turnaround time at this New Orleans main office is usually 45 minutes. Walk-in services for birth certificate requests are available at Parish Health Units in the following parishes: Caddo, Calcasieu, East Baton Rouge, Jefferson, Jefferson - Marrero, Lafayette, Lafourche, Ouachita, Rapides and Tangipahoa. Photo ID required, turnaround time immediate.

Online search: Orders can be placed online at www.vitalchek.com, a state-approved vendor.

Expedited service: If ordered from state, based on only an urgent need basis. You must provide documentation of the emergency with plane tickets, verifications of reservations, or official letters requesting documents by a specific date. A fee of $16.00 is charged for overnight delivery. Phone and online service from www.vitalchek.com includes a $12.95 fee for using a credit card. Turnaround time is 10 days via this agency, 2-3 days via www.vitalchek.com

Death Records

Vital Records Registry, Office of Public Health, PO Box 60630, New Orleans, LA 70160 (Courier address- 325 Loyola Ave Room 102, New Orleans, LA 70112); 504-219-4500, 800-454-9570, 877-605-8562 (VitalChek), Fax- 866-761-1855; 8AM-4PM.

www.dhh.louisiana.gov/offices/?ID=252

This agency refers to expedited service as emergency service

Indexing & Storage: Records available from 1955 on. Records over 50 years old must be obtained from the State Archives. New records available for inquiry immediately.

Searching: Death records are considered confidential for 50 years. Must show how related or have a signed release from immediate family member if for investigative purposes. Include in request- full name, date of death, place of death, relationship to person of record, reason for information request, photo ID. Records older than 50 years must be searched at the State Archives 225-922-1184.

Access by: mail, phone, fax, in person, online.

Fee & Payment: The search fee is $7.00 plus $.50 per transaction for a mail or VitalChek order. Fee payee- Department of Vital Records. Prepayment required. Credit cards accepted for fax and in person requests only. Personal checks, Visa, and MasterCard accepted.

Mail search: Turnaround time- 4-6 weeks. SASE not required.

Phone search: Use the VitalChek number above.

Fax search: Fax requests accepted, use of credit card required.

In person: in person search requires a photo ID. Turnaround time usually 45 minutes.

Online search: Orders can be placed online at www.vitalchek.com, a state-approved vendor.

Expedited service: If ordered from state, based on only an urgent need basis. You must provide documentation of the emergency with plane tickets, verifications of reservations, or official letters requesting documents by a specific date. A fee of $16.00 is charged for overnight delivery. Phone and online service from VitalChek includes a $12.95 fee for using a credit card. Turnaround time is 10 days via this agency, 2-3 days via VitalChek.

Marriage Certificates, Divorce Records

Records not maintained by a state level agency.

Only Orleans Parish marriage records are available from 1948 on at the Registry for a $5.00 fee, same search criteria as others. Include bride name (maiden), groom and date of marriage. Other marriage & all divorce records are found at parish of event.

Marriage Records older than 50 years are open to the public. Use the VitalChek 877-605-8562 for marriage records in Orleans Parish only.

Workers' Compensation Records

Department of Labor, Office of Workers' Compensation, PO Box 94040, Baton Rouge, LA 70804-9040 (Courier address- LA Department of Labor, Office of Workers' Compensation, Baton Rouge, LA 70802); 800-201-3457, Fax- 225-342-7582; 8AM-5PM.

www.laworks.net

Indexing & Storage: Records available from 1983 on an electronic format. Only cases on file are those where the employee lost 7 days or more of work and/or had disputed issues resolved or settlements approved. New records available for inquiry immediately.

Searching: Most records are considered confidential. Public records include decisions, awards, or orders in disputed cases. Include in request- claimant name, SSN, date of accident, reason for information request, specific records that you need copies of. Otherwise, signed release required. All record requests must be in writing. This data not released- pending records.

Access by: mail, fax, in person.

Fee & Payment: Copies are $.25 per page, $1.00 to certify. There is no fee to search. Fee payee- Workers' Compensation Administrative Fund. Prepayment preferred Cash is not accepted. Personal checks accepted, credit cards are not.

Mail search: Turnaround time- 3 days. SASE not required.

Fax search: Records can be requested by fax at no extra fee.

In person: If you request in person, the turnaround time is shortened only by the mail time.

Driver Records

Dept of Public Safety and Corrections, Office of Motor Vehicles, PO Box 64886, Baton Rouge, LA 70896 (Courier address- 7979 Independence Blvd, Baton Rouge, LA 70896); 877-368-5463, 225-925-6388, Fax- 225-925-6915; 7:30AM-4PM.

www.expresslane.org

Copies of tickets may be obtained from the address listed above. The fee is $5.00 per document.

Indexing & Storage: Records available for 3 yrs for moving violations, 10 yrs from DWI conviction date, and 5 or 10 yrs for suspensions. Pre-8/15/01 accidents are displayed 3 yrs from accident date, no fault shown. Accidents after 8/01 shown only if license is suspended. New records available for inquiry in 2 to 3 weeks.

Searching: Casual requesters can obtain driving records with proper release form signed by subject. Include in request- driver's license number, full name, date of birth. It is sometimes helpful to include the race or sex when requesting a record. This data not released- medical data

Access by: mail, in person, online.

Fee & Payment: The fee for mail-in or walk-in requests is $15.00 per name, if accessed electronically then $6.00. The fee is $5.00 for basic driver license information. Fee payee- Office of Motor Vehicles. Prepayment required. Personal checks not accepted. Credit cards accepted at web site only.

Mail search: Turnaround time- 10 working days. SASE not required.

In person: Walk-in requesters may "view" a record for no charge. Casual requesters must present signed form. The fee is for the hard copy. Records can be requested from the Motor Vehicle Offices in Lake Charles, Monroe, Baton Rouge, Shreveport, or Alexandria.

Online search: There are two methods. The commercial requester, interactive mode is available from 7 AM to 9:30 PM daily. There is a minimum order requirement of 2,000 requests per month. A bond or large deposit is required. Fee is $6.00 per record. For more information, call 225-922-001. The 2nd method is for individuals to order their own record at www.expresslane.org. The fee is $17.00 and requires a credit card.

Vehicle Ownership & Registration

Department of Public Safety & Corrections, Office of Motor Vehicles, PO Box 64886, Baton Rouge, LA 70896 (Courier address- 7979 Independence Blvd, Baton Rouge, LA 70806); 225-925-7198, 877-368-5463, Fax- 225-925-4256; 8AM-4PM.

www.expresslane.org

Indexing & Storage: Records available for 7 years. New records available for inquiry in 4-6 weeks.

Searching: Casual requesters can obtain records, but personal information is not released without consent of subject. Include in request- written request stating the nature of the inquiry and VIN. This data not released- SSNs.

Access by: mail.

Fee & Payment: The current fee for VIN, registration, and plate checks is $8.00 to search and $2.00 per page for certification. Fee payee- Office of Motor Vehicles. Prepayment required. Personal checks accepted, credit cards are not.

Mail search: Turnaround time- 4-6 weeks. Mail searches require license plate number or vehicle identification number (VIN). SASE not requested

Accident Reports

Louisiana State Police, Traffic Records Unit - A27, PO Box 66614, Baton Rouge, LA 70896 (Courier address- 7919 Independence Blvd, Baton Rouge, LA 70806); 225-925-6157, Fax- 225-925-4922; 8AM-4PM.

www.lsp.org/safety_crash.html

Send questions to ehardin@dps.state.la.us.

Indexing & Storage: Records available from 2000 to present. New records available for inquiry in 1 to 2 weeks.

Searching: If photos needed, use same PO Box but attention Photo Lab D-3 or call 225-925-3518. The driver name(s), date of accident and parish are needed when ordering.

Access by: mail, phone, in person.

Fee & Payment: The fee is $7.50 per record. Fee payee- Louisiana State Police. Prepayment required. Personal checks are not accepted. No credit cards accepted.

Mail search: Turnaround time- 10 working days. A SASE is requested.

Phone search: Searching by telephone available for ongoing accounts.

In person: Turnaround time is while you wait, if personnel not busy.

Vessel Ownership & Registration

Department of Wildlife & Fisheries, Vessel Records, PO Box 14796, Baton Rouge, LA 70898 (Courier address- 2000 Quail Dr, Baton Rouge, LA 70808); 225-765-2898, Fax- 225-763-5421; 8:15AM-4:15PM.

www.wlf.state.la.us/boating/

Lien information is found at the parish level. Louisiana is not a title state; boats are not titled, only registered.

Indexing & Storage: Records available on paper for three years. Record are indexed on computer from the 1970s to present. All motorized boats and sailboats over 12 ft must be registered. New records available for inquiry in seconds.

Searching: Records not released to the public unless subject has given permission or by subpoena. The hull ID # is not released. Include in request- Louisiana #, name, or hull ID #, and from whom boat was acquired. This data not released- SSN, address.

Access by: mail, fax.

Fee & Payment: There is no fee.

Mail search: Turnaround time- 7 to 10 days. SASE not required.

Fax search: Records may be requested by fax.

Legislation Records

Louisiana House (Senate) Representative, State Capitol, 2nd Floor, PO Box 44486, Baton Rouge, LA 70804; 225-342-2365 (Senate Documents (Rm 205)), 225-342-6458 (House Documents (Rm 207)), 225-342-2456 (Information Help Desk), 800-256-3793 (General Information, In-state); 8AM-5PM. www.legis.state.la.us

Sessions are from the last Monday in April for 60 days in odd numbered years, In March for 85 days in even numbered years. The PO Box above is for the House; the PO Box for Senate bills is 94183.

Indexing & Storage: Records available from 1952 to present, 1997 forward is on Internet.

Searching: Include in request- bill number, year. Call first on the passed bills for location on microfiche. Pending bills are available in hard copy.

Access by: mail, phone, fax, in person, online.

Fee & Payment: Copies are $.25 per page. A minimum of $1.50 for postage applies. Fee payee- LA Legislative Document Services. Will send invoices. Personal checks accepted, credit cards are not.

Mail search: Turnaround time- same day if possible. A minimum of $1.50 postage applies. SASE not required.

Phone search: Public Update Legislative Services Line is known as the PULS Line is available at 225-342-2456 or toll free (Louisiana only) 800-256-3793.

Fax search: The fee is $1.00 per page for items returned by fax.

In person: No fee for request.

Online search: The Internet site has a wealth of information about sessions and bills from 1997 forward. The LA Revised Statutes mat be access via this site also.

Voter Registration

Louisiana Secretary of State, Elections Division, PO Box 94125, Baton Rouge, LA 70804-9125 (Courier address- 8585 Archives Blvd, Baton Rouge, LA 70809); 225-922-0900, Fax- 225-922-0945; 8AM-4:30PM.

www.sos.louisiana.gov/tabid/68/Default.aspx

Although the information is public record, individual searching must be done at the parish level through the Parish Registrar of Voters.

Indexing & Storage: Records available for all currently registered voters.

Searching: The agency will sell the database statewide or by parish. Media formats include email, labels, CD, and lists. There are no restrictions regarding purchasing for marketing purposes. Email questions to mcritchie@sos.louisiana.gov. This data not released- SSNs, DBs.

GED Certificates

Div of Family, Career, and Technical Education, GED Program, PO Box 94064, Baton Rouge, LA 70804-9064; 225-342-0444 (Main Number), Fax- 225-219-4439; 8AM - 4:30PM.

www.louisianaschools.net/lde/family/525.html

Indexing & Storage: New records available for inquiry in 2-3 weeks.

Searching: One may verify a GED. To search, you must use their form, which may be requested via phone or fax. Include in request- name at time of test, year test taken, DOB, SSN. If the request is for pre-employment screening purposes, there must be a signed release.

Access by: mail, fax, in person.

Fee & Payment: There is no fee.

Mail search: Turnaround time- 4-10 working days. SASE not required.

Fax search: Results of a fax search will be mailed, same criteria as mail searches.

In person: in person searchers must have a photo ID. Turnaround time: Immediate.

Hunting & Fishing License Information

Access to Records is Restricted.

Wildlife & Fisheries Department, License Division, PO Box 98000, Baton Rouge, LA 70898-9000 (Courier address- 2000 Quail Dr, Baton Rouge, LA 70808); 225-765-2881, 225-765-2800, Fax- 225-763-3510; 8:AM-4:30PM.

www.wlf.louisiana.gov/licenses/

All license information is subject to the DPPA under US Code 18. At present, not all 14 permissible uses are readily available and use of a subpoena is suggested.

Louisiana State Licensing Agencies

For details about the agency responsible for licensing/certifying/registering an item below or in the Agency Quick Finder section, match an item's number with the number of the agency in the *Licensing Agency Information* section.

Acupuncturist #20 ..... www.lsbme.louisiana.gov/apps/verifications/lookup.aspx
Addiction Counselor #28 ..... www.la-adra.org/database.asp
Alcoholic Beverage Vendor #3 ..... www.atc.rev.state.la.us/licenselookup.html
Architect #50 ..... www.lastbdarchs.com/roster.htm
Architectural Firm #50 ..... www.lastbdarchs.com/roster.htm
Athletic Trainer #20 ..... www.lsbme.louisiana.gov/apps/verifications/lookup.aspx
Auctioneer/Auction Firm #44 ..... www.lalb.org/database.asp
Auto Buyer (In & Out of State) #61 ..... www.lrumvc.louisiana.gov/search/search.htm
Automobile Parts Dealer, Used #61 ..... www.lrumvc.louisiana.gov/search/search.htm
Automotive Dismantler #61 ..... www.lrumvc.louisiana.gov/search/search.htm
Bank #32 ..... www.ofi.state.la.us
Bond For Deed Agency #32 ..... www.ofi.state.la.us
Cemetery #2 ..... www.lcb.state.la.us/search.html
Check Casher #32 ..... www.ofi.state.la.us
Chemical Engineer #40 ..... www.lapels.com/indiv_search.asp
Child Residential Care #35 ..... www.dss.state.la.us/departments/os/child_care_facilities_by_parish.html
Chiropractor #7 ..... www.lachiropracticboard.com/lic-drs.htm
Clinical Lab Personnel #20 ..... www.lsbme.louisiana.gov/apps/verifications/lookup.aspx
Collection Agency #32 ..... www.ofi.state.la.us
Construction Project, +$50000 #41 ..... www.lslbc.louisiana.gov/findcontractor_type.htm
Consumer Credit Grantor #32 ..... www.ofi.state.la.us
Contractor #30 ..... www.lslbc.louisiana.gov/findcontractor.asp
Contractor, General/Subcontractor #41 ..... www.lslbc.louisiana.gov/findcontractor_type.htm
Counselor, Professional (LPC) #46 ..... www.lpcboard.org/lpc_alpha_list.htm
Credit Repair Agency #32 ..... www.ofi.state.la.us
Credit Union #32 ..... www.ofi.state.la.us
Day Care Facility #35 ..... www.dss.state.la.us/departments/os/child_care_facilities_by_parish.html
Dentist / Dental Hygienist #9 ..... www.lsbd.org/DentistSearch.aspx
Dietitian #13 ..... www.lbedn.org/licensee_database.asp
Drug Distributor, Wholesale #64 ..... www.lsbwdd.org
Electrical Engineer #40 ..... www.lapels.com/indiv_search.asp
Emergency Shelter #35 ..... www.dss.state.la.us/departments/os/child_care_facilities_by_parish.html
Engineer/Engineer Intern #40 ..... www.lapels.com/indiv_search.asp
Engineering Firm #40 ..... www.lapels.com/firm_search.asp
Environmental Engineer #40 ..... www.lapels.com/indiv_search.asp
Exercise Physiologist, Clinical #20 ..... www.lsbme.louisiana.gov/apps/verifications/lookup.aspx
Foster Care/Adoption Care #35 ..... www.dss.state.la.us/departments/os/child_care_facilities_by_parish.html
Home Improvem't Cont'r +$75,000 #41 ..... www.lslbc.louisiana.gov/findcontractor_type.htm
Insurance Agent, LHA/PC #33 ..... www.ldi.state.la.us/search_forms/searchforms.htm
Insurance Agent/Broker/Producer #33 ..... www.ldi.state.la.us/search_forms/searchforms.htm
Interior Designer #14 ..... http://lsbid.org/licensees.asp
Land Surveyor Firm #40 ..... www.lapels.com/firm_search.asp
Land Surveyor/Surveyor Intern #40 ..... www.lapels.com/indiv_search.asp
Lender #32 ..... www.ofi.state.la.us
Lobbyist #31 ..... www.ethics.state.la.us/Lobs.pdf
Marriage and Family Therapist #46 ..... www.lpcboard.org/lpc_alpha_list.htm
Medical Doctor #20 ..... www.lsbme.louisiana.gov/apps/verifications/lookup.aspx
Midwife #20 ..... www.lsbme.louisiana.gov/apps/verifications/lookup.aspx
Mold Remediation #41 ..... www.lslbc.louisiana.gov/findcontractor_type.htm
Mortgage Lender/Broker, Residential #32 ..... www.ofi.state.la.us/newrml.htm
Motor Vehicle Crusher/Shredder #61 ..... www.lrumvc.louisiana.gov/search/search.htm
Motor Vehicle Dealer, Used/Mfg/Distr, #61 ..... www.lrumvc.louisiana.gov/search/search.htm
Motor Vehicle Sales Rep./Seller #61 ..... www.lrumvc.louisiana.gov/search/search.htm
Notary Public #54 ..... www.sos.louisiana.gov/tabid/502/Default.aspx
Notification Filer #32 ..... www.ofi.state.la.us/Notification%20Licensees.htm
Nuclear Engineer #40 ..... www.lapels.com/indiv_search.asp
Nuclear Medicine Technologist #16 ..... www.lsrtbe.org/search.cfm
Nurse, RN #21 ..... https://www.lsbn.state.la.us/services/service.asp?s=1&sid=8
Nurse-LPN #25 ..... www.lsbpne.com/license_verification.htm

Nurses' Aide #36 .... www.labenfa.com
Nursing Home Administrator #36 .... www.labenfa.com
Nutritionist #13 .... www.lbedn.org/licensee_database.asp
Occupational Therapist/Technologist #20 .... www.lsbme.louisiana.gov/apps/verifications/lookup.aspx
Optometrist #22 .... www.arbo.org/index.php?action=findanoptometrist
Osteopathic Physician #20 .... www.lsbme.louisiana.gov/apps/verifications/lookup.aspx
Pawnbroker #32 .... www.ofi.state.la.us/newpawn.htm
Payday Lender #32 .... www.ofi.state.la.us/
Pharmacist/Pharmacy/Pharm Tech #23 .... www.labp.com/pbs.html
Pharmacy Intern (College) #23 .... www.labp.com/pbs.html
Pharmacy/Hospital #23 .... www.labp.com/pbs.html
Physical Therapist/Therapist Asst #24 .... www.laptboard.org
Physician Assistant #20 .... www.lsbme.louisiana.gov/apps/verifications/lookup.aspx
Podiatrist #20 .... www.lsbme.louisiana.gov/apps/verifications/lookup.aspx
Prevention Specialist (Social Work) #28 .... www.la-adra.org/database.asp
Private Investigator/PI Company #58 .... www.lsbpie.com
Psychologist #15 .... www.onesimuswebs.com/lsbep_db.asp
Radiation Therapy Technologist #16 .... www.lsrtbe.org/search.cfm
Radiographer/Radiologic Technologist #16 .... www.lsrtbe.org/search.cfm
Radiologic Technologist, Private #20 .... www.lsbme.louisiana.gov/apps/verifications/lookup.aspx
Real Estate Agent/Broker/Sales #60 .... www.lrec.state.la.us/sblist/csblistmain.asp
Real Estate Appraiser #29 .... www.lreasbc.state.la.us/dbfiles/appraiserinfo.htm
Residential Construction +$50,000 #41 .... www.lslbc.louisiana.gov/findcontractor_type.htm
Respiratory Therapist/Therapy Tech. #20 .... http://mt.gov/dli/rcp/
Savings & Loan #32 .... www.ofi.state.la.us/newcus.htm
Social Worker/Supervisor #6 .... www.labswe.org/databases.htm
Solicitor #33 .... www.ldi.state.la.us/search_forms/searchforms.htm
Speech Pathologist/Audiologist #18 .... www.lbespa.org/lbespa_db.asp
Substance Abuse Counselor #28 .... www.la-adra.org/database.asp
Thrift & Loan Company #32 .... www.ofi.state.la.us/newthrift.htm
Vocational Rehabilitation Counselor #63 .... www.lrcboard.org/licensee_database.asp

Louisiana Licensing Quick Finder

Acupuncturist #20 504-568-6820
Addiction Counselor #28 225-922-7700
Adult Education Instructor #42 225-342-3562
Adult Residential Care #35 225-342-9905
Agricultural Consultant #56 225-925-4578
Alarm/Security Company #26 225-272-2310
Alcoholic Beverage Vendor #3 225-925-4041
Amusement Ride Inspector #55 225-925-7045
Amusement Ride Owner/Operator #55 225-925-7045
Arborist/Utility Arborist #39 225-925-3770
Architect #50 225-925-4802
Architectural Firm #50 225-925-4802
Art Therapist #42 225-342-3562
Athletic Trainer #20 504-568-6820
Attorney #49 800-421-5722
Auctioneer/Auction Firm #44 225-922-2329
Auto Buyer (In & Out of State) #61 225-925-3870
Automobile Parts Dealer, Used #61 225-925-3870
Automotive Dismantler #61 225-925-3870
Bank #32 225-925-4660
Barber/Barber Shop/Instrct./Sch'l #4 225-925-1701
Boiler Inspector/Installer #55 225-925-4344
Bond For Deed Agency #32 225-925-4660
Boxing/Wrestling Personnel #27 318-362-4529
Burglar Alarm Contractor #55 225-925-6766
Cemetery #2 504-838-5267
Check Casher #32 225-925-4660
Check Seller #32 225-925-4660
Chemical Engineer #40 225-925-6291
Child Nutrition Program Supvr #42 225-342-3562
Child Residential Care #35 225-342-9905
Chiropractor #7 225-765-2322
Clinical Lab Personnel #20 504-568-6820
Collection Agency #32 225-925-4660
Construction Project, +$50000 #41 225-765-2301
Consumer Credit Grantor #32 225-925-4667
Contractor #30 225-765-2301
Contractor, General/Subcontractor #41 225-765-2301
Cosmetologist/Cosmetology Instructor #8 225-756-3404
Counselor, Professional (LPC) #46 225-765-2515
Court Reporter #37 225-342-2668
Credit Repair Agency #32 225-925-4660
Credit Union #32 225-925-4660
Crematory #12 504-838-5109
Day Care Facility #35 225-342-9905
Dental Hygienist #9 504-568-8574
Dentist #9 504-568-8574
Dietitian #13 225-756-3490
Drug Distributor, Wholesale #64 225-295-8567
Electrical Engineer #40 225-925-6291
Electrologist #10 504-838-5697
Electronics Repairman #34 225-231-4710
Embalmer #12 504-838-5109
Emergency Medical Technician #20 504-568-6820
Emergency Shelter #35 225-342-9905
Engineer/Engineer Intern #40 225-925-6291
Engineering Firm #40 225-925-6291
Environmental Engineer #40 225-925-6291
Equine Dentist #45 225-342-2176
Esthetician #8 225-756-3404
Euthanasia Technician #45 225-342-2176
Exercise Physiologist, Clinical #20 504-568-6820
Explosives Dealer/Handler #38 225-925-6113
Fire Alarm Contractor #55 225-925-6766
Fire Extinguisher Contractor #55 225-925-6766
Fire Protection Sprinkler Contract'r #55 225-925-6766
Fire Suppression Contractor #55 225-925-6766
Florist, Retail/Wholesale #39 225-925-3770
Foster Care/Adoption Care #35 225-342-9905
Funeral Director/Establishment #12 504-838-5109
Funeral Home Internship/Worker #12 504-838-5109
Guidance Counselor #42 225-342-3562
Hearing Aid Dealer #19 318-362-3014
Home Improvem't Cont'r +$75,000 #41 225-765-2301
Horse Owner/Trainer #52 504-483-4000
Horse Racing #52 504-483-4000
Horse Racing-related Profession #52 504-483-4000
Horticulturist #39 225-925-3770
Insurance Agent, LHA/PC #33 225-342-0860
Insurance Agent/Broker/Producer #33. 225-342-0860
Interior Designer #14 225-763-5550
Investment Advisor #53 225-925-4660
Jockey/Apprentice/Jockey Agent #52 504-483-4000
Juvenile Detention #35 225-342-9905
Land Surveyor/Survey Intern/Firm #40 225-925-6291
Landscape Architect/Contractor #39 225-925-3770
Lender #32 225-925-4660
Livestock Branding #43 225-925-3962
Loan Broker #32 225-925-4660
Lobbyist #31 225-763-8777
Lottery #47 225-297-2000
Lottery Claims Center #48 504-889-0031
Manicurist #8 225-756-3404
Marriage and Family Therapist #46 225-765-2515
Massage Therapist #62 225-771-4090
Maternity Home #35 225-342-9905
Medical Doctor #20 504-568-6820
Medical Gas Piping Installer #51 225-756-3434
Midwife #20 504-568-6820
Mold Remediation #41 225-765-2301
Montessori Teacher #42 225-342-3562
Mortgage Lender/Broker, Resid't'l #32 225-925-4662
Motor Vehicle Agent/Sellerman #59 504-838-5207
Motor Vehicle Crusher/Shredder #61 225-925-3870
Motor Vehicle Dealer, Used #61 225-925-3870
Motor Vehicle Dealer; New/Used #59 504-838-5207
Motor Vehicle Inspector #1 225-667-1927
Motor Vehicle Leasing/Rent'l Firm #59 504-838-5207
Motor Vehicle Mfg/Distributor #61 225-925-3870
Motor Vehicle Sales Finance Firm #59 504-838-5207

Motor Vehicle Sales Rep. #61 225-925-3870
Music Therapist #42 225-342-3562
Notary Public #54 225-922-0507
Notification Filer #32 225-992-0634
Nuclear Engineer #40 225-925-6291
Nuclear Medicine Technologist #16 504-838-5231
Nurse (Practical) School #25 504-838-5791
Nurse, RN #21 225-763-3570
Nurse, Student #21 225-763-3570
Nurse-LPN #25 504-838-5791
Nurses' Aide #36 225-295-8575
Nursing Home Administrator #36 225-295-8571
Nursing School #21 225-763-3570
Nutritionist #13 225-756-3490
Occupational Therapist/Technologist #20504-568-6820
Optometrist #22 318-335-2989
Osteopathic Physician #20 504-568-6820
Pari-Mutuel Employee #52 504-483-4000
Pawnbroker #32 225-925-4660
Payday Lender #32 225-925-4660
Personal Care Attendant #35 225-342-9905
Pesticide Ap/Dealer/Operator #56 225-925-4578
Pharmacist/Pharmacy #23 225-925-6496
Pharmacy Intern (College) #23 225-925-6496
Pharmacy Tech #23 225-925-6496
Pharmacy/Hospital #23 225-925-6496
Physical Therapist/Therapist Asst #24. 337-262-1043
Physician Assistant #20 504-568-6820
Plumber Journeyman/Master #51 225-756-3434
Podiatrist #20 504-568-6820
Polygraph Examiner #57 225-744-3531
Prevention Spec'list (Social Work) #28 225-922-7700
Private Investigator/PI Company #58... 225-763-3556
Private Security #26 225-272-2310
Psychologist #15 225-763-3935
Public Accountant-CPA #5 504-566-1244
Radiation Therapy Technologist #16 ... 504-838-5231
Radiographer #16 504-838-5231
Radiologic Technologist #16 504-838-5231
Radiologic Technologist, Private #20... 504-568-6820
Reading Specialist #42 225-342-3562
Real Estate Agent/Broker/Sales #60.... 225-765-0191
Real Estate Appraiser #29 225-765-0191
Real Estate Schl/Instruc/Educator #60 225-765-0191
Residential Construction +$50,000 #41 225-765-2301
Respiratory Therapist/Therapy Tech. #20 504-568-6820
Respite Care #35 225-342-9905
Retort Operator #12 504-838-5109
Sanitarian #17 225-925-7204
Satellite Technician #34 225-231-4710
Savings & Loan #32 225-925-4660
School Counsel'r/Librar'n/Nurse/Princ'p'l/Superint'd'nt #42 225-342-3562
School Psychologist #42 225-342-3562
School Superintendent, Parish or City #42 225-342-3562
School Therapist #42 225-342-3562
Securities Salesperson/Dealer #53 225-925-4660
Security Guard #26 225-272-2310
Shorthand Reporter #37 225-342-2668
Social Worker #6 225-756-3470
Solicitor #33 225-342-0860
Speech Pathologist/Audiologist #18 225-756-5480
Speech/Lang'ge/Hear'ng Teacher #42 225-342-3562
Substance Abuse Counselor #28 225-922-7700
Supervised Independent Living #35 225-342-9905
Teacher, Temporary #42 225-342-3562
Teacher/Teacher's Aide #11 225-342-5840
Thrift & Loan Company #32 225-925-4660
Timeshare Interest Salesperson #60 225-765-0191
TV-Radio Technician #34 225-231-4710
Veterinarian/Veterinary Tech #45 225-342-2176
Vocational Rehabilitation Couns'l'r #63 225-922-1435
Water Supply Piping #51 225-756-3434

Louisiana Licensing Agency Information

#1 State Police Safety & Enforcement, 527 Florida Blvd, Denham Springs, LA 70726; 225-925-6113, Fax- 225-925-4048. www.lsp.org/motorcarrier.html

#2 Cemetery Board, 3445 N Causeway Blvd, #700, Metairie, LA 70002-4946; 504-838-5267, Fax- 504-838-5289. www.lcb.state.la.us

#3 Board of Alcohol & Tobacco, 8585 Archives Ave, Ste 220, PO Box 66404 (70896), Baton Rouge, LA 70809; 225-925-4041, Fax- 225-925-3975. Hours- 8AM-4PM. www.atc.rev.state.la.us Search data at- www.atc.rev.state.la.us/licenselookup.html

#4 Board of Barber Examiners, PO Box 14029 (4626 Jamestown Ave, #1), Baton Rouge, LA 70898-4029; 225-925-1701, Fax- 225-925-1703. Hours- 8AM-4PM. www.legis.state.la.us/boards/board_members.asp?board=18

#5 Board of Certified Public Accountants, 601 Poydras St, #1770, New Orleans, LA 70130; 504-566-1244, Fax- 504-566-1252. www.cpaboard.state.la.us Will sell lists.

#6 Board of Certified Social Work Examiners, 18550 Highland Rd, #B, Baton Rouge, LA 70809; 225-756-3470, Fax- 225-756-3472. www.labswe.org Search data at- www.labswe.org/databases.htm Verifications not available by phone. Use database or submit written request for verification - $5.00 fee.

#7 Board of Chiropractic Examiners, 8621 Summa Ave, Baton Rouge, LA 70809; 225-765-2322, Fax- 225-765-2640. 8:30AM-4:30. www.lachiropracticboard.com/index.htm Search data at- www.lachiropracticboard.com/lic-drs.htm

#8 Board of Cosmetology, 11622 Sunbelt Court, Baton Rouge, LA 70809; 225-756-3404, Fax- 225-756-3410. www.beautyschoolsdirectory.com/faq/license_la.php

#9 Board of Dentistry, 365 Canal Street, #2680, New Orleans, LA 70130; 504-568-8574, Fax- 504-568-8598. www.lsbd.org Search data at- www.lsbd.org/DentistSearch.aspx Lists of all dentists is sold for $500.00; list of dental hygienists is also available for $500.00.

#10 Board of Electrolysis Examiners, PO Box 8648, Metairie, LA 70011-8648; 504-838-5697, Fax- 318-463-3991. www.legis.state.la.us/boards/board_members.asp?board=274

#11 Board of Elementary & Secondary Education, 1201 N 3rd St #5-190, Baton Rouge, LA 70802; 225-342-5840, Fax- 225-342-5843. www.doe.state.la.us/lde/bese/home.html

#12 Board of Embalmers & Funeral Directors, PO Box 8757, Metairie, LA 70011; 888-508-9083 or 504-838-5109, Fax- 504-838-5112. Hours- 9AM-4PM. www.lsbefd.state.la.us

#13 Board of Examiners in Dietetics & Nutrition, 18550 Highland Rd, #B, Baton Rouge, LA 70809; 225-756-3490, Fax- 225-756-3472. 8AM-4:30PM. www.lbedn.org

#14 State Board of Interior Designers, 5222 Summa Court, #358, Baton Rouge, LA 70809; 225-763-5550, Fax- 225-763-5551. http://lsbid.org/Default.htm Search data at- http://lsbid.org/licensees.asp

#15 Board of Examiners of Psychologists, 8280 YMCA Plaza Dr, 1 Oak Sq, Bldg 8B, Baton Rouge, LA 70810; 225-763-3935, Fax- 225-763-3968. www.lsbep.org/index.html Search data at- www.onesimuswebs.com/lsbep_db.asp

#16 Board of Examiners of Radiologic Technologists, 3108 Cleary Ave, #207, Metairie, LA 70002; 504-838-5231, Fax- 504-780-1740. Hours- 8AM-4PM. www.lsrtbe.org Search data at- www.lsrtbe.org/search.cfm

#17 Board of Examiners of Sanitarians, 7173-A Florida Blvd, Baton Rouge, LA 70806; 225-925-7204, Fax- 225-925-7245. Hours- 7:30AM-4PM. www.lsbes.org

#18 Board of Examiners of Speech/Language Pathology & Audiology, 18550 Highland Rd, Suite B, Baton Rouge, LA 70809; 225.756.3480, Fax- 225-756-3472. www.lbespa.org

#19 Board of Hearing Aid Dealers, PO Box 6016, Monroe, LA 71211-6016; 318-362-3014, Fax- 318-362-3019. Hours- 8AM-4PM.

#20 Executive Director, Board of Medical Examiners, 630 Camp St, New Orleans, LA 70130; 504-568-6820, auto response- dial 1, Fax- 504-568-8893. www.lsbme.louisiana.gov/ Search data at- www.lsbme.louisiana.gov/apps/verifications/lookup.aspx Email verification requests accepted.

#21 Board of Nursing, 5207 Essen Ln, # 6, Baton Rouge, LA 70809; 225-763-3570, Fax- 225-763-3580. https://www.lsbn.state.la.us/default.asp Search data at- https://www.lsbn.state.la.us/services/service.asp?s=1&sid=8

#22 Board of Optometry Examiners, 115-B N 13th St, Oakdale, LA 71463; 318-335-2989, Fax- 318-335-2989. Hours- 8AM-5PM. www.arbo.org/index.php? Search at- www.arbo.org/index.php?action=findanoptometrist

#23 Board of Pharmacy, 5615 Corporate Blvd, #8E, Baton Rouge, LA 70808; 225-925-6496, Fax- 225-925-6499. www.labp.com Search data at- www.labp.com/pbs.html

#24 Board of Physical Therapy Examiners, 104 Fairlane Dr, Lafayette, LA 70507-5307; 337-262-1043, Fax- 337-262-1054. www.laptboard.org Search data at- www.laptboard.org

#25 Board of Practical Nurse Examiners, 3421 N Causeway Blvd, #505, Metairie, LA 70002-3711; 504-838-5791, Fax- 504-838-5279. Hours- 7:30AM-3:30PM. www.lsbpne.com

#26 Board of Private Security Examiners, 15703 Old Hammond Hwy, Baton Rouge, LA 70816; 225-272-2310, Fax- 225-272-5816. www.legis.state.la.us/boards/board_members.asp?board=384

#27 Boxing & Wrestling Commission, PO Box 13126, Monroe, LA 71213; 318-362-4529, Fax- 318-362-4628. www.legis.state.la.us/boards/board_members.asp?board=16

#28 Addictive Disorder Regulatory Authority, Licensing and Certification, 628 N. 4th Street, Baton Rouge, LA 70802; 225.342.8941, Fax- 225.342.0441. 8AM-4:30PM. www.la-adra.org Search at- www.la-adra.org/database.asp

#29 Real Estate Commission, Real Estate Appraisers State Board of Certification, 5222 Summa Ct, Baton Rouge, LA 70809-3727; 225-765-0191, in-state toll-free-800-821-4529, Fax- 225-765-0637. www.lreasbc.state.la.us Search data at- www.lreasbc.state.la.us/dbfiles/appraiserinfo.htm

#30 Contractors Licensing Board, PO Box 14419, Baton Rouge, LA 70898; 225-765-2301, Fax- 225-765-2431. www.lslbc.louisiana.gov/ Search data at- www.lslbc.louisiana.gov/findcontractor.asp

#31 Supervisory Committee on Campaign Finance Disclosure, Louisiana Board of Ethics, PO Box 4368 (2415 Quail Dr, 3rd Fl), Baton Rouge, LA 70821; 225-763-8777; 800-842-6630, Fax- 225-763-8780. Hours- 8AM-4:45PM. www.ethics.state.la.us Search data at- www.ethics.state.la.us/Lobs.pdf

#32 Office of Financial Institutions, 8660 United Plaza Blvd, 2nd Fl, Baton Rouge, LA 70809; 225-925-4660, Fax- 225-925-4548. www.ofi.state.la.us

#33 Department of Insurance, Agent's License Division, 1702 N 3rd St, Baton Rouge, LA 70802; 225-342-0860, Fax- 225-219-9322. www.ldi.state.la.us/index.htm Search data at- www.ldi.state.la.us/search_forms/searchforms.htm

#34 Radio And Television Technicians Board, 6554 Florida Blvd, #109, Baton Rouge, LA 70806; 225-231-4710, Fax- 225-231-4711.

#35 Department of Social Services, Bureau of Licensing, PO Box 3078, Baton Rouge, LA 70821; 225-342-9905, Fax- 225-342-9690. www.dss.state.la.us

#36 Examiners of Nursing Facility Administrators, 5647 Superior Dr, Baton Rouge, LA 70816-6049; 225-295-8571, Fax- 225-295-8574. Hours- 7:30AM-4PM. www.labenfa.com

#37 Examiners of Certified Shorthand Reporters, PO Box 3257, Baton Rouge, LA 70821-3257; 225-342-2668, Fax- 225-342-2698. www.lacourtreporterboard.com/

#38 Explosives Control Unit, State Police, POB 66168 Box A-26, Baton Rouge, LA 70896; 225-925-6113, Fax- 225-925-4048. www.lsp.org/tess.html#terials

#39 Department of Agriculture, Agricultural & Environmental Sciences, PO Box 3596, Baton Rouge, LA 70821-3596; 225-925-3770, Fax- 225-925-3760. www.ldaf.state.la.us/portal/

#40 Professional Engineers & Land Surveying Board, 9643 Brookline Ave #121, Baton Rouge, LA 70809-1433; 225-925-6291, Fax- 225-925-6292. www.lapels.com/index.htm Search data at- www.lapels.com/indiv_search.asp Will sell lists.

#41 Licensing Board for Contractors, PO Box 14419, Baton Rouge, LA 70898-4419; 225-765-2301, Fax- 225-765-2431. www.lslbc.louisiana.gov/index.asp

#42 Department of Education, Licensing Bureau of Higher Education Certification, 626 N 4th St, Baton Rouge, LA 70804-9064; 225-342-3562, Fax- 225-342-3499. www.doe.state.la.us/lde/offices/teachercert.html

#43 Dept of Agriculture & Forestry, Livestock Brand Commission, PO Box 1951 (5825 Florida Blvd), Baton Rouge, LA 70821; 225-925-3962, Fax- 225-925-4103. Hours- 7:30AM-4:30PM. www.ldaf.state.la.us/portal/Offices/AnimalHealthServices/LivestockBrandCommission/BrandInspectorsEnforcementOfficers/tabid/231/Default.aspx

#44 Auctioneers Licensing Board, 5222 Summa Ct., Ste 352, Baton Rouge, LA 70809; 225-763-5568, Fax- 225-763-5598. Hours- 8AM-3PM. www.lalb.org Search data at- www.lalb.org/database.asp

#45 Board of Veterinary Medicine, 263 3rd St, #104, Baton Rouge, LA 70801; 225-342-2176, Fax- 225-342-2142. www.lsbvm.org Will sell lists.

#46 Licensed Professional Counselors, Board of Examiners, 8631 Summa Ave, Baton Rouge, LA 70809; 225-765-2515, Fax- 225-765-2514. Hours- 10AM-4PM M-TH. www.lpcboard.org Search - www.lpcboard.org/lpc_alpha_list.htm

#47 Lottery Corporation, State Headquarters, 555 Laurel St, Baton Rouge, LA 70801; 225-297-2000, Fax- 225-297-2005. www.louisianalottery.com/

#48 Lottery Corporation, PO Box 90010, Baton Rouge, LA 70879-0010; 225-297-2350. www.louisianalottery.com

#49 State Bar Association, 601 St Charles Av, New Orleans, LA 70130; 800-421-5722, Fax- 504-566-0930. www.lsba.org/

#50 Board of Architectural Examiners, 9625 Fenway Ave #B, Baton Rouge, LA 70809-1413; 225-925-4802, Fax- 225-925-4804. www.lastbdarchs.com Search data at- www.lastbdarchs.com/roster.htm

#51 Plumbing Board, 12497 Airline Hwy, Baton Rouge, LA 70817; 225-756-3434, Fax- 225-756-3433. Hours- 8:30AM-4:30PM. www.lslbc.louisiana.gov/spb.htm

#52 State Racing Commission, 320 N Carrollton Ave, #2B, New Orleans, LA 70119-5100; 504-483-4000, Fax- 504-483-4898. www.legis.state.la.us/boards/board_members.asp?board=153

#53 Securities Division, Office of Financial Institutions, PO Box 94095 (8660 United Plaza Blvd, 2nd Fl), Baton Rouge, LA 70804; 225-925-4660, Fax- 225-925-4548. www.ofi.state.la.us

#54 Office of Secretary of State, PO Box 94125, Baton Rouge, LA 70804-9125; 225-922-0507, Fax- 225-922-0945. www.sos.louisiana.gov/tabid/70/Default.aspx

#55 Office of the State Fire Marshall, 8181 Independence Blvd, Baton Rouge, LA 70806; 225-925-4911; 800-256-5452, Fax- 225-925-3813. www.dps.state.la.us/sfm/index.htm

#56 Agricultural & Environmental Sciences, Structural Pest Control Commission, PO Box 3596 (5825 Florida Blvd), Baton Rouge, LA 70821; 225-925-4578, Fax- 225-925-3760. www.ldaf.state.la.us/portal/Offices/AgriculturalEnvironmentalSciences/PesticideEnvironmentalPrograms/StructuralPestControlProgram/tabid/369/Default.aspx

#57 Baton Rouge Police Dept., Polygraph Board, 16286 Winding Ridge Dr, Prairieville, LA 70769; 225-744-3531. www.legis.state.la.us/boards/board_members.asp?board=212

#58 Board of Private Investigators Examiners, 2051 Silverside Dr, #190, Baton Rouge, LA 70808; 225-763-3556; 800-299-9696, Fax- 225-763-3536. www.lsbpie.com

#59 Motor Vehicle Commission, 3519 12th Street, Metairie, LA 70002-3427; 504-838-5207, Fax- 504-838-5416. www.lmvc.state.la.us

#60 Real Estate Commission, PO Box 14785 (5222 Summa Court), Baton Rouge, LA 70898-4785; 225-765-0191, in-state toll-free 800-821-4529, Fax- 225-765-0637. www.lrec.state.la.us Search data at- www.lrec.state.la.us/sblist/csblistmain.asp

#61 Used Motor Vehicle & Parts Commission, 3132 Valley Creek Dr, Baton Rouge, LA 70808; 225-925-3870, Fax- 225-925-3869. Hours- 8AM-4:30PM. www.lrumvc.louisiana.gov Search data at- www.lrumvc.louisiana.gov/search/search.htm "New Motored products" include new motorhomes, motorcycles, ATV/Off-road, trailers, boats and boat motors.

#62 Professional Licensing Boards, Board of Massage Therapy, 12022 Plank Rd, Baton Rouge, LA 70811; 225-771-4090, Fax- 225-771-4021. www.lsbmt.org

#63 Board of Examiners, Board of Vocational Rehabilitation Counselors, PO Box 41594, Baton Rouge, LA 70835; 225-922-1435, Fax- 225-922-1352. www.lrcboard.org

#64 Board of Wholesale Drug Distributors, 12046 Justice Ave, #C, Baton Rouge, LA 70816; 225-295-8567, Fax- 225-295-8568. www.lsbwdd.org

Louisiana Federal Courts

The following list indicates the district and division name for each Parish in the state. If the bankruptcy court location is different from the district court, then the location of the bankruptcy court appears in parentheses.

Louisiana Parish/Court Cross Reference

Parish	District	Division
Acadia Parish	Western	Lafayette (Lafayette-Opelousas)
Allen Parish	Western	Lake Charles
Ascension Parish	Middle	Baton Rouge
Assumption Parish	Eastern	New Orleans
Avoyelles Parish	Western	Alexandria
Beauregard Parish	Western	Lake Charles
Bienville Parish	Western	Shreveport
Bossier Parish	Western	Shreveport
Caddo Parish	Western	Shreveport
Calcasieu Parish	Western	Lake Charles
Caldwell Parish	Western	Monroe
Cameron Parish	Western	Lake Charles
Catahoula Parish	Western	Alexandria
Claiborne Parish	Western	Shreveport
Concordia Parish	Western	Alexandria
De Soto Parish	Western	Shreveport
East Baton Rouge Parish	Parish	Middle Baton Rouge
East Carroll Parish	Western	Monroe
East Feliciana Parish	Middle	Baton Rouge
Evangeline Parish	Western	Lafayette (Lafayette-Opelousas)
Franklin Parish	Western	Monroe
Grant Parish	Western	Alexandria
Iberia Parish	Western	Lafayette (Lafayette-Opelousas)
Iberville Parish	Middle	Baton Rouge
Jackson Parish	Western	Monroe
Jefferson Davis Parish	Western	Lake Charles
Jefferson Parish	Eastern	New Orleans
La Salle Parish	Western	Alexandria
Lafayette Parish	Western	Lafayette (Lafayette-Opelousas)
Lafourche Parish	Eastern	New Orleans
Lincoln Parish	Western	Monroe
Livingston Parish	Middle	Baton Rouge
Madison Parish	Western	Monroe
Morehouse Parish	Western	Monroe
Natchitoches Parish	Western	Alexandria
Orleans Parish	Eastern	New Orleans
Ouachita Parish	Western	Monroe
Plaquemines Parish	Eastern	New Orleans
Pointe Coupee Parish	Middle	Baton Rouge
Rapides Parish	Western	Alexandria
Red River Parish	Western	Shreveport
Richland Parish	Western	Monroe
Sabine Parish	Western	Shreveport
St. Bernard Parish	Eastern	New Orleans
St. Charles Parish	Eastern	New Orleans
St. Helena Parish	Middle	Baton Rouge
St. James Parish	Eastern	New Orleans
St. John the Baptist Parish	Parish	EasternNew Orleans
St. Landry Parish	Western	Lafayette (Lafayette-Opelousas)
St. Martin Parish	Western	Lafayette (Lafayette-Opelousas)
St. Mary Parish	Western	Lafayette (Lafayette-Opelousas)
St. Tammany Parish	Eastern	New Orleans
Tangipahoa Parish	Eastern	New Orleans
Tensas Parish	Western	Monroe
Terrebonne Parish	Eastern	New Orleans
Union Parish	Western	Monroe
Vermilion Parish	Western	Lafayette (Lafayette-Opelousas)
Vernon Parish	Western	Alexandria
Washington Parish	Eastern	New Orleans
Webster Parish	Western	Shreveport
West Baton Rouge Parish	Parish	Middle Baton Rouge
West Carroll Parish	Western	Monroe
West Feliciana Parish	Middle	Baton Rouge
Winn Parish	Western	Alexandria

Standards for Federal Courts: Fees are standard unless noted in profile. Search fee is $26.00 per item (one party name or case number). Copy fee is $.50 per page. Certification fee is $9.00 per document, double for exemplification, if available. Most courts require prepayment. Mail requests should enclose a SASE unless otherwise noted. Before releasing records, all courts require prepayment, unless noted.

District courts index by defendant and plaintiff and by case number. Bankruptcy courts usually index by debtor and case number. While most courts now have their indexes on computer, many may still maintain index card files as well. Courts will archive closed case files at different times.

There are numerous public access programs available to online subscribers. Search the U.S. Party/Case Index to find party names and case numbers among all courts. Individual case data is provided on PACER. A search of CM/ECF provides copies of cases filed electronically. For details about PACER, the US Party/Case Index, and CM/ECF see the Appendix or go to http://pacer.psc.uscourts.gov or call 800-676-6856.

US District Court
Louisiana Eastern District

New Orleans Division Clerk of Court, 500 Poydras St, Rm C-151, New Orleans, LA 70130, 504-589-7600/7650; records- 504-589-7671; Fax- 504-589-7698. Hours- 8:30AM-5PM. www.laed.uscourts.gov

Counties/Note: Assumption Parish, Jefferson Parish, Lafourche Parish, Orleans Parish, Plaquemines Parish, St. Bernard Parish, St. Charles Parish, St. James Parish, St. John the Baptist Parish, St. Tammany Parish, Tangipahoa Parish, Terrebonne Parish, Washington Parish.

Searches/Indexing: Search request requires name only. Results do not include SSN or DOB. New cases are in the index 1-2 days after filing date.

Both computer and card indexes maintained. Case files sent to archives 6 months after closed.

Search Access: Only docket info is available by phone. **Mail:** Search usually completed- 3-5 days. Include SASE for return. **Fax:** Fax search requests accepted. **In person:** 6 public terminals available. No self-serve copier.

Payment: Pay by money order, cashier's check. Payee: Clerk, US District Court.

E-Services: Document images available. PACER records go back to 1989. New records online after 1 day. ECF at https://ecf.laed.uscourts.gov

US Bankruptcy Court Louisiana Eastern District

New Orleans Division Clerk of Court, 500 Poydras St, B-601, New Orleans, LA 70130, 504-589-7878. Hours- 8:30AM - 4:30PM. www.laeb.uscourts.gov

Counties/Note: Assumption Parish, Jefferson Parish, Lafourche Parish, Orleans Parish, Plaquemines Parish, St. Bernard Parish, St. Charles Parish, St. James Parish, St. John the Baptist Parish, St. Tammany Parish, Tangipahoa Parish, Terrebonne Parish, Washington Parish.

Searches/Indexing: Helpful in include SSN in search request. Results do not include SSN or DOB. Will not fax back documents. New cases are in the index immediately after filing date. Both computer and card indexes maintained; computer only after 1/2002; 1979 to 1985 on card index. Old records also indexed on microfiche. District-wide searches back to 11/1985 available here on computer.

Search Access: info is available from 8:30AM-4:30PM via phone, without fee for case status information. Only docket data is released. Voice Case Information Service available, call VCIS at 504-589-7879 or 866-375-7879. **Mail:** Search usually completed- same day if possible. Include SASE for return. **In person:** 5 public terminals available. Computer generated copies- $.10 each.

Payment: Pay by credit cards, money order, cashier's check, business check. No debtor personal checks accepted. Payee: Clerk, US Bankruptcy Court.

E-Services: PACER records go back to 1985. New records online immediately. ECF at https://ecf.laeb.uscourts.gov. Search next 2 months court calendar free at https://ecf.laeb.uscourts.gov/cgi-bin/PublicCalendar.pl/. Also, court supplies a list of archive retrieval companies for handling Ft Worth Archive records.

US District Court Louisiana Middle District

Baton Rouge Division Court Clerk, 777 Florida St, #139, Baton Rouge, LA 70801, 225-389-3500; Fax- 225-389-3501. 8AM-4:30PM. www.lamd.uscourts.gov

Counties/Note: Ascension Parish, East Baton Rouge Parish, East Feliciana Parish, Iberville Parish, Livingston Parish, Pointe Coupee Parish, St. Helena Parish, West Baton Rouge Parish, West Feliciana Parish.

Searches/Indexing: Search request requires name only. Results do not include SSN or DOB. Will not fax back documents. New cases are in the index immediately after filing date. Computer index back to 1992 maintained; prior to 1992 on microfiche. Case files sent to archives 1 year after closed.

Search Access: Limited docket info available by phone. **Mail:** Search usually completed- 2-3 days. SASE not required. **In person:** 2 public terminals available. Self-serve computer copies- $.10 each. Copy machine- $.25 per page.

Payment: Pay by Visa/MC, money order, cashier's check, business check. No personal checks. Payee: Clerk, US District Court.

E-Services: Document images available. PACER records go back to 10/1993. New records online after 1 day. ECF at https://ecf.lamd.uscourts.gov. **Opinions Online:** www.lamd.uscourts.gov/Opinions/opinions.asp. **Online Note:** Access courtroom calendars at main website and click on Calendars.

US Bankruptcy Court Louisiana Middle District

Baton Rouge Div. Court Clerk, 707 Florida St, Rm 119, Baton Rouge, LA 70801, 225-389-0211; Fax- 229-389-0410. Hours- 8:30AM-4:30PM. www.lamb.uscourts.gov

Counties/Note: Ascension Parish, East Baton Rouge Parish, East Feliciana Parish, Iberville Parish, Livingston Parish, Pointe Coupee Parish, St. Helena Parish, West Baton Rouge Parish, West Feliciana Parish.

Searches/Indexing: Include name, SSN, address in search request. Results include last 4 SSN digits and address. Will fax back pages $.50 each. New cases are in the index immediately after filing date. Computer index goes back to 1986; in card catalog back to 1950s. All closed paper files have been sent to archives.

Search Access: Only docket info available by phone. Voice Case Information Service available, call VCIS at 225-382-2175. **Mail:** Search usually completed- 1 week. Include SASE for return. **Fax:** Fax search requests accepted. **In person:** 3 public terminals available. Computer self-serve copies- $.10 each.

Payment: Pay by Visa/MC, money order, cashier's check, business check. No personal checks. Payee: Clerk, US Bankruptcy Court.

E-Services: PACER records go back to 5/15/1992. New records online after 1 day. ECF at https://ecf.lamb.uscourts.gov. **Opinions Online:** www.lamb.uscourts.gov/opinions.htm. **Online Note:** Access Unclaimed Funds list at www.lamb.uscourts.gov/publicinfo.htm.

US District Court Louisiana Western District

Alexandria Division Court Clerk, 105 US Post Office and Courthouse, 515 Murray St, Alexandria, LA 71301, 318-473-7415; records-318-676-4273; crim dockets- 318-676-4277; civil dockets- 318-676-4273; Fax- 318-473-7345. 8AM-N, 1-4:30PM. www.lawd.uscourts.gov

Counties: Avoyelles Parish, Catahoula Parish, Concordia Parish, Grant Parish, La Salle Parish, Natchitoches Parish, Rapides Parish, Winn Parish.

Searches/Indexing: Include DOB and SSN in search request. Results do not include SSN or DOB. Will fax back documents for fee. New cases are in the index 3 days after filing date. Cases files now all electronic; never purged.

Search Access: Only docket info is available by phone. **Mail:** Search usually completed- 1-2 days. Include SASE for return. **Fax:** Written fax requests accepted. **In person:** 1 public terminal available. No self-serve copier.

Payment: Pay by money order, cashier's or personal check. No credit cards accepted. Payee: Clerk, US District Court.

E-Services: PACER records go back to 10/1993. ECF at https://ecf.lawd.uscourts.gov

Lafayette Div. Court Clerk, 800 Lafayette St #2100, Lafayette, LA 70501, 337-593-5000; Fax- 337-593-5027. Hours- 8AM-N, 1-4:30PM. www.lawd.uscourts.gov

Counties: Acadia Parish, Evangeline Parish, Iberia Parish, Lafayette Parish, St Landry Parish, St Martin Parish, St Mary Parish, Vermilion Parish.

Searches/Indexing: Include DOB and SSN in search request. Results do not include SSN or DOB. Will not fax back documents. New cases are in the index 1 day after filing date. Certified name searches only available at Shreveport office. Cases files now all electronic; never purged.

Search Access: Only docket info is available by phone. **Mail:** Search usually completed- 1-2 days. Certified name searches only performed from the Shreveport office. Include SASE for return. **In person:** 2 public terminals available. No self-serve copier.

Payment: Pay by Visa/MC, money order, cashier's, business or personal check. Payee: Clerk, US District Court.

E-Services: PACER records go back to 10/1993. ECF at https://ecf.lawd.uscourts.gov

Lake Charles Div. Court Clerk, 611 Broad St, Suite 188, Lake Charles, LA 70601, 337-437-3870; Fax- 337-437-3873. 8AM-N, 1-4:30PM. www.lawd.uscourts.gov

Counties/Note: Allen Parish, Beauregard Parish, Calcasieu Parish, Cameron Parish, Jefferson Davis Parish, Vernon Parish.

Searches/Indexing: Include DOB and SSN in search request. Results do not include SSN or DOB. Will not fax back documents. New cases are in the index 3 days after filing date. Electronically filed records available at this court. Cases files now all electronic; never purged.

Search Access: Only docket info is available by phone. **Mail:** Search usually completed- 1-2 days. Include SASE for return. **In person:** 1 public terminal available. No self-serve copier.

Payment: Pay by Visa/MC, money order, cashier's, business or personal check. Payee: Clerk, US District Court.

E-Services: PACER records go back to 10/1993. New records online after 3 days. ECF at https://ecf.lawd.uscourts.gov

Monroe Division Court Clerk, 201 Jackson St, #215, Monroe, LA 71201, 318-322-6740; Fax-318-387-9661. Hours- 8AM-N, 1-4:30PM. www.lawd.uscourts.gov

Counties/Note: Caldwell Parish, East Carroll Parish, Franklin Parish, Jackson Parish, Lincoln Parish, Madison Parish, Morehouse Parish, Ouachita Parish, Richland Parish, Tensas Parish, Union Parish, West Carroll Parish. Very few case records held at Monroe any longer; search at Shreveport Division.

Searches/Indexing: Include DOB and SSN in search request. Shreveport computerized index used for searching. Results do not include SSN or DOB. Will not fax back documents. New cases are in the index 3 days after filing date. Cases files now all electronic; never purged.

Search Access: Only docket info is available by phone. **Mail:** Search usually completed- 1-2 days. Include SASE for return. **In person:** No self-serve copier.

Payment: Pay by Visa/MC, money order, cashier's, business or personal check. Payee: Clerk, US District Court.

E-Services: PACER records go back to 10/1993. ECF at https://ecf.lawd.uscourts.gov

Shreveport Division Court Clerk, US Courthouse, Suite 1167, 300 Fannin St, Shreveport, LA 71101-3083, 318-676-4273; Fax- 318-676-3962. Hours-8AM-N, 1-4:30PM. www.lawd.uscourts.gov

Counties/Note: Bienville Parish, Bossier Parish, Caddo Parish, Claiborne Parish, De Soto Parish, Red River Parish, Sabine Parish, Webster Parish.

Searches/Indexing: Include DOB and SSN in search request. Results do not include SSN or DOB. Will not fax back documents. New cases are in the index immediately after filing date. Computer index back to 1990 maintained. Computer index for cases filed back to 1977. Copies of closed records pre-1977 available on microfiche. Cases files now all electronic; never purged.

Search Access: Only docket info is available by phone. If case file is at the Federal Records Center, this court will give instructions. **Mail:** Search usually completed- 1-2 days. Include SASE for return. **In person:** No self-serve copier.

Payment: Pay by Visa/MC, money order, cashier's check, business check. Payee: Clerk, US District Court.

E-Services: PACER records go back to 10/1993. ECF at https://ecf.lawd.uscourts.gov

US Bankruptcy Court Louisiana Western District

Alexandria Div. Court Clerk, 300 Jackson St, Suite 116, Alexandria, LA 71301-8357, 318-445-1890. Hours-8AM-5PM. www.lawb.uscourts.gov

Counties/Note: Avoyelles Parish, Catahoula Parish, Concordia Parish, Grant Parish, La Salle Parish, Natchitoches Parish, Rapides Parish, Vernon Parish, Winn Parish. Chapter 7 and 11 cases from the Monroe Division now at Alexandria. Chapter 12 and Chapter 13 continue handled by Shreveport.

Searches/Indexing: Include full name and/or SSN in search request. Results include last 4 SSN digits only. Will not fax back documents. New cases are in the index immediately after filing date. District-wide searches available here back to 1/1986. Case files sent to archives 5 years after closed.

Search Access: Only docket info is available by phone. Voice Case Information Service available, call VCIS at 800-326-4026 or 318-676-4234. **Mail:** Search usually completed- 5 days. SASE not required. **In person:** 2 public terminals available. No self-serve copier. Copy from computer is $.10 per page. Court can recommend an outside vendor to search and make copies, plus cost of postage; copy service will bill law firms.

Payment: Pay by Visa/MC, money order, cashier's or business check. No personal or debtor checks. Payee: Clerk, US Bankruptcy Court.

E-Services: Document images available. PACER records go back to 1992. New records online after 1 day. ECF at https://ecf.lawb.uscourts.gov. Opinions now on ECF system. **Online Note:** Search judge's planning calendars free at www.lawb.uscourts.gov/judge/judge.htm. View Unclaimed Funds reports at www.lawb.uscourts.gov/court/Unclaimed/unclaimed.htm.

Lafayette-Opelousas Division Court Clerk, 214 Jefferson St #110, Lafayette, LA 70501-7050, 337-262-6800; Fax- 337-262-6788. Hours-8AM-5PM. www.lawb.uscourts.gov

Counties/Note: Acadia Parish, Evangeline Parish, Iberia Parish, Lafayette Parish, St. Landry Parish, St. Martin Parish, St. Mary Parish, Vermilion Parish. Office also handles case records for Lake Charles Division.

Searches/Indexing: Include full name and/or SSN in search request. Results include last 4 SSN digits only. Will not fax back documents. New cases are in the index immediately after filing date. Both computer and card indexes maintained. Pre-1987 files on index cards. Older records also on microfiche. District-wide searches available here back to 1/1986. Case files sent to archives 5 years after closed.

Search Access: Only docket info is available by phone. Voice Case Information Service available, call VCIS at 800-326-4026 or 318-676-4234. **Mail:** Search usually completed- 1 day. Include SASE for return. **In person:** Public terminals available. No self-serve copier.

Payment: Pay by Visa/MC, money order, cashier's or business check. No personal or debtor checks. Payee: Clerk, US Bankruptcy Court.

E-Services: Document images available. PACER records go back to 1992. New records online after 1 day. ECF at https://ecf.lawb.uscourts.gov. Opinions now on ECF system. **Online Note:** Search judge's planning calendars free at www.lawb.uscourts.gov/judge/judge.htm. View Unclaimed Funds reports at www.lawb.uscourts.gov/court/Unclaimed/unclaimed.htm.

Lake Charles Div. c/o Lafayette-Opelousas Division, 214 Jefferson St #100, Lafayette, LA 70501-7050, 337-262-6800. Hours- 8AM-5PM. www.lawb.uscourts.gov

Counties/Note: Allen Parish, Beauregard Parish, Calcasieu Parish, Cameron Parish, Jefferson Davis Parish. lake Charles is an unmanned office; records at Lafayette Div.

Searches/Indexing: Include full name and/or SSN in search request. Results include last 4 SSN digits only. Will not fax back documents. New cases are in the index immediately after filing date. District-wide searches available here back to 1/1986. Case files sent to archives 5 years after closed.

Search Access: Only docket info is available by phone. Voice Case Information Service available, call VCIS at 800-326-4026 or 318-676-4234. **Mail:** Include SASE for return. **In person:** Public terminals available. No self-serve copier.

Payment: Pay by Visa/MC, money order, cashier's or business check. No personal or debtor checks. Payee: Clerk, US Bankruptcy Court.

E-Services: Document images available. PACER records go back to 1992. New records online after 1 day. ECF at https://ecf.lawb.uscourts.gov. Opinions now on ECF system. **Online Note:** Search judge's planning calendars free at www.lawb.uscourts.gov/judge/judge.htm. View Unclaimed Funds reports at www.lawb.uscourts.gov/court/Unclaimed/unclaimed.htm.

Monroe Div. c/o Alexandria Division, 300 Jackson St, #116, Alexandria, LA 71301, 318-445-1890. Hours-8AM-5PM. www.lawb.uscourts.gov

Counties/Note: Caldwell Parish, East Carroll Parish, Franklin Parish, Jackson Parish, Lincoln Parish, Madison Parish, Morehouse Parish, Ouachita Parish, Richland Parish, Tensas Parish, Union Parish, West Carroll Parish. Monroe court is unmanned; cases housed as follows: Chapter 7 and Chapter 11 cases to Alexandria (address and phone given here); Chapter 12 and Chapter 13 cases to Shreveport.

Searches/Indexing: Include full name and/or SSN in search request. Results include last 4 SSN digits only. Will not fax back documents. New cases are in the index immediately after filing date. Case files sent to archives 5 years after closed.

Search Access: Only docket info is available by phone. Voice Case Information Service available, call VCIS at 800-326-4026 or 318-676-4234. **Mail:** Include SASE for return. **In person:** Public terminals available. No self-serve copier.

Payment: Pay by Visa/MC, money order, cashier's or business check. No personal or debtor checks. Payee: Clerk, US Bankruptcy Court.

E-Services: Document images available. PACER records go back to 1992. New records online after 1 day. ECF at https://ecf.lawb.uscourts.gov. Opinions now on ECF system. **Online Note:** Search judge's planning calendars free at www.lawb.uscourts.gov/judge/judge.htm. View Unclaimed Funds reports at www.lawb.uscourts.gov/court/Unclaimed/unclaimed.htm.

Shreveport Division Court Clerk, 300 Fannin St, #2201, Shreveport, LA 71101-3089, 318-676-4267; Fax- 318-676-3699. 8AM-5PM. www.lawb.uscourts.gov

Counties/Note: Bienville Parish, Bossier Parish, Caddo Parish, Claiborne Parish, De Soto Parish, Red River Parish, Sabine Parish, Webster Parish. Also has Monroe Div. Chapter 12 and 13 cases.

Searches/Indexing: Include full name and/or SSN in search request. Results include last 4 SSN digits only. Will not fax back documents. New cases are in the index immediately after filing date. District-wide searches available here back to 1/1986. Case files sent to archives 5 years after closed.

Search Access: Only docket info is available by phone. Voice Case Information Service available, call VCIS at 800-326-4026 or 318-676-4234. **Mail:** Search usually completed- 1 day. Include SASE for return. **In person:** 3 public terminals available. No self-serve copier.

Payment: Pay by Visa/MC, money order, cashier's or business check. No personal or debtor checks. Payee: Clerk, US Bankruptcy Court.

E-Services: Document images available. PACER records go back to 1992. New records online after 1 day. ECF at https://ecf.lawb.uscourts.gov. Opinions now on ECF system. **Online Note:** Search judge's planning calendars free at www.lawb.uscourts.gov/judge/judge.htm. View Unclaimed Funds reports at www.lawb.uscourts.gov/court/Unclaimed/unclaimed.htm.

Louisiana Parish Courts

Court	Jurisdiction	No. of Courts	How Organized
District Courts*	General	65	42 Districts
City Courts*	Limited	50	City Boundaries
Parish Courts	Limited	3	
Justice of the Peace Courts	Municipal	390	
Mayor's Courts	Municipal	250	
Family Court	Special	1	East Baton Rouge
Juvenile Courts	Special	4	

* Profiled in this Sourcebook.

Court	CIVIL								
	Tort	Contract	Real Estate	Min. Claim	Max. Claim	Small Claims	Estate	Eviction	Domestic Relations
District Courts*	X	X	X	$0	No Max		X		X
City Courts*	X	X	X	$0	$15,000	$3000			X
Parish Courts	X	X	X	$0	$10,000	$3000		X	X
Justice of the Peace Courts	X	X	X	$0	$3000	$3000		X	
Family Court									X
Juvenile Courts									X

Court	CRIMINAL				
	Felony	Misdemeanor	DWI/DUI	Preliminary Hearing	Juvenile
District Courts*	X	X	X		X
City Courts*		X	X	X	X
Parish Courts		X	X	X	X
Justice of the Peace Courts					
Family Court					X
Juvenile Courts					X

Administration

Judicial Administrator, Judicial Council of the Supreme Court, 400 Royal Street, Suite 1190, New Orleans, LA, 70130; 504-310-2550, Fax: 504-310-2587. (CST) www.lasc.org

Court Structure

The trial court of general jurisdiction in Louisiana is the District Court. A District Court Clerk in each Parish holds all the records for that Parish. Each Parish has its own clerk and courthouse. City Courts are courts of record and generally exercise concurrent jurisdiction with the District Court in civil cases where the amount in controversy does not exceed $15,000. In criminal matters, City Courts generally have jurisdiction over ordinance violations and misdemeanor violations of state law. City judges also handle a large number of traffic cases. Parish Courts exercise jurisdiction in civil cases worth up to $10,000 and criminal cases punishable by fines of $1,000 or less, or imprisonment of six months or less. Cases are appealable from the Parish Courts directly to the courts of appeal. A municipality may have a Mayor's Court which handles traffic cases and minor infractions. Unless noted, all courts require prepayment of fees.

Online Access

Search opinions from the state Supreme Court at www.lasc.org/opinion_search.asp. Online records go back to 1995. There is no statewide system open to the public for trial court dockets, but a number of parishes offer online access.

Searching Tips, Fees, and Other Guidelines

The courts vary widely in terms of fees. Count on at least a $10.00 search fee. 80% of the courts offer a public access terminal.

Acadia Parish

15th District Court PO Box 922, Crowley, LA 70527; 337-788-8881; fax: 337-788-1048; 8:30AM-4:30PM. ***Felony, Misdemeanor, Civil, Probate.*** www.acadiaparishclerk.com

Civil Records: Access: Phone, fax, mail, in person. Both court and visitors may perform in person searches. Search fee: $20.00 per name. Required to search: name, years to search. Civil cases indexed by defendant, plaintiff, on computer from 1985, archived from 1800s. Mail turnaround time civil 1-2 days. Civil PAT goes back to 1999.

Criminal Records: Access: Fax, mail, in person. Both court and visitors may perform in person searches. Search fee: $20.00 per name per year. Required to search: name, years to search, DOB; also helpful: SSN. Criminal records computerized from 1979, archived from 1800s. Note: Copy of check must be faxed with fax request. Mail turnaround time 1-2 days. Criminal PAT goes back to 1979. PAT results show middle initial, DOB. Terminal results include SSN.

General Information: No adoption or juvenile records released. Fee to fax out file $6.00 1st page, $2.00 add'l page; includes copies. Court makes copy: $1.00 per page, $2.00 per page is mailed. Self serve: $.75 per page.If copies are to be returned by mail and you do not provide an SASE, add $1.00 per page mailing fee. Cert fee: $6.00 per doc. Payee: Acadia Parish Clerk of Court. Personal checks accepted; credit cards are not. Mail requests: SASE required.

Allen Parish

33rd District Court PO Box 248, Oberlin, LA 70655; 337-639-4351; criminal fax: 337-639-2030; civil fax: same; 8AM-4:30PM. ***Felony, Misdemeanor, Civil, Probate.***

Probate is in a separate index. Probate fax is same as main fax number.

Civil Records: Access: Mail, in person. Both court and visitors may perform in person searches. Search fee: $10.00 per name. Fee is for a 10 year search. Required to search: name, years to search. Civil cases indexed by defendant, plaintiff, archived back to 1913; on computer back to 1985. Mail turnaround time 2 days. Civil PAT goes back to 1985. PAT civil results show middle initial.

Criminal Records: Access: Mail, in person. Both court and visitors may perform in person searches. Search fee: $10.00 per name. Fee is for a 10 year search. Required to search: name, years to search, DOB, SSN. Criminal records archived back to 1913; on computer back to 7/94. Mail turnaround time 2 days. Criminal PAT goes back to 1994. PAT results show middle initial, DOB. Identifiers on terminal results vary; SSNs may appear.

General Information: No adoption or juvenile records released. Fee to fax out file $5.00 and $2.00 each add'l page. Court makes copy: $1.00 per page. Certification fee: $5.00 per certification. Payee: Allen Parish Clerk of Court. Personal checks accepted; credit cards are not. Mail requests: SASE requested.

Ascension Parish

23rd District Court PO Box 192, Donaldsonville, LA 70346; 225-473-9866; criminal fax: 225-473-8641; civil fax: 225-473-8641; 8:30AM-4:30PM. ***Felony, Misdemeanor, Civil, Probate.***

www.eatel.net/~apcc/Clerk_of_Court/indexx.html

Civil Records: Access: Fax, mail, in person, online. Both court and visitors may perform in person searches. Search fee: $10.00 per name; add $5.00 on search fee if request made by fax. Required to search: name, years to search. Civil cases indexed by defendant, plaintiff, on computer from 1987, index books back to 1800s. Mail turnaround time 2 days. Civil PAT goes back to 1987. Access to civil judgments, etc, available by subscription; $100 set-up charge single user; $250 multiple user up to 5, plus $50.00 monthly and $.50 per image printed; includes recorded document index; see www.ascensionclerk.com/onlineservices.aspx.

Criminal Records: Access: Fax, mail, in person. Both court and visitors may perform in person searches. Search fee: $15.00 per name; add $5.00 on search fee if request made by fax. Required to search: name, years to search, DOB; also helpful: SSN. Criminal Records go back to 1800s; computerized records since 11/86. Mail turnaround time 2 days. Criminal PAT goes back to 11/1986.

General Information: No adoption or juvenile records released. Will fax documents $5.00 1st page, $1.00 each add'l. Court makes copy: $1.00 per page; $.50 per page after 1st 15. Self serve: $.50 per page. Certification fee: $3.00. Payee: Ascension Parish Clerk of Court. In state personal checks accepted. No credit cards accepted. Mail requests: SASE requested.

Assumption Parish

23rd District Court PO Box 249, Napoleonville, LA 70390; 985-369-6653; criminal fax: 985-369-2032; civil fax: same; 8:30AM-4:30PM. ***Felony, Misdemeanor, Civil, Probate.***

www.assumptionclerk.com/

Civil Records: Access: Fax, mail, in person, online. Both court and visitors may perform in person searches. Search fee: $10.00 per name per 7 years; $15.00 for 10 years. Required to search: name, years to search. Civil cases indexed by defendant, plaintiff, archived back to 1800s; on computer back to 1990. Mail turnaround time 1 day. Civil PAT goes back to 1990. After registration you may search civil court records and probate records back to 4/16/2005 at http://97.89.251.18/resolution/ or call 985-369-6653 for info or signup.

Criminal Records: Access: Fax, mail, in person, online. Both court and visitors may perform in person searches. Search fee: $15.00 per name; is for 10 years. Required to search: name, years to search, DOB. Criminal records archived back to 1800s; on computer back to 1994. Mail turnaround time 1 day. Criminal PAT goes back to 1994. After registration you may login to search criminal records at http://97.89.251.18/qGov/Verdict/Criminal/Index.aspx or call 985-369-6653 for info or signup. Registration is free.

General Information: No adoption or juvenile records released. Will fax documents $2.00 1st page, $1.00 each add'l. Court makes copy: $1.00 per page. Self serve: $.75 per page. Certification fee: $5.00 per document. Payee: Assumption Parish Clerk of Court. Personal checks accepted; credit cards are not. Mail requests: SASE requested.

Avoyelles Parish

12th District Court PO Box 219, 300 N Main, Courthouse Bldg, Marksville, LA 71351; 318-253-7523; probate phone: 318-253-7523; 8:30AM-5PM. ***Felony, Misdemeanor, Civil, Probate.***

Civil Records: Access: Mail, in person. Both court and visitors may perform in person searches. Search fee: $10.00 per name. Required to search: name, years to search. Civil cases indexed by defendant, plaintiff, on computer from 1985, microfiche back to 1800s. Mail turnaround time 1 day. Civil PAT goes back to 1985.

Criminal Records: Access: Mail, in person. Both court and visitors may perform in person searches. Search fee: $10.00 per name. Required to search: name, years to search, DOB; also helpful: SSN. Criminal records computerized from 1985, microfiche back to 1800s. Mail turnaround time 1 day. Criminal PAT goes back to 1995.

General Information: No adoption or juvenile records released. Will not fax documents. Court makes copy: $1.00 per page. Self serve: $.50 per page. Certification fee: $3.00 per page. Payee: Clerk of Court. Personal checks accepted; credit cards are not. SASE not required.

Beauregard Parish

36th District Court PO Box 1148, 201 W 1st St, DeRidder, LA 70634; 337-463-8595; fax: 337-462-3916; 8-4:30. ***Felony, Misdemeanor, Civil, Probate.***

Civil Records: Access: Mail, in person. Both court and visitors may perform in person searches. Search fee: $15.00 per name. Fee is per 10 years searched. Required to search: name, years to search. Civil cases indexed by defendant, plaintiff, on computer since 1985, archived from 1913. Mail turnaround time 1 week.

Criminal Records: Access: Mail, in person. Both court and visitors may perform in person searches. Search fee: $15.00 per name. Fee is per 10 years searched. Required to search: name, years to search, DOB; also helpful: SSN. Criminal record index in books. Mail turnaround time 1 week.

General Information: No adoption or juvenile records released. Will not fax documents. Court makes copy: $1.25 per page. Cert fee: $5.00 per doc. Payee: Clerk of Court. Personal checks accepted; credit cards are not. Mail requests: SASE required.

Bienville Parish

2nd District Court 100 Courthouse Dr, Rm 100, Arcadia, LA 71001; 318-263-2123; fax: 318-263-7426; 8:30AM-4:30PM. ***Felony, Misdemeanor, Civil, Probate.***

www.bienvilleparish.org/clerk

Civil Records: Access: Fax, mail, in person, online. Both court and visitors may perform in person searches. Search fee: $10.00 per name. Required to search: name, years to search. Civil cases indexed by defendant, plaintiff, on computer from 1991, index books prior. Mail turnaround time 2-3 days. Public use terminal has civil records back to 1/1996. PAT results show middle initial, DOB. An online subscription service to record images is available. Contact the Clerk of Court for details and pricing.

Criminal Records: Access: Fax, mail, in person. Both court and visitors may perform in person searches. Search fee: $10.00 per name. Required to search: name, years to search, DOB; also helpful: SSN. Criminal records computerized from 1991, index books prior. Mail turnaround time 2-3 days. An online subscription service to record images is available. Contact the Clerk of Court for pricing.

General Information: Online identifiers in results same as on public terminal. No adoption or juvenile records released. Will fax documents $2.00 plus $1.00 per page. Court makes copy: $1.00 per page. Self serve: $.50 per page. Certification fee: $5.00 per cert. Payee: Clerk of Court. Personal checks accepted; credit cards are not. Mail requests: SASE required.

Bossier Parish

26th District Court PO Box 430, 204 Burt Blvd, 3rd Fl, Benton, LA 71006; 318-965-2336; fax: 318-965-2713; 8:30AM-4:30PM. ***Felony, Misdemeanor, Civil, Probate, Traffic.***

www.bossierclerk.com

Civil Records: Access: Mail, in person, online. Both court and visitors may perform in person searches. Search fee: $15.00 per name. Required to search: name, years to search. Civil cases indexed by defendant, plaintiff, on computer from 1987, index books back to 1843. Mail turnaround time same or next day. Civil PAT goes back to 1987. PAT civil results show middle initial. Access to the Parish Clerk of Court online records requires $50 setup fee and $35 monthly flat fee, see www.bossierparishassessor.org/cgi-bin/pro_search.pl Civil, criminal, probate (1982 forward), traffic and domestic index information is by name or case number. Call 318-965-2336 for more information.

Criminal Records: Access: Mail, online, in person. Both court and visitors may perform in person searches. Search fee: $15.00 per name. Required to search: name, years to search: also helpful: DOB. Criminal records on computer since 1982. Mail turnaround time same or next day. Criminal PAT goes back to 1982. PAT results show middle initial, DOB. Online access to criminal records is the same as civil; results show middle initial.

General Information: No adoption or juvenile records released. Will not fax documents. Court makes copy: $.50 per page, self serve same. Certification fee: $2.00. Payee: Clerk of Court. Business checks accepted. No credit cards accepted. Mail requests: SASE requested.

Caddo Parish

1st District Court 501 Texas St, Rm 103, Texas St Courthouse, Shreveport, LA 71101-5408; 318-226-6791; criminal phone: 318-226-6786; civil phone: 318-226-6776; probate phone: 318-226-6778; 8:30AM-5PM. ***Felony, Misdemeanor, Civil, Probate.***

www.caddoclerk.com

Civil Records: Access: Mail, in person, online. Both court and visitors may perform in person searches. Search fee: $10.00 per name. Required to search: name, years to search. Civil cases indexed by defendant, plaintiff, on computer from 1984; images go back to 2000. Mail turnaround time 1-2 days. Civil PAT goes back to 1984. Online access to civil records back to 1994 and name index back to 1984 is through county internet service. Registration and $100 set-up fee and $30 monthly usage fee is required. Marriage and recording information is also available. Online images $.25 each to print. For information and sign-up, call 318-226-6523.

Criminal Records: Access: Mail, in person, online. Both court and visitors may perform in person searches. Search fee: $10.00 per name. For criminal computer printouts, fee is $2.00 for first page and $1.00 each add'l. Required to search: name, years to search, DOB; also helpful: SSN. Criminal records computerized from 1984; images go back to 2000. Mail turnaround time 1-2 days. Criminal PAT goes back to same as civil. Online access to criminal records is the same as civil. Online criminal name index goes back to '80; minutes to '84. Current calendar is also available.

General Information: No adoption or juvenile records released. Will fax documents to local or toll-free number. Court makes copy: $.50 per page. Self serve: $.50 per page. Certification fee: $2.00 per cert. Payee: Clerk of Court. Personal checks accepted. Mail requests: SASE required.

Shreveport City Court Civil Division, 1244 Texas, Shreveport, LA 71101; 318-673-5800; fax: 318-673-5813; 8AM-5PM. ***Civil Actions under $25,000, Small Claims.***
www.ci.shreveport.la.us/dept/CityCourts/cityIndex.htm

Civil Records: Access: Mail, in person. Visitors must perform in person searches themselves. No search fee. Required to search: name, years to search. Civil cases indexed by defendant, plaintiff, on computer back to 1987. Note: Must provide case number for mail searches. Public use terminal has civil records back to 1987. PAT results show middle initial, DOB.

General Information: No sealed records released. Will not fax documents. Court makes copy: $.50 per page. Certification fee: $2.50. Payee: Shreveport City Court. Personal checks and major credit cards accepted. Mail requests: SASE required.

Calcasieu Parish

14th District Court PO Box 1030, 1000 Ryn St, Courthouse, Lake Charles, LA 70602; 337-437-3550; civil phone: x2; fax: 337-437-3833; 8:30AM-4:30PM. ***Felony, Misdemeanor, Civil, Probate.***
www.calclerkofcourt.com

Search fee for each index searched. Probate fax is same as main fax number.

Civil Records: Access: Fax, mail, in person, online. Both court and visitors may perform in person searches. Search fee: $15.00 per name. Additional fee of $1.00 per year after 1st 10 years. Required to search: name, years to search. Civil cases indexed by defendant, plaintiff, on computer back 15 years. Mail turnaround time 24 hours. Civil PAT goes back to 1987. PAT civil results show middle initial. Online access to civil records is the same as criminal, see below.

Criminal Records: Access: Fax, mail, in person, online. Both court and visitors may perform in person searches. Search fee: $15.00 per name. Additional fee of $1.00 per year after 1st 10 years. Required to search: name, years to search, DOB; also helpful: SSN. Criminal records on computer since 1987. Mail turnaround time 24 hours. Criminal PAT goes back to same as civil.PAT results show name, DOB. Online access to court record indices is free at http://207.191.42.34/resolution/. Registration and password required. Full documents requires $100.00 per month subscription. Online results show middle initial, DOB.

General Information: Online identifiers in results same as on public terminal. No adoption or juvenile records released. Will fax documents $5.00 1st page, $.50 each add'l. Court makes copy: $1.00 per page, self serve same. Certification fee: $6.00 per cert. Payee: Clerk of Court. Personal checks accepted; credit cards are not. Mail requests: SASE required.

Lake Charles City Court PO Box 1664, Lake Charles, LA 70602; criminal phone: 337-491-1565; civil phone: 337-491-1564; fax: 337-491-1303; 8AM-4:30PM. ***Misdemeanor, Civil Actions under $25,000, Small Claims.*** www.lccitycourt.org/

Civil Records: Access: Mail, in person. Both court and visitors may perform in person searches. No search fee. Required to search: name, years to search. Civil cases indexed by defendant, plaintiff, kept on paper for 10 years, older records archived on computer. Mail turnaround time 2-5 days. Public use terminal has civil records back to 1989. PAT results show middle initial, DOB, SSN.

Criminal Records: Access: Mail, in person. Both court and visitors may perform in person searches. No search fee. Criminal records kept on paper for 10 years, older records archived on computer. Mail turnaround time 2-3 days.

General Information: No sealed records released. Will not fax documents. Court makes copy: $5.00 per page, self serve same. Certification fee: $5.00. Certification included in copy fee. Payee: Lake Charles City Court. Personal checks and major credit cards accepted.

Caldwell Parish

37th District Court Clerk of Court, PO Box 1327, Columbia, LA 71418; 318-649-2272; criminal fax: 318-649-2037; civil fax: same; 8AM-4:30PM. ***Felony, Misdemeanor, Civil, Probate.***

All record requests must be in writing. Probate fax is same as main fax number.

Civil Records: Access: Fax, mail, in person. Both court and visitors may perform in person searches. Search fee: $10.00 per name if court does search. Required to search: name, years to search. Civil cases indexed by defendant, plaintiff, on books from 1910, computerized since 11/84. Mail turnaround time 1 day. Civil PAT goes back to 11/1984. PAT results show name only.

Criminal Records: Access: Mail, in person. Both court and visitors may perform in person searches. Search fee: $10.00 per name if court does search. Required to search: name, years to search, DOB; also helpful: SSN. Note that some criminal records don't contain DOB or SSN. Criminal records kept on books since 1970. Mail turnaround time 1 day. Criminal PAT goes back to 1/1999; results show name only.

General Information: No adoption or juvenile records released. Will fax documents $3.00 1st page, $1.00 each add'l plus costs for the copies. Court makes copy: $1.00 per page, self serve same. Certification fee: $5.00 per document. Payee: Clerk of Court. Personal checks accepted; credit cards are not. Mail requests: SASE helpful.

Cameron Parish

38th District Court PO Box 549, Cameron, LA 70631; 337-775-5316; fax: 337-775-2838; 8:30AM -4:30PM. ***Felony, Misdemeanor, Civil, Probate.***

Civil Records: Access: Phone, mail, fax, in person. Both court and visitors may perform in person searches. Search fee: $10.00. Required to search: name, years to search. Civil cases indexed by defendant, plaintiff, from 1874; on computer back to 7/1994. Mail turnaround time 2 days. Civil PAT goes back to 1994.

Criminal Records: Access: Fax, mail, in person. Both court and visitors may perform in person searches. Search fee: $10.00 per name. Required to search: name, years to search, DOB. Criminal records from 1874; on computer back to 1980. Mail turnaround time 2 days. Criminal PAT goes back to 1981.

General Information: No adoption, interdiction or juvenile records released. Fee to fax out file $5.00 1st page, $1.00 each add'l. Court makes copy: $1.00 per page, self serve same. Certification fee: $5.00. Payee: Cameron Parish Clerk of Court. Personal checks accepted; credit cards are not. Mail requests: SASE required.

Catahoula Parish

7th District Court PO Box 654, Harrisonburg, LA 71340; 318-744-5497; fax: 318-744-5488; 8AM-4:30PM. ***Felony, Misdemeanor, Civil, Probate.***

Civil Records: Access: Mail, in person. Both court and visitors may perform in person searches. Search fee: $2.00 per name per year. Required to search: name, years to search. Civil cases indexed by defendant, plaintiff, minute entries back to 1800s. Mail turnaround time 1 week. Public use terminal has civil records back to 5/13/1998. PAT results show name only.

Criminal Records: Access: Mail, in person. Both court and visitors may perform in person searches. Search fee: $2.00 per name per year. Required to search: name, years to search, DOB. Criminal records minute entries back to 1800s. Mail turnaround time 1 week. PAT results show name only.

General Information: No adoption or juvenile records released. Will fax documents $5.00 plus $1.00 per page. Court makes copy: $1.00 per page, self serve same. Certification fee: $5.00. Payee: Clerk of Court. Personal checks accepted; credit cards are not. Mail requests: SASE required.

Claiborne Parish

2nd District Court PO Box 330, Homer, LA 71040; 318-927-9601; criminal fax: 318-927-2345; civil fax: same; 8:30AM-4:30PM. ***Felony, Misdemeanor, Civil, Probate.***

Probate is a separate index at this same address. Probate fax is same as main fax number.

Civil Records: Access: Mail, in person. Both court and visitors may perform in person searches. Search fee: $10.00 per name. Required to search: name, years to search. Civil cases indexed by defendant, plaintiff; index on docket books back to early 1900s. Mail turnaround time 1-2 days.

Criminal Records: Access: Mail, in person. Both court and visitors may perform in person searches. Search fee: $10.00 per name. Required to search: name, years to search, DOB; also helpful: SSN. Criminal records on computer 1993 forward. Mail turnaround time 1-2 days.

General Information: No adoption or juvenile records released. Fee to fax out doc $10.00 each. Court makes copy: $1.00 per page. Certification fee: $5.00 per document. Payee: Clerk of Court. Personal checks accepted. Mail requests: SASE required.

Concordia Parish

7th District Court PO Box 790, Vidalia, LA 71373; 318-336-4204; fax: 318-336-8777; 8:30AM-4:30PM. ***Felony, Misdemeanor, Civil, Probate.*** www.concordiaclerk.org

Civil Records: Access: Mail, in person. Visitors must perform in person searches themselves. Search fee: $25.00 per name. Required to search: name, years to search. Civil cases indexed by defendant, plaintiff, on computer from 1983, index books back to 1800s. Mail turnaround time 3-4 days. Civil PAT goes back to 1983. PAT results show name only.

Criminal Records: Access: Mail, in person. Visitors must perform in person searches themselves. Search fee: $15.00 per name. Required to search: name, years to search, DOB; also helpful: SSN. Criminal records computerized from 1983, index books back to 1800s. Mail turnaround time 3-4 days. Criminal PAT goes back to same as civil.PAT results show name, DOB.

General Information: No adoption or juvenile records released. Will fax documents $5.00 per doc plus $1.00 per page. Court makes copy: $1.00 per page, self serve same. Certification fee: $5.00. Payee: Clerk of Court. Personal checks accepted; credit cards are not. SASE not required.

De Soto Parish

11th District Court PO Box 1206, Mansfield, LA 71052; 318-872-3110; criminal phone: 318-872-3181; civil phone: 318-872-3788; fax: 318-872-4202; 8:30AM-4:30PM. ***Felony, Misdemeanor, Civil, Probate.*** www.desotoparishclerk.org/

Probate fax- 318-872-4202

Civil Records: Access: Mail, in person, online. Both court and visitors may perform in person searches. Search fee: $10.00 per name. Required to search: name, years to search. Civil cases indexed by defendant, plaintiff, on computer from 1991, index books back to 1843. Mail turnaround time 1-2 days. Civil PAT goes back to 1991. PAT results show name only. Access index via a web-based subscription service. Search indexes only for $50.00 per month, search index, view, & print image is $100.00 per month, plus a one-time setup fee of $150.00. Contact Jessica or Valerie at 318-872-3110 to set-up an account.
Criminal Records: Access: Mail, in person, online. Both court and visitors may perform in person searches. Search fee: $10.00 per name. Required to search: name, years to search, DOB. Criminal records on computer since 1991, archived or in books to 1950's. Mail turnaround time 1-2 days. Criminal PAT goes back to same as civil. PAT results show name only. Online access same as civil.
General Information: No adoption or juvenile records released. Fee to fax out doc $10.00 plus $1.00 per page. Court makes copy: $1.00 per page. Self serve: $.50 per page. Certification fee: $5.00 per doc. Payee: Clerk of Court. Personal checks accepted; credit cards are not. Mail requests: SASE Required.

East Baton Rouge Parish

Baton Rouge City Court PO Box 3438, 233 St Louis St, Baton Rouge, LA 70802; 225-389-5279; criminal phone: 225-389-5294; civil phone: 225-389-3017; criminal fax: 225-389-7619; civil fax: 225-389-5260; 8AM-5PM. ***Misdemeanors, Civil Actions under $20,000, Small Claims, Criminal Traffic.***
www.brgov.com/dept/citycourt/
Criminal Dept is #145; Civil is on 2nd Fl. Records Dept phone- 225-389-8388.
Civil Records: Access: Mail, in person, fax, online. Visitors must perform in person searches themselves. Search fee: $20.00 per name. Required to search: name, years to search. Civil cases indexed by defendant, plaintiff, on computer back to 1985, microfiche to 1980. Mail turnaround time 2-5 days. Civil PAT goes back to 1989. Access city court's database including attorneys and warrants free at from the web page.
Criminal Records: Access: In person, online. Required to search: name, years to search. Note: Background checks for the City are performed in the Criminal Records Division at the Baton Rouge Police Dept located at 504 Mayflower or at Parish Prison. Criminal PAT goes back to same as civil. PAT results show middle initial, DOB. Public terminal criminal results may also include SSN. Access city court's criminal dockets database and warrants free at http://brgov.com/dept.citycourt.
General Information: No sealed records released. Will fax documents for no fee. Court makes copy: $.50 per page. Certification fee: $1.00 per page. Payee: City of Baton Rouge. Personal checks accepted. Accepts Visa/MC plus 5% surcharge.

East Baton Rouge Parish Clerk of Court County

19th District Court PO Box 1991, Baton Rouge, LA 70821; 225-389-3950; criminal phone: 225-389-3964; probate phone: 225-389-5118; fax: 225-389-3392; 7:30AM-5:30PM. ***Felony, Misdemeanor, Civil, Probate.*** www.ebrclerkofcourt.org
Probate fax- 225-389-2372
Civil Records: Access: Fax, mail, online, in person. Both court and visitors may perform in person searches. Search fee: $22 per name per index, if certificate issued. Required to search: name, years to search. Civil cases indexed by defendant, plaintiff, in index books from 1810. Mail turnaround time 3-5 days. Civil PAT goes back to 1988. Online access to the clerk's database is by subscription. Civil record indexes go back to '88; case tracking of civil and probate back to 1988. Setup fee is $100.00 plus $50.00 per month for 1st password, $25.00 for each add'l passwords. Call MIS Dept at 225-389-5295 for info or visit the website.
Criminal Records: Access: Mail, online, in person. Both court and visitors may perform in person searches. Search fee: $20.00 per name, if certificate issued. Required to search: name, years to search, DOB; also helpful: SSN. Criminal docket on books from 1942; on computer back to 1990. Mail turnaround time 3-5 days. Criminal PAT goes back to 1987. PAT results show name only. Online access to criminal records is the same as civil. Criminal case tracking goes back to 8/1990. Online results show name only.
General Information: No adoption or juvenile records released. Fee to fax out file $5.00 each plus $.50 per page. Court makes copy: $.50 per page, self serve same. Certification fee: $5.00. Payee: East Baton Rouge Parish. Only cashiers checks, business checks, and money orders accepted. Major credit cards accepted. Mail requests: SASE helpful.

East Carroll Parish

6th District Court 400 1st St, Lake Providence, LA 71254; 318-559-2399; fax: 318-559-0037; 8:30-4:30PM. ***Felony, Misdemeanor, Civil, Probate.***
Civil Records: Access: Mail, in person. Both court and visitors may perform in person searches. Search fee: $20.00 per name per 10 years. Required to search: name, years to search. Civil cases indexed by defendant, plaintiff; index on docket books back to 1832. Mail turnaround time same day.
Criminal Records: Access: Mail, in person. Both court and visitors may perform in person searches. Search fee: $20.00 for 10 yr check. Required to search: name, years to search, DOB; also helpful: SSN. Criminal records indexed in books back to 1832. Mail turnaround time same day.
General Information: No adoption or juvenile records released. Will fax documents $5.00 plus $2.00 per page. Court makes copy: $2.00 per page. Certification fee: $5.00 per cert.. Payee: Clerk of Court. No personal checks or credit cards accepted. Mail requests: SASE required.

East Feliciana Parish

20th District Court PO Box 599, Clinton, LA 70722; 225-683-5145; fax: 225-683-3556; ***Felony, Misdemeanor, Civil, Probate.***
www.eastfelicianaclerk.org/court.html
Probate fax is same as main fax number.
Civil Records: Access: Mail, in person, online. Both court and visitors may perform in person searches. Search fee: $10.00 per name per ten years. Required to search: name, years to search; also helpful: address. Civil cases indexed by defendant, plaintiff, on computer from 1980, index books back to 1825. Mail turnaround time 1-2 days. Civil PAT goes back to 1988. Online subscription service is available. $400.00 per quarter permits access to viewable documents; $250 per quarter permits access in indices. This database also includes recordings, conveyances, mortgages, and marriage records.
Criminal Records: Access: Fax, mail, in person. Both court and visitors may perform in person searches. Search fee: $10.00 per name. Required to search: name, years to search, DOB, SSN. Criminal records computerized from 1990, index books back to 1825. Mail turnaround time 1-2 days. Criminal PAT goes back to 1990.
General Information: No adoption or juvenile records released. Will fax documents $5.00 1st page, $1.00 each add'l. Court makes copy: $1.00 per page. Certification fee: $5.00 per doc. Payee: Clerk of Court. Personal checks accepted; credit cards are not. Mail requests: SASE required.

Evangeline Parish

13th District Court PO Drawer 347, Ville Platte, LA 70586; 337-363-5671; criminal fax: 337-363-5780; civil fax: same; 8AM-4:30PM. ***Felony, Misdemeanor, Civil, Probate.***
Probate fax is same as main fax number.
Civil Records: Access: Fax, mail, in person. Both court and visitors may perform in person searches. Search fee: $15.00 per name. Fee is for first 7 years searched. Add $2.00 per add'l year. Required to search: name, years to search. Civil cases indexed by defendant, plaintiff, on computer back to 1989; prior records archived from 1911. Mail turnaround time 1-2 days. Public use terminal has civil records back to 1989. Results include complete name (1st, middle, last name).
Criminal Records: Access: Fax, mail, in person. Both court and visitors may perform in person searches. Search fee: $15.00 per name. Fee is for first 7 years searched. Add $2.00 per add'l year. Required to search: name, years to search; also helpful: DOB, SSN. Criminal records computerized from 1989, prior records archived from 1911. Mail turnaround time 1-2 days.
General Information: No adoption or juvenile records released. Will fax copies $10.00 1st page, $1.00 each add'l. Court makes copy: $.75 per page. Self serve: $.75 per page.To mail copies-$5.00 for 1st 5 pages, $1.00 each add'l page. Certification fee: $2.00 per page includes copy. Payee: Clerk of Court. Personal checks accepted; credit cards are not. SASE not required.

Franklin Parish

5th District Court PO Box 1564, Winnsboro, LA 71295; 318-435-5133; criminal fax: 318-435-6792; civil fax: same; 8:30AM-4:30PM. ***Felony, Misdemeanor, Civil, Probate.***
Probate fax is same as main fax number.
Civil Records: Access: Mail, in person. Both court and visitors may perform in person searches. Search fee: $10.00 per name. Required to search: name, years to search. Civil cases indexed by defendant, plaintiff, on computer from 1989, index books back to 1843. Mail turnaround time 1-2 days.
Criminal Records: Access: Mail, in person. Both court and visitors may perform in person searches. Search fee: $10.00 per name. Fee includes 10 year search. Required to search: name, years to search, DOB; also helpful: SSN. Criminal records on computer since 1995. Mail turnaround 1-2 days.
General Information: No adoption or juvenile records released. Will fax documents $5.00 1st page, $1.00 each add'l. Court makes copy: $1.00 per page. Certification fee: $5.00 per document. Payee: Clerk of Court. Business checks accepted. No credit cards accepted. Mail requests: SASE required.

Grant Parish

35th District Court PO Box 263, Colfax, LA 71417; 318-627-3246; probate phone: same; fax: 318-627-3201; 8:30AM-4:30PM. ***Felony, Misdemeanor, Civil, Probate.***
Civil Records: Access: Phone, fax, mail, in person. Both court and visitors may perform in person searches. Search fee: $5.00 per name. Required to search: name, years to search. Civil cases indexed by defendant, plaintiff, on computer back to 1989; index books back to 1878. Mail turnaround time 1-2 days. Public use terminal has civil records. Terminal shows largely land-related documents.
Criminal Records: Access: Phone, fax, mail, in person. Both court and visitors may perform in person searches. Search fee: $5.00 per name. Required to search: name, years to search, DOB; also helpful: SSN. Criminal index goes back to 1904; on computer back to 1996. Mail turnaround 1-2 days.
General Information: No adoption or juvenile records released without approval of a judge. Will fax documents $5.00 1st page, $2.00 each add'l, prepaid. Court makes copy: $1.00 per page. Self serve: $.50 per page. Certification fee: $5.00. Payee: Grant Parish Clerk of Court. Personal checks accepted; credit cards are not. Mail requests: SASE required.

Iberia Parish

16th District Court PO Drawer 12010, 300 Iberia St, New Iberia, LA 70562-2010; 337-365-7282; criminal fax: 337-365-0737; civil fax: same; 8:30AM-4:30PM. ***Felony, Misdemeanor, Civil, Probate.*** www.iberiaclerk.com
Probate fax is same as main fax number.
Civil Records: Access: Mail, in person. Both court and visitors may perform in person searches. Search fee: $10.00 per name. Required to search: name, years to search, SSN or DOB; also helpful: address. Civil cases indexed by defendant, plaintiff, on computer back to 1974, index books back to 1868. Civil PAT goes back to 30 years.
Criminal Records: Access: Mail, in person. Both court and visitors may perform in person searches. Search fee: $10.00 per name. Required to search: name, years to search, DOB, SSN; also helpful:

address. Criminal records computerized from 1994, index books back to 1868. Criminal PAT goes back to 10 years.
General Information: No adoption or juvenile records released. Will fax specific case file data to local or toll-free number. Civil fax- $5.75 for 1st page, $1.50 each add'l. Court makes copy: $.75 per page. Self serve: $.50 per page. Certification fee: $5.50 per document. Payee: Clerk of Court. Personal checks accepted.

Iberville Parish

18th District Court PO Box 423, 58050 Meriam, Plaquemine, LA 70764; 225-687-5160; fax: 225-687-5260; 8:30AM-4:30PM. ***Felony, Misdemeanor, Civil, Probate.***
Criminal department on 3rd Fl.
Civil Records: Access: Fax, mail, in person, online. Both court and visitors may perform in person searches. Search fee: $10.00 per name. Required to search: name, years to search. Civil cases indexed by defendant, plaintiff, on computer back to 1990, books back to 1800s. Mail turnaround time 1-2 days. Civil PAT goes back to 1990. Access to civil records online by subscription, contact clerk for details.
Criminal Records: Access: Mail, in person. Both court and visitors may perform in person searches. Search fee: $10.00 per name. Required to search: name, years to search, DOB; also helpful: SSN, address. Criminal docket on books back to 1900 or so. Mail turnaround time 1-2 days. Criminal PAT goes back to same as civil. PAT results show name only. Online results show name only.
General Information: No adoption or juvenile records released. Fee to fax out file $5.00 1st page, $1.00 each add'l. Court makes copy: $1.00 per page, self serve same. Certification fee: $5.00 per doc. Payee: Clerk of Court. Personal checks accepted; credit cards are not. Mail requests: SASE required.

Jackson Parish

2nd District Court PO Drawer 730, Jonesboro, LA 71251; 318-259-2424; criminal fax: 318-395-0386; civil fax: same; 8:30AM-4:30PM. ***Felony, Misdemeanor, Civil, Probate.***
www.jacksonparishclerk.org/
Probate fax is same as main fax number.
Civil Records: Access: Phone, mail, in person. Both court and visitors may perform in person searches. Search fee: $10.00 per name. Fee is per 10 years searched. Required to search: name, years to search. Civil cases indexed by defendant, plaintiff; index on docket books from 1880 and on computer since 1988. Mail turnaround time immediate. Civil PAT goes back to 1988.
Criminal Records: Access: Phone, mail, in person. Both court and visitors may perform in person searches. Search fee: $10.00 per name. Fee is per 10 years searched. Required to search: name, years to search, DOB; also helpful: SSN. Criminal records on computer since 1988. Mail turnaround time 1-2 days. Criminal PAT goes back to same as civil.
General Information: No adoption or juvenile records released. Will fax documents $5.00. Court makes copy: $1.00 per page, self serve same. Certification fee: $5.00 per certification. Payee: Clerk of Court. Personal checks accepted; credit cards are not. Mail requests: SASE required.

Jefferson Davis Parish

31st District Court PO Box 799, Jennings, LA 70546; 337-824-8340; fax: 337-824-1354; 8:30-4:30PM. ***Felony, Misdemeanor, Civil, Probate.***
Civil Records: Access: Mail, in person. Both court and visitors may perform in person searches. Search fee: $10.00 per name for 10 years. Required to search: name, years to search; also helpful: address. Civil cases indexed by defendant, plaintiff, archived from 1913, on computer back to 1991. Mail turnaround time 2 days.
Criminal Records: Access: Mail, in person. Both court and visitors may perform in person searches. Search fee: $10.00 per name for 10 years. Required to search: name, years to search; also helpful: DOB, SSN. Include city of residence of subject in your search request. Criminal records archived from 1913, on computer back to 1991. Mail turnaround 2 days.
General Information: No adoption or juvenile records released. Will fax documents $1.00 per page plus $10.00 fax fee. Court makes copy: $1.00 per page. Self serve: $.50 per page. Certification fee: $5.00. Payee: Clerk of Court. Personal checks accepted; credit cards are not. SASE not required.

Jefferson Parish

24th District Court PO Box 10, 200 Derbigny St, Gretna, LA 70054; 504-364-2900; criminal phone: 504-364-2992; civil phone: 504-364-3740/2611; probate phone: same as civil; criminal fax: 504-364-3797; civil fax: 504-364-3780; 8:30AM-4:30PM. ***Felony, Misdemeanor, Civil, Probate.*** www.jpclerkofcourt.us
Civil Records: Access: Phone, fax, mail, online, in person. Both court and visitors may perform in person searches. Search fee: $5.00 per name. Required to search: name, years to search. Civil cases indexed by defendant, plaintiff, on computer from 1986, in index books back to 1972, prior records archived. Note: Phone search requests on computer are free, but only a couple names per request. Mail turnaround time 1-2 days. Civil PAT goes back to 1986 but older cases added as accessed. PAT results show name only. Access to court records on JeffNet is $100, plus $50.00 monthly, $.25 per printed page. Includes recordings, marriage index, and assessor rolls. For further information and sign-up, visit the website and click on "Jeffnet" or call 504-364-2976.
Criminal Records: Access: Mail, fax, online, in person. Both court and visitors may perform in person searches. Search fee: $10.00 per name. Required to search: name, years to search, DOB; also helpful: SSN. Criminal records computerized from 1995 to present, active cases are in books from 1972. Mail turnaround time 1-2 days. Criminal PAT goes back to 5/1995.PAT results show name, DOB. Online access via internet, see civil. Online results show middle initial, DOB.
General Information: No adoption, juvenile or grand jury records released. Will fax documents $5.00 1st page, $1.00 each add'l. Court makes copy: $1.00 per page. Certification fee: $5.00 for pleading; $2.00 per page if copy machine, $.50 if from computer. Payee: Clerk of Court. Only cashiers checks and money orders accepted. No credit cards accepted. Mail requests: SASE required.

La Salle Parish

28th District Court PO Box 1316, Jena, LA 71342; 318-992-2158; fax: 318-992-2157; 8:30-4:30PM. ***Felony, Misdemeanor, Civil, Probate.***
Civil Records: Access: Phone, fax, mail, in person. Both court and visitors may perform in person searches. Search fee: $20.00 1st name, $10.00 additional name. Fee is for 10 year search per name with certificate. Required to search: name, years to search. Civil cases indexed by defendant, plaintiff, archived from 1916; on computer since 6/95. Mail turnaround time 1-2 weeks; will release results sooner by phone. Civil PAT goes back to 1995.
Criminal Records: Access: Phone, fax, mail, in person. Both court and visitors may perform in person searches. Search fee: $20.00 1st name, $10.00 additional name. Fee is for 10 year search per name with certificate. Required to search: name, years to search, DOB; also helpful: SSN. Criminal records archived from 1936; on computer since 1999. Mail turnaround time 1-2 weeks; will release results sooner by phone. Criminal PAT goes back to '99.
General Information: No adoption or juvenile records released. Fee to fax out doc $10.00 each. Court makes copy: $1.00 per page, self serve same. Certification fee: $5.00 per cert. Payee: Clerk of Court. Personal checks accepted; credit cards are not. Mail requests: SASE required.

Lafayette Parish

15th District Court PO Box 2009, c/o Clerk of Court, Lafayette, LA 70502; 337-291-6400; criminal phone: 337-291-6329; civil phone: 337-291-6303; probate phone: 337-291-6303; criminal fax: 337-291-6475; civil fax: 337-291-6480; 8:30AM-4:30PM. ***Felony, Misdemeanor, Civil, Probate.***
www.lafayetteparishclerk.com
Probate fax- 337-291-6480
Civil Records: Access: Phone, fax, mail, online, in person. Both court and visitors may perform in person searches. Search fee: $20.00 per name. Required to search: name, years to search. Civil cases indexed by defendant, plaintiff, archived from 1923; on computer back to 1986. Mail turnaround time 1-2 days. Civil PAT goes back to 1986. Access to the remote online system requires $100 setup fee plus $65 per month. Civil index goes back to 1986. For more info, call Derek C. at 337-291-6433 or see www.lafayetteparishclerk.com/onlineIndex.cfm.
Criminal Records: Access: Phone, fax, mail, in person, online. Both court and visitors may perform in person searches. Search fee: $20.00 per name. Required to search: name, years to search, DOB. Criminal records archived from 1966; on computer back to 1983. Mail turnaround time 1-2 days. Criminal PAT goes back to 1983. Online access to criminal index is the same as civil. May not be available, yet.
General Information: No adoption or juvenile records released. Will fax documents to local or toll free line for $1.00 per page, 2 page minimum. Court makes copy: $1.00 per page. Certification fee: $5.00 per Civil certification; $1.00 for criminal cert. Payee: Clerk of Court. Personal checks accepted. SASE not required.

Lafourche Parish

17th District Court PO Box 818, Thibodaux, LA 70302; 985-447-4841; criminal phone: 985-448-0591; civil phone: 985-447-5550; probate phone: 985-447-5550; criminal fax: 985-447-5800; civil fax: same; 8:30AM-4:30PM. ***Felony, Misdemeanor, Civil, Probate.*** www.lafourcheclerk.com/
Probate is separate index at this same address. Probate fax is same as main fax number.
Civil Records: Access: Fax, mail, in person. Both court and visitors may perform in person searches. Search fee: $20.00 per name. Required to search: name, years to search. Civil cases indexed by defendant, plaintiff, on computer back to 7/1982, microfiche from 1970, index books to early 1800s. Civil PAT goes back to 1813. Results include full name.
Criminal Records: Access: Fax, mail, in person. Both court and visitors may perform in person searches. Search fee: $20.00 per name. Fee is for 10 year search. Required to search: name, years to search, DOB; also helpful: SSN, race, sex. Criminal records computerized from 7/1982, index books back to 1800s. Criminal PAT goes back to 7/82.PAT results show name, DOB. Results include race/sex.
General Information: No adoption or juvenile records released. Fee to fax out file $2.00 per page, includes copy fee. Court makes copy: $1.00 per page. Certification fee: $5.00 per certification plus $1.00 per page. Payee: Lafourche Parish Clerk of Court. Personal checks accepted; credit cards are not. SASE not required.

Lincoln Parish

3rd District Court PO Box 924, Ruston, LA 71273-0924; 318-251-5130; fax: 318-255-6004; 8:30-4:30PM. ***Felony, Misdemeanor, Civil, Probate.***
Civil Records: Access: Mail, in person. Both court and visitors may perform in person searches. Search fee: $10.00 per name. Fee is per 10 years searched. Required to search: name, years to search. Civil cases indexed by defendant, plaintiff, on computer since 1985, index books back to 1800s. Mail turnaround time 1-2 days. Civil PAT goes back to 1984.
Criminal Records: Access: Mail, in person. Both court and visitors may perform in person searches. Search fee: $10.00 per name. Fee is per 10 years searched. Required to search: name, years to search, DOB; also helpful: SSN. Criminal records on computer since 1992. Mail turnaround time 1-2 days. Criminal PAT goes back to same as civil.
General Information: No adoption or juvenile records released. Fee to fax out file $5.00 for 1st page, $1.00 each add'l. Court makes copy: $1.00 per page. Self serve: $.50 per page. Certification fee: $5.00 per doc. Payee: Clerk of Court. No personal checks or credit cards accepted. SASE not required.

Livingston Parish

21st District Court PO Box 1150, Livingston, LA 70754; 225-686-2216; fax: 225-686-1867; 8AM-4:30PM. ***Felony, Misdemeanor, Civil, Probate.***
www.livclerk.org
Civil Records: Access: Mail, in person, online. Visitors must perform in person searches themselves. Search fee: $32.00. Required to search: name, years to search. Civil cases indexed by defendant, plaintiff; index on docket books since 1800s; computerized records past 10 years. Mail turnaround time 1-2 days. Civil PAT goes back to 1989. PAT civil results show middle initial. Online access is available to local attorneys only, with registration, call 225-686-2216 x1107. $50.00 per year fee for online access.
Criminal Records: Access: Mail, in person, online. Visitors must perform in person searches themselves. Search fee: $32.00. Required to search: name, years to search, DOB; also helpful: SSN, race, sex. Criminal records indexed in books since 1800s; computerized records past 10 years. Mail turnaround time 1-2 days. Criminal PAT goes back to same as civil. PAT criminal results show middle initial. Online access is available to local attorneys only, with registration, call 225-686-2216 x1107. $50.00 per year fee for online access. Online results show middle initial.
General Information: No adoption or juvenile records released. Will not fax documents. Court makes copy: $1.00 per page. Self serve: $.50 per page. Certification fee: $5.00 per doc. Payee: 21st District Court. Personal checks accepted. Visa/MC accepted for online copies only.

Madison Parish

6th District Court PO Box 1710, Tallulah, LA 71282; 318-574-0655; fax: 318-574-3961; 8:30-4:30PM. ***Felony, Misdemeanor, Civil, Probate.***
Civil Records: Access: Phone, mail, in person. Both court and visitors may perform in person searches. Search fee: $10.00 per name. Required to search: name, years to search. Civil cases indexed by defendant, plaintiff, kept on computer since 7/93. Mail turnaround time 1-2 days. Civil PAT goes back to 1993.
Criminal Records: Access: Phone, mail, in person, fax. Both court and visitors may perform in person searches. Search fee: $10.00 per name. Required to search: name, years to search, DOB; also helpful: SSN. Criminal records on index, computerized since 1999. Mail turnaround time 1-2 days. Criminal PAT goes back to 1998.
General Information: No adoption or juvenile records released. Will fax documents $2.00 per page. Court makes copy: $2.00 per page if court mails; $1.00 per page no mailing, self serve same. Certification fee: $5.50. Payee: Clerk of Court. Personal checks accepted; credit cards are not. Mail requests: SASE required.

Morehouse Parish

4th District Court PO Box 1543, Bastrop, LA 71221; 318-281-3343; criminal fax: 318-281-3775; civil fax: same; 8:30AM-4:30PM. ***Felony, Misdemeanor, Civil, Probate.***
Probate fax is same as main fax number.
Civil Records: Access: Phone, fax, mail, in person. Both court and visitors may perform in person searches. Search fee: $15.00 per name. Fee is per 10 years searched. Required to search: name, years to search; also helpful: address. Civil cases indexed by defendant, plaintiff, on computer since 1987, in books since 1898, some on microfilm. Mail turnaround time 2-3 days. Civil PAT goes back to 1987. PAT results show name only.
Criminal Records: Access: Phone, fax, mail, in person. Both court and visitors may perform in person searches. Search fee: $15.00 per name. Fee is per 10 years searched. Required to search: name, years to search, DOB; also helpful: address, SSN. Criminal records in books since 1926 and on microfilm since 1974; computerized records go back to 1994. Mail turnaround time 2-3 days. Criminal PAT goes back to 1994.PAT results show name, DOB.
General Information: No adoption, juvenile or judicial commitment records released. Will fax documents $5.00 1st page, $1.00 each add'l. Court makes copy: $1.00 per page, self serve same. Certification fee: $5.00 per document. Payee: Clerk of Court. Personal checks accepted; credit cards are not. Mail requests: SASE required.

Natchitoches Parish

10th District Court PO Box 476, Natchitoches, LA 71458; 318-352-8152; civil phone: 318-357-2293; fax: 318-352-9321; 8:30AM-4:30PM. ***Felony, Misdemeanor, Civil, Small Claims, Probate.***
www.npclerkofcourt.org/
Civil Records: Access: Phone, fax, mail, in person, online. Both court and visitors may perform in person searches. Search fee: $10.00 per name. Required to search: name, years to search. Civil cases indexed by defendant, plaintiff, on computer back to 6/1991, archived from 1950, index books back to 1700s. Mail turnaround time 1 week. Civil PAT goes back to 1986. With username and password to WebView you can search and access civil records, judgments. $50 setup fee, then $50.00 monthly, plus $.50 per image. Includes conveyance and marriage records. Direct subscription inquires to Linda Cockrell at 318-352-8152.
Criminal Records: Access: Phone, mail, in person. Both court and visitors may perform in person searches. Search fee: $10.00 per name. Required to search: name, years to search, DOB; also helpful: SSN. Criminal records computerized from 6/1991, archived from 1950, index books back to 1800s. Mail turnaround time 1 week. Criminal PAT goes back to 1991.
General Information: No adoption or juvenile records released. Will fax civil documents only for $5.00 1st page, $2.00 each add'l. Court makes copy: $1.00 per page, self serve same. Certification fee: $5.00 per document. Payee: Clerk of Court. Personal checks accepted; credit cards are not. Mail requests: SASE required.

Orleans Parish

Civil District Court 421 Loyola Ave, Rm 402, Attn: Clerk of Civil Dist. Ct., New Orleans, LA 70112; 504-592-9100; fax: 504-592-9128; 8:30AM-5PM. ***Civil, Probate, Domestic Relations.***
www.orleanscdc.com/
Civil Records: Access: Phone, mail, online, in person. Both court and visitors may perform in person searches. No search fee. Required to search: name, years to search. Civil cases indexed by defendant, plaintiff, on computer since 1985, in books back to early 1800s. Mail turnaround time 1-2 days. Public use terminal has civil records back to 1985. CDC Remote provides access to civil cases from 1985 and First City Court cases as well as parish mortgage and conveyance indexes. The fee is $500 per year. Call 504-592-9264 for more information. Online results show name only.
General Information: Online identifiers in results same as on public terminal. No adoption or juvenile released. Will not fax documents. Court makes copy: $1.00 per page. Certification fee: $2.00 per page includes copy fee. Payee: Clerk of Court. Only attorneys' checks, cashiers checks and money orders accepted. No credit cards accepted. Mail requests: SASE required.

Criminal District Court 2700 Tulane Ave, Rm 115, New Orleans, LA 70119; 504-658-9000; records- 658-9028; 8:15AM-3PM clerk; 8AM-4PM records. ***Felony, Misdemeanor.***
Records Dept phone- 504-658-9028, open til 4PM.
Criminal Records: Access: Mail, in person. Both court and visitors may perform in person searches. Search fee: $10.00 per name. Required to search: name, DOB, SSN. SSN must be included. If you do not specify the years to search, then the search will include their complete records. Criminal records on computer past 8 years, books and files go back to early 1900s. Note: Only government agencies may fax in requests. Mail turnaround time 2 days.
General Information: No adoption or juvenile records released. Records Rm will fax out documents. Court makes copy: $1.50 per page. Certification fee: $.,50 per page. Payee: Clerk of Court. Business checks accepted. No credit cards accepted. Mail requests: SASE required.

New Orleans City Court 421 Loyola Ave, Rm 201, New Orleans, LA 70112; 504-592-9155; fax: 504-592-9281; 9AM-4PM. ***Civil Actions under $25,000, Small Claims, Eviction.***
www.orleanscdc.com/
Will receive fax docs for $5.00 1st 2 pages then $2.50 each add'l. Small claims phone-504-592-9154.
Civil Records: Access: Mail, in person, online. Both court and visitors may perform in person searches. No search fee. Required to search: name, years to search. Civil cases indexed by defendant, plaintiff, on computer back to 1988. Mail turnaround time 5-10 days. Public use terminal has civil records back to 1988. PAT results show name only. Public terminal includes eviction and small claims records filed in FCC. CDC Remote provides access to First City Court cases from 1988 as well as civil cases, parish mortgage and conveyance indexes. The fee is $250 or $300 per year. Call 504-592-9264 for more information. Online results show middle initial.
General Information: Online identifiers in results same as on public terminal. No sealed records released. Will not fax documents. Court makes copy: $1.00 per page. Certification fee: $3.00 per page. Payee: New Orleans First City Court. No personal checks. Credit cards accepted. Mail requests: SASE requested.

Ouachita Parish

4th District Court PO Box 1862, Monroe, LA 71210-1862; 318-327-1444; fax: 318-327-1462; 8:30AM-5PM. ***Felony, Misdemeanor, Civil, Probate.***
Civil Records: Access: Fax, mail, in person. Both court and visitors may perform in person searches. Search fee: $10.00 per name. Required to search: name, years to search. Civil cases indexed by defendant, plaintiff, on computer from 1991, index books back to 1800s. Mail turnaround time 1-2 days. Civil PAT goes back to 1989.
Criminal Records: Access: Fax, mail, in person. Both court and visitors may perform in person searches. Search fee: $10.00 per name. Required to search: name, years to search, DOB; also helpful: SSN. Criminal records computerized from 1991, index books back to 1800s. Mail turnaround time 1-2 days. Criminal PAT goes back to 1991.
General Information: No adoption or juvenile records released. Will fax documents $2.00 1st page, $1.00 each add'l. Court makes copy: $1.00 per page. Self serve: $.50 per page. Certification fee: $2.00 per page. Payee: Clerk of Court. Business checks accepted. Checks accepted up to $50.00. No credit cards accepted. Mail requests: SASE requested.

Plaquemines Parish

25th District Court PO Box 40, 301 Maine St, Belle Chasse, LA 70037; 504-392-4969; criminal phone: 504-392-4969; civil phone: 504-297-5180; probate phone: 504-297-5180; fax: 504-297-5195; 8:30AM-4:30PM. ***Felony, Misdemeanor, Civil, Probate.*** Probate fax- 504-297-5195
Civil Records: Access: In person only. Visitors must perform in person searches themselves. Required to search: name, years to search. Civil cases indexed by defendant, plaintiff; index on docket books back to 1800s; computerized since 1/1977. Note: Court will search probate records; fee is $10 per name. Civil PAT goes back to 1977. PAT civil results show middle initial.
Criminal Records: Access: In person only. Visitors must perform in person searches themselves. Required to search: name, years to search, DOB. Criminal records indexed in books back to 1966; computerized records go back to 1/1966. Note: Contact the Plaquemines Sheriff's Office (18039 Hwy 15, Pointe-a-LaHache, 70082) for a criminal search, 985-333-5002, fax-985-333-9238. Criminal PAT goes back to 1966 (index only). PAT criminal results show middle initial.
General Information: No adoption or juvenile records released. Will not fax documents. Court makes copy: $.50 per page criminal; Civil- $1.00 per

page. Self serve: No self serve criminal copier; Civil self serve- $.50 each. Certification fee: $5.00 per document. Payee: Clerk of Court. Personal checks accepted; credit cards are not.

Pointe Coupee Parish

18th District Court PO Box 86, New Roads, LA 70760; 225-638-9596; criminal phone: x3; civil phone: x1; fax: 225-638-9590; 8:30AM-4:30PM. ***Felony, Misdemeanor, Civil, Probate.***

Civil Records: Access: Mail, in person. Both court and visitors may perform in person searches. Search fee: $10.00 per name. Required to search: name, years to search. Civil cases indexed by defendant, plaintiff; index on docket books back to 1800s. Mail turnaround time 1-5 days.

Criminal Records: Access: In person only. Visitors must perform in person searches themselves. Required to search: name, years to search, DOB; SSN helpful. Criminal records indexed in books back to 1800s.

General Information: No adoption or juvenile records released. Will fax documents to local or toll free line. Court makes copy: $1.00 per page. Certification fee: $5.00 per doc. Payee: Clerk of Court. Personal checks accepted; credit cards are not. SASE not required.

Rapides Parish

9th District Court PO Box 952, Alexandria, LA 71309; 318-473-8153; criminal phone: 318-619-5860; civil phone: 318-619-5852; probate phone: 318-619-5847; criminal fax: 318-473-4667; civil fax: same; 8:30AM-4:30PM. ***Felony, Misdemeanor, Civil, Probate.*** www.rapidesclerk.org

Probate fax is same as main fax number.

Civil Records: Access: Mail, in person. Both court and visitors may perform in person searches. Search fee: $11.00 per name. Fee is per separate index. Required to search: name, years to search. Civil cases indexed by defendant, plaintiff; index on docket books since 1864, civil in computer since 10/84. Mail turnaround time within 72 hours. Civil PAT goes back to 1984. PAT civil results show middle initial.

Criminal Records: Access: Mail, in person. Both court and visitors may perform in person searches. Search fee: $11.00 per name. Fee is per separate index. Required to search: name, years to search, DOB; also helpful: SSN. Criminal records on computer since 1984; prior records in index books back to 1864. Mail turnaround time 72 hours. Criminal PAT goes back to same as civil. PAT results show middle initial, DOB, SSN.

General Information: No adoption, juvenile, or judicial commitment records released. Will fax documents to local or toll free line. Court makes copy: $1.00 per page, self serve same. Certification fee: $5.00 per cert. Payee: Rapides Parish Clerk of Court. Personal checks accepted; credit cards are not. SASE not required.

Red River Parish

39th District Court PO Box 485, Coushatta, LA 71019; 318-932-6741; fax: 318-932-3126; 8:30AM -4:30PM. ***Felony, Misdemeanor, Civil, Probate.***

Civil Records: Access: Mail, in person. Both court and visitors may perform in person searches. Search fee: $10.00 per name. Required to search: name, years to search. Civil cases indexed by defendant, plaintiff; index on docket books. Mail turnaround time 1-2 days. Public use terminal has civil records back to 2000.

Criminal Records: Access: Mail, in person. Only the court performs in person searches; visitors may not. Search fee: $10.00 per name. Required to search: name, years to search, DOB; also helpful: SSN. The index is kept in the DA's office. Mail turnaround time 1-2 days.

General Information: No adoption or juvenile records released. Will fax documents to local or toll-free number. Court makes copy: $2.00 per page. Self serve: $1.00 per page. Certification fee: $5.00 per document. Payee: Clerk of Court. Personal checks only accepted. No credit cards accepted. Mail requests: SASE required.

Richland Parish

5th District Court PO Box 119, Rayville, LA 71269; 318-728-4171, 318-728-7000; fax: 318-728-7020; 8:30AM-4:30PM. ***Felony, Misdemeanor, Civil, Probate.***

Civil Records: Access: Mail, in person. Both court and visitors may perform in person searches. Search fee: $10.00 per name. Required to search: name, years to search. Civil cases indexed by defendant, plaintiff, on since 1/94, prior on books to 1800s. Mail turnaround time 1-2 days.

Criminal Records: Access: Mail, in person. Both court and visitors may perform in person searches. Search fee: $10.00 per name. Required to search: name, years to search, DOB, SSN. Criminal records on since 1/94, prior on books to 1800s. Mail turnaround time 1-2 days.

General Information: No adoption or juvenile records released. Will fax documents to local or toll free line. Court makes copy: $1.00 per page. Self serve: $.50 per page. Certification fee: $5.00. Payee: Clerk of Court. Personal checks accepted; credit cards are not. Mail requests: SASE required.

Sabine Parish

11th District Court Sabine Clerk of Court, PO Box 419, Many, LA 71449; 318-256-6223; criminal fax: 318-256-9037; civil fax: same; 8AM-4:30PM. ***Felony, Misdemeanor, Civil, Probate.*** www.sabineparishclerk.com/

Probate fax is same as main fax number.

Civil Records: Access: Fax, mail, in person, online. Both court and visitors may perform in person searches. Search fee: $20.00 per name. Required to search: name, years to search. Civil cases indexed by defendant, plaintiff, index on computer back to 1984. Mail turnaround time 5-10 days. Public use terminal has civil records back to 7/1990. Access civil & succession-probate records by subscription at www.sabineparishclerk.com/online.htm. $50.00 one-time setup fee plus $100 per month, includes conveyance, mortgage, marriage records. Civil suits go back to 1/1985; Probate to 1920.

Criminal Records: Access: Fax, mail, in person. Both court and visitors may perform in person searches. Search fee: $20.00 per name. Required to search: name, years to search. Criminal records on computer by name go back to 1990. Mail turnaround time 5-10 days. Access to criminal records online not available.

General Information: No adoption or juvenile records released. Will fax documents $5.00 1st page, $2.00 each add'l. Court makes copy: $1.25 per page. Self serve: $1.00 per page. Certification fee: $5.00 per cert; $10.00 for exemplification. Payee: Sabine Parish Clerk. Personal checks accepted; credit cards are not. Mail requests: SASE required.

St. Bernard Parish

34th District Court PO Box 1746, Chalmette, LA 70044; 504-271-34348:30AM-4:30PM. ***Felony, Misdemeanor, Civil, Probate.*** www.stbclerk.com

Civil Records: Access: Mail, in person, online. Both court and visitors may perform in person searches. Search fee: $10.00 per name. Fee is per 10 years searched. Required to search: name, years to search. Civil cases indexed by defendant, plaintiff; index on docket books back to 1800s, on computer since 1989. Mail turnaround time 2-3 days. Civil PAT goes back to 1989. PAT results show name only. Search Civil suits back to 1/1989 free at www.stbclerk.com/modules.php?name=system&file=records.

Criminal Records: Access: Mail, in person, online. Both court and visitors may perform in person searches. Search fee: $10.00 per name. Fee is per 10 years searched. Required to search: name, years to search, DOB; also helpful: SSN, address. Criminal records indexed in books back to 1800s, on computer since 1989. Mail turnaround time 2-3 days. Criminal PAT goes back to same as civil. Search criminal index back to 1/1989 free at www.stbclerk.com/modules.php?name=system&file=records.

General Information: No adoption or juvenile. Will not fax documents. Court makes copy: $1.00 per page. Certification fee: $5.00. Payee: Clerk of Court. No personal checks or credit cards accepted. Mail requests: SASE required.

St. Charles Parish

29th District Court PO Box 424, 15045 River Rd, Hahnville, LA 70057; 985-783-6632; criminal fax: 985-783-2005; civil fax: same; 8:30AM-4:30PM. ***Felony, Misdemeanor, Civil, Probate.***

Probate is a separate index at this same address. Probate fax is same as main fax number.

Civil Records: Access: Mail, fax, in person. Both court and visitors may perform in person searches. Search fee: $10.00 per name. Required to search: name, years to search. Civil cases indexed by defendant, plaintiff, on computer back to 1982, on index books back to 1890. Mail turnaround time 1 day. Civil PAT goes back to 1982. PAT results show name, DOB.

Criminal Records: Access: Mail, fax, in person. Both court and visitors may perform in person searches. Search fee: $10.00 per name. Required to search: name, years to search, DOB; also helpful: SSN, race, sex. Criminal records computerized from 1981, on index books back to 1900s. Mail turnaround time 1 day. Criminal PAT goes back to 5/1990.PAT results show name, DOB.

General Information: No adoption or juvenile records released. Fee to fax out file $4.00 per page. Court makes copy: $1.00 per page, self serve same. Certification fee: $5.00 per page includes copies. Payee: Clerk of Court. Personal checks accepted; credit cards are not. SASE not required.

St. Helena Parish

21st District Court PO Box 308, 369 Mitnan St, Greensburg, LA 70441; 225-222-4514; criminal fax: 225-222-3443; civil fax: 225-222-3443; 8:30AM-4:30PM. ***Felony, Misdemeanor, Civil, Probate.***

Search fee applies for each division. Probate fax is same as main fax number.

Civil Records: Access: Phone, mail, fax, in person. Both court and visitors may perform in person searches. Search fee: $10.00 per name. Required to search: name, years to search. Civil cases indexed by defendant, plaintiff; index on docket books back to 1800s. Mail turnaround time 1-2 days.

Criminal Records: Access: Mail, in person. Both court and visitors may perform in person searches. Search fee: $10.00 per name. Required to search: name, years to search, DOB; also helpful: SSN. Criminal records indexed in books back to 1800s. Mail turnaround time 1-2 days.

General Information: No adoption or juvenile records released. Will not fax out documents. Court makes copy: $1.00 per page. Self serve: $.50 per page. Certification fee: $5.00 per seal. Payee: Clerk of Court. Personal checks accepted; credit cards are not. Mail requests: SASE required.

St. James Parish

23rd District Court PO Box 63, 5800 Louisiana Hwy 44, River Rd, Convent, LA 70723; 225-562-7496; criminal phone: 225-562-2271; civil phone: 225-562-2360; probate phone: 225-562-2360; criminal fax: 225-562-2383; civil fax: same; 8AM-4:30PM. ***Felony, Misdemeanor, Civil, Probate.***

Probate is a separate index at this same address. Probate fax is same as main fax number.

Civil Records: Access: Mail, in person. Both court and visitors may perform in person searches. Search fee: $15.00 per name. Required to search: name, years to search. Civil cases indexed by defendant, plaintiff; index on docket books back to early 1900s; on computer back to 1988. Mail turnaround time 1-2 days. Civil PAT goes back to 1990. PAT civil results show middle initial.

Criminal Records: Access: Mail, in person. Both court and visitors may perform in person searches. Search fee: $15.00 per name. Required to search: name, years to search, DOB. Criminal records indexed in books back to early 1900s; on computer back to 1988. Mail turnaround time 1-2 days. Criminal PAT goes back to 1990. PAT criminal results show middle initial.

General Information: No adoption or juvenile records released. Will fax documents for $5.00 per doc fee. Court makes copy: $1.00 per page. Certification fee: $5.00 per document. Payee: Clerk of Court. Only cashiers checks and money orders accepted. No credit cards accepted. Mail requests: SASE required.

St. John the Baptist Parish

40th District Court PO Box 280, Edgard, LA 70049; 985-497-3331; fax: 985-497-3972; 8:30AM -4:30PM. ***Felony, Misdemeanor, Civil, Probate.*** www.stjohnclerk.org

Court is planning to offer online searches when technology becomes available again.

Civil Records: Access: Mail, fax, in person. Both court and visitors may perform in person searches. Search fee: $15.00 per name. Fee is for first 15 years. Add $1.00 per add'l year. Required to search: name, years to search. Civil cases indexed by defendant, plaintiff, on computer since 11/2/1982. Mail turnaround time 3-4 days. Civil PAT goes back to 1982. PAT results show name only.

Criminal Records: Access: Mail, fax, in person. Both court and visitors may perform in person searches. Search fee: $15.00 per name. Fee is for first 15 years. Add $1.00 per add'l year. Required to search: name, years to search, DOB; also helpful: SSN. Felony records on computer since 1983, misdemeanors since 3/91. Mail turnaround time 3-4 days. Criminal PAT goes back to same as civil. PAT results show middle initial, DOB.

General Information: No adoption or juvenile records released. Fee to fax out file $5.00 per page. Court makes copy: $2.00 per page. Self serve: $1.00 per page. Certification fee: $5.00 per doc. Payee: Clerk of Court. No personal checks or credit cards accepted. Mail requests: SASE required.

St. Landry Parish

27th District Court PO Box 750, Courthouse, Opelousas, LA 70570; 337-942-5606; fax: 337-948-1653; 8AM-4:30PM. ***Felony, Misdemeanor, Civil, Probate.*** www.stlandry.org

Civil Records: Access: Mail, fax, in person, online. Both court and visitors may perform in person searches. Search fee: $20.00 per name. Additional $1.00 fee per year after 1st 10 years. Required to search: name, years to search. Civil cases indexed by defendant, plaintiff; index on docket books back to 1800s, on computer back to 1992. Mail turnaround time 1-2 days. Civil PAT goes back to 1997. PAT results show name only. Results include plaintiff names. Online subscription access program to civil cases is available. The fee is $50.00 per month. Includes civil court records back to 1997, also land indexes and images. Contact the court or visit the web page for details.

Criminal Records: Access: Mail, fax, in person. Both court and visitors may perform in person searches. Search fee: $20.00 per name. Additional $1.00 fee per year after 1st 10 years. Required to search: name, years to search, DOB; also helpful: SSN. Criminal records indexed in books back to 1800s, on computer back to 1992. Mail turnaround time 1-2 days. Criminal PAT goes back to 1995. PAT results show name only. Online results show name only.

General Information: Online identifiers in results same as on public terminal. No adoption or juvenile records released. Fee to fax out file $5.00 1st page, $1.00 each add'l. Court makes copy: $1.00 per page. Self serve: $.50 per page. Certification fee: $5.50. Payee: Clerk of Court. Personal checks accepted; credit cards are not. Mail requests: SASE required.

St. Martin Parish

16th District Court PO Box 308, St. Martinville, LA 70582; 337-394-2210; fax: 337-394-7772; 8:30AM-4:30PM. ***Felony, Misdemeanor, Civil, Probate.*** www.stmartinparishclerkofcourt.com

Civil Records: Access: In person, online. Both court and visitors may perform in person searches. Search fee: $10.00 per name. Required to search: name, years to search; also helpful: address. Civil cases indexed by defendant, plaintiff, archived from 1760, on computer since 1990. Civil PAT goes back to 1990. PAT results show middle initial, DOB. Court indices to be available at www.stmartinparishclerkofcourt.com.

Criminal Records: Access: In person. Both court and visitors may perform in person searches. Search fee: $10.00 per name. Required to search: name, years to search, DOB; also helpful: address, SSN. Criminal records archived from 1760, on computer since 1990. Criminal PAT goes back to same as civil. PAT results show middle initial, DOB. Online results show middle initial, DOB.

General Information: No adoption, sealed records, expunged or juvenile records released. Will fax documents $.75 per page. Court makes copy: $1.00 per page, self serve same. Certification fee: $6.00 per doc. Payee: Clerk of Court. Personal checks accepted; credit cards are not.

St. Mary Parish

16th Judicial District Court PO Drawer 1231, Franklin, LA 70538; 337-828-4100 X200; fax: 337-828-2509; 8:30AM-4:30PM. ***Felony, Misdemeanor, Civil, Probate.***

Civil Records: Access: In person only. Visitors must perform in person searches themselves. Required to search: name, years to search. Civil cases indexed by defendant, plaintiff; index on docket books back to 1800s. Civil PAT goes back to 1980. PAT results show name only; terminal is in the record room.

Criminal Records: Access: In person only. Visitors must perform in person searches themselves. Required to search: name, years to search, DOB; SSN helpful. Criminal records indexed in books back to 1800s. Criminal PAT goes back to 1983. PAT results show middle initial, DOB. Public terminal is located in record room.

General Information: No adoption or juvenile records released. Will not fax documents. Court makes copy: $1.00 per page. Self serve: $.50 per page. Certification fee: $5.00. Payee: St. Mary Parish Clerk of Court. Personal checks, money order, cash accepted. No credit cards accepted.

St. Tammany Parish

22nd District Court PO Box 1090, Covington, LA 70434; 985-809-8700; criminal fax: 985-809-8777; civil fax: same; 8:30AM-4:30PM. ***Felony, Misdemeanor, Civil, Probate.*** www.sttammanyclerk.org/main/index.asp

Civil Records: Access: Mail, in person, online. Both court and visitors may perform in person searches. No search fee, unless extensive. Required to search: name, years to search. Civil cases indexed by defendant, plaintiff, archived on index books back to 1810, on computer since 1992, document images scanned since 1995. Mail turnaround time 1-2 days. Civil PAT goes back to 1992. PAT results show name only. Internet access to civil records is from the Clerk of Court. $50 initial setup fee, $50.00 per month and $.20 to print a page. For information, call Kristie Howell at 985-809-8787. A non-Internet dial-up s is also available; $100 setup and $.20 per minute. Civil index goes back to 1992; images to 1995. Search index free at https://www.sttammanyclerk.org/liveapp/default.asp.

Criminal Records: Access: Mail, in person, online. Both court and visitors may perform in person searches. No search fee, unless extensive. Required to search: name, years to search, DOB; also helpful: SSN. Criminal records on computer since 10/87. Mail turnaround time 2-3 days. Criminal PAT goes back to 10/1987. PAT results show middle initial, DOB. Internet access to criminal records is the same as civil. Dialup criminal indices go back to 1988. Online results show name, DOB.

General Information: No adoption or juvenile records released. Will fax documents if name search pre-paid. Court makes copy: $.25 per page, self serve same. Certification fee: $4.00 per doc. Payee: Clerk of Court. Personal checks accepted. Credit cards only accepted for online access payments. Mail requests: SASE required.

Tangipahoa Parish

21st District Court PO Box 667, Amite, LA 70422; 985-748-4146; criminal fax: 985-748-6503; civil fax: 985-748-6746; 8:30AM-4:30PM. ***Felony, Misdemeanor, Civil, Probate.*** www.tangiclerk.org

Civil Records: Access: Mail, in person, online. Both court and visitors may perform in person searches. Search fee: $10.00 per name per 10 years. Required to search: name, years to search. Civil cases indexed by defendant, plaintiff, archived back to early 1900s; on computer back to 1974. Mail turnaround time 3-4 days. Civil PAT goes back to 1974. Name & date filed. Online access to Parish notaries index records is $25.00 set-up fee (name only-no history). Index back to 1974. Visit www.tangiclerk.org/OnlineServices/onlineservices.asp for info or call Andi Matheu at 985-748-4146.

Criminal Records: Access: Mail, in person. Both court and visitors may perform in person searches. Search fee: $10.00 per name. Required to search: name, years to search, DOB, SSN. Criminal records archived back to early 1900s; on computer back to 1994. Mail turnaround time 3-4 days. Criminal PAT goes back to same as civil. Results include name and date filed.

General Information: No adoption or juvenile records released. Fee to fax out file $5.00 1st page, $1.00 each add'l. Court makes copy: $1.00 per page, self serve same. Certification fee: $5.00 per document. Payee: Clerk of Court. Personal checks and major credit cards accepted. Mail requests: SASE required.

Tensas Parish

6th District Court PO Box 78, 201 Hancock St, St. Joseph, LA 71366; 318-766-3921; fax: 318-766-3926; 8:30AM-4:30PM. ***Felony, Misdemeanor, Civil, Probate.***

Civil Records: Access: In person only. Visitors must perform in person searches themselves. Required to search: name, years to search. Civil cases indexed by defendant, plaintiff, archived back to 1800s, on computer since mid-1998.

Criminal Records: Access: In person only. Visitors must perform in person searches themselves. Required to search: name, years to search; also helpful: DOB, SSN. Criminal records on computer since 1998; archived back to 1800s.

General Information: No adoption or juvenile records released. Will not fax documents. Court makes copy: $3.00 1st page, $2.00 ea add'l. Certification fee: $5.50. Payee: Clerk of Court. Personal checks accepted; credit cards are not.

Terrebonne Parish

32nd District Court PO Box 1569, 7856 Main St, Houma, LA 70361; 985-868-5660; fax: 985-868-5143; 8:30AM-4:30PM. ***Felony, Misdemeanor, Civil, Probate, Traffic.***

Search fee is per index. Probate is separate index at this same address.

Civil Records: Access: Mail, fax, in person. Both court and visitors may perform in person searches. Search fee: $20.00 per name. Required to search: name, years to search. Civil cases indexed by defendant, plaintiff, on computer since 1986, in books to 1823. Note: Will accept fax search request if prepaid. Mail turnaround time 1 week. Civil PAT available. Public terminal on 1st Fl.

Criminal Records: Access: Mail, in person. Both court and visitors may perform in person searches. Search fee: $20.00 per name. Required to search: name, years to search, DOB; also helpful: SSN, race, sex. Criminal records archived to 1800s. Mail turnaround time 1 week. Criminal PAT available.

General Information: No adoption or juvenile records released. Will fax documents $5.00 fee plus $1.00 per page. Court makes copy: $1.00 per page. Certification fee: $5.00 per cert. Payee: Terrebonne Parish Clerk of Court. Personal checks accepted; credit cards are not. Mail requests: SASE required.

Union Parish

3rd District Court Courthouse Bldg, 100 E Bayou #105, Farmerville, LA 71241; 318-368-3055; fax: 318-368-3861; 8:30AM-4:30PM. ***Felony, Misdemeanor, Civil, Probate.***

Probate fax is same as main fax number.

Civil Records: Access: Mail, in person. Both court and visitors may perform in person searches. Search fee: $10.00 per name. Required to search: name, years to search. Civil cases indexed by defendant, plaintiff; index on docket books back to 1839. Mail turnaround time 2-3 days. Public use terminal has civil records back to 1979.

Criminal Records: Access: Mail, fax, in person. Both court and visitors may perform in person searches. Search fee: $10.00 per name. Required to search: name, years to search, SSN. Criminal records indexed in books back to 1839; computerized records go back to 1982. Mail turnaround time 2-3 days.

General Information: No adoption or juvenile records released. Will fax documents $5.00 per doc. Court makes copy: $2.00 per page. Self serve: $1.00 per page. Certification fee: $5.00 per instrument. Payee: Clerk of Court. Personal checks accepted; credit cards are not. Mail requests: SASE required.

Vermilion Parish

15th District Court 100 N State St, #101, Abbeville, LA 70510; 337-898-1992; civil phone: 337-898-4550; criminal fax: 337-740-8803; civil fax: 337-898-9803; 8:30AM-4:30PM. ***Felony, Misdemeanor, Civil, Probate.***

Civil Records: Access: Phone, fax, mail, in person. Both court and visitors may perform in person searches. Search fee: $20.00 per name. Required to search: name, years to search, DOB, SSN. Civil cases indexed by defendant, plaintiff, on computer since 1983, in books since 1885, on microfilm since 1885. Mail turnaround time 1-2 days after payment.

Criminal Records: Access: Phone, fax, mail, in person. Both court and visitors may perform in person searches. Search fee: $20.00 per name. Required to search: name, years to search; also helpful: SSN, DOB, race, sex. Criminal records on computer since 1983, in books since 1885, on microfilm since 1885. Mail turnaround 1-2 days after payment. Public terminal has crim records back to 1993, results show middle initial, DOB.

General Information: No adoption or juvenile records released. Will fax back documents no fee. Court makes copy: $1.00 per page. Certification fee: $5.00 per cert; if many pages in full docket, the cert fee may be $10.00. Payee: Vermilion Parish Clerk of Court. Personal checks, money order or cash accepted. No credit cards accepted. Mail requests: SASE required.

Vernon Parish

30th District Court PO Box 40, Leesville, LA 71496; 337-238-1384; probate phone: 337-238-4345; fax: 337-238-9902; 8AM-4:30PM. ***Felony, Misdemeanor, Civil, Probate.*** www.vernonclerk.com/

Probate fax is same as main fax number.

Civil Records: Access: Mail, fax, in person. Both court and visitors may perform in person searches. Search fee: $10.00 per name. Required to search: name, years to search. Civil cases indexed by defendant, plaintiff, on computer from 11/1985, archived back to 1900. Mail turnaround time same day. Civil PAT goes back to 1986. PAT civil results show middle initial.

Criminal Records: Access: Mail, in person. Both court and visitors may perform in person searches. Search fee: $10.00 per name. Required to search: name, years to search, DOB, SSN. Criminal records computerized from 11/1985, archived back to 1900. Mail turnaround time same day. Criminal PAT goes back to 11/1985. PAT criminal results show middle initial.

General Information: No adoption or juvenile records released. Will fax documents to local or toll free line. Court makes copy: $1.25 per page. Self serve: $.75 per page. Certification fee: $5.00. Payee: Clerk of Court. Personal checks accepted; credit cards are not. Mail requests: SASE required.

Washington Parish

22nd District Court PO Box 607, Franklinton, LA 70438; 985-839-4663/7821; 8AM-4:30PM. ***Felony, Misdemeanor, Civil, Probate.***

Civil Records: Access: Mail, in person. Both court and visitors may perform in person searches. Search fee: $10.00 per name per index. Required to search: name, years to search. Civil cases indexed by defendant, plaintiff, on computer from 1993, archived 4/1967, index books back to 1800s. Mail turnaround time 1-2 days. Civil PAT goes back to 1988.

Criminal Records: Access: Mail, fax, in person. Both court and visitors may perform in person searches. Search fee: $10.00 per name per index. Required to search: name, years to search, DOB; also helpful- SSN. Criminal records computerized from 1993, archived 4/1967, index books back to 1800s. Mail turnaround time 1-2 days. Criminal PAT goes back to 8/1989; newer cases have show more info.

General Information: No adoption or juvenile records released. Will not fax documents. Court makes copy: $1.00 per page. Self serve: $.50 per page. Certification fee: $5.00. Payee: Washington Parish Clerk of Court. Personal checks accepted; credit cards are not. Mail requests: SASE requested.

Webster Parish

26th District Court PO Box 370, Minden, LA 71058-0370; 318-371-0366; fax: 318-371-0226; 8:30AM-4:30PM. ***Felony, Misdemeanor, Civil, Probate.*** www.websterclerk.org/

Probate is a separate index at this same address.

Civil Records: Access: Fax, mail, in person, online. Both court and visitors may perform in person searches. Search fee: $10.00 per name. Required to search: name, years to search. Civil cases indexed by defendant, plaintiff, archived back to 1800s, on computer since 1986. Mail turnaround time 2-3 days. Civil PAT goes back to 4/1992. Access court records by subscription; fee is $50.00 setup fee plus $35.00 per month for index searches and images. Civil index goes back to 4/16/1992; images back to 2005. Sub includes criminal, probate, civil, traffic, also marriages and conveyances. Login, signup or find more info at www.websterclerk.org/records.html.

Criminal Records: Access: Mail, fax, in person, online. Both court and visitors may perform in person searches. Search fee: $10.00 per name. Required to search: name; also helpful: years to search. Criminal records not on computer, in books to 1871. Mail turnaround time 2-3 days. Criminal PAT goes back to 11/1992. Access to criminal index and images is included in the general subscription service described in the civil section, above. The criminal subscription index goes back to 11/28/1992; images go back to early 2007.

General Information: No adoption or juvenile records released. Will fax documents $5.00 per page. Court makes copy: $1.00 per page. Self serve: $.50 per page. Certification fee: $5.00 per document. Payee: Clerk of Court. Personal checks accepted; credit cards are not. SASE not required.

West Baton Rouge Parish

18th District Court PO Box 107, Port Allen, LA 70767; 225-383-0378; fax: 225-383-3694; 8:30AM -4:30PM. ***Felony, Misdemeanor, Civil, Probate.*** www.wbrclerk.org/

Probate fax is same as main fax number.

Civil Records: Access: Phone, mail, in person. Both court and visitors may perform in person searches. Search fee: $10.00 per name. Required to search: name, years to search. Civil cases indexed by defendant, plaintiff, on computer from 1983. Mail turnaround time 1-2 days. Civil PAT goes back to 1983. PAT results show name only.

Criminal Records: Access: Phone, mail, in person. Both court and visitors may perform in person searches. Search fee: $10.00 per name. Required to search: name, years to search, DOB; also helpful: SSN. Criminal records computerized from 1983. Mail turnaround time 1-2 days. Criminal PAT goes back to same as civil. PAT results show name only.

General Information: No adoption or juvenile records released. Will fax documents $5.00 each. Court makes copy: $1.00 per page. Self serve: $.50 per page. Certification fee: $5.00 per doc. Payee: Clerk of Court. Personal checks accepted; credit cards are not. Mail requests: SASE required.

West Carroll Parish

5th District Court PO Box 1078, Oak Grove, LA 71263; 318-428-3281/2369; fax: 318-428-9896; 8:30-4:30PM. ***Felony, Misdemeanor, Civil, Probate.***

Civil Records: Access: Mail, in person. Both court and visitors may perform in person searches. Search fee: $1.00 per name per year. Required to search: name, years to search. Civil cases indexed by defendant, plaintiff; index on docket books back to 1800s. Mail turnaround time 1-2 days.

Criminal Records: Access: Mail, in person. Both court and visitors may perform in person searches. Search fee: $1.00 per name per year. Required to search: name, years to search, DOB. Criminal records indexed in books back to 1800s. Mail turnaround time 1-2 days. Public use terminal has crim records back to same as civil.PAT results show name, DOB.

General Information: No adoption or juvenile records released. Will fax documents to local or toll free line. Court makes copy: $2.00 per page. Certification fee: $5.00 per certification. Payee: Clerk of Court. Only cashiers checks and money orders accepted. No credit cards accepted. Mail requests: SASE required.

West Feliciana Parish

20th District Court PO Box 1843, St Francisville, LA 70775; 225-635-3794; fax: 225-635-3770; 8:30AM-4:30PM. ***Felony, Misdemeanor, Civil, Probate.***

Civil Records: Access: Mail, in person. Both court and visitors may perform in person searches. Search fee: $10.00 per name. Fee is per 10 years searched. Required to search: name, years to search; also helpful: address. Civil cases indexed by defendant, plaintiff, on computer from 1984, index books back to 1800s. Mail turnaround time 3-5 days. Civil PAT goes back to 1990. PAT civil results show middle initial.

Criminal Records: Access: Mail, in person. Both court and visitors may perform in person searches. Search fee: $10.00 per name. Fee is per 10 years searched. Required to search: name, years to search, DOB; also helpful: address. Criminal records on computer since 1992; prior on cards and dockets back to 1800s. Mail turnaround time 3-5 days. Criminal PAT goes back to 1991. PAT results show middle initial, DOB.

General Information: No adoption, juvenile or juvenile records released. Will fax documents $5.00 1st page, $1.00 ea add'l. Court makes copy: $1.00 per page, self serve same. Certification fee: $5.00. Payee: Clerk of Court. Business checks accepted. No credit cards accepted. Mail requests: SASE required.

Winn Parish

8th District Court 100 Main St, #103, Winnfield, LA 71483; 318-628-3515; fax: 318-628-3527; 8AM-4:30PM. ***Felony, Misdemeanor, Civil, Probate.***

Civil Records: Access: Mail, in person. Both court and visitors may perform in person searches. Search fee: $10.00 per name for 10 year search. Required to search: name, years to search, address. Civil cases indexed by defendant, plaintiff, on books from 1886 to present, on computer from 1988, mortgages since 1981, conveyances since 1993. Mail turnaround time 2-3 days.

Criminal Records: Access: Mail, in person. Both court and visitors may perform in person searches. Search fee: $10.00 per name for 10 year search. Required to search: name, years to search, address, DOB; also helpful: SSN. Criminal records in books since 1886, computerized since 1997. Mail turnaround time 2-3 days.

General Information: No adoption or juvenile records released. Fee to fax out file $5.00 each plus $1.00 per page. Court makes copy: $1.00 per page, self serve same. Certification fee: $5.00. Payee: Winn Parish Clerk of Court. Personal checks accepted; credit cards are not. Mail requests: SASE required.

Louisiana Recording Offices

Organization: 64 parishes, 64 recording offices. The recording officer is the Clerk of Court. One parish – St. Martin – has two non-contiguous segments. In Orleans Parish, deeds are recorded in a different office from mortgages. Louisiana is in the Central Time Zone (CST).

Real Estate Records: Most parishes will perform a mortgage search - $20.00 1st name; $10 each add'l name. Some will provide a record owner search. Copy fees vary, usually $1.00 or $.75 per page. Most parishes' certification fee is $5.00 per doc plus copy fee. Many parishes include tax and other non-UCC liens in mortgage records.

UCC Records: Financing statements are filed with the Parish Clerk of Court and are entered onto a statewide database of UCC financing statements available for searching at any parish office. Most parishes perform UCC searches for $30.00 per debtor name, use form UCC-11. UCC copy fee is $1.00 to $2.00 per page.

Tax Lien Records: All federal and state tax liens are filed with the Clerk of Court. Parishes usually file tax liens on personal property in the same index. However, tax liens are not kept on the same statewide database as UCCs. Most parishes will perform tax lien searches for varying fees. Parishes who still perform these types of searches will automatically include tax liens on personal property in a mortgage certificate search.

Other Liens: Judgments, labor, material, hospital.

Online Access: A number of parishes offer online access to recorded documents. Most are commercial fee systems but newer systems are allowing for free index searching, then a fee for images, usually $1.00 each. A statewide system at www.latax.state.la.us/Menu_ParishTaxRolls/TaxRolls.aspx offers free access to assessor parish tax roll data, but no name searching.

Acadia Parish

Clerk of Court, PO Box 922, Crowley, LA 70526. Recording, R/E & UCC phone-337-788-8881; fax-337-788-1048; 8:30AM-4:30PM (CST) www.acadiaparishclerk.com

Index: Separate indices to search include conveyances, mortgages, miscellaneous. Record index not computerized. Office will perform a UCC search but public must search other records themselves. Search fee- mortgage: $20.00 1st, $10.00 each add'l. Office will provide mortgage certificates. Copy fee $1.50 if clerk makes copy, $.75 per page is public makes copy. $2.00 per page for request to mail copies. Cert fee- $5.50 per cert plus copy fee. Payee- Acadia Parish Clerk of Court. **Other phones:** Treasurer- 337-788-8800; Elections- 337-788-8881; Vital Records- 337-788-8881. **Property tax/Assessing-** PO Box 1329, 500 Court Cr, 2nd Fl, Crowley, LA 70527; 337-788-8871, assessor fax-337-788-0523. hours- 8AM-4PM **Online-** Search tax roll data on statewide website, www.latax.state.la.us/Menu_ParishTaxRolls/TaxRolls.aspx.

Allen Parish

Clerk of Court, PO Box 248, Oberlin, LA 70655. Recording, R/E & UCC phone-337-639-4351; fax-337-639-2030; 8AM-4:30PM (CST)

Index: Separate indices to search include mortgage, conveyance, misc. Records indexed on a public use terminal back to 1/1993. Only the public may search. Copy fee $1.00 per page from computer or if court makes copy, self-service copy fee $.50 per page. Cert fee- $5.00 per doc plus copy fee; exemplification fee varies, call for rates. Payee- Allen Parish Clerk of Court. **Other phones:** Elections- 337-639-4351; Vital Records- 337-639-4351. **Property tax/Assessing-** PO Box 218, Oberlin, LA 70655; 337-639-4391, fax-337-639-4169. **Online** - Search tax roll data on statewide at www.latax.state.la.us/Menu_ParishTaxRolls/TaxRolls.aspx.

Ascension Parish

Clerk of Court, PO Box 192, Donaldsonville, LA 70346. Recording, R/E & UCC phone-225-473-9866; fax-225-473-0758; 8:30AM-4:30PM (CST) www.ascensionclerk.com/default.aspx

Index: Separate indices to search include mortgage, conveyance. Records indexed on computer back to 7/1/70. Only the public may search. Copy fee $1.00 per page; self serve- $.50 per page. Fax back fee- $5.00 plus $1.00 per page after 1st. Cert fee- $5.00 per doc plus copy fee. Payee- Ascension Parish Clerk of Court. **Online access to Real Estate, Deed, Lien, Mortgage, Judgment, Mapping records:** Access available by subscription; $100 set-up charge single user; $250 multiple user up to 5, plus $50.00 monthly and $.50 per image printed; see www.ascensionclerk.com/onlineservices.aspx. **Other phones:** Elections- 225-473-9866. **Property tax/Assessing-** PO Box 544, Donaldsonville, LA 70346; 225-473-9239, assessor fax- 225-473-9333. **Online-** Search tax roll data on statewide website, www.latax.state.la.us/Menu_ParishTaxRolls/TaxRolls.aspx.

Assumption Parish

Clerk of Court, PO Drawer 249, Napoleonville, LA 70390. 985-369-6653; fax-985-369-2032; 8:30AM-4:30PM (CST) www.assumptionclerk.com

Index: Separate indices to search include conveyance and mortgage. Records indexed on a public use terminal back to 1990; back to 1981 for mortgages, 1943 for conveyances. Office personnel or visitors may perform searches. General index search fee $15.00 per name. Office will not search real estate records. Office will not search UCC records. Copy fee $1.00 per page. Cert fee- $5.00 per doc plus copy fee. Payee- Assumption Parish Clerk of Court. **Online access to Mortgage, Probate, Civil, Marriage, Civil Court records:** Online access is by subscription at http://97.89.251.18/resolution/. Civil/Probate goes back to 4/2005. Marriages back to 9/18/1998; mortgages to 1/8/1981. User ID and password required. **Other phones:** Register of Voters- 985-369-7347. **Property tax/Assessing-** PO Box 806, Napoleonville, LA 70390; 985-369-6385, assessor fax- 985-369-7049. **Online access-** Search tax roll data on statewide website, www.latax.state.la.us/Menu_ParishTaxRolls/TaxRolls.aspx.

Avoyelles Parish

Clerk of Court, PO Box 219, Marksville, LA 71351. Recording, R/E & UCC phone-318-253-7523; fax-318-253-4614; hours - 8:30AM-4:30PM (CST) www.avoyellesclerk.com/

Index: Separate indices to search include conveyances, mortgages, oil/gas/mineral. Records indexed on a public use terminal back to 1900's. Office personnel or visitors may perform searches. General search fee- $10.00. UCC's $30.00. Office will search real estate records. Will search UCC records. Copy fee $1.00 per page. Cert fee- $5.00 per doc plus copy fee. Payee- Avoyelles Parish Clerk of Court. **Online access to Real Estate, Land, Deeds, Conveyance, Mortgage, Oil & Gas, Plat records:** Access to land record at www.avoyellesclerk.com/Default.aspx?tabid=110. Application fee is $50.00 and a monthly service fee of $125.00. Contact the Clerk's Office for application at 318-253-7523. **Other phones:** Treasurer- 318-253-9208; Elections- 318-253-7523; Vital Records- 318-253-7523. **Property tax/Assessing-** PO Box806, Marksville, LA 71351; 318-253-4507, fax- 318-253-8828. **Online-** Search tax roll data on statewide website, www.latax.state.la.us/Menu_ParishTaxRolls/TaxRolls.aspx.

Beauregard Parish

Clerk of Court, PO Box 100, De Ridder, LA 70634. 337-463-8595; fax-337-462-3916; 8AM-4:30PM

Index: Separate indices to search include mortgages, conveyances, charters, sheriff deeds, trade names/partnerships. Record index not computerized. Office personnel or visitors may perform searches. Search fee $30.00 UCCs, other searches vary. Office will not search real estate records. Copy fee $1.25 per page. Cert fee- $5.00 per doc plus copy fee. Payee- Beauregard Parish Clerk of Court. For bulk data sales inquiries please contact Bobby Cudd, Assessor. **Property tax/Assessing-** 214 W 2nd St, PO Box 477, DeRidder, LA 70634; 337-463-8945, assessor fax-337-463-8980. hours- 8AM-4PM Public access computer in office for index and records searching. **Online-** Search tax roll data on statewide website, www.latax.state.la.us/Menu_ParishTaxRolls/TaxRolls.aspx.

Bienville Parish

Clerk of Court, 100 Courthouse Dr, Rm 100, Arcadia, LA 71001-3600. Recording, R/E & UCC phone-318-263-2123; fax-318-263-7426; 8:30AM-4:30PM (CST) www.bienvilleparish.org/clerk/

Index: Separate indices to search include (conveyances-1980, mortgage-1988, misc.-2003), (probate, civil-1996). Records indexed on a public use terminal. Office will perform a UCC and Tax lien search but public must search other records themselves. General index search fee $20.00 1st name, $10.00 each add'l name. UCCs $30.00. Office will search mortgage records. Copy fee $1.00 per page. Cert fee- $5.00 per doc plus copy fee. Payee- Bienville Parish Clerk of Court. **Other phones:** Treasurer- 318-263-2019. **Property tax/Assessing-**

100 Courthouse Dr, Arcadia, LA 71001; 318-263-2214. **Online access**- Access to property tax index to be available free at www.bienvilleparish.org, click on Tax Assessor. A fee may apply to access full data, and registration may be required. Search tax roll data on statewide website, www.latax.state.la.us/Menu_ParishTaxRolls/TaxRolls.aspx.

Bossier Parish

Clerk of Court, PO Box 430, Benton, LA 71006. 318-965-2336; fax-318-965-2713; 8:30AM-4:30PM (CST) www.bossierclerk.com
Index: Separate indices to search include separate books by years, alpha sections, then by date. Records indexed on a public use terminal back to 1984. Office personnel or visitors may perform searches. Mortgage certificate search fee $15.00 per name. Office will search real estate records. Will search UCC records. Copy fee $.50 per page. Will fax back docs for $5.00 plus $.50 per page local, $1.00 per page long distance. Cert fee- $2.00 per cert plus copy fee. Payee- Bossier Parish Clerk of Court. Please phone assessor's office for bulk data purchase requests. **Online access to Real Estate, Deed, Marriage, Civil Court records:** Access to the clerk's WebView System is by subscription; one-time signup fee is $50 plus $35 per month, plus small fee per image printed. Monthly billing. Mortgages go back to 1984, marriages to 1843, courts back to 1980s; see http://209.209.204.34/WebInquiry/login.aspx?ReturnUrl=%2fWebInquiry%2fDefault.aspx. **Property tax/Assessing**- 204 Burt Blvd, 3rd Fl, PO Box 325, Benton, LA 71006; 318-965-2213, assessor fax- 318-965-0274. 8AM-4:30PM www.bossierparishassessor.org/meet-the-assessor.html **Online access**- Free public address search available at www.bossierparishassessor.org/cgi-bin/pro_search.pl. Access to full data requires username and login ID, signup online; fee amounts to less than $1.00 per day. For more information, call 318-221-8718. Search tax roll data on statewide website, www.latax.state.la.us/Menu_ParishTaxRolls/TaxRolls.aspx.

Caddo Parish

Clerk of Court, 501 Texas St, #103, Shreveport, LA 71101-5408. Recording, R/E & UCC phone-318-226-6780, UCC recording phone-318-226-6783; fax-318-227-9080; 8:30AM-5PM www.caddoclerk.com
Index: Separate indices to search include mortgages back to 1/1981; conveyances to 6/1983, directs back to 1917. Records indexed on computer. Office will perform a UCC search but public must search other records themselves. UCC search per debtor name- $30.00 for 1st 10 files; $1.00 each add'l on that search. Copy fee $.50 per page; $1.25 if mailed. Cert fee- $2.00 per doc plus copy fee. Payee- Caddo Parish Clerk of Court. For bulk data sales inquiries, please contact Garland Weidner, Chief Deputy. **Online access to Real Estate, Deed, Lien, Marriage, Mortgage records:** Access to the Parish online records requires a $100 set up fee plus $30 monthly fee; $.25 per image. Mortgages and indirect conveyances index dates back to 1981; direct conveyances date back to 1914. Lending agency data is available. Mortgage images back to 1/1995. Also, access marriage licenses free back to 1937; use username "muser" and password "caddo." Signup and info at www.caddoclerk.com/remote.htm or call 318-226-6523. **Other phones:** Treasurer- 318-226-6900; Elections- 318-226-6788. **Property tax/Assessing**- 501 Texas St, #102, Shreveport, LA 71101-5408; 318-226-6702, assessor fax- 318-227-1009. (Appraiser/Auditor- 318-226-6711) hours- 8:30AM-4:55PM Public access computer in office for index and records searches. www.caddoassessor.org **Online access**- Search assessor property free at www.caddoassessor.org/cgi-bin/pub_search.pl; no name searching for free; Annual sub for full data- $1.00 per day. Search tax roll data on statewide website, www.latax.state.la.us/Menu_ParishTaxRolls/TaxRolls.aspx.

Calcasieu Parish

Clerk of Court, PO Box 1030, Lake Charles, LA 70602-1030. 337-437-3550; fax-337-437-3350; 8:30AM-4:30PM (CST) www.calclerkofcourt.com
Index: Several indexes to search. Records indexed on a public use terminal back to 1989 for Misc and conveyances, 1983 for mortgages, 2003 for UCCs. Office will perform a UCC search but public must search other records themselves. UCC search per debtor name- $30.00. Copy fee $1.00 per page. Will fax $5.00 for 1st page, $3 for 2nd, $1 each add'l. Cert fee- $10.00 per cert plus copy fee. Payee- Calcasieu Parish Clerk of Court. **Online access to Real Estate, Deed, Mortgage, Marriage, Court, UCC records:** Online access to court record indices is free at www.calclerkofcourt.com. Registration and password required. Full documents requires $100.00 per month subscription. **Other phones:** Treasurer- 337-437-3680. **Property tax/Assessing**- 337-721-3000. **Online access**- Search tax roll data on statewide website, www.latax.state.la.us/Menu_ParishTaxRolls/TaxRolls.aspx.

Caldwell Parish

Clerk of Court, PO Box 1327, Columbia, LA 71418. Recording, R/E & UCC phone-318-649-2272; fax-318-649-2037; 8AM-4:30PM (CST)
Index: Separate indices to search include mortgage and conveyance indexes, civil and probate indexes, misc indexes, etc. Records indexed on a public use terminal back to 1996; civil back to 1985, criminal back to 1998. Office will perform a UCC search but public must search other records themselves. Search fee $20.00 per name. Copy fee $1.00 per page. Cert fee- $5.00 per doc plus copy fee. Payee- Caldwell Parish Clerk of Court. **Other phones:** Treasurer- 318-649-2681. **Property tax/Assessing**- PO Box 1446, Columbia, LA 71418; 318-649-2636, assessor fax- 318-649-2616. **Online access**- Search tax roll data on statewide website, www.latax.state.la.us/Menu_ParishTaxRolls/TaxRolls.aspx.

Cameron Parish

Clerk of Court, PO Box 549, Cameron, LA 70631. Recording, R/E & UCC phone-337-775-5316; fax-337-775-7172; 8:30AM-4:30PM (CST)
Index: Separate indices to search. Record index computerized back to 1966. Only the public may search. Copy fee $1.00 per page. Cert fee- $5.00 per doc plus copy fee. Payee- Cameron Parish Clerk of Court. **Other phones:** Treasurer- 337-775-5718; Elections- 337-775-5316; Vital Records- 337-775-5316. **Property tax/Assessing**- PO Bow 1100, 119 Smith Circle, Cameron, LA 70631; 337-775-5416, assessor fax- 337-775-7898. hours- 8AM-4PM http://louisianaassessors.org/cgi-bin/laso/as_dsply.cgi?Assessor=Cameron **Online** - Search tax roll data on statewide website, www.latax.state.la.us/Menu_ParishTaxRolls/TaxRolls.aspx.

Catahoula Parish

Clerk of Court, PO Box 654, Harrisonburg, LA 71340. 318-744-5497; fax-318-744-5488; 8:30AM-4:30PM (CST)
Index: Separate indices to search include mortgage, conveyance, charter. Records indexed on a public use terminal back to 1997. Office personnel or visitors may perform searches. Search fee $20.00 per name; $10.00 each add'l; $10.00 each add'l property. Copy fee $1.00 per page. Cert fee- $5.00 per doc plus copy fee. Payee- Catahoula Parish Clerk of Court. **Property tax/Assessing**- PO Box 570, Harrisonburg, LA 71340; 318-744-5291, assessor fax- 318-744-5334. hours- 8AM-N, 12:30PM-4:30PM **Online access**- Search tax roll data on statewide website, www.latax.state.la.us/Menu_ParishTaxRolls/TaxRolls.aspx.

Claiborne Parish

Clerk of Court, PO Box 330, Homer, LA 71040. Recording, R/E & UCC phone-318-927-9601; fax-318-927-2345; 8:30AM-4:30PM (CST)
Index: Separate indices to search. Records indexed on a public use terminal back to 1979, manual indexes back to 1850. Office personnel or visitors may perform searches. Criminal or civil searches $20.00 per name. Office will not search real estate records. Office will not search UCC records. Copy fee $1.00 per page. Cert fee- $5.00 per doc plus copy fee. Payee- Claiborne Parish Clerk of Court. **Other phones:** Treasurer- 318-927-2222; Elections- 318-927-9601; Vital Records- 318-927-9601. **Property tax/Assessing**- 508 E Main St, Homer, LA 71040; 318-927-3022, assessor fax- 318-927-5941. **Online access**- Search tax roll data on statewide website, www.latax.state.la.us/Menu_ParishTaxRolls/TaxRolls.aspx.

Concordia Parish

Clerk of Court, PO Box 790, Vidalia, LA 71373. Recording, R/E & UCC phone-318-336-4204; fax-318-336-8777; 8:30AM-4:30PM (CST) www.concordiaclerk.org
Index: Separate indices to search include conveyance, mtg. Records indexed on a public use terminal back to 1973. Office personnel or visitors may perform searches. Search fee $30.00. Office will search real estate records. UCC searches records from 1990 to date. General copy fee- $1.00 per page. Cert fee- $5.00 per cert plus copy fee. Payee- Concordia Parish Clerk of Court. **Other phones:** Elections- 318-336-4204. **Property tax/Assessing**- 4001 Carter St, #3, Vidalia, LA 71373; 318-336-5122, assessor fax- 318-336-5122. (Appraiser/Auditor- 318-336-5122) hours- 9AM-4PM **Online access**- Search tax roll data on statewide website, www.latax.state.la.us/Menu_ParishTaxRolls/TaxRolls.aspx.

De Soto Parish

Clerk of Court, PO Box 1206, Mansfield, LA 71052. Recording, R/E & UCC phone-318-872-3110; fax-318-872-4202; 8:30AM-4:30PM (CST) www.desotoparishclerk.org
Index: Separate indices to search include civil, criminal, conveyance, mtg, marriage. Records indexed on a public use terminal back to 1958. Office personnel or visitors may perform searches. Search fee $10.00. Office will not search real estate records. Will search UCC records. Copy fee $1.00 per page. Cert fee- $5.00 per cert plus copy fee. Payee- De Soto Parish Clerk of Court. **Online access to Real Estate, Deed, Judgment, Lien, Mortgage records:** Access Clerk of Court records index by subscription at www.desotoparishclerk.org/online.html; set-up fee is $150.00 plus either $50 per month for index only searching or $100 per month for index, doc viewing, and images. **Other phones:** Elections- 318-872-3110; Civil- 318-872-3788; Criminal -318-872-3181. **Property tax/Assessing**- PO Box1168, Mansfield, LA 71052; 318-872-3610, fax- 318-872-9434. **Online**- Search tax roll data on statewide website, www.latax.state.la.us/Menu_ParishTaxRolls/TaxRolls.aspx.

East Baton Rouge Parish

Clerk of Court, PO Box 1991, Baton Rouge, LA 70821-1991. 225-389-3960, -3979 research, R/E recording phone-225-389-3975; fax-225-389-7835; 7:30AM-5:30PM (CST) www.ebrclerkofcourt.org
Has a satellite office at 10500 Coursey Blvd. Index: All in one. Records indexed on a public use terminal at both locations back to 1/100. Office personnel or visitors may perform searches. General index search fee $20.00 1st name. Conveyance certificate search fee $23.10 each. Copy fee $.50 per page. Cert fee- $5.00 per doc plus copy fee. Payee- E. Baton Rouge Parish Clerk of Court. **Online access to Real Estate, Deed, Lien, Marriage, Probate, Court, Judgment, Map Data Index records:** Access to online records requires a $100 set up fee with a $5 monthly fee and $.33 per minute of use. Four years worth of data is kept active on the system. Lending agency data is available. For info, contact Wendy Gibbs at 225-398-5295. **Other phones:** Elections- 225-389-4765. **Property tax/Assessing**- 222 St. Louis St, Rm 126,

Baton Rouge, LA 70802; 225-389-3920. **Online access**- Search tax roll data on statewide website, www.latax.state.la.us/Menu_ParishTaxRolls/TaxRolls.aspx.

East Carroll Parish

Clerk of Court, 400 1st St, Lake Providence, LA 71254. Recording, R/E & UCC phone-318-559-2399; fax-318-559-0037; 8:30AM-4:30PM (CST)
Index: All in one. Record index not computerized. Office will perform a UCC search but public must search other records themselves. Search fee $2.00 per name per year. Office will not search real estate records. UCC search per debtor name- $30.00. Copy fee $2.00 per page. Cert fee- $5.00 per doc plus copy fee. Payee- East Carroll Parish Clerk of Court. **Other phones:** Treasurer- 318-559-2000. **Property tax/Assessing**- 400 1st St, Lake Providence, LA 71254; 318-559-2850, assessor fax- 318-559-2851. **Online access**- Search tax roll data on statewide website, www.latax.state.la.us/Menu_ParishTaxRolls/TaxRolls.aspx.

East Feliciana Parish

Clerk of Court, PO Drawer 599, Clinton, LA 70722. 225-683-5145; fax-225-683-3556; 8:30AM-4:30PM www.eastfelicianaclerk.org/
Index: Separate indices to search include conveyance, mtg, misc, and marriage. Records indexed on a public use terminal, conveyances back to 1962, Mortgages to 1981, Civil suits to 9/88, Marriages to 12/1987, Misc. to 1/84. Office will perform a UCC search (only if ordering a certificate) but public must search other records themselves. General search fee $30.00 per name; Civil- $10.00. All Property searches done by name only. Copy fee $1.00 per page. Cert fee- $5.00 per doc plus copy fee. Conformed copy is $3.00. Payee- East Feliciana Parish Clerk of Court. **Online access to Real Estate, Lien, Mortgage, Marriage, Civil Court records:** Access to online records requires a subscription, $100 set up fee with a $50 monthly usage fee for indices or $100.00 per month for indices plus images, in quarterly advances. Conveyances go back to 1962, mortgages to 1981; viewable back to 6/18/1982. Marriages go back to 1987, viewable free to 1995, and miscellaneous index goes back to 1984. For info, contact clerk's office at 225-683-5145 or visit www.eastfelicianaclerk.org. **Other phones:** Elections- 225-683-5145. **Property tax/Assessing**- PO Box 263, Clinton, LA 70722; 225-683-8945, assessor fax- 225-683-8042. **Online access**- Search tax roll data on statewide website, www.latax.state.la.us but no name searching.

Evangeline Parish

Clerk of Court, PO Drawer 347, Ville Platte, LA 70586. Recording, R/E & UCC phone-337-363-5671; fax-337-363-5780; 8AM-4:30PM (CST)
Index: Separate indices to search include civil, criminal, mortgage, conveyance, corporations, misc, etc. Records indexed on a public use terminal back to 1976 for con, 1966 for mtg, 1989 for civil. Office personnel or visitors may perform searches. Search fee $15.00 per name. Office will search real estate records. Copy fee $1.00 per page, $5.00 1st page, $1.00 each add'l page to mail, $10.00 1st page, $1.00 each add'l page to fax. per page, $5.00 minimum. Cert fee- $2.00 per page includes copy fee. Payee- Evangeline Parish Clerk of Court. **Other phones:** Treasurer- 337-363-5651; Elections- 337-363-5671. **Property tax/Assessing**- 200 Court St, #300, Ville Platte, LA 70586; 337-363-4310, assessor fax- 337-363-4325. **Online access**- Search tax roll data on statewide website, www.latax.state.la.us/Menu_ParishTaxRolls/TaxRolls.aspx.

Franklin Parish

Clerk of Court, PO Box 1564, Winnsboro, LA 71295. Recording, R/E & UCC phone-318-435-5133; fax-318-435-5134; 8:30AM-4:30PM (CST)
Index: All in one. Records indexed on computer back to 1995. Office personnel or visitors may perform searches. Signed release and prepayment required for search. General index search fee $20.00 per name. Office can perform mortgage searches. Property description required. Office will search UCC records, tax liens not included in UCC search. UCC search or tax lien search per debtor name- $30.00. Copy fee $2.00, if tax lien or real estate $1.00 per page. Cert fee- $5.00 per doc plus copy fee. Payee- Franklin Parish Clerk of Court. **Property tax/Assessing**- 6552 Main St, Winnsboro, LA 71295; 318-435-5390, fax-318-438-9217. **Online access**- Search tax roll data on statewide website,, www.latax.state.la.us/Menu_ParishTaxRolls/TaxRolls.aspx.

Grant Parish

Clerk of Court, PO Box 263, Colfax, LA 71417. Recording, R/E & UCC phone-318-627-3246; fax-318-627-3201; 8:30AM-4:30PM (CST)
Index: Separate indices to search include mortgages, conveyances, civil suits, criminal suits, marriage records. Records indexed on computer back to 1992. Office personnel or visitors may perform searches. General index search fee $20.00 per name per index; $10.00 each add'l index. Office will not search real estate records. UCC search per debtor name- $30.00. Copy fee $1.00 per page. SASE requested for free mail return. Cert fee- $5.00 per doc plus copy fee. Payee- Grant Parish Clerk of Court. **Other phones:** Treasurer- 318-627-3157; Elections- 318-627-3246. **Property tax/Assessing**- 200 Main St, Courthouse 318-627-5471, assessor fax- 318-627-5625. www.grantassessor.org **Online access**- Search tax roll data on statewide website, www.latax.state.la.us but no name searching.

Iberia Parish

Clerk of Court, PO Drawer 12010, New Iberia, LA 70562-2010. 337-365-7282; fax-337-365-0737; 8:30AM-4:30PM (CST) www.iberiaclerk.com
Index: Separate indices to search include books conveyance to 1974, mtgs to 1959, marriage to 2000. Records indexed on both computer and public use terminal. Office personnel or visitors may perform searches. Search fees- tax lien $20.00; UCCs $30.00. Copy fee $.75 per page. Cert fee- $5.00 per doc plus copy fee. Payee- Iberia Parish Clerk of Court. **Online access to Real Estate, Conveyance, Deed, Mortgage, Lien, Marriage** Access to the Parish online records requires a $100.00 monthly usage fee. Lending agency data is available. For info, contact Mike Thibodeaux at 337-365-7282. Registration is also required for the Clerk's index search at www.iberiaclerk.com/resolution/default.asp which includes civil, conveyances, criminal, marriages back to 2000, mortgages back to 1959, and probate back thru 2000. **Property tax/Assessing**- 300 Iberia St, #B-100, New Iberia, LA 70560; 337-369-4415, assessor fax- 337-369-4406. www.iberiaassessor.org **Online** - Search tax roll data on statewide website, www.latax.state.la.us/Menu_ParishTaxRolls/TaxRolls.aspx.

Iberville Parish

Clerk of Court, PO Box 423, Plaquemine, LA 70765-0423. 225-687-5160; fax-225-687-5260; 8:30AM-4:30PM (CST) www.ibervilleparish.com
Index: Separate indices to search include conveyances, mortgages, civil records, oath, bonds, misc. Records indexed on a public use terminal back to 1990. Office personnel or visitors may perform searches. General search fee $10.00 per name. Office can perform mortgage searches. Will search UCC records. UCC search per debtor name- $30.00. Copy fee $1.00 per page. Cert fee- $5.00 per doc plus copy fee. Payee- Iberville Parish Clerk of Court. **Online access to Real Estate, Deed records:** Access to records for a fee go to http://ibervilleclerk.com/html_pages/online.html. Monthly subscription fee charged. **Property tax/Assessing**- PO Box 697, 58050 Meriam St, Courthouse, Plaquemine, LA 70764; 225-687-3568, assessor fax- 225-687-3103. **Online access**- Access assessor property tax records free at www.ibervilleassessor.org/Search.aspx.

Jackson Parish

Clerk of Court, PO Box 730, Jonesboro, LA 71251. Recording, R/E & UCC phone-318-259-2424; fax-318-395-0386; 8:30AM-4:30PM (CST) www.jacksonparishclerk.org
Index: Separate indices to search include conveyances, mortgage, UCC, misc. Records indexed on a public use terminal back to 1972. Conveyance back to 1972, Mortgage, Misc back to 1987, Marriage back to 1880. Office personnel or visitors may perform searches. Mortgage index search fee $20.00 per property; UCC per debtor name- $30.00. Office will no do title searches, but will assist. Will search UCC records. Tax liens show up on a mortgage certificate search. Copy fee $1.00 per page. Cert fee- $5.00 per doc plus copy fee. Payee- Jackson Parish Clerk of Court. **Online access to Real Estate, Grantor/Grantee, Deed, Mortgage, Lien, Judgment, Marriage records:** Access to the clerk's WebView Online Records system is available by subscription; $50 installation and account setup fee plus $50.00 per month usage fee; Sub form at http://72.149.195.202/Webinquiry_Jackson/(s2uty0iozzflf45tewwkeb5)/subscribe.aspx. **Other phones:** Elections- 318-259-2424; Police Jury- 318-259-2361. **Property tax/Assessing**- 500 E Court Ave, #101, Courthouse, Jonesboro, LA 71251; 318-259-2151, assessor fax- 318-259-5672. **Online access**- Search tax roll data on statewide website, www.latax.state.la.us/Menu_ParishTaxRolls/TaxRolls.aspx.

Jefferson Davis Parish

Clerk of Court, PO Box 799, Jennings, LA 70546-0799. 337-824-1160/1161, R/E recording phone-337-824-1160; fax-337-824-1354; 8:30AM-4:30PM
Index: Separate indices to search include mortgage, conveyance, sheriff sale, charter, partnership. Records indexed on a public use terminal back to 1978. Office personnel or visitors may perform searches. General index search fee $20.00 per 1st name, $10.00 each add'l name. Office will search real estate mortgage records only. Will search UCC records. UCC search per debtor name- $30.00. Copy fee $2.00, if tax lien or real estate $1.00 per page. Cert fee- $5.00 to $20.00 per cert plus copy fee. Payee- Jefferson Davis Parish Clerk of Court. **Other phones:** Treasurer- 337-824-4792; Elections- 337-824-1160; Vital Records- 337-824-1161; Civil Dept- 337-824-8340. **Property tax/Assessing**- 300 N State St, #103, Jennings, LA 70546; 337-824-3451, assessor fax- 337-824-7681.

Jefferson Parish

Clerk of Court, PO Box 10, Gretna, LA 70054-0010. Recording, R/E & UCC phone-504-364-2943/2944, UCC recording phone-504-364-2881; fax-504-364-2942; 8:30AM-4:30PM (CST) www.jpclerkofcourt.us
Index: All in one. Records indexed on a public use terminal back to 1967. Only the public may search. Copy fee $1.00 per page from book/$.50 per page from image, UCC copy- $2.00 per page. Cert fee- $5.00 per doc includes copy fee. Payee- Jefferson Parish Clerk of Court. **Online access to Real Estate, Deed, Marriage, Civil Court records:** Access to the clerk's JeffNet database is by subscription; set-up fee is $100.00 plus $50.00 monthly and $.50 per image printed. Mortgage and conveyance images go back to 1971 and changing; index to 1967. Marriage and property records go back to 1992. For info, visit https://ssl.jpclerkofcourt.us/JeffnetSetup/default.asp. Also, search inmates and offenders on a private site at https://www.vinelink.com/vinelink/siteInfoAction.do?siteId=19002. **Other phones:** Elections- 504-364-2963. **Property tax/Assessing**- 200 Derbigny St, #2200, General Gov Bldg, Gretna, LA 70053; 504-362-4100, assessor fax- 504-366-4087. **Online access**- Search the assessor property rolls free at www.jpassessor.com. Call Donna Richoux at 504-364-2900 for fee info. Also, Search tax roll data on statewide website at www.latax.state.la.us/Menu_ParishTaxRolls/TaxRolls.aspx.

La Salle Parish

Clerk of Court, PO Box 1316, Jena, LA 71342. Recording, R/E & UCC phone-318-992-2158; fax-318-992-2157; 8:30AM-4:30PM (CST)
Index: Separate indices to search include mtgs, conveyances, civil, criminal. Records indexed on a public use terminal back to 1993. Office personnel or visitors may perform searches. General index search fee $20.00 1st name; $10.00 each add'l name. Office will not search real estate records. Copy fee $1.00 per page. Cert fee- $5.00 per cert; $1.00 per page. Payee- La Salle Parish Clerk of Court. **Other phones:** Elections- 318-992-2158. **Property tax/Assessing-** PO Box 400, Jena, LA 71342; 318-992-8256, assessor fax- 318-992-8257. (Appraiser/Auditor- 318-992-2211) **Online access-** Search tax roll data on statewide website, www.latax.state.la.us/Menu_ParishTaxRolls/TaxRolls.aspx.

Lafayette Parish

Clerk of Court, PO Box 2009, Lafayette, LA 70502. 337-291-6400; fax-337-291-6392; 8:30AM-4:30PM (CST) www.lafayetteparishclerk.com
Index: All in one. Records indexed on computer back to 1966 for vendee, 1956 for vendor. Public access terminal available. Office personnel or visitors may perform searches. Search fee $30.00 UCCs; tax lien $20.00; mortgage certs $20.00 1st name, $10 each add'l. Office will search real estate records. Copy fee $1.00 per page. Cert fee- $5.00 per doc plus copy fee. Payee- Lafayette Parish Clerk of Court. **Online access to Real Estate, Deed, Mortgage, Lien, UCC records:** Access to Parish online records requires a $100 set up fee plus $15 per month and $.50 per minute. Conveyances date back to 1936; mortgages to 1948; other records to 1986. Lending agency data is available. For info, contact Derek Comeaux at 337-291-6433. Tax and UCC lien data is for this parish only. **Other phones:** Treasurer- 337-291-6300; Elections- 337-291-6454; Vital Records- 337-262-5616 x139. **Property tax/Assessing-** PO Box 3225, 1010 Lafayette St, Lafayette, LA 70502; 337-291-7080, assessor fax- 337-291-7086. **Online access-** Search tax roll data on statewide website, www.latax.state.la.us/Menu_ParishTaxRolls/TaxRolls.aspx. Also, assessor property data is free at www.lafayetteassessor.com/search.html but no name searching.

Lafourche Parish

Clerk of Court, PO Box 818, Thibodaux, LA 70302. Recording, R/E & UCC phone-985-447-4841; fax-985-447-5800; 8:30AM-4:30PM (CST)
Index: Separate indices to search include conveyance, mortgage, misc., charter, wills, etc. Records indexed on a public use terminal back to 1958. Office personnel or visitors may perform searches. Mortgage certs $20.00 1st name, $10 each add'l. Office will not search real estate records. Office will search UCC records available on state computer. UCC search per debtor name- $30.00. Copy fee $1.00 per page. UCCs-$2.00 per page. Cert fee- $5.00 per doc plus copy fee. Payee- Lafourche Parish Clerk of Court. **Other phones:** Elections- 985-447-4841. **Property tax/Assessing-** 403 St. Louis St, Thibodaux, LA 70301; 985-447-7242, assessor fax- 985-447-8060. **Online** - Search tax roll data on statewide website, www.latax.state.la.us/Menu_ParishTaxRolls/TaxRolls.aspx.

Lincoln Parish

Clerk of Court, PO Box 924, Ruston, LA 71273-0924. Recording, R/E & UCC phone-318-251-5130; fax-318-255-6004; 8:30AM-4:30PM (CST)
Index: Separate indices to search include conveyance, mortgage, Charter, Oaths, Bonds. Records indexed on a public use terminal back to 1964 for conveyances, 1973 for mortgages. Office will perform a UCC search but public must search other records themselves. Mortgage certificate search fee $20.00, plus $10.00 each add'l name. UCC search per debtor name- $30.00. Copy fee $1.00 per page. Cert fee- $3.00 per doc plus copy fee. Payee- Lincoln Parish Clerk of Court. Bulk data available for purchase, $800.00 for whole county. **Property tax/Assessing-** PO Box 1218, 100 W Texas Ave, Ruston, LA 71273; 318-251-5140. hours- 8AM-4:30PM **Online access-** Access property assessor data at http://assessor.lincolnparish.org/WebTaxRoll/Default.aspx with free registration. Also, search by owner name for parcel and property data free on the GIS-mapping site at http://gis.lincolnparish.org. Search tax roll data on statewide website, www.latax.state.la.us/Menu_ParishTaxRolls/TaxRolls.aspx.

Livingston Parish

Clerk of Court, PO Box 1150, Livingston, LA 70754. 225-686-2216; fax-225-686-1867; 8AM-4:30PM (CST) https://www.livclerk.org
Index: Separate indices to search include conveyances, mortgages, bonds, charters, civil. Records indexed on a public use terminal back to 1875 for conveyances, 1960 for mortgages. Office personnel or visitors may perform searches. Mortgage certificate search fee $20.00 1st name, $10.00 each add'l name. Office will not search real estate records. Search UCCs free on state system via the county terminal here. UCC search per debtor name- $30.00. Copy fee $1.00 per page; self serve- $.50. Cert fee- $5.00 per doc plus copy fee. Payee- Livingston Parish Clerk of Court. **Online access to Real Estate, Deed, Lien, Judgment, UCC, Plat records:** Access the clerk's search pages at www.livclerk.org/combined/Disclaimer.aspx after free registration. User name and password required to search; $1.00 per page fee for images. $50.00 yearly fee for an account. For assistance, call Vanessa Barnett at 225-686-2216 x1107 or 225-505-8200 cell. **Other phones:** Sheriff- 225-686-2241. **Property tax/Assessing-** 20180 Iowa St, PO Box 307, Livingston, LA 70754; 225-686-7278, assessor fax- 225-686-1817. hours- 8AM-4PM Public access terminal available. **Online** - Search tax roll data on statewide website, www.latax.state.la.us/Menu_ParishTaxRolls/TaxRolls.aspx.

Madison Parish

Clerk of Court, PO Box 1710, Tallulah, LA 71282. Recording, R/E & UCC phone-318-574-0655; fax-318-574-3961; 8:30AM-4:30PM (CST)
Index: Separate indices to search include conveyances, mortgages, partnerships, incorporations, bonds. Records indexed on a public use terminal back to 1981, 1983 for images. Office personnel or visitors may perform searches. Search fee $10.00 per name. Will search UCC records. Copy fee $2.00 per page. Cert fee- $5.50 per cert includes copy fee. Payee- Madison Parish Clerk of Court. **Other phones:** Elections- 318-574-0655. **Property tax/Assessing-** 100 N Cedar St, Courthouse, Tallulah, LA 71282; 318-574-0117. hours- 8AM-4:30PM **Online** - Search tax roll data statewide at, www.latax.state.la.us/Menu_ParishTaxRolls/TaxRolls.aspx.

Morehouse Parish

Clerk of Court, PO Box 1543, Bastrop, LA 71221-1543. Recording, R/E & UCC phone-318-281-3343; fax-318-281-3775; 8:30AM-4:30PM (CST)
Index: Separate indices to search include mortgage, conveyance, marriage, UCC - direct and indirect. Records indexed on a public use terminal back to 1970. Office personnel or visitors may perform searches. General index search fee $15.00 per name. Office will search real estate records. UCC search per debtor name- $30.00. Copy fee $1.00 per page. Cert fee- $5.00 per doc plus copy fee. Payee- Morehouse Parish Clerk of Court. **Other phones:** Vital Records- 318-568-5050/361-7281/281-3343. **Property tax/Assessing-** PO Box 1177, 106 E Jefferson, Bastrop, LA 71221-1177; 318-281-1802, assessor fax- 318-281-8601. hours- 8AM-4:30PM www.morehouseassessor.org/default.htm **Online access-** Search tax roll data on statewide website, www.latax.state.la.us/Menu_ParishTaxRolls/TaxRolls.aspx. Also, at www.morehouseassessor.org/propertyinformation.htm,. eTaxroll users are required to register online to obtain a Username and Password. Once registered, you may have limited access (3 searches per day) or register as a commercial user.

Natchitoches Parish

Clerk of Court, PO Box 476, Natchitoches, LA 71458-0476. 318-352-8152; fax-318-352-9321; 8:30AM-4:30PM (CST) www.npclerkofcourt.org/
Civil office- 318-357-2293/94. Index: All in one. Records indexed on a public use terminal back to 1976. Only the public may search files, but office will do computer searches. Search fee $10.00 per name, per year, per book; $35.00 for UCC 11 search. Copy fee $1.00 per page. Cert fee- $5.00 per doc plus copy fee. Payee- Natchitoches Parish Clerk of Court. **Online access to Real Estate, Deed, Marriage, Divorce, Judgment, Wills/Probate, Assumed Name records:** With username and password to WebView you can search and access marriage and property records back to 1976. $50 setup fee, then $50.00 monthly, plus $.50 per image. Direct subscription inquires to Linda Cockrell at 318-352-8152 or visit http://12.197.242.86/WebInquiry_Natchitoches/login.aspx. **Other phones:** Elections- 318-352-8152; Vital Records- 318-357-2243; Civil- 318-357-2293 or 2294. **Property tax/Assessing-** PO Box 201, 200 Church St, New Courthouse, Natchitoches, LA 71458; 318-352-2377, fax- 318-352-9309. www.natchitochesassessor.org **Online access-** Access assessor property data free at www.natchitochesassessor.org/SearchProperty.aspx. Search tax roll data statewide at, www.latax.state.la.us/Menu_ParishTaxRolls/TaxRolls.aspx.

Orleans Parish, Conveyances

Clerk of Court, 1340 Poydras St, 18th Fl; Amoco Bldg, New Orleans, LA 70112. 504-592-9170, R/E recording phone-504-592-9176, UCC recording phone-504-592-9189; fax-504-523-4320; 9AM-4PM (CST) www.orleanscdc.com
Mortgages recorded at a different office (Office of the Recorder of Mortgages) on 4th Fl, call 504-592-9176. Archives at Suite 500, www.notarialarchives.org/, 504-568-8577. Index: Separate indices to search include conveyances, mortgages, vital statistics. Records indexed on computer back to 1986, and some not all from 1985. The public access terminal includes conveyances and mortgage records back to 1986. Office suggests internet search. The office will accept fax and phone requests for name searches of conveyances index on a 1st come 1st served basis. UCC search per debtor name- $30.00. Copy fee $1.00 per page; UCC copy- $2.00 per page. Cert fee- Generally, cert fee is the same as recording fee: $5.00 for UCC; $3.00 for real estate doc. Payee- Orleans Parish Recorder of Mortgages. **Online access to Real Estate, Deed, Mortgage, Lien, Birth, Death records:** Access the Parish online records requires a $300 yearly subscription fee, prorated. Records date back to 1989. Access includes real estate, liens, civil, 1st city court records. For info/signup, phone 504-592-9264. Conveyances back to 1989, mortgages to 9/21/97. **Other phones:** Vital Records- 504-568-5152; City Hall Information- 504-658-4000; Notorial Archives Fax -504-599-1443. **Property tax/Assessing-** 504-592-7050. **Online access-** Access City of New Orleans property data free at www.cityofno.com/pg-137-1.aspx. Access City property data free at www.cityofno.com/pg-137-1.aspx. Search tax roll data on statewide website, www.latax.state.la.us/Menu_ParishTaxRolls/TaxRolls.aspx.

Ouachita Parish

Clerk of Court, PO Box 1862, Monroe, LA 71210-1862. Recording, R/E & UCC phone-318-327-1444; fax-318-327-1462; 8:30AM-5PM (CST)
Index: Separate indices to search include conveyances, mortgages, bonds, charters, partnerships, etc. Records indexed on a public use terminal back to 1996. Office personnel or visitors may perform searches. Mortgage certificate search $20.00 1st name; $10.00 each add'l name. Office will not search real estate records. Office will not search

UCC records. Copy fee $1.00 per page; self serve- $.50 each. Cert fee- $2.00 per page includes copy fee. Payee- Ouachita Parish Clerk of Çourt. **Other phones:** Elections- 318-327-1444; Sheriff/Tax Collector- 318-329-1200. **Property tax/Assessing-** PO Box 1127, 300 St. John St, Rm 103 (71201), Monroe, LA 71210; 318-327-1300, assessor fax- 318-327-1311. A public access terminal is available. www.opassessor.com **Online**- Access to assessor property data is free at www.ouachitaparishassessor.com/online_property_search.htm. Subscription required to view full details, legal description, etc.; fee is determined by number of logins. Also, search tax roll data on statewide website, www.latax.state.la.us/Menu_ParishTaxRolls/TaxRolls.aspx.

Plaquemines Parish

Clerk of Court, PO Box 40, Belle Chasse, LA 70037-0040. Recording, R/E phone-504-297-5180; fax-504-297-5195; 8:30AM-4:30PM www.clerk25th.com/

Index: Separate indices to search include mortgage, conveyance, marriage, criminal, civil, UCC, other miscellaneous. Records indexed on computer back to 1992. Office personnel or visitors may perform searches. General index search fee $20.00 for 1st name, $10.00 each add'l name. Office will search real estate records (mortgage search only). Copy fee $1.00 per page if make by staff, $.50 per page if self serve. Cert fee- $5.00 per doc plus copy fee. Payee- Plaquemines Parish Clerk of Court. **Other phones:** Elections- 504-297-5180. **Property tax/Assessing-** 106 Ave G, Belle Chasse, LA 70037; 504-297-5250, assessor fax- 504-392-9741. **Online**- Search tax roll data on statewide website, www.latax.state.la.us/Menu_ParishTaxRolls/TaxRolls.aspx.

Pointe Coupee Parish

Clerk of Court, PO Box 86, New Roads, LA 70760. Recording, R/E & UCC phone-225-638-9596; fax-225-638-9590; 8:30AM-4:30PM (CST)

Index: Separate indices to search. Records indexed on a public use terminal back to 1981 for conveyances, to 1967 for mortgages. Only the public may search. Office will not search real estate records. Office will not search UCC records. Copy fee $1.25 per page. Cert fee- $5.00 per doc plus copy fee. Payee- Pointe Coupee Parish Clerk of Court. **Property tax/Assessing-** 211 E Main St, New Roads, LA 70760; 225-638-7077, assessor fax- 225-638-4370. **Online** - Search tax roll data on statewide website, www.latax.state.la.us/Menu_ParishTaxRolls/TaxRolls.aspx.

Rapides Parish

Clerk of Court, PO Box 952, Alexandria, LA 71309. Recording, R/E & UCC phone-318-473-8153; fax-318-473-4667; 8:30-4:30PM www.rapidesclerk.org

Index: Separate indices to search include conveyance, UCC, chattel, mortgage, marriage, courts. Records indexed on a public use terminal back to 1984. Office will perform a UCC search or current owner search but public must search other records themselves. UCC Search fee- $30.00 per name. Copy fee $1.00 per page. Cert fee- $5.00 per doc plus copy fee. Payee- Rapides Parish Clerk of Court. **Other phones:** Elections- 318-473-6770. **Property tax/Assessing-** PO Box 2002, 701 Murray St, Alexandria, LA 71309; 318-448-8511, assessor fax- 318-443-7354. hours- 8AM-4PM A public access terminal is available. www.rapidesassessor.org **Online access**- Search tax roll data on statewide website, www.latax.state.la.us/Menu_ParishTaxRolls/TaxRolls.aspx. Also, with registration, username and password you may search the eTaxroll site free at www.rapidesassessor.org/propertyinformation.htm.

Red River Parish

Clerk of Court, PO Box 485, Coushatta, LA 71019-0485. Recording, R/E & UCC phone-318-932-6741; fax-318-932-3126; 8:30AM-4:30PM (CST)

Index: Separate indices to search include conveyance and mortgages. Most records indexes available on a public use terminal back to 1986. Office personnel or visitors may perform searches. Search fee $30.00 UCCs; tax liens $20.00. Office will search real estate records. Will search UCC records. Copy fee $1.00 per page. Cert fee- $5.00 per doc plus copy fee. Payee- Red River Parish Clerk of Court. Weekly recordings available for bulk purchase. **Other phones:** Elections- 318-932-6741. **Property tax/Assessing-** PO Box 509, Coushatta, LA 71019; 318-932-4922, assessor fax- 318-932-6958. A public access terminal is available.

Richland Parish

Clerk of Court, PO Box 119, Rayville, LA 71269. 318-728-4171; fax-318-728-7020; 8:30AM-4:30PM

Index: Separate indices to search include conveyances and mortgages. Records indexed on a public use terminal back to 1980. Office personnel or visitors may perform searches. Search fee $20.00 per name. Office will search real estate records. (Mortgages only). Copy fee $1.00 per page. Cert fee- $5.00 per doc plus copy fee. Payee- Richland Parish Clerk of Court. **Property tax/Assessing-** 708 S Julia St, #115, Rayville, LA 71269; 318-728-4491, assessor fax- 318-728-6478. **Online**- Search tax roll data on statewide website, www.latax.state.la.us/Menu_ParishTaxRolls/TaxRolls.aspx.

Sabine Parish

Clerk of Court, PO Box 419, Many, LA 71449. 318-256-6223; fax-318-256-9037; 8AM-4:30PM www.sabineparishclerk.com/

Index: Separate indices to search include conveyances and mortgages back to 1843; marriage index goes back to 1930. Records indexed on a public use terminal back to 1963. Office personnel or visitors may perform searches. UU search fee $30.00 per name; civil-$20.00. Real estate owner, mortgage, UCC and property transfer searches available. Copy fee $1.00 per page. Cert fee- $5.00 per doc plus copy fee; exemplification- $10.00. Payee- Sabine Parish Clerk of Court. **Online access to Real Estate, Deed, Mortgage, Civil, Probate records:** Access deeds, civil court and succession-probate court records by subscription along with conveyance, mortgage records at www.sabineparishclerk.com/online.htm. $50.00 one-time setup fee plus $100 per month. Conveyance index goes back to 6/1963, images back to 1/1985. Mortgage index goes back to 6/1968; images to 1/1985. Civil suits go back to 1/1985; Probate to 1920. **Other phones:** Treasurer- 318-256-5637; Elections- 318-256-3697; Sheriff- 318-256-9241. **Property tax/Assessing-** 400 S Capitol, #106, Many, LA 71449; 318-256-3482, fax- 318-256-3481.

St. Bernard Parish

Clerk of Court, PO Box 1746, Chalmette, LA 70044. 504-271-3434; fax-504-278-4380; 8:30AM-4:30PM www.stbclerk.com/modules.php?name=system

Index: All in one. Records indexed on a public use terminal back to 1986. Office personnel or visitors may perform searches. $10.00 per name for 10 years for anything 1986 to present. Mortgage certificate fee $20.00; $10.00 each add'l name. UCC records search includes tax liens if requested. Copy fee $1.00 per page. Cert fee- $5.00 per doc plus copy fee. Payee- St. Bernard Parish Clerk of Court. **Online access to Real Estate, Conveyance, Mortgage, Chattel, Bond, Marriage, Partnership, Civil/Criminal Court records:** Search clerk's court and recording records indexes free at www.stbclerk.com/modules.php?name=system&file=records. Mortgages back to 1974, marriages to 4/1938, conveyances and partnerships back to 1974, courts and chattel back to 1/1989, Misc. and bonds and partnerships back to 1974. **Other phones:** Elections- 504-271-3434. **Property tax/Assessing-** 1101 W St. Bernard Hwy, #105, Chalmette, LA 70043; 504-279-6379. A public access terminal is available. **Online access**- Search tax roll data on statewide website, www.latax.state.la.us/Menu_ParishTaxRolls/TaxRolls.aspx.

St. Charles Parish

Clerk of Court, PO Box 424, Hahnville, LA 70057. Recording, R/E & UCC phone-985-783-6632; fax-985-783-2005; 8:30AM-4:30PM (CST)

Index: All in one. Records indexed on a public use terminal back to 1958. Office will perform a UCC search but public must search other records themselves. Search fee $10.00 per name. General copy fee $1.00 per page. Conformed copies- $3.00 per doc. Cert fee- $2.00 per page includes copy fee. Payee- St. Charles Parish Clerk of Court. **Other phones:** Elections- 985-783-5120; Vital Records- 985-783-6632. **Property tax/Assessing-** 15045 River Rd, Courthouse, Hahnville, LA 70057; 985-783-6281, assessor fax- 985-783-6893. **Online access**- Search tax roll data on statewide website, www.latax.state.la.us/Menu_ParishTaxRolls/TaxRolls.aspx.

St. Helena Parish

Clerk of Court, PO Box 308, Greensburg, LA 70441-0308. 225-222-4514, R/E recording phone-225-222-4521, UCC recording phone-225-222-4514; fax-225-222-3443; 8:30AM-4:30PM (CST)

Index: Indexes by record type. Record index not computerized. Office personnel or visitors may perform searches. General index search fee $10.00 per name. Mortgage search $10.00 per name. UCC search per debtor name- $15.00. Copy fee $1.00 per page. Cert fee- $5.00 per doc includes copy fee. Payee- St. Helena Parish Clerk of Court. **Other phones:** Treasurer- 225-222-4549; Elections- 225-222-4440. **Property tax/Assessing-** PO Box 607, 351 Sitman St, Greensburg, LA 70441; 225-222-4540, assessor fax- 225-222-4132. (Appraiser/Auditor- 225-222-4553) hours- 8AM-4PM **Online access**- Search tax roll data on statewide website, www.latax.state.la.us/Menu_ParishTaxRolls/TaxRolls.aspx.

St. James Parish

Clerk of Court, PO Box 63, Convent, LA 70723. Recording, R/E & UCC phone-225-562-7496; fax-225-562-2383; 8AM-4:30PM (CST)

Index: Separate indices to search include conveyances, mortgages, marriage, probate, oaths, bonds, UCC. Conveyances on computer back to 1973; mortgages to 1950. Office personnel or visitors may perform searches. Search fee $15.00 per name. Office will search real estate records. Will search UCC records. Copy fee $1.00 per page. Cert fee- $5.00 per doc plus copy fee. Payee- St. James Parish Clerk of Court. **Other phones:** Treasurer- 504-562-2300; Elections- 225-562-7496. **Property tax/Assessing-** PO Box 55, 5800 LA Hwy 44, Courthouse, Convent, LA 70723; 225-562-2250, assessor fax- 225-562-2249. (Appraiser - 225-562-2251) hours- 8AM-4PM www.stjamesassessor.com **Online** - Search tax roll data on statewide website, www.latax.state.la.us/Menu_ParishTaxRolls/TaxRolls.aspx.

St. John the Baptist Parish

Clerk of Court, PO Box 280, Edgard, LA 70049-0280. 985-497-3331, R/E recording phone-985-497-8836 x246, UCC recording phone-985-497-8836 x242; fax-985-497-3972; 8:30AM-4:30PM (CST) www.stjohnclerk.org

Index: All in one. Records indexed on a public use terminal back to 1958. Office personnel or visitors may perform searches. Mortgage certificate fee $20.00; $10.00 each add'l name. Office will search real estate records. Will search UCC records. Copy fee $2.00 per page; fax back $5.00 for 1st page, $1.00 each add'l page. Cert fee- $5.00 per doc plus copy fee. Payee- St. John the Baptist Parish Clerk of Court. **Other phones:** Elections- 985-497-8836 x247. **Property tax/Assessing-** 2393 Hwy 18, River Rd at E 3rd St, PO Box 8, Edgard, LA 70049; 985-497-8788, assessor fax- 985-497-5501. hours- 9AM-4PM www.stjohnassessor.org **Online access**- Search tax roll data on statewide website, www.latax.state.la.us/Menu_ParishTaxRolls/TaxRolls.aspx. Also, access property data free at www.stjohnassessor.org/PropertySearch.aspx.

St. Landry Parish

Clerk of Court, PO Box 750, Opelousas, LA 70571-0750. 337-942-5606, R/E recording phone-337-942-5606 x121, UCC recording phone-337-942-5606 x122; fax-337-948-7265; 8AM-4:30PM (CST) www.stlandry.org/index.htm
Index: Separate indices to search include mortgages, conveyances. Records indexed on a public use terminal back to 1973. Office personnel or visitors may perform searches. General index search fee $20.00 1st name, $10.00 each add'l name. UCC search fee- $30.00 per name. Copy fee $2.00; if tax lien or real estate $1.00 per page. Cert fee- $1.00 per page plus copy fee. Payee- St. Landry Parish Clerk of Court. **Online access to Real Estate, Deed, Mortgage, Conveyance records:** Access to recorder office land records is by subscription; fee is $35-50 per month. Data includes mortgages and conveyances, also perhaps court records. For registration and password contact Ms Lisa at Clerk of Court office, extension 103. **Other phones:** Elections- 337-942-5606 x133; Vital Records- 337-942-5606 x122. **Property tax/Assessing**- PO Box 39, Opelousas, LA 70571; 337-942-3166, assessor fax- 337-942-3174. **Online** - Search tax roll data on statewide website, www.latax.state.la.us/Menu_ParishTaxRolls/TaxRolls.aspx.

St. Martin Parish

Clerk of Court, PO Box 308, St. Martinville, LA 70582. 337-394-2210; fax-337-394-7772; 8:30AM-4:30PM (CST) www.stmartinparishclerkofcourt.com
Index: Separate indices to search include computer, books. Records indexed on a public use terminal back to 1986. Office will perform a UCC search but public must search other records themselves. Office will perform Mortgage Certificate search- $20.00 per name, $10.00 per add'l name. Copy fee $1.00 per page. Cert fee- $5.50 per doc plus copy fee. Payee- St. Martin Parish Clerk of Court. **Other phones:** Treasurer- 337-394-2200; Elections- 337-394-2210; Vital Records- 337-394-2210. **Property tax/Assessing**- 415 S Main St, #103, St. Martinville, LA 70582-4526; 337-394-2208, assessor fax- 337-394-2209. www.stmartinassessor.org **Online access**- Access parish assessor property records free at www.stmartinassessor.org/propsrch_disclaim.html. TSearch tax roll data on statewide website, www.latax.state.la.us/Menu_ParishTaxRolls/TaxRolls.aspx.

St. Mary Parish

Clerk of Court, PO Drawer 1231, Franklin, LA 70538. 318-828-4100 x200, R/E recording phone-337-828-4100 x200; fax-318-828-2509; 8:30AM-4:30PM (CST)
Index: Separate indices to search include conveyance, mtgs, marriage, Incorp, partnerships. Records indexed on a public use terminal. Office will perform a UCC and Tax lien search but public must search other records themselves. General index search fee $20.00 for 1st name, $10.00 each add'l name. Copy fee $2.00, if tax lien or real estate $1.00 per page. Cert fee- $5.00 per doc plus copy fee. Payee- St. Mary Parish Clerk of Court. **Property tax/Assessing**- PO Box 264, 500 Main St, Franklin, LA 70538; 337-828-4100 x250, assessor fax- 337-828-2122. www.smpassessor.net **Online**- Search tax roll data on statewide website, www.latax.state.la.us/Menu_ParishTaxRolls/TaxRolls.aspx.

St. Tammany Parish

Clerk of Court, PO Box 1090, Covington, LA 70434. 985-809-8700, R/E recording phone-985-809-8740, UCC recording phone-985-809-8740 x27840; fax-985-809-8775; 8:30AM-4:30PM (CST) www.sttammanyclerk.org/main/index.asp
Index: Separate indices to search include COB, MOB, misc. Records indexed on a public use terminal back to 1961. Office personnel or visitors may perform searches. Search fee $15.00 per hour. Office will search a limited index of real estate records. UCC search per debtor name- $30.00. Copy fee $.25 per page. Cert fee- $2.00 per cert plus copy fee. Payee- St. Tammany Parish Clerk of Court. **Online access to Real Estate, Deed, Mortgage, Lien, Marriage, Court, Traffic, Map records:** Full access to clerk's Premium Service requires a $50 per month plus $50.00 start-up fee, plus $.20 per printed page. Records date back to 1961; viewable images on conveyances back to 1980. For info, contact Eli Wilson or Kristie Howell at 985-809-8787. A dialup service is also available; $100 setup and $.10 per minute. Free public access to indices is also at https://www.sttammanyclerk.org/liveapp/main/main.asp. Free access includes marriages, maps, land/mortgage, traffic and court cases. **Other phones:** Elections- 985-809-8743. **Property tax/Assessing**-701 N Columbia St, Covington, LA 70433; 985-809-8180, fax- 985-809-8190. www.stassessor.org/ **Online access**- Search assessor and property value database free at www.stassessor.org/assessor.php. Search tax roll data on statewide website, www.latax.state.la.us/Menu_ParishTaxRolls/TaxRolls.aspx.

Tangipahoa Parish

Clerk of Court, PO Box 667, Amite, LA 70422. 985-748-4146; fax-985-748-6503; 8:30AM-4:30PM (CST) www.tangiclerk.org
Index: Separate indices to search include mortgage, conveyance, misc. Records indexed on a public use terminal back to 1950s. Office personnel or visitors may perform searches. General search fee $10.00. Copy fee $1.00 per page. Cert fee- $5.00 per doc plus copy fee. Conformed copy fee $3.00 per doc plus copy fee. Payee- Tangipahoa Parish Clerk of Court. **Online Real Estate, Lien, Civil, Marriage, Mortgage records:** Access to Parish online records requires registration and a trial membership. Print documents for $1.00 each. One time setup fee is $25.00. Record dates vary though most indexes go back before 1990. Lending agency data is available. For info, contact Andi Matheu at 985-748-4146. Bulk prints also available. Also, access the mapping feature that includes assessor basic property data. **Other phones:** Treasurer- 985-748-4146; Elections- 985-748-4146; Vital Records- 800-454-9570. **Property tax/Assessing**- PO Box 336, Courthouse, Amite, LA 70422; 985-748-7181, assessor fax- 985-748-3995. hours- 8AM-4PM **Online**- Search tax roll data on statewide website, www.latax.state.la.us/Menu_ParishTaxRolls/TaxRolls.aspx. The county offers a subscription service which includes a mapping service with property information.

Tensas Parish

Clerk of Court, PO Box 78, St. Joseph, LA 71366. 318-766-3921; fax-318-766-3926; 8AM-4:30PM
Index: Separate indices to search include conveyance, mortgage, courts records. Record index not computerized. Office personnel or visitors may perform searches. Search fee- $15.00 per name. Real estate owner, mortgage, and property transfer searches available. Tax liens not included in UCC search. General copy fee $3.00 for 1st page, $2.00 each add'l. Cert fee- $10.00 per doc plus copy fee. Payee- Tensas Parish Clerk of Court. **Other phones:** Treasurer- 318-766-3921; Elections- 318-766-3921. **Property tax/Assessing**- PO Box734, 201 Hancock St, St. Joseph, LA 71366; 225-766-3501, fax- 318-766-3503. **Online**- Search tax roll data on statewide website, www.latax.state.la.us/Menu_ParishTaxRolls/TaxRolls.aspx.

Terrebonne Parish

Clerk of Court, PO Box 1569, Houma, LA 70361. 985-868-5660; fax-985-868-5143; 8:30AM-4:30PM
Index: Separate indices to search include computer, index books back to 1800's. Records indexed on a public use terminal back to 1985. Only the public may search. Copy fee $1.00 per page. Cert fee- $5.00 per doc plus copy fee. Payee- Terrebonne Parish Clerk of Court. **Property tax/Assessing**- 8026 Main St, Box 5094, Houma, LA 70361; 985-876-6620. www.tpcg.org/ **Online** - Access to free tax roll data at www.tpcg.org/view.php?f=assessor. This website also has a subscription service for deeper records.

Union Parish

Clerk of Court, 100 E Bayou St, #105; Courthouse, Farmerville, LA 71241. 318-368-3055; fax-318-368-3861; 8:30AM-4:30PM (CST)
Index: Separate indices to search include conveyance, mortgage, civil, probate and misc. Records indexed on a public use terminal back to 9/1/79. Office personnel or visitors may perform searches. Search fee $30.00 per name. Office will not search real estate records. Copy fee $2.00 per page self-serve- $1.00 per page. Cert fee- $5.00 per doc plus copy fee. Payee- Union Parish Clerk of Court. **Other phones:** Vital Records-504-568-8385. **Property tax/Assessing**- 100 E Bayou St, #105, Courthouse, Farmerville, LA 71241; 318-368-3232, assessor fax- 318-368-8010. **Online access**- Access property index free at www.unionparishassessor.com/online_property_search.htm but for full data registration and fees based on usage are required. Search tax roll data on statewide website, www.latax.state.la.us/Menu_ParishTaxRolls/TaxRolls.aspx.

Vermilion Parish

Clerk of Court, 100 N State St, #101; Courthouse Bldg, Abbeville, LA 70510. Recording, R/E & UCC phone-337-898-1992; fax-337-898-0404; 8:30AM-4:30PM (CST)
Index: Separate indices to search include conveyance, mortgage, UCC, chattel, marriage, licenses, civil, criminal. Records indexed on a public use terminal back to 1978 for conveyances, 1960 for mortgages. Office personnel or visitors may perform searches. General index search fee $10.00 per name, $10.00 each add'l name. Real estate owner, mortgage, and property transfer searches available. Will search UCC records. UCC search per debtor name- $30.00. Copy fee $1.00 per page. Cert fee- $5.00 per doc plus copy fee. Payee- Vermilion Parish Clerk of Court. **Other phones:** Treasurer- 337-898-4300; Elections- 337-898-1992; Vital Records- 337-898-1992. **Property tax/Assessing**- 100 N State St, #110, Abbeville, LA 70510; 337-893-2837, assessor fax- 337-893-1221. (Appraiser/Auditor- 337-893-2837) hours- 8:30AM-4PM **Online access**- Search tax roll data on statewide website, www.latax.state.la.us/Menu_ParishTaxRolls/TaxRolls.aspx.

Vernon Parish

Clerk of Court, PO Box 40, Leesville, LA 71496-0040. 337-238-1384, R/E recording phone-337-238-4824, UCC recording phone-337-238-1384; fax-337-238-9902; 8AM-4:30PM www.vernonclerk.com
Index: Separate indices to search include Mtg to 1975 and Conveyance to 1980. Records indexed on a public use terminal back to 1975 and 1980. Office will perform a UCC search but public must search other records themselves. Search fee $30.00. Office will search real estate records. UCC copy fee $2.00 per page.Real estate or tax lien record copy- $1.25 per page. Cert fee- $5.00 per doc plus copy fee. Payee- Vernon Parish Clerk of Court. **Other phones:** Elections- 337-238-1384. **Property tax/Assessing**- PO Box 1535, 301 E Courthouse St, Leesville, LA 71496; 337-239-2167, assessor fax- 337-239-3176. hours- 7:30AM-4PM **Online access**- Search tax roll data on statewide website, www.latax.state.la.us/Menu_ParishTaxRolls/TaxRolls.aspx.

Washington Parish

Clerk of Court, PO Box 607, Franklinton, LA 70438. 985-839-7821; 8AM-4:30PM (CST)
Index: Separate indices to search include conveyance, mortgage, misc. Records indexed on a public use terminal back to 1973. Only the public may search. Copy fee $1.00 per page if clerk makes copy, $.25 if you make your own. per page. Cert fee- $5.00 per doc plus copy fee. Payee- Washington Parish Clerk of Court. **Property tax/Assessing**- 908 Washington, Courthouse Bldg, Franklinton, LA 70438; 985-839-7815, assessor fax- 985-839-7818. hours- 8AM-4PM

Public access terminal available. **Online access**- Search tax roll data on statewide website, www.latax.state.la.us/Menu_ParishTaxRolls/TaxRolls.aspx.

Webster Parish

Clerk of Court, PO Box 370, Minden, LA 71058-0370. Recording, R/E & UCC phone-318-371-0366; fax-318-371-0226; 8:30AM-4:30PM (CST)
Index: Separate indices to search include mortgage, conveyance, charters and plats. Records indexed on a public use terminal back to 1976. Only the public may search. Copy fee $1.00 per page. Cert fee- $5.00 per doc plus copy fee. Payee- Webster Parish Clerk of Court. **Other phones:** Elections- 318-371-0366. **Property tax/Assessing**- PO Box 734, Minden, LA 71058; 318-377-9311, assessor fax- 318-377-3105. **Online** - Search tax roll data on statewide website, www.latax.state.la.us/Menu_ParishTaxRolls/TaxRolls.aspx.

West Baton Rouge Parish

Clerk of Court, PO Box 107, Port Allen, LA 70767. Recording, R/E & UCC phone-225-383-0378; fax-225-383-3694; 8:30AM-4:30PM (CST)
Index: Separate indices to search include conveyance, mortgage, marriage, misc. Records indexed on a public use terminal back to 1984. Office personnel or visitors may perform searches. General search fee $5.00 per name. Office will search real estate records. Will search UCC records. UCC search per debtor name- $30.00. Copy fee $1.00 per page by clerk; $.50 self serve. Cert fee- $5.00 per item plus $2.00 per page plus copy fee. Payee- West Baton Rouge Parish Clerk of Court. **Property tax/Assessing**- PO Box 76, Port Allen, LA 70767; 225-344-6777, assessor fax-225-344-6779. www.wbrassessor.org/ **Online access**- Access property data via the GIS mapping site for free at www.geoportalmaps.com/atlas/wbr/viewer.htm. Click on Search Parcels by owner name. Also, search the View Your Assessment database free at www.wbrassessor.org/Library/Library.asp.

West Carroll Parish

Clerk of Court, PO Box 1078, Oak Grove, LA 71263. 318-428-2369, R/E recording phone-318-428-3281; fax-318-428-9896; 8:30AM-4:30PM (CST)
Index: Separate indices to search include Mortgage, Conveyance, Lease, Charters, Bond, Marriage, UCC. Record index not computerized. Office personnel or visitors may perform searches. Search fee $30.00 UCCs, tax lien $20.00. Office can perform mortgage searches only. Copy fee $2.00 per page. Cert fee- $5.00 per doc plus copy fee. Payee- West Carroll Parish Clerk of Court. **Other phones:** Elections- 318-428-3281. **Property tax/Assessing**- PO Box610, Oak Grove, LA 71266; 318-428-2371, assessor fax- 318-428-4699. **Online access**- Search tax roll data on statewide website, www.latax.state.la.us/Menu_ParishTaxRolls/TaxRolls.aspx.

West Feliciana Parish

Clerk of Court, PO Box 1843, St. Francisville, LA 70775. 225-635-3794; fax-225-635-3770; 8:30AM-4:30PM (CST)
Index: Separate indices to search include conveyance, mortgage. Records indexed on a public use terminal back to 1981. Earlier records are on paper. Office personnel or visitors may perform searches. Search fee $10 per 10 years unless otherwise indicated. Office will search real estate records. Tax liens not included in UCC search. UCC search per debtor name- $30.00. Copy fee $1.00 per page. Cert fee- $5.00 per doc plus copy fee. $3.00 for stamp copy. Payee- West Feliciana Parish Clerk of Court. **Property tax/Assessing**- PO Box 279, St. Francisville, LA 70775; 225-635-3350, assessor fax-225-635-9581. **Online access**- Search tax roll data on statewide website, www.latax.state.la.us/Menu_ParishTaxRolls/TaxRolls.aspx.

Winn Parish

Clerk of Court, 119 W Main St; Courthouse, Winnfield, LA 71483. Recording, R/E & UCC phone-318-628-3515; fax-318-628-3527; 8AM-4:30PM (CST)
Index: Separate indices to search include conveyance, mortgage, oil & gas. Record index not computerized. Only the public may search. Copy fee $1.00 per page. Cert fee- $5.00 per doc plus copy fee. Payee- Winn Parish Clerk of Court. **Other phones:** Treasurer- 318-628-5824. **Property tax/Assessing**- 119 W Main St, Winnfield, LA 71483; 318-628-3267, assessor fax-318-648-7602.

Louisiana County Locator

You will usually be able to find the city name in the City/Parish Cross Reference below. In that case, it is a simple matter to determine the county from the cross reference. However, only the official US Postal Service city names are included in this index. There are an additional 40,000 place names that people use in their addresses. Therefore, we have also included a ZIP/City Cross Reference immediately following the City/Parish Cross Reference.

If you know the ZIP Code but the city name does not appear in the City/Parish Cross Reference index, look up the ZIP Code in the ZIP/City Cross Reference, find the city name, then look up the city name in the City/Parish Cross Reference. For example, you want to know the county for an address of Menands, NY 12204. There is no "Menands" in the City/Parish Cross Reference. The ZIP/City Cross Reference shows that ZIP Codes 12201-12288 are for the city of Albany. Looking back in the City/Parish Cross Reference, Albany is in Albany Parish.

Louisiana City/Parish Cross Reference

ABBEVILLE Vermilion Parish
ABITA SPRINGS St. Tammany Parish
ACME Concordia Parish
ADDIS West Baton Rouge Parish
AIMWELL Catahoula Parish
AKERS Tangipahoa Parish
ALBANY Livingston Parish
ALEXANDRIA Rapides Parish
AMA St. Charles Parish
AMELIA St. Mary Parish
AMITE (70422) Tangipahoa Parish(71), St. Helena Parish(28)
ANACOCO (71403) Vernon Parish(97), Sabine Parish(2)
ANGIE Washington Parish
ANGOLA West Feliciana Parish
ARABI St. Bernard Parish
ARCADIA (71001) Bienville Parish(80), Lincoln Parish(9), Claiborne Parish(9)
ARCHIBALD Richland Parish
ARNAUDVILLE (70512) St. Landry Parish(59), St. Martin Parish(40)
ASHLAND Natchitoches Parish
ATHENS Claiborne Parish
ATLANTA (71404) Grant Parish(50), Winn Parish(49)
AVERY ISLAND Iberia Parish
BAKER East Baton Rouge Parish
BALDWIN St. Mary Parish
BALL Rapides Parish
BARATARIA Jefferson Parish
BARKSDALE AFB Bossier Parish
BASILE (70515) Acadia Parish(59), Evangeline Parish(40)
BASKIN Franklin Parish
BASTROP Morehouse Parish
BATCHELOR Pointe Coupee Parish
BATON ROUGE East Baton Rouge Parish
BAYOU GOULA Iberville Parish
BELCHER Caddo Parish
BELL CITY (70630) Calcasieu Parish(67), Cameron Parish(32)
BELLE CHASSE Plaquemines Parish
BELLE ROSE Assumption Parish
BELMONT Sabine Parish
BENTLEY Grant Parish
BENTON Bossier Parish
BERNICE (71222) Union Parish(81), Claiborne Parish(18)
BERWICK St. Mary Parish
BETHANY Caddo Parish
BIENVILLE Bienville Parish
BIG BEND Avoyelles Parish
BLANCHARD Caddo Parish
BLANKS Pointe Coupee Parish
BOGALUSA (70427) Washington Parish(97), St. Tammany Parish(2)
BOGALUSA Washington Parish
BONITA Morehouse Parish
BOOTHVILLE Plaquemines Parish
BORDELONVILLE Avoyelles Parish
BOSSIER CITY Bossier Parish
BOURG (70343) Terrebonne Parish(82), Lafourche Parish(17)
BOUTTE St. Charles Parish
BOYCE Rapides Parish
BRAITHWAITE Plaquemines Parish
BRANCH Acadia Parish
BREAUX BRIDGE St. Martin Parish
BRITTANY Ascension Parish
BROUSSARD (70518) Lafayette Parish(89), St. Martin Parish(6), Iberia Parish(3)
BRUSLY West Baton Rouge Parish
BRYCELAND Bienville Parish
BUCKEYE Rapides Parish
BUECHE West Baton Rouge Parish
BUNKIE (71322) Avoyelles Parish(86), St. Landry Parish(12), Rapides Parish(1)
BURAS Plaquemines Parish
BURNSIDE Ascension Parish
BUSH St. Tammany Parish
CADE St. Martin Parish
CALHOUN Ouachita Parish
CALVIN Winn Parish
CAMERON Cameron Parish
CAMPTI Natchitoches Parish
CARENCRO (70520) Lafayette Parish(98), St. Landry Parish(1)
CARLISLE Plaquemines Parish
CARVILLE Iberville Parish
CASTOR Bienville Parish
CECILIA St. Martin Parish
CENTER POINT (71323) Avoyelles Parish(98), Rapides Parish(1)
CENTERVILLE St. Mary Parish
CHALMETTE St. Bernard Parish
CHARENTON St. Mary Parish
CHASE Franklin Parish
CHATAIGNIER Evangeline Parish
CHATHAM Jackson Parish
CHAUVIN Terrebonne Parish
CHENEYVILLE (71325) Rapides Parish(67), Evangeline Parish(32)
CHOPIN Natchitoches Parish
CHOUDRANT (71227) Lincoln Parish(65), Jackson Parish(27), Ouachita Parish(6)
CHURCH POINT (70525) Acadia Parish(82), St. Landry Parish(17)
CLARENCE Natchitoches Parish
CLARKS Caldwell Parish
CLAYTON (71326) Catahoula Parish(65), Concordia Parish(33)
CLINTON (70722) East Feliciana Parish(96), East Baton Rouge Parish(3)
CLOUTIERVILLE Natchitoches Parish
COLFAX Grant Parish
COLLINSTON (71229) Morehouse Parish(82), Ouachita Parish(17)
COLUMBIA (71418) Caldwell Parish(86), Richland Parish(8), Ouachita Parish(3), Catahoula Parish(1)
CONVENT St. James Parish
CONVERSE (71419) Sabine Parish(85), De Soto Parish(14)
COTTON VALLEY (71018) Webster Parish(87), Bossier Parish(12)
COTTONPORT Avoyelles Parish
COUSHATTA (71019) Red River Parish(88), Natchitoches Parish(11)
COVINGTON St. Tammany Parish
CREOLE Cameron Parish
CRESTON Natchitoches Parish
CROWLEY Acadia Parish
CROWVILLE Franklin Parish
CULLEN Webster Parish
CUT OFF Lafourche Parish
CYPRESS Natchitoches Parish
DARROW Ascension Parish
DAVANT Plaquemines Parish
DELCAMBRE (70528) Vermilion Parish(77), Iberia Parish(22)
DELHI (71232) Richland Parish(61), Franklin Parish(19), Madison Parish(19)
DELTA Madison Parish
DENHAM SPRINGS (70706) Livingston Parish(89), St. Helena Parish(10)
DENHAM SPRINGS Livingston Parish
DEQUINCY Calcasieu Parish
DERIDDER (70634) Beauregard Parish(91), Vernon Parish(8)
DERRY Natchitoches Parish
DES ALLEMANDS (70030) St. Charles Parish(88), Lafourche Parish(11)
DESTREHAN St. Charles Parish
DEVILLE (71328) Rapides Parish(86), Avoyelles Parish(13)
DODSON Winn Parish
DONALDSONVILLE Ascension Parish
DONNER Terrebonne Parish
DOWNSVILLE (71234) Union Parish(80), Ouachita Parish(14), Lincoln Parish(5)
DOYLINE Webster Parish
DRY CREEK (70637) Beauregard Parish(72), Allen Parish(27)
DRY PRONG (71423) Grant Parish(96), Rapides Parish(3)
DUBACH (71235) Lincoln Parish(98), Claiborne Parish(1)
DUBBERLY (71024) Webster Parish(89), Bienville Parish(10)
DULAC Terrebonne Parish
DUPLESSIS Ascension Parish
DUPONT Avoyelles Parish
DUSON Lafayette Parish
EAST POINT Red River Parish
ECHO Rapides Parish
EDGARD St. John the Baptist Parish
EFFIE (71331) Avoyelles Parish(97), Catahoula Parish(2)
EGAN Acadia Parish
ELIZABETH Allen Parish
ELM GROVE Bossier Parish
ELMER Rapides Parish
ELTON (70532) Jefferson Davis Parish(79), Allen Parish(20)
EMPIRE Plaquemines Parish
ENTERPRISE (71425) Catahoula Parish(68), Rapides Parish(31)
EPPS (71237) West Carroll Parish(83), Madison Parish(13), East Carroll Parish(3)
ERATH Vermilion Parish
EROS (71238) Ouachita Parish(53), Jackson Parish(46)
ERWINVILLE (70729) West Baton Rouge Parish(97), Pointe Coupee Parish(2)
ESTHERWOOD Acadia Parish
ETHEL East Feliciana Parish
EUNICE (70535) St. Landry Parish(94), Acadia Parish(4), Evangeline Parish(1)
EVANGELINE Acadia Parish
EVANS Vernon Parish
EVERGREEN Avoyelles Parish
EXTENSION Franklin Parish
FAIRBANKS Ouachita Parish
FARMERVILLE Union Parish
FENTON Jefferson Davis Parish
FERRIDAY Concordia Parish
FISHER Sabine Parish
FLATWOODS (71427) Rapides Parish(75), Natchitoches Parish(24)
FLORA Natchitoches Parish
FLORIEN Sabine Parish
FLUKER (70436) Tangipahoa Parish(85), St. Helena Parish(14)
FOLSOM St. Tammany Parish
FORDOCHE Pointe Coupee Parish
FOREST West Carroll Parish
FOREST HILL Rapides Parish
FORT NECESSITY Franklin Parish
FRANKLIN St. Mary Parish
FRANKLINTON Washington Parish
FRENCH SETTLEMENT Livingston Parish
FRIERSON De Soto Parish
FROGMORE Concordia Parish
FULLERTON Vernon Parish
GALLIANO Lafourche Parish
GARDEN CITY St. Mary Parish
GARDNER Rapides Parish
GARYVILLE St. John the Baptist Parish
GEISMAR Ascension Parish
GEORGETOWN Grant Parish
GHEENS Lafourche Parish
GIBSLAND Bienville Parish
GIBSON Terrebonne Parish
GILBERT Franklin Parish
GILLIAM Caddo Parish
GLENMORA (71433) Rapides Parish(98), Allen Parish(1)
GLOSTER De Soto Parish
GLYNN (70736) Pointe Coupee Parish(98), West Baton Rouge Parish(1)
GOLDEN MEADOW Lafourche Parish
GOLDONNA (71031) Natchitoches Parish(53), Winn Parish(46)
GONZALES Ascension Parish
GORUM Natchitoches Parish
GOUDEAU Avoyelles Parish
GRAMBLING Lincoln Parish
GRAMERCY St. James Parish
GRAND CANE De Soto Parish
GRAND CHENIER Cameron Parish
GRAND COTEAU St. Landry Parish
GRAND ISLE Jefferson Parish
GRANT Allen Parish

GRAY Terrebonne Parish
GRAYSON (71435) Caldwell Parish(98), Catahoula Parish(1)
GREENSBURG St. Helena Parish
GREENWELL SPRINGS East Baton Rouge Parish
GREENWOOD Caddo Parish
GRETNA Jefferson Parish
GROSSE TETE Iberville Parish
GUEYDAN (70542) Vermilion Parish(95), Cameron Parish(4)
HACKBERRY Cameron Parish
HAHNVILLE St. Charles Parish
HALL SUMMIT Red River Parish
HAMBURG Avoyelles Parish
HAMMOND (70403) Tangipahoa Parish(95), Livingston Parish(4)
HAMMOND Tangipahoa Parish
HARMON Red River Parish
HARRISONBURG Catahoula Parish
HARVEY Jefferson Parish
HAUGHTON Bossier Parish
HAYES Calcasieu Parish
HAYNESVILLE Claiborne Parish
HEBERT Caldwell Parish
HEFLIN (71039) Webster Parish(80), Bienville Parish(19)
HESSMER Avoyelles Parish
HESTER St. James Parish
HICKS Vernon Parish
HINESTON (71438) Rapides Parish(82), Vernon Parish(17)
HODGE Jackson Parish
HOLDEN (70744) Livingston Parish(95), St. Helena Parish(4)
HOMER Claiborne Parish
HORNBECK (71439) Vernon Parish(78), Sabine Parish(21)
HOSSTON Caddo Parish
HOUMA (70364) Terrebonne Parish(81), Lafourche Parish(18)
HOUMA Terrebonne Parish
HUSSER Tangipahoa Parish
IDA Caddo Parish
INDEPENDENCE (70443) Tangipahoa Parish(52), Livingston Parish(29), St. Helena Parish(17)
INNIS Pointe Coupee Parish
IOTA Acadia Parish
IOWA Calcasieu Parish
JACKSON (70748) East Feliciana Parish(76), West Feliciana Parish(21), East Baton Rouge Parish(2)
JAMESTOWN Bienville Parish
JARREAU Pointe Coupee Parish
JEANERETTE (70544) Iberia Parish(84), St. Mary Parish(15)
JENA La Salle Parish
JENNINGS (70546) Jefferson Davis Parish(97), Acadia Parish(2)
JIGGER Franklin Parish
JONES Morehouse Parish
JONESBORO (71251) Jackson Parish(94), Bienville Parish(5)
JONESVILLE (71343) Catahoula Parish(88), Concordia Parish(11)
JOYCE Winn Parish
KAPLAN Vermilion Parish
KEATCHIE De Soto Parish
KEITHVILLE Caddo Parish
KELLY (71441) Caldwell Parish(82), La Salle Parish(17)
KENNER Jefferson Parish
KENTWOOD (70444) Tangipahoa Parish(82), St. Helena Parish(15), Washington Parish(1)
KILBOURNE West Carroll Parish
KILLONA St. Charles Parish
KINDER (70648) Allen Parish(98), Jefferson Davis Parish(1)
KRAEMER Lafourche Parish
KROTZ SPRINGS St. Landry Parish
KURTHWOOD Vernon Parish
LA PLACE (70068) St. John the Baptist Parish(95), St. Charles Parish(4)
LA PLACE St. John the Baptist Parish
LABADIEVILLE Assumption Parish
LABARRE Pointe Coupee Parish
LACAMP Vernon Parish
LACASSINE Jefferson Davis Parish
LACOMBE St. Tammany Parish
LAFAYETTE Lafayette Parish
LAFITTE Jefferson Parish
LAKE ARTHUR (70549) Jefferson Davis Parish(97), Cameron Parish(2)
LAKE CHARLES (70607) Calcasieu Parish(90), Cameron Parish(9)
LAKE CHARLES Calcasieu Parish
LAKE PROVIDENCE East Carroll Parish
LAKELAND Pointe Coupee Parish
LAROSE Lafourche Parish
LARTO Catahoula Parish
LAWTELL St. Landry Parish
LE MOYEN St. Landry Parish
LEANDER Vernon Parish
LEBEAU St. Landry Parish
LEBLANC Allen Parish
LECOMPTE Rapides Parish
LEESVILLE Vernon Parish
LENA (71447) Rapides Parish(54), Natchitoches Parish(45)
LEONVILLE St. Landry Parish
LETTSWORTH Pointe Coupee Parish
LIBUSE Rapides Parish
LILLIE (71256) Union Parish(94), Claiborne Parish(5)
LISBON Claiborne Parish
LIVINGSTON Livingston Parish
LIVONIA Pointe Coupee Parish
LOCKPORT Lafourche Parish
LOGANSPORT De Soto Parish
LONGLEAF Rapides Parish
LONGSTREET De Soto Parish
LONGVILLE Beauregard Parish
LORANGER Tangipahoa Parish
LOREAUVILLE Iberia Parish
LOTTIE Pointe Coupee Parish
LULING St. Charles Parish
LUTCHER St. James Parish
LYDIA Iberia Parish
MADISONVILLE St. Tammany Parish
MAMOU Evangeline Parish
MANDEVILLE St. Tammany Parish
MANGHAM Richland Parish
MANSFIELD De Soto Parish
MANSURA Avoyelles Parish
MANY Sabine Parish
MARINGOUIN Iberville Parish
MARION Union Parish
MARKSVILLE Avoyelles Parish
MARRERO Jefferson Parish
MARTHAVILLE (71450) Natchitoches Parish(68), Sabine Parish(31)
MATHEWS Lafourche Parish
MAUREPAS (70449) Livingston Parish(95), Ascension Parish(4)
MAURICE (70555) Vermilion Parish(96), Lafayette Parish(3)
MELDER Rapides Parish
MELROSE Natchitoches Parish
MELVILLE St. Landry Parish
MER ROUGE Morehouse Parish
MERAUX St. Bernard Parish
MERMENTAU Acadia Parish
MERRYVILLE Beauregard Parish
METAIRIE Jefferson Parish
MILTON Lafayette Parish
MINDEN (71055) Webster Parish(96), Claiborne Parish(2)
MINDEN Webster Parish
MIRA Caddo Parish
MITTIE Allen Parish
MODESTE Ascension Parish
MONROE Ouachita Parish
MONTEGUT (70377) Terrebonne Parish(89), Lafourche Parish(10)
MONTEREY Concordia Parish
MONTGOMERY (71454) Grant Parish(82), Winn Parish(17)
MOORINGSPORT Caddo Parish
MORA (71455) Rapides Parish(98), Natchitoches Parish(1)
MOREAUVILLE Avoyelles Parish
MORGAN CITY (70380) St. Mary Parish(91), Assumption Parish(8)
MORGAN CITY St. Mary Parish
MORGANZA Pointe Coupee Parish
MORROW (71356) St. Landry Parish(57), Avoyelles Parish(42)
MORSE Acadia Parish
MOUNT AIRY St. John the Baptist Parish
MOUNT HERMON Washington Parish
NAPOLEONVILLE Assumption Parish
NATALBANY Tangipahoa Parish
NATCHEZ Natchitoches Parish
NATCHITOCHES (71457) Natchitoches Parish(97), Winn Parish(2)
NATCHITOCHES Natchitoches Parish
NEGREET Sabine Parish
NEW IBERIA Iberia Parish
NEW ORLEANS (70146) Orleans Parish(91), Plaquemines Parish(8)
NEW ORLEANS Jefferson Parish
NEW ORLEANS Orleans Parish
NEW ROADS Pointe Coupee Parish
NEW SARPY St. Charles Parish
NEWELLTON Tensas Parish
NEWLLANO Vernon Parish
NOBLE Sabine Parish
NORCO St. Charles Parish
NORWOOD East Feliciana Parish
OAK GROVE West Carroll Parish
OAK RIDGE (71264) Morehouse Parish(77), Richland Parish(22)
OAKDALE (71463) Allen Parish(88), Evangeline Parish(6), Rapides Parish(4)
OBERLIN Allen Parish
OIL CITY Caddo Parish
OLLA (71465) La Salle Parish(87), Winn Parish(9), Caldwell Parish(2)
OPELOUSAS St. Landry Parish
OSCAR Pointe Coupee Parish
OTIS Rapides Parish
PAINCOURTVILLE Assumption Parish
PALMETTO St. Landry Parish
PARADIS St. Charles Parish
PATTERSON St. Mary Parish
PAULINA St. James Parish
PEARL RIVER St. Tammany Parish
PELICAN De Soto Parish
PERRY Vermilion Parish
PIERRE PART (70339) Assumption Parish(92), St. Martin Parish(7)
PILOTTOWN Plaquemines Parish
PINE GROVE (70453) St. Helena Parish(85), Livingston Parish(14)
PINE PRAIRIE Evangeline Parish
PINEVILLE (71360) Rapides Parish(96), Avoyelles Parish(2), Grant Parish(1)
PINEVILLE Rapides Parish
PIONEER West Carroll Parish
PITKIN (70656) Vernon Parish(62), Rapides Parish(18), Allen Parish(18)
PLAIN DEALING Bossier Parish
PLAQUEMINE Iberville Parish
PLATTENVILLE Assumption Parish
PLAUCHEVILLE Avoyelles Parish
PLEASANT HILL (71065) Sabine Parish(98), Natchitoches Parish(1)
POINTE A LA HACHE Plaquemines Parish
POLLOCK Grant Parish
PONCHATOULA Tangipahoa Parish
PORT ALLEN West Baton Rouge Parish
PORT BARRE St. Landry Parish
PORT SULPHUR Plaquemines Parish
POWHATAN Natchitoches Parish
PRAIRIEVILLE Ascension Parish
PRIDE East Baton Rouge Parish
PRINCETON Bossier Parish
PROVENCAL Natchitoches Parish
QUITMAN (71268) Jackson Parish(79), Bienville Parish(20)
RACELAND Lafourche Parish
RAGLEY (70657) Beauregard Parish(85), Allen Parish(14)
RAYNE (70578) Acadia Parish(90), Vermilion Parish(5), Lafayette Parish(4)
RAYVILLE Richland Parish
REDDELL Evangeline Parish
REEVES Allen Parish
RESERVE St. John the Baptist Parish
RHINEHART Catahoula Parish
RINGGOLD (71068) Bienville Parish(93), Red River Parish(6)
ROANOKE Jefferson Davis Parish
ROBELINE (71469) Natchitoches Parish(75), Sabine Parish(24)
ROBERT Tangipahoa Parish
RODESSA Caddo Parish
ROSA St. Landry Parish
ROSEDALE Iberville Parish
ROSELAND Tangipahoa Parish
ROSEPINE Vernon Parish
ROUGON Pointe Coupee Parish
RUBY Rapides Parish
RUSTON (71270) Lincoln Parish(94), Jackson Parish(5)
RUSTON Lincoln Parish
SAINT AMANT Ascension Parish
SAINT BENEDICT St. Tammany Parish
SAINT BERNARD St. Bernard Parish
SAINT FRANCISVILLE West Feliciana Parish
SAINT GABRIEL Iberville Parish
SAINT JAMES St. James Parish
SAINT JOSEPH Tensas Parish
SAINT LANDRY Evangeline Parish
SAINT MARTINVILLE St. Martin Parish
SAINT MAURICE Winn Parish
SAINT ROSE St. Charles Parish
SALINE (71070) Natchitoches Parish(59), Bienville Parish(40)
SAREPTA (71071) Webster Parish(95), Bossier Parish(4)
SCHRIEVER Terrebonne Parish
SCOTT (70583) Lafayette Parish(94), Acadia Parish(5)
SHONGALOO Webster Parish
SHREVEPORT (71107) Caddo Parish(98), Bossier Parish(1)
SHREVEPORT (71115) Caddo Parish(95), Red River Parish(4)
SHREVEPORT Caddo Parish
SIBLEY Webster Parish
SICILY ISLAND (71368) Catahoula Parish(98), Franklin Parish(1)
SIEPER Rapides Parish
SIKES Winn Parish
SIMMESPORT Avoyelles Parish
SIMPSON Vernon Parish
SIMSBORO (71275) Lincoln Parish(85), Bienville Parish(14)
SINGER Beauregard Parish
SLAGLE Vernon Parish
SLAUGHTER East Feliciana Parish
SLIDELL St. Tammany Parish
SONDHEIMER East Carroll Parish
SORRENTO Ascension Parish
SPEARSVILLE Union Parish
SPRINGFIELD (70462) Livingston Parish(97), Tangipahoa Parish(2)
SPRINGHILL (71075) Webster Parish(96), Bossier Parish(3)
STARKS Calcasieu Parish
START Richland Parish
STERLINGTON (71280) Ouachita Parish(55), Union Parish(44)
STONEWALL De Soto Parish

SUGARTOWN Beauregard Parish
SULPHUR Calcasieu Parish
SUMMERFIELD Claiborne Parish
SUN St. Tammany Parish
SUNSET St. Landry Parish
SUNSHINE Iberville Parish
SWARTZ Ouachita Parish
TALISHEEK St. Tammany Parish
TALLULAH Madison Parish
TANGIPAHOA Tangipahoa Parish
TAYLOR Bienville Parish
THERIOT Terrebonne Parish
THIBODAUX (70301) Lafourche Parish(95), Terrebonne Parish(3)
THIBODAUX Lafourche Parish
TICKFAW Tangipahoa Parish
TIOGA Rapides Parish
TORBERT Pointe Coupee Parish
TRANSYLVANIA East Carroll Parish
TROUT La Salle Parish
TULLOS (71479) Winn Parish(62), La Salle Parish(37)
TUNICA West Feliciana Parish
TURKEY CREEK Evangeline Parish
UNCLE SAM St. James Parish
URANIA La Salle Parish
VACHERIE (70090) St. James Parish(81), St. John the Baptist Parish(18)
VENICE Plaquemines Parish
VENTRESS Pointe Coupee Parish
VERDA Grant Parish
VICK Avoyelles Parish
VIDALIA Concordia Parish
VILLE PLATTE Evangeline Parish
VINTON Calcasieu Parish
VIOLET St. Bernard Parish
VIVIAN Caddo Parish
WAKEFIELD West Feliciana Parish
WALKER Livingston Parish
WASHINGTON (70589) St. Landry Parish(92), Evangeline Parish(7)
WATERPROOF Tensas Parish
WATSON Livingston Parish
WELSH Jefferson Davis Parish
WEST MONROE Ouachita Parish
WESTLAKE Calcasieu Parish
WESTWEGO Jefferson Parish
WEYANOKE West Feliciana Parish
WHITE CASTLE Iberville Parish
WILDSVILLE Concordia Parish
WILSON East Feliciana Parish
WINNFIELD Winn Parish
WINNSBORO Franklin Parish
WISNER Franklin Parish
WOODWORTH Rapides Parish
YOUNGSVILLE (70592) Lafayette Parish(81), Vermilion Parish(11), Iberia Parish(6)
ZACHARY East Baton Rouge Parish
ZWOLLE Sabine Parish

Louisiana ZIP/City Cross Reference

70001-70011 METAIRIE
70030-70030 DES ALLEMANDS
70031-70031 AMA
70032-70032 ARABI
70033-70033 METAIRIE
70036-70036 BARATARIA
70037-70037 BELLE CHASSE
70038-70038 BOOTHVILLE
70039-70039 BOUTTE
70040-70040 BRAITHWAITE
70041-70041 BURAS
70042-70042 CARLISLE
70043-70044 CHALMETTE
70046-70046 DAVANT
70047-70047 DESTREHAN
70049-70049 EDGARD
70050-70050 EMPIRE
70051-70051 GARYVILLE
70052-70052 GRAMERCY
70053-70054 GRETNA
70055-70055 METAIRIE
70056-70056 GRETNA
70057-70057 HAHNVILLE
70058-70059 HARVEY
70060-70060 METAIRIE
70062-70065 KENNER
70066-70066 KILLONA
70067-70067 LAFITTE
70068-70069 LA PLACE
70070-70070 LULING
70071-70071 LUTCHER
70072-70073 MARRERO
70075-70075 MERAUX
70076-70076 MOUNT AIRY
70078-70078 NEW SARPY
70079-70079 NORCO
70080-70080 PARADIS
70081-70081 PILOTTOWN
70082-70082 POINTE A LA HACHE
70083-70083 PORT SULPHUR
70084-70084 RESERVE
70085-70085 SAINT BERNARD
70086-70086 SAINT JAMES
70087-70087 SAINT ROSE
70090-70090 VACHERIE
70091-70091 VENICE
70092-70092 VIOLET
70094-70096 WESTWEGO
70100-70195 NEW ORLEANS
70301-70310 THIBODAUX
70339-70339 PIERRE PART
70340-70340 AMELIA
70341-70341 BELLE ROSE
70342-70342 BERWICK
70343-70343 BOURG
70344-70344 CHAUVIN
70345-70345 CUT OFF
70346-70346 DONALDSONVILLE
70352-70352 DONNER
70353-70353 DULAC
70354-70354 GALLIANO
70355-70355 GHEENS
70356-70356 GIBSON
70357-70357 GOLDEN MEADOW
70358-70358 GRAND ISLE
70359-70359 GRAY
70360-70364 HOUMA
70371-70371 KRAEMER
70372-70372 LABADIEVILLE
70373-70373 LAROSE
70374-70374 LOCKPORT
70375-70375 MATHEWS
70376-70376 MODESTE
70377-70377 MONTEGUT
70380-70381 MORGAN CITY
70390-70390 NAPOLEONVILLE
70391-70391 PAINCOURTVILLE
70392-70392 PATTERSON
70393-70393 PLATTENVILLE
70394-70394 RACELAND
70395-70395 SCHRIEVER
70397-70397 THERIOT
70401-70404 HAMMOND
70420-70420 ABITA SPRINGS
70421-70421 AKERS
70422-70422 AMITE
70426-70426 ANGIE
70427-70429 BOGALUSA
70431-70431 BUSH
70433-70435 COVINGTON
70436-70436 FLUKER
70437-70437 FOLSOM
70438-70438 FRANKLINTON
70441-70441 GREENSBURG
70442-70442 HUSSER
70443-70443 INDEPENDENCE
70444-70444 KENTWOOD
70445-70445 LACOMBE
70446-70446 LORANGER
70447-70447 MADISONVILLE
70448-70448 MANDEVILLE
70449-70449 MAUREPAS
70450-70450 MOUNT HERMON
70451-70451 NATALBANY
70452-70452 PEARL RIVER
70453-70453 PINE GROVE
70454-70454 PONCHATOULA
70455-70455 ROBERT
70456-70456 ROSELAND
70457-70457 SAINT BENEDICT
70458-70461 SLIDELL
70462-70462 SPRINGFIELD
70463-70463 SUN
70464-70464 TALISHEEK
70465-70465 TANGIPAHOA
70466-70466 TICKFAW
70467-70467 ANGIE
70469-70469 SLIDELL
70470-70471 MANDEVILLE
70501-70509 LAFAYETTE
70510-70511 ABBEVILLE
70512-70512 ARNAUDVILLE
70513-70513 AVERY ISLAND
70514-70514 BALDWIN
70515-70515 BASILE
70516-70516 BRANCH
70517-70517 BREAUX BRIDGE
70518-70518 BROUSSARD
70519-70519 CADE
70520-70520 CARENCRO
70521-70521 CECILIA
70522-70522 CENTERVILLE
70523-70523 CHARENTON
70524-70524 CHATAIGNIER
70525-70525 CHURCH POINT
70526-70527 CROWLEY
70528-70528 DELCAMBRE
70529-70529 DUSON
70531-70531 EGAN
70532-70532 ELTON
70533-70533 ERATH
70534-70534 ESTHERWOOD
70535-70535 EUNICE
70537-70537 EVANGELINE
70538-70538 FRANKLIN
70540-70540 GARDEN CITY
70541-70541 GRAND COTEAU
70542-70542 GUEYDAN
70543-70543 IOTA
70544-70544 JEANERETTE
70546-70546 JENNINGS
70548-70548 KAPLAN
70549-70549 LAKE ARTHUR
70550-70550 LAWTELL
70551-70551 LEONVILLE
70552-70552 LOREAUVILLE
70554-70554 MAMOU
70555-70555 MAURICE
70556-70556 MERMENTAU
70558-70558 MILTON
70559-70559 MORSE
70560-70563 NEW IBERIA
70569-70569 LYDIA
70570-70571 OPELOUSAS
70575-70575 PERRY
70576-70576 PINE PRAIRIE
70577-70577 PORT BARRE
70578-70578 RAYNE
70580-70580 REDDELL
70581-70581 ROANOKE
70582-70582 SAINT MARTINVILLE
70583-70583 SCOTT
70584-70584 SUNSET
70585-70585 TURKEY CREEK
70586-70586 VILLE PLATTE
70589-70589 WASHINGTON
70591-70591 WELSH
70592-70592 YOUNGSVILLE
70593-70598 LAFAYETTE
70601-70629 LAKE CHARLES
70630-70630 BELL CITY
70631-70631 CAMERON
70632-70632 CREOLE
70633-70633 DEQUINCY
70634-70634 DERIDDER
70637-70637 DRY CREEK
70638-70638 ELIZABETH
70639-70639 EVANS
70640-70640 FENTON
70642-70642 FULLERTON
70643-70643 GRAND CHENIER
70644-70644 GRANT
70645-70645 HACKBERRY
70646-70646 HAYES
70647-70647 IOWA
70648-70648 KINDER
70650-70650 LACASSINE
70651-70651 LEBLANC
70652-70652 LONGVILLE
70653-70653 MERRYVILLE
70654-70654 MITTIE
70655-70655 OBERLIN
70656-70656 PITKIN
70657-70657 RAGLEY
70658-70658 REEVES
70659-70659 ROSEPINE
70660-70660 SINGER
70661-70661 STARKS
70662-70662 SUGARTOWN
70663-70665 SULPHUR
70668-70668 VINTON
70669-70669 WESTLAKE
70704-70704 BAKER
70706-70706 DENHAM SPRINGS
70707-70707 GONZALES
70710-70710 ADDIS
70711-70711 ALBANY
70712-70712 ANGOLA
70714-70714 BAKER
70715-70715 BATCHELOR
70716-70716 BAYOU GOULA
70717-70717 BLANKS
70718-70718 BRITTANY
70719-70719 BRUSLY
70720-70720 BUECHE
70721-70721 CARVILLE
70722-70722 CLINTON
70723-70723 CONVENT
70725-70725 DARROW
70726-70727 DENHAM SPRINGS
70728-70728 DUPLESSIS
70729-70729 ERWINVILLE
70730-70730 ETHEL
70732-70732 FORDOCHE
70733-70733 FRENCH SETTLEMENT
70734-70734 GEISMAR
70736-70736 GLYNN
70737-70737 GONZALES
70738-70738 BURNSIDE
70739-70739 GREENWELL SPRINGS
70740-70740 GROSSE TETE
70743-70743 HESTER
70744-70744 HOLDEN
70747-70747 INNIS
70748-70748 JACKSON
70749-70749 JARREAU
70750-70750 KROTZ SPRINGS
70751-70751 LABARRE

70752-70752 LAKELAND
70753-70753 LETTSWORTH
70754-70754 LIVINGSTON
70755-70755 LIVONIA
70756-70756 LOTTIE
70757-70757 MARINGOUIN
70759-70759 MORGANZA
70760-70760 NEW ROADS
70761-70761 NORWOOD
70762-70762 OSCAR
70763-70763 PAULINA
70764-70765 PLAQUEMINE
70767-70767 PORT ALLEN
70769-70769 PRAIRIEVILLE
70770-70770 PRIDE
70772-70772 ROSEDALE
70773-70773 ROUGON
70774-70774 SAINT AMANT
70775-70775 SAINT FRANCISVILLE
70776-70776 SAINT GABRIEL
70777-70777 SLAUGHTER
70778-70778 SORRENTO
70780-70780 SUNSHINE
70781-70781 TORBERT
70782-70782 TUNICA
70783-70783 VENTRESS
70784-70784 WAKEFIELD
70785-70785 WALKER
70786-70786 WATSON
70787-70787 WEYANOKE
70788-70788 WHITE CASTLE
70789-70789 WILSON
70791-70791 ZACHARY
70792-70792 UNCLE SAM
70800-70898 BATON ROUGE
71001-71001 ARCADIA
71002-71002 ASHLAND
71003-71003 ATHENS
71004-71004 BELCHER
71006-71006 BENTON
71007-71007 BETHANY
71008-71008 BIENVILLE
71009-71009 BLANCHARD
71014-71014 BRYCELAND
71016-71016 CASTOR
71018-71018 COTTON VALLEY
71019-71019 COUSHATTA
71020-71020 CRESTON
71021-71021 CULLEN
71023-71023 DOYLINE
71024-71024 DUBBERLY
71025-71025 EAST POINT
71027-71027 FRIERSON
71028-71028 GIBSLAND
71029-71029 GILLIAM
71030-71030 GLOSTER
71031-71031 GOLDONNA
71032-71032 GRAND CANE
71033-71033 GREENWOOD
71034-71034 HALL SUMMIT
71036-71036 HARMON
71037-71037 HAUGHTON
71038-71038 HAYNESVILLE
71039-71039 HEFLIN
71040-71040 HOMER
71043-71043 HOSSTON
71044-71044 IDA
71045-71045 JAMESTOWN
71046-71046 KEATCHIE
71047-71047 KEITHVILLE
71048-71048 LISBON
71049-71049 LOGANSPORT
71050-71050 LONGSTREET
71051-71051 ELM GROVE
71052-71052 MANSFIELD
71055-71058 MINDEN
71059-71059 MIRA
71060-71060 MOORINGSPORT
71061-71061 OIL CITY
71063-71063 PELICAN
71064-71064 PLAIN DEALING
71065-71065 PLEASANT HILL
71066-71066 POWHATAN
71067-71067 PRINCETON
71068-71068 RINGGOLD
71069-71069 RODESSA
71070-71070 SALINE
71071-71071 SAREPTA
71072-71072 SHONGALOO
71073-71073 SIBLEY
71075-71075 SPRINGHILL
71078-71078 STONEWALL
71079-71079 SUMMERFIELD
71080-71080 TAYLOR
71082-71082 VIVIAN
71101-71109 SHREVEPORT
71110-71110 BARKSDALE AFB
71111-71113 BOSSIER CITY
71115-71166 SHREVEPORT
71171-71172 BOSSIER CITY
71201-71213 MONROE
71218-71218 ARCHIBALD
71219-71219 BASKIN
71220-71221 BASTROP
71222-71222 BERNICE
71223-71223 BONITA
71225-71225 CALHOUN
71226-71226 CHATHAM
71227-71227 CHOUDRANT
71229-71229 COLLINSTON
71230-71230 CROWVILLE
71232-71232 DELHI
71233-71233 DELTA
71234-71234 DOWNSVILLE
71235-71235 DUBACH
71237-71237 EPPS
71238-71238 EROS
71239-71239 EXTENSION
71240-71240 FAIRBANKS
71241-71241 FARMERVILLE
71242-71242 FOREST
71243-71243 FORT NECESSITY
71245-71245 GRAMBLING
71247-71247 HODGE
71249-71249 JIGGER
71250-71250 JONES
71251-71251 JONESBORO
71253-71253 KILBOURNE
71254-71254 LAKE PROVIDENCE
71256-71256 LILLIE
71259-71259 MANGHAM
71260-71260 MARION
71261-71261 MER ROUGE
71263-71263 OAK GROVE
71264-71264 OAK RIDGE
71266-71266 PIONEER
71268-71268 QUITMAN
71269-71269 RAYVILLE
71270-71273 RUSTON
71275-71275 SIMSBORO
71276-71276 SONDHEIMER
71277-71277 SPEARSVILLE
71279-71279 START
71280-71280 STERLINGTON
71281-71281 SWARTZ
71282-71284 TALLULAH
71286-71286 TRANSYLVANIA
71291-71294 WEST MONROE
71295-71295 WINNSBORO
71301-71315 ALEXANDRIA
71316-71316 ACME
71318-71318 BIG BEND
71320-71320 BORDELONVILLE
71321-71321 BUCKEYE
71322-71322 BUNKIE
71323-71323 CENTER POINT
71324-71324 CHASE
71325-71325 CHENEYVILLE
71326-71326 CLAYTON
71327-71327 COTTONPORT
71328-71328 DEVILLE
71329-71329 DUPONT
71330-71330 ECHO
71331-71331 EFFIE
71333-71333 EVERGREEN
71334-71334 FERRIDAY
71335-71335 FROGMORE
71336-71336 GILBERT
71338-71338 GOUDEAU
71339-71339 HAMBURG
71340-71340 HARRISONBURG
71341-71341 HESSMER
71342-71342 JENA
71343-71343 JONESVILLE
71344-71344 LARTO
71345-71345 LEBEAU
71346-71346 LECOMPTE
71347-71347 LE MOYEN
71348-71348 LIBUSE
71350-71350 MANSURA
71351-71351 MARKSVILLE
71353-71353 MELVILLE
71354-71354 MONTEREY
71355-71355 MOREAUVILLE
71356-71356 MORROW
71357-71357 NEWELLTON
71358-71358 PALMETTO
71359-71361 PINEVILLE
71362-71362 PLAUCHEVILLE
71363-71363 RHINEHART
71364-71364 ROSA
71365-71365 RUBY
71366-71366 SAINT JOSEPH
71367-71367 SAINT LANDRY
71368-71368 SICILY ISLAND
71369-71369 SIMMESPORT
71371-71371 TROUT
71372-71372 VICK
71373-71373 VIDALIA
71375-71375 WATERPROOF
71377-71377 WILDSVILLE
71378-71378 WISNER
71401-71401 AIMWELL
71403-71403 ANACOCO
71404-71404 ATLANTA
71405-71405 BALL
71406-71406 BELMONT
71407-71407 BENTLEY
71409-71409 BOYCE
71410-71410 CALVIN
71411-71411 CAMPTI
71412-71412 CHOPIN
71414-71414 CLARENCE
71415-71415 CLARKS
71416-71416 CLOUTIERVILLE
71417-71417 COLFAX
71418-71418 COLUMBIA
71419-71419 CONVERSE
71420-71420 CYPRESS
71421-71421 DERRY
71422-71422 DODSON
71423-71423 DRY PRONG
71424-71424 ELMER
71425-71425 ENTERPRISE
71426-71426 FISHER
71427-71427 FLATWOODS
71428-71428 FLORA
71429-71429 FLORIEN
71430-71430 FOREST HILL
71431-71431 GARDNER
71432-71432 GEORGETOWN
71433-71433 GLENMORA
71434-71434 GORUM
71435-71435 GRAYSON
71436-71436 HEBERT
71437-71437 HICKS
71438-71438 HINESTON
71439-71439 HORNBECK
71440-71440 JOYCE
71441-71441 KELLY
71443-71443 KURTHWOOD
71444-71444 LACAMP
71445-71445 LEANDER
71446-71446 LEESVILLE
71447-71447 LENA
71448-71448 LONGLEAF
71449-71449 MANY
71450-71450 MARTHAVILLE
71451-71451 MELDER
71452-71452 MELROSE
71454-71454 MONTGOMERY
71455-71455 MORA
71456-71456 NATCHEZ
71457-71458 NATCHITOCHES
71459-71459 LEESVILLE
71460-71460 NEGREET
71461-71461 NEWLLANO
71462-71462 NOBLE
71463-71463 OAKDALE
71465-71465 OLLA
71466-71466 OTIS
71467-71467 POLLOCK
71468-71468 PROVENCAL
71469-71469 ROBELINE
71471-71471 SAINT MAURICE
71472-71472 SIEPER
71473-71473 SIKES
71474-71474 SIMPSON
71475-71475 SLAGLE
71477-71477 TIOGA
71479-71479 TULLOS
71480-71480 URANIA
71481-71481 VERDA
71483-71483 WINNFIELD
71485-71485 WOODWORTH
71486-71486 ZWOLLE
71496-71496 LEESVILLE
71497-71497 NATCHITOCHES

General Help Numbers:

Governor's Office

1 State House Station, Room 236 — 207-287-3531
Augusta, ME 04333-0001 — Fax 207-287-1034
7:30AM-5:30PM
www.maine.gov/governor/baldacci/

Attorney General's Office

6 State House Station — 207-626-8800
Augusta, ME 04333 — Fax 207-626-8828
www.maine.gov/ag/ — 8AM-5PM

Legislative Records

Maine Legislature, Legislative Information Office
100 State House Station, Rm 121 — 207-287-1692
Augusta, ME 04333-0100 — Fax 207-287-1456
http://janus.state.me.us/legis — 8AM-5PM

State Archives

84 State House Station — 207-287-5795
Augusta, ME 04333-0084 — Fax 207-287-5739
www.maine.gov/sos/arc/ — 8:30AM-4PM

State Specifics:

Capital:	Augusta
	Kennebec County
Time Zone:	EST
Number of Counties:	16
Population:	1,316,456
Web Site:	www.maine.gov

State Agencies

Criminal Records

Maine State Police, State Bureau of Identification, State House Station #42, Augusta, ME 04333 (Courier address - 45 Commerce Dr #1, Augusta, 04330); 207-624-7240, Fax- 207-287-3421; 8AM-5PM. http://www10.informe.org/PCR/

Indexing & Storage: Records available from 1937 on. New records available for inquiry in 1 to 2 days. 90% of all arrests in database have final dispositions recorded for arrests within last 5 yrs.

Searching: Requests must be in writing. Will only do FBI fingerprint checks as authorized by Maine Statutes. Records are updated as often as records are submitted to this agency. Include in request-name, date of birth, any aliases. Fingerprints are optional. Include maiden name for females. Also include purpose of the inquiry and name and address of requester. 63% of the records are fingerprint-supported. Fingerprints generally are submitted with arrest information to this agency by the police. This data not released- limited juvenile records. All convictions and all pending cases less than 1 year old are reported, or if the case has not yet been adjudicated in court.

Access by: mail, in person, online.

Fee & Payment: The search fee is $25.00 for either a name check or fingerprint check, unless requester has online account, then $15.00 for a name check. Fee payee- Treasurer, State of Maine. Prepayment Required. Personal checks accepted. Credit cards accepted at website.

Mail search: Turnaround time- 1 week. **In person:** This only saves mail-in time; records are returned by mail.

Online search: One may request a record search from the web. Results are usually returned via e-mail in 2 hours. Fee is $25.00, unless requester is an in-state subscriber to InforME, then fee is $15.00 per record. There is a $75.00 annual fee to be a subscriber.

Statewide Court Records

State Court Administrator, PO Box 4820, Portland, ME 04112-4820; 207-822-0792, Fax- 207-822-0781; 8AM-4PM. www.courts.state.me.us

Access to trial court records is not available from a central location. All trial court record access must be done at the local level. The home page offers a variety of resources and information.

Access by: mail, online.

Fee & Payment: There is a $5.00 handling fee per Supreme Court record ordered by mail.

Mail search: Records of opinions and Supreme Court rulings are available by request.

Online search: The website offers access to Maine Supreme Court opinions and administrative orders, but not all documents are available online. Also, the site offers online access to trial court schedules by region and case type.

Sexual Offender Registry

State Bureau of Investigation, Sex Offender Registry, State House Station #42, Augusta, ME 04333-0042; 207-624-7270, Fax- 207-287-3421; 8AM-5PM. http://sor.informe.org/sor/

Direct question to maine_SOR.help@maine.gov.

Indexing & Storage: Records available from 01/01/82 to present. New records available for inquiry in 1 to 2 days.

Searching: Include in request- name, date of birth, any aliases (if requesting by mail, phone or fax). Once a request is made and a specific subject is brought up, the requester can ask this agency for more information, including personal information, the description of the offense, dates, and sentence imposed. This data not released- juvenile records, unless convicted as an adult. Also, the entire database is not for sale.

Access by: mail, online. **Fee & Payment:** There is no fee.

Mail search: Turnaround time- 1-2 days. A SASE is not required.

Online search: Search at the web page. Information is only provided for those individuals that are required to register pursuant to Title 34-A MRSA, Chapter 15. Records date to 01/01/82 and forward. The date of the last address verification is indicated next to the registrant's address.

Incarceration Records

Maine Department of Corrections, Inmate Records, 111 State House Station, Augusta, ME 04333; 207-287-4376, Fax- 207-287-4370; 8AM-5PM. www.maine.gov/corrections/

Indexing & Storage: Records available on current and former inmates. New records available for inquiry in 1 to 2 days.

Searching: Include in request- name, date of birth, any aliases. Fingerprints are optional. This data not released- SSN, current address.

Access by: mail, phone, fax, online.

Fee & Payment: There is no fee.

Mail search: Turnaround time- 1-2 weeks. A SASE is requested. **Phone search:** Name searching available by phone, either through the agency main number or through Victim Services. **Fax search:** Records are available by fax.

Online search: Do a search by sending an email to Corrections.Webdesk@maine.gov. Include your full name, address, and reasons for the search. Public information is provided. There is no direct online access available at this time (check website for updated information).

Corporation, LP, LLP, LLC, Trademarks/Servicemarks, Assumed Name

Secretary of State, Reports & Information Division, 101 State House Station, Augusta, ME 04333-0101; 207-624-7752, 207-624-7736 (Main Number), Fax- 207-287-5874; 8AM-5PM.

www.maine.gov/sos/cec/corp/

Indexing & Storage: Records available from 1700's on. The older records are in law books. Records on the in-house computer are for all active and some inactive corporations. New records available for inquiry immediately.

Searching: Include in request- full name of business, specific records that you need copies of. In addition to the articles of organization, business entity records available include: Annual Reports (back to 1986), Officers, Directors, Prior (merged) names, Inactive and Reserved names.

Access by: mail, phone, fax, in person, online.

Fee & Payment: Copies are $2.00 per page, additional $5.00 if certified and $10.00 is specially worded. A Certificate of Existence is $30.00 and $10.00 if not for profit. Fee payee- Secretary of State. They will invoice for copies. Personal checks, Visa, and MasterCard accepted.

Mail search: Turnaround time- 1 week. SASE not required. **Phone search:** They will provide names and addresses of officers and directors over the phone. **Fax search:** Records are available by fax.

In person: See expedited service.

Online search: A free search of basic information about the entity including address, corporate ID, agent, and status is found at https://icrs.informe.org/nei-sos-icrs/ICRS. A commercial subscriber account also gives extensive information and ability to download files. Also, search securities Division Enforcement Actions and Consent Agreements free at www.maine.gov/pfr/securities/enforcement.shtml.

Other access: Bulk data purchase is available, a list of available databases for sale if found at the web. Monthly lists of new entities filed with this office are also available. Call 207-624-7752.

Expedited service: Expedited service is available for mail and phone searches. Turnaround time- 24 hours. Add $50.00 per business name. For immediate service, the fee is $100.00 per business name.

Uniform Commercial Code, Federal & State Tax Liens

Secretary of State, UCC Records Section, 101 State House Station, Augusta, ME 04333-0101 (Courier address- Burton M. Cross State Office Bldg, 109 Sewell St, 4th Fl, Augusta, ME 04333); 207-624-7752, Fax- 207-287-5874; 8AM-5PM.

www.maine.gov/sos/cec/ucc/index.html

For questions, email cec.corporations@maine.gov.

Indexing & Storage: Records available from 1964. Records are computerized since 1993. New records available for inquiry in 3 to 4 days.

Searching: Use search request form UCC-11 when needed for certification. The search includes both federal and state tax liens. Include in request- index number or debtor name only. Try to include a middle initial in your request. They will not search by address or collateral or secured party.

Access by: mail, phone, in person, online.

Fee & Payment: Searches cost $20.00 per name, $12.00 if online. Certification is $5.00. Fee payee- Secretary of State Prepayment required. Personal checks and major credit cards accepted.

Mail search: Turnaround time- a maximum of 5 days. If update or certain dates requested, state boldly. SASE not required.

Phone search: Limited information is available by phone. Usually this is limited to only those listed on the filing.

In person: There is one public access terminal. If copies are needed, written request required and fees apply, see expedited services below.

Online search: There is a free search of the index to search only debtor name or name variations at www.maine.gov/sos/cec/corp/debtor_index.shtml. For search and purchase of official UCC documents and fees visit https://www10.informe.org/ucc/search/begin.shtml. If no record found, the fee is still incurred.

Other access: UCC Bulk Database: $1,200 for all; $1,500 for–images; $600 monthly download; $300 weekly download; $500 weekly images.

Expedited service: Expedited service is available for mail searches. The Maine specific UCC-11 request form has a box to check if expedited service requested. Add $10.00 per name for overnight, $25.00 if immediate. If by mail, write and highlight the word "Expedite" on the search request.

Sales Tax Registrations

Maine Revenue Services, Sales, Fuel & Special Tax Division, 24 State House Station, Augusta, ME 04333; 207-624-9693, Fax- 207-287-6628; 8AM-5PM. www.maine.gov/revenue/

Indexing & Storage: Records available from 1993, on computer. New records available for inquiry in up to 2 months.

Searching: This agency will only confirm to a third party or requester without a power of attorney that a business is registered. Include in request- business name, Entity ID, Acct. Written authorization may be required.

Access by: mail, phone, fax, in person.

Mail search: Turnaround time- 7 to 10 days. A SASE is helpful. No fee for mail request.

Phone search: No fee for telephone request.

Fax search: Same criteria as mail searching.

In person: No fee for request. Proper ID required.

Birth Certificates

Department of Health and Human Services, Office of Vital Records, 244 Water St, Station 11, Augusta, ME 04333-0011; 207-287-3181 (Message), 877-523-2659 (VitalChek), 207-287-1919, Fax- 207-287-1093; 8AM-5PM.

www.maine.gov/dhhs/vitalrecords.htm

Website links VitalChek for online ordering.

Indexing & Storage: Records available from 1923 to present. Maine State Archives has records prior to 1923 (call 207-287-5795). Records are indexed on computer from 1975 to present, and on microfiche from 1892 to present. New records available for inquiry in up to one month.

Searching: Must give relationship to person of record and reason for request. Confidential information will not be released except to the person listed on the birth certificate. Include in request- full name, names of parents, mother's maiden name, date of birth, place of birth. Order form is at www.maine.gov/dhhs/bohodr/documents/vrform.pdf. This data not released- illegitimate births or adoption records.

Access by: mail, phone, in person.

Fee & Payment: $15.00 fee for certified copy, $10.00 for uncertified, add $6.00 per name for additional copy of same record. Fee payee- Treasurer, State of Maine. Prepayment required. Personal checks, Visa, and MasterCard accepted.

Mail search: Turnaround time- 1 to 2 weeks. Specific dates are needed to search as well as names (if available). SASE requested.

Phone search: See expedited service.

In person: Turnaround time is while you wait.

Other access: Physical birth lists are available for purchase, excluding restricted information.

Expedited service: Expedited service is available for mail, phone and fax searches. Turnaround time- 1-5 days. Use of credit card is required. Add fee of $29.95 for 1-3 days service or $22.95 for 45 days service or $12.95 for 7-10 day service.

Death Records

Department of Health and Human Services, Office of Vital Records, 244 Water St, Station 11, Augusta, ME 04333-0011; 207-287-3181 (Message), 877-523-2659 (VitalChek), 207-287-1919, Fax- 207-287-1093; 8AM-5PM.

www.maine.gov/dhhs/vitalrecords.htm

Website links VitalChek for online ordering.

Indexing & Storage: Records available from 1923 to present. Maine State Archives has records prior to 1923 (call 207-287-5795). Records are indexed on computer from 1975 to present, and on microfiche from 1892 to present. New records available for inquiry in up to 1 month.

Searching: Access to cause of death is restricted to those with a legitimate interest in the information. All information on certificate of death is confidential, except name, age, date of death, as well as city/town where death occurred. Include in request- full name, date of death, place of death, relationship to person of record. Order form is at www.maine.gov/dhhs/bohodr/documents/vrform.pdf. This data not released- cause of death, unless a direct and legitimate interest.

Access by: mail, phone, in person, online.

Fee & Payment: $15.00 fee for certified copy, $10.00 for uncertified, add $6.00 per name for additional copy of same record. Fee payee- Treasurer, State of Maine. Prepayment required. Personal checks, Visa, and MasterCard accepted.

Mail search: Turnaround time- 1 to 2 weeks. When requesting a search, keep in mind that records are filed by the date of the death, and then by name. SASE required. **Phone search:** See expedited service.

In person: Turnaround time is while you wait.

Online search: Search death records for 1960 thru 1997 from the web page at http://portalx.bisoex.state.me.us/pls/archives_mhsf/archdev.death_archive.search_form. Also, a free genealogy site at http://vitals.rootsweb.ancestry.com/me/death/search.cgi has Death Indexes from 1960-1997. Search by surname, given name, place or year.

Other access: Bulk file purchases are available, with the exclusion of restricted data.

Expedited service: Expedited service is available for mail, phone and fax searches. Turnaround time- 1-5 days. Use of credit card is required. Add fee of $29.95 for 1-3 days service or $22.95 for 4-5 days service or $12.95 for 7-10 day service.

Marriage Certificates

Department of Health and Human Services, Office of Vital Records, 244 Water St, Station 11, Augusta, ME 04333-0011; 207-287-3181 (Message), 877-523-2659 (VitalChek), 207-287-1919, Fax- 207-287-1093; 8AM-5PM.

www.maine.gov/dhhs/vitalrecords.htm

Website links VitalChek for online ordering.

Indexing & Storage: Records available from 1923 to present. Maine State Archives has records prior to 1923 (call 207-287-5795). Records are indexed on microfiche from 1892 to present. New records available for inquiry in up to one month.

Searching: Must give relationship to persons of record and reason for request. Data recorded in the section of the certificate specified as confidential is not released (i.e. race, education, etc.). Include in request- names of husband and wife, date of marriage, place or county of marriage. Order form is at www.maine.gov/dhhs/bohodr/documents/vrform.pdf.

Access by: mail, phone, in person, online.

Fee & Payment: $15.00 fee for certified copy, $10.00 for uncertified, add $6.00 per name for additional copy of same record. Fee payee- Treasurer, State of Maine. Prepayment required. Personal checks, Visa, and MasterCard accepted.

Mail search: Turnaround time- 1 to 2 weeks. SASE requested. **Phone search:** See expedited svc. **In person:** Turnaround time while you wait.

Online search: Records are available at the web page from 1892 thru 1996.

Other access: Bulk file purchasing is available, with restricted data excluded.

Expedited service: Expedited service is available for mail, phone and fax searches. Turnaround time- 1-5 days. Use of credit card is required. Add fee of $29.95 for 1-3 days service or $22.95 for 4-5 days service or $12.95 for 7-10 day service.

Divorce Records

Department of Health and Human Services, Office of Vital Records, 244 Water St, Station 11, Augusta, ME 04333-0011; 207-287-3181 (Message), 877-523-2659 (VitalChek), 207-287-1919, Fax- 207-287-1093; 8AM-5PM.

www.maine.gov/dhhs/vitalrecords.htm

Website links VitalChek for online ordering.

Indexing & Storage: Records available from 1892 to present. New records available for inquiry in 1 month or less.

Searching: Must give relationship to persons of record and reason for request. Include in request- names of husband and wife, date of divorce, place of divorce. Order form is at www.maine.gov/dhhs/bohodr/documents/vrform.pdf.

Access by: mail, phone, in person.

Fee & Payment: $15.00 fee for certified copy, $10.00 for uncertified, add $6.00 per name for additional copy of same record. Fee payee- Treasurer, State of Maine. Prepayment required. Personal checks, Visa, and MasterCard accepted.

Mail search: Turnaround time- 1 to 2 weeks. SASE requested. **Phone search:** See expedited service. **In person:** Turnaround time is while you wait for up to 2 requests.

Other access: Index information is available for bulk purchase.

Expedited service: Expedited service is available for phone requests. Turnaround time- 1-5 days. Use of credit card is required. Add fee of $29.95 for 1-3 days service or $22.95 for 4-5 days service or $12.95 for 7-10 day service.

Workers' Compensation Records

Workers Compensation Board, 27 State House Station, Augusta, ME 04333-0027; 207-287-7071, 207-287-3751, Fax- 207-287-7198; 7:30AM-5PM.

www.maine.gov/wcb/

Both pre AND post employment checks are NOT permitted.

Indexing & Storage: Records available from 1984, indexed on computer. New records available for inquiry in 1 month.

Searching: Records are considered confidential and are released "on a need-to-know basis." Include in request- claimant name, SSN, reason for information request. This data not released- personal information (height, weight, sex, eye color, etc.) or SSNs.

Access by: mail, in person.

Fee & Payment: The research fee is $5.00. Copies are $.50 per page. Fee payee- Trea. State of Maine, Workers' Compensation Board. When remitting payment, please include invoice number on check. Personal checks accepted, credit cards are not.

Mail search: Turnaround time- 3 to 4 weeks. Requests should be addressed to: Linda Larrabee, Workers' Compensation Board, 27 State House Station, Augusta, ME 04333. SASE is requested.

In person: Requests must still be in writing and prior approval is suggested.

Other access: Computer data is available, but requests are screened for purpose.

Driver Records

BMV - Driver License Services, 101 Hospital Street, 29 State House Station, Augusta, ME 04333-0029; 207-624-9000 x52116, Fax- 207-624-9090; 8AM-5PM. www.maine.gov/sos/bmv/

Indexing & Storage: Records available for 3 years for moving violations, DWIs and 3 years after the reinstatement of suspensions. Accidents are indicated on the record. New records available for inquiry in up to 30 days.

Searching: Driving records and ticket information is released per DPPA guidelines. Personal information is not available to the general public unless the subject opts in, or a signed release is presented. The full name and DOB are required for a search. The driver's license number is optional. This data not released- medical info and SSNs.

Access by: mail, fax, in person, online.

Fee & Payment: The fee is $5.00 for a non-certified three-year record and $10.00 for a ten-year record. Add $1.00 for a certification. Add $2.00 if access online. A "no record found" incurs a full charge, except for walk-in requesters. Fee payee- Secretary of State. Prepayment required. Personal checks accepted.

Mail search: Turnaround time- 3 days. SASE not required. **Fax search:** Add $2.00 and results are returned by mail. **In person:** Up to 5 requests can be obtained in-person immediately; additional requests are available the next day.

Online search: Access is through InforME via the Internet. There are two access systems. Casual requesters can obtain records that have personal information cloaked. There is a subscription service for approved requesters, records contain personal information. There is a subscription service for approved requesters, records contain personal information as records are released per DPPA. The fee for either system is $7.00 per request for a 3-year record and $12.00 for a 10-year record. There is a $75.00 annual fee for the subscription service. A myriad of other state government records are available. Visit www.informe.org/bmv/drc/ or call 207-621-2600.

Other access: The state offers "Driver Cross Check" - a program for employers, to provide notification when activity occurs on a specific record.

Vehicle Ownership & Registration

Department of Motor Vehicles, Registration Section, 29 State House Station, Augusta, ME 04333-0029; 207-624-9000 x52149 (Registration), 207-624-9000 x52138 (Titles), Fax- 207-624-9204; 8AM-5PM M-F. www.maine.gov/sos/bmv/

The above fax is for Registration, fax for Title is 207-624-9239.

Indexing & Storage: Records available from 1982, on microfilm. New records available for inquiry in up to 30 days.

Searching: Casual requesters can obtain records, but personal information is not included unless the subject gives authorization. Opt-in is available. Include in request- full name and DOB, or by VIN or by license plate number. It is suggested to become an account holder.

Access by: mail, phone, fax, in person, online.

Fee & Payment: Uncertified records are $5.00. $6.00 for certified Registration record, $33.00 for a certified Title record. Will also fax record back for an additional $2.00. Fee payee- Secretary of State. Prepayment required. Personal checks and credit cards accepted.

Mail search: Turnaround time- 5 days. SASE not required.

Phone search: Telephone searching is available for parties with an established account. They are billed monthly. However, no new accounts are being established. **Fax search:** Established accounts may order by fax, and then have data returned by fax for an additional $2.00. **In person:** Immediate service limited to simple requests.

Online search: Maine offers online access to title and registration records via InforME. Fee is $5.00 per record. Search title records by VIN or title number. Search registration records by name and DOB, or by plate number. Records are available as interactive online or FTP with a subscription account. There are many other services available with the subscription. $75.00 annual fee. Contact InforME at info@informe.org or visit web page.

Accident Reports

Maine State Police, Traffic Division, Station 20, Augusta, ME 04333-0020; 207-624-8944, Fax-207-624-8945; 8AM-5PM.

www.informe.org/mcrs/ Accidents must be reported involving death, injury, or property damage in excess of $1000.00 (combined damage).

Indexing & Storage: Records available from 1975 to 2003 on microfilm. 2003 forward on computer. New records available for inquiry in up to 30 days.

Searching: Most accident records are public information. All requests must be in writing. If a fatality is involved, the fatality report is not released until the court case is concluded. Include in request- full name, date of birth, date of accident, location of accident. Be sure to order by the operator's name, not by vehicle owner name. This data not released- items marked confidential, such as autopsy or medical records.

Access by: mail, in person, online.

Fee & Payment: Fee is $10.00 per Police Traffic report; $5.00 per 25 pages for an Officer's Investigative Report (fatality involved) or an Accident Reconstruction Report or a Vehicle Autopsy Report. A Mapping Report is $10.00, $15.00 if color and $35.00 if plotter. Fee payee-Treasurer, State of Maine. Prepayment required. Personal checks accepted, credit cards are not.

Mail search: Turnaround time is one day if on computer, five days if microfilm. SASE is requested. **In person:** Turnaround time is usually immediate for walk-in requesters.

Online search: Records from 01/2003 forward may be ordered from www.informe.org/mcrs/ for $10.00 per record. If you do not have a subscription to InforME, then a credit card must be used. Resulting reports is either returned by mail, or emailed in a PDF format. Search by name, date of birth, crash location, crash date, or investigating agency (police department). These reports may include officer narratives.

Other access: Subscribers may purchase monthly database updates or use the "Crash Tracker" notification program for no charge.

Vessel Ownership & Registration

Dept of Inland Fisheries & Wildlife, Vessel Records, 41 State House Station, 284 State St, Augusta, ME 04333-0041; 207-287-5232, 207-287-2043, Fax- 207-287-8094; 8AM-5PM.

www.maine.gov/ifw/ All motorized boats must be registered, boats are not required to be titled.

Indexing & Storage: Records available from 1987 to present for registrations that have been continuously renewed. New records available for inquiry in several months.

Searching: The Fish & Wildlife Office in Augusta is the central office for boat registrations and registration records. Many Maine municipal tax collectors or town clerks are Recreational Vehicle Agents for the Fish & Wildlife Department. Include in request- name or registration number. Liens are not shown and must be searched with UCC filings at 207-624-7752.

Access by: mail, phone, fax, in person.

Fee & Payment: The search fee is $5.00 per record for a name search, $2.00 if in person and done yourself. A boat history fee is $25.00. Fee payee- Treasurer, State of Maine. Prepayment required. Personal checks accepted. Visa/MC/Discover accepted.

Mail search: Turnaround time- 1 to 2 weeks. SASE not required. **Phone search:** Results will only be given verbally, if payment is arranged using a credit card. **Fax search:** Turnaround time is within 72 hours. A credit card must be used for all fax searches. **In person:** Counter service available.

Other access: Bulk purchase available from InforME at 207-621-2600 x38

Legislation Records

Maine Legislature, Legislative Information Office, 100 State House Station, Rm 121, Augusta, ME 04333-0100; 207-287-1692 (Bill Status or LD #), 207-287-1408 (Document Room), Fax- 207-287-1580; 8AM-5PM. http://janus.state.me.us/legis/

Indexing & Storage: Records available for the current session and past session only.

Older passed bills are found at the State Law Library, 207-287-1600.

Voter Registration

Access to Records is Restricted.

Secretary of State, Department of Elections, 101 State House Station, 4th Fl, Augusta, ME 04333-0101; 207-624-7650, Fax- 207-287-5428; 8-5PM.

www.maine.gov/sos/cec/elec/

The data is considered public record in Maine, but presently individual searches must be done at the municipality level. This agency has a central, computerized, statewide voter registration system. Although it will sell voter registration lists to approved entities, records may not be used for marketing purposes or any type of solicitations.

GED Certificates

Dept of Education, GED Office, 23 State House Station, Augusta, ME 04333; 207-624-6752, Fax-207-624-6731; 8AM-5PM.

www.maine.gov/education/aded/dev/ged/transcript.htm

Indexing & Storage: Records available from 1949. New records available for inquiry in 2 days.

Searching: Requests for transcripts must be in writing. There is a request form available on the website. To verify, all of the following is required: name, date of birth, and SSN. Also include requester name and telephone number. For transcripts, a signed release is required. This data not released- SSN, DOB.

Access by: mail, phone, fax, in person, online.

Fee & Payment: There are no fees for verification or copy of transcript, but $3.00 for copy of the diploma. Personal checks are accepted.

Mail search: Turnaround time 1-2 days. SASE not required.

Phone search: You can do a verification over the phone. **Fax search:** Turnaround time 1-2 days.

In person: Turnaround time while you wait.

Online search: Email requests can be made by sending email to: lisa.perry@maine.gov

Hunting & Fishing License Information

Inland Fisheries & Wildlife Department, Licensing Division, 284 State St, Augusta, ME 04333; 207-287-8000, Fax- 207-287-8094; 8AM-5PM.

www.maine.gov/ifw/

The state is computerizing license data. Licenses are issued online at the website. Also, licenses are issued by Town Clerks and approved businesses and forwarded monthly to this department. Records available from 1996 to present.

Maine State Licensing Agencies

For details about the agency responsible for licensing/certifying/registering an item below or in the Agency Quick Finder section, match an item's number with the number of the agency in the *Licensing Agency Information* section.

Maine Licenses Searchable Online

Acupuncturist #13 .... http://pfr.informe.org/ALMSOnline/ALMSQuery/Welcome.aspx
Aesthetician #13........ http://pfr.informe.org/ALMSOnline/ALMSQuery/Welcome.aspx
Alcohol/Drug Abuse Counselor #13........ http://pfr.informe.org/ALMSOnline/ALMSQuery/Welcome.aspx
Alcoholic Beverage Distributor #21........ www.maine.gov/dps/liqr/active_licenses.htm
Ambulatory Surgical Ctr #9........ http://pfr.informe.org/ALMSOnline/ALMSQuery/Welcome.aspx
Animal Medical Technician #13........ http://pfr.informe.org/ALMSOnline/ALMSQuery/Welcome.aspx
Appraiser, Resi. Real Estate #13........ http://pfr.informe.org/ALMSOnline/ALMSQuery/Welcome.aspx
Architect #13........ http://pfr.informe.org/ALMSOnline/ALMSQuery/Welcome.aspx
Assisted Living Facility #9........ https://portalxw.bisoex.state.me.us/dhhs-apps/assisted/certificate.asp
Athletic Trainer #13........ http://pfr.informe.org/ALMSOnline/ALMSQuery/Welcome.aspx
Attorney #22........ www.mebaroverseers.org/attorney_search.asp
Auctioneer #13........ http://pfr.informe.org/ALMSOnline/ALMSQuery/Welcome.aspx
Barber #13........ http://pfr.informe.org/ALMSOnline/ALMSQuery/Welcome.aspx
Boiler #13........ http://pfr.informe.org/ALMSOnline/ALMSQuery/Welcome.aspx
Boxer #13........ http://pfr.informe.org/ALMSOnline/ALMSQuery/Welcome.aspx
Charitable Solicitation #13........ http://pfr.informe.org/ALMSOnline/ALMSQuery/Welcome.aspx
Chiropractor #13........ http://pfr.informe.org/ALMSOnline/ALMSQuery/Welcome.aspx
Cosmetologist #13........ http://pfr.informe.org/ALMSOnline/ALMSQuery/Welcome.aspx
Counselor #13........ http://pfr.informe.org/ALMSOnline/ALMSQuery/Welcome.aspx
Dental Hygienist #16........ http://pfr.informe.org/ALMSOnline/ALMSQuery/Welcome.aspx
Dental Radiographer #16........ http://pfr.informe.org/ALMSOnline/ALMSQuery/Welcome.aspx
Dentist #16........ http://pfr.informe.org/ALMSOnline/ALMSQuery/Welcome.aspx
Denturist #16........ http://pfr.informe.org/ALMSOnline/ALMSQuery/Welcome.aspx
Dietitian #13........ http://pfr.informe.org/ALMSOnline/ALMSQuery/Welcome.aspx
Electrician #13........ http://pfr.informe.org/ALMSOnline/ALMSQuery/Welcome.aspx
Elevator/Tramway #13........ http://pfr.informe.org/ALMSOnline/ALMSQuery/Welcome.aspx
Employee Leasing Company #15........ http://pfr.informe.org/ALMSOnline/ALMSQuery/Welcome.aspx
Engineer #17........ https://www.maine.gov/professionalengineers/database.shtml
Engineer Intern #17........ https://www.maine.gov/professionalengineers/database.shtml
Forester #13........ http://pfr.informe.org/ALMSOnline/ALMSQuery/Welcome.aspx
Fund Raiser #13........ http://pfr.informe.org/ALMSOnline/ALMSQuery/Welcome.aspx
Funeral Service #13........ http://pfr.informe.org/ALMSOnline/ALMSQuery/Welcome.aspx
Geologist #13........ http://pfr.informe.org/ALMSOnline/ALMSQuery/Welcome.aspx
Hearing Aid Dealer/Fitter #13........ http://pfr.informe.org/ALMSOnline/ALMSQuery/Welcome.aspx
HMO #15........ www.maine.gov/pfr/insurance/
Home Health Agency #9........ http://pfr.informe.org/ALMSOnline/ALMSQuery/Welcome.aspx
Home Health Care Svc Agency #9........ http://pfr.informe.org/ALMSOnline/ALMSQuery/Welcome.aspx
Hospice #9........ http://pfr.informe.org/ALMSOnline/ALMSQuery/Welcome.aspx
Hospital #9........ http://pfr.informe.org/ALMSOnline/ALMSQuery/Welcome.aspx
Insurance Adjuster #15........ http://pfr.informe.org/ALMSOnline/ALMSQuery/SearchIndividual.aspx
Insurance Advisor/Consultant #13........ http://pfr.informe.org/ALMSOnline/ALMSQuery/Welcome.aspx
Insurance Agent/Agency/Company #13........ http://pfr.informe.org/ALMSOnline/ALMSQuery/Welcome.aspx
Interior Designer #13........ http://pfr.informe.org/ALMSOnline/ALMSQuery/Welcome.aspx
Intermediate Care Facility (Retarded) #9........ http://pfr.informe.org/ALMSOnline/ALMSQuery/Welcome.aspx
Interpreter #13........ http://pfr.informe.org/ALMSOnline/ALMSQuery/Welcome.aspx
Investment Advisor/Representative #12........ http://pfr.informe.org/ALMSOnline/ALMSQuery/Welcome.aspx
Kickboxer #13........ http://pfr.informe.org/ALMSOnline/ALMSQuery/Welcome.aspx
Landscape Architect #13........ http://pfr.informe.org/ALMSOnline/ALMSQuery/Welcome.aspx
Liquor License, On & Off Premise #21........ www.maine.gov/dps/liqr/active_licenses.htm
Liquor Store/Wholesaler #21........ www.maine.gov/dps/liqr/active_agency_liquor_stores.htm
Lobbyist #1........ www.mainecampaignfinance.com/public/entity_list.asp?TYPE=LOB
Lottery Retailer #2........ www.mainelottery.com/players_info/where_to_buy.html
Manicurist #13........ http://pfr.informe.org/ALMSOnline/ALMSQuery/Welcome.aspx
Manufactured Housing #13........ http://pfr.informe.org/ALMSOnline/ALMSQuery/Welcome.aspx
Marriage & Family Therapist #13........ http://pfr.informe.org/ALMSOnline/ALMSQuery/Welcome.aspx
Massage Therapist #13........ http://pfr.informe.org/ALMSOnline/ALMSQuery/Welcome.aspx
Medical Doctor #23........ www.docboard.org/me/licensure/dw_verification.html

Naturopathic Physician #13 .... http://pfr.informe.org/ALMSOnline/ALMSQuery/Welcome.aspx
Notary Public #24 .... www.maine.gov/online/notary/search/
Nurse #8 .... https://portalx.bisoex.state.me.us/pls/msbn_nlv/bnxdev.license_search.main_page
Nurse, Practical #8 .... https://portalx.bisoex.state.me.us/pls/msbn_nlv/bnxdev.license_search.main_page
Nursing Home #9 .... http://pfr.informe.org/ALMSOnline/ALMSQuery/Welcome.aspx
Nursing Home Administrator #13 .... http://pfr.informe.org/ALMSOnline/ALMSQuery/Welcome.aspx
Occupational Therapist #13 .... http://pfr.informe.org/ALMSOnline/ALMSQuery/Welcome.aspx
Oil & Solid Fuel Professional/Firm #13 .... http://pfr.informe.org/ALMSOnline/ALMSQuery/Welcome.aspx
Optometrist #18 .... http://pfr.informe.org/ALMSOnline/ALMSQuery/Welcome.aspx
Osteopathic Physician/Physician Asst #26 .... www.docboard.org/me-osteo/df/index.htm
Osteopathic Resident/Intern #26 .... www.docboard.org/me-osteo/df/index.htm
Pastoral Counselor #13 .... http://pfr.informe.org/ALMSOnline/ALMSQuery/Welcome.aspx
Pesticide Applicator #3 .... www.maine.gov/agriculture/pesticides/cert/index.htm
Pesticide Dealer #3 .... www.maine.gov/agriculture/pesticides/cert/index.htm
Pharmacist #13 .... http://pfr.informe.org/ALMSOnline/ALMSQuery/Welcome.aspx
Physical Therapist #13 .... http://pfr.informe.org/ALMSOnline/ALMSQuery/Welcome.aspx
Physician Assistant #23 .... www.docboard.org/me/licensure/dw_verification.html
Pilot #13 .... http://pfr.informe.org/ALMSOnline/ALMSQuery/Welcome.aspx
Plumber #13 .... http://pfr.informe.org/ALMSOnline/ALMSQuery/Welcome.aspx
Podiatrist #13 .... http://pfr.informe.org/ALMSOnline/ALMSQuery/Welcome.aspx
Preferred Provider Organization #15 .... www.maine.gov/pfr/insurance/
Psychologist #13 .... http://pfr.informe.org/ALMSOnline/ALMSQuery/Welcome.aspx
Public Accountant-CPA #13 .... http://pfr.informe.org/ALMSOnline/ALMSQuery/Welcome.aspx
Radiologic Technician #13 .... http://pfr.informe.org/ALMSOnline/ALMSQuery/Welcome.aspx
Real Estate Appraiser #13 .... http://pfr.informe.org/ALMSOnline/ALMSQuery/Welcome.aspx
Real Estate Broker #13 .... http://pfr.informe.org/ALMSOnline/ALMSQuery/Welcome.aspx
Re-insurer, Approved #15 .... http://pfr.informe.org/ALMSOnline/ALMSQuery/Welcome.aspx
Renal Disease (End Stage) Facility #9 .... http://pfr.informe.org/ALMSOnline/ALMSQuery/Welcome.aspx
Respiratory Care Therapist #13 .... http://pfr.informe.org/ALMSOnline/ALMSQuery/Welcome.aspx
RN, Advanced Practice #8 .... https://portalx.bisoex.state.me.us/pls/msbn_nlv/bnxdev.license_search.main_page
RN, Professional #8 .... https://portalx.bisoex.state.me.us/pls/msbn_nlv/bnxdev.license_search.main_page
Securities Broker-Dealer/Agent #12 .... http://pfr.informe.org/ALMSOnline/ALMSQuery/Welcome.aspx
Social Worker #13 .... http://pfr.informe.org/ALMSOnline/ALMSQuery/Welcome.aspx
Soil Scientist #13 .... http://pfr.informe.org/ALMSOnline/ALMSQuery/Welcome.aspx
Speech Pathologist/Audiologist #13 .... http://pfr.informe.org/ALMSOnline/ALMSQuery/Welcome.aspx
Substance Abuse Counselor #13 .... http://pfr.informe.org/ALMSOnline/ALMSQuery/Welcome.aspx
Surplus Lines Company #15 .... http://pfr.informe.org/ALMSOnline/ALMSQuery/Welcome.aspx
Surveyor, Land #13 .... http://pfr.informe.org/ALMSOnline/ALMSQuery/Welcome.aspx
Utilization Review Entity #15 .... www.maine.gov/pfr/insurance/
Vendor, Itinerant/Transient #13 .... http://pfr.informe.org/ALMSOnline/ALMSQuery/Welcome.aspx
Veterinarian/Veterinary Technician #13 .... http://pfr.informe.org/ALMSOnline/ALMSQuery/Welcome.aspx
Wrestler #13 .... http://pfr.informe.org/ALMSOnline/ALMSQuery/Welcome.aspx

Maine Licensing Quick Finder

Acupuncturist #13 207-624-8603
Adoption Agency #7 207-287-5060
Adult Day Service #9 207-287-9250
Adult/Child Homes, Inspection #20 207-626-3800
Aesthetician #13 207-624-8603
Agricultural Fair #19 207-287-5671
Air Quality Control Business #5 207-287-2437
Alcohol/Drug Abuse Counselor #13 207-624-8603
Alcoholic Beverage Distributor #21 207-624-7220
All-Terrain Vehicle/ATV #11 207-287-2043
Ambulance Attendant #10 207-626-3860
Ambulatory Surgical Ctr #9 207-287-9300
Animal Medical Technician #13 207-624-8603
Appraiser, Resi. Real Estate #13 207-624-8616
Architect #13 207-624-8522
Assisted Living Facility #9 207-287-9250
Athletic Trainer #13 207-624-8624
Attorney #22 207-623-1121
Auctioneer #13 207-624-8521
Bank #14 207-624-8648
Barber #13 207-624-8579
Bed and Breakfast #19 207-287-5671
Beekeeper #3 207-287-3117
Body Piercing Practitioner #19 207-287-5671
Boiler #13 207-624-8606
Bottle Club, Alcohol #21 207-624-7220
Boxer #13 207-624-8603
Brewery/Winery #21 207-624-7220
Campground #19 207-287-5671
Campground, Commercial #19 207-287-5671
Catering Establishment #19 207-287-5671
Catering, Liquor, Special #21 207-624-7220
Charitable Solicitation #13 207-624-8624
Child Care Resource #7 207-287-5060
Chiropractor #13 207-624-8634
Circus/Carnival #20 207-626-3800
Commercial Fishing #27 207-624-6550
Compres'd Air Producer-breathing #19. 207-287-5671
Construction Plan Review #20 207-626-3800
Cosmetologist #13 207-624-8620
Cottage for Lodging #19 207-287-5671
Counselor #13 207-624-8626
Credit Union #14 207-624-8648
Dance Hall, Inspection #20 207-626-3800
Day Care #7 207-287-5060
Dental Hygienist #16 207-287-3333
Dental Radiographer #16 207-287-3333
Dentist #16 207-287-3333
Denturist #16 207-287-3333
Dietitian #13 207-624-8611
Eating Place #19 207-287-5671
Electrician #13 207-624-8611
Electrologist #19 207-287-5671
Elevator/Tramway #13 207-624-8672
Emergency Medical Technician #10 207-626-3860
Employee Leasing Company #15 207-624-8475
Engineer #17 207-287-3236
Engineer Intern #17 207-287-3236
Explosive #20 207-626-3800
Firearm Permit #25 207-624-7210
Fireworks #20 207-626-3800
First Responder #10 207-626-3860
Forester #13 207-624-8521
Foster Care #7 207-287-5060
Fund Raiser #13 207-624-8624
Funeral Service #13 207-624-8623
Games of Chance #25 207-624-7210
Geologist #13 207-624-8627
Hazard's Mat./Solid Waste Oper't'r #6. 207-287-7688

Hearing Aid Dealer/Fitter #13 207-624-8674
HMO #15 207-624-8475
Home Health Agency #9 207-287-9300
Home Health Care Svc Agency #9 207-287-9300
Hospice #9 207-287-9300
Hospital #9 207-287-9300
Insurance Adjuster #15 207-624-8475
Insurance Advisor/Consultant #13 207-624-8545
Insurance Agent/Agency/Firm #13 207-624-8545
Insurance Producer #15 207-624-8475
Interior Designer #13 207-624-8522
Intermediate Care Facility-retarded #9 207-287-9300
Interpreter #13 207-624-8624
Investment Advisor/Represent've #12 207-624-8551
Kickboxer #13 207-624-8603
Landscape Architect #13 207-624-8522
Library Media Specialist #4 207-624-6603
Limited Purpose Bank #14 207-624-8648
Liquor License, On & Off Premise #21 207-624-7220
Liquor Salesperson #21 207-624-7220
Liquor Store/Wholesaler #21 207-624-7220
Lobbyist #1 207-287-6221
Lobster Harvester #27 207-624-6550
Lodging Place #19 207-287-5671
Lottery Retailer #2 207-287-3721
Manicurist #13 207-624-8603
Manufactured Housing #13 207-624-8612
Marine Worm Digger #27 207-624-6550
Marriage & Family Therapist #13 207-624-8626
Mass Gathering #19 207-287-5671
Massage Therapist #13 207-624-8613
Mechanical Ride, Inspection #20 207-626-3800
Medical Doctor #23 207-287-3601
Micropigmentation Practitioner #19 207-287-5671
Mobile Eating Place #19 207-287-5671
Motor Vehicle Race #20 207-626-3800
Naturopathic Physician #13 207-624-8603
Notary Public #24 207-624-7650
Nurse #8 207-287-1133
Nurse, Practical #8 207-287-1133
Nursery School, Inspection #20 207-626-3800
Nursing Home #9 207-287-9300
Nursing Home Administrator #13 207-624-8623
Occupational Therapist #13 207-624-8626
Oil & Solid Fuel Professional/Company #13 207-624-8672
Optometrist #18 207-624-8691
Osteopathic Physician Extender #26 207-287-2480
Osteopathic Physician/Physician Asst #26 207-287-2480
Osteopathic Resident/Intern #26 207-287-2480
Paramedic #10 207-626-3860
Pastoral Counselor #13 207-624-8626
Pesticide Applicator #3 207-287-2731
Pesticide Dealer #3 207-287-2731
Pharmacist #13 207-624-8620
Physical Therapist #13 207-624-8628
Physician Assistant #23 207-287-3601
Pilot #13 207-624-8620
Plumber #13 207-624-8628
Podiatrist #13 207-624-8626
Polygraph Examiner #20 207-626-3800
Preferred Provider Organization #15 207-624-8475
Private Investigator #25 207-624-7210
Propane/Loges Operator/Delivery #13 207-624-8610
Propane/LP Gas Technician #13 207-624-8610
Psychologist #13 207-624-8628
Public Accountant-CPA #13 207-582-8627
Radiologic Technician #13 207-624-8628
Real Estate Appraiser #13 207-624-8616
Real Estate Broker #13 207-624-8603
Recreational Camp #19 207-287-5671
Reinsurance Intermediary #15 207-624-8475
Re-insurer, Approved #15 207-624-8475
Renal Disease (End Stage) Facility #9 207-287-9300
Residential Child Care Provider #7 207-287-5060
Respiratory Care Therapist #13 207-624-8616
Retail/Wholesale Shellfish #27 207-624-6570
Risk Purchasing Group #15 207-624-8475
Risk Retention Group #15 207-624-8475
RN, Advanced Practice #8 207-287-1133
RN, Professional #8 207-287-1133
Savings & Loan #14 207-624-8648
School Feeding #19 207-287-5671
School Guidance Counselor #4 207-624-6603
School Library Media Specialist #4 207-624-6603
School Principal/Superintendent #4 207-624-6603
Sea Urchin Harvester #27 207-624-6550
Seaweed Harvester #27 207-624-6550
Securities Broker-Dealer/Agent #12 207-624-8551
Security Company, Guard/Alarm #25 207-624-7210
Self Insurance Company #15 207-624-8475
Senior Citizen Meal Provider #19 207-287-5671
Snowmobile #11 207-287-2043
Social Worker #13 207-624-8631
Soil Scientist #13 207-624-8603
Speech Pathologist/Audiologist #13 207-624-8634
Storage Tank, Above Ground #20 207-626-3800
Substance Abuse Counselor #13 207-624-8634
Surplus Lines Company #15 207-624-8475
Surveyor, Land #13 207-624-8611
Swimming Pool #19 207-287-5671
Takeout, Food #19 207-287-5671
Tanning Booth #19 207-287-5671
Tattoo Artist #19 207-287-5671
Taxidermist #11 207-287-2751
Teacher #4 207-624-6603
Theatre #20 207-626-3800
Third Party Administrator #15 207-624-8475
Tobacco Retailer #19 207-287-5671
Trust Company #14 207-624-8648
Utilization Review Entity #15 207-624-8475
Vending Machine #19 207-287-5671
Vendor, Itinerant/Transient #13 207-624-8624
Veterinarian/Veterinary Technician #13 207-624-8628
Viatical Settlements Provider #15 207-624-8475
Watercraft #11 207-287-2043
Wrestler #13 207-624-8603
Youth Camp/Children's Camp #19 207-287-5671

Maine Licensing Agency Information

#1 Registrar, Commission on Governmental Ethics & Elections, 135 State House Station, Augusta, ME 04333; 207-287-4179, Fax- 207-287-6775. Hours- 8AM-5PM. www.maine.gov/ethics/ Search data at- www.mainecampaignfinance.com/public/entity_list.asp?TYPE=LOB

#2 Department of Administrative & Financial Services, Bureau of Alcoholic Beverages & Lottery Operations, 8 State House Station, Augusta, ME 04333-0008; 207-287-3721, Fax- 207-287-6769. Hours- 8AM-5PM. www.mainelottery.com Search data at- www.mainelottery.com/players_info/where_to_buy.html

#3 Department of Agriculture, Food & Rural Resources, Board of Pesticides Control, 28 State House Station, Augusta, ME 04332-0028; 207-287-2731, Fax- 207-287-7548. www.maine.gov/agriculture/pesticides/

#4 Department of Education, Certification Office, 23 State House Station, Augusta Complex, Augusta, ME 04333-0023; 207-624-6603, Fax- 207-624-6604. www.maine.gov/education/cert/index.html Make labels for school mailing lists at www.maine.gov/education/labels/labels.htm.

#5 Department of Environmental Protection, Bureau of Air Quality, 17 State House Station, Augusta, ME 04333-0017; 207-287-2437, Fax- 207-287-7641. www.maine.gov/dep/air/

#6 Department of Environmental Protection, Bureau/Hazardous Materials & Solid Waste Control, 17 State House Station, Augusta, ME 04333; 207-287-7688, Fax- 207-287-7826. Hours- 8AM-5PM. www.maine.gov/dep/staff.htm

#7 Department of Human Services, Office of Child Care, 221 State St, 11 State House Station, Augusta, ME 04333-0011; 207-287-5065, Fax- 207-287-5282. www.maine.gov/dhhs/children.shtml#ildcare

#8 Department of Professional & Financial Regulation, Maine State Board of Nursing, 161 Capitol St, 158 State House Station, Augusta, ME 04333-0158; 207-287-1133, Fax- 207-287-1149. Hours- 8AM-4:30PM. www.maine.gov/boardofnursing/ Search data at- https://portalx.bisoex.state.me.us/pls/msbn_nlv/bnxdev.license_search.main_page

#9 Department of Human Services, Division of Licensing and Certification, 11 State House Station, Augusta, ME 04333; 207-287-9300, Fax- 207-287-9304. www.maine.gov/pfr/professionallicensing/index.shtml Search data at- http://pfr.informe.org/ALMSOnline/ALMSQuery/Welcome.aspx

#10 Department of Public Safety, Main Emergency Medical Svcs, 152 State House Station, Augusta, ME 04333-0152; 207-626-3860, Fax- 207-287-6251. Hours- 8AM-5PM. www.maine.gov/dps/ems/

#11 Department of Inland Fisheries & Wildlife, Licensing & Registration Division, 284 State St, 41 Statehouse Station, Augusta, ME 04333-0041; 207-287-8000, Fax- 207-287-8094 or 6395. Hours- 8AM-5PM. www.maine.gov/ifw/licenses_permits/index.htm#censes

#12 Department of Professional & Financial Regulation, Office of Securities, 121 State House Station, Augusta, ME 04333; 207-624-8551, Fax- 207-624-8590. Hours- 8AM-5PM. www.maine.gov/pfr/securities/index.shtml Search data at- http://pfr.informe.org/ALMSOnline/ALMSQuery/Welcome.aspx

#13 Department of Professional & Financial Regulation, Office of Licensing & Registration, 35 State House Station, Augusta, ME 04333-0035; 207-624-8603, Fax- 207-624-8637. www.maine.gov/pfr/professionallicensing/professions.htm Search data at- http://pfr.informe.org/ALMSOnline/ALMSQuery/Welcome.aspx

#14 Department of Professional & Financial Regulation, Bureau of Financial Institutions, 36 State House Station, Augusta, ME 04333-0036; 207-624-8570, Fax- 207-624-8590. www.maine.gov/pfr/financialinstitutions/index.shtml

#15 Department of Professional & Financial Regulation, Bureau of Insurance, #34 State House Station, Augusta, ME 04333-0034; 207-624-8475 or 800-300-5000, Fax- 207-624-8599. www.maine.gov/pfr/insurance/ Search data athttp://pfr.informe.org/almsonline/almsquery/welcome.aspx?board=1040

#16 Board of Dental Examiners, 143 Statehouse Station, 161 Capitol St, Augusta, ME 04333-0143; 207-287-3333, Fax- 207-287-8140. Hours- 8AM-4:30PM. www.mainedental.org Search data at- http://pfr.informe.org/ALMSOnline/ALMSQuery/Welcome.aspx To obtain lists of the above, contact Kim Haggan at 207-287-5459.

#17 Professional Engineers Board of Licensure, 92 State House Station, Augusta, ME 04333; 207-287-3236, Fax- 207-626-2309. 8AM-4:30PM. https://www.maine.gov/professionalengineers/ Search data at- https://www.maine.gov/professionalengineers/database.shtml

#18 Department of Professional & Financial Regulation, Board of Optometry, 113 State House Station, Augusta, ME 04333; 207-624-8691, Fax- 207-624-8692. Hours- 8AM-2PM. www.maine.gov/pfr/auxboards/optometry/ Search data at- http://pfr.informe.org/ALMSOnline/ALMSQuery/Welcome.aspx

#19 Department of Health and Human Services, Division of Environmental Health, 11 State House Station (286 Water St, 3rd Fl), Augusta, ME 04333-0011; 207-287-5671, Fax- 207-287-3165. www.maine.gov/dhhs/eng/el/ Written requests may be mailed or faxed, only.

#20 Department of Public Safety, Administrative Licensing & Permits, 45 Commerce Dr #1, 104 State House Station, Augusta, ME 04333-0042; 207-626-3800, Fax- 207-626-3838. www.maine.gov/dps/lisc.htm

#21 Department of Public Safety, Liquor Licensing & Compliance, 164 State House Station, Augusta, ME 04333-0164; 207-624-7220, Fax- 207-287-3424. www.maine.gov/dps/lisc.htm Search data at- www.maine.gov/dps/liqr/active_licenses.htm

#22 Board of Overseers of the Bar, PO Box 527 (97 Winthrop St), Augusta, ME 04332; 207-623-1121, Fax- 207-623-4175. www.mebaroverseers.org

#23 Medical Doctor & Physician Assistant Licensing & Investigation, Board of Licensure in Medicine, 137 State House Station, 161 Capitol St, Augusta, ME 04333; 207-287-3601, Fax- 207-287-6590. www.docboard.org/me/me_home.htm Search data at- www.docboard.org/me/licensure/dw_verification.html

#24 Secretary of State, Div of Elections & Commissions, Notary Public Section, 101 State House Station, Augusta, ME 04333-0101; 207-624-7650, Fax- 207-287-6545. www.maine.gov/sos/cec/notary/notaries.html Search data at- www.maine.gov/online/notary/search/

#25 Department of Public Safety, State Police Licensing Division, 42 State House Station, 45 Commerce Dr, Augusta, ME 04333-0042; 207-626-3811, Fax- 207-287-3424. www.maine.gov/dps/msp/index.shtml

#26 Board of Osteopathic Licensure, 142 State House Station, 161 Capitol St, Augusta, ME 04333-0142; 207-287-2480, Fax- 207-287-3015. www.maine.gov/osteo/ Search data at- www.docboard.org/me-osteo/df/index.htm

#27 Department of Marine Resources, 21 State House Station, Hallowell Annex-Baker Bldg, Augusta, ME 04333-0021; 207-624-6550, Fax- 207-624-6024. www.maine.gov/dmr/index.htm

Maine Federal Courts

The following list indicates the district and division name for each county in the state. If the bankruptcy court location is different from the district court, then the location of the bankruptcy court appears in parentheses.

County/Court Cross Reference

County	Court	County	Court
Androscoggin	Portland	Oxford	Portland
Aroostook	Bangor	Penobscot	Bangor
Cumberland	Portland	Piscataquis	Bangor
Franklin	Bangor	Sagadahoc	Portland
Hancock	Bangor	Somerset	Bangor
Kennebec	Bangor	Waldo	Bangor
Knox	Portland (Bangor)	Washington	Bangor
Lincoln	Portland (Bangor)	York	Portland

US District Court District of Maine

Bangor Division Court Clerk, 202 Harlow St, Rm 357, Bangor, ME 04401, 207-945-0575; Fax- 207-945-0362. Hours- 8AM - 5PM. www.med.uscourts.gov

Counties/Note: Aroostook, Franklin, Hancock, Kennebec, Penobscot, Piscataquis, Somerset, Waldo, Washington.

Searches/Indexing: Search request requires name only. Results include partial DOB, last 4 SSN digits. Will not fax back documents. New cases are in the index immediately after filing date. Computer index is alpha by name. Records stored by year, then docket number for case files. There is no set date when closed files sent to archives.

Search Access: Any public record info is released via phone including accession number. **Mail:** Search usually completed- 1-2 days. SASE not required. **In person:** 1 public terminal available. No self-serve copier.

Payment: Pay by Visa/MC/Discover, money order, cashier's or personal check. Payee: Clerk, US District Court.

E-Services: PACER records go back to 8/1991. New records online after 1 day. ECF at https://ecf.med.uscourts.gov. **Opinions Online:** www.med.uscourts.gov/rulesandopinions.htm.

Portland Division Court Clerk, 156 Federal St, Portland, ME 04101, 207-780-3356; Fax- 207-780-3772. Hours- 8AM - 4:30PM. www.med.uscourts.gov

Counties: Androscoggin, Cumberland, Knox, Lincoln, Oxford, Sagadahoc, York.

Searches/Indexing: Search request requires name only. Results include partial DOB, last 4 SSN digits. Will not fax back documents. New cases are in the index immediately after filing date. Computer index back to 1990 maintained; index is alpha by name. Records stored by year, then docket number for case files. There is no set date when closed case files sent to archives.

Search Access: Any public record info is released via phone including accession number. **Mail:** Search usually completed- 1-2 days. SASE not required. **In person:** 1 public terminal available. No self-serve copier.

Payment: Pay by Visa/MC/Discover, money order, cashier's or personal check. Payee: Clerk, US District Court.

E-Services: PACER records go back to 8/1991. ECF at https://ecf.med.uscourts.gov. **Opinions:** www.med.uscourts.gov/rulesandopinions.htm.

US Bankruptcy Court District of Maine

Bangor Division Court Clerk, 202 Harlow St #331, Bangor, ME 04401, 207-945-0348; Fax- 207-945-0304. Hours-8:30AM-1PM; 2-4:30PM. www.meb.uscourts.gov

Counties/Note: Aroostook, Franklin, Hancock, Kennebec, Knox, Lincoln, Penobscot, Piscataquis, Somerset, Waldo, Washington.

Searches/Indexing: Include name only in search request. Results include last 4 SSN digits only. Will not fax back documents. New cases are in the index immediately after filing date. Computer index goes back to 1984; prior on index cards to 1984. District-wide searches available here. Case files sent to archives 2 years after closed.

Search Access: Only docket info available by phone. Voice Case Information Service available, call VCIS at 800-650-7253 or 207-780-3755. **Mail:** Search usually completed- 1 week. SASE not required. **In person:** 1 public terminal available. No self-serve copier.

Payment: Pay by Visa/MC, money order, cashier's check, business check. No personal checks. Payee: US Courts. Prepayment required for individual requesters.

E-Services: PACER records go back to 12/1988. New records online immediately. ECF at https://ecf.meb.uscourts.gov. **Opinions Online:** Judges' opinions accessible via the main webpage. **Online Note:** Unclaimed funds info at www.meb.uscourts.gov/w_unclaimed_funds.html.

Portland Division Court Clerk, 537 Congress St, 2nd Fl, Portland, ME 04101, 207-780-3482; Fax- 207-780-3679. 8:30AM-1PM; 2-4:30PM. www.meb.uscourts.gov

Counties: Androscoggin, Cumberland, Oxford, Sagadahoc, York.

Searches/Indexing: Include name only in search request. Results include last 4 SSN digits. Will not fax back documents. New cases are in the index immediately after filing date. Computer index goes back to 1984; prior on index cards to 1984. District-wide searches available here. Information through VCIS and ECF available 24 hours after docketing. Case files sent to archives 2 years after closed.

Search Access: Only docket info available by phone. Voice Case Information Service available, call VCIS at 800-650-7253 or 207-780-3755. **Mail:** Search usually completed- 1 day. Include SASE for return. **In person:** 1 public terminal available. No self-serve copier.

Payment: Pay by Visa/MC, money order, cashier's check, business check. No personal checks. Payee: US Bankruptcy Court. Prepayment required for individual requesters.

E-Services: PACER records go back to 12/1988. New records online after 1 day. ECF at https://ecf.meb.uscourts.gov. **Opinions Online:** Judges' opinions accessible via the main webpage. **Online Note:** Unclaimed funds info at www.meb.uscourts.gov/w_unclaimed_funds.html.

Standards for Federal Courts: Fees are standard unless noted in profile. Search fee is $26.00 per item (one party name or case number). Copy fee is $.50 per page. Certification fee is $9.00 per document, double for exemplification, if available. Most courts require prepayment. Mail requests should enclose a SASE unless otherwise noted. Before releasing records, all courts require prepayment, unless noted.

District courts index by defendant and plaintiff and by case number. Bankruptcy courts usually index by debtor and case number. While most courts now have their indexes on computer, many may still maintain index card files as well. Courts will archive closed case files at different times.

There are numerous public access programs available to online subscribers. Search the U.S. Party/Case Index to find party names and case numbers among all courts. Individual case data is provided on PACER. A search of CM/ECF provides copies of cases filed electronically. For details about PACER, the US Party/Case Index, and CM/ECF see the Appendix or go to http://pacer.psc.uscourts.gov or call 800-676-6856.

Maine County Courts

Court	Jurisdiction	No. of Courts	How Organized
Superior Courts*	General	17	16 Counties
District Courts*	Limited	31	13 Districts
Probate Courts*	Special	16	

* Profiled in this Sourcebook.

	CIVIL								
Court	Tort	Contract	Real Estate	Min. Claim	Max. Claim	Small Claim	Estate	Eviction	Domestic Relations
Superior Courts*	X	X	X	No Min	No Max				X
District Courts*	X	X	X	No Min	No Max	$4500		X	X
Probate Courts*							X		X

	CRIMINAL				
Court	Felony	Misdemeanor	DWI/DUI	Preliminary Hearing	Juvenile
Superior Courts*	X	X	X	X	
District Courts*	X	X	X	X	X
Probate Courts*					

Administration

State Court Administrator, PO Box 4820, Portland, ME, 04112; 207-822-0792, Fax: 207-822-0781. (EST) www.courts.state.me.us

Court Structure

A Superior Court – the court of general jurisdiction – is located in each of Maine's sixteen counties, except for Aroostook County which has two Superior Courts. Both Superior and District Courts handle misdemeanor and felony cases, with jury trials being held in Superior Court only. The District Court hears both civil and criminal and always sits without a jury.

Within the District Court is the Family Division, which hears all divorce and family matters, including child support and paternity cases. The District Court also hears child protection cases, and serves as Maine's juvenile court. Actions for protection from abuse or harassment, mental health, small claims cases, and money judgments are filed in the District Court. Traffic violations are processed primarily through a centralized Violations Bureau, part of the District Court system. Prior to year 2001, District Courts accepted civil cases involving claims less than $30,000. Now, District Courts have jurisdiction concurrent with that of the Superior Court for all civil actions, except cases vested in the Superior Court by statute.

Probate Courts are part of the county court system, not the state system. Although the Probate Court may be housed with other state courts, the court is generally on a different phone system and calls may not be transferred.

Online Access

The website offers access to Maine Supreme Court opinions and administrative orders, but not all documents are available online. Also, the website offers access to trial court schedules by region and case type. Some county level courts are online through a private vendor. Prepayment is required, unless otherwise noted.

Search probate records free at https://www.maineprobate.net/index.html. Images are $2.00 each if you are not registered; $1.00 each if you subscribe.

Searching Tips, Fees, and Other Guidelines

Per administrative order, Maine Superior and District Court search fees are as follows: 1) $15.00 for a search; 2) copy fee: 1st page is $2.00, $1.00 each additional; 3) if your mail request does not include a self-addressed stamped envelope, then add an additional $5.00. Some courts offer a free search if only one name is submitted. Some courts will search both the civil and criminal indices for $15.00.

Most mail requests of a name search for full criminal history record information are returned to the sender, referring them to the State Bureau of Investigation. Mail requests that make a specific inquiry related to an identified case are responded to in writing. You must also include all appropriate copy and attestation fees.

Androscoggin County

Androscoggin Superior Court PO Box 3660, Auburn, ME 04212-3660; 207-783-5450; 8AM-4PM. ***Felony, Misdemeanor, Civil Actions.***

Civil Records: Access: Mail, in person. Only the court performs in person searches; visitors may not. Search fee: $15.00, includes both civil and criminal. Required to search: name, years to search; also helpful: address. Civil cases indexed by defendant, plaintiff; index on cards since 1977. Mail turnaround 1 wk. Public terminal has civil records.

Criminal Records: Access: Mail, in person. Only the court performs in person searches; visitors may not. Search fee: $15.00, includes both civil and criminal. Required to search: name, years to search; also helpful: DOB. Criminal records go back to 1920s; computer to 1998. Mail turnaround 1 wk.

General Information: No adoption, juvenile, impounded by judge, certain domestic matters. Will not fax documents. Court makes copy: $2.00 1st page, $1.00 each add'l. Certification fee: $5.00 per doc. Payee: Androscoggin Superior Court. Personal checks & Visa/MC accepted. Mail requests: SASE required.

Lewiston District Court - South 8 PO Box 1345, 71 Lisbon St, Lewiston, ME 04243-1345; criminal phone: 207-795-4800; civil: 207-795-4801; 8AM-4PM. ***Misdemeanor, Civil Actions, Eviction, Small Claims.***

Civil Records: Access: Mail, in person. Both court and visitors may perform in person searches. Search fee: $15.00, includes both civil and criminal. Required to search: name, years to search; also helpful: address. Civil cases indexed by defendant. Civil index in docket books from 1980-1987; on computer back to 1987. Mail turnaround time up to 2 weeks.
Criminal Records: Access: Mail, in person. Both court and visitors may perform in person searches. Search fee: $15.00, includes both civil and criminal. Required to search: name, years to search, DOB; also helpful: address, SSN. Criminal records computerized from 1987, docket books from 1956-1987. Mail turnaround time up to 2 weeks.
General Information: No juvenile, protective custody records released. Will not fax documents. Court makes copy: $2.00 1st page, $1.00 each add'l. Certification fee: $5.00 per doc. Payee: Maine District Court. Personal checks and major credit cards accepted. Mail requests: SASE required.

Probate Court 2 Turner St, Unit 5, Auburn, ME 04210; 207-782-0281; fax: 207-782-1135; 8:30AM-5PM. ***Probate.*** Search probate records free at https://www.maineprobate.net/index.html. $2 fee for images, $1 if registered.

Aroostook County

Caribou Superior Court 144 Sweden St, #101, Caribou, ME 04736; 207-498-8125; 8AM-4PM. ***Felony, Misdemeanor, Civil Actions.***
Civil Records: Access: Mail, in person. Only the court performs in person searches; visitors may not. Search fee: One name no fee, two or more $15.00 each, includes both civil and criminal. Required to search: name, DOB, years to search. Civil cases indexed by defendant, plaintiff; index on docket books since 1960. All cases 1990 forward stored in Caribou Court. Mail turnaround time 1 week.
Criminal Records: Access: Mail, in person. Only the court performs in person searches; visitors may not. Search fee: One name no fee, two or more $15.00 each, includes both civil and criminal. Required to search: name, years to search; also helpful: DOB. Criminal docket on books since 1960. All cases 1990 forward stored in Caribou Court. Mail turnaround time 1 week.
General Information: No juvenile, protective custody records released. Will not fax documents. Court makes copy: $2.00 1st page, $1.00 each add'l. Certification fee: $5.00. Payee: Treasurer, State of Maine or Superior Court. Personal checks accepted. Credit cards accepted. Mail requests: SASE required.

Houlton Superior Court 144 Sweden St, #101, Caribou, ME 04736; 207-532-6563; 8AM-4PM. ***Felony, Misdemeanor, Civil Actions.***
The Court only holds record prior to 1990. All cases are located at the Superior Court in Caribou, address Given here.

Caribou District Court - East 1 144 Sweden St, Caribou, ME 04736; 207-493-3144; 8AM-4PM. ***Misdemeanor, Civil Actions, Eviction, Small Claims.***
Civil Records: Access: Mail, in person. Only the court performs in person searches; visitors may not. Search fee: First name free, then $15.00, includes both civil and criminal. Required to search: name, years to search. Civil cases indexed by defendant. Civil index on docket books since 1963, on computer from 10/01. Mail turnaround time 1 week.
Criminal Records: Access: Mail, in person. Only the court performs in person searches; visitors may not. Search fee: First name free, then $15.00, includes both civil and criminal. Required to search: name, years to search; also helpful: DOB. Criminal records on computer since 1987 (includes traffic), docket books since 1963. Note: DOB appears on criminal search result. Mail turnaround time 1 week.
General Information: No juvenile or child protective records released. Will not fax documents. Court makes copy: $2.00 1st page, $1.00 each add'l. Certification fee: $5.00 per page. Payee: Maine District Court. Personal checks accepted. Credit cards accepted. Mail requests: SASE required.

District Court 2 PO Box 794, 27 Riverside Dr, Presque Isle, ME 04769; 207-764-2055; fax: 207-764-2057; 8AM-4PM. ***Misdemeanor, Civil Actions, Eviction, Small Claims.***
Civil Records: Access: Mail, in person. Both court and visitors may perform in person searches. Search fee: $15.00 per name. Required to search: name, years to search. Civil cases indexed by defendant. Civil records on computer since 1999, docket books since 1963. Mail turnaround time 1 week.
Criminal Records: Access: Mail, in person. Visitors must perform in person searches themselves. Search fee: $15.00 per name. Required to search: name, years to search; also helpful: DOB. Criminal records on computer since 1987, docket books since 1963. Mail turnaround time 1 week.
General Information: No juvenile or child protective records released. Will not fax documents. Court makes copy: $2.00 1st page, $1.00 each add'l. Certification fee: $5.00. Payee: Maine District Court. Personal checks accepted. Visa/MC accepted. Mail requests: SASE required or $5.00 postage fee.

Fort Kent District Court - District 1 Division of Western Aroostook, PO Box 473, Fort Kent, ME 04743; 207-834-5003; 8AM-4PM. ***Misdemeanor, Civil Actions, Eviction, Small Claims.***
Civil Records: Access: Phone, mail, in person. Only the court performs in person searches; visitors may not. Search fee: $15.00, includes both civil and criminal. Required to search: name, years to search. Civil cases indexed by defendant, plaintiff, are computerized since 8/2001. Mail turnaround time within 5 days.
Criminal Records: Access: Phone, mail, in person. Only the court performs in person searches; visitors may not. Search fee: $15.00, includes both civil and criminal. Required to search: name, years to search. Criminal records computerized from 1988, on docket books from 1960-1988. Mail turnaround time 2-3 days.
General Information: No juvenile, protective custody, impounded, mental health records released. Will not fax documents. Court makes copy: $2.00 1st page, $1.00 each add'l. Certification fee: $5.00 for attestation. Payee: Maine District Court. Personal checks accepted. Credit cards accepted. Mail requests: SASE required.

Houlton District Court - South 2 PO Box 457, Houlton, ME 04730; 207-532-2147; 8AM-4PM. ***Misdemeanor, Civil Actions, Eviction, Small Claims.***
Civil Records: Access: Mail, in person. Both court and visitors may perform in person searches. Search fee: $15.00, includes both civil and criminal. Required to search: name, years to search; also helpful: address. Civil cases indexed by defendant, plaintiff; index on docket books since 1960. Mail turnaround time 5-7 days.
Criminal Records: Access: Mail, in person. Only the court performs in person searches; visitors may not. Search fee: $15.00, includes both civil and criminal. Required to search: name, years to search; also helpful: address, DOB. Criminal records on computer since 6/1987, docket books since 1960. Mail turnaround time 5-7 days.
General Information: No Juvenile or protective custody records released. Will not fax documents. Court makes copy: $1.00 per page. Certification fee: $5.00. Payee: Maine District Court. Personal checks accepted. Credit cards accepted. Mail requests: SASE required.

Madawaska District Court - West c/o Fort Kent District Court, PO Box 473, Fort Kent, ME 04743; 207-728-4700; 8AM-4PM M,T,F. ***Misdemeanor, Civil Actions, Eviction, Small Claims.***
This court, physically located on 645 E Main in Madawaska, is only open 2 days a month. All case files are in Fort Kent; see that District Court to obtain records.

Probate Court 26 Court St #103, Houlton, ME 04730; 207-532-1502; 8AM-4:30PM. ***Probate.***
Search probate records free at https://www.maineprobate.net/index.html. $2 fee for images, $1 if registered.

Cumberland County

Superior Court - Civil 142 Federal St, Portland, ME 04101; 207-822-4105; criminal phone: 207-822-4113; civil phone: 207-822-4105; 8AM-4PM. ***Civil Actions.***
The search fees and copy fees listed are mandatory per administrative rule. If a SASE not supplied for mail searches, court will charge an add'l $5.00.
Civil Records: Access: In person. Both court and visitors may perform in person searches. Search fee: $15.00 per name, but if only one name then free. Required to search: name, years to search. Civil cases indexed by defendant, plaintiff; index on cards since 1975, prior records archived. Note: Court will only answer general questions on filing and hearing dates by phone or mail.
General Information: No juvenile, medical malpractice, impounded records released. Will not fax documents. Court makes copy: $2.00 1st page, $1.00 each add'l. Certification fee: $5.00. Payee: Superior Court. Personal checks and credit cards accepted.

Unified Superior Court - Criminal 142 Federal St, Portland, ME 04101; 207-822-4113; criminal phone: 207-822-4204; 8AM-4PM. ***Felony, Misdemeanor.*** www.cumberlandcounty.org/
Now has records for the old Portland District Court - South 9 Criminal (Misdemeanors). **Criminal Records:** Access: Mail, in person. Both court and visitors may perform in person searches. Search fee: $15.00, includes both felonies and misdemeanors. Required to search: name, years to search, DOB. Criminal records indexed on cards since 1900s, some records from 8/98 to present are computerized. Mail turnaround time 2-3 days. The search includes search of records from the old Portland District Court.
General Information: No juvenile records released. Will not fax documents. Court makes copy: $2.00 1st page, $1.00 each add'l. Certification fee: $5.00. Payee: Clerk of Courts. Personal checks accepted; credit cards are not. Mail requests: SASE required.

Portland District Court - South 9 Civil PO Box 412, 205 Newbury St, Portland, ME 04112; 207-822-4200; 8AM-4PM. ***Civil Actions, Eviction, Small Claims.***
Also see Sagadahoc District Court, which handles cases from eastern Cumberland County. Also see Brighton District Court which handles cases from western Cumberland County.
Civil Records: Access: In person. Both court and visitors may perform in person searches. Search fee: $15.00, includes both civil and criminal. Required to search: name, years to search. Civil cases indexed by defendant. Civil records go back ten years, small claims and eviction five years.
General Information: No child custody records released. Will not fax documents. Court makes copy: $2.00 1st page, $1.00 each add'l. Certification fee: $5.00 per doc. Payee: Maine District Court. Personal checks accepted; credit cards are not. Mail requests: If a SASE not supplied for mail searches, court may charge add'l $5.00.

Bath District Court - East 6 147 New Meadows Rd, West Bath, ME 04530; 207-442-0200; 8AM-4PM. ***Misdemeanor, Civil Actions, Eviction, Small Claims.***
Combined with West Bath District Court 6 in Sagadahoc County.

Bridgton District Court - North 9 3 Chase St, #2, Bridgton, ME 04009; 207-647-3535; 8AM-4PM. ***Misdemeanor, Civil Actions, Eviction, Small Claims.***
Civil Records: Access: Phone, mail, in person. Visitors must perform in person searches themselves. Search fee: $15.00, includes both civil and criminal. Required to search: name, years to search. Civil cases indexed by defendant. Civil records go back to 1965; on computer back to 2001. Mail turnaround time 5 days.
Criminal Records: Access: Phone, mail, in person. Only the court performs in person searches; visitors may not. Search fee: $15.00, includes both civil and criminal. Required to search: name, years to search; also helpful: DOB. Criminal records

computerized from 1986, records go back to 1965. Mail turnaround time 5 days. Public use terminal has crim records back to 1988.PAT results show name, DOB. Terminal is not currently available.
General Information: No juvenile, protective custody, financial affidavits, impounded or domestic records released. Will not fax documents. Court makes copy: $2.00 1st page, $1.00 each add'l. Certification fee: $5.00 per doc. Payee: Maine District Court. Personal checks and major credit cards accepted. Mail requests: SASE required.

Probate Court 142 Federal St, #125, Portland, ME 04101-4196; 207-871-8382; fax: 207-791-2658; 8:30AM-4:15PM. ***Probate.***
www.cumberlandcounty.org Search probate records free at https://www.maineprobate.net/index.html. $2 fee for images, $1 if registered.

Franklin County

Superior Court 140 Main St, Farmington, ME 04938; 207-778-3346; 8AM-4PM. ***Felony, Misdemeanor, Civil Actions.***
Civil Records: Access: Mail, in person. Both court and visitors may perform in person searches. Search fee: $15.00 per name, includes both civil and criminal. Required to search: name, years to search. Civil cases indexed by defendant, plaintiff; index on docket books and index cards since 1900s. Mail turnaround time 1 week.
Criminal Records: Access: Mail, in person. Only the court performs in person searches; visitors may not. Search fee: $15.00 per name, includes both civil and criminal. Required to search: name, years to search; also helpful: DOB, SSN. Criminal docket on books and index cards since 1900s. Mail turnaround time 1 week.
General Information: No juvenile, impounded or medical malpractice records released. Will not fax documents. Court makes copy: $2.00 1st page, $1.00 each add'l. Certification fee: $5.00 per document. Payee: Superior Court. Personal checks accepted. Credit cards accepted. Mail requests: SASE required.

Franklin District Court 12 129 Main St, Farmington, ME 04938; 207-778-8200; 8AM-4PM. ***Misdemeanor, Civil Actions, Eviction, Small Claims.***
The search fees and copy fees listed are mandatory per administrative rule.
Civil Records: Access: Mail, in person. Visitors must perform in person searches themselves. Search fee: $15.00 if request for more than one name. Required to search: name, years to search. Civil cases indexed by defendant. Civil index on docket books since 1965 (index cards in front). Mail turnaround time 1 week.
Criminal Records: Access: Mail, in person. Only the court performs in person searches; visitors may not. Search fee: $15.00 if request for more than one name. Required to search: name, years to search, DOB. Criminal records on computer since 1987, on docket books since 1965 (index cards in front). Mail turnaround time 1 week.
General Information: No impounded records released. Will not fax documents. Court makes copy: $2.00 1st page, $1.00 each add'l. Certification fee: $5.00 per document. Add $1.00 per page copy fee on to cert fee. Payee: Maine District Court. Personal checks accepted. Credit cards accepted.

Probate Court 140 Main St, County Courthouse, Farmington, ME 04938; 207-778-5888; fax: 207-778-5899; 8:30AM-4PM. ***Probate.***
Search probate records free at https://www.maineprobate.net/index.html. $2 fee for images, $1 if registered.

Hancock County

Superior Court 50 State St, Ellsworth, ME 04605-1926; 207-667-7176; 8AM-4PM. ***Felony, Misdemeanor, Civil Actions.***
The search fees and copy fees listed are mandatory per administrative rule.
Civil Records: Access: Mail, in person. Only the court performs in person searches; visitors may not. Search fee: $15.00 per name, if multiples. Required to search: name, years to search. Civil cases indexed by defendant, plaintiff, on card files since 1960. Mail turnaround time 1 day.
Criminal Records: Access: Mail, person only. Only the court performs in person searches; visitors may not. Search fee: $15.00 per name, if multiples. Required to search: name, years to search, DOB. Criminal records on card files since 1960. Mail turnaround time 1 day.
General Information: No protective custody records released. Will not fax documents. Court makes copy: $2.00 1st page, $1.00 each add'l.They will bill you for copies, but search fee must be paid up front. Certification fee: $5.00 per cert. Payee: State of Maine. Personal checks and major credit cards accepted. Mail requests: SASE required.

Ellsworth District Court - Central 5 50 State St #2, Ellsworth, ME 04605; 207-667-7141; 8AM-4PM. ***Misdemeanor, Civil Actions, Eviction, Small Claims.***
The search fees and copy fees listed are mandatory per administrative rule. The Bar Harbor District Court - South 5 merged with this court in July 2005. Records are co-mingled.
Civil Records: Access: Mail, in person. Both court and visitors may perform in person searches. Search fee: $15.00, includes both civil and criminal. Required to search: name, years to search. Civil cases indexed by defendant, plaintiff. Need to know names of both parties to search. Civil index on docket books since 1965; on computer back to 10/01. Mail turnaround 1 week. Public use terminal available.
Criminal Records: Access: Mail, in person. Only the court performs in person searches; visitors may not. Search fee: $15.00, includes both civil and criminal. Required to search: name, years to search, DOB. Criminal records computerized from 1987, docket books since 1965. Mail turnaround time 1 week. Public use terminal available.
General Information: No juvenile, child protection, adoption or mental health records released. Will not fax documents. Court makes copy: $2.00 1st page, $1.00 each add'l. Certification fee: $5.00 per document. Payee: Maine District Court. Personal checks accepted. Visa/MC accepted. Mail requests: SASE required.

Probate Court 50 State St, #6, Ellsworth, ME 04605; 207-667-8434; probate phone: 207-667-9098; fax: 207-667-5316; 8:30AM-4PM. ***Probate.***
Search probate records free at https://www.maineprobate.net/index.html. $2 fee for images, $1 if registered.

Kennebec County

Superior Court 95 State St, Clerk of Court, Augusta, ME 04330; 207-624-5800; fax: 207-287-9057; 8AM-4PM. ***Felony, Misdemeanor, Civil Actions.*** www.courts.state.me.us/mainecourts/superior/superior_augusta.html
The search fees and copy fees listed are mandatory per administrative rule.
Civil Records: Access: In person only. Only the court performs in person searches; visitors may not. Search fee: 1st search free, then $15.00 per case. Required to search: name, years to search. Civil cases indexed by defendant, plaintiff; index on cards since 1977, docket books since 1970, on computer 2 years.
Criminal Records: Access: In person only. Only the court performs in person searches; visitors may not. Search fee: 1st search free, then $15.00 per case. Required to search: name, years to search; also helpful: DOB, docket number. Criminal records indexed on cards since 1977, docket books since 1978, on computer 5 years.
General Information: No protective custody records released. Will not fax documents. Court makes copy: $2.00 1st page, $1.00 each add'l. Certification fee: $5.00 per doc. Payee: Treasurer State of Maine. Personal checks and major credit cards accepted.

Maine District Court 7 Division of Southern Kennebec, 145 State St, Augusta, ME 04330-7495; 207-287-8075; fax: 207-287-8082; 8AM-4PM. ***Misdemeanor, Civil Actions, Eviction, Small Claims.***
Civil Records: Access: Mail, in person. Both court and visitors may perform in person searches. Search fee: $15.00, includes both civil and criminal. Required to search: name, years to search. Civil cases indexed by defendant. Civil records kept 10 years. Mail turnaround time 1 week.
Criminal Records: Access: Mail, in person. Only the court performs in person searches; visitors may not. Search fee: $15.00, includes both civil and criminal. Required to search: name, years to search, DOB; also helpful: SSN. Criminal records computerized from 1987, docket books since 1963. Mail turnaround time 1 week.
General Information: No juvenile, mental health, protective custody and closed proceeding case records released. Will not fax documents. Court makes copy: $2.00 1st page, $1.00 each add'l. Certification fee: $5.00 per doc. Payee: Maine District Court. Personal checks accepted. Visa/MC accepted. Mail requests: SASE required.

Waterville District Court - District 7 18 Colby St, Waterville, ME 04901; 207-873-2103; 8AM-4PM. ***Misdemeanor, Civil Actions, Eviction, Small Claims.***
www.courts.state.me.us/mainecourts/district/district_waterville.html
Civil Records: Access: Mail, in person. Both court and visitors may perform in person searches. Search fee: $15.00, includes both civil and criminal. Required to search: name, years to search; also helpful: address. Civil cases indexed by defendant. Civil records on computer since 2001. Docket books from 1979-1987 are archived. Mail turnaround time 1 week.
Criminal Records: Access: Mail, in person. Both court and visitors may perform in person searches. Search fee: $15.00, includes both civil and criminal. Required to search: name, years to search, DOB; also helpful: address, SSN. Criminal records on computer since 1999. Docket books from 1979-1987 are archived. Mail turnaround time 2 weeks.
General Information: No juvenile, protective custody records released. Court reserves the right to restrict the number of record requests. Will not fax documents. Court makes copy: $2.00 1st page, $1.00 each add'l. Certification fee: $5.00 per doc. Payee: Maine District Court. Personal checks accepted. Credit cards accepted. Mail requests: SASE required.

Probate Court 95 State St, Augusta, ME 04330; 207-622-7558 or 207-622-7559; fax: 207-621-1639; 8AM-4PM. ***Probate.***
www.datamaine.com/probate
Search dockets back to 1995 online at www.datamaine.com/probate/docket.html. Also, search probate records free at https://www.maineprobate.net/index.html. $2 fee for docs, $1 if registered.

Knox County

Superior Court 62 Union St, Rockland, ME 04841-2836; 207-594-2576; fax: 207-596-2251; 8AM-4PM. ***Felony, Misdemeanor, Civil Actions.***
Civil Records: Access: Mail, in person. Only the court performs in person searches; visitors may not. Search fee: $15.00, includes both civil and criminal. Required to search: name, years to search. Civil cases indexed by defendant, plaintiff; index on docket books since 1930s, index cards (in office) since mid-1970s; on computer back to 1999. Mail turnaround time 1 week.
Criminal Records: Access: Mail, in person. Only the court performs in person searches; visitors may not. Search fee: $15.00, includes both civil and criminal. Required to search: name, years to search; also helpful: DOB, middle initial. Criminal docket on books since 1930s, index cards (in office) since mid-1970s; on computer back to 1999. Mail turnaround time 1 week.
General Information: No Impounded or pre-sentence records released. Will not fax documents. Court makes copy: $2.00 1st page, $1.00 each add'l. Certification fee: $5.00. Payee: State Treasurer. Personal checks accepted. Visa/MC accepted. Mail requests: SASE required.

District Court 6 62 Union St, Rockland, ME 04841; 207-596-2240; probate phone: 207-594-0427; 8AM-4PM. ***Misdemeanor, Civil Actions, Eviction, Small Claims.***

Search fee includes both civil and criminal indexes. **Civil Records:** Access: Mail, in person. Only the court performs in person searches; visitors may not. Search fee: First search is free, each add'l search $15.00 per name. Required to search: name, years to search. Civil cases indexed by defendant, plaintiff; index on docket books back to the 1970's. Mail turnaround time 3-4 days.
Criminal Records: Access: Mail, in person. Only the court performs in person searches; visitors may not. Search fee: First search is free, each add'l search $15.00 per name. Required to search: name, years to search, DOB. Criminal docket on books back to 1989. Mail turnaround time 3-4 days.
General Information: No impounded records released. Will not fax documents. Court makes copy: $2.00 1st page, $1.00 each add'l. Certification fee: $5.00 per cert. Payee: Maine District Court. Personal checks accepted. Visa/MC accepted. Mail requests: SASE required.

Probate Court 62 Union St, Rockland, ME 04841; 207-594-0427; fax: 207-594-0863; 8AM-4PM. ***Probate.*** http://knoxcounty.midcoast.com
Search probate records free at https://www.maineprobate.net/index.html. $2 fee for images, $1 if registered.

Lincoln County

Lincoln County Superior Court High St, PO Box 249, Wiscasset, ME 04578; 207-882-7517; fax: 207-882-7741; 8AM-4PM. ***Felony, Misdemeanor, Civil Actions.***
Civil Records: Access: Mail, in person. Only the court performs in person searches; visitors may not. Search fee: No fee to search 1 case per day; each add'l search is $15.00, includes both civil and criminal. Required to search: name, years to search. Civil cases indexed by defendant, plaintiff; index on docket books and index cards since 1960s. Mail turnaround time 1-2 days.
Criminal Records: Access: Mail, in person. Only the court performs in person searches; visitors may not. Search fee: No fee to search 1 case per day; each add'l search is $15.00, includes both civil and criminal. Required to search: name, years to search, DOB. Criminal docket on books and index cards since 1960s. Mail turnaround time 1-2 days.
General Information: No protective custody records released. Will not fax documents. Court makes copy: $2.00 1st page, $1.00 each add'l. Certification fee: $5.00. Payee: Lincoln County Superior Court. Personal checks and major credit cards accepted. Mail requests: SASE required.

District Court 6 32 High St, PO Box 249, Wiscasset, ME 04578; 207-882-6363; criminal fax: 207-882-5980; civil fax: same; 8AM-4PM. ***Misdemeanor, Civil Actions, Eviction, Small Claims.*** www.co.lincoln.me.us
Civil Records: Access: Phone, mail, in person. Both court and visitors may perform in person searches. Search fee: $15.00, includes both civil and criminal. Required to search: name, years to search. Civil cases indexed by defendant, plaintiff; index on docket books since 1965; on computer back to 1987. Mail turnaround time 1 week.
Criminal Records: Access: Mail, in person. Only the court performs in person searches; visitors may not. Search fee: $15.00, includes both civil and criminal. Required to search: name, years to search, DOB or SSN. Criminal records computerized from 1987, docket books since 1960. Mail turnaround time 1 week.
General Information: No juvenile, child protective or impounded records released. Will not fax documents. Court makes copy: $2.00 1st page, $1.00 each add'l. Certification fee: $5.00 per doc. Payee: Maine District Court. Personal checks accepted. Visa/MC accepted. Mail requests: SASE required.

Probate Court 32 High St, PO Box 249, Wiscasset, ME 04578; 207-882-7392; fax: 207-882-4324; 8AM-4PM. ***Probate.*** www.co.lincoln.me.us/dep.html
Search probate records free at https://www.maineprobate.net/index.html. $2 fee for images, $1 if registered.

Oxford County

Superior Court PO Box 179, 26 Western Ave, Courthouse, South Paris, ME 04281-0179; 207-743-8936; fax: 207-743-0544; 8AM-4PM. ***Felony, Misdemeanor, Civil Actions over $30,000.***
The search fees and copy fees listed are mandatory per administrative rule. If a SASE is not supplied for mail searches, court may charge add'l $5.00. The search fee includes both the civil and criminal indexes.
Civil Records: Access: Mail, in person. Both court and visitors may perform in person searches. Search fee: $15.00, includes both civil and criminal. Required to search: name, years to search, DOB. Civil cases indexed by defendant, plaintiff. Criminal records on computer back to 1998; on docket books since 1980. Mail turnaround time 3-4 days.
Criminal Records: Access: Mail, in person. Both court and visitors may perform in person searches. Search fee: $15.00, includes both civil and criminal. Required to search: name, years to search, DOB. Criminal docket on books since 1960. Mail turnaround time 1-2 days.
General Information: No protective custody or protection from abuse records released. Will fax back documents for no fee. Court makes copy: $1.00 per page. Certification fee: $5.00 per doc. Payee: Clerk of Superior Court. Personal checks and major credit cards accepted. Mail requests: SASE requested.

Rumford Dist. Ct. Div. of North Oxford Municipal Bldg, 145 Congress St, Rumford, ME 04276; 207-364-7171; 8AM-4PM. ***Misdemeanor, Civil Actions, Eviction, Small Claims.***
The search fees and copy fees listed are mandatory per administrative rule. Search includes both civil and criminal index. If a SASE is not supplied for mail searches, court may charge add'l $5.00.
Civil Records: Access: Mail, in person. Only the court performs in person searches; visitors may not. Search fee: $15.00 per name. Required to search: name, years to search. Civil cases indexed by defendant, plaintiff; index on docket books since 1966. Mail turnaround time 1 week.
Criminal Records: Access: Mail, in person. Only the court performs in person searches; visitors may not. Search fee: $15.00 per name. Required to search: name, years to search, DOB. Criminal records on computer since 3/1988, docket books since 1966. Mail turnaround time 1 week.
General Information: No impounded records released. Will not fax documents. Court makes copy: $2.00 1st page, $1.00 each add'l. Certification fee: $5.00 per cert. Payee: Maine District Court. Personal checks and major credit cards accepted. Mail requests: SASE required.

South Paris District Court - South 11 26 Western Ave, South Paris, ME 04281; 207-743-8942; 8AM-4PM. ***Misdemeanor, Civil Actions, Eviction, Small Claims.***
Civil Records: Access: Mail, in person. Only the court performs in person searches; visitors may not. Search fee: $15.00, includes both civil and criminal. Required to search: name, years to search. Civil cases indexed by defendant. Civil index on docket books back 5 years. Mail turnaround time 1-2 days.
Criminal Records: Access: Mail, in person. Both court and visitors may perform in person searches. Search fee: $15.00, includes both civil and criminal. Required to search: name, years to search; also helpful: DOB. Criminal records on computer since 4/99, docket books back to 1966. Note: Records after 4/99 cannot be accessed on the public access computer; request a search in writing. Mail turnaround time 1-2 days.
General Information: No juvenile or child protective records released. Will not fax documents. Court makes copy: $2.00 1st page, $1.00 each add'l. Certification fee: $5.00 per document. Payee: Maine District Court. Personal checks and major credit cards accepted. Mail requests: SASE required.

Probate Court PO Box 179, 26 Western Ave, South Paris, ME 04281; 207-743-6671; fax: 207-743-4255; 8AM-4PM. ***Probate.*** www.oxfordcounty.org/probate.htm
Search probate records free at https://www.maineprobate.net/index.html. $2 fee for images, $1 if registered.

Penobscot County

Superior Court 97 Hammond St, Bangor, ME 04401; 207-561-2300; 8AM-4PM. ***Felony, Misdemeanor, Civil Actions.*** www.courts.state.me.us/mainecourts/superior/superior_bangor.html
The search fees and copy fees listed are mandatory per administrative rule. If a SASE is not supplied for mail searches, court may charge add'l $5.00. There is no charge for a single search.
Civil Records: Access: Mail, in person. Only the court performs in person searches; visitors may not. Search fee: $15.00 per name multiple searches only (otherwise no fee for single case) includes both civil and criminal. Required to search: name, years to search. Civil cases indexed by defendant, plaintiff; index on docket books since 1976; on computer back to 2002; archived back to 1927.
Criminal Records: Access: Mail, in person. Only the court performs in person searches; visitors may not. Search fee: $15.00 per name multiple searches only (otherwise no fee for single case) includes both civil and criminal. Required to search: name, years to search, DOB. Criminal docket on books since 1976; on computer back to 1998; archived back to 1927.
General Information: No impounded records released. Will not fax documents. Court makes copy: $2.00 1st page, $1.00 each add'l. Certification fee: $5.00 per doc. Payee: Treasurer, State of Maine. Personal checks accepted. Credit cards accepted. Mail requests: SASE required or pay $5.00 add'l for mail return.

Bangor District Court 73 Hammond St, Bangor, ME 04401; 207-941-3040; 8AM-4PM. ***Misdemeanor, Civil Actions, Eviction, Small Claims.*** Search fee includes both civil and criminal indexes, if asked. **Civil Records:** Access: Mail, in person. Only the court performs in person searches; visitors may not. Search fee: $15.00, includes both civil and criminal. Required to search: name, years to search. Civil cases indexed by defendant. Civil index on docket books since 1962. Note: Court suggests using central state repository. Mail turnaround time 1 week.
Criminal Records: Access: Mail, in person. Only the court performs in person searches; visitors may not. Search fee: 1st name free, then $15.00 each add'l name; includes both civil and criminal. Required to search: name, years to search; also helpful: DOB. Criminal records on computer since late 1988, docket books since 1962. Mail turnaround time 1 week. Public use terminal has crim records back to 12/1986.
General Information: No protective custody records released. Will not fax documents. Court makes copy: $2.00 1st page, $1.00 each add'l. Certification fee: $5.00 per seal. Payee: Maine District Court. Personal checks accepted. Money orders accepted. Visa/MC accepted. Mail requests: SASE required.

Central District Court - Central 13 52 Main St, Lincoln, ME 04457; 207-794-8512; 8AM-4PM. ***Misdemeanor, Civil Actions, Eviction, Small Claims.***
Civil Records: Access: In person only. Only the court performs in person searches; visitors may not. Search fee: $15.00 per name. Required to search: name, years to search. Civil cases indexed by defendant. Civil index on docket books since 1964.
Criminal Records: Access: In person only. Only the court performs in person searches; visitors may not. Search fee: $15.00 per name. Required to search: name, years to search, DOB. Criminal records on computer since 1987, docket books since 1964.
General Information: No juvenile or protective custody records released. Court makes copy: $2.00 1st page, $1.00 each add'l. Certification fee: $5.00 per piece. Payee: Maine District Court. Personal checks accepted. Credit cards accepted.

Millinocket District Court - North 13 207 Penobscot Ave, Millinocket, ME 04462; 207-723-4786; 8AM-4PM. ***Misdemeanor, Civil Actions, Eviction, Small Claims.***

Search fee includes both civil and criminal indexes, if asked. **Civil Records:** Access: In person, online. Both court and visitors may perform in person searches. Search fee: $15.00 per name. Required to search: name, years to search. Civil cases indexed by defendant, plaintiff; index on docket books since 1964; computerized records since 1987. Public terminal civil records go back to 1982. Record searches at www.maine.gov/portal/online_services/

Criminal Records: Access: Mail, in person, online. Both court and visitors may perform in person searches. Search fee: $15.00 per name. No charge if you provide docket numbers. Required to search: name, years to search, DOB. Criminal records on computer since 1987, docket books since 1964. Mail turnaround time 3-6 days. Search records at www.maine.gov/portal/online_services/

General Information: No juvenile or protective custody records released. Will not fax documents. Court makes copy: $2.00 1st page, $1.00 each add'l. Certification fee: $5.00 per doc. Payee: Maine District Court. Personal checks accepted. Visa/MC accepted. Mail requests: SASE requested.

Newport District Court - West 3 12 Water St, Newport, ME 04953; 207-368-5778; fax: 207-368-7724; 8AM-4PM. ***Misdemeanor, Civil Actions, Eviction, Small Claims.***

Civil Records: Access: Mail, in person. Both court and visitors may perform in person searches. Search fee: $15.00, includes both civil and criminal. Required to search: name, years to search. Civil cases indexed by defendant, plaintiff; index on docket books back to 1965; computerized back to 2001. Mail turnaround 1 week. Civil PAT goes back to 2001.

Criminal Records: Access: Mail, in person. Both court and visitors may perform in person searches. Search fee: $15.00, includes both civil and criminal. Required to search: name, years to search, DOB. Criminal records on computer for 5 years, on docket books since 1987. Mail turnaround time 1 week. Criminal PAT goes back to 1987.

General Information: No impounded records released. Will not fax documents. Court makes copy: $2.00 1st page, $1.00 each add'l. Certification fee: $5.00 per cert. Payee: Maine District Court. Personal checks accepted. Credit cards accepted. Mail requests: SASE required.

Probate Court 97 Hammond St, Bangor, ME 04401-4996; 207-942-8769; fax: 207-941-8499; 8AM-4:30PM. ***Probate.*** www.maineprobate.net

Search probate records free at https://www.maineprobate.net/index.html. $2 fee for images, $1 if registered.

Piscataquis County

Superior Court 159 E Main St, Dover-Foxcroft, ME 04426; 207-564-8419; 8AM-4PM. ***Felony, Misdemeanor, Civil Actions.***

Search fee applies to each division. **Civil Records:** Access: Mail, in person. Only the court performs in person searches; visitors may not. Search fee: $15.00 per name includes both civil and criminal. Required to search: name, years to search. Civil cases indexed by defendant, plaintiff; index on docket books since 1960; computerized records since 1998. Mail turnaround time 1 week.

Criminal Records: Access: Mail, in person. Only the court performs in person searches; visitors may not. Search fee: $15.00 per name includes both civil and criminal. Required to search: name, years to search; also helpful: DOB. Criminal docket on books since 1960; computerized records since 1998. Mail turnaround time 1 week.

General Information: No pre-sentence report records released. Will not fax documents. Court makes copy: $2.00 1st page, $1.00 each add'l. Certification fee: $5.00 per cert. Payee: State of Maine Superior Court. Personal checks accepted. Visa/MC accepted. Mail requests: SASE required.

District Court 13 163 E Main St, Dover-Foxcroft, ME 04426; 207-564-2240; 8AM-4PM. ***Misdemeanor, Civil Actions, Eviction, Small Claims.***

Civil Records: Access: Mail, in person. Both court and visitors may perform in person searches. Search fee: $15.00 per name includes both civil and criminal. Required to search: name, years to search. Civil cases indexed by defendant, plaintiff; index on docket books since 1963. Mail turnaround 1 week.

Criminal Records: Access: Mail, in person. Both court and visitors may perform in person searches. Search fee: $15.00 per name includes both civil and criminal. Required to search: name, years to search; also helpful: DOB. Criminal records on computer since 1987, docket books since 1963. Mail turnaround time 1 week.

General Information: No protective custody or juvenile records released. Will not fax documents. Court makes copy: $2.00 1st page, $1.00 each add'l. Certification fee: $5.00 per cert. Payee: Maine District Court. Personal checks and major credit cards accepted. Mail requests: SASE required.

Probate Court 159 E Main St, Dover-Foxcroft, ME 04426; 207-564-2431; fax: 207-564-2431; 8:30AM-4PM. ***Probate.***

Search probate records free at https://www.maineprobate.net/index.html. $2 fee for images, $1 if registered.

Sagadahoc County

Superior Court 147 New Meadows Rd, West Bath, ME 04530; 207-443-9733; 8AM-4:00PM. ***Felony, Misdemeanor, Civil Actions.***

www.courts.state.me.us/mainecourts/superior/superior_bath.html

Civil Records: Access: Mail, in person. Both court and visitors may perform in person searches. Search fee: $15.00, includes both civil and criminal. Required to search: name, years to search. Civil cases indexed by defendant, plaintiff; index on docket books since 1976; on computer back to 1999. Mail turnaround time 7 days.

Criminal Records: Access: Mail, in person. Both court and visitors may perform in person searches. Search fee: $15.00, includes both civil and criminal. Required to search: name, years to search, DOB. Criminal docket on books since 1900s; on computer back to 1999. Mail turnaround time 7 days.

General Information: No impounded records released. Will not fax documents. Court makes copy: $2.00 1st page, $1.00 each add'l. Certification fee: $5.00 per document. Payee: Clerk of Superior Court. Cash, checks, or money orders accepted. Major credit cards accepted. Mail requests: SASE required.

West Bath District Court 6 147 New Meadows Rd, West Bath, ME 04530; 207-442-0200; criminal phone: 207-442-0205; civil phone: 207-442-0204; 8AM-4PM. ***Misdemeanor, Civil Actions, Eviction, Small Claims.***

www.courts.state.me.us/mainecourts/district/district_westbath.html

This court handles the eastern part of Cumberland County and all of Sagadahoc County.

Civil Records: Access: In person only. Both court and visitors may perform in person searches. Search fee: $15.00, includes both civil and criminal. Required to search: name, years to search. Civil cases indexed by defendant, plaintiff; index on docket books since 1980's; prior archived. Note: Search fees and copy fees listed are mandatory per administrative rule. If a SASE not supplied for mail searches, court may charge add'l $5.00.

Criminal Records: Access: In person only. Both court and visitors may perform in person searches. Search fee: $15.00, includes both civil and criminal. Required to search: name, years to search; also helpful: DOB. Criminal records on computer since 1987, docket books back to 1975; prior archived. Note: The search fees and copy fees listed are mandatory per administrative rule.

General Information: No protective custody or juvenile records released. Will not fax documents. Court makes copy: $2.00 1st page, $1.00 each add'l. Certification fee: $5.00. Payee: Maine District Court. Personal checks accepted. Credit cards accepted.

Probate Court 752 High St, Bath, ME 04530; 207-443-8218; fax: 207-443-8217; 8:30AM-4:30PM. ***Probate.***

Search probate records free at https://www.maineprobate.net/index.html. $2 fee for images, $1 if registered.

Somerset County

Superior Court 41 Court Ave, Skowhegan, ME 04976; 207-474-5161; probate phone: 207-474-3322; 8AM-4PM. ***Felony, Misdemeanor, Civil Actions.***

The search fees and copy fees listed are mandatory per administrative rule.

Civil Records: Access: Mail, in person. Only the court performs in person searches; visitors may not. Search fee: $15.00 per name; no fee for searching one name only. Required to search: name, years to search. Civil cases indexed by defendant, plaintiff, archived in Augusta back to 1800s, docket books and index cards back to 1900s. Mail turnaround time 2-3 days; archived records longer. Civil PAT goes back to 1970s. PAT results show name only.

Criminal Records: Access: Mail, in person. Only the court performs in person searches; visitors may not. Search fee: $15.00 per name; no fee for searching one name only. Required to search: name, years to search; also helpful: DOB. Criminal records archived in Augusta back to 1800s, docket books and index cards back to 1900s; on computer back to 1998. Mail turnaround time 2-3 days, longer if record in archives. Criminal PAT available.PAT results show name, DOB.

General Information: No impounded, present investigations, psychological evaluations or child support records released. Will not fax documents. Court makes copy: $2.00 1st page, $1.00 each add'l. Certification fee: $5.00 per doc. Payee: Clerk of Superior Court. Personal checks accepted. Visa/MC accepted.

District Court 12 PO Box 525, 47 Court St, Skowhegan, ME 04976; 207-474-9518; 8AM-4PM. ***Misdemeanor, Civil Actions, Eviction, Small Claims.***

Civil Records: Access: Mail, in person. Both court and visitors may perform in person searches. Search fee: $15.00, includes both civil and criminal. Required to search: name, years to search. Civil cases indexed by defendant. Civil index on docket books since 1960s, divorces since 1970s. Mail turnaround time 2-4 weeks. Civil PAT goes back to 2002.

Criminal Records: Access: Mail, in person. Both court and visitors may perform in person searches. Search fee: $15.00, includes both civil and criminal. Required to search: name, years to search; also helpful: DOB. Criminal records on computer since 1987, docket books since 1960s. Mail turnaround time 2-4 weeks. Criminal PAT goes back to 1987.

General Information: No juvenile records released. Will not fax documents. Court makes copy: $2.00 1st page, $1.00 each add'l. Certification fee: $5.00 per doc. Payee: Maine District Court. Personal checks accepted. Visa/MC accepted. Mail requests: SASE required.

Probate Court 41 Court St, Skowhegan, ME 04976; 207-474-3322; 8:30AM-4:30PM. ***Probate.***

Search probate records free at https://www.maineprobate.net/index.html. $2 fee for images, $1 if registered.

Waldo County

Superior Court/Belfast 103 Church St, Belfast, ME 04915; 207-338-1940; 8AM-4PM. ***Felony, Misdemeanor, Civil Actions.***

Physical add: 137 Church St. **Civil Records:** Access: Mail, in person. Only the court performs in person searches; visitors may not. Search fee: $15.00, includes both civil and criminal. Allows 1 name free search. Required to search: name, years to search. Civil cases indexed by defendant, plaintiff, archived back to 1980 (not in office), on docket books since 1980; on computer back to 12/99. Mail turnaround time 5 days.

Criminal Records: Access: Mail, in person. Only the court performs in person searches; visitors may not. Search fee: $15.00, includes both civil and criminal. Allows 1 name free search. Required to search: name, years to search; also helpful: DOB. Criminal records archived back to 1975 (not in office), on docket books since 1975; on computer back to 12/99. Mail turnaround time 5 days. Request criminal and juvenile crime information www10.informe.org/PCR/. This is a request site, (for the information) not the direct information.

General Information: No protective custody records released. Will not fax documents. Court makes copy: $2.00 1st page, $1.00 each add'l. Certification fee: $5.00 per doc. Payee: State Treasurer. Personal checks accepted. Visa/MC accepted. Mail requests: SASE required.

District Court 5/Belfast 103 Church St, Belfast, ME 04915; 207-338-3107; 8AM-4PM. ***Misdemeanor, Civil Actions, Eviction, Small Claims.***
Civil Records: Access: Mail only. Only the court performs in person searches; visitors may not. Search fee: $15.00, includes both civil and criminal. Required to search: name, years to search. Civil cases indexed by defendant, plaintiff; index on docket books since 1966, computerized since 2001. Mail turnaround time 1 week.
Criminal Records: Access: Mail only. Only the court performs in person searches; visitors may not. Search fee: $15.00, includes both civil and criminal. Required to search: name, years to search, DOB. Criminal records on computer since 1987, docket books since 1966. Mail turnaround 1 week.
General Information: No juvenile or impounded records released. Will not fax documents. Court makes copy: $2.00 1st page, $1.00 each add'l. Certification fee: $5.00 per doc. Payee: Maine District Court. Personal checks accepted. Visa/MC accepted. Mail requests: SASE required.

Probate Court 39A Spring St, PO Box 323, Belfast, ME 04915-0323; 207-338-2780/2963; fax: 207-338-2360; 8AM-4PM. ***Probate.***
Search probate records free at https://www.maineprobate.net/index.html. $2 fee for images, $1 if registered.

Washington County

Superior Court PO Box 526, Clerk of Court, 85 Court St, Machias, ME 04654; 207-255-3044; 8AM-4PM. ***Felony, Misdemeanor, Civil.***
Civil Records: Access: Mail, in person. Both court and visitors may perform in person searches. Search fee: $15.00, includes both civil and criminal. Required to search: name, years to search. Civil cases indexed by defendant, plaintiff; index on docket books and index cards since 1930s. Mail turnaround time 1 week.
Criminal Records: Access: Mail, in person. Both court and visitors may perform in person searches. Search fee: $15.00, includes both civil and criminal. Required to search: name, years to search, DOB. Criminal docket on books and index cards since 1930s. Mail turnaround time 1 week.
General Information: No impounded records released. Will not fax documents. Court makes copy: $2.00 1st page, $1.00 each add'l. Self serve: Self serve copier downstairs in Deeds office. Certification fee: $5.00 per document. Payee: Treasurer, State of Maine. Personal checks accepted. Visa/MC accepted but there is a minimum. Mail requests: SASE required.

Calais District Court - North 4 PO Box 929, Calais, ME 04619; 207-454-2055; TTY# 207-454-0085; 8AM-4PM. ***Misdemeanor, Civil Actions, Eviction, Small Claims.***
Civil Records: Access: In person only. Both court and visitors may perform in person searches. Search fee: $15.00 per name, if more than 1 name. Required to search: name, years to search. Civil cases indexed by defendant, plaintiff; index on docket books since 1988, on computer back to 2001.
Criminal Records: Access: In person only. Both court and visitors may perform in person searches. Search fee: $15.00 per name, if more than 1 name. Required to search: name, years to search, DOB. Criminal records on computer since 1987, docket books since 07/79.
General Information: No juvenile or protective custody records released. Will not fax documents. Court makes copy: $2.00 1st page, $1.00 each add'l. Certification fee: $5.00 per doc. Payee: Maine District Court. Personal checks and credit cards accepted.

Maine District Court 4 47 Court St, PO Box 297, Machias, ME 04654; 207-255-3044; 8AM-4PM. ***Misdemeanor, Civil Actions, Eviction, Small Claims.***
Civil Records: Access: Mail, in person. Only the court performs in person searches; visitors may not. Search fee: 1st name free; add'l $15.00 per name. Required to search: name, years to search. Civil cases indexed by defendant, plaintiff; index on docket books since 1985; on computer back to 2001. Mail turnaround time 4 days.
Criminal Records: Access: Mail, in person. Only the court performs in person searches; visitors may not. Search fee: 1st name free add'l $15.00. Required to search: name, years to search, DOB. Criminal records on computer 1987-1999, docket books since 1985. Mail turnaround time 4 days.
General Information: No protective custody or juvenile records released. Will not fax documents. Court makes copy: $2.00 1st page, $1.00 each add'l. Certification fee: $5.00 per document. Payee: Maine District Court. Personal checks accepted. Mail requests: SASE required.

Probate Court PO Box 297, 47 Court St., Machias, ME 04654; 207-255-6591; fax: 207-255-3999; 8AM-4PM. ***Probate.***
www.washingtoncountymaine.com/probate/
Search probate records free at https://www.maineprobate.net/index.html. $2 fee for images, $1 if registered.

York County

Superior Court Clerk of Court, PO Box 160, Alfred, ME 04002; 207-324-5122; 8AM-4PM. ***Felony, Misdemeanor, Civil Actions.***
Civil Records: Access: Mail, in person. Only the court performs in person searches; visitors may not. Search fee: $15.00, includes both civil and criminal. Required to search: name, years to search. Civil cases indexed by defendant, plaintiff; index on docket books since 1960; computerized records go back to 2002. Note: No faxes are accepted or sent. Mail turnaround time- 1-5 names is 5 days; 6-10 names 30 working days.
Criminal Records: Access: Mail, in person. Only the court performs in person searches; visitors may not. Search fee: $15.00, includes both civil and criminal. Required to search: name, years to search, DOB. Criminal docket on books since 1966; computerized records go back to 1998. Note: No faxes are accepted or sent. Mail turnaround time: 1-5 names is 5 days; 6-10 names 30 working days.
General Information: No juvenile, or protective custody records released. Will not fax documents. Court makes copy: $2.00 1st page, $1.00 each add'l. Certification fee: $5.00 per attestation. Payee: Clerk of Courts. Cashiers checks and money orders accepted. Major credit cards accepted. Mail requests: SASE required.

Biddeford District Court - East 10 25 Adams St, Biddeford, ME 04005; 207-283-1147; 8AM-4PM. ***Misdemeanor, Civil Actions, Eviction, Small Claims.***
Civil Records: Access: Mail, in person. Visitors must perform in person searches themselves. Search fee: $15.00, includes both civil and criminal. Required to search: name, years to search. Civil cases indexed by defendant. Civil index on docket books since 1989, prior on docket books. Note: Court will do up to 3 searches only. Mail turnaround time 4-5 days.
Criminal Records: Access: Mail, in person. Visitors must perform in person searches themselves. Search fee: $15.00, includes both civil and criminal. Required to search: name, years to search; also helpful: DOB. Criminal records on computer since 1986, prior on docket books. Mail turnaround time is 5 days.
General Information: No child protection or juvenile records released. Will not fax documents. Court makes copy: $2.00 1st page, $1.00 each add'l. Certification fee: $5.00 per doc. Payee: Maine District Court. Personal checks accepted. Visa/MC accepted. Mail requests: SASE required.

Springvale District Court - West 10 447 Main St, Springvale, ME 04083; 207-459-1400; 8AM-4PM. ***Misdemeanor, Civil Actions, Eviction, Small Claims.***
Civil Records: Access: Mail, in person. Both court and visitors may perform in person searches. Search fee: $15.00, includes both civil and criminal. Required to search: name, years to search. Civil cases indexed by defendant. Civil records on computer since 1985, docket books since 1985. Mail turnaround time 3-4 days.
Criminal Records: Access: Mail, in person. Both court and visitors may perform in person searches. Search fee: $15.00, includes both civil and criminal. Required to search: name, years to search, DOB. Criminal records on computer since 1997, dockets books since 1980. Mail turnaround time 3-4 days.
General Information: No impounded, juvenile, mental health or protective custody records released. Will not fax documents. Court makes copy: $2.00 1st page, $1.00 each add'l. Certification fee: $5.00 per document includes copies. Payee: Maine District Court. Personal checks and major credit cards accepted. Mail requests: SASE required.

York District Court - South 10 11 Chases Pond Rd, York, ME 03909; 207-363-1230; 8AM-4PM. ***Misdemeanor, Civil Actions, Eviction, Small Claims.***
Civil Records: Access: Mail, in person. Visitors must perform in person searches themselves. Search fee: $15.00, includes both civil and criminal. Allows 1 name free search. Required to search: name, years to search. Civil cases indexed by defendant, plaintiff; index on docket books since 1975; on computer back to 1987. Mail turnaround time 2-4 days.
Criminal Records: Access: Mail, in person. Visitors must perform in person searches themselves. Search fee: $15.00, includes both civil and criminal. Allows 1 name free search. Required to search: name, years to search, DOB. Criminal records computerized from 1987, docket books since 1975. Mail turnaround time 2-4 days.
General Information: No impounded, juvenile and protective custody records released. Will not fax documents. Court makes copy: $2.00 1st page, $1.00 each add'l. Certification fee: $5.00 per doc. Payee: Maine District Court. Personal checks accepted. Visa/MC accepted. Mail requests: SASE required.

Probate Court PO Box 399, 45 Kennebunk Rd, Alfred, ME 04002; 207-324-1577; fax: 207-324-0163; 8AM-4:30PM. ***Probate.***
Search probate records free at https://www.maineprobate.net/index.html. $2 fee for images, $1 if registered

Maine Recording Offices

ORGANIZATION: 16 counties, 18 recording offices. The recording officer is the County Register of Deeds. Counties maintain a general index of all transactions recorded. Aroostook and Oxford Counties each have 2 recording offices. There's no county assessors; each town and city employs its own. Maine is in the Eastern Time Zone (EST).

REAL ESTATE RECORDS: Counties do not perform real estate name searches but some will lookup a name informally. Copy fee in most counties is $1.00 per page. Certification fees vary widely. Assessor and tax records are located at the town/city level.

UCC RECORDS: Only real estate related filings are filed with the Register of Deeds. All other UCC records are with the Secretary of State. Most counties will not search these records, you must hire somone or come in-person. Copy fee is usually $1.00 per page.

TAX LIEN RECORDS: Supposedly all tax liens on personal property are filed with the Secretary of State but counties tend to have some of these. All tax liens on real property and state/federal tax liens are filed with the Register of Deeds.

OTHER LIENS: Municipal, bail bond, mechanics.

ONLINE ACCESS: A number of counties offer online access. Some counties outsource via vendors. Where known, local jusrisdictions with web access to assessment records are indicated in the county profile. There is a statewide Debtor Name Search system at www.maine.gov/sos/cec/corp/debtor_index.shtml.

Androscoggin County

County Register of Deeds, 2 Turner St; Courthouse, Auburn, ME 04210-5978. Recording, R/E & UCC phone-207-782-0191; fax-207-784-3163; 8AM-5PM http://androscoggindeeds.com

Index: All in one. Records indexed on a public use terminal back to 1976. Only the public may search. Copy fee $1.25 per page. Plans- $5.00 per page. Cert fee- None. Payee- Androscoggin County Register of Deeds. **Online access to Real Estate, Deed, Lien records:** Access the Registry index by subscription for a $300.00 annual fee plus $1.25 per page/image printed. Indexes go back to 1976. For info and sign-up, contact Registry of Deeds at 207-782-0191. Search for free at http://androscoggindeeds.com/ALIS/WW400R.PGM. Index goes back to 1976; images to 1/1976 but images cannot be printed. **Other phones:** Treasurer- 207-784-7491. **Other Online Records-** Town of Lisbon assessor data is free at www.mygovnow.com/lisbto/Invision/assessing/index.htm. No name searching. Also City of Auburn tax assessor data is free at http://gis.auburnmaine.gov/PublicAuburnBasemap

Aroostook County (Northern District)

County Register of Deeds, PO Box 47, Fort Kent, ME 04743. 207-834-3925; fax-207-834-3138; 8AM-4:30PM www.aroostook.me.us/deeds.html

See the web page for the assigned townships. Index: All in one. Records indexed on computer back to 1982. Only the public may search. Copy fee $1.00 per page if mailed back.Real estate copy- $.50 per page, $.25 if self serve. Cert fee- $2.00 per doc plus copy fee. Payee- Northern Aroostook County Register of Deeds. **Online access to Real Estate, Deed, Lien, Judgment records:** Remote access via a commercial online system has been replaced by a subscription internet-based system. Data on the internet system includes deeds, mortgages, liens, judgment, and land recording generally. Records go back to 1982. Subscription fee is $100 for North District, $100 for South. For more info and signup, see www.aroostookdeedsnorth.com then click on Access Information button on left side of page. **Other phones:** Treasurer- 207-834-3090; Elections- 207-834-3090; Vital Records- 207-834-3090. **Property tax/Assessing-** 416 W Main St, Fort Kent, ME 04743; 207-834-3090.

Aroostook County (Southern District)

County Register of Deeds, 26 Court St, #102, Houlton, ME 04730. 207-532-1500, R/E recording phone-207-834-3925; fax-207-532-1506; 8AM-4:30PM www.aroostook.me.us/deeds.html

See the web page for the assigned townships. Index: Separate indices to search include computer, pre-1985 books. Records indexed on a public use terminal back to 1985. Only the public may search. Copy fee $.50 per page; $1.00 each if mailed; self serve- $.25 each. Cert fee- none. Payee- Aroostook County Register of Deeds. **Online access to Real Estate, Deed, Lien, Judgment records:** Remote access via a commercial online system has been replaced by a subscription internet-based system. Data includes deeds, mortgages, liens, judgment, and land recording generally. Records go back to 1985. Subscription fee is $100 for North and South Districts. For more info and signup, see www.aroostookdeedsnorth.com then click on Access Information button on left side of page. **Property tax/Assessing-** 21 Water St, Houlton, ME 04730; 207-532-7114. www.houlton-maine.com/contact.php

Cumberland County

County Registry of Deeds, PO Box 7230, Portland, ME 04112. Recording, R/E & UCC phone-207-871-8389; fax-207-772-4162; 8AM-4:30PM

Index: All in one. Records indexed on a public use terminal back to 1/1/1965. Only the public may search. Copy fee $1.50 per page, $10.00 for copy of plat. Cert fee- $2.00 per doc plus copy fee. Payee- Cumberland County Register of Deeds. **Online access to Real Estate, Deed, Lien, Judgment records:** Search Register of Deeds fee site at https://www.mainelandrecords.com/melr_me005/MelrApp/index.jsp. $3.00 fee per doc, or register and pay monthly fee. **Other phones:** Treasurer- 207-871-8392. **Property tax/Assessing-** 290 Tuttle Rd, Cumberland, ME 04021; 207-829-2204, fax- 207-829-2224. www.cumberlandmaine.com/Assessor.cfm **Online access-** Cape Elizabeth data free- www.capeelizabeth.com/taxdata.html. Gray Town assessor data- www.mygovnow.com/grayto/Invision/assessing/index.htm. Portland assessor- www.portlandassessor.com. Scarborough- www.scarborough.me.us/assessing/index.html. Falmouth assessor at http://gis.cdm.com/FalmouthMaineGIS/l. Cumberland, Raymond, Freeport, Gorham, Harpswell, Standish, S. Portland, Westbrook, Windham, Yarmouth town assessors at www.visionappraisal.com/databases/maine/index.htm

Franklin County

County Register of Deeds, 140 Main St,#5, Farmington, ME 04938-1818. 207-778-5889; fax-207-778-5899; 8:30AM-4PM www.franklincountydeedsme.com

Records indexed on a public use terminal back to 1984. Only the public may search. Copy fee $1.00 per financing statement. Cert fee- $.50 per cert plus copy fee. Payee- Franklin County Register of Deeds. **Online access to Real Estate, Deed, Lien, Judgment, UCC records:** Access to recorders data index is free at www.franklincountydeedsme.com. Land index goes back to 1984; images go back to part of 1993 (in process). For full access and to print documents, registration and fees are required.

Hancock County

County Register of Deeds, 50 State St, #9, Ellsworth, ME 04605. Recording, R/E & UCC phone-207-667-8353; fax-207-667-1410; 8:30AM-4PM www.co.hancock.me.us/reg_deeds/index.html

Index: Separate indices to search. Records indexed on a public use terminal back to 1937. Office personnel or visitors may perform searches. No fee for search. Office will search real estate records as time permits. Will search UCC records. Copy fee $1.00 per page. Cert fee- $1.00 per doc plus copy fee. Payee- Hancock County Registry of Deeds. **Online access to Real Estate, Deed, Lien, UCC, Judgment, Will records:** Access to the county registry of deeds database at www.registryofdeeds.com requires registration. Viewing of index back to 1790 is free, but $1.50 per page to print document. For info see website or call 888-833-3979. Also, City of Ellsworth real estate data is free at www.mygovnow.com/ellsci/Invision/assessing/index.htm. Also, free public record searches at www.hancockcountymaineregistryofdeeds.com/public.htm. **Other phones:** Treasurer- 207-667-8272. **Property tax/Assessing-** 1 City Hall Plaza, Ellsworth City Hall, Ellsworth, ME 04605; 207-667-8674. http://cityofellsworthme.org/ **Online access-** Access to Bar Harbor property data is free at http://data.visionappraisal.com/BarHarborME/. Free registration required. Access Mount Desert assessor- http://data.visionappraisal.com/MountDesertME/. Also, access Ellsworth property data free at www.mygovnow.com/ellsci/Invision/assessing/index.htm or download data from http://cityofellsworthme.org/files/reweb.txt.

Kennebec County

County Register of Deeds, PO Box 1053, Augusta, ME 04332-1053. 207-622-0431; fax-207-622-1598; 8AM-4PM www.kennebeccounty.org
Index: Separate indices to search include computer, books. Records indexed on a public use terminal back to 1935. Office will perform a UCC search but public must search other records themselves. Copy fee $1.50 per page. Will not fax back docs. Cert fee- $.50 per cert plus copy fee. Payee- Kennebec County Register of Deeds. **Online access to Real Estate, Deed records:** Register free and search recorder index free at www.kennebec.me.us.landata.com. Fee for images by subscription or pay-per-view. **Other Online Records-** Access Winslow Town Property data free www.winslowmaine.org/assessing.html or http://data.visionappraisal.com/WinslowME/DEFULT.asp. Records on the Town of Waterville Assessor's data is free at http://data.visionappraisal.com/WatervilleME/. Also, search City of Augusta assessor database at http://data.visionappraisal.com/AugustaME/. Free registration for full data. Also, search Winthrop Town and Gardiner Town data free at www.visionappraisal.com/databases/.

Knox County

County Register of Deeds, PO Box 943, Rockland, ME 04841. 207-594-0422; fax-207-594-0446; 8AM-4PM www.knoxcounty.midcoast.com
Index: Separate indices to search include grantor/grantee. Records indexed on a public use terminal back to 1966. Only the public may search. Will not search UCC records. Copy fee $1.00 per page. Cert fee- $1.00 per doc plus copy fee. Payee- Knox County Register of Deeds. **Online access to Real Estate, Grantor/Grantee, Deed, Mortgage, Lien, Judgment, UCC records:** Search property records at mainelandrecords.com. Indexes are available from 1966 to present. Document images are available from 1966 to present; fees for images. $3.00 fee per doc, or register and pay monthly fee. **Other phones:** Treasurer- 207-594-0421. **Other Online Records-** Search Camden, Rockland, Rockport, and South Thomaston town assessors data at www.visionappraisal.com/databases/maine/index.htm.

Lincoln County

County Register of Deeds, PO Box 249, Wiscasset, ME 04578-0249. 207-882-7431; fax-207-882-4061; 8AM-4PM www.lincolncomeregofdeeds.com
Index: All in one. Records indexed on a public use terminal back to 1954. Only the public may search. Copy fee $1.00 per page. Will fax back- $2.20 per page. Cert fee- $1.00 per doc plus copy fee. Payee- Lincoln County Register of Deeds. **Online access to Real Estate, Deed records:** Search Register of Deeds indices and images back to 1954 for free at www.lincolncomeregofdeeds.com. Click on Free Access at left. Images for a fee go back to 1/1981. **Property tax/Assessing**- 32 High St, Courthouse, Wiscasset, ME 04578; see above. **Online access-** Search Town of Boothbay property data free at http://data.visionappraisal.com/BoothbayME/.

Oxford County

County Register of Deeds, PO Box 179, South Paris, ME 04281-0179. 207-743-6211; fax-207-743-2656; 8AM-4PM
www.oxfordcounty.org/registry_of_deeds.htm
Files in this office for all towns except the following: Brownfield, Denmark, Fryeburg, Hiram, Lovell, Porter, Stoneham, Stow, and Sweden. Index: All in one. Records indexed on a public use terminal back to 1969. Only the public may search. Copy fee $1.00 per page. Cert fee- $1.00 per doc plus copy fee. Payee- Oxford County Register of Deeds. **Online access to Real Estate, Grantor/Grantee, Deed, Mortgage, Lien, Judgment records:** Search recording records for the Eastern portion of the county at https://www.mainelandrecords.com/melr_me005/MelrApp/index.jsp. $3.00 fee per doc, or register and pay fee. **Other phones:** Treasurer- 207-743-6359.

Oxford County

Register of Deeds, 38 Portland St, Fryeburg, ME 04037. 207-935-2565; fax-207-935-4183; 9AM-4PM www.oxfordcounty.org/Registry_of_deeds_WD.htm
Files in this office include West District: Stoneham, Stow, Lovell, Fryeburg, Brownfield, Denmark, Porter and Hiram. Index: All in one. Records indexed on a public use terminal back to 1991. Office will perform a UCC search but public must search other records themselves. Copy fee $1.00 per page. Plan copy- $5.00 per page. Cert fee- $1.00 per doc plus copy fee. Payee- Oxford County Register of Deeds. Office does not sell bulk data at this time. **Online access to Real Estate, Grantor/Grantee, Deed, Mortgage, Lien, Judgment records:** Recording records for the Western portion of the county should be available online in 2009, see the website. Images are to be available back 10 1977. **Other phones:** Treasurer- 207-743-6359.

Penobscot County

County Register of Deeds, PO Box 2070, Bangor, ME 04402-2070. 207-942-8797; fax-207-945-4920; 8AM-4:30PM www.penobscotdeeds.com
Index: All in one. Records indexed on a public use terminal back to 1967. Only the public may search. Copy fee $1.00 per page. Cert fee- $1.00 per doc plus copy fee. Payee- Penobscot County Register of Deeds. **Online access to Real Estate, Deed records:** Search the Register of Deeds index back to 1967 and images back to 1967 for free at www.penobscotdeeds.com. A fee is charged for copies and you may not download with registering. **Property tax/Assessing**- 73 Harlow St, Bangor, ME 04401; 207-992-4215, fax- 207-945-4433. www.bangormaine.gov/cg_ca_overview.php **Online access-** Search the City of Old Town real estate database for free at www.old-town.me.us/assessor/rev.asp.

Piscataquis County

County Register of Deeds, 159 E Main St, Dover-Foxcroft, ME 04426. 207-564-2411; fax-207-564-7708; 8:30AM-4PM
Index: All in one. Records indexed on a public use terminal back to 1975. Only the public may search. Copy fee $1.00 per page. Cert fee- $1.00 per page includes copy fee. Payee- Piscataquis County Register of Deeds. **Online Real Estate, Grantor/Grantee, Deed, Mortgage, Lien, Judgment records:** Search free on Register of Deeds site at https://www.mainelandrecords.com. $3.00 fee per doc, or register and pay monthly fee plus $.50 per name search and $.25 per doc. **Property tax/Assessing**- 207-287-2011.

Sagadahoc County

County Register of Deeds, 752 High St, Bath, ME 04530. 207-443-8214; fax-207-443-8216; 8:30AM-4:30PM www.sagadahocdeedsme.com
Index: Separate indices to search include plans. Records indexed on a public use terminal back to 1964. Only the public may search; office will check a name for recent recording. No fee for search. Copy fee $1.00 per page. $6.00 for plans; fax back- $2.00 per page. Cert fee- Cert fee included in copy fee. Payee- Sagadahoc County Register of Deeds. **Online access to Real Estate, Grantor/Grantee, Deed records:** Register of Deeds records are online for a $300.00 per year fee plus $.50 per page to view or copy. Records go back to 1964 on Grantor/Grantee index. Images go back to 03/80. For info and registration, call Register of Deeds. **Other Online Records-** Search records on the City of Bath Assessor database free at http://assessdb.cityofbath.com. Search Topsham assessor property records free at http://data.visionappraisal.com/TopshamME/DEFAULT.asp.

Somerset County

County Register of Deeds, PO Box 248, Skowhegan, ME 04976-0248. 207-474-3421; fax-207-474-2793; 8:30AM-4:30PM
All tax info and vital records managed at municipal level. Index: All in one. Records indexed on a public use terminal back to 1956. Only the public may search. Copy fee $1.00 per page if mailed; copies faxed back- $2.00 per page. Plans are $5.00 per page. Cert fee- $1.00 per document. Payee- Register of Deeds. **Online access to Real Estate, Grantor/Grantee, Deed, Mortgage, Lien, Judgment records:** Access real estate records free at https://www.mainelandrecords.com/melr_me005/MelrApp/index.jsp Registration required for all users. Records goes back to 1956. $3.00 fee per doc, or subscribe and pay monthly fee of $35.00 plus $.50 pr name plus $.25 per document image. **Property tax/Assessing**- 207-474-6903.

Waldo County

Register of Deeds, PO Box D, Belfast, ME 04915. 207-338-1710; fax-207-338-6360; 8AM-4PM
Index: Separate indices to search include books, computer. Records indexed on a public use terminal back to 1981. Office will perform a UCC search but public must search other records themselves. Copy fee $1.00 per page. Cert fee- $1.00 per cert plus copy fee; faxed copies $2.00 per page. Payee- Waldo County Register of Deeds. **Online Real Estate, Grantor/Grantee, Deed, Mortgage, Lien, Judgment records:** Access real estate records by subscription at https://www.mainelandrecords.com/melr_me005/MelrApp/index.jsp. Index back to 1981, images back to 1981. $3.00 fee per doc, or register and pay monthly fee.

Washington County

County Register of Deeds, PO Box 297, Machias, ME 04654-0297. 207-255-6512; fax-207-255-3838; 8AM-4PM
Index: All in one. Records indexed on computer back to 1972. Only the public may search. Office will search UCC records if short searches. Copy fee $1.00 per page. Cert fee- $1.00 per doc plus copy fee. Payee- Washington County Register of Deeds. **Other phones:** Treasurer- 207-255-8354; County Clerk- 207-255-3127. **Property tax/Assessing**- PO Box 418, Machias, ME 04654; 207-255-6621 (Machias area only), assessor fax- 207-255-6492. hours- 9AM04PM

York County

County Register of Deeds, PO Box 339, Alfred, ME 04002-0339. 207-324-1576; fax-207-324-2886; 8:30AM-4:30PM www.york.me.us.landata.com/
Index: Separate indices to search include grantor/grantee, plans. Records indexed on a public use terminal back to 1966. Only the public may search. Copy fee $1.50 per page. Plan copies- $6.00 per page. Cert fee- $5.00 per doc plus copy fee. Payee- York County Register of Deeds. **Online access to Real Estate, Deed records:** Search Register of Deeds records at www.york.me.us.landata.com. Register then search basic index free; get doc copies either by sub @ $1.50 per pg or non-sub @$2.25 per page. **Other phones:** Treasurer- 207-324-1571. **Property tax/Assessing**- PO Box 667, Alfred, ME 04002; 207-363-1005, assessor fax- 207-363-1009. hours- 8AM-4:30PM www.yorkmaine.org/Departments/Assessing/tabid/189/Default.aspx **Online** - Search Kennebunk Town data free at www.kennebunkmaine.us/index.asp; click on Dept then Assessor. Data as pdf or as spreadsheet. Also, Berwick, Cornish, Eliot, Kennebunkport, Kittery, Ogunquit, Old Orchard Beach, Saco, Wells, and York Town assessors data is free at www.visionappraisal.com/databases/maine/index.htm Free registration required.

Maine County Locator

You will usually be able to find the city name in the City/County Cross. Reference below. In that case, it is a simple matter to determine the county from the cross reference. However, only the official US Postal Service city names are included in this index. There are an additional 40,000 place names that people use in their addresses. Therefore, we have also included a ZIP/City Cross. Reference immediately following the City/County Cross. Reference.

If you know the ZIP Code but the city name does not appear in the City/County Cross. Reference index, look up the ZIP Code in the ZIP/City Cross. Reference, find the city name, then look up the city name in the City/County Cross. Reference. For example, you want to know the county for an address of Menands, NY 12204. There is no "Menands" in the City/County Cross. Reference. The ZIP/City Cross. Reference shows that ZIP Codes 12201-12288 are for the city of Albany. Looking back in the City/County Cross. Reference, Albany is in Albany County.

Maine City/County Cross Reference

ABBOT Piscataquis
ABBOT VILLAGE Piscataquis
ACTON York
ADDISON Washington
ALBION Kennebec
ALFRED York
ALNA Lincoln
ANDOVER Oxford
ANSON Somerset
ASHLAND Aroostook
ATHENS Somerset
ATLANTIC Hancock
AUBURN Androscoggin
AUGUSTA Kennebec
AURORA Hancock
BAILEY ISLAND Cumberland
BAILEYVILLE Washington
BANGOR Penobscot
BAR HARBOR Hancock
BAR MILLS York
BASS HARBOR Hancock
BATH Sagadahoc
BAYVILLE Lincoln
BEALS Washington
BELFAST Waldo
BELGRADE Kennebec
BELGRADE LAKES Kennebec
BENEDICTA Aroostook
BERNARD Hancock
BERWICK York
BETHEL Oxford
BIDDEFORD York
BIDDEFORD POOL York
BINGHAM Somerset
BIRCH HARBOR Hancock
BLAINE Aroostook
BLUE HILL Hancock
BLUE HILL FALLS Hancock
BOOTHBAY Lincoln
BOOTHBAY HARBOR Lincoln
BOWDOIN Sagadahoc
BOWDOINHAM Sagadahoc
BRADFORD Penobscot
BRADLEY Penobscot
BREMEN Lincoln
BREWER Penobscot
BRIDGEWATER Aroostook
BRIDGTON Cumberland
BRISTOL Lincoln
BROOKLIN Hancock
BROOKS Waldo
BROOKSVILLE Hancock
BROOKTON Washington
BROWNFIELD Oxford
BROWNVILLE Piscataquis
BROWNVILLE JUNCTION Piscataquis
BRUNSWICK Cumberland
BRYANT POND Oxford
BUCKFIELD Oxford
BUCKS HARBOR Washington
BUCKSPORT Hancock
BURLINGTON Penobscot
BURNHAM Waldo
BUSTINS ISLAND Cumberland
BUXTON York
CALAIS Washington
CAMBRIDGE Somerset
CAMDEN Knox
CANAAN Somerset
CANTON Oxford
CAPE ELIZABETH Cumberland
CAPE NEDDICK York
CAPE PORPOISE York
CARATUNK Somerset
CARDVILLE Penobscot
CARIBOU Aroostook
CARMEL Penobscot
CASCO Cumberland
CASTINE Hancock
CENTER LOVELL Oxford
CHAMBERLAIN Lincoln
CHARLESTON Penobscot
CHEBEAGUE ISLAND Cumberland
CHERRYFIELD Washington
CHINA Kennebec
CHINA VILLAGE Kennebec
CLAYTON LAKE Aroostook
CLIFF ISLAND Cumberland
CLINTON Kennebec
COLUMBIA FALLS Washington
COOPERS MILLS Lincoln
COREA Hancock
CORINNA Penobscot
CORINTH Penobscot
CORNISH York
COSTIGAN Penobscot
CRANBERRY ISLES Hancock
CROUSEVILLE Aroostook
CUMBERLAND CENTER Cumberland
CUMBERLAND FORESIDE Cumberland
CUSHING Knox
CUTLER Washington
DAMARISCOTTA Lincoln
DANFORTH Washington
DANVILLE Androscoggin
DEER ISLE Hancock
DENMARK Oxford
DENNYSVILLE Washington
DETROIT Somerset
DEXTER (04930) Penobscot(97), Somerset(2)
DIXFIELD Oxford
DIXMONT Penobscot
DOVER FOXCROFT Piscataquis
DRESDEN Lincoln
DRYDEN Franklin
DURHAM Androscoggin
EAGLE LAKE Aroostook
EAST ANDOVER Oxford
EAST BALDWIN Cumberland
EAST BLUE HILL Hancock
EAST BOOTHBAY Lincoln
EAST CORINTH Penobscot
EAST DIXFIELD Franklin
EAST LIVERMORE Androscoggin
EAST MACHIAS Washington
EAST MILLINOCKET Penobscot
EAST NEWPORT Penobscot
EAST ORLAND Hancock
EAST PARSONFIELD York
EAST POLAND Androscoggin
EAST STONEHAM Oxford
EAST VASSALBORO Kennebec
EAST WATERBORO York
EAST WATERFORD Oxford
EAST WILTON Franklin
EAST WINTHROP Kennebec
EASTON Aroostook
EASTPORT Washington
EDDINGTON Penobscot
EDGECOMB Lincoln
ELIOT York
ELLSWORTH Hancock
ENFIELD Penobscot
ESTCOURT STATION Aroostook
ETNA Penobscot
EUSTIS Franklin
EXETER Penobscot
FAIRFIELD (04937) Kennebec(97), Somerset(2)
FALMOUTH Cumberland
FARMINGDALE Kennebec
FARMINGTON Franklin
FARMINGTON FALLS Franklin
FORT FAIRFIELD Aroostook
FORT KENT Aroostook
FORT KENT MILLS Aroostook
FRANKFORT Waldo
FRANKLIN Hancock
FREEDOM Waldo
FREEPORT Cumberland
FRENCHBORO Hancock
FRENCHVILLE Aroostook
FRIENDSHIP Knox
FRYE Oxford
FRYEBURG Oxford
GARDINER Kennebec
GARLAND Penobscot
GEORGETOWN Sagadahoc
GLEN COVE Knox
GORHAM Cumberland
GOULDSBORO Hancock
GRAND ISLE Aroostook
GRAND LAKE STREAM Washington
GRAY Cumberland
GREENBUSH Penobscot
GREENE Androscoggin
GREENVILLE Piscataquis
GREENVILLE JUNCTION (04442) Piscataquis(86), Somerset(13)
GREENWOOD Oxford
GROVE Washington
GUILFORD Piscataquis
HALLOWELL Kennebec
HAMPDEN Penobscot
HANCOCK Hancock
HANOVER Oxford
HARBORSIDE Hancock
HARMONY Somerset
HARPSWELL Cumberland
HARRINGTON Washington
HARRISON Cumberland
HARTLAND Somerset
HAYNESVILLE Aroostook
HEBRON Oxford
HINCKLEY Somerset
HIRAM Oxford
HOLDEN (04429) Penobscot(98), Hancock(1)
HOLLIS CENTER York
HOPE Knox
HOULTON Aroostook
HOWLAND Penobscot
HUDSON Penobscot
HULLS COVE Hancock
ISLAND FALLS Aroostook
ISLE AU HAUT Knox
ISLE OF SPRINGS Lincoln
ISLESBORO Waldo
ISLESFORD Hancock
JACKMAN Somerset
JAY Franklin
JEFFERSON Lincoln
JONESBORO Washington
JONESPORT Washington
KENDUSKEAG Penobscot
KENNEBUNK York
KENNEBUNKPORT York
KENTS HILL Kennebec
KINGFIELD Franklin
KINGMAN Penobscot
KITTERY York
KITTERY POINT York
LAGRANGE (04453) Penobscot(98), Piscataquis(1)
LAMBERT LAKE Washington
LEBANON York
LEE Penobscot
LEEDS Androscoggin
LEVANT Penobscot
LEWISTON Androscoggin
LIBERTY Waldo
LILLE Aroostook
LIMERICK York
LIMESTONE Aroostook
LIMINGTON York
LINCOLN Penobscot
LINCOLN CENTER Penobscot
LINCOLNVILLE Waldo
LINCOLNVILLE CENTER Waldo
LISBON Androscoggin
LISBON CENTER Androscoggin
LISBON FALLS Androscoggin
LITCHFIELD Kennebec
LITTLE DEER ISLE Hancock
LIVERMORE Androscoggin
LIVERMORE FALLS Androscoggin
LOCKE MILLS Oxford
LONG ISLAND Cumberland
LOVELL Oxford
LUBEC Washington
MACHIAS Washington

MACHIASPORT Washington
MADAWASKA Aroostook
MADISON Somerset
MANCHESTER Kennebec
MANSET Hancock
MAPLETON Aroostook
MARS HILL Aroostook
MASARDIS Aroostook
MATINICUS Knox
MATTAWAMKEAG Penobscot
MECHANIC FALLS Androscoggin
MEDDYBEMPS Washington
MEDWAY Penobscot
MEREPOINT Cumberland
MEXICO Oxford
MILBRIDGE Washington
MILFORD Penobscot
MILLINOCKET Penobscot
MILO Piscataquis
MINOT Androscoggin
MINTURN Hancock
MONHEGAN Lincoln
MONMOUTH Kennebec
MONROE Waldo
MONSON Piscataquis
MONTICELLO Aroostook
MOODY York
MORRILL Waldo
MOUNT DESERT Hancock
MOUNT VERNON Kennebec
NAPLES Cumberland
NEW GLOUCESTER Cumberland
NEW HARBOR Lincoln
NEW LIMERICK Aroostook
NEW PORTLAND Somerset
NEW SHARON Franklin
NEW SWEDEN Aroostook
NEW VINEYARD Franklin
NEWAGEN Lincoln
NEWCASTLE Lincoln
NEWFIELD York
NEWPORT Penobscot
NEWRY Oxford
NOBLEBORO Lincoln
NORRIDGEWOCK Somerset
NORTH AMITY Aroostook
NORTH ANSON Somerset
NORTH BERWICK York
NORTH BRIDGTON Cumberland
NORTH BROOKLIN Hancock
NORTH FRYEBURG Oxford
NORTH HAVEN Knox
NORTH JAY Franklin
NORTH MONMOUTH Kennebec
NORTH NEW PORTLAND Somerset
NORTH SHAPLEIGH York
NORTH TURNER Androscoggin
NORTH VASSALBORO Kennebec
NORTH WATERBORO York
NORTH WATERFORD Oxford
NORTH YARMOUTH Cumberland
NORTHEAST HARBOR Hancock
NORWAY Oxford
OAKFIELD Aroostook
OAKLAND Kennebec
OCEAN PARK York
OGUNQUIT York
OLAMON Penobscot
OLD ORCHARD BEACH York
OLD TOWN Penobscot
OQUOSSOC Franklin
ORIENT Aroostook
ORLAND Hancock
ORONO Penobscot
ORRINGTON Penobscot
ORRS ISLAND Cumberland
OTTER CREEK Hancock
OWLS HEAD Knox
OXBOW Aroostook
OXFORD Oxford
PALERMO Waldo
PALMYRA Somerset
PARIS Oxford
PARSONSFIELD York
PASSADUMKEAG Penobscot
PATTEN Penobscot
PEAKS ISLAND Cumberland
PEJEPSCOT Sagadahoc
PEMAQUID Lincoln
PEMBROKE Washington
PENOBSCOT Hancock
PERHAM Aroostook
PERRY Washington
PERU Oxford
PHILLIPS Franklin
PHIPPSBURG Sagadahoc
PITTSFIELD Somerset
PLAISTED Aroostook
PLYMOUTH Penobscot
POLAND Androscoggin
PORT CLYDE Knox
PORTAGE Aroostook
PORTER Oxford
PORTLAND Cumberland
POWNAL Cumberland
PRESQUE ISLE Aroostook
PRINCETON Washington
PROSPECT HARBOR Hancock
QUIMBY Aroostook
RANDOLPH Kennebec
RANGELEY Franklin
RAYMOND Cumberland
READFIELD Kennebec
RICHMOND Sagadahoc
ROBBINSTON Washington
ROCKLAND Knox
ROCKPORT Knox
ROCKWOOD (04478) Somerset(86), Piscataquis(13)
ROUND POND Lincoln
ROXBURY Oxford
RUMFORD Oxford
RUMFORD CENTER Oxford
RUMFORD POINT Oxford
SABATTUS Androscoggin
SACO York
SAINT AGATHA Aroostook
SAINT ALBANS Somerset
SAINT DAVID Aroostook
SAINT FRANCIS Aroostook
SAINT GEORGE Knox
SALSBURY COVE Hancock
SANDY POINT Waldo
SANFORD York
SANGERVILLE Piscataquis
SARGENTVILLE Hancock
SCARBOROUGH Cumberland
SEAL COVE Hancock
SEAL HARBOR Hancock
SEARSMONT Waldo
SEARSPORT Waldo
SEBAGO Cumberland
SEBAGO LAKE Cumberland
SEBASCO ESTATES Sagadahoc
SEBEC Piscataquis
SEBEC LAKE Piscataquis
SEDGWICK Hancock
SHAPLEIGH York
SHAWMUT Somerset
SHERIDAN Aroostook
SHERMAN Aroostook
SHERMAN MILLS Aroostook
SHERMAN STATION (04777) Penobscot(90), Aroostook(9)
SHIRLEY MILLS Piscataquis
SINCLAIR Aroostook
SKOWHEGAN Somerset
SMALL POINT Sagadahoc
SMITHFIELD Somerset
SMYRNA MILLS Aroostook
SOLDIER POND Aroostook
SOLON Somerset
SORRENTO Hancock
SOUTH BERWICK York
SOUTH BRISTOL Lincoln
SOUTH CASCO Cumberland
SOUTH CHINA Kennebec
SOUTH FREEPORT Cumberland
SOUTH GARDINER Kennebec
SOUTH GOULDSBORO Hancock
SOUTH HIRAM Oxford
SOUTH PARIS Oxford
SOUTH PORTLAND Cumberland
SOUTH THOMASTON Knox
SOUTH WATERFORD Oxford
SOUTH WINDHAM Cumberland
SOUTHPORT Lincoln
SOUTHWEST HARBOR Hancock
SPRINGFIELD Penobscot
SPRINGVALE York
SPRUCE HEAD Knox
SQUIRREL ISLAND Lincoln
STACYVILLE (04777) Penobscot(90), Aroostook(9)
STACYVILLE Penobscot
STANDISH Cumberland
STEEP FALLS Cumberland
STETSON Penobscot
STEUBEN Washington
STILLWATER Penobscot
STOCKHOLM Aroostook
STOCKTON SPRINGS Waldo
STONEHAM Oxford
STONINGTON Hancock
STRATTON Franklin
STRONG Franklin
SULLIVAN Hancock
SUMNER Oxford
SUNSET Hancock
SURRY Hancock
SWANS ISLAND Hancock
TEMPLE Franklin
TENANTS HARBOR Knox
THOMASTON Knox
THORNDIKE Waldo
TOPSFIELD Washington
TOPSHAM Sagadahoc
TREVETT Lincoln
TROY Waldo
TURNER Androscoggin
TURNER CENTER Androscoggin
UNION Knox
UNITY Waldo
UPPER FRENCHVILLE Aroostook
VAN BUREN Aroostook
VANCEBORO Washington
VASSALBORO Kennebec
VIENNA Kennebec
VINALHAVEN Knox
WAITE Washington
WALDOBORO Lincoln
WALLAGRASS Aroostook
WALPOLE Lincoln
WARREN Knox
WASHBURN Aroostook
WASHINGTON Knox
WATERBORO York
WATERFORD Oxford
WATERVILLE Kennebec
WAYNE Kennebec
WEEKS MILLS Kennebec
WELD Franklin
WELLS York
WESLEY Washington
WEST BALDWIN Cumberland
WEST BETHEL Oxford
WEST BOOTHBAY HARBOR Lincoln
WEST BOWDOIN Sagadahoc
WEST BUXTON York
WEST ENFIELD Penobscot
WEST FARMINGTON Franklin
WEST FORKS Somerset
WEST KENNEBUNK York
WEST MINOT Androscoggin
WEST NEWFIELD York
WEST PARIS Oxford
WEST POLAND Androscoggin
WEST ROCKPORT Knox
WEST SOUTHPORT Lincoln
WEST TREMONT Hancock
WESTBROOK Cumberland
WESTFIELD Aroostook
WHITEFIELD Lincoln
WHITING Washington
WHITNEYVILLE Washington
WILEYS CORNER Knox
WILTON Franklin
WINDHAM Cumberland
WINDSOR Kennebec
WINN Penobscot
WINTER HARBOR Hancock
WINTERPORT Waldo
WINTERVILLE Aroostook
WINTHROP Kennebec
WISCASSET Lincoln
WOODLAND Washington
WOOLWICH Sagadahoc
WYTOPITLOCK Aroostook
YARMOUTH Cumberland
YORK York
YORK BEACH York
YORK HARBOR York

Maine ZIP/City Cross Reference

03901-03901	BERWICK
03902-03902	CAPE NEDDICK
03903-03903	ELIOT
03904-03904	KITTERY
03905-03905	KITTERY POINT
03906-03906	NORTH BERWICK
03907-03907	OGUNQUIT
03908-03908	SOUTH BERWICK
03909-03909	YORK
03910-03910	YORK BEACH
03911-03911	YORK HARBOR
04001-04001	ACTON
04002-04002	ALFRED
04003-04003	BAILEY ISLAND
04004-04004	BAR MILLS
04005-04005	BIDDEFORD
04006-04006	BIDDEFORD POOL
04007-04007	BIDDEFORD
04008-04008	BOWDOINHAM
04009-04009	BRIDGTON
04010-04010	BROWNFIELD
04011-04011	BRUNSWICK
04013-04013	BUSTINS ISLAND
04014-04014	CAPE PORPOISE
04015-04015	CASCO
04016-04016	CENTER LOVELL
04017-04017	CHEBEAGUE ISLAND
04019-04019	CLIFF ISLAND
04020-04020	CORNISH
04021-04021	CUMBERLAND CENTER
04022-04022	DENMARK
04024-04024	EAST BALDWIN
04027-04027	LEBANON
04028-04028	EAST PARSONFIELD
04029-04029	SEBAGO
04030-04030	EAST WATERBORO
04032-04034	FREEPORT
04037-04037	FRYEBURG
04038-04038	GORHAM
04039-04039	GRAY
04040-04040	HARRISON
04041-04041	HIRAM
04042-04042	HOLLIS CENTER
04043-04043	KENNEBUNK
04046-04046	KENNEBUNKPORT
04047-04047	PARSONSFIELD
04048-04048	LIMERICK
04049-04049	LIMINGTON
04050-04050	LONG ISLAND
04051-04051	LOVELL
04053-04053	MEREPOINT
04054-04054	MOODY
04055-04055	NAPLES
04056-04056	NEWFIELD
04057-04057	NORTH BRIDGTON
04058-04058	NORTH FRYEBURG
04060-04060	NORTH SHAPLEIGH
04061-04061	NORTH WATERBORO
04062-04062	WINDHAM
04063-04063	OCEAN PARK
04064-04064	OLD ORCHARD BEACH
04066-04066	ORRS ISLAND
04067-04067	PEJEPSCOT
04068-04068	PORTER
04069-04069	POWNAL
04070-04070	SCARBOROUGH
04071-04071	RAYMOND
04072-04072	SACO
04073-04073	SANFORD
04074-04074	SCARBOROUGH
04075-04075	SEBAGO LAKE
04076-04076	SHAPLEIGH
04077-04077	SOUTH CASCO
04078-04078	SOUTH FREEPORT
04079-04079	HARPSWELL
04080-04080	SOUTH HIRAM
04081-04081	SOUTH WATERFORD
04082-04082	SOUTH WINDHAM
04083-04083	SPRINGVALE
04084-04084	STANDISH
04085-04085	STEEP FALLS
04086-04086	TOPSHAM
04087-04087	WATERBORO
04088-04088	WATERFORD
04090-04090	WELLS
04091-04091	WEST BALDWIN
04092-04092	WESTBROOK
04093-04093	WEST BUXTON
04093-04093	BUXTON
04094-04094	WEST KENNEBUNK
04095-04095	WEST NEWFIELD
04096-04096	YARMOUTH
04097-04097	NORTH YARMOUTH
04098-04098	WESTBROOK
04100-04104	PORTLAND
04105-04105	FALMOUTH
04106-04106	SOUTH PORTLAND
04107-04107	CAPE ELIZABETH
04108-04108	PEAKS ISLAND
04109-04109	PORTLAND
04110-04110	CUMBERLAND FORESIDE
04112-04112	PORTLAND
04116-04116	SOUTH PORTLAND
04122-04124	PORTLAND
04210-04212	AUBURN
04216-04216	ANDOVER
04217-04217	BETHEL
04219-04219	BRYANT POND
04220-04220	BUCKFIELD
04221-04221	CANTON
04222-04222	DURHAM
04223-04223	DANVILLE
04224-04224	DIXFIELD
04225-04225	DRYDEN
04226-04226	EAST ANDOVER
04227-04227	EAST DIXFIELD
04228-04228	EAST LIVERMORE
04230-04230	EAST POLAND
04231-04231	EAST STONEHAM
04231-04231	STONEHAM
04233-04233	EAST WATERFORD
04234-04234	EAST WILTON
04235-04235	FRYE
04236-04236	GREENE
04237-04237	HANOVER
04238-04238	HEBRON
04239-04239	JAY
04240-04243	LEWISTON
04250-04250	LISBON
04251-04251	LISBON CENTER
04252-04252	LISBON FALLS
04253-04253	LIVERMORE
04254-04254	LIVERMORE FALLS
04255-04255	LOCKE MILLS
04255-04255	GREENWOOD
04256-04256	MECHANIC FALLS
04257-04257	MEXICO
04258-04258	MINOT
04259-04259	MONMOUTH
04260-04260	NEW GLOUCESTER
04261-04261	NEWRY
04262-04262	NORTH JAY
04263-04263	LEEDS
04265-04265	NORTH MONMOUTH
04266-04266	NORTH TURNER
04267-04267	NORTH WATERFORD
04268-04268	NORWAY
04270-04270	OXFORD
04271-04271	PARIS
04273-04274	POLAND
04275-04275	ROXBURY
04276-04276	RUMFORD
04278-04278	RUMFORD CENTER
04279-04279	RUMFORD POINT
04280-04280	SABATTUS
04281-04281	SOUTH PARIS
04282-04282	TURNER
04283-04283	TURNER CENTER
04284-04284	WAYNE
04285-04285	WELD
04286-04286	WEST BETHEL
04287-04287	WEST BOWDOIN
04287-04287	BOWDOIN
04288-04288	WEST MINOT
04289-04289	WEST PARIS
04290-04290	PERU
04291-04291	WEST POLAND
04292-04292	SUMNER
04294-04294	WILTON
04330-04338	AUGUSTA
04341-04341	COOPERS MILLS
04342-04342	DRESDEN
04343-04343	EAST WINTHROP
04344-04344	FARMINGDALE
04345-04345	GARDINER
04346-04346	RANDOLPH
04347-04347	HALLOWELL
04348-04348	JEFFERSON
04349-04349	KENTS HILL
04350-04350	LITCHFIELD
04351-04351	MANCHESTER
04352-04352	MOUNT VERNON
04353-04353	WHITEFIELD
04354-04354	PALERMO
04355-04355	READFIELD
04357-04357	RICHMOND
04358-04358	SOUTH CHINA
04359-04359	SOUTH GARDINER
04360-04360	VIENNA
04361-04361	WEEKS MILLS
04362-04362	WHITEFIELD
04363-04363	WINDSOR
04364-04364	WINTHROP
04401-04402	BANGOR
04406-04406	ABBOT VILLAGE
04406-04406	ABBOT
04408-04408	AURORA
04410-04410	BRADFORD
04411-04411	BRADLEY
04412-04412	BREWER
04413-04413	BROOKTON
04414-04414	BROWNVILLE
04415-04415	BROWNVILLE JUNCTION
04416-04416	BUCKSPORT
04417-04417	BURLINGTON
04418-04418	CARDVILLE
04418-04418	GREENBUSH
04419-04419	CARMEL
04420-04421	CASTINE
04422-04422	CHARLESTON
04423-04423	COSTIGAN
04424-04424	DANFORTH
04426-04426	DOVER FOXCROFT
04427-04427	EAST CORINTH
04427-04427	CORINTH
04428-04428	EDDINGTON
04429-04429	HOLDEN
04430-04430	EAST MILLINOCKET
04431-04431	EAST ORLAND
04433-04433	ENFIELD
04434-04434	ETNA
04435-04435	EXETER
04438-04438	FRANKFORT
04441-04441	GREENVILLE
04442-04442	GREENVILLE JUNCTION
04443-04443	GUILFORD
04444-04444	HAMPDEN
04446-04446	HAYNESVILLE
04448-04448	HOWLAND
04449-04449	HUDSON
04450-04450	KENDUSKEAG
04451-04451	KINGMAN
04453-04453	LAGRANGE
04454-04454	LAMBERT LAKE
04455-04455	LEE
04456-04456	LEVANT
04457-04457	LINCOLN
04458-04458	LINCOLN CENTER
04459-04459	MATTAWAMKEAG
04460-04460	MEDWAY
04461-04461	MILFORD
04462-04462	MILLINOCKET
04463-04463	MILO
04464-04464	MONSON
04465-04465	NORTH AMITY
04467-04467	OLAMON
04468-04468	OLD TOWN
04469-04469	ORONO
04471-04471	ORIENT
04472-04472	ORLAND
04473-04473	ORONO
04474-04474	ORRINGTON
04475-04475	PASSADUMKEAG
04476-04476	PENOBSCOT
04478-04478	ROCKWOOD
04479-04479	SANGERVILLE
04481-04481	SEBEC
04482-04482	GUILFORD
04482-04482	SEBEC LAKE
04485-04485	SHIRLEY MILLS
04487-04487	SPRINGFIELD
04488-04488	STETSON
04489-04489	STILLWATER
04490-04490	TOPSFIELD
04491-04491	VANCEBORO
04492-04492	WAITE
04493-04493	WEST ENFIELD
04495-04495	WINN
04496-04496	WINTERPORT
04497-04497	WYTOPITLOCK
04530-04530	BATH
04535-04535	ALNA
04536-04536	BAYVILLE
04537-04537	BOOTHBAY
04538-04538	BOOTHBAY HARBOR
04539-04539	BRISTOL
04541-04541	CHAMBERLAIN
04543-04543	DAMARISCOTTA
04544-04544	EAST BOOTHBAY
04547-04547	FRIENDSHIP
04548-04548	GEORGETOWN
04549-04549	ISLE OF SPRINGS
04551-04551	BREMEN
04552-04552	NEWAGEN
04553-04553	NEWCASTLE
04554-04554	NEW HARBOR
04555-04555	NOBLEBORO
04556-04556	EDGECOMB
04558-04558	PEMAQUID
04562-04562	PHIPPSBURG
04563-04563	CUSHING
04564-04564	ROUND POND
04565-04565	SEBASCO ESTATES
04567-04567	SMALL POINT
04568-04568	SOUTH BRISTOL
04570-04570	SQUIRREL ISLAND
04571-04571	TREVETT
04572-04572	WALDOBORO
04573-04573	WALPOLE
04574-04574	WASHINGTON
04575-04575	WEST BOOTHBAY HARBOR
04576-04576	WEST SOUTHPORT
04576-04576	SOUTHPORT
04578-04578	WISCASSET
04579-04579	WOOLWICH
04605-04605	ELLSWORTH
04606-04606	ADDISON
04607-04607	GOULDSBORO
04608-04608	ATLANTIC
04609-04609	BAR HARBOR
04611-04611	BEALS
04612-04612	BERNARD
04613-04613	BIRCH HARBOR
04614-04614	BLUE HILL
04615-04615	BLUE HILL FALLS
04616-04616	BROOKLIN
04617-04617	BROOKSVILLE
04618-04618	BUCKS HARBOR
04619-04619	CALAIS
04622-04622	CHERRYFIELD

04623-04623 COLUMBIA FALLS
04624-04624 COREA
04625-04625 CRANBERRY ISLES
04626-04626 CUTLER
04627-04627 DEER ISLE
04628-04628 DENNYSVILLE
04629-04629 EAST BLUE HILL
04630-04630 EAST MACHIAS
04631-04631 EASTPORT
04634-04634 FRANKLIN
04635-04635 FRENCHBORO
04637-04637 GRAND LAKE STREAM
04638-04638 GROVE
04640-04640 HANCOCK
04642-04642 HARBORSIDE
04643-04643 HARRINGTON
04644-04644 HULLS COVE
04645-04645 ISLE AU HAUT
04646-04646 ISLESFORD
04648-04648 JONESBORO
04649-04649 JONESPORT
04650-04650 LITTLE DEER ISLE
04652-04652 LUBEC
04653-04653 BASS HARBOR
04654-04654 MACHIAS
04655-04655 MACHIASPORT
04656-04656 MANSET
04657-04657 MEDDYBEMPS
04658-04658 MILBRIDGE
04659-04659 MINTURN
04660-04660 MOUNT DESERT
04661-04661 NORTH BROOKLIN
04662-04662 NORTHEAST HARBOR
04664-04664 SULLIVAN
04665-04665 OTTER CREEK
04666-04666 PEMBROKE
04667-04667 PERRY
04668-04668 PRINCETON
04669-04669 PROSPECT HARBOR
04671-04671 ROBBINSTON
04672-04672 SALSBURY COVE
04673-04673 SARGENTVILLE
04674-04674 SEAL COVE
04675-04675 SEAL HARBOR
04676-04676 SEDGWICK
04677-04677 SORRENTO
04678-04678 SOUTH GOULDSBORO
04679-04679 SOUTHWEST HARBOR
04680-04680 STEUBEN
04681-04681 STONINGTON
04683-04683 SUNSET
04684-04684 SURRY
04685-04685 SWANS ISLAND
04686-04686 WESLEY
04690-04690 WEST TREMONT
04691-04691 WHITING
04692-04692 WHITNEYVILLE
04693-04693 WINTER HARBOR
04694-04694 WOODLAND
04694-04694 BAILEYVILLE
04730-04730 HOULTON
04732-04732 ASHLAND
04733-04733 BENEDICTA
04734-04734 BLAINE
04735-04735 BRIDGEWATER
04736-04736 CARIBOU
04737-04737 CLAYTON LAKE
04738-04738 CROUSEVILLE
04739-04739 EAGLE LAKE
04740-04740 EASTON
04741-04741 ESTCOURT STATION
04742-04742 FORT FAIRFIELD
04743-04743 FORT KENT
04744-04744 FORT KENT MILLS
04745-04745 FRENCHVILLE
04746-04746 GRAND ISLE
04747-04747 ISLAND FALLS
04749-04749 LILLE
04750-04751 LIMESTONE
04756-04756 MADAWASKA
04757-04757 MAPLETON
04758-04758 MARS HILL
04759-04759 MASARDIS
04760-04760 MONTICELLO
04761-04761 NEW LIMERICK
04762-04762 NEW SWEDEN
04763-04763 OAKFIELD
04764-04764 OXBOW
04765-04765 PATTEN
04766-04766 PERHAM
04767-04767 PLAISTED
04768-04768 PORTAGE
04769-04769 PRESQUE ISLE
04770-04770 QUIMBY
04772-04772 SAINT AGATHA
04773-04773 SAINT DAVID
04774-04774 SAINT FRANCIS
04775-04775 SHERIDAN
04776-04776 SHERMAN MILLS
04776-04776 SHERMAN
04777-04777 SHERMAN STATION
04777-04777 STACYVILLE
04779-04779 SINCLAIR
04780-04780 SMYRNA MILLS
04781-04781 SOLDIER POND
04781-04781 WALLAGRASS
04782-04782 STACYVILLE
04783-04783 STOCKHOLM
04784-04784 UPPER FRENCHVILLE
04785-04785 VAN BUREN
04786-04786 WASHBURN
04787-04787 WESTFIELD
04788-04788 WINTERVILLE
04841-04841 ROCKLAND
04843-04843 CAMDEN
04846-04846 GLEN COVE
04847-04847 HOPE
04848-04848 ISLESBORO
04849-04849 LINCOLNVILLE
04850-04850 LINCOLNVILLE CENTER
04851-04851 MATINICUS
04852-04852 MONHEGAN
04853-04853 NORTH HAVEN
04854-04854 OWLS HEAD
04855-04855 PORT CLYDE
04856-04856 ROCKPORT
04857-04857 SAINT GEORGE
04857-04857 WILEYS CORNER
04858-04858 SOUTH THOMASTON
04859-04859 SPRUCE HEAD
04860-04860 TENANTS HARBOR
04861-04861 THOMASTON
04862-04862 UNION
04863-04863 VINALHAVEN
04864-04864 WARREN
04865-04865 WEST ROCKPORT
04901-04903 WATERVILLE
04910-04910 ALBION
04911-04911 ANSON
04912-04912 ATHENS
04915-04915 BELFAST
04917-04917 BELGRADE
04918-04918 BELGRADE LAKES
04920-04920 BINGHAM
04921-04921 BROOKS
04922-04922 BURNHAM
04923-04923 CAMBRIDGE
04924-04924 CANAAN
04925-04925 CARATUNK
04926-04926 CHINA
04926-04926 CHINA VILLAGE
04927-04927 CLINTON
04928-04928 CORINNA
04929-04929 DETROIT
04930-04930 DEXTER
04932-04932 DIXMONT
04933-04933 EAST NEWPORT
04935-04935 EAST VASSALBORO
04936-04936 EUSTIS
04937-04937 FAIRFIELD
04938-04938 FARMINGTON
04939-04939 GARLAND
04940-04940 FARMINGTON FALLS
04941-04941 FREEDOM
04942-04942 HARMONY
04943-04943 HARTLAND
04944-04944 HINCKLEY
04945-04945 JACKMAN
04947-04947 KINGFIELD
04949-04949 LIBERTY
04950-04950 MADISON
04951-04951 MONROE
04952-04952 MORRILL
04953-04953 NEWPORT
04954-04954 NEW PORTLAND
04955-04955 NEW SHARON
04956-04956 NEW VINEYARD
04957-04957 NORRIDGEWOCK
04958-04958 NORTH ANSON
04961-04961 NORTH NEW PORTLAND
04961-04961 NEW PORTLAND
04962-04962 NORTH VASSALBORO
04963-04963 OAKLAND
04964-04964 OQUOSSOC
04965-04965 PALMYRA
04966-04966 PHILLIPS
04967-04967 PITTSFIELD
04969-04969 PLYMOUTH
04970-04970 RANGELEY
04971-04971 SAINT ALBANS
04972-04972 SANDY POINT
04973-04973 SEARSMONT
04974-04974 SEARSPORT
04975-04975 SHAWMUT
04976-04976 SKOWHEGAN
04978-04978 SMITHFIELD
04979-04979 SOLON
04981-04981 STOCKTON SPRINGS
04982-04982 STRATTON
04983-04983 STRONG
04984-04984 TEMPLE
04985-04985 WEST FORKS
04986-04986 THORNDIKE
04987-04987 TROY
04988-04988 UNITY
04989-04989 VASSALBORO
04992-04992 WEST FARMINGTON

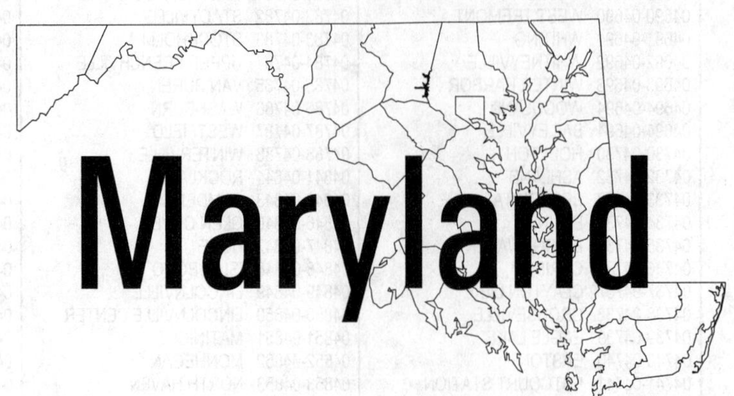

Maryland

General Help Numbers:

Governor's Office

State House, 100 State Circle
Annapolis, MD 21401
www.gov.state.md.us
410-974-3901
Fax 410-974-3275
9AM-5PM

Attorney General's Office

200 St Paul Place
Baltimore, MD 21202
www.oag.state.md.us
410-576-6300
Fax 410-576-6404
8AM-5PM

Legislative Records

Legislative Information Desk, Library & Information Srv
90 State Circle, Basement Level
Annapolis, MD 21401-1991
http://mlis.state.md.us
410-946-5400
Fax 410-946-5405
8AM-5PM

State Archives

Hall of Records
350 Rowe Blvd
Annapolis, MD 21401
www.msa.md.gov/
410-260-6400
Fax 410-974-2525
8AM-4:30PM T-F;
8:30-4:30 SAT

State Specifics:

Capital:	Annapolis Anne Arundel County
Time Zone:	EST
Number of Counties:	23
Population:	5,633,597
Web Site:	www.maryland.gov

State Agencies

Criminal Records

Criminal Justice Information System, Public Safety & Correctional Records, PO Box 32708, Pikeville, MD 21282-5743 (Courier address- 6776 Reisterstown Rd, Rm 102, Baltimore, MD 21215); 410-764-4501, 888-795-0011, Fax- 410-653-5690; 8AM-5PM. www.dpscs.state.md.us

Link to Customer Service Unit via the website in order to download a petition for authorization and return the petition via fax or mail.

Indexing & Storage: Records available from 1978. New records available for inquiry in 10 days if not submitted electronically. 90% of all arrests in database have final dispositions recorded, 97% for those arrests within last 5 years.

Searching: Release of criminal records is restricted. All private parties must first write/fax/phone this office and request a "petition package," then apply for a petition number. Employers are eligible to request a petition number; 3rd parties may not, directly. Include in request- set of fingerprints. A signed release is not necessary but is helpful. When applying for fingerprinting, a photo ID is required. 100% of records are fingerprint-supported. All searches require fingerprints and all require an authorization number including government. Investigators and all 3rd parties are considered as agents of employers and must use employer's authorization. All records released to law enforcement; public receives records with conviction data only. Records with dispositions of acquittal are not released to private entities.

Access by: mail, in person.

Fee & Payment: The fee is $18.00 per request, add $1.00 for a "gold seal." If a statutorily-required FBI fingerprint check is required, add $19.25. Fee payee- CJIS. Prepayment required. Money orders and cashier's checks are preferred. Personal checks accepted, credit cards are not.

Mail search: Turnaround time- 10-15 business days. A SASE is not required.

In person: In person requests are allowed, though signed release and fingerprints are required, and turnaround time is 5 days.

Other access: The State Court Administrator's Office has online access to criminal records from all state district courts, 3 circuit courts, and 1 city court. See that profile for more information.

Expedited service: Will rush expedite your request for no add'l charge, however a written request including a legitimate reason why must be submitted. An FBI check cannot be expedited. Will expedite the return if you provide a prepaid shipper envelope.

Statewide Court Records

Administrative Office of the Courts, 580 Taylor Ave, Annapolis, MD 21401; 410-260-1400, 410-260-1488, Fax- 410-974-5291; 8AM-5PM.

www.courts.state.md.us

For legal reference assistance email mdlaw.library@courts.state.md.us.

Online search: There is a free search of dockets from the trial courts at http://casesearch.courts.state.md.us/inquiry/inquiry-index.jsp. The search includes all district courts and circuit courts. Records are updated daily, but note that case information from Montgomery and Prince George's counties are always lagging one day behind. All case information may be searched by party name or case number. Appellate opinions are available at www.courts.state.md.us/opinions.html.

Other access: Bulk data of civil record information can be requested for a fee at www.courts.state.md.us/district/forms/acct/dca107.pdf.

Sexual Offender Registry

Criminal Justice Information System, PO Box 32708, SOR Unit, Pikeville, MD 21282-5743 (Courier address- 6776 Reisterstown Rd, Baltimore, MD 21215); 410-585-3649, 866-368-8657, Fax- 410-653-5690; 8:30AM-5:00PM.

www.socem.info/

Request the Sexual Offender Registry by email at websiteresponse@dpscs.state.md.us.

Indexing & Storage: Records available from 10/01/95. New records available for inquiry in a week if not submitted electronically.

Searching: This data not released- fingerprints, SSN, or the victim's date of birth.

Access by: mail, online.

Mail search: Turnaround time- 1 to 2 weeks. Include requester's full name, address, and reason for the request.

Online search: Online access is free at www.socem.info/. Search by name or ZIP Code. An interactive map is also available.

Other access: A printout is available of partial or complete SOR. Request must be in writing.

Incarceration Records

DPS and Correctional Services, Maryland Division of Corrections, 6776 Reistertown Road, Suite 310, Baltimore, MD 21215-2342; 410-585-3351, Fax-410-764-4220; 8AM-4:30PM.

www.dpscs.state.md.us

For an inmate's DOC # and location contact Data Processing via methods below or email to cwood@dpscs.state.md.us. To obtain any other information than DOC number you must contact individual institutions.

Indexing & Storage: Records available on current and former inmates. New records available for inquiry in 1 to 2 days.

Searching: Only location and DOC number are released from this agency. Include in request- inmates race, sex, full name, DOB and the SSN if known. Records computerized since 1980. This data not released- medical and certain personal information

Access by: mail, phone, fax, online.

Fee & Payment: No fee for search.

Mail search: Turnaround time- 1-3 days.

Phone search: Name searching available.

Fax search: Can request via the fax.

Online search: Search inmates online at www.dpscs.state.md.us/onlineservs/oil/. The Locator may not list some short sentenced inmates who, although committed to the Commissioner of Correction, are in fact housed at Division of Pretrial and Detention Services facilities.

Corporation, LP, LLP, LLC, Fictitious Name, Trade Name

Department of Assessments and Taxation, Charter Corporation Division, 301 W Preston St, Room 801, Baltimore, MD 21201; 410-767-1340, 410-767-1330, Fax- 410-333-7097; 8AM-4:30PM.

www.dat.state.md.us

Indexing & Storage: Records available from 1908 on. New records available for inquiry immediately.

Searching: Officers and directors info is not immediately available. Include in request- full name of business, corporation file number. The following is available; the Articles of Incorporation, Annual Reports, Officers, Directors, DBA's, Prior names (merged names), Inactive and Reserved names.

Access by: mail, phone, fax, in person, online.

Fee & Payment: An abstract of corporate records is $20.00, a Good Standing is $20.00. Copies are $1.00 per page plus $20.00 to certify. Fee payee- SDAT. Prepayment required. Personal checks, Visa, and MasterCard accepted.

Mail search: Turnaround time- 7 days. Officer and director information takes 2 weeks. Expedited service will improve turnaround time for mail or fax requests. SASE not required.

Phone search: Charter information includes date of incorporation, agent, and status. They will let you know how many pages if you wish to order copies.

Fax search: This is considered expedited service, see below.

In person: The office closes at 5 PM for searchers. Public access terminals are available.

Online search: Search for corporate name and trade name records for free at the main website (see above); also includes real estate statewide (cannot search by name) and UCC records. A Certificate of Good Standing is available online at http://sdatcert1.resiusa.org/certificate/ for the $40.00 fee. Certificates of Status are not available for trade names, name reservations, and sole proprietorships.

Other access: This agency will release information in a bulk output format through a contactor. Obtain priccs, formats, production schedules, etc. from Specprint, Inc. Contact Mr. Joe Jenkins of Specprint, Inc. at 410- 561-9600.

Expedited service: Expedited service is available for mail, phone and fax searches. Turnaround time- 3 days. There is an additional $20.00 fee to expedite a copy or expedite a certificate. A credit card must be used if requesting by fax.

Trademarks/Servicemarks

Secretary of State, Trademarks Division, 16 Francis Street, Jeffrey Bldg, Annapolis, MD 21401; 410-974-5521 x3859, Fax- 410-974-5527; 8:30AM-4:30PM. www.marylandsos.gov

Indexing & Storage: Records available for the past 10 years. Trademarks are registered for 10 years before expiring. New records available for inquiry immediately.

Searching: Include in request- trademark/servicemark name.

Access by: mail, phone, fax, in person, online.

Fee & Payment: There is no search fee. Certification is $5.00, copies are $.30 per page. Fee payee- Secretary of State. Prepayment required. Personal checks accepted, credit cards are not.

Mail search: Turnaround time- 1 week. No fee for mail request.

Phone search: No fee for telephone request. Only limited information is available.

Fax search: Will return information by mail in 1 week.

In person: No fee for request. Call before visiting.

Online search: Online searching is available at the Internet site. Search can be by keyword in the description field, the service or product, the owner, the classification, or the mark name or keyword in the mark name. Site offers application forms to register, renew, or assign trade and service marks, and general info about registration. Click on "Trade & Service Marks" or search at www.sos.state.md.us/Registrations/Trademarks/TMSearch.htm.

Other access: A computer printout of all marks registered, renewed or assigned within a 3 month period is available for $.05 per trademark.

Uniform Commercial Code

UCC Division-Taxpayer's Services, Department of Assessments & Taxation, 301 West Preston St, Baltimore, MD 21201; 410-767-1340, Fax- 410-333-7097; 8:30AM-5PM.

http://sdatcert3.resiusa.org/ucc-charter/

This agency will not do a general name or entity search. A searcher must come in person, hire a retriever, use the Internet, or buy the database.

Indexing & Storage: Records available for all active files.

Searching: Tax liens are not filed here, but are filed with the clerk of the circuit court of the debtor's jurisdiction. For help, email charterhelp@dat.state.md.us.

Access by: mail, in person, online.

Fee & Payment: There is no search fee. The copy fee is $1.00 per page. Certification is $20.00. Fee payee- Department of Assessments & Taxation Prepayment required. Personal checks accepted, credit cards are not.

Mail search: Will not do name searching, but will make copies if exact number of pages paid in advance.

In person: Records can be viewed at no charge on public access terminals.

Online search: The Internet site above or http://sdatcert3.resiusa.org/ucc-charter/ offers free access to UCC index information. Also, there is a related site offering access to real property data for the whole state at www.dat.state.md.us/.

Other access: The agency has available for sale copies of public release master data files including corporation, real estate, and UCC. In addition, they can produce customized files on paper or disk. Visit the website for more information.

Federal & State Tax Liens

Records not maintained by a state level agency.

All tax liens are filed at the county level.

Sales Tax Registrations

Taxpayer Services, Revenue Administration Division, 301 W Preston St #206, Baltimore, MD 21201; 410-767-1313, 410-767-1300, Fax- 410-767-1571; 8AM-5PM. www.comp.state.md.us

Email questions to sut@comp.state.md.us.

Indexing & Storage: Records available on a computer index for the past 4 years of applicants. New records available for inquiry in 7 days.

Searching: This agency will only confirm that a business's number is valid and confirm the name and address of the business. They will provide no other information. The business name and federal ID# or SSN of owner is required to search.

Access by: mail, phone, fax, online.

Fee & Payment: There are no fees.

Mail search: Turnaround time- 7 working days. Records are not returned by mail, they will call you. SASE not required.

Phone search: Call only if you have the permit number.

Fax search: Records are available by fax.

Online search: Using the web, one can determine if a MD sales tax account number is valid.

Birth Certificates

Department of Health, Division of Vital Records, PO Box 68760, Baltimore, MD 21215-0020 (Courier address- 6550 Reisterstown Rd, The Plaza, Baltimore, MD 21215); 410-764-3038, 410-764-3170 (Order), 410-318-6119 (Recording), Fax- 410-358-7381; 8AM-4PM M-F and 3rd Saturday of each month. www.vsa.state.md.us/

Birth certificates for individuals born in Maryland after 1939 are also available for same day service at local health departments in all jurisdictions except Montgomery County, Baltimore City, and Baltimore County.

Indexing & Storage: Records available from 1898 to present for all counties and 1910 to present for City of Baltimore. For prior records, contact the State Archives. New records available for inquiry in 4 to 6 weeks.

Searching: Must have a notarized signed release from person of record or mother or father, unless requester is parent or guardian or person listed. Include in request- full name, names of parents, mother's maiden name, date of birth, place of birth, relationship to person of record. Requester must supply valid photo ID.

Access by: mail, phone, fax, in person, online.

Fee & Payment: The search fee is $12.00. Fee payee- Division of Vital Records. Prepayment required. Cash is accepted for walk in requesters only. Personal checks accepted. Major credit cards accepted as indicated.

Mail search: Turnaround time- 2 to 3 weeks. A SASE is requested.

Phone search: See expedited service. Turnaround time is 3-5 days.

Fax search: See expedited service.

In person: Turnaround time is same day (typically, 15 to 30 minutes). Walk in requesters may pay with cash or check; no credit cards. Presentation of original photo ID is required for walk in requesters.

Online search: Records may be ordered from a designated vendor at www.vitalchek.com. Use of credit card is required and additional $7.00 fee required.

Expedited service: Expedited service is available for online and fax searches from VitalChek. Turnaround time- 2 days. Add $7.00 for use of credit card and express ship fees, if desired.

Death Records

Department of Health, Division of Vital Records, PO Box 68760, Baltimore, MD 21215-0020 (Courier address- 6550 Reisterstown Rd, The Plaza, Baltimore, MD 21215); 410-764-3038, 410-764-3170 (Order), 410-318-6119 (Recording), Fax- 410-358-7381; 8AM-4PM M-F and 3rd Saturday of each month. www.vsa.state.md.us/

Indexing & Storage: Records available from 1969 to present. For records prior to 1969 contact Maryland State Archives, 410-260-6429. New records available for inquiry in 2-3 weeks (if filed at county).

Searching: Must have a signed release from immediate family member. A signature is required from the requester. Include in request- full name, date of death, place of death, relationship to person of record, reason for information request. Request must be signed. Include copy of photo ID with request.

Access by: mail, phone, fax, in person, online.

Fee & Payment: The search fee is $12.00. Fee payee- Division of Vital Records. Prepayment required. Personal checks, money orders accepted. Major credit cards accepted as indicated.

Mail search: Turnaround time- 2 to 4 weeks. A SASE is requested.

Phone search: See expedited service. Turnaround time is 2-3 days.

Fax search: See expedited service.

In person: Turnaround time is same day.

Online search: Records may be ordered from a designated vendor at www.vitalchek.com. Use of credit card is required and additional $7.00 fee required.

Expedited service: Expedited service is available for online and fax searches from VitalChek. Turnaround time- 2 days. Add $7.00 for use of credit card and express ship fees, if desired.

Marriage Certificates

Department of Health, Division of Vital Records, PO Box 68760, Baltimore, MD 21215-0020 (Courier address- 6550 Reisterstown Rd, The Plaza, Baltimore, MD 21215); 410-764-3038, 410-764-3170 (Order), 410-318-6119 (Recording), Fax- 410-358-7381; 8AM-4PM M-F and 3rd Saturday of each month. www.vsa.state.md.us/

Indexing & Storage: Records available from 1990 to present. Prior records must be obtained from the court of record or Archives. New records available for inquiry in 6 months.

Searching: Must have a notarized signed release from persons of record or authorized representative. Include in request- names of husband and wife, date of marriage, place or county of marriage, besides permission letter. Include copy of photo ID with request.

Access by: mail, phone, fax, in person, online.

Fee & Payment: The search fee is $12.00. Fee payee- Division of Vital Records. Prepayment required. Personal checks, money orders accepted. Major credit cards accepted as indicated.

Mail search: Turnaround time- 2 to 3 weeks. A SASE is requested.

Phone search: See expedited service. Turnaround time is 2-3 days.

Fax search: See expedited service.

In person: Turnaround time same day.

Online search: Records may be ordered from a designated vendor at www.vitalchek.com. Use of credit card is required and additional $7.00 fee required.

Expedited service: Expedited service is available for online and fax searches from VitalChek. Turnaround time- 2 days. Add $7.00 for use of credit card and express ship fees, if desired.

Divorce Records

Department of Health, Division of Vital Records, PO Box 68760, Baltimore, MD 21215-0020 (Courier address- 6550 Reisterstown Rd, The Plaza, Baltimore, MD 21215); 410-764-3038, 410-318-6119 (Recording), 800-832-3277, Fax- 410-358-7381; 8AM-4PM M-F and 3rd Saturday of each month.

www.vsa.state.md.us/

This office does not issue a certificate of divorce, but can verify those names involved. The divorce decree must be obtained from the circuit court granting the divorce.

Indexing & Storage: Records available from 1992 to present. MD Archives has records prior to 1973. All others at the local Circuit Court. New records available for inquiry in 6 months.

Searching: Must have a notarized release from persons of record or authorized agent. Include in request- names of husband and wife (maiden name), date of divorce.

Access by: mail, fax, in person, online.

Fee & Payment: There is $12.00 fee to receive a Verification of Report of Divorce and Absolute Annulment. The clerk of the court issuing the decree holds the actual hard copy record. Fee payee- Division of Vital Records. Prepayment required. Personal checks accepted. Major credit cards accepted as indicated.

Mail search: Turnaround time- 2 to 3 weeks. SASE is required.

Fax search: See expedited service.

In person: Turnaround time same day.

Online search: Records may be ordered from a designated vendor at www.vitalchek.com. Use of credit card is required and additional $7.00 fee required.

Expedited service: Expedited service is available for online and fax searches from VitalChek. Turnaround time- 2 days. Add $7.00 for use of credit card and express ship fees, if desired.

Workers' Compensation Records

Workers' Compensation Commission, 10 E Baltimore St, Baltimore, MD 21202; 410-864-5100, 800-492-0479, Fax- 410-864-5301; 8AM-4:30PM. www.wcc.state.md.us

Indexing & Storage: New records available for inquiry immediately.

Searching: Include in request- signed release if not involved, claim number or claimant name, SSN, date of accident, place of employment at time of accident. This data not released- medical records, personal financial records.

Access by: mail, phone, in person, online.

Fee & Payment: Fee for copies is $.50 per page. There is no search fee. Fee payee- Workers' Compensation Commission. Prepayment required. Personal checks accepted, credit cards are not.

Mail search: Turnaround time- 1 week or so. For copies of documents, the claimant's authorization is needed for requesters not an involved party; A SASE is requested.

Phone search: Limited verification information is available by phone, three names only per call. You must have the 6 digit claim number or the name and SSN.

In person: Turnaround time while you wait unless records must be accessed from storage.

Online search: Free access is provided and there is a more in-depth service available for a fee. The free Public Information is found at www.wcc.state.md.us/WFMS/public_inquiry.html. The free access is at Request for online hook-up must be in writing on letterhead. There is no search fee, but programming fees must be paid in advance. The system is open 24 hours a day to only in-state accounts. Write to the Commission at address above, care of Information Technology Division, or at 410-864-5170.

Other access: This agency will sell its entire database depending on the use of the purchaser. Intended use must be validated and approved. Contact the commission for further information.

Driver Records

MVA, Driver Records Unit, Rm 145, 6601 Ritchie Hwy, NE, Glen Burnie, MD 21062; 410-787-7758, Fax- 410-424-3678; 8:15AM-4:30PM.

www.mva.state.md.us

Indexing & Storage: Records available for 3 years for moving violations, 10 years for DWIs, and 5 years for suspensions. Law requires a request from the driver to have violations purged from the driving record. Accidents are indicated. New records available for inquiry in 5 to 10 days.

Searching: Casual requesters cannot obtain records with personal information unless consent of subject is given. Records may not be resold or used for direct mail advertising or selling. Include in request- driver's license number or the name and DOB, and necessary form. A business may request multiple records using Form DL-15. Requesters must submit form DR-057 if an account has not been established or if consent of subject is needed. The forms may be downloaded from the web.

Access by: mail, in person, online.

Fee & Payment: The fee for a driving record is $9.00. There is an additional $3.00 for certification of a non-electronic record. Fee payee- MVA. Prepayment required. Credit cards are not accepted for mail requests. Personal checks, Visa, and MasterCard accepted.

Mail search: Turnaround time- 2 to 3 days. MVA offices statewide will also accept mail-in requests for records. Records not mailed out-of-state unless signature given. A SASE is requested.

In person: Up to 25 requests will be processed in-person, additional requests are available the next day. In-person inquires may be processed at over 25 Motor Vehicle offices throughout the state.

Online search: Under the Direct Access Record System (DARS), participants access driver and vehicle record information via an Internet connection. The system is open 24/6 to qualified and bonded individuals and businesses. Fee is $9.00 per record. Inquiries are processed interactive and require using either the driver's license number, name and date of birth, VIN or tag number. A batch system (VORS) is also available using FTP or tape cartridge.

Other access: Drivers may view their own record online at https://secure.marylandmva.com/emvaservices/VRR/dept.asp after obtaining a PIN. Also, under the License Monitoring System (LMS), transfers of record data to employers can occur via FTP.

Vehicle Ownership & Registration

Department of Motor Vehicles, Vehicle Registration Division, Room 204, 6601 Ritchie Hwy, NE, Glen Burnie, MD 21062; 410-768-7508, Fax- 410-768-7529; 8:30AM-4:30PM.

www.mva.state.md.us

Indexing & Storage: Records available from 1920. New records available for inquiry in 3 to 5 days.

Searching: All vehicle/ownership records are open to the public; however, personal information is not released to casual requesters without consent of subject. Include in request- title, VIN, tag #, full name and DOB. This data not released- medical information.

Access by: mail, in person, online.

Fee & Payment: Fees are $9.00 for non-certified records and $12.00 for certified records. Fee payee- MVA. Prepayment required. Credit cards are only accepted for walk-in requesters. Personal checks accepted. Major credit cards accepted.

Mail search: Turnaround time- 3 to 5 days. Requester can provide prepaid express mail package for faster service. Request on letterhead preferred. SASE not required.

In person: Turnaround time is generally in a few minutes.

Online search: The state offers vehicle and ownership data over the same online network (DARS) utilized for driving record searches. Fee is $9.00 per record. Access by VIN, tag # or full name. The network is available six days a week, 24 hours a day to qualified bonded accounts. Email MVRSdatarequests@mdot.state.md.us for information on setting up an account.

Accident Reports

MSP - Central Records Division, Accident Reports, 1711 Belmont Ave, Baltimore, MD 21244; 410-298-3390, Fax- 410-298-3198; 8AM-5PM. www.mdsp.org/

This agency does not have reports for the City of Baltimore. Call 410-396-2378 or 2663 for those reports.

Indexing & Storage: Records available for 5 years on paper. Records are electronically indexed from 2001 to present. New records available for inquiry in 20 days.

Searching: Include in request- name, location, date, report number if known. If a fatality was involved, please so state in the request.

Access by: mail, in person.

Fee & Payment: The search fee is $4.00 which includes all copies and is non-refundable. Fee payee- Maryland State Police. Prepayment required. Personal checks accepted, credit cards are not.

Mail search: Turnaround time- 3 to 4 weeks. A SASE is requested.

In person: Immediate service limited to simple requests.

Vessel Ownership & Registration

Dept of Natural Resources, Licensing & Registration Service, 1804 West St, #300, Annapolis, MD 21401; 410-260-3220, Fax- 410-260-3239; 8:30AM-4:30PM.

www.dnr.state.md.us

Boat trailers, (only trailers) are registered through the Maryland Motor Vehicle Administration. They can be reached at 1-800-950-1682.

Indexing & Storage: Records available from the 1960s to the present. This is a title state: all motorized boats must be titled and registered. Records are indexed on microfiche or CDs from the 1960s to the present, and on computer for the last 4 years. New records available for inquiry in 24 hours.

Searching: The agency follows the mandates of the DPPA. Only those with a legitimate business use can obtain records with personal information. Casual requesters must have a signed release of subject. Include in request- one of the following is required: Maryland boat #, tidal fish license #, or name and address of boat owner/license holder. There are six additional Regional Service Centers in the state that will process record requests. This data not released- DOB, phone, home address

Access by: mail, in person.

Fee & Payment: Certified true copies are $10.00 each. Microfiche history files are $5.00 each. Current computer file copies are $5.00 each. Fee payee- DNR. Prepayment required. Personal checks accepted, credit cards are not.

Mail search: Turnaround time- 2 weeks. SASE not required.

In person: Turnaround time is immediate depending on staff availability, unless historical records needed.

Legislation Records

Legislative Information Desk, Library & Information Services, 90 State Circle, Basement Level, Annapolis, MD 21401-1991; 410-946-5400 (Bill Status Only), 800-492-7122 (In-state), Fax- 410-946-5405; 8AM-5PM.

http://mlis.state.md.us

Indexing & Storage: Records available from 1996 to present on computer, from 1976-1997 on microfilm, and 1998 forward hard copy. New records available for inquiry immediately.

Searching: Legislative information is provided by phone, e-mail, Internet or face-to-face contact or through the distribution of numerous legislative documents. Include in request- bill number and year.

Access by: mail, phone, in person, online.

Fee & Payment: The copy fee is $.15 per page. Fee payee- Department of Legislative Services Personal checks accepted, credit cards are not.

Mail search: Turnaround time- variable. SASE not required. No search fee for mail requests, copy fee must be paid.

Phone search: No fee for telephone request.

In person: No fee for request.

Online search: The Internet site has complete information regarding bills and status from the 1990's as well as the statutes.

Voter Registration

Access to Records is Restricted.

State Board of Elections, PO Box 6486, Annapolis, MD 21401-0486 (Courier address- 151 West Street, #200, Annapolis, MD 21401); 410-269-2840, 800-222-8683, Fax- 410-974-2019; 8AM-5PM. www.elections.state.md.us

Agency may sell voter registration lists in bulk media for all twenty-four jurisdictions to MD registered voters only. If voter history is requested, then list must be purchased from each local jurisdiction. Commercial use of list is banned. The website offers free access to the campaign finance database for checking campaign contributions and overall summaries and statistics. For questions, email info@elections.state.md.us.

GED Certificates

State Department of Education, GED Office, 200 W Baltimore St, 6th Fl, Baltimore, MD 21201 (Courier address- 4 N Liberty St, Baltimore, MD 21201); 410-767-0538, Fax- 410-333-8435; 8:30AM-4:30PM.

www.umbc.edu/alrc/GED1.html

Indexing & Storage: New records available for inquiry in 30 days.

Searching: Include in request- name, date of birth, SSN, signed release. The signed release is needed for either the verification or transcript copy.

Access by: mail, fax, in person.

Fee & Payment: The fee is $5.00 for a copy of a transcript. There is no fee for a verification. Fee payee- GED Office. Prepayment required. Personal checks accepted, credit cards are not.

Mail search: Turnaround time- 3 to 5 days. SASE not required.

Fax search: For employment purposes requiring diploma verification, fax a release form with the SSN and full signature of the individual to the GED Office at 410-333-8435. Turnaround time is 2-3 days.

In person: Counter service is available from 10AM-2PM at the N Liberty address.

Hunting & Fishing License Information

Department of Natural Resources, Licensing & Registration Service, 1804 West St, #300, Annapolis, MD 21404; 410-260-3220, Fax- 410-260-8217; 8:30AM-4:30PM.

www.dnr.state.md.us

They have a central computer database. Licenses can be issued online at the webpage.

Indexing & Storage: Records available for 10 years. New records available for inquiry in 1-2 days.

Searching: Requests are subject to DPPA. Requests must be in writing, submit as many identifiers as possible. Include in request- full name, DOB, SSN. This data not released- address and phone (can confirm but will not release).

Access by: mail, in person.

Fee & Payment: There is a $5.00 fee per name. Fee payee- Department of Natural Resources. Personal checks accepted.

Mail search: Turnaround time- 7-10 days. Requests are processed as time permits.

In person: Records searched as time permits.

Maryland State Licensing Agencies

For details about the agency responsible for licensing/certifying/registering an item below or in the Agency Quick Finder section, match an item's number with the number of the agency in the *Licensing Agency Information* section.

Maryland Licenses Searchable Online

Architect #23 .... www.dllr.state.md.us/pq/
Architectural Partnership/Corp #12........ www.dllr.state.md.us/pq/
Attorney #3 .... www.courts.state.md.us/cpf/attylist.html
Barber #8 .... www.dllr.state.md.us/pq/
Business, Any Licensed #4.................... www.blis.state.md.us/
Carrier Vehicle #25.............................. http://webapp.psc.state.md.us/intranet/transport/GetCarrier_new.cfm
Charity #16 .... www.sos.state.md.us/charity/charityhome.htm
Collection Agency #13 ....
https://www.dllr.state.md.us/cgi-bin/fin_reg_el/rel2/PQ_Application.cgi?calling_app=Query::PQ_main
Condominium/Timeshare #16................ www.sos.state.md.us/Registrations/condo_TS.htm
Contractor #10 ....
https://www.dllr.state.md.us/cgi-bin/ElectronicLicensing/OP_search/PQ_search.cgi?calling_app=HIC::HIC_qselect
Cosmetologist #8.................................. www.dllr.state.md.us/pq/
CPA-Public Accountant #12.................. www.dllr.state.md.us/pq/
Driver For Hire #25.............................. http://webapp.psc.state.md.us/Intranet/Transport/ForHireDriver_new.cfm
Election #16 .... www.sos.state.md.us/ElectionsInfo.htm
Electrician, Master #12........................ www.dllr.state.md.us/pq/
Electrologist #7 .... http://209.60.234.65/mdbon_weblookup/
Engineer, Examining #12...................... www.dllr.state.md.us/pq/
Engineer, Professional #12.................... www.dllr.state.md.us/pq/
Extradition/Requisition #16.................. www.sos.state.md.us/Services/Extradit.htm
For Hire Carrier Suspended #25.......... http://webapp.psc.state.md.us/Intranet/Transport/ForHireSuspendedCarriers_new.cfm
Forester #12 .... www.dllr.state.md.us/pq/
Fund Raising Counsel #16 .... www.sos.state.md.us/charity/RegisterProfSol.htm
Gem Dealer #12.................................... www.dllr.state.md.us/pq/
Grain Dealer #4 .... www.mda.state.md.us/pdf/grainbrochure2005.pdf
Home Improvement Contractor #12 ...... www.dllr.state.md.us/pq/
Home Improvement Salesperson #10 ...
https://www.dllr.state.md.us/cgi-bin/ElectronicLicensing/OP_search/PQ_search.cgi?calling_app=HIC::HIC_qselect
Home Inspector #12 .... www.dllr.state.md.us/pq/
HVACR Contractor #12.......................... www.dllr.state.md.us/pq/
Interior Designer #12............................ www.dllr.state.md.us/pq/
Land Surveyor #12 .... www.dllr.state.md.us/pq/
Landscape Architect #12........................ www.dllr.state.md.us/pq/
Lead Inspectors/Contractors #6
www.mde.state.md.us/Programs/LandPrograms/LeadCoordination/homeOwners/search/contractor.asp
Limousine Driver #18............................ www.psc.state.md.us/psc/
Lobbyist #14 .... http://ethics.gov.state.md.us/listing.htm
Lobbyist Employer #14.......................... http://ethics.gov.state.md.us/listing.htm
Medical Doctor #22................................ www.mbp.state.md.us/
Mortgage Broker #13..............................
https://www.dllr.state.md.us/cgi-bin/fin_reg_el/rel2/PQ_Application.cgi?calling_app=Query::PQ_main
Notary Public #16 .... www.sos.state.md.us/Notary/NotarySearch.htm
Nurse-RN/LPN/Assistant #24................ http://209.60.234.65/mdbon_weblookup/
Nursery, Plant #4.................................. www.mda.state.md.us/plants-pests/plant_protection_weed_mgmt/nurseries_plant_dealers/
Nursing Occupation #24 .... http://209.60.234.65/mdbon_weblookup/
Optometrist #22.................................... www.arbo.org/index.php?action=findanoptometrist
Pardon/Commutation #16...................... www.sos.state.md.us/Services/Pardons.htm
Pawnbroker #12.................................... www.dllr.state.md.us/pq/
Pesticide Applicator/Operator #4 .... www.mda.state.md.us/plants-pests/pesticide_regulation/pesticide_db.php
Pesticide Business/Dealer #4 .... www.mda.state.md.us/plants-pests/pesticide_regulation/pesticide_db.php
Pesticide Consultant #4 .... www.mda.state.md.us/plants-pests/pesticide_regulation/pesticide_db.php
Pesticide, Private Applicator #4............ www.mda.state.md.us/plants-pests/pesticide_regulation/pesticide_db.php
Pharmacist #22...................................... www.mdbop.org/verifications/index.htm
Plant Broker/Dealer #4 .... www.mda.state.md.us/plants-pests/plant_protection_weed_mgmt/nurseries_plant_dealers/
Plumber #12 .... www.dllr.state.md.us/pq/
Polygraph Examiner/School/Sales #26 . www.mdpolygraph.org/info.htm

Precious Metal & Gem Dealer #12 .... www.dllr.state.md.us/pq/
Public Accountant-CPA #12 .... www.dllr.state.md.us/pq/
Radiation Therapy Technician #22 .... www.mbp.state.md.us/
Real Estate Agent #15 .... https://www.dllr.state.md.us/cgi-bin/ElectronicLicensing/RE/certification/RECertification1.cgi
Real Estate Appraiser #12 .... www.dllr.state.md.us/pq/
Real Estate Broker #15 .... https://www.dllr.state.md.us/cgi-bin/ElectronicLicensing/RE/certification/RECertification1.cgi
Respiratory Care Practitioner #22 .... www.mbp.state.md.us/
Solicitor, Professional #16 .... www.sos.state.md.us/charity/RegisterProfSol.htm#ps
Special Police/Railroad Police #16 .... www.sos.state.md.us/Services/Police.htm
Subcontractor #10 ....
https://www.dllr.state.md.us/cgi-bin/ElectronicLicensing/OP_search/PQ_search.cgi?calling_app=HIC::HIC_qselect
Taxi Driver #18 .... www.psc.state.md.us/psc/
Taxicab #25 .... http://webapp.psc.state.md.us/Intranet/Transport/TaxicabDriver_new.cfm
Transportation Permit Holder #25 .... http://webapp.psc.state.md.us/Intranet/Transport/GetPermitList_new.cfm

Maryland Licensing Quick Finder

Acupuncturist #22 410-764-4766
Airport #19 410-859-7064
Airport License, Public/Private #19 410-859-7137
Alarm Technician #11 .... 410-799-0191 x334
Aquaculture Operation #4 410-260-8323
Architect #23 410-230-6322
Architectural Partnership/Corp #12 410-230-6261
Asbestos-related Company #6 410-537-3200
Athletic Agent #17 410-230-6223
Attorney #3 410-260-1950
Audiologist #22 410-764-4723
Bail Bondsman #21 410-468-2383
Barber #8 410-230-6320
Boxer/Boxing Professional #17 410-230-6223
Bus Driver #18 410-768-7232
Business, Any Licensed #4 .... 888-ChooseMD
Carrier Vehicle #25 410-767-8107
Charity #16 410-974-5534
Chiropractor/Chiropractic Assist. #22 410-764-5902
Collection Agency #13 410-230-6230
Condominium/Timeshare #16 410-974-5521
Contractor #10 410-230-6309
Cosmetologist #8 410-230-6320
Counselor #22 410-764-4732
CPA-Public Accountant #12 410-230-6258
Day Care Provider #2 410-767-0335
Dental Assistant #22 .... 410-402-8500 x4
Dental Hygienist #22 .... 410-402-8500 x4
Dental Teacher #22 .... 410-402-8500 x4
Dentist #22 .... 410-402-8500 x4
Dietitian/Nutritionist #22 410-764-4733
Driver For Hire #25 410-767-8107
Election #16 410-974-5521
Electrician, Master #12 410-230-6231
Electrologist #7 410-585-1952
Embalmer #22 410-764-4792
Engineer, Examining #12 410-230-6231
Engineer, Professional #12 410-230-6322
Esthetician #8 410-230-6320
Extradition/Requisition #16 410-974-5521
Firearms Registration Sect. #11 .... 410-799-0191 x324
For Hire Carrier Suspended #25 410-767-8107
Forester #12 410-230-6231
Franchise, Bus. Op, Multi-level Mktng #20 410-576-7785
Fund Raising Counsel #16 410-974-5534
Funeral Director #22 410-764-4792
Funeral Establishment #22 410-764-4792
Gem Dealer #12 410-230-4640
Grain Dealer #4 410-841-5769
Guidance Counselor #5 410-767-0412
Handgun Permittee #11 .... 410-799-0191 x341
Harness Racing #9 410-230-6330
Hazardous Waste #6 410-537-3343
Hearing Aid Dispenser #22 410-764-4792
Home Improvement Contractor #12 410-230-6209
Home Improvement Salesperson #10 410-230-6309
Home Inspector #12 410-230-6231
Horse Racing #9 410-230-6330
Horse Stable, 5 or more #4 410-841-5861
HVACR Contractor #12 410-230-6200
Insurance Agent #21 410-468-2383
Insurance Broker/Advisor #21 410-468-2383
Interior Designer #12 410-230-6322
Investment Adviser/Represent't've #20 410-576-7048
K-9 Unit #11 .... 410-799-0191 x334
Land Surveyor #12 410-230-6322
Landscape Architect #12 410-230-6322
Lead Inspectors/Contractors #6 410-537-3863
Limousine Driver #18 .... 410-768-7232, PSC 410-767-8000
Lobbyist #14 410-974-2068
Lobbyist Employer #14 410-974-2068
Makeup Artist #8 410-230-6320
Massage Therapist #22 410-764-2431
Medical Doctor #22 410-764-4777
Mining Foreman/Fire Boss #6 410-537-3557
Mortgage Broker #13 410-230-6230
Mortician #22 410-764-4792
Nail Technician #8 410-230-6320
Notary Public #16 410-974-5520
Notice Filing #20 410-576-7050
NPDES Permit #4 410-537-3323
Nurse-RN/LPN/Assistant #24 410-585-1978
Nursery, Plant #4 410-841-5920
Nursing Home Administrator #22 410-764-4750
Nursing Occupation #24 410-585-1990
Nutrient Manager #4 410-841-5959
Occupational Therapist/Assistant #22 410-402-8560
Optometrist #22 410-764-4710
Organic Producer/Handler #4 410-841-5769
Pardon/Commutation #16 410-974-5521
Pawnbroker #12 410-230-4640
Pesticide Applicator/Operator #4 410-841-5710
Pesticide Business/Dealer #4 410-841-5710
Pesticide Consultant #4 410-841-5710
Pesticide, Private Applicator #4 410-841-5710
Pharmacist #22 410-764-4755
Physical Therapist #22 410-764-4752
Physical Therapist Assistant #22 410-764-4752
Pilot #12 410-230-6329
Plant Broker/Dealer #4 410-841-5920
Plumber #12 410-230-6231
Podiatrist #22 410-764-4785
Police Officer, Special #11 .... 410-799-0191 x334
Precious Metal & Gem Dealer #12 410-230-4640
Private Investigator #11 .... 410-799-0191 x331
Psychologist #22 410-764-4787
Psychometrist (Education) #5 410-767-0412
Public Accountant-CPA #12 410-230-6258
Pump Installer #6 .... 410-537-3557 x3510
Pupil Personnel Worker #5 410-767-0412
Radiation Therapy Technician #22 410-764-4775
Reading Specialist #5 410-767-0412
Reading Teacher #5 410-767-0412
Real Estate Agent #15 410-230-6230
Real Estate Appraiser #12 410-230-6165
Real Estate Broker #15 410-230-6230
Referee #17 410-230-6223
Respiratory Care Practitioner #22 410-764-4775
Sanitarian #6 .... 410-537-3557 x3597
School Administrator/Superintend't #5 410-767-0412
School Library Media Gen'l'st/Special't #5 410-767-0412
School Psychologist #5 410-767-0412
Securities Broker/Dealer #20 410-576-6494
Securities Sales Agent #20 410-576-6494
Security Agency/Guard #11 .... 410-799-0191 x340
Security Registration #20 410-576-7050
Sewage Treatment #6 410-537-3510
Social Worker #22 410-764-4788
Solicitor, Professional #16 410-974-5534
Special Police/Railroad Police #16 410-974-5521
Speech Pathologist #22 410-764-4725
Subcontractor #10 410-230-6309
Surface Mine #4 .... 800-633-6101 x3772
Taxi Driver #18 .... 410-768-7232, PSC 410-767-8000
Taxicab #25 410-767-8107
Teacher #5 410-767-0412
Toxic Material Permit #4 410-537-3323
Transportation Permit Holder #25 410-767-8107
Truck Driver #18 410-768-7232
Veterinarian #1 410-841-5862
Veterinary Hospital #1 410-841-5862
Veterinary Technician #1 410-841-5862
Waste Water Treatm't Plant Superin'd't #6 410-537-3167
Water Conditioner Installer #6 410-537-3000
Water Quality Certification #4 .... 800-633-6101 x3772
Water Use Permit #4 410-537-3591
Well Driller #6 410-537-3597
Wetlands Use Permit #4 .... 800-633-6101 x3772

Maryland Licensing Agency Information

#1 Board of Veterinary Medical Examiners, 50 Harry S Truman Pky, Annapolis, AR 21401; 410-841-5862, Fax- 410-841-5999. Hours- 8AM-4:30PM. www.mda.state.md.us/go/vetboard/

#2 Office of Child Care, 200 W Baltimore St, Baltimore, MD 21201; 410-767-0335, Fax- 410-321-2240. www.marylandpublicschools.org/MSDE/divisions/child_care/child_care.htm

#3 Client Protection Fund of the Bar of Maryland, Robert F Sweeney Dist Ct Bldg, 2011 Commerce Park Dr, Annapolis, MD 21401; 410-260-3635, Fax- 410-260-3636. www.courts.state.md.us/cpf/ Search data at- www.courts.state.md.us/cpf/attylist.html The state bar assoc. (MSBA) is a separate organization. MSBA phone number is 410-685-7878, fax 410-685-1016; 520 W Fayette St, Balt. MD 21201.

#4 Department of Agriculture, Pesticide Regulation Section, 50 Harry S Truman Pky, Annapolis, MD 21401; 410-841-5710, Fax- 410-841-2765. www.mda.state.md.us

#5 Department of Education, Division of Certification & Accreditation, 200 W Baltimore St, Baltimore, MD 21201-2595; 410-767-0412, Fax- 410-333-8963. www.marylandpublicschools.org/MSDE/divisions/certification/

#6 Department of Environment, 1800 Washington Blvd, Baltimore, MD 21230; 410-537-3000; 800-633-6101. www.mde.state.md.us Each unit has its own separate fax machine.

#7 Department of Health & Mental Hygiene, Board of Nursing, Electrology Practice Committee, 4201 Patterson Ave, Baltimore, MD 21215; 410-585-1900; 888-202-9861, Fax- 410-358-3530. www.mbon.org/main.php?v=norm&p=0&c=electrology/index.html

#8 Department of Labor, Licensing & Regulation, Board of Barbers & Cosmetologists, 500 N Calvert St, 3rd Fl, Rm 201, Baltimore, MD 21202; 410-230-6320, Fax- 410-230-6314. www.dllr.state.md.us/license/occprof/barber.html Search data at- www.dllr.state.md.us/pq/

#9 Department of Labor, Licensing & Regulation, Racing Commission, 300 E Towsontowne Blvd, Towson, MD 21286; 410-296-9682, Fax- 410-296-9687. www.dllr.state.md.us/racing/

#10 Department of Licensing & Regulation, Home Improvement Commission, 500 N Calvert St, #306, Baltimore, MD 21202-3651; 410-230-6309; 888-218-5925. www.dllr.state.md.us/license/occprof/homeim.html Search data at- https://www.dllr.state.md.us/cgi-bin/ElectronicLicensing/OP_search/PQ_search.cgi?calling_app=HIC::HIC_qselect

#11 State Police, Licensing Division, 7751 Washington Blvd, Jessup, MD 20794; 410-799-0191, Fax- 410-799-5934. Hours- 8AM-5PM. www.mdsp.org

#12 Department of Labor, Licensing & Regulation, Occupational Boards, 500 N Calvert St, 3rd Fl, Baltimore, MD 21202; 410-230-6200, Fax- 410-333-1229. www.dllr.state.md.us/license/occprof/ Search data at- www.dllr.state.md.us/pq/

#13 Department of Licensing & Regulation, Office of Financial Regulations, 500 N Calvert St, #402, Baltimore, MD 21202; 888-218-5925. www.dllr.state.md.us/license/electron.html#nreg Search data at- https://www.dllr.state.md.us/cgi-bin/fin_reg_el/rel2/PQ_Application.cgi?calling_app=Query::PQ_main

#14 State Ethics Commission, 45 Calvert St, 3rd Fl, Annapolis, MD 21401; 877-669-6085, 410-260-7770, Fax- 410-260-7746. Hours- 8AM-4:30PM. http://ethics.gov.state.md.us Search data at- http://ethics.gov.state.md.us/listing.htm Purchase a paper copy of the lobbyist list for $10.00.

#15 Department of Licensing & Regulation, Real Estate Commission, 500 N Calvert St, 3rd Fl, Baltimore, MD 21202-3551; 410-230-6230, Fax-410-333-6314. Hours- 8:30AM-4:30PM. www.dllr.state.md.us/license/occprof/recomm.html Search data at- https://www.dllr.state.md.us/cgi-bin/ElectronicLicensing/RE/certification/REcertification1.cgi

#16 Office of Secretary of State, 16 Francis St, Statehouse, Annapolis, MD 21401; 410-974-5521, Fax- 410-974-5190. Hours- 8:30AM-4:30PM. www.sos.state.md.us

#17 Department of Licensing & Regulation, Athletic Commission, 500 N Calvert St, Rm 304, Baltimore, MD 21202; 410-230-6223, Fax- 410-230-6314. www.dllr.state.md.us/license/occprof/athlet.html

#18 Department of Transportation, Motor Vehicle Administration, 6601 Ritchie Hwy NE, Glen Burnie, MD 21062; 410-768-7232, Fax- 410-333-6088. Hours- 8:30AM-4:30PM. www.marylandmva.com/index.html Taxi and Limo drivers also must have permits from the Public Service Commission.

#19 Department of Transportation, Aviation Administration, PO Box 8766, 3rd Fl, Terminal Bldg, BWI Airport, MD 21240; 410-859-7064, Fax- 410-859-7287. www.marylandaviation.com/

#20 Securities Division, Attorney General's Office, 200 St Paul Pl, 25th Fl, Baltimore, MD 21202; 410-576-6360, Fax- 410-576-6532. www.oag.state.md.us/Securities/

#21 Licensing & Regulation, Insurance Agent/Brokers Licensing & Investigation, 525 St Paul Pl, Baltimore, MD 21202; 410-468-2000, Fax- 410-468-2399. www.mdinsurance.state.md.us

#22 Health Professional Licensing, 4201 Patterson Ave, Baltimore, MD 21215-2299; 410-764-4700, Fax- 410-358-0128. www.dhmh.state.md.us/html/proflicm.htm

#23 Board of Architects, 500 N Calvert St , Rm 308, Baltimore, MD 21202-3651; 888-218-5925, 410-230-6322, Fax- 410-333-0021. www.dllr.state.md.us/license/occprof/arc.html Search data at- www.dllr.state.md.us/pq/ Lists of currently licensed individual architect & firms can be purchased for a fee. Call 410-230-6352.

#24 Board of Nursing, 4140 Patterson Ave, Baltimore, MD 21215; 888-202-9861, 410-585-1900, Fax- 410-358-3530. 8AM-5PM M,T,TH,F; 9:30AM-5PM W. www.mbon.org/main.php Search - http://209.60.234.65/mdbon_weblookup/ A telephone voice response system called IVR is available, 410-585-1978.

#25 Public Service Commission, Transportation Division, 6 St Paul St, 16th Fl, Baltimore, MD 21202; 410-767-8128, Fax- 410-333-6088. http://webapp.psc.state.md.us/intranet/psc/links_new.cfm At the main website, click on transportation.

#26 Polygraph Association, PO Box 221, Linthicum, MD 21090; contact- joy.mpa@comcast.net. www.mdpolygraph.org/ Search data at- www.mdpolygraph.org/info.htm contact Joy Neal, Secretary by email only.

Maryland Federal Courts

The following list indicates the district and division name for each county in the state. If the bankruptcy court location is different from the district court, then the location of the bankruptcy court appears in parentheses.

Maryland County/Court Cross Reference

Allegany....................Baltimore
Anne Arundel............Baltimore
Baltimore....................Baltimore
Baltimore City City....Baltimore
Calvert.......................Greenbelt
Caroline......................Baltimore
Carroll........................Baltimore
Cecil...........................Baltimore
Charles.......................Greenbelt
Dorchester..................Baltimore
Frederick....................Baltimore
Garrett........................Baltimore
Harford.......................Baltimore
Howard.......................Baltimore
Kent............................Baltimore
Montgomery...............Greenbelt
Prince George's.........Greenbelt
Queen Anne's............Baltimore
Somerset....................Baltimore
St. Mary's..................Greenbelt
Talbot.........................Baltimore
Washington................Baltimore
Wicomico...................Baltimore
Worcester...................Baltimore

Standards for Federal Courts: *See the Appendix for standards and fees for searching Federal Courts.*

US District Court
Maryland Northern District

Baltimore (Northern) Division Clerk of Court, 101 W Lombard St, 4th Fl, Rm 4415, Baltimore, MD 21201, 410-962-2600. 9AM-4PM. www.mdd.uscourts.gov

Counties/Note: Allegany, Anne Arundel, Baltimore, City of Baltimore, Caroline, Carroll, Cecil, Dorchester, Frederick, Garrett, Harford, Howard, Kent, Queen Anne's, Somerset, Talbot, Washington, Wicomico, Worcester.

Searches/Indexing: Include name and years to search in search request. Results do not include SSN or DOB. Will not fax back documents. New cases are in the index 1-2 days after filing date. Both computer and card indexes maintained; computer goes back to 1994. Case files sent to archives 3 years after closed.

Search Access: Court will verify questions via phone, but will not read long dockets. **Mail:** Search usually completed- 3-4 working days. Include SASE for return. **Fax:** Fax search requests accepted. **In person:** 3 public terminals available. No self-serve copier.

Payment: Pay by credit cards (in person only), money order, cashier's or personal check. Payee: Clerk, USDC.

E-Services: PACER records go back to 10/1990. New records online after 1 day. ECF at https://ecf.mdd.uscourts.gov. **Opinions Online:** www.mdd.uscourts.gov/publications/opinions/Opinions.asp. Recent opinions only, also public interest cases. **Online Note:** Access calendars free at www.mdd.uscourts.gov/calendar/calendar.html.

Greenbelt (Southern) Division Clerk of Court, 6500 Cherrywood Lane, Rm 200, Greenbelt, MD 20770, 301-344-0660. 9AM-4PM. www.mdd.uscourts.gov

Counties/Note: Calvert, Charles, Montgomery, Prince George's, St. Mary's.

Searches/Indexing: Search request requires name only. Results do not include SSN or DOB. Will not fax back documents. New cases are in the index 1-2 days after filing date. Both computer and card indexes maintained; computer back to 1990. Case files sent to archives 3 years after closed.

Search Access: Court will verify info via phone, but will not read long dockets. **Mail:** Search usually completed- 5 working days. Searches and copy requests must be made in writing to the clerk's office. Include SASE for return. **In person:** 2 public terminals available. Copies made off of computer $.10 each. Court can recommend an outside vendor to so searches and copies.

Payment: Pay by credit cards (in person only), money order, cashier's or personal check. Payee: Clerk, USDC.

E-Services: PACER records go back to 10/1990. New records online immediately. ECF at https://ecf.mdd.uscourts.gov. **Opinions Online:** www.mdd.uscourts.gov/publications/opinions/Opinions.asp. Recent opinions only, also public interest cases. **Online Note:** Access calendars free at www.mdd.uscourts.gov/calendar/calendar.html.

US Bankruptcy Court
District of Maryland

Baltimore (Northern) Division Court Clerk, Garmatz Federal Courthouse, 101 W Lombard St, Ste 8308, Baltimore, MD 21201, 410-962-2688; Fax- 410-962-2110. Hours-8AM-4PM. www.mdb.uscourts.gov

Counties/Note: Anne Arundel, Baltimore, City of Baltimore, Caroline, Carroll, Cecil, Dorchester, Harford, Howard, Kent, Queen Anne's, Somerset, Talbot, Wicomico, Worcester. Open cases originating on the Eastern Shore can be viewed at the Salisbury Div, 129 E Main St #104, however the Salisbury office will not answer mail or phone questions. Cases under Chapters 7, 12 and 13 cases from Caroline, Dorchester, Kent, Queen Anne's, Somerset, Talbot, Wicomico, and Worcester counties are scheduled for Salisbury. By debtor's request, a case in Queen Anne's County may be in Baltimore or Salisbury.

Searches/Indexing: Debtor name required to search; SSN and address helpful. Results do not include SSN or DOB. New cases are in the index 2 days after filing date. Computer index goes back to 2000, but records are incomplete the further back you look. Case files sent to archives 6 months after closed.

Search Access: Only docket info is available by phone. Voice Case Information Service available, call VCIS at 800-829-0145 or 410-962-0733. **Mail:** Search usually completed- 2-4 weeks. SASE not required. **In person:** 3 public terminals available. No self-serve copier but pages can be printed off computer $.10 each.

Payment: No credit cards or debtor, business, or personal checks accepted. Payee: Clerk, US Bankruptcy Court.

E-Services: PACER records go back to mid 1991. New records online after 1 day. ECF at https://ecf.mdb.uscourts.gov. **Opinions Online:** http://207.41.17.84/QryOpinion.aspx?qTarget=Opinion. **Online Note:** Search judgments back through 2002 free at http://207.41.17.84/QryJudgment.aspx?qTarget=Judgment. Access calendars free at https://ecf.mdb.uscourts.gov/cgi-bin/PublicCalendar4.pl.

Greenbelt (Southern) Division Court Clerk, 6500 Cherrywood Ln, #300, Greenbelt, MD 20770, 301-344-8018. Hours- 8AM-4PM. www.mdb.uscourts.gov

Counties/Note: Allegany, Calvert, Charles, Frederick, Garrett, Montgomery, Prince George's, St. Mary's, Washington.

Searches/Indexing: Search requires debtor name. Results do not include SSN or DOB. New cases are in the index 2-3 days after filing date. Case files sent to archives 6 months after closed.

Search Access: Only docket info is available by phone. Voice Case Information Service available, call VCIS at 800-829-0145 or 410-962-0733. **Mail:** Search usually completed- 5 days. Court Clerk can recommend an outside vendor to search open cases. SASE not required. **In person:** Public terminals available. No self-serve copier.

Payment: No credit cards or debtor, business, or personal checks accepted. Payee: Clerk, US Bankruptcy Court. In house copy work (4 pages or less and copies that need to be certified) is done on an "as time permits" basis. Copy work of 5 pages or more is done off premises at less cost.

E-Services: PACER records go back to mid 1991. New records online after 1 day. ECF at https://ecf.mdb.uscourts.gov. **Opinions Online:** http://207.41.17.84/QryOpinion.aspx?qTarget=Opinion. **Online Note:** Search judgments back through 2002 free at http://207.41.17.84/QryJudgment.aspx?qTarget=Judgment. Access calendars free at https://ecf.mdb.uscourts.gov/cgi-bin/PublicCalendar4.pl.

Maryland County Courts

Court	Jurisdiction	No. of Courts	How Organized
Circuit Courts*	General	25	8 Circuits
District Courts*	Limited	26	12 Districts
Orphan's Courts*	Probate	24	Register of Wills

* Profiled in this Sourcebook.

Court	CIVIL Tort	Contract	Real Estate	Min. Claim	Max. Claim	Small Claims	Estate	Eviction	Domestic Relations
Circuit Courts*	X	X	X	$25000	No Max				X
District Courts*	X	X	X	$0	$25000 or $30000	$5000		X	X
Orphan's Court*							X		

Court	CRIMINAL Felony	Misdemeanor	DWI/DUI	Preliminary Hearing	Juvenile
Circuit Courts*	X	X			X
District Courts*		X	X	X	
Orphan's Court*					

Administration

Court Administrator, Administrative Office of the Courts, 580 Taylor Ave, Annapolis, MD, 21401; 410-260-1400, 410-260-1488, Fax: 410-974-5291. (EST) www.courts.state.md.us

Court Structure

Circuit courts generally handle the State's major civil cases and more serious criminal matters, along with juvenile cases, family matters such as divorce, and most appeals from the District Court, orphans' courts and administrative agencies. The circuit courts also can hear cases from the District Court (civil or criminal) in which one of the parties has requested a jury trial, under certain circumstances.

The District Court hears both civil and criminal cases involving claims up to $30,000, and has exclusive jurisdiction over peace order cases and landlord/tenant, replevin (recovery of goods claimed to be wrongfully taken or detained), and other civil cases involving amounts at or less than $5,000. The District Court also handles motor vehicle/boating violations and other misdemeanors and limited felonies, although the circuit courts share jurisdiction if the penalties authorized are three years or more in prison, a fine of $2,500 or more, or both. Both trial courts can hear domestic violence cases. The Circuit Court handles probate in only Montgomery and Harford counties. In other counties, probate is handled by the Register of Wills and is a county, not a court, function.

Note there is a Baltimore County and the City of Baltimore; each has its own courts.

Online Access

Appellate opinions are available from www.courts.state.md.us/opinions.html. There is a free seach of dockets from the trial courts at http://casesearch.courts.state.md.us/inquiry/inquiry-index.jsp. The search includes all district courts and circuit courts. The DOB is shown on some but not all dockets. Records are updated daily, but note that case information from Montgomery and Prince George's counties are always lagging one day behind. All case information may be searched by party name or case number.

Bulk subscription data of civil record available for a fee using a form found at www.courts.state.md.us/district/forms/acct/dca107.pdf. Plans are underway for subscribing parties to access statewide Case Search bulk data and data extracts through a standards-based interface in XML format. Also, there is an attorney Calendar Service that displays information related to an Attorney's trial and hearing schedule such as case number, attorney name, trial or hearing date, defendant name, time, room, etc.

Searching Tips, Fees, and Other Guidelines

In most but not all Circuit Courts and District Courts, copies are $.50 per page. Certification is $5.00. Prepayment required unless noted.

Allegany County

4th Judicial Circuit Court 30 Washington St, Cumberland, MD 21502; 301-777-5922; fax: 301-777-2100; 8AM-4:30PM. ***Felony, Misdemeanor, Civil Actions over $25,000.***

Civil Records: Access: In person, online. Visitors must perform in person searches themselves. Required to search: name, years to search. Civil cases indexed by defendant, plaintiff, on computer since 11/92, archived and indexed from 1790. Civil PAT goes back to 6/1997. PAT civil results show middle initial. Free case look-up at http://casesearch.courts.state.md.us.

Criminal Records: Access: In person, online. Visitors must perform in person searches themselves. Required to search: name, years to search; also helpful: DOB. Criminal records on computer since 9/99, archived and indexed from 1790. Criminal PAT goes back to 6/1996. PAT criminal results show middle initial. Online access to criminal is same as civil. Online results show middle initial, DOB. **General Information:** No adoption, juvenile, sealed, expunged or mental records released. Will not fax documents. Court makes copy: $.50 per page. Self serve: $.25 per page. Certification fee: $5.00 per instrument. Payee: Circuit Court. Personal checks accepted; credit cards are not.

District Court 3 Pershing St, 2nd Fl, Cumberland, MD 21502; 301-723-3100; 8:30AM-4:30PM. ***Misdemeanor, Civil Actions under $25,000, Eviction, Small Claims.***

Civil Records: Access: Online, in person. Visitors must perform in person searches themselves. Required to search: name, years to search. Civil cases indexed by defendant. Civil records on computer from 1990, on index books from 1970. Free case look-up at http://casesearch.courts.state.md.us.

Criminal Records: Access: Online, in person. Visitors must perform in person searches themselves. Required to search: name, years to search; SSN helpful. Criminal records computerized from 1980, index books. Note: Court requires a case number for a search. Online access to criminal is same as civil; results show middle initial, DOB.

General Information: No adoption, juvenile, sealed, expunged or mental records released. Will not fax documents. Court makes copy: $.50 per page. Certification fee: $5.00 per page. Payee: District Court of MD. Personal checks and credit cards accepted.

Register of Wills 59 Prospect Sq. 1st Fl, Cumberland, MD 21502; 301-724-3760, 888-724-0148 in MD; fax: 301-724-1249; 8:30AM-4:30PM. ***Probate.*** www.registers.state.md.us/county/al/html/allegany.html

Anne Arundel County

5th Judicial Circuit Court PO Box 71, 7 Church St, Annapolis, MD 21401; 410-222-1397; criminal phone: 410-222-1420; civil phone: 410-222-1431; 8:30AM-4:30PM; phones- 9AM-3:30PM. ***Felony, Misdemeanor, Civil Actions over $25,000.***

Civil Records: Access: Phone, mail, online, in person. Both court and visitors may perform in person searches. No search fee. Required to search: name, years to search. Civil cases indexed by defendant, plaintiff, on computer from 1991, on index from 1900. Mail turnaround time 2 days. Civil PAT goes back to 1991. Results include name and case number. Free case look-up at http://casesearch.courts.state.md.us. **Criminal Records:** Access: In person, online. Both court and visitors may perform in person searches. No search fee. Required to search: name, years to search; also helpful: SSN. Criminal records computerized from 1988, indexed from 1960, archived from 1900. Note: Results include name, address and case number. Criminal PAT goes back to 1988. PAT results show name, DOB, SSN. Online access to criminal is same as civil. Online results show middle initial, DOB.

General Information: Online identifiers in results same as on public terminal. No adoption, juvenile, sealed, expunged or mental records released. Will not fax documents. Court makes copy: $.50 per page. Certification fee: $5.00 per cert. Payee: Clerk of Circuit Court. Personal checks accepted; credit cards are not. Mail requests: SASE required for civil.

District Court 251 Rowe Blvd, #141, Annapolis, MD 21401; criminal phone: 410-260-1370; civil: 410-260-1800; 8:30AM-4:30PM. ***Misdemeanor, Civil Actions under $25,000, Eviction, Small Claims.***

Civil Records: Access: Mail, in person, online. Both court and visitors may perform in person searches. No search fee. Required to search: name, years to search. Civil cases indexed by defendant. Civil records on computer from 1982, archived and indexed from 1900s. Mail turnaround time 5 days. Civil PAT goes back to 1987. Free case look-up at http://casesearch.courts.state.md.us.

Criminal Records: Access: Mail, online, in person. Both court and visitors may perform in person searches. No search fee. Required to search: name, years to search. Criminal records computerized from 1982, archived and indexed from 1900s. Mail turnaround time 5 days. Criminal PAT goes back to 1982. Online access to criminal is same as civil. Online results show middle initial, DOB.

General Information: Court makes copy: $.50 per page. Certification fee: $5.00 per doc. Payee: District Court. Personal checks, major credit cards accepted. Mail requests: SASE required.

Register of Wills PO Box 2368, 7 1/2 Circuit Courthouse-Church Circle #403, Annapolis, MD 21404-2368; 410-222-1430, 800-679-6665 in MD; fax: 410-222-1467; 8AM-4PM. ***Probate.*** www.registers.state.md.us/county/aa/html/annearundel.html Wills only; no genealogy searches.

Baltimore County

3rd Judicial Circuit Court 401 Bosley Ave, 2nd Fl, Towson, MD 21204; 410-887-2601; criminal phone: 410-887-2627; civil phone: 410-887-2614; fax: 410-887-3062; 8:30AM-4:30PM. ***Felony, Civil Actions over $30,000.***

Civil Records: Access: Online, in person. Visitors must perform in person searches themselves. Required to search: name, years to search; also helpful: address. Civil cases indexed by defendant, plaintiff, in books, file jackets. Civil PAT goes back to 1995. PAT results show name only. Results include case number. Free case look-up at http://casesearch.courts.state.md.us.

Criminal Records: Access: In person, online. Visitors must perform in person searches themselves. Required to search: name, years to search; also helpful: address, DOB, SSN. Criminal records computerized from 1984, prior on books. Note: Results include name, address and case number. Criminal PAT goes back to same as civil. PAT results show name only. Online access to criminal is same as civil. Online results show middle initial, DOB.

General Information: No adoption, juvenile, sealed, expunged or mental records released. Will not fax documents. Court makes copy: $.50 per page. Certification fee: $5.00 per page. Payee: Suzanne Mensh, Clerk. Personal checks accepted. Out of state checks not accepted. No credit cards accepted.

District Court 120 E Chesapeake Ave, Towson, MD 21286-5307; 410-512-2000; criminal phone: x3; civil phone: x2; 8:30AM-4:30PM. ***Misdemeanor, Civil Actions under $30,000, Eviction, Small Claims.*** Court will not search but will provide case file information. This court also holds records for its satelite office.

Civil Records: Access: Online, in person. Visitors must perform in person searches themselves. Required to search: name, years to search; also helpful: address. Civil cases indexed by defendant, plaintiff, on computer from 1985, on microfiche from 1971, archived from 1970, on card index from 1971. Civil PAT goes back to 1985. Addresses are not always available on terminal search results. Free case look-up available online at http://casesearch.courts.state.md.us.

Criminal Records: Access: Online, in person. Visitors must perform in person searches themselves. Required to search: name, years to search. Criminal records on computer since 1981. Criminal PAT goes back to 1981. PAT results show middle initial, DOB, SSN. Online access to criminal is same as civil. Online results show middle initial, DOB.

General Information: No adoption, juvenile, sealed, expunged or medical records released. Will not fax out documents. Court makes copy: $.50 per page. Certification fee: $5.00 per case. Payee: District Court of MD. Personal checks accepted; credit cards are not.

Register of Wills 401 Bosley Ave, Towson, MD 21204-4403; 410-887-6685, 888-642-5387 in MD; fax: 410-583-2517; 8AM-4:30PM. ***Probate.*** www.registers.state.md.us/county/ba/html/baltimore.html

Baltimore City

8th Judicial Circuit Court - Civil Division 111 N Calvert, Rm 462, Baltimore, MD 21202; 410-333-3722; civil phone: 410-369-3045; fax: 410-333-6986; 8:30AM-4:30PM. ***Civil Actions over $25,000.*** www.baltocts.state.md.us

Civil Records: Access: Phone, mail, online, in person. Both court and visitors may perform in person searches. No search fee. Required to search: name, years to search; also helpful: address. Civil cases indexed by defendant. Civil records on computer from 1983. Note: Court conducts searches on a limited basis. Mail turnaround time 5 days. Public use terminal has civil records back to 10 years. PAT results show name only. Results include case number. Free case look-up at http://casesearch.courts.state.md.us. Online results show middle initial, DOB.

General Information: No adoption, juvenile, sealed, expunged or mental records released. Will not fax documents. Court makes copy: $.50 per page. Certification fee: $5.00 per cert. Payee: Clerk of the Circuit Court. Business checks accepted. No credit cards. SASE not required.

8th Judicial Circuit Court - Criminal Division 110 N Calvert Rm 200, Baltimore, MD 21202; 410-333-3750; 8:30AM-4:30PM. ***Felony, Misdemeanor.*** www.mdcourts.gov/baltcity.html

Criminal Records: Access: Online, in person. Visitors must perform in person searches themselves. Required to search: name, years to search; also helpful: address, DOB. Criminal records computerized from 1994, on microfilm from 1972. Search court records free at http://casesearch.courts.state.md.us. Updated nightly. Online results show middle initial, DOB.

General Information: No adoption, juvenile, sealed, expunged or mental records released. Will not fax documents. Court makes copy: $.50 per page, self serve same. Certification fee: $5.00 per case. Payee: Clerk of Circuit Court. Business checks accepted.

District Court - Civil Division 501 E Fayette St, Baltimore, MD 21202; 800-939-4523, 410-878-8900; 8:30AM-4:30PM. ***Civil Actions under $25,000, Eviction, Small Claims.***

Civil Records: Access: Mail, in person, online. Both court and visitors may perform in person searches. No search fee. Required to search: name, years to search. Civil cases indexed by defendant. Civil records on computer from 1986, on card index from 1971. Mail turnaround time 5-10 days. Public use terminal has civil records back to 1991; results show name only. Free case look-up at http://casesearch.courts.state.md.us. Updated nightly.

General Information: No medical or sealed records released. Will not fax documents. Court makes copy: $.50 per page. Certification fee: $5.00 per doc. Payee: District Court of MD. Personal checks accepted; credit cards are not. Mail requests: SASE required.

District Court - Criminal Division 1400 E North Ave., Baltimore, MD 21213; 800-939-4523, 410-878-8000; 8AM-4:30PM. ***Misdemeanor.*** www.mdcourts.gov/baltcity.html

Criminal Records: Access: Mail, online, in person. No search fee. Required to search: name, years to search. Criminal records computerized from 1982, prior on index cards from 1970. Mail turnaround time 1 week. Public use terminal has crim records back to 1982. Public terminal located at 700 E Patapso Ave. Search court records free at http://casesearch.courts.state.md.us. Online results show middle initial, DOB.

General Information: No adoption, juvenile, sealed, expunged, medical or mental records released. Will not fax documents. Court makes copy: $.50 per page. Certification fee: $5.00 per doc. Payee: District Court. Personal checks and major credit cards accepted. Mail requests: SASE required.

Register of Wills 111 N Calvert St, Courthouse East, Rm 352, Baltimore, MD 21202; 410-752-5131, 888-876-0035 in MD; fax: 410-752-3494; 8:30AM-4:30PM. ***Probate.*** www.registers.state.md.us/city/bc/html/baltimorecity.html Phone extension #505 is the Records Room.

Calvert County

7th Judicial Circuit Court 175 Main St Courthouse, Prince Frederick, MD 20678; 410-535-1660; criminal phone: x2266; civil phone: x2404; fax: 410-535-6245; 8:30AM-4:30PM. ***Felony, Misdemeanor, Civil Actions over $25,000.*** www.mdcourts.gov/clerks/calvert

Civil Records: Access: Online, in person. Visitors must perform in person searches themselves. Required to search: name, years to search. Civil cases indexed by defendant, plaintiff, on computer back to 10/1997, prior on index books back to 1959. Civil

PAT goes back to 10/1997. PAT civil results show middle initial. Free case look-up at http://casesearch.courts.state.md.us.
Criminal Records: Access: In person, online. Visitors must perform in person searches themselves. Required to search: name, years to search; SSN helpful. Criminal records computerized from 4/2000; prior in books back to 1967, on CD to 1948. Note: Public is referred to CJIS Central Repository in Pikesville, 888-795-0011, 410-764-4501. Criminal PAT goes back to 4/2000. PAT results show middle initial, DOB. Records from 04/2000 forward. Online access to criminal is same as civil; results show middle initial, DOB.
General Information: Online identifiers in results same as on public terminal. No adoption, juvenile, sealed, expunged or mental records released. Will not fax documents. Court makes copy: $.25 per page, self serve same. Certification fee: $5.00. Payee: Clerk of Circuit Court. Personal checks accepted; credit cards are not.

District Court 200 Duke St Rm 2200, Prince Frederick, MD 20678; 443-550-6700; 8:30AM-4:30PM. ***Misdemeanor, Civil Actions under $25,000, Eviction, Small Claims.***
Civil Records: Access: In person, online. Visitors must perform in person searches themselves. Required to search: name; also helpful: address. Civil cases indexed by defendant. Civil records on computer from mid-80s, archived from 1971 to 1981, prior on Cot index. Civil PAT goes back to 1991. PAT results show name only. Free case look-up at http://casesearch.courts.state.md.us.
Criminal Records: Access: In person, online. Visitors must perform in person searches themselves. Required to search: name; also helpful: address, DOB. Criminal records computerized from 1981, archived from 1971-1981, prior on archived index. Criminal PAT goes back to same as civil. PAT results show middle initial, SSN, and terminal will include DOB if it was provided; and address is usually included. Online access to criminal is same as civil. Online results show middle initial, DOB.
General Information: No adoption, juvenile, sealed, expunged or medical records released. Will not fax documents. Court makes copy: $.50 per page. Certification fee: $5.00 per cert. Payee: District Court of Maryland. Personal checks accepted. Credit cards accepted, fees apply.

Register of Wills 175 Main St, Courthouse, Prince Frederick, MD 20678; 410-535-0121, 888-374-0015 in MD; fax: 410-414-3952; 8:30AM-4:30PM. ***Probate.***
www.registers.state.md.us/county/cv/html/calvert.html

Caroline County

2nd Judicial Circuit Court Box 458, Denton, MD 21629; 410-479-1811; criminal fax: 410-479-1142; civil fax: same; 8:30AM-4:30PM. ***Felony, Misdemeanor, Civil Actions over $25,000.***
Misdemeanor case records held at District Court until appealed, then stored at Circuit Court.
Civil Records: Access: Online, in person. Visitors must perform in person searches themselves. Required to search: name, years to search; also helpful: address. Civil cases indexed by defendant, plaintiff, on computer from 10/98, card index from 1774. Civil PAT goes back to 10/2000. Free case look-up at http://casesearch.courts.state.md.us.
Criminal Records: Access: In person, online. Visitors must perform in person searches themselves. Required to search: name, years to search; also helpful: address, DOB, SSN. Criminal records computerized from 2000, card index from 1774. Criminal PAT goes back to same as civil. Online access to criminal is same as civil. Online results show middle initial, DOB.
General Information: No adoption, juvenile, sealed, expunged or mental records released. Will not fax documents. Court makes copy: $.50 per page. Self serve: $.25 per page. Certification fee: $5.00 per cert. Payee: F Dale Minner, Clerk. Personal checks accepted; credit cards are not.

District Court 207 S 3rd St, Denton, MD 21629; 410-819-4600; 8:30AM-4:30PM. ***Misdemeanor, Civil Actions under $25,000, Eviction, Small Claims.***
Civil Records: Access: Online, in person. Visitors must perform in person searches themselves. Required to search: name, years to search; also helpful: address. Civil cases indexed by defendant. Civil records on cards from 1971, computerized since 1981. Civil PAT goes back to at least 3 years. Public terminal includes traffic records. Identifiers on public terminal results do not always appear. Free case look-up online at http://casesearch.courts.state.md.us.
Criminal Records: Access: Online, in person. Visitors must perform in person searches themselves. Required to search: name, years to search; also helpful: address, DOB. Criminal records on cards from 1971, computerized since 1981. Criminal PAT goes back to at least 3 years. Identifiers on public terminal results do not always appear. Online access to criminal is same as civil. Online results show middle initial, DOB.
General Information: No adoption, juvenile, sealed, expunged or mental records released. Will not fax documents. Court makes copy: $.50 per page. Certification fee: $5.00 per doc. Payee: District Court. Personal checks accepted. AmEx, Discover, MC cards accepted; There is an add'l usage fee if credit card used. Visa cards accepted only if a debit card.

Register of Wills County Courthouse, 109 Market St, Rm 119, PO Box 416, Denton, MD 21629; 410-479-0717, 888-786-0019 in MD; fax: 410-479-4983; 8AM-4:30PM. ***Probate.***
www.registers.state.md.us/county/ca/html/caroline.html

Carroll County

5th Judicial Circuit Court 55 N Court St, Westminster, MD 21157; criminal phone: 410-386-2025; civil phone: 410-386-2326; fax: 410-876-0822; 8:30AM-4:30PM. ***Felony, Misdemeanor, Civil Actions over $25,000.***
www.mdcourts.gov/clerks/carroll/index.html
Civil Records: Access: Online, in person. Visitors must perform in person searches themselves. Required to search: name; also helpful: years to search. Civil cases indexed by defendant, plaintiff, on computer from 1990, on card books from 1837 to 1990. Civil PAT goes back to 1990. Free case look-up at http://casesearch.courts.state.md.us.
Criminal Records: Access: In person, online. Visitors must perform in person searches themselves. Required to search: name; also helpful: years to search. Criminal records computerized from 1990, on card books from 1837 to 1990. Criminal PAT goes back to same as civil. Online access to criminal is same as civil. Online results show middle initial, DOB.
General Information: No adoption, juvenile, sealed, expunged or mental records released. Will not fax documents. Court makes copy: $.50 per page. Self serve: $.25 per page. Certification fee: $5.00 per doc; Exemplification fee- $10.00 per doc. Payee: Clerk of Court. Personal checks accepted; credit cards are not.

District Court 101 N Court St, Westminster, MD 21157; 410-871-3500; 8:30AM-4:30PM. ***Misdemeanor, Civil Actions under $25,000, Eviction, Small Claims.***
Civil Records: Access: Online, in person. Visitors must perform in person searches themselves. Required to search: name, years to search. Civil cases indexed by defendant, plaintiff, on computer back to 1991; on card index from 1971. Civil PAT goes back to 1991. Free case look-up at http://casesearch.courts.state.md.us.
Criminal Records: Access: Online, in person. Visitors must perform in person searches themselves. Required to search: name, years to search; also helpful: DOB. Criminal records computerized from 1982; on card index from 1971. Criminal PAT goes back to 1982. Online access to criminal is same as civil. Online results show middle initial, DOB.
General Information: No adoption, juvenile, sealed, shielded, expunged or mental records released. Will not fax documents. Court makes copy: $.50 per page. Certification fee: $5.00 per document. Payee: District Court. Personal checks accepted. Credit cards accepted.

Register of Wills 55 N Court St, Rm 104, Westminster, MD 21157; 410-848-2586, 888-876-0034 in MD; fax: 410-876-0657; 8:30AM-4:30PM. ***Probate.***
www.registers.state.md.us/county/cr/html/carroll.html

Cecil County

2nd Judicial Circuit Court 129 E Main St, Rm 108, Elkton, MD 21921; 410-996-5325; criminal phone: 410-996-5373; civil phone: 410-996-5369; fax: 410-392-6032; 8:30AM-4:30PM. ***Felony, Misdemeanor, Civil Actions over $25,000.***
www.mdcourts.gov/cecil.html
Civil Records: Access: Online, in person. Visitors must perform in person searches themselves. Required to search: name, years to search. Civil cases indexed by defendant. Civil records on card index from 1948. Civil PAT goes back to 1948. Free case look-up at http://casesearch.courts.state.md.us.
Criminal Records: Access: In person, online. Visitors must perform in person searches themselves. Required to search: name, years to search; also helpful: DOB, SSN. Criminal records on card index from 1948; computerized records since 1993. Criminal PAT goes back to same as civil. PAT results show middle initial, DOB. Online access to criminal is same as civil. Online results show middle initial, DOB.
General Information: Online identifiers in results same as on public terminal. No adoption, juvenile, sealed, expunged or mental records released. Will not fax documents. Court makes copy: $1.00 per page. Self serve: $.50 per page. Certification fee: $5.00 per page. Payee: Clerk of Court. Personal checks accepted; credit cards are not.

District Court 170 E Main St, Elkton, MD 21921; 410-996-2700; 8:30AM-4:30PM. ***Misdemeanor, Civil Actions under $25,000, Eviction, Small Claims.***
Civil Records: Access: Online, in person. Visitors must perform in person searches themselves. Required to search: name, years to search. Civil cases indexed by defendant. Civil records on computer from 1987, on card index from 1971. Civil PAT goes back to 1987. Free case look-up at http://casesearch.courts.state.md.us.
Criminal Records: Access: In person, online. Visitors must perform in person searches themselves. Required to search: name, years to search. Criminal records computerized from 1981, on card index from 1971. Criminal PAT goes back to 1981. Online access to criminal is same as civil. Online results show middle initial, DOB.
General Information: No adoption, juvenile, sealed, expunged or mental records released. Will not fax documents. Court makes copy: $.50 per page. Certification fee: $5.00. Payee: District Court. Personal checks accepted. Credit cards accepted.

Register of Wills PO Box 468, 129 E Main St, Courthouse, #101, Elkton, MD 21922-0468; 410-996-5330, 888-398-0301 in MD; fax: 410-996-1039; 8AM-4:30PM. ***Probate.***
www.registers.state.md.us/county/ce/html/cecil.html

Charles County

Circuit Court for Charles County PO Box 970, 200 Charles Street, La Plata, MD 20646; 301-932-3215; criminal phone: 301-932-3220; 8:30AM-4:30PM. ***Felony, Misdemeanor, Civil Actions over $2,500.***
www.mdcourts.gov/clerks/charles
Civil Records: Access: Online, in person. Visitors must perform in person searches themselves. Required to search: name, years to search. Civil cases indexed by defendant, plaintiff; index on docket books from 1950, on computer back to 1996. Civil PAT goes back to 1996. Free case look-up at http://casesearch.courts.state.md.us.
Criminal Records: Access: In person, online. Visitors must perform in person searches themselves. Required to search: name, years to search. Criminal records indexed in books from 1950, on computer back to 1996. Criminal PAT goes back

to same as civil. Online access to criminal is same as civil. Online results show middle initial, DOB.
General Information: No adoption, juvenile, sealed, expunged or medical records released. Court makes copy: $.50 per page. Self serve: $.25 per page. Certification fee: $5.00 per cert. Payee: Clerk of the Circuit Court. Personal checks accepted.

District Court PO Box 3070, 200 Charles St, La Plata, MD 20646; 301-932-3300; criminal phone: 301-932-3295; civil phone: 301-932-3290; 8:30AM-4:30PM. ***Misdemeanor, Civil Actions under $25,000, Eviction, Small Claims.***
Civil Records: Access: Online, in person. Visitors must perform in person searches themselves. Required to search: name, years to search. Civil cases indexed by defendant, plaintiff, on computer from 1987, on index from 1971. Civil PAT goes back to 1981. Free case look-up at http://casesearch.courts.state.md.us.
Criminal Records: Access: Online, in person. Visitors must perform in person searches themselves. Required to search: name, years to search. Criminal records computerized from 1984, on index from 1971. Criminal PAT goes back to 09/1998. Online access to criminal is same as civil. Online results show middle initial, DOB.
General Information: No confidential info, unserved warrants, medical records released. Will not fax documents. Court makes copy: $.50 per page. Certification fee: $5.00 per doc plus copy fee; triple seal is $10.00. Payee: District Court. Personal checks and major credit cards accepted.

Register of Wills/Orphans' Court PO Box 3080, Courthouse, 200 E Charles St, La Plata, MD 20646; 301-932-3345, 888-256-0054 in MD; fax: 301-932-3349; 8:30AM-4:30PM. ***Probate.***
www.registers.state.md.us/county/ch/html/charles.html

Dorchester County

1st Judicial Circuit Court Box 150, 206 High St, Cambridge, MD 21613; 410-228-0481; fax: 410-228-1860; 8:30AM-4:30PM. ***Felony, Misdemeanor, Civil Actions over $25,000.***
Civil Records: Access: Online, in person. Visitors must perform in person searches themselves. Required to search: name, years to search. Civil cases indexed by defendant, plaintiff, on computer from 1993. Civil PAT goes back to 1993. Results include name and case number. Free case look-up at http://casesearch.courts.state.md.us.
Criminal Records: Access: In person, online. Visitors must perform in person searches themselves. Required to search: name, years to search. Criminal records computerized from 1993. Note: Results include address and case number. Criminal PAT goes back to 1993. PAT results show middle initial, DOB. Results include name and case number. Online access to criminal is same as civil. Online results show middle initial, DOB.
General Information: Online identifiers in results same as on public terminal. No adoption, juvenile, sealed, expunged or mental records released. Court makes copy: $.25 per page, self serve same. Certification fee: $5.00. Payee: Clerk of Circuit Court. Personal checks accepted; credit cards are not.

District Court 310 Gay St, Cambridge, MD 21613; 410-901-1420; 8:30AM-4:30PM. ***Misdemeanor, Civil Actions under $25,000, Eviction, Small Claims.***
Civil Records: Access: Online, in person. Visitors must perform in person searches themselves. Required to search: name, years to search; also helpful: address. Civil cases indexed by defendant. Civil records archived and indexed from 1971; computerized records since 1985. Civil PAT goes back to 1985. Free case look-up at http://casesearch.courts.state.md.us.
Criminal Records: Access: Online, in person. Visitors must perform in person searches themselves. Required to search: name, years to search; also helpful: address, DOB, SSN. Criminal records on card index from 1971; computerized records since 1985. Criminal PAT goes back to same as civil. Online access to criminal is same as civil. Online results show middle initial, DOB.
General Information: No adoption, sealed, juvenile, expunged or mental records released. Will not fax documents. Court makes copy: $.50 per page. Certification fee: $5.00 per page. Payee: District Court. Personal checks accepted. MC, AmEx, Discover accepted; Visa debit cards.

Register of Wills 206 High St, Cambridge, MD 21613; 410-228-4181, 888-242-6257 in MD; fax: 410-228-4988; 8AM-4:30PM; Public- 8:30AM-4:30PM. ***Probate.***
www.registers.state.md.us/county/do/html/dorchester.html

Frederick County

6th Judicial Circuit Court 100 W Patrick St, Frederick, MD 21701; 301-600-1970; criminal phone: 301-600-1973; civil phone: 301-600-1977; fax: 301-600-2245; 8:30AM-4:30PM. ***Felony, Misdemeanor, Civil Actions over $25,000.***
Civil Records: Access: Online, in person. Visitors must perform in person searches themselves. Required to search: name, years to search. Civil cases indexed by defendant, plaintiff, on computer from 2/98, prior on card books. Civil PAT goes back to 1998. Free case look-up at http://casesearch.courts.state.md.us.
Criminal Records: Access: In person, online. Visitors must perform in person searches themselves. Required to search: name, years to search. Criminal records computerized from 12/81, prior on index books. Criminal PAT goes back to 3/2000. PAT results show middle initial, DOB. Online access to criminal is same as civil. Online results show middle initial, DOB.
General Information: No adoption, juvenile, sealed, expunged or mental records released. Will not fax documents. Court makes copy: $.25 per page. Certification fee: $5.00 per doc. Payee: Clerk of Circuit Court. Personal checks accepted; credit cards are not.

District Court 100 W Patrick St, Frederick, MD 21701; 301-600-2000; 8:30AM-4:30PM. ***Misdemeanor, Civil Actions under $25,000, Eviction, Small Claims.***
If the case number is known, the court will supply a copy of the disposition for $1.00 per page; turnaround time is 30 days.
Civil Records: Access: Online, in person. Visitors must perform in person searches themselves. Required to search: name; also helpful: years to search. Civil cases indexed by defendant, plaintiff, on computer and microfiche from 1986, archived and on card index from 1971. Civil PAT goes back to 1986. PAT results show name and case number. Free case look-up at http://casesearch.courts.state.md.us.
Criminal Records: Access: Online, in person. Visitors must perform in person searches themselves. Required to search: name, DOB; also helpful: years to search. Criminal records on computer and microfiche from 1982, archived and on card index from 1971. Note: Results include address and case number. Criminal PAT goes back to 1982. PAT results show middle initial, DOB, SSN. Online access to criminal is same as civil. Online results show middle initial, DOB.
General Information: No adoption, juvenile, sealed, expunged or mental records released. Will not fax documents. Court makes copy: $.50 per page. Certification fee: $5.00 per doc. Payee: District Court. Personal checks accepted. Credit cards accepted.

Register of Wills 100 W Patrick St, Frederick, MD 21701; 301-600-6565, 888-258-0526; fax: 301-600-6580; 8AM-4:30PM. ***Probate.***
www.registers.state.md.us/county/fr/html/frederick.html

Garrett County

4th Judicial Circuit Court PO Box 447, Oakland, MD 21550; 301-334-1937; criminal phone: 301-334-5016; civil phone: 301-334-1944; fax: 301-334-5017; 8:30AM-4:30PM. ***Felony, Civil Actions over $25,000, Criminal, Equity Types.***
Civil Records: Access: Mail, in person, online. Both court and visitors may perform in person searches. No search fee. Required to search: name, years to search. Civil cases indexed by defendant, plaintiff, on computer since 11/97. Mail turnaround time 1 day. Civil PAT goes back to 11/1997. PAT civil results show middle initial. Free case look-up at http://casesearch.courts.state.md.us.
Criminal Records: Access: Mail, in person, online. Both court and visitors may perform in person searches. No search fee. Required to search: name, years to search, DOB. Criminal records on computer since 11/99. Mail turnaround time 1 day. Criminal PAT goes back to 10/25/1999. PAT criminal results show middle initial. Search court records free at http://casesearch.courts.state.md.us. Online results show middle initial, DOB.
General Information: Online identifiers in results same as on public terminal. No adoption, juvenile, sealed, expunged or mental records released. Will not fax documents. Court makes copy: $.50 per page. Self serve: $.25 per page. Certification fee: $5.00 per page. Payee: Sondra R Buckel, Clerk. Personal checks accepted; credit cards are not. SASE not required.

District Court 205 S 3rd St, Oakland, MD 21550; 301-334-8020; 8:30AM-4:30PM. ***Misdemeanor, Civil Actions under $25,000, Eviction, Small Claims.***
Civil Records: Access: In person, online. Visitors must perform in person searches themselves. Required to search: name, years to search. Civil cases indexed by defendant. Civil records on computer from 1990, on index books from 1971. Free case look-up at http://casesearch.courts.state.md.us.
Criminal Records: Access: In person, online. Visitors must perform in person searches themselves. Required to search: name, years to search, DOB. Criminal records computerized from 1981. Online access to criminal is same as civil. Online results show middle initial, DOB.
General Information: No adoption, juvenile, sealed, expunged or mental records released. Will not fax documents. Court makes copy: $.50 per page. Certification fee: $5.00 per page. Payee: District Court. Personal checks accepted. Credit cards accepted.

Register of Wills Courthouse, 313 E Alder St, Rm 103, Oakland, MD 21550; 301-334-1999, 888-334-2203 in MD; fax: 301-334-1984; 8AM-4:30PM. ***Probate.***
www.registers.state.md.us/county/ga/html/garrett.html

Harford County

3rd Judicial Circuit 20 W Courtland St, Bel Air, MD 21014; criminal phone: 410-638-3472; civil phone: 410-638-3430; probate phone: 410-638-3275; fax: 410-636-7615; 8:30AM-4:30PM. ***Felony, Misdemeanor, Civil Actions over $25,000.***
www.mdcourts.gov/clerks/harford
Civil Records: Access: Online, in person. Visitors must perform in person searches themselves. Required to search: name, years to search; also helpful: address. Civil cases indexed by defendant, plaintiff, on computer since 05/04/1998 and on books prior. Civil PAT goes back to 5/4/1998. Results include name and case number. Free case look-up at http://casesearch.courts.state.md.us.
Criminal Records: Access: In person, online. Visitors must perform in person searches themselves. Required to search: name, years to search; also helpful: DOB. Criminal records on computer since 06/1999 and on books prior. Criminal PAT goes back to 6/1999.PAT results show name, DOB. Results include name and case number. Online access to criminal is same as civil. Online results show middle initial, DOB.
General Information: Online identifiers in results same as on public terminal. No adoption, presentence investigations, juvenile, sealed, expunged or mental records released. Will not fax documents. Court makes copy: $.50 per page. Self serve: $.25 per page. Certification fee: $5.00 per cert. Payee: Clerk of the Circuit Court. Only cashiers checks and money orders accepted. No credit cards accepted.

District Court 2 S Bond St, Bel Air, MD 21014; 410-836-4545; 8:30AM-4:30PM. ***Misdemeanor, Civil Actions under $30,000, Eviction, Small Claims.***
Civil Records: Access: Mail, in person, online. Visitors must perform in person searches themselves. No search fee. Required to search: name,

years to search. Civil cases indexed by defendant. Civil records on computer from 1989, on microfiche from 1972, archived from 1900. Civil PAT goes back to 1981. PAT results show name only. Free look-up at http://casesearch.courts.state.md.us.
Criminal Records: Access: Mail, online, in person. Visitors must perform in person searches themselves. No search fee. Required to search: name, years to search; also helpful: address, DOB. Criminal records computerized from 1981, on microfiche from 1972, archived from 1900. Note: Results include name and case number. Mail turnaround time 3-4 days. Criminal PAT goes back to same as civil. PAT results show middle initial, DOB, SSN. Online access to criminal is same as civil. Online results show middle initial, DOB.
General Information: No motor vehicle, sealed, expunged or mental records released. Will not fax documents. Court makes copy: $.50 per page. Certification fee: $5.00. Payee: District Court of MD. Personal checks accepted. Credit cards accepted. Mail requests: SASE required.

Register of Wills 20 W Courtland St, Rm 304, Court House, Bel Air, MD 21014; 410-638-3275, 888-258-0525 in MD; fax: 410-893-3177; 8:30AM-4:00PM. ***Probate.***
www.registers.state.md.us/county/ha/html/harford.html

Howard County

5th Judicial Circuit Court 8360 Court Ave, Ellicott City, MD 21043; 410-313-2111; 888-313-0197; criminal phone: 410-313-3824; civil phone: 410-313-3844; 8:30AM-4:30PM. ***Felony, Misdemeanor, Civil Actions over $25,000.***
www.mdcourts.gov/clerks/howard/
Civil Records: Access: Online, in person. Visitors must perform in person searches themselves. Required to search: name, years to search; also helpful: address. Civil cases indexed by defendant, plaintiff, on computer from 1984, archived from 1900, on card index from 1900. Civil PAT goes back to 1997. Free case look-up at http://casesearch.courts.state.md.us.
Criminal Records: Access: In person, online. Visitors must perform in person searches themselves. Required to search: name, years to search; also helpful: address, DOB, SSN. Criminal records on card index to 1840, on computer since 1984. Criminal PAT goes back to 1998. Online access to criminal is same as civil. Online results show middle initial, DOB.
General Information: No adoption, juvenile, sealed, expunged or mental records released. Will not fax documents. Court makes copy: $.50 per page. Self serve: $.25 per page. Certification fee: $5.00 per page. Payee: Office of Clerk. Personal checks accepted.

District Court 3451 Courthouse Dr, Ellicott City, MD 21043; 410-480-7700; 8:30AM-4:30PM. ***Misdemeanor, Civil Actions under $30,000, Eviction, Small Claims.***
Civil Records: Access: Mail, in person, online. Both court and visitors may perform in person searches. No search fee. Required to search: name, years to search. Civil cases indexed by defendant. Civil records on computer from 1992, on card index prior from 1971. Mail turnaround time before 1989 4-6 weeks, 1989-present 7 days. Civil PAT goes back to 1990. Free case look-up at http://casesearch.courts.state.md.us.
Criminal Records: Access: Mail, online, in person. Both court and visitors may perform in person searches. No search fee. Required to search: name, years to search. Criminal records computerized from 1989, on card index prior from 1971. Mail turnaround time before 1989- 4-6 weeks; 1989-present- 7 days. Criminal PAT goes back to 1985. Online access to criminal is same as civil. Online results show middle initial, DOB.
General Information: No adoption, juvenile, sealed, expunged or mental records released. Will not fax documents. Court makes copy: $.50 per page, self serve same. Certification fee: $5.00. Payee: District Court of MD. Personal checks accepted. Credit cards accepted. Mail requests: SASE required if return receipt requested.

Register of Wills 8360 Court Ave, Ellicott City, MD 21043; 410-313-2133, 888-848-0136 in MD; fax: 410-313-3409; 8:30AM-4:30PM. ***Probate.***
www.registers.state.md.us/county/ho/html/howard.html

Kent County

2nd Judicial Circuit Court 103 N Cross St Courthouse, Chestertown, MD 21620; 410-778-7460; criminal phone: 410-778-7477; civil phone: 410-778-7461; criminal fax: 410-778-7412; civil fax: same; 8:30AM-4:30PM. ***Felony, Misdemeanor, Civil Actions over $25,000.***
www.courts.state.md.us/clerks/kent/records.html
Civil Records: Access: Online, in person. Visitors must perform in person searches themselves. Required to search: name, years to search. Civil cases indexed by defendant, plaintiff, on computer from 1998, on card index from 1656. Civil PAT goes back to 5/1998. Free case look-up at http://casesearch.courts.state.md.us.
Criminal Records: Access: In person, online. Visitors must perform in person searches themselves. Required to search: name, years to search; also helpful: DOB, SSN. Criminal records computerized from 05/2000, on card index from 1949, archived to 1656. Criminal PAT goes back to 5/2000. Online access to criminal is same as civil. Online results show middle initial, DOB.
General Information: No adoption, juvenile, sealed, expunged or mental records released. Will not fax documents. Court makes copy: $.50 per page. Self serve: $.25 per page. Certification fee: $5.00 per cert. Payee: Mark L Mumford, Clerk. Personal checks accepted; credit cards are not.

District Court 103 N Cross St, Chestertown, MD 21620; 410-810-3362; fax: 410-810-3361; 8:30AM-4:30PM. ***Misdemeanor, Civil Actions under $30,000, Eviction, Small Claims, Traffic.***
Civil Records: Access: Online, in person. Visitors must perform in person searches themselves. Required to search: name, years to search. Civil cases indexed by defendant. Civil records on computer from 1989; on card index from 1971. Free case look-up at http://casesearch.courts.state.md.us.
Criminal Records: Access: Online, in person. Visitors must perform in person searches themselves. Required to search: name, years to search, DOB. Criminal records computerized from 1988, on card index from 1971. Online access to criminal is same as civil. Online results show middle initial, DOB.
General Information: No sealed, expunged, mental records or judge's notes released. Will not fax documents. Court makes copy: $.50 per page. Self serve: available for up to 10 copies. Certification fee: $5.00 per document includes copies. Payee: District Court of MD. Personal checks accepted. Credit cards accepted in person only.

Register of Wills 103 N Cross St, Chestertown, MD 21620; 410-778-7466, 888-778-0179 in MD; probate phone: 410-778-7465 & 410-778-7463; fax: 410-778-2466; 8AM-4:30PM. ***Probate.***
www.registers.state.md.us/county/ke/html/kent.html

Montgomery County

Circuit Court 50 Maryland Ave, Rockville, MD 20850; 240-777-9466; criminal phone: 240-777-9440; civil phone: 240-777-9401; criminal fax: 240-777-9444; civil fax: 240-777-9413; 8:30AM-4:30PM. ***Felony, Misdemeanor, Civil Actions over $25,000.***
www.montgomerycountymd.gov/mc/judicial
Copy Rm phone- 240-777-9431.
Civil Records: Access: In person, online. Both court and visitors may perform in person searches. No search fee. Required to search: name, years to search; also helpful: case number. Civil cases indexed by defendant, plaintiff, on computer from 1977, archived from 1900, on card index from 1977. Note: This court will not provide name searches, only copies of specific documents. Civil PAT goes back to 1977. Free case look-up at http://casesearch.courts.state.md.us. Also, the daily calendar is free at www.montgomerycountymd.gov/mc/judicial/circuit/docket.html.
Criminal Records: Access: In person, online. Both court and visitors may perform in person searches. No search fee. Required to search: name, years to search; also helpful: case number. Criminal records computerized from 1973, archived from 1900, on card index from 1977. Note: Court will not perform name searches, only copies of specific documents. Criminal PAT goes back to 1973. Search court records free at http://casesearch.courts.state.md.us. Online results show middle initial, DOB. Address usually appears in online criminal results.
General Information: No adoption, juvenile, sealed, expunged or mental records released. Will not fax documents. Court makes copy: $.50 per page. Certification fee: $5.00 per doc. Payee: Clerk of Circuit Court. Personal checks accepted; credit cards are not.

District Court 8552 Second Ave., Silver Spring, MD 20910; 301-563-8500, 866-873-9785; 8:30AM-4:30PM. ***Misdemeanor, Civil Actions under $25,000, Eviction, Small Claims.***
Civil Records: Access: Mail, in person, online. Both court and visitors may perform in person searches. No search fee. Required to search: name, years to search. Civil cases indexed by defendant, plaintiff, on computer from 1986, in book index and case folder. Mail turnaround time 2-4 weeks. Civil PAT goes back to 1986. Free case look-up at http://casesearch.courts.state.md.us.
Criminal Records: Access: Mail, online, in person. Both court and visitors may perform in person searches. No search fee. Required to search: name, years to search. Criminal records on computer, index book and case folder. Mail turnaround time 2-4 weeks. Criminal PAT goes back to at least 3 years. Online access to criminal is same as civil. Online results show middle initial, DOB.
General Information: No juvenile, sealed, expunged or mental records or judge's notes released. Will not fax documents. Court makes copy: $.50 per page. Self serve: computer printouts- $.50 per page. Certification fee: $5.00 per cert. Payee: District Court. Personal checks accepted; credit cards are not. Mail requests: SASE required.

Rockville District Court 27 Courthouse Square, Rockville, MD 20850; criminal phone: 301-279-1565; civil phone: 301-279-1500; 8:30AM-4:30PM. ***Misdemeanor, Civil Actions under $25,000, Eviction, Small Claims, Traffic.***
Civil Records: Access: Mail, in person, online. Both court and visitors may perform in person searches. No search fee. Required to search: name, years to search. Civil cases indexed by defendant. Civil records go back to 1971; on computer back to 1990, prior in case folder. Mail turnaround time 2-4 weeks. Civil PAT goes back to 1990. Free case look-up at http://casesearch.courts.state.md.us.
Criminal Records: Access: Mail, online, in person. Both court and visitors may perform in person searches. No search fee. Required to search: name, years to search; also helpful: DOB. Criminal records go back to 1971; on computer back to 1987. Mail turnaround time 2-4 weeks. Criminal PAT goes back to 1987. Online access to criminal is same as civil. Online results show middle initial, DOB.
General Information: No juvenile, sealed, expunged, mental records or judge's notes released. Will not fax documents. Court makes copy: $.50 per page. Certification fee: $5.00 per page. Payee: District Court. Personal checks accepted. Mail requests: SASE required.

Register of Wills 50 Maryland Ave, #322, Judicial Ctr., Rockville, MD 20850; 240-777-9600; fax: 240-777-9602; 8:30AM-4:30PM. ***Probate.***
www.registers.state.md.us/county/mo/html/montgomery.html

Prince George's County

District Court 14735 Main St, Rm 173B, Upper Marlboro, MD 20772; 301-952-4080, 800-943-8853; 8:30AM-4:30PM. ***Misdemeanor, Civil Actions under $25,000, Eviction, Small Claims.***
Civil Records: Access: Mail, in person, online. Both court and visitors may perform in person searches. No search fee. Required to search: name, years to search. Civil cases indexed by defendant. Civil

records on computer from 1988, on card index from 1970. Mail turnaround time 1-2 weeks. Civil PAT goes back to 1988. Free case look-up at http://casesearch.courts.state.md.us.
Criminal Records: Access: Mail, online, in person. Visitors must perform in person searches themselves. No search fee. Required to search: name, years to search. Criminal records computerized from 1984, on cards from 1970. Mail turnaround time 1-2 weeks. Criminal PAT goes back to 1984. Online access to criminal is same as civil. Online results show middle initial, DOB.
General Information: No adoption, juvenile, sealed, expunged or mental records released. Will not fax documents. Court makes copy: $.50 per page. Certification fee: $5.00 per page. Payee: District Court of Maryland. Personal checks accepted. Mail requests: SASE required.

7th Judicial Circuit Court 14735 Main St, Upper Marlboro, MD 20772; criminal phone: 301-952-3344; civil phone: 301-952-3240; 8:30AM-4:30PM. ***Felony, Misdemeanor, Civil Actions over $25,000.*** www.co.pg.md.us/Government/JudicialBranch/circuit.asp?nivel=foldmenu(1)
Civil court physical address is Courthouse Annex Bldg, 14701 Gov Odenbolvie Dr.
Civil Records: Access: In person, online. Visitors must perform in person searches themselves. Required to search: name, years to search. Civil cases indexed by defendant, plaintiff, on computer from 1981, on microfiche from 1979, on card index prior. Civil PAT goes back to 1981. For case searches for the state go to http://casesearch.courts.state.md.us/inquiry/inquiry-index.jsp. Includes defendant name, city and state, case number, date of birth, plaintiff name (civil cases only), trial date, charge, case disposition.
Criminal Records: Access: In person, online. Visitors must perform in person searches themselves. Required to search: name, years to search, DOB; SSN helpful. Criminal records computerized from 1981, on microfiche from 1979, on card index prior. Criminal PAT goes back to 1980. For case searches for the state go to http://casesearch.courts.state.md.us/inquiry/inquiry-index.jsp. Includes defendant name, city and state, case number, date of birth, trial date, charge, case disposition. Online results show middle initial, DOB.
General Information: No adoption, juvenile, sealed, expunged or mental records released. Court makes copy: $.50 per page. Certification fee: $5.00 per page. Payee: Clerk of Circuit Court. Personal checks accepted. Visa/MC accepted.

Register of Wills PO Box 1729, 5303 Chrysler Way #300, Upper Marlboro, MD 20773; 301-952-3250, 888-464-4219 in MD; fax: 301-952-4489; 8:30AM-4:30PM; 3:30PM for counter service.. ***Probate*** .www.registers.state.md.us/county/pg/html/princegeorges.html

Queen Anne's County

2nd Judicial Circuit Court Courthouse, 100 Courthouse Sq, Centreville, MD 21617; 410-758-1773, 800-987-7591; 8:30AM-4:30PM. ***Felony, Misdemeanor, Civil Actions over $25,000.***
www.courts.state.md.us/clerks/queenannes/index.html
Misdemeanor case records held at District Court until appealed, then stored at Circuit Court.
Civil Records: Access: Online, in person. Visitors must perform in person searches themselves. Required to search: name, years to search. Civil cases indexed by defendant, plaintiff, on computer from 11/92; on index books from 1978. Civil PAT goes back to 11/1992. Results include name and case number. Free case look-up online at http://casesearch.courts.state.md.us.
Criminal Records: Access: In person, online. Visitors must perform in person searches themselves. Required to search: name, years to search, SSN. Criminal records computerized from 11/92; on index books from 1978. Criminal PAT goes back to same as civil.PAT results show name, DOB. Results include name and case number. Online access to criminal is same as civil. Online results show middle initial, DOB.
General Information: Online identifiers in results same as on public terminal. No adoption, juvenile, sealed, expunged or mental records released. Court makes copy: $.50 per page. Certification fee: $5.00 per cert. Payee: Clerk of Circuit Court. Personal checks accepted; credit cards are not.

District Court 120 Broadway, Centreville, MD 21617; 410-819-4000; fax: 410-819-4001; 8:30AM-4:30PM. ***Misdemeanor, Civil Actions under $30,000, Eviction, Small Claims.***
Civil Records: Access: Online, in person. Visitors must perform in person searches themselves. Required to search: name, years to search; also helpful: address. Civil cases indexed by defendant. Civil records on computer from 1988, archived from 1974, prior on index books. Civil PAT goes back to 1988. Free case look-up at http://casesearch.courts.state.md.us.
Criminal Records: Access: Online, in person. Visitors must perform in person searches themselves. Required to search: name, years to search; also helpful: address, DOB, SSN. Criminal records computerized from 1981, prior on index books. Criminal PAT goes back to 1981. Online access to criminal is same as civil. Online results show middle initial, DOB.
General Information: No adoption, juvenile, sealed, expunged or mental records released. Will not fax documents. Court makes copy: $.50 per page. Certification fee: $5.00. Payee: District Court of Maryland. Personal checks and Visa cards accepted.

Register of Wills Liberty Bldg, 107 N Liberty St #220, PO Box 59, Centreville, MD 21617; 410-758-0585, 888-758-0010 in MD; fax: 410-758-4408; 8AM-4:30PM. ***Probate.*** www.registers.state.md.us/county/qa/html/queenannes.html

Somerset County

1st Judicial Circuit Court PO Box 99, Princess Anne, MD 21853; 410-845-4840; criminal phone: 410-845-4850; civil phone: 410-845-4855; probate phone: 410-651-1696; fax: 410-845-4841; 8AM-4:30PM. ***Felony, Misdemeanor, Civil Actions over $25,000.***
Civil Records: Access: Online, in person. Visitors must perform in person searches themselves. Required to search: name, years to search; also helpful: address. Civil cases indexed by defendant, plaintiff, on computer from 9/93; prior archived and on index books. Civil PAT goes back to 1997. Free look-up at http://casesearch.courts.sta te.md.us.
Criminal Records: Access: In person, online. Visitors must perform in person searches themselves. Required to search: name, years to search; also helpful: address, DOB, SSN. Criminal records computerized from 9/93; prior archived and on index books. Criminal PAT goes back to 1999. Online access to criminal is same as civil. Online results show middle initial, DOB.
General Information: No adoption, juvenile, sealed, expunged or mental records released. Will not fax documents. Court makes copy: $.50 per page. Self serve: $.25 per page. Certification fee: $5.00. Payee: Clerk of Circuit Court. Personal checks accepted; credit cards are not.

District Court 12155 Elm St #C, Princess Anne, MD 21853-1358; 800-939-7306, 410-845-4700; 8:30AM-4:30PM. ***Misdemeanor, Civil Actions under $25,000, Eviction, Small Claims.***
Felony cases go to Circuit Court if preliminary hearing waived or cause found. Records held at court where trial heard.
Civil Records: Access: Online, in person. Visitors must perform in person searches themselves. Required to search: name, years to search. Civil cases indexed by defendant, plaintiff, on computer from 1987, archived and on index books from 1971. Civil PAT goes back to 1987. PAT results show middle initial, DOB. Free case look-up at http://casesearch.courts.state.md.us.
Criminal Records: Access: Online, in person. Visitors must perform in person searches themselves. Required to search: name, years to search; also helpful: SSN. Criminal records computerized from 1987, archived and on index books from 1971. Criminal PAT goes back to same as civil. PAT results show middle initial, DOB. Online access to criminal is same as civil. Online results show middle initial, DOB.
General Information: Online identifiers in results same as on public terminal. No adoption, juvenile, sealed, expunged or mental records released. Will not fax documents. Court makes copy: $.50 per page. Certification fee: $5.00 per doc. Payee: District Court. Personal checks accepted; credit cards are not.

Register of Wills 30512 Prince William St, Princess Anne, MD 21853; 410-651-1696, 888-758-0039 in MD; fax: 410-651-3873; 8AM-4:30PM.
www.registers.state.md.us/county/so/html/somerset.html

St. Mary's County

7th Judicial Circuit Court PO Box 676, 41605 Courthouse Dr., Leonardtown, MD 20650; 301-475-7844 x4; 8:30AM-4:30PM. ***Felony, Misdemeanor, Civil Actions over $30,000.***
Civil Records: Access: Online, in person. Visitors must perform in person searches themselves. Required to search: name, years to search. Civil cases indexed by defendant, plaintiff, on computer from 1987, on card index from 1970. Civil PAT goes back to 1987. PAT results show name only. Free case look-up at http://casesearch.courts.state.md.us.
Criminal Records: Access: In person, online. Visitors must perform in person searches themselves. Required to search: name, years to search; SSN helpful. Criminal records computerized from 1987, on card index from 1970. Criminal PAT goes back to 2000. PAT results show name only. Online access to criminal is same as civil. Online results show middle initial, DOB.
General Information: No adoption, juvenile, sealed, expunged or mental/medical records released. Will not fax documents. Court makes copy: $.50 per page.A self serve copier is also available; you purchase a copier debit card and your copy account is drawn down as you use it. Certification fee: $5.00 per cert. Payee: Clerk of the Circuit Court. Personal checks accepted; credit cards are not.

District Court Carter State Office Bldg, 23110 Leonard Hall Dr, Leonardtown, MD 20650; 301-880-2700; fax: 301-880-2701; 8:30AM-4:30PM. ***Misdemeanor, Civil Actions under $30,000, Eviction, Small Claims*** .www.msa.md.gov/msa/mdmanual/36loc/sm/html/smj.html
Civil Records: Access: Online, in person. Visitors must perform in person searches themselves. Required to search: name, years to search. Civil cases indexed by defendant. Civil records on computer from 1987, archived from 1971. Civil PAT goes back to 1983; results show middle initial, DOB, SSN. Free look-up at http://casesearch.courts.sta te.md.us.
Criminal Records: Access: Online, in person. Visitors must perform in person searches themselves. Required to search: name, years to search; also helpful: DOB. Criminal records computerized from 1985, archived from 1971. Criminal PAT goes back to 1983. PAT results show middle initial, DOB, SSN. Search results may also include physical identifiers. Online access to criminal is same as civil. Online results show middle initial, DOB.
General Information: No adoption, juvenile, sealed, expunged or mental records released. Will not fax out documents. Court makes copy: $.50 per page. Certification fee: $5.00 per doc or triple seal for $10.00. Payee: District Court of Maryland. Personal checks accepted. Credit cards accepted in person; add $6.50 processing fee, $5.50 if debit card.

Register of Wills 41605 Court House Dr, PO Box 602, Leonardtown, MD 20650; 301-475-5566; fax: 301-475-4968; 8:30AM-4:30PM. ***Probate.***
www.registers.state.md.us/county/sm/html/stmarys.html

Talbot County

Circuit Court 11 N Washington St, #16, Easton, MD 21601-3195; 410-822-2611; fax: 410-820-8168; 8:30AM-4:30PM. ***Felony, Misdemeanor, Civil Actions over $25,000.***
www.mdcourts.gov/clerks/talbot/index.html
Civil Records: Access: Online, in person. Visitors must perform in person searches themselves.

Required to search: name, years to search; also helpful: address. Civil cases indexed by defendant, plaintiff, on card index from 1993. Civil PAT goes back to 1997. PAT results show name only. Free look-up at http://casesearch.courts.state.md.us.
Criminal Records: Access: In person, online. Visitors must perform in person searches themselves. Required to search: name, years to search; also helpful: address, DOB, SSN. Criminal records on card index from 1993. Criminal PAT goes back to same as civil. PAT results show name only. Online access to criminal is same as civil. Online results show middle initial, DOB.
General Information: Online identifiers in results same as on public terminal. No adoption, juvenile, sealed, expunged or mental records released. Will not fax documents. Court makes copy: $.50 per page. Certification fee: $5.00. Payee: Mary Ann Shortall, Clerk of Court. Personal checks accepted; credit cards are not. Mail requests: SASE required for mail return of any copies.

District Court 108 W Dover St, Easton, MD 21601; 410-819-5850; 8:30-4:30PM. ***Misdemeanor, Civil under $30,000, Eviction, Small Claims.***
Civil Records: Access: Online, in person. Visitors must perform in person searches themselves. Required to search: name, years to search. Civil cases indexed by defendant. Civil records go back to 1971; on computer back to 1988. Civil PAT goes back to 1988. PAT results show name only. Free case look-up at http://casesearch.courts.state.md.us.
Criminal Records: Access: Online, in person. Visitors must perform in person searches themselves. Required to search: name, years to search. Criminal records go back to 1971; on computer back to 1984. Criminal PAT goes back to 1984. PAT results show name only. Online access to criminal is same as civil. Online results show middle initial, DOB.
General Information: No adoption, juvenile, sealed, expunged or mental records released. Will not fax documents. Court makes copy: $.50 per page. Certification fee: $5.00 per doc. Payee: District Court of MD. Personal checks accepted. MasterCards accepted and VISA debit cards only.

Register of Wills PO Box 816, Courthouse, 11 N Washington St, Easton, MD 21601; 410-770-6700, 888-822-0039 in MD; fax: 410-822-5452; 8AM-4:30PM. ***Probate.*** www.registers.state.md.us/county/ta/html/talbot.html

Washington County

Washington County Circuit Court Box 229, Hagerstown, MD 21741; 301-733-8660; criminal phone: 301-790-7941; civil phone: 301-790-4972; fax: 301-791-1151; 8:30AM-4:30PM. ***Felony, Misdemeanor, Civil Actions over $25,000.***
Records prior to 1900 available at Maryland State Archives.
Civil Records: Access: Online, in person. Visitors must perform in person searches themselves. Required to search: name, years to search. Civil cases indexed by defendant. Civil records on case files, docket books to 1900; on computer back to 1985. Civil PAT goes back to 1996. PAT results show name only. The public access index for "Law" and Criminal" go back to 1954. Search records back to 1997 free at http://casesearch.courts.s tate.md.us.
Criminal Records: Access: In person, online. Visitors must perform in person searches themselves. Required to search: name, years to search; also helpful: DOB. Criminal records on case files, docket books to 1900; on computer back to 1985. Criminal PAT goes back to same as civil. PAT results show name only. The public access index for "Law" and Criminal" go back to 1954. Online access to criminal is same as civil. Online results show middle initial, DOB. Some information "shielded" online but available on public access terminal.
General Information: Online identifiers in results same as on public terminal. No adoption, juvenile, sealed, expunged or mental records released. Will fax documents $3.00 up to 20 pages, then $.10 add'l page. Court makes copy: $.50 per page. Self serve: $.25 per page. Certification fee: $5.00. Payee: Clerk of Circuit Court. Personal checks accepted; credit cards are not.

District Court 36 W Antietam St, Hagerstown, MD 21740; 800-945-1406, 240-420-4600; 8:30AM-4:30PM. ***Misdemeanor, Civil Actions under $25,000, Eviction, Small Claims.***
Civil Records: Access: Phone, mail, online, in person. Both court and visitors may perform in person searches. No search fee. Required to search: name, years to search; also helpful: address. Civil cases indexed by defendant. Civil records on computer from 1986, archived and on index books from 1971. Mail turnaround time 30 days. Civil PAT goes back to 1986. Free case look-up at http://casesearch.courts.state.md.us.
Criminal Records: Access: In person, online. Visitors must perform in person searches themselves. Required to search: name, years to search; also helpful: address, DOB, SSN, case number. Criminal records computerized from 1982, on index books from 1971. Criminal PAT goes back to 1982. Online access to criminal is same as civil. Online results show middle initial, DOB.
General Information: No adoption, juvenile, sealed, expunged or mental records released. Will not fax documents. Court makes copy: $.50 per page. Certification fee: $5.00 per doc. Payee: District Court. Personal checks accepted. Debit cards accepted, also AmEx, Visa. Mail requests: SASE required for civil.

Register of Wills 95 W Washington, Hagerstown, MD 21740; 301-739-3612, 888-739-0013 in MD; fax: 301-733-8636; 8AM-4:30PM. ***Probate.*** www.registers.state.md.us/county/wa/html/washington.html

Wicomico County

1st Judicial Circuit Court PO Box 198, Salisbury, MD 21803-0198; 410-543-6551; fax: 410-546-8590; 8:30AM-4:30PM. ***Felony, Misdemeanor, Civil Actions over $25,000.***
All phone search requests must include case number.
Civil Records: Access: Phone, mail, online, in person. Both court and visitors may perform in person searches. No search fee. Required to search: name, years to search. Civil cases indexed by defendant, plaintiff, on books since 1867, cases filed after 5/93 on computer. Note: All phone requests must include case number. Mail turnaround time 1-2 days. Civil PAT goes back to 1993. Free case look-up at http://casesearch.courts.state.md.us.
Criminal Records: Access: Phone, mail, in person, online. Both court and visitors may perform in person searches. No search fee. Required to search: name, years to search; also helpful: DOB, SSN. Criminal docket on books since 1867, cases filed after 5/93 on computer. Note: Phone requests must include case number. Mail turnaround time 1-2 days. Criminal PAT goes back to same as civil. Online access to criminal is same as civil. Online results show middle initial, DOB.
General Information: No adoption, juvenile, sealed, expunged or mental records released. Court makes copy: $.50 per page. Self serve: $.25 per page. Certification fee: $5.00. Payee: Clerk of Circuit Court. Personal checks accepted. Out of state checks not accepted. No credit cards. SASE not required.

District Court 201 Baptist St, Salisbury, MD 21801; 410-713-3500; 8:30AM-4:30PM. ***Misdemeanor, Civil Actions under $25,000, Eviction, Small Claims.***
Civil Records: Access: Online, in person. Visitors must perform in person searches themselves. Required to search: name, years to search; also helpful: address. Civil cases indexed by defendant, plaintiff, on computer go back to 1985, archived from 1984, on card index from 1971. Civil PAT goes back to 1982. PAT results show name only. Free case look-up at http://casesearch.courts.state.md.us.
Criminal Records: Access: Online, in person. Visitors must perform in person searches themselves. Required to search: name, years to search; also helpful: address, DOB. Criminal records go back to 1971; on computer back 1983. Note: Sometimes the DOB is provided on the public access terminal. Criminal PAT goes back to 1985. PAT results show name only. Online access to criminal is same as civil. Online results show middle initial, DOB.
General Information: No adoption, juvenile, sealed, expunged or mental records released. Will not fax documents. Court makes copy: $.50 per page. Certification fee: $5.00. Payee: District Court. Personal checks accepted; credit cards are not.

Register of Wills 101 N Division St, Rm 102, Salisbury, MD 21801; 410-543-6635, 888-786-0018 in MD; fax: 410-334-3440; 8:30AM-4:30PM. ***Probate.*** www.registers.state.md.us/county/wi/html/wicomico.html

Worcester County

1st Judicial Circuit Court Clerk of Circuit Court, PO Box 40, Snow Hill, MD 21863; criminal phone: 410-632-5502; civil phone: 410-632-5501; 8:30AM-4:30PM. ***Felony, Misdemeanor, Civil Actions over $25,000.***
Civil Records: Access: In person, online. Visitors must perform in person searches themselves. Required to search: name, years to search. Civil cases indexed by defendant. Civil records indexed on computer since 7/93, on docket books prior. Civil PAT goes back to 1993. Free case look-up at http://casesearch.courts.state.md.us.
Criminal Records: Access: In person, online. Visitors must perform in person searches themselves. Required to search: name, years to search. Criminal records indexed on computer since 7/93, on docket books prior. Criminal PAT goes back to same as civil. Online access to criminal is same as civil; results show middle initial, DOB.
General Information: No adoption, juvenile, sealed or expunged records released. Will not fax out case files. Court makes copy: $.50 per page. Self serve: $.25 per page. Certification fee: $5.00. Payee: Clerk of Circuit Court. Personal checks accepted; credit cards are not.

District Court 301 Commerce St, Snow Hill, MD 21863-1007; 800-941-0282, 410-219-7830; fax: 410-219-7840; 8:30-4:30PM. ***Misdemeanor, Civil Actions under $25,000, Eviction, Small Claims.***
Civil Records: Access: Online, in person. Visitors must perform in person searches themselves. Required to search: name, years to search; also helpful: address. Civil cases indexed by defendant. Civil records on computer since 1988. Note: Records can be researched via books in the lobby. Civil PAT goes back to 1993. Free case look-up at http://casesearch.courts.state.md.us.
Criminal Records: Access: Online, in person. Visitors must perform in person searches themselves. Required to search: name, years to search; also helpful: address, DOB, SSN. Criminal records on computer since 1982. Note: Records can be researched via books in the lobby. Criminal PAT goes back to same as civil. Online access to criminal is same as civil. Online results show middle initial, DOB.
General Information: No sealed or juvenile records released. Court makes copy: $.50 per page. Certification fee: $5.00 per page. Payee: District Court. Personal checks accepted. Major credit cards accepted with fee. Mail requests: SASE required for mail return of any copies.

Register of Wills Courthouse, 1 W Market St, Rm 102, Snow Hill, MD 21863-1074; 410-632-1529, 888-256-0047 in MD; fax: 410-632-5600; 8AM-4:30PM. ***Probate.*** www.registers.state.md.us/county/wo/html/worcester.html

Maryland Recording Offices

ORGANIZATION: 23 counties and one independent city; 24 recording offices. The recording officer is the Clerk of the Circuit Court. Baltimore City has a recording office separate from the County of Baltimore - watch for ZIP Codes that include both the city and the county. Maryland is in the Eastern Time Zone (EST).

REAL ESTATE RECORDS: Counties will not perform real estate searches. Copies usually cost $.50 per page and certification fee is $5.00 per document.

UCC RECORDS: Maryland was a dual filing state until July 1995. Since then all new UCC filings except for consumer goods, farm-related and real estate-related filings were submitted only to the central filing office. Starting July, 2001, only real estate related filing are submitted to the Clerk of Circuit Court.

TAX LIEN RECORDS: All tax liens are filed with the county Clerk of Circuit Court. Counties will not perform name searches. You must hire a retriever to search.

OTHER LIENS: Judgment, mechanics, county, hospital, condominium.

ONLINE ACCESS: Search statewide property records data free at http://sdatcert3.resiusa.org/rp_rewrite/. There is no name searching. Also, the Maryland State Dept. of Planning offers MDPropertyview with property maps/parcels and assessments on the web or CD-rom. Registration required; visit www.mdp.state.md.us/tax_mos.htm. There is no name searching. Also, the state launched an experimental Digital Image Retrieval System for Land Record Indices at www.mdlandrec.net/. The Maryland Judiciary, the 24 elected Maryland Court Clerks, and Maryland State Archives have joined in partnership to provide up-to-date access to all verified land record instruments in Maryland. This service is currently provided free to all interested in testing the system.

Also, vendors provide online access in several places. County tax records are at www.taxrecords.com. Land survey, condominium, and survey plats are available free by county at www.plats.net. Use username "Plato" and password "plato#". No name searching.

Allegany County

County Clerk of the Circuit Court, 30 Washington St, Cumberland, MD 21502-2948. 301-777-5922; fax-301-777-2100; 8AM-4:30PM (EST)

Index: All in one. Records indexed on a public use terminal back to 1789. Only the public may search. Copy fee $.50 per page. Cert fee- $5.00 per doc plus copy fee. Payee- Allegany County Clerk of Circuit Court. **Online access to Real Property, Land Survey/Plat records:** Land records online from www.mdlandrec.net/msa/stagser/s1700/s1741/cfm/index.cfm, and www.plats.net (use username "Plato" and password "plato#") and MDPropertyview at www.mdp.state.md.us/data/mdview.htm. **Other phones:** Treasurer- 301-777-5965; Elections- 301-777-5931. **Property tax/Assessing-** 112 Baltimore St, 3rd Fl, PO Box 343, Cumberland, MD 21501; 301-777-2108, assessor fax- 301-777-2052. **Online access-** Search real property data free at http://sdatcert3.resiusa.org/rp_rewrite/. No name searching. See Clerk of Circuit Court recording office for online property search options.

Anne Arundel County

County Clerk of the Circuit Court, PO Box 71, Annapolis, MD 21404. 410-222-1425; fax-410-222-1087; 8:30AM-4:30PM (EST)

Index: Separate indices to search include mainframe, electronic, old books. Records indexed on a public use terminal back to 1600s. Only the public may search. Copy fee $.50 per page. Cert fee- $5.00 per cert plus copy fee. Payee- Clerk of Circuit Court. **Online access to Real Property, Land Survey/Plat records:** Land records online from www.mdlandrec.net/msa/stagser/s1700/s1741/cfm/index.cfm, and www.plats.net (use username "Plato" and password "plato#") and MDPropertyview at www.mdp.state.md.us/data/mdview.htm. **Other phones:** Treasurer- 410-222-1140; Tax Office- 410-222-1144. **Property tax/Assessing-** Dept of Assessments & Taxation, 45 Calvert St, Annapolis, MD 21401; 410-974-5727, assessor fax- 410-974-5738. (Appraiser/Auditor- 410-974-5709) hours- 8AM-5PM **Online access-** Search real property data free at http://sdatcert3.resiusa.org/rp_rewrite/. No name searching. See Clerk of Circuit Court recording office for online property search options.

Baltimore City

City Clerk, 100 N Calvert St, Rm 610, Baltimore, MD 21202. 410-333-3760; 8:30AM-8PM M-Th; 8:30AM-5PM F. (EST)

Index: Separate indices to search include grantor/grantee, block index. Records indexed on computer back to 7/1/72. Only the public may search. Will not search UCC records. Copy fee $.50 per page; $.25 self serve. Cert fee- $5.00 per doc plus copy fee. Payee- Circuit Court for Baltimore City. **Online Real Property, Deed, Land Survey/Plat records:** Land records online at www.mdlandrec.net/msa/stagser/s1700/s1741/cfm/index.cfm, and MDPropertyview at www.mdp.state.md.us/data/mdview.htm. **Other phones:** Treasurer- 410-396-5122; Vital Records- 410-764-5904. **Property tax/Assessing-** 6 St Paul St, 11th Fl, Baltimore, MD 21202; 410-767-8250, assessor fax- 410-333-4626. hours- 8AM-5PM **Online access-** Search real property data free at http://sdatcert3.resiusa.org/rp_rewrite/. No name searching. See Clerk of Circuit Court recording office for online property search options.

Baltimore County

County Clerk of the Circuit Court, PO Box 6754, Baltimore, MD 21285. 410-887-2652, R/E recording phone-410-887-3088; fax-410-887-2834; 8:30AM-4:30PM (EST)

Index: Separate indices to search include notices, judgments, plats, homeowner's assoc. Records indexed on a public use terminal back to 1964. Terminal available until 6PM. Only the public may search. Copy fee $.50 per page. Self serve- $.25 each. Cert fee- $5.00 per cert. Payee- County Clerk of Circuit Court. **Online Real Property, Deed, Land Survey/Plat records:** Land records at www.mdlandrec.net/msa/stagser/s1700/s1741/cfm/index.cfm, and www.plats.net (use username "Plato" and password "plato#") and MDPropertyview at www.mdp.state.md.us/data/mdview.htm. **Other phones:** Treasurer- 410-887-2416; Elections- 410-887-5700; Vital Records- 410-764-3038. **Property tax/Assessing-** 300 E Joppa Rd, #602, Towson, MD 21286; 410-512-4906, assessor fax- 410-321-2119. **Online access-** Search real property data free at http://sdatcert3.resiusa.org/rp_rewrite/. No name searching. See Clerk of Circuit Court recording office for online property search options.

Calvert County

County Clerk of the Circuit Court, 175 Main St; Courthouse, Prince Frederick, MD 20678. 410-535-1660, R/E recording phone-410-535-1600 x2264; 8:30-4:30PM www.courts.state.md.us/clerks/calvert/

Index: Separate indices to search include plats, homeowner depository, miscellaneous. Records indexed on a public use terminal back to 1969. Only the public may search. Will not search UCC records. Copy fee $.50 per page. Cert fee- $5.00 per instrument plus copy fee. Payee- Calvert County Clerk of Circuit Court. **Online access to Real Property, Land Survey/Plat records:** Land records online from www.mdlandrec.net/msa/stagser/s1700/s1741/cfm/index.cfm, and www.plats.net (use username "Plato" and password "plato#") and MDPropertyview at www.mdp.state.md.us/data/mdview.htm. **Other phones:** Treasurer- 410-535-1600 x2272. **Property tax/Assessing-** 200 Duke St, #1200, Prince Frederick, MD 20678; 443-550-6840, assessor fax- 443-550-6850. hours- 8AM-5PM **Online access-** Search real property data free at http://sdatcert3.resiusa.org/rp_rewrite/. No name searching. See Clerk of Circuit Court recording office for online property search options.

Caroline County

County Clerk of the Circuit Court, PO Box 458, Denton, MD 21629. Recording, R/E & UCC phone-410-479-1811; fax-410-479-1142; 8:30AM-4:30PM

Index: All in one. Records indexed on a public use terminal back to 1993. Only the public may search. Copy fee $1.00 per page. Cert fee- $5.00 per cert plus copy fee. Payee- Caroline County Clerk of Circuit Court. **Online access to Real Property, Land Survey/Plat records:** Land records online from www.mdlandrec.net/msa/stagser/s1700/s1741/cfm/index.cfm, and www.plats.net (use username "Plato" and password "plato#") and MDPropertyview at www.mdp.state.md.us/data/mdview.htm. **Other phones:** Treasurer- 410-479-0410. **Property tax/Assessing-** 207 S 3rd St, Denton MultiService Ctr, Denton, MD 21629; 410-819-4450, assessor fax-410-819-4441. hours- 8AM-4:30PM **Online access-** Search real property data free at http://sdatcert3.resiusa.org/rp_rewrite/. No name searching. See Clerk of Circuit Court recording office for online property search options.

Carroll County

County Clerk of the Circuit Court, 55 N Court St, Rm G8, Westminster, MD 21157. 410-386-2026, R/E recording phone-410-386-2022; fax-410-876-0822; 8:30AM-4:30PM
http://mdcourts.gov/clerks/carroll/index.html
Index: All in one. Records indexed on computer back to 1960. Only the public may search. Copy fee $.50 per page. Cert fee- $5.00 per cert plus copy fee. Payee- Carroll County Clerk of Circuit Court. **Online Real Property, Land Survey/Plat records:** Land records online at www.mdlandrec.net/msa/stagser/s1700/s1741/cfm/index.cfm, and www.plats.net (use username "Plato" and password "plato#") and MDPropertyview at www.mdp.state.md.us/data/mdview.htm. **Other phones:** Treasurer- 410-386-2971; Elections- 410-380-3080. **Property tax/Assessing-** 17 E Main St, Winchester Exchange, Rear, Westminster, MD 21157; 410-857-0600, assessor fax- 410-857-0128. (Appraiser/Auditor- 410-857-0600) hours- 8AM-5PM **Online access-** Search real property data free at http://sdatcert3.resiusa.org/rp_rewrite/. No name searching. See Clerk of Circuit Court recording office for online property search options.

Cecil County

County Clerk of the Circuit Court, 129 E Main St, Rm 108, Elkton, MD 21921-5971. 410-996-5375; fax-410-392-6032; 8:30AM-4:30PM (EST)
www.courts.state.md.us/cecil.html
Index: Separate indices to search include liens, plat, financing statements, notices, notary public. Only the public may search. Copy fee $.50 per page. Cert fee- $5.00 per doc plus copy fee. Payee- County Clerk of Circuit Court. **Online access to Real Property, Land Survey/Plat records:** Land records online from www.mdlandrec.net/msa/stagser/s1700/s1741/cfm/index.cfm, and www.plats.net (use username "Plato" and password "plato#") and MDPropertyview at www.mdp.state.md.us/data/mdview.htm. **Other phones:** Treasurer- 410-996-5394. **Property tax/Assessing-** 170 E Main St, Multi-Service Center, Elkton, MD 21921; 410-996-2760, assessor fax- 410-996-2770. hours- 8AM-5PM **Online access-** Search real property data free at http://sdatcert3.resiusa.org/rp_rewrite/. No name searching. See Clerk of Circuit Court recording office for online property search options.

Charles County

County Clerk of the Circuit Court, PO Box 970, La Plata, MD 20646. 301-932-3201; fax-301-932-3339; 8:30-4:30PM www.courts.state.md.us/clerks/charles/
Index: All in one. Records indexed on a public use terminal back to 1658. Only the public may search. Copy fee $.50 per page. Plats- $1.00 per page. Cert fee- $5.00 per cert plus copy fee. Payee- Charles County Clerk of Circuit Court. **Online Real Property, Land Survey/Plat records:** Land records at www.mdlandrec.net/msa/stagser/s1700/s1741/cfm/index.cfm, and www.plats.net (use username "Plato" and password "plato#") and MDPropertyview at www.mdp.state.md.us/data/mdview.htm. **Other phones:** Treasurer- 301-645-0685; Elections- 301-934-8962. **Property tax/Assessing-** PO Box 2726, S Maryland Trade Ctr, 101 Catalpa Dr, #101A, La Plata, MD 20646; 301-932-2440, assessor fax- 301-932-2189. **Online access-** Search real property data free at http://sdatcert3.resiusa.org/rp_rewrite/. No name searching. Also, access property tax data free at www.charlescounty.org/treas/taxes/acctinquiry/selection.jsp. Also, tax sale list search free at www.charlescounty.org/treas/taxes/taxsale/selection.jsp. Also see Clerk of Circuit Court recording office for other online property search options.

Dorchester County

County Clerk of the Circuit Court, PO Box 150, Cambridge, MD 21613. 410-228-0481, R/E recording phone-410-228-0480; fax-410-228-1860; 8:30AM-4:30PM (EST) www.docogonet.com
Index: Separate indices to search include Mdland Recs, Misc., old UCCs, plats. Records indexed on a public use terminal back to 1669. Only the public may search. Copy fee $.25 per page. Plats- $.50 or $2.00 per page. Cert fee- $5.00 per cert plus copy fee. Payee- Dorchester County Clerk of Circuit Court. **Online access to Real Property, Land Survey/Plat records:** Land records online from www.mdlandrec.net/msa/stagser/s1700/s1741/cfm/index.cfm, and www.plats.net (use username "Plato" and password "plato#") and MDPropertyview at www.mdp.state.md.us/data/mdview.htm. **Other phones:** Treasurer- 410-228-4343 (County). **Property tax/Assessing-** PO Box 488, 501 Court Ln, #204, Cambridge, MD 21613; 410-228-3380, assessor fax- 410-228-3704. **Online access-** Search real property data free at http://sdatcert3.resiusa.org/rp_rewrite/. No name searching. See Clerk of Circuit Court recording office for online property search options. Also, access to free property tax information go to http://ww2.paragon-csi.com/dorchester-MD/. Must have property ID, address or map, grid, and parcel codes to look at them.

Frederick County

County Clerk of the Circuit Court, 100 W Patrick St, Frederick, MD 21701. 301-600-1916, R/E recording phone-301-600-1957; fax-301-600-2245; 8:30AM-4:30PM (EST)
Index: All in one. Records indexed on a public use terminal back to 1972. Office will perform a UCC search but public must search other records themselves. Copy fee $.50 per page. Cert fee- $5.00 per doc plus copy fee. Payee- Frederick County Clerk of Circuit Court. **Online access to Real Property, Deed, Land Survey/Plat records:** Land records available by subscription from www.mdlandrec.net/msa/stagser/s1700/s1741/cfm/index.cfm. Also, Property data available from www.plats.net (use username "Plato" and password "plato#") and MDPropertyview at www.mdp.state.md.us/data/mdview.htm. **Other phones:** Treasurer- 301-600-1111; Elections- 301-600-1005. **Property tax/Assessing-** 5310 E Spectrum Dr, Frederick, MD 21703; 301-815-5366, assessor fax- 301-663-8941. hours- 7:30AM-5PM Public access terminal available. **Online access-** Search real property data free at http://sdatcert3.resiusa.org/rp_rewrite/. No name searching.

Garrett County

County Clerk of the Circuit Court, PO Box 447, Oakland, MD 21550-0447. 301-334-1937, R/E recording phone-301-334-1935, UCC recording phone-301-334-5016; fax-301-334-5017; 8:30AM-4:30PM (EST)
Index: All in one. Records indexed on a public use terminal back to 1872. Only the public may search. Copy fee $1.00 per page.Real estate or tax lien copy- $.50 per page. Cert fee- $5.00 per cert plus copy fee. Payee- Garrett County Clerk of Circuit Court. **Online access to Real Property, Land Survey/Plat records:** Land records online from www.mdlandrec.net/msa/stagser/s1700/s1741/cfm/index.cfm, and www.plats.net (use username "Plato" and password "plato#") and MDPropertyview at www.mdp.state.md.us/data/mdview.htm. **Other phones:** Treasurer- 301-334-1965; Elections- 301-334-6987; Vital Records- 301-334-7700. **Property tax/Assessing-** PO Box 388, 203 S 4th St, Rm 106, Oakland, MD 21550; 301-334-1950, assessor fax- 301-334-5018. **Online access-** Search real property data free at http://sdatcert3.resiusa.org/rp_rewrite/. No name searching. See Clerk of Circuit Court recording office for online property search options.

Harford County

County Clerk of the Circuit Court, 20 W Courtland St, Bel Air, MD 21014. 410-638-3474; fax-410-879-6449; 8:30AM-4:30PM (EST)
www.courts.state.md.us/clerks/harford/
Index: Separate indices to search include books, computer. Records indexed on a public use terminal back to 1/1/1970. Images of documents back to 1773. Only the public may search. Copy fee $.50 per page; self serve- $.25 each. Cert fee- $5.00 per cert plus copy fee. Payee- Harford County Clerk of Circuit Court. **Online access to Real Property, Land Survey/Plat records:** Land records online at www.mdlandrec.net/msa/stagser/s1700/s1741/cfm/index.cfm, and www.plats.net (use username "Plato" and password "plato#") and MDPropertyview at www.mdp.state.md.us/data/mdview.htm. **Other phones:** Treasurer- 410-638-3269; Elections- 410-638-3268. **Property tax/Assessing-** 2 S Bond St, Bel Air, MD 21014; 410-836-4800, assessor fax- 410-838-5914. **Online access-** Search real property data free at http://sdatcert3.resiusa.org/rp_rewrite/. No name searching. See Clerk of Circuit Court recording office for online property search options.

Howard County

County Clerk of the Circuit Court, 9250 Bendix Rd, Columbia, MD 21045. 410-313-5850 (Land Records) 8:30AM-4:30PM (EST)
Index: Separate indices to search include computer, index books. Records indexed on computer back to 1850's, images back to 1980s. Only the public may search. Copy fee $.50 per page; self serve $.25. Cert fee- $5.00 per cert plus copy fee. Payee- Howard County Clerk of Circuit Court. **Online Real Property, Deed, Land Survey/Plat records:** Land records at www.mdlandrec.net/msa/stagser/s1700/s1741/cfm/index.cfm, and www.plats.net (use username "Plato" and password "plato#") and MDPropertyview at www.mdp.state.md.us/data/mdview.htm. **Other phones:** Treasurer- 410-313-2063. **Property tax/Assessing-** 3451 Courthouse Dr, Dept of Assessment, District Court Multi Service Ctr, Columbia, MD 21045; 410-480-7940, assessor fax- 410-480-7960. hours- 7:30AM-5PM A public access terminal is available. **Online access-** Search real property data free at http://sdatcert3.resiusa.org/rp_rewrite/. No name searching. See Clerk of Circuit Court recording office for online property search options.

Kent County

Clerk of the Circuit Court, 103 N Cross St, Chestertown, MD 21620. 410-778-7460, 410-778-7415, R/E recording phone-410-778-7460; fax-410-778-7412; 8:30AM-4:30PM (EST)
www.courts.state.md.us./clerks/kent/index.html
Index: Separate indices to search include land records, judgments and plats. Records indexed on a public use terminal back to 1642. Only the public may search. Copy fee $.50 per page; plat copies-$1.00. Cert fee- $5.00 per cert plus copy fee. Payee- Kent County Clerk of Circuit Court. **Online Real Property, Land Survey/Plat records:** Land records online from www.mdlandrec.net/msa/stagser/s1700/s1741/cfm/index.cfm, and www.plats.net (use username "Plato" and password "plato#") and MDPropertyview at www.mdp.state.md.us/data/mdview.htm. **Other phones:** Elections- 410-778-0038; Finance- 410-778-7478. **Property tax/Assessing-** 400 High St, Chestertown, MD 21620; 410-778-7447, assessor fax- 410-778-7411. **Online access-** Search real property data free at http://sdatcert3.resiusa.org/rp_rewrite/. No name searching. See Clerk of Circuit Court recording office for online property search options.

Montgomery County

County Clerk of the Circuit Court, 50 Maryland Ave, Rm 122A; County Courthouse, Rockville, MD 20850. 240-777-9466, R/E recording phone-240-777-9470; fax-240-777-9486; 8:30AM-4:30PM (EST)
www.montgomerycountymd.gov/mc/judicial/
Index: All in one. Records indexed on a public use terminal back to 1977 on the HP, 1999 on ELROI-LRAC. Only the public may search. Office will search UCC records if in land, but not the chattel records that have been effectively closed since July 1, 2001. Copy fee $.50 per page if office makes copies, for self-service copies $.25. Cert fee- $5.00 per cert plus copy fee. Payee- Montgomery County Clerk of Circuit Court. **Online access to Real Property, Land**

Survey/Plat records: Access to clerk records is via JIS Dialup Access; contact Mary Hutchins 410-260-1031. Land records online from www.mdlandrec.net/msa/stagser/s1700/s1741/cfm/index.cfm, and www.plats.net (use username "Plato" and password "plato#") and MDPropertyview at www.mdp.state.md.us/data/mdview.htm. **Other phones:** Treasurer- 240-777-8995; Elections- 240-777-8500; Vital Records- 240-777-1755. **Property tax/Assessing-** 51 Monroe St, #400, Ruckville, MD 20850; 301-279-1701, assessor fax- 301-610-4796. **Online access-** Search real property data for free at http://sdatcert3.resiusa.org/rp_rewrite/. No name searching. Also, access to the assessor's property tax account database is free at https://www.montgomerycountymd.gov/apps/tax/index.asp. Also see Clerk of Circuit Court recording office for other online property search options.

Prince George's County

County Clerk of the Circuit Court, 14735 Main St; Land Records Dept, Upper Marlboro, MD 20772. 301-952-3318; fax-301-952-3768; 8:30AM-4:30PM (EST) www.co.pg.md.us/
Records indexed on computer back to 1980s. Only the public may search. Copy fee $.50 per page; with copy key, self serve $.25 per page. Cert fee- $5.00 per doc plus copy fee. Payee- Prince George's County Clerk of Circuit Court. **Online Real Property, Deed, Land Survey/Plat records:** Land records at www.mdlandrec.net/msa/stagser/s1700/s1741/cfm/index.cfm, and www.plats.net (use username "Plato" and password "plato#") and MDPropertyview at www.mdp.state.md.us/data/mdview.htm. **Other phones:** Treasurer- 301-952-3946. **Property tax/Assessing-** 14735 Main St, Courthouse, Upper Marlboro, MD 20772; 301-952-2500, assessor fax-301-952-2955. Assessor office will search to find property owner name for you. www.co.pg.md.us/Government/AgencyIndex/Assessment/index.asp **Online access-** Search real property data free at http://sdatcert3.resiusa.org/rp_rewrite/. No name searching. See Clerk of Circuit Court recording office for online property search options. Also, search the Treasurer's property tax inquiry system at http://tax-acct-info.goprincegeorgescounty.com/PropertyTaxes/TaxInquiry.aspx.

Queen Anne's County

County Clerk of the Circuit Court, 100 Court House Sq, Centreville, MD 21617. 410-758-1773 x129 or x110; hours - 8:30AM-4:30PM (EST) www.mdcourts.gov/clerks/queenannes/index.html
Index: Separate indices to search include books, computer. Records indexed on a public use terminal back to the beginning. Only the public may search. Will not search UCC records. Copy fee $.50 per page, $.25 per page with copy key. Cert fee- $5.00 per cert plus copy fee. Payee- Queen Anne's County Clerk of Circuit Court. **Online access to Real Property, Deed, Land Survey/Plat records:** Land records online from www.mdlandrec.net/msa/stagser/s1700/s1741/cfm/index.cfm, and www.plats.net (use username "Plato" and password "plato#") and MDPropertyview at www.mdp.state.md.us/data/mdview.htm. **Other phones:** Treasurer- 410-758-0414. **Property tax/Assessing-** 120 Broadway, Centreville, MD 21617; 410-819-4160. **Online** - real property data free at http://sdatcert3.resiusa.org/rp_rewrite/. No name searching. See Clerk of Circuit Court recording office for online property search options.

Somerset County

County Clerk of the Circuit Court, PO Box 99, Princess Anne, MD 21853. 410-845-4840; fax-410-845-4841; 8AM-4:30PM (EST)
Index: All in one. Records indexed on a public use terminal back to 1665. Only the public may search. Copy fee $.50 per page. Cert fee- $5.00 per page plus copy fee. Payee- Somerset County Clerk of Circuit Court. **Online access to Real Property, Land Survey/Plat records:** Land records online from www.mdlandrec.net/msa/stagser/s1700/s1741/cfm/index.cfm, and www.plats.net (use username "Plato" and password "plato#") and MDPropertyview at www.mdp.state.md.us/data/mdview.htm. **Other phones:** Treasurer- 410-651-0440; Elections- 410-651-0767; Vital Records- 410-845-4840. **Property tax/Assessing-** 11545 Somerset Ave, Princess Anne, MD 21853; 410-651-0868, assessor fax- 410-651-1995. **Online access-** Search real property data free at http://sdatcert3.resiusa.org/rp_rewrite/. No name searching. See Clerk of Circuit Court recording office for online property search options.

St. Mary's County

County Clerk of the Circuit Court, PO Box 676; Land Records Division, Leonardtown, MD 20650. 301-475-7844, R/E recording phone-301-475-4554; 8:30AM-4:30PM (EST)
Index: Separate indices to search include land, plats, marriages, miscellaneous. Records indexed on a public use terminal back to 1968. Only the public may search. Copy fee $.50 per page. Self serve- $.25 each. Cert fee- $5.00 per doc plus copy fee. Payee- St. Mary's County Clerk of Circuit Court. **Online Real Property, Deed, Land Survey/Plat records:** Land records online from www.mdlandrec.net/msa/stagser/s1700/s1741/cfm/index.cfm, and www.plats.net (use username "Plato" and password "plato#") and MDPropertyview at www.mdp.state.md.us/data/mdview.htm. **Other phones:** Treasurer- 301-475-4473. **Property tax/Assessing-** PO Box 653, 23110 Leonard Hall Dr, Carter Bldg, Rm 2059, Leonardtown, MD 20650; 301-880-2900, assessor fax- 301-475-4856. hours- 8AM-5PM **Online access-** Search real property data free at http://sdatcert3.resiusa.org/rp_rewrite/. No name searching. See Clerk of Circuit Court recording office for online property search options.

Talbot County

Clerk of the Circuit Court, 11 N Washington St, #16, Easton, MD 21601-3195. 410-822-2611; fax-410-820-9518; hours - 8:30AM-4:30PM (EST) www.courts.state.md.us/clerks/talbot/
Index: All in one. Records indexed on a public use terminal back to 1966. Only the public may search. Copy fee $.50 per page. Cert fee- $5.00 per cert plus copy fee. Payee- Talbot County Clerk of Circuit Court. **Online Real Property, Land Survey/Plat, Judgments/Liens records:** Land records online from www.mdlandrec.net/msa/stagser/s1700/s1741/cfm/index.cfm, and www.plats.net (use username "Plato" and password "plato#") and MDPropertyview at www.mdp.state.md.us/data/mdview.htm. Also, access to state Circuit Court Judgments and Liens for free go to http://casesearch.courts.state.md.us/inquiry/inquiry-index.jsp. **Other phones:** Treasurer- 410-770-8020; Elections- 410-770-8099; Vital Records- 410-764-3038. **Property tax/Assessing-** 215 Bay St, Easton, MD 21601; 410-819-5920, assessor fax- 410-822-0048. **Online access-** Search real property data free at http://sdatcert3.resiusa.org/rp_rewrite/. No name searching. See Clerk of Circuit Court recording office for online property search options.

Washington County

County Clerk of the Circuit Court, PO Box 229, Hagerstown, MD 21741-0229. phone-301-733-8660; fax-301-791-1151; 8AM-4:30PM (EST) www.courts.state.md.us/clerks/washington/index.html
Index: All in one on paper. Records indexed on computer back to 1963. Only the public may search. Copy fee $.50 per page. Cert fee- $5.00 per doc plus copy fee. Payee- Washington County Clerk of Circuit Court. **Online access to Real Property, Land Survey/Plat records:** Land records online from www.mdlandrec.net/msa/stagser/s1700/s1741/cfm/index.cfm, and www.plats.net (use username "Plato" and password "plato#") and MDPropertyview at www.mdp.state.md.us/data/mdview.htm. **Other phones:** Treasurer- 240-313-2110; Elections- 240-313-2050; Vital Records- 301-733-8660. **Property tax/Assessing-** 3 Public Sq, Hagerstown, MD 21741; 301-791-3050, assessor fax- 301-791-2925. **Online access-** Search real property data free at http://sdatcert3.resiusa.org/rp_rewrite/. No name searching. See Clerk of Circuit Court recording office for online property search options.

Wicomico County

County Clerk of the Circuit Court, PO Box 198, Salisbury, MD 21803-0198. 410-543-6551; 8:30AM-4:30PM (EST) www.mdcourts.gov/clerks/wicomico/
Index: All in one. Records indexed on a public use terminal back to 1966. Only the public may search. Office will not search real estate records. Will not search UCC records. Copy fee $.50 per page. Cert fee- $5.00 plus copy fee; Exemplification fee $10.00 plus copy fee. Payee- Wicomico County Clerk of Circuit Court. **Online access to Real Property, Land Survey/Plat records:** Land records online from www.mdlandrec.net/msa/stagser/s1700/s1741/cfm/index.cfm, and www.plats.net (use username "Plato" and password "plato#") and MDPropertyview at www.mdp.state.md.us/data/mdview.htm. **Other phones:** Treasurer- 410-548-4840; Elections- 410-548-4830. **Property tax/Assessing-** 201 Baptist St, Salisbury DC-MSC, Salisbury, MD 21801-4962; 410-713-3560, assessor fax- 410-713-3570. **Online access-** Search real property data free at http://sdatcert3.resiusa.org/rp_rewrite/. No name searching. See Clerk of Circuit Court recording office for online property search options.

Worcester County

County Clerk of the Circuit Court, PO Box 40, Snow Hill, MD 21863-0040. Recording, R/E & UCC phone-410-632-5500, UCC recording phone-410-632-1196; 8:30AM-4:30PM (EST)
Records indexed on a public use terminal back to 1700's. Office will perform a UCC search but public must search other records themselves. Office will not search real estate records. Will not search UCC records. Copy fee $.50 per page, $5.00 minimum. Cert fee- $5.00 per cert plus copy fee. Payee- Worcester County Clerk of Circuit Court. **Online Real Property, Land Survey/Plat records:** Land records at www.mdlandrec.net/msa/stagser/s1700/s1741/cfm/index.cfm, and www.plats.net (use username "Plato" and password "plato#") and MDPropertyview at www.mdp.state.md.us/data/mdview.htm. **Other phones:** Treasurer- 410-623-0686; Elections- 410-632-1320. **Property tax/Assessing-** 1 W Market St, #1202, Snow Hill, MD 21863; 410-632-1196, assessor fax- 410-632-1366. **Online access-** Search real property data free at http://sdatcert3.resiusa.org/rp_rewrite/. No name searching. See Clerk of Circuit Court recording office for online property search options.

Maryland County Locator

You will usually be able to find the city name in the City/County Cross Reference below. In that case, it is a simple matter to determine the county from the cross reference. However, only the official US Postal Service city names are included in this index. There are an additional 40,000 place names that people use in their addresses. Therefore, we have also included a ZIP/City Cross Reference immediately following the City/County Cross Reference.

If you know the ZIP Code but the city name does not appear in the City/County Cross Reference index, look up the ZIP Code in the ZIP/City Cross Reference, find the city name, then look up the city name in the City/County Cross. Reference. For example, you want to know the county for an address of Menands, NY 12204. There is no "Menands" in the City/County Cross Reference. The ZIP/City Cross Reference shows that ZIP Codes 12201-12288 are for the city of Albany. Looking back in the City/County Cross Reference, Albany is in Albany County.

Maryland City/County Cross Reference

ABELL St. Mary's
ABERDEEN Harford
ABERDEEN PROVING GROUND Harford
ABINGDON Harford
ACCIDENT Garrett
ACCOKEEK Prince George's
ADAMSTOWN Frederick
ALESIA (21107) Carroll(59), Baltimore(40)
ALLEN Wicomico
ANDREWS AIR FORCE BASE Prince George's
ANNAPOLIS Anne Arundel
ANNAPOLIS JUNCTION (20701) Howard(77), Anne Arundel(22)
AQUASCO Prince George's
ARNOLD Anne Arundel
ASHTON Montgomery
AVENUE St. Mary's
BALDWIN (21013) Baltimore(70), Harford(29)
BALTIMORE (21209) Baltimore(52), Baltimore City(47)
BALTIMORE (21239) Baltimore City(80), Baltimore(19)
BALTIMORE Anne Arundel
BALTIMORE Baltimore
BALTIMORE Baltimore City
BARCLAY Queen Anne's
BARNESVILLE Montgomery
BARSTOW Calvert
BARTON (21521) Allegany(72), Garrett(27)
BEALLSVILLE Montgomery
BEL AIR Harford
BEL ALTON Charles
BELCAMP Harford
BELTSVILLE Prince George's
BENEDICT Charles
BENSON Harford
BETHESDA Montgomery
BETHLEHEM Caroline
BETTERTON Kent
BIG POOL Washington
BISHOPVILLE Worcester
BITTINGER Garrett
BIVALVE Wicomico
BLADENSBURG Prince George's
BLOOMINGTON Garrett
BOONSBORO Washington
BORING Baltimore
BOWIE Prince George's
BOYDS Montgomery
BOZMAN Talbot
BRADDOCK HEIGHTS Frederick
BRADSHAW Baltimore
BRANDYWINE (20613) Prince George's(88), Charles(11)
BRENTWOOD Prince George's
BRINKLOW Montgomery
BROOKEVILLE (20833) Montgomery(96), Howard(3)
BROOKLANDVILLE Baltimore
BROOKLYN (21225) Baltimore City(54), Anne Arundel(45)
BROOMES ISLAND Calvert
BROWNSVILLE Washington
BRUNSWICK Frederick
BRYANS ROAD Charles
BRYANTOWN Charles
BUCKEYSTOWN Frederick
BURKITTSVILLE Frederick
BURTONSVILLE Montgomery
BUSHWOOD St. Mary's
BUTLER Baltimore
CABIN JOHN Montgomery
CALIFORNIA St. Mary's
CALLAWAY St. Mary's
CAMBRIDGE Dorchester
CAPITOL HEIGHTS Prince George's
CARDIFF Harford
CASCADE (21719) Washington(98), Frederick(1)
CATONSVILLE Baltimore
CAVETOWN Washington
CECILTON Cecil
CENTREVILLE Queen Anne's
CHANCE Somerset
CHAPTICO St. Mary's
CHARLESTOWN Cecil
CHARLOTTE HALL (20622) Charles(64), St. Mary's(35)
CHASE Baltimore
CHELTENHAM Prince George's
CHESAPEAKE BEACH Calvert
CHESAPEAKE CITY Cecil
CHESTER Queen Anne's
CHESTERTOWN (21620) Kent(95), Queen Anne's(4)
CHESTERTOWN Queen Anne's
CHEVY CHASE Montgomery
CHEWSVILLE Washington
CHILDS Cecil
CHURCH CREEK Dorchester
CHURCH HILL Queen Anne's
CHURCHTON Anne Arundel
CHURCHVILLE Harford
CLAIBORNE Talbot
CLARKSBURG (20871) Montgomery(89), Frederick(10)
CLARKSVILLE Howard
CLEAR SPRING Washington
CLEMENTS St. Mary's
CLINTON Prince George's
COBB ISLAND Charles
COCKEYSVILLE Baltimore
COLLEGE PARK Prince George's
COLORA Cecil
COLTONS POINT St. Mary's
COLUMBIA Howard
COMPTON St. Mary's
CONOWINGO Cecil
COOKSVILLE (21723) Howard(85), Carroll(14)
CORDOVA Talbot
CORRIGANVILLE Allegany
CRAPO Dorchester
CRISFIELD Somerset
CROCHERON Dorchester
CROFTON Anne Arundel
CROWNSVILLE Anne Arundel
CRUMPTON Queen Anne's
CUMBERLAND Allegany
CURTIS BAY (21226) Baltimore City(56), Anne Arundel(43)
DAMASCUS Montgomery
DAMERON St. Mary's
DAMES QUARTER Somerset
DARLINGTON Harford
DAVIDSONVILLE Anne Arundel
DAYTON Howard
DEAL ISLAND Somerset
DEALE Anne Arundel
DELMAR Wicomico
DENTON Caroline
DERWOOD Montgomery
DETOUR Carroll
DICKERSON (20842) Montgomery(79), Frederick(20)
DISTRICT HEIGHTS Prince George's
DOWELL Calvert
DRAYDEN St. Mary's
DUNDALK (21222) Baltimore(97), Baltimore City(2)
DUNKIRK (20754) Calvert(90), Anne Arundel(10)
EARLEVILLE Cecil
EAST NEW MARKET Dorchester
EASTON Talbot
ECKHART MINES Allegany
EDEN (21822) Worcester(89), Somerset(10)
EDGEWATER Anne Arundel
EDGEWOOD Harford
ELK MILLS Cecil
ELKRIDGE Howard
ELKTON Cecil
ELLERSLIE Allegany
ELLICOTT CITY (21043) Howard(97), Baltimore(2)
ELLICOTT CITY Howard
EMMITSBURG Frederick
ESSEX Baltimore
EWELL Somerset
FAIRPLAY Washington
FALLSTON Harford
FAULKNER Charles
FEDERALSBURG Caroline
FINKSBURG Carroll
FISHING CREEK Dorchester
FLINTSTONE Allegany
FOREST HILL Harford
FORK Baltimore
FORT GEORGE G MEADE Anne Arundel
FORT HOWARD Baltimore
FORT WASHINGTON Prince George's
FREDERICK Frederick
FREELAND (21107) Carroll(59), Baltimore(40)
FREELAND Baltimore
FRIENDSHIP Anne Arundel
FRIENDSVILLE Garrett
FROSTBURG (21532) Allegany(84), Garrett(15)
FRUITLAND Wicomico
FULTON Howard
FUNKSTOWN Washington
GAITHER Carroll
GAITHERSBURG Montgomery
GALENA Kent
GALESVILLE Anne Arundel
GAMBRILLS Anne Arundel
GAPLAND Washington
GARRETT PARK Montgomery
GARRISON Baltimore
GEORGETOWN Cecil
GERMANTOWN Montgomery
GIBSON ISLAND Anne Arundel
GIRDLETREE Worcester
GLEN ARM Baltimore
GLEN BURNIE Anne Arundel
GLEN ECHO Montgomery
GLENELG Howard
GLENN DALE Prince George's
GLENWOOD Howard
GLYNDON Baltimore
GOLDSBORO Caroline
GRANTSVILLE Garrett
GRASONVILLE Queen Anne's
GREAT MILLS St. Mary's
GREENBELT Prince George's
GREENSBORO Caroline
GUNPOWDER Harford
GWYNN OAK (21207) Baltimore(67), Baltimore City(32)
GWYNN OAK Baltimore
HAGERSTOWN Washington
HALETHORPE (21227) Baltimore(98), Baltimore City(1)
HAMPSTEAD (21074) Carroll(88), Baltimore(11)
HANCOCK Washington
HANOVER (21076) Anne Arundel(91), Howard(8)
HANOVER Anne Arundel
HARMANS Anne Arundel
HARWOOD Anne Arundel
HAVRE DE GRACE Harford
HEBRON Wicomico
HELEN St. Mary's
HENDERSON Caroline
HENRYTON Carroll
HIGHLAND (20777) Howard(95), Montgomery(4)
HILLSBORO Caroline
HOLLYWOOD St. Mary's
HUGHESVILLE Charles
HUNT VALLEY Baltimore
HUNTINGTOWN Calvert
HURLOCK Dorchester
HYATTSVILLE Prince George's
HYDES (21082) Baltimore(96), Harford(3)
IJAMSVILLE Frederick
INDIAN HEAD Charles
INGLESIDE Queen Anne's
IRONSIDES Charles
ISSUE Charles
JARRETTSVILLE Harford

JEFFERSON Frederick
JESSUP (20794) Howard(80), Anne Arundel(19)
JOPPA Harford
KEEDYSVILLE Washington
KENNEDYVILLE Kent
KENSINGTON Montgomery
KEYMAR (21757) Frederick(50), Carroll(49)
KINGSVILLE (21087) Baltimore(79), Harford(20)
KITZMILLER Garrett
KNOXVILLE (21758) Frederick(50), Washington(49)
LA PLATA Charles
LADIESBURG Frederick
LANHAM Prince George's
LAUREL Anne Arundel
LAUREL Howard
LAUREL Prince George's
LEONARDTOWN St. Mary's
LEXINGTON PARK St. Mary's
LIBERTYTOWN Frederick
LINEBORO Carroll
LINEBORO CPO Carroll
LINKWOOD Dorchester
LINTHICUM HEIGHTS Anne Arundel
LINWOOD Carroll
LISBON Howard
LITTLE ORLEANS Allegany
LONACONING (21539) Allegany(67), Garrett(32)
LONG GREEN Baltimore
LOTHIAN Anne Arundel
LOVEVILLE St. Mary's
LUKE Allegany
LUSBY Calvert
LUTHERVILLE TIMONIUM Baltimore
LYNCH Kent
MADISON Dorchester
MAGNOLIA Harford
MANCHESTER (21102) Carroll(98), Baltimore(1)
MANOKIN Somerset
MARBURY Charles
MARDELA SPRINGS Wicomico
MARION STATION Somerset
MARRIOTTSVILLE (21104) Carroll(53), Howard(38), Baltimore(8)
MARYDEL Caroline
MARYLAND LINE Baltimore
MASSEY Kent
MAUGANSVILLE Washington
MAYO Anne Arundel
MC HENRY Garrett
MCDANIEL Talbot
MECHANICSVILLE (20659) St. Mary's(97), Charles(2)
MIDDLE RIVER Baltimore
MIDDLEBURG Carroll
MIDDLETOWN Frederick
MIDLAND Allegany
MIDLOTHIAN Allegany
MILLERS (21107) Carroll(59), Baltimore(40)
MILLERSVILLE Anne Arundel
MILLINGTON (21651) Queen Anne's(59), Kent(40)
MONKTON (21111) Baltimore(87), Harford(12)
MONROVIA Frederick
MONTGOMERY VILLAGE Montgomery
MORGANZA St. Mary's
MOUNT AIRY (21771) Frederick(47), Carroll(39), Howard(11), Montgomery(1)
MOUNT RAINIER Prince George's
MOUNT SAVAGE Allegany
MOUNT VICTORIA Charles
MYERSVILLE Frederick
NANJEMOY Charles
NANTICOKE Wicomico
NEAVITT Talbot
NEW MARKET Frederick
NEW MIDWAY Frederick
NEW WINDSOR (21776) Carroll(82), Frederick(17)
NEWARK Worcester
NEWBURG Charles
NEWCOMB Talbot
NIKEP Allegany
NORTH BEACH (20714) Calvert(87), Anne Arundel(12)
NORTH EAST Cecil
NOTTINGHAM Baltimore
OAKLAND Garrett
OCEAN CITY Worcester
ODENTON Anne Arundel
OLDTOWN Allegany
OLNEY Montgomery
OWINGS Calvert
OWINGS MILLS Baltimore
OXFORD Talbot
OXON HILL Prince George's
PARK HALL St. Mary's
PARKTON Baltimore
PARKVILLE (21234) Baltimore(89), Baltimore City(10)
PARSONSBURG Wicomico
PASADENA Anne Arundel
PATUXENT RIVER St. Mary's
PERRY HALL Baltimore
PERRY POINT Cecil
PERRYMAN Harford
PERRYVILLE Cecil
PHOENIX Baltimore
PIKESVILLE (21208) Baltimore(93), Baltimore City(6)
PINEY POINT St. Mary's
PINTO Allegany
PITTSVILLE Wicomico
POCOMOKE CITY (21851) Worcester(86), Somerset(13)
POINT OF ROCKS Frederick
POMFRET Charles
POOLESVILLE Montgomery
PORT DEPOSIT Cecil
PORT REPUBLIC Calvert
PORT TOBACCO Charles
POTOMAC Montgomery
POWELLVILLE Wicomico
PRESTON Caroline
PRINCE FREDERICK Calvert
PRINCESS ANNE Somerset
PYLESVILLE Harford
QUANTICO Wicomico
QUEEN ANNE Queen Anne's
QUEENSTOWN Queen Anne's
RANDALLSTOWN Baltimore
RAWLINGS Allegany
REHOBETH Somerset
REISTERSTOWN (21136) Baltimore(97), Carroll(2)
RHODES POINT Somerset
RHODESDALE Dorchester
RIDERWOOD Baltimore
RIDGE St. Mary's
RIDGELY Caroline
RISING SUN Cecil
RIVA Anne Arundel
RIVERDALE Prince George's
ROCK HALL Kent
ROCK POINT Charles
ROCKVILLE Montgomery
ROCKY RIDGE Frederick
ROHRERSVILLE Washington
ROSEDALE (21237) Baltimore(96), Baltimore City(3)
ROYAL OAK Talbot
SABILLASVILLE (21780) Frederick(94), Washington(5)
SAINT INIGOES St. Mary's
SAINT JAMES Washington
SAINT LEONARD Calvert
SAINT MARYS CITY St. Mary's
SAINT MICHAELS Talbot
SALISBURY Wicomico
SANDY SPRING Montgomery
SAVAGE Howard
SCOTLAND St. Mary's
SECRETARY Dorchester
SEVERN Anne Arundel
SEVERNA PARK Anne Arundel
SHADY SIDE Anne Arundel
SHARPSBURG Washington
SHARPTOWN Wicomico
SHERWOOD Talbot
SHOWELL Worcester
SILVER SPRING (20903) Montgomery(84), Prince George's(15)
SILVER SPRING Montgomery
SIMPSONVILLE Howard
SMITHSBURG (21783) Washington(79), Frederick(20)
SNOW HILL Worcester
SOLOMONS Calvert
SOUTHERN MD FACILITY Prince George's
SPARKS GLENCOE Baltimore
SPARROWS POINT Baltimore
SPENCERVILLE Montgomery
SPRING GAP Allegany
STEVENSON Baltimore
STEVENSVILLE Queen Anne's
STILL POND Kent
STOCKTON Worcester
STREET Harford
SUBURB MARYLAND FAC Montgomery
SUDLERSVILLE Queen Anne's
SUITLAND Prince George's
SUNDERLAND Calvert
SWANTON Garrett
SYKESVILLE (21784) Carroll(94), Howard(5)
TAKOMA PARK (20912) Montgomery(89), Prince George's(10)
TAKOMA PARK Prince George's
TALL TIMBERS St. Mary's
TANEYTOWN (21787) Carroll(93), Frederick(6)
TAYLORS ISLAND Dorchester
TEMPLE HILLS Prince George's
TEMPLEVILLE Caroline
THURMONT Frederick
TILGHMAN Talbot
TODDVILLE Dorchester
TOWSON Baltimore
TRACYS LANDING Anne Arundel
TRAPPE Talbot
TUSCARORA Frederick
TYASKIN Wicomico
TYLERTON Somerset
UNION BRIDGE (21791) Carroll(52), Frederick(47)
UNIONVILLE Frederick
UPPER FAIRMOUNT Somerset
UPPER FALLS Baltimore
UPPER HILL Somerset
UPPER MARLBORO Prince George's
UPPERCO (21155) Baltimore(90), Carroll(9)
VALLEY LEE St. Mary's
VIENNA Dorchester
WALDORF (20601) Charles(95), Prince George's(4)
WALDORF Charles
WALKERSVILLE Frederick
WARWICK Cecil
WASHINGTON Prince George's
WASHINGTON GROVE Montgomery
WELCOME Charles
WENONA Somerset
WEST FRIENDSHIP Howard
WEST RIVER Anne Arundel
WESTERNPORT Allegany
WESTMINSTER Carroll
WESTOVER Somerset
WHALEYVILLE Worcester
WHITE HALL (21161) Baltimore(57), Harford(42)
WHITE MARSH Baltimore
WHITE PLAINS Charles
WHITEFORD Harford
WILLARDS Wicomico
WILLIAMSPORT Washington
WINDSOR MILL Baltimore
WINGATE Dorchester
WITTMAN Talbot
WOODBINE (21797) Carroll(52), Howard(46)
WOODSBORO Frederick
WOODSTOCK (21163) Baltimore(51), Howard(48)
WOOLFORD Dorchester
WORTON Kent
WYE MILLS Talbot

Maryland ZIP/City Cross Reference

20331-20331	WASHINGTON
20601-20604	WALDORF
20606-20606	ABELL
20607-20607	ACCOKEEK
20608-20608	AQUASCO
20609-20609	AVENUE
20610-20610	BARSTOW
20611-20611	BEL ALTON
20612-20612	BENEDICT
20613-20613	BRANDYWINE
20615-20615	BROOMES ISLAND
20616-20616	BRYANS ROAD
20617-20617	BRYANTOWN
20618-20618	BUSHWOOD
20619-20619	CALIFORNIA
20620-20620	CALLAWAY
20621-20621	CHAPTICO
20622-20622	CHARLOTTE HALL
20623-20623	CHELTENHAM
20624-20624	CLEMENTS
20625-20625	COBB ISLAND
20626-20626	COLTONS POINT
20627-20627	COMPTON
20628-20628	DAMERON
20629-20629	DOWELL
20630-20630	DRAYDEN
20632-20632	FAULKNER
20634-20634	GREAT MILLS
20635-20635	HELEN
20636-20636	HOLLYWOOD
20637-20637	HUGHESVILLE
20639-20639	HUNTINGTOWN
20640-20640	INDIAN HEAD
20643-20643	IRONSIDES
20645-20645	ISSUE
20646-20646	LA PLATA
20650-20650	LEONARDTOWN
20653-20653	LEXINGTON PARK
20656-20656	LOVEVILLE
20657-20657	LUSBY
20658-20658	MARBURY
20659-20659	MECHANICSVILLE
20660-20660	MORGANZA
20661-20661	MOUNT VICTORIA
20662-20662	NANJEMOY
20664-20664	NEWBURG
20667-20667	PARK HALL
20670-20670	PATUXENT RIVER
20674-20674	PINEY POINT
20675-20675	POMFRET
20676-20676	PORT REPUBLIC
20677-20677	PORT TOBACCO
20678-20678	PRINCE FREDERICK
20680-20680	RIDGE
20682-20682	ROCK POINT
20684-20684	SAINT INIGOES
20685-20685	SAINT LEONARD
20686-20686	SAINT MARYS CITY
20687-20687	SCOTLAND
20688-20688	SOLOMONS
20689-20689	SUNDERLAND
20690-20690	TALL TIMBERS
20692-20692	VALLEY LEE
20693-20693	WELCOME
20695-20695	WHITE PLAINS
20697-20697	SOUTHERN MD FACILITY
20701-20701	ANNAPOLIS JUNCTION
20703-20703	LANHAM
20704-20705	BELTSVILLE
20706-20706	LANHAM
20707-20709	LAUREL
20710-20710	BLADENSBURG
20711-20711	LOTHIAN
20712-20712	MOUNT RAINIER
20714-20714	NORTH BEACH
20715-20721	BOWIE
20722-20722	BRENTWOOD
20723-20726	LAUREL
20731-20731	CAPITOL HEIGHTS
20732-20732	CHESAPEAKE BEACH
20733-20733	CHURCHTON
20735-20735	CLINTON
20736-20736	OWINGS
20737-20738	RIVERDALE
20740-20742	COLLEGE PARK
20743-20743	CAPITOL HEIGHTS
20744-20744	FORT WASHINGTON
20745-20745	OXON HILL
20746-20746	SUITLAND
20747-20747	DISTRICT HEIGHTS
20748-20748	TEMPLE HILLS
20749-20749	FORT WASHINGTON
20750-20750	OXON HILL
20751-20751	DEALE
20752-20752	SUITLAND
20753-20753	DISTRICT HEIGHTS
20754-20754	DUNKIRK
20755-20755	FORT GEORGE G MEADE
20757-20757	TEMPLE HILLS
20758-20758	FRIENDSHIP
20759-20759	FULTON
20762-20762	ANDREWS AIR FORCE BASE
20763-20763	SAVAGE
20764-20764	SHADY SIDE
20765-20765	GALESVILLE
20768-20768	GREENBELT
20769-20769	GLENN DALE
20770-20771	GREENBELT
20772-20775	UPPER MARLBORO
20776-20776	HARWOOD
20777-20777	HIGHLAND
20778-20778	WEST RIVER
20779-20779	TRACYS LANDING
20780-20789	HYATTSVILLE
20790-20791	CAPITOL HEIGHTS
20792-20792	UPPER MARLBORO
20794-20794	JESSUP
20797-20797	SOUTHERN MD FACILITY
20799-20799	CAPITOL HEIGHTS
20800-20800	SUBURB MARYLAND FAC
20810-20811	BETHESDA
20812-20812	GLEN ECHO
20813-20814	BETHESDA
20815-20815	CHEVY CHASE
20816-20817	BETHESDA
20818-20818	CABIN JOHN
20824-20824	BETHESDA
20825-20825	CHEVY CHASE
20827-20827	BETHESDA
20830-20832	OLNEY
20833-20833	BROOKEVILLE
20837-20837	POOLESVILLE
20838-20838	BARNESVILLE
20839-20839	BEALLSVILLE
20841-20841	BOYDS
20842-20842	DICKERSON
20847-20853	ROCKVILLE
20854-20854	POTOMAC
20855-20855	DERWOOD
20856-20858	ROCKVILLE
20858-20858	SILVER SPRING
20859-20859	POTOMAC
20860-20860	SANDY SPRING
20861-20861	ASHTON
20862-20862	BRINKLOW
20866-20866	BURTONSVILLE
20868-20868	SPENCERVILLE
20871-20871	CLARKSBURG
20872-20872	DAMASCUS
20874-20876	GERMANTOWN
20877-20879	GAITHERSBURG
20880-20880	WASHINGTON GROVE
20882-20885	GAITHERSBURG
20886-20886	MONTGOMERY VILLAGE
20889-20889	BETHESDA
20890-20890	SUBURB MARYLAND FAC
20891-20891	KENSINGTON
20892-20894	BETHESDA
20895-20895	KENSINGTON
20896-20896	GARRETT PARK
20897-20897	SUBURB MARYLAND FAC
20898-20899	GAITHERSBURG
20900-20911	SILVER SPRING
20912-20913	TAKOMA PARK
20914-20997	SILVER SPRING
21001-21001	ABERDEEN
21005-21005	ABERDEEN PROVING GROUND
21009-21009	ABINGDON
21010-21010	GUNPOWDER
21012-21012	ARNOLD
21013-21013	BALDWIN
21014-21015	BEL AIR
21017-21017	BELCAMP
21018-21018	BENSON
21020-21020	BORING
21021-21021	BRADSHAW
21022-21022	BROOKLANDVILLE
21023-21023	BUTLER
21024-21024	CARDIFF
21027-21027	CHASE
21028-21028	CHURCHVILLE
21029-21029	CLARKSVILLE
21030-21030	COCKEYSVILLE
21031-21031	HUNT VALLEY
21032-21032	CROWNSVILLE
21034-21034	DARLINGTON
21035-21035	DAVIDSONVILLE
21036-21036	DAYTON
21037-21037	EDGEWATER
21040-21040	EDGEWOOD
21041-21043	ELLICOTT CITY
21044-21046	COLUMBIA
21047-21047	FALLSTON
21048-21048	FINKSBURG
21050-21050	FOREST HILL
21051-21051	FORK
21052-21052	FORT HOWARD
21053-21053	FREELAND
21054-21054	GAMBRILLS
21055-21055	GARRISON
21056-21056	GIBSON ISLAND
21057-21057	GLEN ARM
21060-21062	GLEN BURNIE
21065-21065	COCKEYSVILLE
21065-21065	HUNT VALLEY
21071-21071	GLYNDON
21074-21074	HAMPSTEAD
21075-21075	ELKRIDGE
21076-21076	HANOVER
21077-21077	HARMANS
21078-21078	HAVRE DE GRACE
21080-21080	HENRYTON
21082-21082	HYDES
21084-21084	JARRETTSVILLE
21085-21085	JOPPA
21087-21087	KINGSVILLE
21088-21088	LINEBORO
21088-21088	LINEBORO CPO
21090-21090	LINTHICUM HEIGHTS
21092-21092	LONG GREEN
21093-21094	LUTHERVILLE TIMONIUM
21098-21098	HANOVER
21101-21101	MAGNOLIA
21102-21102	MANCHESTER
21104-21104	MARRIOTTSVILLE
21105-21105	MARYLAND LINE
21106-21106	MAYO
21107-21107	ALESIA
21107-21107	FREELAND
21107-21107	MILLERS
21108-21108	MILLERSVILLE
21111-21111	MONKTON
21113-21113	ODENTON
21114-21114	CROFTON
21117-21117	OWINGS MILLS
21120-21120	PARKTON
21122-21123	PASADENA
21128-21128	PERRY HALL
21130-21130	PERRYMAN
21131-21131	PHOENIX
21132-21132	PYLESVILLE
21133-21133	RANDALLSTOWN
21136-21136	REISTERSTOWN
21139-21139	RIDERWOOD
21140-21140	RIVA
21144-21144	SEVERN
21146-21146	SEVERNA PARK
21150-21150	SIMPSONVILLE
21152-21152	SPARKS GLENCOE
21153-21153	STEVENSON
21154-21154	STREET
21155-21155	UPPERCO
21156-21156	UPPER FALLS
21157-21158	WESTMINSTER
21160-21160	WHITEFORD
21161-21161	WHITE HALL
21162-21162	WHITE MARSH
21163-21163	WOODSTOCK
21200-21203	BALTIMORE
21204-21204	TOWSON
21205-21206	BALTIMORE
21207-21207	GWYNN OAK
21208-21208	PIKESVILLE
21209-21218	BALTIMORE
21219-21219	SPARROWS POINT
21220-21220	MIDDLE RIVER
21221-21221	ESSEX
21222-21222	DUNDALK
21223-21224	BALTIMORE
21225-21225	BROOKLYN
21226-21226	CURTIS BAY
21227-21227	HALETHORPE
21228-21228	CATONSVILLE
21229-21233	BALTIMORE
21234-21234	PARKVILLE
21235-21235	BALTIMORE
21236-21236	NOTTINGHAM
21237-21237	ROSEDALE
21239-21241	BALTIMORE
21244-21244	GWYNN OAK
21244-21244	WINDSOR MILL
21250-21285	BALTIMORE
21286-21286	TOWSON
21287-21299	BALTIMORE
21400-21412	ANNAPOLIS
21501-21505	CUMBERLAND
21520-21520	ACCIDENT
21521-21521	BARTON
21522-21522	BITTINGER
21523-21523	BLOOMINGTON
21524-21524	CORRIGANVILLE
21528-21528	ECKHART MINES
21529-21529	ELLERSLIE
21530-21530	FLINTSTONE
21531-21531	FRIENDSVILLE
21532-21532	FROSTBURG
21536-21536	GRANTSVILLE
21538-21538	KITZMILLER
21539-21539	LONACONING
21540-21540	LUKE
21541-21541	MC HENRY
21542-21542	MIDLAND
21543-21543	MIDLOTHIAN
21545-21545	MOUNT SAVAGE
21546-21546	NIKEP
21550-21550	OAKLAND
21555-21555	OLDTOWN
21556-21556	PINTO
21557-21557	RAWLINGS
21560-21560	SPRING GAP
21561-21561	SWANTON
21562-21562	WESTERNPORT
21601-21606	EASTON
21607-21607	BARCLAY

21609-21609 BETHLEHEM
21610-21610 BETTERTON
21612-21612 BOZMAN
21613-21613 CAMBRIDGE
21617-21617 CENTREVILLE
21619-21619 CHESTER
21620-21620 CHESTERTOWN
21622-21622 CHURCH CREEK
21623-21623 CHURCH HILL
21624-21624 CLAIBORNE
21625-21625 CORDOVA
21626-21626 CRAPO
21627-21627 CROCHERON
21628-21628 CRUMPTON
21629-21629 DENTON
21631-21631 EAST NEW MARKET
21632-21632 FEDERALSBURG
21634-21634 FISHING CREEK
21635-21635 GALENA
21636-21636 GOLDSBORO
21637-21637 GALENA
21638-21638 GRASONVILLE
21639-21639 GREENSBORO
21640-21640 HENDERSON
21641-21641 HILLSBORO
21643-21643 HURLOCK
21644-21644 INGLESIDE
21645-21645 KENNEDYVILLE
21646-21646 LYNCH
21647-21647 MCDANIEL
21648-21648 MADISON
21649-21649 MARYDEL
21650-21650 MASSEY
21651-21651 MILLINGTON
21652-21652 NEAVITT
21653-21653 NEWCOMB
21654-21654 OXFORD
21655-21655 PRESTON
21656-21656 CHURCH HILL
21657-21657 QUEEN ANNE
21658-21658 QUEENSTOWN
21659-21659 RHODESDALE
21660-21660 RIDGELY
21661-21661 ROCK HALL
21662-21662 ROYAL OAK
21663-21663 SAINT MICHAELS
21664-21664 SECRETARY
21665-21665 SHERWOOD
21666-21666 STEVENSVILLE
21667-21667 STILL POND
21668-21668 SUDLERSVILLE
21669-21669 TAYLORS ISLAND
21670-21670 TEMPLEVILLE
21671-21671 TILGHMAN
21672-21672 TODDVILLE
21673-21673 TRAPPE
21675-21675 WINGATE
21676-21676 WITTMAN
21677-21677 WOOLFORD
21678-21678 WORTON
21679-21679 WYE MILLS
21681-21688 RIDGELY
21690-21690 CHESTERTOWN
21701-21709 FREDERICK
21710-21710 ADAMSTOWN
21711-21711 BIG POOL
21713-21713 BOONSBORO
21714-21714 BRADDOCK HEIGHTS
21715-21715 BROWNSVILLE
21716-21716 BRUNSWICK
21717-21717 BUCKEYSTOWN
21718-21718 BURKITTSVILLE
21719-21719 CASCADE
21720-21720 CAVETOWN
21721-21721 CHEWSVILLE
21722-21722 CLEAR SPRING
21723-21723 COOKSVILLE
21725-21725 DETOUR
21727-21727 EMMITSBURG
21733-21733 FAIRPLAY
21734-21734 FUNKSTOWN
21735-21735 GAITHER
21736-21736 GAPLAND
21737-21737 GLENELG
21738-21738 GLENWOOD
21740-21749 HAGERSTOWN
21750-21750 HANCOCK
21754-21754 IJAMSVILLE
21755-21755 JEFFERSON
21756-21756 KEEDYSVILLE
21757-21757 KEYMAR
21758-21758 KNOXVILLE
21759-21759 LADIESBURG
21762-21762 LIBERTYTOWN
21764-21764 LINWOOD
21765-21765 LISBON
21766-21766 LITTLE ORLEANS
21767-21767 MAUGANSVILLE
21768-21768 MIDDLEBURG
21769-21769 MIDDLETOWN
21770-21770 MONROVIA
21771-21771 MOUNT AIRY
21773-21773 MYERSVILLE
21774-21774 NEW MARKET
21775-21775 NEW MIDWAY
21776-21776 NEW WINDSOR
21777-21777 POINT OF ROCKS
21778-21778 ROCKY RIDGE
21779-21779 ROHRERSVILLE
21780-21780 SABILLASVILLE
21781-21781 SAINT JAMES
21782-21782 SHARPSBURG
21783-21783 SMITHSBURG
21784-21784 SYKESVILLE
21787-21787 TANEYTOWN
21788-21788 THURMONT
21790-21790 TUSCARORA
21791-21791 UNION BRIDGE
21792-21792 UNIONVILLE
21793-21793 WALKERSVILLE
21794-21794 WEST FRIENDSHIP
21795-21795 WILLIAMSPORT
21797-21797 WOODBINE
21798-21798 WOODSBORO
21801-21804 SALISBURY
21810-21810 ALLEN
21811-21811 BERLIN
21813-21813 BISHOPVILLE
21814-21814 BIVALVE
21816-21816 CHANCE
21817-21817 CRISFIELD
21820-21820 DAMES QUARTER
21821-21821 DEAL ISLAND
21822-21822 EDEN
21824-21824 EWELL
21826-21826 FRUITLAND
21829-21829 GIRDLETREE
21830-21830 HEBRON
21835-21835 LINKWOOD
21836-21836 MANOKIN
21837-21837 MARDELA SPRINGS
21838-21838 MARION STATION
21840-21840 NANTICOKE
21841-21841 NEWARK
21842-21843 OCEAN CITY
21849-21849 PARSONSBURG
21850-21850 PITTSVILLE
21851-21851 POCOMOKE CITY
21852-21852 POWELLVILLE
21853-21853 PRINCESS ANNE
21856-21856 QUANTICO
21857-21857 REHOBETH
21858-21858 RHODES POINT
21861-21861 SHARPTOWN
21862-21862 SHOWELL
21863-21863 SNOW HILL
21864-21864 STOCKTON
21865-21865 TYASKIN
21866-21866 TYLERTON
21867-21867 UPPER FAIRMOUNT
21868-21868 UPPER HILL
21869-21869 VIENNA
21870-21870 WENONA
21871-21871 WESTOVER
21872-21872 WHALEYVILLE
21874-21874 WILLARDS
21875-21875 DELMAR
21890-21890 WESTOVER
21901-21901 NORTH EAST
21902-21902 PERRY POINT
21903-21903 PERRYVILLE
21904-21904 PORT DEPOSIT
21911-21911 RISING SUN
21912-21912 WARWICK
21913-21913 CECILTON
21914-21914 CHARLESTOWN
21915-21915 CHESAPEAKE CITY
21916-21916 CHILDS
21917-21917 COLORA
21918-21918 CONOWINGO
21919-21919 EARLEVILLE
21920-21920 ELK MILLS
21921-21922 ELKTON
21930-21930 GEORGETOWN

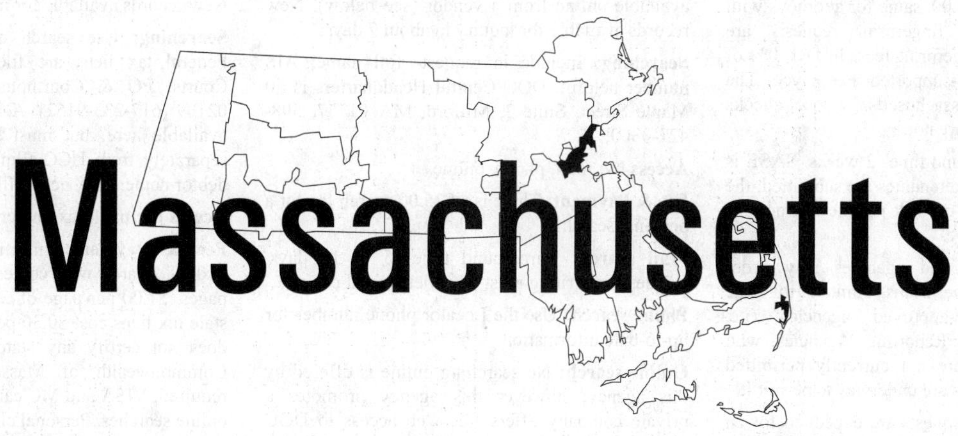

Massachusetts

General Help Numbers:

Governor's Office

State House, Room 360 617- 727-4000
Boston, MA 02133 Fax 617-727-9725
www.state.ma.us/gov 8AM-6PM

Attorney General's Office

One Ashburton Place, Room 2010 617-727-2200
Boston, MA 02108-1698 Fax 617-727-5768
www.ago.state.ma.us 9AM-5PM

Legislative Records

Massachusetts General Court, State House
Beacon St, Room 428 (Document Room) 617-722-2860
Boston, MA 02133
www.mass.gov/legis/ 9AM-5PM

State Archives

Archives Division 617-727-2816
220 Morrissey Blvd Fax 617-288-8429
Boston, MA 02125 9AM-5PM M-F; 9AM-3PM SAT
www.sec.state.ma.us/arc/

State Specifics:

Capital:	Boston Suffolk County
Time Zone:	EST
Number of Counties:	14
Population:	6,497,967
Website:	www.mass.gov

State Agencies

Criminal Records

Criminal History Systems Board, CORI, 200 Arlington Street, #2200, Chelsea, MA 02150; 617-660-4640, Fax- 617-660-4613; 9AM-5PM.

www.mass.gov/chsb/

These CORI searches are offered: 1) Personal, 2) Certified Agency, 3) Publicly Accessible (PUBAC). Certified Agency requests are pre-approved via statute or the Board. PUBAC is open to the public; data is limited.

Indexing & Storage: Records available for at least 50 years. New records available for inquiry in 1 day. 100% of PUBAC records have final dispositions recorded. This agency does not conduct FBI fingerprint searches. Unit provides CORI to Board certified, non-criminal justice agencies such as schools, day care centers, home health aides, youth athletic coaches, and municipal government agencies.

Searching: PUBAC requesters are limited to adult records; the crime must include a sentence of 5 years or more OR sentenced and convicted for any term if, at the time of request, the subject is on probation or has been released within 2 years of felony conviction. Include in request- name, date of birth; please include SSN in request for record matching purposes; SSNs are not shown in results. The Personal request (on one's self) requires a notarized signature. A "certified agency" search is for employers, screening companies, care providers, and others approved by CHSB. Any employer may be approved. CRAs must fill out a Non-Disclosure form. A Certified Agency record includes all conviction & open or pending actions. A PUBAC record contains only convictions.

Access by: mail, online.

Fee & Payment: The Personal request is $25.00. The Certified Agency request is $15.00. The PUBAC request is $30.00; same for attorneys with a court order. No fingerprint requests are permitted, thus no fingerprint fees. In fact, 0% of records are fingerprint-supported. Fee payee- The Commonwealth of Massachusetts. Personal checks accepted, credit cards are not.

Mail search: Turnaround time- 2 weeks. SASE is required. If more than ten names are submitted, the list must be presented on disk per the instructions found on their web page.

Online search: Certified agencies may order $15.00 records online. This limited to 'true employers' and pre-approved agencies (i.e. hospitals). Consumer Reporting Agencies who represent employers are not currently permitted access online, but plans are underway to permit it.

Expedited service: Requests are expedited for an additional $10.00 per record.

Statewide Court Records

Chief Justice for Administration & Management, Two Center Plaza, Room 540, Boston, MA 02108; 617-742-8575, Fax- 617-742-0968; 8:30AM-5PM.

www.mass.gov/courts/admin/index.html

Searching: Opinions to the Mass Supreme and Appellate courts found at http://massreports.com.

Online search: Opinions to the Mass Supreme and Appellate courts can be found at http://massreports.com/. Online access to records on the statewide Trial Courts Information Center website is available to attorneys and law firms at www.ma-trialcourts.org/tcic/welcome.jsp. Contact Peter Nylin by email at nylin_p@jud.state.ma.us. Site is updated daily.

Sexual Offender Registry

Sex Offender Registry Board, PO Box 4547, Salem, MA 01970; 978-740-6400, Fax- 978-740-6464; 8:45AM-5PM. www.mass.gov/sorb/

The Sex Offender Registry Board estimates that there are nearly 18,000 sex offenders living and/or working in the Commonwealth of Massachusetts.

Indexing & Storage: Records back to 08/01/81.

Searching: Information about a sex offender is available to the public only if subject has been classified by the Board as a Level 2 or a Level 3 Offender. The Board suggests that in person requests should be conducted at local law enforcement offices. Requests to this office must be in writing or online access is available from the Internet site.

Access by: mail, online.

Fee & Payment: There is no fee.

Mail search: Turnaround time- 1-2 weeks.

Online search: Search free from links found at the home page. Pursuant to M.G.L. C. 6, §§ 178C - 178P, the individuals who appear on the web page have been designated a Level 3 Sex Offenders by the Sex Offender Registry Board.

Incarceration Records

Massachusetts Executive Office of Public Safety, Department Of Corrections, 50 Maple Street, Suite 3, Chelsea, MA 02150; 508-422-3300, Fax- 508-850-5217; 8AM-5PM.

www.mass.gov/chsb

Indexing & Storage: Records available on current and former inmates by mail. Current inmates, only, available online from a vendor (see below). New records available for inquiry in about 7 days.

Searching: Include in request- full name; AIS number helpful. DOC Central Headquarters is 50 Maple Street, Suite 3, Milford, MA 01757, 508-422-3300;

Access by: mail, phone, online.

Fee & Payment: There is a $25.00 search fee for a personal search.

Mail search: Turnaround time- 5 to 10 days. Requests in writing must be on letterhead paper

Phone search: Use the Locator phone number for up-to-date information.

Online search: No searching online is offered by this agency; however this agency promotes a private company offers free web access to DOC offenders at https://www.vinelink.com/vinelink/siteInfoAction.do?siteId=20000.

Corporation, LLP, LP, LLC, Trademarks/Servicemarks,

Secretary of the Commonwealth, Corporation Division, One Ashburton Pl, 17th Floor, Boston, MA 02108; 617-727-9640 (Corporations), 617-727-2850 (Records), 617-727-8329 (Trademarks), 617-727-9440 (Forms Requests), Fax- 617-742-4538; 8:45AM-5PM.

www.sec.state.ma.us/cor/coridx.htm

Indexing & Storage: Records available for corporations and business entities organized since 1978 on computer. Corporations and business entities organized prior to 1978 may or may not be available. Annual reports are maintained for 10 years. New records available for inquiry immediately.

Searching: Hard copies keep in office 1 year, then stored off site. Include in request- full name of business. In addition to the articles of organization, business entity records available include: Annual Reports, Officers and Directors names and addresses, Prior (merged) names, Inactive and Reserved names and US Tax ID numbers.

Access by: mail, phone, in person, online.

Fee & Payment: Uncertified copies cost $.30 per page. Certified copies cost $7.00 for the first page and $2.00 for each additional page. Certified copies of articles of incorporation are $12.00 per organization. Fee payee- Commonwealth of Massachusetts. Prepayment required. Personal checks accepted. Credit cards accepted for online orders only.

Mail search: Turnaround time- 3 to 5 days. A SASE is requested. **Phone search:** No fee for telephone request. Telephone room hours are 8:45AM-5PM. **In person:** Turnaround time while you wait.

Online search: There is a free Internet lookup from the website. Site also provides UCC info.

Other access: Bulk sale on CD is available.

Uniform Commercial Code, State Tax Liens

UCC Division, Secretary of the Commonwealth, One Ashburton Pl, 17th Fl, Boston, MA 02108; 617-727-9640, Fax- 617-742-4538; 8:45AM-5PM.

www.sec.state.ma.us/cor/corpweb/corucc/uccmain.htm

Indexing & Storage: Records available from 09/01/81 on computer and 01/01/84 on microfiche. New records available for inquiry in 24 hours.

Searching: Use search request form UCC-11. Federal tax liens are filed at the US District Courts, PO & Courthouse Bldg, Boston, MA 02109 (617-233-9152). A list of state tax liens is available here, but must be searched in person separately from UCC filings. Include in request- debtor name. Only active filings are available.

Access by: mail, fax, in person, online.

Fee & Payment: Information listing only is $10.00. Search with copies is $30.00 for first 15 pages, $1.00 per page of copies after 15. Separate state tax liens cost $0.30 per copy made. The state does not certify any state tax lien. Fee payee- Commonwealth of Massachusetts. Prepayment required. VISA and MC cards accepted for fax and online searches. Personal checks accepted.

Mail search: Turnaround time- 2 days. **Fax search:** Requests accepted by fax if credit card given. **In person:** You may request information in person, but turnaround time for certified documents is 24 hours. You may search on an in-house public terminal.

Online search: There is free access to record index from http://corp.sec.state.ma.us/uccfiling/uccSearch/Default.aspx. Search by name, organization or file number.

Other access: Microfiche may be purchased.

Sales Tax Registrations

Revenue Department - Customer Srv. Bureau, Sales Tax Registrations, PO Box 7010, Boston, MA 02204 (Courier address- 200 Arlington Street, 4th Floor, Chelsea, MA 02150); 617-887-6367; 8AM-5PM.

www.mass.gov/?pageID=dorhomepage&L=1&L0=Home&sid=Ador

There are actually 6 offices in the state that allow walk-in researchers. The office in Chelsea will not let you in the building.

Searching: This agency will only confirm that a business is registered. They will provide no other information. Include in request- business name or tax number.

Access by: mail, phone, fax, in person.

Mail search: Turnaround time- 5 to 10 days. A SASE is requested. No fee for mail request. **Phone search:** No fee for telephone request. **Fax search:** They ask that you call first to get the number, they do not wish to publish their fax number. **In person:** No fee for request. Call to find closest office.

Birth Certificates

Registry of Vital Records and Statistics, 150 Mt Vernon St, 1st FL, Dorchester, MA 02125-3105; 617-740-2600, 617-740-2606, Fax- 617-825-7755; 8:45AM-4:45PM.

www.mass.gov/dph/bhsre/rvr/vrcopies.htm

Direct questions to this agency email address vital.recordsrequest@state.ma.us.

Indexing & Storage: Records available from 1911 to present. Records from 1841 to 1905 are located at the Massachusetts Archives, 220 Morrissey Blvd., Boston, MA 02125. Records prior to 1841 are located at the town/city level. New records available for inquiry in 6 months.

Searching: Access to out-of-wedlock birth records and health information is strictly limited. A court order is required for adopted children's records. Otherwise, records are open. Include in request- full name, names of parents, mother's maiden name, date of birth, place of birth. Must present a photo ID or provide a copy of a photo ID to search. Phone and fax searchers must give exact place and date of event.

Access by: mail, phone, fax, in person, online.

Fee & Payment: The fee is $18.00 per certified record if in person and $28.00 by mail. Fee payee- Commonwealth of Massachusetts. Personal checks and major credit cards accepted.

Mail search: Turnaround time- 3 to 4 weeks. A SASE is requested.

Phone search: See expedited service. Must use a credit card. **Fax search:** See expedited service. Must use a credit card.

In person: Turnaround time is immediate. You can also do your own searching of records. First 20 minutes is free, then there is a $9.00 fee. The research center is open 9AM-12PM and 2PM-4:30PM, M-F.

Online search: Orders can be placed via a state designated vendor. Go to www.vitalchek.com. Extra fees are involved.

Expedited service: Expedited service is available for mail, phone, fax, and online orders. Turnaround time- 2 days. The fax number to use is 866-881-9699. Total fee is $42.50 plus cost of express delivery for if ordered by fax, phone or online. If by mail, the total fee is $37.00.

Death Records

Registry of Vital Records and Statistics, 150 Mt Vernon St, 1st FL, Dorchester, MA 02125-3105; 617-740-2600, 617-740-2606, Fax- 617-825-7755; 8:45AM-4:45PM.

www.mass.gov/dph/bhsre/rvr/vrcopies.htm

Direct questions to this agency email address vital.recordsrequest@state.ma.us.

Indexing & Storage: Records available from 1906 to present. Prior records at State Archives to 1841. New records available for inquiry in 4 months.

Searching: Fetal death records are not available. A court order is required to access the originals of amended records. Include in request- full name, date of death, place of death. Name of spouse and age at time of death will help facilitate the search. Phone and fax requesters must supply exact place and date of event.

Access by: mail, phone, fax, in person, onlinc.

Fee & Payment: The fee is $18.00 per certified record if in person and $28.00 by mail. Fee payee- Commonwealth of Massachusetts. Personal checks and major credit cards accepted.

Mail search: Turnaround time- 3 to 4 weeks. A SASE is requested.

Phone search: See expedited service. You must use a credit card.

Fax search: See expedited service.

In person: There is a research center open 9AM-12PM and 2PM-4:30PM M-F. Searching is free the first 20 minutes, then it is $9.00 per hour.

Online search: Orders can be placed via a state designated vendor. Go to www.vitalchek.com. Extra fees are involved.

Expedited service: Expedited service is available for mail, phone, fax, and online orders. Turnaround time- 2 days. The fax number to use is 866-881-9699. Total fee is $42.50 plus cost of express delivery for if ordered by fax, phone or online. If by mail, the total fee is $37.00.

Marriage Certificates

Registry of Vital Records and Statistics, 150 Mt Vernon St, 1st FL, Dorchester, MA 02125-3105; 617-740-2600, 617-740-2606, Fax- 617-825-7755; 8:45AM-4:45PM.

www.mass.gov/dph/bhsre/rvr/vrcopies.htm

Direct questions to this agency email address vital.recordsrequest@state.ma.us.

Indexing & Storage: Records available from 1906 to present. Prior records to 1841 are at State Archives. New records available for inquiry in 5 months.

Searching: A court order is required for originals of amended records. Include in request- names of husband and wife, date of marriage, place or county of marriage. Phone or fax searchers must submit exact place and date of event. Also helpful are parents' names.

Access by: mail, phone, fax, in person, online.

Fee & Payment: The fee is $18.00 per certified record if in person and $28.00 by mail. Fee payee- Commonwealth of Massachusetts. Personal checks and major credit cards accepted.

Mail search: Turnaround time- 3 to 4 weeks. A SASE is requested. See expedited service. **Phone search:** See expedited service. You must use a credit card. **Fax search:** See expedited service.

In person: There is a research center open from 9AM-12PM and 2PM-4:30PM, M-F. The first 20 minutes are free, then a $9.00 per hour fee is charged.

Online search: Orders can be placed via a state designated vendor. Go to www.vitalchek.com. Extra fees are involved.

Expedited service: Expedited service is available for mail, phone, fax, and online orders. Turnaround time- 2 days. The fax number to use is 866-881-9699. Total fee is $42.50 plus cost of express delivery for if ordered by fax, phone or online. If by mail, the total fee is $37.00.

Divorce Records

Access to Records is Restricted.

Registry of Vital Records and Statistics, 150 Mt Vernon St, 1st FL, Dorchester, MA 02125-3105; 617-740-2600, 617-740-2606.

www.mass.gov/dph/bhsre/rvr/vrcopies.htm

Divorce records are found at county of issue. However, this agency maintains an index from 1952 to present. The state will do a search for free by mail only to determine the county. Direct questions to vital.recordsrequest@state.ma.us.

Workers' Compensation Records

Keeper of Records, Department of Industrial Accidents, 600 Washington St, 7th Floor, Boston, MA 02111; 617-727-4900, Fax- 617-727-4440; 8AM-4PM.

www.mass.gov/dia/

Records are under the jurisdiction of Sec of State, per the state public record law.

Indexing & Storage: Records available from 1995 on, and prior records located at State Archives. The index is computerized since 1982. Earlier records may be researched via microfiche for an index number. New records available for inquiry in 24 hours.

Searching: All requests must be submitted in writing. Include in request- claimant name, address and phone, SSN, date of injury, employer, insurance carrier, and other pertinent information. A signed release from claimant is required to receive data regarding medical records, DOB, and SSN. This data not released- medical records, date of birth, SSN, personal data such as home address or phone number, unless authorized by court.

Access by: mail, in person.

Fee & Payment: There is a standard fee of $5.00 prior to release of record(s). Add $.20 per page and $.50 per page if computer generated. They will invoice. Fee payee- Commonwealth of Massachusetts. Prepayment required if lengthy request. Personal checks accepted, credit cards not.

Mail search: Turnaround time- as much as 6 weeks. SASE not required.

In person: Generally, the requester must return to pick up results.

Driver Records-Registry

Registry of Motor Vehicles, Driver Control Unit, PO Box 55889, Boston, MA 02205-5889; 617-351-9213 (Registry), 617-351-4500, Fax- 617-351-9219; 8AM-4:30PM M-T-W-F; 8AM-7PM TH. www.mass.gov/rmv/

The driving records provided by the Registry are for employment or general business use. The Merit Rating Board oversees records for insurance use. Both the Registry and the Merit Rating Board use the same database of driving record histories.

Indexing & Storage: Records available for 6 years plus current year for moving violations. New records available for inquiry in 1 week.

Searching: Casual requesters can only obtain records without personal information. Include in request- full name, driver's license number, date of birth. The address of the requester should also be included. Request forms are found at www.mass.gov/rmv/forms/l21078.pdf and www.mass.gov/rmv/forms/21080.pdf. This data not released- bulk information or lists for commercial purposes.

Access by: mail, phone, in person, online.

Fee & Payment: The fee is $15.00 per record via the Registry, $6.00 if online. Fee payee- Registry of Motor Vehicles. Prepayment required. Personal checks accepted.

Mail search: Turnaround time- 8 working days. SASE not required.

Phone search: For pre-approved accounts, the Registry offers a phone-in request line at 617-351-9213. Orders can be paid with a credit card, results are mailed.

In person: Up to 10 requests will be processed immediately; the rest are available the next day. You may request a record from any field office.

Online search: The driver license number is needed for input. Records are generally available in batch mode (afternoon requests ready early the next morning) or within minutes interactive. Fee is $6.00 per record. Call the above number for further details.

Driver Records-Insurance

Merit Rating Board, Attn: Detailed Driving History Records, PO Box 55889, Boston, MA 02205-5889; 617-351-4400, Fax- 617-351-9660; 8:30AM-5:00PM. www.mass.gov/mrb

The Merit Rating Board's (MRB) maintains an extensive DB of driving records and reports this information to MA auto insurers and government agencies involved in transportation and public safety. Insurers report auto claims & out-of-state records to MRB.

Indexing & Storage: Records available for 6 years for moving violations and at fault accidents (process date). The license number, DOB and name are validated against the Registry of Motor Vehicles (RMV) driver license file. New records available for inquiry in 1 day.

Searching: These records do not include RMV revocation or suspension history. Include in request- driver's license number, full name as whom on DL document, and DOB. All written requests must be on the agency form.

Access by: mail, in person, online.

Fee & Payment: The processing fee is $15.00 per record. Fee payee- Commonwealth of Massachusetts. Prepayment required. Personal checks accepted, credit cards are not.

Mail search: Turnaround time- 2 days. SASE not required.

In person: Counter service is available, turnaround time while you wait.

Online search: An online service is available to authorized insurance companies and agents to view driving records maintained by the MRB. This service is available through the RMV Uninsured Motorist System at www.mass.gov/rmv/ums/. A FTP site is used for file transfer between the MRB and insurers. The MRB transfers SDIP driving history record information to insurers. The information is used to adjust automobile insurance rates. Per statute, this method is not available to the general public.

Vehicle Ownership & Registration

Registry of Motor Vehicles, Document Control, PO Box 55889, Boston, MA 02205-5889; 617-351-4500, Fax- 617-351-9524; 8AM-4:30PM. www.mass.gov/rmv/

Use PO Box 55885 for the Title Dept. In general, license, ownership, and registration information is available to the public. Personal information is not available to casual requesters without consent.

Indexing & Storage: Records available for two years.

Searching: Requesters with a DPPA permissible use should use "A Request for Personal Information In RMV Records." Casual requesters need to submit signed release form "Consent for Release of Highly Restricted Personal Information In RMV Records." Lien information is provided as part of the record.

Access by: mail, fax, in person, online.

Fee & Payment: The current fee is $5.00 for per computer record request of title history; $10 for photocopy of original RMV-1 application. Fee payee- RMV Prepayment required. Personal checks accepted, credit cards are not.

Mail search: Turnaround time- 7 to 10 days. SASE not requested.

Fax search: Records are available by fax to qualifying requesters.

In person: in person requesters may get computer records immediately, but microfiche records take 3 days.

Online search: Searching is limited to Massachusetts based insurance companies and agents for the purpose of issuing or renewing insurance. This system is not open to the public. There is no fee, but line charges will be incurred.

Accident Reports

Crash Records, Registry of Motor Vehicles, PO Box 55889, Boston, MA 02205; 617-351-9434, Fax- 617-351-9524; 8:45AM-5PM.

www.mass.gov/rmv/forms/accident.htm

Accident reports may also be obtained from the local police department in the investigating jurisdiction.

Indexing & Storage: Records available for 2 years to present. Records are indexed on computer. New records available for inquiry in 8 weeks.

Searching: A request form may be downloaded at www.mass.gov/rmv/forms/accrecform.pdf. Items required for search include; full name, date of accident, location of accident, and license or registration number. This data not released- Criminal Offender Record Information (CORI).

Access by: mail.

Fee & Payment: The non-refundable charge is $10.00 per report. Fee payee- Registry of Motor Vehicles. Prepayment required. Personal checks and money orders accepted. No credit cards accepted.

Mail search: Turnaround time- 4 weeks. SASE suggested.

Other access: Quarterly or yearly tapes are available for $2,500.

Vessel Ownership & Registration

Massachusetts Environmental Police, Registration and Titling Bureau, 251 Causeway Street, #101, Boston, MA 02114; 617-626-1610, Fax- 617-626-1630; 8:45AM-4:45PM.

www.mass.gov/dfwele/dle/elereg.htm

Lien information is kept by this agency and appears on the title record.

Indexing & Storage: Records available from 1998 to present. All motor powered boats and jet skis must be registered with this agency. All boats 14ft and over must be titled. Records are indexed on computer.

Searching: Include in request- name or hull number. This data not released- SSNs, DOBs, and phone numbers.

Access by: mail, phone, fax.

Fee & Payment: There is no search fee.

Mail search: Turnaround time- 1 week. SASE not required.

Phone search: Records 2000 to present are available by phone on a limited basis.

Fax search: Turnaround time is usually 2 days, but up to 1 week in busy season.

Other access: To obtain printed lists or CD, contact the Bureau Chief at 617-626-1611. The fee is $50.00 for a CD.

Legislation Records

Massachusetts General Court, State House, Beacon St, Room 428 (Document Room), Boston, MA 02133; 617-722-2860 (Document Room), 617-722-1276 (Senate), 617-722-2356 (House); 9AM-5PM. www.mass.gov/legis/

Records available for usually two years on computer. Older years are available from the State House Library at 617-727-2590. Records are computer indexed from 1995 to present.

Voter Registration

Access to Records is Restricted.

Sec. of the Commonwealth - Elections Division, One Ashburton Place, McCormack Building, Room 1705, Boston, MA 02108; 617-727-2828, Fax- 617-742-3238; 9AM-5PM.

www.sec.state.ma.us/ele/eleidx.htm

The state has a database, but is not available to the public. Records are maintained at the local city and town level. In general, the records are open to the public only on a local basis. Lists must also be purchased from the parties. Direct questions to elections@sec.state.ma.us.

GED Certificates

Massachusetts Dept of Education, GED Records, 350 Main St, Malden, MA 02148; 781-338-6625, 781-338-6604, Fax- 781-338-3089; 9AM-5PM.

www.doe.mass.edu/ged/

Indexing & Storage: New records available for inquiry in 1 month.

Searching: Although this agency is able to verify a GED, they will not release copies of transcripts. You must go to one of the 32 test centers. They can tell you which center to request the copy. Include in request- signed release, DOB, SSN, and name used at time of test. The year and the name of institution are also helpful.

Access by: mail, fax.

Fee & Payment: There is no fee for a simple verification. If a certified letter of verification the fee is $2.00. Fee payee- Commonwealth of Massachusetts. Prepayment required. Only money orders are accepted. Personal checks not accepted. Credit cards not accepted.

Mail search: Turnaround time- 5 to 7 days. SASE not required.

Fax search: Fax requesting is available to all requesters. Use the form found on the web. Turnaround time is 2-3 days.

Hunting & Fishing License Information

Division of Fisheries & Wildlife, Licensing Records, 251 Causeway St #400, Boston, MA 02114-2104; 617-626-1590, Fax- 617-626-1517; 9AM-5PM. www.mass.gov/dfwele/

Records available for 1 year back only. Older records are maintained at one of several locations off premises and take longer to research.

Massachusetts State Licensing Agencies

For details about the agency responsible for licensing/certifying/registering an item below or in the Agency Quick Finder section, match an item's number with the number of the agency in the *Licensing Agency Information* section.

Massachusetts Licenses Searchable Online

Adjuster, Fire Loss #4 .... www.mass.gov/?pageID=ocaconstituent&L=2&L0=Home&L1=Licensee&sid=Eoca
Adoption Center #8 .... www.eec.state.ma.us/adoptSearchResult.aspx?city=&zipcode=&type=ADOPT
Aesthetician #7 .... http://license.reg.state.ma.us/pubLic/licque.asp?color=red&Board=HD
Alarm Installer, Burglar/Fire #7 .... http://license.reg.state.ma.us/pubLic/licque.asp?color=red&Board=EL
Ambulance Service #14 .... http://db.state.ma.us/dph/amb/amb_search.asp
Amusement Device Inspector #27 .... www.mass.gov/?pageID=eopssubtopic&L=3&L0=Home&L1=Consumer+Protection+%26+Business+Licensing&L2=License+Type+by+Business+Area&sid=Eeops
Appraiser, MVR Damage #4 .... www.mass.gov/?pageID=ocaconstituent&L=2&L0=Home&L1=Licensee&sid=Eoca
Architect #18 .... http://license.reg.state.ma.us/pubLic/licque.asp?color=red&Board=AR
Asbestos/Lead Abatement Vocation #24 .. www.mass.gov/?pageID=elwdsubtopic&L=4&L0=Home&L1=Workers+and+Unions&L2=Licensing+and+Certification&L3=Asbestos+Program&sid=Elwd
Athletic Trainer #7 .... http://license.reg.state.ma.us/pubLic/licque.asp?color=red&Board=AH
Attorney #2 .... http://massbbo.org/bbolookup.php
Audiologist #7 .... http://license.reg.state.ma.us/pubLic/licque.asp?color=red&Board=SP
Automobile Repair Shop #4 .... www.aib.org/BDYSHOP/bdshind.htm
Automobile Sales Financer #11 .... www.mass.gov/Eoca/docs/dob/mvlist.xls
Bank & Savings Institution #35 .... http://db.state.ma.us/dob/in-choose.asp
Bank, Cooperative #35 .... http://db.state.ma.us/dob/in-choose.asp
Barber/Barber Shop #7 .... http://license.reg.state.ma.us/pubLic/licque.asp?color=red&Board=BR
Brokerage Firm #10 .... www.finra.org/Investors/ToolsCalculators/BrokerCheck/index.htm
Building Inspector/Local Inspector #3 .... www.mass.gov/?pageID=eopsagencylanding&L=3&L0=Home&L1=Public+Safety+Agencies&L2=Massachusetts+Department+of+Public+Safety&sid=Eeops
Building Producer #3 .... www.mass.gov/?pageID=eopsagencylanding&L=3&L0=Home&L1=Public+Safety+Agencies&L2=Massachusetts+Department+of+Public+Safety&sid=Eeops
Check Casher #11 .... www.mass.gov/Eoca/docs/dob/cclist.xls
Check Casher/Seller #35 .... http://db.state.ma.us/dob/licenseelist.asp
Chiropractor #7 .... http://license.reg.state.ma.us/pubLic/licque.asp?color=red&Board=CH
Collection Agency #35 .... http://db.state.ma.us/dob/licenseelist.asp
Concrete Technician #3 .... www.mass.gov/?pageID=eopsterminal&L=3&L0=Home&L1=Public+Safety+Agencies&L2=Massachusetts+Department+of+Public+Safety&sid=Eeops&b=terminalcontent&f=dps_license_lookup&csid=Eeops
Concrete Testing Laboratory #3 .... www.mass.gov/?pageID=eopsterminal&L=3&L0=Home&L1=Public+Safety+Agencies&L2=Massachusetts+Department+of+Public+Safety&sid=Eeops&b=terminalcontent&f=dps_license_lookup&csid=Eeops
Construction Supervisor #3 .... www.mass.gov/?pageID=eopsagencylanding&L=3&L0=Home&L1=Public+Safety+Agencies&L2=Massachusetts+Department+of+Public+Safety&sid=Eeops
Construction Supervisor, Resid'l #3 .... http://db.state.ma.us/dps/licenseelist.asp
Consumer Credit Grantor #35 .... http://db.state.ma.us/dob/licenseelist.asp
Contractor, Home Improvement #3 .... www.mass.gov/?pageID=eopsagencylanding&L=3&L0=Home&L1=Public+Safety+Agencies&L2=Massachusetts+Department+of+Public+Safety&sid=Eeops
Cosmetologist/Manicurist/Aesthetician #7 http://license.reg.state.ma.us/pubLic/licque.asp?color=red&Board=HD
Credit Union #35 .... http://db.state.ma.us/dob/in-choose.asp
Day Care Center #8 .... www.eec.state.ma.us/oo_licensing.aspx
Debt Collector #11 .... www.mass.gov/Eoca/docs/dob/dclist.xls
Dentist/Dental Hygienist #7 .... http://license.reg.state.ma.us/public/_dhplnewsystem.asp
Electrician #7 .... http://license.reg.state.ma.us/pubLic/licque.asp?color=red&Board=EL
Electrologist #7 .... http://license.reg.state.ma.us/pubLic/licque.asp?color=red&Board=ET
Embalmer #12 .... http://license.reg.state.ma.us/pubLic/licque.asp?color=red&Board=EM
Emergency Medical Technician #14 .... http://db.state.ma.us/dph/emtcert/cert_search.asp
EMS Training Institution #14 .... www.mass.gov/?pageID=eohhs2terminal&&L=5&L0=Home&L1=Government&L2=Departments+and+Divisions&L3=Department+of+Public+Health&L4=Programs+and+Services+K+-+S&sid=Eeohhs2&b=terminalcontent&f=dph_emergency_services_g_about&csid=Eeohhs2
Engineer #7 .... http://license.reg.state.ma.us/pubLic/licque.asp?color=red&Board=EN
Engineers/Fireman School #27 .... www.mass.gov/?pageID=eopssubtopic&L=3&L0=Home&L1=Consumer+Protection+%26+Business+Licensing&L2=License+Type+by+Business+Area&sid=Eeops
Family Child Care Provider #8 .... www.eec.state.ma.us
Finfishing, Commercial #34 .... www.mass.gov/dfwele/dmf/
Fire Sprinkler Contractor/Fitter #27 .... www.mass.gov/?pageID=eopssubtopic&L=3&L0=Home&L1=Consumer+Protection+%26+Business+Licensing&L2=License+Type+by+Business+Area&sid=Eeops

Fireman, 1st/2nd Class #27 .... www.mass.gov/?pageID=eopssubtopic&L=3&L0=Home&L1=Consumer+Protection+%26+Business+Licensing&L2=License+Type+by+Business+Area&sid=Eeops
Firemen / Engineer #27 .... www.mass.gov/?pageID=eopssubtopic&L=3&L0=Home&L1=Consumer+Protection+%26+Business+Licensing&L2=License+Type+by+Business+Area&sid=Eeops
Foreign Transmittal Agency #35 .... http://db.state.ma.us/dob/licenseelist.asp
Foster Care Provider #8 .... www.eec.state.ma.us/fosterSearchResult.aspx?city=&zipcode=&type=FOSTER
Funeral Director #12 .... http://license.reg.state.ma.us/pubLic/licque.asp?color=red&Board=EM
Fur Buyer #34 .... www.mass.gov/dfwele/dfw/
Gas Fitter #7 .... http://license.reg.state.ma.us/pubLic/licque.asp?color=red&Board=PL
Health Insurer #4 .... www.mass.gov/?pageID=ocaagencylanding&L=4&L0=Home&L1=Government&L2=Our+Agencies+and+Divisions&L3=Division+of+Insurance&sid=Eoca
Health Profession, Allied #7 .... http://license.reg.state.ma.us/pubLic/licque.asp?color=red&Board=AH
HMO #4 .... www.mass.gov/?pageID=ocasubtopic&L=7&L0=Home&L1=Consumer&L2=Insurance&L3=Health+ Insurance&L4=Health+Care+Access+Bureau&L5=Group+Products+and+Plans&L6=Currently+Licensed+HMO+Products+Available+in+MA&sid=Eoca
Home Improvement Contractor #3 .... www.mass.gov/?pageID=eopsagencylanding&L=3&L0=Home&L1=Public+Safety+Agencies&L2=Massachusetts+Department+of+Public+Safety&sid=Eeops
Home Improvement Supervisor #3 .... www.mass.gov/?pageID=eopsterminal&L=3&L0=Home&L1=Public+Safety+Agencies&L2=Massachusetts+Department+of+Public+Safety&sid=Eeops&b=terminalcontent&f=dps_license_lookup&csid=Eeops
Home Inspector #7 .... http://license.reg.state.ma.us/pubLic/hi_biz/v_list_hi.asp
Inspection Agency, 3rd Party #3 .... www.mass.gov/?pageID=eopsagencylanding&L=3&L0=Home&L1=Public+Safety+Agencies&L2=Massachusetts+Department+of+Public+Safety&sid=Eeops
Insurance Advisor/Adjuster #4 .... www.mass.gov/?pageID=ocaconstituent&L=2&L0=Home&L1=Licensee&sid=Eoca
Insurance Agent/Broker #4 .... www.mass.gov/?pageID=ocaconstituent&L=2&L0=Home&L1=Licensee&sid=Eoca
Insurance Premium Financer #35 .... http://db.state.ma.us/dob/licenseelist.asp
Insurance, Domestic/Foreign Firm #4 .... www.mass.gov/?pageID=ocaagencylanding&L=4&L0=Home&L1=Government&L2=Our+Agencies+and+Divisions&L3=Division+of+Insurance&sid=Eoca
Investment Advisor #10 .... www.finra.org/Investors/ToolsCalculators/BrokerCheck/index.htm
Land Surveyor #7 .... http://license.reg.state.ma.us/pubLic/licque.asp?color=red&Board=EN
Landscape Architect #18 .... http://license.reg.state.ma.us/pubLic/licque.asp?color=red&Board=LA
Lead Inspector #24 .... www.mass.gov/?pageID=elwdsubtopic&L=5&L0=Home&L1=Workers+and+Unions&L2=Licensing+and+Certification&L3=Lead+Program&L4=Lead+License+Lists&sid=Elwd
Loan Company, Small #11 .... www.mass.gov/Eoca/docs/dob/sllist.xls
Loan Servicer #11 .... www.mass.gov/Eoca/docs/dob/lslist.xls
Lobbyist/Lobbyist Employer #21 .... www.sec.state.ma.us/lobbyist/LobbyistSearch/PublicSearch.asp?action=P
Lobstering #34 .... www.mass.gov/dfwele/dmf/
Lumber Producer, Native #3 .... www.mass.gov/?pageID=eopsagencylanding&L=3&L0=Home&L1=Public+Safety+Agencies&L2=Massachusetts+Department+of+Public+Safety&sid=Eeops
Mammography Radiologic Techl'gist #26 . http://db.state.ma.us/dph/Radtechs/
Manufactured Building Producer #3 .... www.mass.gov/?pageID=eopsagencylanding&L=3&L0=Home&L1=Public+Safety+Agencies&L2=Massachusetts+Department+of+Public+Safety&sid=Eeops
Marriage & Family Therapist #7 .... http://license.reg.state.ma.us/pubLic/licque.asp?query=personal&color=red&board=MH
Medical Doctor #6 .... http://profiles.massmedboard.org/MA-Physician-Profile-Find-Doctor.asp
Mental Health Counselor #7 .... http://license.reg.state.ma.us/pubLic/licque.asp?query=personal&color=red&board=MH
Mental Health/Human Svcs Pro, Allied #7 http://license.reg.state.ma.us/pubLic/licque.asp?query=personal&color=red&board=MH
Mortgage Broker #11 .... www.mass.gov/Eoca/docs/dob/mblist.xls
Mortgage Broker/Lender #11 .... www.mass.gov/Eoca/docs/dob/mclist.xls
Mortgage Lender #11 .... www.mass.gov/Eoca/docs/dob/mllist.xls
Motor Vehicle Sales Financer #35 .... http://db.state.ma.us/dob/licenseelist.asp
Nurse, LPN/RN/Midwife #7 .... http://license.reg.state.ma.us/public/_dhplnewsystem.asp
Nursing Home Administrator #7 .... http://license.reg.state.ma.us/public/licque.asp?color=blue
Nursing Home Health Officer #7 .... http://license.reg.state.ma.us/public/licque.asp?color=blue
Nursing Home Psychologist/Provider #7 .. http://license.reg.state.ma.us/public/licque.asp?color=blue
Occupational Therapist/Assistant #7 .... http://license.reg.state.ma.us/pubLic/licque.asp?color=red&Board=AH
Optician #7 .... http://license.reg.state.ma.us/pubLic/licque.asp?query=personal&color=red&board=DO
Optician, Dispensing #7 .... http://license.reg.state.ma.us/pubLic/licque.asp?color=red&Board=DO
Optometrist #7 .... http://license.reg.state.ma.us/pubLic/licque.asp?color=red&Board=OP
P&C Insurance Agency #4 .... www.mass.gov/?pageID=ocaconstituent&L=2&L0=Home&L1=Licensee&sid=Eoca
Perfusionist #7 .... http://license.reg.state.ma.us/public/_dhplnewsystem.asp
Pharmacist #7 .... http://license.reg.state.ma.us/public/_dhplnewsystem.asp
Physical Therapist/Assistant #7 .... http://license.reg.state.ma.us/pubLic/licque.asp?color=red&Board=AH
Physician Assistant #13 .... www.mass.gov/?pageID=eohhs2subtopic&L=5&L0=Home&L1=Provider&L2=Certification%2c+Licensure%2c+and+Registration&L3=Occupational+and+Professional&L4=Physician+Assistants&sid=Eeohhs2
Pipefitter #27 .... www.mass.gov/?pageID=eopssubtopic&L=3&L0=Home&L1=Consumer+Protection+%26+Business+Licensing&L2=License+Type+by+Business+Area&sid=Eeops

Pipefitter School #27 .... www.mass.gov/?pageID=eopssubtopic&L=3&L0=Home&L1=Consumer+Protection+%26+Business+Licensing&L2=License+Type+by+Business+Area&sid=Eeops
Plumber #7 .... http://license.reg.state.ma.us/pubLic/licque.asp?color=red&Board=PL
Podiatrist #7 .... http://license.reg.state.ma.us/pubLic/licque.asp?color=red&Board=PD
Psychologist, Educational #7 .... http://license.reg.state.ma.us/pubLic/licque.asp?query=personal&color=red&board=MH
Public Accountant-CPA #7 .... http://license.reg.state.ma.us/pubLic/licque.asp?color=red&Board=PA
Radiation Therapy/Radiologic Tech #26 ... http://db.state.ma.us/dph/Radtechs/
Radio & TV Repair Technician #7 .... http://license.reg.state.ma.us/pubLic/licque.asp?color=red&Board=TV
Radiographer #26 .... http://db.state.ma.us/dph/Radtechs/
Radiologic Technologist #26 .... http://db.state.ma.us/dph/Radtechs/
Real Estate Agent/Broker/Sales #7 .... http://license.reg.state.ma.us/pubLic/licque.asp?color=red&Board=RE
Real Estate Appraiser #7 .... http://license.reg.state.ma.us/pubLic/licque.asp?color=red&Board=RA
Refrigeration Technician/Contr./Sch'l #27 www.mass.gov/?pageID=eopssubtopic&L=3&L0=Home&L1=Consumer+Protection+%26+Business+Licensing&L2=License+Type+by+Business+Area&sid=Eeops
Rehabilitation Therapist #7 .... http://license.reg.state.ma.us/pubLic/licque.asp?query=personal&color=red&board=MH
Residential Care, Youth #8 .... www.eec.state.ma.us/oo_adop_res.aspx
Respiratory Care Therapist #7 .... http://license.reg.state.ma.us/public/_dhplnewsystem.asp
Retail Installment Financer #35 .... http://db.state.ma.us/dob/licenseelist.asp
Sales Finance Company #11 .... www.mass.gov/Eoca/docs/dob/mvlist.xls
Sanitarian #18 .... http://license.reg.state.ma.us/pubLic/licque.asp?color=red&Board=SA
School Bus #31 .... http://db.state.ma.us/dpu/qorders/frmTransportation.asp
Seafood Dealer #34 .... www.mass.gov/dfwele/dmf/
Securities Broker/Dealer/Agent #10 .... www.finra.org/Investors/ToolsCalculators/BrokerCheck/index.htm
Shellfishing, Commercial #34 .... www.mass.gov/dfwele/dmf/
Social Worker #7 .... http://license.reg.state.ma.us/pubLic/licque.asp?color=red&Board=SW
Speech-Language Pathologist #7 .... http://license.reg.state.ma.us/pubLic/licque.asp?color=red&Board=SP
Sprinkler Fitting School #27 .... www.mass.gov/?pageID=eopssubtopic&L=3&L0=Home&L1=Consumer+Protection+%26+Business+Licensing&L2=License+Type+by+Business+Area&sid=Eeops
Surplus Lines Broker #4 .... www.mass.gov/?pageID=ocaconstituent&L=2&L0=Home&L1=Licensee&sid=Eoca
Taxidermist #34 .... www.mass.gov/dfwele/dfw/
Trapping #34 .... www.mass.gov/dfwele/dfw/
Trauma Center #14 .... www.facs.org/trauma/verified.html
Trust Company #35 .... http://db.state.ma.us/dob/in-choose.asp
Veterinarian #7 .... http://license.reg.state.ma.us/pubLic/licque.asp?color=red&Board=VT
Water Supply Facility Operator #7 .... http://license.reg.state.ma.us/pubLic/licque.asp?color=red&Board=DW

Massachusetts Licensing Quick Finder

Acupuncturist #5 617-654-9810
Adjuster, Fire Loss #4 617-521-7794
Adoption Center #8 617-988-6600
Aerial Passenger Cable Car #27 .. 617-727-3200 x662
Aesthetician #7 617-727-9940
Aircraft Registration #23 617-973-8883
Airport Manager #23 617-973-8883
Alarm Installer, Burglar/Fire #7 617-727-9931
Alcoh'l Bev/Wine Seller/Broker/Whlse #1 .... 617-727-3040 x21
Alcoh'l Bev/Wine Transport Permit #1 .... 617-727-3040 x21
Alcoholism/Drug Facility #15 617-624-5111
Alcoholism/Drug Program #15 617-624-5111
Ambulance Service #14 617-753-7300
Ambulatory Surgical Ctr #28 617-753-8000
Amusement Device Inspector #27617-727-3200 x607
Appraiser (MVD) #20 617-521-7453
Appraiser, MVR Damage #4 617-521-7447
Architect #18 617-727-3072
Asbestos/Lead Abatem't Vocation #24 . 617-626-6975
Athletic Trainer #7 617-727-3071
Attorney #2 617-728-8800
Auctioneer #30 617-727-3480
Auctioneer School #30 617-727-3480
Audiologist #7 617-727-1747
Automobile Dealer #11 .... 617-956-1500 x501
Automobile Repair Shop #4 617-727-3480
Automobile Sales Financer #11 .. 617-956-1500 x501
Bank & Savings Institution #35 617-956-1500
Bank, Cooperative #35 617-956-1500

Barber/Barber Shop #7 617-727-7367
Birthing Center #28 617-753-8000
Blood Bank #28 617-753-8000
Boiler Engineer #27 617-727-3200
Boiler/Pressure Vessel Inspecor #27 .... 617-727-3200 x607
Boxer #9 .... 617-727-3200 x25257
Boxing Physician #9 .... 617-727-3200 x25257
Boxing Professional #9 .... 617-727-3200 x25257
Brewery/Pub/Sacramen'l Wine #1 .. 617-727-3040 x21
Brewery/Winery Storer/Farmer #1 . 617-727-3040 x21
Brokerage Firm #10 617-727-3548
Building Inspector/Local Inspector #3 .. 617-727-7532
Building Producer #3 617-727-7532
Bus/Motor Coach Driver #31 617-305-3559
Cattle Dealer/Transporter #19 617-626-1700
Chair Lift #27 .... 617-727-3200 x662
Check Casher #11 .... 617-956-1500 x501
Check Casher/Seller #35 617-956-1500
Chiropractor #7 617-727-3093
Cigarette Seller #32 617-887-5090
Clinic #28 617-753-8000
Collection Agency #35 617-956-1500
Concrete Technician #3 617-727-7532
Concrete Testing Laboratory #3 617-727-7532
Construction Supervisor #3 ..... 617-727-7532 x25205
Construction Supervisor, Resid'l #3 617-727-7532
Consumer Credit Grantor #35 617-956-1500
Contractor, Home Improvem't #3 508-821-9375 x502
Cosmetologist/Manicurist/Aesthetician #7 617-727-9940

Credit Union #35 617-956-1500
Day Care Center #8 617-988-6600
Day Care Center Teacher/Director #8 . 617-988-6600
Debt Collector #11 .... 617-956-1500 x501
Dental Examiner #41 617-727-9928
Dentist/Dental Hygienist #7 617-727-9928
Domestics Agency #22 617-626-6970
Electrician #7 617-727-9931
Electrologist #7 617-727-9957
Elevator Construction/Maintenance #27 .... 617-727-3200 x25238
Elevator Operator #27 .... 617-727-3200 x25238
Embalmer #12 617-727-1718
Emergency Medical Technician #14 617-753-7300
Employm't Ag'ncy, Placing/Temp #22 . 617-626-6970
EMS Training Institution #14 617-753-7000
Engineer #7 617-727-9957
Engineers/Fireman School #27 ... 617-727-3200 x607
Exterminator #19 617-626-1776
Family Child Care Assistant #8 617-988-6600
Family Child Care Provider #8 617-988-6600
Finfishing, Commercial #34 617-626-1520
Fire Sprinkler Contract'r/Fitter #27617-727-3200 x607
Fireman, 1st/2nd Class #27 .... 617-727-3200 x607
Firemen / Engineer #27 .... 617-727-3200 x607
Foreign Transmittal Agency #35 617-956-1500
Foster Care Provider #8 617-988-6600
Funeral Director #12 617-727-1718
Fur Buyer #34 617-626-1590
Gas Fitter #7 617-727-9952
Gas Station Owner #30 617-727-3480

Guard Dog/Hearing Dog Business #19 . 617-626-1786
Hairdresser #7 617-727-9940
Health Care Plan, Managed #4 617-521-7372
Health Insurer #4 617-521-7794
Health Profession, Allied #7 617-727-3071
HMO #4 617-521-7794
Hoisting Machinery Operator #27 . 617-727-3200 x607
Home Health Care Provider #22 617-626-6970
Home Improvement Contract'r #3 508-821-9375 x502
Home Improvement Supervisor #3 .... 617-727-7532 x25207
Home Inspector #7 617-727-4459
Horse (Equine) Dealer #19 617-626-1797
Horse/Greyhound #16 617-727-2581
Hospice #28 617-753-8000
Hospital #28 617-753-8000
Inspection Agency, 3rd Party #3 617-727-7532
Insurance Advisor/Adjuster #4 617-521-7794
Insurance Agent/Broker #4 617-521-7794
Insurance Premium Financer #35 617-956-1500
Insurance, Domestic/Foreign Firm #4 .. 617-321-7391
Investment Advisor #10 617-727-3548
Jockey #16 617-727-2581
Justice of the Peace #29 .... 617-725-4016 x5
Laboratory, Medical-related #28 617-753-8000
Land Surveyor #7 617-727-9957
Landscape Architect #18 617-727-3072
Lead Inspector #24 617-626-6975
Library Media Specialist #17 781-338-6600
Loan Company, Small #11 .... 617-956-1500 x501
Loan Servicer #11 .... 617-956-1500 x501
Lobbyist/Lobbyist Employer #21 617-878-3434
Lobstering #34 617-626-1520
Lumber Producer, Native #3 .... 617-727-3636 x561
Mammography Radiologic Technol'gist #26 617-427-2944
Manicurist #7 617-727-9940
Manufactured Building Producer #3 617-727-7532
Marriage & Family Therapist #7 617-727-3071
Medical Doctor #6 617-654-9800
Mental Health Counselor #7 617-727-3071
Mental Health/Human Svcs Pro, Allied #7 ... 617-727-3071
Milk Plant #19 617-626-1811
Modeling Industry/Agency #22 617-626-6970
Mortgage Broker #11 .... 617-956-1500 x501
Mortgage Broker/Lender #11 .... 617-956-1500 x501
Mortgage Lender #11 .... 617-956-1500 x501
Motion Picture Operator #27 ... 617-727-3200 x25223
Motor Vehicle Repair Shop #30 617-727-3480
Motor Vehicle Sales Financer #35 617-956-1500
Nanny Agency #22 617-626-6970
Notary Public #29 617-725-4030
Nuclear Medicine Technologist #26 617-427-2944
Nuclear Plant Engineer/Operator #27 .... 617-727-3200 x607
Nurse, LPN/RN/Midwife #7 617-727-9961
Nursery #19 617-626-1801
Nursery Agent #19 617-626-1801
Nurses' Aide in Long-term Care Facility #28 617-753-8143
Nursing Home Administrator #7 617-727-3074
Nursing Home Health Officer #7 617-727-3074
Nursing Home Psychol'st/Provider #7 .. 617-727-3074
Nursing Home/Rest Home #28 617-753-8000
Occupational Therapist/Assistant #7 617-727-3071
Oil Burner Technician/Contr. #27 . 617-727-3200 x607
Optician #7 617-727-3093
Optician, Dispensing #7 617-727-3093
Optometrist #7 617-727-3093
Out-Patient Rehabilitation Facility #28 . 617-753-8000
Owner/Trainer, Horse/Greyhound #16 . 617-727-2581
P&C Insurance Agency #4 617-521-7794
Pasteurization Plant #19 617-626-1811
Peddler/Hawker #30 617-727-3480
Perfusionist #7 617-727-4499
Personal Agent #27 .... 617-727-3200 x637
Pesticide Applicator/Dealer #19 617-626-1776
Pet Shop #19 617-626-1795
Pharmacist #7 617-727-9953
Physical Therapist/Assistant #7 617-727-3071
Physician Assistant #13 617-973-0806
Pipefitter #27 .... 617-727-3200 x607
Pipefitter School #27 .... 617-727-3200 x607
Plumber #7 617-727-9952
Podiatrist #7 617-727-1747
Private Detective #33 978-538-6128
Private Investigator #33 978-538-6128
Psychologist, Educational #7 617-727-3071
Public Accountant-CPA #7 617-727-1806
Racetrack, Horse/Greyhound #16 617-727-2581
Radiation Therapy/Radiol'g'c Tech #26 617-427-2944
Radio & TV Repair Technician #7 617-727-3074
Radiographer #26 617-427-2944
Radiologic Technologist #26 617-427-2944
Radon Specialist #26 617-427-2944
Real Estate Agent/Broker/Sales #7 617-727-2373
Real Estate Appraiser #7 617-727-3055
Refrigeration Technician/Contr./School #27 .... 617-727-3200 x607
Rehabilitation Therapist #7 617-727-3071
Renal Dialysis, End Stage #28 617-753-8000
Residential Care, Youth #8 617-988-6600
Respiratory Care Therapist #7 617-727-1747
Retail Installment Financer #35 617-956-1500
Riding Instructor/School #19 617-626-1797
Sales Finance Company #11 .... 617-956-1500 x501
Sanitarian #18 617-727-3072
School Administrator #17 781-338-6600
School Bus #31 617-305-3559
School Guidance Counselor #17 781-338-6600
Seafood Dealer #34 617-626-1520
Securities Broker/Dealer/Agent #10 617-727-3548
Security Guard Agency #33 978-538-6128
Shellfishing, Commercial #34 617-626-1520
Simulcast & Inter-Track Wagering #16 617-727-2581
Ski Tow #27 .... 617-727-3200 x662
Skimobile #27 .... 617-727-3200 x662
Social Worker #7 617-727-3073
Speech-Language Pathologist #7 617-727-1747
Sprinkler Fitting School #27 .... 617-727-3200 x607
Stable (Horse & Buggy Operator) #19 . 617-626-1797
Surplus Lines Broker #4 617-521-7794
Swine Dealer #19 617-626-1700
Taxidermist #34 617-626-1590
Teacher #17 781-338-6600
Theatrical Booking Agent #27 .... 617-727-3200 x637
Ticket Reseller #27 .... 617-727-3200 x637
Tramway Inspector #27 .... 617-727-3200 x662
Trapping #34 617-626-1590
Trauma Center #14 617-753-7300
Trust Company #35 617-956-1500
Vending Machine #25 617-983-6712
Vendor, Transient #30 617-727-3480
Veterinarian #7 617-727-3080
Water Supply Facility Operator #7 617-727-3074
Weights & Measures #30 617-727-3480
Wine & Malt Beverage Permit #1 .. 617-727-3040 x21

Massachusetts Licensing Agency Information

#1 Alcoholic Beverages Control Commission, 239 Causeway St, #200, Boston, MA 02114-2130; 617-727-3040, Fax- 617-727-1258. Hours- 9AM-5PM. www.mass.gov/abcc/

#2 Board of Overseers Registry Dept, Board of Bar Examiners, 99 High St, Boston, MA 02110; 617-728-8700, Fax- 617-482-8000. http://massbbo.org

#3 Board of Building Regulations & Standards, Construction-Related Licensing Programs, 1 Ashburton Pl, Rm 1301, Boston, MA 02108; 617-727-7532, Fax- 617-727-1754. www.mass.gov/?pageID=eopsagencylanding&L=3&L0=Home&L1=Public+Safety+Agencies&L2=Massachusetts+Department+of+Public+Safety&sid=Eeops

#4 Division of Insurance, Agents & Brokers Licensing, 1 South Station, 5th Fl, Boston, MA 02110-2208; 617-521-7794, Fax- 617-521-7772. www.mass.gov/doi/ Search data at- www.mass.gov/doi/Consumer/CSS_health.html For searching, this agency provides lists to view or download.

#5 Committee on Acupuncture, Board of Registration in Medicine, 560 Harrison Ave, #G-4, Boston, MA 02118; 617-654-9800, Fax- 617-426-9358. Hours- 8:45AM-5PM. www.massmedboard.org

#6 Board of Registration in Medicine, 560 Harrison Ave, #G4, Boston, MA 02118; 617-654-9800, 800-377-0550, Fax- 617-426-9373. Hours- 8:45AM-5PM. www.massmedboard.org Search data at- http://profiles.massmedboard.org/MA-Physician-Profile-Find-Doctor.asp

#7 Consumer Affairs and Business Regulation, Division of Professional Licensure, 239 Causeway St, #400, Boston, MA 02114-2130; 617-727-3074, Fax- 617-727-7406. www.mass.gov/dpl/boards.htm Search data at- http://license.reg.state.ma.us/pubLic/licque.asp

#8 Department of Early Education and Care, 51 Sleeper St, 4th Fl, Boston, MA 02210; 617-988-6600, Fax- 617-988-2451. www.eec.state.ma.us Use website's "Find Child Care" search box. Excel lists of providers free at website.

#9 Boxing Commission, 1 Ashburton Pl, Rm 1301, Boston, MA 02108; 617-727-3200 x25257, Fax- 617-727-5732.

#10 Securities Division, Licensing and Registration Section, 1 Ashburton Pl, 17th Fl, Boston, MA 02108; 617-727-3548, Fax- 617-248-0177. www.sec.state.ma.us/sct/ Search data at- www.finra.org/Investors/ToolsCalculators/BrokerCheck/index.htm

#11 Consumer Compliance Unit, Division of Banks, 1 South Station, 3rd Fl, Boston, MA 02110; 617-956-1500 x501, Fax- 617-956-1599. www.mass.gov/dob

#12 Division of Registration, Board of Funeral Directors & Embalmers, 239 Causeway St, #500, Boston, MA 02114-2130; 617-727-1718, Fax- 617-727-1627. www.mass.gov/dpl/boards/em/ Search data at- http://license.reg.state.ma.us/pubLic/licque.asp?color=red&Board=EM

#13 Division of Health Profession Licensure, Board of Registration of Physicians Assistants, 239 Causeway St #200, Boston, MA 02114; 617-973-0806, Fax- 617-973-0982. 8:45AM-5PM.

www.mass.gov/dph/boards/ Search data at- www.mass.gov/?pageID=eohhs2subtopic&L=5&L0=Home&L1=Provider&L2=Certification%2c+Licensure%2c+and+Registration&L3=Occupational+and+Professional&L4=Physician+Assistants&sid=Eeohhs2

#14 Office of Emergency Medical Services, 2 Boylston St, 3rd Fl, Boston, MA 02116-4737; 617-753-7300, Fax- 617-753-7320. www.mass.gov/dph/oems/ Search data at- www.mass.gov/dph/oems/

#15 Department of Public Health, Bureau of Substance Abuse Services, 250 Washington St, 3rd Fl, Boston, MA 02108; 800-327-5050, Fax- 617-624-5185. www.mass.gov/dph/bsas/bsas.htm

#16 Consumer Department, Racing Commission, 1 Ashburton Pl, Rm 1313, Boston, MA 02108; 617-727-2581, Fax- 617-227-6062. www.mass.gov/?pageID=ocaagencylanding&L=4&L0=Home&L1=Government&L2=Our+Agencies+and+Divisions&L3=State+Racing+Commission&sid=Eoca

#17 Division of Educational Personnel, Department of Education & Arts, 350 Main St, 3rd Fl, Malden, MA 02148; 781-338-6600, Fax- 781-338-3391. Hours- 8:45AM-4:45PM. www.doe.mass.edu/contact/

#18 Board of Registration of Architects, Division of Professional Licensure, 239 Causeway St #500, Boston, MA 02114; 617-727-3072, Fax- 617-727-1627. www.mass.gov/dpl/boards/ar/

#19 Department of Food & Agriculture, Pesticide Bureau, 251 Causeway St, #500, Boston, MA 02114-2151; 617-626-1776, Fax- 617-626-1850. www.mass.gov/agr/

#20 Division of Insurance, Motor Vehicle Damage Appraisers Licensing Board, 1 South Station, 5th Fl, Boston, MA 02110; 617-521-7447, Fax- 617-521-7576. www.mass.gov/doi/MVDA/Mvda_home.html

#21 Secretary of the Commonwealth, Lobbyist & Lobbyist Employer Directory, 1 Ashburton Pl, Room 1719, Boston, MA 02108; 617-727-2832, Fax- 617-727-5914. www.sec.state.ma.us/lobbyist/LobbyistLoginSystem/LobbyistContact.asp Search data at- www.sec.state.ma.us/lobbyist/LobbyistSearch/PublicSearch.asp?action=P

#22 Division of Occupational Safety, Employment Agency Program, 19 Staniford St, 1st Fl, Boston, MA 02114; 617-626-6970. www.mass.gov/dos/ea/

#23 Aeronautics Commission, 10 Park Plaza, Rm 3190, Boston, MA 02116-3966; 617-973-8881, Fax- 617-973-8889. www.massaeronautics.org

#24 Department of Occupational Safety, Licensing Division, Labor & Workforce Development, 19 Staniford St, 2nd Fl, Boston, MA 02114; 617-626-6975, Fax- 617-626-6944. www.mass.gov/dos/

#25 Department of Public Health, Division of Food & Drugs, 305 South St, Jamaica Plain, MA 02130; 617-983-6712, Fax- 617-524-8062. www.mass.gov/dph/

#26 Radiation Control Program, Department of Public Health, 529 Main St, Charlestown, MA 02129; 617-242-3035, Fax- 617-242-3457. www.mass.gov/?pageID=eohhs2terminal&L=5&L0=Home&L1=Government&L2=Departments+and+Divisions&L3=Department+of+Public+Health&L4=Programs+and+Services+K+-+S&sid=Eeohhs2&b=terminalcontent&f=dph_environmental_radiationcontrol_g_about&csid=Eeohhs2 Search data at- http://db.state.ma.us/dph/Radtechs/

#27 Department of Public Safety, 1 Ashburton Pl, Boston, MA 02108; 617-727-7775, Fax- 617-727-4764. Hours- 8:45AM-5PM. www.mass.gov/dps/ Search data at- www.mass.gov/?pageID=eopssubtopic&L=3&L0=Home&L1=Consumer+Protection+%26+Business+Licensing&L2=License+Type+by+Business+Area&sid=Eeops

#28 Department of Public Health, Health Care Quality, 99 Chauncey St, Boston, MA 02111; 617-753-8000, Fax- 617-753-8095. www.mass.gov/dph/dhcq

#29 Governor's Council, Public Records Division, 1 Ashburton Pl, McCormack Bldg, Rm 1719, Boston, MA 02108; 617-727-2832, Fax- 617-727-5914. Hours- 9AM-5PM. www.sec.state.ma.us/pre/preidx.htm

#30 Division of Standards, Consumer Affairs & Business Regulation, 1 Ashburton Pl, Rm 1115, Boston, MA 02108; 617-727-3480, Fax- 617-727-5705. www.mass.gov/?pageID=ocaagencylanding&L=4&L0=Home&L1=Government&L2=Our+Agencies+and+Divisions&L3=Division+of+Standards&sid=Eoca

#31 Department of Telecommunications and Energy, Transportation Oversight Division, 1 South St, #2, Boston, MA 02110-2208; 617-305-3559, Fax- 617-478-2598. www.mass.gov/?pageID=ocasubtopic&L=6&L0=Home&L1=Government&L2=Our+Agencies+and+Divisions&L3=Department+of+Public+Utilities&L4=DPU+Divisions&L5=Transportation+Oversight+Division&sid=Eoca

#32 Department of Revenue, Excises Unit, PO Box 7012, Boston, MA 02204; 617-887-6774, Fax- 617-887-6962. www.mass.gov/?pageID=dorconstituent&L=2&L0=Home&L1=Businesses&sid=Ador

#33 Department of State Police, Certification Unit, 485 Maple St, Danvers, MA 01923; 978-538-6128, Fax- 978-538-6021.

#34 Department of Fisheries, Wildlife & Environmental Enforcement, Division of Fish & Wildlife, 251 Causeway St, #S-400, Boston, MD 02114-2104; 617-626-1500, Fax- 617-626-1505. www.mass.gov/dfwele/dfw/dfw_toc.htm

#35 Division of Banks & Loan Agencies, 1 South Station, 3rd FL, Boston, MA 02110; 617-956-1500, Fax- 617-956-1599. www.mass.gov/dob

#36 Special Licensing Unit, Department of State Police, 20 Somerset St, 9th Fl, Boston, MA 02108

Massachusetts Federal Courts

The following list indicates the district and division name for each county in the state. If the bankruptcy court location is different from the district court, then the location of the bankruptcy court appears in parentheses.

Massachusetts County/Court Cross Reference

County	Court
Barnstable	Boston
Berkshire	Springfield (Worcester)
Bristol	Boston
Dukes	Boston
Essex	Boston
Franklin	Springfield (Worcester)
Hampden	Springfield (Worcester)
Hampshire	Springfield (Worcester)
Middlesex	Boston
Nantucket	Boston
Norfolk	Boston
Plymouth	Boston
Suffolk	Boston
Worcester	Worcester

Standards for Federal Courts: *See the Appendix for information on standards and fee for searching Federal Courts.*

US District Court

Boston Division Court Clerk, US Courthouse, 1 Courthouse Way Ste 2300, Boston, MA 02210, 617-748-9152; records- 617-748-9086; Fax- 617-748-9096. 8:30AM-5PM. www.mad.uscourts.gov **Counties:** Barnstable, Bristol, Dukes, Middlesex, Essex, Nantucket, Norfolk, Plymouth, Suffolk.

Searches/Indexing: Include full name in search request. Results include last 4 SSN digits. Will not fax back documents. New cases are in the index 1 day after filing date. Computer index maintained; court database dates from the early 1900's. Criminal case files sent to archives 4 years after closed; 3 years for civil.

Search Access: Mail: Search usually completed- 2-4 weeks. SASE not required. **In person:** 3 public terminals available. Self-serve copies $.25. **Payment:** Pay by Visa/MC, money order, cashier's or personal check. Payee: Clerk, US District Court.

E-Svcs: PACER- http://pacer.mad.uscourts.gov. Document images available. PACER records go back to 1/1990. New records online after 1 day. ECF at https://ecf.mad.uscourts.gov. **Opinions:** http://pacer.mad.uscourts.gov/opinion.html.

Springfield Division Court Clerk, 300 State St, Springfield, MA 01105, 413-785-6800, 785-0015; crim dockets- 413-785-0216; civil dockets- 413-785-0215; Fax- 413-785-0204. 8:00-4:30PM. www.mad.uscourts.gov **Counties:** Berkshire, Franklin, Hampden, Hampshire.

Searches/Indexing: Include full name in search request. Results may include last 4 SSN digits, also birth year. New cases are in the index immediately after filing date. Case files sent to archives 2-3 years after closed.

Search Access: Docket info available via phone if clerk has time. **Mail:** Search usually completed- 1-2 days. SASE not required. **Fax:** Will charge for fax search request only if copies and certification requested. **In person:** 1 public terminal available. No self-serve copier. **Payment:** Pay by Visa/MC, money order, cashier's or personal check. Payee: Clerk, US District Court.

E-Svcs: PACER- http://pacer.mad.uscourts.gov. Document images available. PACER records go back to 1/1990. New records online after 1 day. ECF at https://ecf.mad.uscourts.gov. **Opinions:** http://pacer.mad.uscourts.gov/opinion.html.

Worcester Division Court Clerk, 595 Main St, Rm 502, Worcester, MA 01608, 508-929-9900. Hours- 8:30AM-5PM. www.mad.uscourts.gov **Counties/Note:** Worcester.

Searches/Indexing: Include full name in search request. Results include last 4 SSN digits. New cases are in the index immediately after filing date. Indexes on computer from 1988; on microfiche from 1981. Earlier indexes back to early 1900s in storage. Files sent to archive 2-4 years after closed.

Search Access: Only docket info available by phone. **Mail:** Search usually completed- 1-2 days. SASE not required. **Fax:** Fax search requests accepted, invoice will be sent with records copies. **In person:** 1 public terminal available. No self-serve copier. **Payment:** Pay by Visa/MC, money order, cashier's or personal check. Payee: Clerk, US District Court.

E-Svcs: PACER- http://pacer.mad.uscourts.gov. Document images available. PACER records go back to 1/1990. New records online after 1 day. ECF at https://ecf.mad.uscourts.gov. **Opinions:** http://pacer.mad.uscourts.gov/opinion.html.

US Bankruptcy Court

Boston/Eastern Division Court Clerk, 1101 Thomas P. O'Neill, Jr. Federal Bldg, 10 Causeway St, Boston, MA 02222-1074, 617-565-8950; Fax- 617-565-6650; records room fax- 617-565-6651; fax record requests to- 617-565-6651. Hours- 8:30AM-5PM. www.mab.uscourts.gov

Counties/Note: Barnstable, Bristol, Dukes, Essex (except towns assigned to Worcester Division), Nantucket, Norfolk (except towns assigned to Worcester Division), Plymouth, Suffolk, and the following towns in Middlesex: Arlington, Belmont, Burlington, Everett, Lexington, Malden, Medford, Melrose, Newton, North Reading, Reading, Stoneham, Wakefield, Waltham, Watertown, Wilmington, Winchester and Woburn. There is also a Bankruptcy Office in Hyannis, 617-565-6073, but no filings; Boston manages records.

Searches/Indexing: To search, include full name; SSN and DOB may be helpful. Results include SSN last 4 digits only, partial address. Will not fax back documents. New cases are in the index immediately after filing date. Case files sent to archives 6 months after closed.

Search Access: Only general info released via phone. Voice Case Information Service available, call VCIS at 888-201-3572 or 617-565-6025. **Mail:** Search usually completed- 7-10 days. Include SASE for return. **Fax:** Fax search same as mail. **In person:** 3 public terminals available. Self serve copies $.25 each. **Payment:** Pay by money order, cashier's or personal check. No debtor checks/credit cards. Payee: US Bankruptcy Court. Copy fees can be billed after search is completed.

E-Services: Document images available. PACER records go back to 4/1987. New records online immediately. ECF at https://ecf.mab.uscourts.gov. **Opinions:** www.mab.uscourts.gov/mab/node/13.

Springfield/Western Div. Court Clerk, 300 State St, Springfield, MA 01105, 413-785-6900; Fax- 413-781-9477. Hours- 8:30AM-5PM. www.mab.uscourts.gov **Counties:** Berkshire, Franklin, Hampden, Hampshire.

Searches/Indexing: To search, include full name; SSN and DOB may be helpful. Results include SSN last 4 digits only, partial address. Will not fax back documents. New cases are in the index immediately after filing date. Case files sent to archives 1 year after closed.

Search Access: Only docket info is available by phone. Voice Case Information Service available, call VCIS at 888-201-3572 or 617-565-6025. **Mail:** Search usually completed- 7-10 days. Include SASE for return. **Fax:** Fax search same as mail. **In person:** Public terminals available. Self-serve copies $.25 each.

Payment: Pay by money order, cashier's or personal check. No debtor checks/credit cards. Payee: US Bankruptcy Court.

E-Services: Document images available. PACER records go back to 4/1987. New records online after 1 day. ECF at https://ecf.mab.uscourts.gov. **Opinions:** www.mab.uscourts.gov/mab/node/13.

Worcester/Central Division Court Clerk, 595 Main St, Rm 211, Worcester, MA 01608, 508-770-8900; Fax- 508-793-0189; records room fax- 508-770-8958; fax record requests - 508-770-8958 8:30AM-5PM. www.mab.uscourts.gov

Counties/Note: Middlesex (except towns assigned to the Boston Division), Worcester and the following towns: in Essex-Andover, Haverhill, Lawrence, Methuen, North Andover; in Norfolk-Bellingham, Franklin, Medway, Millis, Norfolk.

Searches/Indexing: To search, include full name; SSN and DOB may be helpful. Results include SSN last 4 digits only, partial address. Will not fax back documents. New cases are in the index immediately after filing date. Case files sent to archives 1 year after closed.

Search Access: Only docket info is available by phone. Voice Case Information Service available, call VCIS at 888-201-3572 or 617-565-6025. **Mail:** Search usually completed- 7-10 days. Include SASE for return. **Fax:** Fax search same as mail. **In person:** Public terminals available. Self-serve copies $.25 each.

Payment: Pay by money order, cashier's or personal check. No debtor checks/credit cards. Payee: US Bankruptcy Court.

E-Services: Document images available. PACER records go back to 4/1987. New records online after 1 day. ECF at https://ecf.mab.uscourts.gov. **Opinions:** www.mab.uscourts.gov/mab/node/13.

Massachusetts County Courts

Court	Jurisdiction	No. of Courts	How Organized
Superior Courts*	General	19	14 Counties
District Courts*	General	68	62 Geographic Divisions
Boston Municipal Court*	General	1	
Housing Courts*	General	7	6 Divisions
Probate and Family Courts*	Probate	15	14 Divisions
Juvenile Courts	Special	7	11 Divisions
Land Court	Special	1	

* Profiled in this Sourcebook.

Court	CIVIL Tort	Contract	Real Estate	Min. Claim	Max. Claim	Small Claims	Estate	Eviction	Domestic Relations
Superior Courts*	X	X	X	$25,000	No Max				
District Courts*	X	X	X	$0	No Max	$2000	X	X	X
Boston Municipal Court*	X	X	X	$0	No Max	$2000			X
Housing Courts*			X	$0	No Max	$2000			
Probate and Family Courts*							X		X
Land Court			X						

Court	CRIMINAL Felony	Misdemeanor	DWI/DUI	Preliminary Hearing	Juvenile
Superior Courts*	X				
District Courts*	X	X	X	X	X
Boston Municipal Court*		X	X		
Housing Courts*		X		X	
Probate and Family Courts*					
Juvenile Courts					X

Administration

Chief Justice for Administration and Management, Two Center Plaza, Room 540, Boston, MA, 02108; 617-742-8575, Fax: 617-742-0968. www.mass.gov/courts/admin/index.html

Court Structure

The various court sections are often called "Departments." While Superior Courts and District Courts have concurrent jurisdiction in civil cases, the practice is to assign cases for or less than $25,000 to the District Court and those over $25,000 to Superior Court. In addition to misdemeanors, District Courts and Boston Municipal Courts have jurisdiction over certain minor felonies. District Court criminal jurisdiction extends to all felonies punishable by a sentence up to five years, and many other specific felonies with greater potential penalties; all misdemeanors; and all violations of city and town ordinances and by-laws. The District Court also tries small claims involving up to $2,000 (initially tried to a magistrate, with a defense right of appeal either to a judge or to a jury). Eviction cases may be filed at a county District Court or at the regional "Housing Court." A case may be moved from a District Court to a Housing Court, but never the reverse. Housing Courts also hear misdemeanor "Code Violation" cases and prelims for these. There are five Housing Court Regions - Boston (Suffolk County), Worcester (County), Southeast (Plymouth and Bristol Counties), Northeast (Essex County), and Western (Berkshire, Franklin, Hampden and Hampshire Counties). The Southeast Housing Court has three branches - Brockton, Fall River, and New Bedford.

There are 15 Probate and Family Court locations in Massachusetts - one per county plus two in Bristol.

Online Access

Opinions from the Supreme Court and Appellate Courts can be found at http://massreports.com. Online access to records on the statewide Trial Courts Information Center website with both criminal and civil superior court cases, BUT the site is available to ONLY attorneys and law firms. Visit www.ma-trialcourts.org/tcic/welcome.jsp. Access is free but BBO number is a requisite. Middlesex, Suffolk, Worcester indices go back to 1990s; other counties go back to active cases as of 2000-2001. For more information, contact Peter Nylin by email at nylin_p@jud.state.ma.us or Victoria Palmarcci at victoria.palmacci@jud.state.ma.us. Site is updated daily.

Searching Tips, Fees, and Other Guidelines

Massachusetts courts *attest* or confirm document; a *certificate* is a separate authentification page with a gold seal. Since July 2003, the state mandated the attestation fee be $2.50 per page (includes copy fee) and the copy fee be $1.00 per page for all Superior and District Courts. Most but not all courts follow this schedule.

Barnstable County

Superior Court 3195 Main St, PO Box 425, Barnstable, MA 02630; 508-375-6684; fax: 508-362-1658; 8:30AM-4:30PM. ***Felony, Civil Actions over $25,000.***
Their public access terminal is connected to the statewide Superior Court system.
Call court to recommend document retriever who can perform search for you.
Civil Records: Access: In person, online. Visitors must perform in person searches themselves. Required to search: name, years to search; also helpful: address. Civil cases indexed by defendant, plaintiff, on computer back to 1/2001; on index cards from 1985 and books from 1830s. Civil PAT goes back to 1995. Online only for attorneys and law firms at www.ma-trialcourts.org/tcic/.
Criminal Records: Access: In person, online. Visitors must perform in person searches themselves. Required to search: name, years to search, DOB; also helpful: address, SSN. Criminal records computerized from 1975; books from 1830s. Criminal PAT goes back to 1975. PAT criminal results show middle initial. Online for attorneys and law firms only with registration at www.ma-trialcourts.org/tcic/.
General Information: No victims names released. Will not fax out case files. Court makes copy: $1.00 per page. Self serve: $.50 per page. Certification fee: $2.50. Payee: Barnstable Superior Court. Business checks not accepted. No credit cards accepted. Prepayment required. Mail requests: SASE required for mail return of any copies.

Barnstable District Court PO Box 427, Route 6A, Barnstable, MA 02630; 508-375-6600; criminal phone: 508-375-6776; civil phone: 508-375-6785; fax: 508-362-0213; 8:30AM-4:30PM. ***Felony, Misdemeanor, Civil, Eviction, Small Claims.***
Includes Barnstable, Yarmouth, and Sandwich.
Civil Records: Access: Phone, mail, in person. Only the court performs in person searches; visitors may not. No search fee. Required to search: name, years to search. Civil cases indexed by defendant, plaintiff, indexed on computer; older on cards and docket books. Mail turnaround time 1-2 weeks. Civil PAT goes back to 2003.
Criminal Records: Access: Mail, in person. Only the court performs in person searches; visitors may not. No search fee. Required to search: name, years to search, DOB. Criminal records on computer since 1996; prior records on index cards and docket books. Mail turnaround time 1-2 weeks. Criminal PAT goes back to 2003.
General Information: No impounded records released. Will not fax documents. Court makes copy: $1.00 per page. Certification fee: $2.50 includes copy fee. Payee: District Court. Only cashiers checks and money orders accepted. Visa/MC, Diners, Carte Blanch, JCB cards accepted. Prepayment required. Mail requests: SASE required.

Falmouth District Court 161 Jones Rd, Falmouth, MA 02540; 508-495-1500; criminal phone: x225; civil phone: x230; fax: 508-495-0992; 8:30AM-4:30PM. ***Felony, Misdemeanor, Civil, Eviction, Small Claims.***
Includes Falmouth, Mashpee, and Bourne.
Civil Records: Access: Phone, in person. Only the court performs in person searches; visitors may not. No search fee. Required to search: name, years to search. Civil cases indexed by defendant, plaintiff, computerized since 1996.
Criminal Records: Access: Phone, in person. Only the court performs in person searches; visitors may not. No search fee. Required to search: name, years to search. Criminal records computerized since 1996.
General Information: No impounded records released. Will not fax documents. Court makes copy: $1.00 per page. Certification fee: $2.50. Cert fee includes copies. Payee: Falmouth District Court. Personal checks accepted; credit cards are not. Prepayment required.

Orleans District Court 237 Rock Harbor Rd, Orleans, MA 02653; 508-255-4700; 8:30AM-4:30PM. ***Felony, Misdemeanor, Civil, Eviction, Small Claims.*** Includes Brewster, Chatham, Dennis, Eastham, Orleans, Truro, Wellfleet, Harwich, and Provincetown.
Civil Records: Access: In person only. Visitors must perform in person searches themselves. Required to search: name, years to search. Civil cases indexed by defendant, plaintiff, kept in storage from 1978. Some prior records destroyed. Public use terminal has civil records. PAT results show name only.
Criminal Records: Access: In person only. Visitors must perform in person searches themselves. Required to search: name, years to search. Records in storage from 1978. Some prior records destroyed.
General Information: No impounded records released. Will not fax documents. Court makes copy: $1.00 per page. Certification fee: $2.50. Payee: Orleans District Court. Personal checks accepted; credit cards are not. Prepayment required.

Probate & Family Court PO Box 346, 3195 Main St, Route 6A, Barnstable, MA 02630; 508-375-6710; fax: 508-362-3662; 8:30AM-4PM. ***Probate.***

Berkshire County

Superior Court 76 East St, Pittsfield, MA 01201; 413-499-7487; fax: 413-442-9190; 8:30AM-4:30PM. ***Felony, Civil Actions over $25,000.***
Civil Records: Access: Mail, online. Only the court performs in person searches; visitors may not. No search fee. Required to search: name, years to search. Civil cases indexed by defendant, plaintiff; index on cards from 1900s, on computer back to 2000. Mail turnaround time 3-4 weeks. Civil PAT goes back to 2000. PAT results show name only. Only attorneys and law firms may access records online after registration at www.ma-trialcourts.org/tcic/.
Criminal Records: Access: Mail, in person, online. Only the court performs in person searches; visitors may not. No search fee. Required to search: name, years to search. Criminal records indexed on cards from 1900s, on computer back to 2000. Note: Because their index does not contain DOBs or SSNs, they cannot verify the subject, thus they recommend you contact the Criminal History Board in Boston, MA. Mail turnaround time 3-4 weeks. Criminal PAT available. PAT results show middle initial, DOB, SSN. Only attorneys and law firms may access records online after registration at www.ma-trialcourts.org/tcic/.
General Information: No impounded records released. Will not fax documents. Court makes copy: $1.00 per page. Certification fee: $2.50 per document. Payee: Berkshire Superior Court. Personal checks accepted; credit cards are not. Prepayment required. Mail requests: SASE required.

Northern Berkshire District Court #28 111 Holden St, North Adams, MA 01247; 413-663-5339; fax: 413-664-7209; 8AM-4:30PM. ***Felony, Misdemeanor, Civil, Eviction, Small Claims.***
Handles cases for Adams, Chesire, Clarksburg, Florida, Hancock, New Ashford, North Adams, Savoy, Williamstown, and Windsor. Exercises concurrent jurisdiction over Hancock and Windsor with the Pittsfield Division. Includes cases from closed Court #30.
Civil Records: Access: Fax, mail, in person. Only the court performs in person searches; visitors may not. No search fee. Required to search: name, years to search. Civil cases indexed by defendant, plaintiff; index on cards from 1983, docket books to 1900. Mail turnaround time 1-2 weeks. Public use terminal has civil records back to 2004.
Criminal Records: Access: Fax, mail, in person. Only the court performs in person searches; visitors may not. No search fee. Required to search: name, years to search, DOB, and SSN if available. Criminal records indexed on cards from 1983, docket books to 1900. Mail turnaround time 1-2 weeks.
General Information: No impounded records released. Will fax documents to local or toll free line. Court makes copy: $1.00 per page. Certification fee: $2.50. Payee: District Court. Business checks accepted. No credit cards accepted. Prepayment required. Mail requests: SASE required.

Pittsfield District Court #27 24 Wendell Ave, Pittsfield, MA 01201; criminal phone: 413-442-5468; civil phone: 413-499-0558; criminal fax: 413-499-7327; civil fax: 413-443-7090; 8:30AM-4:30PM. ***Felony, Misdemeanor, Civil, Eviction, Small Claims.*** Includes Becket, Dalton, Hancock, Hinsdale, Lanesborough, Lenox, Peru, Pittsfield, Richmond, Washington and Windsor. This court exercises concurrent jurisdiction over Hancock and Windsor with the North Berkshire Divisions.
Civil Records: Access: Phone, mail, in person. Both court and visitors may perform in person searches. No search fee. Required to search: name, years to search. Civil cases indexed by defendant, plaintiff; index on docket books and in recent years in the computer. Mail turnaround time 1-2 weeks. Civil PAT goes back to 2001.
Criminal Records: Access: Phone, mail, in person. Both court and visitors may perform in person searches. No search fee. Required to search: name, years to search; DOB. Criminal docket on books and in recent years in the computer. Mail turnaround time 1-2 weeks. Criminal PAT goes back to 1999. PAT results may show name, DOB, SSN.
General Information: No juvenile or sealed records released. Will fax documents $1.00 per page. Court makes copy: $1.00 per page, self serve same. Certification fee: $2.50. Payee: Pittsfield District Court. Personal checks accepted; credit cards are not. Prepayment required. Mail requests: SASE required.

Southern Berkshire District Court 9 Gilmore Ave, Great Barrington, MA 01230; 413-528-3520; criminal fax: 413-528-0757; civil fax: same; 8:30AM-4:30PM. ***Felony, Misdemeanor, Civil, Eviction, Small Claims.***
Includes Alford, Becket, Egremont, Great Barrington, Lee, Lenox, Monterey, Mt. Washington, New Marlborough, Otis, Sandisfield, Sheffield, Stockbridge, Tyringham, and West Stockbridge. Shares jurisdiction of Becket and Lenox with Pittsfield Dist. Court.
Civil Records: Access: Fax, mail, in person. Both court and visitors may perform in person searches. No search fee. Required to search: name, years to search. Court will only perform search if given the docket number. Civil cases indexed by defendant,

plaintiff; index on cards from 1984, docket books to 1900. Mail turnaround time 1-2 weeks.
Criminal Records: Access: Fax, mail, in person. Both court and visitors may perform in person searches. No search fee. Required to search: name, years to search, DOB. Criminal records indexed on cards from 1984, docket books to 1900. Note: Court will only do search if given docket number. Mail turnaround time 1-2 weeks.
General Information: No juvenile, impounded records released. Will not fax documents. Court makes copy: $1.00 per page, self serve same. Certification fee: $2.50 per cert. Payee: District Court. Personal checks accepted; credit cards are not. Prepayment required. Mail requests: SASE required.

Probate & Family Court 44 Bank Row, Pittsfield, MA 01201; 413-442-6941; fax: 413-443-3430; 8:30AM-4PM. ***Probate.***

Western Housing Court, MA; ***Eviction, Misdemeanor (Code Violations), Small Claims.***
See Hampden County Western Housing Court for many housing code cases, real estate-related small claims and eviction cases for this county; also see district courts in this county.

Bristol County

Superior Court - Taunton 9 Court St, Taunton, MA 02780; 508-823-6588 x1; 8AM-4:30PM. ***Felony, Civil Actions over $25,000.***
Civil Records: Access: Mail, in person, online. Both court and visitors may perform in person searches. No search fee. Required to search: name, years to search. Civil cases indexed by defendant, plaintiff, on computer link to Boston from 1985, index books from 1935. Mail turnaround time 2 weeks. Civil PAT goes back to 1980.
Criminal Records: Access: Mail, in person, online. Both court and visitors may perform in person searches. No search fee. Required to search: name, years to search; also helpful: DOB. Criminal records on computer link to Boston from 1985, index books from 1935. Mail turnaround time 2 weeks. Criminal PAT goes back to 2000.
General Information: Online only for attorneys and law firms at www.ma-trialcourts.org/tcic/. No impounded records released. Will not fax documents. Court makes copy: $1.00 per page. Certification fee: $2.50 per cert. Payee: Clerk of Superior Court of Bristol County. Personal checks accepted; credit cards are not. Prepayment required.

Attleboro District Court 34 Courthouse, 88 N Main St, Attleboro, MA 02703; 508-222-5900; criminal phone: x390; civil: x392; criminal fax: 508-222-4869; civil fax: 508-222-4869; 8AM-4:30PM. ***Felony, Misdemeanor, Civil, Eviction, Small Claims.*** www.mass.gov/courts/courtsandjudges/courts/attleborodistrictmain.html Includes Attleboro, Mansfield, North Attleboro, and Norton.
Civil Records: Access: Phone, mail, in person. Both court and visitors may perform in person searches. No search fee. Required to search: name, years to search. Civil cases indexed by defendant, plaintiff, on computer since 1995; prior records on index cards from 1983, docket books from 1900. Mail turnaround time 1-2 weeks. Public use terminal has civil records back to 2001.
Criminal Records: Access: Phone, mail, in person. Only the court performs in person searches; visitors may not. No search fee. Required to search: name, years to search, DOB, SSN. Criminal records on computer since 1995; prior records on index cards from 1983, docket books from 1900. Mail turnaround time 1-2 weeks.
General Information: No impounded records released. Will not fax documents. Court makes copy: $1.00 per page. Cert fee: $2.50. Payee: District Court, Attleboro District Court. Business checks accepted. Visa/MC accepted. Prepayment required.

Fall River District Court 45 Rock St, Fall River, MA 02720; 508-679-8161; fax: 508-675-5477; 8:30AM-4:30PM. ***Felony, Misdemeanor, Civil, Eviction, Small Claims.*** www.mass.gov/courts/courtsandjudges/courts/fallriverdistrictmain.html Includes Fall River, Freetown, Somerset, Swansea, and Westport.
Civil Records: Access: In person only. Both court and visitors may perform in person searches. No search fee. Required to search: name, years to search. Civil cases indexed by defendant, plaintiff, on index on computer from 1989, on docket books in vault from 1985. Note: Office may do search; they are short-staffed and may not be able.
Criminal Records: Access: In person only. Both court and visitors may perform in person searches. No search fee. Required to search: name, years to search, DOB or SSN. Criminal records on index on computer from 1991, on docket books in vault from 1985. Note: Office may do search; they are short-staffed and may not be able.
General Information: No sealed, minor, confidential address records released. Fee to fax document $.50 per page. Court makes copy: $1.00 per page. Certification fee: $2.50 per page. Payee: District Court. Only cashiers checks and money orders accepted. No credit cards. Prepayment required.

New Bedford District Court 33 75 N 6th St, New Bedford, MA 02740; 508-999-9700; criminal phone: 508-990-9353; civil phone: 508-990-9351; fax: 508-990-8094; 8AM-4:30PM. ***Felony, Misdemeanor, Civil, Eviction, Small Claims.***
Small claims phone: 508-990-9333. Includes Acushnet, Dartmouth, Fairhaven, Freetown, New Bedford, and Westport.
Civil Records: Access: Mail, in person. Visitors must perform in person searches themselves. No search fee. Required to search: name, years to search. Civil cases indexed by defendant, plaintiff, filed from 1989, prior on docket books; on computer back to 1995. Public use terminal has civil records back to 1995 but only small claims. PAT results show name, DOB. Terminal results also show SSNs.
Criminal Records: Access: Mail, in person, fax. Visitors must perform in person searches themselves. No search fee. Required to search: name, years to search, DOB; also helpful: SSN. Criminal records filed from 1989, prior on docket books; on computer back to 1995. Note: Searches are limited to pending charges; this agency recommends searching elsewhere for closed case files. Mail turnaround time 1-2 weeks.
General Information: No impounded records released. Will not fax documents. Court makes copy: $1.00 per page. Certification fee: $2.50 per cert. Payee: New Bedford District Court. Business checks accepted. No credit cards accepted. Prepayment required. Mail requests: SASE required.

Taunton District Court 120 Cohannet St, Taunton, MA 02780; 508-824-4032; fax: 508-824-2282; 8AM-4:30PM. ***Felony, Misdemeanor, Civil, Eviction, Small Claims.*** Includes Berkley, Dighton, Easton, Raynham, Rehoboth, Seekonk, and Taunton.
Civil Records: Access: Phone, mail, in person. Visitors must perform in person searches themselves. No search fee. Required to search: name, years to search. Civil cases indexed by defendant, plaintiff; index on cards for 6 years.
Criminal Records: Access: Phone, mail, in person. Visitors must perform in person searches themselves. No search fee. Required to search: name, years to search, DOB. Criminal records indexed on cards for 6 year. Mail turnaround time 1-2 days.
General Information: Will fax documents. Court makes copy: $1.00 per page. Cert fee: $2.50. Payee: District Court. Personal checks accepted; credit cards are not. Prepayment required. SASE not required.

New Bedford Probate & Family Court 505 Pleasant St, New Bedford, MA 02740; 508-999-5249; fax: 508-999-1269; 8AM-4:30PM. ***Probate.***

Probate & Family Court 11 Court St, Taunton, MA 02780; 508-824-4004; 9AM-4PM,M-TH, 8:30AM-4PM F. ***Probate.*** www.bcpfc.com

Southeast Housing Court - Fall River 289 Rock St., 2nd FL, Fall River, MA 02720; 508-677-1505; fax: 508-672-9621; 8:30-4:30PM. ***Eviction, Misdemeanor, code violation, small claims.***
Also known as Fall River Trial Court. Includes housing code cases, real estate-related small claims, and many eviction cases for Bristol County except the New Bedford area; also see district courts.

Southeast Housing Ct - New Bedford 139 Hathaway Rd, New Bedford, MA 02740; 508-994-0156; 8:30AM-4:30PM Mon,Fri. ***Eviction, Misdemeanor (Code Violations), Small Claims.***
Open Mondays and Fridays only. Includes many code, real estate-related small claims, and eviction cases for the New Bedford area only; also see area district court.

Dukes County

Superior Court PO Box 1267, Edgartown, MA 02539; 508-627-4668; 8AM-4PM. ***Felony, Civil Actions over $25,000.***
Civil Records: Access: Mail, in person, online. Both court and visitors may perform in person searches. No search fee. Required to search: name, years to search. Civil cases indexed by defendant, plaintiff; index on cards from 1976 and books from 1695. Mail turnaround time 1-2 days. Civil PAT goes back to 1985. Online only for attorneys and law firms at www.ma-trialcourts.org/tcic/.
Criminal Records: Access: Mail, in person, online. Both court and visitors may perform in person searches. No search fee. Required to search: name, years to search. Criminal records indexed on cards from 1976 and books from 1695. Mail turnaround time 1-2 days. Criminal PAT goes back to same as civil. Online for attorneys and law firms only with registration at www.ma-trialcourts.org/tcic/.
General Information: No sealed records released. Will not fax documents. Court makes copy: $1.00 per page. Certification fee: $2.50. Payee: Clerk of Superior Court. Personal checks accepted; credit cards are not. Mail requests: SASE required.

Edgartown District Court PO Box 1284, 81 Main St, Courthouse, Edgartown, MA 02539-1284; 508-627-3751; fax: 508-627-7070; 8:30-4:30PM. ***Felony, Misdemeanor, Civil, Eviction, Small Claims.*** www.mass.gov/courts/courtsandjudges/courts/edgartowndistrictmain.html Includes Edgartown, Oak Bluffs, Tisbury, West Tisbury, Aquinnah (formerly Gay Head), Gosnold, and Elizabeth Islands.
Civil Records: Access: In person only. Both court and visitors may perform in person searches. No search fee. Required to search: name, years to search. Civil cases indexed by defendant, plaintiff; index on cards from 1990, docket books to 2006.
Criminal Records: Access: In person only. Both court and visitors may perform in person searches. No search fee. Required to search: name, years to search, DOB; SSN helpful. Criminal records indexed on cards from 1990, docket books to 2006.
General Information: No sealed records released. Will fax specific case file no add'l fee. Court makes copy: $1.00 per page. Certification fee: $2.50 includes copy fee. Payee: District Court. No personal checks accepted. Visa/MC accepted in person only.

Probate & Family Court PO Box 237, 81 Main St, #104, 1st Fl, Edgartown, MA 02539; 508-627-4703; fax: 508-627-7664; 10AM-3PM. ***Probate, Domestic Relations.***

Essex County

Superior Court - Salem 34 Federal St, Salem, MA 01970; 978-744-5500; criminal phone: x2; civil phone: x1; criminal fax: 978-825-9989; civil fax: 978-741-0691; 8AM-4:30PM. ***Felony, Civil Actions over $25,000.***
Civil Records: Access: Mail, in person, online. Visitors must perform in person searches themselves. No search fee. Required to search: name, years to search. Civil cases indexed by defendant, plaintiff, are entered on computer for civil actions from all three Superior courts in this county. Computer records go back to 1985. Civil PAT goes back to 1985. PAT results show name only. Online access for attorneys and law firms only with registration at www.ma-trialcourts.org/tcic/.
Criminal Records: Access: In person, online. Visitors must perform in person searches themselves. Required to search: name, years to search. Criminal computer records go back to 1985. Criminal PAT goes back to 1990. PAT results show name only. Online access for attorneys and law firms only with registration at www.ma-trialcourts.org/tcic/.

General Information: Impounded cases are not released. Will not fax out documents. Court makes copy: $1.00 per page. Self serve: $1.00 per page. Certification fee: $1.50 per cert. Payee: Clerk of Superior Court. Personal checks accepted; credit cards are not. Mail requests: SASE requested.

Superior Court - Lawrence 43 Appleton Way, Lawrence, MA 01840; 978-687-7463 x4; fax: 978-687-7869; 8AM-4:30PM. ***Civil Actions over $25,000.***

Index cards - records prior to 1985 - are found in the Salem office; criminal records also in Salem Court.

Civil Records: Access: In person, online. Both court and visitors may perform in person searches. No search fee. Required to search: name, years to search. Civil cases indexed by defendant, plaintiff, on computer since 1985; prior records on index cards in Salem office. Public use terminal has civil records back to 10 years. Online only for attorneys and law firms at www.ma-trialcourts.org/tcic/. Online results show name only.

General Information: No impounded records released. Will not fax documents. Court makes copy: $1.00 per page. Certification fee: $2.50 per cert. Payee: Clerk of Superior Court. Personal checks accepted; credit cards are not. Prepayment required.

Superior Court - Newburyport 145 High St, Newburyport, MA 01950; 978-462-4474; fax: 978-462-0432; 8-4:30PM. ***Felony, Civil over $25,000.*** www.mass.gov/courts/courtsandjudges/courts/essexsupmain.html

All finished criminal record files are in Salem and civil case records Session A in Salem, Session B in Newburyport and Session C & D in Lawrence. This court suggest to search at the main office in Salem.

Civil Records: Access: Mail, in person, online. Both court and visitors may perform in person searches. No search fee. Required to search: name, years to search. Civil cases indexed by defendant, plaintiff, on computer back to 1988. Online only for attorneys and law firms at www.ma-trialcourts.org/tcic/.

Criminal Records: Access: In person, online. Both court and visitors may perform in person searches. No search fee. Required to search: name, years to search. Online for attorneys and law firms only with registration at www.ma-trialcourts.org/tcic/.

General Information: No impounded records released. Court makes copy: $1.00 per page. Certification fee: $2.50 per cert. Payee: Clerk of Superior Court. Personal checks accepted; credit cards are not. Prepayment required.

Gloucester District Court 197 Main St, Gloucester, MA 01930; 978-283-2620 x4; fax: 978-283-8784; 8:30AM-4:30PM. ***Felony, Misdemeanor, Civil, Eviction, Small Claims.*** www.mass.gov/courts/courtsandjudges/courts/gloucesterdistrictmain.html

Includes Essex, Gloucester, and Rockport.

Civil Records: Access: Mail, in person. Visitors must perform in person searches themselves. No search fee. Required to search: name, years to search; also helpful: DOB. Civil cases indexed by defendant, plaintiff, go back to 1975. Public use terminal has civil records to 2003; results show name only.

Criminal Records: Access: In person only. Visitors must perform in person searches themselves. Required to search: name, years to search; also helpful: DOB. Criminal records go back to 1975.

General Information: No juvenile records released. Will not fax documents. Court makes copy: $1.00 per page. Certification fee: $2.50 per page. Payee: Gloucester District Court. Personal checks accepted; credit cards are not. Prepayment required.

Haverhill District Court PO Box 1389, Haverhill, MA 01831; 978-373-4151; criminal phone: x111; civil phone: x164; fax: 978-521-6886; 8:30AM-4:30PM. ***Felony, Misdemeanor, Civil, Eviction, Small Claims.*** Includes Boxford, Bradford, Georgetown, Groveland, and Haverhill.

Civil Records: Access: Phone, fax, mail, in person. Only the court performs in person searches; visitors may not. No search fee. Required to search: name, years to search. Civil cases indexed by defendant, plaintiff; index on cards from 1983. Non-active in storage. Mail turnaround time 1-2 weeks. Civil PAT available.

Criminal Records: Access: Phone, fax, mail, in person. Only the court performs in person searches; visitors may not. No search fee. Required to search: name, years to search; also helpful: DOB. Criminal records indexed on cards from 1992, computerized since 2000. Non-active in storage. Mail turnaround time 1-2 weeks. Criminal PAT available.

General Information: No juvenile, sealed cases, confidential records released. Will fax documents to local or toll-free number. Court makes copy: $1.00 per page. Certification fee: $2.50. Payee: District Court. Personal checks accepted; credit cards are not. Prepayment required. Mail requests: SASE required.

Ipswich District Court 188 State St, Newburyport, MA 01950; 978-462-2652; fax: 978-462-5641; 8:30AM-4:30PM. ***Felony, Misdemeanor, Civil, Eviction, Small Claims.***

Includes Hamilton, Ipswich, Topsfield, and Wenham.

Civil Records: Access: In person only. Visitors must perform in person searches themselves. Required to search: name, years to search. Civil cases indexed by defendant, plaintiff; index on cards and computer, small claims from 1984, civil from 1964. Civil on docket books from 1970. Public use terminal has civil records.

Criminal Records: Access: In person only. Visitors must perform in person searches themselves. Required to search: name, years to search; also helpful: DOB. Criminal records indexed on cards from 1979.

General Information: No juvenile records released. Will not fax documents. Court makes copy: $1.00 per page. Certification fee: $2.50 per page. Payee: District Court. Personal checks accepted; credit cards are not. Prepayment required.

Lawrence District Court 2 Appleton St, Lawrence, MA 01840; 978-687-7184; criminal phone: x1; civil phone: x2; criminal fax: 978-687-0794; civil fax: 978-975-3171; 8AM-4:30PM. ***Felony, Misdemeanor, Civil, Eviction, Small Claims.*** www.mass.gov/courts/courtsandjudges/courts/lawrencedistrictmain.html Includes Andover, Lawrence, Methuen, and North Andover.

Civil Records: Access: In person only. Visitors must perform in person searches themselves. Required to search: name, years to search. Civil cases indexed by defendant, plaintiff; index on cards from 1983, docket books from 1900, on computer since 1990. Public use terminal has civil records.

Criminal Records: Access: Mail, in person. Both court and visitors may perform in person searches. No search fee. Required to search: name, years to search, DOB; also helpful: address, SSN. Criminal records indexed on cards from 1983, docket books from 1900, on computer since 1999. Mail turnaround time 1-2 weeks.

General Information: No medical, police reports, impounded, juvenile records released. Will not fax documents. Court makes copy: $1.00 per page. Certification fee: $2.50 per page includes copy fee. Payee: District Court. No personal checks or credit cards accepted. Prepayment required. Mail requests: SASE requested for criminal.

Lynn District Court 580 Essex St, Lynn, MA 01901; 781-598-5200; fax: 781-598-4350; 8AM-4:30PM. ***Felony, Misdemeanor, Civil, Eviction, Small Claims.*** Includes Lynn, Marblehead, Nahant, Saugus, Swampscott.

Civil Records: Access: Mail, in person. Visitors must perform in person searches themselves. No search fee. Required to search: name, years to search. Civil cases indexed by defendant, plaintiff; index on cards from 1983, docket books from approx 1900. Records older than 15 years are difficult to find and may take longer. Public use terminal has civil records back to 2001.

Criminal Records: Access: Mail, in person. Visitors must perform in person searches themselves. No search fee. Required to search: name, years to search; also helpful: DOB, SSN. Criminal records computerized from 1997, on index cards from 1983, docket books from appx 1900. Records older than 15 years are difficult to find an. Mail turnaround 5 days.

General Information: No juvenile, impounded or sealed records released. Will not fax documents. Court makes copy: $1.00 per page. Certification fee: $2.50 per cert. Payee: Lynn District Court. Personal checks accepted; credit cards are not. Prepayment required. Mail requests: SASE required.

Newburyport District Court 22 188 State St, Newburyport, MA 01950; 978-462-2652; fax: 978-463-0438; 8:30AM-4:30PM. ***Felony, Misdemeanor, Civil, Eviction, Small Claims.***

Includes Amesbury, Merrimac, Newbury, Newburyport, Rowley, Salisbury, and West Newbury.

Civil Records: Access: Mail, in person. Both court and visitors may perform in person searches. No search fee. Required to search: name, years to search. Civil cases indexed by defendant, plaintiff; index on cards from 1983, prior archived in Worcester. Mail turnaround time 1-2 weeks. Civil PAT goes back to 1996.

Criminal Records: Access: Mail, in person. Both court and visitors may perform in person searches. No search fee. Required to search: name, years to search, DOB. Criminal records indexed on cards from 1983, prior archived in Worcester. Mail turnaround time 1-2 weeks. Criminal PAT goes back to same as civil.

General Information: No juvenile or impounded records released. Will fax documents to local or toll-free number. Court makes copy: $1.00 per page. Certification fee: $2.50 per cert. Payee: District Court. Personal checks and major credit cards accepted. Prepayment required. SASE not required.

Peabody District Court 86 1 Lowell St, Peabody, MA 01960; 978-532-3100; fax: 978-531-8524; 8:30AM-4:30PM. ***Felony, Misdemeanor, Civil, Eviction, Small Claims.*** www.mass.gov/courts/courtsandjudges/courts/peabodydistrictmain.html Includes Lynnfield, Peabody.

Civil Records: Access: In person only. Visitors must perform in person searches themselves. Required to search: name, years to search. Civil cases indexed by defendant, plaintiff, stored in office for 10 years, prior stored in basement and are difficult to find. Public use terminal has civil records back to 2003.

Criminal Records: Access: Mail, in person. Visitors must perform in person searches themselves. No search fee. Required to search: name, years to search, DOB. Criminal records stored in office for 10 years, prior stored in basement and are difficult to find. Note: Will do mail search for 1 name only.

General Information: No juvenile or impounded records released. Will not fax out documents. Court makes copy: $1.00 per page. Certification fee: $2.50 per cert. Payee: District Court. Personal checks accepted; credit cards are not. Prepayment required.

Salem District Court 36 65 Washington St, Salem, MA 01970; 978-744-1167; fax: 978-744-3211; 8:30AM-4:30PM. ***Felony, Misdemeanor, Civil, Eviction, Small Claims.*** www.mass.gov/courts/courtsandjudges/courts/salemdistrictmain.html Includes Beverly, Danvers, Manchester by the Sea, Middleton, and Salem.

Civil Records: Access: In person only. Visitors must perform in person searches themselves. Required to search: name, years to search. Civil cases indexed by defendant, plaintiff; index on cards and docket books. Note: Visitors must perform in person searches Thursday or Friday 2-4:30PM Civil PAT goes back to 2003; results show middle initial, DOB.

Criminal Records: Access: In person. Visitors must perform in person searches themselves. Required to search: name, years to search, DOB, SSN. Criminal records indexed on cards and docket books. Note: In person criminal searches on Thursday or Friday 2-4:30PM. Criminal PAT goes back to same as civil. PAT results show middle initial, DOB.

General Information: No juvenile or impounded records released. Will fax documents to local or toll-free number. Court makes copy: $1.00 per page. Certification fee: $2.50. Payee: District Court. Personal checks accepted; credit cards are not..

Northeast Housing Court 2 Appleton St, Fenton Judicial Ctr, Lawrence, MA 01840; 978-689-7833; 8:30AM-4:30PM. ***Eviction, Misdemeanor, Code Violations, Housing, Small Claims.***

Includes housing code, real estate small claims and eviction cases for Middlesex County towns Acton, Ayer, Billerica, Chelmsford, Dracut, Dunstable, Groton, Lowell, Pepperell, Shirley, Stow, Tewksbury, Tyngsboro, Westford; also see district courts.

Probate & Family Court 36 Federal St, Salem, MA 01970; 978-744-1020; fax: 978-741-2957; 8AM-4:30PM. ***Probate.***

Franklin County

Superior Court PO Box 1573, 425 Main St, Greenfield, MA 01302; 413-774-5535; criminal fax: 413-774-4770; civil fax: same; 8:30AM-4:30PM. ***Felony, Civil Actions over $25,000.***

Civil Records: Access: Fax, in person, online. Both court and visitors may perform in person searches. No search fee. Required to search: name, years to search. Civil cases indexed by defendant, plaintiff, in files; on computer back 15 years. Civil PAT goes back to 15 years. PAT results show name only. Online only for attorneys and law firms at www.ma-trialcourts.org/tcic/.

Criminal Records: Access: Fax, in person, online. Visitors must perform in person searches themselves. No search fee. Required to search: name, years to search, DOB. Criminal records in files; on computer back 8 years. Criminal PAT goes back to 8 years.PAT results show name, DOB. Online for attorneys and law firms only with registration at www.ma-trialcourts.org/tcic/.

General Information: No impounded or juvenile records released. Will fax documents with toll-free number. Court makes copy: $1.00 per page. Certification fee: $2.50 per page attested includes copy fee. What is known as a certified copy in most states is known as a attested copy in Mass. What Mass. calls a single page "Certificate" with gold seal is $20.00. Payee: Franklin County Superior Court. Personal checks accepted; credit cards are not. Prepayment required.

Greenfield District Court 425 Main St, Greenfield, MA 01301; 413-774-5533; probate phone: 413-774-7011; fax: 413-774-5328; 8:30AM-4:30PM. ***Felony, Misdemeanor, Civil, Eviction, Small Claims.*** Includes Ashfield, Bernardston, Buckland, Charlemont, Colrain, Conway, Deerfield, Gill, Greenfield, Hawley, Heath, Leyden, Monroe, Montague, Northfield, Rowe, Shelburne, Sunderland, and Whately.

Civil Records: Access: In person only. Both court and visitors may perform in person searches. No search fee. Required to search: name, years to search. Civil cases indexed by defendant, plaintiff; index on docket books or index cards; on computer back to 1998. Public use terminal has civil records back to 2004. PAT results show name only.

Criminal Records: Access: In person only. Both court and visitors may perform in person searches. No search fee. Required to search: name, years to search, DOB. Criminal docket on books or index cards; on computer back to 1994.

General Information: No juvenile records released. Will not fax documents. Court makes copy: $1.00 per page. Certification fee: $2.50. Payee: Greenfield District Court. Personal checks accepted; credit cards are not. Prepayment required.

Orange District Court #42 One Court Square, Orange, MA 01364; 978-544-8277; fax: 978-544-5204; 8:30AM-4:30PM. ***Felony, Misdemeanor, Civil, Eviction, Small Claims.***
www.mass.gov/courts/courtsandjudges/courts/orangedistrictmain.html
Includes Athol, Erving, New Salem, Orange, Warwick, and Wendell, Shutesbury, Leverett.

Civil Records: Access: Phone, mail, in person. Both court and visitors may perform in person searches. No search fee. Required to search: name, years to search. Civil cases indexed by defendant, plaintiff; index in docket books from 1975. Mail turnaround 1-2 weeks. Public use terminal has civil records.

Criminal Records: Access: Phone, mail, in person. Only the court performs in person searches; visitors may not. No search fee. Required to search: name, years to search. Criminal docket on books from 1975. Mail turnaround time 1-2 weeks.

General Information: No juvenile records released. Will fax documents to local or toll-free number. Court makes copy: $1.00 per page. Certification fee: $2.50 per page. Payee: District Court. No personal checks accepted. Visa/MC accepted. Prepayment required.

Probate & Family Court PO Box 590, 425 Main St, Greenfield, MA 01302; 413-774-7011; fax: 413-774-3829; 8AM-4:30PM. ***Probate.***

Western Housing Court, MA; ***Eviction, Misdemeanor (Code Violations), Small Claims.*** See Hampden County Western Housing Court for many housing code cases, real estate-related small claims and eviction cases for this county; also see district courts in this county.

Hampden County

Superior Court 50 State St, PO Box 559, Springfield, MA 01102-0559; criminal: 413-735-6017; civil: 413-735-6016; fax: 413-737-1611; 8:30AM-4:30PM. ***Felony, Civil over $25,000.***

Civil Records: Access: Phone, mail, in person, online. Both court and visitors may perform in person searches. No search fee. Required to search: name, years to search. Civil cases indexed by defendant, plaintiff, on computer from 1989 to present; prior on index cards from 1930s, books from 1812. Civil PAT goes back to 1981.

Criminal Records: Access: In person, online. Visitors must perform in person searches themselves. Required to search: name, years to search. Criminal records computerized from 1992 to present; prior on index cards from 1930s. Criminal PAT goes back to 1990.

General Information: Online only for attorneys and law firms at www.ma-trialcourts.org/tcic/. No impounded case records released. Will fax documents. Court makes copy: $1.00 per page. Certification fee: $2.50. Payee: Clerk of Superior Court. Personal checks accepted; credit cards are not. Prepayment required. Mail requests: SASE requested for civil.

Chicopee District Court #20 30 Church St, Chicopee, MA 01020; 413-598-0099; fax: 413-594-6187; 8:30AM-4:30PM. ***Felony, Misdemeanor, Civil, Eviction, Small Claims.***

Civil Records: Access: Phone, mail, in person. Both court and visitors may perform in person searches. No search fee. Required to search: name, years to search. Civil cases indexed by defendant, plaintiff; index on cards from 1983, docket books to 1960; computerized since 2001. Public use terminal has civil records back to 2004.

Criminal Records: Access: In person. Visitors must perform in person searches themselves. Required to search: name, years to search, DOB. Criminal records indexed on cards from 1983, docket books to 1900.

General Information: No juvenile records released. Will not fax documents. Court makes copy: $1.00 per page. Certification fee: $2.50 per cert. Payee: District Court. Personal checks accepted; credit cards are not. Mail requests: SASE required for civil.

Holyoke District Court 20 Court Sq, Holyoke, MA 01041-5075; 413-538-9710; fax: 413-533-7165; 9AM-4:30PM. ***Felony, Misdemeanor, Civil, Eviction, Small Claims.***

Civil Records: Access: Phone, mail, fax, in person. Both court and visitors may perform in person searches. No search fee. Required to search: name, years to search. Civil cases indexed by defendant, plaintiff; index on cards and docket books back to 1989. Mail turnaround 1-2 weeks. Public terminal has civil records back to 1989. PAT results show name only.

Criminal Records: Access: Fax, mail, in person. Only the court performs in person searches; visitors may not. No search fee. Required to search: name, years to search, DOB or SSN, signed release. Criminal records indexed on cards and docket books since 1976; on computer back to 1986. Mail turnaround time 1-2 weeks.

General Information: No juvenile, sealed records released. Will fax documents to local or toll-free number. Court makes copy: $1.00 per page. Certification fee: $2.50. Payee: District Court. Only cashiers checks and money orders accepted. No credit cards accepted. Prepayment required. Mail requests: SASE requested.

Palmer District Court 235 Sykes St, Ste 3, Palmer, MA 01069; 413-283-8916; fax: 413-283-6775; 8:30AM-4:30PM. ***Felony, Misdemeanor, Civil, Eviction, Small Claims.***
www.mass.gov/courts/courtsandjudges/courts/palmerdistrictmain.html
Includes Ludlow, Monson, Wilbraham, Palmer, Wales, Brimfield, Holland, and Hampden.

Civil Records: Access: In person only. Visitors must perform in person searches themselves. Required to search: name, years to search. Civil cases indexed by defendant, plaintiff; index on cards back to 1982. Public use terminal has civil records back to 2002.

Criminal Records: Access: In person only. Visitors must perform in person searches themselves. Required to search: name, years to search. Criminal records indexed on cards for 10 years; on computer back to 1995.

General Information: No sealed or juvenile records released. Will not fax out documents. Court makes copy: $1.00 per page. Certification fee: $2.50 per cert. Payee: Palmer District Court. Personal checks accepted; credit cards are not. Prepayment required.

Springfield District Court PO Box 2421, 50 State St, Springfield, MA 01101-2421; 413-748-8600; criminal phone: 413-748-8694; civil phone: 413-748-8659; criminal fax: 413-747-4842; civil fax: 413-747-4841; 8:30AM-4:30PM. ***Felony, Misdemeanor, Civil, Eviction, Small Claims.***
www.mass.gov/courts/courtsandjudges/courts/springfielddistrictmain.html
Includes Agawam, East Longmeadow, Longmeadow, Springfield, and West Springfield.

Civil Records: Access: In person only. Visitors must perform in person searches themselves. Required to search: name, years to search. Civil cases indexed by defendant, plaintiff; index on cards; computerized records since 7/03, small claims since 2001.

Criminal Records: Access: In person. Visitors must perform in person searches themselves. Required to search: name, years to search. Criminal records indexed on cards; computerized records since 1992.

General Information: No sealed, expunged, or adoption records released. Will not fax out documents. Court makes copy: $1.00 per page. Certification fee: $2.50. Payee: District Court. Business checks accepted. Visa/MC accepted.

Westfield District Court 224 Elm St, Westfield, MA 01085; 413-568-8946; fax: 413-568-4863; 8AM-4PM. ***Felony, Misdemeanor, Civil, Eviction, Small Claims.***
Includes Blandford, Chester, Granville, Montgomery, Russell, Southwick, Tolland, and Westfield.

Civil Records: Access: Mail, in person. Both court and visitors may perform in person searches. No search fee. Required to search: name, years to search. Civil cases indexed by defendant, plaintiff; index on cards and in files. Public use terminal has civil records back to 2004.

Criminal Records: Access: In person only. Both court and visitors may perform in person searches. No search fee. Required to search: name, years to search. Criminal records indexed on cards and in files.

General Information: No sealed or juvenile records released. Will not fax documents. Court makes copy: $1.00 per page. Cert fee: $2.50 per cert. Payee: District Court. Cashiers checks and money orders accepted. Visa/MC accepted. Prepayment required.

Probate & Family Court 50 State St, Springfield, MA 01103-0559; 413-748-7746; fax: 413-781-5605; 8AM-4:25PM. ***Probate.***

Western Housing Court PO Box 559, 01102, 37 Elm St, 01103, Springfield, MA; 413-748-7838; fax: 413-732-4607; 8:30-4:30PM. ***Civil, Eviction, Misdemeanor (Code Violations), Small Claims.***
Includes many housing code cases, real estate-related small claims and eviction cases for counties of Berkshire, Franklin, Hampden, and Hampshire; also see district courts.

Hampshire County

Superior Court PO Box 1119, Northampton, MA 01061; 413-584-5810 x331; probate phone: 413-586-8500; fax: 413-586-8217; 9AM-4PM. ***Felony, Civil Actions over $25,000.***

Civil Records: Access: Mail, fax, in person, online. Both court and visitors may perform in person searches. No search fee. Required to search: name, years to search. Civil cases indexed by defendant, plaintiff, in files, index cards from 1800s; on computer back to 2000. Mail turnaround time 1 week. Civil PAT goes back to 2000. Results include name and docket number. Online only for attorneys and law firms at www.ma-trialcourts.org/tcic/.

Criminal Records: Access: Mail, fax, in person, online. Both court and visitors may perform in person searches. No search fee. Required to search: name, years to search. Criminal records in files, index cards from 1800s; on computer back to 1983. Mail turnaround time 1 week. Criminal PAT goes back to 1983. Results include name and docket number. Online for attorneys and law firms only with registration at www.ma-trialcourts.org/tcic/.

General Information: Online identifiers in results same as on public terminal. No impounded case records released. Will fax documents to local or toll free line. Court makes copy: $1.00 per page. Certification fee: $20.00. Payee: Clerk of Superior Court. Personal checks accepted; credit cards are not. Prepayment required. SASE not required.

Belchertown/Hadley District Court 205 State St, Route 202, Belchertown, MA 01007; 413-323-4056; criminal phone: x2248; civil phone: x2263; fax: 413-323-6803; 8:30AM-4:30PM. ***Felony, Misdemeanor, Civil, Eviction, Small Claims.***

Formerly Hadley Dist. Ct. Includes Amherst, Belchertown, Granby, Hadley, South Hadley, Pelham, Ware, all the MDC Quabbin Reservoir and Watershed Area. Includes cases formerly heard at the closed court in Ware.

Civil Records: Access: Fax, mail, in person. Both court and visitors may perform in person searches. No search fee. Required to search: name, years to search. Civil cases indexed by defendant, plaintiff; index on cards or docket books back to 1960. Some records sent to archives in Worcester. Note: In person searchers may use computer only. Mail turnaround time 1-2 weeks. Public use terminal has civil records back to 1993.

Criminal Records: Access: Fax, mail, in person. Only the court performs in person searches; visitors may not. No search fee. Required to search: name, years to search, DOB, SSN. Criminal records indexed on cards or docket books back to 1920; on computer back to 1996. Some records sent to archives in Worcester. Mail turnaround time 1-2 weeks.

General Information: No sealed, impounded, confidential or juvenile records released. Will not fax documents. Court makes copy: $1.00 per page, self serve same. Certification fee: $2.50. Payee: Eastern Hampshire District Court. Personal checks accepted. Credit cards accepted in person. Prepayment required. Mail requests: SASE helpful.

Northampton District Court Courthouse, 15 Gothic St, Northampton, MA 01060; 413-584-7776; criminal phone: 413-584-7400; civil phone: 413-584-7400; criminal fax: 413-586-1980; civil fax: 413-584-9479; 8:30AM-4:30PM. ***Felony, Misdemeanor, Civil, Eviction, Small Claims.***

Includes Chesterfield, Cummington, Easthampton, Goshen, Hatfield, Huntington, Middlefield, Northampton, Plainfield, Southampton, Westhampton, Williamsburg, and Worthington.

Civil Records: Access: Fax, mail, in person. Both court and visitors may perform in person searches. No search fee. Required to search: name, years to search, address. Civil cases indexed by defendant, plaintiff; index on cards and docket books back to 1970, computerized since 5/02. Mail turnaround time 1-2 weeks. Public use terminal has civil records back to 2001. PAT results show name only.

Criminal Records: Access: Fax, mail, in person. Both court and visitors may perform in person searches. No search fee. Required to search: name, years to search, DOB, SSN. Criminal docket on books go back to 1970, on computer since 1997. Mail turnaround time 1-2 weeks.

General Information: No CHINS-care & protection, show cause-mental health records released. No fee to fax documents. Court makes copy: $1.00 per page, self serve same. Certification fee: $2.50 per page. Payee: District Court. No personal checks. Visa/MC pr debit cards accepted in person only. Prepayment required. Mail requests: SASE requested.

Probate & Family Court 33 King St #3, Northampton, MA 01060-3297; 413-586-8500; fax: 413-584-1132; 8:30AM-4PM. ***Probate.***
www.hampshireprobate.com/

Western Housing Court, MA; ***Eviction, Misdemeanor (Code Violations), Small Claims.***

See Hampden County Western Housing Court for many housing code cases, real estate-related small claims and eviction cases for this county; also see district courts in this county.

Middlesex County

Superior Court - Lowell 360 Gorham St, Lowell, MA 01852; 978-453-0201; criminal phone: x259; civil phone: x280; 8:30AM-4:30PM. ***Felony, Civil Actions over $25,000.***
www.mass.gov/courts/courtsandjudges/courts/middsupmain.html

Civil Records: Access: Mail, in person, online. Both court and visitors may perform in person searches. No search fee. Required to search: name, years to search. Civil cases indexed by defendant, plaintiff, on computer since 1990; prior records kept at East Cambridge Middlesex Superior Court, 40 Thorndike, Cambridge, MA 02141. Mail turnaround time 1-2 days. Online only for attorneys and law firms at www.ma-trialcourts.org/tcic/welcome.jsp.

Criminal Records: Access: Mail, in person, online. Both court and visitors may perform in person searches. No search fee. Required to search: name, years to search. Criminal records on computer since 1990; prior records kept at East Cambridge Middlesex Superior Court, 40 Thorndike, Cambridge, MA 02141. Mail turnaround time 1-2 days. Online for attorneys and law firms only with registration at www.ma-trialcourts.org/tcic/welcome.jsp

General Information: Will not fax documents. Court makes copy: $1.00 per page. Certification fee: $2.50 per page. Payee: Clerk of Superior Court. Personal checks accepted; credit cards are not. Prepayment required.

Superior Court - Woburn 200 TradeCenter, Woburn, MA 01801; 781-939-2700/2800; criminal phone: x4; civil phone: x5; fax: 617-788-8137; 8:30AM-4:30PM. ***Felony, Civil Actions over $25,000.***
www.mass.gov/courts/courtsandjudges/courts/middsupmain.html

Up until 3/17/2008 this court was located in East Cambridge.

Civil Records: Access: Mail, in person, online. Both court and visitors may perform in person searches. No search fee. Required to search: name, years to search; also helpful: address. Civil cases indexed by defendant, plaintiff, on computer from 1986, rest on card indexes to 1986. Mail turnaround time 3-5 days. Civil PAT goes back to 1991. Court is planning to have public internet access. Online for attorneys and law firms only with registration at www.ma-trialcourts.org/tcic/welcome.jsp.

Criminal Records: Access: Mail, in person, online. Both court and visitors may perform in person searches. No search fee. Required to search: name, years to search; also helpful: address. Criminal records computerized from 1991, rest on card indexes to 1986. Mail turnaround time 3-5 days. Criminal PAT goes back to 1991.PAT results show name, DOB. Court plans to have public internet access for attorneys and law firms only with registration at www.ma-trialcourts.org/tcic/welcome.jsp.

General Information: No impounded or those restricted by statute records released. Will not fax documents. Court makes copy: $1.00 per page. Self serve: $.25 per page. Certification fee: $2.50 per page. Payee: Clerk of Superior Court. Personal checks accepted; credit cards are not. Prepayment required.

Ayer District Court 25 E Main St, Ayer, MA 01432; 978-772-2100; fax: 978-772-5345; 8:30AM-4:30PM. ***Felony, Misdemeanor, Civil, Eviction, Small Claims.***
www.mass.gov/courts/courtsandjudges/courts/ayerdistrictmain.html

Includes Ayer, Ashby, Boxborough, Dunstable, Groton, Littleton, Pepperell, Shirley, Townsend, Westford and Devens Regional Enterprise Zone.

Civil Records: Access: Mail, in person. Both court and visitors may perform in person searches. No search fee. Required to search: name, years to search, DOB. Civil cases indexed by defendant, plaintiff; index on cards from 1977 to present; only required to keep records 20 years. Mail turnaround time 1-2 weeks. Public use terminal has civil records back to limited number of years. PAT results show name only.

Criminal Records: Access: Mail, in person. Both court and visitors may perform in person searches. No search fee. Required to search: name, years to search, DOB. Criminal records indexed on cards from 1977 to 1995, computerized 1996 forward; Only required to keep records 10 years. Mail turnaround time 1-2 weeks. No criminal records on public access terminal; only civil and small claims.

General Information: Juvenile records not released. Will not fax documents. Court makes copy: $1.50 per page. Certification fee: $2.50 per page. Payee: Ayer District Court. Personal checks accepted. Major credit cards accepted in person only. Prepayment required. Mail requests: SASE required.

Cambridge District Court 52 PO Box 338, 40 Thorndike St, East Cambridge, MA 02141; 617-494-4095; criminal phone: x134; civil phone: x127; fax: 617-494-9129; 8:30AM-4:30PM. ***Felony, Misdemeanor, Civil, Eviction, Small Claims.***
www.mass.gov/courts/courtsandjudges/courts/cambridgedistrictmain.html

Includes Cambridge, Arlington, Belmont.

Civil Records: Access: In person only. Visitors must perform in person searches themselves. Required to search: name, years to search. Civil cases indexed by defendant, plaintiff; index on cards or docket books. State law requires records be retained 10 years.

Criminal Records: Access: In person only. Visitors must perform in person searches themselves. Required to search: name, years to search, DOB. Criminal records indexed on cards or docket books; computerized records since 1997. State law requires records be retained 10 years.

General Information: No sealed or juvenile records released. Will fax documents to local or toll free line. Court makes copy: $1.00 per page. Certification fee: $2.50 per cert. Payee: District Court. Personal checks accepted. Major credit cards accepted but machine does not always work. Prepayment required.

Concord District Court 47 305 Walden St, Concord, MA 01742; 978-369-0500; fax: 978-371-2945; 8:30AM-4:30PM. ***Felony, Misdemeanor, Civil, Eviction, Small Claims.***
www.mass.gov/courts/courtsandjudges/courts/concorddistrictmain.html

Includes Concord, Carlisle, Lincoln, Lexington, Bedford, Acton, Maynard, Stow and State PD.

Civil Records: Access: Mail, in person. Visitors must perform in person searches themselves. No search fee. Required to search: name, years to search; also helpful: address. Civil cases indexed by defendant, plaintiff, on computer from 1991, index cards and books from 1950, archived from 1643. Note: In person searches performed from 10AM-4PM only. Public use terminal has civil records.

Criminal Records: Access: Mail, in person. Visitors must perform in person searches themselves. No search fee. Required to search: name, years to search; also helpful: address, DOB, SSN. Criminal records index printed from computer from 1998, index cards and books from 1950, archived from 1643. Note: In person searches performed from 10AM-4PM only. Mail turnaround time 1-2 weeks.

General Information: No impounded files released. Will not fax documents. Court makes copy: $1.00 per page. Certification fee: $2.50 per cert. Payee:

Commonwealth of Massachusetts. Personal checks accepted; credit cards are not. Prepayment required. Mail requests: SASE requested.

Framingham District Court PO Box 1969, 600 Concord St, Framingham, MA 01701; 508-875-7461; fax: 508-626-2503; 8:30AM-4:30PM. ***Felony, Misdemeanor, Civil, Eviction, Small Claims.*** www.mass.gov/courts/courtsandjudges/courts/framinghamdistrictmain.html Includes Ashland, Framingham, Holliston, Hopkinton, Sudbury, and Wayland.

Civil Records: Access: Mail, fax, in person. Both court and visitors may perform in person searches. No search fee. Required to search: name, years to search. Civil cases indexed by defendant, plaintiff; index on cards or docket books back to 1900; on computer back to 1986. Note: Special form required for mail request. Mail turnaround time 7 days. Civil PAT goes back to 2002. PAT results show name only.

Criminal Records: Access: Mail, in person, fax. Both court and visitors may perform in person searches. No search fee. Required to search: name, years to search. Criminal records indexed on cards or docket books back to 1900; on computer back to 1986. Note: Special form required for mail request. Mail turnaround time 7 days. Criminal PAT goes back to 2002.PAT results show name, DOB. Terminal results include SSN.

General Information: No sealed, expunged or juvenile records released. Will not fax documents. Court makes copy: $1.00 per page. Certification fee: $2.50 per page. Payee: District Court. Only cashiers checks and money orders accepted. Visa/MC accepted. Prepayment required. Mail requests: SASE requested.

Lowell District Court 41 Hurd St, Lowell, MA 01852; 978-459-4101; criminal phone: X204; civil phone: x235; fax: 978-937-2486; 8:30AM-4:30PM. ***Felony, Misdemeanor, Civil, Eviction, Small Claims.*** www.mass.gov/courts/courtsandjudges/courts/lowelldistrictmain.html Includes Billerica, Chelmsford, Dracut, Lowell, Tewksbury, and Tyngsboro.

Civil Records: Access: In person only. Visitors must perform in person searches themselves. Required to search: name, years to search. Civil cases indexed by defendant, plaintiff; index on cards or docket books. Records retained for 10 years. Public use terminal has civil records.

Criminal Records: Access: In person. Visitors must perform in person searches themselves. Required to search: name, years to search, DOB. Criminal records indexed on cards or docket books. Records retained for 10 years.

General Information: No impounded records released. Will fax documents. Court makes copy: $1.00 per page. Cert fee: $2.50. Payee: District Court, Lowell Division. Business checks accepted. Major credit cards accepted. Prepayment required.

Malden District Court 89 Summer St., Malden, MA 02148; 781-322-7500; criminal phone: x3; civil phone: x4; fax: 781-322-0169; 8:30AM-4:30PM. ***Felony, Misdemeanor, Civil, Eviction, Small Claims.*** www.mass.gov/courts/courtsandjudges/courts/maldendistrictmain.html

Includes Malden, Melrose, Everett, and Wakefield.

Civil Records: Access: Mail, fax, In person. Only the court performs in person searches; visitors may not. No search fee. Required to search: name, years to search. Civil cases indexed by defendant, plaintiff; index on cards or docket books back to 1970; on computer back to 1992. Mail turnaround time 3-5 days. Public use terminal has civil records back to 2001.

Criminal Records: Access: In person only. Both court and visitors may perform in person searches. Required to search: name, years to search, DOB. Criminal records indexed on cards or docket books back to 1970; on computer back to 1999.

General Information: No juvenile records released. Will not fax documents. Court makes copy: $1.00 per page. Certification fee: $2.50 per doc. Payee: District Court. Personal checks accepted; credit cards are not. Prepayment required.

Marlborough District Court 21 45 Williams St, Marlborough, MA 01752; 508-485-3700; fax: 508-485-1575; 8:30AM-4:30PM. ***Felony, Misdemeanor, Civil, Eviction, Small Claims.*** www.mass.gov/courts/courtsandjudges/courts/marlboroughdistrictmain.html

Includes Marlborough and Hudson.

Civil Records: Access: Phone, mail, in person. Both court and visitors may perform in person searches. No search fee. Required to search: name, years to search. Civil cases indexed by defendant, plaintiff; index on cards or docket books. State law requires records be retained for 10 years. Mail turnaround time 1-2 weeks.

Criminal Records: Access: Phone, mail, in person. Both court and visitors may perform in person searches. No search fee. Required to search: name, years to search, DOB. Criminal records indexed on cards or docket books. State law requires records be retained for 10 years. Mail turnaround time 1-2 weeks.

General Information: No juvenile records released. Court makes copy: $1.00 per page. Certification fee: $2.50 per cert. Payee: District Court. Personal checks accepted; credit cards are not. Prepayment required.

Natick District Court 117 E Central St, Natick, MA 01760; 508-653-4332 x1, 653-8100; fax: 508-655-8196; 8:30AM-4:30PM. ***Felony, Misdemeanor, Civil, Eviction, Small Claims.*** www.mass.gov/courts/courtsandjudges/courts/natickdistrictmain.html

Includes Natick and Sherborn.

Civil Records: Access: In person only. Visitors must perform in person searches themselves. Required to search: name, years to search. Civil cases indexed by defendant, plaintiff; index on cards and docket books, back for 10 years.

Criminal Records: Access: In person only. Visitors must perform in person searches themselves. Required to search: name, years to search, DOB. Criminal records indexed on cards and docket books, back for 10 years.

General Information: No juvenile records released. Will not fax documents. Court makes copy: $1.00 per page. Certification fee: $2.50 per cert. Payee: District Court. Personal checks accepted. Visa/MC accepted. Prepayment required.

Newton District Court 1309 Washington St, West Newton, MA 02141; 617-244-3600; fax: 617-243-7291; 8:30AM-4:30PM. ***Felony, Misdemeanor, Civil, Eviction, Small Claims.*** www.state.ma.us/courts/courtsandjudges/courts/newtondistrictmain.html

Civil Records: Access: Mail, fax, in person. Both court and visitors may perform in person searches. No search fee. Required to search: name, years to search. Civil cases indexed by defendant, plaintiff; index on cards back to 1900. Mail turnaround time 1 week. Public use terminal has civil records back to 2002. PAT results show name only.

Criminal Records: Access: Mail, fax, in person. Both court and visitors may perform in person searches. No search fee. Required to search: name, years to search. Criminal records indexed in books back to 1900. Mail turnaround time 1 week.

General Information: No juvenile, (some) 209-A cases or mental health records released. Will not fax documents. Court makes copy: $1.00 per page. Certification fee: $2.50 per cert. Payee: District Court of Newton. Personal checks and major credit cards accepted. Prepayment required.

Somerville District Court 175 Fellsway, Somerville, MA 02145; 617-666-8000; fax: 617-776-2111; 8:30AM-4:30PM. ***Felony, Misdemeanor, Civil, Eviction, Small Claims.*** www.mass.gov/courts/courtsandjudges/courts/somervilledistrictmain.html

Includes Medford and Somerville.

Civil Records: Access: In person only. Visitors must perform in person searches themselves. Required to search: name, years to search. Civil cases indexed by defendant, plaintiff; index on cards or docket books. State law requires records be retained for 20 years.

Criminal Records: Access: In person only. Visitors must perform in person searches themselves. Required to search: name, years to search, DOB. Criminal records on computer since 1997; prior records on index cards or docket books. State law requires records be retained for 20 years.

General Information: No juvenile or impounded records released. Will not fax documents. Court makes copy: $1.00 per page. Certification fee: $2.50 per cert. Payee: District Court. Personal checks accepted; credit cards are not. Prepayment required.

Waltham District Court 51 38 Linden St, Waltham, MA 02452; 781-894-4500 x4; 8:30AM-4:30PM. ***Felony, Misdemeanor, Civil, Eviction, Small Claims.*** www.mass.gov/courts/courtsandjudges/courts/walthamdistrictmain.html

Includes Waltham, Watertown, and Weston.

Civil Records: Access: Mail, in person. Both court and visitors may perform in person searches. No search fee. Required to search: name, years to search. Civil cases indexed by defendant, plaintiff; index on cards and docket books, back for 10 years. Mail turnaround time 1 week. Public use terminal available.

Criminal Records: Access: Mail, in person. Both court and visitors may perform in person searches. No search fee. Required to search: name, years to search; also helpful: DOB. Criminal records indexed on cards and docket books, back for 10 years. Mail turnaround time 1 week. Public use terminal available.

General Information: No juvenile records released. Court makes copy: $1.00 per page. Certification fee: $2.50 per cert. Payee: District Court. Personal checks accepted; credit cards are not. Prepayment required. Mail requests: SASE required.

Woburn District Court 53 30 Pleasant St, Woburn, MA 01801; 781-935-4000; fax: 781-933-4404; 8:30AM-4:30PM. ***Felony, Misdemeanor, Civil, Eviction, Small Claims.*** www.mass.gov/courts/courtsandjudges/courts/woburndistrictmain.html

Includes Burlington, North Reading, Reading, Stoneham, Wilmington, Winchester, and Woburn.

Civil Records: Access: Mail, fax, in person. Both court and visitors may perform in person searches. No search fee. Required to search: name, years to search. Civil cases indexed by defendant, plaintiff; index on cards, computer listing or docket books back 30 years. Mail turnaround time 1-2 weeks. Public use terminal has civil records back to 1996. PAT results show name only.

Criminal Records: Access: Mail, fax, in person. Both court and visitors may perform in person searches. No search fee. Required to search: name, years to search; also helpful: DOB. Criminal records indexed on cards, computer listing or docket books back 30 years. Mail turnaround time 1-2 weeks.

General Information: No statutorily non-public records released. Will not fax documents. Court makes copy: $1.00 per page. Certification fee: $2.50 per cert. Payee: District Court. Personal checks accepted. Visa/MC accepted. Prepayment required. Mail requests: SASE required.

Probate & Family Court 208 Cambridge St, PO Box 410480, East Cambridge, MA 02141-0005; 617-768-5800; fax: 617-225-0781; 8AM-4:30PM. ***Probate.***

Nantucket County

Superior Court PO Box 967, Nantucket, MA 02554; 508-228-2559; fax: 508-228-3725; 8:30AM-4PM. ***Felony, Civil Actions over $25,000.***

Civil Records: Access: Phone, fax, mail, in person, online. Both court and visitors may perform in person searches. No search fee. Required to search: name, years to search. Civil cases indexed by defendant, plaintiff; index on docket books from 1762. Mail turnaround time 1 week. Online only for attorneys and law firms at www.ma-trialcourts.org/tcic/.

Criminal Records: Access: Phone, fax, mail, in person, online. Both court and visitors may perform in person searches. No search fee. Required to search: name, years to search. Criminal records indexed in books from 1762. Mail turnaround time 1

week. Online for attorneys and law firms only with registration at www.ma-trialcourts.org/tcic/.
General Information: No impounded records released. No fee to fax documents; in-state faxing only. Court makes copy: $1.00 per page, self serve same. Certification fee: $2.50 per cert. Payee: Nantucket Superior Court. Personal checks accepted; credit cards are not. Prepayment required. Mail requests: SASE required.

Nantucket District Court 16 Broad St, PO Box 1800, Nantucket, MA 02554; 508-228-0460; fax: 508-325-5759; 8AM-4PM. ***Felony, Misdemeanor, Civil, Eviction, Small Claims.***
Civil Records: Access: In person only. Visitors must perform in person searches themselves. Required to search: name, years to search. Civil cases indexed by defendant, plaintiff; index on cards or docket books. State law requires records be retained for 10 years. Public use terminal has civil records back to 2004. PAT results show name only.
Criminal Records: Access: In person only. Visitors must perform in person searches themselves. Required to search: name, years to search. Criminal records indexed on cards or docket books back to 1917. State law requires records be retained for 10 years.
General Information: Will not fax documents. Court makes copy: $1.00 per page. Certification fee: $2.50 per cert. Payee: Nantucket District Court. Personal checks accepted; credit cards are not.

Probate & Family Court PO Box 1116, 16 Broad St, Nantucket, MA 02554; 508-228-2669; fax: 508-228-3662; 8AM-4PM. ***Probate.***
Send all mail to the PO Box.

Norfolk County

Superior Court 650 High St, Dedham, MA 02026; 781-326-1600; criminal phone: x2; civil phone: x1; criminal fax: 781-320-9726; civil fax: 781-326-3871; 8:30AM-4:30PM. ***Felony, Civil Actions over $25,000.***
www.mass.gov/courts/courtsandjudges/courts/norfsupmain.html
Civil Records: Access: Phone, mail, in person, online. Both court and visitors may perform in person searches. No search fee. Required to search: name, years to search. Civil cases indexed by defendant, plaintiff; index on docket books from 1900, on computer back to 9/2000. Mail turnaround time 1 week; 1-2 days for criminal phone in requests. Civil PAT goes back to 9/2000. PAT results show middle initial, DOB. Online only for attorneys and law firms at www.ma-trialcourts.org/tcic/.
Criminal Records: Access: In person, online. Visitors must perform in person searches themselves. Required to search: name, years to search; also helpful: address, DOB, SSN. Criminal records indexed in books from 1900; on computer back to 9/2000. Criminal PAT goes back to same as civil. PAT results show middle initial, DOB. Online for attorneys and law firms only with registration at www.ma-trialcourts.org/tcic/.
General Information: No impounded records released. No one may view a file of a sex-related crime without authorization from a judge. Will not fax documents. Court makes copy: $1.00 per page. Self serve: $.50 per page. Certification fee: $2.50 per cert. Payee: Clerk of Superior Court. Personal checks accepted for copies only. No credit cards accepted. Prepayment required. SASE not required.

Brookline District Court 360 Washington St, Brookline, MA 02445; 617-232-4660; fax: 617-739-0734; 8:30AM-4:30PM. ***Felony, Misdemeanor, Civil, Eviction, Small Claims.***
Civil Records: Access: In person only. Visitors must perform in person searches themselves. Required to search: name, years to search. Civil cases indexed by defendant, plaintiff; index on cards and docket books back for 10 years.
Criminal Records: Access: In person only. Visitors must perform in person searches themselves. Required to search: name, years to search; also helpful: DOB. Criminal records indexed on cards and docket books back for 10 years.
General Information: No sealed case records released. Will not fax documents. Court makes copy: $1.00 per page. Certification fee: $2.50. Payee: Brookline District Court. Personal checks accepted. Visa/MC accepted in person only. Prepayment required.

Dedham District Court 631 High St, Dedham, MA 02026; 781-329-4777; fax: 781-329-8640; 8:15AM-4:30PM. ***Felony, Misdemeanor, Civil, Eviction, Small Claims.***
Includes Dedham, Dover, Medfield, Needham, Norwood, Wellesley, and Westwood.
Civil Records: Access: In person only. Visitors must perform in person searches themselves. Required to search: name, years to search. Civil cases indexed by defendant, plaintiff, on computer since 1997, and on index cards or docket books prior to that. State law requires records be retained for 10 years.
Criminal Records: Access: In person only. Visitors must perform in person searches themselves. Required to search: name, years to search. Criminal records on computer since 1997, and on index cards or docket books prior to that. State law requires records be retained for 10 years. Note: Public access is available after 10:30AM.
General Information: No juvenile records released. Court makes copy: $1.00 per page. Certification fee: $2.50 per cert. Payee: District Court. Personal checks accepted. Credit cards accepted. Prepayment required.

Quincy District Court One Dennis Ryan Parkway, Quincy, MA 02169; 617-471-1650; fax: 617-472-1924; 8:30AM-4:30PM. ***Felony, Misdemeanor, Civil, Eviction, Small Claims.***
Includes Braintree, Cohasset, Holbrook, Quincy, Randolph, and Weymouth, Quincy. No fax search requests accepted at this court.
Civil Records: Access: In person only. Visitors must perform in person searches themselves. Required to search: name, years to search. Civil cases indexed by defendant, plaintiff; index on cards or docket books. State law requires records be retained for 10 years.
Criminal Records: Access: In person only. Visitors must perform in person searches themselves. Required to search: name, years to search; also helpful: DOB. Criminal records on computer since 1996; prior records on index cards or docket books. State law requires records be retained for 10 years.
General Information: Juvenile records current now with Norfolk Juv. Court; no juvenile records released. Will not fax documents. Court makes copy: $1.00 per page. Certification fee: $2.50 per cert. Payee: District Court. Only cashiers checks and money orders accepted. No credit cards accepted.

Stoughton District Court 1288 Central St, #16, Stoughton, MA 02072; 781-344-2131; fax: 781-341-8744; 8:30AM-4:30PM. ***Felony, Misdemeanor, Crim Supplemental, Civil, Eviction, Small Claims.***
Includes Avon, Canton, Sharon, and Stoughton. All fax search requests must include docket numbers.
Civil Records: Access: Mail, fax, in person. Both court and visitors may perform in person searches. No search fee. Required to search: name, years to search. Civil cases indexed by defendant, plaintiff; index on cards or docket books for 10 years or more. Mail turnaround time 1 week; if archived- 6 weeks. Public use terminal has civil records back to 2005.
Criminal Records: Access: Mail, fax, in person. Only the court performs in person searches; visitors may not. No search fee. Required to search: name, years to search; also helpful: DOB. Criminal records on computer since 1995; prior records on index cards or docket books for 10 years or more. Note: Only the court may perform in person criminal searches for pre-1995 cases. Visitors may search computer 1995 to present. Mail turnaround time 1 week; 6 weeks if archived.
General Information: No juvenile records released. Will fax documents $1.00 per page if prepaid. Court makes copy: $1.00 per page. Certification fee: $2.50 per page. Payee: District Court. Personal checks accepted; credit cards are not. Prepayment required. Mail requests: SASE requested.

Wrentham District Court 60 East St, Wrentham, MA 02093; 508-384-3106; criminal fax: 508-384-5052; civil fax: 508-384-9454; 8:30AM-4:30PM. ***Felony, Misdemeanor, Civil, Eviction, Small Claims.***
Includes Foxborough, Franklin, Medway, Millis, Norfolk, Plainville, Walpole, and Wrentham.
Civil Records: Access: In person only. Visitors must perform in person searches themselves. Required to search: name, years to search. Civil cases indexed by defendant, plaintiff, retained 20 years. Physical records go back to 1985; pre-1985 on docket books.
Criminal Records: Access: In person only. Visitors must perform in person searches themselves. Required to search: name, years to search; also helpful: DOB. Criminal records retained 20 years. Physical records go back to 1985; on computer back to 1999; pre-1985 on docket books.
General Information: No show cause hearing or juvenile records released. Will not fax documents. Court makes copy: $1.00 per page. Certification fee: $2.50 per page. Payee: District Court. Personal checks accepted; credit cards are not. Prepayment required.

Probate & Family Court 35 Shawmut Rd, Canton, MA 02021; 781-830-1200; fax: 781-830-4310; 8:30AM-4:30PM. ***Probate, Divorce, Equity.***
www.ncpfc.com Due to health concerns, Probate was moved from the old location on High St in Dedham in 2003. Should remain at this new Canton location most of 2009. However, the Register of Deeds remains in Dedham at old address.

Plymouth County

Superior Court - Brockton 72 Belmont St, Brockton, MA 02401; 508-583-8250; fax: 508-584-5639; 8:30AM-4:30PM. ***Felony, Civil Actions over $25,000.***
Civil Records: Access: In person, online. Visitors must perform in person searches themselves. Required to search: name, years to search. Civil cases indexed by defendant, plaintiff, for current civil cases are here and Plymouth, closed case are in Plymouth and Brockton; computerized records since 2000. Civil PAT goes back to 2000. Online only for attorneys and law firms at www.ma-trialcourts.org/tcic/.
Criminal Records: Access: In person, online. Visitors must perform in person searches themselves. Required to search: name, years to search. Criminal records here, but some in Plymouth, some pending; computerized records since 2000. Criminal PAT goes back to same as civil. Online for attorneys and law firms only with registration at www.ma-trialcourts.org/tcic/.
General Information: No impounded records released. Court makes copy: $1.00 per page. Certification fee: $2.50 per cert. Payee: Clerk of Superior Court. Personal checks accepted; credit cards are not. Prepayment required.

Superior Court - Plymouth Plymouth Superior Court, Court St, Plymouth, MA 02360; 508-747-8400; fax: 508-830-0676; 8:30AM-4:30PM. ***Felony, Civil Actions over $25,000.***
www.mass.gov/courts/courtsandjudges/courts/plymouthsupmain.html
Civil Records: Access: Phone, mail, in person, online. Only the court performs in person searches; visitors may not. No search fee. Required to search: name, years to search. Civil cases indexed by defendant, plaintiff, for all closed cases are kept here; computerized records since 1983 (approx). Public use terminal available, records go back to 1983 approx. Online only for attorneys and law firms at www.ma-trialcourts.org/tcic/.
Criminal Records: Access: Online, in person only, with exception. Required to search: name, years to search. Criminal records 10 years or older are here; for recent cases go to the Brockton Superior Court. Note: This court's criminal records under ten years old can be searched in person only at Brockton Superior Court, 72 Belmont St, Brockton, 508-583-8250. Public use terminal available, crim records go back to 15 years. Online for attorneys and law firms only with registration at www.ma-trialcourts.org/tcic/.
General Information: No impounded records released. Court makes copy: $1.00 per page. Certification fee: $2.50. Payee: Clerk of Superior

Court. Personal checks accepted; credit cards are not. Prepayment required. Mail requests: SASE requested.

Brockton District Court PO Box 7610, 215 Main St, Brockton, MA 02303-7610; 508-587-8000; 8:30AM-4:30PM. ***Felony, Misdemeanor, Civil, Eviction, Small Claims.***
Includes Abington, Bridgewater, Brockton, East Bridgewater, West Bridgewater, and Whitman.
Civil Records: Access: Mail, in person. Both court and visitors may perform in person searches. No search fee. Required to search: name, years to search. Civil cases indexed by defendant, plaintiff; index on cards or docket books, retained for 10 years; on computer back to 1994. Mail turnaround time 1-2 weeks. Civil PAT goes back to 1995.
Criminal Records: Access: Mail, in person. Both court and visitors may perform in person searches. No search fee. Required to search: name, years to search; also helpful: DOB. Criminal records indexed on cards or docket books, retained for 10 years; on computer back to 1994. Mail turnaround time 1-2 weeks. Criminal PAT goes back to 1994. PAT results show middle initial, DOB. Terminal results include SSN.
General Information: No juvenile or impounded records released. Will not fax documents. Court makes copy: $1.00 per page. Certification fee: $2.50 per page. Payee: District Court. Personal checks accepted. Prepayment required.

Hingham District Court 28 George Washington Blvd, Hingham, MA 02043; 781-749-7000; fax: 781-740-8390; 8:30AM-4:30PM. ***Felony, Misdemeanor, Civil, Eviction, Small Claims.***
Includes Hanover, Hingham, Hull, Norwell, Rockland, and Scituate.
Civil Records: Access: Mail, in person. Both court and visitors may perform in person searches. No search fee. Required to search: name, years to search. Civil cases indexed by defendant, plaintiff; index on cards or docket books, retained for 10 years or more. Mail turnaround time 1-2 weeks.
Criminal Records: Access: Mail, in person. Only the court performs in person searches; visitors may not. No search fee. Required to search: name, years to search; also helpful: DOB. Criminal records indexed on cards or docket books, retained for 10 years or more. Mail turnaround time 1-2 weeks.
General Information: No juvenile records released. Will not fax documents. Court makes copy: $1.00 per page. Certification fee: $2.50 per cert. Payee: District Court. Personal checks accepted; credit cards are not. Prepayment required.

Plymouth 3rd District Court Courthouse, S Russell St, Plymouth, MA 02360; 508-747-0500; fax: 508-830-9303; 8:30AM-4:30PM. ***Felony, Misdemeanor, Civil, Eviction, Small Claims.***
Includes Duxbury, Halifax, Hanson, Kingston, Marshfield, Pembroke, Plymouth, and Plympton.
Civil Records: Access: Mail, in person. Both court and visitors may perform in person searches. No search fee. Required to search: name, years to search. Civil cases indexed by defendant, plaintiff; index on cards or docket books. State law requires records be retained for 10 years. Visitors can only access the index cards. Mail turnaround time 3-4 days.
Criminal Records: Access: Mail, in person. Both court and visitors may perform in person searches. No search fee. Required to search: name, years to search; also helpful: DOB. Criminal records indexed on cards or docket books. State law requires records be retained for 10 years. Visitors can only access the index cards. Mail turnaround time 3-4 days.
General Information: No juvenile or impounded records released. Court makes copy: $1.00 per page. Certification fee: $2.50. Payee: Plymouth District Court. Personal checks accepted; credit cards are not. Prepayment required. Mail requests: SASE required for mail return of any copies.

Wareham District Court 2200 Cranberry Hwy, Junction Routes 28 & 58, West Wareham, MA 02576; 508-295-8300 x315; fax: 508-291-6376; 8AM-4:30PM. ***Felony, Misdemeanor, Civil, Eviction, Small Claims.***
www.mass.gov/courts/courtsandjudges/courts/warehamdistrictmain.html
Includes Carver, Lakeville, Marion, Mattpoinsett, Middleboro, Rochester, and Wareham.
Civil Records: Access: Phone, mail, in person. Both court and visitors may perform in person searches. No search fee. Required to search: name, years to search. Civil cases indexed by defendant, plaintiff. Criminal records back to 1960. Computerized records back to 1995. Mail turnaround time 1-2 weeks. Civil PAT goes back to 2004.
Criminal Records: Access: Phone, mail, in person. Only the court performs in person searches; visitors may not. No search fee. Required to search: name, years to search; also helpful: DOB. Criminal records back to 1960. Computerized records back to 1995. Mail turnaround time 1-2 weeks. Criminal PAT goes back to 2004.
General Information: No juvenile records released. Will not fax documents. Court makes copy: $1.00 per page, self serve same. Certification fee: $2.50 per page includes copy fee. Payee: District Court. Personal checks accepted. Visa/MC accepted. Prepayment required. Mail requests: SASE requested.

Probate & Family Court 52 Obery St, Plymouth, MA 02360; 508-747-6204; fax: 508-746-6846; 8:30AM-4:30PM. ***Probate.***
www.pcpfc.com
There is also a location in Brockton, but records appear on the PATs and index at Plymouth.

Southeast Housing Court PO Box 7520, 215 Main St, 1st Fl, Brockton, MA 02303; 508-894-4170; fax: 508-894-4168; 8:30AM-4:30PM. ***Eviction, Misdemeanor (Code Violations), Small Claims.*** Includes housing code cases, real estate-related small claims, and many eviction cases for Plymouth County; also see district courts.

Suffolk County

Superior Court - Civil 3 Pemberton Sq, Superior Court Clerk, Copy Dept, Boston, MA 02108; 617-788-8175; fax: 617-788-7667; 8:30AM-4:30PM. ***Civil.***
Civil Records: Access: Mail, in person, online. Both court and visitors may perform in person searches. No search fee. Required to search: name, years to search. Civil cases indexed by defendant, plaintiff, on computer from 1991, index cards and books from 1860. Mail turnaround time 1 week. Public use terminal has civil records back to 7/1990. Terminal results may include address. Online only for attorneys and law firms at www.ma-trialcourts.org/tcic/. Online results show middle initial, DOB.
General Information: No impounded records released. Will not fax documents. Court makes copy: $1.00 per page. Self serve: $.25 per page. Certification fee: $2.50. Payee: Clerk of Superior Court. Business checks accepted. No credit cards accepted. Prepayment required.

Superior Court - Criminal Superior Court Clerk, Three Pemberton Sq, 14th Fl, Boston, MA 02108; 617-788-8160; 8:30AM-5PM. ***Felony.***
www.mass.gov/courts/courtsandjudges/courts/suffsupcrimmain.html
Criminal Records: Access: Mail, in person, online. Both court and visitors may perform in person searches. No search fee; fee is determined by number of pages involved. Required to search: name, years to search. Criminal records computerized from 1991, index cards and books from 1950, archived from 1864. Mail turnaround time 1-2 weeks. Public use terminal has crim records back to 1991. Online for attorneys and law firms only with registration at www.ma-trialcourts.org/tcic/.
General Information: Will not fax documents. Court makes copy: $1.00 per page (attested). Certification fee: $20.00. Payee: Superior Court. No personal checks or credit cards accepted. Prepayment required.

Brighton District Court 52 Academy Hill Rd, Brighton, MA 02135; 617-782-6521; fax: 617-254-2127; 8:30AM-4:30PM. ***Felony, Misdemeanor, Civil, Eviction, Small Claims.***
Includes Allston and Brighton.
Civil Records: Access: In person only. Visitors must perform in person searches themselves. Required to search: name, years to search. Civil cases indexed by defendant, plaintiff; index on cards or docket books back to 1980. State law requires records be retained for 10 years. Public use terminal has civil records.
Criminal Records: Access: Phone, mail, in person. Visitors must perform in person searches themselves. No search fee. Required to search: name, years to search, DOB. Computerized records from 1990, criminal records on index cards or docket books back to 1978. State law requires records be retained for 10 years. Mail turnaround time 1-2 weeks.
General Information: No sealed or impounded records released. Will not fax documents. Court makes copy: $1.00 per page. Certification fee: $2.50 per page. Payee: BMC- Brighton. Personal checks accepted; credit cards are not. Prepayment required. Mail requests: SASE required for mail return of any copies.

Charlestown Division Court 3 City Square, Charlestown, MA 02129; 617-242-5400; fax: 617-242-1677; 8:30AM-4:30PM. ***Felony, Misdemeanor, Civil, Eviction, Small Claims.***
www.mass.gov/courts/courtsandjudges/courts/charlestowndistrictmain.html
Civil Records: Access: Fax, mail, in person. Only the court performs in person searches; visitors may not. No search fee. Required to search: name, years to search. Civil cases indexed by defendant, plaintiff; index on cards or docket books. State law requires records be retained for 10 years. Mail turnaround time 1-2 weeks.
Criminal Records: Access: Fax, mail, in person. Only the court performs in person searches; visitors may not. No search fee. Required to search: name, years to search; also helpful: DOB. Criminal records indexed on cards or docket books. State law requires records be retained for 10 years. Mail turnaround time 1-2 weeks.
General Information: No juvenile records released. Will not fax documents. Court makes copy: $1.00 per page. Certification fee: $2.50 per cert. Payee: District Court. Personal checks accepted; credit cards are not. Prepayment required.

Chelsea District Court 120 Broadway, Chelsea, MA 02150; 617-660-9200; fax: 617-660-9215; 8:30AM-4:30PM. ***Felony, Misdemeanor, Civil, Eviction, Small Claims.***
www.mass.gov/courts/courtsandjudges/courts/chelseadistrictmain.html Includes Chelsea and Revere.
Civil Records: Access: Phone, mail, in person. Only the court performs in person searches; visitors may not. No search fee. Required to search: name, years to search. Civil cases indexed by defendant, plaintiff; index on cards or docket books back to 1900; on computer back to 1990. Mail turnaround 1-2 weeks.
Criminal Records: Access: Phone, mail, in person. Only the court performs in person searches; visitors may not. No search fee. Required to search: name, years to search; also helpful: address, DOB. Criminal records indexed on cards or docket books back to 1900; on computer back to 1990. Mail turnaround time 1-2 weeks.
General Information: No closed cases, impounded, sealed, mental health commitment, alcoholic or victim of sexual offense records released. Will not fax documents. Court makes copy: $1.00 per page. Certification fee: $2.50 per page. Payee: District Court. Personal checks accepted; credit cards are not. Prepayment required. Mail requests: SASE required for mail return of any copies.

Dorchester District Court 510 Washington St, Dorchester, MA 02124; 617-288-9500; criminal phone: x239; civil phone: x229; criminal fax: 617-436-8250; civil fax: same; 8:30AM-4:30PM. ***Felony, Misdemeanor, Civil, Eviction, Small Claims.***
Civil Records: Access: Mail, in person. Both court and visitors may perform in person searches. No search fee. Required to search: name, years to search. Civil cases indexed by defendant, plaintiff; index on cards or docket books from 1970. State law requires records be retained for 20 years. Mail turnaround time 1-2 weeks. Civil PAT goes back to 2000.
Criminal Records: Access: Mail, in person. Only the court performs in person searches; visitors may not. No search fee. Required to search: name, years to search, DOB. Criminal records indexed on cards or

docket books to 1950's; on computer since 1998. State law requires records be retained for 20 years. Mail turnaround time 1-2 weeks. Criminal PAT goes back to 2000.
General Information: No juvenile records released. Will fax documents to local or toll free line. Court makes copy: $1.00 per page. Certification fee: $2.50 per page. Payee: District Court. Personal checks accepted; credit cards are not. Prepayment required. Mail requests: SASE required for mail return of any copies.

East Boston District Court 37 Meridian St, East Boston, MA 02128; 617-569-7550; criminal fax: 617-561-4988; civil fax: same; 8:30AM-4:30PM. ***Misdemeanor, Civil Actions under $25,000, Eviction, Small Claims.***
Includes East Boston and Winthrop.
Civil Records: Access: In person. Visitors must perform in person searches themselves. Required to search: name, years to search. Civil cases indexed by defendant, plaintiff; index on cards or docket books since 1965, not computerized. State law requires records be retained for 20 years.
Criminal Records: Access: In person. Visitors must perform in person searches themselves. Required to search: name, years to search. Criminal records indexed on cards or docket books, computerized since 1997. State law requires records be retained 20 years. Public use terminal has crim records back to 1990.
General Information: No juvenile records released. Will fax documents. Court makes copy: $1.00 per page. Certification fee: $2.50 per page. Payee: Boston Municipal Court/ East Boston Division. Personal checks accepted; credit cards are not. Prepayment required. Mail requests: SASE required for mail return of any copies.

Roxbury District Court 85 Warren St, Roxbury, MA 02119; 617-427-7000 x350; fax: 617-541-0286; 8:30AM-4:30PM. ***Felony, Misdemeanor, Civil, Eviction, Small Claims.***
Civil Records: Access: Phone, fax, mail, in person. Only the court performs in person searches; visitors may not. No search fee. Required to search: name, years to search. Civil cases indexed by defendant, plaintiff; index on cards or docket books since 1981; on computer back to 1999. Records retained 10 years. Mail turnaround time 1-2 weeks. Civil PAT goes back to 1999.
Criminal Records: Access: Fax, mail, in person. Only the court performs in person searches; visitors may not. No search fee. Required to search: name, years to search, DOB; also helpful: address. Criminal records indexed on cards or docket books since 1981; on computer back to 1999. Records retained 10 years. Note: Criminal searches restricted at this time; call court for exact search procedure, extension 532. Mail turnaround time 1-2 weeks. Criminal PAT available.
General Information: No juvenile records released. Fee to fax out file $1.00 per page. Court makes copy: $1.00 per page. Certification fee: $2.50 per page. Payee: Roxbury Court. No personal checks accepted. Prepayment required. Mail requests: SASE required for mail return of any copies.

South Boston Division 535 E Broadway #F2, South Boston, MA 02127; 617-268-9292/9293; fax: 617-268-7321; 8:30AM-4:30PM. ***Felony, Misdemeanor, Civil, Eviction, Small Claims.***
www.mass.gov/courts/courtsandjudges/courts/southbostondistrictmain.html
Civil Records: Access: In person only. Visitors must perform in person searches themselves. Required to search: name, years to search, address. Civil cases indexed by defendant, plaintiff; index on cards or docket books. Records go back 20 years.
Criminal Records: Access: In person only. Visitors must perform in person searches themselves. Required to search: name, years to search, address, DOB. Criminal records indexed on cards or docket books. Records go back 20 years; from 2000 on computer.
General Information: No juvenile or medical records released. Will not fax documents. Court makes copy: $1.00 per page. Certification fee: $2.50 per cert. Payee: District Court. Personal checks accepted; credit cards are not. Prepayment required.

West Roxbury District Court 445 Arborway, Courthouse, Jamaica Plain, MA 02130; 617-971-1200; fax: 617-983-0243; 8:30AM-4:30PM. ***Felony, Misdemeanor, Civil, Eviction, Small Claims.***
www.mass.gov/courts/courtsandjudges/courts/westroxburydistrictmain.html Includes West Roxbury, Jamaica Plain, Hyde Park, Roslindale, Parts of Mission Hill, and Mattapan sections of Boston.
Civil Records: Access: In person only. Visitors must perform in person searches themselves. Required to search: name, years to search, type of civil action; also helpful: address. Civil cases indexed by defendant, plaintiff; index on cards or docket books. State law requires records be retained for 10 years.
Criminal Records: Access: In person. Visitors must perform in person searches themselves. Required to search: name, years to search; also helpful: DOB. Criminal records indexed on cards or docket books. State law requires records be retained for 10 years.
General Information: No juvenile records released. Will not fax documents. Court makes copy: $1.00 per page. Certification fee: $2.50 per page. Payee: District Court. Personal checks accepted; credit cards are not. Prepayment required.

Boston Municipal Court - Central Div. Office of Clerk-Magistrate, 24 New Chardon St, 6th Fl, Boston, MA 02114; criminal phone: 617-788-8600; civil phone: 617-788-8400; crim fax: 617-788-8465; civil fax: 617-788-8675; 8:30-4:30PM. ***Misdemeanor, Civil, Small Claims.***
www.mass.gov/courts/courtsandjudges/courts/bostonmunicipalcourt/index.html#jurisdiction
Small Claims phone number 617-788-8411. Misdemeanor records are located on the 6th floor in a separate index.
Civil Records: Access: Mail, in person. Both court and visitors may perform in person searches. No search fee. Required to search: name, years to search. Civil cases indexed by defendant, plaintiff, on computer back to 1995; only court searches those records. Public can search prior records on index cards. Mail turnaround time 1-2 weeks.
Criminal Records: Access: Mail, in person. Both court and visitors may perform in person searches. No search fee. Required to search: name, years to search; also helpful: DOB. Criminal records computerized from 1995; only court searches those records. Public can search prior records on index cards. Mail turnaround time 1-2 weeks.
General Information: No impounded records released. Will fax documents $.00 per page fax fee. Court makes copy: $1.00 per page. Certification fee: $2.50 per page includes copy fee. Payee: District Court. Personal checks accepted. Prepayment required.

Boston Housing Court 24 New Chardon St, 3rd Fl, Edward W Brooke Courthouse, Boston, MA 02114; 617-788-8485; fax: 617-788-8981; 8:30AM-4:30PM. ***Eviction, Misdemeanor (Code Violations) for residential, commercial, industrial property, Housing Civil Unlimited.***
www.mass.gov/courts/courtsandjudges/courts/bostonhousingmain.html
Small claims phone is 617-788-8515. Includes many housing code cases, real estate-related small claims and eviction cases for Suffolk County, except Revere, Winthrop and Chelsea.

Probate & Family Court P.O. Box 9667, Edward W Brooke Courthouse, 24 New Chardon St, 3rd Fl, Boston, MA 02114-4703; 617-788-8300; fax: 617-788-8962; 8AM-5PM. ***Probate.***
www.mass.gov/courts/courtsandjudges/courts/suffprobmain.html Jurisdiction includes Boston, Brighton, Charlestown, Chelsea, Dorchester, East Boston, Hyde Park, Jamaica Plain, Revere, Roslindale, South Boston, Winthrop.

Worcester County

Superior Court 225 Main St, Rm 1008, Worcester, MA 01608; 508-831-2000, 508-770-1899; 8AM-4:30PM. ***Felony, Civil Actions over $25,000.***
www.mass.gov/courts/courtsandjudges/courts/worcsupmain.html
Civil Records: Access: Mail, in person, online. Both court and visitors may perform in person searches. No search fee. Required to search: name, years to search. Civil cases indexed by defendant, plaintiff, on computer from 1990, index books from 1900. Mail turnaround time 1 week. Civil PAT goes back to 1990. Online only for attorneys and law firms at www.ma-trialcourts.org/tcic/.
Criminal Records: Access: Mail, in person, online. Both court and visitors may perform in person searches. No search fee. Required to search: name, years to search. Criminal records computerized from 1990, index books from 1900. Mail turnaround time 1 week. Criminal PAT goes back to same as civil. Online for attorneys and law firms only with registration at www.ma-trialcourts.org/tcic/.
General Information: No impounded or juvenile records released. Will not fax documents. Court makes copy: $1.00 per page. Certification fee: $2.50 per cert. Payee: Clerk of Superior Court. Personal checks accepted; credit cards are not.

Clinton District Court 300 Boylston St, Clinton, MA 01510; 978-368-7811; criminal fax: 978-368-7827; civil fax: same; 8:30AM-4:30PM. ***Felony, Misdemeanor, Civil, Eviction, Small Claims.***
Includes Berlin, Bolton, Boylston, Clinton, Harvard, Lancaster, Sterling, and West Boylston.
Civil Records: Access: Mail, in person. Only the court performs in person searches; visitors may not. No search fee. Required to search: name, years to search; also helpful: DOB, SSN. Civil cases indexed by defendant, plaintiff; index on cards or docket books back to 1987. Mail turnaround 1-2 weeks.
Criminal Records: Access: Mail, in person. Only the court performs in person searches; visitors may not. No search fee. Required to search: name, years to search, address, DOB, SSN, signed release. Criminal records indexed on cards or docket books back to 1987. Mail turnaround time 1-2 weeks.
General Information: No juvenile records released. Will not fax documents. Court makes copy: $1.00 per page, self serve same. Certification fee: $1.50 per page. Payee: Clerk Magistrate. Personal checks accepted; credit cards are not. Prepayment required. Mail requests: SASE required.

Dudley District Court 64 PO Box 100, Dudley, MA 01571; 508-943-7123; fax: 508-949-0015; 8AM-4:30PM. ***Felony, Misdemeanor, Civil, Eviction, Small Claims.*** Includes Charlton, Dudley, Oxford, Southbridge, Sturbridge, and Webster.
Civil Records: Access: Phone, fax, mail, in person. Both court and visitors may perform in person searches. No search fee. Required to search: name, years to search. Civil cases indexed by defendant, plaintiff, on computer back to 2002; prior on index cards or docket books; records retained 10 years. Mail turnaround time 1-2 weeks. Public use terminal has civil records back to 2002. PAT results show name only.
Criminal Records: Access: Phone, fax, mail, in person. Both court and visitors may perform in person searches. No search fee. Required to search: name, years to search, DOB. Criminal records computerized from 6/96; on index cards or docket books back 10 years. Mail turnaround 1-2 weeks.
General Information: No juvenile records released. Court makes copy: $1.00 per page, self serve same. Certification fee: $2.50. Payee: District Court. Business checks accepted. All major credit cards accepted in person only. Prepayment required. SASE not required.

East Brookfield District Court 544 E Main St, East Brookfield, MA 01515-1701; criminal phone: 508-885-6305 x109; civil phone: 508-885-6395 x 107; fax: 508-885-7623; 8:30AM-4:30PM. ***Felony, Misdemeanor, Civil, Eviction, Small Claims.***

Includes Barre, Brookfield, East Brookfield, Hardwick, Leicester, New Braintree, North Brookfield, Oakham, Paxton, Rutland, Spencer, Warren, and West Brookfield.
Civil Records: Access: Mail, in person. Both court and visitors may perform in person searches. No search fee. Required to search: name, years to search. Civil cases indexed by defendant, plaintiff; index on cards or docket books and computer. Mail turnaround time 1-2 weeks; use a retriever when possible suggested. Public use terminal has civil records back to 2004. PAT results show name only. Terminal has small claims & civil records.
Criminal Records: Access: Mail, in person. Both court and visitors may perform in person searches. No search fee. Required to search: name, years to search; also helpful: DOB. Criminal records indexed on cards or docket books to 1945, computerized since 1999. Mail turnaround time 1-2 weeks; strongly suggest to use a retriever when possible.
General Information: No juvenile, mental health records released. Will not fax documents. Court makes copy: $1.00 per page. Certification fee: $2.50 per cert. Payee: District Court. Personal checks and major credit cards accepted. Prepayment required. Mail requests: SASE requested.

Fitchburg District Court 16 100 Elm St, Fitchburg, MA 01420; 978-345-2111; fax: 978-342-2461; 8:30AM-4:30PM. ***Felony, Misdemeanor, Civil, Eviction, Small Claims.***
Includes Fitchburg and Lunenburg.
Civil Records: Access: In person only. Visitors must perform in person searches themselves. Required to search: name, years to search. Civil cases indexed by defendant, plaintiff; index on cards or docket books back 10 years, also on computer. Civil PAT goes back to 2002. PAT results show name only.
Criminal Records: Access: In person only. Visitors must perform in person searches themselves. Required to search: name, years to search. Criminal records indexed on cards or docket books back 10 years; on computer back to 1994. Criminal PAT goes back to 2002. PAT results show middle initial, DOB.
General Information: No juvenile or mental health records released. Will not fax out case files. Court makes copy: $1.00 per page. Certification fee: $2.50. Payee: District Court. Personal checks accepted. Visa/MC/Carte Blanche cards accepted.

Gardner District Court 108 Matthews St, Gardner, MA 01440-0040; 978-632-2373; fax: 978-630-3902; 8:30AM-4:30PM. ***Felony, Misdemeanor, Civil, Small Claims.***
www.mass.gov/courts/courtsandjudges/courts/gardnerdistrictmain.html Includes Gardner, Hubbardston, Petersham, and Westminster.
Civil Records: Access: Mail, in person. Both court and visitors may perform in person searches. No search fee. Required to search: name, years to search, address. Civil cases indexed by defendant, plaintiff; index on cards or docket books back 10 years, also on computer. Mail turnaround time 1-2 weeks; quicker for phone and fax searches. Public use terminal has civil records. PAT results show name only.
Criminal Records: Access: Phone, fax, mail, in person. Both court and visitors may perform in person searches. No search fee. Required to search: name, years to search, DOB. Criminal records indexed on cards or docket books back 10 years. Mail turnaround time 1-2 weeks; quicker for phone and fax verifications.
General Information: No juvenile records released. No fee to fax documents. Court makes copy: $1.00 per page. Certification fee: $2.50 per cert. Payee: District Court. Personal checks accepted; credit cards are not. Prepayment required.

Leominster District Court 25 School St, Leominster, MA 01453; 978-537-3722; fax: 978-537-3970; 8:30AM-4:30PM. ***Felony, Misdemeanor, Civil, Eviction, Small Claims.***
Includes Princeton, Holden and Leominster.
Civil Records: Access: Mail, in person. Both court and visitors may perform in person searches. No search fee. Required to search: name, years to search. Civil cases indexed by defendant, plaintiff; index on cards or docket books back 10 years, also on computer. Mail turnaround time 1-2 weeks. Public use terminal has civil records back to 2005. PAT results show name only.
Criminal Records: Access: Mail, in person. Both court and visitors may perform in person searches. No search fee. Required to search: name, years to search; also helpful: DOB. Criminal records on computer since 1987; index cards or docket books back 10 years. Mail turnaround time 1-2 weeks.
General Information: No juvenile or impounded records released. Will not fax documents. Court makes copy: $1.00 per page. Certification fee: $2.50 per cert. Payee: District Court. Personal checks accepted; credit cards are not. Prepayment required. Mail requests: SASE required.

Milford District Court 161 West St, Milford, MA 01757; 508-473-1260; fax: 508-634-8477; 8:30AM-4:30PM. ***Felony, Misdemeanor, Civil, Eviction, Small Claims.***
www.mass.gov/courts/courtsandjudges/courts/milforddistrictmain.html Includes Mendon, Upton, Hopedale, and Milford in Worcester County; also includes Bellingham in Norfolk County.
Civil Records: Access: In person only. Both court and visitors may perform in person searches. No search fee. Required to search: name, years to search. Civil cases indexed by defendant, plaintiff; index on cards or docket books back 10 years; on computer back to 2004. Public use terminal has civil records back to 2004. PAT results show name only. Terminal has small claims & civil records.
Criminal Records: Access: In person only. Both court and visitors may perform in person searches. No search fee. Required to search: name, years to search, DOB; also helpful: aliases. Criminal records computerized from 1998; prior records on cards & docket books; computer indexes searchable by court.
General Information: No mental health, impounded, alcohol, commitment, sexual abuse victim, waivers of fees or costs for indigents, delinquency, C & P, CHINS, 209A minor or 209A address records released. Will not fax documents. Court makes copy: $1.00 per page. Certification fee: $2.50. Payee: District Court. Business checks accepted. Visa/MC accepted. Prepayment required.

Uxbridge District Court 261 S Main St, Uxbridge, MA 01569; 508-278-2454; fax: 508-278-2929; 8:30AM-4:30PM. ***Felony, Misdemeanor, Civil, Eviction, Small Claims.***
Includes Blackstone, Douglas, Millville, Northbridge, Sutton, and Uxbridge.
Civil Records: Access: Mail, in person. Only the court performs in person searches; visitors may not. No search fee. Required to search: name, years to search. Civil cases indexed by defendant, plaintiff, indexed on computer. Note: All requests must be in writing. Mail turnaround time 1-2 weeks. Public use terminal has civil records back to 7/1/2004. PAT results show name only. Terminal has small claims & civil records.
Criminal Records: Access: Mail, in person. Only the court performs in person searches; visitors may not. No search fee. Required to search: name, years to search; also helpful: DOB. Criminal records indexed on cards or docket books back 10 years. Note: All requests must be in writing. Mail turnaround time 1-2 weeks.
General Information: Will fax documents to local or toll-free number. Court makes copy: $1.00 per page. Certification fee: $2.50 per cert. Payee: District Court. Personal checks accepted; credit cards are not. Prepayment required.

Westborough District Court 186 Oak St, Westborough, MA 01581; 508-366-8266; fax: 508-366-8268; 8AM-4:30PM. ***Felony, Misdemeanor, Civil, Eviction, Small Claims.***
Includes Grafton, Northborough, Shrewsbury, Southborough, and Westborough.
Civil Records: Access: In person only. Both court and visitors may perform in person searches. No search fee. Required to search: name, years to search. Civil cases indexed by defendant, plaintiff; index on cards or docket books back 10 years; also on computer. Public use terminal has civil records back to 2004. PAT results show name only.
Criminal Records: Access: In person only. Both court and visitors may perform in person searches. No search fee. Required to search: name, years to search; also helpful: DOB. Criminal records indexed on cards or docket books back 10 years; also on computer.
General Information: No impounded, juvenile records released. Will not fax documents. Court makes copy: $1.00 per page. Certification fee: $2.50 per cert. Payee: District Court Westborough Division. Personal checks accepted; credit cards are not. Prepayment required.

Winchendon District Court 80 Central St, Winchendon, MA 01475; 978-297-0156; fax: 978-297-0161; 8:30AM-4:30PM. ***Felony, Misdemeanor, Civil, Eviction, Small Claims.***
Includes Ashburnham, Phillipston, Royalston, Templeton, and Winchendon.
Civil Records: Access: Phone, mail, in person. Both court and visitors may perform in person searches. No search fee. Required to search: name, years to search. Civil cases indexed by defendant, plaintiff; index on cards or docket books back 10 years; also on computer. Mail turnaround time 1-2 weeks. Civil PAT goes back to 2004. PAT results show name only. The further back, the less complete the case record database on the public terminal is. Results on terminal includes plaintiff names.
Criminal Records: Access: Mail, in person. Both court and visitors may perform in person searches. No search fee. Required to search: name, years to search; also helpful: DOB, docket number. Criminal records indexed on docket books back 10 years. Mail turnaround time 1-2 weeks. Criminal PAT goes back to 1995. PAT results show name only. The further back, the less complete the case record database on the public terminal is. Results on terminal include PCF#.
General Information: Will not fax documents. Court makes copy: $1.00 per page. Certification fee: $2.50 per page. Payee: District Court. Personal checks accepted; credit cards are not. Prepayment required. Mail requests: SASE required.

Worcester District Court 225 Main St, $m 1019, Worcester, MA 01608; 508-831-2010; fax: 508-797-0716; 8AM-4:30PM. ***Felony, Misdemeanor, Civil, Eviction, Small Claims.***
www.mass.gov/courts/courtsandjudges/courts/worcesterdistrictmain.html
Includes Auburn, Millbury, and Worcester.
Civil Records: Access: Mail, in person. Both court and visitors may perform in person searches. No search fee. Required to search: name, years to search. Civil cases indexed by defendant, plaintiff; index on cards 1987-1998; docket books 1999-2008, also on computer. Mail turnaround time 1-2 weeks. Civil PAT goes back to 2001; results show name only.
Criminal Records: Access: In person only. Both court and visitors may perform in person searches. No search fee. Required to search: name, years to search. Criminal records on computer since 1999; prior records on docket books since 1982. Criminal PAT goes back to 1999. PAT results show middle initial, DOB.
General Information: No sealed, expunged, adoption or sex offense records released. Will not fax documents. Court makes copy: $1.00 per page. Certification fee: $2.50. Payee: District Court. Personal checks accepted. Visa/MC accepted. Prepayment required.

Probate & Family Court 225 Main St, Worcester, MA 01608; 508-831-2200; fax: 508-752-6138; 8AM-4:30PM. ***Probate.***

Worcester Housing Court 225 Main St, Worcester, MA 01608; 508-831-2050; fax: 508-792-1170; 8:30AM-4:30PM. ***Eviction, Misdemeanor (Code Violations), Small Claims.***
Includes housing code cases, real estate-related small claims and many eviction cases for Worcester County; also see district courts.

Massachusetts Recording Offices

ORGANIZATION: 14 counties, 21 recording offices. Berkshire and Bristol counties each have three recording offices. Essex, Middlesex, and Worcester counties each have two recording offices. Cities/towns bearing the same name as a county are Barnstable, Essex, Franklin, Hampden, Nantucket, Norfolk, Plymouth, and Worcester. Some UCC financing statements on personal property collateral were submitted to the 350 cities and towns until June 30, 2001, while real estate recording is handled by the counties. County Register of Deeds (real estate), and Clerk of US District Court (federal tax liens). Massachusetts is in the Eastern Time Zone (EST).

REAL ESTATE RECORDS: Counties will not perform real estate searches, though towns may. Copy fee is usually $1.00 per page. Typically, certification is either $3.00 or $5.00 per doc or $2.00 per seal/page, or sometimes it is included in the copy fee. Exemplification is also available and is oftern confused with certification. Vital records are $6.00 per copy. Each town also has Assessor/Tax Collector/Treasurer offices from which limited real estate ownership and tax information is available.

UCC RECORDS: Massachusetts was a dual filing state until July 1, 2001. Back then, financing statements were usually filed both with the Town/City clerk and at the state level except for real estate related collateral that is recorded at the county Register of Deeds. Now, all filing are at the state except for the real estate related collateral. Most Massachusetts town/city recording offices no longer perform UCC searches.

TAX LIEN RECORDS: Federal tax liens on personal property were filed with the Town/City Clerks prior to 1970. Since that time federal tax liens on personal property are filed with the U.S. District Court in Boston as well as with the towns/cities. The address is: U.S. District Court, 1 Courthouse Way, Boston, MA 02110; 617-748-9152. Searches are available by mail or in person at this federal District Court. Include address of individual names in your search request in order to narrow the results. A mail search costs $26.00 and will take about two weeks. You can do the search yourself at no charge on their public access computer terminal.

State tax liens on personal property are filed with the Town/City Clerk or the Tax Collector. All tax liens against real estate are filed with the county Register of Deeds.

OTHER LIENS: Medical, town/city tax, child support.

ONLINE ACCESS: A large number of towns and several counties offer online access to assessor records via the internet for no charge. Also, a private vendor has placed assessor records from a number of towns online at www.visionappraisal.com/databases/mass/index.htm

Barnstable County

County Register of Deeds, PO Box 368, Barnstable, MA 02630. 508-362-7733; fax-508-362-5065; 8AM-4PM www.bcrd.co.barnstable.ma.us

Record index not computerized. Only the public may search. Copy fee $1.00 per page. Cert fee- $10.00 per doc plus copy fee. Payee- Barnstable County Register of Deeds. **Online access to Real Estate, Deed, Lien records:** Access to County records is free at https://72.8.52.132/ALIS/WW400R.HTM. Search for free, but to print requires a $50 annual fee. Records date back to 1940. Lending agency data is available. **Other phones:** Treasurer- 508-362-4653. **Property tax/Assessing**- 367 Main St, Town Hall, Hyannis, MA 02601; 508-362-4022, assessor fax- 508-862-4722. hours- 8:30AM-4:30PM

Barnstable Town, 367 Main St, Hyannis, MA 02601, 508-862-4044, fax-508-790-6326; 8:30AM-4:30PM **Online-** town assessor records free at www.town.barnstable.ma.us/Vsapps20/PropertyLookUp09/Default.aspx.

Bourne Town, 24 Perry Ave, Town Hall, Buzzards Bay, MA 02532, 508-759-0613x313, fax-508-759-7980; 8:30AM-4:30PM **Online-** Access to property taxes free go to www.townofbourne.com/

Brewster Town, 2198 Main St, Brewster, MA 02631, 508-896-4506, fax-508-896-8089; 8:30AM-4PM **Online-** assessors' property data at www.town.brewster.ma.us/content/category/9/71/97/. Requires free registration, username and password.

Chatham Town, 549 Main St, Chatham, MA 02633, 508-945-5101, fax-508-945-3550; 8AM-4PM **Online-** Free access to assessor database at http://data.visionappraisal.com/ChathamMA/.

Dennis Town, PO Box 2060, South Dennis, MA 02660-1419, (485 Main St, Town Hall, South Dennis, MA 02660) 508-760-6115, fax-508-394-8309; 8:30AM-4:30PM **Online-** Access to assessor property records is free at http://townofdennis.bonsailogic.com/.

Eastham Town, 2500 State Hwy, Eastham, MA 02642, 508-240-5900 x223, fax-508-240-5918; 8AM-4PM A public access terminal is available. www.eastham-ma.gov/ **Online-** Assessor's online database of property card data is free at www.assessedvalues.com/index.zhtml?jurcode=86.

Falmouth Town, 59 Town Hall Sq, Falmouth, MA 02541, 508-548-7611x7360, fax-508-457-2511; 8AM-4:30PM **Online-** Access property data free http://falmouth.patriotproperties.com/default.asp.

Harwich Town, 732 Main St, Harwich, MA 02645-2717, 508-430-7516, fax-508-432-5039; 8:30AM-4PM

Mashpee Town, 16 Great Neck Rd N, Town Hall, Mashpee, MA 02649, 508-539-1400 x561, fax-508-539-1403; 9AM-4PM www.ci.mashpee.ma.us **Online-** Search Mashpee Assessor database free at www.assessedvalues.com/index.zhtml?jurcode=172.

Orleans Town, 19 School Rd, Orleans, MA 02653-3699, 508-240-3700, fax-508-240-3388; 8:30AM-4:30PM A public access terminal is available. www.town.orleans.ma.us **Online-** Search current assessment data free at www.assessedvalues.com/search.zhtml?jurcode=224.

Provincetown Town, 260 Commercial St, Provincetown, MA 02657, 508-487-7013 x528, fax-508-487-9560; 8AM-5PM www.provincetown-ma.gov/assessor.html **Online-** Records on the Provincetown Assessor database including sales are free at www.provincetown-ma.gov/assessor.html.

Sandwich Town, 145 Main St, Sandwich, MA 02563, 508-888-0340, fax-508-888-2497; 8:30AM-4:30PM

Truro Town, PO Box 2030, Truro, MA 02666-2012, (24 Town Hall Rd, West Wing of Town Hall, Truro, MA 02666) 508-349-7004 x14, fax-508-349-5508; 8AM-4PM www.truro-ma.gov/html_pages/offices/office_assessors.php **Online-** Access to Assessor's database for free go to www.assessedvalues.com/INDEX.ZHTML?JURCODE=300

Wellfleet Town, 300 Main St, Wellfleet, MA 02667, 508-349-0301, fax-508-349-0317; 8-4PM **Online-** Access property assessment records free at www.assessedvalues.com/index.zhtml?jurcode=318

Yarmouth Town, 1146 Rte 28, Town Hall, South Yarmouth, MA 02664, 508-398-2231 x216, fax-508-760-4842; 8:30AM-4:30PM http://yarmouth.ma.us/index.asp?NID=70 **Online-** Records on the Assessor's database are free at http://data.visionappraisal.com/yarmouthma/DEFAULT.asp.

Berkshire County (Middle District)

Middle District Register of Deeds, 44 Bank Row, Pittsfield, MA 01201. 413-443-7438; fax-413-448-6025; 8:30AM-4:30PM (No Recording after 3:59PM). www.berkshiremiddledeeds.com, or www.masslandrecords.com

Index: All in one. Records indexed on computer back to 1985. Only the public may search. Copy fee $1.00 per page. Cert fee- $1.00 per page includes copy fee. Payee- Commonwealth of Massachusetts. Contact Andrea F. Nuciforo, Jr. **Online access to Real Estate, Lien records:** Online search- see Berkshire County Southern District. **Property tax/Assessing**- 70 Allen St, #108, Pittsfield, MA 01201; 413-395-0102, assessor fax- 413-496-9887. hours- 8:30AM-4PM Public access terminal available.

Berkshire County (Northern District)

Northern District Register of Deeds, 65 Park St, #1, Adams, MA 01220. Recording, R/E & UCC phone-413-743-0035; fax-413-743-1003; 8:30AM-4:30PM

Index: All in one. Records indexed on a public use terminal back to 1985. Only the public may search. Copy fee $1.00 per page. Cert fee- $1.00 per page plus copy fee. Payee- Commonwealth of Massachusetts. **Online access to Real Estate, Lien records:** Online search- see Berkshire County Southern District. **Other phones:** Treasurer- 413-743-8390 (Town of Adams); Vital Records- 413-743-8320 (Town of Adams). **Property tax/Assessing-** 8 Park St, Adams, MA 01220; 413-743-8350.

Berkshire County (Southern District)

Southern District Register of Deeds, 334 Main St, #2, Great Barrington, MA 01230-1894. 413-528-0146; fax-413-528-6878; 8:30AM-4:30PM; Recording- 8:30AM-4PM www.berkshiresouthdeeds.com
Index: Various indexes back to 1790. Records indexed on a public use terminal back to 1971. Only the public may search. Copy fee $1.00 per page. Cert fee- $1.00 per page includes copy fee. Payee- Southern Berkshire Registry of Deeds or Commonwealth of Massachusetts. **Online Real Estate, Judgment, Deed, Lien, Judgment records:** Access to Southern District Recorder's records is free at www.masslandrecords.com/malr/controller; records date back to 1971. Searchable indices include recorded land, plans, registered land. Lending agency data available. Also, search Register of Deeds Records for all Berkshire districts free at www.masslandrecords.com. Click on appropriate Division on map.

Berkshire County Cities/Towns

Adams Town, 8 Park St, Adams, MA 01220, 413-743-8320, fax-413-743-8316; 8:30AM-4PM

Alford Town, 5 Alford Center Rd, Town Hall, Alford, MA 01230-8914, 413-528-4536, fax-413-528-4581; 8-11AM Th A public access terminal is available. http://townofalford.org/contact-us/ **Online-** Access assessor rolls and property sales free at http://csc-ma.us/AlfordPubAcc/jsp/Home.jsp.

Becket Town, 557 Main St, Jeanne W Pryor, Becket, MA 01223, 413-623-8934, fax-413-623-6036; 8:30AM-4:30PM **Online-** Access to parcel information and maps for free go to www.townofbecket.org/Public_Documents/BecketMA_BComm/assessorboard

Cheshire Town, PO Box S, Cheshire, MA 01225, (80 Church St) 413-743-1690, fax-413-743-0389; 9AM-2PM Tu; 9AM-4PM Th

Clarksburg Town, 111 River Rd, Town Hall, Clarksburg, MA 01247, 413-663-8247, fax-413-664-6575; 2PM-4:30PM M-Th

Dalton Town, 462 Main St, Town Hall, Dalton, MA 01226, 413-684-6111 x14, fax-413-684-6129; 8AM-4PM M-W; 8AM-6PM Th; Closed Fri Public access terminal available.

Egremont Town, PO Box 368, S Egremont, MA 01258-0368, (171 Egremont Plain Rd) 413-528-0182 X11, fax-413-528-5465; 7PM-9PM Tues **Online-** Access assessor rolls and property sales free at http://csc-ma.us/PropertyContent/jsp/Home.jsp?Page=1. Select Egremont Town.

Florida Town, 20 South St, Town Hall, Drury, MA 01343, 413-664-6685, fax-413-664-8640; hours- by appointment

Great Barrington Town, 334 Main St, Great Barrington, MA 01230-1802, 413-528-1619 x3, fax-413-528-2290; 8:30AM-4PM www.townofgb.org/Pages/GBarringtonMA_Assessor/index **Online-** Access assessor rolls and property sales free at http://csc-ma.us/PropertyContent/jsp/Home.jsp?Page=1.

Hancock Town, PO Box 1097, Hancock, MA 01237-1097, (3650 Hancock Rd) 413-738-5225, fax-413-738-5310; 8AM-1PM Tu; 9AM-N Th; 9-11AM 1st Sat of month

Hinsdale Town, PO Box 803, Hinsdale, MA 01235, (Town Hall) 413-655-2301, fax-413-655-8807; 6:30-8PM W-F and by app't. **Online-** Access assessor rolls and property sales free at http://csc-ma.us/PropertyContent/jsp/Home.jsp?Page=1.

Lanesborough Town, PO Box 1492, Lanesborough, MA 01237, (83 N Main St) 413-442-1351, fax-413-443-5811; 8AM-1PM

Lee Town, 32 Main St, Town Hall, Lee, MA 01238, 413-243-5505, fax-413-243-5507; 8:30AM-4PM **Online-** Access assessor rolls and property sales free at http://csc-ma.us/PropertyContent/jsp/Home.jsp?Page=1.

Lenox Town, 6 Walker St, Town Hall, Lenox, MA 01240-2718, 413-637-5506, fax-413-637-5518; 8:30AM-4PM **Online-** Access and search assessor's data free at www.assessedvalues.com/search.zhtml?jurcode=152.

Middlefield Town, PO Box 265, Middlefield, MA 01243, (Town Hall) 413-623-2079, fax-413-623-6108; 7-9PM; 9AM-N Sat

Monterey Town, PO Box 277, Monterey, MA 01245, (Town Hall) 413-528-5175, fax-413-528-9452; 9:30AM-12:30PM Sat, or by appointment A public access terminal is available.

Mt. Washington Town, 118 East St, Mt. Washington, MA 01258, 413-528-2839, fax-413-528-2839; 11AM-5PM-M,11AM-4PM-T

New Ashford Town, 188 Mallory Rd, New Ashford, MA 01237, 413-458-5461, fax-413-458-5461; by appointment

New Marlborough Town, PO Box 99, Mill River, MA 01244, (Town Hall, Mill River-Southfield Rd, Mill River, MA 01244) 413-229-8116, fax-413-229-6674; 9AM-2PM No public access terminal.

North Adams City, 10 Main St, North Adams, MA 01247, 413-662-3015; 8AM-4:30PM

Otis Town, PO Box 237, Otis, MA 01253, (1 N. Main St., Town Hall, Otis, MA 01253) 413-269-0100 x5, fax-413-269-0111; 8AM-3PM T-F; 9AM-N Sat www.townofotisma.com/Pages/OtisMA_Assessor/index **Online-** Search town assessor database at http://data.visionappraisal.com/OtisMA/. Free registration and username required.

Peru Town, PO Box 1175, Hindsdale, MA 01235, (3 E Main Rd) 413-655-8312, fax-413-655-2759; 6-8PM Mondays; by app't

Pittsfield City, 70 Allen St, Rm 103, City Hall, Pittsfield, MA 01201, 413-499-9361, fax-413-499-9363; 8:30AM-4PM www.pittsfield-ma.org/departments.asp?ID=29

Richmond Town, PO Box 81, Richmond, MA 01254, (1529 State Rd) 413-698-3315, fax-413-698-3272; 9AM-N M,T,Th,F **Online-** Access assessor rolls and property sales free at http://csc-ma.us/PropertyContent/jsp/Home.jsp?Page=1.

Rowe Town, Town Hall, Rowe, MA 01367, 413-339-5520, fax-413-339-5316; 8-11AM W www.rowe-ma.gov/Pages/RoweMA_Assessors/index

Sandisfield Town, PO Box 163, Sandisfield, MA 01255, (3 Silverbrook Rd, Town Hall, Sandisfield, MA 01255) 413-258-4711, fax-413-258-4225; 10AM-2PM, 6-8PM M; 10AM-2PM Th or by Appointment

Savoy Town, 720 Main Rd, Town Office, Savoy, MA 01256, 413-743-3759, fax-413-743-4292; 1-5PM T,TH; 10AM-N Sat in winter; by app't only

Sheffield Town, PO Box 175, Sheffield, MA 01257, (21 Depot Sq, Town Hall, Sheffield, MA 01257) 413-229-8752, fax-413-229-7010; 9AM-4PM **Online-** assessor rolls and property sales free at http://csc-ma.us/PropertyContent/jsp/Home.jsp?Page=1

Stockbridge Town, PO Box 417, Stockbridge, MA 01262-0417, (6 Main St) 413-298-4568, fax-413-298-4485; 9AM-4PM

Tyringham Town, 116 Main Rd, Tyringham, MA 01264, 413-243-1749, fax-413-243-4942; 9AM-1PM M-Th or by appointment

Washington Town, 8 Summit Hill Rd, #GA094, Washington, MA 01223, 413-623-8878, fax-413-623-2116; 7-9PM M or by appointment

West Stockbridge Town, PO Box 163, West Stockbridge, MA 01266, (21 State Line Rd) 413-232-0300 x300, fax-413-232-7195; 8AM-3PM M,T,TH,F www.weststockbridge-ma.gov/Pages/WestStockbridgeMA_Tax/index

Williamstown Town, 31 North St, Williamstown, MA 01267, 413-458-9341, fax-413-458-4839; 8:30AM-4:30PM

Windsor Town, PO Box 277, Windsor, MA 01270, (3 Hinsdale Rd) 413-684-3977, fax-413-684-1585; 5-7PM Monday or by app'n't **Online-** assessor rolls and property sales free at http://csc-ma.us/PropertyContent/jsp/Home.jsp?Page=1.

Bristol County (Fall River District)

County Register of Deeds, 441 N Main St, Fall River, MA 02720. 508-673-1651, R/E recording phone-508-673-1651 or 2910; fax-508-673-7633; 8AM-4:30PM www.fallriverdeeds.com
Index: All in one. Records indexed on a public use terminal back to 1986. Only the public may search. Copy fee $1.00 per page. Cert fee- none. Payee- Fall River Registry of Deeds. **Online Real Estate, Deed, Lien, Judgment, Death records:** Access registry documents at https://www.fallriverdeeds.com/. Search index free - click on Free Search - but a subscription is required for pay-per views of images, $1.00 per page, maximum of $5.00 per doc. For add'l online search see Bristol County Southern District. Indexes are 1982 to present. **Property tax/Assessing-** One Gov't Center, Fall River, MA 02720; 508-324-2302.

Bristol County (Northern District)

County Register of Deeds, 11 Court St, Taunton, MA 02780-0248. 508-822-0502; fax-508-880-4975; 8AM-4:00PM www.tauntondeeds.com
Index: All in one. Records indexed on a public use terminal back to 1978. Only the public may search. Copy fee $1.00 per page. Cert fee- none. Payee- Bristol County Register of Deeds. **Online access to Real Estate, Lien records:** Online search- see Bristol County Southern District. **Other phones:** Treasurer- 508-824-4028.

Bristol County (Southern District)

County Register of Deeds, 25 N 6th St, New Bedford, MA 02740. 508-993-2603; fax-508-997-4250; 8AM-4:30PM www.newbedforddeeds.com/mason/main/
Index: Separate indices to search include recorded land, registered land. Records indexed on a public use terminal back to 1978. Office will perform a UCC search but public must search other records themselves. Copy fee $1.00 per page; $.50 self serve. Cert fee- none. Payee- Bristol County Register of Deeds. **Online access to Real Estate, Deed, Lien records:** Access to County records requires a $100 set up fee and $.50 per minute of use. All three districts are on this system; the record dates vary by district. Lending agency data is available. For info, contact Sherrilynn at 508-993-2605 x17. Real Estate searches at www.newbedforddeeds.com/mason/main/search/. **Property tax/Assessing-** 133 William St, City Hall, Rm 109, New Bedford, MA 02740; 508-979-1440, assessor fax- 508-979-1643. hours- 8AM-4PM **Online access-** Access to parcel information for free go to www.newbedford-ma.gov/Assessors/RealProperty/RealpropertyLookup.cfm

Bristol County Cities/Towns

Acushnet Town, 122 Main St, Town Hall, Acushnet, MA 02743, 508-998-0215, fax-508-998-0203; 8AM-4PM Public access terminal available. www.acushnet.ma.us/assessors.htm

Attleboro City, 77 Park St, City Hall, Attleboro, MA 02703, 508-223-2222, fax-508-222-3046; 8:30AM-4:30PM www.cityofattleboro.us/assessor/ **Online-** Property data available free at www.cityofattleboro.us/assessor/ .

Berkley Town, 1 N Main St, Berkley, MA 02779, 508-822-3348, fax-508-822-3511; 9AM-3PM **Online-** assessor rolls and property sales free at http://csc-ma.us/PropertyContent/jsp/Home.jsp?Page=1. Click on Berkley Town.

Dartmouth Town, PO Box 79399, Dartmouth, MA 02747, (400 Slocum Rd, Rm 203, 2nd Fl, Town Hall, Dartmouth, MA 02747) 508-910-1800, fax-508-910-1894; 8:30AM-4:30PM **Online-** Search the town assessor database at http://data.visionappraisal.com/DartmouthMA/.

Dighton Town, 979 Somerset Ave, Dighton, MA 02715-0465, 508-669-5411, fax-508-669-5932; 8AM-4PM M,T,TH; 8AM-5PM W; 8AM-N F www.dighton-ma.gov/Public_Documents/Dighton

MA_Assessor/index **Online-** Access assessor rolls and property sales free at http://csc-ma.us/PropertyContent/jsp/Home.jsp?Page=1.

Easton Town, 136 Elm St, North Easton, MA 02356, 508-230-0530, fax-508-230-0539; 8:30AM-7:30PM M; 8:30AM-4:30AM T-Th; 8:30AM-12:30PM F

Fairhaven Town, 40 Center St, Fairhaven, MA 02719-2999, 508-979-4025, fax-508-979-4079; 8:30AM-4:30PM

Fall River City, One Government Ctr, Fall River, MA 02722, 508-324-2220, fax-508-324-2211; 9AM-5PM **Online-** Access property data free at http://fallriver.patriotproperties.com/default.asp.

Freetown Town, PO Box 438, Assonet, MA 02702, (3 N Main St, Town Hall, Assonet, MA 02702) 508-644-2203, fax-508-644-9826; 9AM-7PM Mon, 9AM-4PM T-F http://freetownma.gov/dept/?DeptID=BOA **Online-** Access property data free http://assessedvalues.com/search.zhtml?jurcode=102.

Mansfield Town, 6 Park Row, Town Hall, Mansfield, MA 02048-2433, 508-261-7345, fax-508-261-1083; 8AM-4PM M, T, Th; 8AM-8PM W; 8AM-N Fri **Online-** town assessor database at http://data.visionappraisal.com/MansfieldMA/.

New Bedford City, 133 William St, New Bedford, MA 02740, 508-979-1450, fax-508-991-6225; 8AM-4PM **Online-** Access to the assessor property database is free at www.newbedford-ma.gov/Assessors/RealProperty/RealpropertyLookup.cfm.

North Attleborough Town, 43 S Washington St, North Attleborough, MA 02761-0871, 508-699-0142, fax-508-699-2354; 8AM-4PM; til 7PM Th **Online-** Search the town assessor database at http://data.visionappraisal.com/NorthAttleboroMA/.

Norton Town, 70 E Main St, Town Hall, Norton, MA 02766, 508-285-0231, fax-508-285-0297; 8:30AM-4:30PM M,T,W,F; 8:30AM-8PM Th

Raynham Town, 53 Orchard St, Raynham, MA 02767-1320, 508-824-2700, fax-508-823-1812; 8:30AM-4:30PM M-Th; 8:30AM-N Fri **Online-** Access the Online Property Viewer free at http://host.appgeo.com/raynham/. Also, access to property data to be available free on a private site at www.appraisalresource.com/OnlineDatabases.aspx.

Rehoboth Town, 148 Peck St, Rehoboth, MA 02769-3099, 508-252-6502, fax-508-252-5342; 8AM-4PM M-Th; 8AM-Noon F

Seekonk Town, 100 Peck St, Seekonk, MA 02771, 508-336-2920, fax-508-336-0764; 8:30AM-4:30PM M,T,Th; 8:30AM-7PM Wed; 8:30AM-N Fri **Online-** Access assessor rolls and property sales free at http://csc-ma.us/PropertyContent/jsp/Home.jsp?Page=1.

Somerset Town, 140 Wood St, Somerset, MA 02726, 508-646-2818, fax-508-646-2802; 8:30AM-4PM **Online-** Access assessor rolls and property sales free at http://csc-ma.us/PropertyContent/jsp/Home.jsp?Page=1. Select Somerset Town.

Swansea Town, 81 Main St, Town Hall, Swansea, MA 02777, 508-678-9389, fax-n/a; 9AM-4PM M,T,Th,F; 9AM-5PM W **Online-** assessor rolls and property sales free at http://csc-ma.us/PropertyContent/jsp/Home.jsp?Page=1. Select Swansea Town.

Taunton City, 15 Summer St, City Hall, Taunton, MA 02780, 508-821-1024, fax-508-821-1098; 9AM-5PM **Online-** Access assessor data free at http://data.visionappraisal.com/TauntonMA/.

Westport Town, 816 Main Rd, Town Hall, Westport, MA 02790, 508-636-1000, fax-508-636-1147; 8:30AM-4PM

Dukes County

County Register of Deeds, PO Box 5231, Edgartown, MA 02539. 508-627-4025; fax-508-627-7821; 8:30AM-4:30PM http://dukescounty.org

This county is comprised of 7 towns; there is no County Assessor, Appraiser, Elections, etc. Index: All in one. Records indexed on a public use terminal back to 1984. Only the public may search. Copy fee $1.00 per page. Cert fee- included in copy fee. Payee- Dukes County Register of Deeds. **Online access to Real Estate, Deed, Lien, Judgment records:** Access to Registry of Deeds data is free at www.masslandrecords.com. Select Dukes County on map. **Other phones:** Treasurer- 508-696-3845. **Property tax/Assessing-** Edgartown Assessor, PO Box 886, 70 Main St, 1st Fl, Town Hall, Edgartown, MA 02539; 508-627-6140, assessor fax- 508-627-6123. There are 7 Assessor's Offices-1 in each town.

Dukes County Cities/Towns

Chilmark Town, PO Box 119, Chilmark, MA 02535, (401 Middle Rd, Town Hall, Chilmark, MA 02535) 508-645-2107, fax-508-645-2110; 9AM-N. Public access terminal available. www.ci.chilmark.ma.us/Pages/ChilmarkMA_Assessor/index

Edgartown Town, PO Box 35, Edgartown, MA 02539-0035, (70 Main St, 1st Fl) 508-627-6110, fax-508-627-6123; 8AM-4PM www.edgartown-ma.us/ **Online-** Search Town assessor's database at http://data.visionappraisal.com/EdgartownMA/DEFAULT.asp. Free registration for full data.

Gosnold Town, 28 Towerhill Rd, Gosnold, MA 02713, (Town Hall) 508-990-7408, fax-508-990-3318; by appointment

Oak Bluffs Town, PO Box 2490, Oak Bluffs, MA 02557-2490, (Town Hall) 508-693-5515, fax-508-693-5124; 8:30AM-4PM **Online-** town assessor data at http://data.visionappraisal.com/OakBluffsMA/. Free registration for full data.

Tisbury Town, PO Box 606, Tisbury, MA 02568-0606, (51 Spring St, Town Hall, Tisbury, MA 02568) 508-696-4215, fax-508-693-5876; 8:30AM-4:30PM **Online-** Search the town assessor data at http://data.visionappraisal.com/TisburyMA/. Free registration for full data.

Town of Aquinnah, 65 State Rd, Aquinnah, MA 02535, (Town Hall) 508-645-2306, fax-508-645-2310; by appointment

West Tisbury Town, Box 278, West Tisbury, MA 02575-0278, (Town Hall) 508-696-0148, fax-508-696-0103; 8:30AM-1:30PM **Online-** Access assessor data at http://data.visionappraisal.com/WestTisburyMA/.

Essex County (Northern District)

County Register of Deeds, 354 Merrimack St, #304, Lawrence, MA 01843-1755. 978-683-2745; fax-978-681-5409; 8AM-4:30PM (recording until 4PM). www.lawrencedeeds.com

Index: All in one. Records indexed on a public use terminal back to 1981. Office will perform a UCC search but public must search other records themselves. Only real estate related UCCs filed here. Copy fee $1.00 per page. Cert fee- $1.00 per page plus copy fee. Payee- Essex County Register of Deeds. **Online access to Real Estate, Grantor/Grantee, Deed, Lien records:** Search the recorder database for free at http://72.72.82.242/alis/ww400r . Also see Andover Town and Essex County Southern District. **Other phones:** Treasurer- 978-683-2745. **Property tax/Assessing-** 200 Common St, Lawrence, MA 01840; 978-794-5790.

Essex County (Southern District)

County Register of Deeds, 36 Federal St, Salem, MA 01970. 978-741-0201; fax-978-744-5865; 8AM-4:30PM www.salemdeeds.com

Index: All in one. Records indexed on a public use terminal back to 1964. Only the public may search. Copy fee $1.00 per page; self serve $.50. Cert fee- $1.00 per page includes copy fee. Payee- Essex County Register of Deeds. **Online access to Real Estate, Grantor/Grantee, Deed, Lien records:** Records on the Essex County South Registry of Deeds database are free at www.salemdeeds.com/goget.asp. Click on "Deeds online". Images start 1/1992; records back to 1/1984. Search by grantee/grantor, town & date, street, or book & page. Search the recorder database for free at www.lawrencedeeds.com/dsSearch.asp. Also see Andover Town and Essex County Northern District. **Property tax/Assessing-** 978-741-0200.

Essex County Cities/Towns

Amesbury Town, 62 Friend St, Town Hall, Amesbury, MA 01913, 978-388-8100, fax-978-388-8150; 8AM-4PM M-Th; 5PM-8PM Th; 8AM-N F http://data.visionappraisal.com/AmesburyMA/. **Online-** Search the town assessor data at http://data.visionappraisal.com/AmesburyMA/. Free registration for full data.

Andover Town, 36 Bartlet St, Andover, MA 01810-3882, 978-623-8255, fax-978-623-8260; 8:30AM-4:30PM http://andoverma.gov/assessors/ **Online-** Property tax records on Assessor's database are free at http://andoverma.gov/assessedvalues/ but no name searching.

Beverly City, 191 Cabot St, Beverly, MA 01915-1031, 978-921-6000 x164, fax-978-921-8511; 8:30AM-4:30PM M,T,W; 8:30AM-7:30PM Th; 8:30AM-1PM **Online-** Access city property data free at http://beverly.patriotproperties.com/default.asp.

Boxford Town, 7A Spofford Rd, Boxford, MA 01921, 978-887-6000 x501, fax-978-887-3546; 8AM-4:30PM M-Th; Closed Fri.

Danvers Town, 1 Sylvan St, Town Hall, Danvers, MA 01923, 978-777-0001, fax-978-777-1025; 8AM-5PM M-W; 8AM-7:30PM Th; 8AM-1:30PM F **Online-** Access property data free at http://danvers.patriotproperties.com/default.asp.

Georgetown Town, 1 Library St, Town Hall, Georgetown, MA 01833, 978-352-5711, fax-978-352-5725; 9-N M,W; 9AM-4PM T-TH; Closed F www.georgetownma.gov/Public_Documents/GeorgetownMA_Assessor/index **Online-** assessor database at http://data.visionappraisal.com/GeorgetownMA/DEFAULT.asp. Registration required.

Gloucester City, 9 Dale Ave, Gloucester, MA 01930-5998, 978-281-9720, fax-978-281-8472; 8:30-4PM M-W,F Winter; 8:30AM-6:30PM Th

Groveland Town, 183 Main St, Town Hall, Groveland, MA 01830, 978-469-5005, fax-978-469-5006; 7AM-2PM

Hamilton Town, PO Box 429, Hamilton, MA 01936, (577 Bay Rd) 978-468-5570, fax-978-468-2682; 8AM-7PM M; 8AM-4:30PM T-TH; Closed F www.hamiltonma.gov **Online-** Real Estate records located at Essex County.

Haverhill City, 4 Summer St, Rm 118, City Hall, Haverhill, MA 01830, 978-374-2312, fax-978-373-8490; 8AM-4PM **Online-** property data free at http://haverhill.patriotproperties.com/default.asp.

Ipswich Town, 25 Green St, Ipswich, MA 01938-2357, 978-356-6600, fax-978-356-6616; 8AM-7PM M; 8AM-4PM T,W,Th; 8AM-N Fri **Online-** Access property data free at http://ipswich.patriotproperties.com/default.asp.

Lawrence City, 200 Common St, Lawrence, MA 01840, 978-794-5803, fax-978-794-1354; 8:30AM-4:30PM

Lynn City, 3 City Hall Sq, Lynn, MA 01901, 781-598-4000, fax-781-477-7032; 8:30AM-4PM M,W,TH; 8:30AM-8PM T; 8:30AM-12:30PM F **Online-** Access property data free at http://lynn.patriotproperties.com/default.asp.

Lynnfield Town, 55 Summer St, Lynnfield, MA 01940-1823, 781-334-3128, fax-781-334-5829; 8AM-4:30PM (F 8AM-1PM) **Online-** Access property data free at http://lynnfield.patriotproperties.com/default.asp.

Manchester-by-the-Sea Town, 10 Central St, Town Hall, Manchester-by-the Sea, MA 01944-1399, (10 Central St, 1st Fl, Rm #4, Town Hall, Manchester-by-the Sea, MA 01944) 978-526-2040, fax-978-526-2001; 9AM-5PM M-W; 9AM-8PM Th **Online-** Search the property assessment data at http://manchester.patriotproperties.com/default.asp.

Marblehead Town, Abbot Hall, Marblehead, MA 01945, 781-631-0528, fax-781-631-8571; 2:30-5PM, M,T,Th; 7:30AM-7:30PM, W; 7:30AM-12:30PM Fri **Online-** Access property data free at http://marblehead.patriotproperties.com/default.asp?br=exp&vr=6.

Merrimac Town, 4 School St, Town Hall, Merrimac, MA 01860, 978-346-8013, fax-978-346-7832; 9AM-4PM, M,T,TH,F A public access terminal is available.

Methuen City, 41 Pleasant St, Rm 112, Methuen, MA 01844, 978-983-8595, fax-978-983-8974; 8AM-4:30PM M-Th; 8AM-N Fri Public access terminal available. www.cityofmethuen.net/index.php **Online-** Search the property assessment data free at http://webpro2005.cityofmethuen.net/default.asp.

Middleton Town, 48 S Main St, Memorial Hall, Middleton, MA 01949, 978-774-6927, fax-978-774-6167; 9AM-4PM M-W-Th; 9AM-1PM F; 6-8PM T

Nahant Town, Town Hall, Nahant, MA 01908-0075, 781-581-0018, fax-781-593-0340; 9AM-N **Online-** Access property data free at http://nahant.patriotproperties.com/default.asp.

Newbury Town, 25 High Rd, Newbury, MA 01951-4799, 978-462-2332, fax-978-465-3064; 8AM-4PM M,,W,Th; 8AM-7PM T; Closed Fri. Public use terminal available. **Online-** Access property tax data free at http://newbury.patriotproperties.com/default.asp.

Newburyport City, PO Box 550, Newburyport, MA 01950, (60 Pleasant St) 978-465-4407, fax-978-462-7936; 8AM-4PM M,T,W; 8AM-8PM TH; 8AM-N F www.cityofnewburyport.com/assessor.htm **Online-** Search city assessor database at http://data.visionappraisal.com/NewBURYPORTMA/. Free registration for full data.

North Andover Town, 120 Main St, North Andover, MA 01845, 978-688-9502, fax-978-688-9557; 8:30AM-4:30PM **Online-** Access assessor rolls and property sales free at http://csc-ma.us/PropertyContent/jsp/Home.jsp?Page=1.

Peabody City, 24 Lowell St, City Hall, Peabody, MA 01960, 978-538-5756, fax-978-538-5985; 8:30AM-4PM M-W; 8:30AM-7PM TH; 8:30AM-12:30PM F **Online-** Access property data free at http://host.appgeo.com/PeabodyMA/

Rockport Town, PO Box 429, Rockport, MA 01966, (34 Broadway) 978-546-6894, fax-978-546-3562; 8AM-4PM

Rowley Town, PO Box 351, Rowley, MA 01969-0351, (139 Main St, 1A Rte) 978-948-2081, fax-978-948-2162; 1-8PM M, 8AM-4:30PM W, 8AM-N T, Th, F **Online-** Search the town assessor data at http://data.visionappraisal.com/RowleyMA/.

Salem City, 93 Washington, City Hall, Salem, MA 01970-3593, 978-745-9595 x5611, fax-978-740-9209; 8AM-4PM M-W; 8AM-7PM Th; 8AM-N Fri **Online-** property data by location or parcel ID at www.salem.com/Pages/SalemMA_WebDocs/maps but no name searching. Also, access property data free at http://salem.patriotproperties.com/default.asp. No name searching.

Salisbury Town, 5 Beach Rd, Salisbury, MA 01952, 978-462-7591, fax-978-462-4176; 8:30AM-6PM M, 8:30AM-4PM T-Th; 8:30AM-1PM F **Online-** Access property data free at http://salisbury.patriotproperties.com/default.asp.

Saugus Town, 298 Central St, Town Hall, Saugus, MA 01906, 781-231-4101, fax-781-231-4109; 8:30AM-7PM M; 8:15AM-5PM T,W,Th; 8:15AM-12:30PM F **Online-** Access assessor rolls and property sales free at http://csc-ma.us/PropertyContent/jsp/Home.jsp?Page=1.

Swampscott Town, 22 Monument Ave, Town Hall, Swampscott, MA 01907, 781-596-8855, fax-781-596-8870; 8AM-4:30PM M-Th; 8AM-N F Public access terminal available. **Online-** Access property data free at http://swampscott.patriotproperties.com/default.asp.

Topsfield Town, 8 W Common St, Town Hall, Topsfield, MA 01983, 978-887-1505, fax-978-887-1507; 8AM-4PM M-TH; 8AM-N Fri www.topsfield-ma.gov/gov/assessor/assessorsboard.shtml

Town of Essex, Martin St, Town Hall, Essex, MA 01929, 978-768-7111; 8:30AM-1PM M,W; 1-4PM T & Th; Closed F

Wenham Town, 138 Main St, Town Hall, Wenham, MA 01984, (5 School St, Town Hall, Wenham, MA 01984) 978-468-5520 x1, fax-978-468-8014; 9:30AM-4:30PM M,W,TH; 9:30AM-7PM T; 9:30AM-1PM F www.wenhamma.gov/dpts_bds_comms/assessors.htm

West Newbury Town, 381 Main St, Town Office Bldg, West Newbury, MA 01985-1499, 978-363-1100 x110, fax-978-363-1117; 8AM-4:30PM M-TH; 8AM-N Fri. www.westnewbury-ma.gov/Public_Documents/WestNewburyMA_Assessor/index

Franklin County

County Register of Deeds, PO Box 1495, Greenfield, MA 01302-1495. 413-772-0239; fax-413-774-7150; 8:30AM-4:30PM (Recording 8:45AM-4PM). http://franklindeeds.com
Index: All in one. Records indexed on a public use terminal back to 1956. Only the public may search. Copy fee $1.00 per page. Cert fee- none. Payee- Commonwealth of Massachusetts. **Online access to Real Estate, Deed, Lien, Judgment records:** Access to Registry of Deeds data is free at www.masslandrecords.com. Select Franklin County on map. **Property tax/Assessing-** 355 E Central St, Municipal Bldg, Franklin, MA 02038; 508-520-4920, assessor fax- 508-520-4923. hours- 8AM-4:00PM M,T,TH; 8AM-6PM W; 8AM-1PM F

Franklin County Cities/Towns

Ashfield Town, PO Box 560, Ashfield, MA 01330-0595, (412 Main St, Town Hall, Ashfield, MA 01330) 413-628-4441, fax-413-628-0228; 8AM-7PM M; 9AM-5PM T; 8:30AM-7:30PM W; 9AM-5PM F

Bernardston Town, PO Box 504, Bernardston, MA 01337-0435, (38 Church St, Town Hall, Bernardston, MA 01337) 413-648-5408, fax-413-648-9318; 9AM-2PM **Online-** Access assessor rolls and property sales free at http://csc-ma.us/PropertyContent/jsp/Home.jsp?Page=1. Select Bernardston Town.

Buckland Town, PO Box 159, Buckland, MA 01338, (17 State St) 413-625-8572, fax-413-625-8570; 9AM-2PM M-Th

Charlemont Town, PO Box 605, Charlemont, MA 01339-0605, (2023 Rte 2) 413-625-6157, fax-413-625-6157; by appointment http://csc-ma.us/Charlemont **Online-** Access assessor rolls and property sales free at http://csc-ma.us/PropertyContent/jsp/Home.jsp?Page=1.

Colrain Town, 55 Main Rd, Colrain, MA 01340, 413-624-3454, fax-413-624-8852; 9AM-4PM M-Th, 7PM-9PM M

Conway Town, PO Box 240, Conway, MA 01341, (32 Main St, Town Office Bldg, Conway, MA 01341) 413-369-4235 x4, fax-413-369-4237; 9AM-N T,Th,F

Deerfield Town, 8 Conway St, South Deerfield, MA 01373, 413-665-2130, fax-413-665-5512; 9AM-4PM A public access terminal is available. Property card may be printed for $1.00. **Online-** Access property data free at http://deerfield.patriotproperties.com/default.asp.

Erving Town, 12 E Main St, Town Hall, Erving, MA 01344, 413-422-2800, fax-413-422-2808; 10AM-2PM

Franklin Town, 355 E Central St, Municipal Bldg Ground Fl, Franklin, MA 02038, 508-520-4900, fax-508-520-4903; 8AM-4PM M,T,TH, 8AM-6PM W; 8AM -1PM F. Public terminal is available. http://franklinma.virtualtownhall.net/Pages/FranklinMA_Assessors/index **Online-** Access property data free at http://franklin.patriotproperties.com/default.asp.

Gill Town, 325 Main Rd, Town Clerk's Office, Gill, MA 01376, 413-863-8103, fax-413-863-7775; 6PM-7:30PM M T; N-5PM F; 9AM-N Sat

Greenfield Town, 14 Court Sq, Town Hall, Greenfield, MA 01301, 413-772-1555 x112, fax-413-772-1542; 8AM-5PM M-Th; 8AM-12:30PM Fri Public access terminal available. **Online-** Access the property search database free at http://75.147.40.237/Assessors/Permitsearch.asp.

Hawley Town, Town Hall, Hawley, MA 01339-9624, 413-339-5518, fax-413-339-4959; 3PM-5PM Wed

Heath Town, 1 E Main St, Town Hall, Heath, MA 01346, 413-337-4934, fax-413-337-8542; 9:30AM-1:30PM M-Th **Online-** Access assessor rolls and property sales free at http://csc-ma.us/PropertyContent/jsp/Home.jsp?Page=1. Select Heath Town.

Leverett Town, PO Box 178, Leverett, MA 01054, (9 Montague Rd, Town Hall, Leverett, MA 01054) 413-548-9150, fax-413-548-9150; 10AM-2:30PM T,W,TH

Leyden Town, Town Hall, Leyden, MA 01337, 413-774-7769, fax-413-772-0146; 8AM-1PM M; 1PM-5PM W

Monroe Town, PO Box 6, Monroe, MA 01350, (Town Hall) 413-424-5272, fax-413-424-7580; 8AM-N M-W **Online-** Access assessor rolls and property sales free at http://csc-ma.us/PropertyContent/jsp/Home.jsp?Page=1.

Montague Town, 1 Ave A, Turners Falls, MA 01376-1128, 413-863-3200 x203, fax-413-863-3224; 8:30AM-4:30PM Public terminal available. **Online-** Access property and assessment data free at http://montague.patriotproperties.com/default.asp?br=exp&vr=6.

New Salem Town, 15 S Main St, Town Hall, New Salem, MA 01355, 978-544-2731, fax-978-544-5775; 6-8PM M; 9-11AM W. No public terminal.

Northfield Town, 69 Main St, Town Hall, Northfield, MA 01360, 413-498-2901, fax-413-498-5103; 9AM-3PM M-T (& 2nd Wed); 9-N, 5-8PM Wed

Orange Town, 6 Prospect St, Orange, MA 01364, 978-544-1100 x101, fax-978-544-1134; 8AM-4PM M-Th; 8AM-1PM F

Shelburne Town, 51 Bridge St, Town Hall, Shelburne, MA 01370, 413-625-0301, fax-413-625-0312; 9AM-5PM M T; 5-8PM Th

Shutesbury Town, PO Box 264, Shutesbury, MA 01072-0264, (1 Cooleyville Rd, Town Hall, Shutesbury, MA 01072) 413-259-1204, fax-413-259-1107; 9AM-1PM M-Th

Sunderland Town, 12 School St, Sunderland, MA 01375-9503, 413-665-1442, fax-413-665-1446; hours - 8AM-4PM M-TH; 8AM-N Fri. www.townofsunderland.us/Assessors.html

Warwick Town, 12 Athol Rd, Town Hall, Warwick, MA 01378, 978-544-8304, fax-978-544-6499; 8AM-2PM, M

Wendell Town, PO Box 18, Wendell Depot, MA 01380, (7 Morse Village Rd) 978-544-6682, fax-978-544-6052; 6:30PM-8:30PM Wed or by appointment

Whately Town, PO Box 89, Whately, MA 01093-0089, (218 Chestnut Plain Rd) 413-665-0054, fax-413-665-9560; N-7PM T; 9AM-4PM M,W,Th,F

Hampden County

County Register of Deeds, 50 State St; Hall of Justice, Springfield, MA 01103. 413-755-1722; fax-413-731-8190; 8:30AM-4:30PM; 9AM-4PM recording. http://registryofdeeds.co.hampden.ma.us
Index: Separate indices to search include recorded land, registered land. Records indexed on computer back to 1960. Only the public may search. Copy fee $1.00 per page; plan copies $3.00 per sheet. Cert fee- none. Payee- Hampden County Registry of Deeds. Bulk data available for purchase, contact Administration Dept. **Online Real Estate, Deed, Lien records:** Access to the county index of land records is free or via sub at http://204.213.242.147/alis/ww400r.pgm. Images can be viewed free, but cannot be printed unless you subscribe and become a remote access customer. (Copies can be printed at $.50 per page, billed monthly. Access to images via dial-up or web requires a $100 annual fee. Records go back to 1960. Lending agency info is available. Searchable indexes are bankruptcy (from PACER), unregistered land site, and registered land site. For info, contact Greg Rogers at 413-755-1722 x149 or Kim Kleis at 413-755-1722 x129. **Property tax/Assessing-** 413-787-6160.

Hampden County Cities/Towns

Agawam Town, 36 Main St, Agawam, MA 01001-1837, 413-786-0400 x215, fax-413-786-9927; 8:30AM-4:30PM www.agawam.ma.us **Online-** Access Property Assessment Data free at http://agawam.patriotproperties.com/default.asp.

Blandford Town, PO Box 101, Blandford, MA 01008, (102 Main St) 413-848-2782, fax-413-848-0908; 6-8PM Mon Evening or by appointment **Online-** Access property data free at www.townofblandford.org/search.aspx#Results.

Brimfield Town, PO Box 508, Brimfield, MA 01010, (21 Main St, Town Hall, Brimfield, MA 01010) 413-245-4101, fax-413-245-4107; 6:30PM-8PM T; 9-11AM Sat

Chester Town, 15 Middlefield Rd, Town Hall, Chester, MA 01011, 413-354-6603, fax-413-354-2268; 6-7PM M www.townofchester.net/chestermass/id9.html **Online-** Access assessor rolls and property sales free at http://csc-ma.us/PropertyContent/jsp/Home.jsp?Page=1. Select Chester Town.

Chicopee City, 17 Springfield St, City Hall, Chicopee, MA 01013, 413-594-1466, fax-413-594-1469; 9AM-5PM

East Longmeadow Town, 60 Center Sq, East Longmeadow, MA 01028-2446, 413-525-5400 x410, fax-413-525-0022; 8AM-4PM

Granville Town, PO Box 247, Granville, MA 01034-0247, (707 Main Rd, Town Hall, Granville, MA 01034) 413-357-8585, fax-413-357-6002; 9AM-1PM, 7-9PM M

Hampden Town, PO Box 215, Hampden, MA 01036, (625 Main St) 413-566-2151 x103, fax-413-566-3513; 9AM-3PM M-TH; Closed F www.hampden.org/dept/boa.html

Holland Town, 27 Sturbridge Rd, Holland, MA 01521-9712, 413-245-7108 x12, fax-413-245-7037; 1PM-4PM M, Th; 1PM-4PM,7:30PM-8:30PM Tues http://town.holland.ma.us/Pages/HollandMA_Assessor/index **Online-** Access assessor data free at www.visionappraisal.com/databases/.

Holyoke City, 536 Dwight St, Rm 2, Holyoke, MA 01040, (City Hall, Rm 2) 413-322-5520, fax-413-322-5521; 8:30AM-4:30PM

Longmeadow Town, 20 Williams St, Town Hall, Longmeadow, MA 01106, 413-565-4103, fax-413-565-4130; 8:15AM-4:30PM M-Th; 8:15AM-Noon F **Online-** Access to tax records is at http://data.visionappraisal.com/LONGMEADOWMA/. Free registration for full data.

Ludlow Town, 488 Chapin St, Ludlow, MA 01056, 413-583-5600, fax-413-583-5603; 8:30AM-4:30PM

Monson Town, 110 Main St, #4, Monson, MA 01057-1332, (110 Main St) 413-267-4115, fax-413-267-3726; 9AM-4PM

Montgomery Town, 161 Main Rd, Town Hall, Montgomery, MA 01085, 413-862-3386, fax-413-862-3204; by appointment

Palmer Town, 4417 Main St, Palmer Town Bldg, Palmer, MA 01069, 413-283-2608, fax-413-283-2637; 9AM-4PM Public access terminals available.

Russell Town, 65 Main St, Town Hall, Russell, MA 01071, 413-862-6207, fax-413-862-3103; 4:30-6:30PM T; 4-6PM F

Southwick Town, 454 College Hwy, Southwick, MA 01077, 413-569-5504, fax-413-569-0667; 8:30AM-4:30PM **Online-** Search town assessor data at http://data.visionappraisal.com/SouthwickMA/. Free registration for full data.

Springfield City, 36 Court St, Springfield, MA 01103, 413-787-6095, fax-413-787-6502; 9AM-4PM (Th open until 6PM) **Online-** Access city assessor property valuations free at www.springfieldcityhall.com/finance/assr-search.0.html. Also, search city GIS-mapping site for property data at http://www2.springfieldcityhall.com/gis/ but no name searching.

Tolland Town, 241 W Granville Rd, Tolland, MA 01034, 413-258-4068, fax-413-258-4048; 8AM-4PM M-T; 8AM-N Wed **Online-** Access property data in pdf format free at www.tolland-ma.gov/Public_Documents/TollandMA_Assessor/property_lookup. Also, access assessor rolls and property sales free at http://csc-ma.us/PropertyContent/jsp/Home.jsp?Page=1.

Wales Town, PO Box 834, Wales, MA 01081-0834, (3 Hollow Rd, Town Hall, Wales, MA 01081) 413-245-7571, fax-413-245-3261; 9AM-3PM M-T

West Springfield Town, 26 Central St, #8, West Springfield, MA 01089-2779, 413-263-3012, fax-413-263-3046; 8AM-4:30PM www.west-springfield.ma.us/Public_Documents/WSpringfieldMA_Assr/index **Online-** Search town assessor database http://data.visionappraisal.com/WestSpringfieldMA/.

Westfield City, 59 Court St, Westfield, MA 01085-3574, 413-572-6235, fax-413-564-3114; 9AM-5PM **Online-** Assessor records can be found free for Westfield City at http://data.visionappraisal.com/WestfieldMA/.

Wilbraham Town, 240 Springfield St, Wilbraham, MA 01095, 413-596-2800 x200, fax-413-596-2830; 8:30-4:30 http://wilbrahamma.virtualtownhall.net/Pages/WilbrahamMA_Assessors/index

Hampshire County

County Register of Deeds, 33 King St, #1; Hall of Records, Northampton, MA 01060. Recording, R/E & UCC phone-413-584-3637; fax-413-584-4136; 8:30AM-4:30PM (Recording ends at 4PM). www.hampshiredeeds.com

Index: All in one. Records indexed on a public use terminal back to 1968. Only the public may search. Copy fee $1.00 per page. Cert fee- none. Payee- Commonwealth of Massachusetts. **Online access to Real Estate, Deed, Lien, Judgment, Will records:** Access to records for free at www.sec.state.ma.us/sec/rod/rodhamp/hampidx.htm; index 1973-present, images 1870-present. Also, Registry of Deeds records are searchable at www.masslandrecords.com. Click on Hampshire on map. Images go back to 1873. **Property tax/Assessing-** 212 Main St, City Hall, Northampton, MA 01060; 413-587-1202, fax- 413-587-1289.

Hampshire County Cities/Towns

Amherst Town, 4 Boltwood Ave, Town Hall, Amherst, MA 01002, 413-259-3035, fax-413-259-2401; 8AM-4:30PM M,T,W,F; Noon-4:30PM TH **Online-** Search the town assessor data at http://data.visionappraisal.com/AmherstMA/. Free registration for full data. Also, the town has a GIS-mapping site but no name searching, free at http://gis.amherstma.gov/public/propertysearch.aspx.

Belchertown Town, PO Box 629, Belchertown, MA 01007-0629, (2 Jabish St) 413-323-0281, fax-413-323-0107; 8AM-5PM www.belchertown.org/departments/assessors/assesshome.htm **Online-** Access property data free at http://belchertown.patriotproperties.com/default.asp.

Chesterfield Town, 422 Main Rd, Box 13, Davenport Bldg, Chesterfield, MA 01012-0013, (422 Main Rd, Davenport Bldg) 413-296-4741, fax-413-296-4394; 7-9PM M or by Appointment

Cummington Town, 585 Berkshire Tr, Cummington, MA 01026, 413-634-5458, fax-413-634-5568; 6-8PM W No public access terminal. www.cummington-ma.gov/Assessor.php

Easthampton City, 50 Payson Ave, #100, Easthampton, MA 01027, (50 Payson Ave) 413-529-1460, fax-413-529-1417; 8AM-4PM M-F; 7-8PM Wwd. Public access terminal available during business hours.

Goshen Town, PO Box 124, Goshen, MA 01032-0124, (40 Main St, Town Offices, Goshen, MA 01032) 413-268-8236, fax-413-268-8237; 7AM-8:30PM Monday

Granby Town, 250 State St, Kellogg Hall, Granby, MA 01033, 413-467-7178, fax-413-467-2080; 9AM-3PM M,T,W,Th; 9AM-N Fri; 7-9PM 1st & 3rd M

Hadley Town, 100 Middle St, Hadley, MA 01035-9517, 413-584-1590, fax-413-586-5661; 9-4PM www.hadleyma.org/offices/assessor.shtml

Hatfield Town, 59 Main St, Hatfield, MA 01038-9702, 413-247-0492, fax-413-347-5029; 8AM-N; 1-4:30PM

Huntington Town, PO Box 523, Office of Town Clerk, Huntington, MA 01050, (24 Russell Rd, Office of Town Clerk, Huntington, MA 01050) 413-667-3186, fax-413-667-3507; 9AM-N Mon; 6-8PM Wed

Northampton City, 210 Main St, Northampton, MA 01060, 413-587-1224, fax-413-587-1220; 8:30-4:30PM www.northamptonma.gov/assessor/ **Online-** Access to property evaluation information for free go to www.northamptonassessor.us/

Pelham Town, 351 Amherst Rd, Rhodes Bldg, Pelham, MA 01002-9753, 413-253-7129, fax-413-256-1061; 8:30AM-4:30PM M-Th

Plainfield Town, 304 Main St, Plainfield, MA 01070, 413-634-5420, fax-413-634-5683; 10AM-Noon Sat

South Hadley Town, 116 Main St, South Hadley, MA 01075-2833, 413-538-5023, fax-413-538-7565; 8:30AM-4:30PM

Southampton Town, PO Box 276, Southampton, MA 01073, (8 East St, Town Hall, Southampton, MA 01073) 413-527-8392, fax-413-529-1006; 8:30AM-4PM M-Th **Online-** assessor property data in spreadsheet format free at www.town.southampton.ma.us/dbcc/files/SOUTHAMPTON%20FY2008%20ASSESSED%20VALUES.xls

Ware Town, 126 Main St, Ware, MA 01082, 413-967-4471, fax-413-967-9600; 8:30AM-4:30PM

Westhampton Town, Town Hall, Westhampton, MA 01027, 413-527-0463, fax-413-527-8655; 7-8:30PM M **Online-** Access assessor rolls and property sales free at http://csc-ma.us/PropertyContent/jsp/Home.jsp?Page=1.

Williamsburg Town, PO Box 447, Haydenville, MA 01039-0447, (141 Main St, Town Office, Haydenville, MA 01039) 413-268-8402, fax-413-268-8409; 9AM-2PM M; 9AM-N T; 9AM-2PM/6PM-8PM TH

Worthington Town, Town Hall, Worthington, MA 01098-0247, (160 Huntington Rd, Town Hall, Worthington, MA 01098) 413-238-5578, fax-413-238-5579; 10AM-Noon Sat.

Middlesex County (Northern District)

County Register of Deeds, 360 Gorham St, Lowell, MA 01852. 978-322-9000; fax-978-322-9001; 8:30AM-4:15PM www.lowelldeeds.com

Index: Separate indices to search include recorded land, registered land, plans. Records indexed on a public use terminal back to 1/2/1976. Only the public may search. Copy fee $1.00 per page. Cert fee- $1.00 per page plus copy fee. Payee- Commonwealth of Massachusetts. Bulk data available for purchase from ACS company,contact Bob Gerenscer. **Online access to Real Estate, Deed, Lien, Judgment, UCC, Will records:** Access Register of Deeds data free at www.masslandrecords.com. Click on North Middlesex on map. **Property tax/Assessing-** 978-970-4200.

Middlesex County (Southern District)

County Registry of Deeds, 208 Cambridge St, Cambridge, MA 02141. Recording, R/E & UCC phone-617-679-6300; fax-617-494-9083; 8AM-4PM www.cambridgedeeds.com/

Index: All in one. Records indexed on a public use terminal back to 1974. Only the public may search. Copy fee $1.00 per page. Cert fee- $1.00 per page includes copy fee. Payee- Commonwealth of Massachusetts. **Online access to Real Estate, Deed, Lien, Judgment records:** Access to Register of Deeds data is free www.masslandrecords.com. Click on South Middlesex on map.

Acton Town, 472 Main St, Town Hall, Acton, MA 01720, 978-264-9615, fax-978-264-9630; 8AM-5PM. Public access terminal available.

Middlesex County Cities/Towns

Arlington Town, 730 Mass Ave, Town Hall, Arlington, MA 02476-9109, 781-316-3073, fax-781-316-3079; 8AM-4PM, M-W, 8AM-7PM,Th, 8-N, Fri **Online-** Search the town assessor database free at http://arlserver.town.arlington.ma.us/Property/.

Ashby Town, 895 Main St, Ashby, MA 01431, 978-386-2424 x10, fax-978-386-2490; 9AM-N M-

TH; 5PM-8PM W **Online-** Access assessor rolls and property sales free at http://csc-ma.us/PropertyContent/jsp/Home.jsp?Page=1. Click on Ashby Town. Also, access to parcel maps for free at www.ci.ashby.ma.us/assessors/maplink.html.

Ashland Town, 101 Main St, Town Hall, Ashland, MA 01721, 508-881-0100 x601, fax-508-231-1503; 8AM-3:30PM M,T,Th; 8AM-7PM W **Online-** Access assessor rolls and property sales free at http://csc-ma.us/PropertyContent/jsp/Home.jsp?Page=1.

Ayer Town, PO Box 308, Ayer, MA 01432, (1 Main St, Town Hall, Ayer, MA 01432) 978-772-8215, fax-978-772-8222; 8:30AM-5PM www.ayer.ma.us **Online-** Access assessor rolls and property sales free at http://csc-ma.us/PropertyContent/jsp/Home.jsp?Page=1. Click on Ayer Town.

Bedford Town, 10 Mudge Way, Town Hall, Bedford, MA 01730-0083, 781-275-0083, fax-781-275-5757; 8AM-4PM www.town.bedford.ma.us/assessors/assessorsindex.html **Online-** Access assessor rolls and property sales free at http://csc-ma.us/PropertyContent/jsp/Home.jsp?Page=1.

Belmont Town, 455 Concord Ave, Town Hall, Belmont, MA 02178-2514, 617-993-2600, fax-617-993-2601; 8AM-4PM **Online-** Access town assessor data free at http://75.69.237.127/Belmont/.

Billerica Town, 365 Boston Rd, Town Hall, Billerica, MA 01821-1885, 978-671-0924, fax-978-663-6510; 8:30AM-4PM **Online-** property data free http://billerica.patriotproperties.com/default.asp. No name searching.

Boxborough Town, 29 Middle Rd, Boxborough, MA 01719-1499, 978-263-1116 x5, fax-978-264-3127; 10AM-2PM & 7-9PM M; 9AM-2PM T-Th, Appt-Fri Public access terminal available.

Burlington Town, 29 Center St, Burlington, MA 01803, 781-270-1660, fax-781-238-4692; 8:30AM-4:30PM www.burlington.org/assessors.htm **Online-** Access property data free at http://burlington.patriotproperties.com/default.asp. Also, access assessor's maps for free at www.burlington.org/engineering/maps.htm.

Cambridge City, 795 Massachusetts Ave, Rm 103, City Hall, Cambridge, MA 02139, 617-349-4260, fax-617-349-4269; 8:30AM-8PM M; 8:30AM-5PM T-TH; 8:30-noon Fri. **Online-** Search city assessor database at www.cambridgema.gov/fiscalaffairs/PropertySearch.cfm. Does not require a username and password, simply click on link.

Carlisle Town, 66 Westford St, Carlisle, MA 01741, 978-369-6155, fax-978-371-0594; 9AM-3PM or by appointment

Chelmsford Town, 50 Billerica Rd, Chelmsford, MA 01824, 978-250-5205, fax-978-2505208; 8:30AM-5PM **Online-** town assessor database at http://data.visionappraisal.com/ChelmsfordMA/. Free registration for full data.

Concord Town, PO Box 535, Concord, MA 01742, (22 Monument Sq) 978-318-3080, fax-978-318-3093; 8AM-4:30PM M-Th; 8AM-N F **Online-** Alpha search residential and commercial assessments at www.concordnet.org/assessor/.

Dracut Town, 62 Arlington St, Rm 4, Dracut, MA 01826, 978-453-0951, fax-978-452-7924; 8:30-4:30 www.dracut-ma.us/departments.aspx?deptid=6 **Online-** Search the town assessor database at http://data.visionappraisal.com/DracutMA/.

Dunstable Town, 511 Main St, Dunstable, MA 01827, 978-649-4514, fax-978-649-4371; 6PM-8PM M; 9AM-3PM T,W,Th http://dunstable-ma.gov/boards/assessors

Everett City, City Hall, Rm 10, Everett, MA 02149, (484 Broadway, Rm 10) 617-394-2225, fax-617-389-0764; 8AM-7:30PM Mon; 8AM-4PM T-Th; 8-11:30AM Fri.

Framingham Town, 150 Concord St, Rm 105, Memorial Bldg, Framingham, MA 01702-8374, 508-532-5520, fax-508-628-1358; 8:30AM-5PM www.framinghamma.gov/index.asp?NID=101 **Online-** assessor rolls and property sales free http://csc-ma.us/PropertyContent/jsp/Home.jsp?Page=1.

Groton Town, 173 Main St, Town Hall, Groton, MA 01450, 978-448-1100, fax-978-448-2030; 8:30AM-7PM M; 8:30AM-4:30PM T-Th; 9-4 F; 9-1 Sat **Online-** Access the property search site for free at http://host.appgeo.com/grotonma/. Also, assessor property records free at www.visionappraisal.com/ coming soon.

Holliston Town, 703 Washington St, Rm 102, Holliston, MA 01746, (703 Washington St, Main Fl, Rm 102, Holliston, MA 01746) 508-429-0601, fax-508-429-0684; 8:30AM-4:30PM www.townofholliston.us/assessors_office.htm **Online-** Access assessor rolls and property sales free at http://csc-ma.us/PropertyContent/jsp/Home.jsp?Page=1. Select Holliston Town. Access to parcel data at http://csc-ma.us/PROPAPP/Opening.do?subAction=NewSearch&town=HollistonPubAcc.

Hopkinton Town, 18 Main St, Hopkinton, MA 01748-1260, 508-497-9710, fax-508-497-9702; 8AM-4:30PM **Online-** Access Board of Assessors maps at www.hopkinton.org/gov/assessor/listing.htm; no name searching. View pdf pages of current assessment reports free at www.hopkinton.org/gov/assessor/pdf/08-appraisal-report.pdf.

Hudson Town, 78 Main St, Town Hall, Hudson, MA 01749, 978-568-9615, fax-978-562-8508; 8AM-4:30PM **Online-** assessor data free at http://data.visionappraisal.com/HudsonMA/DEFAULT.asp.

Lexington Town, 1625 Massachusetts Ave, Town Office Bldg, Lexington, MA 02420, 781-862-0500 x270, fax-781-861-2754; 8:30AM-4:30PM **Online-** Access assessor data free at http://data.visionappraisal.com/LexingtonMA/.

Lincoln Town, PO Box 6353, Lincoln Center, MA 01773-6353, (16 Lincoln Rd) 781-259-2607, fax-781-259-1677; 8:30AM-4:30PM

Littleton Town, PO Box 1305, Littleton, MA 01460, (37 Shattuck St) 978-952-2314, fax-978-952-2321; 9AM-3PM M,T,W,F; 9AM-9PM Th

Lowell City, 375 Merrimack St, City Hall, Lowell, MA 01852, 978-970-4161, fax-978-970-4162; 8AM-5PM **Online-** property assessment data free at www.lowellma.gov/services/gis/.

Malden City, 200 Pleasant St, #323, City Hall, Malden, MA 02148, 781-397-7116, fax-781-388-0610; 8AM-4PM M,W,Th; 8AM-7PM T; 8AM-N Fri A public access terminal is available. www.cityofmalden.org

Marlborough City, 140 Main St, Marlborough, MA 01752-3812, 508-460-3775, fax-508-624-6504; 8:30AM-5PM **Online-** city assessor data at http://data.visionappraisal.com/MarlboroughMA/. Free registration for full data.

Maynard Town, 195 Main St, Town Hall, Maynard, MA 01754-2575, 978-897-8553, fax-978-897-8457; 8AM-4PM **Online-** Access assessor rolls and property sales free at http://csc-ma.us/PropertyContent/jsp/Home.jsp?Page=1.

Medford City, 85 George P Hassett Dr, City Clerk, Medford, MA 02155, 781-393-2425, fax-781-391-1895; 8:30AM-4:30PM M,T,Th; 8:30AM-7:30PM W; 8:30AM-12:30 Fri **Online-** Search the city assessor database at http://data.visionappraisal.com/MedfordMA/.

Melrose City, 562 Main St, Melrose, MA 02176, 781-979-4114, fax-781-979-4149; 8:30AM-4PM M-Th; 8:30AM-12:30PM Fri. **Online-** property data at http://melrose.patriotproperties.com/default.asp.

Natick Town, 13 E Central St, Natick, MA 01760, 508-647-6430, fax-508-655-6715; 8AM-5PM **Online-** Search town assessments free at www.natickma.org/assess/assessinfo.asp.

Newton City, 1000 Commonwealth Ave, Newton Center, MA 02159, 617-796-1200, fax-617-796-1214; 8:30AM-5PM M,W; 8:30AM-8PM Tues **Online-** Records on the City of Newton Fiscal 2003 assessment database are free at www.ci.newton.ma.us/assessors2003/Search.asp. Data represents market value as of January of current year.

North Reading Town, 235 N St, North Reading, MA 01864-1294, 978-664-6030, fax-978-664-4196; 8AM-4PM M-TH; 8AM-1PM F **Online-** Access assessor rolls and property sales free at http://csc-ma.us/NreadingPubAcc/jsp/Home.jsp?Page=1 but no name searching.

Pepperell Town, 1 Main St, Town Hall, Pepperell, MA 01463-1644, 978-433-0339, fax-978-433-0338; hours- 8AM-4:30PM www.town.pepperell.ma.us/TownHall/assessors.html

Reading Town, 16 Lowell St, Reading, MA 01867, 781-942-9050, fax-781-942-9070; 8:30AM-5PM **Online-** Records on Assessor database are free at www.ziplink.net/~reading1/assessor.htm but no name searching.

Sherborn Town, 19 Washington St, Sherborn, MA 01770, 508-651-7853, fax-508-651-0407; 9AM-1PM M-Th & Tues eves 6-8PM

Shirley Town, 7 Keady Way, Shirley, MA 01464, 978-425-2600 x205, fax-978-425-2681; 8:30AMPM-3PM; 6PM-8:30PM Mon & appts **Online-** Access property data free at http://shirley.patriotproperties.com/default.asp.

Somerville City, 93 Highland Ave, Somerville, MA 02143, 617-625-6600 x4100, fax-617-625-4239; 8:30AM-4:30PM M-W; 8:30-7:30PM Th; 8:30-12:30PM Fri. **Online-** Search city assessor data at http://data.visionappraisal.com/SomervilleMA/.

Stoneham Town, 35 Central St, Stoneham, MA 02180, 781-279-2650, fax-781-279-2653; 8AM-4PM M,W-Th; 8AM-7PM T; 8AM-N Fri www.stoneham-ma.gov/Pages/StonehamMA_Assessor/index **Online-** Access property data free at http://stoneham.patriotproperties.com/default.asp?br=exp&vr=6.

Stow Town Clerk, 380 Great Rd, Town Bldg, Stow, MA 01775, 978-897-4514 x1, fax-978-897-4534; 8AM-12:30PM 1PM-4PM M-TH www.stow-ma.gov/Pages/StowMA_Assessor/index

Sudbury Town, 322 Concord Rd, Sudbury, MA 01776-1800, 978-443-8891 x3351, fax-978-443-0264; 9AM-5PM **Online-** Access to the property valuations list for current year is free at www.town.sudbury.ma.us/services/department_home.asp?dept=Assessors. No name searching on this address index list.

Tewksbury Town, 1009 Main St, Town Hall, Tewksbury, MA 01876-2796, 978-640-4355, fax-978-851-8610; 8:30AM-4:30PM **Online-** Search lists of yearly tax assessments free at www.tewksbury.info/assessor/FY2006Assessments.html. Also, address search recent property sales list free at www.tewksbury.net/assessor/sales.html; link to the pdf list is at the bottom of page.

Townsend Town, 272 Main St, Memorial Hall, Townsend, MA 01469, 978-597-1704, fax-978-597-8135; 9AM-4PM; 9AM-8PM T; 9AM-N 1st & 3rd Sat. Public access terminal in Library.

Tyngsborough Town, 25 Bryants Lane, Tyngsborough, MA 01879, 978-649-2300 x129, fax-978-649-2301; 8AM-7PM M; 8:30AM-4PM T-Th; 8-12:30PM Fri. Public terminal in Library.

Wakefield Town, 1 Lafayette St, Town Hall, Wakefield, MA 01880-2383, 781-246-6383, fax-781-246-4155; 8:30AM-5PM **Online-** property data at http://wakefield.patriotproperties.com/default.asp.

Waltham City, 610 Main St, 2nd Fl, Waltham, MA 02452, 781-314-3120, fax-781-314-3130; 8:30AM-4:30PM **Online-** Access property data free at http://waltham.patriotproperties.com/default.asp.

Watertown Town, 149 Main St, Admin Bldg, Watertown, MA 02472, 617-972-6486, fax-617-972-6595; 8:30AM-5PM. **Online-** property data at http://watertown.patriotproperties.com/default.asp.

Wayland Town, 41 Cochituate Rd, Wayland, MA 01778-2697, 508-358-3630 or 3631, fax-508-358-3627; 8:30AM-4:30PM www.wayland.ma.us/assessors/index.htm **Online-** assessor property records at http://data.visionappraisal.com/WAYLANDMA/DEFAULT.asp.

Westford Town, 55 Main St, Town Hall, Westford, MA 01886, 978-692-5515, fax-978-399-2555; 8AM-4PM www.westfordma.gov/ **Online-** town online offerings - property, GIS - free at www.westfordma.gov/pages/onlineservices/gis. Also, access to parcel look-up for free go to www.westfordma.gov/Pages/Government/TownDepartments/WestfordMA_MapsGIS/parcellookup.

Weston Town, PO Box 378, Weston, MA 02493, (11 Town House Rd) 781-893-7320, fax-781-529-0106; 8:30AM-5PM **Online-** Access to property data is free at www.mapsonline.net/westonma/ but no name searching.

Wilmington Town, 121 Glen Rd, Town Hall, Wilmington, MA 01887, 978-658-2030, fax-978-658-3334; 8:30AM-4:30PM

Winchester Town, 71 Mount Vernon St, Town Hall, Winchester, MA 01890, (71 Mount Vernon St, 1st Fl, Town Hall, Winchester, MA 01890) 781-721-7130, fax-781-721-1153; 8AM-4PM www.winchester.us **Online-** property data free at http://winchester.patriotproperties.com/default.asp.

Woburn City, 10 Common St, Woburn, MA 01801-4197, 781-897-5850, fax-781-932-4455; 9AM-4:30PM M-W; 9AM-7PM TH; 9AM-1PM F http://ma-woburn.civicplus.com/index.asp?nid=75 **Online-** Search the city assessor data at http://data.visionappraisal.com/WoburnMA/.

Nantucket County

County Register of Deeds, 16 Broad St, Nantucket, MA 02554. 508-228-7250; fax-508-325-5331; 8AM-4PM; recording: 8AM-N, 1-3:45PM

Index: All in one. Records indexed on a public use terminal back to 1958. Only the public may search. Copy fee $1.00 per page. Cert fee- $1.00 per page plus copy fee. Payee- Nantucket Registry of Deeds. **Online access to Real Estate, Deed, Lien, Mortgage records:** Access land records for free at masslandrecords.com; click Nantucket under "Select a County." . **Other phones:** Treasurer- 508-228-7265; Elections- 508-228-7217; Vital Records- 508-228-7217. **Property tax/Assessing-** 16 Broad St, Nantucket, MA 02554; 508-228-7211, assessor fax-508-228-7210. hours- 8AM-4PM

Nantucket Town, 16 Broad St, Town & County Bldg, Nantucket, MA 02554, 508-228-7217, fax-508-325-5313; 8AM-3:45PM www.nantucket-ma.gov/Pages/NantucketMA_Assessor/index **Online-** Access property data free at http://data.visionappraisal.com/nantucketma/DEFAULT.asp.

Norfolk County

County Register of Deeds, PO Box 69, Dedham, MA 02027-0069. 781-461-6101; fax-781-326-4742; 8:30AM-4:45PM www.norfolkdeeds.org

Index: All in one. Records indexed on a public use terminal back to 1956. Only the public may search. Copy fee $1.00 per page. Cert fee- none. Payee- Norfolk County Register of Deeds. **Online Real Estate, Deed, Lien, Judgment records:** Access to county online records is on two levels, both at http://research.norfolkdeeds.org/ALIS/WW400R.PGM. You may search images and indices free, however, to print requires a subscription; $100 per year plus $1.00 per page. Land records go back to 1956; images to 1793. Land court records go back to 9/1984, with images back to 1901. Customer Svcs- 781-461-6101.

Norfolk County Cities/Towns

Avon Town, Buckley Ctr, Avon, MA 02322, 508-588-0414, fax-508-559-0209; 8:30AM-4:30PM

Bellingham Town, 10 Mechanic St, Bellingham, MA 02019, 508-657-2830, fax-508-657-2832; 8:30AM-4:30PM T,W,Th; 8:30AM-1PM F; 8:30AM-7PM Mon. www.bellinghamma.org/Pages/BellinghamMA_Assessors/index **Online-** property data free at http://bellingham.patriotproperties.com/default.asp.

Braintree Town, 1 JFK Memorial Dr, Braintree, MA 02184-6498, 781-794-8000 x8241, fax-781-794-8259; 8:30AM-4:30PM **Online-** property data at http://braintree.patriotproperties.com/default.asp.

Brookline Town, 333 Washington St, Town Hall, Brookline, MA 02445, 617-730-2010, fax-617-730-2043; 8AM-5PM M-W, 8AM-8PM Th, 8AM-12:30PM F **Online-** Records on the Town of Brookline Assessors database are free at www.brooklinema.gov/assessors/propertylookup1.asp

Canton Town, 801 Washington St, Memorial Hall, Canton, MA 02021, 781-821-5013, fax-781-821-5016; 9AM-5PM **Online-** Access assessed value data at www.town.canton.ma.us/assessors/assessors.htm. No name searching; address only.

Cohasset Town, 41 Highland Ave, Cohasset, MA 02025-1814, 781-383-4100, fax-781-383-1561; 8:30AM-4:30PM M,W,Th; 8:30AM-7PM T; 8:30AM-1PM Fri. Public access terminals available. www.townofcohasset.org/assessor/index.html

Dedham Town, PO Box 306, Dedham, MA 02027, (26 Bryant St) 781-751-9200, fax-781-751-9109; 8:30AM-4:30PM **Online-** Property records on the Assessor's database are free at http://data.visionappraisal.com/dedhamma/. Does not require a username & password, simply click on link. Also, search the GIS mapping site for owner and property data free at www.dedham-ma.gov/index.cfm?pid=12650.

Dover Town, PO Box 250, Dover, MA 02030-0250, (5 Springdale Ave) 508-785-0032, fax-508-785-2341; 9AM-1PM M,W,F; 9AM-4PM T,Th **Online-** Access assessor property values data free at www.doverma.org/assessorsproposedvaluesnew.php. You must open individual tables to search by name.

Foxborough Town, 40 South St, Foxborough, MA 02035-2397, 508-543-1208, fax-508-543-6278; 8:30AM-4PM M,W,TH; 8:30AM-4PM, 5PM-8PM T; 8:30AM-N F Public access terminal available. **Online-** Assessor property records free at www.visionappraisal.com/ coming soon.

Holbrook Town, Town Hall, Holbrook, MA 02343-1502, 781-767-4314, fax-781-767-9054; 8AM-4PM **Online-** Access property data free at http://holbrook.patriotproperties.com/default.asp.

Medfield Town, 459 Main St, Town Hall, Medfield, MA 02052, 508-359-8505, fax-508-359-6182; 8:30AM-4:30PM M-W; 8:30AM-7:30PM Th; 8:30AM-1PM F **Online-** town property data free at http://medfield.patriotproperties.com/default.asp?br=exp&vr=6.

Medway Town, 155 Village St, Medway, MA 02053, 508-533-3204, fax-508-533-3287; 8AM-7:30PM M; 8AM-4PM T-TH; 8AM-1PM Fri. www.townofmedway.org/ **Online-** assessor data free at www.assessedvalues.com/index.zhtml?jurcode=177. Also, Parcel Maps available free via the link on the Assessor webpage.

Millis Town, 900 Main St, Millis, MA 02054-1512, 508-376-7046, fax-508-376-7055; 8:30AM-8PM M; 8:30AM-4:30PM T,W,Th; 8:30AM-12:30PM Fri.

Milton Town, 525 Canton Ave, Town Hall, Milton, MA 02186, 617-898-4859, fax-617-696-6995; 8:30AM-5PM

Needham Town, PO Box 920663, Needham, MA 02492, (1471 Highland Ave) 781-455-7510, fax-781-449-4569; 8:30AM-5PM **Online-** Access assessor rolls and property sales free at http://csc-ma.us/PropertyContent/jsp/Home.jsp?Page=1. Select Needham Town.

Norfolk Town, 1 Liberty Ln, Norfolk, MA 02056, 508-528-1400, fax-508-541-3363; 9AM-6PM M-Th **Online-** Access to town property data is free at http://host.appgeo.com/NorfolkMA/ -no name search.

Norwood Town, PO Box 40, Norwood, MA 02062, (566 Washington St, Municipal Bldg, Norwood, MA 02062) 781-762-1240, fax-781-762-0954; 8AM-4PM

Plainville Town, PO Box 1717, Plainville, MA 02762, (142 South St) 508-695-3142 x20, fax-508-695-1857; 8AM-4:30PM,5PM-8PM M; 8AM-4:30PM T-TH Public access terminal available.

Quincy City, 1305 Hancock St, City Hall, Quincy, MA 02169, 617-376-1136, fax-617-376-1139; 8:30AM-4:30PM **Online-** assessor property data free http://data.visionappraisal.com/QuincyMA/DEFAULt.asp. No name searching. Also a sales look-up.

Randolph Town, 41 S Main St, Randolph, MA 02368, 781-961-0900, fax-781-961-0919; 8:30AM-4:30PM

Sharon Town, 90 S Main St, Town Hall, Sharon, MA 02067, 781-784-1505, fax-781-784-1503; 8:30AM-5PM M-W; 8:30AM-8PM Th; 8:30AM-12:30PM F

Stoughton Town, 10 Pearl St, Town Hall, Stoughton, MA 02072, (10 Pearl St, 1st Fl, Town Hall, Stoughton, MA 02072) 781-341-1300, fax-781-341-1032; 8:30AM-4:30PM M-W; 8:30AM-7PM TH; 8:30AM-N F www.stoughton-ma.gov/main-index.html **Online-** Assessor's database free at http://stoughton.patriotproperties.com/default.asp?br=exp&vr=6

Walpole Town, 135 School St, Town Hall, Walpole, MA 02081-2898, 508-660-7296, fax-508-660-7303; 8AM-4PM M-TH; 8AM-8PM T; 8AM-N, F www.walpole-ma.gov/Assessors.htm **Online-** Search the town assessor database at http://data.visionappraisal.com/WalpoleMA/.

Wellesley Town, 525 Washington St, Town Hall, Wellesley, MA 02482, 781-431-1019 x2250, fax-781-237-5037; 8AM-5PM www.wellesleyma.gov/Pages/WellesleyMA_Assessor/index **Online-** Property tax records from Assessor free at http://wellesleyma.virtualtownhall.net/Pages/WellesleyMA_Assessor/index. Click on Fiscal Year Accessed Values.

Westwood Town, 580 High St, Westwood, MA 02090, 781-326-3964, fax-781-329-8030; 8:30AM-4:30PM M,W,TH; 8:30AM-7PM T; 8:30AM-1PM Fri. www.townhall.westwood.ma.us/index.cfm?pid=10072 **Online-** assessor data at http://data.visionappraisal.com/WestwoodMA/ but no searching.

Weymouth Town, 75 Middle St, Town Hall, East Weymouth, MA 02189, 781-340-5017, fax-781-335-3283; 8:30-4:30PM Public terminal available. www.weymouth.ma.us/mf/index.asp?id=1238 **Online-** Access to property data is free at www.weymouth.ma.us/propview/.

Wrentham Town, 79 South St, Town Hall, Rm 208, Wrentham, MA 02093, 508-384-5415, fax-508-384-5434; 8AM-4PM M-TH; 8AM-1:30PM F www.wrentham.ma.us/index.php?section=39

Plymouth County

Registry of Deeds, 50 Obery St, Plymouth, MA 02360. 508-830-9200, R/E recording phone-508-830-9261; fax-508-830-9280; 8:15AM-4:30PM; recording 8:30AM-4PM). http://plymouthdeeds.org/

Index: Separate indices to search include grantor by year. Records indexed on a public use terminal back to 1971; grantor-grantee back to 1955. Only the public may search. Copy fee $1.00 per page. Cert fee- no cert fee for purchased documents. Payee- Plymouth County Register of Deeds. **Online access to Real Estate, Deed, Lien, Judgment records:** Access to Titleview at http://plymouthdeeds.org/search-records-2.html requires a usage charge of $30.00 per month, plus $1.00 per image page, but guests may do index searches for free, but no image printing. Indices date back to 1955. Access is by dial-up or internet. For info call 508-830-9283. A fax back service is $3 plus $1 per page in county, $5. plus $1 per page, outside.

Plymouth County Cities/Towns

Abington Town, 500 Gliniewicz Way, Abington, MA 02351, 781-982-2112, fax-781-982-2138; 8:30AM-4:30PM http://abingtonmass.com **Online-** Search town assessor database at http://data.visionappraisal.com/AbingtonMA/. Also, search revaluation data free at http://abingtonmass.com/reval.html.

Bridgewater Town, 64 Central Sq, Town Hall, Bridgewater, MA 02324, 508-697-0921, fax-508-697-0941; 8AM-7:30PM Mon; 8AM-4:30PM T,W,Th **Online-** property data free on the GIS site at www.bridgewaterma.org/gisviewer/Index.cfm. No name searching.

Brockton City, 45 School St, Brockton, MA 02301, 508-580-7114, fax-508-580-7104; 8:30AM-4:30PM

Carver Town, 108 Main St, Carver, MA 02330, 508-866-3403, fax-508-866-3408; 8AM-4PM M,W,TH; 8AM-N F, 8AM-7PM T

Duxbury Town, 878 Tremont St, Duxbury, MA 02332-4499, 781-934-1131, fax-781-934-9278; 8AM-4PM. www.town.duxbury.ma.us/Public_Documents/DuxburyMA_BComm/assessors **Online-** assessor rolls and property sales free at http://csc-ma.us/PropertyContent/jsp/Home.jsp?Page=1.

East Bridgewater Town, PO Box 387, East Bridgewater, MA 02333, (175 Central St, Town Hall, East Bridgewater, MA 02333) 508-378-1606, fax-508-378-1638; hours- 8:30AM-8PM Mon;

8:30AM-4:30PM T-TH; 8AM-N Fri www.eastbridgewaterma.org/

Halifax Town, 499 Plymouth St, Halifax, MA 02338-1395, 781-293-7970, fax-781-294-7684; 7AM-4PM; 6:30-8:30PM (Tues-2nd & 4th) (closed Fri) **Online-** Assessor property records free at www.visionappraisal.com/ coming soon.

Hanover Town, 550 Hanover St, Hanover, MA 02339-2217, 781-826-2691, fax-781-826-5239; 8AM-4PM Public access terminal available.

Hanson Town, 542 Liberty St, Town Hall, Hanson, MA 02341, (Town Hall, 542 Liberty St, Hanson, MA 02341) 781-293-2772, fax-781-294-0884; 8AM-5PM M,W,TH; 8-9PM T; closed Fri **Online-** property records free on the GIS-mapping site at http://gis.virtualtownhall.net/hanson/index.htm; no name searching.

Hingham Town, 210 Central St, Hingham, MA 02043, 781-741-1410, fax-781-740-0239; 8:30AM-4:30PM M,W,Th; 8:30AM-7PM T; 8:30AM-1PM Fri **Online-** Search the assessor rolls and property sales free at http://csc-ma.us/HinghamPubAcc/jsp/Home.jsp?. Click on "New Search" or "Sales."

Hull Town, 253 Atlantic Ave, Town Hall, Hull, MA 02045, 781-925-2262, fax-781-925-0224; 8AM-4PM M,W; 8:30AM-7:30PMT, Th www.town.hull.ma.us/Public_Documents/HullMA_Assessors/assessors **Online-** property records free at www.town.hull.ma.us/Public_Documents/HullMA_Assessors/values/HULL%20FIELD%20CARDS

Kingston Town, 26 Evergreen St, Kingston, MA 02364, 781-585-0502, f-781-585-0542; 8:30-4:30

Lakeville Town, 346 Bedford St, Lakeville, MA 02347, 508-946-8814, fax-508-946-3970; 9AM-4PM **Online-** assessor data free at http://data.visionappraisal.com/LakevilleMA/DEFAULT.asp.

Marion Town, 2 Spring St, Marion, MA 02738, 508-748-3502, fax-508-748-9983; 8AM-4:30PM M-Th; 8AM-3:30PM F www.marionma.gov/Pages/MarionMA_Assessors/index **Online-** assessor data at http://data.visionappraisal.com/MarionMA/.

Marshfield Town, 870 Moraine St, Town Hall, Marshfield, MA 02050, 781-834-5540, fax-781-837-7163; 8:30AM-4:30PM **Online-** assessor database at http://marshfield.patriotproperties.com.

Mattapoisett Town, PO Box 89, Mattapoisett, MA 02739-0089, (16 Main St., Town Hall, Mattapoisett, MA 02739) 508-758-4103, fax-508-758-3030; 8AM-4PM **Online-** property data and sales free at http://data.visionappraisal.com/MattapoisettMA/DEFAULT.asp.

Middleborough Town, 20 Centre St, 1st Fl, Middleborough, MA 02346, 508-946-2415, fax-508-946-2308; 8:45AM-5PM **Online-** assessor data at http://data.visionappraisal.com/MiddleboroMA/.

Norwell Town, PO Box 295, Norwell, MA 02061-0295, (345 Main St, Town Hall, Norwell, MA 02061) 781-659-8072, fax-781-659-7795; 8AM-4:15PM M T; 8-7:30PM W; 8-4PM TH; 8-Noon F **Online-** Access assessor property data free at http://data.visionappraisal.com/NorwellMA/.

Pembroke Town, 100 Center St, Pembroke, MA 02359, 781-293-7211, fax-781-293-4650; 8:30AM-4:30PM **Online-** assessor data free at http://pembroke.patriotproperties.com/default.asp?br=exp&vr=6.

Plymouth Town, 11 Lincoln St, Plymouth, MA 02360-3386, 508-747-1620x189, fax-508-830-4062; 8AM-4:30PM **Online-** Access property data free http://plymouth.patriotproperties.com/default.asp.

Plympton Town, 5 Palmer Rd, Plympton, MA 02367-1123, (5 Palmer Rd, Rte 58, Town House, Plympton, MA 02367) 781-585-3220, fax-781-582-1505; 9AM-2PM, 6-8PM M; 9-2PM T-Th.

Rochester Town, 1 Constitution Way, Town Hall, Rochester, MA 02770, 508-763-3866, fax-508-763-4892; 7-9PM M **Online-** property records free at www.visionappraisal.com/ coming soon.

Rockland Town, 242 Union St, Rockland, MA 02370, 781-871-1892 x1, fax-781-871-0386; 8:30AM-4:30PM **Online-** Access to property data to be available free on a private site at www.appraisalresource.com/OnlineDatabases.aspx.

Scituate Town, 600 CJ Cushing Way, Town Hall, Scituate, MA 02066, 781-545-8744, fax-781-545-8704; 8:30AM-4:45PM M,W,Th; 8:30-7:30 T, 8:30-11:45AM F **Online-** Assessor property data for free at www.town.scituate.ma.us/assessor/index.html. Click on "Town of Scituate Property Assessment Data as of…"

Wareham Town, 54 Marion Rd, Wareham, MA 02571, 508-291-3140, fax-508-291-3116; 8:30AM-4:30PM **Online-** town assessor database at http://data.visionappraisal.com/WarehamMA/. Free registration for full data. Also, access GIS-mapping data for free at http://gis.virtualtownhall.net/wareham_new/index.asp

West Bridgewater Town, 65 N Main St, Town Hall, West Bridgewater, MA 02379-1734, 508-894-1200, fax-508-894-1210; 8AM-4PM M,T,TH; 8AM-7PM W; 8AM-1PM Fri

Whitman Town, PO Box 426, Whitman, MA 02382, (54 South Ave) 781-618-9710, fax-781-618-9791; 8AM-4PM M,W,Th-F; 8AM-7:30PM T

Suffolk County

Suffolk Register of Deeds, PO Box 9660, Boston, MA 02114-9660. Recording, R/E & UCC phone-617-788-8575; fax-617-720-4163; 8AM-4:30PM www.suffolkdeeds.com

Index: All in one. Records indexed on a public use terminal back to 1979. Only the public may search. Copy fee $1.00 per page. Cert fee- $1.00 per doc plus copy fee. Payee- Commonwealth of Massachusetts. **Online access to Real Estate, Deed, Lien, Judgment records:** Records on the County Registry of Deeds database are free at www.masslandrecords.com/malr/controller. Search by name, corporation, and grantor/grantee. Recorded land records begin 1978; Registered land, 1983. **Other phones:** Treasurer- 617-788-8575; Elections- 617-788-8575; Vital Records- 617-788-8575. **Property tax/Assessing-** 617-788-8575. **Online access-** Search Boston assessor property records free at www.cityofboston.gov/assessing/search/. City property taxes also available, but no name searching.

Suffolk County Cities/Towns

Boston City, 1 City Hall Plaza, Rm 601, City Hall, Boston, MA 02201, 617-635-4601, fax-617-635-4658; 9AM-5PM **Online-** Records on the City of Boston Assessor database are free at www.cityofboston.gov/assessing/search/. Property tax bill and payment searchable by parcel number free at www.cityofboston.gov/assessing/paysearch.asp.

Chelsea City, 500 Broadway, Rm 209, City Hall, Chelsea, MA 02150, 617-889-8227, fax-617-889-8367; 8AM-4PM M,W,Th; 8AM-7PM T; 8AM-N F **Online-** Search the city assessor database at http://data.visionappraisal.com/ChelseaMA/..

Revere City, 281 Broadway, City Hall, Revere, MA 02151-5087, 781-286-8160, fax-781-286-8135; 8:15AM-5PM M-Th; 8:15AM-N Fri **Online-** Access property data free at http://revere.patriotproperties.com/default.asp.

Winthrop Town, Town Hall, Winthrop, MA 02152-3156, 617-846-1742, fax-617-539-5814; 8AM-7PM M; 8AM-4PM T-Th; 8AM-N Fri

Worcester County (North District)

County Register of Deeds, 166 Boulder Dr, #202, Fitchburg, MA 01420. 978-342-2132; fax-978-345-2865; 8:30AM-4:30PM; Recording- 8:30AM-4PM www.fitchburgdeeds.com/

Index: Separate indices to search include grantor/grantee. Records indexed on computer back to 1973. Only the public may search. Copy fee $.50 per page. Cert fee- $1.00 per page. Payee- Commonwealth of Massachusetts. Bulk data available, contact Donna Duval. **Online access to Real Estate, Deed, Lien, Land Court records:** Access to Registry of Deeds is free at www.fitchburgdeeds.com/. Scroll down left column then click 'Click here to access…' Small fee to copy or certify documents. Land index back to 1973; images to 1868. Also, Also search recorded docs free at www.masslandrecords.com/malr/index.htm. **Property tax/Assessing-** 508-799-1098.

Worcester County (Worcester Dist)

County Register of Deeds, 90 Front St, Worcester, MA 01608. 508-798-7717; fax-508-753-1338; 8:15AM-4:30PM; recording 9AM-N, 1-4PM). www.worcesterdeeds.com

Index: All in one. Records indexed on a public use terminal back to 1966. Only the public may search. Copy fee $1.00 per page. Cert fee- $1.00 per cert plus copy fee. Payee- Worcester County Register of Deeds. **Online access to Real Estate, Grantor/Grantee, Deed, Lien, Judgment, Will records:** Access to the Register of Deeds database is free at www.masslandrecords.com. Click on South Worcester on map. **Other phones:** Treasurer- 508-798-2441. **Property tax/Assessing-** 508-799-1000

Worcester County Cities/Towns

Ashburnham Town, 15 Oakmont Dr, Ashburnham, MA 01430, 978-827-4102, fax-978-827-4105; 8AM-4:30PM (5-7PM 1st & 3rd Mon of month) www.ashburnham-ma.gov/

Athol Town, 584 Main St, Athol, MA 01331, 978-249-4551, fax-978-249-2491; 8AM-5PM M,W,Th; 8AM-8PM T; closed Fri.

Auburn Town, 104 Central St, Auburn, MA 01501, 508-832-7701, fax-508-832-7702; 8-4PM

Barre Town, PO Box 418, Barre, MA 01005, (40 West St, Town Hall, Barre, MA 01005) 978-355-5003, fax-978-355-5025; 9AM-N, 1-4PM T-F; 7-9PM M,W

Berlin Town, 23 Linden St, Box 8, Berlin, MA 01503, (23 Linden St) 978-838-2931, fax-978-838-0014; 12-3PM T,Th; 7-9PM W

Blackstone Town, 15 St Paul St, Municipal Ctr, Blackstone, MA 01504-2295, 508-883-1500 x146, fax-508-883-7043; 9-4:30PM; 5:30-7:30PM Tues www.townofblackstone.com/depts/pages/assessor.php **Online-** Access property data free at http://data.visionappraisal.com/BlackstoneMA/.

Bolton Town, PO Box 278, Bolton, MA 01740, (663 Main St, Rear Entrance, Bolton, MA 01740) 978-779-2771, fax-978-779-5461; 9AM-2:30PM M, W,Th; 9AM-4, 6-8PM T **Online-** Access assessor rolls and property sales free at http://csc-ma.us/PropertyContent/jsp/Home.jsp?Page=1.

Boylston Town, 221 Main St, Boylston, MA 01505, 508-869-2234, fax-508-869-6210; 8AM-2PM M-TH; 6PM-8PM M; Closed Fri. Public access terminals available.

Brookfield Town, 6 Central St, Brookfield, MA 01506, 508-867-2930 x12, fax-508-867-5091; 9AM-3PM M W Th, 9AM-2PM T; 9AM-N F **Online-** assessor rolls and property sales free at http://csc-ma.us/PropertyContent/jsp/Home.jsp?Page=1. Select Brookfield Town.

Charlton Town, 37 Main St, Charlton, MA 01507, 508-248-2249, fax-508-248-2073; 10AM-3PM M-Th; 1st & 3rd Tues of month 6-8PM **Online-** Access property data free at http://charlton.patriotproperties.com/default.asp.

Clinton Town, 242 Church St, Clinton, MA 01510, 978-365-4119, fax-978-895-4130; 8-4PM

Douglas Town, 29 Depot St, Municipal Ctr, Douglas, MA 01516, 508-476-4000 x355, fax-508-476-4012; 9AM-1PM, 1:30PM-4PM M-TH; 6PM-8PM T **Online-** Access to assessor property data is free at www.mapsonline.net/douglasma/.

Dudley Town, 71 W Main St, #207, Dudley Municipal Complex, Dudley, MA 01571, 508-949-8004, fax-508-949-7115; 8AM-N, 12:30-4:30 PM M-Th; 5-7PM Th; 9AM-1PM F **Online-** assessor data at http://data.visionappraisal.com/DudleyMA/.

East Brookfield Town, Town Hall, East Brookfield, MA 01515, 508-867-6769, fax-508-867-4190; 9AM-12 Mon; 11AM-1PM Fri **Online-** assessor rolls and property sales free at http://csc-ma.us/PropertyContent/jsp/Home.jsp?Page=1. Select East Brookfield Town.

Fitchburg City, 718 Main St, Fitchburg, MA 01420-3198, 978-345-9592, fax-978-345-9595;

8:30AM-4:30PM **Online-** Access city property data free at http://216.129.143.192:56789/home/webpro/.

Gardner City, 95 Pleasant St, Rm 118, City Hall, Gardner, MA 01440, 978-630-4008, fax-978-630-2520; 8AM-4:30PM M-Th; 8AM-4PM Fri. **Online-** Search the city assessor data at http://data.visionappraisal.com/GardnerMA/.

Grafton Town, 30 Providence Rd, Municipal Ctr, Grafton, MA 01519-1186, 508-839-5335 x195, fax-508-839-4602; 8:30AM-4:30PM; 8:30AM-7PM Tues **Online-** property data is free at http://csc-ma.us/GraftonPubAcc/jsp/Home.jsp?Page=1; also at http://csc-ma.us/PropertyContent/jsp/Home.jsp?Page=1. Select Grafton Town.

Hardwick Town, PO Box 575, Gilbertville, MA 01031-0575, (307 Main St) 413-477-6197, fax-413-477-6703; 8:30AM-4PM & 6:30-9PM M; 8:30AM-N T,W **Online-** assessor rolls and property sales free at http://csc-ma.us/PropertyContent/jsp/Home.jsp?Page=1. Select Harwick Town.

Harvard Town, 13 Ayer Rd, Town Hall, Harvard, MA 01451-1458, 978-456-4100, fax-978-456-4113; 8:30AM-4PM M-Th **Online-** assessor data at http://data.visionappraisal.com/HARVARDMA/.

Holden Town, 1196 Main St, Town Hall, Holden, MA 01520-1092, 508-829-0265, fax-508-829-0281; 8:30AM-4:30PM; Summer Hr 8AM-4PM **Online-** Search the Town assessor's database free at http://data.visionappraisal.com/HOLDENMA/.

Hopedale Town, PO Box 7, Hopedale, MA 01747, (78 Hopedale S, Town Hall, Hopedale, MA 01747) 508-634-2203 x215, fax-508-634-2200; 9AM-7PM M; 9AM-2PM T-TH www.hopedale-ma.gov/Public_Documents/HopedaleMA_Assessor/index **Online-** assessment data free at http://hopedale.patriotproperties.com/default.asp?br=exp&vr=6.

Hubbardston Town, PO Box H, Hubbardston, MA 01452, (7 Main St, Town Hall, Hubbardston, MA 01452) 978-928-5244, fax-978-928-1402; 2-8PM M; 8AM-4PM T-Th

Lancaster Town, PO Box 97, Town Hall, Lancaster, MA 01523-0097, (695 Main St, Town Hall, Lancaster, MA 01523) 978-365-2542, fax-978-368-4005; 9AM-6PM M; 9AM-4PM T-TH **Online-** assessor rolls and property sales free at http://csc-ma.us/PropertyContent/jsp/Home.jsp?Page=1. Select Lancaster Town.

Leicester Town, 3 Washburn Sq, Leicester, MA 01524, 508-892-7011, fax-508-892-7070; 8:30AM-4PM **Online-** Access property data free at http://leicester.patriotproperties.com/default.asp.

Leominster City, 25 West St, Leominster, MA 01453, 978-534-7536, fax-978-534-7546; 8:30AM-4PM M-W & F; 8:30AM-5:30PM Th **Online-** Search the assessor's database at http://data.visionappraisal.com/leominsterma/..

Lunenburg Town, PO Box 135, Lunenburg, MA 01462, (17 Main St, Town Hall, Lunenburg, MA 01462) 978-582-4130, fax-978-582-4148; 8AM-4PM M,W,TH; 8AM-6:30PM Tues; 8AM-12:30PM Fri. www.lunenburgonline.com/education/dept/dept.php?sectionid=273 **Online-** Access assessor rolls and property sales free at http://csc-ma.us/PropertyContent/jsp/Home.jsp?Page=1.

Mendon Town, PO Box 54, Mendon, MA 01756-0054, (20 Main St) 508-473-1085, fax-508-478-8241; 8:30AM-6PM Mon; 8:30AM-4PM T,TH; 8:30AM-4PM W

Milford Town, 52 Main St, Milford, MA 01757, 508-634-2307, fax-508-634-2324; 8:30AM-4:30PM **Online-** Access property data free at http://milford.patriotproperties.com/default.asp.

Millbury Town, 127 Elm St, Municipal Office Bldg, Millbury, MA 01527, 508-865-9110, fax-508-865-0857; 9AM-4PM **Online-** Access to the town tax assessor info is free at http://data.visionappraisal.com/MillburyMA/.

Millville Town, PO Box 703, Millville, MA 01529-0703, (8 Central St., Municipal Bldg, Millville, MA 01529) 508-883-5849, fax-508-883-2994; 8:30AM-1PM M-Th; 6-8PM W

New Braintree Town, 20 Memorial Dr, Rm 5, New Braintree, MA 01531, 508-867-4952, fax-508-867-4467; 7-9PM M **Online-** Access assessor rolls and property sales free at http://csc-ma.us/PropertyContent/jsp/Home.jsp?Page=1.

North Brookfield Town, 167 N Main St, North Brookfield, MA 01535, 508-867-0203, fax-508-867-0217; Noon-2:30PM 6PM-8PM T; Noon-2:30PM Th; 9AM-N Fri **Online-** Access assessor rolls and property sales free at http://csc-ma.us/PropertyContent/jsp/Home.jsp?Page=1. Select North Brookfield Town.

Northborough Town, 63 Main St, Northborough, MA 01532-1994, 508-393-5001, fax-508-393-6996; 8AM-4PM M,W,Th; 8AM-7PM T; 7AM-N Fri **Online-** assessor rolls and property sales free at http://csc-ma.us/PropertyContent/jsp/Home.jsp?Page=1.

Northbridge Town, 7 Main St, Town Hall, Whitinsville, MA 01588, 508-234-2001, fax-508-234-2001; 8:30AM-7PM M; 8:30AM-4:30PM T-Th; 8:30AM-1PM F

Oakham Town, PO Box 222, Oakham, MA 01068-0222, (2 Coldbrook Rd, Town Hall, Oakham, MA 01068) 508-882-5549, fax-508-882-3060; 9-11:30AM and 7-9PM Mon **Online-** Access assessor rolls and property sales free at http://csc-ma.us/PropertyContent/jsp/Home.jsp?Page=1. Select Oakham Town.

Oxford Town, 325 Main St, Oxford, MA 01540, 508-987-6032, fax-508-987-6048; 9AM-4:30PM www.town.oxford.ma.us/Pages/OxfordMA_Assessor/index **Online-** Search the property assessments by street name for free at Access property data free at https://security.town.oxford.ma.us/.

Paxton Town, 697 Pleasant St, Paxton, MA 01612, 508-799-7347 x15, fax-508-797-0966; 9AM-4PM M-Th **Online-** town assessor database at http://data.visionappraisal.com/PaxtonMA/.

Petersham Town, PO Box 486, Petersham, MA 01366, (3 S Main St, Town Hall, Petersham, MA 01366) 978-724-6649, fax-978-724-3501; 6-8PM Monday

Phillipston Town, 50 The Common, Phillipston, MA 01331, 978-249-1733, fax-same; 12-2PM, 6-8PM M; 5-7PM W; 8:30AM-10AM Sat

Princeton Town, 6 Town Hall Dr, Princeton, MA 01541-1137, 978-464-2103, fax-978-464-2106; 8:30AM-3:30PM M W; 5PM-7PM T; 8AM-Noon Th; closed Fri

Royalston Town, PO Box 127, Royalston, MA 01368, (5 School St) 978-249-0493, fax-978-249-0748; 9:30AM-2:30PM Tuesdays; Summer-Mondays 5-9PM **Online-** Access assessor rolls and property sales free at http://csc-ma.us/PropertyContent/jsp/Home.jsp?Page=1. Select Royalston Town.

Rutland Town, 250 Main St, Rutland, MA 01543, 508-886-4104, fax-508-886-2929; 8:30AM-4:30PM M,W,Th; 8AM-7PM T; Closed Fri **Online-** Access to Rutland town assessor records is free at http://data.visionappraisal.com/RutlandMA/.

Shrewsbury Town, 100 Maple Ave, Town Hall, Shrewsbury, MA 01545, 508-841-8507, fax-508-842-0587; 8AM-4:30PM

Southborough Town, 17 Common St, Town Hall, Southborough, MA 01772, 508-485-0710, fax-508-480-0161; 9AM-5PM **Online-** Access assessor rolls and property sales free at http://csc-ma.us/SouthboroughPubAcc/jsp/Home.jsp?Page=1. No name searching.

Southbridge Town, 41 Elm St, Southbridge, MA 01550, 508-764-5408, fax-508-764-5425; 8AM-4PM M-W; 8AM-8PM Th; 8AM-N Fri **Online-** Access assessor data free with registration at http://data.visionappraisal.com/SouthbridgeMA/DEFAULT.asp.

Spencer Town, 157 Main St, Town Hall, Spencer, MA 01562-2197, 508-885-7500 x150, fax-508-885-7528; 8AM-4PM, 6-8PM M; 8-4 TTh; 8-N, 1-4 W; 8-N Fri.

Sterling Town, 1 Park St, Mary Ellen Butterick Muni Bldg, Sterling, MA 01564, 978-422-8111, fax-978-422-0289; 7:30AM-5PM M-TH; 8AM-6:30PM W; 7:30AM-11:30AM F www.sterling-ma.gov/Pages/SterlingMA_Treasurer/index

Sturbridge Town, 308 Main St, Sturbridge, MA 01566, 508-347-2510, fax-508-347-5886; 8AM-N, 1PM-4PM www.town.sturbridge.ma.us/Public_Documents/SturbridgeMA_Depts/assessor **Online-** Access assessor property data free with registration at http://data.visionappraisal.com/SturbridgeMA/DEFAULT.asp.

Sutton Town, 4 Uxbridge Rd, Town Hall, Sutton, MA 01590, 508-865-8725, fax-508-865-8721; 9AM-4PM M,T,W,Th; 6:30-8:30PM T; 9AM-N Fri Public access terminals available.

Templeton Town, 4 Elm St., Town Office Bldg, Baldwinville, MA 01436, 978-939-8466, fax-978-939-8327; 7:30AM-5PM M; 7:30-3PM T-Th; 7:30-1:30PM Fri **Online-** Access assessor data at http://data.visionappraisal.com/TempletonMA/..

Upton Town, Box 969, Upton, MA 01568, (1 Main St) 508-529-3565, fax-508-529-1010; 9AM-3PM M/W; T&Th 9:15AM-1 & 6-8PM; Fri 9AM - 1PM **Online-** Access property ownership data free at www.appraisalresource.com/Search.aspx?town=Upton.

Uxbridge Town, 21 S Main St, Uxbridge, MA 01569, 508-278-3156, fax-508-278-3154; 8AM-4PM www.uxbridge-ma.gov/Pages/Assessor.php **Online-** assessor rolls and property sales free at http://csc-ma.us/PropertyContent/jsp/Home.jsp?Page=1. Search maps by owner's name or address at www.mapsonline.net/uxbridgema/.

Warren Town, PO Box 603, Warren, MA 01083-0603, (48 High St, Municipal Bldg, Warren, MA 01083) 413-436-5701, fax-413-436-9754; 8:30AM-3:30PM M-W,F; 4-7PM Th

Webster Town, 350 Main St, Webster, MA 01570, 508-949-3850, fax-508-949-3888; 8AM-7PM M, 8AM-4PM T-Th; 8:30AM-N F

West Boylston Town, 127 Hartwell St, #100, West Boylston, MA 01583, 508-835-6240, fax-508-835-4102; 9AM-4PM M-T; 8AM-3PM W; 9AM-2PM TH; 9:15AM-2PM Fri. www.westboylston.com/Pages/WBoylstonMA_Assessors/index

West Brookfield Town, PO Box 766, West Brookfield, MA 01585, (2 E Main, Town Hall, West Brookfield, MA 01585) 508-867-1421 x302, fax-508-867-1401; 9AM-N M-Th; 6PM-8PM T; Closed on F **Online-** Access assessor rolls and property sales free at http://csc-ma.us/PropertyContent/jsp/Home.jsp?Page=1.

Westborough Town, 34 W Main St, Town Hall, Westborough, MA 01581-1998, 508-366-3020, fax-508-366-3012; 8AM-5PM M W TH; 8AM-8PM T; 7:30AM-N F **Online-** property data free at http://westborough.patriotproperties.com/default.asp.

Westminster Town, 11 South St, Westminster, MA 01473, 978-874-7406, fax-978-874-7411; 8AM-4:30PM M-Th; 8AM-1PM F

Winchendon Town, 109 Front St, Winchendon, MA 01475, 978-297-2766, fax-978-297-1616; 8:30AM-6PM M; 8:30AM-4:30PM T-Th; 8:30AM-N Fri

Worcester City, 455 Main St, Rm 206, City Hall, Worcester, MA 01608, 508-799-1128, fax-508-799-1194; 8:45AM-4:15PM T,W,Th,F; 8:45AM-5PM M **Online-** Online access to the City Assessor Valuation Search database is free at www.ci.worcester.ma.us/aso/value_search.htm. Also, assessor property records free at www.visionappraisal.com/ coming soon.

Massachusetts County Locator

You will usually be able to find the city name in the City/County Cross Reference below. In that case, it is a simple matter to determine the county from the cross reference. However, only the official US Postal Service city names are included in this index. There are an additional 40,000 place names that people use in their addresses. Therefore, we have also included a ZIP/City Cross Reference immediately following the City/County Cross Reference.

If you know the ZIP Code but the city name does not appear in the City/County Cross Reference index, look up the ZIP Code in the ZIP/City Cross Reference, find the city name, then look up the city name in the City/County Cross Reference. For example, you want to know the county for an address of Menands, NY 12204. There is no "Menands" in the City/County Cross Reference. The ZIP/City Cross Reference shows that ZIP Codes 12201-12288 are for the city of Albany. Looking back in the City/County Cross Reference, Albany is in Albany County.

Massachusetts City/County Cross Reference

ABINGTON Plymouth
ACCORD Plymouth
ACTON Middlesex
ACUSHNET Bristol
ADAMS Berkshire
AGAWAM Hampden
ALLSTON Suffolk
AMESBURY Essex
AMHERST Hampshire
ANDOVER Essex
ARLINGTON Middlesex
ARLINGTON HEIGHTS Middlesex
ASHBURNHAM Worcester
ASHBY Middlesex
ASHFIELD Franklin
ASHLAND Middlesex
ASHLEY FALLS Berkshire
ASSONET Bristol
ATHOL Worcester
ATTLEBORO Bristol
ATTLEBORO FALLS Bristol
AUBURN Worcester
AUBURNDALE Middlesex
AVON Norfolk
AYER Middlesex
BABSON PARK Norfolk
BALDWINVILLE Worcester
BAR CODE MCCORMACK Suffolk
BARNSTABLE Barnstable
BARRE Worcester
BECKET Berkshire
BEDFORD Middlesex
BELCHERTOWN Hampshire
BELLINGHAM Norfolk
BELMONT Middlesex
BERKLEY Bristol
BERKSHIRE Berkshire
BERLIN Worcester
BERNARDSTON Franklin
BEVERLY Essex
BILLERICA Middlesex
BLACKSTONE Worcester
BLANDFORD Hampden
BOLTON Worcester
BONDSVILLE Hampden
BOSTON Middlesex
BOSTON Suffolk
BOXBOROUGH Middlesex
BOXFORD Essex
BOYLSTON Worcester
BRAINTREE Norfolk
BRANT ROCK Plymouth
BREWSTER Barnstable
BRIDGEWATER Plymouth
BRIGHTON Suffolk
BRIMFIELD Hampden
BROCKTON Plymouth
BROOKFIELD Worcester
BROOKLINE Norfolk
BROOKLINE VILLAGE Norfolk
BRYANTVILLE Plymouth
BUCKLAND Franklin
BURLINGTON Middlesex
BUZZARDS BAY (02532) Barnstable(74), Plymouth(25)
BUZZARDS BAY Barnstable
BYFIELD Essex
CAMBRIDGE Middlesex
CANTON Norfolk
CARLISLE Middlesex
CARVER Plymouth
CATAUMET Barnstable
CENTERVILLE Barnstable
CHARLEMONT Franklin
CHARLESTOWN Suffolk
CHARLTON Worcester
CHARLTON CITY Worcester
CHARLTON DEPOT Worcester
CHARTLEY Bristol
CHATHAM Barnstable
CHELMSFORD Middlesex
CHELSEA Suffolk
CHERRY VALLEY Worcester
CHESHIRE Berkshire
CHESTER (01011) Hampden(89), Hampshire(5), Berkshire(5)
CHESTERFIELD Hampshire
CHESTNUT HILL Middlesex
CHICOPEE Hampden
CHILMARK Dukes
CLINTON Worcester
COHASSET Norfolk
COLRAIN Franklin
CONCORD Middlesex
CONWAY Franklin
COTUIT Barnstable
CUMMAQUID Barnstable
CUMMINGTON Hampshire
CUTTYHUNK Dukes
DALTON Berkshire
DANVERS Essex
DARTMOUTH Bristol
DEDHAM Norfolk
DEERFIELD Franklin
DENNIS Barnstable
DENNIS PORT Barnstable
DEVENS (01434) Worcester(54), Middlesex(45)
DIGHTON Bristol
DOUGLAS Worcester
DOVER Norfolk
DRACUT Middlesex
DRURY Berkshire
DUDLEY Worcester
DUNSTABLE Middlesex
DUXBURY Plymouth
EAST BOSTON Suffolk
EAST BRIDGEWATER Plymouth
EAST BROOKFIELD Worcester
EAST DENNIS Barnstable
EAST FALMOUTH Barnstable
EAST FREETOWN Bristol
EAST LONGMEADOW Hampden
EAST MANSFIELD Bristol
EAST ORLEANS Barnstable
EAST OTIS Berkshire
EAST PRINCETON Worcester
EAST SANDWICH Barnstable
EAST TAUNTON Bristol
EAST TEMPLETON Worcester
EAST WALPOLE Norfolk
EAST WAREHAM Plymouth
EASTHAM Barnstable
EASTHAMPTON Hampshire
EASTON Bristol
EDGARTOWN Dukes
ELMWOOD Plymouth
ERVING Franklin
ESSEX Essex
EVERETT Middlesex
FAIRHAVEN Bristol
FALL RIVER Bristol
FALMOUTH Barnstable
FAYVILLE Worcester
FEEDING HILLS Hampden
FISKDALE Worcester
FITCHBURG Worcester
FLORENCE Hampshire
FORESTDALE Barnstable
FORT DEVENS (01433) Worcester(53), Middlesex(46)
FOXBORO Norfolk
FRAMINGHAM Middlesex
FRANKLIN Norfolk
GARDNER Worcester
GEORGETOWN Essex
GILBERTVILLE Worcester
GLENDALE Berkshire
GLOUCESTER Essex
GOSHEN Hampshire
GRAFTON Worcester
GRANBY Hampshire
GRANVILLE Hampden
GREAT BARRINGTON Berkshire
GREEN HARBOR Plymouth
GREENBUSH Plymouth
GREENFIELD Franklin
GROTON Middlesex
GROVELAND Essex
HADLEY Hampshire
HALIFAX Plymouth
HAMILTON Essex
HAMPDEN Hampden
HANOVER (02339) Plymouth(98), Norfolk(1)
HANOVER Plymouth
HANSCOM AFB Middlesex
HANSON Plymouth
HARDWICK Worcester
HARVARD Worcester
HARWICH Barnstable
HARWICH PORT Barnstable
HATFIELD Hampshire
HATHORNE Essex
HAVERHILL Essex
HAYDENVILLE Hampshire
HEATH Franklin
HINGHAM Plymouth
HINSDALE Berkshire
HOLBROOK Norfolk
HOLDEN Worcester
HOLLAND Hampden
HOLLISTON Middlesex
HOLYOKE Hampden
HOPEDALE Worcester
HOPKINTON Middlesex
HOUSATONIC Berkshire
HUBBARDSTON Worcester
HUDSON Middlesex
HULL Plymouth
HUMAROCK Plymouth
HUNTINGTON (01050) Hampshire(98), Hampden(1)
HYANNIS Barnstable
HYANNIS PORT Barnstable
HYDE PARK Suffolk
INDIAN ORCHARD Hampden
IPSWICH Essex
JAMAICA PLAIN Suffolk
JEFFERSON Worcester
KINGSTON Plymouth
LAKE PLEASANT Franklin
LAKEVILLE Plymouth
LANCASTER Worcester
LANESBORO Berkshire
LAWRENCE Essex
LEE Berkshire
LEEDS Hampshire
LEICESTER Worcester
LENOX Berkshire
LENOX DALE Berkshire
LEOMINSTER Worcester
LEVERETT (01054) Franklin(77), Hampshire(22)
LEXINGTON Middlesex
LINCOLN Middlesex
LINWOOD Worcester
LITTLETON Middlesex
LONGMEADOW Hampden
LOWELL Middlesex
LUDLOW Hampden
LUNENBURG Worcester
LYNN Essex
LYNNFIELD Essex
MALDEN Middlesex
MANCHAUG Worcester
MANCHESTER Essex
MANOMET Plymouth
MANSFIELD Bristol
MARBLEHEAD Essex
MARION Plymouth
MARLBOROUGH Middlesex
MARSHFIELD Plymouth
MARSHFIELD HILLS Plymouth
MARSTONS MILLS Barnstable
MASHPEE Barnstable
MATTAPAN Suffolk
MATTAPOISETT Plymouth
MAYNARD Middlesex
MEDFIELD Norfolk
MEDFORD Middlesex
MEDWAY Norfolk

MELROSE Middlesex
MENDON Worcester
MENEMSHA Dukes
MERRIMAC Essex
METHUEN Essex
MIDDLEBORO Plymouth
MIDDLEFIELD Hampshire
MIDDLETON Essex
MILFORD Worcester
MILL RIVER Berkshire
MILLBURY Worcester
MILLIS Norfolk
MILLVILLE Worcester
MILTON Norfolk
MILTON VILLAGE Norfolk
MINOT Plymouth
MONPONSETT Plymouth
MONROE BRIDGE Franklin
MONSON Hampden
MONTAGUE Franklin
MONTEREY Berkshire
MONUMENT BEACH Barnstable
NAHANT Essex
NANTUCKET Nantucket
NATICK Middlesex
NEEDHAM Norfolk
NEW BEDFORD Bristol
NEW BRAINTREE Worcester
NEW SALEM Franklin
NEW TOWN Middlesex
NEWBURY Essex
NEWBURYPORT Essex
NEWTON Middlesex
NEWTON CENTER Middlesex
NEWTON HIGHLANDS Middlesex
NEWTON LOWER FALLS Middlesex
NEWTON UPPER FALLS Middlesex
NEWTONVILLE Middlesex
NONANTUM Middlesex
NORFOLK Norfolk
NORTH ADAMS Berkshire
NORTH AMHERST Hampshire
NORTH ANDOVER Essex
NORTH ATTLEBORO Bristol
NORTH BILLERICA Middlesex
NORTH BROOKFIELD Worcester
NORTH CARVER Plymouth
NORTH CHATHAM Barnstable
NORTH CHELMSFORD Middlesex
NORTH DARTMOUTH Bristol
NORTH DIGHTON Bristol
NORTH EASTHAM Barnstable
NORTH EASTON Bristol
NORTH EGREMONT Berkshire
NORTH FALMOUTH Barnstable
NORTH GRAFTON Worcester
NORTH HATFIELD Hampshire
NORTH MARSHFIELD Plymouth
NORTH OXFORD Worcester
NORTH PEMBROKE Plymouth
NORTH READING Middlesex
NORTH SCITUATE Plymouth
NORTH TRURO Barnstable
NORTH UXBRIDGE Worcester
NORTH WALTHAM Middlesex
NORTHAMPTON Hampshire
NORTHBOROUGH Worcester
NORTHBRIDGE Worcester
NORTHFIELD Franklin
NORTON Bristol
NORWELL Plymouth
NORWOOD Norfolk
NUTTING LAKE Middlesex
OAK BLUFFS Dukes
OAKDALE Worcester
OAKHAM Worcester
OCEAN BLUFF Plymouth
ONSET Plymouth
ORANGE Franklin
ORLEANS Barnstable
OSTERVILLE Barnstable
OTIS Berkshire
OXFORD Worcester
PALMER Hampden
PAXTON Worcester
PEABODY Essex
PEMBROKE Plymouth
PEPPERELL Middlesex
PETERSHAM (01366) Franklin(51), Worcester(48)
PINEHURST Middlesex
PITTSFIELD Berkshire
PLAINFIELD Hampshire
PLAINVILLE (02762) Norfolk(98), Bristol(1)
PLYMOUTH Plymouth
PLYMPTON Plymouth
POCASSET Barnstable
PRIDES CROSSING Essex
PRINCETON Worcester
PROVINCETOWN Barnstable
QUINCY Norfolk
RANDOLPH Norfolk
RAYNHAM Bristol
RAYNHAM CENTER Bristol
READING Middlesex
READVILLE Suffolk
REHOBOTH Bristol
REVERE Suffolk
RICHMOND Berkshire
ROCHDALE Worcester
ROCHESTER Plymouth
ROCKLAND Plymouth
ROCKPORT Essex
ROSLINDALE Suffolk
ROWE Franklin
ROWLEY Essex
ROYALSTON Worcester
RUSSELL Hampden
RUTLAND Worcester
SAGAMORE Barnstable
SAGAMORE BEACH (02562) Barnstable(98), Plymouth(1)
SALEM Essex
SALISBURY Essex
SANDISFIELD Berkshire
SANDWICH Barnstable
SAUGUS Essex
SAVOY Berkshire
SCITUATE Plymouth
SEARS ROEBUCK Suffolk
SEEKONK Bristol
SHARON Norfolk
SHATTUCKVILLE Franklin
SHEFFIELD Berkshire
SHELBURNE FALLS Franklin
SHELDONVILLE Norfolk
SHERBORN Middlesex
SHIRLEY Middlesex
SHREWSBURY Worcester
SHUTESBURY Franklin
SIASCONSET Nantucket
SILVER BEACH Barnstable
SOMERSET Bristol
SOMERVILLE Middlesex
SOUTH BARRE Worcester
SOUTH CARVER Plymouth
SOUTH CHATHAM Barnstable
SOUTH DARTMOUTH Bristol
SOUTH DEERFIELD Franklin
SOUTH DENNIS Barnstable
SOUTH EASTON Bristol
SOUTH EGREMONT Berkshire
SOUTH GRAFTON Worcester
SOUTH HADLEY Hampshire
SOUTH HAMILTON Essex
SOUTH HARWICH Barnstable
SOUTH LANCASTER Worcester
SOUTH LEE Berkshire
SOUTH ORLEANS Barnstable
SOUTH WALPOLE Norfolk
SOUTH WELLFLEET Barnstable
SOUTH YARMOUTH Barnstable
SOUTHAMPTON Hampshire
SOUTHBOROUGH Worcester
SOUTHBRIDGE Worcester
SOUTHFIELD Berkshire
SOUTHWICK Hampden
SPENCER Worcester
SPRINGFIELD Hampden
STERLING Worcester
STILL RIVER Worcester
STOCKBRIDGE Berkshire
STONEHAM Middlesex
STOUGHTON Norfolk
STOW Middlesex
STURBRIDGE Worcester
SUDBURY Middlesex
SUNDERLAND Franklin
SUTTON Worcester
SWAMPSCOTT Essex
SWANSEA Bristol
TAUNTON Bristol
TEMPLETON Worcester
TEWKSBURY Middlesex
THORNDIKE Hampden
THREE RIVERS Hampden
TOPSFIELD Essex
TOWNSEND Middlesex
TRURO Barnstable
TURNERS FALLS Franklin
TYNGSBORO Middlesex
TYRINGHAM Berkshire
UPTON Worcester
UXBRIDGE Worcester
VILLAGE OF NAGOG WOODS Middlesex
VINEYARD HAVEN Dukes
WABAN Middlesex
WAKEFIELD Middlesex
WALES Hampden
WALPOLE Norfolk
WALTHAM Middlesex
WARE Hampshire
WAREHAM Plymouth
WARREN Worcester
WARWICK Franklin
WATERTOWN Middlesex
WAVERLEY Middlesex
WAYLAND Middlesex
WEBSTER Worcester
WELLESLEY Norfolk
WELLESLEY HILLS Norfolk
WELLFLEET Barnstable
WENDELL Franklin
WENDELL DEPOT Franklin
WENHAM Essex
WEST BARNSTABLE Barnstable
WEST BOXFORD Essex
WEST BOYLSTON Worcester
WEST BRIDGEWATER Plymouth
WEST BROOKFIELD Worcester
WEST CHATHAM Barnstable
WEST CHESTERFIELD Hampshire
WEST DENNIS Barnstable
WEST FALMOUTH Barnstable
WEST GROTON Middlesex
WEST HARWICH Barnstable
WEST HATFIELD (01088) Worcester(98), Hampshire(1)
WEST HYANNISPORT Barnstable
WEST MEDFORD Middlesex
WEST MILLBURY Worcester
WEST NEWBURY Essex
WEST NEWTON Middlesex
WEST ROXBURY Suffolk
WEST SPRINGFIELD Hampden
WEST STOCKBRIDGE Berkshire
WEST TISBURY Dukes
WEST TOWNSEND Middlesex
WEST WAREHAM Plymouth
WEST WARREN Worcester
WEST YARMOUTH Barnstable
WESTBOROUGH Worcester
WESTFIELD Hampden
WESTFORD Middlesex
WESTMINSTER Worcester
WESTON Middlesex
WESTPORT Bristol
WESTPORT POINT Bristol
WESTWOOD Norfolk
WEYMOUTH Norfolk
WHATELY Franklin
WHEELWRIGHT Worcester
WHITE HORSE BEACH Plymouth
WHITINSVILLE Worcester
WHITMAN Plymouth
WILBRAHAM Hampden
WILLIAMSBURG Hampshire
WILLIAMSTOWN Berkshire
WILMINGTON Middlesex
WINCHENDON Worcester
WINCHENDON SPRINGS Worcester
WINCHESTER Middlesex
WINDSOR (01270) Franklin(95), Berkshire(4)
WINTHROP Suffolk
WOBURN Middlesex
WOODS HOLE Barnstable
WOODVILLE Middlesex
WORCESTER Worcester
WORONOCO Hampden
WORTHINGTON Hampshire
WRENTHAM Norfolk
YARMOUTH PORT Barnstable

Massachusetts ZIP/City Cross Reference

01001-01001 AGAWAM
01002-01004 AMHERST
01005-01005 BARRE
01007-01007 BELCHERTOWN
01008-01008 BLANDFORD
01009-01009 BONDSVILLE
01010-01010 BRIMFIELD
01011-01011 CHESTER
01012-01012 CHESTERFIELD
01013-01022 CHICOPEE
01026-01026 CUMMINGTON
01027-01027 EASTHAMPTON
01028-01028 EAST LONGMEADOW
01029-01029 EAST OTIS
01030-01030 FEEDING HILLS
01031-01031 GILBERTVILLE
01032-01032 GOSHEN
01033-01033 GRANBY
01034-01034 GRANVILLE
01035-01035 HADLEY
01036-01036 HAMPDEN
01037-01037 HARDWICK
01038-01038 HATFIELD
01039-01039 HAYDENVILLE
01040-01041 HOLYOKE
01050-01050 HUNTINGTON
01053-01053 LEEDS
01054-01054 LEVERETT
01056-01056 LUDLOW
01057-01057 MONSON
01059-01059 NORTH AMHERST
01060-01061 NORTHAMPTON
01062-01062 FLORENCE
01063-01063 NORTHAMPTON
01066-01066 NORTH HATFIELD
01068-01068 OAKHAM
01069-01069 PALMER
01070-01070 PLAINFIELD
01071-01071 RUSSELL
01072-01072 SHUTESBURY
01073-01073 SOUTHAMPTON
01074-01074 SOUTH BARRE
01075-01075 SOUTH HADLEY
01077-01077 SOUTHWICK
01079-01079 THORNDIKE
01080-01080 THREE RIVERS
01081-01081 WALES
01082-01082 WARE
01083-01083 WARREN
01084-01084 WEST CHESTERFIELD
01085-01086 WESTFIELD
01088-01088 WEST HATFIELD
01089-01090 WEST SPRINGFIELD
01092-01092 WEST WARREN
01093-01093 WHATELY
01094-01094 WHEELWRIGHT
01095-01095 WILBRAHAM
01096-01096 WILLIAMSBURG
01097-01097 WORONOCO
01098-01098 WORTHINGTON
01101-01105 SPRINGFIELD
01106-01106 LONGMEADOW
01107-01115 SPRINGFIELD
01116-01116 LONGMEADOW
01118-01144 SPRINGFIELD
01151-01151 INDIAN ORCHARD
01152-01199 SPRINGFIELD
01201-01203 PITTSFIELD
01220-01220 ADAMS
01222-01222 ASHLEY FALLS
01223-01223 BECKET
01224-01224 BERKSHIRE
01225-01225 CHESHIRE
01226-01227 DALTON
01229-01229 GLENDALE
01230-01230 GREAT BARRINGTON
01235-01235 HINSDALE
01236-01236 HOUSATONIC
01237-01237 LANESBORO
01238-01238 LEE
01240-01240 LENOX
01242-01242 LENOX DALE
01243-01243 MIDDLEFIELD
01244-01244 MILL RIVER
01245-01245 MONTEREY
01247-01247 NORTH ADAMS
01252-01252 NORTH EGREMONT
01253-01253 OTIS
01254-01254 RICHMOND
01255-01255 SANDISFIELD
01256-01256 SAVOY
01257-01257 SHEFFIELD
01258-01258 SOUTH EGREMONT
01259-01259 SOUTHFIELD
01260-01260 SOUTH LEE
01262-01263 STOCKBRIDGE
01264-01264 TYRINGHAM
01266-01266 WEST STOCKBRIDGE
01267-01267 WILLIAMSTOWN
01270-01270 WINDSOR
01301-01302 GREENFIELD
01330-01330 ASHFIELD
01331-01331 ATHOL
01337-01337 BERNARDSTON
01338-01338 BUCKLAND
01339-01339 CHARLEMONT
01340-01340 COLRAIN
01341-01341 CONWAY
01342-01342 DEERFIELD
01343-01343 DRURY
01344-01344 ERVING
01346-01346 HEATH
01347-01347 LAKE PLEASANT
01349-01349 TURNERS FALLS
01350-01350 MONROE BRIDGE
01351-01351 MONTAGUE
01354-01354 NORTHFIELD
01355-01355 NEW SALEM
01360-01360 NORTHFIELD
01364-01364 ORANGE
01366-01366 PETERSHAM
01367-01367 ROWE
01368-01368 ROYALSTON
01369-01369 SHATTUCKVILLE
01370-01370 SHELBURNE FALLS
01373-01373 SOUTH DEERFIELD
01375-01375 SUNDERLAND
01376-01376 TURNERS FALLS
01378-01378 WARWICK
01379-01379 WENDELL
01380-01380 WENDELL DEPOT
01420-01420 FITCHBURG
01430-01430 ASHBURNHAM
01431-01431 ASHBY
01432-01432 AYER
01433-01433 FORT DEVENS
01434-01434 DEVENS
01436-01436 BALDWINVILLE
01438-01438 EAST TEMPLETON
01440-01441 GARDNER
01441-01441 WESTMINSTER
01450-01450 GROTON
01451-01451 HARVARD
01452-01452 HUBBARDSTON
01453-01453 LEOMINSTER
01460-01460 LITTLETON
01462-01462 LUNENBURG
01463-01463 PEPPERELL
01464-01464 SHIRLEY
01466-01466 ASHBURNHAM
01467-01467 STILL RIVER
01468-01468 TEMPLETON
01469-01469 TOWNSEND
01470-01471 GROTON
01472-01472 WEST GROTON
01473-01473 WESTMINSTER
01474-01474 WEST TOWNSEND
01475-01475 WINCHENDON
01477-01477 WINCHENDON SPRINGS
01501-01501 AUBURN
01503-01503 BERLIN
01504-01504 BLACKSTONE
01505-01505 BOYLSTON
01506-01506 BROOKFIELD
01507-01507 CHARLTON
01508-01508 CHARLTON CITY
01509-01509 CHARLTON DEPOT
01510-01510 CLINTON
01515-01515 EAST BROOKFIELD
01516-01516 DOUGLAS
01517-01517 EAST PRINCETON
01518-01518 FISKDALE
01519-01519 GRAFTON
01520-01520 HOLDEN
01521-01521 HOLLAND
01522-01522 JEFFERSON
01523-01523 LANCASTER
01524-01524 LEICESTER
01525-01525 LINWOOD
01526-01526 MANCHAUG
01527-01527 MILLBURY
01529-01529 MILLVILLE
01531-01531 NEW BRAINTREE
01532-01532 NORTHBOROUGH
01534-01534 NORTHBRIDGE
01535-01535 NORTH BROOKFIELD
01536-01536 NORTH GRAFTON
01537-01537 NORTH OXFORD
01538-01538 NORTH UXBRIDGE
01539-01539 OAKDALE
01540-01540 OXFORD
01541-01541 PRINCETON
01542-01542 ROCHDALE
01543-01543 RUTLAND
01545-01546 SHREWSBURY
01549-01549 BERLIN
01550-01550 SOUTHBRIDGE
01560-01560 SOUTH GRAFTON
01561-01561 SOUTH LANCASTER
01562-01562 SPENCER
01564-01564 STERLING
01566-01566 STURBRIDGE
01568-01568 UPTON
01569-01569 UXBRIDGE
01570-01570 WEBSTER
01571-01571 DUDLEY
01580-01582 WESTBOROUGH
01583-01583 WEST BOYLSTON
01585-01585 WEST BROOKFIELD
01586-01586 WEST MILLBURY
01587-01587 UPTON
01588-01588 WHITINSVILLE
01590-01590 SUTTON
01600-01610 WORCESTER
01611-01611 CHERRY VALLEY
01612-01612 PAXTON
01613-01655 WORCESTER
01701-01705 FRAMINGHAM
01718-01718 VILLAGE OF NAGOG WOODS
01719-01719 BOXBOROUGH
01720-01720 ACTON
01721-01721 ASHLAND
01730-01730 BEDFORD
01731-01731 HANSCOM AFB
01740-01740 BOLTON
01741-01741 CARLISLE
01742-01742 CONCORD
01745-01745 FAYVILLE
01746-01746 HOLLISTON
01747-01747 HOPEDALE
01748-01748 HOPKINTON
01749-01749 HUDSON
01752-01752 MARLBOROUGH
01754-01754 MAYNARD
01756-01756 MENDON
01757-01757 MILFORD
01760-01760 NATICK
01770-01770 SHERBORN
01772-01772 SOUTHBOROUGH
01773-01773 LINCOLN
01775-01775 STOW
01776-01776 SUDBURY
01778-01778 WAYLAND
01784-01784 WOODVILLE
01801-01801 WOBURN
01803-01805 BURLINGTON
01806-01808 WOBURN
01810-01812 ANDOVER
01813-01815 WOBURN
01821-01822 BILLERICA
01824-01824 CHELMSFORD
01826-01826 DRACUT
01827-01827 DUNSTABLE
01830-01832 HAVERHILL
01833-01833 GEORGETOWN
01834-01834 GROVELAND
01835-01835 HAVERHILL
01840-01843 LAWRENCE
01844-01844 METHUEN
01845-01845 NORTH ANDOVER
01850-01854 LOWELL
01860-01860 MERRIMAC
01862-01862 NORTH BILLERICA
01863-01863 NORTH CHELMSFORD
01864-01864 NORTH READING
01865-01865 NUTTING LAKE
01866-01866 PINEHURST
01867-01867 READING
01876-01876 TEWKSBURY
01879-01879 TYNGSBORO
01880-01880 WAKEFIELD
01885-01885 WEST BOXFORD
01886-01886 WESTFORD
01887-01887 WILMINGTON
01888-01888 WOBURN
01889-01889 NORTH READING
01890-01890 WINCHESTER
01899-01899 ANDOVER
01901-01905 LYNN
01906-01906 SAUGUS
01907-01907 SWAMPSCOTT
01908-01908 NAHANT
01910-01910 LYNN
01913-01913 AMESBURY
01915-01915 BEVERLY
01921-01921 BOXFORD
01922-01922 BYFIELD
01923-01923 DANVERS
01929-01929 ESSEX
01930-01931 GLOUCESTER
01936-01936 HAMILTON
01937-01937 HATHORNE
01938-01938 IPSWICH
01940-01940 LYNNFIELD
01944-01944 MANCHESTER
01945-01945 MARBLEHEAD
01947-01947 SALEM
01949-01949 MIDDLETON
01950-01950 NEWBURYPORT
01951-01951 NEWBURY
01952-01952 SALISBURY
01960-01964 PEABODY
01965-01965 PRIDES CROSSING
01966-01966 ROCKPORT
01969-01969 ROWLEY
01970-01971 SALEM
01982-01982 SOUTH HAMILTON
01983-01983 TOPSFIELD
01984-01984 WENHAM
01985-01985 WEST NEWBURY
02018-02018 ACCORD
02019-02019 BELLINGHAM
02020-02020 BRANT ROCK
02021-02021 CANTON
02025-02025 COHASSET
02026-02027 DEDHAM
02030-02030 DOVER
02031-02031 EAST MANSFIELD
02032-02032 EAST WALPOLE

02035-02035 FOXBORO
02038-02038 FRANKLIN
02040-02040 GREENBUSH
02041-02041 GREEN HARBOR
02043-02044 HINGHAM
02045-02045 HULL
02047-02047 HUMAROCK
02048-02048 MANSFIELD
02050-02050 MARSHFIELD
02051-02051 MARSHFIELD HILLS
02052-02052 MEDFIELD
02053-02053 MEDWAY
02054-02054 MILLIS
02055-02055 MINOT
02056-02056 NORFOLK
02059-02059 NORTH MARSHFIELD
02060-02060 NORTH SCITUATE
02061-02061 NORWELL
02062-02062 NORWOOD
02065-02065 OCEAN BLUFF
02066-02066 SCITUATE
02067-02067 SHARON
02070-02070 SHELDONVILLE
02071-02071 SOUTH WALPOLE
02072-02072 STOUGHTON
02081-02081 WALPOLE
02090-02090 WESTWOOD
02093-02093 WRENTHAM
02100-02125 BOSTON
02126-02126 MATTAPAN
02127-02128 BOSTON
02129-02129 CHARLESTOWN
02130-02130 JAMAICA PLAIN
02131-02131 ROSLINDALE
02132-02132 WEST ROXBURY
02133-02133 BOSTON
02134-02134 ALLSTON
02135-02135 BRIGHTON
02136-02136 HYDE PARK
02137-02137 READVILLE
02138-02142 CAMBRIDGE
02143-02145 SOMERVILLE
02146-02146 BROOKLINE
02147-02147 BROOKLINE VILLAGE
02148-02148 MALDEN
02149-02149 EVERETT
02150-02150 CHELSEA
02151-02151 REVERE
02152-02152 WINTHROP
02153-02153 MEDFORD
02154-02154 WALTHAM
02155-02155 MEDFORD
02156-02156 WEST MEDFORD
02157-02157 BABSON PARK
02158-02162 NEWTON
02163-02163 BOSTON
02164-02165 NEWTON
02166-02166 AUBURNDALE
02167-02167 CHESTNUT HILL
02168-02168 WABAN
02169-02171 QUINCY
02172-02172 WATERTOWN
02173-02173 LEXINGTON
02174-02174 ARLINGTON
02175-02175 ARLINGTON HEIGHTS
02176-02177 MELROSE
02178-02178 BELMONT
02179-02179 WAVERLEY
02180-02180 STONEHAM
02181-02181 WELLESLEY
02184-02185 BRAINTREE
02186-02186 MILTON
02187-02187 MILTON VILLAGE
02188-02191 WEYMOUTH
02192-02192 NEEDHAM
02193-02193 WESTON
02194-02194 NEEDHAM
02195-02195 NEWTON
02196-02222 BOSTON
02228-02228 EAST BOSTON
02238-02239 CAMBRIDGE
02241-02241 BOSTON
02254-02254 WALTHAM
02258-02258 NEWTON
02266-02266 BOSTON
02269-02269 QUINCY
02272-02277 WATERTOWN
02283-02293 BOSTON
02294-02294 SEARS ROEBUCK
02295-02297 BOSTON
02299-02299 BAR CODE MCCORMACK
02301-02305 BROCKTON
02322-02322 AVON
02324-02325 BRIDGEWATER
02327-02327 BRYANTVILLE
02330-02330 CARVER
02331-02332 DUXBURY
02333-02333 EAST BRIDGEWATER
02334-02334 EASTON
02337-02337 ELMWOOD
02338-02338 HALIFAX
02339-02340 HANOVER
02341-02341 HANSON
02343-02343 HOLBROOK
02344-02344 MIDDLEBORO
02345-02345 MANOMET
02346-02346 MIDDLEBORO
02347-02347 LAKEVILLE
02348-02349 MIDDLEBORO
02350-02350 MONPONSETT
02351-02351 ABINGTON
02355-02355 NORTH CARVER
02356-02357 NORTH EASTON
02358-02358 NORTH PEMBROKE
02359-02359 PEMBROKE
02360-02363 PLYMOUTH
02364-02364 KINGSTON
02366-02366 SOUTH CARVER
02367-02367 PLYMPTON
02368-02368 RANDOLPH
02370-02371 ROCKLAND
02375-02375 SOUTH EASTON
02379-02379 WEST BRIDGEWATER
02381-02381 WHITE HORSE BEACH
02382-02382 WHITMAN
02401-02411 BROCKTON
02420-02421 LEXINGTON
02445-02446 BROOKLINE
02447-02447 BROOKLINE VILLAGE
02451-02454 WALTHAM
02455-02455 NORTH WALTHAM
02456-02456 NEW TOWN
02457-02457 BABSON PARK
02458-02458 NEWTON
02459-02459 NEWTON CENTER
02460-02460 NEWTONVILLE
02461-02461 NEWTON HIGHLANDS
02462-02462 NEWTON LOWER FALLS
02464-02464 NEWTON UPPER FALLS
02465-02465 WEST NEWTON
02466-02466 AUBURNDALE
02467-02467 CHESTNUT HILL
02468-02468 WABAN
02471-02472 WATERTOWN
02474-02474 ARLINGTON
02475-02475 ARLINGTON HEIGHTS
02476-02476 ARLINGTON
02477-02477 WATERTOWN
02478-02478 BELMONT
02479-02479 WAVERLEY
02481-02481 WELLESLEY HILLS
02482-02482 WELLESLEY
02492-02492 NEEDHAM
02493-02493 WESTON
02494-02494 NEEDHAM
02495-02495 NONANTUM
02499-02499 BROCKTON
02532-02532 BUZZARDS BAY
02534-02534 CATAUMET
02535-02535 CHILMARK
02536-02536 EAST FALMOUTH
02537-02537 EAST SANDWICH
02538-02538 EAST WAREHAM
02539-02539 EDGARTOWN
02540-02541 FALMOUTH
02542-02542 BUZZARDS BAY
02543-02543 WOODS HOLE
02552-02552 MENEMSHA
02553-02553 MONUMENT BEACH
02554-02554 NANTUCKET
02556-02556 NORTH FALMOUTH
02557-02557 OAK BLUFFS
02558-02558 ONSET
02559-02559 POCASSET
02561-02561 SAGAMORE
02562-02562 SAGAMORE BEACH
02563-02563 SANDWICH
02564-02564 SIASCONSET
02565-02565 SILVER BEACH
02568-02568 VINEYARD HAVEN
02571-02571 WAREHAM
02573-02573 VINEYARD HAVEN
02574-02574 WEST FALMOUTH
02575-02575 WEST TISBURY
02576-02576 WEST WAREHAM
02584-02584 NANTUCKET
02601-02601 HYANNIS
02630-02630 BARNSTABLE
02631-02631 BREWSTER
02632-02632 CENTERVILLE
02633-02633 CHATHAM
02634-02634 CENTERVILLE
02635-02635 COTUIT
02636-02636 CENTERVILLE
02637-02637 CUMMAQUID
02638-02638 DENNIS
02639-02639 DENNIS PORT
02641-02641 EAST DENNIS
02642-02642 EASTHAM
02643-02643 EAST ORLEANS
02644-02644 FORESTDALE
02645-02645 HARWICH
02646-02646 HARWICH PORT
02647-02647 HYANNIS PORT
02648-02648 MARSTONS MILLS
02649-02649 MASHPEE
02650-02650 NORTH CHATHAM
02651-02651 NORTH EASTHAM
02652-02652 NORTH TRURO
02653-02653 ORLEANS
02655-02655 OSTERVILLE
02657-02657 PROVINCETOWN
02659-02659 SOUTH CHATHAM
02660-02660 SOUTH DENNIS
02661-02661 SOUTH HARWICH
02662-02662 SOUTH ORLEANS
02663-02663 SOUTH WELLFLEET
02664-02664 SOUTH YARMOUTH
02666-02666 TRURO
02667-02667 WELLFLEET
02668-02668 WEST BARNSTABLE
02669-02669 WEST CHATHAM
02670-02670 WEST DENNIS
02671-02671 WEST HARWICH
02672-02672 WEST HYANNISPORT
02673-02673 WEST YARMOUTH
02675-02675 YARMOUTH PORT
02702-02702 ASSONET
02703-02703 ATTLEBORO
02712-02712 CHARTLEY
02713-02713 CUTTYHUNK
02714-02714 DARTMOUTH
02715-02715 DIGHTON
02717-02717 EAST FREETOWN
02718-02718 EAST TAUNTON
02719-02719 FAIRHAVEN
02720-02724 FALL RIVER
02725-02726 SOMERSET
02738-02738 MARION
02739-02739 MATTAPOISETT
02740-02742 NEW BEDFORD
02743-02743 ACUSHNET
02744-02746 NEW BEDFORD
02747-02747 NORTH DARTMOUTH
02748-02748 SOUTH DARTMOUTH
02754-02754 NORTH DIGHTON
02760-02761 NORTH ATTLEBORO
02762-02762 PLAINVILLE
02763-02763 ATTLEBORO FALLS
02764-02764 NORTH DIGHTON
02766-02766 NORTON
02767-02767 RAYNHAM
02768-02768 RAYNHAM CENTER
02769-02769 REHOBOTH
02770-02770 ROCHESTER
02771-02771 SEEKONK
02777-02777 SWANSEA
02779-02779 BERKLEY
02780-02783 TAUNTON
02790-02790 WESTPORT
02791-02791 WESTPORT POINT
05501-05544 ANDOVER

Michigan

General Help Numbers:

Governor's Office
PO Box 30013 — 517-373-3400
Lansing, MI 48909 — Fax 517-335-6863
www.michigan.gov/gov — 8AM-5PM

Attorney General's Office
PO Box 30212 — 517-373-1110
Lansing, MI 48909 — Fax 517-373-3042
www.michigan.gov/ag/ — 8AM-5PM

Legislative Records
Michigan Legislature Document Room
State Capitol, PO Box 30036 — 517-373-0169
Lansing, MI 48909
www.legislature.mi.gov — 8:30AM-5PM

State Archives
Archives of Michigan — 517-373-1408
702 W. Kalamazoo — Fax 517-241-1658
Lansing, MI 48809 — 9AM-1PM M,TH; 1-5PM T,W,F
www.michigan.gov/hal

State Specifics:

Capital:	Lansing Ingham County
Time Zone:	EST*
Number of Counties:	83
Population:	10,003,422
Web Site:	www.michigan.gov

* Four north-western Michigan counties are CST: They are: Dickinson, Gogebic, Iron, Menominee.

State Agencies

Criminal Records

Michigan State Police, Criminal History Section, Criminal Justice Information Center, 7150 Harris Dr, Lansing, MI 48913; 517-322-1956, Fax- 517-322-0635; 8AM-5PM.

www.michigan.gov/msp

All felonies and serious misdemeanors that are punishable by over 93 days are required to be reported to the state repository by law enforcement agencies, prosecutors, and courts in all 83 Michigan counties.

Indexing & Storage: Records available until the subject's DOB indicates 99 years or a death is reported. New records available for inquiry in up to 30 days. 80% of all arrests in database have final dispositions recorded, 87% for those arrests within last 5 years.

Searching: Include in request- full name, sex, race, date of birth. A SSN or maiden name/previous name is very helpful. This data not released- non-conviction information. Effective 2/2006, the general public may receive information on arrest records that do not have a conviction attached. Information regarding warrants and suppressed records are not released. Prior to that date only conviction data was released.

Access by: mail, online.

Fee & Payment: The fee is $30.00 with a fingerprint card, and $49.25 with state and FBI fingerprint cards. Name searches available online for a lesser fee. Registered users may be eligible for a fee waiver on name searches. Fee payee- State of Michigan. Prepayment required. Personal checks accepted. Credit cards accepted for online access.

Mail search: Turnaround time- 4 to 6 weeks. Limited searches with fingerprints available.

Online search: Online access is available at http://apps.michigan.gov/ICHAT/Home.aspx. Fee is $10.00 per name. Call 517-322-1377. You are also allowed up to three variations on one name search. Use of a MasterCard or VISA is required. This is the only method available for a non-fingerprint search.

Statewide Court Records

State Court Administrative Office, PO Box 30048, Lansing, MI 48909 (Courier address- 925 W Ottawa St, Lansing, MI 48913); 517-373-0130, Fax- 517-373-7517; 8:30AM-5PM.

http://courts.michigan.gov/scao/

No trial court records available from this agency.

Online search: Subscribe to email updates of appellate opinions at http://coa.courts.mi.gov/resources/subscribe.htm. There is no fee. Search opinions at http://coa.courts.mi.gov/resources/opinions.htm. There is a wide range of online computerization of the judicial system from "none" to "fairly complete," but there is no statewide court records network.

Other access: Zip files are provided for recent Supreme Court and Court of Appeals releases.

Sexual Offender Registry

Michigan State Police, SOR Section, 7150 Harris Dr, Lansing, MI 48913; 517-322-4938, Fax- 517-322-4957; 8AM-5PM. www.mipsor.state.mi.us

Records may be searched at the local law enforcement level. There are over 38,000 registered sex offenders living in Michigan.

Indexing & Storage: Records available since 1995 and held for duration of the offender. New records available for inquiry in immediate.

Searching: The agency recommends in person searchers to visit local law enforcement offices. Include in request- name and DOB. Only those offenders who have been convicted of a listed offense on or after October 1, 1995 or convicted prior to that date who were still incarcerated, on parole or probation for a listed offense on October 1, 1995 are listed.

Access by: online.

Fee & Payment: There is no search fee.

Online search: One may search the registry at the website, there is no charge.

Incarceration Records

Michigan Department of Corrections, Central Records Office, PO Box 30003, Lansing, MI 48909 (Courier address- 206 E. Michigan Ave., Lansing, MI 48909); 517-373-3651, Fax- 517-373-2558; 8AM-4:30PM.

www.michigan.gov/corrections

Indexing & Storage: Records available on current and former inmates. New records available for inquiry in 2-3 weeks.

Searching: Almost complete computer records go back to 1981. Computer records prior to that year become less complete the further back you search. Include in request- full name or MDOC number. The DOB and SSN are helpful. Location, MDOC number, conviction and sentencing information, physical identifiers, and release dates are provided. This data not released- SSN

Access by: mail, phone, fax, online.

Fee & Payment: There is a fee for copies; usually these are FOIA requests.

Mail search: Turnaround time- 5 to 7 days. A mail search can also be directed through the Attorney General's office (phone 510-682-2007).

Phone search: Name searches are available.

Fax search: Requests may be faxed.

Online search: The online access found at www.state.mi.us/mdoc/asp/otis2.html has many search criteria capabilities. There is also a DOC Most Wanted list at www.state.mi.us/mdoc/MostWanted/MostWanted.asp.

Other access: Bulk sales of database information is available.

Corporation, LLC, LP, LLP, Assumed Name

Department of Labor & Economic Growth, Bureau of Commercial Services - Corp Div, PO Box 30054, Lansing, MI 48909-7554; 517-241-6470, Fax- 517-241-0538; 8AM-5PM.

http://michigan.gov/corporations

Indexing & Storage: Records available from the first corporation in Michigan. Older records were indexed on cards. The index to records for active entities are maintained on computer. New records available for inquiry in 24 hours or less.

Searching: Forms, policies, and procedures may be viewed at their website. The fax listed above is for record requests and copies or certificate orders. Include in request- full name of business, corporation file number. The directors are only listed on the annual report.

Access by: mail, phone, fax, in person, online.

Fee & Payment: There is no search fee. The minimum charge for copies is $6.00 per record and $1.00 per page if over 6 pages. The minimum charge for a certificate (good standing) is $10.00. Fee payee- State of Michigan. Credit cards are accepted for in person requests only. Personal checks, Visa, and MasterCard accepted.

Mail search: Turnaround time- 5 to 7 days. There is no fee unless copies or certificates are needed, then there is a minimum $6.00 fee. SASE not required. Copies cost $1.00 per page.

Phone search: You can order copies or certificates.

Fax search: Same criteria as mail searches.

In person: The agency has a public access terminal for viewing records.

Online search: At the main website, search by company name or file number for records of domestic corporations, limited liability companies, limited partnerships and of foreign corporations, and limited partnerships qualified to transact business in the state. Click on Business Entity Search or go to www.dleg.state.mi.us/bcs_corp/sr_corp.asp.

Other access: The database is for sale by contract.

Expedited service: An expedited fee of 25% of the total cost for copies or certificates is charged for expedited service. Expedited orders are completed by the end of the next business day.

Trademarks/Servicemarks

Dept of labor & Economic Growth, Commercial Svcs - Trademarks & Service Marks, PO Box 30054, Lansing, MI 48909-7554; 517-241-6470, Fax- 517-241-0538; 8AM-5PM.

www.michigan.gov/dleg/0,1607,7-154-35299_35413_35431---,00.html

Indexing & Storage: Records available for current records. The index is available since 1990.

Access by: mail, phone, fax, in person, online.

Fee & Payment: The fee is $5.00 if this agency does the search.

Mail search: They suggest to use the web instead of mail.

Phone search: No fee for telephone request. Search is limited, they will let you know if a wording exists. **Fax search:** Requests accepted.

In person: No fee for request. There is a public access terminal.

Online search: Free searching is available at www.dleg.state.mi.us/bcsc/forms/corp/mark/markcom.pdf. This is a search of a PDF file of their system.

Uniform Commercial Code, Federal & State Tax Liens

MI Department of State, UCC Section, PO Box 30197, Lansing, MI 48909-7697 (Courier address- 7064 Crowner Dr, Dimondale, MI 48821); 517-322-1144, Fax- 517-322-5434; 8AM-5PM.

www.michigan.gov/sosucc

Indexing & Storage: Records available from 1964. Records are computerized since 1990. New records available for inquiry in 2 to 3 days, only hours if online.

Searching: Use UCC-11 request form. The search includes federal and state tax liens. Include in request- debtor name.

Access by: mail, phone, fax, in person, online.

Fee & Payment: The search fee is $6.00. The copy fee is $2.00 per page Certification (official seal) is an additional $6.00. Fee payee- State of Michigan. Personal checks accepted. Credit cards accepted for online access only.

Mail search: Turnaround time- 1 week.

Phone search: phone requesting is available for pre-established billing accounts, results are returned by mail.

Fax search: See expedited services.

In person: Requests are serviced in person, but the agency would prefer that requesters use the online access. See expedited services.

Online search: From the website, click on Login or Register. Conducting a Debtor Name Quick Search is free. No login is needed. Documents may be ordered for a fee. Registration is required. A credit card is necessary unless the requester has an established billing account.

Other access: A monthly subscription service is available for the bulk purchase of UCC filings on microfilm. The fee is $50 or actual cost, whichever is greater. Call 517-322-1144 for additional information.

Expedited service: Expedited service is available for an additional $25.00 fee. Expedited searches are provided on a prepaid account basis at $25.00 + $6.00 per debtor name. If request is received by 11 AM, search is mailed that same day.

Sales Tax Registrations

Access to Records is Restricted.

Michigan Dept of Treasury, Sales, Use, Withholding Tax Division, Registration, Lansing, MI 48922; 517-636-4730, Fax- 517-636-4491; 8AM-4:45PM.

www.michigan.gov/treasury

The agency will only verify or confirm data, no searches provided. Disclosure of tax returns and tax return information to someone other than the taxpayer is statutorily restricted to protect taxpayer confidentiality.

Birth Certificates

Department of Health, Vital Records Requests, PO Box 30721, Lansing, MI 48909 (Courier address- 201 Townsend St, Capitol View Bldg 3rd Fl, Lansing, MI 48913); 517-335-8656 (Instructions), 517-335-8666 (Request Unit), Fax- 517-321-5884; 8AM-5PM.

www.michigan.gov/mdch

Any Michigan vital record can be "verified" for a fee of $10.00. Verification is only a yes-no that record exists. Application for records can be downloaded from the website.

Indexing & Storage: Records available from 1867 on. Affidavits of parentage go back to June 1, 1997. New records available for inquiry in 90 to 120 days after birth.

Searching: Certified copies of birth records are only issued to the individual to whom the record pertains, the parent(s) named on the record, an heir, legal guardian or legal rep. of an eligible person, or through court order, unless record is 110 years old. Include in request- full name, names of parents, mother's maiden name, date of birth, place of birth, relationship to person of record. The signature and relationship to the subject are required items on the request form. Also include copy of photo ID. This data not released- sealed records.

Access by: mail, in person, online.

Fee & Payment: The fee for a certified copy is $26.00 which includes 3 years searched. Each additional year searched is another $12.00. Use of credit card is an additional $8.50. An "Authenticated Copy" is available for $29.00. Fee payee- State of Michigan. Prepayment required. Personal checks accepted. Major credit cards accepted online.

Mail search: Turnaround time- 15 to 20 days. SASE not required.

In person: Turnaround time up to 3 hours. Counter open 8AM to 4:45PM, same day requests must be submitted by 3PM. This is considered rush service.

Online search: Records can be ordered from the web site, credit card is required. Processing time is 2 weeks.

Expedited service: Expedited service is available for in person (same day), mail and online searches. The agency calls this "rush service." Turnaround time- 5 to 10 days. Add credit card fee (online only) and express mail fee. Add $10.00 for rush service.

Death Records

Department of Health, Vital Records Requests, PO Box 30721, Lansing, MI 48909 (Courier address- 201 Townsend St, Capitol View Bldg 3rd Fl, Lansing, MI 48913); 517-335-8656 (Instructions), 517-335-8666 (Request Unit), Fax- 517-321-5884; 8AM-5PM.

www.michigan.gov/mdch

Any Michigan vital record can be "verified" for a fee of $10.00. Verification is only a yes-no that record exists. Application for records can be downloaded from the website.

Indexing & Storage: Records available from 1867 to present. New records available for inquiry immediately.

Searching: Records are open to the public. Include in request- full name, date of death, place of death, relationship to person of record. This data not released- sealed records.

Access by: mail, fax, in person, online.

Fee & Payment: The fee for a certified copy is $26.00 which includes 3 years searched. Each additional year searched is another $12.00. Use of credit card is an additional $8.50. An "Authenticated Copy" is available for $29.00. Fee payee- State of Michigan. Prepayment required. Personal checks, money orders accepted. Major credit cards accepted online.

Mail search: Turnaround time- 15 to 20 days. SASE not required.

Fax search: Records are available by fax from VitalChek at 517-321-5884. See expedited service.

In person: Turnaround time up to 3 hours. Counter open 8AM to 4:45PM, same day requests must be submitted by 3PM. This is considered rush service.

Online search: Records can be ordered from the web site, credit card is required. Processing time is 2 weeks.

Expedited service: Expedited service is available for in person (same day), mail and online searches. The agency calls this "rush service." Turnaround time- 5 to 10 days. Add credit card fee (online only) and express mail fee. Add $10.00 for rush service.

Marriage Certificates

Department of Health, Vital Records Requests, PO Box 30721, Lansing, MI 48909 (Courier address- 201 Townsend St, Capitol View Bldg 3rd Fl, Lansing, MI 48913); 517-335-8656 (Instructions), 517-335-8666 (Requests Unit); 8AM-5PM.

www.michigan.gov/mdch

Any Michigan vital record can be "verified" for a fee of $10.00. Verification is only a yes-no that record exists. Application for records can be downloaded from the website.

Indexing & Storage: Records available from 1867 to present. New records available for inquiry immediately.

Searching: Records are open to the public. There is no bride index for the years 1950 thru 1975. Include in request- names of husband and wife, date of marriage, place or county of marriage.

Access by: mail, fax, in person, online.

Fee & Payment: The fee for a certified copy is $26.00 which includes 3 years searched. Each additional year searched is another $12.00. Use of credit card is an additional $8.50. An "Authenticated Copy" is available for $29.00. Fee payee- State of Michigan. Prepayment required. Personal checks accepted. Major credit cards accepted online.

Mail search: Turnaround time- 15 to 20 days. SASE not required.

Fax search: Records are available by fax from VitalChek at 517-321-5884. See expedited service.

In person: Turnaround time up to 3 hours. Counter open 8AM to 4:45PM, same day requests must be submitted by 3PM. This is considered rush service.

Online search: Records can be ordered from the website; credit card is required. Processing time is 2 weeks.

Expedited service: Expedited service is available for in person (same day), mail and online searches. The agency calls this "rush service." Turnaround time- 1 to 2 business days. Add credit card fee (online only) and express mail fee. Add $10.00 for rush service.

Divorce Records

Department of Health, Vital Records Requests, PO Box 30721, Lansing, MI 48909 (Courier address- 201 Townsend St, Capitol View Bldg 3rd Fl, Lansing, MI 48913); 517-335-8656 (Instructions), 517-335-8666 (Requests Unit), Fax- 517-321-5884; 8AM-5PM.

www.michigan.gov/mdch

Any Michigan vital record can be "verified" for a fee of $10.00. Verification is only a yes-no that record exists. Application for records can be downloaded from the website.

Indexing & Storage: Records available from 1897 to present. New records available for inquiry in 6-10 months.

Searching: Records are not restricted. There are no divorce records for Detroit for 1973 and 1974. There is no "wife index" available prior to 1978. Include in request- names of husband and wife, date of divorce, county where divorce granted.

Access by: mail, fax, in person, online.

Fee & Payment: The fee for a certified copy is $26.00 which includes 3 years searched. Each additional year searched is another $12.00. Use of credit card is an additional $8.50. An "Authenticated Copy" is available for $29.00. Fee payee- State of Michigan. Prepayment required. Personal checks accepted. Major credit cards accepted online.

Mail search: Turnaround time- 15 to 20 days. SASE not required.

Fax search: Records are available by fax from VitalChek at 517-321-5884. See expedited service.

In person: Turnaround time up to 3 hours. Counter open 8AM to 4:45PM, same day requests must be submitted by 3PM. This is considered rush service.

Online search: Records can be ordered from the web site, credit card is required. Processing time is 2 weeks.

Expedited service: Expedited service is available for in person (same day), mail and online searches. The agency calls this "rush service." Turnaround time- 5 to 10 days. Add credit card fee (online only) and express mail fee. Add $10.00 for rush service.

Workers' Compensation Records

Department of Labor & Economic Dev., Workers' Compensation Agency, 7150 Harris Dr, Lansing, MI 48909; 888-396-5041, Fax- 517-322-1808; 8AM-5PM.

www.michigan.gov/wca

In person requests are discouraged due to confidentiality of records and records may not be on site. Injured employee may review their own records, but should call first and make arrangements.

Indexing & Storage: Records available from 1981 on computer and from 1976 to 1981 records on microfilm. You can request by fax, but results are mailed. New records available for inquiry in 1 week.

Searching: Request must be in writing and cannot be for pre-employment screening. Only litigated cases are released. Include in request- claimant name, SSN, and date of injury. This data not released- any records exempt from disclosure under the MI Freedom of Information Act.

Access by: mail, fax, online.

Fee & Payment: Fee is $.25 per page plus postage and research labor cost if over 30 pages. Fee payee- Labor & Economic Growth Prepayment required. Personal checks accepted, credit cards are not.

Mail search: Turnaround time- 1 to 2 weeks. Turnaround time may be longer if records must be searched at archives. SASE not required.

Fax search: Fax requests accepted.

Online search: Go to the website and follow the links to see if an employer has coverage. The site does not allow searching by employee name.

Driver Records

Department of State, Record Lookup Unit, 7064 Crowner Dr, Lansing, MI 48918; 517-322-1624 (Look-up Unit), Fax- 517-322-1181; 8:30AM-4:50PM.

www.michigan.gov/sos

Copies of court abstracts of convictions may be purchased at the same address for a fee of $7.00 per copy. Copies of tickets must be obtained from the courts involved.

Indexing & Storage: Records available for 7 years from conviction date; unless there is an alcohol or controlled substance conviction which will remain on record for 10 years. Accidents are reported on the record only if the driver is cited. New records available for inquiry in 8 days.

Searching: Casual requesters must submit form BDVR-154, with written consent of subject or show a permissible DPPA purpose, to receive records with personal information. Otherwise, records without personal information are released. Include in request- name and either DOB or DL number. This data not released- highly restricted personal information (MCL 257.40b) such as SSN, address, photograph, medical and disability data.

Access by: mail, phone, fax, in person, online.

Fee & Payment: The fee for obtaining a record is $7.00 per search. If certification is needed, there is an additional $1.00 fee. Fee payee- State of Michigan. The fee may accompany the request for mail-in, or a bill can be sent with the records. There is a full charge for a no record found. Credit cards are accepted for fax and phone requests only. Personal checks accepted. Major credit cards accepted.

Mail search: Turnaround time- 10 working days. SASE not required.

Phone search: Call-in accounts are for established, approved accounts or those wishing to obtain their own record. Use of a credit card is required.

Fax search: Established accounts can order by fax, results are returned by mail.

In person: Turnaround time is 24 hours unless you are the actual driver, then the record is immediately available. Also, one may purchase his/her own certified driving record payable by cash, check, or credit card (Discover only) at Secretary of State PLUS and SUPER!Center branch offices.

Online search: Online ordering is available on an interactive or batch basis. The system is open 7 days a week. Ordering is by DL or name and DOB. An account must be established and billing is monthly. Fee is $7.00 per record. A $25,000 surety bond is required. Also, the agency offers an activity notification service for employers who register their drivers. For more information on either program, call 517-322-6281.

Other access: The state offers the license file for bulk purchase to approved requesters. Customized runs are $64 per thousand records; complete database can be purchased for $16 per thousand. A $25,000 surety bond is required. Call 517-322-1042.

Vehicle, Vessel Ownership & Registration

Department of State, Record Lookup Unit, 7064 Crowner Dr, Lansing, MI 48918; 517-322-1624, 888-767-6424, Fax- 517-322-1181; 8AM-4:45PM.

www.michigan.gov/sos

Indexing & Storage: Records available for 10 years to present for title information and 4 years to present for registration information. Vessel titles are on computer since 1974. All motorized boats must be registered, if 20 ft or over they must also be titled. New records available for inquiry in 8 days.

Searching: Requests for vehicle and ownership records of others must be submitted on Form BDVR154. Large volume users or fax requesters must be pre-approved. The request form is available online. Normally, a search requires the plate or VIN. Records to be accessed include mobile homes and boats. This data not released- highly restricted personal information (MCL 257.40b).

Access by: mail, phone, fax, in person, online.

Fee & Payment: The fee is $7.00 per transaction. Certification is $1.00 per record. Fee payee- State of Michigan. Prepayment required, if no account. There is a full charge for a "no record found." Personal checks accepted. Major credit cards accepted for fax and phone requests.

Mail search: Turnaround time- 10 days. A SASE is not requested.

Phone search: Call-in requests are for established, approved accounts only or for those obtaining their own records. Records are mailed.

Fax search: Established accounts or credit card order requesters may order by fax and receive results by mail.

In person: You can make your request in person, but they will mail back the records in 4 or 5 days. Requests must be in writing or on form mentioned above.

Online search: Online searching via the Internet is single inquiry and requires a VIN or plate number (no name searches). An account is required with a $25,000 surety bond. Fee is $7.00 per record. For more information, call 517-322-6281. The program is called Direct Access and details are found on the web. A unique service offered is the Repeat Offender Inquiry. This web search function allows dealers and others to learn if a vehicle purchaser is ineligible for license plates and subject to registration denial under Michigan's Repeat Offender Law. Search results state if the purchaser is eligible, not eligible, or if not on file. The web site is https://services.sos.state.mi.us/RepeatOffender/Inquiry.aspx.

Other access: Michigan offers bulk retrieval from the VIN and plate database. A written request letter, stating purpose, must be submitted and approved. A $25,000 surety bond is required upon approval. Please call 517-322-1042.

Accident Reports

Department of State Police, Criminal Justice Information Center, 7150 Harris Dr, Lansing, MI 48913; 517-322-5509, Fax- 517-322-5350; 8AM-5PM. www.michigan.gov/msp/0,1607,7-123-1593_24055-35982--,00.html

Requests must be in writing or through web page.

Indexing & Storage: Records available from 1983 to present for state police records. UD10's for all law enforcement agencies in Michigan are available for the current year plus 2 years back, first page only. New records available for inquiry in 3 to 4 weeks, 10 days if online.

Searching: Include in request- full name, date of accident, location of accident. This data not released- DOB, SSN, address and phone

Access by: mail, fax, in person, online.

Fee & Payment: Accident reports are $10.00 per report and more if extensive searching required. Fee payee- State of Michigan. Prepayment required. Personal checks accepted. Credit cards accepted only at web page.

Mail search: Turnaround time- 10 days. A SASE is requested.

Fax search: Records are available by fax. Turnaround time is 5 days.

In person: You may request information in person; turnaround time for return is 5 days.

Online search: Records may be requested from the Traffic Crash Purchasing System at https://mdotwas1.mdot.state.mi.us/TCPS/login/welcome.jsp. The fee is $10.00, a credit cards may be used unless billing arrangements are made. Records are available going back 10 years. For specific questions email CrashPurchaseTCPS@michigan.gov.

Legislation Records

Michigan Legislature Document Room, State Capitol, PO Box 30036, Lansing, MI 48909 (Courier address- North Capitol Annex, Lansing, MI 48909); 517-373-0169, 517-373-0169 (Library of Michigan (Journals)); 8:30AM-5PM.

www.legislature.mi.gov

Indexing & Storage: Records available from 1997 on computer. New records available for inquiry in 2 to 3 days. Data on older passed bills, research, and legal reference is handled by the State Law Library, 517-373-0630.

Searching: Search by bill number, sponsor or subject.

Access by: mail, phone, in person, online.

Fee & Payment: There are no fees involved. No credit cards accepted.

Mail search: Turnaround time- 1 day. SASE not required.

Phone search: Only current and past session information is available. Leave a message on the phone.

In person: Simple requests may be processed while you wait.

Online search: Their Internet site is an excellent free resource. Information available includes status of bills, bill text, joint resolution text, journals, calendars, session and committee schedules, and MI complied laws. Also, search MI compiled laws free at the home page.

Voter Registration

Secretary of State, Bureau of Elections, PO Box 20126, Lansing, MI 48901 (Courier address- 430 W Allegan St, 1st Fl, Lansing, MI 48918); 517-373-2540, Fax- 517-241-4785; 8AM-5PM.

www.michigan.gov/sos/1,1607,7-127-1633---,00.html

In general, the records are open to the public. For single name searches go to https://webapps.sos.state.mi.us/mivote/votersearch.aspx. Must have first and last name, birth month and year and residential zip code.

Indexing & Storage: Records available from 08/98 forward. New records available for inquiry in 1 to 2 days.

Searching: All requests must be in writing. The agency will let the requester know the fees. Include in request- name, DOB. The record includes name, address, and the birth year.

Access by: mail, fax.

Fee & Payment: The fee is $7.00 per name, even if identifier matches. If an identifier (such as a DOB) is not given, each common name is $7.00. Fee payee- State of Michigan Prepayment required.

Mail search: Turnaround time- 2 to 3 days. Records are available by mail.

Fax search: Records are available by fax, if request is prepaid.

Other access: The agency will sell district, statewide or customized subsets of the database on CD. Fees are usually $100 to $170, depending on data requested.

Expedited service: If shipping label and account information provided, the agency will expedite.

GED Certificates

MI Department of Labor & Econ Growth, Adult Education - GED Testing, 201 N Washington Square, 3rd Fl, Lansing, MI 48913; 517-373-1692, Fax- 517-335-3461; 7AM-5PM.

www.michigan.gov/adulteducation

Indexing & Storage: Records available from 3/1969 to present. New records available for inquiry in up to 1 week.

Searching: To search, include the SSN, DOB and date and location of test. For a copy of a transcript, also include a signed release.

Access by: mail, phone, fax, in person, online.

Fee & Payment: There are no fees.

Mail search: Turnaround time is 1 week; 3 weeks if record is prior to 1979. SASE not required.

Phone search: You request a verification by leaving a message and fax a signed release. The agency will call or fax back the information.

Fax search: Same criteria as mail searching.

In person: The building is also known as the Victor Building. Office is on third floor.

Online search: Will accept e-mail requests with a scanned signature.

Hunting & Fishing License Information

Access to Records is Restricted.

Dept of Natural Resources, Customer Systems, PO Box 30181, Lansing, MI 48909 (Courier address- 530 W Allegan St, Lansing, MI 48933); 517-241-1919, Fax- 517-241-4278; 8AM-5PM.

www.michigan.gov/dnr

Hunting and fishing license information is no longer released. All FOIA requests are now being denied because records are considered to be purely personal information.

Michigan State Licensing Agencies

For details about the agency responsible for licensing/certifying/registering an item below or in the Agency Quick Finder section, match an item's number with the number of the agency in the *Licensing Agency Information* section.

Michigan Licenses Searchable Online

Adoption Svc/Child Placing Agency #13 ... www.michigan.gov/dhs/0,1607,7-124-5455_27716_27721---,00.html
Adult Foster Care/Homes for Aged #21 ... www.dleg.state.mi.us/brs_afc/sr_afc.asp
Aircraft Dealer #23 ... www.michigan.gov/documents/aero/2006_October_Dealer_web_page_listing_FIN_175448_7.pdf
Airport Manager #23 ... www.michigan.gov/documents/Mgr_List_147366_7.pdf
Alarm System Service #17 ... https://www2.dleg.state.mi.us/colaLicVerify/
Ambulance Attendant #10 ... www.dleg.state.mi.us/free/default.asp
Amusement Ride #8 ... www.dleg.state.mi.us/verify.htm
Appraiser, Real Estate/Gen./Resi'l #8 ... www.dleg.state.mi.us/verify.htm
Aquaculture Operation #2 ... www.michigan.gov/documents/mda/mda_aquaculture_192478_7.pdf
Architect #8 ... www.dleg.state.mi.us/verify.htm
Asbestos Accreditation, Individ'l #11 ... www.dleg.state.mi.us/asbestos_program/sr_individual.asp
Asbestos Contractor #11 ... www.dleg.state.mi.us/asbestos_program/sr_contractor.asp
Asbestos Training Provider #11 ... www.dleg.state.mi.us/asbestos_program/sr_tcp.asp
Atmosphere Storage Operator #2 ... www.michigan.gov/mda/0,1607,7-125-1569_16993_19105-46661--,00.html
Attorney, State Bar #26 ... www.michbar.org/memberdirectory/
Auto Dealer/Mech'/Repair Facility #27 ... www.michigan.gov/sos/0,1607,7-127-1631_8849-51047--,00.html
Bank & Trust Company #14 ... www.dleg.state.mi.us/fis/ind_srch/cht_bank/state_charter_bank_criteria.asp
Barber #8 ... www.dleg.state.mi.us/verify.htm
Barber Shop/School #8 ... www.dleg.state.mi.us/verify.htm
Boxing/Wrestling Occupation #8 ... www.dleg.state.mi.us/verify.htm
Builder, Residential #8 ... www.dleg.state.mi.us/verify.htm
Camp, Child/Adult Foster Care #13 ... www.michigan.gov/dhs/0,1607,7-124-5455_27716_27723---,00.html
Carnival #8 ... www.dleg.state.mi.us/verify.htm
Casino Interest Personnel/Firm #28 ... http://miboecfr.nicusa.com/cgi-bin/cfr/casino_srch.cgi
Cemetery #8 ... www.dleg.state.mi.us/verify.htm
Check Seller #3 ... www.michigan.gov/dleg/0,1607,7-154-10555_13251_13257---,00.html
Child Care Family/Group/Center #13 ... www.michigan.gov/dhs/0,1607,7-124-5455_27716_27718---,00.html
Child Care Institution #25 ... www.michigan.gov/dhs/0,1607,7-124-5455_27716_27719---,00.html
Child Facility, Court Operated #25 ... www.michigan.gov/dhs/0,1607,7-124-5455_27716_27722---,00.html
Child Foster Care Family Home #21 ... www.dleg.state.mi.us/brs_cwl/sr_cf.asp
Chiropractor #15 ... www.dleg.state.mi.us/free/default.asp
Collection Manager #8 ... www.dleg.state.mi.us/verify.htm
Community Planner #8 ... www.dleg.state.mi.us/verify.htm
Community Planner (Mfg. Home) #16 ... https://www2.dleg.state.mi.us/colaLicVerify/
Consumer Financial Service #3 ... www.michigan.gov/dleg/0,1607,7-154-10555_13251_13257---,00.html
Contractor, Residential #8 ... www.dleg.state.mi.us/verify.htm
Cosmetologist #8 ... www.dleg.state.mi.us/verify.htm
Cosmetology Shop/School #8 ... www.dleg.state.mi.us/verify.htm
Counselor #15 ... www.dleg.state.mi.us/free/default.asp
Credit Card Issuer #3 ... www.michigan.gov/dleg/0,1607,7-154-10555_13251_13257---,00.html
Credit Union #14 ... www.dleg.state.mi.us/fis/ind_srch/CreditUnion/Search.asp
Debt Management Firm #12 ... www.michigan.gov/documents/cis_ofis_debtlist_25540_7.pdf
Dental Hygienist #15 ... www.dleg.state.mi.us/free/default.asp
Dentist/Dental Assistant #15 ... www.dleg.state.mi.us/free/default.asp
ElectionCampaign Finance Comm'tee #28 http://miboecfr.nicusa.com/cgi-bin/cfr/mi_com.cgi
Election Candidate Committee #28 ... http://miboecfr.nicusa.com/cgi-bin/cfr/can_search.cgi
Emergency Medical Personnel #15 ... www.dleg.state.mi.us/free/default.asp
Employment Agency, fee only #8 ... www.dleg.state.mi.us/verify.htm
EMT Advanced/Specialist/Instructor #10 .. www.dleg.state.mi.us/free/default.asp
Engineer #9 ... www.dleg.state.mi.us/verify.htm
Flight School #23 ... www.michigan.gov/documents/AERO_Flight_Schools_Aug_2005_134972_7.pdf
Forester #8 ... www.dleg.state.mi.us/verify.htm
Funeral Home #8 ... www.dleg.state.mi.us/verify.htm
Funeral Salesperson #8 ... www.dleg.state.mi.us/verify.htm
Funeral, Prepaid Contract Regis. #8 ... www.dleg.state.mi.us/verify.htm
Grain Dealer #2 ... www.mda.state.mi.us/prodag/GrainDealers/dealers.html
Grain Trucker #2 ... www.mda.state.mi.us/prodag/GrainDealers/dealers.html

Health Facility/Laboratory #15 .... www.dleg.state.mi.us/free/default.asp
Hearing Aid Dealer #8 .... www.dleg.state.mi.us/verify.htm
HMO #5 .... www.michigan.gov/dleg/0,1607,7-154-10555_13251_13262---,00.html
Insurance Adjuster #5 .... www.michigan.gov/dleg/0,1607,7-154-10555_13251_13262---,00.html
Insurance Agent//Solicit/Admin. #5 .... www.michigan.gov/dleg/0,1607,7-154-10555_13251_13262---,00.html
Insurance Counselor #5 .... www.dleg.state.mi.us/fis/ind_srch/ins_agnt/insurance_agent_criteria.asp
Insurance Solicitor #5 .... www.dleg.state.mi.us/fis/ind_srch/ins_agnt/insurance_agent_criteria.asp
Insurance-related Entity #5 .... www.michigan.gov/dleg/0,1607,7-154-10555_13251_13262---,00.html
Investment Adviser #12 .... http://adviserinfo.sec.gov/IAPD/Content/Search/iapd_OrgSearch.aspx
Landscape Architect #8 .... www.dleg.state.mi.us/verify.htm
Liquor Dist./Whlse./Mfg. #6 .... https://www2.dleg.state.mi.us/MWPR/
Liquor Finance Division #6 .... https://www2.dleg.state.mi.us/MWPR/
Liquor Hearings & Appeals #6 .... https://www2.dleg.state.mi.us/MWPR/
Liquor License #6 .... https://www2.dleg.state.mi.us/MWPR/
Liquor Licensing Director #6 .... https://www2.dleg.state.mi.us/MWPR/
Living Care Facility #12 .... www.michigan.gov/documents/cis_ofis_lclist_25541_7.pdf
Lobbyist/Lobbyist Agent #28 .... http://miboecfr.nicusa.com/cgi-bin/cfr/lobby_srch.cgi
Long Term Care Company #5 .... www.michigan.gov/dleg/0,1607,7-154-10555_13251_13262---,00.html
Mammography Facility #15 .... www.dleg.state.mi.us/free/default.asp
Marriage & Family Therapist #15 .... www.dleg.state.mi.us/free/default.asp
Medical Doctor #15 .... www.dleg.state.mi.us/free/default.asp
Medical First Responder #10 .... www.dleg.state.mi.us/free/default.asp
Mortgage Licensee #3 .... www.michigan.gov/dleg/0,1607,7-154-10555_13251_13257---,00.html
Mortuary Science #8 .... www.dleg.state.mi.us/verify.htm
Motor Vehicle Loan Seller/Financer #3 .... www.michigan.gov/dleg/0,1607,7-154-10555_13251_13257---,00.html
Nurse #15 .... www.dleg.state.mi.us/free/default.asp
Nursery Dealer/Grower #2 .... www.mda.state.mi.us/industry/Nursery/license/index.html
Nurses' Aide #15 .... www.dleg.state.mi.us/free/default.asp
Nursing Home #15 .... www.dleg.state.mi.us/bhs_car/sr_car.asp
Nursing Home Administrator #15 .... www.dleg.state.mi.us/free/default.asp
Ocularist #8 .... www.dleg.state.mi.us/verify.htm
Optometrist #15 .... www.dleg.state.mi.us/free/default.asp
Osteopathic Physician #15 .... www.dleg.state.mi.us/free/default.asp
Paramedic #10 .... www.dleg.state.mi.us/free/default.asp
Personnel Agency #17 .... https://www2.dleg.state.mi.us/colaLicVerify/
Pesticide Application Business #2 .... www.mda.state.mi.us/pest/
Pharmacist #15 .... www.dleg.state.mi.us/free/default.asp
Physical Therapist #15 .... www.dleg.state.mi.us/free/default.asp
Physician Assistant #15 .... www.dleg.state.mi.us/free/default.asp
Podiatrist #15 .... www.dleg.state.mi.us/free/default.asp
Political Action Committee #28 .... http://miboecfr.nicusa.com/cgi-bin/cfr/pac_search.cgi
Political Party Committee #28 .... http://miboecfr.nicusa.com/cgi-bin/cfr/mi_com.cgi?com_type=PPY
Polygraph Examiner #8 .... www.dleg.state.mi.us/verify.htm
Potato Dealer #2 .... www.michigan.gov/mda/0,1607,7-125-1566_1733_2321-11149--,00.html
Private Investigator/Detective #17 .... https://www2.dleg.state.mi.us/colaLicVerify/
Private Security/Arrest Author'y #17 .... https://www2.dleg.state.mi.us/colaLicVerify/
Psychologist #15 .... www.dleg.state.mi.us/free/default.asp
Public Accountant-CPA #8 .... www.dleg.state.mi.us/verify.htm
Real Estate Agent/Broker/Seller #9 .... www.dleg.state.mi.us/verify.htm
Regulatory Loan Licensee #3 .... www.michigan.gov/dleg/0,1607,7-154-10555_13251_13257---,00.html
Sanitarian #15 .... www.dleg.state.mi.us/free/default.asp
Savings Bank #14 .... www.dleg.state.mi.us/fis/ind_srch/sav_bank/state_savings_bank_list.asp
Securities Agent #12 .... www.finra.org/index.htm
Securities Broker/Dealer #12 .... www.finra.org/index.htm
Security Agency #17 .... https://www2.dleg.state.mi.us/colaLicVerify/
Security Alarm Installer #17 .... https://www2.dleg.state.mi.us/colaLicVerify/
Security Guard, Private #17 .... https://www2.dleg.state.mi.us/colaLicVerify/
Social Worker #15 .... www.dleg.state.mi.us/free/default.asp
Surety Company #5 .... www.michigan.gov/dleg/0,1607,7-154-10555_13251_13262---,00.html
Surplus Line Broker #5 .... www.michigan.gov/dleg/0,1607,7-154-10555_13251_13262---,00.html
Surveyor, Professional #9 .... www.dleg.state.mi.us/verify.htm
Teacher #19 .... https://mdoe.state.mi.us/teachercert/
Third-Party Administrator #5 .... www.michigan.gov/dleg/0,1607,7-154-10555_13251_13262---,00.html
Veterinarian/Veterinary Technician #15 .... www.dleg.state.mi.us/free/default.asp
Weights & Measures Person/Agency #2 .... www.mda.state.mi.us/industry/lab/service/index.html

Michigan Licensing Quick Finder

Adoption Svc/Child Placing Agcny #13 ... 866-685-0006
Adult Foster Care/Homes for Aged #21 866-685-0006
Aircraft Dealer #23 ... 517-335-9283
Aircraft/Aeronautics Registration #23 ... 517-335-9283
Airport Manager #23 ... 517-335-9283
Airport/Heliport #23 ... 517-335-9283
Alarm System Service #17 ... 517-241-5645
Ambulance Attendant #10 ... 517-241-0179
Amusement Ride #8 ... 517-241-9265
Animal (Dead) Renderer #2 ... 517-373-1077
Animal Control Officer #2 ... 517-373-1077
Animal Feed (Commercial) #2 ... 800-292-3939
Animal Remedy/Animal Shelter #2 ... 517-373-1077
Appraiser, Real Estate/Gen./Resi'l #8 .. 517-241-9201
Aquaculture Operation #2 ... 517-373-1077
Architect #8 ... 517-241-9253
Asbestos Accreditation, Individ'l #11 ... 517-322-1320
Asbestos Contractor #11 ... 517-322-1320
Asbestos Training Provider #11 ... 517-322-1320
Assessor #24 ... 517-373-8320
Athletic Event- Boxing, etc #8 ... 517-241-9246
Atmosphere Storage Operator #2 ... 517-373-1075
Attorney, State Bar #26 ... 800-968-1442
Auto Dealer/Mech'/Repair Facility #27 . 517-636-6400
Bank & Trust Company #14 ... 517-373-0220
Barber #8 ... 517-241-9201
Barber Shop/School #8 ... 517-241-9258
BIDCO #14 ... 517-373-0220
Bingo Operation, Special/Weekly #1 ... 517-335-5600
Boiler Repairer #7 ... 517-241-9334
Boilermaker/Boiler Installer #7 ... 517-241-9334
Boxing/Wrestling Occupation #8 ... 517-241-9246
Builder, Residential #8 ... 517-241-9427
Camp, Child/Adult Foster Care #13 ... 866-685-0006
Carnival #8 ... 517-241-9265
Casino Interest Personnel/Firm #28 ... 517-373-2540
Cemetery #8 ... 517-241-9244
Charitable Gaming (Supplier) #1 ... 517-335-5600
Check Seller #3 ... 877-999-6442
Child Care Family/Group/Center #13 ... 866-685-0006
Child Care Institution #25 ... 517-335-6124
Child Facility, Court Operated #25 ... 517-335-6124
Child Foster Care Family Home #21 ... 866-685-0006
Chiropractor #15 ... 517-241-9427
Collection Manager #8 ... 517-241-9258
Community Planner #8 ... 517-241-9253
Community Planner (Mfg. Home) #16 .. 517-241-9317
Consumer Financial Service #3 ... 877-999-6442
Contractor, Residential #8 ... 517-241-9427
Corrections Officer #18 ... 517-335-1426
Cosmetologist #8 ... 517-241-9201
Cosmetology Shop/School #8 ... 517-241-9258
Counselor #15 ... 517-241-9427
Counselor, School Guidance #19 ... 517-373-6505
Credit Card Issuer #3 ... 877-999-6442
Credit Union #14 ... 517-373-0220
Debt Management Firm #12 ... 877-999-6442, 517-373-0220

Dental Hygienist #15 ... 517-241-9427
Dentist/Dental Assistant #15 ... 517-241-9427
Election Campaign Finance Comm'tee #28 ... 517-373-2540
Election Candidate Committee #28 ... 517-373-2540
Electrician (various types) #7 ... 517-241-9320
Elevator Service #7 ... 517-241-9337
Emergency Medical Personnel #15 ... 517-241-9427
Employment Agency, fee only #8 ... 517-241-9258
EMT Advanced/Specialist/Instructor #10517-241-0179
Engineer #9 ... 517-241-9253
Fertilizer and Liming #2 ... 517.373.1087
Fieldperson (Dairy/Farm related) #2 ... 800-292-3939
Flight School #23 ... 517-335-9283
Food Establishment #2 ... 517-373-1060
Food Service License #2 ... 517-373-1060
Forester #8 ... 517-241-9288
Funeral Home #8 ... 517-241-9252
Funeral Salesperson #8 ... 517-241-9252
Funeral, Prepaid Contract Regis. #8 ... 517-241-9252
Gasoline Seller (Retail) #2 ... 800-292-3939
Grain Dealer #2 ... 517-241-2865
Grain Trucker #2 ... 517-241-2865
Health Facility/Laboratory #15 ... 517-241-2648
Hearing Aid Dealer #8 ... 517-241-9234
HMO #5 ... 877-999-6442
Insurance Adjuster #5 ... 877-999-6442
Insurance Agent/Counsel/Solicit/Admin. #5 ... 877-999-6442
Insurance Counselor #5 ... 877-999-6442
Insurance Solicitor #5 ... 877-999-6442
Insurance-related Entity #5 ... 877-999-6442
Investment Adviser #12877-999-6442, 517-373-0220
Landscape Architect #8 ... 517-241-8364
Liquor Dist./Whlse./Mfg. #6 ... 517-322-1415
Liquor Finance Division #6 ... 517-322-1071
Liquor Hearings & Appeals #6 ... 517-322-1390
Liquor License #6 ... 517-322-1408
Liquor Licensing Director #6 ... 517-322-1408
Livestock Dealer #2 ... 517-373-1077
Living Care Facility #12 877-999-6442, 517-373-0220
Lobbyist/Lobbyist Agent #28 ... 517-373-2540
Long Term Care Company #5 ... 877-999-6442
Lottery Retailer #1 ... 517-335-5600
Mammography Facility #15 ... 517-241-1989
Manufact'd Home Installer/Svcs./Retail #16 ... 517-241-9317
Manufactured Home Community #16 .. 517-241-9317
Marriage & Family Therapist #15 ... 517-241-9427
Mechanical Construction #7 ... 517-241-9325
Medical Doctor #15 ... 517-241-9427
Medical First Responder #10 ... 517-241-0179
Milk Distributor #2 ... 517-373-1060
Milk Facility/Wash Facility #2 ... 517-373-1060
Milk Plant/Hauler/Installer #2 ... 517-373-1060
Millionaire Party/Vegas Night Gaming #1 ... 517-335-5600
Mortgage Licensee #3 ... 877-999-6442

Mortuary Science #8 ... 517-241-9252
Motor Vehicle Loan Seller/Financer #3 877-999-6442
Notary Public #22 ... 517-373-2531
Nurse #15 ... 517-241-9427
Nursery Dealer/Grower #2 ... 517-373-1087
Nurses' Aide #15 ... 517-241-9427
Nursing Home #15 ... 517-334-8408
Nursing Home Administrator #15 ... 517-241-9427
Ocularist #8 ... 517-241-9258
Optometrist #15 ... 517-241-9427
Osteopathic Physician #15 ... 517-241-9427
Paramedic #10 ... 517-241-0179
Personnel Agency #17 ... 517-241-5645
Pesticide Application Business #2 ... 517-373-4095
Pesticide Application Certification #2 ... 517-373-9752
Pet Shop #2 ... 517-373-1077
Pharmacist #15 ... 517-241-9427
Physical Therapist #15 ... 517-241-9427
Physician Assistant #15 ... 517-241-9427
Plumber #7 ... 517-241-9330
Podiatrist #15 ... 517-241-9427
Political Action Committee #28 ... 517-373-2540
Political Party Committee #28 ... 517-373-2540
Polygraph Examiner #8 ... 517-241-9288
Potato Dealer #2 ... 517-373-1075
Private Investigator/Detective #17 ... 517-241-5645
Private Security/arrest author'y #17 ... 517-241-5645
Psychologist #15 ... 517-241-9427
Public Accountant-CPA #8 ... 517-241-9427
Pump Installer #20 ... 517-241-1389
Race Track Employee #4 ... 517-335-1420
Racing Professional #4 ... 517-335-1420
Raffle #1 ... 517-335-5600
Real Estate Agent/Broker/Seller #9 ... 517-241-9288
Regulatory Loan Licensee #3 ... 877-999-6442
Restricted Use Pesticide (RUP) Listing #2 ... 517-373-0946
Riding Stable #2 ... 517-373-1077
Sanitarian #15 ... 517-241-9427
Savings Bank #14 ... 517-373-0220
School Librarian #19 ... 517-373-6505
Securities Agent #12 ... 877-999-6442, 517-373-0220
Securities Broker/Dealer #12 ... 877-999-6442, 517-373-0220
Security Agency #17 ... 517-241-5645
Security Alarm Installer #17 ... 517-241-5645
Security Guard, Private #17 ... 517-241-5645
Seed #2 ... 517-373-0946
Social Worker #15 ... 517-241-9427
Surety Company #5 ... 877-999-6442
Surplus Line Broker #5 ... 877-999-6442
Surveyor, Professional #9 ... 517-241-9253
Teacher #19 ... 517-373-6505
Third-Party Administrator #5 ... 877-999-6442
Veterinarian/Veterinary Technician #15 517-241-9427
Weights/Measures Person/Ag'ncy#2 ... 800-292-3939
Well Contractor #20 ... 517-241-1389

Michigan Licensing Agency Information

#1 Bureau of State Lottery, PO Box 30023 (101 E Hillsdale), Lansing, MI 48909; 517-335-5600, Fax- 517-373-5644. Hours- 7:45AM-4:45PM. www.michigan.gov/lottery

#2 Department of Agriculture, Licensing, Certification & Registration, PO Box 30017 (525 W Alegan, 4th Fl), Lansing, MI 48909; 800-292-3939. www.michigan.gov/mda Food establishment licensing is at the local/county level.

#3 Department of Labor & Economic Growth, Consumer Finance Unit, PO Box 30220 (611 W Ottawa, 3nd Fl), Lansing, MI 48909; 877-999-6442, Fax- 517-335-1501. Hours- 8AM-5PM. www.michigan.gov/ofis Search data at- www.michigan.gov/dleg/0,1607,7-154-10555_13251_13257---,00.html

#4 Department of Agriculture, Office of Racing Commissioner, 37650 Professional Center Dr, Livonia, MI 48154-1100; 517-335-1420, Fax-734-462-2429. www.michigan.gov/mda/0,1607,7-125-1572_2875_31952---,00.html

#5 Department of Labor & Economic Growth, Financial and Insurance Services, PO Box 30165 (7150 Harris Dr), Lansing, MI 48909; 517-373-0220; 877-999-6442, Fax- 517-335-4978. 8AM-5PM. www.michigan.gov/ofis Search data at- www.michigan.gov/dleg/0,1607,7-154-10555_13251_13262---,00.html

#6 Department of Labor & Economic Growth, Liquor Control Commission, PO Box 30005 (7150 Harris Dr), Lansing, MI 48909-7505; 517-322-1420, Fax- 517-322-5046. www.michigan.gov/dleg/0,1607,7-154-10570---,00.html Search data at- https://www2.dleg.state.mi.us/MWPR/ Will sell/provide lists or offer other means of verification.

#7 Department of Consumer & Industry Services, Bureau of Construction Codes, PO Box 30254, Lansing, MI 48909; 517-241-9313, Fax- 517-373-8547. Hours- 8AM-5PM. www.michigan.gov/dleg/0,1607,7-154-10575-92379--,00.html

#8 Department of Consumer & Industry Services, Bureau of Commercial Services/Licensing Division, PO Box 30018, Lansing, MI 48909; 517-241-9288, Fax- 517-241-9280. www.michigan.gov/cis Search data at- www.dleg.state.mi.us/verify.htm Also, search licenses at www.michigan.gov/statelicensesearch/. Also, search licensees lists at http://cis.state.mi.us/bcs_free/default.asp.

#9 Department of Consumer & Industry Services, Bureau of Commercial Services/Licensing Division, PO Box 30018, Lansing, MI 48909; 517-241-9254, Fax- 517-373-2162. www.michigan.gov/cis Search data at- http://cis.state.mi.us/verify.htm

#10 Department of Community Health, Emergency Medical Services and Trauma Systems Section, 201 Townsend, Lansing, MI 48913; 517-241-0179, Fax- 517-241-9458. Hours- 8AM-4:30PM. www.michigan.gov/healthlicense Search data at- www.dleg.state.mi.us/free/default.asp

#11 Department of Labor & Economic Growth, Occupational Safety & Health Admin/Construction Safety & Health Div-Asbestos Program, PO Box 30671 (7150 Harris Dr), Lansing, MI 48909-8171; 517-322-1320, Fax-517-322-1713. Hours- 8AM-5PM. www.michigan.gov/dleg/0,1607,7-154-11407_15333_15369---,00.html Search data at- www.dleg.state.mi.us/asbestos_program/

#12 Department of Financial & Insurance Services, Division of Securities, PO Box 30165 (611 W Ottawa, 3nd Fl), Lansing, MI 48909-8201; 877-999-6442; 517-373-0220, Fax- 517-335-4978. Hours- 7AM-4:30PM. www.michigan.gov/dleg/0,1607,7-154-10555---,00.html

#13 Department Human Svcs, Div of Child Day Care Licensing, Office of Children & Adult Licensing/Div of Child Welfare Licensing, 7109 W Saginaw 2nd Fl, Lansing, MI 48909; 517-335-6124, Fax- 517-335-6121. Hours- 8AM-5PM. www.michigan.gov/dhs

#14 Department of Consumer & Industry Services, Office of Financial and Insurance Regulation (OFIR), PO Box 30165 (7150 Harris Dr), Lansing, MI 48909; 517-373-0220, Fax- 517-335-4978. Hours- 8AM-5PM. www.michigan.gov/cis Search data at- www.michigan.gov/dleg/0,1607,7-154--22352--,00.html

#15 Department of Consumer & Industry Services, Health Services Licensing Division, PO Box 30670 (611 W Ottawa, 1st Fl), Lansing, MI 48909; 517-335-0918, Fax- 517-373-2179. Hours-8AM-5PM. www.michigan.gov/healthlicense Search at- www.dleg.state.mi.us/free/default.asp

#16 Department of Consumer & Industry Services, Manufactured Home & Land Development Division, PO Box 30703, Lansing, MI 48909; 517-241-9317. www.michigan.gov/dleg/0,1607,7-154-10575_17394_17412-42904--,00.html Search data at- https://www2.dleg.state.mi.us/colaLicVerify/

#17 Department of Labor and Economic Growth, Private Security & Investigator Unit, PO Box 30018, Lansing, MI 48909; 517-241-5645, Fax-517-373-2162. Hours- 8AM-5PM. www.michigan.gov/cis Search data at- https://www2.dleg.state.mi.us/colaLicVerify/

#18 Department of Corrections, 206 E Michigan Ave, Lansing, MI 48933; 517-335-1426. www.michigan.gov/corrections

#19 Department of Education, Office of Professional Preparation & Certification, Hannah Bldg, 2nd Fl, Lansing, MI 48909; 517-373-6505, Fax- 517-373-0542. www.michigan.gov/mde Search at- https://mdoe.state.mi.us/teachercert/

#20 Department of Environmental Quality, Drinking Water & Environmental Health Sec., Well Construction, PO Box 30473 (525 W Allegan, 2nd Fl North), Lansing, MI 48909-7773; 517-241-1389, Fax- 517-241-1328. www.michigan.gov/deq

#21 Department of Human Svcs, Div of Child Welfare Licensing, Office of Child and Adult Licensing-Div of Adult Foster Care/Homes for the Aged Licensing, 7109 W Saginaw, 2nd Fl Box 30650, Lansing, MI 48909-8150; 517-335-6108, Fax- 517-335-6121. Hours- 8AM-5PM. www.michigan.gov/dhs

#22 Department of State, Office of the Great Seal, 7064 Crowner Dr, Lansing, MI 48918; 517-373-2531, Fax- 517-373-3706. www.michigan.gov/sos/0,1607,7-127-1638---,00.html

#23 Department of Transportation, Bureau of Aeronautics, 2700 E Airport Service Dr, Lansing, MI 48906; 517-335-9283, Fax- 517-321-6422. www.michigan.gov/aero/

#24 Department of Treasury, State Assessors Board, PO Box 30471, Lansing, MI 48909; 517-373-8320, Fax- 517-241-3583. www.michigan.gov/treasury/0,1607,7-121-1751_2220---,00.html List updated Fridays.

#25 Department of Human Services, Office of Children & Adult Licensing/Div of Child Welfare Licensing, 7109 W Saginaw, 2nd Fl, Lansing, MI 48909-8150; 517-335-6124, Fax- 517-335-6121. Hours- 8AM-5PM. www.michigan.gov/cis

#26 State Bar, 306 Townsend St, Michael Franck Bldg, Lansing, MI 48933; 517-346-6300; 800-968-1442, Fax- 517-482-6248. www.michbar.org Search at- www.michbar.org/memberdirectory/

#27 Licensing Unit, Bureau of Regulatory Services, 430 W Allegan, 3rd Fl, Lansing, MI 48918; 517-636-6400, Fax- 517-335-2810. Hours-8AM-5PM. www.michigan.gov/sos Search data at- www.michigan.gov/sos/0,1607,7-127-1631_8849-51047--,00.html

#28 Bureau of Elections, Campaign Finance & Elections Reporting, PO Box 20126 (430 W Allegan St, Treasury Bldg, 1st Fl), Lansing, MI 48901-0726; 517-373-2540, Fax- 517-241-4785. Hours- 8AM-5PM. http://miboecfr.nicusa.com

Michigan Federal Courts

The following list indicates the district and division name for each county in the state. If the bankruptcy court location is different from the district court, then the location of the bankruptcy court appears in parentheses.

County/Court Cross Reference

County	District	Division
Alcona	Eastern	Bay City
Alger	Western	Marquette-Northern (Marquette)
Allegan	Western	Kalamazoo (Grand Rapids)
Alpena	Eastern	Bay City
Antrim	Western	Grand Rapids
Arenac	Eastern	Bay City
Baraga	Western	Marquette-Northern (Marquette)
Barry	Western	Grand Rapids
Bay	Eastern	Bay City
Benzie	Western	Grand Rapids
Berrien	Western	Kalamazoo (Grand Rapids)
Branch	Western	Lansing (Grand Rapids)
Calhoun	Western	Kalamazoo (Grand Rapids)
Cass	Western	Kalamazoo (Grand Rapids)
Charlevoix	Western	Grand Rapids
Cheboygan	Eastern	Bay City
Chippewa	Western	Marquette-Northern (Marquette)
Clare	Eastern	Bay City
Clinton	Western	Lansing (Grand Rapids)
Crawford	Eastern	Bay City
Delta	Western	Marquette-Northern (Marquette)
Dickinson	Western	Marquette-Northern (Marquette)
Eaton	Western	Lansing (Grand Rapids)
Emmet	Western	Grand Rapids
Genesee	Eastern	Flint
Gladwin	Eastern	Bay City
Gogebic	Western	Marquette-Northern (Marquette)
Grand Traverse	Western	Grand Rapids
Gratiot	Eastern	Bay City
Hillsdale	Western	Lansing (Grand Rapids)
Houghton	Western	Marquette-Northern (Marquette)
Huron	Eastern	Bay City
Ingham	Western	Lansing (Grand Rapids)
Ionia	Western	Grand Rapids
Iosco	Eastern	Bay City
Iron	Western	Marquette-Northern (Marquette)
Isabella	Eastern	Bay City
Jackson	Eastern	Ann Arbor (Detroit)
Kalamazoo	Western	Kalamazoo (Grand Rapids)
Kalkaska	Western	Grand Rapids
Kent	Western	Grand Rapids
Keweenaw	Western	Marquette-Northern (Marquette)
Lake	Western	Grand Rapids
Lapeer	Eastern	Flint
Leelanau	Western	Grand Rapids
Lenawee	Eastern	Ann Arbor (Detroit)
Livingston	Eastern	Flint
Luce	Western	Marquette-Northern (Marquette)
Mackinac	Western	Marquette-Northern (Marquette)
Macomb	Eastern	Detroit
Manistee	Western	Grand Rapids
Marquette	Western	Marquette-Northern (Marquette)
Mason	Western	Grand Rapids
Mecosta	Western	Grand Rapids
Menominee	Western	Marquette-Northern (Marquette)
Midland	Eastern	Bay City
Missaukee	Western	Grand Rapids
Monroe	Eastern	Ann Arbor (Detroit)
Montcalm	Western	Grand Rapids
Montmorency	Eastern	Bay City
Muskegon	Western	Grand Rapids
Newaygo	Western	Grand Rapids
Oakland	Eastern	Ann Arbor (Detroit)
Oceana	Western	Grand Rapids
Ogemaw	Eastern	Bay City
Ontonagon	Western	Marquette-Northern (Marquette)
Osceola	Western	Grand Rapids
Oscoda	Eastern	Bay City
Otsego	Eastern	Bay City
Ottawa	Western	Grand Rapids
Presque Isle	Eastern	Bay City
Roscommon	Eastern	Bay City
Saginaw	Eastern	Bay City
Sanilac	Eastern	Detroit
Schoolcraft	Western	Marquette-Northern (Marquette)
Shiawassee	Eastern	Flint
St. Clair	Eastern	Detroit
St. Joseph	Western	Kalamazoo (Grand Rapids)
Tuscola	Eastern	Bay City
Van Buren	Western	Kalamazoo (Grand Rapids)
Washtenaw	Eastern	Ann Arbor (Detroit)
Wayne	Eastern	Detroit
Wexford	Western	Grand Rapids

Standards for Federal Courts: Fees are standard unless noted in profile. Search fee is $26.00 per item (one party name or case number). Copy fee is $.50 per page. Certification fee is $9.00 per document, double for exemplification, if available. Most courts require prepayment. Mail requests should enclose a SASE unless otherwise noted. Before releasing records, all courts require prepayment, unless noted.

District courts index by defendant and plaintiff and by case number. Bankruptcy courts usually index by debtor and case number. While most courts now have their indexes on computer, many may still maintain index card files as well. Courts will archive closed case files at different times.

There are numerous public access programs available to online subscribers. Search the U.S. Party/Case Index to find party names and case numbers among all courts. Individual case data is provided on PACER. A search of CM/ECF provides copies of cases filed electronically. For details about PACER, the US Party/Case Index, and CM/ECF see the Appendix or go to http://pacer.psc.uscourts.gov or call 800-676-6856.

US District Court Michigan Eastern District

Ann Arbor Division Court Clerk, PO Box 8199, Ann Arbor, MI 48107 (In person: 200 E Liberty St, Rm 120, Ann Arbor), 734-741-2380; Fax- 734-741-2065. Hours- 8:30AM-5PM. www.mied.uscourts.gov

Counties/Note: Jackson, Lenawee, Monroe, Oakland, Washtenaw. Civil cases in these counties are assigned randomly to Detroit, Flint, Ann Arbor, or Port Huron Divisions. Ann Arbor may hear cases assigned from Wayne County (Detroit).

Searches/Indexing: Only full name is required to search; you may include identifiers. Results do not include SSN or DOB. Will not fax back documents. New cases are in the index 2 days after filing date. Both computer and card indexes maintained; computer goes back to 1990. District-wide searches available back to 1985. Closed cases kept electronically; paper files sent to archives. **Search Access:** Only docket info available by phone. **Mail:** Search usually completed- 3 days. SASE not required. **Fax:** Fax requests accepted for searches and case files. **In person:** 1 public terminal available. Computer copies $.10 each. **Payment:** Pay by money order, cashier's or personal check. No credit cards accepted. Payee: Clerk, US District Court.

E-Services: PACER records go back to 1988. New records online after 1 day. ECF at https://ecf.mied.uscourts.gov. **Opinions Online:** www.mied.uscourts.gov/Judges/opinions.cfm.

Note: Record request forms for each division at www.mied.uscourts.gov/Clerk/courtRecords.cfm.

Bay City Division Court Clerk, PO Box 913, Bay City, MI 48707 (In person: 1000 Washington Ave, Rm 304, US Post Office Bldg, Bay City), 989-894-8800; Fax- 989-894-8804. 8AM-5PM. www.mied.uscourts.gov

Counties/Note: Alcona, Alpena, Arenac, Bay, Cheboygan, Clare, Crawford, Gladwin, Gratiot, Huron, Iosco, Isabella, Midland, Montmorency, Ogemaw, Oscoda, Otsego, Presque Isle, Roscommon, Saginaw, Tuscola. There is a Port Huron Hearing Office, but not records there.

Searches/Indexing: Only full name is required to search; you may include identifiers. Results do not include SSN or DOB. Will not fax back documents. New cases are in the index 2 days after filing date. Both computer and card indexes maintained; computer goes back to 1990. District-wide searches available back to 1985. Closed electronic cases never purged.

Search Access: Only docket info available by phone. **Mail:** Search usually completed- 1-2 days. SASE not required. **Fax:** Fax search requests accepted. **In person:** 1 public terminal available. No self-serve copier. **Payment:** Pay by money order, cashier's or personal check. No credit cards accepted. Payee: Clerk, US District Court.

E-Services: PACER records go back to 1988. New records online after 1 day. ECF at https://ecf.mied.uscourts.gov. **Opinions Online:** www.mied.uscourts.gov/Judges/opinions.cfm.

Note: Record request forms for each division at www.mied.uscourts.gov/Clerk/courtRecords.cfm.

Detroit Division Court Clerk, 231 W Lafayette Blvd, Rm 564, Detroit, MI 48226, 313-234-5005; records- 313-234-5010; Fax- 313-234-5393. 8:30AM-5PM. www.mied.uscourts.gov

Counties/Note: Macomb, St. Clair, Sanilac, Wayne (and Oakland County). Civil cases for these counties are assigned randomly among Flint, Ann Arbor and Detroit divisions. Port Huron cases may also be assigned to Detroit. Case files are kept where the case is assigned.

Searches/Indexing: Only full name is required to search; you may include identifiers. Results do not include SSN or DOB. Will not fax back documents. New cases are in the index 2 days after filing date. Both computer and card indexes maintained; computer goes back to 1990. District-wide searches available back to 1985. Closed cases kept electronically.

Search Access: Only docket info on active cases is released via phone. **Mail:** Search usually completed- 3 days. SASE not required. **Fax:** Fax search requests accepted. **In person:** 6 public terminals available. No self-serve copier.

Payment: Pay by Visa/MC (in person only), money order, cashier's or personal check. Payee: Clerk, US District Court. Prepayment required for all copying. Make checks out for exact amount.

E-Services: PACER records go back to 1988. New records online after 1 day. ECF at https://ecf.mied.uscourts.gov. **Opinions Online:** www.mied.uscourts.gov/Judges/opinions.cfm.

Note: Record request forms for each division at www.mied.uscourts.gov/Clerk/courtRecords.cfm.

Flint Division Court Clerk, 600 Church St, Rm 140, Federal Bldg and US Courthouse, Flint, MI 48502, 810-341-7840. Hours- 8:30AM-5PM. www.mied.uscourts.gov

Counties/Note: Genesee, Lapeer, Livingston, Shiawassee. All cases can be accessed electronically in the District index. However, Civil cases may be assigned by draw among the Detroit, Ann Arbor, Bay City and Flint divisions; include Port Huron as a remote possibility. As of 7/1995, depending on case loads, Criminal cases may also be assigned by draw to Detroit, Ann Arbor, Bay City or Flint, but most cases are heard in Flint.

Searches/Indexing: Only full name is required to search; you may include identifiers. Results do not include SSN or DOB. Will not fax back documents. New cases are in the index 2 days after filing date. Computer, microfiche indexes maintained; computer goes back to 1996. Old Flint cases records indexed on cards. District-wide searches available here; record throughput dates vary. A reasonable number of free searches can be requested in person. Search cases on microfiche free. Court personnel can also conduct free searches for cases on computer. Closed electronic cases never purged.

Search Access: Only docket info available by phone. Only a reasonable number of requests per call. All docket info will not be released. **Mail:** Search usually completed- 1-2 days. SASE not required. **Fax:** Fax search requests accepted. **In person:** No self-serve copier. **Payment:** Pay by money order, cashier's or personal check. No credit cards. Payee: Clerk, US District Court.

E-Services: PACER records go back to 1988. New records online after 1 day. ECF at https://ecf.mied.uscourts.gov. **Opinions Online:** www.mied.uscourts.gov/Judges/opinions.cfm.

Note: Record request forms for each division at www.mied.uscourts.gov/Clerk/courtRecords.cfm.

US Bankruptcy Court Michigan Eastern District

Bay City Division Court Clerk, 111 1st St, Bay City, MI 48708, 989-894-8840. Hours-8:30AM-4:30PM. www.mieb.uscourts.gov

Counties/Note: Alcona, Alpena, Arenac, Bay, Cheboygan, Clare, Crawford, Gladwin, Gratiot, Huron, Iosco, Isabella, Midland, Montmorency, Ogemaw, Oscoda, Otsego, Presque Isle, Roscommon, Saginaw, Tuscola.

Searches/Indexing: Include SSN and full name in search request. Results include last 4 SSN digits. Will not fax back documents. New cases are in the index immediately after filing date. Both computer and card indexes maintained. District-wide searches available back to 10/1992. Case files sent to archives 2 years after closed. **Search Access:** Only case number, case name, filing date, chapter, 341 date, attorney and trustee names released. Also, use VCIS to obtain docket information. Voice Case Information Service available, call VCIS at 877-422-3066. **Mail:** Search usually completed- 2 days. Include SASE for return. **In person:** 1 public terminal available. Computer generated copies $.10 each.

Payment: Pay by Visa/MC, money order, cashier's or business check. No personal checks accepted. Payee: US Bankruptcy Court.

E-Services: PACER records go back to 10/1992. New records online after 1 day. ECF at https://ecf.mieb.uscourts.gov. **Opinions Online:** www.mieb.uscourts.gov/courtOpinions/index.html **Online Note:** PDF versions of daily dockets at www.mieb.uscourts.gov/courtDocket/index.html.

Detroit Division Clerk of Court, 211 W Fort St, 21st Fl, Detroit, MI 48226, 313-234-0065; records- 313-234-0051. Hours- 8:30AM-4PM. www.mieb.uscourts.gov

Counties: Jackson, Lenawee, Macomb, Monroe, Oakland, Sanilac, St. Clair, Washtenaw, Wayne.

Searches/Indexing: Include SSN and full name in search request. Results include last 4 SSN digits. Will not fax back documents. New cases are in the index immediately after filing date. Both computer and card indexes maintained. District-wide searches available back to 10/1992. Case files sent to archives 2 years after closed.

Search Access: Only case number, case name, filing date, chapter, 341 date, attorney and trustee names released. Voice Case Information Service available, call VCIS at 877-422-3066. **Mail:** Search usually completed- 2 days. Include SASE for return. **In person:** 4 public terminals available. Computer generated copies $.10 each.

Payment: Pay by Visa/MC, money order, cashier's check, business check. No personal checks. Payee: US Bankruptcy Court.

E-Services: PACER records go back to 10/1992. New records online after 1 day. ECF at https://ecf.mieb.uscourts.gov. **Opinions Online:** www.mieb.uscourts.gov/courtOpinions/index.html **Online Note:** PDF versions of daily dockets at www.mieb.uscourts.gov/courtDocket/index.html.

Flint Division Court Clerk, 226 W 2nd St, Flint, MI 48502, 810-235-4126. 8:30AM-4PM. www.mieb.uscourts.gov **Counties:** Genesee, Lapeer, Livingston, Shiawassee.

Searches/Indexing: Include SSN and full name in search request. Results include last 4 SSN digits. Will not fax back documents. New cases are in the index immediately after filing date. Both computer and card indexes maintained. District-wide searches available back to 10/1992. Case files sent to archives 2 years after closed.

Search Access: Only case number, case name, filing date, chapter, 341 date, attorney and trustee names released. Voice Case Information Service available, call VCIS at 877-422-3066. **Mail:** Search usually completed- 2 days. Include SASE for return. **In person:** 1 public terminal available. Computer generated copies $.10 each.

Payment: Pay by Visa/MC, money order, cashier's check, business check. No personal checks. Payee: Clerk, US Bankruptcy Court.

E-Services: PACER records go back to 10/1992. New records online after 1 day. ECF at https://ecf.mieb.uscourts.gov. **Opinions Online:** www.mieb.uscourts.gov/courtOpinions/index.html **Online Note:** PDF versions of daily dockets at www.mieb.uscourts.gov/courtDocket/index.html.

US District Court Michigan Western District

Grand Rapids Division Court Clerk, 399 Gerald Ford Federal Building, 110 Michigan St NW, Grand Rapids, MI 49503, 616-456-2381; Fax- 616-456-2058. 8:30AM-4:30PM, phones til 5PM. www.miwd.uscourts.gov

Counties/Note: Antrim, Barry, Benzie, Emmet, Charlevoix, Grand Traverse, Ionia, Kalkaska, Kent, Lake, Leelanau, Manistee, Mason, Mecosta, Missaukee, Montcalm, Muskegon, Newaygo, Oceana, Osceola, Ottawa, Wexford. The Lansing and Kalamazoo Divisions may also handle cases from these counties. Cases in these counties may also be tried in the Kalamazoo or Lansing courts.

Searches/Indexing: Full name only identifier required to search. Results do not include SSN or DOB. Will not fax back documents. New cases are in the index 24-48 hours after filing date. Computer goes back to 1988. Closed electronic cases not purged. **Search Access:** Only docket info is available by phone. **Mail:** Search usually completed- 1-2 days. Include SASE for return. **In person:** 1 public terminal. No self-serve copier.

Payment: Pay by Visa/MC/AmEx/Discover, money order, cashier's or personal check. Payee: Clerk, US District Court. Prepayment required, except for law firms.

E-Services: PACER records go back to 9/1989 for civil; to 1992 for criminal. ECF at www.miwd.uscourts.gov/ecf.htm. Written opinions available via ECF/PACER, registration required.

Kalamazoo Division Court Clerk, B-35 Federal Bldg, 410 W Michigan Ave, Kalamazoo, MI 49007, 269-337-5706; Fax- 269-337-5703. Hours- 8:30AM-4:30PM, phones til 5PM. www.miwd.uscourts.gov

Counties/Note: Allegan, Berrien, Calhoun, Cass, Kalamazoo, St. Joseph, Van Buren. Also handle cases from counties in the Grand Rapids Division.

Searches/Indexing: Full name only identifier required to search. Results do not include SSN or DOB. Will not fax back documents. New cases are in the index 24-48 hours after filing date. Computer goes back to 1992. Closed electronic cases not purged. **Search Access:** Only docket info is available by phone. **Mail:** Search usually completed- 1-2 days. Include SASE for return. **In person:** 1 public terminal. No self-serve copier.

Payment: Pay by Visa/MC/AmEx/Discover, money order, cashier's or personal check. Payee: Clerk, US District Court. Prepayment required, except for law firms.

E-Services: PACER records go back to 9/1989 for civil; to 1992 for criminal. ECF at www.mwd.uscourts.gov/ecf.htm. Written opinions available via ECF/PACER, registration required.

Lansing Division Court Clerk, 113 Federal Building, 315 W Allegan St, Lansing, MI 48933, 517-377-1559. Hours-8:30AM-4:30PM, phones til 5PM. www.miwd.uscourts.gov

Counties/Note: Branch, Clinton, Eaton, Hillsdale, Ingham. Also handle cases from the counties in the Grand Rapids Division.

Searches/Indexing: Full name only identifier required to search. Results do not include SSN or DOB. Will not fax back documents. New cases are in the index 24-48 hours after filing date. Closed cases maintained 5 years, then archived.

Search Access: Only docket info is available by phone. **Mail:** Search usually completed- 1-2 days. Include SASE for return. **In person:** 1 public terminal available. No self-serve copier.

Payment: Pay by Visa/MC/AmEx/Discover, money order, cashier's or personal check. Payee: Clerk, US District Court.

E-Services: PACER records go back to 9/1989 for civil; to 1992 for criminal. ECF at www.miwd.uscourts.gov/ecf.htm. Written opinions available via ECF/PACER, registration required.

Marquette- Northern Division Court Clerk, PO Box 698, Marquette, MI 49855 (In person: 229 Federal Bldg, 202 W Washington St, Marquette, MI 49855), 906-226-2021, clerk-226-2117; Fax- 906-226-6735. Hours-8:30AM-4:30PM, phones til 5PM. www.miwd.uscourts.gov

Counties/Note: Alger, Baraga, Chippewa, Delta, Dickinson, Gogebic, Houghton, Iron, Keweenaw, Luce, Mackinac, Marquette, Menominee, Ontonagon, Schoolcraft.

Searches/Indexing: Full name only identifier required to search. Results do not include SSN or DOB. Will not fax back documents. New cases are in the index 24-48 hours after filing date. Computer goes back to 1999. Closed electronic cases not purged. **Search Access:** Use a credit card for telephone searching; copies will be mailed. **Mail:** Search usually completed- 1-2 days. Include SASE for return. **In person:** 1 public terminal available. No self-serve copier.

Payment: Pay by Visa/MC/AmEx/Discover, money order, cashier's or personal check. Payee: Clerk, US District Court. Prepayment required except from businesses and law firms.

E-Services: PACER records go back to 9/1989 for civil; to 1992 for criminal. ECF at www.miwd.uscourts.gov/ecf.htm. Written opinions available via ECF/PACER, registration required.

US Bankruptcy Court Michigan Western District

Grand Rapids (Southern) Division Court Clerk, 1 Division Ave, Rm 200, Grand Rapids, MI 49503, 616-456-2693; Fax- 616-456-2919. Hours-8AM-4PM. www.miwb.uscourts.gov

Counties/Note: Allegan, Antrim, Barry, Benzie, Berrien, Branch, Calhoun, Cass, Charlevoix, Clinton, Eaton, Emmet, Grand Traverse, Hillsdale, Ingham, Ionia, Kalamazoo, Kalkaska, Kent, Lake, Leelanau, Manistee, Mason, Mecosta, Missaukee, Montcalm, Muskegon, Newaygo, Oceana, Osceola, Ottawa, St. Joseph, Van Buren, Wexford. There are also courtrooms in Kalamazoo, Lansing, and Traverse City. Entire Western District bankruptcy records are available electronically on the public access terminal here in Grand Rapids.

Searches/Indexing: SSN, address, tax ID number and company name are helpful in search request. Results include last 4 SSN digits. Will fax back results. New cases are in the index immediately after filing date. Computer index back to 1990 maintained. Call clerk to determine if case is open, closed, or at archives. Case files sent to archives 1 year after closed.

Search Access: Court will only verify by phone whether a case was filed. Voice Case Information Service available, call VCIS at 866-729-9098 or 616-456-2075. **Mail:** Search usually completed- 1 week. Include SASE for return. **Fax:** Will accept fax search request if prepaid. **In person:** 3 public terminals available. No self-serve copier.

Payment: Pay by Visa/MC, money order, cashier's or personal check. No debtor checks accepted. Payee: US Bankruptcy Court.

E-Services: PACER records go back to 9/1989. New records online immediately. ECF at https://ecf.miwb.uscourts.gov. **Opinions Online:** www.miwb.uscourts.gov/content/opinions/.

Online Note: Active motion calendars free at www.miwb.uscourts.gov/content/calendars/. There is also an Unclaimed Funds list; click on Services.

Marquette (Northern) Div. Court Clerk, PO Box 909, Marquette, MI 49855 (In person: 202 W Washington, Rm 314, Marquette, MI 49855), 906-226-2117; Fax- 906-226-7388. 8AM-4PM. www.miwb.uscourts.gov

Counties/Note: Alger, Baraga, Chippewa, Delta, Dickinson, Gogebic, Houghton, Iron, Keweenaw, Luce, Mackinac, Marquette, Menominee, Ontonagon, Schoolcraft. Entire Western District bankruptcy records are available electronically on the public access terminal.

Searches/Indexing: SSN, address, tax ID number and company name are helpful in search request. Results include last 4 SSN digits. Will fax back documents $.50 per page. New cases are in the index immediately after filing date. Computer index back to 1990 maintained.

Search Access: Court will only verify by phone if a case is filed. Voice Case Information Service available, call VCIS at 866-729-9098 or 616-456-2075. **Mail:** Search usually completed- 1 day. For the fee, the following items are sent: case number, list of creditors, first scheduled meeting of creditors. SASE not required. **Fax:** Fax search requests accepted with credit card. **In person:** 1 public terminal available. No self-serve copier.

Payment: Pay by Visa/MC, money order, cashier's or personal check. No debtor checks accepted. Payee: US Bankruptcy Court.

E-Services: PACER records go back to 9/1989. New records online after 1 day. ECF at https://ecf.miwb.uscourts.gov. **Opinions Online:** www.miwb.uscourts.gov/content/opinions/.

Online Note: Active motion calendars free at www.miwb.uscourts.gov/content/calendars/. There is also an Unclaimed Funds list; click on Services.

Michigan County Courts

Court	Jurisdiction	No. of Courts	How Organized
Circuit Courts*	General	83	57 Circuits
District Courts*	Limited	105	98 Districts
Municipal Courts	Municipal	4	
Probate Courts*	Probate	79	83 Counties

* Profiled in this Sourcebook.

	CIVIL								
Court	**Tort**	**Contract**	**Real Estate**	**Min. Claim**	**Max. Claim**	**Small Claims**	**Estate**	**Eviction**	**Domestic Relations**
Circuit Courts*	X	X	X	$25,000	No Max				X
District Courts*	X	X	X	$0	$25,000	$3000		X	
Municipal Courts	X	X	X	$0	$3000				
Probate Courts*							X		

	CRIMINAL				
Court	**Felony**	**Misdemeanor**	**DWI/DUI**	**Preliminary Hearing**	**Juvenile**
Circuit Courts*	X				X
District Courts*		X	X	X	
Municipal Courts		X	X	X	
Probate Courts*					

Administration

State Court Administrator, PO Box 30048, Lansing, MI, 48909; 517-373-0130, Fax: 517-373-7517. http://courts.michigan.gov/scao/

Court Structure

The Circuit Court is the court of general jurisdiction. In general, the Circuit Court handles all civil cases with claims of more than $25,000 and all felony criminal cases (cases where the accused, if found guilty, could be sent to prison). The Family Division of Circuit Ccourt handles all cases regarding divorce, paternity, adoptions, personal protection actions, emancipation of minors, treatment and testing of infectious disease, safe delivery of newborns, name changes, juvenile offenses, and child abuse and neglect. In addition, the Circuit Court hears cases appealed from the other trial courts or from administrative agencies.

The District Court handles most traffic violations, all civil cases with claims up to $25,000, landlord-tenant matters, most traffic tickets, and all misdemeanor criminal cases (generally, cases where the accused, if found guilty, cannot be sentenced to more than one year in jail). In addition, small claims cases are heard by a division of the District Court. In Michigan, a few municipalities have chosen to retain a Municipal Court rather than create a district court. The municipal courts have limited powers and are located in Grosse Pointe, Grosse Pointe Farms, Grosse Pointe Park, and Grosse Point Shores/Grosse Pointe Woods.

A Court of Claims in Lansing that is a function of the 30th Circuit Court has jurisdiction over claims against the State of Michigan.

Several counties (Barry, Berrien, Iron, Isabella, Lake, and Washtenaw) and the 46th Circuit Court are participating in a "Demonstration" pilot project designed to streamline court services and consolidate case management. These courts may refer to themselves as County Trial Courts.

Online Access

There is a wide range of online computerization of the judicial system from "none" to "fairly complete," but there is no statewide court records network. (Note that the Michigan State Police, Criminal Justice Information Center offers a statewide access system.) Some Michigan courts provide public access terminals in clerk's offices, and some courts are developing off-site electronic filing and searching capability. A few offer remote online to the public. Subscribe to free email updates of appellate opinions at http://coa.courts.mi.gov/resources/subscribe.htm. Court of Appeals opinions are free at http://coa.courts.mi.gov/resources/opinions.htm.

Searching Tips, Fees, and Other Guidelines

Court records are considered public except for specific categories: controlled substances, spousal abuse, Holmes youthful trainee, parental kidnapping, set aside convictions and probation, and sealed records. Courts will, however, affirm that cases exist and provide case numbers. Some courts will not perform criminal searches, rather they refer requests to the State Police. Although most courts charge $10.00 for certification, search requirements, and procedures vary widely because each jurisdiction may create its own administrative orders. Prepayment is required unless otherwise noted.

Alcona County

23rd Circuit Court PO Box 308, Harrisville, MI 48740; 989-724-9410; fax: 989-724-9419; 8:30AM-N, 1-4:30PM (EST). ***Felony, Civil Actions over $25,000, Vital Statistics.***

Civil Records: Access: Phone, mail, in person. Only the court performs in person searches; visitors may not. Search fee: $10.00 per name. Required to search: name, years to search. Civil cases indexed by defendant, plaintiff, on computer since 1990, pleading headings in books since 1869. Mail turnaround time 1-2 days.

Criminal Records: Access: Phone, fax, mail, in person. Only the court performs in person searches; visitors may not. Search fee: $10.00 per name. Required to search: name, years to search, DOB. Criminal records on computer since 1990, pleading headings in books since 1869. Mail turnaround time 1-2 days.

General Information: No suppressed, juvenile, sex offenders, mental health, or adoption records released. Will fax documents for no fee if all fees paid. Court makes copy: $1.00 per page. Certification fee: $10.00 plus $1.00 per page copy fee after first page. Payee: Alcona County Clerk. Personal checks accepted. Credit card payments accepted via GPS. Mail requests: SASE required.

81st District Court PO Box 385, Harrisville, MI 48740; 989-724-9500; fax: 989-724-9509; 8:30AM-4:30PM (EST). ***Misdemeanor, Civil Actions under $25,000, Eviction, Small Claims.***

Civil Records: Access: Phone, fax, mail, in person. Only the court performs in person searches; visitors may not. Search fee: $10.00. Required to search: name, years to search. Civil cases indexed by defendant, plaintiff, on books since 1980; on computer back to 1997. Mail turnaround 1 week.

Criminal Records: Access: Fax, mail, in person. Only the court performs in person searches; visitors may not. Search fee: $10.00. Required to search: name, years to search, DOB. Criminal docket on books since 1980; on computer back to 1997. Mail turnaround time 1 week.

General Information: No suppressed, juvenile, sex offenders, mental health, or adoption records released. Fee to fax out doc $10.00 each. Court makes copy: $1.00 per page. Certification fee: $10.00. Payee: 81st District Court. No personal checks or credit cards accepted. Mail requests: SASE required.

Probate Court PO Box 328, 106 Fifth St, Harrisville, MI 48740; 989-724-9490; fax: 989-724-9499; 8:30AM-4:30PM (EST). ***Probate.***
www.alpenacounty.org/Probate.htm

Alger County

11th Circuit Court 101 Court St, PO Box 538, Munising, MI 49862; 906-387-2076; criminal fax: 906-387-2156; civil fax: same; 8AM-4PM ***Felony, Civil Actions over $25,000, Vital Statistics.***

Civil Records: Access: Mail, in person. Only the court performs in person searches; visitors may not. Search fee: $5.00 per name. Required to search: name, years to search. Civil cases indexed by defendant, plaintiff; index on docket books back to 1884; on computer back to 2000. Mail turnaround time 1 week.

Criminal Records: Access: Mail, in person. Only the court performs in person searches; visitors may not. Search fee: $5.00 per name. Required to search: name, years to search. Criminal records indexed in books back to 1884; on computer back to 2000. Mail turnaround time 1 week.

General Information: No juvenile, sex offenders, mental health, or adoption records released. Will fax documents to toll-free number. Court makes copy: $1.00 per page. Certification fee: $10.00 per document. Payee: Alger County Clerk. Personal checks accepted. Mail requests: SASE required.

93rd District Court PO Box 186, Munising, MI 49862; 906-387-3879; criminal fax: 906-387-2688; civil fax: same; 8AM-4PM (EST). ***Misdemeanor, Civil Actions under $25,000, Eviction, Small Claims.***

Civil Records: Access: Mail, in person. Only the court performs in person searches; visitors may not. Search fee: $10.00 per name. Required to search: name, years to search. Civil cases indexed by defendant, plaintiff; index on docket books back 10 years; on computer back to 2000. Mail turnaround time 5-7 days.

Criminal Records: Access: Fax, mail, in person. Only the court performs in person searches; visitors may not. Search fee: $10.00 per name. Required to search: name, years to search, DOB. Criminal records indexed in books back 10 years; on computer back to 2000. Mail turnaround 5-7 days.

General Information: No suppressed records released. Will fax documents to local or toll free line. Court makes copy: $.25 per page. Certification fee: $10.00 per document plus copy fee for any add'l pages. Payee: District Court. Business checks accepted. No credit cards accepted. Mail requests: SASE required.

Probate Court 101 Court St, Munising, MI 49862; 906-387-2080; fax: 906-387-4134; 8AM-N, 1-4PM (EST). ***Probate.***

Allegan County

48th Circuit Court 113 Chestnut St, Allegan, MI 49010; 269-673-0300; probate phone: 269-673-0250; criminal fax: 269-673-0298; civil fax: same; 8AM-5PM (EST). ***Felony, Civil Actions over $25,000, Vital Statistics.***

Civil Records: Access: Mail, fax, in person. Only the court performs in person searches; visitors may not. Search fee: $5.00 per name. Required to search: name, years to search. Civil cases indexed by defendant, plaintiff, on computer since 1985. Mail turnaround time 1-7 days.

Criminal Records: Access: Mail, fax, in person. Only the court performs in person searches; visitors may not. Search fee: $5.00 per name. Required to search: name, years to search, DOB. Criminal records on computer since 1985. Mail turnaround time 1-7 days.

General Information: No suppressed, juvenile, sex offenders, mental health, or adoption records released. Will fax documents to local or toll free line. Court makes copy: $1.00 per page. Certification fee: $10.00 per page. Payee: Allegan County Clerk. Personal checks accepted. Visa/MC accepted for fax filings only. Mail requests: SASE required.

57th District Court 113 Chestnut St, Allegan, MI 49010; 269-673-0400; criminal phone: 269-673-0400; civil phone: 269-673-0355; fax: 269-673-0490; 8:30AM-4:30PM (EST). ***Misdemeanor, Civil Actions under $25,000, Eviction, Small Claims.***
www.allegancounty.org/Government/DC/

Civil Records: Access: In person only. Both court and visitors may perform in person searches. No search fee. Required to search: name, years to search. Civil cases indexed by defendant, plaintiff; index on docket books. Civil PAT goes back to 1980s. PAT civil results show middle initial. Find case number on public terminal, then clerk can retrieve full record. Records on terminal are less complete the further back you look.

Criminal Records: Access: In person only. Both court and visitors may perform in person searches. No search fee. Required to search: name, years to search, DOB. Criminal records indexed in books. Criminal PAT goes back to same as civil. PAT results show middle initial, DOB. Find case number on public terminal, then clerk can retrieve full record. Records on terminal are less complete the further back you look.

General Information: No non-public records released. Will fax documents to local or toll free line. Court makes copy: $1.00 per page. Certification fee: $10.00. Payee: 57th District Court. Personal checks accepted. Major credit cards accepted via GPS. Mail requests: SASE required for mail return of any copies.

Probate Court 2243 33rd St, Allegan, MI 49010; 269-673-0250; fax: 269-673-5875; 8AM-5PM

Alpena County

26th Circuit Court 720 W Chisholm #2, Alpena, MI 49707; 989-354-9520; fax: 989-354-9644; 8:30AM-4:30PM (EST). ***Felony, Civil Actions over $25,000, Vital Statistics.***
www.alpenacounty.org/courts.htm

Civil Records: Access: Fax, mail, in person. Only the court performs in person searches; visitors may not. Search fee: $10.00 per name. Required to search: name, years to search. Civil cases indexed by defendant, plaintiff, on computer since 1988, prior on docket books. Mail turnaround time 3 days or less. Civil PAT goes back to 1988.

Criminal Records: Access: Fax, mail, in person. Only the court performs in person searches; visitors may not. Search fee: $10.00 per name. Required to search: name, years to search. Criminal records on computer since 1988; prior on docket books. Mail turnaround time 2-3 days. Criminal PAT goes back to 1988.

General Information: No suppressed, juvenile, sex offenders, mental health, or adoption records released. Will fax documents $5.00 plus $1.00 per page. Court makes copy: $2.00 per page. Certification fee: $10.00. Payee: County Clerk. Personal checks accepted; credit cards are not. SASE not required.

88th District Court 719 W Chisholm #3, Alpena, MI 49707; 989-354-9678; criminal phone: 989-354-9686; civil phone: 989-354-9685; criminal fax: 989-354-9785; civil fax: same; 8:30AM-4:30PM (EST). ***Misdemeanor, Civil Actions under $25,000, Eviction, Small Claims.***
www.alpenacounty.org/courts.htm

Civil Records: Access: Fax, mail, in person. Only the court performs in person searches; visitors may not. Search fee: $5.00 per name. Required to search: name, years to search. Civil cases indexed by defendant, plaintiff, on computer back to 1989, prior on cards back to 1970s. Mail turnaround 1-2 days.

Criminal Records: Access: Fax, mail, in person. Only the court performs in person searches; visitors may not. Search fee: $5.00 per name. Required to search: name, years to search, DOB; also helpful: SSN. Criminal records computerized from 1989, prior on cards back to 1970s. Mail turnaround time 1-2 days.

General Information: No suppressed, juvenile, sex offenders, mental health, or adoption records released. Will fax documents to local or toll free line. Court makes copy: $1.00 per page. Certification fee: $5.00. Payee: 88th District Court. Only cashiers checks and money orders accepted. No Major credit cards accepted via GPS. Mail requests: SASE required.

Probate Court 719 W Chisholm St, Suite 4, Alpena, MI 49707; 989-354-9650; fax: 989-354-9782; 8:30AM-4:30PM (EST). ***Probate.***
www.alpenacounty.org/courts.htm

Antrim County

13th Circuit Court PO Box 520, Bellaire, MI 49615; 231-533-6353; probate phone: 231-533-6681; fax: 231-533-6935; 8:30AM-5PM (EST). ***Felony, Civil Actions over $25,000, Vital Statistics.***
www.antrimcounty.org/circuitcourt.asp

Civil Records: Access: Fax, mail, in person, online. Both court and visitors may perform in person searches. Search fee: $5.00 per name. Required to search: name, years to search. Civil cases indexed by defendant, plaintiff, on computer since 1977, prior on books. Note: Only court can search on computer, in person searchers may look at old records on docket books. Mail turnaround time 1 week. Access to a record index is at http://online.co.grand-traverse.mi.us/iprod/clerk/cccivil.html.

Criminal Records: Access: Fax, mail, in person, online. Both court and visitors may perform in person searches. Search fee: $5.00 per name. Required to search: name, years to search; also helpful: DOB. Criminal docket on books from 1800s, on computer since 1997. Note: Only court can search on computer, in person searchers may review old docket books. Mail turnaround time 1 week. Access to criminal record index is found at http://online.co.grand-traverse.mi.us/iprod/clerk/cccriminal.html.

General Information: No suppressed, juvenile, sex offenders, mental health, or adoption records released. Will fax documents $5.00 per doc. Court makes copy: $.25 per page. Certification fee: $10.00 plus $1.00 per page. Payee: Antrim County Clerk. Personal checks accepted; credit cards are not. Mail requests: SASE required.

86th District Court PO Box 597, Bellaire, MI 49615; 231-533-6441; criminal phone: same; civil phone: 231-533-6842; criminal fax: 231-533-6322; civil fax: same; 8AM-4:30PM (EST). ***Misdemeanor, Civil Actions under $25,000, Eviction, Small Claims.***
Civil Records: Access: Fax, mail, in person. Only the court performs in person searches; visitors may not. Search fee: $10.00. Required to search: name, years to search. Civil cases indexed by defendant, plaintiff, on computer since 1986, prior on cards. Mail turnaround time usually same day.
Criminal Records: Access: Fax, mail, in person. Only the court performs in person searches; visitors may not. Search fee: $10.00 per name. Required to search: name, years to search, DOB; also helpful: SSN. Criminal records on computer since 1986, prior on cards. Mail turnaround time usually same day.
General Information: No suppressed, sex offenders records released. Will fax documents. Court makes copy: $1.00 per page. Certification fee: $10.00 per doc. Payee: District Court. Business checks accepted. Major Major credit cards accepted via GPS. Mail requests: SASE required.

Probate Court PO Box 130, 205 E Cayuga St, Bellaire, MI 49615; 231-533-6681; fax: 231-533-6600; 8:30AM-N,12:30-4:30PM (EST). ***Probate.*** www.antrimcounty.org/probate.asp

Arenac County

23rd Circuit Court 120 N Grove St, PO Box 747, Standish, MI 48658; 989-846-9186; criminal fax: 989-846-9199; civil fax: same; 9AM-4:30PM ***Felony, Civil Actions over $25,000, Vital Statistics.***
Civil Records: Access: Mail, in person. Both court and visitors may perform in person searches. Search fee: $5.00 per name. Required to search: name, years to search. Civil cases indexed by defendant, plaintiff, go back to 1883, civil records on computer back to 1991, prior on index books. Mail turnaround time 1-5 days. Civil PAT goes back to 1991. PAT results show name only.
Criminal Records: Access: Mail, in person. Both court and visitors may perform in person searches. Search fee: $5.00 per name. Required to search: name, years to search, DOB; also helpful: SSN. Criminal records go back to 1883, Criminal records computerized from 1991, prior on index books. Mail turnaround 1-5 days. Criminal PAT goes back to same as civil; results show middle initial, DOB.
General Information: No suppressed, juvenile, mental health, or adoption records released. Will not fax documents. Court makes copy: $1.00 per page. Certification fee: $10.00 first page, $1.00 ea add'l. Payee: Arenac County Clerk. Personal checks accepted. Major credit cards accepted via GPS. Mail requests: SASE required.

81st District Court PO Box 129, Standish, MI 48658; 989-846-9538; fax: 989-846-2008; 8:30AM-4:30PM (EST). ***Misdemeanor, Civil Actions under $25,000, Eviction, Small Claims.***
Civil Records: Access: Phone, fax, mail, in person. Only the court performs in person searches; visitors may not. Search fee: $10.00. Required to search: name, years to search. Civil cases indexed by defendant, plaintiff, on computer since 1990, prior on docket books. Mail turnaround time 5 days.
Criminal Records: Access: Phone, fax, mail, in person. Only the court performs in person searches; visitors may not. Search fee: $10.00. Required to search: name, years to search, DOB; also helpful: SSN. Criminal records on computer since 1990, prior on cards by name. Mail turnaround time 5 days.
General Information: No suppressed, juvenile, sex offenders, mental health, or adoption records released. Will fax documents $2.00 1st page, $.50 each add'l. No charge for fax cover sheet. Court makes copy: $1.00 1st page, $.25 each add'l. Certification fee: $10.00 per doc. Payee: 81st District Court. Personal checks accepted. Major credit cards accepted via GPS. Mail requests: SASE required.

Probate Court 120 N Grove, PO Box 666, Standish, MI 48658; 989-846-6941; fax: 989-846-6757; 9AM-4:30PM (EST). ***Probate.***
Alternate fax number is 989-846-9199.

Baraga County

12th Circuit Court 16 N 3rd St, L'Anse, MI 49946; 906-524-6183; fax: 906-524-6186; 8:30AM-4:30PM (EST). ***Felony, Civil Actions over $25,000, Vital Statistics.***
Civil Records: Access: Phone, mail, in person. Both court and visitors may perform in person searches. Search fee: $5.00. Required to search: name, years to search. Civil cases indexed by defendant, plaintiff; index on docket books, are computerized since 1998. Mail turnaround time same day. Public use terminal has civil records back to 6/1998.
Criminal Records: Access: Phone, mail, in person. Both court and visitors may perform in person searches. Search fee: $5.00 per name. Required to search: name, years to search, DOB; also helpful: SSN. Criminal docket on books, are computerized since 1998. Mail turnaround time same day.
General Information: No suppressed records released. Will fax documents. Court makes copy: $1.00 per page, self serve same. Certification fee: $10.00 per doc; add copy fee for add'l pages. Payee: County Clerk. Personal checks accepted; credit cards are not. Mail requests: SASE required.

97th District Court 16 N 3rd St, L'Anse, MI 49946; 906-524-6109; fax: 906-524-7017; 8:30AM-N, 1-4:30PM (EST). ***Misdemeanor, Civil Actions under $25,000, Eviction, Small Claims.***
Civil Records: Access: Mail, in person. Only the court performs in person searches; visitors may not. Search fee: $10.00 per name. Required to search: name, years to search. Civil cases indexed by defendant, plaintiff, listed on docket books back 10 years. Mail turnaround time 2-3 days.
Criminal Records: Access: Mail, in person. Only the court performs in person searches; visitors may not. Search fee: $10.00 per name. Required to search: name, years to search, DOB; also helpful: SSN. Criminal records listed on docket books back 10 years. Mail turnaround time 2-3 days.
General Information: No suppressed, sex offenders records released. Will fax documents to local or toll-free number. Court makes copy: $1.00 per page. Cert fee: $10.00 plus $1.00 per page after first. Payee: 97th District Court. Personal checks accepted; credit cards are not. Mail requests: SASE requested.

Probate Court County Courthouse, 16 N 3rd St, L'Anse, MI 49946; 906-524-6390; fax: 906-524-2052; 8:30AM-N, 1-4:30PM (EST). ***Probate.***

Barry County

5th Circuit Court 220 W State St, Hastings, MI 49058; 269-945-1285; criminal fax: 269-945-0209; civil fax: same; 8AM-5PM (EST). ***Felony, Civil Actions over $25,000, Vital Statistics.***
www.barrycounty.org
Civil Records: Access: Fax, mail, in person. Both court and visitors may perform in person searches. Search fee: $5.00 per name; $10.00 per name if prior to 1992. Required to search: name, years to search. Civil cases indexed by defendant, plaintiff, on computer since 1992, card index back to 1977, prior on books. Mail turnaround time 2 days.
Criminal Records: Access: Fax, mail, in person. Both court and visitors may perform in person searches. Search fee: $5.00 per name; $10.00 per name if prior to 1992. Required to search: name, years to search, DOB; also helpful: SSN. Criminal records on computer since 1992, card index back to 1977, prior on books. Mail turnaround time 2 days.
General Information: No suppressed, juvenile, sex offenders, mental health, or adoption records released. Will fax back documents $1.00 per page. Court makes copy: $.25 per page. Certification fee: $10.00 for 1st page, $1.00 each add'l includes copy fee. Payee: County Clerk. Personal checks accepted. Credit card payments accepted via GPS. Mail requests: SASE or toll-free fax number required.

56B District Court 206 W Court St #202, Hastings, MI 49058; 269-945-1404; criminal fax: 269-948-3314; civil fax: same; 8AM-5PM (EST). ***Misdemeanor, Civil Actions under $25,000, Eviction, Small Claims.***
www.barrycounty.org/courts-and-law-enforcement/56b-district-court/
Civil Records: Access: Phone, fax, mail, in person. Only the court performs in person searches; visitors may not. Search fee: $5.00 per name. Required to search: name, years to search. Civil cases indexed by defendant, plaintiff, on computer since 1990, prior on index books. Mail turnaround 2 days.
Criminal Records: Access: Phone, fax, mail, in person. Only the court performs in person searches; visitors may not. Search fee: $5.00 per name. Required to search: name, years to search, DOB. Criminal records on computer since 1990, prior on index books. Mail turnaround time 2 days.
General Information: No suppressed, sex offenders, or mental health records released. Will fax documents $1.00 per page. Court makes copy: $1.00 per page. Certification fee: $10.00 plus $1.00 per page after first. Payee: 56B District Court. Personal checks accepted. Credit card payments accepted via GPS. Mail requests: SASE required.

Probate Court 206 W Court St, #302, Hastings, MI 49058; 269-945-1390; fax: 269-948-3322; 8AM-5PM (EST). ***Probate.*** www.barrycounty.org/
Also handles name change, adoption, emancipations.

Bay County

18th Circuit Court 1230 Washington Ave #725, Bay City, MI 48708-5737; 989-895-4265; fax: 989-895-4099; 8AM-5PM (EST). ***Felony, Civil Actions over $25,000, Vital Statistics.***
http://baycountycourt.com
Civil Records: Access: Phone, fax, mail, in person, online. Both court and visitors may perform in person searches. No search fee. Required to search: Name. Civil cases indexed by defendant, plaintiff, on computer for the last since 1986. Mail turnaround time same day. Civil PAT goes back to 1986. Access the county courts' records for free at http://68.22.255.190/c74/c74_cases.php. Calendar of scheduled cases at http://68.22.255.190/c74/c74_calendar.php.
Criminal Records: Access: Phone, fax, mail, in person, online. Both court and visitors may perform in person searches. Search fee: $10.00. Required to search: Name, DOB. Criminal records on computer for the last since 1986. Mail turnaround time same day. Criminal PAT goes back to same as civil. Access the county courts' records for free at http://68.22.255.190/c74/c74_cases.php. Calendar of scheduled cases at http://68.22.255.190/c74/c74_calendar.php.
General Information: No suppressed records released. Will not fax documents. Court makes copy: $1.00 per page. Certification fee: $10.00, $1.00 each add'l. Payee: 18th Circuit Court. Personal checks accepted; credit cards are not. Mail requests: SASE requested.

74th District Court 1230 Washington Ave, Bay City, MI 48708; 989-895-4232; criminal phone: 989-895-4229; civil phone: 989-895-4203; fax: 989-895-4233; 8AM-5PM (EST). ***Misdemeanor, Civil Actions under $25,000, Eviction, Small Claims.***
www.baycountycourts.com
Civil Records: Access: In person only, online. Visitors must perform in person searches themselves. No search fee. Required to search: name, years to search. Civil cases indexed by defendant, plaintiff, on computer since 1992, listed on index cards prior. Civil PAT goes back to 1994. Access court case files free at http://68.22.255.190/c74/c74_cases.php. Calendar of scheduled cases at http://68.22.255.190/c74/c74_calendar.php.
Criminal Records: Access: In person, online. Visitors must perform in person searches themselves. Required to search: name, years to search, DOB; SSN helpful. Criminal records on computer since 1992, listed on index cards prior. Criminal PAT goes back to 1992. Access court case files free at http://68.22.255.190/c74/c74_cases.php. Calendar of scheduled cases at http://68.22.255.190/c74/c74_calendar.php.
General Information: No suppressed, juvenile, sex offenders, mental health, or adoption records released. Will not fax documents. Court makes copy: $1.00 per page. Self serve: $.25 per page. Certification fee: $10.00. Payee: 74th District Court. Personal checks accepted. Visa/MC accepted.

Probate Court 1230 Washington, #715, Bay City, MI 48708; 989-895-4205; fax: 989-895-4194; 8AM-5PM (EST). ***Probate.***
Access the county courts' calendar of scheduled cases for free at www.baycountycourts.com.

Benzie County

19th Circuit Court PO Box 377, Beulah, MI 49617; 231-882-9671 & 800-315-3593; criminal fax: 231-882-5941; civil fax: same; 8AM-5PM ***Felony, Civil Actions over $25,000, Vital Statistics.***
Civil Records: Access: Phone, fax, mail, in person. Both court and visitors may perform in person searches. No search fee. Required to search: name, years to search. Civil cases indexed by defendant, plaintiff, on computer since 1980, records go back to 1869. Mail turnaround time 1-2 days.
Criminal Records: Access: Phone, fax, mail, in person. Both court and visitors may perform in person searches. No search fee. Required to search: name, years to search. Criminal records on computer since 1980, records go back to 1869. Mail turnaround time 1-2 days.
General Information: No suppressed or home-youthful training case records released. Will fax documents $3.00 1st page, $1.00 each add'l. Court makes copy: $.50 per page. Certification fee: $10.00 plus copy fee beyond 1st page. Payee: Benzie County Clerk. Personal checks accepted. Credit card payments may be accepted via GPS. Mail requests: SASE required.

85th District Court PO Box 377, Beulah, MI 49617; 231-882-0019; fax: 231-882-0022; 9AM-N, 1-5PM (EST). ***Misdemeanor, Civil Actions under $25,000, Eviction, Small Claims.***
Visitors may use the law library to do their in-person searches at no charge.
Civil Records: Access: Mail, in person. Both court and visitors may perform in person searches. Search fee: $3.00 per name. Required to search: name, years to search. Civil cases indexed by defendant, plaintiff, on computer back to 1990, prior on cards to 1965. Mail turnaround time 4 days. Civil PAT goes back to 1990. Use public access terminal to look up by case number.
Criminal Records: Access: Mail, in person. Both court and visitors may perform in person searches. Search fee: $3.00 per name. Required to search: name, years to search, DOB. Criminal records computerized from 1990, prior on cards to 1965. Mail turnaround time 4 days. Criminal PAT goes back to same as civil. Use public access terminal to look up by case number.
General Information: No suppressed, juvenile, sex offenders, mental health, or adoption records released. Will fax documents $3.00 1st page, $1.00 ea add'l. Court makes copy: $1.00 per page. Certification fee: $10.00 per page includes copies. Payee: 85th District Court. Personal checks accepted. Out of state checks accepted. Credit card payments may be accepted via GPS but not by court. Mail requests: SASE required.

Probate Court 448 Court Pl, County Gov't Ctr., Beulah, MI 49617; 231-882-9675; fax: 231-882-5987; 8:30AM-N, 1-5PM (EST). ***Probate.***
www.benzieco.net/dept_probate_court.htm

Berrien County

2nd Circuit Court 811 Port St, St Joseph, MI 49085; 269-983-7111 x8368; criminal phone: x8227; civil phone: x8382; criminal fax: 269-982-8642; civil fax: 269-983-3604; 8:30AM-5PM (EST). ***Felony, Civil Actions over $25,000, Vital Statistics.*** www.berriencounty.org
Civil Records: Access: Mail, in person. Only the court performs in person searches; visitors may not. Search fee: $10.00 per name. Required to search: name, years to search. Civil cases indexed by defendant, plaintiff, on computer since 1981, prior on books (domestic) back to 1835, (civil/crim) back to 1837. Mail turnaround time same or next day.
Criminal Records: Access: Mail, in person. Only the court performs in person searches; visitors may not. Search fee: $10.00 per name. Required to search: name, years to search, DOB; also helpful: SSN. Criminal records on computer since 1981, prior on books to 1837. Mail turnaround time 1-2 days.
General Information: No suppressed, juvenile, mental health, or adoption records released. Will fax documents to local or toll free line. Court makes copy: $1.00 per page. Certification fee: $10.00. Payee: Berrien County Clerk. Personal checks accepted. Credit card payments via GPS. SASE not required.

5th District Court - Trial Ct Criminal Div. Attn: Records, 811 Port St, St Joseph, MI 49085; 269-983-7111; fax: 269-982-8643; 8:30AM-5PM (EST). ***Misdemeanor, Civil Actions under $25,000, Eviction, Small Claims.***
www.berriencounty.org
Civil Records: Access: Mail, in person. Only the court performs in person searches; visitors may not. Search fee: $10.00 per name. Required to search: name, years to search; also helpful: address. Civil cases indexed by defendant, plaintiff, on computer since 1988, on logs from 1976-87, on index cards from 1969-75. Will do civil record check searches for only seven years. Note: In person requesters must call ahead five days in advance; records held for 3 add'l days. Searching is limited and must be supervised. Mail turnaround time 3 days.
Criminal Records: Access: Mail, in person. Only the court performs in person searches; visitors may not. Search fee: $11.00 per name. Required to search: name, years to search, DOB or SSN; also helpful: signed release, address. Criminal records on computer back ten years, on microfiche back to 1970. Note: In person requesters must call ahead 3 days in advance; records held for 3 add'l days. Mail turnaround time 3 days.
General Information: No suppressed or mental health records released. Will fax documents if prepaid. Court makes copy: $1.00 per page; microfilm copies are $2.00 per page. Certification fee: Included in search fee. $10.00 plus $1.00 per page after 1st. Payee: 5th District Court. Personal checks accepted. Credit card accepted via GPS. SASE not required.

Probate Court 811 Port St., St Joseph, MI 49085; 269-983-7111 x8365; fax: 269-982-8644; 8:30AM-5PM (EST). ***Probate.***
www.berriencounty.org/?dept=8&pid=239

Branch County

15th Circuit Court 31 Division St, Coldwater, MI 49036; 517-279-4306; criminal fax: 517-278-5627; civil fax: same; 8AM-5PM (EST). ***Felony, Civil Actions over $25,000, Vital Statistics.***
www.co.branch.mi.us
Civil Records: Access: Mail, in person. Both court and visitors may perform in person searches. Search fee: $10.00 for 10 year search; $1.00 per name per each add'l year. Required to search: name, years to search. Civil cases indexed by defendant, plaintiff, on computer since 1988, prior in books back to 1830s. Mail turnaround time 1-5 days. Civil PAT goes back to 1988; civil results show middle initial.
Criminal Records: Access: Mail, in person. Both court and visitors may perform in person searches. Search fee: $10.00 for 10 year search; $1.00 per name per each add'l year. Required to search: name, years to search, DOB. Criminal records on computer since 1988, prior in books back to 1830s. Mail turnaround time 1-5 days. Criminal PAT goes back to same as civil. PAT results show middle initial, DOB.
General Information: No suppressed records released. Will fax documents if all fees prepaid. Court makes copy: $1.00 per page. Certification fee: $10.00 per document. Payee: Branch County Clerk. Business checks accepted. Mail requests: SASE required.

3A District Court 31 Division St., Coldwater, MI 49036; 517-279-4308; criminal phone: 517-279-4329; civil phone: 517-279-4331; fax: 517-279-4333; 8AM-5PM (EST). ***Misdemeanor, Civil Actions under $25,000, Eviction, Small Claims.***
www.branchcountycourts.com
Small Claims is 279-4330 and Traffic is 279-4328.
Civil Records: Access: Mail, in person. Only the court performs in person searches; visitors may not. Search fee: $10.00 per name. Required to search: name, years to search. Civil cases indexed by defendant, plaintiff, on computer since 6/1991, prior on index books. Mail turnaround time immediate if possible, otherwise 2-3 days.
Criminal Records: Access: Mail, in person. Only the court performs in person searches; visitors may not. Search fee: $10.00 per name. Required to search: name, years to search, DOB; also helpful: SSN. Criminal records on computer since 10/1988. Mail turnaround time immediate if possible, otherwise 2-3 days.
General Information: No suppressed or non-public records released. Will fax documents if search fee prepaid. Court makes copy: $1.00 per page. Certification fee: $10.00 + $1.00 copy fee. Payee: 3A District Court. Personal checks accepted. Visa/MC accepted. Credit card payments accepted via GPS. SASE not required.

Probate Court 31 Division St, Coldwater, MI 49036; 517-279-4318; fax: 517-279-6444; 8AM-N, 1-5PM (EST). ***Probate.***

Calhoun County

37th Circuit Court 161 E Michigan Ave, Battle Creek, MI 49014-4066; 269-969-6518; fax: 269-969-6922; 8AM-5PM (EST). ***Felony, Civil Actions over $25,000, Vital Statistics.***
http://courts.co.calhoun.mi.us/circuit.htm
Expect some delays on phone calls to this jurisdiction.
Civil Records: Access: Mail, in person. Both court and visitors may perform in person searches. Search fee: $5.00 per name. Required to search: name, years to search. Civil cases indexed by defendant, plaintiff, on computer since 1984, prior on microfilm. Note: Court will provide case number, filed date, case title, case status, and date of final judgment for the search fee. Mail turnaround time up to 3 weeks. Civil PAT available.
Criminal Records: Access: In person only. Both court and visitors may perform in person searches. Search fee: $5.00 per name if in person and court does search. Required to search: name, years to search, DOB; SSN helpful. Criminal records on computer since 1984, prior on microfilm. Note: Court prefers requests go to State Police (517-322-5531). Searcher may view public court file if case number known. Criminal PAT available.
General Information: No suppressed, juvenile, sex offenders, mental health, or adoption records released. Will fax documents $3.00 plus $1.00 per copy. Court makes copy: $1.00 per page. $10.00 charge if file is retrieved from storage. Certification fee: $10.00 per doc. Payee: 37th Circuit Court Clerk. Personal checks accepted. Major credit cards accepted via GPS. Mail requests: SASE required for civil.

10th District Court 161 E Michigan Ave, Battle Creek, MI 49014; 269-969-6666; criminal phone: 269-969-6678; civil phone: 269-969-6683; probate phone: 269-969-6794; fax: 269-969-6647; 8AM-4PM (EST). ***Misdemeanor, Civil Actions under $25,000, Eviction, Small Claims.***
http://courts.co.calhoun.mi.us/district.htm
The 10th District Court Marshall Branch's records and administration is now housed here.
Civil Records: Access: Mail, fax, in person. Visitors must perform in person searches themselves. No search fee, unless case is in archives, then $10.00. Required to search: name, years to search. Civil cases indexed by defendant, plaintiff, on computer back to 1986, prior on docket books. Public access terminal searches back to 10/1997. Note: Fax requests must be signed. Mail turnaround time 5 days. Civil PAT goes back to 1997.
Criminal Records: Access: Fax, mail, in person. Visitors must perform in person searches themselves. No search fee, unless case is in archives, then $10.00. Required to search: name, DOB; also helpful-case number. Criminal records computerized from 1986, prior on docket books. Public access terminal searches back to 10/1997. Note: One to five requests per day are accepted. Fax requests must be signed. Mail turnaround time 5 days. Criminal PAT goes back to same as civil.
General Information: No suppressed or non-public records released. Will fax documents $1.00 per page. Court makes copy: $1.00 per page. Certification fee: $10.00 plus $1.00 per page after first. Payee: 10th District Court. Personal checks accepted. Major credit cards accepted via GPS. Mail requests: SASE required.

Probate Court Justice Ctr, 161 E Michigan Ave, Battle Creek, MI 49014; 269-969-6794; fax: 269-969-6797; 8AM-5PM, F 9-5PM (EST). ***Probate.*** http://courts.co.calhoun.mi.us/probate.htm

Cass County

43rd Circuit Court 120 N Broadway, File Room; 60296 M-62, #10, Cassopolis, MI 49031; 269-445-4412; criminal phone: 269-445-4416; civil phone: 269-445-4416; criminal fax: 269-445-4453; civil fax: same; 8AM-5PM (EST). ***Felony, Civil Actions over $25,000, Vital Statistics.***
Civil Records: Access: Phone, fax, mail, in person. Both court and visitors may perform in person searches. Search fee: $10.00 per name. Required to search: name, years to search. Civil cases indexed by defendant, plaintiff, on computer back to 1988; books since 1963. Mail turnaround time 2 weeks by mail.
Criminal Records: Access: Fax, mail, in person. Only the court performs in person searches; visitors may not. Search fee: $10.00 per name. Required to search: name, years to search, DOB. Criminal records computerized from 1988; books since 1963. Mail turnaround time 2 weeks by mail.
General Information: No suppressed, juvenile, sex offenders, mental health, or adoption records released. No fee to fax to a toll-free number. Court makes copy: $1.00 per page. Certification fee: $10.00. Payee: Cass County Clerk. Business checks accepted. No credit cards accepted. Mail requests: SASE required.

4th District Court 60296 M 62 #10, Cassopolis, MI 49031-8716; 269-445-4424; fax: 269-445-4486; 8AM-5PM (EST). ***Misdemeanor, Civil Actions under $25,000, Eviction, Small Claims, Traffic.***
Civil Records: Access: Phone, mail, fax, in person. Only the court performs in person searches; visitors may not. Search fee: $10.00 per name. Required to search: name, years to search; also helpful: address. Civil cases indexed by defendant, plaintiff, on computer since 1988, indexed on cards prior back to 1969. Note: You can fax requests, but results will not be returned by fax. Mail turnaround time 2 weeks.
Criminal Records: Access: Phone, mail, fax, in person. Only the court performs in person searches; visitors may not. Search fee: $10.00 per name. Required to search: name, years to search, DOB; also helpful: address. Criminal records on computer since 1988, indexed on cards prior back to 1969. Mail turnaround time 2 weeks.
General Information: No suppressed, juvenile, sex offenders, mental health, or adoption records released. Will fax documents $10.00 per name. Court makes copy: $1.00 first page, $.50 each add'l. Certification fee: $10.00 plus $1.00 per page after first. Payee: 4th District Court. Personal checks accepted. Credit card payments accepted via GPS. SASE not required.

Probate Court 60296 - M62, #10, Cassopolis, MI 49031; 269-445-4454; fax: 269-445-4453; 8AM-5PM (EST). ***Probate.***

Charlevoix County

33rd Circuit Court 203 Antrim St, Charlevoix, MI 49720; 231-547-7200; criminal phone: 231-547-7200 x11; civil phone: 231-547-7200 x14; criminal fax: 231-547-7217; civil fax: same; 9AM-5PM (EST). ***Felony, Civil Actions over $25,000, Vital Statistics.*** www.charlevoixcounty.org/clerk.asp
Civil Records: Access: Mail, by fax, in person. Only the court performs in person searches; visitors may not. No search fee. Required to search: name, years to search. Civil cases indexed by defendant, plaintiff, on computer from 1990, microfiche and archives from 1868. Mail turnaround time 1 week.
Criminal Records: Access: Mail, by fax, in person. Only the court performs in person searches; visitors may not. No search fee. Required to search: name, years to search, DOB; also helpful: SSN. Criminal records computerized from 1991, microfiche and archives from 1868. Mail turnaround 1 week.
General Information: No suppressed, juvenile, adoption records released. Will fax documents, usually same day. Court makes copy: $1.00 per page. Certification fee: $10.00 first page plus $1.00 each add'l. Payee: Charlevoix County Clerk. Personal checks accepted. Mail requests: SASE requested.

90th District Court 301 State St, Court Bldg, Charlevoix, MI 49720; 231-547-7227; civil phone: 231-547-7254; fax: 231-547-7253; 9AM-5PM (EST). ***Misdemeanor, Civil Actions under $25,000, Eviction, Small Claims.***
Civil Records: Access: Phone, mail, fax, in person. Both court and visitors may perform in person searches. Search fee: $5.00 per name. Required to search: name only. Civil cases indexed by defendant, plaintiff, on computer back to 1987, listed on index cards to 1969. Mail turnaround time 1-2 days.
Criminal Records: Access: Mail, fax, in person. Both court and visitors may perform in person searches. Search fee: $5.00 per name. Required to search: name, DOB. Criminal records computerized from 1987, listed on index cards to 1969. Mail turnaround time 1-2 days.
General Information: No suppressed records released. Will fax documents $5.00 per name. Court makes copy: $1.00 per page. Certification fee: $10.00. Payee: 90th District Court. Personal checks accepted. Credit card payments may be accepted via GPS. SASE not required.

Probate Court 301 State St, County Bldg, Charlevoix, MI 49720; 231-547-7214; 547-7215; fax: 231-547-7256; 9AM-5PM (EST). ***Probate.*** Shares same judge with Emmet County Probate Ct.

Cheboygan County

53rd Circuit Court PO Box 70, Cheboygan, MI 49721; 231-627-8846; fax: 231-627-8453; 8AM-5PM (EST). ***Felony, Civil Actions over $25,000, Vital Statistics.*** www.cheboygancounty.net/
Civil Records: Access: Phone, mail, in person. Both court and visitors may perform in person searches. No search fee. Required to search: name, years to search. Civil cases indexed by defendant, plaintiff, on computer from 1987, index books from 1886. Mail turnaround time 3-4 days. Civil PAT goes back to 1987. PAT civil results show middle initial.
Criminal Records: Access: Phone, mail, in person. Both court and visitors may perform in person searches. No search fee. Required to search: name, years to search, DOB. Criminal records computerized from 1987, index books from 1886. Mail turnaround time 3-4 days. Criminal PAT goes back to same as civil. PAT criminal results show middle initial.
General Information: No suppressed records released. Will fax document for $1.00 prepaid. Court makes copy: $1.00 per page. Certification fee: $10.00 1st page plus $1.00 each add'l page. Cert fee includes copies. Payee: County Clerk. Personal checks accepted. Mail requests: SASE required.

89th District Court PO Box 70, Cheboygan, MI 49721; 231-627-8809; criminal phone: 231-627-8840; civil phone: 231-627-8839; fax: 231-627-8444; 8:30AM-4PM (EST). ***Misdemeanor, Civil Actions under $25,000, Eviction, Small Claims.*** www.89thdistrictcourt.org
Civil Records: Access: Phone, fax, mail, in person. Both court and visitors may perform in person searches. Search fee: $5.00 per name. Required to search: name, years to search. Civil cases indexed by defendant, plaintiff, on computer back to 1988, microfilmed prior. Mail turnaround time 3-4 days. Civil PAT goes back to 1988. Dockets for 2 weeks ahead are available at www.89thdistrictcourt.org/scheduling.htm.
Criminal Records: Access: Phone, fax, mail, in person. Both court and visitors may perform in person searches. Search fee: $5.00 per name. Required to search: name, years to search, DOB, address. Criminal records computerized from 1985. Mail turnaround time 3-4 days. Criminal PAT goes back to 1985. PAT results show middle initial, DOB. Terminal results include SSN. Dockets for 2 weeks ahead are available at www.89thdistrictcourt.org/scheduling.htm. Dispositions also.
General Information: No suppressed, juvenile, sex offenders, mental health, or adoption records released. Will fax out documents $1.00 1st page, $.25 each add'l. Court makes copy: $1.00 1st page, $.25 each add'l. Certification fee: $10.00 per doc. Payee: 89th District Court. Personal checks accepted. Credit cards accepted. Mail requests: SASE required.

Probate Court 870 S Main St, PO Box 70, Cheboygan, MI 49721; 231-627-8823; fax: 231-627-8868; 8:30AM-4:30PM (EST). ***Probate.***

Chippewa County

50th Circuit Court 319 Court St, Sault Ste Marie, MI 49783; 906-635-6300; criminal fax: 906-635-6851; civil fax: same; 8AM-5PM (EST). ***Felony, Civil Actions over $25,000, Vital Statistics.***
Civil Records: Access: Mail, in person. Only the court performs in person searches; visitors may not. Search fee: $5.00 per name. Fee is for 10 year search. Required to search: name, years to search. Civil cases indexed by defendant, plaintiff, on computer since 1990, prior on index books to late 1800s. Mail turnaround time 1-2 days.
Criminal Records: Access: Mail, in person. Only the court performs in person searches; visitors may not. Search fee: $5.00 per name. Fee is for 10 year search. Required to search: name, years to search, DOB; also helpful: SSN. Criminal records on computer since 1990, prior on index books to late 1800s. Mail turnaround time 1-2 days.
General Information: No suppressed, juvenile, sex offenders, mental health, or adoption records released. Will fax documents to local or toll free line. Court makes copy: $1.00 per page. Certification fee: $10.00 plus $1.00 per page after first. Payee: County Clerk. Personal checks accepted. Credit card payments accepted via GPS.

91st District Court 325 Court St, Sault Ste Marie, MI 49783; 906-635-6320; criminal phone: 906-635-6322; civil phone: 906-635-7614; criminal fax: 906-635-7605; civil fax: same; 9AM-4:30PM (EST). ***Misdemeanor, Civil Actions under $25,000, Eviction, Small Claims.***
Call before faxing for instructions.
Civil Records: Access: Mail, fax, in person. Both court and visitors may perform in person searches. Search fee: $5.00 per name. Required to search: name, years to search. Civil cases indexed by defendant, plaintiff, on computer since 1989, prior on index books to 1969. Mail turnaround time 10 days. Civil PAT goes back to 1989.
Criminal Records: Access: Mail, fax, in person. Both court and visitors may perform in person searches. Search fee: $5.00 per name. Required to search: name, years to search, DOB; also helpful: SSN. Criminal records on computer since 1989, prior on index books to 1969. Mail turnaround time 10 days. Criminal PAT goes back to 1989. PAT results show middle initial, DOB.
General Information: No suppressed records released. Will fax documents to toll-free number. Court makes copy: $1.00 per page. Certification fee: $10.00 plus copy fee after 1st page. Payee: 91st District Court. Only cashiers checks and money orders accepted. No credit cards accepted. Mail requests: SASE required.

Probate Court 319 Court St, Sault Ste Marie, MI 49783; 906-635-6314; fax: 906-635-6852; 9AM-5PM (EST). ***Probate.***

Clare County

55th Circuit Court 225 W Main St, PO Box 438, Harrison, MI 48625; 989-539-7131; criminal fax: 989-539-6616; civil fax: same; 8AM-4:30PM ***Felony, Civil Actions over $25,000, Vital Statistics.***
Civil Records: Access: Mail, in person. Only the court performs in person searches; visitors may not. Search fee: $6.00 per name. Add $1.00 per year if more than five. Required to search: name, years to search DOB. Civil cases indexed by defendant, plaintiff, on computer since 1992, on books from 1925; visitors can access the books themselves, not computer. Mail turnaround time 1-5 days.
Criminal Records: Access: Mail, in person. Only the court performs in person searches; visitors may not. Search fee: $6.00 per name. Add $1.00 per year if more than five. Required to search: name, years to search, DOB. Criminal records on computer since 1992, on books from 1925, visitors can access the books themselves, not computer. Mail turnaround time 1-5 days.
General Information: No suppressed, juvenile, sex offenders, mental health, or adoption records released.

Will fax out documents to toll-free numbers only. Court makes copy: $1.00 per page. Certification fee: $10.00 per document plus $1.00 per page. Payee: Clare County Clerk. Personal checks accepted. No credit cards accepted at this office. Mail requests: SASE required.

80th District Court 225 W. Main St, Harrison, MI 48625; 989-539-7173; criminal fax: 989-539-4036; civil fax: same; 8AM-4:30PM (EST). ***Misdemeanor, Civil Actions under $25,000, Eviction, Small Claims.***

Civil Records: Access: Mail, fax, in person. Only the court performs in person searches; visitors may not. Search fee: $6.00 per name; $1.00 per yr over 5 years. Required to search: name, years to search. Civil cases indexed by defendant, plaintiff, go back to 1969; on computer back to 1988. Mail turnaround 5 days.

Criminal Records: Access: Mail, fax, in person. Only the court performs in person searches; visitors may not. Search fee: $6.00 per name; $1.00 per yr over 5 years. Required to search: name, years to search, DOB, SSN. Criminal records go back to 1969; on computer back to 1988. Mail turnaround 5 days.

General Information: No suppressed, juvenile, sex offenders, mental health, or adoption records released. Will fax documents. Court makes copy: $1.00 per page. Cert fee: $10.00 per doc includes copy fee. Payee: 80th District Court. Personal checks accepted; credit cards are not. Mail requests: SASE required.

Probate and Family Court 225 W Main St., PO Box 96, Harrison, MI 48625; 989-539-7109; 8AM-4:30PM (EST). ***Probate, Family.*** This is combined with Gladwin County Probate Court.

Clinton County

29th Circuit Court 100 E State St, #2500, St Johns, MI 48879-1580; 989-224-5140; criminal fax: 989-227-6421; civil fax: same; 8AM-5PM (EST). ***Felony, Civil Actions over $25,000, Vital Statistics.*** www.clinton-county.org

Civil Records: Access: Mail, in person. Both court and visitors may perform in person searches. Search fee: $10.00 per name. Fee is for 10 year search. Required to search: name, years to search. Civil cases indexed by defendant, plaintiff, in calendar books since 1800s, some on microfiche; on computer since 1996. Mail turnaround time 24 hours. Civil PAT goes back to 1996; results show name only.

Criminal Records: Access: Mail, in person. Both court and visitors may perform in person searches. Search fee: $10.00 per name. Fee is for 10 year search. Required to search: name, years to search; also helpful: DOB. Criminal records in calendar books since 1800s, some on microfiche; on computer since 1996. Mail turnaround time 24 hours. Criminal PAT goes back to 1996; results show name, DOB.

General Information: No suppressed or non public records released. Will fax documents $3.00 up to 20 pages. Court makes copy: $1.00 per page 1st 10, $.50 each add'l. Certification fee: $10.00 per document. Payee: Clinton County Clerk. Personal checks accepted. Credit card payments accepted via GPS. Mail requests: SASE requested.

65th District Court 100 E State St, #3400, St Johns, MI 48879-1571; 989-224-5150; criminal phone: 989-224-5153; civil phone: 989-224-5152; criminal fax: 989-224-5154; civil fax: same; 8AM-5PM (EST). ***Misdemeanor, Civil Actions under $25,000, Eviction, Small Claims.*** www.clinton-county.org

Civil Records: Access: In person only. Visitors must perform in person searches themselves. Required to search: name, years to search. Civil cases indexed by defendant, plaintiff, on computer since 1989-90. Civil PAT goes back to 1996+. Terminal results show middle initial if it's available.

Criminal Records: Access: In person only. Visitors must perform in person searches themselves. Required to search: name, years to search, DOB, SSN. Criminal records on computer since 1986. Criminal PAT goes back to 1996+. Terminal results show middle initial if available.

General Information: No suppressed, juvenile, sex offenders, mental health, or adoption records released. Will not fax out case files. Court makes copy: $1.00 per page. Certification fee: $10.00 per document. Payee: 65th District Court. Personal checks accepted. Major credit cards accepted via GPS.

Probate Court 100 E State St #4300, St Johns, MI 48879; 989-224-5190; fax: 989-227-6565; 8AM-5PM (EST). ***Probate.*** www.clinton-county.org

Crawford County

46th Circuit Court 200 W Michigan Ave, Grayling, MI 49738; 989-348-2841; criminal fax: 989-344-3223; civil fax: same; 8:30AM-N, 1PM-4:30PM (EST). ***Felony, Civil Actions over $25,000, Vital Statistics.*** www.Circuit46.org

Civil Records: Access: Mail, in person, online. Only the court performs in person searches; visitors may not. Search fee: $5.00 per name. Required to search: name, years to search. Civil cases indexed by defendant, plaintiff, on computer since 1990, prior on books to 1930s. Mail turnaround time 2-3 days. Online access to court case records (closed cases for 90 days only) is free at http://66.129.39.149/c46_Cases.php.

Criminal Records: Access: Mail, in person, online, phone, fax. Only the court performs in person searches; visitors may not. Search fee: $5.00 per name. Required to search: name, years to search, DOB. Criminal records on computer since 1990, prior on books to 1960. Mail turnaround 2-3 days. Online access to criminal records is the same as civil.

General Information: No suppressed records released. Will fax documents $3.00 per page or to toll-free number at no charge. Court makes copy: $1.00 per page. Certification fee: $10.00. Payee: Crawford County. Personal checks and major credit cards accepted. Mail requests: SASE required.

46th Circuit Trial Court - District Division 200 W Michigan Ave., Grayling, MI 49738; 989-348-2841 X242; fax: 989-344-3290; 8AM-4:30PM (EST). ***Misdemeanor, Civil Actions under $25,000, Eviction, Small Claims.*** www.Circuit46.org

Civil Records: Access: Phone, mail, fax, in person, online. Only the court performs in person searches; visitors may not. No search fee. Required to search: name, years to search. Civil cases indexed by defendant, plaintiff, on computer since 1990, books from 1969. Mail turnaround time 1-4 days. Online access to limited index of court records is free at http://66.129.39.149/c46_Cases.php.

Criminal Records: Access: Phone, mail, fax, in person, online. Only the court performs in person searches; visitors may not. No search fee. Required to search: name, years to search, DOB. Criminal records on computer since 1989. Mail turnaround time 1-4 days. Online access to criminal records is the same as civil. There are limitations, this system is not meant to be used for background checks; it is supplemental only.

General Information: No suppressed, juvenile, sex offenders, mental health, or adoption records released. Will not fax documents. Court makes copy: $1.00 per page, self serve same. Certification fee: $10.00 plus $1.00 each add'l page. Payee: District Division Court. Personal checks accepted; credit cards are not. Mail requests: SASE required.

Probate Court 200 W Michigan Ave., Grayling, MI 49738; 989-344-3237; fax: 989-344-3277; 8AM-4:30PM (EST). ***Probate.*** www.Circuit46.org

Delta County

47th Circuit Court 310 Ludington St, Escanaba, MI 49829; 906-789-5105; criminal fax: 906-789-5196; civil fax: same; 8AM-4PM (EST). ***Felony, Civil Actions over $25,000, Vital Statistics.***

Civil Records: Access: Mail, in person. Both court and visitors may perform in person searches. Search fee: $10.00 per name. Required to search: name; also helpful: years to search, address. Civil cases indexed by defendant, plaintiff, on computer from 1986, archived into 1800s. Mail turnaround time same day.

Criminal Records: Access: Mail, in person. Both court and visitors may perform in person searches. Search fee: $20.00 per name. Required to search: name; also helpful: years to search, DOB, SSN. Criminal records computerized from 1989, archived into 1800s. Mail turnaround time same day.

General Information: No suppressed, juvenile, sex offenders, mental health, or adoption records released. Will fax documents no add'l fee. Court makes copy: $1.00 per page. Certification fee: $10.00 plus $1.00 per page after first. Payee: Delta County. Personal checks accepted. Credit card payments accepted via GPS. Mail requests: SASE required.

94th District Court 310 Ludington St., Escanaba, MI 49829; criminal phone: 906-789-5108; civil phone: 906-789-5106; fax: 906-789-5198; 8AM-4PM (EST). ***Misdemeanor, Civil Actions under $25,000, Eviction, Small Claims.***

Civil Records: Access: Mail, in person. Only the court performs in person searches; visitors may not. Search fee: $5.00. Required to search: name, years to search; also helpful: address. Civil cases indexed by defendant, plaintiff, on computer back to 1988, prior on books to 1968. Mail turnaround time 3 days.

Criminal Records: Access: Mail, in person. Only the court performs in person searches; visitors may not. Search fee: $10.00 per name. Required to search: name, years to search, DOB; also helpful: address, SSN. Criminal records computerized from 1988, prior on books to 1968. Mail turnaround time 3 days.

General Information: No suppressed, juvenile, sex offenders, mental health, or adoption records released. Will fax documents to toll-free number. Court makes copy: $.25 per page. Certification fee: $10.00 per document. Payee: 94th District Court. Personal checks accepted. Major credit cards accepted via GPS. Mail requests: SASE required.

Probate Court 310 Ludington St., Escanaba, MI 49829; 906-789-5112; fax: 906-789-5140; 8AM-N, 1-4PM (EST). ***Probate.***

Dickinson County

41st Circuit Court PO Box 609, 705 S Stephenson, Iron Mountain, MI 49801; 906-774-0988; criminal fax: 906-774-4660; civil fax: same; 8AM-4:30PM (CST). ***Felony, Civil Actions over $25,000, Vital Statistics.*** www.dickinsoncountymi.gov/courts.html

Civil Records: Access: Mail, in person. Both court and visitors may perform in person searches. Search fee: $15.00 per name. Fee is for 10 year search. Required to search: name, years to search. Civil cases indexed by defendant, plaintiff; index on docket books since 1891; on computer since 5/95. Mail turnaround time 1-2 days.

Criminal Records: Access: Mail, in person. Both court and visitors may perform in person searches. Search fee: $5.00 per name. Fee is for 10 year search. Required to search: name, years to search, DOB; also helpful: SSN. Criminal docket on books since 1891; on computer since 5/95. Mail turnaround 1-2 days.

General Information: No suppressed, juvenile, sex offenders, mental health, or adoption records released. Fee to fax back $1.50 per page. Court makes copy: $1.00 per page. Certification fee: $10.00 per doc. Payee: County Clerk. Business checks accepted. Credit card payments accepted via GPS. Mail requests: SASE required if results to be mailed.

95 B District Court County Courthouse, PO Box 609, Iron Mountain, MI 49801; 906-774-0506; criminal fax: 906-774-8560; civil fax: same; 8AM-4:30PM (CST). ***Misdemeanor, Civil Actions under $25,000, Eviction, Small Claims.***

May require a signed release for certain records.

Civil Records: Access: Phone, mail, fax. Only the court performs in person searches; visitors may not. Search fee: $5.00 per name. Required to search: name, years to search; also helpful: address. Civil cases indexed by defendant, plaintiff; index on cards from 1981; on computer back to 2/1995. Mail turnaround time 1 week. **Criminal Records:** Access: Mail, fax, in person. Only the court performs in person searches; visitors may not. Search fee: $5.00 per name. Required to search: name, years to search, DOB; also helpful: address, SSN. Criminal records indexed on cards from 1981; computer back to 2/1995. Mail turnaround 1 week.

General Information: No suppressed, juvenile, sex offenders, mental health, or adoption records released. Will fax documents for no fee. Court makes copy: $1.00 1st page; $.50 each add'l. Certification fee:

$10.00 per document. Payee: 95-B District Court. Only cashiers checks and money orders accepted. No credit cards accepted. Mail requests: SASE required.

Probate Court PO Box 609, 705 S Stephenson, Iron Mountain, MI 49801; 906-774-1555; fax: 906-774-1561; 8AM-4:30PM (CST). ***Probate.*** www.dickinsoncountymi.gov/countyInfo/courthouse.html

Eaton County

56th Circuit Court 1045 Independence Blvd, Charlotte, MI 48813; 517-543-7500 x4335; criminal fax: 517-543-4475; civil fax: same; 8AM-5PM (EST). ***Felony, Civil Actions over $25,000, Vital Statistics.*** www.eatoncountycourts.org/courts.html Email questions to CircuitCourtClerk@eatoncounty.org.
Civil Records: Access: Phone, fax, mail, in person. Both court and visitors may perform in person searches. Search fee: $8.00 per name if by fax or mail. Required to search: name, years to search. Civil cases indexed by defendant, plaintiff, on computer back to 1988, microfilm since 1930s, books from 1848. Note: If faxing in a search request, also fax copy of your payment check. Mail turnaround time 1-3 days. Recent day divorce decrees at www.eatoncounty.org/Departments/Circuit_Court_Clerk/COUNTY_SERVICES.htm.
Criminal Records: Access: Fax, mail, in person, online. Both court and visitors may perform in person searches. Search fee: $8.00 per name if by fax or mail. Required to search: name, years to search, DOB; also helpful: SSN. Criminal records computerized from 1969, microfilm since 1930s, books from 1860s. Note: There is no charge to do a name search if in person. If faxing request, also fax copy of your payment check. Mail turnaround time 1-3 days. Last 12-13 months of criminal case dispositions listed at www.eatoncounty.org/Departments/Circuit_Court_Clerk/COUNTY_SERVICES.htm
General Information: No suppressed, juvenile, sex offenders, mental health, or adoption records released. Will fax documents. Court makes copy: $1.00 first page, $.50 each add'l. Certification fee: $10.00 for 1st page, $1.00 each add'l page. Payee: Eaton County Circuit Court Clerk. Personal checks accepted. Mail requests: SASE required.

56A District Court 1045 Independence Blvd, Charlotte, MI 48813; 517-543-7500; criminal phone: x4042; civil phone: x4064; fax: 517-543-1469; 8AM-5PM (EST). ***Misdemeanor, Civil Actions under $25,000, Eviction, Small Claims.*** www.eatoncountycourts.org/courts.html
Civil Records: Access: In person only. Visitors must perform in person searches themselves. Required to search: name, years to search. Civil cases indexed by defendant, plaintiff, on computer back to 1990; prior in books. Civil PAT goes back to 1990. PAT results show middle initial, DOB. **Criminal Records:** Access: In person only. Visitors must perform in person searches themselves. Required to search: name, years to search, DOB. Criminal records computerized from 1990. Criminal PAT goes back to same as civil; results show middle initial, DOB.
General Information: No suppressed, sex offenders, mental health, or adoption records released. Will not fax documents. Court makes copy: $.30 per page. Certification fee: $10.00 per doc. Payee: 56A District Court. Personal checks accepted. Visa/MC accepted in person only.

Probate Court 1045 Independence Blvd, Probate Court, Charlotte, MI 48813; 517-543-7500 x1234; fax: 517-543-8439; 8AM-5PM (EST). ***Probate.*** www.eatoncounty.org/Courts/Eaton_County_56th_Probate_Court.htm

Emmet County

57th Circuit Court 200 Division St, Petoskey, MI 49770; 231-348-1744; fax: 231-348-0602; 7:30AM-6PM (EST). ***Felony, Civil Actions over $25,000, Vital Statistics.*** www.co.emmet.mi.us/circuit/
The search fee includes the civil and criminal indexes.
Civil Records: Access: Mail, in person. Only the court performs in person searches; visitors may not. Search fee: $5.00 per name. Required to search: name, years to search. Civil cases indexed by defendant, plaintiff, on computer from 1867 to present. Mail turnaround time 5 days.
Criminal Records: Access: Mail, in person. Only the court performs in person searches; visitors may not. Search fee: $5.00 per name. Required to search: name, years to search, DOB. Criminal records computerized from 1867 to present. Mail turnaround time 5 days.
General Information: No suppressed records released. Will not fax documents. Court makes copy: $.50 per page. Certification fee: $10.00 per cert plus $1.00 per page, includes copy fee. Payee: Emmet County Clerk. Local personal checks accepted. No credit cards accepted. Mail requests: SASE required.

90th District Court 200 Division St., Petoskey, MI 49770; 231-348-1750; criminal phone: 231-348-1752; civil phone: 231-348-1753; fax: 231-348-0616; 8AM-5PM (EST). ***Misdemeanor, Civil Actions under $25,000, Eviction, Small Claims.***
Civil Records: Access: Fax, mail, in person. Only the court performs in person searches; visitors may not. Search fee: $5.00 per name. Required to search: name, years to search. Civil cases indexed by defendant, plaintiff, on computer since 1981, prior listed in books. Mail turnaround time 48 hours.
Criminal Records: Access: Fax, mail, in person. Only the court performs in person searches; visitors may not. Search fee: $5.00 per name. Required to search: name, years to search, DOB. Criminal records on computer since 1981, prior listed on microfiche. Mail turnaround time on all Division searches is 48 hours.
General Information: No suppressed, juvenile, sex offenders, mental health, or adoption records released. Will fax documents $6.00 1st page, $1.00 each add'l. Court makes copy: $1.00 per page. Certification fee: $10.00. Payee: 90th District Court. Business checks accepted. Major credit cards accepted via GPS. SASE not required.

Probate Court 200 Division St., Petoskey, MI 49770; 231-348-1764; fax: 231-348-0672; 8AM-5PM (EST). ***Probate.*** Shares the same judge with Charlevoix County Probate Court.

Genesee County

7th Circuit Court 900 S Saginaw, Flint, MI 48502; 810-257-3220; 8AM-4PM (EST). ***Felony, Civil Actions over $25,000, Vital Statistics.*** www.co.genesee.mi.us
Cases files could be located at one of seven lower courts in the county. Probate court is located in a separate office at the same address.
Civil Records: Access: Mail, in person, online. Both court and visitors may perform in person searches. Search fee: $5.00 per name. Required to search: name, years to search. Civil cases indexed by defendant, plaintiff, on computer since 1979, prior on index cards. Mail turnaround time 1-2 weeks. Civil PAT goes back to 1979. Online access to court records is free at www.co.genesee.mi.us/clerk/#; click on "Circuit Court Records."
Criminal Records: Access: Mail, in person, online. Both court and visitors may perform in person searches. Search fee: $5.00 per name. Required to search: name, years to search, DOB; also helpful: race, sex. Criminal records on computer since 1979, prior on index cards. Mail turnaround 1-2 weeks. Criminal PAT goes back to same as civil. Online access to criminal records is the same as civil.
General Information: No suppressed, juvenile, adoption, or mental health records released. Will not fax documents. Court makes copy: $1.00 per page. Certification fee: $10.00 per doc. Payee: Genesee County Clerk. Business checks and money orders accepted. Credit card payments accepted via GPS. Mail requests: SASE required.

67th District Court 630 S Saginaw, Flint, MI 48502; 810-257-3170; 8AM-4PM (EST). ***Misdemeanor, Civil Actions under $25,000, Eviction, Small Claims.*** www.co.genesee.mi.us/districtcourt/
Cases files can be located at any one of 7 district courts in the county. The Clerk's index will indicate the exact location.
Civil Records: Access: Mail, in person, online. Only the court performs in person searches; visitors may not. Search fee: $15.00 per name, $2.00 for a computer printout. Required to search: name, years to search; also helpful: address. Civil cases indexed by defendant, plaintiff, on computer since 1983, on microfilm since 1969, prior archived. Mail turnaround 1 week. Search by name at www.co.genesee.mi.us/districtcourt/recordschk.htm.
Criminal Records: Access: Mail, in person, online. Only the court performs in person searches; visitors may not. Search fee: $15.00 per name, $2.00 for a computer printout. Required to search: name, years to search, DOB, offense; also helpful: address. Criminal records on computer since 1983, on microfilm since 1969, prior archived. Mail turnaround time 1 week. Search by name at www.co.genesee.mi.us/districtcourt/recordschk.htm. Also includes traffic.
General Information: No drug related case records released. Will not fax documents. Court makes copy: $1.00 per page. Certification fee: $10.00. Payee: 67th District Court. Cashiers checks, business checks, and money orders accepted. Major credit cards accepted in person only. Mail requests: SASE helpful.

68th District Court 630 S Saginaw, Flint, MI 48502; 810-766-8968; criminal phone: 810-766-8968 x1; civil phone: 810-766-8968 x2; fax: 810-766-8967; 8AM-4PM (EST). ***Misdemeanor, Civil Actions under $25,000, Eviction, Small Claims.*** www.ci.flint.mi.us/68th/68th.asp
The 68th District Court consists of the City of Flint and is a district of the third class with five judges.
Civil Records: Access: Mail, in person. Only the court performs in person searches; visitors may not. Search fee: $15.00 per name, $2.00 for a computer printout. Required to search: name, years to search; also helpful: address. Civil cases indexed by defendant, plaintiff, on computer since 1983, on microfilm since 1969, prior archived. Mail turnaround time 1 week.
Criminal Records: Access: Mail, in person. Only the court performs in person searches; visitors may not. Search fee: $15.00 per name, $2.00 for a computer printout. Required to search: name, years to search, DOB, offense; also helpful: address, SSN. Criminal records on computer since 1983, on microfilm since 1969, prior archived. Note: Court has jurisdiction over felony arraignments and criminal cases punishable by one year or less in jail. Mail turnaround time 1 week.
General Information: No drug related case records released. Will fax documents. Court makes copy: $1.00 per page. Certification fee: $15.00. Payee: 68th District Court. Only cashiers checks, business checks, and money orders accepted. Credit card payments accepted via GPS. Mail requests: SASE helpful.

Probate Court 900 S Saginaw St #502, Flint, MI 48502; 810-257-3528; fax: 810-257-2713; 8AM-4PM (EST). ***Probate.*** www.co.genesee.mi.us/probate/index.htm
Access records free at www.co.genesee.mi.us/probate/index.htm -click on Probate Court Records,

Gladwin County

55th Circuit Court 401 W Cedar, Gladwin, MI 48624; 989-426-7351; criminal fax: 989-426-6917; civil fax: same; 8:30AM-3:30PM (EST). ***Felony, Civil Actions over $25,000, Vital Statistics.***
Civil Records: Access: Fax, mail. Only the court performs in person searches; visitors may not. No search fee, but if search requirements are not met, fee is $5.00. Required to search: name, years to search. Civil cases indexed by defendant, plaintiff, on computer since 1994, prior on books. Mail turnaround time 2-3 days.
Criminal Records: Access: Fax, mail. Only the court performs in person searches; visitors may not. No search fee, but if search requirements are not met, fee is $5.00. Required to search: name, years to search, DOB; also helpful: SSN. Criminal records on computer since 1994, prior on books. Mail turnaround time 2-3 days.
General Information: No suppressed, juvenile, sex offenders, mental health, or adoption records released. Will fax documents. Court makes copy: $1.00 per

page. Certification fee: $10.00 1st page, $1.00 each add'l page. Payee: Gladwin County Clerk. No personal checks accepted. Credit card payments accepted via GPS. Mail requests: SASE required.

80th District Court 401 W Cedar, Gladwin, MI 48624; 989-426-9207; fax: 989-246-0894; 8:30AM-4:30PM (EST). ***Misdemeanor, Civil Actions under $25,000, Eviction, Small Claims.***
www.gladwinco.com/d80.htm
Civil Records: Access: Mail, fax, in person. Only the court performs in person searches; visitors may not. No search fee. Required to search: name, years to search. Civil cases indexed by defendant, plaintiff, on computer since 1988, prior on index cards and docket books, archived to late 1968. Mail turnaround time same day when possible.
Criminal Records: Access: Mail, fax, in person. Only the court performs in person searches; visitors may not. Search fee: $1.00 per summery; $5.00 per case documents. Required to search: name, years to search, DOB; also helpful: SSN. Criminal records on computer since 1988, prior on index cards and docket books, archived to late 1968. Mail turnaround time same day if possible.
General Information: No suppressed, juvenile, sex offenders, mental health, or adoption records released. Will fax documents to local or toll-free number. Court makes copy: $1.00 per page. Certification fee: $10.00 per doc plus copy fee for add'l pages. Payee: 80th District Court. Personal checks accepted; credit cards are not. Mail requests: SASE required.

Probate Court 401 W Cedar, Gladwin, MI 48624; 989-426-7451; fax: 989-426-6936; 8:30AM-4:30PM (EST). ***Probate.***
This is combined with Clare County Probate Court.

Gogebic County

32nd Circuit Court 200 N Moore St, Bessemer, MI 49911; 906-663-4518; probate phone: 906-667-0421; fax: 906-663-4660; 8:30AM-4:30PM (CST). ***Felony, Civil Actions over $25,000, Vital Statistics.***
www.gogebic.org/circuit.htm
Probate fax is same as main fax number. District Court phone#: 906-663-4611.
Civil Records: Access: Fax, mail, in person. Only the court performs in person searches; visitors may not. Search fee: $25.00 per name per 7 year search. Required to search: name, years to search. Civil cases indexed by defendant, plaintiff, in books since 1887, computerized since 1997. Mail turnaround 1-2 days.
Criminal Records: Access: Fax, mail, in person. Only the court performs in person searches; visitors may not. Search fee: $25.00 per name per 7 year search. Required to search: name, years to search, DOB. Criminal records in books since 1887, computerized since 1997. Mail turnaround 1-2 days.
General Information: No suppressed, juvenile, sex offenders, mental health, or adoption records released. Will fax documents $1.50 per page. Court makes copy: $1.00 per page. Certification fee: $10.00 per doc. Payee: Gogebic County Clerk's Office. Personal checks accepted; credit cards are not. Mail requests: SASE required.

98th District Court 200 N Moore St, Bessemer, MI 49911; 906-663-4611; fax: 906-667-1102; 8:30AM-N, 1-4:30PM (CST). ***Misdemeanor, Civil Actions under $25,000, Eviction, Small Claims.***
www.gogebic.org/district.htm
Civil Records: Access: Mail, in person. Only the court performs in person searches; visitors may not. Search fee: $25.00 per name. Required to search: name, years to search. Civil cases indexed by defendant, plaintiff, on computer since 6/88. Mail turnaround time 10 days.
Criminal Records: Access: Mail, in person. Only the court performs in person searches; visitors may not. Search fee: $25.00 per name. Required to search: name, years to search, DOB, SSN. Criminal records on computer since 6/88. Mail turnaround 10 days.
General Information: No suppressed, juvenile, sex offenders, mental health, or adoption records released. Court makes copy: $1.00 per page. Cert fee: $10.00 per doc. Payee: District Ct. Business checks accepted. No credit cards accepted. SASE not required.

Probate Court 200 N Moore St., Bessemer, MI 49911; 906-667-0421; fax: 906-663-4660; 8:30AM-N, 1-4:30PM (CST). ***Probate.***
www.gogebic.org/probate.htm

Grand Traverse County

13th Circuit Court 328 Washington St, Traverse City, MI 49684; 231-922-4710; 8AM-5PM (EST). ***Felony, Civil Actions over $25,000, Vital Statistics.***
www.co.grand-traverse.mi.us
Family Division records now located at 280 Washington St, #206. Their phone# is 231-922-4679.
Civil Records: Access: Phone, mail, in person, online. Only the court performs in person searches; visitors may not. Search fee: $10.00 per name. Required to search: name, years to search. Civil cases indexed by defendant, plaintiff, on computer since 1971, prior on books since 1859. Mail turnaround time 1 week. Search civil records free at http://online.co.grand-traverse.mi.us/iprod/clerk/cccivil.html. 1981 through 1985 contain only index information. 1986 to present include case information and register of actions. Database updated nightly.
Criminal Records: Access: Phone, mail, in person, online. Only the court performs in person searches; visitors may not. Search fee: $10.00 per name. Required to search: name, years to search; also helpful: DOB, SSN. Criminal records on computer since 1977. Mail turnaround time 1 week. Access to a record index is found at http://online.co.grand-traverse.mi.us/iprod/clerk/cccriminal.html.
General Information: No suppressed records released. Will fax documents. Court makes copy: $1.00 first page, $.25 each add'l. Certification fee: $10.00 plus $1.00 per page after first. Payee: 13th Circuit Court. Personal checks accepted. Mail requests: SASE required.

86th District Court 280 Washington St., Traverse City, MI 49684; 231-922-4580; fax: 231-922-4454; 8AM-5PM (EST). ***Misdemeanor, Civil Actions under $25,000, Eviction, Small Claims.***
Criminal at #114B; Civil at #114C; Traffic at #114A
Civil Records: Access: Phone, mail, in person. Only the court performs in person searches; visitors may not. No search fee. Required to search: name, years to search. Civil cases indexed by defendant, plaintiff, on computer since 1988, prior on books. Mail turnaround time 2-3 days. Civil PAT available. 2 PATs available in the lobby.
Criminal Records: Access: Phone, mail, in person. Only the court performs in person searches; visitors may not. No search fee. Required to search: name, years to search, DOB; also helpful: SSN. Most criminal records on computer. Mail turnaround time 2-3 days. Criminal PAT available. 2 PATs available in the lobby.
General Information: No suppressed, juvenile, sex offenders, mental health, or adoption records released. Will fax documents to local or toll-free number. Court makes copy: $1.00 per page. Certification fee: $10.00 per doc. Payee: 86th District Court. Business checks accepted. Credit card payments accepted via GPS. Mail requests: SASE required.

Probate Court 280 Washington St #223, Traverse City, MI 49684; 231-922-6862; fax: 231-922-4458; 8AM-5PM (EST). ***Probate.***

Gratiot County

29th Circuit Court 214 E Center St, Ithaca, MI 48847; 989-875-5215; fax: 989-875-5254; 8AM-N, 1-4:30PM (EST). ***Felony, Civil Actions over $25,000, Vital Statistics.***
www.co.gratiot.mi.us/circuitcourt/index.htm
Civil Records: Access: Mail, in person. Only the court performs in person searches; visitors may not. Search fee: $12.00 per name. Fee is for 10 years, $1.00 each additional year. Required to search: name, years to search. Civil cases indexed by defendant, plaintiff. Records computerized back 10 years. Mail turnaround time 1-3 days.
Criminal Records: Access: Mail, in person. Only the court performs in person searches; visitors may not. Search fee: $12.00 per name. Fee is for 10 years, $1.00 each additional year. Required to search: name, years to search. Records computerized back 10 years. Mail turnaround time 1-3 days.
General Information: No suppressed, juvenile, sex offenders, mental health, or adoption records released. Will fax documents to local or toll free line. Court makes copy: $1.00 per page. Certification fee: $10.00 per doc. Payee: Gratiot County Clerk. Personal checks accepted. All major credit cards accepted. Mail requests: SASE required.

65-B District Court 245 E Newark St, Ithaca, MI 48847; 989-875-5240; criminal phone: same; criminal fax: 989-875-5290; civil fax: same; 8AM-4:30PM (EST). ***Misdemeanor, Civil Actions under $25,000, Eviction, Small Claims.***
www.co.gratiot.mi.us/
Civil Records: Access: In person only. Visitors must perform in person searches themselves. Required to search: name, years to search. Civil cases indexed by defendant, plaintiff; index on docket books from 1969 to present, computerized since 1996. Civil PAT goes back to 1996. PAT results show name only.
Criminal Records: Access: In person only. Visitors must perform in person searches themselves. Required to search: name, years to search, DOB. Criminal records on computer since 2/20/96, in books since 1969. Criminal PAT goes back to same as civil. PAT results show middle initial, DOB.
General Information: No non-public records released. Will not fax out case files. Court makes copy: $1.00 per page. Certification fee: $10.00 plus $1.00 per page after first. Payee: 65B District Court. Personal checks accepted; credit cards are not.

Probate Court PO Box 217, 214 E Center St, Ithaca, MI 48847; 989-875-5231; fax: 989-875-5331; 8AM-N, 1PM-4:30PM (EST). ***Probate.***
www.co.gratiot.mi.us/probate/index.htm

Hillsdale County

1st Circuit Court 29 N Howell, Hillsdale, MI 49242; 517-437-3391; fax: 517-437-3392; 8:30AM-5PM (EST). ***Felony, Civil Actions over $25,000, Vital Statistics.***
Civil Records: Access: Mail, in person. Only the court performs in person searches; visitors may not. Search fee: $1.00 per name per year. Required to search: name, years to search. Civil cases indexed by defendant, plaintiff, on computer back to 1844. Mail turnaround time 1-2 days.
Criminal Records: Access: Mail, in person. Only the court performs in person searches; visitors may not. Search fee: $1.00 per name per year. Required to search: name, years to search, DOB; also helpful: SSN. Criminal records computerized from 1844. Mail turnaround time 1-2 days.
General Information: No suppressed, juvenile, sex offenders, mental health, or adoption records released. Will fax documents to local or toll free line. Court makes copy: $.50 per page. Certification fee: $10.00 per doc plus $1 each add'l page. Payee: Hillsdale County Clerk. Personal checks accepted; out-of-state personal checks not accepted. No credit cards accepted. Mail requests: SASE required.

2nd District Court 49 N Howell, Hillsdale, MI 49242; 517-437-7329; fax: 517-437-2908; 8AM-4:30PM; 8AM-5PM Traffic (EST). ***Misdemeanor, Civil Actions under $25,000, Eviction, Small Claims.***
www.co.hillsdale.mi.us/
Civil Records: Access: Phone, mail, in person. Only the court performs in person searches; visitors may not. Search fee: $10.00. Required to search: name, years to search. Civil cases indexed by defendant, plaintiff, kept in docket books back to 1969; on computer back to 2001. Note: A request in writing may be required. Mail turnaround time 1 week.
Criminal Records: Access: Phone, mail, in person. Only the court performs in person searches; visitors may not. Search fee: $10.00. Required to search: name, years to search, DOB. Criminal records kept in docket books back to 1969; on computer back to 2001. Mail turnaround time 1 week.
General Information: No suppressed records released. Will fax documents to local or toll free line. Court makes copy: $.25 per page. Certification fee: $10.00 plus $1.00 each add'l page. Payee: Hillsdale District Court. Personal checks accepted.

Probate Court 29 N Howell, Hillsdale, MI 49242; 517-437-4643; fax: 517-437-4148; 8:30AM-N, 1-5PM (EST). ***Probate.***

Houghton County

12th Circuit Court 401 E Houghton Ave, Houghton, MI 49931; 906-482-5420; criminal fax: 906-483-0364; civil fax: same; 8AM-4:30PM ***Felony, Civil Actions over $25,000, Vital Statistics.*** www.houghtoncounty.net/directory-12jcc.shtml

Civil Records: Access: Mail, in person. Only the court performs in person searches; visitors may not. Search fee: $20.00 per name. Required to search: name, years to search. Civil cases indexed by defendant, plaintiff, kept on docket books, cards since 6/76; are computerized as of 1997. Mail turnaround time 1-2 days.

Criminal Records: Access: Mail, in person. Only the court performs in person searches; visitors may not. Search fee: $20.00 per name. Required to search: name, years to search, DOB; also helpful: SSN. Criminal records kept on docket books, cards since 11/63; are computerized as of 1997. Mail turnaround time 1-2 days.

General Information: No suppressed, juvenile, sex offenders, mental health, or adoption records released. Will fax documents to local or toll free line. Court makes copy: $1.00 per page. Certification fee: $10.00. Payee: Clerk of Circuit Court. Personal checks accepted; credit cards are not. SASE not required.

97th District Court 401 E Houghton Ave., Houghton, MI 49931; 906-482-4980; fax: 906-482-5270; 8AM-4:30PM (EST). ***Misdemeanor, Civil Actions under $25,000, Eviction, Small Claims.***

Civil Records: Access: Mail, fax, in person. Only the court performs in person searches; visitors may not. Search fee: $20.00 per name. Required to search: name, years to search; also helpful: address. Civil cases indexed by defendant, plaintiff, listed in "Registers of Actions." Records on computer back to 1998; others back to 1969. Mail turnaround time up to 1 week.

Criminal Records: Access: Mail, fax, in person. Only the court performs in person searches; visitors may not. Search fee: $20.00 per name. Required to search: name, years to search, DOB, SSN; also helpful: address, signed release. Criminal records listed in "Registers of Actions." Records on computer back to 1998; others back to 1969. Mail turnaround time up to 1 week.

General Information: Will not fax documents. Court makes copy: $1.00 first page, $.50 each add'l. Certification fee: $10.00. Payee: 97th District Court. Business checks accepted. No credit cards accepted. Mail requests: SASE required.

Probate Court 401 E. Houghton Ave., Houghton, MI 49931; 906-482-3120; fax: 906-487-5964; 8AM-4:30PM (EST). ***Probate.***

Huron County

52nd Circuit Court 250 E Huron Ave, Bad Axe, MI 48413; 989-269-9942; probate phone: 989-269-9944; fax: 989-269-6160; 8:30AM-5PM (EST). ***Felony, Civil Actions over $25,000, Vital Statistics.***

Civil Records: Access: Fax, In person. Both court and visitors may perform in person searches. Search fee: $5.00 per name. Required to search: name, years to search. Civil cases indexed by defendant, plaintiff, on computer since 1992, prior on books to 1867. Note: Fax requests accepted but results not released until payment received. Mail turnaround time 2-3 days.

Criminal Records: Access: Mail, fax, in person. Both court and visitors may perform in person searches. Search fee: $5.00 per name. Required to search: name, years to search, DOB; also helpful: SSN. Criminal records on computer since 1992, prior on books to 1867. Note: Fax requests accepted but results not released until payment received. Mail turnaround time 2-3 days.

General Information: No suppressed, juvenile, sex offenders, mental health, or adoption records released. Will fax documents to local or toll free line. Court makes copy: $1.00 per page. Certification fee: $15.00 per doc. Payee: Huron County Clerk. Personal checks accepted; credit cards are not. SASE not required.

73B District Court 250 E Huron Ave., Bad Axe, MI 48413; 989-269-9987; fax: 989-269-6167; 8:30AM-5PM (EST). ***Misdemeanor, Civil Actions under $25,000, Eviction, Small Claims.***

Civil Records: Access: Phone, fax, mail, in person. Only the court performs in person searches; visitors may not. Search fee: $5.00 per name. Required to search: name, years to search. Civil cases indexed by defendant, plaintiff, on computer since 6/1992, prior on books since 1969. Mail turnaround time 1-5 days.

Criminal Records: Access: Phone, fax, mail, in person. Only the court performs in person searches; visitors may not. Search fee: $5.00 per name. Required to search: name, years to search, DOB. Criminal records on computer since 6/1992, prior on books since 1969. Mail turnaround time 1-5 days.

General Information: No suppressed, juvenile, sex offenders, mental health, or adoption records released. No fee to fax documents. Court makes copy: $1.00 per page. Certification fee: $10.00. Payee: 73B District Court. Business checks accepted. Mail requests: SASE required.

Probate Court 250 E. Huron Ave., Rm 206, Bad Axe, MI 48413; 989-269-9944; fax: 989-269-0004; 8:30AM-N, 1-5PM (EST). ***Probate.***

Ingham County

30th Circuit Court PO Box 40771, 313 W. Kalamazoo, Lansing, MI 48933; 517-483-6500; fax: 517-483-6501; 9:00AM-5:00PM (EST). ***Felony, Civil Actions over $25,000, Vital Statistics.*** www.ingham.org/cc/circuit.htm

Civil Records: Access: Phone, mail, in person, online. Both court and visitors may perform in person searches. Search fee: $8.00 per name search fee for records after 1986. Required to search: name, years to search. Civil cases indexed by defendant, plaintiff, on computer since 1986. Mail turnaround time 1-2 days; if file is in storage, then 1 week. Civil PAT goes back to 1986. Results include name. Access court records and schedules at https://courts.ingham.org/. Schedules search free; record search is not; register or search by credit card, $8 + $2 convenience fee per court and $2.50 for each Register of Action viewed. Cases go back to 1986.

Criminal Records: Access: Mail, in person, online. Both court and visitors may perform in person searches. Search fee: $8.00 per name. Required to search: name, years to search; also helpful: DOB. Criminal records on computer since 1986. Mail turnaround time 1-2 days; if file is in storage, then 1 week. Criminal PAT goes back to same as civil.PAT results show name, DOB. Access to criminal records online is same as civil, see above.

General Information: All circuit court files are public record unless specifically suppressed by Law. Will not fax documents. Court makes copy: $1.00 per page. Certification fee: $10.00. Payee: Ingham County Circuit Court. Personal checks accepted. Credit card payments accepted via GPS. Mail requests: SASE required.

54 A District Court 124 W Michigan Ave, Lansing, MI 48933; 517-483-4433; criminal phone: 517-483-4445; civil phone: 517-483-4426; fax: 517-483-4108; 8AM-4:30PM (EST). ***Misdemeanor, Civil Actions under $25,000, Eviction, Small Claims.*** www.lansingcourt.com

This court covers the City of Lansing.

Civil Records: Access: In person, online. Visitors must perform in person searches themselves. Required to search: name, years to search. Civil cases indexed by defendant, plaintiff, on computer since 1990, microfiche from 1985, prior archived. Civil PAT goes back to 1990. Access court records and schedules at https://courts.ingham.org/. Schedules search free; record search is not; register or search by credit card, $8 + $2 convenience fee per court and $2.50 for each Register of Action viewed. Cases go back to 1999.

Criminal Records: Access: In person, online. Visitors must perform in person searches themselves. Required to search: name, years to search, DOB, offense, date of offense. Criminal records on computer since 1990, microfiche from 1985, prior not archived may be available on microfiche before 1969. Criminal PAT goes back to same as civil. Access to criminal records online is same as civil, see above.

General Information: No suppressed, juvenile, sex offenders, mental health, or adoption, non-public records released. Will not fax out case files. Court makes copy: $1.00 per page. Certification fee: $10.00 plus $1.00 per page after first. Payee: 54A District Court. No personal checks accepted. Visa/MC accepted. Credit card payments accepted via Western Union Speedpay.

54 B District Court 101 Linden, East Lansing, MI 48823; 517-351-7000; criminal phone: 517-336-8630; civil phone: 517-351-1730; fax: 517-351-3371; 8AM-4:30PM (EST). ***Misdemeanor, Civil Actions under $25,000, Eviction, Small Claims.*** http://cityofeastlansing.com

This court covers the City of East Lansing.

Civil Records: Access: Mail, in person, online. Both court and visitors may perform in person searches. No search fee. Required to search: name, years to search, also helpful- case number. Civil cases indexed by defendant, plaintiff, case number. Civil records on computer since 1991. Roe's also on computer but not accessible by the public. Note: Older records must be searched by court personnel and can take 1-3 days. Mail turnaround time 1 hour to 1 week; depends on availability. Civil PAT goes back to 1991. PAT results show name only. Access court records & schedules at https://courts.ingham.org/. Schedules search free; record search is not; register or search by credit card, $8 + $2 convenience fee per court and $2.50 for each Register of Action viewed. Cases go back to 1999.

Criminal Records: Access: Mail, in person, online. Both court and visitors may perform in person searches. No search fee. Required to search: name, DOB; if prior to 1989 give years needed. Criminal records on computer since 1989. ROA's also on computer but not accessible by the public. Mail turnaround time 1 hour to 1 week; depends on file availability. Criminal PAT goes back to 1989. PAT results show name only. PAT results may show vehicle info. Access to criminal records online is same as civil, see above.

General Information: No suppressed, juvenile, sex offenders, mental health, or adoption records released. Will not fax documents. Court makes copy: $.25 per page. Certification fee: $10.00 plus $1.00 per page after first. Payee: 54-B District Court. No 2-party or payroll checks accepted. Debit cards, Visa/MC accepted. Credit card payments accepted via GPS. Mail requests: SASE required.

55th District Court 700 Buhl St., Mason, MI 48854; 517-676-8400; civil phone: 517-676-8401; fax: 517-676-8241; 8:30AM-5PM (EST). ***Misdemeanor, Civil under $25,000, Eviction, Small Claims.*** www.ingham.org/dc/district.htm

This court covers all of Ingham County except for Lansing and East Lansing.

Civil Records: Access: Mail, in person, online. Both court and visitors may perform in person searches. No search fee. Required to search: name, years to search. Civil records on computer since 11/91, prior listed in index books. Mail turnaround time varies. Civil PAT goes back to 11/1991. Access court records & schedules at https://courts.ingham.org/. Schedules search free; record search is not; register or search by credit card, $8 + $2 convenience fee per court and $2.50 for each Register of Action viewed. Cases go back to 1999.

Criminal Records: Access: Mail, in person, online. Both court and visitors may perform in person searches. No search fee. Required to search: name, years to search, DOB; case number; also helpful: SSN. Criminal records on computer since 1994, prior on books. Mail turnaround time varies. Criminal PAT goes back to 1994. Access to criminal records online is same as civil, see above.

General Information: No suppressed, juvenile, sex offenders, mental health, or adoption records released. Will fax documents $1.00 per page. Court makes copy: $1.00 per page. Certification fee: $10.00 plus $1.00 each add'l page. Payee: 55th District Court. Personal checks and major credit cards accepted. Mail requests: SASE helpful.

Lansing Probate Court 313 W Kalamazoo St, Veterans Memorial Courthouse, Lansing, MI 48933; 517-483-6300 x8; fax: 517-483-6150; 8AM-N, 1-5PM (EST). ***Probate.***
The probate court located in Mason was closed; all of their records reside here. Schedules search free online at https://courts.ingham.org/. Record search back to 1986 online is not; register or search by credit card, $8 + $2 convenience fee.

Ionia County

8th Circuit Court 100 Main, Ionia, MI 48846; 616-527-5322; probate phone: 616-527-5326; criminal fax: 616-527-8201; civil fax: same; 8:30AM-5PM (EST). ***Felony, Civil Actions over $25,000, Vital Statistics.***
www.ioniacounty.org/Circuit/Circuit-Home.asp
Probate fax is same as main fax number.
Civil Records: Access: Fax, mail, in person. Only the court performs in person searches; visitors may not. Search fee: $5.00 per name. Required to search: name, years to search. Civil cases indexed by defendant, plaintiff, on computer since 1990; prior records kept in books and files, archived to 1800s. Mail turnaround time 1 week.
Criminal Records: Access: Fax, mail, in person. Only the court performs in person searches; visitors may not. Search fee: $5.00 per name. Required to search: name, years to search; also helpful: DOB, SSN. Criminal records on computer since 6/84; in books and files prior. Mail turnaround time 1 week.
General Information: No suppressed records released. Will fax documents. Court makes copy: $1.00 per page. Certification fee: $10.00 plus $1.00 per page copy fee after first. Payee: Ionia County Clerk. Personal checks accepted. Credit card payments accepted via GPS only. SASE not required.

64 A District Court 101 W Main, Ionia, MI 48846; 616-527-5346; fax: 616-527-5343; 8AM-5PM (EST). ***Misdemeanor, Civil Actions under $25,000, Eviction, Small Claims.***
www.ioniacounty.org/district/home1.asp
Civil Records: Access: Fax, mail, in person. Only the court performs in person searches; visitors may not. Search fee: $3.00 per name. Required to search: name, years to search. Civil cases indexed by defendant, plaintiff, in files and books available since 1969. Note: Fax request must be followed up by originals. Mail turnaround time 10 days.
Criminal Records: Access: Fax, mail, in person. Only the court performs in person searches; visitors may not. Search fee: $3.00 per name. Required to search: name, years to search, DOB; also helpful: address. Criminal records in files and books available since 1969. Note: Fax must be followed up by originals. Mail turnaround time 10 days.
General Information: No suppressed, juvenile, sex offenders, mental health, or adoption records released. Will fax documents to local or toll-free number. Court makes copy: $.50 per page. Certification fee: $10.00 plus $1.00 per page after first. Payee: 64-A District Court. Personal checks accepted. Mail requests: SASE requested.

Probate Court 100 Main St, Ionia, MI 48846; 616-527-5326; fax: 616-527-5321; 8:30AM-5PM (EST). ***Probate.***
www.ioniacounty.org/Probate/Probate_home.asp

Iosco County

23rd Circuit Court PO Box 838, Tawas City, MI 48764; 989-362-3497; criminal fax: 989-984-1012; civil fax: same; 9AM-5PM (EST). ***Felony, Civil Actions over $25,000, Vital Statistics.*** www.iosco.net
Civil Records: Access: Phone, mail, in person. Only the court performs in person searches; visitors may not. Search fee: $10.00 per name per record found. Required to search: name, years to search. Civil cases indexed by defendant, plaintiff, on computer since 1987, prior on books. Mail turnaround time 1 week.
Criminal Records: Access: Phone, mail, in person. Only the court performs in person searches; visitors may not. Search fee: $10.00 per name per record found. Required to search: name, years to search, DOB; also helpful: SSN. Criminal records on computer since 1983. Mail turnaround time 1 week.
General Information: No suppressed, parental waivers, mental health, or adoption records released. Will not fax documents. Court makes copy: $1.00 per page. Certification fee: $10.00 plus $1.00 per page. Payee: Iosco County Clerk. Cashiers checks and money orders accepted. Credit cards accepted through GPS, 888-604-7888. SASE not required.

81st District Court PO Box 388, 422 Lake St, Tawas City, MI 48764; 989-362-4441; fax: 989-984-1021; 8:30AM-4:30PM (EST). ***Misdemeanor, Civil Actions under $25,000, Eviction, Small Claims.***
Civil Records: Access: Mail, in person. Only the court performs in person searches; visitors may not. Search fee: $10.00. Required to search: name, years to search. Civil cases indexed by defendant, plaintiff, on computer since 1987, prior on books. Mail turnaround time 2-3 days.
Criminal Records: Access: Mail, in person. Only the court performs in person searches; visitors may not. Search fee: $5.00. Required to search: name, years to search, DOB; also helpful: SSN. Criminal records on computer since 1987, prior on books. Mail turnaround time 2-3 days.
General Information: No suppressed, juvenile, sex offenders, mental health, or adoption records released. Will fax documents to local or toll free line. Court makes copy: $2.00 first page, $1.00 each add'l. Certification fee: $10.00 plus $1.00 per page after first. Payee: 81st District Court. No personal checks. Major Major credit cards accepted via GPS. Mail requests: SASE required.

Probate Court PO Box 421, 422 Lake St, Tawas City, MI 48764; 989-362-3991; fax: 989-984-1035; 8AM-5PM (EST). ***Probate.***

Iron County

41st Circuit Court 2 South 6th St #9, Crystal Falls, MI 49920; 906-875-3221; fax: 906-875-6775; 8AM-N; 12:30-4PM (CST). ***Felony, Civil Actions over $25,000, Vital Statistics.***
www.iron.org/edc/gov-clerk.php
Search fee includes civil and criminal indexes.
Civil Records: Access: Fax, mail, in person. Only the court performs in person searches; visitors may not. Search fee: $15.00 per name. Required to search: name, years to search. Civil cases indexed by defendant, plaintiff. Most records on books, on microfiche 1958-67. Mail turnaround time 2-3 days.
Criminal Records: Access: Fax, mail, in person. Only the court performs in person searches; visitors may not. Search fee: $15.00 per name. Required to search: name, years to search, DOB. Most records on books, on microfiche 1958-67. Mail turnaround time 2-3 days.
General Information: No suppressed, juvenile, sex offenders, mental health, or adoption records released. Will fax documents $1.50 per page. Court makes copy: $.25 per page. Certification fee: $10.00 plus $1.00 per page after first. Payee: Iron County Clerk. Personal checks accepted. Credit card payments accepted via GPS. Mail requests: SASE requested.

95 B District Court 2 S 6th St., Crystal Falls, MI 49920; 906-875-0619; fax: 906-875-0656; 8AM-4PM (CST). ***Misdemeanor, Civil Actions under $25,000, Eviction, Small Claims.*** www.iron.org
Civil Records: Access: Mail, in person. Only the court performs in person searches; visitors may not. Search fee: $10.00. Required to search: name, years to search. Civil cases indexed by defendant, plaintiff, computerized since 1999, earlier records index kept on cards, accessible from 1970. Note: There is no search fee if a name and DOB are submitted for a Yes or No answer. The fee kicks in for accessing details of the case. Mail turnaround time 1 week.
Criminal Records: Access: Mail, in person. Only the court performs in person searches; visitors may not. Search fee: $10.00. Required to search: name, years to search, DOB; also helpful: SSN. Criminal records computerized since 1999, earlier records index kept on cards, accessible from 1970. Note: There is no search fee if a name and DOB are submitted for a Yes or No answer. The fee kick in for accessing details of the case. Mail turnaround time 1 week.
General Information: No suppressed, juvenile, sex offenders, mental health, or adoption records released. Will fax documents $1.00 per page. Court makes copy: $.25 per page. Certification fee: $10.00 plus $1.00 per page after first. Payee: 95-B District Court. Personal checks accepted. Credit card payments accepted via GPS. SASE not required.

Probate Court 2 S 6th St, #10, Crystal Falls, MI 49920; 906-875-0659; fax: 906-875-0656; 8AM-N, 12:30-4PM (CST). ***Probate.*** www.iron.org

Isabella County

21st Circuit Court 200 N Main St, Mount Pleasant, MI 48858; 989-772-0911 X346; fax: 989-779-8022; 8AM-4:30PM (EST). ***Felony, Civil Actions over $25,000, Vital Statistics.***
www.isabellacounty.org/trial.html
Civil Records: Access: Mail, in person. Both court and visitors may perform in person searches. Search fee: $5.00 from 1980 to present. Prior years $1.00 per year. Required to search: name, years to search. Civil cases indexed by defendant, plaintiff, on computer since 1980, archived from 1900. Mail turnaround time 1-2 weeks. Civil PAT available. PAT results show middle initial, DOB, SSN.
Criminal Records: Access: Mail, in person. Both court and visitors may perform in person searches. Search fee: $5.00 from 1980 to present. Prior years $1.00 per year. Required to search: name, years to search, DOB; also helpful: SSN. Criminal records on computer since 1980, archived from 1900. Mail turnaround time 1-2 weeks. Criminal PAT goes back to 1986. PAT results show middle initial, DOB, SSN.
General Information: No suppressed, juvenile, sex offenders, mental health, or adoption records released. Will fax to local or toll-free line. Court makes copy: $1.00 per page. Cert fee: $10.00 plus $1.00 per page after first. Payee: Isabella County Court. Personal checks accepted. Mail requests: SASE helpful.

76th District Court 300 N Main St., Mount Pleasant, MI 48858; 989-772-0911 X490; probate phone: x316; fax: 989-779-8022; 8AM-4:30PM (EST). ***Misdemeanor, Civil Actions under $25,000, Eviction, Small Claims.***
www.isabellacounty.org/trial.html
Civil Records: Access: Mail, in person. Both court and visitors may perform in person searches. Search fee: $5.00 per name. Required to search: name, years to search. Civil cases indexed by defendant, plaintiff, on computer since 1988, on books since 1969. Mail turnaround time 5-7 days. Civil PAT available.
Criminal Records: Access: Mail, in person. Both court and visitors may perform in person searches. Search fee: $5.00 per name. Required to search: name, years to search, DOB; also helpful: SSN. Criminal records on computer back 10 years, on books since 1969. Mail turnaround time 5-7 days. Criminal PAT available.
General Information: No suppressed, juvenile, sex offenders, or adoption records released. Will fax documents. Court makes copy: $1.00 per page. Certification fee: $10.00 1st page; $1.00 each add'l. Payee: Isabella County Trial Court. Business checks accepted. Credit card payments accepted via GPS. Mail requests: SASE required.

Probate Court 300 N Main St, Mount Pleasant, MI 48858; 989-772-0911 x316 (or x276); fax: 989-779-8022; 8AM-4:30PM (EST). ***Probate.***
www.isabellacounty.org

Jackson County

4th Circuit Court 312 S Jackson St, Jackson, MI 49201; 517-788-4268; criminal fax: 517-788-4601; civil fax: same; 8AM-5PM (EST). ***Felony, Civil Actions over $25,000, Vital Statistics.***
www.co.jackson.mi.us/CCinfo.asp
Civil Records: Access: Phone, mail, in person, online. Only the court performs in person searches; visitors may not. Search fee: $10.00 per hour. Required to search: name, years to search. Civil cases indexed by defendant, plaintiff, on computer since

1982, prior on index cards and docket books since 1800s. Mail turnaround 1 week. Access records free at http://96.61.192.32/c12/c12_cases.php.
Criminal Records: Access: Phone, mail, in person, online. Only the court performs in person searches; visitors may not. Search fee: $10.00 per hour. Required to search: name, years to search; also helpful: DOB, SSN. Criminal records on computer since 1982, prior on index cards and docket books since 1800s. Mail turnaround 1 week. Access records at http://96.61.192.32/c12/c12_cases.php.
General Information: No adoption or juvenile records released. Will fax documents $3.00 1st page, $1.00 each add'l. Court makes copy: $.50 per page. Certification fee: $10.00 plus $2.00 per page after first;. Payee: Jackson County Clerk. Cashiers checks and money orders accepted. Visa/MC accepted. Prepayment of fax and mail service required. Fees billed to Attorneys.

12th District Court 312 S Jackson St., Jackson, MI 49201; 517-788-4260; criminal phone: 517-788-4260; civil phone: 517-788-4037; criminal fax: 517-788-4262; civil fax: 517-780-4704; 7AM-6PM (EST). ***Misdemeanor, Civil Actions under $25,000, Eviction, Small Claims.*** www.d12.com
Civil Records: Access: Fax, mail, in person, online. Only the court performs in person searches; visitors may not. No search fee. Required to search: name, years to search. Civil cases indexed by defendant, plaintiff, on computer since 1986; microfilm to 1969. Mail turnaround time 5 days. Access court records free at http://96.61.192.32/c12/c12_cases.php.
Criminal Records: Access: Fax, mail, in person, online. Only the court performs in person searches; visitors may not. No search fee. Required to search: name, years to search, DOB; also helpful: SSN. Criminal records on computer since 1986; microfilm from 1969. Mail turnaround time 5 days. PAT results show middle initial, DOB. Access records free at http://96.61.192.32/c12/c12_cases.php.
General Information: No suppressed, juvenile, sex offenders, mental health, or probation records released. Will fax documents $5.00 1st page, $1.00 each add'l. Court makes copy: $.25 per page, first 10 free to county resident. Certification fee: $10.00 plus $1.00 per page after first. Payee: 12th District Court. Personal checks accepted. Visa/MC accepted. Mail requests: SASE helpful.

Probate Court 312 S Jackson St, 1st Fl, Jackson, MI 49201; 517-788-4290; fax: 517-788-4291; 8AM-5PM (EST). ***Probate.*** www.co.jackson.mi.us/CCinfo.asp Access probate records free at http://96.61.192.32/c12/c12_cases.php.

Kalamazoo County

9th Circuit Court 227 W Michigan Ave, Kalamazoo, MI 49007; 269-383-8837; fax: 269-383-8647; 8AM-5PM (EST). ***Felony, Civil over $25,000, Vital Stats.*** www.kalcounty.com/courts/
Civil Records: Access: Mail, in person. Visitors must perform in person searches themselves. Search fee: $1.00 per name. Required to search: name, years to search. Civil cases indexed by defendant, plaintiff, stored as hard copies, some records kept off-site; computerized records go back to 1984. Mail turnaround time 3 days. Civil PAT goes back to 1984. PAT civil results show middle initial. Terminal has index of case numbers only.
Criminal Records: Access: Mail, in person. Visitors must perform in person searches themselves. Search fee: $1.00 per name. Required to search: name, years to search, DOB. Criminal records stored as hard copies, some records kept off-site; computerized records go back to 1984. Mail turnaround time 3 days. Criminal PAT goes back to same as civil. PAT results show middle initial, DOB. Results also show race and gender. Public terminal has index of case numbers only.
General Information: No suppressed or non-public records released. Will not fax documents. Court makes copy: $1.00 per page. Certification fee: $13.00 per doc for seal includes copy fee. Payee: Circuit Court Clerk. Personal checks accepted except for criminal payments. Major Major credit cards accepted via GPS. Mail requests: SASE required.

8th District Court - Crosstown 150 E Crosstown Parkway, Kalamazoo, MI 49001; 269-384-8171; fax: 269-383-8899; 8AM-5PM (EST). ***Misdemeanor, Civil Actions under $25,000, Eviction, Small Claims.*** www.kalcounty.com
This court covers City of Kalamazoo.
Civil Records: Access: In person only. Visitors must perform in person searches themselves. Required to search: name, years to search. Civil cases indexed by defendant, plaintiff, on computer back to 1998, prior on index books to 1969. Note: All requests to review files or obtain document copies must be made on the File/Copy Request Form. Each requester may only request 5 case files per day. Civil PAT goes back to 1/1999.
Criminal Records: Access: In person only. Visitors must perform in person searches themselves. Required to search: name, years to search, DOB. Some Criminal records computerized from 1991, prior on books to 1969. Note: All requests to review files or obtain document copies must be made on the File/Copy Request Form. Criminal PAT goes back to 1991.PAT results show name, DOB.
General Information: No suppressed or non-public records released. No fee to fax documents. Court makes copy: $1.00 per page. Cert fee: $10.00 1st page plus copy fee for add'l pages. Payee: 8th District Court. Personal checks accepted; credit cards are not.

8th District Court - North 227 W Michigan Ave, Kalamazoo, MI 49007; 269-384-8171; fax: 269-384-8047; 8AM-5PM (EST). ***Misdemeanor, Civil under $25,000, Eviction, Small Claims.*** www.kalcounty.com
This court covers Kalamazoo County.
Civil Records: Access: In person only. Visitors must perform in person searches themselves. Required to search: name, years to search. Civil cases indexed by defendant, plaintiff, on computer back to 1998, prior on index books to 1969. Note: All requests to review files or obtain document copies must be made on the File/Copy Request Form. Each requester may only request 5 case files per day. Civil PAT goes back to 1/1999.
Criminal Records: Access: In person only. Visitors must perform in person searches themselves. Required to search: name, years to search, DOB. Some Criminal records computerized from 1991, prior on books to 1969. Note: All requests to review files or obtain document copies must be made on the File/Copy Request Form. Each requester may only request 5 case files per day. Criminal PAT goes back to 1991.PAT results show name, DOB.
General Information: No suppressed or non-public records released. No fee to fax documents. Court makes copy: $1.00 per page. Cert fee: $10.00 1st page plus copy fee for add'l pages. Payee: 8th District Court. Personal checks accepted; credit cards are not.

8th District Court - South 7810 Shaver Rd., Portage, MI 49024; 269-383-6460; criminal phone: x2; criminal fax: 269-321-3645; civil fax: same; 8AM-5PM (EST). ***Misdemeanor, Civil Actions under $25,000, Eviction, Small Claims.*** This court covers Kalamazoo County South of N Ave/Kilgore.
Civil Records: Access: In person only. Visitors must perform in person searches themselves. Required to search: name, years to search. Civil cases indexed by defendant, plaintiff, on computer back to 1998, prior on index books to 1969. Civil PAT goes back to 1/1999.
Criminal Records: Access: Fax, mail, in person. Visitors must perform in person searches themselves. No search fee. Required to search: name, years to search, DOB. Some Criminal records computerized from 1991, prior on books to 1969. Note: All requests to review files or obtain document copies must be made on the File/Copy Request Form. Mail turnaround time 5 days. Criminal PAT goes back to 1991. PAT results show middle initial, DOB, SSN.
General Information: No suppressed or non-public records released. Will not fax out documents. Court makes copy: $1.00 per page. Certification fee: $10.00 1st page plus copy fee for add'l pages. Payee: 8th District Court. Personal checks accepted. Visa/MC cards accepted. Credit card payments accepted via GPS. Mail requests: SASE requested.

Probate Court 150 E Crosstown Parkway, Kalamazoo, MI 49001; 269-383-8666; fax: 269-383-8685; 9AM-N, 1-5PM (EST). ***Probate.*** www.kalcounty.com/courts/probate/default.asp

Kalkaska County

46th Circuit Court PO Box 10, Kalkaska, MI 49646; 231-258-3300; probate phone: 231-258-3314; criminal fax: 231-258-3337; civil fax: same; 9AM-5PM (EST). ***Felony, Civil Actions over $25,000, Vital Statistics.*** www.Circuit46.org
Probate records located at 605 N Birch St.
Civil Records: Access: Mail, in person, online. Only the court performs in person searches; visitors may not. No search fee. Required to search: name, years to search. Civil cases indexed by defendant, plaintiff, on computer since 1989, prior on books, indexed to late 1800s. Mail turnaround 1-3 days. Online access to court case records (open or closed cases for 90 days) free at http://66.129.39.149/c46_Cases.php.
Criminal Records: Access: Mail, in person, online. Only the court performs in person searches; visitors may not. No search fee. Required to search: name, years to search, DOB; also helpful: SSN. Criminal records on computer since 1989, prior on books, indexed to 1800s. Mail turnaround 1-3 days. Online access to criminal records is same as civil.
General Information: No suppressed records released. Will fax documents $5.00 plus $1.00 per page. Not all docs can be returned by fax. Court makes copy: $1.00 per page. Certification fee: $10.00 per document. Payee: Kalkaska County Clerk. Personal checks accepted; credit cards are not. Mail requests: SASE required.

46th Circuit Trial Court - District Court 605 N Birch St., Kalkaska, MI 49646; 231-258-9031; fax: 231-258-2424; 8AM-4:30PM (EST). ***Misdemeanor, Civil Actions under $25,000, Eviction, Small Claims, Traffic.*** www.Circuit46.org
Civil Records: Access: Phone, mail, in person, online. Both court and visitors may perform in person searches. No search fee. Required to search: name, years to search. Civil cases indexed by defendant, plaintiff, on computer since 1989, prior on books. Mail turnaround time 4 days plus mailing time. Civil PAT goes back to 1989. PAT civil results show middle initial. Public terminal is in a secured area, available by approved appointment only. Access to limited index of court records is free at http://66.129.39.149/c46_Cases.php.
Criminal Records: Access: Phone, mail, in person, online. Both court and visitors may perform in person searches. No search fee. Required to search: name, years to search, DOB. Criminal records on computer since 1989, prior on books. Mail turnaround time 4 days plus mailing time. Criminal PAT goes back to same as civil. PAT results show middle initial, DOB. Public terminal is in a secured area, available by approved appointment only. Online access to criminal records is the same as civil. There are limitations, this system is not meant to be used for background checks, it is supplemental only. Online results show middle initial, DOB.
General Information: Online identifiers in results same as on public terminal. No suppressed records released. Will fax documents to local or toll free line. Court makes copy: $1.00 per page. Certification fee: $10.00 plus $1.00 per page after first. Payee: 46th Circuit Trial Court. Cashiers checks and money orders accepted. No credit cards accepted. Mail requests: SASE required.

Circuit Trial Court - Probate Division 605 N Birch, Kalkaska, MI 49646; 231-258-3330 x2; fax: 231-258-3329; 8-4:30PM (EST). ***Probate.*** www.Circuit46.org Search cases by name free at http://66.129.39.149/c46_Cases.php.

Kent County

17th Circuit Court 180 Ottawa Ave NW, #2400, Grand Rapids, MI 49503; 616-632-5480; criminal fax: 616-632-5458; civil fax: same; 8AM-5PM ***Felony, Civil Actions over $25,000, Vital Statistics.*** www.accesskent.com/CourtsAndLawEnforcement/17thCircuitCourt/17cc_index.htm
Search fee includes both civil and criminal indexes.

Civil Records: Access: Mail, in person, online. Only the court performs in person searches; visitors may not. Search fee: $5.00 per name. Required to search: name, DOB, years to search. Civil cases indexed by defendant, plaintiff, on computer since 1986, prior on books. Mail turnaround time 2-3 days. Search for $6.00 per name at https://www.accesskent.com/CourtNameSearch/. DOB not required but credit card is for record found. Also, search hearings schedule free at https://www.accesskent.com/CCHearing/
Criminal Records: Access: Mail, in person, online. Only the court performs in person searches; visitors may not. Search fee: $5.00 per name. Required to search: name, years to search, DOB. Criminal records on computer since 1986, prior on books. Mail turnaround 2-3 days. Search for $6.00 per name at https://www.accesskent.com/CourtNameSearch/. DOB and credit card required for results. Search accident reports $3.00 per name at https://www.accesskent.com/AccidentReports/
General Information: No suppressed records released. Will not fax documents. Court makes copy: $1.00 per page. Certification fee: $10.00 plus copy fee after 1st page. Payee: Kent County Clerk. Personal checks accepted; credit cards are not. Mail requests: SASE required.

59th District Court - Walker 4343 Remembrance Rd NW, Walker, MI 49534; 616-453-5765; fax: 616-791-6851; 8AM--5PM (EST). ***Misdemeanor, Civil Actions under $25,000, Eviction, Small Claims.***
Civil Records: Access: Mail, in person. Only the court performs in person searches; visitors may not. Search fee: $1.00 per name. Add $1.00 per add'l year requested. Required to search: name, years to search; also helpful: address. Civil cases indexed by defendant, plaintiff, on computer from 1989, docket books and cards prior. Mail turnaround time varies.
Criminal Records: Access: Mail, in person. Only the court performs in person searches; visitors may not. Search fee: $1.00 per name. Add $1.00 per add'l year requested. Required to search: name, years to search, DOB; also helpful: address, SSN. Criminal records computerized from 1989, docket books and cards prior. Mail turnaround time varies.
General Information: No suppressed, juvenile, sex offenders, mental health, or adoption records released. Will fax documents $1.00 per name. Court makes copy: $1.00 per page. Certification fee: $10.00 plus $1.00 per page after first. Payee: 59th District Court. Personal checks accepted. Major credit cards accepted via GPS. Mail requests: SASE required.

59th District Court - Grandville 3161 Wilson Ave SW, Grandville, MI 49418; 616-538-9660; criminal fax: 616-538-5144; civil fax: same; 8:30AM-5PM (EST). ***Misdemeanor, Civil Actions under $25,000, Eviction, Small Claims.***www.cityofgrandville.com/Services/Courts/OverviewCourts.htm
Civil Records: Access: Mail, in person. Only the court performs in person searches; visitors may not. Search fee: $8.00. Required to search: name, years to search; also helpful: address. Civil cases indexed by defendant, plaintiff, on computer from 1986, docket books and cards prior. Mail turnaround time 1-2 days.
Criminal Records: Access: Mail, in person. Only the court performs in person searches; visitors may not. Search fee: $8.00. Required to search: name, years to search, DOB; also helpful: address. Criminal records computerized from 1986, docket books and cards prior. Mail turnaround time 1-2 days.
General Information: No suppressed, juvenile, sex offenders, mental health, or adoption records released. Court makes copy: $1.00 per page. Certification fee: $10.00 plus $1.00 per page after first. Payee: 59th District Court. Personal checks accepted. Mail requests: SASE helpful.

61st District Court - Grand Rapids 180 Ottawa Ave NW #1400, County Courthouse, Grand Rapids, MI 49503; 616-632-5700; criminal phone: 616-632-5700 x1; civil phone: 616-632-5700 x2; criminal fax: 616-632-5592; civil fax: 616-632-5583; 7:45AM-4:45PM (EST). ***Misdemeanor, Civil Actions under $25,000, Eviction, Small Claims.*** www.grcourt.org/
Civil Records: Access: Mail, fax, in person, online. Both court and visitors may perform in person searches. No search fee. Required to search: name, years to search. Civil cases indexed by defendant, plaintiff, kept in files and books, computerized since 1999. Mail turnaround time 7-10 days. Civil PAT goes back to 10/1999. PAT civil results show middle initial. Search online at https://www.grcourt.org/CourtPayments/
Criminal Records: Access: Mail, fax, in person, online. Both court and visitors may perform in person searches. No search fee. Required to search: name, years to search, DOB; also helpful: SSN. Criminal records are automated from 1999, images on microfiche from 1980. Mail turnaround time 7-10 days. Criminal PAT goes back to same as civil.PAT results show name, DOB. Search at https://www.grcourt.org/CourtPayments/ Online results show middle initial, DOB.
General Information: No suppressed, juvenile, sex offenders, mental health, or adoption records released. Will fax documents to local or toll-free number. Court makes copy: $1.00 first page, $.50 each add'l. Certification fee: $10.00 plus $1.00 per page after first. Payee: 61st District Court. Personal checks accepted. Credit card payments accepted via GPS. Prepayment mail service. SASE not required.

62 A District Court - Wyoming 2650 De Hoop Ave SW, Wyoming, MI 49509; 616-257-9814; criminal phone: 616-257-9814; civil phone: 616-530-7382; fax: 616-249-3419; 8AM-5PM (EST). ***Misdemeanor, Civil Actions under $25,000, Eviction, Small Claims.***
www.ci.wyoming.mi.us/DistrictCourt/d-court.asp
Civil Records: Access: Mail, fax, in person. Both court and visitors may perform in person searches. Search fee: $1.00 per name & $.50 per year. Required to search: name, years to search. Civil cases indexed by defendant, plaintiff, kept on docket books since 1980; on computer back to 1997. Note: The judge must approve all requests from collection agencies. Mail turnaround time 2-3 days. Civil PAT goes back to 1997.
Criminal Records: Access: Mail, fax, in person. Both court and visitors may perform in person searches. Search fee: $1.00 per name & $.50 per year. Required to search: name, years to search, DOB; also helpful: Case #. Criminal docket books kept since 1980; on computer back to 1997. Note: The court suggests mail requests be sent to the state police. Mail turnaround time 2-3 days. Criminal PAT goes back to same as civil. PAT results show middle initial, DOB.
General Information: No suppressed, juvenile, sex offenders, mental health, or adoption records released. Will not fax documents. Court makes copy: $1.00 per page. Certification fee: $10.00 plus $1.00 per page after first. Payee: 62 A District Court. Personal checks accepted. Accepts Visa credit cards in person only. Mail requests: SASE required.

62 B District Court - Kentwood 4740 Walma Ave, Kentwood, MI 49512; 616-698-9310; fax: 616-698-8199; 8AM-5PM (EST). ***Misdemeanor, Civil Actions under $25,000, Eviction, Small Claims.***
Civil Records: Access: Mail, in person. Both court and visitors may perform in person searches. Search fee: $5.00 per name. Required to search: name, years to search. Civil cases indexed by defendant, plaintiff, on computer since 11/88, prior on books. Mail turnaround time 1-2 days. Civil PAT goes back to 11/1988; results show name only.
Criminal Records: Access: Mail, in person. Both court and visitors may perform in person searches. Search fee: $5.00 per name. Required to search: name, years to search, DOB. Criminal records on computer since 11/88, prior on books. Mail turnaround time 1-2 days. Criminal PAT goes back to same as civil. PAT results show name only.
General Information: No suppressed, juvenile, sex offenders, mental health, or adoption records released. Will not fax documents. Court makes copy: $2.00 1st page, $.25 each add'l, self serve same. Certification fee: $10.00. Payee: 62 B District Court. Personal checks accepted. Visa/MC accepted. Credit card payments also accepted via GPS. Mail requests: SASE helpful.

63rd District Court - 1st Division 105 Maple St, Rockford, MI 49341; 616-866-1576; fax: 616-866-3080; 8AM-5PM ***Misdemeanor, Civil under $25,000, Eviction, Small Claims.***
Civil Records: Access: In person only. Visitors must perform in person searches themselves. Required to search: n/a. Civil cases indexed by defendant, plaintiff, on computer since 8/94, prior on books. Civil PAT goes back to 1996.
Criminal Records: Access: In person only. Visitors must perform in person searches themselves. Required to search: n/a. Criminal records on computer since 8/94, prior on books. Criminal PAT goes back to same as civil.
General Information: No suppressed, juvenile, sex offenders, mental health, or adoption records released. Will not fax documents. Court makes copy: $1.00 per page. Certification fee: $10.00. Payee: 63rd District Court. Personal checks & major credit cards accepted.

Probate Court 180 Ottawa Ave NW #2500, Grand Rapids, MI 49503; 616-632-5440; fax: 616-632-5430; 8AM-4:30PM (EST). ***Probate.*** www.accesskent.com/CourtsAndLawEnforcement/ProbateCourt/probate_index.htm

Keweenaw County

12th Circuit Court 5095 4th St., Eagle River, MI 49950-9624; 906-337-2229; criminal fax: 906-337-2795; civil fax: same; 9AM-4PM (EST). ***Felony, Civil Actions over $25,000, Vital Statistics.***
Civil Records: Access: Mail, in person. Only the court performs in person searches; visitors may not. Search fee: $10.00. Required to search: name, years to search. Civil cases indexed by defendant, plaintiff, kept on index books since 1963. Mail turnaround time 1-2 days.
Criminal Records: Access: Mail, in person. Only the court performs in person searches; visitors may not. Search fee: $10.00. Required to search: name, years to search, DOB. Criminal index on books since 1964. Mail turnaround time 1-2 days.
General Information: No suppressed, juvenile, sex offenders, mental health, or adoption records released. Will fax documents. Court makes copy: $1.00 per page, self serve same. Certification fee: $10.00 per document. Payee: Keweenaw County. Personal checks accepted; credit cards are not. Mail requests: SASE requested.

97th District Court 5095 4th St., Eagle River, MI 49950; 906-337-2229; criminal fax: 906-337-2795; civil fax: same; 9AM-4PM (EST). ***Misdemeanor, Civil Actions under $25,000, Eviction, Small Claims.***
Civil Records: Access: Fax, mail, in person. Only the court performs in person searches; visitors may not. Search fee: $10.00 per name. Required to search: name, years to search. Civil cases indexed by defendant, plaintiff, kept on books to 1970's. Note: Results cannot be faxed. Mail turnaround 1-2 days.
Criminal Records: Access: Fax, mail, in person. Only the court performs in person searches; visitors may not. Search fee: $10.00 per name. Required to search: name, years to search, DOB; also helpful: SSN. Criminal records kept on books to 1970's. Mail turnaround time 1-2 days.
General Information: No suppressed, juvenile, sex offenders, mental health, or adoption records released. Will fax documents but search results cannot be faxed. Court makes copy: $1.00 per page, self serve same. Certification fee: $10.00 per document. Payee: Keweenaw County. Personal checks accepted. Mail requests: SASE required.

Probate Court 5095 4th St, Eagle River, MI 49950; 906-337-1927; fax: 906-337-2795; 9AM-4PM (EST). ***Probate.***

Lake County

Lake County Trial Court 800 10th St, #300, Baldwin, MI 49304; 231-745-4614; criminal phone: same; fax: 231-745-6232; 8AM--5PM (EST). ***Felony, Misdemeanor, Civil Actions, Eviction, Small Claims, Probate, Vital Statistics.***
Civil Records: Access: Mail, in person. Only the court performs in person searches; visitors may not. Search fee: $5.00 per name per year. Required to

search: name, years to search. Civil cases indexed by defendant, plaintiff, on computer since 7/89, prior on books to 1876. Mail turnaround time 1-2 days.
Criminal Records: Access: Mail, in person. Only the court performs in person searches; visitors may not. Search fee: $5.00 per name per year. Required to search: name, years to search, DOB; also helpful: SSN. Criminal records on computer since 7/89, prior on books to 1876. Mail turnaround time 1-2 days.
General Information: No suppressed, sex offenders, mental health, or adoption records released. Fee to fax document $1.00 each. Court makes copy: $1.00 per page. Certification fee: $10.00. Payee: Lake County Trial Court. Personal checks accepted. Major credit cards accepted via GPS. SASE not required.

Lapeer County

40th Circuit Court 255 Clay St, Lapeer, MI 48446; 810-667-0358; fax: 810-667-0264; 8AM-5PM, counter til 4:30 (EST). ***Felony, Civil Actions over $25,000, Vital Statistics.***
www.lapeercountyweb.org/court.htm
Civil Records: Access: Mail, in person. Visitors must perform in person searches themselves. Search fee: $5.00 search fee covers 10 year span. Required to search: name, years to search. Civil cases indexed by defendant, plaintiff, on computer since 1994, prior on index cards and books. Mail turnaround time 48 hours. Civil PAT goes back to 1994. PAT results show name only.
Criminal Records: Access: Mail, in person. Visitors must perform in person searches themselves. Search fee: $5.00 search fee covers 10 year span. Required to search: name, years to search; DOB. Criminal records on computer since 1996, prior on index cards and books. Mail turnaround time 48 hours. Criminal PAT goes back to 1996. PAT results show name only.
General Information: No suppressed records released. Will not fax documents. Court makes copy: $1.00 per page. Cert fee: $10.00 1st page; $1.00 per page after first. Payee: 40th Circuit Court. Personal checks accepted. Mail requests: SASE required.

71 A District Court 255 Clay St., Lapeer, MI 48446; 810-667-0314; criminal phone: x2; civil phone: x3; 8AM-5PM (EST). ***Misdemeanor, Civil Actions under $25,000, Eviction, Small Claims.***
Civil Records: Access: Mail, in person. Only the court performs in person searches; visitors may not. Search fee: $5.00 per name. Required to search: name, years to search. Civil cases indexed by defendant, plaintiff, on computer since 1992, cards and dockets from 1969. Mail turnaround 10 days.
Criminal Records: Access: Mail, in person. Only the court performs in person searches; visitors may not. Search fee: $5.00 per name. Required to search: name, years to search, DOB; also helpful: SSN. Criminal records on computer since 1992, cards and dockets from 1969. Mail turnaround time 10 days.
General Information: No suppressed, juvenile, sex offenders, mental health, or adoption records released. Will not fax documents. Court makes copy: $1.00 per page. Certification fee: $10.00 plus $1.00 per page after first. Payee: 71 A District Court. Third party checks not accepted. Visa/MC cards accepted. Credit card payments accepted via GPS. Mail requests: SASE required.

Probate Court 255 Clay St., Lapeer, MI 48446; 810-667-0261; fax: 810-667-0271; 8AM-5PM (EST). ***Probate.***

Leelanau County

13th Circuit Court 8527 E Gov't Ctr Dr, #103, Suttons Bay, MI 49682; 231-256-9824; fax: 231-256-8295; 9AM-5PM (EST). ***Felony, Civil Actions over $25,000, Vital Statistics.***
Formerly located in Leland.
Civil Records: Access: Mail, fax, in person, online. Both court and visitors may perform in person searches. Search fee: $3.00 per name. Required to search: name, years to search. Civil cases indexed by defendant, plaintiff, on computer since 1/93, prior on docket books. Mail turnaround 2-3 days. Access to a record index is at http://online.co.grand-traverse.mi.us/iprod/clerk/cccivil.html. Family court records also included.
Criminal Records: Access: Mail, fax, in person, online. Both court and visitors may perform in person searches. Search fee: $3.00 per name. Required to search: name, years to search. Criminal records on computer since 1/97; prior records on books. Mail turnaround time 2-3 days. Access to a record index is found at http://online.co.grand-traverse.mi.us/iprod/clerk/cccriminal.html. Search by name or case number to 1981.
General Information: No suppressed, juvenile, sex offenders, mental health, or adoption records released. Will fax documents $2.50 1st page, $2.50 each add'l. Court makes copy: $.50 per page. Certification fee: $10.00 plus $1.00 per page. Payee: County Clerk. Personal checks accepted; credit cards are not. Mail requests: SASE required.

86th District Court PO Box 486, 301 E Cedar St, Leland, MI 49654; 231-256-8250; criminal fax: 231-256-8275; civil fax: same; 8AM-4PM (EST). ***Misdemeanor, Civil Actions under $25,000, Eviction, Small Claims.***
www.co.leelanau.mi.us/government0254.asp
Civil Records: Access: Fax, mail, in person. Only the court performs in person searches; visitors may not. No search fee. Required to search: name, years to search. Civil cases indexed by defendant, plaintiff, on computer since 1991, prior on books to 1969. Public access terminal goes back to 1990; terminal results include DOB. Mail turnaround time 3 days.
Criminal Records: Access: Phone, fax, mail, in person. Only the court performs in person searches; visitors may not. No search fee. Required to search: name, years to search, DOB; also helpful: SSN. Criminal records on computer since 1991, prior on books to 1969. Public access terminal goes back to 1990; terminal results include DOB. Mail turnaround time 3 days.
General Information: No suppressed, sex offenders records released. Fee to fax document $.25 per page. Court makes copy: $1.00 per page. Certification fee: $10.00 per document. Payee: 86th District Court. Business checks accepted. Credit cards accepted; usage fee applies. Credit card payments accepted via GPS. Mail requests: SASE requested.

Family Court 8527 E Gov't Center Dr, #203, Suttons Bay, MI 496682; 231-256-9803; fax: 231-256-9845; 9AM-5PM (EST). ***Probate, Family.***
Formerly located in Leland.

Lenawee County

39th Circuit Court 425 N Main St, Adrian, MI 49221; 517-264-4597; fax: 517-264-4790; 8AM-4:30PM (EST). ***Felony, Civil Actions over $25,000, Vital Statistics.***
Civil Records: Access: Mail, in person. Both court and visitors may perform in person searches. Search fee: $10.00 per name. Fee is for ten years. Required to search: name, years to search. Civil cases indexed by defendant, plaintiff, on computer back to 1/89, prior on books. Mail turnaround time 1-2 days. Civil PAT goes back to 1989.
Criminal Records: Access: Mail, in person. Both court and visitors may perform in person searches. Search fee: $10.00 per name. Fee is for 10 years. Required to search: name, years to search. Criminal records computerized from 1/89, prior on books. Mail turnaround time 1-2 days. Criminal PAT goes back to same as civil.
General Information: No suppressed, juvenile, sex offenders, mental health, or adoption records released. Will fax documents. Court makes copy: $1.00 per page. Certification fee: $13.00 per doc includes copy fee. Payee: Lenawee County Clerk or 39th Circuit Court. Personal checks accepted. Mail requests: SASE helpful.

2A District Court 425 N Main St., Rex B Martin Courthouse, Adrian, MI 49221; 517-264-4668; criminal phone: 517-264-4673; civil phone: 517-264-4662; fax: 517-264-4665; 8AM-4:30PM (EST). ***Misdemeanor, Civil Actions under $25,000, Eviction, Small Claims.***
Civil and criminal indexes are separate search fees.
Civil Records: Access: Fax, mail, in person. Both court and visitors may perform in person searches. Search fee: $10.00 per name. Required to search: name, years to search. Civil cases indexed by defendant, plaintiff, on computer since 1988, prior on index books, cards and microfilm back to 1968. Mail turnaround time 2 days. Civil PAT goes back to 1987. PAT results show middle initial, DOB, SSN.
Criminal Records: Access: Fax, mail, in person. Both court and visitors may perform in person searches. Search fee: $10.00 per name. Required to search: name, years to search, DOB. Criminal records on computer since 1988, prior on index books, cards and microfilm back to 1969. Mail turnaround time 2 days. Criminal PAT goes back to 1987. PAT results show middle initial, DOB, SSN.
General Information: No suppressed, juvenile, sex offenders, mental health, or adoption records released. Will fax documents to local or toll free line. Court makes copy: $.25 per page. Certification fee: $10.00 per doc. Payee: 2A District Court. Personal checks & Visa/MC accepted. Mail requests: SASE required.

Probate Court 425 N Main St, Adrian, MI 49221; 517-264-4614; fax: 517-264-4616; 8AM-4:30PM (EST). ***Probate.***

Livingston County

44th Circuit Court 204 S Highlander Way #4, Howell, MI 48843; 517-546-9816; probate phone: 517-546-3750; criminal fax: 517-548-4219; civil fax: same; 8AM-5PM (EST). ***Felony, Civil Actions over $25,000, Vital Stats***. www.co.livingston.mi.us
Juvenile Unit records at 517-546-1500. Probate in a separate index at this same address. Probate fax- 517-552-2510
Civil Records: Access: Mail, in person, online. Both court and visitors may perform in person searches. Search fee: $6.00 record verification fee per name. Required to search: name, years to search. Civil cases indexed by defendant, plaintiff, computerized from 1987, on microfiche and archived from 1900s. Mail turnaround time 5 days. Civil PAT goes back to 1987. Access civil records online free or by subscription at https://www.livingstonlive.org/CourtRecordValidation/.
Criminal Records: Access: Mail, in person, online. Both court and visitors may perform in person searches. Search fee: $6.00 record verification fee per name. Required to search: name, years to search. Criminal records computerized from 1987, microfiche and archived from 1900s. Mail turnaround time 5 days. Criminal PAT goes back to same as civil. Access criminal records back to 1997 free or by subscription at https://www.livingstonlive.org/CourtRecordValidation/ but a DOB is required to search on the free access.
General Information: All records released, none are restricted. Will fax documents to local or toll free line. Court makes copy: $1.00 per page. Certification fee: $10.00 per document. Payee: Livingston County Clerk. Personal checks accepted if in state. Mail requests: SASE required.

53 A District Court 204 S Highlander Way #1, Howell, MI 48843; 517-548-1000; criminal phone: 517-548-1000 x7642; civil phone: 517-548-1000 x7648; fax: 517-548-9445; 8AM-5PM (EST). ***Misdemeanor, Civil Actions under $25,000, Eviction, Small Claims.***
http://co.livingston.mi.us/DistrictCourt
Civil Records: Access: Mail, in person, online. Visitors must perform in person searches themselves. No search fee. Required to search: name, years to search; also helpful: address. Civil cases indexed by defendant, plaintiff, on computer since 1982. Civil PAT goes back to 10 years. Access civil records after registration or by subscription at https://www.livingstonlive.org/CourtRecordValidation/. **Criminal Records:** Access: In person, online. Visitors must perform in person searches themselves. Required to search: name, years to search, DOB; also helpful: address, SSN. Criminal records on computer since 1982. Criminal PAT goes back to same as civil. The PAT here also has Brighton records. Access criminal records back to 1997 after registration or by subscription at https://www.livingstonlive.org/CourtRecordValidation/ but a DOB is required to search on the free access. **General Information:** No suppressed, juvenile, sex offenders, mental health, or adoption records released. Will fax documents to local or toll-

free number. Court makes copy: $1.00 per page. Certification fee: $10.00. Payee: 53 District Court. Personal checks accepted. Major Major credit cards accepted via GPS. SASE not required.

53 B District Court 224 N1st St, Brighton, MI 48116; 810-229-6615; criminal phone: x6; civil phone: x7; fax: 810-229-1770; 8-11:30AM, 1:30-5PM (EST). ***Misdemeanor, Civil Actions under $25,000, Eviction, Small Claims.***
http://co.livingston.mi.us/DistrictCourt/brighton.htm
This Brighton Court's records also appear on the Howell Division public access terminals.
Civil Records: Access: Mail, in person, online. Only the court performs in person searches; visitors may not. No search fee. Required to search: name, years to search. Civil cases indexed by defendant, plaintiff, on computer since 1985, prior on index books. Mail turnaround time 1 week. Civil PAT goes back to 10 years. Access civil records after registration or by subscription at https://www.livingstonlive.org/CourtRecordValidation/.
Criminal Records: Access: In person, online. Visitors must perform in person searches themselves. Required to search: name, years to search, DOB; also helpful: SSN. Criminal records on computer since 1985, prior on index books. Criminal PAT goes back to same as civil. Access criminal records back to 1997 after registration or by subscription at https://www.livingstonlive.org/CourtRecordValidation/ but a DOB is required to search on the free access.
General Information: No suppressed, juvenile, sex offenders, mental health, or adoption records released. Will not fax documents. Court makes copy: $1.00 per page. Certification fee: $10.00. Payee: 53rd District Court. Personal checks accepted. Credit card payments accepted via GPS. Mail requests: SASE required for civil.

Probate Court 204 S. Highlander Way #2, Howell, MI 48843; 517-546-3750; fax: 517-552-2510; 8AM-5PM (EST). ***Probate.***
www.co.livingston.mi.us/probatecourt/

Luce County

11th Circuit Court 407 W Harrie, Newberry, MI 49868; 906-293-5521; probate phone: 906-293-5601; fax: 906-293-5553; 8AM-4PM (EST). ***Felony, Civil Actions over $25,000, Vital Statistics.***
Civil Records: Access: Mail, in person. Only the court performs in person searches; visitors may not. No search fee. Required to search: name, years to search. Civil cases indexed by defendant, plaintiff, on cards since 1876. Mail turnaround 4-5 days.
Criminal Records: Access: Mail, in person. Only the court performs in person searches; visitors may not. No search fee. Required to search: name, years to search, DOB. Criminal records listed on cards since 1876. Mail turnaround time 4-5 days.
General Information: No suppressed, juvenile, sex offenders, mental health, or adoption records released. Will fax documents $1.00 per page plus $1.00 fax fee. Court makes copy: $1.00 per page. Certification fee: $10.00. Payee: 11th Circuit Court. Personal checks accepted. Credit card payments accepted via GPS. Mail requests: SASE required.

92nd District Court 407 W Harrie, Newberry, MI 49868; 906-293-5531; fax: 906-293-5773; 8AM-4PM (EST). ***Misdemeanor, Civil Actions under $25,000, Eviction, Small Claims.***
Civil Records: Access: Phone, fax, mail, in person. Only the court performs in person searches; visitors may not. No search fee. Required to search: name, years to search. Civil cases indexed by defendant, plaintiff, to 1969, some on computer. Mail turnaround time 1 week.
Criminal Records: Access: Phone, fax, mail, in person. Only the court performs in person searches; visitors may not. No search fee. Required to search: name, years to search, DOB; also helpful: SSN. Criminal records to 1969, some on computer. Mail turnaround time 1 week.
General Information: Will fax documents $1.00 per page. Court makes copy: $1.00 per page. Certification fee: $10.00. Payee: 92nd District Court. In state personal checks accepted. Credit card payments accepted via GPS. Government Payment Services plan participant. Mail requests: SASE preferred.

Probate Court 407 W. Harrie, Newberry, MI 49868; 906-293-5601; fax: 906-293-3581; 8AM-N, 1-4PM (EST). ***Probate.*** This is a combined court with Mackinac County Probate Court.

Mackinac County

11th Circuit Court 100 S Marley St, Rm 10, St Ignace, MI 49781; 906-643-7300; fax: 906-643-7302; 8:30AM-4:30PM (EST). ***Felony, Civil Actions over $25,000, Vital Statistics.***
Civil Records: Access: Mail, in person. Only the court performs in person searches; visitors may not. Search fee: $10.00. Required to search: name, years to search. Civil cases indexed by defendant, plaintiff, on docket book; on computer back to 1998. Mail turnaround time 10 days.
Criminal Records: Access: Mail, in person. Only the court performs in person searches; visitors may not. Search fee: $10.00. Required to search: name, years to search, DOB. Criminal records on docket book; on computer back to 1998. Mail turnaround time 10 days.
General Information: No suppressed, juvenile, sex offenders, mental health, or adoption records released. Will not fax documents. Court makes copy: $1.00 per page. Cert fee: $10.00 per cert. Payee: County Clerk. Personal checks okay. Mail request: SASE required.

92nd District Court 100 S Marley, Rm 55, St Ignace, MI 49781; 906-643-7321; fax: 906-643-7326; 8:30AM-4:30PM (EST). ***Misdemeanor, Civil Actions under $25,000, Eviction, Small Claims.***
Civil Records: Access: Mail, in person, fax, phone. Visitors must perform in person searches themselves. No search fee. Required to search: name, years to search. Civil cases indexed by defendant. Civil records on computer since 11/92, prior in files to 1969.
Criminal Records: Access: Fax, mail, in person. Visitors must perform in person searches themselves. No search fee. Required to search: name, years to search, DOB. Criminal records on computer since 11/92, prior in files to 1969. Mail turnaround time 1 week.
General Information: No suppressed, juvenile, sex offenders, mental health, or adoption records released. Will fax documents $10.00 per name. Court makes copy: $1.00 per page. Certification fee: $10.00. Payee: 92nd District Court. Personal checks accepted. Credit card payments accepted via GPS, pay location code 1432. Mail requests: SASE required.

Probate Court 100 S Marley St Rm. 15, St Ignace, MI 49781; 906-643-7303; fax: 906-643-8861; 8:30AM-N, 1-4:30PM (EST). ***Probate.***
This is a combined court with Luce County Probate.

Macomb County

16th Circuit Court 40 N Main St, Mount Clemens, MI 48043; 586-469-5351; fax: 586-783-8184; 8AM-4:30PM (EST). ***Felony, Civil Actions over $25,000, Vital Statistics.***
www.macombcountymi.gov/clerksoffice/
Civil Records: Access: Mail, fax, in person, online. Both court and visitors may perform in person searches. No search fee. Required to search: name or case number. Civil cases indexed by defendant, plaintiff, on computer since 1977, on microfiche to 1969, prior to 1800s archived. Mail turnaround time 1 week. Civil PAT goes back to 1980. PAT results show name only. Civil online access is the same as criminal, see below. Online records include divorces.
Criminal Records: Access: Mail, fax, in person, online. Both court and visitors may perform in person searches. No search fee. Required to search: name or case number. Criminal records on computer since 1970, on microfiche to 1969, prior to 1800s archived. Mail turnaround time 1 week. Criminal PAT goes back to same as civil. PAT criminal results show middle initial. Access Circuit Court index for free at http://macombcountymi.gov/pa/. Fee for full records and copies. Online results show middle initial.
General Information: Online identifiers in results same as on public terminal. No suppressed, juvenile, sex offenders, mental health, or adoption records released. Will fax documents $10.00 plus $1.00 per page. Court makes copy: $.40 per page. Certification fee: $10.00 per doc plus $1.00 per page. Payee: Macomb County Clerk. Personal checks and major credit cards accepted. Mail requests: SASE required.

37th District Court - Center Line 7070 E Ten Mile Rd, Center Line, MI 48015; 586-757-8333; fax: 586-759-9611; 8:30AM-4:30PM (EST). ***Misdemeanor, Civil Actions under $25,000, Eviction, Small Claims.*** http://37thdistrictcourt.net/
Shares 37th District with Warren. Each court has to be searched separately.
Civil Records: Access: Mail, in person. Only the court performs in person searches; visitors may not. Search fee: $10.00 per name. Required to search: name, years to search. Civil cases indexed by defendant, plaintiff, on computer since 1992, prior on index cards. Mail turnaround time 2 weeks.
Criminal Records: Access: Mail, in person, fax. Only the court performs in person searches; visitors may not. Search fee: $10.00 per name. Required to search: name, years to search, DOB; also helpful: SSN. Criminal records on computer since 1992, prior on index cards. Mail turnaround 2 wks.
General Information: No suppressed, juvenile, sex offenders, mental health, or adoption records released. Will not fax documents. Court makes copy: $1.00 per page. Certification fee: $10.00. Payee: 37th District Court. Personal checks and major credit cards accepted. No credit cards accepted for bonds. SASE not required.

37th District Court - Warren 8300 Common Rd., Warren, MI 48093; 586-574-4900; fax: 586-574-4932; 8:30AM-4:30PM (EST). ***Misdemeanor, Civil Actions under $25,000, Eviction, Small Claims.***
http://37thdistrictcourt.net/
Shares 37th District with Center Line. Each court has to be searched separately.
Civil Records: Access: Mail, in person. Only the court performs in person searches; visitors may not. Search fee: $10.00 per name. Required to search: name, years to search. Civil cases indexed by defendant, plaintiff, on computer since 1992, prior on index cards. Mail turnaround time 2 weeks.
Criminal Records: Access: Mail, in person, fax. Only the court performs in person searches; visitors may not. Search fee: $10.00 per name. Required to search: name, years to search, DOB; also helpful: SSN. Criminal records on computer since '92, prior on index cards. Mail turnaround 2 weeks.
General Information: No suppressed, juvenile, sex offenders, mental health, or adoption records released. Will not fax documents. Court makes copy: $1.00 per page. Certification fee: $10.00. Payee: 37th District Court. Personal checks and major credit cards accepted. SASE not required.

38th District Court - Eastpointe 16101 Nine Mile Rd, Eastpointe, MI 48021; 586-445-5020; fax: 586-445-5060; 8AM-4:30PM (EST). ***Misdemeanor, Civil Actions under $25,000, Eviction, Small Claims.*** www.38thdistrictcourt.org/
Civil Records: Access: Mail, in person, online. Both court and visitors may perform in person searches. No search fee. Required to search: name, years to search. Civil cases indexed by defendant, plaintiff, on computer since 1996, prior on index cards. Mail turnaround time 10 days. Civil PAT goes back to 1997. PAT results show name only. Name look-ups free at https://secure.courts.michigan.gov/jis/
Criminal Records: Access: Mail, in person, online. Both court and visitors may perform in person searches. No search fee. Required to search: name, years to search, DOB. Criminal records on computer since 1996, prior on index cards. Mail turnaround time 10 days. Criminal PAT goes back to 1997. Access name look-ups at https://secure.courts.michigan.gov/jis/ Online results show name only.
General Information: No suppressed, sex offenders, mental health records released. Will fax documents to local or toll-free number. Court makes copy: $.25 per page. Certification fee: $10.00. Payee: 38th District Court. Personal checks accepted. Major credit cards accepted via GPS. Mail requests: SASE required.

39th B District Court - Fraser PO Box 10, 33000 Garfield, Fraser, MI 48026; 586-293-3137; fax: 586-296-8499; 8AM-4:30PM ***Misdemeanor, Infractions.*** www.macombcountymi.gov/district_court/court39b.htm
All civil actions, eviction, and small claims cases now handled by 39-A District Court in Roseville.
Criminal Records: Access: Mail, in person. Only the court performs in person searches; visitors may not. No search fee. Required to search: name, years to search, DOB; also helpful: SSN. Criminal records on computer since 1988, prior on microfilm. Mail turnaround time 1-2 days.
General Information: No suppressed, juvenile, sex offenders, mental health, or adoption records released. Will fax documents to local or toll-free number. Court makes copy: $1.00 per page, $2.00 if on microfilm. Certification fee: $10.00 per doc. Payee: 39th District Court. Personal checks accepted. Credit card payments accepted via GPS. SASE not required.

39th District Court - Roseville 29733 Gratiot Ave, Roseville, MI 48066; 586-773-2010; criminal phone: 586-447-4430; civil phone: 586-447-4420; criminal fax: 586-445-5070; civil fax: same; 8AM-4:30PM (EST). ***Misdemeanor, Civil Actions under $25,000, Eviction, Small Claims.***
www.macombcountymi.gov/district_court/index.htm
All civil actions, eviction, and small claims cases from the Fraser location are now located here.
Civil Records: Access: Mail, in person. Only the court performs in person searches; visitors may not. No search fee. Required to search: name, years to search. Civil cases indexed by defendant, plaintiff, on computer since 1985, prior on microfilm. Mail turnaround time 1-2 days.
Criminal Records: Access: Mail, in person. Only the court performs in person searches; visitors may not. No search fee. Required to search: name, years to search, DOB; also helpful: SSN. Criminal records on computer since 1985, prior on microfilm. Mail turnaround time 1-2 days.
General Information: No suppressed, juvenile, sex offenders, mental health, or adoption records released. Will fax documents to local or toll-free number. Court makes copy: $1.00 per page, $2.00 if on microfilm. No certification fee. Payee: 39th District Court. Personal checks accepted; credit cards are not. SASE not required.

40th District Court - St. Clair Shores 27701 Jefferson, St. Clair Shores, MI 48081; 586-445-5280; criminal phone: 586-445-5281; civil phone: 586-445-5282; fax: 586-445-4003; 8:30AM-4:30PM (EST). ***Misdemeanor, Civil Actions under $25,000, Eviction, Small Claims.*** http://macombcountymi.gov/district_court/court40.htm
Civil Records: Access: Mail, in person. Visitors must perform in person searches themselves. Search fee: $10.00 per name. Required to search: name, years to search. Civil cases indexed by defendant, plaintiff, on computer since 1991; prior records on index books. Note: The court has a request form that must be used with all searches. Mail turnaround time 2 weeks.
Criminal Records: Access: Mail, in person, fax. Only the court performs in person searches; visitors may not. Search fee: $10.00 per name. Required to search: name, years to search, DOB; also helpful: SSN. Criminal records on computer since 1991; prior records on index books. Note: Mail requests must have case number. The court has a request form that must be used with all searches. Mail turnaround time 2 weeks.
General Information: No suppressed, juvenile, sex offenders, mental health, or adoption records released. Will not fax documents. Court makes copy: $1.00 per page. Cert fee: $10.00 per certification. Payee: 40th District Court. Personal checks accepted. Credit card payments accepted via GPS. SASE not required.

41 A District Court - Shelby 51660 Van Dyke, Shelby Township, MI 48316; 586-739-7325; criminal phone: 586-739-7325 x5; civil phone: 586-739-7325 x6; fax: 586-726-4555; 8AM-Noon; 1-4PM (EST). ***Misdemeanor, Civil Actions under $25,000, Eviction, Small Claims.***
www.macombcountymi.gov/district_court/index.htm
Serving Macomb Township, Shelby Township, Utica.
Civil Records: Access: Mail, in person. Both court and visitors may perform in person searches. No search fee. Required to search: name, years to search. Civil cases indexed by defendant, plaintiff, on computer since 1992, prior on index cards. Civil PAT goes back to 1997. Public terminal available M,T,TH from 9AM-1PM/1 hour limit.
Criminal Records: Access: Mail, in person. Both court and visitors may perform in person searches. No search fee. Required to search: name, years to search, DOB. Criminal records on computer since 1992, prior on index cards. Criminal PAT goes back to same as civil. Public terminal available M,T,TH from 9AM-1PM/1 hour limit.
General Information: No suppressed, sex offenders, mental health records released. Will fax documents to local or toll-free number. Court makes copy: $1.00 per page. Certification fee: $10.00 1st page, $1.00 each add'l page. Payee: 41A District Court. Personal checks accepted. Visa/MC accepted.

41 A District Court - Sterling Heights 40111 Dodge Park, Sterling Heights, MI 48313; 586-446-2500; criminal phone: 586-446-2550; civil phone: 586-446-2535; fax: 586-276-4074; 8:30AM-4:30PM (EST). ***Misdemeanor, Civil Actions under $25,000, Eviction, Small Claims.***
www.macombcountymi.gov/district_court/index.htm
Civil Records: Access: Mail, in person. Only the court performs in person searches; visitors may not. No search fee. Required to search: name, years to search. Civil cases indexed by defendant, plaintiff, on computer since 1992; prior records on books. Mail turnaround time 1 week.
Criminal Records: Access: Mail, in person. Only the court performs in person searches; visitors may not. No search fee. Required to search: name, years to search, DOB; also helpful: SSN. Criminal records on computer since 1986; prior records on books. Mail turnaround time 1 week.
General Information: No suppressed, juvenile, sex offenders, mental health, or adoption records released. Will fax documents to local or toll-free number. Court makes copy: $1.00 per page. Certification fee: $10.00. Payee: 41A District Court. Personal checks accepted. Credit card payments may be accepted via GPS but not at court. Mail requests: SASE required.

41 B District Court 22380 Starks Dr, Clinton Township, MI 48036; 586-469-9300; fax: 586-469-1651; 8:30AM-4:30PM (EST). ***Misdemeanor, Civil Actions under $25,000, Eviction, Small Claims, Traffic.*** www.41bdistrictcourt.com/
Serving Clinton Township, Harrison Township, Mount Clemens. Civil records at the Mount Clemens location are now here.
Criminal Records: Access: In person only. Both court and visitors may perform in person searches. No search fee. Required to search: name, years to search, DOB. Criminal records computerized from 1996, prior on microfilm to 1970s. Public use terminal has crim records back to 1996. PAT results show middle initial, DOB.
General Information: No suppressed, juvenile, sex offenders, mental health, or adoption records released. Will not fax documents. Court makes copy: $.50 per page. Certification fee: $10.00. Payee: 41 B District Court. Personal or cashiers checks and money orders accepted. Visa/MC accepted. Credit card payments accepted via GPS.

42nd District Court Division 1 PO Box 6, 14713 Thirty-three Mile Rd, Romeo, MI 48065; 586-752-9679; fax: 586-752-1906; 8:30AM-4:45PM (EST). ***Misdemeanor, Civil Actions under $25,000, Eviction, Small Claims.***
www.macombcountymi.gov/district_court/index.htm
Serving Armada and Armada Township, Bruce Township, Memphis, Ray Township, Richmond and Richmond Township, Romeo, Washington Township.
Civil Records: Access: Mail, in person. Only the court performs in person searches; visitors may not. Search fee: $10.00 per name. Required to search: name, years to search. Civil cases indexed by defendant, plaintiff, on computer since 1990, prior on index books. Mail turnaround time 2-3 days.
Criminal Records: Access: Mail, in person. Only the court performs in person searches; visitors may not. Search fee: $10.00 per name. Required to search: name, years to search, DOB; also helpful: SSN, sex, signed release. Criminal records on computer since 1990, prior on index books. Mail turnaround time 2-3 days.
General Information: Will not fax documents. Court makes copy: $.35 per page. Certification fee: $10.00. Payee: 42-1 District Court. Personal checks accepted. Visa/MC accepted; Call ahead for instructions. Credit card payments accepted via GPS. Mail requests: SASE requested.

42nd District Court Division 2 35071 Twenty-three Mile Rd, New Baltimore, MI 48047; 586-725-9500; criminal phone: 586-469-5046; civil phone: 586-493-0567; criminal fax: 586-725-1404; civil fax: same; 8:30AM-5PM (EST). ***Misdemeanor, Civil Actions under $25,000, Eviction, Small Claims.***
www.macombcountymi.gov/district_court/index.htm
Includes City of New Baltimore, Village of New Haven, and townships of Lenox and Chesterfield.
Civil Records: Access: Mail, in person. Only the court performs in person searches; visitors may not. No search fee. Required to search: name, years to search. Civil cases indexed by defendant, plaintiff, on computer back to 1990. Mail turnaround time 1 week. Civil PAT goes back to 1990.
Criminal Records: Access: Mail, in person. Only the court performs in person searches; visitors may not. No search fee. Required to search: name, years to search, DOB; also helpful: SSN. Criminal records computerized from 1990. Mail turnaround time 1 week. Criminal PAT goes back to 1990.
General Information: Will fax case file $.50 per page. Court makes copy: $1.00 per page. Certification fee: $10.00 per doc includes copies. Payee: 42nd District Court. No Personal checks and major credit cards accepted. Prepayment of mail search required. Mail requests: SASE required.

41 B District Court - Mt Clemens, MI; ***Civil Actions under $25,000, Eviction, Small Claims.***
Court combined with 41 B District Ct - Clinton TWP.

Probate Court 21850 Dunham Rd, Mount Clemens, MI 48043-1075; 586-469-5290; fax: 586-783-0971; 8:30AM-4:30PM (EST). ***Probate.***
www.macombcountymi.gov

Manistee County

19th Circuit Court 415 3rd St, Manistee, MI 49660; 231-723-3331; criminal fax: 231-723-1492; civil fax: same; 8:30AM-5PM (EST). ***Felony, Civil Actions over $25,000, Vital Statistics.***
Civil Records: Access: Mail, in person. Only the court performs in person searches; visitors may not. Search fee: $5.00 per name. Required to search: name, years to search. Civil cases indexed by defendant, plaintiff, on computer since 7/90, index books from 1867. Mail turnaround time 2-3 days.
Criminal Records: Access: Mail, in person. Only the court performs in person searches; visitors may not. Search fee: $5.00 per name. Required to search: name, years to search, DOB. Criminal records on computer since 7/90, index books from 1867. Mail turnaround time 2-3 days.
General Information: No suppressed, juvenile, sex offenders, mental health, or adoption records released. Will fax documents $2.00 per page. Court makes copy: $.50 per page. Certification fee: $13.00 1st page, includes copy fee. Add $2.00 each add'l page. Payee: Manistee County Clerk. Personal checks accepted. SASE not required.

85th District Court 415 3rd St, Manistee, MI 49660; 231-723-5010; criminal fax: 231-723-1491; civil fax: same; 8:30AM-N, 1-5PM (EST). ***Misdemeanor, Civil Actions under $25,000, Eviction, Small Claims.*** www.manisteecounty.net
Civil Records: Access: Fax, mail, in person. Both court and visitors may perform in person searches. Search fee: $5.00 per name. Required to search: name, years to search. Civil cases indexed by defendant, plaintiff, on computer since 4/89, prior on index books. Mail turnaround time 21 days maximum. Civil PAT goes back to 4/1989. PAT results show name only.
Criminal Records: Access: Fax, mail, in person. Both court and visitors may perform in person searches. Search fee: $5.00 per name. Required to

search: name, years to search, DOB. Criminal records on computer since 4/89, prior on index books. Mail turnaround time 5-7 days; 21 days max. Criminal PAT goes back to same as civil.PAT results show name, DOB.
General Information: No suppressed, juvenile, sex offenders, mental health, or adoption records released. Will fax documents no fee. Court makes copy: $1.00 per page. Certification fee: $10.00 per document. Payee: 85th District Court. Personal checks accepted; credit cards are not. Mail requests: SASE required.

Probate Court 415 3rd St, Manistee, MI 49660; 231-723-3261; fax: 231-398-3558; 8:30AM-N, 1-5PM (EST). ***Probate.*** http://manisteecounty.net/

Marquette County

25th Circuit Court 234 W Baraga Ave, Marquette, MI 49855; 906-225-8330; fax: 906-228-1572; 8AM-5PM (EST). ***Felony, Civil Actions over $25,000, Vital Statistics.***
Civil Records: Access: Mail, in person. Only the court performs in person searches; visitors may not. Search fee: $10.00 per name. Required to search: name, years to search. Civil cases indexed by defendant, plaintiff, on books since 1852, on computer from 4/95. Mail turnaround time 1-2 days.
Criminal Records: Access: Mail, in person. Only the court performs in person searches; visitors may not. Search fee: $10.00 per name. Required to search: name, years to search, DOB. Criminal docket on books since 1852, on computer from 4/95. Mail turnaround time 1-2 days.
General Information: No suppressed, juvenile, sex offenders, mental health, or adoption records released. Will fax documents to local or toll free line. Court makes copy: $1.00 per page. Certification fee: $10.00 plus $1.00 per page. Payee: County Clerk. Personal checks accepted; credit cards are not. SASE not required.

96th District Court County Courthouse, Marquette, MI 49855; 906-225-8235; fax: 906-225-8255; 8AM-5PM (EST). ***Misdemeanor, Civil Actions under $25,000, Eviction, Small Claims.***
Civil Records: Access: Fax, mail, in person. Only the court performs in person searches; visitors may not. Search fee: $5.00 per name by mail, $10.00 by fax. Required to search: name, years to search; also helpful: address. Civil cases indexed by defendant, plaintiff, on computer since 1995, prior on docket books and microfiche. Mail turnaround 1-2 weeks.
Criminal Records: Access: Fax, mail, in person. Only the court performs in person searches; visitors may not. Search fee: $5.00 per name by mail, $10.00 by fax. Required to search: name, years to search, DOB. Criminal records on computer since 1995, prior on docket books and microfiche. Mail turnaround time 1-2 weeks.
General Information: No suppressed records released. Will fax documents for add'l $5.00 fee. Court makes copy: $1.00 per page. Certification fee: $10.00 plus $1.00 per page after first. Payee: 96th District Court. Business checks accepted. Credit cards accepted, extra fees involved. Credit card payments accepted via GPS. Mail requests: SASE required.

Probate Court 234 W Baraga, Marquette, MI 49855; 906-225-8300; fax: 906-228-1533; 8AM-5PM (EST). ***Probate.*** Copy fee is $1.00 per page.

Mason County

51st Circuit Court 304 E Ludington Ave, Ludington, MI 49431; 231-845-1445; fax: 231-843-1972; 8AM-5PM (EST). ***Felony, Civil Actions over $25,000, Vital Statistics.***
Civil Records: Access: Phone, fax, mail, in person. Only the court performs in person searches; visitors may not. No search fee. Required to search: name, years to search. Civil cases indexed by defendant, plaintiff, on file since 1867. Mail turnaround time 1 week.
Criminal Records: Access: Phone, fax, mail, in person. Only the court performs in person searches; visitors may not. No search fee. Required to search: name, years to search, DOB. Criminal records on file since 1867. Mail turnaround time 1 week.
General Information: No suppressed, juvenile, sex offenders, mental health, or adoption records released. Court makes copy: $1.00 per page, but can vary w/type of doc, self serve same. Certification fee: $10.00 per doc. Payee: Mason County Clerk. Personal checks accepted. Credit card payments accepted via GPS. Prepayment of mail service required. Mail requests: SASE required.

79th District Court County Court, 304 E Ludington Ave, Ludington, MI 49431; 231-843-4130; fax: 231-845-9076; 9AM-5PM (EST). ***Misdemeanor, Civil Actions under $25,000, Eviction, Small Claims.***
Civil Records: Access: In person only. Only the court performs in person searches; visitors may not. No search fee. Required to search: name, years to search. Civil cases indexed by defendant, plaintiff, on Register of Action Cards since 1969, computerized since 10/96. Civil PAT goes back to 1996.
Criminal Records: Access: In person only. Only the court performs in person searches; visitors may not. No search fee. Required to search: name, years to search, DOB. Criminal records on Register of Action Docket Cards since 1969, computerized since 10/96. Criminal PAT goes back to 1996.
General Information: No suppressed, juvenile, sex offenders, mental health, or adoption records released. No fee to fax documents locally only. Court makes copy: $1.00 per page. Certification fee: $10.00 plus $1.00 per page after first. Payee: 79th District Court. Only cashiers checks and money orders accepted. Credit card payments accepted via GPS.

Probate Court 304 E Ludington Ave, Ludington, MI 49431; 231-843-8666; fax: 231-843-1972; 9AM-N, 1-5PM (EST). ***Probate.***

Mecosta County

49th Circuit Court 400 Elm, Big Rapids, MI 49307; 231-592-0783; fax: 231-592-0193; 8:30AM-5PM (EST). ***Felony, Civil Actions over $25,000, Vital Statistics.***
www.co.mecosta.mi.us/circuit.asp
Vital records available at www.co.mecosta.mi.us/clerk.asp for a fee.
Civil Records: Access: Fax, mail, in person. Only the court performs in person searches; visitors may not. Search fee: $5.00 per name. Required to search: name, years to search. Civil cases indexed by defendant, plaintiff, on computer since 10/70, archived and microfiche since 1900s. Mail turnaround time 1 week.
Criminal Records: Access: Fax, mail, in person. Only the court performs in person searches; visitors may not. Search fee: $5.00 per name. Required to search: name, years to search. Criminal records on computer since 10/70, archived and microfiche since 1900s. Mail turnaround 1 week.
General Information: No suppressed, juvenile, mental health, or adoption records released. Will fax documents to local or toll free line. Court makes copy: $1.00 per page. Certification fee: $10.00 per page includes copy fee. Payee: Mecosta County Clerk. No personal checks; money orders and cashiers checks preferred. Mail requests: SASE required.

77th District Court 400 Elm, Big Rapids, MI 49307; 231-592-0799; civil phone: 231-592-0796; fax: 231-796-2180; 8:30AM-4:30PM (EST). ***Misdemeanor, Civil Actions under $25,000, Eviction, Small Claims.***
Civil Records: Access: Mail, fax, in person. Only the court performs in person searches; visitors may not. Search fee: $5.00 per name. Required to search: name, years to search. Civil cases indexed by defendant, plaintiff, on computer to 1995. Mail turnaround time 7 days.
Criminal Records: Access: Mail, in person. Only the court performs in person searches; visitors may not. Search fee: $5.00 per name. Required to search: name, years to search, DOB. Criminal records on computer for 10 years, archived and microfiche prior. Note: Signed release required if request is for employment screening purposes. Mail turnaround time 7 days.
General Information: No suppressed, juvenile, sex offenders, mental health, or adoption records released. Will fax documents to local or toll free line. Court makes copy: $1.00 per page. Certification fee: $10.00. Payee: 77th District Court. Business checks accepted. Major credit cards accepted via GPS. Mail requests: SASE required.

Probate Court 400 Elm St, Big Rapids, MI 49307; 231-592-0135; fax: 231-592-0191; 8:30AM-5PM T,TH,F (EST). ***Probate.*** www.co.mecosta.mi.us/probate.asp Shares the same judge with Osceola County Probate Court.

Menominee County

41st Circuit Court 839 10th Ave, Menominee, MI 49858; 906-863-9968; criminal fax: 906-863-8839; civil fax: same; 8AM-4:30PM (CST). ***Felony, Civil Actions over $25,000, Vital Statistics.***
www.menomineecounty.com/
Civil Records: Access: Mail, in person. Only the court performs in person searches; visitors may not. Search fee: $1.00 per year per person (as plaintiff or defendant). Required to search: name, years to search. Civil cases indexed by defendant, plaintiff, kept by docket entry in file folders, archived to 1900, computerized since 1998. Mail turnaround 2-3 days.
Criminal Records: Access: Mail, in person. Only the court performs in person searches; visitors may not. Search fee: $5.00 per person for the first 5 years (minimum search), $1.00 each add'l year. Required to search: name, years to search, DOB; also helpful: SSN. Criminal records kept by docket entry in file folders to 1900; on computer back to 1998. Mail turnaround time 2-3 days.
General Information: No suppressed, juvenile, sex offenders, mental health, or adoption records released. Will fax documents for no fee. Court makes copy: $1.00 per page. Certification fee: $10.00 per document. Payee: 41st Circuit Court. Personal checks accepted. Credit card payments accepted via GPS.

95 A District Court 839 10th Ave, Menominee, MI 49858; 906-863-8532; criminal fax: 906-863-2023; civil fax: same; 8AM-4:30PM (CST). ***Misdemeanor, Civil Actions under $25,000, Eviction, Small Claims.***
Civil Records: Access: Fax, mail, in person. Only the court performs in person searches; visitors may not. Search fee: $5.00 per name. Required to search: name, years to search. Civil cases indexed by defendant, plaintiff; index on docket books since 1969. Mail turnaround time 1 week.
Criminal Records: Access: Fax, mail, in person. Only the court performs in person searches; visitors may not. Search fee: $5.00 per name. Required to search: name, years to search, DOB. Criminal records indexed in books since 1969. Mail turnaround time 1 week.
General Information: No suppressed, juvenile, sex offenders, mental health, or adoption records released. Will fax documents $.20 per page. Court makes copy: $.25 per page. Certification fee: $10.00. Payee: District Court 95A. Personal checks accepted; credit cards are not. Mail requests: SASE required for mail return of any copies.

Probate Court 839 10th Ave., Menominee, MI 49858; 906-863-2634; fax: 906-863-9904; 8AM-4:30PM (CST). ***Probate, Juvenile.***

Midland County

42nd Circuit Court Courthouse, 301 W Main St, Midland, MI 48640; 989-832-6735; fax: 989-832-6610; 8AM-5PM (EST). ***Felony, Civil Actions over $25,000, Vital Statistics.***
http://co.midland.mi.us/departments/home.php?id=4
Civil Records: Access: Phone, mail, in person. Only the court performs in person searches; visitors may not. Search fee: $5.00 per name. Required to search: name, years to search. Civil cases indexed by defendant, plaintiff, on computer from 1985, prior on books since 1800s. Mail turnaround time same day. Search court calendars free at http://co.midland.mi.us/court_calendar.php.
Criminal Records: Access: Phone, mail, in person. Only the court performs in person searches; visitors may not. Search fee: $5.00 per name. Required to search: name, years to search, DOB. Criminal records computerized from 1985, prior on books since 1800s. Mail turnaround time same day. Search court calendars free at http://co.midland.mi.us/court_calendar.php.

General Information: No suppressed records released. Will fax documents $1.00 per page. Court makes copy: $1.00 per page. Certification fee: $15.00 plus $1.00 per page. Payee: Clerk of Circuit Court. Personal checks accepted. Visa/MC accepted. Credit card payments accepted via GPS. Mail requests: SASE required.

75th District Court - Criminal Division 301 W Main St, Midland, MI 48640-5183; 989-832-6702 (6714-traffic); criminal phone: 989-832-6718; fax: 989-832-6601; 8:30AM-5PM (EST). ***Misdemeanor.***
Criminal Records: Access: Mail, in person. Only the court performs in person searches; visitors may not. Search fee: $5.00 per name per year (includes cert if asked for). Required to search: name, years to search, DOB. Criminal records on computer since 1991, prior on docket books and paper index. Mail turnaround time 1 week. Search court calendars free at http://co.midland.mi.us/court_calendar.php.
General Information: No suppressed, sex offenders or mental health records released. Will fax documents. Court makes copy: $1.00 per page after 5 pages. Certification fee: $5.00 per name. Payee: 75th District Court. Personal checks accepted. Credit card payments accepted via GPS. SASE not required.

75th District Court - Civil Division 301 W Main St, Midland, MI 48640; 989-832-6701; 8:30AM-5PM (EST). ***Civil Actions under $25,000, Eviction, Small Claims.***
Small Claims can be reached at 989-832-6717.
Civil Records: Access: Mail, in person. Both court and visitors may perform in person searches. Search fee: $1.00 per name per year. Required to search: name, years to search; also helpful: address. Civil cases indexed by defendant, plaintiff, on computer since 6/89; on index books until 6/89. Mail turnaround time 5-7 days.
General Information: No suppressed, juvenile, sex offenders, mental health, or adoption records released. Will not fax documents. Court makes copy: $1.00 per page. Certification fee: $10.00 1st page, $1.00 each add'l. Payee: 75th District Court. Personal checks accepted. Credit card payments accepted via GPS. Credit card payments accepted for criminal & traffic only. Mail requests: SASE required.

Probate Court 301 W Main St, Midland, MI 48640; 989-832-6880; fax: 989-832-6607; 8AM-5PM (EST). ***Probate.***
http://co.midland.mi.us/departments/home.php?id=23
Search court calendars free at http://co.midland.mi.us/court_calendar.php.

Missaukee County

28th Circuit Court PO Box 800, Lake City, MI 49651; 231-839-4967; criminal fax: 231-839-3684; civil fax: same; 9AM-5PM (EST). ***Felony, Civil Actions over $25,000, Vital Statistics.***
www.missaukee.org/court.htm?
Civil Records: Access: Phone, fax, mail, in person. Both court and visitors may perform in person searches. Search fee: $5.00 per name. Required to search: name, years to search. Civil cases indexed by defendant, plaintiff, on computer since 1965, prior on books. Mail turnaround time 2 days. Civil PAT goes back to 1965. PAT results show name only.
Criminal Records: Access: Phone, fax, mail, in person. Both court and visitors may perform in person searches. Search fee: $5.00 per name. Required to search: name, years to search; also helpful: DOB, SSN. Criminal records on computer since 1988, prior on books. Mail turnaround time 2 days. Criminal PAT goes back to 1988. PAT results show name only.
General Information: No suppressed, juvenile, sex offenders, mental health, or adoption records released. Will fax documents $5.00 1st page, $1.00 each add'l. Court makes copy: $1.00 per page. Self serve: available. Certification fee: $10.00 per document. Payee: Missaukee County Clerk. Personal checks accepted. Credit card payments accepted via GPS. Mail requests: SASE required.

84th District Court PO Box 800, Lake City, MI 49651; criminal phone: 231-839-5851; civil phone: 231-839-4590; fax: 231-839-8821; 9AM-5PM (EST). ***Misdemeanor, Civil Actions under $25,000, Eviction, Small Claims.***
Civil Records: Access: Fax, mail, in person. Only the court performs in person searches; visitors may not. Search fee: $5.00 per name. Required to search: name, years to search. Civil cases indexed by defendant, plaintiff, on computer since 1989. Mail turnaround time 1 week.
Criminal Records: Access: Fax, mail, in person. Only the court performs in person searches; visitors may not. No search fee. Required to search: name, years to search, DOB, SSN. Criminal records on computer since 1988. Mail turnaround 1 week.
General Information: No suppressed, juvenile, sex offenders, mental health, or adoption records released. Will fax documents to local or toll free line. Court makes copy: $1.00 per page. Certification fee: $10.00 plus $1.00 per page after first. Payee: District Court. Personal checks accepted. Credit card payments accepted via GPS. Mail requests: SASE required.

Probate Court PO Box 800, 111 S Canal St, Lake City, MI 49651; 231-839-2266; fax: 231-839-5856; 9AM-N, 1-5PM (EST). ***Probate.*** Will accept email search requests to probate@missaukee.org

Monroe County

38th Circuit Court 106 E 1st St, Monroe, MI 48161; 734-240-7020; fax: 734-240-7045; 8:30AM-5PM (EST). ***Felony, Civil Actions over $25,000, Vital Statistics.*** www.co.monroe.mi.us/monroe/default.aspx?PageId=380
Civil Records: Access: Mail, in person. Both court and visitors may perform in person searches. Search fee: $8.00 per name. Fee is per name per 5 years. Required to search: name, years to search. Civil cases indexed by defendant, plaintiff, on computer back to 1991; prior on docket books. Mail turnaround time same or next day Civil PAT goes back to 1991. PAT results show name only.
Criminal Records: Access: Mail, in person. Both court and visitors may perform in person searches. Search fee: $8.00 per name. Fee is per name per 5 years. Required to search: name, years to search, DOB. Criminal records computerized from 1991; prior on docket books. Mail turnaround time same or next day. Criminal PAT goes back to 1991. PAT results show middle initial, DOB.
General Information: No suppressed records released. Will not fax documents. Court makes copy: $1.00 per page. Certification fee: $3.00. Payee: 38th Circuit Court. No personal checks or credit cards accepted. SASE not required.

1st District Court 106 E 1st St, Monroe, MI 48161; 734-240-7075; criminal phone: 734-240-7080; civil phone: 734-240-7090; criminal fax: 734-240-7098; civil fax: same; 8AM-4:45PM (EST). ***Misdemeanor, Civil Actions under $25,000, Eviction, Small Claims.***
www.co.monroe.mi.us/monroe/default.aspx
Civil Records: Access: Mail, in person. Both court and visitors may perform in person searches. No search fee. Required to search: name, years to search, address. Civil cases indexed by defendant, plaintiff, on computer since 1993; prior records to 1969 on microfiche. Mail turnaround time 1 week. Civil PAT goes back to 10 years. PAT results show middle initial, DOB.
Criminal Records: Access: Mail, in person. Both court and visitors may perform in person searches. No search fee. Required to search: name, years to search, DOB; also helpful: address, SSN. Criminal records on computer since 1993; prior records to 1969 on microfiche. Mail turnaround time 1 week. Criminal PAT goes back to 10 years. PAT results show middle initial, DOB.
General Information: No suppressed, juvenile, sex offenders, mental health, or adoption records released. Will not fax documents. Court makes copy: $1.00 per page; 3 page minimum for criminal, 2 for civil. Certification fee: $10.00 per page. Payee: 1st District Court. Business checks accepted. Mail requests: SASE required.

Probate Court 106 E 1st St, Monroe, MI 48161; 734-240-7346; fax: 734-240-7354; 9AM-N, 1-5PM www.co.monroe.mi.us/Monroe/default.aspx?PageId=382

Montcalm County

8th Circuit Court 639 N State St, Stanton, MI 48888; 989-831-3520; fax: 989-831-3525; 8AM-5PM (EST). ***Felony, Civil Actions over $25,000, Vital Statistics.*** www.montcalm.org
The office closes for lunch hour at noon.
Civil Records: Access: Mail, in person. Only the court performs in person searches; visitors may not. Search fee: $10.00 for 1st. yr. $1.00 each yr after. Required to search: name, years to search. Civil cases indexed by defendant, plaintiff; index on docket books to 1867, computerized since 1990. Mail turnaround time 1-3 days.
Criminal Records: Access: Mail, in person, fax. Only the court performs in person searches; visitors may not. Search fee: $10.00 for 1st. yr. $1.00 each yr after. Required to search: name, years to search, DOB. Criminal docket on books to 1867, computerized since 1990. Mail turnaround time 1-3 days.
General Information: No suppressed, juvenile, sex offenders, mental health, adoption, birth or DD214 records released. Will fax documents to local or toll-free number. Court makes copy: $1.00 per page. Certification fee: $10.00 plus $1.00 per page after first. Payee: Montcalm County Clerk. Personal checks accepted. Credit card payments accepted via GPS. Mail requests: SASE required.

64 B District Court 617 N State Rd, Stanton, MI 48888; criminal phone: 989-831-7450; civil phone: 989-831-7452; fax: 989-831-7453; 8AM-5PM (EST). ***Misdemeanor, Civil Actions under $25,000, Eviction, Small Claims.***
Probation phone- 989-831-7434.
Civil Records: Access: Mail, in person. Only the court performs in person searches; visitors may not. Search fee: $1.00 per name. Required to search: name, years to search. Civil cases indexed by defendant, plaintiff, on computer back 15 years, prior on books and microfiche. Mail turnaround 7 days.
Criminal Records: Access: Mail, in person, fax. Only the court performs in person searches; visitors may not. Search fee: $1.00 per name. Required to search: name, years to search, DOB; also helpful: SSN. Criminal records on computer since 1989, prior on books and microfiche. Mail turnaround time 7 days.
General Information: No suppressed records released. Will fax out documents. Court makes copy: $1.00 per page, self serve same. Certification fee: $10.00 plus $1.00 each add'l page. Payee: 64 B District Court. Personal checks accepted. Mail requests: SASE required.

Probate Court 625 N State St., Stanton, MI 48888; 989-831-7316; fax: 989-831-7314; 8AM-5PM (EST). ***Probate.***

Montmorency County

26th Circuit Court PO Box 789, Atlanta, MI 49709; 989-785-8022; probate phone: 989-785-8064; criminal fax: 989-785-8023; civil fax: same; 8:30AM-N, 1-4:30PM (EST). ***Felony, Civil Actions over $25,000, Vital Statistics.***
Civil Records: Access: Mail, in person. Both court and visitors may perform in person searches. Search fee: $5.00 per name. Required to search: name, years to search. Civil cases indexed by defendant, plaintiff, on computer since 1990, prior on books since 1940s, microfiche to 1970. Note: For in person searches, call ahead two days in advance. Mail turnaround time 3-5 days.
Criminal Records: Access: Mail, in person. Both court and visitors may perform in person searches. Search fee: $5.00 per name. Required to search: name, years to search; also helpful: DOB. Criminal records on computer since 1990, prior on books since 1940s. Note: For in person searches, call ahead two days in advance. Mail turnaround time 3-5 days.
General Information: No suppressed, birth certificate (except to heir or parent) adoption records released. Fee to fax out file $1.00 per page. Court makes copy: $1.00 per page. Certification fee: $10.00 plus $1.00 each add'l page. Payee: County Clerk. Personal checks accepted. Credit card payments may

be accepted via GPS but not by court. Mail requests: SASE required.

88-2 District Court County Courthouse, PO Box 789 (12265 M32), Atlanta, MI 49709; 989-785-8035; criminal fax: 989-785-8036; civil fax: same; 8:30AM-N, 1-4:30PM ***Misdemeanor, Civil Actions under $25,000, Eviction, Small Claims, Traffic.***
www.montmorencycountymichigan.us/DistrictCourt.html
Civil Records: Access: Mail, in person. Only the court performs in person searches; visitors may not. Search fee: $5.00 per name. Required to search: name, years to search; also helpful: address. Civil cases indexed by defendant, plaintiff, on computer back to 1990, prior on books and card file since 1969. Mail turnaround time 2-5 days.
Criminal Records: Access: Mail, in person. Only the court performs in person searches; visitors may not. Search fee: $5.00 per name. Required to search: name, years to search, DOB; also helpful: address, SSN, signed release. Criminal records computerized from 1990, prior on books and card file since 1969. Mail turnaround time 2-5 days.
General Information: No suppressed, juvenile, sex offenders, mental health, or adoption records released. Fee to fax back doc $1.00 each. Court makes copy: $1.00 per page, self serve same. Certification fee: $10.00 per page. Payee: 88th District Court-Montmorency County. Personal checks accepted. Major credit cards accepted via GPS. Mail requests: SASE required.

Probate Court PO Box 789, 12265 M-32, Judicial Annex, Atlanta, MI 49709-0789; 989-785-8064; fax: 989-785-8065; 8:30AM-N, 1-4:30PM.
www.montmorencycountymichigan.us/PROBATE.html

Muskegon County

14th Circuit Court County Bldg, 6th Fl, 990 Terrace St, Muskegon, MI 49442; 231-724-6251; criminal phone: 231-724-1124; civil phone: 231-724-6173; fax: 231-724-6695; 8AM-5PM (EST). ***Felony, Civil Actions over $25,000, Vital Statistics.***
Phone numbers for divorce is 231-724-6453 and for support 231-724-6447.
Civil Records: Access: Phone, mail, fax, in person. Both court and visitors may perform in person searches. No search fee. Required to search: name, years to search. Civil cases indexed by defendant, plaintiff, on computer back to 1984, prior on books since 1853. Mail turnaround time 2-3 days. Civil PAT goes back to 1984.
Criminal Records: Access: Phone, mail, fax, in person. Both court and visitors may perform in person searches. Search fee: $10.00 per name. Required to search: name, years to search, DOB; also helpful: SSN. Criminal records computerized from 1984, prior on books since 1853. Mail turnaround time 2-3 days. Criminal PAT goes back to same as civil.
General Information: No suppressed, juvenile, sex offenders, mental health, or adoption records released. Fee to fax out file $1.00 per page. Court makes copy: $1.00 per page. Certification fee: $10.00 plus $1.00 per page after first. Payee: Circuit Court Records. No personal checks. Major credit cards accepted via GPS. Mail requests: SASE required.

60th District Court 990 Terrace, 1st Fl, Muskegon, MI 49442; 231-724-6294; criminal phone: 231-724-6258; fax: 231-724-3489; 8:30AM-4:30PM (EST). ***Misdemeanor, Civil Actions under $25,000, Eviction, Small Claims.***
www.co.muskegon.mi.us/60thdistrict/
Civil Records: Access: Mail, in person. Both court and visitors may perform in person searches. No search fee. Required to search: name, years to search. Civil cases indexed by defendant, plaintiff, on computer since 5/93, prior on hard copy. Mail turnaround time 3 days. Civil PAT goes back to 5/1993. Online access to the court weekly docket is free at www.co.muskegon.mi.us/60thdistrict/docket.htm.
Criminal Records: Access: Mail, in person, online. Both court and visitors may perform in person searches. No search fee. Required to search: name, years to search, DOB. Criminal records on computer since 5/93, prior on hard copy. Mail turnaround time 3 days. Criminal PAT goes back to same as civil. Online access to court weekly docket is free at www.co.muskegon.mi.us/60thdistrict/docket.htm.
General Information: No suppressed, juvenile, sex offenders, mental health, or adoption records released. Will not fax documents. Court makes copy: $1.00 per page. Certification fee: $10.00. Payee: 60th District Court. Personal checks accepted. Mail requests: SASE required.

Probate Court 990 Terrace St, 5th Fl, Muskegon, MI 49442; 231-724-6241; fax: 231-724-6232; 8AM-N, 1-5PM (EST). ***Probate.***
www.co.muskegon.mi.us/probatecourt/

Newaygo County

27th Circuit Court PO Box 885, White Cloud, MI 49349-0885; 231-689-7269; criminal phone: 231-689-7236; civil phone: same; criminal fax: 231-689-7007; civil fax: same; 8AM-N; 1-5PM (EST). ***Felony, Civil Actions over $25,000, Vital Statistics.***
www.countyofnewaygo.com/Clerk/ClerkHome.htm
Civil Records: Access: Mail, fax, in person. Only the court performs in person searches; visitors may not. No search fee. Required to search: name, years to search. Civil cases indexed by defendant, plaintiff, archived since 1880s; on computer since 7/1994. Mail turnaround time 2-5 days.
Criminal Records: Access: Mail, fax, in person. Only the court performs in person searches; visitors may not. No search fee. Required to search: name, years to search; also helpful: DOB. Criminal records archived since 1880s; on computer since 7/1994. Mail turnaround time 2-5 days.
General Information: No suppressed records released. Will fax documents to toll-free number. Court makes copy: $1.00 per page. Certification fee: $10.00 plus $1.00 per page for copy after first. Payee: County Circuit Court Clerk. Personal checks accepted. Mail requests: SASE requested.

78th District Court 1092 Newell St, White Cloud, MI 49349; 231-689-7257; fax: 231-689-7258; 8AM-N, 1-5PM (EST). ***Misdemeanor, Civil Actions under $25,000, Eviction, Small Claims.***
www.countyofnewaygo.com/Courts/District/DCHome.htm
Civil Records: Access: Fax, mail, in person. Both court and visitors may perform in person searches. No search fee. Required to search: name, years to search; also helpful: address. Civil cases indexed by defendant, plaintiff, on computer since 7/27/89, prior in folders. Mail turnaround time 7-10 days. Civil PAT goes back to 1989. PAT civil results show middle initial.
Criminal Records: Access: Fax, mail, in person. Both court and visitors may perform in person searches. No search fee. Required to search: name, years to search, DOB; also helpful: address. Criminal records on computer since 7/27/89, prior in folders. Mail turnaround time 7-10 days. Criminal PAT goes back to same as civil. PAT results show middle initial, DOB.
General Information: No suppressed records released. No fee to fax documents. Court makes copy: $1.00 per page, self serve same. Certification fee: $10.00 plus $1.00 per page after first. Payee: 78th District Court. Personal checks accepted. Credit card payments accepted via GPS. Visa/MC/Discover/AmEx cards accepted. Mail requests: SASE required.

Probate Court PO Box 885, 1092 Newell St., White Cloud, MI 49349; 231-689-7270; fax: 231-689-7276; 8AM-N, 1-5PM (EST). ***Probate.***
www.countyofnewaygo.com/Courts/Probate/ProbateHome.htm

Oakland County

6th Circuit Court County Clerk of the Court, 1200 N Telegraph Rd, Pontiac, MI 48341; 248-858-0581; fax: 248-452-9221; 8AM-4:30PM (EST). ***Felony, Civil Actions over $25,000, Vital Statistics.***
www.oakgov.com/courts/
Email questions to clerklegal@oakgov.com.
Civil Records: Access: Mail, in person, online. Both court and visitors may perform in person searches. Search fee: $1.00 per name. Required to search: name, years to search. Civil cases indexed by defendant, plaintiff, on computer since 1963, prior on microfilm. Mail turnaround time 7 days. Civil PAT goes back to 1963. Register of Actions free at www.oakgov.com/clerkrod/courtexplorer. Order document copies online, plus enhanced access fee starting at $2.50.
Criminal Records: Access: Mail, in person, online. Both court and visitors may perform in person searches. Search fee: $1.00 per name. Required to search: name; also helpful: years to search, DOB, SSN. Criminal records on computer since 1963, prior on microfilm & books. Mail turnaround time 7 days. Criminal PAT goes back to same as civil. Personal identifiers include name and birth year only. Online criminal access is the same as civil see above.
General Information: No suppressed, non-public, sex offenders or mental health records released. Will fax documents to local or toll free line. Court makes copy: $1.00 per page, self serve same.Copies can be mailed or emailed to requester. Certification fee: $10.00 plus $1.00 per page after first. Payee: Oakland County Clerk's Office. Personal checks not accepted. Major credit cards accepted. Mail requests: SASE required.

43rd District Court 43 E Nine Mile Rd, Hazel Park, MI 48030; 248-547-3034; fax: 248-546-4088; 8AM-4:15PM (EST). ***Misdemeanor, Civil Actions under $25,000, Eviction, Small Claims.***
www.oakgov.com/courts/
Civil Records: Access: In person only. Both court and visitors may perform in person searches. No search fee. Required to search: name, years to search. Civil cases indexed by defendant, plaintiff, on computer since 1989, prior on books since 1970.
Criminal Records: Access: In person only. Both court and visitors may perform in person searches. No search fee. Required to search: name, years to search, DOB. Criminal records on computer since 1989, prior on books since 1970.
General Information: No suppressed, juvenile, sex offenders, mental health, or adoption records released. Court makes copy: $1.00 per page. Certification fee: $10.00 per doc includes copy fee. Payee: 43rd District Court. Only cashiers checks, cash or money orders accepted. Credit card payments accepted via GPS.

44th District Court - Royal Oak 400 E Eleven Mile Rd, Royal Oak, MI 48067; 248-246-3600; criminal fax: 248-246-3601; civil fax: same; 8AM-4:30PM (EST). ***Misdemeanor, Civil Actions under $25,000, Eviction, Small Claims.***
www.oakgov.com/courts/
Civil Records: Access: Mail, in person. Only the court performs in person searches; visitors may not. Search fee: $10.00 per name. Required to search: name, years to search. Civil cases indexed by defendant, plaintiff, on computer since 1983s, prior on docket books and index cards. Mail turnaround time 5 days.
Criminal Records: Access: Mail, in person. Only the court performs in person searches; visitors may not. Search fee: $10.00 per name. Required to search: name, years to search, DOB, signed release, offense; also helpful: address. Criminal records on computer since 1983s, prior on docket books and index cards. Mail turnaround time 5 days.
General Information: No suppressed, juvenile, sex offenders, mental health, or adoption records released. Will not fax documents. Court makes copy: $1.00 per page. Certification fee: $10.00 per page, includes copy fee. Payee: 44th District Court. Personal checks accepted. Major credit cards accepted via GPS. Mail requests: SASE required.

45 A District Court - Berkley 3338 Coolidge, Berkley, MI 48072; 248-544-3300; criminal phone: 248-544-3300; civil phone: 248-544-3301; criminal fax: 248-546-2416; civil fax: same; 8:30AM-4:45PM (EST). ***Misdemeanor, Civil Actions under $25,000, Eviction, Small Claims.***
www.oakgov.com/courts/
Civil Records: Access: Mail, in person. Only the court performs in person searches; visitors may not. Search fee: $1.00 per name, per search. Required to search: name, years to search. Civil cases indexed

by defendant, plaintiff, on computer since 1989 prior on books. Mail turnaround time 1 week.
Criminal Records: Access: Mail, in person. Only the court performs in person searches; visitors may not. Search fee: $1.00 per name, per search. Required to search: name, years to search, DOB; also helpful: SSN. Criminal records on computer since 1989, prior on books. Mail turnaround time 1 week.
General Information: No suppressed records released. Will fax documents. Court makes copy: $1.00 per page. Certification fee: $10.00 per request. Payee: 45 A District Court. Personal checks accepted; credit cards are not. Mail requests: SASE required.

45 B District Court 13600 Oak Park Blvd, Oak Park, MI 48237; 248-691-7440; criminal phone: 248-691-7429; civil phone: 248-691-7427; fax: 248-691-7158; 9AM-5PM (EST). ***Misdemeanor, Civil Actions under $25,000, Eviction, Small Claims.***
www.oakgov.com/courts/
Court covers Huntington Woods, Oak Park, Pleasant Ridge, and Royal Oak Township.
Civil Records: Access: Mail, in person. Both court and visitors may perform in person searches. No search fee. Required to search: name, years to search. Civil cases indexed by defendant, plaintiff, on computer back to 1988. Docket books and index cards back to 1987. Mail turnaround time varies. Civil PAT goes back to 1988.
Criminal Records: Access: Mail, in person. Both court and visitors may perform in person searches. No search fee. Required to search: name, years to search, DOB. Criminal records computerized from 1993. Docket books and index cards go back to 1988. Mail turnaround time varies. Criminal PAT goes back to 1988.
General Information: No suppressed records released. Will not fax documents. Court makes copy: $1.00 per page. Certification fee: $10.00. Payee: 45 B District Court. Business checks accepted. Major Major credit cards accepted via GPS. Mail requests: SASE required.

46th District Court - Southfield 26000 Evergreen Rd, Southfield, MI 48076; 248-796-5800; criminal phone: 248-796-5880; civil phone: 248-796-5870; criminal fax: 248-796-5875; civil fax: same; 8AM-4:30PM (counter) (EST). ***Misdemeanor, Civil Actions under $25,000, Eviction, Small Claims.***
www.oakgov.com/courts/
Civil Records: Access: Mail, in person. Both court and visitors may perform in person searches. Search fee: $1.00 per name. Required to search: name or case number. Civil cases indexed by defendant, plaintiff, prior to 1992 are on microfilm; most recent records are computerized. Mail turnaround time varies. Public use terminal available.
Criminal Records: Access: Mail, in person. Both court and visitors may perform in person searches. Search fee: $1.00 per name. Required to search: name, years to search, DOB. Criminal records on computer since 1992, prior on microfiche. Mail turnaround time varies. Public use terminal available.
General Information: No suppressed or "non-public" records released, such as juvenile, sex offenders, mental health, or adoption records. Will not fax documents. Court makes copy: $.50 per page.If copies are made from microfilm, the copy fee is $1.00 per page. Certification fee: $10.00 per document. Payee: 46th District Court. Personal checks accepted. Major credit cards accepted via GPS. Mail requests: SASE not requested.

47th District Court - Farmington, Farmington Hills 31605 W 11 Mile Rd, Farmington Hills, MI 48336; 248-871-2900; criminal phone: 248-871-2920; civil phone: 248-871-2910; 8:30AM-4:30PM (EST). ***Misdemeanor, Civil Actions under $25,000, Eviction, Small Claims.***
www.oakgov.com/courts/
Civil Records: Access: In person only. Visitors must perform in person searches themselves. Required to search: name, years to search, case number. Civil cases indexed by defendant, plaintiff, on computer since 7/19/93; prior on microfiche since 1975. Civil PAT goes back to 7/19/93.
Criminal Records: Access: In person only. Visitors must perform in person searches themselves. Required to search: name, years to search, case number DOB; also helpful: offense. Criminal records on computer since 7/19/93; prior on microfiche since 1975. Criminal PAT goes back to same as civil.
General Information: No suppressed, sex offenders or mental health records released. Court makes copy: $1.00 per page. Certification fee: $10.00 plus $1.00 per page after first. Payee: 47th District Court. Personal checks accepted. Major credit cards accepted via GPS.

48th District Court - Bloomfield Hills PO Box 3200, 4280 Telegraph Rd, Bloomfield Hills, MI 48302; 248-647-1141; civil phone: 248-433-9343; fax: 248-647-8955; 8:30AM-4:30PM (EST). ***Misdemeanor, Civil Actions under $25,000, Eviction, Small Claims.***
www.oakgov.com/dc48/index.html
Civil Records: Access: Phone, mail, in person. Both court and visitors may perform in person searches. No search fee. Required to search: name, years to search, address. Civil cases indexed by defendant, plaintiff, on computer since 1980. Mail turnaround time varies. Civil PAT goes back to 1980. PAT civil results show middle initial. Terminal results may or may not show full name.
Criminal Records: Access: Phone, mail, in person. Both court and visitors may perform in person searches. No search fee. Required to search: name, years to search, address, DOB. Criminal records on computer since 1980. Mail turnaround time varies. Criminal PAT goes back to same as civil. PAT results show middle initial, DOB. Terminal results may or may not show full name.
General Information: No suppressed, juvenile, sex offenders, mental health, victim or adoption records released. Will not fax documents. Court makes copy: $1.00 per page. Certification fee: $10.00 plus $1.00 per page after first - this applies to civil, eviction and small claims cases only. No fee to certify a criminal record. Payee: 48th District Court. Personal checks accepted. Credit cards accepted vai GPS, call 888-604-7888.

50th District Court - Pontiac Criminal Division 70 N Saginaw, Pontiac, MI 48342; 248-758-3820; criminal phone: x3; 8:30AM-4:30PM ***Misdemeanor.*** www.pontiac.mi.us/Court/index.html
Criminal Records: Access: Mail, in person. Both court and visitors may perform in person searches. Search fee: $1.00 per name. Required to search: name, years to search, DOB; also helpful: SSN. Criminal records on computer since 1984, prior on index cards since 1975. Mail turnaround 2-3 days. Public terminal has crim records back to 4/2004.
General Information: No suppressed, juvenile, sex offenders, mental health, or adoption records released. Will fax documents to local or toll free line. Court makes copy: $1.00 first page, $.25 each add'l, self serve same. Certification fee: $10.00 per doc. Payee: 50th District Court. Business checks accepted. Credit card payments accepted via GPS.

51st District Court - Waterford 5100 Civic Center Dr, Waterford, MI 48329; 248-674-4655; criminal phone: x6; civil phone: x4; 8:30AM-4:45PM (EST). ***Misdemeanor, Civil Actions under $25,000, Eviction, Small Claims.***
www.twp.waterford.mi.us/court/
Search the docket online free at www.twp.waterford.mi.us/court/dockets/index.htm.
Civil Records: Access: Mail, in person. Only the court performs in person searches; visitors may not. Search fee: $1.00 per name. Required to search: name, years to search. Civil cases indexed by defendant, plaintiff, on computer since 1980s, prior on docket books and index cards back 10 years. Mail turnaround time 10 days.
Criminal Records: Access: Mail, in person. Only the court performs in person searches; visitors may not. Search fee: $1.00 per name. Required to search: name, years to search, DOB; also helpful: SSN. Criminal records on computer since 1980s, prior on docket books and index cards to 1985. Mail turnaround time 10 days.
General Information: No suppressed, juvenile, sex offenders, mental health, or adoption records released. Will fax documents to local number. Court makes copy: $1.00 per page. Certification fee: $10.00 per doc. Payee: 51st District Court. Personal checks accepted. Major credit cards accepted via GPS.

52nd District Court - Division 1, Novi 48150 Grand River, Novi, MI 48374; criminal phone: 248-305-6460; civil phone: 248-305-6080; 8AM-4:15PM (EST). ***Misdemeanor, Civil Actions under $25,000, Eviction, Small Claims.***
www.52-1districtcourt.com
Civil Records: Access: Phone, mail, in person. Only the court performs in person searches; visitors may not. Search fee: $1.00 per name. Prefers to do large name lists on Tuesday & Friday. Required to search: name, years to search. Civil cases indexed by defendant, plaintiff, on computer since 1987, prior on books. Mail turnaround time 1 month.
Criminal Records: Access: Phone, mail, in person. Only the court performs in person searches; visitors may not. Search fee: $1.00 per name. Best to do large name lists on Thursday & Friday. Required to search: name, years to search; also helpful: DOB. Criminal records on computer since 1987, prior on books. Mail turnaround time 1 month.
General Information: No suppressed, juvenile, sex offenders or mental health records released. Will not fax documents. Court makes copy: $1.00 per page. Certification fee: $10.00. Payee: 52-1 District Court. Personal checks accepted. Visa/MC/Discover Major credit cards accepted via GPS. Mail requests: SASE required.

52nd District Court - Division 2 5850 Lorac, Clarkston, MI 48346; 248-625-4880; fax: 248-625-5602; 8:30AM-4:30PM (EST). ***Misdemeanor, Civil Actions under $25,000, Eviction, Small Claims.***
www.oakgov.com/courts/
Court covers Springfield, Holly, Groveland, Brandon, Independence, Clarkston & Ortonville and townships of White Lake and Rose.
Civil Records: Access: Phone, fax, mail, in person. Only the court performs in person searches; visitors may not. Search fee: $1.00 per name. Required to search: name, years to search. Civil cases indexed by defendant, plaintiff, on computer since 1982, prior on microfiche since 1976. Mail turnaround time 3-5 days.
Criminal Records: Access: Phone, fax, mail, in person. Only the court performs in person searches; visitors may not. Search fee: $1.00 per name. Required to search: name, years to search, DOB. Criminal records on computer since 1982, prior on microfiche since 1976. Mail turnaround 3-5 days.
General Information: No suppressed, juvenile or sex offender records released. Fax service and fee is under consideration. Court makes copy: $1.00 per page. Certification fee: $10.00. No personal checks accepted. Visa/MC accepted in person only. Mail requests: SASE required.

52nd District Court - Division 3 700 Barclay Circle, Rochester Hills, MI 48307; 248-853-5553; fax: 248-853-3277; 8:15AM-4:30PM (EST). ***Misdemeanor, Civil Actions under $25,000, Eviction, Small Claims.***
www.oakgov.com/courts/
Civil Records: Access: Phone, fax, mail, in person. Only the court performs in person searches; visitors may not. Search fee: $1.00 per name. Required to search: name; also helpful: years to search. Civil cases indexed by defendant, plaintiff, on computer for 10 years, prior on docket books and index cards. Mail turnaround time varies.
Criminal Records: Access: Phone, fax, mail, in person. Only the court performs in person searches; visitors may not. Search fee: $1.00 per name. Required to search: name, DOB; also helpful: years to search. Criminal records on computer for 10 years, prior on docket books and index cards. Mail turnaround time varies.
General Information: No suppressed records released. Will not fax documents. Court makes copy: $1.00 per page. Certification fee: $10.00. Payee: 52-3 District Court. Personal checks accepted. Credit cards accepted in person only.

52nd District Court - Division 4 520 W Big Beaver Rd, Troy, MI 48084; 248-528-0400; civil phone: 248-528-0404; fax: 248-528-3588; 8:15AM-4:15PM ***Misdemeanor, Civil under $25,000, Eviction, Small Claims.*** www.oakgov.com/courts/
Division 4 is Troy, Clawson.
Civil Records: Access: Mail, fax, in person. Only the court performs in person searches; visitors may not. Search fee: $1.00 per name. Required to search: name, years to search. Civil cases indexed by defendant, plaintiff, go back to 1995. Mail turnaround time 1 week.
Criminal Records: Access: Fax, mail, in person. Only the court performs in person searches; visitors may not. Search fee: $1.00 per name. Required to search: name; also helpful: years to search, DOB, SSN. Mail turnaround time 1 week.
General Information: No suppressed, juvenile, sex offenders, mental health, or adoption records released. No fee to fax documents for criminal records and local calls only. Court makes copy: $1.00 per page. Certification fee: $10.00 per doc. Payee: 52-4 District Court. Personal checks accepted. Visa/MC/AmEx accepted. Mail requests: SASE required.

50th District Court - Pontiac Civil Division 70 N Saginaw, Pontiac, MI 48342; 248-758-3820 x4; civil phone: 248-758-3880; fax: 248-758-3888; 8AM-4:30PM (EST). ***Civil Actions under $25,000, Eviction, Small Claims.***
www.pontiac.mi.us/Court/index.html
Civil Records: Access: Fax, mail, in person. Both court and visitors may perform in person searches. Search fee: $1.00 per name. Required to search: name, years to search. Civil cases indexed by defendant, plaintiff, on computer since 1985. Mail turnaround time 3-4 days. Public use terminal has civil records back to 2004.
General Information: No suppressed, juvenile, sex offenders, mental health, or adoption records released. Court makes copy: $1.00 1st page, $.25 each add'l. Certification fee: $10.00 per doc includes copies. Payee: 50th District Court. Personal checks accepted. Credit card payments accepted via GPS.

Probate Court 1200 N Telegraph Rd, 1st Fl, Oakland County Complex, East Wing, Pontiac, MI 48341; 248-858-0260; fax: 248-452-2016; 8AM-5PM (EST). ***Probate.***
www.oakgov.com/courts/

Oceana County

27th Circuit Court 100 State St, #M-34, Hart, MI 49420; 231-873-3977; 9AM-5PM (EST). ***Felony, Civil Actions over $25,000, Vital Statistics.***
Civil Records: Access: Mail, in person. Only the court performs in person searches; visitors may not. Search fee: $5.00 per name. Required to search: name, years to search. Civil cases indexed by defendant, plaintiff, on computer since 1994, paper records to 1800s. Mail turnaround time same day.
Criminal Records: Access: Mail, in person. Only the court performs in person searches; visitors may not. Search fee: $5.00 per name. Required to search: name, years to search; also helpful: DOB. Criminal records on computer since 1994, paper records to 1800s. Mail turnaround time same day.
General Information: No suppressed, juvenile, sex offenders, mental health, or adoption records released. Will not fax documents. Court makes copy: $1.00 per page. Certification fee: $10.00 plus $1.00 per page. Payee: Oceana County Circuit Court. Personal checks accepted if in-state. Mail requests: SASE requested.

78th District Court PO Box 471, Hart, MI 49420; 231-873-4530; fax: 231-873-1861; 8AM-5PM (EST). ***Misdemeanor, Civil Actions under $25,000, Eviction, Small Claims.***
Civil Records: Access: Fax, mail, in person. Only the court performs in person searches; visitors may not. Search fee: $1.00 per charge found. Required to search: name, years to search. Civil cases indexed by plaintiff. Civil records on file cards and in file folders since 1967; on computer back to 1999. Mail turnaround time same day.
Criminal Records: Access: Fax, mail, in person. Only the court performs in person searches; visitors may not. Search fee: $1.00 per charge found. Required to search: name, years to search, DOB. Criminal records on file cards and in file folders since 1967; on computer back to 1999. Mail turnaround time same day.
General Information: No suppressed records released. Will fax documents to local or toll-free number on Fridays only. Court makes copy: $5.00 for 1st page; $1.00 each add'l; Civil- $1.00 per page. Certification fee: $10.00 1st page $1.00 each add'l page. Payee: 78th District Court. No personal checks or credit cards accepted. SASE not required.

Probate Court County Bldg, 100 S State St, #M-10, Hart, MI 49420; 231-873-3666; fax: 231-873-1943; 9AM-5PM (EST). ***Probate.***

Ogemaw County

34th Circuit Court 806 W Houghton, #101, West Branch, MI 48661; 989-345-0215; fax: 989-345-7223; 8:30AM-4:30PM (EST). ***Felony, Civil Actions over $25,000, Vital Statistics.***
Civil Records: Access: Phone, fax, mail, in person. Only the court performs in person searches; visitors may not. Search fee: $10.00 per name for search of records prior to 1990, otherwise no charge. Required to search: name, years to search. Civil cases indexed by defendant, plaintiff; index on cards since 1970, library books in vault since 1960; on computer back to 1993. Mail turnaround time 1-3 weeks.
Criminal Records: Access: Phone, fax, mail, in person. Only the court performs in person searches; visitors may not. Search fee: $10.00 per name for search of records prior to 1990, otherwise no charge. Required to search: name, years to search, DOB; also helpful: SSN. Criminal records indexed on cards since 1970, library books in vault since 1960; on computer back to 1990. Mail turnaround time 1-3 weeks.
General Information: No suppressed, juvenile, sex offenders, mental health, or adoption records released. Will fax documents $2.00 1st page, $1.00 each add'l. Court makes copy: $.50 per page. Certification fee: $10.00 plus $1.00 per page. Payee: Ogermaw County Clerk. Personal checks accepted; credit cards are not. Mail requests: SASE required.

82nd District Court PO Box 365, West Branch, MI 48661; 989-345-5040; criminal fax: 989-345-5910; civil fax: same; 8:30AM-4:30PM (EST). ***Misdemeanor, Civil Actions under $25,000, Eviction, Small Claims.***
Civil Records: Access: Fax, mail, in person. Only the court performs in person searches; visitors may not. Search fee: $5.00 per name. Required to search: name, years to search. Civil cases indexed by defendant, plaintiff, on computer since 1990, prior on books since 1969. Mail turnaround time 2-3 days.
Criminal Records: Access: Fax, mail, in person. Only the court performs in person searches; visitors may not. Search fee: $5.00 per name. Required to search: name, years to search, DOB. Criminal records on computer since 1990, prior on books since 1969. Mail turnaround time 2-3 days.
General Information: No suppressed records released. No fee to fax documents. Court makes copy: $.50 per page. Certification fee: $10.00 per case includes copy fee. Payee: 82nd District Court. Personal checks accepted. Credit card payments accepted via Paytrust Solutions. Prepayment of mail search required. Mail requests: SASE requested.

Probate Court County Courthouse, Rm 203, 806 W Houghton Ave, West Branch, MI 48661; 989-345-0145; fax: 989-345-5901; 8:30AM-N, 1-4:30PM
www.ogemawcountymi.gov/probate/index.php

Ontonagon County

32nd Circuit Court 725 Greenland Rd, Ontonagon, MI 49953; 906-884-4255; criminal fax: 906-884-6796; civil fax: same; 8:30AM-4:30PM (EST). ***Felony, Civil Actions over $25,000, Vital Statistics.***
Civil Records: Access: Mail, fax, in person. Both court and visitors may perform in person searches. Search fee: $5.00 per name. Required to search: name, years to search. Civil cases indexed by defendant, plaintiff; index on docket books and in folders. Mail turnaround time 2-3 days.
Criminal Records: Access: Mail, fax, in person. Both court and visitors may perform in person searches. Search fee: $5.00 per name. Required to search: name, years to search. Criminal records in folders. Mail turnaround time 2-3 days.
General Information: No suppressed records released. Will fax documents $2.00 each. Court makes copy: $1.00 per page, self serve same. Certification fee: $10.00. Payee: County Clerk. Personal checks accepted; credit cards are not. SASE not required.

98th District Court 725 Greenland Rd, Ontonagon, MI 49953; 906-884-2865; criminal fax: 906-884-2865; civil fax: same; 8:30AM-4:30PM (EST). ***Misdemeanor, Civil Actions under $25,000, Eviction, Small Claims.***
Civil Records: Access: Mail, in person. Only the court performs in person searches; visitors may not. Search fee: $5.00 each name. Required to search: name, years to search. Civil cases indexed by defendant, plaintiff, kept for 10 years then destroyed. Small claims kept 6 years only. Mail turnaround time 1 week.
Criminal Records: Access: Mail, in person. Only the court performs in person searches; visitors may not. Search fee: $5.00 each name. Required to search: name, years to search, DOB. Criminal records kept for 10 years then destroyed. Mail turnaround time 1 week.
General Information: No suppressed records released. Will fax documents. Court makes copy: $1.00 per page. Certification fee: $10.00 plus $1.00 each additional copy. Payee: 98th District Court. Business checks accepted. No credit cards accepted. Mail requests: SASE required.

Probate Court 725 Greenland Rd, Ontonagon, MI 49953; 906-884-4117; fax: 906-884-2916; 8:30AM-N, 1-4:30PM (EST). ***Probate.***

Osceola County

49th Circuit Court 301 W Upton, Reed City, MI 49677; 231-832-6103; fax: 231-832-6149; 9AM-5PM (EST). ***Felony, Civil Actions over $25,000, Vital Statistics.***
Civil Records: Access: Phone, fax, mail, in person. Both court and visitors may perform in person searches. Search fee: $5.00 per name. Required to search: name, years to search. Civil cases indexed by defendant, plaintiff, on computer since 1992, prior on docket books. Mail turnaround time 1-2 days.
Criminal Records: Access: Phone, fax, mail, in person. Both court and visitors may perform in person searches. Search fee: $5.00 per name. Required to search: name, years to search, DOB. Criminal records on computer since 1992, prior on docket books back to 1967. Mail turnaround time 1-2 days.
General Information: No suppressed or adoption records released. Will fax uncertified pages $1.00 1st 5, $.50 each add'l. Court makes copy: $1.00 per page. Certification fee: $10.00 plus $1.00 per page after first. Payee: 49th Circuit Court. Personal checks accepted. Credit cards payments accepted via GPS. Mail requests: SASE required.

77th District Court 410 W Upton, Reed City, MI 49677; 231-832-6155; fax: 231-832-9190; 8:30AM-4:30PM (EST). ***Misdemeanor, Civil Actions under $25,000, Eviction, Small Claims.***
Civil Records: Access: Phone, mail, fax, in person. Only the court performs in person searches; visitors may not. Search fee: $5.00 per name. Required to search: name, years to search. Civil cases indexed by defendant, plaintiff, on computer since 6/91. Mail turnaround time 2 days.
Criminal Records: Access: Phone, mail, fax, in person. Only the court performs in person searches; visitors may not. Search fee: $5.00 per name. Required to search: name, DOB. Criminal records on computer since 6/91. Mail turnaround time 2 days.
General Information: No suppressed records released. Will fax documents for no fee. Court makes copy: $1.00 per page. Certification fee: $10.00 per doc includes copy fee. Payee: 77th District Court. Only cashiers checks and money orders accepted. Credit card payments accepted via GPS. Can pay by phone for a $10.00 fee. Mail requests: SASE required.

Probate Court 410 W Upton, Reed City, MI 49677; 231-832-6124; fax: 231-832-6181; 8:30AM-N, 1-4:30PM (EST). ***Probate.*** Shares the same judge with Mecosta County Probate Court.

Oscoda County

23rd Circuit Court PO Box 399, 311 Morenci Ave, Mio, MI 48647; 989-826-1110; probate phone: 989-826-1107; fax: 989-826-1136; 8:30AM-4:30PM (EST). ***Felony, Civil Actions over $25,000, Vital Statistics.*** www.oscodacountymi.com Probate fax- 989-826-1158

Civil Records: Access: Mail, in person. Only the court performs in person searches; visitors may not. Search fee: $10.00 per name per year. Required to search: name, years to search. Civil cases indexed by defendant, plaintiff, on computer since 1989, prior on docket books to 1880s. Mail turnaround 2-3 wks.

Criminal Records: Access: Mail, in person. Only the court performs in person searches; visitors may not. Search fee: $10.00 per name per year. Required to search: name, years to search, DOB. Criminal records on computer since 1989, prior on docket books to 1880s. Mail turnaround time 2-3 weeks.

General Information: No suppressed records released. Will fax documents $5.00 1st page, $2.00 each add'l. Court makes copy: $1.00 per page. Certification fee: $10.00 plus $1.00 per page copy fee after first. Payee: Oscoda County Clerk. Personal checks accepted. Credit card payments accepted via GPS. Mail requests: SASE required.

81st District Court PO Box 625, Mio, MI 48647; criminal phone: 989-826-1105; civil phone: 989-826-1106; fax: 989-826-1188; 8:30AM-4:30PM (EST). ***Misdemeanor, Civil Actions under $25,000, Eviction, Small Claims.***

Civil Records: Access: Mail, in person. Only the court performs in person searches; visitors may not. Search fee: $10.00 per name. Required to search: name, years to search. Civil cases indexed by defendant, plaintiff, on computer back to 1990, prior on index cards. Mail turnaround time 1-2 days.

Criminal Records: Access: Mail, in person. Only the court performs in person searches; visitors may not. Search fee: $10.00 per name. Required to search: name, years to search, DOB. Criminal records computerized from 1990, prior on index cards. Mail turnaround time 1-2 days.

General Information: No suppressed records released. Will fax documents to local or toll free line. Court makes copy: $.50 per page. Certification fee: $10.00 plus $1.00 per page after first. Payee: 81st District Court. No personal checks. Credit card payments accepted via GPS. Mail requests: SASE required.

Probate Court PO Box 399, 105 S Court St, Mio, MI 48647; 989-826-1107; fax: 989-826-1158; 8:30AM-N, 1-4:30PM (EST). ***Probate.*** www.oscodacountyprobatecourt.com

Otsego County

46th Circuit Court 225 Main St, Gaylord, MI 49735; 989-731-7500(Clerk); criminal fax: 989-731-7519; civil fax: same; 8AM-4:30PM (EST). ***Felony, Civil Actions over $25,000, Vital Statistics.*** www.Circuit46.org

Civil Records: Access: Mail, in person, online. Both court and visitors may perform in person searches. Search fee: $1.00 per name. Required to search: name, years to search. Civil cases indexed by defendant, plaintiff, on computer since 1988, prior on indexes since 1800s. Mail turnaround time varies. Online access to court case records (closed cases for 90 days only) is free at http://66.129.39.149/c46_Cases.php.

Criminal Records: Access: Mail, in person, online. Both court and visitors may perform in person searches. Search fee: $1.00 per name. Required to search: name, years to search, DOB. Criminal records on computer since 1988, prior on indexes since 1800s. Mail turnaround time varies. Online access to criminal records is the same as civil.

General Information: No suppressed, juvenile, mental health, or adoption records released. Will fax documents to local or toll-free number; all others $5.00 fee per page. Court makes copy: $1.00 per page. Certification fee: $10.00 per document. Payee: Otsego County Clerk. Personal checks accepted. Credit card payments accepted via GPS. Mail requests: SASE required.

46th Circuit Trial Court - District Court 800 Livingston Blvd, #1C, Gaylord, MI 49735; 989-731-0201; fax: 989-732-5130; 8AM-4:30PM (EST). ***Misdemeanor, Civil Actions under $25,000, Eviction, Small Claims.*** www.circuit46.org

Civil Records: Access: Mail, in person, online. Both court and visitors may perform in person searches. No search fee. Required to search: name, years to search. Civil cases indexed by defendant, plaintiff, on computer since 1985, prior index cards. Mail turnaround time 4 days. Civil PAT goes back to 1985. PAT results show name only. Online access to limited index of court records is free at http://66.129.39.149/c46_Cases.php.

Criminal Records: Access: Mail, fax, in person, online. Both court and visitors may perform in person searches. No search fee. Required to search: name, years to search, DOB. Criminal records on computer since 1985, prior index cards to 1969. Mail turnaround time 4 days. Criminal PAT goes back to same as civil. PAT results show middle initial, DOB. Access to online criminal records is the same as civil. There are limitations, this system is not meant to be used for background checks, it is supplemental only.

General Information: No suppressed records released. Will fax documents $1.00 per page. Court makes copy: $1.00 per page. Certification fee: $10.00 plus $1.00 per page after first. Payee: 46th Circuit Trial Court. Personal checks accepted. Visa/MC accepted. Mail requests: SASE required.

Probate Court 800 Livingston Blvd, #1C, Gaylord, MI 49735; 989-731-0204, 989-731-0201; fax: 989-732-5130; 8AM-4:30PM (EST). ***Probate.*** www.Circuit46.org

Online access to limited index of court records is free at http://66.129.39.149/c46_Cases.php.

Ottawa County

20th Circuit Court 414 Washington Ave, Grand Haven, MI 49417; 616-846-8315; fax: 616-846-8138; 8AM-5PM M; 9AM-5PM T-F (EST). ***Felony, Civil Actions over $25,000, Vital Statistics.*** www.co.ottawa.mi.us/CoGov/Clerk/clerkcourt.htm

Civil Records: Access: Mail, fax, in person. Visitors must perform in person searches themselves. Search fee: $10.00 per name per decade. No fee if you provide case number. Required to search: name, years to search. Civil cases indexed by defendant, plaintiff, number. Civil records on computer since 1989. Mail turnaround time 2-3 days; phone search - 24 hours. Civil PAT goes back to 1990. PAT results show middle initial, DOB.

Criminal Records: Access: Mail, fax, in person. Visitors must perform in person searches themselves. Search fee: $10.00 per name per decade. No fee if you provide case number. Required to search: name, years to search, DOB; also helpful: SSN. Criminal records on computer since 1990. Mail turnaround time 2-3 days; phone search - 24 hours. Criminal PAT goes back to same as civil. PAT results show middle initial, DOB.

General Information: No suppressed, juvenile, sex offenders, mental health, or adoption records released. Will not fax documents. Court makes copy: $.50 per page, self serve same. Certification fee: $10.00 per doc plus $1.00 per page. Payee: Ottawa County Clerk. No personal checks accepted. Major credit cards accepted via GPS. Mail requests: SASE requested.

58th District Court - Grand Haven 414 Washington Ave, Grand Haven, MI 49417; 616-846-8280; criminal phone: 616-846-8127; civil phone: 616-846-8289; criminal fax: 616-846-8291; civil fax: 616-846-8035; 8AM-5PM (EST). ***Misdemeanor, Civil Actions under $25,000, Eviction, Small Claims.*** www.co.ottawa.mi.us/CourtsLE/58thDistrict/

Search fee includes both civil and criminal indexes

Civil Records: Access: Mail, fax, in person. Both court and visitors may perform in person searches. Search fee: $3.00. Required to search: name, years to search. Civil cases indexed by defendant, plaintiff, on computer back to 1993, prior on index cards since 1969. Mail turnaround time 4 days. Civil PAT goes back to 1993. PAT results show name only.

Criminal Records: Access: Mail, fax, in person. Both court and visitors may perform in person searches. Search fee: $3.00. Required to search: name, years to search, DOB. Criminal records computerized from 1990, prior on index cards since 1969. Mail turnaround time 4 days. Criminal PAT goes back to 1990. PAT results show middle initial, DOB, SSN.

General Information: No suppressed records released. Will fax documents $3.00 per page. Court makes copy: $1.00 per page. Certification fee: $10.00 plus $1.00 per page after first. Payee: 58th District Court. Personal checks accepted, but not out-of-state. Major credit cards accepted via GPS. Mail requests: SASE required.

58th District Court - Holland 85 W 8th St, Holland, MI 49423; 616-392-6991; fax: 616-392-5013; 8AM-5PM (EST). ***Misdemeanor, Civil Actions under $25,000, Eviction, Small Claims.*** www.co.ottawa.mi.us/CoGov/Clerk/clerkcourt.htm

Records Dept phone- 616-355-4306

Civil Records: Access: Fax, mail, in person. Only the court performs in person searches; visitors may not. Search fee: $3.00 per name. Required to search: name, years to search. Civil cases indexed by defendant, plaintiff, on computer since 1988, prior on books since 1969. Mail turnaround time varies. Civil PAT available.

Criminal Records: Access: Fax, mail, in person. Only the court performs in person searches; visitors may not. Search fee: $3.00 per name. Required to search: name, years to search, DOB; also helpful: SSN. Criminal records on computer since 1988, prior on books since 1969. Mail turnaround time varies. Criminal PAT available.

General Information: No suppressed records released. Will not fax out documents. Court makes copy: $1.00 per page. Certification fee: $10.00 per doc includes copies. Payee: 58th District Court. Personal checks accepted. Out of state checks not accepted. Visa/MC accepted. Mail requests: SASE required.

58th District Court - Hudsonville 3100 Port Sheldon, Hudsonville, MI 49426; 616-662-3100 x2; fax: 616-669-2950; 8AM-Noon; 1-5PM (EST). ***Misdemeanor, Civil Actions under $25,000, Eviction, Small Claims.*** www.co.ottawa.mi.us/CoGov/Clerk/clerkcourt.htm

Civil Records: Access: Mail, in person. Only the court performs in person searches; visitors may not. Search fee: $3.00 per name. Required to search: name, years to search; also helpful: address. Civil cases indexed by defendant, plaintiff, on computer since 7/1993, prior on index file. Mail turnaround time 2 days. Civil PAT goes back to 1990.

Criminal Records: Access: Mail, in person. Only the court performs in person searches; visitors may not. Search fee: $3.00 per name. Required to search: name, years to search, DOB; also helpful: address. Criminal records on computer since 1990. Mail turnaround time 2 days. Criminal PAT goes back to 1990.

General Information: No suppressed records released. Will fax documents $3.00 per name. Court makes copy: $1.00 per page. Certification fee: $10.00. Payee: 58th District Court. Personal checks accepted. Credit card payments accepted via GPS. SASE not required.

Probate Court 12120 Fillmore St, West Olive, MI 49460; 616-786-4110; fax: 616-738-4624; 7AM-6PM M; 8AM-5PM T-TH (EST). ***Probate.*** www.co.ottawa.mi.us/CourtsLE/Probate/

Presque Isle County

53rd Circuit Court PO Box 110, 151 E Huron, Rogers City, MI 49779; 989-734-3288; probate phone: 989-734-3268; fax: 989-734-7635; 8:30AM-4:30PM (EST). ***Felony, Civil Actions over $25,000, Vital Statistics.***

Civil Records: Access: Phone, fax, mail, in person. Only the court performs in person searches; visitors may not. No search fee. Required to search: name, years to search. Civil cases indexed by defendant, plaintiff; index on docket books since 1871. Mail turnaround time 1 week.

Criminal Records: Access: Phone, fax, mail, in person. Only the court performs in person searches; visitors may not. No search fee. Required to search: name, years to search, DOB. Criminal docket on books since 1871. Mail turnaround time 1 week.

General Information: No suppressed, juvenile, mental health, or adoption records released. Will fax documents $1.00 per page id prepaid. Court makes copy: $1.00 per page. Certification fee: $10.00 1st page, $1.00 ea add'l. Payee: Presque Isle County Clerk. Personal checks accepted up to $249.99. Credit card payments may be accepted via GPS but not by court. Mail requests: SASE required.

89th District Court PO Box 110, Rogers City, MI 49779; 989-734-2411; fax: 989-734-3400; 8AM-4PM (EST). ***Misdemeanor, Civil Actions under $25,000, Eviction, Small Claims.***
www.89thdistrictcourt.org/

Civil Records: Access: Mail, in person. Only the court performs in person searches; visitors may not. Search fee: $5.00. Required to search: name, years to search. Civil cases indexed by defendant, plaintiff, on computer since 7/94, prior on index books. Mail turnaround time 2 weeks. Dockets for 2 weeks ahead are available at www.89thdistrictcourt.org/scheduling.htm.

Criminal Records: Access: Mail, in person. Only the court performs in person searches; visitors may not. Search fee: $5.00. Required to search: name, years to search, DOB. Criminal records on computer since 7/94, prior on index books. Mail turnaround time 2 weeks or less. Dockets for 2 weeks ahead are at www.89thdistrictcourt.org/scheduling.htm.

General Information: No suppressed records released. Will not fax documents. Court makes copy: $1.00 first page, $.50 each add'l, self serve same. Certification fee: $10.00 plus $1.00 per page after first. Payee: 89th District Court. Personal checks accepted; credit cards are not. Mail requests: SASE required.

Probate Court 151 Huron Ave, PO Box 110, Rogers City, MI 49779; 989-734-3268; fax: 989-734-4420; 8:30AM-4:30PM (EST). ***Probate.***

Roscommon County

34th Circuit Court 500 Lake St #1, Attn: County Clerk Reg of Deeds, Roscommon, MI 48653; 989-275-1902; fax: 989-275-0602; 8:30AM-4:30PM (EST). ***Felony, Civil Actions over $25,000, Vital Statistics.***

Civil Records: Access: Fax, mail, in person. Both court and visitors may perform in person searches. Search fee: $5.00 per name. Required to search: name, years to search. Civil records on computer since 3/94, prior on docket books and cards. Mail turnaround time 24 hours. Civil PAT available.

Criminal Records: Access: Fax, mail, in person. Both court and visitors may perform in person searches. Search fee: $5.00 per name. Required to search: name, years to search, DOB. Criminal records on computer since 3/94, prior on docket books and cards. Mail turnaround time 24 hours. Criminal PAT available.

General Information: No suppressed, sex offenders or mental health records released. Fee to fax out file $3.00 1st page, $1.00 each add'l. Court makes copy: $.50 per page. Certification fee: $11.00 plus $1.00 per page after first. Payee: 34th Circuit Court. Personal checks accepted; credit cards are not. Mail requests: SASE required.

83rd District Court 500 Lake St, Roscommon, MI 48653; 989-275-5312; criminal fax: 989-275-6033; civil fax: same; 8:30AM-4:30PM (EST). ***Misdemeanor, Civil Actions under $25,000, Eviction, Small Claims.***

Civil Records: Access: Phone, fax, mail, in person. Only the court performs in person searches; visitors may not. No search fee. Required to search: name, years to search. Civil cases indexed by defendant, plaintiff, on computer since 1988, prior on index cards since 1969. Mail turnaround time same day.

Criminal Records: Access: Phone, fax, mail, in person. Only the court performs in person searches; visitors may not. No search fee. Required to search: name, years to search, DOB; also helpful: SSN. Criminal records on computer since 1988, prior on index cards since 1969. Mail turnaround time same day.

General Information: No suppressed, juvenile, sex offenders, mental health, or adoption records released. No fee to fax documents. Court makes copy: $.50 per page. No certification fee. Payee: 83rd District Court. Personal checks accepted. Credit card payments accepted via GPS.

Probate Court 500 Lake St, Roscommon, MI 48653; 989-275-5221; fax: 989-275-8537; 8:30AM-4:30PM (EST). ***Probate.***

Saginaw County

10th Circuit Court 111 S Michigan Ave, Saginaw, MI 48602; 989-790-5541; probate phone: 989-790-5233; fax: 989-790-5248; 8AM-5:00PM (EST). ***Felony, Civil Actions over $25,000, Vital Statistics.***
www.saginawcounty.com/clerk/court/index.html

Civil Records: Access: Mail, in person, online. Both court and visitors may perform in person searches. No search fee at this time. Required to search: name, years to search. Civil cases indexed by defendant, plaintiff, on computer since 1985, prior on index books, microfilm. Mail turnaround time 2 days. Civil PAT goes back to 1986. PAT results show middle initial, DOB. Search civil records free at www.saginawcounty.com/clerk/circuit_civil_records.html. Calendars may be searched at www.saginawcounty.com/clerk/docket/index.html.

Criminal Records: Access: Mail, in person, online. Both court and visitors may perform in person searches. No search fee at this time. Required to search: name, years to search, DOB. Criminal records on computer since 1986, prior on index books. Mail turnaround time 2 days. Criminal PAT goes back to same as civil. PAT results show middle initial, DOB. Search criminal records online free at www.saginawcounty.com/clerk/circuit_criminal_records.html.

General Information: No suppressed, sex offenders, mental health or guardianship records released. Will fax documents, up to 5 pages. Court makes copy: $1.00 per page. Certification fee: $10.00 plus $1.00 per page. Payee: Saginaw County Clerk. Personal checks accepted. Credit card payments accepted via GPS and online. In person searches limited to debit cards only. Mail requests: SASE required.

70th District Court - Criminal Division 111 S Michigan Ave, Saginaw, MI 48602; 989-790-5385; fax: 989-790-5589; 8AM-4:45PM (EST). ***Misdemeanor.***
www.saginawcounty.com/DistrictCourt/

Criminal Records: Access: Fax, mail, in person. Only the court performs in person searches; visitors may not. Search fee: $10.00 per name. Required to search: name, years to search, DOB, signed release; also helpful: address. Criminal records computerized from 1987, prior on microfiche since 1972. Note: Fax information received only if pre-paid. Mail turnaround time 1 week. Public use terminal has crim records.PAT results show name, DOB.

General Information: No suppressed, juvenile, sex offenders, mental health, or adoption records released. Will fax documents to local or toll free line for a fee depending on how many pages. Prepayment required of $10.00 plus fax fee. Court makes copy: $1.00 per page. Certification fee: $10.00 for 1st page, $1.00 per page after. Payee: 70th District Court. Business checks accepted. Major credit cards accepted in person only. Mail requests: SASE required.

70th District Court - Civil Division 111 S Michigan Ave, Saginaw, MI 48602; 989-790-5380; fax: 989-790-5562; 8AM-4:45PM (EST). ***Civil Actions under $25,000, Eviction, Small Claims.***
www.saginawcounty.com/districtcourt

Civil Records: Access: Mail, in person. Only the court performs in person searches; visitors may not. Search fee: $10.00 per name. Required to search: name, years to search. Civil cases indexed by defendant, plaintiff, on computer since 1982, prior on docket books. Mail turnaround time 1 week. Public use terminal has civil records back to 1988. PAT civil results show middle initial. Terminal results show middle initial if one was provided.

General Information: No suppressed records released. Will fax documents to local or toll free line for a fax fee. Court makes copy: $1.00 per page. Certification fee: $10.00. Payee: 70th District court. Personal checks accepted; credit cards are not. Mail requests: SASE required.

Probate/Family Court 111 S Michigan St, 2nd Fl, Rm 204, Saginaw, MI 48602; 989-790-5320; fax: 989-790-5328; 8AM-5PM (EST). ***Probate.***
www.saginawcounty.com/probate

Sanilac County

24th Circuit Court 60 W Sanilac, Rm 203, Sandusky, MI 48471; 810-648-3212 x8227; fax: 810-648-5466; 8AM-4:30PM (EST). ***Felony, Civil Actions over $25,000, Vital Statistics.***
www.sanilaccounty.net/office.asp?id=circuitcou

Civil Records: Access: Mail, in person. Both court and visitors may perform in person searches. Search fee: $10.00 per name. Required to search: name, years to search. Civil cases indexed by defendant, plaintiff, on computer since 1993. Mail turnaround time 2-3 days. PAT results show name only.

Criminal Records: Access: Mail, in person. Both court and visitors may perform in person searches. Search fee: $10.00, per name. Required to search: name, years to search. Criminal records on computer since 1993. Mail turnaround time 2-3 days. PAT results show name only.

General Information: No suppressed, juvenile, sex offenders, mental health, or adoption records released. Will fax documents to local or toll free line. Court makes copy: $1.00 per page, self serve same. Certification fee: $10.00. Payee: Sanilac County Clerk. Personal checks accepted. Credit card payments go through GPS. Mail requests: SASE required.

73A District Court 60 W Sanilac, Sandusky, MI 48471; 810-648-3250; civil phone: 810-648-3250; fax: 810-648-3271; 8AM-4:30PM (EST). ***Misdemeanor, Civil Actions under $25,000, Eviction, Small Claims.***
Traffic phone is 810-648-3424.

Civil Records: Access: Mail, in person. Only the court performs in person searches; visitors may not. Search fee: $1.00 per name per year. Required to search: name, years to search; also helpful: address. Civil cases indexed by defendant, plaintiff, on computer back to 1989, prior on docket books to 1969. Mail turnaround time 1 week.

Criminal Records: Access: Mail, in person. Only the court performs in person searches; visitors may not. Search fee: $1.00 per name per year. Required to search: name, years to search, DOB; also helpful: address. Criminal records computerized from 1989, prior on docket books to 1969. Mail turnaround time 1 week.

General Information: No suppressed records released. Will fax documents to local or toll free line. Fax fee included in search. Court makes copy: $1.00 per page. Certification fee: $10.00 plus $1.00 per page after first. Payee: 73A District Court. Personal checks accepted; credit cards are not. Mail requests: SASE required.

Probate Court 60 W Sanilac Ave, Rm 106, Sandusky, MI 48471-1096; 810-648-3221; fax: 810-648-2900; 8AM-N, 1-4:30PM (EST). ***Probate.***

Schoolcraft County

11th Circuit Court 300 Walnut St, Rm 164, Manistique, MI 49854; 906-341-3618; probate phone: 906-341-3644; criminal fax: 906-341-5680; civil fax: same; 8AM-4PM (EST). ***Felony, Civil Actions over $25,000, Vital Statistics.***
Probate is a separate index in Rm 129. Probate fax-906-341-3627

Civil Records: Access: Phone, fax, mail, in person. Both court and visitors may perform in person searches. Search fee: $10.00 per name. Required to search: name, years to search. Civil cases indexed by defendant, plaintiff; index on docket books and index since 1881. Mail turnaround time 2-3 days.
Criminal Records: Access: Phone, fax, mail, in person. Only the court performs in person searches; visitors may not. Search fee: $10.00 per name. Required to search: name, years to search. Criminal docket on books and index since 1881. Mail turnaround time 2-3 days.
General Information: No suppressed, juvenile, sex offenders, mental health, or adoption records released. Will fax documents to local or toll free line. Court makes copy: $1.00 per page. Certification fee: $10.00 per document. Payee: Schoolcraft County Clerk. Personal checks accepted. Credit card payments accepted via GPS. SASE not required.

93rd District Court 300 Walnut St, Rm 135, Manistique, MI 49854; 906-341-3630; criminal fax: 906-341-8006; civil fax: same; 8AM-4PM (EST). ***Misdemeanor, Civil Actions under $25,000, Eviction, Small Claims.***
Civil Records: Access: Mail, in person. Both court and visitors may perform in person searches. Search fee: $10.00. Required to search: name, years to search. Civil cases indexed by defendant, plaintiff, kept on index cards. Mail turnaround time 2-3 days.
Criminal Records: Access: Mail, in person. Only the court performs in person searches; visitors may not. Search fee: $10.00. Required to search: name, years to search, DOB; also helpful: SSN. Criminal records kept on index cards. Mail turnaround time 2-3 days.
General Information: No suppressed, sex offenders or mental health records released. Will fax documents. Court makes copy: $1.00 per page, self serve same. Certification fee: $10.00 plus copy fee if more than 1 page. Payee: 93rd District Court. Business checks accepted. No credit cards accepted. Mail requests: SASE required.

Probate Court 300 Walnut St, Rm 129, Manistique, MI 49854; 906-341-3641; fax: 906-341-3627; 8AM-N, 1-4PM (EST). ***Probate.***

Shiawassee County

35th Circuit Court 208 N Shiawassee St, Corunna, MI 48817; 989-743-2262; fax: 989-743-2241; 8AM-5PM, may close for lunch hour (EST). ***Felony, Civil Actions over $25,000, Vital Statistics.***
Civil Records: Access: Phone, fax, mail, in person. Both court and visitors may perform in person searches. Search fee: $10.00 for up to 10 years. Required to search: name, years to search. Civil cases indexed by defendant, plaintiff, on computer since 9/87, prior on docket books and cards. Mail turnaround time 1 week.
Criminal Records: Access: Phone, fax, mail, in person. Both court and visitors may perform in person searches. Search fee: $10.00 for up to 10 years. Required to search: name, years to search, DOB. Criminal records on computer since 10/93; prior on docket books. Mail turnaround time 1 week.
General Information: No suppressed records released. Will fax documents for $10.00 fee. Court makes copy: $1.00 per page 1st 5 pages; $.15 each add'l. Certification fee: $10.00 per document. A Register of Action fee is $10.00. Payee: 35th Circuit Court. Personal checks accepted; credit cards are not. Mail requests: SASE required.

66th District Court 110 E Mack St, Corunna, MI 48817; 989-743-2395; criminal fax: 989-743-2469; civil fax: same; 8AM-5PM (EST). ***Misdemeanor, Civil Actions under $25,000, Eviction, Small Claims.***
Civil Records: Access: Phone, fax, mail, in person. Both court and visitors may perform in person searches. No search fee. Required to search: name, years to search; also helpful: DOB, SSN. Civil cases indexed by defendant, plaintiff, on computer back to 1995, prior on microfiche. Mail turnaround time 1 week. Civil PAT goes back to 1995.
Criminal Records: Access: Phone, fax, mail, in person. Both court and visitors may perform in person searches. No search fee. Required to search: name, years to search, DOB. Case number required for pre-1995 research. Criminal records computerized from 1995, prior on microfiche to 1969. Mail turnaround time 1 week. Criminal PAT goes back to same as civil.
General Information: No suppressed records released. Faxes out documents Fridays only. Court makes copy: $1.00 per page. Certification fee: $10.00 includes copy fee. Payee: 66th District Court. Personal checks accepted. Mail requests: SASE required.

Probate Court 110 E Mack St, Corunna, MI 48817; 989-743-2211; fax: 989-743-2349; 8AM-5PM (EST). ***Probate.***

St. Clair County

31st Circuit Court 201 McMorran Blvd, Port Huron, MI 48060; 810-985-2200; fax: 810-985-4796; 8AM-4:30PM (EST). ***Felony, Civil Actions over $25,000, Vital Statistics.***
www.stclaircounty.org/Offices/courts
Civil Records: Access: Mail, fax, in person, online. Both court and visitors may perform in person searches. No search fee. Required to search: name, years to search; also helpful: address. Civil cases indexed by defendant, plaintiff, on computer back to 1987, non computerized records back to 1936. Mail turnaround time 24 hours. Civil PAT available. A index of records can be viewed at www.stclaircounty.org/Offices/courts/circuit/records.asp.
Criminal Records: Access: Mail, fax, in person, online. Both court and visitors may perform in person searches. No search fee. Required to search: name, years to search, DOB; also helpful: address. Criminal records computerized from 1987, non computerized records back to 1936. Mail turnaround time 24 hours. Criminal PAT available. Records index can be viewed at www.stclaircounty.org/Offices/courts/circuit/records.asp.
General Information: No suppressed, juvenile, mental health, or adoption records released. Will fax documents $10.00 per searched name. Court makes copy: $1.00 per page. Certification fee: $10.00. Payee: St. Clair Clerk of Court. Will accept In state checks. Credit cards accepted. Mail requests: SASE required.

72nd District Court 201 McMorran Blvd, Rm 2900, Port Huron, MI 48060; 810-985-2076; criminal phone: 810-985-2072; civil phone: 810-985-2077; fax: 810-982-1260; 8AM-4:30PM M-TH; 9AM-4:30PM (EST). ***Misdemeanor, Civil Actions under $25,000, Eviction, Small Claims.***
www.stclaircounty.org/offices/courts/
Civil Records: Access: In person, online. Visitors must perform in person searches themselves. Required to search: name, years to search. Civil cases indexed by defendant, plaintiff, on computer since 1987, prior on docket books back to 1969. Civil PAT goes back to 1989. PAT results show name only. Access court case index free at www.stclaircounty.org/DCS/search.aspx.
Criminal Records: Access: In person, online. Visitors must perform in person searches themselves. Required to search: name, years to search, DOB; SSN helpful. Criminal records on computer since 1987, prior on docket books back to 1969. Criminal PAT goes back to same as civil. PAT results show name only. Access court case index free at www.stclaircounty.org/DCS/search.aspx.
General Information: No suppressed records released. Will fax documents $1.00 per page. Court makes copy: $1.00 per page. Certification fee: $10.00 per doc includes copy fee. Payee: 72nd District Court. Personal checks and major credit cards accepted. Mail requests: SASE required for mail return of any copies.

Probate Court 201 McMorran Blvd, Rm 2600, Port Huron, MI 48060; 810-985-2066; fax: 810-985-2179; 8AM-4:30PM (EST). ***Probate.***
www.stclaircounty.org/Offices/courts/probate/
Probate cases may be included in the online search at www.stclaircounty.org/DCS/search.aspx.

St. Joseph County

45th Circuit Court PO Box 189, Centreville, MI 49032; 269-467-5531; criminal fax: 269-467-5628; civil fax: same; 9AM-5PM (EST). ***Felony, Civil Actions over $25,000, Vital Statistics.***
www.stjosephcountymi.org/ccircuit.htm
Civil Records: Access: Mail, in person. Both court and visitors may perform in person searches. Search fee: $1.00 per name. For records prior to 1988, fee is $1.00 per year searched. Required to search: name, years to search. Civil cases indexed by defendant, plaintiff, on computer since 1988, prior on books from 1900, earlier in archives. Note: Visitors can do in person searches after 1988. Mail turnaround time 1 day. Civil PAT goes back to 1988. PAT civil results show middle initial.
Criminal Records: Access: Mail, in person. Both court and visitors may perform in person searches. Search fee: $1.00 per name. For records prior to 1988, fee is $1.00 per year searched. Required to search: name, years to search. Criminal records on computer since 1988, prior on books from 1900, earlier in archives. Note: Court can do in person searches of indexes after 1988. Mail turnaround time same day. Criminal PAT goes back to same as civil. PAT results show middle initial, DOB.
General Information: No suppressed records released. Will fax documents $2.00 1st page, $1.00 each add'l. Court makes copy: $1.00 per page. Certification fee: $10.00 per certification plus $1.00 per page. Payee: St. Joseph County Clerk. Business checks accepted. Credit card payments accepted via GPS. SASE not required.

3-B District Court PO Box 67, Centreville, MI 49032; 269-467-5627; criminal phone: 269-467-5585; civil phone: 269-467-5623; fax: 269-467-5611; 8:30AM-5PM (EST). ***Misdemeanor, Civil Actions under $25,000, Eviction, Small Claims.***
www.stjosephcountymi.org/cdistrict.htm
Civil Records: Access: Phone, mail, in person. Both court and visitors may perform in person searches. No search fee. Required to search: name, years to search; also helpful: address. Civil cases indexed by defendant, plaintiff, on computer since 1987, prior in archives. Note: Phone search access limited. Mail turnaround time minimum 72 hours. Civil PAT goes back to 9/1987. PAT results show middle initial, DOB.
Criminal Records: Access: Fax, mail, in person. Both court and visitors may perform in person searches. No search fee. Required to search: name, years to search, DOB, date of offense. Criminal records on computer since 1987, prior in archives. Note: Signed release required for some searches. Mail turnaround time minimum 72 hours. Criminal PAT goes back to same as civil. PAT results show middle initial, DOB.
General Information: No suppressed records released. Will not fax documents. Court makes copy: $.15 per page. Certification fee: $10.00 per doc. Payee: 3-B District Court. Business checks accepted. Credit card payments accepted via GPS. SASE not required.

Probate Court PO Box 190, 125 W Main, Centreville, MI 49032; 269-467-5538; fax: 269-467-5560; 8AM-5PM (EST). ***Probate.***
www.stjosephcountymi.org/cprobate.htm

Tuscola County

54th Circuit Court 440 N State St, Caro, MI 48723; 989-673-3330; 989-672-3780 county clerk; criminal phone: 989-672-3776; civil phone: 989-672-3775; probate phone: 989-672-3850; fax: 989-672-4266; 8AM-N, 1-4:30PM (EST). ***Felony, Civil Actions over $25,000, Vital Statistics.***
www.tuscolacounty.org
Civil Records: Access: Mail, in person. Only the court performs in person searches; visitors may not. Search fee: $5.00 per name. Fee is $1.00 for each year prior to 1989. Required to search: name, years to search. Civil cases indexed by defendant, plaintiff, on computer since 1989, prior on books since beginning. Mail turnaround time 3-4 days.
Criminal Records: Access: Mail, in person. Only the court performs in person searches; visitors may

not. Search fee: $5.00 per name. Fee is $1.00 for each year prior to 1989. Required to search: name, years to search, DOB; also helpful: SSN. Criminal records on computer since 1989, prior on books since beginning. Mail turnaround time 3-4 days.
General Information: No suppressed, juvenile, sex offenders, mental health, or adoption records released. Will not fax documents. Court makes copy: $1.00 per page. Certification fee: $10.00 plus $1.00 per page after first. Payee: County Clerk. No personal checks. Credit card payments accepted via GPS. Mail requests: SASE required.

71 B District Court 440 N State St., Caro, MI 48723; 989-672-3800; criminal phone: 989-672-3790; civil phone: 989-672-3800; criminal fax: 989-672-4526; civil fax: 989-673-0451; 8AM-4:30PM (EST). ***Misdemeanor, Civil Actions under $25,000, Eviction, Small Claims.***
Civil Records: Access: Mail, in person. Only the court performs in person searches; visitors may not. No search fee. Required to search: name, years to search. Civil cases indexed by defendant, plaintiff, on computer since 1998, prior on cards. Mail turnaround time 5-10 days. Public use terminal available, records go back to 1998. Must schedule in advance for Public Access Terminal.
Criminal Records: Access: Mail, in person. Only the court performs in person searches; visitors may not. No search fee. Required to search: name, years to search, DOB; also helpful: SSN. Criminal records on computer since 1998; others back to 1969. Mail turnaround time 1-3 days. Public use terminal available. Must schedule in advance for Public Access Terminal.
General Information: No suppressed records released. Will not fax documents. Court makes copy: $.50 per page. Certification fee: $10.00 plus $1.00 per page after first. Payee: 71 B District Court. Personal checks accepted. Credit cards accepted; a surcharge applies. Credit card payments accepted via GPS. Mail requests: SASE required.

Probate Court 440 N State St, Caro, MI 48723; 989-672-3850; fax: 989-672-2057; 8AM-N, 1-4:30PM (EST). ***Probate.***

Van Buren County

36th Circuit Court 212 Paw Paw St #101, Paw Paw, MI 49079; 269-657-8218 #6; criminal fax: 269-657-8298; civil fax: 269-657-0719; 8:30AM-5PM (EST). ***Felony, Civil Actions over $25,000, Vital Statistics.***
www.vbco.org/government0093.asp
Civil Records: Access: Mail, in person. Only the court performs in person searches; visitors may not. Search fee: $1.00 per name per year. Fee includes combined civil and criminal search. Required to search: name, years to search. Civil cases indexed by defendant, plaintiff, on computer back to 1990, prior on docket books since 1800s. Mail turnaround time 1 day.
Criminal Records: Access: Mail, in person. Only the court performs in person searches; visitors may not. Search fee: $1.00 per name per year. Required to search: name, years to search, DOB, signed release. Criminal records computerized from 1990, prior on docket books since 1800s. Mail turnaround time 1 day.
General Information: No suppressed, sex offender records released. Will phone when documents ready if toll-free number provided. Court makes copy: $1.00 per page. Certification fee: $10.00 plus $1.00 per page after first. Payee: Van Buren County Clerk. Personal checks accepted. Credit card payments accepted via GPS. Mail requests: SASE required.

7th District Court - East 212 Paw Paw St, #130, Paw Paw, MI 49079; 269-657-8222; fax: 269-657-0719; 9AM-4:30PM (EST). ***Misdemeanor, Civil Actions under $25,000, Eviction, Small Claims.***
www.vbco.org/government0093.asp
Civil Records: Access: Mail, fax, in person. Both court and visitors may perform in person searches. No search fee. Required to search: name, years to search. Civil cases indexed by defendant, plaintiff, kept in file folder; computerized records since 1999. Mail turnaround time 1-2 days.
Criminal Records: Access: Mail, fax, in person. Both court and visitors may perform in person searches. No search fee. Required to search: name, years to search, DOB, SSN. Criminal records kept in file folder; computerized since 1999. Mail turnaround time 1-2 days.
General Information: No suppressed records released. Court makes copy: $1.00 per page. Certification fee: $10.00 per doc. Payee: 7th District Court. No personal checks accepted. Credit card payments accepted via GPS. Mail requests: SASE required.

7th District Court - West Division 1007 E Wells, PO Box 311, South Haven, MI 49090; 269-637-5258; fax: 269-639-4517; 8:30AM-4:30PM (EST). ***Misdemeanor, Civil Actions under $25,000, Eviction, Small Claims.***
www.vbco.org/government0093.asp
Civil Records: Access: Mail, in person. Only the court performs in person searches; visitors may not. Search fee: $1.00 per name. Required to search: name, years to search. Civil cases indexed by defendant, plaintiff, on computer since 1991, prior on index cards since 1982. Mail turnaround 3 days.
Criminal Records: Access: Mail, in person. Only the court performs in person searches; visitors may not. Search fee: $1.00 per name. Required to search: name, years to search, DOB; also helpful: SSN. Criminal records on computer since 1991, prior on index cards since 1982. Mail turnaround time 3 days.
General Information: No suppressed, juvenile, sex offenders, mental health, or adoption records released. Court makes copy: $1.00 per page. Self serve: $.25 per page. Certification fee: $10.00 plus $1.00 per page after first. Payee: 7th District Court. Personal checks accepted. Credit card payments accepted via GPS. Mail requests: SASE required.

Probate Court 212 Paw Paw St, Ste 220, Paw Paw, MI 49079; 269-657-8225; fax: 269-657-7573; 8:30AM-5PM (EST). ***Probate.***
www.vbco.org/government0093.asp

Washtenaw County

22nd Circuit Court PO Box 8645, 101 E Huron St, Ann Arbor, MI 48107-8645; 734-222-3001; fax: 734-222-3089; 8:30AM-4:30PM (EST). ***Felony, Civil Actions over $25,000, Vital Statistics.***
www.washtenawtrialcourt.org
Weekly court dockets listed by judge are free at http://washtenawtrialcourt.org/calendar.
Civil Records: Access: Mail, in person, online. Both court and visitors may perform in person searches. Search fee: $5.00 per name from 1979 to present; $1.00 per name per year prior to 1979. Required to search: name, years to search. Civil cases indexed by defendant, plaintiff, kept as originals in file folders, records go back to 1900; computerized since 1979. Note: Fax requests not accepted without prepayment. Mail turnaround time 2-3 weeks. Civil PAT goes back to 1979. PAT results show middle initial, SSN, but results from PAT do not always include DOB or address. Only signed orders back 30 days are free online at http://washtenawtrialcourt.org/signed_orders; search by judge.
Criminal Records: Access: Mail, in person, online. Both court and visitors may perform in person searches. Search fee: $5.00 per name from 1979 to present; $1.00 per name per year prior to 1979. Required to search: name, years to search, DOB. Criminal records kept as originals in file folders, records go back to 1900; computerized since 1979. Note: Fax requests not accepted without prepayment. Mail turnaround time 2-3 weeks. Criminal PAT goes back to 1979. PAT results show middle initial, SSN but results from PAT do not always include DOB or address. Only signed orders back 30 days are free online at http://washtenawtrialcourt.org/signed_orders; search by judge.
General Information: No suppressed records released. Will not fax documents. Court makes copy: $1.00 per page. Certification fee: $10.00 per doc. Payee: Washtenaw County Clerk. Personal checks accepted. Mail requests: SASE required.

14A1 District Court 4133 Washtenaw, Ann Arbor, MI 48107-8645; 734-973-4545; criminal fax: 734-973-4693; civil fax: same; 8AM-4:30PM (EST). ***Misdemeanor, Civil Actions under $25,000, Eviction, Small Claims.***
www.14adistrictcourt.org
Civil Records: Access: Mail, in person, online. Both court and visitors may perform in person searches. No search fee. Required to search: name, years to search. Civil cases indexed by defendant, plaintiff, on computer since 1985, prior on index cards. Mail turnaround time 1-2 weeks. Civil PAT goes back to 1985. Dockets and calendars are searchable at www.14adistrictcourt.org/cases.
Criminal Records: Access: Mail, in person, online. Both court and visitors may perform in person searches. No search fee. Required to search: name, years to search, DOB. Criminal records on computer since 1985, prior on index cards. Mail turnaround time 1-2 weeks. Criminal PAT goes back to same as civil. PAT results show middle initial, DOB. Dockets and calendars are searchable at www.14adistrictcourt.org/cases. Online results show middle initial.
General Information: No suppressed records released. Will fax documents to local number. Court makes copy: $1.00 per page. Certification fee: $10.00 per doc. Payee: 14 A District Court. Personal checks accepted. Visa/MC, Discover accepted. Mail requests: SASE required.

14A2 District Court 415 W Michigan Ave, Ypsilanti, MI 48197; 734-484-6690; fax: 734-484-6697; 8AM-4:30PM (EST). ***Misdemeanor, Civil Actions under $25,000, Eviction, Small Claims.***
www.14adistrictcourt.org
Civil Records: Access: Mail, in person, online. Only the court performs in person searches; visitors may not. No search fee. Required to search: name, years to search. Civil cases indexed by defendant, plaintiff, on computer since 1985, prior on file cards since 1969. Note: Specific docket information must be given; court will not do name searches. Mail turnaround time 1 week; phone turnaround can be immediate up to 2 days. Only dockets and calendars are searchable online at www.14adistrictcourt.org/cases.
Criminal Records: Access: Mail, in person, online. Only the court performs in person searches; visitors may not. No search fee. Required to search: name, years to search, DOB. Criminal records on computer since 1985, prior on file cards since 1969. Note: This court will not do name searches. Mail turnaround time 1 week; phone turnaround immediate up to 2 days. Only dockets and calendars are searchable online at www.14adistrictcourt.org/cases.
General Information: No suppressed, juvenile, sex offenders, mental health, or adoption records released. Will not fax documents. Court makes copy: $.25 per page. Certification fee: $10.00 per case plus $1.00 per page. Payee: 14 A-2 District Court. Personal checks accepted. Major credit cards accepted; $10.00 minimum. Credit card payments accepted via GPS. Mail requests: SASE requested.

14A3 District Court 122 S Main St, Chelsea, MI 48118; 734-475-8606; fax: 734-475-0460; 8AM-4:30PM (EST). ***Misdemeanor, Civil Actions under $25,000, Eviction, Small Claims.***
www.14adistrictcourt.org
Civil Records: Access: Mail, fax, in person, online. Both court and visitors may perform in person searches. No search fee. Required to search: name, years to search. Civil cases indexed by defendant, plaintiff, on computer since 1986; prior on index cards. Note: Court will perform search time permitting. Civil PAT available. PAT results show name only. Dockets and calendars are searchable at www.14adistrictcourt.org/cases.
Criminal Records: Access: In person, online. Both court and visitors may perform in person searches. No search fee. Required to search: name, years to search, DOB; SSN helpful. Criminal records on computer since 1986; prior on index cards. Criminal PAT available. PAT results show name only. Dockets and calendars are searchable at www.14adistrictcourt.org/cases.

General Information: No suppressed records released. Will not fax documents. Court makes copy: $1.00 for 1st copy, $.25 each add'l. Certification fee: $10.00 per doc. Payee: 14A District Court. Personal checks and major credit cards accepted. Mail requests: SASE required for civil.

14B District Court - Civil Division 7200 S Huron River Dr, Ypsilanti, MI 48197; 734-483-5300; fax: 734-483-3630; 8AM-5PM (EST). ***Civil Actions under $25,000, Eviction, Small Claims.***

Civil Records: Access: Mail, in person. Only the court performs in person searches; visitors may not. No search fee. Required to search: name, years to search. Civil cases indexed by defendant, plaintiff, on computer since 1990, prior on card files from 1985-1989. Mail turnaround time 1 week, phone turnaround is 1 day.

General Information: No suppressed, juvenile, sex offenders, probation, mental health, or adoption records released. Will not fax documents. Court makes copy: $.50 per page. Certification fee: $10.00 per doc. Payee: 14-B District Court. Business checks accepted. Major Major credit cards accepted via GPS. SASE not required.

14B District Court - Criminal Division 7200 S Huron River Dr, Ypsilanti, MI 48197; 734-483-1333; fax: 734-483-3630; 8AM-5PM (EST). ***Misdemeanor.***

Criminal Records: Access: Fax, mail, in person. Only the court performs in person searches; visitors may not. No search fee. Required to search: name, years to search, DOB; also helpful: SSN. Criminal records on computer since 1990, prior records kept by name. Mail turnaround time 1 week; phone turnaround 1 day.

General Information: No suppressed, probation, juvenile, sex offenders, probation, mental health, or adoption records released. Will not fax documents. Court makes copy: $.50 per page. Certification fee: $10.00 per doc. Payee: 14-B District Court. Personal checks accepted. Major Major credit cards accepted via GPS. SASE not required.

15th District Court - Civil Division PO Box 8650, 101 E Huron St, Ann Arbor, MI 48107; 734-222-3389; fax: 734-222-3335; 8AM-4:30PM (EST). ***Civil Actions under $25,000, Eviction, Small Claims.***
www.15thdistrictcourt.org
Criminal Traffic phone- 734-222-3380.

Civil Records: Access: Phone, fax, mail, in person, online. Only the court performs in person searches; visitors may not. No search fee. Required to search: name, years to search. Civil cases indexed by defendant, plaintiff, on computer since 1990, prior on docket books. Mail turnaround time 2-3 days. Public use terminal has civil records. PAT results show name only. Access court records free at https://secure.courts.michigan.gov/jis/. Online results show name only.

General Information: No suppressed records released. Will not fax documents. Court makes copy: $.25 per page. Certification fee: $10.00 per doc plus $1.00 per page. Payee: 15th District Court. Personal checks and major credit cards accepted. Mail requests: SASE required for civil.

15th District Court - Criminal Division PO Box 8650, 101 E Huron St, Ann Arbor, MI 48107-8650; 734-222-3380; fax: 734-222-3335; 8AM-4:30PM (EST). ***Misdemeanor, Traffic.***
www.15thdistrictcourt.org

Criminal Records: Access: Mail, fax, in person, online. Only the court performs in person searches; visitors may not. No search fee. Required to search: name, years to search, DOB; also helpful: offense. Criminal records computerized back to 1996; prior on docket cards since 1969. Note: The court will not do a name search; either a case number or charge and incident date is required. Mail turnaround time 2-3 days. Access court records free at https://secure.courts.michigan.gov/jis/. Online results include address. Online records of open case records back to 8/6/2006 available, with searches for case numbers available on closed cases. Online results show name only.

General Information: No suppressed, juvenile, sex offenders, mental health, or adoption records released. Will not fax documents. Court makes copy: $.25 per page. Certification fee: $10.00 per doc plus $1.00 per page. Payee: 15th District Court. Checks accepted. Major credit cards accepted. Mail requests: SASE required.

Probate Court PO Box 8645, 101 E Huron St, Ann Arbor, MI 48107; 734-222-3072 x2; fax: 734-222-3019; 8AM-4:30PM (EST). ***Probate.***
http://courts.ewashtenaw.org

Wayne County

Frank Murphy Hall of Justice 1441 St Antoine, Rm 904, Detroit, MI 48226; 313-224-2500; criminal phone: 313-224-2502/2503; fax: 313-224-2786; 8AM-4:30PM (EST). ***Felony.***

Criminal Records: Access: Mail, in person. Both court and visitors may perform in person searches. Search fee: $5.00 per name. Required to search: name, years to search, DOB; also helpful: city where crime occurred, aliases. Criminal records on computer since mid 1974, prior on microfiche through 1976, archives off-site 1800s to 2000. Mail turnaround time 3-4 days. Public use terminal has crim records back to mid-1974. PAT results show middle initial, DOB.

General Information: No suppressed, juvenile, sex offenders, mental health, or adoption records released. Will not fax documents. Court makes copy: $1.00 per page. Certification fee: $10.00 per doc. Payee: Wayne County Clerk. No personal checks accepted. Credit card payments accepted via GPS. Mail requests: SASE required.

36th District Court 421 Madison, Detroit, MI 48226; 313-965-2200; criminal phone: 313-965-5029; civil phone: 313-965-6098; fax: 313-965-3951; 8AM-4:30PM (EST). ***Felony, Misdemeanor, Civil Actions under $25,000, Eviction, Small Claims Under $3000.***
www.36thdistrictcourt.org/
Small Claims phone number is 313-965-5972.

Civil Records: Access: In person only. Visitors must perform in person searches themselves. Required to search: name, years to search, address. Civil cases indexed by name, case number. Civil records on computer since 1985, prior kept in file folders. Note: If a case number is provided, then court will retrieve records. Civil PAT goes back to 1981. Civil records public terminal is on 2nd Fl.

Criminal Records: Access: In person only. Both court and visitors may perform in person searches. No search fee. Required to search: name, DOB; SSN helpful. Criminal records go back to 1987. Note: Will do a single name search over the phone to let you know index numbers, if any. Criminal PAT available. Criminal public terminal on 1st Fl.

General Information: No suppressed records released. Will not fax documents. Court makes copy: $1.00 per page. Certification fee: $10.00 plus $1.00 per page after first. Payee: 36th District Court. Personal checks accepted. Visa/MC/Discover Major credit cards accepted via GPS.

16th District Court 15140 Farmington Rd, Livonia, MI 48154-5498; 734-466-2500; 466-2550 Probation; criminal phone: X3452; civil phone: X3541; 8:30AM-4:30PM (EST). ***Misdemeanor, Civil Actions under $25,000, Eviction, Small Claims.***
www.ci.livonia.mi.us/

Civil Records: Access: Mail, in person. Both court and visitors may perform in person searches. No search fee. Required to search: name, years to search. Civil cases indexed by defendant, plaintiff, on computer since 1990, prior on microfiche. Mail turnaround time 1 week. Civil PAT goes back to 1990.

Criminal Records: Access: In person only. Visitors must perform in person searches themselves. Required to search: name, years to search, DOB; also helpful: offense, date of offense, case number. Criminal records on computer since 1991, prior on microfiche. Note: Court will process request is case number is provided. Criminal PAT goes back to 1991.

General Information: No suppressed records released. Will fax documents to local or toll free line. Court makes copy: $1.00 per page. Certification fee: $10.00 per cert. Payee: 16th District Court. Personal checks accepted. Visa/MC accepted. Credit card payments accepted via GPS. Mail requests: SASE required for civil.

17th District Court 15111 Beech-Daly Rd, Redford, MI 48239; 313-387-2790; civil phone: 313-387-2796; fax: 313-387-2712; 8:30AM-4:15PM (EST). ***Misdemeanor, Civil Actions under $25,000, Eviction, Small Claims.***

Civil Records: Access: Phone, mail, in person. Only the court performs in person searches; visitors may not. No search fee. Required to search: name, years to search. Civil cases indexed by defendant, plaintiff, on computer since 1990, prior on index cards. Note: Will do single name lookups over the phone. Mail turnaround time 2 days. Civil PAT goes back to 1996.

Criminal Records: Access: Fax, mail, in person. Only the court performs in person searches; visitors may not. Search fee: $10.00 per name. Required to search: name, years to search, DOB, SSN. Criminal records on computer since 1990, prior on index cards. Mail turnaround time 2 days. Criminal PAT goes back to 1996.

General Information: No suppressed, child and spousal abuse records released. Court makes copy: $1.00 per page. Certification fee: $10.00 per doc. Payee: 17th District Court. Personal checks accepted. Visa/MC and debit cards accepted. Mail requests: SASE required.

18th District Court 36675 Ford Rd, Westland, MI 48185; 734-595-8720; fax: 734-595-0160; 8AM-4PM, till 5:30 on TH (EST). ***Misdemeanor, Civil Actions under $25,000, Eviction, Small Claims.***
www.18thdistrictcourt.com

Civil Records: Access: Phone, mail, fax, in person. Only the court performs in person searches; visitors may not. No search fee. Required to search: name, years to search; also helpful: case number or title. Civil cases indexed by defendant, plaintiff, on computer since 1987, prior on microfilm back to 1969. Note: Will name search free, but cert fee applied to copy. Mail turnaround time 1-2 weeks.

Criminal Records: Access: Phone, mail, in person. Only the court performs in person searches; visitors may not. No search fee. Required to search: name, years to search, DOB; also helpful: case number. Criminal records on computer since 1992, prior on microfilm back to 1969. Note: Will name search free, but cert fee applied to copy. Mail turnaround time 1-2 weeks.

General Information: No suppressed records released. Will fax documents to local or toll free line. Court makes copy: $1.00 per page. Certification fee: $10.00 per doc. Payee: 18th District Court. Personal checks accepted. Credit card payments accepted via GPS. Mail requests: SASE required.

19th District Court 16077 Michigan Ave, Dearborn, MI 48126; 313-943-2060; criminal phone: 313-943-3033; civil phone: 313-943-2056; fax: 313-943-3071; 8AM-4:30PM (EST). ***Misdemeanor, Civil Actions under $25,000, Eviction, Small Claims.***
www.cityofdearborn.org

Civil Records: Access: Fax, mail, in person. Only the court performs in person searches; visitors may not. No search fee. Required to search: name, years to search. Civil cases indexed by defendant, plaintiff, on computer since 1986. Mail turnaround time 3 days.

Criminal Records: Access: Fax, mail, in person. Only the court performs in person searches; visitors may not. No search fee. Required to search: name, years to search, DOB, offense, date of offense. Criminal records on computer since 1987, prior on docket books. Mail turnaround time 3 days.

General Information: No suppressed records released. Court makes copy: $1.00 per page. Certification fee: $10.00. Payee: 19th District Court. Cashiers checks and money orders accepted. Visa/MC accepted. Credit card payments accepted via GPS. Also, pay online at www.officialpayments.com. Mail requests: SASE helpful.

20th District Court 25637 Michigan Ave, Dearborn Heights, MI 48125; 313-277-7480; criminal phone: 313-277-7480 x2; civil phone: 313-277-7480 x6; fax: 313-277-7141; 9AM-5PM (EST). ***Misdemeanor, Civil Actions under $25,000, Eviction, Small Claims.***

Civil Records: Access: In person only. Only the court performs in person searches; visitors may not. Required to search: name, years to search; also helpful: address. Civil cases indexed by defendant, plaintiff, on computer since 4/1991, prior records on microfiche or books. Civil PAT goes back to 2000.

Criminal Records: Access: In person only. Only the court performs in person searches; visitors may not. Required to search: name, years to search, DOB; also helpful: SSN. Criminal records on computer since 4/1991, prior records on microfiche or books. Criminal PAT available.

General Information: No suppressed, juvenile, sex offenders, mental health, or adoption records released. Will fax documents. Court makes copy: $1.00 per page, self serve same. Certification fee: $10.00. Payee: 20th District Court. Business checks accepted. Visa/MC accepted. Credit card payments accepted via GPS.

21st District Court 6000 Middlebelt Rd, Garden City, MI 48135; 734-793-1680; criminal phone: x1; civil phone: x2; criminal fax: 734-793-1681; civil fax: same; 8:30AM-5PM (EST). ***Misdemeanor, Civil Actions under $25,000, Eviction, Small Claims.***

Civil Records: Access: Mail, in person. Only the court performs in person searches; visitors may not. No search fee. Required to search: name, years to search. Civil cases indexed by defendant, plaintiff, on computer back to 1989, prior on books, microfilm, and cards. Note: In person searchers must fill out a "File/copy Request Form." Visitors can search the printed case index to locate a case number. Mail turnaround time 1-2 days.

Criminal Records: Access: Mail, in person. Only the court performs in person searches; visitors may not. No search fee. Required to search: name, years to search, DOB. Criminal records computerized from 1989, prior on books, microfilm, and cards. Note: In person searchers must fill out a "File/copy Request Form." Visitors can first search the printed case index to locate a criminal case number. Mail turnaround time 1-2 days.

General Information: No suppressed records released. Will not fax documents. Court makes copy: $1.00 per page. Certification fee: $10.00 per cert includes copies. Payee: 21st District Court. Personal checks accepted. Credit card payments accepted via GPS. Mail requests: SASE required.

22nd District Court 27331 S River Park Dr, Inkster, MI 48141; 313-277-8200; fax: 313-277-8221; 8:30AM-4:30PM (EST). ***Misdemeanor, Civil Actions under $25,000, Eviction, Small Claims.***

Civil Records: Access: Mail, in person. Only the court performs in person searches; visitors may not. Search fee: Search fee determined on case by case basis. Required to search: name, years to search. Civil cases indexed by defendant, plaintiff, on computer since 1996, prior on docket books. Mail turnaround time 2 weeks.

Criminal Records: Access: Mail, in person. Only the court performs in person searches; visitors may not. Search fee: Search fee determined on case by case basis. Required to search: name, years to search, DOB; also helpful: SSN. Criminal records on computer since 1996, prior on books. Mail turnaround time 2 weeks.

General Information: No suppressed records released. Will not fax out documents. Court makes copy: $1.00 per page. Certification fee: $10.00 per doc. Payee: 22nd District Court. Personal checks accepted. Credit card payments accepted via GPS. Mail requests: SASE required.

23rd District Court 23365 Goddard Rd, Taylor, MI 48180; 734-374-1334; criminal phone: 734-374-1334; civil phone: 734-374-1328; fax: 734-374-1303; 8:15AM-4:45PM (EST). ***Misdemeanor, Civil Actions under $25,000, Eviction, Small Claims.***

Civil Records: Access: Mail, in person. Only the court performs in person searches; visitors may not. No search fee. Required to search: name, years to search. Civil cases indexed by defendant, plaintiff, on computer since 1993, prior on books. Mail turnaround time 1-2 days.

Criminal Records: Access: Mail, in person. Only the court performs in person searches; visitors may not. No search fee. Required to search: name, years to search, DOB; also helpful: SSN. Criminal records on computer since 1993, prior on index cards. Mail turnaround time 1-2 days.

General Information: No suppressed, sexual abuse or drug abuse records released. Will fax documents $1.00 per page if long distance call; local no fax fee. Court makes copy: $1.00 per page. Certification fee: $10.00. Payee: 23rd District Court. Personal checks accepted. Visa/MC/Discover credit cards accepted in criminal division only. SASE not required.

24th District Court - Allen Park & Melvindale 6515 Roosevelt, Allen Park, MI 48101-2524; 313-928-0535; criminal phone: x225 or x226; civil phone: 313-928-1899; criminal fax: 313-928-1860; civil fax: same; 8:30AM-4:30PM (EST). ***Misdemeanor, Civil Actions under $25,000, Eviction, Small Claims.***

www.24thdiscourt.org

Civil Records: Access: Phone, mail, fax, in person. Only the court performs in person searches; visitors may not. No search fee. Required to search: name, years to search, case number. Civil cases indexed by defendant, plaintiff, on computer since 1992, prior records stored as hard-copies. Mail turnaround time 1 week.

Criminal Records: Access: Fax, mail, in person. Only the court performs in person searches; visitors may not. No search fee. Required to search: name, years to search, DOB. Criminal records on computer since 1993, prior records stored as hard-copies. Mail turnaround time 1 week.

General Information: No non-public records, including driving and probation records, released. Will fax documents to local or toll free line. Court makes copy: $.50 per page, self serve same. Certification fee: $10.00. Payee: 24th District Court. Personal checks accepted. Credit cards accepted in person. Credit card payments accepted via GPS. Mail requests: SASE required if return mail requested.

25th District Court 1475 Cleophus, Lincoln Park, MI 48146; 313-382-8603; criminal phone: 313-382-8600; civil phone: 313-382-9365; fax: 313-382-9361; 9AM-4:30PM (EST). ***Misdemeanor, Civil Actions under $25,000, Eviction, Small Claims.***

Civil Records: Access: Mail, phone, fax, in person. Only the court performs in person searches; visitors may not. No search fee. Required to search: name, years to search. Civil cases indexed by defendant, plaintiff, on computer since 1988, prior records stored as hard-copies. Mail turnaround time 1 week.

Criminal Records: Access: Mail, phone, fax, in person. Only the court performs in person searches; visitors may not. No search fee. Required to search: name, years to search, DOB. Criminal records on computer since 1987, prior on docket books and cards. Mail turnaround time 1 week.

General Information: No suppressed or expunged records released. Will fax documents for no fee. Court makes copy: $1.00 per page. Certification fee: $11.00 per doc. Payee: 25th District Court. Personal checks accepted. Visa/MC cards accepted. Credit card payments accepted via GPS. Mail requests: SASE required.

26-1 District Court 10600 W Jefferson, River Rouge, MI 48218; 313-842-7819; criminal phone: 313-297-0024; civil phone: 313-297-0023; fax: 313-842-5923; 8:30AM-4:30PM (EST). ***Misdemeanor, Civil Actions under $25,000, Eviction, Small Claims.***

Civil Records: Access: Fax, mail, in person. Only the court performs in person searches; visitors may not. No search fee. Required to search: name, years to search. Civil cases indexed by defendant, plaintiff, on computer since 11/93; prior records on cards. Mail turnaround time 1 week.

Criminal Records: Access: Fax, mail, in person. Only the court performs in person searches; visitors may not. No search fee. Required to search: name, years to search, DOB. Criminal records on computer since 1993, prior on index cards. Mail turnaround time 1 week.

General Information: No suppressed records released. Will fax documents $2.00. Court makes copy: $1.00 per page, self serve same. Certification fee: $10.00 per doc. Payee: 26-1 District Court. No personal checks or credit cards accepted. Mail requests: SASE helpful.

26-2 District Court 3869 W Jefferson, Ecorse, MI 48229; 313-386-7900; fax: 313-928-5956; 9AM-4PM (EST). ***Misdemeanor, Civil Actions under $25,000, Eviction, Small Claims.***

Civil Records: Access: Mail, in person. Only the court performs in person searches; visitors may not. Search fee: $25.00. Required to search: name, years to search. Civil cases indexed by defendant, plaintiff, on computer back to 1992, prior on index cards. Mail turnaround 1 wk. Civil PAT available.

Criminal Records: Access: Mail, in person. Only the court performs in person searches; visitors may not. Search fee: $25.00. Required to search: name, years to search, DOB; also helpful: SSN. Criminal records computerized from 1992, prior on index cards. Mail turnaround 1 week. Criminal PAT available.

General Information: No suppressed records released. Will fax documents $2.00 per page. Court makes copy: $1.00 per page. Certification fee: $10.00 per doc. Payee: 26-2 District Court. Business checks accepted. Credit card payments accepted via GPS. SASE not required.

27th District Court 2015 Biddle Ave, Wyandotte, MI 48192; 734-324-4475; criminal phone: 734-324-4477; civil phone: 734-324-4491; criminal fax: 734-324-4472; civil fax: same; 8:30AM-4:15PM (EST). ***Misdemeanor, Civil Actions under $25,000, Eviction, Small Claims.***

www.wyandotte.net/27thdistrictcourt/index.htm

The 27-2 District Court in Riverview was closed as of 12/31/02. All of their records are at this court.

Civil Records: Access: Mail, in person. Only the court performs in person searches; visitors may not. Search fee: $1.00. Required to search: name, years to search. Civil cases indexed by defendant, plaintiff, on computer since 1988, prior on index cards. Mail turnaround time varies.

Criminal Records: Access: Mail, in person. Only the court performs in person searches; visitors may not. Search fee: $1.00. Required to search: name, years to search, DOB. Criminal records on computer since 1988, prior on index cards. Mail turnaround time varies.

General Information: No suppressed records released. Will fax documents to local or toll free line. Court makes copy: $1.00 per page. Certification fee: $10.00 plus copy fee for add'l pages. Payee: 27th District Court. Money order or in person cash accepted. Credit card payments accepted via GPS. Mail requests: SASE required.

28th District Court 14720 Reaume Parkway, Southgate, MI 48195; 734-258-3068; criminal phone: x3631; civil phone: x3632; fax: 734-246-1405; 8:30AM-4:30PM (EST). ***Misdemeanor, Civil Actions under $25,000, Eviction, Small Claims.***

www.28dc.com

GPS by phone 888-604-7888 #1227.

Civil Records: Access: In person only. Both court and visitors may perform in person searches. No search fee. Required to search: name, years to search; also helpful: address. Civil cases indexed by defendant, plaintiff, on computer back to 1987, prior on card files by party back to 1979.

Criminal Records: Access: In person only. Only the court performs in person searches; visitors may not. No search fee. Required to search: name, years to search, DOB; also helpful: address, case number. Criminal records go back to 1979; on computer back to 1986.

General Information: No suppressed, probation, sex offenders, or mental health records released. Will not fax out case files. Court makes copy: $1.00 per page. Certification fee: $10.00 per document includes copies. Payee: 28th District Court. Cash, cashiers check or money order accepted. Major credit cards accepted in person and by phone. Credit card payments accepted via GPS.

29th District Court 34808 Sims Ave, Wayne, MI 48184; 734-722-5220; fax: 734-722-7003; 8AM-4PM (EST). ***Misdemeanor, Civil Actions under $25,000, Eviction, Small Claims.*** www.ci.wayne.mi.us/court.php

Civil Records: Access: Phone, mail, in person. Only the court performs in person searches; visitors may not. No search fee. Required to search: name, years to search. Civil cases indexed by defendant, plaintiff, on computer since 1990. Note: Will name search free, but a copy fee applies. Mail turnaround 1 week.

Criminal Records: Access: Phone, mail, in person. Only the court performs in person searches; visitors may not. No search fee. Required to search: name, years to search, DOB; also helpful: address. Criminal records on computer since 1990. Mail turnaround time 1 week, phone turnaround 1 day.

General Information: No suppressed, juvenile, sex offenders, mental health, or adoption records released. Will fax documents to local or toll free line. Court makes copy: $.50 per page. Certification fee: $10.00. Payee: 29th District Court. Personal checks accepted. Visa/MC accepted. Credit card payments accepted via GPS. Mail requests: SASE required.

30th District Court 12050 Wood Ward Ave, Highland Park, MI 48203; 313-252-0300; fax: 313-865-1115; 8AM-4:30PM (EST). ***Misdemeanor, Civil Actions under $25,000, Eviction, Small Claims.***

Civil Records: Access: Mail, in person. Both court and visitors may perform in person searches. Search fee: $5.00 per name. Required to search: name, years to search, DOB. Civil cases indexed by defendant, plaintiff, on computer since 1989, prior on index cards or docket books. Mail turnaround time 1-2 weeks.

Criminal Records: Access: Mail, in person. Both court and visitors may perform in person searches. Search fee: $5.00 per name. Required to search: name, years to search, DOB. Criminal records on computer since 1989, prior on index cards or docket books. Mail turnaround time 1-2 weeks.

General Information: No suppressed records released. Will fax documents. Court makes copy: $1.00 per page. Certification fee: $5.00. Payee: 30th District Court. Personal checks accepted; credit cards are not. Mail requests: SASE required.

31st District Court 3401 Evaline Ave, Hamtramck, MI 48212; 313-876-7710; fax: 313-876-7724; 8AM-4PM (EST). ***Misdemeanor, Civil Actions under $25,000, Eviction, Small Claims.***

Civil Records: Access: Mail, in person. Only the court performs in person searches; visitors may not. No search fee. Required to search: name, years to search. Civil cases indexed by defendant, plaintiff, on computer since 1989, prior on index cards. Mail turnaround time 1-2 days.

Criminal Records: Access: Mail, in person. Only the court performs in person searches; visitors may not. No search fee. Required to search: name, years to search, DOB. Criminal records on computer since 1989, prior on index cards. Mail turnaround time 1-2 days.

General Information: No suppressed records released. Will fax documents $1.00 per page. Court makes copy: $1.00 per page. Self serve: none. Certification fee: $10.00 plus copy fee after first page. Payee: 31st District Court. Personal checks and major credit cards accepted. Mail requests: SASE required.

32 A District Court 19617 Harper Ave, Harper Woods, MI 48225; 313-343-2590; civil phone: 313-343-2592; fax: 313-343-2594; 8:30AM-4:30PM (EST). ***Misdemeanor, Civil Actions under $25,000, Small Claims.***

Civil Records: Access: Phone, fax, mail, in person. Only the court performs in person searches; visitors may not. No search fee. Required to search: name, years to search. Civil cases indexed by defendant, plaintiff, indexed by name and case number on computer, microfiche, and paper. Mail turnaround time same day.

Criminal Records: Access: Phone, fax, mail, in person. Only the court performs in person searches; visitors may not. No search fee. Required to search: name, years to search. Criminal records indexed by name and case number on computer, microfiche, and paper. Mail turnaround time same day.

General Information: No suppressed records released. Will fax documents, no fee. Court makes copy: $.50 per page. Certification fee: $11.00 per doc. Payee: 32A District Court. Personal checks accepted. Visa/MC accepted. Mail requests: SASE requested.

33rd District Court 19000 Van Horn Rd, Woodhaven, MI 48183; 734-671-0201; criminal phone: 734-671-0201; civil phone: 734-671-0225; fax: 734-671-0307; 8:30AM-4:30PM (EST). ***Misdemeanor, Civil Actions under $25,000, Eviction, Small Claims.***

Civil Records: Access: In person only. Visitors must perform in person searches themselves. Required to search: name, years to search. Civil cases indexed by defendant, plaintiff, on computer since 1999, prior on microfilm and microfiche but only court can search on these. Civil PAT goes back to 1999. PAT results show name only.

Criminal Records: Access: In person only. Both court and visitors may perform in person searches. No search fee. Required to search: name, years to search, DOB. Criminal records on computer since 1995, prior on microfilm and microfiche. Criminal PAT goes back to same as civil. PAT results show name only.

General Information: No suppressed records released. Will not fax documents. Court makes copy: $.25 per page. Certification fee: $10.00 plus $1.00 per page after first. Payee: 33rd District Court. Business checks accepted. Major credit cards accepted.

34th District Court 11131 S Wayne Rd, Romulus, MI 48174; 734-941-4462; fax: 734-941-7530; 8:30AM-4PM (EST). ***Misdemeanor, Civil Actions under $25,000, Eviction, Small Claims.***

Civil Records: Access: Mail, in person. Only the court performs in person searches; visitors may not. No search fee. Required to search: name, years to search. Civil cases indexed by defendant, plaintiff, on computer since 1984, prior on index cards and docket books. Mail turnaround time 2 weeks.

Criminal Records: Access: Mail, in person. Only the court performs in person searches; visitors may not. No search fee. Required to search: name, years to search, DOB; also helpful: SSN. Criminal records on computer since 1984, prior on index cards and docket books. Mail turnaround time 1 week.

General Information: No suppressed records released. Will fax documents to local or toll-free number. Court makes copy: $1.00 per page. Certification fee: $10.00 per page includes copy fee. Payee: 34th District Court. No personal checks accepted. Credit card payments accepted. Mail requests: SASE required.

35th District Court 660 Plymouth Rd, Plymouth, MI 48170; 734-459-4740; fax: 734-454-9303; 8AM-4:30PM (EST). ***Misdemeanor, Civil Infractions, Civil Actions under $25,000, Eviction, Small Claims.*** www.35thdistrictcourt.org

Civil Records: Access: Fax, mail, in person. Both court and visitors may perform in person searches. No search fee. Required to search: name, years to search. Civil cases indexed by defendant, plaintiff, on computer since 1990. Mail turnaround time 1 week. Civil PAT goes back to 1998.

Criminal Records: Access: Fax, mail, in person. Both court and visitors may perform in person searches. No search fee. Required to search: name, years to search, DOB; also helpful: SSN, sex, signed release. Criminal records on computer since 1990. Mail turnaround time 1 week. Criminal PAT goes back to same as civil.

General Information: No suppressed, juvenile, sex offenders, mental health, or adoption records released. Fee to fax document $1.00 each. Court makes copy: $1.00 per page. Certification fee: $10.00 per cert includes copies. Payee: 35th District Court. Third party checks not accepted. Visa/MC and debit cards accepted.

3rd Circuit Court 2 Woodward Ave, Coleman A Young Municipal Ctr, Detroit, MI 48226; 313-224-5530; 8AM-4:30PM (EST). ***Civil Actions over $25,000, Vital Statistics.*** www.3rdcc.org

Civil Records: Access: Mail, in person. Both court and visitors may perform in person searches. Search fee: $1.00 per name. Required to search: name, years to search. Civil cases indexed by defendant, plaintiff, on computer since 1984, prior on index cards. Mail turnaround time 1 week. Public use terminal has civil records back to 1985. PAT civil results show middle initial.

General Information: No suppressed records released. Will not fax documents. Court makes copy: $2.25 per page. Certification fee: $10.00 plus $1.00 per page. Payee: 3rd Circuit Court. Business checks accepted. No credit cards accepted.

Probate Court Coleman A Young Muni. Ctr, 13th Fl, 2 Woodland Ave, #1307, Detroit, MI 48226; 313-224-5706; 8AM-4:30PM (EST). ***Probate.*** www.wcpc.us/ Search probate records at http://public.wcpc.us/pa/pa.urd/pamw6500.display. Summary, party, event, docket, disposition, costs available. Records go back into 1980s.

Wexford County

28th Circuit Court PO Box 490, Cadillac, MI 49601; 231-779-9450; fax: 231-779-0447; 8:30AM-5PM (EST). ***Felony, Civil Actions over $25,000, Vital Statistics.*** www.wexfordcounty.org

Civil Records: Access: Mail, in person. Only the court performs in person searches; visitors may not. Search fee: $5.00 per name for 10 year search. Required to search: name, years to search. Civil cases indexed by defendant, plaintiff, go back to 1868, civil records on computer since 1977. Mail turnaround time same day if possible.

Criminal Records: Access: Mail, in person. Only the court performs in person searches; visitors may not. Search fee: $5.00 per name for 10 year search. Required to search: name, years to search. Criminal records go back to 1868, criminal records on computer since 1977. Mail turnaround same day.

General Information: No suppressed, YTA files, juvenile, sex offenders, mental health, or adoption records released. Will not fax documents. Court makes copy: $1.00 per page. Certification fee: $10.00, plus $1.00 each add'l page. Payee: Wexford County Clerk. Checks and money orders accepted. Credit card payments accepted via Vitalchek. Mail requests: SASE required.

84th District Court 437 E Division St, Cadillac, MI 49601; 231-779-9515; fax: 231-779-5396; 8:30AM-5PM (EST). ***Misdemeanor, Civil Actions under $25,000, Eviction, Small Claims.***

Civil Records: Access: Phone, fax, mail, in person. Both court and visitors may perform in person searches. Search fee: $1.00 per page found. Required to search: name, years to search. Civil cases indexed by defendant, plaintiff, on computer since 1984; on index from 1969 to 1984. Mail turnaround 1 week.

Criminal Records: Access: Mail, fax, in person. Both court and visitors may perform in person searches. Search fee: $1.00 per name found. Required to search: name, years to search, DOB; also helpful: SSN. Criminal records on computer since 1984; prior records on blue cards. Mail turnaround time 1 week.

General Information: No suppressed, juvenile, sex offenders, mental health, or adoption records released. Will fax documents to local or toll-free number. Court makes copy: $1.00 per page. Certification fee: $10.00 per doc. Payee: 84th District Court. Personal checks accepted; credit cards are not. Mail requests: SASE required.

Probate Court 437 E Division, Cadillac, MI 49601; 231-779-9510; probate phone: 231-779-9511; fax: 231-779-9485; 8:30AM-5PM (EST). ***Probate***

Michigan Recording Offices

ORGANIZATION: 83 counties, 83 recording offices. The recording officer is the County Register of Deeds. 79 Michigan counties are in the Eastern Time Zone (EST) and 4 counties that border on Wisconsin – Gogebic, Iron, Dickinson, Menominee – are in the Central Time Zone (CST).

REAL ESTATE RECORDS: Some counties will perform real estate searches. A copy usually costs $1.00 per page. Certification fee is $1.00 per cert plus copy fee. Ownership records are located at the Equalization Office, designated as "Assessor" or "Equalization" in this section. Tax records are located at the Treasurer's Office.

UCC RECORDS: Financing statements are all filed at the state level except for real estate-related collateral which are filed with the County Register. Prior to July, 2001, consumer goods and farm collateral were also filed at the County Register and these older records can be searched here if active.

TAX LIEN RECORDS: Federal and state tax liens on personal property of businesses are filed with the Secretary of State. Other federal and state tax liens are filed with the Register of Deeds. Most counties search each tax lien index separately. Some charge one fee to search both while others charge a separate fee for each one. When combining a UCC and tax lien search, total fee is usually $9.00 for all three searches. Some counties require tax identification number as well as name before performing a search.

OTHER LIENS: Construction, lis pendens.

ONLINE ACCESS: Search UCC data statewide at www.michigan.gov/sosucc. There is no statewide online access to recorded land data but a number of counties, including Wayne, offer free access to Assessor and Register of Deeds records. At www.dleg.state.mi.us/platmaps/sr_subs.asp is free access to digital images, with print capability, of the plats and related documents of land subdivisions in the State of Michigan's construction plat files.

Alcona County

County Register of Deeds, PO Box 269, Harrisville, MI 48740-0269. Recording, R/E & UCC phone-989-724-9450; fax-989-724-9459; 8:30AM-4:30PM www.alconacountymi.com/content/section/12/58/

Index: All in one except birth records. Records indexed in a book available to the public. Office personnel or visitors may perform searches. Search fee $10.00 per name. Office will not search real estate records. Will not search UCC records. Copy fee $1.00 per page. Cert fee- $2.00 per cert includes copy fee. Payee- Alcona County Register of Deeds. Bulk data available for purchase. **Other phones:** Treasurer- 989-724-9420; Elections- 989-724-9410; Vital Records- 989-724-9410. **Property tax/Assessing-** PO Box 322, Harrisville, MI 48740; 989-724-9430, assessor fax- 989-724-9439. **Online** - Access to property and GIS/mapping is free at www.alconacountymi.com/component/option,com_docman/Itemid,42/

Alger County

Register of Deeds, PO Box 538, Munising, MI 49862. 906-387-2076; fax-906-387-2156; 8AM-4PM (EST)

Index: Separate indices to search include deeds, mortgages. Records indexed on computer back to 1/05. Office personnel or visitors may perform searches. Search fee $6.00 per name. Copy fee $1.00 per page. Cert fee- $1.00 per cert plus copy fee. Payee- Alger County Register of Deeds. **Other phones:** Treasurer- 906-387-4535; Elections/Vitals- 906-387-2076. **Property tax/Assessing-** 101 Court St, Munising, MI 49862; 906-387-2567.

Allegan County

County Register of Deeds, 113 Chestnut St; County Courthouse, Allegan, MI 49010-1360. Recording, R/E & UCC phone-269-673-0390; fax-269-673-0289; 8AM-5PM (EST) www.allegancounty.org

Index: All in one. Records indexed. Office personnel or visitors may perform searches. General index search fee $6.00 per search. Office will perform real estate to locate specific document only. Copy fee $1.00 per page; $2.00 per plat page. Cert fee- $1.00 per page plus copy fee. Payee- Allegan County Register of Deeds. Tiff images in bulk format available to purchase, contact Patty Faks 269-963-0390. **Other phones:** Treasurer- 269-673-0260; Elections- 269-673-0450; Vital Records- 269-673-0450. **Property tax/Assessing-** 113 Chestnut St, County Courthouse, Equalization Department, Allegan, MI 49010-1360; 269-673-0230, assessor fax- 269-673-0312. www.allegancounty.org **Online access-** Search index by name or address at https://is.bsasoftware.c om/bsa.is/SelectUnit.aspx. The site includes Cities of Otsego, Plainwell, Douglas, and Saugatuck Township. Search tax index or foreclosures by name or address at www.allegancounty.org/Government/TR/TaxSearch.asp?pt= or https://is.bsasoftware.co m/bsa.is/SelectUnit.aspx w/ Cities of Otsego, Town-ships ofPlainwell, Wayland, Douglas, Saugatuck.

Alpena County

County Register of Deeds, 720 W Chisholm St, #4; Courthouse, Alpena, MI 49707-2487. 989-354-9547; fax-989-354-9646; 8:30AM-4:30PM (EST) www.alpenacounty.org/co_deeds.htm

Index: Separate indices to search. Records indexed on a public use terminal back to 1993. Office personnel or visitors may perform searches. Search fee $12.00 per name; will search real estate for $.50 per year. Copy fee $1.00 per page. Cert fee- $1.00 per cert plus copy fee. Payee- Alpena County Register of Deeds. Bulk data available for purchase at $1.00 per page. **Other phones:** Treasurer- 989-354-9534; Elections- 989-354-9520; Vital Records- 989-354-9520. **Property tax/Assessing-** 720 W Chisholm St, #5, Alpena, MI 49707; 989-354-9560, fax- 989-354-9647. www.alpenacounty.org/equalization.htm **Online access-** Search the assessor property tax data free at www.alpena.mi.govern.com/parcelquery.php. Access property data and GIS-maps free at www.alpenacounty.org/local_maps.htm

Antrim County

County Register of Deeds, PO Box 376, Bellaire, MI 49615. 231-533-6683; 533-6170 abstracting dept, R/E recording phone-231-533-6683; fax-231-533-8317; 8:30AM-5PM; 10AM-4PM searches. (EST) www.antrimcounty.org

Abstracting Dept offers 1-10 yr search for $30.00; a 10-40 yr search for $40.00; plus $2.00 each transaction; call 231-533-6238. Index: Separate indices to search include computer, grantor/grantee books. Records indexed on a public use terminal back to 1993. Office personnel or visitors may perform searches. General index search fee $5.00 minimum plus $.50 per year. Copy fee $1.00 per page. Cert fee- $1.00 per doc plus copy fee; self serve same. Payee- Antrim County Register of Deeds. **Other phones:** Treasurer- 231-533-6720. **Property tax/Assessing-** 203 E Cayuga St, PO Box 541, Bellaire, MI 49615; 231-533-6320, assessor fax- 231-533-5907. www.antrimcounty.org/equalization.asp **Online access-** Search parcel data information free at www.antrimcounty.org/parcelsearch.asp.

Arenac County

County Register of Deeds, PO Box 296, Standish, MI 48658. 989-846-9201, R/E recording phone-517-846-9201; 8:30AM-5PM (EST)

Index: All in one. Records indexed on a public use terminal back to 1992. Office will perform a UCC search but public must search other records themselves. No fee for search. Copy fee $1.00 per page. Cert fee- $1.00 per cert plus copy fee. Payee- Arenac County Register of Deeds. **Other phones:** Treasurer- 517-846-4106; Elections/Vitals- 517-846-4626; **Property tax/Assessing-** 517-846-6246.

Baraga County

County Register of Deeds, 16 N 3rd St; Courthouse, L'Anse, MI 49946-1085. 906-524-6183; fax-906-524-6186; 8:30AM-4:30PM www.baragacounty.org

Index: All in one as of 2005, prior indexed by mortgages, deeds, misc, surveys. Records indexed on a public use terminal back to 2000. Office will perform a UCC search but public must search other records themselves. Search fee $5.00 per name. Copy fee $2.00 per page. Cert fee- $7.00 per doc plus copy fee. Payee- Baraga County Register of Deeds. **Other phones:** Treasurer- 906-524-7773; Elections- 906-524-6183; Vital Records- 906-524-6183. **Property tax/Assessing-** 12 N 3rd St, L'Anse, MI 49946; 906-524-7331, assessor fax- 906-524-7303. www.baragacounty.org/indexeq.htm

Barry County

County Register of Deeds, PO Box 7, Hastings, MI 49058-0007. phone-269-945-1289; fax-269-945-1298; 8AM-5PM (EST) www.barrycounty.org

Index: Separate indices to search. Records indexed on a public use terminal back to 03/93. Office personnel or visitors may perform searches. Search fee $6.00 per name. Office will not search real estate records. Office will search UCC records. Copy fee $1.00 per page. Cert fee- $1.00 per cert plus copy fee. Payee- Barry County Register of Deeds. Paper copies of bulk data available; contact Darla Burghdoff, Register. **Online access to Real Estate, Deed, Lien, Mortgage, Judgment records:** Access recorded Indexes back to 4/1993 free at www.barrycounty.org/online-services/register-of-deeds-image-search/. Pre 1993 images being added. **Other phones:** Treasurer- 269-945-1287; Elections- 269-945-1285; Vital Records- 269-945-1285. **Property tax/Assessing**- 220 W State St, Hastings, MI 49058; 269-945-1292, assessor fax- 269-948-4833. **Online access**- Access to county parcel data is free at www.barrycounty.org/online-services/parcel-search/. County property Index is from 12/95 to 12/2005; assessment rolls should not be used for a title search or legal description. Also, Search Vital Records data free at http://internal.barrycounty.org/clerkweb/. Access county property data free on the tax parcel lookup at http://barryco.readyhosting.com/ParcelMaps.htm.

Bay County

County Register of Deeds, 515 Center Ave, #102, Bay City, MI 48708-5994. Recording, R/E & UCC phone-989-895-4228; fax-989-895-4296; 8AM-5PM (EST) www.baycounty-mi.gov/ROD/

Documents sent for recording require a SASE for return. Index: Index complete on computer back to 1985; index on card file 1984-1958; before 1958 on old books. Records indexed on a public use terminal back to 1985. Office will perform a UCC search but public must search other records themselves. UCC search or combined tax lien search per debtor name- $6.00. General copy fee $1.00 per page. Cert fee- $3.00 per cert plus copy fee. Payee- Bay County Register of Deeds. Bulk data available for purchase, contact Vicki Roupe, Register of Deeds. **Online access to Real Estate, Deed, Lien records:** Access the register's land records data after registration, logon with username and password at http://rod.baycounty-mi.gov/. Index goes back to 1985; no images. **Other phones:** Treasurer- 989-895-4285; Elections- 989-895-4280; Vital Records- 989-895-4280. **Property tax/Assessing**- 515 Center Ave #602, Bay City, MI 48708-5994; 989-895-4075, assessor fax- 989-895-4078. www.baycounty-mi.gov/Equalization/ **Online access**- Access county property tax data for free at http://ptq.baycounty-mi.gov/. Do a general property search free at www.baygis.org/. Also search residential sales, interactive map. Also, access tax data for City of Essexville and Hampton Township at https://is.bsasoftware.com/bsa.is/SelectUnit.aspx.

Benzie County

County Register of Deeds, 448 Court Pl, Beulah, MI 49617. 231-882-0016; fax-231-882-0167; 8AM-N, 1-5PM www.benzieco.net/dept_register_of_deeds.htm

Index: Separate indices prior to 2004 to search include grantor/grantee, mortgage, discharge mortgage, tax liens. Records indexed on a public use terminal back to 1982. Office personnel or visitors may perform searches. General index search fee $5.00 minimum. Office will not search real estate records unless document specified. Tax liens not included in UCC search. UCC search per debtor name-$6.00. Copy fee $1.00 per page; $2.00 per page for UCC. Cert fee- $1.00 per seal plus copy fee. Payee- Benzie County Register of Deeds. **Online access to Real Estate, Deed, Lien, Parcel records:** Recorder land data by subscription on either the Laredo system using subscription and fees or the Tapestry System using credit card, http://tapestry.fidlar.com; $3.99 search; $.50 per image. Index goes back to 1982, images to 7/1998. **Other phones:** Treasurer- 231-882-0011; Elections- 231-882-0001; Vital Records- 231-882-0001. **Property tax/Assessing**- 231-882-0015. **Online** - Access Almira land and property tax data free https://is.bsasoftware.com/bsa.is/SelectUnit.aspx.

Berrien County

County Register of Deeds, 701 Main St; Berrien County Admin Ctr, St. Joseph, MI 49085. 616-983-7111 x8562, R/E recording phone-269-983-7111 x8562; fax-616-982-8659; 8:30AM-5PM (EST) www.berriencounty.org/?dept=24

Index: All in one. Records indexed on a public use terminal back to 7/75. Office personnel or visitors may perform searches. Search fee $.50 per name per year, $5.00 minimum. UCC search per debtor name- $6.00 per name. UCC copy fee $2.00 per page.Real estate record copy- $1.00 per page. Cert fee- $1.00 per doc plus copy fee. Payee- Berrien County Register of Deeds. **Other phones:** Treasurer- 269-983-7111 x8208; Elections- 269-983-7111 x8233; Vital Records- 269-983-7111 x8233. **Property tax/Assessing**- 701 Main St, Joseph, MI 49085; 269-983-7111 x8215. **Online access**- Access to City of Niles property data is free with registration at https://is.bsasoftware.com/bsa.is/SelectUnit.aspx.

Branch County

County Register of Deeds, 23 E Pearl St, Coldwater, MI 49036. 517-279-4320; fax-517-279-6458; 8AM-5PM (EST) www.co.branch.mi.us

Index: 1997-present on computer; grantor/grantee index and cards back to 1974; before 1974 in books. Records indexed on a public use terminal back to 1997. Office will perform a UCC search but public must search other records themselves. Search fee- $5.00 per name. Copy fee $1.00 per page. Cert fee- $1.00 per cert plus copy fee. Payee- Branch County Register of Deeds. Bulk data available for purchase, contact Register of Deeds. **Online access to Real Estate, Deed, Lien, Business Name records:** Recorder land data by subscription on either the Laredo system using subscription and fees or the Tapestry2 System using credit card, https://tapestry.fidlar.com/Tapestry2/Default.aspx. $5.95 search; $.50 per image. Index and images go back to 1/1/1997. Search business names and DBAs at www.co.branch.mi.us/dbasearch.taf. **Other phones:** Treasurer- 517-279-4321; Elections- 517-279-4306; Vital Records- 517-279-4306. **Property tax/Assessing**- Equalization, 23 E Pearl St, Coldwater, MI 49036; 517-279-4312. **Online access**- Access City of Coldwater and Township of Coldwater property tax/special assessments free after registration at https://is.bsasoftware.com/bsa.is/SelectUnit.aspx. Search the county death records only free at www.co.branch.mi.us/deathsearch.taf.

Calhoun County

County Register of Deeds, 315 W Green St, Marshall, MI 49068. 269-781-0718; fax-269-781-0721; 8AM-5PM (EST) http://co.calhoun.mi.us

Index: Separate indices to search include books, card files, computer back to 1980. Records indexed on computer back to 1982. Office will perform a UCC and tax lien search but public must search other records themselves. Search fee $6.00 per name. Copy fee $1.00 per page. Cert fee- $1.00 per doc plus copy fee. Payee- Calhoun County Register of Deeds. Bulk data available for purchase for $1.00 per entry; contact Diane Withers. **Online access to Real Estate, Grantor/Grantee, Deed, Lien, Parcel records:** Access the recorder's Index free back to 1/3/1980 at http://rod.co.calhoun.mi.us/indexsearch.html. **Other phones:** Treasurer- 269-969-6910/616-781-0807; Elections- 269-781-0988; Vital Records- 269-781-0718. **Property tax/Assessing**- 315 W Green St, Marshall, MI 49068; 269-781-0745. **Online access**- Access to data for Cities of Albion, Battle Creek, Marshall, Springfield and Townships of Marshall, Newton, and Sheridan is free with registration at https://is.bsasoftware.com/bsa.is/SelectUnit.aspx.

Cass County

County Register of Deeds, PO Box 355, Cassopolis, MI 49031-0355. Recording, R/E & UCC phone-269-445-4464; fax-269-445-4406; 8AM-5PM (EST) www.casscountymi.org

Index: All in one. Records indexed on computer from 1994 to present. Office personnel or visitors may perform searches. Search fee $5.00 per name. Office will search limited real estate records. Office will not search UCC records. Tax lien or real estate copy $1.00 per page; $2.00 per page for UCC. Cert fee- $1.00 per cert plus copy fee. Payee- Cass County Clerk/Register. Bulk data available for purchase, contact Monica Kennedy. **Online access to Real Estate, Grantor/Grantee, Deed records:** Access to recorded records for free go to http://index.casscountymi.org/recorder/web/. **Other phones:** Treasurer- 269-445-4468; Elections- 269-445-4464; Vital Records- 269-445-4464. **Property tax/Assessing**- . **Online access**- Access county property tax records free at www.cass.mi.gov ern.com/parcelquery.php. Also access to GIS-mapping for free go to http://maps.casscountymi.org/

Charlevoix County

County Register of Deeds, 301 State St; County Bldg, Charlevoix, MI 49720. 231-547-7204; fax-231-237-0106; 9AM-5PM (EST) www.charlevoixcounty.org

Index: Separate indices to search are books, computer back to 1989. Records indexed on a public use terminal back to 1989. Public may search on the computer terminal. Office will not search real estate records. Copy fee $1.00 per page. Cert fee- $1.00 per cert plus copy fee. Payee- Charlevoix County Register of Deeds. Index records available for purchase, usually for credit purposes. **Online access to Real Estate, Deed records:** Register of Deeds records free back to 1/2005 only at http://12.150.40.69/rodweb/ . **Other phones:** Treasurer- 231-547-7202; Elections- 231-547-7200 clerk's ofc; Vital Records- 231-547-7200. **Property tax/Assessing**- 301 State St, Charlevoix, MI 49720; 231-547-7230, assessor fax- 231-547-7232. www.charlevoixcounty.org/equal.asp **Online access**- Access the assessor's basic property data or property tax payment free at www.charlevoixcounty.org/. Also, access county and Township of Evangeline tax data free with registration at https://is.bsasoftware.com/bsa.is/SelectUnit.aspx. Index search is free but registration is required to view and print documents for $2.00 each.

Cheboygan County

County Register of Deeds, PO Box 70, Cheboygan, MI 49721. 231-627-8808, R/E recording phone-231-627-8866; fax-231-627-8453; 8:30AM-5PM (EST) www.cheboygancounty.net/pages/county_clerk/

Index: All in one. Records indexed on computer back to 1982. Office personnel or visitors may perform searches. Will not guarantee searches. Search fee $5.00 per name. Office will search real estate records. Copy fee $1.00 per page. Will fax back $1.00 per page. Cert fee- $1.00 per cert plus copy fee. Payee- Cheboygan County Register of Deeds. **Other phones:** Treasurer- 231-627-8821; Elections- 231-627-8808; Vital Records- 231-627-8808. **Property tax/Assessing**- 870 S Main St, Cheboygan County Bldg, 1st Fl, Rm #108, Cheboygan, MI 49721; 231-627-8811, assessor fax- 231-627-8403. hours- 8AM-4PM www.cheboygancounty.net/pages/equalization/ **Online access**- Access to assessor property index is free at www.cheboyganequalization.com/.

Chippewa County

County Register of Deeds, 319 Court St; Courthouse, Sault Ste. Marie, MI 49783. Recording, R/E & UCC phone-906-635-6312; fax-906-635-6855; 8AM-5PM (EST) www.chippewacountymi.gov

Index: All in one. Records indexed on a public use terminal back to 1987. Office personnel (depending on time involved and available manpower) or visitors may perform searches. Search fee $5.00 minimum plus $.50 per year plus copy fee. Office will sometimes search real estate records. Will search UCC records. Copy fee $1.00 per page. $3.00 per plat page. Cert fee- $1.00 per cert plus copy fee. Payee- Chippewa County Register of Deeds. **Other phones:** Treasurer- 906-635-6308; Elections- 906-635-6300; Vital Records- 906-635-6300. **Property tax/Assessing**- 319 Court St, Sault Ste. Marie, MI 49783; 906-635-6304, assessor fax- 906-635-6372. hours- 8AM-4:30PM A public terminal available.

Clare County

County Register of Deeds, PO Box 438, Harrison, MI 48625. Recording, R/E & UCC phone-989-539-7131; fax-989-539-6616; 8AM-4:30PM www.clareco.net
Index: Separate indices to search include grantor/grantee, mortgage, tract/land, and UCC. Records indexed on a public use terminal back to 1981. Office will perform a tax lien index name search but public must name search other indexes themselves. Record search fee $50.00 initial fee, $10.00 per entry if real estate. Separate federal/state tax lien search- $3.00 per debtor. Copy fee $1.00 per page; UCC $2.00 per page. Cert fee- $1.00 per cert plus copy fee. Payee- Clare County Register of Deeds. **Other phones:** Treasurer- 989-539-7801; Elections- 989-539-7131; Vital Records- 989-539-7131. **Property tax/Assessing**- 225 W Main St, Board of Equalization, Harrison, MI 48625; 989-539-7894, assessor fax- 989-539-7208. Public terminal available.

Clinton County

County Register of Deeds, PO Box 435, St. Johns, MI 48879-0435. Recording, R/E & UCC phone-989-224-5270; fax-989-227-6473; 8AM-5PM (EST) www.clinton-county.org/rod/register_of_deeds.htm
Index: All in one. Records indexed on a public use terminal back to 8/93. Office personnel or visitors may perform searches. Office personnel will only search for out-of-state requesters, as a general rule. Search fee $.50 per year, $5.00 minimum. Office will search real estate records. Will search UCC records for info only. Separate federal or state tax lien search- $3.00 per debtor. Copy fee $2.00 per UCC or Plat page; if tax lien or real estate $1.00 per page. Cert fee- $1.00 per cert plus copy fee. Payee- Clinton County Register of Deeds. **Online access to Real Estate, Deed, Judgment, Lien, Assumed Name records:** Register to search free on the recorders database at www.clinton-county.org/rod/index_search.htm. Username and password is required. Also, search fictitious business names free at www.clinton-county.org/clerk/dba_search.asp. **Other phones:** Treasurer- 989-224-5280. **Property tax/Assessing**- 100 E State St, #1200, St Johns, MI 48879; 989-224-5170, assessor fax- 989-227-6497. www.clinton-county.org/equal/equalization.htm **Online access**- Access DeWitt, Eagle, Victor, and Watertown tax data, utility bills, and assessments free with registration at https://is.bsasoftware.com/bsa.is/SelectUnit.aspx. Property data available at http://maps.clinton-county.org/ClintonCountyCX/Disclaimer.htm, no name searching. Property tax data by sub at www.clinton-county.org/treasurer/delq_tax_search.htm, $20 process fee & $.25 per parcel.

Crawford County

County Register of Deeds, 200 W Michigan Ave, Grayling, MI 49738. 989-348-2841, R/E recording phone-989-344-3203; fax-989-344-3223; 8:30AM-4:30PM (EST) www.crawfordco.org/deeds/deeds.htm
Index: Separate indices to search. Records indexed on a public use terminal back to 1994. Office personnel or visitors may perform searches. Search fee $5.00 per name. Office will not search real estate records. Copy fee $1.00 per page. Cert fee- $1.00 per doc plus copy fee. Payee- Crawford County Register of Deeds. **Other phones:** Treasurer- 989-344-3229; Elections- 989-344-3200; Vital Records- 989-344-3207. **Property tax/Assessing**- 200 W Michigan, Grayling, MI 49738; 989-344-3235. (Auditor- 989-344-3234)

Delta County

County Register of Deeds, 310 Ludington St, #104, Escanaba, MI 49829-4039. Recording, R/E & UCC phone-906-789-5116; fax-906-789-5196; 8AM-4PM
Index: All in one. Records indexed on a public use terminal back to 9/84. Book indices 1986-civil war era (1862). Office personnel or visitors may perform searches. Search fee $6.00 for UCC per name, lien search etc $3.00 each type: federal, state, unemployment. Office will search real estate records, but will not do a "title search". UCC copy fee $2.00 per page.Real estate record- $1.00 per page. Cert fee- $3.00 per cert plus copy fee. Payee- Register of Deeds. **Other phones:** Treasurer- 906-789-5117; Elections- 906-789-5105; Vital Records- 906-789-5105. **Property tax/Assessing**- 310 Ludington St, #247, Escanaba, MI 49829; 906-789-5109. (Appraiser/Auditor- 906-789-5109);

Dickinson County

County Register of Deeds, PO Box 609, Iron Mountain, MI 49801. 906-774-0955; fax-906-774-4660; 8AM-4:30PM (CST)
Index: Separate indices to search include computer, pre-1994 tract books. Records indexed on a public use terminal back to 1994. Office personnel or visitors may perform searches. General search fee $5.00 per name. UCC search per debtor name- $6.00. Tax lien search fee- $3.00 per debtor. Copy fee $1.00 per page. UCC copy- $2.00 per page. Cert fee- $1.00 per doc plus copy fee. Payee- Dickinson County Register of Deeds. **Other phones:** Treasurer- 906-774-8130. **Property tax/Assessing**- 705 S Stephenson Ave, PO Box 609, Iron Mountain, MI 49801; 906-774-2515, assessor fax- 906-774-3686. **Online access**- Access City of Iron Mountain land and property tax data free with registration at https://is.bsasoftware.com/bsa.is/SelectUnit.aspx. County plans to have Register of Deeds records online.

Eaton County

County Register of Deeds, 1045 Independence Blvd, Rm 104, Charlotte, MI 48813-1095. 517-543-4203, R/E recording phone-517-543-7500 x4203, UCC recording phone-517-543-7500 x1231; fax-517-543-4134; 8AM-5PM (EST) www.eatoncounty.org/Departments/Eaton_County_Register_of_Deeds.htm
Records indexed on computer back to 1990, cards back to 1965, and books back to 1836. Only the public may search. Copy fee $2.00, if UCC or real estate $1.00 per page. Cert fee- $1.00 per cert plus copy fee. Payee- Eaton County Register of Deeds. **Online Marriage License, New Business records:** Access marriage license filings free at http://207.74.121.30/VitalStats/Marriage.aspx. Search new business filings- http://207.74.121.30/VitalStats/NewBus.aspx. **Other phones:** Treasurer- 517-543-4262; Elections- 517-543-7500 x2488; Vital Records- 517-543-7500 x2426; Information Systems- 517-543-7500 x4704. **Property tax/Assessing**- Equalization Dept, 1045 Independence Blvd, Charlotte, MI 48813; 517-543-4104, assessor fax- 517-543-7377. (Appraiser/Auditor- 517-543-7500 x4124) **Online access**- Search access property and tax data for Cities of Charlotte, Eaton Rapids, Grand Ledge, and Townships of Carmel and Delta for free at https://is.bsasoftware.com/bsa.is/SelectUnit.aspx. Images are $2.00 each. Includes access to delinquent tax data. Free registration and password required to access parcel data on the GIS-mapping site at http://207.74.121.41/imsweb/. For delinquent tax data, see Assessor listing for Eaton County.

Emmet County

County Register of Deeds, 200 Division St, #150, Petoskey, MI 49770. Recording, R/E & UCC phone-231-348-1761; fax-231-348-1773; 8:30AM-5PM (EST) www.co.emmet.mi.us/deeds/
Index: All in one. Records indexed on a public use terminal back to 101/56. Office will perform a UCC search but public must search other records themselves. Search fee $6.00 per name. UCC copy fee $2.00 per page.Real estate record copy- $1.00 per page. Cert fee- $1.00 per cert plus copy fee. Payee- Emmet County Register of Deeds. **Online access to Real Estate, Deed, Lien records:** Access recorder land records for free at www.co.emmet.mi.us/equalization/propsrcheq.htm Also, search marriages, deaths, and assumed names free at www.co.emmet.mi.us/clerk/. **Other phones:** Treasurer- 231-348-1715; Elections- 231-348-1744; Vital Records- 231-348-1744. **Property tax/Assessing**- 200 Division St, #180, Petoskey, MI 49770; 231-348-1708, assessor fax- 231-348-1768. www.co.emmet.mi.us/equalization/ **Online access**- Access assessor property records free at www.co.emmet.mi.us/equalization/propsrcheq.htm. Use username "general" and password "general". Also, access county property tax, land, animal licenses, and delinquent taxes free with registration at https://is.bsasoftware.com/bsa.is/SelectUnit.aspx.

Genesee County

County Register of Deeds, 1101 Beach St; Admin Bldg, Flint, MI 48502. Recording, R/E & UCC phone-810-257-3060; fax-810-768-7965; 8AM-5PM (EST) www.co.genesee.mi.us/registerdeeds/
Index: All in one. Records indexed on a public use terminal back to 1990. Office will perform a UCC search but public must search other records themselves. Search fee $6.00 per name. Office will not search real estate records. Copy fee $2.00, if real estate $1.00 per page. Cert fee- $1.00 per cert plus copy fee. Payee- Genesee County Register of Deeds. **Online access to Real Estate, Deed, Marriage, Death records:** Access to Register of Deeds database is free at www.co.genesee.mi.us/rod/. But to view documents back to 10/2000, there is a fee, and user ID and password required. Also, online access to the county clerk's marriage (back to 1963) and death (back to 1930) indexes are free at www.co.genesee.mi.us/vitalrec/. **Other phones:** Treasurer- 810-257-3054; Elections- 810-257-3283; Vital Records- 810-257-3225. **Property tax/Assessing**- 1101 Beach St, #206, Flint, MI 48502; 810-257-3017, assessor fax- 810-768-7954. hours- 8AM-N, 1PM-5PM www.co.genesee.mi.us/equal/index.htm **Online access**- Search property index at www.co.genesee.mi.us/cgi-bin/gweb.exe?mode=7800&sessionname=gentax&command=connect. Also, access property data for the county and for Cities of Burton, Linden and townships of Fenton, Davison, Grand Blanc, and Vienna free with registration at https://is.bsasoftware.com/bsa.is/SelectUnit.aspx.

Gladwin County

County Register of Deeds, 401 W Cedar Ave, #7, Gladwin, MI 48624-2093. 989-426-7551; fax-989-426-6902; 8:30AM-4:30PM www.gladwinco.com
Office will fax back results for add'l $1.00 per page, prepaid. Index: Separate indices to search include books, computer. Records indexed on computer being added to. Office personnel or visitors may perform searches. General index search fee $.50 per year per name; $5.00 minimum. Office will only search real estate records on computer since 3/14/1991. UCC or tax lien search per debtor name- $10.00. Copy fee $1.00 per page. Cert fee- $1.00 per cert plus copy fee. Payee- Gladwin County Register of Deeds. **Other phones:** Treasurer- 989-426-7251; Elections- 989-426-7351; Vital Records- 989-426-7351. **Property tax/Assessing**- 989-426-9327. **Online access**- Access City of Gladwin property data free with registration at https://is.bsasoftware.com/bsa.is/SelectUnit.aspx.

Gogebic County

County Register of Deeds, 200 N Moore St; Courthouse, Bessemer, MI 49911. Recording, R/E & UCC phone-906-667-0381; fax-906-663-4660; 8:30AM-4:30PM (CST) www.gogebic.org
Index: All in one. Records indexed on a public use terminal back to 1988. Office will perform a UCC search but public must search other records themselves. Search fee-$6.00 per name searched. Copy fee $1.00 per page. Cert fee- $5.00 per cert plus copy fee. Payee- Gogebic County Register of Deeds. Register of Deed's CD images in bulk and printed reports are available for purchase. **Other phones:** Treasurer- 906-667-4517; Elections- 906-667-4518; Vital Records- 906-667-4518. **Property tax/Assessing**- 200 N Moore St, Courthouse, Bessemer, MI 49911; 906-663-4414, assessor fax- 906-663-4105.

Grand Traverse County

County Register of Deeds, 400 Boardman Ave, Traverse City, MI 49684-2577. 231-922-4753, R/E recording phone-231-922-4750; fax-231-922-2770;

8AM-5PM (vault closes at 4:30PM). www.co.grand-traverse.mi.us/departments/Register_of_Deeds.htm
Index: Separate indices to search arranged by date. Records indexed on a public use terminal back to mid-1985. Only the public may search; office rarely. Office search fee $6.00 per name. UCC search per debtor name- $15.00. Copy fee $1.00 per page. Cert fee- $1.00 per cert plus copy fee. Payee- Grand Traverse County Register of Deeds. **Online access to Real Estate, Deed, Tax Lien, Judgment, Assumed Name, Construction Permit, Marriage, Death records:** Recorder's document index search back to 1986 is free at www.co.grand-traverse.mi.us/services/online_records.htm. Images require fee; pay by credit card. Deaths go back to 1867; marriages to 1853. Also, access death and marriage indices free at www.tcnet.org/gtcounty/index.html or via the county online svcs page. Also, recording data by sub on Laredo system or Tapestry credit card system at http://tapestry.fidlar.com; $3.99 search; $.50 per image back to 1986. Also, access tax & special assessments free at https://is.bsasoftware.com/bsa.is/. **Other phones:** Treasurer- 231-922-4735; Elections- 231-922-4760; Vital Records- 231-922-4760. **Property tax/Assessing**- 400 Boardman Ave, 1st Fl, Governmental Ctr, Traverse City, MI 49684-2577; 231-922-4772, assessor fax- 231-922-4658. Attached to the GIS-mapping department. www.co.grand-traverse.mi.us/departments/Equalization_G_I_S_.htm **Online** - Access property tax and special assessments at https://is.bsasoftware.com/bsa.is/SelectUnit.aspx.

Gratiot County

County Register of Deeds, PO Box 5, Ithaca, MI 48847. 989-875-5217; fax-989-875-5235; 8AM-4:30PM (EST)
Index: All in one. Records indexed on a public use terminal back to 1000. Only the public may search. Copy fee $1.00 per page. Cert fee- $1.00 per cert plus copy fee. Payee- Gratiot County Register of Deeds. Custom printouts available- $.50 per page plus $10.00 setup fee; contact Linda. **Other phones:** Treasurer- 989-875-5220; Elections- 989-875-5215 county clerk; Vitals- 989-875-5215. **Property tax/Assessing**- 214 E Center St, Ithaca, MI 48847; 989-875-5203.

Hillsdale County

County Register of Deeds, 29 N Howell, Rm 3; Courthouse, Hillsdale, MI 49242. Recording, R/E & UCC phone-517-437-2231; fax-517-437-3139; 8:30AM-5PM (EST) www.co.hillsdale.mi.us
Index: All in one. Records indexed on a public use terminal back to 1984. Office personnel or visitors may perform searches. Search fee $6.00 per name. Office will search real estate records-request must be in writing accompanied by the minimum statutory fee of $5.00 (name only). Will not search UCC records. UCC copy fee $2.00 per page.Real estate record copy- $1.00 per page. Cert fee- $1.00 per cert plus copy fee. Payee- Hillsdale County Register of Deeds. **Online access to Real Estate, Deed, Judgment, Lien, UCC records:** Access to the recorder's index is free but images available only by sub. Records go back to 9/1984 and more being added. Fee is $300.00 for recorder, or $50.00 for just the assessor's equalization records. Copies included. Call recorder for signup. Also, access to recorders index is free via a private firm at http://counties.recordfusion.com/countyweb/login.jsp?countyname=Hillsdale.
Search free as Guest; registration and fees for full data. Fees to view images. **Other phones:** Treasurer- 517-437-4700; Elections- 517-437-3391; Vitals- 517-437-3391. **Property tax/Assessing**- 29 N Howell, #12, Hillsdale, 49242; 517-439-9166, fax- 517-439-9502. www.hillsdalecounty.info/government0094.asp **Online access**- Search parcels free at www.hillsdalecounty.info/parcelsearch.asp but no name searching. Access Hillsdale tax records free at https://is.bsasoftware.com/bsa.is/SelectUnit.aspx.
Map searching is available at www.gis.hillsdale.us. See County Register of Deeds section for subscription info for county assessment data.

Houghton County

County Register of Deeds, 401 E Houghton Ave, Houghton, MI 49931. 906-482-1311; fax-906-483-0364; 8AM-4:30PM (EST) www.houghtoncounty.net/directory-hcdeeds.shtml
Index: Separate indices to search- tract books, computer. Records indexed on a public use terminal back to 1997. Only the public may search. Copy fee $1.00 per page. Cert fee- $8.00 per doc plus copy fee. Payee- Houghton County Register of Deeds. Custom mortgage reports available for purchase; $100 setup fee; $50 per hour runtime fee. **Online Real Estate, Deed, Lien, Mortgage, UCC, Plat records:** recording index free at http://fidlar.houghtoncounty.net/websense/default.aspx. **Other phones:** Treasurer- 906-482-0560; Elections- 906-482-1150; Vital- 906-482-1150. **Property tax/Assessing**- 401 E Houghton Ave, Houghton, MI 49931; 906-482-0250. www.houghtoncounty.net/directory-hceq.shtml

Huron County

County Register of Deeds, 250 E Huron Ave, Bad Axe, MI 48413. Recording, R/E & UCC phone-989-269-9941; fax-989-269-8786; 8:30AM-5PM (EST) www.infomi.com/county/huron/
Index: All in one. Records indexed on computer back to 1984. Office personnel or visitors may perform searches. Search fee $6.00 per name. Office will not search real estate records. UCC search includes tax liens if requested. Copy fee $1.00 per page; $2.00 for plats. Cert fee- $1.00 per cert plus copy fee. Payee- Huron County Register of Deeds. Treasurer- 989-269-9238; Elections- 989-269-9942; Vital Records- 989-269-9942. **Property tax/ Assessing**- 250 E Huron Ave, #309, Bad Axe, MI 48413; 989-269-6497, assessor fax- 989-269-0012.

Ingham County

County Register of Deeds, PO Box 195, Mason, MI 48854-0195. Recording, R/E & UCC phone-517-676-7216; fax-517-676-7287; 8AM-5PM (EST) www.ingham.org/rd/rodindex.htm
Index: All in one. Records indexed on a public use terminal back to 1956. Only the public may search. Copy fee $1.00 per page. Cert fee- $1.00 per cert plus copy fee. Payee- Ingham County Register of Deeds. **Online access to Real Estate, Grantor/Grantee, Deed, Marriage, Fictitious Name records:** Access the Register of Deeds database indexes back to 1956 - after free registration at https://qdocs.ingham.org/recorder/web/login.jsp?submit=Enter+Eagle+Web.
Also, marriage applicants can be searched by the week for free at www.ingham.org/CL/Vital_Records/Marriage_Weekly_Lists.htm. Search fictitious names and campaign finance filings free at www.ingham.org/cl/Business_Filings/DBA_Lists.htm. **Other phones:** Treasurer- 517-676-7220; Elections- 517-676-7205; Vital Records- 517-676-7201. **Property tax/Assessing**- Equilization/ Mapping, 341 S Jefferson, Courthouse, Mason, MI 48854; 517-676-7212, assessor fax- 517-676-7272. 8AM-N 1PM-5PM www.ingham.org/eq/eqindex.htm **Online access**- Access land, tax, utility records and more free with registration for Cities of East Lansing, Lansing, Leslie, Mason and townships of Aurelius, Lansing, Vevay, and Village of Stockbridge at https://is.bsasoftware.com/bsa.is/SelectUnit.aspx.

Ionia County

County Register of Deeds, PO Box 35, Ionia, MI 48846. 616-527-5320; fax-616-527-8234; 8:30AM-N, 1-5PM (EST) www.ioniacounty.org
Index: All in one. Records indexed on a public use terminal back to 1994. Office will perform a real estate search but public must search other records themselves. Search fee $60.00 unless otherwise indicated. The offices' abstractor will search real estate records for a fee. Will not search UCC records. Copy fee $1.00 per page. Cert fee- $1.00 per cert plus copy fee. Payee- Ionia County Register of Deeds. **Online access to Real Estate, Deed, Judgment, Lien, Will, Death records:** Access recorder records free at http://counties2.recordfusion.com/countyweb/login.jsp?countyname=Ionia. Login as "guest" for free name search. **Other phones:** Treasurer- 616-527-5329; Elections- 616-527-5322; Vital Records- 616-527-5322. **Property tax/Assessing**- 100 W Main St, Courthouse, Ionia, MI 48846; 616-527-5376. **Online access**- Access county property data free at www.ioniacounty.org/taxweb/viewparcels.asp. Also, access City of Belding and Ionia City and Lyons Town land and property records free with registration at https://is.bsasoftware.com/bsa.is/SelectUnit.aspx. Use www.ioniacounty.org under the heading "online parcel information" to search tax records online.

Iosco County

County Register of Deeds, PO Box 367, Tawas City, MI 48764. phone-989-362-2021; fax-989-984-1101; 9AM-5PM (EST) www.iosco.net
Index: Pre-1986 records indexed by grantor/grantee and mortgage. Records indexed on a public use terminal back to 1987. Office personnel or visitors may perform searches. Search fee $6.00 per name. Real estate owner, mortgage, and property transfer searches available only over phone or in person. UCC search includes tax liens if requested. Copy fee $1.25 per page. Cert fee- $1.00 per cert plus copy fee. Payee- Iosco County Register of Deeds. **Other phones:** Treasurer- 989-362-4409; Elections- 989-362-3497; Vital Records- 989-362-3497. **Property tax/Assessing**- PO Box 327, Tawas City, MI 48764; 989-984-1111, assessor fax- 989-984-1122. **Online access**- Three jurisdictions are available free at https://is.bsasoftware.com/bsa.is/SelectUnit.aspx - City of East Tawas, and Oscoda, Plainfield, and Baldwin Townships.

Iron County

Register of Deeds, 2 S 6th St, #11, Crystal Falls, MI 49920-1413. 906-875-3321; fax-906-875-0658; 8AM-N, 12:30-4PM (CST) www.iron.org/edc/gov-register-of-deeds.php
Index: Separate indices to search include grantee/grantor, Mortgagor/Mortgagee, and Books. Records indexed on computer back to 1992. Visitors or office personnel may search. General index search fee $.50 per year with $5.00 minimum. Office will do limited searches of real estate records. Office will not search UCC records. Copy fee $1.00 per page, UCC record and plat copies are $2.00 per page. Cert fee- $1.00 per cert plus copy fee. Payee- Iron County Register of Deeds. Bulk images of documents available for purchase. **Other phones:** Treasurer- 906-875-3362; Vital Records- 906-875-3221. **Property tax/Assessing**- 2 S 6th St, #13, Crystal Falls, MI 49920; 906-875-6502. www.iron.org/edc/gov-equalization.php

Isabella County

County Register of Deeds, 200 N Main St, Mt. Pleasant, MI 48858. Recording, R/E & UCC phone-989-772-0911 x253; fax-989-953-7219; 8AM-4:30PM (EST) www.isabellacounty.org
Will name search mail requests for $5.00 for 10 years. Need exact name, doc approx date, doc type; need name of person requesting search, name of company and how to return. Add'l $5.00 if faxed back. Fees must be prepaid. Index: All in one. (Certified copies of judgements that effect real property.) Records indexed on a public use terminal back to 1940. Office personnel or visitors may perform searches. Search fee $5.00 for 10 years. Office will not search UCC records. Copy fee $1.00 per page. Cert fee- $1.00 per cert plus copy fee. Payee- County Register of Deeds. Bulk data available for purchase for all copies at $1.00 per page (no matter of amount copied). **Online access to Real Estate, Grantor/Grantee, Deed, Lien, Mortgage, UCC records:** Access recorder land data back to 1940 on ACS at https://mi.uslandrecords.com/milr/MilrApp/index.jsp.
Other phones: Treasurer- 989-772-0911 x258; Elections- 989-772-0911 x259; Vital Records- 989-772-0911 x259. **Property tax/Assessing**- 200 N Main St, Mt. Pleasant, MI 48858; 989-772-0911 x242. **Online access**- Access to City of Mt Pleasant

property and tax data is free with registration at https://is.bsasoftware.com/bsa.is/SelectUnit.aspx.

Jackson County

County Register of Deeds, 120 W Michigan Ave, 11th Fl, Jackson, MI 49201. 517-788-4350; fax-517-788-4686; 8AM-5PM www.co.jackson.mi.us/rod/

Index: Separate indices to search include computer, tract books. Records indexed on a public use terminal back to 1984. Only the public may search. Copy fee $1.00 per page. UCC copy $2.00 per page. Cert fee- $1.00 per page plus copy fee. Payee- Jackson County Register of Deeds. **Online access to Real Estate, Grantor/Grantee, Deed, Lien, Divorce Judgment, Death, UCC records:** recorded documents at http://counties2.recordfusion.com/countyweb/login.jsp?countyname=Jackson with a fee for add'l services. **Other phones:** Treasurer- 517-788-4418. **Property tax/Assessing**- 120 W Michigan Ave, 12th Fl, County Equalization Dept, Jackson, MI 49201; 517-788-4378, fax- 517-768-6747. www.co.jackson.mi.us/departments/eq/index.asp **Online** - Access property, tax and land data for the county and City of Jackson and townships of Columbia and Rives for free at https://is.bsasoftware.com/bsa.is/SelectUnit.aspx. Search for Columbia utility bills as well. Also, search Gis-mapping site for property free at www.co.jackson.mi.us/CCinfo.asp. Click Here under Jackson County GIS. Search tax sale data free at www.jacksoncountytaxsale.com/.

Kalamazoo County

County Register of Deeds, 201 W Kalamazoo Ave, #102, Kalamazoo, MI 49007. 269-383-8970; fax-none; 8AM-4PM (EST) www.kalcounty.com

Index: Separate indices to search include computer, old file folders. Deed and mortgage records indexed on a public use terminal back to 1985. Office will perform a UCC search ($6.00) or 1 current owner search (free) but public must search other records themselves. The assessor or treasurer office will perform a property lookup if you provide name. General copy fee $1.00 per page. UCC copy $2.00 per page. Cert fee- $1.00 per doc plus copy fee. Payee- Kalamazoo County Register of Deeds. Office will sell reports and lists by subject and date range, $1.00 per page; contact Jo. **Other phones:** Treasurer- 269-384-8124; Elections- 269-383-8840; Vital Records- 269-383-8840. **Property tax/Assessing**- Equalization Dept, 201 W Kalamazoo Ave, #101, Kalamazoo, MI 49007; 269-383-8960, fax- 269-383-8962. 8AM-5PM There are 19 units in the county and assessor for each. www.kalcounty.com/equalization/index.htm **Online access**- Access property assessor data free at www.kalcounty.com/equalization/parcel_search.php. Also, access property, land, and tax data for Cities of Kalamazoo, Parchment, Portage and the townships of Alamo, Brady, Comstock, Kalamazoo, Oshtemo,. Pavilion, Ross, Schoolcraft, and Wakeshma for free with registration at https://is.bsasoftware.com/bsa.is/SelectUnit.aspx. Search treasurer's delinquent taxes at https://is.bsasoftware.com/bsa.is/default.aspx.

Kalkaska County

County Register of Deeds, 605 N Birch St, Kalkaska, MI 49646. Recording, R/E & UCC phone-231-258-3315; fax-231-258-3345; 9AM-5PM (EST)

Index: Separate indices to search are by computer back to 1992; grantor/grantee and tracts back to 1800s. Records indexed on a public use terminal back to 5/20/96. Office personnel or visitors may perform searches. Search fee $55.00 per hour. These searches are usually for the older archived records only. Office will not search real estate records. Copy fee $1.00 per page. Cert fee- $1.00 per page plus copy fee. Payee- Kalkaska County Register of Deeds. Office sells bulk data as reports, usually mortgages; $.20 per entry. **Other phones:** Treasurer- 231-258-3310; Elections- 231-258-3300; Vital Records- 231-258-3300. **Property tax/Assessing**- Equalization Dept, 605 N Birch St, #110, Kalkaska, MI 49646; 231-258-3340, assessor fax- 231-258-3341. hours- 8AM-5PM A public access terminal is available.

Kent County

County Register of Deeds, 300 Monroe Ave NW, Grand Rapids, MI 49503-2286. 616-632-7610; fax-616-632-7615; 8AM-5PM www.accesskent.com/YourGovernment/RegisterofDeeds/deeds_index.htm

Index: Separate indices to search. Records indexed on a 10 public use terminals back to 1980. Office will perform a UCC search but public must search other records themselves. Copy fee $1.00 per page. Cert fee- $1.00 per doc plus copy fee. Payee- Kent County Register of Deeds. Office sells pulk data as custom reports; contact Register of Deeds. **Online access to Real Estate, Deed, Lien, Fictitious Name records:** Access Kent deeds index free at https://www.accesskent.com/deeds/. Fee for document $2.00 per page plus a $.50 convenience fee. Search and purchase accident reports $3.00 at https://www.accesskent.com/AccidentReports/. Search fictitious business names free at https://www.accesskent.com/BusinessNames/. **Other phones:** Treasurer- 616-632-7501; Elections- 616-632-7650; Vital Records- 616-632-7640. **Property tax/Assessing**- 300 Monroe Ave NW, Grand Rapids, MI 49503; 616-632-7520, assessor fax- 616-632-7545. Order vital statistic records $7 at https://www.accesskent.com/servlet/VitalRec. **Online** County parcel data free at https://www.accesskent.com/Property/. View records- $1; subscribe- $75 per yr; 616-632-6516. Search Grand Rapids property at www.ci.grand-rapids.mi.us/22. Walker City assessor and more- https://is.bsasoftware.com/bsa.is/SelectUnit.aspx free registration. Search Ada, Bowne, Caledonia, Courtland, Grand Rapids, Lowell, Vergennes assessments- www.addorio.com/netparcel.htm.

Keweenaw County

County Register of Deeds, 5095 4th St, Eagle River, MI 49950-9744. Recording, R/E & UCC phone-906-337-2229; fax-906-337-2795; 9AM-4PM (EST)

Index: Separate indices to search include mortgage, misc., deed. Record index not computerized. Office personnel or visitors may perform searches. Search fee $3.00 per name. Office will not search real estate records. UCC search includes tax liens if requested. Copy fee $1.00 per page. Cert fee- $10.00 per cert plus copy fee. Payee- Keweenaw County Register of Deeds. **Other phones:** Treasurer- 906-337-1625; Elections- 906-337-2229; Vital Records- 906-337-2229. **Property tax/Assessing**- 5095 4th St, Eagle River, MI 49950-9624; 906-337-3471, assessor fax-906-337-2795.

Lake County

County Register of Deeds, 800 10th St, #200, Baldwin, MI 49304. Recording, R/E & UCC phone-231-745-4641; fax-231-745-8632; 8:30AM-5PM

Index: All in one. Records indexed on a public use terminal back to 1990. Office personnel or visitors may perform searches. Search fee $.50 per name per year plus copy fee. Office will search real estate records prior to 1990, if request is in writing. Office will search UCC records prior to 7/2001 and current fixture (land) files. UCC search includes tax liens if requested. Tax lien search- $3.00 per debtor. Copy fee $1.00 per page. Cert fee- $1.00 per cert plus copy fee. Payee- Lake County Register of Deeds. **Other phones:** Treasurer- 231-745-4622; Elections- 231-745-2725; Vital Records- 231-745-4641. **Property tax/Assessing**- 800 10th St, #230, Baldwin, MI 49304; 231-745-2723, assessor fax- 231-745-2241. A public access terminal available.

Lapeer County

County Register of Deeds, 279 N Court St, Lapeer, MI 48446. 810-667-0211; fax-810-667-0293; 8AM-5PM (EST) www.county.lapeer.org/deeds/

Index: Separate indices to search include general, surveys, plats, land records. Records indexed on a public use terminal; indexed images go back to 1946. Office will perform a UCC search but public must search other records themselves. Search fee-$6.00 per name. Copy fee $2.00 for UCC; tax lien or real estate $1.00 per page. Cert fee- $1.00 per cert plus copy fee. Payee- Lapeer County Register of Deeds. **Online access to Real Estate, Deed, Lien, Judgment records:** Access recorder data free by name by clicking on "Guest Login" at http://207.72.70.14/scripts/landweb.dll. Registration and fees required for full search. Pop-up blocker must be off. Indexed images may go back to 1946. **Other phones:** Treasurer- 810-667-0239; Elections- 810-667-0356; Vital Records- 810-667-0356. **Property tax/Assessing**- 576 Liberty Park, City Hall, Lapeer, MI 48446; 810-664-2902, assessor fax- 810-667-7157. www.ci.lapeer.mi.us/assessor.htm **Online access**- Access property, land and tax data for Cities of Lapeer and Imlay, and townships of Almont, Imlay, Mayfield for free with registration at https://is.bsasoftware.com/bsa.is/SelectUnit.aspx. Also has special assessment records for Lapeer.

Leelanau County

County Register of Deeds, 8527 E Gov't Center Dr, Ste. 105, Suttons Bay, MI 49682. 231-256-9682, 866-256-9711, R/E recording phone-231-256-9682; fax-231-256-8149; 9AM-5PM (EST) www.leelanau.cc

Index: Separate indices to search. Records indexed on computer back to 1991. Office personnel or visitors may perform searches; office will do a name check on computer back to 1991 only. Search fee $5.00 minimum. Copy fee $1.00 per page. Cert fee- $1.00 per cert plus copy fee. Payee- Leelanau County Register of Deeds. Monthly lender reports available for $.10 per entry. **Online access to Real Estate, Deed, Lien, Mortgage, Judgment records:** Access the recorders database of indexes free at www.leelanau.cc/RODSearch.asp. Records go back past 1/1991 to 1980 but may be subject to errors and omissions. Subscription service for full data and images; $1.25 per page or $200 per month unlimited. **Other phones:** Treasurer- 231-256-9838; Elections- 231-256-9824; Vital Records- 231-256-9824. **Property tax/Assessing**- 8527 E Gov't Center Dr, Ste. 101, Suttons Bay, MI 49682; 231-256-9823, assessor fax- 231-256-8159. (Appraiser/Auditor- 231-256-9823) **Online access**- Access assessor property data free at www.leelanau.cc/PropertySearch.asp.

Lenawee County

County Register of Deeds, 301 N Main St, Adrian, MI 49221. 517-264-4538, UCC recording phone-517-264-4541; fax-517-264-4543; 8AM-4:30PM (EST) www.lenawee.mi.us/register_of_deeds/index.html

Index: All in one. Records indexed on a public use terminal back to 1968 (deeds) and 1969 (mortgages). Only the public may search. General copy fee $1.00 per page. Copy fee for plats or UCCs $2.00 per page. Cert fee- $1.00 per cert plus copy fee. Payee- Lenawee County Register of Deeds. **Online access to Real Estate, Deed, Will, Lien records:** Access to recording records available by subscription, $700 per month, $50. per hour, but nre contracts are not being taken. Some other type of online access is planned for the future. **Other phones:** Treasurer- 517-264-4554; Elections- 517-264-4595; Vital Records- 517-264-4595. **Property tax/Assessing**- 301 N Main St, Adrian, MI 49221; 517-264-4522, fax- 517-264-4529. www.lenawee.mi.us/equalization/index.html **Online access**- Search assessing/property data free at http://lenaweeco.is.bsasoftware.com/. Also, access to City of Tecumseh data including animal licensing is free with registration at https://is.bsasoftware.com/bsa.is/SelectUnit.aspx

Livingston County

County Register of Deeds, 200 E Grand River; Courthouse, Howell, MI 48843. 517-546-0270; fax-517-546-5966; 8AM-5PM (EST) www.co.livingston.mi.us/RegisterofDeeds/

Index: Separate indices to search include tract, grantor/grantee. Records indexed on a public use terminal back to 10/1984. Office personnel or visitors may perform searches. General search fee $5.00. Office will search real estate records. Office will not search UCC records. Separate federal/state combined tax lien search- $6.00 per debtor. Copy fee $2.00 per page for plats; tax lien or real estate $1.00 per page. Cert fee- $1.00 per cert plus copy fee. Payee- Livingston County Register of Deeds. **Online access to Real Estate, Deed, Lien, Death records:** Web access to county records back to 1984 available to occasional users; a dedicated line is available for professionals for $1200 fee. Annual fee for occasional use- $400. Records date back to 1984. See https://www.livingstonlive.org/Deeds/ or contact IT Dept at 517-548-3230. Also, search the county death indices to 1948 for free at www.livgenmi.com/deathlisting.htm. **Other phones:** Treasurer- 517-546-7010; Elections- 517-546-0500; Vital Records- 517-546-0500. **Property tax/Assessing**- 304 E Grand River, #102, Howell, MI 48843; 517-546-4182, assessor fax- 517-552-2322. www.livingstonlive.org **Online access**- Access property, tax, and other civil data for Cities of Brighton, Howell, and Townships of Brighton, Handy, Hartland, Putnam free with registration at https://is.bsasoftware.com/bsa.is/SelectUnit.aspx. Includes Village of Fowler property tax data.

Luce County

County Clerk, Register of Deeds, 407 W Harrie St; County Gov't Bldg, Newberry, MI 49868. Recording, R/E & UCC phone-906-293-5521; fax-906-293-5553; 8AM-4PM (EST)

Index: Separate indices to search include computer, grantor/grantee books. Records indexed on a public use terminal back to 1994. Only the public may search. Copy fee $1.00 per page. Cert fee- $10.00 per copy plus copy fee. Payee- Luce County Register of Deeds. **Other phones:** Treasurer- 906-293-8171; Elections- 906-293-5521; Vital Records- 906-293-5521. **Property tax/Assessing**- 407 W Harrie St, County Gov't Bldg, Newberry, MI 49868; 906-293-5611, assessor fax- 906-293-4890. A public access terminal available.

Mackinac County

County Register of Deeds, 100 Marley St, Saint Ignace, MI 49781. Recording, R/E & UCC phone-906-643-7306; fax-906-643-7302; 8:30AM-4:30PM

Index: Separate indexes to search. Records indexed on a public use terminal back to 1990. Only the public may search. Copy fee $1.00 per page. Cert fee- $1.00 per cert plus copy fee. Payee- Mackinac County Register of Deeds. **Other phones:** Treasurer- 906-643-7317; Elections- 906-643-7300; Vital Records-906-643-7300. **Property tax/Assessing**- 100 Marley St, Saint Ignance, MI 49781; 906-643-7310.

Macomb County

County Register of Deeds, 10 N Main, Mt. Clemens, MI 48043. 586-469-7953, R/E recording phone-586-469-5309, UCC recording phone-586-469-5342; fax-586-469-5130; hours - 8:30AM-5PM (EST) http://macombcountymi.gov/clerksoffice/index.asp

Treasurer office located at 1 S Main St. Index: All in one. Records indexed on computer from 10/1/81 to present, card file from 4/1/65 to 9/30/81, and old books divided by blocks or years back to 4/1/65. Office personnel or visitors may perform searches free. General index search fee $5.00 minimum (10 years) $.50 each year thereafter. Real estate record owner and mortgage searches available. Office will search UCC records prior to 7/2001 and current fixture (land) files. Will search tax liens. UCC search per debtor name- $12.00. Copy fee $1.00 per page. Cert fee- $1.00 per page plus copy fee. Payee- Macomb County Register of Deeds. Bulk data available for purchase on film or FTP, contact ACS at 800-800-0323. **Online access to Real Estate, Deed, Business Registration records:** Property records database found at www.landaccess.com/index.jsp?content=register. Free registration for password and user name. Subscription by month or purchase on pay-per-view basis. Search business registrations free at https://macombvitals.macombcountymi.gov/dba.php. Also, county recorder images from a private source at www.courthousedirect.com. Fees/registration required. **Other phones:** Treasurer- 586-469-5190; Elections- 586-469-5209; Vital Records- 586-469-5120; Search- 586-469-7953. **Property tax/Assessing**- 1 S Main St, Mt Clemens, MI 48043; 586-469-5312, assessor fax- 586-307-8290. **Online access**- 13 cities' and towns' property, tax, and certain other civil records are free with registration at https://is.bsasoftware.com/bsa.is/SelectUnit.aspx. Also, death records at https://macombvitals.macombcountymi.gov/death.php by name or date.

Manistee County

Register of Deeds, 415 3rd St; Courthouse, Manistee, MI 49660-1606. 231-723-2146; fax-231-398-3544; 8:30AM-5PM (EST) www.manisteecountymi.gov/

Index: Separate indices to search. Records indexed on a public use terminal back to 8/19/91. Office will perform a UCC search but public must search other records themselves. Search fee $6.00 per name. UCC copy fee $2.00 per page.Real estate record copy- $1.00 per page. Cert fee- $2.00 per cert plus copy fee. Payee- Manistee County Register of Deeds. **Other phones:** Treasurer- 231-723-3173; Elections- 231-723-3331; Vital Records- 231-723-3331. **Property tax/Assessing**- Equalization Department, 415 3rd St, Manistee, MI 49660; 231-723-5957, assessor fax- 231-398-3531. www.manisteecountymi.gov/ **Online access**- Access property records free at www.liaa.org/manisteeparcels/propertysearch.asp.

Marquette County

County Register of Deeds, 234 W Baraga Ave, #C-105, Marquette, MI 49855. Recording, R/E & UCC phone-906-225-8415; fax-906-225-8420; 8AM-5PM (EST) www.co.marquette.mi.us/register.htm

Index: Separate indices to search go back to 1854. All searchable by name or legal description. Records indexed on a public use terminal back to 1988. Office personnel or visitors may perform searches. General search fee $5.00. Only "minor" real estate record searches performed by office. UCC search includes tax liens if requested. UCC search or tax lien search per debtor name- $6.00. General copy fee $1.00 per page. UCC copy $2.00 per page. Cert fee- $1.00 per cert plus copy fee. Payee- Marquette County Register of Deeds. **Online access to Real Estate, Deed, Lien records:** Recorder land data by subscription on either the Laredo system using subscription and fees or the Tapestry System using credit card, http://tapestry.fidlar.com; $3.99 search; $.50 per image. Index and images go back to 1988. **Other phones:** Treasurer- 906-225-8425; Elections- 906-225-8330; Vital Records- 906-225-8330. **Property tax/Assessing**- 234 W Baraga Ave, Equalization Department, County Courthouse, Marquette, MI 49855; 906-225-8405, fax- 906-228-1564. (Auditor-906-225-8405) www.co.marquette.mi.us/equaliza.htm **Online access**- Access City of Marquette only property, tax, and building records free at https://is.bsasoftware.com/bsa.is/SelectUnit.aspx.

Mason County

County Register of Deeds, 304 E Ludington Ave, Ludington, MI 49431. 231-843-4466; fax-231-845-7977; 9AM-5PM (EST) www.masoncounty.net/

Index: Separate indices to search are by computer, grantor/grantee, tract cards back to 1940s. Records indexed on a public use terminal back to 10/1994. Office personnel or visitors may perform searches. Current owner search only $.50 per name per year, $5.00 minimum. Office will do last deed only searches. Copy fee $1.00 per page. Cert fee- $1.00 per doc plus copy fee. Payee- Mason County Register of Deeds. Bulk dta available for purchase as reports; contact Diane. **Online Real Estate, Deed, Lien records:** 3 options available to search county Register database at www.masoncounty.net/content.aspx?Page=Online%20Services&departmentID=10. Search the Websense index free; other two require registration and fees. Other methods require subscription on either the Laredo system using subscription and fees or the Tapestry System using credit card, http://tapestry.fidlar.com/. Data goes back to 10/1994. **Other phones:** Treasurer- 231-843-2989; Elections- 231-843-8202; Vital Records- 231-843-8202. **Property tax/Assessing**- 304 E Ludington Ave, Ludington, 49431; 231-845-6288, assessor fax-231-845-6289. www.masoncounty.net/content.aspx?departmentid=7&page=home **Online**- Access county property data at www.liaa.org/masonparcels/propertysearch.asp. Access City of Ludington parcels and tax data free at https://is.bsasoftware.com/bsa.is/SelectUnit.aspx. Ditto for Hamlin Township property, and ditto for Pere Marquette Township property and utility bills.

Mecosta County

County Register of Deeds, PO Box 718, Big Rapids, MI 49307. 231-592-0148; 8:30AM-5PM (EST) www.co.mecosta.mi.us

Index: All in one. Records indexed on a public use terminal back to 1980. Office will perform a UCC search but public must search other records themselves. Copy fee $1.00 per page; larger plat and condos- $2.00 per page. Cert fee- $1.00 per cert plus copy fee. Payee- Mecosta County Register of Deeds. **Other phones:** Treasurer- 231-592-0169. **Property tax/Assessing**- 231-592-0108. **Online access**- Access county property, land, and tax data index free at https://is.bsasoftware.com/bsa.is/SelectUnit.aspx. May charge fees to view images. Data includes City of Big Rapids and Animal License, Special Assessments, Delinquent Taxes.

Menominee County

Register of Deeds, 839 10th Ave, Menominee, MI 49858. 906-863-2822; fax-906-863-8839; 8AM-4:30PM (CST) www.menomineecounty.com/

Fax number is for entire courthouse; be sure to attach a cover sheet with specifics. Index: All in one back to 1/2000; prior indices were deeds and mortgages. Records indexed on a public use terminal back to 1/1/1993. Office personnel or visitors may perform searches. Office searches are minimal. General index search fee minimum of $5.00. Property transfer searches available. Copy fee $1.00 per page; plat copies $2.00. Cert fee- $1.00 per page plus copy fee. Payee- Register of Deeds. **Online access to Real Estate, Deed records:** Access to land records free at www.menomineecounty.com/online_services/category_general/ then click on County Land Records. Search is free - use "Guest Login." Document images may be ordered by fax for $1.50 each or mail for $1.00 each. Subscriptions available for full data. **Other phones:** Treasurer- 906-863-5548; Elections-906-863-9968; Vitals- 906-863-9968; Equalization-906-863-2683. **Property tax/Assessing**- County Treasurer, 839 10th Ave, 2nd Fl, Menominee, MI 49858; 906-863-5548, assessor fax- 906-863-8839. A public access terminal available. **Online**- Access property tax and land data for City of Menominee and Township of Menominee free with registration at https://is.bsasoftware.com/bsa.is/SelectUnit.aspx.

Midland County

County Register of Deeds, 220 W Ellsworth St; County Services Bldg, Midland, MI 48640-5194. 989-832-6820; fax-932-832-6842; 8AM-5PM (EST) www.co.midland.mi.us

Index: All in one. Records indexed on a public use terminal back to 1984. Only the public may search. Copy fee $1.00 per page. Cert fee- $1.00 per doc plus copy fee. Payee- Midland County Register of Deeds. Computer printout of reception book at $.25 per page. **Online access to Real Estate, Deed, Lien, Judgment, Mortgage records:** Access the county register's land records search system free at http://webapps.co.midland.mi.us/landweb.dll and login as Guest. Subscription required for full data; call for signup and usage fees. **Other phones:** Treasurer-989-832-6850; Elections- 989-832-6739; Vital Records- 989-832-6739. **Property tax/Assessing**-220 W Ellsworth St, 3rd Fl, Midland, MI 48640; 989-832-6844, assessor fax- 989-832-6849. www.co.midland.mi.us/departments/home.php?id=11 **Online access**- Access the county and City of

Midland property data free with registration at https://is.bsasoftware.com/bsa.is/SelectUnit.aspx. County access via www.co.midland.mi.us also includes delinquent tax and animal license data.

Missaukee County

County Register of Deeds, PO Box 800, Lake City, MI 49651. Recording, R/E & UCC phone-231-839-4967; fax-231-839-3684; 9AM-5PM (EST) www.missaukee.org/regdept.htm

Index: All in one. Records indexed on a public use terminal back to 1989. Office personnel (will show public how to do their own searches) or visitors may perform searches. General index search fee $.50 per year per document with a minimum of $5.00. Office will search limited real estate records. Office will search limited UCC records. Copy fee $2.00, if tax lien or real estate $1.00 per page. Cert fee- $8.00 per cert includes copy fee. Payee- Missaukee County Register of Deeds. Treasurer- 231-839-2169; Elections- 231-839-4967; Vital Records- 231-839-4967. **Property tax/Assessing**- 231-839-2702.

Monroe County

Register of Deeds, 51 S Macomb St, Monroe, MI 48161. phone-734-240-7390; 8:30AM-4PM (EST) www.co.monroe.mi.us/monroe/default.aspx

Index: All in one. Records indexed on a public use terminal back to 02/27/1991. Only the public may search. Will not search UCC records. Copy fee $1.00 per page. Cert fee- $1.00 per page includes copy fee. Payee- Monroe County Register of Deeds. Data available in bulk through website only. Also, voter data on CD-rom is $20.00 each. **Online access to Real Estate, Deed, Lien, Fictitious Name records:** Recorder land data by subscription on either the Laredo system using subscription and fees or the Tapestry System using credit card, http://tapestry.fidlar.com; $5.95 search; $.50 per image printed. Index goes back to 2/15/91, images to 1980. Access fictitious business names free at https://www.co.monroe.mi.us/egov/searchdbanames.aspx. **Other phones:** Treasurer- 734-240-7365; County Clerk- 734-240-7020. **Property tax/Assessing**- 51 S Macomb St, Monroe, MI 48161; 734-240-7235, assessor fax- 734-240-7244. hours- 8:30AM-5PM www.co.monroe.mi.us/Monroe/default.aspx?PageId=535 **Online access**- Access assessment database land index free at https://www.co.monroe.mi.us/egov/landrecords/. Printing of images requires credit card payment. Also, access county tax bill and delinquent tax data free at https://is.bsasoftware.com/bsa.is/SelectUnit.aspx. This also offers access to City of Monroe Property, tax, and utility bill data.

Montcalm County

County Register of Deeds, PO Box 188, Stanton, MI 48888. 989-831-7337; fax-989-831-7320; 8AM-N, 1-5PM (EST) www.montcalm.org

Index: All in one. Records indexed on 4 public use terminals back to approximately 1970. Office personnel or visitors may perform searches. Direct search requests to abstract office. General index search fee $10.00 per name. UCC copy fee $2.00 per page.Real estate record copy- $1.00 per page. Cert fee- $1.00 per doc plus copy fee. Payee- Montcalm County Register of Deeds. Office sell bulk data in report format; bulk images- $.50-$.75 per page depending on data type. **Online access to Real Estate, Deed, Lien records:** Access to recorders index is free via a private firm at http://counties.recordfusion.com/countyweb/login.jsp?countyname=Montcalm. Search free as Guest; registration and fees for full data. Fee to view images. **Other phones:** Treasurer- 989-831-7334; Elections- 989-831-7339; Vital Records- 989-831-7339. **Property tax/Assessing**- 989-831-5226 x203. **Online access**- Assessor property tax data is free at www.montcalm.org/taxweb/viewparcels.asp. Search tax roll and tax sale data free at www.co.whatcom.wa.us/treasurer/index.jsp. Access to Cities of Greenville property, tax, and land data at https://is.bsasoftware.com/bsa.is/SelectUnit.aspx.

Montmorency County

County Register of Deeds, PO Box 789, Atlanta, MI 49709. Recording, R/E & UCC phone-989-785-8079; fax-989-785-8080; 8:30AM-N, 1PM-4:30PM (EST) www.montmorencycountymichigan.us/RegisterofDeeds.html

Index: Separate indices to search include deeds, mortgages, liens, judgments/lps, surveys, land corners, deaths, oil & gas. Records indexed on a public use terminal back to 8/87. Office personnel or visitors may perform searches. Search fee-$5.00 per name. Office will search for specific of real estate records only. Will not search UCC records. Copy fee $2.00, if tax lien or real estate $1.00 per page. Cert fee- $3.00 per cert plus copy fee. Payee- Montmorency County Register of Deeds. Bulk data available for purchase in print form only. Contact Teresa Walker, Register. **Other phones:** Treasurer- 989-785-8086; Elections- 989-785-8022; Vital Records- 989-785-8022. **Property tax/Assessing**- PO Box 789 - Equalization Dept, Atlanta, MI 49709; 989-785-8046, assessor fax- 989-785-8094. A public access terminal available. www.montmorencycountymichigan.us/EQUALIZATIONDEPARTMENT.html

Muskegon County

County Register of Deeds, 990 Terrace St, 2nd Fl, Muskegon, MI 49442. 231-724-6271; fax-231-724-6842; 8AM-5PM; recording hours: 8AM-4:30PM (EST) www.co.muskegon.mi.us/deeds/

Index: Separate indices to search are by computer back to 8/1978; prior in grantor/grantee index, tract books. Records indexed on a public use terminal back to 1978. Office personnel or visitors may perform searches. Search fee $5.00 per name. Copy fee $1.00 per page. Office can fax back docs. Cert fee- $1.00 per page plus copy fee. Payee- Muskegon County Register of Deeds. Office sells bulk data reports; $5.00 per page; usually 15 entries per page. **Online access to Real Estate, Grantor/Grantee, Deed, Mortgage, Lien records:** Login as Great, password Muskegon, to search recorder land records free at www.co.muskegon.mi.us/deeds/record_search.htm. Registration and fees apply in access images. **Other phones:** Treasurer- 231-724-6261; Elections- 231-724-6221; Vital Records- 231-724-6221. **Property tax/Assessing**- 173 E Apple Ave, Bldg C, Muskegon, MI 49442; 231-724-6386, fax- 231-724-1129. hours- 8AM-5PM www.co.muskegon.mi.us/equalization/ **Online access**- Access to the city of Norton Shores tax data is free with registration at https://is.bsasoftware.com/bsa.is/SelectUnit.aspx. Also at this site you may access City of Roosevelt property and tax data. Access the county genealogical death index system for free at www.co.muskegon.mi.us/clerk/websearch.cfm. Records 1867-1965.

Newaygo County

County Register of Deeds, PO Box 885, White Cloud, MI 49349. Recording, R/E & UCC phone-231-689-7246; fax-231-689-7271; 8:30AM-N, 1-4:30PM (EST) www.countyofnewaygo.com

Index: All in one. Records indexed on a public use terminal back to 1989. Only the public may search. Copy fee $1.00 per page. Will fax back $5.00 per copy. Cert fee- $1.00 per doc plus copy fee. Payee- Newaygo County Register of Deeds. **Online access to Real Estate, Deed, Lien, Judgment records:** Access the county land records search system free at http://rod.countyofnewaygo.com/landweb.dll. Login as Guest. Subscription required for full access, $500 monthly plus $1 per page. **Other phones:** Treasurer- 231-689-7230; Elections- 231-689-7235; Vital Records- 231-689-7235; Sheriff- 231-689-6623. **Property tax/Assessing**- PO Box 885, White Cloud, MI 49349; 231-689-7244, assessor fax- 231-689-7032. hours- 8AM-5PM A public terminal available. www.countyofnewaygo.com/Equal/EqualHome.htm **Online access**- Search property data free on the GIS-mapping site at http://gis.countyofnewaygo.com/MapViews/Public%5FV2/Newaygo/viewer.htm but no name searching. A subscription version offering various options is available, call 231-689-7281 or see. Also, access City of Fremont land/property data free at https://is.bsasoftware.com/bsa.is/SelectUnit.aspx.

Oakland County

County Register of Deeds, 1200 N Telegraph Rd, Dept 480, Pontiac, MI 48341-0480. 248-858-0605/0606, R/E recording phone-248-858-0597, UCC recording phone-248-858-0600; fax-248-858-7466; 8AM-4:30PM (EST) www.oakgov.com/clerkrod/

Index: Separate indices to search include land, UCC records. Records indexed on a public use terminal back to 1983. Office personnel or visitors may perform searches. Search fee index only- $5.00 per name; UCC search $9.00. Copy fee $1.00 per page. Small plats- $2.50 per page, large $3.00. Cert fee- $1.00 per doc plus copy fee. Payee- Oakland County Register of Deeds. Foreclusure lists are avaialble for purchase once a week, $5.00. **Online access to Real Estate, Deed, Lien, Mortgage, Assumed Name records:** Access to Oakland recorded land data is by subscription at www.landaccess.com/, available $40.00 monthly (lowest fee) or $5.00 per search plus $1.00 per doc view. Search fictitious/assumed names for free at www.oakgov.com/crts0003/main. **Other phones:** Treasurer- 248-858-0611; Elections- 248-858-0564; Vital Records- 248-858-0571. **Property tax/Assessing**- 248-858-0740. **Online access**- Access to Oakland property data is by subscription, available monthly or per use. For info visit www.oakgov.com/index.html (click on "Access Oakland") or call Information Services at 248-858-0861. Search Rochester Hills assessor data at http://64.7.183.246/Services/TaxandAssessing/SearchOverview.asp. No name searching. Also access 8 municipalities land, property tax records and more at https://is.bsasoftware.com/bsa.is/SelectUnit.aspx.

Oceana County

County Register of Deeds, PO Box 111, Hart, MI 49420. Recording, R/E & UCC phone-231-873-4158; fax-231-873-9218; 9AM-5PM www.oceana.mi.us/

Index: Separate indices to search include from 2002 to present on computer, 1961 - 2002 index cards, before 1961-books. Records indexed on a public use terminal back to 2002; more being added. Office will perform a UCC search but public must search other records themselves. Search fee-$5.00 per name. Office will not search real estate records, but office personnel will assist. Copy fee $1.00 per page; UCC copy $2.00 per page. Cert fee- $1.00 per page plus copy fee. Payee- Oceana County Register of Deeds. **Online access to Real Estate, Deed records:** Access the record index back to 1/2002 free at http://mi-oceana-recorder.governmaxa.com/recordmax/record40.asp. No images currently available. **Other phones:** Treasurer- 231-873-3980; Elections- 231-873-4328; Vital Records- 231-873-4328. **Property tax/Assessing**- PO Box 191, Courthouse, 100 State St, Hart, MI 49420; 231-873-4609, assessor fax- 231-873-3710. 8AM-5PM www.oceana.mi.us/equalizer/ **Online access**- Access property tax and land records for Hart Township for free with registration at https://is.bsasoftware.com/bsa.is/SelectUnit.aspx. Also, access property data at http://mi-oceana-equalization.governmax.com/collectmax/collect30.asp. All Townships are included in the database except Hart - (64-007) and Benona - (64-011).

Ogemaw County

County Register of Deeds, 806 W Houghton Ave, Rm 104, West Branch, MI 48661. Recording, R/E & UCC phone-989-345-0728; fax-989-345-6221; 8:30AM-4:30PM (EST) http://ogemawcountymi.gov

Index: All in one. Records indexed on a public use terminal back to 12/1984. Office will perform a UCC search but public must search other records themselves. Office will not search real estate records. UCC search per debtor name- $6.00. Copy fee $2.00, if tax lien or real estate $1.00 per page; $1.50 if mailed. Cert fee- $1.00 per cert plus copy fee. Payee- Ogemaw County Register of Deeds. **Other phones:** Treasurer- 989-345-0084; Elections- 989-345-0215; Vital Records- 989-345-0215. **Property tax/ Assessing-** 806 W Houghton Ave, Rm 105, Equalization Dept, West Branch, 48661; 989-345-0328, fax- 989-345-4939. **Online** - Access assessor equalization data free at http://ogemaw.mi.govern.com/parcelquery.php. Also, access property data free at http://ogemawgis.com/parcelquery/website/.

Ontonagon County

Register of Deeds, 725 Greenland Rd, Ontonagon, MI 49953-1492. Recording, R/E & UCC phone-906-884-4255; fax-906-884-6796; 8:30AM-4:30PM (EST)
Index: Separate indices to search include deeds, mortgage, misc. Records indexed on a public use terminal back to 1995. Office personnel or visitors may perform searches. General index search fee $5.00 per name; will search deeds if year given. Office will not search real estate records or do title work. Will not search UCC records. Copy fee $1.00 per page. Cert fee- $1.00 per cert plus copy fee. Payee- Ontonagon County Register of Deeds. Bulk data available for purchase; each township CD $20 or $220 for the whole county. **Other phones:** Treasurer- 906-884-4665; Elections- 906-884-4255; Vital Records- 906-884-4255. **Property tax/Assessing-** 725 Greenland Rd, Ontonagon, MI 49953-1492; 906-884-2765. (Appraiser/Auditor- 906-884-2765) hours- 8:30AM-N, 1PM-4:30PM A public access terminal available.

Osceola County

Register of Deeds, 301 W Upton Ave, Reed City, MI 49677-0208. 231-832-6113; 9AM-5PM (EST)
Index: Separate indices to search include grantor/grantee, mtgor/mtgee, 1856-2002. Records indexed on a public use terminal back to 2000. Only the public may search. Office will not search real estate records. Will not search UCC records. Copy fee $1.00 per page. Cert fee- $1.00 per doc plus copy fee. Payee- Osceola County Register of Deeds. Paper copies of bulk data available for purchase. **Other phones:** Treasurer- 231-832-6110; Vital Records- 231-832-6101. **Property tax/Assessing-** 301 W Upton Ave, Reed City, MI 49677-0208; 231-832-6119, assessor fax- 231-832-6149. A public access terminal available in the treasurer's office.

Oscoda County

County Register of Deeds, PO Box 399, Mio, MI 48647. 989-826-1116; fax-989-826-1156; 8:30AM-4:30PM (EST) www.oscodacountymi.com/Register%20of%20Deeds.htm
Index: All in one. Records indexed on a public use terminal back to 1992. Only the public may search. Copy fee $1.00 per page, UCC copy fee $2.00 per page. Cert fee- $1.00 per cert plus copy fee. Payee- Oscoda County Register of Deeds. **Online access to Real Estate, Deed, Lien, UCC, Mortgage, Plat, Judgment records:** Recorder land data by subscription on either the Laredo system using subscription and fees or the Tapestry2 System using credit card, https://tapestry.fidlar.com/Tapestry2/LoggedOut.aspx. Also, access to land records (name only) for free go to http://65.111.217.227/FreeWebSearch/CriteriaPage.aspx. **Other phones:** Treasurer- 989-826-1112; Elections- 989-826-1110. **Property tax/Assessing-** PO Box 399, Mio, MI 48647; 989-826-1104, assessor fax- 989-826-1138.

Otsego County

County Register of Deeds, 225 W Main St, Rm 108, Gaylord, MI 49735. Recording, R/E & UCC phone-989-731-7550, UCC recording phone-989-731-7552; fax-989-731-7519; 8AM-4:30PM (EST)
Requests must be in writing along with money up front. Index: All in one. Records indexed on a public use terminal back to 1984. Office personnel or visitors may perform searches. Search fee $5.00 (or UCC $6.00 on UCC form) in writing or prepaid, back to 1984; prior years $.50 per year. Office will search real estate records. Will search UCC records. Copy fee $1.00 per page; UCC, tax lien and plat copies are $2.00 each. Cert fee- $1.00 per doc plus copy fee. Payee- Otsego County Register of Deeds. Bulk data is available for purchase (printed only at $.20 per doc), contact Judy Seelinger at Register of Deeds, 989-731-7550. **Other phones:** Treasurer- 989-731-7560; Elections- 989-731-7501; Vital Records- 989-731-7500. **Property tax/Assessing-** 1064 Cross St, Gaylord, 49735; 989-731-7410, fax- 989-731-7418. www.otsegocountymi.gov/equalization/equalization.htm **Online access-** Search property and assessment data on the Equalization Dept search site at http://maps.otsegocountymi.gov/

Ottawa County

County Register of Deeds, PO Box 265, Grand Haven, MI 49417-0265. 616-846-8346; fax-616-846-8131; 8AM-5PM (EST) www.miottawa.org/
Index: All in one. Records indexed on a public use terminal back to 10/16/58. Office will perform a UCC search but public must search other records themselves. Search fee-$.50 each year the grantor/grantee searches are made with a $5.00 minimum except for tract. Office will not search real estate records. Copy fee $1.00 per page. $3.00 per page for a plat. Cert fee- $1.00 per cert plus copy fee. Payee- Ottawa County Register of Deeds. Bulk images availalbe for purchase by FTP site, contact Gary Scholten at 616-846-8237. **Online Real Estate, Deed, Lien, Mortgage, Judgment records:** Search recorded index and property data free at https://www.miottawa.org/Property/noLogin.do but a fee applies to view docs, purchase by subscription or with credit card. Also access recorder records by subscription at https://www.landaccess.com/ottawa/sub.jsp?county=miottawa. Fee- $80.00 per month plus $1.00 per page to view and print; maximum $10.00 per doc. Credit card search only. **Other phones:** Treasurer- 616-846-8230; Elections- 616-846-8310; Vital Records- 616-846-8310. **Property tax/Assessing-** 13300 168th St, Township Hall, Grand Haven, MI 49417; 616-842-5988, assessor fax-616-842-9419. **Online-** Holland City land/tax data at https://is.bsasoftware.com/bsa.is/SelectUnit.aspx. Also, access property and tax records for 8 municipalities free with registration as well. Includes some building and assessment data. Also, free online mapping service with parcel ID at www.gis.co.ottawa.mi.us/ottawacounty/. No name searching. 2nd interactive mapping site free/fee at http://miottawa.org/CoGov/Depts/GIS/mapping.htm.

Presque Isle County

County Register of Deeds, PO Box 110, Rogers City, MI 49779-0110. 989-734-2676; fax-989-734-0506; 8:30AM-4:30PM (EST)
Index: All in one. Records indexed on a public use terminal back to 1992. Only the public may search. Copy fee $1.00 per page. Cert fee- $1.00 per cert includes copy fee. Payee- Presque Isle County Register of Deeds. **Other phones:** Treasurer- 989-734-4075; Elections- 989-734-3288; Vital Records- 989-734-3288. **Property tax/Assessing-** PO Box 110, Rogers City, MI 49779-0110; 989-734-3810, assessor fax- 989-734-2777. www.presqueislecounty.org/equalization_department.htm **Online access-** Search property tax data free at www.presqueisle.mi.gove rn.com/parcelquery.php.

Roscommon County

County Register of Deeds, 500 Lake St, Roscommon, MI 48653. 989-275-5931, R/E recording phone-517-275-5931; fax-989-275-8640; 8:30AM-4:30PM
Index: Separate indices to search include computer and various pre-1985 indices. Records indexed on computer back to 1985. Office will perform a UCC search but public must search other records themselves. Search fee-$5.00 for a specific document. UCC search request with SS/TIN (per name)- $6.00, $12.00 without. Separate federal or state tax lien search- $3.00 per debtor. Copy fee $1.00 per page. UCC copy $2.00 per page. Cert fee- $1.00 per cert plus copy fee. Payee- Roscommon County Register of Deeds. **Online access to Real Estate, Deed, Lien, Mortgage records:** Access land recorded index free at https://mi.uslandrecords.com/milr/controller. Select Roscommon. **Other phones:** Treasurer- 989-275-5823; Elections- 989-275-5923; Vital Records- 989-275-5923. **Property tax/Assessing-** 500 Lake St, Roscommon, MI 48653; 989-275-8121, assessor fax-989-275-7037. A public access terminal available.

Saginaw County

County Register of Deeds, 111 S Michigan Ave, Saginaw, MI 48602. 989-790-5270; fax-989-790-5278; 8AM-5PM (EST) www.saginawcounty.com
Index: All in one. Records indexed on a public use terminal back to 1982; $1.00 to print image. Office personnel or visitors may perform searches. Current owner search fee $5.00 per name. Office will not do title work. Copy fee $1.00 per page. Cert fee- $1.00 per doc plus copy fee. Payee- Saginaw County Register of Deeds. Office sells reports on grantor/grantee, mortgages, etc, but these are sparse, often no address. Bulk fee- $1.00 per page. **Online Real Estate, Grantor/Grantee, Deed, Assumed Business Name, Marriage, Death, Election records:** Search the Register of Deeds index at www.saginawcounty.com/ROD/Simple.htm. Images are $1.00 to print, plus a $5.00 convenience fee if credit card used. Access county clerks assumed names, marriages, death free at www.saginawcounty.com/clerk/search/index.html. Vital statistic records go back to 1995. **Other phones:** Treasurer- 989-790-5225; Elections- 989-790-5251; Vital Records- 989-790-5251. **Property tax/ Assessing-** 111 S Michigan Ave, Saginaw, MI 48602; 989-790-5260, assessor fax- 989-792-4994. www.saginawcounty.com/equ/index.html **Online access-** Search equalization board tax records at www.saginawcounty.com/equ/prop_info.htm. Also, a general property and sales search on the GIS site is free at www.sagagis.org/search/.

Sanilac County

County Register of Deeds, Box 168, Sandusky, MI 48471-0168. Recording, R/E & UCC phone-810-648-2313; fax-810-648-5461; 8AM-N, 1-4:30PM (EST) www.sanilaccounty.net
Index: Separate indices to search include computer back to 1/1982 (deeds only); previous on grantor/grantee books. Records indexed on computer, anything before 1991 is indexed in grantor/grantee indexes. Are currently working on entering recordings before 1991 into the computer. Office personnel or visitors may perform searches. General index search fee $.50 per name per year. Real estate record owner and property searches available. Office will search UCC records prior to 7/2001. UCC search includes tax liens if requested. UCC search per debtor name- $6.00. Separate state tax lien search- $3.00 per debtor. Separate federal tax lien search- $6.00 per debtor. UCC copy fee $2.00 per copy.Real estate record copy- $1.00 per copy. Cert fee- $1.00 per cert plus copy fee. Payee- Sanilac County Register of Deeds. **Other phones:** Treasurer- 810-648-2127; Elections- 810-648-3212; Vital Records- 810-648-3212. **Property tax/Assessing-** 60 W Sanilac Ave, Rm 209, Sandusky, MI 48471; 810-648-2955, assessor fax- 810-648-5459. hours- 8AM-4:30PM. **Online-** Access parcel data at www.sanilaccounty.net/PublicPages/Parcels.aspx. Also, access county land and property tax records free at https://is.bsasoftware.com/bsa.is/SelectUnit.aspx. Access Argyle Township and Moore Township property records for free there also.

Schoolcraft County

County Register of Deeds, 300 Walnut St, Rm 164, Manistique, MI 49854. phone-906-341-3618; fax-906-341-5680; 8AM-4PM (EST)
Index: Separate indices to search include deeds, mortgages, liens, land corners. Records indexed on a public use terminal back to 1997. Office will perform a UCC search but public must search other records themselves. Copy fee $1.00 per page. Cert fee- $1.00

per cert plus copy fee. Payee- Schoolcraft County Register of Deeds. **Other phones:** Treasurer- 906-341-3622; Elections- 906-341-3618; Vital Records-906-341-3618. **Property tax/Assessing-** 300 Walnut St, Rm 207, Manistique, MI 49854; 906-341-3677, assessor fax- 906-341-0282. hours- 9AM-4PM

Shiawassee County

Register of Deeds, PO Box 103, Corunna, MI 48817. 989-743-2216; fax-989-743-2459; 8AM-5PM (EST)
Index: Separate indices to search are computer, tract. Records indexed on 5 public use terminals back to 1980. Office will perform a tax lien search but public must search other records themselves. Search fee $3.00 for state, $3.00 for federal per name. Copy fee $1.00 per page; UCC copy $2.00 per page. Cert fee-$1.00 per cert plus copy fee. Payee- Shiawassee County Register of Deeds. Office will sell reports, mortgage for instance, $1.00 per page. **Other phones:** Treasurer- 989-743-2224; Elections- 989-743-2242; Vital Records- 989-743-2242. **Property tax/Assessing-** 989-743-2263. **Online access-** Access land and property tax data for Cities of Laingsburg and Perry, and Caledonia Township for free at https://is.bsasoftware.com/bsa.is/SelectUnit.aspx. Also here is property tax data for Venice Township.

St. Clair County

County Register of Deeds, 200 Grand River Blvd, Rm 103, Port Huron, MI 48060. 810-989-6930; fax-810-985-4795; 8AM-4:30PM (EST) www.stclaircounty.org/Offices/register_of_deeds/
Index: All in one. Records indexed on a public use terminal back to 1984. Office will perform a UCC search but public must search other records themselves. Copy fee $1.00 per page. Cert fee- $1.00 per doc plus copy fee. Payee- St. Clair County Register of Deeds. **Online Real Estate, Deed, Lien, Death records:** Access register of deeds database free at https://publicdeeds.stclaircounty.org:444/. Click on OPR. Online records go back to 05/1984. **Other phones:** Treasurer- 810-989-6915. **Property tax/Assessing-** 200 Grand River, #105, County Equalization Dept, Port Huron, MI 48060; 810-985-6925, assessor fax- 810-989-6328. www.stclaircounty.org **Online access-** Search tax equalization data free at www.stclaircounty.org/offices/equalization/search.aspx. Also, land data may be at http://gis.stclaircounty.org/landmanagement/ on the map site. Also, access land and property tax data for Cities of Algonac, Marysville, St Clair also Townships of Clay, Cottleville, East China, and Ira for free with registration at https://is.bsasoftware.com/bsa.is/SelectUnit.aspx.

St. Joseph County

County Register of Deeds, PO Box 388, Centreville, MI 49032-0388. 269-467-5552; fax-269-467-5593; 8AM-5PM (EST) www.stjosephcountymi.org/deeds/
Index: Separate indices to search. Records indexed on a public use terminal back to 1993. Office will perform a UCC search but public must search other records themselves. General search fee $5.00 minimum for real estate records. UCC search per debtor name- $6.00. Copy fee $1.00 per page; UCC copy $2.00 per page. Cert fee- $1.00 per cert plus copy fee. Payee- St. Joseph County Register of Deeds. Office does sell bulk data, contact Cynthia. **Other phones:** Treasurer- 269-467-5528. **Property tax/Assessing-** PO Box 276, 115 S Dean St, Equilization Dept, Centreville, MI 49032; 269-467-5576, assessor fax- 269-467-5672. www.stjosephcountymi.org/lrc/ **Online access-** Search assessor records for free at www.stjosephcountymi.org/taxsearch/default.asp. Also offered is a subscription service with additional features. Also, property tax and delinquent tax data and City of Sturgis land data for free with registration at https://is.bsasoftware.com/bsa.is/SelectUnit.aspx.

Tuscola County

County Register of Deeds, 440 N State St, Caro, MI 48723. phone-989-672-3840; fax-989-672-3844; 8AM-N, 1-4:30PM (EST) www.tuscolacounty.org
Index: All in one. Records indexed on a public use terminal back to 1992. Only the public may search. General copy fee $1.00 per page; UCCs or plats-$2.00 per page. Cert fee- $1.00 per cert plus copy fee. Payee- Tuscola County Register of Deeds. Office sells reports for $1.00 per page, plus $.50 per entry. **Online Real Estate, Grantor/Grantee, Deed, Lien, Mtg, Judgment, UCC records:** recorder's index free at www.landaccess.com/sites/mi/tuscola/index.php. **Other phones:** Treasurer- 989-672-3890; Elections-989-672-3780; Vital Records- 989-672-3780. **Property tax/Assessing-** 989-672-3830.

Van Buren County

County Register of Deeds, 219 Paw Paw St, #102, Paw Paw, MI 49079. Recording, R/E & UCC phone-269-657-8242; fax-269-657-0674; 8:30AM-5PM (EST) www.vbco.org/government0104.asp
Index: All in one. Records indexed on a public use terminal back to 1000. Office personnel or visitors may perform searches. Search fee- as state law allows. Office will search real estate records only if on UCC side. Office will not search UCC records. Copy fee $1.00 per page. Cert fee- $1.00 per cert plus copy fee. Payee- Van Buren County Register of Deeds. Real Estate records available on CD; $.23 per image, contact Carole. **Other phones:** Treasurer- 269-657-8228; Elections- 269-657-8218; Vital Records- 269-657-8218. **Property tax/Assessing-** 219 Paw Paw St, #302, Equalization Dept, Paw Paw, MI 49079; 269-657-8234, assessor fax- 269-657-0579. **Online access-** Access City/Township of South Haven property tax, land, and special assessment data for free at https://is.bsasoftware.com/bsa.is/SelectUnit.aspx. Also includes property records for Townships of Antwerp and Paw Paw.

Washtenaw County

County Register of Deeds, PO Box 8645, Ann Arbor, MI 48107. Recording, R/E & UCC phone-734-222-6710; fax-734-222-6819; 8:30AM-5PM (EST) www.ewashtenaw.org/government/clerk_register
Index: In lower level, search separate indices-computer back to 1986; microfilm back 1964-86; prior on books to 1824. Records indexed on a public use terminal back to 1986. Except for and in person current owner search, only the public may search. Search fee $5.00 current owner search only. Copy fee $1.00 per page. Cert fee- $1.00 per doc plus copy fee. Payee- Washtenaw County Register of Deeds. Office will sell lists and reports, contact Linda Clark. **Online access to Real Estate, Deed, Lien, Judgment, Death, Marriage, Business Name records:** Access a menu of searchable databases at www.ewashtenaw.org/online. $1.00 fee for real estate images from Register of Deeds search page; click on Deeds Document Search. **Other phones:** Treasurer-734-222-6600; Elections- 734-222-6730; Vital Records- 734-222-6700. **Property tax/Assessing-** PO Box 8645, 200 N Main St, #210, Equalization Dept Suite 210, Ann Arbor, MI 48107-; 734-994-2511. Ann Arbor City Assessor- 734-994-2650. **Online access-** Search land and property tax data and more for Cities of Ann Arbor, Chelsea, Milan, Saline, Ypsilanti, and townships of Ann Arbor, Augusta, Bridgewater, Dexter, Lodi, Pittsfield, Superior, Webster, York, Ypsilanti and Village of Dexter. for free with registration at https://is.bsasoftware.com/bsa.is/SelectUnit.aspx. Also, free Property/Parcel Lookup at http://secure.ewashtenaw.org/ecommerce/property/pStart.do.

Wayne County

County Register of Deeds, 400 Monroe, 7th Fl, Rm 620, Detroit, MI 48226. 313-224-5860, search dept-224-5866; fax-313-224-5884; 8AM-4:30PM (EST) www.waynecounty.com/register/
Index: Separate indices to search include computer, old tracts, old grantor/grantee. Records indexed on a public use terminal back to 1986. Office personnel or visitors may perform searches. Index search fee for last owner- $5.00 in person; by mail-$15.00. Office will not name search real estate records. UCC search per debtor name- $6.00. General copy fee $1.00. Plat copy- $5.00 per page. Cert fee- $10.00 per doc plus copy fee. Payee- Wayne County Register of Deeds. The 5th Fl Treasurer office sells lists of foreclusures, 313-224-5990. **Online access to Real Estate, Deed, Judgment, Lien, Assumed Name records:** Search county recorder land records database for free back to '86 at www.waynecountylandrecords.com. A full data on-demand svc and a business svc available for a fee, call 313-967-6857 for info/sign-up or see www.waynecountylandrecords.com/. Search assumed names at www.waynecounty.com/clerk/AssumedNames/. **Other phones:** Treasurer- 313-224-5990 (on 5th Fl); Elections- 313-224-5525/6262; Vital Records- 313-224-5525/6262. **Property tax/Assessing-** 2 Woodward Ave, Detroit, MI 48226; 313-224-3560/3035. **Online access-** Property and tax data and more for 16 municipalities free at https://is.bsasoftware.com/bsa.is/SelectUnit.aspx. Search delinquent tax list at www.waynecounty.com/pta/Disclaimer.asp. Dearborn property data free at www.dearbornfordcenter.com/dbnassessor/. No name searching. Also, City of Livona property data is free at www.ci.livonia.mi.us/. No name searching. Also, search Wyandotte City tax billings free at http://click2gov.wyan.org/Click2GovTX/Index.jsp?selection=Owner.

Wexford County

County Register of Deeds, 437 E Division St; PO Box 303, Cadillac, MI 49601. 231-779-9455; fax-231-779-5352; 8:30AM-5PM (vault hours 8:30AM-4PM). (EST) www.wexfordcounty.org/
Index: All in one. Records indexed on a public use terminal back to 00. Office personnel or visitors may perform searches. General search fee $5.00 min. Office will not search real estate records. Will search UCC records. UCC search per debtor name-$6.00. Separate federal/state combined tax lien search- $6.00 per debtor. Copy fee $1.00 per page. UCC copy fee $2.00 per page. Cert fee- $1.00 per cert plus copy fee. Payee- County Register of Deeds. **Other phones:** Treasurer- 231-779-9475; Elections- 231-779-9450. **Property tax/Assessing-** 437 E Division St, Cadillac, MI 49601; 231-779-9531. hours- 8:30AM-5PM **Online-** Access the land parcel and Assessment roll site free at www.liaa.info/wexford/propertysearch.asp.

Michigan County Locator

You will usually be able to find the city name in the City/County Cross Reference below. In that case, it is a simple matter to determine the county from the cross reference. However, only the official US Postal Service city names are included in this index. There are an additional 40,000 place names that people use in their addresses. Therefore, we have also included a ZIP/City Cross Reference immediately following the City/County Cross Reference.

If you know the ZIP Code but the city name does not appear in the City/County Cross Reference index, look up the ZIP Code in the ZIP/City Cross Reference, find the city name, then look up the city name in the City/County Cross Reference. For example, you want to know the county for an address of Menands, NY 12204. There is no "Menands" in the City/County Cross Reference. The ZIP/City Cross Reference shows that ZIP Codes 12201-12288 are for the city of Albany. Looking back in the City/County Cross Reference, Albany is in Albany County.

Michigan City/County Cross Reference

ACME Grand Traverse
ADA Kent
ADDISON Lenawee
ADRIAN Lenawee
AFTON Cheboygan
AHMEEK Keweenaw
AKRON Tuscola
ALANSON (49706) Emmet(82), Cheboygan(17)
ALBA Antrim
ALBION Calhoun
ALDEN (49612) Antrim(69), Kalkaska(30)
ALGER (48610) Arenac(34), Ogemaw(33), Gladwin(32)
ALGONAC St. Clair
ALLEGAN Allegan
ALLEN Hillsdale
ALLEN PARK Wayne
ALLENDALE Ottawa
ALLENTON St. Clair
ALLOUEZ Keweenaw
ALMA Gratiot
ALMONT Lapeer
ALPENA (49707) Alpena(97), Presque Isle(2)
ALPHA Iron
ALTO Kent
AMASA Iron
ANCHORVILLE St. Clair
ANN ARBOR Washtenaw
APPLEGATE Sanilac
ARCADIA (49613) Manistee(79), Benzie(20)
ARGYLE Sanilac
ARMADA (48005) Macomb(96), St. Clair(3)
ARNOLD Marquette
ASHLEY Gratiot
ATHENS (49011) Calhoun(96), St. Joseph(1), Branch(1)
ATLANTA Montmorency
ATLANTIC MINE Houghton
ATLAS Genesee
ATTICA Lapeer
AU GRES Arenac
AU TRAIN Alger
AUBURN Bay
AUBURN HILLS Oakland
AUGUSTA Kalamazoo
AVOCA St. Clair
AZALIA Monroe
BAD AXE Huron
BAILEY (49303) Muskegon(86), Newaygo(12)
BALDWIN Lake
BANCROFT Shiawassee
BANGOR Van Buren
BANNISTER (48807) Gratiot(63), Saginaw(34), Clinton(1)
BARAGA Baraga
BARBEAU Chippewa
BARK RIVER (49807) Delta(47), Dickinson(33), Menominee(19)
BARODA Berrien
BARRYTON (49305) Mecosta(93), Isabella(6)
BARTON CITY Alcona
BATH Clinton
BATTLE CREEK Calhoun
BAY CITY Bay
BAY PORT Huron
BAY SHORE Charlevoix
BEAR LAKE Manistee
BEAVER ISLAND Charlevoix
BEAVERTON (48612) Gladwin(96), Clare(2), Midland(1)
BEDFORD Calhoun
BELDING (48809) Ionia(90), Kent(9)
BELLAIRE Antrim
BELLEVILLE Wayne
BELLEVUE (49021) Eaton(63), Barry(27), Calhoun(9)
BELMONT Kent
BENTLEY (48613) Bay(88), Gladwin(9), Arenac(1)
BENTON HARBOR (49022) Berrien(98), Van Buren(1)
BENTON HARBOR Berrien
BENZONIA Benzie
BERGLAND Ontonagon
BERKLEY Oakland
BERRIEN CENTER (49102) Berrien(98), Cass(1)
BERRIEN SPRINGS Berrien
BESSEMER Gogebic
BEULAH Benzie
BIG BAY Marquette
BIG RAPIDS (49307) Mecosta(97), Newaygo(2)
BIRCH RUN (48415) Saginaw(97), Tuscola(1), Genesee(1)
BIRMINGHAM Oakland
BITELY (49309) Newaygo(90), Lake(9)
BLACK RIVER Alcona
BLANCHARD (49310) Isabella(63), Mecosta(33), Montcalm(3)
BLISSFIELD Lenawee
BLOOMFIELD HILLS Oakland
BLOOMINGDALE (49026) Van Buren(89), Allegan(10)
BOON Wexford
BOYNE CITY (49712) Charlevoix(97), Antrim(2)
BOYNE FALLS (49713) Charlevoix(92), Emmet(7)
BRADLEY Allegan
BRANCH (49402) Mason(51), Lake(45), Oceana(3)
BRANT Saginaw
BRECKENRIDGE (48615) Gratiot(73), Midland(26)
BREEDSVILLE Van Buren
BRETHREN Manistee
BRIDGEPORT Saginaw
BRIDGEWATER Washtenaw
BRIDGMAN Berrien
BRIGHTON Livingston
BRIMLEY Chippewa
BRITTON (49229) Lenawee(89), Monroe(8), Washtenaw(1)
BROHMAN Newaygo
BRONSON Branch
BROOKLYN Jackson
BROWN CITY (48416) Sanilac(57), Lapeer(36), St. Clair(5)
BRUCE CROSSING Ontonagon
BRUNSWICK (49313) Muskegon(77), Newaygo(22)
BRUTUS (49716) Emmet(56), Cheboygan(43)
BUCHANAN Berrien
BUCKLEY (49620) Wexford(56), Grand Traverse(43)
BURLINGTON Calhoun
BURNIPS Allegan
BURR OAK (49030) St. Joseph(90), Branch(9)
BURT Saginaw
BURT LAKE Cheboygan
BURTON Genesee
BYRON (48418) Shiawassee(67), Genesee(23), Livingston(9)
BYRON CENTER (49315) Kent(94), Ottawa(3), Allegan(1)
CADILLAC (49601) Wexford(98), Missaukee(1)
CADMUS Lenawee
CALEDONIA (49316) Kent(88), Allegan(8), Barry(3)
CALUMET Houghton
CAMDEN Hillsdale
CANNONSBURG Kent
CANTON Wayne
CAPAC (48014) St. Clair(98), Lapeer(1)
CARLETON Monroe
CARNEY Menominee
CARO Tuscola
CARP LAKE (49718) Emmet(70), Cheboygan(29)
CARROLLTON Saginaw
CARSON CITY (48811) Montcalm(75), Gratiot(24)
CARSONVILLE Sanilac
CASCO St. Clair
CASEVILLE Huron
CASNOVIA (49318) Muskegon(66), Newaygo(22), Kent(10)
CASPIAN Iron
CASS CITY (48726) Tuscola(84), Sanilac(12), Huron(3)
CASSOPOLIS Cass
CEDAR Leelanau
CEDAR LAKE Montcalm
CEDAR RIVER Menominee
CEDAR SPRINGS Kent
CEDARVILLE Mackinac
CEMENT CITY (49233) Lenawee(77), Jackson(22)
CENTER LINE Macomb
CENTRAL LAKE Antrim
CENTREVILLE St. Joseph
CERESCO Calhoun
CHAMPION Marquette
CHANNING Dickinson
CHARLEVOIX (49720) Charlevoix(98), Antrim(1)
CHARLOTTE Eaton
CHASE Lake
CHASSELL Houghton
CHATHAM Alger
CHEBOYGAN Cheboygan
CHELSEA Washtenaw
CHESANING Saginaw
CHIPPEWA LAKE Mecosta
CLARE (48617) Clare(79), Isabella(20)
CLARKLAKE Jackson
CLARKSTON Oakland
CLARKSVILLE (48815) Ionia(97), Kent(2)
CLAWSON Oakland
CLAYTON Lenawee
CLIFFORD (48727) Lapeer(50), Tuscola(49)
CLIMAX Kalamazoo
CLINTON (49236) Lenawee(83), Washtenaw(16)
CLINTON TOWNSHIP Macomb
CLIO (48420) Genesee(97), Tuscola(1)
CLOVERDALE Barry
COHOCTAH Livingston
COLDWATER Branch
COLEMAN (48618) Midland(83), Isabella(13), Gladwin(2)
COLOMA (49038) Berrien(94), Van Buren(5)
COLON (49040) St. Joseph(89), Branch(10)
COLUMBIAVILLE (48421) Lapeer(95), Genesee(4)
COLUMBUS St. Clair
COMINS (48619) Oscoda(78), Montmorency(21)
COMMERCE TOWNSHIP Oakland
COMSTOCK Kalamazoo
COMSTOCK PARK Kent
CONCORD Jackson
CONKLIN (49403) Ottawa(91), Muskegon(4), Kent(3)
CONSTANTINE (49042) St. Joseph(98), Cass(1)
CONWAY Emmet
COOKS (49817) Delta(56), Schoolcraft(43)
COOPERSVILLE (49404) Ottawa(96), Muskegon(3)
COPEMISH (49625) Manistee(92), Wexford(7)
COPPER CITY Houghton
COPPER HARBOR Keweenaw
CORAL Montcalm
CORNELL (49818) Delta(86), Marquette(13)
CORUNNA Shiawassee
COVERT Van Buren
COVINGTON Baraga
CROSS VILLAGE Emmet
CROSWELL Sanilac
CRYSTAL Montcalm
CRYSTAL FALLS Iron
CURRAN (48728) Alcona(87), Oscoda(12)
CURTIS Mackinac
CUSTER Mason
DAFTER Chippewa

DAGGETT Menominee
DANSVILLE Ingham
DAVISBURG Oakland
DAVISON Genesee
DE TOUR VILLAGE Chippewa
DEARBORN Wayne
DEARBORN HEIGHTS Wayne
DECATUR (49045) Van Buren(90), Cass(8)
DECKER (48426) Sanilac(91), Tuscola(8)
DECKERVILLE Sanilac
DEERFIELD Lenawee
DEERTON (49822) Alger(96), Marquette(3)
DEFORD (48729) Tuscola(98), Sanilac(1)
DELTON Barry
DETROIT Wayne
DEWITT Clinton
DEXTER Washtenaw
DIMONDALE (48821) Eaton(95), Ingham(4)
DODGEVILLE Houghton
DOLLAR BAY Houghton
DORR (49323) Allegan(98), Ottawa(1)
DOUGLAS Allegan
DOWAGIAC (49047) Cass(93), Van Buren(6)
DOWLING Barry
DRAYTON PLAINS Oakland
DRUMMOND ISLAND Chippewa
DRYDEN (48428) Lapeer(97), Oakland(2)
DUNDEE Monroe
DURAND (48429) Shiawassee(97), Genesee(2)
EAGLE Clinton
EAGLE RIVER Keweenaw
EAST CHINA St. Clair
EAST JORDAN (49727) Charlevoix(68), Antrim(31)
EAST LANSING (48823) Ingham(84), Clinton(15)
EAST LANSING Ingham
EAST LEROY Calhoun
EAST TAWAS Iosco
EASTLAKE Manistee
EASTPOINTE Macomb
EASTPORT Antrim
EATON RAPIDS (48827) Eaton(93), Ingham(6)
EAU CLAIRE (49111) Berrien(90), Cass(9)
EBEN JUNCTION Alger
ECKERMAN Chippewa
ECORSE Wayne
EDENVILLE Midland
EDMORE (48829) Montcalm(98), Isabella(1)
EDWARDSBURG Cass
ELBERTA Benzie
ELK RAPIDS Antrim
ELKTON Huron
ELLSWORTH (49729) Antrim(88), Charlevoix(11)
ELM HALL Gratiot
ELMIRA (49730) Antrim(70), Otsego(22), Charlevoix(6)
ELSIE (48831) Clinton(58), Shiawassee(20), Saginaw(17), Gratiot(3)
ELWELL Gratiot
EMMETT St. Clair
EMPIRE (49630) Leelanau(98), Benzie(1)
ENGADINE Mackinac
ERIE Monroe
ESCANABA Delta
ESSEXVILLE Bay
EUREKA Clinton
EVART (49631) Osceola(92), Mecosta(7)
EWEN Ontonagon
FAIR HAVEN St. Clair
FAIRGROVE Tuscola
FAIRVIEW Oscoda
FALMOUTH Missaukee
FARMINGTON Oakland
FARWELL (48622) Clare(82), Isabella(17)
FELCH (49831) Dickinson(82), Marquette(17)
FENNVILLE Allegan
FENTON (48430) Genesee(65), Livingston(30), Oakland(4)
FENWICK (48834) Montcalm(64), Ionia(35)
FERNDALE Oakland
FERRYSBURG Ottawa
FIFE LAKE (49633) Kalkaska(60), Grand Traverse(32), Wexford(4), Missaukee(2)
FILER CITY Manistee
FILION Huron
FLAT ROCK Wayne
FLINT Genesee
FLUSHING Genesee
FORESTVILLE Sanilac
FORT GRATIOT St. Clair
FOSTER CITY Dickinson
FOSTORIA (48435) Tuscola(56), Lapeer(43)
FOUNTAIN Mason
FOWLER (48835) Clinton(98), Gratiot(1)
FOWLERVILLE Livingston
FRANKENMUTH (48734) Saginaw(97), Tuscola(2)
FRANKENMUTH Saginaw
FRANKFORT Benzie
FRANKLIN Oakland
FRASER Macomb
FREDERIC (49733) Crawford(78), Otsego(21)
FREE SOIL (49411) Mason(97), Manistee(2)
FREELAND (48623) Saginaw(81), Midland(10), Bay(8)
FREEPORT (49325) Barry(77), Ionia(13), Kent(9)
FREMONT (49412) Newaygo(96), Oceana(2)
FREMONT Newaygo
FRONTIER Hillsdale
FRUITPORT (49415) Muskegon(89), Ottawa(10)
FULTON (49052) Kalamazoo(78), Calhoun(17), St. Joseph(4)
GAASTRA Iron
GAGETOWN (48735) Tuscola(60), Huron(39)
GAINES (48436) Genesee(90), Shiawassee(9)
GALESBURG Kalamazoo
GALIEN Berrien
GARDEN Delta
GARDEN CITY Wayne
GAYLORD Otsego
GENESEE Genesee
GERMFASK (49836) Schoolcraft(57), Mackinac(42)
GILFORD Tuscola
GLADSTONE Delta
GLADWIN (48624) Gladwin(91), Clare(5), Roscommon(1)
GLEN ARBOR Leelanau
GLENN Allegan
GLENNIE (48737) Alcona(91), Iosco(8)
GOBLES (49055) Van Buren(92), Allegan(7)
GOETZVILLE Chippewa
GOOD HART Emmet
GOODELLS St. Clair
GOODRICH (48438) Genesee(81), Lapeer(18)
GOULD CITY Mackinac
GOWEN (49326) Kent(71), Montcalm(28)
GRAND BLANC (48439) Genesee(98), Oakland(1)
GRAND BLANC Genesee
GRAND HAVEN Ottawa
GRAND JUNCTION (49056) Van Buren(75), Allegan(24)
GRAND LEDGE (48837) Eaton(89), Clinton(9)
GRAND MARAIS Alger
GRAND RAPIDS (49544) Kent(72), Ottawa(27)
GRAND RAPIDS Kent
GRANDVILLE (49418) Kent(84), Ottawa(15)
GRANDVILLE Kent
GRANT Newaygo
GRASS LAKE (49240) Jackson(91), Washtenaw(8)
GRAWN Grand Traverse
GRAYLING (49738) Crawford(95), Kalkaska(3)
GRAYLING Crawford
GREENBUSH (48738) Alcona(90), Iosco(9)
GREENLAND Ontonagon
GREENVILLE (48838) Montcalm(89), Kent(10)
GREGORY (48137) Livingston(98), Washtenaw(1)
GROSSE ILE Wayne
GROSSE POINTE Wayne
GULLIVER Schoolcraft
GWINN Marquette
HADLEY Lapeer
HAGAR SHORES Berrien
HALE (48739) Iosco(75), Ogemaw(24)
HAMBURG Livingston
HAMILTON Allegan
HAMTRAMCK Wayne
HANCOCK Houghton
HANOVER Jackson
HARBERT Berrien
HARBOR BEACH Huron
HARBOR SPRINGS Emmet
HARPER WOODS Wayne
HARRIETTA (49638) Wexford(91), Manistee(8)
HARRIS Menominee
HARRISON Clare
HARRISON TOWNSHIP Macomb
HARRISVILLE Alcona
HARSENS ISLAND St. Clair
HART Oceana
HARTFORD Van Buren
HARTLAND Livingston
HASLETT (48840) Ingham(94), Clinton(5)
HASTINGS Barry
HAWKS Presque Isle
HAZEL PARK Oakland
HEMLOCK (48626) Saginaw(95), Midland(4)
HENDERSON (48841) Shiawassee(82), Saginaw(17)
HERMANSVILLE Menominee
HERRON Alpena
HERSEY (49639) Osceola(78), Mecosta(21)
HESPERIA (49421) Oceana(70), Newaygo(29)
HESSEL Mackinac
HICKORY CORNERS (49060) Barry(66), Kalamazoo(33)
HIGGINS LAKE Roscommon
HIGHLAND Oakland
HIGHLAND PARK Wayne
HILLMAN (49746) Montmorency(88), Alpena(11)
HILLSDALE Hillsdale
HOLLAND (49423) Ottawa(66), Allegan(33)
HOLLAND Ottawa
HOLLY (48442) Oakland(93), Genesee(5), Livingston(1)
HOLT Ingham
HOLTON (49425) Muskegon(83), Oceana(10), Newaygo(6)
HOMER Calhoun
HONOR Benzie
HOPE (48628) Midland(82), Gladwin(17)
HOPKINS Allegan
HORTON (49246) Jackson(96), Hillsdale(3)
HOUGHTON Houghton
HOUGHTON LAKE Roscommon
HOUGHTON LAKE HEIGHTS Roscommon
HOWARD CITY (49329) Montcalm(84), Newaygo(15)
HOWELL Livingston
HUBBARD LAKE (49747) Alpena(50), Alcona(49)
HUBBARDSTON (48845) Ionia(59), Clinton(20), Montcalm(14), Gratiot(6)
HUBBELL Houghton
HUDSON (49247) Lenawee(72), Hillsdale(27)
HUDSONVILLE Ottawa
HULBERT Chippewa
HUNTINGTON WOODS Oakland
IDA Monroe
IDLEWILD Lake
IMLAY CITY (48444) Lapeer(97), St. Clair(2)
INDIAN RIVER Cheboygan
INGALLS Menominee
INKSTER Wayne
INTERLOCHEN (49643) Grand Traverse(67), Benzie(32)
IONIA Ionia
IRON MOUNTAIN Dickinson
IRON RIVER Iron
IRONS (49644) Lake(79), Manistee(19)
IRONWOOD Gogebic
ISHPEMING Marquette
ITHACA Gratiot
JACKSON Jackson
JAMESTOWN Ottawa
JASPER Lenawee
JEDDO (48032) St. Clair(81), Sanilac(18)
JENISON Ottawa
JEROME (49249) Hillsdale(95), Jackson(4)
JOHANNESBURG (49751) Otsego(93), Montmorency(6)
JONES Cass
JONESVILLE Hillsdale
KALAMAZOO Kalamazoo
KALEVA Manistee
KALKASKA Kalkaska
KARLIN Grand Traverse
KAWKAWLIN Bay
KEARSARGE Houghton
KEEGO HARBOR Oakland
KENDALL Van Buren
KENT CITY (49330) Kent(91), Newaygo(5), Ottawa(1), Muskegon(1)
KENTON Houghton
KEWADIN Antrim
KINCHELOE Chippewa
KINDE Huron
KINGSFORD Dickinson
KINGSLEY (49649) Grand Traverse(96), Wexford(3)
KINGSTON (48741) Tuscola(93), Sanilac(6)
KINROSS Chippewa
LA SALLE Monroe
LACHINE Alpena
LACOTA Van Buren
LAINGSBURG (48848) Shiawassee(67), Clinton(32)
LAKE (48632) Clare(76), Isabella(22), Osceola(1)
LAKE ANN Benzie
LAKE CITY Missaukee
LAKE GEORGE Clare
LAKE LEELANAU Leelanau
LAKE LINDEN (49945) Houghton(97), Keweenaw(2)
LAKE ODESSA (48849) Ionia(81), Barry(14), Eaton(3)
LAKE ORION Oakland
LAKELAND Livingston
LAKESIDE Berrien
LAKEVIEW (48850) Montcalm(81), Mecosta(18)
LAKEVILLE Oakland

LAMBERTVILLE Monroe
LAMONT Ottawa
LANSE Baraga
LANSING (48917) Eaton(81), Ingham(18)
LANSING (48906) Ingham(60), Clinton(37), Eaton(2)
LANSING (48911) Ingham(87), Eaton(12)
LANSING Eaton
LANSING Ingham
LAPEER Lapeer
LAWRENCE Van Buren
LAWTON Van Buren
LELAND Leelanau
LENNON (48449) Shiawassee(57), Genesee(42)
LEONARD Oakland
LEONIDAS St. Joseph
LEROY (49655) Osceola(93), Lake(6)
LESLIE Ingham
LEVERING (49755) Emmet(64), Cheboygan(35)
LEWISTON (49756) Montmorency(50), Oscoda(47), Otsego(1)
LEXINGTON Sanilac
LINCOLN Alcona
LINCOLN PARK Wayne
LINDEN (48451) Genesee(90), Livingston(9)
LINWOOD Bay
LITCHFIELD (49252) Hillsdale(91), Jackson(3), Branch(2), Calhoun(2)
LITTLE LAKE Marquette
LIVONIA Wayne
LONG LAKE (48743) Iosco(92), Ogemaw(8)
LORETTO Dickinson
LOWELL (49331) Kent(89), Ionia(10)
LUDINGTON Mason
LUNA PIER Monroe
LUPTON Ogemaw
LUTHER Lake
LUZERNE Oscoda
LYONS Ionia
MACATAWA Ottawa
MACKINAC ISLAND Mackinac
MACKINAW CITY (49701) Emmet(63), Cheboygan(36)
MACOMB Macomb
MADISON HEIGHTS Oakland
MANCELONA (49659) Antrim(78), Kalkaska(21)
MANCHESTER Washtenaw
MANISTEE (49660) Manistee(96), Mason(3)
MANISTIQUE (49854) Schoolcraft(98), Delta(1)
MANITOU BEACH Lenawee
MANTON (49663) Wexford(79), Missaukee(20)
MAPLE CITY Leelanau
MAPLE RAPIDS Clinton
MARCELLUS (49067) Cass(63), St. Joseph(24), Van Buren(11)
MARENISCO (49947) Gogebic(66), Ontonagon(33)
MARINE CITY St. Clair
MARION (49665) Osceola(83), Clare(11), Missaukee(4)
MARLETTE (48453) Sanilac(88), Lapeer(7), Tuscola(4)
MARNE (49435) Ottawa(96), Kent(3)
MARQUETTE Marquette
MARSHALL Calhoun
MARTIN Allegan
MARYSVILLE St. Clair
MASON Ingham
MASS CITY Ontonagon
MATTAWAN (49071) Van Buren(83), Kalamazoo(16)
MAYBEE Monroe
MAYFIELD Grand Traverse
MAYVILLE (48744) Tuscola(89), Lapeer(10)
MC BAIN Missaukee
MC MILLAN Luce
MCBRIDES Montcalm
MEARS Oceana
MECOSTA Mecosta
MELVIN Sanilac
MELVINDALE Wayne
MEMPHIS (48041) St. Clair(74), Macomb(25)
MENDON St. Joseph
MENOMINEE Menominee
MERRILL (48637) Saginaw(73), Midland(14), Gratiot(12)
MERRITT Missaukee
MESICK (49668) Wexford(98), Manistee(1)
METAMORA (48455) Lapeer(98), Oakland(1)
MICHIGAMME (49861) Baraga(59), Marquette(40)
MICHIGAN CENTER Jackson
MIDDLETON Gratiot
MIDDLEVILLE (49333) Barry(97), Kent(1)
MIDLAND (48642) Midland(96), Bay(3)
MIDLAND Midland
MIKADO (48745) Alcona(94), Iosco(5)
MILAN (48160) Washtenaw(70), Monroe(29)
MILFORD (48380) Oakland(73), Livingston(26)
MILFORD Oakland
MILLBROOK Mecosta
MILLERSBURG Presque Isle
MILLINGTON (48746) Tuscola(89), Genesee(10)
MINDEN CITY (48456) Sanilac(79), Huron(20)
MIO Oscoda
MOHAWK Keweenaw
MOLINE Allegan
MONTAGUE (49437) Muskegon(84), Oceana(15)
MONTGOMERY (49255) Branch(96), Hillsdale(3)
MONTROSE (48457) Genesee(78), Saginaw(21)
MORAN Mackinac
MORENCI Lenawee
MORLEY (49336) Mecosta(92), Montcalm(7)
MORRICE Shiawassee
MOSCOW Hillsdale
MOSHERVILLE Hillsdale
MOUNT CLEMENS Macomb
MOUNT MORRIS Genesee
MOUNT PLEASANT Isabella
MUIR Ionia
MULLETT LAKE Cheboygan
MULLIKEN (48861) Eaton(89), Ionia(10)
MUNGER (48747) Bay(96), Saginaw(3)
MUNISING Alger
MUNITH Jackson
MUSKEGON Muskegon
NADEAU Menominee
NAHMA Delta
NAPOLEON Jackson
NASHVILLE (49073) Barry(90), Eaton(9)
NATIONAL CITY Iosco
NATIONAL MINE Marquette
NAUBINWAY Mackinac
NAZARETH Kalamazoo
NEGAUNEE Marquette
NEW BALTIMORE Macomb
NEW BOSTON Wayne
NEW BUFFALO Berrien
NEW ERA Oceana
NEW HAVEN Macomb
NEW HUDSON Oakland
NEW LOTHROP (48460) Shiawassee(60), Saginaw(34), Genesee(5)
NEW RICHMOND Allegan
NEW TROY Berrien
NEWAYGO (49337) Newaygo(96), Montcalm(2), Mecosta(1)
NEWBERRY Luce
NEWPORT Monroe
NILES (49120) Berrien(82), Cass(17)
NILES Berrien
NISULA Houghton
NORTH ADAMS Hillsdale
NORTH BRANCH Lapeer
NORTH STAR Gratiot
NORTH STREET St. Clair
NORTHLAND Marquette
NORTHPORT Leelanau
NORTHVILLE (48167) Wayne(61), Oakland(31), Washtenaw(6)
NORVELL Jackson
NORWAY Dickinson
NOTTAWA St. Joseph
NOVI Oakland
NUNICA (49448) Ottawa(86), Muskegon(13)
OAK GROVE Livingston
OAK PARK Oakland
OAKLAND Oakland
OAKLEY (48649) Saginaw(95), Shiawassee(4)
ODEN Emmet
OKEMOS Ingham
OLD MISSION Grand Traverse
OLIVET (49076) Eaton(71), Calhoun(28)
OMENA Leelanau
OMER Arenac
ONAWAY (49765) Presque Isle(66), Cheboygan(33)
ONEKAMA Manistee
ONONDAGA (49264) Ingham(65), Jackson(30), Eaton(4)
ONSTED Lenawee
ONTONAGON Ontonagon
ORLEANS Ionia
ORTONVILLE (48462) Oakland(95), Lapeer(3)
OSCODA Iosco
OSHTEMO Kalamazoo
OSSEO Hillsdale
OSSINEKE Alpena
OTISVILLE (48463) Genesee(98), Lapeer(1)
OTSEGO (49078) Allegan(92), Kalamazoo(5), Van Buren(2)
OTTAWA LAKE (49267) Monroe(83), Lenawee(16)
OTTER LAKE (48464) Lapeer(82), Genesee(9), Tuscola(8)
OVID (48866) Clinton(64), Shiawassee(35)
OWENDALE Huron
OWOSSO Shiawassee
OXFORD (48371) Oakland(94), Lapeer(5)
OXFORD Oakland
PAINESDALE Houghton
PALMER Marquette
PALMS Sanilac
PALMYRA Lenawee
PALO Ionia
PARADISE Chippewa
PARIS (49338) Mecosta(63), Newaygo(29), Osceola(6)
PARMA Jackson
PAW PAW Van Buren
PECK Sanilac
PELKIE (49958) Houghton(80), Baraga(20)
PELLSTON (49769) Emmet(86), Cheboygan(13)
PENTWATER (49449) Oceana(80), Mason(19)
PERKINS Delta
PERRINTON Gratiot
PERRONVILLE (49873) Menominee(87), Dickinson(12)
PERRY (48872) Shiawassee(92), Ingham(6)
PETERSBURG Monroe
PETOSKEY Emmet
PEWAMO (48873) Ionia(72), Clinton(27)
PICKFORD (49774) Chippewa(91), Mackinac(8)
PIERSON Montcalm
PIGEON Huron
PINCKNEY Livingston
PINCONNING (48650) Bay(95), Arenac(4)
PITTSFORD Hillsdale
PLAINWELL (49080) Allegan(69), Barry(20), Kalamazoo(9)
PLEASANT LAKE Jackson
PLEASANT RIDGE Oakland
PLYMOUTH (48170) Wayne(95), Washtenaw(4)
POINTE AUX PINS Mackinac
POMPEII Gratiot
PONTIAC Oakland
PORT AUSTIN Huron
PORT HOPE Huron
PORT HURON St. Clair
PORT SANILAC Sanilac
PORTAGE Kalamazoo
PORTLAND (48875) Ionia(93), Clinton(6)
POSEN (49776) Presque Isle(74), Alpena(25)
POTTERVILLE Eaton
POWERS Menominee
PRATTVILLE Hillsdale
PRESCOTT Ogemaw
PRESQUE ISLE Presque Isle
PRUDENVILLE Roscommon
PULLMAN Allegan
QUINCY (49082) Branch(91), Hillsdale(8)
QUINNESEC Dickinson
RALPH Dickinson
RAMSAY Gogebic
RAPID CITY (49676) Kalkaska(61), Antrim(38)
RAPID RIVER (49878) Delta(91), Alger(8)
RAVENNA (49451) Muskegon(96), Ottawa(3)
RAY Macomb
READING Hillsdale
REDFORD Wayne
REED CITY (49677) Osceola(82), Lake(14), Newaygo(2)
REESE (48757) Tuscola(68), Saginaw(28), Bay(3)
REMUS (49340) Mecosta(66), Isabella(33)
REPUBLIC Marquette
RHODES (48652) Gladwin(58), Bay(26), Midland(15)
RICHLAND Kalamazoo
RICHMOND Macomb
RICHVILLE Tuscola
RIDGEWAY Lenawee
RIGA (49276) Lenawee(70), Monroe(29)
RIVER ROUGE Wayne
RIVERDALE (48877) Gratiot(57), Montcalm(31), Isabella(11)
RIVERSIDE Berrien
RIVES JUNCTION Jackson
ROCHESTER (48306) Oakland(97), Macomb(2)
ROCHESTER Oakland
ROCK (49880) Delta(68), Marquette(31)
ROCKFORD Kent
ROCKLAND Ontonagon
ROCKWOOD Wayne
RODNEY Mecosta
ROGERS CITY Presque Isle
ROLLIN Lenawee
ROMEO Macomb
ROMULUS Wayne
ROSCOMMON (48653) Roscommon(80), Crawford(19)
ROSE CITY (48654) Ogemaw(81), Oscoda(18)
ROSEBUSH Isabella
ROSEVILLE Macomb

ROTHBURY Oceana
ROYAL OAK Oakland
RUDYARD (49780) Chippewa(95), Mackinac(4)
RUMELY Alger
RUTH (48470) Huron(98), Sanilac(1)
SAGINAW Saginaw
SAGOLA Dickinson
SAINT CHARLES Saginaw
SAINT CLAIR St. Clair
SAINT CLAIR SHORES Macomb
SAINT HELEN Roscommon
SAINT IGNACE Mackinac
SAINT JOHNS Clinton
SAINT JOSEPH Berrien
SAINT LOUIS (48880) Gratiot(91), Midland(8)
SALEM Washtenaw
SALINE Washtenaw
SAMARIA Monroe
SAND CREEK Lenawee
SAND LAKE (49343) Kent(60), Newaygo(22), Montcalm(16)
SANDUSKY Sanilac
SANFORD Midland
SARANAC Ionia
SAUGATUCK Allegan
SAULT SAINTE MARIE Chippewa
SAWYER Berrien
SCHOOLCRAFT (49087) Kalamazoo(96), Van Buren(2)
SCOTTS Kalamazoo
SCOTTVILLE Mason
SEARS Osceola
SEBEWAING (48759) Huron(98), Tuscola(1)
SENECA Lenawee
SENEY (49883) Alger(60), Schoolcraft(39)
SHAFTSBURG Shiawassee
SHELBY Oceana
SHELBYVILLE (49344) Barry(51), Allegan(48)
SHEPHERD (48883) Isabella(75), Midland(23), Gratiot(1)
SHERIDAN Montcalm
SHERWOOD Branch
SHINGLETON (49884) Alger(97), Schoolcraft(2)
SIDNAW Houghton
SIDNEY Montcalm
SILVERWOOD (48760) Tuscola(59), Lapeer(40)
SIX LAKES (48886) Montcalm(98), Mecosta(1)
SKANDIA (49885) Marquette(78), Alger(21)
SKANEE Baraga
SMITHS CREEK St. Clair
SMYRNA Ionia
SNOVER Sanilac
SODUS Berrien
SOMERSET Hillsdale
SOMERSET CENTER Hillsdale
SOUTH BOARDMAN Kalkaska
SOUTH BRANCH (48761) Iosco(41), Ogemaw(28), Alcona(27), Oscoda(2)
SOUTH HAVEN (49090) Van Buren(95), Allegan(4)
SOUTH LYON (48178) Oakland(65), Livingston(23), Washtenaw(10)
SOUTH RANGE Houghton
SOUTH ROCKWOOD Monroe
SOUTHFIELD Oakland
SOUTHGATE Wayne
SPALDING Menominee
SPARTA Kent
SPRING ARBOR Jackson
SPRING LAKE (49456) Ottawa(95), Muskegon(4)
SPRINGPORT (49284) Jackson(60), Calhoun(30), Eaton(9)
SPRUCE (48762) Alcona(89), Alpena(10)
STALWART Chippewa
STAMBAUGH Iron
STANDISH (48658) Arenac(95), Bay(4)
STANTON Montcalm
STANWOOD Mecosta
STEPHENSON Menominee
STERLING (48659) Arenac(95), Bay(4)
STERLING HEIGHTS Macomb
STEVENSVILLE Berrien
STOCKBRIDGE (49285) Ingham(87), Jackson(4), Livingston(4), Washtenaw(3)
STRONGS Chippewa
STURGIS St. Joseph
SUMNER (48889) Gratiot(98), Montcalm(1)
SUNFIELD (48890) Eaton(61), Ionia(38)
SUTTONS BAY Leelanau
SWARTZ CREEK Genesee
TAWAS CITY (48763) Iosco(94), Arenac(5)
TAWAS CITY Iosco
TAYLOR Wayne
TECUMSEH Lenawee
TEKONSHA (49092) Calhoun(83), Branch(16)
TEMPERANCE Monroe
THOMPSONVILLE (49683) Benzie(61), Manistee(31), Grand Traverse(6)
THREE OAKS Berrien
THREE RIVERS St. Joseph
TIPTON Lenawee
TOIVOLA (49965) Houghton(94), Ontonagon(5)
TOPINABEE Cheboygan
TOWER Cheboygan
TRAUNIK Alger
TRAVERSE CITY (49684) Grand Traverse(79), Leelanau(20)
TRAVERSE CITY Grand Traverse
TRENARY Alger
TRENTON Wayne
TROUT CREEK (49967) Ontonagon(58), Houghton(34), Iron(7)
TROUT LAKE Chippewa
TROY Oakland
TRUFANT (49347) Montcalm(94), Kent(5)
TURNER (48765) Arenac(65), Iosco(34)
TUSCOLA Tuscola
TUSTIN (49688) Osceola(91), Lake(5), Wexford(2)
TWIN LAKE Muskegon
TWINING (48766) Arenac(96), Iosco(3)
UBLY (48475) Huron(64), Sanilac(35)
UNION Cass
UNION CITY (49094) Branch(97), Calhoun(2)
UNION LAKE Oakland
UNION PIER Berrien
UNIONVILLE (48767) Tuscola(97), Huron(2)
UNIVERSITY CENTER Bay
UTICA Macomb
VANDALIA Cass
VANDERBILT (49795) Otsego(81), Cheboygan(15), Charlevoix(3)
VASSAR Tuscola
VERMONTVILLE Eaton
VERNON Shiawassee
VESTABURG Montcalm
VICKSBURG (49097) Kalamazoo(97), St. Joseph(2)
VULCAN (49892) Dickinson(76), Menominee(23)
WABANINGO Muskegon
WAKEFIELD Gogebic
WALDRON Hillsdale
WALHALLA Mason
WALKERVILLE (49459) Oceana(90), Newaygo(9)
WALLACE Menominee
WALLED LAKE Oakland
WALLOON LAKE Charlevoix
WARREN Macomb
WASHINGTON Macomb
WATERFORD Oakland
WATERS Otsego
WATERSMEET Gogebic
WATERVLIET (49098) Berrien(91), Van Buren(8)
WATTON Baraga
WAYLAND (49348) Allegan(78), Barry(21)
WAYNE Wayne
WEBBERVILLE (48892) Ingham(78), Livingston(21)
WEIDMAN Isabella
WELLS Delta
WELLSTON (49689) Manistee(86), Wexford(13)
WEST BLOOMFIELD Oakland
WEST BRANCH Ogemaw
WEST OLIVE Ottawa
WESTLAND Wayne
WESTON Lenawee
WESTPHALIA Clinton
WETMORE (49895) Alger(65), Delta(29), Schoolcraft(4)
WHEELER (48662) Gratiot(85), Midland(14)
WHITE CLOUD Newaygo
WHITE LAKE Oakland
WHITE PIGEON (49099) St. Joseph(87), Cass(12)
WHITE PINE Ontonagon
WHITEHALL Muskegon
WHITMORE LAKE (48189) Washtenaw(54), Livingston(45)
WHITTAKER Washtenaw
WHITTEMORE (48770) Iosco(96), Ogemaw(2), Arenac(1)
WILLIAMSBURG (49690) Grand Traverse(87), Antrim(7), Kalkaska(5)
WILLIAMSTON Ingham
WILLIS Washtenaw
WILSON Menominee
WINN Isabella
WIXOM Oakland
WOLVERINE Cheboygan
WOODLAND Barry
WYANDOTTE Wayne
WYOMING Kent
YALE (48097) St. Clair(82), Sanilac(17)
YPSILANTI Washtenaw
ZEELAND Ottawa

Michigan ZIP/City Cross Reference

48001-48001 ALGONAC
48002-48002 ALLENTON
48003-48003 ALMONT
48004-48004 ANCHORVILLE
48005-48005 ARMADA
48006-48006 AVOCA
48007-48007 TROY
48009-48012 BIRMINGHAM
48014-48014 CAPAC
48015-48015 CENTER LINE
48017-48017 CLAWSON
48021-48021 EASTPOINTE
48022-48022 EMMETT
48023-48023 FAIR HAVEN
48025-48025 FRANKLIN
48026-48026 FRASER
48027-48027 GOODELLS
48028-48028 HARSENS ISLAND
48030-48030 HAZEL PARK
48032-48032 JEDDO
48034-48034 SOUTHFIELD
48035-48036 CLINTON TOWNSHIP
48037-48037 SOUTHFIELD
48038-48038 CLINTON TOWNSHIP
48039-48039 MARINE CITY
48040-48040 MARYSVILLE
48041-48041 MEMPHIS
48042-48042 MACOMB
48043-48043 MOUNT CLEMENS
48044-48044 MACOMB
48045-48045 HARRISON TOWNSHIP
48046-48046 MOUNT CLEMENS
48047-48047 NEW BALTIMORE
48048-48048 NEW HAVEN
48049-48049 NORTH STREET
48050-48050 NEW HAVEN
48051-48051 NEW BALTIMORE
48052-48052 ALGONAC
48054-48054 EAST CHINA
48059-48059 FORT GRATIOT
48060-48061 PORT HURON
48062-48062 RICHMOND
48063-48063 COLUMBUS
48064-48064 CASCO
48065-48065 ROMEO
48066-48066 ROSEVILLE
48067-48068 ROYAL OAK
48069-48069 PLEASANT RIDGE
48070-48070 HUNTINGTON WOODS
48071-48071 MADISON HEIGHTS
48072-48072 BERKLEY
48073-48073 ROYAL OAK
48074-48074 SMITHS CREEK
48075-48076 SOUTHFIELD
48079-48079 SAINT CLAIR
48080-48082 SAINT CLAIR SHORES
48083-48085 TROY
48086-48086 SOUTHFIELD
48088-48093 WARREN
48094-48095 WASHINGTON
48096-48096 RAY
48097-48097 YALE
48098-48099 TROY
48101-48102 ALLEN PARK
48103-48109 ANN ARBOR
48110-48110 AZALIA
48111-48112 BELLEVILLE
48113-48113 ANN ARBOR
48114-48114 BRIGHTON
48115-48115 BRIDGEWATER
48116-48116 BRIGHTON
48117-48117 CARLETON
48118-48118 CHELSEA
48120-48121 DEARBORN
48122-48122 MELVINDALE
48123-48124 DEARBORN
48125-48125 DEARBORN HEIGHTS
48126-48126 DEARBORN
48127-48127 DEARBORN HEIGHTS
48128-48128 DEARBORN
48130-48130 DEXTER
48131-48131 DUNDEE
48133-48133 ERIE
48134-48134 FLAT ROCK
48135-48136 GARDEN CITY
48137-48137 GREGORY
48138-48138 GROSSE ILE
48139-48139 HAMBURG
48140-48140 IDA
48141-48141 INKSTER
48143-48143 LAKELAND
48144-48144 LAMBERTVILLE

48145-48145 LA SALLE
48146-48146 LINCOLN PARK
48150-48154 LIVONIA
48157-48157 LUNA PIER
48158-48158 MANCHESTER
48159-48159 MAYBEE
48160-48160 MILAN
48161-48162 MONROE
48164-48164 NEW BOSTON
48165-48165 NEW HUDSON
48166-48166 NEWPORT
48167-48168 NORTHVILLE
48169-48169 PINCKNEY
48170-48170 PLYMOUTH
48173-48173 ROCKWOOD
48174-48174 ROMULUS
48175-48175 SALEM
48176-48176 SALINE
48177-48177 SAMARIA
48178-48178 SOUTH LYON
48179-48179 SOUTH ROCKWOOD
48180-48180 TAYLOR
48182-48182 TEMPERANCE
48183-48183 TRENTON
48184-48184 WAYNE
48185-48186 WESTLAND
48187-48188 CANTON
48189-48189 WHITMORE LAKE
48190-48190 WHITTAKER
48191-48191 WILLIS
48192-48193 WYANDOTTE
48195-48195 SOUTHGATE
48197-48198 YPSILANTI
48200-48202 DETROIT
48203-48203 HIGHLAND PARK
48204-48211 DETROIT
48212-48212 HAMTRAMCK
48213-48217 DETROIT
48218-48218 RIVER ROUGE
48219-48219 DETROIT
48220-48220 FERNDALE
48221-48224 DETROIT
48225-48225 HARPER WOODS
48226-48228 DETROIT
48229-48229 ECORSE
48230-48230 GROSSE POINTE
48231-48235 DETROIT
48236-48236 GROSSE POINTE
48237-48237 OAK PARK
48238-48238 DETROIT
48239-48240 REDFORD
48242-48299 DETROIT
48301-48304 BLOOMFIELD HILLS
48306-48309 ROCHESTER
48310-48314 STERLING HEIGHTS
48315-48318 UTICA
48320-48320 KEEGO HARBOR
48321-48321 AUBURN HILLS
48322-48325 WEST BLOOMFIELD
48326-48326 AUBURN HILLS
48327-48329 WATERFORD
48330-48330 DRAYTON PLAINS
48331-48336 FARMINGTON
48340-48343 PONTIAC
48346-48348 CLARKSTON
48350-48350 DAVISBURG
48353-48353 HARTLAND
48356-48357 HIGHLAND
48359-48362 LAKE ORION
48363-48363 OAKLAND
48366-48366 LAKEVILLE
48367-48367 LEONARD
48370-48371 OXFORD
48374-48377 NOVI
48380-48381 MILFORD
48382-48382 COMMERCE TOWNSHIP
48383-48386 WHITE LAKE
48387-48387 UNION LAKE
48390-48391 WALLED LAKE
48393-48393 WIXOM
48397-48397 WARREN
48398-48398 CLAWSON
48401-48401 APPLEGATE
48410-48410 ARGYLE
48411-48411 ATLAS
48412-48412 ATTICA
48413-48413 BAD AXE
48414-48414 BANCROFT
48415-48415 BIRCH RUN
48416-48416 BROWN CITY
48417-48417 BURT
48418-48418 BYRON
48419-48419 CARSONVILLE
48420-48420 CLIO
48421-48421 COLUMBIAVILLE
48422-48422 CROSWELL
48423-48423 DAVISON
48426-48426 DECKER
48427-48427 DECKERVILLE
48428-48428 DRYDEN
48429-48429 DURAND
48430-48430 FENTON
48432-48432 FILION
48433-48433 FLUSHING
48434-48434 FORESTVILLE
48435-48435 FOSTORIA
48436-48436 GAINES
48437-48437 GENESEE
48438-48438 GOODRICH
48439-48439 GRAND BLANC
48440-48440 HADLEY
48441-48441 HARBOR BEACH
48442-48442 HOLLY
48444-48444 IMLAY CITY
48445-48445 KINDE
48446-48446 LAPEER
48449-48449 LENNON
48450-48450 LEXINGTON
48451-48451 LINDEN
48452-48452 ATTICA
48453-48453 MARLETTE
48454-48454 MELVIN
48455-48455 METAMORA
48456-48456 MINDEN CITY
48457-48457 MONTROSE
48458-48458 MOUNT MORRIS
48460-48460 NEW LOTHROP
48461-48461 NORTH BRANCH
48462-48462 ORTONVILLE
48463-48463 OTISVILLE
48464-48464 OTTER LAKE
48465-48465 PALMS
48466-48466 PECK
48467-48467 PORT AUSTIN
48468-48468 PORT HOPE
48469-48469 PORT SANILAC
48470-48470 RUTH
48471-48471 SANDUSKY
48472-48472 SNOVER
48473-48473 SWARTZ CREEK
48475-48475 UBLY
48476-48476 VERNON
48480-48480 GRAND BLANC
48500-48507 FLINT
48509-48529 BURTON
48531-48559 FLINT
48601-48609 SAGINAW
48610-48610 ALGER
48611-48611 AUBURN
48612-48612 BEAVERTON
48613-48613 BENTLEY
48614-48614 BRANT
48615-48615 BRECKENRIDGE
48616-48616 CHESANING
48617-48617 CLARE
48618-48618 COLEMAN
48619-48619 COMINS
48620-48620 EDENVILLE
48621-48621 FAIRVIEW
48622-48622 FARWELL
48623-48623 FREELAND
48624-48624 GLADWIN
48625-48625 HARRISON
48626-48626 HEMLOCK
48627-48627 HIGGINS LAKE
48628-48628 HOPE
48629-48629 HOUGHTON LAKE
48630-48630 HOUGHTON LAKE HEIGHTS
48631-48631 KAWKAWLIN
48632-48632 LAKE
48633-48633 LAKE GEORGE
48634-48634 LINWOOD
48635-48635 LUPTON
48636-48636 LUZERNE
48637-48637 MERRILL
48638-48638 SAGINAW
48640-48642 MIDLAND
48647-48647 MIO
48649-48649 OAKLEY
48650-48650 PINCONNING
48651-48651 PRUDENVILLE
48652-48652 RHODES
48653-48653 ROSCOMMON
48654-48654 ROSE CITY
48655-48655 SAINT CHARLES
48656-48656 SAINT HELEN
48657-48657 SANFORD
48658-48658 STANDISH
48659-48659 STERLING
48661-48661 WEST BRANCH
48662-48662 WHEELER
48663-48663 SAGINAW
48667-48686 MIDLAND
48701-48701 AKRON
48703-48703 AU GRES
48705-48705 BARTON CITY
48706-48708 BAY CITY
48710-48710 UNIVERSITY CENTER
48720-48720 BAY PORT
48721-48721 BLACK RIVER
48722-48722 BRIDGEPORT
48723-48723 CARO
48724-48724 CARROLLTON
48725-48725 CASEVILLE
48726-48726 CASS CITY
48727-48727 CLIFFORD
48728-48728 CURRAN
48729-48729 DEFORD
48730-48730 EAST TAWAS
48731-48731 ELKTON
48732-48732 ESSEXVILLE
48733-48733 FAIRGROVE
48734-48734 FRANKENMUTH
48735-48735 GAGETOWN
48736-48736 GILFORD
48737-48737 GLENNIE
48738-48738 GREENBUSH
48739-48739 HALE
48740-48740 HARRISVILLE
48741-48741 KINGSTON
48742-48742 LINCOLN
48743-48743 LONG LAKE
48744-48744 MAYVILLE
48745-48745 MIKADO
48746-48746 MILLINGTON
48747-48747 MUNGER
48748-48748 NATIONAL CITY
48749-48749 OMER
48750-48753 OSCODA
48754-48754 OWENDALE
48755-48755 PIGEON
48756-48756 PRESCOTT
48757-48757 REESE
48758-48758 RICHVILLE
48759-48759 SEBEWAING
48760-48760 SILVERWOOD
48761-48761 SOUTH BRANCH
48762-48762 SPRUCE
48763-48764 TAWAS CITY
48765-48765 TURNER
48766-48766 TWINING
48767-48767 UNIONVILLE
48768-48768 VASSAR
48769-48769 TUSCOLA
48770-48770 WHITTEMORE
48787-48787 FRANKENMUTH
48801-48802 ALMA
48804-48804 MOUNT PLEASANT
48805-48805 OKEMOS
48806-48806 ASHLEY
48807-48807 BANNISTER
48808-48808 BATH
48809-48809 BELDING
48811-48811 CARSON CITY
48812-48812 CEDAR LAKE
48813-48813 CHARLOTTE
48815-48815 CLARKSVILLE
48816-48816 COHOCTAH
48817-48817 CORUNNA
48818-48818 CRYSTAL
48819-48819 DANSVILLE
48820-48820 DEWITT
48821-48821 DIMONDALE
48822-48822 EAGLE
48823-48826 EAST LANSING
48827-48827 EATON RAPIDS
48829-48829 EDMORE
48830-48830 ELM HALL
48831-48831 ELSIE
48832-48832 ELWELL
48833-48833 EUREKA
48834-48834 FENWICK
48835-48835 FOWLER
48836-48836 FOWLERVILLE
48837-48837 GRAND LEDGE
48838-48838 GREENVILLE
48840-48840 HASLETT
48841-48841 HENDERSON
48842-48842 HOLT
48843-48844 HOWELL
48845-48845 HUBBARDSTON
48846-48846 IONIA
48847-48847 ITHACA
48848-48848 LAINGSBURG
48849-48849 LAKE ODESSA
48850-48850 LAKEVIEW
48851-48851 LYONS
48852-48852 MCBRIDES
48853-48853 MAPLE RAPIDS
48854-48854 MASON
48855-48855 HOWELL
48856-48856 MIDDLETON
48857-48857 MORRICE
48858-48859 MOUNT PLEASANT
48860-48860 MUIR
48861-48861 MULLIKEN
48862-48862 NORTH STAR
48863-48863 OAK GROVE
48864-48864 OKEMOS
48865-48865 ORLEANS
48866-48866 OVID
48867-48867 OWOSSO
48870-48870 PALO
48871-48871 PERRINTON
48872-48872 PERRY
48873-48873 PEWAMO
48874-48874 POMPEII
48875-48875 PORTLAND
48876-48876 POTTERVILLE
48877-48877 RIVERDALE
48878-48878 ROSEBUSH
48879-48879 SAINT JOHNS
48880-48880 SAINT LOUIS
48881-48881 SARANAC
48882-48882 SHAFTSBURG
48883-48883 SHEPHERD
48884-48884 SHERIDAN
48885-48885 SIDNEY
48886-48886 SIX LAKES
48887-48887 SMYRNA
48888-48888 STANTON
48889-48889 SUMNER
48890-48890 SUNFIELD
48891-48891 VESTABURG
48892-48892 WEBBERVILLE
48893-48893 WEIDMAN
48894-48894 WESTPHALIA
48895-48895 WILLIAMSTON

48896-48896 WINN
48897-48897 WOODLAND
48900-48980 LANSING
49001-49001 KALAMAZOO
49002-49002 PORTAGE
49003-49009 KALAMAZOO
49010-49010 ALLEGAN
49011-49011 ATHENS
49012-49012 AUGUSTA
49013-49013 BANGOR
49014-49018 BATTLE CREEK
49019-49019 KALAMAZOO
49020-49020 BEDFORD
49021-49021 BELLEVUE
49022-49023 BENTON HARBOR
49024-49024 PORTAGE
49026-49026 BLOOMINGDALE
49027-49027 BREEDSVILLE
49028-49028 BRONSON
49029-49029 BURLINGTON
49030-49030 BURR OAK
49031-49031 CASSOPOLIS
49032-49032 CENTREVILLE
49033-49033 CERESCO
49034-49034 CLIMAX
49035-49035 CLOVERDALE
49036-49036 COLDWATER
49038-49038 COLOMA
49039-49039 HAGAR SHORES
49040-49040 COLON
49041-49041 COMSTOCK
49042-49042 CONSTANTINE
49043-49043 COVERT
49045-49045 DECATUR
49046-49046 DELTON
49047-49047 DOWAGIAC
49048-49048 KALAMAZOO
49050-49050 DOWLING
49051-49051 EAST LEROY
49052-49052 FULTON
49053-49053 GALESBURG
49055-49055 GOBLES
49056-49056 GRAND JUNCTION
49057-49057 HARTFORD
49058-49058 HASTINGS
49060-49060 HICKORY CORNERS
49061-49061 JONES
49062-49062 KENDALL
49063-49063 LACOTA
49064-49064 LAWRENCE
49065-49065 LAWTON
49066-49066 LEONIDAS
49067-49067 MARCELLUS
49068-49069 MARSHALL
49070-49070 MARTIN
49071-49071 MATTAWAN
49072-49072 MENDON
49073-49073 NASHVILLE
49074-49074 NAZARETH
49075-49075 NOTTAWA
49076-49076 OLIVET
49077-49077 OSHTEMO
49078-49078 OTSEGO
49079-49079 PAW PAW
49080-49080 PLAINWELL
49081-49081 PORTAGE
49082-49082 QUINCY
49083-49083 RICHLAND
49084-49084 RIVERSIDE
49085-49085 SAINT JOSEPH
49087-49087 SCHOOLCRAFT
49088-49088 SCOTTS
49089-49089 SHERWOOD
49090-49090 SOUTH HAVEN
49091-49091 STURGIS
49092-49092 TEKONSHA
49093-49093 THREE RIVERS
49094-49094 UNION CITY
49095-49095 VANDALIA
49096-49096 VERMONTVILLE
49097-49097 VICKSBURG
49098-49098 WATERVLIET
49099-49099 WHITE PIGEON
49101-49101 BARODA
49102-49102 BERRIEN CENTER
49103-49104 BERRIEN SPRINGS
49106-49106 BRIDGMAN
49107-49107 BUCHANAN
49111-49111 EAU CLAIRE
49112-49112 EDWARDSBURG
49113-49113 GALIEN
49115-49115 HARBERT
49116-49116 LAKESIDE
49117-49117 NEW BUFFALO
49119-49119 NEW TROY
49120-49121 NILES
49125-49125 SAWYER
49126-49126 SODUS
49127-49127 STEVENSVILLE
49128-49128 THREE OAKS
49129-49129 UNION PIER
49130-49130 UNION
49201-49204 JACKSON
49220-49220 ADDISON
49221-49221 ADRIAN
49224-49224 ALBION
49227-49227 ALLEN
49228-49228 BLISSFIELD
49229-49229 BRITTON
49230-49230 BROOKLYN
49231-49231 CADMUS
49232-49232 CAMDEN
49233-49233 CEMENT CITY
49234-49234 CLARKLAKE
49235-49235 CLAYTON
49236-49236 CLINTON
49237-49237 CONCORD
49238-49238 DEERFIELD
49239-49239 FRONTIER
49240-49240 GRASS LAKE
49241-49241 HANOVER
49242-49242 HILLSDALE
49245-49245 HOMER
49246-49246 HORTON
49247-49247 HUDSON
49248-49248 JASPER
49249-49249 JEROME
49250-49250 JONESVILLE
49251-49251 LESLIE
49252-49252 LITCHFIELD
49253-49253 MANITOU BEACH
49254-49254 MICHIGAN CENTER
49255-49255 MONTGOMERY
49256-49256 MORENCI
49257-49257 MOSCOW
49258-49258 MOSHERVILLE
49259-49259 MUNITH
49261-49261 NAPOLEON
49262-49262 NORTH ADAMS
49263-49263 NORVELL
49264-49264 ONONDAGA
49265-49265 ONSTED
49266-49266 OSSEO
49267-49267 OTTAWA LAKE
49268-49268 PALMYRA
49269-49269 PARMA
49270-49270 PETERSBURG
49271-49271 PITTSFORD
49272-49272 PLEASANT LAKE
49273-49273 PRATTVILLE
49274-49274 READING
49275-49275 RIDGEWAY
49276-49276 RIGA
49277-49277 RIVES JUNCTION
49278-49278 ROLLIN
49279-49279 SAND CREEK
49280-49280 SENECA
49281-49281 SOMERSET
49282-49282 SOMERSET CENTER
49283-49283 SPRING ARBOR
49284-49284 SPRINGPORT
49285-49285 STOCKBRIDGE
49286-49286 TECUMSEH
49287-49287 TIPTON
49288-49288 WALDRON
49289-49289 WESTON
49301-49301 ADA
49302-49302 ALTO
49303-49303 BAILEY
49304-49304 BALDWIN
49305-49305 BARRYTON
49306-49306 BELMONT
49307-49307 BIG RAPIDS
49309-49309 BITELY
49310-49310 BLANCHARD
49311-49311 BRADLEY
49312-49312 BROHMAN
49313-49313 BRUNSWICK
49314-49314 BURNIPS
49315-49315 BYRON CENTER
49316-49316 CALEDONIA
49317-49317 CANNONSBURG
49318-49318 CASNOVIA
49319-49319 CEDAR SPRINGS
49320-49320 CHIPPEWA LAKE
49321-49321 COMSTOCK PARK
49322-49322 CORAL
49323-49323 DORR
49325-49325 FREEPORT
49326-49326 GOWEN
49327-49327 GRANT
49328-49328 HOPKINS
49329-49329 HOWARD CITY
49330-49330 KENT CITY
49331-49331 LOWELL
49332-49332 MECOSTA
49333-49333 MIDDLEVILLE
49334-49334 MILLBROOK
49335-49335 MOLINE
49336-49336 MORLEY
49337-49337 NEWAYGO
49338-49338 PARIS
49339-49339 PIERSON
49340-49340 REMUS
49341-49341 ROCKFORD
49342-49342 RODNEY
49343-49343 SAND LAKE
49344-49344 SHELBYVILLE
49345-49345 SPARTA
49346-49346 STANWOOD
49347-49347 TRUFANT
49348-49348 WAYLAND
49349-49349 WHITE CLOUD
49351-49351 ROCKFORD
49355-49357 ADA
49401-49401 ALLENDALE
49402-49402 BRANCH
49403-49403 CONKLIN
49404-49404 COOPERSVILLE
49405-49405 CUSTER
49406-49406 DOUGLAS
49408-49408 FENNVILLE
49409-49409 FERRYSBURG
49410-49410 FOUNTAIN
49411-49411 FREE SOIL
49412-49413 FREMONT
49415-49415 FRUITPORT
49416-49416 GLENN
49417-49417 GRAND HAVEN
49418-49418 GRANDVILLE
49419-49419 HAMILTON
49420-49420 HART
49421-49421 HESPERIA
49422-49424 HOLLAND
49425-49425 HOLTON
49426-49426 HUDSONVILLE
49427-49427 JAMESTOWN
49428-49429 JENISON
49430-49430 LAMONT
49431-49431 LUDINGTON
49434-49434 MACATAWA
49435-49435 MARNE
49436-49436 MEARS
49437-49437 MONTAGUE
49440-49445 MUSKEGON
49446-49446 NEW ERA
49447-49447 NEW RICHMOND
49448-49448 NUNICA
49449-49449 PENTWATER
49450-49450 PULLMAN
49451-49451 RAVENNA
49452-49452 ROTHBURY
49453-49453 SAUGATUCK
49454-49454 SCOTTVILLE
49455-49455 SHELBY
49456-49456 SPRING LAKE
49457-49457 TWIN LAKE
49458-49458 WALHALLA
49459-49459 WALKERVILLE
49460-49460 WEST OLIVE
49461-49461 WHITEHALL
49463-49463 WABANINGO
49464-49464 ZEELAND
49468-49468 GRANDVILLE
49500-49518 GRAND RAPIDS
49519-49519 WYOMING
49523-49599 GRAND RAPIDS
49601-49601 CADILLAC
49610-49610 ACME
49611-49611 ALBA
49612-49612 ALDEN
49613-49613 ARCADIA
49614-49614 BEAR LAKE
49615-49615 BELLAIRE
49616-49616 BENZONIA
49617-49617 BEULAH
49618-49618 BOON
49619-49619 BRETHREN
49620-49620 BUCKLEY
49621-49621 CEDAR
49622-49622 CENTRAL LAKE
49623-49623 CHASE
49625-49625 COPEMISH
49626-49626 EASTLAKE
49627-49627 EASTPORT
49628-49628 ELBERTA
49629-49629 ELK RAPIDS
49630-49630 EMPIRE
49631-49631 EVART
49632-49632 FALMOUTH
49633-49633 FIFE LAKE
49634-49634 FILER CITY
49635-49635 FRANKFORT
49636-49636 GLEN ARBOR
49637-49637 GRAWN
49638-49638 HARRIETTA
49639-49639 HERSEY
49640-49640 HONOR
49642-49642 IDLEWILD
49643-49643 INTERLOCHEN
49644-49644 IRONS
49645-49645 KALEVA
49646-49646 KALKASKA
49647-49647 KARLIN
49648-49648 KEWADIN
49649-49649 KINGSLEY
49650-49650 LAKE ANN
49651-49651 LAKE CITY
49653-49653 LAKE LEELANAU
49654-49654 LELAND
49655-49655 LEROY
49656-49656 LUTHER
49657-49657 MC BAIN
49659-49659 MANCELONA
49660-49660 MANISTEE
49663-49663 MANTON
49664-49664 MAPLE CITY
49665-49665 MARION
49666-49666 MAYFIELD
49667-49667 MERRITT
49668-49668 MESICK
49670-49670 NORTHPORT
49673-49673 OLD MISSION
49674-49674 OMENA
49675-49675 ONEKAMA
49676-49676 RAPID CITY
49677-49677 REED CITY
49679-49679 SEARS

49680-49680 SOUTH BOARDMAN
49682-49682 SUTTONS BAY
49683-49683 THOMPSONVILLE
49684-49686 TRAVERSE CITY
49688-49688 TUSTIN
49689-49689 WELLSTON
49690-49690 WILLIAMSBURG
49696-49696 TRAVERSE CITY
49701-49701 MACKINAW CITY
49705-49705 AFTON
49706-49706 ALANSON
49707-49707 ALPENA
49709-49709 ATLANTA
49710-49710 BARBEAU
49711-49711 BAY SHORE
49712-49712 BOYNE CITY
49713-49713 BOYNE FALLS
49715-49715 BRIMLEY
49716-49716 BRUTUS
49717-49717 BURT LAKE
49718-49718 CARP LAKE
49719-49719 CEDARVILLE
49720-49720 CHARLEVOIX
49721-49721 CHEBOYGAN
49722-49722 CONWAY
49723-49723 CROSS VILLAGE
49724-49724 DAFTER
49725-49725 DE TOUR VILLAGE
49726-49726 DRUMMOND ISLAND
49727-49727 EAST JORDAN
49728-49728 ECKERMAN
49729-49729 ELLSWORTH
49730-49730 ELMIRA
49733-49733 FREDERIC
49734-49735 GAYLORD
49736-49736 GOETZVILLE
49737-49737 GOOD HART
49738-49739 GRAYLING
49740-49740 HARBOR SPRINGS
49743-49743 HAWKS
49744-49744 HERRON
49745-49745 HESSEL
49746-49746 HILLMAN
49747-49747 HUBBARD LAKE
49748-49748 HULBERT
49749-49749 INDIAN RIVER
49751-49751 JOHANNESBURG
49752-49752 KINROSS
49753-49753 LACHINE
49755-49755 LEVERING
49756-49756 LEWISTON
49757-49757 MACKINAC ISLAND
49759-49759 MILLERSBURG
49760-49760 MORAN
49761-49761 MULLETT LAKE
49762-49762 NAUBINWAY
49764-49764 ODEN
49765-49765 ONAWAY
49766-49766 OSSINEKE
49768-49768 PARADISE
49769-49769 PELLSTON
49770-49770 PETOSKEY
49774-49774 PICKFORD
49775-49775 POINTE AUX PINS
49776-49776 POSEN
49777-49777 PRESQUE ISLE
49778-49778 BRIMLEY
49779-49779 ROGERS CITY
49780-49780 RUDYARD
49781-49781 SAINT IGNACE
49782-49782 BEAVER ISLAND
49783-49783 SAULT SAINTE MARIE
49784-49788 KINCHELOE
49789-49789 STALWART
49790-49790 STRONGS
49791-49791 TOPINABEE
49792-49792 TOWER
49793-49793 TROUT LAKE
49795-49795 VANDERBILT
49796-49796 WALLOON LAKE
49797-49797 WATERS
49799-49799 WOLVERINE
49801-49801 IRON MOUNTAIN
49802-49802 KINGSFORD
49805-49805 ALLOUEZ
49806-49806 AU TRAIN
49807-49807 BARK RIVER
49808-49808 BIG BAY
49812-49812 CARNEY
49813-49813 CEDAR RIVER
49814-49814 CHAMPION
49815-49815 CHANNING
49816-49816 CHATHAM
49817-49817 COOKS
49818-49818 CORNELL
49819-49819 ARNOLD
49820-49820 CURTIS
49821-49821 DAGGETT
49822-49822 DEERTON
49825-49825 EBEN JUNCTION
49826-49826 RUMELY
49827-49827 ENGADINE
49829-49829 ESCANABA
49831-49831 FELCH
49833-49833 LITTLE LAKE
49834-49834 FOSTER CITY
49835-49835 GARDEN
49836-49836 GERMFASK
49837-49837 GLADSTONE
49838-49838 GOULD CITY
49839-49839 GRAND MARAIS
49840-49840 GULLIVER
49841-49843 GWINN
49845-49845 HARRIS
49847-49847 HERMANSVILLE
49848-49848 INGALLS
49849-49849 ISHPEMING
49852-49852 LORETTO
49853-49853 MC MILLAN
49854-49854 MANISTIQUE
49855-49855 MARQUETTE
49858-49858 MENOMINEE
49861-49861 MICHIGAMME
49862-49862 MUNISING
49863-49863 NADEAU
49864-49864 NAHMA
49865-49865 NATIONAL MINE
49866-49866 NEGAUNEE
49868-49868 NEWBERRY
49869-49869 NORTHLAND
49870-49870 NORWAY
49871-49871 PALMER
49872-49872 PERKINS
49873-49873 PERRONVILLE
49874-49874 POWERS
49876-49876 QUINNESEC
49877-49877 RALPH
49878-49878 RAPID RIVER
49879-49879 REPUBLIC
49880-49880 ROCK
49881-49881 SAGOLA
49883-49883 SENEY
49884-49884 SHINGLETON
49885-49885 SKANDIA
49886-49886 SPALDING
49887-49887 STEPHENSON
49890-49890 TRAUNIK
49891-49891 TRENARY
49892-49892 VULCAN
49893-49893 WALLACE
49894-49894 WELLS
49895-49895 WETMORE
49896-49896 WILSON
49901-49901 AHMEEK
49902-49902 ALPHA
49903-49903 AMASA
49905-49905 ATLANTIC MINE
49908-49908 BARAGA
49909-49909 IRON RIVER
49910-49910 BERGLAND
49911-49911 BESSEMER
49912-49912 BRUCE CROSSING
49913-49913 CALUMET
49915-49915 CASPIAN
49916-49916 CHASSELL
49917-49917 COPPER CITY
49918-49918 COPPER HARBOR
49919-49919 COVINGTON
49920-49920 CRYSTAL FALLS
49921-49921 DODGEVILLE
49922-49922 DOLLAR BAY
49924-49924 EAGLE RIVER
49925-49925 EWEN
49927-49927 GAASTRA
49929-49929 GREENLAND
49930-49930 HANCOCK
49931-49931 HOUGHTON
49934-49934 HUBBELL
49935-49935 IRON RIVER
49938-49938 IRONWOOD
49942-49942 KEARSARGE
49943-49943 KENTON
49945-49945 LAKE LINDEN
49946-49946 LANSE
49947-49947 MARENISCO
49948-49948 MASS CITY
49950-49950 MOHAWK
49952-49952 NISULA
49953-49953 ONTONAGON
49955-49955 PAINESDALE
49958-49958 PELKIE
49959-49959 RAMSAY
49960-49960 ROCKLAND
49961-49961 SIDNAW
49962-49962 SKANEE
49963-49963 SOUTH RANGE
49964-49964 STAMBAUGH
49965-49965 TOIVOLA
49967-49967 TROUT CREEK
49968-49968 WAKEFIELD
49969-49969 WATERSMEET
49970-49970 WATTON
49971-49971 WHITE PINE

Minnesota

General Help Numbers:

Governor's Office

130 State Capitol 75, Dr ML King Jr. Blvd. 651-296-3391
St Paul, MN 55155 Fax 651-296-2089
www.governor.state.mn.us 7:30AM-5PM

Attorney General's Office

1400 Bremer Tower 651-296-3353
445 Minnesota St Fax 651-297-4193
St Paul, MN 55101 8AM-5PM
www.ag.state.mn.us

Legislative Records

Minnesota Legislature, State Capitol
House-Room 211, Senate-Room 231 651-296-2887
St Paul, MN 55155 Fax 651-651-296-1563
www.leg.state.mn.us 8AM-5PM

State Archives

Division of Library & Archives 651-259-3300
345 Kellogg Blvd West Fax 651-297-9961
St Paul, MN 55102-1906 9AM-5PM W-F; N-8PM T
www.mnhs.org 9AM-4PM SAT (Closed SU-M)

State Specifics:

Capital: St. Paul
Ramsey County

Time Zone: CST

Number of Counties: 87

Population: 5,220,393

Web Site: www.state.mn.us

State Agencies

Criminal Records

Bureau of Criminal Apprehension, CJIS - Criminal History Access Unit, 1430 Maryland Ave E, St Paul, MN 55106; 651-793-2400, Fax- 651-793-2401; 8AM-4:30PM.

www.bca.state.mn.us/CJIS/Documents/cjis-intro.html

State statutes require all law enforcement agencies to report juvenile felony and gross misdemeanor arrests, and adult felony, gross misdemeanor, enhanced gross misdemeanor and targeted misdemeanor arrests to BCA. Other misdemeanors are sometimes reported

Indexing & Storage: Records available from 1924. New records available for inquiry in 1 day. Per a U.S. DOJ Survey, 41% of all arrests in database have final dispositions recorded, 55% for those arrests within last 5 years.

Searching: For most requesters, to obtain the entire adult history, including all arrests, you must have a notarized release form signed by person of record. To get a 15-year record of convictions only, a consent form is not required. Include in request- name, date of birth, and sex. Include signed release for a complete record. Fingerprint searches are not permitted. However, 100% of records are fingerprint-supported. This data not released- juvenile records. With consent, all records are released, including those without dispositions. If no consent then only conviction records released. Targeted misdemeanors (violent, DV, DUI, etc, where a jail sentence may be imposed) are released; other misdemeanors are if received.

Access by: mail, in person, online.

Fee & Payment: The fee for the full adult history is $15.00 (with consent), for non-profits the fee is $8.00. The fee for the 15-year public record (without consent) is $4.00, and free from the web. Fee payee- BCA. Prepayment required. Business checks, personal checks, money orders and certified funds are accepted.

Mail search: Turnaround time- 1 to 2 weeks. A SASE is requested.

In person: Using a public access terminal, a copy of a public record is available for $4.00 per name. For the full adult history the turnaround time is 2 days, unless you are the person of record, then it is immediate. The counter closes at 4:15 PM.

Online search: Access to the public criminal history record (15 year, no consent) is available free at https://cch.state.mn.us/.

Other access: A public database is available on CD-ROM. Monthly updates can be purchased. Data is in ASCII format and is raw data. Fee is $40.00

Statewide Court Records

State Court Administrator, 25 Rev ML King Blvd, #135, St Paul, MN 55155; 651-296-2474, Fax- 651-297-5636; 8AM-4:30PM.

www.mncourts.gov/default.aspx

Except for certain online research capabilities, all court record access must be done at the local level.

Online search: Minnesota offers the Trial Court Public Access (MPA) at http://pa.courts.state.mn.us/default.aspx. Search statewide or by county. Records available include criminal, civil, family, and probate. Searches can be performed using a case number or by name. But there are a number of caveats - many publicly-accessible case records viewable at the courthouse cannot be viewed online. This is a supplementary database; use with caution if true due diligence is required. Appellate and District court calendars are viewable at www.mncourts.gov/default.aspx?page=512. Also, Appellate and Supreme Court opinions are available from a link on the home page.

Other access: http://pa.courts.state.mn.us/default.aspx

Sexual Offender Registry

Bureau of Criminal Apprehension, Minnesota Predatory Offender Program, 1430 Maryland Ave E, St Paul, MN 55106; 651-793-7070, 888-234-1248, Fax- 651-793-7071; 8AM-4:30PM.

https://por.state.mn.us/

This is not a notification state. The state does not permit public access to this information beyond the Level 3 names and non-compliant offenders age 16 and older found on the web.

Indexing & Storage: New records available for inquiry in minutes.

Searching: This means local law enforcement offices cannot give the public access to all names.

Fee & Payment: There is no fee.

Online search: Offenders and non-compliant offender if 16 or older may be searched at https://por.state.mn.us/OffenderSearch.aspx. Risk level 3 search available at DOC site www.doc.state.mn.us/level3/Search.asp.

Incarceration Records

Minnesota Department of Corrections, Records Management Unit, 1450 Energy Park Drive, Suite 200, St. Paul, MN 55108; 651-361-7200, Fax- 651-643-3588; 8AM-5PM.

www.corr.state.mn.us

Main fax number for the DOC is 651-642-0223.

Indexing & Storage: Records available on current and former inmates; however, the online search is limited to those either still in prison or under probation. New records available for inquiry in about 7 days.

Searching: Records are computerized since 1978. Include in request- name and DOB. Location, OID number, physical identifiers, conviction and sentencing information, and release dates are provided.

Access by: mail, phone, fax, online.

Fee & Payment: There is a $10.00 retrieval fee and a copy fee of $.25 per page. Personal checks accepted.

Mail search: Turnaround time- 2-4 days.

Phone search: Searching is available via telephone.

Fax search: Fax requires full name and DOB.

Online search: Search at the web to retrieve public information about adult offenders who have been committed to the Commissioner of Corrections, and who are still under our jurisdiction (i.e. in prison, or released from prison and still under supervision). Search by name, with or without DOB, or by OID number at http://info.doc.state.mn.us/publicviewer/main.asp. Also, there is a separate search for Level 3 offender/predatory information.

Corporation, LLC, LP, Assumed Name, Trademarks/Servicemarks

Business Services, Secretary of State, 60 Empire Dr, #100, St Paul, MN 55103; 651-296-2803 (Information), Fax- 651-297-7067; 8AM-4:30PM.

www.sos.state.mn.us/home/index.asp

Records are also held for non-profits.

Indexing & Storage: Records available from 1850's on. All records are indexed together. New records available for inquiry in one day.

Searching: Part II of foreign corporation annual reports are not released. Include in request- full name of business, corporation file number. In addition to articles of incorporation, corporation records include the following information: Annual Reports, Prior (merged) names, Inactive and Reserved names.

Access by: mail, phone, in person, online.

Fee & Payment: Copies of most documents are $3.00 per page, $6.00 if original document plus amendments requested. Add $5.00 for certification. Fee payee- Secretary of State. Prepayment required. Personal checks accepted. Credit cards accepted online only.

Mail search: Turnaround time- 10 business days. SASE not required.

Phone search: Phone hours are 9AM to 4PM. Limited verification information is given over the phone.

In person: The counter closes at 4PM. There is no fee to view the database or microfilm.

Online search: Go to www.sos.state.mn.us/home/index.asp?page=6. This Internet site permits free look-ups of business names and corporation files. Also, a commercial program called Direct Access is available 24 hours. There is an annual subscription fee of $75.00. Record copies or certificates may be ordered for an additional $10.00 fee using Express Service.

Other access: Information can be purchased in bulk format. Call for more information.

Uniform Commercial Code, Federal & State Tax Liens

UCC Division, Secretary of State, 60 Empire Dr #100, St Paul, MN 55103; 651-296-2803, Fax- 651-215-1009; 8AM-4:30PM.

www.sos.state.mn.us/home/index.asp?page=89

Information about tax liens is found at www.sos.state.mn.us/home/index.asp?page=91.

Indexing & Storage: Records available from 1966 on computer. Tax liens are on microfilm. New records available for inquiry in 48 hours.

Searching: Use search request form UCC-11 for UCC filings. Use a separate UCC-12 request form to obtain federal and state tax liens on businesses. Note that federal tax liens can also be filed at the county. Include in request- debtor name, type of debtor, organization or individual.

Access by: mail, fax, in person, online.

Fee & Payment: The fee for a debtor name search is $20.00 per name. The search fee includes all copies if requested. Otherwise, ordering copies by file are $1.00 per page. Fee payee- Secretary of State. Prepayment required. Personal checks accepted.

Mail search: Turnaround time- 2 days. SASE not required.

Fax search: Same criteria as mail searches.

In person: A free public access terminal is available since this agency does not provide counter service for searches. If specific documents are ordered in person, there documents will be mailed within 2-3 days.

Online search: There is a free look-up by filing number available from the website. A fee is charged for a name search. A comprehensive commercial program called Direct Access is available 24 hours. There is an annual subscription fee of $75.00 per year, plus $5.00 per debtor name. Call 651-296-2803 for more information.

Other access: This agency will provide information in bulk form on CD. Call 651-296-2803 or 877-551-6767 for more information.

Sales Tax Registrations

Minnesota Revenue Dept, Sale and Use Tax, 600 N Robert Street MS:6330, St Paul, MN 55146-6330; 651-296-6181, 800-657-3777, Fax- 651-556-3102; 7:30AM-5PM.

www.taxes.state.mn.us

Indexing & Storage: Records available from 1967 on computer, generally records go back 15 years. New records available for inquiry in 3 days.

Searching: This agency will only confirm that a business or person has a MN sales tax number and if it is active. They can't provide any other information. Include in request- business name and MN city.

Access by: mail, phone, fax, in person, online.

Fee & Payment: There is no fee. No credit cards accepted.

Mail search: Turnaround time- 7-10 days. SASE not required.

Phone search: Record information will be given over the phone.

Fax search: Fax searching available.

In person: Service is while you wait, or can be returned via mail.

Online search: Email requests are accepted at business.registration@state.mn.us.

Birth Certificates

Minnesota Department of Health, Vital Records, PO Box 64882, St Paul, MN 55164 (Courier address- 85 East 7th Place, St Paul, MN 55101); 651-201-5970, Fax- 651-201-5740; 8AM-4:30PM.

www.health.state.mn.us/divs/chs/osr/birth.html

For information pertaining to adoption records, call 651-201-5970 If other questions, email osr1@health.state.mn.us.

Indexing & Storage: Records available from 1900 on. Prior records must be obtained from the county level. New records available for inquiry in 1 month or less.

Searching: Only those with a "tangible interest" may request a certified record, but a notarized signature of the requester is needed. Include in request- full name, date of birth, place of birth, names of parents, mother's maiden name. Also, requester's signature must be notarized. Anyone may order a non-certified record and notarized signature is not required unless it is a birth to unmarried parents. This data not released- birth medical information is only released to the mother of the child.

Access by: mail, fax, in person, online.

Fee & Payment: Fees are $13.00 for a non-certified copy, $16.00 for a certified copy. Fee payee- Minnesota Department of Health. Prepayment required. Credit cards may be used for fax requesters. Personal checks accepted. Major credit cards accepted.

Mail search: Turnaround time- 1 to 2 weeks. SASE not required.

Fax search: See expedited services. Credit card is required.

In person: The MDH no longer handles in-person requests. Visitors may make in-person requests at local registrar offices.

Online search: Search for a marriage certificate fee at www.mncounty.com/Modules/Certificates/Marriage/Default.aspx but not all counties are on the MOMS system yet. Also, search the Birth Certificates Index free from 1900 to 1934 at http://people.mnhs.org/bci/Search.cfm?bhcp=1.

Other access: Bulk lists and files of information, if public record, are available on paper and in electronic format. Call Cheri Denardo at 651-201-5970 for details.

Expedited service: Expedited service is available for faxed or mailed searches. Turnaround time- 24-72 hours. Add $20.00 plus $6.00 for use of credit card and $16.00 for overnight delivery.

Death Records

Minnesota Department of Health, Vital Records, PO Box 64882, St Paul, MN 55164 (Courier address- 85 East 7th Place, St Paul, MN 55101); 651-201-5970, Fax- 651-201-5740; 8AM-4:30PM.

www.health.state.mn.us/divs/chs/osr/death.html

If questions, email osr1@health.state.mn.us.

Indexing & Storage: Records available from 1908 on. Prior records must be obtained at the county level. New records available for inquiry in 1 month or less.

Searching: Only those with a "tangible interest" may request a certified record. Those without such interest made receive non-certified. In person requests must be made at local registrar offices. Include in request- full name, date of death, place of death. Also, requester's signature must be notarized. If date or place not known, include last year known to be alive.

Access by: mail, fax, online.

Fee & Payment: Fees are $13.00 for a non-certified copy and $6.00 for each additional copy of the same name requested at same time. Fee payee- Minnesota Department of Health. Prepayment required. Credit cards may be used for ordering by fax only. Personal checks accepted. Major credit cards accepted.

Mail search: Turnaround time- 1 to 2 weeks. SASE not required.

Fax search: See expedited services. Credit card is required.

Online search: No official online access available from this agency. However the State Historical Society offers a free Death Certificate Search at http://people.mnhs.org/dci/Search.cfm?bhcp=1. Records are from 1906 to 1996.

Other access: Bulk lists and files of information, if public record, are available on paper and in electronic format. Call Cheri Denardo at 651-201-5970 for details.

Expedited service: Expedited service is available for faxed or mailed searches. Turnaround time- 24-72 hours. Add $20.00 plus $6.00 for use of credit card and $16.00 for overnight delivery.

Marriage Certificates, Divorce Records

Records not maintained by a state level agency.

Marriage and divorce records are found at the county level. The Section of Vital Records has an index and they will direct you to the proper county (Marriage since 1958, Divorce since 1970). Call the Section of Vital Records at 651-201-5970.

Workers' Compensation Records

Labor & Industry Department, Workers Compensation Division - File Review, 443 Lafayette Rd, St Paul, MN 55155; 651-284-5200, Fax- 651-284-5731; 8AM-4:30PM.

www.doli.state.mn.us/workcomp.html

Indexing & Storage: Records available on microfilm or image and paper for 18 years after file closure. New records available for inquiry immediately.

Searching: Must have a signed release from claimant to obtain all files. Include in request- claimant name, SSN or case number, signed release.

Access by: mail, phone, fax, in person.

Fee & Payment: There is no search fee or for a yes/no. Copies are $.65 each. Add 6.5% tax. Fee payee- Department of Labor & Industry. Prepayment required. Personal checks accepted, credit cards are not.

Mail search: Turnaround time- 1 to 2 weeks. SASE not required.

Phone search: phone searching is limited to employees involved within a case. **Fax search:** This office will accept fax search requests.

In person: If you request in person, they provide copies onsite if files available; otherwise will mail requested copies.

Driver Records

Driver & Vehicle Services, Records Section, 445 Minnesota St, #161, St Paul, MN 55101; 651-215-1335; 8AM-4:30PM. www.mndriveinfo.org

Copies of tickets can be requested from the same address. The fee is $4.00 per page, up to 3 tickets per page, $5.00 if certified.

Indexing & Storage: Records available for 5 years minimum for moving violations and suspensions; 10 years for open revocation; retained indefinitely for DWIs for 2 or more convictions. Accidents and up to 10 mph over in a 55 zone on interstate roads are not shown. New records available for inquiry in no more than 15 days.

Searching: A casual requester must provided notarized consent of the driver in order to obtain personal information. However, records without personal information are available. The driver's license number or full name and DOB is required for a search. Surrendered licenses will be purged after one year if clear; after five years if the record has convictions. This data not released- medical information.

Access by: mail, in person, online.

Fee & Payment: The fee is $9.50 per non-certified record or $9.00 if requester is obtaining own record. Add $1.00 for certification. Online fee is $1.25. Fee payee- Department of Public Safety. Prepayment required. Personal checks accepted, credit cards are not.

Mail search: Turnaround time- 1 week or more. SASE not required.

In person: Number of immediate requests processed depends on workload.

Online search: Online access costs $1.25 per record. Online inquiries can be processed either as interactive or as batch files (overnight) 24 hours a day, 7 days a week. Requesters operate from a "bank." Records are accessed by either DL number or full name and DOB. Call Data Services at 651-297-5352 for more information. A free view of a DL status report is found at the home page above. The DL# is needed, no personal information is released.

Other access: Minnesota will sell its entire database of driving record information with monthly updates per DPPA guidelines. Customized request sorts are available. Fees vary by type with programming and computer time and are quite reasonable.

Vehicle Ownership & Registration

Driver & Vehicle Services, Vehicle Record Requests, 445 Minnesota St, #161, St Paul, MN 55101; 651-297-5352; 8AM-4:30PM.

www.dps.state.mn.us/dvs/index.html

The necessary record request forms can be downloaded from the website.

Indexing & Storage: Records available for past 7 years. New records available for inquiry in 5 days.

Searching: The agency adopted the 14 permissible uses of DPPA. Casual requesters can obtain records without personal information. If consent is given, then personal information is released.

Access by: mail, in person, online.

Fee & Payment: The fee is $9.50 ($9.00 if ordering own record) per "display record" (print screen). Add $1.00 per printed page if mailed. Certification is an additional $1.00. Fee payee- Department of Public Safety. Prepayment required. Personal checks accepted, credit cards are not.

Mail search: Turnaround time- 1 week. A SASE is requested.

In person: Turnaround time is immediate for walk-in requesters for up to three requests.

Online search: Online access costs $5.00 per record. There is an additional monthly charge for dial-in access. The system, the same as described for driving record requests, is open 24/7. Search by name, plate, VIN or title number. Lien holder information is included. Users, who must qualify per DPPA, will receive address information. Call Records & Management Information 651-297-5352 for more information. Also, to obtain a renewal status report on a plate go to https://dutchelm.dps.state.mn.us/dvsinfo/mainframepublic.asp. Need the plate number and the last four digits of the VIN.

Accident Reports

Driver & Vehicle Services, Accident Records, 445 Minnesota St, Suite 161, St Paul, MN 55101-5181; 651-215-1335, Fax- 651-282-5512; 8AM-4:30PM.

www.mndriveinfo.org

Indexing & Storage: Records available from 998 to present (records are electronically imaged). New records available for inquiry in 3 weeks from date of accident.

Searching: Police reports may be obtained with the written and signed authorization from the person involved in the accident. Include in request- date of accident, full name, date of birth, driver's license number, license plate number, and signed release. Records are indexed by driver names. A request form is found at www.dps.state.mn.us/dvs/PDFForms/DVSFormFrame.htm.

Access by: mail, fax, in person.

Fee & Payment: The fee is $5.00 per report. Fee payee- Driver and Vehicle Srvs Prepayment required. Personal checks accepted, credit cards are not.

Mail search: Turnaround time- 1 week. A SASE is requested.

Fax search: Fax requests require an account with the agency. Turnaround time 3 days if the request is received after the file has become available.

In person: Walk-in requesters may obtain copies of accident reports with the authorization of the individual(s) involved in the accident. Turnaround time: while you wait (typically, 5 to 10 minutes).

Vessel Ownership & Registration

Department of Natural Resources, License Center, 500 Lafayette Rd, St Paul, MN 55155-4026; 651-296-2316, 877-348-8851, 651-297-1230, Fax-651-297-8851; 8AM-4:30PM.

www.dnr.state.mn.us/licenses/watercraft/index.html

This agency uses the DPPA as its guidelines for data access. Thus only pre-determined permissible users may access record data unless written consent is given.

Indexing & Storage: Records available for the last 15 yrs. Records maintained for watercraft, snowmobiles, off-highway vehicles (all terrain) and off-highway motorcycles. A watercraft must be titled if over 16 ft and 1980 model or newer; registered if over 9 ft. New records available for inquiry in 1 month.

Searching: The agency maintains liens on titled watercraft. Lines on other watercraft and snowmobiles, etc., are filed with the UCCs at the state. Include in request- name and hull number or registration number. Use of the DNR ELS Records Request Form is advised. The is required to complete a search.

Access by: mail, in person.

Fee & Payment: There is no search fee.

Mail search: Turnaround time- 1 week.

In person: Turnaround time is usually immediate.

Other access: Bulk requests are offered in several media types to approved entities. Call 651-296-0930 for more information.

Legislation Records

Minnesota Legislature, 211 State Capitol, House-Room 211, Senate-Room 231, St Paul, MN 55155; 651-296-0504 (Senate Information), 651-296-2146 (House Information), 651-296-8338 (Reference), Fax- 651-296-1563; 8AM-5PM.

www.leg.state.mn.us

When sessions, the hours are extended to 5:30 PM. Sessions start in January in odd numbered years and in February in even numbered years.

Indexing & Storage: Records available for current session only. For Senate bill status & general legis. questions, call 651-296-0504; Senate bill copies, 651-296-2343. For historical records, call the Legislative Reference Library at 651-296-3398, a fee is involved.

Searching: Include in request- bill number.

Access by: mail, phone, in person, online.

Fee & Payment: There is no search fee. There is no expedited service; however, they will help requesters who have Federal Express accounts.

Mail search: Turnaround time- variable. SASE not required.

Phone search: No fee for telephone request.

In person: No fee for request.

Online search: Information available through the Internet site includes full text of bills, status, previous 8 years of bills, a bill tracking service, and the state statutes.

Voter Registration

Access to Records is Restricted.

Secretary of State-Election Division, 180 State Office Bldg, 100 Rev. Dr Martin L King Jr. Blvd, St Paul, MN 55155; 651-215-1440, 877-600-8683, Fax- 651-296-9073; 8AM-4:30PM.

www.sos.state.mn.us/home/index.asp?page=4

Records are sold by the state only for political, election, or law enforcement purposes and only to MN registered voters. Some counties will honor record requests, but only for the same purposes.

GED Certificates

Department of Education, GED Testing, 1500 Highway 36 West, Roseville, MN 55113-4266; 651-582-8446, 651-582-8445 (Instructions), Fax-651-582-8458; 8AM-4:30PM.

http://education.state.mn.us/mde/index.html

At the web page, under Learning Support click on "adult education."

Indexing & Storage: Records available from 1970 and permanently maintained (not destroyed over time). New records available for inquiry in 3 weeks.

Searching: Include in request- name when test taken, DOB, last four digits of SSN, and signed release. The year of the test is helpful. A signed release is needed for a either a copy of a transcript or a verification.

Access by: mail, fax.

Fee & Payment: There is no fee.

Mail search: Turnaround time- 1 to 2 days. SASE not required.

Fax search: Same criteria as mail searching.

Hunting & Fishing License Information

MN Dept of Natural Resources, License Center, 500 Lafayette Rd, St Paul, MN 55155-4026; 651-297-1230, 888-646-6367, Fax- 651-297-8851; 8AM-4:30PM.

www.dnr.state.mn.us/index.html

Records are open, but access to address and other personal information is restricted.

Searching: The agency populates and updates licensing data with content from the MN DMV. This content generally includes the DL# and address information. Therefore, the data is subject to DPPA. Include in request- DNR ELS Records Request form (call to obtain, not available from web). If requester does not have a permissible use per DPPA, then written consent of the subject is required.

Access by: mail, phone, in person.

Fee & Payment: Fees are only charged for bulk purchase.

Mail search: Hard copies cannot be mailed without use of form or consent. Use the request form mentioned above.

Phone search: Limited verification information is only given.

In person: Limited data may be viewed.

Minnesota State Licensing Agencies

For details about the agency responsible for licensing/certifying/registering an item below or in the Agency Quick Finder section, match an item's number with the number of the agency in the *Licensing Agency Information* section.

Minnesota Licenses Searchable Online

Abstractor/Abstractor Company #25
... www.state.mn.us/mn/externalDocs/Commerce/Abstractors_Enforcement_Actions_040208010433_AbstractorsActions.htm
Acupuncturist #9 ... www.docboard.org/mn/df/mndf.htm
Adjuster #23 ... www.commerce.state.mn.us/LicenseLookupMain.html
Alcohol/Drug Counselor #29 ... www.health.state.mn.us/divs/hpsc/hop/adc/index.html
Ambulance Svc/Personnel #28 ... www.emsrb.state.mn.us/cert.asp?p=s
Appraiser #23 ... www.commerce.state.mn.us/LicenseLookupMain.html
Architect #37 ... www.aelslagid.state.mn.us/roster.html
Athletic Trainer #9 ... www.docboard.org/mn/df/mndf.htm
Attorney #40 ... www.mncourts.gov/mars/default.aspx
Barber #2 ... https://www.hlb.state.mn.us/mnbce/glsuiteweb/clients/mnboc/public/License_Verifications.aspx
Barber Instructor/School #2 ... https://www.hlb.state.mn.us/mnbce/glsuiteweb/clients/mnboc/public/License_Verifications.aspx
Bingo Operation #35 ... www.gcb.state.mn.us/
Boiler Inspector #36 ... www.doli.state.mn.us/stateinspectors.html
Bondsman (Insurance) #23 ... www.commerce.state.mn.us/LicenseLookupMain.html
Building Contractor, Residen'l #23 ... www.commerce.state.mn.us/LicenseLookupMain.html
Campground Membership Agent #23 ... www.commerce.state.mn.us/LicenseLookupMain.html
Chiropractor #4 ... https://www.hlb.state.mn.us/chi/publicaccess/search.asp
Collection Agency #23 ... www.commerce.state.mn.us/LicenseLookupMain.html
Consumer Credit/Payday Lender #24 ... www.commerce.state.mn.us/LicenseLookupMain.html
Contract'r/Remodeler, Resid'l #23 ... www.commerce.state.mn.us/LicenseLookupMain.html
Controlled Substance #13 ... https://www.hlb.state.mn.us/mnbop/glsuiteweb/homeframe.aspx
Cosmelotogist #2 ... https://www.hlb.state.mn.us/mnbce/glsuiteweb/clients/mnboc/public/License_Verifications.aspx
Cosmetologist #23 ... www.commerce.state.mn.us/LicenseLookupMain.html
Cosmetology Instr'r/School #2 ... https://www.hlb.state.mn.us/mnbce/glsuiteweb/clients/mnboc/public/License_Verifications.aspx
Cosmetology School/Shop #23 ... www.commerce.state.mn.us/LicenseLookupMain.html
CPA #39 ... www.boa.state.mn.us/Licensees/LicenseeList.aspx
CPA Firm #39 ... www.boa.state.mn.us/Licensees/FirmList.aspx
Credit Union #24 ... www.commerce.state.mn.us/LicenseLookupMain.html
Crematory #27 ... www.health.state.mn.us/divs/hpsc/mortsci/mortscielect.cfm
Currency Exchange #23 ... www.commerce.state.mn.us/LicenseLookupMain.html
Debt Collector #23 ... www.commerce.state.mn.us/LicenseLookupMain.html
Debt Prorate Company #24 ... www.commerce.state.mn.us/LicenseLookupMain.html
Dental Assistant #5 ... https://www.hlb.state.mn.us/mnbod/glsuiteweb/homeframe.aspx
Dental Hygienist #5 ... https://www.hlb.state.mn.us/mnbod/glsuiteweb/homeframe.aspx
Dentist #5 ... https://www.hlb.state.mn.us/mnbod/glsuiteweb/homeframe.aspx
Dietitian #33 ... www.dieteticsnutritionboard.state.mn.us/Default.aspx?tabid=1001
Drug Mfg./Whlse./Dist. #13 ... https://www.hlb.state.mn.us/mnbop/glsuiteweb/homeframe.aspx
Electrical Contractor #6 ... www.electricity.state.mn.us/contractor_directory.html
Electrical Inspector #6 ... www.electricity.state.mn.us/pdf/ElectricalInspectorDirectory.pdf
Electric Technology System Contractor #6 www.electricity.state.mn.us/contractor_directory.html
Elevator Contractor #6 ... www.electricity.state.mn.us/pdf/LicensedElevatorContractors.pdf
Emergency Medical Technician #28 ... www.emsrb.state.mn.us/cert.asp?p=s
EMS Examiner #28 ... www.emsrb.state.mn.us/examiner.asp?p=s
Engineer #37 ... www.aelslagid.state.mn.us/roster.html
Esthetician #23 ... www.commerce.state.mn.us/LicenseLookupMain.html
Funeral Director #27 ... www.health.state.mn.us/divs/hpsc/mortsci/mortscielect.cfm
Funeral Establishment #27 ... www.health.state.mn.us/divs/hpsc/mortsci/mortscielect.cfm
Gambling Equipment Distributor #35 ... www.gcb.state.mn.us/
Gambling Equipment Manufacturer #35 ... www.gcb.state.mn.us/
Gambling, Lawful Organization #35 ... www.gcb.state.mn.us/
Geologist #37 ... www.aelslagid.state.mn.us/roster.html
Grain Licensing #21 ... http://www2.mda.state.mn.us/webapp/lis/default.jsp
High Pressure Inspector #36 ... www.doli.state.mn.us/stateinspectors.html
Insurance Agency #23 ... www.commerce.state.mn.us/LicenseLookupMain.html
Insurance Agent/Seller #23 ... www.commerce.state.mn.us/LicenseLookupMain.html

Interior Designer #37 .... www.aelslagid.state.mn.us/roster.html
Landscape Architect #37 .... www.aelslagid.state.mn.us/roster.html
Lawyer, Discipline #40 .... www.mncourts.gov/lprb/SearchLawyer.aspx
Lender, Small #24 .... www.commerce.state.mn.us/LicenseLookupMain.html
Liquor On-sale Retail #34 .... www.dps.state.mn.us/age/?118,23
Liquor Store, On-sale Retail/Mun'ip'l #34 . www.dps.state.mn.us/age/?118,23
Livestock Dealer/Market/Weigher #21 ...... http://www2.mda.state.mn.us/webapp/lis/default.jsp
Loan Company #24 .... www.commerce.state.mn.us/LicenseLookupMain.html
Lobbyist #19 .... www.cfboard.state.mn.us/lob_lists.html
Lottery Retailer #42 .... www.lottery.state.mn.us/retailer/lookup.html
Managing General Agent #23 .... www.commerce.state.mn.us/LicenseLookupMain.html
Manicurist #23 .... www.commerce.state.mn.us/LicenseLookupMain.html
Medical Doctor #9 .... www.docboard.org/mn/df/mndf.htm
Medical Gas Mfg./Whlse./Dist. #13 .... https://www.hlb.state.mn.us/mnbop/glsuiteweb/homeframe.aspx
Medical Professional Firm #9 .... www.docboard.org/mn/df/mndf.htm
Midwife #9 .... www.docboard.org/mn/df/mndf.htm
Mortgage Originator/Servicer, Resid'l #24 www.doli.state.mn.us/license_search.html?action=lookupForm
Mortician #27 .... www.health.state.mn.us/divs/hpsc/mortsci/mortsciselect.cfm
Motor Vehicle Financer #24 .... www.commerce.state.mn.us/LicenseLookupMain.html
Notary Public #23 .... www.commerce.state.mn.us/LicenseLookupMain.html
Nurse-LPN #10 .... https://www.hlb.state.mn.us/mbn/Portal/DesktopDefault.aspx?tabindex=0&tabid=41
Nurse-RN #10 .... https://www.hlb.state.mn.us/mbn/Portal/DesktopDefault.aspx?tabindex=0&tabid=41
Nursing Home Administrator #7 .... www.benha.state.mn.us/beta/Default.aspx?tabid=782
Nutritionist #33 .... www.dieteticsnutritionboard.state.mn.us/Default.aspx?tabid=1001
Occupational Therapist #29 .... www.health.state.mn.us/divs/hpsc/hop/otp/licprac.html
Optometrist #11 .... www.optometryboard.state.mn.us/Default.aspx?tabid=799
Pesticide Applicator Company #22 .... www.mda.state.mn.us/licensing/online/default.htm
Pesticide Applicator, Private #22 .... www.mda.state.mn.us/licensing/online/default.htm
Pharmaceutical Technician #13 .... https://www.hlb.state.mn.us/mnbop/glsuiteweb/homeframe.aspx
Pharmacist #13 .... https://www.hlb.state.mn.us/mnbop/glsuiteweb/homeframe.aspx
Pharmacy #13 .... https://www.hlb.state.mn.us/mnbop/glsuiteweb/homeframe.aspx
Physician Assistant #9 .... www.docboard.org/mn/df/mndf.htm
Podiatrist #14 .... https://www.hlb.state.mn.us/sblmonline/public/default.aspx
Political Action Committee #19 .... www.cfboard.state.mn.us/campfin/pcfatoz.html
Political Candidate #19 .... www.cfboard.state.mn.us/cand_lists.html
Preceptor #13 .... https://www.hlb.state.mn.us/mnbop/glsuiteweb/homeframe.aspx
Real Estate Agent/Broker/Dealer #23 .... www.commerce.state.mn.us/LicenseLookupMain.html
Re-Insurance Intermediary #23 .... www.commerce.state.mn.us/LicenseLookupMain.html
Respiratory Care Practitioner #9 .... www.docboard.org/mn/df/mndf.htm
Securities Seller/Inves't Advisor #23 .... www.commerce.state.mn.us/LicenseLookupMain.html
Social Worker #16 .... https://www.hlb.state.mn.us/BOSW/Online/DesktopModules/ServiceForm.aspx?svid=21&mid=164
Soil Scientist #37 .... www.aelslagid.state.mn.us/roster.html
Surgeon #9 .... www.docboard.org/mn/df/mndf.htm
Surveyor, Land #37 .... www.aelslagid.state.mn.us/roster.html
Teacher #17
... http://education.state.mn.us/mde/Teacher_Support/Educator_Licensing/View_an_Individual_Educators_License/index.html
Telemedicine #9 .... www.docboard.org/mn/df/mndf.htm
Thrift/Industrial Loan Company #24 .... www.commerce.state.mn.us/LicenseLookupMain.html
Undergr'nd Storage Tank Contr./Supr. #43 www.pca.state.mn.us/cleanup/ust.html#certification
Veterinarian #18 .... www.vetmed.state.mn.us/Default.aspx?tabid=801

Minnesota Licensing Quick Finder

Abstractor/Abstractor Company #25
.... 800-657-3978, 651-296-6319
Acupuncturist #9 612-617-2130
Adjuster #23 651-296-6319
Adoption Assistance Program #30 651-431-4656
Alarm/Com. System Contr./Installer #6 651-284-5064
Alcohol/Drug Counselor #29 651-282-5619
Alcohol/Drug Counselor #30 651-201-2758
All-Terrain Vehicle/ATV #32 651-296-2316
Ambulance Svc/Personnel #28 612-627-6000
Appraiser #23 651-296-6319
Architect #37 651-296-2388
Asbestos Contractor/Worker #26 651-215-0900
Assessor, Accredited/Certified #1 651-556-6086

Assessor/Assessor Specialist #1 651-556-6086
Athletic Trainer #9 612-617-2130
Attorney #40 651-296-2254
Attorney Specialist Bar Member #31 651-297-1857
Background Study & Investg'n #30 651-296-3971
Bank #24 651-297-3779
Barber #2 651-201-2742
Barber Instructor/School #2 651-201-2742
Bingo Operation #35 651-639-4000
Boat & Canoe Registration #32 651-296-2316
Boat Title #32 651-296-2316
Boats for Hire #36 651-284-5080
Boiler Inspector #36 651-284-5188
Bondsman (Insurance) #23 651-296-6319

Building Contractor, Residen'l #23 651-296-6319
Campground Membership Agent #23 .. 651-296-6319
Chemical & Mental Health #30 651-431-2460
Child Care Facility #30 651-296-3971
Children's Service #30 651-297-3840
Chiropractor #4 651-201-2850
Collection Agency #23 651-296-6319
Consumer Credit/Payday Lender #24 .. 651-296-2297
Contract'r/Remodeler, Resid'l #23 651-296-6319
Controlled Substance #13 612-617-2201
Cosmelotogist #2 651-201-2742
Cosmetologist #23 651-296-6319
Cosmetology Instr'r/School #2 651-201-2742
Cosmetology School/Shop #23 651-296-6319

County Fair #41 952-496-7950
CPA #39 651-296-7938
CPA Firm #39 651-296-7938
Credit Union #24 651-296-2297
Crematory #27 651-282-3829
Currency Exchange #23 651-296-6319
Debt Collector #23 651-296-6319
Debt Prorate Company #24 651-296-2297
Dental Assistant #5...... 888-240-4762, 612-617-2250
Dental Hygienist #5...... 888-240-4762, 612-617-2250
Dentist #5.................. 888-240-4762, 612-617-2250
Developmental Disability License #30... 651-582-1998
Dietitian #33 612-699-3438
Disability Services Division #30 651-431-2400
Drug Mfg./Whlse./Dist. #13 612-617-2201
Electrical Contractor #6 651-642-0800
Electrical Inspector #6 651-284-5064
Electrical Technology System Contractor #6 651-284-5064
Electrician #6 651-284-5064
Elevator Contractor #6 651-284-5064
Emergency Medical Technician #28 612-627-6000
EMS Examiner #28 612-627-6000
Engineer #37 651-296-2388
Esthetician #23 651-296-6319
Food Manager #26 651-215-0870
Foster Care Program #30 651-296-3971
Funeral Director #27 651-282-3829
Funeral Establishment #27 651-282-3829
Gambling Equipment Distributor #35 ... 651-639-4000
Gambling Equipment Manufact'r #35 651-639-4000
Gambling, Lawful Organization #35 651-639-4000
Geologist #37 651-296-2388
Grain Licensing #21 651-201-6176
Hearing Aid Dispenser #29 651-282-5620
High Pressure Inspector #36 651-284-5088
Insurance Agency #23 651-296-6319
Insurance Agent/Seller #23 651-296-6319
Interior Designer #37 651-296-2388
Landscape Architect #37 651-296-2388
Lawyer, Discipline #40 651-296-2254
Lender, Small #24 651-296-2297
Liquor and Wine Offsale Retail #34...... 651-201-7510
Liquor Consumption & Display Info #34651-201-7512
Liquor On-sale Retail #34 651-201-7504
Liquor Store, On-sale Retail/Municipal #34 651-201-7504
Liquor Whlse/Mfg./Label'r/Importer #34 651-201-7506
Livestock Dealer/Market/Weigher #21 . 651-201-6509
Loan Company #24 651-296-2297
Lobbyist #19 651-296-5615
Lottery Retailer #42 651-635-8119
Managing General Agent #23 651-296-6319
Manicurist #23 800-657-3978
Manufactured Home Installer #38 651-284-5849
Manufactured Home Mfg./Dealer #38 .. 651-284-5849
Manufactured Structures Section #38 .. 651-284-5849
Marriage & Family Therapist #8 612-617-2220
Medical Doctor #9 612-617-2130
Medical Gas Mfg./Whlse./Dist. #13 612-617-2201
Medical Professional Firm #9 612-617-2130
Mental Health Practitioner, Unlicensed #29 651-282-5621
Mental Health, Chem'l Depend'cy Prof #30 651-582-1990
Midwife #9 612-617-2130
Mortgage Originator/Servicer, Resid'l #24 651-282-9855
Mortician #27 651-282-3829
Motor Vehicle Financer #24 651-296-2297
Notary Public #23 651-296-6319
Nurse-LPN #10 612-617-2270
Nurse-RN #10 612-617-2270
Nursing Home Administrator #7 612-617-2117
Nutritionist #33 612-642-1825
Occupational Therapist #29 651-282-5624
Occupational Therapy Assistant #29 ... 651-282-5624
Off-Highway Motorcycle #32 651-296-2316
Off-Road Vehicle #32 651-296-2316
Optometrist #11 612-617-2173
Pesticide Applicator Company #22 651-201-6548
Pesticide Applicator, Private #22 651-201-6548
Pharmaceutical Technician #13 612-617-2201
Pharmacist #13 612-617-2201
Pharmacy #13 612-617-2201
Physician Assistant #9 612-617-2130
Plumber #26 651-215-0836
Podiatrist #14 612-617-2200
Police/Peace Officer #12 651-643-3060
Political Action Committee #19 651-296-5615
Political Candidate #19 651-296-5615
Preceptor #13 612-617-2201
Private Detective #44 651-793-2666
Private Investigator #44 651-793-2666
Psychological Practitioner #15 651-617-2230
Psychologist #15 651-617-2230
Racetrack/Card Club Operator #41 952-496-7950
Racing (Racing ClassA -Track Owner) #41 952-496-7950
Racing/Card Club Occupation #41 952-496-7950
Real Estate Agent/Broker/Dealer #23 .. 651-296-6319
Re-Insurance Intermediary #23 651-296-6319
Respiratory Care Practitioner #9 612-617-2130
Sanitarian #26 651-215-0870
Securities Salesperson/Inves't Advisor #23 651-296-2283
Security Agent/Protective Agent #44 ... 651-793-2666
Snowmobile Registration #32 651-296-2316
Social Worker #16 612-617-2100
Soil Scientist #37 651-296-2388
Speech-Language Audiologist #29 651-282-5629
Speech-Language Pathologist #29 651-282-5629
Surgeon #9 612-617-2130
Surveyor, Land #37 651-296-2388
Teacher #17 651-582-8691
Telemedicine #9 612-617-2130
Thrift/Industrial Loan Company #24 651-296-2297
Undergr'nd Storage Tank Contr./Supvr. #43 651-297-8616
Veterinarian #18 612-617-2170
Waste Disposal Facility Inspector #43 . 651-296-6300
Waste Water Disposal Facility Oper't'r #43 651-296-6300
Water Conditioning Installer/Contractor #26 651-215-0836
Water Supply Operator #26 651-215-0770
Water Well Contractor #26 651-215-0811
Watercraft #32 651-296-2316
X-ray Operator #20 651-201-4545

Minnesota Licensing Agency Information

#1 Board of Assessors, 600 N Robert St, St Paul, MN 55101; 651-556-6086, Fax- 651-556-3128. Hours- 8AM-4:30PM. www.taxes.state.mn.us/taxes/property_tax_administrators/other_supporting_content/assess.shtml

#2 Board of Barber & Cosmelotogist Examiners, 2829 University Ave SE, #710, Minneapolis, MN 55414; 651-201-2742, Fax- 651-617-2601. www.bceboard.state.mn.us/

#4 Board of Chiropractic Examiners, 2829 University Ave SE, #300, Minneapolis, MN 55414-3220; 651-201-2850, Fax- 651-201-2852. Hours- 8AM-4:30PM. www.mn-chiroboard.state.mn.us Search data at- https://www.hlb.state.mn.us/chi/publicaccess/search.asp

#5 Board of Dentistry, 2829 University Ave SE, #450, Minneapolis, MN 55414; 888-240-4762, 612-617-2250, Fax- 612-617-2260. www.dentalboard.state.mn.us Search data at- https://www.hlb.state.mn.us/mnbod/glsuiteweb/homeframe.aspx

#6 Electrical Licensing and Inspection, 443 Lafayette Rd N, St Paul, MN 55155-4342; 651-284-5064, Fax- 651-284-5743. www.electricity.state.mn.us For Disciplinary actions, revocations, suspensions go to www.electricity.state.mn.us/disciplinary_actions.html.

#7 Board of Examiners for Nursing Home Administrators, 2829 University Ave SE, #440, Minneapolis, MN 55414; 612-201-2730. www.benha.state.mn.us Search data at- www.benha.state.mn.us/beta/Default.aspx?tabid=782

#8 Board of Marriage & Family Therapy, 2829 University Ave SE, #330, Minneapolis, MN 55414-3222; 612-617-2220, Fax- 612-617-2221. www.bmft.state.mn.us $10.00 fee for each verification request.

#9 Board of Medical Practice, 2829 University Ave SE, #500, Minneapolis, MN 55414-3246; 612-617-2130, Fax- 612-617-2166. 8AM-4:30PM. www.state.mn.us/portal/mn/jsp/home.do?agency=BMP Search data at- www.docboard.org/mn/df/mndf.htm

#10 Board of Nursing, 2829 University Ave SE, #200, Minneapolis, MN 55414; 612-617-2270, Fax- 612-617-2190. Hours- 8AM-4:30PM. www.state.mn.us/portal/mn/jsp/home.do?agency=NursingBoard Search data at- https://www.hlb.state.mn.us/mbn/Portal/DesktopDefault.aspx?tabindex=0&tabid=41

#11 Board of Optometry, 2829 University Av SE, #550, Minneapolis, MN 55414; 651-201-2762, Fax- 651-201-2763. www.optometryboard.state.mn.us Search data at- www.optometryboard.state.mn.us/Default.aspx?tabid=799

#12 Board of Peace Officers Standards & Training, 1600 University Ave, #200, St Paul, MN 55104-3825; 651-643-3060, Fax- 651-643-3072. Hours- 8AM-4:30PM. www.post.state.mn.us

#13 Board of Pharmacy, 2829 University Ave SE, #530, Minneapolis, MN 55414-3251; 651-201-2825, Fax- 651-201-2837. Hours- 8AM-4:30PM. www.phcybrd.state.mn.us Search data at- https://www.hlb.state.mn.us/mnbop/glsuiteweb/homeframe.aspx

#14 Board of Podiatric Medicine, 2829 University Ave SE, #430, Minneapolis, MN 55414; 612-617-2200, Fax- 612-617-2698. www.podiatry.state.mn.us Search data at- https://www.hlb.state.mn.us/sblmonline/public/default.aspx

#15 Board of Psychology, 2829 University Ave SE, #320, Minneapolis, MN 55414-3237; 612-612-2230, Fax- 612-617-2240. www.psychologyboard.state.mn.us Written requests only. There is a $20 per name verification fee. For copy of the request form go to www.psychologyboard.state.mn.us/licforms.asp?docid=36.

#16 Board of Social Work, 2829 University Ave SE, #340, Minneapolis, MN 55414-3239; 612-617-2100, Fax- 612-617-2103. www.socialwork.state.mn.us Search data at- https://www.hlb.state.mn.us/BOSW/Online/DesktopModules/ServiceForm.aspx?svid=21&mid=164

#17 Licensing Unit, Department of Education, Board of Teaching, 1500 Highway 36 W, Roseville, MN 55113-4266; 651-582-8691, Fax- 651-582-8809. http://education.state.mn.us/mde/Teacher_Support/Educator_Licensing/index.html Search data at- http://education.state.mn.us/mde/Teacher_Support/Educator_Licensing/View_an_Individual_Educators_License/index.html

#18 Board of Veterinary Medicine, 2829 University Ave Sem #540, Minneapolis, MN 55414; 651-201-2844, Fax- 651-201-2842. www.vetmed.state.mn.us Search data at- www.vetmed.state.mn.us/Default.aspx?tabid=801

#19 Campaign Finance Board, 658 Cedar St, 190 Centennial Office Bldg, St Paul, MN 55155; 651-296-5148, Fax- 651-296-1722. Hours- 8AM-4:30PM. www.cfboard.state.mn.us

#20 Department of Health, Radiation Control, PO Box 64975 (625 Robert St N), St Paul, MN 55164-0975; 651-201-4545, Fax- 651-201-4606. www.health.state.mn.us/divs/eh/radiation/

#21 Department of Agriculture, Livestock Weighing & Licensing, 625 Robert St N, St Paul, MN 55155-2538; 651-201-6000. www.mda.state.mn.us Search data at- http://www2.mda.state.mn.us/webapp/lis/default.jsp

#22 Department of Agriculture, Pesticide Registration, 90 W Plato Blvd, St Paul, MN 55107; 651-201-6548. www.mda.state.mn.us Search data at- www.mda.state.mn.us/licensing/online/default.htm

#23 Department of Commerce, Licenses, Registration, Certification Division, 85 7th Place E, #500, St Paul, MN 55101-2198; 800-657-3978, Fax- 651-284-4107. Hours- 8AM-4:15pm. www.state.mn.us/portal/mn/jsp/home.do?agency=Commerce Search data at- www.commerce.state.mn.us/LicenseLookupMain.html For securities registration requests, email securities.commerce@state.mn.us.

#24 Department of Commerce, Division of Financial Examinations, 85 7th Place E, #500, St Paul, MN 55101; 651-296-4026, Fax- 651-284-4107. www.state.mn.us/portal/mn/jsp/home.do?agency=Commerce Search data at- www.doli.state.mn.us/license_search.html?action=lookupForm

#25 Department of Commerce, Licensing Unit for Abstractors, 85 7th Place E, #600, St Paul, MN 55101-2198; 800-657-3978, Fax- 651-284-4107. www.state.mn.us/portal/mn/jsp/home.do?agency=Commerce Search data at- www.state.mn.us/mn/externalDocs/Commerce/Abstractors_Enforcement_Actions_040208010433_AbstractorsActions.htm

#26 Department of Health, Environmental Health Division, 121 E 7th Pl, #230, St Paul, MN 55164-0975; 651-215-0700, Fax- 651-215-0979. www.health.state.mn.us/divs/eh/

#27 Department of Health, Mortuary Science Section, PO Box 64882 (85 E 7th Pl, #300), St Paul, MN 55164-0882; 651-282-3829, Fax- 651-282-3839. www.health.state.mn.us/divs/hpsc/mortsci/mortsci.htm Search data at- www.health.state.mn.us/divs/hpsc/mortsci/finda.htm

#28 Emergency Medical Services, Regulatory Board, 2829 University Ave SE #310, Minneapolis, MN 55414-3222; 651-201-2800, Fax- 651-201-2812. www.emsrb.state.mn.us Search data at- www.emsrb.state.mn.us

#29 Health Occupation Programs, Health Policy & Systems Compliance, PO Box 64882, St Paul, MN 55164-0882; 651-201-3730, Fax- 651-282-5628. www.health.state.mn.us/divs/hpsc/hop/ Online searching is under construction at website.

#30 Department of Human Services, 444 Lafayette Rd, St Paul, MN 55155; 651-431-2000, Fax- 651-297-1490. www.dhs.state.mn.us

#31 State Board of Law Examiners, Board of Legal Certification, 180 E 5th St, #950, St Paul, MN 55101; 651-297-1857, Fax- 651-296-5866. www.blc.state.mn.us/Specialty_Fields/specialty_fields.html The web search features only Bar Association members.

#32 Department of Natural Resources, License Bureau, 500 Lafayette Rd, St Paul, MN 55155-4026; 651-296-2316, Fax- 651-297-8851. Hours- 8AM-4:30PM. www.dnr.state.mn.us/rlp/index.html

#33 Board of Dietetics & Nutrition Practice, 2829 University Ave SE, #555, Minneapolis, MN 55414-3250; 651-201-2764, Fax- 651-201-2763. www.dieteticsnutritionboard.state.mn.us Search data at- www.dieteticsnutritionboard.state.mn.us/Default.aspx?tabid=1001

#34 Department of Public Safety, Alcohol & Gambling Enforcement, 444 Cedar St, #133, St Paul, MN 55101-5133; 651-201-7507, Fax- 651-297-5259. www.dps.state.mn.us/alcgamb/alcenf/alcenf.html Search data at- www.dps.state.mn.us/age/?118,23 Also, search the liquor license database at www.dps.state.mn.us/alcgamb/New_Folder/search1.asp.

#35 Gambling Control Board, 1711 W County Rd B, #300B, Roseville, MN 55113; 651-639-4000. Hours- 8AM-4:30PM. www.gcb.state.mn.us Search data at- www.gcb.state.mn.us/

#36 Department of Labor & Industry, Code Administration & Inspection Services, 443 Lafayette Rd, St Paul, MN 55155-4304; 651-284-5080, Fax- 651-284-5737. www.doli.state.mn.us/code.html Search data at- http://workplace.doli.state.mn.us/codesearch/

#37 Board of AELSLAGID, Licensing Boards, 85 E 7th Pl, #160, St Paul, MN 55101; 651-296-2388, Fax- 651-297-5310. Hours- 8AM-04:30PM. www.aelslagid.state.mn.us Search data at- www.aelslagid.state.mn.us/roster.html

#38 Building Codes & Standards Division, Manufactured Structures Section, 443 Lafayette Road N, St Paul, MN 55155; 651-284-5068, Fax- 651-284-5749. www.doli.state.mn.us/bc_manufactured.html

#39 Board of Accountancy, 85 E 7th Pl, #125, St Paul, MN 55101-2143; 651-296-7938, Fax- 651-282-2644. Hours- 8AM-4:30PM. www.boa.state.mn.us Search data at- www.boa.state.mn.us/Licensees/LicenseeList.aspx

#40 Supreme Court, Attorney Registration, 25 Rev. Martin Luther King Jr. Blvd. #305, St Paul, MN 55155; 651-296-2254, Fax- 651-297-4149. Hours- 8AM-4:30PM. www.mncourts.gov/?page=302 Search data at- www.mncourts.gov/mars/default.aspx Lists also available to download free at the search page.

#41 Racing Commission, PO Box 630 (1100 Canterbury Rd), Shakopee, MN 55379; 952-496-7950, Fax- 952-496-7954. www.mnrace.commission.state.mn.us

#42 State Lottery, 2645 Long Lake Rd, Roseville, MN 55113; 651-635-8273, Fax- 651-297-7498. www.lottery.state.mn.us Search data at- www.lottery.state.mn.us/retailer/lookup.html Search online by city.

#43 Pollution Control Agency, 520 Lafayette Rd, St Paul, MN 55155-4194; 651-296-6300, Fax-651-297-8676. www.pca.state.mn.us

#44 Private Detective & Protective Agent Services Board, 1430 E Maryland Ave E, St Paul, MN 55106; 651-793-2666, Fax- 651-793-7065. www.dps.state.mn.us/pdb/

Minnesota Federal Courts

The following list indicates the district and division name for each county in the state. If the bankruptcy court location is different from the district court, then the location of the bankruptcy court appears in parentheses.

County/Court Cross Reference

County	Court	County	Court
Aitkin	Duluth	Martin	Minneapolis (St Paul)
Anoka	Minneapolis	McLeod	Minneapolis
Becker	Minneapolis (Fergus Falls)	Meeker	Minneapolis
Beltrami	Minneapolis (Fergus Falls)	Mille Lacs	Duluth
Benton	Duluth	Morrison	Duluth
Big Stone	Minneapolis (Fergus Falls)	Mower	Minneapolis (St Paul)
Blue Earth	Minneapolis (St Paul)	Murray	Minneapolis (St Paul)
Brown	Minneapolis (St Paul)	Nicollet	Minneapolis (St Paul)
Carlton	Duluth	Nobles	Minneapolis (St Paul)
Carver	Minneapolis	Norman	Minneapolis (Fergus Falls)
Cass	Duluth	Olmsted	Minneapolis (St Paul)
Chippewa	Minneapolis	Otter Tail	Minneapolis (Fergus Falls)
Chisago	Minneapolis (St Paul)	Pennington	Minneapolis (Fergus Falls)
Clay	Minneapolis (Fergus Falls)	Pine	Duluth
Clearwater	Minneapolis (Fergus Falls)	Pipestone	Minneapolis (St Paul)
Cook	Duluth	Polk	Minneapolis (Fergus Falls)
Cottonwood	Minneapolis (St Paul)	Pope	Minneapolis (Fergus Falls)
Crow Wing	Duluth	Ramsey	St Paul
Dakota	Minneapolis (St Paul)	Red Lake	Minneapolis (Fergus Falls)
Dodge	Minneapolis (St Paul)	Redwood	Minneapolis (St Paul)
Douglas	Minneapolis (Fergus Falls)	Renville	Minneapolis
Faribault	Minneapolis (St Paul)	Rice	Minneapolis (St Paul)
Fillmore	Minneapolis (St Paul)	Rock	Minneapolis (St Paul)
Freeborn	Minneapolis (St Paul)	Roseau	Minneapolis (Fergus Falls)
Goodhue	Minneapolis (St Paul)	Scott	Minneapolis (St Paul)
Grant	Minneapolis (Fergus Falls)	Sherburne	Minneapolis
Hennepin	Minneapolis	Sibley	Minneapolis (St Paul)
Houston	Minneapolis (St Paul)	St. Louis	Duluth
Hubbard	Minneapolis (Fergus Falls)	Stearns	Minneapolis (Fergus Falls)
Isanti	Minneapolis	Steele	Minneapolis (St Paul)
Itasca	Duluth	Stevens	Minneapolis (Fergus Falls)
Jackson	Minneapolis (St Paul)	Swift	Minneapolis
Kanabec	Duluth	Todd	Minneapolis (Fergus Falls)
Kandiyohi	Minneapolis	Traverse	Minneapolis (Fergus Falls)
Kittson	Minneapolis (Fergus Falls)	Wabasha	Minneapolis (St Paul)
Koochiching	Duluth	Wadena	Minneapolis (Fergus Falls)
Lac qui Parle	Minneapolis (St Paul)	Waseca	Minneapolis (St Paul)
Lake	Duluth	Washington	Minneapolis (St Paul)
Lake of the Woods	Minneapolis (Fergus Falls)	Watonwan	Minneapolis (St Paul)
Le Sueur	Minneapolis (St Paul)	Wilkin	Minneapolis (Fergus Falls)
Lincoln	Minneapolis (St Paul)	Winona	Minneapolis (St Paul)
Lyon	Minneapolis (St Paul)	Wright	Minneapolis
Mahnomen	Minneapolis (Fergus Falls)	Yellow Medicine	Minneapolis (St Paul)
Marshall	Minneapolis (Fergus Falls)		

Standards for Federal Courts: Fees are standard unless noted in profile. Search fee is $26.00 per item (one party name or case number). Copy fee is $.50 per page. Certification fee is $9.00 per document, double for exemplification, if available. Most courts require prepayment. Mail requests should enclose a SASE unless otherwise noted. Before releasing records, all courts require prepayment, unless noted.

District courts index by defendant and plaintiff and by case number. Bankruptcy courts usually index by debtor and case number. While most courts now have their indexes on computer, many may still maintain index card files as well. Courts will archive closed case files at different times.

There are numerous public access programs available to online subscribers. Search the U.S. Party/Case Index to find party names and case numbers among all courts. Individual case data is provided on PACER. A search of CM/ECF provides copies of cases filed electronically. For details about PACER, the US Party/Case Index, and CM/ECF see the Appendix or go to http://pacer.psc.uscourts.gov or call 800-676-6856.

US District Court District of Minnesota

Duluth Division Court Clerk, Clerk's Office, 417 Federal Bldg, 515 W 1st St, Duluth, MN 55802-1397, 218-529-3500; Fax- 218-529-3505. Hours-8AM-5PM. www.mnd.uscourts.gov

Counties/Note: Aitkin, Becker*, Beltrami*, Benton, Big Stone*, Carlton, Cass, Clay*, Clearwater*, Cook, Crow Wing, Douglas*, Grant*, Hubbard*, Itasca, Kanabec, Kittson*, Koochiching, Lake, Lake of the Woods*, Mahnomen*, Marshall*, Mille Lacs, Morrison, Norman*, Otter Tail,* Pennington*, Pine, Polk*, Pope*, Red Lake*, Roseau*, Stearns*, Stevens*, St. Louis, Todd*, Traverse*, Wadena*, Wilkin*. From 3/1995 to 1998, cases from the counties marked with an asterisk (*) were heard at Duluth. Before and after that period, cases were and are allocated between St. Paul and Minneapolis.

Searches/Indexing: Search request requires name only. Results do not include SSN or DOB. Will not fax back documents. New cases are in the index immediately after filing date. Computer index maintained back to 1990.

Search Access: Only case number and parties involved released via phone. **Mail:** Search usually completed- 24 hours. SASE not required. **Fax:** Fax search requests accepted, prepayment required; use the credit card authorization form at www.mnd.uscourts.gov/FORMS/ecfforms/creditcardform.doc. **In person:** 2 public terminals available. No self-serve copier. **Payment:** Pay by money order, cashier's or personal check. No credit cards accepted. Payee: Clerk, US District Ct.

E-Services: PACER online at http://pacer.mnd.uscourts.gov. PACER records go back to 2/1990. New records online after 1 day. ECF at https://ecf.mnd.uscourts.gov. **Opinions:** www.nysd.uscourts.gov/courtweb/PubMain.htm.

Online Note: Search recent filings at www.mnd.uscourts.gov/ncs/caselist.html.

Minneapolis Division Court Clerk, Court Clerk, Rm 202, 300 S 4th St, Minneapolis, MN 55415, 612-664-5000; Fax- 612-664-5033. Hours-8AM-5PM. www.mnd.uscourts.gov

Counties/Note: Cases are allocated between Minneapolis and St Paul. Cases from the Fergus Falls Branch are located in Minneapolis.

Searches/Indexing: Include SSN or DOB in request; this may help the office make a proper identification. Results do not include SSN or DOB. Will not fax back documents. New cases are in the index immediately after filing. Computer, microfiche and card indexes maintained.

Search Access: Only case number and parties involved released via phone. **Mail:** Search usually completed- 1-2 days. SASE not required. **Fax:** Fax search requests accepted, prepayment required; use the credit card authorization form at www.mnd.uscourts.gov/FORMS/ecfforms/creditcardform.doc. **In person:** 4 public terminals available. No self-serve copier. **Payment:** Pay by Visa/MC/AmEx, money order, cashier's or personal check. Payee: Clerk, US District Court.

E-Svcs: PACER- http://pacer.mnd.uscourts.gov. PACER records go back to 2/1990. New records online after 1 day. ECF at https://ecf.mnd.uscourts.gov. **Opinions:** www.nysd.uscourts.gov/courtweb/PubMain.htm. **Online Note:** Search recent filings at www.mnd.uscourts.gov/ncs/caselist.html.

St Paul Division Court Clerk, 100 Federal Bldg, 316 N Robert St, St Paul, MN 55101, 651-848-1100; Fax- 651-848-1109. Hours-8AM-5PM. www.mnd.uscourts.gov

Counties/Note: All counties not covered by the Duluth Division. Cases are allocated between Minneapolis and St Paul. See listing for Minneapolis District Ct.

Searches/Indexing: Include SSN or DOB in request; this may help the office make a proper identification. Results do not include SSN or DOB. Will not fax back documents. New cases are in the index immediately after filing. Computer, microfiche and card indexes maintained.

Search Access: Only case number and parties involved released via phone. **Mail:** Search usually completed- 24 hours. SASE not required. **Fax:** Fax search requests accepted; prepayment required; use the credit card authorization form at www.mnd.uscourts.gov/FORMS/ecfforms/creditcardform.doc. **In person:** 2 public terminals available. No self-serve copier. **Payment:** Pay by Visa/MC/AmEx, money order, cashier's or personal check. Payee: Clerk, US District Court.

E-Svcs: PACER- http://pacer.mnd.uscourts.gov. PACER records go back to 2/1990. New records online after 1 day. ECF at https://ecf.mnd.uscourts.gov. **Opinions:** www.nysd.uscourts.gov/courtweb/PubMain.htm. **Online Note:** Search recent filings at www.mnd.uscourts.gov/ncs/caselist.html.

US Bankruptcy Court District of Minnesota

Duluth Division Court Clerk, 515 W 1st St, 416 US Courthouse, Duluth, MN 55802, 218-529-3600; Fax- 218-529-3606. Hours-8AM-4:30PM. www.mnb.uscourts.gov

Counties/Note: Aitkin, Benton*, Carlton, Cass, Cook, Crow Wing, Itasca, Kanabec*, Koochiching, Lake, Mille Lacs*, Morrison*, Pine*, St. Louis. A petition commencing Chapter 11 or 12 proceedings may initially be filed in any of the 4 divisions, but may be assigned to another division. (*) Chapter 7 and 13 cases in Benton, Kanabec, Mille Lacs, Morrison and Pine may also be filed in St. Paul.

Searches/Indexing: Search request requires name only. Results do not include SSN or DOB. Will not fax back documents. New cases are in the index 1-2 days after filing date.

Search Access: Only docket info is available by phone. Voice Case Information Service available, call VCIS at 800-959-9002. **Mail:** Search usually completed- 3 days. SASE not required. **In person:** 2 public terminals available.

Payment: Pay by Visa/MC, money order, personal check. Payee: Clerk, US Bankruptcy Court.

E-Services: PACER records go back to 1/1993. New records online after 1 day. ECF at https://ecf.mnb.uscourts.gov. **Opinions Online:** www.mnb.uscourts.gov/Newsite/Judge_Office/indexJudge.html. **Online Note:** Judges calendars at www.w2.mnb.uscourts.gov/cgi-bin/mnb3CalDisplay.pl.

Fergus Falls Division Court Clerk, 118 S Mill St, 204 US Courthouse, Fergus Falls, MN 56537, 218-739-4671. Hours-8AM-5PM. www.mnb.uscourts.gov

Counties/Note: Becker, Beltrami, Big Stone, Clay, Clearwater, Douglas, Grant, Hubbard, Kittson, Lake of the Woods, Mahnomen, Marshall, Norman, Otter Tail, Pennington, Polk, Pope, Red Lake, Roseau, Stearns, Stevens, Todd, Traverse, Wadena, Wilkin. Stearns County may file in Minneapolis or Fergus Falls. A petition commencing Chapter 11 or 12 proceedings may be filed initially in any of the four divisions, but may then be assigned to another division.

Searches/Indexing: Search request requires name only. Results do not include SSN or DOB. Will not fax back documents. New cases are in the index immediately after filing date.

Search Access: Only docket info is available by phone. Voice Case Information Service available, call VCIS at 800-959-9002. **Mail:** Search usually completed- 1-7 days. SASE not required. **In person:** 1 public terminal available. No self-serve copier.

Payment: Pay by Visa/MC, money order, cashier's or personal check. Payee: Clerk, Bankruptcy Ct.

E-Services: PACER records go back to 1/1993. New records online after 1 day. ECF at https://ecf.mnb.uscourts.gov. **Opinions Online:** www.mnb.uscourts.gov/Newsite/Judge_Office/indexJudge.html. **Online Note:** Judges calendars at www.w2.mnb.uscourts.gov/cgi-bin/mnb3CalDisplay.pl.

Minneapolis Division Court Clerk, 300 S 4th St, 301 US Courthouse, Minneapolis, MN 55415, 612-664-5200; records- 612-664-5209. Hours-8AM-5PM. www.mnb.uscourts.gov

Counties/Note: Anoka, Carver, Chippewa, Hennepin, Isanti, Kandiyohi, McLeod, Meeker, Renville, Sherburne, Swift, Wright. Stearns County cases may be in Minneapolis or Fergus Falls. Initial petitions for Chapter 11 or 12 may be filed initially at any of the 4 divisions, but may then be assigned to a judge in another division.

Searches/Indexing: Search request requires name only. Results do not include SSN or DOB. Will not fax back documents. New cases are in the index immediately after filing date. Computer and microfiche indexes maintained. District-wide searches available back to 1/1992 from Minneapolis; holds closed cases from St. Paul for 4 years but no indexing available at this office.

Search Access: Only docket info is available by phone. Voice Case Information Service available, call VCIS at 800-959-9002. **Mail:** Search usually completed- same day if possible. SASE not required. **In person:** 1 public terminal available. Self-serve copies $.15 each.

Payment: Pay by Visa/MC, money order, cashier's or personal check. Payee: Clerk, Bankruptcy Ct.

E-Services: PACER records go back to 1/1993. New records online after 1 day. ECF at https://ecf.mnb.uscourts.gov. **Opinions Online:** www.mnb.uscourts.gov/Newsite/Judge_Office/indexJudge.html. **Online Note:** Judges calendars at www.w2.mnb.uscourts.gov/cgi-bin/mnb3CalDisplay.pl.

St Paul Division Court Clerk, 200 Warren E Burger Federal Bldg & US Courthouse, 316 N Roberts St, St. Paul, MN 55101, 651-848-1000. Hours-8AM-5PM. www.mnb.uscourts.gov

Counties/Note: St Paul courthouse re-opened in St. Paul, 2008. Blue Earth, Brown, Chisago, Cottonwood, Dakota, Dodge, Faribault, Fillmore, Freeborn, Goodhue, Houston, Jackson, Lac qui Parle, Le Sueur, Lincoln, Lyon, Martin, Mower, Murray, Nicollet, Nobles, Olmsted, Pipestone, Ramsey, Redwood, Rice, Rock, Scott, Sibley, Steele, Wabasha, Waseca, Washington, Watonwan, Winona, Yellow Medicine. Cases from Benton, Kanabec, Mille Lacs, Morrison and Pine may be heard at St Paul or Duluth. A petition commencing Chapter 11 or 12 proceedings may be filed initially with any of the four divisions, but may then be assigned to another division.

Searches/Indexing: Search request requires name only. Results do not include SSN or DOB. Will not fax back documents. New cases are in the index immediately after filing date.

Search Access: Only docket info is available by phone. Voice Case Information Service available, call VCIS at 800-959-9002. **Mail:** Search usually completed- 2-3 days. SASE not required. **In person:** 1 public terminal available. No self-serve copier.

Payment: Pay by Visa/MC, money order, cashier's or personal check. Payee: Clerk, Bankruptcy Ct.

E-Services: PACER records go back to 1/1993. New records online after 1 day. ECF at https://ecf.mnb.uscourts.gov. **Opinions Online:** www.mnb.uscourts.gov/Newsite/Judge_Office/indexJudge.html. **Online Note:** Judges calendars at www.w2.mnb.uscourts.gov/cgi-bin/mnb3CalDisplay.pl.

Minnesota County Courts

Court	Jurisdiction	No. of Courts	How Organized
District Courts*	General	97	10 Districts

* Profiled in this Sourcebook.

Court	CIVIL								
	Tort	Contract	Real Estate	Min. Claim	Max. Claim	Small Claims	Estate	Eviction	Domestic Relations
District Courts*	X	X	X	$0	No Max	$7500	X	X	X

Court	CRIMINAL				
	Felony	Misdemeanor	DWI/DUI	Preliminary Hearing	Juvenile
District Courts*	X	X	X		X

Administration

State Court Adminstrator, 25 Rev. Dr. Martin Luther King Jr. Blvd., St Paul, MN, 55155; Telephone: 651-296-2474, Fax: 651-297-5636. (CST) www.mncourts.gov/default.aspx

Court Structure

There are 97 District Courts (some counties gave divisional courts) comprising 10 judicial districts. The limit for small claims is $7500 unless the case involves a consumer credit transaction then the limit is $4000.

Online Access

Minnesota offers the Trial Court Public Access (MPA) at http://pa.courts.state.mn.us/default.aspx. Search statewide or by county. Records available include criminal, civil, family, and probate. Searches can be performed using a case number or by name. But there are a number of caveats - certain publicly-accessible case records cannot be viewed online. For example, the federal Violence Against Women Act (VAWA) prevents the state from displaying harassment and domestic abuse case records online, but these convictions are available at the courthouse. Comment fields for all case types are not available online but are available at the courthouse. Party street address and name searches on criminal, traffic, and petty misdemeanor pre-conviction case records are not accessible, but are at the courthouse. A criminal/traffic/petty search excludes all Hennepin County and Ramsey County payable citations except: 1) those that result in a court appearance; and 2) Ramsey DNR payable citations. Also, Party street address and name searches on criminal pre-conviction case records are publicly accessible and available at the courthouse, but not online. Online users are not notified when such public data is restricted from online viewing. The public access terminals found at the courthouses do not use this system.

The bottom line is the public access terminals found at courthouses are still the most accurate searching locations. In Judicial Districts (arranged by number and often covering several counties) many court's public access terminals contain court records for that entire district. The online system is supplemental at best.

Appellate and District court calenders are viewable at www.mncourts.gov/default.aspx?page=512. Appellate and Supreme Court opinions are at www.mncourts.gov/default.aspx?page=1650. An approved bail bond agent list search is also free.

Searching Tips, Fees, and Other Guidelines

In general, the search, copy and certification fees each are $5.00. Some courts charge an additional $10.00 plus the copy free. Most Judicial Districts no longer perform criminal record name searches for the public, but may do civil name searches.

An exact name is required to search, e.g., a request for "Robert Smith" will not result in finding "Bob Smith." The requester must request both names and pay two search and copy fees. When a search is permitted by "plaintiff or defendant," most jurisdictions state that a case is indexed by only the first plaintiff or defendant. Second or third party names would not be sufficient information for a search.

Most courts take personal checks. Exceptions are noted. Prepayment of fees are required unless otherwise noted.

Aitkin County

9th Judicial District Court 209 Second St NW, Aitkin, MN 56431; 218-927-7350; fax: 218-927-4535; 8AM-4:30PM. ***Felony, Misdemeanor, Civil, Eviction, Small Claims, Probate.***

www.mncourts.gov/district/9/

Week ahead court calendars available online.

Civil Records: Access: Mail, in person, online. Both court and visitors may perform in person searches. Search fee: $5.00 per name. Required to search: name, years to search. Civil cases indexed by defendant, plaintiff, on computer from 2/90, cards to 1982, index books prior. Mail turnaround time 1 week. Civil PAT goes back to 2/1990. PAT results show name only. Limited search of civil, family and probate records are found at http://pa.courts.state.mn.us/default.aspx. Electronic filings and abuse cases not shown.

Criminal Records: Access: Mail, in person, online. Both court and visitors may perform in person searches. Search fee: $5.00 per name. Required to search: name, years to search, DOB. Criminal records computerized from 2/90, cards to 1982, index books prior. Mail turnaround time 1 week. Criminal PAT goes back to 2/1990.PAT results show name, DOB. Public terminal allows for a statewide search. Limited search of criminal record index at http://pa.courts.state.mn.us/default.aspx. Online results show middle initial, DOB.

General Information: No adoption, juvenile, sex offender or sealed records released. Fee to fax back-$25.00 per doc up to 25 pgs. Court makes copy: $5.00 per doc. Certification fee: $10.00 per doc. Payee: Aitkin District Court. Personal checks accepted; credit cards are not. Mail requests: SASE required.

Anoka County

10th Judicial District Court Attn: File Room, 325 E Main St, Anoka, MN 55303; 763-422-7350; criminal phone: 763-422-7385; civil phone: 763-323-5939; probate phone: 763-422-7471; criminal fax: 763-422-6919; civil fax: 763-422-6919; 8AM-4:30PM. ***Felony, Misdemeanor, Civil, Eviction, Small Claims, Probate.***

www.co.anoka.mn.us/departments/courts/index.htm

Probate fax- 763-422-7085.

Civil Records: Access: Mail, in person, online. Both court and visitors may perform in person searches. No search fee. Required to search: name, years to search. Civil cases indexed by defendant, plaintiff, on computer from 1985, prior on microfiche. Weekly calendars free at www.mncourts.gov/district/10/?page=1326. Mail turnaround time 2 weeks. Civil PAT goes back to 1985. PAT civil

results show middle initial. Limited search of civil, family and probate records are found at http://pa.courts.state.mn.us/default.aspx. Electronic filings and abuse cases not shown.
Criminal Records: Access: In person, online. Visitors must perform in person searches themselves. Required to search: name, years to search, DOB. Criminal records computerized from 1985, prior on microfiche. Criminal PAT goes back to 1985. PAT results show middle initial, DOB. Public terminal allows for a statewide search. Limited search of criminal record index at http://pa.courts.state.mn.us/default.aspx. Only cases with dispositions appear in results. Electronic filings and abuse cases not shown. Weekly calendars free at www.mncourts.gov/district/10/?page=1326. Online results show middle initial, DOB.
General Information: No adoption, juvenile, sex offender or sealed records released. Will not fax documents. Court makes copy: $5.00 per doc; exemplification $10.00. Certification fee: $10.00 per doc and includes copies. Payee: Court Administrator. Personal checks accepted. Credit cards accepted.

Becker County

7th Judicial District Court PO Box 787, Detroit Lakes, MN 56502; 218-846-7305; probate phone: same; fax: 218-847-7620; 8AM-4:30PM. ***Felony, Misdemeanor, Civil, Eviction, Small Claims, Probate.*** www.mncourts.gov/district/7/
Civil Records: Access: In person, online. Both court and visitors may perform in person searches. No search fee. Required to search: name; also helpful: years to search. Civil cases indexed by defendant, plaintiff, on computer from 8/86, prior on books from 1891. Civil PAT goes back to 1986. PAT civil results show middle initial. Limited search of civil, family and probate records are found at http://pa.courts.state.mn.us/default.aspx. Search by case number or by name.
Criminal Records: Access: In person, online. Visitors must perform in person searches themselves. Required to search: name, years to search. Criminal records computerized from 8/86, prior on books from 1891. Criminal PAT goes back to 1986. PAT results show middle initial, DOB. Public terminal allows for a statewide search. Limited search of criminal record index at http://pa.courts.state.mn.us/default.aspx. Only cases with dispositions appear in results. Online results show middle initial, DOB.
General Information: No adoption, juvenile, sex offender or sealed records released. Fee to fax back- $25.00 per doc up to 25 pgs. Court makes copy: $5.00 per doc w/ judge's signature; $.25 per page all other docs. Certification fee: $10.00 per doc. Payee: Becker County. Personal checks/major credit cards accepted.

Beltrami County

District Court c/o Court Admin, Judicial Ctr, 600 Minnesota Ave NW, #108, Bemidji, MN 56601; 218-333-4120; criminal phone: 281-333-4125; civil phone: 218-333-4128; probate phone: 218-333-4123; criminal fax: 218-333-4209; civil fax: same; 8AM-4:30PM. ***Felony, Misdemeanor, Civil, Eviction, Small Claims, Probate.*** www.mncourts.gov/district/9/
Probate fax is same as main fax number. Week ahead court calendars available online.
Civil Records: Access: Mail, in person, online. Both court and visitors may perform in person searches. Search fee: $5.00 per name. Required to search: name, years to search. Civil cases indexed by defendant, plaintiff, on computer back to 1983. Mail turnaround time 1-5 days. Civil PAT goes back to 1983. Limited search of civil, family and probate at http://pa.courts.state.mn.us/default.aspx.
Criminal Records: Access: In person, online. Visitors must perform in person searches themselves. Required to search: name, years to search, DOB. Criminal records computerized from 1983. Criminal PAT goes back to 1983. Public terminal allows for a statewide search. Limited search of criminal record index at http://pa.courts.state.mn.us/default.aspx. Online results show middle initial, DOB.
General Information: No adoption, juvenile, sex offender or sealed records released. Will fax documents to local or toll free line. Court makes copy: $5.00 per doc. Certification fee: $10.00 per doc. Payee: Court Administrator. Personal checks and major credit cards accepted. Mail requests: SASE required for civil.

Benton County

7th Judicial District Court 615 Highway 23, PO Box 189, Foley, MN 56329-0189; 320-968-5205; fax: 320-968-5353; 8AM-4:30PM. ***Felony, Misdemeanor, Civil, Eviction, Small Claims, Probate, Family.*** www.mncourts.gov/district/7/
Civil Records: Access: In person, online. Visitors must perform in person searches themselves. Required to search: name, years to search. Civil cases indexed by defendant, plaintiff, on computer from 1986. Civil PAT goes back to 1986. Limited search of civil, family and probate records are found at http://pa.courts.state.mn.us/default.aspx. Electronic filings and abuse cases not shown.
Criminal Records: Access: In person, online. Visitors must perform in person searches themselves. Required to search: name, years to search, DOB. Criminal records computerized from 1986. Court recommends searching via the BCA at 651-642-0610. Criminal PAT goes back to 1986. Public terminal allows for a statewide search. Limited search of criminal record index at http://pa.courts.state.mn.us/default.aspx. Online results show middle initial, DOB.
General Information: No adoption, juvenile records released. Will not fax out case files. Court makes copy: $5.00 per doc. Self serve: no charge if off computer. Certification fee: $10.00 per doc. Payee: Court Administrator. Personal checks accepted. Visa/MC accepted.

Big Stone County

Big Stone District Court 20 2nd St SE, #107, Ortonville, MN 56278; 320-839-2536; probate 320-839-2536; fax: 320-839-2537; 8-4:30PM. ***Felony, Misdemeanor, Civil, Eviction, Small Claims, Probate.*** www.mncourts.gov/district/8/
Probate fax is same as main fax number.
Civil Records: Access: Mail, in person, online. Both court and visitors may perform in person searches. Search fee: $5.00. Required to search: name, years to search. Civil cases indexed by defendant, plaintiff, on computer from 1989, prior on cards and in books. Civil PAT goes back to 1990. This court is on the MNCIS system; records can be accessed by public terminal from other counties. Limited search of civil, family and probate records are found at http://pa.courts.state.mn.us/default.aspx. Electronic filings and abuse cases not shown.
Criminal Records: Access: In person, online. Visitors must perform in person searches themselves. Required to search: name, years to search, DOB; SSN helpful. Criminal records computerized from 1989, prior on cards and in books. Criminal PAT goes back to 1990. his court is on the MNCIS system; records can be accessed by public terminal from other counties. Limited search of criminal record index at http://pa.courts.state.mn.us/default.aspx. Online results show middle initial, DOB.
General Information: No adoption, juvenile, sex offender or sealed records released. Will not fax documents. Court makes copy: $5.00 per doc. Certification fee: $10.00 per doc. Payee: Court Administrator. Personal checks accepted. Visa/MC accepted. Mail requests: SASE required for civil.

Blue Earth County

5th Judicial District Court 204 S 5th St, Mankato, MN 56001; 507-304-4050; fax: 507-304-4437; 8AM-4:30PM. ***Felony, Misdemeanor, Civil, Eviction, Small Claims, Probate.*** www.co.blue-earth.mn.us/dept/courts.php
Civil Records: Access: Mail, in person, online. Both court and visitors may perform in person searches. Search fee: $5.00 per name. Required to search: name, exact dates to search. Civil cases indexed by defendant, plaintiff, on computer from 8/85, prior in books and cards. Mail turnaround time 7-10 days. Civil PAT goes back to 1985. PAT results show name only. Limited search of civil, family and probate records are found at http://pa.courts.state.mn.us/default.aspx. Electronic filings and abuse cases not shown.
Criminal Records: Access: In person, online. Visitors must perform in person searches themselves. Required to search: name, exact dates to search; also helpful: DOB. Criminal records computerized from 8/85, prior in books and cards. The county forwards mail requests to State Bureau of Criminal Apprehension. Criminal PAT goes back to 1985. PAT results show DOB and middle initials only if they were on the original complaint. Public terminal allows for a statewide search. Limited search of criminal record index at http://pa.courts.state.mn.us/default.aspx. Online results show middle initial, DOB.
General Information: No juvenile, adoption, sealed records released. Fee to fax back- $25.00 per doc up to 25 pgs. Court makes copy: $5.00 per doc. Certification fee: $10.00 per doc. Payee: Court Administrator. Personal checks accepted. Visa/MC accepted. SASE not required.

Brown County

5th Judicial District Court PO Box 248, 14 S State St, New Ulm, MN 56073-0248; 507-233-6670; fax: 507-359-9562; 8AM-5PM. ***Felony, Misdemeanor, Civil, Eviction, Small Claims, Probate.*** www.mncourts.gov/district/5/
Civil Records: Access: Mail, in person, online. Both court and visitors may perform in person searches. Search fee: $5.00 per name. Required to search: name, years to search. Civil cases indexed by defendant, plaintiff, on computer from 1988, microfiche 1981-1988, prior on books. Mail turnaround time 3 days. Civil PAT goes back to 1988. Records available at any 5th District courthouse public access terminals. Results may show DOB or address but not always. Limited search of civil, family and probate records are found at http://pa.courts.state.mn.us/default.aspx. Electronic filings and abuse cases not shown.
Criminal Records: Access: In person, online. Visitors must perform in person searches themselves. Required to search: name, years to search. Criminal records computerized from 1988, microfiche 1981-1988, prior on books. Make written requests to the State Bureau of Criminal Apprehension. Criminal PAT goes back to 1988. Records available at any 5th District courthouse public access terminals. Public terminal allows for a statewide search. Results may show DOB or address but not always. Limited search of criminal record index at http://pa.courts.state.mn.us/default.aspx. Online results show middle initial, DOB.
General Information: No adoption, juvenile, sex offender or sealed records released. Fee to fax back- $25.00 per doc up to 25 pgs. Court makes copy: $5.00 per doc. Certification fee: $10.00 per doc includes copies. Payee: Court Administrator. Personal checks accepted. Credit cards accepted. Mail requests: SASE required for civil.

Carlton County

6th Judicial District Court PO Box 190 (301 Walnut St), Carlton, MN 55718; 218-384-4281; criminal phone: 218-384-9109; civil phone: 218-384-9139; probate phone: 218-384-9113; criminal fax: 218-384-9182; civil fax: 218-384-9577; 8AM-4PM. ***Felony, Misdemeanor, Civil, Eviction, Small Claims, Probate.*** www.mncourts.gov/district/6/
Civil Records: Access: Mail, fax, in person, online. Both court and visitors may perform in person searches. Search fee: $5.00 per name. Required to search: name, years to search; also helpful: address. Civil cases indexed by defendant, plaintiff, on computer from 1985, in books from 1982. Mail turnaround time 3 days. Civil PAT goes back to 1986. PAT results show middle initial, DOB. Limited search of civil, family and probate records are found at http://pa.courts.state.mn.us/default.aspx. Electronic filings and abuse cases not shown.
Criminal Records: Access: In person, online. Visitors must perform in person searches

themselves. Required to search: name, years to search; also helpful: address, DOB. Criminal records computerized from 1985, in books from 1972. If you cannot come to the courthouse, the court recommends using a retriever or contact the state Bureau of Criminal Apprehension. Criminal PAT goes back to 1986. PAT results show middle initial, DOB. Public terminal allows for a statewide search. Limited search of criminal record index at http://pa.courts.state.mn.us/default.aspx. Only cases with dispositions appear in results. Online results show middle initial, DOB.
General Information: No adoption, juvenile, sex offender or sealed records released. Fee to fax back- $25.00 per doc up to 25 pgs. Court makes copy: $5.00 per doc. Cert fee: $10.00 per doc. Payee: Court Admin. Personal checks accepted. Most credit cards accepted. Mail requests: SASE required for civil.

Carver County

1st Judicial District Court 604 E 4th St, Chaska, MN 55318-2183; 952-361-1420; fax: 952-361-1491; 8AM-4:30PM. ***Felony, Misdemeanor, Civil, Eviction, Small Claims, Probate.*** www.mncourts.gov/district/1/
Civil Records: Access: In person, online. Visitors must perform in person searches themselves. Civil cases indexed by defendant, plaintiff, on computer from 2/92, prior on books. Public use terminal available, records go back to 1992. Results include name, city, state, zip. Limited search of civil, family and probate records are found at http://pa.courts.state.mn.us/default.aspx. Electronic filings and abuse cases not shown.
Criminal Records: Access: In person, online. Visitors must perform in person searches themselves. Criminal records computerized from 2/92, prior on books. Results include name, city, state, zip. Public use terminal available, crim records go back to 1992. Results include name, city, state, zip. Public terminal allows for a statewide search. Limited search of criminal record index at http://pa.courts.state.mn.us/default.aspx. Online results show middle initial, DOB.
General Information: No adoption, juvenile, sex offender or sealed records released. Will not fax documents. Court makes copy: $5.00 per doc. Cert fee: $10.00 per doc. Payee: Court Administrator. Personal checks accepted. Visa/MC accepted.

Cass County

9th Judicial District Court PO Box 3000, 300 Minnesota Ave, Walker, MN 56484; 218-547-7200; fax: 218-547-1904; 8AM-4:30PM. ***Felony, Misdemeanor, Civil, Eviction, Small Claims, Probate.*** www.mncourts.gov/district/9/
Week ahead court calendars available online.
Civil Records: Access: Mail, in person, online. Visitors must perform in person searches themselves. Search fee: $5.00 per name. Required to search: full name, years to search; also helpful: address. Civil cases indexed by defendant, plaintiff, on computer from mid-1990, on index cards from 1983-1990, on books to 1983-1900. Mail turnaround time 5 days Civil PAT goes back to mid-1990. Limited search of civil, family and probate records found at http://pa.courts.state.mn.us/defau lt.aspx. Electronic filings and abuse cases not shown.
Criminal Records: Access: In person, online. Visitors must perform in person searches themselves. Criminal records computerized from mid-1990, on index cards from 1983-1990, on books to 1983-1900. Criminal PAT goes back to mid-1990. Public terminal allows for a statewide search. Limited search of criminal record index at http://pa.courts.state.mn.us/default.aspx. Only cases with dispositions appear in results. Online results show middle initial, DOB.
General Information: No adoption, juvenile or sealed records released. Fee to fax back- $25.00 per doc up to 25 pgs. Court makes copy: $5.00 per doc. Certification fee: $10.00 per doc. Payee: District Court. Personal checks accepted. Credit cards accepted. Mail requests: SASE required for civil.

Chippewa County

8th Judicial District Court Chippewa County Court Administer, 629 N 11th St, Montevideo, MN 56265; 320-269-7774; fax: 320-269-7733; 8AM-4:30PM. ***Felony, Misdemeanor, Civil, Eviction, Small Claims, Probate.*** www.mncourts.gov/district/8/
Civil Records: Access: Mail, in person, online. Both court and visitors may perform in person searches. Search fee: $5.00 per name. Required to search: name, years to search. Civil cases indexed by defendant, plaintiff, on computer from 1988, but regularly purged, in books from 1870 (probate only). Mail turnaround time 1 week. Civil PAT goes back to 1988. Limited search of civil, family and probate at http://pa.courts.state.mn.us/default.aspx. Electronic filings and abuse cases not shown.
Criminal Records: Access: Mail, in person, online. Both court and visitors may perform in person searches. Search fee: $5.00 per name. Required to search: name, years to search, DOB. Criminal records computerized from 1988. Mail turnaround time 1 week. Criminal PAT goes back to 1988. Public terminal allows for a statewide search. Limited search of criminal record index at http://pa.courts.state.mn.us/default.aspx. Online results show middle initial, DOB.
General Information: No adoption, juvenile, sex offender or sealed records released. Will not fax documents. Court makes copy: $5.00 per doc. Certification fee: $10.00 per doc. Payee: Court Administrator. Personal checks accepted. Mail requests: SASE required for civil.

Chisago County

10th Judicial District Court 313 N Main St, Rm 358, Center City, MN 55012; 651-213-8650; fax: 651-213-8651; 8AM-4:30PM. ***Felony, Misdemeanor, Civil, Eviction, Small Claims, Probate.*** www.mncourts.gov/district/10/
Civil Records: Access: Mail, in person, online. Both court and visitors may perform in person searches. Search fee: $5.00 per name. Required to search: name, years to search. Civil cases indexed by defendant, plaintiff, on computer from 09/1984, prior on index cards. Weekly calendars free at www.mncourts.gov/district/10/?page=1326. Civil PAT goes back to late 1980s. PAT results show middle initial, DOB. Limited search of civil, family and probate records are found at http://pa.courts.state.mn.us/default.aspx. Electronic filings and abuse cases not shown.
Criminal Records: Access: In person, online. Visitors must perform in person searches themselves. Required to search: name, years to search; also helpful: DOB. Criminal records computerized from 09/1984, prior on index cards. Criminal PAT goes back to late 1980s. PAT results show middle initial, DOB. Public terminal allows for a statewide search. Limited search of criminal record index at http://pa.courts.state.mn.us/default.aspx. Weekly calendars free at www.mncourts.gov/district/10/?page=1326. Online results show middle initial, DOB.
General Information: No adoption, juvenile, sex offender or sealed records released. Fee to fax back- $25.00 per doc up to 25 pgs. Court makes copy: $5.00 per doc; $.25 per page if not date stamped.Only the court can make a copy of a file, but visitors can make copies of copies free in the Law Library. Certification fee: $10.00 per doc includes copy fee. Payee: Court Administrator. Personal checks accepted. Credit cards accepted. Mail requests: SASE required for civil.

Clay County

7th Judicial District Court PO Box 280, 807 11th St N, Clay County Ct Admin, Moorhead, MN 56561; 218-299-5065; fax: 218-299-7307; 8AM-4:30PM. ***Felony, Misdemeanor, Civil, Eviction, Small Claims, Probate.*** www.co.clay.mn.us/Depts/CourtAdm/CourtAdm.htm
Civil Records: Access: Mail, in person, online. Visitors must perform in person searches themselves. No search fee. Required to search: name; also helpful: years to search. Civil cases indexed by defendant, plaintiff, on computer back to 1982; prior on microfiche, microfilm and docket books. Civil PAT goes back to 1982. PAT civil results show middle initial. Limited search of civil, family and probate at http://pa.courts.state.mn.us/default.aspx. Electronic filings and abuse cases not shown.
Criminal Records: Access: In person, online. Visitors must perform in person searches themselves. Required to search: name, years to search, DOB. Criminal records computerized from 1982; prior on microfiche and microfilm. Criminal PAT goes back to 1982. PAT results show middle initial, DOB. Public terminal allows for a statewide search. Limited search of criminal record index at http://pa.courts.state.mn.us/default.aspx. Online results show middle initial, DOB.
General Information: No adoption or sealed records released. Fee to fax back- $25.00 per doc up to 25 pgs. Court makes copy: $5.00 per doc. Certification fee: $10.00 per doc. Payee: Court Administrator. Personal checks accepted. Credit cards accepted. SASE not required.

Clearwater County

9th Judicial District Court 213 Main Ave North, Dept 303, Bagley, MN 56621; 218-694-6177; probate phone: same; fax: 218-694-6213; 8AM-4:30PM. ***Felony, Misdemeanor, Civil, Eviction, Small Claims, Probate.*** www.mncourts.gov/district/9/
Week ahead court calendars available online.
Civil Records: Access: Mail, in person, online. Both court and visitors may perform in person searches. Search fee: $5.00 per name, by court. Required to search: name, years to search. Civil cases indexed by defendant, plaintiff, on computer from 1990, on cards and books prior back to 1903. Mail turnaround time 1 week. Civil PAT goes back to 1990. Limited search of civil, family and probate records are found at http://pa.courts.state.mn.us/default.aspx. Electronic filings and abuse cases not shown.
Criminal Records: Access: In person, online. Visitors must perform in person searches themselves. Required to search: name, years to search; also helpful: DOB. Criminal records computerized from 1990, on cards and books prior back to 1903. Court personnel will not perform name searches. Requests are referred to the state criminal agency. Criminal PAT goes back to 1990. Public terminal allows for a statewide search. Limited search of criminal record index at http://pa.courts.state.mn.us/default.aspx. Online results show middle initial, DOB.
General Information: No adoption, juvenile or sealed records released. Fee to fax back- $25.00 per doc up to 25 pgs. Court makes copy: $5.00 per doc. Certification fee: $10.00 per doc. Payee: Court Administrator. Personal checks and major credit cards accepted. SASE not required.

Cook County

6th Judicial District Court 411 W 2nd St, Grand Marais, MN 55604-2307; 218-387-3610; fax: 218-387-3007; 8AM-4PM. ***Felony, Misdemeanor, Civil, Eviction, Small Claims, Probate, Traffic.*** www.mncourts.gov/district/6/
Civil Records: Access: In person, online. Visitors must perform in person searches themselves. Required to search: name, years to search. Civil cases indexed by defendant, plaintiff, on computer back to 2/91, prior on card files. Civil PAT goes back to 1991. PAT results show name only. Limited search of civil, family and probate records are found at http://pa.courts.state.mn.us/default.aspx. Electronic filings not shown.
Criminal Records: Access: In person, online. Visitors must perform in person searches themselves. Required to search: name, years to search, DOB. Criminal records computerized from 2/91, prior on card files. Criminal PAT goes back to 1991. PAT results show name only. Public terminal allows for a statewide search. Limited search of criminal record index at http://pa.courts.state.mn.us/default.aspx. Only cases with dispositions in results. Electronic filings not shown. Online results show middle initial, DOB.
General Information: No adoption, juvenile, sex offender or sealed records released. Fee to fax back- $25.00 per doc up to 25 pgs. Court makes copy: $5.00 per doc. Cert fee: $10.00 per doc. Payee: Court Admin. Business checks accepted. Visa/MC accepted.

Cottonwood County

5th Judicial District Court PO Box 97, Windom, MN 56101; 507-831-4551; fax: 507-831-1425; 8AM-4:30PM. ***Felony, Misdemeanor, Civil, Eviction, Small Claims, Probate.***
www.mncourts.gov/district/5/
Civil Records: Access: Mail, fax, in person, online. Both court and visitors may perform in person searches. Search fee: $10.00 per name. Required to search: name; also helpful: years to search. Civil cases indexed by defendant, plaintiff, on computer back to 1989; probate on microfilm. There is a $5.00 fee to certify a judgment search done on computer. Mail turnaround time 2-3 days. Civil PAT goes back to 1989. Limited search of civil, family and probate records are found at http://pa.courts.state.mn.us/default.aspx. Electronic filings and abuse cases not shown.
Criminal Records: Access: Mail, fax, in person, online. Both court and visitors may perform in person searches. Search fee: $10.00 per name. Required to search: name, years to search, DOB. Criminal records computerized from 1989; prior records on card file. Court will only do searches if caseload permits. Mail turnaround time 2-3 days. Criminal PAT goes back to 1989. Public terminal allows for a statewide search. Limited search of criminal record index at http://pa.courts.state.mn.us/default.aspx. Online results show middle initial, DOB.
General Information: No adoption, juvenile, sex offender or sealed records released. Will fax documents to local or toll free line. Court makes copy: $5.00 per doc. Certification fee: $10.00 per doc includes copy fee. Payee: Court Administrator. Personal checks accepted. Visa/MC accepted. Mail requests: SASE required.

Crow Wing County

District Court Crow Wing County Judicial Center, 213 Laurel St, #11, Brainerd, MN 56401; 218-824-1310; fax: 218-824-1311; 8AM-5PM. ***Felony, Misdemeanor, Civil, Eviction, Small Claims, Probate.*** www.mncourts.gov/district/9/
Week ahead court calendars available online.
Civil Records: Access: Mail, in person, online. Both court and visitors may perform in person searches. Search fee: $5.00 per name. Required to search: name, years to search. Civil cases indexed by defendant, plaintiff, on computer from 1989, prior in books from 1873. Mail turnaround time 5 days Civil PAT goes back to 1989. PAT results show name, DOB. Limited search of civil, family and probate records are found at http://pa.courts.state.mn.us/default.aspx. Electronic filings and abuse cases not shown.
Criminal Records: Access: In person, online. Both court and visitors may perform in person searches. Search fee: $5.00 per name. Required to search: name, years to search; also helpful: DOB. Criminal records computerized from 1989, prior in books from 1873. Criminal PAT goes back to 1989.PAT results show name, DOB. Public terminal allows for a statewide search. Limited search of criminal record index at http://pa.courts.state.mn.us/default.aspx. Online results show middle initial, DOB.
General Information: No adoption, juvenile, sex offender or sealed records released. Will not fax documents. Court makes copy: $5.00 per doc. Certification fee: $10.00 per doc. Payee: Court Administrator. Personal checks accepted; credit cards are not. Mail requests: SASE required for civil.

Dakota County

1st Judicial District Court - Apple Valley 14955 Galaxie Ave, Apple Valley, MN 55124; 952-891-7256; criminal phone: 952-891-7239; civil phone: 952-891-7244; criminal fax: 952-891-7312; civil fax: 952-891-7285; 8AM-4:30PM. ***Misdemeanor, Civil, Eviction, Small Claims, Traffic.*** www.mncourts.gov/default.aspx?siteID=1
Send criminal record faxes to attention Cindy.
Civil Records: Access: In person, online. Visitors must perform in person searches themselves. Required to search: name, years to search. Civil cases indexed by defendant, plaintiff, on computer back to 1988, prior in files in index books back to 1969. Civil PAT goes back to 1988. Limited search of civil, family and probate records are found at http://pa.courts.state.mn.us/default.aspx. Electronic filings and abuse cases not shown.
Criminal Records: Access: In person, online. Visitors must perform in person searches themselves. Required to search: name, years to search, DOB. Criminal records computerized from 1988, prior in files to 1987 if not destroyed. Criminal PAT goes back to 1988. Public terminal allows for a statewide search. Limited search of criminal record index at http://pa.courts.state.mn.us/default.aspx. Online results show middle initial, DOB.
General Information: No adoption, juvenile, sex offender or sealed records released. Fee to fax back-$25.00 per doc up to 25 pgs. Court makes copy: $5.00 per doc. Self serve: $.50 per page. Certification fee: $10.00 per doc. Payee: District Court. Personal checks accepted. Credit cards accepted.

1st Judicial District Court - Division 3 1 Mendota Rd West, #140, West St Paul, MN 55118-4767; 651-554-6200; criminal fax: 651-554-6226; civil fax: same; 8AM-4:30PM. ***Misdemeanor, Civil, Eviction, Small Claims.***
www.mncourts.gov/default.aspx?siteID=1
Formerly located at 125 3rd Ave North, S. St. Paul.
Civil Records: Access: In person, online. Visitors must perform in person searches themselves. Required to search: name, years to search. Civil cases indexed by defendant, plaintiff, on computer from 12/87, prior on ledgers. Civil PAT goes back to 1/1988. PAT results show middle initial, DOB, SSN. Limited search of civil, family and probate records are found at http://pa.courts.state.mn.us/default.aspx. Electronic filings and abuse cases not shown.
Criminal Records: Access: In person, online. Visitors must perform in person searches themselves. Required to search: name, years to search. Criminal records computerized from 12/87, prior on ledgers. Criminal PAT goes back to 1/1988. PAT results show middle initial, DOB. Public terminal allows for a statewide search. Limited search of criminal record index at http://pa.courts.state.mn.us/default.aspx. Online results show middle initial, DOB.
General Information: No adoption, juvenile, sex offender or sealed records released. Will not fax out case files. Court makes copy: $5.00 per doc. Cert fee: $10.00 per doc. Payee: Court Administrator. Personal checks and major credit cards accepted.

District Court Judicial Center, 1560 Hwy 55, Hastings, MN 55033; 651-438-8100; criminal fax: 651-438-8160; civil fax: 651-438-8162; 8AM-4:30PM. ***Felony, Misdemeanor, Civil, Eviction, Small Claims, Probate.***
www.mncourts.gov/default.aspx?siteID=1
Probate fax- 651-438-8161
Civil Records: Access: In person, online. Visitors must perform in person searches themselves. Required to search: name, years to search. Civil cases indexed by defendant, plaintiff, on computer from 1/88, on ledgers prior. Civil PAT goes back to 1/1988. PAT results show name only. Public terminals at 3 locations- Judicial Ctr, 1560 W Hwy 55 in Hastings; Western Svc Ctr, 14955 Galaxies Ave in Apple Valley; Northern Svc Ctr, 1 Mendota Rd W, #140 in West St Paul. Limited search of civil, family and probate records are found at http://pa.courts.state.mn.us/default.aspx. Electronic filings and abuse cases not shown.
Criminal Records: Access: In person, online. Visitors must perform in person searches themselves. Required to search: name, years to search. Criminal records computerized from 1/88, on ledgers prior. Criminal PAT goes back to 1/1988. PAT results show middle initial, DOB. Public terminals at 3 locations- Judicial Ctr, 1560 W Hwy 55 in Hastings; Western Svc Ctr, 14955 Galaxie Ave in Apple Valley; Northern Svc Ctr, 1 Mendot Rd W, #140 in West St Paul. Public terminal allows for a statewide search. Limited search of criminal record index at http://pa.courts.state.mn.us/default.aspx. Online results show middle initial, DOB.
General Information: No adoption, juvenile, sealed records released. Will not fax out case files. Court makes copy: $5.00 per doc. Certification fee: $10.00 per doc. Payee: District Court. Personal checks accepted. Credit cards accepted.

Dodge County

3rd Judicial District Court 22 Sixth St E, Dept. 12, Mantorville, MN 55955; 507-635-6260; fax: 507-635-6271; 8AM-4:30PM. ***Felony, Misdemeanor, Civil, Eviction, Small Claims, Probate.*** www.mncourts.gov/district/3/
Civil Records: Access: Fax, mail, in person, online. Visitors must perform in person searches themselves. Search fee: $5.00 per name. Required to search: name, years to search. Civil cases indexed by defendant, plaintiff, on computer back to 1989, on cards from 1984, on books from 1972. Mail turnaround time 3 days. Civil PAT goes back to 1989. PAT results show name only. Limited search of civil, family and probate records are found at http://pa.courts.state.mn.us/default.aspx. Daily Court calendar is posted at www.mncourts.gov/default.aspx?page=512.
Criminal Records: Access: In person, online. Visitors must perform in person searches themselves. Required to search: name, years to search, DOB. Criminal records computerized from 1984, on cards from 1984, on books from 1972. Criminal PAT goes back to 1989. PAT results show middle initial, DOB. Public terminal allows for a statewide search. Limited search of criminal record index at http://pa.courts.state.mn.us/default.aspx. Online results show middle initial, DOB.
General Information: No adoption, juvenile, sex offender or sealed records released. Fee to fax back-$25.00 per doc up to 25 pgs. Court makes copy: $5.00 per doc. Cert fee: $10.00 per doc. Payee: Court Administrator. Personal checks accepted. Visa/MC accepted. Mail requests: SASE required for civil.

Douglas County

7th Judicial District Court 305 8th Ave West, Alexandria, MN 56308; 320-762-3882; criminal fax: 320-762-8863; civil fax: same; 8AM-4:30PM. ***Felony, Misdemeanor, Civil, Eviction, Small Claims, Probate.*** www.mncourts.gov/district/7/
Probate fax is same as main fax number.
Civil Records: Access: In person, online. Both court and visitors may perform in person searches. No search fee. Required to search: name, years to search. Civil cases indexed by defendant, plaintiff, on computer from 1987, on microfiche from 1951, books prior. The books are grouped by letter, but not alphabetized. Civil PAT goes back to 1987. Limited search of civil, family and probate records are found at http://pa.courts.state.mn.us/default.aspx. Electronic filings and abuse cases not shown.
Criminal Records: Access: In person, online. Visitors must perform in person searches themselves. Required to search: name. Criminal records computerized from 1987, on microfiche from 1951, books prior. The books are grouped by letter, but not alphabetized. Court recommends search through BCA. Criminal PAT goes back to 1987. Public terminal allows for a statewide search. Limited search of criminal record index at http://pa.courts.state.mn.us/default.aspx. Online results show middle initial, DOB.
General Information: No adoption, juvenile or sealed records released. Will not fax documents. Court makes copy: $5.00 per doc. Cert fee: $10.00 plus $5.00 copy fee. Payee: Court Administrator. Personal checks accepted. Visa/MC accepted.

Faribault County

5th Judicial District Court PO Box 130, Blue Earth, MN 56013; 507-526-6273; fax: 507-526-3054; 8AM-4:30PM. ***Felony, Misdemeanor, Civil, Eviction, Small Claims, Probate.***
www.mncourts.gov/district/5/
Civil Records: Access: Mail, in person, online. Both court and visitors may perform in person searches. Search fee: $5.00 per name. Required to search: name, years to search. Civil cases indexed by defendant, plaintiff, on computer from 1989, in books

from 1870. Mail turnaround time 1 week. Civil PAT goes back to 1989. Limited search of civil, family and probate records are found at http://pa.courts.state.mn.us/default.aspx. Electronic filings and abuse cases not shown.
Criminal Records: Access: In person, online. Visitors must perform in person searches themselves. Required to search: name, years to search; also helpful: DOB. Criminal records computerized from 1989, in books from 1870. The county suggests sending requests to the state Bureau of Criminal Apprehension. Criminal PAT goes back to 1989. Public terminal allows for a statewide search. Limited search of criminal record index at http://pa.courts.state.mn.us/default.aspx. Online results show middle initial, DOB.
General Information: No adoption, juvenile, sex offender or sealed records released. Fee to fax back- $25.00 per doc up to 25 pgs. Court makes copy: $5.00 per doc. Cert fee: $10.00 per doc. Payee: Court Administrator. Personal checks and major credit cards accepted. Mail requests: SASE required for civil.

Fillmore County

3rd Judicial District Court 101 Fillmore St, PO Box 436, Preston, MN 55965; 507-765-4483; criminal fax: 507-765-4571; civil fax: same; 8AM-4:30PM. ***Felony, Misdemeanor, Civil, Eviction, Small Claims, Probate.*** www.mncourts.gov/district/3/
Probate fax is same as main fax number.
Civil Records: Access: Mail, in person, online. Both court and visitors may perform in person searches. Search fee: $5.00 per name. Required to search: name, years to search. Civil cases indexed by defendant, plaintiff, on computer from 1990, books from 1860s. Mail turnaround time 1-2 days. Civil PAT goes back to 1990. PAT results show name only. Limited search of civil, family and probate records at http://pa.courts.state.mn.us/default.aspx. Electronic filings and abuse cases not shown.
Criminal Records: Access: In person, online. Visitors must perform in person searches themselves. Required to search: name, years to search, DOB. Criminal records computerized from 1990, books from 1860s. Criminal PAT goes back to 1990. PAT results show middle initial, DOB. Public terminal allows for a statewide search. Limited search of criminal record index at http://pa.courts.state.mn.us/default.aspx. Online results show middle initial, DOB.
General Information: No adoption, juvenile or sealed records released. Fee to fax back- $25.00 per doc up to 25 pgs. Court makes copy: $5.00 per doc. Certification fee: $10.00 per doc. Payee: Court Administrator. Personal checks accepted. Credit cards accepted. SASE not required.

Freeborn County

3rd Judicial District Court 411 S Broadway, Albert Lea, MN 56007; 507-377-5153; fax: 507-377-5260; 8AM-5PM. ***Felony, Misdemeanor, Civil, Eviction, Small Claims, Probate.***
www.mncourts.gov/district/3/
Civil Records: Access: Mail, in person, online. Both court and visitors may perform in person searches. Search fee: $5.00 per name. Required to search: name, years to search. Civil cases indexed by defendant, plaintiff, on computer from 11/89. Civil PAT goes back to 11/1989. Limited search of civil, family and probate records are found at http://pa.courts.state.mn.us/default.aspx. Electronic filings and abuse cases not shown.
Criminal Records: Access: In person, online. Visitors must perform in person searches themselves. Required to search: name, years to search, DOB. Criminal records computerized from 11/89. Criminal PAT goes back to 11/1989. Public terminal allows for a statewide search. Limited search of criminal record index at http://pa.courts.state.mn.us/default.aspx. Online results show middle initial, DOB.
General Information: No adoption, juvenile, sex offender or sealed records released. Will not fax documents. Court makes copy: $5.00 per doc. Certification fee: $10.00 per doc. Payee: Court Administrator. Personal checks accepted. Visa/MC accepted. Mail requests: SASE required for civil.

Goodhue County

1st Judicial District Court 454 W 6th St, Red Wing, MN 55066; 651-267-4800; probate phone: 651-267-4810; criminal fax: 651-267-4989; civil fax: same; 8AM-4:30PM. ***Felony, Misdemeanor, Civil, Eviction, Small Claims, Probate.***
www.mncourts.gov/district/1/
Probate fax is same as main fax number.
Civil Records: Access: Mail, in person, online. Both court and visitors may perform in person searches. No search fee. Required to search: name, years to search. Civil cases indexed by defendant, plaintiff, on computer from 3/92, prior records on docket books. Mail turnaround time less than 1 week. Civil PAT goes back to 1992. PAT results show name only. Limited search of civil, family and probate records are at http://pa.courts.state.mn.us/default.aspx. Electronic filings and abuse cases not shown.
Criminal Records: Access: In person, online. Visitors must perform in person searches themselves. Required to search: name. Criminal records computerized from 3/92, prior records on docket books. Criminal PAT goes back to 1992.PAT results show name, DOB. Public terminal allows for a statewide search. Limited search of criminal record index at http://pa.courts.state.mn.us/default.aspx. Online results show middle initial, DOB.
General Information: No adoption, juvenile, sex offender or sealed records released. Fee to fax back- $25.00 per doc up to 25 pgs. Court makes copy: $5.00 per doc. Certification fee: $10.00 per doc. Payee: Court Administrator. Personal checks accepted. Visa/MC accepted. SASE not required.

Grant County

8th Judicial District Court PO Box 1007, 10 2nd St NE, Elbow Lake, MN 56531; 218-685-4825; fax: 218-685-5349; 8AM-4PM; till 7PM TH. ***Felony, Misdemeanor, Civil, Eviction, Small Claims, Probate.*** www.mncourts.gov/district/8/
Civil Records: Access: Mail, in person, online. Both court and visitors may perform in person searches. Search fee: $5.00 per name. Required to search: name, years to search. Civil cases indexed by defendant, plaintiff, on computer from 6/89, on cards from 1930, prior at Historical Society. Mail turnaround time 3-4 days. Civil PAT goes back to 1989. Limited search of civil, family and probate records are found at http://pa.courts.state.mn.u s/default.aspx. Electronic filings and abuse cases not shown.
Criminal Records: Access: In person, online. Visitors must perform in person searches themselves. Required to search: name, years to search; also helpful: DOB. Criminal records computerized from 6/89, on cards from 1930, prior at Historical Society. Criminal PAT goes back to 1989. Public terminal allows for a statewide search. Limited search of criminal record index at http://pa.courts.state.mn.us/default.aspx. Online results show middle initial, DOB.
General Information: No adoption, juvenile, sex offender or sealed records released. Fee to fax back- $25.00 per doc up to 20 pgs. Court makes copy: $5.00 per doc. Cert fee: $10.00 per doc. Payee: Court Administrator. Personal checks accepted. Visa/MC accepted. Mail requests: SASE required for civil.

Hennepin County

4th Judicial Dist. Court - Division 1 Civil 1251 C Government Ctr, 300 S 6th St, Minneapolis, MN 55487; 612-348-3164; fax: 612-348-2131; 8AM-4:30PM (closed Wed at 1:30). ***Civil, Small Claims, Eviction.*** www.mncourts.gov/district/4/
The Housing Court handles evictions and is located here, #A-1700, phone 612-348-5186; Housing Court handles cases countywide. Conciliation Court (Small Claims Court) is in #306, 612-348-2713.
Civil Records: Access: Fax, mail, in person, online. Both court and visitors may perform in person searches. Search fee: $5.00 per name by mail, no fee if in person using terminal. Required to search: name, years to search. Civil cases indexed by defendant, plaintiff, on computer from 1978, prior on microfilm. Mail turnaround time 7-10 days. Public use terminal has civil records back to 1978. PAT civil results show middle initial. No address, DOB generally not available. PAT is countywide. Search civil, family and probate records free at http://pa.courts.state.mn.us/default.aspx. Electronic filings and abuse cases not shown. Search judgments free at http://pa.courts.state.mn.us/default.aspx. Plaintiff, defendant search of small claims is free at www2.co.hennepin.mn.us/ccourt/ccsrch.jsp. See records center webpage for record specifics at www.mncourts.gov/district/4/?page=1865. Online results show middle initial, DOB.
General Information: No sex offender or sealed records released, domestic abuse and paternity cases are limited. Will fax documents no fee. Court makes copy: $5.00 per doc. Cert fee: $10.00 per doc. Payee: Court Administrator. Personal checks accepted; credit cards are not. Mail requests: SASE required.

4th Judicial Dist. Court - Div. 1 Criminal 300 S 6th St, PSL-2nd Floor HCGC, Minneapolis, MN 55487; 612-348-2612; fax: 612-348-6099; 8AM-4:30PM. ***Felony, Misdemeanor.***
www.mncourts.gov/district/4/
See records center webpage for record specifics at www.mncourts.gov/district/4/?page=1865.
Criminal Records: Access: Fax, mail, in person, online. Both court and visitors may perform in person searches. Search fee: $10.00 per name (uncertified). Required to search: name, years to search, DOB. Felony record index back to 1886. Computerized records back to 1978. Files copies held up to 30 years per state law. Online info about criminal searching at www.mncourts.gov/district/4/?page=1865. Mail turnaround time 14-21 days. Public use terminal has crim records back to 1989. PAT results show middle initial, DOB. PAT is countywide. Limited search of criminal record index at http://pa.courts.state.mn.us/default.aspx. Only cases with dispositions appear in results. Electronic filings and abuse cases not shown. Online results show middle initial, DOB.
General Information: No adoption, juvenile, sex offender or sealed records released. Will fax documents. Court makes copy: $5.00 per doc. Certification fee: $10.00 per case. Cert fee includes search fee. Payee: Court Administrator. Personal checks accepted. Credit cards accepted in person. Mail requests: SASE required.

4th Judicial Dist. Ct - Div. 2 Brookdale 6125 Shingle Creek Parkway #200, Brooklyn Center, MN 55430; 612-543-2150; criminal phone: 612-348-2040 district-wide; fax: 763-569-3697; 8AM-4:30PM M,T,TH,F; Thurs til 1:30PM. ***Misdemeanor, Traffic.*** www.mncourts.gov/district/4/
Making copies a problem here: PAT can't print, clerk may not retrieve, web can't certify. Jurisdiction area- Brooklyn Ctr, Brooklyn Park, Champlin, Corcoran, Crystal, Dayton, Greenfield, Hanover, Hassan, New Hope, Osseo, Robbinsdale, Rockford, Rogers.
Criminal Records: Access: In person, online. Both court and visitors may perform in person searches. Search fee: $5.00 per name. Required to search: name, years to search, DOB. Criminal records on computer since 1987. If file is not onsite, it is ordered on the 15th and the end of each month. Public use terminal has crim records back to 1985. PAT is located in lobby but it cannot print out documents; is countywide. Public terminal allows for a statewide search. Limited search of criminal record index at http://pa.courts.state.mn.us/default.aspx. Only cases with dispositions appear in results. Electronic filings and abuse cases not shown. See record center page for record specifics www.mncourts.gov/district/4/?page=1865. Online results show middle initial, DOB.
General Information: No juvenile court, conciliation court, unlawful detainers or sealed records released. Fee to fax back- $25.00 per doc up to 25 pgs. Court makes copy: $5.00 per doc, if the clerk agrees to make copies. Certification fee: $10.00 per doc. Payee: Hennepin County District Court. Personal checks accepted. Visa/MC accepted. Mail requests: SASE required.

4th Judicial Dist. Ct - Div. 3 Ridgedale 12601 Ridgedale Dr, Minnetonka, MN 55305-1912; 612-543-1400; fax: 952-541-6297; 8AM-4:30PM. ***Misdemeanor, Traffic.***
www.mncourts.gov/district/4/
Juris- Deephaven, Eden Prairie, Excelsior, Golden Vly, Greenwood, Hopkins, Independence, Long Lk, Loretto, Maple Grove, Maple Plain, Medina, Minnetonka, Minnetrista, Mound, Orono, Plymouth, Shorewood, Spring Pk, St Bonifacius, Tonka Bay, Wayzata, Woodland
Criminal Records: Access: Phone, fax, mail, in person, online. Both court and visitors may perform in person searches. Search fee: $5.00 per name. Required to search: name, years to search; also helpful: DOB. Criminal records on computer since 1989; prior records on microfiche. Phone requests are limited to 1 name only. Making copies a problem here: PAT can't print, clerk may not retrieve, web can't certify. Mail turnaround time 3-4 weeks. Public use terminal has crim records back to 1986. PAT results show middle initial, DOB, SSN. Public terminal, which does not always work, has limited data available. Limited search of criminal record index at http://pa.courts.state.mn.us/default.aspx. Only cases with dispositions appear in results. Electronic filings and abuse cases not shown. See records center for record specifics at www.mncourts.gov/district/4/?page=1865. Online results show middle initial, DOB.
General Information: No police reports, juvenile or sealed records released. Will not fax out documents. Court makes copy: $5.00 per doc. Certification fee: $10.00 per doc. Payee: Hennepin County District Court. Personal checks accepted. Credit cards accepted in person only. Mail requests: SASE required.

4th Judicial Dist. Ct. - Div. 4 Southdale 7009 York Ave South, Edina, MN 55435; 612-543-0400; fax: 952-830-4993; 8AM-4:30PM, W- 8AM-1:30PM. ***Misdemeanor, Traffic.***
www.mncourts.gov/district/4/
Making copies a problem here: PAT can't print, clerk might not retrieve, web can't certify. Jurisdictional area- Airport (MAC), Bloomington, Edina, Richfield, St Louis Pk.
Criminal Records: Access: Mail, in person, online. Visitors must perform in person searches themselves. No search fee. Required to search: name, years to search, DOB; also helpful: offense, date of offense. Criminal records on computer since late 1970s, felonies on computer earlier. In person search with court assistance $10.00. Mail turnaround time 1 week. Public use terminal has crim records back to the date the court opened. Terminal located in lobby, is countywide. Public terminal allows for a statewide search. Limited search of criminal record index at http://pa.courts.state.mn.us/default.aspx. Only cases with dispositions appear in results. Electronic filings and abuse cases not shown. Online results show middle initial, DOB.
General Information: No juvenile or sealed records released. Will not fax documents. Court makes copy: $5.00 per doc. Certification fee: $10.00 per doc. Payee: Hennepin County District Court. Personal checks accepted. Visa/MC accepted. Mail requests: SASE required.

4th Judicial District Court - Division 1 C400 Government Ctr, 300 S 6th St, Minneapolis, MN 55487-0340; 612-348-3244; fax: 612-348-2130; 8:30AM-4:30PM. ***Probate.***
www.mncourts.gov/district/4/
Search Probate and Family cases free at http://pa.courts.state.mn.us/default.aspx. See records center webpage for record specifics at www.mncourts.gov/district/4/?page=1865.

Houston County

3rd Judicial District Court 304 S Marshall, Rm 204, Caledonia, MN 55921; 507-725-5806; criminal phone: 507-725-5828; fax: 507-725-5550; 8AM-4:30PM. ***Felony, Misdemeanor, Civil, Eviction, Small Claims, Probate.***
www.mncourts.gov/district/3/
Civil Records: Access: Mail, in person, online. Both court and visitors may perform in person searches. Search fee: $5.00 per name. Required to search: name, years to search, DOB. Civil cases indexed by defendant, plaintiff, on computer back to 8/89, prior on cards and books. Probate on microfilm to 1990. Mail turnaround time 2 days. Civil PAT goes back to 1989. PAT results show name, DOB. Limited search of civil, family and probate records are found at http://pa.courts.state.mn.us/default.aspx. Electronic filings and abuse cases not shown.
Criminal Records: Access: In person, online. Visitors must perform in person searches themselves. Required to search: name, years to search; also helpful: DOB. Criminal records computerized from 8/89, prior on cards and books. Criminal PAT goes back to 1989. Public terminal allows for a statewide search. Limited search of criminal record index at http://pa.courts.state.mn.us/default.aspx. Online results show middle initial, DOB.
General Information: No adoption, juvenile, sex offender or sealed records released. Fee to fax back-$25.00 per doc up to 25 pgs. Court makes copy: $5.00 per doc. Cert fee: $10.00 per doc. Payee: Court Administrator. Personal checks accepted. Visa/MC accepted. Mail requests: SASE required for civil.

Hubbard County

9th Judicial District Court 301 Court Ave, Park Rapids, MN 56470; 218-732-5286; fax: 218-732-0137; 8AM-4:30PM. ***Felony, Misdemeanor, Civil, Eviction, Small Claims, Probate.***
www.courts.state.mn.us
Week ahead court calendars available online.
Civil Records: Access: Mail, in person, online. Visitors must perform in person searches themselves. Search fee: $5.00 per name. Required to search: name, years to search. Civil cases indexed by defendant, plaintiff, on computer since 1990, prior on index cards. Civil PAT goes back to 1990. Limited search of civil, family and probate records are found at http://pa.courts.state.mn.us/default.aspx. Electronic filings and abuse cases not shown.
Criminal Records: Access: In person, online. Visitors must perform in person searches themselves. Required to search: name, DOB. Criminal records on computer since 1990, prior on index cards. Criminal PAT goes back to 1990. Public terminal allows for a statewide search. Limited search of criminal record index at http://pa.courts.state.mn.us/default.aspx. Online results show middle initial, DOB.
General Information: No adoption, juvenile, sex offender or sealed records released. Fee to fax back-$25.00 per doc up to 25 pgs. Court makes copy: $5.00 per doc. Certification fee: $10.00 per doc. Payee: Court Administrator. Personal checks accepted; credit cards are not. SASE not required.

Isanti County

10th Judicial District Court 7533 Sunwood Dr NW #306, Ramsey, MN 55303-5186; 763-689-2292; criminal fax: 763-689-8340; civil fax: same; 8AM-4:30PM. ***Felony, Misdemeanor, Civil, Eviction, Small Claims, Probate.***
www.mncourts.gov/district/10/
Probate fax is same as main fax number.
Civil Records: Access: Mail, in person, online. Both court and visitors may perform in person searches. No search fee. Required to search: name, years to search. Civil cases indexed by defendant, plaintiff, on computer from 12/84, prior on microfiche. Weekly calendars free at www.mncourts.gov/district/10/?page=1326. Civil PAT goes back to 1985. Limited search of civil, family and probate records are at http://pa.courts.state.mn.us/default.aspx. Electronic filings and abuse cases not shown.
Criminal Records: Access: In person, online. Visitors must perform in person searches themselves. Required to search: name, years to search. Criminal records computerized from 12/84, prior on microfiche. Criminal PAT goes back to 1985. Public terminal allows for a statewide search. Limited search of criminal record index at http://pa.courts.state.mn.us/default.aspx. Weekly calendars free at www.mncourts.gov/district/10/?page=1326. Online results show middle initial, DOB.
General Information: No adoption, juvenile, sex offender or sealed records released. Will fax free to local or toll-free numbers. Court makes copy: $10.00 per doc for certification or exemplification. Certification fee: $10.00 per doc. Payee: Court Administrator. Personal checks accepted. Visa/MC accepted. Mail requests: SASE required for civil.

Itasca County

9th Judicial District Court 123 4th St NE, Grand Rapids, MN 55744-2600; 218-327-2870; fax: 218-327-2897; 8AM-4PM. ***Felony, Misdemeanor, Civil, Eviction, Small Claims, Probate, Family.***
www.co.itasca.mn.us/Court/Gov_cou.htm
Week ahead court calendars available online.
Civil Records: Access: Mail, in person, online. Both court and visitors may perform in person searches. Search fee: $5.00 per name. Required to search: name, years to search, DOB. Civil cases indexed by defendant, plaintiff, on computer from 4-87, on microfiche to 1982, on books prior. Mail turnaround time 20 days, 24 hours more to pull from off-site storage. Civil PAT goes back to 4/1987. Limited search of civil, family and probate records are found at http://pa.courts.state.mn.us/default.aspx. Electronic filings and abuse cases not shown.
Criminal Records: Access: In person, online. Visitors must perform in person searches themselves. Required to search: name, years to search, DOB. Criminal records computerized from 4-87, on microfiche to 1982, on books prior. This agency will not perform a record search. Record checks should made through the Bureau of Criminal Apprehension; see state section on criminal records. Criminal PAT goes back to 4/1987. PAT results show middle initial, DOB. Public terminal allows for a statewide search. Limited search of criminal record index at http://pa.courts.state.mn.us/default.aspx. Online results show middle initial, DOB.
General Information: No adoption, juvenile or sealed records released. Fee to fax back- $25.00 per doc up to 25 pgs. Court makes copy: $5.00 per doc. Certification fee: $10.00 plus $5.00 copy fee. Payee: Court Administrator. Personal checks accepted. Visa/MC accepted. SASE not required.

Jackson County

5th Judicial District Court PO Box 177, Jackson, MN 56143; criminal phone: 507-847-2566; civil phone: 507-847-4400; fax: 507-847-5433; 8AM-4:30PM. ***Felony, Misdemeanor, Civil, Eviction, Small Claims, Probate.***
www.mncourts.gov/district/5/
Probate is a separate index at this same address.
Civil Records: Access: Fax, mail, in person, online. Both court and visitors may perform in person searches. Search fee: $10.00 per name. Required to search: name, years to search, address. Civil cases indexed by defendant, plaintiff, on computer from 5/89. Probate on microfiche from 1870. Mail turnaround time 2-3 days. Civil PAT goes back to 5/1989. Limited search of civil, family and probate records at http://pa.courts.state.mn.us/default.aspx. Electronic filings and abuse cases not shown.
Criminal Records: Access: Fax, mail, in person, online. Visitors must perform in person searches themselves. Search fee: $10.00 per name if referred to BCA state agency. Required to search: name, years to search, DOB. Criminal records computerized from 5/89. Probate on microfiche from 1870. Mail turnaround time 2-3 days. Criminal PAT goes back to 5/1989. Public terminal allows for a statewide search. Limited search of criminal record index at http://pa.courts.state.mn.us/default.aspx. Online results show middle initial, DOB.
General Information: No adoption, juvenile, sex offender or sealed records released. Fee to fax back-$25.00 per doc up to 25 pgs. Court makes copy: $5.00 per doc. Self serve: No fee for self serve copies. Certification fee: $10.00 per doc. Payee: Court Administrator. Personal checks and major credit cards accepted. SASE not required.

Kanabec County

District Court 18 N Vine, #318, Mora, MN 55051-1385; 320-679-6400; fax: 320-679-6411; 8AM-4:30PM. ***Felony, Misdemeanor, Civil, Eviction, Small Claims, Probate.*** www.mncourts.gov/district/10/

Civil Records: Access: In person, online. Visitors must perform in person searches themselves. Required to search: name, years to search. Civil cases indexed by defendant, plaintiff, on computer from 1986, prior on books and microfiche. Weekly calendars free at www.mncourts.gov/district/10/?page=1326. Civil PAT goes back to 1986. PAT results show middle initial, DOB, SSN. Limited search of civil, family and probate records are at http://pa.courts.state.mn.us/default.aspx. Electronic filings and abuse cases not shown.

Criminal Records: Access: In person, online. Visitors must perform in person searches themselves. Required to search: name, years to search; also helpful: DOB. Criminal records computerized from 1986, prior on books and microfiche. Criminal PAT goes back to 1986. PAT results show middle initial, DOB, SSN. Public terminal allows for a statewide search. Limited search of criminal record index at http://pa.courts.state.mn.us/default.aspx. Weekly calendars free at www.mncourts.gov/district/10/?page=1326. Online results show middle initial, DOB.

General Information: No adoption, juvenile or sealed records released. Will not fax documents. Court makes copy: $5.00 per doc; exemplification $10.00. Certification fee: $10.00 per doc. Payee: Court Administrator. Personal checks accepted. Visa/MC accepted.

Kandiyohi County

Kandiyohi District Court 505 Becker Ave SW, Willmar, MN 56201; 320-231-6206; fax: 320-231-6276; 8AM-4:30PM. ***Felony, Misdemeanor, Civil, Eviction, Small Claims, Probate.*** www.mncourts.gov/district/8/

Civil Records: Access: Mail, in person, online. Both court and visitors may perform in person searches. Search fee: $5.00 per name. Required to search: name, years to search. Civil cases indexed by defendant, plaintiff, on computer from 1986, prior on microfilm. Mail turnaround time 48 hours. Civil PAT goes back to 1986. PAT civil results show middle initial. Limited search of civil, family and probate records at http://pa.courts.state.mn.us/default.aspx. Electronic filings/abuse cases not shown.

Criminal Records: Access: In person, online. Visitors must perform in person searches themselves. Required to search: name, years to search; DOB helpful. Criminal records computerized from 1986, prior on microfilm. Criminal PAT goes back to 1986. PAT results show middle initial, DOB. Public terminal allows for a statewide search. Limited search of criminal record index at http://pa.courts.state.mn.us/default.aspx. Online results show middle initial, DOB.

General Information: No adoption, juvenile, sex offender or sealed records released. Fee to fax back-$25.00 per doc up to 25 pgs. Court makes copy: $5.00 per doc. Certification fee: $10.00 per doc. Payee: Court Administrator. Personal checks accepted. Visa/MC accepted. SASE not required.

Kittson County

9th Judicial District Court 410 Fifth St S, #204, Hallock, MN 56728; 218-843-3632; fax: 218-843-3634; 8AM-4:30PM. ***Felony, Misdemeanor, Civil, Eviction, Small Claims, Probate.*** www.mncourts.gov/district/9/

Week ahead court calendars available online.

Civil Records: Access: In person, online. Both court and visitors may perform in person searches. Search fee: $5.00 per name. Will charge $20.00 per hour for extensive searches. Required to search: name, years to search. Civil cases indexed by defendant, plaintiff, on computer from 9/90, prior on books and index cards. Visitors may look at judgment docket. Civil PAT goes back to 1990. PAT results show name only. Limited search of civil, family and probate records are found at http://pa.courts.state.mn.us/default.aspx. Electronic filings and abuse cases not shown.

Criminal Records: Access: In person, online. Visitors must perform in person searches themselves. Required to search: name, years to search, DOB, offense. Criminal records computerized from 9/90, prior on books and index cards. Criminal PAT goes back to 1990. PAT results show name only. Public terminal allows for a statewide search. Limited search of criminal record index at http://pa.courts.state.mn.us/default.aspx. Online results show middle initial, DOB.

General Information: No adoption, juvenile, sex offender or sealed records released. Fee to fax back-$25.00 per doc up to 25 pgs. Court makes copy: $5.00 per doc. Certification fee: $10.00 per doc. Payee: Court Administrator. Personal checks and major credit cards accepted.

Koochiching County

9th Judicial District Court Court House, 715 4th St, International Falls, MN 56649; criminal phone: 218-283-1163; civil phone: 218-283-1160; probate phone: 218-283-1160; fax: 218-283-1162; 8AM-4PM. ***Felony, Misdemeanor, Civil, Eviction, Small Claims, Probate.*** www.mncourts.gov/district/9/

Week ahead court calendars available online. Misdemeanor records- 218-283-1163. Probate fax is same as main fax number.

Civil Records: Access: Mail, in person, online. Both court and visitors may perform in person searches. Search fee: $5.00 per name. Required to search: name, years to search, DOB. Civil cases indexed by defendant, plaintiff, on computer from 8/90, on TCIS cards from 1984, on books from 1906. Search daily court calendar at the website. Civil PAT goes back to 8/1990. Limited search of civil, family and probate records are found at http://pa.courts.state.mn.us/default.aspx. Electronic filings and abuse cases not shown.

Criminal Records: Access: In person, online. Visitors must perform in person searches themselves. Required to search: name, years to search, DOB. Criminal records computerized from 8/90, on TCIS cards from 1984, on books from 1906. Criminal record checks can be done via BCA. Criminal PAT goes back to 8/1990. Public terminal allows for a statewide search. Limited search of criminal record index at http://pa.courts.state.mn.us/default.aspx. Online results show middle initial, DOB.

General Information: No adoption, juvenile, sex offender or sealed records released. Fee to fax back-$25.00 per doc up to 25 pgs. Court makes copy: $5.00 per doc. Certification fee: $10.00 per doc. Payee: Court Administrator. Personal checks accepted; credit cards are not. Mail requests: SASE required for civil.

Lac qui Parle County

8th Judicial District Court PO Box 36, 600 6th St, Madison, MN 56256; 320-598-3536; fax: 320-598-3915; 8AM-4:30PM. ***Felony, Misdemeanor, Civil, Eviction, Small Claims, Probate.*** www.mncourts.gov/district/8/

Civil Records: Access: Fax, phone, mail, in person. Both court and visitors may perform in person searches. Search fee: $5.00 per name. Required to search: name, years to search. Civil cases indexed by defendant, plaintiff, on computer from 1988, prior on index cards. Mail turnaround time 2-3 days. Civil PAT goes back to 1988. Limited search of civil, family and probate records are found at http://pa.courts.state.mn.us/default.aspx. Electronic filings and abuse cases not shown.

Criminal Records: Access: In person, online. Both court and visitors may perform in person searches. No search fee. Required to search: name, years to search, DOB; SSN helpful. Criminal records computerized from 1988, prior on index cards. Court may refer criminal searches requests to the sheriff's office, 320-598-3720. Sheriff address is 600 6th St. Criminal PAT goes back to 1988. Public terminal allows for a statewide search. Limited search of criminal record index at http://pa.courts.state.mn.us/default.aspx. Online results show middle initial, DOB.

General Information: No adoption, juvenile, sex offender or sealed records released. Fee to fax back-$25.00 per doc up to 25 pgs. Court makes copy: $5.00 per doc. Certification fee: $10.00 per doc. Payee: Court Administrator. Personal checks accepted. Visa/MC accepted for fine payments only. Mail requests: SASE required for civil.

Lake County

6th Judicial District Court 601 3rd Ave, Two Harbors, MN 55616; 218-834-8330; probate phone: 218-834-8329; criminal fax: 218-834-8397; civil fax: same; 8AM-4:30PM. ***Felony, Misdemeanor, Civil, Eviction, Small Claims, Probate.*** www.mncourts.gov/district/6/

Probate fax is same as main fax number.

Civil Records: Access: Fax, mail, in person, online. Both court and visitors may perform in person searches. Search fee: $5.00 per name. Required to search: name, years to search. Civil cases indexed by defendant, plaintiff, on computer back to 1991, prior on index cards. Mail turnaround time 2-3 days. Civil PAT goes back to 1991. PAT results show name only. Limited search of civil, family and probate records are at http://pa.courts.state.mn.us/default.aspx. Electronic filings are not shown.

Criminal Records: Access: In person, online. Visitors must perform in person searches themselves. Required to search: name, years to search, DOB. Criminal records computerized from 1991, prior on index cards. Criminal PAT goes back to 1991. PAT results show name only. Public terminal allows for a statewide search. Limited search of criminal record index at http://pa.courts.state.mn.us/default.aspx. Only cases with dispositions appear in results. Electronic filings are not shown. Online results show middle initial, DOB.

General Information: No adoption, juvenile, sex offender or sealed records released. Fee to fax back-$25.00 per doc up to 25 pgs. Court makes copy: $5.00 per doc. Cert fee: $10.00 per doc. Payee: Court Administrator. Personal checks accepted. Credit cards accepted. Mail requests: SASE required for civil.

Lake of the Woods County

9th Judicial District Court 206 8th Ave SE, #250, Baudette, MN 56623; 218-634-1451; fax: 218-634-9444; 7:30AM-4PM. ***Felony, Misdemeanor, Civil, Eviction, Small Claims, Probate.*** www.mncourts.gov/district/9/

Week ahead court calendars available online.

Civil Records: Access: Fax, mail, in person, online. Both court and visitors may perform in person searches. Search fee: $10.00 per name. Required to search: name, years to search. Civil cases indexed by defendant, plaintiff, on computer back to 1990; on microfilm to 1923. Mail turnaround time 2 days. Civil PAT goes back to 1990. Limited search of civil, family and probate records are found at http://pa.courts.state.mn.us/default.aspx. Electronic filings and abuse cases not shown.

Criminal Records: Access: In person, online. Visitors must perform in person searches themselves. Required to search: name, years to search, DOB. Criminal records computerized from 1990; on microfilm back to 1923. Criminal searches referred to B.C.A. Criminal PAT goes back to 1990. Public terminal allows for a statewide search. Limited search of criminal record index at http://pa.courts.state.mn.us/default.aspx. Online results show middle initial, DOB.

General Information: No adoption, juvenile, sex offender or sealed records released. No fee to fax documents. Court makes copy: $5.00 per doc. Certification fee: $10.00 per doc plus $5.00 copy fee. Payee: Court Administrator. Personal checks accepted; credit cards are not. SASE not required.

Le Sueur County

1st Judicial District Court 88 S Park Ave, Le Center, MN 56057; 507-357-8252; fax: 507-357-6433; 8AM-4:30PM. ***Felony, Misdemeanor, Civil, Eviction, Small Claims, Probate.*** www.mncourts.gov/district/1/

Civil Records: Access: In person, online. Both court and visitors may perform in person searches.

Required to search: name. Civil cases indexed by defendant, plaintiff, on computer from 1994, prior on books. Civil PAT goes back to 1992. PAT civil results show middle initial. Limited search of civil, family and probate records are found at http://pa.courts.state.mn.us/default.aspx. Electronic filings and abuse cases not shown.
Criminal Records: Access: In person, online. Visitors must perform in person searches themselves. Required to search: name, DOB. Criminal records computerized from 1992, prior on books. Criminal PAT goes back to 1992. PAT results show middle initial, DOB. Public terminal allows for a statewide search. Limited search of criminal record index at http://pa.courts.state.mn.us/default.aspx. Online results show middle initial, DOB.
General Information: No adoption, juvenile, sex offender or sealed records released. Will fax documents. Court makes copy: $5.00 per doc. Certification fee: $10.00 per doc includes copies. Payee: Court Administrator. Personal checks accepted. Visa/MC accepted.

Lincoln County

5th Judicial District Court PO Box 15, 319 N Rebecca St, Ivanhoe, MN 56142-0015; 507-694-1355 or 507-694-1505; probate phone: 507-694-1355; fax: 507-694-1717; 8AM-4:30PM. ***Felony, Misdemeanor, Civil, Eviction, Small Claims, Probate, Family.*** www.mncourts.gov/district/5/
Probate fax is same as main fax number.
Civil Records: Access: Mail, in person, online. Both court and visitors may perform in person searches. Search fee: $5.00 per name. Required to search: name, years to search. Civil cases indexed by defendant, plaintiff. Public terminal is available to access cases from 1/1989, on TCIS manual index cards from 12/82, on books from late 1800. Civil PAT goes back to 1989. PAT results show middle initial, DOB. Limited search of civil, family and probate records are at http://pa.courts.state.mn.us/default.aspx. Electronic filings are not shown.
Criminal Records: Access: In person, online. Both court and visitors may perform in person searches. No search fee. Required to search: name, years to search, DOB. Criminal records computerized from 1989, on TCIS from 12/82, on books from late 1800. All written requests for criminal records are referred to statewide BCA; call for form, 650-793-2420, but if you have a case number, this court will pull the public file for you for inspection. Criminal PAT goes back to 1989. PAT results show middle initial, DOB, SSN. Public terminal allows for a statewide search. Limited search of criminal record index at http://pa.courts.state.mn.us/default.aspx. Online results show middle initial, DOB, SSN.
General Information: No adoption, juvenile, sex offender or sealed records released. Fee to fax back-$25.00 per doc up to 25 pgs. Court makes copy: $5.00 per doc. Cert fee: $10.00 per doc. Payee: Court Administrator. Personal checks accepted. Visa/MC accepted. Mail requests: SASE required for civil.

Lyon County

5th Judicial District Court 607 W Main, Marshall, MN 56258; 507-537-6734; fax: 507-537-6150; 8:30AM-4:30PM. ***Felony, Misdemeanor, Civil, Eviction, Small Claims, Probate.*** www.mncourts.gov/district/5/
Civil Records: Access: Mail, in person, online. Both court and visitors may perform in person searches. Search fee: $10.00. Required to search: name, years to search. Civil cases indexed by defendant, plaintiff, on computer from 1987, prior on index cards. Mail turnaround time 1 week Civil PAT goes back to 1997. PAT results show name, DOB. Limited search of civil, family and probate records are found at http://pa.courts.state.mn.us/default.aspx. Electronic filings and abuse cases not shown.
Criminal Records: Access: In person, online. Visitors must perform in person searches themselves. Criminal records go back to 1987. The court asks requests be sent to the state Bureau of Criminal Apprehension. Criminal PAT goes back to 1997.PAT results show name, DOB. Public terminal allows for a statewide search. Limited search of criminal record index at http://pa.courts.state.mn.us/default.aspx. Online results show middle initial, DOB.
General Information: No adoption, juvenile, sex offender or sealed records released. Will not fax documents. Court makes copy: $5.00 per doc. Certification fee: $10.00 per doc. Payee: Court Administrator. Personal checks accepted. Credit cards accepted. Mail requests: SASE required for civil.

Mahnomen County

9th Judicial District Court PO Box 459, 311 N Main, Mahnomen, MN 56557; 218-935-2251; fax: 218-935-2851; 8AM-4:30PM. ***Felony, Misdemeanor, Civil, Eviction, Small Claims, Probate.*** www.mncourts.gov/district/9/
Week ahead court calendars available online.
Civil Records: Access: In person, online. Both court and visitors may perform in person searches. Search fee: $5.00 per name. Required to search: name, years to search. Civil cases indexed by defendant, plaintiff, on computer from 8/90, prior on books from 1907. Civil PAT goes back to 1990. Limited search of civil, family and probate records are at http://pa.courts.state.mn.us/default.aspx. Electronic filings and abuse cases not shown.
Criminal Records: Access: In person, online. Both court and visitors may perform in person searches. Search fee: $5.00 per name. Required to search: name, years to search. Criminal records computerized from 8/90, prior on books from 1907. Criminal PAT goes back to 1990. Public terminal allows for a statewide search. Limited search of criminal record index at http://pa.courts.state.mn.us/default.aspx. Online results show middle initial, DOB.
General Information: No adoption, juvenile, sex offender or sealed records released. Will not fax documents. Court makes copy: $5.00 per doc. Cert fee: $10.00 per doc. Payee: Court Administrator. Personal checks accepted. Visa/MC accepted.

Marshall County

9th Judicial District Court Court Administrator - Records, 208 E Colvin, Ste 18, Warren, MN 56762; 218-745-4921; fax: 218-745-4343; 8AM-4:30PM. ***Felony, Misdemeanor, Civil, Eviction, Small Claims, Probate.*** www.mncourts.gov/district/9/
Week ahead court calendars available online.
Civil Records: Access: Mail, in person, online. Both court and visitors may perform in person searches. Search fee: $5.00 per name. Required to search: name, years to search; also helpful: address. Civil cases indexed by defendant, plaintiff, on computer from 5/90, on cards from 1982, on books from 1885. Mail turnaround time same day. Civil PAT goes back to 1990. PAT results show name only. Limited search of civil, family and probate records are at http://pa.courts.state.mn.us/default.aspx. Electronic filings and abuse cases not shown.
Criminal Records: Access: Mail, in person, online. Visitors must perform in person searches themselves. Search fee: $5.00 per name. Required to search: name, years to search; also helpful: address, DOB. Criminal records computerized from 5/90, on cards from 1982, on books from 1885. Most name searchers with written requests are asked to contact the BCA State repository. Mail turnaround time same day. Criminal PAT goes back to 1990. PAT results show name only. Public terminal allows for a statewide search. Limited search of criminal record index at http://pa.courts.state.mn.us/default.aspx. Online results show middle initial, DOB.
General Information: No adoption, juvenile, sex offender or sealed records released. Will not fax documents. Court makes copy: $5.00 per doc. Certification fee: $10.00 per doc. Payee: Court Administrator. Personal checks and major credit cards accepted. Mail requests: SASE required.

Martin County

5th Judicial District Court 201 Lake Ave, Rm 304, Martin County Court Admin., Fairmont, MN 56031; 507-238-3205; probate phone: same; fax: 507-238-1913; 8AM-5PM. ***Felony, Misdemeanor, Civil, Eviction, Small Claims, Probate.*** www.mncourts.gov/district/5/
Probate fax is same as main fax number.
Civil Records: Access: Mail, in person, online. Both court and visitors may perform in person searches. Search fee: $10.00 per name. Required to search: name, years to search; also helpful: address. Civil cases indexed by defendant, plaintiff, on computer from 7/89, on cards from 1986, on books from 1800s. Mail turnaround time 2 weeks. Civil PAT goes back to 7/1989. Limited search of civil, family and probate records are at http://pa.courts.state.mn.us/default.aspx. Electronic filings and abuse cases not shown.
Criminal Records: Access: In person, online. Visitors must perform in person searches themselves. Required to search: name, years to search, DOB; also helpful: address, SSN. Criminal records computerized from 7/89, on cards from 1986, on books from 1800s. Court suggests sending requests to State Bureau of Criminal Apprehension. Criminal PAT goes back to 7/1989. Public terminal allows for a statewide search. Limited search of criminal record index at http://pa.courts.state.mn.us/default.aspx. Online results show middle initial, DOB.
General Information: No adoption, most juvenile, or sealed records released. Will fax civil search results or specific case files for $25.00 per fax if prepaid. Court makes copy: $5.00 per doc. Certification fee: $10.00 per doc. Payee: Court Administrator. Personal checks accepted. Credit cards accepted. Mail requests: SASE required for civil.

McLeod County

1st Judicial District Court 830 E 11th, Glencoe, MN 55336; 320-864-1281; probate phone: same; fax: 320-864-5905; 8AM-4:30PM. ***Felony, Misdemeanor, Civil, Eviction, Small Claims, Probate.*** www.co.mcleod.mn.us/mcleodco.cfm?pageID=14&sub=yes
Civil Records: Access: Mail, in person, online. Both court and visitors may perform in person searches. No search fee. Required to search: name, years to search. Civil records on computer from 4/92, prior on books. Mail turnaround time 3-5 days. Civil PAT goes back to 1991. Limited search of civil, family and probate records are found at http://pa.courts.state.mn.us/default.aspx. Electronic filings and abuse cases not shown.
Criminal Records: Access: In person, online. Visitors must perform in person searches themselves. Required to search: name, years to search. Criminal records computerized from 4/92, prior on books. Criminal PAT goes back to 1991. Public terminal allows for a statewide search. Limited search of criminal record index at http://pa.courts.state.mn.us/default.aspx. Online results show middle initial, DOB.
General Information: No adoption, juvenile, sex offender or sealed records released. Will not fax documents. Court makes copy: $5.00 per doc. Certification fee: $10.00 per doc. Payee: Court Administrator. Personal checks accepted. Visa/MC accepted. Mail requests: SASE required for civil.

Meeker County

8th Judicial District Court 325 N Sibley, Litchfield, MN 55355; 320-693-5230; fax: 320-693-5254; 8AM-4:30PM. ***Felony, Misdemeanor, Civil, Eviction, Small Claims, Probate.*** www.mncourts.gov/district/8/
Civil Records: Access: Mail, in person, online. Both court and visitors may perform in person searches. Search fee: $5.00 per name. Required to search: name; also helpful: years to search, address. Civil cases indexed by defendant, plaintiff, on computer from 11/88, prior on index cards. Mail turnaround time 2-3 days. Civil PAT goes back to 11/1988. Limited search of civil, family and probate records

may be at http://pa.courts.state.mn.us/default.aspx. Electronic filings and abuse cases not shown.
Criminal Records: Access: In person, online. Visitors must perform in person searches themselves. Required to search: name; also helpful: years to search, DOB. Criminal records computerized from 11/88, prior on index cards back to 1880s. Criminal PAT goes back to 11/1988. Public terminal allows for a statewide search. Limited search of criminal record index at http://pa.courts.state.mn.us/default.aspx. Online results show middle initial, DOB.
General Information: No adoption, juvenile, sex offender or sealed records released. Fee to fax back- $25.00 per doc up to 25 pgs. Court makes copy: $5.00 per doc. Certification fee: $10.00 per doc. Payee: Court Administrator. Personal checks accepted. Visa/MC accepted. Mail requests: SASE required for civil.

Mille Lacs County

7th Judicial District Court Courthouse, 635 2nd St SE, Milaca, MN 56353; 320-983-8313; fax: 320-983-8384; 8AM-4:30PM. ***Felony, Misdemeanor, Civil, Eviction, Small Claims, Probate.*** www.mncourts.gov/district/7/
Civil Records: Access: Mail, in person, online. Both court and visitors may perform in person searches. Search fee: $5.00. Required to search: name, years to search. Civil cases indexed by defendant, plaintiff, on computer from 4/86, cards from 1981, books prior. Mail turnaround time 2 weeks. Civil PAT goes back to 1986. Limited search of civil, family and probate records are found at http://pa.courts.state.mn.us/default.aspx. Electronic filings and abuse cases not shown.
Criminal Records: Access: In person, online. Visitors must perform in person searches themselves. Required to search: name, years to search. Criminal records computerized from 4/86, cards from 1981, books prior. Criminal PAT goes back to 1986. Public terminal allows for a statewide search. Limited search of criminal record index at http://pa.courts.state.mn.us/default.aspx. Online results show middle initial, DOB.
General Information: No adoption, juvenile, sex offender or sealed records released. Fee to fax back- $25.00 per doc up to 25 pgs. Court makes copy: $5.00 per doc. Certification fee: $10.00 per doc. Payee: District Court. Personal checks accepted. Visa/MC accepted. Mail requests: SASE required for civil.

Morrison County

7th Judicial District Court 213 SE 1st Ave, Little Falls, MN 56345; 320-632-0327; probate phone: 320-632-0327; fax: 320-632-0340; 8AM-4:30PM. ***Felony, Misdemeanor, Civil, Eviction, Small Claims, Probate.*** www.mncourts.gov/district/7/
Civil Records: Access: Fax, mail, in person, online. Both court and visitors may perform in person searches. No search fee. Required to search: name, years to search. Civil cases indexed by defendant, plaintiff, on computer from 5/86, prior on cards and books. Civil PAT goes back to 5/1986. PAT results show middle initial, DOB, SSN. Limited search of civil, family and probate records are found at http://pa.courts.state.mn.us/default.aspx. Electronic filings and abuse cases not shown.
Criminal Records: Access: In person, online. Visitors must perform in person searches themselves. Required to search: name, years to search, DOB. Criminal records computerized from 5/86, prior on cards and books. Criminal PAT goes back to 5/1986. PAT results show middle initial, DOB. Public terminal allows for a statewide search. Limited search of criminal record index at http://pa.courts.state.mn.us/default.aspx. Online results show middle initial, DOB.
General Information: No adoption, juvenile, sex offender or sealed records released. Fee to fax back- $25.00 per doc up to 25 pgs. Court makes copy: $5.00 per doc. Certification fee: $10.00 per doc. Payee: Court Administrator. Personal checks and major credit cards accepted. Mail requests: SASE required for civil.

Mower County

Mower County District Court 201 1st St NE, Austin, MN 55912; 507-437-9465; fax: 507-434-2702; 8AM-4:30PM. ***Felony, Misdemeanor, Civil, Eviction, Small Claims, Probate, Family.*** www.mncourts.gov/district/3/
Civil Records: Access: Mail, in person, online. Both court and visitors may perform in person searches. Search fee: $5.00. Required to search: name, years to search. Civil cases indexed by defendant, plaintiff, on computer from 1989. Civil PAT goes back to 1989. PAT results show middle initial, DOB, SSN. Limited search of civil, family and probate records are at http://pa.courts.state.mn.us/default.aspx. Electronic filings and abuse cases not shown.
Criminal Records: Access: In person, online. Visitors must perform in person searches themselves. Required to search: name, years to search, DOB. Criminal records computerized from 1989. Criminal PAT goes back to 1989. PAT results show middle initial, DOB. Public terminal allows for a statewide search. Limited search of criminal record index at http://pa.courts.state.mn.us/default.aspx. Online results show middle initial, DOB.
General Information: No adoption, juvenile, paternity or sealed records released. Fee to fax back- $25.00 per doc up to 25 pgs. Court makes copy: $5.00 per doc. Cert fee: $10.00 per doc. Payee: Court Administrator. Personal checks and major credit cards accepted. Mail requests: SASE required for civil.

Murray County

5th Judicial District Court PO Box 57, Slayton, MN 56172-0057; 507-836-6163; fax: 507-836-6019; 8AM-5PM. ***Felony, Misdemeanor, Civil, Eviction, Small Claims, Probate.*** www.mncourts.gov/district/5/
Civil Records: Access: Fax, mail, in person, online. Both court and visitors may perform in person searches. Search fee: $5.00 per name. Required to search: name, years to search. Civil cases indexed by defendant, plaintiff, on computer from 7/88. Mail turnaround time 7 days Civil PAT available. Limited search of civil, family and probate records are at http://pa.courts.state.mn.us/default.aspx. Electronic filings and abuse cases not shown.
Criminal Records: Access: In person, online. Visitors must perform in person searches themselves. Required to search: name, years to search; SSN helpful. Criminal records computerized from 7/88. The court suggests sending requests to Bureau of Criminal Apprehension. Criminal PAT available. Public terminal allows for a statewide search. Limited search of criminal record index at http://pa.courts.state.mn.us/default.aspx. Online results show middle initial, DOB.
General Information: No adoption, juvenile, or sealed records released. Fee to fax back- $25.00 per doc up to 25 pgs. Court makes copy: $5.00 per doc. Cert fee: $10.00 per doc. Payee: Court Administrator. Personal checks accepted. Visa/MC accepted.

Nicollet County

5th Judicial District Court PO Box 496, St Peter, MN 56082; 507-931-6800; criminal phone: 507-934-0388; civil phone: 507-934-0386; probate phone: 507-934-0380; fax: 507-931-4278; 8AM-5PM. ***Felony, Misdemeanor, Civil, Eviction, Small Claims, Probate.*** www.mncourts.gov/district/5/
Fine Inquiry telephone is 507-934-7503. The court in North Mankato is closed. All records from that District Court branch are located here.
Civil Records: Access: Mail, in person, online. Both court and visitors may perform in person searches. Search fee: $5.00 per name. Required to search: name, years to search. Civil cases indexed by defendant, plaintiff, on computer from 9/25/88, on books from 1890. The civil records prior to 9/25/88 for the entire county are located here. Mail turnaround time 2 weeks. Civil PAT goes back to 1988. PAT results show name only. Limited search of civil, family and probate records are found at http://pa.courts.state.mn.us/default.aspx. Electronic filings and abuse cases not shown.
Criminal Records: Access: In person, online. Visitors must perform in person searches themselves. Required to search: name, years to search, DOB. Criminal records on computer since 9/25/88. Prior records for this court only are located here on books and cards. The court will not do criminal searches. Criminal PAT goes back to 1988. PAT results show name only. Public terminal allows for a statewide search. Limited search of criminal record index at http://pa.courts.state.mn.us/default.aspx. Online results show middle initial, DOB.
General Information: No adoption, juvenile, sex offender or sealed records released. Will not fax documents. Court makes copy: $5.00 per doc. Certification fee: $10.00 per doc includes copies. Payee: Court Administrator. Personal checks accepted. Visa/MC accepted. Mail requests: SASE required for civil.

Nobles County

5th Judicial District Court PO Box 547, 1530 Airport Rd, Worthington, MN 56187; 507-372-8263; probate phone: same; fax: 507-372-4994; 8AM-4:30PM. ***Felony, Misdemeanor, Civil, Eviction, Small Claims, Probate.*** www.mncourts.gov/district/5/
Civil Records: Access: Mail, in person, online. Both court and visitors may perform in person searches. Search fee: $5.00 per name. Required to search: name, years to search. Civil cases indexed by defendant, plaintiff, on computer from 7/88, on books and index cards prior. Mail turnaround time 5 days Civil PAT goes back to 7/1988. Limited search of civil, family and probate records are found at http://pa.courts.state.mn.us/default.aspx. Electronic filings and abuse cases not shown.
Criminal Records: Access: In person, online. Visitors must perform in person searches themselves. Required to search: name, years to search; SSN helpful. Criminal records computerized from 7/88, on books and index cards prior. The court suggests sending requests to the state Bureau of Criminal Apprehension. Criminal PAT goes back to 7/1988. Public terminal allows for a statewide search. Limited search of criminal record index at http://pa.courts.state.mn.us/default.aspx. Online results show middle initial, DOB.
General Information: No adoption, juvenile, sex offender or sealed records released. Will not fax documents. Court makes copy: $5.00 per doc. Self serve: No self serve criminal copier; Civil self serve- $1.00 each. Certification fee: $10.00 per doc. Payee: Court Administrator. Personal checks accepted. Credit cards accepted in person only. Mail requests: SASE required for civil.

Norman County

9th Judicial District Court 16 3rd Ave E, Courthouse, Ada, MN 56510-0146; 218-784-5458; fax: 218-784-3110; 8AM-4:30PM. ***Felony, Misdemeanor, Civil, Eviction, Small Claims, Probate.*** www.mncourts.gov/district/9/
Week ahead court calendars available online. Probate fax is same as main fax number.
Civil Records: Access: Mail, in person, online. Both court and visitors may perform in person searches. Search fee: $5.00 per name. Required to search: name, years to search. Civil records on computer since 5/1990, prior on index cards. Civil PAT goes back to 1990. Limited search of civil, family and probate records are at http://pa.courts.state.mn.us/default.aspx. Electronic filings and abuse cases not shown.
Criminal Records: Access: In person, online. Visitors must perform in person searches themselves. Required to search: name, years to search, DOB. Criminal records on computer since 5/90, prior on index cards. Criminal searches directed to BCA- 1-800-832-6446, fax 218-935-9999. Criminal PAT goes back to 1990. Public terminal allows for a statewide search. Limited search of criminal record index at http://pa.courts.state.mn.us/default.aspx. Online results show middle initial, DOB.
General Information: No adoption, juvenile, sex offender or sealed records released. Fee to fax back-

$25.00 per doc up to 25 pgs. Court makes copy: $5.00 per doc. Certification fee: $10.00 per doc includes copies. Payee: Court Administrator. Business checks accepted. Visa/MC accepted. SASE not required.

Olmsted County

Olmsted County District Court 151 4th St SE, Rochester, MN 55904; criminal phone: 507-206-2496; civil phone: 507-206-2499; probate phone: 507-206-2489; fax: 507-285-8996; 9AM-4:30PM. ***Felony, Misdemeanor, Civil, Eviction, Small Claims, Probate.*** www.mncourts.gov/district/3/

Civil Records: Access: In person, online. Both court and visitors may perform in person searches. No search fee. Required to search: name, years to search. Civil cases indexed by defendant, plaintiff, on computer from mid-1989, prior to 1856 on index cards. Probate files vary greatly, but most contain date and place of death, list of heirs, copy of will (if one was written), inventory of personal property, and final disposition of the estate. Civil PAT goes back to 1983. Limited search of civil, family and probate records are found at http://pa.courts.state.mn.us/default.aspx. Electronic filings and abuse cases not shown.

Criminal Records: Access: In person, online. Visitors must perform in person searches themselves. Required to search: name, DOB. Criminal records computerized from mid-1989, prior to 1856 on index cards. Access the daily court calendar at the website. Criminal PAT goes back to 1983. Public terminal allows for a statewide search. Limited search of criminal record index at http://pa.courts.state.mn.us/default.aspx. Online results show middle initial, DOB.

General Information: No adoption, juvenile, sex offender or sealed records released. Fee to fax back-$25.00 per doc up to 25 pgs. Court makes copy: $5.00 per doc. Certification fee: $10.00 per doc. Payee: Court Administrator. Personal checks accepted. Visa/MC accepted.

Otter Tail County

Otter Tail County District Court 121 W Junius Ave #310, Fergus Falls, MN 56538-0417; 218-998-8420; 8AM-4:30PM. ***Felony, Misdemeanor, Civil, Eviction, Small Claims, Probate, Traffic.*** www.mncourts.gov/district/7/

A fax fee applies whether they tell you or not.

Civil Records: Access: Mail, in person, online. Both court and visitors may perform in person searches. Search fee: $5.00 per name. Required to search: name; also helpful: years to search. Civil cases indexed by defendant, plaintiff, on computer from 1987, prior on index books. Civil PAT goes back to 10/1986. PAT results show name only. Limited search of civil, family and probate records are found at http://pa.courts.state.mn.us/default.aspx. Electronic filings and abuse cases not shown.

Criminal Records: Access: In person, online. Visitors must perform in person searches themselves. Required to search: name, years to search, DOB; also helpful: address. Criminal records computerized from 1987, prior on index books. Criminal PAT goes back to 10/1986. PAT results show name only. Public terminal allows for a statewide search. Limited search of criminal record index at http://pa.courts.state.mn.us/default.aspx. Online results show middle initial, DOB.

General Information: No adoption, certain juvenile or sealed records released. Fee to fax back- $25.00 per doc up to 25 pgs. Court makes copy: $5.00 per doc. Certification fee: $10.00 per doc. Payee: Court Administrator. Personal checks accepted. Mail requests: SASE required for civil.

Pennington County

9th Judicial District Court Court Admin Office, PO Box 619, Thief River Falls, MN 56701; 218-683-7023; fax: 218-681-0907; 8AM-4:30PM. ***Felony, Misdemeanor, Civil, Eviction, Small Claims, Probate.*** www.mncourts.gov/district/9/

Week ahead court calendars available online.

Civil Records: Access: In person, online. Both court and visitors may perform in person searches. Search fee: $5.00 per name. Required to search: name, years to search. Civil cases indexed by defendant, plaintiff, on computer back to 1990, prior on TCIS cards and books to 1911. Civil PAT goes back to 1990. PAT civil results show middle initial. Limited search of civil, family and probate records are found at http://pa.courts.state.mn.us/default.aspx. Electronic filings and abuse cases not shown.

Criminal Records: Access: In person, online. Visitors must perform in person searches themselves. Required to search: name, years to search, DOB. Criminal records computerized from 1990, prior on TCIS cards and books to 1911. Criminal PAT goes back to 1990. PAT results show middle initial, DOB. Public terminal allows for a statewide search. Limited search of criminal record index at http://pa.courts.state.mn.us/default.aspx. Online results show middle initial, DOB.

General Information: No adoption, juvenile, sex offender or sealed records released. Fee to fax back-$25.00 per doc up to 25 pgs. Court makes copy: $5.00 per doc, self serve same. Certification fee: $10.00 per doc. Payee: Court Administrator. Personal checks and major credit cards accepted.

Pine County

10th Judicial District Court 635 Northridge Dr NW, #320, Pine City, MN 55063; 320-591-1500; fax: 320-591-1524; 8AM-4:30PM. ***Felony, Misdemeanor, Civil, Eviction, Small Claims, Probate.*** www.mncourts.gov/district/10/

Civil Records: Access: Mail, In person, online. Visitors must perform in person searches themselves. Search fee: No civil searches, but judgment search is $5.00 per name. Required to search: name, years to search. Civil cases indexed by defendant, plaintiff, on computer from 2/85. Weekly calendars free at www.mncourts.gov/district/10/?page=1326. Civil PAT goes back to 2/1985. PAT civil results show middle initial. Limited search of civil, family and probate records are found at http://pa.courts.state.mn.us/default.aspx. Electronic filings and abuse cases not shown.

Criminal Records: Access: In person, online. Visitors must perform in person searches themselves. Required to search: name, years to search. Criminal records computerized from 2/85. Criminal PAT goes back to 2/1985. PAT criminal results show middle initial. Public terminal allows for statewide search. Limited search crim record index at http://pa.courts.state.mn.us/default.aspx. Weekly calendars free at www.mncourts.gov/district/10/?page=1326. Online results show middle initial, DOB.

General Information: No adoption, juvenile, or sealed records released. Will fax documents. Court makes copy: $5.00 per doc; exemplification $10.00. Certification fee: $10.00 per doc. Payee: Court Admin. Personal checks accepted. Visa/MC accepted.

Pipestone County

5th Judicial District Court PO Box 337, 416 S Hiawatha Ave, Pipestone, MN 56164; 507-825-6730; fax: 507-825-6733; 8:30AM-4:30PM. ***Felony, Misdemeanor, Civil, Eviction, Small Claims, Probate.*** www.mncourts.gov/district/5/

Civil Records: Access: Mail, in person, online. Both court and visitors may perform in person searches. Search fee: $5.00 per name. Required to search: name, years to search. Civil cases indexed by defendant, plaintiff, on computer from 1989, prior on books. Mail turnaround time 7 days Civil PAT goes back to 1989. Search civil, family and probate records and calendars at http://pa.courts.state.mn.us/default.aspx. Electronic filings and abuse cases not shown.

Criminal Records: Access: In person, online. Visitors must perform in person searches themselves. Required to search: name, years to search. Criminal records computerized from 1989, prior on books. Court suggests sending requests to State Bureau of Criminal Apprehension. Criminal PAT goes back to 1989. Public terminal allows for a statewide search. Limited search of criminal record index at http://pa.courts.state.mn.us/default.aspx. Online results show middle initial, DOB.

General Information: No adoption, juvenile, sex offender victims or sealed records released. Fee to fax back- $25.00 per doc up to 25 pgs. Court makes copy: $5.00 per doc. Certification fee: $10.00 per doc. Payee: Court Administrator. Personal checks accepted. Visa/MC accepted. Mail requests: SASE required for civil.

Polk County

9th Judicial District Court Court Administrator, 816 Marin Ave, #210, Crookston, MN 56716; 218-281-2332; fax: 218-281-2204; 8AM-4:30PM. ***Felony, Misdemeanor, Civil, Eviction, Small Claims, Probate.*** www.mncourts.gov/district/9/

Week ahead court calendars available online.

Civil Records: Access: Mail, in person, online. Visitors must perform in person searches themselves. Search fee: $5.00 per name. Required to search: name, years to search. Civil cases indexed by defendant, plaintiff, on computer from 1990, prior on index cards or books. Child protection and child service cases are available since 7/1/2002. Mail turnaround time 3-5 days. Civil PAT goes back to 1990. PAT results show middle initial, DOB. Limited search of civil, family and probate records are at http://pa.courts.state.mn.us/default.aspx. Electronic filings and abuse cases not shown.

Criminal Records: Access: Mail, in person, online. Visitors must perform in person searches themselves. Search fee: $5.00 per name. Required to search: name, years to search, DOB. Criminal records computerized from 1990, prior on index cards or books. Mail turnaround time 3-5 days. Criminal PAT goes back to 1990. PAT results show middle initial, DOB. Public terminal allows for a statewide search. Limited search of criminal record index at http://pa.courts.state.mn.us/default.aspx. Online results show middle initial, DOB.

General Information: No adoption, non-felony under age 16 juvenile or sealed records released. Fee to fax back- $25.00 per doc up to 25 pgs. Court makes copy: $5.00 per doc. Cert fee: $10.00 per doc. Payee: Court Administrator. Personal checks accepted. Visa/MC accepted. Mail requests: SASE required.

Pope County

8th Judicial District Court 130 E Minnesota Ave, Glenwood, MN 56334; 320-634-5222; fax: 320-634-5527; 8AM-4:30PM. ***Felony, Misdemeanor, Civil, Eviction, Small Claims, Probate.*** www.mncourts.gov/district/8/

Civil Records: Access: Mail, in person, online. Both court and visitors may perform in person searches. Search fee: $5.00 per name. Required to search: name, years to search. Civil cases indexed by defendant, plaintiff, on computer from 1988, prior on TCIS cards ad books. Mail turnaround time 1 week Civil PAT goes back to 1990. Limited search of civil, family and probate records are found at http://pa.courts.state.mn.us/default.aspx. Electronic filings and abuse cases not shown.

Criminal Records: Access: In person, online. Visitors must perform in person searches themselves. Required to search: name, years to search. Criminal records computerized from 1988, prior on TCIS cards ad books. Criminal PAT goes back to 1990. PAT results show middle initial, DOB. Public terminal allows for a statewide search. Limited search of criminal record index at http://pa.courts.state.mn.us/default.aspx. Online results show middle initial, DOB.

General Information: No adoption, juvenile, sex offender or sealed records released. Will fax documents to local or toll-free number. Court makes copy: $5.00 per doc. Certification fee: $10.00 per doc. Payee: Court Administrator. Personal checks and major credit cards accepted. Mail requests: SASE required for civil.

Ramsey County

2nd Judicial District Court 1700 Ramsey County Courthouse, 15 Kellogg Blvd West, St Paul, MN 55102; criminal phone: 651-266-8180; civil phone: 651-266-8253; criminal fax: 651-266-8172; civil fax: 651-266-8263; 8AM-4:30PM. ***Felony, Misdemeanor, Civil, Probate.*** www.mncourts.gov/district/2/

Civil Records: Access: Mail, in person, online. Both court and visitors may perform in person searches.

Search fee: $10.00 per name. Required to search: name, years to search. Civil cases indexed by defendant, plaintiff, on computer from 5/88, prior on books. Mail turnaround time 1-2 days. Civil PAT goes back to 1988. PAT civil results show middle initial. Limited search of civil, family and probate records at http://pa.courts.state.mn.us/default.aspx. Electronic filings and abuse cases not shown.
Criminal Records: Access: In person, online. Visitors must perform in person searches themselves. Required to search: name, years to search, DOB. Felony records on computer go back to 1987; misdemeanors go back to 1985, prior on books to 1953 felonies only. Criminal PAT goes back to 1987. Public terminal allows for a statewide search. Limited search of criminal record index at http://pa.courts.state.mn.us/default.aspx. Online results show middle initial, DOB.
General Information: No adoption, juvenile, sex offender or sealed records released. Fee to fax back- $25.00 per doc up to 25 pgs. Court makes copy: $5.00 per doc; name printouts- $.50 each. Certification fee: $10.00 per doc. Payee: Court Administrator. Personal checks accepted. Visa/MC accepted. Mail requests: SASE required for civil.

2nd Judicial Dist. Ct - Maplewood Area 2050 White Bear Ave, Maplewood, MN 55109; 651-266-1999; fax: 651-266-1978; 8AM-4:30PM. ***Misdemeanor.*** www.mncourts.gov/district/2/
This court holds the records for the closed New Brighton Court.
Criminal Records: Access: In person, online. Visitors must perform in person searches themselves. Required to search: name; also helpful: address, DOB, offense, date of offense. Criminal records computerized from 11/90. Public use terminal has crim records back to 11/1990. PAT results show middle initial, DOB. Terminal results include date of offense. Public terminal allows for a statewide search. Limited search of criminal record index at http://pa.courts.state.mn.us/default.aspx. Online results show middle initial, DOB.
General Information: No adoption, juvenile, sex offender victim, sealed or medical records released. Will not fax documents. Court makes copy: $5.00 per doc. Certification fee: $10.00 per doc. Payee: Ramsey County District Court. Personal checks accepted. Credit cards accepted but not over phone.

Red Lake County

9th Judicial District Court PO Box 339, Red Lake Falls, MN 56750; 218-253-4281; criminal fax: 218-253-4287; civil fax: same; 8AM-4:30PM. ***Felony, Misdemeanor, Civil, Eviction, Small Claims, Probate.*** www.mncourts.gov/district/9/
Week ahead court calendars available online. Probate fax is same as main fax number.
Civil Records: Access: Mail, in person, online. Both court and visitors may perform in person searches. Search fee: $5.00 per name. Required to search: name, years to search. Civil cases indexed by defendant, plaintiff, on computer and microfiche from 1990, on books from 1897. Mail turnaround time 2-5 days. Civil PAT goes back to 1990. Limited search of civil, family and probate records are found at http://pa.courts.state.mn.us/default.aspx. Electronic filings and abuse cases not shown.
Criminal Records: Access: In person, online. Visitors must perform in person searches themselves. Required to search: name, years to search, DOB. Criminal records on computer and microfiche from 1990, on books from 1897. Court suggest you perform criminal search through BCA. Criminal PAT goes back to 1990.PAT results show name, DOB. Public terminal allows for a statewide search. Limited search of criminal record index at http://pa.courts.state.mn.us/default.aspx. Online results show middle initial, DOB.
General Information: No adoption, juvenile, sex offender or sealed records released. Will not fax documents. Court makes copy: $5.00 per doc. Certification fee: $10.00 per doc includes search fee. Payee: Court Administrator. Personal checks and major credit cards accepted. Mail requests: SASE required for civil.

Redwood County

5th Judicial District Court PO Box 130, 250th 3rd & Jefferson, Redwood Falls, MN 56283; 507-637-4020; probate phone: 507-637-4018; fax: 507-637-4021; 8AM-4:30PM. ***Felony, Misdemeanor, Civil, Eviction, Small Claims, Probate.*** www.mncourts.gov/district/5/
Probate fax is same as main fax number.
Civil Records: Access: In person, online. Both court and visitors may perform in person searches. No search fee. Required to search: name, years to search. Civil cases indexed by defendant, plaintiff, on computer from 11/88, prior on card and books. Civil PAT goes back to 1988. Limited search of civil, family and probate records are found at http://pa.courts.state.mn.us/default.aspx. Electronic filings and abuse cases not shown.
Criminal Records: Access: In person, online. Visitors must perform in person searches themselves. Required to search: name, years to search. Criminal records computerized from 11/88, prior on card and books. No felony or gross misdemeanor searches will be performed. Criminal PAT goes back to 1988. Public terminal allows for a statewide search. Limited search of criminal record index at http://pa.courts.state.mn.us/default.aspx. Online results show middle initial, DOB.
General Information: No adoption, juvenile, sex offender or sealed records released. Fee to fax back- $25.00 per doc up to 25 pgs. Court makes copy: $5.00 per doc. Certification fee: $10.00 per doc. Payee: Court Administrator. Personal checks and major credit cards accepted.

Renville County

8th Judicial District Court 500 E DePue Ave, 3rd level, Olivia, MN 56277; 320-523-3680; fax: 320-523-3689; 8AM-4:30PM. ***Felony, Misdemeanor, Civil, Eviction, Small Claims, Probate.*** www.mncourts.gov/district/8/
Civil Records: Access: Mail, in person, online. Both court and visitors may perform in person searches. Search fee: $5.00 per name. Required to search: name, years to search. Civil cases indexed by defendant, plaintiff, on computer from 1988, prior on index cards. Civil PAT goes back to 1/1988. Limited search of civil, family and probate records are at http://pa.courts.state.mn.us/default.aspx. Electronic filings and abuse cases not shown.
Criminal Records: Access: In person, online. Visitors must perform in person searches themselves. Required to search: name. Criminal records computerized from 1988, prior on index cards. Court recommends that written requests be submitted to the MN Bureau of Criminal Apprehension. Criminal PAT goes back to 1/1988. Public terminal allows for a statewide search. Limited search of criminal record index at http://pa.courts.state.mn.us/default.aspx. Online results show middle initial, DOB.
General Information: No adoption, juvenile or sealed records released. Fee to fax back- $25.00 per doc up to 20 pgs. Court makes copy: $5.00 per doc. Certification fee: $10.00 per doc. Payee: Court Administrator. Personal checks accepted; credit cards are not. Mail requests: SASE required for civil.

Rice County

3rd Judicial District Court 218 NW 3rd St, Faribault, MN 55021; 507-332-6107; probate phone: same; fax: 507-332-6199; 8AM-4:30PM. ***Felony, Misdemeanor, Civil, Eviction, Small Claims, Probate.*** www.mncourts.gov/district/3/
Civil Records: Access: Mail, in person, online. Both court and visitors may perform in person searches. Search fee: $5.00 per name. Required to search: name, years to search. Civil cases indexed by defendant, plaintiff, on computer from 1990, prior on index cards. Mail turnaround time 3 days. Civil PAT available. Public terminal connects to statewide online system. Limited search of civil, family and probate records are found at http://pa.courts.state.mn.us/default.aspx. Electronic filings and abuse cases not shown.
Criminal Records: Access: In person, online. Visitors must perform in person searches themselves. Required to search: name, years to search; SSN helpful. Criminal records computerized from 1990, prior on index cards. Criminal PAT available. Public terminal connects to statewide online system. Limited search of criminal record index at http://pa.courts.state.mn.us/default.aspx. Online results show middle initial, DOB.
General Information: Online identifiers in results same as on public terminal. No adoption, juvenile, sex offender or sealed records released. Will fax documents for $5.00 fee. Court makes copy: $5.00 per doc. Certification fee: $10.00 per doc. Payee: Court Administrator. Personal checks accepted. Visa/MC accepted. Mail requests: SASE required for civil.

Rock County

5th Judicial District Court PO Box 745, Luverne, MN 56156; 507-283-5020; criminal fax: 507-283-5017; civil fax: same; 8AM-5PM. ***Felony, Misdemeanor, Civil, Eviction, Small Claims, Probate.*** www.mncourts.gov/district/5/
Probate fax is same as main fax number.
Civil Records: Access: Mail, in person, online. Both court and visitors may perform in person searches. Search fee: $10.00 per name. Required to search: name, years to search. Civil cases indexed by defendant, plaintiff, on computer from 1989, prior on books. Visitors may search in books for records prior to 1985. Mail turnaround time same day if possible. Civil PAT goes back to 1989. Limited search of civil, family and probate records are found at http://pa.courts.state.mn.us/default.aspx. Electronic filings and abuse cases not shown.
Criminal Records: Access: Mail, in person, online. Both court and visitors may perform in person searches. Search fee: $10.00 per name. Required to search: name, years to search; also helpful: SSN. Criminal records computerized from 1989, prior on books. Visitors may search in books for records prior to 1985. Mail turnaround time same day if possible. Criminal PAT goes back to 1989. Public terminal allows for a statewide search. Limited search of criminal record index at http://pa.courts.state.mn.us/default.aspx. Online results show middle initial, DOB. Online results also show city and state of residence.
General Information: No adoption, juvenile, sex offender or sealed records released. Fee to fax back- $25.00 per doc up to 25 pgs. Court makes copy: $5.00 per doc. Certification fee: $10.00 (includes the copy fee, if ordered at same time). Payee: Court Administrator. Personal checks accepted. Visa/MC accepted. Mail requests: SASE required.

Roseau County

9th Judicial District Court 606 5th Ave SW Rm 20, Roseau, MN 56751; 218-463-2541; probate phone: same; fax: 218-463-1889; 8AM-4:30PM. ***Felony, Misdemeanor, Civil, Eviction, Small Claims, Probate.*** www.mncourts.gov/district/9/
Week ahead court calendars available online.
Civil Records: Access: Mail, in person, online. Both court and visitors may perform in person searches. Search fee: $5.00 per name. Required to search: name, years to search. Civil cases indexed by defendant, plaintiff, on computer back to 1990, prior on index cards or imaging to 1895. Mail turnaround time same day if possible. Civil PAT goes back to 1991. Public access terminal is made available to ongoing, experienced requesters. Limited search of civil, family and probate records are found at http://pa.courts.state.mn.us/default.aspx. Electronic filings and abuse cases not shown.
Criminal Records: Access: In person, online. Visitors must perform in person searches themselves. Required to search: name, years to search; also helpful: DOB. Criminal records computerized from 1990, prior on imaging or thru state historical society. Court will perform only statutorily required criminal searches. Criminal PAT goes back to 1991. Public access terminal is made available to ongoing, experienced requesters. Public terminal allows for a statewide search. Limited search of criminal record index at http://pa.courts.state.mn.us/default.aspx. Online results show middle initial, DOB.

General Information: No adoption, juvenile, paternity or sealed records released. Will fax documents to toll-free number. Court makes copy: $5.00 per doc. Certification fee: $10.00 per doc includes copy fee. Payee: Court Administrator. Personal checks accepted. Visa/MC accepted. Mail requests: SASE required for civil.

Scott County

1st Judicial District Court Scott County Justice Ctr, 200 Fourth Ave W, Shakopee, MN 55379; 952-496-8200; fax: 952-496-8211; 8AM-4:30PM. ***Felony, Misdemeanor, Civil, Eviction, Small Claims, Probate.*** www.mncourts.gov/district/1/

Civil Records: Access: Mail, in person, online. Both court and visitors may perform in person searches. Search fee: $5.00 per name. Required to search: name, years to search. Civil cases indexed by defendant, plaintiff, on computer from 1981, prior on books. Mail turnaround time 5 days Civil PAT goes back to 1996. Public terminal located in Library. Limited civil, family and probate records are at http://pa.courts.state.mn.us/default.aspx. Electronic filings and abuse cases not shown.

Criminal Records: Access: Mail, in person, online. Both court and visitors may perform in person searches. Search fee: $5.00 per name. Required to search: name, years to search, DOB. Criminal records computerized from 1981, prior on books. Criminal PAT goes back to 1996. Public terminal located in Library. Public terminal allows for a statewide search. Limited search of criminal record index at http://pa.courts.state.mn.us/default.aspx. Online results show middle initial, DOB.

General Information: No adoption, juvenile or sealed records released. Fee to fax back- $25.00 per doc up to 25 pgs. Court makes copy: $5.00 per doc. Certification fee: $10.00 per doc. Payee: Scott County District Court. Personal checks accepted. Credit cards accepted. Mail requests: SASE required.

Sherburne County

10th Judicial District Court Sherburne County Government Ctr, 13880 Hwy 10 West, Business Ctr Dr, Elk River, MN 55330-4608; 763-241-2800; fax: 763-241-2816; 8AM-4:30PM. ***Felony, Misdemeanor, Civil, Eviction, Small Claims, Probate.*** www.mncourts.gov/district/10/

Civil Records: Access: Mail, in person, online. Both court and visitors may perform in person searches. Search fee: $5.00 per name. Required to search: name, years to search. Civil cases indexed by defendant, plaintiff, on computer from 1985, prior on books. Weekly calendars free at www.mncourts.gov/district/10/?page=1326. Mail turnaround time 1 week Civil PAT goes back to 1985. PAT results show name only. Limited search of civil, family and probate records are found at http://pa.courts.state.mn.us/default.aspx. Electronic filings and abuse cases not shown.

Criminal Records: Access: In person, online. Both court and visitors may perform in person searches. Search fee: $5.00 per name. Required to search: name, years to search, DOB. Criminal records computerized from 1985, prior on books back to 1930s. Criminal PAT goes back to 1985. PAT results show name only. Public terminal allows for a statewide search. Limited search of criminal record index at http://pa.courts.state.mn.us/default.aspx. Weekly calendars free at www.mncourts.gov/district/10/?page=1326. Online results show middle initial, DOB.

General Information: No adoption, juvenile, confidential or sealed records released. Will not fax documents. Court makes copy: $5.00 per doc; exemplification $10.00. Certification fee: $10.00 per doc includes copy fee. Payee: Court Administrator. Personal checks accepted. Visa/MC accepted. Mail requests: SASE required for civil.

Sibley County

1st Judicial District Court PO Box 867, 400 Court St, Gaylord, MN 55334; 507-237-4051; criminal fax: 507-237-4062; civil fax: same; 8AM-4:30PM. ***Felony, Misdemeanor, Civil, Eviction, Small Claims, Probate.*** www.mncourts.gov/district/1/ Probate fax is same as main fax number.

Civil Records: Access: Mail, in person, online. Both court and visitors may perform in person searches. Search fee: $5.00 per name. Required to search: name, years to search. Civil cases indexed by defendant, plaintiff, on computer from 5/92, prior on books to 1800s. Mail turnaround time 2-3 weeks. Civil PAT goes back to 1992. Limited search of civil, family and probate records are found at http://pa.courts.state.mn.us/default.aspx. Search by case number or by name; Electronic filings and abuse cases not shown.

Criminal Records: Access: Mail, in person, online. Both court and visitors may perform in person searches. Search fee: $5.00 per name. Required to search: name, years to search, DOB. Criminal records computerized from 5/92, prior on books to 1800s. Mail turnaround time 2-3 weeks. Criminal PAT goes back to 1992. Public terminal allows for a statewide search. Limited search of criminal record index at http://pa.courts.state.mn.us/default.aspx. Only cases with dispositions appear in results; Electronic filings and abuse cases not shown. Online results show middle initial, DOB.

General Information: No adoption, juvenile, or sealed records released. Fee to fax back- $25.00 per doc up to 25 pgs. Court makes copy: $5.00 per doc. Certification fee: $10.00 per doc. Payee: Court Administrator. Personal checks accepted. Visa/MC accepted. Mail requests: SASE required.

St. Louis County

6th Judicial District Court 100 N 5th Ave W, Rm 320, Duluth, MN 55802-1294; 218-726-2469; probate phone: 218-726-2521; criminal fax: 218-726-2473; civil fax: 218-725-5074; 8AM-4:30PM. ***Felony, Misdemeanor, Civil, Eviction, Small Claims, Probate.*** www.mncourts.gov/district/6/

All 3 St Louis County courts can access computer records for the county and direct you to the appropriate court to get the physical file. Probate fax is same as main fax number.

Civil Records: Access: Mail, in person, online. Both court and visitors may perform in person searches. Search fee: $5.00 per name. Required to search: name, years to search. Civil cases indexed by defendant, plaintiff, on computer from 1976. Mail turnaround time 1 week. Civil PAT goes back to 1976. PAT results show middle initial, DOB, SSN. Limited search of civil, family and probate records are at http://pa.courts.state.mn.us/default.aspx. Electronic filings and abuse cases not shown.

Criminal Records: Access: In person, online. Visitors must perform in person searches themselves. Required to search: name. Criminal records computerized from 1976. Criminal PAT goes back to 1976. Public terminal allows for a statewide search. Limited search of criminal record index at http://pa.courts.state.mn.us/default.aspx. Online results show middle initial, DOB.

General Information: No adoption, juvenile, juvenile victim of sex offense, sealed records released. Will not fax documents. Court makes copy: $5.00 per doc. Certification fee: $10.00 (includes search fee). Payee: Court Administrator. Personal checks accepted; credit cards are not. SASE not required.

6th Judicial Dist CT - Hibbing Branch 1810 12th Ave East, Hibbing, MN 55746; 218-262-0105; probate phone: 218-726-2400; criminal fax: 218-262-0219; civil fax: same; 8AM-4:30PM. ***Felony, Misdemeanor, Civil, Eviction, Small Claims, Probate.*** www.mncourts.gov/district/6/

All 3 St Louis County courts can access county computer records and direct you to the appropriate court for the physical file. Probate fax is same as main fax number.

Civil Records: Access: Mail, in person, online. Both court and visitors may perform in person searches. Search fee: $5.00 per name/per judgment. Required to search: name, years to search. Civil cases indexed by defendant, plaintiff, on computer from 1985, prior on card or books. Civil PAT goes back to 1991. Not all terminal results include address, middle name or initial. Limited search of civil, family and probate records at http://pa.courts.state.mn.us/default.aspx. Electronic filings and abuse cases not shown.

Criminal Records: Access: In person, online. Visitors must perform in person searches themselves. Required to search: name, years to search. Criminal records computerized from 1985, prior on card or books. Criminal PAT goes back to 1991. PAT results show middle initial, DOB, SSN. Results include charges. Public terminal allows for a statewide search. Limited search of criminal record index at http://pa.courts.state.mn.us/default.aspx. Online results show middle initial, DOB.

General Information: No adoption, juvenile, sex offender or sealed records released. Fee to fax back- $25.00 per doc up to 25 pgs. Court makes copy: $5.00 per doc. Certification fee: $10.00 per doc. Payee: Court Administrator. Personal checks accepted. Credit cards not accepted for copies or searches. Mail requests: SASE required for civil.

6th Judicial Dist. Ct. - Virginia Branch 300 S 5th Ave, Virginia, MN 55792; 218-749-7106; fax: 218-749-7109; 8AM-4:30PM. ***Felony, Misdemeanor, Civil, Eviction, Small Claims, Probate.*** www.mncourts.gov/district/6/

All three St Louis County courts can access computer records for the county and direct you to the appropriate court for the physical files.

Civil Records: Access: Mail, in person, online. Both court and visitors may perform in person searches. Search fee: $5.00 per name. Required to search: name, years to search. Civil cases indexed by defendant, plaintiff, on computer back 15 years, prior on books. Mail turnaround time 1-2 days. Civil PAT goes back to 1990. PAT civil results show middle initial. Limited search of civil, family and probate records are found at http://pa.courts.state.mn.us/default.aspx. Electronic filings and abuse cases not shown.

Criminal Records: Access: In person, online. Visitors must perform in person searches themselves. Required to search: name, years to search, DOB. Criminal records on computer back 15 years, prior on books. Criminal PAT goes back to 1990. PAT criminal results show middle initial. Public terminal allows for a statewide search. Limited search of criminal record index at http://pa.courts.state.mn.us/default.aspx. Online results show middle initial, DOB.

General Information: No adoption, juvenile, sex offender or sealed records released. Fee to fax back- $25.00 per doc up to 25 pgs. Court makes copy: $5.00 per doc. Certification fee: $10.00 per doc. Payee: Court Administrator. Personal checks accepted; credit cards are not. SASE not required.

Stearns County

Stearns County District Court 725 Courthouse Square, St Cloud, MN 56303; 320-656-3620; fax: 320-656-6335; 8AM-4:30PM. ***Felony, Misdemeanor, Civil, Small Claims, Eviction, Probate, Traffic.*** www.mncourts.gov/district/7/ Court calendars free at website.

Civil Records: Access: Mail, in person, online. Both court and visitors may perform in person searches. Search fee: $5.00 per name. Required to search: name, years to search. Civil cases indexed by defendant, plaintiff, on computer back to 1984, on books from the 1920s. Civil PAT goes back to 1984. PAT results show middle initial, DOB. Limited search of civil, family and probate records are at http://pa.courts.state.mn.us/default.aspx. Electronic filings and abuse cases not shown.

Criminal Records: Access: In person, online. Both court and visitors may perform in person searches. No search fee. Required to search: name. Criminal records computerized from 1984, on books from the 1920s. Criminal PAT goes back to 1984. PAT results show middle initial, DOB. Public terminal allows for a statewide search. Limited search of criminal record index at http://pa.courts.state.mn.us/default.aspx. Online results show middle initial, DOB.

General Information: No adoption or other sealed records released without court petition. Fee to fax back- $25.00 per doc up to 25 pgs. Court makes copy: $5.00 per doc. Certification fee: $10.00. Payee: District Court. Personal checks accepted. Visa/MC accepted. SASE not required.

Steele County

3rd Judicial District Court PO Box 487 (111 E Main St), Owatonna, MN 55060; 507-444-7700; probate phone: 507-444-7707; fax: 507-444-7491; 8AM-4:30PM. ***Felony, Misdemeanor, Civil, Eviction, Small Claims, Probate.*** www.mncourts.gov/district/3/

Civil Records: Access: Mail, in person, online. Both court and visitors may perform in person searches. Search fee: $5.00. Required to search: name, years to search. Civil cases indexed by defendant, plaintiff, on computer from 1990, on books from 1870. Civil PAT goes back to 1990. Limited search of civil, family and probate records are found at http://pa.courts.state.mn.us/default.aspx. Electronic filings and abuse cases not shown.

Criminal Records: Access: In person, online. Visitors must perform in person searches themselves. Required to search: name, years to search; SSN helpful. Criminal records computerized from 1990, on books from 1870. Criminal PAT goes back to 1990. Public terminal allows for a statewide search. Limited search of criminal record index at http://pa.courts.state.mn.us/default.aspx. Online results show middle initial, DOB.

General Information: No adoption, juvenile, sex offender or sealed records released. Will not fax documents. Court makes copy: $5.00 per doc. Certification fee: $10.00 per doc. Payee: Court Administrator. Personal checks accepted. Visa/MC accepted. Mail requests: SASE required for civil.

Stevens County

8th Judicial District Court PO Box 530, 400 Colorado, Morris, MN 56267; 320-589-7287; probate phone: same; fax: 320-589-7288; 8AM-4:30PM (8AM-4PM Summer hours). ***Felony, Misdemeanor, Civil, Eviction, Small Claims, Probate.*** www.mncourts.gov/district/8/

Civil Records: Access: Mail, in person, online. Both court and visitors may perform in person searches. Search fee: $5.00 per name. Required to search: name, years to search. Civil cases indexed by defendant, plaintiff, on computer from 2/89, on cards from 5/86, on books from 1900. Mail turnaround time 2 days. Civil PAT goes back to 2/1989. PAT results show name only. Limited search of civil, family and probate records are found at http://pa.courts.state.mn.us/default.aspx. Electronic filings and abuse cases not shown.

Criminal Records: Access: In person, online. Visitors must perform in person searches themselves. Required to search: name, years to search. Criminal records computerized from 2/89, on cards from 5/86, on books from 1900. For access to criminal history information, the court recommends the BCA at 651-642-0610. Criminal PAT goes back to 2/1989. PAT results show name only. Public terminal allows for a statewide search. Limited search of criminal record index at http://pa.courts.state.mn.us/default.aspx. Online results show middle initial, DOB.

General Information: No adoption, juvenile, sex offender or sealed records released. Will fax documents to local or toll free line. Court makes copy: $5.00 per doc. Certification fee: $10.00 per doc. Payee: Court Administrator. Personal checks and major credit cards accepted. Mail requests: SASE required for civil.

Swift County

8th Judicial District Court PO Box 110, Benson, MN 56215; 320-843-2744; criminal fax: 320-843-4124; civil fax: same; 8AM-4:30PM. ***Felony, Misdemeanor, Civil, Eviction, Small Claims, Probate.*** www.mncourts.gov/district/8/

Probate records prior to 1983 are in a separate index. Probate fax is same as main fax number.

Civil Records: Access: Phone, fax, mail, in person, online. Both court and visitors may perform in person searches. No search fee. Required to search: name, years to search. Civil cases indexed by defendant, plaintiff, on computer back to 8/1988, prior in files and books from 1800s. Mail turnaround time 1-2 weeks Civil PAT goes back to 8/1988. PAT results show name only. Limited search of civil and family are found at http://pa.courts.state.mn.us/default.aspx. Electronic filings and abuse cases not shown.

Criminal Records: Access: Mail, in person, online. Visitors must perform in person searches themselves. Search fee: $5.00 per name. Required to search: name, years to search; also helpful: DOB. Criminal records computerized from 1988, prior in files and books from 1800s except those destroyed per retention schedule. Criminal PAT goes back to 8/1988. Public terminal allows for a statewide search. Limited search of criminal record index at http://pa.courts.state.mn.us/default.aspx. Online results show middle initial, DOB.

General Information: No adoption, juvenile, minor victim of sex offense, sealed records released. Fee to fax back- $25.00 per doc up to 25 pgs. Court makes copy: $5.00 per doc. Certification fee: $10.00 per doc. Payee: Court Administrator. Personal checks and major credit cards accepted. Mail requests: SASE required for civil.

Todd County

7th Judicial District Court 221 1st Ave South, #100, Long Prairie, MN 56347; 320-732-7800; criminal fax: 320-732-2506; civil fax: same; 8AM-4:30PM. ***Felony, Misdemeanor, Civil, Eviction, Small Claims, Probate.*** www.mncourts.gov/district/7/

Probate fax is same as main fax number.

Civil Records: Access: Mail, in person, online. Both court and visitors may perform in person searches. Search fee: $5.00 per name. Required to search: name, years to search, address. Civil cases indexed by defendant, plaintiff, on computer 7/86, prior on index cards and books. Mail turnaround time 5-7 days. Civil PAT goes back to 1986. PAT civil results show middle initial. Limited search of civil, family and probate records are found at http://pa.courts.state.mn.us/default.aspx. Electronic filings and abuse cases not shown.

Criminal Records: Access: Mail, in person, online. Both court and visitors may perform in person searches. Search fee: $5.00 per name. Required to search: name, years to search, address, DOB. Criminal records on computer 7/86, prior on index cards and books. Mail turnaround time 5-7 days. Criminal PAT goes back to 1986. PAT criminal results show middle initial. Public terminal allows for a statewide search. Limited search of criminal record index at http://pa.courts.state.mn.us/default.aspx. Online results show middle initial, DOB.

General Information: No adoption, juvenile or sealed records released. Fee to fax back- $25.00 per doc up to 25 pgs. Court makes copy: $5.00 per doc. Certification fee: $10.00 per document, includes copy fee. Payee: Court Administrator. Personal checks accepted. Visa/MC accepted. Mail requests: SASE required.

Traverse County

8th Judicial District Court 702 2nd Ave N, PO Box 867, Wheaton, MN 56296; 320-563-4343; criminal fax: 320-563-4311; civil fax: same; 8AM-N, 12:30-4:30PM. ***Felony, Misdemeanor, Civil, Eviction, Small Claims, Probate.*** www.mncourts.gov/district/8/

Probate fax is same as main fax number.

Civil Records: Access: Mail, in person, online. Both court and visitors may perform in person searches. Search fee: $5.00 per name. Required to search: name, years to search. Civil cases indexed by defendant, plaintiff, on computer from 6/89, prior on index cards and books, and on images. Only judgment searches accepted by mail. Mail turnaround time 1-2 days. Civil PAT goes back to 6/1989. Limited search of civil, family and probate records at http://pa.courts.state.mn.us/default.aspx. Electronic filings and abuse cases not shown.

Criminal Records: Access: In person, online. Visitors must perform in person searches themselves. Required to search: name, years to search. Criminal records computerized from 6/89, prior on index cards and books. Criminal PAT goes back to 6/1989. Public terminal allows for a statewide search. Limited search of criminal record index at http://pa.courts.state.mn.us/default.aspx. Online results show middle initial, DOB.

General Information: No adoption, juvenile, sex offender or sealed records released. Fee to fax back- $25.00 per doc up to 25 pgs. Court makes copy: $5.00 per doc. Certification fee: $10.00 per document. Payee: Court Administrator. Personal checks accepted. Visa/MC accepted. Mail requests: SASE required for civil.

Wabasha County

3rd Judicial District Court 625 Jefferson Ave, Wabasha, MN 55981; 651-565-3012; criminal phone: 651-565-3010/3524/3097; civil phone: 651-565-3579/3087/3051; probate phone: 651-565-3051/3579/3087; criminal fax: 651-565-8214; civil fax: same; 8AM-4:30PM. ***Felony, Misdemeanor, Civil, Eviction, Small Claims, Probate.*** www.mncourts.gov/district/3/

Probate fax is same as main fax number.

Civil Records: Access: Phone, fax, mail, in person, online. Both court and visitors may perform in person searches. Search fee: $5.00 for judgment searches. Required to search: name, years to search. Civil cases indexed by defendant, plaintiff, on computer from 6/89, prior on index cards and books. Search daily court calendar at the website. Civil PAT goes back to 6/1989. Limited search of civil, family and probate records are found at http://pa.courts.state.mn.us/default.aspx. Electronic filings and abuse cases not shown.

Criminal Records: Access: In person, online. Visitors must perform in person searches themselves. Required to search: name, years to search; also helpful: DOB. Criminal records computerized from 6/89, prior on index cards and books. View weekly court calendar at the website. Criminal PAT goes back to 6/1989. Public terminal allows for a statewide search. Limited search of criminal record index at http://pa.courts.state.mn.us/default.aspx. Online results show middle initial, DOB.

General Information: No adoption, juvenile, sex offender or sealed records released. Fee to fax back- $25.00 per doc up to 25 pgs. Court makes copy: $5.00 per doc. Certification fee: $10.00 per doc. Payee: Wabasha District Court. Personal checks accepted. Credit cards accepted. Mail requests: SASE requested.

Wadena County

7th Judicial District Court County Courthouse, 415 S Jefferson St, Wadena, MN 56482; 218-631-7633; fax: 218-631-7635; 8AM-4:30PM. ***Felony, Misdemeanor, Civil, Eviction, Small Claims, Probate.*** www.mncourts.gov/district/7/

Note that the search fee is $5.00 and the copy fee is an additional $5.00.

Civil Records: Access: Mail, in person, online. Both court and visitors may perform in person searches. Search fee: $5.00 per name. Required to search: name, years to search. Civil cases indexed by defendant, plaintiff, on computer from 7/86; prior on books, cards and microfiche. Mail turnaround time 7 to 10 days. Civil PAT goes back to 7/1986. Limited search of civil, family and probate records are at http://pa.courts.state.mn.us/default.aspx. Electronic filings and abuse cases not shown.

Criminal Records: Access: Mail, in person, online. Both court and visitors may perform in person searches. Search fee: $5.00 per name. Required to search: name, years to search, DOB; also helpful: address. Criminal records computerized from 7/86; prior on books, cards and microfiche. Mail turnaround time 7-10 days. Criminal PAT goes back to 7/1986. Public terminal allows for a statewide search. Limited search of criminal record index at http://pa.courts.state.mn.us/default.aspx. Online results show middle initial, DOB.

General Information: No adoption, juvenile, or sealed records released. Fee to fax back- $25.00 per doc up to 25 pgs. Court makes copy: $5.00 per doc, $1.00 if terminal printout. Certification fee: $10.00, includes copy fee. Payee: Court Administrator. Personal checks accepted. Visa/MC accepted.

Waseca County

3rd Judicial District Court 307 N State St, Waseca, MN 56093; 507-835-0540; fax: 507-837-5317; 8AM-4:30PM; closed 8AM-12:30PM TH. ***Felony, Misdemeanor, Civil, Eviction, Small Claims, Probate, Family.***
www.mncourts.gov/district/3/

Civil Records: Access: Mail, in person, online. Both court and visitors may perform in person searches. Search fee: $5.00 per name. Required to search: name, years to search. Civil cases indexed by defendant, plaintiff, on computer from 1990, prior on TCIS cards and books. Mail turnaround time 5 days. Civil PAT goes back to 1990. PAT results show name, DOB. Limited search of civil, family and probate records are found at http://pa.courts.state.mn.us/default.aspx. Electronic filings and abuse cases not shown.

Criminal Records: Access: In person, online. Visitors must perform in person searches themselves. Required to search: name, years to search, DOB. Criminal records computerized from 1990, prior on TCIS cards and books. Criminal PAT goes back to 1990. PAT results show middle initial, DOB. Public terminal allows for a statewide search. Limited search of criminal record index at http://pa.courts.state.mn.us/default.aspx. Online results show middle initial, DOB.

General Information: No adoption, juvenile, sex offender victim or sealed records released. Fee to fax back- $25.00 per doc up to 25 pgs. Court makes copy: $5.00 per doc. Certification fee: $10.00 per doc. Payee: Court Administrator. Personal checks accepted. Visa/MC accepted. Mail requests: SASE required for civil.

Washington County

10th Judicial District Court 14949 62nd St North, PO Box 3802, Stillwater, MN 55082-3802; 651-430-6263; fax: 651-430-6300; 8:30AM-5PM. ***Felony, Misdemeanor, Civil, Eviction, Small Claims, Probate.*** www.mncourts.gov/district/10/

Civil Records: Access: Mail, in person, online. Both court and visitors may perform in person searches. Search fee: $5.00 per name. Required to search: name, years to search. Civil cases indexed by defendant, plaintiff, on computer back to 12/83, prior on books. Weekly calendars free at www.mncourts.gov/district/10/?page=1326. Civil PAT goes back to 1991. Limited search of civil, family and probate records are found at http://pa.courts.state.mn.us/default.aspx. Electronic filings and abuse cases not shown.

Criminal Records: Access: In person, online. Visitors must perform in person searches themselves. Required to search: name, years to search, DOB. Criminal records computerized from 12/83, prior on books. Fax and mail access limited to statute requirements. Criminal PAT goes back to 1991. Public terminal allows for a statewide search. Limited search of criminal record index at http://pa.courts.state.mn.us/default.aspx. Weekly calendars free at www.mncourts.gov/district/10/?page=1326. Online results show middle initial, DOB.

General Information: No adoption, juvenile, sex offender or sealed records released. Will not fax documents. Court makes copy: $5.00 per doc; exemplification $20.00. Certification fee: $10.00 per doc. Payee: Court Administrator. Personal checks accepted. Credit cards accepted. SASE not required.

Watonwan County

5th Judicial District Court PO Box 518, 710 2nd Ave South, St James, MN 56081; 507-375-1236; criminal phone: x1; civil phone: x2; probate phone: x2; fax: 507-375-5010; 8AM-5PM. ***Felony, Misdemeanor, Civil, Eviction, Small Claims, Probate.*** www.mncourts.gov/district/5/
The Jury Office can be reached at 507-375-1236.

Civil Records: Access: Fax, mail, in person, online. Both court and visitors may perform in person searches. Search fee: $5.00 per name. Required to search: name, years to search. Civil cases indexed by defendant, plaintiff, on computer from 5/89, prior on index cards. Mail turnaround time 5 business days. Civil PAT goes back to 4/1988. PAT results show middle initial, DOB, SSN. Limited search of civil, family and probate records are found at http://pa.courts.state.mn.us/default.aspx. Search by case number or by name.

Criminal Records: Access: Mail, in person, online. Visitors must perform in person searches themselves. Search fee: $15.00 per name. Required to search: name, years to search; also helpful: DOB. Criminal records computerized from 5/89, prior on index cards. Mail turnaround time 5 business days. Criminal PAT goes back to 4/1988. PAT results show middle initial, DOB, SSN. Public terminal allows for a statewide search. Limited search of criminal record index at http://pa.courts.state.mn.us/default.aspx. Only cases with dispositions appear in results. Online results show middle initial, DOB.

General Information: No adoption, juvenile, sex offender or sealed records released. Fee to fax back- $5.00 per doc. Court makes copy: $5.00 per doc. Certification fee: $10.00 per doc includes copy fee. Payee: Court Administrator. Personal checks and major credit cards accepted. Mail requests: SASE required for civil.

Wilkin County

8th Judicial District Court PO Box 219, Breckenridge, MN 56520; 218-643-7172; probate phone: same; fax: 218-643-7167; 8AM-4:30PM. ***Felony, Misdemeanor, Civil, Eviction, Small Claims, Probate.*** www.mncourts.gov/district/8/

Civil Records: Access: Phone, mail, in person, online. Both court and visitors may perform in person searches. No search fee. Required to search: name; also helpful: years to search. Civil cases indexed by defendant, plaintiff, on computer from 1989, prior on books. Mail turnaround time 7-14 days. Civil PAT goes back to 1989. Limited search of civil, family and probate records are found at http://pa.courts.state.mn.us/default.aspx. Electronic filings and abuse cases not shown.

Criminal Records: Access: In person, online. Both court and visitors may perform in person searches. Required to search: name; also helpful: years to search. Criminal records computerized from 1989, prior on books. Criminal PAT goes back to 1989. Public terminal allows for a statewide search. Limited search of criminal record index at http://pa.courts.state.mn.us/default.aspx. Online results show middle initial, DOB.

General Information: No adoption, juvenile, sex offender or sealed records released. Fee to fax back- $25.00 per doc up to 25 pgs. Court makes copy: $5.00 per doc. Certification fee: $10.00 per doc. Payee: Court Administrator. Personal checks accepted. Visa/MC accepted. Mail requests: SASE required.

Winona County

3rd Judicial District Court 171 W 3rd St, Winona, MN 55987; 507-457-6385; fax: 507-457-6392; 8AM-4:30PM. ***Felony, Misdemeanor, Civil, Eviction, Small Claims, Probate.***
www.mncourts.gov/district/3/

Civil Records: Access: Mail, in person, online. Both court and visitors may perform in person searches. Search fee: $10.00 per hour. Required to search: name, years to search. Civil cases indexed by defendant, plaintiff, on computer from 1986, on books from 1962. Only in person civil searches by public computer, not older book indices. Mail turnaround time 5-10 working days. Civil PAT goes back to 1986. PAT civil results show middle initial. identifiers on terminal results vary by case type. Limited search of civil, family and probate records are at http://pa.courts.state.mn.us/default.aspx. Electronic filings and abuse cases not shown.

Criminal Records: Access: In person, online. Visitors must perform in person searches themselves. Required to search: name, years to search, DOB. Criminal records computerized from 1986, on books from 1962. Criminal searchers are usually referred to the MN State BCA. Court accepts phone requests to lookup specific offenses, 502-457-6570; case number very helpful. Criminal PAT goes back to 1986. PAT results show middle initial, DOB. Terminal results can include addresses. Public terminal allows for a statewide search. Limited search of criminal record index at http://pa.courts.state.mn.us/default.aspx. Only cases with dispositions appear in results. Online results show middle initial, DOB.

General Information: No adoption, juvenile or sealed records released. Will not fax documents. Court makes copy: $5.00 per doc. Certification fee: $10.00 per case. Cert fee includes original $5.00 search fee. Payee: Court Administrator. Personal checks accepted. Visa/MC accepted. SASE not required.

Wright County

10th Judicial District Court 10 NW 2nd St, Rm 201, Buffalo, MN 55313-1192; 763-682-7549; fax: 763-682-7300; 8AM-4:30PM. ***Felony, Misdemeanor, Civil, Eviction, Small Claims, Probate.***
www.mncourts.gov/district/10/

Civil Records: Access: In person, online. Visitors must perform in person searches themselves. Required to search: name, years to search, approx. date. Civil cases indexed by defendant, plaintiff, on computer from 8/84, prior on books, cards & microfiche. Certificates for outstanding docketed money judgments may be requested by mail. Each name variation requires $5.00 fee. Weekly calendars are online free at www.mncourts.gov/district/10/?page=1326. Civil PAT goes back to 1984. PAT results show middle initial; also DOB and full name may be on party record. Limited search of civil, family and probate records at http://pa.courts.state.mn.us/default.aspx. Electronic filings and abuse cases not shown.

Criminal Records: Access: In person, online. Visitors must perform in person searches themselves. Required to search: name, years to search; also helpful: DOB, approx. date. Criminal records computerized from 8/84, prior on books, cards & microfiche. Criminal PAT goes back to 1984. PAT results show middle initial, DOB. Public terminal allows for a statewide search. Limited search of criminal record index at http://pa.courts.state.mn.us/default.aspx. Weekly calendars free at www.mncourts.gov/district/10/?page=1326. Online results show middle initial, DOB.

General Information: No adoption, juvenile, confidential or sealed records released. Fee to fax back- $25.00 per doc up to 25 pgs; prepay by credit card. Court makes copy: $5.00 per doc; exemplification $10.00. Certification fee: $10.00 per doc. Payee: Court Administrator. Personal checks and major credit cards accepted.

Yellow Medicine County

8th Judicial District Court 415 9th Ave, #103, Granite Falls, MN 56241; 320-564-3325; fax: 320-564-4435; 8AM-4PM. ***Felony, Misdemeanor, Civil, Eviction, Small Claims, Probate.***
www.mncourts.gov/district/8/

Civil Records: Access: Mail, in person, online. Both court and visitors may perform in person searches. Search fee: $10.00 for certified search. Required to search: name, years to search; also helpful: address. Civil cases indexed by defendant, plaintiff, on computer from 1988. Civil PAT goes back to 1988. Limited search of civil, family and probate records are at http://pa.courts.state.mn.us/default.aspx. Electronic filings and abuse cases not shown.

Criminal Records: Access: In person, online. Visitors must perform in person searches themselves. Required to search: name, years to search. Criminal records computerized from 1988. Criminal PAT goes back to 1988. Public terminal allows for a statewide search. Limited search of criminal record index at http://pa.courts.state.mn.us/default.aspx. Online results show middle initial, DOB.

General Information: No adoption, juvenile or sealed records released. Fee to fax back- $25.00 per doc up to 25 pgs. Court makes copy: $5.00 per doc. Certification fee: $10.00 per doc. Payee: Court Administrator. Personal checks and major credit cards accepted. Mail requests: SASE required for civil.

Minnesota Recording Offices

ORGANIZATION: 87 counties, 87 recording offices. The recording officer is the County Recorder. Minnesota is in the Central Time Zone (CST)

REAL ESTATE RECORDS: Many Minnesota counties will perform real estate searches, including over the phone if kept to short questions. Uncertified copy fees vary. Certification fee is usually $10.00 per doc which includes the copy fee.

UCC RECORDS: The only UCC filings recorded by the County Recorder are real estate related collateral. Most counties will perform searches of these records, fees vary.

TAX LIEN RECORDS: Federal and state tax liens on personal property of businesses are filed with the Secretary of State. Other federal and state tax liens are filed with the County Recorder. A special search form UCC-12 is used for separate tax lien searches. Some counties search each tax lien index separately, and charge $15.00 or $20.00 fee to search both indexes, but others charge a separate fee for each index searched. Search fees vary.

OTHER LIENS: Mechanics, hospital, judgment, attorneys, divorce-related real estate recordings.

ONLINE ACCESS: There is no statewide system but a number of counties offer web access to assessor data and recorded deeds, but you may search UCC data on the Secretary of State website at www.sos.state.mn.us/home/index.asp?page=1171

Aitkin County

County Recorder, 209 2nd St NW, Rm 205, Aitkin, MN 56431. Recording, R/E & UCC phone-218-927-7336; fax-218-927-7324; 8AM-4:30PM (CST) www.co.aitkin.mn.us/departments/Recorder/recorder.htm

Index: Separate indices to search. Records indexed on a public use terminal back to 1985. Office personnel or visitors may perform searches. Search fee $20.00 per name. Office will do a quick search of real estate records, nothing definite. General copy fee $1.00 per page after 10 pages.Real estate or tax lien copy- $.25 per page. Cert fee- $1.00 per page, $5.00 minimum, includes copy fee. Payee- Aitkin County Recorder. **Other phones:** Treasurer- 218-927-7325; Elections- 218-927-7354; Vital Records- 218-927-7336; Marriage Records -218-927-7325. **Property tax/Assessing**- 209 2nd St NW, Rm 111, Aitkin, MN 56431; 218-927-7327, assessor fax- 218-927-7379. (Appraiser/Auditor- 218-927-7327) A public access terminal available. **Online access**- Access property data free at http://gisweb.co.aitkin.mn.us/wf2_aitkinpublic/Default.aspx. Click on Search to search by name.

Anoka County

County Recorder, 2100 3rd Ave, Anoka, MN 55303-2265. 763-323-5400, R/E recording phone-763-323-5413; fax-763-323-5421; 8AM-4:30PM (CST) www.co.anoka.mn.us/

Recording and property tax departments - called Property Records and Taxation - are combined in this county. Index: All in one. Records indexed on a public use terminal back to 1994; historical tract is indexed back to 1950. Office personnel or visitors may perform searches. General copy fee $1.00 per page up to 10 pages.Real estate record copy- $.55 per page uncertified. Cert fee- $1.00 per page, $5.00 minimum. Payee- Anoka County Recorder. Bulk data available for $.10 per page; contact Pam Leblanc at 763-323-5424. **Online access to Real Estate, Deed records:** Access to the County online records requires an annual fee of $35 and a $25 monthly fee and $.25 per transaction. Records date back to 1995. Lending agency data is available. For info, contact Pam LeBlanc at 763-323-5424. There is also a dial-up property information system at 763-323-5400. **Other phones:** Treasurer- 763-323-5400. **Property tax/Assessing**- 2100 3rd Ave, Anoka, MN 55303-2265; 763-323-5400, assessor fax- 763-323-5421. A public access terminal is available. www.anokacounty.us **Online access**- Access property data at https://prtinfo.co.anoka.mn.us/.

Becker County

County Recorder, PO Box 787, Detroit Lakes, MN 56502. Recording, R/E & UCC phone-218-846-7304; fax-218-846-7323; 8AM-4:30PM (CST) www.co.becker.mn.us/dept/recorder/default.aspx

Index: All in one. Records indexed on a public use terminal back to 1993. Office personnel or visitors may perform searches. Search fee $15.00 per name. Office will not search real estate records. Office will not search UCC records. General copy fee $1.00 per page after 5 pages. Fax back- $5.00 per doc.Cert fee- $10.00 up to 10 pages plus copy fee. Payee- Becker County Recorder. Office does sell bulk data on CD's, contact Darlene Maneval. **Other phones:** Treasurer- 218-846-7311; Elections- 218-846-7301; Vital Records- 218-846-7304. **Property tax/Assessing**- PO Box 787, 913 Lake Ave, 2nd Fl, Courthouse, Detroit Lakes, MN 56502; 218-846-7300, assessor fax- 218-846-7257. (Appraiser/Auditor- 218-846-7301) www.co.becker.mn.us/dept/assessor/default.aspx **Online** - Access to the assessor property data is free at http://gis-server.co.becker.mn.us/website/beckerpublic/Default.aspx. Also, search plat images free at www.co.becker.mn.us/dept/recorder/plats_online.aspx.

Beltrami County

County Recorder, 701 Minnesota Ave, #120, Bemidji, MN 56601. Recording, R/E & UCC phone-218-333-4170, UCC recording phone-218-333-4137; 8AM-4:30PM (CST) www.co.beltrami.mn.us

Index: Separate indices to search include books and computer. Records indexed on a public use terminal back to 1987. Office personnel or visitors may perform searches. Search fee $30.00 per hour. Office will search real estate records as time allows. Office will not search UCC records. Copy fee $1.00 per page.Cert fee- $10.00 per cert includes copy fee. Payee- Beltrami County Recorder. **Online access to Real Estate, Deed, Lien records:** Recorder land data by subscription on either the Laredo system using subscription and fees or the Tapestry System using credit card, see http://tapestry.fidlar.com; $3.99 search; $.50 per image. Index goes back to 1985, images to 2002. **Other phones:** Treasurer- 218-333-4175; Elections- 218-333-8448; Vital Records- 218-333-8040. **Property tax/Assessing**- 701 Minnesota Ave, #130, Bemidji, MN 56601; 218-333-4116.

Benton County

County Recorder, PO Box 129, Foley, MN 56329. Recording, R/E & UCC phone-320-968-5037; fax-320-968-5306; 8AM-4:30PM (CST) www.co.benton.mn.us

Index: Separate indices to search include through 07/31/2005, records are on microfiche. Records indexed on a public use terminal back to 0801/2005. Office personnel or visitors may perform searches. Search fee $20.00 per name. Office will search real estate records back 6 months or last deed only. Will search UCC records. General copy fee $.25 per page.Cert fee- $10.00 per page includes copy fee. Payee- Benton County Recorder. Bulk data available for purchase of mortgage reports. Talk to anyone in Recorder's office. **Online access to Plats/Tract records:** Access to plats/tract available for free at www.co.benton.mn.us/Recorder/plats.asp. **Other phones:** Treasurer- 320-968-5006; Elections- 320-968-5027; Vital Records- 320-968-5037. **Property tax/Assessing**- PO Box 129, 531 Dewey St, Foley, MN 56329; 320-968-5019, assessor fax- 320-968-5329. www.co.benton.mn.us/Assessor/index.htm **Online access**- Free search of Auditor property tax data at http://benton.visualgov.com/ParcelSearch.aspx but no name searching.

Big Stone County

County Recorder, 20 2nd St SE, #106, Ortonville, MN 56278. Recording, R/E phone-320-839-6390, UCC recording phone- 320-839-2308; fax- 320-839-6394; hours - 8AM-4:30PM (CST) www.bigstonecounty.org/RecorderInfo.htm

Index: All in one. Records indexed on a public use terminal back to 2003. Only the public may search. Copy fee $.50 per page. Real estate copy- $2.00 minimum per document. Cert fee- $10.00 per doc. Payee- Big Stone County Recorder. **Other phones:** Treasurer- 320-839-6395; Vital Records- 320-839-6390; Auditor- 320-839-6366. **Property tax/Assessing**- 20 SE 2nd St, Ortonville, MN 56278; 320-839-6360, assessor fax- 320-839-6364. (Appraiser/Auditor- 320-839-6366);

Blue Earth County

County Recorder, PO Box 3567, Mankato, MN 56002-3567. Recording, R/E & UCC phone-507-304-4251, UCC recording phone-507-304-4469; fax-507-304-4079; 8AM-5PM www.co.blue-earth.mn.us

Index: All in one. Records indexed on computer back to 2004. Office personnel or visitors may perform searches. Search fee $5.00 per name. Real estate owner, mortgage, and property transfer searches available. Will search back 1 year; legal description required. Office will not search UCC records. Copy fee $3.00 per page; self serve- $1.00.Cert fee- $10.00 per doc. Payee- Blue Earth Taxpayer Services. Mapping available, $25.00. **Other phones:** Treasurer- 507-304-4251; Elections- 507-304-4341; Vital Records- 507-304-4343. **Property tax/Assessing**- PO Box 3567, Mankato, MN 56002-3567; 507-304-4251, assessor fax- 507-304-4079. **Online access**- Access to the property data search database is free at www.co.blue-earth.mn.us/tax/. Also, you may search at www.blueearth.minnesotaassessors.com. No name searching at either site, but a subscription service is available at the latter.

Brown County

County Recorder, PO Box 248, New Ulm, MN 56073-0248. Recording, R/E & UCC phone-507-233-6653, UCC recording phone-507-233-6657; fax-507-233-6668; 8AM-5PM (CST) www.co.brown.mn.us

Index: All in one. Records indexed on a public use terminal back to 1987. Office personnel or visitors may perform searches. Search fee $15.00 per name base fee. Real estate owner, mortgage, and property transfer searches available. Tax liens not included in UCC search. UCC search per debtor, including 10 copies/listings- $20.00. Tax lien search- $2.00 per debtor. Copy fee $1.00 per page.Cert fee- $10.00 per doc plus copy fee. Payee- Brown County Recorder. **Online access to Real Estate, Grantor/Grantee, Deed, Tract records:** Real Estate, Grantor/Grantee Index and Tract index to be available 2009. **Other phones:** Treasurer- 507-233-6617; Elections- 507-233-6617; Vital Records- 507-233-6657. **Property tax/ Assessing**- PO Box 248, New Ulm, MN 56073-0248; 507-233-6609, assessor fax- 507-359-1430. (Appraiser/Auditor- 507-233-6609) www.co.brown.mn.us/departments/Crthouse/Assessr/Assessr.htm **Online** - Search property maps for assessment data at www.co.brown.mn.us/brown_mn/gismain.htm. No name search.

Carlton County

County Recorder, PO Box 70, Carlton, MN 55718. Recording, R/E & UCC phone-218-384-9122, UCC recording phone-218-384-9156; fax-218-384-9157; 8AM-4PM (CST) www.co.carlton.mn.us

Index: Separate indices to search include computer, books. Records indexed on a public use terminal back to 1989. Office personnel or visitors may perform searches. General index search fee $20.00 for 2 hour search, and $10.00 per add'l hour up to four. Legal description required to retrieve real estate records; office can assist with search training only. Office will search UCC records and tax liens if on proper forms. Copy fee $1.00 per page.Cert fee- $1.00 per page, $5.00 minimum. Payee- Carlton County Treasurer. **Online access to Real Estate, Deed, Lien records:** Access recorder land records via the Laredo/Tapestry subscription web system. Fees start at $50 per month; $.35 to print an image. Index goes back to 1989, images to 2003 with earlier being added. Also a per search service; pay with credit card. **Other phones:** Treasurer- 218-384-9594; Vital Records- 218-384-9156. **Property tax/Assessing**- PO Box 129, County Courthouse, Rm 114, Carlton, MN 55718; 218-384-9142, assessor fax- 218-384-9157. www.co.carlton.mn.us/Departments/Assessor/Assessor_Home.htm

Carver County

County Recorder, 600 E 4th St; Carver County Gov't Ctr, Admin Bldg, Chaska, MN 55318-2158. 952-361-1930; fax-952-361-1931; 8AM-4:30PM (CST) www.co.carver.mn.us

Index: All in one. Records indexed on a public use terminal back to 1988. Only the public may search. Copy fee $1.00 per page after 10 pages.Cert fee- $1.00 per page, $5.00 minimum. Payee- Carver County Treasurer. **Online access to Real Estate, Grantor/Grantee, Deed, Lien records:** Access to recorder land records available by subscription at http://landshark.co.carver.mn.us/LandShark/login.jsp. **Other phones:** Treasurer- 952-361-1980; Elections- 952-361-1910; Vital Records- 952-361-1930. **Property tax/Assessing**- 600 E 4th St, Chaska, MN 55318; 952-361-1960, assessor fax- 952-361-1959. **Online** - Access property and tax roll data free at https://www.co.carver.mn.us/carvercountyrecap/ParcelSearch.aspx but no name searching. Also search the GIS-mapping site free at. http://gis.co.carver.mn.us/website/gishome/disclaimer_parcel_search.html but no name searching.

Cass County

County Recorder, PO Box 3000, Walker, MN 56484. 218-547-7381, R/E recording phone-218-547-7381/7249, UCC recording phone-218-547-7233; fax-218-547-7292; 8AM-4:30PM (CST) www.co.cass.mn.us

Index: Separate indices to search include abstract and Torrens. Records indexed on public use terminal back to 4/1/87. Office personnel or visitors may perform searches. Search fee $20.00 per name for UCC's. Office will search real estate records-2 years only. Will search UCC records. Copy fee $1.00 per page.Cert fee- $10.00 per doc includes copy fee. Payee- Cass County Recorder. **Online access to Real Estate, Deed, Lien records:** Real estate data available by subscription on either the Laredo system using subscription and fees or the Tapestry System using credit card, http://tapestry.fidlar.com; $5.99 search; $.50 per image. Index goes back to 4/1/87; images to 5/5/1965. **Other phones:** Treasurer- 218-547-7290; Elections- 218-547-7281; Vital Records- 218-547-7247; Auditor- 218-547-7260. **Property tax/Assessing**- PO Box 3000, 300 Minnesota Ave, Main Fl, Walker, MN 56484; 218-547-7298, fax-218-547-7272. www.co.cass.mn.us/assessor/assessor_home.html **Online** - Access property data at www.co.cass.mn.us/cassmnpublicreports/taxsearch/search.aspx but no name searching. View GIS-mapping data free at www.co.cass.mn.us/website/cass/viewer.asp?theValue=cassparcel&Cmd=INIT. No name searching.

Chippewa County

County Recorder, 629 N 11th St, Montevideo, MN 56265. Recording, R/E & UCC phone-320-269-9431; fax-320-269-7168; 8AM-4:30PM (CST) www.co.chippewa.mn.us/

Index: Separate indices to search include tract index by descriptions, images are in books or computer. Records indexed on a public use terminal back to 1997. Office personnel or visitors may perform searches. General index search fee $20.00 per hour. Office will not search real estate records. Tax liens not included in UCC search. UCC search fee- $20.00 per hour. Separate federal tax lien search- $2.00 per debtor. Copy fee $.50 per page.Cert fee- $10.00 minimum. Payee- Chippewa County Recorder. **Online access to Real Estate, Deed, Lien records:** Recorder land data by subscription on either the Laredo system using subscription or the Tapestry System using credit card, http://tapestry.fidlar.com; $3.99 search; $.50 per image. Index goes back to 1991; images to 1998. **Other phones:** Treasurer- 320-269-7447; Elections- 320-269-7447; Vital Records- 320-269-9431. **Property tax/Assessing**- 629 N 11th St, #3, Montevideo, MN 56265; 320-269-7696, fax-320-269-6137. www.co.chippewa.mn.us/assessor.htm Access property tax records at www.co.chippewa.mn.us/taxdisclaim.htm but no name searching.

Chisago County

County Recorder, 313 N Main St, Rm 277; Government Ctr, Center City, MN 55012-9663. 651-213-8580; fax-651-213-8581; 8AM-4:30PM (CST) www.co.chisago.mn.us

Index: Separate indices to search include grantor/grantee, tracts. Records indexed on a public use terminal back to 1988, some earlier. Only the public may search. Copy fee $1.00 per page, will fax doc $5.00 per doc.Cert fee- $10.00 per doc includes copy fee. Payee- Chisago County Recorder. Contact Auditors office. **Online access to Real Estate, Grantor/Grantee, Deed records:** Access to the recorder's real property data back to 1988 is by subscription with LandShark, see http://24.56.144.170/LandShark/login.jsp. **Other phones:** Treasurer- 651-213-8540; Elections- 651-213-8500; Vital Records- 651-213-8580. **Property tax/Assessing**- 313 N Main, Rm 246, Center City, MN 55012; 651-213-8550, assessor fax- 651-213-8551. A public access terminal is available. www.co.chisago.mn.us **Online access**- Search the treasurer's property search site at http://24.56.144.168/chisagocountyrecap/. Also, access parcel data at the GIS-mapping site at http://24.56.144.170/wf2_chisagopublic/Default.aspx, but no name searching at either site.

Clay County

County Recorder, PO Box 280, Moorhead, MN 56561-0280. Recording, R/E & UCC phone-218-299-5031; fax-218-299-7500; 8AM-4:30PM (CST) www.co.clay.mn.us

Index: Separate indices to search include Torrens and abstract, UCC/CNS, marriage, birth & death. Records indexed on a public use terminal back to 1987 (grantor/grantee). Office personnel or visitors may perform searches. Search fee $20.00 per name. Office will not search real estate records; all records online. Will not search old UCC records, only active ones. Copy fee $1.00 per page for real estate docs except plats (free on-line).Cert fee- $10.00 flat fee regardless of pages. Payee- Clay County Recorder. **Online access to Real Estate, Deed, Lien, Plat, Corner Certificate records:** Access recorder land data by subscription on either the Laredo system using sub and fees or the Tapestry System using credit card, http://tapestry.fidlar.com; $5.95 search; $.50 per image. Index goes back to 1987; images to 1976. Plats and corner certificates online free at www.co.clay.mn.us/depts/recorder/laredo/rerrol.htm. **Other phones:** Treasurer- 218-299-5011; Elections- 218-299-5006; Vital Records- 218-299-5031. **Property tax/Assessing**- PO Box 280, 807 N 11th St, Courthouse, 2nd FL, Moorhead, MN 56561-0280; 218-299-5017, assessor fax- 218-299-5195. www.co.clay.mn.us/Depts/Assessor/Assessor.htm **Online access**- Search property tax data free at www.tax.co.clay.mn.us/claycountymn/ but not name searching. Also, search property data on the GIS site at www.maps.co.clay.mn.us/map/Clay/disclaimer.htm but no name searching.

Clearwater County

County Recorder, 213 Main Ave N, Dept 207, Bagley, MN 56621. Recording, R/E & UCC phone-218-694-6129; fax-218-694-6179; 8AM-4:30PM

Index: All in one. Records indexed on a public use terminal back to 1987. Office personnel or visitors may perform searches. Search fee $20.00 for UCC. Office will search real estate records. Will search UCC records. Copy fee $2.00 per doc.Cert fee- $5.00 per doc plus copy fee. Payee- Clearwater County Recorder. **Other phones:** Treasurer- 218-694-6130; Vital Records- 218-694-6129. **Property tax/Assessing**- 213 Main Ave N, Dept 203, Bagley, MN 56621; 218-694-6260, assessor fax- 218-694-6244. A public access terminal is available. **Online access**- Search property records free at taxinfo.co.clearwater.mn.us by address or parcel number. Access free online maps at www.co.clearwater.mn.us/website/clearwaterpublic/main.php.

Cook County

County Recorder, 411 W 2nd St, Grand Marais, MN 55604-2307. Recording, R/E & UCC phone-218-387-3660; fax-218-387-3043; 8AM-4PM (CST) www.co.cook.mn.us

Index: Separate indices to search include grantee/grantor, Tract. Records indexed on a public use terminal back to 1983. Office personnel or visitors may perform searches. Search fee $20.00 UCCs, $5.00 tax liens. Office will search real estate records. Copy fee: abstract $1.00 for 1st page, $.50 per page each add'l page.Cert fee- $10.00 minimum. Payee-

Cook County Recorder. **Online access to Real Estate, Deed, Lien records:** Recorder land data by subscription on either the Laredo system using subscription and fees or the Tapestry System using credit card, http://tapestry.fidlar.com; $3.99 search; $.50 per image. Abstracts go back to 1983, Torrens to 1970. **Other phones:** Treasurer- 218-387-3640; Elections- 218-387-3640; Vital Records- 218-387-3660. **Property tax/Assessing**- 411 W 2nd St, Grand Marais, MN 55604; 218-387-3650. www.co.cook.mn.us/index.php/assessor-home **Online access**- Access Cook County property and assessment data free at www.co.cook.mn.us/index.php/property-information.

Cottonwood County

County Recorder, PO Box 326, Windom, MN 56101. Recording, R/E & UCC phone-507-831-1458; fax-507-831-3675; 8AM-4:30PM (CST) www.co.cottonwood.mn.us/countyrecorder.html
Index: All in one. Records indexed on a public use terminal back to 00; computer index is not complete. Office will perform a UCC search but public must search other records themselves. Search fee $20.00. Office will not search real estate records. Copy fee $.50 per page.Cert fee- $10.00 per doc includes copy fee. Payee- Cottonwood County Recorder. **Online access to Real Estate, Deed, Lien records:** Recorder land data by subscription on either the Laredo system using subscription and fees or the Tapestry System using credit card, http://tapestry.fidlar.com; $3.99 search; $.50 per image. Index and images go back to 9/12/2000. **Other phones:** Treasurer- 507-831-1342; Elections- 507-831-1905; Vital Records- 507-831-1458. **Property tax/Assessing**- 900 3rd Ave, Windom, MN 56101; 507-831-2458, assessor fax-507-831-1804. A public access terminal is available in Recorders office.

Crow Wing County

County Recorder, PO Box 383, Brainerd, MN 55401. Recording, R/E & UCC phone-218-824-1280; fax-218-824-1281; 8AM-5PM (CST) www.co.crow-wing.mn.us
Index: All in one. Records indexed on a public use terminal back to 1989. Only the public may search. Copy fee $1.00 per page.Cert fee- $10.00 per doc includes copy fee. Payee- Crow Wing County Recorder. **Online access to Real Estate, Deed, Lien records:** Access to recorder data is available by subscription, $50.00 per month and $.25 per image. Email the County Recorder at kathyl@co.crow-wing.mn.us for info and signup, or login at http://erecord.co.crow-wing.mn.us/LandShark/login.jsp. **Other phones:** Treasurer- 218-824-1300; Elections- 218-824-1050; Vital Records- 218-824-1300. **Property tax/Assessing**- 326 Laurel St, Courthouse, Brainerd, MN 55401; 218-824-1010, assessor fax- 218-824-1011. www.co.crow-wing.mn.us/assessor/ **Online access**- Access assessor data free at www.taxdata.co.crow-wing.mn.us/taxdata/ but no name searching. Access county plat maps free at www.co.crow-wing.mn.us/surveyor/crow_wing_county_plat_maps.html.

Dakota County

County Recorder, 1590 Hwy 55, Hastings, MN 55033. 651-438-4355; fax-651-438-8176; 8AM-4:30PM (CST) www.co.dakota.mn.us/default.htm
Index: All in one. Records indexed on a public use terminal back to 1990. Only the public may search. Copy fee $1.00 per page after 10 pages.Cert fee-$1.00 per page, $5.00 minimum. Payee- Dakota County Recorder. Bulk data available for purchase. **Online access to Real Estate, Deed, Lien, Mortgage records:** access to recorded documents requires a subscription and an escrow account set up with Property Taxation & Records. Fee is 100/month and $0.50/image viewed. To obtain a Login ID and Password, contact 651-438-4355. **Other phones:** Treasurer- 651-438-4576. **Property tax/Assessing**- 1590 Hwy 55, Hastings, MN 55033-2372; 651-438-4576, assessor fax- 651-438-4469. A public access terminal is available. **Online access**- Real Estate Inquiry records database is free at http://gis.co.dakota.mn.us/scripts/esrimap.dll?Name=webq1&Cmd=Map&. Includes address, estimated value, taxes, last sale price, building details. Also, search foreclosure data free by address at http://services.co.dakota.mn.us/foreclosure/.

Dodge County

County Recorder, 22 6th St E, Dept 101, Mantorville, MN 55955. Recording, R/E & UCC phone-507-635-6250; fax-507-635-6255; 8AM-4:30PM (CST) www.co.dodge.mn.us
Index: Separate indices to search include books, computer. Records indexed on a public use terminal back to 11/601. Office personnel or visitors may perform searches. Search fee $11.00 per name unless otherwise indicated. Office will search real estate records. Will not search UCC records. Copy fee $1.00 per page, fax fee $2.00. Cert fee- $10.00 per doc includes copy fee. Payee- Dodge County Recorder. Bulk data (all recorded documents after 11/6/01) available for purchase, contact Sue Alberts. **Other phones:** Treasurer- 507-635-6239; Elections- 507-635-6239; Vital Records- 507-635-6250. **Property tax/Assessing**- 22 6th St E, Dept 44, Mantorville, MN 55955; 507-635-6245, assessor fax- 502-635-6255. A public access terminal is available. www.co.dodge.mn.us/ **Online access**- Access to property tax records is free at http://secure.co.dodge.mn.us/dodgeCounty/.

Douglas County

County Recorder, 305 8th Ave W; Courthouse, Alexandria, MN 56308. Recording, R/E & UCC phone-320-762-3877; fax-320-762-2389; 8AM-4:30PM (CST) www.co.douglas.mn.us
Index: All in one. Records indexed on a public use terminal back to 7/91. Office personnel or visitors may perform searches. Search fee-$20.00. Office will do a brief search of real estate records. No title searches. Will search UCC records. Copy fee $.50 per page; mailing $5.00; faxing $12.00.Cert fee- $10.00 per doc. Payee- Douglas County Recorder. **Other phones:** Treasurer- 320-762-3077; Elections- 320-762-3077; Vital Records- 320-762-3877. **Property tax/Assessing**- 305 8th Ave W, Courthouse, Alexandria, MN 56308; 320-762-3884, assessor fax-320-762-2968. A public access terminal is available. **Online access**- Look-up assessor property tax data free at http://morris.state.mn.us/tax/.

Faribault County

County Recorder, PO Box 130, Blue Earth, MN 56013. Recording, R/E & UCC phone-507-526-6252; fax-507-526-6227; 8AM-4:30PM (CST)
Index: Separate indices to search include real estate, Torrens, tax liens, UCC, CRS, notaries, etc. Records indexed on a public use terminal back to 1/1995. Only the public may search. Copy fee $1.00 per page.Cert fee- $1.00 per page, $5.00 minimum. Payee- Faribault County Recorder. **Online access to Real Estate, Deed, Lien records:** Recorder land data by subscription on either the Laredo system using subscription and fees or the Tapestry System using credit card, http://tapestry.fidlar.com; $3.99 search; $.50 per image. Index back to 1995; images to 9/15/03. **Other phones:** Treasurer- 507-526-6260; Elections- 507-526-6212; Vital Records- 507-526-6252. **Property tax/Assessing**- PO Box 130, 415 N Main St, Blue Earth, MN 56013; 507-526-6201, assessor fax- 507-526-6227. (Appraiser/Auditor- 507-526-6201)

Fillmore County

County Recorder, Box 465, Preston, MN 55965-0465. Recording, R/E & UCC phone-507-765-3852; fax-507-765-2802; 8AM-4:30PM (CST) www.co.fillmore.mn.us
Index: Separate indices to search. Records indexed on a public use terminal back to 1996. Office personnel or visitors may perform searches. Search fee $35.00 unless otherwise indicated. Office will search real estate records. Will search UCC records. Copy fee $1.00 per page.Cert fee- $10.00 per cert plus copy fee. Payee- Fillmore County Recorder. **Online access to GIS-Mapping records:** Access to GIS-mapping records for free go to www.co.fillmore.mn.us/. **Other phones:** Treasurer-507-765-3811; Elections- 507-765-4701; Vital Records- 507-765-5339. **Property tax/ Assessing**- PO Box 67, Preston, MN 55965-0067; 507-765-3868, assessor fax- 507-765-2802. A public access terminal is available.

Freeborn County

County Recorder, 411 S Broadway; Courthouse, Albert Lea, MN 56007-4506. Recording, R/E & UCC phone-507-377-5130; fax-507-377-5265; 8AM-5PM (CST) www.co.freeborn.mn.us/recorder/default.aspx
Index: Separate indices to search include tract and grantor/grantee. Records indexed on a public use terminal back to 11/95. Only the public may search. Copies included in search fee. Real estate or tax lien copy- $1.00 per page uncertified. Cert fee- $10.00 per doc includes copy fee. Payee- Freeborn County Recorder. **Other phones:** Treasurer- 507-377-5117; Elections- 507-377-5116; Vital Records- 507-377-5130. **Property tax/Assessing**- PO Box 1147, 411 S Broadway, Albert Lea, MN 56007; 507-377-5176, assessor fax- 507-377-5259. A public access terminal is available. **Online access**- Online access to property records is available at http://qpublic.net/mn/freeborn/.

Goodhue County

County Recorder, PO Box 408, Red Wing, MN 55066. Recording, R/E & UCC phone-651-385-3150, UCC recording phone-651-385-3148; fax-651-385-3119; 8AM-4:30PM (CST) www.co.goodhue.mn.us
Index: All in one. Records indexed on a public use terminal back to 1987. Office personnel or visitors may perform searches. Search fee $20.00 per name. Office will not search real estate records. Copy fee $1.00 per page.Cert fee- $10.00 per doc includes copy fee. Payee- Goodhue County Recorder. Will sell customize lists based on document type, call Sue Huber for info- 651-385-3152. **Online access to Real Estate, Deed, Lien records:** Access to recorder's land records is by LandShark at http://156.99.35.20/LandShark/login.jsp. Fees $50.00 monthly. Username, and password required. **Other phones:** Treasurer- 651-385-3032; Elections- 651-385-3032; Vitals- 651-385-3148. **Property tax/ Assessing**- 509 W 5th St, Red Wing, 55066; 651-385-3006. www.co.goodhue.mn.us/departments/assessor/ **Online access**- Access property and sales data free at www.co.goodhue.mn.us/goodhuecountyrecap/ but no name searching. Search property data free on GIS site at http://goodhuecounty.plansightgis.com/launch.htm but no name searching. Also, forfeited land list at www.co.goodhue.mn.us/departments/auditortreasurer/ForfeitedLandList.aspx.

Grant County

County Recorder, PO Box 1007, Elbow Lake, MN 56531-1007. Recording, R/E & UCC phone-218-685-4133; fax-218-685-4178; 8AM-4PM (CST) www.co.grant.mn.us
Index: All in one. Records indexed on a public use terminal back to 2005. Office will perform a UCC search but public must search other records themselves. General search fee $20.00 per hour. Copies included in search fee. Cert fee- $10.00 per document. Payee- Grant County Recorder. **Other phones:** Treasurer- 218-685-4655; Elections- 218-685-4520; Vital Records- 218-685-4655. **Property tax/Assessing**- 10 2nd St NE, PO Box 1007, Courthouse, Elbow Lake, MN 56531; 218-685-4644, assessor fax- 218-685-5346. A public access terminal is available. www.co.grant.mn.us/licensing.asp#Assessor **Online access**- Look-up assessor property tax data free at http://morris.state.mn.us/tax/ or. also, search current property tax free at http://206.145.187.205/tax/disclaimer.asp?cid=26 but no name searching.

Hennepin County

County Recorder & REgistrar of Titles, 300 S 6th St, #A-500 Gov't Ctr, Minneapolis, MN 55487. 612-348-5139; fax-612-348-4948; 8AM-4:30PM (CST) www.co.hennepin.mn.us

A 2nd fax number is 612-317-6293. Index: Separate indices to search include Torrens, abstract. Pre-1988 indexes on microfilm. Records indexed on a public use terminal back to 1988. Only the public may search. Copy fee $1.00 per page.Cert fee- $10.00 per doc includes copy fee. Payee- Hennepin County Recorder. Bulk data available for purchase, contact 612-673-2394, or contact supervisor. **Online access to Real Estate, Deed, Lien records:** Access to Hennepin County online records requires a $35 annual fee with a charge of $5 per hour from 7AM-7PM, or $4.15 per hour at other times. Records date back to 1988. Only lending agency data is available. An Automated phone system is also available; 612-348-3011. **Other phones:** Treasurer- 612-348-3011; Elections- 612-348-5151; Vital Records- 612-348-8240. **Property tax/Assessing**- 309 2nd Ave S, Minneapolis, MN 55401; 612-673-2382, assessor fax-612-673-3538. A public access terminal is available. **Online access**- Search parcel property tax records on county Property Information Search database free at http://www16.co.hennepin.mn.us/pins/.

Houston County

County Recorder, PO Box 29, Caledonia, MN 55921-0029. Recording, R/E & UCC phone-507-725-5813; fax-507-725-2647; 8AM-4:30PM (CST) www.houstoncounty.govoffice2.com

Index: Separate indices to search include legal description, grantor/grantee, document number, date of recording. Records indexed on a public use terminal back to 1996. Office personnel or visitors may perform searches. Office staff does limited searches for $16.80 per hour plus copies. Office will search only what is on the state computer. Copy fee $1.00 per page. If copies are bigger than 8 1/2 x 14, fees vary depending on size.Cert fee- $10.00 per cert includes copy fee. Payee- Houston County Recorder. **Other phones:** Treasurer- 507-725-5815; Vital Records- 507-725-5813; Auditor- 507-725-5803; GIS -507-725-5827. **Property tax/Assessing**- 304 S Marshall St, Rm 109, Caledonia, MN 55921; 507-725-5801, assessor fax- 507-725-2647. (Appraiser/Auditor- 507-725-5801) A public access terminal is available. **Online access**- Online access to property records is available at http://beacon.schneidercorp.com/.

Hubbard County

County Recorder, 301 Court Ave, Park Rapids, MN 56470. 218-732-3552; fax-218-732-3645; 8AM-4:30PM (CST) www.co.hubbard.mn.us/Recorder.htm

Index: Separate indices to search include grantor/grantee, abstract, Torrens, tract, etc. Records indexed on a public use terminal for abstract 1/92; for Torrens 00. Office personnel or visitors may perform searches. General index search fee $15.00 per name (for tax liens). Office will search real estate records back to last deed. Office will not search UCC records. Copy fee $10.00 for 1st page, $.50 each add'l page per doc.Cert fee- $10.00 per doc includes copy fee. Payee- Hubbard County Recorder. **Online access to Real Estate, Deed, Lien records:** Recorder land data by subscription on either the Laredo system using subscription and fees or the Tapestry System using credit card, http://tapestry.fidlar.com; $3.99 search; $.50 per image. Index and images go back to 6/1992. **Other phones:** Treasurer- 218-732-4348; Elections-218-732-3196; Vital Records- 218-732-3552; Auditor- 218-732-3196. **Property tax/Assessing**- 301 Court Ave, Park Rapids, MN 56470; 218-732-3452, assessor fax- 218-732-3645. A public access terminal is available. **Online** - Access property tax data free at www.co.hubbard.mn.us/wf2_hubbardpublic/Default.aspx.

Isanti County

County Recorder, 555 18th Ave SW, Courthouse, Cambridge, MN 55008. 763-689-1191, R/E recording phone-612-689-1191, UCC recording phone-763-689-1191; fax-none; 8AM-4:30PM (CST) www.co.isanti.mn.us

Index: All in one. Records indexed on computer from 1996 to present, books prior to 1996. Only the public may search. General copy fee $1.00 per page.Cert fee-$10.00 per doc. Payee- Isanti County Recorder. Bulk data available for purchase. **Other phones:** Treasurer-763-689-1781; Elections- 763-689-1644; Vital Records- 763-689-1191. **Property tax/Assessing**-Same address as recording office. 763-689-2752. (Appraiser/Auditor- 763-689-1644) A public access terminal is available. **Online access**- Search assessor property and tax data free at http://isanti.visualgov.com/ no name searching. Access monthly sales sheets by Town for free at www.co.isanti.mn.us/depart.htm#assess. Access property data free on the GIS-mapping site at http://204.73.107.41/isanti7/index.htm. No name searching.

Itasca County

County Recorder, 123 NE 4th St, Grand Rapids, MN 55744-2600. Recording, R/E & UCC phone-218-327-2856; fax-218-327-0689; 8AM-4:30PM (CST) www.co.itasca.mn.us

Index: Separate indices to search include computer, microfilm. Records indexed on a public use terminal back to 1987 for Grantor/Grantee index, 1995 for images. Office personnel or visitors may perform searches. General index search fee $12.00 per search if over an hour; $20.00 is searching UCCs. Copy fee $1.00 per page.Cert fee- $10.00 per copy; $5.00 per cert if Torrens, plus copy fee. Payee- Itasca County Recorder. **Online access to Real Estate, Deed, Lien records:** Access recorder land data by sub on either the Laredo system using subscription and fees or the Tapestry System using credit card, http://tapestry.fidlar.com; $3.99 search; $.50 per image. Index goes back to 4/87; images to 10/15/93. **Other phones:** Treasurer- 218-327-2859; Elections-218-327-2849; Vital Records- 218-327-7327. **Property tax/Assessing**- 123 NE 4th St, Grand Rapids, MN 55744; 218-327-2861, assessor fax- 218-327-7343. (Appraiser/Auditor- 218-327-2860) **Online access**- Access property and parcel data free from a private company at www.parcelinfo.com/parcels/.

Jackson County

County Recorder, PO Box 209; Jackson County Recorder, Jackson, MN 56143. 507-328-7644, R/E recording phone-507-328-7635, UCC recording phone-507-328-7634; fax-507-328-7964; 8AM-4:30PM (CST) www.co.jackson.mn.us

Index: All in one. Records indexed on a public use terminal back to 199. Office personnel or visitors may perform searches. Search fee $20.00. Copy fee $.25 per page. Plats- $10.00.Cert fee- $10.00 per doc includes copy fee. Payee- Jackson County Recorder. Certificates of Real Estate Value available for purchase on CD; contact Bryan Eder at 507-328-7649. **Other phones:** Treasurer- 507-328-7636; Elections- 507-328-7650; Vital Records- 507-328-7660. **Property tax/Assessing**- 405 4th St, Jackson, 56143; 507-328-7670. (Appraiser- 507-328-7670);

Kanabec County

County Recorder, 18 N Vine St, Ste 261B, Mora, MN 55051. 320-679-6466; fax-320-679-6431; 8AM-4:30PM (CST) www.kanabeccounty.org

Index: Separate indices to search include 10 separate indexes and public cubicles. Records indexed on a public use terminal back to 1985. Only the public may search. Copy fee $1.00 per page. Fax back- $5.00 per page.Cert fee- $10.00 per doc includes copy fee. Payee- Kanabec County Recorder. Bulk data available for purchase, contact Karen McClellan. 320-679-6460. **Other phones:** Treasurer- 320-679-6430; Elections- 320-679-6431; Vital Records- 320-679-6466. **Property tax/Assessing**- 18 N Vine St, Mora, MN 55051; 320-679-6420, assessor fax- 320-679-6421. A public access terminal is available. **Online access**- Online access to property records is available at www.qpublic.net/mn/kanabec/.

Kandiyohi County

County Recorder, PO Box 736, Willmar, MN 56201-0736. Recording, R/E & UCC phone-320-231-6223; fax-320-231-6284; 8AM-4:30PM (CST) www.co.kandiyohi.mn.us

Index: All in one. Records indexed on a public use terminal back to 3/2/87. Office personnel or visitors may perform searches. Search fee $20.00 per name. Will not search UCC records. General copy fee $1.00 per page.Cert fee- $10.00 per cert includes copy fee. Payee- Kandiyohi County Recorder. Bulk data available for purchase. 320-231-6204. **Online access to Real Estate, Deed, Lien records:** Access recorder land data by subscription on either the Laredo system using subscription w/ fees, www.fidler.com or the Tapestry System using credit card, http://tapestry.fidlar.com/. $5.95 search; $.50 per image. Index back to 3/1987; images to 1/1998. **Other phones:** Treasurer- 320-231-6200; Elections-320-231-6202 x6338; Vital Records- 320-231-6532. **Property tax/Assessing**- 400 Benson Ave SW, Willmar, MN 56201; 320-231-6200, assessor fax-320-231-6263. (Appraiser/Auditor- 320-231-6202) A public access terminal is available. **Online access**-Look-up assessor property tax data free at http://morris.state.mn.us/tax/.

Kittson County

Recorder, 410 5th St, #202, Hallock, MN 56728. 218-843-2842; fax-218-843-2538; 8:30AM-4:30PM

Index: All in one. Records indexed on a public use terminal back to 9/87. Office personnel or visitors may perform searches. Search fee $46.00. Office will search real estate records. Will not search UCC records. Copy fee $1.00 per page after 10 pages.Cert fee- $10.00 per cert plus copy fee. Payee- Kittson County Recorder. Bulk data available for purchase in e-mail and CD. **Other phones:** Treasurer- 218-843-3432; Elections- 218-843-2655; Vital Records- 218-843-2842. **Property tax/Assessing**- 410 S 5th St, #214, Hallock, MN 56728; 218-843-3615, assessor fax- 218-843-3616.

Koochiching County

County Recorder, 715 4th St; Courthouse, International Falls, MN 56649. Recording, R/E & UCC phone-218-283-1193; fax-218-283-1194; 8AM-5PM (CST) www.co.koochiching.mn.us

Index: All in one. Records indexed on a public use terminal back to 1990. Office personnel or visitors may perform searches. Search fee-$20.00 per name. Office will not search real estate records. Copy fee $1.00 per page.Cert fee- $10.00 per doc includes copy fee. Payee- Koochiching County Treasurer. Bulk data available for purchase at $.25 per image, concatc Stephanie at 218-283-1171. **Online access to Real Estate, Deed, Lien records:** Access recorder land data by subscription on either the Laredo system using sub and fees or the Tapestry System using credit card, http://tapestry.fidlar.com; $3.99 search; $.50 per image. Index goes back to 1980, images to 3//2000. **Other phones:** Treasurer- 218-283-1112; Elections-218-283-1101; Vital Records- 218-283-1193. **Property tax/Assessing**- 715 4th St, Courthouse, International Falls, MN 56649; 218-283-1121, assessor fax- 218-283-1125. A public access terminal is available. www.co.koochiching.mn.us/ **Online access**- Access to property and parcel data is free from a private company at www.parcelinfo.com.

Lac qui Parle County

County Recorder, PO Box 132, Madison, MN 56256-0132. Recording, R/E & UCC phone-320-598-3724, UCC recording phone-380-598-3724; fax-320-598-3125; 8:30AM-4:30PM (CST) www.lqpco.com

Index: All in one. Records indexed on a public use terminal back to 1990. Office personnel or visitors may perform searches. Search fee-$20.00 per name.

Real estate owner, mortgage, and property transfer searches available. Will search UCC records. Must use UCC request form. Copy fee $.25 per page in office. $1.00 per page if emailed or faxed by office. Plats copy $10.00 each.Cert fee- $10.00 per cert includes copy fee. Payee- Lac qui Parle County Recorder. Bulk data available for purchase, contact ori Schwendemann. **Other phones:** Treasurer- 320-598-3648; Elections- 320-598-7444; Vital Records- 320-598-3724. **Property tax/Assessing-** 600 6th St, Courthouse, Madison, 56256; 320-598-3187, assessor fax- 320-598-3125. www.lqpco.com/assessor.php

Lake County

County Recorder, 601 3rd Ave, Two Harbors, MN 55616. Recording, R/E & UCC phone-218-834-8347; fax-218-834-8493; 8AM-4:30PM www.co.lake.mn.us
Index: Separate indices to search include abstracts, torrens, vitals, liens. Real estate records indexed on a public use terminal back to 1996. Office will perform a UCC search but public must search other records themselves. Search fee $20.00, with appropriate request forms and fees prepaid. Copy fee $1.00 per page.Cert fee- $10.00 per doc includes copy fee. Payee- Lake County Recorder. **Online access to Real Estate, Deed, Lien, Mortgage, Misc. records:** Recorder land data by subscription on either the Laredo system using subscription and fees or the Tapestry System using credit card, http://tapestry.fidlar.com; $3.99 search; $.50 per image. Links available through county website. Index goes back to 1996; images to 1997. **Other phones:** Treasurer- 218-834-8344; Elections- 218-834-8318; Vital Records- 218-834-8301; Court administrator- 218-834-8330. **Property tax/Assessing-** Same address as recording office. 218-834-8313, assessor fax- 218-834-8302. A public access terminal is available. **Online access-** Access property data free at www.parcelinfo.com; click on Lake County Users Click Here. Also can access via the county website www.co.lake.mn.us/.

Lake of the Woods County

County Recorder, 206 SE 8th Ave, #280, Baudette, MN 56623. 218-634-1902; fax-218-634-2509; 7:30-4PM www.co.lake-of-the-woods.mn.us/recorder.htm
Index: All in one. Records indexed on a public use terminal back to 2002. Office personnel or visitors may perform searches. No fee for search. Office will search real estate records. Will not search UCC records. Copy fee $1.00 per page.Cert fee- $5.00 per doc plus copy fee. Payee- Lake of the Woods County Recorder. **Online access to Plat/Tract records:** Access to Plat book for free go to www.co.lake-of-the-woods.mn.us/maps.htm. **Other phones:** Treasurer- 218-634-2361; Elections- 218-634-2836; Vital Records- 218-634-1902. **Property tax/ Assessing-** 206 SE 8th Ave, Baudette. MN 56623; 218-634-2536, assessor fax- 218-634-2509. A public access terminal is available in the Recorders office.

Le Sueur County

County Recorder, 88 S Park Ave; Courthouse, Le Center, MN 56057-1620. 507-357-8235, R/E recording phone-507-357-2251; fax-507-357-6375; 8AM-4:30PM www.co.le-sueur.mn.us/Recorder.html
Records indexed on a public use terminal back to 1992. Office personnel or visitors may perform searches. General search fee $6.00 per name. UCC search per debtor- $20.00. Copy fee $1.00 per page after 10 pages.Cert fee- $10.00 per cert includes copy fee. Payee- Le Sueur County Recorder. **Online access to Real Estate, Deed records:** Access to recorder's land records is by subscription through LandShark at http://156.99.35.20/LandShark/login.jsp. Fees of $50.00 installation, $2.00 per doc viewed, username, and password required. **Property tax/Assessing-** 88 S Park St, Le Center, MN 56057; 507-357-2251, fax-507-357-6375. A public access terminal is available.

Lincoln County

County Recorder, PO Box 29, Ivanhoe, MN 56142. Recording, R/E & UCC phone-507-694-1360 or 1430, fax-507-694-1198; 8:30AM-4:30PM (CST) www.mncounties3.org/lincoln/
Index: All in one. Records indexed on a public use terminal back to 1998. Office personnel or visitors may perform searches. Search fee $10.00 per name. Office will tract index search, but will not search mortgages or titles records. Will not search UCC records. General copy fee-$.25 per page.Cert fee- $5.00 per doc plus copy fee. Payee- Lincoln County Recorder. **Online access to Real Estate, Deed, Lien records:** Recorder land data by subscription on either the Laredo system using subscription and fees or the Tapestry System using credit card, http://tapestry.fidlar.com; $3.99 search; $.50 per image. Index and images go back 1/1997. **Other phones:** Treasurer- 507-694-1550; Elections- 507-694-1529; Vital Records- 507-694-1360 or 1430. **Property tax/Assessing-** PO Box 29, 319 N Rebecca, Ivanhoe, MN 56142; 507-694-1522, assessor fax-507-694-1198. hours- 7AM-4:30PM

Lyon County

County Recorder, 607 W Main St, Marshall, MN 56258. Recording, R/E & UCC phone-507-537-6722; fax-507-537-7988; 8:30-4:30PM www.lyonco.org
Index: All in one. Records indexed on a public use terminal back to 1987. Office will perform a UCC search but public must search other records themselves. Only telephone searches performed for real estate records. UCC search per debtor name-$20.00. Copies included in search fee. Cert fee-$10.00 per page includes copy fee. For certified copies by mail include $2.50 postage. Payee- Lyon County Recorder. **Online access to Real Estate, Deed, Lien records:** Recorder land data by subscription on either the Laredo system using subscription and fees or the Tapestry System using credit card, http://tapestry.fidlar.com; $3.99 search; $.50 per image. Index back to 1987; images to 1998. **Other phones:** Treasurer- 507-537-6724; Vital Records- 507-537-6722. **Property tax/Assessing-** 607 W Main St, Marshall, MN 56258; 507-537-6731, assessor fax- 507-537-6091. **Online access-** Look-up assessor property tax data free at http://morris.state.mn.us/tax/.

Mahnomen County

County Recorder, PO Box 380, Mahnomen, MN 56557. Recording, R/E & UCC phone-218-935-5528; fax-218-935-5946; 8AM-4:30PM M-T. (CST)
Index: All in one. Records indexed on a public use terminal back to 1974. Office personnel or visitors may perform searches. Search fee $15.00 per name. Office will search real estate records. Office will not search UCC records. General copy fee $.25 per page.Cert fee- $5.00 per doc plus copy fee. Payee- Mahnomen County Recorder. **Other phones:** Treasurer- 218-935-2545; Elections- 218-935-5669. **Property tax/Assessing-** 311 N Main, Courthouse, Mahnomen, MN 56557; 218-935-2417, assessor fax-218-935-5946. (Appraiser/Auditor- 218-935-2417) A public access terminal is available.

Marshall County

County Recorder, 208 E Colvin, #7, Warren, MN 56762; 218-745-4801; fax-218-745-5013; 8AM-4:30PM (CST) www.co.marshall.mn.us
Index: All in one. Records indexed on a public use terminal back to 1993. Office personnel or visitors may perform searches. Search fee $13.00 per name. Office will search real estate records for $30.00 per hour minimum real estate research fee. UCC search per debtor $20.00. Copy fee $1.00 per page.Cert fee- $10.00 per doc. Payee- Marshall County Recorder. Bulk data available for purchase. **Other phones:** Treasurer- 218-745-4831; Elections- 218-745-4801; Vital Records- 218-745-4801. **Property tax/ Assessing-** 208 E Colvin Ave, Ste13, Warren, MN 56762; 218-745-5331, assessor fax- 218-745-4338. **Online access-** Look-up assessor property tax data free at http://morris.state.mn.us/tax/.

Martin County

County Recorder, 201 Lake Ave, #203, Fairmont, MN 56031-1851. Recording, R/E & UCC phone-507-238-3213; fax-507-235-8537; 8AM-5PM (CST) www.co.martin.mn.us
Index: Separate indices to search include books before 1982, after on computer. Records indexed on a public use terminal back to 1982. Office personnel or visitors may perform searches. Search fee $20.00 per hour. Office will search real estate and UCC records. Copy fee $1.00 per page.Cert fee- $10.00 per cert includes copy fee. Payee- Martin County Recorder. Bulk data available for purchase. **Online access to Real Estate, Deed, Lien records:** Recorder land data by subscription on either the Laredo system using sub and fees or the Tapestry System using credit card, http://tapestry.fidlar.com; $5.95 search; $.50 per image. Index and images go back to 1982. **Other phones:** Treasurer- 507-238-3211; Elections- 507-238-3211; Vital Records- 507-238-3213. **Property tax/Assessing-** 201 Lake Ave, Rm326, Fairmont, MN 56031; 507-238-3210, assessor fax- 507-238-4601. hours- 7AM-5PM A public access terminal is available. **Online-** Online access to property records is available at http://beacon.schneidercorp.com/.

McLeod County

County Recorder, 2389 Hennepin Ave N, Glencoe, MN 55336. 320-864-1327; fax-320-864-1295; 8AM-4:30PM (CST) www.co.mcleod.mn.us/
Index: Separate indices to search include paper and computer. Records indexed on a public use terminal back to 4/93. Only the public may search. Copy fee $1.00 per page.Cert fee- $5.00 per name plus copy fee. Payee- McLeod County Recorder. **Online Real Estate, Deed records:** recorder data by subscription at http://landshark.co.mcleod.mn.us/LandShark/login.jsp. Set-up $50 plus $50.00 per month, plus $2.00 per image. **Other phones:** Treasurer- 320-864-1203; Vital Records- 320-864-1311. **Property tax/Assessing-** 830 E 11th St, Glencoe, MN 55336; 320-864-1254, assessor fax- 320-864-1295. www.co.mcleod.mn.us/mcleodco.cfm?pageID=9&sub=yes **Online access-** Access to property records and tax information for free go to www.co.mcleod.mn.us/. Check property taxes and delinquent taxes online at www.co.mcleod.mn.us. Click on the link to the right of the county logo in the middle of the page. Info goes back to 1993.

Meeker County

County Recorder, 325 N Sibley Ave; Courthouse, Litchfield, MN 55355. Recording, R/E & UCC phone-320-693-5440; fax-320-693-5444; 8AM-4:30PM (CST) www.co.meeker.mn.us
Index: All in one. Records indexed on a public use terminal back to 1993. Office personnel or visitors may perform searches. Office will search real estate records. Office will not search UCC records. General copy fee $.50 per page.Cert fee- $10.00 per cert plus copy fee. Payee- Meeker County Recorder. **Other phones:** Treasurer- 320-693-5345; Elections- 320-693-5212; Vital Records- 320-693-5345. **Property tax/Assessing-** 325 N Sibley Ave, Courthouse, Litchfield, MN 55355; 320-693-5205, assessor fax-320-693-5294. A public access terminal is available. **Online access-** Look-up assessor property tax data free at http://morris.state.mn.us/tax/.

Mille Lacs County

County Recorder, 635 2nd St SE, Milaca, MN 56353. Recording, R/E & UCC phone-320-983-8308, UCC recording phone-320-983-8309; fax-320-983-8388; 8AM-4:30PM (CST) www.co.mille-lacs.mn.us
Index: All in one. Records indexed on a public use terminal back to 9/96. Office personnel or visitors may perform searches. Search fee $20.00 per name. Office will not search real estate records. Copy fee $1.00 per page.Cert fee- $10.00 per doc includes copies. Payee- Mille Lacs County Recorder. **Other**

phones: Treasurer- 320-983-8310; Elections- 320-983-8301; Vital Records- 320-983-8236. **Property tax/Assessing**- 635 2nd St SE, Milaca, MN 56353; 320-983-8311, assessor fax- 320-983-8280. (Appraiser/Auditor- 320-983-8281) A public access terminal is available. **Online**- Look-up assessor property tax data free at http://morris.state.mn.us/tax/.

Morrison County

County Recorder, 213 SE 1st Ave; Admin Bldg, Little Falls, MN 56345. 320-632-0145, R/E recording phone-320-632-0145,0142, 0146, 0143, 0144 or 0147; fax-320-632-0141; 8AM-4:30PM (CST) www.co.morrison.mn.us

Files UCCs in their office. Index: Books, computer, microfilm for deeds, tracts. Records indexed on a public use terminal back to 1/1987. Office personnel or visitors may perform searches. Charge only for lengthy searches; fee $30.00. Office will only search computerized real estate index back to 1996. Will search UCC records. Copy fee $1.00 per page.Cert fee- $10.00 per page plus copy fee. Payee- Morrison County Recorder. Bulk data available for purchase, contact Irene Trettel. **Online access to Real Estate, Deed, Lien records:** Access is via a subscription dial-up service; $50 setup plus $50 monthly charged annually, and $25 de-activation fee if you quit. Info and Signup with Bunny at 320-632-0145. **Other phones:** Treasurer- 320-632-0150; Elections- 320-632-0132; Vital Records- 320-632-0146; Auditor- 320-632-0130. **Property tax/Assessing**- 213 SE 1st Ave, Admin Bldg, Little Falls, MN 56345; 320-632-0101, assessor fax- 320-632-7804. (Appraiser/Auditor- 320-632-0101) A public access terminal is available. **Online access**- Search for property data on a GIS-mapping site free at http://beacon.schneidercorp.com/. Search delinquent taxes at www.co.morrison.mn.us/category.aspx?Id=2B87D349-BED5-40F5-9E73-705EDC6A8880.

Mower County

County Recorder, 201 1st St NE, Austin, MN 55912-3475. 507-437-9446; fax-507-437-9471; 8AM-5PM (CST) www.co.mower.mn.us/Recorder01.htm

Payments must be paid in advance or an account set up with a security deposit for copies mailed or faxed. Index: Separate indices to search include document number, date, grantor/grantee, reception book. Records indexed on a public use terminal back to 1/15/88. Office will perform a UCC search but public must search other records themselves. Search fee $20.00 per debtor. Copy fee $1.00 per page.Cert fee- $10.00 per doc includes copy fee. Payee- Mower County Recorder. **Online access to Real Estate, Grantor/Grantee, Deed, Lien records:** Access recorder land data for fee on either the Laredo system using subscription and fees or the Tapestry System using credit card, http://tapestry.fidlar.com; $3.99 search; $.50 per image. Index back to 1988; images to 8/1999. **Other phones:** Treasurer- 507-437-9456; Elections- 507-437-9536; Vital Records- 507-437-9456; Auditor- 507-437-9456; Information -507-437-9493. **Property tax/Assessing**- 201 1st St NE, Austin, MN 55912; 507-437-9440, assessor fax- 507-437-9471. (Appraiser/Auditor- 507-437-9440) A public access terminal is available. **Online access**- Search property assessor data free at www.mower.min nesotaassessors.com. No name searching for free; a sub service available which does.

Murray County

County Recorder, PO Box 57, Slayton, MN 56172-0057. Recording, R/E & UCC phone-507-836-6148 x144, UCC recording phone-507-836-6148 x143; fax-507-836-8904; 8AM-4:30PM (CST) www.murray-countymn.com

Index: Separate indices to search include print out indexes for computer, index books before the computer. Records indexed on a public use terminal back to 11/1/2002. Only the public may search. If customer has a specific document number, will search for this or some general searches. No O & E reports. Copy fee $1.00 per page.Cert fee- $10.00 per cert includes copy fee. Payee- Murray County Recorder. **Other phones:** Treasurer- 507-836-6148 x150; Elections- 507-836-6148 x147; Vital Records- 507-836-6148 x150. **Property tax/Assessing**- 2500 28th St, Slayton, MN 56172; 507-836-6148 x152, assessor fax- 507-836-8904. www.murray-countymn.com/ **Online access**- Access to property tax search for free go to http://morris.state.mn.us/tax/

Nicollet County

County Recorder, PO Box 493, St. Peter, MN 56082-0493. phone-507-934-0320; fax-507-934-4487; 8AM-5PM (CST) www.co.nicollet.mn.us/

Index: All in one. Records indexed on a public use terminal back to 1991. Office personnel or visitors may perform searches. Search fees-vary. Office will search real estate records (1 year). UCC search per debtor name $20.00. Separate federal/state combined tax lien search- $2.00 per debtor. General copy fee $1.00 per page.$3.00 per large page. Cert fee- $10.00 per cert includes copy fee. Payee- Nicollet County Recorder. **Other phones:** Treasurer- 507-934-0335; Elections- 507-935-0348; Vital Records- 507-934-0325. **Property tax/Assessing**- 501 S Minnesota Ave, St. Peter, MN 56082; 507-934-0246, assessor fax- 507-934-0438. www.co.nicollet.mn.us/

Nobles County

County Recorder, PO Box 757, Worthington, MN 56187. 507-295-5268; fax-507-372-8235; 8AM-4:30PM (CST) www.co.nobles.mn.us

Index: All in one. Records indexed on a public use terminal back to 1999. Office will perform a UCC search but public must search other records themselves. Search fee $20.00 per debtor. General copy fee $.50 per page; $1.00 per page if copied from microfilm.Cert fee- $10.00 per doc includes copy fee. Payee- Nobles County Recorder. **Other phones:** Treasurer- 507-295-5268. **Property tax/Assessing**- 315 10th St, 2nd Fl, Worthington, MN 56187; 507-372-8234, assessor fax- 507-372-8238. A public access terminal is available. **Online access**- Look-up assessor property tax data free at http://morris.state.mn.us/tax/.

Norman County

County Recorder, PO Box 146, Ada, MN 56510. Recording, R/E & UCC phone-218-784-5481; fax-218-784-2399; 8:30AM-4:30PM (CST)

Index: Separate indices. Record index not computerized. Office personnel or visitors may perform searches. Search fee- UCCs $20.00 per name. Office will search real estate records. Office will not search UCC records. Real estate or tax lien copy $2.00 per doc.Cert fee- $10.00 per cert includes copy fee. Payee- Norman County Recorder. **Other phones:** Treasurer- 218-784-5473; Elections- 218-784-5471; Vital Records- 218-784-5481. **Property tax/ Assessing**- 16 E 3rd Ave, Ada, MN 56510; 218-784-5487, assessor fax- 218-784-3441. **Online access**- Look-up assessor property tax data free at http://morris.state.mn.us/tax/.

Olmsted County

County Recorder, Property Records & Licensing, 151 4th St SE, Rochester, MN 55904. 507-328-7670; 8:30AM-5PM (CST) www.co.olmsted.mn.us/departments/licensing/index.asp

Index: Separate indices to search include computer, books by legal description, and miscellaneous. Records indexed on a public use terminal back to 11/12/1993. Office personnel or visitors may perform searches. Name search fee $4.00; $5.00 minimum on judgments and tax liens. Real estate searches- $40.00 per hour, minimum 1 hr. Office will not search UCC records. Copy fee $2.00 per page.Cert fee- $10.00 per cert includes copy fee. Payee- Olmsted County Property Records & Licensing. Bulk data available for purchase,contact Bryan Eder. **Online access to Real Estate, Deed, Mortgage records:** Assessor recording office land info by subscription via Landshark at http://landshark.co.olmsted.mn.us/LandShark/login.jsp. Yearly or monthly signup required, plus escrow account for usage. **Other phones:** Elections- 507-328-7650; Vital Records- 507-328-7660. **Property tax/Assessing**- 151 4th St SE, Rochester, MN 55904; 507-328-7670, assessor fax- 507-328-7964. (Appraiser/Auditor- 507-285-8124) hours- 8AM-5PM A public access terminal is available. **Online access**- Property records and GIS-map data is available free at https://webapp.co.olmsted.mn.us/propertytax/Site/Default.aspx

Otter Tail County

County Recorder, PO Box 867, Fergus Falls, MN 56538. Recording, R/E -218-998-8140; fax-218-998-8147; 8AM-5PM www.co.otter-tail.mn.us

Index: All in one. Records indexed on a public use terminal back to 1997. Office personnel or visitors may perform searches. Real estate owner, mortgage, and property transfer searches available. Office will not search UCC records. Tax lien search fee- $20.00 per debtor. UCC copy fee $1.00 per page.Real estate record copy- $2.00 per page. Cert fee- $1.00 per page, $5.00 minimum. Payee- Otter Tail County Recorder. **Online access to Real Estate, Deed records:** Access recorder office real estate data by subscription at www.co.otter-tail.mn.us/LandShark/login.jsp. User name and login required. Call recorder office for details and sign-up . **Other phones:** Treasurer- 218-998-8295. **Property tax/Assessing**- 505 Fir Ave W, Fergus Falls, MN 56537; 218-998-8010, assessor fax-218-998-8305. A public access terminal is available. www.co.otter-tail.mn.us/assessor/default.php **Online**- Search property tax data at www.co.otter-tail.mn.us/taxes/. Parcel searching or map searching only.

Pennington County

County Recorder, PO Box 616, Thief River Falls, MN 56701. 218-683-7027; fax-218-683-7026; 8AM-4:30PM (CST)

Index: Separate indices to search. Records indexed on a public use terminal back to 1989. Office personnel or visitors may perform searches. Search fee- No charge for quick search, $20.00 per hour for lengthly searches. Office will give recent real estate documents related to a property location. Copy fee $.50 per page.Cert fee- $10.00 per document per statute. No page fee. Payee- Pennington County Recorder. Bulk data available for purchase. **Other phones:** Treasurer- 218-683-7022; Elections- 218-683-7000; Vital Records- 218-683-7027. **Property tax/Assessing**- 101 Main Ave N, Thief River Falls, MN 56701; 218-683-7029, fax- 218-683-7026.

Pine County

County Recorder, 635 Northridge Dr NW #250, Pine City, MN 55063. Recording, R/E & UCC phone-320-591-1642, UCC recording phone-320-629-6781; fax-320-591-1640; 8AM-4:30PM http://co.pine.mn.us/

Index: All in one. Records indexed on a public use terminal back to 1995. Office personnel or visitors may perform searches. Search fee $5.00 per name. Office will not search real estate records. Office will not search UCC records. Copy fee $1.00 per page.Cert fee- $10.00 per doc includes copy fee. Payee- Pine County Recorder. **Other phones:** Treasurer- 320-591-1660; Elections- 320-591-1670; Vital Records- 320-591-1670. **Property tax/Assessing**- 635 Northridge Dr NW, Pine City, MN 55063; 320-591-1632. A public access terminal is available. http://co.pine.mn.us/

Pipestone County

County Recorder, 416 Hiawatha Ave S, Pipestone, MN 56164. Recording, R/E & UCC phone-507-825-6755; fax-507-825-6767; 8AM-4:30PM (CST) www.pipestone-county.com/

Index: All in one. Records indexed on a public use terminal back to 1986. Office personnel or visitors may perform searches. Search fee $20.00. Office will search real estate records. Office will not search UCC records. Copy fee $1.00 per page.Cert fee- $10.00 per page includes copy fee. Payee- Pipestone County Recorder. Bulk data available for purchase. **Other phones:** Treasurer- 507-825-6745; Elections- 507-

825-6740; Vital Records- 507-825-6755. **Property tax/Assessing-** 416 Hiawatha Ave S, Pipestone, MN 56164; 507-825-6750, assessor fax- 507-825-6741.

Polk County

County Recorder, PO Box 397, Crookston, MN 56716. 218-281-3464; fax-218-281-1636; 8AM-4:30PM www.co.polk.mn.us/list_departments/recordersOffice/index.aspx
Index: All in one. Records indexed on computer back to 1974. Office personnel or visitors may perform searches. Search fee $20.00 per name. Office will search real estate records. Tax liens not included in UCC search. Copy fee $1.00 per page.Cert fee- $10.00 per doc includes copy fee. Payee- Polk County Recorder. **Other phones:** Treasurer- 218-281-2554; Elections- 218-281-2554; Vital Records- 218-281-3464. **Property tax/Assessing-** 612 N Broadway, #201, Crookston, MN 56716; 218-281-4186, assessor fax- 218-281-3669. Public terminal is available. www.co.polk.mn.us/list_departments/assessor/index.aspx

Pope County

County Recorder, 130 E Minnesota Ave, #206, Glenwood, MN 56334. Recording, R/E & UCC phone-320-634-5723; fax-320-634-5717; 8AM-4:30PM (CST) www.co.pope.mn.us/Recorders.htm
Index: All in one. Records indexed on a public use terminal back to 1987. Office personnel (limited search) or visitors may perform searches. Search fee $20.00 per name. Office will search real estate records one year back only. Copy fee $.25 per page for real estate doc, $5.00 for fax fee.Cert fee- $10.00 per cert includes copy fee. Payee- Pope County Recorder. Bulk data available for purchase, contact Donna Quandt. **Online access to Real Estate, Deed, Lien records:** Recorder land data by subscription on either the Laredo system using subscription and fees or the Tapestry System using credit card, http://tapestry.fidlar.com; $5.99 search; $.50 per image. Index and images goes back to 11/1987. **Other phones:** Treasurer- 320-634-5705; Elections-320-634-5705; Vital Records- 320-634-5723; Auditor- 320-634-5705. **Property tax/Assessing-** 130 E Minnesota Ave, #222, Glenwood, MN 56334; 320-634-5728, assessor fax- 320-634-3087. (Appraiser/Auditor- 320-634-5728) A public access terminal is available. **Online access-** Look-up assessor property tax data free at http://morris.state.mn.us/tax/disclaimer.asp?cid=61. Also, access to county property/parcel data is free at http://morris.state.mn.us/tax/.

Ramsey County

County Recorder, 90 W Plato Blvd, St. Paul, MN 55107. 651-266-2000; fax-651-266-2066; 8-4:30PM www.co.ramsey.mn.us/prr/recorder/index.htm
Index: Separate indices. Records indexed on a public use terminal back to 1993. Office personnel or visitors may perform searches. Search fee $55.00 per hour for detailed search. Office will search real estate records for current owner/lst entry for no fee. Office will not search UCC records. Copy fee $1.00 per page.Cert fee- $10.00 per cert minimum; add $1 per pg over 5. Payee- Ramsey County Recorder. Bulk data available for purchase- index of documents, lender/borrower-$20.00, or data made to order. **Online Real Estate, Deed records:** This agency's extensive search product including recorded documents is by subscription; see http://rrinfo.co.ramsey.mn.us/public/document/index.asp. **Other phones:** Treasurer- 651-266-2000; Elections- 651-266-2171; Vital Records- 651-266-1333. **Property tax/Assessing-** 90 W Plato Blvd 651-266-2131. **Online** - Search the property assessment rolls free at http://rrinfo.co.ramsey.mn.us/public/characteristic/index.aspx but no name searching.

Red Lake County

County Recorder, PO Box 3, Red Lake Falls, MN 56750-0003. Recording, R/E & UCC phone-218-253-2997; fax-218-253-2052; 9AM-5PM (CST)
Index: Separate indices to search include Torrens certificate, abstract. Records indexed on a public use terminal back to 1986. Office personnel or visitors may perform searches. Search fee $20.00 per name. Real estate searches by office are not certifiable. Copy fee $1.00 per document.Cert fee- $10.00 per cert plus copy fee. Payee- Red Lake County Recorder. **Other phones:** Treasurer- 218-253-2797; Vitals- 218-253-2997. **Property tax/ Assessing-** PO Box 458, Courthouse, Red Lake Falls, 56750; 218-253-2596, assessor fax- 218-253-2052.

Redwood County

County Recorder, PO Box 130, Redwood Falls, MN 56283. 507-637-4032; fax-507-637-4064; 8AM-4:30PM (CST) www.mncounties2.org/redwood/
Index: All in one. Records indexed on a public use terminal back to 6/1/95. Office personnel or visitors may perform searches. Search fee-$4.00 per name. Office will not search real estate records. UCC search includes tax liens if requested. Copy fee $1.00 per page.Cert fee- $1.00 per page, $10.00 minimum includes copy fee. Payee- Redwood County Recorder. **Other phones:** Treasurer- 507-637-4013; Elections-507-637-4069; Vital Records- 507-637-4032. **Property tax/Assessing-** 250 S Jefferson, Courthouse Sq, Redwood Falls, MN 56283; 507-637-4008, assessor fax- 507-637-4009. A public access terminal is available. **Online access-** Look-up assessor property tax data free at http://morris.state.mn.us/tax/.

Renville County

County Recorder, 500 E DePue, 2nd Fl, Olivia, MN 56277. 320-523-3669; fax-320-523-3650; 8AM-4:30PM (CST) www.co.renville.mn.us
Index: All in one. Records indexed on a public use terminal back to 1986. Office personnel or visitors may perform searches. Search fee $20.00 per name. Office will search UCC records by computer. General copy fee $1.00 per page.Cert fee- $10.00 per doc includes copy fee. Payee- Renville County Recorder. Bulk data available for purchase. **Other phones:** Treasurer- 320-523-2071; Elections- 320-523-2071; Vital Records- 320-523-3669. **Property tax/ Assessing-** 500 E DePue, 2nd Fl, Courthouse, Olivia, MN 56277; 320-523-3645, assessor fax- 320-523-3679. (Appraiser/Auditor- 320-523-3645) A public access terminal is available. **Online access-** Look-up assessor property tax data free at http://morris.state.mn.us/tax/.

Rice County

County Recorder, 320 NW 3rd St, #10, Faribault, MN 55021-6146. Recording, R/E & UCC phone-507-332-6114; fax-507-333-3754; 8AM-4:30PM (CST) www.co.rice.mn.us
Index: All in one. Records indexed on a public use terminal back to 01/1992. Office personnel or visitors may perform searches. Office will search real estate records depending on search wanted. UCC-11 search per debtor name- $20.00. General copy fee $1.00 per page.Real estate record copy- $.50 per page. Cert fee- $10.00 per doc includes copy fee. Payee- Rice County Recorder. **Other phones:** Treasurer- 507-332-6104; Elections- 507-332-6104; Vital Records- 507-332-6114. **Property tax/Assessing-** 320 NW 3rd St, #10, Fairbault, MN 55021; 507-332-6102. (Appraiser/Auditor- 507-332-6102) A public access terminal is available. **Online access-** Search assessor property data free on the GIS system at http://beacon.schneidercorp.com/ but no name searching. Search parcel data and residential/commercial sales data free at www.rice.minnesotaassessors.com. No name searching for free but a sub service is also available with name searching.

Rock County

County Recorder, PO Box 509, Luverne, MN 56156. Recording, R/E & UCC phone-507-283-5014; fax-507-283-1343; 8AM-5PM (CST) www.co.rock.mn.us
Index: Separate indices to search include Torrens, State tax liens, federal tax liens. Records indexed on a public use terminal back to 1992. Office personnel or visitors may perform searches. General search fee $25.00 per hour; $10.00 minimum. Office will search real estate records. UCC search includes tax liens if requested. UCC search per debtor, including 10 copies/listings- $20.00 fixed. Copy fee $.25 per page; fax and email copy fee $1.00. Cert fee- $10.00 per doc includes copy fee. Payee- Rock County Recorder. Bulk data available for purchase. **Online access to Real Estate, Deed, Lien records:** Access Recorder land data by subscription on either the Laredo system using subscription and fees or the Tapestry System using credit card, http://tapestry.fidlar.com; $3.99 search; $.50 per image. Index and images goes back to 10/1992. **Other phones:** Treasurer- 507-283-5055; Elections- 507-283-5060; Vital Records- 507-283-5060. **Property tax/Assessing-** 204 E Brown, Luverne, MN 56156; 507-283-5022, assessor fax- 507-283-1343. A public access terminal is available. **Online access-** Look-up assessor property tax data free at http://morris.state.mn.us/tax/.

Roseau County

County Recorder, 606 5th Ave SW, Rm 170, Roseau, MN 56751-1477. Recording, R/E & UCC phone-218-463-2061; fax-218-463-4294; 8AM-4:30PM (CST)
Index: All in one. Records indexed on a public use terminal back to 1892. Office will perform a UCC search but public must search other records themselves. Copy fee $1.00 per page after 10 pages.Cert fee- $10.00. Payee- Roseau County Recorder. Bulk data available for purchase. **Other phones:** Treasurer- 218-463-1215; Elections- 218-463-1282; Vital Records- 218-463-1215. **Property tax/Assessing-** 606 5th Ave SW, Roseau, MN 56751; 218-463-1861, assessor fax- 218-463-4218. A public access terminal is available. **Online access-** Online access to property records is available at http://136.234.18.34/website/roseau/main.php. For access, please contact Trish Harren at trish.harren@co.roseau.mn.us or at (218) 463-4248.

Scott County

Recorder, 200 4th Ave W, Shakopee, MN 55379. 952-496-8150; fax-952-496-8769; 8AM-4:30PM (CST) www.co.scott.mn.us/wps/portal/ScottCounty/
Index: All in one. Records indexed on a public use terminal back to 1985. Office personnel or visitors may perform searches. Office will search real estate records back 3 years or 3 entries. Office will not search UCC records. Copy fee $1.00 per page.Cert fee- $10.00 per page. Payee- Scott County Recorder. **Other phones:** Treasurer- 952-496-8150; Elections-952-496-8161; Vital Records- 952-496-8150. **Property tax/Assessing-** 200 4th Ave W, Shakopee, MN 55379; 952-496-8115, assessor fax- 952-496-8135. (Appraiser/Auditor- 952-496-8150) **Online access-** Search assessor and a variety of property data free at http://www2.co.scott.mn.us/stellent/idcplg/records/pxs?IdcService=SC_PROPERTYTAX_HOME but no name searching. Search the county property databases free by link at www.co.scott.mn.us/wps/portal/ScottCounty/. There is also a free online document subscription service and GIS mapping.

Sherburne County

County Recorder, 13880 Hwy 10, Elk River, MN 55330. 763-241-2915, 800-719-2826, R/E recording phone-800-719-2826; fax-763-241-2995; 8AM-4:30PM (CST) www.co.sherburne.mn.us
Index: All in one. Records indexed on a public use terminal back to 1986. Only the public may search. General copy fee $.50 per page. Fee to fax back-$2.50 1st page, $.50 each add'l page.Real estate or tax lien copy- $2.00 1st page, $.50 each add'l page. Cert fee- $10.00 per doc includes copy fee. Payee-Sherburne County Recorder. Bulk data available for purchase, contact Holly, Betty or Samantha. **Other phones:** Treasurer- 800-438-0575; Elections- 800-719-2826; Vital Records- 800-719-2826. **Property tax/Assessing-** 13880 Hwy 10, Elk River, MN 55330; 763-241-2880, assessor fax- 763-241-7195. www.co.sherburne.mn.us/assessor/default.htm

Online access- Property records from the county tax assessor database free at http://beacon.schneidercorp.com/?site=SherburneCountyMN. However, to perform a name search, you must subscribe; fee is $25.00 setup, $300.00 per year.

Sibley County

County Recorder, PO Box 44, Gaylord, MN 55334-0044. 507-237-4080; fax-507-237-4306; 8AM-4:30PM http://co.sibley.mn.us/Dept_Frame.htm
Index: All in one. Records indexed on a public use terminal back to 8/94. Office personnel or visitors may perform searches. Search fee $40.00 for deed forward; $4.00 for each add'l RE entry. Fee for UCC search-$20.00 per name. Office will search real estate records. Will search UCC records. Tax lien search fee- $5.00 per debtor. Copy fee $1.00 per page; $3.00 per page if found in books.Cert fee- $1.00 per page, $10.00 minimum. Payee- Sibley County Recorder. **Other phones:** Treasurer- 507-237-4084; Elections- 507-237-4070; Vitals- 507-237-4080. **Property tax/Assessing**- PO Box 532, Gaylord, MN 55334-0532; 507-237-4078, assessor fax- 507-237-4078. A public access terminal is available.

St. Louis County

County Recorder, PO Box 157, Duluth, MN 55801-0157. Recording, R/E & UCC phone-218-726-2677; fax-218-725-5052; 8AM-4:30PM (CST) www.co.st-louis.mn.us/slcportal/
Index: Separate indices to search include abstract and Torrens title. Records indexed on a public use terminal back to 1987 for abstracts, all for Torrens. Office will perform a UCC search but public must search other records themselves. Search fee $20.00 per debtor. Office will search UCC records in writing only for $20.00 per debtor name. Copy fee $1.00 per page. Minimum copy fee $3.00.Cert fee- $10.00 per doc includes copy fee. Payee- St. Louis County Recorder. Bulk data available for purchase, contact Recorder Mark Monacelli for subscription info. **Online access to Real Estate, Grantor/Grantee, Deed, Lien, Mortgage records:** Access the recorder database by subscription. Fee is $120 monthly and includes assessment records. Contact the Auditor or Recorder office for sign up, or visit the Recorder office website and click on Online Contract. **Other phones:** Treasurer- 218-726-2380; Elections- 218-726-2385; Vital Records- 218-726-2559; Torrens Division- 218-726-2680. **Property tax/Assessing**- 100 N 5th Ave W, Rm 212, Duluth, MN 55802-1291; 218-726-2304, assessor fax- 218-725-5053. (Appraiser/Auditor- 218-726-2304) A public access terminal is available. **Online access**- Access auditor tax records for tax professionals database by subscription. Fee is $120 monthly. For info or sign-up, contact Pam Palen at 218-726-2380 or email to palenp@co.st-louis.mn.us. Also, search auditor info for free at www.co.st-louis.mn.us/auditor/parcelinfo2005//. Also, search the City of Duluth property assessor data free at www.duluthmn.gov/assessor/search/index.cfm.

Stearns County

County Recorder, 705 Courthouse Sq, Rm 131, Admin Ctr, St. Cloud, MN 56303. 320-656-3855, R/E recording phone-320-259-3855; fax-320-656-3916; 8AM-4:30PM (CST) www.co.stearns.mn.us
Index: All in one. Records indexed on a public use terminal back to 1995. Office will perform a UCC search but public must search other records themselves. UCC search per debtor name- $20.00. Copy fee $1.00 per page.Cert fee- $1.00 per page, $5.00 minimum. Payee- Stearns County Recorder. **Other phones:** Treasurer- 320-656-3870; Elections- 320-656-3920. **Property tax/Assessing**- 705 Courthouse Sq, Admin Ctr, St. Cloud, MN 56303; 320-656-3680, assessor fax- 320-656-3977. A public access terminal is available. **Online access**- Records from the county tax assessor database are free at http://secure.co.stearns.mn.us/. No name searching.

Steele County

County Recorder, PO Box 890, Owatonna, MN 55060. Recording, R/E & UCC phone-507-444-7450; fax-507-444-7470; 8AM-5PM www.co.steele.mn.us
Index: All in one. Records indexed on a public use terminal from 1991 to present. Only the public may search. Copy fee $1.00 per page. A SASE is required.Cert fee- $10.00 per doc includes copy fee. Prepayment required. Payee- Steele County Recorder. Bulk data available for purchase (computer printouts @$2.00 per page), contact Glen Purdie. **Online access to Real Estate, Deed, Lien records:** Access recorder land data by subscription on either the Laredo system using sub and fees or the Tapestry System using credit card, http://tapestry.fidlar.com; $3.99 search; $.50 per image. Index goes back to 1/1991; images back to 1/1991. **Other phones:** Treasurer- 507-444-7420; Elections- 507-444-7410; Vital Records- 507-444-7490. **Property tax/Assessing**- 630 Florence Ave, Owatonna, MN 55060; 507-444-7435, assessor fax- 507-444-7446. A public access terminal is available. **Online access**- Search parcel data, sales, and GIS-mapping site free at www.co.steele.mn.us/Administration/Auditor/Auditor.html

Stevens County

County Recorder, PO Box 530, Morris, MN 56267. 320-589-7414; fax-320-589-7112; 8:30AM-4:30PM (Summer Hours 8AM-4PM). www.co.stevens.mn.us/
Index: All in one. Records indexed on computer back to 1996. Office personnel or visitors may perform searches. Search fee $20.00 per hour. Office will search real estate records. Office will not search UCC records. Copy fee $1.00 per page.Cert fee- $10.00 per doc plus copy fee. Payee- Stevens County Recorder. **Other phones:** Treasurer- 320-589-7418; Elections- 320-589-7409; Vital Records- 320-589-7414. **Property tax/Assessing**- 5th & Colorado, Morris, MN 56267; 320-589-7407. hours- 8AM-4:30PM www.co.stevens.mn.us/ **Online access**- Look-up assessor property tax data free at http://morris.state.mn.us/tax/.

Swift County

County Recorder, PO Box 246, Benson, MN 56215. Recording, R/E & UCC phone-320-843-3377; fax-320-843-6105; 8AM-4:30PM www.swiftcounty.com/
Index: Separate indices to search include Torrens, abstract, State & Fed tax liens. Records indexed on a public use terminal back to 1987. Office personnel or visitors may perform searches. Search fee varies. Office will search real estate records. Real estate copy fee $2.00 per doc.Cert fee- $10.00 per doc plus copy fee. Payee- Swift County Recorder. **Other phones:** Treasurer- 320-843-3544; Elections- 320-843-4069; Vital Records- 320-843-3544. **Property tax/Assessing**- PO Box 274, Benson, MN 56215; 320-842-5891, assessor fax- 320-843-2275. **Online access**- Access parcel data by address, ID, or book/page for free at http://morris.state.mn.us/tax/.

Todd County

County Recorder, 221 1st Ave S, #300, Long Prairie, MN 56347-1391. Recording, R/E & UCC phone-320-732-4428; fax-320-732-4001; 8AM-4:30PM (CST) www.co.todd.mn.us/Recorder/recorder.htm
Index: All in one. Records indexed on a public use terminal back to 1993. Office personnel or visitors may perform searches. Search fee $35.00 per hour. Office will search real estate records. Office will not search UCC records. Copy fee $1.00 per page.Cert fee- $10.00 per doc includes copy fee. Payee- Todd County Recorder. Bulk data available for purchase. **Other phones:** Treasurer- 320-732-4471; Elections- 320-732-4471; Vital Records- 320-732-4428. **Property tax/Assessing**- 221 1st Ave S, #400, Long Prairie, MN 56347; 320-732-4430, assessor fax- 320-732-4001. (Appraiser/Auditor- 320-732-4430) **Online access**- Access property data on the GIS-mapping site free at www.co.todd.mn.us/TODDCOUNTY/propertyinfo0003.asp but no name or address searching. Also, look-up assessor property tax data free at http://morris.state.mn.us/tax/. Search buildings at www.co.todd.mn.us/TODDCOUNTY/propertyinfo0012.asp. Also, access to county property/parcel data is free at http://morris.state.mn.us/tax/.

Traverse County

County Recorder, PO Box 487, Wheaton, MN 56296-0487. 320-563-4622, R/E recording phone-320-563-4242, UCC recording phone-320-563-4622; fax-320-563-4424; 8AM-4:30PM (CST)
Index: All in one. Records indexed on a public use terminal back to 2004. Office personnel or visitors may perform searches. Search of general index performed by phone is free. General search fee- $20.00 per name. Office will search real estate records. Office will not search UCC records. Copy fee $1.00 per page after 10 pages.Cert fee- $10.00 per doc plus copy fee. Payee- Traverse County Recorder. **Other phones:** Treasurer- 320-563-4616; Elections- 320-563-4622; Vital Records- 320-563-4622. **Property tax/Assessing**- PO Box 813, Wheaton, MN 56296; 320-563-4113, assessor fax- 320-563-4229.

Wabasha County

County Recorder, 625 Jefferson Ave, Wabasha, MN 55981. 651-565-3623, R/E recording phone-612-565-3623; fax-651-565-2774; 8AM-4PM (CST)
Index: Separate indices to search include 6/6, tracts. Records indexed on a public use terminal back to 1994. Office will perform a UCC search but public must search other records themselves. General search fee $20.00 per name. Copy fee $.50 per page, $1.00 minimum.Cert fee- $10.00 per doc includes copy fee. Payee- Wabasha County Recorder. **Other phones:** Treasurer- 651-565-3669. **Property tax/Assessing**- 625 Jefferson Ave, Wabasha, 55981; 651-565-3669, assessor fax- 651-565-2774. www.co.wabasha.mn.us/ **Online** - Access property information free at www.co.wabasha.mn.us/index.php?option=com_wrapper&Itemid=108.

Wadena County

County Recorder, 415 Jefferson St S, Wadena, MN 56482. Recording, R/E & UCC phone-218-631-7622; fax-218-631-5709; 8AM-4:30PM (CST) www.co.wadena.mn.us
Index: Separate indices to search. Records indexed on computer back to 1995. Office personnel or visitors may perform searches. UCC Info request search fee $20.00 per debtor. Office will search real estate records. Will search UCC records. Copy fee $1.00 per page.Cert fee- $10.00 per doc includes copy fee. Payee- Wadena County Recorder. **Other phones:** Treasurer- 218-631-7621; Elections- 218-631-7650; Vital Records- 218-631-7788; Auditor- 218-631-7785. **Property tax/Assessing**- 415 Jefferson St S, Courthouse, Wadena, MN 56482; 218-631-7628, assessor fax- 218-631-7754. (Appraiser/Auditor- 218-631-7628) A public access terminal is available. www.co.wadena.mn.us/assessor.htm **Online access**- Search tax parcels free at www.co.wadena.mn.us/website/wadenapublic/main.php but no name searching.

Waseca County

County Recorder, 307 N State St, Waseca, MN 56093. 507-835-0670; fax-507-837-5333; 8AM-4:30PM (CST) www.co.waseca.mn.us/recorder.htm
Index: All in one. Records indexed on a public use terminal back to 1/199. Only the public may search. Copy fee $1.00 per page; old large book page- $3.00 per copy.Cert fee- $10.00 per doc includes copy fee. Payee- Waseca County Recorder. **Online access to Real Estate, Deed, Mortgage. records:** With registration, username and password you may access recording data on LandShark system at http://landshark.co.waseca.mn.us/LandShark/login.jsp . Fee is $50.00 per month, plus copy fee for images. **Other phones:** Treasurer- 507-835-0620; Elections- 507-835-0610; Vital Records- 507-835-0625. **Property tax/Assessing**- Same address as recording office. 507-835-0640, assessor fax- 507-835-0633. A public access terminal is available. www.co.waseca.mn.us/assessor.htm

Washington County

County Recorder, PO Box 6; 14949 N 62nd St, Stillwater, MN 55082. Recording, R/E & UCC phone-651-430-6175, UCC recording phone-651-275-7061; fax-651-275-7060; 8AM-5PM (CST) www.co.washington.mn.us
Index: All in one. Records index on a public use terminal back to 1984. Images on public use terminal-Torrens-1927; abstract-late 1800's (with some gaps). Only the public may search. Copy fee $1.00 per page.Cert fee- $10.00 for documents per cert includes copy fee; $15.00 for plats per cert includes copy fee. Payee- Washington County. **Online access to Real Estate, Deed, Lien, Mortgage, Plat, Tract records:** Access to county tract records requires a $50.00 set up fee and $30.00 monthly fee; abstract images go back to 7/1994; Torrens images to 10/1989; tracts to 1984. UCC and Torrens cert. data is not on this system. **Other phones:** Treasurer- 651-430-6175; Elections-651-430-6175; Vital Records- 651-275-7057; Torrens Division- 651-430-6175. **Property tax/Assessing-** 14949 62nd St N, Stillwater, 55082; 651-430-6175. www.co.washington.mn.us/info_for_residents/atse/assessment__values/ **Online access-** Access to property tax records is free at http://www2.co.was hington.mn.us/opip/; no name searching - property ID or address required.

Watonwan County

County Recorder, PO Box 518, St. James, MN 56081. Recording, R/E & UCC phone-507-375-1216; fax-507-375-1215; 8:30AM-N, 1-5PM (CST)
Index: All in one. Records indexed on a public use terminal back to 2000. Only the public may search. Tax lien search fee- $15.00 per debtor. Copy fee $1.00 per page.Cert fee- $10.00 per doc includes copy fee. Payee- Watonwan County Recorder. **Other phones:** Treasurer- 507-375-1213; Elections- 507-375-1210; Vital Records- 507-375-1216. **Property tax/Assessing-** Courthouse, St. James, MN 56081; 507-375-1205, assessor fax- 507-375-3547. hours-8AM-5PM

Wilkin County

County Recorder, PO Box 29, Breckenridge, MN 56520. Recording, R/E & UCC phone-218-643-7164; fax-218-643-7170; 8AM-4:30PM (CST) www.wilkincountymn.govoffice2.com/index.asp
Index: All in one. Records indexed on a public use terminal back to 1994. Office personnel or visitors may perform searches. General index search fee $20.00 per hour. Office will search real estate records. Copy fee $1.00 per page.Real estate record copy-$3.00 1st 2 pages; $.50 each add'l page. Cert fee-$10.00 per cert includes copy fee. Payee- Wilkin County Recorder. Bulk data available for purchase, contact Renae Niemi. **Other phones:** Treasurer- 218-643-7112; Elections- 218 643-7165; Vital Records-218-643-7112. **Property tax/Assessing-** 300 5th St S,, Courthouse, 1st Fl, Breckenridge, MN 56520; 218-643-7162, assessor fax- 218-643-7169. **Online access-** Access parcel data free at http://morris.state.mn.us/tax/disclaimer_value.asp?cid=84 but no name searching.

Winona County

County Recorder, 177 Main St, Winona, MN 55987. Recording, R/E & UCC phone-507-457-6340, UCC recording phone-507-457-6396; fax-507-454-9371; 8AM-4:30PM (CST) www.co.winona.mn.us
Index: All in one. Records indexed on a public use terminal back to 1987. Office personnel or visitors may perform searches. Search fee $20.00. Office will search real estate records. Office will not search UCC records. Copy fee $2.00 per doc.Cert fee- $10.00 per doc includes copy fee. Payee- Winona County Recorder. Bulk data available for purchase, contact anyone in the office. **Other phones:** Treasurer- 507-457-6450; Elections- 507-457-6420; Vital Records-507-457-6395. **Property tax/Assessing-** 177 Main St, Winona, MN 55987; 507-457-6330, assessor fax-507-457-9365.

Wright County

County Recorder, 10 2nd St NW, Rm 210, Buffalo, MN 55313-1196. Recording, R/E & UCC phone-763-682-7357, UCC recording phone-763-684-4551; fax-763-684-4558; 8AM-4:30PM www.co.wright.mn.us
Index: Separate indices to search include microfilm, tract books, computer. Records indexed on a public use terminal back to 1991. Office will perform a UCC search for a fee, but public must search other records themselves. Copy fee $1.00 per page.Cert fee- $1.00 per page, $5.00 minimum, includes copy fee. Payee-Wright County Recorder. **Online access to Real Estate, Grantor/Grantee, Deed, Lien records:** Access to Land Title database is free at www.co.wright.mn.us/department/recorder/landtitle/index.htm. **Other phones:** Treasurer- 763-682-7578; Elections- 763-682-7578; Vital Records- 763-682-7594. **Property tax/Assessing-** 10 2nd St NW, Buffalo, MN 55313; 763-682-7367, assessor fax-763-684-4553. hours- 8AM04:30PM **Online access-** Search the property tax database for free at www.co.wright.mn.us/department/audtreas/proptax/default.asp.

Yellow Medicine County

County Recorder, 415 9th Ave #10, Granite Falls, MN 56241. 320-564-2529; fax-320-564-3670; 8AM-4PM (CST) http://yellowmedicine.govoffice.com
Index: Book, computer. Records indexed on a public use terminal back to 11/1996. Office personnel or visitors may perform searches. Search fee $20.00. Office will only search real estate records back 5 years. Office will not search UCC records. Copy fee $1.00 per page.Cert fee- $10.00 per doc. Payee-Yellow Medicine County Recorder. Mortgage and Deed reports available, contact anyone at the county recorder's office. **Other phones:** Elections- 320-564-3132; Vital Records- 320-564-2529; Auditor/Treasurer- 320-564-3132. **Property tax/Assessing-** 415 9th Ave, Courthouse 320-564-3628, assessor fax- 320-564-3670. **Online access-** Look-up assessor property tax data free at http://morris.state.mn.us/tax/.

Minnesota County Locator

You will usually be able to find the city name in the City/County Cross Reference below. In that case, it is a simple matter to determine the county from the cross reference. However, only the official US Postal Service city names are included in this index. There are an additional 40,000 place names that people use in their addresses. Therefore, we have also included a ZIP/City Cross Reference immediately following the City/County Cross Reference.

If you know the ZIP Code but the city name does not appear in the City/County Cross Reference index, look up the ZIP Code in the ZIP/City Cross Reference, find the city name, then look up the city name in the City/County Cross Reference. For example, you want to know the county for an address of Menands, NY 12204. There is no "Menands" in the City/County Cross Reference. The ZIP/City Cross Reference shows that ZIP Codes 12201-12288 are for the city of Albany. Looking back in the City/County Cross Reference, Albany is in Albany County.

Minnesota City/County Cross Reference

ADA Norman
ADAMS Mower
ADOLPH St. Louis
ADRIAN Nobles
AFTON Washington
AH GWAH CHING Cass
AITKIN (56431) Aitkin(69), Crow Wing(30)
AKELEY (56433) Hubbard(84), Cass(15)
ALBANY Stearns
ALBERT LEA Freeborn
ALBERTA (56207) Stevens(98), Swift(1)
ALBERTVILLE Wright
ALBORN St. Louis
ALDEN Freeborn
ALDRICH (56434) Todd(67), Wadena(32)
ALEXANDRIA Douglas
ALMELUND Chisago
ALPHA (56111) Martin(60), Jackson(39)
ALTURA (55910) Winona(86), Wabasha(14)
ALVARADO (56710) Marshall(85), Polk(14)
AMBOY (56010) Blue Earth(97), Faribault(1)
AMIRET Lyon
ANGLE INLET Lake of the Woods
ANGORA St. Louis
ANGUS Polk
ANNANDALE Wright
ANOKA Anoka
APPLETON (56208) Swift(91), Lac qui Parle(5), Big Stone(2)
ARCO (56113) Lincoln(81), Lyon(18)
ARGYLE Marshall
ARLINGTON Sibley
ASHBY (56309) Grant(64), Otter Tail(29), Douglas(6)
ASKOV Pine
ATWATER (56209) Kandiyohi(83), Meeker(16)
AUDUBON Becker
AURORA St. Louis
AUSTIN (55912) Mower(94), Freeborn(5)
AVOCA Murray
AVON Stearns
BABBITT St. Louis
BACKUS (56435) Cass(96), Crow Wing(3)
BADGER Roseau
BAGLEY (56621) Clearwater(94), Polk(5)
BAKER Clay
BALATON (56115) Lyon(56), Murray(43)
BANGOR Pope
BARNESVILLE (56514) Clay(90), Wilkin(8)
BARNUM Carlton
BARRETT Grant
BARRY Big Stone
BATTLE LAKE Otter Tail
BAUDETTE (56623) Lake of the Woods(84), Koochiching(15)
BAXTER Crow Wing
BAYPORT Washington
BEARDSLEY (56211) Big Stone(72), Traverse(27)
BEAVER BAY Lake
BEAVER CREEK Rock
BECIDA Hubbard
BECKER Sherburne
BEJOU (56516) Mahnomen(77), Norman(22)
BELGRADE (56312) Stearns(67), Kandiyohi(32)
BELLE PLAINE (56011) Scott(78), Sibley(13), Le Sueur(4), Carver(2)
BELLINGHAM Lac qui Parle
BELTRAMI (56517) Polk(98), Norman(1)
BELVIEW (56214) Redwood(90), Yellow Medicine(9)
BEMIDJI (56601) Beltrami(93), Hubbard(6)
BEMIDJI Beltrami
BENA Cass
BENEDICT Hubbard
BENSON (56215) Swift(95), Pope(4)
BEROUN Pine
BERTHA (56437) Todd(85), Otter Tail(14)
BETHEL (55005) Anoka(97), Isanti(2)
BIG FALLS Koochiching
BIG LAKE Sherburne
BIGELOW Nobles
BIGFORK Itasca
BINGHAM LAKE (56118) Cottonwood(92), Jackson(7)
BIRCHDALE Koochiching
BIRD ISLAND Renville
BIWABIK St. Louis
BLACKDUCK (56630) Itasca(42), Aitkin(41), Beltrami(16)
BLOMKEST Kandiyohi
BLOOMING PRAIRIE (55917) Steele(65), Dodge(19), Mower(8), Freeborn(6)
BLUE EARTH (56013) Faribault(97), Martin(2)
BLUFFTON Otter Tail
BOCK Mille Lacs
BORUP (56519) Norman(58), Clay(42)
BOVEY Itasca
BOWLUS (56314) Morrison(95), Stearns(4)
BOWSTRING Itasca
BOY RIVER Cass
BOYD (56218) Lac qui Parle(61), Yellow Medicine(38)
BRAHAM (55006) Isanti(35), Washington(31), Pine(13), Kanabec(11)
BRAINERD (56401) Crow Wing(94), Cass(5)
BRANDON (56315) Douglas(96), Otter Tail(3)
BRECKENRIDGE Wilkin
BREWSTER (56119) Nobles(68), Jackson(31)
BRICELYN Faribault
BRIMSON (55602) St. Louis(93), Lake(6)
BRITT St. Louis
BROOK PARK (55007) Pine(98), Kanabec(1)
BROOKS (56715) Red Lake(97), Polk(2)
BROOKSTON St. Louis
BROOTEN (56316) Stearns(88), Kandiyohi(10)
BROWERVILLE Todd
BROWNS VALLEY (56219) Traverse(95), Big Stone(4)
BROWNSDALE Mower
BROWNSVILLE Houston
BROWNTON McLeod
BRUNO Pine
BUCKMAN Morrison
BUFFALO Wright
BUFFALO LAKE (55314) Renville(81), Sibley(18)
BUHL St. Louis
BURNSVILLE Dakota
BURTRUM (56318) Todd(71), Morrison(28)
BUTTERFIELD (56120) Watonwan(59), Cottonwood(40)
BYRON (55920) Olmsted(98), Dodge(1)
CALEDONIA Houston
CALLAWAY Becker
CALUMET Itasca
CAMBRIDGE Isanti
CAMPBELL (56522) Wilkin(88), Otter Tail(9), Grant(2)
CANBY (56220) Yellow Medicine(80), Lac qui Parle(11), Lincoln(7)
CANNON FALLS (55009) Goodhue(92), Dakota(7)
CANTON Fillmore
CANYON St. Louis
CARLOS Douglas
CARLTON Carlton
CARVER Carver
CASS LAKE (56633) Cass(69), Beltrami(26), Hubbard(3)
CASTLE ROCK Dakota
CEDAR Anoka
CENTER CITY Chisago
CEYLON Martin
CHAMPLIN Hennepin
CHANDLER Murray
CHANHASSEN Carver
CHASKA Carver
CHATFIELD (55923) Fillmore(53), Olmsted(46)
CHISAGO CITY Chisago
CHISHOLM St. Louis
CHOKIO (56221) Stevens(90), Big Stone(8), Traverse(1)
CIRCLE PINES Anoka
CLARA CITY Chippewa
CLAREMONT (55924) Dodge(72), Steele(27)
CLARISSA Todd
CLARKFIELD (56223) Yellow Medicine(98), Lac qui Parle(1)
CLARKS GROVE Freeborn
CLEAR LAKE Sherburne
CLEARBROOK (56634) Clearwater(55), Polk(44)
CLEARWATER (55320) Wright(61), Stearns(38)
CLEMENTS Redwood
CLEVELAND Le Sueur
CLIMAX Polk
CLINTON Big Stone
CLITHERALL Otter Tail
CLONTARF (56226) Swift(85), Pope(14)
CLOQUET (55720) Carlton(90), St. Louis(9)
COHASSET Itasca
COKATO Wright
COLD SPRING Stearns
COLERAINE Itasca
COLLEGEVILLE Stearns
COLOGNE Carver
COMFREY (56019) Brown(64), Cottonwood(27), Watonwan(7)
COMSTOCK Clay
CONGER Freeborn
COOK (55788) Itasca(77), St. Louis(22)
COOK (55723) St. Louis(78), Itasca(21)
CORRELL Big Stone
COSMOS (56228) Meeker(94), Renville(5)
COTTAGE GROVE Washington
COTTON St. Louis
COTTONWOOD (56229) Lyon(78), Yellow Medicine(20)
COURTLAND Nicollet
CRANE LAKE St. Louis
CROMWELL Carlton
CROOKSTON Polk
CROSBY Crow Wing
CROSSLAKE Crow Wing
CRYSTAL BAY Hennepin
CULVER St. Louis
CURRIE Murray
CUSHING (56443) Morrison(77), Todd(22)
CYRUS (56323) Pope(86), Stevens(13)
DAKOTA Winona
DALBO Isanti
DALTON (56324) Otter Tail(97), Grant(2)
DANUBE Renville
DANVERS Swift
DARFUR Watonwan
DARWIN Meeker
DASSEL Meeker
DAWSON Lac qui Parle
DAYTON Hennepin
DE GRAFF (56233) Swift(82), Chippewa(17)
DEBS Beltrami
DEER CREEK Otter Tail
DEER RIVER (56636) Itasca(92), Cass(7)
DEERWOOD Crow Wing
DELANO (55328) Wright(97), Carver(2)
DELAVAN Faribault
DELFT Cottonwood
DENHAM Pine
DENHAM St. Louis
DENNISON (55018) Goodhue(86), Rice(12)
DENT Otter Tail
DETROIT LAKES (56501) Becker(97), Otter Tail(2)

DETROIT LAKES Becker
DEXTER Mower
DILWORTH Clay
DODGE CENTER Dodge
DONALDSON Kittson
DONNELLY (56235) Grant(53), Stevens(46)
DOVER Olmsted
DOVRAY Murray
DULUTH (55810) St. Louis(97), Carlton(2)
DULUTH St. Louis
DUMONT (56236) Traverse(70), Big Stone(29)
DUNDAS Rice
DUNDEE (56126) Nobles(65), Cottonwood(18), Murray(12), Jackson(3)
DUNNELL Martin
DUQUETTE Pine
EAGLE BEND (56446) Todd(93), Douglas(6)
EAGLE LAKE Blue Earth
EAST GRAND FORKS Polk
EASTON Faribault
ECHO Yellow Medicine
EDEN PRAIRIE Hennepin
EDEN VALLEY (55329) Stearns(50), Meeker(49)
EDGERTON (56128) Pipestone(76), Nobles(16), Rock(6)
EFFIE (56639) Itasca(93), Koochiching(6)
EITZEN Houston
ELBOW LAKE Grant
ELGIN (55932) Wabasha(55), Olmsted(44)
ELIZABETH Otter Tail
ELK RIVER (55330) Sherburne(76), Wright(17), Anoka(5)
ELKO Scott
ELKTON Mower
ELLENDALE (56026) Steele(57), Freeborn(41), Waseca(1)
ELLSWORTH (56129) Nobles(84), Rock(14), Lyon(1)
ELMORE (56027) Faribault(96), Martin(3)
ELROSA Stearns
ELY (55731) St. Louis(88), Lake(11)
ELYSIAN (56028) Le Sueur(92), Waseca(7)
EMBARRASS St. Louis
EMILY Crow Wing
EMMONS Freeborn
ERHARD Otter Tail
ERSKINE (56535) Polk(96), Red Lake(3)
ESKO (55733) Carlton(96), St. Louis(3)
ESSIG Brown
EUCLID Polk
EVAN (56238) Redwood(75), Brown(25)
EVANSVILLE (56326) Douglas(85), Otter Tail(11), Grant(3)
EVELETH St. Louis
EXCELSIOR (55331) Hennepin(98), Carver(1)
EYOTA Olmsted
FAIRFAX (55332) Renville(85), Nicollet(13), Sibley(1)
FAIRMONT Martin
FARIBAULT Rice
FARMINGTON Dakota
FARWELL (56327) Douglas(56), Pope(43)
FEDERAL DAM Cass
FELTON Clay
FERGUS FALLS Otter Tail
FERTILE (56540) Polk(93), Norman(6)
FIFTY LAKES Crow Wing
FINLAND Lake
FINLAYSON (55735) Pine(75), Aitkin(24)
FISHER Polk
FLENSBURG Morrison
FLOM Norman
FLOODWOOD (55736) St. Louis(93), Itasca(6)
FOLEY (56329) Benton(94), Morrison(5)
FORBES St. Louis
FOREST LAKE (55025) Washington(78), Anoka(12), Chisago(9)
FORESTON (56330) Mille Lacs(77), Benton(22)
FORT RIPLEY (56449) Crow Wing(84), Morrison(15)
FOSSTON (56542) Polk(95), Mahnomen(4)
FOUNTAIN Fillmore
FOXHOME Wilkin
FRANKLIN (55333) Renville(92), Redwood(4), Brown(3)
FRAZEE (56544) Becker(83), Otter Tail(16)
FREEBORN Freeborn
FREEPORT (56331) Stearns(98), Todd(1)
FRONTENAC Goodhue
FROST Faribault
FULDA (56131) Murray(84), Nobles(10), Cottonwood(5)
GARDEN CITY Blue Earth
GARFIELD Douglas
GARRISON (56450) Crow Wing(60), Mille Lacs(39)
GARVIN Lyon
GARY Norman
GATZKE (56724) Marshall(98), Roseau(1)
GAYLORD (55334) Sibley(93), Nicollet(6)
GENEVA Freeborn
GEORGETOWN Clay
GHENT Lyon
GIBBON (55335) Sibley(78), Nicollet(21)
GILBERT St. Louis
GILMAN Benton
GLENCOE (55336) McLeod(93), Sibley(6)
GLENVILLE Freeborn
GLENWOOD Pope
GLYNDON Clay
GONVICK (56644) Clearwater(84), Polk(15)
GOOD THUNDER Blue Earth
GOODHUE (55027) Goodhue(97), Wabasha(2)
GOODLAND Itasca
GOODRIDGE (56725) Pennington(71), Marshall(27)
GRACEVILLE (56240) Big Stone(75), Traverse(24)
GRANADA (56039) Martin(97), Faribault(2)
GRAND MARAIS Cook
GRAND MEADOW Mower
GRAND PORTAGE Cook
GRAND RAPIDS Itasca
GRANDY Isanti
GRANGER Fillmore
GRANITE FALLS (56241) Yellow Medicine(83), Chippewa(11), Renville(4)
GRASSTON (55030) Pine(91), Kanabec(8)
GREEN ISLE (55338) Sibley(96), Carver(3)
GREENBUSH Roseau
GREENWALD Stearns
GREY EAGLE Todd
GROVE CITY Meeker
GRYGLA (56727) Beltrami(59), Marshall(40)
GULLY (56646) Polk(95), Clearwater(4)
HACKENSACK Cass
HADLEY Murray
HALLOCK Kittson
HALMA Kittson
HALSTAD Norman
HAMBURG (55339) Carver(69), Sibley(26), McLeod(4)
HAMEL Hennepin
HAMMOND Wabasha
HAMPTON Dakota
HANCOCK (56244) Stevens(68), Pope(29), Swift(2)
HANLEY FALLS Yellow Medicine
HANOVER (55341) Wright(76), Hennepin(23)
HANSKA (56041) Brown(98), Watonwan(1)
HARDWICK Rock
HARMONY Fillmore
HARRIS Chisago
HARTLAND (56042) Freeborn(95), Waseca(4)
HASTINGS (55033) Dakota(91), Washington(8)
HAWICK Kandiyohi
HAWLEY Clay
HAYFIELD (55940) Dodge(81), Olmsted(17), Mower(1)
HAYWARD Freeborn
HAZEL RUN Yellow Medicine
HECTOR (55342) Renville(95), Sibley(3)
HENDERSON (56044) Sibley(88), Le Sueur(10)
HENDRICKS (56136) Lincoln(97), Dodge(2)
HENDRUM Norman
HENNING Otter Tail
HENRIETTE Pine
HERMAN (56248) Grant(87), Traverse(6), Stevens(5)
HERON LAKE (56137) Jackson(74), Cottonwood(19), Nobles(5)
HEWITT (56453) Todd(79), Otter Tail(20)
HIBBING (55746) St. Louis(98), Itasca(1)
HIBBING St. Louis
HILL CITY (55748) Aitkin(68), Itasca(31)
HILLMAN (56338) Morrison(95), Crow Wing(4)
HILLS Rock
HINCKLEY (55037) Pine(97), Kanabec(2)
HINES Beltrami
HITTERDAL (56552) Clay(79), Becker(20)
HOFFMAN (56339) Grant(88), Douglas(11)
HOKAH Houston
HOLDINGFORD Stearns
HOLLAND Pipestone
HOLLANDALE Freeborn
HOLLOWAY Swift
HOLMES CITY Douglas
HOLYOKE (55749) Carlton(71), Pine(28)
HOMER Winona
HOPE Steele
HOPKINS Hennepin
HOUSTON (55943) Houston(84), Winona(15)
HOVLAND Cook
HOWARD LAKE Hennepin
HOWARD LAKE Wright
HOYT LAKES St. Louis
HUGO (55038) Washington(67), Anoka(32)
HUMBOLDT Kittson
HUNTLEY Faribault
HUTCHINSON (55350) McLeod(91), Renville(5), Meeker(3)
IHLEN Pipestone
INTERNATIONAL FALLS Koochiching
INVER GROVE HEIGHTS Dakota
IONA (56141) Murray(90), Nobles(10)
IRON St. Louis
IRONTON Crow Wing
ISABELLA Lake
ISANTI Isanti
ISLE (56342) Mille Lacs(74), Kanabec(18), Aitkin(6)
IVANHOE Lincoln
JACOBSON (55752) Itasca(82), Aitkin(17)
JANESVILLE (56048) Waseca(98), Blue Earth(1)
JASPER (56144) Rock(77), Pipestone(18), Murray(3), Mower(1)
JEFFERS Cottonwood
JENKINS Crow Wing
JOHNSON (56250) Big Stone(70), Traverse(29)
JORDAN Scott
KABETOGAMA (56669) Koochiching(60), St. Louis(39)
KANARANZI (56146) Nobles(96), Rock(3)
KANDIYOHI Kandiyohi
KARLSTAD (56732) Kittson(89), Marshall(6), Roseau(4)
KASOTA (56050) Le Sueur(97), Blue Earth(2)
KASSON (55944) Dodge(94), Olmsted(5)
KEEWATIN Itasca
KELLIHER Beltrami
KELLOGG Wabasha
KELSEY St. Louis
KENNEDY Kittson
KENNETH (56147) Rock(72), Nobles(27)
KENSINGTON (56343) Douglas(69), Pope(15), Stevens(7), Grant(6)
KENT Wilkin
KENYON (55946) Goodhue(83), Rice(12), Dodge(3), Steele(1)
KERKHOVEN (56252) Kandiyohi(58), Swift(32), Chippewa(9)
KERRICK (55756) Pine(92), Carlton(7)
KETTLE RIVER Carlton
KIESTER (56051) Faribault(97), Freeborn(2)
KILKENNY (56052) Rice(66), Le Sueur(33)
KIMBALL (55353) Stearns(76), Meeker(23)
KINNEY St. Louis
KLOSSNER Nicollet
KNIFE RIVER Lake
LA CRESCENT (55947) Houston(88), Winona(11)
LA SALLE Watonwan
LAFAYETTE (56054) Nicollet(90), Sibley(9)
LAKE BENTON (56149) Lincoln(97), Pipestone(2)
LAKE BRONSON Kittson
LAKE CITY (55041) Wabasha(84), Goodhue(15)
LAKE CRYSTAL Blue Earth
LAKE ELMO Washington
LAKE GEORGE Hubbard
LAKE HUBERT Crow Wing
LAKE ITASCA Clearwater
LAKE LILLIAN Kandiyohi
LAKE PARK (56554) Becker(95), Clay(4)
LAKE WILSON Murray
LAKEFIELD Jackson
LAKELAND Washington
LAKEVILLE (55044) Dakota(86), Scott(13)
LAMBERTON (56152) Redwood(81), Cottonwood(18)
LANCASTER (56735) Kittson(97), Roseau(2)
LANESBORO Fillmore
LANSING Mower
LAPORTE (56461) Hubbard(94), Cass(5)
LASTRUP Morrison
LE CENTER Le Sueur
LE ROY (55951) Rice(60), Fillmore(40)
LE SUEUR (56058) Le Sueur(84), Sibley(11), Nicollet(3)
LENGBY (56651) Mahnomen(61), Polk(38)
LEONARD (56652) Clearwater(97), Beltrami(2)
LEOTA Nobles
LESTER PRAIRIE McLeod
LEWISTON Winona
LEWISVILLE (56060) Watonwan(87), Blue Earth(12)
LINDSTROM Chisago
LISMORE Nobles
LITCHFIELD Meeker
LITTLE FALLS Morrison
LITTLEFORK Koochiching
LOMAN Koochiching
LONDON Freeborn
LONG LAKE Hennepin
LONG PRAIRIE (56347) Todd(98), Morrison(1)
LONG PRAIRIE Todd
LONGVILLE Cass
LONSDALE Rice
LORETTO Hennepin
LOUISBURG Lac qui Parle
LOWRY (56349) Pope(84), Douglas(15)
LUCAN Redwood

LUTSEN Cook
LUVERNE Rock
LYLE (55953) Mower(80), Rice(14), Freeborn(4)
LYND Lyon
MABEL (55954) Fillmore(89), Houston(10)
MADELIA (56062) Watonwan(91), Brown(8)
MADISON Lac qui Parle
MADISON LAKE (56063) Blue Earth(59), Waseca(28), Le Sueur(11)
MAGNOLIA (56158) Rock(75), Nobles(25)
MAHNOMEN (56557) Mahnomen(95), Clearwater(2), Norman(2)
MAHTOWA Carlton
MAKINEN St. Louis
MANCHESTER Freeborn
MANHATTAN BEACH Crow Wing
MANKATO Blue Earth
MANKATO Nicollet
MANTORVILLE Dodge
MAPLE LAKE Wright
MAPLE PLAIN Hennepin
MAPLE PLAIN Wright
MAPLETON (56065) Blue Earth(56), Faribault(32), Waseca(11)
MARBLE Itasca
MARCELL Itasca
MARGIE Koochiching
MARIETTA (56257) Lac qui Parle(98), Grant(1)
MARINE ON SAINT CROIX Washington
MARSHALL Lyon
MAX Itasca
MAYER Carver
MAYNARD (56260) Chippewa(70), Renville(29)
MAZEPPA (55956) Wabasha(74), Goodhue(24), Olmsted(1)
MC GRATH Aitkin
MC KINLEY St. Louis
MCGREGOR Aitkin
MCINTOSH Polk
MEADOWLANDS St. Louis
MEDFORD (55049) Steele(89), Rice(10)
MELROSE Stearns
MELRUDE St. Louis
MENAHGA (56464) Wadena(52), Becker(29), Hubbard(15), Otter Tail(2)
MENDOTA Dakota
MENTOR (56736) Polk(88), Red Lake(11)
MERIDEN (56067) Waseca(69), Steele(30)
MERRIFIELD Crow Wing
MIDDLE RIVER Marshall
MILACA (56353) Mille Lacs(97), Isanti(2)
MILAN (56262) Chippewa(83), Swift(16)
MILLVILLE Wabasha
MILROY (56263) Redwood(83), Lyon(16)
MILTONA Douglas
MINNEAPOLIS Anoka
MINNEAPOLIS Carver
MINNEAPOLIS Hennepin
MINNEOTA (56264) Lyon(87), Yellow Medicine(11), Lincoln(1)
MINNESOTA CITY Winona
MINNESOTA LAKE (56068) Waseca(44), Faribault(43), Blue Earth(11)
MINNETONKA Hennepin
MINNETONKA BEACH Hennepin
MIZPAH Koochiching
MONTEVIDEO (56265) Chippewa(88), Lac qui Parle(8), Yellow Medicine(3)
MONTGOMERY (56069) Le Sueur(61), Rice(38)
MONTICELLO Carver
MONTICELLO Wright
MONTROSE (55363) Wright(98), Carver(1)
MOORHEAD Clay
MOOSE LAKE (55767) Carlton(80), Pine(19)
MORA Kanabec
MORGAN (56266) Redwood(75), Brown(24)
MORRIS Stevens
MORRISTOWN (55052) Rice(94), Waseca(5)
MORTON (56270) Renville(52), Redwood(47)
MOTLEY (56466) Morrison(48), Cass(40), Todd(11)
MOUND Hennepin
MOUNTAIN IRON St. Louis
MOUNTAIN LAKE (56159) Cottonwood(95), Jackson(3)
MURDOCK (56271) Swift(84), Chippewa(15)
MYRTLE Freeborn
NASHUA (56565) Wilkin(80), Grant(19)
NASHWAUK Itasca
NASSAU Lac qui Parle
NAVARRE Hennepin
NAYTAHWAUSH Mahnomen
NELSON Douglas
NERSTRAND (55053) Rice(80), Goodhue(19)
NETT LAKE St. Louis
NEVIS Hubbard
NEW AUBURN Sibley
NEW GERMANY Carver
NEW LONDON Kandiyohi
NEW MARKET Scott
NEW MUNICH Stearns
NEW PRAGUE (56071) Scott(55), Le Sueur(41), Rice(3)
NEW RICHLAND (56072) Waseca(90), Freeborn(9)
NEW ULM (56073) Brown(86), Nicollet(12), Blue Earth(1)
NEW YORK MILLS Otter Tail
NEWFOLDEN Marshall
NEWPORT Washington
NICOLLET Nicollet
NIELSVILLE (56568) Polk(92), Norman(7)
NIMROD Wadena
NISSWA (56468) Crow Wing(69), Cass(30)
NORCROSS (56274) Grant(68), Traverse(31)
NORTH BRANCH (55056) Chisago(79), Isanti(20)
NORTHFIELD (55057) Rice(81), Dakota(18)
NORTHOME (56661) Itasca(51), Koochiching(36), Beltrami(12)
NORTHROP Martin
NORWOOD (55368) Carver(97), McLeod(2)
NORWOOD Carver
NOYES Kittson
OAK ISLAND Lake of the Woods
OAK PARK Benton
OAKLAND Freeborn
ODESSA (56276) Big Stone(74), Lac qui Parle(25)
ODIN (56160) Watonwan(41), Martin(36), Jackson(21)
OGEMA Becker
OGILVIE (56358) Kanabec(88), Mille Lacs(11)
OKABENA Jackson
OKLEE (56742) Red Lake(79), Pennington(16), Polk(3)
OLIVIA Renville
ONAMIA Mille Lacs
ORMSBY (56162) Martin(55), Watonwan(44)
ORONOCO Olmsted
ORR (55771) St. Louis(91), Koochiching(8)
ORTONVILLE (56278) Big Stone(98), Lac qui Parle(1)
OSAGE Becker
OSAKIS (56360) Todd(57), Douglas(42)
OSLO (56744) Marshall(57), Polk(24), Mower(15), Crow Wing(3)
OSSEO Hennepin
OSTRANDER (55961) Mower(66), Fillmore(33)
OTISCO Waseca
OTTERTAIL Otter Tail
OUTING Cass
OWATONNA Steele
PALISADE Aitkin
PARK RAPIDS (56470) Hubbard(88), Becker(11)
PARKERS PRAIRIE (56361) Otter Tail(63), Douglas(36)
PARKVILLE St. Louis
PAYNESVILLE (56362) Stearns(89), Meeker(6), Kandiyohi(3)
PEASE Mille Lacs
PELICAN RAPIDS (56572) Otter Tail(95), Becker(2), Clay(1)
PEMBERTON (56078) Waseca(73), Blue Earth(26)
PENGILLY Itasca
PENNINGTON Beltrami
PENNOCK Kandiyohi
PEQUOT LAKES (56472) Crow Wing(76), Cass(23)
PERHAM Otter Tail
PERLEY (56574) Norman(95), Clay(4)
PETERSON (55962) Fillmore(94), Winona(5)
PIERZ (56364) Morrison(97), Crow Wing(2)
PILLAGER Cass
PINE CITY Pine
PINE ISLAND (55963) Goodhue(51), Olmsted(31), Dodge(17)
PINE RIVER (56474) Cass(95), Crow Wing(4)
PIPESTONE (56164) Pipestone(97), Lincoln(2)
PITT Lake of the Woods
PLAINVIEW (55964) Wabasha(96), Olmsted(2), Winona(1)
PLATO McLeod
PLUMMER (56748) Red Lake(90), Pennington(9)
PONEMAH Beltrami
PONSFORD Becker
PORTER (56280) Yellow Medicine(63), Lincoln(36)
PRESTON Fillmore
PRINCETON (55371) Mille Lacs(59), Sherburne(23), Isanti(15), Benton(1)
PRINSBURG Kandiyohi
PRIOR LAKE Scott
PUPOSKY Beltrami
RACINE Mower
RANDALL Morrison
RANDOLPH Dakota
RANIER Koochiching
RAY (56669) Koochiching(60), St. Louis(39)
RAYMOND (56282) Kandiyohi(81), Chippewa(18)
READING Nobles
READS LANDING Wabasha
RED LAKE FALLS (56750) Red Lake(94), Polk(3), Pennington(2)
RED WING Goodhue
REDBY Beltrami
REDLAKE Beltrami
REDWOOD FALLS (56283) Redwood(95), Renville(4)
REMER Cass
RENVILLE (56284) Renville(86), Kandiyohi(10), Redwood(2)
REVERE (56166) Redwood(74), Cottonwood(25)
RICE (56367) Benton(82), Stearns(16)
RICHMOND Stearns
RICHVILLE Otter Tail
RICHWOOD Becker
ROCHERT Becker
ROCHESTER Olmsted
ROCK CREEK Pine
ROCKFORD (55373) Wright(65), Hennepin(34)
ROCKFORD Hennepin
ROCKVILLE Stearns
ROGERS (55374) Hennepin(94), Wright(5)
ROLLINGSTONE Winona
ROOSEVELT (56673) Roseau(83), Lake of the Woods(16)
ROSCOE Stearns
ROSE CREEK Mower
ROSEAU Roseau
ROSEMOUNT Dakota
ROTHSAY (56579) Wilkin(63), Otter Tail(36)
ROUND LAKE (56167) Nobles(54), Jackson(45)
ROYALTON (56373) Morrison(89), Benton(10)
RUSH CITY (55069) Chisago(95), Pine(4)
RUSHFORD (55971) Fillmore(82), Houston(10), Winona(6)
RUSHMORE Nobles
RUSSELL Lyon
RUTHTON (56170) Pipestone(73), Lyon(13), Murray(10), Lincoln(2)
RUTLEDGE Pine
SABIN Clay
SACRED HEART Renville
SAGINAW St. Louis
SAINT BONIFACIUS (55375) Hennepin(98), Carver(1)
SAINT CHARLES (55972) Winona(85), Olmsted(14)
SAINT CLAIR Blue Earth
SAINT CLOUD (56304) Sherburne(50), Benton(49)
SAINT CLOUD Stearns
SAINT FRANCIS (55070) Anoka(90), Isanti(9)
SAINT HILAIRE (56754) Pennington(87), Red Lake(12)
SAINT JAMES (56081) Watonwan(98), Brown(1)
SAINT JOSEPH Stearns
SAINT LEO Yellow Medicine
SAINT MARTIN Stearns
SAINT MICHAEL Wright
SAINT PAUL (55118) Dakota(98), Ramsey(1)
SAINT PAUL (55110) Ramsey(85), Washington(13), Anoka(1)
SAINT PAUL (55126) Ramsey(98), Anoka(1)
SAINT PAUL Dakota
SAINT PAUL Hennepin
SAINT PAUL Ramsey
SAINT PAUL Washington
SAINT PAUL PARK Washington
SAINT PETER (56082) Nicollet(89), Le Sueur(10)
SAINT STEPHEN Stearns
SAINT VINCENT Kittson
SALOL Roseau
SANBORN (56083) Redwood(54), Cottonwood(29), Brown(15)
SANDSTONE (55072) Pine(83), Kanabec(15)
SANTIAGO Sherburne
SARGEANT (55973) Mower(96), Dodge(3)
SARTELL (56377) Stearns(79), Benton(20)
SAUK CENTRE (56378) Stearns(80), Todd(19)
SAUK RAPIDS (56379) Benton(98), Stearns(1)
SAUM Beltrami
SAVAGE Scott
SAWYER Carlton
SCANDIA (55073) Washington(62), Chisago(37)
SCHROEDER Cook
SEAFORTH Redwood

SEARLES Brown
SEBEKA (56477) Wadena(80), Otter Tail(19)
SEDAN Pope
SHAFER Chisago
SHAKOPEE Scott
SHELLY Norman
SHERBURN Martin
SHEVLIN (56676) Beltrami(54), Clearwater(45)
SIDE LAKE St. Louis
SILVER BAY Lake
SILVER CREEK Wright
SILVER LAKE McLeod
SLAYTON Murray
SLEEPY EYE (56085) Brown(97), Redwood(2)
SOLWAY (56678) Hubbard(74), Beltrami(24)
SOUDAN St. Louis
SOUTH HAVEN (55382) Stearns(46), Wright(45), Meeker(7)
SOUTH INTERNATIONAL FALLS Koochiching
SOUTH SAINT PAUL Dakota
SPICER Kandiyohi
SPRING GROVE (55974) Houston(98), Fillmore(1)
SPRING LAKE Itasca
SPRING PARK Hennepin
SPRING VALLEY (55975) Fillmore(87), Mower(12)
SPRINGFIELD (56087) Brown(90), Redwood(9)
SQUAW LAKE Itasca
STACY (55079) Chisago(48), Anoka(31), Isanti(20)
STACY (55078) Washington(80), Chisago(20)
STANCHFIELD (55080) Isanti(63), Chisago(36)
STAPLES (56479) Todd(67), Wadena(32)
STARBUCK Pope
STEEN (56173) Rock(71), Polk(28)
STEPHEN (56757) Marshall(98), Kittson(1)
STEWART (55385) McLeod(53), Renville(33), Sibley(12)
STEWARTVILLE (55976) Olmsted(96), Mower(2), Fillmore(1)
STILLWATER Washington
STOCKTON Winona
STORDEN Cottonwood
STRANDQUIST Marshall
STRATHCONA (56759) Roseau(73), Marshall(26)
STURGEON LAKE (55783) Pine(97), Carlton(2)
SUNBURG (56289) Kandiyohi(75), Swift(22), Pope(1)
SWAN RIVER Itasca
SWANVILLE (56382) Morrison(58), Todd(41)
SWATARA (55785) Cass(53), Aitkin(46)
SWIFT Roseau
TACONITE Itasca
TALMOON Itasca
TAMARACK (55787) Aitkin(79), Carlton(20)
TAOPI Mower
TAUNTON (56291) Lyon(46), Yellow Medicine(34), Lincoln(18)
TAYLORS FALLS Chisago
TENSTRIKE Beltrami
THEILMAN Wabasha
THIEF RIVER FALLS (56701) Pennington(95), Marshall(4)
TINTAH (56583) Wilkin(86), Traverse(13)
TOFTE Cook
TOWER St. Louis
TRACY (56175) Lyon(92), Redwood(7)
TRAIL (56684) Pennington(57), Polk(28), Red Lake(13)
TRIMONT Martin
TROSKY Pipestone
TRUMAN (56088) Martin(71), Watonwan(24), Blue Earth(4)
TWIG St. Louis
TWIN LAKES Freeborn
TWIN VALLEY Norman
TWO HARBORS Lake
TYLER (56178) Lincoln(89), Lyon(10)
ULEN (56585) Clay(76), Becker(21), Norman(1)
UNDERWOOD Otter Tail
UPSALA Morrison
UTICA (55979) Winona(98), Fillmore(1)
VERDI (56179) Lincoln(92), Pipestone(7)
VERGAS Otter Tail
VERMILLION Dakota
VERNDALE (56481) Wadena(78), Todd(18), Cass(2)
VERNON CENTER Blue Earth
VESTA (56292) Redwood(97), Yellow Medicine(2)
VICTORIA Carver
VIKING (56760) Marshall(98), Pennington(1)
VILLARD (56385) Pope(57), Stearns(37), Douglas(5)
VINING Otter Tail
VIRGINIA St. Louis
WABASHA Wabasha
WABASSO Redwood
WACONIA (55387) Carver(98), Hennepin(1)
WADENA (56482) Wadena(81), Otter Tail(17)
WAHKON Mille Lacs
WAITE PARK Stearns
WALDORF Waseca
WALKER Cass
WALNUT GROVE (56180) Redwood(81), Cottonwood(12), Murray(6)
WALTERS (56092) Faribault(92), Freeborn(7)
WALTHAM (55982) Mower(98), Dodge(1)
WANAMINGO Goodhue
WANDA Redwood
WANNASKA (56761) Roseau(95), Marshall(3)
WARBA Itasca
WARREN (56762) Marshall(70), Polk(29)
WARROAD Roseau
WARSAW Rice
WASECA (56093) Waseca(96), Steele(3)
WASKISH Beltrami
WATERTOWN (55388) Carver(85), Wright(12), Hennepin(2)
WATERVILLE (56096) Le Sueur(84), Rice(7), Waseca(7)
WATKINS (55389) Meeker(80), Stearns(20)
WATSON Chippewa
WAUBUN (56589) Becker(98), Mahnomen(1)
WAVERLY Wright
WAWINA Itasca
WAYZATA Hennepin
WEBSTER (55088) Rice(68), Scott(30)
WELCH (55089) Goodhue(88), Dakota(11)
WELCOME Martin
WELLS (56097) Faribault(86), Freeborn(11), Waseca(2)
WENDELL (56590) Grant(98), Otter Tail(1)
WEST CONCORD Dodge
WEST UNION Todd
WESTBROOK (56183) Cottonwood(92), Murray(7)
WHALAN Fillmore
WHEATON Traverse
WHIPHOLT Cass
WHITE EARTH Becker
WILLERNIE Washington
WILLIAMS Lake of the Woods
WILLMAR Kandiyohi
WILLOW RIVER Pine
WILMONT Nobles
WILTON Beltrami
WINDOM (56101) Cottonwood(84), Jackson(15)
WINGER (56592) Polk(97), Mahnomen(2)
WINNEBAGO (56098) Faribault(89), Martin(10)
WINONA Winona
WINSTED (55395) McLeod(91), Carver(8)
WINTHROP Sibley
WINTON St. Louis
WIRT Itasca
WOLF LAKE Becker
WOLVERTON Wilkin
WOOD LAKE (56297) Yellow Medicine(94), Redwood(3), Lyon(1)
WOODSTOCK (56186) Murray(79), Pipestone(20)
WORTHINGTON (56187) Nobles(98), Jackson(1)
WRENSHALL (55797) Carlton(94), Pine(5)
WRIGHT Carlton
WYKOFF Fillmore
WYOMING (55092) Chisago(60), Anoka(40)
YOUNG AMERICA Carver
YOUNG AMERICA Hennepin
ZIM St. Louis
ZIMMERMAN (55398) Sherburne(90), Isanti(9)
ZUMBRO FALLS (55991) Wabasha(90), Olmsted(9)
ZUMBROTA Goodhue

Minnesota ZIP/City Cross Reference

55001-55001 AFTON
55002-55002 ALMELUND
55003-55003 BAYPORT
55004-55004 BEROUN
55005-55005 BETHEL
55006-55006 BRAHAM
55007-55007 BROOK PARK
55008-55008 CAMBRIDGE
55009-55009 CANNON FALLS
55010-55010 CASTLE ROCK
55011-55011 CEDAR
55012-55012 CENTER CITY
55013-55013 CHISAGO CITY
55014-55014 CIRCLE PINES
55016-55016 COTTAGE GROVE
55017-55017 DALBO
55018-55018 DENNISON
55019-55019 DUNDAS
55020-55020 ELKO
55021-55021 FARIBAULT
55024-55024 FARMINGTON
55025-55025 FOREST LAKE
55026-55026 FRONTENAC
55027-55027 GOODHUE
55029-55029 GRANDY
55030-55030 GRASSTON
55031-55031 HAMPTON
55032-55032 HARRIS
55033-55033 HASTINGS
55036-55036 HENRIETTE
55037-55037 HINCKLEY
55038-55038 HUGO
55040-55040 ISANTI
55041-55041 LAKE CITY
55042-55042 LAKE ELMO
55043-55043 LAKELAND
55044-55044 LAKEVILLE
55045-55045 LINDSTROM
55046-55046 LONSDALE
55047-55047 MARINE ON SAINT CROIX
55049-55049 MEDFORD
55051-55051 MORA
55052-55052 MORRISTOWN
55053-55053 NERSTRAND
55054-55054 NEW MARKET
55055-55055 NEWPORT
55056-55056 NORTH BRANCH
55057-55057 NORTHFIELD
55060-55060 OWATONNA
55063-55063 PINE CITY
55065-55065 RANDOLPH
55066-55066 RED WING
55067-55067 ROCK CREEK
55068-55068 ROSEMOUNT
55069-55069 RUSH CITY
55070-55070 SAINT FRANCIS
55071-55071 SAINT PAUL PARK
55072-55072 SANDSTONE
55073-55073 SCANDIA
55074-55074 SHAFER
55075-55075 SOUTH SAINT PAUL
55076-55077 INVER GROVE HEIGHTS
55078-55079 STACY
55080-55080 STANCHFIELD
55082-55083 STILLWATER
55084-55084 TAYLORS FALLS
55085-55085 VERMILLION
55087-55087 WARSAW
55088-55088 WEBSTER
55089-55089 WELCH
55090-55090 WILLERNIE
55092-55092 WYOMING
55100-55146 SAINT PAUL
55150-55150 MENDOTA
55155-55199 SAINT PAUL
55301-55301 ALBERTVILLE
55302-55302 ANNANDALE
55303-55304 ANOKA
55305-55305 HOPKINS
55306-55306 BURNSVILLE
55307-55307 ARLINGTON
55308-55308 BECKER
55309-55309 BIG LAKE
55310-55310 BIRD ISLAND
55311-55311 OSSEO
55312-55312 BROWNTON
55313-55313 BUFFALO
55314-55314 BUFFALO LAKE
55315-55315 CARVER
55316-55316 CHAMPLIN
55317-55317 CHANHASSEN
55318-55318 CHASKA
55319-55319 CLEAR LAKE
55320-55320 CLEARWATER
55321-55321 COKATO
55322-55322 COLOGNE
55323-55323 CRYSTAL BAY
55324-55324 DARWIN
55325-55325 DASSEL
55327-55327 DAYTON
55328-55328 DELANO
55329-55329 EDEN VALLEY
55330-55330 ELK RIVER
55331-55331 EXCELSIOR
55332-55332 FAIRFAX
55333-55333 FRANKLIN
55334-55334 GAYLORD
55335-55335 GIBBON

55336-55336	GLENCOE
55337-55337	BURNSVILLE
55338-55338	GREEN ISLE
55339-55339	HAMBURG
55340-55340	HAMEL
55341-55341	HANOVER
55342-55342	HECTOR
55343-55343	HOPKINS
55344-55344	EDEN PRAIRIE
55345-55345	MINNETONKA
55346-55347	EDEN PRAIRIE
55348-55348	MAPLE PLAIN
55349-55349	HOWARD LAKE
55350-55350	HUTCHINSON
55351-55351	YOUNG AMERICA
55352-55352	JORDAN
55353-55353	KIMBALL
55354-55354	LESTER PRAIRIE
55355-55355	LITCHFIELD
55356-55356	LONG LAKE
55357-55357	LORETTO
55358-55358	MAPLE LAKE
55359-55359	MAPLE PLAIN
55360-55360	MAYER
55361-55361	MINNETONKA BEACH
55362-55362	MONTICELLO
55363-55363	MONTROSE
55364-55364	MOUND
55365-55365	MONTICELLO
55366-55366	NEW AUBURN
55367-55367	NEW GERMANY
55368-55368	NORWOOD
55369-55369	OSSEO
55370-55370	PLATO
55371-55371	PRINCETON
55372-55372	PRIOR LAKE
55373-55373	ROCKFORD
55374-55374	ROGERS
55375-55375	SAINT BONIFACIUS
55376-55376	SAINT MICHAEL
55377-55377	SANTIAGO
55378-55378	SAVAGE
55379-55379	SHAKOPEE
55380-55380	SILVER CREEK
55381-55381	SILVER LAKE
55382-55382	SOUTH HAVEN
55383-55383	NORWOOD
55384-55384	SPRING PARK
55385-55385	STEWART
55386-55386	VICTORIA
55387-55387	WACONIA
55388-55388	WATERTOWN
55389-55389	WATKINS
55390-55390	WAVERLY
55391-55391	WAYZATA
55392-55392	NAVARRE
55393-55393	MAPLE PLAIN
55394-55394	YOUNG AMERICA
55395-55395	WINSTED
55396-55396	WINTHROP
55397-55397	YOUNG AMERICA
55398-55398	ZIMMERMAN
55399-55399	YOUNG AMERICA
55400-55488	MINNEAPOLIS
55550-55554	YOUNG AMERICA
55554-55554	NORWOOD
55555-55560	YOUNG AMERICA
55561-55561	MONTICELLO
55562-55562	YOUNG AMERICA
55563-55563	MONTICELLO
55564-55564	YOUNG AMERICA
55565-55565	MONTICELLO
55566-55568	YOUNG AMERICA
55569-55569	OSSEO
55570-55572	MAPLE PLAIN
55572-55572	ROCKFORD
55573-55573	YOUNG AMERICA
55574-55574	MAPLE PLAIN
55575-55575	HOWARD LAKE
55576-55577	MAPLE PLAIN
55577-55577	ROCKFORD
55578-55579	MAPLE PLAIN
55580-55582	MONTICELLO
55583-55583	NORWOOD
55584-55591	MONTICELLO
55592-55593	MAPLE PLAIN
55594-55594	YOUNG AMERICA
55595-55599	LORETTO
55601-55601	BEAVER BAY
55602-55602	BRIMSON
55603-55603	FINLAND
55604-55604	GRAND MARAIS
55605-55605	GRAND PORTAGE
55606-55606	HOVLAND
55607-55607	ISABELLA
55609-55609	KNIFE RIVER
55612-55612	LUTSEN
55613-55613	SCHROEDER
55614-55614	SILVER BAY
55615-55615	TOFTE
55616-55616	TWO HARBORS
55701-55701	ADOLPH
55702-55702	ALBORN
55703-55703	ANGORA
55704-55704	ASKOV
55705-55705	AURORA
55706-55706	BABBITT
55707-55707	BARNUM
55708-55708	BIWABIK
55709-55709	BOVEY
55710-55710	BRITT
55711-55711	BROOKSTON
55712-55712	BRUNO
55713-55713	BUHL
55716-55716	CALUMET
55717-55717	CANYON
55718-55718	CARLTON
55719-55719	CHISHOLM
55720-55720	CLOQUET
55721-55721	COHASSET
55722-55722	COLERAINE
55723-55723	COOK
55724-55724	COTTON
55725-55725	CRANE LAKE
55726-55726	CROMWELL
55727-55727	CULVER
55728-55728	DENHAM
55729-55729	DUQUETTE
55730-55730	GRAND RAPIDS
55731-55731	ELY
55732-55732	EMBARRASS
55733-55733	ESKO
55734-55734	EVELETH
55735-55735	FINLAYSON
55736-55736	FLOODWOOD
55738-55738	FORBES
55740-55740	DENHAM
55741-55741	GILBERT
55742-55742	GOODLAND
55744-55745	GRAND RAPIDS
55746-55747	HIBBING
55748-55748	HILL CITY
55749-55749	HOLYOKE
55750-55750	HOYT LAKES
55751-55751	IRON
55752-55752	JACOBSON
55753-55753	KEEWATIN
55754-55754	HIBBING
55755-55755	KELSEY
55756-55756	KERRICK
55757-55757	KETTLE RIVER
55758-55758	KINNEY
55760-55760	MCGREGOR
55761-55761	MC KINLEY
55762-55762	MAHTOWA
55763-55763	MAKINEN
55764-55764	MARBLE
55765-55765	MEADOWLANDS
55766-55766	MELRUDE
55767-55767	MOOSE LAKE
55768-55768	MOUNTAIN IRON
55769-55769	NASHWAUK
55771-55771	ORR
55772-55772	NETT LAKE
55773-55773	PARKVILLE
55775-55775	PENGILLY
55777-55777	VIRGINIA
55778-55778	RUTLEDGE
55779-55779	SAGINAW
55780-55780	SAWYER
55781-55781	SIDE LAKE
55782-55782	SOUDAN
55783-55783	STURGEON LAKE
55784-55784	SWAN RIVER
55785-55785	SWATARA
55786-55786	TACONITE
55787-55787	TAMARACK
55788-55788	COOK
55789-55789	MEADOWLANDS
55790-55790	TOWER
55791-55791	TWIG
55792-55792	VIRGINIA
55793-55793	WARBA
55794-55794	WAWINA
55795-55795	WILLOW RIVER
55796-55796	WINTON
55797-55797	WRENSHALL
55798-55798	WRIGHT
55799-55799	ZIM
55800-55816	DULUTH
55901-55906	ROCHESTER
55909-55909	ADAMS
55910-55910	ALTURA
55912-55912	AUSTIN
55917-55917	BLOOMING PRAIRIE
55918-55918	BROWNSDALE
55919-55919	BROWNSVILLE
55920-55920	BYRON
55921-55921	CALEDONIA
55922-55922	CANTON
55923-55923	CHATFIELD
55924-55924	CLAREMONT
55925-55925	DAKOTA
55926-55926	DEXTER
55927-55927	DODGE CENTER
55929-55929	DOVER
55931-55931	EITZEN
55932-55932	ELGIN
55933-55933	ELKTON
55934-55934	EYOTA
55935-55935	FOUNTAIN
55936-55936	GRAND MEADOW
55937-55937	GRANGER
55938-55938	HAMMOND
55939-55939	HARMONY
55940-55940	HAYFIELD
55941-55941	HOKAH
55942-55942	HOMER
55943-55943	HOUSTON
55944-55944	KASSON
55945-55945	KELLOGG
55946-55946	KENYON
55947-55947	LA CRESCENT
55949-55949	LANESBORO
55950-55950	LANSING
55951-55951	LE ROY
55952-55952	LEWISTON
55953-55953	LYLE
55954-55954	MABEL
55955-55955	MANTORVILLE
55956-55956	MAZEPPA
55957-55957	MILLVILLE
55959-55959	MINNESOTA CITY
55960-55960	ORONOCO
55961-55961	OSTRANDER
55962-55962	PETERSON
55963-55963	PINE ISLAND
55964-55964	PLAINVIEW
55965-55965	PRESTON
55967-55967	RACINE
55968-55968	READS LANDING
55969-55969	ROLLINGSTONE
55970-55970	ROSE CREEK
55971-55971	RUSHFORD
55972-55972	SAINT CHARLES
55973-55973	SARGEANT
55974-55974	SPRING GROVE
55975-55975	SPRING VALLEY
55976-55976	STEWARTVILLE
55977-55977	TAOPI
55978-55978	THEILMAN
55979-55979	UTICA
55981-55981	WABASHA
55982-55982	WALTHAM
55983-55983	WANAMINGO
55985-55985	WEST CONCORD
55986-55986	WHALAN
55987-55987	WINONA
55988-55988	STOCKTON
55990-55990	WYKOFF
55991-55991	ZUMBRO FALLS
55992-55992	ZUMBROTA
56001-56006	MANKATO
56007-56007	ALBERT LEA
56009-56009	ALDEN
56010-56010	AMBOY
56011-56011	BELLE PLAINE
56013-56013	BLUE EARTH
56014-56014	BRICELYN
56016-56016	CLARKS GROVE
56017-56017	CLEVELAND
56019-56019	COMFREY
56020-56020	CONGER
56021-56021	COURTLAND
56022-56022	DARFUR
56023-56023	DELAVAN
56024-56024	EAGLE LAKE
56025-56025	EASTON
56026-56026	ELLENDALE
56027-56027	ELMORE
56028-56028	ELYSIAN
56029-56029	EMMONS
56030-56030	ESSIG
56031-56031	FAIRMONT
56032-56032	FREEBORN
56033-56033	FROST
56034-56034	GARDEN CITY
56035-56035	GENEVA
56036-56036	GLENVILLE
56037-56037	GOOD THUNDER
56039-56039	GRANADA
56041-56041	HANSKA
56042-56042	HARTLAND
56043-56043	HAYWARD
56044-56044	HENDERSON
56045-56045	HOLLANDALE
56046-56046	HOPE
56047-56047	HUNTLEY
56048-56048	JANESVILLE
56050-56050	KASOTA
56051-56051	KIESTER
56052-56052	KILKENNY
56053-56053	KLOSSNER
56054-56054	LAFAYETTE
56055-56055	LAKE CRYSTAL
56056-56056	LA SALLE
56057-56057	LE CENTER
56058-56058	LE SUEUR
56060-56060	LEWISVILLE
56061-56061	LONDON
56062-56062	MADELIA
56063-56063	MADISON LAKE
56064-56064	MANCHESTER
56065-56065	MAPLETON
56067-56067	MERIDEN
56068-56068	MINNESOTA LAKE
56069-56069	MONTGOMERY
56070-56070	MYRTLE
56071-56071	NEW PRAGUE
56072-56072	NEW RICHLAND
56073-56073	NEW ULM
56074-56074	NICOLLET
56075-56075	NORTHROP
56076-56076	OAKLAND
56077-56077	OTISCO
56078-56078	PEMBERTON
56080-56080	SAINT CLAIR
56081-56081	SAINT JAMES

56082-56082 SAINT PETER
56083-56083 SANBORN
56084-56084 SEARLES
56085-56085 SLEEPY EYE
56087-56087 SPRINGFIELD
56088-56088 TRUMAN
56089-56089 TWIN LAKES
56090-56090 VERNON CENTER
56091-56091 WALDORF
56092-56092 WALTERS
56093-56093 WASECA
56096-56096 WATERVILLE
56097-56097 WELLS
56098-56098 WINNEBAGO
56101-56101 WINDOM
56110-56110 ADRIAN
56111-56111 ALPHA
56112-56112 AMIRET
56113-56113 ARCO
56114-56114 AVOCA
56115-56115 BALATON
56116-56116 BEAVER CREEK
56117-56117 BIGELOW
56118-56118 BINGHAM LAKE
56119-56119 BREWSTER
56120-56120 BUTTERFIELD
56121-56121 CEYLON
56122-56122 CHANDLER
56123-56123 CURRIE
56124-56124 DELFT
56125-56125 DOVRAY
56126-56126 DUNDEE
56127-56127 DUNNELL
56128-56128 EDGERTON
56129-56129 ELLSWORTH
56131-56131 FULDA
56132-56132 GARVIN
56133-56133 HADLEY
56134-56134 HARDWICK
56136-56136 HENDRICKS
56137-56137 HERON LAKE
56138-56138 HILLS
56139-56139 HOLLAND
56140-56140 IHLEN
56141-56141 IONA
56142-56142 IVANHOE
56143-56143 JACKSON
56144-56144 JASPER
56145-56145 JEFFERS
56146-56146 KANARANZI
56147-56147 KENNETH
56149-56149 LAKE BENTON
56150-56150 LAKEFIELD
56151-56151 LAKE WILSON
56152-56152 LAMBERTON
56153-56153 LEOTA
56155-56155 LISMORE
56156-56156 LUVERNE
56157-56157 LYND
56158-56158 MAGNOLIA
56159-56159 MOUNTAIN LAKE
56160-56160 ODIN
56161-56161 OKABENA
56162-56162 ORMSBY
56164-56164 PIPESTONE
56165-56165 READING
56166-56166 REVERE
56167-56167 ROUND LAKE
56168-56168 RUSHMORE
56169-56169 RUSSELL
56170-56170 RUTHTON
56171-56171 SHERBURN
56172-56172 SLAYTON
56173-56173 STEEN
56174-56174 STORDEN
56175-56175 TRACY
56176-56176 TRIMONT
56177-56177 TROSKY
56178-56178 TYLER
56179-56179 VERDI
56180-56180 WALNUT GROVE
56181-56181 WELCOME
56183-56183 WESTBROOK
56185-56185 WILMONT
56186-56186 WOODSTOCK
56187-56187 WORTHINGTON
56201-56201 WILLMAR
56207-56207 ALBERTA
56208-56208 APPLETON
56209-56209 ATWATER
56210-56210 BARRY
56211-56211 BEARDSLEY
56212-56212 BELLINGHAM
56214-56214 BELVIEW
56215-56215 BENSON
56216-56216 BLOMKEST
56218-56218 BOYD
56219-56219 BROWNS VALLEY
56220-56220 CANBY
56221-56221 CHOKIO
56222-56222 CLARA CITY
56223-56223 CLARKFIELD
56224-56224 CLEMENTS
56225-56225 CLINTON
56226-56226 CLONTARF
56227-56227 CORRELL
56228-56228 COSMOS
56229-56229 COTTONWOOD
56230-56230 DANUBE
56231-56231 DANVERS
56232-56232 DAWSON
56233-56233 DE GRAFF
56235-56235 DONNELLY
56236-56236 DUMONT
56237-56237 ECHO
56238-56238 EVAN
56239-56239 GHENT
56240-56240 GRACEVILLE
56241-56241 GRANITE FALLS
56243-56243 GROVE CITY
56244-56244 HANCOCK
56245-56245 HANLEY FALLS
56246-56246 HAWICK
56247-56247 HAZEL RUN
56248-56248 HERMAN
56249-56249 HOLLOWAY
56250-56250 JOHNSON
56251-56251 KANDIYOHI
56252-56252 KERKHOVEN
56253-56253 LAKE LILLIAN
56254-56254 LOUISBURG
56255-56255 LUCAN
56256-56256 MADISON
56257-56257 MARIETTA
56258-56258 MARSHALL
56260-56260 MAYNARD
56262-56262 MILAN
56263-56263 MILROY
56264-56264 MINNEOTA
56265-56265 MONTEVIDEO
56266-56266 MORGAN
56267-56267 MORRIS
56270-56270 MORTON
56271-56271 MURDOCK
56272-56272 NASSAU
56273-56273 NEW LONDON
56274-56274 NORCROSS
56276-56276 ODESSA
56277-56277 OLIVIA
56278-56278 ORTONVILLE
56279-56279 PENNOCK
56280-56280 PORTER
56281-56281 PRINSBURG
56282-56282 RAYMOND
56283-56283 REDWOOD FALLS
56284-56284 RENVILLE
56285-56285 SACRED HEART
56286-56286 SAINT LEO
56287-56287 SEAFORTH
56288-56288 SPICER
56289-56289 SUNBURG
56291-56291 TAUNTON
56292-56292 VESTA
56293-56293 WABASSO
56294-56294 WANDA
56295-56295 WATSON
56296-56296 WHEATON
56297-56297 WOOD LAKE
56301-56304 SAINT CLOUD
56307-56307 ALBANY
56308-56308 ALEXANDRIA
56309-56309 ASHBY
56310-56310 AVON
56311-56311 BARRETT
56312-56312 BELGRADE
56313-56313 BOCK
56314-56314 BOWLUS
56315-56315 BRANDON
56316-56316 BROOTEN
56317-56317 BUCKMAN
56318-56318 BURTRUM
56319-56319 CARLOS
56320-56320 COLD SPRING
56321-56321 COLLEGEVILLE
56323-56323 CYRUS
56324-56324 DALTON
56325-56325 ELROSA
56326-56326 EVANSVILLE
56327-56327 FARWELL
56328-56328 FLENSBURG
56329-56329 FOLEY
56330-56330 FORESTON
56331-56331 FREEPORT
56332-56332 GARFIELD
56333-56333 GILMAN
56334-56334 GLENWOOD
56335-56335 GREENWALD
56336-56336 GREY EAGLE
56338-56338 HILLMAN
56339-56339 HOFFMAN
56340-56340 HOLDINGFORD
56341-56341 HOLMES CITY
56342-56342 ISLE
56343-56343 KENSINGTON
56344-56344 LASTRUP
56345-56345 LITTLE FALLS
56346-56347 LONG PRAIRIE
56349-56349 LOWRY
56350-56350 MC GRATH
56352-56352 MELROSE
56353-56353 MILACA
56354-56354 MILTONA
56355-56355 NELSON
56356-56356 NEW MUNICH
56357-56357 OAK PARK
56358-56358 OGILVIE
56359-56359 ONAMIA
56360-56360 OSAKIS
56361-56361 PARKERS PRAIRIE
56362-56362 PAYNESVILLE
56363-56363 PEASE
56364-56364 PIERZ
56367-56367 RICE
56368-56368 RICHMOND
56369-56369 ROCKVILLE
56371-56371 ROSCOE
56372-56372 SAINT CLOUD
56373-56373 ROYALTON
56374-56374 SAINT JOSEPH
56375-56375 SAINT STEPHEN
56376-56376 SAINT MARTIN
56377-56377 SARTELL
56378-56378 SAUK CENTRE
56379-56379 SAUK RAPIDS
56380-56380 BANGOR
56380-56380 SEDAN
56381-56381 STARBUCK
56382-56382 SWANVILLE
56384-56384 UPSALA
56385-56385 VILLARD
56386-56386 WAHKON
56387-56388 WAITE PARK
56389-56389 WEST UNION
56393-56399 SAINT CLOUD
56401-56401 BRAINERD
56425-56425 BAXTER
56430-56430 AH GWAH CHING
56431-56431 AITKIN
56433-56433 AKELEY
56434-56434 ALDRICH
56435-56435 BACKUS
56436-56436 BENEDICT
56437-56437 BERTHA
56438-56438 BROWERVILLE
56440-56440 CLARISSA
56441-56441 CROSBY
56442-56442 CROSSLAKE
56443-56443 CUSHING
56444-56444 DEERWOOD
56446-56446 EAGLE BEND
56447-56447 EMILY
56448-56448 FIFTY LAKES
56449-56449 FORT RIPLEY
56450-56450 GARRISON
56452-56452 HACKENSACK
56453-56453 HEWITT
56455-56455 IRONTON
56456-56456 JENKINS
56458-56458 LAKE GEORGE
56459-56459 LAKE HUBERT
56460-56460 LAKE ITASCA
56461-56461 LAPORTE
56463-56463 MANHATTAN BEACH
56464-56464 MENAHGA
56465-56465 MERRIFIELD
56466-56466 MOTLEY
56467-56467 NEVIS
56468-56468 NISSWA
56469-56469 PALISADE
56470-56470 PARK RAPIDS
56472-56472 PEQUOT LAKES
56473-56473 PILLAGER
56474-56474 PINE RIVER
56475-56475 RANDALL
56477-56477 SEBEKA
56478-56478 NIMROD
56479-56479 STAPLES
56481-56481 VERNDALE
56482-56482 WADENA
56484-56484 WALKER
56485-56485 WHIPHOLT
56501-56502 DETROIT LAKES
56510-56510 ADA
56511-56511 AUDUBON
56513-56513 BAKER
56514-56514 BARNESVILLE
56515-56515 BATTLE LAKE
56516-56516 BEJOU
56517-56517 BELTRAMI
56518-56518 BLUFFTON
56519-56519 BORUP
56520-56520 BRECKENRIDGE
56521-56521 CALLAWAY
56522-56522 CAMPBELL
56523-56523 CLIMAX
56524-56524 CLITHERALL
56525-56525 COMSTOCK
56527-56527 DEER CREEK
56528-56528 DENT
56529-56529 DILWORTH
56531-56531 ELBOW LAKE
56533-56533 ELIZABETH
56534-56534 ERHARD
56535-56535 ERSKINE
56536-56536 FELTON
56537-56538 FERGUS FALLS
56540-56540 FERTILE
56541-56541 FLOM
56542-56542 FOSSTON
56543-56543 FOXHOME
56544-56544 FRAZEE
56545-56545 GARY
56546-56546 GEORGETOWN
56547-56547 GLYNDON
56548-56548 HALSTAD
56549-56549 HAWLEY
56550-56550 HENDRUM
56551-56551 HENNING

56552-56552	HITTERDAL
56553-56553	KENT
56554-56554	LAKE PARK
56556-56556	MCINTOSH
56557-56557	MAHNOMEN
56560-56563	MOORHEAD
56565-56565	NASHUA
56566-56566	NAYTAHWAUSH
56567-56567	NEW YORK MILLS
56568-56568	NIELSVILLE
56569-56569	OGEMA
56570-56570	OSAGE
56571-56571	OTTERTAIL
56572-56572	PELICAN RAPIDS
56573-56573	PERHAM
56574-56574	PERLEY
56575-56575	PONSFORD
56576-56576	RICHVILLE
56577-56577	RICHWOOD
56578-56578	ROCHERT
56579-56579	ROTHSAY
56580-56580	SABIN
56581-56581	SHELLY
56583-56583	TINTAH
56584-56584	TWIN VALLEY
56585-56585	ULEN
56586-56586	UNDERWOOD
56587-56587	VERGAS
56588-56588	VINING
56589-56589	WAUBUN
56590-56590	WENDELL
56591-56591	WHITE EARTH
56592-56592	WINGER
56593-56593	WOLF LAKE
56594-56594	WOLVERTON
56601-56619	BEMIDJI
56621-56621	BAGLEY
56623-56623	BAUDETTE
56625-56625	BECIDA
56626-56626	BENA
56627-56627	BIG FALLS
56628-56628	BIGFORK
56629-56629	BIRCHDALE
56630-56630	BLACKDUCK
56631-56631	BOWSTRING
56632-56632	BOY RIVER
56633-56633	CASS LAKE
56634-56634	CLEARBROOK
56636-56636	DEER RIVER
56637-56637	TALMOON
56639-56639	EFFIE
56641-56641	FEDERAL DAM
56644-56644	GONVICK
56646-56646	GULLY
56647-56647	HINES
56649-56649	INTERNATIONAL FALLS
56650-56650	KELLIHER
56651-56651	LENGBY
56652-56652	LEONARD
56653-56653	LITTLEFORK
56654-56654	LOMAN
56655-56655	LONGVILLE
56657-56657	MARCELL
56658-56658	MARGIE
56659-56659	MAX
56660-56660	MIZPAH
56661-56661	NORTHOME
56662-56662	OUTING
56663-56663	PENNINGTON
56664-56664	DEBS
56665-56665	PITT
56666-56666	PONEMAH
56667-56667	PUPOSKY
56668-56668	RANIER
56669-56669	RAY
56669-56669	KABETOGAMA
56670-56670	REDBY
56671-56671	REDLAKE
56672-56672	REMER
56673-56673	ROOSEVELT
56674-56674	SAUM
56676-56676	SHEVLIN
56678-56678	SOLWAY
56679-56679	SOUTH INTERNATIONAL FALLS
56680-56680	SPRING LAKE
56681-56681	SQUAW LAKE
56682-56682	SWIFT
56683-56683	TENSTRIKE
56684-56684	TRAIL
56685-56685	WASKISH
56686-56686	WILLIAMS
56687-56687	WILTON
56688-56688	WIRT
56701-56701	THIEF RIVER FALLS
56710-56710	ALVARADO
56711-56711	ANGLE INLET
56712-56712	ANGUS
56713-56713	ARGYLE
56714-56714	BADGER
56715-56715	BROOKS
56716-56716	CROOKSTON
56720-56720	DONALDSON
56721-56721	EAST GRAND FORKS
56722-56722	EUCLID
56723-56723	FISHER
56724-56724	GATZKE
56725-56725	GOODRIDGE
56726-56726	GREENBUSH
56727-56727	GRYGLA
56728-56728	HALLOCK
56729-56729	HALMA
56731-56731	HUMBOLDT
56732-56732	KARLSTAD
56733-56733	KENNEDY
56734-56734	LAKE BRONSON
56735-56735	LANCASTER
56736-56736	MENTOR
56737-56737	MIDDLE RIVER
56738-56738	NEWFOLDEN
56740-56740	NOYES
56741-56741	OAK ISLAND
56742-56742	OKLEE
56744-56744	OSLO
56748-56748	PLUMMER
56750-56750	RED LAKE FALLS
56751-56751	ROSEAU
56754-56754	SAINT HILAIRE
56755-56755	SAINT VINCENT
56756-56756	SALOL
56757-56757	STEPHEN
56758-56758	STRANDQUIST
56759-56759	STRATHCONA
56760-56760	VIKING
56761-56761	WANNASKA
56762-56762	WARREN
56763-56763	WARROAD

Mississippi

General Help Numbers:

Governor's Office

PO Box 139 — 601-359-3150
Jackson, MS 39201 — Fax 601-359-3741
www.governor.state.ms.us — 8AM-5PM
www.governorbarbour.com/

Attorney General's Office

PO Box 220 — 601-359-3680
Jackson, MS 39205 — Fax 601-359-3796
www.ago.state.ms.us — 8AM-5PM

Legislative Records

PO Box 1018 — 601-359-3229
Jackson, MS 39215 — Fax 601-359-3935
http://billstatus.ls.state.ms.us/ — 8:30AM-5PM

State Archives

Archives & Library Division — 601-576-6850
PO Box 571 — Fax 601-576-6975
Jackson, MS 39205-0571
www.mdah.state.ms.us — 9AM-5PM M; 8AM-5PM T-F; 8AM-1PM SAT

State Specifics:

Capital: Jackson, Hinds County

Time Zone: CST

Number of Counties: 82

Population: 2,938,618

Web Site: www.mississippi.gov

State Agencies

Criminal Records

Criminal Information Center, Dept. of Public Safety, Bureau of Investigation, PO Box 958, Jackson, MS 39205 (Courier address- 3891 Highway 468W, Pearl, MS 39208); 601-933-2600, Fax- 601-933-2660; 8AM-5PM.

www.dps.state.ms.us/dps/dps.nsf/Divisions/ci?OpenDocument

CIC permits access to their state criminal records with the subject's expressed written consent on the state's Release Form, and to entities with purposes provided for by state statute, in health care, banking/finance, military, childcare and schools.

Indexing & Storage: Records available for all criminal records information in the possession of or accessible by the Justice Information Center. Dispositions are available for less than half of records; a county-level court search may be necessary.The records on file are 100% fingerprint supported. 40% of the records contain dispositions.

Searching: Approved requestors must submit fingerprint cards, the subject need not. The agency, which is not equipped to handle large numbers of subject requests, still suggests employers and public obtain information at the county level. Include in request- name, current address, SSN, DOB, race, sex, subject's phone number, and witness to subject's signature, notary preferred. In request (the state form), specify if the background check is to be fingerprint-based or name-based. Send the Release Information Request form to the attention of the Special Process Unit. The subject may specify to whom and where to send the results. Charges and convictions shown on results.

Access by: mail, fax.

Fee & Payment: No fee for search.

Mail search: A SASE is required. Same as fax requests. Mail request to the Pearl, MS address.

Fax search: Request must be submitted by the subject, on state Authorization to Release Form. Call the agency and request they fax a blank form.

Statewide Court Records

Administrative Office of Courts, PO Box 117, Jackson, MS 39205 (Courier address- 450 High St, Jackson, MS 39205); 601-576-4630, Fax- 601-576-; 8AM-5PM. www.mssc.state.ms.us

A fax subscription service is available for county level records. The online look-up is only for Supreme Court case dockets.

Indexing & Storage: New records available for inquiry in 30 days or so.

Access by: fax, online.

Fee & Payment: For the fax request system there is a $25.00 start-up fee and a $5.00 per name search fee.

Fax search: The agency provides a statewide fax request service with a 24 hour turnaround time. Felony, civil, and probate case information are provided. Misdemeanor records are not. Call 601-576-4630 or fax 601-576-4639 for details.

Online search: The website offers searching of the MS Supreme Court and Court of Appeals Decisions and dockets.

Sexual Offender Registry

DPS- MS Bureau of Investigations, Sexual Offender Registry, PO Box 958, Jackson, MS 39205; 601-987-1540, Fax- 601-933-2695; 8AM-5PM. www.sor.mdps.state.ms.us

Direct questions to msor@mdps.state.ms.us.

Indexing & Storage: Records available from 07/01/95.

Searching: Searches may also be directed to the local sheriff's office. This data not released- victim information.

Access by: mail, phone, online.

Mail search: Turnaround time- 1 to 2 weeks.

Phone search: Time permitting.

Online search: The state Sex Offender Registry can be accessed at the website. Search by last name, city, county, or ZIP Code.

Incarceration Records

Mississippi Department of Corrections, Records Department, 421 W Pascagoula, Jackson, MS 39205; 601-933-2889 (Central Records Office), Fax- 601-973-3879; 8AM-5PM.

www.mdoc.state.ms.us

Indexing & Storage: Records available on current and former inmates. New records available for inquiry in less than 72 hours.

Searching: Computer records go back to 1978. Include in request- provide full name. The inmate #, county of crime and DOB are helpful.

Access by: mail, phone, online.

Fee & Payment: There is no fee.

Mail search: Turnaround time- 1-2 weeks. SASE not required.

Phone search: Name searching available.

Online search: Search online by name only from the website. Click on Inmate Search. Also, search the Parole Board records (click on Parole Board and follow instructions).

Corporation, LP, LLP, LLC, Trademarks/Servicemarks

Secretary of State, Business Services, PO Box 136, Jackson, MS 39205-0136; 601-359-1633, 800-256-3494, 601-359-1350, Fax- 601-359-1607; 8AM-5PM.

www.sos.state.ms.us/busserv/index.asp

Indexing & Storage: Records available from the 1800's, computerized since 1995. New records available for inquiry immediately.

Searching: Include in request- full name of business. In addition to the articles of organization, business entity records available include: Annual Reports, Officers, Directors, Prior (merged) names, Inactive and Reserved names. This data not released- phone numbers.

Access by: mail, phone, fax, in person, online.

Fee & Payment: There is no search fee. The certification of authenticity fee is $1.00. Copies are $1.00 per page, $.25 per page for administrative procedures. A Good Standing is $25.00, and $27.00 if ordered online. Fee payee- Secretary of State. Prepayment required. You must prepay if the invoice amount is over $50.00. If under $50.00 they will invoice. Personal checks, Visa, and MasterCard accepted.

Mail search: Turnaround time- 1 to 2 days.

Phone search: Will only verify if record exists. **Fax search:** Requests only are accepted, will return to toll-free fax numbers. A second fax line is 601-359-1499.

In person: Computer screen prints are free.

Online search: A variety of online search services are available at https://secure.sos.state.ms.us/busserv/corp/soskb/csearch.asp. There is no fee to view records, including officers and registered agents. A Good Standing can be ordered. Download images for no charge. Also, search securities companies, charities, fundraisers, and pre-needs registered with the state at www.sos.state.ms.us/regenf/ifs/.

Other access: The Data Division offers bulk release of information on an annual subscription basis ($1500). Monthly subscription to list of new corporations and new qualifications is $25.00.

Uniform Commercial Code, Federal & State Tax Liens

Secretary of State, Business Services - UCC, PO Box 136, Jackson, MS 39205-0136 (Courier address- 700 N Jackson St, Jackson, MS 39202); 601-359-1633, 800-256-3494, Fax- 601-359-1607; 8AM-5PM.

www.sos.state.ms.us/busserv/ucc/ucc.asp

Indexing & Storage: Records available from 1968. Records are computerized since 1987. New records available for inquiry in 24-48 hours.

Searching: Use search request form UCC-11. The search includes tax liens. Include in request- debtor name. Images of liens are available by subscription only. This data not released- SSNs.

Access by: mail, phone, in person, online.

Fee & Payment: The search fee is $5.00, copies are $2.00 each, financing statements are $2.00 each. Fee payee- Secretary of State. Prepayment required. The state offers ACH accounts for regular requesters. Personal checks accepted. Credit card only accepted for filing costs.

Mail search: Turnaround time- 1 to 2 days. SASE not required. **Phone search:** Limited information is released over the phone. **In person:** Simple requests are processed, time permitting.

Online search: Free searching for UCC debtors is at www.sos.state.ms.us/busserv/ucc/soskb/SearchStandardRA9.asp.

Other access: A monthly list of farm liens is available for purchase.

Sales Tax Registrations

Office of Revenue, Sales and Use Tax Bureau, PO Box 1033, Jackson, MS 39215 (Courier address- 1577 Springridge Rd, Raymond, MS 39154); 601-923-7000, Fax- 601-923-7034; 8AM-5PM.

www.mstc.state.ms.us

Indexing & Storage: Records available for the most current 3 years and are computerized. New records available for inquiry minutes after set-up.

Searching: will only verify if a business is registered and will not release ownership data. Email requests to sales@mstc.state.ms.us. Include in request- business name. Will also search by tax permit number.

Access by: mail, phone, fax, in person.

Fee & Payment: Prepayment required. Fee payee- Revenue Bureau. Personal checks accepted, credit cards are not.

Mail search: Turnaround time- 5 to 10 working days. SASE not required. No fee for mail request. Copies cost $2.00 per page.

Phone search: No fee for telephone request. **Fax search:** Same criteria as phone or mail searches.

In person: No fee for request. Copies cost $2.00 per page.

Birth Certificates

State Department of Health, Vital Statistics & Records, PO Box 1700, Jackson, MS 39215-1700 (Courier address- 571 Stadium Dr, Jackson, MS 39216); 601-576-7960, 601-576-7988 (VitalChek), Fax- 601-576-7505; 8AM-5PM.

www.msdh.state.ms.us/phs/index.htm

Indexing & Storage: Records available from November 1, 1912 to present. New records available for inquiry immediately.

Searching: Employers need written release from person of record. Records are not public access documents, they are only available to persons with legitimate and tangible interest. Include in request- full name, names of parents, mother's maiden name, date of birth, place of birth, relationship to person of record, reason for information request. Records may be ordered online via a vendor at www.vitalchek.com. This data not released- original records of adoption.

Access by: mail, phone, fax, in person, online.

Fee & Payment: The fee for the certified form is $15.00, plus is a $3.00 per for each additional copy. There is a $7.00 charge for no record found. Fee payee- Mississippi Vital Records Prepayment required. Personal checks accepted; Major credit cards accepted for expedited srv.

Mail search: Turnaround time- 7 to 10 days. SASE not required.

Phone search: Must use a credit card for an additional $7.50 fee. Turnaround time 3 to 5 days.

Fax search: Same criteria as phone searching. Use 601-351-0013 for VitalChek, an approved vendor.

In person: Turnaround time for Short Form-while you wait, Long Form- 3 to 5 days.

Online search: Orders can be placed via a state designated vendor. Go to www.vitalchek.com. Extra fees are involved.

Expedited service: Expedited service is available for mail, phone and fax searches, via www.vitalchek.com. Turnaround time- 3 to 5 days. Add a $7.50 credit card fee and $$ for overnight shipping if desired.

Death Records

State Department of Health, Vital Statistics & Records, PO Box 1700, Jackson, MS 39215-1700 (Courier address- 571 Stadium Dr, Jackson, MS 39215); 601-576-7960, 601-576-7988 (VitalChek), Fax- 601-576-7505; 8AM-5PM.

www.msdh.state.ms.us/phs/index.htm

Indexing & Storage: Records available from November 1, 1912 to present. New records available for inquiry immediately.

Searching: Employers need written release from immediate family member. Records are not considered public access documents. They are only available to persons with legitimate and tangible interest. Include in request- full name, date of death, place of death, SSN, relationship to person of record, reason for information request. Records may be ordered online via a vendor at www.vitalchek.com.

Access by: mail, phone, fax, in person, online.

Fee & Payment: Fee is $10.00 if you want a certified copy, and an additional $2.00 for each additional copy ordered at same time. If no record is found, the fee is $6.00. Fee payee- Mississippi Vital Records Prepayment required. Personal checks accepted. Major credit cards accepted for expedited srv.

Mail search: Turnaround time- 7 to 10 days. SASE not required.

Phone search: Must use a credit card for an additional $7.50 fee. Turnaround time 3 to 5 days.

Fax search: Same criteria as phone searching. Use 601-351-0013 for VitalChek, an approved vendor.

In person: Turnaround time 3 to 5 days.

Online search: Orders can be placed via a state designated vendor. Go to www.vitalchek.com. Extra fees are involved.

Expedited service: Expedited service is available for mail, phone and fax searches, via www.vitalchek.com. Turnaround time- 3 to 5 days. Add $7.50 credit card fee and $$ for overnight shipping if desired.

Marriage Certificates

State Department of Health, Vital Statistics & Records, PO Box 1700, Jackson, MS 39215-1700 (Courier address- 571 Stadium Dr, Jackson, MS 39215); 601-576-7960, 601-576-7988 (VitalChek), Fax- 601-576-7505; 8AM-5PM.

www.msdh.state.ms.us/phs/index.htm

Records are also available at the county level, including those records from 1938 to 1942.

Indexing & Storage: Records available from January 1926 to June 1938 and January 1942 to present. New records available for inquiry immediately.

Searching: Employers need written release from persons of record. Records are not considered public access documents. They are only available to persons with legitimate and tangible interest. Include in request- names of husband and wife, date of marriage, place or county of marriage, relationship to person of record, reason for information request, wife's maiden name. Records may be ordered online via a vendor at www.vitalchek.com.

Access by: mail, phone, fax, in person, online.

Fee & Payment: The fee is $10.00 and $2.00 for each additional copy ordered at same time. If record not found fee is $6.00. Fee payee- Mississippi Vital Records Prepayment required. Personal checks accepted. Major credit cards accepted for expedited srv.

Mail search: Turnaround time- 5 to 10 days. SASE not required.

Phone search: Must use a credit card for an additional $7.50 fee. Turnaround time 3 to 5 days.

Fax search: Same criteria as phone searching. Use 601-351-0013 for VitalChek, an approved vendor.

In person: Search costs $10.00 per request. Turnaround time 3 to 5 days.

Online search: Orders can be placed via a state designated vendor. Go to www.vitalchek.com. Extra fees are involved.

Expedited service: Expedited service is available for mail, phone and fax searches, via www.vitalchek.com. Turnaround time- 1 day. Add a $7.50 credit card fee and $$ for overnight shipping if desired.

Divorce Records

State Department of Health, Vital Statistics & Records, PO Box 1700, Jackson, MS 39215-1700 (Courier address- 571 Stadium Dr, Jackson, MS 39215); 601-576-7960, 601-576-7988 (VitalChek), Fax- 601-576-7505; 8AM-5PM.

www.msdh.state.ms.us/phs/index.htm

The state maintains a statewide index and can refer to book and page number in county records. Requests for copies must be made to the county of record.

Indexing & Storage: Records available from 01/1926 thru 06/1938 and 01/1942 to present. New records available for inquiry in 2-3 months.

Searching: Employers need written release from person of record. Records are not public access documents and are available only to persons with legitimate and tangible interest. Include in request- names of husband and wife, date of divorce, year divorce case began, case number (if known), relationship to person of record, reason for information request. Records may be ordered online via a vendor at www.vitalchek.com.

Access by: mail, in person.

Fee & Payment: The fee to do an index search is $6.00. Copies are not released from this agency. Fee payee- Mississippi Vital Records Prepayment required. Personal checks accepted.

Mail search: Turnaround time- 7 to 10 days. SASE not required. **In person:** Turnaround time depends on staff availability.

Workers' Compensation Records

Workers Compensation Commission, PO Box 5300, Jackson, MS 39296-5300 (Courier address- 1428 Lakeland Dr, Jackson, MS 39216); 601-987-4200; 8AM-5PM. www.mwcc.state.ms.us

Indexing & Storage: Records available for 10 years back to present. New records available for inquiry immediately.

Searching: All requests must be in writing. Claimant's attorney must have contract or medical authorization. Employer/carrier must be party to action to obtain records. They do not conduct searches for pre-employment screening. Include in request- claimant name, SSN, case number, place of employment at time of accident, date of injury. Data not released- privileged medical information.

Access by: mail, in person, online.

Fee & Payment: For party of record, copy is $.10 a page, for non-party of record copy fee is $.50 a page. There is a $5.00 minimum. A certified copy is $1.00 a page copy fee and a $3.50 certification fee, also the $5.00 minimum applies. Fee payee- Mississippi Workers' Compensation Commission. They will invoice. Personal checks accepted, credit cards are not.

Mail search: Turnaround time- 10 working days. SASE not required.

In person: Anyone can come in to view. Medical information is not made available and copies cannot be made unless there is written authorization by party of record.

Online search: The First Report of Injury and other documents are available via the web. There is no fee, but users must register.

Driver Records

Department of Public Safety, Driver Services, PO Box 958, Jackson, MS 39205 (Courier address- 1900 E Woodrow Wilson, Jackson, MS 39216); 601-987-1275; 8AM-5PM.

www.dps.state.ms.us/dps/dps.nsf/main?OpenForm

Copies of tickets may be obtained from the same address for a fee of $5.00 per record and notarized signature.

Indexing & Storage: Records available for 3 years for moving violations, DUIs and suspensions. Accidents and non-moving violations do not appear on MVRs. The driver's address is provided on the record. New records available for inquiry in 45 days or more.

Searching: Casual requesters can obtain personal information only with notarized consent of subject. The state adopted the provisions of the DPPA. Request form is available at the web page. Include in request- full name, license number, and/or DOB. The electronic system requires only the driver's last name and number (first name and DOB are optional). Surrendered license records can only be obtained by a manual search.

Access by: mail, in person, online.

Fee & Payment: The fee for a driving record is $11.00 per request. A copy of a driver license application is $5.00; a copy of a letter of suspension or reinstatement is also $5.00. Fee payee- D of Public Safety. Prepayment required. No personal checks or credit cards accepted.

Mail search: Turnaround time- 2 days. A SASE is requested.

In person: Walk-in requesters may submit up to 10 requests for immediate delivery; the rest are available the next day.

Online search: Both interactive and batch delivery is offer for high volume users only. Billing is monthly. Hook-up is through the Advantis System, fees apply. Lookup is by name only; not by driver license number. Fee is $11.00 per record. For more information, call the Director's office. Another service is available. Drivers may view their own record online at https://www.ms.gov/hp/drivers/license/motorVehicleReportBegin.do. The MVR shows the current status of the license and the moving violations on record. Use of credit card required.

Other access: Overnight batch delivery by tape is available.

Vehicle Ownership & Registration

Mississippi State Tax Commission, Registration Department, PO Box 1140, Jackson, MS 39215 (Courier address- 1577 Springridge Rd, Raymond, MS 39154); 601-923-7100 (Registration), 601-923-7200 (Titles), Fax- 601-923-7134; 8AM-5PM.

www.mstc.state.ms.us/mvl/main.htm

Please note that title information (liens, histories) requests are processed by a different section than registration information. For mail requests, use PO Box 1033 for the Title Department.

Indexing & Storage: Records available from July 1, 1969 to present. Title records are computer indexed from July 1, 1969 to present, and on microfiche from July 1, 1969 to present. New records available for inquiry in 6 to 8 weeks.

Searching: Personal information is not released to casual requesters without consent from the subject. State suggests to use their disclosure form found at www.mstc.state.ms.us/title/forms/77969ALLN1.pdf. The turnaround time will be one week longer if the request requires a search farther back than 5 years.

Access by: mail, fax, in person, online.

Fee & Payment: Fees are $8.00 per search for title, $3.00 per search for VIN or registration, and $5.00 for lien history. Fee payee- Mississippi State Tax Commission. Prepayment required. No cash will be accepted for mail requests. Personal checks accepted, credit cards are not.

Mail search: Turnaround time- up to 14 days.

Fax search: Fax requests are accepted by account holders.

In person: Turnaround time is immediate.

Online search: Internet access to vehicle records is available to approved, DPPA compliant entities. Accounts must pay an annual $100 registration fee, record search fees are the same as listed above. Access is via the web.

Other access: Mississippi offers some standardized files as well as some customization for bulk requesters of VIN and registration information. For more information, contact MLVB at the address listed above.

Accident Reports

Safety Responsibility, Accident Records, PO Box 958, Jackson, MS 39205 (Courier address- 1900 E Woodrow Wilson, Jackson, MS 39216); 601-987-1255; 8AM-5PM.

www.dps.state.ms.us/dps/dps.nsf/main?OpenForm

The above address is for Highway Patrol accident investigations only. Reports require authorization from person involved. You must go to the agency that did the investigation for reports not found with the Highway Patrol.

Indexing & Storage: Records available for 2003 to present on main computer. Records are on microfiche from 1990 to present. New records available for inquiry in 7 to 14 days.

Searching: Must have authorization from individuals involved in the accident. Accident reports are only available to persons involved, their legal counsel and their insurance representative. A request form is available. Include in request- date of accident, location of accident, full name of driver, written authorization. DL needed for older records. Requests must be in writing. In person requests are returned by mail.

Access by: mail, in person.

Fee & Payment: The fee is $10.00 per record. Fee payee- Department of Public Safety. Prepayment required. No personal checks or credit cards.

Mail search: Turnaround time- 5 days. A SASE is requested, use $.65 for postage.

In person: Two reports at a time may be requested in person.

Vessel Ownership & Registration

Wildlife, Fisheries, & Parks Dept, Boating Registration, PO Box 451, Jackson, MS 39205; 601-432-2066, Fax- 601-432-2071; 8AM-5PM.

http://home.mdwfp.com/fishing.aspx

All motorized vessels and all sailboats have to be registered. Liens are recorded if the vessel has been titled. Since July 1998, boats have been titled at the option of the owner/lender.

Indexing & Storage: Records available from 1981 to present. Records are indexed on computer from 1985 to present. New records available for inquiry in 2 weeks or so.

Searching: This agency follows the mandates of the DPPA, allowing access to record information for those with a legitimate business interest. Casual requesters must present a signed release before info is released. Include in request- name or DL number or MS number or hull number.

Access by: mail, phone, fax, in person, online.

Fee & Payment: There is no search fee.

Mail search: Turnaround time is the same day, except during the summer, which can take 3-4 weeks. A SASE is requested.

Phone search: Records are available by phone.

Fax search: Results will be mailed back usually the same day.

In person: Turnaround time is usually immediate.

Online search: One may do a search at the registration renewal site https://www.ms.gov/gf/boating/renewRegistration.jsp. There is no name searching; both the MI Number and Serial (VIN) must be input.

Other access: agency makes records available electronically and on printed lists. Fees vary.

Legislation Records

Mississippi Legislature, PO Box 1018, Jackson, MS 39215 (Courier address- New Capitol, 3rd Floor, Jackson, MS 39215-1018); 601-359-3229 (Senate), 601-359-3360 (House), 601-359-3135 (Legislative Reference Bureau), Fax- 601-359-3935; 8:30AM-5PM.

http://billstatus.ls.state.ms.us/

The room number for Senate documents is 308, the room number for House documents is 305. The session begins the 1st Tuesday after the 1st Monday in January and usually lasts 3 months. Senate Records fax 601-359-3935, House Records fax 601-359-3728.

Records available from the beginning of the Legislature. Bills from 1991 to present are on computer, prior bills are in file books.

Online search: The Internet site has an excellent bill status and measure information program. Data includes current and to at least 1997. State Code is found at www.sos.state.ms.us/ed_pubs/mscode/.

Voter Registration

Secretary of State, Elections Division, PO Box 136, Jackson, MS 39205-0136 (Courier address- 401 Mississippi Street, 1st Floor, Jackson, MS 39201); 800-829-6786, 601-576-2550, Fax- 601-359-5019; 8AM-5PM.

www.sos.state.ms.us/elections/elections.asp

All material kept by the Secretary of State relating to elections in Mississippi is open to the public. However, name searches must be done at the county level. Lists may be purchased here or at the county level.

Searching: This data not released- DOB

Other access: Lists are available for purchase. Call for details.

GED Certificates

State Board for Community & Jr Colleges, GED Office, 3825 Ridgewood Rd, Jackson, MS 39211; 601-432-6338, Fax- 601-432-6890; 8AM-5PM.

www.colin.edu/gedonline/

Searching: Verifications and transcripts are only available by written request. A request form may be downloaded from the web. The form designates where the transcript is to be mailed. Include in request- a signed release, name, date of birth, SSN, date of text. If known, the diploma number is helpful.

Access by: mail, in person.

Fee & Payment: The fee is $5.00 for either a verification or a transcript. Prepayment required. Personal checks not accepted. Credit cards not accepted.

Mail search: Turnaround time- 3 days. Turnaround time is longer in July and August. SASE not required.

In person: The agency will only release information to the test taker, not to a third party or employer.

Hunting & Fishing License Information

Department of Wildlife, Fisheries & Parks, PO Box 451, Jackson, MS 39205 (Courier address- 1505 Eastover Dri, Jackson, MS 39211); 601-432-2055 (License Division), 601-432-2041 (Data Processing Div), Fax- 601-432-2071; 8AM-5PM.

http://home.mdwfp.com/

Indexing & Storage: Records available for present data only. New records available for inquiry in 1 week.

Searching: Records are open to the public. They hold records on "sportsman" license holders which is a combination of hunting and fishing. Temporary license information is not maintained. One can search using the name or driver's license number.

Access by: mail, phone, fax, in person.

Mail or Fax search: Turnaround time- 10 days. SASE not required.

Phone search: Records are available by phone.

In person: You can make the request in person but they will mail back your response.

Other access: They offer bulk sale of various license groups in a variety of media methods. Visit the website for more information, or call 601-432-2025.

Mississippi State Licensing Agencies

For details about the agency responsible for licensing/certifying/registering an item below or in the Agency Quick Finder section, match an item's number with the number of the agency in the *Licensing Agency Information* section.

Mississippi Licenses Searchable Online

Architect #3	www.archbd.state.ms.us/main_find_licensee.html
Attorney/Attorney Firm #27	www.msbar.org/lawyerdirectory.php
Camp, Youth #38	www.msdh.state.ms.us/msdhsite/index.cfm/30,332,183,html
Charity #32	www.sos.state.ms.us/regenf/ifs/
Child Care Facility #38	www.msdh.state.ms.us/msdhsite/_static/30,332,183.html
Child Residential Home #38	www.msdh.state.ms.us/msdhsite/index.cfm/30,332,183,html
Chiropractor #35	www.msbce.ms.gov/msbce/msbce.nsf/Search?OpenForm
Contractor, Commercial #6	www.msboc.us/search.cfm
Contractor, Residential #6	www.msboc.us/search.cfm
Counselor, Professional #10	www.lpc.state.ms.us/html/search.html
CPA-Certified Public Accountant #19	www.msbpa.state.ms.us/licsearch.html
Dental Hygienist #8	www.msbde.state.ms.us/msbde/msbdesearch.nsf/WebStart?OpenFOrm
Dental Radiologist #8	www.msbde.state.ms.us/msbde/msbdesearch.nsf/WebStart?OpenFOrm
Dentist #8	www.msbde.state.ms.us/msbde/msbdesearch.nsf/WebStart?OpenFOrm
Domestic Insurance Company #25	www.mid.state.ms.us/licapp/
Engineer #9	www.pepls.state.ms.us/roster.htm
Fund Raiser #32	www.sos.state.ms.us/regenf/ifs/
Funeral Director #11	www.msbfs.ms.gov/msbfs/roster.nsf/webpage/FS_1?editdocument
Funeral Service Practitioner #11	www.msbfs.ms.gov/msbfs/roster.nsf/webpage/FS_1?editdocument
Geologist #23	www.msbrpg.state.ms.us/rpg.htm
Home Inspector #34	http://appserver.mrec.ms.gov/findlicensee.asp
Insurance Agent/Solicitor/Advisor #25	www.mid.state.ms.us/licensing/licensing.htm
Insurance Company #25	www.mid.state.ms.us/licapp/
Landscape Architect #3	www.archbd.state.ms.us/main_find_licensee.html
Lobbyist #31	www.sos.state.ms.us/elections/Lobbying/Lobbyist_Dir.asp
Marriage & Family Therapist #28	www.swmft.ms.gov/swmft/Roster.nsf/webpage/Therapist_1?editdocument
Notary Public #31	www.sos.state.ms.us/busserv/notaries/notaries.asp
Nurse-LPN #13	https://www.ms.gov/msbn/inquiry_disclaimer.do
Nurse-RN #13	https://www.ms.gov/msbn/inquiry_disclaimer.do
Nursing Home Administrator #14	www.bnha.state.ms.us/msbnha/roster.nsf/webpage/bnha_1?editDocument
Optometrist #15	www.msbo.ms.gov/msbo/OptoRoster.nsf/webpage/Opto_1?editdocument
Pharmacist #16	www.mbp.state.ms.us/mbop/PharmRoster.nsf/webpage/Pharm_1?editdocument
Pharmacy #16	www.mbp.state.ms.us/mbop/PharmRoster.nsf/webpage/Pharm_1?editdocument
Pharmacy Intern/Technician #16	www.mbp.state.ms.us/mbop/PharmRoster.nsf/webpage/Pharm_1?editdocument
Psychologist #18	www.psychologyboard.state.ms.us/msbp/msbp.nsf/Search?OpenForm
Real Estate Agent/Seller #34	http://appserver.mrec.ms.gov/findlicensee.asp
Real Estate Appraiser #30	http://appserver.mrec.ms.gov/findappraiser.asp
Real Estate Broker #34	http://appserver.mrec.ms.gov/findlicensee.asp
Social Worker #28	www.swmft.ms.gov/swmft/Roster.nsf/webpage/Therapist_1?editdocument
Surveyor, Land #9	www.pepls.state.ms.us/roster.htm
Veterinarian #29	www.msvet.org/index.php?pr=Find_A_Vet

Mississippi Licensing Quick Finder

Air Monitor #22	601-961-5100
Alcohol Beverage Employee #26	601-856-1330
Alcoholic Beverage Retailer #2	601-856-1330
Animal/Veterinary Technician #29	662-323-5057
Architect #3	601-856-4652
Art Therapist #33	601-576-7400
Asbestos Contr./Insp./Supv. #22	601-961-5100
Asbestos Project Designer/Planner #22	601-961-5100
Asbestos Worker #22	601-961-5100
Athletic Trainer #37	601-364-7360
Athletic Trainer #33	601-576-7400
Attorney/Attorney Firm #27	601-948-4471
Audiologist #21	601-576-7260
Bank #4	601-359-1031
Barber Instructor/School #5	601-359-1015
Barber/Barber Shop #5	601-359-1015
Beauty Shop/Salon #7	601-354-5315
Body Piercing Operator #33	601-576-7400
Boiler & Pressure Vessel Inspec #37	601-576-7917
Camp, Youth #38	601-576-7613
Charity #32	601-359-1371
Child Care Facility #38	601-576-7613
Child Residential Home #38	601-576-7613
Chiropractor #35	662-773-4433
Contractor, Commercial #6	601-354-6161
Contractor, Residential #6	601-354-6161
Cosmetologist #7	601-354-5315
Cosmetology Instructor #7	601-354-5315
Counselor, Professional #10	662-716-3932
CPA-Certified Public Accountant #19	601-354-7320

Dental Hygienist #8....601-944-9622
Dental Radiologist #8....601-944-9622
Dentist #8....601-944-9622
Dietician #33....601-576-7400
Dietitian #37....601-364-7360
Domestic Insurance Company #25....601-359-3582
Educator, Citizen/Emerg'y/non-Lic's'd #36 601-359-3483
Emergency Medical Technician #37....601-576-7380
Engineer #9....601-359-6160
Esthetician #7....601-354-5315
Eye Enucleator #37....601-364-7360
Eye Enucleator #33....601-576-7400
Finance Company #4....601-359-1031
Fishing, Commercial #24....601-432-2400
Fund Raiser #32....601-359-6371
Funeral Director #11....601-932-1973
Funeral Pre-Need Contractor #32....601-359-6371
Funeral Service Practitioner #11....601-932-1973
Gaming #26....601-351-2800
Geologist #23....601-354-6370
Health Facility #1....601-364-1100
Hearing Aid Dealer #33....601-576-7400
Hearing Aid Dealer (Specialist) #37....601-364-7360
HMO #25....601-359-3582
Home Inspector #34....601-932-9191
Insurance Agent/Solicitor/Advisor #25....601-359-3582
Insurance Company #25....601-359-3582
Investment Advisor #32....601-359-6363
Landscape Architect #3....601-856-4652
Liquor Control #2....601-856-1330
Lobbyist #31....601-359-6353
Long Term Care Insurance Firm #25....601-359-3582
Manicurist #7....601-354-5315
Marriage & Family Therapist #28....601-987-6806
Medical Doctor #12....601-987-3079
Medical Radiation Technician #33....601-576-7400
Mortgage Lender/Company #4....601-359-1031
Notary Public #31....601-359-1633
Nurse-LPN #13....601-987-4188
Nurse-RN #13....601-987-4188
Nursing Home Administrator #14....601-932-1442
Occupational Therapist/Assistant #33....601-364-7360
Optometrist #15....601-853-4338
Osteopathic Physician #12....601-987-3079
Pawn Shop #4....601-359-1031
Pharmacist #16....601-605-5388
Pharmacy #16....601-605-5388
Pharmacy Intern/Technician #16....601-605-5388
Physical Therapist #33....601-939-5124
Physical Therapy Assistant #33....601-939-5124
Podiatrist #12....601-987-3079
Polygraph Examiner #17....601-987-1212
Psychologist #18....662-716-3934
Radiation Technician #37....601-576-7260
Real Estate Agent/Seller #34....601-932-9191
Real Estate Appraiser #30....601-932-6770
Real Estate Broker #34....601-932-9191
Respiratory Care Therapist #33....601-576-7400
Savings Institution #4....601-359-1031
School Administrator #36....601-359-3483
Securities Agent #32....601-359-6363
Securities Broker/Dealer #32....601-359-6363
Security Offering #32....601-359-6369
Septic Tank Installer #37....601-576-7260
Shorthand Reporter #20....601-354-6056
Social Worker #28....601-987-6806
Speech-Language Pathologist #21....601-576-7260
Surplus Lines Insurer #25....601-359-3582
Surveyor, Land #9....601-359-6160
Tattoo Artist #37....601-364-7360
Tattoo Operator #33....601-576-7400
Teacher #36....601-359-3483
Title & Loan Company #4....601-359-1031
Veterinarian #29....662-323-5057
Veterinary Facility #29....662-323-5057
Wigologist #7....601-354-5315

Mississippi Licensing Agency Information

#1 Department of Health, Health Facilities Licensure & Certification, 143B Lefleur's Square, Jackson, MS 39216; 601-364-1100. www.msdh.state.ms.us/msdhsite/_static/30,0,83.html

#2 Office of Alcoholic Beverage Control, PO Box 540 (1286 Gluckstadt Rd), Madison, MS 39130-0540; 601-856-1301, Fax- 601-856-1390. www.mstc.state.ms.us

#3 Board of Architecture, 2 Professional Parkway #2B, Ridgeland, MS 39157; 601-856-4652, Fax- 601-856-1510. www.archbd.state.ms.us Search data at- www.archbd.state.ms.us/main_find_licensee.html

#4 Department of Banking & Consumer Finance, Board of Banking Review, PO Box 23729 (501 N West St, 901 Woolfolk Bldg #A), Jackson, MS 39225-3729; 601-359-1031, Fax- 601-359-3557. www.dbcf.state.ms.us/review.htm

#5 Board of Barber Examiners, PO Box 603 (510 George St, Rm 240), Jackson, MS 39204-0603; 601-359-1015, Fax- 601-359-1050.

#6 Board of Contractors, 215 Woodline Dr, B, Jackson, MS 39232; 601-354-6161, Fax- 601-354-6715. Hours- 8AM-5PM. www.msboc.us/ Search data at- www.msboc.us/search.cfm

#7 Board of Cosmetology, PO Box 55689 (2 Old River Pl #B), Jackson, MS 39296-5689; 601-354-5315, Fax- 601-354-6639. www.msbc.state.ms.us/msbc/Cosmetology.nsf

#8 Board of Dental Examiners, 600 E Amite St #100, Jackson, MS 39201-2801; 601-944-9622, Fax- 601-924-9624. www.msbde.state.ms.us/msbde/msbde.nsf Search data at- www.msbde.state.ms.us/msbde/msbdesearch.nsf/WebStart?OpenFOrm $125.00 fee for list or labels; $150.00 fee for diskette.

#9 Board of Engineers & Land Surveyors, PO Box 3 (239 N Lamar St, #501), Jackson, MS 39205-0003; 601-359-6160, Fax- 601-359-6159. www.pepls.state.ms.us Search data at- www.pepls.state.ms.us/roster.htm

#10 Board of Examiners for Licensed Professional Counselors, PO Box 1497 (129 E Jefferson St), Yazoo City, MS 39194; 662-716-3932, Fax- 662-716-3021. www.lpc.state.ms.us Search data at- www.lpc.state.ms.us/html/search.html

#11 Board of Funeral Service, 3010 Lakeland Cove #W, Flowood, MS 39232; 601-932-1973, Fax- 601-932-1901. www.msbfs.ms.gov/msbfs/web.nsf Website will soon list funeral homes.

#12 Board of Medical Licensure, 1867 Crane Ridge Dr #200-B, Jackson, MS 39216; 601-987-3079, Fax- 601-987-4159. Hours- 8AM-5PM. www.msbml.state.ms.us

#13 Board of Nursing, 1935 Lakeland Dr #B, Jackson, MS 39216-5014; 601-987-4188, Fax- 601-364-2352. www.msbn.state.ms.us Search at- https://www.ms.gov/msbn/inquiry_disclaimer.do

#14 Board of Nursing Home Administrators, 1755 Lelia Dr #305, Jackson, MS 39216; 601-362-6914, Fax- 601-362-6925. www.bnha.state.ms.us/msbnha/web.nsf/ Search data at- www.bnha.state.ms.us/msbnha/roster.nsf/webpage/bnha_1?editDocument

#15 Board of Optometry, PO Box 12370, Jackson, MS 39236; 601-919-1343, Fax- 601-919-1432. Hours- 8:30AM-4:30PM. www.msbo.ms.gov/msbo/opto.nsf Search data at- www.msbo.ms.gov/msbo/OptoRoster.nsf/webpage/Opto_1?editdocument

#16 Board of Pharmacy, 204 Key Dr, Suite D, Madison, MS 39110; 601-605-5388, Fax- 601-605-9546. www.mbp.state.ms.us/mbop/pharmacy.nsf Search data at- www.mbp.state.ms.us/mbop/PharmRoster.nsf/webpage/Pharm_1?editdocument Click on "Licensing".

#17 Board of Polygraph Examiners, Department of Public Safety, PO Box 958, Jackson, MS 39205; 601-987-1212.

#18 Board of Psychology, 2395 Deerfield Road, Yazoo City, MS 39194; 662-716-3934, Fax- 662-716-0336. www.psychologyboard.state.ms.us/msbp/msbp.nsf Search data at- www.psychologyboard.state.ms.us/msbp/msbp.nsf/Search?OpenForm

#19 Board of Public Accountancy, 5 Old River Place #104, Jackson, MS 39202; 601-354-7320, Fax- 601-354-7290. www.msbpa.state.ms.us Search data at- www.msbpa.state.ms.us/licsearch.html

#20 Board of Certified Court Reporters, PO Box 369 (450 High St, 39201), Jackson, MS 39205-0369; 601-576-4622, Fax- 601-576-4622. www.mssc.state.ms.us/cle_bccr/cle_bccr.html

#21 Department of Health, Speech Pathology/Audiology, PO Box 1700 (570 Woodrow Wilson, 39216), Jackson, MS 39215-1700; 601-576-7260, Fax- 601-576-7267. Hours- 8AM-5PM. www.msdh.state.ms.us

#22 Department of Environmental Quality, Pollution Control, PO Box 2261, Jackson, MS 39225; 601-961-5171, Fax- 601-354-6612. Hours- 8AM-5PM. www.deq.state.ms.us/MDEQ.nsf/page/Main_Home?OpenDocument Search data at- http://opc.deq.state.ms.us/default.aspx

#23 Board of Registered Professional Geologists, PO Box 22742 (931 Hwy 80 West), Jackson, MS 39225-2742; 601-354-6370, Fax- 601-354-6032. www.msbrpg.state.ms.us Search data at- www.msbrpg.state.ms.us/rpg.htm

#24 Department of Wildlife, Fisheries & Parks, 1505 Eastover Dr, Jackson, MS 39211; 601-432-2400, Fax- 601-432-2024. http://home.mdwfp.com/

#25 Insurance Department, Licensing Division, PO Box 79, 501 N West St (39201), Jackson, MS 39205; 601-359-3582, Fax- 601-359-1951. www.mid.state.ms.us/licensing/licensing.htm Company lists also available on diskette.

#26 Gaming Commission, 620 North St #200, Jackson, MS 39205; 601-576-3800, Fax- 601-576-3929. www.mgc.state.ms.us

#27 Board of Bar Admissions, PO Box 2168 (643 N State St), Jackson, MS 39225; 601-948-4471, Fax- 601-355-8635. 8AM-5PM. www.msbar.org Search data at- www.msbar.org/lawyerdirectory.php

#28 Marriage & Family Therapists, Board of Examiners for Social Workers, PO Box 4508 (350 W Woodrow Wilson Ave 3rd Fl #3635), Jackson, MS 39296-4508; 601-987-6806, Fax- 601-987-6808. www.swmft.ms.gov/swmft/web.nsf Search data at- www.swmft.ms.gov/swmft/Roster.nsf/webpage/Therapist_1?editdocument

#29 Board of Veterinary Medicine, 209 S Lafayette St, Starkville, MS 39759; 662-323-5057, Fax- 662-323-5057. Hours- 8:30AM-2:30PM. www.msvet.org/

#30 Real Estate Appraisal Board, Licensing & Certification, PO Box 12685 (2506 Lakeland Dr, #300), Jackson, MS 39236-2685; 601-932-6770, Fax- 601-932-2990. www.mrec.ms.gov/mab/index_mab.html Search data at- http://appserver.mrec.ms.gov/findappraiser.asp

#31 Office of Secretary of State, Regulation & Enforcement, PO Box 136 (700 North St), Jackson, MS 39205-0136; 601-359-1350, Fax- 601-359-2663. www.sos.state.ms.us

#32 Office of Secretary of State, Business Regulation & Enforcement Division, PO Box 136 (700 North St), Jackson, MS 39205-0136; 601-359-1350, Fax- 601-359-2663. www.sos.state.ms.us Will provide lists.

#33 Department of Health, Professional Licensure Division, 570 E Woodrow Wilson Dr, Jackson, MS 39216; 800-227-7308, Fax- 601-576-7267. Hours- 8AM-5PM. www.msdh.state.ms.us/msdhsite/_static/30,0,82.html

#34 Real Estate Commission, Licensing & Certification, PO Box 12685 (2506 Lakeland Dr, #300), Jackson, MS 39236; 601-932-6770, Fax- 601-932-2990. www.mrec.state.ms.us Search data at- http://appserver.mrec.ms.gov/findlicensee.asp

#35 Board of Chiropractic Examiners, PO Box 775 (405 W Main St), Louisville, MS 39339; 662-773-4478, Fax- 662-773-4433. www.msbce.ms.gov/msbce/msbce.nsf/webpages/1?OpenDocument Search data at- www.msbce.ms.gov/msbce/msbce.nsf/Search?OpenForm

#36 Department of Education, Teacher Licensure/Certification, PO Box 771 (359 N West St), Jackson, MS 39205; 601-359-3483, Fax- 601-359-2778. www.mde.k12.ms.us

#37 Department of Health, Licensing Division, 570 E Woodrow Wilson, Jackson, MS 39215; 601-364-7360, Fax- 601-576-7923. www.msdh.state.ms.us

#38 Department of Health, Childcare Facilities Licensure, 570 E Woodrow Wilson Dr, Jackson, MS 39215; 601-576-7613, Fax- 601-576-7813. Hours- 8AM-5PM. www.msdh.state.ms.us/msdhsite/_static/30.html

Mississippi Federal Courts

The following list indicates the district and division name for each county in the state. If the bankruptcy court location is different from the district court, then the location of the bankruptcy court appears in parentheses.

County/Court Cross Reference

County	District	Division
Adams	Southern	Vicksburg (Jackson)
Alcorn	Northern	Aberdeen-Eastern (Aberdeen)
Amite	Southern	Jackson
Attala	Northern	Aberdeen-Eastern (Aberdeen)
Benton	Northern	Oxford-Northern (Aberdeen)
Bolivar	Northern	Clarksdale/Delta (Aberdeen)
Calhoun	Northern	Oxford-Northern (Aberdeen)
Carroll	Northern	Greenville (Aberdeen)
Chickasaw	Northern	Aberdeen-Eastern (Aberdeen)
Choctaw	Northern	Aberdeen-Eastern (Aberdeen)
Claiborne	Southern	Vicksburg (Jackson)
Clarke	Southern	Meridian (Biloxi)
Clay	Northern	Aberdeen-Eastern (Aberdeen)
Coahoma	Northern	Clarksdale/Delta (Aberdeen)
Copiah	Southern	Jackson
Covington	Southern	Hattiesburg (Biloxi)
De Soto	Northern	Clarksdale/Delta (Aberdeen)
Forrest	Southern	Hattiesburg (Biloxi)
Franklin	Southern	Jackson
George	Southern	Biloxi-Southern (Biloxi)
Greene	Southern	Hattiesburg (Biloxi)
Grenada	Northern	Oxford-Northern (Aberdeen)
Hancock	Southern	Biloxi-Southern (Biloxi)
Harrison	Southern	Biloxi-Southern (Biloxi)
Hinds	Southern	Jackson
Holmes	Southern	Jackson
Humphreys	Northern	Greenville (Aberdeen)
Issaquena	Southern	Vicksburg (Jackson)
Itawamba	Northern	Aberdeen-Eastern (Aberdeen)
Jackson	Southern	Biloxi-Southern (Biloxi)
Jasper	Southern	Meridian (Biloxi)
Jefferson	Southern	Vicksburg (Jackson)
Jefferson Davis	Southern	Hattiesburg (Biloxi)
Jones	Southern	Hattiesburg (Biloxi)
Kemper	Southern	Meridian (Biloxi)
Lafayette	Northern	Oxford-Northern (Aberdeen)
Lamar	Southern	Hattiesburg (Biloxi)
Lauderdale	Southern	Meridian (Biloxi)
Lawrence	Southern	Hattiesburg (Biloxi)
Leake	Southern	Jackson
Lee	Northern	Aberdeen-Eastern (Aberdeen)
Leflore	Northern	Greenville (Aberdeen)
Lincoln	Southern	Jackson
Lowndes	Northern	Aberdeen-Eastern (Aberdeen)
Madison	Southern	Jackson
Marion	Southern	Hattiesburg (Jackson)
Marshall	Northern	Oxford-Northern (Aberdeen)
Monroe	Northern	Aberdeen-Eastern (Aberdeen)
Montgomery	Northern	Oxford-Northern (Aberdeen)
Neshoba	Southern	Meridian (Biloxi)
Newton	Southern	Meridian (Biloxi)
Noxubee	Southern	Meridian (Biloxi)
Oktibbeha	Northern	Aberdeen-Eastern (Aberdeen)
Panola	Northern	Clarksdale/Delta (Aberdeen)
Pearl River	Southern	Biloxi-Southern (Biloxi)
Perry	Southern	Hattiesburg (Biloxi)
Pike	Southern	Jackson
Pontotoc	Northern	Oxford-Northern (Aberdeen)
Prentiss	Northern	Aberdeen-Eastern (Aberdeen)
Quitman	Northern	Clarksdale/Delta (Aberdeen)
Rankin	Southern	Jackson
Scott	Southern	Jackson
Sharkey	Southern	Vicksburg (Jackson)
Simpson	Southern	Jackson
Smith	Southern	Jackson
Stone	Southern	Biloxi-Southern (Biloxi)
Sunflower	Northern	Greenville (Aberdeen)
Tallahatchie	Northern	Clarksdale/Delta (Aberdeen)
Tate	Northern	Clarksdale/Delta (Aberdeen)
Tippah	Northern	Oxford-Northern (Aberdeen)
Tishomingo	Northern	Aberdeen-Eastern (Aberdeen)
Tunica	Northern	Clarksdale/Delta (Aberdeen)
Union	Northern	Oxford-Northern (Aberdeen)
Walthall	Southern	Hattiesburg (Biloxi)
Warren	Southern	Vicksburg (Jackson)
Washington	Northern	Greenville (Aberdeen)
Wayne	Southern	Meridian (Biloxi)
Webster	Northern	Oxford-Northern (Aberdeen)
Wilkinson	Southern	Vicksburg (Jackson)
Winston	Northern	Aberdeen-Eastern (Aberdeen)
Yalobusha	Northern	Oxford-Northern (Aberdeen)
Yazoo	Southern	Vicksburg (Jackson)

Standards for Federal Courts: Fees are standard unless noted in profile. Search fee is $26.00 per item (one party name or case number). Copy fee is $.50 per page. Certification fee is $9.00 per document, double for exemplification, if available. Most courts require prepayment. Mail requests should enclose a SASE unless otherwise noted. Before releasing records, all courts require prepayment, unless noted.

District courts index by defendant and plaintiff and by case number. Bankruptcy courts usually index by debtor and case number. While most courts now have their indexes on computer, many may still maintain index card files as well. Courts will archive closed case files at different times.

There are numerous public access programs available to online subscribers. Search the U.S. Party/Case Index to find party names and case numbers among all courts. Individual case data is provided on PACER. A search of CM/ECF provides copies of cases filed electronically. For details about PACER, the US Party/Case Index, and CM/ECF see the Appendix or go to http://pacer.psc.uscourts.gov or call 800-676-6856.

US District Court Mississippi Northern District

Aberdeen-Eastern Division Court Clerk, PO Box 704, Aberdeen, MS 39730 (In person: 301 W Commerce, Rm 310, Aberdeen, MS 39730), 662-369-4952. Hours- 8AM-12, 1-5PM. www.msnd.uscourts.gov

Counties/Note: Alcorn, Attala, Chickasaw, Choctaw, Clay, Itawamba, Lee, Lowndes, Monroe, Oktibbeha, Prentiss, Tishomingo, Winston.

Searches/Indexing: Include full party names in search requests. Results do not include SSN or DOB. Will not fax back documents. New cases are in the index 48 hours after filing date. Both computer and card indexes maintained; computer goes back to 1992. Civil cases sent to archives 5 years after disposition; 10 years for criminal.

Search Access: Limited search; if case number is provided via phone, this court will verify that case number. **Mail:** Search usually completed- 1-2 days. Include SASE for return. **In person:** 1 public terminal available. Self-serve copies $.25 each.

Payment: Pay by Visa/MC/AmEx, money order, cashier's check. No personal checks. Payee: Clerk, US District Court.

E-Services: PACER records go back to 1990. New records online after 1 day. ECF at https://ecf.msnd.uscourts.gov. **Opinions Online:** www.msnd.uscourts.gov/opinions.htm. Opinions may only be up to 4/15/2005 only.

Delta Division c/o Oxford-Northern Division, 911 Jackson Ave, Rm 359, Oxford, MS 38655, 662-234-1971; records- 662-234-1351. Hours-8AM-5PM. www.msnd.uscourts.gov

Counties/Note: Bolivar, Coahoma, De Soto, Panola, Quitman, Tallahatchie, Tate, Tunica. Formerly known as the Clarksdale/Delta Division, records are managed now by the Oxford Division, address and phone given above.

Searches/Indexing: Only the party name required in a search request. Results do not include SSN or DOB. Will not fax back documents. Both computer and card indexes maintained; computer goes back to 1992. Civil cases sent to archives 5 years after disposition; 10 years for criminal.

Search Access: Mail: Include SASE for return. **In person:** 1 public terminal available. No self-serve copier.

Payment: Pay by Visa/MC/AmEx, money order, cashier's check. No business or personal checks accepted. Payee: Clerk, US District Court.

E-Services: PACER records go back to 1990. New records online after 1 day. ECF at https://ecf.msnd.uscourts.gov. **Opinions Online:** www.msnd.uscourts.gov/opinions.htm. Opinions may only be up to 4/15/2005 only.

Greenville Division Court Clerk, 305 Main St. #329, US Post Office and Federal Bldg, Greenville, MS 38701, 662-234-1971. Hours-by appointment only. www.msnd.uscourts.gov

Counties/Note: Carroll, Humphreys, Leflore, Sunflower, Washington. Phone above is for the Main Office in Oxford. You may still send email requests to the Greenville address given here.

Searches/Indexing: Include full party names in search requests. Results do not include SSN or DOB. Will not fax back documents. New cases are in the index immediately after filing date. Computer index maintained back to 11/04. Civil cases sent to archives 5 years after disposition; 10 years for criminal.

Search Access: Limited search; if case number is provided via phone, this court will verify that case number. **Mail:** Search usually completed- 1-2 days. Include SASE for return. **In person:** 1 public terminal available. Self-serve copies $.25 each.

Payment: Pay by Visa/MC/AmEx, money order, cashier's check. No personal checks. Payee: Clerk, US District Court.

E-Services: PACER records go back to 1990. New records online after 1 day. ECF at https://ecf.msnd.uscourts.gov. **Opinions Online:** www.msnd.uscourts.gov/opinions.htm. Opinions may only be up to 4/15/2005 only.

Oxford-Northern Division Court Clerk, 911 Jackson Ave, Rm 359, Oxford, MS 38655, 662-234-1971; records- 662-234-1351. 8AM-5PM. www.msnd.uscourts.gov

Counties/Note: Benton, Calhoun, Grenada, Lafayette, Marshall, Montgomery, Pontotoc, Tippah, Union, Webster, Yalobusha. All criminal records for Northern Dist. maintained at Oxford.

Searches/Indexing: Include full party names in search requests. Results do not include SSN or DOB. Will not fax back documents. New cases are in the index 48 hours after filing date. Computer, microfiche and card indexes maintained. Civil cases sent to archives 5 years after disposition; 10 years for criminal.

Search Access: Limited search; if case number is provided via phone, this court will verify that case number. **Mail:** Search usually completed- 2 days. Include SASE for return. **In person:** 1 public terminal available. Self-serve copies $.25 each.

Payment: Pay by Visa/MC/AmEx, money order, cashier's check. No personal checks. Payee: Clerk, US District Court.

E-Services: All records after 11/1/2004 available on ECF. PACER records go back to 1990. New records online after 1 day. ECF at https://ecf.msnd.uscourts.gov. **Opinions Online:** www.msnd.uscourts.gov/opinions.htm. Opinions may only be up to 4/15/2005 only.

US Bankruptcy Court Mississippi Northern District

Aberdeen Division Court Clerk, 703 Hwy 145 N, Rm 178, Thad Cochran US Courthouse, Aberdeen, MS 39730, 662-369-2596. Hours-8AM-12, 1-5PM. www.msnb.uscourts.gov

Counties: Alcorn, Attala, Benton, Bolivar, Clay, Calhoun, Carroll, Chickasaw, Choctaw, Coahoma, De Soto, Grenada, Humphreys, Itawamba, Lafayette, Lee, Leflore, Lowndes, Marshall, Monroe, Montgomery, Oktibbeha, Panola, Pontotoc, Prentiss, Quitman, Sunflower, Tallahatchie, Tate, Tippah, Tishomingo, Tunica, Union, Washington, Webster, Winston, Yalobusha.

Searches/Indexing: Search request requires name only. Results include last 4 SSN digits. Will not fax back documents. New cases are in the index immediately after filing date.

Search Access: Only docket info is available by phone. Voice Case Information Service available, call VCIS at 800-392-8653 or 662-369-8147. **Mail:** Search usually completed- soon as work load permits. Include SASE for return. **Fax:** Written fax requests accepted, prepaid. **In person:** 1 public terminal available. Self-serve copies- $.50 each. You may not take case files from the court to make copies.

Payment: Pay by Visa/MC (in person only), money order, cashier's or personal check. Payee: Clerk, US Bankruptcy Court, Northern District.

E-Services: PACER records go back to 4/1987. New records online immediately. ECF at https://ecf.msnb.uscourts.gov. **Opinions Online:** www.msnd.uscourts.gov/bk/opinions.cfm. **Online Note:** Daily upcoming calendars at www.msnb.uscourts.gov/Calendars.htm.

US District Court Mississippi Southern District

Eastern Division Court Clerk, c/o Jackson Division, PO Box 23552, Jackson, MS 39225-3552 (In person: c/o Jackson Division, 245 E Capitol St, #316, Jackson, MS 39201), 601-965-4439. Hours-8AM-5PM. www.mssd.uscourts.gov

Counties/Note: Clarke, Jasper, Kemper, Lauderdale, Neshoba, Newton, Noxubee, Wayne.

Searches/Indexing: Include full name only in search request; court does not keep SSN or DOB. Results do not include SSN or DOB. Documents faxed back only with clerk's special permission; $1.00 per page. New cases are in the index 2-3 days after filing date. Computer, microfiche, and card indexes maintained. Electronic docket for civil goes back to 1992; 1994 for criminal.

Search Access: Mail: Search usually completed- 1-2 days. Include SASE for return. **Fax:** Any fax must be pre-approved. **In person:** 2 public terminals available. No self-serve copier.

Payment: Pay by money order, cashier's, business or personal check. No credit cards accepted except for electronic filing of Notices of Appeal. Payee: Clerk, US District Court.

E-Services: PACER records go back to 1992. New records online after 1 day. ECF at https://ecf.mssd.uscourts.gov. **Opinions Online:** www.mssd.uscourts.gov/insurance.htm. These are orders and opinions related to Hurricane Katrina.

Hattiesburg Division

Court Clerk, 701 Main St, #200, Hattiesburg, MS 39401, 601-583-2433; Fax- 601-544-8335. Hours- 8AM-5PM. www.mssd.uscourts.gov

Counties/Note: Covington, Forrest, Greene, Jefferson Davis, Jones, Lamar, Lawrence, Marion, Perry, Walthall.

Searches/Indexing: Include full name only in search request; court does not keep SSN or DOB. Results do not include SSN or DOB. Documents faxed back only with clerk's special permission; $1.00 per page. New cases are in the index 48 hours after filing date. Computer, microfiche, and card indexes maintained. Electronic docket for civil goes back to 1992; 1994 for criminal.

Search Access: Limited docket info is available by case number via phone. **Mail:** Search usually completed- 3-4 working days. Include SASE for return. **Fax:** Any fax must be pre-approved. **In person:** 2 public terminals available. Self-serve copies $.25 each.

Payment: Pay by money order, cashier's or personal check. No credit cards accepted except for electronic filing of Notices of Appeal. Payee: Clerk, US District Court.

E-Services: PACER records go back to 1992. New records online after 1 day. ECF at https://ecf.mssd.uscourts.gov. **Opinions Online:** www.mssd.uscourts.gov/insurance.htm. These are orders and opinions related to Hurricane Katrina.

Jackson Division

Court Clerk, PO Box 23552, Jackson, MS 39225-3552 (In person: 245 E Capitol St, # 316, Jackson), 601-965-4439. Hours- 8AM-5PM. www.mssd.uscourts.gov

Counties/Note: Amite, Copiah, Franklin, Hinds, Holmes, Leake, Lincoln, Madison, Pike, Rankin, Scott, Simpson, Smith.

Searches/Indexing: Include full name only in search request; court does not keep SSN or DOB. Results do not include SSN or DOB. Documents faxed back only with clerk's special permission; $1.00 per page. New cases are in the index 48 hours after filing date. Computer, microfiche and card indexes maintained. Open records located at this court; electronic docket- civil back to 1992, criminal to 1994.

Search Access: Mail: Search usually completed- 1-2 days. Include SASE for return. **In person:** 2 public terminals available. Self-serve copies $.25.

Payment: Pay by money order, cashier's check, personal or business check. No credit cards accepted except for electronic filing of Notices of Appeal. Payee: Clerk, US District Court.

E-Services: PACER records go back to 1992. New records online after 1 day. ECF at https://ecf.mssd.uscourts.gov. **Opinions Online:** www.mssd.uscourts.gov/insurance.htm. These are orders and opinions related to Hurricane Katrina.

Southern Division

Court Clerk, 2012 15th S, Rm 403, Gulfport, MS 39501, 228-563-1700. Hours-8AM-5PM. www.mssd.uscourts.gov

Counties/Note: George, Hancock, Harrison, Jackson, Pearl River, Stone.

Searches/Indexing: Include full name only in search request; court does not keep SSN or DOB. Results do not include SSN or DOB. Will fax back documents $1.00 per page but only in emergencies and a low page count. New cases are in the index 48 hours after filing date. Computer, microfiche, and card indexes maintained. Electronic docket for civil goes back to 1992; 1994 for criminal.

Search Access: Limited docket info is available by case number via phone. **Mail:** Search usually completed- 1-2 days. Include SASE for return. **Fax:** Any fax must be pre-approved. **In person:** 3 public terminals available. Self-serve copies $.25.

Payment: Pay by money order, cashier's or personal check. No credit cards accepted except for electronic filing of Notices of Appeal. Payee: Clerk, US District Court.

E-Services: PACER records go back to 1992. New records online after 1 day. ECF at https://ecf.mssd.uscourts.gov. **Opinions Online:** www.mssd.uscourts.gov/insurance.htm. These are orders and opinions related to Hurricane Katrina.

Western Division

Court Clerk, PO Box 23552, Jackson, MS 39225-3552 (In person: Jackson Division, 245 E Capitol St, Suite 316, Jackson, MS), 601-965-4439. 8AM-5PM. www.mssd.uscourts.gov

Counties/Note: Adams, Claiborne, Issaquena, Jefferson, Sharkey, Warren, Wilkinson, Yazoo.

Searches/Indexing: Include full name only in search request; court does not keep SSN or DOB. Results do not include SSN or DOB. Documents faxed back only with clerk's special permission; $1.00 per page. New cases are in the index 2-3 days after filing date. Computer, microfiche, and card indexes maintained. Electronic docket for civil goes back to 1992; 1994 for criminal.

Search Access: Mail: Search usually completed- 1-2 days. Include SASE for return. **Fax:** Any fax must be pre-approved. **In person:** 2 public terminals available. No self-serve copier.

Payment: Pay by money order, cashier's, business or personal check. No credit cards accepted except for electronic filing of Notices of Appeal. Payee: Clerk, US District Court.

E-Services: PACER records go back to 1992. New records online after 1 day. ECF at https://ecf.mssd.uscourts.gov. **Opinions Online:** www.mssd.uscourts.gov/insurance.htm. These are orders and opinions related to Hurricane Katrina.

US Bankruptcy Court
Mississippi Southern District

Biloxi Division

Court Clerk, Dan M Russell, Jr U S Courthouse, 2012 15th St, #244, Gulfport, MS 39501, 228-563-1790. Hours-8AM-4:30PM. www.mssb.uscourts.gov

Counties/Note: Formerly located in Biloxi. Clarke, Covington, Forrest, George, Greene, Hancock, Harrison, Jackson, Jasper, Jefferson Davis, Jones, Kemper, Lamar, Lauderdale, Lawrence, Marion, Neshoba, Newton, Noxubee, Pearl River, Perry, Stone, Walthall, Wayne.

Searches/Indexing: Include SSN and address in search request. Results show name only; court can verify using address or SSN. Will not fax back documents. New cases are in the index a few hours after filing date.

Search Access: Voice Case Information Service available, call VCIS at 800-601-8859 or 601-965-6106. **Mail:** Search usually completed- within 1 day. Include SASE for return. **In person:** 3 public terminals available. No self-serve copier.

Payment: Pay by Visa/MC, money order, cashier's or personal check. Payee: Clerk, Bankruptcy Ct.

E-Svcs: PACER- https://pacer.login.uscourts.gov/cgi-bin/login.pl?court_id=mssbk. PACER records go back to 1986. New records online after 1 day. ECF at https://ecf.mssb.uscourts.gov. **Opinions:** www.mssb.uscourts.gov/Opinions/OpinionsList.htm. **Online Note:** Judges calendars free at www.mssb.uscourts.gov/Calendars.htm.

Jackson Division

Court Clerk, PO Box 2448, Jackson, MS 39225-2448 (In person: 100 E Capitol St #100, Jackson), 601-965-5301. Hours- 8AM-5PM. www.mssb.uscourts.gov

Counties: Adams, Amite, Claiborne, Copiah, Franklin, Hinds, Holmes, Issaquena, Jefferson, Leake, Lincoln, Madison, Pike, Rankin, Scott, Sharkey, Simpson, Smith, Warren, Wilkinson, Yazoo.

Searches/Indexing: Include SSN and address in search request. Results show name only; court can verify using address or SSN. Will not fax back documents. New cases are in the index a few hours after filing. Computer & card indexes maintained.

Search Access: Voice Case Information Service available, call VCIS at 800-601-8859 or 601-965-6106. **Mail:** Search usually completed- 5 days. Include SASE for return. **In person:** Computer generated copies $.10 each.

Payment: Pay by Visa/MC, money order, cashier's or personal check. Payee: Clerk, Bankruptcy Ct.

E-Svcs: PACER- https://pacer.login.uscourts.gov/cgi-bin/login.pl?court_id=mssbk. New records online after 1 day. ECF at https://ecf.mssb.uscourts.gov. **Opinions Online:** www.mssb.uscourts.gov/Opinions/OpinionsList.htm. **Online Note:** Judges calendars free at www.mssb.uscourts.gov/Calendars.htm.

Mississippi County Courts

Court	Jurisdiction	No. of Courts	How Organized
Circuit Courts*	General	70	22 Districts
County Courts*	Limited	3	19 Counties
Combined Courts*		20	
Chancery Courts*	General	91	20 Districts
Justice Courts	Limited	82	
Municipal Courts	Municipal	223	

* Profiled in this Sourcebook.

Court	CIVIL								
	Tort	Contract	Real Estate	Min. Claim	Max. Claim	Small Claims	Estate	Eviction	Domestic Relations
Circuit Courts*	X	X	X	$0	No Max			X	X
County Courts*	X	X	X	$0	$200,000			X	X
Combined Courts*	X	X	X					X	X
Chancery Court*	X	X	X	$0	No Max		X		X
Justice Courts*	X	X	X	$0	$3500	$3500		X	
Municipal Courts								X	

Court	CRIMINAL				
	Felony	Misdemeanor	DWI/DUI	Preliminary Hearing	Juvenile
Circuit Courts*	X				
County Courts*		X	X	X	X
Combined Courts*	X	X	X	X	X
Chancery Court*					X
Justice Courts*		X	X	X	
Municipal Courts		X	X	X	

Administration

Court Administrator, Supreme Court, Box 117, Jackson, MS, 39205; 601-354-7406, Fax: 601-354-7459. (CST) www.mssc.state.ms.us

Court Structure

The court of general jurisdiction is the Circuit Court with 70 courts in 22 districts. Chancery Courts have jurisdiction over disputes in matters involving equity; domestic matters including adoptions, custody disputes and divorces; guardianships; sanity hearings; wills; and challenges to constitutionality of state laws. Land records are filed in Chancery Court. Chancery Courts have jurisdiction over juvenile matters in counties which have no County Court.

County Courts have exclusive jurisdiction over eminent domain proceedings and juvenile matters, among other things. In counties which have a County Court, a County Court judge also serves as the Youth Court judge. County Courts share jurisdiction with Circuit and Chancery Courts in some civil matters. The jurisdictional limit of County Courts is up to $200,000, The traditional limit is $75,000 max for a County Court, but this is not adhered to at all counties. County Courts may handle non-capital felony cases transferred from Circuit Court. Civil cases under $3500 are usually found in Justice Courts as filing fees are less there than at Circuit Courts. Jasper County added a 2nd Justice Court in 5/2008; it is located in City of Paulding. Effective July 2008, a $3500 case limit (formerly $2500) applies for both civil and small claims cases at the Justice Courts. Circuit and County Courts are usually combined, except in Harrison County.

Probate matters are handled by the Chancery Courts, as are property matters. Civil cases involving land - in property and estate matters - can be found here.

Online Access

A statewide online computer system is in use internally for court personnel. The website offers searching of the MS Supreme Court and Court of Appeals Decisions and dockets.

Searching Tips, Fees, and Other Guidelines

A number of Mississippi counties have two Circuit Court Districts. A search of either court in will include the index from the other court. Full name is a search requirement for all courts. DOB and SSN are very helpful for differentiating between like-named individuals.

The Administrative Office of Courts offers a statewide search of civil, probate, or felony records by a fax request with a 24 hour turnaround time. Only criminal felony cases with dispositions are reported, misdemeanor cases are not. Request should include the name, DOB and full or partial SSN. The results report the county and docket number of the case. There is a $25.00 start-up fee and a $5.00 fee per name search. Call 601-576-4630 or fax 601-576-4639 for details.

Adams County

Circuit & County Court PO Box 1224, 115 S Wall, Natchez, MS 39121; 601-446-6326; fax: 601-445-7955; 8AM-5PM. ***Felony, Misdemeanor, Civil (usually over $3,500).***

Civil Records: Access: Mail, in person, online. Both court and visitors may perform in person searches. Search fee: $10.00 per name. Required to search: name, years to search. Civil cases indexed by defendant, plaintiff, on computer; docket books to 1950s; records stored in basement to 1799. Mail turnaround time 1-2 days if on computer. Civil PAT goes back to 1997. The Circuit Court Case and Judgment Roll Information is $25/monthly or $275/yearly. A user account must be created and subscription purchased to use this service at www.deltacomputersystems.com/MS/MS01/

Criminal Records: Access: Mail, in person, online. Both court and visitors may perform in person searches. Search fee: $10.00 per name. Required to search: name, years to search; also helpful: SSN. Criminal records on computer; docket books to 1950s; records stored in basement to 1799. Mail turnaround time 1-2 days if on computer. Criminal PAT goes back to same as civil. The Circuit Court Case and Judgment Roll Information will be $25/monthly or $275/yearly. A user account must be created and subscription purchased to use this service at www.deltacomputersystems.com/MS/MS01/

General Information: No sealed, adoptions, mental health, juvenile, sex, or expunged records released. Will not fax documents. Court makes copy: $1.00 per page. Certification fee: $2.00 per cert. Payee: Circuit Clerk. Personal checks accepted; credit cards are not. Mail requests: SASE required.

Justice Court 115 S Wall St, Natchez, MS 39121; 601-446-6326; fax: 601-445-7955; 8AM-5PM. ***Misdemeanor, Civil Actions under $3,500, Eviction, Small Claims.***

Chancery Court PO Box 1006, 1 Courthouse Sq, Natchez, MS 39121; 601-446-6684; fax: 601-445-7913; 8-5PM. ***Probate, Civil Land, Divorce, Family.***

Alcorn County

Circuit Court PO Box 430 Attn: Circuit Clerk, Corinth, MS 38835; 662-286-7740; fax: 662-286-7767; 8-5PM. ***Felony, Civil (usually over $3,500).***

Civil Records: Access: Mail, fax, in person. Both court and visitors may perform in person searches. Search fee: $10.00 per name. Required to search: name, years to search. Civil cases indexed by defendant, plaintiff; index in docket books from the 1930s. Mail turnaround time varies. Civil PAT goes back to 2/1003. Results include address if given by attorneys.

Criminal Records: Access: Mail, fax, in person. Both court and visitors may perform in person searches. Search fee: $10.00 per name. Required to search: name, years to search, DOB; also helpful: SSN, sex. Criminal docket on books from the 1930s. Mail turnaround time varies. Criminal PAT goes back same as civil; results show middle initial.

General Information: No sealed, adoptions, mental health, juvenile, sex, or expunged records released. Fee to fax document $1.00 each. Court makes copy: $1.00 per page. Self serve: $.50 per page. No certification fee. Payee: Circuit Clerk. Personal checks accepted; credit cards are not. Mail requests: SASE required.

Justice Court PO Box 226, 600 E Waldron St, Corinth, MS 38835; 662-286-7776; fax: 662-286-2157; 8AM-5PM. ***Misdemeanor, Civil Actions under $3,500, Eviction, Small Claims.*** www.alcorncounty.org/justice.aspx

Chancery Court PO Box 69, 501 Waldron St, Corinth, MS 38835-0069; 662-286-7702; fax: 662-286-7706; 8-5PM. ***Probate, Civil Land, Divorce, Family.***

Amite County

Circuit Court PO Box 312, 243 W Main St, Liberty, MS 39645; 601-657-8932; criminal fax: 601-657-1082; civil fax: same; 8AM-5PM. ***Felony, Civil (usually over $3,500).***

Civil Records: Access: Phone, fax, mail, in person. Both court and visitors may perform in person searches. Search fee: $10.00 per name. Required to search: name, years to search. Civil cases indexed by defendant, plaintiff; index on docket books since 1976; judgments on computer back to 1990. Mail turnaround time same day.

Criminal Records: Access: Fax, mail, in person. Both court and visitors may perform in person searches. Search fee: $10.00 per name. Required to search: name, years to search, DOB; also helpful: SSN. Criminal docket on books since 1976. Mail turnaround time same day.

General Information: Marriage records from 1809 - present. Will fax documents $3.00. Court makes copy: $.50 per page. Self serve: $.25 per page. Certification fee: $10.00 per document. Payee: Circuit Clerk. Personal checks accepted; credit cards are not.

Justice Court PO Box 362, 243 Broad St, Liberty, MS 39645; 601-657-4527; fax: 601-657-8604; 8AM-4:30PM. ***Misdemeanor, Civil Actions under $3,500, Eviction, Small Claims.***

Chancery Court PO Box 680, 243 W Main, Liberty, MS 39645; 601-657-8022; fax: 601-657-8288; 8-5PM. ***Probate, Civil Land, Divorce, Family.***

Attala County

Circuit Court 100 Courthouse, #1, Kosciusko, MS 39090; 662-289-1471; fax: 662-289-7666; 8AM-5PM. ***Felony, Civil (usually over $3,500).***

Civil Records: Access: Fax, mail, in person. Both court and visitors may perform in person searches. Search fee: $10.00 per name. Required to search: name, years to search. Civil cases indexed by defendant, plaintiff, kept on docket books since 1915. Mail turnaround time same day.

Criminal Records: Access: Fax, mail, in person. Both court and visitors may perform in person searches. Search fee: $10.00 per name. Required to search: name, years to search, DOB; also helpful: SSN. Criminal docket books kept since 1915. Mail turnaround time same day.

General Information: Will fax documents. Court makes copy: $.50 per page, self serve same. Certification fee: $1.00 per doc. Payee: Circuit Clerk. Business checks accepted. No credit cards accepted. Mail requests: SASE required.

Justice Court 100 Courthouse, #4, Kosciusko, MS 39090; 662-289-7272; fax: 662-289-0105; 8AM-5PM. ***Misdemeanor, Civil Actions under $3,500, Eviction, Small Claims.***

Chancery Ct 230 W. Washington, Kosciusko, MS 39090; 662-289-2921; fax: 662-289-2347; 8AM-5PM. ***Probate, Civil Land, Divorce, Family.***

Benton County

Circuit Court PO Box 262, Ashland, MS 38603; 662-224-6310; fax: 662-224-6312; 8AM-5PM. ***Felony, Civil (usually over $3,500).***

Civil Records: Access: Mail, in person. Both court and visitors may perform in person searches. Search fee: $10.00 per name. Required to search: name, years to search, address. Civil cases indexed by defendant, plaintiff, kept on index books since 1871. Mail turnaround time same day. Civil PAT goes back to 1999. PAT results show name only.

Criminal Records: Access: Mail, in person. Both court and visitors may perform in person searches. Search fee: $10.00 per name. Required to search: name, years to search, DOB; also helpful: SSN. Criminal records kept on index books since 1871. Mail turnaround time same day. Criminal PAT goes back same as civil; results show name only.

General Information: No sealed, adoptions, mental health, juvenile, sex, or expunged records released. Will fax documents for fee. Court makes copy: $1.00 per page. Self serve: $.25 per page. Certification fee: $1.00. Payee: Circuit Court. Only cashiers checks and money orders accepted. No credit cards accepted. Mail requests: SASE required.

Justice Court PO Box 152, 190 Ripley Ave, Ashland, MS 38603; 662-224-6320; fax: 662-224-6313; 8AM-5PM. ***Misdemeanor, Civil Actions under $3,500, Eviction, Small Claims.***

Chancery Court PO Box 218, 190 Ripley Ave, Ashland, MS 38603; 662-224-6300; fax: 662-224-6303; 8-5PM. ***Probate, Civil Land, Divorce, Family.***

Bolivar County

Circuit & County Court - 1st District PO Box 205, 801 Main St, Rosedale, MS 38769; 662-759-6521; fax: 662-759-3717; 8AM-N, 1PM-5PM. ***Felony, Misdemeanor, Civil (usually over $3,500).***

Civil Records: Access: mail, in person. Visitors must perform in person searches themselves. Search fee: $10.00 per name for 7 year search. Required to search: name, years to search. Civil cases indexed by defendant, plaintiff; index on docket books since 1900s. Mail turnaround 2-3 days. Civil PAT goes back to 2002. PAT results show name only. Name listed is name given by filing party.

Criminal Records: Access: Mail, in person. Both court and visitors may perform in person searches. Search fee: $10.00 per name for 7 year search. Required to search: name, years to search. Criminal docket on books since 1900s. Mail turnaround time 2-3 days. Criminal PAT goes back to same as civil. PAT results show name only. Name listed is name given by filing party.

General Information: No sealed, juvenile, sex, or expunged records released. Will fax documents to local or toll-free number. Court makes copy: $.50 per page. Self serve: $.25 per page. Certification fee: $1.50. Payee: Circuit Clerk. Only agency checks and money orders accepted. No credit cards accepted. Mail requests: SASE required for criminal.

Circuit & County Court - 2nd District PO Box 670, Cleveland, MS 38732; 662-843-2061; fax: 662-846-2943; 8AM-5PM. ***Felony, Misdemeanor, Civil (usually over $3,500).***

Civil Records: Access: In person only. Visitors must perform in person searches themselves. Required to search: name, years to search. Civil cases indexed by defendant, plaintiff; index on docket books since 1940. Civil PAT goes back to 2002.

Criminal Records: Access: Mail, in person. Both court and visitors may perform in person searches. Search fee: $10.00 per name; fee is for 7 year search. Required to search: name, years to search. Criminal docket on books since 1940. Mail turnaround time 2-3 days. Criminal PAT goes back to 1992.

General Information: No sealed, juvenile or expunged records released. Will fax documents to local or toll-free number. Court makes copy: $.50 per page. Self serve: $.25 per page. Cert fee: $1.50 per cert. Payee: Circuit Clerk. No personal checks or credit cards accepted. Mail requests: SASE required for criminal record return.

Justice Court PO Box 1507, 404 MLK Dr, Cleveland, MS 38732; 662-843-4008; fax: 662-846-6783; 8AM-5PM. ***Misdemeanor, Civil Actions under $3,500, Eviction, Small Claims.***

Cleveland Chancery Ct PO Box 789, 200 Court St, Cleveland, MS 38732; 662-843-2071; fax: 662-846-2940; 8AM-5PM. ***Probate, Divorce, Family.***

Rosedale Chancery Ct PO Box 238, 801 Main St, Rosedale, MS 38769; 662-759-3762; fax: 662-759-3467; 8AM-N, 1-5PM. ***Probate, Divorce, Family.***

Calhoun County

Circuit Court PO Box 25, Pittsboro, MS 38951; 662-412-3101; fax: 662-412-3103; 8AM-5PM. ***Felony, Civil (usually over $3,500).***

Civil Records: Access: Mail, in person. Both court and visitors may perform in person searches. Search fee: $10.00 per name. Required to search: name, years to search, DOB or SSN. Civil cases indexed by defendant, plaintiff; index on docket books since 1922; computerized records go back to 1922. Mail turnaround time 1 day. Civil PAT goes back to 12 years; civil results show middle initial.

Criminal Records: Access: Mail, in person. Both court and visitors may perform in person searches. Search fee: $10.00 per name. Required to search: name, years to search, DOB; also helpful: SSN. Criminal docket on books since 1922; computerized records go back to 1922. Mail turnaround time 1 day; phone search info released after payment received. Criminal PAT goes back to same as civil. PAT criminal results show middle initial.

General Information: No sealed, mental health, juvenile, sex, or expunged records released. Fee to fax out file $2.00 per page. Court makes copy: $1.00 per page. Self serve: $.25 per page. Certification fee: $1.50. Payee: Circuit Clerk. Personal checks accepted; credit cards are not. SASE not required.

Justice Court PO Box 7, Hwy 9 Courthouse Sq, Pittsboro, MS 38951; 662-412-3134; fax: 662-412-3136; 8AM-5PM. ***Misdemeanor, Civil Actions under $3,500, Eviction, Small Claims.***

Chancery Court PO Box 8, 103 W Main, Pittsboro, MS 38951; 662-412-3117; fax: 662-412-3128; 8-5PM. ***Probate, Civil Land, Divorce, Family.***

Carroll County

Circuit Court PO Box 6, Vaiden, MS 39176; 662-464-5476; fax: 662-464-5407; 8AM-5PM. ***Felony, Civil (usually over $3,500).***

Civil Records: Access: Mail, in person. Both court and visitors may perform in person searches. Search fee: $10.00 per name. Required to search: name, years to search. Civil cases indexed by defendant, plaintiff, on books since 1900s. Mail turnaround time 2 days.

Criminal Records: Access: Mail, in person. Both court and visitors may perform in person searches. Search fee: $10.00 per name. Required to search: name, years to search; also helpful: SSN. Criminal docket on books since 1900s. Mail turnaround time 2 days.

General Information: No adoption, mental health or juvenile records released. Will fax documents to local or toll free line. Court makes copy: $.50 per page. Self serve: $.25 per page. Certification fee: $2.00. Payee: Circuit Court. Personal checks accepted; credit cards are not. Mail requests: SASE required.

Justice Court PO Box 10, Courthouse, Lexington St, Carrollton, MS 38917; 662-237-9285; fax: 662-237-6833; 8AM-5PM. ***Misdemeanor, Civil Actions under $3,500, Eviction, Small Claims.***

Chancery Court PO Box 60, 600 Lexington St, Carrollton, MS 38917; 662-237-9274; fax: 662-237-9642; 8AM-N; 1-5PM. ***Probate, Civil Land, Divorce, Family.***

Chickasaw County

Circuit Court - 1st District 1 Pinson Sq, Rm 2, Houston, MS 38851; 662-456-2331; fax: 662-456-4831; 8-5PM. ***Felony, Civil (usually over $3,500).***

Civil Records: Access: Mail, in person. Both court and visitors may perform in person searches. Search fee: $10.00 per name. There is no fee if the visitor performs the search. Required to search: name, years to search; also helpful: address, DOB, DL. Civil cases indexed by defendant, plaintiff; index on docket books since mid-1800s. Mail turnaround time 2-3 days. Civil PAT goes back to 2004. PAT results show name only.

Criminal Records: Access: Mail, in person. Both court and visitors may perform in person searches. Search fee: $10.00 per name. Required to search: name, years to search, DOB; also helpful: address, SSN. Criminal docket on books since 1900. Mail turnaround time 2-3 days. Criminal PAT goes back to same as civil.PAT results show name, DOB.

General Information: No sealed, adoptions, mental health, juvenile, sex, or expunged records released. Will fax documents $1.00 per page. Court makes copy: $1.00 per page. Certification fee: $1.00 plus $.50 per page after first. Payee: Circuit Clerk. Business checks accepted. No credit cards accepted. Mail requests: SASE required.

Circuit Court - 2nd District Courthouse, 234 W Main St Rm #203, Okolona, MS 38860; 662-447-2838; fax: 662-447-2504; 8AM-5PM. ***Felony, Civil (usually over $3,500).***

Civil Records: Access: Fax, mail, in person. Both court and visitors may perform in person searches. Search fee: $10.00 per name. Required to search: name, years to search; also helpful: address. Civil cases indexed by defendant, plaintiff, on computer. Mail turnaround time 2-3 days. Civil PAT goes back to 2003.

Criminal Records: Access: Fax, mail, in person. Both court and visitors may perform in person searches. Search fee: $10.00 per name. Required to search: name, years to search, DOB; also helpful: SSN. Criminal records on computer. Mail turnaround time 2-3 days. Criminal PAT goes back to 2002.

General Information: No sealed, adoptions, mental health, juvenile, sex, or expunged records released. Will fax documents to local or toll free line. Court makes copy: $1.00 per page. Self serve: $.50 per page. Certification fee: $1.00 plus $.50 per page after first. Payee: Circuit Clerk. Business checks accepted. No credit cards accepted. Mail requests: SASE required.

Justice Court District 1 Courthouse, 1 Pinson Sq, Houston, MS 38851; 662-456-3941; fax: 662-448-8122; 8AM-5PM. ***Misdemeanor, Civil Actions under $3,500, Eviction, Small Claims.***

Justice Court District 2 236 W Main, Okolona, MS 38860; 662-447-3402; fax: 662-447-5020; 8AM-N; 1-5PM. ***Misdemeanor, Civil Actions under $3,500, Eviction, Small Claims.*** Research fee- $10.00 per name.

Chancery Court - District 1 Courthouse Bldg, 1 Pinson Square, Houston, MS 38851; 662-456-2513; fax: 662-456-5295; 8AM-5PM. ***Probate, Divorce, Family.***

Chancery Court - District 2 234 W Main, Rm 201, Okolona, MS 38860-1438; 662-447-2092; fax: 662-447-5024; 8AM-N; 1-5PM. ***Probate, Divorce, Family.***

Choctaw County

Circuit Court PO Box 34, Ackerman, MS 39735; 662-285-6245; fax: 662-285-2196; 8AM-5PM. ***Felony, Civil (usually over $3,500).***

Civil Records: Access: Mail, in person. Both court and visitors may perform in person searches. Search fee: $10.00 per name. Required to search: name, years to search. Civil cases indexed by defendant, plaintiff, in books back to 1926. Mail turnaround time 14 days legal maximum. Civil PAT goes back to 2003.

Criminal Records: Access: Mail, in person. Both court and visitors may perform in person searches. Search fee: $10.00 per name. Same fee for in person search. Required to search: name, years to search; also helpful: DOB, SSN. Criminal records in books back to 1926. Mail turnaround time 14 days legal maximum. Criminal PAT goes back to 2003.

General Information: No sealed, adoptions, mental health, juvenile, sex, or expunged records released. Will fax documents to local or toll free line. Court makes copy: $1.00 per page. Self serve: $.50 per page. Certification fee: $1.00 per page. Payee: Choctaw County Circuit Clerk. Personal checks accepted; credit cards are not. Mail requests: SASE required.

Justice Court 140 Jailhouse Rd, Ackerman, MS 39735; 662-285-3599; fax: 662-285-9039; 8AM-5PM. ***Misdemeanor, Civil Actions under $3,500, Eviction, Small Claims.***

Chancery Court PO Box 250, 22 Quinn St, Ackerman, MS 39735; 662-285-6329; fax: 662-285-3444; 8AM-5PM. ***Probate, Civil Land, Divorce, Family.***

Claiborne County

Circuit Court PO Box 549, Port Gibson, MS 39150; 601-437-5841; criminal fax: 601-437-4543; civil fax: same; 8AM-5PM. ***Felony, Civil (usually over $3,500).***

Civil Records: Access: Mail, in person. Both court and visitors may perform in person searches. Search fee: $10.00 per name. Required to search: name, years to search, address. Civil cases indexed by defendant, plaintiff; index on docket books since 1820. Mail turnaround time varies.

Criminal Records: Access: Mail, in person. Both court and visitors may perform in person searches. Search fee: $10.00 per name. Required to search: name, years to search, address, DOB, signed release. Criminal docket on books since 1820. Mail turnaround time varies.

General Information: No sealed, adoptions, mental health, juvenile, sex, or expunged records released. Will fax documents $2.00 per page, if not extensive. Court makes copy: $1.00 per page; docket sheets $2.00 per page. Cert fee: $1.50 per case. Payee: Sammie L Good, Circuit Clerk. Personal checks accepted; credit cards are not.

Justice Court PO Box 497, 510 Market St, Port Gibson, MS 39150; 601-437-4478; criminal fax: 601-437-3833; civil fax: same; 8AM-5PM. ***Misdemeanor, Civil Actions under $3,500, Eviction, Small Claims.***

Chancery Court PO Box 449, 410 Market St, Port Gibson, MS 39150; 601-437-4992; fax: 601-437-3137; 8AM-5PM. ***Probate, Civil Land, Divorce, Family.***

Clarke County

Circuit Court PO Box 216, 101 S Archusa Ave, Quitman, MS 39355; 601-776-3111; fax: 601-776-1001; 8-5PM. ***Felony, Civil (usually over $3,500).***

Civil Records: Access: Fax, mail, in person. Both court and visitors may perform in person searches. Search fee: $10.00 per name. Required to search: name, years to search; also helpful: address. Civil cases indexed by defendant, plaintiff, kept on docket books since 1950s. Mail turnaround time 1 day. Public use terminal has civil records back to 1995. PAT civil results show middle initial. Results sometimes include the SSN.

Criminal Records: Access: Fax, mail, in person. Both court and visitors may perform in person searches. Search fee: $10.00 per name. Required to search: name, years to search; also helpful: address, DOB, SSN, sex. Criminal docket books kept since 1950s. Mail turnaround time 1 day.

General Information: No sealed, adoptions, mental health, juvenile, sex, or expunged records released. No fee to fax documents. Court makes copy: $.50 per page. Self serve: $.25 per page. Certification fee: $1.50 per doc. Payee: Circuit Clerk. Personal checks accepted; credit cards are not.

Justice Court PO Box 4, 100 E Church St, Quitman, MS 39355; 601-776-5371; fax: 601-776-1014; 8AM-5PM. ***Misdemeanor, Civil Actions under $3,500, Eviction, Small Claims.***

Chancery Court PO Box 689, 101 S Archusa, Quitman, MS 39355; 601-776-2126; fax: 601-776-2756; 8-5PM. ***Probate, Civil Land, Divorce, Family.***

Clay County

Circuit Court PO Box 364, West Point, MS 39773; 662-494-3384; fax: 662-495-2057; 8AM-5PM. ***Felony, Civil (usually over $3,500).***

Civil Records: Access: Phone, mail, in person. Both court and visitors may perform in person searches. Search fee: $10.00 per name. Required to search: name, years to search. Civil cases indexed by defendant, plaintiff; index on docket books back to 1962; archived since mid-1800s. Mail turnaround time same day.

Criminal Records: Access: Mail, in person. Both court and visitors may perform in person searches. Search fee: $10.00 per name. Required to search: name, years to search, address, DOB; also helpful: SSN. Criminal docket on books back to 1962; archived since mid-1800s. Mail turnaround time same day.
General Information: No sealed, adoptions, mental health, juvenile, sex, or expunged records released. Will fax documents. Court makes copy: $1.00 per page. Self serve: $.25 per page. Certification fee: $1.00 per page. Payee: Clay County Circuit Clerk. Personal checks accepted; credit cards are not. SASE not required.

Justice Court PO Box 674, 218 W Broad St, West Point, MS 39773; 662-494-6141; fax: 662-494-6141; 8AM-5PM. ***Misdemeanor, Civil Actions under $3,500, Eviction, Small Claims.***

Chancery Court PO Box 815, 205 Court St, West Point, MS 39773; 662-494-3124; fax: 662-492-4059; 8AM-5PM. ***Probate, Civil Land, Divorce, Family.*** Send faxes to Attention Chancery Court. A private company permits online access to civil records; go to www.recordsusa.com or call Rob at 888-633-4748 x17 for info and demo.

Coahoma County

Circuit & County Court PO Box 849, Clarksdale, MS 38614-0849; 662-624-3014; fax: 662-624-3075; 8AM-5PM. ***Felony, Civil (usually over $3,500).***
Civil Records: Access: Fax, mail, in person. Both court and visitors may perform in person searches. Search fee: $10.00 per name. Required to search: name, years to search, address. Civil cases indexed by defendant, plaintiff, on dockets since 1950, archived since 1836. Note: Will also search judgment rolls. Mail turnaround time 2 days.
Criminal Records: Access: Fax, mail, in person. Both court and visitors may perform in person searches. Search fee: $10.00 per name. Required to search: name, years to search, DOB, signed release; also helpful: address, SSN. Criminal records on dockets since 1910, archived since 1836. Mail turnaround time 2 days.
General Information: No sealed, adoptions, mental health, juvenile, sex, or expunged records released. No fee to fax documents. Court makes copy: $1.00 per page. Self serve: $.50 per page. Certification fee: $1.00. Payee: Circuit Clerk. Personal checks accepted. SASE not required.

Justice Court 144 Ritch St, Clarksdale, MS 38614; 662-624-3060; fax: 662-624-5528; 8AM-5PM. ***Misdemeanor, Civil Actions under $3,500, Eviction, Small Claims.***

Chancery Ct PO Box 98, 115 1st St, Clarksdale, MS 38614; 662-624-3000; fax: 662-624-3040; 8AM-5PM. ***Probate, Civil Land, Divorce, Family.***

Copiah County

Circuit Court PO Box 467, Hazlehurst, MS 39083; 601-894-1241; fax: 601-894-3026; 8AM-5PM. ***Felony, Civil (usually over $3,500).***
Also, use 601-894-3301 for the 22nd Circuit Court District.
Civil Records: Access: Fax, mail, in person. Both court and visitors may perform in person searches. Search fee: $10.00 per name. Required to search: name, years to search. Civil cases indexed by defendant. Civil index on docket books since late 1800s. Mail turnaround time 1-2 days.
Criminal Records: Access: Fax, mail, in person. Both court and visitors may perform in person searches. Search fee: $10.00 per name. Required to search: name, years to search; also helpful: DOB, SSN. Criminal docket on books since late 1800s. Mail turnaround time 1-2 days.
General Information: No sealed, adoptions, mental health, juvenile, sex, or expunged records released. No fee to fax documents. Court makes copy: $.50 per page. Self serve: $.25 per page. Certification fee: $1.50. Payee: Circuit Clerk. Business checks accepted. No credit cards. SASE not required.

Justice Court PO Box 798, 121 W Frost St, Hazlehurst, MS 39083; 601-894-3218; fax: 601-894-6038; 8AM-5PM. ***Misdemeanor, Civil Actions under $3,500, Eviction, Small Claims.***

Chancery Court PO Box 507, 122 S Lowe St, Hazlehurst, MS 39083; 601-894-3021; fax: 601-894-4081; 8AM-5PM. ***Probate, Civil Land, Divorce, Family.***

Covington County

Circuit Court PO Box 667, Collins, MS 39428; 601-765-6506; fax: 601-765-5012; 8AM-5PM. ***Felony, Civil (usually over $3,500).***
Civil Records: Access: Fax, mail, in person. Both court and visitors may perform in person searches. Search fee: $10.00 per name. Required to search: name, years to search. Civil cases indexed by defendant, plaintiff; index on docket books since 1915. Mail turnaround time 2-3 days.
Criminal Records: Access: Fax, mail, in person. Both court and visitors may perform in person searches. Search fee: $10.00 per name. Required to search: name, years to search, DOB; also helpful: SSN. Criminal docket on books since 1915. Mail turnaround time 2-3 days.
General Information: No sealed, adoptions, mental health, juvenile, sex, or expunged records released. No fee to fax documents. Court makes copy: $.50 per page. Self serve: $.25 per page. Certification fee: $3.00. Payee: Circuit Clerk. Personal checks accepted; credit cards are not. Mail requests: SASE required.

Justice Court PO Box 665, 101 Dogwood St, Collins, MS 39428; 601-765-6581; fax: 601-765-5014; 8AM-5PM. ***Misdemeanor, Civil Actions under $3,500, Eviction, Small Claims.***

Chancery Court PO Box 1679, 101 S Elm St, Collins, MS 39428; 601-765-4242; fax: 601-765-5016; 8-5PM. ***Probate, Civil Land, Divorce, Family.***

De Soto County

Circuit & County Court 2535 Hwy 51 South, Hernando, MS 38632; 662-429-1325; criminal phone: 662-429-1325; civil phone: 662-429-1326; criminal fax: 662-449-1416; civil fax: 662-449-1415; 8AM-5PM. ***Felony, Misdemeanor, Civil (usually over $3,500).***
www.desotoms.com
Civil Records: Access: Mail, in person, online. Both court and visitors may perform in person searches. Search fee: $10.00 per name. Required to search: name, years to search; also helpful: address. Civil cases indexed by defendant, plaintiff; index on docket books since 1972. Mail turnaround time 3 days. Civil PAT goes back to 1990-2002; partial from 2003 forward. Search docket information, records and judgments free at www.desotoms.info/.
Criminal Records: Access: Mail, in person, online. Both court and visitors may perform in person searches. Search fee: $10.00 per name. Required to search: name, years to search, DOB; also helpful: SSN. Criminal docket on books since 1972. Mail turnaround time 3 days. Criminal PAT goes back to same as civil. Search docket info and records free at www.desotoms.info/.
General Information: No sealed, juvenile, sex, or expunged records released. Will not fax documents. Court makes copy: $1.00 per page, self serve same. Certification fee: $2.50 per doc. No personal checks accepted. Cash or money order only. No credit cards accepted. SASE not required.

Justice Court 8525 Highway 51 North, Southaven, MS 38671; 662-393-5810; fax: 662-393-5859; 8AM-5PM. ***Misdemeanor, Civil Actions under $3,500, Eviction, Small Claims.***
www.desotoms.com/justice_court.htm
Records maintained since 1984, search fee is $5.00.

Chancery Court PO Box 949, Rm 100, 2535 Hwy 51 South, Hernando, MS 38632; 662-429-1320; fax: 662-449-1420; 8AM-5PM. ***Probate, Civil Land, Divorce, Family.***
www.desotoms.com/directory.htm

Forrest County

Circuit & County Court PO Box 992, 630 Main St, Hattiesburg, MS 39403; 601-582-3213; fax: 601-545-6065; 8AM-5PM. ***Felony, Civil (usually over $3,500).***
Civil Records: Access: Phone, mail, in person. Both court and visitors may perform in person searches. Search fee: $10.00 per name includes copies and cert. Required to search: name, years to search; also helpful: address. Civil cases indexed by defendant, plaintiff; index on docket books since 1900s. Note: Limited phone access. Mail turnaround time 10 days. Civil PAT goes back to 2000.
Criminal Records: Access: Mail, in person. Both court and visitors may perform in person searches. Search fee: $10.00 per name includes copies and cert. Required to search: name, years to search, DOB, SSN; also helpful: address. Criminal docket on books since 1900s; on computer since 1995. Mail turnaround time 10 days. Criminal PAT goes back to same as civil.
General Information: No juvenile or expunged records released. Will fax back documents no fee. Court makes copy: $1.00 per page. Self serve: $.50 per page. Certification fee: $1.50 per cert plus copy fee; is included in copy fee. Payee: Circuit Clerk. Business checks or attorney checks accepted. No credit cards accepted.

Justice Court 700 Main St, Hattiesburg, MS 39401; 601-544-3136 x500; fax: 601-545-6114; 8AM-5PM. ***Misdemeanor, Civil Actions under $3,500, Eviction, Small Claims.***
Searches performed by the court only on Thursdays, or after 2PM rest of week.

Chancery Court PO Box 951, 641 Main St, Hattiesburg, MS 39403; 601-545-6040; fax: 601-545-6043; 8AM-5PM. ***Probate, Civil Land, Divorce, Family.***

Franklin County

Circuit Court PO Box 267, Meadville, MS 39653; 601-384-2320; fax: 601-384-8244; 8AM-5PM. ***Felony, Civil (usually over $3,500).***
Civil Records: Access: Phone, fax, mail, in person. Both court and visitors may perform in person searches. Search fee: $10.00 per name. Required to search: name, years to search. Civil cases indexed by defendant, plaintiff, on books since 1944. Mail turnaround time 2-3 days. Public use terminal has civil records. Judgments only on public access terminal.
Criminal Records: Access: Fax, mail, in person. Both court and visitors may perform in person searches. Search fee: $10.00 per name. Required to search: name, years to search, DOB or SSN; also helpful: address. Criminal docket on books since 1944. Mail turnaround time 2-3 days.
General Information: No sealed, adoptions, mental health, juvenile, sex, or expunged records released. Will fax documents to local or toll free line. Court makes copy: $1.00 per page. Self serve: $.50 per page. Certification fee: $.50 per page. Payee: Circuit Clerk. Personal checks accepted; credit cards are not. SASE not required.

Justice Court PO Box 365, Courthouse Sq/Main, Meadville, MS 39653; 601-384-2002; fax: 601-384-2253; 8AM-5PM. ***Misdemeanor, Civil Actions under $3,500, Eviction, Small Claims.***

Chancery Court PO Box 297, 36 Main St E, Meadville, MS 39653; 601-384-2330; fax: 601-384-5864; 8-5PM. ***Probate, Civil Land, Divorce, Family.***

George County

Circuit Court 355 Cox St, #C, Lucedale, MS 39452; 601-947-4881; fax: 601-947-8804; 8AM-5PM M-F, 9AM-N Sat. ***Felony, Civil (usually over $3,500).***
Civil Records: Access: Fax, mail, in person. Both court and visitors may perform in person searches. Search fee: $10.00 per name. Required to search: name, years to search. Civil cases indexed by defendant, plaintiff; index on docket books since 1910. Mail turnaround time 1-2 days.

Criminal Records: Access: Fax, mail, in person. Both court and visitors may perform in person searches. Search fee: $10.00 per name. Required to search: name, years to search; also helpful: SSN. Criminal docket on books since 1910. Mail turnaround time 1-2 days.
General Information: No sealed, adoptions, mental health, juvenile, sex, or expunged records released. Will fax documents for no add'l fee. Court makes copy: $1.00 per page. Certification fee: $2.00 per cert. Payee: Circuit Clerk. Personal checks accepted; credit cards are not. Mail requests: SASE requested.

Justice Court 368 Cox St, Lucedale, MS 39452; 601-947-4834; fax: 601-947-1911; 8AM-5PM. ***Misdemeanor, Civil Actions under $3,500, Eviction, Small Claims.*** Records on computer (5/92 forward) are $4.00 per name. Prior to 5/92, searches are $20 for first 1/2 hour then $5.00 each 1/4 hour.

Chancery Court 355 Cox St, #A, Lucedale, MS 39452; 601-947-4801; fax: 601-947-1300; 8AM-5PM. ***Probate, Civil Land, Divorce, Family.***

Greene County

Circuit Court PO Box 310, Leakesville, MS 39451; 601-394-2379; fax: 601-394-2334; 8AM-5PM. ***Felony, Civil (usually over $3,500).***
Civil Records: Access: Phone, fax, mail, in person. Both court and visitors may perform in person searches. Search fee: $10.00 per name. Required to search: name, years to search; also helpful: address. Civil cases indexed by defendant, plaintiff; index on docket books since early 1900s. Mail turnaround time 1-2 days.
Criminal Records: Access: Phone, fax, mail, in person. Both court and visitors may perform in person searches. Search fee: $10.00 per name. Required to search: name, years to search; also helpful: SSN. Criminal docket on books since early 1900s. Note: Misdemeanor records are kept in Greene County Justice Court, 601-394-2347. Mail turnaround time 1-2 days.
General Information: No sealed, adoptions, mental health, juvenile, sex, or expunged records released. No fee to fax documents. Court makes copy: $.50 per page. Self serve: $.25 per page. Certification fee: $1.00. Payee: Circuit Clerk. Personal checks accepted; credit cards are not. Mail requests: SASE requested.

Justice Court PO Box 547, 407 Greene Ave, Leakesville, MS 39451; 601-394-2347; fax: 601-394-2114; 8AM-5PM. ***Misdemeanor, Civil Actions under $3,500, Eviction, Small Claims.***

Chancery Ct POB 610, 400 Main St, Leakesville, MS 39451; 601-394-2377; fax: 601-394-4445; 8AM-5PM. ***Probate, Civil Land, Divorce, Family.***

Grenada County

Circuit Court PO Box 1517, Grenada, MS 38902-1517; 662-226-1941; fax: 662-227-2865; 8AM-5PM. ***Felony, Civil (usually over $3,500).***
Public access terminal has only civil judgments.
Civil Records: Access: In person only. Visitors must perform in person searches themselves. Required to search: name, years to search. Civil cases indexed by defendant, plaintiff; index on docket books since mid-1970s. Public use terminal has civil records back to 1999. PAT results show name only. Use terminal to search for judgments.
Criminal Records: Access: In person only. Visitors must perform in person searches themselves. Required to search: name, years to search. Criminal docket on books since mid-1970s.
General Information: No sealed, juvenile, or expunged records released. Will not fax documents. Court makes copy: $1.00 per page. Self serve: $.25 per page. Certification fee: $2.00. Payee: Circuit Clerk. No personal checks or credit cards accepted.

Justice Court 16 First St, Grenada, MS 38901; 662-226-3331; fax: 662-227-5513; 8AM-5PM. ***Misdemeanor, Civil Actions under $3,500, Eviction, Small Claims.***

Chancery Ct PO Box 1208, 59 Green St, Rm 1, Grenada, MS 38902; 662-226-1821; fax: 662-227-2860; 8-5PM. ***Probate, Civil Land, Divorce, Family.***

Hancock County

Circuit Court 3068 Longfellow Dr, Bldg 7, Bay St. Louis, MS 39520; 228-467-5265; probate phone: 228-467-5404; fax: 228-467-2779; 8AM-5PM. ***Felony, Civil (usually over $3,500).***
Civil Records: Access: Mail, in person. Both court and visitors may perform in person searches. Search fee: $10.00 per name. Required to search: name, years to search. Civil cases indexed by defendant, plaintiff; index on docket books since 1975. Mail turnaround time 2 days to 1 week. Civil PAT goes back to 1970. PAT results show name only.
Criminal Records: Access: Mail, in person. Both court and visitors may perform in person searches. Search fee: $10.00 per name. Required to search: name, years to search, DOB; also helpful: SSN. Criminal docket on books since 1970. Mail turnaround time 2 days to 1 week. Criminal PAT goes back same as civil; results show name only.
General Information: No sealed, adoptions, mental health, juvenile, sex, or expunged records released. Will not fax documents. Court makes copy: $1.00 per page, self serve same. Certification fee: $1.50 per page. Payee: Circuit Clerk. Personal checks accepted; credit cards are not. SASE not required.

Justice Court PO Box 698, 17343 Hiway 603, Kiln, MS 39556; 228-467-5573; fax: 228-255-5851; 8AM-5PM. ***Misdemeanor, Civil Actions under $3,500, Eviction, Small Claims.***

Chancery Court 3068 Longfellow Dr, #2B, Bay St. Louis, MS 39520; 228-467-5404; fax: 228-467-3159; 8-5PM. ***Probate, Civil Land, Divorce, Family.***

Harrison County

Circuit Court - 1st District PO Box 998, 1801 23rd Av, Gulfport, MS 39502; 228-865-4147; fax: 228-865-4009; 8AM-5PM. ***Felony, Civil Actions over $200,000.***
Civil Records: Access: Fax, mail, in person, online. Both court and visitors may perform in person searches. Search fee: $10.00 per name. Required to search: name, years to search. Civil cases indexed by defendant, plaintiff, on computer back to 7/1991, prior on docket books, older records are archived. Mail turnaround time 2-3 days. Civil PAT goes back to 10 years. PAT results show middle initial, DOB. Access to Judicial District judgments are free at http://co.harrison.ms.us/departments/circlerk/rolls/. Search current court dockets free at http://co.harrison.ms.us/dockets/.
Criminal Records: Access: Fax, mail, in person, online. Both court and visitors may perform in person searches. Search fee: $10.00 per name. Required to search: name, years to search, DOB; also helpful: SSN. Criminal records computerized from 7/1991, prior on docket books, older records are archived. Mail turnaround time 2-3 days. Criminal PAT goes back to same as civil. PAT results show middle initial, DOB. Search current court dockets free at http://co.harrison.ms.us/dockets/.
General Information: No sealed, adoptions, mental health, juvenile, sex, or expunged records released. Will fax documents $10.00 per doc. Court makes copy: $.50 per page. Self serve: $.25 per page. Certification fee: $2.50 per cert. Payee: Circuit Clerk. Attorney's business checks, money orders, cash or certified checks accepted. No credit cards accepted. Mail requests: SASE requested.

Circuit Court - 2nd District PO Box 235, 730 Martin Luther King Jr Blvd, Biloxi, MS 39533; 228-435-8258; fax: 228-435-8277; 8AM-5PM. ***Felony, Civil Actions over $200,000.***
Civil Records: Access: Fax, mail, in person, online. Both court and visitors may perform in person searches. Search fee: $10.00 per name. Required to search: name, years to search. Civil cases indexed by defendant, plaintiff, on computer since 7/1991. Mail turnaround time 3 days. Civil PAT goes back to 1995. Access Judicial District judgments free at http://co.harrison.ms.us/departments/circlerk/rolls/. Search current court dockets free at http://co.harrison.ms.us/dockets/.
Criminal Records: Access: Fax, mail, in person, online. Both court and visitors may perform in person searches. Search fee: $10.00 per name. Required to search: name, years to search, DOB; also helpful: SSN. Criminal records on computer since 3/91. Mail turnaround time 3 days. Criminal PAT goes back to same as civil. Search current court dockets free at http://co.harrison.ms.us/dockets/.
General Information: No sealed or expunged records released. Will fax documents $.50 per page. Court makes copy: $.50 per page. Self serve: $.25 per page. Certification fee: $1.50 per cert. Payee: Circuit Clerk. Business checks or attorney checks accepted. No credit cards. Mail requests: SASE required.

County Court - 1st District PO Box 998, 1801 23rd Ave, Gulfport, MS 39502; 228-865-4010; criminal phone: 228-865-4010; fax: 228-867-6523; 8AM-5PM. ***Misdemeanor, Civil Actions (usually over $3,500).***
Civil Records: Access: Mail, in person, online. Both court and visitors may perform in person searches. Search fee: $10.00 per name. Required to search: name, years to search. Civil cases indexed by defendant, plaintiff, on computer since 1991, prior on docket books since early 1900s. Mail turnaround 1-2 days. Civil PAT goes back to 9/1991. PAT civil results show middle initial. Search current court dockets free at http://co.harrison.ms.us/dockets/.
Criminal Records: Access: Mail, in person, online. Both court and visitors may perform in person searches. Search fee: $10.00 per name. Required to search: name, years to search; also helpful: DOB. Criminal records on computer since 1991, prior on docket books since early 1900s. Mail turnaround time 1-2 days. Criminal PAT goes back to same as civil. PAT criminal results show middle initial. Search current court dockets free at http://co.harrison.ms.us/dockets/.
General Information: No sealed, adoptions, mental health, juvenile, sex, or expunged records released. Will fax documents to local or toll-free number. Court makes copy: $.50 per page. Self serve: $.25 per page. Certification fee: $1.00 per cert. Payee: County Clerk. Business checks accepted. No credit cards accepted. Mail requests: SASE helpful.

County Court - 2nd District PO Box 235, 730 Martin Luther King Jr Blvd, Biloxi, MS 39533; 228-435-8293/8232; fax: 228-435-8277; 8AM-5PM. ***Misdemeanor, Civil Actions (usually over $3,500).***
Civil Records: Access: Fax, mail, in person, online. Both court and visitors may perform in person searches. Search fee: $10.00 per name. Required to search: name, years to search. Civil cases indexed by defendant, plaintiff, on computer since 3/91, prior on books. Mail turnaround time 24 hours. Civil PAT goes back to 2005. PAT results show name only. Search current court dockets free at http://co.harrison.ms.us/dockets/.
Criminal Records: Access: Fax, mail, in person, online. Both court and visitors may perform in person searches. Search fee: $10.00 per name. Required to search: name, years to search, DOB; also helpful: SSN, aliases. Criminal records on computer since 3/91, prior on books. Mail turnaround time 24 hours. Criminal PAT goes back to same as civil.PAT results show name, DOB. Terminal results include SSN. Search current court dockets free at http://co.harrison.ms.us/dockets/.
General Information: No sealed or expunged records released. No fee to fax documents. Court makes copy: $.50 per page. Self serve: $.25 per page on your paper. Certification fee: $1.00 per doc. Payee: Circuit Clerk. Business checks or attorney checks accepted. No credit cards accepted. Mail requests: SASE required.

Justice Court District 1 PO Box 1754, 1620 23rd Ave., Gulfport, MS 39502; 228-865-4213; criminal phone: 228-865-4214; civil: 228-865-4193; fax: 228-865-4216; 8AM-5PM. ***Misdemeanor, Civil Actions under $3,500, Eviction, Small Claims.***
http://co.harrison.ms.us/departments/justice/cntdst1.asp
Search Justice court tickets free at http://co.harrison.ms.us/departments/justice/tickets/index.asp.

Justice Court District 2 PO Box 1141, 190 Lameuse St, Biloxi, MS 39533; criminal phone: 228-435-8251; civil phone: 228-435-8250; fax: 228-435-8279; 8AM-5PM. ***Misdemeanor, Civil Actions under $3,500, Eviction, Small Claims.***
http://co.harrison.ms.us/departments/justice/cntdst2.asp
Search Justice court tickets free at http://co.harrison.ms.us/departments/justice/tickets/index.asp.

Biloxi Chancery Court PO Box 544, 730 Martin Luther King Jr Blvd, Biloxi, MS 39533; 228-435-8228; fax: 228-435-8281; 8AM-5PM. ***Probate, Divorce, Family.***
http://co.harrison.ms.us/departments/chanclerk/court.asp
Search Chancery Court dockets for free at http://co.harrison.ms.us/dockets/.

Gulfport Chancery Court PO Drawer CC, 1801 23rd Ave, Gulfport, MS 39502; 228-865-4092; fax: 228-865-4054; 8-5. ***Probate, Divorce, Family.***
http://co.harrison.ms.us/departments/chanclerk/court.asp
Search Chancery Court dockets for free at http://co.harrison.ms.us/dockets/.

Hinds County

Circuit & County Court - 1st District PO Box 327, Jackson, MS 39205; 601-968-6628; fax: 601-973-5547; 8AM-5PM. ***Felony, Misdemeanor, Civil (usually over $3,500).***
www.co.hinds.ms.us/pgs/index.asp
Civil Records: Access: Mail, in person. Both court and visitors may perform in person searches. Search fee: $9.00 per name. Required to search: name, years to search. Civil cases indexed by defendant, plaintiff; index on docket books back to 1900s. Mail turnaround time 14 days. Civil PAT goes back to 1990.
Criminal Records: Access: Mail, in person. Both court and visitors may perform in person searches. Search fee: $9.00 per name. Required to search: name, years to search, DOB; also helpful: SSN. Criminal docket on books back to 1900s. Mail turnaround time 14 days. Criminal PAT goes back to same as civil.
General Information: No sealed, adoptions, mental health, juvenile, sex, or expunged records released. Will not fax documents. Court makes copy: $1.00 per page. Self serve: $.50 per page. Certification fee: $1.00. Payee: Circuit Clerk. Personal checks accepted; credit cards are not. Mail requests: SASE required.

Circuit & County Court - 2nd District PO Box 999, Raymond, MS 39154; 601-857-8038; fax: 601-857-0535; 8AM-N, 1-5PM. ***Felony, Misdemeanor, Civil (usually over $3,500).***
www.co.hinds.ms.us/pgs/index.asp
Civil Records: Access: In person, online. Visitors must perform in person searches themselves. Required to search: name, years to search. Civil cases indexed by defendant, plaintiff, on computer since 1994, prior on docket books since late 1800s. Access the clerk's judgment rolls free at www.co.hinds.ms.us/pgs/apps/jridx_query.asp.
Criminal Records: Access: Mail, in person. Both court and visitors may perform in person searches. Search fee: $9.00 per name. Required to search: name, years to search; also helpful: DOB, SSN. Criminal records on computer since 1994, prior on docket books since late 1800s. Mail turnaround time 1 week.
General Information: No sealed, adoptions, mental health, juvenile, sex, expunged or some preliminary criminal records released. Will fax documents $1.00 per page prepaid. Court makes copy: $1.00 per page. Self serve: $.50 per page. Certification fee: $1.50 per cert. Payee: Circuit Clerk. Personal checks accepted; credit cards are not. Mail requests: SASE requested.

Justice Court 407 E Pascagoula, 3rd Fl, PO Box 3490, Jackson, MS 39207; 601-965-8800; civil phone: x3; fax: 601-973-5532; 8-5. ***Misdemeanor, Civil Actions under $3,500, Eviction, Small Claims.***

Chancery Court - Jackson PO Box 686, 316 S President St, Jackson, MS 39205; 601-968-6540; fax: 601-973-5554; 8-5. ***Probate, Divorce, Family.***

Chancery Court - Raymond PO Box 88, 127 W Main, Raymond, MS 39154; 601-857-8055; fax: 601-857-4953; 8-5. ***Probate, Divorce, Family.***

Holmes County

Circuit Court PO Box 718, Lexington, MS 39095; 662-834-2476; fax: 662-834-3870; 8AM-5PM. ***Felony, Civil (usually over $3,500).***
Civil Records: Access: Fax, mail, in person. Both court and visitors may perform in person searches. Search fee: $10.00 per name. Required to search: name, years to search. Civil cases indexed by defendant, plaintiff; index on docket books since 1940s. Mail turnaround time 1-2 days.
Criminal Records: Access: Fax, mail, in person. Both court and visitors may perform in person searches. Search fee: $10.00 per name. Required to search: name, years to search; also helpful: DOB, SSN. Criminal docket on books since 1940s. Mail turnaround time 1-2 days.
General Information: No sealed or expunged records released. No fee to fax documents. Court makes copy: $1.00 per page. Self serve: $.50 per page. Certification fee: $1.50 plus copy fee; Exemplification fee $30.00. Payee: Holmes County Circuit Clerk. Business checks accepted. No credit cards accepted.

Justice Court PO Box 99, 200 Court St, Lexington, MS 39095; 662-834-4565; fax: 662-834-1402; 8AM-5PM. ***Misdemeanor, Civil Actions under $3,500, Eviction, Small Claims.***

Chancery Court PO Box 239, 2 Court Sq, Lexington, MS 39095; 662-834-2508; fax: 662-834-1872; 8-5PM. ***Probate, Civil Land, Divorce, Family.***

Humphreys County

Circuit Court PO Box 696, Belzoni, MS 39038; 662-247-3065; fax: 662-247-3906; 8AM-5PM. ***Felony, Civil (usually over $3,500).***
Civil Records: Access: Fax, mail, in person. Both court and visitors may perform in person searches. Search fee: $10.00 per name. Required to search: name, years to search. Civil cases indexed by defendant, plaintiff, on books since 1918. Mail turnaround time 1 day.
Criminal Records: Access: Fax, mail, in person. Both court and visitors may perform in person searches. Search fee: $10.00 per name. Required to search: name, years to search; also helpful: DOB, SSN. Criminal docket on books since 1918. Mail turnaround 1 day; phone turnaround 30 minutes.
General Information: No sealed, adoptions, mental health, juvenile, sex, or expunged records released. Will fax documents $1.00. Court makes copy: $1.00 per page. Self serve: $.50 per page. Certification fee: $1.00 per page if you perform search. No cert fee if court performs search. Payee: Circuit Clerk. Personal checks accepted; credit cards are not. Mail requests: SASE required.

Justice Court 102 Castleman St, Belzoni, MS 39038; 662-247-4337; fax: 662-247-1095; 8AM-5PM. ***Misdemeanor, Civil Actions under $3,500, Eviction, Small Claims.***

Chancery Court PO Box 547, 102 Castleman St, Belzoni, MS 39038; 662-247-1740; fax: 662-247-0101; 8AM-N, 1-5PM. ***Probate, Civil Land, Divorce, Family.***

Issaquena County

Circuit Court PO Box 27, Mayersville, MS 39113; 662-873-2761; fax: 662-873-2061; 8AM-Noon; 1-5PM. ***Felony, Civil (usually over $3,500).***
Civil Records: Access: Fax, mail, in person. Both court and visitors may perform in person searches. Search fee: $20.00 per name. Required to search: name, years to search. Civil cases indexed by defendant, plaintiff; index on docket books since 1846. Mail turnaround time 1 week.
Criminal Records: Access: Fax, mail, in person. Both court and visitors may perform in person searches. Search fee: $20.00 per name. Required to search: name, years to search; also helpful: DOB, SSN. Criminal docket on books since 1846. Mail turnaround time 1 week.
General Information: No sealed, adoptions, mental health, juvenile, sex, or expunged records released. Will fax documents to local or toll free line. Court makes copy: $.50 per page. Self serve: $.25 per page. Certification fee: $1.00 per cert. Payee: Circuit Clerk. Personal checks accepted; credit cards are not. Mail requests: SASE requested.

Justice Court PO Box 58, 129 Court St, Mayersville, MS 39113; 662-873-6287; fax: 662-873-2094; 8AM-N, 1-5PM. ***Misdemeanor, Civil Actions under $3,500, Eviction, Small Claims.***

Chancery Court PO Box 27, 129 Court St, Mayersville, MS 39113; 662-873-2761; fax: 662-873-2061; 8AM-N, 1-5PM. ***Probate, Civil Land, Divorce, Family.***

Itawamba County

Circuit Court 201 W Main, Fulton, MS 38843; 662-862-3511; fax: 662-862-4006; 8AM-5PM. ***Felony, Civil (usually over $3,500).***
Civil Records: Access: Phone, fax, mail, in person. Both court and visitors may perform in person searches. Search fee: $10.00 with a written request. Required to search: name, years to search. Civil cases indexed by defendant, plaintiff, on books since 1940s, index may be viewed on judgment roll. Mail turnaround time 1 week.
Criminal Records: Access: Phone, fax, mail, in person. Both court and visitors may perform in person searches. Search fee: $10.00 with a written request. Required to search: name, years to search, DOB; also helpful: SSN. Criminal docket on books since 1940s. Mail turnaround time 1 week.
General Information: Will fax documents to local or toll free line. Court makes copy: $.25 per page. No certification fee. Payee: Itawamba County Circuit Court. No personal checks or credit cards accepted. Mail requests: SASE required.

Justice Court 304 D W Wiygul St., Fulton, MS 38843; 662-862-4315; fax: 662-862-5805; 8AM-5PM. ***Misdemeanor, Civil Actions under $3,500, Eviction, Small Claims.***

Chancery Court PO Box 776, 201 W Main, Fulton, MS 38843; 662-862-3421; fax: 662-862-3421; 8AM-5PM M-F; 8AM-N Sat. ***Probate, Civil Land, Divorce, Family.***

Jackson County

Circuit Court PO Box 998, Pascagoula, MS 39568-0998; 228-769-3025; fax: 228-769-3180; 8AM-5PM. ***Felony, Civil (usually over $3,500).***
www.co.jackson.ms.us/DS/CircuitCourt.html
Civil Records: Access: Mail, in person, online. Both court and visitors may perform in person searches. Search fee: $10.00 per name per 10 years searched. Required to search: name, years to search. Civil cases indexed by defendant, plaintiff, on computer back to 1993, prior on docket books since 1920s. Mail turnaround time varies. Civil PAT goes back to 1992. Access to only Circuit Court monthly dockets is free at www.co.jackson.ms.us/DS/CircuitDockets.html.
Criminal Records: Access: Mail, in person, online. Both court and visitors may perform in person searches. Search fee: $10.00 per name, per 10 years searched. Required to search: name, years to search, DOB; also helpful: SSN. Criminal records computerized from 1992, prior on docket books since 1920s. Mail turnaround time varies. Criminal PAT goes back to same as civil. Online access to criminal dockets only is the same as civil.
General Information: No sealed or expunged records released. Will not fax documents. Court makes copy: $1.00 per page. Self serve: $.25 per page. Certification fee: $2.00 per page. Payee: Circuit Clerk. Business checks accepted. No credit cards accepted. Mail requests: SASE required.

County Court PO Box 998, 3104 Magnolia St, Pascagoula, MS 39568; 228-769-3181; fax: 228-769-3180; 8AM-5PM. ***Misdemeanor, Civil Actions (usually over $3,500).***
www.co.jackson.ms.us/DS/CountyCourt.html
Civil Records: Access: Mail, in person. Both court and visitors may perform in person searches.

Search fee: $10.00 per name per 10 years. Required to search: name, years to search. Civil cases indexed by defendant, plaintiff, files go back 20 years; on computer back to 2001. Mail turnaround time 1 week. Civil PAT goes back to 2001.
Criminal Records: Access: Mail, in person. Both court and visitors may perform in person searches. Search fee: $10.00 per name per 10 years. Required to search: name, years to search, DOB. Criminal records go back 12 years; on computer back to 2000. Mail turnaround 1 week. Crim PAT goes back to 2000.
General Information: No sealed, adoptions, mental health, juvenile, sex, or expunged records released. Will not fax documents. Court makes copy: $1.00 per page. Self serve: $.25 per page. Certification fee: $2.00. Payee: Clerk of County Court. Only cashiers checks and money orders accepted. No credit cards accepted. SASE not required.

Justice Court 5343 Jefferson St, Moss Point, MS 39563; criminal phone: 228-769-3097; civil: 228-769-3087; fax: 228-769-3364; 8-5PM. ***Misdemeanor, Civil Actions under $3,500, Eviction, Small Claims.***
www.co.jackson.ms.us/DS/JusticeCourt.html

Chancery Court PO Box 998, 3104 Magnolia St, Pascagoula, MS 39568; 228-769-3124, 769-3125; fax: 228-769-3397; 8AM-5PM. ***Probate, Civil Land, Divorce, Family.***
Access Chancery Court monthly dockets free at www.co.jackson.ms.us/DS/ChanceryDockets.html. Also, access cases and schedule free at www.deltacomputersystems.com/MS/MS30/INDEX.HTML.

Jasper County

Circuit Court - 1st District PO Box 58, Paulding, MS 39348; 601-727-4941; fax: 601-727-4475; 8AM-5PM. ***Felony, Civil (usually over $3,500).***
Civil Records: Access: Fax, mail, in person. Both court and visitors may perform in person searches. Search fee: $10.00 per name. Fee includes a search of both districts in the county. Required to search: name, years to search. Civil cases indexed by defendant, plaintiff; index on docket books since 1932. Mail turnaround time 1 week.
Criminal Records: Access: Fax, mail, in person. Both court and visitors may perform in person searches. Search fee: $10.00 per name. Fee includes a search of both districts in the county. Required to search: name, years to search; also helpful: DOB, SSN. Criminal docket on books since 1932. Mail turnaround time 1 week.
General Information: No sealed or expunged records released. Will fax documents $5.00 per doc. Court makes copy: $.50 per page. Self serve: $.25 per page. Certification fee: $1.50. Payee: Circuit Clerk. Personal checks accepted; credit cards are not. Mail requests: SASE required.

Circuit Court - 2nd District PO Box 447, Bay Springs, MS 39422; 601-764-2245; criminal fax: 601-764-3078; civil fax: same; 8AM-5PM. ***Felony, Civil (usually over $3,500).***
Civil Records: Access: Mail, in person. Both court and visitors may perform in person searches. Search fee: $10.00 per name. Fee includes a search of both districts in the county. Required to search: name, years to search. Civil cases indexed by defendant, plaintiff; index on docket books since 1932. Mail turnaround time 1-2 days. Public use terminal has civil records. Search for judgments only.
Criminal Records: Access: Mail, in person, fax. Both court and visitors may perform in person searches. Search fee: $10.00 per name. Fee includes a search of both districts in the county. Required to search: name, years to search; also helpful: SSN. Criminal docket on books since 1932. Mail turnaround time 1-2 days.
General Information: No sealed, adoptions, mental health, juvenile, sex, or expunged records released. Will fax documents to local or toll free line. Court makes copy: $1.00 per page. Self serve: $.25 per page. Certification fee: $2.00 per page. Payee: Circuit Clerk. Personal checks accepted; credit cards are not. Mail requests: SASE requested.

Justice Court District 1 PO Box 39, 1782 Highway 503, Community Center, Paulding, MS 39338; 601-727-2247; 8AM-5PM. ***Misdemeanor, Civil Actions under $3,500, Eviction, Small Claims.***
www.co.jasper.ms.us/courthouses.html
This court is new as of 5/1/08. Prior to that date, all records are found at Justice Court District 2 in Bay Springs. Paulding has only new cases of 5/1/08.

Justice Court District 2 PO Box 1054, 27 W 8th Ave, Bay Springs, MS 39422; 601-764-2065; fax: 601-764-3402; 8AM-5PM. ***Misdemeanor, Civil Actions under $3,500, Eviction, Small Claims.***
www.co.jasper.ms.us/courthouses.html
This is the original Justice Court for Jasper County. As of 5/1/2008, a second Justice Court was added in Paulding. All Justice Court records prior to that date are at Justice Court District 2.

Bay Springs Chancery Court PO Box 1047, 27 W 8th Ave, Bay Springs, MS 39422; 601-764-3368; fax: 601-764-3999; 8AM-5PM. ***Probate, Divorce, Family, Civil Land.***

Paulding Chancery PO Box 38, 1782 Highway 503, Paulding, MS 39348; 601-727-4941; fax: 601-727-4475; 8AM-5PM. ***Probate, Divorce, Family.***

Jefferson County

Circuit Court PO Box 305, Fayette, MS 39069; 601-786-3422; fax: 601-786-9676; 8AM-5PM. ***Felony, Civil (usually over $3,500).***
Civil Records: Access: Phone, mail, in person. Both court and visitors may perform in person searches. Search fee: $10.00 per name. Required to search: name, years to search, DOB; also helpful: SSN, sex, signed release. Civil cases indexed by defendant, plaintiff; index on docket books since 1966, prior archived. Mail turnaround time same day. Civil PAT goes back to 1971.
Criminal Records: Access: Phone, mail, in person. Both court and visitors may perform in person searches. Search fee: $10.00 per name. Required to search: name, years to search, DOB; also helpful: SSN. Criminal docket on books since 1971, prior archived. Mail turnaround time same day. Criminal PAT goes back to 1971.
General Information: No sealed, adoptions, mental health, juvenile, sex, or expunged records released. Will fax documents to local or toll free line. Court makes copy: $.50 per page criminal; Civil- $1.00 per page. Self serve: $.50 per page. Certification fee: $1.50. Payee: Jefferson County Circuit Court. Business checks accepted. No credit cards accepted. Mail requests: SASE required.

Justice Court PO Box 1047, 307 S Main St, Fayette, MS 39069; 601-786-8594; criminal phone: 601-786-3423; civil phone: 601-786-3423; fax: 601-786-6017; 8AM-5PM. ***Misdemeanor, Civil Actions under $3,500, Eviction, Small Claims.***

Chancery Court PO Box 145, 1483 Main St, Fayette, MS 39069; 601-786-3021; 8AM-5PM. ***Probate, Civil Land, Divorce, Family.***

Jefferson Davis County

Circuit Court PO Box 1090, Prentiss, MS 39474; 601-792-4231; fax: 601-792-4957; 8AM-5PM. ***Felony, Civil (usually over $3,500).***
Civil Records: Access: Phone, fax, mail, in person. Both court and visitors may perform in person searches. Search fee: $10.00 per name. Required to search: name, years to search. Civil cases indexed by defendant, plaintiff; index on docket books since 1906. Mail turnaround time 1-2 days.
Criminal Records: Access: Phone, fax, mail, in person. Both court and visitors may perform in person searches. Search fee: $10.00 per name. Required to search: name, years to search; also helpful: SSN. Criminal docket on books since 1906. Mail turnaround time 1-2 days.
General Information: No sealed, adoptions, mental health, juvenile, sex, or expunged records released. Fee to fax out file $1.00 per page. Court makes copy: $.50 per page. Self serve: $.25 per page. Certification fee: $2.00. Payee: Circuit Clerk. Personal checks accepted; credit cards are not.

Justice Court PO Box 1407, 2335 Columbia Ave, Prentiss, MS 39474; 601-792-5129; fax: 601-792-5128; 8AM-N, 1-5PM. ***Misdemeanor, Civil Actions under $3,500, Eviction, Small Claims.***

Chancery Court PO Box 1137, 2426 Pearl Ave, Prentiss, MS 39474; 601-792-4204; fax: 601-792-2894; 8-5PM. ***Probate, Civil Land, Divorce, Family.***

Jones County

Circuit & County Court - 1st District 101 N. Court St., #B, Ellisville, MS 39437; 601-477-8538; fax: 601-477-8539; 8AM-5PM. ***Felony, Misdemeanor, Civil (usually over $3,500).***
Civil Records: Access: Mail, fax, in person, online. Visitors must perform in person searches themselves. Search fee: $10.00. Required to search: name, years to search. Civil cases indexed by defendant, plaintiff; index on docket books since 1960s. Mail turnaround time 1-2 days. Access the circuit court judgment roll free at www.deltacomputersystems.com/MS/MS34/INDEX.HTML.
Criminal Records: Access: Mail, fax, in person. Both court and visitors may perform in person searches. Search fee: $10.00 per name. Required to search: name, years to search. Criminal docket on books since 1960s. Mail turnaround time 1-2 days.
General Information: No sealed, adoptions, mental health, juvenile, sex, or expunged records released. Will fax documents to local or toll free line. Court makes copy: $1.00 per page. Self serve: $.25 per page. Certification fee: $2.00. Payee: Circuit Clerk. Personal checks accepted; credit cards are not. Mail requests: SASE required.

Circuit & County Court - 2nd District PO Box 1336, Laurel, MS 39441; 601-425-2556; fax: 601-399-4774; 8AM-5PM. ***Felony, Misdemeanor, Civil (usually over $3,500).***
www.co.jones.ms.us
Civil Records: Access: In person, online. Visitors must perform in person searches themselves. Required to search: name, years to search. Civil cases indexed by defendant, plaintiff; index on docket books since 1960s. Civil PAT goes back to 2003. Access the circuit court judgment roll free at www.deltacomputersystems.com/MS/MS34/INDEX.HTML.
Criminal Records: Access: Mail, in person. Both court and visitors may perform in person searches. Search fee: $10.00 per name. Fee is per district. Required to search: name, years to search; also helpful: SSN. Criminal docket on books since 1960s. Mail turnaround time 2 days. Criminal PAT goes back to 2003.
General Information: No sealed or Juvenile Youth Court records released. Will fax documents to local or toll free line. Court makes copy: $1.00 per page. Self serve: $.25 per page. Certification fee: $1.50. Payee: Jones County Circuit Clerk. Personal checks accepted; credit cards are not. Mail requests: SASE required for criminal.

Justice Court PO Box 1997, 402 Central Ave, Laurel, MS 39441; 601-428-3137; fax: 601-428-0526; 8AM-5PM. ***Misdemeanor, Civil Actions under $3,500, Eviction, Small Claims.***
This Justice Court houses all the Justices for Jones County.

Ellisville Chancery Court 101 N Court St. #D, PO Box 248, Ellisville, MS 39437; 601-477-3307; fax: 601-477-1240; 8-5. ***Probate, Divorce, Family.***

Laurel Chancery Court PO Box 1468, 415 N 5th Ave, Laurel, MS 39441; 601-428-3182, 601-428-0527; probate phone: 602-428-3182; fax: 601-428-3610; 8AM-5PM. ***Probate, Divorce, Family.***

Kemper County

Circuit Court PO Box 130, De Kalb, MS 39328; 601-743-2224; fax: 601-743-4173; 8AM-5PM. ***Felony, Civil (usually over $3,500).***
Civil Records: Access: Phone, fax, mail, in person. Both court and visitors may perform in person searches. Search fee: $10.00 per name. Required to search: name, years to search, address. Civil cases

indexed by defendant, plaintiff; index on docket books since 1960s, archived since 1912. Mail turnaround time 1 week.
Criminal Records: Access: Fax, mail, in person. Both court and visitors may perform in person searches. Search fee: $10.00 per name. Required to search: name, years to search, address, DOB; also helpful: SSN. Criminal docket on books since 1960s, archived since 1912. Mail turnaround time 1 week.
General Information: No sealed, adoptions, mental health, juvenile, sex, or expunged records released. Will fax documents $.25 per page. Court makes copy: $.50 per page. Self serve: $.25 per page. Certification fee: $1.00 per page. Payee: Circuit Clerk. Business checks accepted. No credit cards accepted. Mail requests: SASE requested.

Justice Court PO Box 661, Courthouse, Hwy 39, Main St, De Kalb, MS 39328; 601-743-2793; fax: 601-743-4893; 8AM-5PM. ***Misdemeanor, Civil Actions under $3,500, Eviction, Small Claims.***

Chancery Court PO Box 188, Main St Courthouse, De Kalb, MS 39328; 601-743-2460; fax: 601-743-2789; 8AM-5PM. ***Probate, Civil Land, Divorce, Family.***

Lafayette County

Circuit Court LaFayette County Courthouse, One Courthouse Sq, #201, Oxford, MS 38655; 662-234-4951; fax: 662-236-0238; 8AM-5PM. ***Felony, Civil (usually over $3,500).***
Civil Records: Access: Mail, in person. Both court and visitors may perform in person searches. Search fee: $10.00 per name. Fee is per 10 years searched. Required to search: name, years to search; also helpful: address. Civil cases indexed by defendant, plaintiff; index in docket books from 1900; on computer back to 1997. Mail turnaround time next day. Civil PAT goes back to 1997.
Criminal Records: Access: Mail, in person. Both court and visitors may perform in person searches. Search fee: $10.00 per name. Fee is per 10 years searched. Required to search: name, years to search, DOB; also helpful: address, SSN. Criminal docket on books from 1900, on computer back to 1995. Mail turnaround time 1-2 days. Criminal PAT goes back to 1995; results show middle initial, DOB, SSN.
General Information: No sealed, adoptions, mental health, juvenile, or expunged records released. Will fax documents to local or toll free line. Court makes copy: $1.00 per page. Self serve: $.25 per page. Certification fee: $1.50. Payee: Circuit Clerk. Business checks accepted. No credit cards accepted.

Justice Court 713 Jackson Ave, Oxford, MS 38655; 662-234-1545; fax: 662-238-7990; 8AM-5PM. ***Misdemeanor, Civil Actions under $3,500, Eviction, Small Claims.***

Chancery Court PO Box 1240, 300 N Lamar Blvd, Oxford, MS 38655; 662-234-2131; fax: 662-234-5038; 8AM-5PM. ***Probate, Civil Land, Divorce, Family.*** www.lafayettecoms.com/HTML/Main.html?Chancery%20Court%20Page

Lamar County

Circuit Court PO Box 369, Purvis, MS 39475; 601-794-8504; fax: 601-794-3905; 8AM-5PM. ***Felony, Civil (usually over $3,500).***
Civil Records: Access: Mail, in person. Both court and visitors may perform in person searches. Search fee: $10.00 per name. Required to search: name, years to search. Civil cases indexed by defendant, plaintiff; index on docket books since 1904. Mail turnaround time 1-2 days.
Criminal Records: Access: Mail, in person. Both court and visitors may perform in person searches. Search fee: $10.00 per name. Required to search: name, years to search; also helpful: SSN. Criminal docket on books since 1904. Mail turnaround time 1-2 days.
General Information: No sealed, adoptions, mental health, juvenile, sex, or expunged records released. Will not fax documents. Court makes copy: $1.00 per page. Self serve: $.25 per page. No certification fee. Payee: Circuit Clerk. Business checks & major credit cards accepted. Mail requests: SASE requested.

Justice Court PO Box 1010, 205 Main St, #A, Purvis, MS 39475; 601-794-2950; fax: 601-794-1076; 8AM-5PM. ***Misdemeanor, Civil Actions under $3,500, Eviction, Small Claims.***

Chancery Court PO Box 247, 403 Main St, Purvis, MS 39475; 601-794-8504; fax: 601-794-3903; 8-5PM. ***Probate, Civil Land, Divorce, Family.***

Lauderdale County

Circuit & County Court PO Box 1005, Meridian, MS 39302-1005; 601-482-9738; fax: 601-484-3970; 8AM-5PM. ***Felony, Civil (usually over $3,500).*** County Court phone is 601-482-9715.
Civil Records: Access: Phone, mail, fax, in person. Both court and visitors may perform in person searches. Search fee: $10.00 per name. Required to search: name, years to search, SSN. Civil cases indexed by defendant, plaintiff; index on docket books back to 1950s, on computer back to 1992. Court will only search computer records. Mail turnaround 1 week. Civil PAT goes back to 1992.
Criminal Records: Access: Mail, fax, in person. Both court and visitors may perform in person searches. Search fee: $10.00 per name. Required to search: name, years to search, DOB; also helpful: SSN. Criminal records on computer (Felony) back to 1965. Mail turnaround 1 week, phone turnaround 1 week. Criminal PAT goes back to 1965.
General Information: No sealed, adoptions, mental health, juvenile, sex, or expunged records released. Will fax documents to local or toll-free number. Court makes copy: $.50 per page. Self serve: $.25 per page. No certification fee. Payee: Circuit Clerk. Business checks accepted. No credit cards. Will bill complete files to attorneys. Mail requests: SASE requested.

Justice Court PO Box 5126, Meridian, MS 39302; 601-482-9879; fax: 601-482-9813; 8AM-5PM. ***Misdemeanor, Civil Actions under $3,500, Eviction, Small Claims, Traffic.*** Physical Address: 410 Constitution Ave, 6th Fl, Meridian, MS 39301.

Chancery Court PO Box 1587, 500 Constitution Ave, #105, Meridian, MS 39302; 601-482-9701; fax: 601-486-4921; 8AM-5PM. ***Probate, Civil Land, Divorce, Family.***

Lawrence County

Circuit Court PO Box 1249, Monticello, MS 39654; 601-587-4791; fax: 601-587-4405; civil 8AM-5PM. ***Felony, Civil (usually over $3,500).***
Civil Records: Access: Phone, fax, mail, in person. Both court and visitors may perform in person searches. Search fee: $10.00 per name. Required to search: name, years to search; also helpful: address. Civil cases indexed by defendant, plaintiff; index on docket books since late 1970's. Note: For fax request, fax copy of check for fee. Mail turnaround time 1 week.
Criminal Records: Access: Phone, fax, mail, in person. Both court and visitors may perform in person searches. Search fee: $10.00 per name. Required to search: name, years to search, DOB; also helpful: address, SSN. Criminal docket on books since late 1970's. Note: In fax request send copy of payment check Mail turnaround time 1 week, phone turnaround 1-2 days.
General Information: No sealed, adoptions, mental health, juvenile, sex, or expunged records released. Will fax documents $10.00 per doc. Court makes copy: $1.00 per page. Self serve: none. Cert fee: $1.50. Payee: Circuit Clerk. Personal checks accepted; credit cards are not. Mail requests: SASE helpful.

Justice Court PO Box 903, 435 Brinson St, Monticello, MS 39654; 601-587-7183, 587-4854; civil phone: 601-587-4854/7183; fax: 601-587-0755; 8AM-5PM. ***Misdemeanor, Civil Actions under $3,500, Eviction, Small Claims.***

Chancery Court PO Box 821, 517 E Broad St, Courthouse Sq, Monticello, MS 39654; 601-587-7162; fax: 601-587-0767; 8AM-5PM. ***Probate, Civil Land, Divorce, Family.***

Leake County

Circuit Court PO Box 67, Carthage, MS 39051; 601-267-8357; fax: 601-267-8889; 8AM-5PM. ***Felony, Civil (usually over $3,500).***
Civil Records: Access: In person only. Visitors must perform in person searches themselves. Required to search: name, years to search. Civil cases indexed by defendant, plaintiff; index on docket books since 1970s. Public use terminal has civil records. Public terminal has voting and Judgments only.
Criminal Records: Access: Mail, in person. Both court and visitors may perform in person searches. Search fee: $10.00 per name. Required to search: name, years to search, DOB; also helpful: SSN. Criminal docket on books since 1977. Mail turnaround time 1-2 days.
General Information: No sealed, adoptions, mental health, juvenile, sex, or expunged records released. Court makes copy: $1.00 per page. Self serve: $.25 per page. Certification fee: $1.50. Payee: Circuit Clerk. No credit cards accepted. Mail requests: SASE required for criminal.

Justice Court PO Box 69, 121 W Main St, Carthage, MS 39051; 601-267-5677; fax: 601-267-6134; 8AM-5PM. ***Misdemeanor, Civil Actions under $3,500, Eviction, Small Claims.***

Chancery Court PO Box 72, County Courthouse, Court Sq, Carthage, MS 39051; 601-267-7371/72; fax: 601-267-6137; 8AM-5PM. ***Probate, Civil Land, Divorce, Family.*** www.co.leake.ms.us Records also include divorce, custody, land disputes, mental and drug commitments.

Lee County

Circuit & County Court PO Box 762, Circuit Court, Tupelo, MS 38802; 662-841-9022/9023(Circuit) 9730 (County); fax: 662-680-6089; 8AM-5PM. ***Felony, Civil (usually over $3,500).*** Mailing address for County Court - PO Box 736. The courts are separate.
Civil Records: Access: Mail, in person. Both court and visitors may perform in person searches. Search fee: $10.00 per name. Required to search: name, years to search. Civil cases indexed by defendant, plaintiff. Circuit records on computer since 1990, others on docket books since 1987. County records not on computer. Mail turnaround time 1-2 days. Civil PAT goes back to 2003.
Criminal Records: Access: Mail, in person. Both court and visitors may perform in person searches. Search fee: $10.00 per name. Required to search: name, years to search; also helpful: DOB, SSN. Circuit records on computer since 1990, others on docket books since 1987. County records not on computer. Mail turnaround time 1-2 days. Criminal PAT goes back to same as civil.
General Information: No sealed or expunged records released. Will not fax documents. Court makes copy: $.25 per page. Certification fee: $3.00. Payee: Lee County & Circuit Court. Business checks accepted. No credit cards accepted. Mail requests: SASE required.

Justice Court PO Box 108, 331 N Broadway St, Tupelo, MS 38802; 662-841-9014; fax: 662-680-6021; 8-11:30AM, 12:30-5PM. ***Misdemeanor, Civil Actions under $3,500, Eviction, Small Claims.***

Chancery Court PO Box 7127, 200 W Jefferson, Tupelo, MS 38802; 662-841-9100; fax: 662-680-6091; 8-5PM. ***Probate, Civil Land, Divorce, Family.***

Leflore County

Circuit & County Court PO Box 1953, 310 W Market, Greenwood, MS 38935-1953; 662-453-1435; criminal fax: 662-455-1278; civil fax: same; 8AM-5PM. ***Felony, Civil (usually over $3,500).***
Civil Records: Access: Phone, fax, mail, in person, online. Both court and visitors may perform in person searches. Search fee: $10.00 per name. Required to search: name, years to search. Civil cases indexed by defendant, plaintiff, on computer index goes back 10 years; prior records on docket books since mid-1800s. Mail turnaround time 1-2 days. Civil PAT goes back to 10 years. A private company permits online access to civil records

back to 2004; go to www.recordsusa.com or call Rob at 888-633-4748 x17 for info and demo.
Criminal Records: Access: Fax, mail, in person. Both court and visitors may perform in person searches. Search fee: $10.00 per name. Required to search: name, years to search; also helpful: DOB, SSN. Criminal records on computer index goes back 10 years; prior records on docket books since mid-1800s. Mail turnaround time 1-2 days. Criminal PAT goes back to same as civil.
General Information: No sealed or expunged records released. Call for fax fee. Court makes copy: $1.00 per page. Self serve: $.50 per page. Certification fee: $2.00. Payee: Circuit Clerk. Personal checks accepted; credit cards are not.

Justice Court PO Box 8056, 3600 CR 540 - Baldwin Rd, Greenwood, MS 38935; 662-453-1605; fax: 662-455-8759; 8AM-5PM. ***Misdemeanor, Civil Actions under $3,500, Eviction, Small Claims.***

Chancery Court PO Box 1579, 310 W Market St, County Courthouse, Greenwood, MS 38935-1579; 662-453-1432; fax: 662-455-7959; 8AM-5PM. ***Probate, Civil Land, Divorce, Family.*** www.7chancerycourt.com/

Lincoln County

Circuit Court PO Box 357, Brookhaven, MS 39602; 601-835-3435; fax: 601-835-3482; 8AM-5PM. ***Felony, Civil (usually over $3,500).***
Civil Records: Access: Mail, in person. Both court and visitors may perform in person searches. Search fee: $10.00 per name. Required to search: name, years to search. Civil cases indexed by defendant, plaintiff, on computer since 1986, prior on docket books. Mail turnaround time 1-2 days. Civil PAT goes back to 1982.
Criminal Records: Access: Mail, in person. Both court and visitors may perform in person searches. Search fee: $10.00 per name. Required to search: name, years to search; also helpful: DOB, SSN. Criminal records on computer since 1982, prior on docket books. Mail turnaround time 1-2 days. Criminal PAT goes back to same as civil.
General Information: No sealed or expunged records released. Will fax documents $10.00 per doc. Court makes copy: $1.00 per page. Self serve: $.50 per page. Certification fee: $1.00 per page includes copy. Payee: Circuit Clerk. Personal checks accepted. Out of state checks not accepted. Visa/MC accepted.

Justice Court PO Box 767, Brookhaven, MS 39602; 601-835-3474; fax: 601-835-3494; 8AM-5PM. ***Misdemeanor, Civil Actions under $3,500, Eviction, Small Claims.*** Physical Address: 308 S. 2nd St, Brookhaven, MS 39601

Chancery Court PO Box 555, 300 S First St, Brookhaven, MS 39602; 601-835-3412; fax: 601-835-3423; 8AM-5PM. ***Probate, Civil Land, Divorce, Family.*** www.15thchancerydistrictms.org

Lowndes County

Circuit & County Court PO Box 31, Columbus, MS 39703; 662-329-5900; 8AM-5PM. ***Felony, Civil (usually over $3,500).***
Civil Records: Access: Mail, in person. Both court and visitors may perform in person searches. Search fee: $10.00 per name. Required to search: name, years to search. Civil cases indexed by defendant, plaintiff, on computer from 2/94, on docket books from 1900s. Mail turnaround time 7 to 14 days. Civil PAT goes back to 1996.
Criminal Records: Access: Mail, in person. Both court and visitors may perform in person searches. Search fee: $10.00 per name. Required to search: name, years to search, DOB; also helpful: SSN. Criminal records on computer since 11/93; prior on docket books. Mail turnaround time 14 days. Criminal PAT goes back to 1993.
General Information: No sealed, adoption, mental health, juvenile, sex or expunged cases released. Will fax documents to local or toll free line. Court makes copy: $1.00 per page. Self serve: No self serve criminal copier; Civil self serve- $.25 each. Certification fee: $1.00. Payee: Clerk of Court. Personal checks accepted; credit cards are not. Mail requests: SASE required.

Justice Court 11 Airline Rd, Columbus, MS 39702; 662-329-5929; fax: 662-245-4619; 8AM-5PM. ***Misdemeanor, Civil Actions under $3,500, Eviction, Small Claims.***

Chancery Court PO Box 684, 505 S 2nd Ave North, Columbus, MS 39703; 662-329-5800; 8AM-5PM. ***Probate, Civil Land, Divorce, Family.***

Madison County

Circuit & County Court PO Box 1626, Canton, MS 39046; 601-859-4365; fax: 601-859-8555; 8AM-5PM. ***Felony, Civil (usually over $3,500).***
Civil Records: Access: Phone, fax, mail, in person. Both court and visitors may perform in person searches. No search fee. Required to search: name, years to search. Civil cases indexed by defendant, plaintiff, on computer since 1987, prior on docket books since 1950. Mail turnaround time 1 week. Civil PAT goes back to 1989. PAT civil results show middle initial.
Criminal Records: Access: Mail, in person. Both court and visitors may perform in person searches. Search fee: $10.00 per name. Required to search: name, years to search. Criminal records on computer since 1992, prior on docket books since 1945. Mail turnaround time 1 week. Criminal PAT goes back to 1984. PAT results show middle initial, DOB. Terminal results include SSN.
General Information: No sealed, adoptions, mental health, juvenile, sex, or expunged records released. Will fax documents to local or toll free line. Court makes copy: $.50 per page. Self serve: $.25 per page. Certification fee: $1.50. Payee: Circuit Clerk. Personal checks accepted; credit cards are not. Mail requests: SASE requested.

Justice Court 2961 N Liberty Street, Canton, MS 39046; 601-859-6337; fax: 601-859-5878; 8AM-5PM. ***Misdemeanor, Civil Actions under $3,500, Eviction, Small Claims.***
Request for history must be in writing with a $6.00 fee made out to Madison County Justice Court.

Chancery Court PO Box 404, 146 W Center St, Canton, MS 39046; 601-859-1177; fax: 601-855-5759; 8AM-5PM. ***Probate, Civil Land, Divorce, Family.*** Search chancery cases free at www.madison-co.com/elected_offices/chancery_clerk/court_house_search/case_file_inquiry.php, also docket descriptions www.madison-co.com/elected_offices/chancery_clerk/court_house_search/search_docket_descriptions.php.

Marion County

Circuit Court 250 Broad St, #1, Columbia, MS 39429; 601-736-8246; fax: 601-731-6344; 8AM-5PM. ***Felony, Civil (usually over $3,500).***
Civil Records: Access: Mail, in person. Both court and visitors may perform in person searches. Search fee: $10.00 per name. Required to search: name, years to search. Civil cases indexed by defendant, plaintiff; index on docket books since 1800s. Mail turnaround time 3 days.
Criminal Records: Access: Mail, in person, fax. Both court and visitors may perform in person searches. Search fee: $10.00 per name. Required to search: name, years to search; also helpful: SSN. Criminal docket on books since 1800s. Mail turnaround time 1-2 days.
General Information: No sealed, adoptions, mental health, juvenile, sex, or expunged records released. Will fax documents to local or toll free line. Court makes copy: $.50 per page. Self serve: $.25 per page. No certification fee. Payee: Circuit Clerk. Personal checks accepted; credit cards are not. Mail requests: SASE required.

Justice Court 500 Courthouse Square #2, Columbia, MS 39429; 601-736-2572; fax: 601-731-3781; 8AM-5PM. ***Misdemeanor, Civil Actions under $3,500, Eviction, Small Claims.***

Chancery Court 250 Broad St, #2, Columbia, MS 39429; 601-444-0205; civil phone: 601-736-2691; fax: 601-444-0206; 8AM-5PM. ***Probate, Civil Land, Divorce, Family.*** Court records and calendars online at www.deltacomputersystems.com/MS/MS46/INDEX.html.

Marshall County

Circuit Court PO Box 459, 128 E Vandorn Ave, Holly Springs, MS 38635; 662-252-3434; fax: 662-252-5951; 8-5. ***Felony, Civil (usually over $3,500).*** Fax requests- include copy of payment check.
Civil Records: Access: Fax, mail, in person. Both court and visitors may perform in person searches. Search fee: $10.00 per name. Required to search: name, years to search. Civil cases indexed by defendant, plaintiff; index on docket books since 1960s; computerized records go back to 1999. Mail turnaround 1-2 days. Civil PAT goes back to 1999.
Criminal Records: Access: Fax, mail, in person, fax. Both court and visitors may perform in person searches. Search fee: $10.00 per name. Required to search: name, years to search; also helpful: DOB, SSN. Criminal docket on books since 1960s; computerized records go back to 1999. Mail turnaround time 1-2 days. Criminal PAT goes back to same as civil.
General Information: No sealed or expunged records released. No fee to fax back document; prepay or fax copy of your search fee check. Court makes copy: $1.00 per page. Self serve: $.50 per page. Certification fee: $3.50 per cert. Payee: Circuit Court Clerk. Personal checks accepted; credit cards are not. Mail requests: SASE requested.

Justice Court - North & South Districts PO Box 729, 819 West St, Holly Springs, MS 38635; 662-252-3585; fax: 662-252-0028; 8AM-5PM. ***Misdemeanor, Civil Actions under $3,500, Eviction, Small Claims.***

Chancery Court PO Box 219, 128 E Van Dorn, Court Sq, Holly Springs, MS 38635; 662-252-4431; fax: 662-551-3302; 8AM-5PM. ***Probate, Civil Land, Divorce, Family.***

Monroe County

Circuit Court PO Box 843, Aberdeen, MS 39730; 662-369-2732; fax: 662-319-5993; 8AM-5PM. ***Felony, Civil (usually over $3,500).***
Civil Records: Access: In person only. Visitors must perform in person searches themselves. Required to search: name, years to search; also helpful: address. Civil cases indexed by defendant, plaintiff; index on docket books since 1821. Civil PAT goes back to 2002. PAT results show name only.
Criminal Records: Access: In person only. Visitors must perform in person searches themselves. Required to search: name, years to search, DOB; also helpful: address, SSN. Criminal docket on books since 1821. Criminal PAT goes back to 2002. PAT results show name only.
General Information: No sealed, adoptions, mental health, juvenile, sex, or expunged records released. Will not fax out case files. Court makes copy: $1.00 per page. Self serve: $.25 per page. Certification fee: $3.00. Payee: Monroe County Circuit Clerk. Only cashiers checks and money orders accepted. No credit cards accepted.

Justice Court PO Box 518, 1619 Hwy 25 N, Amory, MS 38821; 662-256-8493; fax: 662-256-7876; 8AM-5PM. ***Misdemeanor, Civil Actions under $3,500, Eviction, Small Claims.***
Aberdeen Justice Court Dist. 2 is closed; records here.

Chancery Court PO Box 578, 201 W Commerce St, Aberdeen, MS 39730; 662-369-8143; fax: 662-369-7928; 8AM-5PM. ***Probate, Civil Land, Divorce, Family.***

Montgomery County

Circuit Court PO Box 765, Winona, MS 38967; 662-283-4161; fax: 662-283-3363; 8AM-5PM. ***Felony, Civil (usually over $3,500).***
Civil Records: Access: Mail, in person. Both court and visitors may perform in person searches. Search fee: $10.00 per name. Required to search: name, years to search. Civil cases indexed by defendant, plaintiff; index on docket books since early 1900s. Mail turnaround time 1-2 days.
Criminal Records: Access: Mail, in person. Both court and visitors may perform in person searches. Search fee: $10.00 per name. Required to search:

name, years to search. Criminal docket on books since early 1900s. Mail turnaround time 1-2 days.
General Information: No sealed or expunged records released. Will fax documents to local or toll free line. Court makes copy: $1.00 per page. Self serve: $.25 per page. Certification fee: $2.00. Payee: Circuit Clerk. Personal checks accepted; credit cards are not. Mail requests: SASE required.

Justice Court PO Box 229, 614 Summit St, Winona, MS 38967; 662-283-2290; fax: 662-283-2052; 8AM-5PM. ***Misdemeanor, Civil Actions under $3,500, Eviction, Small Claims.***

Chancery Court PO Box 71, 614 Summit St, Winona, MS 38967; 662-283-2333; fax: 662-283-2233; 8-5PM. ***Probate, Civil Land, Divorce, Family.***

Neshoba County

Circuit Court 401 E Beacon St #110, Philadelphia, MS 39350; 601-656-4781; fax: 601-650-3997; 8AM-5PM. ***Felony, Civil (usually over $3,500).***
Civil Records: Access: Mail, in person. Both court and visitors may perform in person searches. Search fee: $10.00 per name. Required to search: name, years to search. Civil cases indexed by defendant. Civil records in-house back 10 years; indexed back 50 years. Mail turnaround 1-2 days. Public terminal has civil records back to 1993.
Criminal Records: Access: Mail, in person. Both court and visitors may perform in person searches. Search fee: $10.00 per name. Required to search: name, years to search, DOB; also helpful: SSN. Criminal records in-house back 20 years; on docket books back 50 years. Mail turnaround 1-2 days.
General Information: No sealed, adoptions, mental health, juvenile, sex, or expunged records released. Will fax out documents. Court makes copy: $1.00 per page. Certification fee: $2.00. Payee: Circuit Clerk. Business checks accepted. No credit cards accepted. Mail requests: SASE requested.

Justice Court 200 Byrd Ave, Philadelphia, MS 39350; 601-656-5361/1101; fax: 601-656-6482; 8AM-5PM. ***Misdemeanor, Civil Actions under $3,500, Eviction, Small Claims.***

Chancery Ct 401 Beacon St #107, Philadelphia, MS 39350; 601-656-3581; fax: 601-656-5915; 8AM-5PM. ***Probate, Civil Land, Divorce, Family.***

Newton County

Circuit Court PO Box 447, Decatur, MS 39327; 601-635-2368; fax: 601-635-3210; 8AM-5PM. ***Felony, Civil (usually over $3,500).***
Civil Records: Access: Mail, in person. Both court and visitors may perform in person searches. Search fee: $10.00 per name. Required to search: name, years to search. Civil cases indexed by defendant, plaintiff; index on docket books since 1968. Mail turnaround time same day. Civil PAT goes back to 2003; results show middle initial.
Criminal Records: Access: Mail, in person. Both court and visitors may perform in person searches. Search fee: $10.00 per name. Required to search: name, years to search, DOB; also helpful: SSN. Criminal docket on books since 1968. Mail turnaround time same day. Criminal PAT goes back to same as civil. PAT criminal results show middle initial. Some terminal results do no include full name.
General Information: No sealed, adoptions, mental health, juvenile, sex, or expunged records released. Will fax documents to local or toll free line. Court makes copy: $.50 per page. Self serve: $.25 per page. Certification fee: $1.50 per cert. Payee: Circuit Court. Personal checks accepted; credit cards are not. Mail requests: SASE required.

Justice Court PO Box 69, 11 4th Ave, Decatur, MS 39327; 601-635-2740; fax: 601-635-4047; 8AM-5PM. ***Misdemeanor, Civil Actions under $3,500, Eviction, Small Claims.***

Chancery Clerk Office PO Box 68, 92 W Broad St, Decatur, MS 39327; 601-635-2367; civil phone: 601-635-3370; fax: 601-635-3479; 8AM-5PM. ***Probate, Divorce, Family.***

Noxubee County

Circuit Court PO Box 431, Macon, MS 39341; 662-726-5737; fax: 662-726-6041; 8AM-5PM. ***Felony, Civil (usually over $3,500).***
Civil Records: Access: Mail, fax, in person. Both court and visitors may perform in person searches. Search fee: $10.00 per name. Required to search: name, years to search. Civil cases indexed by defendant. Civil index on docket books since 1800s. Mail turnaround time 1 week. Civil PAT goes back to 1970.
Criminal Records: Access: Mail, fax, in person. Both court and visitors may perform in person searches. Search fee: $10.00 per name. Required to search: name, years to search; also helpful: SSN. Criminal docket on books since 1800s. Mail turnaround 1 week. Criminal PAT back to 1965.
General Information: No sealed, adoptions, mental health, juvenile, sex, or expunged records released. Will not fax documents. Court makes copy: $.50 per page. Self serve: $.25 per page. Certification fee: $5.00. Payee: Circuit Clerk. Business checks accepted. No credit cards accepted. Mail requests: SASE required.

Justice Court - North & South Districts 507 S Jefferson, PO Box 550, Macon, MS 39341; 662-726-5834; fax: 662-726-2944; 8AM-5PM. ***Misdemeanor, Civil Actions under $3,500, Eviction, Small Claims.***

Chancery Court PO Box 147, County Courthouse, 505 S Jefferson St, Macon, MS 39341; 662-726-4243; fax: 662-726-2272; 8AM-5PM. ***Probate, Civil Land, Divorce, Family.***

Oktibbeha County

Circuit Court 108 W Main, #118, Starkville, MS 39759; 662-323-1400, 662-323-1356; fax: 662-323-1121; 8-5. ***Felony, Civil (usually over $3,500).*** www.oktibbehacountyms.org/circuit_clerk/index.htm
Civil Records: Access: Mail, fax, in person, online. Both court and visitors may perform in person searches. Search fee: $10.00 per name. Required to search: name, years to search; also helpful: address. Civil cases indexed by defendant, plaintiff; index on docket books since 1938. Mail turnaround time 1 week. Civil PAT goes back to 1990. Access the county civil circuit records back to 1997 free at www.deltacomputersystems.com/MS/MS53/mclinkquerycc.html. Access the county judgment roll free at www.deltacomputersystems.com/MS/MS53/jrlinkquerym.html.
Criminal Records: Access: Mail, fax, in person, online. Both court and visitors may perform in person searches. Search fee: $10.00 per name. Required to search: name, years to search; also helpful: DOB, SSN. Criminal records on docket since 1950. Mail turnaround time 1 week. Criminal PAT goes back to 1997. Access the county criminal circuit records back to 1997 free at www.deltacomputersystems.com/MS/MS53/mclinkquerycr.html.
General Information: No sealed, adoptions, mental health, juvenile, sex, or expunged records released. Will fax out documents no fee. Court makes copy: $1.00 per page. Self serve: $.25 per page. Certification fee: $1.50. Payee: Circuit Clerk. No personal checks or credit cards accepted. Mail requests: SASE required.

Justice Court - Districts 1-3 104 Felix Long Dr, Starkville, MS 39759; 662-324-3032; criminal phone: 662-324-3040; fax: 662-338-1078; 8AM-5PM. ***Misdemeanor, Civil Actions under $3,500, Eviction, Small Claims.***

Chancery Court Courthouse, 101 E Main, Starkville, MS 39759; 662-323-5834; civil phone: same; probate phone: same; fax: 662-338-1064; 8AM-5PM. ***Probate, Civil Land, Divorce, Family.*** www.oktibbehachanceryclerk.com/index.php

Panola County

Circuit Court - 1st District 215 S Pocahontas St, Sardis, MS 38666; 662-487-2073; fax: 662-487-3595; 8-5. ***Felony, Civil (usually over $3,500).***
Civil Records: Access: Fax, mail, in person. Both court and visitors may perform in person searches. Search fee: $10.00 per name. Fee is for each district searched. Required to search: name, years to search. Civil cases indexed by defendant, plaintiff; index on docket books since 1970s, archived since 1925. Mail turnaround time 1-2 days.
Criminal Records: Access: Fax, mail, in person. Both court and visitors may perform in person searches. Search fee: $10.00 per name. Fee is for each district searched. Required to search: name, years to search, DOB; also helpful: SSN. Criminal docket on books since 1970, archived since 1925, records are not computerized. Mail turnaround time 1-2 days.
General Information: No sealed, adoptions, mental health, juvenile, sex, or expunged records released. No fee to fax documents. Prepay or fax copy of your search fee check. Court makes copy: $1.00 per page criminal; Civil $.50 per page. Self serve: $.50 per page criminal; Civil self serve- $.25 each. Certification fee: $1.50. Payee: Circuit Clerk. Business checks accepted. No credit cards accepted. Mail requests: SASE required.

Circuit Court - 2nd District PO Box 346, 151 Public Sq, Batesville, MS 38606; 662-563-6210; fax: 662-563-8233; 8AM-5PM. ***Felony, Civil (usually over $3,500).***
Civil Records: Access: Phone, fax, mail, in person. Both court and visitors may perform in person searches. Search fee: $10.00 per name. Fee is per district. Required to search: name, years to search. Civil cases indexed by defendant, plaintiff, on computer go back to 2004, Civil records on docket books since 1900. Mail turnaround time same day.
Criminal Records: Access: Fax, mail, in person. Both court and visitors may perform in person searches. Search fee: $10.00 per name. Fee is per district. Required to search: name, years to search, address, DOB; also helpful: SSN. Criminal records on computer go back to 2004, Criminal records on docket books since 1900. Mail turnaround time same day.
General Information: No sealed, adoptions, mental health, juvenile, sex, or expunged records released. Will fax documents $1.00 per page. Court makes copy: $1.00 per page criminal; Civil $.50 per page. Self serve: $.25 per page. Certification fee: $1.50 per cert. Payee: Circuit Clerk's Office. Personal checks accepted; credit cards are not. Mail requests: SASE required.

Justice Court PO Box 249, 215 S Pocahontas, Sardis, MS 38666; 662-487-2080; criminal phone: 662-487-2080; civil phone: 662-487-2082; fax: 662-487-2008; 8AM-5PM. ***Misdemeanor, Civil Actions under $3,500, Eviction, Small Claims.*** This Justice Court houses all the Justices for Panola County.

Panola County Chancery Clerk 151 Public Square, Batesville, MS 38606; 662-563-6205; fax: 662-563-6277; 8-5. ***Probate, Divorce, Family.***

Sardis Chancery Court 215 S Pocahontas St, Sardis, MS 38666; 662-487-2070; fax: 662-487-3559; 8AM-N, 1-5PM. ***Probate, Divorce, Family.***

Pearl River County

Circuit Court Courthouse, Poplarville, MS 39470; 601-403-2300; criminal phone: x323; civil phone: Ext 324; fax: 601-403-2327; 8AM-5PM. ***Felony, Civil (usually over $3,500).*** www.pearlrivercounty.net/circuit/index.htm
Civil Records: Access: Mail, fax, in person. Both court and visitors may perform in person searches. Search fee: $10.00 per name. Required to search: name, years to search, DOB, SSN. Civil cases indexed by defendant, plaintiff; index on docket books since 1890. Mail turnaround time 1-2 days. Civil PAT goes back to 2003. PAT civil results show middle initial.
Criminal Records: Access: Mail, fax, in person. Both court and visitors may perform in person searches. Search fee: $10.00 per name. Required to search: name, years to search. Criminal records on computer since late 1960s, prior on docket books since 1890. Mail turnaround time 1-2 days. Criminal PAT goes back to same as civil. PAT

results show middle initial; DOB and SSN shown only if provided by the arresting agency.
General Information: No sealed, adoptions, mental health, juvenile, sex, or expunged records released. Will fax documents to local or toll free line. Court makes copy: $1.00 per page. Self serve: $.50 per page. Certification fee: $2.50. Payee: Circuit Clerk. Personal checks accepted; credit cards are not. SASE not required.

Justice Ct - Northern, SE & SW Districts 169 Savannah Millard Rd, Ste A, Poplarville, MS 39470; 601-403-2500; fax: 601-403-2553; 8AM-5PM. ***Misdemeanor, Civil Actions under $3,500, Eviction, Small Claims.*** www.pearlrivercounty.net/

Chancery Court PO Box 431, 200 S Main St, Poplarville, MS 39470; 601-403-2300 X316; fax: 601-403-2317; 8AM-5PM. ***Probate, Civil Land, Divorce, Family.*** Search court cases free at www.deltacomputersystems.com/search.html and click on Pearl River.

Perry County

Circuit Court PO Box 198, New Augusta, MS 39462; 601-964-8663; fax: 601-964-8740; 8AM-5PM. ***Felony, Civil (usually over $3,500).***
Civil Records: Access: Mail, fax, in person. Both court and visitors may perform in person searches. Search fee: $10.00 per name. Fee is per 10 years searched. Required to search: name, years to search. Civil cases indexed by defendant, plaintiff; index on docket books since 1980. Mail turnaround 1-2 days.
Criminal Records: Access: Mail, fax, in person. Both court and visitors may perform in person searches. Search fee: $10.00 per name. Fee is per 10 years searched. Required to search: name, years to search, DOB; also helpful: SSN, sex, signed release. Criminal docket on books since 1971; on computer since. Mail turnaround time 1-2 days.
General Information: No sealed, adoptions, mental health, juvenile, sex, or expunged records released. Will fax documents to local or toll free line. Court makes copy: $.50 per page. Self serve: $.25 per page. Certification fee: $2.50 per document. Payee: Circuit Clerk. Personal checks accepted; credit cards are not. Mail requests: SASE required.

Justice Court PO Box 455, 103 1st St W, New Augusta, MS 39462; 601-964-8366; fax: 601-964-8368; 8AM-5PM. ***Misdemeanor, Civil Actions under $3,500, Eviction, Small Claims.*** Civil Actions Limit raised from $2500 to 3500 7/1/2008.

Chancery Court PO Box 198, 103 Main St, New Augusta, MS 39462; 601-964-8398; fax: 601-964-8746; 8-5PM. ***Probate, Civil Land, Divorce, Family.***

Pike County

Circuit & County Court PO Drawer 31, Magnolia, MS 39652; 601-783-2581; fax: 601-783-6322; 8-5. ***Felony, Civil (usually over $3,500).***
Civil Records: Access: Fax, mail, in person. Both court and visitors may perform in person searches. Search fee: $6.00 per name. Required to search: name, years to search. Civil cases indexed by defendant, plaintiff; index on docket books since 1950s; on computer from 2000 to present. Mail turnaround 1-2 days. Civil PAT goes back to 1971.
Criminal Records: Access: Fax, mail, in person. Both court and visitors may perform in person searches. Search fee: $6.00 per name. Required to search: name, years to search, DOB; also helpful: SSN. Criminal docket on books and computerized since 1960s. Mail turnaround time 1-2 days. Criminal PAT goes back to same as civil.
General Information: No sealed, adoptions, mental health, juvenile, sex, or expunged records released. Will fax documents to local or toll-free number. Court makes copy: $1.00 per page, self serve same. Certification fee: $1.50 per cert. Payee: Circuit Clerk. Personal checks accepted; credit cards are not. Mail requests: SASE required.

Justice Court - Divisions 1-3 PO Box 509, 2109 Jesse Hall Memorial Dr, Magnolia, MS 39652; 601-783-5333; fax: 601-783-4181; 8AM-5PM. ***Misdemeanor, Civil Actions under $3,500, Eviction, Small Claims.***

Chancery Court PO Box 309, 175 S Cherry St, Magnolia, MS 39652; 601-783-3362; fax: 601-783-5982; 8-5. ***Probate, Civil Land, Divorce, Family.***

Pontotoc County

Circuit Court PO Box 428, Pontotoc, MS 38863; 662-489-3908; fax: 662-489-2318; 8AM-5PM. ***Felony, Civil (usually over $3,500).***
Civil Records: Access: Mail, in person. Both court and visitors may perform in person searches. Search fee: $5.00 per name. Required to search: name, years to search. Civil cases indexed by defendant, plaintiff, on books from 1849. Mail turnaround 1 week. Civil PAT goes back to 2003.
Criminal Records: Access: Mail, in person. Both court and visitors may perform in person searches. Search fee: $5.00 per name. Required to search: name, years to search, DOB; also helpful: SSN. Criminal docket on books from 1849. Records are not computerized. Mail turnaround time 1 week. Criminal PAT goes back to same as civil.
General Information: No sealed, adoptions, mental health, juvenile, sex, or expunged records released. Will fax documents to local or toll free line. Court makes copy: $.50 per page, self serve same. No cert fee. Payee: Circuit Clerk. No personal checks or credit cards accepted. Mail requests: SASE required.

Justice Court - East & West Districts 29 E Washington St, Pontotoc, MS 38863; 662-489-3920; fax: 662-488-2986; 8-5PM. ***Misdemeanor, Civil Actions under $3,500, Eviction, Small Claims.***

Chancery Court PO Box 209, 34 S Liberty, Pontotoc, MS 38863; 662-489-3900; fax: 662-489-3940; 8-5PM. ***Probate, Civil Land, Divorce, Family.***

Prentiss County

Circuit Court PO Box 727, 101 N Main St, Booneville, MS 38829; 662-728-4611; criminal fax: 662-728-2006; civil fax: same; 8AM-5PM. ***Felony, Civil (usually over $3,500).***
Civil Records: Access: Mail, in person. Both court and visitors may perform in person searches. Search fee: $10.00 per name. Required to search: name, years to search. Civil cases indexed by defendant, plaintiff; index on docket books; judgments only on computer since 1985. Mail turnaround time varies. Public use terminal available, records go back to 2007.
Criminal Records: Access: Fax, mail, in person. Both court and visitors may perform in person searches. Search fee: $10.00 per name. Required to search: name, years to search; also helpful: DOB, SSN. Criminal docket on books. Mail turnaround time varies. Public use terminal available, crim records go back to 2007.
General Information: No sealed, adoptions, mental health, juvenile, sex, or expunged records released. Will fax documents. Court makes copy: $.50 per page. Self serve: $.25 per page. Certification fee: $2.00. Payee: Circuit Clerk. Personal checks accepted; credit cards are not. Mail requests: SASE required.

Justice Court 1901C E Chambers Dr, Booneville, MS 38829; 662-728-8696; civil phone: 662-728-2011; fax: 662-728-2009; 8AM-5PM. ***Misdemeanor, Civil Actions under $3,500, Eviction, Small Claims.***

Chancery Court PO Box 477, 100 N Main St, Booneville, MS 38829; 662-728-8151; fax: 662-728-2007; 8AM-5PM. ***Probate, Civil Land, Divorce, Family.***

Quitman County

Circuit Court Courthouse, 230 Chestnut St, #4, Marks, MS 38646; 662-326-8003; criminal fax: 662-326-8004; civil fax: same; 8AM-5PM. ***Felony, Civil (usually over $3,500).***
Civil Records: Access: Fax, mail, in person. Both court and visitors may perform in person searches. Search fee: $10.00 per name. Required to search: name, years to search. Civil cases indexed by defendant, plaintiff, on books and files since 1890. Mail turnaround 2 days; phone results 10 minutes.
Criminal Records: Access: Fax, mail, in person. Both court and visitors may perform in person searches. Search fee: $10.00 per name. Required to search: name, years to search, DOB; also helpful: SSN. Criminal docket on books and files since 1890. Mail turnaround 2 days; phone results- 10 minutes.
General Information: No sealed, adoptions, mental health, juvenile, sex, or expunged records released. No fax fee when $10.00 has been paid. Court makes copy: $.50 per page. Self serve: $.25 per page. Certification fee: $1.50 per document. Payee: Circuit Clerk. Business checks accepted. No credit cards accepted. SASE not required.

Justice Court - Districts 1 & 2 275 E Main St, Marks, MS 38646; 662-326-2104/7906; fax: 662-326-2330; 8AM-N, 1-5PM. ***Misdemeanor, Civil Actions under $3,500, Eviction, Small Claims.***

Chancery Court 220 Chestnut St, Ste 2, Marks, MS 38646; 662-326-2661; fax: 662-326-8004; 8-N, 1-5PM. ***Probate, Civil Land, Divorce, Family.***

Rankin County

Circuit & County Court PO Drawer 1599, 215 E Government St, Brandon, MS 39043; 601-825-1466; criminal fax: 601-824-2582; civil fax: 601-825-1465; 8AM-5PM. ***Felony, Misdemeanor, Civil (usually over $3,500).*** www.rankincounty.org
Civil Records: Access: Mail, in person. Both court and visitors may perform in person searches. Search fee: $10.00 per name. Required to search: name, years to search. Civil cases indexed by defendant, plaintiff, on computer since 1990, prior on docket books. Mail turnaround time 1-2 days. Civil PAT goes back to 1990.
Criminal Records: Access: Mail, in person. Both court and visitors may perform in person searches. Search fee: $10.00 per name. Required to search: name, years to search; also helpful: DOB, SSN. Criminal records on computer since 1990, prior on docket books. Mail turnaround time 1-2 days. Criminal PAT goes back to same as civil.
General Information: No sealed or expunged records released. Will fax documents to local or toll free line. Court makes copy: $1.00 per page. Self serve: No self serve criminal copier; Civil self serve-$.25 each. Certification fee: $1.50. Payee: Circuit Clerk. Personal checks accepted; credit cards are not. Mail requests: SASE required.

Justice Court - Districts 1-4 117 N. Timber, Brandon, MS 39042; 601-824-2665; fax: 601-824-2668; 8AM-5PM. ***Misdemeanor, Civil Actions under $3,500, Eviction, Small Claims.***

Chancery Court 203 Town Sq, Brandon, MS 39042; 601-825-1649; 8-5. ***Probate, Civil Land, Divorce, Family.*** www.rankincounty.org/chcourt/

Scott County

Circuit Court PO Box 371, Forest, MS 39074; 601-469-3601; 8AM-5PM. ***Felony, Civil (usually over $3,500).***
Civil Records: Access: Mail, in person. Both court and visitors may perform in person searches. Search fee: $10.00 per name. Fee is for 7 year search. Required to search: name, years to search. Civil cases indexed by defendant, plaintiff; index on docket books since 1865. Mail turnaround 1 week. Public use terminal available, records go back to 2002.
Criminal Records: Access: Mail, in person. Both court and visitors may perform in person searches. Search fee: $10.00 per name. Fee is for 7 year search. Required to search: name, years to search, DOB; also helpful: SSN. Criminal docket on books since 1865. Mail turnaround time 1 week. Public use terminal available, crim records go back to 2002.
General Information: No sealed, adoptions, mental health, juvenile, sex, or expunged records released. Will fax documents to local or toll free line. Court makes copy: $.50 per page. Self serve: $.25 per page. Certification fee: $1.50 per page. Payee: Circuit Clerk. Personal checks accepted; credit cards are not. Mail requests: SASE required.

Justice Court PO Box 371, 100 Main St, Forest, MS 39074; 601-469-4555; fax: 601-469-5193; 8AM-5PM. ***Misdemeanor, Civil Actions under $3,500, Eviction, Small Claims.***

Chancery Court 100 Main St, PO Box 630, Forest, MS 39074; 601-469-1922, 601-469-1927; fax: 601-469-5180; 8AM-5PM. ***Probate, Civil Land, Divorce, Family.***

Sharkey County

Circuit Court PO Box 218 (120 Locust St), Rolling Fork, MS 39159; 662-873-2766; criminal phone: 662-873-2755; civil phone: 662-873-2755; criminal fax: 662-873-6045; civil fax: same; 8AM-N, 1-5PM. ***Felony, Civil (usually over $3,500).***

Civil Records: Access: Fax, mail, in person. Both court and visitors may perform in person searches. Search fee: $10.00 per name. Required to search: name, years to search. Civil cases indexed by defendant, plaintiff; index on docket books since 1893. Mail turnaround time 1 week.

Criminal Records: Access: Fax, mail, in person. Both court and visitors may perform in person searches. Search fee: $10.00 per name. Required to search: name, years to search, DOB; also helpful: SSN. Criminal docket on books since 1893. Mail turnaround time 1 week.

General Information: No sealed, adoptions, mental health, juvenile, sex, or expunged records released. Fee to fax out file $2.00 per page. Court makes copy: $.50 per page. Self serve: $.25 per page. Certification fee: $2.00 per document. Payee: Circuit Clerk. Business checks accepted. No credit cards accepted. Mail requests: SASE required.

Justice Court PO Box 235, 120 Locust St, Rolling Fork, MS 39159; 662-873-6140; fax: 662-873-0154; 8AM-N, 1-5PM. ***Misdemeanor, Civil Actions under $3,500, Eviction, Small Claims.***

Chancery Court 120 Locust St, PO Box 218, Rolling Fork, MS 39159; 662-873-2755; fax: 662-873-6045; 8AM-N,1-5PM. ***Probate, Civil Land, Divorce, Family.***

Simpson County

Circuit Court PO Box 307, Mendenhall, MS 39114; 601-847-2474; criminal fax: 601-847-4011; civil fax: same; 8AM-5PM. ***Felony, Civil (usually over $3,500).***

Civil Records: Access: Fax, mail, in person. Both court and visitors may perform in person searches. Search fee: $10.00 per name. Required to search: name, years to search. Civil cases indexed by defendant, plaintiff; index on docket books since 1978. Mail turnaround time 1-2 days.

Criminal Records: Access: Fax, mail, in person. Both court and visitors may perform in person searches. Search fee: $10.00 per name. Required to search: name, years to search; also helpful: DOB, SSN. Criminal docket on books since 1978. Mail turnaround time 1-2 days.

General Information: No sealed or expunged records released. No fee to fax documents. Court makes copy: $.50 per page. Self serve: $.25 per page. Certification fee: $1.50 per page. Payee: Circuit Clerk. Business checks accepted. No credit cards accepted.

Justice Court 1498 Simpson Highway 149, Mendenhall, MS 39114; 601-847-5848; fax: 601-847-5856; 8AM-4:45PM. ***Misdemeanor, Civil Actions under $3,500, Eviction, Small Claims.***

Chancery Court PO Box 367, 111 W Pine, Mendenhall, MS 39114; 601-847-2626; fax: 601-847-7016; 8AM-5PM. ***Probate, Civil Land, Divorce, Family.***

Smith County

Circuit Court PO Box 517, 123 Main St, Raleigh, MS 39153; 601-782-4751; criminal fax: 601-782-4007; civil fax: same; 8AM-5PM. ***Felony, Civil (usually over $3,500).***

Civil Records: Access: Mail, in person. Both court and visitors may perform in person searches. Search fee: $10.00 per name. Required to search: name, years to search. Civil cases indexed by defendant, plaintiff; index on docket books since 1912. Mail turnaround time 2 days. Civil PAT goes back to 1997.

Criminal Records: Access: Mail, in person. Both court and visitors may perform in person searches. Search fee: $10.00 per name. Required to search: name, years to search, DOB; also helpful: SSN. Criminal docket on books since 1912. Mail turnaround time 2 days. Criminal PAT goes back to 1997.

General Information: No sealed or expunged records released. Fee to fax out file $5.00 1st page, $1.00 each add'l. Court makes copy: $1.00 per page. Self serve: $.25 per page. Certification fee: $5.00 per document. Payee: Circuit Clerk. Personal checks accepted; credit cards are not. Mail requests: SASE required.

Justice Court PO Box 171, 212 Sylvarena Ave #4, Raleigh, MS 39153; 601-782-4334; fax: 601-782-4005; 8AM-5PM. ***Misdemeanor, Civil Actions under $3,500, Eviction, Small Claims.***

Chancery Court 123 Main St, PO Box 39, Raleigh, MS 39153; 601-782-9811; fax: 601-782-4690; 8AM-5PM. ***Probate, Civil Land, Divorce, Family.***

Stone County

Circuit Court Courthouse, 323 Cavers Ave, Wiggins, MS 39577; 601-928-5246; fax: 601-928-5248; 8AM-5PM. ***Felony, Civil (usually over $3,500).***

Civil Records: Access: Fax, mail, in person. Both court and visitors may perform in person searches. Search fee: $10.00 per name. Required to search: name, years to search. Civil cases indexed by defendant, plaintiff; index on docket books since 1945. Mail turnaround time same day.

Criminal Records: Access: Fax, mail, in person. Both court and visitors may perform in person searches. Search fee: $10.00 per name. Required to search: name, years to search, DOB, notarized release; also helpful: SSN. Criminal docket on books since 1945. Mail turnaround time same day.

General Information: No sealed, adoptions, mental health, juvenile, sex, or expunged records released. Will fax documents $3.00 1st page, $.50 each add'l. Court makes copy: $.50 per page. Certification fee: $1.50. Payee: Circuit Clerk. Business checks accepted. No credit cards accepted. Mail requests: SASE required.

Justice Court 231 3rd St South, Wiggins, MS 39577-2808; 601-928-4415; fax: 601-928-2114; 8AM-5PM. ***Misdemeanor, Civil Actions under $3,500, Eviction, Small Claims.***

Chancery Court 323 E Cavers, PO Drawer 7, Wiggins, MS 39577; 601-928-5266; fax: 601-928-6464; 8AM-5PM. ***Probate, Civil Land, Divorce, Family.***

Sunflower County

Circuit Court PO Box 880, Indianola, MS 38751; 662-887-1252; criminal fax: 662-887-7077; civil fax: same; 8AM-5PM. ***Felony, Civil (usually over $3,500).***

Civil Records: Access: Mail, in person. Both court and visitors may perform in person searches. Search fee: $10.00 per name. Fee is for 7 year search. Required to search: name, years to search. Civil cases indexed by defendant, plaintiff; index on docket books since 1881; on computer since 2000. Mail turnaround time 2 days. Civil PAT goes back to 2000. Public terminal also has partial civil records back to 1996.

Criminal Records: Access: Mail, in person. Both court and visitors may perform in person searches. Search fee: $10.00 per name. Fee is for 7 year search. Required to search: name, years to search, DOB; also helpful: SSN. Criminal docket on books since 1913; on computer since 2000. Mail turnaround time 1-3 days. Criminal PAT goes back to 10/1999. Public terminal also has partial criminal records back to 1996.

General Information: No sealed, adoptions, mental health, juvenile, sex, or expunged records released. Fee to fax out file $1.00 per page. Court makes copy: $.50 per page. Self serve: $.25 per page. Certification fee: $1.50 per document. Payee: Circuit Clerk. Personal checks accepted; credit cards are not. Mail requests: SASE required.

Justice Court - Northern District PO Box 52, 119 N Chester, Ruleville, MS 38771; 662-756-2835; fax: 662-756-4175; 8AM-N, 1-5PM. ***Misdemeanor, Eviction, Small Claims.***

Justice Court - Southern District PO Box 487, 202 Main St, Indianola, MS 38751; 662-887-6921; fax: 662-887-2798; 8AM-N, 1-5PM. ***Misdemeanor, Civil Actions under $3,500, Eviction, Small Claims.***

Chancery Court 200 Main St, PO Box 988, Indianola, MS 38751; 662-887-4703; 8AM-5PM. ***Probate, Civil Land, Divorce, Family.***

Tallahatchie County

Charleston Circuit Court PO Box 86, Charleston, MS 38921; 662-647-8758; probate phone: 662-647-5551; fax: 662-647-8490; 8AM-5PM. ***Felony, Civil (usually over $3,500).***

Civil Records: Access: Fax, mail, in person. Both court and visitors may perform in person searches. Search fee: $10.00 per name. Required to search: name, years to search. Civil cases indexed by defendant, plaintiff, on books since 1920s. Mail turnaround time 3 days.

Criminal Records: Access: Fax, mail, in person. Both court and visitors may perform in person searches. Search fee: $10.00 per name. Required to search: name, years to search, DOB; also helpful: SSN. Criminal docket on books since 1920s. Mail turnaround time 3 days.

General Information: No sealed, adoptions, mental health, juvenile, sex, or expunged records released. Will fax documents for fee. Court makes copy: $.50 per page. Certification fee: $3.00 per cert. Payee: Circuit Clerk. Personal checks accepted; credit cards are not. Mail requests: SASE requested.

Tallahatchie Justice Court District 1 PO Box 440, 1 Main St, 2nd Fl, Charleston, MS 38921; 662-647-3478; fax: 662-647-3478; 8AM-5PM. ***Misdemeanor, Civil Actions under $3,500, Eviction, Small Claims.***

Court is located upstairs of the Charleston Circuit Court; records are not co-mingled.

Tallahatchie Justice Court District 2 PO Box 155, 401 Court Sq, Sumner, MS 38957; 662-375-9452; fax: 662-375-8200; 8AM-N; 1-5PM. ***Misdemeanor, Civil Actions under $3,500, Eviction, Small Claims.***

Also known as Sumner Justice Court.

Charleston Chancery Court #1 Court Sq, PO Box 350, Charleston, MS 38921; 662-647-5551; fax: 662-647-3702; 8AM-5PM. ***Probate, Divorce, Family.***

Sumner Chancery Court PO Box 180, 100 N Main Court Square, Sumner, MS 38957; 662-375-8731; fax: 662-375-7252; 8AM-N, 1-5PM. ***Probate, Divorce, Family.***

Tate County

Circuit Court 201 Ward St, Senatobia, MS 38668; 662-562-5211; criminal fax: 662-562-7486; civil fax: same; 8AM-5PM. ***Felony, Civil (usually over $3,500).***

Civil Records: Access: Mail, in person. Both court and visitors may perform in person searches. Search fee: $10.00 per name. Required to search: name, years to search. Civil cases indexed by defendant, plaintiff, on books since 1872. Mail turnaround time same day. Civil PAT goes back to 1990.

Criminal Records: Access: Mail, in person. Both court and visitors may perform in person searches. Search fee: $10.00 per name. Required to search: name, years to search; also helpful: SSN. Criminal docket on books since 1872. Mail turnaround time same day. Criminal PAT goes back to same as civil.

General Information: No sealed, adoptions, mental health, juvenile, sex, or expunged records released. Will not fax documents. Court makes copy: $.50 first page, $.25 each add'l. Self serve: $.25 per page. Certification fee: $1.00 per page. Payee: Circuit Clerk.

Personal checks accepted; credit cards are not. Mail requests: SASE requested.

Justice Court 103 Preston McCay Dr, Senatobia, MS 38668; 662-562-7626; fax: 662-562-7663; 8AM-N,1-5PM. ***Misdemeanor, Civil Actions under $3,500, Eviction, Small Claims.***

Chancery Court 201 Ward St, PO Box 309, Senatobia, MS 38668; 662-562-5661; fax: 662-560-6205; 8AM-5PM. ***Probate, Civil Land, Divorce, Family.***

Tippah County

Circuit Court Courthouse, 102A N Main St, Ripley, MS 38663; 662-837-7370; criminal fax: 662-837-1030; civil fax: same; 8AM-5PM. ***Felony, Civil (usually over $3,500).***
Probate fax is same as main fax number.
Civil Records: Access: Phone, fax, mail, in person. Both court and visitors may perform in person searches. Search fee: $5.00 per name. Required to search: name, years to search. Civil cases indexed by defendant. Civil index on docket books since 1800s. Mail turnaround time 1 week; phone turnaround 30 minutes.
Criminal Records: Access: Phone, fax, mail, in person. Both court and visitors may perform in person searches. Search fee: $5.00 per name. Required to search: name, years to search, DOB; also helpful: SSN. Criminal docket on books since 1800s. Mail turnaround time 1 week; phone turnaround 30 minutes.
General Information: No sealed, adoptions, mental health, juvenile, sex or expunged records released. Will fax documents $1.00 per page. Court makes copy: civil court- no charge; criminal court $.50 per page. Self serve: Criminal self serve copy $.25 per page; No civil self serve. No certification fee. Payee: Circuit Clerk. Personal checks accepted; credit cards are not. Mail requests: SASE required.

Justice Court Justice Court, 205-B Spring Ave, Ripley, MS 38663; 662-837-8842; fax: 662-837-1398; 8AM-5PM. ***Misdemeanor, Civil Actions under $3,500, Eviction, Small Claims.***

Chancery Court 101 Spring St, Ripley, MS 38663; 662-837-7374; probate phone: 662-837-3607; fax: 662-837-7148; 8AM-5PM. ***Probate, Civil Land, Divorce, Family.***

Tishomingo County

Circuit Court 1008 Battleground Dr, Iuka, MS 38852; 662-423-7026; criminal fax: 662-423-1667; civil fax: same; 8AM-5PM. ***Felony, Civil (usually over $3,500).***
Civil Records: Access: Mail, in person. Both court and visitors may perform in person searches. Search fee: $10.00 per name. Required to search: name, years to search. Civil cases indexed by defendant, plaintiff, on computer back to 2000, in docket books since 1950s, others in storage. Mail turnaround time 1-2 days. Civil PAT goes back to 2000. PAT results show name only.
Criminal Records: Access: Mail, in person. Both court and visitors may perform in person searches. Search fee: $10.00 per name. Required to search: name, years to search, DOB; also helpful: SSN, signed release. Criminal records computerized from 2000, in docket books since 1950s, others in storage. Mail turnaround time 1-2 days. Criminal PAT goes back to same as civil; results show name only.
General Information: No sealed, adoptions, mental health, juvenile, sex, or expunged records released. Will fax documents $10.00 per name. Court makes copy: $1.00 per page. Self serve: $.25 per page. Certification fee: $1.00 per page. Payee: Circuit Clerk. Business checks accepted. No credit cards accepted. Mail requests: SASE requested.

Justice Court - North & South Districts 1008 Battleground Drive, Rm 212, Iuka, MS 38852; 662-423-7033; fax: 662-423-7094; 8AM-5PM. ***Misdemeanor, Civil Actions under $3,500, Eviction, Small Claims.***

Chancery Court 1008 Battleground Dr, Iuka, MS 38852; 662-423-7010; fax: 662-423-7005; 8AM-5PM. ***Probate, Civil Land, Divorce, Family.***

Tunica County

Circuit Court PO Box 184, Tunica, MS 38676; 662-363-2842; fax: 662-363-2413; 8AM-5PM. ***Felony, Civil (usually over $3,500).***
Civil Records: Access: Mail, in person. Both court and visitors may perform in person searches. Search fee: $10.00 per name. Required to search: name, years to search. Civil cases indexed by defendant, plaintiff; index on docket books for 10 years; archived prior. Mail turnaround time 1 week.
Criminal Records: Access: Mail, in person. Both court and visitors may perform in person searches. Search fee: $10.00 per name. Required to search: name, years to search, DOB; also helpful: SSN. Criminal docket on books for 10 years. Mail turnaround time 1 week.
General Information: No sealed, adoptions, mental health, juvenile, sex, or expunged records released. Will fax documents to local or toll free line. Court makes copy: $.50 per page, add'l fee for postage. Self serve: $.25 per page. Certification fee: $3.50. Payee: Circuit Clerk. Personal checks accepted; credit cards are not. Mail requests: SASE requested.

Justice Court 5130 Old Moon Landing Rd., Tunica, MS 38676; 662-363-2178; fax: 662-363-4234; 8AM-5PM. ***Misdemeanor, Civil Actions under $3,500, Eviction, Small Claims.***

Chancery Court PO Box 217, 1300 School St, Rm 104, Tunica, MS 38676; 662-363-2451; fax: 662-357-5934; 8AM-N, 1-5PM. ***Probate, Civil Land, Divorce, Family.***

Union County

Circuit Court PO Box 298, New Albany, MS 38652; 662-534-1910; fax: 662-534-2059; 8AM-5PM. ***Felony, Civil (usually over $3,500).***
Civil Records: Access: Fax, mail, in person. Both court and visitors may perform in person searches. Search fee: $10.00 per name. Includes certification fee. Required to search: name, years to search, address. Civil cases indexed by defendant, plaintiff; index on docket books since early 1900s. Mail turnaround time 1 week. Civil PAT goes back to 2000.
Criminal Records: Access: Fax, mail, in person. Both court and visitors may perform in person searches. Search fee: $10.00 per name. Fee includes certification. Required to search: name, years to search, DOB; also helpful: SSN. Criminal docket on books since early 1900s. Mail turnaround time 1 week. Criminal PAT goes back to 2000.
General Information: No adoption, mental health or juvenile records released. No fee to fax documents. Court makes copy: $.50 per page. Self serve: $.25 per page. Certification fee: $10.00 per doc. Payee: Union County Circuit Clerk. Personal checks accepted; credit cards are not. Mail requests: SASE requested.

Justice Court - East & West Posts PO Box 27, 300 Carter Ave, New Albany, MS 38652; 662-534-1951; fax: 662-534-1935; 8-5. ***Misdemeanor, Civil Actions under $3,500, Eviction, Small Claims.***

Chancery Court PO Box 847, 109 E Main St, New Albany, MS 38652; 662-534-1900; fax: 662-534-1907; 8AM-5PM. ***Probate, Civil Land, Divorce, Family.***
Misdemeanor records phone is 662-534-1951.

Walthall County

Circuit Court 200 Ball Ave, Tylertown, MS 39667; 601-876-5677; criminal fax: 601-876-4077; civil fax: same; 8AM-N; 1-5PM. ***Felony, Civil (usually over $3,500).***
Civil Records: Access: Mail, in person. Both court and visitors may perform in person searches. Search fee: $10.00 per name includes copies. Required to search: name, years to search. Civil cases indexed by defendant, plaintiff; index on docket books since 1914. Mail turnaround time 1-2 days.
Criminal Records: Access: Mail, in person. Both court and visitors may perform in person searches. Search fee: $10.00 per name includes copies. Required to search: name, years to search; also helpful: SSN. Criminal docket on books since 1914. Mail turnaround time 1-2 days.
General Information: No sealed, adoptions, mental health, juvenile, sex, or expunged records released. Will fax documents. Court makes copy: $.50 per page. Self serve: $.25 per page. Certification fee: $1.50 per document. Payee: Circuit Clerk. Personal checks accepted; credit cards are not.

Justice Court - Districts 1 & 2 PO Box 507, 807 Magnolia Ave, Tylertown, MS 39667; 601-876-2311; fax: 601-876-6866; 8AM-N, 1-5PM. ***Misdemeanor, Civil Actions under $3,500, Eviction, Small Claims.***

Chancery Court PO Box 351, 200 Ball Ave, Tylertown, MS 39667; 601-876-3553; fax: 601-876-6026; 8AM-5PM. ***Probate, Civil Land, Divorce, Family.***

Warren County

Circuit & County Court PO Box 351, Vicksburg, MS 39181; 601-636-3961; fax: 601-630-4100; 8AM-5PM. ***Felony, Misdemeanor, Civil (usually over $3,500).***
Civil Records: Access: Mail, in person. Both court and visitors may perform in person searches. Search fee: $10.00 per name. Required to search: name, years to search. Civil cases indexed by defendant, plaintiff, on books since 1970s. Mail turnaround time 1 day. Civil PAT goes back to 2002.
Criminal Records: Access: Mail, in person. Both court and visitors may perform in person searches. Search fee: $10.00 per name. Required to search: name, years to search; also helpful: DOB, SSN. Criminal docket on books since 1970s. Mail turnaround time 1 day. Criminal PAT goes back to same as civil.
General Information: No sealed or expunged records released. Will fax documents $5.00 per page. Court makes copy: $1.00 per page. Self serve: $.25 per page. Certification fee: $1.00 per page. Payee: Circuit Clerk. No personal checks or credit cards accepted. Mail requests: SASE required.

Justice Court - Northern, Central & Southern Districts PO Box 1598, 919 Farmer St, Vicksburg, MS 39181; 601-634-6402; fax: 601-630-8015; 8AM-5PM. ***Misdemeanor, Civil Actions under $3,500, Eviction, Small Claims.***

Chancery Court PO Box 351, 1009 Cherry St, Vicksburg, MS 39181; 601-636-4415; fax: 601-630-8016; 8AM-5PM. ***Probate, Civil Land, Divorce, Family.*** Also handles adoption, divorce, lunacy, Uresa, and minor settlements

Washington County

Circuit & County Court PO Box 1276, Greenville, MS 38702; 662-378-2747; criminal fax: 662-334-2698; civil fax: same; 8AM-5PM. ***Felony, Misdemeanor, Civil (usually over $3,500).***
Civil Records: Access: Fax, mail, in person. Both court and visitors may perform in person searches. Search fee: $10.00 per name. Required to search: name, years to search. Civil cases indexed by defendant, plaintiff, on books since 1964. Mail turnaround time 5-10 days. Public use terminal available, records go back to 9/2006.
Criminal Records: Access: Fax, mail, in person. Both court and visitors may perform in person searches. Search fee: $10.00 per name for 7 years, $1.00 each add'l year. Required to search: name, years to search; also helpful: DOB, SSN. Criminal docket on books since 1964. Mail turnaround time 5-10 days. Public use terminal available, crim records go back to same as civil.
General Information: No sealed or expunged records released. No fee to fax documents. Court makes copy: $1.00 per page. Self serve: $.25 per page. Certification fee: $1.50. Payee: Circuit Clerk. Business checks accepted. No credit cards accepted. Mail requests: SASE required.

Justice Court - Districts 1-3 905 W Alexander, Greenville, MS 38701; 662-332-0633;

fax: 662-390-4760; 8AM-5PM. ***Misdemeanor, Civil Actions under $3,500, Eviction, Small Claims.***

Chancery Court PO Box 309, 900 Washington Ave, Greenville, MS 38702-0309; 662-332-1595; fax: 662-334-2725; 8AM-5PM. ***Probate, Civil Land, Divorce, Family.***

Wayne County

Circuit Court PO Box 428, Waynesboro, MS 39367; 601-735-1171; criminal fax: 601-735-6261; civil fax: same; 8AM-5PM. ***Felony, Civil (usually over $3,500).***
This court is in process of computerizing their records.
Civil Records: Access: Phone, fax, mail, in person. Both court and visitors may perform in person searches. Search fee: $10.00 per name. Required to search: name, years to search. Civil cases indexed by defendant, plaintiff; index on docket books since 1980, others in storage. Mail turnaround time 1-2 days. Civil PAT goes back to 1999.
Criminal Records: Access: Fax, mail, in person. Both court and visitors may perform in person searches. Search fee: $10.00 per name. Required to search: name, years to search; also helpful: DOB, SSN, signed release. Criminal docket on books since 1980, others in storage. Mail turnaround time 1-2 days. Criminal PAT goes back to 1996.
General Information: No sealed or expunged records released. Fee to fax out file $1.00 per page. Court makes copy: $.50 per page. Self serve: $.25 per page. Certification fee: $1.50. Payee: Circuit Clerk. Business checks accepted. No credit cards accepted. Mail requests: SASE required.

Justice Court - Posts 1 & 2 810 Chickasawhay St, #C, Waynesboro, MS 39367; 601-735-3118; fax: 601-735-6266; 8AM-5PM. ***Misdemeanor, Civil Actions under $3,500, Eviction, Small Claims.***

Chancery Court Courthouse, 609 Azalea Dr, Waynesboro, MS 39367; 601-735-2873; fax: 601-735-6224; 8AM-5PM. ***Probate, Civil Land, Divorce, Family.***

Webster County

Circuit Court PO Box 308, 515 Carroll St, Walthall, MS 39771; 662-258-6287; fax: 662-258-7686; 8-5. ***Felony, Civil (usually over $3,500).***
Civil Records: Access: Phone, fax, mail, in person. Both court and visitors may perform in person searches. Search fee: $10.00 per name. Required to search: name, years to search. Civil cases indexed by defendant, plaintiff; index on docket books since 1874. Mail turnaround time 1-2 days.
Criminal Records: Access: Fax, mail, in person. Both court and visitors may perform in person searches. Search fee: $10.00 per name. Required to search: name, years to search, DOB; also helpful: SSN. Criminal docket on books since 1874. Mail turnaround time 1-2 days.
General Information: No sealed, adoptions, mental health, juvenile, sex, or expunged records released. No fee to fax documents. Court makes copy: $1.00 per page. Self serve: $.50 per page. Certification fee: $1.00 per page. Payee: Circuit Clerk. Business checks accepted. No credit cards accepted.

Justice Court - Districts 1 & 2 24 E Fox Ave, Eupora, MS 39744; 662-258-2590; fax: 662-258-3093; 8AM-5PM. ***Misdemeanor, Civil Actions under $3,500, Eviction, Small Claims.***

Chancery Court PO Box 398, 101 Main St, Walthall, MS 39771; 662-258-4131; fax: 662-258-6657; 8-5. ***Probate, Civil Land, Divorce, Family.***

Wilkinson County

Circuit Court PO Box 327, Woodville, MS 39669; 601-888-6697; fax: 601-888-6984; 8AM-5PM. ***Felony, Civil (usually over $3,500).***
Civil Records: Access: Mail, in person. Both court and visitors may perform in person searches. Search fee: $10.00 per name. Required to search: name, years to search. Civil cases indexed by defendant, plaintiff; index on docket books since 1940s. Mail turnaround time 1-2 days.
Criminal Records: Access: Mail, in person. Both court and visitors may perform in person searches. Search fee: $10.00 per name. Required to search: name, years to search; also helpful: DOB, SSN. Criminal docket on books since 1940s. Mail turnaround time 1-2 days.
General Information: No sealed or expunged records released. Will fax documents $5.00 per page. Court makes copy: $.50 per page. Self serve: $.25 per page. Certification fee: $10.00 per doc. Payee: Circuit Clerk. Personal checks accepted; credit cards are not.

Justice Court PO Box 40, 1389 Highway 61 South, Woodville, MS 39669; 601-888-3538, 601-888-3972; fax: 601-888-7591; 8-5. ***Misdemeanor, Civil Actions under $3,500, Eviction, Small Claims.***

Chancery Court PO Box 516, 525 Main St, Woodville, MS 39669; 601-888-4381; fax: 601-888-6776; 8AM-5PM. ***Probate, Civil Land, Divorce, Family.***

Winston County

Circuit Court PO Drawer 785, Louisville, MS 39339; 662-773-3581; criminal fax: 662-773-7192; civil fax: same; 8AM-5PM. ***Felony, Civil (usually over $3,500).***
You may email requests to kim@winstoncounty.org.
Civil Records: Access: Phone, fax, mail, in person. Both court and visitors may perform in person searches. Search fee: $10.00 per name. Required to search: name, years to search. Civil cases indexed by defendant, plaintiff; index on docket books since early 1950s; some on computer back to 1994; all since 2000. Mail turnaround time 14 day maximum. Civil PAT goes back to 2000.
Criminal Records: Access: Fax, mail, in person. Both court and visitors may perform in person searches. Search fee: $10.00 per name. Required to search: name, years to search, DOB; also helpful: SSN. Criminal docket on books since early 1800s; on computer back to 2000. Mail turnaround time 14 day maximum. Criminal PAT goes back to same as civil.
General Information: No sealed, adoptions, or expunged records released. Will fax documents $5.00 1st page, $1.00 each add'l. Court makes copy: $1.00 per page. Self serve: $.25 per page. Certification fee: $2.00. Payee: Circuit Clerk. Personal checks accepted; credit cards are not. Mail requests: SASE requested.

Justice Court PO Box 327, 115 S Court St, Louisville, MS 39339; 662-773-6016; fax: 662-773-8817; 8AM-5PM. ***Misdemeanor, Civil Actions under $3,500, Eviction, Small Claims.***

Chancery Court PO Drawer 69, 115 S Court St, Louisville, MS 39339; 662-773-3631; fax: 662-773-8814; 8-5. ***Probate, Civil Land, Divorce, Family.***

Yalobusha County

Coffeeville Circuit Court PO Box 260, Coffeeville, MS 38922; 662-675-8187; criminal fax: 662-675-8004; civil fax: same; 8AM-5PM. ***Felony, Civil (usually over $3,500).***
Civil Records: Access: Phone, fax, mail, in person. Both court and visitors may perform in person searches. Search fee: $10.00 per name. May mail request with check or fax request with copy of check to be mailed. Required to search: name, years to search. Civil cases indexed by defendant, plaintiff; index on docket books since 1930s. Mail turnaround time 1-2 days.
Criminal Records: Access: Phone, fax, mail, in person. Both court and visitors may perform in person searches. Search fee: $10.00 per name. May mail request with check or fax request with copy of check to be mailed. Required to search: name, years to search; also helpful: DOB. Criminal docket on books since 1930s. Mail turnaround time 1-2 days.
General Information: No sealed, adoptions, mental health, juvenile, sex, or expunged records released. Will fax documents to local or toll free line. Court makes copy: $.50 per page. Self serve: $.25 per page. Certification fee: $10.00. Payee: Circuit Clerk. Personal checks accepted; credit cards are not. Mail requests: SASE requested.

Water Valley Circuit Court PO Box 1431, Water Valley, MS 38965; 662-473-1341; fax: 662-473-5020; 8-5. ***Felony, Civil (usually over $3,500).***
Civil Records: Access: Fax, mail, in person. Both court and visitors may perform in person searches. Search fee: $10.00 per name. Includes certification fee. Required to search: name, years to search. Civil cases indexed by defendant, plaintiff; index on docket books since 1930s. Mail turnaround time 1 week.
Criminal Records: Access: Fax, mail, in person. Both court and visitors may perform in person searches. Search fee: $10.00 per name. Fee includes certification. Required to search: name, years to search, DOB; also helpful: SSN. Criminal docket on books since 1930s. Mail turnaround time 1 week.
General Information: No sealed, adoptions, mental health, juvenile, sex, or expunged records released. No fee to fax documents. Court makes copy: $.50 per page. Self serve: $.25 per page. Certification fee: $10.00 per docket. Payee: Circuit Clerk. Personal checks accepted; credit cards are not.

Justice Court - District 1 PO Box 218, 14400 Main Street, Coffeeville, MS 38922; 662-675-8115; fax: 662-675-8452; 8AM-5PM. ***Misdemeanor, Civil Actions under $3,500, Eviction, Small Claims.***

Justice Court - Division 2 PO Box 918, 205 Blackmur Dr, Water Valley, MS 38965; 662-473-4502; fax: 662-473-5016; 8-5. ***Misdemeanor, Civil Actions under $3,500, Eviction, Small Claims.***

Chancery Court PO Box 664, 201 Blackmur Dr, Water Valley, MS 38965; 662-473-2091; fax: 662-473-3622; 8AM-N, 1-5PM. ***Probate, Civil Land, Divorce, Family.***

Chancery Court PO Box 260, 14400 Main St, Coffeeville, MS 38922; 662-675-2716; fax: 662-675-8004; 8AM-N, 1-5PM. ***Probate, Civil Land, Divorce, Family.***

Yazoo County

Circuit & County Court PO Box 108, 211 E Broadway, Yazoo City, MS 39194; 662-746-1872; fax: 662-716-0113; 8AM-5PM. ***Felony, Misdemeanor, Civil (usually over $3,500).***
Civil Records: Access: Mail, in person. Both court and visitors may perform in person searches. Search fee: $10.00 per name. Required to search: name, years to search. Civil cases indexed by defendant, plaintiff, for Civil Circuit on docket books since 1973; for Civil County on docket books since 1977. Mail turnaround time 1 day.
Criminal Records: Access: Mail, in person. Both court and visitors may perform in person searches. Search fee: $10.00 per name. Required to search: name, years to search, DOB; also helpful: SSN. Criminal records for Criminal Circuit from 1975; Criminal County on docket books since 1975. Mail turnaround time 1 day.
General Information: No sealed, adoptions, mental health, juvenile, sex, or expunged records released. Will fax documents. Court makes copy: $.50 per page. Self serve: $.25 per page. Certification fee: $1.00 per page. Payee: Circuit Clerk. Business checks accepted. No credit cards accepted. Mail requests: SASE required.

Justice Court - Northern & Southern Districts PO Box 798, 211 E Broadway, Yazoo City, MS 39194; 662-746-8181; fax: 662-746-2186; 8AM-5PM. ***Misdemeanor, Civil Actions under $3,500, Eviction, Small Claims.***

Chancery Court PO Box 68, 211 E Broadway, Yazoo City, MS 39194; 662-746-2661; fax: 662-746-3893; 8AM-5PM. ***Probate, Civil Land, Divorce, Family.*** Physical address for court is 209 E Broadway.

Mississippi Recording Offices

ORGANIZATION: 82 counties, 92 recording offices. The recording officers are Chancery Clerk, and Clerk of Circuit Court for state tax liens. Ten counties have two separate recording offices - Bolivar, Carroll, Chickasaw, Harrison, Hinds, Jasper, Jones, Panola, Tallahatchie, Yalobusha. Mississippi is in the Central Time Zone (CST).

REAL ESTATE RECORDS: Very few counties will perform real estate searches. Copies usually cost $.50 per page and certification fee $1.00 per cert/seal. Self serve copies are $.25 each; some counties require an account be setup to quality for the $.25 rate.

UCC RECORDS: This was a dual filing state. Until July, 2001, financing statements were filed both at the state level and with the Chancery Clerk, except for consumer goods, farm-related and real estate-related filings which were filed only with the Chancery Clerk. Now, only real estate-related filings are filed at the county level. A dwindling number of counties will perform UCC searches. Use search request form UCC-11 or the state form. UCC search fee is usually $5.00 per debtor name (or $10.00 on non-standard form); copy fees vary from $.50 to $2.00 per page.

TAX LIEN RECORDS: Federal tax liens on personal property of businesses are filed with the Secretary of State. Federal tax liens on personal property of individuals are filed with the county Chancery Clerk. State tax liens on personal property are filed with the county Clerk of Circuit Court. State tax liens on real property are filed with the Chancery Clerk. Chancery Clerk offices may perform a federal tax lien search for a $5.00 fee per name.

OTHER LIENS: Mechanics, lis pendens, judgment (Circuit Court), construction.

ONLINE ACCESS: A limited number of counties offer online access to records; there is no statewide system except for the Secretary of State's UCC access, and the State Tax Commission Property Tax Landrolls by County at www.mstc.state.ms.us/taxareas/property/countylr07.htm. Search free for UCC debtors is at www.sos.state.ms.us/busserv/ucc/soskb/SearchStandardRA9.asp.

Adams County

Chancery Clerk, PO Box 1006, Natchez, MS 39121. Recording, R/E & UCC phone-601-446-6684; fax-601-445-7913; 8AM-5PM.
Index: All in one. Records indexed on a public use terminal back to 8/93. Only the public may search. Copy fee $.50 per page, self service $.25. Cert fee- $1.00 per cert plus copy fee. Payee- Chancery Clerk. **Online access to Judgment, Circuit Court, Voter Registration records:** Access judgments, voter registration, circuit courts (go back to 1997, scanned 12/02 to present) for a fee go to www.deltacomputersystems.com/search.html. **Other phones:** Elections- 601-446-6326. **Property tax/Assessing**- PO Box 1026, 200 Wall St, Natchez, MS 39121; 601-442-6732, assessor fax- 601-445-7963. A public access terminal is available. **Online access**- Assess assessor property and map data free at www.emapsplus.com/MSAdams/maps/.

Alcorn County

Chancery Clerk, PO Box 69, Corinth, MS 38835-0069. phone-662-286-7700; fax-662-286-7706; 8AM-5PM. http://alcorncounty.org/chancery.aspx
Index: Separate indices to search include computer (with canned images), mortgages, warranty deeds. Records indexed on a public use terminal back to 2/05. Office will perform a UCC search but public must search other records themselves. Will search UCC records if on request form- fee $5.00 per name plus copy fee. Copy fee $2.00 per page; $.25 self serve. Cert fee- $1.00 per cert plus copy fee. Payee- Chancery Clerk. **Other phones:** Elections- 662-286-7740. **Property tax/Assessing**- 600 Waldron St, Courthouse, Corinth, MS 38834; 662-286-7733, assessor fax- 662-286-2548. http://alcorncounty.org/assessor.aspx **Online**- Access free at www.deltacomputersystems.com/MS/MS02/index.html

Amite County

Chancery Clerk, PO Box 680, Liberty, MS 39645-0680. 601-657-8022; fax-601-657-8288; 8AM-5PM.
Index: Separate indices to search include computer, books back to 1810. Records indexed on a public use terminal back to 1990. Only the public may search. Copy fee $.50 per page if clerk makes copy, $.25 per page self serve. Cert fee- $1.00 per doc plus $1.00 per copy. Payee- Amite County Chancery Clerk. **Other phones:** Treasurer- 601-657-8932; Elections- 601-657-8932. **Property tax/Assessing**- PO Box 356, 243 W Main St, Liberty, 39645; 601-657-8973, assessor fax- 601-657-1083. Public access computer available.

Attala County

Chancery Clerk, 230 W Washington St; Chancery Court Bldg, Kosciusko, MS 39090. 662-289-2921; fax-662-289-7662; 8AM-5PM.
Index: Separate indices to search include books by date. Record index not computerized. Only the public may search. Copy fee $.50 per page if clerk makes copy, $.25 per page self serve. Cert fee- $1.00 per doc plus copy fee. Payee- Attala County Chancery Clerk. **Other phones:** Elections- 662-289-1471. **Property tax/Assessing**- 230 W Washington St, Kosciusko, MS 39090; 662-289-5731.

Benton County

Chancery Clerk, PO Box 218, Ashland, MS 38603. 662-224-6300; fax-662-224-6303; 8AM-5PM.
Index: Separate indices to search include computer, books. Records indexed on a public use terminal back to 1995. Office will perform a UCC search but public must search other records themselves. UCC/Tax search per debtor name- $10.00. Copy fee $2.00 for UCC, $.50 per page if clerk makes copy, $.25 per page self serve. Cert fee- $1.00 per doc plus copy fee. Payee- Benton County Chancery Clerk. Bulk data sale available through Delta Computer Systems, call 228-868-2350. **Other phones:** Elections- 662-224-6310. **Property tax/Assessing**- PO Box 337, 190 Ripley St, Ashland, MS 38603; 662-224-6315, assessor fax-662-224-6303. Public access computer available.

Bolivar County (1st District)

Chancery Clerk, PO Box 238, Rosedale, MS 38769. 662-759-3762; fax-662-759-3467; 8AM-N, 1-5PM.
Two recording offices; their indexes are combined on their public access terminals, but physical records are at their respective offices. Index: All in one. Records indexed on a public use terminal back to 1985. Only the public may search. Copy fee $.50 per page; $.25 self serve. Cert fee- $1.00 per cert plus copy fee. Payee- Bolivar County Chancery Clerk. **Other phones:** Treasurer- 662-843-2531; Elections- 662-843-2061. **Property tax/Assessing**- PO Box 339, Rosedale, MS 38769-0339; 662-759-3467, assessor fax- 662-759-3467.

Bolivar County (2nd District)

Chancery Clerk, PO Box 789, Cleveland, MS 38732. phone-662-843-2071; fax-662-846-2940; 8AM-5PM. www.co.bolivar.ms.us/chanceryclerk.htm
Two recording offices; their indexes are combined on their public access terminals, but physical records are at their respective offices. Index: Separate indices to search include grantor/grantee, sectional, subdivision. Records indexed on a public use terminal back to 1985. Only the public may search. Copy fee $.50 per page; $.25 self serve. Cert fee- $1.00 per doc plus copy fee. Payee- Brenett N Haynes- Chancery Clerk. Treasurer- 662-843-2071; Elections- 662-843-2061. **Property tax/Assessing**- PO Box 248, 200 Court St, Cleveland, MS 38732; 662-843-3926, assessor fax-662-843-2936. www.co.bolivar.ms.us/taxassessor.htm

Calhoun County

Chancery Clerk, PO Box 8, Pittsboro, MS 38951. Recording, R/E phone-662-412-3117, UCC recording phone-662-412-3121; fax-662-412-3128; 8AM-5PM (CST)
Index: Separate indices to search include deed, deed tract. Records indexed on a public use terminal back to 00. Office will perform a UCC search but public must search other records themselves. Search fee $10.00 per name. Copy fee $.50 per page; UCC copy $2.00. Cert fee- $5.00 per page. Payee- Calhoun County Clerk of the Chancery Court. **Other phones:** Treasurer- 662-412-3117; Elections- 662-412-3101; Vital Records- 662-412-3101. **Property tax/Assessing**- PO Box 6, 103 W Main, Pittsboro, MS 38951; 662-412-3140, assessor fax- 662-412-0143. (Appraiser/Auditor- 662-412-3146) A public access terminal is available.

Carroll County (1st District)

Chancery Clerk, PO Box 60, Carrollton, MS 38917. 662-237-9274, R/E recording phone-662-237-9217; fax-662-237-9642; 8AM-N, 1PM-5PM.
Carroll County's 2 recording offices must be searched separately. Index: Separate indices to search include deeds in books, deeds of trust in books. Records indexed on a public use terminal back to 11/03. Books go back to 1834. Only the public may search. Copy fee $.50 per page if clerk make copy, $.25 per page self serve. Cert fee- $1.00 per doc plus copy fee. Payee- Carroll County Chancery Clerk. **Other phones:** Elections- 662-464-5476. **Property tax/Assessing-** PO Box 193, Carrollton, MS 38917; 662-237-9217, assessor fax- 662-237-4659.

Carroll County (2nd District)

Chancery Clerk, PO Box 6, Vaiden, MS 39176. 662-464-5476; fax-662-464-5407; 8AM-5PM (CST)
2nd district is split by section, township and range. Carroll County's 2 recording offices must be searched separately. Index: All in one. Record index not computerized. Only the public may search. Copy fee $.25 per page. Cert fee- $1.00 per doc plus copy fee. Payee- Carroll County Clerk of the Chancery Court. **Other phones:** Elections- 662-464-5476. **Property tax/Assessing-** PO Box 193, Carrollton, MS 38923; 662-464-8852, assessor fax- 662-237-4659.

Chickasaw County (1st District)

Chancery Clerk, 1 Pinson Sq, Houston, MS 38851. 662-456-2513; fax-662-456-5295; 8AM-N, 1-5PM.
Prior to 1988, all county land records here. 1988-1999 land records for 2nd District (Okolona) are only at Okolona. Both on public access terminal starting 1999. Records indexed on a public use terminal back to 1999. Only the public may search. Copy fee $2.00 per page. Cert fee- $1.00 per cert plus copy fee. Payee- Chancery Clerk. **Other phones:** Elections- 662-456-2331. **Property tax/Assessing-** 1 Pinson Sq, Houston, MS 38851; 662-456-3327.

Chickasaw County (2nd District)

Chancery Clerk, 234 Main St, Rm 201, Okolona, MS 38860-1438. 662-447-2092; fax-662-447-5024; 8AM-N 1PM-5PM.
Prior to 1988, all county land records here. 1988-1999 land records for 2nd District (Okolona) are only at Okolona. Both on public access terminal starting 1999. Index: Separate indices to search include 2 computer systems, then to book indexes. Records indexed on a public use terminal back to 1990 (approx). Only the public may search. Copy fee $.50 per page. Cert fee- $1.00 per page plus copy fee. Payee- Chancery Clerk. **Other phones:** Treasurer- 662-456-2513; Elections- 662-456-2331. **Property tax/Assessing-** 234 W Main St #204, Okolona, MS 38860; 662-447-2242, assessor fax- 662-447-5022. hours- 8AM-5PM No public access terminal.

Choctaw County

Chancery Clerk, PO Box 250, Ackerman, MS 39735-0250. 662-285-6329; fax-662-285-3444; 8AM-5PM.
Index: Separate indices to search include land deed-direct/reverse (1881-beginning 2003). Records indexed on a public use terminal back to 2/28/03. Only the public may search. Copy fee $1.00 per page. Cert fee- $2.00 per cert included copy fee. Payee- Choctaw County Chancery Clerk. Elections- 662-285-6245. **Property tax/Assessing-** PO Box 907, Ackerman, MS 39735; 662-285-6320.

Claiborne County

Chancery Clerk, PO Box 449, Port Gibson, MS 39150. Recording, R/E & UCC phone-601-437-4992; fax-601-437-3137; 8AM-5PM (CST)
Index: Separate indices to search include mortgages, land deeds, chancery court. Records indexed on computer back to 1981 for deeds and mortgages. Only the public may search. Copy fee $.50 per page if clerk makes copy $.25 self serve. Cert fee- $1.00 per doc plus copy fee. Payee- Claiborne County Clerk of the Chancery Court. Contact office with bulk data sales inquiries. **Other phones:** Treasurer- 601-437-4992; Elections- 601-437-5841; Vital Records- 601-437-5841. **Property tax/Assessing-** PO Box 469, 410 Main St, Port Gibson, MS 39150; 601-437-5591, assessor fax- 601-437-3419. (Appraiser/Auditor- 601-437-5591) Public access computer in office.

Clarke County

Chancery Clerk, PO Box 689, Quitman, MS 39355. Recording, R/E & UCC phone-601-776-2126; fax-601-776-2756; 8AM-5PM (CST)
Index: All in one. Record index not computerized. Only the public may search. UCC copy fee $2.00 per page.Real estate record copy- $.50 per page. Cert fee- $1.00 per cert plus copy fee. Payee- Clarke County Clerk of the Chancery Court. **Other phones:** Treasurer- 601-776-2126; Elections- 601-776-3111. **Property tax/Assessing-** 101 S Archusa St, Courthouse, Quitman, MS 39355; 601-776-6931. (Appraiser/Auditor- 601-776-5085) **Online-** Access property and appraisal data free at www.deltacomputersystems.com/MS/MS12/INDEX.HTML.

Clay County

Chancery Clerk, PO Box 815, West Point, MS 39773. Recording, R/E & UCC phone-662-494-3124; fax-662-492-4059; 8AM-5PM (CST)
Index: Separate indices to search include general deed index, general land mortgage index. Record index not computerized. Office will perform a UCC search but public must search other records themselves. Copy fee $2.00 for UCC, $.50 per page if clerk makes copy, $.25 per page self serve. Cert fee- $1.00 per page plus copy fee. Payee- Clay County Clerk of the Chancery Court. Contact Becky Coe with bulk data sales inquiries. **Other phones:** Elections- 662-494-3384. **Property tax/Assessing-** PO Box 795, 205 Court St, West Point, MS 39773; 662-494-3432, assessor fax- 662-494-7452. (Appraiser/Auditor- 662-494-3432) **Online access-** Tax rolls may be available at the statewide website at www.mstc.state.ms.us/.

Coahoma County

Chancery Clerk, PO Box 98, Clarksdale, MS 38614. Recording, R/E & UCC phone-662-624-3000; fax-662-624-3040; 8AM-5PM (CST)
Index: General index for both land deeds and mtgs. Records indexed on a public use terminal back to 1/11/2005. Office will perform a UCC search but public must search other records themselves. Search fee $5.00 per name plus $2.00 per page and $2.00 per listing. Copy fee $.50 per page. Cert fee- $1.00 per instrument plus copy fee. Payee- Coahoma County Chancery Clerk. **Other phones:** Treasurer- 662-624-3000; Elections- 662-624-3014; Vital Records- 601-576-7988. **Property tax/Assessing-** PO Box 219, 115 1st St, Clarksdale, MS 38614; 662-624-3006, assessor fax- 662-624-5179. A public access computer in office.

Copiah County

Chancery Clerk, PO Box 507, Hazlehurst, MS 39083-0507. Recording, R/E & UCC phone-601-894-3021; fax-601-894-4081; hours- 8AM-5PM (CST) www.copiahcounty.org
Index: All in one. Records indexed on a public use terminal back to 1995. Only the public may search. Copy fee $2.00 per page.Real estate or tax lien copy- $.50 per page. Cert fee- $1.00 per cert plus copy fee. Payee- Chancery Clerk. **Other phones:** Elections- 601-894-1241. **Property tax/Assessing-** PO Box 7301, 122 S Lowe St, Hazelhurst, MS 39083; 601-894-2721, assessor fax- 601-894-3026.

Covington County

Chancery Clerk, PO Box 1679, Collins, MS 39428. 601-765-4242; fax-601-765-5016; 8AM-5PM (CST)
Index: Separate indices to search include books. Records indexed on a public use terminal back to 1991. Only the public may search. Copy fee $.50 per page if clerk makes copy, $.25 per page self serve. Cert fee- $1.00 per doc plus copy fee. Payee- Covington County Clerk of the Chancery Court. **Other phones:** Elections- 601-765-6506. **Property tax/Assessing-** PO Box 1537, 101 Elm St, Collins, MS 39428; 601-765-6232, assessor fax- 601-765-1052. **Online access-** Tax rolls may be available at the statewide website at www.mstc.state.ms.us/.

De Soto County

Chancery Clerk, PO Box 949, Hernando, MS 38632. 662-429-1320(court records) 429-1318(land records), R/E recording phone-662-429-1318; fax-662-449-1420; 8AM-5PM (CST) www.desotoms.info
Index: Separate indices to search include Liens, Bankruptcies, Incorporations, Substitutions, Lis Pendens, Miscellaneous, Warranty Deeds, Trust Deeds, Subdivisions, Military Discharges. Records indexed on a public use terminal back to mid-1995. Only the public may search. Copy fee $.50 per page. Cert fee- $1.00 per cert plus $.50 per page. Payee- De Soto County Clerk of the Chancery Court. **Online access to Real Estate, Grantor/Grantee, Deed, Voter Registration, Foreclosure, Subdivision, Marriage records:** Access to Chancery Clerk grantor/grantee index is available at www.desotoms.info; click on "Chancery Clerk." For voter registration data, click on Circuit Clerk and then Voter Registration tab. Also available, county board and planning commission minutes. For courts and marriages, click on Circuit Clerk. **Other phones:** Elections- 662-429-1325; Tax Collector- 662-429-1340; Chancery Court Records -662-429-1320. **Property tax/Assessing-** 365 Losher St, #100, Hernando, 38632; 662-429-1335. Public access computer terminal in office. www.desotoms.com/tax_assessor.htm **Online access-** Access to assessor property data and tax collector data is free at www.desotoms.info. Click on "Tax Assessor." GIS-mapping site is also available.

Forrest County

Chancery Clerk, PO Box 951, Hattiesburg, MS 39403. 601-545-6017, R/E recording phone-601-545-6014; fax-601-545-6095; 8AM-5PM.
Index: All in one. Records indexed on a public use terminal back to 1974. Office will perform a UCC search but public must search other records themselves. Copy fee $.50 per page. UCC copy $2.00 per page. Cert fee- $1.00 per instrument plus copy fee. Payee- Chancery Clerk. **Other phones:** Treasurer- 601-582-8228; Elections- 601-582-3213; Vital Records- 601-576-7960. **Property tax/Assessing-** PO Box 1626, 601 Main St, Hattiesburg, MS 39401; 601-545-6130, assessor fax- 601-545-6180. Public access computer in office. **Online access-** Access property tax or appraisal records free at www.deltacomputersystems.com/MS/MS18/INDEX.HTML.

Franklin County

Chancery Clerk, PO Box 297, Meadville, MS 39653-0297. 601-384-2330; fax-601-384-5864; 8AM-5PM.
Index: Separate indices to search include books. Records indexed on a public use terminal back to 1988. Office will perform a UCC search but public must search other records themselves. Search fee- $10.00 per name. $2.00 per each UCC found and copied. Office will not search real estate records. Copy fee $2.00 per page for UCC, $.50 per page if clerk makes copy, $.25 per page self serve. Cert fee- $1.00 per doc plus copy fee. Payee- Franklin County Chancery Clerk. Contact the chancery clerks office with bulk data sales inquiries. **Other phones:** Elections- 601-384-2320; Tax Collector- 601-384-2359. **Property tax/Assessing-** PO Box 456, 36 Main St, East, Meadville, MS 39653-0297; 601-384-2359, assessor fax- 601-384-3040. A public access terminal is available.

George County

Chancery Clerk, 355 Cox St, Lucedale, MS 39452. Recording, R/E & UCC phone-601-947-4801; 8AM-5PM; 9AM-N Sat. (CST)
Index: All in one. Records indexed on a public use terminal back to 1993. Only the public may search. Copy fee $.50 per page; UCC copy fee- $1.00 per page. Cert fee- $1.00 per cert plus copy fee. Payee- George County Clerk of the Chancery Court. **Online Access to Real Estate, Deed Records:** A private company permits online access by subscription; www.recordsusa.com or call Rob at 888-633-4748 x17 for info and demo. **Other phones:** Treasurer- 601-947-3766; Elections- 601-947-4881. **Property tax/Assessing-** 355 Cox St, Lucedale, MS 39452; 601-947-7541. (Appraiser/Auditor- 601-947-7541) **Online** - Access to the property tax records is free at www.deltacomputersystems.com/MS/MS20/plinkquerym.html.

Greene County

Chancery Clerk, PO Box 610, Leakesville, MS 39451. 601-394-2377; fax-601-394-2334; 8AM-5PM
Records indexed on a public use terminal (deeds only) back to the 1800's. Only the public may search. Copy fee $.50 per page if clerk makes copy, $.25 per page self serve. Cert fee- $1.00 per doc plus copy fee. Payee- Greene County Chancery Clerk. **Other phones:** Treasurer- 601-394-2377; Elections- 601-394-2379. **Property tax/Assessing-** PO Box 477, 405 McKinnis Ave, Leakesville, MS 39451; 601-394-2378, assessor fax- 601-394-6199. Public access terminal goes back 10 years. **Online access-** Access property and appraisal data free at www.deltacomputersystems.com/MS/MS21/INDEX.HTML.

Grenada County

Chancery Clerk, PO Drawer 1208, Grenada, MS 38902-1208. 662-226-1821; fax-662-227-2860; 8AM-5PM (CST)
Index: All in one. Records indexed on computer since 5/2006. Only the public may search. UCC copy fee $2.00 per page.Real estate record copy- $.50 per page. Cert fee- $1.00 per cert plus copy fee. Payee- Grenada County Clerk of the Chancery Court. **Other phones:** Treasurer- 662-226-1821; Elections- 662-226-1941; Tax Collector- 662-226-1741. **Property tax/Assessing-** PO Box 1488, Grenada, MS 38902; 662-226-1741, assessor fax- 662-226-3701. **Online access-** Search assessor real property and tax sale free at www.tscmaps.com/mg/ms/grenada/index.asp but no name searching.

Hancock County

Chancery Clerk, 3068 Longfellow Dr, Bldg 1, #A, Bay Saint Louis, MS 39520. Recording, R/E & UCC phone-228-467-0455; fax-228-466-6236; 8AM-5PM. www.hancockcountyms.gov
Index: All in one. All records indexed on a public use terminal. Terminal located in the Search Room in the trailer. Office will perform a UCC search but public must search other records themselves. UCC search back 5 years per debtor name $5.00. Copy fee $.50 per page if clerk make copy, $.25 per page self serve. Cert fee- $1.00 per doc plus copy fee. Payee- Chancery Clerk. Contact office with bulk data sales inquiries. **Other phones:** Treasurer- 228-467-4425; Elections- 228-467-5265; Tax Collector- 228-467-4425. **Property tax/Assessing-** 3068 Longfellow Dr, Bldg 9-12, Bay Saint Louis, MS 39520; 228-467-5727, assessor fax- 228-466-6239. (Appraiser/Auditor- 228-467-0130) Public access computer in office. www.hancockcountyms.org **Online access-** Access property data free through the GIS-mapping site owner search page free at www.geoportalmaps.com/atlas/hancock/asp/owner.asp. Search parcel data generally on mapping site free at www.geoportalmaps.com/atlas/hancock/viewer.htm.

Harrison County (1st District)

Chancery Clerk, PO Drawer CC, Gulfport, MS 39502. Recording, R/E & UCC phone-228-865-4036, UCC recording phone-228-865-4235; fax-228-214-1513; 8AM-5PM. http://co.harrison.ms.us
Except for the searchable website, Harrison County's two district's records are not co-mingled. Index: Separate indices to search include deeds, mortgages, liens, UCCs. Records indexed on a public use terminal back to 1985, but no Biloxi (2nd District) records on it. Office personnel or visitors may perform searches. Search fee-$5.00 per name. Office will not search real estate records. Office will search UCC and federal tax lien records. General copy fee $.50 per page; UCC or tax lien- $2.00 per page. Cert fee- $1.00 per doc plus copy fee. Payee- Chancery Clerk. **Online access to Real Estate, Grantor/Grantee, Deed, UCC, Voter Registration, Marriage, Judgment records:** Access all records through the county portal at http://co.harrison.ms.us. Also, search chancery clerk Deed & Record index back 20 years. Also, search voter registration and marriage licenses. Search circuit court judgment rolls at http://co.harrison.ms.us/departments/circlerk/rolls/. **Other phones:** Elections- 228-865-4049; Vital Records- 228-960-7981; Tax Collector- 228-865-4040. **Property tax/Assessing-** PO Box 462, 1801 23rd Ave, Gulfport, MS 39305; 228-865-4043, assessor fax- 228-865-4076. (Appraiser/Auditor- 228-865-4044) A public access terminal is available. **Online access-** Access property tax data free at www.deltacomputersystems.com/MS/MS24DELTA/DATALINK.html or http://co.harrison.ms.us/departments/chanclerk/proplink.asp.

Harrison County (2nd District)

Chancery Clerk, PO Box 544, Biloxi, MS 39533. Recording, R/E & UCC phone-228-435-8220; fax-228-435-8292; 8AM-5PM. http://co.harrison.ms.us
Except for the searchable website, Harrison County's two district's records are not co-mingled. Index: Separate indices to search include computer and books. Records indexed on a public use terminal back to 8/85, but no Gulfport (1st District) records on it. Office will perform a UCC search but public must search other records themselves. Search fee $5.00 per name. Office will not search real estate records. Copy fee $.50 per page, self serve $.25 per page; $2.00 for UCC/tax liens. Cert fee- $1.00 per cert. Payee- Chancery Clerk. **Online access to Real Estate, Grantor/Grantee, Deed, Lien, UCC, Voter Registration, Marriage, Judgment records:** Access to property data is free at www.deltacomputersystems.com/MS/MS24DELTA/DATALINK.html or http://co.harrison.ms.us. You may also choose to search chancery clerk Deed & Record index back 15 years. Also search voter registration and marriage licenses. Also, search circuit court judgment rolls at http://co.harrison.ms.us/departments/circlerk/rolls/. **Other phones:** Elections- 228-865-4167. **Property tax/Assessing-** 730 Dr Martin Luther King Jr Blvd, Biloxi, MS 39530; 228-435-8265, assessor fax- 228-435-8267. A public access terminal is available. Access property tax data at www.deltacomputersystems.com/MS/MS24DELTA/DATALINK.html or http://co.harrison.ms.us/departments/chanclerk/proplink.asp.

Hinds County (1st District)

Chancery Clerk, PO Box 686, Jackson, MS 39205-0686. phone-601-968-6508, UCC recording phone-601-968-6516; fax-601-973-5535; 8AM-5PM. www.co.hinds.ms.us/pgs/elected/chanceryclerk.asp
District has 2 offices; their indexes are combined on the internet, but physical records must be searched at their respective offices. Index: All in one. Records indexed on a public use terminal back to 1987. Office will perform a UCC search but public must search other records themselves. Search fee $5.00 per name. Office will not search real estate records. UCC copy fee $2.00 per page, $.50 per page if clerk make copy, self serve $.25 each. Cert fee- $1.00 per doc plus copy fee. Payee- Hinds County Chancery. **Online access to Real Estate, Grantor/Grantee, Deed, Lien, Judgment records:** Access county records databases free at www.co.hinds.ms.us/pgs/apps/gindex.asp. **Other phones:** Treasurer- 601-968-6588; Elections- 601-968-6628; Tax Collector- 601-968-6588. **Property tax/Assessing-** PO Box 22908, 316 S President St, Jackson, MS 39225-2908; 601-968-6616. **Online-** Search assessor land rolls free also judgments, acreage, condos, and subdivisions free at www.co.hinds.ms.us/pgs/apps/landroll_query.asp. Also, search the Real Property Billing Roll free at www.co.hinds.ms.us/pgs/apps/real_property_billing_roll_query.asp.

Hinds County (2nd District)

Chancery Clerk, PO Box 88, Raymond, MS 39154. 601-857-8055; fax-601-857-4953; 8AM-5PM (CST) www.co.hinds.ms.us/pgs/elected/chanceryclerk.asp
District has 2 offices; their indexes are combined on the internet, but physical records must be searched separately. 2nd District- all towns/cities outside of Jackson: Bolton, part of Clinton, Edwards, Learned, Raymond, part of Terry, Utica. Index: Separate indices to search include computer, books prior to 11/87. Records indexed on computer back to 11/87. Only the public may search. UCC copy fee $2.00 per page, $.50 per page if clerk make copy, $.25 per page self serve. Cert fee- $1.00 per doc plus copy fee. Payee- Hinds County Clerk of the Chancery Court. **Online Real Estate, Grantor/Grantee, Deed, Judgment records:** Access county clerk index free at www.co.hinds.ms.us/pgs/apps/gindex.asp. Chose to search general index, land roll, judgments, acreage, subdivision, condominiums. **Other phones:** Treasurer- 601-857-5574; Elections- 601-968-6628; Tax Collector- 601-857-5574. **Property tax/Assessing-** PO Box 549, 127 W Main St, Raymond, 39154; 601-857-8787. No public computer available. www.co.hinds.ms.us/pgs/elected/taxassessor.asp **Online access-** Access tax roll, property, and other assessor related data free at www.co.hinds.ms.us/pgs/apps/gindex.asp or at www.co.hinds.ms.us/pgs/apps/landroll_query.asp. Also, search the Real Property Billing Roll free at www.co.hinds.ms.us/pgs/apps/real_property_billing_roll_query.asp.

Holmes County

Chancery Clerk, PO Box 239, Lexington, MS 39095. 662-834-2281, R/E recording phone-662-834-0005; fax-662-834-3020; 8-5PM. www.holmescounty.com
Index: All in one. Records indexed on a public use terminal back to 4/00. Only the public may search. Copy fee $.50 per page; self serve- $.25 each. Cert fee- $1.00 per page plus copy fee. Payee- Holmes Cuonty Chancery Clerk. **Other phones:** Treasurer- 662-834-0005; Elections- 662-834-2476; Vital Records- 662-834-2476. **Property tax/Assessing-** 2 Court Sq, Courthouse, Lexington, MS 39095; 662-834-2865. (Appraiser/Auditor- 662-834-3737)

Humphreys County

Chancery Clerk, PO Box 547, Belzoni, MS 39038. 662-247-1740; fax-662-247-0101; 8AM-N,1PM-5PM
Index: Separate indices to search include computer, books by years. Records indexed on a public use terminal back to 2004. Only the public may search. UCC copy fee $2.00 per page.Real estate record copy- $.50 per page. Cert fee- $1.00 per cert plus copy fee. Payee- Humphreys County Clerk of the Chancery Court. **Other phones:** Treasurer- 662-247-2552; Elections- 662-247-3065; Tax Collector- 662-247-2552. **Property tax/Assessing-** 102 Castleman St, Courthouse, Belzoni, MS 39038; 662-247-3174, assessor fax- 662-247-5657. (Appraiser/Auditor- 662-247-0106) hours- 8AM-5PM

Issaquena County

Chancery Clerk, PO Box 27, Mayersville, MS 39113-0027. Recording, R/E & UCC phone-662-873-2761; fax-662-873-2061; 8AM-N; 1-5PM.
Index: Separate indices to search include alphabetical and sectionals. Records indexed on a public use

terminal. Only the public may search. Copy fee $2.00 per page. Cert fee- $1.00 per instrument includes copy fee. Payee- Chancery Clerk. **Other phones:** Treasurer- 662-873-2761; Elections- 662-873-2761; Marriages/Divorces -662-873-2761. **Property tax/Assessing**- PO Box 67, 129 Court St, Mayersville, MS 39113; 662-873-4665, assessor fax- 662-873-2600. No public access computer available.

Itawamba County

Chancery Clerk, PO Box 776, Fulton, MS 38843. Recording, R/E & UCC phone-662-862-3421; fax- 662-862-3421; 8AM-5PM M-F; 8AM-N Sat.

Records indexed on a public use terminal back to about 2000. Only the public may search. Copy fee $2.00 per page for UCC, $.50 per page if clerk make copy, self serve $.25 each. Cert fee- $1.00 per cert. For bulk data sales, call Delta Computer Service at: 228-868-3250. **Other phones:** Elections- 662-862-3511; Vital Records- 662-862-3511. **Property tax/Assessing**- PO Box 158, 201 W Main St, Fulton, MS 38843; 662-862-7598. (Appraiser/Auditor- 662-862-7598) hours- 8AM-5PM Public access computer in office for index and records searching.

Jackson County

Chancery Clerk, PO Box 998, Pascagoula, MS 39568. 228-769-1680; fax-228-769-3397; 8AM-5PM. www.co.jackson.ms.us/DS/ChanceryClerk.html

Due to Hurricane Katrina land record office is now at Civic Center on Vega St in Pascagoula. Index: Separate indices to search include computer, books. Records indexed on a public use terminal back to 7/02. Office personnel or visitors may perform searches. Search fee $5.00 per name. Office will not search real estate records. Copy fee $2.00 per page for UCC, $.50 of clerk make copy, $.25 per page self serve. Cert fee- $1.00 per doc plus copy fee. Payee- Jackson County Chancery Clerk. For bulk data sales, please contact Greta Hearndon. **Other phones:** Treasurer- 228-769-3131; Elections- 228-769-3040. **Property tax/Assessing**- PO Box 998, 2902 Shortcut Rd, Padcagoula, MS 39568; 228-769-3070, assessor fax- 228-769-3005.

Jasper County (1st District)

Chancery Clerk, PO Box 38, Paulding, MS 39348-0038. 601-727-4941, R/E recording phone-601-764-3368; fax-601-727-4475; 8AM-5PM (CST)

Each district office must be searched separately. Index: Separate indices to search include direct/reverse by name, sectional index, federal tax liens, power attorneys and more. Records indexed on a public use terminal back to 2004. Office will perform a UCC search but public must search other records themselves. Search fee-$10.00 per name. UCC search on a limited basis as time permits. Copy fee real estate $.50 per page; $2.00 if tax lien. Cert fee- $1.00 per page. Payee- Jasper County Clerk of the Chancery Court. **Other phones:** Elections- 601-764-2245; Tax Collector- 601-727-4971 or 764-2813. **Property tax/Assessing**- 601-764-2813.

Jasper County (2nd District)

Chancery Clerk, PO Box 1047, Bay Springs, MS 39422. 601-764-3026; fax-601-764-3999; 8AM-5PM.

Each district office must be searched separately. Index: All in one. Records indexed on a public use terminal back to 1990s. Only the public may search. Copy fee $.50 per page; self serve $.25 each. Cert fee- $1.00 per doc plus copy fee. Payee- Chancery Clerk- Jasper County. **Other phones:** Treasurer- 601-764-3469; Elections- 601-764-2245. **Property tax/Assessing**- PO Box 372, 27 W 8th St, Courthouse, Bay Springs, MS 39422; 601-764-2813, assessor fax- 601-764-6519. Public access computer in office.

Jefferson County

Chancery Clerk, PO Box 145, Fayette, MS 39069. Recording, R/E & UCC phone-601-786-3021, UCC recording phone-601-359-1350; fax-601-786-6009; 8AM-5PM.

Index: Separate indices to search include deeds, oil & gas, POA, affidavits, judgments, deeds of trust, cancellations, assignments. Record index not computerized. Office will perform a UCC search but public must search other records themselves. UCC search per debtor name- $10.00. Copy fee $2.00 for UCC/tax liens; general $.50 per page. Cert fee- $1.00 per doc plus copy fee. Payee- Chancery Clerk. **Other phones:** Elections- 601-786-3422; Tax Collector- 601-786-3781. **Property tax/Assessing**- 601-786-3781. (Appraiser/Auditor- 601-786-3781)

Jefferson Davis County

Chancery Clerk, PO Box 1137, Prentiss, MS 39474. 601-792-4204; fax-601-792-2894; 8AM-5PM.

Index: Separate indices to search. Records indexed on a public use terminal back to 11/19/1995. Only the public may search. General copy fee $.50 per page. Cert fee- $1.00 per page. Payee- Chancery Clerk. **Other phones:** Treasurer- 601-792-4291; Elections- 601-792-4231. **Property tax/Assessing**- PO Box 547, 1025 3rd St, Prentiss, MS 39474; 601-792-4291, assessor fax- 601-792-2276. Public access computer in office for index and records searching.

Jones County (1st District)

Chancery Clerk, 101 N Court St; County Courthouse, Ellisville, MS 39437. 601-477-3307; fax-601-477-1240; 8AM-5PM (CST)

Each district office must be searched separately. Index: All in one. Records indexed on computer back to 1/06 only. Office personnel or visitors may perform searches. Search fee $5.00 per name. Office will not search real estate records. Will not search UCC records. Copy fee $.50 per page. UCC copy fee- $2.00. Cert fee- $1.00 per page plus copy fee. Payee- Jones County Chancery Clerk. **Online access to Judgment records:** Access county judgment roll free www.deltacomputersystems.com/MS/MS34/INDEX.HTML. **Other phones:** Elections- 601-425-2556. **Property tax/Assessing**- 101 N Court St, #A, Ellisville, MS 39437; 601-477-3261, assessor fax- 601-477-3042. The main assessor office is in Laurel. www.co.jones.ms.us/taxcollect.html **Online access**- County appraisal and tax records are available by subscription at www.deltacomputersystems.com/MS/MS34/INDEX.HTML for $25.00 monthly or $275.00 annually.

Jones County (2nd District)

Chancery Clerk, PO Box 1468, Laurel, MS 39441. Recording, R/E & UCC phone-601-428-0527, UCC recording phone-601-428-3131; fax-601-428-3610; 8AM-5PM.

Each district office must be searched separately. Index: Separate indices to search include deeds, deeds of trust. Record index not computerized. Office may perform a UCC search but public must search other records themselves. Copy fee $.50 per page; $.25 self serve. Cert fee- $1.00 per page plus copy fee. Payee- Chancery Clerk. **Online access to Judgment records:** Access county judgment roll free at www.deltacomputersystems.com/MS/MS34/INDEX.HTML. **Other phones:** Treasurer- 501-428-3128; Elections- 601-425-2556; Vital Records- 601-576-7981. **Property tax/Assessing**- PO Box 511, 501 N 5th Ave, Laurel, MS 39441; 601-428-3248; RE 601-649-1636, assessor fax- 601-428-3605. (Appraiser/Auditor- 601-649-1896) **Online access**- County appraisal and tax records are available by subscription at www.deltacomputersystems.com/MS/MS34/INDEX.HTML for $25.00 monthly or $275.00 annually.

Kemper County

Chancery Clerk, PO Box 188, De Kalb, MS 39328. 601-743-2560, R/E recording phone-601-743-2460; fax-601-743-2789; 8-5PM. http://co.kemper.ms.us

Index: All in one. Record index not computerized. Only the public may search. Copy fee $2.00 for UCC, $.50 if clerk make copies, self serve $.25 each. Cert fee- $1.00 per doc. Payee- Chancery Clerk. **Other phones:** Treasurer- 601-743-4290; Elections- 601-743-2224; Vital Records- 601-743-2224. **Property tax/Assessing**- PO Box 328, 100 Main St, Courthouse Sq, De Kalb, MS 39328; 601-743-2693, assessor fax- 601-743-9119. (Appraiser/Auditor- 601-743-2693) No public terminal.

Lafayette County

Chancery Clerk, PO Box 1240, Oxford, MS 38655. Recording, R/E & UCC phone-662-234-2131; fax- 662-234-5038; 8AM-5PM (CST)

Index: Separate indices to search. Records indexed on a public use terminal back to 00. Only the public may search. Copy fee $.50 if clerk make copies, self serve $.25 each. Cert fee- $1.00 plus copy fee. Payee- Lafayette County Clerk of the Chancery Court. **Other phones:** Elections- 662-234-4951; Vital Records- 662-656-2569. **Property tax/Assessing**- 300 N Lamar St, Oxford, MS 38655; 662-234-6006, assessor fax- 662-238-7992. (Appraiser/Auditor- 662-234-5562) A public access terminal is available. **Online access**- Access to property data is free at www.deltacomputersystems.com/ms/ms36/plinkquerym.html. Also, access City of Oxford real property tax data free at www.deltacomputersystems.com/MC/MC04/INDEX.HTML.

Lamar County

Chancery Clerk, PO Box 247, Purvis, MS 39475. 601-794-8504; fax-601-794-3903; 8AM-5PM.

Index: Separate indices to search include books. Records indexed on a public use terminal back to 1000. Office personnel or visitors may perform searches. Search fee $5.00 per name. Office will not search real estate records. Copy fee $2.00 per page for UCC. $.50 if clerk makes copy, $.25 if you make your own. Cert fee- $1.00 per cert. Payee- Lamar County Chancery Clerk. **Other phones:** Elections- 601-794-8504. **Property tax/Assessing**- PO Box 309, 109 Main St, Purvis, MS 39475; 601-794-1020, assessor fax- 601-794-1064. Public access computer in office. **Online access**- Access to property data is free at www.deltacomputersystems.com/MS/MS37/INDEX.html

Lauderdale County

Chancery Clerk, PO Box 1587, Meridian, MS 39302-1587. Recording, R/E & UCC phone-601-482-9701, UCC recording phone-601-482-9710; fax-601-486-4943; 8AM-5PM (CST) www.lauderdalecounty.org

Index: Separate indices to search include deeds, mortgages. Records indexed on a public use terminal back to 0600. Only the public may search. General copy fee $.50 per page. UCC copy fee $2.00 per page. Cert fee- $1.00 per doc plus copy fee. Payee- Lauderdale County Clerk of the Chancery Court. **Other phones:** Treasurer- 601-482-4701; Elections- 601-482-9731. **Property tax/Assessing**- Same address as recording office. 601-482-9779. **Online access**- Access property data free at www.deltacomputersystems.com/MS/MS38/INDEX.html.

Lawrence County

Chancery Clerk, PO Box 821, Monticello, MS 39654. Recording, R/E & UCC phone-601-587-7162; fax- 601-587-0767; 8AM-5PM (CST)

Index: Separate indices to search include Direct/Reverse, Sentinel. Record index not computerized. Office will perform a UCC search but public must search other records themselves. Search fee $10.00. Copy fee $.50 per copy. Cert fee- $2.00 per copy plus copy fee. Payee- Lawrence County Chancery Clerk. Contact office with bulk data sales inquiries. **Other phones:** Treasurer- 601-587-2211; Elections- 601-587-4791; Tax Collector- 601-587-2211. **Property tax/Assessing**- PO Box 812, 523 Brinson, Monticello, MS 39654; 601-587-2211, assessor fax- 601-587-0768. Public access computer in office. **Online access**- Search appraisal, Real Property Tax, and tax sales lists free at www.tscmaps.com/mg/ms/lawrence/index.asp.

Leake County

Chancery Clerk, PO Box 72, Carthage, MS 39051. 601-267-7371; fax-601-267-6137; 8AM-5PM. www.leakems.com/

Index: All in one. Records indexed on a public use terminal. Only the public may search. Copy fee $1.00 per page. Cert fee- $1.00 per cert plus copy fee. Payee- Leake County Leake County. **Other phones:** Treasurer- 601-267-7371; Elections- 601-267-8357. **Property tax/Assessing**- 601-267-3021.

Lee County

Chancery Clerk, PO Box 7127, Tupelo, MS 38802. 662-841-9100; fax-662-680-6091; 8AM-5PM.

Index: All in one. Records indexed on a public use terminal back to 1994. Office personnel or visitors may perform searches. Search fee $5.00 per name. Office will not search real estate records. Copy fee $2.00 per page. Cert fee- $1.00 per doc plus copy fee. **Other phones:** Treasurer- 662-841-9100; Elections- 662-841-9024. **Property tax/Assessing**- 662-841-9030. **Online** - Access is to property records is free at www.deltacomputersystems.com/MS/MS41/pappraisalm.html.

Leflore County

Chancery Clerk, PO Box 250, Greenwood, MS 38935-0250. 662-455-7912; fax-662-455-7965; 8AM-5PM.

Index: Separate indices to search include sectional books. Record index not computerized. Only the public may search. General copy fee $.50 per page; self serve- $.25 each; UCC copy- $2.00 per page. Cert fee- $1.00 per seal plus copy fee. Payee- Sam Abraham, Chancery Clerk. **Other phones:** Elections- 662-453-1435. **Property tax/Assessing**- 310 W Market St, Greenwood, MS 38935; 662-455-7900. **Online access**- Access real property data for free at http://cdms.datasysmgt.com/dsmh/WWREALH1.

Lincoln County

Chancery Clerk, PO Box 555, Brookhaven, MS 39602. 601-835-3411; fax-601-835-3423; 8AM-5PM

Index: Separate indices to search include sectional books up to 2007, computer. Records indexed on a public use terminal back to 1987. Office personnel or visitors may perform searches. Search fee $5.00 per name. Office will not search real estate records. General copy fee $.50 per page; self serve- $.25 each. Cert fee- $1.00 per page plus copy fee. Payee- Lincoln County Clerk of the Chancery Court. **Online access to Real Estate, Grantor/Grantee, Deed records:** Access to county deed records is free at www.deltacomputersystems.com/MS/MS43/drlinkquerym.html. **Other phones:** Treasurer- 601-835-3412; Elections- 601-835-3435. **Property tax/Assessing**- 301 S 1st St, Rm 109, Brookhaven, MS 39601; 601-835-3427, assessor fax- 601-835-3424.

Lowndes County

Chancery Clerk, PO Box 684, Columbus, MS 39703. Recording, R/E & UCC phone-662-329-5800, UCC recording phone-662-329-5807; 8AM-5PM (CST)

Index: All in one. Records indexed on a public use terminal back to 2/11/02. Office will perform a UCC search but public must search other records themselves. Request for UCC search must be in writing. UCC search per debtor name- $5.00. Copy fee $.50 per page. Cert fee- $1.00 per cert plus copy fee. Payee- Lowndes County Chancery Clerk. Bulk data available for purchase. **Online Access to Real Estate, Deed, and land records**: A private company permits online access by subscription; go to www.recordsusa.com or call Rob at 888-633-4748 x17 for info and demo. **Other phones:** Treasurer- 662-329-5700; Elections- 662-329-5900; Vital Records- 601-576-7960. **Property tax/Assessing**- PO Box 1077, 505 2nd Ave N, Columbus, MS 39703; 662-329-5700, assessor fax- 662-241-1935. (Appraiser/Auditor- 662-329-5701) A public access terminal is available. www.lowndesassessor.com/ **Online access**- Access property assessor data free at www.lowndesassessor.com/mappage.asp.

Madison County

Chancery Clerk, PO Box 404, Canton, MS 39046. 800 428-0584, 601-859-1177, R/E recording phone-601-859-1177; fax-601-859-0337; 8AM-5PM (CST) www.madison-co.com/elected_offices/chancery_clerk/

Index: Separate indices to search include deeds, Lis Pendens, Const. Lien, subdivision and sectional books. Records indexed on a public use terminal back to 6/88. Office will perform a UCC and/or tax lien search but public must search other records themselves. Search fee $5.00 per name. Office will not search real estate records. UCC copy fee $2.00 per page; all other copies are $.50 per page. Cert fee- $1.00 per cert plus copy fee. Payee- Madison County Chancery Clerk. Bulk data available for purchase, contact Kay Jerome. **Online access to Real Estate, Deed, Mortgage, Federal Lien, Plat, Covenant records:** Access the Chancery clerks recorded land records free at www.madison-co.com/elected_offices/chancery_clerk/. Other databases available. Also, search at www.madison-co.com/online_services/index.php for Federal Lien, Chancery Ct, Plat, Covenant, and more. **Other phones:** Treasurer- 601-855-5581; Elections- 601-352-2049; Vital Records- 601-576-7980. **Property tax/Assessing**- PO Box 292, 140 W Peace St, Canton, MS 39046; 601-859-1921, assessor fax- 601-859-2899. A public access terminal is available. www.madison-co.com/elected_offices/tax_assessor **Online access**- Access Land Roll data free at www.madison-co.com/elected_offices/tax_assessor/real_property_search.php. Also, search personal property tax data free at www.madison-co.com/elected_offices/tax_assessor/personal-property-tax-roll.php. Also, search parcels/property on the GIS-mapping site free at www.tscmaps.com/mg/ms/madison/mappage.asp?county=43.

Marion County

Chancery Clerk, 250 Broad St, #2, Columbia, MS 39429. Recording, R/E & UCC phone-601-736-2691; fax-601-444-0206; 8AM-5PM (CST)

Index: All in one. Records indexed on a public use terminal back to 8/97. Office personnel or visitors may perform searches. Search fee $5.00 per name. Office will search limited real estate records. Copy fee $.50 per page; $.25 self serve. Cert fee- $1.00 per instrument plus copy fee. Payee- Chancery Clerk. Bulk data available for purchase. **Online access to Real Estate, Deed, Probate, Judgment, Redemption records:** Access county records free at www.deltacomputersystems.com/MS/MS46/INDEX.HTML. Says it is a subscription service, but searching is free. Recorder index goes back to 5/1997; no images. **Other phones:** Treasurer- 601-736-2692; Elections- 601-736-8246; Vital Records- 601-736-2691. **Property tax/Assessing**- 250 Broad St, #3, Columbia, MS 39429; 601-736-8256, assessor fax-601-731-2304. A public access terminal is available. **Online access**- Access property data free at www.deltacomputersystems.com/MS/MS46/pappraisalm.html

Marshall County

Chancery Clerk, PO Box 219, Holly Springs, MS 38635. 662-252-4431; fax-662-551-3302; 8AM-5PM.

Index: Separate indices to search include sectional books, direct, reverse by year, will, deeds of trust, etc. Records indexed on a public use terminal. Only the public may search. Copy fee $.50 per page; self serve-$.25 per page. Cert fee- $1.00 per doc plus copy fee. Payee- Chancery Clerk. **Other phones:** Elections-662-252-3434; Tax Collector- 662-252-3661. **Property tax/Assessing**- PO Box 40, 103A S Market, Holly Springs, MS 38635; 662-252-7906, assessor fax- 662-252-1881. Public access terminal available. **Online**- Access to property tax records is free at www.deltacomputersystems.com/MS/MS47/INDEX.html.

Monroe County

Chancery Clerk, PO Box 578, Aberdeen, MS 39730. Recording, R/E & UCC phone-662-369-8143; fax-662-369-7928; 8AM-5PM.

Index: Separate indices to search. Records indexed on a public use terminal back to 1998. Only the public may search. General copy fee- $.50 per page; self serve- $.25 each; UCC- $2.00 per copy. Cert fee- $1.00 per doc plus copy fee. Payee- Chancery Clerk. **Other phones:** Treasurer- 662-369-8143; Elections-662-369-8695. **Property tax/Assessing**- PO Box 636, 301 S Chestnut St, Aberdeen, MS 39730; 662-369-2033, assessor fax- 662-369-4429. **Online access**- Access property records free on the mapping site at www.tscmaps.com/mg/ms/monroe/index.asp.

Montgomery County

Chancery Clerk, PO Box 71, Winona, MS 38967. 662-283-2333; fax-662-283-2233; 8AM-5PM.

Index: Separate indices to search include sectional books. Record index not computerized. Only the public may search. general copy fee- $.50 per page; self serve- $.25 each; UCC copy- $2.00 per page. Cert fee- $1.00 per cert plus copy fee. Payee- Montgomery County Chancery Clerk. Elections- 662-283-4161. **Property tax/Assessing**- 662-283-2112.

Neshoba County

Chancery Clerk, 401 Beacon St, #107, Philadelphia, MS 39350. 601-656-3581; fax-601-656-5915; 8AM-5PM (CST)

Index: Separate indices to search include sectional books, computer. Records indexed on a public use terminal back to 11/2005. Only the public may search. General copy fee $.50 per page; self serve- $.25 each; UCC copy- $2.00 per page. Cert fee- $1.00 per page. Payee- Neshoba County Clerk of the Chancery Court. **Other phones:** Elections- 601-656-4781. **Property tax/Assessing**- 401 Beacon St, #105, Philadelphia, MS 39350; 601-656-4541, assessor fax- 601-656-5121. **Online** - Access to property data free at www.deltacomputersystems.com/MS/MS50/index.html.

Newton County

Chancery Clerk, PO Box 68, Decatur, MS 39327. 601-635-2367; fax-601-635-3479;

Index: All in one. Records indexed on a public use terminal back to 5/00. Office will perform a UCC search but public must search other records themselves. UCC search per debtor name- $5.00. Green Bar printouts- $2.00 per page or $20.00 per hour. Copy fee $.50 per sheet; self serve- $.25 each. Cert fee- $1.00 per cert plus copy fee. Payee- Newton County Chancery Clerk. Elections- 601-635-2368. **Property tax/Assessing**- 601-635-2367.

Noxubee County

Chancery Clerk, PO Box 147, Macon, MS 39341. Recording, R/E & UCC phone-662-726-4243; fax-662-726-2272; 8AM-5PM (CST)

Index: Separate indices to search include direct, indirect, sections. Records indexed on a public use terminal back to 1800's. Office personnel or visitors may perform searches. Search fee $5.00 per name. Office will not search real estate records. Will not search UCC records. Copy fee $.75 per page; UCC copy- $2.00 per page. Cert fee- $1.00 per page plus copy fee. Payee- Noxubee County Clerk of the Chancery Court. **Other phones:** Treasurer- 662-726-4243; Elections- 662-726-5737; Vital Records- 601-576-7981. **Property tax/Assessing**- 505 S Jefferson, Macon, MS 39341; 662-726-4744, assessor fax- 662-726-2679. (Appraiser/Auditor- 662-726-2772) A public access terminal is available.

Oktibbeha County

Chancery Clerk, 101 E Main; Courthouse, Starkville, MS 39759. Recording, R/E & UCC phone- 662-323-5834; fax-662-338-1064; 8AM-5PM (CST) www.oktibbehachanceryclerk.com/index.php

Index: Separate indices to search include computer and books. Records indexed on a public use terminal back to 1960s. Office will perform a UCC search but public must search other records themselves. Tax liens not included in UCC search. UCC search per debtor name- $5.00. General copy fee- $.50 per page; self serve- $.25 each; UCC copy- $1.00. Cert fee- $1.00 per cert plus copy fee. Payee- Oktibbeha County Clerk of the Chancery Court. **Online access to Real Estate, Deed, Lien, Marriage, Judgment records:** Search county information at www.oktibbehachanceryclerk.com/online-search/index.php. An account with username and password is required to login; call Larry Bellipani at 601-583-7373. Also, search the marriage index free at www.deltacomputersystems.com/MS/MS53/mllinkquerym2.html. Also, search the Judgment Roll free at www.deltacomputersystems.com/MS/MS53/jrlinkquerym.html. **Other phones:** Elections- 662-323-1356. **Property tax/Assessing**- 101 E Main, #103, Courthouse, Starkville, MS 39759; 662-323-1273, assessor fax- 662-323-8171. (Appraiser/Auditor- 662-323-1273) A public access terminal is available. www.oktibbehacountyms.org/tax_assessor/index.htm **Online access**- property records, appraisals, tax sale lists free at www.tscmaps.com/mg/ms/oktibbeha/index.asp. Also, assess the Land Redemption database free at www.deltacomputersystems.com/MS/MS53/landredemptionm.html.

Panola County (1st District)

Chancery Clerk, 215 S Pocahontas St, Sardis, MS 38666. 662-487-2070; fax-662-487-3559; 8AM-N, 1PM-5PM.

Public terminal has index for both districts; older records available only at their respective district office. Index: Separate indices to search. Records indexed on a public use terminal back 1990s and earlier images are being added back 35 years. Office will perform a UCC search but public must search other records themselves. Copy fee $.50 per page. Cert fee- $1.00 per cert plus copy fee. Payee- Panola County Clerk. **Other phones:** Treasurer- 662-487-6215; Elections- 662-563-6210; Tax Collector- 662-487-2092/2093. **Property tax/Assessing**- 151 Public Sq, County Courthouse, Batesville, MS 38606; 662-563-6201, assessor fax- 662-563-6237.

Panola County (2nd District)

Chancery Clerk, 151 Public Sq, Batesville, MS 38606. 662-563-6206, 6238, R/E recording phone-662-563-6205; fax-662-563-6277; 8AM-5PM.

Public terminal has index for both districts; older records available only at their respective district office. Index: Separate indices to search include direct, reverse, sectional. Records indexed on a public use terminal back to 1994. Office will perform a UCC search (UCC form required) but public must search other records themselves. General copy fee $.50 per page; self-serve $.25; UCC copy fee- $2.00 per page. Cert fee- $1.00 per cert plus copy fee. Payee- Panola County Chancery Clerk. **Other phones:** Treasurer-662-563-6215; Elections- 662-563-6210. **Property tax/Assessing**- 151 Public Sq, Batesville, MS 38606; 662-563-6270.

Pearl River County

Chancery Clerk, PO Box 431, Poplarville, MS 39470. 601-403-2300 or 749-7700, R/E recording phone-601-403-2316, UCCs-601-403-2312; fax-601-403-2317; 8AM-5PM (CST) www.pearlrivercounty.net

Index: All in one. Records indexed on a public use terminal. Office will perform a UCC search but public must search other records themselves. General copy fee- $2.00 per page.Real estate record copy- $.50 per page. Cert fee- $1.00 per cert plus copy fee. Payee- Pearl River County Clerk of the Chancery Court. **Other phones:** Treasurer- 601-403-2302; Elections-601-403-2318. **Property tax/Assessing**- PO Box 509, 406 S Main St, Poplarville, MS 39470; 601-403-2300, assessor fax- 601-403-2229. A public access terminal is available. www.pearlrivercounty.net/tax/index.htm **Online access**- Access to property data is free at www.pearlrivercounty.net/tax/index.htm

Perry County

Chancery Clerk, PO Box 198, New Augusta, MS 39462. Recording, R/E & UCC phone-601-964-8398; fax-601-964-8265; 8AM-5PM.

Records indexed on a public use terminal. Office will perform a UCC search but public must search other records themselves. UCC search per debtor name- $10.00. Copy fee $.50 per page. Cert fee- $1.00 per doc plus copy fee. Payee- Vickie Walters-Clerk. **Other phones:** Elections- 601-964-8663. **Property tax/Assessing**- 103 Main St, New Augusta, MS 39462; 601-964-3398. (Appraiser/Auditor- 601-964-3400) **Online access**- Access property and personal property and appraisal data free at www.deltacomputersystems.com/MS/MS56/INDEX.HTML.

Pike County

Chancery Clerk, PO Box 309, Magnolia, MS 39652. Recording, R/E & UCC phone-601-783-3362; fax-601-783-5982; 8AM-5PM. www.co.pike.ms.us

Index: Separate indices to search include grantor/grantee, sectional indexes. Records indexed on a public use terminal back to 1000. Only the public may search. Copy fee $.50 per page; self serve- $.25 each. Cert fee- $1.00 per doc plus copy fee. Payee- Pike County Chancery Clerk. Bulk data available for purchase, contact 601-783-5289. **Online access to Real Estate, Grantor/Grantee, Deed records:** Access to county Deeds & Records is free at www.co.pike.ms.us/drlinkquery.html. **Other phones:** Treasurer- 601-783-5289; Elections- 601-783-2581. **Property tax/Assessing**- PO Box 111, Magnolia, MS 39652; 601-783-5511, assessor fax- 601-783-3784. **Online access**- Search property assessor and tax records free at www.co.pike.ms.us/plinkquery.html.

Pontotoc County

Chancery Clerk, PO Box 209, Pontotoc, MS 38863. Recording, R/E & UCC phone-662-489-3900; fax-662-489-3940; 8AM-5PM (CST)

Index: Separate indices to search include deeds, deed of trust, federal tax lien, power of attorneys, UCCs. Records indexed on a public use terminal back to 02/1400 (for land records only). Only the public may search. Copy fee $4.00 per page. Cert fee- $1.00 per page includes copy fee. Payee- Pontotoc County Clerk of the Chancery Court. **Other phones:** Treasurer- 662-489-3904; Elections- 662-489-3908; Tax Collector- 662-489-3904. **Property tax/Assessing**- 11 E Washington St, Pontotoc, MS 38863; 662-489-3903, assessor fax- 662-489-3917. (Appraiser/Auditor- 662-489-3903) A public access terminal is available.

Prentiss County

Chancery Clerk, PO Box 477, Booneville, MS 38829. Recording, R/E & UCC phone-662-728-8151; fax-662-728-2007; 8AM-5PM.

Index: Separate indices to search include warranty deeds, trust deeds. Records indexed on a public use terminal. Only the public may search. Copy fee $.50 per page; self serve $.25 each with account. UCC copy- $1.00 per page. Cert fee- $1.00 per doc plus copy fee. Payee- Chancery Clerk. **Other phones:** Treasurer- 662-728-8151; Elections- 662-728-4611. **Property tax/Assessing**- PO Box 342, 100 N Main St, Booneville, MS 38829; 662-728-4349, assessor fax- 662-728-4472. (Appraiser/Auditor- 662-728-4349) A public access terminal is available.

Quitman County

Chancery Clerk, 220 Chestnut St, #2; Courthouse, Marks, MS 38646. Recording, R/E & UCC phone-662-326-2661; fax-662-326-8004; 8AM-N, 1PM-5PM (CST)

Index: Separate indices to search include computer and some hand written. Construction liens, tax liens, judgments. Records indexed on computer back to 1996. Office personnel or visitors may perform searches. Search fee $5.00 per name. Copy fee $.50 per page. Cert fee- $1.00 per cert plus copy fee. Payee- Chancery Clerk. **Other phones:** Treasurer-662-326-2661; Elections- 662-326-8003. **Property tax/Assessing**- 220 Chestnut St, #1, Courthouse, Marks, MS 38646; 662-326-8928, assessor fax- 662-326-8004. (Appraiser/Auditor- 662-326-8928) hours- 8AM-5PM A public access terminal is available.

Rankin County

Chancery Clerk, PO Box 700, Brandon, MS 39043. 601-825-1469; fax-601-824-7116; 8AM-5PM. www.rankincounty.org

Index: Old and new computer indices to search. Records indexed on a public use terminal back to 2004 (new), 1980-2003 (old). Office personnel or visitors may perform searches. Search fee $5.00 per name. Add $2.00 to search fee for each UCC finding. Office will not search real estate records. General copy fee $.50 per page; self serve $.25 each; UCC- $2.00 each. Cert fee- $1.00 per doc plus copy fee. Payee- Chancery Clerk. Bulk data available for purchase, contact aymond Reed. **Other phones:** Treasurer- 601-825-1366; Elections- 601-825-1466. **Property tax/Assessing**- 211 E Government St, #C, Brandon, MS 39043; 601-825-1470, assessor fax- 601-824-2457. A public access terminal is available. **Online** - Records on the Land Roll database are free at www.rankincounty.org/TA/LandRollDB.asp.

Scott County

Chancery Clerk, PO Box 630, Forest, MS 39074. 601-469-1922; fax-601-469-5180; 8AM-5PM.

Index: Separate indices to search include sectional books, direct, reverse. Records indexed on a public use terminal back to 1200. Only the public may search. General copy fee $.50 per page; self serve- $.50 each; UCCs- $2.00 per page. Cert fee- $1.00 per doc plus copy fee. Payee- Chancery Clerk. **Other phones:** Elections- 601-469-3601; Tax Collector- 601-469-4051. **Property tax/Assessing**- 100 E 1st St, Forest, MS 39074; 601-469-4051, assessor fax- 601-469-5184. (Appraiser/Auditor- 601-469-4051) A public access terminal is available. **Online access**- Tax rolls may be available at the statewide website at www.mstc.state.ms.us/. Also, access assessor and appraiser property data free at www.deltacomputersystems.com/MS/MS62/INDEX.HTML.

Sharkey County

Chancery Clerk, PO Box 218, Rolling Fork, MS 39159. 662-873-2755; fax-662-873-6045; 8AM-5PM.

Index: All in one. Record index not computerized. Office will perform a UCC search but public must search other records themselves. Search fee $10.00 per name. Office will not search real estate records. Copy fee $.50 per page. Cert fee- $2.00 per doc plus copy fee. Payee- Sharkey County Clerk. **Other phones:** Elections- 662-873-2755; Tax Collector- 662-873-4317. **Property tax/Assessing**- 662-873-4317.

Simpson County

Chancery Clerk, PO Box 367, Mendenhall, MS 39114. 601-847-2626, R/E recording phone-601-847-2624, UCC recording phone-601-847-2626; fax-601-847-7016; 8AM-5PM.

Index: All in one. Records indexed on a public use terminal back to 1994. Only the public may search. Copy fee $.50 per page. Cert fee- $1.00 per page plus copy fee. Payee- Simpson County Chancery Clerk. **Other phones:** Elections- 601-847-2474. **Property tax/Assessing**- 111 W Pine Ave, Mendenhall, MS 39114; 601-847-1744.

Smith County

Chancery Clerk, PO Box 39, Raleigh, MS 39153. Recording, R/E & UCC phone-601-782-9811; fax-601-782-4690; 8AM-5PM.

Index: Separate indices to search include sectional books, direct, reverse, wills. Record index not computerized. Office will perform a UCC search but public must search other records themselves. Copy fee $.50 per page; self serve- $.25 each. Cert fee- $1.00 per doc plus copy fee. Payee- Chancery Clerk. **Other phones:** Treasurer- 601-782-9811; Elections- 601-782-4751. **Property tax/Assessing**- 601-782-9803.

Stone County

Chancery Clerk, PO Drawer 7, Wiggins, MS 39577. 601-928-5266; fax-601-928-6464; 8AM-5PM.
Index: Separate indices to search include land records, liens, LIS, trust deeds, chattel, charters, pendens, federal judgments. Current land roll indexed on a public use terminal. Only the public may search. General copy fee $.50 per page; self serve $.25 each; UCCs- $2.00 per copy. Cert fee- $1.00 per doc plus copy fee. Payee- Stone County Chancery Clerk. **Other phones:** Treasurer- 601-928-5266; Elections- 601-928-5246. **Property tax/Assessing**- 308 Court St, Wiggins, MS 39577; 601-928-3121, assessor fax- 601-928-2507. **Online**- property tax records free at www.deltacomputersystems.com/MS/MS66/INDEX.HTML.

Sunflower County

Chancery Clerk, PO Box 988, Indianola, MS 38751-0988. Recording, R/E & UCC phone-662-887-4703; fax-662-887-7054; 8AM-5PM.
Index: Separate indices to search go back to 1800s. Deed records indexed on a public use terminal. Office personnel or visitors may perform searches. Search fee $5.00 per name. Office will not search real estate records. Copy fee $.50 per page; with self-serve account- $.25 each. Cert fee- $1.00 per doc plus copy fee. Payee- Chanceery Clerk. **Other phones:** Treasurer- 662-887-4703; Elections- 662-887-1252; Vital Records- 662-887-1252. **Property tax/ Assessing**- 200 Main St, Courthouse, Indianola, MS 38751-0988; 662-887-1454, assessor fax- 662-887-7423. (Appraiser/Auditor- 662-887-1454);

Tallahatchie County (1st District)

Chancery Clerk, PO Box 350, Charleston, MS 38921. Recording, R/E & UCC phone-662-647-5551; fax-662-647-3702; 8AM-N,1-5PM (CST)
Districts have to be searched separately; that changes when public access terminal becomes operational.
Index: Separate indices to search include land deed records, deeds of trust and Mtgs. Record index to be computerized in 2009; Charleston to have a public access terminal with index for entire county. Office will perform a UCC search but public must search other records themselves. Search fee $5.00 standard UCC form, $10.00 non-standard forms. Copy fee $.50 per page. Cert fee- $1.00 per page plus copy fee. Payee- Tallahatchie County Clerk of the Chancery Court. **Other phones:** Elections- 662-647-8758. **Property tax/Assessing**- PO Box 307, Charleston, MS 38921; 662-647-8922, assessor fax- 662-647-3703. hours- 8AM-5PM Public terminal is available.

Tallahatchie County (2nd District)

Chancery Clerk, PO Box 180, Sumner, MS 38957. Recording, R/E & UCC phone-662-375-8731; fax-662-375-7252; 8AM-5PM (CST)
Districts have to be searched separately; that changes when public access terminal becomes operational.
Index: All in one. Record index to be computerized in 2009; Sumnerr might not have a public access terminal with index for entire county, just 2nd District. Office personnel or visitors may perform searches. Search fee $5.00 per name. Office will not search real estate records. Will search UCC records. Copy fee $.50 per page, $2.00 for UCC. Cert fee- $1.00 per cert plus copy fee. Payee- Tallahatchie County Clerk of the Chancery Court. **Other phones:** Elections- 662-375-8515. **Property tax/Assessing**- PO Box 87, Sumner, MS 38957; 662-375-8386, assessor fax- 662-375-7252.

Tate County

Chancery Clerk, PO Box 309, Senatobia, MS 38668. 662-562-5661; fax-662-560-6205; 8AM-5PM.
Index: More than one index. Deed records indexed on a public use terminal back to 1973; D/Ts back to 2001. Office will perform a UCC search but public must search other records themselves. UCC search or Fed tax lien search $5.00 per debtor name. Copy fee $.50 per page; UCC copies- $2.00 per each UCC.Real estate record copy- $1.00 per page. Will fax back. Cert fee- $1.00 per doc plus copy fee. Payee- Tate Co Chancery Clerk. **Other phones:** Elections- 662-562-5211; Tax Collector- 662-562-4404. **Property tax/Assessing**- 201 Ward St, Senatobia, MS 38668; 662-562-6011, assessor fax- 662-562-6702. **Online access**- Access real property data for free at http://cdms.datasysmgt.com/dsmh/WWREALH1.

Tippah County

Chancery Clerk, 101 E Spring St, Ripley, MS 38663. 662-837-7374; fax-662-837-7148; 8AM-5PM.
Index: Separate index books to search include deed, trust deed. Records indexed on a public use terminal. Only the public may search. Office will not search real estate records. Will not search UCC records. General copy fee $.50 per page; $.25 self serve. Cert fee- $1.00 per page plus copy fee. Payee- Tippah Chancery Clerk. **Other phones:** Treasurer- 662-837-7374; Elections- 662-837-7370; Tax Collector- 662-837-9410. **Property tax/ Assessing**- County Courthouse, Ripley, MS 38663; 662-837-9956, assessor fax- 662-837-1030.

Tishomingo County

Chancery Clerk, 1008 Battleground Dr; Courthouse, Iuka, MS 38852. 662-423-7010; fax-662-423-7005; 8AM-5PM (CST)
Index: Separate indices to search include deed and TR deed books, direct and reverse; UCC book. Records indexed on a public use terminal. In books back to 1887. Only the public may search. Copy fee $.50 per page; self serve- $.25 per page. Cert fee- $1.00 per cert includes copy fee. Payee- Chancery Clerk. **Other phones:** Treasurer- 662-423-7032; Elections- 662-423-7026. **Property tax/Assessing**- 1008 Battleground Dr, Courthouse, Iuka, MS 38852; 662-423-7059, assessor fax- 662-423-9544. A public access terminal is available.

Tunica County

Chancery Clerk, PO Box 217, Tunica, MS 38676. 662-363-2451; fax-662-357-5934; 8AM-N, 1-5PM
Index: Separate indices to search include land deeds, mortgage books. Record index not computerized. Only the public may search. Copy fee- $.25 per page; UCC copy- $2.00 per doc. Cert fee- $1.00 per doc plus copy fee. Payee- Tunica County Clerk of the Chancery Court. **Other phones:** Treasurer- 662-363-1465; Elections- 662-363-2842. **Property tax/Assessing**- PO Box 655, 1052 S Court St, Tunica, MS 38676; 662-363-1266, assessor fax- 662-357-5933. hours- 8AM-5PM

Union County

Chancery Clerk, PO Box 847, New Albany, MS 38652. 662-534-1900; fax-662-534-1907; 8AM-5PM
Index: All in one. Records indexed on a public use terminal back to 1999. Office will perform a UCC search but public must search other records themselves. Search fee varies by nature of request. Copy fee $.50 per copy. Cert fee- $1.00 per doc plus copy fee. Payee- Chancery Clerk. Bulk data available for purchase, contact Delta computer system. **Other phones:** Treasurer- 662-534-1900; Elections- 662-534-1910; Tax Collector- 662-534-1973. **Property tax/Assessing**- PO Box 862, 114 E Bankand St, New Albany, MS 38652; 662-534-1972, assessor fax- 662-534-1971. A public access terminal is available. **Online access**- Access property tax records free at www.deltacomputersystems.com/MS/MS73/INDEX.HTML.

Walthall County

Chancery Clerk, PO Box 351, Tylertown, MS 39667. 601-876-3553; fax-601-876-6026; 8AM-5PM. www.walthallcountychamber.org
Index: Separate indices to search include sectional, forward and reverse. Record index not computerized. Only the public may search. Copy fee $.50 per page; self serve- $.25 each. Cert fee- $1.00 per instrument. Payee- Chancery Clerk. **Other phones:** Elections-601-876-5677. **Property tax/Assessing**- 200 Ball Ave, Tylertown, MS 39667; 601-876-4349, assessor fax- 601-876-9255. (Appraiser/Auditor- 601-876-4349);

Warren County

Chancery Clerk, PO Box 351, Vicksburg, MS 39181. Recording, R/E & UCC phone-601-636-4415; fax-601-630-8016; 8AM-5PM. www.co.warren.ms.us/ChanceryClerk/ChanceryClerk.htm
Index: Separate indices to search include Land documents and Chancery Court. Records indexed on a public use terminal back to 1984. Office will perform a UCC search but public must search other records themselves. Search fee $5.00 per name. General copy fee $.50 per page; self serve- $.25 each; UCC copy- $2.00 per page. Cert fee- $1.00 per page plus copy fee. Payee- Chancery Clerk. Bulk data available for purchase, contact Delta computer systems. **Other phones:** Treasurer- 601-638-6181; Elections- 601-636-3961; Tax Collector- 601-638-6181. **Property tax/Assessing**- 1009 Cherry St, Vicksburg, MS 39181; 601-638-6161, assessor fax- 601-630-8034. (Appraiser/Auditor- 601-638-6161) **Online access**- Access is free at www.deltacomputersystems.com/MS/MS75/INDEX.html.

Washington County

Chancery Clerk, PO Box 309, Greenville, MS 38702-0309. Recording, R/E & UCC phone-662-332-1595; fax-662-334-2725; 8AM-5PM (CST)
Index: Separate indices to search include sectional books. Records indexed on a public use terminal. Only the public may search. General copy fee $.50 per page; self serve- $.25 each; UCC copy- $2.00 per page. Cert fee- $1.00 per page. Payee- Washington County Clerk of the Chancery Court. Treasurer- 662-332-2922; Elections- 662-378-2747. **Property tax/Assessing**- 900 Washington St, Greenville, MS 38701; 662-332-2651. (Appraiser - 662-332-2651) **Online access**- Access is free at www.deltacomputersystems.com/MS/MS76/INDEX.html.

Wayne County

Chancery Clerk, 609 Azalea Dr; Courthouse, Waynesboro, MS 39367. Recording, R/E & UCC phone-601-735-2873; fax-601-735-6224; 8AM-5PM.
Index: All in one. Records indexed on a public use terminal. Only the public may search. Office will search UCC records if you send a UCC-11 form. Copy fee $.50 per copy. UCCs- $2.00 per page. Cert fee- $.50 per page plus copy fee. Payee- Wayne County Chancery Clerk. **Other phones:** Treasurer-601-735-2588; Elections- 601-735-1171. **Property tax/Assessing**- 609 Azalea Dr, Courthouse, Waynesboro, MS 39367; 601-735-3381, assessor fax-601-735-6272. (Appraiser/Auditor- 601-735-3381) **Online**- Access property tax and appraisal data free at http://deltacomputersystems.com/MS/MS77/INDEX.HTML.

Webster County

Chancery Clerk, PO Box 398, Walthall, MS 39771. 662-258-4131; fax-662-258-9635; 8AM-5PM.
Index: Separate indices to search include deeds of trust. Record index not computerized. Office personnel or visitors may perform searches. Search fee $5.00 per name. Office will not search real estate records. Will search UCC records. Copy fee $.50 per page. Cert fee- $1.00 per cert plus copy fee. Payee-Webster County Clerk. **Other phones:** Elections-662-258-6287. **Property tax/Assessing**- 662-258-6446.

Wilkinson County

Chancery Clerk, PO Box 516, Woodville, MS 39669. Recording, R/E & UCC phone-601-888-4381; fax-601-888-6776; 8AM-5PM.
Index: Separate indices to search include deeds, mortgages, oil & gas, probate. Records indexed on a public use terminal. Only the public may search. Copy fee $2.00 per page. Cert fee- $1.00 per cert plus copy fee. Payee- Wilkinson County Chancery Clerk. **Other phones:** Treasurer- 601-888-4381; Elections- 601-

888-6697; Vital Records- 601-960-7960. **Property tax/Assessing-** PO Box 695, 532 Commercial Row, Woodville, MS 39669; 601-888-4562, assessor fax- 601-888-7335. (Appraiser/Auditor- 601-888-6146);

Winston County

Chancery Clerk, PO Drawer 69, Louisville, MS 39339. 662-773-3631; fax-662-773-8814; 8AM-5PM. Index: Separate indices to search include sectional books. Current land roll and tax records indexed on a public use terminal; deeds added in 2007. Only the public may search. Copy fee $.50 per page; self serve- $.25 each. Cert fee- None. Payee- Winston County Chancery Clerk. **Other phones:** Treasurer- 662-773-3631; Elections- 662-773-3581. **Property tax/Assessing-** 113 W Main, Louisville, MS 39339; 662-773-3694, assessor fax- 662-773-8816. **Online access-** Access real property data for free at http://cdms.datasysmgt.com/dsmh/WWREALH1.

Yalobusha County (1st District)

Chancery Clerk, PO Box 260, Coffeeville, MS 38922. Recording, R/E & UCC phone-662-675-2716; fax-662-675-8004; 8AM-N; 1-5PM.
Countywide recording index can be seen on the 1st District public terminal, but the 2nd District cannot see 1st District index, only its own 2nd District. Index: Separate indices to search include deeds, deeds of trust, power of attorneys, federal tax liens, general chancery docket, construction Liens. Records indexed on a public use terminal back to 7/2/07. Office personnel or visitors may perform searches. Search fee $5.00 per name. Will not search UCC records. Copy fee $.50 per page. Cert fee- $1.00 per cert plus copy fee. Payee- Amy F McMinn, Chancery Clerk. **Other phones:** Elections- 662-473-1341. **Property tax/Assessing-** PO Box 260, Coffeeville, MS 38922; 662-675-8707. (Appraiser/Auditor- 662-423-1235)

Yalobusha County (2nd District)

Chancery Clerk, PO Box 664, Water Valley, MS 38965. Recording, R/E & UCC phone-662-473-2091; fax-662-473-3622; 8AM-N, 1-5PM.
Countywide recording index can be seen on the 1st District public terminal, but the 2nd District cannot see 1st District index, only its own 2nd District. The Water Valley office is the larger of the two. Index: Separate indices to search include deed, trust, reverse, direct. Records indexed on a public use terminal back to 7/2/07. Office will perform a UCC search but public must search other records themselves. Search fee $5.00 per name. Copy fee $.50 per page. UCC copy $2.00 per page. Cert fee- $1.00 per doc plus copy fee. Payee- Chancery Clerk. **Other phones:** Treasurer- 662-473-2092; Elections- 662-473-1341; Vital Records- 601-576-7960. **Property tax/Assessing-** PO Box 1552, 201 Blackmur Dr, Water Valley, MS 38965; 662-473-1235, assessor fax- 662-473-3622. (Appraiser - 662-473-1235).

Yazoo County

Chancery Clerk, PO Box 68, Yazoo City, MS 39194. phone-662-746-2661; fax-662-746-3893; 8AM-5PM www.natchezbelle.org/ahgp-ms/yazoo/index.htm
Index: Separate category indices to search. Records (land only, not court records) indexed on a public use terminal back to 1984. Office personnel or visitors may perform searches. Search fee $5.00, faxing or postage is extra depending on size of request searches. UCC copy fee $2.00 per page.Real estate record copy- $.50 per page. Cert fee- $1.00 per cert plus copy fee. Payee- Yazoo County Clerk of the Chancery Court. Bulk data available for purchase, contact Bruce Templeton. **Other phones:** Treasurer- 662-746-2661; Elections- 662-746-1872. **Property tax/Assessing-** PO Box 108, 112 E Broadway, Yazoo City, MS 39194; 662-746-2642, assessor fax- 662-751-8734. (Appraiser/Auditor- 662-746-2642) A public access terminal is available.

Mississippi County Locator

You will usually be able to find the city name in the City/County Cross Reference below. In that case, it is a simple matter to determine the county from the cross reference. However, only the official US Postal Service city names are included in this index. We have also included a ZIP/City Cross Reference immediately following the City/County Cross Reference. If you know the ZIP Code but the city name does not appear in the City/County Cross Reference index, look up the ZIP Code in the ZIP/City Cross Reference, find the city name, then look up the city name in the City/County Cross Reference.

Mississippi City/County Cross Reference

ABBEVILLE Lafayette
ABERDEEN Monroe
ACKERMAN Choctaw
ALGOMA Pontotoc
ALLIGATOR (38720) Bolivar(67), Coahoma(32)
AMORY Monroe
ANGUILLA Sharkey
ARCOLA Washington
ARKABUTLA Tate
ARTESIA Lowndes
ASHLAND (38603) Benton(97), Tippah(2)
AVALON Carroll
AVON Washington
BAILEY (39320) Lauderdale(81), Kemper(18)
BALDWYN (38824) Prentiss(47), Lee(31), Itawamba(14), Union(4)
BANNER (38913) Calhoun(91), Lafayette(8)
BASSFIELD (39421) Jefferson Davis(77), Marion(22)
BATESVILLE Panola
BAY SAINT LOUIS Hancock
BAY SPRINGS (39422) Jasper(72), Smith(27)
BEAUMONT Perry
BECKER Monroe
BELDEN (38826) Lee(55), Pontotoc(44)
BELEN Quitman
BELLEFONTAINE Webster
BELMONT Tishomingo
BELZONI (39038) Humphreys(90), Holmes(7), Leflore(1)
BENOIT Bolivar
BENTON Yazoo
BENTONIA Yazoo
BEULAH Bolivar
BIG CREEK Calhoun
BIGBEE VALLEY Noxubee
BILOXI (39532) Harrison(71), Jackson(28)
BILOXI Harrison
BLUE MOUNTAIN (38610) Tippah(85), Benton(7), Union(6)
BLUE SPRINGS Union
BOGUE CHITTO Lincoln
BOLTON Hinds
BOONEVILLE (38829) Prentiss(94), Tippah(5)
BOYLE Bolivar
BRANDON Rankin
BRAXTON (39044) Simpson(77), Rankin(22)
BROOKHAVEN (39601) Lincoln(97), Franklin(2)
BROOKHAVEN Lincoln
BROOKLYN (39425) Forrest(55), Perry(44)
BROOKSVILLE Noxubee
BRUCE Calhoun
BUCKATUNNA Wayne
BUDE Franklin
BURNSVILLE (38833) Tishomingo(89), Prentiss(5), Alcorn(4)
BYHALIA (38611) Marshall(81), De Soto(18)
BYRAM Hinds
CALEDONIA (39740) Lowndes(90), Monroe(9)
CALHOUN CITY (38916) Calhoun(97), Webster(2)
CAMDEN Madison
CANTON Madison
CARLISLE Claiborne
CARRIERE Pearl River
CARSON Jefferson Davis
CARTHAGE (39051) Leake(94), Neshoba(3), Attala(1)
CARY Sharkey
CASCILLA (38920) Grenada(82), Tallahatchie(17)
CEDARBLUFF Clay
CENTREVILLE (39631) Wilkinson(77), Amite(22)
CHARLESTON Tallahatchie
CHATAWA Pike
CHATHAM Washington
CHUNKY (39323) Newton(79), Lauderdale(20)
CHURCH HILL Jefferson
CLARA Wayne
CLARKSDALE Coahoma
CLEVELAND (38732) Bolivar(96), Sunflower(3)
CLEVELAND Bolivar
CLINTON Hinds
COAHOMA (38617) Coahoma(91), Quitman(8)
COFFEEVILLE (38922) Yalobusha(86), Grenada(13)
COILA Carroll
COLDWATER Tate
COLLINS Covington
COLLINSVILLE (39325) Lauderdale(68), Neshoba(13), Kemper(9), Newton(8)
COLUMBUS Lowndes
COMO (38619) Panola(81), Lafayette(12), Tate(6)
CONEHATTA (39057) Newton(87), Scott(12)
CORINTH Alcorn
COURTLAND Panola
CRAWFORD (39743) Lowndes(74), Oktibbeha(21), Noxubee(4)
CRENSHAW (38621) Panola(75), Quitman(24)
CROSBY (39633) Wilkinson(75), Amite(24)
CROWDER Quitman
CRUGER (38924) Holmes(81), Leflore(11), Carroll(7)
CRYSTAL SPRINGS (39059) Copiah(96), Hinds(3)
D LO Simpson
DALEVILLE (39326) Lauderdale(71), Kemper(28)
DARLING Quitman
DE KALB (39328) Kemper(52), Neshoba(31), Noxubee(15)
DECATUR Newton
DELTA CITY Sharkey
DENNIS Tishomingo
DERMA Calhoun
DIAMONDHEAD Hancock
DIBERVILLE Harrison
DODDSVILLE (38736) Sunflower(57), Leflore(42)
DREW (38737) Sunflower(98), Tallahatchie(1)
DUBLIN Coahoma
DUCK HILL (38925) Montgomery(69), Grenada(30)
DUMAS (38625) Tippah(83), Union(16)
DUNCAN Bolivar
DUNDEE (38626) Tunica(73), Coahoma(26)
DURANT Holmes
EASTABUCHIE Jones
EBENEZER Holmes
ECRU (38841) Pontotoc(97), Union(2)
EDWARDS Hinds
ELLIOTT Grenada
ELLISVILLE Jones
ENID (38927) Tallahatchie(82), Panola(16)
ENTERPRISE (39330) Clarke(85), Lauderdale(8), Jasper(3), Newton(2)
ESCATAWPA Jackson
ETHEL Attala
ETTA Union
EUPORA (39744) Webster(91), Choctaw(6), Calhoun(2)
FALCON Quitman
FALKNER (38629) Tippah(77), Benton(22)
FARRELL Coahoma
FAYETTE Jefferson
FERNWOOD Pike
FITLER Issaquena
FLORA (39071) Madison(96), Hinds(3)
FLORENCE Rankin
FLOWOOD Rankin
FOREST (39074) Scott(90), Smith(9)
FORKVILLE Scott
FOXWORTH (39483) Marion(97), Walthall(2)
FRENCH CAMP (39745) Choctaw(46), Montgomery(38), Attala(15)
FRIARS POINT Coahoma
FULTON Itawamba
GALLMAN Copiah
GATTMAN Monroe
GAUTIER Jackson
GEORGETOWN Copiah
GLEN (38846) Alcorn(84), Tishomingo(15)
GLEN ALLAN Washington
GLENDORA Tallahatchie
GLOSTER Amite
GOLDEN (38847) Itawamba(88), Tishomingo(11)
GOODMAN (39079) Holmes(92), Attala(4), Madison(3)
GORE SPRINGS (38929) Grenada(89), Webster(5), Calhoun(5)
GRACE Issaquena
GREENVILLE Bolivar
GREENVILLE Washington
GREENWOOD Leflore
GREENWOOD SPRINGS (38848) Monroe(98), Itawamba(1)
GRENADA Grenada
GULFPORT Harrison
GUNNISON Bolivar
GUNTOWN (38849) Lee(89), Union(8), Itawamba(1)
HAMILTON Monroe
HARPERVILLE Scott
HARRISTON Jefferson
HARRISVILLE Simpson
HATTIESBURG (39402) Lamar(66), Forrest(33)
HATTIESBURG Forrest
HAZLEHURST Copiah
HEIDELBERG (39439) Jasper(66), Jones(21), Clarke(9), Wayne(3)
HERMANVILLE (39086) Claiborne(78), Copiah(21)
HERNANDO De Soto
HICKORY (39332) Newton(89), Jasper(10)
HICKORY FLAT (38633) Benton(90), Union(9)
HILLSBORO Scott
HOLCOMB (38940) Grenada(93), Carroll(3), Tallahatchie(2)
HOLLANDALE (38748) Washington(90), Sharkey(9)
HOLLY BLUFF Yazoo
HOLLY RIDGE Sunflower
HOLLY SPRINGS (38635) Marshall(89), Benton(6), Tate(3)
HOLLY SPRINGS Marshall
HORN LAKE De Soto
HOULKA (38850) Chickasaw(56), Pontotoc(29), Calhoun(13)
HOUSTON Chickasaw
HURLEY Jackson
INDEPENDENCE Tate
INDIANOLA Sunflower
INVERNESS (38753) Sunflower(93), Humphreys(6)
ISOLA (38754) Humphreys(85), Sunflower(14)
ITTA BENA Leflore
IUKA Tishomingo
JACKSON (39213) Hinds(98), Madison(1)
JACKSON Hinds
JACKSON Rankin
JAYESS (39641) Lawrence(52), Walthall(37), Pike(7), Lincoln(1)
JONESTOWN Coahoma
KILMICHAEL (39747) Montgomery(97), Attala(2)
KILN Hancock
KOKOMO (39643) Marion(85), Walthall(14)
KOSCIUSKO (39090) Attala(84), Leake(15)
LAKE (39092) Scott(71), Newton(25), Smith(3)
LAKE CORMORANT De Soto
LAKESHORE Hancock
LAMAR (38642) Benton(58), Marshall(41)
LAMBERT (38643) Quitman(97), Tallahatchie(2)
LAUDERDALE (39335) Lauderdale(93), Kemper(6)
LAUREL (39443) Jones(86), Jasper(8), Wayne(4)
LAUREL Jones
LAWRENCE Newton
LEAKESVILLE Greene
LELAND Washington
LENA (39094) Leake(53), Scott(38), Rankin(7)
LEXINGTON (39095) Holmes(98), Yazoo(1)
LIBERTY Amite
LITTLE ROCK (39337) Newton(95), Neshoba(4)
LONG BEACH Harrison
LORMAN (39096) Jefferson(64), Claiborne(35)
LOUIN (39338) Jasper(51), Smith(48)
LOUISE Humphreys
LOUISVILLE Winston

LUCEDALE (39452) George(83), Jackson(16)
LUDLOW Scott
LULA Coahoma
LUMBERTON (39455) Lamar(44), Pearl River(42), Stone(11)
LYON Coahoma
MABEN (39750) Webster(77), Oktibbeha(15), Clay(6)
MACON (39341) Noxubee(88), Winston(11)
MADDEN Leake
MAGEE Simpson
MAGNOLIA (39652) Pike(87), Amite(12)
MANTACHIE (38855) Itawamba(98), Lee(1)
MANTEE (39751) Clay(63), Webster(25), Chickasaw(9), Calhoun(2)
MARIETTA (38856) Itawamba(70), Prentiss(29)
MARION Lauderdale
MARKS (38646) Quitman(98), Panola(1)
MATHISTON (39752) Webster(95), Choctaw(4)
MATTSON Coahoma
MAYERSVILLE Issaquena
MAYHEW Lowndes
MC ADAMS Attala
MC CALL CREEK (39647) Franklin(96), Lincoln(2), Wilkinson(1)
MC CARLEY Carroll
MC COMB Pike
MC CONDY Chickasaw
MC COOL (39108) Winston(40), Attala(37), Choctaw(21)
MC HENRY Stone
MC LAIN (39456) Greene(68), Perry(30)
MC NEILL Pearl River
MEADVILLE (39653) Franklin(97), Jefferson(1)
MENDENHALL (39114) Simpson(93), Rankin(6)
MERIDIAN (39301) Lauderdale(89), Clarke(10)
MERIDIAN Lauderdale
MERIGOLD (38759) Sunflower(85), Bolivar(14)
METCALFE Washington
MICHIGAN CITY Benton
MIDNIGHT Humphreys
MINERAL WELLS De Soto
MINTER CITY Leflore
MISSISSIPPI STATE Oktibbeha
MIZE Smith
MONEY Leflore
MONTICELLO (39654) Lawrence(98), Lincoln(1)
MONTPELIER Clay
MOOREVILLE Lee
MOORHEAD Sunflower
MORGAN CITY Leflore
MORGANTOWN Marion
MORTON (39117) Scott(77), Smith(19), Rankin(2)
MOSELLE Jones
MOSS Jasper
MOSS POINT Jackson
MOUND BAYOU Bolivar
MOUNT OLIVE (39119) Covington(50), Simpson(25), Smith(14), Jefferson Davis(8)
MOUNT PLEASANT Marshall
MYRTLE (38650) Union(91), Benton(7)
NATCHEZ (39120) Adams(90), Jefferson(9)
NATCHEZ Adams
NEELY Greene
NESBIT De Soto
NETTLETON (38858) Itawamba(42), Monroe(31), Lee(26)
NEW ALBANY Union
NEW AUGUSTA Perry
NEW SITE Prentiss
NEWHEBRON (39140) Lawrence(91), Jefferson Davis(8)
NEWTON Newton
NICHOLSON Pearl River
NITTA YUMA Sharkey
NORTH CARROLLTON Carroll
NOXAPATER Winston
OAK VALE (39656) Jefferson Davis(80), Lawrence(19)
OAKLAND (38948) Yalobusha(89), Tallahatchie(10)
OCEAN SPRINGS Jackson
OKOLONA (38860) Chickasaw(82), Monroe(8), Lee(7), Pontotoc(1)
OLIVE BRANCH De Soto
OSYKA (39657) Pike(70), Amite(26), Walthall(3)
OVETT (39464) Jones(91), Perry(8)
OXFORD Lafayette
PACE Bolivar
PACHUTA (39347) Jasper(68), Clarke(31)
PANTHER BURN Sharkey
PARCHMAN Sunflower
PARIS Lafayette
PASCAGOULA Jackson
PASS CHRISTIAN (39571) Harrison(97), Hancock(2)
PATTISON (39144) Claiborne(80), Jefferson(14), Copiah(5)
PAULDING Jasper
PEARL Rankin
PEARLINGTON Hancock
PELAHATCHIE (39145) Rankin(95), Scott(4)
PERKINSTON (39573) Stone(59), Hancock(28), George(5), Pearl River(3)
PETAL (39465) Forrest(89), Perry(10)
PHEBA (39755) Clay(91), Oktibbeha(8)
PHILADELPHIA Neshoba
PHILIPP (38950) Tallahatchie(71), Leflore(28)
PICAYUNE Pearl River
PICKENS (39146) Yazoo(66), Madison(31), Holmes(2)
PINEY WOODS Rankin
PINOLA Simpson
PITTSBORO Calhoun
PLANTERSVILLE Lee
PLEASANT GROVE Panola
POCAHONTAS Hinds
PONTOTOC Pontotoc
POPE Panola
POPLARVILLE (39470) Pearl River(98), Hancock(1)
PORT GIBSON Claiborne
PORTERVILLE Kemper
POTTS CAMP (38659) Marshall(82), Benton(17)
PRAIRIE (39756) Clay(75), Monroe(20), Chickasaw(4)
PRAIRIE POINT Noxubee
PRENTISS Jefferson Davis
PRESTON (39354) Kemper(61), Winston(32), Neshoba(4), Noxubee(1)
PUCKETT Rankin
PULASKI (39152) Smith(66), Scott(33)
PURVIS Lamar
QUITMAN Clarke
RALEIGH Smith
RANDOLPH (38864) Pontotoc(95), Calhoun(4)
RAYMOND Hinds
RED BANKS Marshall
REDWOOD Warren
REFORM Choctaw
RENA LARA Coahoma
RICH Coahoma
RICHTON (39476) Perry(94), Wayne(5)
RIDGELAND Madison
RIENZI Alcorn
RIPLEY Tippah
ROBINSONVILLE Tunica
ROLLING FORK Sharkey
ROME Sunflower
ROSE HILL Jasper
ROSEDALE Bolivar
ROXIE (39661) Franklin(89), Adams(8), Jefferson(1)
RULEVILLE Sunflower
RUTH (39662) Lincoln(63), Pike(29), Lawrence(7)
SALLIS Attala
SALTILLO Lee
SANATORIUM Simpson
SANDERSVILLE Jones
SANDHILL Rankin
SANDY HOOK (39478) Marion(56), Walthall(43)
SARAH (38665) Tate(79), Panola(19), Tunica(1)
SARDIS Panola
SATARTIA (39162) Warren(95), Yazoo(4)
SAUCIER Harrison
SCHLATER Leflore
SCOBEY (38953) Yalobusha(52), Grenada(32), Tallahatchie(14)
SCOOBA Kemper
SCOTT Bolivar
SEBASTOPOL Scott
SEMINARY Covington
SENATOBIA Tate
SHANNON (38868) Lee(84), Pontotoc(10), Monroe(3), Chickasaw(1)
SHARON Madison
SHAW (38773) Bolivar(75), Sunflower(24)
SHELBY Bolivar
SHERARD Coahoma
SHERMAN Pontotoc
SHUBUTA (39360) Clarke(78), Wayne(21)
SHUQUALAK Noxubee
SIBLEY Adams
SIDON (38954) Leflore(93), Carroll(5), Holmes(1)
SILVER CITY Humphreys
SILVER CREEK (39663) Lawrence(97), Jefferson Davis(2)
SKENE Bolivar
SLATE SPRING Calhoun
SLEDGE (38670) Quitman(79), Tunica(19)
SMITHDALE (39664) Franklin(59), Amite(33), Lincoln(7)
SMITHVILLE (38870) Monroe(90), Itawamba(9)
SONTAG (39665) Lawrence(80), Lincoln(19)
SOSO (39480) Jones(97), Smith(2)
SOUTHAVEN De Soto
STAR Rankin
STARKVILLE Oktibbeha
STATE LINE (39362) Greene(64), Wayne(35)
STEENS Lowndes
STENNIS SPACE CENTER Hancock
STEWART (39767) Montgomery(41), Webster(37), Choctaw(21)
STONEVILLE Washington
STONEWALL Clarke
STRINGER Jasper
STURGIS (39769) Oktibbeha(79), Winston(19), Choctaw(1)
SUMMIT (39666) Pike(72), Amite(17), Lincoln(9)
SUMNER Tallahatchie
SUMRALL (39482) Lamar(94), Jefferson Davis(3), Marion(2)
SUNFLOWER Sunflower
SWAN LAKE Tallahatchie
SWIFTOWN Leflore
TAYLOR Lafayette
TAYLORSVILLE (39168) Smith(83), Jones(14), Covington(2)
TCHULA Holmes
TERRY Hinds
THAXTON (38871) Pontotoc(87), Lafayette(10), Union(1)
THOMASTOWN Leake
THORNTON Holmes
TIE PLANT Grenada
TILLATOBA (38961) Yalobusha(83), Tallahatchie(15), Grenada(1)
TINSLEY Yazoo
TIPLERSVILLE Tippah
TIPPO Tallahatchie
TISHOMINGO (38873) Tishomingo(91), Prentiss(8)
TOCCOPOLA Lafayette
TOOMSUBA Lauderdale
TOUGALOO (39174) Hinds(91), Madison(8)
TREBLOC Chickasaw
TREMONT Itawamba
TRIBBETT Washington
TULA Lafayette
TUNICA Tunica
TUPELO (38801) Lee(93), Pontotoc(6)
TUPELO (38804) Lee(98), Itawamba(1)
TUPELO Lee
TUTWILER (38963) Coahoma(79), Tallahatchie(18), Sunflower(2)
TYLERTOWN (39667) Walthall(91), Pike(5), Marion(2)
UNION (39365) Neshoba(70), Newton(28), Leake(1)
UNION CHURCH (39668) Jefferson(81), Lincoln(10), Copiah(4), Franklin(3)
UNIVERSITY Lafayette
UTICA (39175) Hinds(82), Copiah(8), Claiborne(8)
VAIDEN (39176) Carroll(65), Attala(29), Montgomery(4)
VALLEY PARK Issaquena
VAN VLEET Chickasaw
VANCE (38964) Quitman(87), Tallahatchie(12)
VARDAMAN (38878) Calhoun(95), Chickasaw(4)
VAUGHAN Yazoo
VERONA Lee
VICKSBURG Warren
VICTORIA Marshall
VOSSBURG (39366) Clarke(63), Jasper(36)
WALLS De Soto
WALNUT (38683) Tippah(79), Alcorn(15), Benton(5)
WALNUT GROVE (39189) Leake(76), Scott(23)
WALTHALL Webster
WASHINGTON Adams
WATER VALLEY (38965) Yalobusha(92), Panola(4), Lafayette(2)
WATERFORD (38685) Marshall(92), Lafayette(7)
WAVELAND Hancock
WAYNESBORO (39367) Wayne(97), Clarke(2)
WAYSIDE Washington
WEBB Tallahatchie
WEIR Choctaw
WESSON (39191) Copiah(58), Lincoln(40)
WEST (39192) Holmes(81), Attala(17), Carroll(1)
WEST POINT (39773) Clay(97), Monroe(2)
WHEELER Prentiss
WHITFIELD Rankin
WIGGINS (39577) Stone(84), Forrest(8), Perry(6)
WINONA (38967) Montgomery(95), Carroll(4)
WINSTONVILLE Bolivar
WINTERVILLE Washington
WOODLAND (39776) Chickasaw(77), Clay(22)
WOODVILLE Wilkinson
YAZOO CITY Yazoo

Mississippi ZIP/City Cross Reference

ZIP	City
38601-38601	ABBEVILLE
38602-38602	ARKABUTLA
38603-38603	ASHLAND
38606-38606	BATESVILLE
38609-38609	BELEN
38610-38610	BLUE MOUNTAIN
38611-38611	BYHALIA
38614-38614	CLARKSDALE
38617-38617	COAHOMA
38618-38618	COLDWATER
38619-38619	COMO
38620-38620	COURTLAND
38621-38621	CRENSHAW
38622-38622	CROWDER
38623-38623	DARLING
38625-38625	DUMAS
38626-38626	DUNDEE
38627-38627	ETTA
38628-38628	FALCON
38629-38629	FALKNER
38630-38630	FARRELL
38631-38631	FRIARS POINT
38632-38632	HERNANDO
38633-38633	HICKORY FLAT
38634-38635	HOLLY SPRINGS
38637-38637	HORN LAKE
38638-38638	INDEPENDENCE
38639-38639	JONESTOWN
38641-38641	LAKE CORMORANT
38642-38642	LAMAR
38643-38643	LAMBERT
38644-38644	LULA
38645-38645	LYON
38646-38646	MARKS
38647-38647	MICHIGAN CITY
38648-38648	MINERAL WELLS
38649-38649	MOUNT PLEASANT
38650-38650	MYRTLE
38651-38651	NESBIT
38652-38652	NEW ALBANY
38654-38654	OLIVE BRANCH
38655-38655	OXFORD
38657-38657	PLEASANT GROVE
38658-38658	POPE
38659-38659	POTTS CAMP
38661-38661	RED BANKS
38662-38662	RICH
38663-38663	RIPLEY
38664-38664	ROBINSONVILLE
38665-38665	SARAH
38666-38666	SARDIS
38668-38668	SENATOBIA
38669-38669	SHERARD
38670-38670	SLEDGE
38671-38672	SOUTHAVEN
38673-38673	TAYLOR
38674-38674	TIPLERSVILLE
38675-38675	TULA
38676-38676	TUNICA
38677-38677	UNIVERSITY
38679-38679	VICTORIA
38680-38680	WALLS
38683-38683	WALNUT
38685-38685	WATERFORD
38686-38686	WALLS
38701-38704	GREENVILLE
38720-38720	ALLIGATOR
38721-38721	ANGUILLA
38722-38722	ARCOLA
38723-38723	AVON
38725-38725	BENOIT
38726-38726	BEULAH
38730-38730	BOYLE
38731-38731	CHATHAM
38732-38733	CLEVELAND
38736-38736	DODDSVILLE
38737-38737	DREW
38738-38738	PARCHMAN
38739-38739	DUBLIN
38740-38740	DUNCAN
38744-38744	GLEN ALLAN
38745-38745	GRACE
38746-38746	GUNNISON
38748-38748	HOLLANDALE
38749-38749	HOLLY RIDGE
38751-38751	INDIANOLA
38753-38753	INVERNESS
38754-38754	ISOLA
38755-38755	GREENVILLE
38756-38756	LELAND
38758-38758	MATTSON
38759-38759	MERIGOLD
38760-38760	METCALFE
38761-38761	MOORHEAD
38762-38762	MOUND BAYOU
38763-38763	NITTA YUMA
38764-38764	PACE
38765-38765	PANTHER BURN
38767-38767	RENA LARA
38768-38768	ROME
38769-38769	ROSEDALE
38771-38771	RULEVILLE
38772-38772	SCOTT
38773-38773	SHAW
38774-38774	SHELBY
38775-38775	SKENE
38776-38776	STONEVILLE
38778-38778	SUNFLOWER
38779-38779	TRIBBETT
38780-38780	WAYSIDE
38781-38781	WINSTONVILLE
38782-38782	WINTERVILLE
38801-38804	TUPELO
38820-38820	ALGOMA
38821-38821	AMORY
38824-38824	BALDWYN
38825-38825	BECKER
38826-38826	BELDEN
38827-38827	BELMONT
38828-38828	BLUE SPRINGS
38829-38829	BOONEVILLE
38833-38833	BURNSVILLE
38834-38835	CORINTH
38838-38838	DENNIS
38839-38839	DERMA
38841-38841	ECRU
38843-38843	FULTON
38844-38844	GATTMAN
38846-38846	GLEN
38847-38847	GOLDEN
38848-38848	GREENWOOD SPRINGS
38849-38849	GUNTOWN
38850-38850	HOULKA
38851-38851	HOUSTON
38852-38852	IUKA
38854-38854	MC CONDY
38855-38855	MANTACHIE
38856-38856	MARIETTA
38857-38857	MOOREVILLE
38858-38858	NETTLETON
38859-38859	NEW SITE
38860-38860	OKOLONA
38862-38862	PLANTERSVILLE
38863-38863	PONTOTOC
38864-38864	RANDOLPH
38865-38865	RIENZI
38866-38866	SALTILLO
38868-38868	SHANNON
38869-38869	SHERMAN
38870-38870	SMITHVILLE
38871-38871	THAXTON
38873-38873	TISHOMINGO
38874-38874	TOCCOPOLA
38875-38875	TREBLOC
38876-38876	TREMONT
38877-38877	VAN VLEET
38878-38878	VARDAMAN
38879-38879	VERONA
38880-38880	WHEELER
38901-38902	GRENADA
38912-38912	AVALON
38913-38913	BANNER
38914-38914	BIG CREEK
38915-38915	BRUCE
38916-38916	CALHOUN CITY
38917-38917	CARROLLTON
38920-38920	CASCILLA
38921-38921	CHARLESTON
38922-38922	COFFEEVILLE
38923-38923	COILA
38924-38924	CRUGER
38925-38925	DUCK HILL
38926-38926	ELLIOTT
38927-38927	ENID
38928-38928	GLENDORA
38929-38929	GORE SPRINGS
38930-38935	GREENWOOD
38940-38940	HOLCOMB
38941-38941	ITTA BENA
38943-38943	MC CARLEY
38944-38944	MINTER CITY
38945-38945	MONEY
38946-38946	MORGAN CITY
38947-38947	NORTH CARROLLTON
38948-38948	OAKLAND
38949-38949	PARIS
38950-38950	PHILIPP
38951-38951	PITTSBORO
38952-38952	SCHLATER
38953-38953	SCOBEY
38954-38954	SIDON
38955-38955	SLATE SPRING
38957-38957	SUMNER
38958-38958	SWAN LAKE
38959-38959	SWIFTOWN
38960-38960	TIE PLANT
38961-38961	TILLATOBA
38962-38962	TIPPO
38963-38963	TUTWILER
38964-38964	VANCE
38965-38965	WATER VALLEY
38966-38966	WEBB
38967-38967	WINONA
39038-39038	BELZONI
39039-39039	BENTON
39040-39040	BENTONIA
39041-39041	BOLTON
39042-39043	BRANDON
39044-39044	BRAXTON
39045-39045	CAMDEN
39046-39046	CANTON
39047-39047	BRANDON
39049-39049	CARLISLE
39051-39051	CARTHAGE
39054-39054	CARY
39055-39055	CHURCH HILL
39056-39056	CLINTON
39057-39057	CONEHATTA
39058-39058	CLINTON
39059-39059	CRYSTAL SPRINGS
39060-39060	CLINTON
39061-39061	DELTA CITY
39062-39062	D LO
39063-39063	DURANT
39064-39064	EBENEZER
39066-39066	EDWARDS
39067-39067	ETHEL
39069-39069	FAYETTE
39070-39070	FITLER
39071-39071	FLORA
39072-39072	POCAHONTAS
39073-39073	FLORENCE
39074-39074	FOREST
39076-39076	FORKVILLE
39077-39077	GALLMAN
39078-39078	GEORGETOWN
39079-39079	GOODMAN
39080-39080	HARPERVILLE
39081-39081	HARRISTON
39082-39082	HARRISVILLE
39083-39083	HAZLEHURST
39086-39086	HERMANVILLE
39087-39087	HILLSBORO
39088-39088	HOLLY BLUFF
39090-39090	KOSCIUSKO
39092-39092	LAKE
39094-39094	LENA
39095-39095	LEXINGTON
39096-39096	LORMAN
39097-39097	LOUISE
39098-39098	LUDLOW
39107-39107	MC ADAMS
39108-39108	MC COOL
39109-39109	MADDEN
39110-39110	MADISON
39111-39111	MAGEE
39112-39112	SANATORIUM
39113-39113	MAYERSVILLE
39114-39114	MENDENHALL
39115-39115	MIDNIGHT
39116-39116	MIZE
39117-39117	MORTON
39119-39119	MOUNT OLIVE
39120-39122	NATCHEZ
39130-39130	MADISON
39140-39140	NEWHEBRON
39144-39144	PATTISON
39145-39145	PELAHATCHIE
39146-39146	PICKENS
39148-39148	PINEY WOODS
39149-39149	PINOLA
39150-39150	PORT GIBSON
39151-39151	PUCKETT
39152-39152	PULASKI
39153-39153	RALEIGH
39154-39154	RAYMOND
39156-39156	REDWOOD
39157-39158	RIDGELAND
39159-39159	ROLLING FORK
39160-39160	SALLIS
39161-39161	SANDHILL
39162-39162	SATARTIA
39163-39163	SHARON
39165-39165	SIBLEY
39166-39166	SILVER CITY
39167-39167	STAR
39168-39168	TAYLORSVILLE
39169-39169	TCHULA
39170-39170	TERRY
39171-39171	THOMASTOWN
39172-39172	THORNTON
39173-39173	TINSLEY
39174-39174	TOUGALOO
39175-39175	UTICA
39176-39176	VAIDEN
39177-39177	VALLEY PARK
39179-39179	VAUGHAN
39180-39183	VICKSBURG
39189-39189	WALNUT GROVE
39190-39190	WASHINGTON
39191-39191	WESSON
39192-39192	WEST
39193-39193	WHITFIELD
39194-39194	YAZOO CITY
39200-39208	JACKSON
39208-39208	PEARL
39209-39232	JACKSON
39232-39232	FLOWOOD
39235-39272	JACKSON
39272-39272	BYRAM
39282-39298	JACKSON
39301-39309	MERIDIAN
39320-39320	BAILEY
39322-39322	BUCKATUNNA
39323-39323	CHUNKY
39324-39324	CLARA

Zip Code	City
39325-39325	COLLINSVILLE
39326-39326	DALEVILLE
39327-39327	DECATUR
39328-39328	DE KALB
39330-39330	ENTERPRISE
39332-39332	HICKORY
39335-39335	LAUDERDALE
39336-39336	LAWRENCE
39337-39337	LITTLE ROCK
39338-39338	LOUIN
39339-39339	LOUISVILLE
39341-39341	MACON
39342-39342	MARION
39345-39345	NEWTON
39346-39346	NOXAPATER
39347-39347	PACHUTA
39348-39348	PAULDING
39350-39350	PHILADELPHIA
39352-39352	PORTERVILLE
39353-39353	PRAIRIE POINT
39354-39354	PRESTON
39355-39355	QUITMAN
39356-39356	ROSE HILL
39358-39358	SCOOBA
39359-39359	SEBASTOPOL
39360-39360	SHUBUTA
39361-39361	SHUQUALAK
39362-39362	STATE LINE
39363-39363	STONEWALL
39364-39364	TOOMSUBA
39365-39365	UNION
39366-39366	VOSSBURG
39367-39367	WAYNESBORO
39400-39407	HATTIESBURG
39421-39421	BASSFIELD
39422-39422	BAY SPRINGS
39423-39423	BEAUMONT
39425-39425	BROOKLYN
39426-39426	CARRIERE
39427-39427	CARSON
39428-39428	COLLINS
39429-39429	COLUMBIA
39436-39436	EASTABUCHIE
39437-39437	ELLISVILLE
39439-39439	HEIDELBERG
39440-39443	LAUREL
39451-39451	LEAKESVILLE
39452-39452	LUCEDALE
39455-39455	LUMBERTON
39456-39456	MC LAIN
39457-39457	MC NEILL
39459-39459	MOSELLE
39460-39460	MOSS
39461-39461	NEELY
39462-39462	NEW AUGUSTA
39463-39463	NICHOLSON
39464-39464	OVETT
39465-39465	PETAL
39466-39466	PICAYUNE
39470-39470	POPLARVILLE
39474-39474	PRENTISS
39475-39475	PURVIS
39476-39476	RICHTON
39477-39477	SANDERSVILLE
39478-39478	SANDY HOOK
39479-39479	SEMINARY
39480-39480	SOSO
39481-39481	STRINGER
39482-39482	SUMRALL
39483-39483	FOXWORTH
39484-39484	MORGANTOWN
39500-39507	GULFPORT
39520-39522	BAY SAINT LOUIS
39522-39522	STENNIS SPACE CENTER
39525-39525	DIAMONDHEAD
39529-39529	BAY SAINT LOUIS
39530-39535	BILOXI
39540-39540	DIBERVILLE
39552-39552	ESCATAWPA
39553-39553	GAUTIER
39555-39555	HURLEY
39556-39556	KILN
39558-39558	LAKESHORE
39560-39560	LONG BEACH
39561-39561	MC HENRY
39562-39563	MOSS POINT
39564-39566	OCEAN SPRINGS
39567-39569	PASCAGOULA
39571-39571	PASS CHRISTIAN
39572-39572	PEARLINGTON
39573-39573	PERKINSTON
39574-39574	SAUCIER
39576-39576	WAVELAND
39577-39577	WIGGINS
39581-39595	PASCAGOULA
39601-39603	BROOKHAVEN
39629-39629	BOGUE CHITTO
39630-39630	BUDE
39631-39631	CENTREVILLE
39632-39632	CHATAWA
39633-39633	CROSBY
39635-39635	FERNWOOD
39638-39638	GLOSTER
39641-39641	JAYESS
39643-39643	KOKOMO
39645-39645	LIBERTY
39647-39647	MC CALL CREEK
39648-39649	MC COMB
39652-39652	MAGNOLIA
39653-39653	MEADVILLE
39654-39654	MONTICELLO
39656-39656	OAK VALE
39657-39657	OSYKA
39661-39661	ROXIE
39662-39662	RUTH
39663-39663	SILVER CREEK
39664-39664	SMITHDALE
39665-39665	SONTAG
39666-39666	SUMMIT
39667-39667	TYLERTOWN
39668-39668	UNION CHURCH
39669-39669	WOODVILLE
39701-39710	COLUMBUS
39730-39730	ABERDEEN
39735-39735	ACKERMAN
39736-39736	ARTESIA
39737-39737	BELLEFONTAINE
39738-39738	BIGBEE VALLEY
39739-39739	BROOKSVILLE
39740-39740	CALEDONIA
39741-39741	CEDARBLUFF
39743-39743	CRAWFORD
39744-39744	EUPORA
39745-39745	FRENCH CAMP
39746-39746	HAMILTON
39747-39747	KILMICHAEL
39750-39750	MABEN
39751-39751	MANTEE
39752-39752	MATHISTON
39753-39753	MAYHEW
39754-39754	MONTPELIER
39755-39755	PHEBA
39756-39756	PRAIRIE
39757-39757	REFORM
39759-39760	STARKVILLE
39762-39762	MISSISSIPPI STATE
39766-39766	STEENS
39767-39767	STEWART
39769-39769	STURGIS
39771-39771	WALTHALL
39772-39772	WEIR
39773-39773	WEST POINT
39776-39776	WOODLAND

Missouri

General Help Numbers:

Governor's Office
PO Box 720 — 573-751-3222
Jefferson City, MO 65102-0720 — Fax 573-751-1495
www.mo.gov/mo/govoffices.htm — 8AM-5PM

Attorney General's Office
PO Box 899 — 573-751-3321
Jefferson City, MO 65102 — Fax 573-751-0774
http://ago.mo.gov/ — 8AM-5PM

Legislative Records
Legislative Library
117A State Capitol — 573-751-4633
Jefferson City, MO 65101
www.moga.mo.gov/ — 8:30AM-4:30PM

State Archives
Missouri State Archives — 573-751-3280
PO Box 1747 — Fax 573-526-7333
Jefferson City, MO 65101 — 8AM-5PM M-F
www.sos.mo.gov/archives/ — (till 9PM on TH); 8:30AM-3:30PM SAT

State Specifics:

Capital:	Jefferson City Cole County
Time Zone:	CST
Number of Counties:	114
Population:	5,911,605
Web Site:	www.mo.gov

State Agencies

Criminal Records

Missouri State Highway Patrol, Criminal Record & Identification Division, 1510 E Elm St, Jefferson City, MO 65102; 573-526-6153, Fax-573-751-9382; 8AM-4 PM M-F.

www.mshp.dps.missouri.gov/MSHPWeb/Root/index.html

Indexing & Storage: Records available from 1970 on. New records available for inquiry in 5 weeks. Per a 2003 DOJ Study, 76% of all arrests in database have final dispositions recorded, 54% for those arrests within last 5 years.

Searching: Youth service providers must have signature of the subject. Include in request- full name, date of birth, sex, race, SSN. Fingerprints are an option. A request form can be downloaded from the website. Records are 100% fingerprint-supported. Open records are accessible by the public. These are convictions or arrests less than 30 days old unless charges are sought, or suspended imposition of sentence during probation period. Certain entities may access closed record files in accordance with state statute, with submission of fingerprints and required fee.

Access by: mail, in person.

Fee & Payment: A name-based search is $9.00 per request. A fingerprint search is $20.00, except certain mandated request purposes are $14.00 per request. Add $19.25.00 if the fingerprint search to include an FBI fingerprint check. Fee payee- State of Missouri Criminal Record System Fund Prepayment required. Personal checks accepted, credit cards are not.

Mail search: Turnaround time- 5 to 10 business days. SASE not required.

In person: Turnaround time is normally within 30 minutes unless lists presented. Electronic (by diskette) request submissions for name-based searches are also acceptable and are encouraged when an entity or business is regularly submitting five or more name-based search requests.

Other access: Bulk/multiple requests can be submitted on diskette; prior arrangement and agency approval required. Responses are printed out, checked for accuracy and returned; however they cannot be returned on diskette. Alias or maiden names require separate search.

Statewide Court Records

Court Administrator, 2112 Industrial Drive - PO Box 104480, Jefferson City, MO 65110; 573-751-4377, Fax- 573-751-5540; 8AM-5PM.

www.courts.mo.gov

Contact local courts for trial court records or see online below.

Indexing & Storage: New records available for inquiry in immediately.

Searching: Include in request- name, case number or date filed.

Online search: Available at https://www.courts.mo.gov/casenet/base/welcome.do. Look up by name or docket number. CaseNet search results show year of birth and address. The system includes all 115 Circuit Courts and City of St. Louis as well as the Eastern, Western, and Southern Appellate Courts, the Supreme Court, and Fine Collection Center. Cases can be searched by case number, filing date, or litigant name from 6AM-1AM M-F. One may search supreme and appellate court opinions at the home page. Some counties only offer probate case data.

Sexual Offender Registry

Missouri State Highway Patrol, Sexual Offender Registry, PO Box 9500, Jefferson City, MO 65102-0568 (Courier address- 1510 E Elm St, Jefferson City, MO 65102); 573-526-6153, 888-767-6747, Fax- 573-751-9382; 8AM-5PM.

www.mshp.dps.mo.gov/CJ38/search.jsp

The Revised Statutes of Missouri, Sections 589.400 to 589.425 and 43.650, RSMO., mandate that the Missouri State Highway Patrol shall maintain a sex offender database and a web site on the Internet that is accessible to the public.

Indexing & Storage: Records available from 01/01/95. New records available for inquiry in 24 hours.

Searching: Registry information is available from the sheriff (or CLEO) in the county, or city not within a county, where the offender resides. The county list may be released to any person upon request. A myriad of information about the offender is available including photograph and physical description of offender, physical description of vehicles owned by offender, any known alias, and nature of all offenses. This data not released- SSN

Access by: phone, online.

Phone search: Record requests accepted over the toll-free telephone line.

Online search: The name index can be searched at the website, by name, county or ZIP Code. The web page also gives links lists to the county sheriffs who have online access.

Other access: Look at bottom of disclaimer page for access to Excel spreadsheet.

Incarceration Records

Missouri Department of Corrections, Offender Inquiry, 2729 Plaza Drive, Jefferson City, MO 65102; 573-751-2389, 573-751-8488 (Probation & Parole), Fax- 573-751-4099; 8AM-5PM.

www.doc.missouri.gov

Email questions- constituentservices@doc.mo.gov.

Indexing & Storage: Records available on current and former inmates. Will release limited information on former inmates. New records available for inquiry in about 30 days.

Searching: Include in request- full name, DOB; SSN helpful. Location, conviction and sentencing information are released.

Access by: mail, phone, fax, online.

Fee & Payment: There is no fee.

Mail search: Turnaround time- 4-6 days. Record requests must include reason for request.

Phone search: Searching available by phone.

Fax search: Same criteria as mail search.

Online search: Inmate searching is offered at https://web.mo.gov/doc/offSearchWeb/.

Corporation, LLC, LP, Fictitious/Assumed Name, Trademarks/Servicemarks

Secretary of State, Corporation Services, PO Box 778, Jefferson City, MO 65102 (Courier address- 600 W Main, Jefferson City, MO 65101); 573-751-4153, 866-223-6535, Fax- 573-751-5841; 8AM-5PM.

www.sos.mo.gov/business/corporations/

Trademarks and Servicemarks are handled by the Corporations Division within Sec. of State and can be reached at the same phone number.

Indexing & Storage: Records available from the 1800s. New records available for inquiry immediately.

Searching: Include in request- full name of business, specific records that you need copies of. In addition to the articles of organization, business entity records available include: Annual Reports, Officers, Directors, DBAs, Prior (merged) names, Inactive and Reserved names. This data not released- SSNs and tax ID numbers.

Access by: mail, phone, fax, in person, online.

Fee & Payment: The fee for an abstract is $10.00, including a Good Standing. An uncertified copy of a record is $.50 per page, a certified copy of a record is $10.00 certification fee plus $.50 per page. A trademark or servicemark search is $5.00. Fee payee- Department of Revenue. Prepayment required. Personal checks and major credit cards accepted.

Mail search: Turnaround time- 2 to 3 days. SASE not required.

Phone search: Status, registered agent, type of entity, and historical information is given over the phone at no charge.

Fax search: Same criteria as mail searching. Records are returned by mail.

In person: Results are returned by mail, if numerous searches involved.

Online search: Search free online at https://www.sos.mo.gov/BusinessEntity/soskb/csearch.asp. The corporate name, the agent name or the charter number is required to search. The site indicates the currency of the data. Many business entity type searches are available.

Uniform Commercial Code

UCC Division, Attn: Records, PO Box 1747, Jefferson City, MO 65102 (Courier address- 600 W Main St, Rm 302, Jefferson City, MO 65101); 573-751-9047 (Local Records), 573-751-3319 (Records Management), Fax- 573-751-3855; 8AM-5PM. www.sos.mo.gov/ucc/

All SSNs have been redacted from images and files. Identification must be made using the name and address.

Indexing & Storage: Records available from 1965. Records are on microfiche from 7-1-80 to present. New records available for inquiry in 1 minute.

Searching: Use search request form UCC-11. Please note that all tax liens are filed at the county level. Include in request- debtor name. This data not released- SSN

Access by: mail, phone, in person, online.

Fee & Payment: A UCC-11 search is $27.00 plus $1.00 per page for copies. UCC-3's are not listed on the summary; order copies to review them. Fee payee- Director of Revenue Prepayment required. Personal checks and major credit cards accepted.

Mail search: Turnaround time- 2 weeks.

Phone search: General information is available without charge.

In person: You may request information in person, but must use their form.

Online search: Free searching for debtor names is available on the Internet at www.sos.mo.gov/ucc/search_notice.asp. However the agency is in the midst of redacting records with SSNs. These images are not available. For an electronic copy of the image of the UCC filing, send an e-mail to UCCMail@sos.mo.gov. The e-mail must contain the File #, name, and address of the filing.

Other access: The agency will release information for bulk purchase, call for procedures and pricing.

Federal & State Tax Liens

Records not maintained by a state level agency.

All tax liens are filed at the county level.

Sales Tax Registrations

Access to Records is Restricted.

Department of Revenue, Business Tax, PO Box 3300, Jefferson City, MO 65105-3300; 573-751-5860, 573-751-2836, Fax- 573-522-1722; 7:30AM-5:30PM.

http://dor.mo.gov/tax/

This agency will neither confirm nor supply any information. Confidential information is only released to owners or corporate officers registered with the Department. They suggest requesters to check at the city level.

Birth Certificates

Department of Health & Senior Svcs, Bureau of Vital Records, PO Box 570, Jefferson City, MO 65102-0570 (Courier address- 930 Wildwood, Jefferson City, MO 65109); 573-751-6387, 573-751-6400 (Message Number), 877-817-7363 (Orders), Fax- 573-526-3846; 8AM-5PM.

www.dhss.mo.gov

Indexing & Storage: Records available from 1910 on. Older records archived or see online below. New records available for inquiry immediately.

Searching: Records are only released to person of record or legal representative of immediate family member. Must have a signed release from person of record or immediate family member for investigative purposes. Include in request- full name, names of parents, mother's maiden name, date of birth, place of birth, relationship to person of record, reason for information request.

Access by: mail, phone, in person, online.

Fee & Payment: Search fee is $15.00 per 5 years searched. Fee is charged regardless if record is found. Emergency requests using a credit card pay an additional $9.95 fee. Fee payee- Missouri Department of Health & Senior Srvs. Prepayment required. Personal checks and major credit cards accepted.

Mail search: Turnaround time- 2 to 3 weeks. A SASE is required.

Phone search: See expedited service.

In person: Turnaround time is usually 10 minutes.

Online search: Orders may be placed online at www.vitalchek.com. Records prior to 1910 are available by county at www.sos.mo.gov/archives/resources/birthdeath/.

Expedited service: Expedited service is available for online and phone searches via www.vitalchek.com. Turnaround time- 1-3 days. Add $9.95 fee for use of credit and additional fee for express delivery.

Death Records

Department of Health & Senior Svcs, Bureau of Vital Records, PO Box 570, Jefferson City, MO 65102-0570 (Courier address- 930 Wildwood, Jefferson City, MO 65109); 573-751-6387, 573-751-6400 (Message Number), 877-817-7363 (Orders), Fax- 573-526-3846; 8AM-5PM.

www.dhss.mo.gov

Indexing & Storage: Records available from 1910 on. Older records archived or see online below. New records available for inquiry immediately.

Searching: Records are only released to legal representative of person of record or immediate family member. Must have a signed release from immediate family member for investigative purposes. Include in request- full name, date of death, place of death, relationship to person of record, reason for information request.

Access by: mail, phone, in person, online.

Fee & Payment: The $13.00 search fee is for 5 years searched. Fee is charged regardless if record is found. Use of credit card is additional $9.95. Fee payee- Missouri Department of Health & Senior Srvs. Prepayment required. Personal checks and major credit cards accepted.

Mail search: Turnaround time- 2 to 3 weeks. A SASE is required.

Phone search: See expedited service.

In person: Turnaround time is usually 10 minutes.

Online search: Orders accepted online only at www.vitalchek.com. Records 50 years and older can be searched at www.sos.mo.gov/archives/resources/birthdeath/.

Expedited service: Expedited service is available for online and phone searches via www.vitalchek.com. Turnaround time- 1-3 days. Add $9.95 fee for use of credit and additional fee for express delivery.

Marriage Certificates, Divorce Records

Records not maintained by a state level agency.

Actual marriage and divorce records are found at county of issue. For marriage, contact the Record of Deeds in the county where license was issued. For divorce decrees, visit the Clerk of the county where issued.

Workers' Compensation Records

Labor & Industrial Relations Department, Workers Compensation Division, PO Box 58, Jefferson City, MO 65102-0058 (Courier address- 3315 W Truman Blvd, Jefferson City, MO 65101); 573-751-4231 x5, 573-751-4091, Fax- 573-751-2012; 8AM-4:30PM.

www.dolir.mo.gov/wc/index.htm

Direct questions to workerscomp@dolir.mo.gov.

Indexing & Storage: Records available from 1945. Records are computerized since 1994. New records available for inquiry in 1 day.

Searching: Report of injury and medical records released only with a release form. All other records are open. Include in request- claimant name, SSN, date of accident.

Access by: mail, fax, in person, online.

Fee & Payment: The search fee is $5.00. Fee payee- Workers Compensation Division. Personal checks accepted, credit cards are not.

Mail search: Turnaround time- 1 to 2 days. SASE not required.

Fax search: The initial fax must include a written request for the search. Turnaround time is 1 to 2 days.

In person: To search in person, you must be party to the case in question or possess written authorization.

Online search: Online access is available to claimants using a pre-assigned PIN.

Driver Records

Department of Revenue, Customer Service Division, PO Box 2167, Jefferson City, MO 65105-0200 (Courier address- Harry S Truman Bldg, 301 W High St, Room 360, Jefferson City, MO 65101); 573-751-4600, 573-751-4300 (Record Sales), Fax- 573-526-7367; 7:30AM-5:30PM.

http://dor.mo.gov/mvdl/drivers/

Copies of tickets are available from the same address. Requests must be in writing, include the name, DOB, license number, and specific violation information. The cost is $5.88 per ticket.

Indexing & Storage: Records available for 3 yrs for moving violations, 5 yrs for suspensions, permanent for alcohol-related, disq's and mand. ins. 0-point violations are not shown on non-CDL record. Accidents are not shown on driving record unless suspension/revocation action taken. New records available for inquiry in 24 hours or less.

Searching: Casual requesters receive records without personal information. If for DPPA purpose of written, notarized consent of subject is provided then personal info is provided. Frequent requesters should establish an account for electronic access. Include in request- full name, DOB and DL or SSN. Forms are found at web page. This data not released- SSN, medical info, eye exams

Access by: mail, phone, fax, in person, online.

Fee & Payment: The fee is $5.88 per record for manual process, electronic access is different. Records may be certified for no additional fee if requested by mail or in-person. Add a 3% surcharge for credit cards and 2.5% for debit cards Fee payee- Department of Revenue. Prepayment required. Cashier's check and money orders preferred. Personal checks and credit cards accepted.

Mail search: Turnaround time- 2 days. A SASE is requested.

Phone search: Order records by use of touchtone phone. Records faxed or mailed within 24 hours. PIN required.

Fax search: Pre-approved accounts may order records and receive by fax for an additional $.50 per page.

In person: Counter service available. Most Contract Offices in the state also process requests, but there is a $2.00 additional fee.

Online search: Online access of Information Exchange costs is only available to those ordering thousands of records in bulk, fee is $.0382 per record plus network charge. Batch processing is not offered. Online inquiries with extensive requests can be put in Missouri's "mailbox" any time of the day. These inquiries are then picked up at 2 AM the following morning, and the resulting MVR's are sent back to each customer's "mailbox" approx. 2 hours later.

Vehicle, Vessel Ownership & Registration

Department of Revenue, Motor Vehicle Bureau, PO Box 100, Jefferson City, MO 65105-0100 (Courier address- Harry S Truman Bldg, 301 W High St, Jefferson City, MO 65105); 573-526-3669, 573-751-4509, Fax- 573-751-7060; 7:30AM-5:30PM.

http://dor.mo.gov/

Lien information shows on the title records. The prices for records were schedule to be changed, but a preliminary injunction has placed the price increase on hold for bulk record sales.

Indexing & Storage: Records available from 1968 to present. Records are indexed on microfiche from 1968 to present, and microfilm from 1981 to present. All motorized boats 12 ft or longer must be titled and registered. New records available for inquiry in 24-48 hrs for vehicle and 2 weeks for marine.

Searching: Ownership and vehicle information is available with no restrictions to access, if request complies with DPPA. Casual requesters must have consent of subject to obtain records with personal information, otherwise this data is blocked. Include in request- year, make, VIN. Current registration/title records are on computer. Records are purged from the computer files after 2 years of no activity. However, the records will remain on microfiche. This data not released- SSN, medical and vision data

Access by: mail, fax, in person, online.

Fee & Payment: The fee is $5.88 per record for walk-in or mail requests with a 3% surcharge for credit cards and 2.5% for debit cards. There is an additional $2.00 fee if request processed at a contract license office. The fee for electronic access is $.0382. Fee payee- Department of Revenue. Prepayment required. Personal checks and major credit cards accepted.

Mail search: Turnaround time- 2 to 4 weeks.

Fax search: The service is available to authorized entities. Use of credit card required. There is an additional $.50 fee added to the request fee.

In person: You may request records in person, go to Room 370.

Online search: Online record searches are available to registered entities who have a DPPA security access code issued by the Department. The fee is $.0382 per record and is automatically withdrawn through the requestor's ACH account. Access is via the Internet. Visit the web page for more information.

Other access: Missouri has an extensive range of records and information available on magnetic tape, labels or paper. Besides offering license, vehicle, title, dealer, and marine records, specific public report data is also available.

Expedited service: The cost is the same as stated above. Depending on the type of request, turnaround time could be the same or next day.

Accident Reports

Missouri State Highway Patrol, Traffic Division, PO Box 568, Jefferson City, MO 65102-0568 (Courier address- 1510 E Elm St, Jefferson City, MO 65101); 573-526-6113, Fax- 573-751-9921; 8AM-5PM.

www.mshp.dps.missouri.gov/MSHPWeb/PatrolDivisions/TFD/index.html

Indexing & Storage: Records available from 1997 to present on computer. Records are indexed on an in-house computer. Records are on a document imaging system or microfilm from 1941. New records available for inquiry in 14 to 30 days.

Searching: Record requests must be in writing. Generally, these records are open to the public. Include in request- full name, date of accident, location of accident, relationship of requester to the subject. There is no telephone searching, but you can call to determine if an accident is on file.

Access by: mail, fax, in person, online.

Fee & Payment: There is a $3.25 fee for a standard 4-page report on record. Fee payee- DPS - Missouri State Highway Patrol Prepayment required. Personal checks are accepted. Credit cards not accepted.

Mail search: Turnaround time- 3 to 4 working days. A SASE is requested.

Fax search: Fax requests are accepted from ongoing requesters, if prepaid.

In person: Turnaround time is immediate.

Online search: Information on accidents investigated by the Highway Patrol for the most recent 29 days only are found at www.mshp.dps.mo.gov/HP68/search.jsp.

Other access: Some crash reconstruction reports may be available via CD, depending on date of crash. CD includes photos and other attachments.

Legislation Records

Legislative Library, Legislation Records, 117A State Capitol, Jefferson City, MO 65101; 573-751-4633; 8:30AM-4:30PM.

www.moga.mo.gov

Sessions are from January to May.

Indexing & Storage: Records available from 1993 to present on computer, from 1909-1972 and 1985 to 2000 on microfiche, and from 1973 to 1984 in books. New records available for inquiry in less than 1 day.

Searching: Include in request- bill number, year.

Access by: mail, phone, fax, in person, online.

Fee & Payment: There is no search fee, but there is a $.10 copy fee per page. Fees must be paid in advance.

Mail search: Turnaround time- 1 week to 10 days. SASE not required.

Phone search: No fee for telephone request. If the requests involves much time/paper, it will be refused.

Fax search: Records may be requested by fax.

In person: Simple requests may be processed while you wait.

Online search: The website offers access to bills and statutes. One can search or track bills by key words, bill number, or sponsors. Go to www.house.mo.gov/billcentral.aspx. Request can be made via email to library@lr.mo.gov. The state statutes are listed at www.moga.mo.gov/statutesearch/.

Voter Registration

Access to Records is Restricted.

Secretary of State, Division of Elections, PO Box 1767, Jefferson City, MO 65102; 573-751-2301, 888-488-8683, Fax- 573-526-3242; 8AM-5PM.

www.sos.mo.gov/elections/

Records are sold in various media formats for political purposes, but not for commercial marketing purposes. For individual look-ups, the agency recommends searching at the county level by the County Clerks.

GED Certificates

GED Office, PO Box 480, Jefferson City, MO 65102; 573-751-3504; 8AM-4:30PM.

http://dese.mo.gov/divcareered/ged_index.htm

Indexing & Storage: Records available from 1960 to present. New records available for inquiry in 2 to 3 weeks.

Searching: Include in request- signed release, date of birth, SSN. The year and location of the test are very helpful and should also be included in the request.

Access by: mail, in person.

Fee & Payment: The fee is $2.00 for either a verification or a transcript. Fee payee- Treasurer, State of Missouri. Prepayment required. Personal checks accepted.

Mail search: Turnaround time- same day. SASE not required.

In person: $2.00 fee per request.

Hunting & Fishing License Information

Conservation Department, Custodian of Records, PO Box 180, Jefferson City, MO 65102-0180 (Courier address- 2901 W Truman Blvd, Jefferson City, MO 65109); 573-751-4115, Fax- 573-751-4467; 8AM-5PM.

http://mdc.mo.gov/

Hunting and fishing permits issued and records of recorded deer and turkey kills are public records and available upon written request. Agency arrest records also available; only close cases released. SSNs are redacted prior to release.

Indexing & Storage: Records available for 5 years, then are archived. There may be a hourly fee for retrieval of archive records, usually if the request requires computer programming or use of another department's staff.

Searching: Names and privileges may be released. Include in request- full name, DOB; any add'l identifiers are helpful- SSN, DR, address, etc. Agency adheres to Missouri's Sunshine Laws for public access. Email record requests to records@mdc.mo.gov.

Access by: mail, fax, in person.

Fee & Payment: Written request required. A fee may be charged based upon type of service provided. Fee payee- Missouri Conservation Department. Prepayment required. Personal checks accepted, credit cards are not.

Mail search: Turnaround time- 3 days. SASE is helpful.

Fax search: Record requests may be faxed. Agency will fax back for no fee.

In person: In person searching is discouraged.

Other access: Mailing lists of the hunting and fishing permit vendors are available. The cost is about $50..

Missouri State Licensing Agencies

For details about the agency responsible for licensing/certifying/registering an item below or in the Agency Quick Finder section, match an item's number with the number of the agency in the *Licensing Agency Information* section.

Missouri Licenses Searchable Online

Acupuncturist #45 .... http://pr.mo.gov/listings.asp
Anesthesia Permit, Dental #17 .... http://pr.mo.gov/listings.asp
Animal Technician #31 .... http://pr.mo.gov/listings.asp
Ankle Specialist #10 .... http://pr.mo.gov/listings.asp
Announcer, Athletic Event/Ring #44 .... http://pr.mo.gov/listings.asp
Architect #2 .... http://pr.mo.gov/listings.asp
Athletic Trainer #11 .... http://pr.mo.gov/listings.asp
Attorney #40 .... http://members.mobar.org/members/LawyerSearch/GSSearch.aspx
Audiologist #11 .... http://pr.mo.gov/listings.asp
Audiologist, Clinical #16 .... http://pr.mo.gov/listings.asp
Audiologist/Speech Path'gist, Clinical #16 .... http://pr.mo.gov/listings.asp
Barber Instructor/School #3 .... http://pr.mo.gov/listings.asp
Barber/Barber Shop #3 .... http://pr.mo.gov/listings.asp
Beauty Shop #5 .... http://pr.mo.gov/listings.asp
Body Piercer #13 .... http://pr.mo.gov/listings.asp
Body Piercing/Branding Estab. #13 .... http://pr.mo.gov/listings.asp
Boxer/Boxing Professional #44 .... http://pr.mo.gov/listings.asp
Brander #13 .... http://pr.mo.gov/listings.asp
Cemetery #25 .... http://pr.mo.gov/listings.asp
Chiropractor #4 .... http://pr.mo.gov/listings.asp
Cosmetologist #5 .... http://pr.mo.gov/listings.asp
Cosmetology School/Instruct/Shop #5 .... http://pr.mo.gov/listings.asp
Counselor, Professional/Trainee #23 .... http://pr.mo.gov/listings.asp
Dental Hygienist #17 .... http://pr.mo.gov/listings.asp
Dental Specialist #17 .... http://pr.mo.gov/listings.asp
Dentist #17 .... http://pr.mo.gov/listings.asp
Drug Distributor #9 .... http://pr.mo.gov/listings.asp
DSGA Permit/Site Certificate #17 .... http://pr.mo.gov/listings.asp
ECS Permit/Site Certificate #17 .... http://pr.mo.gov/listings.asp
Embalmer #6 .... http://pr.mo.gov/listings.asp
Engineer #2 .... http://pr.mo.gov/listings.asp
Esthetician #5 .... http://pr.mo.gov/listings.asp
Funeral Director/Establishment #6 .... http://pr.mo.gov/listings.asp
Funeral Pre-Need Provider/Seller #6 .... http://pr.mo.gov/listings.asp
General Anesthesia Permit #17 .... http://pr.mo.gov/listings.asp
Geologist #26 .... http://pr.mo.gov/listings.asp
Geologist Registrant in Training #26 .... http://pr.mo.gov/listings.asp
Hairdresser #5 .... http://pr.mo.gov/listings.asp
Hearing Instrument Specialist #27 .... http://pr.mo.gov/listings.asp
Insurance Agent/Broker #20 .... www.insurance.mo.gov/industry/producer/agtstatus.htm
Insurance Consultant, Chiropractic #4 .... http://pr.mo.gov/listings.asp
Interior Designer #22 .... http://pr.mo.gov/listings.asp
Interpreter for the Deaf #12 .... http://pr.mo.gov/listings.asp
Landscape Architect #2 .... http://pr.mo.gov/listings.asp
Lobbyist Report #46 .... www.mec.mo.gov/Ethics/Lobbying/LobElecReports.aspx
Manicurist #5 .... http://pr.mo.gov/listings.asp
Marital & Family Therapist #43 .... http://pr.mo.gov/listings.asp
Martial Artist/Martial Art Occupation #44 .... http://pr.mo.gov/listings.asp
Massage Therapist #28 .... http://pr.mo.gov/listings.asp
Massage Therapy Business #28 .... http://pr.mo.gov/listings.asp
Medical Doctor #11 .... http://pr.mo.gov/listings.asp
Notary Public #33 .... www.sos.mo.gov/Notary/NotarySearch/NotarySearch.aspx
Nurse Midwife #7 .... http://pr.mo.gov/listings.asp
Nurse, Advanced Practical #7 .... http://pr.mo.gov/listings.asp
Nurse, Registered #7 .... http://pr.mo.gov/listings.asp
Nurse, Specialist #7 .... http://pr.mo.gov/listings.asp

Nurse-LPN #7 .... http://pr.mo.gov/listings.asp
Nursing Home Administrator #32 .... www.dhss.mo.gov/BNHA/
Nursing School #7 .... http://pr.mo.gov/listings.asp
Occupation'l Therapist/Therapist Ass't #41 .... http://pr.mo.gov/listings.asp
Optometrist #8 .... http://pr.mo.gov/listings.asp
Osteopathic Physician #11 .... http://pr.mo.gov/listings.asp
Parentaral Conscious Sedation #17 .... http://pr.mo.gov/listings.asp
PCS Permit/Site Certificate #17 .... http://pr.mo.gov/listings.asp
Perfusionist #11 .... http://pr.mo.gov/listings.asp
Pesticide Applicator/Technician #18 .... www.kellysolutions.com/MO/Applicators/index.asp
Pesticide Dealer #18 .... www.kellysolutions.com/MO/
Pesticide Technician #18 .... www.kellysolutions.com/MO/
Pharmacist/Pharmacy Intern/Techn. #9 .... http://pr.mo.gov/listings.asp
Pharmacy #9 .... http://pr.mo.gov/listings.asp
Physical Therapist #11 .... http://pr.mo.gov/listings.asp
Physical Therapist Assistant #11 .... http://pr.mo.gov/listings.asp
Physician Assistant #11 .... http://pr.mo.gov/listings.asp
Physician, Athletic Event #44 .... http://pr.mo.gov/listings.asp
Podiatrist #10 .... http://pr.mo.gov/listings.asp
Pre-Need Provider/Seller, Funeral #6 .... http://pr.mo.gov/listings.asp
Psychologist #36 .... http://pr.mo.gov/listings.asp
Public Accountant Partnership #1 .... http://pr.mo.gov/listings.asp
Public Accountant-CPA #1 .... http://pr.mo.gov/listings.asp
Real Estate Agent/Seller #35 .... http://pr.mo.gov/listings.asp
Real Estate Appraiser #14 .... http://pr.mo.gov/listings.asp
Real Estate Broker/Partner/Assoc. #35 .... http://pr.mo.gov/listings.asp
Real Estate Instructor/School #35 .... http://pr.mo.gov/listings.asp
Real Estate Officer/Corp/Association #35 .... http://pr.mo.gov/listings.asp
Respiratory Care Practitioner #42 .... http://pr.mo.gov/listings.asp
School Nurse #7 .... http://pr.mo.gov/listings.asp
Social Worker .... http://pr.mo.gov/listings.asp
Speech-Language Pathologist #16 .... http://pr.mo.gov/listings.asp
State/Legis. Candidate Committee #46 .... www.mec.mo.gov/Ethics/CampaignFinance/CF_PublicSearch.aspx?Candidate
Surveyor, Land #2 .... http://pr.mo.gov/listings.asp
Tattoo Artist #13 .... http://pr.mo.gov/listings.asp
Tattoo Establishment #13 .... http://pr.mo.gov/listings.asp
Teacher #24 .... https://k12apps.dese.mo.gov/webapps/tcertsearch/tc_search1.asp
Timekeeper, Athletic Event #44 .... http://pr.mo.gov/listings.asp
Veterinarian/Veterinary Technician #31 .... http://pr.mo.gov/listings.asp
Veterinary Facility #31 .... http://pr.mo.gov/listings.asp
Wrestler/Wrestling Professional #44 .... http://pr.mo.gov/listings.asp

Missouri Licensing Quick Finder

Acupuncturist #45 573-526-1555
Alcohol & Tobacco Control #21 573-751-5446
Alcohol Brand/Label #21 573-751-5446
Alcohol Suspension #21 573-751-5446
Anesthesia Permit, Dental #17 573-751-0040
Animal Technician #31 573-751-0031
Ankle Specialist #10 573-751-0873
Announcer, Athletic Event/Ring #44 573-751-0243
Architect #2 573-751-0047
Athletic Trainer #11 573-751-0108
Attorney #40 573-635-4128
Audiologist #11 573-751-0108
Audiologist, Clinical #16 573-751-0108
Audiologist/Speech Path'gist, Clinical #16 573-751-0108
Barber Instructor/School #3 573-751-0805
Barber/Barber Shop #3 573-751-0805
Beauty Shop #5 573-751-1053
Bingo Worker/Officer/Operation #30 573-526-5370
Body Piercer #13 573-526-8288
Body Piercing/Branding Estab. #13 573-526-8288
Boxer/Boxing Professional #44 573-751-0243
Brander #13 573-526-8288
Cemetery #25 573-751-0849
Child Care Facility #29 573-751-2450
Chiropractor #4 573-751-2104
Cosmetologist #5 573-751-1053
Cosmetology School/Instruct/Shop #5 573-751-1053
Counselor, Professional/Trainee #23 573-751-0018
Counselor, Substance Abuse #39 573-751-9211
Court Reporter #12 573-751-4144
Dental Hygienist #17 573-751-0040
Dental Specialist #17 573-751-0040
Dentist #17 573-751-0040
Drug Distributor #9 573-751-0091
DSGA Permit/Site Certificate #17 573-751-0040
ECS Permit/Site Certificate #17 573-751-0040
Embalmer #6 573-751-0813
Emergency Med. Technic'n, Basic #19 573-751-6356
Engineer #2 573-751-0047
Esthetician #5 573-751-1053
Funeral Director/Establishment #6 573-751-0813
Funeral Pre-Need Provider/Seller #6 573-751-0813
Gaming Occupation #30 573-526-4092
Gaming Property, Boat #30 573-526-4092
Gaming Supply #30 573-526-4092
General Anesthesia Permit #17 573-751-0040
Geologist #26 573-526-7625
Geologist Registrant in Training #26 573-526-7625
Hairdresser #5 573-751-1053
Hearing Instrument Specialist #27 573-751-0240
Insurance Agent/Broker #20 573-751-3518
Insurance Consultant, Chiropractic #4 573-751-2104
Interior Designer #22 573-522-4683
Interpreter for the Deaf #12 573-526-7787
Investment Advisor #34 573-751-2061
Landfill #37 573-751-5401
Landfill Operator #37 573-751-5401
Landscape Architect #2 573-751-0047
Lobbyist Report #46 573-751-2020
Manicurist #5 573-751-1053
Marital & Family Therapist #43 573-751-0870
Martial Artist/Martial Art Occupat'n #44 573-751-0243
Massage Therapist #28 573-522-6277
Massage Therapy Business #28 573-522-6277
Medical Doctor #11 573-751-0108
Notary Public #33 573-751-2783
Nurse Midwife #7 573-751-0681
Nurse, Advanced Practical #7 573-751-0681
Nurse, Registered #7 573-751-0681
Nurse, Specialist #7 573-751-0681
Nurse-LPN #7 573-751-0681

Nursing Home Administrator #32 573-751-3511
Nursing School #7 573-751-0681
Occupation'l Therapist/Therapist Ass't #41 573-751-0877
Optometrist #8 573-751-0814
Osteopathic Physician #11 573-751-0108
Parentaral Conscious Sedation #17 573-751-0040
PCS Permit/Site Certificate #17 573-751-0040
Perfusionist #11 573-751-0108
Pesticide Applicator/Technician #18 573-751-5504
Pesticide Dealer #18 573-751-5504
Pesticide Technician #18 573-751-5504
Pharmacist/Pharmacy Intern/Tech #9 573-751-0091
Pharmacy #9 573-751-0091
Physical Therapist #11 573-751-0108
Physical Therapist Assistant #11 573-751-0108
Physician Assistant #11 573-751-0108
Physician, Athletic Event #44 573-751-0243
Podiatrist #10 573-751-0873
Pre-Need Provider/Seller, Funeral #6 573-751-0813
Prevention Special't (Social Work) #39 573-751-9211
Psychologist #36 573-751-0099
Public Accountant Partnership #1 573-751-0012
Public Accountant-CPA #1 573-751-0012
Real Estate Agent/Seller #35 573-751-2628
Real Estate Appraiser #14 573-751-0038
Real Estate Broker/Partner/Assoc. #35 573-751-2628
Real Estate Instructor/School #35 573-751-2628
Real Estate Officer/Corp/Assoc. #35 573-751-2628
Respiratory Care Practitioner #42 573-522-2864
School Librarian #24 573-751-4369
School Nurse #7 573-751-0681
Securities Agent #34 573-751-2061
Securities Broker/Dealer #34 573-751-2061
Social Worker, Baccalaureate #15 573-751-0885
Social Worker, Clinical #15 573-751-0885
Speech-Language Pathologist #16 573-751-0108
Statewide/Legis. Candidate Committee #46 573-751-2020
Substance Abuse Assoc -Training #39. 573-751-9211
Substance Abuse Counselor #39 573-751-9211
Surveyor, Land #2 573-751-0047
Tattoo Artist #13 573-526-8288
Tattoo Establishment #13 573-526-8288
Teacher #24 .... 573-751-0051, 751-4369
Timekeeper, Athletic Event #44 573-751-0243
Transfer Station #37 573-751-5401
Veterinarian/Veterinary Technician #31 573-751-0031
Veterinary Facility #31 573-751-0031
Waste Tire End User/Site #37 573-751-5401
Waste Tire Processor/Hauler #37 573-751-5401
Waste Water System Operator #38 573-751-6892
Water Supply Operator #38 573-751-6892
Wrestler/Wrestling Professional #44 573-751-0243

Missouri Licensing Agency Information

#1 Board of Accountancy, PO Box 613 (3605 Missouri Blvd), Jefferson City, MO 65102-0613; 573-751-0012, Fax- 573-751-0890. http://pr.mo.gov/accountancy.asp Search data at- http://pr.mo.gov/listings.asp

#2 Engineers, Land Survey & Landscape Architects, Board of Architects, 3605 Missouri Blvd, #380, Jefferson City, MO 65102; 573-751-0047, Fax- 573-751-8046. Hours- 8AM-5PM. http://pr.mo.gov/apelsla.asp Search data at- http://pr.mo.gov/listings.asp

#3 Board of Barber Examiners, 3605 Missouri Blvd (PO Box 1062), Jefferson City, MO 65102-1335; 573-751-1052, Fax- 573-751-8167. Hours- 8AM-5PM. http://pr.mo.gov/contact-us.asp Search data at- http://pr.mo.gov/listings.asp

#4 Board of Chiropractic Examiners, PO Box 672 (3605 Missouri Blvd), Jefferson City, MO 65102-0672; 573-751-2104, Fax- 573-751-0735. Hours- 8AM-5PM. http://pr.mo.gov/chiropractors.asp Search data at- http://pr.mo.gov/listings.asp

#5 Board of Cosmetology, 3605 Missouri Blvd (PO Box 1062), Jefferson City, MO 65102; 573-751-1052, Fax- 573-751-8167. Hours- 8AM-5PM. http://pr.mo.gov/contact-us.asp Search data at- http://pr.mo.gov/listings.asp

#6 Board of Embalmers & Funeral Directors, PO Box 423 (3605 Missouri Blvd), Jefferson City, MO 65102-0423; 573-751-0813, Fax- 573-751-1155. Hours- 8AM-5PM. www.pr.mo.gov/embalmers.asp Search data at- http://pr.mo.gov/listings.asp

#7 Board of Nursing, PO Box 656 (3605 Missouri Blvd), Jefferson City, MO 65102; 573-751-0681, Fax- 573-751-0075. Hours- 8AM-5PM. www.pr.mo.gov/nursing.asp Search data at- http://pr.mo.gov/listings.asp

#8 Board of Optometry, PO Box 1335 (3605 Missouri Blvd), Jefferson City, MO 65102-1335; 573-751-0814, Fax- 573-751-8216. Hours- 8AM-5PM. http://pr.mo.gov/optometrists.asp Search data at- http://pr.mo.gov/listings.asp

#9 Board of Pharmacy, PO Box 625 (3605 Missouri Blvd), Jefferson City, MO 65102; 573-751-0091, Fax- 573-526-3464. Hours- 8AM-5PM. www.pr.mo.gov/pharmacists.asp Search data at- http://pr.mo.gov/listings.asp

#10 Board of Podiatric Medicine, PO Box 423 (3605 Missouri Blvd), Jefferson City, MO 65102; 573-751-0873, Fax- 573-751-1155. Hours- 8AM-5PM. http://pr.mo.gov/podiatrists.asp Search data at- http://pr.mo.gov/listings.asp

#11 Board of Registration for Healing Arts, PO Box 4 (3605 Missouri Blvd), Jefferson City, MO 65102; 573-751-0098, Fax- 573-751-3166. www.pr.mo.gov/healingarts.asp Search data at- http://pr.mo.gov/listings.asp

#12 Committee of Interpreters, PO Box 1335 (3605 Missouri Blvd), Jefferson City, MO 65102-1335; 573-526-7787, Fax- 573-526-0661. http://pr.mo.gov/interpreters.asp Search data at- http://pr.mo.gov/listings.asp

#13 Office of Tattooing, Body Piercing and Branding, PO Box 1335 (3605 Missouri Blvd), Jefferson City, MO 65102-1335; 573-526-8288, Fax- 573-526-3489. Hours- 8AM-5PM. http://pr.mo.gov/tattooing.asp Search data at- http://pr.mo.gov/listings.asp

#14 Commission of Real Estate Appraisers, PO Box 1335 (3605 Missouri Blvd), Jefferson City, MO 65109; 573-751-0038, Fax- 573-526-3489. http://pr.mo.gov/appraisers.asp Search data at- http://pr.mo.gov/listings.asp

#15 Division of Professional Registration, State Committee for Licensed Clinical Social Workers, PO Box 1335 (3605 Missouri Blvd), Jefferson City, MO 65102; 573-751-0885, Fax- 573-526-3489. Hours- 8AM-5PM. http://pr.mo.gov/socialworkers.asp Search data at- http://pr.mo.gov/listings.asp

#16 Committee of Speech Pathology & Audiology, PO Box 4 (3605 Missouri Blvd), Jefferson City, MO 65102; 573-751-0098, Fax- 573-751-3166. http://pr.mo.gov/speech.asp Search data at- http://pr.mo.gov/listings.asp

#17 Dental Board, PO Box 1367 (3605 Missouri Blvd), Jefferson City, MO 65102-1367; 573-751-0040, Fax- 573-751-8216. Hours- 8AM-5PM. http://pr.mo.gov/dental.asp Search data at- http://pr.mo.gov/listings.asp

#18 Department of Agriculture, Division of Plant Industries, Bureau of Pesticide, PO Box 630 (1616 Missouri Blvd), Jefferson City, MO 65102; 573-751-5504, Fax- 573-751-0005. www.mda.mo.gov Search data at- www.kellysolutions.com/MO/

#19 Department of Health, Emergency Medical Services, PO Box 570 (912 Wildwood Dr), Jefferson City, MO 65102-0570; 573-751-6356, Fax- 573-751-6348. www.dhss.mo.gov/EMS/ Search - www.dhss.mo.gov/EMS/Directories.html

#20 Department of Insurance, Licensing Section, PO Box 690 (301 W High St), Jefferson City, MO 65102-0690; 573-751-4126, Fax- 573-526-3416. www.insurance.mo.gov Search data at- www.insurance.mo.gov/industry/producer/agtstatus.htm

#21 Department of Public Safety, Division of Alcohol & Tobacco Control, 1738 E Elm St, Lower Level, East Door, Jefferson City, MO 65101; 573-751-5446, Fax- 573-526-4540. www.atc.dps.mo.gov

#22 Interior Design Council, PO Box 1335 (3605 Missouri Blvd), Jefferson City, MO 65109; 573-522-4683, Fax- 573-526-3489. http://pr.mo.gov/interior.asp Search data at- http://pr.mo.gov/listings.asp

#23 Division of Professional Regulation, Committee for Professional Counselors, PO Box 1335 (3605 Missouri Blvd), Jefferson City, MO 65102-1335; 573-751-0018, Fax- 573-751-0735. http://pr.mo.gov/counselors.asp Search data at- http://pr.mo.gov/listings.asp Lists available at http://pr.mo.gov/listings.asp.

#24 Department of Elementary & Secondary Education, Division of Teacher Quality & Urban Education, PO Box 480 (205 Jefferson St), Jefferson City, MO 65102-0480; 573-751-2931, Fax- 573-526-3580. Hours- 8AM-4:30PM. http://dese.mo.gov/divteachqual/ Search data at- https://k12apps.dese.mo.gov/webapps/tcertsearch/tc_search1.asp

#25 Endowed Care Cemeteries Registration, Div. of Professional Registration, PO Box 1335 (3605 Missouri Blvd), Jefferson City, MO 65102-1335; 573-751-0849, Fax- 573-526-3489. http://pr.mo.gov/endowedcare.asp Search data at- http://pr.mo.gov/listings.asp

#26 Board of Geologist Registration, PO Box 1335, 3605 Missouri Blvd, Jefferson City, MO 65102-1335; 573-526-7625, Fax- 573-526-0661. http://pr.mo.gov/geologists.asp Search data at- http://pr.mo.gov/listings.asp

#27 Board of Hearing Instrument Specialists, PO Box 1335 (3605 Missouri Blvd), Jefferson City,

MO 65102-1335; 573-751-0240, Fax- 573-526-3856. www.pr.mo.gov/hearing.asp Search data at- http://pr.mo.gov/listings.asp

#28 State Board of Therapeutic Massage, PO Box 1335 (3605 Missouri Blvd), Jefferson City, MO 65102-1335; 573-522-6277, Fax- 573-751-0735. Hours- 8AM-5PM. http://pr.mo.gov/massage.asp Search data at- http://pr.mo.gov/listings.asp

#29 Department of Health, Bureau of Child Care Safety & Licensure, 1715 S Ridge, Jefferson City, MO 65109; 573-751-2450, Fax- 573-526-5345. http://nrc.uchsc.edu/STATES/MO/missouri.htm

#30 Gaming Commission, PO Box 1847 (3417 Knipp Dr), Jefferson City, MO 65102; 573-526-4080, Fax- 573-526-1999. Hours- 8AM-5PM. www.mgc.dps.mo.gov

#31 Veterinary Medical Board, PO Box 633 (3605 Missouri Blvd), Jefferson City, MO 65102-0633; 573-751-0031, Fax- 573-526-3856. http://pr.mo.gov/veterinarian.asp Search data at- http://pr.mo.gov/listings.asp

#32 Board of Nursing Home Administrators, PO Box 570 (3418 Knipp Dr), Jefferson City, MO 65102-0570; 573-751-3511, Fax- 573-526-4314. Hours- 8AM-5PM. www.dhss.mo.gov/BNHA/

#33 Office of Secretary of State, State Information Center, 600 W Main St, #322, Jefferson City, MO 65101; 866-223-6535, 573-751-2783, Fax- 573-751-8199. www.sos.mo.gov Search data at- www.sos.mo.gov/Notary/NotarySearch/NotarySearch.aspx

#34 Secretary of State, Securities Division, 600 W Main St, #229, Jefferson City, MO 65101-1276; 573-751-4136, Fax- 573-526-3124. www.sos.mo.gov/securities/

#35 Real Estate Commission, PO Box 1339 (3605 Missouri Blvd), Jefferson City, MO 65102-1339; 573-751-2628, Fax- 573-751-2777. http://pr.mo.gov/realestate.asp Search data at- http://pr.mo.gov/listings.asp

#36 Committee of Psychology, PO Box 1335 (3605 Missouri Blvd), Jefferson City, MO 65102-1335; 573-751-0099, Fax- 573-526-0661. http://pr.mo.gov/psychologists.asp Search data at- http://pr.mo.gov/listings.asp

#37 Department of Natural Resources, Div of Environmental Quality, Solid Waste Mgmt, PO Box 176 (1738 E Elm), Jefferson City, MO 65102-0176; 573-751-5401, Fax- 573-526-3902. www.dnr.mo.gov/env/swmp/index.html

#38 Department of Natural Resources, Environmental Assistance Program, PO Box 176 (1659 Elm St), Jefferson City, MO 65102; 573-751-6892, Fax- 573-526-5808. www.dnr.mo.gov/env/

#39 Substance Abuse Counselors Certification Board, PO Box 1250, Jefferson City, MO 65102; 573-751-9211, Fax- 573-522-2073. http://pr.mo.gov

#40 The Missouri Bar, PO Box 119 (326 Monroe St), Jefferson City, MO 65102-0119; 573-635-4128, Fax- 573-635-2811. www.mobar.org Search data at- http://members.mobar.org/members/LawyerSearch/GSSearch.aspx

#41 Division of Professional Registration, Board of Occupational Therapy, PO Box 1335 (3605 Missouri Blvd), Jefferson City, MO 65102-1335; 573-751-0877, Fax- 573-526-3489. http://pr.mo.gov/octherapy.asp Search data at- http://pr.mo.gov/listings.asp

#42 Board for Respiratory Care, PO Box 1335 (3605 Missouri Blvd), Jefferson City, MO 65102-1335; 573-522-5864, Fax- 573-526-3489. www.pr.mo.gov/respiratorycare.asp Search data at- http://pr.mo.gov/listings.asp

#43 Committee of Marital & Family Therapists, PO Box 1335 (3605 Missouri Blvd), Jefferson City, MO 65102-1335; 573-751-0870, Fax- 573-751-0735. http://pr.mo.gov/marital.asp Search data at- http://pr.mo.gov/listings.asp

#44 Office of Athletics, PO Box 1335 (3605 Missouri Blvd), Jefferson City, MO 65102-1335; 573-751-0243, Fax- 573-751-5649. http://pr.mo.gov/athletics.asp Search data at- http://pr.mo.gov/listings.asp

#45 Acupuncturist Advisory Committee, PO Box 1335 (3605 Missouri Blvd), Jefferson City, MO 65102-0672; 573-526-1555, Fax- 573-751-0735. Hours- 8AM-5PM. http://pr.mo.gov/acupuncturist.asp Search data at- http://pr.mo.gov/listings.asp

#46 Ethics Commission, PO Box 1370 (3411-A Knipp Dr), Jefferson City, MO 65102; 573-751-2020, Fax- 573-526-4506. www.mec.mo.gov/Ethics/GeneralInfo/GeneralInfo.aspx Search data at- www.mec.mo.gov/Ethics/Lobbying/LobElecReports.aspx

Missouri Federal Courts

The following list indicates the district and division name for each county in the state. If the bankruptcy court location is different from the district court, then the location of the bankruptcy court appears in parentheses.

Missouri County/Court Cross Reference

County	District	Division
Adair	Eastern	Hannibal (St Louis)
Andrew	Western	St Joseph (Kansas City - Western)
Atchison	Western	St Joseph (Kansas City - Western)
Audrain	Eastern	Hannibal (St Louis)
Barry	Western	Joplin-Southwestern (Kansas City)
Barton	Western	Joplin-Southwestern (Kansas City)
Bates	Western	Kansas City - Western
Benton	Western	Jefferson City-Central (Kansas City)
Bollinger	Eastern	Cape Girardeau (St Louis)
Boone	Western	Jefferson City-Central (Kansas City)
Buchanan	Western	St Joseph (Kansas City - Western)
Butler	Eastern	Cape Girardeau (St Louis)
Caldwell	Western	St Joseph (Kansas City - Western)
Callaway	Western	Jefferson City-Central (Kansas City)
Camden	Western	Jefferson City-Central (Kansas City)
Cape Girardeau	Eastern	Cape Girardeau (St Louis)
Carroll	Western	Kansas City - Western
Carter	Eastern	Cape Girardeau (St Louis)
Cass	Western	Kansas City - Western
Cedar	Western	Springfield-Southern (Kansas City)
Chariton	Eastern	Hannibal (St Louis)
Christian	Western	Springfield-Southern (Kansas City)
Clark	Eastern	Hannibal (St Louis)
Clay	Western	Kansas City - Western
Clinton	Western	St Joseph (Kansas City - Western)
Cole	Western	Jefferson City-Central (Kansas City)
Cooper	Western	Jefferson City-Central (Kansas City)
Crawford	Eastern	St Louis
Dade	Western	Springfield-Southern (Kansas City)
Dallas	Western	Springfield-Southern (Kansas City)
Daviess	Western	St Joseph (Kansas City - Western)
De Kalb	Western	St Joseph (Kansas City - Western)
Dent	Eastern	St Louis
Douglas	Western	Springfield-Southern ((Kansas City)
Dunklin	Eastern	Cape Girardeau (St Louis)
Franklin	Eastern	St Louis
Gasconade	Eastern	St Louis
Gentry	Western	St Joseph (Kansas City - Western)
Greene	Western	Springfield-Southern (Kansas City)
Grundy	Western	St Joseph (Kansas City - Western)
Harrison	Western	St Joseph (Kansas City - Western)
Henry	Western	Kansas City - Western
Hickory	Western	Jefferson City-Central (Kansas City)
Holt	Western	St Joseph (Kansas City - Western)
Howard	Western	Jefferson City-Central (Kansas City)
Howell	Western	Springfield-Southern (Kansas City)
Iron	Eastern	St Louis
Jackson	Western	Kansas City – Western
Jasper	Western	Joplin-Southwestern (Kansas City)
Jefferson	Eastern	St Louis
Johnson	Western	Kansas City - Western
Knox	Eastern	Hannibal (St Louis)
Laclede	Western	Springfield-Southern (Kansas City
Lafayette	Western	Kansas City - Western
Lawrence	Western	Joplin-Southwestern (Kansas City)
Lewis	Eastern	Hannibal (St Louis)
Lincoln	Eastern	St Louis
Linn	Eastern	Hannibal (St Louis)
Livingston	Western	St Joseph (Kansas City - Western)
Macon	Eastern	Hannibal (St Louis)
Madison	Eastern	Cape Girardeau (St Louis)
Maries	Eastern	St Louis
Marion	Eastern	Hannibal (St Louis)
McDonald	Western	Joplin-Southwestern (Kansas City)
Mercer	Western	St Joseph (Kansas City - Western)
Miller	Western	Jefferson City-Central (Kansas City)
Mississippi	Eastern	Cape Girardeau (St Louis)
Moniteau	Western	Jefferson City-Central (Kansas City)
Monroe	Eastern	Hannibal (St Louis)
Montgomery	Eastern	Hannibal (St Louis)
Morgan	Western	Jefferson City-Central (Kansas City)
New Madrid	Eastern	Cape Girardeau (St Louis)
Newton	Western	Joplin-Southwestern (Kansas City)
Nodaway	Western	St Joseph (Kansas City - Western)
Oregon	Western	Springfield-Southern (Kansas City)
Osage	Western	Jefferson City-Central (Kansas City)
Ozark	Western	Springfield-Southern (Kansas City)
Pemiscot	Eastern	Cape Girardeau (St Louis)
Perry	Eastern	Cape Girardeau (St Louis)
Pettis	Western	Jefferson City-Central (Kansas City)
Phelps	Eastern	St Louis
Pike	Eastern	Hannibal (St Louis)
Platte	Western	St Joseph (Kansas City - Western)
Polk	Western	Springfield-Southern (Kansas City)
Pulaski	Western	Springfield-Southern (Kansas City)
Putnam	Western	St Joseph (Kansas City - Western)
Ralls	Eastern	Hannibal (St Louis)
Randolph	Eastern	Hannibal (St Louis)
Ray	Western	Kansas City - Western)
Reynolds	Eastern	Cape Girardeau (St Louis)
Ripley	Eastern	Cape Girardeau (St Louis)
Saline	Western	Kansas City - Western
Schuyler	Eastern	Hannibal (St Louis)
Scotland	Eastern	Hannibal (St Louis)
Scott	Eastern	Cape Girardeau (St Louis)
Shannon	Eastern	Cape Girardeau (St Louis)
Shelby	Eastern	Hannibal (St Louis)
St. Charles	Eastern	St Louis
St. Clair	Western	Kansas City - Western
St. Francois	Eastern	St Louis

County	District	Division
St. Louis	Eastern	St Louis
St. Louis City City	Eastern	St Louis
Ste. Genevieve	Eastern	St Louis
Stoddard	Eastern	Cape Girardeau (St Louis)
Stone	Western	Joplin-Southwestern (Kansas City)
Sullivan	Western	St Joseph (Kansas City - Western)
Taney	Western	Springfield-Southern (Kansas City)
Texas	Western	Springfield-Southern (Kansas City)
Vernon	Western	Joplin-Southwestern (Kansas City)
Warren	Eastern	St Louis
Washington	Eastern	St Louis
Wayne	Eastern	Cape Girardeau (St Louis)
Webster	Western	Springfield-Southern (Kansas City)
Worth	Western	St Joseph (Kansas City - Western)
Wright	Western	Springfield-Southern (Kansas City)

Standards for Federal Courts: Fees are standard unless noted in profile. Search fee is $26.00 per item (one party name or case number). Copy fee is $.50 per page. Certification fee is $9.00 per document, double for exemplification, if available. Most courts require prepayment. Mail requests should enclose a SASE unless otherwise noted. Before releasing records, all courts require prepayment, unless noted.

District courts index by defendant and plaintiff and by case number. Bankruptcy courts usually index by debtor and case number. While most courts now have their indexes on computer, many may still maintain index card files as well. Courts will archive closed case files at different times.

There are numerous public access programs available to online subscribers. Search the U.S. Party/Case Index to find party names and case numbers among all courts. Individual case data is provided on PACER. A search of CM/ECF provides copies of cases filed electronically. For details about PACER, the US Party/Case Index, and CM/ECF see the Appendix or go to http://pacer.psc.uscourts.gov or call 800-676-6856.

US District Court
Missouri Eastern District

Cape Girardeau Division Court Clerk, 339 Broadway, Rm 240, Cape Girardeau, MO 63701, 573-331-8800; Fax- 314-244-7909. Hours- 8:30AM-5PM. www.moed.uscourts.gov

Counties/Note: Bollinger, Butler, Cape Girardeau, Carter, Dunklin, Madison, Mississippi, New Madrid, Pemiscot, Perry, Reynolds, Ripley, Scott, Shannon, Stoddard, Wayne.

Searches/Indexing: Search request requires name only. Results do not include SSN or DOB, but they may verify over phone. Will fax back documents $.50 per page. New cases are in the index 1-2 days after filing date. Records indexed on computer back to 1993 for crim, 1992 civil. Index in docket books 1982-1993; also on microfilm. District-wide searches available on computer. Case files sent to archives 4 years after closed.

Search Access: Only docket info is available by phone. **Mail:** Search usually completed- 1-2 days. SASE not required. **Fax:** Faxed requests for docket info accepted; also, for searches if prepaid. The fax number is for the St Louis Office who will fulfill the fax request. **In person:** 1 public terminal available. No self-serve copier.

Payment: Pay by Visa/MC, money order, cashier's or personal check. Payee: Clerk, US District Court.

E-Services: PACER records go back to 1992. New records online after 1 day. ECF at https://ecf.moed.uscourts.gov. **Opinions:** https://ecf.moed.uscourts.gov/documents/index.html. **Note:** Copy request form at www.moed.uscourts.gov/Forms/general/Copy_Request.pdf.

St Louis Division Court Clerk, 111 S 10th St, Ste 3-300, St Louis, MO 63102, 314-244-7900; Fax- 314-244-7909. Hours- 8:30AM-4:30PM. www.moed.uscourts.gov

Counties/Note: Adair, Audrain, Chariton, Clark, Crawford, Dent, Franklin, Gasconade, Iron, Jefferson, Knox, Lewis, Lincoln, Linn, Macon, Maries, Marion, Monroe, Montgomery, Phelps, Pike, Ralls, Randolph, Schuyler, Scotland, Shelby, St. Charles, St. Francois, St. Louis, St. Louis City, Ste. Genevieve, Warren, Washington, This court also holds records for the Hannibal Division. 2nd fax number for this court is 314-244-7969.

Searches/Indexing: Search request requires name only. Results do not include SSN or DOB, but they may verify over phone. Will fax back documents $.50 per page. New cases are in the index immediately after filing date. Records indexed on computer back to 1993 for crim, 1992 civil. Index in docket books 1982-1993; also on microfilm. District-wide searches available on computer. Case files sent to archives 4 years after closed.

Search Access: Only docket info is available by phone. **Mail:** Search usually completed- 1-2 days. SASE not required. **Fax:** Faxed requests for docket info accepted; also, for searches if prepaid. **In person:** 3 or 4 public terminals available. No self-serve copier.

Payment: Pay by Visa/MC, money order, cashier's or personal check. Payee: Clerk, US District Court.

E-Services: PACER records go back to 1992. New records online after 1 day. ECF at https://ecf.moed.uscourts.gov. **Opinions:** https://ecf.moed.uscourts.gov/documents/index.html. **Note:** Copy request form at www.moed.uscourts.gov/Forms/general/Copy_Request.pdf.

US Bankruptcy Court
Missouri Eastern District

St Louis Division Court Clerk, 111 S 10th St, 4th Fl, Thomas Eagleton Courthouse, St Louis, MO 63102-2734, 314-244-4500; Fax- 314-244-4990. 8:30AM-4:30PM. www.moeb.uscourts.gov

Counties/Note: Adair, Audrain, Bollinger, Butler, Cape Girardeau, Carter, Chariton, Clark, Crawford, Dent, Dunklin, Franklin, Gasconade, Iron, Jefferson, Knox, Lewis, Lincoln, Linn, Macon, Madison, Maries, Marion, Mississippi, Monroe, Montgomery, New Madrid, Pemiscot, Perry, Phelps, Pike, Ralls, Randolph, Reynolds, Ripley, Schuyler, Scotland, Scott, Shannon, Shelby, St. Charles, St. Francois, St. Louis, St. Louis City, Ste. Genevieve, Stoddard, Warren, Washington, Wayne.

Searches/Indexing: Include name, SSN, address in search requests. Results include last 4 SSN digits, address. Will not fax back documents. New cases are in the index 24 hours after filing date. Records on computer back 20 years; earlier on index cards to 1960s Case files sent to archives 4-5 years after closed.

Search Access: Voice Case Information Service available, call VCIS at 888-223-6431. **Mail:** Search usually completed- 1-2 days. SASE not required. **In person:** 4 public terminals available. No self-serve copier.

Payment: Pay by Visa/MC, money order, cashier's or personal check. No debtor checks accepted. Payee: Clerk, US Bankruptcy Court.

E-Services: Document images available. PACER records go back to 1/1991. New records online after 1 day. ECF at https://ecf.moeb.uscourts.gov. **Opinions:** www.moeb.uscourts.gov/opin_search.htm. **Online Note:** All records on RACER have been transferred to the CM/ECF system. Also, access calendars free at www.moeb.uscourts.gov/calendars.htm.

US District Court
Missouri Western District

Jefferson City-Central Division Court Clerk, 131 W High St, Jefferson City, MO 65101, 573-636-4015; Fax- 573-636-3456. 9AM-4:30PM. www.mow.uscourts.gov

Counties/Note: Benton, Boone, Callaway, Camden, Cole, Cooper, Hickory, Howard, Miller, Moniteau, Morgan, Osage, Pettis.

Searches/Indexing: Search request requires name, also DOB. Results do not include SSN or DOB. New cases are in the index 1-2 days after filing date. Records indexed on computer and microfiche; computer images back to 2003, index to 1997. District-wide searches available at Springfield, Kansas City, and Jefferson City. Case files sent to archives as deemed necessary.

Search Access: Only docket info is available by phone. **Mail:** Search usually completed- 1-2 days. Include SASE for return. **Fax:** Fax search requests accepted, prepaid. **In person:** 1 public terminal available. Self-serve copies- $.10 each.

Payment: Pay by money order, cashier's or personal check. Visa/MC accepted in person only. Payee: Clerk, US District Court.

E-Services: PACER records go back to 5/1989. ECF at https://ecf.mowd.uscourts.gov. **Opinions:** www.mow.uscourts.gov/New_Opinions.html.

Joplin-Southwestern Division c/o Kansas City Division, Charles Evans Whittaker Courthouse, 400 E 9th St, Kansas City, MO 64106, 816-512-5000; Fax- 816-512-5078. Hours-9AM-4:30PM. www.mow.uscourts.gov

Counties/Note: Barry, Barton, Jasper, Lawrence, McDonald, Newton, Stone, Vernon.

Searches/Indexing: Search request requires name only. Results do not include SSN or DOB. New cases are in the index 2 days after filing date. District-wide searches available at Springfield, Kansas City, and Jefferson City.

Search Access: Mail: Search usually completed- 7 days. SASE not required. **Fax:** Fax search requests accepted, prepaid. **In person:** .

Payment: Pay by money order, cashier's or personal check. Visa/MC accepted in person only. No business checks. Payee: Clerk of Court.

E-Services: PACER records go back to 5/1989. ECF at https://ecf.mowd.uscourts.gov. **Opinions:** www.mow.uscourts.gov/New_Opinions.html.

Kansas City-Western Division Court Clerk, Clerk of Court, Rm 1510, 400 E 9th St, Kansas City, MO 64106, 816-512-5000; records- 816-512-5068; Fax- 816-512-5078. Hours-9AM-4:30PM. www.mow.uscourts.gov

Counties/Note: Bates, Carroll, Cass, Clay, Henry, Jackson, Johnson, Lafayette, Ray, St. Clair, Saline.

Searches/Indexing: Search request requires name, also DOB. Results do not include SSN or DOB. New cases are in the index 1-2 days after filing date. Records indexed on computer and microfiche; computer images back to 2003, index to 1997. District-wide searches available at Springfield, Kansas City, and Jefferson City. Case files sent to archives as deemed necessary.

Search Access: Only docket info is available by phone. **Mail:** Search usually completed- 1 week. SASE not required. **Fax:** Fax search requests accepted, prepaid. **In person:** 1 public terminal available. Self-serve copies- $.10 each.

Payment: Pay by money order, cashier's or personal check. Visa/MC accepted in person only. Payee: US District Court Clerk.

E-Services: PACER records go back to 5/1989. ECF at https://ecf.mowd.uscourts.gov. **Opinions:** www.mow.uscourts.gov/New_Opinions.html.

Springfield-Southern Div. Court Clerk, 222 N John Q Hammons Pkwy, Suite 1400, Springfield, MO 65806, 417-865-3869; Fax- 417-865-7719. Hours- 9AM - 4:30PM. www.mow.uscourts.gov

Counties: Cedar, Christian, Dade, Dallas, Douglas, Greene, Howell, Laclede, Oregon, Ozark, Polk, Pulaski, Taney, Texas, Webster, Wright.

Searches/Indexing: Search request requires name, also DOB. Results do not include SSN or DOB. New cases are in the index immediately after filing date. Records indexed on computer and microfiche; computer images back to 2003, index to 1997. District-wide searches available at Springfield, Kansas City, and Jefferson City. Case files sent to archives as deemed necessary.

Search Access: Only docket info is available by phone. **Mail:** Search usually completed- 1 week. Include SASE for return. **Fax:** Fax search requests accepted, prepaid. **In person:** 1 public terminal available. Self-serve copies- $.10 each.

Payment: Pay by money order, cashier's or personal check. Visa/MC accepted in person only. Payee: Clerk, US District Court.

E-Services: PACER records go back to 5/1989. ECF at https://ecf.mowb.uscourts.gov. **Opinions:** www.mow.uscourts.gov/New_Opinions.html.

St Joseph Division c/o Kansas City Division, Clerk of Court, 201 US Courthouse,, 400 E 9th St, Kansas City, MO 64106, 816-512-5000; Fax- 816-512-5078. Hours- 9AM-4:30PM. www.mow.uscourts.gov

Counties/Note: Andrew, Atchison, Buchanan, Caldwell, Clinton, Daviess, De Kalb, Gentry, Grundy, Harrison, Holt, Livingston, Mercer, Nodaway, Platte, Putnam, Sullivan, Worth.

Searches/Indexing: Search request requires name only. Results do not include SSN or DOB. Will fax back documents $.50 per page, prepaid. New cases are in the index immediately after filing date. District-wide searches available at Springfield, Kansas City, and Jefferson City.

Search Access: Only docket info is available by phone. **Mail:** Search usually completed- 1-2 days. SASE not required. **Fax:** Fax search requests accepted, prepaid. **In person:** .

Payment: Pay by money order, cashier's or personal check. Visa/MC accepted in person only. Payee: Clerk, US District Court.

E-Services: PACER records go back to 5/1989. ECF at https://ecf.mowd.uscourts.gov. **Opinions:** www.mow.uscourts.gov/New_Opinions.html.

US Bankruptcy Court Missouri Western District

Kansas City - Western Division Court Clerk, 400 E 9th St, Rm 1510, Kansas City, MO 64106, 816-512-1800; records- 816-512-1800 x6. Hours-9AM-4:30PM. www.mow.uscourts.gov

Counties/Note: Andrew, Atchison, Barry, Barton, Bates, Benton, Boone, Buchanan, Caldwell, Callaway, Camden, Carroll, Cass, Cedar, Christian, Clay, Clinton, Cole, Cooper, Dade, Dallas, Daviess, De Kalb, Douglas, Gentry, Greene, Grundy, Harrison, Henry, Hickory, Holt, Howard, Howell, Jackson, Jasper, Johnson, Laclede, Lafayette, Lawrence, Livingston, McDonald, Mercer, Miller, Moniteau, Morgan, Newton, Nodaway, Oregon, Osage, Ozark, Pettis, Platte, Polk, Pulaski, Putnam, Ray, Saline, St. Clair, Stone, Sullivan, Taney, Texas, Vernon, Webster, Worth, Wright.

Searches/Indexing: Include name only in search request. Results include last 4 SSN digits. Will not fax back documents. New cases are in the index immediately after filing date. Older records indexed on microfiche. District-wide searches available here back to 6/1989. Case files prior to 3/2001 are in the archives.

Search Access: Voice Case Information Service available, call VCIS at 888-205-2527. **Mail:** Search usually completed- 24 hours. Include SASE for return. **In person:** 3 public terminals available. Computer generated copies $.10 each.

Payment: Pay by money order, cashier's or personal check. No credit cards except attorneys' cards online. Payee: Clerk, US Bankruptcy Court.

E-Services: New records online immediately. ECF at https://ecf.mowb.uscourts.gov. **Opinions:** www.mow.uscourts.gov/New_Opinions.html.

Missouri County Courts

Court	Jurisdiction	No. of Courts	How Organized
Circuit Courts*	General	65	45 Circuits
Associate Circuit Courts*	Limited	52	45 Circuits
Consolidated Courts*		60	45 Circuits
Probate Courts*	Probate	5	
Municipal Courts	Municipal	473	
Family Courts	Special	8	

* Profiled in this Sourcebook.

Court	CIVIL Tort	Contract	Real Estate	Min. Claim	Max. Claim	Small Claims	Estate	Eviction	Domestic Relations
Circuit Courts*	X	X	X	$25,000	No Max				X
Associate Circuit Courts*	X	X	X	$0	$25,000	$3000		X	
Municipal Courts									
Probate Courts*							X		
Family Courts									X

Court	CRIMINAL Felony	Misdemeanor	DWI/DUI	Preliminary Hearing	Juvenile
Circuit Courts*	X		X (if Felony)		
Associate Circuit Courts*		X	X (Misd)	X	
Family Courts					X
Municipal Courts			X		

Administration

State Court Administrator, 2112 Industrial Dr., PO Box 104480, Jefferson City, MO, 65109; 573-751-4377, Fax: 573-751-5540. (CST) www.courts.mo.gov

Court Structure

The Circuit Court is the court of general jurisdiction. There are 45 circuits comprised of 115 county Circuit Courts and one independent City Court. There are also Associate Circuit Courts with limited jurisdiction. A growing trend is to form Combined Courts. Municipal Courts only have jurisdiction over traffic and ordinance violations.

Online Access

Available at https://www.courts.mo.gov/casenet/cases/searchCases.do is Missouri Casenet, an online system for access to docket data. The system includes all Circuit Courts, City of St. Louis, the Eastern, Western, and Southern Appellate Courts, the Supreme Court, and Fine Collection Center. Some counties only offer probate case data. Cases can be searched case number, filing date, or litigant name from 6AM-1AM M-F. CaseNet search results show full name, address, and year of birth only (click on Parties and Attorneys at case result page). Also, search Supreme Court and Appellate Court opinions at www.courts.mo.gov/page.asp?id=1944.

Searching Tips, Fees, and Other Guidelines

Many Circuit Courts and Associate Courts no longer accept mail or fax requests to perform criminal record searches. Instead, the courts instruct requesters to mail criminal search request to the MO State Highway Patrol Criminal Records Division. Note that most courts participate in the Missouri CaseNet online system where record searches can be perfomed for free on the internet.

While the Missouri State Statutes set the Civil Case limit at $25,000 for the Associate Courts, and over $25,000 for the Circuit Courts, a great many county courts have adopted their own Local Court Rules regarding civil cases and the monetary limits. Presumably, Local Court Rules are setup to allow the county to choose which Court - Circuit or Associate - to send a case. This may depend on the court's case load, but generally the cases are assigned more by "the nature of the case" and less by the monetary amount involved. Often, Local Court Rules are found where both the Circuit Court and the Associate Court are located in the same building, or share the same offices and even the same phones. A suggestion is to call the County's Court Clerk to determine the court location of the case.

Adair County

Circuit Court PO Box 690, 106 W Washington, Kirksville, MO 63501; 660-665-2552; fax: 660-665-3420; 8-5PM. ***Felony, Civil Actions over $25,000.***
www.courts.mo.gov/page.asp?id=1534
Civil Records: Access: In person, online. Only the court performs in person searches; visitors may not. Required to search: name, years to search. Civil cases indexed by defendant, plaintiff. Prior on index cards. Access case lookup at https://www.courts.mo.gov/casenet/base/welcome.do. Online records go back to 9/6/2005.
Criminal Records: Access: In person, online. Visitors must perform in person searches themselves. Required to search: name, years to search. Criminal records on computer since 1991, prior on index cards. Note: Criminal search requests are forwarded to MO State Highway Patrol. Online access to criminal records same as civil, above and show year of birth only. Court's public terminal may show add'l, often older data.
General Information: Online identifiers in results same as on public terminal. No juvenile, mental, expunged, sealed, dismissed or suspended records released. Will not fax documents. Court makes copy: $.10 per page. Certification fee: $1.00 per cert. Payee: Circuit Clerk. Personal checks accepted; credit cards are not. Prepayment required.

Associate Circuit Division 106 W Washington, Courthouse, Kirksville, MO 63501; 660-665-3877; fax: 660-785-3222; 8AM-5PM. ***Misdemeanor, Civil Actions under $25,000, Small Claims, Probate.***
www.courts.mo.gov/page.asp?id=1534
Civil Records: Access: In person, online. Visitors must perform in person searches themselves. Required to search: name, years to search. Civil cases indexed by defendant, plaintiff, on computer back to 1990; probate records on microfilm since 1840. Civil PAT goes back to 2005. Access case lookup at https://www.courts.mo.gov/casenet/base/welcome.do. Online records go back to 9/6/2005.
Criminal Records: Access: In person, online. Visitors must perform in person searches themselves. Criminal records computerized from 1990; prior records in files. Criminal PAT goes back to 2005. Online access to criminal records same as civil, above and show year of birth only. Court's public terminal may show add'l, often older data.
General Information: Online identifiers in results same as on public terminal. No juvenile, mental, expunged, sealed, dismissed or suspended imposition of case records released. Will not fax documents. Court makes copy: $1.00 per page. Certification fee: $1.00 per doc. Payee: Associate Circuit Court. Personal checks accepted; credit cards are not. Prepayment required.

Andrew County

Circuit Court PO Box 208 Division I, Savannah, MO 64485; 816-324-4221; fax: 816-324-5667; 8AM-5PM. ***Felony, Civil Actions over $45,000.***
www.courts.mo.gov/page.asp?id=1561
Civil Records: Access: In person, online. Both court and visitors may perform in person searches. No search fee. Required to search: name, years to search. Civil cases indexed by defendant, plaintiff; index on cards since 1976, archived since 1850, computerized since 6/00. Civil PAT goes back to 2001. Case lookup at https://www.courts.mo.gov/casenet/base/welcome.do. Online records go back to 1993.
Criminal Records: Access: In person, online. Visitors must perform in person searches themselves. Required to search: name, years to search; also helpful: DOB. Criminal records on computer since 6/00, archived from 1841. Criminal PAT goes back to same as civil. Online access to criminal records same as civil, above and show year of birth only. Court's public terminal may show add'l, often older data.
General Information: Online identifiers in results same as on public terminal. No juvenile, mental, expunged, sealed, dismissed or suspended imposition of sentence records released. Will not fax documents. Court makes copy: $.25 per page. Cert fee: $2.50 per cert. Payee: Andrew County. Personal checks accepted; no credit cards. Prepayment required.

Associate Circuit Division PO Box 49, 5th & Main, Savannah, MO 64485; 816-324-3921; probate phone: same; fax: 816-324-3191; 8AM-5PM. ***Misdemeanor, Civil Actions under $45,000, Eviction, Small Claims, Probate.***
www.courts.mo.gov/page.asp?id=1561
Civil Records: Access: Mail, in person, online. Both court and visitors may perform in person searches. No search fee. Required to search: name, years to search. Civil cases indexed by defendant, plaintiff, on card file, archived from 1950. Mail turnaround time varies. Civil PAT goes back to 1993. Public terminal in Circuit Ct Div. Access case lookup at https://www.courts.mo.gov/casenet/base/welcome.do. Online records go back to 1993.
Criminal Records: Access: In person, online. Both court and visitors may perform in person searches. No search fee. Required to search: name, years to search. Criminal records on computer since mid-1993. Criminal PAT goes back to 1993. Public terminal in Circuit Court Division. Online access to criminal records same as civil, above and show year of birth only. Court's public terminal may show add'l, often older data.
General Information: Online identifiers in results same as on public terminal. No juvenile, mental, expunged, sealed, dismissed or suspended imposition of sentence records released. Court makes copy: $.25 per page. Certification fee: $1.50 plus $.25 each add'l page. Payee: Associate Circuit Court. Personal checks accepted; credit cards are not. Prepayment required. Mail requests: SASE required for civil.

Atchison County

Combined Circuit Court PO Box 280, Rock Port, MO 64482; 660-744-2707, 660-744-2700; fax: 660-744-5705; 8:30AM-4:30PM. ***Felony, Misdemeanor, Civil Actions, Small Claims, Eviction, Probate, Traffic.***
www.courts.mo.gov/page.asp?id=1543
Combined with the Associate Circuit Ct 2/2009.
Civil Records: Access: In person, online. Visitors must perform in person searches themselves. Required to search: name, years to search. Civil cases indexed by defendant, plaintiff; index on docket books, and archived from 1845. Civil PAT available. PAT results show middle initial, DOB. Case lookup at https://www.courts.mo.gov/casenet/base/welcome.do. Online records go back to 3/20/2006.
Criminal Records: Access: In person, online. Visitors must perform in person searches themselves. Required to search: name, years to search. Criminal records indexed in books, and archived from 1845. Note: Court recommends to search at MO State Highway Patrol, 573-526-6153. Criminal PAT available. PAT results show middle initial, DOB. Online access to criminal records same as civil, above and show year of birth only. Online results show middle initial, DOB. The online system does not always include the DOB. Court's public terminal may show add'l, often older data, like judgments.
General Information: Online identifiers in results same as on public terminal. No juvenile, mental, expunged, sealed, dismissed or suspended imposition of sentence records released. Will fax documents to local or toll free line. Court makes copy: $1.00 per page. Certification fee: $1.00. Payee: Circuit Clerk. Personal checks accepted; credit cards are not. Prepayment required. Mail requests: SASE helpful for mail return of any copies.

Audrain County

Circuit Court Courthouse, 101 N Jefferson, Mexico, MO 65265; criminal phone: 573-473-5840; civil phone: 573-473-5842; fax: 573-581-3237; 8AM-5PM. ***Felony, Civil Actions over $25,000.***
www.courts.mo.gov/page.asp?id=1592
Civil Records: Access: In person, online. Visitors must perform in person searches themselves. Required to search: name, years to search. Civil cases indexed by defendant, plaintiff, on computer since 8/92, prior on index cards, older records archived at Genealogy Club in Mexico, MO. Civil PAT goes back to 1992. Participates in state online court record system at https://www.courts.mo.gov/casenet/base/welcome.do. Online records go back to 5/19/2003.
Criminal Records: Access: In person, online. Visitors must perform in person searches themselves. Required to search: name, years to search; also SSN, case number. Criminal records on computer since 8/92, stored for 25 years on site then archived (back to 1800s). Criminal PAT goes back to same as civil. Online access to criminal records same as civil, above and show year of birth only. Court's public terminal may show add'l, often older data.
General Information: Online identifiers in results same as on public terminal. No juvenile, mental, expunged, sealed, dismissed or suspended imposition of sentence records released. Will not fax documents. Court makes copy: $.25 per page. Certification fee: $1.50 for first 2 pages; $.25 each add'l. Payee: Circuit Clerk. Personal checks accepted; credit cards are not. Prepayment required. Mail requests: SASE required for mail return of any copies.

Associate Circuit Division 101 N Jefferson, Rm 205, Courthouse, Mexico, MO 65265; 573-473-5850; probate phone: 573-473-5854; fax: 573-581-3364; 8AM-5PM. ***Misdemeanor, Civil Actions under $25,000, Small Claims, Probate.***
www.courts.mo.gov/page.asp?id=1592
Civil Records: Access: Mail, in person, online. Both court and visitors may perform in person searches. No search fee. Required to search: name, years to search. Civil cases indexed by defendant, plaintiff, on computer since 9/93, prior on cards, archived to 1800s. Mail turnaround time 1 week. Civil PAT goes back to 2003. PAT results show middle initial, DOB. Participates in state online court record system at https://www.courts.mo.gov/casenet/base/welcome.do. Online records go back to 5/19/2003.
Criminal Records: Access: Mail, in person, online. Both court and visitors may perform in person searches. No search fee. Required to search: name, years to search, DOB, SSN, signed release. Criminal records on computer since 9/93, prior on cards, archived to 1800s. Mail turnaround time 1 week. Criminal PAT goes back to 2003. PAT results show middle initial, DOB. Online access to criminal records same as civil, above and show year of birth only. Court's public terminal may show add'l, often older data.
General Information: Online identifiers in results same as on public terminal. No juvenile, mental, expunged, sealed, dismissed or suspended imposition of sentence records released. Will fax documents to toll-free number. Court makes copy: $.15 per page. Certification fee: $1.50 first page, $1.00 each add'l. Payee: Circuit Court Division II. Only cashiers checks and money orders accepted. No credit cards accepted. Prepayment required.

Barry County

Combined Circuit Court 102 West St #1 (Criminal Div) #2 (Civil Div), Barry County Judicial Center, Cassville, MO 65625; 417-847-3133, 417-847-6557; criminal: x2627; civil: x2626; criminal fax: 417-847-6298; civil fax: 417-847-0182; 8AM-4PM. ***Felony, Misdemeanor, Civil Actions, Eviction, Small Claims, Probate.***
www.courts.mo.gov/page.asp?id=1660 The Circuit Court and Assoc Circuit Court combined 1/2007.
Civil Records: Access: Mail, fax, in person, online. Both court and visitors may perform in person searches. No search fee. Required to search: name, years to search. Civil cases indexed by defendant, plaintiff; index on cards, archived since mid-1800s. Civil PAT goes back to 2005. Lookup cases at https://www.courts.mo.gov/casenet/base/welcome.do. Online records go back to 7/11/2005.
Criminal Records: Access: In person, online (Mail, fax if case number known). Both court and visitors may perform in person searches. No search fee. Required to search: case number. Criminal records indexed on cards, archived since mid-1800s; on computer back to 1995. Note: Call ahead for approval of a mail or fax request, and fee. Often,

this court directs requests to Highway Patrol for criminal background checks. Criminal PAT goes back to 2005. PAT results show name, SSN. but results show DOB year of birth only. Online access to criminal records same as civil, above and show year of birth only. Court's public terminal may show add'l, often older data.
General Information: Online identifiers in results same as on public terminal. No juvenile, mental expunged, sealed, dismissed or suspended imposition of sentence records released. Will fax documents. Court makes copy: $.25 per page. Certification fee: $1.00 per doc. Payee: Circuit Clerk. No personal checks or credit cards accepted. Prepayment required. Mail requests: SASE required for civil.

Barton County

Consolidated Circuit Court 1007 Broadway, Rm 204, County Courthouse, Lamar, MO 64759; 417-682-2444; fax: 417-682-2960; 8AM-N, 1-4:30PM. ***Felony, Misdemeanor, Civil, Eviction, Small Claims, Probate.***
www.courts.mo.gov/page.asp?id=1633
Civil Records: Access: Mail, in person, online. Both court and visitors may perform in person searches. No search fee. Required to search: name, years to search; also helpful: address. Civil cases indexed by defendant, plaintiff, on computer since 1999; prior from 1880 on books or archived. Mail turnaround time 2 weeks. Civil PAT goes back to 1880. PAT civil results show middle initial. Access case lookup at https://www.courts.mo.gov/casenet/base/welcome.do. Results show DOB day and month only. Online records go back to 4/1/1999.
Criminal Records: Access: Mail, online, in person. Both court and visitors may perform in person searches. No search fee. Required to search: name, years to search; also helpful: address, DOB, SSN. Criminal records on computer since 1993; prior from 1880on books or archived. Mail turnaround time 2 weeks. Criminal PAT goes back to 1999. PAT criminal results show middle initial. Online access to criminal same as civil, above. Court's public terminal may show add'l, often older data.
General Information: Online identifiers in results same as on public terminal. No juvenile, mental, expunged, dismissed, or suspended imposition of sentence records released. Will fax out documents $1.00 1st page, $.50 each add'l. Court makes copy: $.10 per page. Self serve copy: Criminal self serve copy $.10 per page; No civil self serve. Certification fee: $2.50. Payee: Circuit Court. Personal checks accepted; credit cards are not. Prepayment required. Mail requests: SASE required.

Bates County

Consolidated Circuit Court 1 N Delaware St, Bates County Courthouse, Butler, MO 64730; 660-679-5171 or 3311; fax: 660-679-4446; 8AM-4:30PM. ***Felony, Misdemeanor, Civil, Eviction, Small Claims, Probate.***
http://tacnet.missouri.org/~court27/
Civil Records: Access: Fax, mail, in person, online. Both court and visitors may perform in person searches. No search fee. Required to search: name, years to search. Civil cases indexed by defendant, plaintiff, on computer since 9/1/92, prior on books since 1858. Mail turnaround time within 48 hours. Civil PAT goes back to 8/13/2003. Access case lookup at https://www.courts.mo.gov/casenet/base/welcome.do. Online records go back to 8/18/2003.
Criminal Records: Access: Fax, mail, in person, online. Both court and visitors may perform in person searches. No search fee. Required to search: name, years to search. Criminal records on computer since 9/1/92, prior on books since 1858. Mail turnaround time within 48 hours. Criminal PAT goes back to same as civil. Online access to criminal same as civil, above. Court's public terminal may show add'l, often older data.
General Information: Online identifiers in results same as on public terminal. No juvenile, mental, expunged, dismissed, or suspended imposition of sentence records released. No fee to fax documents. Court makes copy: $.25 per page, self serve same. Certification fee: $1.50 per certification. Payee: Circuit Court. Only cashiers checks and money orders accepted. No credit cards accepted. Prepayment required. Mail requests: SASE required.

Benton County

Consolidated Circuit Court PO Box 37, 316 Van Buren, Warsaw, MO 65355; 660-438-7712; fax: 660-438-5755; 8-5PM. ***Felony, Misdemeanor, Civil, Eviction, Small Claims, Probate.***
http://home.positech.net/~dcourt/
Associate Division clerk phone is 660-438-6231.
Civil Records: Access: Mail, in person, online. Visitors must perform in person searches themselves. No search fee. Required to search: name, years to search. Civil cases indexed by defendant, plaintiff, on computer since 1993, prior on index cards since 1800. Civil PAT goes back to 11/2001. Participates in the statewide Casenet system at https://www.courts.mo.gov/casenet/base/welcome.do. Online records go back to 11/13/2001.
Criminal Records: Access: In person, online. Visitors must perform in person searches themselves. Required to search: name, years to search, DOB; also helpful: SSN. Criminal records on computer since 1993, prior on index cards since 1800. Note: Court may perform search if time permits. Court will only indicate if subject is on probation or has open case. Court recommends criminal searches at MO State Hwy Patrol, 573-526-6288. Criminal PAT goes back to same as civil. Online access to criminal same as civil, above. Court's public terminal may show add'l, often older data.
General Information: Online identifiers in results same as on public terminal. No juvenile, mental, expunged, dismissed, or suspended imposition of sentence records released. Will fax back documents. Court makes copy: $.10 per page, self serve same. Certification fee: $2.50 per cert. Payee: Clerk of Circuit Court. Personal checks accepted; credit cards are not. Prepayment required.

Bollinger County

Circuit Court PO Box 949, 204 High St, Marble Hill, MO 63764; 573-238-1900 x6; fax: 573-238-2773; 8-4PM. ***Felony, Civil Actions over $25,000.***
www.courts.mo.gov/page.asp?id=1640
Civil Records: Access: In person, online. Visitors must perform in person searches themselves. Required to search: name, years to search. Civil cases indexed by defendant, plaintiff, on computer since 1990, prior on index cards 1976-1990. Civil PAT goes back to 1992. PAT results show middle initial, DOB. Access to civil records is free at https://www.courts.mo.gov/casenet/base/welcome.do. Online records go back to 7/1/2001, judgments to 8/23/1993.
Criminal Records: Access: In person, online. Visitors must perform in person searches themselves. Required to search: name, years to search. Criminal records on computer since 1990, prior on index cards 1976-1990. Criminal PAT goes back to same as civil. PAT results show middle initial, DOB. Online access to criminal records same as civil, above and show year of birth only. Court's public terminal may show add'l, often older data.
General Information: Online identifiers in results same as on public terminal. No juvenile, mental, expunged, dismissed, or suspended imposition of sentence records released. Will not fax documents. Court makes copy: $1.00 per page, self serve same. Certification fee: $1.00 per cert. Payee: Circuit Clerk. Personal checks accepted; credit cards are not. Prepayment required.

Associate Circuit Division PO Box 1040, Marble Hill, MO 63764-1040; 573-238-1900 x4; criminal fax: 573-238-4511; civil fax: same; 8AM-4PM. ***Misdemeanor, Civil Actions under $25,000, Eviction, Small Claims, Probate.***
www.courts.mo.gov/page.asp?id=1640
Probate fax is same as main fax number.
Civil Records: Access: In person, online. Visitors must perform in person searches themselves. Required to search: name, years to search. Civil cases indexed by defendant, plaintiff, on computer back to 1995, prior on books, archived to 1890. Civil PAT goes back to 7/2001. Access case lookup at https://www.courts.mo.gov/casenet/base/welcome.do. Online records go back to 7/1/2001, judgments to 8/23/1993.
Criminal Records: Access: In person, online. Visitors must perform in person searches themselves. Required to search: name, years to search. Criminal records computerized from 1995, prior on books, archived to 1890. Criminal PAT goes back to 6/1994. Online access to criminal records same as civil, above and show year of birth only. Court's public terminal may show add'l, often older data.
General Information: Online identifiers in results same as on public terminal. No juvenile, mental, expunged, dismissed, or suspended imposition of sentence records released. Will fax documents. Court makes copy: $1.00 per page, self serve same. Certification fee: $1.00 per certification. Payee: Circuit Court Division V. Personal checks accepted; credit cards are not. Prepayment required.

Boone County

Consolidated Circuit Court 705 E Walnut, Columbia, MO 65201; 573-886-4000; probate phone: 573-886-4090; fax: 573-886-4044; 8AM-5PM. ***Felony, Misdemeanor, Civil, Eviction, Small Claims, Probate.***
www.courts.mo.gov/hosted/circuit13/
Civil Records: Access: In person, online. Visitors must perform in person searches themselves. Required to search: name, years to search. Civil cases indexed by defendant, plaintiff, on computer for recent cases, others on books. Civil PAT goes back to 1985. Access case lookup at https://www.courts.mo.gov/casenet/base/welcome.do. Online civil records go back to 1986; probate back to 1986.
Criminal Records: Access: In person, online. Visitors must perform in person searches themselves. Required to search: name, years to search, DOB. Criminal records on computer for recent cases, others on books. Criminal PAT goes back to same as civil. Online access to criminal same as civil, above, criminal records go back to 1983. Court's public terminal may show add'l, often older data.
General Information: Online identifiers in results same as on public terminal. No juvenile, mental, paternity, expunged, dismissed, or suspended imposition of sentence records released. Will not fax documents. Court makes copy: $1.00 1st page; $.10 each add'l. Certification fee: $1.00 per cert. Payee: Boone County Circuit Clerk. Business checks accepted. Visa/MC accepted. Prepayment required.

Buchanan County

Consolidated Circuit Court 411 Jules St, Rm 331, St Joseph, MO 64501; 816-271-1462; fax: 816-271-1538; 8AM-5PM. ***Felony, Misdemeanor, Civil, Eviction, Small Claims.***
www.courts.mo.gov/page.asp?id=1563
Civil Records: Access: In person, online. Visitors must perform in person searches themselves. Required to search: name, years to search. Civil cases indexed by defendant, plaintiff, on computer since 2/92, on index cards since 1976, prior archived. Civil PAT goes back to 1992. PAT civil results show middle initial. Access case lookup at https://www.courts.mo.gov/casenet/base/welcome.do. Online records go back to 2000.
Criminal Records: Access: In person, online. Visitors must perform in person searches themselves. Required to search: name, years to search. Criminal records on computer since 2/92, on index cards since 1976, prior archived. Criminal PAT goes back to same as civil. PAT criminal results show middle initial. Online access to criminal same as civil, above, criminal records go back to 1992. Court's public terminal may show add'l, often older data.
General Information: Online identifiers in results same as on public terminal. No juvenile, mental, expunged, dismissed, or suspended imposition of sentence records released. Will fax documents $1.00 per page. Court makes copy: $.25 per page, self serve same. Certification fee: $2.50. Payee: Buchanan

Circuit Clerk. Personal checks accepted; credit cards are not. Prepayment required.

Probate Court Buchanan County Courthouse, 411 Jules St, Rm 333, St Joseph, MO 64501; 816-271-1477; fax: 816-271-1538; 8AM-5PM. ***Probate.*** www.courts.mo.gov/page.asp?id=1563

Butler County

Consolidated Circuit Court Courthouse, Poplar Bluff, MO 63901; criminal: 573-686-8087; civil: 573-686-8082; probate phone: 573-686-8073; criminal fax: 573-686-8093; civil fax: 573-686-8094; 8AM-4PM. ***Felony, Misdemeanor, Civil, Eviction, Small Claims, Probate.***
www.courts.mo.gov/page.asp?id=1650
Circuit and Associate courts combined 12/1/2004. Probate fax- 573-686-0056

Civil Records: Access: Fax, mail, in person, online. Visitors must perform in person searches themselves. Search fee: $1.00 per name per year. Required to search: name, years to search. Civil cases indexed by defendant, plaintiff, on computer since 9/91, prior on cards and books since 1865. Civil PAT goes back to 1992. Access case lookup at https://www.courts.mo.gov/casenet/base/welcome.do, records from 9/2005.

Criminal Records: Access: In person, fax, mail, online. Visitors must perform in person searches themselves. Search fee: $1.00 per name per year. Required to search: name, years to search. Criminal records on computer since 9/91, prior on cards and books since 1865. Mail turnaround time is 1-3 days. Criminal PAT goes back to same as civil. Online access to criminal records same as civil, above and show year of birth only. Court's public terminal may show add'l, often older data.

General Information: Online identifiers in results same as on public terminal. No juvenile, mental, expunged, dismissed, or suspended imposition of sentence records released. Will fax documents $1.00 per page. Court makes copy: $.25 per page, self serve same. Certification fee: $2.50. Payee: Clerk of Circuit Court. Business checks accepted. No credit cards accepted. Prepayment required. SASE not required.

Caldwell County

Consolidated Circuit Court PO Box 68, 49 E Main, Kingston, MO 64650; 816-586-2581; fax: 816-586-2333; 7:30AM-4:30PM. ***Felony, Misdemeanor, Civil, Eviction, Small Claims, Probate.***
www.courts.mo.gov/page.asp?id=1673

Civil Records: Access: Phone, mail, in person, online. Both court and visitors may perform in person searches. No search fee. Required to search: name, years to search. Civil cases indexed by defendant, plaintiff, on computer back to 1995. Mail turnaround time 3 days. Civil PAT goes back to 1995. PAT results show middle initial, DOB. Access case lookup at https://www.courts.mo.gov/casenet/base/welcome.do. Online records go back to 1/23/2006.

Criminal Records: Access: Phone, mail, in person, online. Both court and visitors may perform in person searches. No search fee. Required to search: name, years to search. Criminal records computerized from 1995. Mail turnaround time 3 days. Criminal PAT goes back to 2006. PAT results show middle initial, DOB. Online access to criminal records same as civil, above and show year of birth only. Court's public terminal may show add'l, often older data.

General Information: Online identifiers in results same as on public terminal. No juvenile, mental, expunged, dismissed, or suspended imposition of sentence records released. Will fax documents $1.00 per fax. Court makes copy: $1.00 per page. Certification fee: $1.50 per page. Payee: Circuit Clerk. Personal checks accepted; credit cards are not. Prepayment required. Mail requests: SASE required.

Callaway County

Consolidated Circuit Court 10 E 5th St, Fulton, MO 65251; 573-642-0780; probate phone: 573-642-7080; fax: 573-642-0700; 8AM-5PM. ***Felony, Misdemeanor, Civil, Eviction, Small Claims, Probate.***
www.courts.mo.gov/hosted/circuit13/

Civil Records: Access: Fax, mail, in person, online. Both court and visitors may perform in person searches. No search fee. Required to search: name, years to search. Civil cases indexed by defendant, plaintiff; index on docket books and cards since 1821. Note: Court will only perform searches as time permits Mail turnaround time 5 days. Civil PAT goes back to 2000. Access case lookup at https://www.courts.mo.gov/casenet/base/welcome.do. Online cases go back to 2000; online probate to 1977.

Criminal Records: Access: In person, online. Visitors must perform in person searches themselves. Required to search: name, years to search; also helpful: DOB, SSN. Criminal records on computer since 1993, prior on index books and cards since 1821. Criminal PAT goes back to same as civil. Online access to criminal records same as civil, above and show year of birth only. Court's public terminal may show add'l, often older data.

General Information: Online identifiers in results same as on public terminal. No juvenile, mental, expunged, dismissed, or suspended imposition of sentence records released. Will fax documents $.10 per page to local phone. Court makes copy: $.10 per page, $1.00 minimum. Self serve copy: $.10 per page. Certification fee: $1.50. Payee: Circuit Clerk. Business checks accepted. Attorney/law firm checks accepted. Major credit cards accepted. Prepayment required. SASE not required.

Camden County

Consolidated Circuit Court 1 Court Circle, #8, Camdenton, MO 65020; 573-346-4440; fax: 573-346-5422; 8:30AM-4:30PM. ***Felony, Misdemeanor, Civil, Eviction, Small Claims, Probate.*** www.courts.mo.gov/page.asp?id=1628 2nd website- www.camdenmo.org/circuitcourt/index.htm

Civil Records: Access: Mail, in person, online. Both court and visitors may perform in person searches. No search fee. Required to search: name, years to search. Civil cases indexed by defendant, plaintiff, on computer since 1989, on index cards from 1965 to 1989, prior on index books since 1903. Mail turnaround time 1 day. Civil PAT goes back to 1988. Access case lookup at https://www.courts.mo.gov/casenet/base/welcome.do. Online records go back to 11/28/2005.

Criminal Records: Access: In person, online. Both court and visitors may perform in person searches. No search fee. Required to search: name, years to search; also helpful: DOB, SSN. Criminal records on computer since 1989, on index cards from 1965 to 1989, prior on index books since 1903. Criminal PAT goes back to same as civil. PAT results show name only. Online access to criminal records same as civil, above and show year of birth only. Court's public terminal may show add'l, often older data.

General Information: Online identifiers in results same as on public terminal. No juvenile, mental, expunged, dismissed, or suspended imposition of sentence records released. Will fax documents $1.00 per page. Court makes copy: $.25 per page. Certification fee: $1.50 per cert. Payee: Circuit Clerk. Only cashiers checks and money orders accepted. No credit cards accepted.

Cape Girardeau County

Circuit Court - Civil Division 44 N Lorimier, Cape Girardeau, MO 63702; 573-335-8253; fax: 573-331-2565; 8AM-4:30PM. ***Civil, Eviction, Small Claims, Probate.***
www.courts.mo.gov/page.asp?id=1641
This court should also have records for the Associate Court in Jackson, 573-243-8446. Probate located here at a separate court, 573-334-6249, and online.

Civil Records: Access: Mail, in person, online. Both court and visitors may perform in person searches. No search fee. Required to search: name, years to search. Civil cases indexed by defendant, plaintiff, on computer since 1994, prior on index cards since 10/75. Mail turnaround time 1 week. Public use terminal has civil records back to 1994. Results include last name and first name. Access civil records free at https://www.courts.mo.gov/casenet/base/welcome.do. Online records go back to 7/1/2001.

General Information: Online identifiers in results same as on public terminal. No juvenile, mental, expunged, dismissed, or suspended imposition of sentence, paternity, cases where one party on AFDC records released. Will fax documents to local or toll free line. Court makes copy: $1.00 per page. Certification fee: $1.00 per cert. Payee: Circuit Clerk. Personal checks accepted; credit cards are not. Prepayment required. Mail requests: SASE required.

Circuit Court - Criminal Division I & II 100 Court St, Jackson, MO 63755; 573-243-8446 (misdemeanors); criminal phone: 573-243-1755 (felony); fax: 573-204-2405; 8AM-4:30PM. ***Felony, Misdemeanor.***
www.courts.mo.gov/page.asp?id=1641

Criminal Records: Access: Mail, in person, online. Both court and visitors may perform in person searches. Search fee: $10.00 per name. Required to search: name, years to search. Criminal records on computer since 1991, prior on books. Mail turnaround time 1 week. Public use terminal has crim records back to 8/23/93. PAT criminal results show middle initial. Access criminal records free at www.courts.mo.gov/casenet/base/welcome.do. Online public case records go back to 7/1/01; Circuit court criminal judgments to 8/23/1993.

General Information: Online identifiers in results same as on public terminal. No juvenile, mental, expunged, dismissed, or suspended imposition of sentence records released. Will fax documents to local or toll free line. Court makes copy: $1.00 per page, self serve same. Certification fee: $1.00 per cert seal. Payee: Circuit Clerk. Personal checks accepted; credit cards are not. Prepayment required. Mail requests: SASE required.

Carroll County

Circuit Court PO Box 245, 8 S Main St, Carrollton, MO 64633; 660-542-1466; criminal fax: 660-542-1444; civil fax: same; 8:30AM-4:30PM. ***Felony, Civil Actions over $25,000.***
www.courts.mo.gov/page.asp?id=1568

Civil Records: Access: Fax, mail, in person, online. Both court and visitors may perform in person searches. No search fee. Required to search: name, years to search. Civil cases indexed by defendant, plaintiff, on books since 1833. Mail turnaround time varies. Civil PAT goes back to 2001. Case lookup at https://www.courts.mo.gov/casenet/base/welcome.do. Online records go back to 9/19/01.

Criminal Records: Access: Fax, mail, in person, online. Both court and visitors may perform in person searches. No search fee. Required to search: name, years to search. Criminal docket on books since 1833. Mail turnaround time varies. Criminal PAT available. 2001. Online access to criminal same as civil, above. Court's public terminal may show add'l, often older data.

General Information: Online identifiers in results same as on public terminal. No juvenile, mental, expunged, dismissed, or suspended imposition of sentence records released. Will not fax out documents. Court makes copy: $.35 per page, self serve same. Certification fee: $2.00 per document includes copy fee. Payee: Circuit Clerk. Personal checks accepted. Prepayment required. SASE not required.

Associate Circuit Division Courthouse, 8 S Main, #1, Carrollton, MO 64633; 660-542-1818; criminal phone: 660-542-2494; civil phone: 660-542-1818; probate phone: 660-542-1818; criminal fax: 660-542-1877; civil fax: same; 8:30AM-4:30PM. ***Misdemeanor, Civil Actions under $25,000, Eviction, Small Claims, Probate.***
www.courts.mo.gov/page.asp?id=1568
Probate fax is same as main fax number.

Civil Records: Access: Mail, in person, online. Visitors must perform in person searches themselves. No search fee. Required to search: name,

years to search, address. Civil cases indexed by defendant, plaintiff, go back to 1990; on computer back to 12/2001. Civil PAT goes back to 12/2001. PAT results show middle initial, DOB. Case lookup at https://www.courts.mo.gov/casenet/base/welcome.do. Online records go back to 09/19/01.
Criminal Records: Access: In person, online. Visitors must perform in person searches themselves. Required to search: name, years to search, address, DOB. Criminal records go back to 1990; on computer back to 12/2001. Criminal PAT goes back to same as civil. PAT results show middle initial, DOB. Online access to criminal records same as civil, above and show year of birth only. Court's public terminal may show add'l, often older data.
General Information: Online identifiers in results same as on public terminal. No juvenile, mental, expunged, dismissed, or suspended imposition of sentence records released. Will fax documents for no fee. Court makes copy: $.35 per page. Certification fee: $1.50 per document. Payee: Associate Circuit Court. Only cashiers checks and money orders accepted. No credit cards accepted. Prepayment required. Mail requests: SASE required for mail return of any copies.

Carter County

Circuit Court PO Box 578, 105 Main St, Van Buren, MO 63965; 573-323-4513; fax: 573-323-4885; 8AM-4PM. ***Felony, Civil Actions over $20,000.***
www.courts.mo.gov/page.asp?id=1652
Civil Records: Access: Mail, in person, online. Both court and visitors may perform in person searches. No search fee. Required to search: name, years to search. Civil cases indexed by defendant, plaintiff, on computer since 1979, on index cards since 1988, archived since late-1800s. Access case lookup at https://www.courts.mo.gov/casenet/base/welcome.do. Online records go back to 4/17/2000.
Criminal Records: Access: Mail, in person, online. Visitors must perform in person searches themselves. No search fee. Required to search: name, years to search. Criminal records on computer since 1979, on index cards since 1988, archived since late-1800s. Online access to criminal same as civil, above. Court's public terminal may show add'l, often older data.
General Information: Online identifiers in results same as on public terminal. No juvenile, mental, paternity, expunged, dismissed, or suspended imposition of sentence records released. Will fax document for $2.00 per doc plus $1.00 each add'l page. Court makes copy: $.25 per page. Certification fee: $1.00 per cert. Payee: Circuit Clerk. Personal checks accepted; credit cards are not. Prepayment required. Mail requests: SASE required.

Associate Circuit Division PO Box 578, 105 Main St, Van Buren, MO 63965; 573-323-4513; ; 8AM-4PM. ***Misdemeanor, Civil Actions under $20,000, Eviction, Small Claims, Probate.***
www.courts.mo.gov/page.asp?id=1652
Civil Records: Access: In person, online. Only the court performs in person searches; visitors may not. Required to search: name, years to search. Civil cases indexed by defendant, plaintiff, on index since 1994, prior on docket sheets. Access case lookup at https://www.courts.mo.gov/casenet/base/welcome.do. Online records go back to 4/17/2000.
Criminal Records: Access: In person, online. Only the court performs in person searches; visitors may not. Required to search: name, years to search. Criminal records on index since 1999, prior on docket sheets. Online access to criminal records same as civil, above and show year of birth only. Court's public terminal may show add'l, often older data.
General Information: Online identifiers in results same as on public terminal. No juvenile, mental, expunged, dismissed, or suspended imposition of sentence records released. Will not fax documents. Court makes copy: $.25 per page. No certification fee. Payee: Circuit Court Division II. Personal checks accepted. Prepayment required.

Cass County

Circuit Court 2501 W Wall, Harrisonville, MO 64701; 816-380-8227; probate phone: 816-380-8218; criminal fax: 816-380-8225; civil fax: same; 8AM-5:00PM. ***Felony, Civil Actions over $25,000.***
www.courts.mo.gov/page.asp?id=1902
Civil Records: Access: Phone, mail, in person, online. Both court and visitors may perform in person searches. No search fee. Required to search: name, years to search. Civil cases indexed by defendant, plaintiff, on computer since 1992, on index cards since 1976, prior on judgment books since 1800s. Mail turnaround time 1 week. Civil PAT goes back to 1992. Access case lookup at https://www.courts.mo.gov/casenet/base/welcome.do. Online records go back to 6/6/2005.
Criminal Records: Access: Phone, mail, in person, online. Both court and visitors may perform in person searches. No search fee. Required to search: name, years to search. Criminal records on computer since 1992, on index cards since 1976, prior on judgment books since 1800s. Mail turnaround time 1 week. Criminal PAT goes back to same as civil. Online access to criminal records same as civil, above and show year of birth only. Court's public terminal may show add'l, often older data.
General Information: Online identifiers in results same as on public terminal. No juvenile, mental, expunged, dismissed, or suspended imposition of sentence records released. Will fax documents $.25 per page. Court makes copy: $.25 per page. Certification fee: $1.50 per page. Payee: Cass County Circuit Clerk. No personal checks or credit cards accepted. Prepayment required. Mail requests: SASE required.

Associate Circuit Division 2501 W Wall St, Harrisonville, MO 64701; 816-380-8200; fax: 816-380-8195; 8AM-4:30PM. ***Misdemeanor, Civil Actions under $25,000, Eviction, Small Claims.***
www.courts.mo.gov/page.asp?id=1902
Civil Records: Access: Mail, in person, online. Visitors must perform in person searches themselves. No search fee. Required to search: name, years to search. Civil cases indexed by defendant, plaintiff, go back to 1986; on index cards since 1983. Note: in person searches must look through cards. Mail turnaround time 1-2 days. Case lookup at https://www.courts.mo.gov/casenet/base/welcome.do. Online records go back to 6/6/2005.
Criminal Records: Access: Mail, in person, online. Visitors must perform in person searches themselves. No search fee. Required to search: name, years to search, signed release. Criminal records go back to 1960s; on index cards since 1983; on computer back to 1995. Note: In person searcher must look through cards. Mail turnaround time varies. Online access to criminal records same as civil, above and show year of birth only. Court's public terminal may show add'l, often older data.
General Information: Online identifiers in results same as on public terminal. No juvenile, mental, expunged, dismissed, or suspended imposition of sentence records released. Will not fax documents. Court makes copy: $.25 per page. No certification fee. Payee: Division III. Business checks accepted. No credit cards accepted. Prepayment required. Mail requests: SASE required.

Probate Court 2501 W. Wall St, Harrisonville, MO 64701; 816-380-8217; fax: 816-380-8215; 8AM-N, 1-4:30PM. ***Probate.***
Participates in the free state online court record system at https://www.courts.mo.gov/casenet. Online records go back to 6/6/2005.

Cedar County

Consolidated Circuit Court PO Box 665, 113 South St, Stockton, MO 65785; 417-276-6700; fax: 417-276-5001; 8AM-4:30PM. ***Felony, Misdemeanor, Civil, Eviction, Small Claims, Probate.***
www.courts.mo.gov/page.asp?id=1635
Civil Records: Access: Fax, mail, in person, online. Visitors must perform in person searches themselves. No search fee. Required to search: name, years to search. Civil cases indexed by defendant, plaintiff; index on cards since 1979, prior on docket books to 1830. Civil PAT goes back to 9/11/2000. Access case lookup at https://www.courts.mo.gov/casenet/base/welcome.do. Online records go back to 9/11/2000. Online include Probate.
Criminal Records: Access: In person, online. Visitors must perform in person searches themselves. Required to search: name, years to search. Criminal records indexed on cards since 1979, prior on docket books. Criminal PAT goes back to same as civil. Online access to criminal records same as civil, above and show year of birth only. Court's public terminal may show add'l, often older data.
General Information: Online identifiers in results same as on public terminal. No juvenile, mental, expunged, dismissed, or suspended imposition of sentence records released. Fee to fax out file $1.00 per page. Court makes copy: $.25 per page; Probate $1.00 per page. Self serve copy: $.25 per page. Certification fee: $1.50 per cert. Payee: Cedar County Circuit Court. Personal checks accepted; credit cards are not. Prepayment required.

Chariton County

Consolidated Circuit Court 306 S Cherry, Keytesville, MO 65261; 660-288-3602; criminal phone: 660-288-3271; civil phone: 660-288-3602; criminal fax: 660-288-3763; civil fax: same; 8:30AM-4:30PM. ***Felony, Misdemeanor, Civil, Eviction, Small Claims, Probate.***
www.courts.mo.gov/page.asp?id=1570
The Circuit Court and Associate Division consolidated on 1/1/2006.
Civil Records: Access: Fax, mail, in person, online. Both court and visitors may perform in person searches. Search fee: $4.00 per name. Required to search: name, years to search. Civil cases indexed by defendant, plaintiff, computerized since 5/13/2002; on index books since 1975, prior on docket books to 1827. Mail turnaround time same day. Civil PAT goes back to 2002. PAT results show name only. Participates in free online court records system at https://www.courts.mo.gov/casenet/base/welcome.do. Online records go back to 5/13/2002.
Criminal Records: Access: Fax, mail, in person, online. Both court and visitors may perform in person searches. Search fee: $4.00 per name. Required to search: name, years to search; also helpful: DOB, SSN. Criminal records computerized since 5/13/2002; on index books since 1975, prior on docket books to 1827. Mail turnaround time same day. Criminal PAT goes back to same as civil. PAT results show name only. Online access to criminal same as civil, above. Court's public terminal may show add'l, often older data.
General Information: Online identifiers in results same as on public terminal. No juvenile, mental, expunged, dismissed, or suspended imposition of sentence records released. Fee to fax out file $1.00 per page. Court makes copy: $1.00 per page, self serve same. Certification fee: $1.50 per page. Payee: Chariton County Circuit Clerk. Personal checks accepted; credit cards are not. Prepayment required. Mail requests: SASE required.

Christian County

Circuit Court PO Box 278, Ozark, MO 65721; 417-581-6372; probate phone: 417-581-4523; fax: 417-581-0391; 8AM-4:30PM. ***Felony, Civil Actions over $25,000.***
www.courts.mo.gov/page.asp?id=1656
Add'l website at www.geocities.com/circuit38/
Civil Records: Access: Mail, in person, online. Both court and visitors may perform in person searches. Search fee: $6.00 per name. Required to search: name, years to search. Civil cases indexed by defendant, plaintiff, on computer since 9/97, judgments since 1991; pending cases indexed on computer. Old case card files back to 1979. Note: Results include full name and/or case number. Mail turnaround time 1 week. Civil PAT goes back to 1991. PAT civil results show middle initial. Access case lookup at https://www.courts.mo.gov/casenet/base/welcome.do. Online records go back to 6/13/03.

Criminal Records: Access: Mail, in person, online. Both court and visitors may perform in person searches. Search fee: $6.00 per name. Required to search: name, years to search. Criminal records on computer since 9/97, pending cases indexed in card files. Old case card files back to 1979. Note: Results include full name and/or case number. Mail turnaround time 1 week. Criminal PAT goes back to same as civil. PAT criminal results show middle initial. Online access to criminal same as civil, above. Court's public terminal may show add'l, often older data.
General Information: Online identifiers in results same as on public terminal. No juvenile, mental, expunged, dismissed, or suspended imposition or execution of sentence records released. Will fax documents $.50 per page. Court makes copy: $.30 per page. Certification fee: $1.00. Payee: Christian County Circuit Clerk. No personal checks or credit cards accepted. Prepayment required. Mail requests: SASE required.

Associate Circuit Div. - Civil Div. 1 110 W Elm St, Rm 203, Ozark, MO 65721; 417-581-2425; fax: 417-581-0391; 8AM-4:30PM. ***Civil Actions under $2,500, Eviction, Small Claims.***
www.courts.mo.gov/page.asp?id=1656
Division #1 is Civil, #2 is criminal.
Civil Records: Access: Phone, mail, fax, in person, online. Both court and visitors may perform in person searches. No search fee. Required to search: name, years to search. Civil cases indexed by defendant. Civil records on computer since 7/91. Mail turnaround time 5 days by mail. Public use terminal has civil records back to 7/1991. Case lookup at https://www.courts.mo.gov/casenet/base/welcome.do. Records go back to 6/16/2003.
General Information: Online identifiers in results same as on public terminal. No juvenile, mental, expunged or dismissed records released. Will fax out documents but only if they are no lengthy. Court makes copy: none, but if lengthy $.50 per page. Self serve copy: none. No certification fee. Payee: Associate Division I. Personal checks accepted; credit cards are not. Prepayment required. Mail requests: SASE required.

Associate Circuit Division - Criminal Division 2 110 W Elm St, Rm 105, Ozark, MO 65721; 417-581-4523; fax: 417-581-1443; 8AM-4:30PM. ***Misdemeanor, Probate.***
www.courts.mo.gov/page.asp?id=1656
This court will not perform name searches and asks searchers to contact MSHP at 573-526-6288.
Criminal Records: Access: In person, online. Visitors must perform in person searches themselves. Required to search: name, years to search. Criminal records on computer since 6/2003; some prior on index cards. Note: Will accept phone requests from attorneys and law enforcement officials. Public use terminal has crim records back to 6/2003. Probate records on public terminal back to 6/2003. Terminal located in Circuit Clerk's Office. Participates in free state court system at www.courts.mo.gov/casenet/base/welcome.do. Records go back to 6/16/2003.
General Information: Online identifiers in results same as on public terminal. No juvenile, mental, expunged or dismissed records released. Will not fax documents. Court makes copy: $.30 per page. Self serve copy: $.30 per page. Certification fee: $1.50. Payee: Associate Division 2. No personal checks or credit cards accepted. Prepayment required.

Clark County

Circuit Court 111 E Court, #2, Kahoka, MO 63445; 660-727-3292; fax: 660-727-1051; 8AM-4PM. ***Felony, Civil Actions over $45,000.***
www.courts.mo.gov/page.asp?id=1518
Civil Records: Access: Phone, fax, mail, in person, online. Both court and visitors may perform in person searches. No search fee. Required to search: name, years to search. Civil cases indexed by defendant, plaintiff, on books since 1991, prior archived since 1836. Mail turnaround time 4 days. Civil PAT goes back to 9/19/2001. PAT results show name only. Access case lookup at https://www.courts.mo.gov/casenet/base/welcome.do. Online records go back to 09/19/01.
Criminal Records: Access: Phone, fax, mail, in person, online. Both court and visitors may perform in person searches. No search fee. Required to search: name, years to search. Criminal docket on books since 1991, prior archived since 1836. Mail turnaround time 4 days. Criminal PAT goes back to same as civil. PAT results show name only. Online access to criminal same as civil, above. Court's public terminal may show add'l, often older data.
General Information: Online identifiers in results same as on public terminal. No juvenile, mental, expunged, dismissed, or suspended imposition of sentence records released. Fee to fax out file $1.00 per page. Court makes copy: $.50 per page, self serve same. Certification fee: $3.00 per document. Payee: Clerk of Circuit Court. Personal checks accepted; credit cards are not. Prepayment required. Mail requests: SASE required.

Associate Circuit Division 113 W Court, Kahoka, MO 63445; 660-727-3628; fax: 660-727-2600; 8AM-4PM. ***Misdemeanor, Civil Actions under $45,000, Eviction, Small Claims, Probate.***
www.courts.mo.gov/page.asp?id=1518
Civil Records: Access: Mail, fax, in person, online. Both court and visitors may perform in person searches. No search fee. Required to search: name, years to search. Civil cases indexed by defendant, plaintiff; index on cards, archived since 1836. Mail turnaround time 1-10 days. Access case lookup at https://www.courts.mo.gov/casenet/base/welcome.do. Online records go back to 09/19/01.
Criminal Records: Access: Mail, fax, in person, online. Both court and visitors may perform in person searches. No search fee. Required to search: name, years to search. Criminal records on computer since 1988, prior archived since 1836. Mail turnaround time 1-10 days. Public use terminal has crim records back to 1988. PAT results show middle initial, DOB. Online access to criminal records same as civil, above and show year of birth only. Court's public terminal may show add'l, often older data.
General Information: Online identifiers in results same as on public terminal. No juvenile, mental, expunged, dismissed, or suspended imposition of sentence records released. Will not fax documents. Court makes copy: $.25 per page. Certification fee: $1.50 plus $1.00 per add'l page. Payee: Associate Circuit Court. Personal checks accepted; credit cards are not. Prepayment required. Mail requests: SASE required.

Clay County

Consolidated Circuit Court 11 S Water St, Liberty, MO 64068; 816-407-3900; fax: 816-407-3888; 8AM-5PM. ***Felony, Misdemeanor, Civil, Eviction, Small Claims, Probate.***
www.circuit7.net
Civil Records: Access: Mail, in person, online. Both court and visitors may perform in person searches. No search fee. Required to search: name, years to search. Civil cases indexed by defendant, plaintiff, on computer since 1987; prior records on index. Civil PAT goes back to 1987. PAT results show name only. Access case lookup at https://www.courts.mo.gov/casenet/base/welcome.do. Online index dates back to 1978 for civil and 1977 for probate.
Criminal Records: Access: In person, online. Visitors must perform in person searches themselves. Required to search: name, years to search, DOB. Criminal records on computer since 1994, prior on index cards. Criminal PAT goes back to 1992. PAT results show name only. Online access to criminal same as civil, above, record index dates back to 1995. Court's public terminal may show add'l, often older data.
General Information: Online identifiers in results same as on public terminal. No juvenile, mental, expunged, dismissed, or suspended imposition of sentence records released. Will fax documents; cannot fax certified copies. Court makes copy: $.25 per page. Certification fee: $5.00 per cert. Payee: Clay County Circuit Clerk. No personal checks or credit cards accepted. Prepayment required. Mail requests: SASE required for civil.

Clinton County

Consolidated Circuit Court PO Box 275, Plattsburg, MO 64477; criminal phone: 816-539-3755; civil phone: 816-539-3731; fax: 816-539-3893; 8AM-5PM. ***Felony, Misdemeanor, Civil, Eviction, Small Claims, Probate.***
www.courts.mo.gov/page.asp?id=1674
The Associate Division and Circuit Court consolidated in 10/2005.
Civil Records: Access: Mail, fax, in person, online. Visitors must perform in person searches themselves. No search fee. Required to search: name, years to search. Civil cases indexed by defendant, plaintiff, (Judgments) on computer from 1976, archived since 1833. Civil PAT goes back to 1976. Access case lookup at https://www.courts.mo.gov/casenet/base/welcome.do. Online records go back to 1/23/2006.
Criminal Records: Access: Mail, fax, in person, online. Visitors must perform in person searches themselves. No search fee. Required to search: name, years to search. Criminal records (Judgments) on computer from 1976, archived since 1833. Mail turnaround time 2 days. Criminal PAT goes back to same as civil. Online access to criminal same as civil, above. Court's public terminal may show add'l, often older data.
General Information: Online identifiers in results same as on public terminal. No juvenile, mental, expunged, dismissed, or suspended imposition of sentence records released. Will fax documents $2.00 per page. Court makes copy: $1.00 per page. Certification fee: $1.50. Payee: Circuit Clerk. No personal checks or credit cards accepted. Prepayment required.

Cole County

Consolidated Circuit Court PO Box 1870, 301 E High St, Jefferson City, MO 65102-1870; 573-634-9155; criminal phone: 573-634-9171; civil phone: 573-634-9151; fax: 573-635-0796; 7:30AM-4:30PM. ***Felony, Misdemeanor, Civil, Eviction, Small Claims, Probate.***
www.courts.mo.gov/page.asp?id=1905
The Circuit Court and Associate Division consolidated on 01/01.
Civil Records: Access: Fax, mail, in person, online. Both court and visitors may perform in person searches. No search fee. Required to search: name, years to search. Civil cases indexed by defendant, plaintiff, (pending) on computer, on books since 1820. Mail turnaround time 2-5 days. Civil PAT goes back to 2000. Access case lookup at https://www.courts.mo.gov/casenet/base/welcome.do. Online records go back to 1/1980; probate to 6/2/72.
Criminal Records: Access: In person, online. Both court and visitors may perform in person searches. Required to search: name, years to search; also helpful: DOB, SSN. Criminal records on computer since 1989, prior on book since 1820. Note: Online results include name and case number. Criminal PAT goes back to same as civil. Online access to criminal same as civil, above. Court's public terminal may show add'l, often older data.
General Information: Online identifiers in results same as on public terminal. No juvenile, mental, expunged, dismissed, or suspended imposition of sentence records released. Other access to criminal records: the court prefers that requesters go to the state highway patrol. Will fax documents to local or toll-free number. Court makes copy: $.40 per page. Certification fee: $1.00 per page. Payee: Cole County Circuit Clerk. No personal checks or credit cards accepted. Prepayment required. Mail requests: SASE requested for civil.

Cooper County

Consolidated Circuit Court 200 Main St, Rm 26, Boonville, MO 65233; 660-882-2232 Circuit; 660-882-5604 Associate; fax: 660-882-2043; 8:30AM-5PM. ***Felony, Misdemeanor, Civil, Eviction, Small Claims, Probate.***
www.courts.mo.gov/page.asp?id=1614

Civil Records: Access: Phone, fax, mail, in person, online. Both court and visitors may perform in person searches. No search fee. Required to search: name, years to search. Civil cases indexed by defendant, plaintiff, on cards since 1975, case files from 1819 forward; on computer back to 2001. Mail turnaround time 1-2 days. Can tell if record is available and cost over phone. Civil PAT goes back to 4/2001. Access to civil records is free at https://www.courts.mo.gov/casenet/base/welcome.do. Online records go back to 4/2001.
Criminal Records: Access: In person, online. Both court and visitors may perform in person searches. No search fee. Required to search: name, years to search, DOB; also helpful: SSN. Criminal records on cards since 1975, case files from 1819 forward; on computer back to 2001 for Circuit, mid-1990s for Associate Ct. Note: Court can say if record is available and cost over phone. Criminal PAT goes back to same as civil. Online access to criminal same as civil, above. Court's public terminal may show add'l, often older data.
General Information: Online identifiers in results same as on public terminal. No juvenile, mental, expunged, dismissed, or suspended imposition of sentence records released. Will fax out documents $1.00 per page. Court makes copy: $1.00 per page. Certification fee: $1.50 per cert. Payee: Circuit Clerk. No personal checks or credit cards accepted. Prepayment required. Mail requests: SASE required for civil.

Crawford County

Circuit Court PO Box 177, Steelville, MO 65565; 573-775-2866; criminal fax: 573-775-2452; civil fax: same; 8AM-4:30PM. ***Felony, Civil Actions over $25,000.***
www.courts.mo.gov/page.asp?id=1668
Civil Records: Access: Mail, in person, online. Both court and visitors may perform in person searches. No search fee. Required to search: name, years to search. Civil cases indexed by defendant, plaintiff, on computer from 3/02/92 for judgments only, archived from 1800s, some records on index cards and books. Mail turnaround time as time permits. Civil PAT goes back to 3/1992. PAT results show middle initial, DOB. Terminal results also show SSNs. Participates in the state court record system at https://www.courts.mo.gov/casenet/base/welcome.do. Online records go back to 4/9/2001.
Criminal Records: Access: Mail, in person, online. Both court and visitors may perform in person searches. No search fee. Required to search: name, years to search, offense, date of offense. Criminal records on computer since 3/02/92, prior on cards. Mail turnaround time as time permits. Criminal PAT goes back to same as civil. PAT results show middle initial, DOB. Terminal results include SSN. Online access to criminal same as civil, above. Court's public terminal may show add'l, often older data.
General Information: Online identifiers in results same as on public terminal. No juvenile, mental, expunged, dismissed, or suspended imposition of sentence records released. Will fax documents $1.00 per page. Court makes copy: $.30 per page, self serve same. Certification fee: $1.00 per seal. Payee: Crawford County Circuit Clerk. No personal checks or credit cards accepted. Prepayment required. Mail requests: SASE required.

Associate Circuit Division PO Box B.C., 111 Third St, Steelville, MO 65565; 573-775-2149; criminal fax: 573-775-4010; civil fax: same; 8AM-5PM. ***Misdemeanor, Civil Actions under $25,000, Eviction, Small Claims, Probate.***
www.courts.mo.gov/page.asp?id=1668
The court will not do record searches, however the court will look up specific case file is case number given. Probate fax is same as main fax number.
Civil Records: Access: In person, online. Visitors must perform in person searches themselves. Required to search: name, years to search. Civil cases indexed by defendant, plaintiff, kept since 1989 on paper, prior destroyed. Civil PAT goes back to 4/2001. Participates in the state court record system at https://www.courts.mo.gov/casenet/base/welcome.do. Online records go back to 4/9/2001.
Criminal Records: Access: In person, Online. Visitors must perform in person searches themselves. Criminal records kept since 1996, prior destroyed. Note: Per judge's orders, court will not accept search requests or perform criminal record searches. Criminal PAT goes back to same as civil. Online access to criminal records same as civil, above and show year of birth only. Court's public terminal may show add'l, often older data.
General Information: Online identifiers in results same as on public terminal. No sealed records released. Will fax out specific case files. Court makes copy: $.30 per page, self serve same. Certification fee: $2.50 per page. Payee: Associate Circuit Court. Personal checks and major credit cards accepted. Prepayment required. Mail requests: SASE required for mail return of any copies.

Dade County

Consolidated Circuit Court Courthouse, Greenfield, MO 65661; 417-637-2271; fax: 417-637-5055; 8AM-4PM. ***Felony, Misdemeanor, Civil, Eviction, Small Claims, Probate.***
www.courts.mo.gov/page.asp?id=1636
Civil Records: Access: Mail, in person, online. Both court and visitors may perform in person searches. Search fee: $5.00. Required to search: name, years to search. Civil cases indexed by defendant, plaintiff, in index cards since 1982, prior on books to 1800s; on computer back to 2000. Mail turnaround time 2-3 days. Civil PAT goes back to 2000. PAT results show middle initial, DOB. Terminal results also show SSNs. Access case lookup at https://www.courts.mo.gov/casenet/base/welcome.do. Online records go back to 9/20/1999. Online records include Probate Court.
Criminal Records: Access: Mail, in person, online. Both court and visitors may perform in person searches. Search fee: $5.00. Required to search: name, years to search; also helpful-DOB, SSN, signed release. Criminal records in index cards since 1982, prior on book to 1800s; on computer back to 2000. Mail turnaround time 2-3 days. Criminal PAT goes back to same as civil. PAT results show middle initial, DOB. Terminal results include SSN. Online access to criminal same as civil, above. Court's public terminal may show add'l, often older data.
General Information: Online identifiers in results same as on public terminal. No juvenile, mental, expunged, dismissed, or suspended imposition of sentence records released. Will fax documents. Court makes copy: $.10 per page, self serve same. Certification fee: $2.50. Payee: Dade County Circuit Clerk. Personal checks accepted; credit cards are not. Prepayment required. Mail requests: SASE required.

Dallas County

Circuit Court PO Box 373, 108 S Maple St, Buffalo, MO 65622; 417-345-2243; fax: 417-345-5539; 7:30AM-4PM. ***Felony, Civil Actions over $25,000.***
Civil Records: Access: In person, online. Visitors must perform in person searches themselves. Required to search: name, years to search. Civil cases indexed by defendant, plaintiff, on computer since 1991, prior on book since 1951. Civil PAT goes back to 11/13/01. Access case lookup at https://www.courts.mo.gov/casenet/base/welcome.do. Online records go back to 11/13/2001.
Criminal Records: Access: In person, online. Visitors must perform in person searches themselves. Required to search: name, years to search; also helpful: DOB. Criminal records on computer since 1992, prior on book since 1951. Criminal PAT goes back to same as civil. Online access to criminal same as civil, above. Court's public terminal may show add'l, often older data.
General Information: Online identifiers in results same as on public terminal. No juvenile, mental, expunged, dismissed, or suspended imposition of sentence records released. Fee to fax out file $1.00 per page, 10 page limit. Court makes copy: $.25 per page, self serve same. Certification fee: $1.00 per document. Payee: Circuit Clerk. Personal checks accepted; credit cards are not. Prepayment required.

Associate Circuit Division PO Box 1150, 108 S Maple, Buffalo, MO 65622; 417-345-7641; fax: 417-345-5358; 7:30AM-N, 1-4PM. ***Misdemeanor, Civil Actions under $25,000, Eviction, Small Claims, Probate.***
http://home.positech.net/~dcourt/
Civil Records: Access: In person, online. Both court and visitors may perform in person searches. No search fee. Required to search: name, years to search. Civil cases indexed by defendant, plaintiff; index on cards since 1800s; computerized since 1990. Civil PAT goes back to 11/2000. Public terminal located in main Circuit Court Clerk office. Case lookup at https://www.courts.mo.gov/casenet/base/welcome.do. Online records go back to 1992.
Criminal Records: Access: In person, online. Visitors must perform in person searches themselves. Required to search: name, years to search. Criminal records on computer since 1990, on index cards since 1800s. Note: Court will do a single name search only, maybe. Criminal PAT goes back to 1991. Public terminal located in main Circuit Court Clerk office. Online access to criminal records same as civil, above and show year of birth only. Court's public terminal may show add'l, often older data.
General Information: Online identifiers in results same as on public terminal. No juvenile, mental, expunged, dismissed, or suspended imposition of sentence records released. Will not fax documents. Court makes copy: $.25 per page. Certification fee: $1.00 per page. Payee: Associate Circuit Court. Only cashiers checks and money orders accepted. No credit cards accepted. Prepayment required.

Daviess County

Circuit Court PO Box 337, Gallatin, MO 64640; 660-663-2932; fax: 660-663-3876; 8AM-4:30PM. ***Felony, Civil Actions over $25,000.***
www.courts.mo.gov/page.asp?id=1675
Civil Records: Access: Phone, fax, mail, in person, online. Both court and visitors may perform in person searches. Search fee: $10.00 per name. Required to search: name, years to search. Civil cases indexed by defendant, plaintiff, on records books since 1839. Mail turnaround time 1 day; phone turnaround 1 day with request filed. Civil PAT goes back to 1/2006. Results include name, year filed, type of case. Access case lookup at https://www.courts.mo.gov/casenet/base/welcome.do. Online records go back to 1/23/2006.
Criminal Records: Access: Phone, fax, mail, in person, online. Both court and visitors may perform in person searches. Search fee: $10.00 per name. Required to search: name, years to search, DOB. Criminal records on records books since 1839. Note: Results include name, year filed, type of case. Mail turnaround time 1 day; phone turnaround 1 day after request filed. Criminal PAT goes back to 1/2006. Results include name, year filed, type of case. Online access to criminal same as civil, above. Court's public terminal may show add'l, often older data.
General Information: Online identifiers in results same as on public terminal. No juvenile, mental, expunged, dismissed, or suspended imposition of sentence records released. Will fax documents $2.00 per page. Court makes copy: $1.00 per page. Certification fee: $2.00. Payee: Daviess County Circuit Clerk. Business checks accepted. No credit cards accepted. Prepayment required. Mail requests: SASE required.

Associate Circuit Division PO Box 233, 102 N Main St, Courthouse #6, Gallatin, MO 64640; 660-663-2532; probate phone: 660-663-2532; fax: 660-663-2646; 8AM-4:30PM. ***Misdemeanor, Civil Actions under $25,000, Eviction, Small Claims, Probate.*** www.courts.mo.gov/page.asp?id=1675
Probate records are unavailable before 1890 due to Courthouse fire.
Civil Records: Access: Fax, phone, in person, online. Only the court performs in person searches; visitors may not. No search fee. Required to search: name, years to search. Civil cases indexed by defendant, plaintiff, index cards since 9/84, prior on judgment books. Civil PAT goes back to 1/2006. Terminal in Circuit Clerk office. Case lookup at

https://www.courts.mo.gov/casenet/base/welcome.do. Online records go back to 1/23/2006.
Criminal Records: Access: Mail, in person, online. Only the court performs in person searches; visitors may not. No search fee. Required to search: name, years to search. Criminal records indexed on cards since 1979, prior on judgment books. Mail turnaround time 1-2 days. Criminal PAT goes back to 1/2006. Terminal in Circuit Clerk office. Online access to criminal records same as civil, above and show year of birth only. Court's public terminal may show older data.
General Information: Online identifiers in results same as on public terminal. No juvenile, mental, expunged, dismissed, or suspended imposition of sentence records released. Will fax documents $2.00. Court makes copy: $1.00 per page. Certification fee: $1.50. Payee: Associate Division Court. Only cashiers checks and money orders accepted. No credit cards accepted. Prepayment required. Mail requests: SASE required.

De Kalb County

Circuit Court PO Box 248, 109 W Main, Maysville, MO 64469; 816-449-2602; probate phone: 816-449-5400; 8AM-4:30PM. ***Felony, Civil Actions over $45,000.***
www.courts.mo.gov/page.asp?id=1676
Civil Records: Access: In person, online. Visitors must perform in person searches themselves. Required to search: name, years to search. Civil cases indexed by defendant, plaintiff; index on cards since 1970, computerized since 2003. Access case lookup free at https://www.courts.mo.gov/casenet/base/welcome.do. Online records go back to 1/23/2006.
Criminal Records: Access: In person, online. Visitors must perform in person searches themselves. Required to search: name, years to search. Criminal records indexed on cards since 1970, computerized since 2003. Online access to criminal same as civil, above. Court's public terminal may show add'l, often older data.
General Information: Online identifiers in results same as on public terminal. No juvenile or suspended imposition of sentence records released. Will fax specific case file for $1.00. Court makes copy: $1.00 per page, self serve same. Certification fee: $1.00. Payee: Clifton DeShon, Circuit Clerk. Personal checks accepted; credit cards are not. Prepayment required.

Associate Circuit Division PO Box 248, Maysville, MO 64469; 816-449-5400; probate phone: 816-449-5400; criminal fax: 816-449-2440; civil fax: same; 8:30AM-N, 1-4:30PM. ***Misdemeanor, Civil Actions under $45,000, Eviction, Small Claims, Probate.***
www.courts.mo.gov/page.asp?id=1676
Court personnel will not do name searches. Probate index is separate index at this same address. Probate fax is same as main fax number.
Civil Records: Access: In person, online. Visitors must perform in person searches themselves. Required to search: name, years to search. Civil cases indexed by defendant, plaintiff; index on cards since 1960s. Civil PAT goes back to - 2 years. Case lookup at https://www.courts.mo.gov/casenet/base/welcome.do. Online records go back to 1/23/2006.
Criminal Records: Access: In person, online. Visitors must perform in person searches themselves. Required to search: name, years to search; DOB; also helpful-SSN, case number. Criminal records indexed on cards since 1980s. Criminal PAT goes back to - 2 years. Online access to criminal records same as civil, above and show year of birth only. Court's public terminal may show add'l, often older data.
General Information: Online identifiers in results same as on public terminal. No juvenile, mental, expunged, dismissed, or suspended imposition of sentence records released. Will fax specific case file, but not certified. Court makes copy: $1.00 per page, self serve same. Certification fee: $1.50 per cert. Payee: Associate Circuit Court. Only cashiers checks and money orders accepted. No credit cards accepted. Prepayment required.

Dent County

Circuit Court 112 E 5th St, Salem, MO 65560; 573-729-3931; fax: 573-729-9414; 8AM-4:30PM. ***Felony, Civil Actions over $25,000.***
www.courts.mo.gov/page.asp?id=1669
Civil Records: Access: Mail, fax, in person, online. Both court and visitors may perform in person searches. No search fee. Required to search: name, years to search. Civil cases indexed by defendant, plaintiff, on computer since 1993, on index cards since 1978. Mail turnaround time 2 days. Civil PAT goes back to 1996. PAT results show middle initial, DOB. Case lookup at https://www.courts.mo.gov/casenet/base/welcome.do. Online records go back to 4/9/2001.
Criminal Records: Access: In person, online. Visitors must perform in person searches themselves. Required to search: name, years to search. Criminal records on computer since 1993, on index cards since 1978. Criminal PAT goes back to same as civil. PAT results show middle initial, DOB. Online access to criminal same as civil, above. Court's public terminal may show add'l, often older data.
General Information: Online identifiers in results same as on public terminal. No juvenile, mental, expunged, dismissed, or suspended imposition of sentence records released. Will not fax documents. Court makes copy: $.25 per page. Certification fee: $2.00 per cert. Payee: Dent County Circuit Clerk. Only cashiers checks and money orders accepted. No credit cards accepted. Prepayment required. Mail requests: SASE required for civil.

Associate Circuit Division 112 E 5th St, Salem, MO 65560; 573-729-3134; probate phone: 573-729-3134; fax: 573-729-5172; 8AM-4:30PM. ***Misdemeanor, Civil Actions under $25,000, Eviction, Small Claims, Probate.***
www.courts.mo.gov/page.asp?id=1669
Small Claims and Probate fax is 573-729-5172.
Civil Records: Access: Mail, fax, in person, online. Both court and visitors may perform in person searches. No search fee. Required to search: name, years to search. Civil cases indexed by defendant, plaintiff, on computer since 1985, prior on index cards. Mail turnaround time 2-3 days. Civil PAT goes back to 2001. PAT results show middle initial, DOB, SSN. Case lookup at https://www.courts.mo.gov/casenet/base/welcome.do. Online records go back to 4/9/2001.
Criminal Records: Access: Mail, fax, in person, online. Both court and visitors may perform in person searches. No search fee. Required to search: name, years to search, DOB, signed release. Criminal records on computer since 1985, prior on index cards. Note: Results include address. Mail turnaround time 2-3 days. Criminal PAT goes back to 2001. PAT results show middle initial, DOB, SSN. Online access to criminal same as civil, above. Court's public terminal may show add'l, often older data.
General Information: Online identifiers in results same as on public terminal. No juvenile, mental, expunged, dismissed, or suspended imposition of sentence records released. Will not fax documents. Court makes copy: $.25 per page. Certification fee: $2.00. Payee: Associate Circuit Court or Probate Court. Business checks accepted. No credit cards accepted. Prepayment required. Mail requests: SASE required.

Douglas County

Circuit Court PO Box 249, Ava, MO 65608; 417-683-4713; fax: 417-683-2794; 8AM-4:30PM. ***Felony, Civil Actions over $25,000.***
www.courts.mo.gov/page.asp?id=1678
Civil Records: Access: Phone, mail, in person, online. Visitors must perform in person searches themselves. Search fee: $10.00 per hour. Required to search: name, years to search. Civil cases indexed by defendant, plaintiff, on alpha cards since 1977. Mail turnaround time 1 week. Civil PAT goes back to 2006. Case lookup at https://www.courts.mo.gov/casenet/base/welcome.do. Civil results give address. Online records go back to 2/20/2006.
Criminal Records: Access: Phone, mail, in person, online. Visitors must perform in person searches themselves. Search fee: $10.00 per hour. Required to search: name, years to search; also helpful: DOB, SSN. Criminal records on alpha cards since 1977. Mail turnaround time 1 week. Criminal PAT goes back to 5 years. Online access to criminal records same as civil, above and show year of birth only, but online criminal search gives DOB and address in results. Court's public terminal may show add'l, often older data.
General Information: Online identifiers in results same as on public terminal. No juvenile, mental, expunged, dismissed, or suspended imposition of sentence records released. Will fax documents to local or toll free line. Court makes copy: $.25 per page. Certification fee: $2.50. Payee: Circuit Clerk. Personal checks accepted; credit cards are not. Prepayment required. Mail requests: SASE required.

Associate Circuit Division PO Box 276, 203 SE 2nd Ave, Ava, MO 65608; 417-683-2114; ; 8AM-4:30PM. ***Misdemeanor, Civil Actions under $25,000, Eviction, Small Claims, Probate.***
www.courts.mo.gov/page.asp?id=1678
Civil Records: Access: Mail, in person, online. Only the court performs in person searches; visitors may not. No search fee. Required to search: name, years to search. Civil cases indexed by defendant, plaintiff; index on cards and computer. Mail turnaround time 2 days. Case lookup at https://www.courts.mo.gov/casenet/base/welcome.do. Online records go back to 2/20/2006 and includes probate.
Criminal Records: Access: In person, online. Only the court performs in person searches; visitors may not. No search fee. Required to search: name, years to search; SSN helpful. Criminal records computerized from 1991. Note: Court rarely allows for mail requests. Online access to criminal same as civil, above. Court's public terminal may show add'l, often older data.
General Information: Online identifiers in results same as on public terminal. No juvenile, mental, expunged, dismissed, or suspended imposition of sentence records released. Will not fax documents. Court makes copy: $.25 per page. Certification fee: $1.50 per cert. Payee: Associate Circuit Court. Personal checks accepted; credit cards are not. Prepayment required. Mail requests: SASE required for civil.

Dunklin County

Consolidated Circuit Court PO Box 567, Kennett, MO 63857; 573-888-2456; civil phone: 573-888-3378; probate phone: 573-888-3272; fax: 573-888-0319; 8:30AM-4:30PM. ***Felony, Misdemeanor, Civil, Eviction, Small Claims, Probate.***
www.courts.mo.gov/page.asp?id=1647
All searches require a written request, and requests can be faxed to the court. The Circuit Court and Associate Division consolidated 01/01/2006. Probate and Juvenile #202, Criminal #301/302, Civil #103.
Civil Records: Access: In person, online. Visitors must perform in person searches themselves. Required to search: name, years to search. Civil cases indexed by defendant, plaintiff; index on cards back to 1900; on computer back to 1990. Civil PAT goes back to 1990. Access to civil records is free at https://www.courts.mo.gov/casenet/base/welcome.do. Online records go back to 7/1/2001.
Criminal Records: Access: In person, online. Visitors must perform in person searches themselves. Required to search: name, years to search, DOB, SSN. Criminal records computerized from 8/1994. Note: Court only performs records searches for Law Enforcement Agencies. Criminal PAT goes back to 8/1994. Online access to criminal same as civil, above. Court's public terminal may show add'l, often older data.
General Information: Online identifiers in results same as on public terminal. No juvenile, mental, expunged or dismissed records released. Will fax documents $1.00 per page. Court makes copy: $.50 per page. Self serve copy: $.25 per page. Certification fee: $2.00 per document. Payee: Circuit Clerk. Personal checks accepted. Prepayment

required. Will bill attorneys, courts and abstract companies.

Franklin County

Consolidated Circuit Court 401 E Main St, #100, Union, MO 63084; criminal phone: 636-583-7365; civil phone: 636-583-7366; probate phone: 636-583-6312; ; 8AM-4:30PM. ***Felony, Misdemeanor, Civil Actions, Eviction, Small Claims, Probate.*** www.courts.mo.gov/page.asp?id=1616

Consolidated May, 2008. Assoc. Circuit and Probate courts now also located here. Probate fax- 636-583-7368. For criminal searches, this court refers you to Casenet or the state criminal record repository- 573-526-6153; 751-9382-fax.

Civil Records: Access: Online, in person. Visitors must perform in person searches themselves. Required to search: name, years to search. Civil cases indexed by defendant, plaintiff, on computer back to 1995; others filed as originals to 1821. Civil PAT goes back to 1995. Case lookup at https://www.courts.mo.gov/casenet/base/welcome.do. Online records go back to 1/1995.

Criminal Records: Access: Online, in person. Visitors must perform in person searches themselves. Required to search: name, years to search, DOB. Criminal records computerized from 1995; others filed as originals to 1940. Criminal PAT goes back to same as civil. Online access to criminal same as civil, above. Court's public terminal may show add'l, often older data.

General Information: Online identifiers in results same as on public terminal. No juvenile, mental, expunged, dismissed, or suspended imposition of sentence records released. Will not fax documents. Court makes copy: $.25 per page, self serve same. Certification fee: $1.00. Payee: Circuit Clerk. Personal checks accepted; credit cards are not. Prepayment required.

Associate Circuit Division, ***Misdemeanor, Civil Actions under $25,000, Eviction, Small Claims, Probate.***

This Associate Division has been Consolidated with the Circuit Court, May, 2008. Probate court joins these courts in a new courthouse.

Gasconade County

Circuit Court 119 E 1st St, Rm 6, Hermann, MO 65041-1182; 573-486-2632; criminal fax: 573-486-5812; civil fax: same; 8AM-4:30PM. ***Felony, Civil Actions over $25,000.*** www.courts.mo.gov/page.asp?id=1617

Civil Records: Access: Mail, in person, online. Both court and visitors may perform in person searches. No search fee. Required to search: name, years to search. Civil cases indexed by defendant, plaintiff; index on cards since 1976, prior on books stored in vault; online since 9/2000. Mail turnaround time 2-3 days. Civil PAT goes back to 1990. PAT civil results show middle initial. Case lookup at https://www.courts.mo.gov/casenet/base/welcome.do. Online records go back to 7/31/2000,

Criminal Records: Access: In person, online. Visitors must perform in person searches themselves. Required to search: name, years to search. Criminal records indexed on cards since 1976, prior on books stored in vault; online since 9/2000. Criminal PAT goes back to same as civil. PAT results show middle initial, DOB. Online access to criminal same as civil, above. Court's public terminal may show add'l, often older data.

General Information: Online identifiers in results same as on public terminal. No juvenile, mental, expunged, dismissed, or suspended imposition of sentence records released. Will fax documents $2.00 1st page, $1.00 each add'l. Court makes copy: $2.00 for 1st page, $1.00 each add'l per doc. Self serve copy: $.50 per page. Certification fee: $1.00 per cert seal. Payee: Gasconade Circuit Court. Personal checks accepted; credit cards are not. Prepayment required. Mail requests: SASE required.

Associate Circuit Division 119 E. 1st St. Rm 3, Hermann, MO 65041; 573-486-2632; fax: 573-486-5812; 8AM-4:30PM. ***Misdemeanor, Civil Actions under $25,000, Eviction, Small Claims, Probate.*** www.courts.mo.gov/page.asp?id=1617

Civil Records: Access: In person, online. Both court and visitors may perform in person searches. No search fee. Required to search: name, years to search. Civil cases indexed by defendant, plaintiff, on computer since 9/00, prior on index cards since 1979. Note: Only the court performs in person searches for records prior to 09/00. Civil PAT goes back to 2000. Public terminal is in Circuit Court office. Case lookup at https://www.courts.mo.gov/casenet/base/welcome.do. Online records go back to 7/31/2000.

Criminal Records: Access: Online, in person. Both court and visitors may perform in person searches. No search fee. Required to search: name, years to search. Criminal records on computer since 1988, prior on index cards since 1979. Note: Both court and visitors may perform in person searches of records before 9/2000. Criminal PAT goes back to same as civil. Public terminal is in Circuit Court office. Online access to criminal same as civil, above. Court's public terminal may show add'l, often older data.

General Information: Online identifiers in results same as on public terminal. No juvenile, mental, expunged, dismissed, or suspended imposition of sentence records released. Court makes copy: $.10 per page. Certification fee: $2.50 per cert. Payee: Associate Circuit Court. Personal checks accepted; credit cards are not. Prepayment required. Will bill probate fees. Mail requests: SASE required for mail return of any copies.

Gentry County

Circuit Court PO Box 27, 200 W Clay St, Albany, MO 64402; 660-726-3618; fax: 660-726-4102; 8AM-4:30PM. ***Felony, Civil Actions over $25,000.*** www.courts.mo.gov/page.asp?id=1544

Civil Records: Access: Mail, fax, in person, online. Both court and visitors may perform in person searches. Search fee: $5.00 per name. Required to search: name, years to search. Civil cases indexed by defendant, plaintiff, archived since 1885. Mail turnaround time 5 working days. Civil PAT goes back to 3/2006. Case lookup at https://www.courts.mo.gov/casenet/base/welcome.do. Online records go back to 3/20/2006.

Criminal Records: Access: Mail, in person, online. Both court and visitors may perform in person searches. Search fee: $5.00 per name. Required to search: name, years to search; also helpful: DOB, SSN. Criminal records archived since 1885. Mail turnaround time 5 working days. Criminal PAT goes back to 3/2006. Online access to criminal same as civil, above. Court's public terminal may show add'l, often older data.

General Information: Online identifiers in results same as on public terminal. No juvenile, mental, expunged, dismissed, or suspended imposition of sentence records released. Fee to fax out file $1.00 per page. Court makes copy: $.30 per page, self serve same. Certification fee: $1.00 per page. Payee: Circuit Clerk. Personal checks accepted; credit cards are not. Prepayment required. Mail requests: SASE required.

Associate Circuit Division 200 W Clay St, Albany, MO 64402; 660-726-3411; fax: 660-726-3130; 8AM-4:30PM. ***Misdemeanor, Civil Actions under $25,000, Eviction, Small Claims, Probate.*** www.courts.mo.gov/page.asp?id=1544

Civil Records: Access: In person, online. Visitors must perform in person searches themselves. Required to search: name, years to search. Civil cases indexed by defendant, plaintiff; index on cards. Civil PAT goes back to 3/2006. Case lookup at https://www.courts.mo.gov/casenet/base/welcome.do. Online records go back to 3/20/2006.

Criminal Records: Access: Fax, mail, in person, online. Both court and visitors may perform in person searches. Search fee: $5.00 per name. Required to search: name, years to search. Criminal records indexed on cards. Mail turnaround time 7 days. Criminal PAT goes back to 3/2006. Online access to criminal same as civil, above. Court's public terminal may show add'l, often older data.

General Information: Online identifiers in results same as on public terminal. No juvenile, mental, expunged, dismissed, or suspended imposition of sentence records released. Will not fax documents. Court makes copy: $1.00 per page; not-open file- $.25 per page. Certification fee: $1.50 per cert. Payee: Associate Circuit Court. Personal checks accepted; credit cards are not. Prepayment required. Mail requests: SASE required for criminal.

Greene County

Circuit Court 1010 Booneville, Springfield, MO 65802; 417-868-4074; criminal phone: x4; civil: x2; 8AM-5AM. ***Felony, Civil Actions over $25,000.*** www.greenecountymo.org/circuit_clerk/index.php

This court combined with the Assoc. Circuit Court in 2007. A criminal search now includes felony and misdemeanor; Civil includes all civil records. Add'l phones- Domestic- x4, Traffic- x5.

Civil Records: Access: Mail, in person, online. Both court and visitors may perform in person searches. No search fee. Required to search: name, years to search. Civil cases indexed by defendant, plaintiff, on computer back to 7/89, prior on index cards. Mail turnaround time 1 week. Civil PAT goes back to 1989. Public terminal does not always include address. Access records back to 1990 at https://www.courts.mo.gov/casenet/base/welcome.do.

Criminal Records: Access: Mail, in person, online. Both court and visitors may perform in person searches. Search fee: $5.00 per name. Required to search: name, years to search; also helpful: address, DOB, SSN. Criminal records computerized from 7/89, prior on index cards. Mail turnaround time 1 week. Criminal PAT goes back to same as civil. Access records back to 1990 at https://www.courts.mo.gov/casenet/base/welcome.do. Court's public terminal may show add'l, often older data.

General Information: Online identifiers in results same as on public terminal. No juvenile, mental, expunged, sealed, dismissed or suspended imposition of sentence records released. Will not fax documents. Court makes copy: $.10 per page, self serve same. Certification fee: $1.50 per seal. Payee: Circuit Clerk. Business checks accepted. No credit cards accepted. Prepayment required. Mail requests: SASE required.

Associate Circuit Division 1010 N Boonville, Springfield, MO 65802; 417-868-4074; criminal phone: 417-829-6567; civil phone: 417-829-6562; probate phone: 417-868-4027; criminal fax: 417-868-4186; civil fax: 417-868-4883; 8AM-5PM. ***Misdemeanor, Civil Actions under $25,000, Eviction, Small Claims, Probate.*** www.greenecountymo.org/circuit_clerk/index.php

This court combined with the Circuit Court in 2007. A criminal search now includes felony and misdemeanor; Civil includes all civil records. Probate is a separate court at the same address.

Civil Records: Access: Mail, in person, online. Both court and visitors may perform in person searches. No search fee. Required to search: name, years to search. Civil cases indexed by defendant, plaintiff, on computer since mid-1989, prior on index cards. Mail turnaround time 1 week. Civil PAT goes back to 1989. Public terminal does not always include address. Access records back to 1990 at https://www.courts.mo.gov/casenet/base/welcome.do.

Criminal Records: Access: Mail, in person, online. Both court and visitors may perform in person searches. Search fee: $5.00 per name. Required to search: name, years to search; also helpful: address, DOB, SSN. Criminal records on computer since mid-1989, prior on index cards. Mail turnaround time 1 week. Criminal PAT goes back to same as civil. Access records back to 1990 at https://www.courts.mo.gov/casenet/base/welcome.do. Court's public terminal may show add'l, often older data.

General Information: Online identifiers in results same as on public terminal. No, mental, expunged, sealed, dismissed or suspended imposition of sentence records released. Will not fax documents. Court makes copy: $.10 per page, self serve same. Certification fee: $1.50 per seal. Payee: Circuit Clerk.

Business checks accepted. No credit cards accepted. Prepayment required. Mail requests: SASE required.

Grundy County

Circuit Court Courthouse, 700 Main St, PO Box 196, Trenton, MO 64683; 660-359-6605; fax: 660-359-6604; 8:30AM-4:30PM. ***Felony, Civil Actions over $25,000, Eviction.***
www.courts.mo.gov/page.asp?id=1538
Civil Records: Access: In person, online. Visitors must perform in person searches themselves. Required to search: name, years to search. Civil cases indexed by defendant, plaintiff, archived since 1841; on computer back to 2000. Civil PAT goes back to 3/2000. PAT results show middle initial, DOB, SSN. Case lookup at https://www.courts.mo.gov/casenet/base/welcome.do. Online records go back to 3/2000.
Criminal Records: Access: In person, online. Visitors must perform in person searches themselves. Required to search: name, years to search. Criminal records archived since 1841; on computer back to 2000. Criminal PAT goes back to same as civil. PAT results show middle initial, DOB, SSN. Online access to criminal same as civil, above. Court's public terminal may show add'l, often older data.
General Information: Online identifiers in results same as on public terminal. No juvenile, Title 4D, child support, mental, expunged, dismissed, or suspended imposition of sentence cases. Will fax specific file data for $2.00 per document. Court makes copy: $.25 per page. Certification fee: $2.50 per cert. Payee: Circuit Clerk. Personal checks accepted; credit cards are not. Prepayment required. Mail requests: SASE required for mail return of any copies.

Associate Circuit Division PO Box 26 (700 Main St), Trenton, MO 64683; 660-359-6606/6909; fax: 660-359-6604; 8AM-4:30PM. ***Misdemeanor, Civil Actions under $25,000, Small Claims, Probate, Traffic.***
www.courts.mo.gov/page.asp?id=1538
Civil Records: Access: Mail, in person, online. Visitors must perform in person searches themselves. No search fee. Required to search: name, years to search. Civil cases indexed by defendant, plaintiff; index on cards, probate records archived. Mail turnaround time 2-5 days. Civil PAT goes back to 2000. Case lookup at https://www.courts.mo.gov/casenet/base/welcome.do. Online records go back to 3/29/2000.
Criminal Records: Access: In person, online. Visitors must perform in person searches themselves. Required to search: name, years to search. Criminal records indexed on cards, probate records archived. Criminal PAT goes back to same as civil. Online access to criminal records same as civil, above and show year of birth only. Court's public terminal may show add'l, often older data.
General Information: Online identifiers in results same as on public terminal. No juvenile, mental, expunged, dismissed, or suspended imposition of sentence records released. Will not fax documents. Court makes copy: $1.00 per page. Certification fee: $2.50 per doc. Payee: Grundy County Circuit Court Division II. Business checks accepted. No credit cards accepted. Prepayment required. Mail requests: SASE required for civil.

Harrison County

Consolidated Circuit Court PO Box 189, 1500 Central, Bethany, MO 64424; 660-425-6425/6432; fax: 660-425-6390; 8AM-4:30PM. ***Felony, Misdemeanor, Civil, Eviction, Small Claims, Probate.***
www.courts.mo.gov/page.asp?id=1539
Civil Records: Access: Mail, in person, online. Both court and visitors may perform in person searches. No search fee. Required to search: name, years to search. Civil cases indexed by defendant, plaintiff; index on cards since 1979, prior on index books. Mail turnaround time 2 days. Civil PAT goes back to 2000. PAT results show middle initial, DOB. Case lookup at https://www.courts.mo.gov/casenet/base/welcome.do. Online records go back to 3/29/2000.
Criminal Records: Access: In person, online. Visitors must perform in person searches themselves. Required to search: name, years to search. Criminal records indexed on cards since 1979, prior on index books. Criminal PAT goes back to same as civil. Online access to criminal same as civil, above. Court's public terminal may show add'l, often older data.
General Information: Online identifiers in results same as on public terminal. No juvenile, mental, expunged, dismissed, or suspended imposition of sentence records released. Will not fax documents. Court makes copy: $.25 per page. Certification fee: $1.00. Payee: Harrison County Circuit Court. Personal checks accepted; credit cards are not. Prepayment required. Mail requests: SASE required for civil.

Henry County

Consolidated Circuit Court PO Box 487, Clinton, MO 64735; 660-885-7232; fax: 660-885-8247; 8AM-4:30PM. ***Felony, Misdemeanor, Civil, Eviction, Small Claims, Probate.***
http://tacnet.missouri.org/~court27/
The Circuit Court and Associate Division consolidated as of 01/03.
Civil Records: Access: Mail, in person, online. Both court and visitors may perform in person searches. No search fee. Required to search: name, years to search. Civil cases indexed by defendant, plaintiff, on computer since 8/92, on index cards since 1979, archived since 1877. Mail turnaround time 5-10 days Civil PAT goes back to 2003. Case lookup at https://www.courts.mo.gov/casenet/base/welcome.do. Online records go back to 8/18/2003.
Criminal Records: Access: In person, online. Only the court performs in person searches; visitors may not. No search fee. Required to search: name, years to search. Criminal records on computer since 8/92, on index cards since 1979, archived since 1877. Note: This court tends to forward criminal search requests to the MO Highway Patrol, but the court does do searches occasionally. Criminal PAT available. Online access to criminal same as civil, above. Court's public terminal may show add'l, often older data.
General Information: Online identifiers in results same as on public terminal. No juvenile, mental, expunged, dismissed, or suspended imposition of sentence records released. Will not fax documents. Court makes copy: $.25 per page. $2.50 fee for records copied from big books. Certification fee: $1.50. Payee: Henry County Circuit Court. Personal checks accepted. Prepayment required. Copy fees may be billed. Mail requests: SASE required for civil.

Hickory County

Circuit Court PO Box 101, Hermitage, MO 65668; 417-745-6421; fax: 417-745-6670; 8AM-N, 12:30-4PM. ***Felony, Civil Actions over $45,000.***
www.positech.net/~dcourt/
Civil Records: Access: In person, online. Both court and visitors may perform in person searches. No search fee. Required to search: name, years to search. Civil cases indexed by defendant, plaintiff, on computer since 1992, prior on index books since 1976. Civil PAT goes back to 2001. Case lookup at https://www.courts.mo.gov/casenet/base/welcome.do. Online records go back to 11/13/2001.
Criminal Records: Access: In person, online. Both court and visitors may perform in person searches. No search fee. Required to search: name, years to search, signed release. Criminal records on computer since 1992, prior on index books since 1976. Criminal PAT goes back to same as civil. Online access to criminal same as civil, above. Court's public terminal may show add'l, often older data.
General Information: Online identifiers in results same as on public terminal. No juvenile, mental, expunged, dismissed, or suspended imposition of sentence records released. Fee to fax back is $1.00 per page. Court makes copy: $1.00 per page microfilm; $.25 per page paper. Certification fee: $1.00 per page. Payee: Hickory County Circuit Clerk. Personal checks accepted; credit cards are not. Prepayment required.

Associate Circuit Division PO Box 75, Courthouse Sq, Hermitage, MO 65668; 417-745-6822; fax: 417-745-0136; 8AM-N; 12:30PM-4:30PM. ***Misdemeanor, Civil Actions under $45,000, Eviction, Small Claims, Probate.***
www.positech.net/~dcourt/
Civil Records: Access: In person, online. Both court and visitors may perform in person searches. No search fee. Required to search: name, years to search. Civil cases indexed by defendant, plaintiff; index on cards since 1980. Civil PAT goes back to 2001. PAT results show middle initial, DOB. Case lookup at https://www.courts.mo.gov/casenet/base/welcome.do. Online records go back to 11/13/2001.
Criminal Records: Access: In person, online. Both court and visitors may perform in person searches. No search fee. Required to search: name, years to search, DOB. Criminal records indexed on cards since 1980. Criminal PAT goes back to same as civil. PAT results show middle initial, DOB. Online access to criminal records same as civil, above and show year of birth only. Court's public terminal may show add'l, often older data.
General Information: Online identifiers in results same as on public terminal. No juvenile, mental, expunged, dismissed, or suspended imposition of sentence records released. Will not fax out documents. Court makes copy: $.25 per page, self serve same. Certification fee: $1.00 per cert. Payee: Associate Circuit Court. No personal checks or credit cards accepted. Prepayment required.

Holt County

Circuit Court PO Box 318, Oregon, MO 64473; 660-446-3301; fax: 660-446-3328; 8AM-4:30PM. ***Felony, Civil Actions over $25,000.***
www.courts.mo.gov/page.asp?id=1547
Civil Records: Access: Mail, in person, online. Only the court performs in person searches; visitors may not. Search fee: $4.00. Required to search: name, years to search. Civil cases indexed by defendant, plaintiff, on books. Mail turnaround time varies. Civil PAT goes back to 3/20/06. PAT results show name, DOB. Participates in the statewide MO Casenet record system at https://www.courts.mo.gov/casenet/base/welcome.do. Online records go back to 3/20/2006.
Criminal Records: Access: Mail, in person, online. Only the court performs in person searches; visitors may not. Search fee: $4.00. Required to search: name, years to search. Criminal docket on books. Mail turnaround time varies. Criminal PAT goes back to 3/20/2006.PAT results show name, DOB. Online access to criminal same as civil, above. Court's public terminal may show add'l, often older data.
General Information: Online identifiers in results same as on public terminal. No juvenile, mental, expunged, dismissed, or suspended imposition of sentence records released. Will fax documents $2.00 each. Court makes copy: $1.00 per page. Certification fee: $1.00 per page. Payee: Recorder. Personal checks accepted; credit cards are not. Prepayment required. Mail requests: SASE required.

Associate Circuit Division PO Box 173, Oregon, MO 64473; 660-446-3380; fax: 660-446-3588; 8:30AM-4:30PM. ***Misdemeanor, Civil Actions under $25,000, Eviction, Small Claims, Probate.***
www.courts.mo.gov/page.asp?id=1547
Civil Records: Access: Mail, fax, in person, online. Both court and visitors may perform in person searches. No search fee. Required to search: name, years to search. Civil cases indexed by defendant, plaintiff; index on cards since 1979. Mail turnaround time 2 days. Civil PAT goes back to 3/2006. Case lookup at https://www.courts.mo.gov/casenet/base/welcome.do. Online records go back to 3/20/2006.
Criminal Records: Access: In person, online. Visitors must perform in person searches themselves. Required to search: name, years to search. Criminal records on computer since 1991, prior on index cards since 1979. Criminal PAT goes back to 3/2006. Online access to criminal records same as civil, above and show year of birth only.

Court's public terminal may show add'l, often older data.
General Information: Online identifiers in results same as on public terminal. No juvenile, mental, expunged, dismissed, or suspended imposition of sentence records released. Will not fax documents. Court makes copy: $.25 per page. Certification fee: $1.50 per cert plus $1.00 per page. Payee: Associate Circuit Court. Personal checks accepted; credit cards are not. Prepayment required. Mail requests: SASE required for civil.

Howard County

Circuit Court 1 Courthouse Square, Fayette, MO 65248; 660-248-2194; fax: 660-248-5009; 8:30-4:30PM. ***Felony, Civil Actions over $30,000.***
www.courts.mo.gov/page.asp?id=1599
Office will not do certified searches, only simple searches to see if a name exists.
Civil Records: Access: Mail, fax, in person, online. Visitors must perform in person searches themselves. No search fee. Required to search: name, years to search. Civil cases indexed by defendant, plaintiff; index on cards; computer records go back to the 1970's. Civil PAT goes back to 1970s. PAT civil results show middle initial. Case lookup at https://www.courts.mo.gov/casenet/base/welcome.do. Online records go back to 10/01.
Criminal Records: Access: In person, online, mail, fax. Visitors must perform in person searches themselves. No search fee. Required to search: name, years to search. Criminal records indexed on cards; computer records go back to the 1970's. Note: Results include address. Criminal PAT goes back to same as civil. PAT criminal results show middle initial. Online access to criminal same as civil, above. Court's public terminal may show add'l, often older data.
General Information: Online identifiers in results same as on public terminal. No juvenile, mental, expunged, dismissed, or suspended imposition of sentence records released. Will fax out specific case files for $2.00 per document. Court makes copy: $.25 per page, self serve same. Certification fee: $2.00. Payee: Circuit Clerk. Personal checks accepted; credit cards are not. Prepayment required. Mail requests: SASE required.

Associate Circuit Division PO Box 370, Fayette, MO 65248; 660-248-3326; probate phone: 660-248-3326.; fax: 660-248-1075; 8:30AM-4:30PM. ***Misdemeanor, Civil Actions under $45,000, Eviction, Small Claims, Probate.***
www.courts.mo.gov/page.asp?id=1599
Civil Records: Access: In person, online. Visitors must perform in person searches themselves. Required to search: name, years to search. Civil cases indexed by defendant, plaintiff, go back to 1975. Civil PAT goes back to 2001. Case lookup at https://www.courts.mo.gov/casenet/base/welcome.do. Records go back to 10/31/2001. Includes Probate and Traffic records.
Criminal Records: Access: In person, online. Visitors must perform in person searches themselves. Required to search: name, years to search, DOB. Criminal records go back to 1975. Criminal PAT goes back to same as civil. Online access to criminal records same as civil, above and show year of birth only. Court's public terminal may show older data.
General Information: Online identifiers in results same as on public terminal. No juvenile, mental, expunged, dismissed, or suspended imposition of sentence records released. Will fax documents to local or toll-free number. Court makes copy: $.25 per page. Certification fee: $1.50 per cert. Payee: Associate Circuit Court. Personal checks accepted. Prepayment required.

Howell County

Circuit Court PO Box 967, West Plains, MO 65775; 417-256-3741; fax: 417-256-4650; 8AM-4:30PM. ***Felony, Civil Actions over $25,000.***
www.courts.mo.gov/page.asp?id=1653
Civil Records: Access: Phone, fax, mail, in person, online. Both court and visitors may perform in person searches. No search fee. Required to search: name, years to search. Civil cases indexed by defendant, plaintiff; index on cards since 1977. Mail turnaround 2 days. Civil PAT goes back to 8/1991. PAT results show name only. Case lookup at https://www.courts.mo.gov/casenet/base/welcome.do. Online records go back to 4/17/2000.
Criminal Records: Access: In person, online. Visitors must perform in person searches themselves. Required to search: name, years to search. Criminal records indexed on cards since 1977. Criminal PAT goes back to 8/1991. PAT results show name only. Online access to criminal records same as civil, above and show year of birth only. Court's public terminal may show add'l, often older data.
General Information: Online identifiers in results same as on public terminal. No juvenile, mental, expunged, dismissed, or suspended imposition of sentence records released. Will fax documents $1.00 per page. Court makes copy: $.10 per page. Certification fee: $1.50. Payee: Howell County Circuit Clerk. Personal checks accepted; credit cards are not. Prepayment required. Will bill to attorneys. Mail requests: SASE required for civil.

Associate Circuit Division 222 Courthouse, West Plains, MO 65775; 417-256-4050; criminal fax: 417-256-5826; civil fax: same; 8AM-4:30PM. ***Misdemeanor, Civil Actions under $25,000, Eviction, Small Claims, Probate.***
www.courts.mo.gov/page.asp?id=1653
Probate fax is same as main fax number.
Civil Records: Access: Mail, in person, online. Both court and visitors may perform in person searches. No search fee. Required to search: name, years to search. Civil cases indexed by defendant, plaintiff; index on cards since 1/1/79, computerized since 4/2000. Mail turnaround time ASAP. Case lookup at https://www.courts.mo.gov/casenet/base/welcome.do. Online records go back to 1990.
Criminal Records: Access: Mail, in person, online. Both court and visitors may perform in person searches. No search fee. Required to search: name, years to search, DOB; also helpful: SSN. Criminal records on computer since early 1991, on index cards since 1/1/79, prior on books. Mail turnaround time ASAP. Online access to criminal records same as civil, above and show year of birth only. Court's public terminal may show add'l, often older data.
General Information: Online identifiers in results same as on public terminal. No juvenile, mental, expunged, dismissed, or suspended imposition of sentence records released. Will not fax documents. Court makes copy: $.10 per page, self serve same. Certification fee: $1.50 per document. Payee: Associate/Probate Court. Only cashiers checks and money orders accepted. Prepayment required. Mail requests: SASE required.

Iron County

Circuit Court PO Box 24, 250 S Main, Ironton, MO 63650; 573-546-2811; fax: 573-546-2166; 8AM-4PM. ***Felony, Civil Actions over $25,000.***
www.courts.mo.gov/page.asp?id=1670
Civil Records: Access: In person, online. Visitors must perform in person searches themselves. Required to search: name, years to search. Civil cases indexed by defendant, plaintiff; index on cards since 1976, prior on books. Note: Files requested by case number take 10 days turnaround. Civil PAT goes back to 4/2001. Case lookup at https://www.courts.mo.gov/casenet/base/welcome.do. Online records go back to 4/9/2001.
Criminal Records: Access: In person, online. Visitors must perform in person searches themselves. Required to search: name, years to search. Criminal records indexed on cards since 1976, prior on books to 1856. Note: 10 day turnaround on files requested by case number. Criminal PAT goes back to 4/2001. Participates in the free statewide Casenet court record system at www.courts.mo.gov/casenet/base/welcome.do. Online records go back to 4/9/2001. Court's public terminal may show add'l, often older data.
General Information: Online identifiers in results same as on public terminal. No juvenile, mental, expunged, dismissed, or suspended imposition of sentence records released. Will fax documents for $5.00 fee. Court makes copy: $1.00 per page. Certification fee: $2.00. Payee: Iron County Circuit Clerk. Personal checks accepted; credit cards are not. Prepayment required.

Associate Circuit Division PO Box 325, 250 S Main St, Courthouse, Ironton, MO 63650; 573-546-2511; fax: 573-546-6006; 8:30AM-4:30PM. ***Misdemeanor, Civil Actions under $25,000, Eviction, Small Claims, Probate.***
www.courts.mo.gov/page.asp?id=1670
Probate fax is same as main fax number.
Civil Records: Access: Mail, in person, online. Both court and visitors may perform in person searches. No search fee. Required to search: name, years to search; also helpful: address. Civil cases indexed by defendant, plaintiff; index on cards since 1979, computerized from 4/01. Mail turnaround time 5 days. Civil PAT goes back to 4/2001. PAT results show name only. Case lookup at https://www.courts.mo.gov/casenet/base/welcome.do. Online records go back to 4/9/2001.
Criminal Records: Access: Fax, mail, in person, online. Both court and visitors may perform in person searches. No search fee. Required to search: name, years to search, DOB; also helpful: address, signed release. Criminal records computerized from 4/01. Mail turnaround time 5 days. Criminal PAT goes back to same as civil. PAT results show name only. Online access to criminal records same as civil, above and show year of birth only. Court's public terminal may show add'l, often older data.
General Information: Online identifiers in results same as on public terminal. No juvenile, mental, expunged, dismissed, or suspended imposition of sentence records released. Will fax documents. Court makes copy: $.30 per page, self serve same. Certification fee: $1.50 plus $1.00 per page includes copies. Payee: Associate Circuit Court. Personal checks accepted if in-state. No credit cards accepted. Prepayment required. Mail requests: SASE required.

Jackson County

Circuit Court - Civil Division 415 E 12th, 3rd Fl, Kansas City, MO 64106; 816-881-3522; probate phone: 816-881-3755; fax: 816-881-4327; 8AM-5PM. ***Civil, Eviction, Small Claims, Probate.***
www.16thcircuit.org
There is a combined computer system with the Independence civil court.
Civil Records: Access: Online, in person. Visitors must perform in person searches themselves. Required to search: name, years to search. Civil cases indexed by defendant, plaintiff, on computer since 1973, some records on microfiche and books, older records archived off-site. Public use terminal has civil records back to 1989. PAT results show name only. Case lookup at https://www.courts.mo.gov/casenet/base/welcome.do. Jackson Casenet records go back to 1/1989, but judgments only go back to 2/15/1989. Probate Court also participates in the Casenet system; also, access probate records at www.16thcircuit.org/publicaccess.asp.
General Information: Online identifiers in results same as on public terminal. No juvenile, mental, expunged, dismissed, or suspended imposition of sentence records released. Will not fax documents. Court makes copy: $.50 per page. Certification fee: $2.50 per cert. Payee: Dept of Civil Records. Business checks accepted. No credit cards accepted. Prepayment required.

Independence Circuit Ct. - Civil Annex 308 W Kansas #310, Independence, MO 64050; 816-881-4573; probate phone: 816-881-4552; fax: 816-881-4410; 8AM-5PM. ***Civil, Eviction, Small Claims, Probate.***
www.16thcircuit.org
Direct civil search requests to Rm 204. This court on the same computer system as Kansas City for civil cases, but files maintained separately.
Civil Records: Access: In person, online. Visitors must perform in person searches themselves. Required to search: name, years to search. Civil cases indexed by defendant, plaintiff, on computer since 1989. Note: The court will not do background checks, except for attorneys. You must have case number if the court is to pull a record. Public use

terminal has civil records back to 1989. PAT civil results show middle initial. Case lookup at https://www.courts.mo.gov/casenet/base/welcome.do. Online records go back to 1/1989. Online access to probate records is free at www.16thcircuit.org/publicaccess.asp. This includes private process servers, jury verdicts, criminal traffic, and criminal sureties.
General Information: Online identifiers in results same as on public terminal. No sealed records released. Will not fax documents. Court makes copy: $.50 per page. Certification fee: $2.50 per cert. Payee: Civil Records. Only cashiers checks and money orders accepted. No credit cards accepted. Prepayment required. Mail requests: SASE required for mail return of any copies.

Circuit Court - Criminal Division 1315 Locust, Kansas City, MO 64106-2937; 816-881-4350; fax: 816-881-3420; 8AM-5PM. ***Felony, Misdemeanor.*** www.16thcircuit.org
All background checks (name searches) are sent to the Missouri Highway Patrol in Jefferson City. Court will only pull file or give copies if a specific case number is given.
Criminal Records: Access: Online, mail, in person. Visitors must perform in person searches themselves. No search fee. Criminal records on computer since 1968 for felonies, 1980 for misdemeanors. Note: With a case or file number, you can request a copy of a document via mail. Mail turnaround time 10-14 days. Participates in the free state online court record system at www.courts.mo.gov/casenet/base/welcome.do. Online records go back to 1/1989. Also, current criminal docket calendar is available from the home page.
General Information: Online identifiers in results same as on public terminal. Will not fax documents. Court makes copy: $.25 per page. No certification fee. Only cashiers checks and money orders accepted. No credit cards accepted. Prepayment required. Mail requests: SASE required.

Jasper County

Carthage Circuit Court Courthouse, Rm 303, 302 S Main St, Carthage, MO 64836; 417-358-0441; criminal fax: 417-358-0461; civil fax: same; 8AM-5PM. ***Felony, Civil Actions over $25,000.***
www.courts.mo.gov/page.asp?id=1638
Although the Carthage Circuit and Associate Division merged, the records are only co-mingled from 7/2000 forward. Each of the 4 courts in the county must be searched for an accurate overall search. Probate is separate index, separate address.
Civil Records: Access: Mail, in person, online. Both court and visitors may perform in person searches. No search fee. Required to search: name, years to search. Civil cases indexed by defendant, plaintiff, on computer since 7/1/91, prior on cards since 1975. Mail turnaround time 1 week. Civil PAT goes back to 1991. Case lookup at https://www.courts.mo.gov/casenet/base/welcome.do. Online records go back to 6/26/2000.
Criminal Records: Access: Mail, in person, online. Both court and visitors may perform in person searches. No search fee. Required to search: name, years to search. Criminal records on computer since 7/1/91, prior on cards since 1975. Mail turnaround time 1 week. Criminal PAT goes back to same as civil. Online access to criminal records same as civil, above and show year of birth only. Court's public terminal may show add'l, often older data.
General Information: Online identifiers in results same as on public terminal. No juvenile, mental, expunged, dismissed, or suspended imposition of sentence records released. Will fax documents to local number only. Court makes copy: $.25 per page, self serve same. Certification fee: $1.50 per page plus copy fee; Exemplification fee- $3.00. Payee: Jasper County Circuit Clerk. Business checks accepted. No credit cards accepted. Prepayment required. Mail requests: SASE required.

Joplin Circuit Court Courthouse, 3rd Fl, 601 S Pearl, Rm 300, Joplin, MO 64801; 417-625-4310; criminal fax: 417-782-7172; civil fax: same; 8:30AM-N, 1PM-4:30PM. ***Felony, Civil Actions over $25,000.***
www.courts.mo.gov/page.asp?id=1638
Although the Joplin Circuit and Associate Division merged, the records are only co-mingled from 07/00 forward. Each of the 4 courts in the county must be searched for an accurate overall search.
Civil Records: Access: In person, online. Visitors must perform in person searches themselves. Required to search: name, years to search. Civil cases indexed by defendant, plaintiff, on computer since 7/1/91, prior on cards since 1975. Civil PAT goes back to 1991. PAT civil results show middle initial. Case lookup at https://www.courts.mo.gov/casenet/base/welcome.do. Online records go back to 6/26/2000.
Criminal Records: Access: In person, online. Visitors must perform in person searches themselves. Required to search: name, years to search. Criminal records computerized from 1991, prior on cards back to 1975. Criminal PAT goes back to same as civil. PAT criminal results show middle initial. Online access to criminal same as civil, above. Court's public terminal may show add'l, often older data.
General Information: Online identifiers in results same as on public terminal. No juvenile, mental, expunged, dismissed, or suspended imposition of sentence records released. Will fax out specific case files. Court makes copy: $.25 per page. Certification fee: $1.50 per page. Payee: Jasper County Circuit Clerk. No personal checks or credit cards accepted. Prepayment required.

Carthage Associate Division Court Courthouse, Rm 304, 302 S. Main St, Carthage, MO 64836; 417-358-0450; fax: 417-358-0460; 8:30AM-N, 1-4:30PM. ***Misdemeanor, Civil Actions under $45,000, Eviction, Small Claims, Probate.***
www.courts.mo.gov/page.asp?id=1638
Although Carthage Circuit and Associate Division merged, the records are co-mingled from 7/2000 forward only. Each of the 4 courts in the county must be searched for an accurate overall search.
Civil Records: Access: In person, online. Visitors must perform in person searches themselves. Required to search: name, years to search. Civil cases indexed by defendant, plaintiff, on computer back to 2000, prior on cards back to 1979. Civil PAT goes back to 1999. PAT civil results show middle initial. Participates in the free statewide Casenet record system at https://www.courts.mo.gov/casenet/base/welcome.do. Online records go back to 6/26/2000.
Criminal Records: Access: In person, online. Visitors must perform in person searches themselves. Required to search: name, years to search. Criminal records computerized from 2000, prior on cards back to 1979. Criminal PAT goes back to same as civil. PAT criminal results show middle initial. Online access to criminal same as civil. Court's public terminal may show add'l, often older data.
General Information: Online identifiers in results same as on public terminal. No juvenile, mental, expunged, dismissed, or suspended imposition of sentence records released. Will not fax documents. Court makes copy: $.25 per page. Certification fee: $1.75 per cert includes copy fee. Payee: Associate Court. No personal checks or credit cards accepted. Prepayment required.

Joplin Associate Division Court Courthouse, 2nd Fl, 601 S Pearl, Joplin, MO 64801; 417-625-4316; fax: 417-625-4340; 8AM-N, 1-4:30PM. ***Misdemeanor, Civil Actions under $45,000, Eviction, Small Claims, Probate.***
www.courts.mo.gov/page.asp?id=1638
Although the Joplin Circuit and Associate Division merged, records are only co-mingled from 7/2000 forward. Each of the 4 courts in the county must be searched for an overall search. Probate fax- 417-358-0404
Civil Records: Access: Mail, fax, in person, online. Both court and visitors may perform in person searches. No search fee. Required to search: name, years to search. Civil cases indexed by defendant, plaintiff, on computer back to 1993, prior on cards back to mid-1970s. Mail turnaround time 1-3 days. Civil PAT goes back to 2000. Case lookup at https://www.courts.mo.gov/casenet/base/welcome.do. Online records go back to 6/26/2000.
Criminal Records: Access: Mail, fax, in person, online. Both court and visitors may perform in person searches. No search fee. Required to search: name, years to search. Criminal records computerized from 1993, prior on cards back to mid-1970s. Mail turnaround time 1-3 days. Criminal PAT goes back to same as civil. Online access to criminal same as civil, see above. Court's public terminal may show add'l, often older data.
General Information: Online identifiers in results same as on public terminal. No juvenile, mental, expunged, dismissed, or suspended imposition of sentence records released. Will not fax out documents. Court makes copy: $.25 per page. Certification fee: $1.75 per cert. Payee: Associate Circuit Court. No personal checks or credit cards accepted. Prepayment required. Mail requests: SASE required.

Jefferson County

Circuit Court - Civil Division PO Box 100, 300 2nd St, Hillsboro, MO 63050; 636-797-5443, 636-797-5060; fax: 636-797-5073; 8AM-5PM. ***Civil Actions, Eviction, Small Claims, Probate.***
www.courts.mo.gov/page.asp?id=1620
Civil Records: Access: Phone, fax, mail, in person, online. Both court and visitors may perform in person searches. Search fee: $1.00 per name. Required to search: name, years to search. Civil cases indexed by defendant, plaintiff, on computer since 10/90, prior on books since 1966. Mail turnaround time 1-2 days. Public use terminal has civil records back to 1985. Case lookup at https://www.courts.mo.gov/casenet/base/welcome.do. Records go back to 5/9/2006.
General Information: Online identifiers in results same as on public terminal. No juvenile, mental, expunged, dismissed, or suspended imposition of sentence records released. Court makes copy: $1.00 per page. Certification fee: $.50 per page. Payee: Circuit Clerk. Business checks accepted. No credit cards accepted. Prepayment required. Mail requests: SASE required.

Circuit Court - Criminal Division PO Box 100, 300 2nd St, Hillsboro, MO 63050; 636-797-5370; fax: 636-797-5073; 8AM-4:30PM. ***Felony, Misdemeanor.***
www.courts.mo.gov/page.asp?id=1620
Criminal Records: Access: In person, online. Both court and visitors may perform in person searches. Search fee: $10.00 per name if court performs your in person search. Required to search: name, years to search, signed release, DOB or SSN. Criminal records on computer since 1989, on index cards 1976 to 1988, prior on books or microfilm. Public use terminal has crim records back to 1989. Participates in the free state online court record system at www.courts.mo.gov/casenet/base/welcome.do. Online records go back to 5/9/2006.
General Information: Online identifiers in results same as on public terminal. No juvenile, mental, expunged, dismissed, or suspended imposition of sentence records released. Will not fax documents. Court makes copy: $1.00 per page. Certification fee: $.50 per file. Payee: Circuit Clerk. Business checks accepted. No credit cards accepted. Prepayment required. Mail requests: SASE required for civil.

Johnson County

Consolidated Circuit Court Johnson County Justice Ctr, 101 W Market, Warrensburg, MO 64093; 660-422-7413/or/7410; fax: 660-422-7417; 8AM-4:30PM. ***Felony, Misdemeanor, Civil, Eviction, Small Claims, Probate.***
www.courts.mo.gov/page.asp?id=1610
Civil Records: Access: Mail, fax, in person, online. Visitors must perform in person searches themselves. Search fee: $10.00 per name. Required to search: name, years to search. Civil cases indexed by defendant, plaintiff, on file since 1800s, microfilmed from 1950s to 1988. Note: Only the court can pull records prior to 1976. Mail

turnaround time 1 week. Civil PAT goes back to 1994. Case lookup at https://www.courts.mo.gov/casenet/base/welcome.do. Online records go back to 6/6/2005.

Criminal Records: Access: Mail, fax, in person, online. Visitors must perform in person searches themselves. Search fee: $10.00 per name. Required to search: name, years to search, DOB, SSN. Criminal records on file since 1800s, microfilmed through 1988. Note: Court will perform search if prior to 1976. Mail turnaround time 1 week. Criminal PAT goes back to same as civil. Online access to criminal records same as civil, above and show year of birth only. Court's public terminal may show add'l, often older data.

General Information: Online identifiers in results same as on public terminal. No juvenile, adoptions, mental, expunged, dismissed, or suspended imposition of sentence records released. Will fax documents $3.00 1st page; $1.00 ea add'l page. Court makes copy: $.50 per page. Self serve copy: $.25 per page. Certification fee: $1.50 per cert. Payee: Circuit Clerk. No personal checks or credit cards accepted. Prepayment required.

Knox County

Consolidated Circuit Court PO Box 116, Edina, MO 63537; 660-397-2305; fax: 660-397-3331; 8:30AM-N, 1-4PM. ***Felony, Misdemeanor, Civil, Eviction, Small Claims, Probate.***
www.courts.mo.gov/page.asp?id=1535

The Circuit Court and Associate Division consolidated 3/01/2006. Records keeping is still separated at this location however.

Civil Records: Access: Mail, in person, online. Both court and visitors may perform in person searches. No search fee. Required to search: name, years to search. Civil cases indexed by defendant, plaintiff, on microfiche since 3/83, archived since 1845, no computerization. Mail turnaround time same day. Civil PAT goes back to 9/6/2005. PAT civil results show middle initial. The public access terminal uses the Casenet System. Case lookup at https://www.courts.mo.gov/casenet/base/welcome.do. Online records go back to 9/6/2005.

Criminal Records: Access: Mail, in person, online. Both court and visitors may perform in person searches. No search fee. Required to search: name, years to search. Criminal records archived since 1845, no computerization. Mail turnaround time same day. Criminal PAT goes back to same as civil. PAT criminal results show middle initial. The public access terminal uses the Casenet System. Online access to criminal records same as civil, above and show year of birth only. Court's public terminal may show add'l, often older data.

General Information: Online identifiers in results same as on public terminal. No juvenile, mental, expunged, dismissed, or suspended imposition of sentence records released. Will fax documents; fee varies but usually $3.50 per doc. Court makes copy: $1.00 per page, self serve same. Certification fee: $2.00. Payee: Circuit Court. Personal checks accepted; credit cards are not. Prepayment required. SASE not required.

Laclede County

Consolidated Circuit Court 200 N Adams St, Lebanon, MO 65536; 417-532-2471, 532-9196; criminal phone: 417-532-2471; criminal fax: 417-532-3683; civil fax: same; 8AM-4PM. ***Felony, Misdemeanor, Civil. Eviction, Small Claims, Probate.*** www.courts.mo.gov/page.asp?id=1629

Probate is a separate index at this same address. Probate fax is same as main fax number.

Civil Records: Access: Phone, fax, mail, in person, online. Both court and visitors may perform in person searches. No search fee. Required to search: name, years to search. Civil cases indexed by defendant, plaintiff, on cards since 1976, prior on books. Mail turnaround time varies. Civil PAT goes back to 1995; judgment index only. PAT results show name, DOB, SSN. Results include SSN and case number. Case lookup at https://www.courts.mo.gov/casenet/base/welcome.do. Online records go back to 11/28/2005.

Criminal Records: Access: Phone, fax, mail, in person, online. Both court and visitors may perform in person searches. No search fee. Required to search: name, years to search; also helpful: SSN. Criminal records on cards since 1976, prior on books. Mail turnaround time varies. Criminal PAT available. PAT results show name, DOB, SSN. Results include SSN and case number. Online access to criminal records same as civil, above and show year of birth only. Court's public terminal may show add'l, often older data.

General Information: Online identifiers in results same as on public terminal. No juvenile, mental, expunged, dismissed, or suspended imposition of sentence records released. Will fax documents $3.00 1st page, $1.00 each add'l. Court makes copy: $.25 per page, self serve same. Certification fee: $1.50 per document. Payee: Laclede County Circuit Clerk. Personal checks accepted; credit cards are not. Prepayment required. Copy fees may be billed to Attorneys only. Mail requests: SASE required.

Lafayette County

Consolidated Circuit Court PO Box 10, County Clerk's Office, Lexington, MO 64067; 660-259-6101; probate phone: 660-259-2324; criminal fax: 660-259-6148; civil fax: same; 8AM-4:30PM. ***Felony, Misdemeanor, Civil, Eviction, Small Claims, Probate.***
www.courts.mo.gov/page.asp?id=1605

The Circuit Court and Associate Division consolidated as of 9/2004. Probate fax- 660-259-4997

Civil Records: Access: Mail, fax, in person, online. Both court and visitors may perform in person searches. No search fee. Required to search: name, years to search. Civil cases indexed by defendant, plaintiff, case number. Civil records on books, archived since 1821; on computer back to 1987. Note: All search requests to clerk must be in writing. Forms available online. Mail turnaround time 3-5 days. Civil PAT goes back to 1994. PAT results show name only. Case lookup at https://www.courts.mo.gov/casenet/base/welcome.do. Online records go back to 04/01/02.

Criminal Records: Access: In person, online. Both court and visitors may perform in person searches. No search fee. Required to search: name, years to search; also helpful-case number. Criminal docket on books, archived since 1823; on computer back to 1987. Criminal PAT goes back to same as civil. PAT results show name only. Online access to criminal records same as civil, above and show year of birth only. Court's public terminal may show add'l, often older data.

General Information: Online identifiers in results same as on public terminal. No juvenile, mental, expunged, dismissed, or suspended imposition of sentence records released. Will fax back documents $1.00 per page. Court makes copy: $.25 per page; Probate- $1.00 per page, self serve same. Certification fee: $2.50 per document. Payee: Circuit Clerk. No personal checks accepted; money orders only. Visa/MC accepted for payment of court costs only. Attorney of record and copy fees may be billed. Mail requests: SASE required.

Lawrence County

Circuit Court 1 Courthouse Sq, #201, Mt Vernon, MO 65712; 417-466-2471; fax: 417-466-7899; 8AM-4:30PM. ***Felony, Civil Actions over $25,000.***
www.courts.mo.gov/page.asp?id=1661

Court is consolidated with Associated Circuit Court but they maintain separate addresses at the courthouse until 2009.

Civil Records: Access: Mail, in person, online. Both court and visitors may perform in person searches. Search fee: $5.00 per name. Required to search: name, years to search. Civil cases indexed by defendant, plaintiff, on computer back to 7/1991. Mail turnaround time 1 week. Civil PAT goes back to 7/1991. Case lookup at https://www.courts.mo.gov/casenet/base/welcome.do. Online records go back to 7/11/2005.

Criminal Records: Access: Mail, in person, online. Both court and visitors may perform in person searches. Search fee: $5.00 per name. Required to search: name, years to search, DOB; also helpful: SSN. Criminal records computerized from July 1, 1991. Mail turnaround time 1 week. Criminal PAT goes back to same as civil. Online access to criminal records same as civil, above and show year of birth only. Court's public terminal may show add'l, often older data.

General Information: Online identifiers in results same as on public terminal. No juvenile, mental, expunged, dismissed, or suspended imposition of sentence records released. Will fax out documents if all fees prepaid and not a lot of copies to fax. Court makes copy: $.25 per page, self serve same. Certification fee: $2.00 per cert. Payee: Circuit Court. Business checks or money orders accepted. No credit cards accepted. Prepayment required. Mail requests: SASE helpful.

Associate Circuit Division 1 Courthouse Sq, #102, Mt Vernon, MO 65712; 417-466-2463; probate phone: 417-466-2105; fax: 417-466-7899; 8:30AM-5PM. ***Misdemeanor, Civil Actions under $45,000, Eviction, Small Claims, Probate, Traffic.***
www.courts.mo.gov/page.asp?id=1661

Court is consolidated with Circuit Court but they maintain separate addresses at the courthouse until 2009. Probate records are indexed in a separate database, but at same address.

Civil Records: Access: In person, online. Visitors must perform in person searches themselves. Required to search: name, years to search. Civil cases indexed by defendant, plaintiff; index on cards since 1979, prior on books. Civil PAT goes back to 1991. PAT results show name, DOB. Case lookup at https://www.courts.mo.gov/casenet/base/welcome.do. Online records go back to 7/11/2005 and includes probate.

Criminal Records: Access: In person, online. Visitors must perform in person searches themselves. Required to search: name, years to search; also helpful: DOB, SSN. Criminal records indexed on cards since 1979, prior on books. Criminal PAT goes back to 1991.PAT results show name, DOB. Online access to criminal records same as civil, above and show year of birth only. Court's public terminal may show add'l, often older data.

General Information: Online identifiers in results same as on public terminal. No juvenile, mental, expunged, dismissed, or suspended imposition of sentence records released. Will not fax documents. Court makes copy: $.35 per page, self serve same. No certification fee. Payee: Associate Circuit Court. Personal checks accepted; credit cards are not. Prepayment required.

Lewis County

Consolidated Circuit Court PO Box 8, Monticello, MO 63457; 573-767-5232; fax: 573-767-5342; 8AM-N,1-4PM. ***Felony, Misdemeanor, Civil, Eviction, Small Claims, Probate.***
www.courts.mo.gov/page.asp?id=1537

Consolidated court on 4-1-03.

Civil Records: Access: Mail, in person, online. Visitors must perform in person searches themselves. No search fee. Required to search: name, years to search. Civil cases indexed by defendant, plaintiff, on computer back to 1976 (judgments) and index books, archived since 1830s. Civil PAT goes back to 9/6/05. PAT civil results show middle initial. Case lookup at https://www.courts.mo.gov/casenet/base/welcome.do. Online records go back to 9/6/2005.

Criminal Records: Access: In person, online. Visitors must perform in person searches themselves. Required to search: name, years to search. Criminal records on computer and index books, archived since 1830s. Criminal PAT goes back to same as civil. PAT criminal results show middle initial. Online access to criminal records same as civil, above and show year of birth only. Court's public terminal may show add'l, often older data.

General Information: Online identifiers in results same as on public terminal. No juvenile, mental, expunged, dismissed, or suspended imposition of sentence records released. Will fax documents. Court makes copy: $.10 per page plus $.20 per minute. Self serve copy: $.10 per page. Certification fee: $2.50.

Payee: Lewis County Circuit Court. Personal checks accepted; credit cards are not. Prepayment required.

Lincoln County

Consolidated Circuit Court Lincoln County Justice Ctr, 45 Business park Dr, Troy, MO 63379; 636-528-6300; fax: 636-528-9168; 8AM-4:30PM. ***Felony, Misdemeanor, Civil, Eviction, Small Claims, Probate.***
www.courts.mo.gov/page.asp?id=1682
Civil Records: Access: In person, online. Visitors must perform in person searches themselves. Required to search: name, years to search. Civil cases indexed by defendant, plaintiff, on computer since 8/92, prior on index cards since 1978. Civil PAT goes back to 4/2002. Record access free at https://www.courts.mo.gov/casenet/base/welcome.do. Online records go back to 04/03/02.
Criminal Records: Access: In person, online. Visitors must perform in person searches themselves. Required to search: name, years to search. Criminal records on computer since 8/92, prior on index cards since 1978. Criminal PAT goes back to same as civil. PAT criminal results show middle initial. Online access to criminal records same as civil, above and show year of birth only. Court's public terminal may show add'l, often older data.
General Information: Online identifiers in results same as on public terminal. No juvenile, mental, expunged, dismissed, or suspended imposition of sentence records released. Will fax specific case file only; not search documents. Court makes copy: $.25 per page, self serve same. Certification fee: $.50 per page includes copies. Payee: Lincoln County Circuit Clerk. Personal checks accepted; credit cards are not. Prepayment required.

Linn County

Consolidated Circuit Court PO Box 84, 108 N High St, Linneus, MO 64653-0084; 660-895-5212; fax: 660-895-5277; 8AM-N, 1-4:30PM. ***Felony, Misdemeanor, Civil, Eviction, Small Claims, Probate.***
www.courts.mo.gov/page.asp?id=1573
Civil Records: Access: Fax, mail, in person, online. Both court and visitors may perform in person searches. No search fee. Required to search: name, years to search. Civil cases indexed by defendant, plaintiff, on books. Mail turnaround time 1 week. Civil PAT goes back to 5/2001. Case lookup at https://www.courts.mo.gov/casenet/base/welcome.do. Online records go back to 5/13/2002.
Criminal Records: Access: Fax, mail, in person, online. Both court and visitors may perform in person searches. No search fee. Required to search: name, years to search. Criminal docket on books. Mail turnaround time 1 week. Criminal PAT goes back to same as civil. Online access to criminal records same as civil, above and show year of birth only. Court's public terminal may show add'l, often older data.
General Information: Online identifiers in results same as on public terminal. No juvenile, mental, expunged, dismissed, or suspended imposition of sentence records released. No fee to fax documents. Court makes copy: $1.00 per page. Certification fee: $1.50 per page includes copies. Payee: Linn County Circuit Court. Only cashiers checks and money orders accepted. No credit cards accepted. Prepayment required. Mail requests: SASE required.

Livingston County

Circuit Court 700 Webster St, Chillicothe, MO 64601; 660-646-8000 x305; civil phone: 660-646-8000; fax: 660-646-2734; 8AM-5PM. ***Felony, Civil Actions over $25,000.***
www.courts.mo.gov/page.asp?id=1677
Civil Records: Access: Mail, fax, in person, online. Visitors must perform in person searches themselves. No search fee. Required to search: name, years to search, any personal identifiers. Civil cases indexed by defendant, plaintiff; index on cards since 1974, prior on record books. Civil PAT goes back to 1/23/2006. PAT results show name, DOB. Case lookup at https://www.courts.mo.gov/casenet/base/welcome.do. Online records go back to 1/23/2006.
Criminal Records: Access: Mail, fax, in person, online. Visitors must perform in person searches themselves. No search fee. Required to search: name, years to search, any personal identifiers. Criminal records indexed on cards since 1974, prior on record books. Criminal PAT goes back to 1/23/2006. PAT results show middle initial, DOB. Terminal results include SSN. Online access to criminal records same as civil, above and show year of birth only. Court's public terminal may show add'l, often older data.
General Information: Online identifiers in results same as on public terminal. No juvenile, mental, expunged, dismissed, or suspended imposition of sentence records released. Will fax documents to local or toll free line. Court makes copy: $1.00 per page, self serve same. Certification fee: $1.50. Payee: Livingston County Circuit Clerk. Personal checks accepted; credit cards are not. Prepayment required. Attorneys may be billed for copy fees. Mail requests: SASE required.

Associate Circuit Division Livingston County Courthouse, #8, Chillicothe, MO 64601; 660-646-8000 x1; criminal phone: x1; civil phone: same; probate phone: 660-646-8000; fax: 660-646-8014; Public- 8:30AM-4:30PM; Office- 8AM-5PM. ***Misdemeanor, Civil Actions under $25,000, Eviction, Small Claims, Probate.***
www.courts.mo.gov/page.asp?id=1677
Civil Records: Access: Phone, fax, mail, in person, online. Both court and visitors may perform in person searches. No search fee. Required to search: name, years to search; also helpful: address; Signed release required for closed records. Civil cases indexed by defendant, plaintiff; index on cards and record books since 1975, prior on record books. Mail turnaround time 5 days. Civil PAT goes back to 2006. Case lookup at https://www.courts.mo.gov/casenet/base/welcome.do. Online records go back to 1/23/2006.
Criminal Records: Access: Phone, fax, mail, in person, online. Both court and visitors may perform in person searches. No search fee. Required to search: name, years to search, DOB; Signed release required for closed records. Criminal records indexed on cards and record books since 1975, prior on record books. Mail turnaround time 5 days. Criminal PAT goes back to 2006. Participates in the free state online court record system at www.courts.mo.gov/casenet/base/welcome.do. Online records go back to 1/23/2006. Court's public terminal may show add'l, often older data.
General Information: Online identifiers in results same as on public terminal. No juvenile, mental, expunged, dismissed, or suspended imposition of sentence records released. Call for fax fee. Court makes copy: $1.00 per page. Self serve copy: $.10 per page. Certification fee: $1.50. Payee: Associate Circuit Court. Personal checks accepted; credit cards are not. Prepayment required. Mail requests: SASE required.

Macon County

Circuit Court PO Box 382, 101 E Washington St, Macon, MO 63552; 660-385-4631; criminal phone: 660-385-4631; civil phone: 660-385-4631; fax: 660-385-4235; 8AM-4:30PM. ***Felony, Civil Actions over $25,000.***
www.maconcountymo.com/Government/CircuitCourt/tabid/88/Default.aspx
Civil Records: Access: Fax, mail, in person, online. Both court and visitors may perform in person searches. No search fee. Required to search: name, years to search. Civil cases indexed by defendant, plaintiff, on computer since 1/1/91, on index cards from 1976-1990, prior on books. Mail turnaround time 2-5 days. Civil PAT goes back to 1991. PAT results show name only. Case lookup at https://www.courts.mo.gov/casenet/base/welcome.do. Online records go back to 4/17/2000.
Criminal Records: Access: In person, online. Both court and visitors may perform in person searches. No search fee. Required to search: name, years to search. Criminal records on computer since 1/1/91, on index cards from 1976-1990, prior on books. Note: Court directs criminal name search requests to Casenet or the MO State Hiway Patrol. Criminal PAT goes back to same as civil. PAT results show name only. Online access to criminal records same as civil, above and show year of birth only. Court's public terminal may show add'l, often older data.
General Information: Online identifiers in results same as on public terminal. No juvenile, mental, expunged, dismissed, or suspended imposition of sentence records released. Will fax documents $1.00 1st page, $.25 each add'l. Court makes copy: $.25 per page, self serve same. Certification fee: $3.00 per doc. Payee: Clerk of Circuit Court. Personal checks accepted; credit cards are not. Prepayment required. Mail requests: SASE required.

Associate Circuit Division PO Box 491, 101 E Washington, Bldg 2, Macon, MO 63552; 660-385-3531; probate phone: 660-385-3531; criminal fax: 660-385-3132; civil fax: same; 8AM-4:30PM. ***Misdemeanor, Civil Actions under $25,000, Eviction, Small Claims, Probate.***
www.courts.mo.gov/page.asp?id=1666
Probate fax is same as main fax number.
Civil Records: Access: Fax, mail, in person, online. Both court and visitors may perform in person searches. No search fee. Required to search: name, years to search. Civil cases indexed by defendant, plaintiff; index on cards and books; on computer back to 1992. Civil PAT goes back to 1976. Older civil records on public terminal are incomplete. Case lookup at https://www.courts.mo.gov/casenet/base/welcome.do. Online records go back to 4/17/2003.
Criminal Records: Access: Fax, in person, online. Visitors must perform in person searches themselves. No search fee. Required to search: name, years to search, DOB. Criminal records on computer since 1992, prior on index cards back to 1989. Note: Records over 2 years old not held on site, court clerk needs 1-2 days to retrieve. Criminal PAT goes back to 1992. Online access to criminal records same as civil, above and show year of birth only. Court's public terminal may show add'l, often older data.
General Information: Online identifiers in results same as on public terminal. No juvenile, mental, expunged, dismissed, or suspended imposition of sentence records released. Will not fax documents. Court makes copy: n/a. Self serve copy: $.25 per page. Certification fee: $1.50. Payee: Circuit Court Division II or Probate Court. No personal checks or credit cards accepted. Prepayment required. Mail requests: SASE required for civil.

Madison County

Consolidated Circuit Court PO Box 470, Fredericktown, MO 63645-0470; 573-783-2102; fax: 573-783-5920; 8AM-5PM. ***Felony, Misdemeanor, Civil, Small Claims, Probate.***
www.courts.mo.gov/page.asp?id=1624
The Associates court was merged into the Circuit Court effective 01/01/2006. All records are co-mingled.
Civil Records: Access: In person, online. Visitors must perform in person searches themselves. Required to search: name, years to search. Civil cases indexed by defendant, plaintiff, on computer back to 1993, prior on index cards from 1979-1992. Civil PAT goes back to 1993. PAT results show name only. Online case lookup at https://www.courts.mo.gov/casenet/base/welcome.do. Records go back to 11/01/00.
Criminal Records: Access: In person, online. Visitors must perform in person searches themselves. Required to search: name, years to search. Criminal records computerized from 1993, prior on index cards from 1979-1993. Criminal PAT goes back to same as civil. PAT results show name only. Online access to criminal records same as civil, above and show year of birth only. Court's public terminal may show add'l, often older data.
General Information: Online identifiers in results same as on public terminal. No juvenile, mental, expunged, dismissed, or suspended imposition of sentence records released. Will not fax documents. Court makes copy: $1.00 per page. Certification fee: $2.00 per page includes copy. Payee: Madison County Circuit Clerk. Personal checks accepted;

credit cards are not. Prepayment required. Mail requests: SASE required for mail return of any copies.

Maries County

Circuit Court PO Box 213, Vienna, MO 65582; 573-422-3338; fax: 573-422-3976; 8AM-4PM. ***Felony, Civil Actions over $25,000.***
www.courts.mo.gov/page.asp?id=4754
Civil Records: Access: Fax, mail, in person, online. Both court and visitors may perform in person searches. No search fee. Required to search: name, years to search. Civil cases indexed by defendant, plaintiff, go back to 1940. Mail turnaround time 1-3 days. Civil PAT goes back to 1/07. PAT results show name only. Judgments only. Case lookup at https://www.courts.mo.gov/casenet/base/welcome.do. Records go back to 1/22/2007.
Criminal Records: Access: Fax, mail, in person, online. Both court and visitors may perform in person searches. No search fee. Required to search: name, years to search. Criminal records go back 10 1940. Mail turnaround time 1-3 days. Criminal PAT goes back to same. Online access to criminal records same as civil, above and show year of birth only. Court's public terminal may show add'l, often older data.
General Information: Online identifiers in results same as on public terminal. No juvenile, mental, expunged, dismissed, or suspended imposition of sentence records released. Will fax documents $1.00 per page. Court makes copy: $.25 per page, self serve same. Certification fee: $1.50 per cert. Payee: Maries County Circuit Clerk. Personal checks accepted; credit cards are not. Prepayment required. Mail requests: SASE required.

Associate Circuit Division PO Box 490, Vienna, MO 65582; 573-422-3303; fax: 573-422-9917; 8AM-4PM. ***Misdemeanor, Civil Actions under $25,000, Eviction, Small Claims, Probate.***
www.courts.mo.gov/page.asp?id=4754
Most civil cases are directed to the Circuit Court regardless of limit.
Civil Records: Access: Mail, fax, in person, online. Both court and visitors may perform in person searches. No search fee. Required to search: name, years to search. Cases indexed by defendant, plaintiff; index on cards since 1985, archived since 1868. Civil PAT goes back to 2007. Case lookup at https://www.courts.mo.gov/casenet/base/welcome.do. Records go back to 1/22/2007.
Criminal Records: Access: In person, online. Only the court performs in person searches; visitors may not. No search fee. Required to search: name, years to search, DOB, signed release; also helpful-SSN. Criminal records indexed on cards since 1985, archived since 1868. Criminal PAT available. Participates in free state online court record system at www.courts.mo.gov/casenet/base/welcome.do. Records go back to 1/22/2007. Court's public terminal may show add'l, often older data.
General Information: Online identifiers in results same as on public terminal. No juvenile, mental, expunged, dismissed, or suspended imposition of sentence records released. Will not fax documents. Court makes copy: $.25 per page. Certification fee: $1.50 per cert. Payee: Maries County Associate Court. Only cashiers checks and money orders accepted. No credit cards accepted. Prepayment required. Mail requests: SASE required for civil.

Marion County

Consolidated Circuit Court District 1 PO Box 431, 100 S Main St, Palmyra, MO 63461; 573-769-2550; fax: 573-769-4558; 8AM-5PM. ***Felony, Civil Actions, Eviction, Small Claims, Probate.***
www.courts.mo.gov/page.asp?id=1580
Civil Records: Access: In person, online. Visitors must perform in person searches themselves. Required to search: name, years to search. Civil cases indexed by defendant, plaintiff; index on cards since 1977, prior on judgment books. Civil PAT goes back to 1987. Onbline case lookup at https://www.courts.mo.gov/casenet/base/welcome.do. Online records go back to 9/12/2005.
Criminal Records: Access: In person, online. Visitors must perform in person searches themselves. Required to search: name, years to search, DOB. Criminal records indexed on cards since 1977, prior on judgment books. Criminal PAT goes back to 1995. Public access and online system show same results after 9/05. Online access to criminal records same as civil, above and show year of birth only. Court's public terminal may show add'l, often older data.
General Information: Online identifiers in results same as on public terminal. No juvenile, mental, expunged, dismissed, or suspended imposition of sentence records released. Will not fax documents. Court makes copy: $.25 per page, self serve same. Certification fee: $2.00 per cert. Payee: Marion County Circuit Clerk of Division I. Business checks accepted. No credit cards accepted. Prepayment required. Mail requests: SASE required for mail return of any copies.

Consolidated Circuit Court District 2 906 Broadway, Rm 105, Hannibal, MO 63401; 573-221-0198; fax: 573-221-9328; 8AM-Noon, 1-5PM. ***Felony, Misdemeanor, Civil, Eviction, Small Claims, Probate.***
www.courts.mo.gov/page.asp?id=1580
Jurisdiction is Twps of Miller and Mason only. The Associate Circuit Court consolidate with this court in July 2005.
Civil Records: Access: Fax, mail, in person, online. Both court and visitors may perform in person searches. No search fee. Required to search: name, years to search. Civil cases indexed by defendant, plaintiff, on computer since 1991, prior on index cards. Mail turnaround time 5 days. Civil PAT goes back to 1976. Case lookup at https://www.courts.mo.gov/casenet/base/welcome.do. Online records go back to 9/12/2005.
Criminal Records: Access: In person, online. Visitors must perform in person searches themselves. Required to search: name, years to search. Criminal records on computer. Criminal PAT goes back to same as civil. Online access to criminal records same as civil, above and show year of birth only. Court's public terminal may show add'l, often older data.
General Information: Online identifiers in results same as on public terminal. No juvenile, mental, expunged, dismissed, or suspended imposition of sentence records released. Will not fax out documents. Court makes copy: $.50 per page. Certification fee: $5.00 per document. Payee: Circuit Clerk District II. No personal checks accepted. Cash, money orders or cashier checks only accepted. No credit cards accepted.

McDonald County

Consolidated Circuit Court PO Box 157, Pineville, MO 64856; 417-223-7515; fax: 417-223-4125; 8AM-4:30PM. ***Felony, Misdemeanor, Civil, Small Claims, Probate.***
www.courts.mo.gov/page.asp?id=1663
Civil Records: Access: Fax, mail, in person, online. Visitors must perform in person searches themselves. No search fee. Required to search: name, years to search. Civil cases indexed by defendant, plaintiff, on computer since 1991, on index cards since 1979, prior on index cards. Civil PAT goes back to 8/1991. PAT civil results show middle initial. Online case lookup at https://www.courts.mo.gov/casenet/base/welcome.do. Online records go back to 1/21/2004
Criminal Records: Access: In person, online. Visitors must perform in person searches themselves. Required to search: name, years to search. Criminal records on computer since 1991, on index cards since 1979, prior on index cards. Note: Criminal search requests are directed to the MO Highway Patrol. Criminal PAT goes back to 10/1991. PAT criminal results show middle initial. Online access to criminal records same as civil, above and show year of birth only. Court's public terminal may show add'l, often older data.
General Information: Online identifiers in results same as on public terminal. No juvenile, mental, expunged, dismissed, paternity or suspended imposition of sentence records released. Court makes copy: $.25 per page. Certification fee: $2.00; Probate $1.50 per page. Payee: McDonald County Circuit Clerk. Business checks accepted. No credit cards accepted. Prepayment required. Mail requests: SASE required.

Mercer County

Circuit Court Courthouse, 802 E Main, Princeton, MO 64673; 660-748-4335; fax: 660-748-4339; 8:30AM-N, 1-4:30PM. ***Felony, Civil Actions over $45,000.***
www.courts.mo.gov/page.asp?id=1540
Civil Records: Access: In person, online. Visitors must perform in person searches themselves. Required to search: name, years to search. Civil cases indexed by defendant, plaintiff, on computer since 1991, on index cards since 1977, prior on books. Civil PAT goes back to 1999. Case lookup at https://www.courts.mo.gov/casenet/base/welcome.do. Online records go back to 3/29/2000.
Criminal Records: Access: In person, online. Visitors must perform in person searches themselves. Required to search: name, years to search, DOB. Criminal records on computer since 1991, on index cards since 1977, prior on books. Criminal PAT goes back to same as civil. Online access to criminal records same as civil, above and show year of birth only. Court's public terminal may show add'l, often older data.
General Information: Online identifiers in results same as on public terminal. No juvenile, mental, expunged, dismissed, or suspended imposition of sentence records released. Will fax documents $1.00 per page. Court makes copy: $.25 per page, self serve same. Certification fee: $1.50. Payee: Mercer County Circuit Clerk. Personal checks not accepted if out of state; money orders preferred. No credit cards accepted. Prepayment required. Mail requests: SASE required for mail return of any copies.

Associate Circuit Division Mercer County Courthouse, 802 E Main St, Princeton, MO 64673; 660-748-4232; criminal fax: 660-748-4292; civil fax: same; 8:30AM-N, 1-4:30PM. ***Misdemeanor, Civil Actions under $45,000, Eviction, Small Claims, Probate, Traffic.***
www.courts.mo.gov/page.asp?id=1540
Probate fax is same as main fax number.
Civil Records: Access: In person, online. Visitors must perform in person searches themselves. Required to search: name, years to search. Civil cases indexed by defendant. Civil records indexed. Civil PAT goes back to 3/2000. PAT results show middle initial, DOB. Public terminal located in Circuit Clerk's office. Case lookup at https://www.courts.mo.gov/casenet/base/welcome.do. Online records go back to 3/2000.
Criminal Records: Access: In person, online. Visitors must perform in person searches themselves. Required to search: name, years to search; also helpful: DOB, SSN. Criminal records on index. Criminal PAT goes back to same as civil. PAT results show middle initial, DOB. Public terminal located in Circuit Clerk's office. Online access to criminal records same as civil, above and show year of birth only. Court's public terminal may show add'l, often older data.
General Information: Online identifiers in results same as on public terminal. No juvenile, mental, expunged, dismissed, or suspended imposition of sentence records released. Will fax documents $1.00 per page. Court makes copy: $.25 per page. Certification fee: $1.50 plus $1.00 per page. Payee: Circuit Court Division II. Personal checks accepted; credit cards are not. Prepayment required. Mail requests: SASE required for mail return of any copies.

Miller County

Consolidated Circuit Court PO Box 11, Tuscumbia, MO 65082; 573-369-1980; fax: 573-369-1894; 8AM-4:30PM. ***Felony, Misdemeanor, Civil, Small Claims, Eviction, Probate.***
www.courts.mo.gov/page.asp?id=1630
The Circuit Court and Associate Division consolidated 11/28/2005.
Civil Records: Access: Phone, fax, mail, in person, online. Both court and visitors may perform in person searches. Search fee: $4.00 per name. Required to search: name, years to search. Civil cases

indexed by defendant, plaintiff; index on cards since 1976, prior on books. Civil PAT goes back to 1991. PAT results show name only. Case lookup at https://www.courts.mo.gov/casenet/base/welcome.do. Online records go back to 11/28/2005.
Criminal Records: Access: In person, online. Visitors must perform in person searches themselves. Required to search: name, years to search. Criminal records indexed on cards since 1976, prior on books. Note: Court refers background checkers to the State Highway Patrol. Criminal PAT goes back to same as civil. PAT results show name only. Online access to criminal records same as civil, above and show year of birth only. Court's public terminal may show add'l, often older data.
General Information: Online identifiers in results same as on public terminal. No juvenile, mental, expunged, dismissed, or suspended imposition of sentence records released. No fee to fax documents if other fees prepaid. Will fax to local and toll-free numbers only. Court makes copy: $.50 per page, self serve same. Certification fee: $2.00. Payee: Miller County Circuit Court. Personal checks accepted; credit cards are not. Prepayment required. Mail requests: SASE required for civil.

Mississippi County

Consolidated Circuit Court PO Box 369, Charleston, MO 63834; 573-683-2146 x1; fax: 573-683-7696; 8AM-5PM. ***Felony, Misdemeanor, Civil, Small Claims, Eviction, Probate.***
www.courts.mo.gov/page.asp?id=1643
Civil Records: Access: In person, online. Visitors must perform in person searches themselves. Required to search: name, years to search. Civil cases indexed by defendant, plaintiff, in case files since 1976. Civil PAT goes back to 1979. Access to civil records is free at https://www.courts.mo.gov/casenet/base/welcome.do. Online records go back to 6/15/2001.
Criminal Records: Access: In person, online. Visitors must perform in person searches themselves. Required to search: name, years to search, DOB. Criminal records in case files since 1951. Criminal PAT goes back to same as civil. Online access to criminal records same as civil, above and show year of birth only. Court's public terminal may show add'l, often older data.
General Information: Online identifiers in results same as on public terminal. No juvenile, mental, expunged, dismissed, or suspended imposition of sentence records released. Will fax out specific case files. Court makes copy: $1.00 1st page; $.25 each add'l page. Certification fee: $.50 per cert. Payee: Circuit Clerk. Personal checks accepted; credit cards are not. Prepayment required.

Moniteau County

Circuit Court 200 E Main, California, MO 65018; 573-796-2071; fax: 573-796-2591; 8AM-N, 1-4:30PM. ***Felony, Civil Actions over $25,000.***
www.courts.mo.gov/page.asp?id=1631
Civil Records: Access: In person, online. Both court and visitors may perform in person searches. No search fee. Required to search: name, years to search; also helpful: case number. Civil cases indexed by defendant, plaintiff, on computer since 1992, prior on index cards and books. Civil PAT goes back to 1992. Online case lookup at https://www.courts.mo.gov/casenet/base/welcome.do. Online records go back to 11/28/2005.
Criminal Records: Access: In person, online. Both court and visitors may perform in person searches. No search fee. Required to search: name, years to search; also helpful: case number. Criminal records on computer since 1980, prior on index cards and books to 1845. Criminal PAT goes back to 1992. Online access to criminal records same as civil, above and show year of birth only. Court's public terminal may show add'l, often older data.
General Information: Online identifiers in results same as on public terminal. No juvenile, mental, expunged, dismissed, or suspended imposition of sentence records released. Will not fax out case files. Court makes copy: $.50 per page, self serve same. Certification fee: $1.00 per doc. Payee: Moniteau County Circuit Court. Personal checks accepted; credit cards are not. Prepayment required.

Associate Circuit Division 200 E Main, California, MO 65018; 573-796-4671; probate phone: 573-796-2814; ; 8AM-4:30PM. ***Misdemeanor, Civil Actions under $25,000, Eviction, Small Claims, Probate.***
www.courts.mo.gov/page.asp?id=1631
The court will not do probate record searches.
Civil Records: Access: Phone, in person, online. Visitors must perform in person searches themselves. No search fee. Required to search: name, years to search. Civil cases indexed by defendant, plaintiff; index on cards since 1979, prior on index books from 1948 to 1979, archived before. Civil PAT available. Case lookup at https://www.courts.mo.gov/casenet/base/welcome.do. Online records go back to 11/28/2005 and includes probate.
Criminal Records: Access: In person, online. Visitors must perform in person searches themselves. Required to search: name, years to search. Criminal records indexed on cards since 1979, prior on index books from 1948 to 1979, archived before. Criminal PAT available. Online access to criminal records same as civil, above and show year of birth only. Court's public terminal may show add'l, often older data.
General Information: Online identifiers in results same as on public terminal. No juvenile, mental, expunged, dismissed, or suspended imposition of sentence records released. Will not fax documents. Court makes copy: $.25 per page, self serve same. Certification fee: $1.50 for 1st page, $1.00 each add'l. Payee: Moniteau Court. Personal checks accepted; credit cards are not. Prepayment required.

Monroe County

Consolidated Circuit Court PO Box 227, 300 N Main, Paris, MO 65275; 660-327-5204; criminal fax: 660-327-5781; civil fax: same; 8AM-4:30PM. ***Felony, Misdemeanor, Civil, Small Claims, Eviction, Probate, Traffic.***
www.courts.mo.gov/page.asp?id=1582
Civil Records: Access: Mail, in person, online. Both court and visitors may perform in person searches. Search fee: $14.00 per name. Required to search: name, years to search. Civil cases indexed by defendant, plaintiff, on computer since 1996; index cards since 1979, prior on index books. Mail turnaround time 1 week. Public use terminal available, records go back to 7/1/05. Case lookup at https://www.courts.mo.gov/casenet/base/welcome.do. Online records go back to 9/12/2005.
Criminal Records: Access: Mail, in person, online. Both court and visitors may perform in person searches. Search fee: $14.00 per name. Required to search: name, years to search, SSN, signed release. Criminal records on computer since 1996, on index cards from 1979 to 1990. Mail turnaround time 1 week. Public use terminal available, crim records go back to same. Online access to criminal records same as civil, above and show year of birth only. Court's public terminal may show add'l, often older data.
General Information: Online identifiers in results same as on public terminal. No juvenile, mental, expunged, dismissed, or suspended imposition of sentence records released. Fee to fax out file $1.00 per page. Court makes copy: $1.00 per page. Self serve copy: $.50 per page. Certification fee: $2.00. Payee: Monroe County Circuit Court. Personal checks accepted; credit cards are not. Prepayment required. Mail requests: SASE required.

Montgomery County

Circuit Court 211 E 3rd, #301, Montgomery City, MO 63361; 573-564-3341; fax: 573-564-3914; 8AM-4:30PM. ***Felony, Civil Actions over $25,000.***
www.courts.mo.gov/page.asp?id=1593
Civil Records: Access: Online, in person. Visitors must perform in person searches themselves. Required to search: name, years to search. Civil cases indexed by defendant, plaintiff, on computer since 1987 for judgments, on index cards since 1979, prior on books to 1864. Civil PAT goes back to 1996. Results include name, action, docket entries, case number, parties. Case lookup at https://www.courts.mo.gov/casenet/base/welcome.do. Online records go back to 7/1/1997.
Criminal Records: Access: Online, in person. Visitors must perform in person searches themselves. Required to search: name, years to search. Criminal records on computer since 1987 for judgments, on index cards since 1979, prior on books. Criminal PAT goes back to same as civil. Results include name, action, docket entries, case number, parties. Online access to criminal same as civil, above, criminal records go back to 8/18/1997. Court's public terminal may show add'l, often older data.
General Information: Online identifiers in results same as on public terminal. No juvenile, mental, expunged, dismissed, or suspended imposition of sentence records released. Will fax documents $5.00 1st page, $2.00 each add'l page. Court makes copy: $.25 per page, self serve same. Certification fee: $1.50 plus $.25 per page. Payee: Montgomery County Circuit Court. Personal checks accepted; credit cards are not. Prepayment required.

Associate Circuit Division 211 E 3rd St, Montgomery City, MO 63361; 573-564-3348; fax: 573-564-8081; 8AM-4:30PM. ***Misdemeanor, Civil Actions under $25,000, Eviction, Small Claims, Probate.*** www.courts.mo.gov/page.asp?id=1593
Civil Records: Access: Online, in person. Visitors must perform in person searches themselves. Required to search: name, years to search. Civil cases indexed by defendant, plaintiff, on computer back to 1976, prior on index cards. Case lookup at https://www.courts.mo.gov/casenet/base/welcome.do. Online civil records go back to 7/1/1997.
Criminal Records: Access: Online, in person. Visitors must perform in person searches themselves. Required to search: name, years to search, DOB. Criminal records computerized from 1976, prior on index cards. Online access to criminal same as civil, above, records go back to 8/18/1997. Court's public terminal may show add'l, often older data.
General Information: Online identifiers in results same as on public terminal. No juvenile, mental, expunged, dismissed, or suspended imposition of sentence records released. Court makes copy: $.25 per page. Certification fee: $1.50 per page. Payee: Montgomery Circuit Court Div 2. No checks accepted. No credit cards accepted. Prepayment required. Mail requests: SASE required for mail return of any copies.

Morgan County

Circuit Court 211 E Newton, Versailles, MO 65084; 573-378-4413; fax: 573-378-5356; 8AM-5PM. ***Felony, Civil Actions over $25,000.***
www.courts.mo.gov/page.asp?id=1632
Civil Records: Access: Phone, mail, in person, online. Visitors must perform in person searches themselves. No search fee. Required to search: name, years to search. Civil cases indexed by defendant, plaintiff, on computer since 1992, on index cards since 1979, prior archived since mid-1800s. Civil PAT goes back to 1984. PAT results show name only. Online case lookup at https://www.courts.mo.gov/casenet/base/welcome.do. Online records go back to 11/28/2005.
Criminal Records: Access: Phone, mail, in person, online. Visitors must perform in person searches themselves. No search fee. Required to search: name, years to search. Criminal records on computer since 1992, on index cards since 1979, prior archived since mid-1800s. Mail turnaround time 1 week; phone turnaround immediate. Criminal PAT goes back to same as civil. PAT results show middle initial, DOB. Online access to criminal same as civil, above. Court's public terminal may show add'l, often older data.
General Information: Online identifiers in results same as on public terminal. No juvenile, mental, expunged, dismissed, or suspended imposition of sentence records released. Will not fax documents. Court makes copy: $.50 per page. Self serve copy: $.25 per page. Certification fee: $1.50. Payee: Circuit Court. Personal checks accepted; credit cards are not.

Prepayment required. Copy fees may be billed. Mail requests: SASE required.

Associate Circuit Division 211 E Newton St, Versailles, MO 65084; 573-378-4235; criminal phone: 573-378-4060; civil phone: 573-378-4235; probate phone: 573-378-4235; criminal fax: 573-378-5356; civil fax: 573-378-6847; 8AM-5PM. ***Misdemeanor, Civil Actions under $25,000, Eviction, Small Claims, Probate.***
www.courts.mo.gov/page.asp?id=1632
Probate has a separate index. Probate fax- 573-378-6847. Traffic is with the criminal division.
Civil Records: Access: Phone, mail, in person, online. Both court and visitors may perform in person searches. No search fee. Required to search: name, years to search. Civil cases indexed by defendant, plaintiff, on computer since 1991, prior on index to 1970. Mail turnaround time 2-3 days. Public use terminal available. PAT civil results show middle initial. Case lookup at https://www.courts.mo.gov/casenet/base/welcome.do. Online records go back to 11/28/2005 and includes probate.
Criminal Records: Access: Phone, mail, in person, online. Only the court performs in person searches; visitors may not. No search fee. Required to search: name, years to search; also helpful: address, DOB, SSN, singed release. Criminal records on computer since 1989, prior on index to 1970. Note: Signed release required for some searches. Mail turnaround time 2-3 days. Public use terminal available. PAT criminal results show middle initial. Online access to criminal records same as civil, above and show year of birth only. Court's public terminal may show add'l, often older data.
General Information: Online identifiers in results same as on public terminal. No juvenile, mental, expunged, dismissed, or suspended imposition of sentence records released. Will fax documents. Court makes copy: $1.00 per page. Self serve copy: $.50 per page. Certification fee: $1.50 per page. Payee: Associate Circuit Court or Probate Court. Only cashiers checks and money orders accepted. No credit cards accepted. Prepayment required. Mail requests: SASE required.

New Madrid County

Consolidated Circuit Court County Courthouse, 450 Main St, New Madrid, MO 63869; 573-748-2228; fax: 573-748-5409; 8AM-4:30PM. ***Felony, Misdemeanor, Civil, Eviction, Small Claims, Probate.***
www.courts.mo.gov/page.asp?id=1645
Civil Records: Access: In person, online. Visitors must perform in person searches themselves. Required to search: name, years to search. Civil cases indexed by defendant, plaintiff, on Cot index since 1979, prior on books. Civil PAT goes back to 2/2001. PAT results show middle initial, DOB. Access to civil records is free at https://www.courts.mo.gov/casenet/base/welcome.do. Online records go back to 2/7/2001.
Criminal Records: Access: In person, online. Visitors must perform in person searches themselves. Required to search: name, years to search. Criminal records on Cott index since 1979, prior on books. Criminal PAT goes back to same as civil. PAT results show middle initial, DOB. Online access to criminal same as civil, above. Court's public terminal may show add'l, often older data.
General Information: Online identifiers in results same as on public terminal. No juvenile, mental, expunged, dismissed, or suspended imposition of sentence records released. Will fax out specific case files. Court makes copy: $1.00 per page. Certification fee: $5.00 per doc. Payee: Circuit Clerk. No personal checks or credit cards accepted. Prepayment required.

Newton County

Consolidated Circuit Court PO Box 170, Criminal Div. (PO Box 130 for civil), 101 S Wood St, Courthouse, Neosho, MO 64850; 417-451-8210; criminal fax: 417-451-8272; civil fax: 417-451-8298; 8AM-5PM. ***Felony, Misdemeanor, Civil, Eviction, Small Claims, Probate.***
www.courts.mo.gov/page.asp?id=1664
Probate is a separate division; probate address is 101 S Wood, #204. Probate fax- 417-451-8265
Civil Records: Access: In person, online. Visitors must perform in person searches themselves. Civil cases indexed by defendant, plaintiff, on computer since 1991, microfilm since 1860, prior on index cards and books. Civil PAT goes back to 1991. PAT results show name, DOB. Case lookup at https://www.courts.mo.gov/casenet/base/welcome.do. Online records go back to 1/21/2004.
Criminal Records: Access: In person, online. Visitors must perform in person searches themselves. Required to search: name, years to search. Criminal records on computer since 1991, microfilm since 1860, prior on index cards and books. Criminal PAT goes back to same as civil.PAT results show name, DOB. Online access to criminal same as civil, above. Court's public terminal may show add'l, often older data.
General Information: Online identifiers in results same as on public terminal. No juvenile, mental, expunged, dismissed, or suspended imposition of sentence records released. Will not fax documents. Court makes copy: $.25 per page. Certification fee: $1.00 per document. Payee: Newton County Circuit Clerk. Business checks accepted. No credit cards accepted. Prepayment required.

Nodaway County

Consolidated Circuit Court 303 N Market, Maryville, MO 64468; 660-582-5431; probate phone: 660-582-4221; fax: 660-582-2047; 8AM-4:30PM. ***Felony, Misdemeanor, Civil, Eviction, Small Claims, Probate.***
www.courts.mo.gov/page.asp?id=1549
The Circuit Court and Associate Division consolidated 10/2005.
Civil Records: Access: Phone, mail, in person, online. Visitors must perform in person searches themselves. No search fee. Required to search: name, years to search. Civil cases indexed by defendant, plaintiff, on computer back to 5/91, archived since 1845. Civil PAT goes back to 5/1991. PAT results show name only. Case lookup at https://www.courts.mo.gov/casenet/base/welcome.do. Online records go back to 3/20/2006.
Criminal Records: Access: In person, online. Visitors must perform in person searches themselves. Required to search: name, years to search, DOB. Criminal records computerized from 5/91, archived since 1845. Criminal PAT goes back to same as civil. PAT results show name only. Online access to criminal same as civil, above. Court's public terminal may show add'l, often older data.
General Information: Online identifiers in results same as on public terminal. No juvenile, mental, expunged, dismissed, or suspended imposition of sentence records released. Fee to fax out file $1.00 per page. Court makes copy: $.25 per page. Certification fee: $.50. Payee: Circuit Clerk. Personal checks accepted; credit cards are not. Prepayment required. Mail requests: SASE required.

Oregon County

Circuit Court PO Box 406, Courthouse Sq, Alton, MO 65606; 417-778-7460; fax: 417-778-7206; 8AM-4PM. ***Felony, Civil Actions over $25,000.***
www.courts.mo.gov/page.asp?id=1654
Civil Records: Access: In person, online. Both court and visitors may perform in person searches. No search fee. Required to search: name, years to search. Civil cases indexed by defendant, plaintiff, on books. Civil PAT goes back to 1991. PAT civil results show middle initial. Case lookup at https://www.courts.mo.gov/casenet/base/welcome.do. Online records go back to 1991.
Criminal Records: Access: In person, online. Both court and visitors may perform in person searches. No search fee. Required to search: name, years to search. Criminal docket on books. Note: Court will only search if not busy, and may refer you to State Highway Patrol. Criminal PAT goes back to same as civil. PAT criminal results show middle initial. Online access to criminal same as civil, above. Court's public terminal may show add'l, often older data.
General Information: Online identifiers in results same as on public terminal. No juvenile, mental, expunged, dismissed, or suspended imposition of sentence records released. Will fax documents $1.00 1st page, $.50 each add'l. Court makes copy: $.25 per page. Certification fee: $2.00 per cert. Payee: Circuit Court. Personal checks and cash accepted. No credit cards accepted. Prepayment required.

Associate Circuit Division PO Box 211, Courthouse Sq, Alton, MO 65606; 417-778-7461; fax: 417-778-6209; 8AM-4PM. ***Misdemeanor, Civil Actions under $45,000, Eviction, Small Claims, Probate.***
www.courts.mo.gov/page.asp?id=1654
Civil Records: Access: In person, online. Both court and visitors may perform in person searches. No search fee. Required to search: name, years to search. Civil cases indexed by defendant, plaintiff; index on cards, archived since 1850. Civil PAT goes back to 2000. Online case lookup at https://www.courts.mo.gov/casenet/base/welcome.do. Online records go back to 1991.
Criminal Records: Access: In person, online. Both court and visitors may perform in person searches. No search fee. Required to search: name, years to search. Criminal records on computer since 3/11/92, prior on files. Criminal PAT goes back to 3/22/1992. Online access to criminal records same as civil, above and show year of birth only. Court's public terminal may show add'l, often older data.
General Information: Online identifiers in results same as on public terminal. No juvenile, mental, expunged, or dismissed records released. (Suspended Imposition of Sentence only available during probationary period.). Will fax out docs $1.00 per page. Court makes copy: $1.00 per page. Self serve copy: $.10 per page. Certification fee: $2.00 per cert. Payee: Associate Circuit Court. Business checks accepted. No credit cards accepted. Prepayment required.

Osage County

Consolidated Circuit Court PO Box 825, Linn, MO 65051; 573-897-3114; fax: 573-897-4075; 8AM-4:30PM. ***Felony, Misdemeanor, Civil, Eviction, Small Claims, Probate.***
www.courts.mo.gov/page.asp?id=1618
The Associate Division consolidated into the Circuit Court on 01/01/2006.
Civil Records: Access: Phone, mail, in person, online. Both court and visitors may perform in person searches. No search fee. Required to search: name, years to search. Civil cases indexed by defendant, plaintiff; index on cards and books. Mail turnaround time ASAP. Civil PAT goes back to 1992, some to 2000. PAT results show name, DOB. Probate is on terminal back to 2000. Case lookup at https://www.courts.mo.gov/casenet/base/welcome.do. Online civil records go back to 9/01/2000.
Criminal Records: Access: Phone, mail, fax, in person, online. Both court and visitors may perform in person searches. No search fee. Required to search: name, years to search, DOB; also helpful: SSN. Criminal records indexed on cards and books, computerized since 1992. Mail turnaround time ASAP. Criminal PAT goes back to same as civil. PAT results show middle initial, DOB. Online access to criminal same as civil, above. Online criminal records go back to 8/28/1992. Court's public terminal may show add'l, often older data.
General Information: Online identifiers in results same as on public terminal. No juvenile, mental, expunged, dismissed, or suspended imposition of sentence records released. Fee to fax out file $1.00 per page. Court makes copy: $.25 per page, self serve same. Certification fee: $2.00 per cert. Payee: Circuit Clerk. Personal checks and major credit cards accepted. Prepayment required. Mail requests: SASE required.

Ozark County

Circuit Court PO Box 36, Gainesville, MO 65655; 417-679-4232; fax: 417-679-4554; 8AM-N, 12:30-4:30PM. ***Felony, Civil Actions over $25,000.***
www.courts.mo.gov/page.asp?id=1679

Civil Records: Access: Mail, in person, online. Only the court performs in person searches; visitors may not. No search fee. Required to search: name, years to search. Civil cases indexed by defendant, plaintiff; index on cards since 1979, archived since 1933. Civil PAT goes back to 2/1006. Case lookup at https://www.courts.mo.gov/casenet/base/welcome.do. Online records go back to 2/20/2006.
Criminal Records: Access: In person, online. Only the court performs in person searches; visitors may not. No search fee. Required to search: name, years to search, DOB. Criminal records indexed on cards since 1979, archived since 1933. Criminal PAT available. Online access to criminal same as civil, above. Court's public terminal may show add'l, often older data.
General Information: Online identifiers in results same as on public terminal. No juvenile, mental, expunged, dismissed, or suspended imposition of sentence records released. Will fax documents $.50 per page. Court makes copy: $.25 per page. Certification fee: $1.50. Payee: Ozark County Circuit Court. Personal checks accepted; credit cards are not. Prepayment required.

Associate Circuit Division PO Box 278, Courthouse Sq, Gainesville, MO 65655; 417-679-4611; fax: 417-679-2099; 8AM-4:30PM. ***Misdemeanor, Civil Actions under $25,000, Eviction, Small Claims, Probate.***
www.courts.mo.gov/page.asp?id=1679
Civil Records: Access: Fax, mail, in person, online. Only the court performs in person searches; visitors may not. No search fee. Required to search: name, years to search. Civil cases indexed by defendant, plaintiff, on case files. Public use terminal available, records go back to 2006. PAT civil results show middle initial. Case lookup at https://www.courts.mo.gov/casenet/base/welcome.do. Online records go back to 2/20/2006 and includes probate.
Criminal Records: Access: In person, online. Only the court performs in person searches; visitors may not. No search fee. Required to search: name, years to search, DOB, signed release; SSN helpful. Criminal records on computer since 1990. Public use terminal available. PAT criminal results show middle initial. Online access to criminal records same as civil, above and show year of birth only. Court's public terminal may show add'l, often older data.
General Information: Online identifiers in results same as on public terminal. No juvenile, mental, expunged, dismissed, or suspended imposition of sentence records released. Will fax documents $1.00 per page. Court makes copy: $1.00 per page. Certification fee: $1.50 per cert. Payee: Associate Circuit Court. Personal checks accepted if local. No credit cards accepted. Prepayment required. Mail requests: SASE required for civil.

Pemiscot County

Circuit Court County Courthouse, PO Box 34, Caruthersville, MO 63830; 573-333-0182; fax: 573-333-1272; 8AM-4:30PM. ***Felony, Civil Actions over $25,000.***
www.courts.mo.gov/page.asp?id=1646
Civil Records: Access: In person, online. Visitors must perform in person searches themselves. Required to search: name, years to search. Civil cases indexed by defendant, plaintiff; index on cards since 1979, prior on books. Civil PAT goes back to 1/7/2001. PAT results show name only. Case lookup at https://www.courts.mo.gov/casenet/base/welcome.do. Online records go back to 2/7/2001.
Criminal Records: Access: In person, online. Visitors must perform in person searches themselves. Required to search: name, years to search. Criminal records indexed on cards since 1979, prior on books. Criminal PAT goes back to same as civil. PAT results show name only. Online access to criminal same as civil, above. Court's public terminal may show add'l, often older data.
General Information: Online identifiers in results same as on public terminal. No juvenile, mental, expunged, dismissed, or suspended imposition of sentence records released. Will not fax documents. Court makes copy: $.50 per page. No certification fee. Payee: Pemiscot County Circuit Clerk. No personal checks accepted. Prepayment required.

Associate Circuit Division PO Drawer 228, 800 Ward Ave, County Courthouse, Caruthersville, MO 63830; 573-333-2784; fax: 573-333-4722; 8AM-4:30PM. ***Misdemeanor, Civil Actions under $45,000, Eviction, Small Claims, Probate.***
www.courts.mo.gov/page.asp?id=1646
Civil Records: Access: In person, online. Only the court performs in person searches; visitors may not. Required to search: name, years to search. Civil cases indexed by defendant, plaintiff, on computer back to 2001, index cards since 1979, prior on books. Case lookup at https://www.courts.mo.gov/casenet/base/welcome.do. Online records go back to 2/14/2001.
Criminal Records: Access: In person, online. Only the court performs in person searches; visitors may not. Required to search: name, years to search. Criminal records on computer since 5/90, on index cards from 1979-1990, prior on books. Online access to criminal same as civil, above, criminal record access goes back to 1990. Court's public terminal may show add'l, often older data.
General Information: Online identifiers in results same as on public terminal. No juvenile, mental, expunged, dismissed, or suspended imposition of sentence records released. Will fax documents to local or toll-free number. Court makes copy: $1.00 per page. No certification fee. Payee: Pemiscot County Clerk. Only cashiers checks and money orders accepted. No credit cards accepted. Prepayment required.

Perry County

Consolidated Circuit Court 15 W Saint Maries St #2, Perryville, MO 63775-1399; 573-547-6581; criminal phone: x5; civil phone: x3; probate phone: x7; fax: 573-547-9323; 8AM-5PM. ***Felony, Misdemeanor, Civil, Eviction, Small Claims, Probate.***
www.courts.mo.gov/page.asp?id=1642
The Associate Division consolidated into the Circuit Court on 07/01/2003.
Civil Records: Access: In person, online. Visitors must perform in person searches themselves. Required to search: name, years to search. Civil cases indexed by defendant, plaintiff, on computer since 1994, prior on index cards. Civil PAT goes back to 1994. Results include name and case number. Access to civil records is free at https://www.courts.mo.gov/casenet/base/welcome.do. Online civil records go back to 7/1/2001.
Criminal Records: Access: In person, online. Both court and visitors may perform in person searches. No search fee. Required to search: name, years to search. Criminal records on computer since 1993, prior on index cards. Criminal PAT goes back to same as civil. Online access to criminal same as civil, above, criminal case records go back to 1993. Court's public terminal may show add'l, often older data.
General Information: Online identifiers in results same as on public terminal. No juvenile, mental, paternity (except final judgment), expunged, dismissed, or suspended imposition of sentence records released. Will fax documents $1.00 per page. Court makes copy: $1.00 per page. Certification fee: $1.00 per cert. Payee: Perry County Circuit Clerk. Personal checks accepted; credit cards are not. Prepayment required.

Pettis County

Circuit Court - Civil 415 S Ohio, Sedalia, MO 65301; 660-826-5000 x926; probate phone: x924; criminal fax: 660-826-4520; civil fax: same; 8AM-5PM. ***Civil Actions, Eviction, Small Claims, Probate.***
www.courts.mo.gov/page.asp?id=1615
Civil Records: Access: Phone, fax, mail, in person, online. Both court and visitors may perform in person searches. No search fee. Required to search: name, years to search. Civil cases indexed by defendant, plaintiff; index on docket books since 9/75, prior on judgment books. Mail turnaround time 1-2 days. Civil PAT goes back to 4/2001; judgments back to 1991. Access to civil records is free at https://www.courts.mo.gov/casenet/base/welcome.do back to 4/1/2001.
General Information: Online identifiers in results same as on public terminal. No juvenile, mental, expunged, dismissed, or suspended imposition of sentence records released. Will fax documents $2.50 1st page, $1.50 each add'l. Court makes copy: $1.00 1st page, $.50 each add'l. Certification fee: $1.50. Payee: Pettis County Circuit Clerk. Personal checks accepted; credit cards are not. Prepayment required. Mail requests: SASE required.

Circuit Court - Criminal 415 S Ohio, Sedalia, MO 65301; 660-826-5000 x924; fax: 660-827-8613; 7:30AM-5PM. ***Felony, Misdemeanor, Traffic.***
www.courts.mo.gov/page.asp?id=1615
Criminal Records: Access: Phone, fax, mail, in person, online. Both court and visitors may perform in person searches. No search fee. Required to search: name, years to search, DOB, SSN; on some cases: signed release. Criminal records computerized from 1993, on index cards from 1975-1993, prior on judgment books. Mail turnaround time 1-2 weeks. Criminal PAT goes back to 1995. Access to criminal records is free at https://www.courts.mo.gov/casenet/base/welcome.do back to 1/1992.
General Information: Online identifiers in results same as on public terminal. No juvenile, mental, expunged, dismissed, or suspended imposition of sentence records released. Will fax documents for free. Court makes copy: $1.00 1st page; $.50 each add'l. Certification fee: $1.50 per page. Payee: Circuit Clerk. Only cashiers checks and money orders accepted. No credit cards accepted. Prepayment required. Mail requests: SASE required.

Probate Court 415 S. Ohio St, Sedalia, MO 65301; 660-826-5000 x470; fax: 660-827-8613; 8AM-5PM. ***Probate.***
Access to probate records is available free at https://www.courts.mo.gov/casenet.

Phelps County

Consolidated Circuit Court 200 N Main St, Rolla, MO 65401; 573-458-6210; criminal phone: 573-458-6202; civil phone: 573-458-6215; probate phone: 573-458-6245; fax: 573-458-6224; 8AM-5PM. ***Felony, Misdemeanor, Civil, Small Claims, Eviction, Probate.***
www.courts.mo.gov/page.asp?id=4755
Probate fax- 573-458-6235
Civil Records: Access: In person, online. Visitors must perform in person searches themselves. Required to search: name, years to search. Civil cases indexed by defendant, plaintiff, on computer since 1992; prior on books to 1957. Civil PAT goes back to 1992. PAT civil results show middle initial. Case lookup at https://www.courts.mo.gov/casenet/base/welcome.do. Online records go back to 1/22/2007.
Criminal Records: Access: In person, online. Visitors must perform in person searches themselves. Required to search: names, years to search. Criminal records computerized since 1991, prior indexed on books to 1957. Criminal PAT goes back to same as civil. PAT criminal results show middle initial. Online access to criminal same as civil, above. Court's public terminal may show add'l, often older data.
General Information: Online identifiers in results same as on public terminal. No juvenile, mental, expunged or dismissed records released. Will fax documents $1.00 per page. Court makes copy: $.25 per page, self serve same. Certification fee: $1.00 per page does include copies. Payee: Circuit Clerk. No out-of-state checks accepted. No credit cards accepted. Prepayment required. Mail requests: SASE required for mail return of any copies.

Pike County

Consolidated Circuit Court 115 W Main, Bowling Green, MO 63334; 573-324-3112; fax: 573-324-3150; 8AM-4:30PM. ***Felony, Misdemeanor, Civil, Small Claims, Eviction, Probate, Traffic.***
www.courts.mo.gov/page.asp?id=1683
This court consolidated with the Associate Court in June 2006.

Civil Records: Access: Mail, in person, online. Visitors must perform in person searches themselves. No search fee. Required to search: name, years to search; also helpful: address. Civil cases indexed by defendant, plaintiff; index on cards since 1977, prior on books; Associate court records indexed on cards since 1979, archived since 1819. Note: Court will help with simple searches only, will not do judgments of lien searches. Civil PAT goes back to 1992. PAT civil results show middle initial. Online case lookup at https://www.courts.mo.gov/casenet/base/welcome.do. Online records go back 4/2002.
Criminal Records: Access: In person, online. Visitors must perform in person searches themselves. Required to search: name, years to search; also helpful: DOB. Criminal records indexed on cards since 1977, prior on books; Associate court records indexed on cards since 1979, archived since 1819. Note: Criminal searches should be directed to the MO Highway Patrol. Criminal PAT goes back to same as civil. PAT criminal results show middle initial. Online access to criminal same as civil, above. Court's public terminal may show add'l, often older data.
General Information: Online identifiers in results same as on public terminal. No juvenile, mental, expunged, dismissed, or suspended imposition of sentence records released. Will fax documents to local or toll-free number; will not fax certified documents. Court makes copy: $.50 per page, self serve same. Certification fee: $1.00 per page and $1.00 per doc. Fee for certified copy of Judgment of Dissolution-$10.00. Payee: Pike County Circuit Clerk. Personal checks accepted; credit cards are not. Prepayment required. Mail requests: SASE required for civil.

Platte County

Consolidated Circuit Court 415 Third St #5, Platte City, MO 64079; 816-858-2232; fax: 816-858-3392; 8AM-5PM. ***Felony, Misdemeanor, Civil, Eviction, Small Claims.***
www.courts.mo.gov/page.asp?id=1567
Associate court consolidated with Circuit court in 2006.
Civil Records: Access: Online, in person. Visitors must perform in person searches themselves. Required to search: name, years to search. Civil cases indexed by defendant, plaintiff, on computer since 10/91. Civil PAT goes back to 10/1991. PAT results show name, DOB. The public access terminal provides the same screen as Casenet online system. Case lookup at https://www.courts.mo.gov/casenet/base/welcome.do. Cases go back to 1/1/1991.
Criminal Records: Access: Online, in person. Visitors must perform in person searches themselves. Required to search: name, years to search, DOB; also helpful: SSN. Criminal records on computer since 10/91. Criminal PAT goes back to 10/1991.PAT results show name, DOB. The public access terminal provides the same screen as Casenet online system. Online access to criminal records same as civil, above and show year of birth only. Court's public terminal may show add'l, often older data.
General Information: Online identifiers in results same as on public terminal. No juvenile, mental, expunged, dismissed, or suspended imposition of sentence records released. Will not fax documents. Court makes copy: $.25 per page. Certification fee: $1.00. Payee: Platte County Circuit Clerk. Only cashiers checks and money orders accepted. No credit cards accepted. Prepayment required.

Probate Court 415 Third St, #95, Platte City, MO 64079; 816-858-3438; probate phone: 816-858-3440; fax: 816-858-3392; 8AM-5PM. ***Probate.***
Can search by name or case number at https://www.courts.mo.gov/casenet. Cases go back to 1/1/1991.

Polk County

Consolidated Circuit Court 102 E Broadway, Rm 14, Bolivar, MO 65613; 417-326-4912; fax: 417-326-4194; 8AM-5PM. ***Felony, Misdemeanor, Civil, Eviction, Small Claims, Probate.*** www.positech.net/~dcourt/
The Circuit Court and Associate Division consolidated as of 01/03.
Civil Records: Access: In person, online. Visitors must perform in person searches themselves. Required to search: name, years to search. Civil cases indexed by defendant, plaintiff, on computer since 1991, prior on card index since 1979. Civil PAT goes back to 2001. Case lookup at https://www.courts.mo.gov/casenet/base/welcome.do. Online records go back to 11/13/2001.
Criminal Records: Access: In person, online. Visitors must perform in person searches themselves. Required to search: name, years to search. Criminal records on computer since 1991, prior on card index since 1979. Criminal PAT goes back to same as civil. Online access to criminal records same as civil, above and show year of birth only. Court's public terminal may show add'l, often older data.
General Information: Online identifiers in results same as on public terminal. No juvenile, mental, expunged, dismissed, or suspended imposition of sentence records released. Will fax documents to local or toll-free number. Court makes copy: $.25 per page. Self serve copy: $.10 per page. Certification fee: $2.00 per cert. Payee: Circuit Clerk. Personal checks accepted; credit cards are not. Prepayment required. Mail requests: SASE required for mail return of any copies.

Pulaski County

Consolidated Circuit Court 301 Historic Rt 66 E, #202, Waynesville, MO 65583; 573-774-4755; probate phone: 573-774-4784; fax: 573-774-6967; 8AM-4:30PM. ***Felony, Misdemeanor, Civil, Eviction, Small Claims.***
www.courts.mo.gov/page.asp?id=4756
Civil Records: Access: In person, online. Visitors must perform in person searches themselves. Required to search: name, years to search; also helpful: address. Civil cases indexed by defendant, plaintiff, on computer since 1990, prior on books since 1903. Civil PAT goes back to 1991. Case lookup at https://www.courts.mo.gov/casenet/base/welcome.do. Online records go back to 1/22/2007
Criminal Records: Access: In person, online. Visitors must perform in person searches themselves. Required to search: name, years to search; also helpful: DOB, SSN. Criminal records on computer since 1990, prior on books since 1903. Criminal PAT goes back to same as civil. Participates in free state online court record system at www.courts.mo.gov/casenet/base/welcome.do. Online records go back to 1/22/2007 Court's public terminal may show add'l, often older data.
General Information: Online identifiers in results same as on public terminal. No juvenile, mental, paternity, expunged, dismissed, or suspended imposition of sentence records released. Will fax specific case files for $2.00 per 5 pages. Court makes copy: $.25 per page. Certification fee: $2.00 per cert. Payee: Circuit Clerk. Business checks accepted. Prepayment required.

Probate Court 301 Historic 66 East, #316, Waynesville, MO 65583; 573-774-4784; fax: 573-774-6673; 8AM-4:30PM. ***Probate.***
Participates in the free state online court record system at https://www.courts.mo.gov/casenet.

Putnam County

Circuit Court Courthouse Rm 202, Unionville, MO 63565; 660-947-2071; fax: 660-947-2320; 8AM-N; 1-5PM. ***Felony, Civil Actions over $45,000.***
www.courts.mo.gov/page.asp?id=1541
Civil Records: Access: Mail, in person, online. Both court and visitors may perform in person searches. No search fee. Required to search: name, years to search. Civil cases indexed by defendant, plaintiff; index on cards since 1848; on computer since 3/00. Mail turnaround time same day. Civil PAT goes back to 1990. Case lookup at https://www.courts.mo.gov/casenet/base/welcome.do. Online records go back to 3/29/2000.
Criminal Records: Access: In person, online. Visitors must perform in person searches themselves. Required to search: name, years to search. Criminal records indexed on cards since 1848; on computer since 3/00. Note: No criminal histories are researched by court staff. Requesters referred to the State Hwy Patrol. Criminal PAT goes back to same as civil. Online access to criminal records same as civil, above and show year of birth only. Court's public terminal may show add'l, often older data.
General Information: Online identifiers in results same as on public terminal. No juvenile, mental, expunged, dismissed, or suspended imposition of sentence records released. Will fax documents $1.00 1st page; $50 each add'l;. Court makes copy: $.25 per page, self serve same. Certification fee: $1.00. Payee: Circuit Clerk. Business checks accepted. No credit cards accepted. Prepayment required. Mail requests: SASE required for civil.

Associate Circuit Division Courthouse Rm 101, 1601 W Main, Unionville, MO 63565; 660-947-2117; fax: 660-947-7348; 9AM-5PM. ***Misdemeanor, Civil Actions under $45,000, Eviction, Small Claims, Probate.***
www.courts.mo.gov/page.asp?id=1541
Civil Records: Access: Mail, in person, online. Both court and visitors may perform in person searches. No search fee. Required to search: name, years to search. Civil cases indexed by defendant, plaintiff, on computer since 1994, prior on books. Mail turnaround time as long as 30-60 days. Civil PAT goes back to 3/29/2000. PAT civil results show middle initial. Case lookup at https://www.courts.mo.gov/casenet/base/welcome.do. Online records go back to 3/29/2000.
Criminal Records: Access: Mail, in person, online. Both court and visitors may perform in person searches. No search fee. Required to search: name, years to search, DOB, SSN. Criminal records on computer since 1994, prior on books. Mail turnaround time as long as 30-60 days. Criminal PAT goes back to 1994. PAT criminal results show middle initial. Online access to criminal records same as civil, above and show year of birth only. Court's public terminal may show add'l, often older data.
General Information: Online identifiers in results same as on public terminal. No mental, expunged, dismissed, or suspended imposition of sentence records released. Will fax documents. Court makes copy: $1.00 per page, self serve same. Certification fee: $1.50. Payee: Associate Circuit Court. Checks accepted for search fee payment. No credit cards accepted. Prepayment required. Mail requests: SASE required.

Ralls County

Consolidated Circuit Court PO Box 466, New London, MO 63459; criminal phone: 573-985-5641; civil phone: 573-985-5633; fax: 573-985-3446; 8:30AM-N, 1-4:30PM. ***Felony, Misdemeanor, Civil, Eviction, Small Claims, Probate.***
www.courts.mo.gov/page.asp?id=1585
The Associate Division consolidated into this court on 08/01/2005.
Civil Records: Access: Mail, in person, online. Both court and visitors may perform in person searches. No search fee. Required to search: name, years to search, DOB, SSN and signed release. Civil cases indexed by defendant, plaintiff; index on cards since 1976, prior on books. Mail turnaround time varies. Public use terminal has civil records back to 1990. PAT results show name only. Case lookup at https://www.courts.mo.gov/casenet/base/welcome.do. Online records go back to 9/12/2005.
Criminal Records: Access: In person, online. Visitors must perform in person searches themselves. Required to search: name, years to search, signed release and SSN. Criminal records indexed on cards since 1976, prior on books. PAT results show middle initial, DOB. Online access to criminal records same as civil, above and show

year of birth only. Court's public terminal may show add'l, often older data.
General Information: Online identifiers in results same as on public terminal. No juvenile, mental, expunged, dismissed, or suspended imposition of sentence records released. Court makes copy: $.25 per page, self serve same. Certification fee: $1.00. Payee: Ralls County Circuit Court. In-state personal checks accepted. No credit cards accepted. Prepayment required. Mail requests: SASE required for civil.

Randolph County

Consolidated Circuit Court 372 Highway JJ, Huntsville, MO 65259; 660-277-4601; fax: 660-277-4636; 8AM-4:30PM. ***Felony, Misdemeanor, Civil, Eviction, Small Claims, Probate.***
www.courts.mo.gov/page.asp?id=1600
Court formerly located in Moberly.
Civil Records: Access: Fax, mail, in person, online. Both court and visitors may perform in person searches. No search fee. Required to search: name, years to search, address. Civil cases indexed by defendant, plaintiff. On index cards since 1975, prior on record books. Mail turnaround time 1 week. Public use terminal available. PAT civil results show middle initial. Participates in free record system at https://www.courts.mo.gov/casenet/base/welcome.do. Online civil records go back to 10/31/2001.
Criminal Records: Access: Fax, mail, in person, online. Both court and visitors may perform in person searches. No search fee. Required to search: name, years to search, address, DOB; also helpful-SSN. Criminal records computerized from 1994, prior on index books. Mail turnaround time 1 week. Public use terminal available. PAT criminal results show middle initial. Give them the DOB, they will verify. Participates in the free court record system at www.courts.mo.gov/casenet/base/welcome.do. Online criminal records go back to 5/1/1994. Court's public terminal may show add'l, often older data.
General Information: Online identifiers in results same as on public terminal. No juvenile, mental, expunged, dismissed, or suspended imposition of sentence records released. Will fax out document $4.00 per page. Court makes copy: $.25 per page. Certification fee: $1.50 per page. Payee: Randolph County Circuit Clerk. No personal checks or credit cards accepted. Prepayment required. Mail requests: SASE required.

Ray County

Consolidated Circuit Court PO Box 594, Richmond, MO 64085; 816-776-3377; fax: 816-776-6016; 8AM-4PM. ***Felony, Misdemeanor, Civil, Eviction, Small Claims, Probate.***
www.courts.mo.gov/page.asp?id=1569
The Associate Division consolidated into this court on 01/01/2006.
Civil Records: Access: Phone, fax, mail, in person, online. Both court and visitors may perform in person searches. No search fee. Required to search: name, years to search. Civil cases indexed by defendant, plaintiff; index on cards since 1977, prior on judgment books. Probate records are in a separate index. Mail turnaround time 2-4 weeks. Civil PAT goes back to 12/2001. PAT results show name only. Online case lookup at https://www.courts.mo.gov/casenet/base/welcome.do. Online records go back to 2001.
Criminal Records: Access: In person, online. Both court and visitors may perform in person searches. No search fee. Required to search: name, years to search; also helpful: DOB, SSN. Criminal records indexed on cards since 1977, prior on judgment books. Note: The court refers criminal record search requesters to contact the MO Highway Patrol, 573-751-3313. Criminal PAT goes back to same as civil. PAT results show name only. Online access to criminal records same as civil, above and show year of birth only. Court's public terminal may show add'l, often older data.
General Information: Online identifiers in results same as on public terminal. No juvenile, mental, expunged, dismissed, or suspended imposition of sentence records released. Fee to fax out file $1.00 per page. Court makes copy: $.25 per page. Certification fee: $1.50 per cert. Payee: Ray County Circuit Clerk. Business checks accepted. No credit cards accepted. Prepayment required. Mail requests: SASE required for civil.

Reynolds County

Circuit Court PO Box 76, Centerville, MO 63633; 573-648-2494 x34; criminal fax: 573-648-2503; civil fax: same; 8AM-4PM. ***Felony, Civil Actions over $45,000.***
www.courts.mo.gov/page.asp?id=1671
Civil Records: Access: Phone, mail, in person, online. Both court and visitors may perform in person searches. Search fee: $10.00. Required to search: name, years to search. Civil cases indexed by defendant, plaintiff, on cards and books, archived since 1872. Mail turnaround time 2 days. Civil PAT goes back to 2001. Case lookup at https://www.courts.mo.gov/casenet/base/welcome.do. Online records go back to 4/9/2001.
Criminal Records: Access: Phone, mail, in person, online. Both court and visitors may perform in person searches. Search fee: $10.00. Required to search: name, years to search, DOB; also helpful: SSN, sex, signed release. Criminal records on cards and books, archived since 1872. Mail turnaround time 2 days. Criminal PAT goes back to same as civil. Online access to criminal records same as civil, above and show year of birth only. Court's public terminal may show add'l, often older data.
General Information: Online identifiers in results same as on public terminal. No juvenile, mental, expunged, dismissed, or suspended imposition of sentence records released. Fee to fax out file $2.00 each plus $1.00 per page. Court makes copy: $2.00 per doc. Self serve copy: $.50 per page. Certification fee: $2.00 per document. Payee: Randy L Cowin. Personal checks accepted. Prepayment required. Mail requests: SASE required.

Associate Circuit Division PO Box 39, Centerville, MO 63633; 573-648-2494 X31; probate phone: x35; criminal fax: 573-648-2503; civil fax: same; 8AM-4PM. ***Misdemeanor, Civil Actions under $45,000, Eviction, Small Claims, Probate.***
www.courts.mo.gov/page.asp?id=1671
Probate fax is same as main fax number.
Civil Records: Access: Phone, mail, in person, online. Both court and visitors may perform in person searches. No search fee. Required to search: name, years to search. Civil cases indexed by defendant, plaintiff; index on cards and files (probate in books); on computer back to 2000. Mail turnaround time 2 days. Civil PAT goes back to 2001. Online case lookup at https://www.courts.mo.gov/casenet/base/welcome.do. Online records go back to 4/9/2001.
Criminal Records: Access: In person, online. Both court and visitors may perform in person searches. No search fee. Required to search: name, years to search. Criminal records indexed on cards and files back to early 1970's; on computer back to 2000. Criminal PAT goes back to same as civil. Online access to criminal records same as civil, above and show year of birth only. Court's public terminal may show add'l, often older data.
General Information: Online identifiers in results same as on public terminal. No juvenile, mental, expunged, dismissed, or suspended imposition of sentence records released. Will fax documents. Court makes copy: $1.00 per page. Certification fee: $2.00. Payee: Circuit Court Division III. Personal checks accepted; credit cards are not. Prepayment required. SASE not required.

Ripley County

Consolidated Circuit Court 100 Courthouse Sq, Doniphan, MO 63935; 573-996-2818, 573-996-2013; probate phone: 573-996-2013; fax: 573-996-5014; 7:30AM-4PM. ***Felony, Misdemeanor, Civil, Eviction, Small Claims, Probate.***
www.courts.mo.gov/page.asp?id=1651
This court consolidated on 12/1/2004. 2nd fax number is 573-996-5014. Probate is a separate index at this same address.
Civil Records: Access: In person, online. Visitors must perform in person searches themselves. Required to search: name, years to search. Civil cases indexed by defendant, plaintiff, on cards and books since 1976, archived since 1850s. Civil PAT goes back to 1993. PAT results show middle initial, DOB. Terminal results also show SSNs. Case lookup at https://www.courts.mo.gov/casenet/base/welcome.do. Online records go back to 9/26/05.
Criminal Records: Access: In person, online. Visitors must perform in person searches themselves. Required to search: name, years to search, DOB. Criminal records on cards and books since 1976, archived since 1850s. Criminal PAT goes back to 2003. PAT results show middle initial, DOB. Terminal results include SSN. Online access to criminal records same as civil, above and show year of birth only. Court's public terminal may show add'l, often older data.
General Information: Online identifiers in results same as on public terminal. No juvenile, mental, expunged, dismissed, or suspended imposition of sentence records released. Will not fax documents. Court makes copy: $.25 per page, self serve same. Certification fee: $2.00 if done by in-person searcher. Cert fee included in search fee. Payee: Circuit Clerk. Personal checks accepted; credit cards are not. Prepayment required.

Saline County

Circuit Court PO Box 597, 101 E Arrow St #205, Marshall, MO 65340; 660-886-2300; fax: 660-831-5360; 8AM-4:30PM. ***Felony, Civil Actions over $25,000.***
www.courts.mo.gov/page.asp?id=1607
Civil Records: Access: Mail, in person, online. Visitors must perform in person searches themselves. No search fee. Required to search: name, years to search. Civil cases indexed by defendant, plaintiff; index on cards since 1974, prior on books since 1820. Civil PAT goes back to 1985. Search free on state online court record system at www.courts.mo.gov/casenet/cases/nameSearch.do. Online records go back to 4/2002.
Criminal Records: Access: In person, online. Visitors must perform in person searches themselves. Required to search: name, years to search. Criminal records indexed on cards since 1974, prior on books since 1820. Criminal PAT goes back to same as civil. Online access to criminal same as civil, above. Court's public terminal may show add'l, often older data.
General Information: Online identifiers in results same as on public terminal. No juvenile, mental, expunged, dismissed, or suspended imposition of sentence records released. Will fax documents $1.00 per page. Court makes copy: $.25 per page, self serve same. Certification fee: $1.50 per cert. Payee: Saline County Circuit Court. Personal checks accepted; credit cards are not. Prepayment required.

Associate Circuit Division PO Box 751, Marshall, MO 65340; 660-886-6988; probate phone: 660-886-8808; fax: 660-886-2919; 8AM-4:30PM. ***Misdemeanor, Civil Actions under $25,000, Eviction, Small Claims.***
www.courts.mo.gov/page.asp?id=1607
Civil Records: Access: Phone, mail, in person, online. Only the court performs in person searches; visitors may not. No search fee. Required to search: name, years to search. Civil cases indexed by defendant, plaintiff; index on cards since 1979, prior on books. Mail turnaround time 1-2 days. Case lookup at https://www.courts.mo.gov/casenet/base/welcome.do. Online records go back to 4/1/2002.
Criminal Records: Access: Phone, mail, in person, online. Only the court performs in person searches; visitors may not. No search fee. Required to search: name, years to search. Criminal records on computer since 1993, prior on cards and books. Mail turnaround time 1-2 days. Online access to criminal same as civil, above. Court's public terminal may show add'l, often older data.
General Information: Online identifiers in results same as on public terminal. No juvenile, mental, expunged, dismissed, or suspended imposition of sentence records released. Will fax documents, no fax

fee. Court makes copy for no fee.No certification fee. Mail requests: SASE required.

Schuyler County

Circuit Court PO Box 186, Lancaster, MO 63548; 660-457-3784; fax: 660-457-3016; 8AM-4PM. ***Felony, Civil Actions over $25,000.***
www.courts.mo.gov/page.asp?id=1521
Misdemeanor and probate phone is 660-457-3755.
Civil Records: Access: Mail, in person, online. Both court and visitors may perform in person searches. Search fee: $14.00 per name. Required to search: name, years to search. Civil cases indexed by defendant, plaintiff; index on cards & books. Mail turnaround time 1-2 days. Civil PAT goes back to 9/19/01. Case lookup at https://www.courts.mo.gov/casenet/base/welcome.do. Online records go back to 9/19/01.
Criminal Records: Access: Mail, in person, online. Both court and visitors may perform in person searches. Search fee: $14.00 per name. Required to search: name, years to search. Criminal records indexed on cards & books. Note: Phone request callers are referred to the MO Highway Patrol. Mail turnaround time 1-2 days. Criminal PAT goes back to same as civil. Online access to criminal same as civil, above. Court's public terminal may show add'l, often older data.
General Information: Online identifiers in results same as on public terminal. No juvenile, mental, expunged, dismissed, or suspended imposition of sentence records released. Will fax documents $2.00 plus $1.00 per page. Court makes copy: $1.00 per page, self serve same. Certification fee: $1.00. Payee: Schuyler County Circuit Clerk. Personal checks accepted; credit cards are not. Prepayment required. Mail requests: SASE required.

Associate Circuit Division Box 158, Lancaster, MO 63548; 660-457-3755; fax: 660-457-3016; 8AM-4PM. ***Misdemeanor, Civil Actions under $25,000, Eviction, Small Claims, Probate.***
www.courts.mo.gov/page.asp?id=1521
Civil Records: Access: Mail, fax, in person, online. Both court and visitors may perform in person searches. Search fee: $5.00 per name. Required to search: name, years to search. Civil cases indexed by defendant, plaintiff; index on cards since 1976; computerized records go back to 1992. Mail turnaround time 4 days. Civil PAT goes back to 9/19/2001. Online case lookup at https://www.courts.mo.gov/casenet/base/welcome.do. Online records go back to 09/19/01.
Criminal Records: Access: Mail, fax, in person, online. Both court and visitors may perform in person searches. Search fee: $5.00 per name. Required to search: name, years to search, SSN, DOB. Criminal records on computer since 5/92, prior on index cards. Mail turnaround time 4 days. Criminal PAT goes back to same as civil. Online access to criminal same as civil, above. Court's public terminal may show add'l, often older data.
General Information: Online identifiers in results same as on public terminal. No juvenile, mental, expunged, dismissed, or suspended imposition of sentence records released. Will fax documents $1.00 per page. Court makes copy: $1.00 per page. Self serve copy: $.25 per page. Certification fee: $1.50. Payee: Associate Circuit Court. Business checks accepted. Prepayment required. Mail requests: SASE required.

Scotland County

Consolidated Circuit Court Courthouse, Rm 106, 117 S Market, Memphis, MO 63555; 660-465-2404, 660-465-8605; probate phone: 660-465-2404; fax: 660-465-8673; 8AM-4PM. ***Felony, Misdemeanor, Civil, Eviction, Small Claims, Probate.***
www.courts.mo.gov/page.asp?id=1527
Circuit Ct consolidated with Associate Ct 1/2007.
Civil Records: Access: Mail, fax, in person, online. Both court and visitors may perform in person searches. No search fee. Required to search: name, years to search. Civil cases indexed by defendant, plaintiff, on computer since 1993, prior civil back to 1947 on cards and books to 1841, probate back to 1841. Mail turnaround time 2-7 days. Civil PAT goes back to 2001. PAT civil results show middle initial. Public terminal located in main Circuit Court Clerk office. Case lookup at https://www.courts.mo.gov/casenet/base/welcome.do. Online records go back to 09/19/01.
Criminal Records: Access: Mail, fax, in person, online. Both court and visitors may perform in person searches. No search fee. Required to search: name, years to search. Criminal records on computer since 1993, prior on cards and books to 1847. Mail turnaround time ASAP. Criminal PAT goes back to same as civil. PAT results show middle initial, DOB. Public terminal located in main Circuit Court Clerk office. Online access to criminal same as civil, above. Court's public terminal may show add'l, often older data.
General Information: Online identifiers in results same as on public terminal. No juvenile, mental, expunged, dismissed, or suspended imposition of sentence records released. Fee to fax out file $1.00 per page, prepaid. Court makes copy: $.25 per page, self serve same. Certification fee: $1.50 plus $.25 per page; $1.00 per cert for Probate page. Payee: Scotland County Circuit Clerk. Personal checks accepted; credit cards are not. Prepayment required. Mail requests: SASE required.

Scott County

Consolidated Circuit Court PO Box 587, 131 S Winchester, Benton, MO 63736; 573-545-3596; criminal phone: 573-545-3576; civil phone: 573-545-3596- Assoc Ct; probate phone: 573-545-3511; criminal fax: 573-545-3597; civil fax: 573-545-4231- Assoc fax; 8AM-N, 1-5PM. ***Felony, Misdemeanor, Civil, Eviction, Small Claims, Probate.***
www.courts.mo.gov/page.asp?id=1644
The Associate Circuit and the Circuit Court were consolidated 1/2006. Generally, the staff of the Associate Court became the new Criminal Division; and Circuit Court became the Civil Division. Probate fax- 573-545-3685.
Civil Records: Access: In person, online. Visitors must perform in person searches themselves. Required to search: name, years to search. Civil cases indexed by defendant, plaintiff, on computer back to 1980, prior on index cards and books. Civil PAT goes back to 1980. PAT results show name only. Access to civil records is free at https://www.courts.mo.gov/casenet/base/welcome.do. Online records go back to 6/15/2001.
Criminal Records: Access: In person, online. Visitors must perform in person searches themselves. Required to search: name, years to search, DOB. Criminal records on computer since 1980, prior on index cards and books. Criminal PAT goes back to 1980. PAT results show middle initial, DOB. Access to criminal records is free at https://www.courts.mo.gov/casenet/base/welcome.do. Online records go back to 6/15/2001. Court's public terminal may show add'l, often older data.
General Information: Online identifiers in results same as on public terminal. No juvenile, mental, expunged, dismissed, or suspended imposition of sentence records released. Will fax out documents but only if small number of pages. Court makes copy: $1.00 first page, $.25 each add'l (Probate- $.50 each add'l). Certification fee: $3.00 per doc. Payee: Clerk of Court. Personal checks accepted, credit cards may are not. Prepayment required.

Shannon County

Consolidated Circuit Court PO Box 148, Courthouse, South Side Entrance, Eminence, MO 65466; 573-226-3315; fax: 573-226-5321; 8AM-4:30PM. ***Felony, Misdemeanor, Civil, Eviction, Small Claims, Probate.***
www.courts.mo.gov/page.asp?id=1655
The Associate Division consolidated with this court on 08/01/2005.
Civil Records: Access: Mail, in person, online. Both court and visitors may perform in person searches. No search fee. Required to search: name, years to search. Civil cases indexed by defendant, plaintiff; index on cards and books. Record index on computer back to 1980. Note: Also, visitors may perform in person probate records searches themselves. Mail turnaround time 1 week. Civil PAT goes back to 4/2000. Online case lookup at https://www.courts.mo.gov/casenet/base/welcome.do. Online records go back to 1992.
Criminal Records: Access: Mail, in person, online. Both court and visitors may perform in person searches. No search fee. Required to search: name, years to search, offense. Criminal records indexed on cards and books. Record index on computer back to 1980. Mail turnaround time 1 week. Criminal PAT goes back to same as civil. Online access to criminal records same as civil, above and show year of birth only. Court's public terminal may show add'l, often older data.
General Information: Online identifiers in results same as on public terminal. No juvenile, mental, expunged, dismissed, or suspended imposition of sentence records released. Fee to fax out file $2.00 per page. Court makes copy: $.25 per page. Certification fee: $2.00 per cert. Payee: Shannon County Circuit Clerk. Personal checks accepted; credit cards are not. Prepayment required. Mail requests: SASE required.

Shelby County

Consolidated Circuit Court PO Box 176, Shelbyville, MO 63469; 573-633-2151; criminal fax: 573-633-1004; civil fax: same; 8AM-4:30PM. ***Felony, Misdemeanor, Civil, Eviction, Small Claims, Probate.***
www.courts.mo.gov/page.asp?id=1667
The Associate Division consolidated with this court on 01/01/2006.
Civil Records: Access: Mail, fax, in person, online. Both court and visitors may perform in person searches. No search fee. Required to search: name, years to search. Civil cases indexed by defendant, plaintiff; index on cards since 1975, prior on books since 1835. Mail turnaround time 1 day. Public use terminal available. PAT civil results show middle initial. Online case lookup at https://www.courts.mo.gov/casenet/base/welcome.do. Online records go back to 4/17/2000.
Criminal Records: Access: Mail, fax, in person, online. Both court and visitors may perform in person searches. No search fee. Required to search: name, years to search. Criminal records indexed on cards since 1975, prior on books since 1835. Mail turnaround time 1 day. Public use terminal available. PAT criminal results show middle initial. Online access to criminal records same as civil, above and show year of birth only. Court's public terminal may show add'l, often older data.
General Information: Online identifiers in results same as on public terminal. No juvenile, mental, expunged, dismissed, or suspended imposition of sentence records released. Fee to fax out file $3.00 each. Court makes copy: $.25 per page. Self serve copy: $.10 per page. Certification fee: $1.50 per cert. Payee: Shelby County Circuit Clerk. Personal checks accepted; credit cards are not. Prepayment required. Mail requests: SASE required.

St. Charles County

Consolidated Circuit Court 300 N 2nd St, St. Charles, MO 63301; 636-949-7900 x3098; criminal phone: 636-949-7380; probate phone: 636-949-3086; fax: 636-949-7390; 8:30AM-5PM. ***Felony, Misdemeanor, Civil, Eviction, Small Claims, Probate.***
www.courts.mo.gov/page.asp?id=1588
The Circuit Court and Associate Division consolidated as of 01/03. Traffic Court is reached at 636-949-7385. Probate fax- 636-949-3070
Civil Records: Access: Mail, in person, online. Both court and visitors may perform in person searches. No search fee. Required to search: name, years to search. Civil cases indexed by defendant, plaintiff; index on cards since 1971, prior on books; judgment records (A-M) on computer since 1987. Mail turnaround time 1 day. Civil PAT goes back to 1994. PAT results show middle initial, DOB. Case lookup at https://www.courts.mo.gov/casenet/base/welcome.do. Online civil records form 01/1994 forward. Probate data from 10/10/2000 forward. Municipal court cases now on CaseNet.

Criminal Records: Access: In person, online. Visitors must perform in person searches themselves. Required to search: name, years to search; also helpful: DOB. Criminal records indexed on cards since 1971, prior on books; judgment records (A-M) on computer since 1987. Criminal PAT goes back to 1992. PAT results show middle initial, DOB. Online access to criminal records is the same as civil. Online criminal records back to 10/1992. Misdemeanor and traffic back to 01/1996. Municipal court cases now on CaseNet. Court's public terminal may show add'l, often older data.
General Information: Online identifiers in results same as on public terminal. No juvenile, mental, expunged, dismissed, or suspended imposition of sentence records released. Will fax documents. Court makes copy: $.10 per page. Certification fee: $1.50. Payee: St. Charles Circuit Clerk. No personal checks or credit cards accepted. Prepayment required. Mail requests: SASE required for civil.

St. Clair County

Consolidated Circuit Court PO Box 493, Osceola, MO 64776; 417-646-2226; fax: 417-646-2401; 8AM-4:30PM. ***Felony, Misdemeanor, Civil, Eviction, Small Claims, Probate.***
http://tacnet.missouri.org/~court27/
Civil Records: Access: Mail, in person, online. Both court and visitors may perform in person searches. Search fee: $2.00 per name. Required to search: name, years to search. Civil cases indexed by defendant, plaintiff. Civil judgment records on computer since 1991, on index cards since 1980, prior records on index books. Mail turnaround time 1-2 days. Civil PAT goes back to 8/2003; Casenet from 2003. Online case lookup at https://www.courts.mo.gov/casenet/base/welcome.do. Index goes back to 8/18/2003.
Criminal Records: Access: Mail, in person, online. Both court and visitors may perform in person searches. Search fee: $2.00 per name. Required to search: name, years to search, DOB. Criminal records on computer since 1991, on index cards since 1980, prior records on index books. Mail turnaround time 1-2 days. Criminal PAT goes back to same as civil. Online access to criminal records same as civil, above and show year of birth only. Court's public terminal may show add'l, often older data.
General Information: Online identifiers in results same as on public terminal. No juvenile, mental, expunged, dismissed, or suspended imposition of sentence records released. Will fax documents. Court makes copy: $1.00 per page. Certification fee: $.50 per document. Payee: St Clair County Circuit Clerk. Personal checks accepted; credit cards are not. Prepayment required. Mail requests: SASE required.

St. Francois County

Circuit Court - Division I & II 1 N Washington, Rm 303, Farmington, MO 63640; 573-756-4551; fax: 573-756-3733; 8AM-5PM. ***Felony, Civil Actions over $25,000.***
www.courts.mo.gov/page.asp?id=1626
Civil Records: Access: Fax, mail, in person, online. Both court and visitors may perform in person searches. No search fee. Required to search: name, years to search. Civil cases indexed by defendant, plaintiff, on computer since 6/90, on microfiche since 1970, archived since 1821. Mail turnaround time 1-2 weeks. Civil PAT goes back to 6/1990. Case lookup at https://www.courts.mo.gov/casenet/base/welcome.do. Online records go back to 11/01/00.
Criminal Records: Access: In person, online. Both court and visitors may perform in person searches. No search fee. Required to search: name, years to search; also helpful: DOB, SSN. Criminal records on computer since 3/1/93. Criminal PAT goes back to 3/1993. Online access to criminal records same as civil, above and show year of birth only. Court's public terminal may show add'l, often older data.
General Information: Online identifiers in results same as on public terminal. No juvenile, mental, expunged, dismissed, or suspended imposition of sentence records released. Will not fax documents. Court makes copy: $.25 per page, self serve same. Attorney copy fee is $1.00 per page. Certification fee: $1.50 per document. Payee: Clerk of Circuit Court. Business checks accepted. No credit cards accepted. Prepayment required. Mail requests: SASE required for civil.

Associate Circuit Division County Courthouse, 3rd Fl, 1 N Washington, Rm 301, Farmington, MO 63640; 573-756-5755; civil phone: same; probate phone: x42; criminal fax: 573-756-8173; civil fax: same; 8AM-5PM. ***Misdemeanor, Civil Actions under $25,000, Small Claims, Probate.***
www.courts.mo.gov/page.asp?id=1626
Probate in a separate office at this same address.
Civil Records: Access: In person, online. Only the court performs in person searches; visitors may not. Required to search: name, years to search. Civil cases indexed by defendant, plaintiff; index on cards since 1979; on computer back to 1990. Note: This court has been known to perform civil lookups over the phone. Case lookup at https://www.courts.mo.gov/casenet/base/welcome.do. Online records go back to 1992.
Criminal Records: Access: In person, online. Only the court performs in person searches; visitors may not. Required to search: name, years to search. Criminal records computerized from 1990; other records go back to 1980. Online access to criminal same as civil, above, criminal records go back to 1992. Court's public terminal may show add'l, often older data.
General Information: Online identifiers in results same as on public terminal. No juvenile, mental, expunged, dismissed, or suspended imposition of sentence records released. Will not fax documents. Court makes copy: $.30 per page. No certification fee. Payee: Circuit Court Division III. Business checks accepted. No credit cards accepted. Prepayment required.

St. Louis County

Circuit Court of St. Louis County - Civil 7900 Carondelet, Clayton, MO 63105-1766; 314-615-8029; fax: 314-615-8739; 8AM-5PM. ***Civil Actions over $25,000.***
www.stlouisco.com/circuitcourt
Records Rm phone- 314-615-8034. When faxing a search request, fax to "Attn Certified Copies."
Civil Records: Access: Phone, fax, mail, in person, online. Both court and visitors may perform in person searches. No search fee. Required to search: name, years to search; also helpful: address. Civil cases indexed by defendant, plaintiff, on computer back to 1978, prior on index cards. Case files archived for 25 years. Mail turnaround time up to 3 days. Civil PAT goes back to 1978. PAT civil results show middle initial. Access court records free at https://www.courts.mo.gov/casenet/base/welcome.do - records go back to 10/1/2007. Search probate index free at www.stlouisco.com/CourtCaseSearch/frmProbateSearch.aspx?TabId=pr.
General Information: Online identifiers in results same as on public terminal. No juvenile, paternity, mental, expunged, dismissed, or suspended imposition of sentence records released. Will not fax documents. Court makes copy: $.30 per page. Certification fee: $1.50 per cert. Payee: Circuit Clerk. Personal checks accepted. Credit cards accepted in person only. Prepayment required. SASE not required.

Associate Circuit - Civil Division 7900 Carondolet, Clayton, MO 63105; 314-615-8090; probate phone: 314-615-2629; fax: 314-615-2689; 8AM-5PM. ***Civil Actions under $25,000, Eviction, Small Claims, Probate.***
www.stlouisco.com/circuitcourt
Small claims court phone- 314-615-2658. Probate office is on 5th Fl.
Civil Records: Access: Phone, mail, in person, online. Both court and visitors may perform in person searches. No search fee. Required to search: name, years to search. Civil cases indexed by defendant, plaintiff, on computer since 1986, prior on cards. Mail turnaround time 1 week. Public use terminal has civil records back to 1986. PAT results show name only. Access Court records back to 7/6/2004 free on the state court system at https://www.courts.mo.gov/casenet/base/welcome.do. Search probate index up to 12/10/2004 free at www.stlouisco.com/CourtCaseSearch/frmProbateSearch.aspx?TabId=pr.
General Information: Online identifiers in results same as on public terminal. No juvenile, mental, expunged, dismissed, paternity, suspended imposition of sentence records released. Will not fax documents. Court makes copy: $.30 per page. Self serve copy: $.10 per page. Certification fee: $1.50 per cert. Payee: Circuit Clerk-Civil Division. Personal checks accepted. Major credit cards accepted in person only, not over the phone. Prepayment required. Mail requests: SASE required.

Circuit Court of St. Louis County - Criminal 7900 Carondelet Av, Clayton, MO 63105; 314-615-2675; fax: 314-615-2689; 8AM-5PM. ***Felony, Misdemeanor, Traffic.***
www.stlouisco.com/circuitcourt
Criminal Records: Access: Phone, mail, fax, in person, online. Both court and visitors may perform in person searches. No search fee. Required to search: name, years to search, DOB, offense, date of offense. Criminal records computerized from 1986, prior on index cards. Permanent records on microfiche since 1978, earlier in books. Case files archived for. Mail turnaround time varies. Public use terminal has crim records back to 1986. PAT criminal results show middle initial. Participates in the free state online court record system at www.courts.mo.gov/casenet/base/welcome.do. Online records go back to 6/4/2007.
General Information: Online identifiers in results same as on public terminal. No juvenile, mental, expunged, dismissed, or suspended imposition of sentence records released. Will not fax documents. Court makes copy: $.30 per page. Certification fee: $1.50. Payee: Circuit Clerk. Personal checks and major credit cards accepted. Prepayment required. Mail requests: SASE required.

St. Louis City

Circuit Courts - Civil 10 N Tucker Blvd, Civil Courts Bldg, St Louis, MO 63101; 314-622-4405; probate phone: 314-622-4301; fax: 314-622-4537; 8AM-5PM. ***Civil, Eviction, Small Claims, Probate.***
www.courts.mo.gov/hosted/circuit22/
Small Claims telephone number is 314-622-3788. Probate is located on the 10th Fl. Circuit Clerk's website is www.stlcitycircuitcourt.com/.
Civil Records: Access: Mail, in person, online. Both court and visitors may perform in person searches. No search fee. Required to search: name, years to search. Civil cases indexed by defendant, plaintiff, on computer since 1/80, on index cards since early 1800s. Mail turnaround time usually 1 week. Public use terminal has civil records back to 1982. Online access to civil records back to 10/1/2007 is free at http://https://www.courts.mo.gov/casenet/base/welcome.do. Remote access is also through MoBar Net and is open only to attorneys. Call 314-535-1950 for information. Also, probate records are free online at www.courts.mo.gov/casenet/base/welcome.do. Online probate records go back to 1/1990.
General Information: Online identifiers in results same as on public terminal. No sealed or confidential records released. Will not fax documents. Court makes copy: $.30 per page. Certification fee: $3.50 for 1st page; $.50 each add'l. Payee: City of St. Louis Circuit Clerk. Only cashiers checks and money orders accepted. No credit cards accepted. Prepayment required. Mail requests: SASE required.

City of St Louis Circuit Court - Criminal 1114 Market St, 2nd Fl, Carnahan Courthouse, Attn: Case Records/File Section, St Louis, MO 63101; 314-622-4773 (gen info); criminal phone: 314-622-4485 or 4486 (felony), 314-622-4548 (misd.); fax: 314-622-4537; 8AM-5PM. ***Felony, Misdemeanor.***
www.courts.mo.gov/hosted/circuit22/
The Court Clerk's Admin. Office and Civil Div. is located 10 N Tucker, www.stlcitycircuitcourt.com/.
Criminal Records: Access: In person, mail, fax, online. Both court and visitors may perform in person searches. No search fee. Required to search: name, years to search, DOB, signed release; also

helpful: address, SSN. Criminal records on computer since 1990 for misdemeanor; since 1992 for felony. Note: Courts criminal case records/copy section telephone is 714-613-4156 or 4408. Fax is given above. Public use terminal has crim records back to 1980. Public access terminal on the 3rd Fl has limited case information. Participates in the free state online court record system at www.courts.mo.gov/casenet/base/welcome.do.
General Information: Online identifiers in results same as on public terminal. No juvenile, mental, expunged, dismissed, or suspended imposition of sentence records released. Will fax documents to local or toll-free number. Court makes copy: $.30 per page. Certification fee: $3.50. Payee: City of St. Louis Circuit Clerk. Business checks accepted. No credit cards accepted. Prepayment required. Mail requests: SASE required.

Ste. Genevieve County

Circuit Court 55 S 3rd, Rm 23, Ste Genevieve, MO 63670; 573-883-2705; fax: 573-883-9351; 8AM-5PM. ***Felony, Civil Actions over $25,000.***
www.courts.mo.gov/page.asp?id=1625
Civil Records: Access: In person, online. Visitors must perform in person searches themselves. Required to search: name, years to search. Civil cases indexed by defendant, plaintiff, on books since early 1800s, recent civil records (1995) computerized. Civil PAT goes back to 1993. PAT civil results show middle initial. Online case lookup at https://www.courts.mo.gov/casenet/base/welcome.do. Online records go back to 11/06/00.
Criminal Records: Access: In person, online. Visitors must perform in person searches themselves. Required to search: name, years to search. Criminal Record indexes on books, not computerized. Criminal PAT goes back to same as civil. PAT criminal results show middle initial. Online access to criminal records same as civil, above and show year of birth only. Court's public terminal may show add'l, often older data.
General Information: Online identifiers in results same as on public terminal. No juvenile, mental, expunged, paternity, dismissed, or suspended imposition of sentence records released. Will fax documents to local or toll-free number. Court makes copy: $1.00 per page. Self serve copy: $.25 per page. Certification fee: $1.50 per cert. Payee: St Genevieve County Circuit Clerk. Business checks accepted. No credit cards accepted. Prepayment required. Mail requests: SASE required for mail return of any copies.

Associate Circuit Division 55 S 3rd St, Ste Genevieve, MO 63670; 573-883-2265; fax: 573-883-9351; 8AM-5PM. ***Misdemeanor, Civil Actions under $45,000, Eviction, Small Claims, Probate.***
www.courts.mo.gov/page.asp?id=1625
The court will not make copies of documents for the public.
Civil Records: Access: In person, online. Visitors must perform in person searches themselves. Required to search: name, years to search. Civil cases indexed by defendant, plaintiff, on books. Civil PAT goes back to 1997. PAT results show middle initial, DOB. Online case lookup at https://www.courts.mo.gov/casenet/base/welcome.do. Online records go back to 11/06/00.
Criminal Records: Access: In person, online. Visitors must perform in person searches themselves. Required to search: name, years to search. Criminal docket on books. Criminal PAT goes back to 1994. PAT results show middle initial, DOB. Online access to criminal records same as civil, above and show year of birth only. Court's public terminal may show add'l, often older data.
General Information: Online identifiers in results same as on public terminal. No juvenile, mental, expunged, dismissed, or suspended imposition of sentence records released. Will fax documents. Court makes copy: n/a. Self serve copy: $.25 per page. Certification fee: $2.50. Payee: Circuit Court Div III. Only cashiers checks and money orders accepted. No credit cards accepted.

Stoddard County

Consolidated Circuit Court PO Box 30, Bloomfield, MO 63825; 573-568-4640; probate phone: x3; fax: 573-568-2271; 8AM-4:30PM. ***Felony, Misdemeanor, Civil Actions, Eviction, Small Claims, Probate.***
www.courts.mo.gov/page.asp?id=1648
Civil, criminal, and probate divisions are combined into one consolidated unit, 2008.
Civil Records: Access: Fax, mail, in person, online. Both court and visitors may perform in person searches. No search fee. Required to search: name, years to search. Civil cases indexed by defendant, plaintiff, on computer since 1991, prior on cards and books. Mail turnaround time 1-3 days. Civil PAT goes back to 1991. PAT results show middle initial, DOB. Access to civil records is free at https://www.courts.mo.gov/casenet/base/welcome.do. Online records go back to 7/1/2001.
Criminal Records: Access: Mail, in person, online. Both court and visitors may perform in person searches. No search fee. Required to search: name, years to search; also helpful: DOB, SSN. Criminal records on computer since 1991, prior on cards and books. Mail turnaround time 1-3 days. Criminal PAT goes back to 1991. PAT results show middle initial, DOB. Online access to criminal records same as civil, above and show year of birth only. Court's public terminal may show add'l, often older data.
General Information: Online identifiers in results same as on public terminal. No juvenile, mental, expunged, dismissed, or suspended imposition of sentence records released. Will fax documents to local or toll-free number. Court makes copy: $.10 per page. Certification fee: $1.50. Payee: Stoddard County Circuit Clerk. Personal checks accepted; credit cards are not. Prepayment required. Mail requests: SASE required.

Stone County

Consolidated Circuit Court PO Box 18, 110 S Maple, Judicial Ctr, 2nd Fl, Galena, MO 65656; 417-357-6114; fax: 417-357-6163; 7:30AM-N; 12:30PM-4:00PM. ***Felony, Misdemeanor, Civil, Eviction, Small Claims, Probate.***
www.courts.mo.gov/page.asp?id=1662
Consolidated with Divisions II and III in 2007.
Civil Records: Access: Phone, fax, mail, in person, online. Both court and visitors may perform in person searches. No search fee. Required to search: name, years to search. Civil cases indexed by defendant, plaintiff, on cards and books, archived since 1852; computerized records since 1992. Mail turnaround time 1 week. Civil PAT goes back to 1992. Case lookup at https://www.courts.mo.gov/casenet/base/welcome.do. Online records go back to 7/11/2005 and includes probate.
Criminal Records: Access: Phone, fax, mail, in person, online. Both court and visitors may perform in person searches. No search fee. Required to search: name, years to search; also helpful: DOB, SSN. Criminal records on cards and books, archived since 1852; computerized records since 1992. Mail turnaround time 1 week. Criminal PAT goes back to same as civil. Online access to criminal records same as civil, above and show year of birth only. Court's public terminal may show add'l, often older data.
General Information: Online identifiers in results same as on public terminal. No juvenile, mental, expunged, dismissed, or suspended imposition of sentence records released. Will not fax out documents. Court makes copy: $.25 per page. Certification fee: $1.50 per cert. Payee: Circuit Court. No personal checks or credit cards accepted. Prepayment required. Mail requests: SASE required.

Sullivan County

Consolidated Circuit Court 109 N Main, Courthouse, Milan, MO 63556-1358; 660-265-4717; criminal phone: 660-265-3303; civil phone: 660-265-4717; probate phone: 660-265-3303; fax: 660-265-5071; 9:00AM-4:30PM. ***Felony, Misdemeanor, Civil, Eviction, Small Claims, Probate.***
www.courts.mo.gov/page.asp?id=1576
Civil Records: Access: In person, online. Visitors must perform in person searches themselves. Required to search: name, years to search. Civil cases indexed by defendant, plaintiff; index on cards since 1979, prior on books. Civil PAT goes back to 2002. Participates in the statewide Casenet court record system at https://www.courts.mo.gov/casenet/base/welcome.do. Online records go back to 5/13/2002.
Criminal Records: Access: In person, online. Visitors must perform in person searches themselves. Required to search: name, years to search; also helpful: DOB, SSN. Criminal records indexed on cards since 1979, prior on books. Criminal PAT goes back to same as civil. PAT results show middle initial, DOB. Online access to criminal records same as civil, above and show year of birth only. Court's public terminal may show add'l, often older data.
General Information: Online identifiers in results same as on public terminal. No juvenile, mental, expunged, dismissed, or suspended imposition of sentence records released. Will not fax documents. Court makes copy: $1.00 per page. Self serve copy: $.25 per page. Certification fee: $1.50. Payee: Consolidated Circuit Court of Sullivan County. Personal checks accepted; credit cards are not. Prepayment required.

Taney County

Circuit Court PO Box 335, Forsyth, MO 65653; 417-546-7230; fax: 417-546-6133; 8AM-5PM. ***Felony, Civil Actions over $25.000, Probate.***
www.courts.mo.gov/page.asp?id=1658
The Associate Division is now consolidated with this court.
Civil Records: Access: Mail, in person, online. Visitors must perform in person searches themselves. Search fee: $4.00 per name. Required to search: name, years to search. Civil cases indexed by defendant, plaintiff, on computer since 1/95, prior on index cards and books since 1885. Civil PAT goes back to 1995. Participates in state court record system at https://www.courts.mo.gov/casenet/base/welcome.do. Online records include probate court.
Criminal Records: Access: In person, online. Visitors must perform in person searches themselves. Required to search: name, years to search, DOB. Criminal records on computer since 1/95, prior on index cards and books since 1885. Note: For information on criminal records call MO State Highway Patrol at 573-526-6153. Criminal PAT goes back to same as civil. Online access to criminal records same as civil, above and show year of birth only. Court's public terminal may show add'l, often older data.
General Information: Online identifiers in results same as on public terminal. No juvenile, mental, expunged, dismissed, or suspended imposition of sentence records released. Will fax documents. Court makes copy: $.25 per page. Certification fee: $1.50 per cert. Payee: Circuit Clerk. Personal checks accepted; credit cards are not. Prepayment required. Mail requests: SASE required for mail return of any copies.

Associate Circuit Court PO Box 129, 110 W Elm, Forsyth, MO 65653; criminal phone: 417-546-7212; civil phone: 417-546-7206; criminal fax: 417-546-4513; civil fax: 417-546-5821; 8AM-5PM. ***Misdemeanors, Civil Actions under $25,000, Eviction, Small Claims.***
www.courts.mo.gov/page.asp?id=1658
Civil Division mailing address is PO Box 1030.
Civil Records: Access: Mail, in person, online. Both court and visitors may perform in person searches. Search fee: $4.00 per name. Required to search: name, years to search. Civil cases indexed by defendant, plaintiff, on computer since 1984, prior on cards and books. Mail turnaround time 2 days, more if busy. Public use terminal has civil records. Public terminal located in Circuit Ct office. Participates in the statewide MO Casenet record system at https://www.courts.mo.gov/casenet/base/welcome.do. Online records go back to 6/2003.
Criminal Records: Access: Mail, In person, online. No search fee. Required to search: Name, years to

search, DOB. Computerized records go back to about 1984. Mail turnaround time 2 days, more if busy. Criminal access is same as civil, see above. Court's public terminal may show add'l, often older data.
General Information: Online identifiers in results same as on public terminal. No juvenile, mental, expunged, dismissed, or suspended imposition of sentence records released. Will fax documents to local or toll-free number if less than 5 pages. Court makes copy: $.25 per page, self serve same. Certification fee: $1.50. Payee: Associate Circuit Court. Personal checks accepted; credit cards are not. Prepayment required. Mail requests: SASE required.

Texas County

Circuit Court PO Box 287, 210 N Grand, Houston, MO 65483; 417-967-3742; fax: 417-967-4220; 8:30-N; 12:30PM-4:30PM. ***Felony, Civil Actions over $25,000.***
www.courts.mo.gov/page.asp?id=4757
Civil Records: Access: In person, online. Visitors must perform in person searches themselves. Required to search: name, years to search. Civil cases indexed by defendant, plaintiff; index on docket books since 1900s. Participates in state online court record system at https://www.courts.mo.gov/casenet/base/welcome.do. Online records go back to 1/22/2007.
Criminal Records: Access: In person, online. Visitors must perform in person searches themselves. Required to search: name, years to search. Criminal records indexed in books since 1900s. Participates in the free state online court record system at www.courts.mo.gov/casenet/base/welcome.do. Records go back to 1/22/2007. Court's public terminal may show add'l, often older data.
General Information: Online identifiers in results same as on public terminal. No juvenile, mental, expunged, dismissed, or suspended imposition of sentence records released. Will not fax documents. Court makes copy: $1.00 per page. Certification fee: $2.00. Payee: Texas County Circuit Clerk. Personal checks accepted; credit cards are not. Prepayment required.

Associate Circuit Division County Courthouse, 210 N Grand, #302, Houston, MO 65483; 417-967-3663; probate phone: 417-967-2100; criminal fax: 417-967-4128; civil fax: same; 8AM-N; 1-5PM. ***Misdemeanor, Civil Actions under $25,000, Eviction, Small Claims, Probate.***
www.courts.mo.gov/page.asp?id=4757
Probate is a separate index at this address. Probate fax is same as main fax number.
Civil Records: Access: Phone, fax, mail, in person, online. Only the court performs in person searches; visitors may not. No search fee. Required to search: name, years to search. Civil cases indexed by defendant, plaintiff; index on cards since 1979, prior on cards and books. Mail turnaround time 7-10 days Civil PAT available. Participates in state online court record system at https://www.courts.mo.gov/casenet/base/welcome.do. Online records go back to 1/22/2007.
Criminal Records: Access: Phone, fax, mail, in person, online. Only the court performs in person searches; visitors may not. No search fee. Required to search: name, years to search, SSN. Criminal records indexed on cards since 1979, prior on cards and books. Note: For information on criminal records call MO State Highway Patrol at 573 526 6153. Mail turnaround time 7-10 days. Criminal PAT available. Participates in the free state online court record system at www.courts.mo.gov/casenet/base/welcome.do. Records go back to 1/22/2007. Court's public terminal may show add'l, often older data.
General Information: Online identifiers in results same as on public terminal. No juvenile, mental, expunged, dismissed, or suspended imposition of sentence records released. Will not fax out documents. Court makes copy: $1.00 per page. Certification fee: $2.50. Payee: Associate Circuit Court. Business checks accepted. No credit cards accepted. Prepayment required. Mail requests: SASE required.

Vernon County

Consolidated Circuit Court Courthouse, Suite 15, 100 W Cherry St, Nevada, MO 64772; 417-448-2525/2550; criminal fax: 417-448-2512; civil fax: same; 8AM-4:30PM. ***Felony, Misdemeanor, Civil, Eviction, Small Claims, Probate.***
www.courts.mo.gov/page.asp?id=1637
Probate fax is same as main fax number.
Civil Records: Access: In person, online, email. Visitors must perform in person searches themselves. No search fee. Required to search: name, years to search. Civil cases indexed by defendant, plaintiff, go back to 1863; on computer back to 2000. Judgments on index cards up until 1992. Civil PAT goes back to 1990. PAT results show middle initial, DOB. Terminal results also show SSNs. Participates in state online court record system at https://www.courts.mo.gov/casenet/base/welcome.do. Online records go back to 9/11/2000. Online records include probate court. Direct email civil search requests to vicki.erwin@courts.mo.gov.
Criminal Records: Access: Mail, in person, online. Visitors must perform in person searches themselves. Search fee: $5.00 per name. Required to search: name, years to search, DOB. Criminal records go back to 1863; on computer back to 1990 for Assoc. Court records, back to 2000 for Circuit Court records. Criminal PAT goes back to 1990. PAT results show middle initial, DOB. Terminal results include SSN. Online access to criminal records same as civil, above and show year of birth only. Online results show middle initial, DOB, SSN. Court's public terminal may show add'l, often older data.
General Information: Online identifiers in results same as on public terminal. No juvenile, mental, expunged, dismissed, or suspended imposition of sentence records released. Will fax documents. Court makes copy: $.20 per page; microfilmed records $1.00 per page. Self serve copy: $.20 per page. Certification fee: $1.50. Payee: Vernon County Circuit Clerk. Personal checks accepted; credit cards are not. Prepayment required. SASE not required.

Warren County

Consolidated Circuit Court 104 W Main, Warrenton, MO 63383; 636-456-3363, 636-456-3375; probate phone: same; fax: 636-456-2422; 8AM-4:30PM. ***Felony, Misdemeanor, Civil, Eviction, Small Claims, Probate.***
www.courts.mo.gov/page.asp?id=1595
The Associated Circuit Court has consolidated with the main Circuit Court. Probate fax is same as main fax number.
Civil Records: Access: Online, in person. Visitors must perform in person searches themselves. Required to search: name, years to search. Civil cases indexed by defendant, plaintiff; index on cards since 1976, prior on books. Public use terminal available, records go back to 1975 Circuit; 5/2003 Assoc. PAT results show middle initial, DOB, SSN. Participates in state online court record system at https://www.courts.mo.gov/casenet/base/welcome.do. Online records go back to 9/20/1999.
Criminal Records: Access: Online, in person. Visitors must perform in person searches themselves. Required to search: name, years to search. Criminal records indexed on cards since 1976, prior on books. Public use terminal available, crim records go back to 1975 Circuit; 5/2003 Assoc. PAT results show middle initial, DOB. Online access to criminal records same as civil, above and show year of birth only. Court's public terminal may show add'l, often older data.
General Information: Online identifiers in results same as on public terminal. No juvenile, mental, expunged, dismissed, or suspended imposition of sentence records released. Will fax documents to local or toll-free number. Court makes copy: $.50 per page. Certification fee: $1.00 per certification. Payee: Warren County Circuit Clerk. Attorney checks accepted. Major credit cards accepted; $4.00 courtesy fee applies for credit or debit cards. Prepayment required.

Washington County

Circuit Court PO Box 216, Potosi, MO 63664; 573-438-6111; fax: 573-438-7900; 8AM-5PM. ***Felony, Civil Actions over $45,000.***
www.courts.mo.gov/page.asp?id=1627
Civil Records: Access: Mail, in person, online. Both court and visitors may perform in person searches. No search fee. Required to search: name, years to search. Civil cases indexed by defendant, plaintiff; index on cards since 1976, prior on books. Mail turnaround time 5-10 days. Civil PAT goes back to 1988. For older records not on the public terminal, there is a card file open to the public to view. Participates in state online court record system at https://www.courts.mo.gov/casenet/base/welcome.do. Online records go back to 11/09/00.
Criminal Records: Access: Mail, in person, online. Both court and visitors may perform in person searches. No search fee. Required to search: name, years to search. Criminal records indexed on cards since 1976, prior on books. Mail turnaround time 5-10 days. Criminal PAT goes back to 11/2000. For older records not on the public terminal, there is a card file open to the public to view. Online access to criminal records same as civil, above and show year of birth only. Court's public terminal may show add'l, often older data.
General Information: Online identifiers in results same as on public terminal. No juvenile, mental, expunged, dismissed, or suspended imposition of sentence records released. Will not fax documents. Court makes copy: $.50 per page. Certification fee: $2.00. Payee: Washington County Circuit Clerk. Personal checks accepted; credit cards are not. Prepayment required. Mail requests: SASE required.

Associate Circuit Division 102 N Missouri St, Potosi, MO 63664; 573-438-6111, 438-3691; criminal fax: 573-438-7900; civil fax: same; 8AM-5PM. ***Misdemeanor, Civil Actions under $45,000, Eviction, Small Claims, Probate.***
www.courts.mo.gov/page.asp?id=1627
Probate is a separate index as this same address. Probate fax is same as main fax number.
Civil Records: Access: mail, in person, online. Only the court performs in person searches; visitors may not. No search fee. Required to search: name, years to search. Civil cases indexed by defendant, plaintiff, computerized since 1996, older records archived. Mail turnaround time 2-3 weeks. Civil PAT goes back to 2000. Participates in the statewide Casenet court record system at https://www.courts.mo.gov/casenet/base/welcome.do. Online records go back to 11/00.
Criminal Records: Access: Mail, in person, online. Only the court performs in person searches; visitors may not. No search fee. Required to search: name, years to search; also helpful: DOB, SSN. Criminal records computerized since 1996, older records archived. Mail turnaround time 2-3 week. Criminal PAT available. Online access to criminal records same as civil, above and show year of birth only. Court's public terminal may show add'l, often older data.
General Information: Online identifiers in results same as on public terminal. No juvenile, mental, expunged, dismissed, or suspended imposition of sentence records released. Will not fax documents. Court makes copy: $.50 per page. Certification fee: $2.50 per cert. Payee: Associate Circuit Clerk. Personal checks accepted; credit cards are not. Prepayment required. Mail requests: SASE required.

Wayne County

Consolidated Circuit Court PO Box 78, 109 Walnut St, Greenville, MO 63944; 573-224-3014; fax: 573-224-3225; 8AM-5PM. ***Felony, Misdemeanor, Civil, Eviction, Small Claims, Probate.*** www.courts.mo.gov/page.asp?id=1672
Divisions were consolidated 10/2005.
Civil Records: Access: Mail, in person, online. Both court and visitors may perform in person searches. No search fee. Required to search: name, years to search. Civil cases indexed by defendant, plaintiff; index on cards since 1978, prior on books. Mail turnaround time 1 week. Civil PAT goes back to 2001. PAT results show name only. Participates in

the statewide Casenet court record system at https://www.courts.mo.gov/casenet/base/welcome.do. Online records go back to 4/9/2001.
Criminal Records: Access: In person, online. Both court and visitors may perform in person searches. No search fee. Required to search: name, years to search; also helpful: DOB. Criminal records indexed on cards since 1978, prior on books. Criminal PAT goes back to 2000. PAT results show middle initial, DOB. Online access to criminal same as civil, above, criminal records go back to 4/9/2001. Court's public terminal may show add'l, often older data.
General Information: Online identifiers in results same as on public terminal. No juvenile, mental, expunged, dismissed, or suspended imposition of sentence records released. Will not fax out documents. Court makes copy: $.50 per page. Certification fee: $2.00 per cert. Payee: Wayne County Circuit Clerk. Personal checks accepted; credit cards are not. Prepayment required. Mail requests: SASE required for civil.

Webster County

Circuit Court - Civil PO Box B, Courthouse, Marshfield, MO 65706; 417-859-2006; fax: 417-859-6265; 8AM-5PM. ***Civil Actions, Eviction, Small Claims, Probate.*** http://home.positech.net/~dcourt/
Civil Records: Access: Fax, mail, in person, online. Both court and visitors may perform in person searches. No search fee. Required to search: name, years to search. Civil cases indexed by defendant, plaintiff, on computer since 1976 (judgment index). Mail turnaround time 5 days Public use terminal has civil records back to 1976, judgments only. PAT results show name only. Access to civil records back to 11/13/2001 is free at https://www.courts.mo.gov/casenet/base/welcome.do.
General Information: Online identifiers in results same as on public terminal. No juvenile, mental, expunged, dismissed, or suspended imposition of sentence records released. Will fax documents $2.00 per page. Court makes copy: $.25 per page, self serve same. Certification fee: $2.00. Payee: Webster County Circuit Clerk. Personal checks accepted; credit cards are not. Prepayment required. Mail requests: SASE required.

Circuit Court - Criminal PO Box B, Courthouse, Marshfield, MO 65706; 417-859-2041; fax: 417-859-6265; 8-5PM. ***Felony, Misdemeanor.*** http://home.positech.net/~dcourt/
Criminal Records: Access: Mail, in person, online. Only the court performs in person searches; visitors may not. No search fee. Required to search: name, years to search; also helpful: DOB, SSN. Criminal records on computer since 1992. Mail turnaround time varies. Public use terminal has crim records back to 1992. Access to criminal records back to 11/13/2001 is free at https://www.courts.mo.gov/casenet/base/welcome.do. Online search results include year of birth only.
General Information: Online identifiers in results same as on public terminal. No juvenile, mental, expunged, dismissed, or suspended imposition of sentence records released. Will not fax documents. Court makes copy: $.35 per page. Certification fee: No certification fee. Payee: Associate Circuit Court. Only cashiers checks and money orders accepted. No credit cards accepted. Prepayment required. Mail requests: SASE required.

Worth County

Circuit Court PO Box 350, 11 W 4th St, Grant City, MO 64456; 660-564-2210; fax: 660-564-3394; 7AM-4:30PM. ***Felony, Civil over $45,000.*** www.courts.mo.gov/page.asp?id=1558
Civil Records: Access: Fax, mail, in person, online. Both court and visitors may perform in person searches. Search fee: $5.00 per name. Required to search: name, years to search. Civil cases indexed by defendant, plaintiff, on computer since 1990, prior on index cards. Mail turnaround time same day. Civil PAT goes back to 1996. Participates in the statewide MO Casenet record system at https://www.courts.mo.gov/casenet/base/welcome.do. Online records go back to 3/20/2006.
Criminal Records: Access: Fax, mail, in person, online. Both court and visitors may perform in person searches. Search fee: $5.00 per name. Required to search: name, years to search. Criminal records on computer since 1990, prior on index cards. Mail turnaround time same day. Criminal PAT goes back to same as civil. Participates in the statewide MO Casenet record system at www.courts.mo.gov/casenet/base/welcome.do. Online records go back to 3/20/2006. Court's public terminal may show add'l, often older data.
General Information: Online identifiers in results same as on public terminal. No juvenile, mental, expunged, dismissed, or suspended imposition of sentence records released. Will fax documents to local or toll-free number. Court makes copy: $.20 per page. Certification fee: $2.50 per cert. Payee: Worth County Circuit Clerk. Personal checks accepted; credit cards are not. Prepayment required. Mail requests: SASE required.

Associate Circuit Division PO Box 350, 11 W 4th St, Grant City, MO 64456; 660-564-2152; fax: 660-564-3394; 9AM-4:30PM. ***Misdemeanor, Civil Actions under $45,000, Eviction, Small Claims, Probate.*** www.courts.mo.gov/page.asp?id=1558
This court is consolidated with the Circuit Ct but records management remains the same as always.
Civil Records: Access: In person, online. Visitors must perform in person searches themselves. Required to search: name, years to search. Civil cases indexed by defendant, plaintiff; index on cards since 1979, prior on index books. Participates in state online court record system at https://www.courts.mo.gov/casenet/base/welcome.do. Online records go back to 3/20/2006.
Criminal Records: Access: In person, online. Both court and visitors may perform in person searches. No search fee. Required to search: name, years to search. Criminal records indexed on cards since 1979, prior on index books. Online access to criminal records same as civil, above and show year of birth only. Court's public terminal may show add'l, often older data.
General Information: Online identifiers in results same as on public terminal. No juvenile, mental, expunged, dismissed, or suspended imposition of sentence records released. Will not fax documents. Court makes copy: $1.00 per page. Certification fee: $2.50 per cert. Payee: Associate Circuit Court. Personal checks accepted; credit cards are not. Prepayment required. Mail requests: SASE required for mail return of any copies.

Wright County

Circuit Court PO Box 39, Hartville, MO 65667; 417-741-7121; fax: 417-741-7504; 8AM-4:30PM. ***Felony, Civil Actions over $25,000.*** www.courts.mo.gov/page.asp?id=1680
Civil Records: Access: Mail, in person, online. Both court and visitors may perform in person searches. No search fee. Required to search: name, years to search. Civil cases indexed by defendant, plaintiff; index on cards since 1979, prior on books to 1900s. Mail turnaround time 1 day. Public use terminal has civil records back to 2/20/06. PAT results show name only. Judgment index, court records available on public access terminal since 2/20/06. Participates in state online court record system at https://www.courts.mo.gov/casenet/base/welcome.do. Online records go back to 2/20/2006.
Criminal Records: Access: Mail, in person, online. Both court and visitors may perform in person searches. No search fee. Required to search: name, years to search. Criminal records indexed on cards since 1979, prior on books to 1900s. Mail turnaround time 1 day. Online access to criminal records same as civil, above and show year of birth only. For criminal searches contact Highway Patrol at 573-526-6153. Court's public terminal may show add'l, often older data.
General Information: Online identifiers in results same as on public terminal. No juvenile, mental, expunged, dismissed, or suspended imposition of sentence records released. Will fax documents $5.00. Court makes copy: $.25 per page, self serve same. Certification fee: $2.00. Payee: Wright County Circuit Clerk. Personal checks accepted; credit cards are not. Prepayment required. SASE not required.

Associate Circuit Division PO Box 58, Hartville, MO 65667; 417-741-6450; criminal fax: 417-741-7120; civil fax: same; 8AM-4:30PM. ***Misdemeanor, Civil Actions under $25,000, Eviction, Small Claims, Probate.*** www.courts.mo.gov/page.asp?id=1680
Probate fax is same as main fax number.
Civil Records: Access: Phone, fax, mail, in person, online. Only the court performs in person searches; visitors may not. No search fee. Required to search: name, years to search. Civil cases indexed by defendant, plaintiff; index on cards since 1979, prior on books. Mail turnaround time approx. 1 week. Participates in state online court record system at https://www.courts.mo.gov/casenet/base/welcome.do. Online records go back to 2/20/2006 and include probate. Visitors can use internet at Public Library downstairs for lookups.
Criminal Records: Access: Phone, fax, mail, in person, online. Only the court performs in person searches; visitors may not. No search fee. Required to search: name, years to search; also helpful: DOB, SSN. Criminal records on computer since 1990, prior on cards and books; on computer back to 1990. Mail turnaround time 1 week. Online access to criminal records same as civil, above and show year of birth only. Visitors can use internet at Public Library downstairs for lookups. Court's public terminal may show add'l, often older data.
General Information: Online identifiers in results same as on public terminal. No juvenile, mental, expunged, or dismissed records released. Fee to fax out file $1.00 per page. Court makes copy: $.25 per page, self serve same. Certification fee: $1.00 per page includes copy fee. Payee: Associate Circuit Court. Only cashiers checks and money orders accepted. No credit cards accepted. Prepayment required. Mail requests: SASE required.

Missouri Recording Offices

ORGANIZATION: 114 counties and one independent city; 115 recording offices. The recording officer is the Recorder of Deeds. City of St. Louis has its own recording office. Watch for ZIP Codes that may be City of St. Louis or County of St. Louis. Missouri is in the Central Time Zone.

REAL ESTATE RECORDS: A few counties will perform real estate searches. Copy fee is usually $1.00 per page, but many counties charge $2.00 for 1st page. Certification fees are usually $1.00 per cert/seal, but many counties charge more. Marriage License with certification fee $9.00.

UCC RECORDS: Missouri was a dual filing state; until July, 2001, financing statements were filed both at the state level and with the Recorder of Deeds except for consumer goods, farm related and real estate-related filings which were filed only with the Recorder. Now only real estate relating filings are filed at the county level. In counties that will still perform a UCC search, the fee is usually $14.00 per debtor name without copies.

TAX LIEN RECORDS: All federal and state tax liens are filed with the county Recorder of Deeds. Tax liens are usually indexed together. Some, not many, counties will perform tax lien searches. Search and copy fees vary widely.

OTHER LIENS: Mechanics, judgment, child support.

ONLINE ACCESS: A number of counties offer online access. UCCs are available online from the Secretary of State. Free searching for debtor names is at www.sos.mo.gov/ucc/search_notice.asp.

Adair County

Recorder of Deeds, 106 W Washington St; Courthouse, Kirksville, MO 63501. 660-665-3890; fax-660-785-3212; 8:30AM-N, 1-4:30PM
Index: Separate indices to search include documents prior to April, 1985. In one index from April, 1985 to current. Records indexed on a public use terminal back to 4/85. Only the public may search. Copy fee $1.00 per page. Cert fee- $1.00 per cert plus copy fee. Payee- Adair County Recorder of Deeds. **Other phones:** Treasurer- 660-665-6755; Elections- 660-665-3350; Health Dept- Vital Records -660-665-8491. **Property tax/Assessing-** 106 W Washington St, Courthouse, Kirksville, MO 63501; 660-665-4423, assessor fax- 660-665-0349. (Appraiser/Auditor- 660-665-4423) hours- 8AM-4:30PM

Andrew County

Recorder of Deeds, PO Box 208, Savannah, MO 64485. Recording, R/E & UCC phone-816-324-4221; fax-816-324-5667; 8AM-5PM
Index: All in one. Records indexed on a public use terminal back to 2003. Only the public may search. Copy fee $2.00 1st page; $1.00 each add'l. per page after 10 pages. Cert fee- $1.00 per doc plus copy fee. Payee- Andrew County Recorder of Deeds. **Other phones:** Treasurer- 816-324-3614; Elections- 816-324-3624. **Property tax/Assessing-** 816-324-3023.

Atchison County

Recorder of Deeds, PO Box 280, Rock Port, MO 64482. 660-744-2707, R/E recording phone-660-744-2707/2705; fax-660-744-5705; 8:30AM-N, 1PM-4:30PM www.morecorders.com
Index: Separate indices to search. Record index not computerized. Only the public may search. Will not search UCC records. Copy fee $1.00 per page. Cert fee- $1.00 per cert plus copy fee. Payee- Atchison County Recorder of Deeds. Bulk data available for purchase contact Julie. **Other phones:** Treasurer- 660-744-2800; Elections- 660-744-6214. **Property tax/Assessing-** PO Box 280, 400 Washington St, Rock Port, MO 64482; 660-744-2948, assessor fax- 660-744-5705. No public terminal available.

Audrain County

Recorder of Deeds, 101 N Jefferson, Rm 105; County Courthouse, Mexico, MO 65265. 573-473-5830; fax-573-581-8087; 8AM-5PM www.audraincounty.org
Index: Separate indices to search include deed trust, UCC. Records indexed on a public use terminal back to 6/88. Office will perform a UCC search but public must search other records themselves. UCC search per debtor name $14.00. Office will not search real estate records. Copy fee $1.00 per page; Surveys/plats $2.50. Cert fee- $1.00 per cert plus copy fee. Payee- Audrain County Recorder of Deeds. Bulk Data available for purchase, contact Marsha Peery. **Property tax/Assessing-** 101 N Jefferson, #106, Mexico, MO 65265; 573-473-5827, assessor fax- 573-581-2534. No public terminal available. www.audraincounty.org/offices/assessor/index.html **Online-** Search assessor property data for a fee on the GIS system at http://beacon.schneidercorp.com. Registration and username required. At the default website, choose Missouri then Audrain County, then register.

Barry County

Recorder of Deeds, PO Box 340, Cassville, MO 65625. 417-847-2914; fax-417-847-8740; 8AM-4PM
Index: All in one. Records indexed on a public use terminal back to 1992. Only the public may search. Tax lien search fee- $4.00 per debtor. General copy fee $.25 per page. Cert fee- $1.00 per page plus $1.00 per doc. Payee- Barry County Recorder of Deeds. **Other phones:** Treasurer- 417-847-2019; Elections- 417-847-2561. **Property tax/Assessing-** Courthouse, Cassville, MO 65625; 417-847-4589.

Barton County

Recorder of Deeds, 1004 Gulf, Rm 107; Courthouse, Lamar, MO 64759. Recording, R/E & UCC phone-417-682-2110; fax-417-682-4102; 8:30AM-4:30PM
Index: Separate indices to search include land, UCCs, tax liens. Records indexed on computer back to 9/00. Only the public may search. Will not search UCC records. Copy fee $1.00 per doc. Cert fee- $1.00 per cert plus copy fee. Payee- Barton County Recorder of Deeds. **Other phones:** Treasurer- 417-682-5881; Elections- 417-682-3529; Vital Records- 417-682-3363; Circuit Court- 417-682-2444; Historical Soc - 417-682-4141 after 1. **Property tax/Assessing-** 1004 Gulf, Rm 109, Lamar, MO 64759; 417-682-3553, assessor fax- 417-681-0176. hours- 8AM-4:30PM No public terminal available.

Bates County

Recorder of Deeds, PO Box 186, Butler, MO 64730. Recording, R/E & UCC phone-660-679-3611; fax-660-679-3903; 8:30AM-N, 1-4:30PM
Index: All in one. Records indexed on a public use terminal back to 1998. Only the public may search. Will not search UCC records. Copy fee $1.00 per page. Cert fee- $1.00 per instrument includes copy fee. Payee- Bates County Recorder of Deeds. Bulk data available for purchase, contact Lucille Mundey, Recorder. **Other phones:** Treasurer- 660-679-3341; Elections- 660-679-3371. **Property tax/Assessing-** 1 N Delaware, Butler, MO 64730; 660-679-3157, assessor fax- 660-679-4935.

Benton County

Recorder of Deeds, PO Box 37, Warsaw, MO 65355. Recording, R/E & UCC phone-660-438-5732; fax-660-438-3652; 8AM-N, 1-4:30PM
Index: All in one. Records indexed on a public use terminal back to 2/92. Only the public may search. Will not search UCC records. Copy fee $1.00 per page. Cert fee- $2.00 per cert plus copy fee. Payee- Benton County Recorder of Deeds. **Other phones:** Treasurer- 660-438-6313; Elections- 660-438-7326. **Property tax/Assessing-** PO Box 40, Warsaw, MO 65355; 660-438-5323.

Bollinger County

Recorder of Deeds, PO Box 49, Marble Hill, MO 63764. Recording, R/E & UCC phone-573-238-1900 x7; fax-573-238-2674; 8AM-4PM
Index: All in one. Records indexed on a public use terminal back to 1993. Office will perform a UCC search but public must search other records themselves. UCC records with a filed search request and a fee of $14.00. Copy fee $2.00 for 1st page; $1.00 each add'l. For certified copy of Marriage record fee is $9.00. Cert fee- $2.00 includes copy fee. Payee- Bollinger County Recorder of Deeds. Bulk data available for purchase as print outs. **Other phones:** Treasurer- 573-238-1900 x8; Elections- 573-238-1900 x5. **Property tax/Assessing-** PO Box 164, 204 High St, Marble Hill, MO 63764; 573-238-1900 x1, assessor fax- 573-238-2674.

Boone County

Recorder of Deeds, 801 E Walnut, Rm 132; Boone County Gov't Ctr, Columbia, MO 65201-7728. Recording, R/E & UCC phone-573-886-4345, UCC recording phone-573-886-4355; fax-573-886-4359; 8AM-5PM www.showmeboone.com/RECORDER/
Index: All in one. Records indexed on a public use terminal back to 1986. Only the public may search. Copy fee $1.00 per page. Cert fee- $1.00 per cert plus copy fee. Payee- Boone County Recorder of Deeds. Bulk data available for purchase, contact Bettie Johnson. **Online access to Real Estate, Lien,**

Marriage, UCC records: Access to the recorder database is free at www.showmeboone.com/recorder/. **Other phones:** Treasurer- 573-886-4365; Elections- 573-886-4295; Vital Records- 573-751-6400; Marriage License -573-886-4350. **Property tax/Assessing**- 801 E Walnut, Rm 143, Boone County Gov't Ctr, Columbia, MO 65201; 573-886-4270, fax- 573-886-4254. (Appraiser/Auditor- 573-886-4270) www.showmeboone.com/ASSESSOR/ **Online access**- Assessor data of real and personal property is free at www.showmeboone.com/assessor/. Free registration and password required.

Buchanan County

Recorder of Deeds, 411 Jules St, Rm 103; Courthouse, St. Joseph, MO 64501-1789. Recording, R/E & UCC phone-816-271-1437; fax-816-271-1582; 8AM-4:30PM www.co.buchanan.mo.us/
Index: All in one. Records indexed on a public use terminal back to 1990. Only the public may search. Real estate record copy- $2.00 1st page, $1.00 per page thereafter. Cert fee- $1.00 per doc plus copy fee. Payee- Buchanan County Recorder of Deeds. **Online access to Real Estate, Deed, Lien, UCC, Marriage, Judgment, Will records:** Access the recorder database for a fee at www.co.buchanan.mo.us. Fee for database is $250.00 per month by contract agreement. **Other phones:** Treasurer- 816-271-1432; Elections- 816-271-1412. **Property tax/Assessing**- 411 Jules St, Courthouse, St. Joseph, MO 64501; 816-271-1469. (Auditor- 816-271-1520) www.co.buchanan.mo.us/ **Online access**- Search the GIS-mapping site for property data free at www.buchanancomogis.com but no name searching.

Butler County

Recorder of Deeds, 100 N Main St; Courthouse, Poplar Bluff, MO 63901. Recording, R/E & UCC phone-573-686-8086; 8AM-4PM
Index: Separate indices. Records indexed on a public use terminal back to 1995. Only the public may search. Copy fee $.50 per page after 10 pages.Real estate or tax lien copy- $2.00 1st page, $1.00 per page thereafter. Cert fee- $1.00 per cert plus copy fee. Payee- Butler County Recorder of Deeds. Bulk data available for purchase; contact Marion Tibbs. **Other phones:** Treasurer- 573-686-8083; Elections- 573-686-8050; Vital Records- 573-686-8086. **Property tax/Assessing**- 100 N Main St, Courthouse, Poplar Bluff, MO 63901; 573-686-8084, assessor fax- 573-686-8068. (Appraiser/Auditor- 573-686-8084);

Caldwell County

Recorder of Deeds, PO Box 65, Kingston, MO 64650. Recording, R/E & UCC phone-816-586-3080; fax-816-586-1252; 8AM-4:30PM
Index: Separate indexes to search include transfers of real estate, deed of trust, misc, et al. Record index not computerized. Office will perform a UCC search but public must search other records themselves. Copy fee $2.00 1st page; $1.00 each add'l. Cert fee- $1.00 per doc plus copy fee. Payee- Caldwell County Recorder of Deeds. **Other phones:** Treasurer- 816-586-2781; Elections- 816-586-2571. **Property tax/Assessing**- Courthouse, Kingston, MO 84650; 816-586-5261, assessor fax- 816-586-3600.

Callaway County

Recorder of Deeds, PO Box 406, Fulton, MO 65251. 573-642-0787; fax-573-642-1491; 8AM-5PM
Index: Separate indices to search include deeds, and deeds of trust. Records indexed on a public use terminal back to 1996. Only the public may search. Copy fee $1.00 per page. Cert fee- $1.00 per cert plus copy fee. Payee- Callaway County Recorder of Deeds. Bulk data available for purchase; contact Vicky. **Online access to Real Estate, Liens, Judgment, Grantor/Grantee, Marriage records:** Access to records for a fee go to http://callaway.missouri.org/recorder/index.html . **Other phones:** Treasurer- 573-642-0770; Elections- 573-642-0730. **Property tax/Assessing**- 10 E 5th St, Fulton, MO 65251; 573-642-0766, assessor fax- 573-642-7929.

Camden County

Recorder of Deeds, 1 Court Circle, #5, Camdenton, MO 65020. 573-346-4440, R/E recording phone-573-317-3880; fax-573-346-8367; 8:30AM-4:30PM
Index: Separate indices to search. Records indexed on a public use terminal back to 1970. Only the public may search. Copy fee $1.00 per page. Copy fee for plats $5.00 per page. Cert fee- $1.00 per doc plus copy fee. Payee- Camden County Recorder of Deeds. **Other phones:** Treasurer- 573-317-3880. **Property tax/Assessing**- 1 Court Circle, Camdenton, MO 65020; 573-346-4440 x1269, fax- 573-317-3964.

Cape Girardeau County

Recorder of Deeds, PO Box 248, Jackson, MO 63755. 573-243-8123; fax-573-204-2477; 8AM-4:30PM
Index: All in one. Records indexed on computer back to 1989. Only the public may search. Real estate record copy- $2.00 for 1st page; $1.00 each add'l. Cert fee- $1.00 per cert plus copy fee. Payee- Cape Girardeau County Recorder of Deeds. Office does sell bulk data, contact Eric McGowan. **Online access to Real Estate, Deed, Lien records:** Recorder land data by subscription on either the Laredo system using subscription and fees or the Tapestry System using credit card, http://tapestry.fidlar.com; $5.99 search; $.50 per image. Index goes back to 1/1989; images to 1995. **Other phones:** Treasurer- 573-243-3720. **Property tax/Assessing**- 1 Barton Sq, 2nd Fl, Jackson, MO 63755; 573-243-2468, assessor fax- 573-204-2525.
www.showme.net/CapeCounty/assr.htm

Carroll County

Recorder of Deeds, PO Box 245, Carrollton, MO 64633. 660-542-1466; fax-660-542-1444; 8:30AM-4:30PM
Index: All in one. Record index not computerized. Only the public may search. Copy fee $1.00 per page after 10 pages. Cert fee- $2.00 per page plus copy fee. Payee- Carroll County Recorder of Deeds. **Other phones:** Treasurer- 660-542-1977. **Property tax/Assessing**- 8 S Main St, #4, Carrollton, MO 64633; 660-542-2184, assessor fax- 660-542-3491.

Carter County

Recorder of Deeds, PO Box 1107, Van Buren, MO 63965. Recording, R/E & UCC phone-573-323-9656; fax-573-323-4885; 8AM-N, 1-4PM
Index: All in one. Record index not computerized. Office will perform a UCC search but public must search other records themselves. Search fee $14.00. Copy fee $1.00 per page. Cert fee- $1.00 per page plus copy fee. Payee- Carter County Recorder of Deeds. **Other phones:** Treasurer- 573-323-8271; Elections- 573-323-4527. **Property tax/Assessing**- 105 Main St, Van Buren, MO 63965; 573-323-4709.

Cass County

Recorder of Deeds, 102 E Wall St;, Harrisonville, MO 64701. 816-380-8123; fax-816-380-4086; 8AM-4:30PM www.casscounty.com/cassfr.htm
Prepaid fax accounts available; contact Sandy Gregory at 816-380-8123. Index: All in one. Records indexed on a public use terminal back to 1991. Only the public may search. Will not search UCC records. Copy fee $2.00 1st per page, $1.00 each add'l. Plats- $5.00 each. Marriage certs- $9.00. Cert fee- $1.00 per seal plus copy fee. Payee- Cass County Recorder of Deeds. Bulk data available for purchase; contact Leone Blank. **Online access to Real Estate, Deed, Lien records:** Access to the recorders official records database at http://207.14.218.122/or_wb1/ requires a username and password; inquire through the Recorder's office. **Property tax/Assessing**- 102 E Wall St, 2nd Fl, Harrisonville, MO 64701; 816-380-8179, assessor fax- 816-380-8165. **Online** - Access assessor property data for free at http://beacon.schneidercorp.com/?site=CassCountyMO. Also, search for property tax records free at http://mylocalgov.com/cassountymo/pubbizing21.asp?countyname2=cass. Look up tax bills free at https://mylocalgov.com/mcca/index.asp?countyname=cass.

Cedar County

Recorder of Deeds, 113 South St; Courthouse, Stockton, MO 65785. 417-276-6700 x246; fax-417-276-5499; 8AM-N, 1-4PM
Index: Separate indices to search include records from 1999 to present on computer, prior to 1980 on film. Records indexed on a public use terminal back to 1980. Only the public may search. Copy fee $1.00 per page. Nothing faxed back without payment first. Cert fee- $1.00 per cert plus copy fee. Payee- Cedar County Recorder of Deeds. **Other phones:** Treasurer- 417-276-6700 x245; Elections- 417-276-6700 x221. **Property tax/Assessing**- 113 South St, Stockton, MO 65785; 417-276-6700 x3, assessor fax- 417-276-2207.

Chariton County

Recorder of Deeds, 306 S Cherry St, Keytesville, MO 65261. 660-288-1005; fax-660-288-3763; 8:30AM-N, 1-4:30PM
Index: Separate indices to search include books from 1827 to 2/1/1998. Land records indexed on computer from 020198 to present; marriages on computer from 1827 to 1930 and from 02/0198 to present. Office personnel or visitors may perform searches. Search fee $4.00 per name. Office will not search real estate records. Office will not search tax liens. UCC search per debtor name- $14.00. Copy fee $1.00 per page. Cert fee- $1.50 per cert plus copy fee. Payee- Chariton County Recorder of Deeds. **Other phones:** Treasurer- 660-288-3789; Elections- 660-288-3273; Circuit Clerk- 660-288-3602. **Property tax/Assessing**- 306 S Cherry St, Keytesville, MO 65261; 660-288-3873, assessor fax- 660-288-1503.

Christian County

Recorder of Deeds, PO Box 358, Ozark, MO 65721. 417-581-9941; fax-417-581-9943; 8AM-4:30PM www.christiancountymo.gov
Index: All in one. Records indexed on a public use terminal back to 1994. Only the public may search. Copy fee $1.00 per page. Cert fee- $1.00 per doc, does not include copy fee. Payee- Christian County Recorder of Deeds. **Online access to Real Estate, Deed, Marriage, Tax Lien records:** Access the recording office records free at http://landrecords.christiancountymo.gov. Real estate, marriage, and UCC records go back to 10/1994; tax liens to 1/3/2000. Username and password is Public. **Property tax/Assessing**- 100 W Church St, Rm 301, Ozark, MO 65721; 417-581-2440, assessor fax- 417-581-3029. www.christiancountymo.gov/assessor.htm **Online**- Search tax payment lookup at www.christiancountycollector.com/christian-payment.php.

Clark County

Recorder of Deeds, 111 E Court, #2; Courthouse, Kahoka, MO 63445. Recording, R/E & UCC phone-660-727-3292; fax-660-727-1051; 8AM-N,1-4PM
Index: Separate indices to search. Records indexed on a public use terminal back to 1995. Only the public may search. Copy fee $1.00 per page. Cert fee- $3.00 per doc plus copy fee. Payee- Clark County Recorder of Deeds. **Other phones:** Treasurer- 660-727-3272; Elections- 660-727-3283. **Property tax/Assessing**- 111 E Court, Courthouse, Kahoka, MO 63445; 660-727-3023. www.accessclarkcounty.com/assessor/

Clay County

Recorder of Deeds, PO Box 238, Liberty, MO 64069. 816-407-3550; fax-816-407-3601; 8AM-4PM http://recorder.claycogov.com/pages/index.asp
Best not to fax to them, the fax is located in different office. Index: All in one. Records indexed on public use terminal back to 7/00. Only the public may search. Copy fee $2.00 per page and $1.00 each add'l for RE and tax liens. Cert fee- $1.00 per cert plus copy fee. Payee- Clay County Recorder of Deeds. **Online access to Real Estate, Deed, RE UCCs, Marriage,**

Military Discharge records: Access to recorder's database is free at http://recorder.claycogov.com/pages/online_access.asp. Overall index goes back to 7/1986; images back to 1986. Real estate only UCCs back to 1986. No images for marriages, discharges, just data. **Other phones:** Treasurer- 816-407-3540; Main Switchboard- 816-407-3600. **Property tax/Assessing**- 1 Courthouse Sq, Liberty, MO 64068; 816-407-3500, assessor fax- 816-407-3501. www.claycogov.com/county/county.php **Online**- Access assessor property records free at http://gisweb.claycogov.com/realEstate/realEstate.jsp but no name searching. Also, access real estate records from Collector's Office free at https://collector.claycogov.com. Also, search county property manually on the GIS-mapping site free at http://gisweb.claycogov.com/gis/viewer.htm.

Clinton County

Recorder of Deeds, PO Box 275, Plattsburg, MO 64477. 816-539-3719; fax-816-539-3893; 8-4:30PM

Records indexed on a public use terminal back to 1993. Office will perform a UCC search but public must search other records themselves. Search fee $14.00. UCC copy fee $2.00 per page after 10 pages.Real estate or tax lien copy- $2.00; $1.00 add'l. Cert fee- $3.00 per cert plus copy fee. Payee- Clinton County Recorder of Deeds. Bulk data available for purchase; contact Linda. **Other phones:** Treasurer- 816-539-3724; Elections- 816-539-3713. **Property tax/Assessing**- PO Box 436, 207 N Main, Plattsburg, MO 64477; 816-539-3716, assessor fax- 816-539-3097. hours- 8:30AM-4:30PM

Cole County

Recorder of Deeds, PO Box 353, Jefferson City, MO 65102. 573-634-9115; fax-573-634-4631; 8AM-4:30PM

www.colecounty.org/cole1/cole/recorder/index.html

Index: All in one. Records indexed on a public use terminal back to 1986. Office personnel or visitors may perform searches. Office will search real estate records. Office will not search UCC records. Copy fee $1.00 per page after 1st 10 pages. Cert fee- $1.00 per cert plus copy fee. Payee- Cole County Recorder of Deeds. **Other phones:** Treasurer- 573-634-9121; County Clerk- 573-634-9185. **Property tax/Assessing**- 210 Adams St, Jefferson City, MO 65101; 573-634-9131, fax- 573-634-9139. (Appraiser/- 573-634-9122) www.colecounty.org/assessor/ **Online access**- Access property and other mapping data free at www.midmogis.org/InteractiveMapIndex.html. There is a add'l GIS-mapping site, but subscription is required at www.midmogis.org/website/colecounty/

Cooper County

Recorder of Deeds, 200 Main St, Rm 26; Courthouse, Boonville, MO 65233-1276. 660-882-2161; fax-660-882-2155; 8:30AM-5PM

Index: All in one. Records indexed on a public use terminal back to 1994. Only the public may search. Copy fee $1.00 per page. Cert fee- $1.50 per cert plus copy fee. Payee- Cooper County Recorder of Deeds. **Other phones:** Elections- 660-882-2114. **Property tax/Assessing**- 200 Main St, Rm 22, Boonville, MO 65233; 660-882-2646, assessor fax- 660-882-2640. www.mo-river.net/government/cooper/assessor.htm

Crawford County

Recorder of Deeds, PO Box 236, Steelville, MO 65565-0235. Recording, R/E & UCC phone-573-775-5048; fax-573-775-3365; 8AM-4:30PM

Index: Books and Computer. Records indexed on a public use terminal back to WD-1984, TD-1900. Office will perform a UCC search but public must search other records themselves. Search fee $14.00. Copy fee $.50 per page; UCC records copy fee $.50 per page after 10 pages. Cert fee- $2.00 per cert plus copy fee. For 18 x 24 fee is $5.00. Payee- Crawford County Recorder of Deeds. **Other phones:** Treasurer- 573-775-2897; Elections- x 2376; Vital Records- x 2555. **Property tax/Assessing**- PO Box 149, 302 Main St, Steelville, MO 65565; 573-775-2065.

Dade County

Recorder of Deeds, Courthouse, Greenfield, MO 65661. Recording, R/E & UCC phone-417-637-5373; fax-417-637-1006; 8AM-N, 1-4PM

Index: All in one. Records indexed on computer back to 1997. Office will perform a UCC search but public must search other records themselves. Copy fee $1.00 per page. Cert fee- $1.00 per doc includes copy fee. Payee- Dade County Recorder of Deeds. **Other phones:** Treasurer- 417-637-2732; Elections- 417-637-2724. **Property tax/Assessing**- 300 N Water St, Greenfield, MO 65661; 417-637-2224, assessor fax- 417-637-0424. hours- 8AM-4PM

Dallas County

Recorder of Deeds, PO Box 406, Buffalo, MO 65622. Recording, R/E & UCC phone-417-345-2242; fax-417-345-2230; 8AM-N,1-4PM

Index: All in one. Land records indexed on computer back to 1992; marriage records back to 1867. Only the public may search. Copy fee $1.00 per page. Cert fee- $1.00 per cert plus copy fee. Payee- Dallas County Recorder of Deeds. Bulk data available for purchase in CDs, 2006 to present, $50.00 per book. Contact Stacy Satterfield. **Other phones:** Treasurer- 417-345-2020; Elections- 417-345-2632; Tax Collector- 417-345-7836. **Property tax/Assessing**- 417-345-8774.

Daviess County

Recorder of Deeds, PO Box 132, Gallatin, MO 64640. 660-663-3183; fax-660-663-3376; 8AM-N, 1-4:30PM

Index: Separate indices to search include mortgage trust deeds, general & miscellaneous deeds, tax liens and request for notice. Record index not computerized. Only the public may search. Will not search UCC records. Copy fee $2.00 per deed, $1.00 each add'l. Cert fee- $4.00 per doc includes copy fee. Payee- Daviess County Recorder of Deeds. **Other phones:** Treasurer- 660-663-2432. **Property tax/Assessing**- 102 N Main, Courthouse, Gallatin, MO 64640; 660-663-3300.

De Kalb County

Recorder of Deeds, PO Box 248, Maysville, MO 64469-0248. Recording, R/E phone-816-449-5010, UCCs-816-449-2602; fax-816-449-2440; 8-4:30PM

Index: All in one. Records indexed on a public use terminal back to 1992. Only the public may search. Copy fee $1.00 per page per page. Cert fee- $1.00 per cert plus copy fee. Payee- De Kalb County Recorder of Deeds. Treasurer- 816-449-5810. **Property tax/Assessing**- PO Box 248, 109 W Main St, Maysville, 64469; 816-449-2212, fax- 816-449-5915. **Online access**- Search assessor property data for a fee on the GIS system at http://beacon.schneidercorp.com/. Registration and username required.

Dent County

Recorder of Deeds, 112 E 5th St, Salem, MO 65560. 573-729-2198; fax-573-729-9414; 8AM-4:30PM

www.salemmo.com/county/RecorderOfDeeds.asp

Index: Separate indices to search include computer. Records indexed on a public use terminal back to 1955. Office personnel or visitors may perform searches. Search fee $1.00 per name per year. Office will search real estate records. Will not search UCC records. General copy fee $1.00 per page.Real estate record copy- $.25 per page. Cert fee- $1.00 per cert plus copy fee. Payee- Dent County Recorder of Deeds. Office does sell bulk data, contact the office. **Other phones:** Treasurer- 573-729-8260; Elections- 573-729-4144. **Property tax/Assessing**- 400 N Main St, Salem, MO 65560; 573-729-6010, fax- 573-729-6106. www.salemmo.com/county/Assessor.asp

Douglas County

Recorder of Deeds, PO Box 249, Ava, MO 65608. Recording, R/E & UCC phone-417-683-4713; fax-417-683-2794; 8AM-4:30PM

Index: All in one. Records indexed on a public use terminal back to 1995. Only the public may search. Recorded documents copy fee $1.00 per page. Cert fee- $2.50 per page plus copy fee. Payee- Douglas County Recorder of Deeds. **Online access to Real Estate, Deed, Lien records:** Recorder land data by subscription on either the Laredo system using subscription and fees or the Tapestry System using credit card, http://tapestry.fidlar.com; $3.99 search; $.50 per image. Index and images go back to 1995. **Other phones:** Treasurer- 417-683-2183; Elections- 417-683-4714; Collector- 417-683-4314. **Property tax/Assessing**- 203 SE 2nd Ave, PO Box 92, Ava, MO 65608; 417-683-2829.

Dunklin County

Recorder of Deeds, PO Box 389, Kennett, MO 63857. Recording, R/E & UCC phone-573-888-3468; fax-573-888-8956; 8:30AM-N, 1-4:30PM

Index: All in one. Records indexed on a public use terminal back to 1990. Only the public may search. Copy fee $1.00 per page after 10 pages. Cert fee- $1.00 per cert plus copy fee. Payee- Dunklin County Recorder of Deeds. Bulk data available for purchase, contact Susan Luce. **Property tax/Assessing**- PO Box 727, Kennett, MO 63857; 573-888-1409, assessor fax- 573-888-4771.

Franklin County

Recorder of Deeds, 400 E Locust, Rm 102, Union, MO 63084. 636-583-6367; fax-636-583-7330; 8AM-4:30PM www.franklinmo.org

Index: All in one. Records indexed on a public use terminal back to 1982. Only the public may search. Real estate- $2.00 1st page, $1.00 each add'l page. Cert fee- $1.00 per cert plus copy fee. Payee- Franklin County Recorder of Deeds. Bulk data available in microfilm images only, paper copies of indexes; contact Trudy Ronsick. **Online access to Real Estate, Deed, Lien records:** Recorder land data by subscription on either the Laredo system using subscription and fees or the Tapestry System using credit card, http://tapestry.fidlar.com; $3.99 search; $.50 per image. Index and images go back to 1/1982. **Other phones:** Treasurer- 636-583-6392; Elections- 636-583-7382; Vital Records- 636-583-7300. **Property tax/Assessing**- 400 E Locust, Rm 105A, Union, 63084; 636-583-6348, fax- 636-583-6383. www.franklinmo.org/Assessor/assessor_main.htm

Gasconade County

Recorder of Deeds, 119 E 1st St, Rm 6, Hermann, MO 65041-1182. Recording, R/E & UCC phone-573-486-2632; fax-573-486-5812; 8AM-4:30PM

Index: All in one. Records indexed on computer back to January, 1989. Only the public may search. Copy fee $2.00 1st page, $1.00 each add'l. Surveys/plats- $5.00. Cert fee- $1.00 per page plus copy fee. Payee- Gasconade County Recorder of Deeds. Office does sell bulk data, contact Lisa Dibal. **Other phones:** Treasurer- 573-486-2411; Elections- 573-486-5427. **Property tax/Assessing**- 119 E 1st St, Rm 23, Hermann, MO 65041; 573-486-3100, assessor fax- 573-486-3693. (Appraiser/Auditor- 573-486-3100) Public access terminal at Collector's office.

Gentry County

Recorder of Deeds, PO Box 27, Albany, MO 64402. 660-726-3618; fax-660-726-4102; 8AM-4:30PM

Index: All in one. Records indexed on computer back to 4/5/05. Only the public may search. Copy fee $1.00 per page. Cert fee- $1.00 per doc plus copy fee. Payee- Gentry County Recorder of Deeds. Bulk data available for purchase; contact Sheryl Coburn. **Other phones:** Treasurer- 660-726-3319; Elections- 660-726-3525. **Property tax/Assessing**- 200 W Clay, Albany, MO 64402; 660-726-5289, assessor fax- 660-726-5810. hours- 9AM-4:30PM

Greene County

Recorder of Deeds, 940 Boonville, Rm 100, Springfield, MO 65802. Recording, R/E & UCC phone-417-868-4068; fax-417-868-4807; 8AM-4:30PM www.greenecountymo.org

Index: All in one. Records indexed on a public use terminal back to 1988. Only the public may search. Copy fee $1.00 per page. Cert fee- $1.00 per cert plus copy fee. Payee- Recorder of Deeds. Bulk data (index and images) available for purchase, contact Linda Montgomery, Recorder of Deeds. **Online access to Real Estate, Recoding, Deed, Lien, UCC records:** Search the recorder database for free at www.greenecountymo.org/recorder/realsearch.php. Search UCCs and tax liens at www.greenecountymo.org/recorder/ucctaxsearch.php. **Other phones:** Treasurer- 417-868-4051; Elections- 417-868-4055. **Property tax/Assessing-** 940 Boonville, Springfield, MO 65802; assessor phone-417-868-4101, assessor fax- 417-868-4844. www.greenecountyassessor.org/Home.asp?mnu=Home **Online access-** Search assessor data free at www.greenecountyassessor.org/OwnerSearch.asp.

Grundy County

Recorder of Deeds, PO Box 196, Trenton, MO 64683. 660-359-5409, R/E recording phone-660-359-4040 x257; fax-660-359-6604; 8:30AM-4:30PM
Index: All in one. Records indexed on computer back to 2004. Office will perform a UCC search but public must search other records themselves. Search fee $14.00 per name. General copy fee $1.00 per page after 10 pages.Real estate record copy- $.25 per page. Cert fee- $2.00 per doc plus copy fee. Payee- Grundy County Recorder of Deeds. Office does sell bulk data, contact the office. **Other phones:** Treasurer- 660-359-4040 x263; Elections- 660-359-4040 x221. **Property tax/Assessing-** 700 Main St, Trenton,MO 64683; 660-359-4040 x241, fax- 660-339-7637.

Harrison County

Recorder of Deeds, PO Box 525, Bethany, MO 64424. Recording, R/E & UCC phone-660-425-6425; fax-660-425-3772; 8AM-N, 1-4:30PM
Index: All in one. Records indexed on a public use terminal back to 2000. Only the public may search. Copy fee $1.00 per page after 10 pages. Cert fee- $1.00 per cert plus copy fee. Payee- Harrison County Recorder of Deeds. Bulk data available for purchase; contact Lila Craig. **Other phones:** Treasurer- 660-425-6442. **Property tax/Assessing-** PO Box 525, 1500 Central, Bethany, MO 64424; 660-425-2313, assessor fax- 660-425-0127.

Henry County

Recorder of Deeds, 100 W Franklin, #4; Courthouse, Clinton, MO 64735. phone-660-885-6963 x7210; fax-660-885-2264; 8:30AM-4:30PM
Index: All in one. Records indexed on a public use terminal back to 7/89. Only the public may search. Copy fee $1.00 per page. Cert fee- $1.00 per page plus copy fee. Payee- Henry County Recorder of Deeds. **Other phones:** Treasurer- 660-885-6963 x7208; Elections- 660-885-6963 x7206. **Property tax/Assessing-** 100 W Franklin, Clinton, MO 64735; 660-885-7213.

Hickory County

Recorder of Deeds, PO Box 101, Hermitage, MO 65668. 417-745-6421; fax-417-745-6670; 8AM-N, 12:30-4:30PM
Index: All in one. Records indexed on a public use terminal back to 1998. Only the public may search. Copy fee $1.00 per page after 10 pages. Cert fee- $1.00 per page. Payee- Hickory County Recorder of Deeds. **Other phones:** Treasurer- 417-745-6310; Elections- 417-745-6450. **Property tax/Assessing-** PO Box 97, Hermitage, MO 65668; 417-745-6346, assessor fax- 417-745-6715. (Appraiser/Auditor- 417-745-6957) hours- 8AM-N, 1-4:30PM

Holt County

Recorder of Deeds, PO Box 318, Oregon, MO 64473. phone-660-446-3301; 8:30AM-N, 1-4:30PM
Index: All in one. Record index not computerized. Office personnel or visitors may perform searches. Search fee $14.00 per name. Office will search real estate records (1 specific item with approx date). Will search UCC records (1 specific item with approx date). UCC search per debtor name- $4.00. Copy fee $1.00 per page. Cert fee- $1.00 per cert plus copy fee. Payee- Holt County Recorder of Deeds. Office does sell bulk data, contact Carla Markt. **Other phones:** Treasurer- 660-446-3397; Elections- 660-446-3303. **Property tax/Assessing-** PO Box 366, 102 W Nodaway, Oregon, MO 64473; 660-446-3329, assessor fax- 660-446-3092. 9AM-N, 1-4:30PM

Howard County

Recorder of Deeds, 1 Courthouse Sq, Fayette, MO 65248. Recording, R/E & UCC phone-660-248-2194; fax-660-248-5009; 8:30AM-4:30PM
Index: All in one. Records indexed on a public use terminal back to 1994. Only the public may search. General copy fee $2.00 per doc or $.25 per page. Cert fee- $3.00 per cert includes copy fee. Payee- Howard County Recorder of Deeds. Treasurer- 660-248-2196. **Property tax/Assessing-** 660-248-3400.

Howell County

Recorder of Deeds, PO Box 967, West Plains, MO 65775. 417-256-3750; 8AM-4:30PM
Index: All in one. Records indexed on a public use terminal back to 1/1/1991. Only the public may search. Copy fee $1.00 per page. Cert fee- $1.50 per cert plus copy fee. Payee- Howell County Recorder of Deeds. **Online access to Real Estate, Deed, Lien records:** Access recorder land data by subscription on either the Laredo system using subscription and fees or Tapestry System using credit card, http://tapestry.fidlar.com; $3.99 search; $.50 per image. Index goes back to 1991; images to 1/1998. **Other phones:** Treasurer- 417-256-4261. **Property tax/Assessing-** 101 Courthouse, West Plains, MO 65775; 417-256-8284, assessor fax- 417-256-8266. hours- 8:30AM-4:30PM

Iron County

Recorder of Deeds, PO Box 24, Ironton, MO 63650. phone-573-546-2811; fax-573-546-2166; 8AM-4:30PM http://ironcounty.homestead.com/CountyGovernment.html
Index: All in one. Records on a public use terminal. Office will perform a UCC search but public must search other records themselves. Office will not search real estate records. UCC search per debtor name- $14.00. UCC search & copy request (including 10 pages of copies)- $28.00. Copy fee $.40 per page. Cert fee- $2.00 per cert plus copy fee. Payee- Iron County Recorder of Deeds. Office does sell bulk data of daily recordings for $.40 per page. **Other phones:** Treasurer- 573-546-7611; Elections- 573-546-2912; Vitals- 573-546-2811. **Property tax/ Assessing-** 202 S Sheperd, Ironton, MO 63650; 573-546-7319, assessor fax- 573-546-4129. hours- 9AM-4PM

Jackson County (Kansas City)

Recorder of Deeds, 415 E 12th St, Rm 104, Kansas City, MO 64106-2706. 816-881-3192, R/E recording phone-816-881-3048; fax-816-881-3719; 8AM-5PM www.jacksongov.org
Has another office in Independence, which covers the eastern part of the county. It is not necessary to file proper documents in that office for the eastern section of the county. Call for more details. Index: All in one. Records indexed on a public use terminal back to 1968. Visitors may perform searches, office will also perform searches, but not real estate or UCCs. Search fee $8.00 per name. Office will assist in search of real estate records. Real estate copy fee $2.00 per page for the 1st page, $1.00 each add'l page. Cert fee- $1.00 per cert plus copy fee. Payee- Jackson County Recorder of Deeds. CD subscription $25.00 annual, call 816-881-3191. **Online access to Real Estate, Grantor/Grantee, Deed, Lien, Marriage, Judgment, UCC records:** Search the recorder Grantor/Grantee database for free at http://records.co.jackson.mo.us/search.asp?cabinet=opr. Also, access recording office land data at www.etitlesearch.com; registration required, fee based on usage. Also, search Kansas City land data free at http://kivaweb.kcmo.org/kivanet/2/land/lookup/index.cfm?fa=dslladdr. Search the marriage records free at http://records.co.jackson.mo.us/search.asp?cabinet=marriage. Search the UCC database at http://records.co.jackson.mo.us/search.asp?cabinet=ucc. **Other phones:** Treasurer- 816-881-3232; Elections- 816-881-4820; Vital Records- 816-513-6309. **Property tax/Assessing-** 415 E 12th St, Kansas City, MO 64106; 816-881-3530. (Appraiser/Auditor- 816-881-3091) **Online access-** Search property tax data free at www.jacksongov.org/TaxSrch/.

Jasper County

Recorder of Deeds, PO Box 387, Carthage, MO 64836-0387. 417-358-0432; fax-417-359-1200; 8:30AM-4:30PM http://recorder.jaspercounty.org/
Index: All in one. Records indexed on a public use terminal back to 1989. Only the public may search. Copy fee $1.00 per page. Cert fee- $1.00 per cert plus copy fee. Payee- Jasper County Recorder of Deeds. Bulk data available for purchase, contact Donna Grove-Recorder. **Other phones:** Treasurer- 417-358-0448. **Property tax/Assessing-** 302 S Main, Carthage, MO 64836; 417-358-0440, assessor fax-417-237-1098. Public access terminal available.

Jefferson County

Recorder of Deeds, PO Box 100, Hillsboro, MO 63050. Recording, R/E & UCC phone-636-797-5414, UCC recording phone-636-797-5499; fax-636-797-6310; 8AM-5PM www.jeffcomo.org
Index: All in one. Records indexed on a public use terminal back to 1985. Only the public may search. Copy fee $2.00 1st page, $1.00 each add'l. Cert fee- $1.00 per doc plus copy fee. Payee- Jefferson County Recorder of Deeds. **Online access to Real Estate, Deed, Lien records:** Access recording office land data at www.etitlesearch.com; registration required, fee based on usage; call 870-856-3055 for info. Also, recorder land data by subscription on either the Laredo system using subscription and fees or Tapestry System using credit card, http://tapestry.fidlar.com; $3.99 search; $.50 per image. Index goes back to 1/1985; images to 6/17/2002. **Other phones:** Treasurer- 636-797-5368; Elections- 636-797-5486; Birth & Death Records- 636-789-3372. **Property tax/Assessing-** 729 Maple St, Admin Ctr, Hillsboro, MO 63050; 636-797-5466, assessor fax- 636-797-5083. (Appraiser - 636-797-5474) www.jcao.org/ **Online access-** Search assessor property data for free at www.jcao.org/.

Johnson County

Recorder of Deeds, 300 N Holden St, #305, Warrensburg, MO 64093. 660-747-6811; fax-660-747-0062; 8:30AM-4:30PM
Index: All in one. Records indexed on a public use terminal back to 1991. Office will perform a UCC search but public must search other records themselves. UCC info request- $14.00 per debtor. Copy fee $1.00 per page. Plats and surveys- $5.00 per page. UCC copy request- $14.00 per name per doc. Cert fee- $1.00 per page plus copy fee. Payee- Johnson County Recorder of Deeds. **Other phones:** Treasurer- 660-747-7411. **Property tax/Assessing-** 300 N Holden St, #204, Warrensburg, MO 64093-1704; 660-747-9822.

Knox County

Recorder of Deeds, 107 N 4th St, Edina, MO 63537. 660-397-4005; fax-660-397-3331; 8:30-N, 1-4PM
Index: Separate indices include grantor and grantee. Record index not computerized. Only the public may search. Copy fee $1.00 per page. Cert fee- $1.50 per cert plus copy fee. Payee- Knox County Recorder of Deeds. **Other phones:** Treasurer- 660-397-3364; Elections- 660-397-2184.

Laclede County

Recorder of Deeds, 200 N Adams, Lebanon, MO 65536-3046. 417-532-4011; fax-417-532-3852; 8AM-4PM http://lacledecountymissouri.org/recorder/
Index: All in one. Records indexed on a public use

terminal back to 04/1992. Only the public may search. Office will not search real estate records. Office will not search UCC records. Copy fee $1.00 per page. Cert fee- $.50 per cert plus copy fee. Payee- Laclede County Recorder of Deeds. Office does sell bulk data, contact Phyllis Swearingen. **Online Real Estate, Grantor/Grantee, Deed, Marriage, Tax Lien, Plat, Survey records:** Access to recorders documents indexes is free at http://69.68.214.114/search.php but registration and fees for images. **Other phones:** Treasurer- 417-532-4741; Elections- 417-532-5471; Vital Records- 417-532-2134 (Birth); 4011 (Marriage); Collector- 417-532-4301. **Property tax/Assessing**- 200 N Adams Ave, Lebanon, MO 65536; 417-532-7163, assessor fax- 417-533-7417. (Appraiser - 417-532-7163);

Lafayette County

Recorder of Deeds, PO Box 416, Lexington, MO 64067. 660-259-6178; fax-660-259-2918; 8:30AM-4:30PM

Index: All in one. Records indexed on a public use terminal back to 1991. Only the public may search. Copy fee $1.00 per page. Cert fee- $1.00 per cert plus copy fee. Payee- Lafayette County Recorder of Deeds. Treasurer- 660-259-3711; Elections- 660-259-4315. **Property tax/Assessing**- 1001 Main St, Lexington, MO 64067; 660-259-6158, assessor fax-660-259-4482. A public access terminal is available.

Lawrence County

Recorder of Deeds, PO Box 449, Mount Vernon, MO 65712. Recording, R/E & UCC phone-417-466-2670; fax-417-466-4995; 9AM-5PM

Index: Separate indices to search include before 1992 there are 2 indexes: 1 for trust deeds; 1 for misc. land records. Records indexed on a public use terminal back to 1992. Only the public may search. Copy fee $1.00 per doc. Cert fee- $2.00 per doc includes copy fee. Payee- Lawrence County Recorder of Deeds. **Other phones:** Treasurer- 417-466-2662. **Property tax/Assessing**- Courthouse on the Sq, Mount Vernon, MO 65712; 417-466-2831.

Lewis County

Recorder of Deeds, PO Box 97, Monticello, MO 63457-0097. 573-767-5440; fax-573-767-5378; 8AM-N,1-4PM

Index: All in one. Records indexed on a public use terminal back to 7/91. Office will perform a UCC search but public must search other records themselves. Office will not search real estate records. UCC search per debtor name- $14.00. Copy fee $1.00 per page after 10 pages. Cert fee- $1.00 per doc plus copy fee. Payee- Lewis County Recorder of Deeds. **Other phones:** Treasurer- 573-767-5446; Elections-573-767-5205. **Property tax/Assessing**- 100 E Lafayette, Monticello, MO 63457; 573-767-5209.

Lincoln County

Recorder of Deeds, 201 Main St, Troy, MO 63379. 636-528-6300, R/E recording phone-636-528-6300 or 528-0325; fax-636-528-2665; 8AM-4:30PM www.lincoln.mo.us.landata.com

Index: All in one. Records indexed on a public use terminal back to 1988. Only the public may search. Copy fee $.50 per page. Cert fee- $1.00 per cert plus copy fee. Payee- Lincoln County Recorder of Deeds. **Online Real Estate, Deed, Tax Lien, UCC records:** Access recording real estate and UCC records after registering at www.lincoln.mo.us.landata.com. Click on New To This Site to register. Index search is free; there is a fee to purchase documents; credit cards accepted. Real estate records index goes back to 1/1/1988; Tax liens back to 10/1/2001. **Other phones:** Treasurer- 636-528-6300; Elections- 636-528-6300; Vital Records- 636-528-6300. **Property tax/Assessing**- 201 Main St, Troy, MO 63379; 636-528-0320, assessor fax- 636-528-1327. Public access terminal available. www.lincolncoassessor.com/ **Online** - For free parcel searches go to www.lincolncomogis.com/lincoln/. Click on Parcel Search.

Linn County

Recorder of Deeds, PO Box 151, Linneus, MO 64653. 660-895-5216, R/E recording phone-660-895-5216/ Real Estate Records; fax-660-895-5379; 9AM-N, 1-4:30PM

Index: All in one. Records indexed on a public use terminal back to 11/1992. Only the public may search. Will not search UCC records. Copy fee $1.00 per page. Cert fee- $1.00 per doc plus copy fee. Payee- Linn County Recorder of Deeds. **Online access to Real Estate, Deed, Lien records:** Recorder land data by subscription on either the Laredo system using subscription and fees or the Tapestry System using credit card, http://tapestry.fidlar.com; $3.99 search; $.50 per image. Index and images go back to 1995. **Other phones:** Treasurer- 660-895-5410; County Clerk- 660-895-5417. **Property tax/Assessing**- 660-895-5387.

Livingston County

Recorder of Deeds, 700 Webster St, #6; Courthouse, Chillicothe, MO 64601. 660-646-8000 x6; fax-660-646-5402; 8:30AM-N, 1-4:30PM

Index: Separate indices to search include standard docs, D of T, Release Deeds, Power of Attorney. Records indexed on a public use terminal back to 1/0/2002. Only the public may search. Will not search UCC records. Copy fee $1.00 per page. Cert fee-$2.00 per doc plus copy fee. Payee- Livingston County Recorder of Deeds. **Other phones:** Treasurer-660-646-8000 x7; Elections- 660-646-8000 x3. **Property tax/Assessing**- 700 Webster St, Courthouse, Chillicothe, 64601; 660-646-8000 x2.

Macon County

Recorder of Deeds, PO Box 382, Macon, MO 63552. 660-385-2732; fax-660-385-4235; 8:30AM-4PM www.maconcountymo.com

Index: Separate indices to search include microfilm, books, index cards, marriages, discharges. Records indexed on a public use terminal back to 1984. Only the public may search. Copy fee $.25 per page; microfilm- $.50 per page. Cert fee- $1.00 per cert includes copy fee. Payee- Macon County Recorder of Deeds. **Other phones:** Treasurer- 660-385-2713; Elections- 660-385-2913. **Property tax/Assessing**-101 E Washington, Bldg 3, Macon, MO 63552; 660-385-2416, assessor fax- 660-385-3140.

Madison County

Recorder of Deeds, One Court House Sq, Fredericktown, MO 63645-1137. 573-783-3410; fax-573-783-2715; 8AM-5PM

Index: All in one. Records indexed on a public use terminal back to 1998. Only the public may search. Copy fee $1.00 per doc plus $.10 per page. Cert fee-$2.00 per cert plus copy fee. Payee- Madison County Recorder of Deeds. Office does sell bulk data, contact the office. **Other phones:** Treasurer- 573-783-3325. **Property tax/ Assessing**- One Court House Sq, Fredericktown, MO 63645; 573-783-3325. hours-8AM-4PM

Maries County

Recorder of Deeds, PO Box 213, Vienna, MO 65582. Recording, R/E & UCC phone-573-422-3338; fax-573-422-3976; 8AM-4PM

Index: All in one. Book and page index computerized. Office will perform a UCC search if time allows, but public must search other records themselves. Copy fee $.25 per page. Will fax back $1.00 per page. Cert fee-$1.50 per cert includes copy fee (1 copy). Payee-Maries County Recorder of Deeds. Bulk data is available for purchase; contact the Recorder. **Other phones:** Treasurer- 573-422-3311; Elections- 573-422-3388; Vital Records- 573-422-3338; Collector-573-422-3343. **Property tax/Assessing**- Courthouse, Vienna, MO 65582; 573-422-3540, assessor fax- 573-422-3859.

Marion County

Recorder of Deeds, PO Box 392, Palmyra, MO 63461. 573-769-7001; fax-573-769-6012; 8AM-5PM

Index: All in one. Records indexed on a public use terminal back to 1997. Only the public may search. Copy fee $.50 per page after 10 pages. Deeds- $2.00 per doc. Cert fee- $2.00 per cert plus copy fee. Payee-Marion County Recorder of Deeds. **Online access to Real Estate. Deed, Lien records:** Access to real estate records at http://tapestry.fidlar.com/ for a fee. Also, Recorder land data by subscription on either the Laredo system using subscription and fees or the Tapestry System using credit card, http://tapestry.fidlar.com; $3.99 search; $.50 per image. Index and images go back to 1995. **Other phones:** Treasurer- 573-769-2552; Elections- 573-729-2549. **Property tax/Assessing**- 906 Broadway, Hannibal 63401; 573-221-0589, assessor fax- 573-221-4250.

McDonald County

Recorder of Deeds, PO Box 157, Pineville, MO 64856. Recording, R/E & UCC phone-417-223-7523; fax-417-223-4125; 8AM-4PM

Index: All in one. Records indexed on computer from 1999 to present. Only the public may search. Office will look up deeds if you have date. Office will not name search real estate records. Will not search UCC records. Copy fee $1.00 per instrument. Cert fee-$2.00 per doc includes copy fee. Payee- McDonald County Recorder of Deeds. **Other phones:** Treasurer-417-223-4462; Elections- 417-223-4717; Vital Records- 417-223-4351. **Property tax/Assessing**- PO Box 726, 606 N Main, Pineville, MO 64856; 417-223-4361, assessor fax- 417-223-7432.

Mercer County

Recorder of Deeds, 802 E Main St, Princeton, MO 64673. 660-748-4335; fax-660-748-4339; 8:30AM-N, 1-4:30PM

Index: Separate indices to search. Record index not computerized. Only the public may search. Copy fee $1.00 per page. Cert fee- $1.00 per cert plus copy fee. Payee- Mercer County Recorder of Deeds. **Other phones:** Treasurer- 660-748-3435. **Property tax/Assessing**- 802 E Main St, Courthouse, Princeton, MO 64673; 660-748-3511.

Miller County

Recorder of Deeds, PO Box 11, Tuscumbia, MO 65082. 573-369-1935; fax-573-369-1939; 8:30-4:30 www.millercountymissouri.org/Recorder.html

Index: All in one. Records indexed on a public use terminal back to 11/1/1993. Only the public may search. Office will look up deeds and give basic info only. Copy fee $.50 per page. Plats or surveys copied on wide format copier- $5.00 1st page, $3.00 each add'l page. Cert fee- $2.00 per cert plus copy fee. Payee- Miller County Recorder. **Other phones:** Treasurer- 573-369-1920; Elections- 573-369-1911; Vitals- 573-751-6387. **Property tax/Assessing**- PO Box 207, Tuscumbia, MO 65082; 573-369-1960, assessor fax- 573-369-1906.

Mississippi County

County Recorder, PO Box 369, Charleston, MO 63834. 573-683-2146, R/E recording phone-573-683-2146 x226; fax-573-683-7696; 8AM-5PM.

Index: All in one. Records indexed on a public use terminal back to 1992. Only the public may search. Will not search UCC records. Copy fee $1.00 per page. Cert fee- $2.00 1st page $1.00 add'l, copy fee included. Payee- Recorder of Deeds. **Online access to Real Estate, Deed records:** Access land records at http://etitlesearch.com. You can do a name search; choose from $200.00 monthly subscription or per click account. **Other phones:** Treasurer- 573-683-2146 x235; Elections- 573-683-2146 x222. **Property tax/Assessing**- PO Box 369, Charleston, MO 63834; 573-683-2146 x238.

Moniteau County

Circuit Clerk and Recorder, 200 E Main St, California, MO 65018. 573-796-2071, R/E recording phone-573-796-4822; fax-573-796-2591; 8-4:30PM
Index: All in one. Records indexed on a public use terminal back to 1996. Only the public may search. Copy fee $.50 per page. Cert fee- $1.00 per doc plus copy fee. Payee- Recorder of Deeds. **Other phones:** Treasurer- 573-796-4608; Elections- 573-796-4661; Vitals- 573-796-4671. **Property tax/Assessing-** 200 E Main St, California, MO 65018; 573-796-4637, assessor fax- 573-796-3082.

Monroe County

Recorder of Deeds, PO Box 246, Paris, MO 65275. 660-327-1131; fax-660-327-1130; 8AM-4:30PM.
Index: All in one. Records indexed on a public use terminal back to 1996. Only the public may search. Copy fee $.50 per page after 10 pages. Cert fee- $2.00 per doc plus copy fee. Payee- Monroe County Recorder. **Other phones:** Treasurer- 660-327-4711; Elections- 660-327-5106. **Property tax/Assessing-** 300 N Main, Rm 107, Paris, Missouri 65275-1399; 660-327-5607, assessor fax- 660-327-5119.

Montgomery County

Recorder of Deeds, 310 Salisbury St, #A, Montgomery City, MO 63361. 573-564-3157; 8AM-4:30PM. www.montgomerycountymo.org
Index: All in one. Records indexed on a public use terminal back to 1996. Only the public may search. Will not search UCC records. Copy fee $1.00 per page. Cert fee- $1.50 per page plus copy fee. Payee- Montgomery County Recorder. **Other phones:** Treasurer- 573-564-2319; Elections- 573-564-3357. **Property tax/Assessing-** 310 Salisbury St #B, Montgomery City, MO 63361; 573-564-2445.

Morgan County

County Recorder, 100 E Newton St; Courthouse, Versailles, MO 65084. 573-378-4029; fax-573-378-6431; 8AM-4:30PM.
Index: All in one. Records indexed on a public use terminal back to 1992. Office will perform a UCC search but public must search other records themselves. Search fee $14.00 per name. Copy fee $.50 per page. Cert fee- $.50 per page plus copy fee. Payee- Morgan County Recorder. Bulk purchase of data available for purchase on CD. **Other phones:** Treasurer- 573-378-4404; Elections- 573-378-5436. **Property tax/Assessing-** 573-378-5459.

New Madrid County

Recorder of Deeds, PO Box 217, New Madrid, MO 63869. 573-748-5146; fax-573-748-8969; 8:30AM-N, 1-4:30PM
Index: All in one. Records indexed from 1804 to present in many books. Records indexed on computer back to April 28, 2003. Only the public may search. General copy fee- $2.00 1st page, $1.00 each add'l. Cert fee- $1.00 per cert plus copy fee. Payee- New Madrid County Recorder of Deeds. **Online access to Real Estate, Deed records:** Land records may be available at http://etitlesearch.com. You can do a name search; choose from $200.00 monthly subscription or per click account. **Other phones:** Elections- 573-748-2524. **Property tax/Assessing-** 450 Main St, New Madrid, 63869; 573-748-2387.

Newton County

Recorder of Deeds, PO Box 604, Neosho, MO 64850. 417-451-8224, R/E recording phone-417-451-8224 or 8225, UCC recording phone-417-451-8225; fax-417-451-8273; 8:30AM-5PM www.ncrecorder.org
Index: Separate indices to search include grantor/grantee, WD books. Records indexed on a public use terminal back to 1994. Office will perform a UCC search but public must search other records themselves. Office will lookup deed but not search all docs. UCC search per debtor name- $14.00. Copy fee $1.00 per page. Cert fee- $1.00 1st page plus copy fee. Payee- Recorder of Deeds. **Online access to Real Estate, Deed, Mortgage, UCC, Lien, Vital Statistic records:** Search the index free back to 1994 at www.ncrecorder.org/searchaccess.htm. **Other phones:** Treasurer- 417-451-8226; Elections- 417-451-8220; Vital Records- 573-751-6387; Mapping-417-451-8229; Health Dept (Birth & Death) -417-451-3743. **Property tax/Assessing-** 101 S Wood St, #205, Neosho, MO 64850; 417-451-8228 or 8218, assessor fax- 417-451-8259. (Appraiser/Auditor- 417-451-8379) 8:00-5:00PM No public access terminal.

Nodaway County

Recorder of Deeds, 305 N Main, Rm 104, Maryville, MO 64468. 660-582-5711; fax-660-582-5282; 8:30AM-4:30PM
Index: All in one. Records indexed on computer back to 1977. Only the public may search. Copy fee $1.00 per page. Cert fee- $2.00 per cert. Payee- Recorder of Deeds. **Other phones:** Treasurer- 660-582-4302; Elections- 660-582-2251. **Property tax/Assessing-** 305 N Main, Rm 106, Maryville, MO 64468; 660-582-7633, assessor fax- 660-562-8175. (Appraiser/Auditor- 660-582-3374) Office will assist on their office computer. No public access terminal.

Oregon County

Recorder of Deeds, PO Box 406, Alton, MO 65606. 417-778-7460; fax-417-778-2007; 8AM-4PM.
Index: Separate indices to search include warranty deed, misc, trust deed. Record index not computerized. Office will perform a UCC search but public must search other records themselves. Copy fee $.25 per page. Cert fee- $1.00 per instrument includes copy fee. Payee- Recorder of Deeds. **Other phones:** Treasurer- 417-778-6303; Elections- 417-778-7475. **Property tax/Assessing-** PO Box 361, Alton, MO 65606; 417-778-7471, assessor fax- 417-778-7441. hours- 8AM-N, 1PM-4PM Public access terminal at Collector's office.

Osage County

Recorder of Deeds, PO Box 825, Linn, MO 65051-0825. Recording, R/E & UCC phone-573-897-3114; fax-573-897-4075; 8AM-4:30PM
Index: All in one. Records indexed on computer back to 11/93. Office will perform a UCC search but public must search other records themselves. Copy fee $.50 per page. Cert fee- $2.00 per cert plus copy fee. Payee- Osage County Recorder of Deeds. **Other phones:** Treasurer- 573-897-3095; Elections- 573-897-2139; Vitals- 573-751-6001. **Property tax/Assessing-** PO Box 409, Linn, MO; 573-897-2217.

Ozark County

Circuit Clerk & Recorder, PO Box 36, Gainesville, MO 65655. phone-417-679-4232; fax-417-679-4554; 8AM-N, 12:30-4:30PM
Records indexed on a public use terminal back to 1992. Deeds back to 1982. Only the public may search. Copy fee $1.00 per doc; UCC copy fee after 1st 10 pages- $.50 per page. Cert fee- $1.50 per deed plus copy fee. Payee- Clerk. **Other phones:** Treasurer- 417-679-3553; Elections- 417-679-3516. **Property tax/Assessing-** #1 Courthouse, Gainesville, MO 65655; 417-679-4705.

Pemiscot County

Recorder of Deeds, 610 Ward Ave, Ste 1A; County Courthouse, Caruthersville, MO 63830. Recording, R/E & UCC phone-573-333-2204; 8:30AM-4:30PM
Index: Separate indices to search include deed of trust, warranty & miscellaneous. Record index not computerized. Office will perform a UCC search but public must search other records themselves. Office will not search real estate records. UCC search per debtor name- $14.00 for search plus $14.00 for copy request. 1st 10 UCC copies free, then copy fee $.50 per page.Real estate record copy- $1.00 per page. Cert fee- $1.00 per doc plus copy fee. Payee- Pemiscot County Recorder of Deeds. **Online access to Real Estate, Deed records:** Access land records at http://etitlesearch.com. You can do a name search; choose from $200.00 monthly subscription or per click account. **Other phones:** Treasurer- 573-333-4171. **Property tax/Assessing-** 573-333-1390.

Perry County

Recorder of Deeds, 15 W Ste. Marie St, #1, Perryville, MO 63775. Recording, R/E & UCC phone-573-547-1611; fax-573-547-3879; 8AM-5PM
Index: All in one. Records indexed on a public use terminal back to 1989. Office will perform a UCC search but public must search other records themselves. Search fee $14.00 per name. Copy fee after 1st 10 pages is $.50 per page. UCC copy- $14.00 up to 10 copies. Real estate or tax lien copy- $2.00 1st page; $1.00 each add'l. Cert fee- $1.00 per doc plus copy fee. Payee- Perry County recorder. **Online access to Real Estate, Deed, Lien records:** Recorder land data by subscription on either the Laredo system using subscription and fees or the Tapestry System using credit card, http://tapestry.fidlar.com; $5.95 search; $.50 per image. Index goes back to 1989; images to 12/99. **Other phones:** Treasurer- 573-547-4502; Elections- 573-547-4242. **Property tax/Assessing-** 321 N Main St, Perryville, MO 63775; 573-547-4422. No public terminal available.

Pettis County

Recorder of Deeds, 415 S. Ohio, Sedalia, MO 65301. 660-826-5000 x431, R/E recording phone-x431; fax-660-829-4479; 8AM-5PM www.pettiscomo.com
Index: All in one. Records indexed on a public use terminal back to 1993. Only the public may search. Office will not search real estate records. Copy fee $1.00 per page. Plats/surveys- $5.00 each. Cert fee- $1.00 per doc plus copy fee. Payee- Recorder of Deeds. **Online access to Real Estate, Deed, Lien records:** Recorder land data by subscription on either the Laredo system using subscription and fees or the Tapestry System using credit card, http://tapestry.fidlar.com; $3.99 search; $.50 per image. Index and images go back to 7/1/93. **Other phones:** Treasurer- x408; Elections- x400; Vital Records- x431. **Property tax/Assessing-** 415 S Ohio, 2nd Fl, Sedalia, MO 65301; 660-826-5000. hours- 9AM-5PM Personal Property--X417, Mapper--X421, Real Estate--X422. www.pettiscomo.com/assr.html **Online access-** Search assessor property data for a fee on the GIS system at http://beacon.schneidercorp.com/ with registration and username required.

Phelps County

Recorder of Deeds, 200 N Main, #133; Courthouse, Rolla, MO 65401. 573-458-6095; fax-573-458-6098; 8AM-5PM. www.phelpscounty.org/
Index: All in one. Records indexed on a public use terminal back to 1/85. Office will perform a UCC search but public must search other records themselves. Search fee $14.00 for UCC. Office will not search real estate records. Copy fee $1.00 per page. Cert fee- $2.00 per page includes copy fee. Payee- Phelps County Recorder. **Other phones:** Treasurer- 573-458-6130; Elections- 573-458-6100; Vitals- 573-458-6123. **Property tax/Assessing-** 200 N Main #126, Rolla, MO 65401; 573-458-6140.

Pike County

Recorder of Deeds, 115 W Main St, Bowling Green, MO 63334. 573-324-5567, R/E recording phone-573-324-3261, UCC recording phone-573-324-5567; fax-573-324-5210; 8AM-4:30PM
Index: All in one. Records indexed on a public use terminal back to 1995. Only the public may search. Copy fee $1.00 per page. Cert fee- $1.00 per cert plus copy fee. Payee- Pike County Recorder of Deeds. **Other phones:** Treasurer- 573-324-2102; Elections-573-324-2412. **Property tax/Assessing-** 115 W Main St 1st Fl, Courthouse, Bowling Green, MO 63334; 573-324-3261, assessor fax- 573-324-5919. www.pikecountymo.org/courthouse.htm#Assessor

Platte County

Recorder of Deeds, 415 3rd St, #70, Platte City, MO 64079. 816-858-3326, R/E recording phone-816-858-3320, UCC recording phone-816-858-1832; fax-816-

858-2379; 8AM-5PM. www.co.platte.mo.us/county_offices_departments/recorder.html
Index: Separate indices to search include deeds, durable power of attorney, request for notice. Records indexed on a public use terminal back to 11/90, prior in index books. Office will perform a UCC search only if you have proper request document, but public must search other records themselves. Office will not search real estate records. UCC search per debtor name- $14.00 plus $14.00 for copies. Copy fee $1.00 per page. Cert fee- $1.00 per doc plus copy fee. Payee- Recorder of Deeds. Bulk data available for purchase; contact Steve. **Online access to Real Estate, Lien, UCC, Marriage records:** To access recorder's indexes online, complete the online deed form and a password will be issued to you; no fee at this time. **Other phones:** Treasurer- 816-858-3318; Elections- 816-858-4400. **Property tax/Assessing-** 415 3rd St, #20, Platte City, MO 64079; 816-858-3306, assessor fax- 816-858-3314. www.co.platte.mo.us **Online access-** Assessor data available free at http://maps.co.platte.mo.us/. Also, access the Collector's tax payments data free at www.plattecountycollector.com/platte-payment.php but parcel ID or account number required.

Polk County

Recorder of Deeds, 102 E Broadway; Courthouse, Bolivar, MO 65613-1502. Recording, R/E & UCC phone-417-326-4924; fax-417-326-6898; 8AM-5PM.
Index: Separate indices to search include grantor/grantee. Records indexed on a public use terminal back to 0101/1994. Office will perform a UCC search but public must search other records themselves. General search fee $14.00 per name. Office will not search real estate records. Tax liens not included in UCC search. Copy fee $1.00 per page. Cert fee- $2.00 per doc plus copy fee. Payee- Recorder. Bulk data available for purchase in CD form by month ($350.00 per month). **Other phones:** Treasurer- 417-326-4913; Elections- 417-326-4031; Vital - 417-326-4031. **Property tax/Assessing-** 102 E Broadway, Courthouse, Rm 9, Bolivar, MO 65613; 417-326-4643, assessor fax- 417-326-3131. (Appraiser/Auditor- 417-326-4346) Public access terminal available.

Pulaski County

Recorder of Deeds, 301 Historic Rte 66 E, #202, Waynesville, MO 65583. 573-774-4760, R/E recording phone-573-774-4752; fax-573-774-6967; 8AM-4:30PM
www.pulaskicountyrecorderofdeeds.org/
Index: Separate indices to search include anything before 1991 can be searched in books. Records indexed on a public use terminal back to 1991. Only the public may search. Copy fee $1.00 per page. Cert fee- $1.00 per doc plus copy fee. Payee- Pulaski County Recorder of Deeds. **Other phones:** Treasurer- 573-774-6609 x124. **Property tax/Assessing-** 573-774-6609 x117.

Putnam County

Recorder of Deeds, Courthouse, Rm 202, Unionville, MO 63565-1659. 660-947-2071; fax-660-947-2320; 8AM-N, 1PM-5PM.
Give them book and page, they can make a doc copy $1.00 per page, prepaid. Index: All in one. Records indexed on a public use terminal back to 1996. Only the public may search. Copy fee $1.00 per page. Cert fee- $1.00 per doc plus copy fee. Payee- Rutnam County Recorder. **Other phones:** Treasurer- 660-947-2095; Elections- 660-947-2674. **Property tax/Assessing-** 1601 W Main, Courthouse, Rm 201, Unionville, MO 63565; 660-947-3900, assessor fax- 660-947-3902. hours- 8:30AM-N, 1PM-4:30PM Public access terminal available. http://putnam.missouriassessors.com/ **Online access-** Free parcel search at http://putnam.missouriassessors.com/search.php?mode=search.

Ralls County

Recorder of Deeds, PO Box 466, New London, MO 63459-0455. Recording, R/E & UCC phone-573-985-5631; 8:30AM-N, 1-4:30PM
Index: Separate indices to search include computer and books. Records indexed on a public use terminal back to 1989. Only the public may search. Copy fee $1.00 per page for deeds, other records $25 per page. Cert fee- $1.00 per cert plus copy fee. Payee- Ralls County Recorder of Deeds. **Other phones:** Treasurer- 573-985-7151; Elections- 573-985-7111; Circuit Court Civil- 573-985-5633. **Property tax/Assessing-** 573-985-5671.

Randolph County

Recorder of Deeds, 110 S Main St; Courthouse, Huntsville, MO 65259. Recording, R/E & UCC phone-660-277-4718; fax-660-277-4273; 8AM-4PM.
Index: Indices by year. Records indexed on a public use terminal back to 1996. Only the public may search. Copy fee $2.00 1st page, $1.00 each add'l. Cert fee- $1.00 per page plus copy fee. Payee- Recorder of Deeds. **Other phones:** Treasurer- 660-277-4714; Elections- 660-277-4717. **Property tax/Assessing-** 110 S Main St, Courthouse, Huntsville, MO 65259; 660-277-4716.

Ray County

Recorder of Deeds, PO Box 167, Richmond, MO 64085. 816-776-4500; 8AM-N, 1-4PM
Index: All in one. Records indexed on a public use terminal back to 7/03. Only the public may search. Copy fee $1.00 per page after 10 pages. Cert fee- $1.00 per page plus copy fee. Payee- Ray County Recorder of Deeds. **Other phones:** Treasurer- 660-776-6140. **Property tax/Assessing-** 100 W Main, Courthouse, 2nd Fl, Richmond, MO 64085; 816-776-2676, assessor fax- 816-776-4521. Public use terminal available. http://ray.missouriassessors.com/ **Online access-** Free assessor parcel search at http://ray.missouriassessors.com/search.php?mode=search.

Reynolds County

Recorder of Deeds, PO Box 76, Centerville, MO 63633-0076. 573-648-2494, R/E recording phone-573-648-2494 x34; fax-573-648-2503; 8AM-4PM.
Index: Books in alpha order to 2/2003. Records indexed on a public use terminal back to 2000. Office personnel or visitors may perform searches. Search fee $14.00 for UCC search. Office will not search real estate records. Office will not search UCC records. Copy fee $2.00 per document. Cert fee- $4.00 per doc plus copy fee. Payee- Reynolds County Recorder. **Other phones:** Treasurer- 573-648-2494 x37; Elections- 573- 648-2494 x12; Vital Records- 573-648-2494 x12. **Property tax/Assessing-** Courthouse, Centerville, MO 63633; 573-648-2494 x18.

Ripley County

Recorder of Deeds, 100 Courthouse Sq, #3, Doniphan, MO 63935. 573-996-7941; 8AM-4PM.
Index: All in one by years/dates. Record index not computerized. Office personnel or visitors may perform searches. Search fee varies. Office will briefly search real estate records. Office will search UCC records. General copy fee $1.00 per page. Cert fee- $1.00 per page plus copy fee. Payee- Recorder of Deeds. **Other phones:** Treasurer- 573-996-3903. **Property tax/Assessing-** 100 Courthouse Sq, #9, Doniphan, MO 63935; 573-996-7113, assessor fax- 573-996-5187.

Saline County

Recorder of Deeds, Courthouse, Rm 206, Marshall, MO 65340. Recording, R/E & UCC phone-660-886-2677; fax-660-886-2603; 8AM-4:30PM
Index: Separate indices to search include land, UCC, marriage. Records indexed on a public use terminal back to 1992. Only the public may search. Copy fee $1.00 per page for real estate. Cert fee- $1.00 per page plus copy fee. Payee- Saline County Recorder of Deeds. **Online access to Real Estate, Grantor/Grantee, Deed, Lien records:** Recorder land data by subscription on either the Laredo system using subscription and fees or the Tapestry System using credit card, http://tapestry.fidlar.com; $3.99 search; $.50 per image. Index goes back to 1992; images to 1996. **Other phones:** Treasurer- 660-886-3636; Elections- 660-886-3331; Vital Records- 660-886-3434. **Property tax/Assessing-** 660-335-3111.

Schuyler County

Recorder of Deeds, PO Box 186, Lancaster, MO 63548. 660-457-3784; fax-660-457-3016; 8AM-4PM
Index: Separate indices to search include land transfers, financials. Record index not computerized. Only the public may search. Will not search UCC records. Copy fee $1.00 per page. Cert fee- $1.00 per doc plus copy fee. Payee- Recorder of Deeds. **Other phones:** Treasurer- 660-457-3825; Elections- 660-457-3842. **Property tax/Assessing-** PO Box 418, #1 Courthouse Sq #13, Lancaster, MO 63548; 660-457-3211, assessor fax- 660-457-3016. hours- 9AM-N, 1-4PM

Scotland County

Recorder of Deeds, 117 S Market St, #106, Memphis, MO 63555-1449. 660-465-2284, R/E recording phone-660-465-8605, UCC recording phone-660-465-2284; fax-660-465-2408; 8AM-4PM
Index: Separate indices to search include direct and indirect. Records indexed on computer back to 1993. Only the public may search. Office will not search real estate records. Will not search UCC records. Copy fee $1.00 per page. Cert fee- $2.00 per cert plus copy fee. Payee- Scotland County Recorder of Deeds. **Other phones:** Treasurer- 660-465-2529. **Property tax/Assessing-** 117 S Market St, Memphis, MO 63555; 660-465-2269, assessor fax- 660-465-2408. hours- 8:30AM-4PM

Scott County

Recorder of Deeds, PO Box 78, Benton, MO 63736. 573-545-3551; fax-573-545-3551; 8:30AM-5PM
Index: Separate indices. Records indexed on a public use terminal back to 1999. Only the public may search. General copy fee $1.00 per page after 10 pages. Real estate copy- $2.00 1st page, $1.00 each add'l. Cert fee- $2.00 per cert 1st. $1.00 each add'l page. Payee- Scott County Recorder of Deeds. **Online access to Real Estate, Deed records:** Access recording office land data at www.etitlesearch.com; registration required, fee based on usage. **Other phones:** Treasurer- 573-545-3543. **Property tax/Assessing-** PO Box 245, 131 S Winchester St, Benton, MO 63736; 573-545-3535, assessor fax- 573-545-3536. hours- 8AM-4:30PM Public use terminal available. www.scottcountymo.com/assessor.html

Shannon County

Recorder of Deeds, PO Box 148, Eminence, MO 65466. 573-226-3315, R/E recording phone-573-226-3313; fax-573-226-5321; 8AM-N, 12:30PM-4:30PM
Index: Separate indices to search include 1881-1995 books; 1955-present on imaging system. Records indexed on a public use terminal back to 5/95. Only the public may search. Copy fee $.25 per page. Cert fee- $2.00 per cert plus copy fee. Payee- Shannon County Recorder of Deeds. **Other phones:** Treasurer- 573-226-3051. **Property tax/Assessing-** County Collector, 106 Main, Courthouse, Eminence, MO 65466; 573-226-3416.

Shelby County

Recorder of Deeds, PO Box 176, Shelbyville, MO 63469. 573-633-2151, R/E recording phone-573-633-2821; fax-573-633-1004; 8AM-N, 1PM-4PM.
Index: Separate indices to search include deeds, UCCs, Marriage, Surveys, Tax Liens. Records indexed on a public use terminal back to 2002. Only the public may search. Copy fee $1.00 per UCC. $1.00 per deed up to 6 pages, $2.00 each add'l page. Cert fee- $3.00 per page plus copy fee. Payee- Shelby Co. Recorder. **Other phones:** Treasurer- 573-633-2574; Elections- 573-633-2181; Vital Records- 573-

633-2353. **Property tax/Assessing**- PO Box 165, 100 E Main, Shelbyville, MO 63469; 573-633-2521, assessor fax- 573-633-1004.

St. Charles County

Recorder of Deeds, 201 N 2nd St, #529, St. Charles, MO 63301. Recording, R/E & UCC phone-636-949-7505, UCC phone-636-949-7508; fax-636-949-7512; 8AM-5PM http://recorder.sccmo.org/recorder/
Index: All in one. Records indexed on a public use terminal back to 1972. Office will perform a UCC search but public must search other records themselves. Copy fee $2.00 1st page, $1.00 each add'l; $1.00 each self serve. Cert fee- $1.00 per cert plus copy fee. Payee- St Charles County Recorder of Deeds. Yearly indexes on roll film available for purchase, contact Jeanne Callaway. **Other phones:** Elections- 636-949-7550; Vital Records- 636-949-7558. **Property tax/Assessing**- 201 N 2nd St, Rm 247, St. Charles, MO 63301; 636-949-7425, assessor fax- 636-949-7435. (Appraiser/Auditor- 636-949-7431) A public access terminal is available. http://assessor.sccmo.org/assessor/ **Online access**- Access recorder records free at http://scharles.landrecordsonline.com/. Search index free; images -$1.00 per page. Also, search property assessment data free at http://assessor.sccmo.org/assessor/index.php?option=com_assessordb&Itemid=49. No name searching.

St. Clair County

Recorder of Deeds, PO Box 323, Osceola, MO 64776-0493. 417-646-2950; fax-417-646-2951; 8AM-4:30PM
Index: All in one. Records indexed on a public use terminal back to 4/77 for real estate, 1924 for marriage. Only the public may search. Copy fee $1.00 per page. Cert fee- $1.00 per cert plus copy fee. Payee- St. Clair Recorder. **Other phones:** Treasurer- 417-646-8068; Elections- 417-646-2315. **Property tax/Assessing**- PO Box 95, 655 2nd St, Osceola, MO 64776; 417-646-8880 or 2449, fax- 417-646-5523. http://stclaircountymissouri.com/stclaircountymissouricomassessorcom.aspx

St. Francois County

Recorder of Deeds, 1 W Liberty, #100, Farmington, MO 63640. 573-756-2323; 8-4PM www.sfcgov.org
Index: All in one. Records indexed on a public use terminal back to 1994. Only the public may search. Copy fee $.50 per page after 10 pages. Cert fee- $1.00 per cert plus copy fee. Payee- St. Francois County Recorder of Deeds. **Online access to Real Estate, Deed, Lien records:** Recorder land data by subscription on the Tapestry System using credit card, http://tapestry.fidlar.com; $3.99 search; $.50 per image. Index goes back to 1994; images to 2005. **Other phones:** Treasurer- 573-756-3349. **Property tax/Assessing**- 1W Liberty, Rm 200, Farmington, MO 63640; 573-756-2509 x1, assessor fax- 573-756-5687. www.sfcassessor.org/index.html **Online access**- Access property assessor data free at www.sfcassessor.org/parcel_search.html.

St. Genevieve County

Recorder of Deeds, 55 S 3rd St, Rm 3; Courthouse, Ste. Genevieve, MO 63670. 573-883-2706; fax-573-883-5312; 8AM-4:30PM
Index: All in one. Records indexed on a public use terminal back to 1900's. Only the public may search. Copy fee $.50 per page. Cert fee- $2.00 per cert. Payee- Recorder of Deeds. **Other phones:** Treasurer- 573-883-3000; Elections- 573-883-5589. **Property tax/Assessing**- 55 S 3rd St, Rm 3, Courthouse, PO Box 26, Ste. Genevieve, MO 63670; 573-883-2333, assessor fax- 573-883-5312.

St. Louis City

Recorder of Deeds, 1200 Market St, Rm 126, St. Louis, MO 63103. 314-622-3259 or 3260, R/E recording phone-314-622-3260; fax-314-622-4175; 8AM-5PM. www.stlouiscity.com
Index: Separate indices to search include vital statistics, land. Records indexed on a public use terminal back to 1981. Terminal located in room 128; another in archives unit. Office personnel or visitors may perform searches. No charge for fax or phone current owner search, please provide date. Archives searches (older records, pre-1981) fee $8.00 per name. Office will not search real estate records. Will not search UCC records. Copy fee $3.00 1st page; $2.00 each add'l, from microfilm. Cert fee- $2.00 per cert plus copy fee. Payee- Recorder of Deeds. **Online access to Real Estate, Deed, Lien records:** Recorder land data by subscription on either the Laredo system using subscription and fees or the Tapestry System using credit card, http://tapestry.fidlar.com; $3.99 search; $.50 per image. Index goes back to 1/1881. Images are only available with a Laredo subscription, or via the recorder office. **Other phones:** Treasurer- 314-622-2062; Vital Records- 314-622-3016; Marriage License- 314-622-4328; Births; Deaths - 314-622-3017; 314-622-3019. **Property tax/Assessing**- 1200 Market, Rm 120, St. Louis, MO 63103; 314-622-4050. Bulk GIS-related data for purchase on CD-rom. http://stlouis.missouri.org/citygov/assessor/index.htm **Online**- Access the mapping site free at www.co.st-louis.mo.us/plan/gis/. Search personal property by account number, address, name at http://revenue.stlouisco.com/Collection/ppInfo/.

St. Louis County

Recorder of Deeds, 41 S Central Ave, 4th Fl, Clayton, MO 63105. 314-615-2500; fax-314-615-4964; 8AM-5PM www.stlouisco.com
Index: All in one. Records indexed on a public use terminal back to 1974. Only the public may search. General copy fee-$2.00 1st page, $1.00 each add'l page per doc. UCC copy fee $.50 per page after 10 pages. Cert fee- $1.00 per cert plus copy fee. Payee- St. Louis County Recorder of Deeds. **Other phones:** Vital Records- 314-615-1684. **Property tax/Assessing**- 41 S. Central Ave, 3rd Fl, Admin Bldg, St. Louis, MO 63103; 314-615-4225, assessor fax- 316-615-5135. **Online access**- Access county property data free at http://revenue.stlouisco.com/ias/. Search personal property tax data free at http://revenue.stlouisco.com/Collection/ppInfo/.

Stoddard County

Recorder of Deeds, PO Box 217, Bloomfield, MO 63825-0217. Recording, R/E & UCC phone-573-568-3444; fax-573-568-2545; 8:30AM-4:30PM
Index: Separate indices to search include computer and books by year. Records indexed on computer back to 4/06. Only the public may search. Copy fee $.50 per pages. Cert fee- $1.00 per doc plus copy fee. Payee- Recorder of Deeds. **Other phones:** Treasurer- 573-568-3327; Elections- 573-568-3339. **Property tax/Assessing**- 310 Courthouse Sq, Bloomfield, MO 63825; 573-568-3163, assessor fax- 573-568-2051.

Stone County

Recorder of Deeds, PO Box 186, Galena, MO 65656. Recording, R/E & UCC phone-417-357-6362; fax-417-357-8131; 8AM-4PM www.stoneco-mo.us
Index: All in one. Records indexed on a public use terminal back to 1/1/1993. Images back to 1997. Only the public may search. Copy fee $.25; if real estate or other recorded document- $2.00 per page. Cert fee- $1.00 per doc plus copy fee. Payee- Stone County Recorder. **Online access to Real Estate, Grantor/Grantee, Deed, UCC, Subdivision, Condominium records:** Access to recorder data is free through land access.com at www.landaccess.com/sites/mo/stone/index.php?mostone. **Other phones:** Treasurer- 417-357-6131; Elections- 417-357-6127. **Property tax/Assessing**- PO Box 135, 108 E 4th St, 2nd Fl, Galena, MO 65656; 417-357-6141, assessor fax- 417-357-6369. (Appraiser/Auditor- 417-294-0890) www.stoneco-mo.us/assessor.htm **Online access**- Access property data from the GIS interactive map at www.stoneco-mo.us/disclaim.htm. Download the MapGuide viewer first.

Sullivan County

Recorder of Deeds, Courthouse, Milan, MO 63556. 660-265-3630; fax-660-265-5071; 9AM-N; 1PM-4:30PM
Index: All in one. Records indexed on a public use terminal back to 2003. Only the public may search. Copy fee $1.00 per page. Cert fee- $1.00 per doc plus copy fee. Payee- Recorder of Deeds. **Other phones:** Treasurer- 660-265-4514; Elections- 660-265-3786. **Property tax/Assessing**- 109 N Main #36, Milan, MO 63556; 660-265-4474, assessor fax- 660-265-4037. No public access terminal.

Taney County

Recorder of Deeds, PO Box 428, Forsyth, MO 65653. 417-546-7234; fax-417-546-9021; 8AM-5PM www.co.taney.mo.us
Index: All in one. Records indexed on a public use terminal back to 1983. Only the public may search. Copy fee $1.00 per page. Cert fee- $1.50 per cert plus copy fee. Payee- Taney County Recorder of Deeds. Bulk data available for purchase, contact Robert Dixon, Recorder. **Online access to Real Estate, Deed, Lien records:** Recorder land data by subscription on either the Laredo system using subscription and fees or the Tapestry System using credit card, http://tapestry.fidlar.com; $5.99 search; $.50 per image. Index and images go back to 7/1/1994. **Other phones:** Treasurer- 417-546-7207. **Property tax/Assessing**- 417-546-7240. **Online access**- Search assessor property data free on the GIS system at http://beacon.schneidercorp.com.

Texas County

Recorder of Deeds, PO Box 287, Houston, MO 65483. 417-967-3742; fax-417-967-4220; 8AM-5PM
Index: All in one. Records indexed on a public use terminal back to 1996. Only the public may search. Copy fee $1.00 per page. Cert fee- $3.00. Payee- Recorder of Deeds. **Other phones:** Treasurer- 417-967-2589. **Property tax/Assessing**- 210 N Grand Ave, Houston, MO 65483; 417-967-4709, assessor fax- 417-967-2091.

Vernon County

Recorder of Deeds, 100 W Cherry, Rm 11; Courthouse, Nevada, MO 64772. Recording, R/E & UCC phone-417-448-2520; fax-417-448-2524; 8:30AM-N, 1-4:30PM http://vernoncountymo.org
Index: All in one. Records indexed on a public use terminal back to 1994. Images from 4/00. Only the public may search. Copy fee $1.00 per page after 10 pages. Cert fee- $1.00 per cert plus copy fee. Payee- Vernon County Recorder of Deeds. **Other phones:** Treasurer- 417-448-2510; Elections- 417-448-2500; Recorder of Deeds- 417-448-2520. **Property tax/Assessing**- 100 W Cherry, Courthouse, Rm 100, Nevada, MO 64772; 417-448-2530, assessor fax- 417-667-8360. http://vernoncountymo.org

Warren County

Recorder of Deeds, 104 W Boone's Lick Rd, Warrenton, MO 63383. 636-456-9800; 8AM-4:30PM
Index: Pre-1990 records in hand written books; 1990 forward on computer. Records indexed on a public use terminal back to 1990. Only the public may search. Copy fee $1.00 per page. Cert fee- $1.00 per doc plus copy fee. Payee- Warren County Recorder of Deeds. **Online access to Real Estate, Deed, Lien records:** Recorder land data by subscription on either the Laredo system using subscription and fees or the Tapestry System using credit card, http://tapestry.fidlar.com; $3.99 search; $.50 per image. **Other phones:** Treasurer- 636-456-3389. **Property tax/Assessing**- 105 S Market, Warrenton, MO 63383; 636-456-8885, assessor fax- 636-456-

9024. Public access computer in office for index and records searching.

Washington County

Recorder of Deeds, 102 N Missouri St, Potosi, MO 63664. Recording, R/E & UCC phone-573-438-6111; 8AM-4:30PM.

Index: Separate indices to search. Records indexed on a public use terminal back to 1999. Only the public may search. Copy fee $1.00 per page.Real estate record copy- $.50 per page. Cert fee- $2.00 for cert and $.50 per page plus copy fee. Payee- Recorder of Deeds. **Other phones:** Treasurer- 573-438-6111; Elections- 573-438-6111. **Property tax/Assessing-** 102 N Missouri St, Potosi, MO 63664; 573-438-4992.

Wayne County

Recorder of Deeds, PO Box 78, Greenville, MO 63944. 573-224-3015; fax-573-224-3225; 8:30AM-N; 1PM-4:30PM.

Index: Books. Records indexed on computer back to 1/27/03. Office will perform a UCC search but public must search other records themselves. Search fee $14.00. Copy fee $.50 per page. Cert fee- $2.00 per page includes copy fee. Payee- Recorder of Deeds. **Other phones:** Treasurer- 573-224-3019; Elections- 573-224-3011. **Property tax/Assessing-** PO Box 54, 109 Walnut, Greenville, MO 63944; 573-224-3006, assessor fax- 573-224-3446.

Webster County

Recorder of Deeds, PO Box 546, Marshfield, MO 65706. Recording, R/E & UCC phone-417-859-5882; fax-417-468-3843; 8AM-5PM

Index: Separate indices to search include land, UCCs, State & Fed tax liens, marriage. Records indexed on a public use terminal back to 1985. Only the public may search. Copy fee $1.00 per page. Cert fee- $1.00 per doc plus copy fee. **Online access to Real Estate, Deed, Lien, UCC records:** Access to recorded data is by subscription; $200.00 per month. Get info and register through the recorder's office. **Other phones:** Treasurer- 417-468-2108; Elections- 417-859-8683. **Property tax/Assessing-** 101 Crittendon, Marshfield, MO 65706; 417-859-2169.

Worth County

Recorder of Deeds, PO Box 14, Grant City, MO 64456. 660-564-2484; fax-660-564-2432; 8AM-4PM.

Index: Separate indices to search by type. Record index not computerized. Office personnel or visitors may perform searches. General search fee $4.00 per name. Office will not search real estate records. Will not search UCC records. UCC search per debtor name- $14.00. UCC search & copy request (including 10 pages of copies)- $28.00. Copy fee $1.00 per page. Cert fee- None. Payee- Worth County Recorder of Deeds. **Other phones:** Treasurer- 660-564-2154. **Property tax/Assessing-** 660-564-2153. hours- 8:30AM-4:30PM

Wright County

County Recorder, PO Box 39, Hartville, MO 65667. Recording, R/E & UCC phone-417-741-7322; fax-417-741-7504; 8AM-4:30PM.

Index: Separate indices to search include computer and books. Records indexed on a public use terminal back to 1993, books up to 1993. Only the public may search. Copy fee $1.00 per page. Cert fee- $2.00 per doc plus copy fee. Payee- Wright County Recorder. **Other phones:** Treasurer- 417-741-7225; Elections- 417-741-6661; Vital - 573-751-6400. **Property tax/Assessing-** 417-741-6400.

Missouri County Locator

You will usually be able to find the city name in the City/County Cross Reference below. In that case, it is a simple matter to determine the county from the cross reference. However, only the official US Postal Service city names are included in this index. There are an additional 40,000 place names that people use in their addresses. Therefore, we have also included a ZIP/City Cross Reference immediately following the City/County Cross Reference.

Missouri City/County Cross Reference

ADRIAN Bates
ADVANCE (63730) Stoddard(78), Cape Girardeau(16), Bollinger(5)
AGENCY Buchanan
ALBA Jasper
ALBANY Gentry
ALDRICH (65601) Polk(70), Dade(28), Cedar(1)
ALEXANDRIA Clark
ALLENDALE Worth
ALLENTON St. Louis
ALMA Lafayette
ALTAMONT Daviess
ALTENBURG (63732) Cape Girardeau(95), Perry(4)
ALTON Oregon
AMAZONIA Andrew
AMITY De Kalb
AMORET Bates
AMSTERDAM Bates
ANABEL Macon
ANDERSON McDonald
ANNADA Pike
ANNAPOLIS (63620) Iron(56), Madison(32), Reynolds(10)
ANNISTON Mississippi
APPLETON CITY (64724) St. Clair(93), Bates(6)
ARBELA (63432) Scotland(88), Clark(11)
ARBYRD Dunklin
ARCADIA (63621) Iron(79), Madison(20)
ARCHIE Cass
ARCOLA (65603) Dade(97), Cedar(2)
ARGYLE (65001) Osage(61), Maries(38)
ARMSTRONG (65230) Howard(86), Randolph(13)
ARNOLD Jefferson
ARROW ROCK Saline
ASBURY (64832) Barton(83), Jasper(16)
ASH GROVE (65604) Greene(65), Lawrence(32), Dade(1)
ASHBURN Pike
ASHLAND Boone
ATLANTA Macon
AUGUSTA St. Charles
AURORA (65605) Lawrence(90), Barry(9)
AUXVASSE (65231) Callaway(98), Audrain(1)
AVA (65608) Douglas(90), Taney(9)
AVALON Livingston
AVILLA Jasper
BAKERSFIELD (65609) Ozark(77), Howell(22)
BALLWIN St. Louis
BARING (63531) Knox(59), Scotland(40)
BARNARD Nodaway
BARNETT (65011) Morgan(94), Moniteau(5)
BARNHART Jefferson
BATES CITY (64011) Lafayette(92), Johnson(7)
BEAUFORT Franklin
BELGRADE Washington
BELL CITY (63735) Stoddard(91), Scott(8)
BELLE (65013) Maries(68), Osage(31)
BELLEVIEW (63623) Iron(97), Reynolds(2)
BELLFLOWER (63333) Montgomery(96), Lincoln(3)
BELTON Cass
BENDAVIS Texas
BENTON Scott
BENTON CITY Audrain
BERGER Franklin
BERNIE (63822) Stoddard(95), Dunklin(4)
BERTRAND (63823) Mississippi(90), Scott(9)
BETHANY Harrison
BETHEL Shelby
BEULAH (65436) Phelps(87), Texas(8), Pulaski(3)
BEVIER Macon
BILLINGS (65610) Christian(95), Lawrence(3)
BIRCH TREE (65438) Shannon(74), Oregon(25)
BISMARCK (63624) St. Francois(70), Washington(25), Iron(4)
BIXBY Iron
BLACK (63625) Reynolds(89), Iron(10)
BLACKBURN (65321) Saline(61), Lafayette(38)
BLACKWATER Cooper
BLACKWELL (63626) Washington(80), St. Francois(19)
BLAIRSTOWN Henry
BLAND (65014) Gasconade(68), Osage(25), Maries(6)
BLODGETT Scott
BLOOMFIELD Stoddard
BLOOMSDALE (63627) Ste. Genevieve(90), Jefferson(9)
BLUE EYE (65611) Stone(95), Taney(4)
BLUE SPRINGS Jackson
BLYTHEDALE Harrison
BOGARD Carroll
BOIS D ARC (65612) Greene(93), Lawrence(6)
BOLCKOW (64427) Andrew(83), Nodaway(16)
BOLIVAR Polk
BONNE TERRE (63628) St. Francois(94), Ste. Genevieve(2), Washington(2)
BONNOTS MILL Osage
BOONVILLE Cooper
BOSS (65440) Dent(59), Reynolds(31), Iron(9)
BOSWORTH Carroll
BOURBON (65441) Crawford(95), Washington(3)
BOWLING GREEN (63334) Pike(98), Lincoln(1)
BRADLEYVILLE (65614) Taney(90), Christian(9)
BRAGG CITY Pemiscot
BRAGGADOCIO Pemiscot
BRANDSVILLE Howell
BRANSON (65616) Taney(93), Stone(6)
BRANSON Taney
BRASHEAR Adair
BRAYMER (64624) Caldwell(69), Carroll(14), Ray(12), Livingston(3)
BRAZEAU Perry
BRECKENRIDGE (64625) Caldwell(82), Livingston(8), Daviess(8)
BRIAR Ripley
BRIDGETON St. Louis
BRIGHTON Polk
BRINKTOWN Maries
BRIXEY Ozark
BRONAUGH (64728) Vernon(73), Barton(26)
BROOKFIELD (64628) Linn(96), Chariton(3)
BROOKLINE STATION Greene
BROSELEY Butler
BROWNING (64630) Linn(64), Sullivan(35)
BROWNWOOD Stoddard
BRUMLEY Miller
BRUNER (65620) Christian(98), Douglas(1)
BRUNSWICK Chariton
BUCKLIN (64631) Linn(79), Macon(20)
BUCKNER Jackson
BUCYRUS Texas
BUFFALO (65622) Dallas(97), Polk(2)
BUNCETON Cooper
BUNKER (63629) Reynolds(66), Dent(25), Shannon(7)
BURFORDVILLE Cape Girardeau
BURLINGTON JUNCTION Nodaway
BUTLER Bates
BUTTERFIELD Barry
CABOOL (65689) Howell(72), Texas(25), Douglas(2)
CADET Washington
CAINSVILLE (64632) Harrison(70), Mercer(29)
CAIRO Randolph
CALEDONIA Washington
CALHOUN Henry
CALIFORNIA (65018) Moniteau(96), Cooper(3)
CALLAO Macon
CAMDEN Ray
CAMDEN POINT Platte
CAMDENTON Camden
CAMERON (64429) Clinton(68), De Kalb(29), Daviess(1)
CAMPBELL Dunklin
CANALOU New Madrid
CANTON (63435) Lewis(94), Clark(5)
CAPE FAIR (65624) Stone(95), Barry(3)
CAPE GIRARDEAU Cape Girardeau
CAPLINGER MILLS Cedar
CARDWELL Dunklin
CARL JUNCTION Jasper
CARTERVILLE Jasper
CARTHAGE Jasper
CARUTHERSVILLE Pemiscot
CASCADE Wayne
CASSVILLE Barry
CATAWISSA (63015) Franklin(75), Jefferson(24)
CATRON New Madrid
CAULFIELD (65626) Howell(66), Ozark(33)
CEDAR CITY Callaway
CEDAR HILL Jefferson
CEDARCREEK Taney
CENSUS BUREAU Boone
CENTER Ralls
CENTERTOWN (65023) Cole(83), Moniteau(16)
CENTERVIEW Johnson
CENTERVILLE Reynolds
CENTRALIA (65240) Boone(72), Audrain(25), Callaway(1)
CHADWICK (65629) Christian(98), Douglas(1)
CHAFFEE Scott
CHAMOIS Osage
CHARLESTON (63834) Mississippi(94), Scott(5)
CHERRYVILLE Crawford
CHESTERFIELD St. Louis
CHESTNUTRIDGE Christian
CHILHOWEE (64733) Johnson(70), Henry(24), Jackson(4)
CHILLICOTHE (64601) Livingston(98), Sullivan(1)
CHULA (64635) Livingston(79), Linn(11), Grundy(9)
CLARENCE (63437) Shelby(88), Macon(6), Monroe(4)
CLARK (65243) Randolph(40), Boone(29), Audrain(22), Howard(5)
CLARKSBURG (65025) Moniteau(57), Cooper(42)
CLARKSDALE De Kalb
CLARKSVILLE Pike
CLARKTON Dunklin
CLEARMONT Nodaway
CLEVELAND Cass
CLEVER Christian
CLIFTON HILL (65244) Randolph(96), Chariton(3)
CLIMAX SPRINGS Camden
CLINTON (64735) Henry(95), Benton(4)
CLUBB Wayne
CLYDE Nodaway
COATSVILLE (63535) Schuyler(56), Putnam(43)
COFFEY (64636) Daviess(93), Harrison(6)
COLE CAMP (65325) Benton(90), Morgan(6), Pettis(3)
COLLINS St. Clair
COLUMBIA Boone
COMMERCE Scott
CONCEPTION Nodaway
CONCEPTION JUNCTION Nodaway
CONCORDIA (64020) Lafayette(90), Johnson(8), Saline(1)
CONRAN New Madrid
CONTEL CORPORATION St. Charles
CONWAY (65632) Laclede(54), Webster(27), Dallas(18)
COOK STATION (65449) Crawford(97), Phelps(2)
COOTER Pemiscot
CORDER Lafayette
CORNING Holt
COSBY Andrew
COTTLEVILLE St. Charles
COUCH Oregon
COWGILL (64637) Caldwell(78), Ray(21)
CRAIG Holt
CRANE (65633) Stone(93), Barry(6)
CREIGHTON (64739) Henry(77), Cass(22)
CROCKER (65452) Pulaski(95), Miller(4)
CROSS TIMBERS (65634) Hickory(89), Benton(9), Camden(1)
CRYSTAL CITY Jefferson
CUBA Crawford
CURRYVILLE Pike
DADEVILLE Dade
DAISY Cape Girardeau
DALTON Chariton
DARDENNE St. Charles
DARLINGTON Gentry
DAVISVILLE (65456) Crawford(98), Iron(2)
DAWN (64638) Livingston(72), Carroll(27)

DE KALB Buchanan
DE SOTO Jefferson
DE WITT Carroll
DEARBORN Platte
DEEPWATER (64740) Henry(71), St. Clair(28)
DEERFIELD Vernon
DEERING Pemiscot
DEFIANCE St. Charles
DELTA Cape Girardeau
DENVER (64441) Worth(50), Gentry(49)
DES ARC (63636) Iron(66), Madison(29), Wayne(3)
DEVILS ELBOW (65457) Pulaski(95), Phelps(4)
DEXTER Stoddard
DIAMOND (64840) Newton(98), Jasper(1)
DIGGINS Webster
DITTMER Jefferson
DIXON (65459) Pulaski(74), Maries(23), Miller(2)
DOE RUN St. Francois
DONIPHAN (63935) Ripley(95), Carter(1), Oregon(1)
DORA (65637) Ozark(63), Howell(22), Douglas(14)
DOVER Lafayette
DOWNING (63536) Schuyler(73), Scotland(26)
DREXEL (64742) Cass(87), Bates(12)
DRURY (65638) Douglas(89), Ozark(10)
DUDLEY Stoddard
DUENWEG Jasper
DUKE (65461) Phelps(95), Pulaski(4)
DUNNEGAN (65640) Polk(92), Cedar(7)
DURHAM (63438) Lewis(66), Marion(33)
DUTCHTOWN Cape Girardeau
DUTZOW Warren
EAGLE ROCK Barry
EAGLEVILLE Harrison
EARTH CITY St. Louis
EAST LYNNE Cass
EAST PRAIRIE Mississippi
EASTON Buchanan
EDGAR SPRINGS (65462) Phelps(97), Dent(2)
EDGERTON (64444) Platte(93), Buchanan(6)
EDINA Knox
EDWARDS (65326) Benton(58), Camden(40)
EL DORADO SPRINGS (64744) Cedar(90), Vernon(5), St. Clair(3)
ELDON (65026) Miller(95), Morgan(4)
ELDRIDGE Laclede
ELK CREEK Texas
ELKLAND (65644) Webster(56), Dallas(43)
ELLINGTON (63638) Reynolds(94), Shannon(3), Carter(1)
ELLSINORE (63937) Carter(84), Butler(15)
ELMER Macon
ELMO Nodaway
ELSBERRY (63343) Lincoln(96), Pike(3)
EMDEN (63439) Shelby(65), Marion(34)
EMINENCE Shannon
EMMA Lafayette
EOLIA (63344) Pike(62), Lincoln(37)
ESSEX Stoddard
ETHEL Macon
ETTERVILLE Miller
EUDORA Polk
EUGENE (65032) Cole(66), Miller(33)
EUNICE Texas
EUREKA (63025) St. Louis(66), Jefferson(33)
EVERTON (65646) Dade(61), Lawrence(38)
EWING (63440) Lewis(70), Marion(25), Shelby(4)
EXCELLO Macon
EXCELSIOR SPRINGS (64024) Clay(73), Ray(26)
EXETER (65647) Barry(78), Newton(19), McDonald(1)
FAGUS Butler
FAIR GROVE (65648) Greene(77), Dallas(12), Webster(9)
FAIR PLAY (65649) Polk(95), Cedar(4)
FAIRDEALING Ripley
FAIRFAX (64446) Atchison(94), Holt(5)
FAIRPORT De Kalb
FAIRVIEW (64842) Newton(97), Barry(1)
FALCON (65470) Laclede(82), Wright(16)
FARBER Audrain
FARLEY Platte
FARMINGTON (63640) St. Francois(98), Ste. Genevieve(1)
FARRAR Perry
FAUCETT Buchanan
FAYETTE Howard
FENTON (63026) St. Louis(51), Jefferson(48)
FENTON St. Louis
FESTUS (63028) Jefferson(93), Ste. Genevieve(6)
FILLMORE Andrew
FISK Butler
FLEMINGTON (65650) Polk(51), Hickory(48)
FLETCHER (63030) Washington(57), Jefferson(42)
FLINTHILL St. Charles
FLORENCE Morgan
FLORISSANT St. Louis
FOLEY Lincoln
FORDLAND (65652) Webster(91), Christian(7), Douglas(1)
FOREST CITY Holt
FORISTELL (63348) St. Charles(66), Warren(30), Lincoln(3)
FORSYTH (65653) Taney(98), Christian(2)
FORT LEONARD WOOD Pulaski
FORTESCUE Holt
FORTUNA (65034) Morgan(63), Moniteau(36)
FOSTER Bates
FRANKFORD (63441) Pike(97), Ralls(2)
FRANKLIN Howard
FREDERICKTOWN (63645) Madison(97), Ste. Genevieve(1)
FREEBURG Osage
FREEMAN Cass
FREISTATT Lawrence
FREMONT (63941) Carter(62), Oregon(25), Ripley(11)
FRENCH VILLAGE (63036) St. Francois(74), Ste. Genevieve(25)
FRIEDHEIM Cape Girardeau
FROHNA Perry
FULTON Callaway
GAINESVILLE Ozark
GALENA (65656) Stone(77), Christian(22)
GALLATIN Daviess
GALT (64641) Grundy(79), Sullivan(20)
GARDEN CITY Cass
GARRISON (65657) Christian(98), Taney(1)
GASCONADE Gasconade
GATEWOOD Ripley
GENTRY Gentry
GERALD Franklin
GIBBS Adair
GIBSON Dunklin
GIDEON (63848) New Madrid(62), Pemiscot(37)
GILLIAM Saline
GILMAN CITY (64642) Harrison(76), Daviess(15), Grundy(8)
GIPSY Bollinger
GLASGOW (65254) Howard(95), Chariton(4)
GLENALLEN Bollinger
GLENCOE St. Louis
GLENWOOD Schuyler
GLOVER Iron
GOBLER (63849) Dunklin(63), Pemiscot(36)
GOLDEN Barry
GOLDEN CITY (64748) Barton(63), Jasper(21), Dade(15)
GOODMAN (64843) McDonald(73), Newton(26)
GOODSON Polk
GORDONVILLE Cape Girardeau
GORIN (63543) Scotland(96), Knox(2)
GOWER (64454) Buchanan(53), Clinton(46)
GRAFF Wright
GRAHAM (64455) Nodaway(95), Andrew(4)
GRAIN VALLEY Jackson
GRANBY Newton
GRANDIN (63943) Carter(79), Ripley(20)
GRANDVIEW Jackson
GRANGER Scotland
GRANT CITY (64456) Worth(98), Harrison(1)
GRASSY Bollinger
GRAVOIS MILLS (65037) Morgan(78), Camden(21)
GRAY SUMMIT Franklin
GRAYRIDGE Stoddard
GREEN CASTLE (63544) Sullivan(48), Adair(44), Putnam(6)
GREEN CITY Sullivan
GREEN RIDGE Pettis
GREENFIELD Dade
GREENTOP (63546) Adair(83), Schuyler(14), Scotland(1)
GREENVILLE Wayne
GREENWOOD (64034) Jackson(91), Cass(8)
GROVER St. Louis
GROVESPRING (65662) Wright(79), Laclede(19)
GRUBVILLE (63041) Franklin(85), Jefferson(14)
GUILFORD Nodaway
HALE (64643) Carroll(56), Livingston(43)
HALF WAY Polk
HALLSVILLE Boone
HALLTOWN Lawrence
HAMILTON (64644) Caldwell(84), Daviess(15)
HANNIBAL (63401) Marion(83), Ralls(16)
HARDENVILLE Ozark
HARDIN (64035) Ray(95), Carroll(4)
HARRIS (64645) Sullivan(85), Mercer(14)
HARRISBURG (65256) Boone(87), Howard(12)
HARRISONVILLE Cass
HARTSBURG (65039) Boone(93), Callaway(6)
HARTSHORN (65479) Texas(92), Shannon(7)
HARTVILLE Wright
HARVIELL (63945) Butler(97), Ripley(2)
HARWOOD Vernon
HATFIELD (64458) Harrison(96), Worth(3)
HAWK POINT (63349) Lincoln(98), Warren(1)
HAYTI Pemiscot
HAZELWOOD St. Louis
HELENA Andrew
HEMATITE Jefferson
HENLEY (65040) Cole(91), Miller(8)
HENRIETTA Ray
HERCULANEUM Jefferson
HERMANN (65041) Gasconade(84), Montgomery(13), Warren(1)
HERMANN Montgomery
HERMITAGE Hickory
HIGBEE (65257) Randolph(72), Howard(27)
HIGGINSVILLE Lafayette
HIGH HILL Montgomery
HIGH POINT Moniteau
HIGH RIDGE (63049) Jefferson(96), St. Louis(3)
HIGHLANDVILLE (65669) Christian(87), Stone(12)
HILLSBORO Jefferson
HIRAM Wayne
HOLCOMB (63852) Dunklin(98), Pemiscot(1)
HOLDEN Johnson
HOLLAND (63853) Pemiscot(92), Dunklin(7)
HOLLIDAY Monroe
HOLLISTER Taney
HOLT Clay
HOLTS SUMMIT Callaway
HOPKINS Nodaway
HORNERSVILLE Dunklin
HORTON Vernon
HOUSE SPRINGS Jefferson
HOUSTON Texas
HOUSTONIA (65333) Pettis(97), Saline(2)
HUGGINS Texas
HUGHESVILLE Pettis
HUMANSVILLE (65674) Polk(81), Cedar(13), Hickory(2), St. Clair(2)
HUME (64752) Bates(72), Vernon(27)
HUMPHREYS (64646) Sullivan(88), Linn(11)
HUNNEWELL (63443) Shelby(38), Monroe(31), Marion(29)
HUNTSVILLE Randolph
HURDLAND (63547) Knox(95), Adair(4)
HURLEY Stone
IBERIA Miller
IMPERIAL Jefferson
INDEPENDENCE Jackson
IONIA (65335) Pettis(66), Benton(33)
IRONDALE (63648) St. Francois(60), Washington(39)
IRONTON (63650) Iron(82), St. Francois(15), Madison(2)
ISABELLA Ozark
JACKSON Cape Girardeau
JACKSONVILLE (65260) Macon(62), Randolph(27), Monroe(9)
JADWIN Dent
JAMESON Daviess
JAMESPORT (64648) Daviess(97), Livingston(2)
JAMESTOWN (65046) Moniteau(92), Cooper(7)
JASPER (64755) Jasper(91), Barton(8)
JEFFERSON CITY Cole
JERICO SPRINGS (64756) Cedar(91), Dade(8)
JEROME Phelps
JONESBURG (63351) Montgomery(56), Warren(43)
JOPLIN Jasper
KAHOKA Clark
KAISER (65047) Miller(97), Camden(2)
KANSAS CITY (64188) Clay(92), Jackson(7)
KANSAS CITY (64147) Jackson(74), Cass(25)
KANSAS CITY (64164) Platte(98), Clay(1)
KANSAS CITY Clay
KANSAS CITY Jackson
KANSAS CITY Platte
KEARNEY Clay
KELSO Scott
KENNETT Dunklin
KEWANEE New Madrid
KEYTESVILLE Chariton
KIDDER (64649) Caldwell(73), Daviess(26)
KIMBERLING CITY Stone
KIMMSWICK Jefferson
KING CITY (64463) Gentry(94), De Kalb(3), Andrew(1)
KINGDOM CITY Callaway
KINGSTON Caldwell

KINGSVILLE (64061) Johnson(98), Jackson(1)
KIRBYVILLE Taney
KIRKSVILLE Adair
KISSEE MILLS Taney
KNOB LICK St. Francois
KNOB NOSTER (65336) Johnson(91), Pettis(8)
KNOX CITY (63446) Knox(90), Lewis(9)
KOELTZTOWN Osage
KOSHKONONG (65692) Oregon(53), Howell(46)
LA BELLE (63447) Lewis(97), Knox(2)
LA GRANGE Lewis
LA MONTE Pettis
LA PLATA (63549) Macon(95), Adair(3)
LA RUSSELL (64848) Lawrence(93), Jasper(6)
LABADIE Franklin
LACLEDE Linn
LADDONIA (63352) Audrain(93), Ralls(6)
LAKE OZARK (65049) Camden(72), Miller(27)
LAKE SAINT LOUIS St. Charles
LAKE SPRING Dent
LAMAR Barton
LAMPE Stone
LANAGAN McDonald
LANCASTER Schuyler
LAQUEY (65534) Pulaski(84), Laclede(15)
LAREDO (64652) Grundy(97), Sullivan(1)
LATHAM Moniteau
LATHROP (64465) Clinton(90), Caldwell(9)
LATOUR (64760) Johnson(50), Cass(49)
LAURIE Morgan
LAWSON (64062) Ray(66), Clay(17), Clinton(16)
LEADWOOD St. Francois
LEASBURG Crawford
LEBANON (65536) Laclede(98), Dallas(1)
LECOMA (65540) Dent(70), Phelps(29)
LEES SUMMIT (64082) Jackson(89), Cass(10)
LEES SUMMIT Jackson
LEETON (64761) Johnson(92), Henry(7)
LENOX Dent
LENTNER (63450) Shelby(70), Monroe(29)
LEONARD (63451) Shelby(95), Knox(2), Macon(2)
LEOPOLD Bollinger
LESLIE Franklin
LESTERVILLE (63654) Reynolds(89), Iron(10)
LEVASY Jackson
LEWISTOWN Lewis
LEXINGTON Lafayette
LIBERAL Barton
LIBERTY Clay
LICKING Texas
LIGUORI Jefferson
LILBOURN (63862) Bollinger(77), New Madrid(22)
LINCOLN Benton
LINN Osage
LINN CREEK Camden
LINNEUS Linn
LIVONIA Putnam
LOCK SPRINGS Daviess
LOCKWOOD (65682) Dade(83), Lawrence(10), Barton(5)
LODI Wayne
LOHMAN Cole
LONE JACK (64070) Jackson(96), Johnson(3)
LONEDELL Franklin
LONG LANE Dallas
LOOSE CREEK Osage
LOUISBURG (65685) Dallas(97), Polk(2)
LOUISIANA Pike
LOWNDES Wayne
LOWRY CITY St. Clair
LUCERNE (64655) Putnam(98), Sullivan(1)
LUDLOW Livingston
LUEBBERING Franklin
LURAY Clark
LYNCHBURG Laclede
MACKS CREEK (65786) Camden(98), Dallas(1)
MACOMB (65702) Wright(72), Douglas(27)
MADISON (65263) Monroe(95), Randolph(3)
MAITLAND Holt
MALDEN (63863) Dunklin(98), New Madrid(1)
MALTA BEND Saline
MANSFIELD (65704) Wright(95), Douglas(4)
MAPAVILLE Jefferson
MARBLE HILL (63764) Bollinger(91), Cape Girardeau(8)
MARCELINE (64658) Linn(68), Chariton(31)
MARIONVILLE (65705) Lawrence(81), Stone(18)
MARQUAND (63655) Madison(74), Bollinger(24), Wayne(1)
MARSHALL (65340) Saline(96), Pettis(3)
MARSHFIELD Webster
MARSTON New Madrid
MARTHASVILLE (63357) Warren(93), St. Charles(6)
MARTINSBURG (65264) Audrain(75), Callaway(21), Montgomery(3)
MARTINSVILLE Harrison
MARYLAND HEIGHTS St. Louis
MARYVILLE Nodaway
MATTHEWS New Madrid
MAYSVILLE De Kalb
MAYVIEW Lafayette
MAYWOOD (63454) Marion(68), Lewis(31)
MC BRIDE Perry
MC CLURG (65701) Taney(71), Douglas(28)
MC FALL (64657) Gentry(65), Harrison(25), Daviess(8)
MC GEE Wayne
MC GIRK Moniteau
MEADVILLE Linn
MEMPHIS Scotland
MENDON Chariton
MENFRO Perry
MERCER Mercer
META (65058) Maries(51), Osage(29), Miller(12), Cole(5)
METZ Vernon
MEXICO (65265) Audrain(98), Monroe(1)
MIAMI Saline
MID MISSOURI Boone
MIDDLE BROOK (63656) Iron(85), Reynolds(14)
MIDDLETOWN (63359) Pike(57), Montgomery(31), Lincoln(6), Audrain(4)
MILAN Sullivan
MILFORD Barton
MILL SPRING Wayne
MILLER Lawrence
MILLERSVILLE (63766) Cape Girardeau(88), Bollinger(11)
MILO Vernon
MINDENMINES Barton
MINERAL POINT Washington
MISSOURI CITY Clay
MISSOURI STATE LOTTERY COMM Cole
MOBERLY Randolph
MOKANE Callaway
MONETT (65708) Barry(58), Lawrence(41)
MONROE CITY (63456) Monroe(46), Marion(33), Ralls(19)
MONTGOMERY CITY (63361) Montgomery(82), Callaway(17)
MONTICELLO Lewis
MONTIER Shannon
MONTREAL Camden
MONTROSE (64770) Henry(90), Bates(8)
MOODY Howell
MOORESVILLE (64664) Livingston(98), Sullivan(1)
MORA (65345) Pettis(64), Benton(23), Morgan(11)
MOREHOUSE New Madrid
MORLEY Scott
MORRISON (65061) Gasconade(86), Osage(13)
MORRISVILLE Polk
MORSE MILL Jefferson
MOSBY Clay
MOSCOW MILLS Lincoln
MOUND CITY Holt
MOUNDVILLE Vernon
MOUNT MORIAH Harrison
MOUNT STERLING (65062) Gasconade(69), Ozark(21), Osage(9)
MOUNT VERNON Lawrence
MOUNTAIN GROVE (65711) Wright(94), Douglas(4)
MOUNTAIN VIEW (65548) Howell(95), Shannon(3)
MYRTLE Oregon
NAPOLEON Lafayette
NAYLOR (63953) Ripley(96), Butler(3)
NECK CITY Jasper
NEELYVILLE (63954) Butler(96), Ripley(3)
NELSON (65347) Pettis(46), Saline(31), Cooper(22)
NEOSHO Newton
NEVADA Vernon
NEW BLOOMFIELD Callaway
NEW BOSTON (63557) Linn(67), Macon(29), Sullivan(1)
NEW CAMBRIA (63558) Macon(83), Chariton(16)
NEW FLORENCE (63363) Montgomery(88), Warren(11)
NEW FRANKLIN Howard
NEW HAMPTON (64471) Harrison(93), Gentry(6)
NEW HARTFORD Pike
NEW HAVEN (63068) Franklin(98), Gasconade(1)
NEW LONDON (63459) Ralls(93), Pike(6)
NEW MADRID New Madrid
NEW MELLE St. Charles
NEW OFFENBURG Ste. Genevieve
NEWARK Knox
NEWBURG Phelps
NEWTONIA Newton
NEWTOWN (64667) Sullivan(77), Mercer(15), Putnam(7)
NIANGUA (65713) Webster(89), Wright(10)
NIXA (65714) Christian(94), Stone(5)
NOBLE Ozark
NOEL McDonald
NORBORNE (64668) Carroll(78), Ray(21)
NORWOOD (65717) Wright(86), Douglas(13)
NOVELTY Knox
NOVINGER (63559) Adair(51), Putnam(48)
O FALLON St. Charles
OAK GROVE (64075) Jackson(89), Lafayette(10)
OAK RIDGE Cape Girardeau
ODESSA (64076) Lafayette(98), Johnson(1)
OLD APPLETON (63770) Cape Girardeau(63), Perry(36)
OLD MONROE Lincoln
OLDFIELD (65720) Christian(78), Douglas(21)
OLEAN Miller
OLNEY Lincoln
ORAN (63771) Scott(82), Stoddard(16)
OREGON Holt
ORONOGO (64855) Jasper(95), Barton(4)
ORRICK (64077) Ray(74), Clay(25)
OSAGE BEACH Camden
OSBORN (64474) De Kalb(97), Clinton(2)
OSCEOLA (64776) St. Clair(97), Benton(2)
OTTERVILLE (65348) Cooper(85), Morgan(11), Pettis(3)
OWENSVILLE (65066) Gasconade(92), Crawford(7)
OXLY Ripley
OZARK (65721) Christian(98), Greene(1)
PACIFIC (63069) Franklin(67), Jefferson(16), St. Louis(15)
PAINTON Stoddard
PALMYRA Marion
PARIS Monroe
PARK HILLS St. Francois
PARMA (63870) Stoddard(83), New Madrid(16)
PARNELL (64475) Nodaway(88), Worth(9), Gentry(2)
PASCOLA Pemiscot
PASSAIC Bates
PATTERSON Wayne
PATTON Bollinger
PATTONSBURG (64670) Daviess(79), De Kalb(13), Harrison(4), Gentry(2)
PAYNESVILLE Pike
PEACE VALLEY (65788) Howell(95), Oregon(4)
PECULIAR Cass
PERKINS Scott
PERRY (63462) Ralls(79), Monroe(20)
PERRYVILLE Perry
PEVELY Jefferson
PHILADELPHIA (63463) Marion(97), Shelby(2)
PHILLIPSBURG (65722) Laclede(87), Dallas(12)
PICKERING Nodaway
PIEDMONT Wayne
PIERCE CITY (65723) Lawrence(90), Newton(6), Barry(3)
PILOT GROVE Cooper
PILOT KNOB Iron
PINEVILLE McDonald
PITTSBURG Hickory
PLATO (65552) Texas(98), Laclede(1)
PLATTE CITY Platte
PLATTSBURG Clinton
PLEASANT HILL (64080) Cass(96), Jackson(3)
PLEASANT HOPE (65725) Greene(89), Polk(10)
PLEVNA (63464) Knox(76), Marion(23)
POCAHONTAS Cape Girardeau
POINT LOOKOUT Taney
POLK (65727) Polk(87), Hickory(12)
POLLOCK (63560) Sullivan(92), Putnam(7)
POLO (64671) Caldwell(70), Ray(29)
POMONA Howell
PONCE DE LEON (65728) Christian(75), Stone(24)
PONTIAC Ozark
POPLAR BLUFF Butler
PORTAGE DES SIOUX St. Charles
PORTAGEVILLE (63873) New Madrid(84), Pemiscot(15)
PORTLAND Callaway
POTOSI Washington
POTTERSVILLE (65790) Howell(88), Ozark(11)
POWELL McDonald
POWERSITE Taney
POWERSVILLE (64672) Putnam(97), Mercer(2)
PRAIRIE HOME Cooper
PRESTON (65732) Hickory(94), Dallas(5)
PRINCETON Mercer
PROTEM Taney
PURCELL Jasper
PURDIN Linn
PURDY Barry
PUXICO (63960) Stoddard(96), Bollinger(3)
QUEEN CITY Schuyler

QUINCY (65735) Hickory(68), Benton(24), St. Clair(6)
QUITMAN Nodaway
QULIN Butler
RACINE Newton
RAVENWOOD (64479) Nodaway(95), Gentry(4)
RAYMONDVILLE Texas
RAYMORE Cass
RAYVILLE Ray
REA Andrew
REDFORD Reynolds
REEDS Jasper
REEDS SPRING (65737) Stone(98), Taney(1)
RENICK Randolph
REPUBLIC (65738) Greene(85), Christian(14)
REVERE Clark
REYNOLDS Reynolds
RHINELAND (65069) Montgomery(86), Callaway(13)
RICH HILL (64779) Bates(93), Vernon(6)
RICHARDS Vernon
RICHLAND (65556) Pulaski(61), Laclede(20), Camden(18)
RICHMOND Ray
RICHWOODS (63071) Washington(88), Jefferson(11)
RIDGEDALE Taney
RIDGEWAY Harrison
RISCO New Madrid
RIVES Dunklin
ROACH Camden
ROBERTSVILLE (63072) Franklin(96), Jefferson(3)
ROBY Texas
ROCHEPORT (65279) Boone(86), Howard(13)
ROCK PORT Atchison
ROCKAWAY BEACH Taney
ROCKBRIDGE Ozark
ROCKVILLE (64780) St. Clair(62), Bates(37)
ROCKY COMFORT (64861) McDonald(92), Newton(5), Barry(1)
ROCKY MOUNT (65072) Morgan(85), Miller(14)
ROGERSVILLE (65742) Webster(53), Greene(46)
ROLLA Phelps
ROMBAUER Butler
ROSCOE St. Clair
ROSEBUD (63091) Gasconade(73), Franklin(26)
ROSENDALE Andrew
ROTHVILLE Chariton
RUETER Taney
RUSH HILL Audrain
RUSHVILLE (64484) Buchanan(74), Platte(25)
RUSSELLVILLE (65074) Cole(68), Moniteau(29), Miller(1)
RUTLEDGE (63563) Scotland(56), Knox(43)
SAGINAW Newton
SAINT ALBANS Franklin
SAINT ANN St. Louis
SAINT CATHARINE Linn
SAINT CATHERINE Linn
SAINT CHARLES St. Charles
SAINT CLAIR Franklin
SAINT ELIZABETH Miller
SAINT JAMES (65559) Phelps(98), Maries(1)
SAINT JOSEPH (64506) Buchanan(97), Andrew(2)
SAINT JOSEPH Buchanan
SAINT LOUIS (63143) St. Louis(88), St. Louis City(11)
SAINT LOUIS (63120) St. Louis City(89), St. Louis(10)
SAINT LOUIS St. Louis
SAINT LOUIS St. Louis City
SAINT MARY Ste. Genevieve
SAINT PATRICK Clark
SAINT PETERS St. Charles
SAINT ROBERT Pulaski
SAINT THOMAS (65076) Cole(83), Osage(16)
SAINTE GENEVIEVE Ste. Genevieve
SALEM (65560) Dent(98), Shannon(1)
SALISBURY (65281) Chariton(98), Howard(1)
SANTA FE Monroe
SARCOXIE (64862) Jasper(87), Lawrence(8), Newton(4)
SAVANNAH Andrew
SAVERTON Ralls
SCHELL CITY (64783) Vernon(58), St. Clair(41)
SCOTT CITY Scott
SEDALIA Pettis
SEDGEWICKVILLE (63781) Bollinger(77), Perry(20), Cape Girardeau(2)
SELIGMAN Barry
SENATH Dunklin
SENECA (64865) Newton(89), McDonald(10)
SEYMOUR (65746) Webster(98), Douglas(1)
SHELBINA (63468) Shelby(80), Monroe(19)
SHELBYVILLE (63469) Shelby(98), Knox(1)
SHELDON (64784) Vernon(74), Barton(16), Cedar(7)
SHELL KNOB (65747) Stone(56), Barry(43)
SHERIDAN (64486) Worth(54), Nodaway(45)
SHOOK Wayne
SIBLEY Jackson
SIKESTON (63801) Scott(94), New Madrid(4)
SILEX Lincoln
SILVA (63964) Wayne(88), Madison(11)
SKIDMORE (64487) Nodaway(93), Holt(6)
SLATER Saline
SMITHTON (65350) Pettis(93), Morgan(5)
SMITHVILLE (64089) Clay(98), Platte(1)
SOLO Texas
SOUTH FORK Howell
SOUTH GREENFIELD (65752) Dade(67), Lawrence(32)
SOUTH WEST CITY McDonald
SPARTA (65753) Christian(98), Douglas(1)
SPICKARD (64679) Grundy(89), Mercer(10)
SPOKANE (65754) Christian(84), Stone(15)
SPRINGFIELD Greene
SQUIRES (65755) Douglas(53), Ozark(46)
ST CATHARINE Linn
ST JOSEPH Buchanan
STANBERRY (64489) Gentry(98), Nodaway(1)
STANTON Franklin
STARK CITY Newton
STEEDMAN Callaway
STEELE (63877) Pemiscot(97), Dunklin(2)
STEELVILLE (65565) Crawford(96), Washington(2)
STEFFENVILLE (63470) Lewis(93), Shelby(6)
STELLA (64867) Newton(90), McDonald(9)
STET Carroll
STEWARTSVILLE (64490) De Kalb(56), Clinton(38), Buchanan(4)
STOCKTON (65785) Cedar(98), St. Clair(1)
STOTTS CITY Lawrence
STOUTLAND (65567) Laclede(62), Camden(37)
STOUTSVILLE Monroe
STOVER (65078) Morgan(98), Benton(1)
STRAFFORD (65757) Greene(77), Webster(22)
STRASBURG Cass
STURDIVANT Bollinger
STURGEON (65284) Boone(95), Audrain(4)
SUCCESS Texas
SULLIVAN (63080) Franklin(82), Crawford(12), Washington(4)
SULPHUR SPRINGS Jefferson
SUMMERSVILLE (65571) Texas(83), Shannon(16)
SUMNER (64681) Linn(51), Chariton(48)
SUNRISE BEACH (65079) Camden(87), Morgan(12)
SWEDEBORG Pulaski
SWEET SPRINGS (65351) Saline(76), Pettis(22), Johnson(1)
SYRACUSE (65354) Morgan(89), Cooper(10)
TALLAPOOSA New Madrid
TANEYVILLE Taney
TARKIO Atchison
TAYLOR (63471) Marion(93), Lewis(6)
TEBBETTS Callaway
TECUMSEH Ozark
TERESITA Shannon
THAYER Oregon
THEODOSIA (65761) Ozark(75), Taney(25)
THOMPSON (65285) Audrain(98), Monroe(1)
THORNFIELD Ozark
TIFF Washington
TIFF CITY McDonald
TINA Carroll
TIPTON (65081) Moniteau(89), Cooper(9), Morgan(1)
TRELOAR Warren
TRENTON Grundy
TRIMBLE Clinton
TRIPLETT Chariton
TROY Lincoln
TRUXTON (63381) Lincoln(45), Warren(40), Montgomery(13)
TUNAS Dallas
TURNERS Greene
TURNEY Clinton
TUSCUMBIA Miller
UDALL Ozark
ULMAN Miller
UNION Franklin
UNION STAR De Kalb
UNIONTOWN Perry
UNIONVILLE (63565) Putnam(89), Sullivan(10)
URBANA (65767) Dallas(83), Hickory(15)
URICH (64788) Henry(82), Bates(17)
UTICA Livingston
VALLES MINES (63087) St. Francois(90), Jefferson(9)
VALLEY PARK St. Louis
VAN BUREN (63965) Carter(93), Reynolds(6)
VANDALIA (63382) Audrain(80), Ralls(10), Pike(8)
VANDUSER Scott
VANZANT Douglas
VERONA (65769) Lawrence(78), Barry(21)
VERSAILLES Morgan
VIBURNUM Iron
VICHY Maries
VIENNA Maries
VILLA RIDGE Franklin
VISTA St. Clair
VULCAN (63675) Iron(92), Washington(4), Reynolds(2)
WACO Jasper
WAKENDA Carroll
WALDRON Platte
WALKER Vernon
WALNUT GROVE Greene
WALNUT SHADE Taney
WAPPAPELLO (63966) Butler(67), Wayne(32)
WARDELL (63879) Pemiscot(98), New Madrid(1)
WARRENSBURG Johnson
WARRENTON (63383) Warren(97), Lincoln(2)
WARSAW Benton
WASHBURN (65772) Barry(93), McDonald(6)
WASHINGTON Franklin
WASOLA Ozark
WATSON Atchison
WAVERLY (64096) Lafayette(98), Saline(1)
WAYLAND Clark
WAYNESVILLE Pulaski
WEATHERBY (64497) De Kalb(69), Daviess(30)
WEAUBLEAU (65774) Hickory(90), St. Clair(9)
WEBB CITY Jasper
WELDON SPRING St. Charles
WELLINGTON Lafayette
WELLSVILLE (63384) Montgomery(88), Audrain(9), Callaway(1)
WENTWORTH (64873) Lawrence(66), Newton(33)
WENTZVILLE St. Charles
WESCO Crawford
WEST ALTON St. Charles
WEST PLAINS Howell
WESTBORO Atchison
WESTON Platte
WESTPHALIA Osage
WHEATLAND (65779) Hickory(85), Benton(14)
WHEATON Barry
WHEELING (64688) Livingston(77), Linn(22)
WHITEMAN AIR FORCE BASE Johnson
WHITEOAK Dunklin
WHITESIDE Lincoln
WHITEWATER Cape Girardeau
WILLARD Greene
WILLIAMSBURG Callaway
WILLIAMSTOWN (63473) Lewis(76), Clark(23)
WILLIAMSVILLE (63967) Butler(58), Wayne(41)
WILLOW SPRINGS (65793) Howell(95), Texas(4)
WINDSOR (65360) Henry(51), Pettis(25), Benton(12), Johnson(9)
WINDYVILLE Dallas
WINFIELD Lincoln
WINIGAN (63566) Linn(80), Sullivan(19)
WINONA (65588) Shannon(93), Oregon(6)
WINSTON Daviess
WITTENBERG Perry
WOLF ISLAND Mississippi
WOOLDRIDGE (65287) Cooper(79), Moniteau(20)
WORTH (64499) Worth(75), Gentry(24)
WORTHINGTON Putnam
WRIGHT CITY (63390) Warren(90), Lincoln(9)
WYACONDA (63474) Clark(91), Scotland(5), Lewis(3)
WYATT Mississippi
YUKON Texas
ZALMA (63787) Bollinger(94), Wayne(5)
ZALMA Bollinger
ZANONI Ozark

Missouri ZIP/City Cross Reference

63001-63001 ALLENTON
63005-63006 CHESTERFIELD
63010-63010 ARNOLD
63011-63011 BALLWIN
63012-63012 BARNHART
63013-63013 BEAUFORT
63014-63014 BERGER
63015-63015 CATAWISSA
63016-63016 CEDAR HILL
63017-63017 CHESTERFIELD
63019-63019 CRYSTAL CITY
63020-63020 DE SOTO
63021-63022 BALLWIN
63023-63023 DITTMER
63024-63024 BALLWIN
63025-63025 EUREKA
63026-63026 FENTON
63028-63028 FESTUS
63030-63030 FLETCHER
63031-63034 FLORISSANT
63036-63036 FRENCH VILLAGE
63037-63037 GERALD
63038-63038 GLENCOE
63039-63039 GRAY SUMMIT
63040-63040 GROVER
63041-63041 GRUBVILLE
63042-63042 HAZELWOOD
63043-63043 MARYLAND HEIGHTS
63044-63044 BRIDGETON
63045-63045 EARTH CITY
63047-63047 HEMATITE
63048-63048 HERCULANEUM
63049-63049 HIGH RIDGE
63050-63050 HILLSBORO
63051-63051 HOUSE SPRINGS
63052-63052 IMPERIAL
63053-63053 KIMMSWICK
63055-63055 LABADIE
63056-63056 LESLIE
63057-63057 LIGUORI
63060-63060 LONEDELL
63061-63061 LUEBBERING
63065-63065 MAPAVILLE
63066-63066 MORSE MILL
63068-63068 NEW HAVEN
63069-63069 PACIFIC
63070-63070 PEVELY
63071-63071 RICHWOODS
63072-63072 ROBERTSVILLE
63073-63073 SAINT ALBANS
63074-63074 SAINT ANN
63077-63077 SAINT CLAIR
63079-63079 STANTON
63080-63080 SULLIVAN
63083-63083 SULPHUR SPRINGS
63084-63084 UNION
63087-63087 VALLES MINES
63088-63088 VALLEY PARK
63089-63089 VILLA RIDGE
63090-63090 WASHINGTON
63091-63091 ROSEBUD
63099-63099 FENTON
63100-63199 SAINT LOUIS
63301-63304 SAINT CHARLES
63330-63330 ANNADA
63332-63332 AUGUSTA
63333-63333 BELLFLOWER
63334-63334 BOWLING GREEN
63336-63336 CLARKSVILLE
63338-63338 COTTLEVILLE
63339-63339 CURRYVILLE
63341-63341 DEFIANCE
63342-63342 DUTZOW
63343-63343 ELSBERRY
63344-63344 EOLIA
63345-63345 FARBER
63346-63346 FLINTHILL
63347-63347 FOLEY
63348-63348 FORISTELL
63349-63349 HAWK POINT
63350-63350 HIGH HILL
63351-63351 JONESBURG
63352-63352 LADDONIA
63353-63353 LOUISIANA
63357-63357 MARTHASVILLE
63359-63359 MIDDLETOWN
63361-63361 MONTGOMERY CITY
63362-63362 MOSCOW MILLS
63363-63363 NEW FLORENCE
63364-63364 NEW HARTFORD
63365-63365 NEW MELLE
63366-63366 O FALLON
63367-63367 LAKE SAINT LOUIS
63368-63368 DARDENNE
63369-63369 OLD MONROE
63370-63370 OLNEY
63371-63371 PAYNESVILLE
63373-63373 PORTAGE DES SIOUX
63376-63376 SAINT PETERS
63377-63377 SILEX
63378-63378 TRELOAR
63379-63379 TROY
63381-63381 TRUXTON
63382-63382 VANDALIA
63383-63383 WARRENTON
63384-63384 WELLSVILLE
63385-63385 WENTZVILLE
63386-63386 WEST ALTON
63387-63387 WHITESIDE
63388-63388 WILLIAMSBURG
63389-63389 WINFIELD
63390-63390 WRIGHT CITY
63394-63394 CONTEL CORPORATION
63401-63401 HANNIBAL
63430-63430 ALEXANDRIA
63431-63431 ANABEL
63432-63432 ARBELA
63433-63433 ASHBURN
63434-63434 BETHEL
63435-63435 CANTON
63436-63436 CENTER
63437-63437 CLARENCE
63438-63438 DURHAM
63439-63439 EMDEN
63440-63440 EWING
63441-63441 FRANKFORD
63442-63442 GRANGER
63443-63443 HUNNEWELL
63445-63445 KAHOKA
63446-63446 KNOX CITY
63447-63447 LA BELLE
63448-63448 LA GRANGE
63450-63450 LENTNER
63451-63451 LEONARD
63452-63452 LEWISTOWN
63453-63453 LURAY
63454-63454 MAYWOOD
63456-63456 MONROE CITY
63457-63457 MONTICELLO
63458-63458 NEWARK
63459-63459 NEW LONDON
63460-63460 NOVELTY
63461-63461 PALMYRA
63462-63462 PERRY
63463-63463 PHILADELPHIA
63464-63464 PLEVNA
63465-63465 REVERE
63466-63466 SAINT PATRICK
63467-63467 SAVERTON
63468-63468 SHELBINA
63469-63469 SHELBYVILLE
63470-63470 STEFFENVILLE
63471-63471 TAYLOR
63472-63472 WAYLAND
63473-63473 WILLIAMSTOWN
63474-63474 WYACONDA
63501-63501 KIRKSVILLE
63530-63530 ATLANTA
63531-63531 BARING
63532-63532 BEVIER
63533-63533 BRASHEAR
63534-63534 CALLAO
63535-63535 COATSVILLE
63536-63536 DOWNING
63537-63537 EDINA
63538-63538 ELMER
63539-63539 ETHEL
63540-63540 GIBBS
63541-63541 GLENWOOD
63543-63543 GORIN
63544-63544 GREEN CASTLE
63545-63545 GREEN CITY
63546-63546 GREENTOP
63547-63547 HURDLAND
63548-63548 LANCASTER
63549-63549 LA PLATA
63551-63551 LIVONIA
63552-63552 MACON
63555-63555 MEMPHIS
63556-63556 MILAN
63557-63557 NEW BOSTON
63558-63558 NEW CAMBRIA
63559-63559 NOVINGER
63560-63560 POLLOCK
63561-63561 QUEEN CITY
63563-63563 RUTLEDGE
63565-63565 UNIONVILLE
63566-63566 WINIGAN
63567-63567 WORTHINGTON
63601-63601 PARK HILLS
63620-63620 ANNAPOLIS
63621-63621 ARCADIA
63622-63622 BELGRADE
63623-63623 BELLEVIEW
63624-63624 BISMARCK
63625-63625 BLACK
63626-63626 BLACKWELL
63627-63627 BLOOMSDALE
63628-63628 BONNE TERRE
63629-63629 BUNKER
63630-63630 CADET
63631-63631 CALEDONIA
63632-63632 CASCADE
63633-63633 CENTERVILLE
63636-63636 DES ARC
63637-63637 DOE RUN
63638-63638 ELLINGTON
63640-63640 FARMINGTON
63644-63644 PARK HILLS
63645-63645 FREDERICKTOWN
63646-63646 GLOVER
63648-63648 IRONDALE
63650-63650 IRONTON
63651-63651 KNOB LICK
63653-63653 LEADWOOD
63654-63654 LESTERVILLE
63655-63655 MARQUAND
63656-63656 MIDDLE BROOK
63660-63660 MINERAL POINT
63661-63661 NEW OFFENBURG
63662-63662 PATTON
63663-63663 PILOT KNOB
63664-63664 POTOSI
63665-63665 REDFORD
63666-63666 REYNOLDS
63670-63670 SAINTE GENEVIEVE
63673-63673 SAINT MARY
63674-63674 TIFF
63675-63675 VULCAN
63701-63705 CAPE GIRARDEAU
63730-63730 ADVANCE
63732-63732 ALTENBURG
63733-63733 ZALMA
63735-63735 BELL CITY
63736-63736 BENTON
63737-63737 BRAZEAU
63738-63738 BROWNWOOD
63739-63739 BURFORDVILLE
63740-63740 CHAFFEE
63742-63742 COMMERCE
63743-63743 DAISY
63744-63744 DELTA
63745-63745 DUTCHTOWN
63746-63746 FARRAR
63747-63747 FRIEDHEIM
63748-63748 FROHNA
63750-63750 GIPSY
63751-63751 GLENALLEN
63752-63752 GORDONVILLE
63753-63753 GRASSY
63755-63755 JACKSON
63758-63758 KELSO
63760-63760 LEOPOLD
63763-63763 MC GEE
63764-63764 MARBLE HILL
63765-63765 MENFRO
63766-63766 MILLERSVILLE
63767-63767 MORLEY
63769-63769 OAK RIDGE
63770-63770 OLD APPLETON
63771-63771 ORAN
63772-63772 PAINTON
63774-63774 PERKINS
63775-63775 PERRYVILLE
63776-63776 MC BRIDE
63779-63779 POCAHONTAS
63780-63780 SCOTT CITY
63781-63781 SEDGEWICKVILLE
63782-63782 STURDIVANT
63783-63783 UNIONTOWN
63784-63784 VANDUSER
63785-63785 WHITEWATER
63786-63786 WITTENBERG
63787-63787 ZALMA
63801-63801 SIKESTON
63820-63820 ANNISTON
63821-63821 ARBYRD
63822-63822 BERNIE
63823-63823 BERTRAND
63824-63824 BLODGETT
63825-63825 BLOOMFIELD
63826-63826 BRAGGADOCIO
63827-63827 BRAGG CITY
63828-63828 CANALOU
63829-63829 CARDWELL
63830-63830 CARUTHERSVILLE
63833-63833 CATRON
63834-63834 CHARLESTON
63837-63837 CLARKTON
63838-63838 CONRAN
63839-63839 COOTER
63840-63840 DEERING
63841-63841 DEXTER
63845-63845 EAST PRAIRIE
63846-63846 ESSEX
63847-63847 GIBSON
63848-63848 GIDEON
63849-63849 GOBLER
63850-63850 GRAYRIDGE
63851-63851 HAYTI
63852-63852 HOLCOMB
63853-63853 HOLLAND
63855-63855 HORNERSVILLE
63857-63857 KENNETT
63860-63860 KEWANEE
63862-63862 LILBOURN
63863-63863 MALDEN
63866-63866 MARSTON
63867-63867 MATTHEWS
63868-63868 MOREHOUSE
63869-63869 NEW MADRID
63870-63870 PARMA
63871-63871 PASCOLA
63873-63873 PORTAGEVILLE
63874-63874 RISCO
63875-63875 RIVES
63876-63876 SENATH
63877-63877 STEELE
63878-63878 TALLAPOOSA
63879-63879 WARDELL
63880-63880 WHITEOAK
63881-63881 WOLF ISLAND
63882-63882 WYATT
63901-63902 POPLAR BLUFF
63931-63931 BRIAR
63932-63932 BROSELEY
63933-63933 CAMPBELL
63934-63934 CLUBB
63935-63935 DONIPHAN
63936-63936 DUDLEY
63937-63937 ELLSINORE
63938-63938 FAGUS
63939-63939 FAIRDEALING
63940-63940 FISK
63941-63941 FREMONT
63942-63942 GATEWOOD
63943-63943 GRANDIN
63944-63944 GREENVILLE
63945-63945 HARVIELL
63947-63947 HIRAM
63950-63950 LODI
63951-63951 LOWNDES
63952-63952 MILL SPRING
63953-63953 NAYLOR

Zip	City
63954-63954	NEELYVILLE
63955-63955	OXLY
63956-63956	PATTERSON
63957-63957	PIEDMONT
63960-63960	PUXICO
63961-63961	QULIN
63962-63962	ROMBAUER
63963-63963	SHOOK
63964-63964	SILVA
63965-63965	VAN BUREN
63966-63966	WAPPAPELLO
63967-63967	WILLIAMSVILLE
64001-64001	ALMA
64011-64011	BATES CITY
64012-64012	BELTON
64013-64015	BLUE SPRINGS
64016-64016	BUCKNER
64017-64017	CAMDEN
64018-64018	CAMDEN POINT
64019-64019	CENTERVIEW
64020-64020	CONCORDIA
64021-64021	CORDER
64022-64022	DOVER
64024-64024	EXCELSIOR SPRINGS
64028-64028	FARLEY
64029-64029	GRAIN VALLEY
64030-64030	GRANDVIEW
64034-64034	GREENWOOD
64035-64035	HARDIN
64036-64036	HENRIETTA
64037-64037	HIGGINSVILLE
64040-64040	HOLDEN
64048-64048	HOLT
64050-64058	INDEPENDENCE
64060-64060	KEARNEY
64061-64061	KINGSVILLE
64062-64062	LAWSON
64063-64065	LEES SUMMIT
64066-64066	LEVASY
64067-64067	LEXINGTON
64068-64069	LIBERTY
64070-64070	LONE JACK
64071-64071	MAYVIEW
64072-64072	MISSOURI CITY
64073-64073	MOSBY
64074-64074	NAPOLEON
64075-64075	OAK GROVE
64076-64076	ODESSA
64077-64077	ORRICK
64078-64078	PECULIAR
64079-64079	PLATTE CITY
64080-64080	PLEASANT HILL
64081-64082	LEES SUMMIT
64083-64083	RAYMORE
64084-64084	RAYVILLE
64085-64085	RICHMOND
64086-64086	LEES SUMMIT
64087-64087	LIBERTY
64088-64088	SIBLEY
64089-64089	SMITHVILLE
64090-64090	STRASBURG
64092-64092	WALDRON
64093-64093	WARRENSBURG
64096-64096	WAVERLY
64097-64097	WELLINGTON
64098-64098	WESTON
64100-64199	KANSAS CITY
64401-64401	AGENCY
64402-64402	ALBANY
64420-64420	ALLENDALE
64421-64421	AMAZONIA
64422-64422	AMITY
64423-64423	BARNARD
64424-64424	BETHANY
64426-64426	BLYTHEDALE
64427-64427	BOLCKOW
64428-64428	BURLINGTON JUNCTION
64429-64429	CAMERON
64430-64430	CLARKSDALE
64431-64431	CLEARMONT
64432-64432	CLYDE
64433-64433	CONCEPTION
64434-64434	CONCEPTION JUNCTION
64435-64435	CORNING
64436-64436	COSBY
64437-64437	CRAIG
64438-64438	DARLINGTON
64439-64439	DEARBORN
64440-64440	DE KALB
64441-64441	DENVER
64442-64442	EAGLEVILLE
64443-64443	EASTON
64444-64444	EDGERTON
64445-64445	ELMO
64446-64446	FAIRFAX
64447-64447	FAIRPORT
64448-64448	FAUCETT
64449-64449	FILLMORE
64451-64451	FOREST CITY
64452-64452	FORTESCUE
64453-64453	GENTRY
64454-64454	GOWER
64455-64455	GRAHAM
64456-64456	GRANT CITY
64457-64457	GUILFORD
64458-64458	HATFIELD
64459-64459	HELENA
64461-64461	HOPKINS
64463-64463	KING CITY
64465-64465	LATHROP
64466-64466	MAITLAND
64467-64467	MARTINSVILLE
64468-64468	MARYVILLE
64469-64469	MAYSVILLE
64470-64470	MOUND CITY
64471-64471	NEW HAMPTON
64473-64473	OREGON
64474-64474	OSBORN
64475-64475	PARNELL
64476-64476	PICKERING
64477-64477	PLATTSBURG
64478-64478	QUITMAN
64479-64479	RAVENWOOD
64480-64480	REA
64481-64481	RIDGEWAY
64482-64482	ROCK PORT
64483-64483	ROSENDALE
64484-64484	RUSHVILLE
64485-64485	SAVANNAH
64486-64486	SHERIDAN
64487-64487	SKIDMORE
64489-64489	STANBERRY
64490-64490	STEWARTSVILLE
64491-64491	TARKIO
64492-64492	TRIMBLE
64493-64493	TURNEY
64494-64494	UNION STAR
64496-64496	WATSON
64497-64497	WEATHERBY
64498-64498	WESTBORO
64499-64499	WORTH
64500-64500	SAINT JOSEPH
64500-64500	ST JOSEPH
64501-64508	SAINT JOSEPH
64601-64601	CHILLICOTHE
64620-64620	ALTAMONT
64621-64621	AVALON
64622-64622	BOGARD
64623-64623	BOSWORTH
64624-64624	BRAYMER
64625-64625	BRECKENRIDGE
64628-64628	BROOKFIELD
64630-64630	BROWNING
64631-64631	BUCKLIN
64632-64632	CAINSVILLE
64633-64633	CARROLLTON
64635-64635	CHULA
64636-64636	COFFEY
64637-64637	COWGILL
64638-64638	DAWN
64639-64639	DE WITT
64640-64640	GALLATIN
64641-64641	GALT
64642-64642	GILMAN CITY
64643-64643	HALE
64644-64644	HAMILTON
64645-64645	HARRIS
64646-64646	HUMPHREYS
64647-64647	JAMESON
64648-64648	JAMESPORT
64649-64649	KIDDER
64650-64650	KINGSTON
64651-64651	LACLEDE
64652-64652	LAREDO
64653-64653	LINNEUS
64654-64654	LOCK SPRINGS
64655-64655	LUCERNE
64656-64656	LUDLOW
64657-64657	MC FALL
64658-64658	MARCELINE
64659-64659	MEADVILLE
64660-64660	MENDON
64661-64661	MERCER
64664-64664	MOORESVILLE
64665-64665	MOUNT MORIAH
64667-64667	NEWTOWN
64668-64668	NORBORNE
64670-64670	PATTONSBURG
64671-64671	POLO
64672-64672	POWERSVILLE
64673-64673	PRINCETON
64674-64674	PURDIN
64676-64676	ROTHVILLE
64677-64677	SAINT CATHERINE
64677-64677	SAINT CATHARINE
64677-64677	ST CATHARINE
64679-64679	SPICKARD
64680-64680	STET
64681-64681	SUMNER
64682-64682	TINA
64683-64683	TRENTON
64686-64686	UTICA
64687-64687	WAKENDA
64688-64688	WHEELING
64689-64689	WINSTON
64701-64701	HARRISONVILLE
64720-64720	ADRIAN
64722-64722	AMORET
64723-64723	AMSTERDAM
64724-64724	APPLETON CITY
64725-64725	ARCHIE
64726-64726	BLAIRSTOWN
64728-64728	BRONAUGH
64730-64730	BUTLER
64733-64733	CHILHOWEE
64734-64734	CLEVELAND
64735-64735	CLINTON
64738-64738	COLLINS
64739-64739	CREIGHTON
64740-64740	DEEPWATER
64741-64741	DEERFIELD
64742-64742	DREXEL
64743-64743	EAST LYNNE
64744-64744	EL DORADO SPRINGS
64745-64745	FOSTER
64746-64746	FREEMAN
64747-64747	GARDEN CITY
64748-64748	GOLDEN CITY
64750-64750	HARWOOD
64751-64751	HORTON
64752-64752	HUME
64755-64755	JASPER
64756-64756	JERICO SPRINGS
64759-64759	LAMAR
64760-64760	LATOUR
64761-64761	LEETON
64762-64762	LIBERAL
64763-64763	LOWRY CITY
64765-64765	METZ
64766-64766	MILFORD
64767-64767	MILO
64769-64769	MINDENMINES
64770-64770	MONTROSE
64771-64771	MOUNDVILLE
64772-64772	NEVADA
64776-64776	OSCEOLA
64777-64777	PASSAIC
64778-64778	RICHARDS
64779-64779	RICH HILL
64780-64780	ROCKVILLE
64781-64781	ROSCOE
64783-64783	SCHELL CITY
64784-64784	SHELDON
64788-64788	URICH
64789-64789	VISTA
64790-64790	WALKER
64801-64804	JOPLIN
64830-64830	ALBA
64831-64831	ANDERSON
64832-64832	ASBURY
64833-64833	AVILLA
64834-64834	CARL JUNCTION
64835-64835	CARTERVILLE
64836-64836	CARTHAGE
64840-64840	DIAMOND
64841-64841	DUENWEG
64842-64842	FAIRVIEW
64843-64843	GOODMAN
64844-64844	GRANBY
64847-64847	LANAGAN
64848-64848	LA RUSSELL
64849-64849	NECK CITY
64850-64850	NEOSHO
64853-64853	NEWTONIA
64854-64854	NOEL
64855-64855	ORONOGO
64856-64856	PINEVILLE
64857-64857	PURCELL
64858-64858	RACINE
64859-64859	REEDS
64861-64861	ROCKY COMFORT
64862-64862	SARCOXIE
64863-64863	SOUTH WEST CITY
64864-64864	SAGINAW
64865-64865	SENECA
64866-64866	STARK CITY
64867-64867	STELLA
64868-64868	TIFF CITY
64869-64869	WACO
64870-64870	WEBB CITY
64873-64873	WENTWORTH
64874-64874	WHEATON
64944-64999	KANSAS CITY
65001-65001	ARGYLE
65010-65010	ASHLAND
65011-65011	BARNETT
65013-65013	BELLE
65014-65014	BLAND
65016-65016	BONNOTS MILL
65017-65017	BRUMLEY
65018-65018	CALIFORNIA
65020-65020	CAMDENTON
65022-65022	CEDAR CITY
65023-65023	CENTERTOWN
65024-65024	CHAMOIS
65025-65025	CLARKSBURG
65026-65026	ELDON
65031-65031	ETTERVILLE
65032-65032	EUGENE
65034-65034	FORTUNA
65035-65035	FREEBURG
65036-65036	GASCONADE
65037-65037	GRAVOIS MILLS
65038-65038	LAURIE
65039-65039	HARTSBURG
65040-65040	HENLEY
65041-65041	HERMANN
65042-65042	HIGH POINT
65043-65043	HOLTS SUMMIT
65046-65046	JAMESTOWN
65047-65047	KAISER
65048-65048	KOELTZTOWN
65049-65049	LAKE OZARK
65050-65050	LATHAM
65051-65051	LINN
65052-65052	LINN CREEK
65053-65053	LOHMAN
65054-65054	LOOSE CREEK
65055-65055	MC GIRK
65056-65056	HERMANN
65058-65058	META
65059-65059	MOKANE
65061-65061	MORRISON
65062-65062	MOUNT STERLING
65063-65063	NEW BLOOMFIELD
65064-65064	OLEAN
65065-65065	OSAGE BEACH
65066-65066	OWENSVILLE
65067-65067	PORTLAND
65068-65068	PRAIRIE HOME
65069-65069	RHINELAND
65072-65072	ROCKY MOUNT
65074-65074	RUSSELLVILLE
65075-65075	SAINT ELIZABETH
65076-65076	SAINT THOMAS
65077-65077	STEEDMAN
65078-65078	STOVER
65079-65079	SUNRISE BEACH
65080-65080	TEBBETTS
65081-65081	TIPTON
65082-65082	TUSCUMBIA
65083-65083	ULMAN
65084-65084	VERSAILLES
65085-65085	WESTPHALIA
65101-65111	JEFFERSON CITY

65199-65199 MISSOURI STATE LOTTERY COMM
65201-65218 COLUMBIA
65230-65230 ARMSTRONG
65231-65231 AUXVASSE
65232-65232 BENTON CITY
65233-65233 BOONVILLE
65236-65236 BRUNSWICK
65237-65237 BUNCETON
65239-65239 CAIRO
65240-65240 CENTRALIA
65243-65243 CLARK
65244-65244 CLIFTON HILL
65246-65246 DALTON
65247-65247 EXCELLO
65248-65248 FAYETTE
65250-65250 FRANKLIN
65251-65251 FULTON
65254-65254 GLASGOW
65255-65255 HALLSVILLE
65256-65256 HARRISBURG
65257-65257 HIGBEE
65258-65258 HOLLIDAY
65259-65259 HUNTSVILLE
65260-65260 JACKSONVILLE
65261-65261 KEYTESVILLE
65262-65262 KINGDOM CITY
65263-65263 MADISON
65264-65264 MARTINSBURG
65265-65265 MEXICO
65270-65270 MOBERLY
65274-65274 NEW FRANKLIN
65275-65275 PARIS
65276-65276 PILOT GROVE
65278-65278 RENICK
65279-65279 ROCHEPORT
65280-65280 RUSH HILL
65281-65281 SALISBURY
65282-65282 SANTA FE
65283-65283 STOUTSVILLE
65284-65284 STURGEON
65285-65285 THOMPSON
65286-65286 TRIPLETT
65287-65287 WOOLDRIDGE
65291-65291 CENSUS BUREAU
65299-65299 MID MISSOURI
65299-65299 COLUMBIA
65301-65302 SEDALIA
65305-65305 WHITEMAN AIR FORCE BASE
65320-65320 ARROW ROCK
65321-65321 BLACKBURN
65322-65322 BLACKWATER
65323-65323 CALHOUN
65324-65324 CLIMAX SPRINGS
65325-65325 COLE CAMP
65326-65326 EDWARDS
65327-65327 EMMA
65329-65329 FLORENCE
65330-65330 GILLIAM
65332-65332 GREEN RIDGE
65333-65333 HOUSTONIA
65334-65334 HUGHESVILLE
65335-65335 IONIA
65336-65336 KNOB NOSTER
65337-65337 LA MONTE
65338-65338 LINCOLN
65339-65339 MALTA BEND
65340-65340 MARSHALL
65344-65344 MIAMI
65345-65345 MORA
65347-65347 NELSON
65348-65348 OTTERVILLE
65349-65349 SLATER
65350-65350 SMITHTON
65351-65351 SWEET SPRINGS
65354-65354 SYRACUSE
65355-65355 WARSAW
65360-65360 WINDSOR
65401-65409 ROLLA
65433-65433 BENDAVIS
65436-65436 BEULAH
65438-65438 BIRCH TREE
65439-65439 BIXBY
65440-65440 BOSS
65441-65441 BOURBON
65443-65443 BRINKTOWN
65444-65444 BUCYRUS
65446-65446 CHERRYVILLE
65449-65449 COOK STATION
65452-65452 CROCKER
65453-65453 CUBA
65456-65456 DAVISVILLE
65457-65457 DEVILS ELBOW
65459-65459 DIXON
65461-65461 DUKE
65462-65462 EDGAR SPRINGS
65463-65463 ELDRIDGE
65464-65464 ELK CREEK
65466-65466 EMINENCE
65468-65468 EUNICE
65470-65470 FALCON
65473-65473 FORT LEONARD WOOD
65479-65479 HARTSHORN
65483-65483 HOUSTON
65484-65484 HUGGINS
65486-65486 IBERIA
65501-65501 JADWIN
65529-65529 JEROME
65532-65532 LAKE SPRING
65534-65534 LAQUEY
65535-65535 LEASBURG
65536-65536 LEBANON
65540-65540 LECOMA
65541-65541 LENOX
65542-65542 LICKING
65543-65543 LYNCHBURG
65546-65546 MONTIER
65548-65548 MOUNTAIN VIEW
65550-65550 NEWBURG
65552-65552 PLATO
65555-65555 RAYMONDVILLE
65556-65556 RICHLAND
65557-65557 ROBY
65559-65559 SAINT JAMES
65560-65560 SALEM
65564-65564 SOLO
65565-65565 STEELVILLE
65566-65566 VIBURNUM
65567-65567 STOUTLAND
65570-65570 SUCCESS
65571-65571 SUMMERSVILLE
65572-65572 SWEDEBORG
65573-65573 TERESITA
65580-65580 VICHY
65582-65582 VIENNA
65583-65583 WAYNESVILLE
65584-65584 SAINT ROBERT
65586-65586 WESCO
65588-65588 WINONA
65589-65589 YUKON
65590-65590 LONG LANE
65591-65591 MONTREAL
65601-65601 ALDRICH
65603-65603 ARCOLA
65604-65604 ASH GROVE
65605-65605 AURORA
65606-65606 ALTON
65607-65607 CAPLINGER MILLS
65608-65608 AVA
65609-65609 BAKERSFIELD
65610-65610 BILLINGS
65611-65611 BLUE EYE
65612-65612 BOIS D ARC
65613-65613 BOLIVAR
65614-65614 BRADLEYVILLE
65615-65616 BRANSON
65617-65617 BRIGHTON
65618-65618 BRIXEY
65619-65619 BROOKLINE STATION
65620-65620 BRUNER
65622-65622 BUFFALO
65623-65623 BUTTERFIELD
65624-65624 CAPE FAIR
65625-65625 CASSVILLE
65626-65626 CAULFIELD
65627-65627 CEDARCREEK
65629-65629 CHADWICK
65630-65630 CHESTNUTRIDGE
65631-65631 CLEVER
65632-65632 CONWAY
65633-65633 CRANE
65634-65634 CROSS TIMBERS
65635-65635 DADEVILLE
65636-65636 DIGGINS
65637-65637 DORA
65638-65638 DRURY
65640-65640 DUNNEGAN
65641-65641 EAGLE ROCK
65644-65644 ELKLAND
65645-65645 EUDORA
65646-65646 EVERTON
65647-65647 EXETER
65648-65648 FAIR GROVE
65649-65649 FAIR PLAY
65650-65650 FLEMINGTON
65652-65652 FORDLAND
65653-65653 FORSYTH
65654-65654 FREISTATT
65655-65655 GAINESVILLE
65656-65656 GALENA
65657-65657 GARRISON
65658-65658 GOLDEN
65659-65659 GOODSON
65660-65660 GRAFF
65661-65661 GREENFIELD
65662-65662 GROVESPRING
65663-65663 HALF WAY
65664-65664 HALLTOWN
65666-65666 HARDENVILLE
65667-65667 HARTVILLE
65668-65668 HERMITAGE
65669-65669 HIGHLANDVILLE
65672-65673 HOLLISTER
65674-65674 HUMANSVILLE
65675-65675 HURLEY
65676-65676 ISABELLA
65679-65679 KIRBYVILLE
65680-65680 KISSEE MILLS
65681-65681 LAMPE
65682-65682 LOCKWOOD
65685-65685 LOUISBURG
65686-65686 KIMBERLING CITY
65688-65688 BRANDSVILLE
65689-65689 CABOOL
65690-65690 COUCH
65692-65692 KOSHKONONG
65701-65701 MC CLURG
65702-65702 MACOMB
65704-65704 MANSFIELD
65705-65705 MARIONVILLE
65706-65706 MARSHFIELD
65707-65707 MILLER
65708-65708 MONETT
65710-65710 MORRISVILLE
65711-65711 MOUNTAIN GROVE
65712-65712 MOUNT VERNON
65713-65713 NIANGUA
65714-65714 NIXA
65715-65715 NOBLE
65717-65717 NORWOOD
65720-65720 OLDFIELD
65721-65721 OZARK
65722-65722 PHILLIPSBURG
65723-65723 PIERCE CITY
65724-65724 PITTSBURG
65725-65725 PLEASANT HOPE
65726-65726 POINT LOOKOUT
65727-65727 POLK
65728-65728 PONCE DE LEON
65729-65729 PONTIAC
65730-65730 POWELL
65731-65731 POWERSITE
65732-65732 PRESTON
65733-65733 PROTEM
65734-65734 PURDY
65735-65735 QUINCY
65737-65737 REEDS SPRING
65738-65738 REPUBLIC
65739-65739 RIDGEDALE
65740-65740 ROCKAWAY BEACH
65741-65741 ROCKBRIDGE
65742-65742 ROGERSVILLE
65744-65744 RUETER
65745-65745 SELIGMAN
65746-65746 SEYMOUR
65747-65747 SHELL KNOB
65752-65752 SOUTH GREENFIELD
65753-65753 SPARTA
65754-65754 SPOKANE
65755-65755 SQUIRES
65756-65756 STOTTS CITY
65757-65757 STRAFFORD
65758-65758 GAINESVILLE
65759-65759 TANEYVILLE
65760-65760 TECUMSEH
65761-65761 THEODOSIA
65762-65762 THORNFIELD
65764-65764 TUNAS
65765-65765 TURNERS
65766-65766 UDALL
65767-65767 URBANA
65768-65768 VANZANT
65769-65769 VERONA
65770-65770 WALNUT GROVE
65771-65771 WALNUT SHADE
65772-65772 WASHBURN
65773-65773 WASOLA
65774-65774 WEAUBLEAU
65775-65775 WEST PLAINS
65776-65776 SOUTH FORK
65777-65777 MOODY
65778-65778 MYRTLE
65779-65779 WHEATLAND
65781-65781 WILLARD
65783-65783 WINDYVILLE
65784-65784 ZANONI
65785-65785 STOCKTON
65786-65786 MACKS CREEK
65787-65787 ROACH
65788-65788 PEACE VALLEY
65789-65789 POMONA
65790-65790 POTTERSVILLE
65791-65791 THAYER
65793-65793 WILLOW SPRINGS
65800-65899 SPRINGFIELD

Montana

General Help Numbers:

Governor's Office

PO Box 200801, State Capitol 406-444-3111
Helena, MT 59620-0801 Fax 406-444-5529
http://mt.gov/gov2/ 8AM-5PM

Attorney General's Office

PO Box 201401 406-444-2026
Helena, MT 59620 Fax 406-444-3549
www.doj.mt.gov/resources/attorneygeneral.asp 8AM-5PM

Legislative Records

State Capitol, Rm 10 406-444-3064
PO Box 201706 406-444-3660 (Research)
Helena, MT 59620-1706 Fax 406-444-2588
http://leg.mt.gov/css/default.asp 8AM-5PM

State Archives

Historical Society, Library/Archives Div. 406-444-2681
PO Box 201201, 225 N Roberts St Fax 406-444-5297
Helena, MT 59620-1201 9AM-4:30PM T-F
and 1st SA each month 9AM-1PM
www.his.state.mt.us/research/library/collections.asp

State Specifics:

Capital: Helena
Lewis and Clark County

Time Zone: MST

Number of Counties: 56

Population: 967,440

Web Site: http://mt.gov/

State Agencies

Criminal Records

Department of Justice, Criminal Records, PO Box 201403, Helena, MT 59620-1403 (Courier address- 303 N Roberts, 4th Floor, Helena, MT 59620); 406-444-3625, Fax- 406-444-0689; 8AM-5PM. http://doj.mt.gov/

Email questions to dojitsdpublicrecords@mt.gov.

Indexing & Storage: Records available from 1950's on and are 100% computerized. New records available for inquiry in 1 week to 1 month. 85% of all arrests in database have final dispositions recorded.

Searching: Account status to approved screening firms. Include in request- name, alias, date of birth. The SSN and any aliases are helpful. Place written requests on letterhead. Fingerprint searches are optional. 100% of records are fingerprint-supported. This data not released- traffic offenses, unless felony driving under the influence of alcohol. All felonies and misdemeanors (except traffic violations) are released. Records without dispositions are released; the agency attempts to locate the disposition prior to public release. Deferred impositions that have been dismissed are not released.

Access by: mail, in person, online.

Fee & Payment: The fee is $10.00 per individual for a name check or fingerprint check, $11.50 for name check online. Add $24.00 for an FBI fingerprint check if required by statute for child care or schools. Fee payee- Montana Criminal Records Prepayment required. Personal checks accepted, credit cards are not.

Mail search: Turnaround time- 5-10 days. A SASE is requested.

In person: This agency will create the individual's fingerprint card needed for a fingerprint check for a $5.00 fee plus the search fee of $10.00. Turnaround time is usually immediate, unless there is a record or "hit."

Online search: Access is available for "public users" or "registered users" at https://app.mt.gov/choprs/. Fee is $11.00 per record. Registered users must pay a $75 annual fee and have access to other data. Search using the name and DOB. The SSN is helpful but not required. Results include up to 4 aliases, dispositions, detentions, sentences, and correctional status.

Statewide Court Records

Office of The Court Administrator, P.O. Box 203005, Helena, Montana 59620-3005 (Courier address- 301 S. Park, Room 328, Park Avenue Building, Helena, MT 59620); 406-841-2950, Fax- 406-841-2955; 8AM-5PM. http://courts.mt.gov/

All trial court record access must be done at the local level. The Clerk of the Supreme Court is at 406-444-3858.

Online search: Current Montana Supreme Court opinions are available at http://fnweb1.isd.doa.state.mt.us/idmws/custom/sll/sll_fn_home.htm.

Sexual Offender Registry

Department of Justice, Sexual and Violent Offender Registry, PO Box 201417, Helena, MT 59620-1417; 406-444-2497, 406-444-9479, Fax- 406-444-2759; 8AM-5PM.

http://doj.mt.gov/svor/search.asp

There are over 3,900 registered offenders in the database. There are three Tier Levels of offenders, 1 being the lowest and 3 being the highest. Level 3 also indicates the offender is a sexually violent predator.

Indexing & Storage: Records available from 1989 forward. Tier Levels were instituted in 1997. New records available for inquiry in 1 week to 1 month.

Searching: Submit questions to dojsvor@mt.gov. Include in request- city or county or ZIP or name.

Access by: online.

Fee & Payment: There is no fee to search.

Online search: The state sexual offender list is available at the website. You can search for this information by name, by city or county, or by ZIP Code. The percent sign (%) may be used as a wildcard character in the Last Name field to represent one or more other characters.

Other access: The entire database may be purchased as a download for $300.00.

Incarceration Records

Montana Department of Corrections, Directors Office, PO Box 201301, Helena, MT 59620-1301 (Courier address- 1539 11th Ave, Helena, MT 59620); 406-444-3930, 406-444-7461 (Information Officer), Fax- 406-444-4920; 8:30AM-4:30PM. www.cor.state.mt.us

Indexing & Storage: Records available on current and former inmates. Computerized records go back to 1980. Older records sent to Historical Society. New records available for inquiry in up to 120 days.

Searching: Location, physical identifiers, conviction and sentencing information, and release dates are provided. Include in request- name; and DOB. Computer records go back to 1978. This data not released- SSN and medical information.

Access by: mail, phone, fax, online.

Fee & Payment: There is no fee.

Mail search: Turnaround time- 10 to 40 days. SASE not required.

Phone search: Name searching is permitted.

Fax search: Fax requests are accepted, depending on complexity of search.

Online search: Search current or former inmates on the ConWeb system at http://app.mt.gov/conweb/. Search by ID# or name.

Other access: Entire offender database is available for purchase for $100.00; call Discovering Montana, 406-449-3468. Academic or social researchers can acquire the same database for no charge.

Corporation, LLC, LP, Fictitious/Assumed Name, Trademarks/Servicemarks

Business Services Bureau, Secretary of State, PO Box 202801, Helena, MT 59620-2801 (Courier address- 1306 6th Ave, Capital Bldg, Rm 260, Helena, MT 59620); 406-444-3665, Fax- 406-444-3976; 8AM-5PM.

www.sos.mt.gov/Business/index.asp

Indexing & Storage: Records available from the 1860s. New records available for inquiry immediately.

Searching: Include in request- full name of business, specific records that you need copies of. In addition to the articles of organization, business entity records available include: Annual Reports, Officers, Directors, DBAs, Prior (merged) names, Inactive and Reserved names.

Access by: mail, phone, fax, in person, online.

Fee & Payment: There is no search fee, but there is a flat fee of $10.00 for all copies within a file; records are certified for this price. May also be ordered online. Fee payee- Secretary of State. Prepayment required. Prepaid accounts may be established. Personal checks accepted. Credit cards accepted when purchasing copies online.

Mail search: Turnaround time- 2 weeks. A SASE is requested.

Phone search: Limit of three requests per call.

Fax search: Documents or copies returned by fax are priced at $5.00 per file, flat rate.

In person: Counter service is available.

Online search: Visit http://app.mt.gov/bes/ for free searches of MT business entities. Certified copies may be ordered online for $10.00 using a credit card. There is a commercial service for finding registered principles. Go to http://app.mt.gov/registered/.

Other access: One may purchase a download, customized, of all MT business entities. Go to https://app.mt.gov/corprecords/. Also, lists of new corporations per month are available.

Expedited service: Expedited service is available for mail, phone and in person searches. Turnaround time- 1 day to 1 hour. Add $20.00 per search for 24 hour service; $100 for 1 hour service.

Uniform Commercial Code, Federal Tax Liens

Business Services Division, Secretary of State, Rm 260, PO Box 202801, Helena, MT 59620-2801 (Courier address- 1301 6th Ave, Rm 260, State Capitol, Helena, MT 59601); 406-444-2468, Fax- 406-444-3976; 8AM-5PM.

www.sos.mt.gov/Business/UCC.asp

Indexing & Storage: Records available from 1965, indexed on computer and on microfiche. Terminated or expired financing statements are not available prior to 6/30/01, with the exception of notices of federal tax liens. New records available for inquiry in one day.

Searching: Use search request form UCC-11. The search includes notice of federal tax liens on businesses and individuals. All state tax liens are filed at the county level. Include in request- debtor exact name and any fictitious names. This data not released- SSN.

Access by: mail, fax, in person, online.

Fee & Payment: The search fee is $7.00 per debtor name, copies are $5.00 per search/file. Fee payee- Secretary of State. The state will accept prepaid accounts. Personal checks accepted, credit cards are not.

Mail search: Turnaround time- 1 to 3 days.

Fax search: To fax back, there is an additional fee of $5.00 (flat rate).

In person: Counter service is 1 to 3 days unless expedite fee is paid.

Online search: A web-based subscription service provides information about all active liens filed with the office. To use the service you need to establish an account with Discovering Montana for a fee of $25 per month. See https://app.mt.gov/uccs/. Contact Discovering Montana at 101 N Rodney #3, Helena MT 59601, or call 866-449-3468, or visit website at http://mt.gov/default.asp.

Other access: The agency offers farm bill filings lists on a monthly basis for $5.00 per category on paper or microfiche. A CD-Rom for all Farm Products is available for $20.00. There is a proposed rule for flat $10.00 fee for paper and microfiche.

Expedited service: Turnaround time- 1 day. Add $20.00 per search.

State Tax Liens

Records not maintained by a state level agency.

Records are at the county level.

Sales Tax Registrations

State does not impose sales tax.

Birth Certificates

Montana Department of Health, Vital Records, PO Box 4210, Helena, MT 59604 (Courier address- 111 N Sanders, Rm 209, Helena, MT 59601); 406-444-2685, Fax- 866-696-1912; 8AM-5PM.

http://vhsp.dphhs.mt.gov/certificates/ordercertificates.shtml

A non-certified informational record is available for $10.00, providing the birth occurred over 30 years ago.

Indexing & Storage: Records available from 1907 on. New records available for inquiry in 3 months.

Searching: Must be able to show direct and tangible interest of records. The decision if you can get copies of records will be up to the staff of the Vital Records department. Include in request- full name, names of parents, mother's maiden name, date of birth, place of birth, relationship to person of record, reason for information request. Must include copy of guardianship papers, if you are guardian. All requesters must include photo ID and phone number.

Access by: mail, fax, in person, online.

Fee & Payment: A certified copy is $12.00. If year not known, then add a search fee of $10.00 for 5 years searched and $1.00 each add'l year. A non-certified "informational" record is $10.00. Fee payee- Montana Vital Records. Prepayment required. Personal checks and major credit cards accepted.

Mail search: Turnaround time- 10 days. SASE not required.

Fax search: Through a vendor, see expedited service

In person: Turnaround time same day.

Online search: Orders can be placed via a state designated vendor. Go to www.vitalchek.com. Extra fees are involved.

Expedited service: Expedited service is available for fax and online orders from VitalChek. Vendor fee is $10.50, plus cost of express shipment if desired. Turnaround time- overnight delivery.

Death Records

Montana Department of Health, Vital Records, PO Box 4210, Helena, MT 59604 (Courier address- 111 N Sanders, Rm 209, Helena, MT 59601); 406-444-2685, Fax- 866-696-1912; 8AM-5PM.

http://vhsp.dphhs.mt.gov/certificates/ordercertificates.shtml

Indexing & Storage: Records available from 1908, archived from 1860. New records available for inquiry in 3 months.

Searching: Records are open. Include in request- full name, date of death, place of death, relationship to person of record, reason for information request. Requesters must include a copy of picture ID and phone number.

Access by: mail, fax, in person, online.

Fee & Payment: A certified copy is $12.00. If year not known, then add a search fee of $10.00 for 5 years searched and $1.00 each add'l year. A non-certified "informational" record is $10.00. Fee payee- Montana Vital Records. Prepayment required. Personal checks and major credit cards accepted.

Mail search: Turnaround time- 10 days.

Fax search: Through a vendor, see expedited service

In person: Turnaround time same day.

Online search: Orders can be placed via a state designated vendor. Go to www.vitalchek.com. Extra fees are involved.

Expedited service: Expedited service is available for fax and online orders from VitalChek. Vendor fee is $10.50, plus cost of express shipment if desired. Turnaround time- overnight delivery.

Marriage Certificates, Divorce Records

Access to Records is Restricted.

Montana Department of Health, Vital Records, PO Box 4210, Helena, MT 59604 (Courier address- 111 N Sanders, Rm 209, Helena, MT 59601); 406-444-2685, 888-877-1946 (VitalChek), Fax- 866-696-1912.

Marriage and divorce records are found at county of issue. This agency is required by law to maintain an index of these records. The index is from 1943 to present. The State can direct you to the correct county for a fee of $10.00 per 5 years searched.

Workers' Compensation Records

Montana State Fund, General Legal Inquiries, PO Box 4759, Helena, MT 59604-4759 (Courier address- 5 S. Last Chance Gulch, Helena, MT 59601); 406-444-6500, Fax- 406-444-5963; 8AM-5PM.

www.montanastatefund.com/wps/portal

Indexing & Storage: Records available from mid 1980's to 1995 on microfiche. Records 1996 forward are computerized. New records available for inquiry in 30 days.

Searching: Put request in writing, including reason for the request. They will determine whether the request is legitimate, unless you include a signed release form. Include in request- claimant name, SSN, date of accident, employer.

Access by: mail, fax, in person.

Fee & Payment: Copy fees are $.35 per page if from computer, $.50 per page if from microfiche. There is no search fee. Fee payee- Montana State Fund. Prepayment required. Personal checks accepted, credit cards are not.

Mail search: Turnaround time- 7 days. SASE not required.

Fax search: Same criteria as mail searches.

In person: Walk-ins treated like mail requesters.

Driver Records

Motor Vehicle Division, Driver's Services, PO Box 201430, Helena, MT 59620-1430 (Courier address- Records Unit, 303 N Roberts, Room 260, Helena, MT 59620); 406-444-4590, Fax- 406-444-7623; 8AM-5PM.

www.doj.mt.gov/driving/default.asp

Indexing & Storage: Records available for lifetime. New records available for inquiry in up to 45 days.

Searching: Anyone may order a driving record; however, personal information including address is not released. Opt out is not necessary. Use of the State Form 34-0100 is required. The form can be downloaded at the website. Include in request- driver's full name, DOB, and/or license number. In person and mail requests must have notarized signature of requester or present a state-issued ID. This data not released- SSN, address, photo, and medical information.

Access by: mail, in person, online.

Fee & Payment: The fee is $4.00 per three-year record history, $7.25 if processed electronically, and $10.00 for a certified history. Fee payee- Motor Vehicle Division. Prepayment required. Billing or draw accounts available. Personal checks accepted. Credit cards accepted online.

Mail search: Turnaround time- 3 days. Requests must be in writing, stating purpose and on letterhead. Use of state form described above is highly recommended. A SASE is requested.

In person: Simple requests processed immediately. Up to 5 records may be requested in person for immediate delivery at this location. Use of forms are required.

Online search: There are two methods offered, one for Public User requests and a subscription service. The fee is $7.25. The Public Access results do not offer address information. For registered subscribers, an agreement must be signed and there is an annual $75.00 registration fee. Services online also include a License Status Conviction Activity batch or monitoring search, at a reduced price. For more about online services visit https://app.mt.gov/dojdrs/ or call 406-449-3468.

Expedited service: Fax return service is available for an additional $3.00 per page.

Vehicle, Vessel Ownership & Registration

Department of Justice, Title and Registration Bureau, 1003 Buckskin Drive, Deer Lodge, MT 59722; 406-846-6000, Fax- 406-846-6039; 8AM-5PM.

http://doj.mt.gov/driving/vehicletitleregistration.asp

Lien information appears on the title record. General questions are directed to mvdtitleinfo@mt.gov.

Indexing & Storage: Records available from 1976 to present on microfiche. Watercraft data is available from 1988. New records available for inquiry in 5 to 10 days for imaging.

Searching: Casual requesters may not obtain records without written consent of the subject. DPPA requirements enforced. MV210 Form - Release of Motor Vehicle Records - can be downloaded from the website. Requires notarization of the requester or copy of DL. Items required for search could include full name, VIN, plate number, or title number. Cannot look up information by plate alone; must have second identifier.

Access by: mail, in person, online.

Fee & Payment: The fee is $6.00 per vehicle/vessel or name search; $25.00 for title or odometer history. Other fees are in place for online access (see below). Fee payee- State of Montana Prepayment required. Personal checks accepted, credit cards are not.

Mail search: Turnaround time- 5 to 7 days. Requests must be in writing, signed and notarized. Use of the state form is required. SASE not required.

In person: Simple requests may be processed while you wait, if staffing available.

Online search: Both "Public User" and Registered User" interfaces are offered at https://app.mt.gov/dojvs. The Registered User system is for ongoing registered accounts approved by the Motor Vehicle Division. Depending on the level of authority granted, the following is available: Vehicle Information, License Plate Information, Vehicle Owner Information, Lien History, Title History and Registration Information. The fee is $2.00 per search. There is an annual $75.00 registration fee for 10 users. The "Public User" system is designed for Montana citizens or users with an occasional need to know the ownership history of a pre-owned car. Sensitive information, such as the SSN or home address is not released. A $5.00 fee applies and a credit card must be used.

Other access: Bulk or batch ordering of registration information is available on tape, disk, or paper. The user must fill out a specific form, which gives the user the capability of customization. For further information, contact the Registrar at address above.

Accident Reports

Montana Highway Patrol, Crash Records, 2550 Prospect Ave, Helena, MT 59620-1419; 406-444-3278, Fax- 406-444-4169; 8AM-5PM.

www.doj.mt.gov/enforcement/highwaypatrol/default.asp

Digital images are available with previous year's data.

Indexing & Storage: Records available for 10 years to present. Computer indexing since 1996. Digital images are available starting with the year 1995. New records available for inquiry in 10 to 14 days after the accident.

Searching: Records are only released to persons involved in crash, owner, attorney or insurance representing someone or estate of those involved in the case, or by a signed released. Witness statements are released. A Crash Release Form available on web. Include in request- location of accident, date of accident, full name(s) of drivers, signature of requester.

Access by: mail, in person.

Fee & Payment: The search fee is $2.00 per report, non-fundable. Photos are available in CD format for $10.00. Order form is on the web. Fee payee- Montana Highway Patrol. Prepayment required. Personal checks accepted, credit cards are not.

Mail search: Turnaround time- 3 to 4 working days. Requests must be submitted in writing following guidelines mentioned above. SASE not required.

In person: Records will be released if proper authorization is shown.

Other access: Statistics, are available, call 406-444-3298.

Legislation Records

State Legislature of Montana, State Capitol, Rm 110, PO Box 201706, Helena, MT 59620-1706; 406-444-3064, 406-444-3660 (Research), Fax- 406-444-2588; 8AM-5PM.

http://leg.mt.gov/css/default.asp

Indexing & Storage: Records available from 1983 to present, on microfiche 1987 to 1997, on computer since 1997. New records available for inquiry in 1 week.

Searching: Include in request- bill number, year.

Access by: mail, phone, in person, online.

Fee & Payment: Copy fee is $.15 per page. Fee payee- Montana Legislative Services Division. Personal checks and major credit cards accepted.

Mail search: Turnaround time- variable. SASE not required.

Phone search: No fee for telephone request.

In person: No fee for search request, $.15 per copy.

Online search: Search Code at http://data.opi.mt.gov/bills/mca_toc/index.htm. Bill and Session info from 1999 forward are available on the Internet. State statutes and codes may be researched from http://data.opi.state.mt.us/bills/mca_toc/index.htm. Bills by year at http://leg.mt.gov/css/bills/default.asp.

Other access: Current session bills and resolutions are available on CD-ROM for $150; other products include the Montana Code, House and Senate Journals, and Annotations, among others.

Voter Registration

Secretary of State, Elections Bureau, PO Box 202801, Helena, MT 59620-2801; 406-444-5376, Fax- 406-444-2023; 8AM-5PM.

www.sos.mt.gov/Elections/index.asp

Searching by state personnel depends on the voter file system workload.

Indexing & Storage: Records available back to 2006. Counties will update the state database daily. New records available for inquiry in 1 to 7 days.

Searching: This data not released- SSNs and driver license numbers.

Access by: mail, phone, fax, in person, online.

Fee & Payment: There are no fees for searches unless large lists or bulk records needed.

Mail search: Turnaround time- 2 to 4 days. SASE not required.

Phone search: Records are available by phone.

Fax search: Fax searching available.

In person: Simple requests may be processed immediately.

Online search: Access records at http://app.mt.gov/voterfile/select_criteria.html. Records can be purchased for non-commercial use only.

Other access: This agency database or customized portions can be purchased on disk or CD-ROM. Fee to purchase database is $1,000 or $5,000 for subscription with updates. For more information, contact Lisa Kimmet.

GED Certificates

Office of Public Instruction, GED Program, PO Box 202501, Helena, MT 59620-2501; 406-444-4438, Fax- 406-444-1373; 6:30AM-2:30PM.

www.opi.mt.gov/

Indexing & Storage: New records available for inquiry in three weeks.

Searching: The agency will not issue duplicate diplomas. Include in request- name, SSN, DOB, approximate year of test, SASE. If the information is going to a third party (employer or screening company) include a signed release from the subject and indicate where to send the documentation.

Access by: mail, in person.

Fee & Payment: There is no search fee for either a verification or transcript. The fee is the cost of the stamped envelope.

Mail search: Turnaround time 1 week. A SASE is required.

In person: No fee for request. Turnaround time same day.

Hunting & Fishing License Information

Fish, Wildlife & Parks Department, Licensing Records, PO Box 200701, Helena, MT 59620-0701 (Courier address- 1420 E 6th Ave, Helena, MT 59620); 406-444-2950, Fax- 406-444-3707; 8AM-5PM.

http://fwp.mt.gov/default.html

Indexing & Storage: Records available from 1976 for the special resident and non-resident permits and the general permits go back for 5 years.

Searching: The agency will verify if a person has purchased a license. Include in request- full name, date of birth, SSN. This data not released- phone number and SSN.

Access by: mail, phone, in person.

Fee & Payment: There is no search fee.

Mail search: Turnaround time- 1 week or more. A SASE is requested.

Phone search: Records are available by phone.

In person: Simple requests may be processed immediately.

Other access: A master list showing names, address, and types of licenses purchased can be ordered from this agency. The cost is $100.00. Since 2005, licensees have the choice of opting in/out to have their names distributed, thus the master list is shrinking.

Montana State Licensing Agencies

For details about the agency responsible for licensing/certifying/registering an item below or in the Agency Quick Finder section, match an item's number with the number of the agency in the *Licensing Agency Information* section.

Montana Licenses Searchable Online

Acupuncturist #33 .... http://app.mt.gov/lookup/
Adoption Agency #4 .... www.dphhs.mt.gov/cfsd/adoption/privateadoptionagencies.shtml
Alarm Response Runner #9 .... http://app.mt.gov/lookup/
Architect #10 .... http://app.mt.gov/lookup/
Athletic Event/Event Timekeeper #3 .... http://app.mt.gov/lookup/
Audiologist #21 .... http://mt.gov/dli/slp/
Barber/Barber Shop/Instruct'r #2 .... http://app.mt.gov/lookup/
Boxer/Boxing Professional #3 .... http://app.mt.gov/lookup/
Boxing Mgr/Promoter/Judge #3 .... http://app.mt.gov/lookup/
Cemetery, Privately Owned #3 .... http://app.mt.gov/lookup/
Chemical Dependency Counselor #19 .... http://app.mt.gov/lookup/
Child Care Provider #26 .... http://oraweb.hhs.state.mt.us:9999/ccrd/plsql/ccrd_provider.startup
Chiropractor #3 .... http://app.mt.gov/lookup/
Clinical Nurse Specialist #32 .... http://app.mt.gov/lookup/
Clinical Social Worker #17 .... http://app.mt.gov/lookup/
Construction Blaster #18 .... http://app.mt.gov/lookup/
Cosmetologist/Cosmetl'y Instr./Sch'l #2 .... http://app.mt.gov/lookup/
CP Installer/Designer #31 .... http://deq.mt.gov/UST/licensees.asp
Crematory/Crematory Oper./Tech. #3 .... http://app.mt.gov/lookup/
Day Care Center #26 .... http://oraweb.hhs.state.mt.us:9999/ccrd/plsql/ccrd_provider.startup
Dental Hygienist #5 .... http://app.mt.gov/lookup/
Dentist/Dental Assistant #5 .... http://app.mt.gov/lookup/
Denturist #5 .... http://app.mt.gov/lookup/
Drug Registration, Dangerous #7 .... http://app.mt.gov/lookup/
Drug Wholesaler #7 .... http://app.mt.gov/lookup/
Electrician #8 .... http://app.mt.gov/lookup/
Electrologist #2 .... http://app.mt.gov/lookup/
Emergency Medical Technician #33 .... http://app.mt.gov/lookup/
Engineer #10 .... http://app.mt.gov/lookup/
Esthetician #2 .... http://app.mt.gov/lookup/
Firearms Instructor #9 .... http://app.mt.gov/lookup/
Funeral Director #3 .... http://app.mt.gov/lookup/
Guide #6 .... http://app.mt.gov/lookup/
Hearing Aid Dispenser #3 .... http://app.mt.gov/lookup/
Insurance Adjuster #37 .... http://sao.mt.gov/insurance/findagent.asp
Insurance Producer #37 .... http://sao.mt.gov/insurance/findagent.asp
Land Surveyor #10 .... http://app.mt.gov/lookup/
Landscape Architect #3 .... http://app.mt.gov/lookup/
Living Trust Seller #38 .... www.sao.mt.gov
Lobbying Principal #24 .... http://app.mt.gov/cgi-bin/camptrack/lobbysearch/lobbySearch.cgi
Lobbyist #24 .... http://app.mt.gov/cgi-bin/camptrack/lobbysearch/lobbySearch.cgi
Manicurist #2 .... http://app.mt.gov/lookup/
Medical Doctor #33 .... http://app.mt.gov/lookup/
Midwife Nurse #32 .... http://app.mt.gov/lookup/
Midwife, Direct Entry/Apprentice #1 .... http://app.mt.gov/lookup/
Monitoring Well Installer #31 .... http://deq.mt.gov/UST/licensees.asp
Mortuary/Mortician #3 .... http://app.mt.gov/lookup/
Multi-level Marketing Company #38 .... www.sao.mt.gov
Naturopathic Physician #1 .... http://app.mt.gov/lookup/
Nurse Anesthetist #32 .... http://app.mt.gov/lookup/
Nurse Practitioner #32 .... http://app.mt.gov/lookup/
Nurse-RN/LPN #32 .... http://app.mt.gov/lookup/
Nutritionist #33 .... http://app.mt.gov/lookup/
Occupational Therapist #21 .... http://mt.gov/dli/otp/
Optometrist #7 .... http://app.mt.gov/lookup/
Osteopathic Physician #33 .... http://app.mt.gov/lookup/
Outfitter, Hunting/Fishing #6 .... http://app.mt.gov/lookup/

Pharmacist #7	http://app.mt.gov/lookup/
Physical Therapist #17	http://app.mt.gov/lookup/
Physician Assistant #33	http://app.mt.gov/lookup/
Plumber #8	http://app.mt.gov/lookup/
Podiatrist #33	http://app.mt.gov/lookup/
Private Investigator/Trainee #9	http://app.mt.gov/lookup/
Private Placement Offering #38	www.sao.mt.gov
Private Security Guard #9	http://app.mt.gov/lookup/
Process Server #9	http://app.mt.gov/lookup/
Property Manager #15	http://mt.gov/dli/rre/
Psychologist #11	http://app.mt.gov/lookup/
Public Accountant #12	http://mt.gov/dli/pac/
Radiologic Technologist #21	http://mt.gov/dli/rts/
Real Estate Agent/Broker/Sales #15	http://mt.gov/dli/rre/
Real Estate Appraiser #14	http://mt.gov/dli/rea/
Referee #3	http://app.mt.gov/lookup/
Resident Manager #9	http://app.mt.gov/lookup/
Respiratory Care Practitioner #21	http://mt.gov/dli/rcp/
SchoolCounselor/Psycholog'st #35	http://data.opi.state.mt.us/edcredentials/index.asp
School Principal #35	http://data.opi.state.mt.us/edcredentials/index.asp
School Superintendent #35	http://data.opi.state.mt.us/edcredentials/index.asp
Securities Broker/Seller #38	www.sao.mt.gov
Security Alarm Installer #9	http://app.mt.gov/lookup/
Security Company/Organization #9	http://app.mt.gov/lookup/
Security Org., Proprietary #9	http://app.mt.gov/lookup/
Social Worker, LSW #17	http://app.mt.gov/lookup/
Speech Pathologist #21	http://mt.gov/dli/slp/
Surveyor, Land #10	http://app.mt.gov/lookup/
Teacher #35	http://data.opi.state.mt.us/edcredentials/index.asp
Telephone, Customer-Owned, Coin #38	www.sao.mt.gov
Timeshare Broker/Salesperson #15	http://mt.gov/dli/rre/
Underground Tank Inspector #31	http://deq.mt.gov/UST/licensees.asp
Underground Tank Instal/remov'r #31	http://deq.mt.gov/UST/licensees.asp
Variable Annuities Seller #38	www.sao.mt.gov
Veterinarian #11	http://app.mt.gov/lookup/
Wrestler #3	http://app.mt.gov/lookup/
X-ray Technician #21	http://mt.gov/dli/rts/

Montana Licensing Quick Finder

Acupuncturist #33	406-841-2364
Adoption Agency #4	406-444-5916
Alarm Response Runner #9	406-841-2387
Apiary #20	406-444-5400
Architect #10	406-841-2367
Asbestos Contr./Supvr./Supplier #25	406-444-3490
Asbestos Inspector/Worker #25	406-444-3490
Asbestos Project Designer/Plann'r #25	406-444-3490
Athletic Event/Event Timekeeper #3	406-841-2370
Attorney #16	406-442-7660
Audiologist #21	406-841-2385
Barber/Barber Shop/Instruct'r #2	406-841-2300
Boxer/Boxing Professional #3	406-841-2370
Boxing Mgr/Promoter/Judge #3	406-841-2370
Brand (Livestock) #29	406-444-2045
Brand Inspector #29	406-444-2045
Candidates, Political #24	406-444-2942
Card Contractor/Card Tourney #28	406-444-1971
Card Dealer #28	406-444-1971
Card Table, Live #28	406-444-1971
Casino Night #28	406-444-1971
Cemetery, Privately Owned #3	406-841-2394
Chemical Dependency Counselor #19	406-444-2827
Child Care Agency #4	406-444-1675
Child Care Provider #26	406-444-2012
Chiropractor #3	406-841-2390
Clinical Nurse Specialist #32	406-841-2340
Clinical Social Worker #17	406-841-2369
Commodity Dealer #20	406-444-5400
Construction Blaster #18	406-841-2367
Contractor, Public/Independent #36	406-444-7734
Contractor, Revoked License #36	406-444-7734
Cosmetologist/Cosm'tol'y Inst./Sch'l #2	406-841-2300
CP Installer/Designer #31	406-444-0493
Crematory/Crematory Oper./Tech. #3	406-841-2394
Dam Safety Operation Permit #34	406-444-6601
Day Care Center #26	406-444-2012
Dental Hygienist #5	406-841-2390
Dentist/Dental Assistant #5	406-841-2390
Denturist #5	406-841-2390
Drug Registration, Dangerous #7	406-841-2356
Drug Wholesaler #7	406-841-2356
Electrician #8	406-841-2299
Electrologist #2	406-841-2300
Emergency Medical Technician #33	406-841-2380
Engineer #10	406-841-2367
Esthetician #2	406-841-2300
Feed Dealer #20	406-444-5400
Fertilizer Dealer #20	406-444-5400
Firearms Instructor #9	406-841-2387
Foster Care Home/Program #4	406-444-1675
Funeral Director #3	406-841-2394
Fur/Hide Dealer #27	406-444-2452
Gambling Machine, Video/Electr'c #28	406-444-1971
Gambling Operator #28	406-444-1971
Gaming Device Mfg./Dist. #28	406-444-1971
Grain Elevator #20	406-444-5400
Group Home, Youth #30	406-444-0507
Guide #6	406-841-2304
Hearing Aid Dispenser #3	406-841-2395
Horse Racing Occupation #22	406-444-4287
Insurance Adjuster #37	406-444-2040
Insurance Producer #37	406-444-2040
Jockey #22	406-444-4287
Land Surveyor #10	406-841-2367
Landscape Architect #3	406-841-2395
Livestock Dealer #29	406-444-2045
Living Trust Seller #38	406-444-2040
Lobbying Principal #24	406-444-2942
Lobbyist #24	406-444-2942
Lottery Retailer #23	406-444-5825
Manicurist #2	406-841-2300
Meat and Poultry #29	406-444-5202
Medical Doctor #33	406-841-2364
Medical Gas Endorsem't, Plumber #8	406-841-2299
Midwife Nurse #32	406-841-2340
Midwife, Direct Entry/Apprentice #1	406-841-2394
Mint Oil Producer #20	406-444-5400
Monitoring Well Installer #31	406-444-0493
Mortuary/Mortician #3	406-841-2394
Multi-level Marketing Company #38	406-444-2040
Naturopathic Physician #1	406-841-2394
Notary Public #13	406-444-5379
Nurse Anesthetist #32	406-841-2340
Nurse Practitioner #32	406-841-2340
Nurse-RN/LPN #32	406-841-2340
Nurseryman #20	406-444-5400

Nutritionist #33 406-841-2364
Occupational Therapist #21 406-841-2385
Optometrist #7 406-841-2390
Osteopathic Physician #33 406-841-2364
Outfitter, Hunting/Fishing #6 406-841-2373
Pesticide Applicator/Dealer #20 406-444-5400
Pharmacist #7 406-841-2356
Physical Therapist #17 406-841-2391
Physician Assistant #33 406-841-2361
Plumber #8 406-841-2299
Podiatrist #33 406-841-2364
Private Investigator/Trainee #9 406-841-2387
Private Placement Offering #38 406-444-2040
Private Security Guard #9 406-841-2387
Process Server #9 406-841-2387
Produce Licensee #20 406-444-5400
Property Manager #15 406-841-2325
Psychologist #11 406-841-2394
Public Accountant #12 406-841-2320
Radiologic Technologist #21 406-841-2385
Real Estate Agent/Broker/Sales #15 406-841-2325
Real Estate Appraiser #14 406-841-2325
Referee #3 406-841-2370
Resident Manager #9 406-841-2387
Respiratory Care Practitioner #21 406-841-2385
School Guidance Couns'r/Psycholog'st #35 406-444-3150
School Principal #35 406-444-3150
School Superintendent #35 406-444-3150
Securities Broker/Seller #38 406-444-2040
Security Alarm Installer #9 406-841-2387
Security Company/Organization #9 406-841-2387
Security Org., Proprietary #9 406-841-2387
Seed Dealer #20 406-444-5400
Septic Tank Cleaner #25 406-444-5294
Social Worker, LSW #17 406-841-2369
Speech Pathologist #21 406-841-2385
Surveyor, Land #10 406-841-2367
Taxidermist #27 406-444-2452
Teacher #35 406-444-3150
Telephone, customer-owned, Coin #38 406-444-2040
Timeshare Broker/Salesperson #15 406-841-2325
Underground Tank Inspector #31 406-444-0493
Underground Tank Instal/remov'r #31 . 406-444-0493
Variable Annuities Seller #38 406-444-2040
Veterinarian #11 406-841-2394
Water & Sewage Plant Operator #25 406-444-5294
Weather Modifier #34 406-444-6601
Well Driller #34 406-444-6601
Wrestler #3 406-841-2370
X-ray Technician #21 406-841-2385

Montana Licensing Agency Information

#1 Board of Alternative Health Care, Health Care License Bureau, PO Box 200513 (301 S Park Ave, #430), Helena, MT 59620-0513; 406-841-2365, Fax- 406-841-2305. http://mt.gov/dli/ahc/ Search data at- http://app.mt.gov/lookup/

#2 Board of Barbers & Cosmetologists, Division of Professional & Occupational Licensing, PO Box 200513 (301 S Park Av, #430), Helena, MT 59620-0513; 406-841-2320, Fax- 406-841-2323. http://mt.gov/dli/bsd/license/bsd_boards/cos_board/board_page.asp Search data at- http://app.mt.gov/lookup/ Download licensee lists after purchase and after selecting Board type at www.mt.gov/dli/bsd/license/bus_index.asp.

#3 Boards: Chiropractor, Funerary, Hearing, Landscape Architect, Athletic Events, Division of Professional & Occupational Licensing, PO Box 200513 (301 S Park, Rm 430), Helena, MT 59620-0513; 406-841-2393, Fax- 406-841-2343. http://mt.gov/dli/bsd/ Search data at- http://app.mt.gov/lookup/ Download licensee lists after purchase and after selecting Board type at www.mt.gov/dli/bsd/license/bus_index.asp.

#4 Department of Public Health Human Services, Child & Family Services Division, PO Box 8005 (1400 Broadway), Helena, MT 59604; 406-444-5900, Fax- 406-444-5956. www.dphhs.mt.gov/cfsd/index.shtml

#5 Board of Dentistry, Division of Health Care Licensing, PO Box 200513 (301 S Park 4th Fl), Helena, MT 59620-0513; 406-841-2390, Fax- 406-841-2305. Hours- 7:30AM-4:30PM. http://mt.gov/dli/den/ Search data at- http://app.mt.gov/lookup/ Records available online back to 7/1996. Also, download licensee lists after purchase and after selecting Board type at www.mt.gov/dli/bsd/license/bus_index.asp.

#6 Board of Outfitters, Division of Professional & Occupational Licensing, PO Box 200513 (301 S Park Ave 4th Fl), Helena, MT 59620-0513; 406-841-2373, Fax- 406-841-2309. http://mt.gov/DLI/BSD/license/bsd_boards/out_board/licenses/out/pdf/Outfitter_Application.pdf Search data at- http://app.mt.gov/lookup/ Download licensee lists after purchase and after selecting Board type at www.mt.gov/dli/bsd/license/bus_index.asp.

#7 Board of Optometry, Board of Pharmacy, Division of Professional & Occupational Licensing, PO Box 200513 (301 S Park 4th Fl), Helena, MT 59620-0513; 406-841-2390, Fax- 406-841-2305. http://mt.gov/dli/bsd/license/bsd_boards/opt_board/board_page.asp Search data at- http://app.mt.gov/lookup/ Download licensee lists after purchase and after selecting Board type at www.mt.gov/dli/bsd/license/bus_index.asp.

#8 Plumbing and Electrical Board, Division of Professional & Occupational Licensing, PO Box 200513 (301 S Park #430), Helena, MT 59620-0513; 406-841-2299, Fax- 406-841-2309. Hours- 8AM-5PM M-F. www.mt.gov/dli/bsd/ Search data at- http://app.mt.gov/lookup/ Download licensee lists after purchase and after selecting Board type at www.mt.gov/dli/bsd/license/bus_index.asp.

#9 Board of Private Security Patrol Officers & Invest., Division of Professional & Occupational Licensing, PO Box 200513 (301 S Park Ave 4th Fl), Helena, MT 59620-0513; 406-841-2334, Fax- 406-841-2309. http://mt.gov/dli/bsd/license/license.asp Search data at- http://app.mt.gov/lookup/ Physical Therapy Board (406-841-2369) is separate but at the same address. Physical Therapy Board email- dlibsdptp@state.mt.us. Also, download licensee lists after purchase and after selecting Board type at www.mt.gov/dli/bsd/license/bus_index.asp.

#10 Boards of Architects, Engineers & Land Surveyors, Division of Professional & Occupational Licensing, PO Box 200513 (301 S Park Ave 4th Fl), Helena, MT 59620-0513; 406-841-2017, Fax- 406-841-2309. http://mt.gov/dli/bsd/license/license.asp Search data at- http://app.mt.gov/lookup/ Download licensee lists after purchase and after selecting Board type at www.mt.gov/dli/bsd/license/bus_index.asp.

#11 Veterinary Board, Board of Psychologists, PO Box 200513 (301 S Park 4th Fl), Helena, MT 59620-0513; 406-841-2394, Fax- 406-841-2305. http://mt.gov/dli/bsd/license/bsd_boards/vet_board/board_page.asp Search data at- http://app.mt.gov/lookup/ Individual websites- Psychology Board is http://mt.gov/dli/bsd/license/bsd_boards/psy_board/board_page.asp. Vet Board is http://mt.gov/dli/bsd/license/bsd_boards/vet_board/board_page.asp.

#12 Board of Public Accountants, PO Box 200513 (301 S Park Ave 4th Fl), Helena, MT 59620-0513; 406-841-2389, Fax- 406-841-2323. http://mt.gov/dli/pac/ Search data at- http://mt.gov/dli/pac/ Download licensee lists after purchase and after selecting Board type at www.mt.gov/dli/bsd/license/bus_index.asp.

#13 Notary Division, Secretary of State, PO Box 202801 (1306 6th Ave, Rm 260, Helena, MT 59620; 406-444-5379, Fax- 406-444-4263. http://sos.mt.gov/Notary/

#14 Board of Real Estate Appraisers, PO Box 200513 (301 S Park Ave 4th Fl), Helena, MT 59620-0513; 406-841-2320, Fax- 406-841-2323. http://mt.gov/dli/rea/ Search data at- http://mt.gov/dli/rea/ Download licensee lists after purchase and after selecting Board type at www.mt.gov/dli/bsd/license/bus_index.asp.

#15 Board of Realty Regulation, PO Box 200513 (301 S Park 4th Fl), Helena, MT 59620-0513; 406-841-2961, Fax- 406-841-2323. http://mt.gov/dli/rre/ Download licensee lists after purchase and after selecting Board type at www.mt.gov/dli/bsd/license/bus_index.asp.

#16 State Bar of Montana, PO Box 577 (7 W 6th Ave, #2B), Helena, MT 59624; 406-442-7660, Fax- 406-442-7763. www.montanabar.org Use email cwood@montanabar.org to request to confirm an attorney's membership.

#17 Physical Therapy Board, Division of Professional & Occupational Licensing, PO Box 200513 (301 S Park Av, #430), Helena, MT 59620-0513; 406-841-2391, Fax- 406-841-2305. http://mt.gov/dli/bsd/contact.asp Search data at- http://app.mt.gov/lookup/ Download licensee lists after purchase and after selecting Board type at www.mt.gov/dli/bsd/license/bus_index.asp.

#18 Construction Blasters, Division of Professional & Occupational Licensing, PO Box 200513 (301 S Park Av, #430), Helena, MT 59620-0513; 406-841-2368, Fax- 406-841-2309. http://mt.gov/dli/bsd/license/bsd_boards/bla_prg/board_page.asp Search data at- http://app.mt.gov/lookup/ Download licensee lists after purchase and after selecting Board type at www.mt.gov/dli/bsd/license/bus_index.asp.

#19 Chemical Dependency Counselors Board, Division of Professional & Occupational Licensing, PO Box 200513 (301 S Park), Helena, MT 59620-0513;
406-444-2392, Fax- 406-841-2305. http://mt.gov/dli/bsd/license/bsd_boards/swp_board/board_page.asp Search data at- http://app.mt.gov/lookup/

#20 Department of Agriculture, Licensing and Registration, PO Box 200201 (303 N Roberts St), Helena, MT 59620; 406-444-5400, Fax- 406-444-7336. www.agr.mt.gov/licensing/commercial.asp

#21 Department of Commerce, Licensing Boards, PO Box 200513 (301 S Park #430), Helena, MT 59620-0513; 406-841-2385, Fax- 406-841-2305. Hours- 7:30AM-4:30PM. http://mt.gov/dli/bsd/license/license.asp

#22 Department of Livestock, Board of Horse Racing, PO Box 200512, Helena, MT 59620-0512; 406-444-4287, Fax- 406-444-4305. www.simulcast.com/board_of_horse_racing.htm

#23 Department of Commerce, Montana Lottery, 2525 N Montana Ave, Helena, MT 59601; 406-444-5825, Fax- 406-444-5830. www.montanalottery.com

#24 Commissioner of Political Practices, PO Box 202401 (1205 8th Ave), Helena, MT 59620; 406-444-2942, Fax- 406-444-1643. Hours- 8AM-5PM. www.politicalpractices.mt.gov/default.mcpx

#25 Department of Environmental Quality, Permitting & Compliance Division, 1520 E 6th Ave, PO Box 200901, Helena, MT 59620-0901; 406-444-4323, Fax- 406-444-1374. http://deq.mt.gov/pcd/

#26 Department of Health & Human Services, Quality Assurance Division, PO Box 202953 (1400 Broadway, Helena), Helena, MT 59620; 406-444-2012, Fax- 406-444-1742. www.dphhs.mt.gov/programsservices/childcare.shtml

#27 Department of Fish, Wildlife & Parks, Licensing/Data Bureau, PO Box 200701 (1420 E 6th Ave), Helena, MT 59620-0701; 406-444-2535, Fax- 406-444-4952. http://fwp.mt.gov/hunting/trapping/default.html

#28 Department of Justice, Gambling Control Division, PO Box 201424 (2550 Prospect Ave), Helena, MT 59620-1424; 406-444-1971, Fax- 406-444-9157. http://doj.mt.gov/gaming/

#29 Department of Livestock, Brand Enforcement, PO Box 202001, Helena, MT 59620-2001; 406-444-2045, Fax- 406-444-2877. http://liv.mt.gov/liv/public/goals/be.asp

#30 Department of Public Health Human Services, Research & Planning Bureau, 2401 Colonial Drive, Helena, MT 59620-4001; 406-444-0507, Fax- 406-444-5956. www.dphhs.mt.gov/qad/youthcarefacilities/youthgrouphomepacket.shtml

#31 Department of Environmental Quality, Waste and Underground Tanks Division, PO Box 200901, Helena, MT 59620-0901; 406-444-3840, Fax- 406-444-1374. http://deq.mt.gov/ust/ Search data at- http://deq.mt.gov/UST/licensees.asp

#32 Board of Nursing, Division of Professional & Occupational Licensing, PO Box 200513 (301 S Park #430), Helena, MT 59620-0513; 406-841-2345, Fax- 406-841-2305. http://mt.gov/dli/bsd/license/bsd_boards/nur_board/board_page.asp Search data at- http://app.mt.gov/lookup/ Download licensee lists after purchase and after selecting Board type at www.mt.gov/dli/bsd/license/bus_index.asp.

#33 Board of Medical Examiners, PO Box 200513 (301 S Park, 4th Fl), Helena, MT 59620-0513; 406-841-2364, Fax- 406-841-2305. 8AM-5PM. http://mt.gov/dli/bsd/license/bsd_boards/med_board/board_page.asp Search data at- http://app.mt.gov/lookup/ Lists provided for a fee if offering continuing educational credits.

#34 Department of Natural Resources & Conservation, Water Resources Division, PO Box 201601 (1424 9th Ave), Helena, MT 59620-1601; 406-444-6601, Fax- 406-444-5918. http://dnrc.mt.gov/wrd/ Will not provide lists.

#35 Certification Division, Office of Public Instruction, PO Box 202501, Helena, MT 59620-2501; 406-444-3150, Fax- 406-444-0743. Hours- 8AM-5PM. www.opi.mt.gov Search data at- http://data.opi.state.mt.us/edcredentials/index.asp

#36 Public Contractors Licensing, Department of Labor, PO Box 8011, Helena, MT 59604; 406-444-7734, Fax- 406-444-3465.

#37 Insurance Division, State Auditor's Office, 840 Helena Ave, Helena, MT 59601; 406-444-2040. http://sao.mt.gov Search data at- http://sao.mt.gov/insurance/findagent.asp

#38 Securities Division, State Auditor's Office, 840 Helena Ave, Helena, MT 59601; 406-444-2040, Fax- 406-444-3497. Hours- 8AM-5PM. http://sao.mt.gov/

Montana Federal Courts

The following list indicates the district and division name for each county in the state. If the bankruptcy court location is different from the district court, then the location of the bankruptcy court appears in parentheses.

County/Court Cross Reference

County	Court
Beaverhead	Butte
Big Horn	Billings (Butte)
Blaine	Great Falls (Butte)
Broadwater	Helena (Butte)
Carbon	Billings (Butte)
Carter	Billings (Butte)
Cascade	Great Falls (Butte)
Chouteau	Great Falls (Butte)
Custer	Billings (Butte)
Daniels	Billings (Butte)
Dawson	Billings (Butte)
Deer Lodge	Butte
Fallon	Billings (Butte)
Fergus	Great Falls (Butte)
Flathead	Missoula (Butte)
Gallatin	Butte
Garfield	Billings (Butte)
Glacier	Great Falls (Butte)
Golden Valley	Billings (Butte)
Granite	Missoula (Butte)
Hill	Great Falls (Butte)
Jefferson	Helena (Butte)
Judith Basin	Great Falls (Butte)
Lake	Missoula (Butte)
Lewis and Clark	Helena (Butte)
Liberty	Great Falls (Butte)
Lincoln	Missoula (Butte)
Madison	Butte
McCone	Billings (Butte)
Meagher	Helena (Butte)
Mineral	Missoula (Butte)
Missoula	Missoula (Butte)
Musselshell	Billings (Butte)
Park	Billings (Butte)
Petroleum	Billings (Butte)
Phillips	Billings (Butte)
Pondera	Great Falls (Butte)
Powder River	Billings (Butte)
Powell	Helena (Butte)
Prairie	Billings (Butte)
Ravalli	Missoula (Butte)
Richland	Billings (Butte)
Roosevelt	Billings (Butte)
Rosebud	Billings (Butte)
Sanders	Missoula (Butte)
Sheridan	Billings (Butte)
Silver Bow	Butte
Stillwater	Billings (Butte)
Sweet Grass	Billings (Butte)
Teton	Great Falls (Butte)
Toole	Great Falls (Butte)
Treasure	Billings (Butte)
Valley	Billings (Butte)
Wheatland	Billings (Butte)
Wibaux	Billings (Butte)
Yellowstone	Billings (Butte)
Yellowstone Nat. Park (part)	Billings (Butte)

Standards for Federal Courts: Fees are standard unless noted in profile. Search fee is $26.00 per item (one party name or case number). Copy fee is $.50 per page. Certification fee is $9.00 per document, double for exemplification, if available. Most courts require prepayment. Mail requests should enclose a SASE unless otherwise noted. Before releasing records, all courts require prepayment, unless noted.

District courts index by defendant and plaintiff and by case number. Bankruptcy courts usually index by debtor and case number. While most courts now have their indexes on computer, many may still maintain index card files as well. Courts will archive closed case files at different times.

There are numerous public access programs available to online subscribers. Search the U.S. Party/Case Index to find party names and case numbers among all courts. Individual case data is provided on PACER. A search of CM/ECF provides copies of cases filed electronically. For details about PACER, the US Party/Case Index, and CM/ECF see the Appendix, go to http://pacer.psc.uscourts.gov or call 800-676-6856.

US District Court District of Montana

Billings Division Court Clerk, James Battin Courthouse, 316 N 26th St, Billings, MT 59101, 406-247-7000; Fax- 406-247-7008. Hours-8:30AM-5PM. www.mtd.uscourts.gov

Counties/Note: Big Horn, Carbon, Carter, Custer, Daniels, Dawson, Fallon, Garfield, Golden Valley, McCone, Musselshell, Park, Petroleum, Powder River, Prairie, Richland, Rosebud, Sheridan, Stillwater, Sweet Grass, Treasure, Wheatland, Wibaux, Yellowstone, Yellowstone National Park.

Searches/Indexing: Search request requires name only. Results do not include SSN or DOB. Will fax back documents for $.50 per page. New cases are in the index 1-2 days after filing date. Computer index maintained back to 1996. District-wide searches available here. Case files sent to archives 4-5 years after closed.

Search Access: Only docket info is available by phone. **Mail:** Search usually completed- 1 week. SASE not required. **Fax:** Fax search and case file requests accepted. **In person:** 1 public terminal available. No self-serve copier.

Payment: Pay by Visa/MC, money order, cashier's or personal check. Payee: Clerk, US District Court.

E-Services: PACER records go back to 1992. New records online after 1 day. ECF at https://ecf.mtd.uscourts.gov. **Opinions:** www.mtd.uscourts.gov/opinions.htm. **Note:** Calendars for 3 weeks at www.mtd.uscourts.gov/calendar.htm.

Butte Division Court Clerk, US District Court, 400 N Main, Butte, MT 59701, 406-782-0432; Fax- 406-782-0537; records room fax- 406-782-9045; fax record requests to- 406-782-9045. Hours-8:30AM-5PM. www.mtd.uscourts.gov

Counties: Beaverhead, Deer Lodge, Gallatin, Madison, Silver Bow.

Searches/Indexing: Search request requires name only. Results do not include SSN or DOB. Will fax back documents for $.50 per page. New cases are in the index 1-2 days after filing date. Computer index maintained back to 1996. District-wide searches available here. Case files sent to archives 4-5 years after closed.

Search Access: Mail: Search usually completed- 1-2 days. SASE not required. **In person:** 1 public terminal available. No self-serve copier.

Payment: Pay by Visa/MC, money order, cashier's or personal check. Payee: Clerk, US District Court.

E-Services: PACER records go back to 1992. New records online after 1 day. ECF at https://ecf.mtd.uscourts.gov. **Opinions:** www.mtd.uscourts.gov/opinions.htm. **Note:** Calendars for 3 weeks at www.mtd.uscourts.gov/calendar.htm.

Great Falls Division Court Clerk, Post Office Bldg, 215 1st Ave N, Great Falls, MT 59401, 406-727-1922; Fax- 406-727-7648. Hours-8:30AM-5PM. www.mtd.uscourts.gov

Counties/Note: Blaine, Cascade, Chouteau, Daniels, Fergus, Glacier, Hill, Judith Basin, Liberty, Phillips, Pondera, Roosevelt, Sheridan, Teton, Toole, Valley.

Searches/Indexing: Search request requires name only. Results do not include SSN or DOB. Will fax back documents for $.50 per page. New cases are in the index immediately after filing date. Computer index maintained back to 1996. District-wide searches available here. Case files sent to archives 4-5 years after closed.

Search Access: Only docket info available; provide case number. **Mail:** Search usually completed- 1 day. Include SASE for return. **In person:** 1 public terminal available. No self-serve copier.

Payment: Pay by Visa/MC, money order, cashier's or personal check. No out-of-state attorney checks accepted. Payee: Clerk, US District Court.

E-Services: PACER records go back to 1992. New records online after 1 day. ECF at https://ecf.mtd.uscourts.gov. **Opinions:** www.mtd.uscourts.gov/opinions.htm. **Note:** Calendars for 3 weeks at www.mtd.uscourts.gov/calendar.htm.

Helena Division Court Clerk, Paul G Hatfield Courthouse, 901 Front St, #2100, Helena, MT 59626, 406-441-1355; records- 406-441-4921; Fax- 406-441-1357. Hours- 8:30AM-5PM. www.mtd.uscourts.gov

Counties/Note: Broadwater, Jefferson, Lewis and Clark, Meagher, Powell.

Searches/Indexing: Include name, cause number in search request. Results do not include SSN or DOB. Will fax back documents for $.50 per page. New cases are in the index same day if possible after filing date. Both computer and card indexes maintained. District-wide searches available here. Case files sent to archives 4-5 years after closed.

Search Access: Mail: Search usually completed- soon as work load permits. Include SASE for return. **Fax:** Fax search and case file requests accepted. **In person:** 1 public terminal available. No self-serve copier.

Payment: Pay by Visa/MC, money order, cashier's or personal check. Payee: Clerk, US District Court.

E-Services: PACER records go back to 1992. New records online after 1 day. ECF at https://ecf.mtd.uscourts.gov. **Opinions:** www.mtd.uscourts.gov/opinions.htm. **Note:** Calendars for 3 weeks at www.mtd.uscourts.gov/calendar.htm.

Missoula Division Court Clerk, Russell Smith Courthouse, 201 E Broadway, Missoula, MT 59801, 406-542-7260; Fax- 406-542-7272. Hours-8:30AM-5PM. www.mtd.uscourts.gov

Counties/Note: Flathead, Granite, Lake, Lincoln, Mineral, Missoula, Ravalli, Sanders.

Searches/Indexing: Search request requires name only. Results do not include SSN or DOB. Will fax back documents for $.50 per page. New cases are in the index 1-2 days after filing date. Computer index maintained back to 1996. District-wide searches available here. Cases in this district originate here; after closing, cases held here 3 years for civil, 5 for criminal, then sent to Records Center.

Search Access: Only docket info is available by phone. **Mail:** Search usually completed- 1-2 days. SASE not required. **Fax:** Fax search and case file requests accepted. **In person:** 1 public terminal available. No self-serve copier.

Payment: Pay by Visa/MC, money order, cashier's or personal check. Payee: Clerk, US District Court.

E-Services: PACER records go back to 1992. New records online after 1 day. ECF at https://ecf.mtd.uscourts.gov. **Opinions:** www.mtd.uscourts.gov/opinions.htm. **Note:** Calendars for 3 weeks at www.mtd.uscourts.gov/calendar.htm.

US Bankruptcy Court District of Montana

Butte Division Court Clerk, 303 Federal Bldg, 400 N Main St, Butte, MT 59701, 406-782-3354; Fax- 406-782-0537. Hours- 8AM-4:30PM. www.mtb.uscourts.gov

Counties/Note: All counties in Montana. There are hearing locations in Great Falls, Billings, Missoula, Kalispell as well as Butte.

Searches/Indexing: Search request requires name only. Results include last 4 SSN digits. Will fax back documents $1.00 per page. New cases are in the index immediately after filing date.

Search Access: Only docket info is available by phone. Voice Case Information Service available, call VCIS at 888-879-0071 or 406-782-1060. **Mail:** Search usually completed- 2-3 days. SASE not required. **Fax:** Fax search requests accepted. **In person:** 1 public terminal available. No self-serve copier.

Payment: Pay by Visa/MC, money order, cashier's or attorney checks. No debtor checks/credit cards accepted. Payee: Clerk, US Bankruptcy Court.

E-Services: PACER records go back to 1986. New records online after 1 day. ECF at https://ecf.mtb.uscourts.gov. Calendars on ECF system. **Opinions Online:** www.mtb.uscourts.gov/mtb_opinions.asp. Judge's Decisions posted here are selected by the judges to inform the public. **Online Note:** Court calendar can be checked via 'Quick Links' at the main website.

Montana County Courts

Court	Jurisdiction	No. of Courts	How Organized
District Courts*	General	56	22 Districts
Limited Jurisdiction Courts*	Limited	66	56 Counties
City Courts	Limited	81	
Municipal Court	Municipal	5	
Water Courts	Special		4 Divisions
Workers' Compensation Court	Special	1	

* Profiled in this Sourcebook.

Court	CIVIL								
	Tort	Contract	Real Estate	Min. Claim	Max. Claim	Small Claims	Estate	Eviction	Domestic Relations
District Courts*	X	X	X	$5000-7000	No Max		X		X
Justice Courts*	X	X	X	$0	$7000	$3000		X	
City Courts	X	X	X	$0	$7000	$3000			
Municipal Court	X	X	X	$0	$7000	$3000			
Water Courts			X						

Court	CRIMINAL				
	Felony	Misdemeanor	DWI/DUI	Preliminary Hearing	Juvenile
District Courts*	X			X	X
Justice Courts*		X	X	X	
City Courts		X	X	X	
Municipal Court		X	X	X	

Administration

Court Administrator, Park Avenue Building, Room 328 (PO Box 203005), Helena, MT, 59620; 406-841-2950, Fax: 406-841-2955. http://courts.mt/gov

Court Structure

The District Courts are courts of general jurisdiction and handle all felony cases, all probate cases, most civil cases at law and in equity, certain special actions and proceedings. The courts of limited jurisdiction are Justice Courts, City Courts and Municipal Courts. Although the jurisdiction of these courts differs slightly, collectively they address cases involving misdemeanor offenses, civil cases for amounts up to $7,000, small claims valued up to $3,000, landlord/tenant disputes, local ordinances, forcible entry and detainer, protection orders, certain issues involving juveniles, and other matters. Some Justice Courts and City Courts have consolidated.

Many Montana Justices of the Peace maintain case record indexes on their personal computers, which does speed the retrieval process.

Online Access

Supreme Court opinions, orders, and recently filed briefs may be found at http://searchcourts.mt.gov. There is no statewide access to docket information from the trial courts.

Searching Tips, Fees, and Other Guidelines

Most District Courts charge $2.00 per name per year, first 7 years, then $1.00 per year for searching. Copies are usally $1.00 per page first 10 pages, then $.50 per page after. Certification is usually $2.00. A document titled *Access to Court Records* is found at http://courts.mt.gov/crt_records/faq.asp. The document advises that all documents filed with the court should not contain the full DOB, unless required by law.

Beaverhead County

District Court Beaverhead County Courthouse, 2 S Pacific St, Dillon, MT 59725; 406-683-3725; criminal fax: 406-683-3728; civil fax: same; 8AM-5PM (MST). ***Felony, Civil Actions over $7,000, Probate.*** Probate fax is same as main fax number.

Civil Records: Access: Fax, mail, in person. Both court and visitors may perform in person searches. Search fee: $2.00 per name per year, first 7 years, then $1.00 per year. Required to search: name, years to search. Civil cases indexed by defendant, plaintiff, in books back to 1870s; on computer since 1997. Note: For fax access, include fax copy of check for fee. Mail turnaround time 1-2 days. Civil PAT goes back to 7/1997. PAT results show name only.

Criminal Records: Access: Fax, mail, in person. Both court and visitors may perform in person searches. Search fee: $2.00 per name per year, first 7 years, then $1.00 per year. Required to search: name, years to search. Criminal records in books back to 1870s; on computer since 1997. Note: For fax request, include copy of check for fee. Mail turnaround time 1-2 days. Criminal PAT goes back to same as civil. PAT results show name only.

General Information: No adoption, juvenile, sanity, paternity or dismissed criminal records released. Will fax documents $1.00 per page. Court makes copy:

$1.00 per page 1st 10 pages, then $.50 each add'l, self serve same. Certification fee: $2.00. Payee: Clerk of Court. No personal checks or credit cards accepted. Prepayment required. Mail requests: SASE required.

County Justice Court 2 S Pacific, Cluster #16, Dillon, MT 59725; 406-683-3755; fax: 406-683-3736; 8AM-3PM (MST). ***Misdemeanor, Civil Actions under $7,000, Eviction, Small Claims.*** www.beaverheadcounty.org

Big Horn County

District Court 121 W 3rd St, Rm 221, PO Box 908, Hardin, MT 59034; 406-665-9750; fax: 406-665-9755; 8AM-5PM (MST). ***Felony, Civil Actions over $7,000, Probate.***

Civil Records: Access: Fax, mail, in person. Both court and visitors may perform in person searches. Search fee: $2.00 per name per year, first 7 years, then $1.00 per year. Required to search: name, years to search. Civil cases indexed by defendant, plaintiff, in books, microfilm, and computer back to 1913. Mail turnaround time same day. Civil PAT goes back to 1913. PAT civil results show middle initial.

Criminal Records: Access: Fax, mail, in person. Both court and visitors may perform in person searches. Search fee: $2.00 per name per year, first 7 years, then $1.00 per year. Required to search: name, years to search, DOB; also helpful, SSN. Criminal records in books and on microfilm back to 1913; on computer back to 1913. Note: Court order required for confidential information. Mail turnaround time same day. Criminal PAT goes back to same as civil. PAT criminal results show middle initial.

General Information: No adoption, sanity, pre-sentence, psychiatric evaluation, dependent & neglected, or confidential criminal justice records released. Fee to fax out file $1.00 per page. Court makes copy: $1.00 per page 1st 10 pages, then $.50 each add'l, self serve same. Certification fee: $2.00. Payee: Clerk of Court. No personal checks or credit cards accepted. Prepayment required. Will bill government agencies. Mail requests: SASE required.

Justice Court PO Box 908, 121 W 3rd, Hardin, MT 59034; 406-665-9760; fax: 406-665-9764; 8AM-5PM (MST). ***Misdemeanor, Civil Actions under $7,000, Eviction, Small Claims.***

This court is a combined City and Justice Court.

Blaine County

District Court PO Box 969, Chinook, MT 59523; 406-357-3230; criminal fax: 406-357-3109; civil fax: same; 8AM-5PM (MST). ***Felony, Civil Actions over $5,000, Eviction, Probate.***

Probate fax is same as main fax number.

Civil Records: Access: Fax, mail, in person. Both court and visitors may perform in person searches. Search fee: $2.00 per name per year, first 7 years, then $1.00 per year. Required to search: name, years to search. Civil cases indexed by defendant, plaintiff, in books from 1912; on computer back to 1995. Mail turnaround time same day. Civil PAT goes back to 1995. PAT results show name only.

Criminal Records: Access: Fax, mail, in person. Both court and visitors may perform in person searches. Search fee: $2.00 per name per year, first 7 years, then $1.00 per year. Required to search: name, years to search, signed release. Criminal records in books from 1912; on computer back to 1995. Mail turnaround time same day. Criminal PAT goes back to same as civil. PAT results show name only.

General Information: No adoption, juvenile or sanity records released. Fee to fax out file $1.00 per page. Court makes copy: $1.00 per page 1st 10 pages, then $.50 each add'l. Certification fee: $2.00 per certification. Payee: Clerk of Court. No personal checks or credit cards accepted. Prepayment required. Mail requests: SASE required.

Chinook Justice Court PO Box 1266, 420 Ohio St, Chinook, MT 59523; 406-357-2335; fax: 406-357-2361; 8AM-5PM (MST). ***Misdemeanor, Civil Actions under $7,000, Small Claims.***

Eviction and Ordinance Violations are not handled here. There is also a Harlem Justice Court, at Harlem City Hall, 406-353-4971, only open 10AM-N every 1st and 3rd Wednesday.

Broadwater County

District Court 515 Broadway, Townsend, MT 59644; 406-266-9236; fax: 406-266-4720; 8AM-N, 1-5PM (MST). ***Felony, Civil Actions over $7,000, Probate.***

Civil Records: Access: Fax, mail, in person. Both court and visitors may perform in person searches. Search fee: $2.00 per name per year, first 7 years, then $1.00 per year. Required to search: name, years to search, DOB. Civil cases indexed by defendant, plaintiff, on microfiche and archives back to 1897; on computer back to 1997. Mail turnaround time same day. Civil PAT goes back to 1997. PAT civil results show middle initial.

Criminal Records: Access: Fax, mail, in person. Both court and visitors may perform in person searches. Search fee: $2.00 per name per year, first 7 years, then $1.00 per year. Required to search: name, years to search, DOB. Criminal records on microfiche and archives back to 1897; on computer back to 1997. Mail turnaround time same day. Criminal PAT goes back to same as civil. PAT criminal results show middle initial.

General Information: No adoption, juvenile or sanity records released. Will fax documents. Court makes copy: $1.00 per page 1st 10 pages, then $.50 each add'l. Self serve: $1.00 per page. Certification fee: $2.00. Payee: Clerk of Court. Personal checks accepted; credit cards are not. Prepayment required. Mail requests: SASE required.

Justice Court 515 Broadway, Townsend, MT 59644; 406-266-9231; fax: 406-266-4720; 8AM-5PM (MST). ***Misdemeanor, Civil Actions under $7,000, Eviction, Small Claims.***

Carbon County

District Court PO Box 948, Red Lodge, MT 59068; 406-446-1225; fax: 406-446-1911; 8AM-5PM (MST). ***Felony, Civil Actions, Probate.***

Civil Records: Access: Phone, fax, mail, in person. Both court and visitors may perform in person searches. Search fee: $2.00 per name per year, first 7 years, then $1.00 per year. Required to search: name, years to search. Civil cases indexed by defendant, plaintiff; index in docket books from 1895; on computer back to 1997. Mail turnaround time 1-2 days.

Criminal Records: Access: Fax, mail, in person. Only the court performs in person searches; visitors may not. Search fee: $2.00 per name per year, first 7 years, then $1.00 per year. Required to search: name, years to search. Criminal docket on books from 1895; on computer back to 1997. Mail turnaround time 1-2 days.

General Information: No adoption, juvenile or sanity records released. Will fax documents $1.00 per page; no charge to toll free number. Court makes copy: $1.00 per page 1st 10 pages, then $.50 each add'l. Certification fee: $2.00. Payee: Clerk of Court. Personal checks accepted; credit cards are not. Prepayment required. Mail requests: SASE required.

Carbon County Justice Court PO Box 2, 102 N Broadway, Red Lodge, MT 59068; 406-446-1440; fax: 406-446-9175; 8AM-5PM (MST). ***Misdemeanor, Civil Actions under $7,000, Eviction, Small Claims.*** www.co.carbon.mt.us

Joliet City Court PO Box 210, Joliet, MT 59041; 406-962-3567; 8AM-N Wed only (MST). ***Misdemeanor, Civil Actions under $7,000.***

Carter County

District Court PO Box 322, Ekalaka, MT 59324; 406-775-8714; fax: 406-775-8703; 8AM-5PM (MST). ***Felony, Civil Actions over $5,000, Eviction, Probate.***

Probate is separate index at this same address.

Civil Records: Access: Phone, fax, mail, in person. Both court and visitors may perform in person searches. Search fee: $2.00 per name per year, first 7 years, then $1.00 per year. Required to search: name, years to search. Civil cases indexed by defendant, plaintiff, in books from 1917; computerized back to 1996. Mail turnaround time same or next day.

Criminal Records: Access: Phone, fax, mail, in person. Only the court performs in person searches; visitors may not. Search fee: $2.00 per name per year, first 7 years, then $1.00 per year. Required to search: name, years to search, signed release; also helpful: SSN. Criminal records in books from 1917; computerized back to 1996. Mail turnaround time 1-2 days; same or next day for phone requests.

General Information: No adoption, juvenile or sanity records released. Will fax documents $1.00 per page. Court makes copy: $1.00 per page 1st 10 pages, then $.50 each add'l, self serve same. Certification fee: $2.00 per instrument. Payee: Clerk of Court. Personal checks accepted. Prepayment required. Mail requests: SASE required.

Justice Court PO Box 72, Ekalaka, MT 59324-0072; 406-775-8754, 406-775-8838; fax: 406-775-8703; 8AM-5PM 1st,2nd,3rd W of month; 10AM-3:PM 4th W (MST). ***Misdemeanor, Small Claims, Eviction, Ordinance.***

Cascade County

District Court County Courthouse, 415 2nd Ave North, Great Falls, MT 59401; 406-454-6780 x4; criminal phone: 406-454-6786; civil phone: 406-454-6785; fax: 406-454-6907; 8AM-5PM (MST). ***Felony, Civil Actions over $7,000, Probate.*** www.co.cascade.mt.us/

Civil Records: Access: Fax, mail, in person. Both court and visitors may perform in person searches. Search fee: $2.00 per name per year, first 7 years, then $1.00 per year. Required to search: name, years to search. Civil cases indexed by defendant, plaintiff, on computer from 1987; on docket books to 1889. Mail turnaround time 1-2 days. Civil PAT goes back to 1987. PAT results show name only.

Criminal Records: Access: Fax, mail, in person. Both court and visitors may perform in person searches. Search fee: $2.00 per name per year, first 7 years, then $1.00 per year. Required to search: name, years to search. Criminal records computerized from 1987; on docket books to 1889. Mail turnaround time 1-2 days. Criminal PAT goes back to same as civil. PAT results show name only.

General Information: No adoption or sanity records released. Will not fax documents. Court makes copy: $1.00 per page; $.50 per page after 1st 10. Certification fee: $2.00 per cert. Payee: Clerk of Court. Business checks accepted. No credit cards accepted. Prepayment required. Mail requests: SASE required.

Cascade Justice Court Cascade County Courthouse, 415 2nd Ave N, Great Falls, MT 59401; 406-454-6870; fax: 406-454-6877; 8AM-5PM (MST). ***Misdemeanor, Civil Actions under $7,000, Eviction, Small Claims.***

Chouteau County

District Court PO Box 459, Ft Benton, MT 59442; 406-622-5024; fax: 406-622-3028; 8AM-5PM (MST). ***Felony, Civil Actions over $5,000, Eviction, Probate.***

Civil Records: Access: Fax, mail, in person. Both court and visitors may perform in person searches. Search fee: $2.00 per name per year, first 7 years, then $1.00 per year. Required to search: name, years to search. Civil cases indexed by defendant, plaintiff, on books from 1886; on computer back for 10 years. Mail turnaround time 1 day. Civil PAT goes back to 1997.

Criminal Records: Access: Fax, mail, in person. Both court and visitors may perform in person searches. Search fee: $2.00 per name per year, first 7 years, then $1.00 per year. Required to search: name, years to search. Criminal docket on books from 1886; on computer back for 10 years. Mail turnaround time 1 day. Criminal PAT goes back to same as civil.

General Information: No adoption, paternity, juvenile or sanity records released. Will fax documents $2.00 1st page, $1.00 each add'l. Court makes copy: $1.00 per page 1st 10 pages, then $.50 each add'l. Certification fee: $2.00 per cert. Payee: Clerk of Court. Business and personal checks accepted. No credit cards accepted. Prepayment required. Mail requests: SASE required.

Chouteau County Justice Court PO Box 459, 1215 Washington, Ft Benton, MT 59442; 406-622-5502; fax: 406-622-3815; 9AM-4PM (MST). ***Misdemeanor, Civil Actions under $7,000, Eviction, Small Claims, Ordinance.***
As of 12/02, the records from the former Justice Court in Big Sandy are housed at this location.

Custer County

District Court 1010 Main, Miles City, MT 59301-3419; 406-874-3326; criminal fax: 406-874-3451; civil fax: same; 8AM-5PM (MST). ***Felony, Civil Actions over $5,000, Probate.***
Probate fax is same as main fax number.
Civil Records: Access: Phone, fax, mail, in person. Both court and visitors may perform in person searches. Search fee: $2.00 per name per year, first 7 years, then $1.00 per year. Required to search: name, years to search. Civil cases indexed by defendant, plaintiff, on computer back to 1990; also in books. Mail turnaround time 1-2 days. Civil PAT goes back to 1990. PAT civil results show middle initial.
Criminal Records: Access: Mail, in person. Both court and visitors may perform in person searches. Search fee: $2.00 per name per year, first 7 years, then $1.00 per name per year. Required to search: name, years to search. Criminal records computerized from 1990; also in books. Mail turnaround time 1-2 days. Criminal PAT goes back to same as civil. PAT criminal results show middle initial.
General Information: No dependent & neglected, juvenile or sanity records released. Will fax documents $1.00 per page. Court makes copy: $1.00 per page 1st 10 pages, then $.50 each add'l. Certification fee: $2.00 per document. Payee: Clerk of District Court. Personal checks accepted; credit cards are not. Prepayment required. Mail requests: SASE required.

Justice Court 1010 Main St, Miles City, MT 59301; 406-874-3408; fax: 406-874-3452; 8AM-5PM (MST). ***Misdemeanor, Civil Actions under $7,000, Eviction, Small Claims, Traffic.*** www.co.custer.mt.us
Record search request must be in writing, fee is $25.00 per search.

Daniels County

District Court PO Box 67, Scobey, MT 59263; 406-487-2651; criminal fax: 406-487-5432; civil fax: same; 8AM-N, 1-5PM (MST). ***Felony, Civil Actions over $5,000, Probate.***
Probate fax is same as main fax number.
Civil Records: Access: Phone, mail, in person. Both court and visitors may perform in person searches. Search fee: $2.00 per name per year, first 7 years, then $1.00 per year. Required to search: name, years to search. Civil cases indexed by defendant, plaintiff, on books since 1920; on computer back to 1997. Mail turnaround time same day.
Criminal Records: Access: Mail, in person, fax. Only the court performs in person searches; visitors may not. Search fee: $2.00 per name per year, first 7 years, then $1.00 per year. Required to search: name, years to search. Criminal docket on books since 1920; on computer back to 1986. Mail turnaround time 1-2 days.
General Information: No adoption, juvenile or sanity records released. Fee to fax document $.50 per page. Court makes copy: $1.00 per page 1st 10 pages, then $.50 each add'l. Certification fee: $2.00 per document. Payee: Clerk of Court. Personal checks accepted; credit cards are not. Prepayment required. Mail requests: SASE required.

Justice Court PO Box 838, County Courthouse, Upstairs, Scobey, MT 59263; 406-487-5432; fax: 406-487-5432; 8AM-10AM (MST). ***Misdemeanor, Civil Actions under $7,000, Eviction, Small Claims.***

Dawson County

District Court 207 W Bell, Glendive, MT 59330; 406-377-3967; fax: 406-377-7280; 8AM-5PM (MST). ***Felony, Civil Actions over $3,000, Probate.*** www.dawsoncountymontana.com/clerk_of_court.htm
Civil Records: Access: Mail, in person. Both court and visitors may perform in person searches. Search fee: $2.00 per name per year, first 7 years, then $1.00 per year. Required to search: name, years to search. Civil cases indexed by defendant, plaintiff, on computer from 1997, on card index prior. Mail turnaround time usually same or next day. Civil PAT goes back to 1997.
Criminal Records: Access: Mail, in person. Both court and visitors may perform in person searches. Search fee: $2.00 per name per year, first 7 years, then $1.00 per year. Required to search: name, years to search, DOB, SSN. Criminal records computerized from 1997, on card index prior. Mail turnaround time usually same or next day. Criminal PAT goes back to same as civil.
General Information: No adoption, juvenile, sanity or expunged records released. Will fax documents to local or toll free line. Court makes copy: $1.00 per page 1st 10 pages, then $.50 each add'l, self serve same.Marriage license copy-$5.00 plus cert fee; divorce decree copy-$10.00 plus cert fee. Certification fee: $2.00 per document. If they prepare authenticated copies fee is $6.00 for seal. Payee: Clerk of District Court. Only cashiers checks and money orders accepted. No credit cards accepted. Prepayment required. Mail requests: SASE required.

Justice Court 207 W Bell, Glendive, MT 59330; 406-377-5425; fax: 406-377-1869; 8AM-5PM (MST). ***Misdemeanor, Civil Actions under $7,000, Eviction, Small Claims.***

Deer Lodge County

District Court 800 S Main, Anaconda, MT 59711; 406-563-4041; fax: 406-563-4077; 8AM-5PM (MST). ***Felony, Civil Actions over $5,000, Eviction, Probate.***
Civil Records: Access: Phone, mail, in person. Both court and visitors may perform in person searches. Search fee: $2.00 per name per year, first 7 years, then $1.00 per year. Required to search: name, years to search. Civil cases indexed by defendant, plaintiff, in archives and index books; on computer back to 1993. Mail turnaround time 2-3 days. Civil PAT goes back to 1993.
Criminal Records: Access: Mail, in person. Both court and visitors may perform in person searches. Search fee: $2.00 per name per year, first 7 years, then $1.00 per year. Required to search: name, years to search. Criminal records in archives and index books; on computer back to 1993. Mail turnaround time 2-3 days. Criminal PAT goes back to same as civil.
General Information: No adoption, juvenile or sanity records released. Fee to fax out file $4.00 each. Court makes copy: $1.00 per page 1st 10 pages, then $.50 each add'l. Certification fee: $2.00. Payee: Clerk of Court. Personal checks accepted; credit cards are not. Prepayment required. Mail requests: SASE required.

Justice Court 800 S Main, Anaconda, MT 59711; 406-563-4025; fax: 406-563-4028; 8AM-N, 1-5PM (MST). ***Misdemeanor, Civil Actions under $7,000, Eviction, Small Claims.***

Fallon County

District Court PO Box 1521, Baker, MT 59313; 406-778-8114; criminal fax: 406-778-2815; civil fax: same; 8AM-5PM (MST). ***Felony, Civil Actions over $5,000, Eviction, Probate.***
Probate fax is same as main fax number.
Civil Records: Access: Mail, in person. Both court and visitors may perform in person searches. Search fee: $2.00 per name per year, first 7 years, then $1.00 per year. Required to search: name, years to search, address. Civil cases indexed by defendant, plaintiff, in books. Mail turnaround time same day. Civil PAT goes back to 1913. PAT results show name only.
Criminal Records: Access: Mail, in person. Both court and visitors may perform in person searches. Search fee: $2.00 per name per year, first 7 years, then $1.00 per year. Required to search: name, years to search. Criminal records in books. Mail turnaround time same day. Criminal PAT goes back to 1914. PAT results show name only.
General Information: No confidential records released. Fee to fax out file $1.00 per page. Court makes copy: $1.00 per page 1st 10 pages, then $.50 each add'l. Certification fee: $2.00. Payee: Clerk of Court. Personal checks accepted; credit cards are not. Prepayment required. Mail requests: SASE required.

Justice Court Box 846, 10 W Fallon, Baker, MT 59313; 406-778-7128; fax: 406-778-2815; 11AM-4PM T,W,TH (MST). ***Misdemeanor, Civil Actions under $7,000, Eviction, Small Claims.***

Fergus County

District Court PO Box 1074, 712 W Main, Lewistown, MT 59457; 406-535-5026; criminal fax: 406-535-6076; civil fax: same; 8AM-5PM (MST). ***Felony, Civil Actions over $7,000, Eviction, Probate.*** www.co.fergus.mt.us
Probate fax is same as main fax number.
Civil Records: Access: Phone, fax, mail, in person. Both court and visitors may perform in person searches. Search fee: $2.00 per name per year, first 7 years, then $1.00 per year. Required to search: name, years to search. Civil cases indexed by defendant, plaintiff, on computer back to 1997; prior on docket books, microfiche. Mail turnaround time 1 day. Civil PAT goes back to 1996.
Criminal Records: Access: Phone, fax, mail, in person. Both court and visitors may perform in person searches. Search fee: $2.00 per name per year, first 7 years, then $1.00 per year. Required to search: name, years to search. Criminal records computerized from 1997; prior on docket books, microfiche. Mail turnaround time 1 day. Criminal PAT goes back to same as civil.
General Information: No adoption, juvenile, sanity or expunged records released. Fee to fax out file $1.00 per page. Court makes copy: $1.00 per page 1st 10 pages, then $.50 each add'l, self serve same. Certification fee: $2.00 per document. Payee: Clerk of Court. Personal checks accepted; credit cards are not. Prepayment required. Mail requests: SASE required.

Justice Court 121 8th Ave South, Lewistown, MT 59457; 406-535-5418; fax: 406-535-3860; 9AM-4PM (MST). ***Misdemeanor, Eviction, Small Claims under $3000, Ordinance.***
You may email requests to jpcourt@co.fergus.mt.us

Flathead County

District Court 800 S Main, Kalispell, MT 59901; 406-758-5660; fax: 406-758-5652; 8AM-5PM (MST). ***Felony, Civil Actions over $5,000, Probate.*** www.co.flathead.mt.us/clkcrt/index.html
Court clerk location is 920 S. Main, 3rd Fl.
Civil Records: Access: Mail, in person. Both court and visitors may perform in person searches. Search fee: $2.00 per name per year, first 7 years, then $1.00 per year. Required to search: name, years to search. Civil cases indexed by defendant, plaintiff, on computer since 1990; records go back to 1893. Mail turnaround time 24-48 hours. Civil PAT goes back to 1990. Public terminal results do not always include identifiers.
Criminal Records: Access: Mail, in person. Only the court performs in person searches; visitors may not. Search fee: $2.00 per name per year, first 7 years, then $1.00 per year. Required to search: name, years to search. Criminal records on computer since 1990; records go back to 1893. Note: In person searchers will not be able to view confidential criminal records without permission. Mail turnaround time 3 days. Criminal PAT goes back to 1990. Public terminal results do not always include identifiers.
General Information: No adoption, dependent/neglected children or sanity records released. Fee to fax out file $1.00 per page. Court makes copy: $1.00 per page; $.50 per page after first 10. Certification fee: $2.00 per doc. Payee: Clerk of Court. Personal checks accepted; credit cards are not. Prepayment required. Mail requests: SASE required.

County Justice Court 920 S Main St, Kalispell, MT 59901; 406-758-5643; fax: 406-758-5842; 8AM-5PM (MST). ***Misdemeanor, Civil Actions under $7,000, Eviction, Small Claims.*** www.co.flathead.mt.us/justice/index.html

Gallatin County

Clerk of District Court 615 S 16th St, Rm 302, Bozeman, MT 59715; 406-582-2165; fax: 406-582-2176; 8AM-5PM (MST). ***Felony, Civil Actions over $7,000, Probate.*** www.gallatin.mt.gov

Civil Records: Access: Phone, mail, fax, in person. Both court and visitors may perform in person searches. Search fee: $2.00 per name per year, first 7 years, then $1.00 per year. Required to search: name, years to search. Civil cases indexed by defendant, plaintiff, on computer back to 1985; docket books back to 1860. Mail turnaround time 1-3 days. Civil PAT goes back to 1985. PAT results show name only. 2 access terminal available.

Criminal Records: Access: Mail, in person. Both court and visitors may perform in person searches. Search fee: $2.00 per name per year, first 7 years, then $1.00 per year. Required to search: name, years to search. Criminal records computerized from 1985; docket books back to 1860. Mail turnaround time 1-3 days. Criminal PAT goes back to same as civil. PAT results show name only.

General Information: No adoption or sanity records released. Fee to fax out file $2.00 1st page, $1.00 ea add'l page. Court makes copy: $1.00 per page; $.50 per page after 1st 10 pages. Certification fee: $2.00. Payee: Clerk of Court. Personal checks accepted; credit cards are not. Prepayment required. If not sure of correct check amount, leave amount blank and put in 'not to exceed $30.00.'. Mail requests: SASE required.

Belgrade City Court 91 E Central, Belgrade, MT 59714; 406-388-3774; fax: 406-388-3779; 8AM-N; 1PM-5PM (MST). ***Misdemeanor, Civil Actions under $7,000, Eviction, Ordinance.*** www.ci.belgrade.mt.us

Formerly Belgrade Justice and City Court.

Bozeman Justice Court 615 S 16th St, Rm 168, Bozeman, MT 59715; 406-582-2191; fax: 406-582-2163; 8AM-4PM (MST). ***Misdemeanor, Civil Actions under $7,000, Eviction, Small Claims.*** www.gallatin.mt.gov/Public_Documents/gallatincomt_justice/justcourt

Garfield County

District Court PO Box 8, 352 Leavitt Ave, Jordan, MT 59337; 406-557-6254; fax: 406-557-2323; 8AM-5PM (MST). ***Felony, Civil Actions over $5,000, Eviction, Probate.***

Civil Records: Access: Phone, mail, in person. Both court and visitors may perform in person searches. Search fee: $2.00 per name per year, first 7 years, then $1.00 per year. Required to search: name, years to search. Civil cases indexed by plaintiff. Civil records in books from early 1900s; computerized records go back to 1998. Note: Some records lost due to fire in December, 1997. Mail turnaround time 1 week.

Criminal Records: Access: Phone, mail, in person. Both court and visitors may perform in person searches. Search fee: $2.00 per name per year, first 7 years, then $1.00 per year. Required to search: name, years to search; also helpful: DOB. Criminal records in books from early 1900s, computerized records go back to 1998. Note: Some records lost due to fire in December, 1997. Mail turnaround time 1 week.

General Information: No adoption, juvenile or sanity records released. Will fax documents to local or toll free line. Court makes copy: $1.00 per page 1st 10 pages, then $.50 each add'l. Certification fee: $2.00 per cert. Payee: Clerk of Court. Personal checks accepted; credit cards are not. Prepayment required. SASE not required.

Justice Court PO Box 482, 352 Leavitt St, Jordan, MT 59337; 406-557-2733; fax: 406-557-2735; 8AM-5PM W (MST). ***Misdemeanor, Civil Actions under $7,000, Eviction, Small Claims.***

Glacier County

District Court 512 E Main St, Cut Bank, MT 59427; 406-873-3619; criminal fax: 406-873-5627; civil fax: same; 8AM-5PM (MST). ***Felony, Civil Actions, Probate.***

Probate fax is same as main fax number.

Civil Records: Access: Phone, fax, mail, in person, email. Both court and visitors may perform in person searches. Search fee: $2.00 per name per year, first 7 years, then $1.00 per year. Required to search: name, years to search. Civil cases indexed by defendant, plaintiff, in books from 1919; on computer since 1992. Note: Direct email search requests to dianderson@state.mt.us. Mail turnaround time usually same day, 2-3 hours for phone requests depending on workload. Civil PAT goes back to 1919.

Criminal Records: Access: Fax, mail, in person. Both court and visitors may perform in person searches. Search fee: $2.00 per name per year, first 7 years, then $1.00 per year. Required to search: name, years to search, DOB, SSN. Criminal records in books from 1919; on computer since 1992. Note: Written request required. Mail turnaround time usually same day, 2-3 hours for phone requests depending on workload. Criminal PAT goes back to 1919.

General Information: No adoption, juvenile, sanity or paternity records released without court order. Fee to fax out file $1.00 per page. Court makes copy: $1.00 per page 1st 10 pages, then $.50 each add'l. Self serve: $1.00 per page. Certification fee: $2.00 per cert. Payee: Clerk of District Court. Personal checks accepted; credit cards are not. Prepayment required. Mail requests: SASE requested.

Justice Court 512 E Main St, Cut Bank, MT 59427; 406-873-3631; fax: 406-873-3659; 8AM-N, 1-5PM (MST). ***Misdemeanor, Civil Actions under $7,000, Eviction, Small Claims.***

Golden Valley County

District Court PO Box 10, Ryegate, MT 59074; 406-568-2231; fax: 406-568-2428; 8AM-5PM (MST). ***Felony, Civil Actions over $5,000, Eviction, Probate.***

Civil Records: Access: Fax, mail, in person. Only the court performs in person searches; visitors may not. Search fee: $2.00 per name per year, first 7 years, then $1.00 per year. Required to search: name, years to search, signed release. Civil cases indexed by defendant, plaintiff, on books back to 1923. Computerized records back to 1997. Mail turnaround time 2-3 days.

Criminal Records: Access: Fax, mail, in person. Only the court performs in person searches; visitors may not. Search fee: $2.00 per name per year, first 7 years, then $1.00 per year. Required to search: name, years to search, signed release. Criminal docket on books to 1923. Computerized records go back to 1997. Mail turnaround time 2-3 days.

General Information: No adoption, juvenile or sanity records released. Will fax documents $1.00 per page. Same fee applies to send them a fax. Court makes copy: $1.00 per page 1st 10 pages, then $.50 each add'l, self serve same. Certification fee: $2.00. Payee: Clerk of Court. Personal checks accepted; credit cards are not. Prepayment required. Mail requests: SASE required.

Justice Court PO Box 10, 104 Kemp, Ryegate, MT 59074; 406-568-2102; fax: 406-568-2428; 9AM-5PM Tues (MST). ***Misdemeanor, Civil Actions under $7,000, Eviction, Small Claims.***

Granite County

District Court PO Box 399, Philipsburg, MT 59858-0399; 406-859-3712; fax: 406-859-3817; 8AM-N, 1-5PM (MST). ***Felony, Civil Actions over $7,000, Eviction, Probate.***

Civil Records: Access: Phone, fax, mail, in person. Both court and visitors may perform in person searches. Search fee: $2.00 per name per year, first 7 years, then $1.00 per year. Required to search: name, years to search. Civil cases indexed by defendant, plaintiff; index on docket books since 1893. Mail turnaround time 1-4 days. Civil PAT goes back to 1990. PAT results show name only.

Criminal Records: Access: Phone, fax, mail, in person. Both court and visitors may perform in person searches. Search fee: $2.00 per name per year, first 7 years, then $1.00 per year. Required to search: name, years to search. Criminal docket on books since 1893. Mail turnaround time 1-4 days. Criminal PAT goes back to same as civil. PAT results show name only.

General Information: No adoption, juvenile or sanity records released. Will fax documents $1.00 per page. Court makes copy: $1.00 per page 1st 10 pages, then $.50 each add'l, self serve same. Certification fee: $2.00. Payee: Clerk of Court. Personal checks accepted; credit cards are not. Prepayment required. Mail requests: SASE required.

Drummond Justice Court #2 PO Box 159, 202 E Front St, Drummond, MT 59832; 406-288-3446; fax: 406-288-3050; 9AM-N, 1-4PM M,W,F (MST). ***Misdemeanor, Civil Actions under $7,000, Eviction, Small Claims.***

Philipsburg Justice Court PO Box 356, 330 N Sansom, Philipsburg, MT 59858; 406-859-3006; fax: 406-859-3817; 11AM-N, 1-5PM M,W,F (MST). ***Misdemeanor, Civil Actions under $7,000, Eviction, Small Claims.***

Hill County

District Court 315 Fourth St, Havre, MT 59501; 406-265-5481 X224; fax: 406-265-3693; 8AM-5PM (MST). ***Felony, Civil Actions over $5,000, Eviction, Probate.*** http://co.hill.mt.us

Civil Records: Access: Phone, fax, mail, in person. Both court and visitors may perform in person searches. Search fee: $2.00 per name per year, first 7 years, then $1.00 per year. Required to search: name, years to search; also very helpful- maiden name. Civil cases indexed by defendant, plaintiff, on computer since 1985; prior records on docket books to 1912. Mail turnaround time same day. Civil PAT goes back to 1985. PAT civil results show middle initial.

Criminal Records: Access: Fax, mail, in person. Both court and visitors may perform in person searches. Search fee: $2.00 per name per year, first 7 years, then $1.00 per year. Required to search: name, years to search; also helpful: maiden name. Criminal records on computer since 1988; prior records on docket books to 1912. Note: Absolutely no criminal record checks by phone. Mail turnaround time same day. Criminal PAT goes back to 1988. PAT criminal results show middle initial.

General Information: No adoption, juvenile, paternity, sanity records released. Will fax documents $1.00 per page. Court makes copy: $1.00 per page 1st 10 pages, then $.50 each add'l. Certification fee: $2.00. Payee: Clerk of Court. Business checks accepted. No credit cards accepted. Prepayment required. Mail requests: SASE required.

Justice Court Hill County Courthouse, 315 4th St, Havre, MT 59501; 406-265-5481 X240; fax: 406-262-9441; 8AM-5PM (MST). ***Misdemeanor, Civil Actions under $7,000, Eviction, Small Claims.*** http://co.hill.mt.us

Also known as a Limited Jurisdiction Court.

Jefferson County

District Court PO Box H, Boulder, MT 59632; 406-225-4041 & 4042; fax: 406-225-4044; 8AM-N, 1-5PM (MST). ***Felony, Civil Actions over $7,000, Eviction, Probate.***

Civil Records: Access: Mail, fax, in person. Both court and visitors may perform in person searches. Search fee: $2.00 per name per year, first 7 years, then $1.00 per year. Required to search: name, years to search. Civil cases indexed by defendant, plaintiff, on computer since 1993, on microfilm since 1925. Mail turnaround time same day. Civil PAT goes back to 1993. PAT civil results show middle initial.

Criminal Records: Access: Mail, fax, in person. Both court and visitors may perform in person searches. Search fee: $2.00 per name per year, first 7 years, then $1.00 per year. Required to search: name, years to search. Criminal records on computer since 1992, on microfilm since 1925. Mail turnaround

time same day. Criminal PAT goes back to 1992. PAT criminal results show middle initial.
General Information: Juvenile, sanity or adoption records not released. Will fax documents to local or toll-free number, otherwise $1.00 per page. Court makes copy: $1.00 per page 1st 10 pages, then $.50 each add'l. Certification fee: $2.00. Payee: Clerk of Court. Personal checks accepted; credit cards are not. Prepayment required. Mail requests: SASE required.

Justice Court PO Box H, 108 S Washington, Boulder, MT 59632; 406-225-4055; fax: 406-225-4088; 8AM-N, 1-5PM (MST). ***Misdemeanor, Civil Actions under $7,000, Eviction, Small Claims.***

Judith Basin County

District Court PO Box 307, Stanford, MT 59479; 406-566-2277 X113; criminal fax: 406-566-2211; civil fax: same; 8AM-5PM (MST). ***Felony, Civil Actions over $5,000, Probate.***
Probate is a separate index at this same address. Probate fax is same as main fax number.
Civil Records: Access: Phone, fax, mail, in person. Both court and visitors may perform in person searches. Search fee: $2.00 per name per year, first 7 years, then $1.00 per year. Required to search: name, years to search. Civil cases indexed by defendant, plaintiff, on books back to 1920; on computer back to 1996. Mail turnaround time 10 days.
Criminal Records: Access: Phone, mail, in person. Both court and visitors may perform in person searches. Search fee: $2.00 per name per year, first 7 years, then $1.00 per year. Required to search: name, years to search, signed release. Criminal docket on books back to 1920; on computer back to 1996. Mail turnaround time 10 days.
General Information: No adoption, sanity records released. Will fax documents. Court makes copy: $1.00 per page 1st 10 pages, then $.50 each add'l. Self serve: Criminal self serve copy $1.00 per page; No civil self serve. Certification fee: $2.00 per document. Payee: Clerk of Court. Business checks accepted. No credit cards accepted. Prepayment required. Mail requests: SASE required.

Justice Court PO Box 339, 91Third St North, Stanford, MT 59479; 406-566-2277 X117; fax: 406-566-2211; 8AM-5PM (MST). ***Misdemeanor, Civil Actions under $7,000, Eviction, Small Claims.***

Lake County

District Court Clerk of District Court Office, 106 4th Ave E, Polson, MT 59860; 406-883-7254; fax: 406-883-8582; 8AM-5PM (MST). ***Felony, Civil Actions over $7,000, Probate.***
Civil Records: Access: Phone, fax, mail, in person. Both court and visitors may perform in person searches. Search fee: $2.00 per name per year, first 7 years, then $1.00 per year. Required to search: name, years to search. Civil cases indexed by defendant, plaintiff, on books since 1923; on computer since 1990. Mail turnaround time 3 days; 2 hours for phone requests. Civil PAT goes back to 1989. PAT results show name only.
Criminal Records: Access: Phone, fax, mail, in person. Both court and visitors may perform in person searches. Search fee: $2.00 per name per year, first 7 years, then $1.00 per year. Required to search: name, years to search. Criminal docket on books since 1923; on computer since 1990. Mail turnaround time 3 days; 2 hours for phone requests. Criminal PAT goes back to same as civil. PAT results show name only.
General Information: No adoption, juvenile, sanity or expunged records released. Will fax documents $1.00 per page. Court makes copy: $1.00 per page 1st 10 pages, then $.50 each add'l. Certification fee: $2.00. Payee: Clerk of Court. Business checks accepted. No credit cards accepted. Prepayment required. Mail requests: SASE required.

Justice Court 106 4th Ave E, Polson, MT 59860; 406-883-7258; fax: 406-883-7343; 8AM-5PM (MST). ***Misdemeanor, Civil Actions under $7,000, Eviction, Small Claims.***

Lewis and Clark County

District Court 228 Broadway, PO Box 158, Helena, MT 59624; 406-447-8216; fax: 406-447-8275; 8AM-5PM (MST). ***Felony, Civil Actions over $5,000, Eviction, Probate, Small Claims.***
www.co.lewis-clark.mt.us
No search fee if you perform search yourself in office.
Civil Records: Access: Fax, mail, in person, email. Both court and visitors may perform in person searches. Search fee: $2.00 per name per year, first 7 years, then $1.00 per year. Required to search: name, years to search. Civil cases indexed by defendant, plaintiff, on computer since 1991, microfilm prior to 1/96. Mail turnaround time 2 days. Civil PAT goes back to 1991. PAT results show name only. Will accept email record requests to lkallio@co.lewis-clark.mt.us.
Criminal Records: Access: Fax, mail, in person, email. Both court and visitors may perform in person searches. Search fee: $2.00 per name per year, first 7 years, then $1.00 per year. Required to search: name, years to search. Criminal records on computer since 1993, microfilm prior to 1/97. Mail turnaround time 2 days. Criminal PAT goes back to 1993. Will accept email record requests to lkallio@co.lewis-clark.mt.us. Online results show name only.
General Information: No adoption or sanity records released. Fee to fax out file $1.00 per page. Court makes copy: $1.00 per page 1st 10 pages, then $.50 each add'l, self serve same. Certification fee: $2.00. Payee: Clerk of Court. Personal checks accepted. Visa/MC accepted. Prepayment required. Mail requests: SASE required.

Justice Court 228 Broadway, Helena, MT 59623; 406-447-8201; criminal phone: 406-447-8201; civil phone: 406-447-8202; criminal fax: 406-447-8269; civil fax: same; 8AM-N; 1PM-4PM (MST). ***Misdemeanor, Civil Actions under $7,000, Eviction, Small Claims, Ordinance.***
www.co.lewis-clark.mt.us/
Formerly a Limited Jurisdiction Court.

Liberty County

District Court PO Box 549, Chester, MT 59522; 406-759-5615; fax: 406-759-5996; 8AM-5PM (MST). ***Felony, Civil Actions over $5,000, Eviction, Probate.***
With fax requests, include copy of your check.
Civil Records: Access: Fax, mail, in person. Both court and visitors may perform in person searches. Search fee: $2.00 per name per year, first 7 years, then $1.00 per year. Required to search: name, years to search, address. Civil cases indexed by defendant, plaintiff, on books since 1920. Mail turnaround time 2-3 days.
Criminal Records: Access: Fax, mail, in person, fax. Both court and visitors may perform in person searches. Search fee: $2.00 per name per year, first 7 years, then $1.00 per year. Required to search: name, years to search, signed release. Criminal docket on books since 1920. Mail turnaround time 2-3 days.
General Information: No adoption, juvenile or sanity records released. Will fax documents to local or toll free line. Court makes copy: $1.00 per page 1st 10 pages, then $.50 each add'l. Certification fee: $2.00 per cert. Payee: Clerk of Court. Personal checks accepted; credit cards are not. Prepayment required. Mail requests: SASE required.

Justice Court PO Box 170, 311 1/2 Adams Ave, Chester, MT 59522; 406-759-5215; fax: 406-759-5455; 9AM-N, 1-5PM Tues (MST). ***Misdemeanor, Civil Actions under $7,000, Eviction, Small Claims.***

Lincoln County

District Court 512 California Ave, Libby, MT 59923; 406-293-7781; probate phone: x224; fax: 406-293-9816; 8AM-5PM (MST). ***Felony, Civil Actions over $7,000, Probate.***
Civil Records: Access: Mail, in person. Both court and visitors may perform in person searches. Search fee: $2.00 per name per year, first 7 years, then $1.00 per year. Required to search: name, years to search. Civil cases indexed by defendant, plaintiff, on computer from 1991, prior on docket books. Mail turnaround time 1 week. Civil PAT goes back to 1996. PAT results show name only.
Criminal Records: Access: Mail, in person. Both court and visitors may perform in person searches. Search fee: $2.00 per name per year, first 7 years, then $1.00 per year. Required to search: name, years to search. Criminal records computerized from 1996, prior on docket books. Mail turnaround time 1 week. Criminal PAT goes back to same as civil. PAT results show name only.
General Information: No adoption, juvenile or sanity records released. Will fax out results at no extra fee. Court makes copy: $1.00 per page, divorce decree- $10.00. Certification fee: $2.00. Payee: Clerk of Court. Personal checks accepted; credit cards are not. Mail requests: SASE required.

Eureka Justice Court #2 PO Box 403, 152 Hwy 37, Eureka, MT 59917; 406-297-2622; fax: 406-297-3829; 8AM-N, 1-5PM (MST). ***Misdemeanor, Civil Actions under $7,000, Eviction, Small Claims.***

Libby Justice Court #1 418 Mineral Ave, Libby, MT 59923; 406-293-7781 x236, x235, X259; criminal phone: x259 & 236; civil phone: x235; fax: 406-293-5948; 8AM-5PM (MST). ***Misdemeanor, Civil Actions under $7,000, Eviction, Small Claims.***

Madison County

District Court PO Box 185, Virginia City, MT 59755; 406-843-4230; fax: 406-843-5207; 8AM-5PM (MST). ***Felony, Civil Actions over $5,000, Eviction, Probate.***
www.madison.mt.gov/departments/clerk_dcourt/clerk_dcourt.asp
Civil Records: Access: Phone, fax, mail, in person. Both court and visitors may perform in person searches. Search fee: $2.00 per name per year, first 7 years, then $1.00 per year. Required to search: name, years to search. Civil cases indexed by defendant, plaintiff, on books since 1864; on computer back to 1990. Mail turnaround time 1 week. Civil PAT goes back to 1990.
Criminal Records: Access: Fax, mail, in person. Both court and visitors may perform in person searches. Search fee: $2.00 per name per year, first 7 years, then $1.00 per year. Required to search: name, years to search. Criminal docket on books since 1864; on computer back to 1990. Mail turnaround time 1 week. Criminal PAT goes back to same as civil.
General Information: No adoption, juvenile or sanity records released. Fee to fax out file $4.00 1st page, $1.00 each add'l. Court makes copy: $1.00 per page 1st 10 pages, then $.50 each add'l, self serve same. Certification fee: $2.00. Payee: Clerk of Court. Personal checks accepted; credit cards are not. Prepayment required. Mail requests: SASE required for mail return of any copies.

Madison County Justice Court PO Box 277, 100 W Wallace St, Virginia City, MT 59755; 406-843-4237; fax: 406-843-4219; 8AM-5PM (MST). ***Misdemeanor, Civil Actions under $7,000, Eviction, Small Claims.*** www.madison.mt.gov/departments/justice_court/justice_ct.asp

McCone County

District Court PO Box 199, Circle, MT 59215; 406-485-3410; fax: 406-485-3410; 8AM-5PM (MST). ***Felony, Civil Actions over $5,000, Eviction, Probate.***
Civil Records: Access: Mail, in person. Only the court performs in person searches; visitors may not. Search fee: $2.00 per name per year, first 7 years, then $1.00 per year. Required to search: name, years to search. Civil cases indexed by defendant, plaintiff, in books from 1919, computerized since 1996. Mail turnaround time 1-2 days.
Criminal Records: Access: Mail, in person. Only the court performs in person searches; visitors may not. Search fee: $2.00 per name per year, first 7 years, then $1.00 per year. Required to search: name, years to search. Criminal records in books and microfilm since 1919, computerized since 1996. Mail turnaround time 1-2 days.

General Information: No adoption, juvenile, sanity or mental health records released. Will fax documents to local or toll free line. Court makes copy: $1.00 per page 1st 10 pages, then $.50 each add'l. Certification fee: $2.00 per cert. Payee: Clerk of Court. Personal checks accepted; credit cards are not. Prepayment required. Mail requests: SASE helpful.

Justice Court PO Box 192, 1004 C Ave, Circle, MT 59215; 406-485-3548; fax: 406-485-2689; 9AM-N Tues& W (MST). ***Misdemeanor, Civil Actions under $7,000, Eviction, Small Claims.***

Meagher County

District Court PO Box 443, White Sulphur Springs, MT 59645; 406-547-3612 x110; fax: 406-547-3836; 7:30AM-4PM (MST). ***Felony, Civil Actions over $5,000, Eviction, Probate.***

Civil Records: Access: Phone, mail, fax, in person. Both court and visitors may perform in person searches. Search fee: $2.00 per name per year, first 7 years, then $1.00 per year. Required to search: name, years to search. Civil cases indexed by defendant, plaintiff; index on docket books or microfiche to 1900; on computer back to 1996. Mail turnaround time 1 day or same day.

Criminal Records: Access: Phone, mail, fax, in person. Both court and visitors may perform in person searches. Search fee: $2.00 per name per year, first 7 years, then $1.00 per year. Required to search: name, years to search, DOB. Criminal docket on books or microfiche to 1900; on computer back to 1996. Mail turnaround time 3 days.

General Information: No adoption, juvenile or sanity records released. Will fax documents to local or toll-free number. Court makes copy: $1.00 per page 1st 10 pages, then $.50 each add'l. Certification fee: $2.00. Payee: Clerk of Court. Personal checks accepted; credit cards are not. Prepayment required. Mail requests: SASE required.

Justice Court PO Box 698, Justice Court, 15 W Main St, White Sulphur Springs, MT 59645; 406-547-3954 X115; fax: 406-547-3961; 8AM-N (MST). ***Misdemeanor, Civil Actions under $7,000, Eviction, Small Claims.*** 2nd fax #- - 406-547-3836.

Mineral County

District Court PO Box 129, Superior, MT 59872; 406-822-3538; fax: 406-822-3579; 8AM-N,1-5PM (MST). ***Felony, Civil Actions over $7,000, Probate.*** Probate is a separate index at this same address.

Civil Records: Access: Fax, mail, in person. Both court and visitors may perform in person searches. Search fee: $2.00 per name per year, first 7 years, then $1.00 per year. Required to search: name, years to search. Civil cases indexed by defendant, plaintiff; index in docket books from 1914, on computer back to 1990. Mail turnaround time same day after payment received.

Criminal Records: Access: Fax, mail, in person. Both court and visitors may perform in person searches. Search fee: $2.00 per name per year, first 7 years, then $1.00 per year. Required to search: name, years to search. Criminal docket on books from 1914, on computer back to 1990. Mail turnaround time same day after payment received.

General Information: No adoption, sanity records released. Fee to fax out file $5.00 each. You must fax request with copy of payment check. Court makes copy: $1.00 per page 1st 10 pages, then $.50 each add'l. Certification fee: $2.00 per document. Payee: Clerk of Court. Personal checks accepted; credit cards are not. Mail requests: SASE required.

Justice Court PO Box 658, 300 River St, Superior, MT 59872; 406-822-3550; fax: 406-822-3821; 8AM-N, 1-5PM (MST). ***Misdemeanor, Civil Actions under $7,000, Eviction, Small Claims.***

Missoula County

District Court 200 W Broadway, Missoula, MT 59802; 406-258-4780; fax: 406-258-4899; 8AM-5PM (MST). ***Felony, Civil Actions over $7,000, Probate.*** www.co.missoula.mt.us/coc

Images on the public access terminals can be printed out, also emailed.

Civil Records: Access: Fax, mail, in person. Both court and visitors may perform in person searches. Search fee: $2.00 per name per year, first 7 years, then $1.00 per year. Required to search: name, years to search. Civil cases indexed by defendant, plaintiff, on computer from 10/89, microfilm from 1970s, archived to late 1800s. Mail turnaround time up to 2 weeks. Civil PAT goes back to 1989. PAT civil results show middle initial.

Criminal Records: Access: Fax, mail, in person. Both court and visitors may perform in person searches. Search fee: $2.00 per name per year, first 7 years, then $1.00 per year. Required to search: name, years to search. Criminal records computerized from 10/89, microfilm from 1970s, archived to late 1800s. Mail turnaround time up to 2 weeks. Criminal PAT goes back to same as civil. PAT criminal results show middle initial.

General Information: No adoption, juvenile, sealed, expunged or pre-sentence psychiatric records released. Will fax documents $2.00 each; no fee if returning on toll free line. Court makes copy: $1.00 per page 1st 10 pages, then $.50 each add'l. Certification fee: $2.00. Exemplification fee- $4.00. Payee: Clerk of Court. Personal checks accepted. Credit cards accepted. Prepayment required. Mail requests: SASE requested.

Limited Jurisdiction Court - Dept 1 200 W Broadway, Missoula County Courthouse, 3rd Fl, Missoula, MT 59802; 406-258-4871; fax: 406-258-3935; 8AM-5PM (MST). ***Misdemeanor, Civil Actions under $7,000, Eviction, Small Claims.*** www.co.missoula.mt.us/jp1/

Musselshell County

District Court 506 Main St, Roundup, MT 59072; 406-323-1413; criminal fax: 406-323-1710; civil fax: same; 8AM-N, 1-5PM (MST). ***Felony, Civil Actions over $5,000, Eviction, Probate.***

Include copy of the fees check with any fax requests. Probate fax is same as main fax number.

Civil Records: Access: Mail, fax, in person. Both court and visitors may perform in person searches. Search fee: $2.00 per name per year, first 7 years, then $1.00 per year. Required to search: name, years to search. Civil cases indexed by defendant, plaintiff. Computerized records from 7/96, civil records on docket books from 1911. Mail turnaround 2-3 days.

Criminal Records: Access: Mail, fax, in person. Both court and visitors may perform in person searches. Search fee: $2.00 per name per year, first 7 years, then $1.00 per year. Required to search: name, years to search. Criminal docket on books from 1911. Mail turnaround time 2-3 days.

General Information: No adoption, (some) juvenile or sanity records released. Will fax documents to local or toll free line. Court makes copy: $1.00 per page 1st 10 pages, then $.50 each add'l, self serve same. Certification fee: $2.00 per document. Payee: Clerk of Court. Personal checks accepted; credit cards are not. Prepayment required. Mail requests: SASE required.

Justice Court PO Box 660, 34 2nd Ave W, Roundup, MT 59072; 406-323-1078; fax: 406-323-1734; 9AM-4PM (MST). ***Misdemeanor, Civil Actions under $7,000, Eviction, Small Claims.***

Park County

District Court PO Box 437, Livingston, MT 59047; 406-222-4125; fax: 406-222-4128; 8AM-5PM (MST). ***Felony, Civil Actions over $7,000, Eviction, Probate.***

Civil Records: Access: Fax, mail, in person. Both court and visitors may perform in person searches. Search fee: $2.00 per name per year, first 7 years, then $1.00 per year. Required to search: name, years to search. Civil cases indexed by defendant, plaintiff, on computer, microfiche, and docket books from 1889 to present. Mail turnaround time 1-2 days for all requests. Civil PAT goes back to 1980. PAT results show name only.

Criminal Records: Access: Fax, mail, in person. Both court and visitors may perform in person searches. Search fee: $2.00 per name per year, first 7 years, then $1.00 per year. Required to search: name, years to search. Criminal records on computer, microfiche, and docket books from 1889 to present. Mail turnaround time 1-2 days for all requests. Criminal PAT goes back to 1996. PAT results show name only.

General Information: No adoption, juvenile or sanity records released. Court makes copy: $1.00 per page first 10 pages, then $.50 each add'l. Certification fee: $2.00. Payee: Clerk of Court. Personal checks accepted; credit cards are not. Prepayment required. SASE not required.

Justice Court 414 E Callender, Livingston, MT 59047; 406-222-4169/4170; civil phone: 406-222-4149; fax: 406-222-4103; 8AM-N, 1-5:00PM (MST). ***Misdemeanor, Civil Actions under $7,000, Eviction, Small Claims.*** www.parkcounty.org/JP/jp.html

Petroleum County

District Court PO Box 226, Winnett, MT 59087; 406-429-5311; fax: 406-429-6328; 8AM-4PM (MST). ***Felony, Civil Actions over $5,000, Eviction, Probate.***

Civil Records: Access: Phone, mail, in person. Both court and visitors may perform in person searches. Search fee: $2.00 per name per year, first 7 years, then $1.00 per year. Required to search: name, years to search. Civil cases indexed by defendant, plaintiff; index in docket books from 1924. Mail turnaround time 1 day.

Criminal Records: Access: Phone, mail, in person. Only the court performs in person searches; visitors may not. Search fee: $2.00 per name per year, first 7 years, then $1.00 per year. Required to search: name, years to search. Criminal docket on books from 1924. Mail turnaround time 1 day.

General Information: No adoption, juvenile or sanity records released. Will fax documents to local or toll free line. Court makes copy: $1.00 per page 1st 10 pages, then $.50 each add'l, self serve same. Certification fee: $2.00. Payee: Clerk of Court. Personal checks accepted; credit cards are not. Prepayment required. Mail requests: SASE required.

Justice Court PO Box 226, 201 E Main, Winnett, MT 59087; 406-429-5311; fax: 406-429-6328; 9AM-4PM TH (MST). ***Misdemeanor, Civil Actions under $7,000, Eviction, Small Claims.***

Phillips County

District Court PO Box 530, Malta, MT 59538; 406-654-1023; criminal fax: 406-654-1023; civil fax: same; 8AM-5PM (MST). ***Felony, Civil Actions over $5,000, Eviction, Probate.***

Probate fax is same as main fax number.

Civil Records: Access: Mail, in person. Only the court performs in person searches; visitors may not. Search fee: $2.00 per name per year, first 7 years, then $1.00 per year. Required to search: name, years to search; also helpful: address. Civil cases indexed by defendant, plaintiff, on computer back to 1997; prior on books. Mail turnaround time 1-2 days.

Criminal Records: Access: Mail, in person. Only the court performs in person searches; visitors may not. Search fee: $2.00 per name per year, first 7 years, then $1.00 per year. Required to search: name, years to search, signed release, DOB or SSN; also helpful: address. Criminal records computerized from 1997; books, microfilm back to 1915. Mail turnaround time 1-2 days.

General Information: No adoption, juvenile or sanity records released. Will fax documents $5.00; no charge to toll free number. Court makes copy: $1.00 per page 1st 10 pages, then $.50 each add'l. Certification fee: $2.00 per document. Payee: Clerk of Court. Personal checks accepted; credit cards are not. Prepayment required. Mail requests: SASE required.

Justice Court PO Box 1396, 314 S 2nd Ave West, Malta, MT 59538; 406-654-1118; fax: 406-

654-1213; 9AM-3PM M-TH (MST). ***Misdemeanor, Civil Actions under $7,000, Eviction, Small Claims.***

Pondera County

District Court 20 Fourth Ave SW, Conrad, MT 59425; 406-271-4026; criminal fax: 406-271-4081; civil fax: same; 8AM-5PM (MST). ***Felony, Civil Actions over $5,000, Eviction, Probate.***
Probate fax is same as main fax number.
Civil Records: Access: Fax, mail, in person. Both court and visitors may perform in person searches. Search fee: $2.00 per name per year, first 7 years, then $1.00 per year. Required to search: name, years to search. Civil cases indexed by defendant, plaintiff; index in docket books from 1919; on computer back to 1995. Mail turnaround time 2-3 days.
Criminal Records: Access: Fax, mail, in person. Both court and visitors may perform in person searches. Search fee: $2.00 per name per year, first 7 years, then $1.00 per year. Required to search: name, years to search. Criminal docket on books from 1919; on computer back to 1995. Mail turnaround time 2-3 days.
General Information: No adoption, neglect, or sanity records released. Will fax documents $3.00 1st page, $1.00 ea add'l. Court makes copy: $1.00 per page 1st 10 pages, then $.50 each add'l. Certification fee: $2.00 per document. Payee: Clerk of Court. Personal checks accepted, some restrictions apply. No credit cards accepted. Prepayment required. Mail requests: SASE required.

Justice Court 20 Fourth Ave SW, Conrad, MT 59425; 406-271-4030; fax: 406-271-4031; 9AM-N, 1-4PM (MST). ***Misdemeanor, Civil Actions under $7,000, Eviction, Small Claims.***

Powder River County

District Court PO Box 239, Broadus, MT 59317; 406-436-2320; criminal fax: 406-436-2325; civil fax: same; 8AM-N, 1-5PM (MST). ***Felony, Civil Actions over $5,000, Probate.***
http://prco.mt.gov/departments/ClerkofDistrictCourt.asp
Probate is a separate index at this same address. Probate fax is same as main fax number.
Civil Records: Access: Fax, mail, in person. Both court and visitors may perform in person searches. Search fee: $2.00 per name per year, first 7 years, then $1.00 per year. Required to search: name, years to search. Civil cases indexed by defendant, plaintiff, on computer since 1993, microfiche since 1974, and books since 1919. Mail turnaround time same day. Civil PAT goes back to 1993. PAT results show name only.
Criminal Records: Access: Fax, mail, in person. Both court and visitors may perform in person searches. Search fee: $2.00 per name per year, first 7 years, then $1.00 per year. Required to search: name, years to search. Criminal records on computer since 1993, microfiche since 1974, and books since 1919. Mail turnaround time same day if prepaid. Criminal PAT goes back to same as civil. PAT results show name only.
General Information: No adoption, juvenile, sanity, dismissed criminal records released. Fee to fax out file $1.00 per page. Court makes copy: $1.00 per page 1st 10 pages, then $.50 each add'l. Certification fee: $2.00 per cert. Payee: Clerk of Court. Only cashiers checks and money orders accepted. No credit cards accepted. Prepayment required. Mail requests: SASE required.

Justice Court PO Box 692, Courthouse Sq, Broadus, MT 59317; 406-436-2503; fax: 406-436-2866; 8AM-5PM M-W, 8AM-N W (MST). ***Misdemeanor, Civil Actions under $7,000, Eviction, Small Claims.***
Record requests must in writing on letterhead. $.25 per copy plus postage, but minimum cost is $3.00, prepaid.

Powell County

District Court 409 Missouri Ave, Deer Lodge, MT 59722; 406-846-3680 X234/235; fax: 406-846-2784; 8AM-5PM (MST). ***Felony, Civil Actions over $5,000, Eviction, Probate.***
Civil Records: Access: Mail, in person. Both court and visitors may perform in person searches. Search fee: $2.00 per name per year, first 7 years, then $1.00 per year. Required to search: name, years to search. Civil cases indexed by defendant, plaintiff; index on docket books since turn of century, on computer since 1996. Mail turnaround time 2-3 days. Civil PAT goes back to 1996. PAT results show name only.
Criminal Records: Access: Mail, in person. Both court and visitors may perform in person searches. Search fee: $2.00 per name per year, first 7 years, then $1.00 per year. Required to search: name, years to search, DOB, SSN. Criminal docket on books since turn of century, on computer since 1996. Mail turnaround time 2-3 days. Criminal PAT goes back to same as civil. PAT results show name only.
General Information: No adoption, juvenile or sanity records released. Will fax documents $1.00 per page. Court makes copy: $1.00 per page 1st 10 pages, then $.50 each add'l. Certification fee: $2.00. Payee: Clerk of Court. Personal checks accepted; credit cards are not. Prepayment required. Mail requests: SASE required.

Justice Court, City Court 409 Missouri, Powell County Courthouse, Deer Lodge, MT 59722; 406-846-3680; fax: 406-846-1031; 8AM-5PM (MST). ***Misdemeanor, Civil Actions under $7,000, Eviction, Small Claims, Ordinance.***
$25.00 per name fee per 7 years for court to record search, even if request is in person; includes both courts.

Prairie County

District Court PO Box 125, Terry, MT 59349; 406-635-5575; fax: 406-635-5576; 8AM-N; 1PM-5PM (MST). ***Felony, Civil Actions over $5,000, Eviction, Probate.***
Civil Records: Access: Fax, mail, in person. Both court and visitors may perform in person searches. Search fee: $2.00 per name per year, first 7 years, then $1.00 per year. Required to search: name, years to search. Civil cases indexed by defendant, plaintiff, on books since 1915; computerized records go back to 1997. Mail turnaround time 5 days.
Criminal Records: Access: Fax, mail, in person. Both court and visitors may perform in person searches. Search fee: $2.00 per name per year, first 7 years, then $1.00 per year. Required to search: name, years to search, DOB, SSN. Criminal docket on books since 1915; computerized records go back to 1997. Mail turnaround time 5 days.
General Information: No adoption, juvenile or sanity records released. Will fax documents to local or toll free line. Court makes copy: $1.00 1st 10 pages, $.50 each add'l page, self serve same. Certification fee: $2.00 per cert. Payee: Clerk of Court. Personal checks accepted; credit cards are not. Prepayment required. Mail requests: SASE requested.

Justice Court PO Box 124, 217 Park, Terry, MT 59349; 406-635-4466; fax: 406-635-4126; 12:30-3:30PM (MST). ***Misdemeanor, Civil Actions under $7,000, Eviction, Small Claims, Ordinance.***

Ravalli County

District Court Ravalli County Courthouse, 205 Bedford St. #D, Hamilton, MT 59840; 406-375-6710; criminal fax: 406-375-6721; civil fax: same; 9AM-5PM (MST). ***Felony, Civil Actions over $7,000, Probate.***
www.ravallicounty.mt.gov/clerkofcourt/
Probate fax is same as main fax number.
Civil Records: Access: Mail, in person. Both court and visitors may perform in person searches. Search fee: $2.00 per name per year, first 7 years, then $1.00 per year. Required to search: name, years to search. Civil cases indexed by defendant, plaintiff, on microfiche (1989), docket books (1914). Mail turnaround time 4-5 days. Civil PAT goes back to 1996.
Criminal Records: Access: Mail, in person. Both court and visitors may perform in person searches. Search fee: $2.00 per name per year, first 7 years, then $1.00 per year. Required to search: name, years to search. Criminal records on microfiche (1989), docket books (1914). Mail turnaround time 4-5 days. Criminal PAT goes back to same as civil.
General Information: No adoption, juvenile, psychological, medical or expunged records released. Will fax documents $1.00 per page. Court makes copy: $1.00 per page 1st 10 pages, then $.50 each add'l, self serve same. Certification fee: $2.00 per cert plus copy fee; authentication or exemplification fee $6.00. Payee: Clerk of Court. Personal checks accepted; credit cards are not. Prepayment required. Mail requests: SASE required.

Justice Court Dept. #1 and #2 205 Bedford St., Hamilton, MT 59840; 406-375-6755; fax: 406-375-6759; 9AM-5PM (MST). ***Misdemeanor, Civil Actions under $7,000, Eviction, Small Claims.***
www.ravallicounty.mt.gov/justicecourt/justice.htm
Dept #2, Judge Jim Bailey is in Ste F; Dept #1, Judge Rubin Clue is in Ste E.

Richland County

District Court 201 W Main, Sidney, MT 59270; 406-433-1709; criminal fax: 406-433-6945; civil fax: same; 8AM-5PM (MST). ***Felony, Civil Actions over $5,000, Probate.***
Probate fax is same as main fax number. Evictions are handled by Justice and Small Claims Court, 406-433-2815.
Civil Records: Access: Phone, fax, mail, in person. Both court and visitors may perform in person searches. Search fee: $2.00 per name per year, first 7 years, then $1.00 per year. Required to search: name, years to search. Civil cases indexed by defendant, plaintiff, in books since 1914; on computer back to 1997. Mail turnaround time 1-3 days.
Criminal Records: Access: Phone, fax, mail, in person. Both court and visitors may perform in person searches. Search fee: $2.00 per name per year, first 7 years, then $1.00 per year. Required to search: name, years to search. Criminal records in books since 1914; on computer back to 1997. Mail turnaround time 1-3 days.
General Information: No adoption, juvenile, paternity, sanity, dismissed or expunged records released. Will fax documents $1.00 per page. Court makes copy: $1.00 per page 1st 10 pages, then $.50 each add'l, self serve same. Certification fee: $2.00 per seal. Payee: Clerk of Court. Personal checks accepted; credit cards are not. Prepayment required. Mail requests: SASE required.

Justice Court 123 W Main, Sidney, MT 59270; 406-433-2815; fax: 406-433-6885; 8AM-5PM (MST). ***Misdemeanor, Civil Actions under $7,000, Eviction, Small Claims.***

Roosevelt County

District Court County Courthouse, 400 2nd Ave S, Wolf Point, MT 59201; 406-653-6266; probate phone: same; fax: 406-653-6203; 8AM-5PM (MST). ***Felony, Civil Actions over $5,000, Eviction, Probate.***
Civil Records: Access: Phone, fax, mail, in person. Both court and visitors may perform in person searches. Search fee: $2.00 per name per year, first 7 years, then $1.00 per year. Required to search: name, years to search. Civil cases indexed by defendant, plaintiff, on books and microfiche back to 1919, computerized back to 1996. Mail turnaround time 2-3 days after payment receipt.
Criminal Records: Access: Fax, mail, in person. Only the court performs in person searches; visitors may not. Search fee: $2.00 per name per year, first 7 years, then $1.00 per year. Required to search: name, years to search; also helpful: DOB. Criminal docket on books and microfiche back to 1919, computerized back to 1996. Mail turnaround time 2-3 days after payment received.
General Information: No adoption, juvenile or sanity records released. Will fax documents $3.00 plus $1.00 per page. Court makes copy: $1.00 per page 1st 10 pages, then $.50 each add'l. Certification fee: $2.00. Payee: Clerk of Court. Personal checks accepted; credit cards are not. Prepayment required. Mail requests: SASE required.

Culbertson Justice Court Post #2 PO Box 421, 212 Broadway, Culbertson, MT 59218; 406-787-6607; fax: 406-787-6608; 9AM-3PM M-TH

(MST). ***Misdemeanor, Civil Actions under $7,000, Eviction, Small Claims.***

Wolf Point Justice Court Post #1 County Courthouse, 400 Second Ave. S., Wolf Point, MT 59201; 406-653-6261, 406-653-6258; fax: 406-653-6236; 8AM-N (MST). ***Misdemeanor, Civil Actions under $7,000, Eviction, Small Claims, County Ordinance.***
This location is also home to Wolf Point City Court where city ordinances.

Rosebud County

District Court PO Box 48, 120 Main St, Forsyth, MT 59327; 406-346-7322; fax: 406-346-2719; 8AM-5PM (MST). ***Felony, Civil Actions over $5,000, Eviction, Probate.***
Search fee includes both civil and criminal indexes.
Civil Records: Access: Fax, mail, in person. Only the court performs in person searches; visitors may not. Search fee: $2.00 per name per year, first 7 years, then $1.00 per year. Written requests only. Required to search: name, years to search. Civil cases indexed by defendant, plaintiff, in books, on microfiche back to 1901; on computer back to 1996. Mail turnaround time 2 days. Civil PAT goes back to 1996. PAT results show name only.
Criminal Records: Access: Fax, mail, in person. Both court and visitors may perform in person searches. Search fee: $2.00 per name per year, first 7 years, then $1.00 per year. Written requests only. Required to search: name, years to search, signed release. Criminal records in books, on microfiche back to 1901; on computer back to 1996. Mail turnaround time 2 days. Criminal PAT goes back to 1996. PAT results show name only.
General Information: No adoption, juvenile, sanity or sealed records released. Will fax out documents. Court makes copy: $1.00 per page 1st 10 doc pages, then $.50 each add'l, self serve same. Certification fee: $2.00 per doc. Payee: Clerk of Court. No personal checks or credit cards accepted. Prepayment required. Mail requests: SASE required.

Limited Jurisdiction Court #1 PO Box 504, 1200 Main St, County Courthouse, Forsyth, MT 59327; 406-346-2638; fax: 406-346-7551; 8AM-5PM (MST). ***Misdemeanor, Civil Actions under $7,000, Eviction, Small Claims.***
Also has records for the Limited Jurisdiction Court in Colstrip, which was closed in 2006. The clerk expects to have all Colstrip records eventually; now only has Colstrip records back to 2003.

Limited Jurisdiction Court #2, Colstrip, MT; 406-346-2638; fax: 406-346-7551. ***Misdemeanor, Civil Actions under $7,000, Eviction, Small Claims.***
Court closed 2006; records back to 2003 at Limited Jurisdiction Court #1 in Forsyth, phone numbers given here. All records available at Forsyth.

Sanders County

District Court PO Box 519, 1111 Main St, Thompson Falls, MT 59873; 406-827-6962; probate phone: same; fax: 406-827-6973; 8AM-5PM (MST). ***Felony, Civil Actions over $7,000, Eviction, Probate.***
Civil Records: Access: Mail, in person. Both court and visitors may perform in person searches. Search fee: $2.00 per name per year, first 7 years, then $1.00 per year. Required to search: name, years to search. Civil cases indexed by defendant, plaintiff; index on docket books since 1906, on computer since 1999. Mail turnaround time 1-4 days. Civil PAT goes back to 1999. PAT results show name only.
Criminal Records: Access: Mail, in person. Both court and visitors may perform in person searches. Search fee: $2.00 per name per year, first 7 years, then $1.00 per year. Required to search: name, years to search. Criminal docket on books since 1906, on computer since 1999. Mail turnaround time 1-4 days. Criminal PAT goes back to same as civil. PAT results show name only.
General Information: No adoption, juvenile, sanity or pre-sentence investigation records released. Will fax documents to local or toll free line. Court makes copy: $1.00 per page 1st 10 pages, then $.50 each add'l, self serve same. Certification fee: $2.00. Payee: Clerk of Court. Personal checks accepted; credit cards are not. Prepayment required. Mail requests: SASE required.

Justice Court PO Box 519, 1111 Main St, Thompson Falls, MT 59873; 406-827-6941; fax: 406-827-6987; 8AM-N, 1-5PM (MST). ***Misdemeanor, Civil Actions under $7,000, Eviction, Small Claims, Traffic.***

Sheridan County

District Court 100 W Laurel, Plentywood, MT 59254; 406-765-3404; fax: 406-765-2602; 8AM-N, 1-5PM (MST). ***Felony, Civil Actions over $5,000, Eviction, Probate.***
www.co.sheridan.mt.us
Civil Records: Access: Phone, mail, in person. Both court and visitors may perform in person searches. Search fee: $2.00 per name per year, first 7 years, then $1.00 per year. Required to search: name, years to search. Civil cases indexed by defendant, plaintiff; index on docket books since 1913. Mail turnaround time 1-2 days.
Criminal Records: Access: Phone, mail, in person. Both court and visitors may perform in person searches. Search fee: $2.00 per name per year, first 7 years, then $1.00 per year. Required to search: name, years to search. Criminal docket on books since 1913. Mail turnaround time 1-2 days.
General Information: No adoption, juvenile or sanity records released. Will fax documents to toll free line if prepaid. Court makes copy: $1.00 per page 1st 10 pages, then $.50 each add'l. Certification fee: $2.00. Payee: Clerk of District Court. Personal checks accepted; credit cards are not. Prepayment required. Mail requests: SASE required.

Justice Court 100 W Laurel, Plentywood, MT 59254; 406-765-3409; fax: 406-765-3489; 8AM-5PM (MST). ***Misdemeanor, Civil Actions under $7,000, Eviction, Small Claims.***

Silver Bow County

District Court 155 W Granite St, Rm 313, Butte, MT 59701; 406-497-6350; fax: 406-497-6358; 8AM-5PM (MST). ***Felony, Civil Actions over $7,000, Probate.***
Civil Records: Access: Fax, mail, in person. Both court and visitors may perform in person searches. Search fee: $2.00 per name per year, first 7 years, then $1.00 per year. Required to search: name, years to search. Civil cases indexed by defendant, plaintiff, in original files since 1970, on microfilm back to 1887; on computer back to 1996. Mail turnaround time 3 days. Civil PAT goes back to 1996. PAT civil results show middle initial.
Criminal Records: Access: Fax, mail, in person. Both court and visitors may perform in person searches. Search fee: $2.00 per name per year, first 7 years, then $1.00 per year. Required to search: name, years to search. Criminal records in original files since 1970, on microfilm back to 1887; on computer back to 1995. Mail turnaround time 1-3 days; will not do phone searches. Criminal PAT goes back to 1996. PAT criminal results show middle initial.
General Information: No adoption, juvenile or sanity records released. Fee to fax out file $1.00 per page. Court makes copy: $1.00 per page 1st 10 pages, then $.50 each add'l. Certification fee: $2.00. Payee: Clerk of Court. Personal checks accepted; credit cards are not. Prepayment required. Mail requests: SASE required.

Limited Jurisdiction Court #1 & #2 155 W Granite St, Rm 305, Silver Bow County Courthouse, Butte, MT 59701; 406-497-6391/6392; criminal phone: 406-497-6390; civil phone: 406-497-6390; criminal fax: 406-497-6468; civil fax: same; 8AM-5PM (MST). ***Misdemeanor, Civil Actions under $7,000, Eviction, Small Claims.***
There are two Justice Courts at this location. Both courts must be searched for records.

Stillwater County

District Court PO Box 367, Columbus, MT 59019; 406-322-8030; fax: 406-322-8048; 8AM-N, 1-5PM (MST). ***Felony, Civil Actions over $5,000, Probate.***
Search Evictions at local courts.
Civil Records: Access: Phone, mail, in person. Both court and visitors may perform in person searches. Search fee: $2.00 per name per year, first 7 years, then $1.00 per year. Required to search: name, years to search. Civil cases indexed by defendant, plaintiff; index on docket books since 1913; on computer back to 1994. Mail turnaround time 1-2 days. Public use terminal available, records go back to 1994. PAT results show name only.
Criminal Records: Access: Phone, mail, in person. Both court and visitors may perform in person searches. Search fee: $2.00 per name per year, first 7 years, then $1.00 per year. Required to search: name, years to search. Criminal docket on books since 1913; on computer back to 1994. Mail turnaround time 1-2 days. Public use terminal available, crim records go back to 1994. PAT results show name only.
General Information: No adoption, juvenile or sanity records released. Will fax documents $1.00 per page. Court makes copy: $1.00 per page 1st 10 pages, then $.50 each add'l. Certification fee: $2.00. Payee: Clerk of Court. Personal checks accepted; credit cards are not. Prepayment required. Mail requests: SASE required.

Justice Court PO Box 77, 400 E 3rd Ave N, Columbus, MT 59019; 406-322-8040; fax: 406-322-8048; 8AM-N, 1-5PM (MST). ***Misdemeanor, Civil Actions under $7,000, Eviction, Small Claims.***

Sweet Grass County

District Court PO Box 698, Big Timber, MT 59011; 406-932-5154; criminal fax: 406-932-5433; civil fax: same; 8AM-N, 1-5PM (MST). ***Felony, Civil Actions over $5,000, Eviction, Probate.***
Probate records in a separate index at same address. Probate fax is same as main fax number.
Civil Records: Access: Phone, mail, in person. Only the court performs in person searches; visitors may not. Search fee: $2.00 per name per year, first 7 years, then $1.00 per year. Required to search: name, years to search. Civil cases indexed by defendant, plaintiff, in books since 1895, on microfiche since 1972, computerized since 1996. Mail turnaround time 1 day.
Criminal Records: Access: Phone, mail, in person. Only the court performs in person searches; visitors may not. Search fee: $2.00 per name per year, first 7 years, then $1.00 per year. Required to search: name, years to search. Criminal records in books since 1895, on microfiche since 1972, computerized since 1996. Mail turnaround time 1 day.
General Information: No adoption, juvenile or sanity records released. Will fax documents free locally, add $1.50 if not a toll free number. Court makes copy: $1.00 per page 1st 10 pages, then $.50 each add'l. Certification fee: $2.00 per document. Payee: Clerk of Court. Personal checks accepted; credit cards are not. Prepayment required. Mail requests: SASE required.

Justice Court PO Box 1432, 200 West 1st, Big Timber, MT 59011; 406-932-5150; fax: 406-932-5433; 8AM-5PM (MST). ***Misdemeanor, Traffic Complaints, Civil Actions under $7,000, Eviction, Small Claims.***

Teton County

District Court PO Box 487, Choteau, MT 59422; 406-466-2909; fax: 406-466-2910; 8AM-N, 1-5PM (MST). ***Felony, Civil Actions over $5,000, Eviction, Probate.***
Civil Records: Access: Phone, fax, mail, in person. Only the court performs in person searches; visitors may not. Search fee: $2.00 per name per year, first 7 years, then $1.00 per year. Required to search: name, years to search. Civil cases indexed by defendant, plaintiff, on books from 1893; on computer back to 1995. Mail turnaround time 1 day.

Criminal Records: Access: Phone, mail, in person. Only the court performs in person searches; visitors may not. Search fee: $2.00 per name per year, first 7 years, then $1.00 per year. Required to search: name, years to search. Criminal docket on books from 1893; on computer back to 1995. Mail turnaround time 1 day.
General Information: No adoption, juvenile or sanity records released. Fee to fax out file $1.00 per page. Court makes copy: $1.00 per page 1st 10, $.50 each add'l. Certification fee: $2.00 per document. Payee: Clerk of Court. Personal checks accepted; credit cards are not. Prepayment required. Mail requests: SASE required.

Justice Court PO Box 337, 1 Main Ave S, Choteau, MT 59422; 406-466-5611; fax: 406-466-2138; 8AM-N, 1-5PM (MST). ***Misdemeanor, Civil Actions under $7,000, Eviction, Small Claims.***

Toole County

District Court PO Box 850, Shelby, MT 59474; 406-424-8330; criminal fax: 406-424-8331; civil fax: same; 8AM-5PM (MST). ***Felony, Civil Actions over $5,000, Probate.***
Probate fax is same as main fax number. Eviction at local level.
Civil Records: Access: Phone, fax, mail, in person. Both court and visitors may perform in person searches. Search fee: $2.00 per name per year, first 7 years, then $1.00 per year. Required to search: name, years to search. Civil cases indexed by defendant, plaintiff, in books from 1914; on computer since 1997. Mail turnaround time same day as request received.
Criminal Records: Access: Phone, fax, mail, in person. Both court and visitors may perform in person searches. Search fee: $2.00 per name per year, first 7 years, then $1.00 per year. Required to search: name, years to search, DOB. Criminal records in books from 1914; on computer since 1997. Mail turnaround time same day as received.
General Information: No adoption, juvenile or sanity records released. Will fax documents $.50 per page. Court makes copy: $1.00 per page 1st 10 pages, then $.50 each add'l. Self serve: $1.00 per page. Certification fee: $2.00 per document. Payee: Clerk of Court. Personal checks accepted; credit cards are not. Prepayment required. Mail requests: SASE required.

Justice Court PO Box 738, 226 1st St S, Rm 104, Shelby, MT 59474; 406-424-8315; fax: 406-424-8316; 8AM-5PM (MST). ***Misdemeanor, Civil Actions under $7,000, Eviction, Small Claims.***

Treasure County

District Court PO Box 392, Hysham, MT 59038; 406-342-5547; fax: 406-342-5445; 8AM-5PM (MST). ***Felony, Civil Actions over $5,000, Eviction, Probate.***
Civil Records: Access: Fax, mail, in person. Both court and visitors may perform in person searches. Search fee: $2.00 per name per year, first 7 years, then $1.00 per year. Required to search: name, years to search. Civil cases indexed by defendant, plaintiff, on books since 1919, on microfilm from 1985 to present; on computer back to 1996. Mail turnaround time usually 1 day.
Criminal Records: Access: Fax, mail, in person. Both court and visitors may perform in person searches. Search fee: $2.00 per name per year, first 7 years, then $1.00 per year. Required to search: name, years to search, DOB. Criminal docket on books since 1919, on microfilm from 1985 to present; on computer back to 1996. Mail turnaround time 1 week.
General Information: No adoption or sanity records released. Fee to fax out file- $1.50 per page. Court makes copy: $1.00 per page 1st 10 pages, then $.50 each add'l. Certification fee: $2.00. Payee: Clerk of Court. Personal checks accepted; credit cards are not. Prepayment required. Mail requests: SASE required.

Justice Court PO Box 297, 307 Rapelje Ave, Hysham, MT 59038-0297; 406-342-5532; fax: 406-342-5532; 9AM-N (MST). ***Misdemeanor, Civil Actions under $7,000, Eviction, Small Claims.***

Valley County

Clerk of District Court 501 Court Sq #6, Glasgow, MT 59230; 406-228-6268; criminal fax: 406-228-6212; civil fax: same; 8AM-5PM (MST). ***Felony, Civil Actions over $5,000, Eviction, Probate.***
Probate fax is same as main fax number.
Civil Records: Access: Phone, fax, mail, in person. Only the court performs in person searches; visitors may not. Search fee: $2.00 per name per year, first 7 years, then $1.00 per year. Required to search: name, years to search. Civil cases indexed by defendant, plaintiff, in books since 1893; on computer back to 1996. Mail turnaround time same day.
Criminal Records: Access: Fax, mail, in person. Only the court performs in person searches; visitors may not. Search fee: $2.00 per name per year, first 7 years, then $1.00 per year. Required to search: name, years to search, signed release. Criminal records in books since 1893; on computer back to 1996. Mail turnaround time same day.
General Information: No adoption, juvenile or sanity records released. Fee to fax out file $1.00 per page. Court makes copy: $1.00 per page 1st 10 pages, then $.50 each add'l. Certification fee: $2.00 per document. Payee: Clerk of Court. Business checks accepted. No credit cards accepted. Prepayment required. Mail requests: SASE required.

Justice Court 501 Court Sq #10, Glasgow, MT 59230; 406-228-6271; fax: 406-228-4601; 8AM-N (MST). ***Misdemeanor, Civil Actions under $7,000, Eviction, Small Claims.***

Wheatland County

District Court Box 227, Harlowton, MT 59036; 406-632-4893; probate phone: same; fax: 406-632-4873; 8AM-N, 1-5PM (MST). ***Felony, Civil Actions over $5,000, Eviction, Probate.***
Probate fax is same as main fax number.
Civil Records: Access: Fax, mail, in person. Both court and visitors may perform in person searches. Search fee: $2.00 per name per year, first 7 years, then $1.00 per year. Required to search: name, years to search. Civil cases indexed by defendant, plaintiff. Computerized records back to 1996, civil records on docket books since 1917, probate on microfiche from 1984. Mail turnaround time next day.
Criminal Records: Access: Mail, in person. Both court and visitors may perform in person searches. Search fee: $2.00 per name per year, first 7 years, then $1.00 per year. Required to search: name, years to search. Computerized records back to 1996, criminal records on docket books since 1917, probate on microfiche from 1984. Mail turnaround time next day.
General Information: No adoption, juvenile or sanity records released. Will fax documents to local or toll free line. Court makes copy: $1.00 per page 1st 10 pages, then $.50 each add'l. Certification fee: $2.00. Payee: Clerk of Court. Personal checks accepted; credit cards are not. Prepayment required. Mail requests: SASE required.

Justice Court PO Box 524, 201 A Ave NW, Harlowton, MT 59036; 406-632-4821; fax: 406-632-4880; 10AM-1PM T,TH (MST). ***Misdemeanor, Civil Actions under $7,000, Eviction, Small Claims.***

Wibaux County

District Court PO Box 292, 200 S Wilbaux St, Courthouse, Wibaux, MT 59353; 406-796-2484; fax: 406-796-2484; 8AM-N, 1-5PM (MST). ***Felony, Civil Actions over $5,000, Eviction, Probate.***
Civil Records: Access: Phone, fax, mail, in person. Both court and visitors may perform in person searches. Search fee: $2.00 per name per year, first 7 years, then $1.00 per year. Required to search: name, years to search. Civil cases indexed by defendant, plaintiff; index on docket books since 1914, on computer since 1/97. Mail turnaround time 1 week.
Criminal Records: Access: Phone, fax, mail, in person. Only the court performs in person searches; visitors may not. Search fee: $2.00 per name per year, first 7 years, then $1.00 per year. Required to search: name, years to search. Criminal docket on books since 1914, on computer since 1/97. Mail turnaround time 1 week.
General Information: No adoption, juvenile or sanity records released. Will fax documents $2.00 1st page, $.50 each add'l, turnaround time is 2-3 days. Court makes copy: $1.00 per page 1st 10 pages, then $.50 each add'l. Self serve: No self serve criminal copier; Civil self serve- $.15 each. Certification fee: $2.00 per doc. Payee: Clerk of Court. Personal checks accepted; credit cards are not. Prepayment required. Arrangements must first be made for payment for fax and phone requests. Mail requests: SASE required.

Justice Court PO Box 445, 203 S Wibaux St, Wibaux, MT 59353; 406-796-7671; fax: 406-796-2484; 1-5PM Mon,Wed; 8AM-N Fri. (MST). ***Misdemeanor, Civil Actions under $7,000, Eviction, Small Claims.***

Yellowstone County

District Court PO Box 35030, 217 N 27 St, 7th Fl, Billings, MT 59107; 406-256-2862; criminal phone: 406-256-2860; civil phone: 406-256-2851; probate phone: 406-256-2865; fax: 406-256-2995; 8AM-5PM (MST). ***Felony, Civil Actions over $7,000, Probate.***
www.co.yellowstone.mt.us/clerk%5Fcourt/
Civil Records: Access: Mail, in person. Both court and visitors may perform in person searches. Search fee: $2.00 per name per year, first 7 years, then $1.00 per year. Required to search: name, years to search. Civil cases indexed by defendant, plaintiff, in books, on microfilm back to 1800s; on computer back to 1992. Mail turnaround time 1 day if record less than 10 years old. Civil PAT goes back to 1990. PAT results show name only.
Criminal Records: Access: Mail, in person. Both court and visitors may perform in person searches. Search fee: $2.00 per name per year, first 7 years, then $1.00 per year. Required to search: name, years to search. Criminal records in books, on microfilm back to 1800s; on computer back to 1990. Mail turnaround time 1 day if record less than 10 years old. Criminal PAT goes back to same as civil. PAT results show name only.
General Information: No adoption, juvenile or sanity records released. Will not fax documents. Court makes copy: $1.00 per page 1st 10 pages, then $.50 each add'l. Certification fee: $2.00 per cert. Payee: Clerk of Court. No personal checks or credit cards accepted. Prepayment required. Mail requests: SASE required.

Justice Court PO Box 35032, 217 N 27th, Rm 603, Billings, MT 59107; 406-256-2998; fax: 406-256-2898; 9AM-5PM (MST). ***Misdemeanor, Civil Actions under $7,000, Eviction, Small Claims.***
www.co.yellowstone.mt.gov/justicecourt/

Montana Recording Offices

ORGANIZATION: 57 counties, 56 recording offices. Yellowstone National Park is considered a county but is not included as a filing location. The recording officer is the County Clerk and Recorder, and Clerk of District Court for state tax liens. Montana is in the Mountain Time Zone (MST)

REAL ESTATE RECORDS: Many Montana counties will perform real estate searches. Copy fee is usually $.50 1st page, $.25 each add'l. Certification fee is usually $2.00 per document plus copy fee.

UCC RECORDS: Financing statements are filed at the state level except for real estate related collateral which are filed with the Clerk and Recorder. However, prior to July, 2001, consumer goods collateral were also filed at the county and these older records can be searched there. UCC search fee is usually $7.00 per debtor name.

TAX LIEN RECORDS: Federal tax liens on personal property of businesses are filed with the Secretary of State. Other federal tax liens are filed with the county Clerk and Recorder. State tax liens are filed with the Clerk of District Court. Usually tax liens on personal property filed with the Clerk and Recorder are in the same index with UCC financing statements. Most counties will perform tax lien searches, some as part of a UCC search and others for a separate fee, usually $7.00 per name. Copy fees vary.

OTHER LIENS: Mechanics, thresherman, judgment, lis pendens, construction, logger.

ONLINE ACCESS: Search for a for a Montana property owner by name and county on the Montana Cadastral Mapping Project GIS mapping database at http://gis.mt.gov. The Secretary of State offers a web-based subscription service of active liens filed with their office.

Beaverhead County

Clerk and Recorder, 2 S Pacific, Dillon, MT 59725-2799. Recording, R/E & UCC phone-406-683-3720; fax-406-683-3778; 8AM-5PM (MST)

Index: Separate indices to search include deeds, mortgages, POA, cert of survey & plats, mining claim locations, mining claim work. Records indexed on a public use terminal back to 4/02. Only the public may search. Copy fee $.50 per page. Cert fee- $2.00 per cert plus copy fee. Payee- Beaverhead County Clerk and Recorder. Treasurer- 406-683-5821; Elections- 406-683-3720; Vital Records- 406-683-3720. **Other Online Records-** Name search on the statewide Cadastral database free at http://gis.mt.gov.

Big Horn County

Clerk and Recorder, PO Box 908, Hardin, MT 59034. Recording, R/E & UCC phone-406-665-9730, UCC recording phone-406-665-9732; fax-406-665-9738; 8AM-5PM.

Index: All in one since 7/01/01. Records indexed on a public use terminal back to 7/1/02. Office personnel or visitors may perform searches. Search fee $7.00. Basic name search free. Copy fee $.50 1st page, $.25 each add'l. Cert fee- $2.00 per doc includes copy fee. Payee- Clerk - Recorder. For Title companies. Treasurer- 406-665-9830; Elections- 406-665-9730; Vital Records- 406-665-9730. **Property tax/Assessing-** 406-665-9710. (Appraiser/Auditor- 406-665-9710) **Online access-** Name search on the statewide Cadastral database free at http://gis.mt.gov

Blaine County

Clerk and Recorder, PO Box 278, Chinook, MT 59523. 406-357-3240; fax-406-357-2199; 8AM-5PM. http://mt.gov/maco/Counties/BLAINE.htm

Index: Separate indices to search include deeds, Mortgages, Misc, Oil & Gas, Satis/&/Assign. Records indexed on a public use terminal back to 2004. Office will perform current UCC's searches but public must search other records themselves. Search fee $7.00 per name. Copy fee $.25 per page. Cert fee- $2.00 per doc plus copy fee. Payee- Blaine County Clerk & Recorder. Treasurer- 406-357-3280; Elections- 406-357-3240; Vital Records- 406-357-3240. **Property tax/Assessing-** 420 Ohio, Chinook, MT 59523; 406-357-3210. (Appraiser/Auditor- 406-357-3210) **Online access-** Name search on the statewide Cadastral database free at http://gis.mt.gov.

Broadwater County

Clerk and Recorder, 515 Broadway, Townsend, MT 59644. Recording, R/E & UCC phone-406-266-3443; fax-406-266-3674; 8AM-5PM.

Index: All in one. Records indexed on a public use terminal back to 1995. Office will perform a UCC search and very limited real estate search, but public must search other records themselves. Search fee $7.00 per name. Copy fee $.50 1st page, $.25 each add'l. Cert fee- $2.00 per doc plus copy fee. Payee- Broadwater County Clerk. Treasurer- 406-266-3445; Elections- 406-266-3443; Vital Records- 406-266-3443. **Property tax/Assessing-** 515 Broadway, Townsend, MT 59644; 406-266-3430, assessor fax-406-266-3674. (Appraiser/Auditor- 406-266-3430) **Online access-** Name search on the statewide Cadastral database free at http://gis.mt.gov.

Carbon County

Clerk and Recorder, PO Box 887, Red Lodge, MT 59068. Recording, R/E & UCC phone-406-446-1220; fax-406-446-2640; 7AM-5:30PM (MST) www.co.carbon.mt.us

Index: All in one. Records indexed back to May, 1995. Office personnel or visitors may perform searches. Search fee $7.00 per name. Copy fee $.25 per page, $1.00 minimum if real estate. Cert fee- $2.00 per doc includes copy fee. Payee- Clerk and Recorder. CD-rom of recorded docs and plats available,- scanned images only. Contact Linda Ladvala 406-446-1220. Treasurer- 406-446-1221; Elections- 406-446-1595; Vital Records- 406-446-1220. **Property tax/Assessing-** PO Box 647, 17 W 11th St, Courthouse, Red Lodge, MT 59068; 406-466-1221/23, assessor fax- 406-446-2640. (Appraiser/Auditor- 406-446-1224) hours- 8AM-5PM Public access terminal in Recorder's office. **Online access-** Name search on the statewide Cadastral database free at http://gis.mt.gov

Carter County

Clerk and Recorder, PO Box 315, Ekalaka, MT 59324-0315. 406-775-8749; fax-406-775-8750; 8AM-N, 1-5PM.

Index: Separate indices to search include deed, mortgage, misc. Records indexed on a public use terminal back to 2/02. Only the public may index search, generally. Office will search if provided book and page number. General index search fee $7.00 per name. Copy fee $.50 1st page; $.25 each add'l. Cert fee- $2.00 per doc plus copy fee. Payee- Carter County Clerk. **Other phones:** Treasurer- 406-775-8735; Elections- 406-775-8749; Vital Records- 406-775-8749. **Property tax/Assessing-** 406-775-8717. **Online access-** Name search on the statewide Cadastral database free at http://gis.mt.gov.

Cascade County

Clerk and Recorder, PO Box 2867, Great Falls, MT 59403-2867. 406-454-6802, R/E recording phone-406-454-6801; fax-406-454-6703; 8AM-5PM. http://clerkrecorder.co.cascade.mt.us/Recorder/web/

Index: All in one. Records indexed on a public use terminal back to 1988. Office personnel or visitors may perform searches. Search fee $7.00 per name. Office will not search real estate or UCC records. Copy fee $.50 1st page; $.25 each add'l page. Cert fee- $2.00 per doc plus copy fee. Payee- Clerk & Recorder. **Online access to Real Estate, Deed records:** Recording office land data available at http://clerkrecorder.co.cascade.mt.us/Recorder/web/. Registration and fees required. **Other phones:** Treasurer- 406-454-6850; Elections- 406-454-6803; Vital Records- 406-454-6718. **Property tax/Assessing-** 300 Central Ave, Ste 520, Great Falls, MT 59401; 406-454-7460. (Appraiser/Auditor- 406-454-7460) **Online access-** Name search free on the statewide cadastral mapping site at http://cadastral.mt.gov/ (incomplete tax data)

Chouteau County

Clerk and Recorder, PO Box 459, Fort Benton, MT 59442-0459. 406-622-5151; fax-406-622-3012; 8AM-5PM (MST)

Index: Separate indices to search include deeds, mortgages, assignments, leases, misc., royalty transfers, judgments, lis pendens. Records indexed on a public use terminal back to 4/95. Office personnel or visitors may perform searches. General index search fee $5.00 per name per book. Copy fee $.50 for first page, $.25 per page there after. Cert fee- $2.00 per cert plus copy fee. Payee- Chouteau County Clerk and Recorder. Treasurer- 406-622-5032; Elections- 406-622-5151; Vitals- 406-622-5151. **Property tax/ Assessing-** 406-622-5261. **Online access-** Name search on the statewide Cadastral database free at http://gis.mt.gov.

Custer County

Clerk and Recorder, 1010 Main St, Miles City, MT 59301-1010. Recording, R/E & UCC phone-406-874-3343; fax-406-874-3452; 8AM-5PM (MST)
Index: Separate indices to search. Records indexed on a public use terminal back to 6/94. Office will perform a UCC search but public must search other records themselves. Search fee $7.00 per book per 10 years. Copy fee $.50 for first page, $.25 each additional. Cert fee- $2.00 per cert plus copy fee. Payee- Custer County Clerk and Recorder. Treasurer- 406-874-3427; Elections- 406-874-3343; Vital Records- 406-444-4228. **Property tax/Assessing**- 1010 Main St, Miles City, MT 59301-1010; 406-232-1295. (Appraiser/Auditor- 406-232-6437) **Online access**- Name search on the statewide Cadastral database free at http://gis.mt.gov.

Daniels County

Clerk and Recorder, PO Box 247, Scobey, MT 59263. Recording, R/E & UCC phone-406-487-5561; fax-406-487-5583; 8AM-5PM (MST)
Index: Separate indices to search include deeds, mortgages, misc. Public use terminal not available. Office personnel or visitors may perform searches. Search fee $.50 per year unless otherwise indicated. UCC or tax lien searches $7.00. Copy fee $.50 1st page, $.25 each add'l. Cert fee- $2.00 per cert plus copy fee. Payee- Daniels County Clerk and Recorder. Treasurer- 406-487-2671; Elections- 406-487-5561; Vital Records- 406-487-5561. **Property tax/Assessing**- PO Box 397, 213 Main St, Scobey, MT 59263; 406-487-2791. (Appraiser/Auditor- 406-487-2791) **Online access**- Name search on the statewide Cadastral database free at http://gis.mt.gov. Links to parcel search and property mapping.

Dawson County

Clerk and Recorder, 207 W Bell, Glendive, MT 59330. Recording, R/E & UCC phone-406-377-3058; fax-406-377-1717; 8AM-5PM. www.dawsoncountymontana.com/clerk_&_recorder.htm
Index: Separate indices to search include computer back to 3/21/2000, various books before that date. Records indexed on computer by document number. Only the public may search. Copy fee $.50 1st page; $.25 each add'l. Cert fee- $2.00 per doc plus $.50 1st page, $.25 each add'l page includes copy fee. Payee- Clerk and Recorder. Treasurer- 406-377-3026; Elections- 406-377-3058; Vital Records- 406-377-3058. **Property tax/Assessing**- 207 W Bell, Glendive, MT 59330; 406-377-4256, assessor fax- 406-377-4500. (Appraiser/Auditor- 406-377-4256) www.dawsoncountymontana.org/ **Online access**- Statewide cadastral mapping site found at http://gis.mt.gov/. Links to parcel search and property maps. Search by GEO code, owner, or subdivision.

Deer Lodge County

Clerk and Recorder, 800 Main St; Courthouse, Anaconda, MT 59711-2999. 406-563-4060, R/E phone-406-563-4061; fax-406-563-4001; 8AM-5PM.
Index: All in one. Records indexed on a public use terminal back to 1988. Office personnel or visitors may perform searches. General index search fee $.50 per name per year. Copy fee $.50 1st page; $.25 each add'l page. Fee to fax doc is $5.00. Cert fee- $2.00 per doc plus copy fee. **Online access to Real Estate, Deed records:** Recording office land data to be available at a later date at www.etitlesearch.com; registration and fees required. **Other phones:** Treasurer- 406-563-4051; Elections- 406-563-4060; Vital Records- 406-563-4062. **Property tax/Assessing**- 800 Main St, Anaconda, MT 59711-2999; 406-563-4045, assessor fax- 406-563-4043. (Appraiser/Auditor- 406-563-4045) **access**- Access property data and maps free at www.cadastral.mt.gov.

Fallon County

Clerk and Recorder, PO Box 846, Baker, MT 59313-0846. Recording, R/E & UCC phone-406-778-7106; fax-406-778-2048; 8AM-5PM. www.falloncounty.net
Index: Separate indices in books to search include deeds, misc, mtgs, satisifaction of mtgs and assignments. Newer records indexed on computer. Office personnel or visitors may perform searches. General index search fee $7.00 per debtor. Office will search real estate records. Will search UCC records. Copy fee $.50 per page; $.25 each add'l of same doc. Cert fee- $2.00 per doc plus copy fee. Payee- Clerk and Recorder. Treasurer- 406-778-7109; Elections-406-778-8105; Vital Records- 406-778-7106. **Property tax/Assessing**- PO Box 787, 10 W Fallon, Baker, MT 59313-0787; 406-778-7109, assessor fax-406-778-3209. (Appraiser/Auditor- 406-778-7172) No public use computer in office. **Online access**- Statewide cadastral mapping site found at http://gis.mt.gov/. Links to parcel search and property maps. Search by GEO code, owner, or subdivision.

Fergus County

Clerk and Recorder, 712 W Main, Lewistown, MT 59457. 406-535-5242; fax-406-535-9023; 8AM-5PM. www.co.fergus.mt.us
Index: All in one. Records indexed on computer since 1989, otherwise indexed by document type in separate book indexes. Office personnel or visitors may perform searches. Search fee $7.00 per name. Office will not search real estate records. UCC search includes tax liens if requested. Copy fee $.50 1st page, $.25 each add'l page. Cert fee- $2.00 per doc plus copy fee. Payee- Clerk Recorder. **Online access to Real Estate, Deed records:** Recording office land data to be available at a later date at www.etitlesearch.com; registration and fees required. **Other phones:** Treasurer- 406-535-9220; Elections-406-535-5242; Vital Records- 406-535-5242. **Property tax/Assessing**- 712 W Main, Lewistown, MT 59457; 406-538-5723, assessor fax- 406-538-2483. (Appraiser/Auditor- 406-538-5723) **Online access**- Statewide cadastral mapping site found at http://gis.mt.gov/. Links to parcel search and property maps. Search by GEO code, owner, or subdivision.

Flathead County

Clerk and Recorder, 800 S Main, 2nd Fl; Courthouse, Kalispell, MT 59901-5400. 406-758-5534, R/E recording phone-406-758-5698; fax-406-758-5865; 8-5PM (MST) http://flathead.mt.gov/clerk_recorder/
Index: All in one. Records indexed on a public use terminal back to 1/1/1984. Office personnel or visitors may perform searches. Search fee $7.00 per name. Copy fee $.50 for 1st page, $.25 each add'l. Cert fee-$2.00 per doc plus copy fee. Payee- Flathead County Clerk and Recorder. **Online access to Real Estate, Grantor/Grantee, Deed, Mortgage, Lien, Judgment records:** Access recorded lard records by subscribing to the idoc system at www.co.flathead.mt.us/idoc/. Annual fee is $180.00; contact the Clerk and Recorder's office for info and signup, or visit the web. **Other phones:** Treasurer-406-758-5688; Elections- 406-758-5535; Vital Records- 406-758-5527; Recording information- 406-758-5801; General Office -406-758-5533. **Property tax/Assessing**- 800 S Main, Kallspell, MT 59901; 406-758-5524. http://flathead.mt.gov/auditor/ **Online access**- Name search on the statewide Cadastral database free at http://gis.mt.gov. Flathead County does not have an assessing office.

Gallatin County

Clerk and Recorder, 311 W Main, Rm 204, Bozeman, MT 59715. Recording, R/E & UCC phone-406-582-3050; fax-406-582-3196; 8AM-5PM (MST) www.gallatin.mt.gov
Index: All in one. Records indexed on a public use terminal back to 1/1/1990. Office personnel or visitors may perform searches. Search fee $.50 per year/per name/per real estate index. UCC search fee- $7.00 per name. Office will search real estate records. Will search UCC records. Copy fee $.50 1st page; $.25 each add'l, $1.00 minimum. Cert fee- $2.00 per doc plus copy fee. Payee- Gallatin County Clerk and Recorder. Office does not sell bulk data, but GIS Department will. **Online access to Real Estate, Deed records:** Recording office land data to be available at a later date at www.etitlesearch.com; registration and fees required. **Other phones:** Treasurer- 406-582-3030; Elections- 406-582-3060; Vital Records- 406-582-3050; State tax liens/district court- 406-582-2165. **Property tax/Assessing**- 2273 Boothill Ct, #100, Bozeman, MT 59715; 406-582-3400, assessor fax-406-582-3420. (Appraiser/Auditor- 406-582 3400) Public use computer available. **Online access**- Statewide cadastral mapping site found at http://gis.mt.gov/. Links to parcel search and property maps. Search parcel by GEO code, owner, or subdivision. Also search property data free at http://webapps.gallatin.mt.gov/proptax/. Also, search property on the GIS-mapping site free at http://webapps.gallatin.mt.gov/mappers/ but no name searching.

Garfield County

Clerk and Recorder, PO Box 7, Jordan, MT 59337-0007. Recording, R/E & UCC phone-406-557-2760; fax-406-557-2765; 8AM-5PM.
Index: Separate indices to search include deeds, mtgs, misc. pre-1/2005. Records indexed on a public use terminal back to 10/1/2005. Office will perform a UCC search but public must search other records themselves. Search fee $7.00 per name. Copy fee $.50 1st page, $.25 each add'l. Cert fee- $2.00 per doc plus copy fee. Payee- Garfield Clerk and Recorder. Bulk data is available for purchase, contact Janet Sherer at Clerk/Recorder office. Treasurer- 406-557-2233; Elections- 406-557-2760; Vital Records- 406-557-2760. **Property tax/Assessing**- 406-557-6164, assessor fax- 406-557-2625. (Appraiser/Auditor- 406-557-2772) **Online access**- Name search on the statewide Cadastral database free at http://gis.mt.gov.

Glacier County

Clerk and Recorder, 512 E Main, Cut Bank, MT 59427. 406-873-3610; fax-406-873-3613; 8AM-5PM. www.glaciercountygov.com/mc/page.do
Index: Separate indices to search include deed, mortgage (various), liens, UCC, misc, O/G (various). Records indexed on a public use terminal back to 7/92. Office personnel or visitors may perform searches. Search fee $7.00 per name. UCC search includes tax liens if requested. Copy fee $.50 per page. Cert fee- $2.00 per doc plus copy fee. Payee-Glacier Clerk & Recorder. Treasurer- 406-873-3625; Elections- 406-873-3607; Vital Records- 406-873-3610. **Property tax/Assessing**- 512 E Main, Cut Bank, MT 59427; 406-873-3637. (Appraiser/Auditor-406-873-3637) **Online access**- Statewide cadastral mapping site found at http://gis.mt.gov/. Links to parcel search and property maps. Search parcel by GEO code, owner, or subdivision. Glacier County has a Clerk & Recorders' Office only, no Assessing Ofc.

Golden Valley County

Clerk and Recorder, PO Box 10, Ryegate, MT 59074. 406-568-2231; 8AM-5PM (MST) www.co.golden-valley.mt.us/html/clerk.html
Index: Separate indices to search. Record index not computerized. Office personnel or visitors may perform searches. Search fee $2.00 per name per year. UCC search per debtor name- $7.00 per year. Copy fee $.50 per page. Cert fee- $2.00 per doc includes copy fee. Payee- Clerk/ Recorder/ Clerk of Court. Treasurer- 406-586-2342; Elections- 406-568-2231; Vital Records- 406-568-2231. **Property tax/Assessing**- 107 Kemp, PO Box 10, Ryegate, MT 59074; 406-568-2371, assessor fax- 406-568-2428. **Online access**- Statewide cadastral mapping site found at http://gis.mt.gov/. Links to parcel search and property maps. Search parcel by GEO code, owner, or subdivision. Golden Valley County has a Department of Revenue office only, no assessing office.

Granite County

Clerk and Recorder, PO Box 925, Philipsburg, MT 59858. Recording, R/E & UCC phone-406-859-3771; fax-406-859-3817; 8AM-5PM.
Records indexed on a public use terminal back to 1100. Office personnel or visitors may perform

searches. Search fee $7.00. Office will perform a minimal real estate search. Will search UCC records. Copy fee $.50 1st page; $.25 each add'l. Cert fee- $2.00 per doc plus copy fee. Payee- Clerk & Recorder. Treasurer- 406-859-3831; Elections- 406-859-3771; Vital Records- 406-859-3771. **Property tax/Assessing-** PO Box 38, Philipsburg, MT 59858; 406-859-3521. **Online access-** Statewide cadastral mapping site found at http://gis.mt.gov/. Links to parcel search and property maps. Search parcel by GEO code, owner, or subdivision. Granite County has a Dept of Revenue office only, no Assessing Office.

Hill County

Clerk and Recorder, 315 4th St; Courthouse, Havre, MT 59501. 406-265-5481, R/E recording phone-406-265-5481 x221,222,223; fax-406-265-2445; 8AM-5PM (MST) http://co.hill.mt.us

Index: Separate indices to search include deed, mortgage, misc, leases, satisfactions, UCCs, liens. Records indexed on computer since 10/1/2001. Above records in alphabetical order in prior main indexes. Office will perform a UCC search but public must search other records themselves. No fee for search. UCC search only through last 5 years. Copy fee $.50 1st page, $.25 each add'l. Cert fee- $2.00 per doc plus copy fee. Payee- Hill County Clerk and Recorder. Treasurer- 406-265-5481 x259; Elections- 406-265-5481 x221, 222, 223; Vital Records- 406-265-5481 x221, 222, 223. **Property tax/Assessing-** 315 4th St, Courthouse, Havre, MT 59501; 406-265-5481 x210, assessor fax- 406-265-1305. **Online access-** Name search on the statewide Cadastral database free at http://gis.mt.gov, or at http://cadastral.mt.gov.

Jefferson County

Clerk and Recorder, PO Box H, Boulder, MT 59632. 406-225-4020; fax-406-225-4149; 8AM-N, 1-5PM (MST) www.jeffco.mt.gov/county/records.html

Index: Separate indices to search. Records indexed on a public use terminal back to 11/1989. Office will perform a UCC search but public must search other records themselves. Search fee $7.00 for UCC. Copy fee $.50 1st page, $.25 each add'l. Cert fee- $2.00 per doc plus copy fee. Payee- Jefferson County Clerk & Recorder. Treasurer- 406-225-4103; Elections- 406-225-4018; Vital Records- 406-225-4020. **Property tax/Assessing-** 104 Centennial St, Boulder, MT 59632; 406-225-4001. (Appraiser/Auditor- 406-225-4001) hours- 8AM-5PM **Online access-** Name search on the statewide Cadastral database free at http://gis.mt.gov.

Judith Basin County

Clerk and Recorder, PO Box 427, Stanford, MT 59479. Recording, R/E & UCC phone-406-566-2277; fax-406-566-2211; 8AM-5PM (MST)

Index: Numerous indices to search. Records indexed on a public use terminal back to 1/1/2002. Office personnel or visitors may perform searches. Search fee $7.00 per name. Real estate searches are subject to limitations. Will search UCC records. Copy fee $.50 1st page; $.25 each add'l. Cert fee- $2.00 per page plus copy fee. Payee- Clerk & Recorder. **Online access to Real Estate, Deed records:** Recording office land data to be available at a later date at www.etitlesearch.com; registration and fees required. **Other phones:** Treasurer- 406-566-2277; Elections-406-566-2277; Vitals- 406-566-2277. **Property tax/Assessing-** PO Box 160, Stanford, MT 59479; 406-566-2291. (Appraiser/Auditor- 406-566-2291)

Lake County

Clerk and Recorder, 106 4th Ave E, Polson, MT 59860. 406-883-7210, R/E recording phone-406-883-7208, UCC recording phone-406-883-7210; fax-406-883-7283; 8AM-5PM www.lakecounty-mt.org

Index: All in one. Records indexed on a public use terminal back to 1/1/89. Office personnel or visitors may perform searches. General index search fee $7.00 per name. Limited Real Estate searches available. Mortgage searches available. Will search UCC records. Copy fee $.50 1st page; $.25 each add'l page. Cert fee- $2.00 per cert plus copy fee. If they have to go back to old microfilm, there is an add'l $2.00 fee per doc. Payee- Lake County Clerk and Recorder. **Online access to Real Estate, Deed, Map, Survey records:** Real estate doc images, COS's, maps, and surveys can be downloaded free from the ftp site at ftp://lakecounty-mt.org. Folders by type and month. **Other phones:** Treasurer- 406-883-7224; Elections-406-883-7268; Vital Records- 406-883-7208; Clerk of Court (tax liens)- 406-883-7254. **Property tax/Assessing-** 201 3rd Ave E #B, Polson, MT 59860; 406-883-7227, assessor fax- 406-883-7293. (Appraiser/Auditor- 406-883-7227) **Online access-** Access the Web Tax System at www.lakecounty-mt.org but password is required. Statewide cadastral mapping site found at http://gis.mt.gov/. Links to parcel search and property maps. Search parcel by GEO code, owner, or subdivision. Also, search treasurer's tax payment list after registration at www.lakecounty-mt.org/scripts/xworks.exe.

Lewis and Clark County

Clerk and Recorder, PO Box 1721, Helena, MT 59624. 406-447-8337; fax-406-457-8598; 8AM-5PM (MST) www.co.lewis-clark.mt.us

Index: All in one. Records indexed on a public use terminal back to 2001. Only the public may search. General copy fee $.50 1st page, $.25 each add'l. Cert fee- $2.00 per cert plus copy fee. Payee- Lewis and Clark County Clerk and Recorder. Bulk data available for purchase, contact Paulette DeHart at 406-447-8334. **Online access to Real Estate, Grantor/Grantee, Deed, Lien records:** Search Grantor/Grantee index and recorder records free at http://records.co.lewis-clark.mt.us/icris/splash.jsp. Search free with userID PUBLIC and password RECORD. Registration recommended. This new automation includes document imaging via subscription online service. Records go back to 4/2001. **Other phones:** Treasurer- 406-447-8329; Elections- 406-447-8338. **Property tax/Assessing-** 316 N Park Ave, Rm 106, Helena, MT 59601; 406-444-4000, assessor fax- 406-444-2980. Public use computer available. **Online access-** Search property tax data free at http://webtax.csa-inc.net/lewisandclarkmt/. Statewide cadastral mapping site found at http://gis.mt.gov/. Links to parcel search and property maps. Search parcel by GEO code, owner, or subdivision.

Liberty County

Clerk and Recorder, PO Box 459, Chester, MT 59522-0459. 406-759-5365; fax-406-759-5395; 8AM-5PM (MST) www.co.liberty.mt.us/

Index: Separate indices to search include deeds, Assets, Oil and Gas leases, mtgs, misc. Records indexed on a public use terminal back to 2000. Office personnel or visitors may perform searches. Search fee $7.00 per name. Office will not search real estate records. Will search UCC records. Copy fee $.50, if real estate $.25 per page. Cert fee- $2.00 per doc, plus $.50 per page, plus copy fee. Payee- Clerk & Recorder. Treasurer- 406-759-5455; Elections- 406-759-5365; Vital Records- 406-759-5365. **Property tax/Assessing-** PO Box 685, Chester, MT 59522-0459; 406-759-5455, assessor fax- 406-759-5396. (Appraiser/Auditor- 406-759-5126) **Online access-** Statewide cadastral mapping site found at http://gis.mt.gov/. Links to parcel search and property maps. Search by GEO code, owner, or subdivision.

Lincoln County

Recorder, 512 California Ave, Libby, MT 59923. 406-293-7781, R/E recording phone- x205; fax-406-293-8577; 8AM-5PM. www.lincolncountymt.us

Index: All in one. Records indexed on a public use terminal back to 1992. Office personnel or visitors may perform searches. Search fee $7.00 per name. Copy fee $.50 per page. Cert fee- $2.00 per doc plus copy fee. Payee- Clerk/Recorder. Bulk data on CD"s available for purchase; Contact Jill (406) 293-7781 ext. 206. Treasurer- 406-293-7781 x253; Elections- x283; Vitals- x205; Clerk of Court- x243. **Property tax/Assessing-** 952 E Spruce #600, Libby, MT 59923; 406-293-6898, assessor fax- 406-293-5487. (Appraiser/Auditor- 406-293-6898) **Online access-** Name search on the statewide Cadastral database free at http://gis.mt.gov.

Madison County

Clerk and Recorder, PO Box 366, Virginia City, MT 59755. 406-843-4270; 8AM-5PM (MST)

Index: Separate indices to search include computer, books. Records indexed on a public use terminal. Records back to 1993. Only the public may search. Copy fee $.50 1st page; $.25 each add'l. Cert fee- $2.00 per doc plus copy fee. Payee- Madison County Clerk and Recorder. **Online access to Real Estate, Deed records:** Recording office land data to be available at a later date at www.etitlesearch.com; registration and fees required. **Other phones:** Treasurer- 406-843-4212. **Property tax/Assessing-** PO Box 307, 100 W Wallace, Virginia City, MT 59755; 406-843-5335. (Appraiser/Auditor- 406-843-5335) Office will perform name lookups free; fee applies to print images.

McCone County

Clerk and Recorder, PO Box 199, Circle, MT 59215-0199. Recording, R/E & UCC phone-406-485-3505; fax-406-485-2689; 8AM-5PM (MST)

Index: Separate indices to search include deed, misc, mortgages, satisfaction of mortgages, liens, UCCs, tract books. Record index not computerized. Office personnel or visitors may perform searches. Search fee $7.00 per name. Office will search real estate records. Will search UCC records. Copy fee $.25 per page. Cert fee- $2.00 per cert plus copy fee. Payee- McCone County Clerk and Recorder. Treasurer- 406-485-3590; Elections- 406-485-3505; Vital Records-406-485-3505. **Property tax/Assessing-** PO Box 179, Circle, MT 59215 406-485-3565. (Appraiser/Auditor-406-485-3432) **Online access-** Name search on the statewide Cadastral database free at http://gis.mt.gov.

Meagher County

Clerk & Recorder, PO Box 309, White Sulphur Springs, MT 59645. Recording, R/E & UCC phone-406-547-3612; fax-406-547-3388; 9AM-4PM.

Index: Separate indices to search include deeds, mortgages, miscellaneous. Records indexed on computer back to 1995. Office personnel or visitors may perform searches. Search fee $5.00 per name. Office will search real estate records. Will search UCC records. Copy fee $.50 1st page; $.25 each add'l. Cert fee- $2.00 per cert plus copy fee. Payee-Meagher County Clerk & Recorder. Treasurer- 406-547-3641; Elections- 406-547-3612; Vitals- 406-547-3612. **Property tax/Assessing-** 15 W Main, White Sulphur Springs, 59645; 406-547-3653. (Appraiser - 406-547-3653) **Online access-** Name search on the statewide Cadastral database free at http://gis.mt.gov.

Mineral County

Clerk and Recorder, PO Box 550, Superior, MT 59872. 406-822-3520; fax-406-822-3579; 8AM-5PM.

Index: All in one. Records indexed on a public use terminal back to 1998. Office will perform a UCC search but public must search other records themselves. UCC search per debtor name- $7.00. Copy fee $.50 1st page; $.25 each add'l. Cert fee- $2.00 per doc plus copy fee. Payee- Clerk & Recorder. **Online access to Real Estate, Deed records:** Recording office land data to be available at a later date at www.etitlesearch.com; registration and fees required. **Other phones:** Treasurer- 406-822-3530; Elections- 406-822-3520; Vital Records- 406-822-3520. **Property tax/Assessing-** PO Box 669, 300 River St, Superior, MT 59872; 406-822-3540, assessor fax- 406-822-3837. (Appraiser/Auditor- 406-822-3540) No public terminal available. **Online access-** Name search on the statewide Cadastral database free at http://gis.mt.gov.

Missoula County

Clerk and Recorder, 200 W Broadway, Missoula, MT 59802. 406-258-4752; fax-406-258-3913; 8AM-5PM. www.co.missoula.mt.us

Index: All in one. Records indexed on a public use terminal back to 1982. Office will perform a UCC search but public must search other records themselves. Search fee $7.00 per name. Office will not search real estate records. Copy fee $.50 per page. Cert fee- $2.00 per doc plus copy fee. Payee- Missoula Clerk & Recorder. Recording data is available for purchase on CD-rom and microfilm; contact Debbe at 406-258-4911. **Online access to Real Estate, Deed records:** Recording office land data to be available at a later date at www.etitlesearch.com; registration and fees required. **Other phones:** Treasurer- 406-258-4847; Elections- 406-258-4751; Vital Records- 406-258-4752. **Property tax/Assessing**- 2681 Palmer St, Ste I, Missoula, MT 59808; 406-329-1400, assessor fax- 406-329-1449. (Appraiser/Auditor- 406-329-1400) http://co.missoula.mt.us. **Online access**- Statewide cadastral mapping site found at http://gis.mt.gov/. Links to parcel search and property maps. Search parcel by GEO code, owner, or subdivision. Access the county property data system free at www.co.missoula.mt.us/owner/. Property search by Address, Tax ID, Geocode, Map. Records search by Tax ID, Geocode, Book/Page. No name searching.

Musselshell County

Clerk and Recorder, 506 Main St; Courthouse, Roundup, MT 59072. Recording, R/E & UCC phone-406-323-1104; fax-406-323-3303; 8AM-5PM (MST)

Index: All in one 1995 to current. Older docs in separate indexes. Records indexed on a public use terminal back to 1995. Office will perform a UCC or tax lien search but public must search other records themselves. Search fee $7.00 per name. Copy fee $.50 per page. Cert fee- $2.00 per doc plus copy fee. Payee- Musselshell County. Treasurer- 406-323-2504; Elections- 406-323-1104; Vital Records- 406-323-1104. **Property tax/Assessing**- 506 Main St, Courthouse Bldg, Roundup, MT 59072; 406-323-1513, assessor fax- 406-323-3303. (Appraiser/Auditor- 406-323-1513) hours- 8AM-N, 1-5PM No public access computer in office. **Online access**- Statewide cadastral mapping site found at http://gis.mt.gov/. Links to parcel search and property maps. Search by GEO code, owner, or subdivision.

Park County

Clerk and Recorder, 414 E Callendar, Livingston, MT 59047. 406-222-4110; fax-406-222-4193; 8AM-5PM (MST) www.parkcounty.org/

Index: All in one. Records indexed on a public use terminal back to 1989. Office personnel or visitors may perform searches. Office will not search real estate records. Will search UCC records. General copy fee $.50 per page. Cert fee- $2.00 per cert plus copy fee. Payee- Park County Clerk and Recorder. **Online access to Real Estate, Grantor/Grantee, Deed, Lien records:** Access to document searches at www.parkcounty.org/idoc/. The computer document indexing begins from January 1, 1989. Users are required to sign a user contract & pay a yearly user's fee payable on a prorated schedule and payable on January 1 each year. Treasurer- 406-222-4119; Elections- 406-222-4111; Vital Records- 406-222-4111. **Property tax/Assessing**- 414 E Callendar, Livingston, MT 59047; 406-222-4113, assessor fax- 406-222-4124. No public access computer at office. **Online access**- Statewide cadastral mapping site at http://gis.mt.gov/. Links to parcel search and property maps. Search by GEO code, owner, or subdivision.

Petroleum County

Clerk and Recorder, PO Box 226, Winnett, MT 59087. 406-429-5311; fax-406-429-6328; 8AM-5PM

Index: Separate indices to search include deeds, mortgages, leases, conveys, liens, assignments, water logs. Record index not computerized. Office personnel or visitors may perform searches. Search fee $7.00 per name. Office can perform mortgage searches but will not search other real estate. Will search UCC records. Copy fee $.50 1st page; $.25 each add'l page. Cert fee- $2.00 per doc plus copy fee. Payee- Petroleum County Clerk and Recorder. Treasurer- 406-429-5551; Elections- 406-429-5311; Vital Records- 406-429-5311. **Property tax/Assessing**- PO Box 226, 301 E Main St, Courthouse, Winnett, MT 59087; 406-429-5551, assessor fax- 406-429-6328. (Appraiser/Auditor- 406-429-5231) hours- 8AM-N, 1PM-5PM No public terminal available. **Online** - Name search on the statewide Cadastral database free at http://gis.mt.gov.

Phillips County

Recorder, PO Box 360, Malta, MT 59538. Recording, R/E & UCC phone-406-654-2423; fax-406-654-2429; 8AM-5PM (MST)

Index: All in one. Records indexed on a public use terminal back to 0800. Office personnel or visitors may perform searches. Search fee $7.00 per name/ plus $.50 for the 1st page and $.25 for each add'l page of the same document. Office will not search real estate records. UCC search includes tax liens if requested. Copy fee $.50 1st page, $.25 each add'l. Cert fee- $2.00 per doc plus copy fee. Payee- Clerk & Recorder. Treasurer- 406-654-1742; Elections- 406-654-2423; Vital Records- 406-654-2423; Marriage License -406-654-1023. **Property tax/Assessing**- PO Box 1734, 314 2nd Ave W, Malta, MT 59538; 406-654-2123, assessor fax- 406-654-2335. No public terminal available in office. **Online access**- Statewide cadastral mapping site found at http://gis.mt.gov/. Links to parcel search and property maps. Search parcel by GEO code, owner, or subdivision.

Pondera County

Clerk and Recorder, 20 4th Ave SW, Conrad, MT 59425. 406-271-4000, R/E recording phone-406-271-4001; fax-406-271-4070; hours- 8AM-5PM. http://ponderacountymontana.org

Index: Separate indices to search include deeds, mortgages, UCCs, satisfactions, leases, liens, releases, Misc. Records indexed on a public use terminal back to 1997. Office personnel or visitors may perform searches. Search fee $7.00 per name. Copy fee $.25 per page. Cert fee- $2.00 per doc plus copy fee. Payee- Clerk & Recorder. Treasurer- 406-271-4015; Elections- 406-271-4000; Vital Records- 406-271-4026; Clerk of Court- 406-271-4026. **Property tax/Assessing**- 20 4th Ave SW, Conrad, MT 59425; 406-271-4015, assessor fax- 406-271-4070. (Appraiser/Auditor- 406-271-4012) No public terminal available in office. **Online access**- Statewide cadastral mapping site found at http://gis.mt.gov/. Links to parcel search and property maps. Search parcel by GEO code, owner, or subdivision.

Powder River County

Clerk and Recorder, PO Box 270, Broadus, MT 59317-0270. Recording, R/E & UCC phone-406-436-2361; fax-406-436-2151; 8AM-5PM (MST)

Index: Separate indices to search include deeds, mortgages, assignments, Misc & Filed, but these are now all consolidated on computer as of 1999. Records indexed on a public use terminal back to 1999. Only the public may search. Copy fee $.50 $.50 1st page, $.25 each add'l. Cert fee- $2.00 per cert plus copy fee. Payee- Powder River County Clerk and Recorder. Treasurer- 406-436-2444; Elections- 406-436-2361; Vital Records- 406-436-2361. **Property tax/Assessing**- PO Box 200, Clerk and Recorder, Powder River County Courthouse, Broadus, MT 59317; 406-436-2407. **Online** - Name search on the statewide Cadastral database free at http://gis.mt.gov.

Powell County

Clerk and Recorder, 409 Missouri Ave, Deer Lodge, MT 59722. 406-846-3680 x222; fax-406-846-3891; 8AM-5PM (MST)

Index: All in one. Records indexed on a public use terminal back to 100. Only the public may search. Copy fee $.25 per page. Cert fee- $2.50 per cert 1st page, plus copy fee. Payee- Powell County Clerk and Recorder. Treasurer- 406-846-3680 x226; Elections- 406-846-3680 x223; Vital Records- 406-846-3680 x222. **Property tax/Assessing**- 409 Missouri Ave, Deer Lodge, MT 59722; 406-846-3680 x230, assessor fax- 406-846-2784. (Appraiser/Auditor- 406-846-3680 x211) **Online access**- Statewide cadastral mapping site found at http://gis.mt.gov/. Links to parcel search and property maps. Search by GEO code, owner, or subdivision. (Incomplete tax records).

Prairie County

Clerk and Recorder, PO Box 125, Terry, MT 59349. 406-635-5575; fax-406-635-5576; 8AM-N; 1-5PM. www.prairie.mt.gov/pages/clerk_recorder.htm

Index: All in one. Records indexed on a public use terminal back to 04/2003. Office personnel or visitors may perform searches. Search fee $2.00 per name per year. Office will search real estate records. Will not search UCC records. Copy fee $.25 per page. $.50 per page for microfilm. Cert fee- $2.00 per doc plus copy fee. Payee- Clerk and Recorder. Treasurer- 406-635-5577; Elections- 406-635-5575; Vitals- 406-635-5575. **Property tax/Assessing**- PO Box 628, Terry, 59349; 406-635-5560. **Online access**- Name search statewide Cadastral database free at http://gis.mt.gov.

Ravalli County

Clerk and Recorder, 215 S 4th St, #C, Hamilton, MT 59840. 406-375-6555; fax-406-375-6554; 9AM-5PM. www.ravallicounty.mt.gov/clerkrecorder/default.htm

Index: All in one. Records indexed on a public use terminal back to 1988. Office personnel or visitors may perform searches. Search fee $7.00 per name. UCC search fee- $35.00 per hour. Copy fee $.50 1st page of doc $.25 each add'l. Cert fee- $2.50 per doc includes copy fees. Payee- Clerk & Recorder. **Online Property, Real Estate, Deed, Property records:** Access property tax and recorded document info at www.ravallicounty.mt.gov/clerkrecorder/access.htm. Signed Access Authorization Memo with the County required; must pay the annual fee, either $120 yearly for companies of 5 or less, or $400 for large companies. Call IT office for info and sign-up at 406-375-6700. **Other phones:** Treasurer- 406-375-6600; Elections- 406-375-6550; Vital Records- 406-375-6555; Clerk of Court- 406-375-6710. **Property tax/Assessing**- 406-375-6585. (Appraiser/Auditor- 406-375-2710) **Online access**- Name search on the statewide Cadastral database free at http://gis.mt.gov. Access property tax and recorded document info at www.ravallicounty.mt.gov/clerkrecorder/access.htm. Signed Access Authorization Memo with the County required; must pay the annual fee. Call IT office for info and sign-up at 406-375-6700.

Richland County

Clerk and Recorder, 201 W Main St, Sidney, MT 59270. Recording, R/E & UCC phone-406-433-1708; fax-406-433-3731; 8AM-5PM www.richland.org

Index: Separate indexes to search include deeds, mortgages, misc, tracking indexes, town. Records indexed on computer back to 6/03. Only the public may search. Copy fee $.50 per page self serve; $.25 if the lucky copy machine used. Will fax document $1.00 per page. Cert fee- $2.00 per doc plus copy fee. Payee- Richland County Clerk and Recorder. Treasurer- 406-433-1707; Elections- 406-433-1708; Vitals- 406-433-1708. **Property tax/Assessing**- 201 W Main St, Sidney, MT 59270; 406-433-1203, assessor fax- 406-433-6837. (Appraiser/Auditor- 406-433-2850) **Online access**- Name search on the statewide Cadastral database free at http://gis.mt.gov.

Roosevelt County

Clerk and Recorder, 400 2nd Ave S, Wolf Point, MT 59201. Recording, R/E & UCC phone-406-653-6250; fax-406-653-6289; 8AM-5PM.

Index: Separate indices to search include tract, ownership. Records indexed on computer back to 10/95. Office will perform a limited UCC search but public must search other records themselves. UCC or tax lien search per debtor name- $7.00. Copy fee $.50

per page. Cert fee- $2.00 per doc plus copy fee. Payee- Clerk & Recorder. Treasurer- 406-653-6239; Elections- 406-653-6229; Vital Records- 406-653-6252; 406-653-6233. **Property tax/Assessing-** 400 2nd Ave S, Wolf Point, MT 59201; 406-653-6256. (Appraiser - 406-653-6257) **Online-** Search statewide cadastral website free at http://gis.doa.mt.gov/

Rosebud County

Clerk and Recorder, PO Box 47, Forsyth, MT 59327. 406-346-2251; fax-406-346-7551; 8AM-5PM.
Index: All in one. Records indexed on a public use terminal back to 11/1993. Only the public may search. Copy fee $.50 1st page, $.25 each add'l. Cert fee- $2.00 per doc plus copy fee. Payee- Rosebud County. Treasurer- 406-346-7661; Elections- 406-346-7318; Vital Records- 406-444-4228. **Property tax/ Assessing-** 1200 Main St, PO Box 66, Forsyth, MT 59327; 406-346-2516, assessor fax- 406-346-7551. (Appraiser/Auditor- 406-346-2516) **Online access-** Name search on the statewide Cadastral database free at http://gis.mt.gov.

Sanders County

Clerk and Recorder, PO Box 519, Thompson Falls, MT 59873. Recording, R/E & UCC phone-406-827-6922; fax-406-827-6970; 8AM-5PM (MST) www.sanderscounty.mt.gov
Index: All in one. Records indexed on a public use terminal back to 1991. Office will perform a UCC search but public must search other records themselves. Search fee $7.00. Copy fee $.25 per page. Cert fee- $2.00 per doc plus copy fee. Payee- Sanders County Clerk. Bulk data available for purchase, web dox & web tax, contact Jennine Robbins. Treasurer- 406-827-6924; Elections- 406-827-6922; Vital Records- 406-827-6922. **Property tax/Assessing-** PO Box 267, Thompson Falls, MT 59873; 406-827-6932, assessor fax- 406-827-0372. (Appraiser/Auditor- 406-827-6932) **Online access-** Name search on the statewide Cadastral database free at http://gis.mt.gov.

Sheridan County

Clerk and Recorder, 100 W Laurel Ave, Plentywood, MT 59254. 406-765-3403; fax-406-765-2609; 8AM-5PM. www.co.sheridan.mt.us
Index: All in one. Records indexed on computer back to 1993. Only the public may search. Copy fee $.25 per page. Cert fee- $2.00 per doc plus copy fee. Payee- Sheridan County Clerk & Recorder. Treasurer- 406-765-3414; Elections- 406-765-3403; Vital Records- 406-765-3403. **Property tax/ Assessing-** 100 W Laurel Ave, Plentywood, MT 59254; 406-765-2291, assessor fax- 406-765-3492. (Appraiser/Auditor- 406-765-2291) **Online access-** Search the statewide cadastral mapping site free at http://gis.doa.mt.gov/. Also, access the parcel look-ups page at http://gis.doa.state.mt.us/index.html.

Silver Bow County

Clerk and Recorder, 155 W Granite St, #208, Butte, MT 59701. 406-497-6335, R/E recording phone-406-497-6338, UCC phone-406-497-6339; fax-406-497-6328; 8AM-5PM (MST) www.co.silverbow.mt.us/
Index: Indexes- tax liens, UCC, notice of attachments, mining claim, misc. lease. Records indexed on a public use terminal back to 1996. Only the public may search. Copy fee $.50 1st page, $.25 each add'l. Cert fee- $2.00 per doc plus copy fee. Payee- Clerk and Recorder. Treasurer- 406-497-6300; Elections- 406-497-6344; Vital Records- 406-497-6340. **Property tax/Assessing-** 155 W Granite St, #203, Butte, MT 59701; 406-497-6290, assessor fax- 406-496-4331. No public use computer in office. **Online-** Name search statewide Cadastral data at http://gis.mt.gov. Search by owner name and GEO code.

Stillwater County

Clerk and Recorder, PO Box 149, Columbus, MT 59019. 406-322-8000; fax-406-322-8007; 8AM-5PM http://co.stillwater.mt.us
Index: All in one. Records indexed on a public use terminal back to 1997. Office will perform a UCC search (for a fee), but public must search other records themselves. Copy fee $.50 1st page, $.25 each add'l page. Cert fee- $2.00 per doc plus copy fee. Payee- Stillwater County Clerk and Recorder. Treasurer- 406-322-8020; Elections- 406-322-8000; Vital Records- 406-322-8000. **Property tax/Assessing-** 400 3rd Ave N, PO Box 359, Columbus, MT 59019; 406-322-8015, assessor fax- 406-322-8009. (Appraiser/Auditor- 406-322-8015) **Online access-** Name search on the statewide Cadastral database free at http://gis.mt.gov.

Sweet Grass County

Clerk and Recorder, PO Box 888, Big Timber, MT 59011. 406-932-5152; 8AM-5PM.
Index: Separate indices to search include deeds, mortgages, satisfactions, misc. Records indexed on computer back to 1999. Only the public may search. Copy fee $.25 per page. Cert fee- $2.50 1st page; $.25 each add'l plus copy fee. Payee- Sweet Grass County. Deed data available for purchase on CD; contact Sherry Bjorndal. Treasurer- 406-932-5151; Elections- 406-932-5152; Vital Records- 406-932-5152. **Property tax/Assessing-** PO Box 888, 200 W 1st Ave, Big Timber, MT 59011; 406-932-5149. (Appraiser/Auditor- 406-932-5149) hours- 8AM-3PM Public access computer in treasurer's office, 8-5pm. **Online access-** Name search on the statewide Cadastral database free at http://gis.mt.gov.

Teton County

Clerk and Recorder, PO Box 610, Choteau, MT 59422. Recording, R/E & UCC phone-406-466-2693; fax-406-466-3244; 8AM-5PM. www.tetoncomt.org
Index: All in one. Records indexed on a public use terminal back to 2000. Only the public may search. Copy fee $.50 1st page; $.25 each add'l. Cert fee- $2.50 per doc plus copy fee. Treasurer- 406-466-2694; Elections- 406-466-2693; Vital Records- 406-466-2693. **Property tax/Assessing-** 101 S Main, Courthouse, PO Box 616, Choteau, MT 59422; 406-466-2908, assessor fax- 406-466-5820. (Appraiser/Auditor- 406-466-2908) **Online access-** Name search on the statewide Cadastral database free at http://gis.mt.gov.

Toole County

Clerk and Recorder, 226 1st St S, Shelby, MT 59474. Recording, R/E & UCC phone-406-424-8300; fax-406-424-8301; 8AM-5PM.
Index: All in one. Records indexed on a public use terminal back to 1995. Only the public may search. Copy fee $.50 per page. Cert fee- $2.00 per doc includes copy fee. Treasurer- 406-424-8320; Elections- 406-424-8300; Vital Records- 406-424-8300. **Property tax/Assessing-** 226 1st St S, Ste 206, Shelby, MT 59474; 406-424-8370, assessor fax- 406-424-8371. (Appraiser/Auditor- 406-424-8370) **Online access-** Name search on the statewide Cadastral database free at http://gis.mt.gov.

Treasure County

Clerk and Recorder, PO Box 392, Hysham, MT 59038. 406-342-5547; fax-406-342-5547; 8AM-N,1-5PM (MST)
Index: Separate indices to search include grantor/grantee, misc book, deed book, tract index. Record index not computerized. Office personnel or visitors may perform searches. Search fee $7.00 per name. Office will search real estate records. Will search UCC records. Copy fee $.50 1st page; $.25 each add'l. Cert fee- $2.00 per doc plus copy fee. Payee- Treasure County Clerk and Recorder. Treasurer- 406-342-5545; Elections- 406-342-5547; Vital Records- 406-342-5547. **Property tax/Assessing-** 307 Rapelje Ave, PO Box 191, Hysham, MT 59038; 406-342-5540, assessor fax- 406-342-5445. (Appraiser/Auditor- 406-342-5540) hours- Varies **Online access-** Name search on the statewide Cadastral database free at http://gis.mt.gov.

Valley County

Clerk and Recorder, 501 Court Sq #2, Glasgow, MT 59230. Recording, R/E & UCC phone-406-228-6220; fax-406-228-9027; 8AM-5PM (MST)
Index: Separate indices to search include as of 5/1/2005 by doc number & refer to instrument type; before 5/1/2005-deeds, mortgages, real estate, misc, liens, misc numbers, misc records. Records indexed on a public use terminal back to 99. Office personnel or visitors may perform searches. Search fee $7.00 per name. Office will only assist with real estate record searches. UCC search up to 5 years previous only. Copy fee $.50 per page. Cert fee- $2.50 1st page, $.25 each add'l page plus copy fee. Payee- Clerk and Recorder. Treasurer- 406-228-6231; Elections- 406-228-6220; Vital Records- 406-228-6268; Dept of Revenue- 406-228-6233. **Property tax/Assessing-** 501 Courthouse Sq, #7, Glasgow, MT 59230; 406-228-6250, fax- 406-228-9027. (Appraiser/Auditor- 406-228-6250) **Online access-** Name search on the statewide Cadastral database free at http://gis.mt.gov.

Wheatland County

Clerk and Recorder, PO Box 1903, Harlowton, MT 59036. 406-632-4891; fax-406-632-4880; 8AM-N, 1-5PM (MST)
Index: Separate indices to search include deed, mortgage, assignments, lease, contract, military, misc. Record index not computerized. Only the public may search. Will not search UCC records. Copy fee $.50 1st page; $.25 each add'l. Cert fee- $2.00 per doc includes copy fee. Payee- County Clerk & Recorder. Treasurer- 406-632-4892; Elections- 406-632-4891; Vital Records- 406-632-4891. **Property tax/Assessing-** 201 A Ave NW, Harlowton, MT 59036; 406-632-4894, assessor fax- 406-632-4880. **Online access-** Name search on the statewide Cadastral database free at http://gis.mt.gov.

Wibaux County

Clerk and Recorder, PO Box 199, Wibaux, MT 59353-0199. Recording, R/E & UCC phone-406-796-2481; fax-406-796-2625; 8AM-5PM (MST)
Index: Separate indices to search. Record index not computerized. Only the public may search. Copy fee $.10 per page. Cert fee- $2.00 per doc and $.25 each add'l page plus copy fee. Payee- Clerk & Recorder. Treasurer- 406-796-2482; Elections- 406-796-2481; Vital Records- 406-796-2481. **Property tax/Assessing-** PO Box 197, 203 S Wilbaux, Wibaux, MT 59353-0197; 406-796-2483, assessor fax- 406-796-2625. **Online access-** Name search on the statewide Cadastral database free at http://gis.mt.gov.

Yellowstone County

Clerk and Recorder, PO Box 35001, Billings, MT 59107. Recording, R/E & UCC phone-406-256-2785; fax-406-256-2736; hours- 8AM-5PM (MST) www.co.yellowstone.mt.us/clerk/
Index: All in one. Records indexed on a public use terminal back to 98. Office personnel or visitors may perform searches. Search fee $.50 per year per debtor. Office will not search real estate records. UCC search per debtor name- $7.00. Copy fee $.50 per page. Cert fee- $2.00 per cert plus copy fee. Payee- Yellowstone County Clerk and Recorder. **Online Real Estate, Grantor/Grantee, Deed, Lien, Mortgage records:** Access county clerk & recorder documents free at https://secure.co.yellowstone.mt.us/clerk/. Click on Free Service Search or you may register and login for full data for a fee. **Other phones:** Treasurer- 406-256-2785; Elections- 406-256-2743; Vital Records- 406-256-2788. **Property tax/Assessing-** 175 N 27th St, Rm 108, PO Box 35010, Billings, MT 59107; 406-256-2802, assessor fax- 406-896-4070. www.co.yellowstone.mt.gov/gis/index.asp **Online access-** Access tax assessor records free at www.co.yellowstone.mt.us/gis/. Also, name search on the statewide Cadastral database free at http://gis.mt.gov.

Montana County Locator

You will usually be able to find the city name in the City/County Cross Reference below. In that case, it is a simple matter to determine the county from the cross reference. However, only the official US Postal Service city names are included in this index. There are an additional 40,000 place names that people use in their addresses. Therefore, we have also included a ZIP/City Cross Reference immediately following the City/County Cross Reference.

If you know the ZIP Code but the city name does not appear in the City/County Cross Reference index, look up the ZIP Code in the ZIP/City Cross Reference, find the city name, then look up the city name in the City/County Cross Reference. For example, you want to know the county for an address of Menands, NY 12204. There is no "Menands" in the City/County Cross Reference. The ZIP/City Cross Reference shows that ZIP Codes 12201-12288 are for the city of Albany. Looking back in the City/County Cross Reference, Albany is in Albany County.

Montana City/County Cross Reference

ABSAROKEE Stillwater
ACTON Yellowstone
ALBERTON (59820) Missoula(58), Mineral(41)
ALDER Madison
ALZADA Carter
ANACONDA (59711) Deer Lodge(87), Granite(9), Silver Bow(2)
ANGELA (59312) Garfield(66), Rosebud(33)
ANTELOPE Sheridan
ARLEE (59821) Lake(69), Missoula(28), Sanders(2)
ASHLAND Rosebud
AUGUSTA Lewis and Clark
AVON Powell
BABB Glacier
BAINVILLE Roosevelt
BAKER Fallon
BALLANTINE Yellowstone
BASIN Jefferson
BEARCREEK Carbon
BELFRY Carbon
BELGRADE Gallatin
BELT Cascade
BIDDLE Powder River
BIG ARM Lake
BIG SANDY Chouteau
BIG SKY Gallatin
BIG TIMBER Sweet Grass
BIGFORK (59911) Flathead(57), Lake(42)
BIGHORN Treasure
BILLINGS Yellowstone
BIRNEY Rosebud
BLACK EAGLE Cascade
BLOOMFIELD Dawson
BONNER Missoula
BOULDER Jefferson
BOX ELDER Hill
BOYD Carbon
BOYES Carter
BOZEMAN Gallatin
BRADY (59416) Pondera(55), Chouteau(39), Teton(4), Liberty(1)
BRIDGER Carbon
BROADUS Powder River
BROADVIEW (59015) Yellowstone(67), Musselshell(20), Stillwater(11)
BROCKTON Roosevelt
BROCKWAY (59214) McCone(86), Prairie(13)
BROWNING Glacier
BRUSETT Garfield
BUFFALO Fergus
BUSBY Big Horn
BUTTE Silver Bow
BYNUM Teton
CAMERON Madison
CANYON CREEK Lewis and Clark
CAPITOL Carter
CARDWELL (59721) Madison(53), Jefferson(46)
CARTER Chouteau
CASCADE Cascade
CAT CREEK Petroleum
CHARLO Lake
CHESTER Liberty
CHINOOK (59523) Blaine(91), Hill(8)
CHOTEAU Teton
CIRCLE (59215) McCone(93), Dawson(6)
CLANCY Jefferson
CLINTON (59825) Missoula(84), Granite(15)
CLYDE PARK Park
COFFEE CREEK Fergus
COHAGEN Garfield
COLSTRIP Rosebud
COLUMBIA FALLS Flathead
COLUMBUS Stillwater
CONDON Missoula
CONNER Ravalli
CONRAD (59425) Pondera(98), Teton(1)
COOKE CITY Park
CORAM Flathead
CORVALLIS Ravalli
CORWIN SPRINGS Park
CRANE Richland
CROW AGENCY Big Horn
CULBERTSON Roosevelt
CUSTER Yellowstone
CUT BANK Glacier
DAGMAR Sheridan
DARBY Ravalli
DAYTON (59914) Flathead(69), Lake(30)
DE BORGIA Mineral
DECKER Big Horn
DEER LODGE (59722) Powell(92), Deer Lodge(7)
DELL Beaverhead
DENTON Fergus
DILLON Beaverhead
DIVIDE Silver Bow
DIXON Sanders
DODSON (59524) Phillips(88), Blaine(11)
DRUMMOND Granite
DUPUYER Pondera
DUTTON Teton
EAST GLACIER PARK Glacier
EAST HELENA (59635) Lewis and Clark(93), Jefferson(3), Broadwater(3)
EDGAR Carbon
EKALAKA Carter
ELLISTON Powell
ELMO Lake
EMIGRANT Park
ENNIS Madison
ESSEX Flathead
ETHRIDGE Toole
EUREKA Lincoln
FAIRFIELD Teton
FAIRVIEW Richland
FALLON Prairie
FISHTAIL Stillwater
FLAXVILLE Daniels
FLORENCE (59833) Ravalli(64), Missoula(35)
FLOWEREE (59440) Chouteau(73), Cascade(26)
FORESTGROVE Fergus
FORSYTH Rosebud
FORT BENTON Chouteau
FORT HARRISON Lewis and Clark
FORT PECK Valley
FORT SHAW (59443) Cascade(92), Teton(7)
FORTINE Lincoln
FOUR BUTTES Daniels
FRAZER Valley
FRENCHTOWN Missoula
FROID (59226) Roosevelt(78), Sheridan(21)
FROMBERG Carbon
GALATA (59444) Toole(76), Liberty(23)
GALLATIN GATEWAY Gallatin
GARDINER Park
GARNEILL Fergus
GARRISON Powell
GARRYOWEN Big Horn
GERALDINE Chouteau
GEYSER (59447) Judith Basin(96), Chouteau(4)
GILDFORD Hill
GLASGOW Valley
GLEN Beaverhead
GLENDIVE Dawson
GLENTANA Valley
GOLD CREEK Powell
GRANTSDALE Ravalli
GRASS RANGE Fergus
GREAT FALLS Cascade
GREENOUGH Missoula
GREYCLIFF Sweet Grass
HALL Granite
HAMILTON Ravalli
HAMMOND Carter
HARDIN Big Horn
HARLEM Blaine
HARLOWTON Wheatland
HARRISON Madison
HATHAWAY Rosebud
HAUGAN Mineral
HAVRE Hill
HAYS Blaine
HEART BUTTE Pondera
HELENA Lewis and Clark
HELMVILLE Powell
HERON Sanders
HIGHWOOD Chouteau
HILGER Fergus
HINGHAM Hill
HINSDALE Valley
HOBSON Judith Basin
HOGELAND Blaine
HOMESTEAD (59242) Sheridan(83), Roosevelt(16)
HOT SPRINGS (59845) Sanders(86), Lake(9), Flathead(4)
HUNGRY HORSE Flathead
HUNTLEY (59037) Yellowstone(98), Big Horn(1)
HUSON Missoula
HYSHAM Treasure
INGOMAR Rosebud
INVERNESS (59530) Hill(97), Liberty(2)
ISMAY (59336) Custer(42), Fallon(40), Prairie(11), Carter(5)
JACKSON Beaverhead
JEFFERSON CITY Jefferson
JOLIET Carbon
JOPLIN (59531) Liberty(84), Hill(15)
JORDAN Garfield
JUDITH GAP (59453) Fergus(55), Wheatland(44)
KALISPELL Flathead
KEVIN Toole
KILA Flathead
KINSEY Custer
KREMLIN Hill
LAKE MC DONALD Flathead
LAKESIDE (59922) Flathead(73), Lake(26)
LAMBERT Richland
LAME DEER Rosebud
LARSLAN Valley
LAUREL (59044) Yellowstone(97), Carbon(2)
LAVINA Golden Valley
LEDGER (59456) Pondera(52), Liberty(31), Toole(15)
LEWISTOWN Fergus
LIBBY Lincoln
LIMA Beaverhead
LINCOLN (59639) Powell(73), Lewis and Clark(26)
LINDSAY (59339) Dawson(92), Prairie(7)
LIVINGSTON Park
LLOYD Blaine
LODGE GRASS Big Horn
LOLO Missoula
LOMA Chouteau
LONEPINE Sanders
LORING Phillips
LOTHAIR Liberty
LUTHER Carbon
MALMSTROM A F B Cascade
MALTA Phillips
MANHATTAN Gallatin
MARION Flathead
MARTIN CITY Flathead
MARTINSDALE Meagher
MARYSVILLE Lewis and Clark
MC ALLISTER Madison
MC CABE Roosevelt
MC LEOD (59052) Sweet Grass(80), Park(19)
MEDICINE LAKE Sheridan
MELROSE Silver Bow
MELSTONE Musselshell
MELVILLE Sweet Grass
MILDRED Prairie
MILES CITY Custer
MILL IRON Carter

MILLTOWN Missoula
MISSOULA Missoula
MOCCASIN Judith Basin
MOLT (59057) Yellowstone(72), Stillwater(27)
MONARCH Cascade
MOORE Fergus
MOSBY Garfield
MUSSELSHELL Musselshell
NASHUA Valley
NEIHART Cascade
NIARADA (59852) Sanders(85), Flathead(14)
NORRIS Madison
NOXON Sanders
NYE Stillwater
OILMONT Toole
OLIVE Powder River
OLNEY Flathead
OPHEIM Valley
OTTER (59062) Powder River(86), Rosebud(13)
OUTLOOK Sheridan
OVANDO Powell
PABLO Lake
PARADISE Sanders
PARK CITY Stillwater
PEERLESS Daniels
PENDROY Teton
PHILIPSBURG Granite
PINESDALE Ravalli
PLAINS Sanders
PLENTYWOOD Sheridan
PLEVNA Fallon
POLARIS Beaverhead
POLEBRIDGE Flathead
POLSON Lake
POMPEYS PILLAR Yellowstone
PONY Madison
POPLAR Roosevelt
POWDERVILLE Powder River
POWER (59468) Teton(83), Cascade(15)
PRAY Park
PROCTOR Lake
PRYOR Big Horn
RADERSBURG Broadwater
RAMSAY Silver Bow
RAPELJE Stillwater
RAVALLI Lake
RAYMOND Sheridan
RAYNESFORD Judith Basin
RED LODGE Carbon
REDSTONE Sheridan
REED POINT (59069) Stillwater(71), Sweet Grass(28)
REEDPOINT (59069) Stillwater(71), Sweet Grass(28)
RESERVE (59258) Sheridan(88), Roosevelt(11)
REXFORD Lincoln
RICHEY Dawson
RICHLAND Valley
RINGLING Meagher
ROBERTS Carbon
ROLLINS (59931) Flathead(89), Lake(10)
RONAN Lake
ROSCOE Carbon
ROSEBUD (59347) Rosebud(97), Custer(2)
ROUNDUP Musselshell
ROY Fergus
RUDYARD (59540) Hill(86), Chouteau(13)
RYEGATE (59074) Golden Valley(96), Stillwater(3)
SACO Phillips
SAINT IGNATIUS Lake
SAINT MARIE Valley
SAINT REGIS Mineral
SAINT XAVIER Big Horn
SALTESE Mineral
SAND COULEE Cascade
SAND SPRINGS Garfield
SANDERS Treasure
SANTA RITA Glacier
SAVAGE (59262) Richland(60), Dawson(39)
SCOBEY Daniels
SEELEY LAKE Missoula
SHAWMUT Wheatland
SHELBY Toole
SHEPHERD Yellowstone
SHERIDAN Madison
SIDNEY Richland
SILVER GATE Park
SILVER STAR Madison
SIMMS Cascade
SOMERS Flathead
SONNETTE Powder River
SPRINGDALE Park
STANFORD Judith Basin
STEVENSVILLE Ravalli
STOCKETT Cascade
STRYKER Lincoln
SULA Ravalli
SUMATRA Rosebud
SUN RIVER Cascade
SUNBURST Toole
SUPERIOR Mineral
SWEET GRASS Toole
SWEETGRASS Toole
TEIGEN (59084) Petroleum(80), Fergus(20)
TERRY (59349) Prairie(86), Custer(13)
THOMPSON FALLS Sanders
THREE FORKS (59752) Gallatin(88), Broadwater(10)
TOSTON Broadwater
TOWNSEND Broadwater
TREGO Lincoln
TROUT CREEK Sanders
TURNER Blaine
TWIN BRIDGES Madison
TWO DOT Wheatland
TWODOT Wheatland
ULM Cascade
VALIER Pondera
VANDALIA Valley
VAUGHN (59487) Cascade(93), Teton(6)
VICTOR Ravalli
VIDA McCone
VIRGINIA CITY Madison
VOLBORG Custer
WARM SPRINGS Deer Lodge
WARMSPRINGS Deer Lodge
WEST GLACIER Flathead
WEST YELLOWSTONE Gallatin
WESTBY Sheridan
WHITE SULPHUR SPRINGS Meagher
WHITEFISH Flathead
WHITEHALL (59759) Jefferson(84), Madison(15)
WHITETAIL Daniels
WHITEWATER Phillips
WHITLASH Liberty
WIBAUX Wibaux
WILLARD Fallon
WILLOW CREEK Gallatin
WILSALL (59086) Park(79), Gallatin(19), Meagher(1)
WINIFRED Fergus
WINNETT Petroleum
WINSTON Broadwater
WISDOM Beaverhead
WISE RIVER (59762) Beaverhead(53), Deer Lodge(46)
WOLF CREEK Lewis and Clark
WOLF POINT Roosevelt
WORDEN Yellowstone
WYOLA Big Horn
YELLOWTAIL Big Horn
ZORTMAN Phillips
ZURICH Blaine

Montana ZIP/City Cross Reference

59001-59001 ABSAROKEE
59002-59002 ACTON
59003-59004 ASHLAND
59006-59006 BALLANTINE
59007-59007 BEARCREEK
59008-59008 BELFRY
59010-59010 BIGHORN
59011-59011 BIG TIMBER
59012-59012 BIRNEY
59013-59013 BOYD
59014-59014 BRIDGER
59015-59015 BROADVIEW
59016-59016 BUSBY
59017-59017 CAT CREEK
59018-59018 CLYDE PARK
59019-59019 COLUMBUS
59020-59020 COOKE CITY
59021-59021 CORWIN SPRINGS
59022-59022 CROW AGENCY
59024-59024 CUSTER
59025-59025 DECKER
59026-59026 EDGAR
59027-59027 EMIGRANT
59028-59028 FISHTAIL
59029-59029 FROMBERG
59030-59030 GARDINER
59031-59031 GARRYOWEN
59032-59032 GRASS RANGE
59033-59033 GREYCLIFF
59034-59034 HARDIN
59035-59035 YELLOWTAIL
59036-59036 HARLOWTON
59037-59037 HUNTLEY
59038-59038 HYSHAM
59039-59039 INGOMAR
59041-59041 JOLIET
59043-59043 LAME DEER
59044-59044 LAUREL
59046-59046 LAVINA
59047-59047 LIVINGSTON
59050-59050 LODGE GRASS
59051-59051 LUTHER
59052-59052 MC LEOD
59053-59053 MARTINSDALE
59054-59054 MELSTONE
59055-59055 MELVILLE
59057-59057 MOLT
59058-59058 MOSBY
59059-59059 MUSSELSHELL
59061-59061 NYE
59062-59062 OTTER
59063-59063 PARK CITY
59064-59064 POMPEYS PILLAR
59065-59065 PRAY
59066-59066 PRYOR
59067-59067 RAPELJE
59068-59068 RED LODGE
59069-59069 REEDPOINT
59069-59069 REED POINT
59070-59070 ROBERTS
59071-59071 ROSCOE
59072-59073 ROUNDUP
59074-59074 RYEGATE
59075-59075 SAINT XAVIER
59076-59076 SANDERS
59077-59077 SAND SPRINGS
59078-59078 SHAWMUT
59079-59079 SHEPHERD
59080-59080 JOLIET
59081-59081 SILVER GATE
59082-59082 SPRINGDALE
59083-59083 SUMATRA
59084-59084 TEIGEN
59085-59085 TWODOT
59085-59085 TWO DOT
59086-59086 WILSALL
59087-59087 WINNETT
59088-59088 WORDEN
59089-59089 WYOLA
59100-59117 BILLINGS
59201-59201 WOLF POINT
59211-59211 ANTELOPE
59212-59212 BAINVILLE
59213-59213 BROCKTON
59214-59214 BROCKWAY
59215-59215 CIRCLE
59217-59217 CRANE
59218-59218 CULBERTSON
59219-59219 DAGMAR
59221-59221 FAIRVIEW
59222-59222 FLAXVILLE
59223-59223 FORT PECK
59224-59224 FOUR BUTTES
59225-59225 FRAZER
59226-59226 FROID
59230-59230 GLASGOW
59231-59231 SAINT MARIE
59240-59240 GLENTANA
59241-59241 HINSDALE
59242-59242 HOMESTEAD
59243-59243 LAMBERT
59244-59244 LARSLAN
59245-59245 MC CABE
59247-59247 MEDICINE LAKE
59248-59248 NASHUA
59250-59250 OPHEIM
59252-59252 OUTLOOK
59253-59253 PEERLESS
59254-59254 PLENTYWOOD
59255-59255 POPLAR
59256-59256 RAYMOND
59257-59257 REDSTONE
59258-59258 RESERVE
59259-59259 RICHEY
59260-59260 RICHLAND
59261-59261 SACO
59262-59262 SAVAGE
59263-59263 SCOBEY
59270-59270 SIDNEY
59273-59273 VANDALIA
59274-59274 VIDA
59275-59275 WESTBY
59276-59276 WHITETAIL
59301-59301 MILES CITY
59311-59311 ALZADA
59312-59312 ANGELA
59313-59313 BAKER
59314-59314 BIDDLE
59315-59315 BLOOMFIELD
59316-59316 BOYES
59317-59317 BROADUS
59318-59318 BRUSETT
59319-59319 CAPITOL
59322-59322 COHAGEN
59323-59323 COLSTRIP
59324-59324 EKALAKA
59326-59326 FALLON
59327-59327 FORSYTH
59330-59330 GLENDIVE
59332-59332 HAMMOND
59333-59333 HATHAWAY
59336-59336 ISMAY
59337-59337 JORDAN
59338-59338 KINSEY

59339-59339 LINDSAY
59341-59341 MILDRED
59342-59342 MILL IRON
59343-59343 OLIVE
59344-59344 PLEVNA
59345-59345 POWDERVILLE
59347-59347 ROSEBUD
59348-59348 SONNETTE
59349-59349 TERRY
59351-59351 VOLBORG
59353-59353 WIBAUX
59354-59354 WILLARD
59401-59401 GREAT FALLS
59402-59402 MALMSTROM A F B
59403-59406 GREAT FALLS
59410-59410 AUGUSTA
59411-59411 BABB
59412-59412 BELT
59414-59414 BLACK EAGLE
59416-59416 BRADY
59417-59417 BROWNING
59418-59418 BUFFALO
59419-59419 BYNUM
59420-59420 CARTER
59421-59421 CASCADE
59422-59422 CHOTEAU
59424-59424 COFFEE CREEK
59425-59425 CONRAD
59427-59427 CUT BANK
59430-59430 DENTON
59432-59432 DUPUYER
59433-59433 DUTTON
59434-59434 EAST GLACIER PARK
59435-59435 ETHRIDGE
59436-59436 FAIRFIELD
59440-59440 FLOWEREE
59441-59441 FORESTGROVE
59442-59442 FORT BENTON
59443-59443 FORT SHAW
59444-59444 GALATA
59445-59445 GARNEILL
59446-59446 GERALDINE
59447-59447 GEYSER
59448-59448 HEART BUTTE
59450-59450 HIGHWOOD
59451-59451 HILGER
59452-59452 HOBSON
59453-59453 JUDITH GAP
59454-59454 KEVIN
59456-59456 LEDGER
59457-59457 LEWISTOWN
59460-59460 LOMA
59461-59461 LOTHAIR
59462-59462 MOCCASIN
59463-59463 MONARCH
59464-59464 MOORE
59465-59465 NEIHART
59466-59466 OILMONT
59467-59467 PENDROY
59468-59468 POWER
59469-59469 RAYNESFORD
59471-59471 ROY
59472-59472 SAND COULEE
59473-59473 SANTA RITA
59474-59474 SHELBY
59477-59477 SIMMS
59479-59479 STANFORD
59480-59480 STOCKETT
59482-59482 SUNBURST
59483-59483 SUN RIVER
59484-59484 SWEETGRASS
59484-59484 SWEET GRASS
59485-59485 ULM
59486-59486 VALIER
59487-59487 VAUGHN
59489-59489 WINIFRED
59501-59501 HAVRE
59520-59520 BIG SANDY
59521-59521 BOX ELDER
59522-59522 CHESTER
59523-59523 CHINOOK
59524-59524 DODSON
59525-59525 GILDFORD
59526-59526 HARLEM
59527-59527 HAYS
59528-59528 HINGHAM
59529-59529 HOGELAND
59530-59530 INVERNESS
59531-59531 JOPLIN
59532-59532 KREMLIN
59535-59535 LLOYD
59537-59537 LORING
59538-59538 MALTA
59540-59540 RUDYARD
59542-59542 TURNER
59544-59544 WHITEWATER
59545-59545 WHITLASH
59546-59546 ZORTMAN
59547-59547 ZURICH
59601-59626 HELENA
59631-59631 BASIN
59632-59632 BOULDER
59633-59633 CANYON CREEK
59634-59634 CLANCY
59635-59635 EAST HELENA
59636-59636 FORT HARRISON
59638-59638 JEFFERSON CITY
59639-59639 LINCOLN
59640-59640 MARYSVILLE
59641-59641 RADERSBURG
59642-59642 RINGLING
59643-59643 TOSTON
59644-59644 TOWNSEND
59645-59645 WHITE SULPHUR SPRINGS
59647-59647 WINSTON
59648-59648 WOLF CREEK
59701-59707 BUTTE
59710-59710 ALDER
59711-59711 ANACONDA
59713-59713 AVON
59714-59714 BELGRADE
59715-59715 BOZEMAN
59716-59716 BIG SKY
59717-59719 BOZEMAN
59720-59720 CAMERON
59721-59721 CARDWELL
59722-59722 DEER LODGE
59724-59724 DELL
59725-59725 DILLON
59727-59727 DIVIDE
59728-59728 ELLISTON
59729-59729 ENNIS
59730-59730 GALLATIN GATEWAY
59731-59731 GARRISON
59732-59732 GLEN
59733-59733 GOLD CREEK
59735-59735 HARRISON
59736-59736 JACKSON
59739-59739 LIMA
59740-59740 MC ALLISTER
59741-59741 MANHATTAN
59743-59743 MELROSE
59745-59745 NORRIS
59746-59746 POLARIS
59747-59747 PONY
59748-59748 RAMSAY
59749-59749 SHERIDAN
59750-59750 BUTTE
59751-59751 SILVER STAR
59752-59752 THREE FORKS
59754-59754 TWIN BRIDGES
59755-59755 VIRGINIA CITY
59756-59756 WARMSPRINGS
59756-59756 WARM SPRINGS
59758-59758 WEST YELLOWSTONE
59759-59759 WHITEHALL
59760-59760 WILLOW CREEK
59761-59761 WISDOM
59762-59762 WISE RIVER
59771-59773 BOZEMAN
59801-59812 MISSOULA
59820-59820 ALBERTON
59821-59821 ARLEE
59823-59823 BONNER
59824-59824 CHARLO
59825-59825 CLINTON
59826-59826 CONDON
59827-59827 CONNER
59828-59828 CORVALLIS
59829-59829 DARBY
59830-59830 DE BORGIA
59831-59831 DIXON
59832-59832 DRUMMOND
59833-59833 FLORENCE
59834-59834 FRENCHTOWN
59835-59835 GRANTSDALE
59836-59836 GREENOUGH
59837-59837 HALL
59840-59840 HAMILTON
59841-59841 PINESDALE
59842-59842 HAUGAN
59843-59843 HELMVILLE
59844-59844 HERON
59845-59845 HOT SPRINGS
59846-59846 HUSON
59847-59847 LOLO
59848-59848 LONEPINE
59851-59851 MILLTOWN
59852-59852 NIARADA
59853-59853 NOXON
59854-59854 OVANDO
59855-59855 PABLO
59856-59856 PARADISE
59858-59858 PHILIPSBURG
59859-59859 PLAINS
59860-59860 POLSON
59863-59863 RAVALLI
59864-59864 RONAN
59865-59865 SAINT IGNATIUS
59866-59866 SAINT REGIS
59867-59867 SALTESE
59868-59868 SEELEY LAKE
59870-59870 STEVENSVILLE
59871-59871 SULA
59872-59872 SUPERIOR
59873-59873 THOMPSON FALLS
59874-59874 TROUT CREEK
59875-59875 VICTOR
59901-59904 KALISPELL
59910-59910 BIG ARM
59911-59911 BIGFORK
59912-59912 COLUMBIA FALLS
59913-59913 CORAM
59914-59914 DAYTON
59915-59915 ELMO
59916-59916 ESSEX
59917-59917 EUREKA
59918-59918 FORTINE
59919-59919 HUNGRY HORSE
59920-59920 KILA
59921-59921 LAKE MC DONALD
59922-59922 LAKESIDE
59923-59923 LIBBY
59925-59925 MARION
59926-59926 MARTIN CITY
59927-59927 OLNEY
59928-59928 POLEBRIDGE
59929-59929 PROCTOR
59930-59930 REXFORD
59931-59931 ROLLINS
59932-59932 SOMERS
59933-59933 STRYKER
59934-59934 TREGO
59935-59935 TROY
59936-59936 WEST GLACIER
59937-59937 WHITEFISH

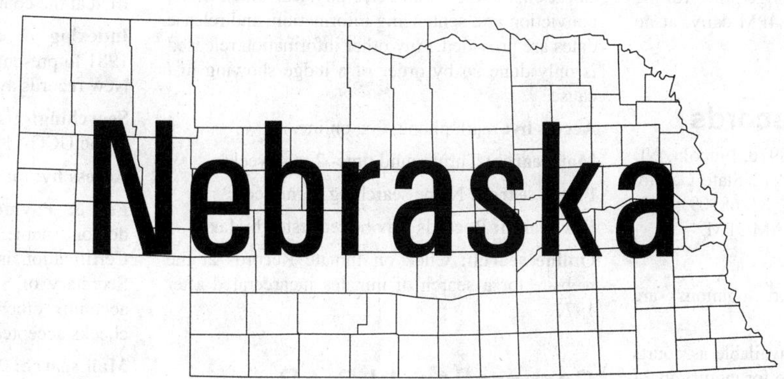

General Help Numbers:

Governor's Office

PO Box 94848 | 402-471-2244
Lincoln, NE 68509-4848 | Fax 402-471-6031
www.governor.nebraska.gov/ | 8AM-5PM

Attorney General's Office

2115 State Capitol | 402-471-2682
Lincoln, NE 68509 | Fax 402-471-3297
www.ago.state.ne.us/ | 8AM-5PM

Legislative Records

Clerk of Legislature Office
PO Box 94604 | 402-471-2271
Lincoln, NE 68509-4604 | Fax 402-471-2126
www.unicam.state.ne.us | 8AM-5PM

State Archives

Archives | 402-471-4771
PO Box 82554 | Fax 402-471-8922
Lincoln, NE 68501-2554 | 9:30AM-4:30PM M-F;
www.nebraskahistory.org | 8-5 SA; 1:30PM-5PM SU

State Specifics:

Capital: Lincoln
Lancaster County

Time Zone: CST*

* Nebraska's nineteen western-most counties are MST: They are: Arthur, Banner, Box Butte, Chase, Cherry, Cheyenne, Dawes, Deuel, Dundy, Garden, Grant, Hooker, Keith, Kimball, Morrill, Perkins, Scotts. Bluff, Sheridan, Sioux.

Number of Counties: 93

Population: 1,783,432

Web Site: www.nebraska.gov/

State Agencies

Criminal Records

Nebraska State Patrol, CID, PO Box 94907, Lincoln, NE 68509-4907 (Courier address- 233 S 10th St, Lincoln, NE 68508); 402-471-4545, Fax-402-479-4002; 8AM-5PM.
www.nsp.state.ne.us

Indexing & Storage: Records available from 1937 to present.62% of all arrests in database have final dispositions recorded, 57% for those arrests within last 5 years.

Searching: Include in request- full name, disposition, date of birth, SSN, sex, race. Fingerprints required for certain state occupation checks; this includes an FBI fingerprint search. State keeps record of requesters and will inform the person of record if asked. 100% of records are fingerprint-supported. Felonies are required to be submitted this agency, though not all misdemeanors are. Agency will refer you to the proper county. This data not released- juvenile records. Records without dispositions are not released, except if an arrest without disposition is less than one year old.

Access by: mail, fax, in person.

Fee & Payment: The search fee is $15.00 per name. Fee payee- Nebraska State Patrol. Prepayment required. Personal checks accepted, credit cards are not.

Mail search: Turnaround time- 2 to 5 days. SASE not required.

Fax search: Requests by fax are accepted, if pre-paid.

In person: They accept requests in person and turnaround is 15 minutes, but they will mail back the report if it is lengthy or incomplete (unless it is the requester's own report). Fingerprint rolling service is offered from 8AM to 4PM daily, at no charge.

Statewide Court Records

Court Administrator, PO Box 98910, Lincoln, NE 68509-8910 (Courier address- 1213 State Capitol Building, 1445 K Street, Lincoln, NE 68509); 402-471-3730, Fax- 402-471-2197; 8AM-5PM.

http://court.nol.org/

Appellate and Supreme Court opinions are available from the website.

Indexing & Storage: Records available as courts enter data. New records available for inquiry in 24 hours.

Online search: An online access subscription service is available for all Nebraska County Courts and all District Courts except Douglas County District Court (which has its own system). The system starts with a name search and resulting list gives full DOB. Then a click on the case for complete case details, all party listings, payments. Search for criminal, civil, probate, juvenile, and traffic. A onetime search is $15.00. But ongoing users can set up a subscription account with Nebraska.gov. There is a $50 annual, then record access is either $1.00 per record or a $300 flat rate per month. Other types of records are also available from this system, including motor vehicle and UCC. Go to www.nebraska.gov/faqs/justice/ or call 402-471-7810. Supreme Court opinions are available from http://court.nol.org/opinions/.

Sexual Offender Registry

Nebraska State Patrol, Sexual Offender Registry, PO Box 94907, Lincoln, NE 68509-4907 (Courier address- 1500 Nebraska Highway 2, Lincoln, NE 68502); 402-471-8647, Fax- 402-471-8496; 8AM-5PM. www.nsp.state.ne.us/sor/

The public is only granted access to sex offenders who are classified as high risk/Level 3 sex offenders. As of June 2007, there were over 2575 active registered sex offenders in the state of Nebraska.

Indexing & Storage: Records available from 1997 to present. New records available for inquiry in 24 hours or less.

Searching: This data not released- on low risk offenders.

Access by: phone, online.

Phone search: Limited searching by telephone.

Online search: A Level 3 sexual offender registry search is available at the website. The records may be searched by either ZIP Code, last name, city, or county. Search or review the entire list of names.

Incarceration Records

Nebraska Department of Correctional Services, Central Records Office, PO Box 94661, Lincoln, NE 68509-4661; 402-479-5273, Fax- 402-479-5913; 8AM-5PM. www.corrections.state.ne.us

Indexing & Storage: Records available on current and former inmates back to 1977. New records available for inquiry in 1 day.

Searching: Include in request- full name or DOC inmate #. The DOB and SSN number are helpful. To search online, only the name is needed. Location, DOC number, physical identifiers, conviction and sentencing information, and release dates are provided. Any other information released is only done so by order of a judge showing just cause.

Access by: mail, phone, fax, online.

Mail search: Turnaround time- 2 to 4 weeks.

Phone search: Name searching permitted.

Fax search: Records may be requested by fax.

Online search: Click on Inmate Records at the website for a search of inmates incarcerated after 1977.

Corporation, LLC, LP, Trade Names, Trademarks/Servicemarks

Secretary of State, Corporation Division, 1301 State Capitol Bldg - PO Box 94608, Lincoln, NE 68509; 402-471-4079, Fax- 402-471-3666; 8AM-5PM.

www.sos.state.ne.us/business/corp_serv/

Indexing & Storage: Records available from the beginning of state corporation filings. New records available for inquiry in less than one week.

Searching: Include in request- full name of business. In addition to the articles of organization, business entity records available include: Reports, Officers, Directors, Prior (merged) names, Inactive and Reserved names and Occupation Tax records for the last 5 years.

Access by: mail, phone, fax, in person, online.

Fee & Payment: No search fee, copies are $1.00 per page, $.45 for copies ordered online. Fee payee- Secretary of State. Prepayment required. Personal checks accepted. Credit cards accepted for online purchases.

Mail search: Turnaround time- 2 days. SASE not required.

Phone search: Records are available by phone.

Fax search: Fax searching available.

In person: Simple requests may be processed immediately.

Online search: There are two levels of service. The free lookup at https://www.nebraska.gov/sos/corp/corpsearch.cgi?nav=search provides general information to obtain information on the status of corporations and other business entities registered in this state. The state has designated Nebraska.gov (800-747-8177) to facilitate online retrieval of records. This access to records requires fees and the lookup can be accessed from the same webpage. Also, search securities companies registered with the state at www.ndbf.ne.gov/searches/securities.shtml.

Other access: Nebraska.gov has the capability of offering database purchases.

Uniform Commercial Code, Federal & State Tax Liens

UCC Division, Secretary of State, Rm 1301, PO Box 95104, Lincoln, NE 68509-5104 (Courier address- 1301 State Capitol Bldg, 1445 "K" Street, Lincoln, NE 68509); 402-471-4080, Fax- 402-471-4429; 8AM-5PM.

www.sos.state.ne.us/business/ucc/

Since July 1, 1999, all federal and state tax liens are filed at this agency. Previously tax liens were filed at the county level.

Indexing & Storage: Records available from 1981 to present, on both computer and microfiche. New records available for inquiry in only minutes.

Searching: Use search request Nebraska version of the UCC-11 form.

Access by: mail, fax, in person, online.

Fee & Payment: The search fee is $4.50 per debtor name. Copies are $.50 per page. Certification is an additional $10.00. Fee payee- Secretary of State. They will invoice established accounts, otherwise prepayment required. Personal checks accepted, credit cards are not.

Mail search: Turnaround time- 1 day. A SASE is requested.

Fax search: The fee is $4.50 per debtor. Use the Nebraska Search Form (UCC-11). Turnaround time is 4 hours or less.

In person: Records are generally available with a short wait.

Online search: Access is outsourced to Nebraska.gov To set an account, go to www.nebraska.gov/subscribe.phtml. The system is available 24 hours daily. There is an annual $50.00 fee in addition to charges to view records. Call 800-747-8177 for more information.

Other access: Check with Nebrask@ Online for bulk purchase programs.

Sales Tax Registrations

Revenue Department, Taxpayer Assistance, PO Box 94818, Lincoln, NE 68509-4818 (Courier address- 301 Centennial Mall South, Lincoln, NE 68509); 402-471-5729, Fax- 402-471-5990; 8AM-5PM. www.revenue.state.ne.us/salestax.htm

Indexing & Storage: Records available from 1967.

Searching: This office will confirm that a business is registered and supply requester with name, address and date of license. Include in request- business name. They will also search by tax permit number or by federal tax ID.

Access by: mail, phone, in person.

Mail search: A SASE is requested. No fee for mail request.

Phone search: No fee for telephone request.

In person: Simple requests may be processed immediately.

Other access: Bulk data on registered businesses and new businesses is available for purchase.

Birth Certificates

Health & Human Services System, Vital Statistics Section, PO Box 95065, Lincoln, NE 68509-5065 (Courier address- 1033 "O" Street, #130, Lincoln, 68508); 402-471-2871, 402-471-6440 (Expedited Orders), Fax- 402-471-8230; 8AM-5PM.

www.hhs.state.ne.us/VitalRecords/

Records may also be ordered at regional offices in Omaha, Kearney, North Platte, Norfolk, and Gering.

Indexing & Storage: Records available from 1904 to present. Records are indexed by Soundex code, year and county. Records are indexed by computer since 1912, and can be found on microfiche from 1912 to 1977. New records available for inquiry in 30 days.

Searching: Non-family members must have a notarized, signed release from person of record or immediate family member for investigative purposes. If the birth certificate is more than 50 years old, a release form is not required. Closed records are not released. Include in request- full name, date of birth, place of birth, names of parents, mother's maiden name, relationship to person of record, reason for information request. If adopted, indicate so. Also, all requesters must include copy of government-issued photo ID. A request form may be downloaded from the web. This data not released- original records of adoption or sealed records.

Access by: mail, phone, fax, in person, online.

Fee & Payment: The fee is $12.00 per record. Fee payee- Vital Records. Prepayment required. Credit cards may only be used for expedited searches by walk in or calling in. The file search fee is non-refundable if no records are found. Personal checks accepted. Major credit cards accepted for walkin or expedited svc.

Mail search: Turnaround time- 2 to 3 weeks. If the agency receives the request by overnight mail, they will mail it back within 2 to 3 days. A SASE is requested.

Phone search: See expedited service.

Fax search: See expedited service.

In person: Walk-in requests are taken at Gold's Building, 1033 O Street, #130, Lincoln. Turnaround time is 20 to 30 minutes.

Online search: Records may be ordered online via the web page. For Internet requests, fax to 402-471-8230 the indicating name(s) on the record(s) requested and the Internet confirmation number.

Expedited service: Expedited service is available by phone via a vendor - vitalchek.com. Fee is $35.00 and includes overnight delivery and fee for required use of credit card. Fax the ID to 402-471-8238. It will take a while to connect, be patient. Turnaround time- overnight delivery. This expedited service is only available between 9AM and 3PM Central Time.

Death Records

Health and Human Services System, Vital Statistics Section, PO Box 95065, Lincoln, NE 68509-5065 (Courier address- 1033 "O" Street, #130, Lincoln, NE 68508); 402-471-2871, 402-471-6440 (Expedited Orders), Fax- 402-471-8230; 8AM-5PM.

www.hhs.state.ne.us/VitalRecords/

If a certificate is more than 50 years in the past, release form is not required.

Indexing & Storage: Records available from 1904 to present. New records available for inquiry in 30 days.

Searching: Must have a notarized, signed release from immediate family member for investigative purposes. Include in request- full name, date of death, place of death, relationship to person of record, reason for information request. Also, all requesters must include copy of government-issued photo ID. A request form may be downloaded from the web.

Access by: mail, phone, fax, in person, online.

Fee & Payment: Fee is $11.00 per record. Fee payee- Vital Records. Prepayment required. Credit cards may only be used for phone or walk-in expedited service. The file search fee is non-refundable if no records are found. Personal checks accepted. Major credit cards accepted for walkin or expedited srv.

Mail search: Turnaround time- 2 to 3 weeks. If the agency receives a search request by overnight mail, they will mail the response within 2 to 3 days. A SASE is requested.

Phone search: See expedited service.

Fax search: See expedited service.

In person: Walk-in requests are taken at Gold's Building, 1033 O Street, #130, Lincoln. Turnaround time is 20 to 30 minutes.

Online search: Records may be ordered online the web page. For Internet requests, fax to 402-471-8230 the indicating name(s) on the record(s) requested and the Internet confirmation number.

Expedited service: Expedited service is available by phone via a vendor - vitalchek.com. Fee is $34.00 and includes overnight delivery and fee for required use of credit card. Fax the ID to 402-471-8238. It will take a while to connect, be patient. Turnaround time- overnight delivery. This expedited service is only available between 9AM and 3PM Central Time.

Marriage Certificates

Health and Human Services System, Vital Statistics Section, PO Box 95065, Lincoln, NE 68509-5065 (Courier address- 1033 "O" Street, #130, Lincoln, NE 68508); 402-471-2871, 402-471-6440 (Expedited Orders), Fax- 402-471-8230; 8AM-5PM.

www.hhs.state.ne.us/VitalRecords/

If a certificate is more than 50 years old, a release is not required.

Indexing & Storage: Records available from 1909 to present. Records are indexed by Soundex code, year and county and are on microfilm from 1956 to present. New records available for inquiry in 30 days.

Searching: Must have a notarized, signed release from persons of record or immediate family member for investigative purposes. Include in request- names of husband and wife, date of marriage, place or county of marriage, relationship to person of record, reason for information request, wife's maiden name. Also, all requesters must include copy of government-issued photo ID. A request form may be downloaded from the web.

Access by: mail, phone, fax, in person, online.

Fee & Payment: Fee is $11.00 per record. Fee payee- Vital Records. Prepayment required. Credit cards may only be used for phone expedited service. The file search fee is non-refundable if no records are found. Personal checks accepted. Major credit cards accepted for walkin or expedited srv.

Mail search: Turnaround time- 2 to 3 weeks. If this agency receives a search request by overnight mail, they will mail a response within 2 to 3 days. A SASE is requested.

Phone search: See expedited service.

Fax search: See expedited service.

In person: Walk-in requests are taken at Gold's Building, 1033 O Street, #130, Lincoln. Turnaround time is 30 minutes.

Online search: Records may be ordered online the web page. For Internet requests, fax to 402-471-8230 the indicating name(s) on the record(s) requested and the Internet confirmation number.

Expedited service: Expedited service is available by phone via a vendor - vitalchek.com. Fee is $34.00 and includes overnight delivery and fee for required use of credit card. Fax the ID to 402-471-8238. It will take a while to connect, be patient. Turnaround time- overnight delivery. This expedited service is only available between 9AM and 3PM Central Time.

Divorce Records

Health and Human Services System, Vital Statistics Section, PO Box 95065, Lincoln, NE 68509-5065 (Courier address- 1033 "O" Street, #130, Lincoln, NE 68508); 402-471-2871, 402-471-6440 (Expedited Orders), Fax- 402-471-8230; 8AM-5PM.

www.hhs.state.ne.us/VitalRecords/

If a certificate is more than 50 years, a release is not required.

Indexing & Storage: Records available from 1909 to present. Records are indexed by Soundex code, year and county and are on microfilm from 1956. New records available for inquiry in 30 days.

Searching: Must have a signed release from person of record or immediate family member for investigative purposes. Include in request- names of husband and wife, date of divorce, relationship to person of record, reason for information request, county where divorce was granted. Also, all requesters must include copy of government-issued photo ID. A request form may be downloaded from the web.

Access by: mail, phone, fax, in person, online.

Fee & Payment: Fee is $11.00 per record. Fee payee- Vital Records. Prepayment required. Credit cards may only be used for phone expedited service. The file search fee is non-refundable if no records are found. Personal checks accepted. Major credit cards accepted for walkin or expedited srv.

Mail search: Turnaround time- 2 to 3 weeks. If this agency receives a request by overnight mail, they will mail a response within 2-3 days. A SASE is requested.

Phone search: See expedited service.

Fax search: See expedited service.

In person: Walk-in requests are taken at Gold's Building, 1033 O Street, #130, Lincoln. Turnaround time is 20-30 minutes.

Online search: Records may be ordered online the web page. For Internet requests, fax to 402-471-8230 the indicating name(s) on the record(s) requested and the Internet confirmation number. Fees start at $11.00.

Expedited service: Expedited service is available by phone via a vendor - vitalchek.com. Fee is $34.00 and includes overnight delivery and fee for required use of credit card. Fax the ID to 402-471-8238. It will take a while to connect, be patient. Turnaround time- overnight delivery. This expedited service is only available between 9AM and 3PM Central Time.

Workers' Compensation Records

Workers' Compensation Court, PO Box 98908, Lincoln, NE 68509-8908 (Courier address- State Capitol, 13th Floor, Lincoln, NE 68509); 402-471-6468, 800-599-5155 (In-state), Fax- 402-471-2700; 8AM-5PM. www.wcc.ne.gov

Indexing & Storage: Records available from 1972 on microfilm, also on printout sheets (SS# & name only) and computer. New records available for inquiry in 5days.

Searching: Basic information is public record. Include in request- claimant name, SSN, date of birth, date of accident, and docket number if available. A date of injury is required for searches going back more than 10 years. This data not released- SSN, medical information, unless release given.

Access by: mail, fax, in person, online.

Fee & Payment: The agency will charge fees if retrieval and copying fees exceed $20.00 This is at the discretion of the Court, If costs will exceed $50.00 a deposit is required. Fee payee- Workers' Compensation Court. Personal checks accepted, credit cards are not.

Mail search: Turnaround time- 4 days. SASE not required.

Fax search: Records may be requested by fax.

In person: Agency will mail results.

Online search: This is for requesting records, not viewing online. Record requests may be made at https://www.nebraska.gov/WC/records.phtml. Unless specifically requested, responses will be limited to first and subsequent reports filed within the last five (5) years. First reports will include the original report of injury and the current status of the report if updated information has been filed. Same fee schedule above applies.

Driver Records

Department of Motor Vehicles, Driver & Vehicle Records Division, PO Box 94789, Lincoln, NE 68509-4789 (Courier address- 301 Centennial Mall, South, Lincoln, NE 68508); 402-471-3918, Fax- 402-471-8694; 8AM-5PM.

www.dmv.ne.gov/

It is suggested you obtain copies of tickets at the local courts.

Indexing & Storage: Records available for 5 years for moving violations and suspensions; lifetime for DWIs. Accidents are reported on the record, but fault is not indicated. Surrendered licenses are purged one year after expiration date. New records available for inquiry in 30 days.

Searching: SSNs will not be released. Only exempt, approved requesters receive the driver's address. The general public cannot get personal data unless notarized authorization from subject and requester presented. Include in request- two of the following; driver's full name, DOB, driver license number. Occasional requesters with a permissible use should use the Application for Copy of Driving Record form. This data not released- medical or vision info

Access by: mail, in person, online.

Fee & Payment: The fee is $3.00 per record. Fee payee- Department of Motor Vehicles. Prepayment required. Personal checks accepted, credit cards are not.

Mail search: Turnaround time- 24 hours. A SASE is requested.

In person: Walk-in requesters must produce photo ID.

Online search: Nebraska outsources all electronic record requests to Nebraska.gov at www.nebraska.gov/subscribe.phtml or call 402-471-7810 The system is interactive and open 24 hours a day, 7 days a week. Fee is $3.00 per record. There is an annual fee of $50.00 and a $.12 per minute connect fee or no connect fee if through the Internet. An online status check is offered at https://www.nebraska.gov/dmv/reinstatements/client.cgi. Enter the full name, dob and either the DL or SSN. There is no fee.

Other access: Bulk requesters must be authorized by state officials. Purpose of the request and subsequent usage are reviewed. For information, call 402-471-3885.

Vehicle Title & Registration, Vessel Title

Department of Motor Vehicles, Driver & Vehicle Records Division, PO Box 94789, Lincoln, NE 68509-4789 (Courier address- 301 Centennial Mall, S, Lincoln, NE 68509); 402-471-3918, Fax- 402-471-8694; 8AM-5PM. www.dmv.ne.gov/

Boats are registered and titled at the county level by the County Treasurer. The DMV has access to the title index and registration index and some images, but does not hold the records or record the liens. Parks and Game owns the registration data.

Indexing & Storage: Records available from 1939. Boat titles available from 1997. All motorized boats manufactured after 11/1/72 must be titled. New records available for inquiry in less than 1 day.

Searching: Only permissible use requesters receive full record data. The general public cannot obtain records, with or without obtain personal data, unless written notarized consent of the subject is provided. Typical items required for search include; full name, VIN or plate number, and year and make. This data not released- historical data unless litigation pending or in progress.

Access by: mail, in person, online.

Fee & Payment: The fee is $1.00 per record. Lien information appears on the record. Fee payee- Department of Motor Vehicles. Prepayment required. Personal checks accepted, credit cards are not.

Mail search: Turnaround time- 5 to 7 days. A SASE is requested.

In person: Turnaround time is while you wait. Requesters must show photo ID.

Online search: Electronic access is through Nebraska.gov www.nebraska.gov/subscribe.phtml. There is a start-up fee addition to the $1.00 per record fee. The system is open 24 hours a day, 7 days a week. Call 800-747-8177 for more information.

Other access: Bulk requesters must be authorized by state officials. Purpose of the request and subsequent usage are reviewed. For more information, call 402-471-3885

Accident Reports

Department of Roads, Accident Records Bureau, Box 94669, Lincoln, NE 68509 (Courier address-1500 Nebraska Highway 2, Lincoln, NE 68502); 402-479-4645, Fax- 402-479-3637; 8AM-5PM. www.dor.state.ne.us

Accident reports are required for incidents with property damage in excess of $1,000 or if death or injury.

Indexing & Storage: Records available on hard copy for current year, then on document imaging 1998 to present. On microfilm 19778-94, on CDs 1995-1997. Fatal accidents are on microfilm since 1956. Records are computerized since 1988. New records available for inquiry in 10 days or more.

Searching: Individual driver's own reports are not released. Include in request- full name, date of accident, county. This data not released- driver's accident report.

Access by: mail, fax, in person.

Fee & Payment: The fee is $6.00 per record. Fee payee- Accident Records Bureau. Prepayment required. Personal checks accepted, credit cards are not.

Mail search: Turnaround time- 1 week to 10 days. SASE not required.

Fax search: Records may be requested by fax.

In person: Simple requests may be processed immediately.

Other access: Records can be purchased in bulk from the computer database (1988 to present).

Vessel Registration

Watercraft Registration, Games and Park Commission, 2200 N. 33rd St, Lincoln, NE 68503; 402-471-5579, Fax- 402-471-8694; 8AM-5PM.

www.ngpc.state.ne.us/boating/

Nebraska motorboat registrations are issued only from the county treasurer of the boater's county of residence, but this agency is responsible for the records. All motorized boats must be registered, unless temporarily in state (60 days or less).

Indexing & Storage: Records available from 1977. Not that all motorized boats manufactured after 11/1/72 must be titled and records are at the DMV. New records available for inquiry in less than 1 day.

Searching: Requesters are asked for reason of request. If purpose is termed legitimate, then record is released. Include in request- name, and registration number if known. The SSN is not entered into the database. The DOB has not been entered into the database since late 2006.

Access by: mail, phone, in person.

Fee & Payment: There is no fee for searching or copies, unless extensive lists provided. Prepayment required. Personal checks accepted, credit cards are not.

Mail search: Turnaround time- 1 to 3 days. A SASE is not required, but helpful.

Phone search: Verifications and simple requests are handled by phone, if reason for request is valid.

In person: Turnaround time is while you wait. Requesters must show photo ID.

Legislation Records

Clerk of Legislature Office, PO Box 94604, Lincoln, NE 68509-4604 (Courier address- State Capitol, 1445 K Street, Rm 2018, Lincoln, NE 68508); 402-471-2271, Fax- 402-471-2126; 8AM-5PM. www.unicam.state.ne.us

Indexing & Storage: Records available from 1961 to present (floor debate). They can pull histories on bills back to 1937. New records available for inquiry in 1-3 days.

Searching: Include in request- bill number, year, statute number if possible.

Access by: mail, phone, fax, in person, online.

Fee & Payment: There is no charge for a copy of a bill. A legislative history of a bill costs $.15 per page. Fee payee- State of Nebraska. Prepayment required. Personal checks accepted, credit cards are not.

Mail search: Turnaround time- 3 to 5 days. Bill number and year required to perform mail searches. SASE not required.

Phone search: You may call for information.

Fax search: Fee is $1.00 per page. Turnaround time is same day if possible or 1-2 days.

In person: Counter service available.

Online search: The website features the state statutes, legislative bills for the present session and a legislative journal. You can search by bill number or subject. A Bill Tracker is found at www.nebraska.gov/billtracker/.

Voter Registration

Access to Records is Restricted.

Secretary of State, Elections Division-Records, PO Box 94608, Lincoln, NE 68509-4608 (Courier address- Nebraska State Capitol, 1445 K Street, 3rd Fl, Lincoln, NE 68509); 402-471-2555, Fax-402-471-7834; 8AM-5PM.

www.sos.state.ne.us/elec/

Record lists are available, but only for political purposes. Individual name searches can be done online, but look-ups must be done at the county level.

GED Certificates

NE Dept of Education, Adult Education, PO Box 94987, Lincoln, NE 68509 (Courier address- 301 Centennial Mall S, Lincoln, NE 68509); 402-471-2475, Fax- 402-471-8127; 8AM-5PM.

www.nde.state.ne.us/ADED/home.htm

Indexing & Storage: Records available for past 40 years or so. New records available for inquiry in 30 days.

Searching: To search, all of the following is required: a signed release, date of birth, all last names used, and SSN. If known, the year and city of test are helpful.

Access by: mail, fax, in person.

Fee & Payment: There is no fee for verification. Copies of transcripts are $2.00. Fee payee- NE Dept of Education. Prepayment required. Money orders are accepted. Personal checks accepted, credit cards are not.

Mail search: Turnaround time- 2 to 3 days. SASE not required.

Fax search: Same criteria as mail searching.

In person: Turnaround time is immediate in most instances.

Other access: Form for duplicate copy of GED diploma for $2.00 each is at www.nde.state.ne.us/ADED/text/duplicate_GED_request.htm.

Expedited service: Will expedite delivery if prepaid overnight envelope is provided.

Hunting & Fishing License Information

Game & Parks Commission, PO Box 30370, Lincoln, NE 68503 (Courier address- 2200 N 33rd St, Lincoln, NE 68503); 402-471-5455, Fax- 402-471-6586; 8AM-5PM.

www.outdoornebraska.org

Indexing & Storage: Records available from 1988 to 2000 on microfiche for Big Game, and 1999 to current year for other hunting and fishing. New records available for inquiry in weeks.

Searching: All information on the face of the license is public information, except for release of SSNs. Include in request- date of birth, name. Date of application helpful. This data not released- SSN

Access by: mail, phone, fax, in person.

Fee & Payment: There is no search fee for an individual record. Fees are charged for database sales.

Mail search: Turnaround time- 1 to 2 days. A SASE is requested.

Phone search: Records are available by phone, when personnel available.

Fax search: Records are available by fax.

In person: Turnaround immediate, time permitting.

Other access: Database purchase of information is available.

Nebraska State Licensing Agencies

For details about the agency responsible for licensing/certifying/registering an item below or in the Agency Quick Finder section, match an item's number with the number of the agency in the *Licensing Agency Information* section.

Nebraska Licenses Searchable Online

Abstracting Company #4 .... www.abe.state.ne.us/local/company_search.phtml
Abstractor #4 .... www.abe.state.ne.us/local/license_search.phtml
Adult Day Care #30 .... www.hhs.state.ne.us/crl/rosters.htm
Alcohol/Drug Tester #30 .... www.nebraska.gov/LISSearch/search.cgi
Animal Technician #30 .... www.nebraska.gov/LISSearch/search.cgi
Architect #2 .... www.ea.state.ne.us/search/search.php
Asbestos-related Occupation #30 .... www.nebraska.gov/LISSearch/search.cgi
Assisted Living Facility #30 .... www.hhs.state.ne.us/crl/rosters.htm
Athletic Trainer #30 .... www.nebraska.gov/LISSearch/search.cgi
Attorney #15 .... www.nebar.com/publicinfo/lawyersearch.asp
Audiologist #30 .... www.nebraska.gov/LISSearch/search.cgi
Bank #31 .... www.ndbf.ne.gov/searches/fisearch.shtml
Barber School #1 .... www.barbers.state.ne.us/
Boxer #28 .... www.athcomm.state.ne.us/certificationcourses.html
Check Seller #31 .... www.ndbf.ne.gov/searches/fisearch.shtml
Child Care Center #30 .... www.hhs.state.ne.us/crl/rosters.htm
Child Caring/Placing Agency #30 .... www.hhs.state.ne.us/crl/rosters.htm
Chiropractor #30 .... www.nebraska.gov/LISSearch/search.cgi
Club, Amateur #28 .... www.athcomm.state.ne.us/certificationcourses.html
Collection Agency #26 .... www.sos.state.ne.us/licensing/collection/pdf/col_agn.pdf
Contestant, Athletic Event #28 .... www.athcomm.state.ne.us/certificationcourses.html
Cosmetologist #30 .... www.nebraska.gov/LISSearch/search.cgi
Cosmetology Salon/School #30 .... www.nebraska.gov/LISSearch/search.cgi
Credit Union #31 .... www.ndbf.ne.gov/searches/fisearch.shtml
Debt Management Agency #26 .... www.sos.state.ne.us/business/pdf/debt_list.pdf
Delayed Deposit Service #31 .... www.ndbf.ne.gov/searches/fisearch.shtml
Dental Anesthesia Permit #30 .... www.nebraska.gov/LISSearch/search.cgi
Dental Hygienist #30 .... www.nebraska.gov/LISSearch/search.cgi
Dentist #30 .... www.nebraska.gov/LISSearch/search.cgi
Developmentally Disabled Center #30 .... www.hhs.state.ne.us/crl/rosters.htm
Drug Distributor, Wholesale #30 .... www.hhs.state.ne.us/crl/rosters.htm
Drug Wholesale Facility #30 .... www.hhs.state.ne.us/crl/rosters.htm
Electrologist #30 .... www.nebraska.gov/LISSearch/search.cgi
Electrology Facility #30 .... www.nebraska.gov/LISSearch/search.cgi
Embalmer #30 .... www.nebraska.gov/LISSearch/search.cgi
Emergency Medical Care Facility #30 .... www.nebraska.gov/LISSearch/search.cgi
Engineer #2 .... www.ea.state.ne.us/search/search.php
Esthetician #30 .... www.nebraska.gov/LISSearch/search.cgi
Esthetician Establishment #30 .... www.nebraska.gov/LISSearch/search.cgi
Fund Transmission #31 .... www.ndbf.ne.gov/searches/fisearch.shtml
Funeral Director #30 .... www.nebraska.gov/LISSearch/search.cgi
Funeral Establishment #30 .... www.nebraska.gov/LISSearch/search.cgi
Geologist #7 .... www.geology.state.ne.us/pdf/roster.pdf
Health Clinic #30 .... www.nebraska.gov/LISSearch/search.cgi
Hearing Aid Dispenser/Fitter #30 .... www.nebraska.gov/LISSearch/search.cgi
Home Health Agency #30 .... www.hhs.state.ne.us/crl/rosters.htm
Hospice #30 .... www.hhs.state.ne.us/crl/rosters.htm
Hospital #30 .... www.nlc.state.ne.us/docs/pilot/pubs/h.html
Insurance Firm/Agent/Broker/Prod. #14 .... www.doi.ne.gov/appointments/search/index.cgi
Insurance Company #14 .... www.doi.ne.gov/appointments/search/index.cgi
Insurance Consultant #14 .... www.doi.ne.gov/appointments/search/index.cgi
Intermediate Care Facility (retarded) #30 .... www.hhs.state.ne.us/crl/rosters.htm
Investigator, Plainclothes #26 .... www.sos.state.ne.us/licensing/private_eye/pdf/PDA%20Apr2008.pdf
Investment Advisor/Advisor Rep. #11 .... www.ndbf.org/searches/fisearch.shtml
Judge, Athletic Event #28 .... www.athcomm.state.ne.us/certificationcourses.html
Labor/Delivery Service/Clinic #30 .... www.hhs.state.ne.us/crl/rosters.htm

Laboratory #30 .... www.hhs.state.ne.us/crl/rosters.htm
Landscape Architect #23 .... www.landarch.state.ne.us/registrants.pdf
Liquor Retailers/ Whlse/Shipper #19 .... www.lcc.ne.gov/license_search/licsearch.cgi
Lobbyist #8 .... www.nebraskalegislature.gov/
Local Anesthesia Certification #30 .... www.nebraska.gov/LISSearch/search.cgi
Long Term Care Center #30 .... www.hhs.state.ne.us/crl/rosters.htm
Manager, Athletic Event #28 .... www.athcomm.state.ne.us/certificationcourses.html
Marriage & Family Therapist #30 .... www.nebraska.gov/LISSearch/search.cgi
Massage Establishment #30 .... www.nebraska.gov/LISSearch/search.cgi
Massage Therapy School #30 .... www.nebraska.gov/LISSearch/search.cgi
Medical Doctor #30 .... www.nebraska.gov/LISSearch/search.cgi
Mental Health Center #30 .... www.nebraska.gov/LISSearch/search.cgi
Mentally Retarded Care Service #30 .... www.hhs.state.ne.us/crl/rosters.htm
Nail Technologist #30 .... www.nebraska.gov/LISSearch/search.cgi
Nurse #30 .... www.nebraska.gov/LISSearch/search.cgi
Nursing Home #30 .... www.nebraska.gov/LISSearch/search.cgi
Nursing Home Administrator #30 .... www.nebraska.gov/LISSearch/search.cgi
Nutrition Therapy, Medical #30 .... www.nebraska.gov/LISSearch/search.cgi
Occupational Therapist #30 .... www.nebraska.gov/LISSearch/search.cgi
Optometrist #30 .... www.nebraska.gov/LISSearch/search.cgi
Osteopathic Physician #30 .... www.nebraska.gov/LISSearch/search.cgi
Pesticide Applicator/Dealer #18 .... www.kellysolutions.com/ne/
Pharmacist #30 .... www.nebraska.gov/LISSearch/search.cgi
Pharmacy #30 .... www.nebraska.gov/LISSearch/search.cgi
Pharmacy, Mail Order #30 .... www.nebraska.gov/LISSearch/search.cgi
Physical Therapist #30 .... www.nebraska.gov/LISSearch/search.cgi
Physician #30 .... www.nebraska.gov/LISSearch/search.cgi
Physician Assistant #30 .... www.nebraska.gov/LISSearch/search.cgi
Physician, Athletic Event #28 .... www.athcomm.state.ne.us/certificationcourses.html
Plant Nursery/Nursery Professional #18 .... www.agr.state.ne.us/division/bpi/bpi.htm
Podiatrist #30 .... www.nebraska.gov/LISSearch/search.cgi
Polygraph Examiner, Private #26 .... www.sos.state.ne.us/licensing/poly_menu.html
Polygraph Examiner, Public #26 .... www.sos.state.ne.us/licensing/poly_menu.html
Preschool #30 .... www.hhs.state.ne.us/crl/rosters.htm
Private Detective #26 .... www.sos.state.ne.us/licensing/private_eye/pdf/PD%20Apr2008.pdf
Private Detective Agency #26 .... www.sos.state.ne.us/licensing/private_eye/pdf/PDA%20Apr2008.pdf
Psychologist #30 .... www.nebraska.gov/LISSearch/search.cgi
Public Accountant-CPA #5 .... www.nbpa.ne.gov/search/index.phtml
Radiographer #30 .... www.nebraska.gov/LISSearch/search.cgi
Real Estate Agent/Seller #25 .... www.nrec.state.ne.us/licinfodb/index.cgi
Real Estate Appraiser #22 .... www.appraiser.ne.gov/appraiser_listing.html
Real Estate Broker #25 .... www.nrec.state.ne.us/licinfodb/index.cgi
Referee #28 .... www.athcomm.state.ne.us/certificationcourses.html
Rehabilitation Agency #30 .... www.hhs.state.ne.us/crl/rosters.htm
Respiratory Care Practitioner #30 .... www.nebraska.gov/LISSearch/search.cgi
Respite Care Service #30 .... www.hhs.state.ne.us/crl/rosters.htm
Sales Finance Company #31 .... www.ndbf.ne.gov/searches/fisearch.shtml
Saving & Loan #31 .... www.ndbf.ne.gov/searches/fisearch.shtml
Second, Athletic Event #28 .... www.athcomm.state.ne.us/certificationcourses.html
Securities Agent/Broker/Dealer #11 .... www.ndbf.org/searches/fisearch.shtml
Social Worker #30 .... www.nebraska.gov/LISSearch/search.cgi
Speech-Language Pathologist #30 .... www.nebraska.gov/LISSearch/search.cgi
Substance Abuse Treatment Ctr #30 .... www.nlc.state.ne.us/docs/pilot/pubs/h.html
Surplus Lines Seller #14 .... www.doi.ne.gov/appointments/search/index.cgi
Surveyor, Land #3 .... www.sso.state.ne.us/bels/lsalpha.html
Swimming Pool Operator #30 .... www.nebraska.gov/LISSearch/search.cgi
Teacher #13 .... www.nde.state.ne.us/tcert/
Timekeeper, Athletic Event #28 .... www.athcomm.state.ne.us/certificationcourses.html
Trust Company #31 .... www.ndbf.ne.gov/searches/fisearch.shtml
Veterinarian/Veterinary Technician #30 .... www.nebraska.gov/LISSearch/search.cgi
Voice Stress Examiner/Analyzer #26 .... www.sos.state.ne.us/licensing/poly_menu.html
Water Operator #30 .... www.nebraska.gov/LISSearch/search.cgi
Wrestler #28 .... www.athcomm.state.ne.us/certificationcourses.html
Wrestling/Boxing Matches #28 .... www.athcomm.state.ne.us/certificationcourses.html
X-ray Unit Portable #30 .... www.nebraska.gov/LISSearch/search.cgi

Nebraska Licensing Quick Finder

Abstracting Company #4 ... 402-471-2383
Abstractor #4 ... 402-471-2383
Adult Day Care #30 ... 402-471-2115
Aerial Applicator, Pesticide #10 ... 402-471-2371
Air Cond./Heat'g Cont'r (Lincoln) #12 ... 402-441-7508
Alcohol/Drug Tester #30 ... 402-471-2118
Amusement Ride Inspector #21 ... 402-471-2239
Animal Herd Regulation #18 ... 402-471-2394
Animal Technician #30 ... 402-471-2118
Announcer, Athletic Event #28 ... 402-471-2009
Architect #2 ... 402-471-2021
Asbestos Worker/Profession'l #17 ... 402-471-2299
Asbestos-related Occupation #30 ... 402-471-2299
Assisted Living Facility #30 ... 402-471-4970
Athletic Trainer #30 ... 402-471-2299
Attorney #15 ... 800-927-0117, 402-475-7091
Auctioneer #6 ... 402-441-7437
Audiologist #30 ... 402-471-2115
Bank #31 ... 402-471-2171
Barber #1 ... 402-471-2051
Barber School #1 ... 402-471-2051
Boiler & Pressure Vessel Inspec #16 ... 402-471-4721
Boiler Inspection #21 ... 402-471-2230
Boxer #28 ... 402-471-2009
Boxing Promoter #28 ... 402-471-2009
Chauffeur #6 ... 402-441-7437
Check Seller #31 ... 402-471-2171
Child Caring/Placing Agency/Ctr #30 ... 402-471-2115
Child Labor #21 ... 402-471-2230
Chiropractor #30 ... 402-471-2299
Club, Amateur #28 ... 402-471-2009
Collection Agency #26 ... 402-471-8606
Contestant, Athletic Event #28 ... 402-471-2009
Contractor Registration #21 ... 402-595-3095
Contractor, Building (Lincoln) #12 ... 402-441-6456
Cosmetologist #30 ... 402-471-2115
Cosmetology Salon/School #30 ... 402-471-2115
Credit Union #31 ... 402-471-2171
Dairy/Food Facility #18 ... 402-471-2394
Debt Management Agency #26 ... 402-471-8606
Delayed Deposit Service #31 ... 402-471-2171
Dental Anesthesia Permit #30 ... 402-471-2118
Denntist / Dental Hygienist #30 ... 402-471-2118
Developmentally Disabled Center #30 ... 402-471-2115
Drug Distributor, Wholesale #30 ... 402-471-2118
Drug Wholesale Facility #30 ... 402-471-2115
Education'l Media Spe'l'st/Librar'n #13 ... 402-471-0739
Electrician #29 ... 402-471-1058
Electrologist #30 ... 402-471-2115
Electrology Facility #30 ... 402-471-2115
Elevator Inspector/Inspection Mgr #21 ... 402-595-2523
Embalmer #30 ... 402-471-2115
Emergency Medical Care Facility #30 ... 402-471-2115
Employment Agency #21 ... 402-595-3095
Engineer #2 ... 402-471-2021
Environmental Health Specialist #17 ... 402-471-2299
Esthetician #30 ... 402-471-2115
Esthetician Establishment #30 ... 402-471-2115
Farm Labor Contractor #21 ... 402-595-3095
Fertilizer Professional/Business #18 ... 402-471-2394
Fire Protect'n Sprinkler Cont'r (Lincoln) #12 ... 402-441-6456
Fund Transmission #31 ... 402-471-2171
Funeral Director #30 ... 402-471-2115
Funeral Establishment #30 ... 402-471-2115
Geologist #7 ... 402-471-8383
Health Clinic #30 ... 402-471-2115
Hearing Aid Dispenser/Fitter #30 ... 402-471-2299
Hearing Quality Assurance Screen #9 ... 402-471-3593
Home Health Agency #30 ... 402-471-2115
Hospice #30 ... 402-471-2115
Hospital #30 ... 402-471-2115
Insurance Agency/Agent/Broker/Prod. #14 ... 402-471-2201
Insurance Company #14 ... 402-471-2201
Insurance Consultant #14 ... 402-471-2201
Insurance Utilizat'n Review Agent #14 ... 402-471-2201
Intermediate Care Facility (for retarded) #30 ... 402-471-2115
Interpreter for the Deaf #9 ... 402-471-3593
Investigator, Plainclothes #26 ... 402-471-8606
Investment Advisor/Advisor Rep. #11 ... 402-471-3445
Jewelry Dealer, Secondhand #6 ... 402-441-7437
Judge, Athletic Event #28 ... 402-471-2009
Labor/Delivery Service/Clinic #30 ... 402-471-2115
Laboratory #30 ... 402-471-2115
Landscape Architect #23 ... 402-471-2407
Law Enforcement Officer #20 ... 308-385-6030
Lead Abatement Worker, etc. #17 ... 402-471-2299
Liquor Retailers/ Whlse/Shipper #19 ... 402-471-2571
Lobbyist #8 ... 402-471-2608
Local Anesthesia Certification #30 ... 402-471-2118
Long Term Care Center #30 ... 402-471-2115
Manager, Athletic Event #28 ... 402-471-2009
Marriage & Family Therapist #30 ... 402-471-2115
Massage Establishment #30 ... 402-471-2115
Massage Therapy School #30 ... 402-471-2115
Matchmaker #28 ... 402-471-2009
Medical Doctor #30 ... 402-471-2118
Mental Health Center #30 ... 402-471-2115
Mentally Retarded Care Service #30 ... 402-471-2115
Nail Technologist #30 ... 402-471-2115
Notary Public #27 ... 402-471-2558
Noxious Weed Control #18 ... 402-471-2394
Nurse #30 ... 402-471-2115
Nursing Education Program #30 ... 402-471-2115
Nursing Home #30 ... 402-471-2115
Nursing Home Administrator #30 ... 402-471-2115
Nutrition Therapy, Medical #30 ... 402-471-2115
Occupational Therapist #30 ... 402-471-2299
Optometrist #30 ... 402-471-2118
Osteopathic Physician #30 ... 402-471-2118
Pawnbroker #6 ... 402-441-7437
Pesticide Applicator/Dealer #18 ... 402-471-2394
Pharmacist #30 ... 402-471-2118
Pharmacy #30 ... 402-471-2115
Pharmacy, Mail Order #30 ... 402-471-2115
Physical Therapist #30 ... 402-471-2299
Physician #30 ... 402-471-2118
Physician Assistant #30 ... 402-471-2118
Physician, Athletic Event #28 ... 402-471-2009
Plant Nursery/Nursery Profession'l #18 402-471-2394
Plumber (Lincoln) #12 ... 402-441-6456
Podiatrist #30 ... 402-471-2118
Polygraph Examiner, Private #26 ... 402-471-8606
Polygraph Examiner, Public #26 ... 402-471-8606
Pre-need Seller #14 ... 402-471-2201
Preschool #30 ... 402-471-2115
Private Detective #26 ... 402-471-8606
Private Detective Agency #26 ... 402-471-8606
Psychologist #30 ... 402-471-4905
Public Accountant-CPA #5 ... 402-471-3595
Racing Event/Professional #24 ... 402-471-4155
Radiographer #30 ... 402-471-2118
Radon Mitigation Specialist/Technician #17 ... 402-471-2299
Real Estate Agent/Seller/Broker #25 ... 402-471-2004
Real Estate Appraiser #22 ... 402-471-9015
Referee #28 ... 402-471-2009
Rehabilitation Agency #30 ... 402-471-2115
Respiratory Care Practitioner #30 ... 402-471-2299
Respite Care Service #30 ... 402-471-2115
Sales Finance Company #31 ... 402-471-2171
Saving & Loan #31 ... 402-471-2171
School Administrator/Supervisor #13 ... 402-471-0739
School Nurse #13 ... 402-471-0739
Second, Athletic Event #28 ... 402-471-2009
Securities Agent #11 ... 402-471-3445
Securities Broker/Dealer #11 ... 402-471-3445
Skin Care Salon #30 ... 402-471-2115
Social Worker #30 ... 402-471-2115
Speech-Language Pathologist #30 ... 402-471-2115
Substance Abuse Treatment Ctr #30 ... 402-471-2115
Surplus Lines Seller #14 ... 402-471-2201
Surveyor, Land #3 ... 402-471-2566
Swimming Pool Operator #30 ... 402-471-2299
Taxi Driver #6 ... 402-441-7437
Teacher #13 ... 402-471-0739
Timekeeper, Athletic Event #28 ... 402-471-2009
Trust Company #31 ... 402-471-2171
Veterinarian #30 ... 402-471-2118
Veterinary (dog, cat, kennels) #18 ... 402-471-2394
Veterinary Technician #30 ... 402-471-2115
Voice Stress Examiner/Analyzer #26 ... 402-471-8606
Water Operator #30 ... 402-471-2299
Water Treatment Plant Operator #17 ... 402-471-2299
Weights & Measures Regulation #18 ... 402-471-2394
Well Driller/Pump Installer #17 ... 402-471-2299
Wrestler #28 ... 402-471-2009
Wrestling/Boxing Matches #28 ... 402-471-2009
X-ray Unit Portable #30 ... 402-471-2115

Nebraska Licensing Agency Information

#1 Board of Barber Examiners, 301 Centennial Mall S, 6th Fl (PO Box 94723), Lincoln, NE 68509-4723; 402-471-2051, Fax- 402-471-2052. www.barbers.state.ne.us

#2 Board of Examiners for Engineers & Architects, PO Box 95165, 215 Centennial Mall S #400, Lincoln, NE 68509-5165; 402-471-2021, Fax- 402-471-0787. www.ea.state.ne.us

#3 Board of Examiners for Land Surveyors, 555 N Cotner Blvd, Lower Level, Lincoln, NE 68505; 402-471-2566, Fax- 402-471-3057. www.sso.state.ne.us/bels/

#4 Abstractors Board of Examiners, PO Box 94944 (1200 N St), Lincoln, NE 68509; 402-471-2383, Fax- 402-471-6575. www.abe.state.ne.us

#5 Board of Public Accountancy, PO Box 94725 (140 N 8th St #290), Lincoln, NE 68509-4725; 402-471-3595, Fax- 402-471-4484. www.nbpa.ne.gov Search data at- www.nbpa.ne.gov/search/index.phtml

#6 Applications & Permits, City Clerk's Office, 555 S 10th St, Lincoln, NE 68508; 402-441-7437, Fax- 402-441-8325. www.lincoln.ne.gov

#7 Board of Geologists, PO Box 94844 (215 Centennial Mall S #400), Lincoln, NE 68509; 402-471-8383, Fax- 402-471-0787. www.geology.state.ne.us Search data at- www.geology.state.ne.us/pdf/roster.pdf

#8 Clerk of the Legislature, PO Box 94604 (Rm 2018, State Capitol), Lincoln, NE 68509-4604; 402-471-2271, Fax- 402-471-2126. 8AM-5PM. www.nebraskalegislature.gov/reports/lobby.php

#9 Commission for the Deaf & Hard of Hearing, 4600 Valley Rd #420, Lincoln, NE 68510-4844; 402-471-3593, Fax- 402-471-3067. Hours- 8AM-5PM. www.ncdhh.ne.gov

#10 Department of Aeronautics, 3431 Aviation Rd #150, Lincoln, NE 68524; 402-471-2371, Fax- 402-471-2906. www.aero.state.ne.us Kearney Office: 5065 Airport Road, Kearney, NE 68847; 308-865-5696; 308 865 5697-Fax.

#11 Department of Banking & Finance, Bureau of Securities, PO Box 95006 (1230 'O' St #400), Lincoln, NE 68509-5006; 402-471-3445. www.ndbf.ne.gov/ Search data at- www.ndbf.org/searches/fisearch.shtml

#12 Department of Building & Safety, City of Lincoln, 555 S 10th St #203, Lincoln, NE 68508; 402-441-7521, Fax- 402-441-8214. Hours- 8AM-4PM. www.lincoln.ne.gov/city/build/index.htm

#13 Department of Education, Teacher Accreditation/Certification Division, PO Box 94987 (Centennial Mall S), Lincoln, NE 68509-4987; 402-471-2295, Fax- 402-471-9735. www.nde.state.ne.us Search data at- www.nde.state.ne.us/tcert/

#14 Department of Insurance, 941 O St #400, Lincoln, NE 68508-3639; 402-471-2201, Fax- 402-471-6559. Hours- 8AM-5PM. www.doi.ne.gov Search data at- www.doi.ne.gov/appointments/search/index.cgi

#15 Bar Association, PO Box 81809 (635 S 14th St), Lincoln, NE 68501-1809; 800-927-0117, 402-475-7091, Fax- 402-475-7098. www.nebar.com Search data at- www.nebar.com/publicinfo/lawyersearch.asp

#16 Division of Safety & Labor Standards, Boiler Inspectors Section, PO Box 95024 (301 Centennial Mall S- Lower Level), Lincoln, NE 68509; 402-471-4721, Fax- 402-471-5039. www.dol.state.ne.us/nwd/center.cfm?PRICAT=2&SUBCAT=2C&ACTION=boiler

#17 Drinking Water & Environmental Sanitation, Credentialing Division, PO Box 95007 (301 Centennial Mall S), Lincoln, NE 68509; 402-471-2299, Fax- 402-471-3577. www.hhs.state.ne.us

#18 Department of Agriculture, Bureau of Plant Industry, PO Box 94756 (301 Centennial Mall South), Lincoln, NE 68509; 402-471-2394, Fax- 402-471-6892. www.agr.state.ne.us/division/bpi/bpi.htm

#19 Liquor Control Commission, PO Box 95046 (301 Centennial Mall S), Lincoln, NE 68509-5046; 402-471-2571, Fax- 402-471-2814. www.lcc.ne.gov Search data at- www.lcc.ne.gov/license_search/licsearch.cgi

#20 Crime Commission, PO Box 94946 (301 Centennial Mall S), Lincoln, NE 68509; 402-471-2194, Fax- 402-471-2837. www.ncc.state.ne.us/CC.htm

#21 Department of Labor, Office of Safety & Labor Standards, 301 Centennial Mall S, Lower Level (PO Box 95024), Lincoln, NE 68509-5024; 402-471-9926, Fax- 402-471-5039. 8AM-5PM. www.dol.state.ne.us/nwd/center.cfm?PRICAT=4&SUBCAT=4F

#22 Real Estate Appraiser Board, PO Box 94963 (301 Centennial Mall, Lower Level), Lincoln, NE 68509-4963; 402-471-9015, Fax- 402-471-9017. Hours- 6:30AM-5PM. www.appraiser.ne.gov

#23 Board of Landscape Architects, PO Box 95165 (215 Centennial Mall S #400), Lincoln, NE 68509-5165; 402-471-2407, Fax- 402-471-0787. www.landarch.state.ne.us Search data at- www.landarch.state.ne.us/registrants.pdf

#24 Racing Commission, PO Box 95014 (301 Centennial Mall S), Lincoln, NE 68509-5014; 402-471-4155, Fax- 402-471-2339. www.horseracing.state.ne.us

#25 Real Estate Commission, PO Box 94667 (1200 N St #402), Lincoln, NE 68509-4667; 402-471-2004, Fax- 402-471-4492. Hours- 8AM-5PM. www.nrec.state.ne.us Search data at- www.nrec.state.ne.us/licinfodb/index.cgi

#26 Secretary of State, Business Services, Licensing Division, PO Box 94608 (1445 K St #1305), Lincoln, NE 68509-4608; 402-471-8606, Fax- 402-471-2530. Hours- 8AM-5PM. www.sos.state.ne.us

#27 Secretary of State, Notary Division, PO Box 95104, Rm 1301, State Capitol Bldg, Lincoln, NE 68509-5104; 402-471-2558, Fax- 402-471-4429. Hours- 8AM-5PM. www.sos.state.ne.us/business/notary/

#28 Athletic Commission, PO Box 94743 (301 Centennial Mall S, 1st Fl), Lincoln, NE 68509-4743; 402-471-2009, Fax- 402-471-3396. Hours- 9AM-3PM. www.athcomm.state.ne.us Search data at- www.athcomm.state.ne.us/certificationcourses.html

#29 Electrical Division, PO Box 95066 (800 S 13th St #109), Lincoln, NE 68509; 402-471-3550, Fax- 402-471-4297. Hours- 8AM-5PM. www.electrical.state.ne.us

#30 Health & Human Svcs Regulation & Licensure, Credentialing Division, PO Box 94986, Lincoln, NE 68509-4986; 402-471-2115, Fax- 402-471-3577. www.hhs.state.ne.us/crl/profindex1.htm Search data at- www.nebraska.gov/LISSearch/search.cgi Boarding Homes do not need a license as of 1/1/2001. Domiciliary Facility and Residential Care Facility are now combined into Assisted Living Facility.

#31 Department of Banking & Finance, Financial Institutions Division, PO Box 95006 (1230 'O' St. #400), Lincoln, NE 68509-5006; 402-471-2171. www.ndbf.ne.gov/ Search data at- www.ndbf.ne.gov/searches/fisearch.shtml

Nebraska Federal Courts

The following list indicates the district and division name for each county in the state.

County/Court Cross Reference

County	Court	County	Court
Adams	Lincoln	Jefferson	Lincoln
Antelope	Lincoln	Johnson	Lincoln
Arthur	North Platte	Kearney	Lincoln
Banner	North Platte	Keith	North Platte
Blaine	North Platte	Keya Paha	North Platte
Boone	Lincoln	Kimball	North Platte
Box Butte	North Platte	Knox	Omaha
Boyd	Lincoln	Lancaster	Lincoln
Brown	North Platte	Lincoln	North Platte
Buffalo	Lincoln	Logan	North Platte
Burt	Omaha	Loup	North Platte
Butler	Lincoln	Madison	Lincoln
Cass	Lincoln (Omaha)	McPherson	North Platte
Cedar	Omaha	Merrick	Lincoln
Chase	North Platte	Morrill	North Platte
Cherry	North Platte	Nance	Lincoln
Cheyenne	North Platte	Nemaha	Lincoln
Clay	Lincoln	Nuckolls	Lincoln
Colfax	Lincoln	Otoe	Lincoln
Cuming	Omaha	Pawnee	Lincoln
Custer	North Platte	Perkins	North Platte
Dakota	Omaha	Phelps	Lincoln
Dawes	North Platte	Pierce	Omaha
Dawson	North Platte	Platte	Lincoln
Deuel	North Platte	Polk	Lincoln
Dixon	Omaha	Red Willow	North Platte
Dodge	Omaha	Richardson	Lincoln
Douglas	Omaha	Rock	North Platte
Dundy	North Platte	Saline	Lincoln
Fillmore	Lincoln	Sarpy	Omaha
Franklin	Lincoln	Saunders	Lincoln
Frontier	North Platte	Scotts. Bluff	North Platte
Furnas	North Platte	Seward	Lincoln
Gage	Lincoln	Sheridan	North Platte
Garden	North Platte	Sherman	Lincoln
Garfield	North Platte	Sioux	North Platte
Gosper	North Platte	Stanton	Omaha (Lincoln)
Grant	North Platte	Thayer	Lincoln
Greeley	Lincoln	Thomas	North Platte
Hall	Lincoln	Thurston	Omaha
Hamilton	Lincoln	Valley	North Platte
Harlan	Lincoln	Washington	Omaha
Hayes	North Platte	Wayne	Omaha
Hitchcock	North Platte	Webster	Lincoln
Holt	Lincoln	Wheeler	Lincoln
Hooker	North Platte	York	Lincoln
Howard	Lincoln		

Standards for Federal Courts: Fees are standard unless noted in profile. Search fee is $26.00 per item (one party name or case number). Copy fee is $.50 per page. Certification fee is $9.00 per document, double for exemplification, if available. Most courts require prepayment. Mail requests should enclose a SASE unless otherwise noted. Before releasing records, all courts require prepayment, unless noted.

District courts index by defendant and plaintiff and by case number. Bankruptcy courts usually index by debtor and case number. While most courts now have their indexes on computer, many may still maintain index card files as well. Courts will archive closed case files at different times.

There are numerous public access programs available to online subscribers. Search the U.S. Party/Case Index to find party names and case numbers among all courts. Individual case data is provided on PACER. A search of CM/ECF provides copies of cases filed electronically. For details about PACER, the US Party/Case Index, and CM/ECF see the Appendix or go to http://pacer.psc.uscourts.gov or call 800-676-6856.

US District Court District of Nebraska

Lincoln Division Court Clerk, 593 Federal Bldg, 100 Centennial Mall N, Lincoln, NE 68508-3803, 402-437-5225, 866-220-4379; Fax- 402-437-5651. 8AM-4:30PM. www.ned.uscourts.gov

Counties/Note: Nebraska cases may be filed in any of 3 courts at the attorney's option, except filings in North Platte must be during its trial session. This Lincoln Division holds most North Platte Division records.

Searches/Indexing: Search request requires name only. Results do not include SSN or DOB or gender; Pre-2004 cases may provide some identifiers. Will fax back docs $1.00 per page. New cases are in the index 1-2 days after filing date. Computer index goes back to 1990, some cases to 1985. District-wide searches available at Omaha or Lincoln. Case files sent to archives approx. 1 year after closed.

Search Access: Only docket info available by phone. **Mail:** Search usually completed- 1-2 days. Include SASE for return. **Fax:** Fax search requests accepted. **In person:** 2 public terminals available. Self-serve copier $.25 per page in public area.

Payment: Pay by Visa/MC, money order, cashier's or personal check. Payee: Clerk, US District Court.

E-Services: PACER records go back to late 1990. New records online after 1 day. ECF at https://ecf.ned.uscourts.gov. **Opinions Online:** www.nebar.com/resources/opinions/usdist/index.htm. **Online Note:** Court calendars on ECF system.

North Platte Division c/o Lincoln Division, 593 Federal Bldg, 100 Centennial Mall N, Lincoln, NE 68508, 402-437-5225, 866-220-4379; Fax- 402-437-5651. 8-4:30PM. www.ned.uscourts.gov

Counties/Note: Nebraska cases may be filed in any of 3 courts at the attorney's option, except filings in North Platte must be during its trial session. Some case records may be in the Omaha Division as well as Lincoln Division.

Searches/Indexing: Search request requires name only. Results do not include SSN or DOB or gender; Pre-2004 cases may provide some identifiers. Will fax back docs $1.00 per page. New cases are in the index 1-2 days after filing date. Computer index goes back to 1990, some cases to 1985. District-wide searches available at Omaha or Lincoln. Case files sent to archives approx. 1 year after closed.

Search Access: Mail: Search usually completed- 4 days. Include SASE for return. **Fax:** Fax search requests accepted. **In person:** No public access terminals available in North Platte. Self-serve copier $.25 per page in public access area.

Payment: Pay by Visa/MC, money order, cashier's or personal check. Payee: Clerk, US District Court.

E-Services: PACER records go back to late 1990. New records online after 1 day. ECF at https://ecf.ned.uscourts.gov. **Opinions Online:** www.nebar.com/resources/opinions/usdist/index.htm. **Online Note:** Court calendars on ECF system.

Omaha Division Court Clerk, 111 S 18th Plaza, #1152, Omaha, NE 68102, 402-661-7350, 866-220-4381; Fax- 402-661-7387. Hours-8AM-4:30PM. www.ned.uscourts.gov

Counties/Note: Nebraska cases may be filed in any of 3 courts at the attorney's option, except filings in North Platte must be during its trial session.

Searches/Indexing: Search request requires name only. Results do not include SSN or DOB or gender; Pre-2004 cases may provide some identifiers. Will fax back docs $1.00 per page. New cases are in the index 1-2 days after filing date. Computer index goes back to 1990, some cases to 1985. District-wide searches available at Omaha or Lincoln. Case files sent to archives approx. 1 year after closed.

Search Access: Mail: Search usually completed- 1-2 days. Include SASE for return. **Fax:** Fax search requests accepted. **In person:** 2 public terminals available. No self-serve copier.

Payment: Pay by Visa/MC, money order, cashier's or personal check. Payee: Clerk, US District Court.

E-Services: PACER records go back to late 1990. New records online after 1 day. ECF at https://ecf.ned.uscourts.gov. **Opinions Online:** www.nebar.com/resources/opinions/usdist/index.htm. **Online Note:** Court calendars on ECF system.

US Bankruptcy Court District of Nebraska

Lincoln Division Court Clerk, 460 Federal Bldg, 100 Centennial Mall N, Lincoln, NE 68508, 402-437-5100; Fax- 402-437-5454. 8AM-4:30PM. www.neb.uscourts.gov

Counties/Note: Adams, Antelope, Boone, Boyd, Buffalo, Butler, Clay, Colfax, Fillmore, Franklin, Gage, Greeley, Hall, Hamilton, Harlan, Holt, Howard, Jefferson, Johnson, Kearney, Lancaster, Madison, Merrick, Nance, Nemaha, Nuckolls, Otoe, Pawnee, Phelps, Platte, Polk, Richardson, Saline, Saunders, Seward, Sherman, Stanton, Thayer, Webster, Wheeler, York. Cases from the North Platte Division assigned to Lincoln.

Searches/Indexing: Search request requires name only. Results include last 4 SSN digits, address. Will not fax back documents. New cases are in the index 1 day after filing date. All debtor names are indexed for files back to 9/89. Only computer files maintained here. Maintains records for main bankruptcy office in Omaha. District-wide searches available here. Case files sent to archives 6 months after closed.

Search Access: Only debtor's name, case number, date filed, 341 information, and date discharged and closed is released. Voice Case Information Service available, call VCIS at 800-829-0112 or 402-221-3757. **Mail:** Search usually completed- 1-2 days. SASE not required. **In person:** 2 public terminals available. Self-serve copies from computer terminal- $.10 each.

Payment: Pay by Visa/MC, money order, cashier's check. No business/personal checks accepted; no debtor credit cards. Payee: Clerk, US Bankruptcy Court.

E-Services: PACER records go back to 9/1989. New records online after 1 day. ECF at https://ecf.neb.uscourts.gov. **Opinions Online:** www.neb.uscourts.gov. Click on Case Info, then Nebraska Bankruptcy Opinions.

North Platte Division c/o Lincoln Division, 460 Federal Bldg, 100 Centennial Mall North, Lincoln, NE 68508, 402-437-5100; Fax- 402-437-5454. 8AM-4:30PM. www.neb.uscourts.gov

Counties/Note: Arthur, Banner, Blaine, Box Butte, Brown, Chase, Cherry, Cheyenne, Custer, Dawes, Dawson, Deuel, Dundy, Frontier, Furnas, Garden, Garfield, Gosper, Grant, Hayes, Hitchcock, Hooker, Keith, Keya Paha, Kimball, Lincoln, Logan, Loup, McPherson, Morrill, Perkins, Red Willow, Rock, Scotts Bluff, Sheridan, Sioux, Thomas, Valley. Cases are assigned to Lincoln Division.

Searches/Indexing: Search request requires name only. Results include last 4 SSN digits, address. Will not fax back documents. New cases are in the index 1 day after filing date. All debtor names are indexed for files back to 9/89. Only computer files maintained here. Case files sent to archives 6 months after closed.

Search Access: Only docket info is available by phone. Voice Case Information Service available, call VCIS at 800-829-0112 or 402-221-3757. **Mail:** Search usually completed- 1-2 days. SASE not required. **In person:** 2 public terminals available. Copies from computer terminal $.10.

Payment: Pay by Visa/MC, money order, cashier's check. No business or personal checks accepted; no debtor credit cards. Payee: Clerk, US Bankruptcy Court.

E-Services: PACER records go back to 9/1989. New records online after 1 day. ECF at https://ecf.neb.uscourts.gov. **Opinions Online:** www.neb.uscourts.gov. Click on Case Info, then Nebraska Bankruptcy Opinions.

Omaha Division Court Clerk, 111 S 18th Plaza, Ste 1125, Omaha, NE 68102, 402-661-7444; Fax- 402-661-7492. Hours-8AM-4:30PM. www.neb.uscourts.gov

Counties/Note: Burt, Cedar, Cass, Cuming, Dakota, Dixon, Dodge, Douglas, Knox, Pierce, Sarpy, Thurston, Washington, Wayne.

Searches/Indexing: Search request requires name only. Results include last 4 SSN digits, address. Will not fax back documents. New cases are in the index 1 day after filing date. All debtor names are indexed for files back to 9/89. Only computer files maintained here. Ppre-2002 paper files kept 1 year after closing, then archived at Kansas City.

Search Access: Only docket info is available by phone. Voice Case Information Service available, call VCIS at 800-829-0112 or 402-221-3757. **Mail:** Search usually completed- 1-2 days. SASE not required. **Fax:** Will not accept fax search requests, but will process a case file request if pre-approved by staff. **In person:** 2 public terminals available. Computer generated copies are $.10.

Payment: Pay by Visa/MC, money order, cashier's check. No business or personal checks accepted; no debtor credit cards. Payee: Clerk, US Bankruptcy Court.

E-Services: PACER records go back to 9/1989. New records online after 1 day. ECF at https://ecf.neb.uscourts.gov. **Opinions Online:** www.neb.uscourts.gov. Click on Case Info, then Nebraska Bankruptcy Opinions.

Nebraska County Courts

Court	Jurisdiction	No. of Courts	How Organized
District Courts*	General	93	12 Districts
County Courts*	Limited	93	12 Districts
Juvenile Courts	Special	3	3 Counties
Workers' Compensation Court	Special	1	

* Profiled in this Sourcebook.

Court	CIVIL: Tort	Contract	Real Estate	Min. Claim	Max. Claim	Small Claims	Estate	Eviction	Domestic Relations
District Courts*	X	X	X	$51,000	No Max				X
County Courts*	X	X	X	$0	$51,000	$2700	X	X	X
Juvenile Courts									

Court	CRIMINAL: Felony	Misdemeanor	DWI/DUI	Preliminary Hearing	Juvenile
District Courts*	X	X			
County Courts*		X	X	X	X
Juvenile Courts					X

Administration

Court Administrator, PO Box 98910, Lincoln, NE, 68509-8910; 402-471-3730, Fax: 402-471-2197 http://court.nol.org/

Court Structure

District Courts have original jurisdiction in all felony cases, equity cases, domestic relations cases, and civil cases where the amount in controversy involves more than $51,000. District Courts also have appellate jurisdiction in certain matters arising out of County Courts. Prior to the current level, historically the state raised the County Court limit on civil matters from $15,000 to $45,000 Sept. 1, 2001. County Courts have original jurisdiction in probate matters, violations of city or village ordinances, juvenile court matters without a separate juvenile court, adoptions, preliminary hearings in felony cases, and eminent domain proceedings. The County Courts have concurrent jurisdiction in civil matters when the amount in controversy is $51,000 or less, criminal matters classified as misdemeanors or infractions, some domestic relations matters, and paternity actions. Nearly all misdemeanor cases are tried in the County Courts. As a rule of thumb, only District Courts can enter a sentence which incarcerates a defendant for more than one year.

County Courts have juvenile jurisdiction in all but 3 counties. Douglas, Lancaster, and Sarpy counties have separate Juvenile Courts.

Online Access

An online access subscription service is available for all Nebraska County Courts and all District Courts except Douglas County District Court. Case details, all party listings, payments, and actions taken for criminal, civil, probate, juvenile, and traffic is available. The system starts with a name search and resulting list gives full DOB. A onetime search is $15.00. Ongoing users must be registered with Nebraska.gov, and have access to other records. There is a start-up fee, but the access fee is $.60 per record or a flat rate of $300.00 per month. Go to www.nebraska.gov/faqs/justice or call 402-471-7810 for more info and data on how far back records go per county. Supreme Court opinions are available from http://court.nol.org/opinions.

Searching Tips, Fees, and Other Guidelines

Most Nebraska courts require the public to do their own in person searches and will not respond to written search requests. The State Attorney General has recommended that courts not perform searches because of the time involved and concerns about legal liability. In general, the copy fee is $.25 per page and the certification fee is $1.00.

Adams County

District Court PO Box 9, Hastings, NE 68902; 402-461-7264; criminal fax: 402-461-7269; civil fax: same; 8:30AM-5PM (CST). ***Felony, Civil Actions over $51,000.***

www.adamscounty.org/courts/index.htm

Civil Records: Access: In person, online. Visitors must perform in person searches themselves. Required to search: name, years to search. Civil cases indexed by defendant, plaintiff; index on microfiche from 1800s, 5 yrs on index cards, on docket books from 1800s. Civil PAT goes back to 7/1997. Civil records online - see criminal access. Online records date from 07/97.

Criminal Records: Access: In person, online. Visitors must perform in person searches themselves. Required to search: name, years to search. Criminal records on microfiche from 1800s, 5 yrs on index cards, on docket books from 1800s. Criminal PAT available. Single use or subscribe at https://www.nebraska.gov/justicecc/ccname.cgi for court access. Single use is $15.00 a record or open an account for $1 per record plus $50 annual fee. Online records date from 07/97. Online results show middle initial, DOB.

General Information: No juvenile, search warrants or mental health records released. Will not fax documents. Court makes copy: $.25 per page. Certification fee: $1.00 per page. Payee: Clerk of District Court. Personal checks accepted; credit cards are not. Prepayment required.

County Court PO Box 95, Hastings, NE 68902-0095; 402-461-7143; fax: 402-461-7144; 8AM-5PM (CST). ***Misdemeanor, Civil Actions under $51,000, Eviction, Small Claims, Probate.***
www.district10.us/

Civil Records: Access: In person, online. Visitors must perform in person searches themselves. Required to search: name, years to search; also helpful: address. Civil cases indexed by defendant. Civil index on cards and files from 1970s. Civil PAT goes back to 1999. Civil records online - see criminal access. Online civil records date from 10/99 forward, probate from 05/98.

Criminal Records: Access: In person, online. Visitors must perform in person searches themselves. Required to search: name, years to search; also helpful: DOB, SSN. Criminal records indexed on cards and files from 1970s. Criminal PAT goes back to same as civil. Single use or subscribe at https://www.nebraska.gov/justicecc/ccname.cgi for court access. Single use is $15.00 a record or open an account for $1 per record plus $50 annual fee. Online criminal and traffic records date from 07/97. Online results show middle initial, DOB.

General Information: No adoption or juvenile records released. Will not fax documents. Court makes copy: $.25 per page. Self serve: same. Certification fee: $1.00 per page. Payee: Adams County Court. Business checks accepted. No credit cards accepted. Prepayment required.

Antelope County

District Court PO Box 45, Neligh, NE 68756; 402-887-4508; criminal fax: 402-887-4870; civil fax: same; 8AM-4:30PM (CST). ***Felony, Civil Actions over $51,000.***

Civil Records: Access: In person, online. Visitors must perform in person searches themselves. Required to search: name, years to search. Civil cases indexed by defendant, plaintiff. Civil index on docket books from 1872, computerized since 1999. Civil PAT goes back to 1999. PAT results show middle initial, DOB, SSN. Civil records online - see criminal access. Online records date from 03/99.

Criminal Records: Access: In person, online. Visitors must perform in person searches themselves. Required to search: name, years to search. Criminal records indexed in books from 1872, computerized since 1999. Criminal PAT goes back to same as civil. PAT results show middle initial, DOB. Single use or subscribe at https://www.nebraska.gov/justicecc/ccname.cgi for court access. Single use is $15.00 a record or open an account for $1 per record plus $50 annual fee. Online records date from 03/99. Online results show middle initial, DOB, SSN.

General Information: No juvenile, sealed, search warrants, or mental health record released. Will fax specific case file for $1.00 per page. Court makes copy: $.25 per page. Self serve: same. Certification fee: $1.00 per page. Payee: Clerk of District Court. Personal checks accepted; credit cards are not. Prepayment required.

Antelope County Court 501 Main, Neligh, NE 68756; 402-887-4650; criminal fax: 402-887-4160; civil fax: same; 8:30AM-5PM (CST). ***Misdemeanor, Civil Actions under $51,000, Eviction, Small Claims, Probate.***
Probate fax is same as main fax number.

Civil Records: Access: In person, online. Visitors must perform in person searches themselves. Required to search: name, years to search. Civil cases indexed by defendant, plaintiff; index on computer from 1999, probate on microfiche from 1876, civil and small claims indexed from 1983. Public use terminal available. PAT results show name, DOB. Civil records online - see criminal access. Online civil and probate records date from 12/99 forward.

Criminal Records: Access: In person, online. Visitors must perform in person searches themselves. Required to search: name, years to search, DOB, signed release. Criminal index on computer from 1999, indexed from 1800s. Public use terminal available.PAT results show name, DOB. Single use or subscribe at https://www.nebraska.gov/justicecc/ccname.cgi for court access. Single use is $15.00 a record or open an account for $1 per record plus $50 annual fee. Online criminal and traffic records date from 12/99. Online results show middle initial, DOB.

General Information: No adoption, or sealed records released. Will fax out specific case files for $1.00 per page. Court makes copy: $.25 per page. Self serve: same. Certification fee: $1.00 plus $.25 per page. Payee: Antelope County Court. Personal checks accepted; credit cards are not. Prepayment required.

Arthur County

District & County Court PO Box 126, 205 Fir St., Arthur, NE 69121; 308-764-2203; fax: 308-764-2216; 8AM-4PM (MST). ***Felony, Misdemeanor, Civil, Eviction, Small Claims, Probate.***

Civil Records: Access: In person, online. Both court and visitors may perform in person searches. No search fee. Required to search: name, years to search. Civil cases indexed by defendant, plaintiff. Civil index on docket books from 1987, on docket books from 1913. Civil PAT goes back to 1999. PAT results show name only. Civil records online - see criminal access. County court online records date from 09/99 forward; District Court records from 06/00.

Criminal Records: Access: In person, online. Both court and visitors may perform in person searches. No search fee. Required to search: name, years to search. Criminal records indexed in books from 1987, on docket books from 1913. Criminal PAT goes back to same as civil. PAT results show name only. Single use or subscribe at https://www.nebraska.gov/justicecc/ccname.cgi for court access. Single use is $15.00 a record or open an account for $1 per record plus $50 annual fee. Online criminal and traffic records date from 09/99 forward; District Court records from 6/2000. Online results show middle initial, DOB.

General Information: No search warrants, juvenile, adoption, mental health, or sealed records released. Will fax documents $1.00 per page. Court makes copy: $.20 per page if mailed. Self serve: $.10 per page. Certification fee: $1.50 first page; $.50 each add'l. Payee: Arthur County Clerk. Personal checks accepted; credit cards are not. Prepayment required.

Banner County

District Court PO Box 67, 206 State St, Harrisburg, NE 69345; 308-436-5265; fax: 308-436-4180; 8AM-5PM (MST). ***Felony, Civil Actions over $51,000.***

Civil Records: Access: Fax, mail, in person, online. Both court and visitors may perform in person searches. No search fee. Required to search: name, years to search; also helpful: address. Civil cases indexed by defendant, plaintiff. Civil index in docket books from 1800s. Mail turnaround time 5-7 days. Civil PAT goes back to 2001. Civil records online - see criminal access. Online civil records date from 06/00 forward.

Criminal Records: Access: Fax, mail, in person, online. Both court and visitors may perform in person searches. No search fee. Required to search: name, years to search, DOB; also helpful: address. Criminal docket on books from 1800s. Mail turnaround time 5-7 days. Criminal PAT goes back to same as civil. Single use or subscribe at https://www.nebraska.gov/justicecc/ccname.cgi for court access. Single use is $15.00 a record or open an account for $1 per record plus $50 annual fee. Online records date from 06/00 forward. Online results show middle initial, DOB.

General Information: No search warrants, mental health, or sealed records released. Will fax documents $.50 per page. Court makes copy: $1.00 per page. Certification fee: $1.50 per cert. Payee: Banner County Clerk. Personal checks accepted; credit cards are not. Prepayment required. Mail requests: SASE required.

Banner County Court PO Box 2, Harrisburg, NE 69345; 308-436-5268; probate phone: 308-436-5268.; fax: 308-436-4180; 8AM-Noon, 1PM-5PM (MST). ***Misdemeanor, Civil Actions under $51,000, Eviction, Small Claims, Probate.***

Civil Records: Access: In person, online. Both court and visitors may perform in person searches. No search fee. Required to search: name, years to search. Civil cases indexed by defendant, plaintiff; index on register of action cards from 1992, prior on docket books, on computer from 12/2000. Civil records online - see criminal access. Online civil and probate records date from 01/01 forward.

Criminal Records: Access: In person, online. Both court and visitors may perform in person searches. No search fee. Required to search: name, years to search, signed release; also helpful: address, DOB. Criminal records on register of action cards from 1992, prior on docket books, on computer from 6/2000. Single use or subscribe at https://www.nebraska.gov/justicecc/ccname.cgi for court access. Single use is $15.00 a record or open an account for $1 per record plus $50 annual fee. Online criminal and traffic records date from 04/00. Online results show middle initial, DOB.

General Information: No adoption, sealed records released. Court makes copy: $.25 per page. Self serve: same. Certification fee: $1.00. Payee: Banner County Court. Personal checks accepted; credit cards are not. Prepayment required.

Blaine County

District Court 145 Lincoln Ave, Brewster, NE 68821; 308-547-2222 x201; criminal fax: 308-547-2228; civil fax: same; 8AM-4PM (CST). ***Felony, Civil Actions over $51,000.***
http://dc8.nol.org

Civil Records: Access: Fax, mail, in person, online. Search fee: $1.00 per name. Required to search: name, years to search. Civil cases indexed by defendant, plaintiff. Civil index on docket books from late 1800s. Mail turnaround time 1-2 days. Civil PAT goes back to 6/2000. PAT results show name only. Civil records online - see criminal access. Online records date from 06/00 forward.

Criminal Records: Access: Fax, mail, in person, online. Both court and visitors may perform in person searches. Search fee: $1.00 per name. Required to search: name, years to search, DOB. Criminal records indexed in books from late 1800s. Mail turnaround time 1-2 days. Criminal PAT goes back to same as civil. PAT results show name only. Single use or subscribe at https://www.nebraska.gov/justicecc/ccname.cgi for court access. Single use is $15.00 a record or open an account for $1 per record plus $50 annual fee. Online records date from 06/00 forward. Online results show name only.

General Information: No search warrants, mental health, or sealed records released. Will fax documents $3.00 1st page. $1.00 ea add'l. Court makes copy: $.25 per page. Certification fee: $1.50. Payee: Blaine County Clerk. Personal checks accepted; credit cards are not. Prepayment required. Mail requests: SASE required.

Blaine County Court 145 Lincoln Ave, Brewster, NE 68821; 308-547-2222 x202; probate phone: x202; criminal fax: 308-547-2228; civil fax: same; 8AM-4PM (CST). ***Misdemeanor, Civil Actions under $51,000, Eviction, Small Claims, Probate.***
Probate fax is same as main fax number.

Civil Records: Access: Phone, fax, mail, in person, online. Only the court performs in person searches; visitors may not. No search fee. Required to search: name, years to search; also helpful: address. Civil cases indexed by defendant, plaintiff. Civil index on docket books from 1960. on microfiche prior to 1960. Mail turnaround time 2 days. Civil records online - see criminal access. Online civil and probate records date from 01/01 forward.

Criminal Records: Access: Phone, fax, mail, in person, online. Only the court performs in person searches; visitors may not. No search fee. Required to search: name, years to search; also helpful: address, DOB, SSN. Criminal records indexed in books from 1960. on microfiche prior to 1960. Mail turnaround time 2 days. Single use or subscribe at https://www.nebraska.gov/justicecc/ccname.cgi for court access. Single use is $15.00 a record or open an account for $1 per record plus $50 annual fee. Online criminal and traffic records date from 08/00. Online results show middle initial, DOB.

General Information: No juvenile, adoption, or sealed records released. Will fax documents $1.00 per page. Court makes copy: $.25 per page. Self serve: same. Certification fee: $1.00 per page. Payee: Blaine County Court. Personal checks accepted; credit cards are not. Prepayment required. Mail requests: SASE required.

Boone County

District Court 222 S 4th St, Albion, NE 68620; 402-395-2057; fax: 402-395-6592; 8:30AM-5PM (CST). ***Felony, Civil Actions over $51,000.***

Civil Records: Access: In person, online. Visitors must perform in person searches themselves. Required to search: name, years to search. Civil cases indexed by defendant, plaintiff. Civil records in general index and dockets from 1800s, computerized records since 2001. Civil PAT goes back to 2000. Civil records online; see criminal access. Online records date from 12/99 forward.

Criminal Records: Access: In person, online. Visitors must perform in person searches themselves. Required to search: name, years to search; also helpful: DOB. Criminal records in general index and dockets from 1800s, computerized records since 2001. Criminal PAT goes back to same as civil. Single use or subscribe at https://www.nebraska.gov/justicecc/ccname.cgi for court access. Single use is $15.00 a record or open an account for $1 per record plus $50 annual fee. Online records date from 12/99. Online results show middle initial, DOB.

General Information: No search warrants, mental health, or sealed records released. Will fax documents $3.00 1st page, $1.00 each add'l. Court makes copy: $.25 per page. Certification fee: $1.00 per page. Payee: Clerk of District Court. Personal checks accepted; credit cards are not. Prepayment required.

Boone County Court 222 S 4th St, Albion, NE 68620; 402-395-6184; fax: 402-395-6592; 8AM-5PM (CST). ***Misdemeanor, Civil Actions under $51,000, Eviction, Small Claims, Probate.***

Civil Records: Access: Fax, mail, in person, online. Both court and visitors may perform in person searches. No search fee. Required to search: name, years to search. Civil cases indexed by defendant, plaintiff; index on general index and docket books from late 1800s; computerized back to 2000; probate on microfiche from 1970. Mail turnaround time 1-2 days. SASE required for large requests. Civil PAT goes back to 6/2000. Civil records online - see criminal access. Online civil records date from 10/00 forward, probate from 01/01.

Criminal Records: Access: In person, online. Visitors must perform in person searches themselves. Required to search: name, years to search; also helpful: DOB. Criminal records on general index and docket books from late 1800s; computerized back to 2000; probate on microfiche from 1970. Criminal PAT goes back to same as civil. Single use or subscribe at https://www.nebraska.gov/justicecc/ccname.cgi for court access. Single use is $15.00 a record or open an account for $1 per record plus $50 annual fee. Online criminal and traffic records date from 06/00. Online results show middle initial, DOB.

General Information: Online identifiers in results same as on public terminal. No adoption, or sealed records released. No fee to fax documents. Court makes copy: $.25 per page. Self serve: same. Certification fee: $1.00. Payee: Clerk of County Court. Personal checks accepted; credit cards are not. Prepayment required. Mail requests: SASE required for civil.

Box Butte County

District Court 515 Box Butte #300, Alliance, NE 69301; 308-762-6293; criminal fax: 308-762-5700; civil fax: same; 9AM-4PM (MST). ***Felony, Civil Actions over $51,000.***

Civil Records: Access: In person, online. Visitors must perform in person searches themselves. Required to search: name, years to search. Civil cases indexed by defendant, plaintiff. Civil general index and docket books from late 1800s. Civil PAT goes back to 1890. PAT results show name, DOB. Civil records online - see criminal access. Online records date from 10/97.

Criminal Records: Access: In person, online. Visitors must perform in person searches themselves. Required to search: name, years to search. Criminal records on general index and docket books from late 1800s. Criminal PAT goes back to 1890.PAT results show name, DOB. Single use or subscribe at https://www.nebraska.gov/justicecc/ccname.cgi for court access. Single use is $15.00 a record or open an account for $1 per record plus $50 annual fee. Online records date from 10/97. Online results show middle initial, DOB.

General Information: No mental health, or sealed records released. Will fax out specific case files for $1.00 per page. Court makes copy: $.25 per page. Self serve: same. Certification fee: $1.00 per page. Personal checks accepted; credit cards are not. Prepayment required.

Box Butte County Court PO Box 613, Alliance, NE 69301; 308-762-6800; fax: 308-762-2650; 8:30AM-5PM (MST). ***Misdemeanor, Civil Actions under $51,000, Eviction, Small Claims, Probate.***

Civil Records: Access: in person, online. Visitors must perform in person searches themselves. Required to search: name, years to search. Civil cases indexed by defendant, plaintiff; index on microfiche for 10 years, on index cards to docket books from late 1800s; computerized records since 2000. Civil PAT goes back to 4/2000. PAT civil results show middle initial. Civil records online - see criminal access. Online records date from 11/00 forward.

Criminal Records: Access: In person, online. Visitors must perform in person searches themselves. Required to search: name, years to search, DOB. Criminal records on microfiche for 10 years, on index cards to docket books from late 1800s; computerized records since 2000. Criminal PAT goes back to same as civil. PAT criminal results show middle initial. Single use or subscribe at https://www.nebraska.gov/justicecc/ccname.cgi for court access. Single use is $15.00 a record or open an account for $1 per record plus $50 annual fee. Online criminal and traffic records date from 04/00. Online results show middle initial, DOB.

General Information: No adoption or sealed records released. Will fax documents $2.75 per page. Court makes copy: $.25 per page. Certification fee: $1.00. Payee: Box Butte County Court. Personal checks accepted; credit cards are not. Prepayment required.

Boyd County

District Court PO Box 26, Butte, NE 68722; 402-775-2391; fax: 402-775-2146; 8:15AM-4PM (CST). ***Felony, Civil Actions over $51,000.***

Civil Records: Access: Mail, fax, in person, online. Both court and visitors may perform in person searches. Search fee: $3.00 per name. Required to search: name, years to search, address. Civil cases indexed by defendant, plaintiff. Civil general index and docket books from late 1800s. Mail turnaround time 3-4 days. Civil PAT goes back to 2000. PAT results show name, DOB. Civil records online - see criminal access. Online records date from 07/00.

Criminal Records: Access: Mail, fax, in person, online. Both court and visitors may perform in person searches. Search fee: $3.00 per name. Required to search: name, years to search, address. Criminal records on general index and docket books from late 1800s. Mail turnaround time 3-4 days. Criminal PAT goes back to same as civil.PAT results show name, DOB. Single use or subscribe at https://www.nebraska.gov/justicecc/ccname.cgi for court access. Single use is $15.00 a record or open an account for $1 per record plus $50 annual fee. Online records date from 07/00 forward. Online results show middle initial, DOB.

General Information: No search warrants, mental health, or sealed records released. Will fax documents $3.00 1st page, $1.00 ea add'l. Court makes copy: $.25 per page. Self serve: same. Certification fee: $1.50. Payee: Boyd County Clerk. Personal checks accepted; credit cards are not. Prepayment required. Mail requests: SASE required.

Boyd County Court PO Box 396, Butte, NE 68722; 402-775-2211; probate phone: 402-775-2211; fax: 402-775-2211; 8AM-4PM M,W; TH- AM (CST). ***Misdemeanor, Civil Actions under $51,000, Eviction, Small Claims, Probate.***

Civil Records: Access: In person, online. Visitors must perform in person searches themselves. Required to search: name, years to search; also helpful: address. Civil cases indexed by defendant, plaintiff. Civil general index and docket books from late 1800s. Civil PAT available. Online subscription service - see criminal access. Online civil records date from 11/00 forward, probate from 10/00.

Criminal Records: Access: In person, online. Visitors must perform in person searches themselves. Required to search: name, years to search; also helpful: address, DOB, SSN. Criminal records on general index and docket books from late 1800s. Criminal PAT available. Single use or subscribe at https://www.nebraska.gov/justicecc/ccname.cgi for court access. Single use is $15.00 a record or open an account for $1 per record plus $50 annual fee. Online criminal and traffic records date from 08/00. Online results show middle initial, DOB.

General Information: No adoption, juvenile, or sealed records released. Will fax documents for no fee. Court makes copy: $.25 per page. Certification fee: $1.00. Payee: Boyd County Court. Personal checks accepted. Prepayment required.

Brown County

District Court 148 W Fourth St, Ainsworth, NE 69210; 402-387-2705; fax: 402-387-0918; 8AM-5PM (CST). ***Felony, Civil Actions over $51,000.***

Civil Records: Access: Phone, fax, mail, in person, online. Both court and visitors may perform in person searches. No search fee. Required to search: name, years to search; also helpful: address. Civil cases indexed by defendant, plaintiff; index on general index and docket books from late 1886s; on computer back to 2000. Mail turnaround time 3-4 days. Civil PAT goes back to 2001. Civil records online - see criminal access. Online records date from 02/00.

Criminal Records: Access: Fax, mail, in person, online. Both court and visitors may perform in person searches. No search fee. Required to search: name, years to search, signed release; also helpful: address, DOB, SSN. Criminal records on general index and docket books from late 1886; on computer back to 2000. Mail turnaround time 3-4 days. Criminal PAT goes back to 2001. Single use or subscribe at https://www.nebraska.gov/justicecc/ccname.cgi for court access. Single use is $15.00 a record or open an account for $1 per record plus $50 annual fee. Online records date from 02/00. Online results show middle initial, DOB.

General Information: No search warrants, mental health, or sealed records released. Fee to fax out file $3.00 per page. Court makes copy: $.25 per page. Self serve: $.25 per page. Certification fee: $2.00 per cert includes copies. Payee: Clerk of District Court, Brown County. Personal checks accepted; credit cards are not. Prepayment required. Mail requests: SASE required.

Brown County Court 148 W Fourth St, Ainsworth, NE 69210; 402-387-2864; fax: 402-387-0918; 8AM-4:30PM (CST). ***Misdemeanor, Civil Actions under $51,000, Eviction, Small Claims, Probate.***

Civil Records: Access: In person, online. Both court and visitors may perform in person searches. No search fee. Required to search: name, years to search. Civil cases indexed by defendant, plaintiff. Civil records in boxes in office since 1980; on computer since 2001. Civil PAT goes back to 2000. Civil records online - see criminal access. Online civil records date from 04/01 forward, probate from 03/01.

Criminal Records: Access: In person, online. Both court and visitors may perform in person searches. No search fee. Required to search: name, years to search, DOB. Criminal records in boxes in office since 1979; on computer since 2000. Criminal PAT goes back to same as civil. Single use or subscribe at https://www.nebraska.gov/justicecc/ccname.cgi for court access. Single use is $15.00 a record or open an account for $1 per record plus $50 annual

fee. Online criminal and traffic records date from 08/00. Online results show middle initial, DOB.
General Information: No adoption, juvenile, or sealed records released. Will not fax documents. Court makes copy: $.25 per page. Certification fee: $1.00 per page. Payee: Brown County Court. Personal checks accepted; credit cards are not. Prepayment required.

Buffalo County

District Court PO Box 520, Kearney, NE 68848; 308-236-1246; fax: 308-233-3693; 8AM-5PM (CST). ***Felony, Civil Actions over $51,000.***
Civil Records: Access: In person, online. Visitors must perform in person searches themselves. Required to search: name only. Civil cases indexed by defendant, plaintiff; index on computer from 1993, on microfiche through 1991, on books from 1800s. Civil PAT goes back to 1997. PAT results show name only. Public terminal in courthouse lobby. Civil records online - see criminal access. Online records date from 05/97.
Criminal Records: Access: In person, online. Visitors must perform in person searches themselves. Required to search: name, DOB. Criminal records computerized from 1997; on microfiche 1991-current; on books from 1800s. Criminal PAT goes back to same as civil. PAT results show name only. Public terminal in courthouse lobby. Single use or subscribe at https://www.nebraska.gov/justicecc/ccname.cgi for court access. Single use is $15.00 a record or open an account for $1 per record plus $50 annual fee. Online records date from 05/97. Online results show middle initial, DOB.
General Information: No juvenile, mental health, search warrants or sealed records released. Will fax out specific case files for $3.00 for 1st page, $1.00 each add'l. Court makes copy: $.25 per page. Self serve: same. Certification fee: $1.00 per doc. Payee: Clerk of District Court. Business checks accepted. No credit cards accepted. Prepayment required.

Buffalo County Court PO Box 520, Kearney, NE 68848; 308-236-1228; criminal phone: 308-236-1231; civil phone: 308-236-3633; probate phone: 308-236-1231; criminal fax: 308-236-1243; civil fax: same; 8AM-5PM (CST). ***Misdemeanor, Civil Actions under $51,000, Eviction, Small Claims, Probate.***
Probate fax is same as main fax number.
Civil Records: Access: In person, online. Visitors must perform in person searches themselves. Required to search: name, years to search. Civil cases indexed by defendant, plaintiff; index on computer from 4/94, on microfiche, general index, and docket books from late 1800s. Public use terminal available. Civil records online - see criminal access. Online civil and probate records date from 04/94.
Criminal Records: Access: In person, online. Visitors must perform in person searches themselves. Required to search: name, years to search. Criminal records computerized from 4/94, on microfiche, general index, and docket books from late 1800s. Public use terminal available. Single use or subscribe at https://www.nebraska.gov/justicecc/ccname.cgi for court access. Single use is $15.00 a record or open an account for $1 per record plus $50 annual fee. Online criminal and traffic records date from 04/94. Online results show middle initial, DOB.
General Information: No adoption, or sealed records released. Will not fax documents. Court makes copy: $.25 per page. Certification fee: $1.00 per seal. Payee: County Court. Personal checks accepted; credit cards are not. Prepayment required.

Burt County

District Court 111 N 13th St #11, Tekamah, NE 68061; 402-374-2905; fax: 402-374-2906; 8AM-4:30PM (CST). ***Felony, Civil Actions over $51,000.***
Civil Records: Access: In person, online. Both court and visitors may perform in person searches. No search fee. Required to search: name, years to search. Civil cases indexed by defendant, plaintiff; index on books from 1800s. Civil PAT goes back to 1999. Civil records online - see criminal access. Online records date from 3/1999.
Criminal Records: Access: In person, online. Both court and visitors may perform in person searches. No search fee. Required to search: name, years to search; also helpful: DOB, SSN. Criminal docket on books from 1800s. Criminal PAT goes back to same as civil. Single use or subscribe at https://www.nebraska.gov/justicecc/ccname.cgi for court access. Single use is $15.00 a record or open an account for $1 per record plus $50 annual fee. Online records date from 3/1999. Online results show middle initial, DOB.
General Information: No mental health records released. Will fax documents to local or toll free line. Court makes copy: $.25 per page. Certification fee: $1.00 per cert includes copies. Payee: Clerk of District Court. Personal checks accepted; credit cards are not. Prepayment required. Mail requests: SASE required for mail return of any copies.

Burt County Court 111 N 13th St, #9, Tekamah, NE 68061; 402-374-2950; fax: 402-374-2951; 8AM-4:30PM (CST). ***Misdemeanor, Civil Actions under $51,000, Eviction, Small Claims, Probate.***
Civil Records: Access: In person, online. Visitors must perform in person searches themselves. Required to search: name, years to search, address. Civil cases indexed by defendant, plaintiff. Civil index on cards back to 1867, computerized back to 1998. Civil PAT goes back to 1998. PAT civil results show middle initial. Civil records online - see criminal access. Online civil records date from 03/00 forward, probate from 05/98.
Criminal Records: Access: In person, online. Visitors must perform in person searches themselves. Required to search: name, years to search, address, DOB. Criminal records indexed on cards back to 1867, computerized back to 1998. Criminal PAT goes back to same as civil. PAT results show middle initial, DOB. Single use or subscribe at https://www.nebraska.gov/justicecc/ccname.cgi for court access. Single use is $15.00 a record or open an account for $1 per record plus $50 annual fee. Online criminal and traffic records date from 02/98. Online results show middle initial, DOB.
General Information: Online identifiers in results same as on public terminal. No adoption records released. Will not fax documents. Court makes copy: $.25 per page. Self serve: same. Certification fee: $1.00 per page. Payee: County Court. No personal checks or credit cards accepted. Prepayment required.

Butler County

District Court 451 5th St, David City, NE 68632-1666; 402-367-7460; criminal fax: 402-367-3249; civil fax: same; 8:30AM-5PM (CST). ***Felony, Civil Actions over $51,000.***
Civil Records: Access: Mail, in person, online. Both court and visitors may perform in person searches. Search fee: $2.00 per name. Required to search: name, years to search. Civil cases indexed by defendant, plaintiff; index on books. Mail turnaround time 1-2 days. Civil PAT goes back to 2001. Civil records online - see criminal access. Online records date from 03/99.
Criminal Records: Access: Mail, in person, online. Both court and visitors may perform in person searches. Search fee: $2.00 per name. Required to search: name, years to search; also helpful: DOB, SSN. Criminal docket on books. Mail turnaround time 1-2 days. Criminal PAT goes back to same. Single use or subscribe at https://www.nebraska.gov/justicecc/ccname.cgi for court access. Single use is $15.00 a record or open an account for $1 per record plus $50 annual fee. Online records date from 03/99. Online results show middle initial, DOB.
General Information: No juvenile or mental health records released. No fee to fax documents. Court makes copy: $.25 per page. Self serve: $.10 per page. Certification fee: $1.50 per document. Payee: District Court. Personal checks accepted; credit cards are not. Prepayment required. Mail requests: SASE required.

Butler County Court 451 5th St, David City, NE 68632-1666; 402-367-7480; fax: 402-367-3249; 8AM-N, 1-5PM (CST). ***Misdemeanor, Civil Actions under $51,000, Eviction, Small Claims, Probate.***
Civil Records: Access: In person, online. Visitors must perform in person searches themselves. Required to search: name, years to search. Civil cases indexed by defendant, plaintiff; index on computer since 1998, docket books from late 1800s, probate on microfiche. Note: They can refer requestors to parties who perform searches at the court. Civil PAT goes back to 1998. PAT results show name, DOB. Civil records online - see criminal access. Online civil records date from 10/99 forward, probate from 03/98.
Criminal Records: Access: In person, online. Visitors must perform in person searches themselves. Required to search: name, years to search; also helpful: DOB. Criminal records on computer since 1998, docket books from late 1800s, probate on microfiche. Note: Court can refer requestors to parties who perform searches at the court. Criminal PAT goes back to same as civil.PAT results show name, DOB. Results include drivers license number. Single use or subscribe at https://www.nebraska.gov/justicecc/ccname.cgi for court access. Single use is $15.00 a record or open an account for $1 per record plus $50 annual fee. Online criminal and traffic records date from 03/98. Online results show middle initial, DOB.
General Information: Online identifiers in results same as on public terminal. No adoption records released. Some juvenile requires signed release. Will fax case file $3.00 if pre-paid. Court makes copy: $.25 per page. Certification fee: $1.00. Payee: Butler County Court. Personal checks accepted; credit cards are not. Prepayment required. Mail requests: SASE required for mail return of any copies.

Cass County

District Court Cass County Courthouse, 346 Main St, Plattsmouth, NE 68048; 402-296-9339; criminal fax: 402-296-9345; civil fax: same; 8AM-5PM (CST). ***Felony, Civil Actions over $51,000.***
www.cassne.org/distcourt.html
Civil Records: Access: In person, online. Visitors must perform in person searches themselves. Required to search: name, years to search. Civil cases indexed by defendant, plaintiff. Civil index on docket books from 1860s, index on computer since 9/97. Civil PAT goes back to 8/1997. PAT results show name only. Civil records online - see criminal access. Online records date from 08/97.
Criminal Records: Access: In person, online. Visitors must perform in person searches themselves. Required to search: name, years to search. Criminal records indexed in books from 1860s, index on computer since 9/97. Criminal PAT goes back to 8/1997. PAT results show name only. Single use or subscribe at https://www.nebraska.gov/justicecc/ccname.cgi for court access. Single use is $15.00 a record or open an account for $1 per record plus $50 annual fee. Online records date from 08/97. Online results show middle initial, DOB.
General Information: Online identifiers in results same as on public terminal. Will fax out specific case files for $1.50 1st page; $.50 each add'l. Court makes copy: $.25 per page. Certification fee: $1.00 per seal. Payee: Clerk of District Court. Personal checks accepted; credit cards are not. Prepayment required.

Cass County Court Cass County Courthouse, 346 Main St Rm 301, Plattsmouth, NE 68048; 402-296-9334; probate phone: 402-296-9334; fax: 402-296-9545; 8AM-5PM (CST). ***Misdemeanor, Civil Actions under $51,000, Eviction, Small Claims, Probate.***
Civil Records: Access: In person, online. Visitors must perform in person searches themselves. Required to search: name, years to search. Civil cases indexed by defendant, plaintiff. Civil index on cards for 5 years then sent to Capital for storage; computerized records since 2000. Civil PAT goes back to 2000. PAT results show name only. Civil records online - see criminal access. Online civil records date from 01/00 forward, probate from 05/98.
Criminal Records: Access: In person, online. Visitors must perform in person searches

themselves. Required to search: name, years to search. Criminal records on computer since 1/97. Criminal PAT goes back to 2000. PAT results show name only. Single use or subscribe at https://www.nebraska.gov/justicecc/ccname.cgi for court access. Single use is $15.00 a record or open an account for $1 per record plus $50 annual fee. Online criminal and traffic records date from 01/97. Online results show middle initial, DOB.
General Information: Will not fax documents. Court makes copy: $.25 per page. Certification fee: $1.25. Payee: Cass County Court. No personal checks or credit cards accepted. Prepayment required.

Cedar County

District Court PO Box 796, Hartington, NE 68739-0796; 402-254-6957; fax: 402-254-6954; 8AM-5PM (CST). ***Felony, Civil Actions over $51,000.***
Civil Records: Access: In person, online. Visitors must perform in person searches themselves. Required to search: name, years to search. Civil cases indexed by defendant, plaintiff. Civil records in books from 1890. Civil PAT goes back to 11/1999. Civil records online - see criminal access. Online records date from 11/99.
Criminal Records: Access: In person, online. Visitors must perform in person searches themselves. Required to search: name, years to search; also helpful: SSN. Criminal records in books from 1890. Criminal PAT goes back to same as civil. Single use or subscribe at https://www.nebraska.gov/justicecc/ccname.cgi for court access. Single use is $15.00 a record or open an account for $1 per record plus $50 annual fee. Online records date from 11/99. Online results show middle initial, DOB.
General Information: Online identifiers in results same as on public terminal. No mental health records released. Will not fax documents. Court makes copy: $.25 per page. Certification fee: $1.00. Payee: District Court. Personal checks accepted; credit cards are not. Prepayment required.

Cedar County Court P O Box 695, Hartington, NE 68739; 402-254-7441; fax: 402-254-7447; 8AM-5PM (CST). ***Misdemeanor, Civil Actions under $51,000, Eviction, Small Claims, Probate.***
Civil Records: Access: In person, online. Visitors must perform in person searches themselves. Required to search: name, years to search. Civil cases indexed by defendant. Civil records on general index, docket books 15 years; some on microfiche to 1983. Civil PAT goes back to 2000. PAT results show middle initial, DOB. Civil records online - see criminal access. Online civil and probate records from 11/00 forward.
Criminal Records: Access: In person, online. Visitors must perform in person searches themselves. Required to search: name, years to search, offense; also helpful: DOB. Criminal records indexed in books since 1983, some on microfiche. Computerized records go back to 2000. Criminal PAT goes back to same as civil. PAT results show middle initial, DOB. Subscribe to JUSTICE at https://www.nebraska.gov/justicecc/ccname.cgi for court access. Single use is $15.00 a record or open an account for $1 per record plus $50 annual fee. Online criminal and traffic records date from 6/200. Online results show middle initial, DOB.
General Information: Online identifiers in results same as on public terminal. No juvenile or judge sealed records released. Will fax out specific case files for $3.00 for 1st page, $1.00 each add'l. Court makes copy: $.25 per page. Self serve: same. Certification fee: $1.00. Payee: Cedar County Court. Personal checks accepted; credit cards are not. Prepayment required. Mail requests: SASE required for mail return of any copies.

Chase County

District Court PO Box 1299, Imperial, NE 69033; 308-882-7500; fax: 308-882-7552; 8AM-4PM (MST). ***Felony, Civil Actions over $51,000.***
Civil Records: Access: Phone, fax, mail, in person, online. Both court and visitors may perform in person searches. No search fee. Required to search: name, years to search. Civil cases indexed by defendant, plaintiff. Civil records general index, docket books from early 1900s. Mail turnaround time 5 days. Civil PAT goes back to 2000. Civil records online - see criminal access. Online records date from 05/00.
Criminal Records: Access: Phone, fax, mail, in person, online. Both court and visitors may perform in person searches. No search fee. Required to search: name, years to search; also helpful: DOB, SSN. Criminal records general index, docket books from early 1900s, computerized since 2000. Mail turnaround time 5 days. Criminal PAT goes back to same as civil. PAT results show middle initial, DOB, SSN. Results include some drivers license numbers. Single use or subscribe at https://www.nebraska.gov/justicecc/ccname.cgi for court access. Single use is $15.00 a record or open an account for $1 per record plus $50 annual fee. Online records date from 05/00. Online results show middle initial, DOB.
General Information: Online identifiers in results same as on public terminal. Will fax documents $1.00 per page. Court makes copy: $.25 per page. Self serve: same. Certification fee: $1.00 plus copy fee for each document. Payee: Chase County Clerk. Personal checks accepted; credit cards are not. Prepayment required. Mail requests: SASE required.

Chase County Court PO Box 1299, 921 Broadway, Imperial, NE 69033; 308-882-7519; fax: 308-882-7554; 8AM-4PM (MST). ***Misdemeanor, Civil Actions under $51,000, Eviction, Small Claims, Probate.***
Civil Records: Access: In person, online. Both court and visitors may perform in person searches. No search fee. Required to search: name, years to search. Civil records on general index, docket books from 1910; prior incomplete. Some probate on microfiche. Civil PAT goes back to 1/2001. Public access terminal located at courthouse. Civil records online - see criminal access. Online civil and probate records date from 1/2001 forward.
Criminal Records: Access: In person, online. Both court and visitors may perform in person searches. No search fee. Required to search: name, years to search, DOB. Criminal records indexed in books from 1910; prior incomplete. Some probate on microfiche. Criminal PAT goes back to 9/2000. Public access terminal located at courthouse. Single use or subscribe at https://www.nebraska.gov/justicecc/ccname.cgi for court access. Single use is $15.00 a record or open an account for $1 per record plus $50 annual fee. Online criminal and traffic records date from 09/00. Online results show middle initial, DOB.
General Information: No adoption, juvenile. Will fax documents to local or toll free line. Court makes copy: $.25 per page. Certification fee: $1.00 per doc. Payee: Chase County Court. Personal checks accepted; credit cards are not. Prepayment required.

Cherry County

District Court 365 N Main St, Valentine, NE 69201; 402-376-1840; fax: 402-376-3830; 8AM-4:30PM (MST). ***Felony, Civil Actions over $51,000.***
Civil Records: Access: In person, online. Visitors must perform in person searches themselves. Required to search: name, years to search; also helpful: address. Civil cases indexed by petitioner, respondent. Civil index on docket books from late 1800s. Civil PAT goes back to 3/1999. Civil records online - see criminal access. Justice records date from 03/99.
Criminal Records: Access: In person, online. Visitors must perform in person searches themselves. Required to search: name, years to search. Criminal records indexed in books from late 1800s; computerized records since 1999. Criminal PAT goes back to same as civil. Single use or subscribe at https://www.nebraska.gov/justicecc/ccname.cgi for court access. Single use is $15.00 a record or open an account for $1 per record plus $50 annual fee. Online records date from 03/99. Online results show middle initial, DOB.
General Information: No juvenile records. Will not fax documents. Court makes copy: $.25 per page. Certification fee: $1.00 per page. Payee: Clerk of District Court. Personal checks accepted; credit cards are not. Prepayment required.

Cherry County Court 365 N Main St, Valentine, NE 69201; 402-376-2590; fax: 402-376-5942; 8AM-5PM (CST). ***Misdemeanor, Civil Actions under $51,000, Eviction, Small Claims, Probate.***
Civil Records: Access: In person, online. Visitors must perform in person searches themselves. Required to search: name, years to search. Civil cases indexed by defendant. Civil records on docket card file from 1986, general index prior from late 1800s. Civil PAT goes back to 11/2000. Civil records online - see criminal access. Online civil and probate records from 11/00 forward.
Criminal Records: Access: In person, online. Visitors must perform in person searches themselves. Required to search: name, years to search, DOB. Criminal records on docket card file from 1986, general index prior from late 1800s; on computer since 8/2000. Criminal PAT goes back to 8/2000. PAT results show middle initial, DOB. Single use or subscribe at https://www.nebraska.gov/justicecc/ccname.cgi for court access. Single use is $15.00 a record or open an account for $1 per record plus $50 annual fee. Online criminal and traffic records date from 08/20 Online results show middle initial, DOB.
General Information: Online identifiers in results same as on public terminal. No adoption records released. Juvenile released only to parties involved. Will fax out docs no add'l fee. Court makes copy: $.25 per page. Self serve: same. Certification fee: $1.25. Payee: Cherry County Court. Personal checks accepted; credit cards are not. Prepayment required.

Cheyenne County

District Court PO Box 217, 1000 10th Ave, Sidney, NE 69162; 308-254-2814; fax: 308-254-7832; 8AM-N,1-5PM (MST). ***Felony, Civil Actions over $51,000.***
Civil Records: Access: In person, online. Visitors must perform in person searches themselves. Required to search: name, years to search. Civil cases indexed by defendant, plaintiff; index on general index, docket books going back to late 1800s, on computer since 9/98. Civil PAT goes back to 1997. Civil records online - see criminal access. Online records date from 08/98.
Criminal Records: Access: In person, online. Visitors must perform in person searches themselves. Required to search: name, years to search; also helpful: DOB, SSN. Criminal records indexed in books going back to late 1800s, on computer since 9/98. Criminal PAT goes back to same as civil. Single use or subscribe at https://www.nebraska.gov/justicecc/ccname.cgi for court access. Single use is $15.00 a record or open an account for $1 per record plus $50 annual fee. Online records date from 08/98. Online results show middle initial, DOB.
General Information: No mental health or search warrants released. Will fax out specific case files to local or toll free line. Court makes copy: $.50 per page. Certification fee: $1.00 per doc. Payee: Clerk of District Court. No personal checks. No credit cards accepted. Prepayment required. Attorneys may be billed.

Cheyenne County Court 1000 10th Ave, Sidney, NE 69162; 308-254-2929; fax: 308-254-2312; 8AM-5PM (MST). ***Misdemeanor, Civil Actions under $51,000, Eviction, Small Claims, Probate.***
Must first receive permission to fax to the court.
Civil Records: Access: Fax, mail, in person, online. Both court and visitors may perform in person searches. No search fee. Required to search: name, years to search. Civil cases indexed by defendant, plaintiff. Civil index on docket books from late 1800s. Mail turnaround time within 1 week. Civil PAT goes back to 6/2000. Civil records online - see criminal access. Online records date from 12/00, including probate.
Criminal Records: Access: Fax, mail, in person, online. Both court and visitors may perform in person searches. No search fee. Required to search:

name, years to search; also helpful: DOB. Criminal records indexed in books from late 1800s; computerized records since 2000. Mail turnaround time within 1 week. Criminal PAT goes back to same as civil. Single use or subscribe at https://www.nebraska.gov/justicecc/ccname.cgi for court access. Single use is $15.00 a record or open an account for $1 per record plus $50 annual fee. Online criminal and traffic records date from 06/00. Online results show middle initial, DOB.
General Information: No adoption, juvenile, confidential records released. Court makes copy: $.25 per page. Certification fee: $1.00 per page. Payee: Cheyenne County Court. Personal checks accepted; credit cards are not. Prepayment required. Mail requests: SASE required.

Clay County

District Court Clerk of The District Court, 111 W Fairfield St, Clay Center, NE 68933; 402-762-3595; fax: 402-762-3604; 8:30AM-5PM (CST). ***Felony, Civil Actions over $51,000.***
www.claycounty.ne.gov/court.html
Civil Records: Access: In person, online. Visitors must perform in person searches themselves. Required to search: name; also helpful: years to search. Civil cases indexed by defendant, plaintiff. Civil index on docket books from late 1800s, on microfiche from 1986, computerized since 1998. Civil PAT goes back to 1998. Civil records online - see criminal access. Online records date from 09/98.
Criminal Records: Access: In person, online. Visitors must perform in person searches themselves. Required to search: name, DOB; also helpful: years to search, SSN. Criminal records indexed in books from late 1800s, on microfiche from 1986, computerized since 1998. Criminal PAT goes back to 9/1998. Single use or subscribe at https://www.nebraska.gov/justicecc/ccname.cgi for court access. Single use is $15.00 a record or open an account for $1 per record plus $50 annual fee. Online records date from 09/98. Online results show middle initial, DOB.
General Information: Online identifiers in results same as on public terminal. No mental health records released. Will fax documents $3.00 1st page, $1.00 ea add'l. Court makes copy: $.25 per page. Certification fee: $1.00. Payee: Clerk of District Court. Personal checks accepted; credit cards are not. Prepayment required.

Clay County Court 111 W Fairfield St, Clay Center, NE 68933; 402-762-3651; fax: 402-762-3250; 8:30AM-5PM (CST). ***Misdemeanor, Civil Actions under $51,000, Eviction, Small Claims, Probate, Traffic.***
www.claycounty.ne.gov/county_court.html
Alternative website - www.district10.us/.
Civil Records: Access: In person, online. Visitors must perform in person searches themselves. Required to search: name, years to search. Civil cases indexed by defendant. Civil records in index books from late 1800s, on computer from 4/2000. Civil PAT goes back to 4/2000. PAT civil results show middle initial. Civil records online - see criminal access. Online records date from 4/2000, including probate.
Criminal Records: Access: In person, online. Visitors must perform in person searches themselves. Required to search: name, years to search; also helpful: DOB, SSN. Criminal docket on books back 15 years from judgment. Criminal PAT goes back to same as civil. PAT results show middle initial, DOB. Single use or subscribe at https://www.nebraska.gov/justicecc/ccname.cgi for court access. Single use is $15.00 a record or open an account for $1 per record plus $50 annual fee. Online criminal and traffic records date from 4/2000. Online results show middle initial, DOB.
General Information: Online identifiers in results same as on public terminal. No adoption or juvenile records released. Will not fax documents. Court makes copy: $.25 per page. Self serve: same. Certification fee: $1.00. Payee: Clay County. Personal checks accepted; credit cards are not. Prepayment required.

Colfax County

District Court 411 E 11th St, Schuyler, NE 68661; 402-352-8506; criminal fax: 402-352-8550; civil fax: same; 8:30AM-4:30PM (CST). ***Felony, Civil Actions over $51,000.***
www.colfaxcounty.ne.gov
The court and clerk only have the record files, not the indexes. The indexes are located in the NE State Historical Society Archives, 1500 R St, Lincoln, NE 68501.
Civil Records: Access: In person, online. Visitors must perform in person searches themselves. Required to search: name, years to search; also helpful: address. Civil cases indexed by defendant, plaintiff. Civil index on docket books back to 1880. Civil PAT goes back to 4/1997. Civil records online - see criminal access. Online records date back to 4/97.
Criminal Records: Access: In person, online. Visitors must perform in person searches themselves. Required to search: name, years to search; also helpful: address, DOB, SSN. Criminal records indexed in books back to 1880. Criminal PAT goes back to same as civil. Single use or subscribe at https://www.nebraska.gov/justicecc/ccname.cgi for court access. Single use is $15.00 a record or open an account for $1 per record plus $50 annual fee. Online records date back to 4/97. Online results show middle initial, DOB.
General Information: No juvenile or mental health records released. Will fax out specific case files for $1.00 per page. Court makes copy: $.30 per page. Certification fee: $1.50. Payee: Clerk of District Court. Business checks and local personal checks accepted. Prepayment required.

Colfax County Court 411 E 11th St, Box 191, Schuyler, NE 68661; 402-352-8511; fax: 402-352-8535; 8AM-4:30PM (CST). ***Misdemeanor, Civil Actions under $51,000, Eviction, Small Claims, Probate.***
Civil Records: Access: In person, online. Visitors must perform in person searches themselves. Required to search: name, years to search. Civil cases indexed by defendant, plaintiff. Civil index on docket books from 1880s; computerized records since 1996. Civil PAT goes back to 1997. Civil records online - see criminal access. Online civil records date from 10/99 forward, probate from 05/98.
Criminal Records: Access: Fax, mail, in person, online. Visitors must perform in person searches themselves. No search fee. Required to search: name, years to search; also helpful: DOB, SSN. Criminal records indexed in books from 1880s; computerized records since 1996. Criminal PAT goes back to same as civil. Single use or subscribe at https://www.nebraska.gov/justicecc/ccname.cgi for court access. Single use is $15.00 a record or open an account for $1 per record plus $50 annual fee. Online criminal and traffic records date from 10/96. Online results show middle initial, DOB.
General Information: No juvenile records released. Will not fax documents. Court makes copy: $.25 per page. Certification fee: $1.00. Payee: Colfax County Court. Personal checks accepted; credit cards are not. Prepayment required.

Cuming County

District Court 200 S Lincoln, Rm 200, West Point, NE 68788; 402-372-6004; fax: 402-372-6017; 8:30AM-4:30PM (CST). ***Felony, Civil Actions over $51,000.***
Civil Records: Access: Mail, fax, in person, online. Visitors must perform in person searches themselves. No search fee. Required to search: name, years to search. Civil cases indexed by defendant, plaintiff. Civil records in books from 1939; on computer back to 2000. Mail turnaround time 24 hours. Civil PAT goes back to 11/1999. PAT results show name only. Civil records online - see criminal access. Online records date from 11/99.
Criminal Records: Access: Fax, in person, online. Visitors must perform in person searches themselves. No search fee. Required to search: name, years to search. Criminal records in books from 1939; on computer back to 2000. Mail turnaround time 24 hours. Criminal PAT goes back to same as civil. PAT results show name, DOB, SSN. Single use or subscribe at https://www.nebraska.gov/justicecc/ccname.cgi for court access. Single use is $15.00 a record or open an account for $1 per record plus $50 annual fee. Online records date from 11/99. Online results show middle initial, DOB.
General Information: No mental health records released. Will fax documents if you provide copy of your check for services. Court makes copy: $.25 per page. Self serve: same. Certification fee: $1.00. Payee: Clerk of District Court. No personal checks or credit cards accepted. Prepayment required.

Cuming County Court 200 S Lincoln, Rm 103, West Point, NE 68788; 402-372-6003; probate phone: 402-372-6003; fax: 402-372-6030; 8:30AM-4:30PM (CST). ***Misdemeanor, Civil Actions under $51,000, Eviction, Small Claims Under $2700, Probate, Traffic.***
www.co.cuming.ne.us/county_court.html
Civil Records: Access: In person, online. Visitors must perform in person searches themselves. Required to search: name, years to search. Civil cases indexed by defendant, plaintiff. Civil index on cards, also on computer since 4/2000. Civil PAT goes back to 1991. Public terminal located in the District Court office. Civil records online - see criminal access. Online records date from 4/2000, including probate.
Criminal Records: Access: In person, online. Visitors must perform in person searches themselves. Required to search: name, years to search; also helpful: DOB, SSN. Criminal records indexed on cards, also on computer since 4/2000. Criminal PAT goes back to 1984. Public terminal located in the District Court office. Single use or subscribe at https://www.nebraska.gov/justicecc/ccname.cgi for court access. Single use is $15.00 a record or open an account for $1 per record plus $50 annual fee. Online criminal and traffic records date from 3/2000. Online results show middle initial, DOB.
General Information: Online identifiers in results same as on public terminal. No mental health records released. Will not fax documents. Court makes copy: $.25 per page. Certification fee: $1.00. Personal checks accepted; ID required. No credit cards accepted. Prepayment required.

Custer County

District Court 431 S 10th Ave, Broken Bow, NE 68822; 308-872-2121; criminal fax: 308-872-5826; civil fax: same; 9AM-5PM (CST). ***Felony, Civil Actions over $51,000.***
Civil Records: Access: Phone, fax, mail, in person, online. Both court and visitors may perform in person searches. No search fee. Required to search: name, years to search; also helpful: address. Civil cases indexed by defendant, plaintiff. Civil index on docket books and docket books from late 1800s; on computer back to 4/1998. Mail turnaround time 3-4 days. Civil PAT goes back to 4/1998. PAT civil results show middle initial. Civil records online - see criminal access. Online records date from 03/98.
Criminal Records: Access: Phone, fax, mail, in person, online. Both court and visitors may perform in person searches. No search fee. Required to search: name, years to search; also helpful: address, DOB, SSN. Criminal records indexed in books and docket books from late 1800s; on computer back to 4/1998. Mail turnaround time 3-4 days. Criminal PAT goes back to same as civil. PAT results show middle initial, DOB. Results include charges. Single use or subscribe at https://www.nebraska.gov/justicecc/ccname.cgi for court access. Single use is $15.00 a record or open an account for $1 per record plus $50 annual fee. Online records date from 03/98. Online results show middle initial, DOB.
General Information: No search warrants, mental health, or sealed records released. Fee to fax out file $3.00 per page. Court makes copy: $.25 per page. Self serve: same. Certification fee: $1.25 per page. Payee: Clerk of District Court. Business checks accepted. No credit cards accepted. Prepayment required. Mail requests: SASE required.

Custer County Court 431 S 10th Ave, Broken Bow, NE 68822; 308-872-5761; criminal fax: 308-872-6052; civil fax: same; 8AM-N, 1-5PM (CST). ***Misdemeanor, Civil Actions under $51,000, Eviction, Small Claims, Probate.***
Probate fax is same as main fax number.
Civil Records: Access: In person, online. Visitors must perform in person searches themselves. Required to search: name, years to search. Civil cases indexed by defendant, plaintiff; index on computer back to 2000, on index books from 1988, probate from 1986, balance are archived. Civil PAT goes back to 2000. Civil records online - see criminal access. Online records date from 1/01, including probate.
Criminal Records: Access: In person, online. Visitors must perform in person searches themselves. Required to search: name, years to search. Criminal records computerized from 2000, index books from 1988, probate from 1986, balance are archived. Criminal PAT goes back to 2000. Single use or subscribe at https://www.nebraska.gov/justicecc/ccname.cgi for court access. Single use is $15.00 a record or open an account for $1 per record plus $50 annual fee. Online criminal and traffic records date from 7/17/00. Online results show middle initial, DOB.
General Information: No adoption records released. Will not fax documents. Court makes copy: $.25 per page. Self serve: $.25 per page. Certification fee: $1.00. Payee: Custer County Court. Personal checks accepted; credit cards are not. Prepayment required.

Dakota County

District Court PO Box 66, Dakota City, NE 68731; 402-987-2115; fax: 402-987-2117; 8AM-4:30PM (CST). ***Felony, Civil Actions over $51,000.***
This office will not do name searches.
Civil Records: Access: In person, online. Visitors must perform in person searches themselves. Required to search: name, years to search. Civil cases indexed by defendant, plaintiff. Civil index on docket books from 1985, prior records archived at NE State Historical Society, Lincoln, NE; computerized records since 1998. Civil PAT goes back to 1988. Civil records online - see criminal access. Online records date from 03/98.
Criminal Records: Access: Online, in person, mail, fax. Visitors must perform in person searches themselves. No search fee. Required to search: name, years to search. Criminal records indexed in books from 1985, prior records archived at NE State Historical Society, Lincoln, NE; computerized records since 1998. Criminal PAT goes back to same as civil. Single use or subscribe at https://www.nebraska.gov/justicecc/ccname.cgi for court access. Single use is $15.00 a record or open an account for $1 per record plus $50 annual fee. Online records date from 03/98. Online results show middle initial, DOB.
General Information: No juvenile or mental health records released. Court makes copy: $.25 per page. Self serve: $.10 per page. Certification fee: $1.00. Payee: Clerk of District Court. Personal checks accepted; credit cards are not. Prepayment required. Mail requests: SASE required.

Dakota County Court PO Box 385, 1601 Broadway, Dakota City, NE 68731; 402-987-2145; fax: 402-987-2185; 8AM-4:30PM (CST). ***Misdemeanor, Civil Actions under $51,000, Eviction, Small Claims, Probate.***
Civil Records: Access: In person, online, mail, fax. Visitors must perform in person searches themselves. No search fee. Required to search: name, years to search. Civil cases indexed by defendant, plaintiff. Civil index on docket books from late 1800s. Mail turnaround time 1 days. Civil PAT goes back to 1998. Civil records online - see criminal access. Online civil records date from 10/99 forward, probate from 05/98.
Criminal Records: Access: In person, online, mail, fax. Visitors must perform in person searches themselves. No search fee. Required to search: name, years to search. Criminal records indexed in books from late 1800s. Mail turnaround time 1 days. Criminal PAT goes back to same as civil. Single use or subscribe at https://www.nebraska.gov/justicecc/ccname.cgi for court access. Single use is $15.00 a record or open an account for $1 per record plus $50 annual fee. Online criminal and traffic records date from 10/97. Online results show middle initial, DOB.
General Information: No adoption or juvenile records released. Will fax out documents. Court makes copy: $.25 per page. Certification fee: $1.00. Payee: Dakota County Court. Business checks accepted. No credit cards accepted. Prepayment required.

Dawes County

District Court 451 Main St, Chadron, NE 69337; 308-432-0109; fax: 308-432-0110; 8:30AM-4:30PM (MST). ***Felony, Civil Actions over $51,000.***
Civil Records: Access: In person, online. Visitors must perform in person searches themselves. Required to search: name, years to search. Civil cases indexed by defendant, plaintiff; index on general index, docket books from 1886. Civil PAT goes back to 2001. PAT results show name only. Civil records online - see criminal access. Online records date from 08/98.
Criminal Records: Access: Fax, mail, in person, online. Visitors must perform in person searches themselves. Search fee: $10.00 per name. Required to search: name, years to search. Criminal records indexed in books from 1886. Criminal PAT goes back to same as civil. PAT results show name only. Single use or subscribe at https://www.nebraska.gov/justicecc/ccname.cgi for court access. Single use is $15.00 a record or open an account for $1 per record plus $50 annual fee. Online records date from 08/98. Online results show name only.
General Information: No mental health records released. Will fax documents to local or toll-free number. Court makes copy: $.25 per page. Certification fee: $1.00. Payee: Clerk of District Court. Personal checks accepted; credit cards are not. Prepayment required. Mail requests: SASE required for mail return of any copies.

Dawes County Court PO Box 806, Chadron, NE 69337; 308-432-0116; fax: 308-432-0118; 7:30AM-4:30PM (MST). ***Misdemeanor, Civil Actions under $51,000, Eviction, Small Claims, Probate.***
Civil Records: Access: In person, online. Visitors must perform in person searches themselves. Required to search: name, years to search. Civil cases indexed by defendant, plaintiff; index on case cards, case files kept since 1993; on computer back to 2001. Civil PAT goes back to 11/2000. PAT results show name only. Civil records online - see criminal access. Online civil and probate records from 11/00 forward.
Criminal Records: Access: In person, online. Visitors must perform in person searches themselves. Required to search: name, years to search, DOB; also helpful: address. Criminal records on case cards, case files kept since 11991; on computer back to 2000. Criminal PAT goes back to 4/2000.PAT results show name, DOB. Single use or subscribe at https://www.nebraska.gov/justicecc/ccname.cgi for court access. Single use is $15.00 a record or open an account for $1 per record plus $50 annual fee. Online criminal and traffic records date from 04/00. Online results show middle initial, DOB.
General Information: Online identifiers in results same as on public terminal. No confidential records released. Will fax out documents. Court makes copy: $.25 per page. Self serve: same. Certification fee: $1.00. Payee: Dawes County Court. Personal checks accepted; credit cards are not. Prepayment required. Mail requests: SASE required for mail return of any copies.

Dawson County

District Court 700 N Washington 3rd Fl, Rm E, Lexington, NE 68850; 308-324-4261; fax: 308-324-9876; 8AM-N, 1-5PM (CST). ***Felony, Civil Actions over $51,000.***
www.dawsoncdc.ne.gov/
Civil Records: Access: Fax, mail, in person, online. Visitors must perform in person searches themselves. No search fee. Required to search: name, years to search. Civil cases indexed by defendant, plaintiff. Recent civil records on microfiche, some older records on microfilm, index books date to late 1800s. Mail turnaround time 2 days. Civil PAT goes back to 5/1997. PAT civil results show middle initial. Civil records online - see criminal access. Online records date from 06/97.
Criminal Records: Access: Fax, mail, in person, online. Visitors must perform in person searches themselves. No search fee. Required to search: name, years to search. Recent records on microfiche, some older records on microfilm, index books date to late 1800s. Mail turnaround time 2 days. Criminal PAT goes back to same as civil. PAT results show middle initial, DOB. Single use or subscribe at https://www.nebraska.gov/justicecc/ccname.cgi for court access. Single use is $15.00 a record or open an account for $1 per record plus $50 annual fee. Online records date from 6/1997. Online results show middle initial, DOB.
General Information: No juvenile or mental health records released. Will fax out documents. Court makes copy: $.25 per page. Certification fee: $1.00. Payee: Clerk of District Court. Personal checks accepted; credit cards are not. Prepayment required. Mail requests: SASE required.

Dawson County Court 700 N Washington St, Rm J, Lexington, NE 68850; 308-324-5606; fax: 308-324-9837; 8AM-5PM (CST). ***Misdemeanor, Civil Actions under $51,000, Eviction, Small Claims, Probate.***
www.supremecourt.ne.gov/county-court/county-court-website/dawson.shtml
Court personnel will only search records if specific case # given; turnaround time is 3-5 days.
Civil Records: Access: In person, online. Visitors must perform in person searches themselves. Required to search: name, years to search; also helpful: address. Civil cases indexed by defendant, plaintiff; index on books from late 1800s, docket books 15 years back; on computer since 1998. Civil PAT goes back to late 1997. Civil records online - see criminal access. Online civil records date from 10/99 forward, probate from 05/98.
Criminal Records: Access: In person, online. Visitors must perform in person searches themselves. Required to search: name, years to search, offense, DOB; also helpful: address. Criminal docket on books from late 1800s, docket books 15 years back; on computer since 1998. Criminal PAT goes back to same as civil. Single use or subscribe at https://www.nebraska.gov/justicecc/ccname.cgi for court access. Single use is $15.00 a record or open an account for $1 per record plus $50 annual fee. Online criminal and traffic records date from 05/00. Online results show middle initial, DOB.
General Information: No adoption or juvenile records released. Will fax specific case for $3.00 1st page, $1.00 ea add'l. Court makes copy: $.25 per page. Self serve: same. Certification fee: $1.00. Payee: Dawson County Court. Personal checks accepted; credit cards are not. Prepayment required. Mail requests: SASE required for mail return of any copies.

Deuel County

District Court PO Box 327, 718 Third St, Chappell, NE 69129; 308-874-3308/2818; fax: 308-874-3472; 8AM-4PM (MST). ***Felony, Civil Actions over $51,000.***
Civil Records: Access: Phone, fax, mail, in person, online. Both court and visitors may perform in person searches. No search fee. Required to search: name; also helpful: years to search. Civil cases indexed by defendant, plaintiff; index on general index and docket books from late 1800s. Mail turnaround time 1 week. Civil PAT goes back to 2000. Civil records online - see criminal access. Online records date from 05/00.
Criminal Records: Access: Phone, fax, mail, in person, online. Both court and visitors may perform in person searches. No search fee. Required to search: name; also helpful: years to search, DOB, SSN. Criminal records on general index and docket books from late 1800s. Mail turnaround time 1 week. Criminal PAT goes back to same as civil. Single

use or subscribe at https://www.nebraska.gov/justicecc/ccname.cgi for court access. Single use is $15.00 a record or open an account for $1 per record plus $50 annual fee. Online records date from 05/00. Online results show middle initial, DOB.
General Information: No mental health or service discharge records released. No fee to fax documents. Court makes copy: $.50 per page. Self serve: $.25 per page. Certification fee: $1.50 per page. Payee: Clerk of District Court. Personal checks accepted; credit cards are not. Prepayment required. Mail requests: SASE required.

Deuel County Court PO Box 514, Chappell, NE 69129; 308-874-2909; fax: 308-874-3472; 8AM-4PM (MST). ***Misdemeanor, Civil Actions under $51,000, Eviction, Small Claims, Probate.***
Civil Records: Access: In person, online. Visitors must perform in person searches themselves. Required to search: name only. Civil cases indexed by defendant, plaintiff. Civil index on cards from 1989, computerized since 2001. Civil PAT goes back to 12/2000. PAT civil results show middle initial. Civil records online - see criminal access. Online civil and probate records from 12/00 forward.
Criminal Records: Access: In person, online. Visitors must perform in person searches themselves. Required to search: name, DOB. Criminal records indexed on cards from 1989, computerized since 2001. Criminal PAT goes back to same as civil. PAT results show middle initial, DOB. Single use or subscribe at https://www.nebraska.gov/justicecc/ccname.cgi for court access. Single use is $15.00 a record or open an account for $1 per record plus $50 annual fee. Online criminal and traffic records date from 12/00. Online results show middle initial, DOB.
General Information: Online identifiers in results same as on public terminal. No juvenile records released. Will fax documents. Court makes copy: $.50 per page. Self serve: same. Certification fee: $1.00 per seal plus $.25 per page. Payee: Deuel County Court. Personal checks accepted; credit cards are not. Prepayment required.

Dixon County

District Court PO Box 395, Ponca, NE 68770; 402-755-5604; criminal fax: 402-755-5651; civil fax: same; 8AM-N, 1-5PM (CST). ***Felony, Civil Actions over $51,000.***
Civil Records: Access: In person, online. Visitors must perform in person searches themselves. Required to search: name, years to search. Civil cases indexed by defendant, plaintiff; index on books from 1876; computerized records go back to 1999. Civil PAT goes back to 1999. PAT results show name only. Civil records online - see criminal access. Online records date from 11/99.
Criminal Records: Access: In person, online. Visitors must perform in person searches themselves. Required to search: name, years to search, DOB. Criminal docket on books from 1876; computerized records go back to 1999. Criminal PAT goes back to same as civil. PAT results show name only. Single use or subscribe at https://www.nebraska.gov/justicecc/ccname.cgi for court access. Single use is $15.00 a record or open an account for $1 per record plus $50 annual fee. Online records date from 11/99. Online results show middle initial, DOB.
General Information: No mental health records released. Will fax out documents. Court makes copy: $.25 per page. Self serve: same. Certification fee: $1.00 per page. Payee: Clerk of District Court. Personal checks accepted; credit cards are not. Will bill copy fees.

Dixon County Court PO Box 497, Ponca, NE 68770; 402-755-5607; fax: 402-755-5651; 8AM-4:30PM (CST). ***Misdemeanor, Civil Actions under $51,000, Eviction, Small Claims, Probate.***
Civil Records: Access: In person, online. Visitors must perform in person searches themselves. Required to search: name, years to search. Civil cases indexed by defendant, plaintiff; index on cards from 1987, prior in dockets from 1876, computerized since 2000. Public use terminal available, records go back to 2000. Civil records online - see criminal access. Online civil records date from 11/01 forward, probate from 1/2001.
Criminal Records: Access: In person, online. Visitors must perform in person searches themselves. Required to search: name, years to search, DOB. Criminal records in files, cards from 1987, prior in dockets from 1876, computerized since 2000. Public use terminal available, crim records go back to same. Single use or subscribe at https://www.nebraska.gov/justicecc/ccname.cgi for court access. Single use is $15.00 a record or open an account for $1 per record plus $50 annual fee. Online criminal and traffic records date from 7/2000. Online results show middle initial, DOB.
General Information: No adoption or juvenile records released. Will not fax documents. Court makes copy: $.25 per page. Certification fee: $1.00. Payee: Dixon County Court. Personal checks accepted; credit cards are not. Prepayment required.

Dodge County

District Court PO Box 1237, Fremont, NE 68026; 402-727-2780; fax: 402-727-2773; 8:30AM-4:30PM (CST). ***Felony, Civil Actions over $51,000, Divorce.***
Civil Records: Access: In person, online. Visitors must perform in person searches themselves. Required to search: name, years to search. Civil cases indexed by defendant, plaintiff; index on general index, docket books from late 1800s; computerized records since 1997. Civil PAT goes back to 7/1997. Civil records online - see criminal access. Online records date from 7/1997.
Criminal Records: Access: In person, online. Visitors must perform in person searches themselves. Required to search: name, years to search. Criminal records indexed in books from late 1800s; computerized records since 1997. Criminal PAT goes back to same as civil. Single use or subscribe at https://www.nebraska.gov/justicecc/ccname.cgi for court access. Single use is $15.00 a record or open an account for $1 per record plus $50 annual fee. Online records date from 7/1997. Online results show middle initial, DOB.
General Information: No mental health records released. Will fax documents $2.00 each in state; $5.00 out of state. Court makes copy: $.25 per page. Certification fee: $1.50. Payee: District Court. Personal checks accepted; credit cards are not. Prepayment required.

Dodge County Court 428 N Broad St, Fremont, NE 68025; 402-727-2755; criminal phone: 402-727-2758; civil phone: 402-727-2756; probate phone: 402-727-2755; fax: 402-727-2762; 8AM-5PM (CST). ***Misdemeanor, Civil Actions under $51,000, Eviction, Small Claims, Probate.***
Probate is separate index at this same address. Probate fax is same as main fax number.
Civil Records: Access: In person, online. Visitors must perform in person searches themselves. Required to search: name, years to search. Civil cases indexed by defendant. Civil records on general index; on computer back to 1998. Probate on microfilm from early 1900s. Civil PAT goes back to 1998. PAT results show name only. Civil records online - see criminal access. Online civil records date from 01/00 forward, probate from 05/98.
Criminal Records: Access: In person, online. Visitors must perform in person searches themselves. Required to search: name, years to search; also helpful: DOB. Criminal records on general index; on computer back to 1998. Criminal PAT goes back to same as civil. PAT results show middle initial, DOB. Single use or subscribe at https://www.nebraska.gov/justicecc/ccname.cgi for court access. Single use is $15.00 a record or open an account for $1 per record plus $50 annual fee. Online criminal and traffic records date from 1/20/97. Online results show middle initial, DOB.
General Information: Online identifiers in results same as on public terminal. No adoption or juvenile records released. Will fax documents $3.00 1st page, $1.00 ea add'l page. Court makes copy: $.25 per page. Self serve: same. Certification fee: $1.00 per document. Payee: Dodge County Court. Personal checks accepted; credit cards are not. Prepayment required.

Douglas County

District Court 1701 Farnam, Hall of Justice, Rm 300, Omaha, NE 68183; 402-444-7018; fax: 402-444-1757; 8AM-4:30PM (CST). ***Felony, Civil Actions over $51,000.***
www.co.douglas.ne.us
Civil Records: Access: Mail, in person, online. Both court and visitors may perform in person searches. Search fee: $5.00 per name. Required to search: name, years to search; also helpful: address. Civil cases indexed by defendant, plaintiff; index on computer from 1980, on books back to late 1800s. Mail turnaround time 1-2 days. Civil PAT goes back to 1974. Access to the Internet system at www.dotcomm.org/cpan/index.htm requires registration and password. System can be searched by name or case number. Fees start with a minimum of $30 per month for 250 transactions. Tier pricing offered for high volume accounts. The system contains both court information and recorder's office data. System can be searched by name or case number, partial DOBs are provided. Call 402-444-6374 for more information.
Criminal Records: Access: Mail, in person, online. Visitors must perform in person searches themselves. Search fee: $5.00 per name. Required to search: name, years to search; also helpful: address, DOB, SSN. Criminal records computerized from 1980, on books back to late 1800s. Mail turnaround time 1-2 days. Criminal PAT goes back to 1981. See description above about online access to criminal records. Online results show middle initial, DOB.
General Information: No juvenile records released. Will not fax documents. Court makes copy: $.50 per page. $1.00 minimum. Add $.50 postage fee. Certification fee: $3.50 for 1-5 pages, $.50 each add'l. Payee: Clerk of District Court. Personal checks accepted; credit cards are not. Prepayment required. Mail requests: SASE required.

County Court Civil 1819 Farnam, #F03, Hall of Justice, Omaha, NE 68183; 402-444-5424; fax: 402-996-8326; 8AM-4:30PM (CST). ***Civil Actions under $51,000, Eviction, Small Claims.***
www.co.douglas.ne.us
Civil Records: Access: Mail, in person, online. Visitors must perform in person searches themselves. No search fee. Required to search: name, years to search. Civil cases indexed by defendant, plaintiff; index on computer from 1987 (small claims), from 1983 (civil). Civil records are purged after about 20 years. Public use terminal has civil records. Access at www.dotcomm.org/cpan/ requires registration and password. Call CPAN at 402-444-7117 for more info. Online results show middle initial, DOB.
General Information: Will not fax documents. Court makes copy: $.25 per page. Certification fee: $1.00; Authentication is $3.00. Payee: Douglas County Court. Personal checks accepted.

County Court Criminal 1701 Farnham St, 2 East, Omaha, NE 68183; 402-444-5387; fax: 402-444-3608; 8AM-4:30PM (CST). ***Misdemeanor, Traffic.***
www.co.douglas.ne.us
Court handles criminal traffic.
Criminal Records: Access: In person, online. Visitors must perform in person searches themselves. Required to search: name, years to search; also helpful: DOB. Criminal records computerized from 1980s. Public use terminal has crim records back to 4/1996. Access at www.dotcomm.org/cpan/ requires registration and password. Call CPAN at 402-444-7117 for more info. Online results show middle initial, DOB.
General Information: Online identifiers in results same as on public terminal. Will not fax documents. Court makes copy: $.25 per page. Certification fee: $1.00; Authentication is $3.00. Payee: Douglas County Court. Personal checks accepted; credit cards are not. Prepayment required.

County Court Probate 1701 Farnam, 3 West, Omaha, NE 68183; 402-444-7152; fax: 402-444-4019; 8AM-4:30PM (CST). ***Probate.***
www.co.douglas.ne.us
Copies are $25 each.

Dundy County

District Court PO Box 506, 112 Seventh Ave, Benkelman, NE 69021; 308-423-2058; fax: 308-423-2325; 8AM-4PM (MST). ***Felony, Civil Actions over $51,000.***
Civil Records: Access: Phone, mail, in person, online. Both court and visitors may perform in person searches. No search fee. Required to search: name, years to search; also helpful: address. Civil cases indexed by defendant, plaintiff. Civil index on docket books from late 1800s. Mail turnaround time 1 day. Civil PAT goes back to 8/2000. Civil records online - see criminal access. Online records date from 8/2000.
Criminal Records: Access: Mail, in person, online. Both court and visitors may perform in person searches. No search fee. Required to search: name, years to search; also helpful: address, DOB, SSN. Criminal records indexed in books from late 1800s. Mail turnaround time 1 day. Criminal PAT goes back to same as civil. Single use or subscribe at https://www.nebraska.gov/justicecc/ccname.cgi for court access. Single use is $15.00 a record or open an account for $1 per record plus $50 annual fee. Online records date from 8/2000. Online results show middle initial, DOB.
General Information: No juvenile records released. Will not fax documents. Court makes copy: $1.00 per page. Self serve: available. Certification fee: $1.50 plus $.50 each add'l page. Payee: Clerk of District Court. Personal checks accepted; credit cards are not. Prepayment required.

Dundy County Court PO Box 378, Benkelman, NE 69021; 308-423-2374; fax: 308-423-2325; 8AM-4PM (MST). ***Misdemeanor, Civil Actions under $51,000, Eviction, Small Claims, Probate.***
Civil Records: Access: In person, online. Visitors must perform in person searches themselves. Required to search: name, years to search. Civil cases indexed by defendant, plaintiff; index on general index, docket books from late 1800s; some probate, civil on microfiche. Civil PAT goes back to 2000. PAT results show middle initial, DOB. Civil records online - see criminal access. Online civil records date from 11/00 forward, probate from 12/00.
Criminal Records: Access: In person, online. Visitors must perform in person searches themselves. Required to search: name, years to search, DOB, signed release; also helpful: address. Criminal records indexed in books from late 1800s, computerized since 2001. Criminal PAT goes back to 2001. PAT results show middle initial, DOB. Single use or subscribe at https://www.nebraska.gov/justicecc/ccname.cgi for court access. Single use is $15.00 a record or open an account for $1 per record plus $50 annual fee. Online criminal and traffic records date from 08/00. Online results show middle initial, DOB.
General Information: No adoption or juvenile records released. Will fax out specific case files for $3.00 charge for 1st page, $1.00 each add'l. Court makes copy: $.25 per page. Certification fee: $1.00 per document. Payee: Dundy County Court. Business checks accepted. No credit cards accepted. Prepayment required.

Fillmore County

District Court PO Box 147, 900 G St, Geneva, NE 68361-0147; 402-759-3811; fax: 402-759-4440; 8AM-N, 1-5PM (CST). ***Felony, Civil Actions over $51,000.***
www.fillmorecounty.org/webpages/district_court/district_court.htm
Civil Records: Access: Fax, mail, in person, online, email. Both court and visitors may perform in person searches. No search fee. Required to search: name, years to search. Civil cases indexed by defendant, plaintiff. Civil index on docket books to late 1800s, on computer since 1998. Mail turnaround time 1-5 days. Civil PAT goes back to 1998. PAT civil results show middle initial. Civil records online - see criminal access. Online records date from 06/98. Email requests should be directed to DistrictCourt@fillmore.nacone.org.
Criminal Records: Access: Fax, mail, in person, online, email. Both court and visitors may perform in person searches. No search fee. Required to search: name, years to search, DOB. Criminal records indexed in books to late 1800s, on computer since 1998. Mail turnaround time 1-5 days. Criminal PAT goes back to same as civil. PAT criminal results show middle initial. Single use or subscribe at https://www.nebraska.gov/justicecc/ccname.cgi for court access. Single use is $15.00 a record or open an account for $1 per record plus $50 annual fee. Online records date from 06/98. Email requests should be directed to DistrictCourt@fillmore.nacone.org. Online results show middle initial, DOB.
General Information: No juvenile or mental health records released. Will fax documents $2.00 1st page, $1.00 ea add'l, prepaid. Court makes copy: $.50 per page. Self serve: $.35 per page. Certification fee: $1.00 plus copy fees. Payee: Clerk of District Court. Personal checks accepted; credit cards are not. Prepayment required. Mail requests: SASE required.

Fillmore County Court PO Box 66, 900 G St, Geneva, NE 68361; 402-759-3514; probate phone: same; fax: 402-759-4440; 8AM-5PM (CST). ***Misdemeanor, Civil Actions under $51,000, Eviction, Small Claims, Probate.***
www.district10.us/
Civil Records: Access: In person, online. Both court and visitors may perform in person searches. No search fee. Required to search: name, years to search. Civil cases indexed by defendant, plaintiff; index on general index, docket books from late 1800s; probate on microfiche. Civil PAT goes back to 2000. Civil records online - see criminal access. Online civil and probate records from 02/00 forward.
Criminal Records: Access: In person, online. Both court and visitors may perform in person searches. No search fee. Required to search: name, years to search. Criminal records indexed in books from late 1800s; probate on microfiche. Criminal PAT goes back to same as civil. Single use or subscribe at https://www.nebraska.gov/justicecc/ccname.cgi for court access. Single use is $15.00 a record or open an account for $1 per record plus $50 annual fee. Online criminal and traffic records date from 02/00. Online results show middle initial, DOB.
General Information: No adoption or juvenile records released. Will fax documents $2.00 1st page, $1.00 each add'l. Court makes copy: $.25 per page. Certification fee: $1.25. Payee: County Court. Personal checks accepted; credit cards are not. Prepayment required.

Franklin County

District Court PO Box 146, 405 15th Ave, Franklin, NE 68939; 308-425-6202; fax: 308-425-6093; 8:30AM-4:30PM (CST). ***Felony, Civil Actions over $51,000.***
Civil Records: Access: In person, online. Visitors must perform in person searches themselves. Required to search: name, years to search. Civil cases indexed by defendant, plaintiff. Civil index on docket books back to turn of century; on computer back to 2/2000. Civil PAT goes back to 2000. Civil records online - see criminal access. Online records date from 02/00.
Criminal Records: Access: In person, online. Visitors must perform in person searches themselves. Required to search: name, years to search. Criminal records indexed in books back to turn of century; on computer back to 2/2000. Criminal PAT goes back to same as civil. Single use or subscribe at https://www.nebraska.gov/justicecc/ccname.cgi for court access. Single use is $15.00 a record or open an account for $1 per record plus $50 annual fee. Online records date from 02/00. Online results show middle initial, DOB.
General Information: No adoption or juvenile records released. Will fax documents $1.50 per page. Court makes copy: $1.00 per page. Self serve: $.25 per page. Certification fee: $1.00. Payee: Clerk of District Court or County Clerk. Personal checks accepted; credit cards are not. Prepayment required.

Franklin County Court PO Box 174, 405 15th Ave, Franklin, NE 68939; 308-425-6288; fax: 308-425-6289; 8AM-5PM (CST). ***Misdemeanor, Civil Actions under $51,000, Eviction, Small Claims, Probate.***
www.district10.us/franklin_county.htm
Court personnel not permitted to do record searches.
Civil Records: Access: In person, online. Visitors must perform in person searches themselves. Required to search: name, years to search. Civil cases indexed by defendant, plaintiff; index on computer since 5/2000, on docket cards since 1988, prior on docket books. Civil PAT goes back to 5/2000. Civil records online - see criminal access. Online civil and probate records from 05/00 forward.
Criminal Records: Access: In person, online. Visitors must perform in person searches themselves. Required to search: name, years to search. Criminal records on computer since 5/2000, docket cards since 1988, prior on docket books. Criminal PAT goes back to same as civil. Single use or subscribe at https://www.nebraska.gov/justicecc/ccname.cgi for court access. Single use is $15.00 a record or open an account for $1 per record plus $50 annual fee. Online criminal and traffic records date from 05/00. Online results show middle initial, DOB.
General Information: No juvenile, adoption records released. Will not fax documents. Court makes copy: $.25 per page. Certification fee: $1.25. Payee: Franklin County Court. Personal checks accepted. Major credit cards accepted online. Prepayment required.

Frontier County

District Court PO Box 40, Stockville, NE 69042; 308-367-8641; fax: 308-367-8730; 9AM-4:30PM (CST). ***Felony, Civil Actions over $51,000.***
www.co.frontier.ne.us/court.html
Civil Records: Access: Mail, in person, online. Both court and visitors may perform in person searches. No search fee. Required to search: name, years to search. Civil cases indexed by defendant, plaintiff; index on general index, docket books from late 1800s; computerized records since 6/00. Mail turnaround time 5 days. Civil PAT goes back to 6/2000. Civil records online - see criminal access. Online records date from 06/00.
Criminal Records: Access: Mail, in person, online. Both court and visitors may perform in person searches. No search fee. Required to search: name, years to search, DOB, signed release. Criminal records indexed in books from late 1800s; computerized records since 6/00. Mail turnaround time 5 days. Criminal PAT goes back to same as civil. Single use or subscribe at https://www.nebraska.gov/justicecc/ccname.cgi for court access. Single use is $15.00 a record or open an account for $1 per record plus $50 annual fee. Online records date from 06/00. Online results show middle initial, DOB.
General Information: Will fax documents $3.00 per page. Court makes copy: $.25 per page. Self serve: same. Certification fee: $1.00 per page. Payee: Clerk of District Court. Only cashiers checks and money orders accepted. No credit cards accepted. Prepayment required. Mail requests: SASE required.

Frontier County Court PO Box 38, Stockville, NE 69042; 308-367-8629; fax: 308-367-8730; 9AM-4:30PM (CST). ***Misdemeanor, Civil Actions under $51,000, Eviction, Small Claims, Probate.***
Civil Records: Access: Fax, mail, in person, online. Both court and visitors may perform in person searches. No search fee. Required to search: name, years to search. Civil cases indexed by plaintiff. Civil records on general index, docket books from late 1800s; on computer back to 10/2000. Mail turnaround time 5 days. Civil PAT goes back to 10/2000. PAT results show name only. Civil records online - see criminal access. Online civil and probate records from 09/00 forward.
Criminal Records: Access: Fax, mail, in person, online. Both court and visitors may perform in

person searches. No search fee. Required to search: name, years to search, DOB; also helpful-signed release. Criminal records indexed in books from late 1800s; on computer back to 10/2000. Mail turnaround time 5 days. Criminal PAT goes back to same as civil.PAT results show name, DOB. Results sometimes include address. Single use or subscribe at https://www.nebraska.gov/justicecc/ccname.cgi for court access. Single use is $15.00 a record or open an account for $1 per record plus $50 annual fee. Online criminal and traffic records date from 09/00. Online results show middle initial, DOB.
General Information: No adoption or juvenile records released. Fee to fax out file $3.00 per page then $1.00 ea add'l. Court makes copy: $.25 per page. Self serve: same. Certification fee: $1.00 per copy. Payee: County Court. Only cashiers checks and money orders accepted. No credit cards accepted. Prepayment required. Mail requests: SASE required.

Furnas County

District Court PO Box 413, Beaver City, NE 68926; 308-268-4015; fax: 308-268-4015; 10AM-N, 1-3PM (CST). ***Felony, Civil Actions over $51,000.***
Civil Records: Access: In person, online. Both court and visitors may perform in person searches. No search fee. Required to search: name, years to search. Civil cases indexed by defendant, plaintiff. Civil records in general index books and files from late 1800s. Civil PAT goes back to 2000. PAT results show name only. Civil records online - see criminal access. Online records date from 04/00.
Criminal Records: Access: In person, online. Both court and visitors may perform in person searches. No search fee. Required to search: name, years to search. Criminal records in general index books and files from late 1800s. Criminal PAT goes back to same as civil. PAT results show name only. Single use or subscribe at https://www.nebraska.gov/justicecc/ccname.cgi for court access. Single use is $15.00 a record or open an account for $1 per record plus $50 annual fee. Online records date from 04/00. Online results show middle initial, DOB.
General Information: No mental health records released. Will fax documents. Court makes copy: $.25 per page. Self serve: same. Certification fee: $1.00. Payee: Clerk of District Court. Personal checks accepted; credit cards are not. Prepayment required.

Furnas County Court PO Box 373, 912 R St, Beaver City, NE 68926; 308-268-4025; fax: 308-268-4025; 8AM-4PM (CST). ***Misdemeanor, Civil Actions under $51,000, Eviction, Small Claims, Probate.***
www.furnascounty.ne.gov/index_html?page=content/magistrate.html
Civil Records: Access: In person, online. Visitors must perform in person searches themselves. Required to search: name, years to search. Civil cases indexed by defendant, plaintiff; index on card system from 1984, docket books back to late 1800s. Note: Court will search only if you provide a case number. Civil PAT goes back to 9/2000. PAT results show name only. Civil records online- see criminal access. Online civil and probate records from 01/01 forward.
Criminal Records: Access: In person, online. Visitors must perform in person searches themselves. Required to search: name, years to search; also helpful: DOB. Criminal records on card system from 1984, docket books back to late 1800s. Note: Court will search only if you provide a case number. Criminal PAT goes back to same as civil. PAT results show name only. Single use or subscribe at https://www.nebraska.gov/justicecc/ccname.cgi for court access. Single use is $15.00 a record or open an account for $1 per record plus $50 annual fee. Online criminal and traffic records date from 09/00. Online results show middle initial, DOB.
General Information: No adoption, juvenile or sealed records released. Court makes copy: $.25 per page. Self serve: same. Certification fee: $1.00 per page. Payee: County Court. Personal checks accepted; credit cards are not. Prepayment required.

Gage County

District Court 612 Grant St, #11, Beatrice, NE 68310-2946; 402-223-1332; fax: 402-223-1313; 8AM-5PM (CST). ***Felony, Civil Actions over $51,000.***
Civil Records: Access: In person, online. Both court and visitors may perform in person searches. No search fee. Required to search: name, years to search. Civil cases indexed by defendant, plaintiff. Civil index on docket books from late 1800s; on computer back to 1997. Civil PAT goes back to 1997. Public terminal search results may include DOB or address. Civil records online - see criminal access. Online records date from 11/96.
Criminal Records: Access: In person, online. Both court and visitors may perform in person searches. No search fee. Required to search: name, years to search, DOB. Criminal records indexed in books from late 1800s; on computer back to 1997. Criminal PAT goes back to same as civil. Public terminal search results may include DOB or address. Single use or subscribe at https://www.nebraska.gov/justicecc/ccname.cgi for court access. Single use is $15.00 a record or open an account for $1 per record plus $50 annual fee. Online records date from 11/96. Online results show middle initial, DOB.
General Information: No juvenile or mental health records released. Will fax documents for no fee. Court makes copy: $.50 per page. Certification fee: $1.00 per cert. Payee: Clerk of District Court. Personal checks accepted; credit cards are not. Prepayment required.

Gage County Court 612 Grant St, #17, Beatrice, NE 68310-2946; 402-223-1323; criminal phone: 402-223-1325; civil phone: 402-223-1328; probate phone: 402-223-1327; fax: 402-223-1374; 8AM-5PM (CST). ***Misdemeanor, Civil Actions under $51,000, Eviction, Small Claims, Probate.***
Civil Records: Access: In person, online. Visitors must perform in person searches themselves. Required to search: name, years to search. Civil cases indexed by defendant, plaintiff. Civil records go back to 1987; on computer back to 1999. Probate records from 1860, probate on microfiche. Note: Court personnel will not perform name searches. Civil PAT goes back to 9/1996. Civil records online - see criminal access. Online civil records date from 11/16/98 forward, probate from 05/98.
Criminal Records: Access: Mail, in person, online. Visitors must perform in person searches themselves. No search fee. Required to search: name, years to search, DOB. Criminal records go back to 1976; on computer back to 1996. Note: Court personnel will not perform name searches. Mail turnaround time 1-3 weeks. Criminal PAT goes back to same as civil. Single use or subscribe at https://www.nebraska.gov/justicecc/ccname.cgi for court access. Single use is $15.00 a record or open an account for $1 per record plus $50 annual fee. Online criminal and traffic records date from 09/09/96. Online results show middle initial, DOB.
General Information: Online identifiers in results same as on public terminal. No adoption or juvenile records released. Will not fax documents. Court makes copy: $.25 per page. Certification fee: $1.00. Payee: Gage County Court. Personal checks accepted; credit cards are not. Prepayment required. Mail requests: SASE required.

Garden County

District Court PO Box 486, Oshkosh, NE 69154; 308-772-3924; fax: 308-772-0124; 8AM-4PM (MST). ***Felony, Civil Actions over $51,000.***
Civil Records: Access: Fax, mail, in person, online. Both court and visitors may perform in person searches. Search fee: $5.00. Required to search: name, years to search. Civil cases indexed by defendant, plaintiff. Civil records in files, docket books back to 1910; on computer back to 1998. Mail turnaround time same day. Civil PAT goes back to 1998. Civil records online - see criminal access. Online records date from 08/98.
Criminal Records: Access: Fax, mail, in person, online. Both court and visitors may perform in person searches. Search fee: $5.00. Required to search: name, years to search. Criminal records in files, docket books back to 1910; on computer back to 1998. Mail turnaround time same day. Criminal PAT goes back to same as civil. Single use or subscribe at https://www.nebraska.gov/justicecc/ccname.cgi for court access. Single use is $15.00 a record or open an account for $1 per record plus $50 annual fee. Online records date from 08/98. Online results show middle initial, DOB.
General Information: No confidential records released. Will fax documents $2.00 1st page, $1.00 each add'l. Court makes copy: $.50 per page. Self serve: $.25 per page. Certification fee: $5.00. Payee: Clerk of District Court. Personal checks accepted; credit cards are not. Prepayment required. Mail requests: SASE required.

Garden County Court PO Box 465, Oshkosh, NE 69154; 308-772-3696; fax: 308-772-0149; 8AM-4PM (MST). ***Misdemeanor, Civil Actions under $51,000, Eviction, Small Claims, Probate.***
Civil Records: Access: In person, online. Visitors must perform in person searches themselves. Required to search: name, years to search. Civil cases indexed by defendant, plaintiff; index on general index, docket books from 1993, computerized since 1998. Note: Phone access limited to short searches. Civil records online - see criminal access. Online civil and probate records from 01/01 forward.
Criminal Records: Access: In person, online. Visitors must perform in person searches themselves. Required to search: name, years to search. Criminal records indexed in books from 1992, computerized since 1998. Single use or subscribe at https://www.nebraska.gov/justicecc/ccname.cgi for court access. Single use is $15.00 a record or open an account for $1 per record plus $50 annual fee. Online criminal and traffic records date from 06/00. Online results show middle initial, DOB.
General Information: No adoption or juvenile records released. Will fax documents $.25 per page fee. Court makes copy: $1.00 per page. Self serve: $.50 per page. Certification fee: $1.25. Payee: Garden County Court. Personal checks accepted; credit cards are not. Prepayment required.

Garfield County

District Court PO Box 218, 250 S 8 Ave, Burwell, NE 68823; 308-346-4161; fax: 308-346-4651; 9AM-5PM (CST). ***Felony, Civil Actions over $51,000.***
Civil Records: Access: Mail, in person, online. Only the court performs in person searches; visitors may not. Search fee: $5.00 per name may be charged to search. Required to search: name, years to search; also helpful: address. Civil cases indexed by defendant, plaintiff. Civil index on docket books from 1885. Mail turnaround time 3-4 days. Civil PAT available. Public terminal search results may include DOB or address. Civil records online - see criminal access. Online records date from 07/00.
Criminal Records: Access: In person, online. Only the court performs in person searches; visitors may not. Required to search: name, years to search; also helpful: address, DOB, SSN. Criminal records indexed in books from 1885. Criminal PAT available. Public terminal search results may include DOB or address. Single use or subscribe at https://www.nebraska.gov/justicecc/ccname.cgi for court access. Single use is $15.00 a record or open an account for $1 per record plus $50 annual fee. Online records date from 07/00. Online results show middle initial, DOB.
General Information: Will fax documents $5.00 per page. Court makes copy: $.25 per page. Self serve: same. Certification fee: $1.50 per page. Payee: Clerk of District Court. Personal checks accepted; credit cards are not. Prepayment required. Mail requests: SASE required with civil search request.

Garfield County Court PO Box 431, Burwell, NE 68823; 308-346-4123; fax: 308-346-5064; 9AM-4PM (CST). ***Misdemeanor, Civil Actions under $51,000, Eviction, Small Claims, Probate.***
Civil Records: Access: In person, online. Both court and visitors may perform in person searches. No search fee. Required to search: name, years to search. Civil cases indexed by defendant. Civil index on

docket books, from 1885 (probate), 25 years for civil; on computer back to 2000. Civil PAT goes back to 2000. Civil records online - see criminal access. Online civil and probate records from 10/00 forward.
Criminal Records: Access: In person, online. Both court and visitors may perform in person searches. No search fee. Required to search: name, years to search. Criminal record keeping back for 25 years; on computer back to 2000. Criminal PAT goes back to same as civil. Single use or subscribe at https://www.nebraska.gov/justicecc/ccname.cgi for court access. Single use is $15.00 a record or open an account for $1 per record plus $50 annual fee. Online criminal and traffic records date from 07/00. Online results show middle initial, DOB.
General Information: No juvenile records released. Will fax documents $3.00 1st page, $1.00 each add'l. Court makes copy: $.25 per page. Certification fee: $1.00. Payee: County Court. Personal checks accepted. Prepayment required.

Gosper County

District Court PO Box 136, 507 Smith St, Elwood, NE 68937; 308-785-2611; fax: 308-785-2300; 8:30AM-4:30PM (CST). ***Felony, Civil Actions over $51,000.***
www.co.gosper.ne.us/webpages/district_court/district_court.htm
Civil Records: Access: Fax, mail, in person, online. Visitors must perform in person searches themselves. No search fee. Required to search: name, years to search. Civil cases indexed by defendant, plaintiff. Civil records in general index books since late 1800s. Civil PAT goes back to 2000. PAT civil results show middle initial. Civil records online - see criminal access. Online records date from 07/00.
Criminal Records: Access: Fax, mail, in person, online. Visitors must perform in person searches themselves. No search fee. Required to search: name, years to search; also helpful: DOB. Criminal records in general index books since late 1800s. Criminal PAT goes back to same as civil. PAT results show middle initial, DOB. Single use or subscribe at https://www.nebraska.gov/justicecc/ccname.cgi for court access. Single use is $15.00 a record or open an account for $1 per record plus $50 annual fee. Online records date from 07/00. Online results show middle initial, DOB.
General Information: Online identifiers in results same as on public terminal. No juvenile records or search warrants released. Will fax documents for $2.00 per page. Court makes copy: $.25 per page. Self serve: same. Certification fee: $1.00 per page. Payee: Clerk of District Court. Personal checks accepted; credit cards are not. Prepayment required. Mail requests: SASE requested.

Gosper County Court PO Box 55, 507 Smith St, Elwood, NE 68937; 308-785-2531; probate phone: same; fax: 308-785-2300; 8:30AM-4:30PM (CST). ***Misdemeanor, Civil Actions under $51,000, Eviction, Small Claims, Probate.***
Always call before faxing.
Civil Records: Access: In person, online. Visitors must perform in person searches themselves. Required to search: name, years to search. Civil cases indexed by defendant, plaintiff. Civil index on cards, docket books kept for 10 years (civil), to late 1800s (probate). Note: Mail access limited to short searches. Civil PAT goes back to 2000. PAT civil results show middle initial. Civil records online - see criminal access. Online civil and probate records from 11/00 forward.
Criminal Records: Access: In person, online. Visitors must perform in person searches themselves. Required to search: name, years to search, DOB. Criminal record keeping back for 15 years, computerized back to 2001. Criminal PAT goes back to same as civil. PAT results show middle initial, DOB. Single use or subscribe at https://www.nebraska.gov/justicecc/ccname.cgi for court access. Single use is $15.00 a record or open an account for $1 per record plus $50 annual fee. Online criminal and traffic records date from 02/00. Online results show middle initial, DOB.
General Information: No adoption or juvenile records released. Will fax documents $3.00 1st page, $1.00 ea add'l. Court makes copy: $.25 per page. Self serve: same. Certification fee: $1.00. Payee: Gosper County Court. Personal checks accepted. Out of state checks not accepted. No credit cards accepted. Prepayment required.

Grant County

District Court PO Box 139, Hyannis, NE 69350; 308-458-2488; fax: 308-458-2780; 8AM-4PM (MST). ***Felony, Civil Actions over $51,000.***
Civil Records: Access: Fax, mail, in person, online. Both court and visitors may perform in person searches. No search fee. Required to search: name, years to search. Civil cases indexed by defendant, plaintiff. Civil index on docket books from 1888. Mail turnaround time 3-4 days. Public use terminal available, records go back to 2000. Civil records online - see criminal access. Online records date from 06/00.
Criminal Records: Access: Fax, mail, in person, online. Both court and visitors may perform in person searches. No search fee. Required to search: name, years to search. Criminal records indexed in books from 1888. Mail turnaround time 3-4 days. Public use terminal available, crim records go back to 2000. Single use or subscribe at https://www.nebraska.gov/justicecc/ccname.cgi for court access. Single use is $15.00 a record or open an account for $1 per record plus $50 annual fee. Online records date from 06/00. Online results show middle initial, DOB.
General Information: No mental health records released. Will fax documents $.20 per page. Court makes copy: $.20 per page; $.50 if to be mailed. Self serve: same. Certification fee: $1.50 includes copy fee. Payee: Grant County Clerk. Personal checks accepted; credit cards are not. Prepayment required. Mail requests: SASE required.

Grant County Court PO Box 437, Hyannis, NE 69350; 308-458-2433; fax: 308-327-5623; 10AM-4PM only on 2nd T of month (MST). ***Misdemeanor, Civil Actions under $51,000, Eviction, Small Claims, Probate.***
This court administered by Sheridan County by Julie Krotz at 308-327-5656. Court will not do record searches by name, etc. but will send and certify copies of specific records.
Civil Records: Access: in person, online. Visitors must perform in person searches themselves. Required to search: name, years to search; also helpful: address. Civil cases indexed by defendant, plaintiff. Civil records in files, docket books from 1888, computerized since 7/00. Note: Limited phone searching for specific records. Civil records online - see criminal access. Online civil records date from 11/00 forward, probate from 01/01.
Criminal Records: Access: In person, online. Visitors must perform in person searches themselves. Required to search: name, years to search, DOB; also helpful: address. Criminal records in files, docket books from 1888, computerized since 7/00. Note: Limited phone searching for specific records. Single use or subscribe at https://www.nebraska.gov/justicecc/ccname.cgi for court access. Single use is $15.00 a record or open an account for $1 per record plus $50 annual fee. Online criminal and traffic records date from 07/00. Online results show middle initial, DOB.
General Information: No adoption records released without court order. Will not fax documents. Court makes copy for no fee. Certification fee: $1.00. Payee: Grant County Court. Personal checks accepted; credit cards are not. Prepayment required.

Greeley County

District Court PO Box 287, 101 S Kildare, Greeley, NE 68842; 308-428-3625; fax: 308-428-3022; 8AM-N; 1PM-4PM (CST). ***Felony, Civil Actions over $51,000.***
Civil Records: Access: Mail, in person, online. Visitors must perform in person searches themselves. No search fee. Required to search: name, years to search, address. Civil cases indexed by defendant, plaintiff; index on general index books from late 1800s. Mail turnaround time 1 day. Civil PAT goes back to 7/2000. PAT results show name only. Civil records online - see criminal access. Online records date from 07/00.
Criminal Records: Access: Fax, mail, in person, online. Visitors must perform in person searches themselves. No search fee. Required to search: name, years to search, DOB, signed release. Criminal records on general index books from late 1800s. Mail turnaround time 1 day. Criminal PAT goes back to same as civil. Single use or subscribe at https://www.nebraska.gov/justicecc/ccname.cgi for court access. Single use is $15.00 a record or open an account for $1 per record plus $50 annual fee. Online records date from 07/00. Online results show middle initial, DOB.
General Information: No mental health records released. Will fax back docs $1.00 per page. Court makes copy: $.25 per page. Self serve: same. Certification fee: $1.50 plus $.25 per page. Payee: Clerk of District Court. Only cashiers checks and money orders accepted. No credit cards accepted. Prepayment required. Mail requests: SASE required.

Greeley County Court PO Box 302, 2 Kildare, Greeley, NE 68842; 308-428-2705; criminal phone: 308-428-3995; civil phone: 308-428-3995; probate phone: 308-428-3995; fax: 308-428-6500; 8AM-5PM (CST). ***Misdemeanor, Civil Actions under $51,000, Eviction, Small Claims, Probate.***
Probate fax is same as main fax number.
Civil Records: Access: In person, online. Visitors must perform in person searches themselves. Required to search: name, years to search. Civil cases indexed by defendant, plaintiff. Civil index on cards, kept from late 1800s, computerized since 5/2000. Civil PAT goes back to 5/2000. Civil records online - see criminal access. Online civil and probate records from 5/2000 forward.
Criminal Records: Access: In person, online. Visitors must perform in person searches themselves. Required to search: name, years to search. Criminal records indexed on cards, kept from late 1800s, computerized since 5/2000. Criminal PAT goes back to 5/2000. Single use or subscribe at https://www.nebraska.gov/justicecc/ccname.cgi for court access. Single use is $15.00 a record or open an account for $1 per record plus $50 annual fee. Online criminal and traffic records date from 05/00. Online results show middle initial, DOB.
General Information: No adoption records released. Will fax out specific case files; fee varies by job. Court makes copy: $.25 per page. Certification fee: $1.00 per page. Payee: County Court. Only cashiers checks and money orders accepted. No credit cards accepted. Prepayment required. Mail requests: SASE required for mail return of any copies.

Hall County

District Court 111 W First St, Box 1926, Grand Island, NE 68802; 308-385-5144; fax: 308-385-5110; 8AM-5PM (CST). ***Felony, Civil Actions over $51,000.***
Also, 800-508-0064.
Civil Records: Access: Fax, mail, in person, online. Visitors must perform in person searches themselves. No search fee. Required to search: name, years to search. Civil cases indexed by defendant, plaintiff. Many records on computer since 1985, some on microfilm, original index books back to late 1800s. Note: Court performs searches for government/law enforcement only. Mail turnaround time 3-4 days. Civil PAT goes back to 1989. PAT results show name only. Civil records online - see criminal access. Online records date from 10/97.
Criminal Records: Access: Fax, mail, in person, online. Visitors must perform in person searches themselves. No search fee. Required to search: name, years to search. Many records on computer since 1985, some on microfilm, original index books back to late 1800s. Note: Court performs searches for government/law enforcement only. Mail turnaround time 3-4 days. Criminal PAT goes back to same as civil. PAT results show name only. Single use or subscribe at https://www.nebraska.gov/justicecc/ccname.cgi for court access. Single use is $15.00 a record or open an account for $1 per record plus $50 annual fee.

Online records date from 10/97. Online results show middle initial, DOB.
General Information: No mental health records released. Fee to fax out file $3.00 1st page, $1.00 each add'l. Court makes copy: $.25 per page. Certification fee: $1.00 per cert. Payee: Clerk of District Court. Personal checks accepted; credit cards are not. Prepayment required. Mail requests: SASE required.

Hall County Court 111 W 1st #1, Grand Island, NE 68801; 308-385-5135; fax: 308-385-5138; 8AM-5PM (CST). ***Misdemeanor, Civil Actions under $51,000, Eviction, Small Claims, Probate.***
Civil Records: Access: In person, online. Visitors must perform in person searches themselves. Required to search: name, years to search. Civil cases indexed by defendant. Civil index on docket books, on computer after 1/24/00. Civil PAT goes back to 1/2000. Civil records online - see criminal access. Online civil records date from 01/00 forward, probate from 08/98.
Criminal Records: Access: Fax, mail, in person, online. Visitors must perform in person searches themselves. No search fee. Required to search: name, years to search, DOB. Criminal records indexed in books; on computer after 5/19/97. Mail turnaround time 1 day. Criminal PAT goes back to 5/1997. Single use or subscribe at https://www.nebraska.gov/justicecc/ccname.cgi for court access. Single use is $15.00 a record or open an account for $1 per record plus $50 annual fee. Online criminal and traffic records date from 05/97. Online results show middle initial, DOB.
General Information: No confidential records released. Will not fax documents. Court makes copy: $.25 per page. Certification fee: $1.00. Payee: County Court. Personal checks accepted; credit cards are not. Prepayment required.

Hamilton County

District Court PO Box 201, Aurora, NE 68818-0201; 402-694-3533; fax: 402-694-2250; 8AM-5PM (CST). ***Felony, Civil Actions over $51,000.***
Civil Records: Access: In person, online. Visitors must perform in person searches themselves. Required to search: name, years to search. Civil cases indexed by defendant, plaintiff. Civil index on docket books and files from late 1800s. Civil PAT goes back to 1998. Civil records online - see criminal access. Online records date from 03/98.
Criminal Records: Access: In person, online. Visitors must perform in person searches themselves. Required to search: name, years to search. Criminal records indexed in books and files from late 1800s. Criminal PAT goes back to same as civil. Single use or subscribe at https://www.nebraska.gov/justicecc/ccname.cgi for court access. Single use is $15.00 a record or open an account for $1 per record plus $50 annual fee. Online records date from 03/98. Online results show middle initial, DOB.
General Information: No mental health board hearing records released. Will fax documents $1.00 per page. Court makes copy: $.25 per page. Self serve: same. Certification fee: $1.00. Payee: Clerk of District Court. Personal checks accepted; credit cards are not. Prepayment required.

Hamilton County Court PO Box 323, 1111 13th St, Aurora, NE 68818; 402-694-6188; fax: 402-694-2250; 8AM-5PM (CST). ***Misdemeanor, Civil Actions under $51,000, Eviction, Small Claims, Probate.***
Will not do name searches but will provide specific docs.
Civil Records: Access: In person, online. Visitors must perform in person searches themselves. Required to search: name, years to search. Civil cases indexed by defendant, plaintiff. Civil records computerized since 1998, older on docket cards, probate on microfiche from late 1800s. Civil PAT goes back to 4/1998. PAT results show name only. Civil records online - see criminal access. Online civil records date from 10/99 forward, probate from 05/98.
Criminal Records: Access: Fax, mail, in person, online. Visitors must perform in person searches themselves. No search fee. Required to search: name, years to search. Computerized since 1997. Criminal PAT goes back to same as civil. PAT results show name only. Single use or subscribe at https://www.nebraska.gov/justicecc/ccname.cgi for court access. Single use is $15.00 a record or open an account for $1 per record plus $50 annual fee. Online criminal and traffic records date from 07/97. Online results show name only.
General Information: No adoption records released. Will not fax documents. Court makes copy: $.25 per page. Certification fee: $1.00 per page. Payee: Hamilton County Court. Personal checks accepted; credit cards are not. Prepayment required.

Harlan County

District Court PO Box 698, Alma, NE 68920; 308-928-2173; fax: 308-928-2079; 8:30AM-4:30PM (CST). ***Felony, Civil Actions over $51,000.***
Civil Records: Access: Phone, mail, in person, online. Both court and visitors may perform in person searches. Search fee: $5.00 per name. Required to search: name, years to search. Civil cases indexed by defendant, plaintiff; index on books and in files from late 1800s, on computer back to 3/2000. Mail turnaround time 1 day. Civil PAT goes back to 3/2000. Civil records online - see criminal access. Online records date from 04/00.
Criminal Records: Access: Phone, mail, in person, online. Both court and visitors may perform in person searches. Search fee: $5.00 per name. Required to search: name, years to search. Criminal docket on books and in files from late 1800s; on computer back to 3/2000. Mail turnaround time 1 day. Criminal PAT goes back to same as civil. Single use or subscribe at https://www.nebraska.gov/justicecc/ccname.cgi for court access. Single use is $15.00 a record or open an account for $1 per record plus $50 annual fee. Online records date from 4/2000. Online results show middle initial, DOB.
General Information: No juvenile records released. Will fax documents $1.00 per page. Court makes copy: $.25 per page. Self serve: same. Certification fee: $1.00. Payee: Clerk of District Court. Personal checks accepted; credit cards are not. Prepayment required.

Harlan County Court PO Box 379, 706 2nd St, Alma, NE 68920; 308-928-2179; fax: 308-928-2170; 8AM-5PM (CST). ***Misdemeanor, Civil Actions under $51,000, Eviction, Small Claims, Probate.***
www.district10.us/harlan_county.htm
Civil Records: Access: In person, online. Visitors must perform in person searches themselves. Required to search: name, years to search; also helpful: address. Civil cases indexed by defendant. Civil index on cards from 1900; computerized since 2000. Civil PAT goes back to 2000. Public data available on CD-ROM for legal research only. Civil records online - see criminal access. Online civil and probate records from 11/00 forward.
Criminal Records: Access: In person, online. Visitors must perform in person searches themselves. Required to search: name, years to search; also helpful: address, DOB. Criminal records indexed on cards from 1900, computerized since 2000. Criminal PAT goes back to same as civil. Public data available on CD-ROM for legal research only. Single use or subscribe at https://www.nebraska.gov/justicecc/ccname.cgi for court access. Single use is $15.00 a record or open an account for $1 per record plus $50 annual fee. Online criminal and traffic records date from 03/00. Online results show middle initial, DOB.
General Information: No adoption records released. Limited access to juvenile records. Will not fax documents. Court makes copy: $.25 per page. Self serve: same. Certification fee: $1.00. Payee: Harlan County Court. Business checks accepted. Visa/MC or debit card accepted. Prepayment required. Payment is required at time of search.

Hayes County

District Court PO Box 370, Hayes Center, NE 69032; 308-286-3413; fax: 308-286-3208; 8AM-4PM (CST). ***Felony, Civil Actions over $51,000.***
Civil Records: Access: Fax, mail, in person, online. Visitors must perform in person searches themselves. No search fee. Required to search: name; also helpful: years to search, address. Civil cases indexed by defendant, plaintiff. Civil index on docket books back to late 1800s. Mail turnaround time 2 days. Civil PAT goes back to 6/2000. PAT civil results show middle initial. Civil records online - see criminal access. Online records date from 06/00.
Criminal Records: Access: Fax, mail, in person, online. Visitors must perform in person searches themselves. No search fee. Required to search: name; also helpful: years to search, address, DOB, SSN. Criminal records indexed in books back to late 1800s. Mail turnaround time 2 days. Criminal PAT goes back to same as civil. PAT criminal results show middle initial. Single use or subscribe at https://www.nebraska.gov/justicecc/ccname.cgi for court access. Single use is $15.00 a record or open an account for $1 per record plus $50 annual fee. Online records date from 6/2000. Online results show middle initial, DOB.
General Information: Online identifiers in results same as on public terminal. No sealed records released. Will fax documents to local or toll free line. Court makes copy: $.25 per page. Self serve: same. Certification fee: $4.00. Payee: Clerk of District Court. Personal checks accepted; credit cards are not. Prepayment required. Mail requests: SASE required.

Hayes County Court PO Box 370, Hayes Center, NE 69032; 308-286-3315; fax: 308-286-3208; 9AM-N, 1-4PM Tues (Clerk's hours), or Fri; call for hours. (CST). ***Misdemeanor, Civil Actions under $51,000, Eviction, Small Claims, Probate.***
Civil Records: Access: In person, online. Visitors must perform in person searches themselves. Required to search: name, years to search. Civil cases indexed by defendant, plaintiff; index on general index books and files back to late 1800s; on computer back to mid-2000. PAT civil results show middle initial. Civil records online - see criminal access. Online civil records date from 11/00 forward, probate from 12/00.
Criminal Records: Access: In person, online. Visitors must perform in person searches themselves. Required to search: name, years to search, DOB. Criminal records on general index books and files back to late 1800s; on computer back to mid-2000. PAT results show middle initial, DOB. Single use or subscribe at https://www.nebraska.gov/justicecc/ccname.cgi for court access. Single use is $15.00 a record or open an account for $1 per record plus $50 annual fee. Online criminal and traffic records date from 08/00. Online results show middle initial, DOB.
General Information: No juvenile or adoption records released. Will not fax documents. Court makes copy: $.25 per page. Self serve: same. Certification fee: $1.00. Payee: County Court. Personal checks accepted; credit cards are not. Prepayment required. Mail requests: SASE required for mail return of any copies.

Hitchcock County

District Court PO Box 248, 229 E "D" St, Trenton, NE 69044; 308-334-5646; fax: 308-334-5398; 8:30AM-4PM (CST). ***Felony, Civil Actions over $51,000.***
www.co.hitchcock.ne.us/court.html
Civil Records: Access: Phone, fax, mail, in person, online. Both court and visitors may perform in person searches. No search fee. Required to search: name, years to search. Civil cases indexed by defendant, plaintiff; index on books from late 1800s; on computer back to 1999. Mail turnaround time 2 days. Civil PAT goes back to 2000. PAT civil results show middle initial. Civil records online - see criminal access. Online records date from 06/00.
Criminal Records: Access: Phone, fax, mail, in person, online. Both court and visitors may perform in person searches. No search fee. Required to search: name, years to search. Criminal docket on books from late 1800s; on computer back to 1999. Mail turnaround time 2 days. Criminal PAT goes back to same as civil. PAT criminal results show

middle initial. Single use or subscribe at https://www.nebraska.gov/justicecc/ccname.cgi for court access. Single use is $15.00 a record or open an account for $1 per record plus $50 annual fee. Online records date from 6/2000. Online results show middle initial, DOB.
General Information: No sealed records released. Will fax documents $3.00 1st page, $1.50 each add'l. Court makes copy: $.50 per page. Certification fee: $1.00 per cert. Payee: Clerk of District Court. Personal checks accepted; credit cards are not. Prepayment required. Mail requests: SASE required.

Hitchcock County Court PO Box 248, Trenton, NE 69044; 308-334-5383; fax: 308-334-5398; 8:30AM-4:30PM (CST). ***Misdemeanor, Civil Actions under $51,000, Eviction, Small Claims, Probate.***
Probate is a separate index at this same address.
Civil Records: Access: In person, online. Both court and visitors may perform in person searches. No search fee. Required to search: name, years to search. Civil cases indexed by defendant, plaintiff. Civil index on docket books, cards go back to 1960s; on computer back to 2000. Probate records go back to late 1800s. Civil PAT goes back to 2000. Public terminal is across the hall. Civil records online - see criminal access. Online civil and probate records from 1/2001 forward.
Criminal Records: Access: In person, online. Both court and visitors may perform in person searches. No search fee. Required to search: name, years to search, DOB. Criminal records go back to 1989 approx. on docket books, cards; on computer back to 2000. Criminal PAT goes back to 2000. Public terminal is across the hall. Single use or subscribe at https://www.nebraska.gov/justicecc/ccname.cgi for court access. Single use is $15.00 a record or open an account for $1 per record plus $50 annual fee. Online criminal and traffic records date from 09/00. Online results show middle initial, DOB.
General Information: No adoption or juvenile records released. Will not fax documents. Court makes copy: $.25 per page. Self serve: same. Certification fee: $1.00. Payee: County Court. Personal checks accepted. Prepayment required.

Holt County

District Court PO Box 755, 204 N 4th St, O'Neill, NE 68763; 402-336-2840; fax: 402-336-3601; 8AM-4:30PM (CST). ***Felony, Civil Actions over $51,000.***
Civil Records: Access: Phone, fax, mail, in person, online. Both court and visitors may perform in person searches. No search fee. Required to search: name, years to search; also helpful: address. Civil cases indexed by defendant, plaintiff. Civil index on docket books and general index books since late 1800, search last 15 years only. Mail turnaround time 1 week or less. Civil PAT goes back to 1980s. PAT results show middle initial, DOB. Civil records online - see criminal access. Online records date from 6/98.
Criminal Records: Access: Phone, fax, mail, in person, online. Both court and visitors may perform in person searches. No search fee. Required to search: name, years to search, DOB. Criminal docket on books and general index books archived since late 1800s, search last 15 years only. Mail turnaround time 1 week or less. Criminal PAT goes back to 1997. PAT results show middle initial, DOB. Single use or subscribe at https://www.nebraska.gov/justicecc/ccname.cgi for court access. Single use is $15.00 a record or open an account for $1 per record plus $50 annual fee. Online records date from 6/98. Online results show middle initial, DOB.
General Information: No juvenile or mental health records released. Will fax documents $3.00 1st page, $1.00 each add'l. Court makes copy: $.20 per page. Self serve: same. Certification fee: $1.00 per page. Payee: Clerk of District Court. Personal checks accepted; credit cards are not. Prepayment required. Mail requests: SASE required.

Holt County Court 204 N 4th St, O'Neill, NE 68763; 402-336-1662; fax: 402-336-1663; 8AM-4:30PM (CST). ***Misdemeanor, Civil Actions under $51,000, Eviction, Small Claims, Probate.***
Probate fax is 402-336-1663.
Civil Records: Access: In person, online. Visitors must perform in person searches themselves. Required to search: name, years to search. Civil cases indexed by defendant. Civil records go back to 1970; on computer back to 2000; probate from 1880. Civil PAT goes back to 7/2000. Civil records online - see criminal access. Online civil records date from 10/00 forward, probate from 11/00.
Criminal Records: Access: In person, online. Visitors must perform in person searches themselves. Required to search: name, years to search, DOB. Criminal records go back to 1885, on computer back to 2000. Criminal PAT goes back to same as civil. Single use or subscribe at https://www.nebraska.gov/justicecc/ccname.cgi for court access. Single use is $15.00 a record or open an account for $1 per record plus $50 annual fee. Online criminal and traffic records date from 07/00. Online results show middle initial, DOB.
General Information: No adoption records released. Will not fax documents. Court makes copy: $.25 per page. Certification fee: $1.00 per doc. Payee: Holt County Court. Personal checks accepted; credit cards are not. Prepayment required. Mail requests: SASE required for mail return of any copies.

Hooker County

District Court PO Box 184, Mullen, NE 69152; 308-546-2244; fax: 308-546-2490; 8:30AM-N, 1-4:30PM (MST). ***Felony, Civil Actions over $51,000.***
Civil Records: Access: In person, online. Visitors must perform in person searches themselves. Required to search: name, years to search. Civil cases indexed by defendant, plaintiff. Civil index on docket books since late 1800s. Civil PAT goes back to 6/2000. Civil records online - see criminal access. Online records date from 06/00.
Criminal Records: Access: In person, online. Visitors must perform in person searches themselves. Required to search: name, years to search. Criminal records indexed in books since late 1800s. Criminal PAT goes back to same as civil. Single use or subscribe at https://www.nebraska.gov/justicecc/ccname.cgi for court access. Single use is $15.00 a record or open an account for $1 per record plus $50 annual fee. Online records date from 6/2000. Online results show middle initial, DOB.
General Information: No mental health records released. Will fax documents $2.00 fee per page. Court makes copy: $1.00 per page. Self serve: $.25 per page. Certification fee: $1.50 per cert. Payee: Clerk of District Court. Personal checks accepted; credit cards are not. Prepayment required.

Hooker County Court PO Box 184, 305 NW 1st St, Mullen, NE 69152; 308-546-2249; fax: 308-546-2490; 8:30AM-3:00PM (MST). ***Misdemeanor, Civil Actions under $51,000, Eviction, Small Claims, Probate.***
Fax number is for sheriff's office.
Civil Records: Access: In person, online. Only the court performs in person searches; visitors may not. Required to search: name, years to search. Civil cases indexed by defendant, plaintiff. Civil index on cards and books from late 1800s. Civil PAT available. Terminal is located in County Clerk Office. Civil records online - see criminal access. Online civil records date from 11/99 forward, probate from 08/98.
Criminal Records: Access: In person, online. Both court and visitors may perform in person searches. No search fee. Required to search: name, years to search; also helpful: DOB, SSN. Criminal records indexed on cards and books from late 1800s, computerized 1998. Criminal PAT available. Terminal is located in County Clerk Office. Single use or subscribe at https://www.nebraska.gov/justicecc/ccname.cgi for court access. Single use is $15.00 a record or open an account for $1 per record plus $50 annual fee. Online criminal and traffic records date from 08/98. Online results show middle initial, DOB.
General Information: No adoption or juvenile records released. No fee to fax out. Court makes copy: $.25 per page. Certification fee: $1.00 per cert. Payee: County Court. Business checks accepted. No credit cards accepted. Prepayment required.

Howard County

District Court PO Box 25, 612 Indian St, St Paul, NE 68873; 308-754-4343; fax: 308-754-4266; 8AM-5PM (CST). ***Felony, Civil Actions over $51,000.***
Civil Records: Access: In person, online. Both court and visitors may perform in person searches. No search fee. Required to search: name, years to search. Civil cases indexed by defendant, plaintiff; index on microfiche from 1986, books prior. Civil PAT goes back to 2002. Civil records online - see criminal access. Online records date from 06/98.
Criminal Records: Access: Fax, mail, in person, online. Both court and visitors may perform in person searches. Required to search: name, years to search, DOB. Criminal records on microfiche from 1986, books prior; on computer back to 9/1998. Criminal PAT goes back to 9/1998. PAT results show name only. Single use or subscribe at https://www.nebraska.gov/justicecc/ccname.cgi for court access. Single use is $15.00 a record or open an account for $1 per record plus $50 annual fee. Online records date from 06/98. Online results show middle initial, DOB.
General Information: No pending case records released. Will not fax documents. Court makes copy: $.25 per page. Certification fee: $5.00 per cert. Payee: Clerk of District Court. Personal checks accepted; credit cards are not. Prepayment required.

Howard County Court 612 Indian St #6, St Paul, NE 68873; 308-754-4192; fax: 308-754-4727; 8AM-N; 1PM-4PM (CST). ***Misdemeanor, Civil Actions under $51,000, Eviction, Small Claims, Probate.***
Civil Records: Access: In person, online. Visitors must perform in person searches themselves. Required to search: name, years to search. Civil cases indexed by defendant. Civil records on docket cards since 1982; computerized records since 2000. Civil PAT goes back to 2000. Civil records online - see criminal access. Online civil records date from 05/01 forward, probate from 08/00.
Criminal Records: Access: In person, online. Visitors must perform in person searches themselves. Required to search: name, years to search; also helpful: DOB. Criminal records on docket cards since 1982; computerized records since 2000. Criminal PAT goes back to same as civil. Single use or subscribe at https://www.nebraska.gov/justicecc/ccname.cgi for court access. Single use is $15.00 a record or open an account for $1 per record plus $50 annual fee. Online criminal and traffic records date from 08/00. Online results show middle initial, DOB.
General Information: Will not fax documents. Court makes copy: $.25 per page. Certification fee: $1.00 per page. Payee: Howard County Court. Business checks accepted. Major credit cards accepted online for traffic only. Prepayment required.

Jefferson County

District Court Jefferson County Courthouse, 411 Fourth St, Fairbury, NE 68352; 402-729-6807; fax: 402-729-6808; 9AM-5PM (CST). ***Felony, Civil Actions over $51,000.***
Civil Records: Access: Fax, mail, in person, online. Both court and visitors may perform in person searches. No search fee. Required to search: name, years to search. Civil cases indexed by defendant, plaintiff. Civil index on docket books from 1870s; on computer back to 1996. Mail turnaround time 1-3 days. Civil PAT goes back to 1996. PAT results show name only. Civil records online - see criminal access. Online records date from 11/96.
Criminal Records: Access: In person, online. Visitors must perform in person searches themselves. Required to search: name, years to search, DOB. Criminal records indexed in books from 1870s; on computer back to 1996. Criminal PAT goes back to 1996. PAT results show middle initial, DOB, SSN. Single use or subscribe at https://www.nebraska.gov/justicecc/ccname.cgi for court access. Single use is $15.00 a record or open

an account for $1 per record plus $50 annual fee. Online records date from 11/96. Online results show name only.
General Information: No mental health records released. Fee to fax out file $2.00 per page. Court makes copy: $.25 per page. Certification fee: $1.00. Payee: Clerk of District Court. Personal checks accepted; credit cards are not. Prepayment required. Mail requests: SASE required for civil.

Jefferson County Court 411 Fourth St, Fairbury, NE 68352; 402-729-6801; fax: 402-729-6802; 8AM-N, 1-5PM (CST). ***Misdemeanor, Civil Actions under $51,000, Eviction, Small Claims, Probate.***
http://court.nol.org/
County Court employees will not search for court records or provide information or documentation of court records for any person or agency.
Civil Records: Access: In person, online. Visitors must perform in person searches themselves. Required to search: name, years to search. Civil cases indexed by defendant, plaintiff; index on cards from 1988, prior on docket books; computerized records from 10/1999. Civil PAT goes back to 1999. PAT results show name only. Civil records online - see criminal access. Online civil records date from 10/99 forward, probate from 05/98.
Criminal Records: Access: In person, online. Visitors must perform in person searches themselves. Required to search: name, years to search, DOB, signed release. Criminal records on cards from 1988, prior on docket books; computerized records from 9/1996. Criminal PAT goes back to 1996. PAT results show middle initial, DOB. Single use or subscribe at https://www.nebraska.gov/justicecc/ccname.cgi for court access. Single use is $15.00 a record or open an account for $1 per record plus $50 annual fee. Phone number in Lincoln for subscription is 402-471-7185 or 800-747-8177. Online criminal and traffic records date from 09/96. Online results show middle initial, DOB.
General Information: No adoption or sealed records released. Will fax back documents for $2.00 per page. Court makes copy: $.25 per page. Certification fee: $1.00 per seal. Payee: County Court. Personal checks accepted. Major credit cards accepted online only. Prepayment required.

Johnson County

District Court PO Box 416, Tecumseh, NE 68450; 402-335-6301; fax: 402-335-6311; 8AM-N, 1-4:30PM (CST). ***Felony, Civil Actions over $51,000.***
Civil Records: Access: Mail, in person, online. Both court and visitors may perform in person searches. No search fee. Required to search: name, years to search. Civil cases indexed by defendant, plaintiff; index on index and docket books from late 1800s, microfiche back 7 years. Civil PAT goes back to 1998. Civil records online - see criminal access. Online civil and probate records from 04/01 forward.
Criminal Records: Access: In person, online. Both court and visitors may perform in person searches. No search fee. Required to search: name, years to search. Criminal records on index and docket books from late 1800s, microfiche back 7 years. Criminal PAT goes back to same as civil. Single use or subscribe at https://www.nebraska.gov/justicecc/ccname.cgi for court access. Single use is $15.00 a record or open an account for $1 per record plus $50 annual fee. Online records date from 4/2000. Online results show middle initial, DOB.
General Information: No juvenile records released. Fee to fax out file $2.00 each. Court makes copy: $.50 per page. Self serve: same. Certification fee: $1.50. Payee: Clerk of District Court. Personal checks accepted; credit cards are not. Prepayment required.

Johnson County Court PO Box 285, 3rd and Broadway, Tecumseh, NE 68450; 402-335-6313; fax: 402-335-6314; 8AM-4:30PM (CST). ***Misdemeanor, Civil Actions under $51,000, Eviction, Small Claims, Probate.***
The court is in the process of computerizing their records.
Civil Records: Access: Mail, in person, online. Both court and visitors may perform in person searches. No search fee. Required to search: name, years to search; also helpful: address. Civil cases indexed by defendant, plaintiff. Civil index on cards back 15 years, microfiche back to late 1800s for probate. Mail turnaround time 1 day. Civil PAT goes back to 4/2000. Civil records online - see criminal access. Online records date from 02/98.
Criminal Records: Access: Mail, in person, online. Both court and visitors may perform in person searches. No search fee. Required to search: name, years to search, DOB, signed release; also helpful: address, SSN. Criminal records indexed on cards back 15 years. Mail turnaround time 1 day. Criminal PAT goes back to same as civil. Single use or subscribe at https://www.nebraska.gov/justicecc/ccname.cgi for court access. Single use is $15.00 a record or open an account for $1 per record plus $50 annual fee. Online criminal and traffic records date from 02/98. Online results show middle initial, DOB.
General Information: No adoption or juvenile records released. Will not fax documents. Court makes copy: $.25 per page. Certification fee: $1.00 per page. Payee: County Court. Personal checks accepted; credit cards are not. Prepayment required.

Kearney County

District Court PO Box 208, Minden, NE 68959; 308-832-1742; fax: 308-832-0636; 8:30AM-5PM (CST). ***Felony, Civil Actions over $51,000.***
www.kearneycounty.ne.gov/index_html?page=content/court.html
Civil Records: Access: In person, online. Visitors must perform in person searches themselves. Required to search: name, years to search. Civil cases indexed by defendant, plaintiff. All records on microfilm since 1800s; on computer back to 9/1998. Note: Mail access to attorneys only. Civil PAT goes back to 9/1998. PAT results show middle initial, DOB. Civil records online - see criminal access. Online records date from 08/98.
Criminal Records: Access: In person, online. Visitors must perform in person searches themselves. Required to search: name, years to search. Criminal records on microfilm since 1800s; on computer back to 9/1998. Criminal PAT available. PAT results show middle initial, DOB. Single use or subscribe at https://www.nebraska.gov/justicecc/ccname.cgi for court access. Single use is $15.00 a record or open an account for $1 per record plus $50 annual fee. Online records date from 08/98. Online results show middle initial, DOB.
General Information: Online identifiers in results same as on public terminal. No mental health records released. Court makes copy: $.25 per page. Certification fee: $1.00. Payee: Clerk of District Court. Personal checks accepted; credit cards are not. Prepayment required.

Kearney County Court PO Box 377, 426 N Colorado, Minden, NE 68959; 308-832-2719; fax: 308-832-0636; 8AM-N, 1-5PM (CST). ***Misdemeanor, Civil Actions under $51,000, Eviction, Small Claims, Probate.***
www.district10.us/kearney_county.htm
Civil Records: Access: In person, online. Visitors must perform in person searches themselves. Required to search: name, years to search. Civil cases indexed by defendant. Civil records computerized since 10/99, rest on index cards, some probate on microfiche. Public use terminal available. Civil records online - see criminal access. Online civil records date from 10/99 forward, probate from 05/98.
Criminal Records: Access: Mail, in person, online. Visitors must perform in person searches themselves. No search fee. Required to search: name, years to search. Criminal records computerized since 3/97, indexes available since 1988. Mail turnaround time 1 week. Public use terminal available. Single use or subscribe at https://www.nebraska.gov/justicecc/ccname.cgi for court access. Single use is $15.00 a record or open an account for $1 per record plus $50 annual fee. Online criminal and traffic records date from 03/97. Online results show middle initial, DOB.
General Information: Court makes copy: $.25 per page. Certification fee: $1.00. Payee: Kearney County Court. Personal checks accepted. Prepayment required. Mail requests: SASE requested.

Keith County

District Court 511 N Spruce St, #202, Ogallala, NE 69153; 308-284-3849; fax: 308-284-3978; 8AM-4PM (MST). ***Felony, Civil Actions over $51,000.***
Civil Records: Access: Fax, mail, in person, online. Both court and visitors may perform in person searches. No search fee. Required to search: name, years to search, DOB. Civil cases indexed by defendant, plaintiff. Civil index on docket books from late 1800s; on computer back to 1975. Mail turnaround time 2-3 days. Civil PAT goes back to 1975. Civil records online - see criminal access. Online records date from 06/97.
Criminal Records: Access: Fax, mail, in person, online. Both court and visitors may perform in person searches. No search fee. Required to search: name, years to search, DOB. Criminal records indexed in books from late 1800s; on computer back to 1975. Mail turnaround time 2-3 days. Criminal PAT goes back to same as civil. PAT results show middle initial, DOB. Single use or subscribe at https://www.nebraska.gov/justicecc/ccname.cgi for court access. Single use is $15.00 a record or open an account for $1 per record plus $50 annual fee. Online records date from 06/97. Online results show middle initial, DOB.
General Information: No juvenile or mental health records released. No fee to fax documents. Fee is charged if long distance. Court makes copy: $.25 per page. Self serve: same. Certification fee: $1.00 per cert. Payee: Clerk of District Court. Personal checks accepted; credit cards are not. Prepayment required.

Keith County Court PO Box 358, 511 N Spruce, Ogallala, NE 69153; 308-284-3693; fax: 308-284-6825; 7:30AM-4:30PM (MST). ***Misdemeanor, Civil Actions under $51,000, Eviction, Small Claims, Probate.***
Civil Records: Access: In person, online. Visitors must perform in person searches themselves. Required to search: name, years to search. Civil cases indexed by defendant, plaintiff. Civil index on cards, files; computerized records since 1997. Civil PAT goes back to 2000. PAT results show name, DOB. Civil records online - see criminal access. Online civil records date from 10/99 forward, probate from 05/98.
Criminal Records: Access: In person, online. Visitors must perform in person searches themselves. Required to search: name, years to search. Criminal records indexed on cards, files; computerized records since 1997. Criminal PAT goes back to 2000.PAT results show name, DOB. Single use or subscribe at https://www.nebraska.gov/justicecc/ccname.cgi for court access. Single use is $15.00 a record or open an account for $1 per record plus $50 annual fee. Online criminal and traffic records date from 06/97. Online results show middle initial, DOB.
General Information: No adoption records released. Will fax documents $2.00 per page. Court makes copy: $.25 per page. Certification fee: $1.25. Payee: County Court. Local checks accepted only. No credit cards accepted. Prepayment required.

Keya Paha County

District Court PO Box 349, Springview, NE 68778; 402-497-3791; fax: 402-497-3799; 8AM-5PM (CST). ***Felony, Civil Actions over $51,000.***
www.co.keya-paha.ne.us
Civil Records: Access: Fax, mail, in person, online. Both court and visitors may perform in person searches. No search fee. Required to search: name, years to search. Civil cases indexed by defendant, plaintiff; index on microfiche 7-9 years, on docket books since late 1800s. Mail turnaround time 3-4 days. Civil PAT goes back to 1999. Civil records online - see criminal access. Online records date from 07/00.
Criminal Records: Access: Fax, mail, in person, online. Both court and visitors may perform in person searches. No search fee. Required to search:

name, years to search. Computerized back to 2000, criminal records on microfiche 7-9 years, on docket books since late 1800s. Mail turnaround time 3-4 days. Criminal PAT goes back to same as civil. Single use or subscribe at https://www.nebraska.gov/justicecc/ccname.cgi for court access. Single use is $15.00 a record or open an account for $1 per record plus $50 annual fee. Online records date from 7/2000. Online results show middle initial, DOB.
General Information: No confidential records released. Will fax documents $2.00 1st page, $1.00 each add'l. Court makes copy: $.25 per page. Legal size- $.30 per page. Self serve: same. Certification fee: $4.00 per document includes copies. Payee: Clerk of District Court. Personal checks accepted; credit cards are not. Prepayment required. Mail requests: SASE required.

Keya Paha County Court PO Box 275, Courthouse Ln, Springview, NE 68778; 402-497-3021; probate phone: 402-684-3021; fax: 402-497-3799; every 2nd Friday, 8AM-4:30PM (CST). ***Misdemeanor, Civil Actions under $51,000, Eviction, Small Claims, Probate.***
Court Ofc is rarely manned. Clerk is usually at Brown County Courthouse. To search at Keya Paha, contact Roxanne Philben, 402-387-2864; she will call the treasurer and instruct them to let you in Keya Paha court to perform your in person search.
Civil Records: Access: In person, online. Visitors must perform in person searches themselves. Required to search: name, years to search; also helpful: address. Civil cases indexed by defendant, plaintiff. Civil records in index books and files, many records on microfiche, back to late 1800s. Civil PAT goes back to 2000. Civil records online - see criminal access. Online civil and probate records from 01/01 forward.
Criminal Records: Access: In person, online. Visitors must perform in person searches themselves. Required to search: name, years to search; also helpful: address, DOB, SSN. Criminal docket on books and files, many records on microfiche, back to late 1800s. Criminal PAT goes back to same as civil. Single use or subscribe at https://www.nebraska.gov/justicecc/ccname.cgi for court access. Single use is $15.00 a record or open an account for $1 per record plus $50 annual fee. Online criminal and traffic records date from 08/00. Online results show middle initial, DOB.
General Information: No juvenile records released. Will not fax documents. Court makes copy: $.25 per page. Certification fee: $1.00 per page. Payee: County Clerk. Personal checks accepted; credit cards are not. Prepayment required.

Kimball County

District Court 114 E 3rd St, #7, Kimball, NE 69145; 308-235-3591; fax: 308-235-3190; 8AM-5PM M-TH, 8AM-4PM F (MST). ***Felony, Civil Actions over $51,000.***
Civil Records: Access: In person, online. Visitors must perform in person searches themselves. Required to search: name, years to search. Civil cases indexed by defendant, plaintiff; index on microfiche from 1960 forward, prior in books from early 1900s, computerized since 10/97. Civil PAT goes back to 10/1997. PAT results show middle initial, DOB, SSN. Civil records online - see criminal access.
Criminal Records: Access: In person, online. Visitors must perform in person searches themselves. Required to search: name, years to search; also helpful: DOB. Criminal records on microfiche from 1960 forward, prior in books from early 1900s, computerized since 10/97. Criminal PAT goes back to 10/1997. PAT results show middle initial, DOB, SSN. Single use or subscribe at https://www.nebraska.gov/justicecc/ccname.cgi for court access. Single use is $15.00 a record or open an account for $1 per record plus $50 annual fee. Also, for $15.00 fee per search, you may access the JUSTICE Court Case system statewide at https://www.nebraska.gov/justicecc/ccname.cgi. Online results show middle initial, DOB.
General Information: No mental health records released. Will fax documents $3.00 1st page, $1.00 ea add'l page. Court makes copy: $.50 per page in person, $1.00 if mailed. Certification fee: $1.50. Payee: Clerk of District Court. Personal checks accepted; credit cards are not. Prepayment required.

Kimball County Court 114 E 3rd St, Kimball, NE 69145; 308-235-2831; fax: 308-235-3927; 8AM-N, 1-5PM, closes 4PM F (MST). ***Misdemeanor, Civil Actions under $51,000, Small Claims, Probate, Traffic.***
Civil Records: Access: In person, online. Visitors must perform in person searches themselves. Required to search: name, years to search. Civil cases indexed by defendant, plaintiff. Civil index on cards and original files, also state computer. Civil PAT goes back to 2000. Civil records online - see criminal access. Online civil and probate records from 11/00 forward.
Criminal Records: Access: In person, online. Visitors must perform in person searches themselves. Required to search: name, years to search. Criminal records indexed on cards and original files. Criminal PAT goes back to 2000. Single use or subscribe at https://www.nebraska.gov/justicecc/ccname.cgi for court access. Single use is $15.00 a record or open an account for $1 per record plus $50 annual fee. Online criminal and traffic records date from 04/00. Online results show middle initial, DOB.
General Information: Will not fax documents as a rule. Court makes copy: $.25 per page. Certification fee: $1.00 per doc. Payee: County Court. Personal checks accepted; credit cards are not. Prepayment required.

Knox County

District Court PO Box 126, 206 Main St, Center, NE 68724; 402-288-5606; fax: 402-288-5609; 8:30AM-4:30PM (CST). ***Felony, Civil Actions over $51,000.***
Civil Records: Access: Online, in person. Visitors must perform in person searches themselves. Required to search: name, years to search. Civil cases indexed by defendant, plaintiff. Civil index on docket books from 1874; on computer back to 9/98. Civil PAT goes back to 9/1998. Civil records online - see criminal access. Online records date from 09/98.
Criminal Records: Access: In person, online. Visitors must perform in person searches themselves. Required to search: name, years to search; also helpful: DOB. Criminal records indexed in books from 1874; on computer back to 9/1998. Criminal PAT goes back to same as civil. Single use or subscribe at https://www.nebraska.gov/justicecc/ccname.cgi for court access. Single use is $15.00 a record or open an account for $1 per record plus $50 annual fee. Online records date from 09/98. Online results show middle initial, DOB.
General Information: No mental health records released. Will fax documents $.25 per page. Court makes copy: $.25 per page. Self serve: $.10 per page. Certification fee: $1.00. Payee: Clerk of District Court. Personal checks accepted; credit cards are not. Prepayment required.

Knox County Court PO Box 125, Center, NE 68724; 402-288-5607; fax: 402-288-5609; 8:30AM-4:30PM (CST). ***Misdemeanor, Civil Actions under $51,000, Eviction, Small Claims, Probate.***
www.supremecourt.ne.gov
Civil Records: Access: In person, online. Visitors must perform in person searches themselves. Required to search: name, years to search. Civil cases indexed by defendant, plaintiff. Civil index on cards and general docket books from late 1800s; on computer from 8/2000. Civil PAT goes back to 8/2000. Civil records online - see criminal access. Online civil records date from 11/00 forward, probate from 09/00.
Criminal Records: Access: In person, online. Visitors must perform in person searches themselves. Required to search: name, years to search; also helpful: DOB. Criminal records indexed on cards and general docket books from late 1800s; on computer from 8/2000. Criminal PAT goes back to same as civil.PAT results show name, DOB. Single use or subscribe at https://www.nebraska.gov/justicecc/ccname.cgi for court access. Single use is $15.00 a record or open an account for $1 per record plus $50 annual fee. Online criminal and traffic records date from 08/00. Online results show middle initial, DOB.
General Information: Online identifiers in results same as on public terminal. No adoption records released. Will not fax documents. Court makes copy: $.25 per page. Self serve: same. Certification fee: $1.00. Payee: County Court. Personal checks accepted; credit cards are not. Prepayment required.

Lancaster County

District Court 575 S Tenth St, Lincoln, NE 68508-2810; 402-441-7328; fax: 402-441-6190; 8AM-4:30PM (CST). ***Felony, Civil Actions over $51,000.***
www.ci.lincoln.ne.us/cnty/discrt/index.htm
Civil Records: Access: Mail, in person, online. Both court and visitors may perform in person searches. Search fee: No search fee 1st half hour; add $4.25 per each 15 minutes add'l; with $20 deposit required for jobs estimated over half hour. Required to search: name, years to search. Civil cases indexed by defendant, plaintiff; index on computer from 1984, microfiche 1972 to 12/1975, docket books 1865 to 1984. Mail turnaround time 5 days. Civil PAT goes back to 1984. PAT results show name only. Civil records online - see criminal access. Online records date from 06/99.
Criminal Records: Access: Mail, in person, online. Both court and visitors may perform in person searches. Search fee: No search fee 1st half hour; add $4.25 per each 15 minutes add'l; with $20 deposit required for jobs estimated over half hour. Required to search: name, years to search, DOB. Criminal records computerized from 1984, microfiche 1972 to 12/1975, docket books 1865 to 1984. Mail turnaround time 5 days. Criminal PAT goes back to same as civil. PAT results show name only. Online access requires a subscription. Visit https://www.nebraska.gov/justicecc/ccname.cgi. Basics fees for court access are $.60 per record or $300 per month flat rate. Online records date from 06/99. Online results show name only.
General Information: Online identifiers in results same as on public terminal. No mental health or grand jury records released. Will fax documents $5.00 fee. Court makes copy: $.50 per page. Certification fee: $1.00 per cert. Payee: Clerk of District Court. Personal checks accepted; credit cards are not. Prepayment required. Mail requests: SASE requested.

Lancaster County Court 575 S 10th, Lincoln, NE 68508; 402-441-7291; criminal phone: 402-441-8959; civil phone: 402-441-7271; probate phone: 402-441-7443; 8AM-4:30PM (CST). ***Misdemeanor, Civil Actions under $51,000, Eviction, Small Claims, Probate.***
Civil Records: Access: Mail, in person, online. Visitors must perform in person searches themselves. No search fee. Required to search: name, years to search. Civil cases indexed by Defendant, Plaintiff. Civil index on docket books back to 1988, computerized since 11/98. Civil PAT goes back to 1995. Single use or subscribe at https://www.nebraska.gov/justicecc/ccname.cgi for court access. Single use is $15.00 a record or pay a monthly flat rate. Online civil records go back to 11/16/98, probate back to 05/98.
Criminal Records: Access: Mail, in person, online. Visitors must perform in person searches themselves. No search fee. Required to search: name, years to search, DOB. Criminal records on computer since 2/95; prior records are available if the case number is known. Note: Only mailed criminal records requested will be accepted. Mail turnaround time 7-10 working days. Criminal PAT goes back to same as civil. Online access to criminal records is the same as civil. Online criminal and traffic records date from 2/28/95. Online results show middle initial, DOB.
General Information: No adoption records released. Will not fax documents. Court makes copy: $.25 per page. Certification fee: $1.00 per cert. Payee: Lancaster County Court. Personal checks accepted. Visa/MC accepted. Prepayment required.

Lincoln County

District Court PO Box 1616, 301 N Jeffers 3rd Fl, North Platte, NE 69103-1616; 308-534-4350 X301 & X303; 8AM-5PM (CST). ***Felony, Civil Actions over $51,000.***
www.co.lincoln.ne.us/content/clrk_dist_crt/index.html
Civil Records: Access: In person, online. Visitors must perform in person searches themselves. Required to search: name, years to search. Civil cases indexed by defendant, plaintiff; index on computer back to 5/1997; books from 1866. Civil PAT goes back to 1997. Civil records online - see criminal access. Online records date from 04/97.
Criminal Records: Access: In person, online. Visitors must perform in person searches themselves. Required to search: name, years to search. Criminal records computerized from 5/1997; books from 1866. Criminal PAT goes back to 1997. Single use or subscribe at https://www.nebraska.gov/justicecc/ccname.cgi for court access. Single use is $15.00 a record or open an account for $1 per record plus $50 annual fee. Online records date from 04/97. Online results show middle initial, DOB.
General Information: No sealed, court ordered or mental health records released. Will fax documents to local or toll-free number. Court makes copy: $.25 per page. Certification fee: $1.00. Payee: Clerk of District Court. Personal checks accepted; credit cards are not. Prepayment required.

Lincoln County Court PO Box 519, 311 N Dewey St, 2nd Fl, North Platte, NE 69103; 308-534-4350; criminal phone: x240; civil phone: x237; probate phone: x186; fax: 308-535-3525; 8AM-5PM (CST). ***Misdemeanor, Civil Actions under $51,000, Eviction, Small Claims, Probate.***
Civil Records: Access: In person, online. Visitors must perform in person searches themselves. Required to search: name, years to search. Civil cases indexed by defendant, plaintiff. Civil records kept on index books back 20-25 years. Civil PAT goes back to 1997. PAT results show middle initial, DOB, SSN. Civil records online - see criminal access. Online civil records date from 10/99 forward, probate from 05/98.
Criminal Records: Access: Mail, fax, in person, online. Visitors must perform in person searches themselves. No search fee. Required to search: name, years to search, DOB. Criminal records on computer since 4/97. Note: No fee if record printed from public access terminal. Criminal PAT goes back to same as civil. PAT results show middle initial, DOB, SSN. Single use or subscribe at https://www.nebraska.gov/justicecc/ccname.cgi for court access. Single use is $15.00 a record or open an account for $1 per record plus $50 annual fee. Online criminal and traffic records date from 04/97. Online results show middle initial, DOB.
General Information: No adoption records released. Will fax documents for fee. Court makes copy: $.25 per page, free if printed from public access terminal. Certification fee: $1.00 per doc. Payee: County Court. Personal checks accepted. Visa, MC, Discover accepted. Prepayment required.

Logan County

District Court PO Box 8, 317 Main St, Stapleton, NE 69163; 308-636-2311; fax: 308-636-2333; 8:30AM-N; 1-4:30PM M-TH; 8:30AM-N; 1PM-4PM F (CST). ***Felony, Civil Actions over $51,000.***
Civil Records: Access: Fax, mail, in person, online. Both court and visitors may perform in person searches. No search fee. Required to search: name, years to search. Civil cases indexed by defendant, plaintiff. Civil index on docket books; computerized records since 2000. Mail turnaround time same day. Civil PAT goes back to 1997. Civil records online - see criminal access. Online records date from 04/97.
Criminal Records: Access: Fax, mail, in person, online. Both court and visitors may perform in person searches. No search fee. Required to search: name, years to search. Criminal docket on books; computerized records since 2000. Mail turnaround time same day. Criminal PAT goes back to same as civil. Single use or subscribe at https://www.nebraska.gov/justicecc/ccname.cgi for court access. Single use is $15.00 a record or open an account for $1 per record plus $50 annual fee. Online records date from 04/97. Online results show middle initial, DOB.
General Information: Will fax documents $2.50 1st page, $1.00 each add'l. Court makes copy: $.25 per page. Certification fee: $1.00 per cert plus $.50 per page includes copy. Payee: Clerk of the District Court. Personal checks accepted; credit cards are not. Prepayment required. Mail requests: SASE helpful.

Logan County Court PO Box 8, 317 Main St, Stapleton, NE 69163; 308-636-2677; 8AM-4:30PM W (CST). ***Misdemeanor, Civil Actions under $51,000, Eviction, Small Claims, Probate.***
Civil Records: Access: In person, online. Both court and visitors may perform in person searches. No search fee. Required to search: name, years to search; also helpful: address. Civil cases indexed by defendant, plaintiff. Civil index on docket books since 1837. Civil records online - see criminal access. Online civil records date from 01/00 forward, probate from 09/98.
Criminal Records: Access: In person, online. Both court and visitors may perform in person searches. No search fee. Required to search: name, years to search, signed release; also helpful: DOB. Criminal docket on books since 1837. Public use terminal has crim records back to 1998. PAT results show name only. Single use or subscribe at https://www.nebraska.gov/justicecc/ccname.cgi for court access. Single use is $15.00 a record or open an account for $1 per record plus $50 annual fee. Online criminal and traffic records date from 09/98. Online results show middle initial, DOB.
General Information: Adoption and juvenile records are not released. Fee to fax out file $3.00 1st page, $1.00 each add'l. Court makes copy: $.25 per page. Certification fee: $1.00. Payee: County Court. Personal checks accepted. Visa/MC accepted for traffic only. Prepayment required.

Loup County

District Court PO Box 187, Taylor, NE 68879; 308-942-3135; fax: 308-942-3103; 8:30AM-5PM M-TH, 8:30AM-N F (CST). ***Felony, Civil Actions over $51,000.***
Civil Records: Access: In person, online. Visitors must perform in person searches themselves. Required to search: name, years to search. Civil cases indexed by defendant, plaintiff. Civil records in index books from late 1800s. Civil PAT goes back to 2000. Civil records online - see criminal access. Online records date from 06/00.
Criminal Records: Access: In person, online. Visitors must perform in person searches themselves. Required to search: name, years to search; also helpful: address, DOB, SSN. Criminal docket on books from late 1800s. Criminal PAT goes back to same as civil. Single use or subscribe at https://www.nebraska.gov/justicecc/ccname.cgi for court access. Single use is $15.00 a record or open an account for $1 per record plus $50 annual fee. Online records date from 6/2000. Online results show middle initial, DOB.
General Information: No juvenile or adoption records released. Will not fax documents. Court makes copy: $.25 per page. Self serve: same. Certification fee: $1.00. Payee: Clerk of District Court. Personal checks accepted; credit cards are not. Prepayment required.

Loup County Court PO Box 146, Taylor, NE 68879; 308-942-6035; fax: 308-942-3103; 8-11AM Tues & TH (CST). ***Misdemeanor, Civil Actions under $51,000, Eviction, Small Claims, Probate.***
Civil Records: Access: In person, online. Visitors must perform in person searches themselves. Required to search: name, years to search. Civil cases indexed by defendant, plaintiff. Civil index on docket books since late 1800s. Some records have been filmed and forwarded to state archives. Civil PAT goes back to 2000. Civil records online - see criminal access. Online civil records date from 10/00 forward, probate from 11/00.
Criminal Records: Access: In person, online. Visitors must perform in person searches themselves. Required to search: name, years to search. Criminal records indexed in books since late 1800s. Some records have been filmed and forwarded to state archives. Criminal PAT goes back to 2000. Single use or subscribe at https://www.nebraska.gov/justicecc/ccname.cgi for court access. Single use is $15.00 a record or open an account for $1 per record plus $50 annual fee. Online criminal and traffic records date from 08/00. Online results show middle initial, DOB.
General Information: Will not fax documents. Court makes copy: $.25 per page. Self serve: same. Certification fee: $1.00. Payee: County Court. Personal checks accepted; credit cards are not. Prepayment required.

Madison County

District Court PO Box 249, Madison, NE 68748; 402-454-3311 X140; fax: 402-454-6528; 8AM-5PM (CST). ***Felony, Civil Actions over $51,000.***
http://co.madison.ne.us/clerkdiscrt.htm
Civil Records: Access: In person, online. Visitors must perform in person searches themselves. Required to search: name, years to search. Civil cases indexed by defendant, plaintiff; index on microfiche from late 1970s, prior on docket books from 1800s; computerized records go back to 1987. Civil PAT goes back to 9/1997. PAT civil results show middle initial. Civil records online - see criminal access. Online records date from 09/97.
Criminal Records: Access: In person, online. Visitors must perform in person searches themselves. Required to search: name, years to search. Criminal records on microfiche from late 1970s, prior on docket books from 1800s; computerized records go back to 1987. Criminal PAT goes back to same as civil. PAT results show middle initial, DOB. Single use or subscribe at https://www.nebraska.gov/justicecc/ccname.cgi for court access. Single use is $15.00 a record or open an account for $1 per record plus $50 annual fee. Online records date from 09/97. Online results show middle initial, DOB.
General Information: Online identifiers in results same as on public terminal. No mental health records released. Will fax out specific case files for $1.00 per page if prepaid. Court makes copy: $.25 per page. Certification fee: $1.50. Payee: Clerk of District Court. Personal checks and major credit cards accepted. Prepayment required.

Madison County Court PO Box 230, Madison, NE 68748; 402-454-3311; criminal phone: x181; civil phone: x142; probate phone: x165; fax: 402-454-3438; 8:30AM-5PM (CST). ***Misdemeanor, Civil Actions under $51,000, Eviction, Small Claims, Probate.***
Probate fax is same as main fax number.
Civil Records: Access: In person, online. Visitors must perform in person searches themselves. Required to search: name, years to search. Civil cases indexed by defendant, plaintiff; index on computer since 1986, prior on docket book, cards. Civil PAT goes back to 2000. PAT results show name only. The terminal is located at the District Court. Civil records online - see criminal access. Online civil records date from 01/99 forward, probate from 05/98.
Criminal Records: Access: In person, online. Visitors must perform in person searches themselves. Required to search: name, years to search, DOB. Criminal records computerized from 1986. Criminal PAT goes back to 2000. PAT results show middle initial, DOB. The terminal is located at the District Court. Single use or subscribe at https://www.nebraska.gov/justicecc/ccname.cgi for court access. Single use is $15.00 a record or open an account for $1 per record plus $50 annual fee. Online criminal and traffic records date from 10/96. Online results show middle initial, DOB.
General Information: No adoption records released. Will fax documents to local or toll free line. Court makes copy: $.25 per page. Self serve: same. Certification fee: $1.00 per certification. Payee: Madison County Court. Personal checks accepted; credit cards are not. Prepayment required.

McPherson County

District Court PO Box 122, Tryon, NE 69167; 308-587-2363; fax: 308-587-2363; 8:30AM-N, 1-4:30PM (CST). ***Felony, Civil Actions over $51,000.*** Call before faxing.

Civil Records: Access: In person, online. Both court and visitors may perform in person searches. No search fee. Required to search: name, years to search; also helpful: address. Civil cases indexed by defendant, plaintiff. Civil index on docket books since late 1800s. Civil PAT goes back to 6/2000. Civil records online - see criminal access. Online records date from 06/00.

Criminal Records: Access: In person, online. Both court and visitors may perform in person searches. No search fee. Required to search: name, years to search; also helpful: address, DOB, SSN. Criminal records indexed in books since late 1800s. Criminal PAT goes back to 6/2000. Single use or subscribe at https://www.nebraska.gov/justicecc/ccname.cgi for court access. Single use is $15.00 a record or open an account for $1 per record plus $50 annual fee. 800-747-8177 or 402-471-7185. Online records date from 6/2000. Online results show middle initial, DOB.

General Information: No adoption records released. Will fax documents $2.00 1st page, $1.00 each add'l. Court makes copy: $.50 per page. Self serve: same. Certification fee: $1.50 per page. Payee: Clerk of District Court. Business checks accepted. No credit cards accepted. Prepayment required. Mail requests: SASE required for mail return of any copies.

McPherson County Court PO Box 122, 500 Anderson, Tryon, NE 69167; 308-587-2363; fax: 308-587-2363; 8:30AM-N, 1-4:30PM (CST). ***Misdemeanor, Civil Actions under $51,000, Eviction, Small Claims, Probate.*** Call before faxing.

Civil Records: Access: In person, online. Both court and visitors may perform in person searches. No search fee. Required to search: name, years to search; also helpful: address. Civil cases indexed by defendant, plaintiff. Civil records computerized since 6/99, rest on index cards, are not computerized. Civil records online - see criminal access. Online civil records date from 01/009 forward, probate from 08/98.

Criminal Records: Access: In person, online. Both court and visitors may perform in person searches. No search fee. Required to search: name, years to search, signed release; also helpful: address, DOB. Criminal records computerized since 8/98. Public use terminal has crim records. Single use or subscribe at https://www.nebraska.gov/justicecc/ccname.cgi for court access. Single use is $15.00 a record or open an account for $1 per record plus $50 annual fee. Online criminal and traffic records date from 08/98. Online results show middle initial, DOB.

General Information: Adoption and juvenile records are not released. Fee to fax out file $2.00 1st page, $1.00 each add'l. Court makes copy: $.50 per page. Self serve: same. Certification fee: $1.25. Payee: County Court. Personal checks accepted; credit cards are not. Prepayment required.

Merrick County

District Court PO Box 27, Central City, NE 68826; 308-946-2461; fax: 308-946-3692; 8AM-5PM (CST). ***Felony, Civil Actions over $51,000.***

Civil Records: Access: In person, online. Visitors must perform in person searches themselves. Required to search: name, years to search. Civil cases indexed by defendant, plaintiff. Civil index on docket books from 1860; on computer back to 1994. Civil PAT goes back to 7/1994. PAT civil results show middle initial. Terminal results also show SSNs. Civil records online - see criminal access. Online records date from 07/94.

Criminal Records: Access: In person, online. Visitors must perform in person searches themselves. Required to search: name, years to search, signed release. Criminal records indexed in books from 1860; on computer back to 1994. Criminal PAT goes back to same as civil. PAT results show middle initial, DOB. Single use or subscribe at https://www.nebraska.gov/justicecc/ccname.cgi for court access. Single use is $15.00 a record or open an account for $1 per record plus $50 annual fee. Online records date from 07/94. Online results show middle initial, DOB.

General Information: No probation or mental health records released. Will fax out specific case files. Court makes copy: $.25 per page. Self serve: same. Certification fee: $1.00. Payee: Clerk of District Court. Personal checks accepted; credit cards are not. Prepayment required.

Merrick County Court County Courthouse, PO Box 27, Central City, NE 68826; 308-946-2812; fax: 308-946-3838; 8AM-5PM (CST). ***Misdemeanor, Civil Actions under $51,000, Eviction, Small Claims, Probate.***

Civil Records: Access: In person, online. Visitors must perform in person searches themselves. Required to search: name, years to search. Civil cases indexed by defendant, plaintiff. Civil index on docket books also on computer back to 1994. Civil PAT goes back to 1/1994. Civil records online - see criminal access. Online civil and probate records from 03/94 forward.

Criminal Records: Access: In person, online. Visitors must perform in person searches themselves. Required to search: name, years to search, DOB. Criminal records indexed in books from 1860; on computer back to 1994. Criminal PAT goes back to same as civil. Single use or subscribe at https://www.nebraska.gov/justicecc/ccname.cgi for court access. Single use is $15.00 a record or open an account for $1 per record plus $50 annual fee. Online criminal and traffic records date from 01/94. Online results show middle initial, DOB.

General Information: No financial affidavits or sealed records released. Will not fax documents. Court makes copy: $.25 per page. Certification fee: $1.00. Payee: County Court. Personal checks accepted; credit cards are not. Prepayment required.

Morrill County

District Court PO Box 824, Bridgeport, NE 69336; 308-262-1261; fax: 308-262-1799; 8AM-N, 1-4:30PM (MST). ***Felony, Civil Actions over $51,000.***

Civil Records: Access: In person, online. Visitors must perform in person searches themselves. Required to search: name, years to search. Civil cases indexed by defendant, plaintiff. Computerized records back to 11/97; civil records on microfilm, books dating back to early 1900. Civil PAT goes back to 1997. Civil records online - see criminal access. Online records date from 10/97.

Criminal Records: Access: In person, online. Visitors must perform in person searches themselves. Required to search: name, years to search. Criminal records on microfilm, books dating back to early 1900. Criminal PAT goes back to same as civil. Single use or subscribe at https://www.nebraska.gov/justicecc/ccname.cgi for court access. Single use is $15.00 a record or open an account for $1 per record plus $50 annual fee. Online records date from 10/97. Online results show middle initial, DOB.

General Information: No mental health records released. Will not fax documents. Court makes copy: $.25 per page. Certification fee: $1.00. Payee: Clerk of District Court. Personal checks accepted; credit cards are not. Prepayment required.

Morrill County Court PO Box 418, Bridgeport, NE 69336; 308-262-0812; 8AM-4:30PM (MST). ***Misdemeanor, Civil Actions under $51,000, Eviction, Small Claims, Probate.***

Civil Records: Access: In person, online. Visitors must perform in person searches themselves. Required to search: name, years to search. Civil cases indexed by defendant, plaintiff. Civil index on docket books to 1908; probate on microfiche. Public use terminal available. Civil records online - see criminal access. Online civil and probate records from 01/01 forward.

Criminal Records: Access: In person, online. Visitors must perform in person searches themselves. Required to search: name, years to search. Criminal records indexed in books to 1908; probate on microfiche. Public use terminal available. Single use or subscribe at https://www.nebraska.gov/justicecc/ccname.cgi for court access. Single use is $15.00 a record or open an account for $1 per record plus $50 annual fee. Online criminal and traffic records date from 04/00. Online results show middle initial, DOB.

General Information: No adoption records released. Court makes copy: $.25 per page. Certification fee: $1.00. Payee: County Court. Personal checks accepted; credit cards are not. Prepayment required.

Nance County

District Court PO Box 338, Fullerton, NE 68638; 308-536-2365; fax: 308-536-2742; 8AM-5PM (CST). ***Felony, Civil Actions over $51,000.*** www.supremecourt.ne.gov/district-court/district-court-website/nance.shtml

Civil Records: Access: Phone, fax, mail, in person, online. Both court and visitors may perform in person searches. No search fee. Required to search: name, years to search; also helpful: address. Civil cases indexed by defendant, plaintiff. Civil index on docket books from late 1800s. Mail turnaround time 1 day. Civil PAT goes back to 1999. Public terminal in District Court Office- County staff will perform searches. Civil records online - see criminal access. Online records date from 12/99.

Criminal Records: Access: In person, online. Both court and visitors may perform in person searches. No search fee. Required to search: name, years to search; also helpful: address, DOB, SSN. Criminal records indexed in books from late 1800s. Criminal PAT goes back to same as civil. Public terminal in District Court Office- County staff will perform searches. Single use or subscribe at https://www.nebraska.gov/justicecc/ccname.cgi for court access. Single use is $15.00 a record or open an account for $1 per record plus $50 annual fee. Online records date from 12/99. Online results show middle initial, DOB.

General Information: No mental health records released. Will fax out documents $2.50 1st page, $1.50 each add'l. Court makes copy: $.25 per page. Certification fee: $1.00. Payee: Clerk of District Court. Personal checks accepted; credit cards are not. Prepayment required. Mail requests: SASE required for civil.

Nance County Court PO Box 837, Fullerton, NE 68638; 308-536-2675; fax: 308-536-2742; 8AM-5PM (CST). ***Misdemeanor, Civil Actions under $51,000, Eviction, Small Claims, Probate.***

Civil Records: Access: Fax, mail, in person, online. Both court and visitors may perform in person searches. No search fee. Required to search: name, years to search; also helpful: address. Civil cases indexed by defendant, plaintiff. Civil index on cards since late 1800s, computerized since 1/01, probate on microfilm. Mail turnaround time 10-14 days. Civil PAT goes back to 2001. PAT results show name only. Civil records online - see criminal access. Online civil and probate records from 08/00 forward.

Criminal Records: Access: In person, online. Both court and visitors may perform in person searches. No search fee. Required to search: name, years to search; also helpful: address, DOB. Criminal records available since 1985, computerized since 2002, probate on microfilm. Note: Court will not pull records unless provided a case number. Criminal PAT goes back to same as civil. PAT results show name only. Single use or subscribe at https://www.nebraska.gov/justicecc/ccname.cgi for court access. Single use is $15.00 a record or open an account for $1 per record plus $50 annual fee. Online criminal and traffic records date from 08/00.Also, for $15.00 fee per search, you may access the JUSTICE Court Case system statewide at https://www.nebraska.gov/justicecc/ccname.cgi. Online results show middle initial, DOB.

General Information: Online identifiers in results same as on public terminal. No juvenile, psychological reports or adoption records released. Will not fax documents. Court makes copy: $.25 per page. Certification fee: $1.00 per cert. Payee: County Court. Personal checks accepted; credit cards are not.

Prepayment required. Mail requests: SASE required for civil.

Nemaha County

District Court 1824 N St, Auburn, NE 68305; 402-274-3616; fax: 402-274-5583; 8AM-N, 1-5PM (CST). ***Felony, Civil Actions over $51,000.***

Civil Records: Access: In person, mail, online. Both court and visitors may perform in person searches. No search fee. Required to search: name, years to search; also helpful: address. Civil cases indexed by defendant, plaintiff; index on general index and docket books since the late 1800s; computerized records go back to 1998. Note: Court will search on a time available basis Mail Turnaround time 1 to 3 days, more if busy. Civil PAT goes back to 6/1998. PAT civil results show middle initial. Civil records online - see criminal access. Online records date from 6/98.

Criminal Records: Access: In person, mail, online. Both court and visitors may perform in person searches. No search fee. Required to search: name, years to search; also helpful: address, DOB, SSN. Criminal records on general index and docket books since1950; computerized records go back to 1998. Note: Court will only criminal search time permitting. Mail turnaround time 1 to 3 days, more if busy. Criminal PAT goes back to same as civil. PAT results show middle initial, DOB. Single use or subscribe at https://www.nebraska.gov/justicecc/ccname.cgi for court access. Single use is $15.00 a record or open an account for $1 per record plus $50 annual fee. Online records date from 6/98. Online results show middle initial, DOB.

General Information: Online identifiers in results same as on public terminal. No mental, juvenile records released. Will fax documents to local or toll free line. Court makes copy: $.25 per page. Certification fee: $1.00. Payee: Clerk of District Court. Personal checks accepted; credit cards are not. Prepayment required.

Nemaha County Court 1824 N St, Auburn, NE 68305; 402-274-3008; fax: 402-274-4605; 8AM-N, 1-5PM (CST). ***Misdemeanor, Civil Actions under $51,000, Eviction, Small Claims, Probate.***

This court also handles adoption, juvenile, and preliminary felony hearings. Probate fax is same as main fax number.

Civil Records: Access: In person, online. Visitors must perform in person searches themselves. Required to search: name, years to search. Civil cases indexed by defendant, plaintiff. Civil index on docket books since late 1800s, computerized records go back to 4/2000. Civil records online - see criminal access. Online civil and probate records from 04/00 forward.

Criminal Records: Access: In person, online. Visitors must perform in person searches themselves. Required to search: name, years to search; also helpful: DOB, SSN. Criminal records indexed in books since late 1800s, computerized records go back to 4/2000. Public use terminal has crim records back to 4/2000. Single use or subscribe at https://www.nebraska.gov/justicecc/ccname.cgi for court access. Single use is $15.00 a record or open an account for $1 per record plus $50 annual fee. Online criminal and traffic records date from 04/00. Online results show middle initial, DOB.

General Information: No adoption records released. Will not fax documents. Court makes copy: $.25 per page. Certification fee: $1.00 per page. Payee: Clerk of County Court. Personal checks accepted; credit cards are not. Prepayment required. Mail requests: SASE required for mail return of any copies.

Nuckolls County

District Court PO Box 362, 150 S Main, Nelson, NE 68961; 402-225-4341; fax: 402-225-2373; 8:30AM-4:30PM (CST). ***Felony, Civil Actions over $51,000.***

www.nuckollscounty.ne.gov

Court's search services not available to employers using employment agencies.

Civil Records: Access: In person, online. Visitors must perform in person searches themselves. Required to search: name, years to search. Civil cases indexed by defendant, plaintiff. Civil index on docket books since late 1800s, computerized since 2000. Civil PAT goes back to 2000. Civil records online - see criminal access. Online records date from 03/00.

Criminal Records: Access: In person, online. Visitors must perform in person searches themselves. Required to search: name, years to search. Criminal records indexed in books since late 1800s, computerized since 2000. Criminal PAT goes back to same as civil. Single use or subscribe at https://www.nebraska.gov/justicecc/ccname.cgi for court access. Single use is $15.00 a record or open an account for $1 per record plus $50 annual fee. Online records date from 03/00. Online results show middle initial, DOB.

General Information: Will fax documents $3.00 1st page, $1.00 ea add'l. Court makes copy: $.25 per page. Self serve: same. Certification fee: $1.00 per cert. Payee: Clerk of District Court. Personal checks accepted; credit cards are not. Prepayment required.

Nuckolls County Court PO Box 372, 105 S Main, Nelson, NE 68961; 402-225-2371; fax: 402-225-2373; 8AM-4:30PM (CST). ***Misdemeanor, Civil Actions under $51,000, Eviction, Small Claims, Probate.***

www.district10.us/

Mail access limited to short searches.

Civil Records: Access: In person, online. Visitors must perform in person searches themselves. Required to search: name, years to search. Civil cases indexed by defendant, plaintiff. Civil index on cards, probate on microfilm. Civil PAT goes back to 2000. Civil records online - see criminal access. Online civil records date from 12/00 forward, probate from 01/01.

Criminal Records: Access: In person, online. Visitors must perform in person searches themselves. Required to search: name, years to search. Criminal records indexed on cards, probate on microfilm. Criminal PAT goes back to same as civil. Single use or subscribe at https://www.nebraska.gov/justicecc/ccname.cgi for court access. Single use is $15.00 a record or open an account for $1 per record plus $50 annual fee. Online criminal and traffic records date from 08/00. Online results show middle initial, DOB.

General Information: No adoption or juvenile records released. Will fax out documents $3.00 per page. Court makes copy: $.25 per page. Self serve: same. Certification fee: $1.00 per cert. Payee: County Court. Personal checks and major credit cards accepted. Prepayment required.

Otoe County

District Court 1021 Central Ave, Rm 209, PO Box 726, Nebraska City, NE 68410; 402-873-9550; fax: 402-873-9583; 8AM-5PM Courthouse doors close at 4:30PM (CST). ***Felony, Dissolutions, Civil Actions over $51,000.***

www.co.otoe.ne.us/court.html

Civil Records: Access: In person, online. Visitors must perform in person searches themselves. Required to search: name, years to search, address. Civil cases indexed by defendant, plaintiff. Civil index on docket books from late 1800s, computerized from 8/97. Civil PAT goes back to 8/1997. PAT civil results show middle initial. Civil records online - see criminal access. Online records date from 08/97.

Criminal Records: Access: In person, online. Visitors must perform in person searches themselves. Required to search: name, years to search. Criminal records indexed in books from late 1800s, computerized from 8/97. Criminal PAT goes back to same as civil. PAT results show middle initial, DOB. Single use or subscribe at https://www.nebraska.gov/justicecc/ccname.cgi for court access. Single use is $15.00 a record or open an account for $1 per record plus $50 annual fee. Online records date from 08/97. Online results show middle initial, DOB.

General Information: Online identifiers in results same as on public terminal. Will fax documents if fees prepaid. Court makes copy: $.25 per page. Self serve: same. Certification fee: $1.00. Payee: Clerk of District Court. Personal checks accepted; credit cards are not. Prepayment required. Mail requests: SASE required for mail return of any copies.

Otoe County Court 1021 Central Ave, Rm 109, PO Box 487, Nebraska City, NE 68410-0487; 402-873-9575; fax: 402-873-9030; 8AM-5PM (CST). ***Misdemeanor, Civil Actions under $51,000, Eviction, Small Claims, Probate.***

Civil Records: Access: Phone, fax, mail, in person, online. Only the court performs in person searches; visitors may not. No search fee. Required to search: name, years to search. Civil cases indexed by defendant, plaintiff. Civil records go back to 1974; computerized records go to 1999. Mail turnaround time 2-3 days. Civil PAT goes back to 2000. Civil records online - see criminal access. Online civil records date from 10/99 forward, probate from 05/98.

Criminal Records: Access: Fax, mail, in person, online. Both court and visitors may perform in person searches. No search fee. Required to search: name, offense; also helpful: years to search, address, DOB. Criminal records go back to 1981; computerized since 1997. Mail turnaround time 2-3 days. Criminal PAT goes back to 1997.PAT results show name, DOB. Public access terminal is at the District Court terminal. Results for older cases do not always include DOB. Single use or subscribe at https://www.nebraska.gov/justicecc/ccname.cgi for court access. Single use is $15.00 a record or open an account for $1 per record plus $50 annual fee. Online criminal and traffic records date from 02/97. Online results show middle initial, DOB.

General Information: No adoption records released without court order; juvenile records only released with signed release statement. Will fax documents $1.00 per page. Court makes copy: $.25 per page. Certification fee: $1.00 per cert. Payee: County Court. Personal checks accepted; credit cards are not. Prepayment required. Mail requests: SASE required.

Pawnee County

District Court PO Box 431, Pawnee City, NE 68420; 402-852-2963; criminal phone: 402-852-2969; 8AM-4PM (CST). ***Felony, Civil Actions over $51,000.***

Civil Records: Access: In person, online. Both court and visitors may perform in person searches. No search fee. Civil cases indexed by defendant, plaintiff. Civil index on docket books since late 1800s. Public use terminal available. Civil records online - see criminal access. Online records date from 03/98.

Criminal Records: Access: In person, online. Visitors must perform in person searches themselves. Criminal records indexed in books since late 1800s. Public use terminal available. Single use or subscribe at https://www.nebraska.gov/justicecc/ccname.cgi for court access. Single use is $15.00 a record or open an account for $1 per record plus $50 annual fee. Online records date from 03/98. Online results show middle initial, DOB.

General Information: No mental health records released. Will not fax documents. Court makes copy: $.25 per page. Self serve: $.25 per page. Certification fee: $1.00. Payee: Clerk of District Court. Personal checks accepted; credit cards are not. Prepayment required.

Pawnee County Court PO Box 471, Pawnee City, NE 68420; 402-852-2388; 8AM-Noon (CST). ***Misdemeanor, Civil Actions under $51,000, Eviction, Small Claims, Probate.***

Probate requests are accepted by mail with prepayment.

Civil Records: Access: In person, online. Visitors must perform in person searches themselves. Required to search: name, years to search; also helpful: address. Civil cases indexed by defendant, plaintiff; index on computer since late 1980s and books back to late 1800s. Civil PAT goes back to 7/2000. Civil records online - see criminal access. Online civil and probate records from 06/00 forward.

Criminal Records: Access: In person, online. Visitors must perform in person searches themselves. Required to search: name, years to

search, DOB; also helpful: SSN. Criminal records indexed on computer since late 1980s and books back to late 1800s. Criminal PAT goes back to same as civil. Single use or subscribe at https://www.nebraska.gov/justicecc/ccname.cgi for court access. Single use is $15.00 a record or open an account for $1 per record plus $50 annual fee. Online criminal and traffic records date from 06/00. Online results show middle initial, DOB.
General Information: No adoption records released. Will not fax documents. Court makes copy: $.25 per page. Self serve: same. Certification fee: $1.00. Payee: Pawnee County Court. Personal checks accepted; credit cards are not. Prepayment required.

Perkins County

District Court PO Box 156, 200 Lincoln Ave, Grant, NE 69140; 308-352-4643; fax: 308-352-2455; 8AM-4PM (MST). ***Felony, Civil Actions over $51,000.***
Court requests no phone calls please.
Civil Records: Access: Fax, mail, in person, online. Both court and visitors may perform in person searches. No search fee. Required to search: name, years to search. Civil cases indexed by defendant, plaintiff. Civil index on docket books since late 1800s. Mail turnaround time 2-4 days. Civil PAT goes back to 2000. PAT results show name only. Civil records online - see criminal access. Online records date from 06/00.
Criminal Records: Access: Fax, mail, in person, online. Both court and visitors may perform in person searches. No search fee. Required to search: name, years to search. Criminal records indexed in books since late 1800s. Mail turnaround time 2-4 days. Criminal PAT goes back to same as civil. PAT results show name only. Single use or subscribe at https://www.nebraska.gov/justicecc/ccname.cgi for court access. Single use is $15.00 a record or open an account for $1 per record plus $50 annual fee. Online records date from 6/2000. Online results show middle initial, DOB.
General Information: All records public. Will fax documents $3.00 prepaid. Court makes copy: $.50 per page. Self serve: same. Certification fee: $1.75 per cert. Payee: Clerk of District Court. Personal checks accepted; credit cards are not. Prepayment required. Mail requests: SASE required.

Perkins County Court PO Box 222, 200 Lincoln Ave, Grant, NE 69140; 308-352-4415; probate phone: same; 9AM-2PM M-TH (MST). ***Misdemeanor, Civil Actions under $51,000, Eviction, Small Claims, Probate.***
Civil Records: Access: In person, online. Visitors must perform in person searches themselves. Required to search: name, years to search. Civil cases indexed by defendant, plaintiff. Civil index on cards from 1987, prior on books; probate on microfilm & hard copy. Civil PAT goes back to 6/2000. Civil records online - see criminal access. Online civil and probate records from 11/00 forward.
Criminal Records: Access: In person, online. Visitors must perform in person searches themselves. Required to search: name, years to search; also helpful: DOB. Criminal records indexed on cards from 1987, prior on books; probate on microfilm & hard copy. Criminal PAT goes back to same as civil. Single use or subscribe at https://www.nebraska.gov/justicecc/ccname.cgi for court access. Single use is $15.00 a record or open an account for $1 per record plus $50 annual fee. Online criminal and traffic records date from 06/00. Online results show middle initial, DOB.
General Information: No sealed records released. Court makes copy: $.25 per page. Certification fee: $1.00. Payee: Perkins County Court. Personal checks accepted; credit cards are not. Prepayment required.

Phelps County

District Court PO Box 462, Holdrege, NE 68949; 308-995-2281; fax: 308-995-2282; 9AM-5PM (CST). ***Felony, Civil Actions over $51,000.***
Civil Records: Access: In person, online. Visitors must perform in person searches themselves. Required to search: name, years to search. Civil cases indexed by defendant, plaintiff; index on computer from 3/1998, on books back to 1885. Public use terminal available, records go back to 3/1998. Civil records online - see criminal access. Online records date from 03/98.
Criminal Records: Access: In person, online. Visitors must perform in person searches themselves. Required to search: name, years to search; also helpful: DOB. Criminal records computerized from 3/1998, on books prior back to 1885. Public use terminal available, crim records go back to 3/1998. Single use or subscribe at https://www.nebraska.gov/justicecc/ccname.cgi for court access. Single use is $15.00 a record or open an account for $1 per record plus $50 annual fee. Online records date from 03/98. Online results show middle initial, DOB.
General Information: No mental health, sealed records released. Will fax specific case files to local or toll-free number. Court makes copy: $.25 per page. Certification fee: $1.00. Payee: Clerk of District Court. Personal checks accepted; credit cards are not. Prepayment required.

Phelps County Court PO Box 255, 715 Fifth Ave, Holdrege, NE 68949; 308-995-6561; fax: 308-995-6562; 8AM-N, 1-5PM (CST). ***Misdemeanor, Civil Actions under $51,000, Eviction, Small Claims, Probate.***
www.district10.us/
Requests for specific record files must be placed in writing. These documents will be mailed within one week.
Civil Records: Access: In person, online. Visitors must perform in person searches themselves. Required to search: name, years to search. Civil cases indexed by defendant, plaintiff. Civil records computerized since 1999, on index cards going back to late 1970s; probate on microfiche to late 1800s. Civil PAT goes back to 3/1998. Civil records online - see criminal access. Online civil records date from 10/99 forward, probate from 06/98. Results include name and address only.
Criminal Records: Access: In person, online. Visitors must perform in person searches themselves. Required to search: name, years to search, DOB. Criminal records computerized since 1998, in files to 1987. Criminal PAT goes back to same as civil.PAT results show name, DOB. Single use or subscribe at https://www.nebraska.gov/justicecc/ccname.cgi for court access. Single use is $15.00 a record or open an account for $1 per record plus $50 annual fee. Online criminal and traffic records date from 06/98. Online results show middle initial, DOB.
General Information: Online identifiers in results same as on public terminal. No adoption records released. Will not fax documents. Court makes copy: $.25 per page. Self serve: same. Certification fee: $1.00 per cert. Payee: Phelps County Court. Personal checks accepted; credit cards are not. Prepayment required. Mail requests: SASE required for mail return of any copies.

Pierce County

District Court 111 W Court St, Rm 12, Pierce, NE 68767; 402-329-4335; fax: 402-329-6412; 8:30AM-4:30PM (CST). ***Felony, Civil Actions over $51,000.***
Civil Records: Access: In person, online. Visitors must perform in person searches themselves. Required to search: name, years to search. Civil cases indexed by defendant, plaintiff. Civil index on docket books from 1870s; on computer back to 3/1999. Civil PAT goes back to 3/1999. Civil records online - see criminal access. Online records date from 03/99.
Criminal Records: Access: In person, online. Visitors must perform in person searches themselves. Required to search: name, years to search; also helpful: address, DOB, SSN. Criminal records indexed in books from 1870s; on computer back to 3/1999. Criminal PAT goes back to same as civil. Subscribe to JUSTICE at https://www.nebraska.gov/justicecc/ccname.cgi for court access. Single use is $15.00 a record or open an account for $1 per record plus $50 annual fee. Online records date from 03/99. Also, you may access the JUSTICE Court Case system statewide at https://www.nebraska.gov/justicecc/ccname.cgi. Online results show middle initial, DOB.
General Information: No mental health records released. Will fax out documents $3.00 1st page, $1.00 each add'l. Court makes copy: $.25 per page. Certification fee: $1.00. Payee: Clerk of District Court. Personal checks accepted; credit cards are not. Prepayment required. Mail requests: SASE required for mail return of any copies.

Pierce County Court 111 W Court St, Rm 11, Pierce, NE 68767; 402-329-6245; fax: 402-329-6412; 8:30AM-4:30PM (CST). ***Misdemeanor, Civil Actions under $51,000, Eviction, Small Claims, Probate.***
Civil Records: Access: In person, online. Visitors must perform in person searches themselves. Required to search: name, years to search. Civil cases indexed by defendant, plaintiff. Civil index on docket books back about 15 years, computerized since 5/2000. Civil PAT goes back to 5/2000. PAT civil results show middle initial. Civil records online - see criminal access. Online civil and probate records from 05/00 forward.
Criminal Records: Access: In person, online. Visitors must perform in person searches themselves. Required to search: name, years to search. Criminal records indexed in books back about 15 years, computerized since 5/00. Criminal PAT goes back to same as civil. PAT results show middle initial, DOB. Single use or subscribe at https://www.nebraska.gov/justicecc/ccname.cgi for court access. Single use is $15.00 a record or open an account for $1 per record plus $50 annual fee. Online criminal and traffic records date from 05/00. Online results show middle initial, DOB.
General Information: Online identifiers in results same as on public terminal. No adoption records released. Will not fax documents. Court makes copy: $.25 per page. Self serve: same. Certification fee: $1.00. Payee: County Court. Personal checks accepted; credit cards are not. Prepayment required.

Platte County

District Court PO Box 1188, Columbus, NE 68602-1188; 402-563-4906; fax: 402-562-6718; 8:30AM-5PM (CST). ***Felony, Civil Actions over $51,000.***
www.plattecounty.net/district.htm
Civil Records: Access: In person, online. Visitors must perform in person searches themselves. Required to search: name, years to search. Civil cases indexed by defendant, plaintiff. Civil records go back to 1800, civil records filed as hard copies; also on computer after 8/1/97. Civil PAT goes back to 1997. Civil records online - see criminal access. Online records date from 09/97. Court Calendar for month available at www.plattecounty.net/district/calendar.htm.
Criminal Records: Access: In person, online. Visitors must perform in person searches themselves. Required to search: name, years to search, DOB. Criminal records go back to 1880's, criminal records filed as hard copies; also on computer after 8/1/97. Criminal PAT goes back to same as civil.PAT results show name, DOB. Single use or subscribe at https://www.nebraska.gov/justicecc/ccname.cgi for court access. Single use is $15.00 a record or open an account for $1 per record plus $50 annual fee. Online records date from 09/97. Court Calendar for month available at www.plattecounty.net/district/calendar.htm. Online results show middle initial, DOB.
General Information: Online identifiers in results same as on public terminal. No juvenile or sealed records released. Will not fax documents. Court makes copy: $.25 per page. Certification fee: $1.00 per certification. Payee: District Court. Only cashiers checks and money orders accepted. No credit cards accepted. Prepayment required.

Platte County Court PO Box 538, 2610 14th St, Columbus, NE 68602-0538; 402-563-4905; fax: 402-562-8158; 8AM-5PM (CST). ***Misdemeanor, Civil Actions under $51,000, Eviction, Small Claims, Probate.***
Probate fax is same as main fax number.

Civil Records: Access: In person, online. Visitors must perform in person searches themselves. Required to search: name, years to search. Civil cases indexed by defendant, plaintiff. Civil index on docket books from 1980; on computer back to 1996. Civil PAT goes back to 10/1999. PAT results show name and may also include address. Civil records online - see criminal access. Online civil records date from 10/99 forward, probate from 05/98.
Criminal Records: Access: In person, online. Visitors must perform in person searches themselves. Required to search: name, years to search, DOB. Criminal records indexed in books from 1980; on computer back to 1996. Criminal PAT goes back to 10/1996. PAT results show middle initial, DOB. Terminal results may also include address. Single use or subscribe at https://www.nebraska.gov/justicecc/ccname.cgi for court access. Single use is $15.00 a record or open an account for $1 per record plus $50 annual fee. Online criminal and traffic records date from 10/96. Online results show middle initial, DOB.
General Information: No adoption records released. Will not fax documents. Court makes copy: $.25 per page. Certification fee: $1.00 per seal. Payee: Platte County Court. Personal checks accepted; credit cards are not. Prepayment required.

Polk County

District Court PO Box 447, Osceola, NE 68651; 402-747-3487; fax: 402-747-8299; 8AM-N,1-5PM (CST). ***Felony, Civil Actions over $51,000.***
Civil Records: Access: In person, online. Visitors must perform in person searches themselves. Required to search: name, years to search. Civil cases indexed by defendant, plaintiff. Civil index on docket books from 1871. Civil PAT goes back to 4/9/1998. PAT civil results show middle initial. Civil records online - see criminal access. Online records date from 04/98.
Criminal Records: Access: In person, online. Visitors must perform in person searches themselves. Required to search: name. Criminal records indexed in books from 1871. Criminal PAT goes back to 4/1998. PAT results show middle initial, DOB. Single use or subscribe at https://www.nebraska.gov/justicecc/ccname.cgi for court access. Single use is $15.00 a record or open an account for $1 per record plus $50 annual fee. Online records date from 04/98. Online results show middle initial, DOB.
General Information: Will fax documents $1.00 1st page, $.50 ea add'l. Court makes copy: $.25 per page. Certification fee: $1.00. Payee: Clerk of District Court. Personal checks accepted; credit cards are not. Prepayment required.

Polk County Court PO Box 506, Osceola, NE 68651; 402-747-5371; fax: 402-747-2656; 8AM-5PM (CST). ***Misdemeanor, Civil Actions under $51,000, Eviction, Small Claims, Probate.***
Probate is a separate index at this same address. Probate fax is same as main fax number.
Civil Records: Access: In person, online. Visitors must perform in person searches themselves. Required to search: name, years to search. Civil cases indexed by defendant, plaintiff. Civil index on cards back to late 1970s; probate records back to late 1800s. Civil PAT goes back to 2000. PAT results show middle initial, DOB. Civil records online - see criminal access. Online civil and probate records from 01/01 forward.
Criminal Records: Access: In person, online. Visitors must perform in person searches themselves. Required to search: name, years to search, DOB. Criminal records indexed on cards back to late 1970s; on computer back to 8/2000. Criminal PAT goes back to same as civil. PAT results show middle initial, DOB. Single use or subscribe at https://www.nebraska.gov/justicecc/ccname.cgi for court access. Single use is $15.00 a record or open an account for $1 per record plus $50 annual fee. Online criminal and traffic records date from 08/00. Online results show middle initial, DOB.
General Information: Online identifiers in results same as on public terminal. No adoption, juvenile records released. Will fax out specific case files. Court makes copy: $.25 per page. Self serve: same. Certification fee: $1.00 per seal. Payee: County Court. Personal checks accepted; credit cards are not. Prepayment required. Mail requests: SASE required for mail return of any copies.

Red Willow County

District Court PO Box 847, 520 Norris Ave, McCook, NE 69001; 308-345-4583; fax: 308-345-7907; 8AM-4PM (CST). ***Felony, Civil Actions over $51,000.***
www.co.red-willow.ne.us/court.html
Civil Records: Access: Mail, in person, online. Both court and visitors may perform in person searches. No search fee. Required to search: name, years to search. Civil cases indexed by defendant, plaintiff. Civil index on docket books since 1871, on microfiche since mid 1980s, computerized since 1998. Mail turnaround time 2-4 days. Civil PAT goes back to 1998. PAT civil results show middle initial. Civil records online - see criminal access. Online records date from 06/98.
Criminal Records: Access: Mail, in person, online. Both court and visitors may perform in person searches. No search fee. Required to search: name, years to search. Criminal records indexed in books since 1871, on microfiche since mid 1980s, computerized since 1998. Mail turnaround time 2-4 days. Criminal PAT goes back to same as civil. PAT criminal results show middle initial. Single use or subscribe at https://www.nebraska.gov/justicecc/ccname.cgi for court access. Single use is $15.00 a record or open an account for $1 per record plus $50 annual fee. Online records date from 06/98. Online results show middle initial, DOB.
General Information: Online identifiers in results same as on public terminal. Will fax documents $3.00 1st page, $1.00 each add'l. Court makes copy: $.50 per page. Certification fee: $1.00. Payee: Clerk of District Court. Personal checks accepted; credit cards are not. Prepayment required. Mail requests: SASE required.

Red Willow County Court PO Box 199, 502 Norris Ave, McCook, NE 69001; 308-345-1904; fax: 308-345-1904; 8AM-5PM (CST). ***Misdemeanor, Civil Actions under $51,000, Eviction, Small Claims, Probate.***
Civil Records: Access: In person, online. Visitors must perform in person searches themselves. Required to search: name, years to search, case number. Civil cases indexed by defendant, plaintiff; index on case files and docket cards since 1984, probate on microfilm since 1977; on computer back to 1998. Civil PAT goes back to 1998. PAT civil results show middle initial. Civil records online - see criminal access. Online civil records date from 01/00 forward, probate from 08/98.
Criminal Records: Access: In person, online. Visitors must perform in person searches themselves. Required to search: name, years to search, DOB, case number. Criminal docket on books since 1984; on computer back to 1998. Criminal PAT goes back to same as civil. PAT results show middle initial, DOB. Subscribe to NOL at https://www.nebraska.gov/justicecc/ccname.cgi for court access. $.60 a record fee or $300 per month flat rate. Online criminal and traffic records date from 06/98. Online results show middle initial, DOB.
General Information: Online identifiers in results same as on public terminal. No adoption, juvenile, convictions set aside on misdemeanor offense, sealed records released. Will fax documents to local or toll-free number. Court makes copy: $.25 per page. Certification fee: $1.00 per cert. Payee: County Court. Personal checks accepted; credit cards are not. Prepayment required.

Richardson County

District Court 1700 Stone St, Falls City, NE 68355; 402-245-2023; fax: 402-245-3725; 8:30AM-5PM (CST). ***Felony, Civil Actions over $51,000.***
Civil Records: Access: In person, online. Visitors must perform in person searches themselves. Required to search: name, years to search. Civil cases indexed by defendant, plaintiff; index on microfiche and at state archives to 1930; on computer back to 1998. Civil PAT goes back to 1998. Civil records online - see criminal access. Online records date from 02/98.
Criminal Records: Access: In person, online. Visitors must perform in person searches themselves. Required to search: name, years to search, DOB, signed release. Criminal records on microfiche and at state archives to 1930; on computer back to 1998. Criminal PAT goes back to 1998. Single use or subscribe at https://www.nebraska.gov/justicecc/ccname.cgi for court access. Single use is $15.00 a record or open an account for $1 per record plus $50 annual fee. Online records date from 02/98. Online results show middle initial, DOB.
General Information: No sealed records released. Will not fax documents. Court makes copy: $.25 per page. Certification fee: $1.00. Payee: Clerk of District Court. Personal checks accepted; credit cards are not. Prepayment required.

Richardson County Court 1700 Stone St Rm 205, Falls City, NE 68355; 402-245-2812; fax: 402-245-3352; 8AM-N, 1-5PM (CST). ***Misdemeanor, Civil Actions under $51,000, Eviction, Small Claims, Probate.***
Civil Records: Access: In person, online. Visitors must perform in person searches themselves. Required to search: name, years to search. Civil cases indexed by defendant, plaintiff. Civil index on cards back to 1970s. Civil PAT goes back to 2000. Civil records online - see criminal access. Online civil and probate records from 11/00 forward.
Criminal Records: Access: In person, online. Visitors must perform in person searches themselves. Required to search: name, years to search; also helpful: DOB. Criminal records indexed on cards back to 1970s. Criminal PAT goes back to same as civil. Single use or subscribe at https://www.nebraska.gov/justicecc/ccname.cgi for court access. Single use is $15.00 a record or open an account for $1 per record plus $50 annual fee. Online criminal and traffic records date from 06/00. Online results show middle initial, DOB.
General Information: No adoption records released. Will not fax documents. Court makes copy: $.25 per page. Certification fee: $1.00 per cert. Payee: County Court. Only cashiers checks and money orders accepted. No credit cards accepted except for traffic fines. Prepayment required.

Rock County

District Court PO Box 367, 400 State St, Bassett, NE 68714; 402-684-3933; fax: 402-684-2741; 9AM-5PM (CST). ***Felony, Civil Actions over $51,000.***
Civil Records: Access: Fax, mail, in person, online. Both court and visitors may perform in person searches. No search fee. Required to search: name, years to search. Civil cases indexed by defendant, plaintiff. Civil index on docket books since 1800s. Mail turnaround time 1-2 days. Civil PAT goes back to 1996. PAT results show name only. Civil records online - see criminal access. Online records date from 08/00.
Criminal Records: Acccss: Fax, mail, in person, online. Both court and visitors may perform in person searches. No search fee. Required to search: name, years to search, DOB. Criminal records indexed in books since 1800s. Mail turnaround time 1-2 days. Criminal PAT goes back to 1996. PAT results show name only. Single use or subscribe at https://www.nebraska.gov/justicecc/ccname.cgi for court access. Single use is $15.00 a record or open an account for $1 per record plus $50 annual fee. Online records date from 8/2000. Online results show name only.
General Information: No juvenile or sealed records released. Will fax documents $2.00 1st page, $1.00 each add'l. Court makes copy: $.25 per page. Certification fee: $1.50 per cert. Payee: Clerk of District Court. Personal checks accepted; credit cards are not. Prepayment required. Mail requests: SASE required.

Rock County Court PO Box 249, 400 State St, Bassett, NE 68714; 402-684-3601; fax: 402-684-

2741; 8AM-5PM M,W,F (CST). ***Misdemeanor, Civil Actions under $51,000, Eviction, Small Claims, Probate.***

Civil Records: Access: In person, online. Visitors must perform in person searches themselves. Required to search: name, years to search. Civil cases indexed by defendant, plaintiff. Civil index on docket books from 1800s, index cards from 1985; on computer back to 8/2000. Civil PAT goes back to 2000. Civil records online - see criminal access. Online civil and probate records from 10/00 forward.

Criminal Records: Access: In person, online. Visitors must perform in person searches themselves. Required to search: name, years to search, DOB. Criminal records indexed in books from 1800s, index cards from 1985; on computer back to 8/2000. Criminal PAT goes back to same as civil. Single use or subscribe at https://www.nebraska.gov/justicecc/ccname.cgi for court access. Single use is $15.00 a record or open an account for $1 per record plus $50 annual fee. Online criminal and traffic records date from 08/00. Online results show middle initial, DOB.

General Information: Will not fax documents. Court makes copy: $.25 per page. Certification fee: $1.50 per cert. Payee: County Court. Personal checks accepted; credit cards are not. Prepayment required.

Saline County

District Court Clerk of District Court, PO Box 865, Wilber, NE 68465; 402-821-2823; fax: 402-821-3179; 8AM-N, 1-5PM (CST). ***Felony, Civil Actions over $51,000.***

This court will not perform name searches.

Civil Records: Access: In person, online. Visitors must perform in person searches themselves. Required to search: name, years to search. Civil cases indexed by defendant, plaintiff. Civil records being entered on computer beginning 8/94, index in dockets books from 1800s. Civil PAT goes back to 8/1994. PAT results show name only. Civil records online - see criminal access. Online records date from 7/94.

Criminal Records: Access: In person, online. Visitors must perform in person searches themselves. Required to search: name, years to search; also helpful: DOB. Criminal records being entered on computer beginning 8/94, index in dockets books from 1800s. Criminal PAT goes back to 8/1994. PAT results show name only. Single use or subscribe at https://www.nebraska.gov/justicecc/ccname.cgi for court access. Single use is $15.00 a record or open an account for $1 per record plus $50 annual fee. Online records date from 7/94. Online results show name only.

General Information: No sealed or mental health records released. Will fax specific case for $1.00 1st page $.25 ea add'l, but not name-search results. Court makes copy: $.25 per page. Self serve: same. Certification fee: $1.00. Payee: Clerk of District Court. Personal checks accepted; credit cards are not. Prepayment required. Mail requests: SASE required for mail return of any copies.

Saline County Court PO Box 865, 215 S High St, Wilber, NE 68465; 402-821-2131; fax: 402-821-2132; 8AM-N; 1PM-5PM (CST). ***Misdemeanor, Civil Actions under $51,000, Eviction, Small Claims, Probate.***

Search fee includes both civil and criminal indexes.

Civil Records: Access: Fax, mail, in person, online. Both court and visitors may perform in person searches. Search fee: $3.00 per name. Required to search: name, years to search. Civil cases indexed by defendant, plaintiff. Civil index on docket books from 1860s; computerized records since 1994. Mail turnaround time- up to 2 weeks, no guarantees Civil PAT goes back to 1994. PAT results show name only. Public terminal available in District Court. Civil records online - see criminal access. Online civil and probate records from 06/94 forward.

Criminal Records: Access: Fax, mail, in person, online. Both court and visitors may perform in person searches. Search fee: $3.00 per name. Required to search: name, years to search. Criminal records indexed in books from 1860s; computerized records since 1994. Mail turnaround time 2-3 days. Criminal PAT goes back to same as civil. PAT results show name only. Public terminal available in District Court. Single use or subscribe at https://www.nebraska.gov/justicecc/ccname.cgi for court access. Single use is $15.00 a record or open an account for $1 per record plus $50 annual fee. Online criminal and traffic records date from 07/94. Online results show middle initial, DOB.

General Information: No juvenile or sealed records released. No fee to fax documents. Court makes copy: $.25 per page. Certification fee: $1.00 per cert. Payee: County Court. Personal checks accepted; credit cards are not. Prepayment required. Mail requests: SASE required.

Sarpy County

District Court 1210 Golden Gate Dr, #3141, Papillion, NE 68046; 402-593-2267; fax: 402-593-4403; 8AM-4:45PM (CST). ***Felony, Civil Actions over $51,000.***

www.sarpy.com

Civil Records: Access: Phone, mail, in person, online. Both court and visitors may perform in person searches. No search fee. Required to search: name, years to search. Civil cases indexed by defendant, plaintiff; index on computer from 1979 forward, on books prior. Mail turnaround time 1-2 days. Civil PAT goes back to 1979. Civil records online - see criminal access. Online records date from 12/98.

Criminal Records: Access: Phone, mail, in person, online. Both court and visitors may perform in person searches. No search fee. Required to search: name, years to search. Criminal records computerized from 1979 forward, on books prior. Note: For phone requests, will only verify from computer index. Mail turnaround time 1-2 days. Criminal PAT goes back to same as civil. Single use or subscribe at https://www.nebraska.gov/justicecc/ccname.cgi for court access. Single use is $15.00 a record or open an account for $1 per record plus $50 annual fee. Online records date from 12/98. Online results show middle initial, DOB.

General Information: No mental health or search warrant records released. Will not fax documents. Court makes copy: $.75 first page, $.25 each add'l (per pleading). Certification fee: $1.00. Payee: Clerk of District Court. Only cashiers checks and money orders accepted. No credit cards accepted. Prepayment required. Mail requests: SASE required.

Sarpy County Court 1210 Golden Gate Dr, #3142, Papillion, NE 68046; 402-593-5775; fax: 402-593-2193; 8AM-4:45PM (CST). ***Misdemeanor, Civil Actions under $50,000, Eviction, Small Claims, Probate.***

www.sarpy.com

Civil Records: Access: Fax, mail, in person, online. Visitors must perform in person searches themselves. No search fee. Required to search: name, years to search. Civil cases indexed by defendant, plaintiff; index on computer since 8/97; prior records on docket books and cards from 1800s. Mail turnaround time 1 day. Civil PAT goes back to 1997. Single use or subscribe at https://www.nebraska.gov/justicecc/ccname.cgi for court access. Single use is $15.00 a record or pay a monthly flat rate.

Criminal Records: Access: Fax, mail, in person, online. Visitors must perform in person searches themselves. No search fee. Required to search: name, years to search, DOB. Criminal records on computer since 8/97; prior records on docket books and cards from 1800s. Mail turnaround time 1 day. Criminal PAT goes back to same as civil. Online access to criminal records is the same as civil. Online criminal and traffic records date from 8/97. Online results show middle initial, DOB.

General Information: No adoption records released. Will not fax documents. Court makes copy: $.25 per page. Certification fee: $1.00 per cert. Payee: County Court. Personal checks accepted. Visa/MC accepted. Prepayment required.

Saunders County

District Court County Courthouse, 433 N Chestnut St, Wahoo, NE 68066; 402-443-8113; fax: 402-443-8170; 8AM-5PM (CST). ***Felony, Civil Actions over $51,000.***

Civil Records: Access: In person, online. Visitors must perform in person searches themselves. Required to search: name, years to search. Civil cases indexed by defendant, plaintiff. Civil index on docket books to late 1800s; on computer back to 1998. Civil PAT goes back to 1998. No SSNs should appear, but results can show whatever identifiers the attorney puts in. Civil records online - see criminal access. Online records date from 6/98.

Criminal Records: Access: In person, online. Visitors must perform in person searches themselves. Required to search: name, years to search; also helpful: DOB, SSN. Criminal records indexed in books to late 1800s; on computer back to 1998. Criminal PAT goes back to 1998.PAT results show name, DOB. Single use or subscribe at https://www.nebraska.gov/justicecc/ccname.cgi for court access. Single use is $15.00 a record or open an account for $1 per record plus $50 annual fee. Online records date from 6/98. Online results show name only.

General Information: No mental health records released. Will fax documents $3.00 1st page; $1.00 each add'l pg, prepaid. Court makes copy: $.25 per page. Self serve: $.25 per page. Certification fee: $1.00 per copy fee. Payee: Clerk of District Court. Personal checks accepted; credit cards are not. Prepayment required.

Saunders County Court 433 N Chestnut, Wahoo, NE 68066; 402-443-8119; fax: 402-443-8121; 8AM-5PM (CST). ***Misdemeanor, Civil Actions under $51,000, Eviction, Small Claims, Probate.***

Civil Records: Access: In person, online. Visitors must perform in person searches themselves. Required to search: name, years to search. Civil cases indexed by defendant, plaintiff. Civil index on docket books. Civil PAT goes back to 2001. Civil records online - see criminal access. Online civil and probate records from 11/00 forward.

Criminal Records: Access: In person, online. Visitors must perform in person searches themselves. Required to search: name, years to search. Criminal records indexed in books. Criminal PAT goes back to 2000. Single use or subscribe at https://www.nebraska.gov/justicecc/ccname.cgi for court access. Single use is $15.00 a record or open an account for $1 per record plus $50 annual fee. Online criminal and traffic records date from 06/26/00. Online results show middle initial, DOB.

General Information: No adoption or sealed records released. Will fax documents $3.00 per page. Court makes copy: $.25 per page. Self serve: same. Certification fee: $1.00. Payee: County Court. Personal checks accepted; credit cards are not. Prepayment required.

Scotts Bluff County

District Court 1725 10th St, PO Box 47, Gering, NE 69341-0047; 308-436-6641; fax: 308-436-6759; 8AM-4:30PM (MST). ***Felony, Civil Actions over $51,000.***

Civil Records: Access: In person, online. Visitors must perform in person searches themselves. Required to search: name, years to search. Civil cases indexed by defendant, plaintiff. Civil index on docket books to 1800s; on computer back to 1997. Note: Mail search done only if case number provided. Civil PAT goes back to 1997. PAT results show name only. Results include judgment information. Civil records online - see criminal access.

Criminal Records: Access: In person, online. Visitors must perform in person searches themselves. Required to search: name. Criminal records indexed in books to 1800s; on computer back to 1997. Note: Results include judgment information. Mail search done only if case number provided. Criminal PAT goes back to same as civil. PAT results show name only. Results include judgment information. Single use or subscribe at https://www.nebraska.gov/justicecc/ccname.cgi for court access. Single use is $15.00 a record or open an account for $1 per record plus $50 annual fee. Also, for $15.00 fee per search, you may access the JUSTICE Court Case system statewide at https://www.nebraska.gov/justicecc/ccname.cgi. Online results show name only.

General Information: No juvenile or mental health records released. Will fax out specific case files for $3.50. Court makes copy: $.25 per page. Certification fee: $1.00 per page. Exemplification fee is $3.00. Payee: Clerk of District Court. Business checks accepted. No credit cards accepted. Prepayment required.

Scotts Bluff County Court 1725 10th St, Gering, NE 69341; 308-436-6648; criminal phone: 308-436-6649; civil phone: 308-436-6770; fax: 308-436-6782; 7:30AM-4:30PM (MST). ***Misdemeanor, Civil Actions under $51,000, Eviction, Small Claims, Probate.***

Civil Records: Access: In person, online. Visitors must perform in person searches themselves. Required to search: name, years to search. Civil cases indexed by defendant, plaintiff. Civil records computerized since 2000. Civil PAT goes back to 5/2000. Civil records online - see criminal access. Online civil and probate records from 03/01 forward.

Criminal Records: Access: In person, online. Visitors must perform in person searches themselves. Required to search: name, years to search, DOB. Criminal records computerized since 2000. Criminal PAT goes back to same as civil. Single use or subscribe at https://www.nebraska.gov/justicecc/ccname.cgi for court access. Single use is $15.00 a record or open an account for $1 per record plus $50 annual fee. Online criminal and traffic records date from 05/00. Online results show middle initial, DOB.

General Information: No adoption records released. Will not fax out documents. Court makes copy: $.25 per page. Certification fee: $1.00 per cert. Payee: County Court. Personal checks accepted; credit cards are not. Prepayment required.

Seward County

District Court PO Box 36, Seward, NE 68434; 402-643-4895; fax: 402-643-2950; 8AM-5PM (CST). ***Felony, Civil Actions over $51,000.***

Civil Records: Access: In person, online. Visitors must perform in person searches themselves. Required to search: name, years to search. Civil cases indexed by defendant, plaintiff. Civil index on docket books since late 1800s; computerized since 6/98. Public use terminal available, records go back to 6/98. Civil records online - see criminal access. Online records date from 06/98.

Criminal Records: Access: In person, online. Visitors must perform in person searches themselves. Required to search: name, years to search. Criminal records indexed in books since late 1800s; computerized since 6/98. Public use terminal available, crim records go back to same. Single use or subscribe at https://www.nebraska.gov/justicecc/ccname.cgi for court access. Single use is $15.00 a record or open an account for $1 per record plus $50 annual fee. Online records date from 06/98. Online results show middle initial, DOB.

General Information: Will fax out specific case files for $3.00 1st page, $1.00 each add'l. Court makes copy: $.30 per page. Certification fee: $1.00. Payee: Clerk of District Court. No personal checks. No credit cards accepted. Prepayment required.

Seward County Court PO Box 37, 529 Seward St, Seward, NE 68434; 402-643-3341; fax: 402-643-2950; 8AM-5PM (CST). ***Misdemeanor, Civil Actions under $51,000, Eviction, Small Claims, Probate.***

Civil Records: Access: Mail, in person, online. Both court and visitors may perform in person searches. No search fee. Required to search: name, years to search. Civil cases indexed by defendant, plaintiff. Civil index on docket books, cards back to 1975, computerized back to 1997. Mail turnaround time 1 day. Civil PAT goes back to 1997. Civil records online - see criminal access. Online civil records date from 10/99 forward, probate from 05/98.

Criminal Records: Access: Mail, in person, online. Both court and visitors may perform in person searches. No search fee. Required to search: name, years to search. Criminal records indexed in books, cards back to 1950. Mail turnaround time 1 day. Criminal PAT goes back to same as civil. Single use or subscribe at https://www.nebraska.gov/justicecc/ccname.cgi for court access. Single use is $15.00 a record or open an account for $1 per record plus $50 annual fee. Online criminal and traffic records date from 03/97. Online results show middle initial, DOB.

General Information: No adoption, juvenile or sealed records released. Will not fax documents. Court makes copy: $.25 per page. Certification fee: $1.00 per page. Payee: County Court. Personal checks accepted; credit cards are not. Prepayment required.

Sheridan County

District Court PO Box 581, Rushville, NE 69360; 308-327-5654; fax: 308-327-5618; 8:30AM-4:30PM (MST). ***Felony, Civil Actions over $51,000.***

Civil Records: Access: Mail, fax, in person, online. Both court and visitors may perform in person searches. Search fee: $5.00 per name. Required to search: name, years to search. Civil cases indexed by defendant, plaintiff; index on index and docket books since 1800s, computerized since 1998. Mail turnaround time 1-2 days. Civil PAT goes back to 8/1998. Civil records online - see criminal access. Online records date from 08/98.

Criminal Records: Access: Mail, fax, in person, online. Both court and visitors may perform in person searches. Search fee: $5.00 per name. Required to search: name, years to search, signed release; also helpful: DOB. Criminal records on index and docket books since 1800s, computerized since 1998. Mail turnaround time 1-2 days. Criminal PAT goes back to same as civil. Single use or subscribe at https://www.nebraska.gov/justicecc/ccname.cgi for court access. Single use is $15.00 a record or open an account for $1 per record plus $50 annual fee. Online records date from 08/98. Online results show middle initial, DOB.

General Information: No mental health, grand jury records released. Will fax documents to local and toll free lines. Court makes copy: $.10 per page. Self serve: same. Certification fee: $1.00 per case. Payee: Clerk of District Court. Personal checks accepted; credit cards are not. Mail requests: SASE required.

Sheridan County Court PO Box 430, 303 E 2nd St, Rushville, NE 69360; 308-327-5656; fax: 308-327-5623; 8AM-4:30PM (MST). ***Misdemeanor, Civil Actions under $51,000, Eviction, Small Claims, Probate.***

Civil Records: Access: In person, online. Visitors must perform in person searches themselves. Required to search: name, years to search. Civil cases indexed by defendant, plaintiff. Civil index on docket books, on microfiche from 1920 forward; on computer back to 6/2000. Civil PAT goes back to 1/2001. PAT results show name only. Civil records online - see criminal access. Online civil and probate records from 11/00 forward.

Criminal Records: Access: In person, online. Visitors must perform in person searches themselves. Required to search: name, years to search. Criminal records indexed in books, on microfiche from 1920 forward; on computer back to 6/2000. Criminal PAT goes back to 6/12/2000. PAT results show name only. Single use or subscribe at https://www.nebraska.gov/justicecc/ccname.cgi for court access. Single use is $15.00 a record or open an account for $1 per record plus $50 annual fee. Online criminal and traffic records date from 06/00. Online results show name only.

General Information: Online identifiers in results same as on public terminal. No adoption or confidential records released. No fee to fax back documents. Court makes copy for no fee. Certification fee: $1.00 per cert. Payee: Sheridan County Court. Personal checks accepted; credit cards are not. Prepayment required.

Sherman County

District Court 630 O St, PO Box 456, Loup City, NE 68853; 308-745-1513 x103; fax: 308-745-0157; 8:30AM-4:30PM (CST). ***Felony, Civil Actions over $51,000.***

Civil Records: Access: In person, online. Visitors must perform in person searches themselves. Required to search: name, years to search. Civil cases indexed by defendant, plaintiff; index on index and docket books since late 1800s; on computer back to 4/2000. Civil PAT goes back to 4/17/2000. Civil records online - see criminal access. Online records date from 04/00.

Criminal Records: Access: In person, online. Visitors must perform in person searches themselves. Required to search: name, years to search. Criminal records on index and docket books since late 1800s; on computer back to 4/2000. Criminal PAT goes back to same as civil. PAT results show middle initial, DOB. DL, sex, hair, eyes, etc., also used as identifiers. Single use or subscribe at https://www.nebraska.gov/justicecc/ccname.cgi for court access. Single use is $15.00 a record or open an account for $1 per record plus $50 annual fee. Online records date from 04/00. Online results show middle initial, DOB.

General Information: Online identifiers in results same as on public terminal. No mental health records released. Will not fax documents. Court makes copy: $.50 per page. Self serve: $.25 per page. Certification fee: $1.00. Payee: Clerk of District Court. Personal checks accepted; credit cards are not. Prepayment required.

Sherman County Court 630 O St, PO Box 55, Loup City, NE 68853; 308-745-1513 x102; fax: 308-745-1510; 8:30AM-4:30PM (CST). ***Misdemeanor, Civil Actions under $51,000, Eviction, Small Claims, Probate.***

Civil Records: Access: In person, online. Visitors must perform in person searches themselves. Required to search: name, years to search. Civil cases indexed by defendant only. Civil index on docket books from late 1800s; on computer back to 5/2000 in DC office. Newer names indexed by defendant only. Civil PAT goes back to 4/2000. PAT civil results show middle initial. Public terminal located in District Court Office. Civil records online - see criminal access. Online civil and probate records from 05/00 forward.

Criminal Records: Access: In person, online. Visitors must perform in person searches themselves. Required to search: name, years to search, DOB. Criminal records indexed in books from late 1800s; on computer back to 5/2000. Newer names indexed by defendant only. Criminal PAT goes back to same as civil. PAT results show middle initial, DOB. Public terminal located in District Court Office. Single use or subscribe at https://www.nebraska.gov/justicecc/ccname.cgi for court access. Single use is $15.00 a record or open an account for $1 per record plus $50 annual fee. Online criminal and traffic records date from 05/00. Online results show name only.

General Information: No adoption records released. Fee to fax out file $3.00 1st page; $1.00 each add'l. Court makes copy: $.25 per page. Self serve: $.25 per page. Certification fee: $1.00 for seal, $.25 per page. Payee: Sherman County Court. Business checks accepted. No credit cards accepted. Prepayment required.

Sioux County

District Court PO Box 158, 325 Main St, Harrison, NE 69346; 308-668-2443; 8AM-4:30PM (MST). ***Felony, Civil Actions over $51,000.***

Civil Records: Access: In person, online. Both court and visitors may perform in person searches. No search fee. Required to search: name, years to search. Civil cases indexed by defendant, plaintiff. Civil records in index and docket books since 1800s; computerized records since 1992. Civil PAT goes back to 1992. Civil records online - see criminal access. Online records date from 06/00.

Criminal Records: Access: In person, online. Both court and visitors may perform in person searches. No search fee. Required to search: name, years to search; also helpful: DOB, SSN. Criminal records in index and docket books since 1800s; computerized records since 1992. Criminal PAT goes back to same as civil. Single use or subscribe at https://www.nebraska.gov/justicecc/ccname.cgi for court access. Single use is $15.00 a record or open

an account for $1 per record plus $50 annual fee. Online records date from 06/00. Online results show middle initial, DOB.
General Information: No adoption or sealed records released. Will fax documents $1.00 per page. Court makes copy: $1.00 per page. Self serve: same. Certification fee: $6.00 per page. Payee: Clerk of District Court. Personal checks accepted; credit cards are not. Prepayment required.

Sioux County Court PO Box 158, 325 Main St, Harrison, NE 69346; 308-668-2443; fax: 308-668-2443; 8AM-4:30PM (MST). ***Misdemeanor, Civil Actions under $51,000, Eviction, Small Claims, Probate.***
Civil Records: Access: In person, online. Both court and visitors may perform in person searches. No search fee. Required to search: name, years to search. Civil cases indexed by defendant, plaintiff. Civil index on docket books from late 1800s. Note: This court prefers to take phone requests. Very few civil cases handled each year. Civil PAT goes back to 1992. Civil records online - see criminal access. Online civil and probate records are from 01/01 forward.
Criminal Records: Access: In person, online. Both court and visitors may perform in person searches. No search fee. Required to search: name, years to search. Criminal records indexed in books from late 1800s. Criminal PAT goes back to same as civil. Single use or subscribe at https://www.nebraska.gov/justicecc/ccname.cgi for court access. Single use is $15.00 a record or open an account for $1 per record plus $50 annual fee. Online criminal and traffic records date from 08/00. Online results show middle initial, DOB.
General Information: No sealed, expunged, or adoption records released. Will fax documents $1.00 per page. Court makes copy: $1.00 per page. Self serve: same. Certification fee: $1.00 per document. Payee: County Court. Personal checks accepted; credit cards are not. Prepayment required.

Stanton County

District Court PO Box 347, Stanton, NE 68779; 402-439-2222; fax: 402-439-2200; 8:30AM-4:30PM (CST). ***Felony, Civil Actions over $51,000.***
Civil Records: Access: Fax, mail, in person, online. Visitors must perform in person searches themselves. No search fee. Required to search: name, years to search. Civil cases indexed by defendant, plaintiff; index on books from 1867, on computer from 12/1999. Mail turnaround time 3-4 days. Civil PAT goes back to 12/1999. PAT civil results show middle initial. Civil records online - see criminal access. Online records date from 12/99.
Criminal Records: Access: Fax, mail, in person, online. Visitors must perform in person searches themselves. No search fee. Required to search: name, years to search; also helpful: address, DOB, SSN. Criminal docket on books from 1867, on computer from 12/1999. Mail turnaround time 3-4 days. Criminal PAT goes back to same as civil. PAT criminal results show middle initial. Single use or subscribe at https://www.nebraska.gov/justicecc/ccname.cgi for court access. Single use is $15.00 a record or open an account for $1 per record plus $50 annual fee. Online records date from 12/99. Online results show middle initial, DOB.
General Information: Online identifiers in results same as on public terminal. No juvenile records released. Will fax documents $2.50 1st page, $1.00 each add'l. Court makes copy: $.25 per page. Self serve: same. Certification fee: $1.00 per page. Payee: Clerk of District Court. Personal checks accepted; credit cards are not. Prepayment required. Mail requests: SASE required.

Stanton County Court 804 Ivy St, PO Box 536, Stanton, NE 68779; 402-439-2221; probate phone: 402-439-2221; fax: 402-439-2227; 8:30AM-4:30PM (CST). ***Misdemeanor, Civil Actions under $51,000, Eviction, Small Claims, Probate.***
www.co.stanton.ne.us/cntycourt.html
Civil Records: Access: In person, online. Visitors must perform in person searches themselves. Required to search: name, years to search. Civil cases indexed by defendant, plaintiff; index on docket cards and books back to 1950s; criminal records go back to 1999, probate on microfilm. Civil PAT goes back to 7/2000. PAT results show name only. Civil records online - see criminal access. Online civil and probate records from 10/00 forward.
Criminal Records: Access: In person, online. Visitors must perform in person searches themselves. Required to search: name, years to search, DOB. Criminal records on docket cards and books back to 1900s; criminal records computerized back to 1999, probate on microfilm. Criminal PAT goes back to same as civil.PAT results show name, DOB. Single use or subscribe at https://www.nebraska.gov/justicecc/ccname.cgi for court access. Single use is $15.00 a record or open an account for $1 per record plus $50 annual fee. Online criminal and traffic records date from 06/00. Online results show name only.
General Information: No adoption records released. Will not fax documents. Court makes copy: $.25 per page. Certification fee: $1.00. Payee: Stanton County. Personal checks accepted; credit cards are not. Prepayment required. Mail requests: SASE required for mail return of any copies.

Thayer County

District Court 225 N 4th St Rm 302, Hebron, NE 68370; 402-768-6116; fax: 402-768-6128; 7:30AM-N, 1:00PM-4:30PM (CST). ***Felony, Civil Actions over $51,000.***
Civil Records: Access: In person, online. Visitors must perform in person searches themselves. Required to search: name, years to search. Civil cases indexed by defendant, plaintiff; index on books from 1900s; computerized records go back 3/2000. Civil PAT goes back to 3/2000. Results include name and case number. Civil records online - see criminal access. Online records date from 03/00.
Criminal Records: Access: In person, online. Visitors must perform in person searches themselves. Required to search: name, years to search. Criminal docket on books from 1900; computerized records go back 3/2000. Criminal PAT goes back to same as civil. Results include name and case number. Single use or subscribe at https://www.nebraska.gov/justicecc/ccname.cgi for court access. Single use is $15.00 a record or open an account for $1 per record plus $50 annual fee. Online records date from 03/00. Online results show middle initial, DOB.
General Information: No mental health or sealed records released. Will not fax documents. Court makes copy: $.25 per page. Certification fee: $1.00. Payee: Thayer County District Court. Personal checks accepted; credit cards are not. Mail requests: SASE required for Naturalization Records only.

Thayer County Court PO Box 94, Hebron, NE 68370; 402-768-6325; fax: 402-768-7232; 7:30AM-4:30PM (CST). ***Misdemeanor, Civil Actions under $51,000, Eviction, Small Claims, Probate.***
Civil Records: Access: In person, online. Visitors must perform in person searches themselves. Required to search: name, years to search, address. Civil cases indexed by defendant, plaintiff; index on docket cards from 1871; probate on microfiche. Civil PAT goes back to 2000. Civil records online - see criminal access. Online civil and probate records from 02/00 forward.
Criminal Records: Access: In person, online. Visitors must perform in person searches themselves. Required to search: name, years to search, DOB. Criminal records on docket cards from 1871; probate on microfiche. Criminal PAT goes back to same as civil. Single use or subscribe at https://www.nebraska.gov/justicecc/ccname.cgi for court access. Single use is $15.00 a record or open an account for $1 per record plus $50 annual fee. Online criminal and traffic records date from 02/00. Online results show middle initial, DOB.
General Information: No adoption or juvenile records released. Will not fax documents. Court makes copy: $.25 per page. Certification fee: $1.00. Payee: County Court. No personal checks or credit cards accepted. Prepayment required.

Thomas County

District Court PO Box 226, 503 Main St, Thedford, NE 69166; 308-645-2261; fax: 308-645-2623; 8AM-N, 1-4PM (CST). ***Felony, Civil Actions over $51,000.***
The District Court no longer performs searches.
Civil Records: Access: In person, online. Visitors must perform in person searches themselves. Required to search: name, years to search. Civil cases indexed by defendant, plaintiff; index in books and in case files since 1800s; on computer back to 6/2000. Civil PAT goes back to 6/2000. Civil records online - see criminal access. Online records date from 06/00.
Criminal Records: Access: In person, online. Visitors must perform in person searches themselves. Required to search: name, years to search, DOB; also helpful- SSN, signed release. Criminal records indexed in books and in case files since 1800s; on computer back to 6/2000. Criminal PAT goes back to same as civil. Single use or subscribe at https://www.nebraska.gov/justicecc/ccname.cgi for court access. Single use is $15.00 a record or open an account for $1 per record plus $50 annual fee. Online records date from 06/00. Online results show middle initial, DOB.
General Information: No sealed or juvenile records released. Will fax documents $5.00 per fax. Court makes copy: $.50 per page. Self serve: same. Certification fee: $5.00 per cert. Payee: Clerk of District Court. Personal checks accepted; credit cards are not. Prepayment required.

Thomas County Court PO Box 233, 503 Main St, Thedford, NE 69166; 308-645-2266 or 2273; fax: 308-645-2623; 8AM-N, 1-4PM (CST). ***Misdemeanor, Civil Actions under $51,000, Eviction, Small Claims, Probate.***
Civil Records: Access: Phone, fax, mail, in person, online. Both court and visitors may perform in person searches. No search fee. Required to search: name, years to search. Civil cases indexed by defendant, plaintiff. Civil index on cards and books from late 1800s. Mail turnaround time 2 days. Civil PAT goes back to 6/2000. Civil records online - see criminal access. Online civil records date from 10/99 forward, probate from 07/98.
Criminal Records: Access: Fax, mail, in person, online. Both court and visitors may perform in person searches. No search fee. Required to search: name, years to search, DOB, signed release. Criminal records indexed on cards and books from late 1800s. Mail turnaround time 2 days. Criminal PAT goes back to same as civil. Single use or subscribe at https://www.nebraska.gov/justicecc/ccname.cgi for court access. Single use is $15.00 a record or open an account for $1 per record plus $50 annual fee. Online criminal and traffic records date from 07/98. Online results show middle initial, DOB.
General Information: No adoption or juvenile records released. Will not fax documents. Court makes copy: $.25 per page. Self serve: same. Certification fee: $1.00 per cert. Payee: County Court. Personal checks accepted. Visa/MC accepted. Prepayment required. Mail requests: SASE required.

Thurston County

District Court PO Box 216, Pender, NE 68047; 402-385-3318; fax: 402-385-2762; 8:30AM-N, 1-5PM (CST). ***Felony, Civil Actions over $51,000.***
Civil Records: Access: In person, online. Visitors must perform in person searches themselves. Required to search: name, years to search. Civil cases indexed by defendant, plaintiff. Civil index on docket books from late 1800s; on computer back to 1998. Civil PAT goes back to 1998. PAT civil results show middle initial. Civil records online - see criminal access. Online records date from 03/98.
Criminal Records: Access: In person, online. Visitors must perform in person searches themselves. Required to search: name, years to search. Criminal records indexed in books from late 1800s; on computer back to 1998. Criminal PAT goes back to same as civil. PAT criminal results show middle initial. Single use or subscribe at https://www.nebraska.gov/justicecc/ccname.cgi for court access. Single use is $15.00 a record or open

an account for $1 per record plus $50 annual fee. Online records date from 03/98. Online results show middle initial, DOB.

General Information: No mental health records released. Will not fax documents. Court makes copy: $.25 per page. Self serve: same. Certification fee: $1.00 per certification. Payee: Clerk of District Court. No personal checks or credit cards accepted. Prepayment required.

Thurston County Court County Courthouse, PO Box 129, Pender, NE 68047; 402-385-3136; fax: 402-385-3143; 8AM-N,1-5PM (CST). ***Misdemeanor, Civil Actions under $51,000, Eviction, Small Claims, Probate.***

Probate fax is same as main fax number.

Civil Records: Access: In person, online. Visitors must perform in person searches themselves. Required to search: name, years to search. Civil cases indexed by defendant, plaintiff; index on books; probate on microfiche since 1800s; on computer back to 1/2000. Civil PAT goes back to 1/2000. Civil records online - see criminal access. Online civil and probate records from 01/00 forward.

Criminal Records: Access: In person, online. Visitors must perform in person searches themselves. Required to search: name, years to search. Criminal docket on books per state requirement; on computer back to 1/2000. Criminal PAT goes back to same as civil. Single use or subscribe at https://www.nebraska.gov/justicecc/ccname.cgi for court access. Single use is $15.00 a record or open an account for $1 per record plus $50 annual fee. Online criminal and traffic records date from 01/00. Online results show middle initial, DOB.

General Information: Online identifiers in results same as on public terminal. No adoption or juvenile records released. Will not fax documents. Court makes copy: $.25 per page. Self serve: $.10 per page. Certification fee: $1.00 per seal. Payee: County Court. Personal checks accepted. Out of state personal checks not accepted. No credit cards accepted. Prepayment required.

Valley County

District Court 125 S 15th St, Ord, NE 68862; 308-728-3700; fax: 308-728-7725; 8AM-5PM (CST). ***Felony, Civil Actions over $51,000.***

Civil Records: Access: In person, online. Both court and visitors may perform in person searches. No search fee. Required to search: name, years to search. Civil cases indexed by defendant, plaintiff. Civil records in general index books since late 1800s. Civil PAT goes back to 3/2000. PAT results show name only. Civil records online - see criminal access. Online records date from 3/2000.

Criminal Records: Access: In person, online. Both court and visitors may perform in person searches. No search fee. Required to search: name, years to search; also helpful: DOB, SSN. Criminal records in general index books since late 1800s; on computer back to 3/2000. Criminal PAT goes back to same as civil.PAT results show name, DOB. Single use or subscribe at https://www.nebraska.gov/justicecc/ccname.cgi for court access. Single use is $15.00 a record or open an account for $1 per record plus $50 annual fee. Online records date from 3/2000. Online results show middle initial, DOB.

General Information: Will fax to toll-free number. Court makes copy: $.10 per page; $.15 per page legal size. Self serve: same. Certification fee: $1.00 per page. Payee: Valley County Clerk. Personal checks accepted; credit cards are not. Prepayment required.

Valley County Court 125 S 15th St, Ord, NE 68862; 308-728-3831; fax: 308-728-7725; 8AM-5PM (CST). ***Misdemeanor, Civil Actions under $51,000, Eviction, Small Claims, Probate.***

Civil Records: Access: Phone, fax, mail, in person, online. Both court and visitors may perform in person searches. No search fee. Required to search: name, years to search. Civil cases indexed by defendant, plaintiff; index on books and in files since 1890s; probate on microfiche. Mail turnaround time 1 week. Civil PAT goes back to 7 years. Civil records online - see criminal access. Online civil and probate records from 05/00 forward.

Criminal Records: Access: Phone, fax, mail, in person, online. Both court and visitors may perform in person searches. No search fee. Required to search: name, years to search. Criminal docket on books and in files since 1890s; probate on microfiche. Mail turnaround time 1 week. Criminal PAT goes back to same as civil. Single use or subscribe at https://www.nebraska.gov/justicecc/ccname.cgi for court access. Single use is $15.00 a record or open an account for $1 per record plus $50 annual fee. Online criminal and traffic records date from 05/00. Online results show middle initial, DOB.

General Information: No adoption records released. Will fax documents $3.00 1st page, $1.00 each add'l. Court makes copy: $.25 per page. Self serve: same. Certification fee: $1.25. Payee: Valley County Court. Personal checks accepted. Prepayment required. Mail requests: SASE required.

Washington County

District Court PO Box 431, Blair, NE 68008; 402-426-6899; fax: 402-426-6898; 8AM-N; 1PM-4:30PM (CST). ***Felony, Civil Actions over $51,000.***

Civil Records: Access: In person, online. Visitors must perform in person searches themselves. Required to search: name, years to search. Civil cases indexed by defendant, plaintiff. Civil index on docket books and in files since 1930s; computerized records since 1997, prior sent to capitol. Civil PAT goes back to 7/1997. PAT results show middle initial, DOB. Civil records online - see criminal access. Online records date from 06/97.

Criminal Records: Access: In person, online. Visitors must perform in person searches themselves. Required to search: name, years to search, DOB. Criminal records indexed in books and in files since 1930s; computerized records since 1997, prior sent to capitol. Criminal PAT goes back to same as civil. PAT results show middle initial, DOB. Single use or subscribe at https://www.nebraska.gov/justicecc/ccname.cgi for court access. Single use is $15.00 a record or open an account for $1 per record plus $50 annual fee. Online records date from 06/97. Online results show middle initial, DOB.

General Information: No juvenile, mental health records released. Will fax documents $3.00 1st page, $1.00 ea add'l. Court makes copy: $.25 per page. Certification fee: $1.00. Payee: Clerk of District Court. Personal checks accepted; credit cards are not. Prepayment required.

Washington County Court 1555 Colfax St, Blair, NE 68008; 402-426-6833; fax: 402-426-6840; 8AM-4:30PM (CST). ***Misdemeanor, Civil Actions under $51,000, Eviction, Small Claims, Probate.***

Probate records are on a separate index at this address. Probate fax is same as main fax number.

Civil Records: Access: In person, online. Visitors must perform in person searches themselves. Required to search: name, years to search. Civil cases indexed by defendant, plaintiff. Civil index on docket books, cards; probate on microfilm since 1867; on computer back to 1997. Civil PAT goes back to 12/1999. PAT civil results show middle initial. Civil records online - see criminal access. Online civil records date from 12/99 forward, probate from 5/98.

Criminal Records: Access: In person, online. Visitors must perform in person searches themselves. Required to search: name, years to search, DOB, SSN. Criminal records indexed in books, cards; probate on microfilm since 1867; on computer back to 1997. Criminal PAT goes back to 2/1997. PAT results show middle initial, DOB. Single use or subscribe at https://www.nebraska.gov/justicecc/ccname.cgi for court access. Single use is $15.00 a record or open an account for $1 per record plus $50 annual fee. Online criminal and traffic records date from 2/97. Online results show middle initial, DOB.

General Information: Online identifiers in results same as on public terminal. No adoption records released. Will not fax documents. Court makes copy: $.25 per page. Self serve: same. Certification fee: $1.00 per certification. Payee: Washington County Court. No personal checks. No credit cards accepted. Prepayment required.

Wayne County

District Court 510 Pearl St, #6, Wayne, NE 68787; 402-375-2260; fax: 402-375-0103; 8:30AM-5PM (CST). ***Felony, Civil Actions over $51,000.***

http://county.waynene.org/court_system

Court personnel will not do searches for the public.

Civil Records: Access: In person, online. Visitors must perform in person searches themselves. Required to search: name, years to search. Civil cases indexed by defendant, plaintiff. Civil index on docket books from late 1800s, computerized since 3/99. Civil PAT goes back to 3/1999. Not all records show personal identifiers. Civil records online - see criminal access. Online records date from 03/99.

Criminal Records: Access: In person, online. Visitors must perform in person searches themselves. Required to search: name, years to search. Criminal records indexed in books from late 1800s, computerized since 3/99. Criminal PAT goes back to same as civil. Not all records show personal identifiers. Subscribe to JUSTICE at https://www.nebraska.gov/justicecc/ccname.cgi for court access. Online results show middle initial, DOB.

General Information: No mental health records released. Will fax out documents $2.00 1st page, $1.00 each add'l, prepaid. Court makes copy: $.25 per page. Self serve: same. Certification fee: $1.00. Payee: Clerk of District Court. Only cashiers checks and money orders accepted. No credit cards accepted. Prepayment required.

Wayne County Court 510 Pearl St, #B, Wayne, NE 68787; 402-375-1622; fax: 402-375-2342; 8AM-5PM (CST). ***Misdemeanor, Civil Actions under $51,000, Eviction, Small Claims, Probate.***

http://county.waynene.org/court_system

Civil Records: Access: In person, online. Visitors must perform in person searches themselves. Required to search: name, years to search. Civil cases indexed by defendant, plaintiff. Civil index on docket books, cards from late 1800s. Civil PAT goes back to 1999. Civil records online - see criminal access. Online civil and probate records from 2/2000 forward.

Criminal Records: Access: In person, online. Visitors must perform in person searches themselves. Required to search: name, years to search. Criminal records indexed in books, cards from late 1800s. Criminal PAT goes back to same as civil. Single use or subscribe at https://www.nebraska.gov/justicecc/ccname.cgi for court access. Single use is $15.00 a record or open an account for $1 per record plus $50 annual fee. Online criminal and traffic records date from 2/2000. Online results show middle initial, DOB.

General Information: No adoption records released. Will not fax documents. Court makes copy: $.25 per page. Self serve: $.25 per page. Certification fee: $1.00. Payee: County Court. Personal checks accepted; credit cards are not. Prepayment required.

Webster County

District Court 621 N Cedar, Red Cloud, NE 68970; 402-746-2716; fax: 402-746-2710; 8:30AM-4:30PM (CST). ***Felony, Civil Actions over $51,000.***

Civil Records: Access: Fax, mail, in person, online. Visitors must perform in person searches themselves. No search fee. Required to search: name, years to search. Civil cases indexed by defendant, plaintiff; index on microfiche; in files back to 1800s. Civil PAT goes back to 10/2000. Civil records online - see criminal access. Online records date from 10/00.

Criminal Records: Access: Fax, mail, in person, online. Visitors must perform in person searches themselves. No search fee. Required to search: name, years to search; also helpful: address, DOB, SSN. Criminal records indexed on microfiche; in files back to 1800s. Criminal PAT goes back to same as civil. Single use or subscribe at https://www.nebraska.gov/justicecc/ccname.cgi for

court access. Single use is $15.00 a record or open an account for $1 per record plus $50 annual fee. Online records date from 10/2000. Online results show middle initial, DOB.
General Information: No mental health records released. Will not fax documents. Court makes copy: $1.00 per page. Certification fee: $1.50 per cert. Payee: Clerk of District Court. Personal checks accepted. Visa/MC accepted. Prepayment required.

Webster County Court 621 N Cedar, Red Cloud, NE 68970; 402-746-2777; fax: 402-746-2771; 8AM-4:30PM (CST). ***Misdemeanor, Civil Actions under $51,000, Eviction, Small Claims, Probate.***
www.district10.us/
Probate fax is same as main fax number.
Civil Records: Access: In person, online. Visitors must perform in person searches themselves. Required to search: name, years to search; also helpful: address. Civil cases indexed by defendant. Civil index on cards and books; probate on microfiche since late 1930, indexed on computer since 7/00. Civil PAT goes back to 1/2001. PAT results show name only. Civil records online - see criminal access. Online civil records date from 01/00 forward, probate from 02/00.
Criminal Records: Access: In person, online. Visitors must perform in person searches themselves. Required to search: name, years to search, DOB. Criminal records indexed on cards and books; probate on microfiche since late 1930, indexed on computer since 7/00. Criminal PAT goes back to 7/2000.PAT results show name, DOB. Single use or subscribe at https://www.nebraska.gov/justicecc/ccname.cgi for court access. Single use is $15.00 a record or open an account for $1 per record plus $50 annual fee. Online criminal and traffic records date from 07/00. Online results show middle initial, DOB.
General Information: Online identifiers in results same as on public terminal. No adoption or juvenile records released. Will fax out specific case files for $3.00 for 1st page; $1.00 each add'l. Court makes copy: $.25 per page. Self serve: same. Certification fee: $1.00. Payee: County Court. Business checks accepted. No credit cards accepted. Prepayment required.

Wheeler County

District Court PO Box 127, Bartlett, NE 68622; 308-654-3235; 9AM-N, 1-5PM (CST). ***Felony, Civil Actions over $51,000.***
Civil Records: Access: Mail, in person, online. Visitors must perform in person searches themselves. No search fee. Required to search: name, years to search. Civil cases indexed by defendant, plaintiff. Civil index on docket books from late 1800s. Note: Mail access limited to short searches. Civil PAT goes back to 2000. Civil records online - see criminal access.
Criminal Records: Access: In person, online. Visitors must perform in person searches themselves. Required to search: name, years to search. Criminal records indexed in books from late 1800s. Criminal PAT goes back to 2000. Single use or subscribe at https://www.nebraska.gov/justicecc/ccname.cgi for court access. Single use is $15.00 a record or open an account for $1 per record plus $50 annual fee. Online records date from 7/2000. Online results show middle initial, DOB.
General Information: No juvenile or adoption records released. Will fax out specific case files for $3.00. Court makes copy: $.50 per page. Certification fee: $5.00. Payee: Clerk of District Court. Personal checks accepted; credit cards are not. Prepayment required.

Wheeler County Court PO Box 127, Bartlett, NE 68622; 308-654-3376; probate phone: same; fax: 308-654-3470; 10AM-3PM TH; and 1st & 2nd M (CST). ***Misdemeanor, Civil Actions under $51,000, Eviction, Small Claims, Probate.***
Court clerk also serves Garfield County Court and may be contacted there, 308-346-4123
Civil Records: Access: In person, online. Only the court performs in person searches; visitors may not. Required to search: name, years to search. Civil cases indexed by defendant, plaintiff. Civil index on docket books from late 1800s. Public use terminal has civil records back to 2000. PAT results show name only. Civil records online - see criminal access. Online civil records date from 1/2001 forward, probate from 1/02.
Criminal Records: Access: In person, online. Visitors must perform in person searches themselves. Required to search: name, years to search. Criminal records indexed in books from late 1800s. Single use or subscribe at https://www.nebraska.gov/justicecc/ccname.cgi for court access. Single use is $15.00 a record or open an account for $1 per record plus $50 annual fee. Online criminal and traffic records date from 7/2000. Online results show middle initial, DOB.
General Information: No adoption records released. Will fax documents $3.00 1st page; $1.00 each add'l. Court makes copy: $.25 per page. Self serve: same. Certification fee: $1.00. Payee: County Court. Personal checks accepted; credit cards are not. Prepayment required.

York County

District Court 510 Lincoln Ave, York, NE 68467; 402-362-4038; fax: 402-362-2577; 8:30AM-5PM (CST). ***Felony, Civil Actions over $51,000.***
The SSN does not show up in the computer index, but will show in the case files.
Civil Records: Access: In person, online. Visitors must perform in person searches themselves. Required to search: name, years to search. Civil cases indexed by defendant, plaintiff. Civil index on docket books and in files from 1875, computerized go back to 1998. Civil PAT goes back to 1998. Civil records online - see criminal access. Online records date from 06/98.
Criminal Records: Access: In person, online. Visitors must perform in person searches themselves. Required to search: name, years to search. Criminal records indexed in books and in files from 1875, computerized records go back to 1998. Criminal PAT goes back to 1998. PAT results show middle initial, DOB, SSN. Single use or subscribe at https://www.nebraska.gov/justicecc/ccname.cgi for court access. Single use is $15.00 a record or open an account for $1 per record plus $50 annual fee. Online records date from 06/98. Online results show middle initial, DOB.
General Information: Online identifiers in results same as on public terminal. Will fax documents. Court makes copy: $.25 per page. Self serve: same. Certification fee: $1.00. Payee: Clerk of District Court. Personal checks accepted; credit cards are not. Prepayment required.

York County Court 510 Lincoln Ave, York, NE 68467; 402-362-4925; fax: 402-362-2577; 8AM-5PM (CST). ***Misdemeanor, Civil Actions under $51,000, Eviction, Small Claims, Probate.***
Civil Records: Access: In person, online. Visitors must perform in person searches themselves. Required to search: name, years to search. Civil cases indexed by defendant, plaintiff; index on docket cards, files from 1875. Civil PAT goes back to 1995. Civil records online - see criminal access. Online civil records date from 10/99 forward, probate from 05/98.
Criminal Records: Access: In person, online. Visitors must perform in person searches themselves. Required to search: name, years to search. Criminal records on docket cards, files from 1875. Criminal PAT goes back to 3/1997. Single use or subscribe at https://www.nebraska.gov/justicecc/ccname.cgi for court access. Single use is $15.00 a record or open an account for $1 per record plus $50 annual fee. Online criminal and traffic records date from 03/97. Online results show middle initial, DOB.
General Information: No adoption or sealed records released. Will not fax documents. Court makes copy: $.25 per page. Certification fee: $1.00. Payee: York County Court. Personal checks accepted; credit cards are not. Prepayment required.

Nebraska Recording Offices

ORGANIZATION: 93 counties, 109 recording offices. The recording officers are County Clerk (UCCs and some state tax liens) and Register of Deeds (real estate and most tax liens). Most counties have a combined Clerk/Register office that is designated as "County Clerk" for our purposes. Still, in combined offices, the Register of Deeds is frequently a different person from the County Clerk. Sixteen counties have separate offices for real estate recording and UCC records - Adams, Cass, Dakota, Dawson, Dodge, Douglas, Gage, Hall, Lancaster, Lincoln, Madison, Otoe, Platte, Sarpy, Saunders, and Scotts Bluff.

74 Nebraska counties are in the Central Time Zone (CST) and the 19 westernmost counties are in the Mountain Time Zone (MST).

REAL ESTATE RECORDS: Some Nebraska counties will perform real estate searches (including owner of record) when provided with the legal description of the property. Address search requests and make checks payable to the Register of Deeds, not the County Clerk. Real Estate search fees vary.

UCC RECORDS: Financing statements are filed at the state level and real estate related collateral are filed with the County Clerk. Previously, financing statements could be filed at any county. All non-real estate UCC filings are entered into a statewide database that is accessible from any county office. A declining number of counties will perform UCC searches. Use UCC-11 request. UCC statute allows for phone searching. UCC search fee is usually $4.50 per debtor name.

TAX LIEN RECORDS: Most federal and state tax liens are filed with the County Register of Deeds. Some state tax liens on personal property are filed with the County Clerk. Some federal tax liens on individuals are filed at the Sec. of State's office. Most counties will perform tax lien searches, some as part of a UCC search, and others for a separate fee.

OTHER LIENS: Mechanics, artisans, judgment, motor vehicle, agricultural.

ONLINE ACCESS: Nebrask@online offers online access to Secretary of State's UCC database; registration and a usage fee is required. For information, visit www.sos.state.ne.us/business/ucc/. Access real estate or personal property data at www.nebraskataxesonline.us/ free for at least 50 counties.

Adams County Clerk

County Clerk, PO Box 203, Hastings, NE 68902-0203. 402-461-7148; fax-402-461-7154; 9AM-5PM (CST) www.adamscounty.org

See Register of Deeds for real estate records. Index: All in one. Record index not computerized. Office will perform a UCC search but public must search other records themselves. Search fee-$1.00 per name. Copy fee $.50 per page. Cert fee- $1.50 per page includes copy fee. Payee- Adams County Register of Deeds. **Other phones:** Treasurer- 402-461-7120; Elections- 402-461-7107.

Adams County Register of Deeds

Register of Deeds, PO Box 203, Hastings, NE 68902. 402-461-7148; fax-402-461-7154; 9AM-5PM (CST) www.adamscounty.org

Index: All in one. Records indexed on a public use terminal back to 1991. Office personnel or visitors may perform searches. Search fee $1.00 per name per search. Office will not search real estate records. Office will not search UCC records. Copy fee $1.00 per page for fax, $.50 per page for mail or in-person. Cert fee- $1.50 per page includes copy fee. Payee- Adams County Register of Deeds. **Other phones:** Treasurer- 402-461-7120; Elections- 402-461-7165; Vitals- 402-471-2871. **Property tax/Assessing-** 500 W 4th St, Rm 107, Hastings, NE 68901; 402-461-7116, assessor fax- 402-461-7215. (Appraiser - 402-461-7116) www.adamscounty.org/assessor/index.htm **Online access-** Access real estate or personal property data free at www.nebraskataxesonline.us/taxcollpage1.aspx?county=Adams.

Antelope County

County Clerk, PO Box 26, Neligh, NE 68756-0026. 402-887-4410; fax-402-887-4719; 8:30AM-5PM.

Records not filed here since 2001. Index: All in one. Records indexed on a public use terminal back to 1996. Only the public may search. Copy fee $.25 per page. $1.00 per page to fax back. Cert fee- $5.00 per doc plus copy fee. Payee- Antelope County Clerk. **Other phones:** Treasurer- 402-887-4247; Elections- 402-887-4410. **Property tax/Assessing-** 501 Main St, Rm 7, Neligh, NE 68756-1473; 402-887-4515, assessor fax- 402-887-4215. 8AM-4:30PM No public access terminal. www.co.antelope.ne.us/assessor.html **Online access-** Access to property search for free go to www.antelope.assessor.gisworkshop.com/

Arthur County

County Clerk, PO Box 126, Arthur, NE 69121-0126. 308-764-2203; fax-308-764-2216; 8AM-N, 1-4PM.

Index: All in one. Records indexed on a public use terminal back to 1990. Office personnel or visitors may perform searches. Search fee $5.00 per name. Office will not search real estate records. Copy fee $.20 per page. Cert fee- $5.00 per cert. Payee- Arthur County Clerk. **Property tax/Assessing-** PO Box 126, 205 Fir St, Arthur, NE 69121; 308-764-2203.

Banner County

County Clerk, PO Box 67, Harrisburg, NE 69345-0002. 308-436-5265; fax-308-436-4180; 8AM-N, 1-5PM (MST)

Index: All in one. Records indexed on a public use terminal back to 2004. Office personnel or visitors may perform searches. Search fee $3.00 per name. Office will not search real estate records. Copy fee $.50 per page. Cert fee- $5.00 1st page, $1.00 each add'l page plus copy fee. Payee- Banner County Clerk. **Other phones:** Treasurer- 308-436-5260. **Property tax/Assessing-** PO Box 67, 204 State St, Courthouse, Harrisburg, NE 69345; 308-436-5265. www.co.banner.ne.us/assessor.html

Blaine County

County Clerk, 145 Lincoln Ave, Brewster, NE 68821. 308-547-2222, R/E recording phone-308-547-2222 ext 201, UCC recording phone-308-547-2222; fax-308-547-2228; hours- 8AM-4PM (CST) www.blainecounty.ne.gov

Index: All in one. Records indexed on computer. Office personnel or visitors may perform searches. General index search fee $1.00 per page. Copy fee $.20 per page. Cert fee- $1.50 per page plus copy fee. Payee- Blaine County Clerk. **Other phones:** Treasurer- 308-547-2222 ext 202; Elections- 308-547-2222; Vital Records- 308-547-2222. **Property tax/Assessing-** 145 Lincoln Ave, Brewster, NE 68821; 308-547-2222 ext 201, assessor fax- 308-547-2228. www.blainecounty.ne.gov/assessor.html

Boone County

County Clerk, 222 S 4th St, Albion, NE 68620-1247. Recording, R/E & UCC phone-402-395-2055, UCC recording phone-402-471-4080; fax-402-395-2055; 8:30AM-5PM (CST) www.co.boone.ne.us

Index: Separate indices to search include deed, mortgage, misc, liens, roads. Record index not computerized. Only the public may search. Copy fee $.50 per page; $.50 if mailed. Cert fee- $1.50 per page plus copy fee. Payee- Boone County Clerk. **Other phones:** Treasurer- 402-395-2513; Elections- 402-395-2055; Vital Records- 402-471-2871/3121. **Property tax/Assessing-** 222 S 4th St, Albion, NE 68620; 402-395-2045, assessor fax- 402-395-2045. **Online access-** Access real estate or personal property data free at www.nebraskataxesonline.us.

Box Butte County

County Clerk, PO Box 678, Alliance, NE 69301-0678. 308-762-6565, UCC recording phone-402-471-4080 (Sec of State); fax-308-762-2867; 8:30AM-4:30PM (MST) www.co.box-butte.ne.us

Recording officers are County Clerk (state tax liens), Register of Deeds (real estate and most tax liens). Index: Separate indices to search include deeds, mortgages, miscellaneous, mech liens, incorporations. Record index not computerized. Only the public may search. Copy fee $1.00 per page. Cert fee- $1.50 per page includes copy fee. Payee- Box Butte County Clerk. **Other phones:** Treasurer- 308-762-6975; Elections- 308-762-6565; Vital Records- 402-471-2871. **Property tax/Assessing-** 515 Box Butte Ave, Ste 100, Alliance, NE 69301; 308-762-6101. www.co.box-butte.ne.us/assessor.html **Online access-** Access real estate or personal property data free at www.nebraskataxesonline.us/taxcollpage1.aspx?county=BoxB.

Boyd County

County Clerk, PO Box 26, Butte, NE 68722. 402-775-2391; fax-402-775-2146; 8:15AM-4PM.
Index: Deeds, mortgages, misc. Record index not computerized. Office will perform a UCC search but public must search other records themselves. Copy fee $.25 per copy. Cert fee- $5.00 per page includes copy fee. Payee- County Clerk. **Other phones:** Treasurer- 402-775-2581; Elections- 402-775-2391; Vital Records- 402-775-2391. **Property tax/Assessing**- PO Box 2, 401 Thayer St, Butte, NE 68722; 402-775-2311, assessor fax- 402-775-2146.

Brown County

County Clerk, 148 W 4th St; Courthouse, Ainsworth, NE 69210. 402-387-2705; fax-402-387-0918; 8AM-5PM.
Index: All in one. Record index not computerized. Only the public may search. Copy fee $.50, if real estate $.25 per page. Cert fee- $5.00 first page, $1.50 each add'l, includes copy fee. Payee- Brown County Clerk. **Other phones:** Treasurer- 402-387-2650; Elections- 402-387-2705; Secretary of State (UCC)- 402-471-2554. **Property tax/Assessing**- 148 W 4th St, #6, Ainsworth, NE 69210-1658; 402-387-1621, fax- 402-387-0918. No public access terminal.

Buffalo County

Register of Deeds, PO Box 1270, Kearney, NE 68848-1270. Recording, R/E & UCC phone-308-236-1239, UCC recording phone-402-471-2558; fax-308-236-1291; 8AM-5PM.
Index: All in one. Records indexed on a public use terminal back to 2002. Only the public may search. Copy fee $.50 per page. Cert fee- $1.50 per page plus copy fee. Payee- Buffalo County Register of Deeds. **Other phones:** Treasurer- 308-236-1250; Elections- 308-236-1233. **Property tax/Assessing**- PO Box 1270, 1512 Central Ave, Kearney, NE 68848; 308-236-1205, fax- 308-233-3713. Public access terminal is available. www.buffalogov.org/offices/Assessor/

Burt County

County Clerk, PO Box 87, Tekamah, NE 68061. 402-374-2955; fax-402-374-2956; 8AM-4:30PM (CST) www.burtcounty.ne.gov/clerk.html
Index: All in one. Records indexed on computer back 2 years. Office personnel or visitors may perform searches. Search fee $4.50 per name. Office will not search real estate records. Copy fee $.50 per page. Cert fee- $3.50 per page, includes copy fee. Payee- Burt County Clerk. **Other phones:** Treasurer- 402-374-2911; Elections- 402-374-2955; Vital Records- 402-471-2871. **Property tax/Assessing**- 111 N 13th St, #10, Tekamah, NE 68061; 402-374-2926. www.burtcounty.ne.gov/assessor.html

Butler County

County Clerk, PO Box 289, David City, NE 68632-0289. 402-367-7430, R/E recording phone-402-367-7431, UCC recording phone-402-471-4080; fax-402-367-3329; hours- 8:30AM-5PM (CST) www.co.butler.ne.us/webpages/clerk/clerk.htm
Index: All in one. Record index not computerized. Only the public may search. Copy fee $1.00 per page (copied & faxed). In courthouse/clerk's office $.25 per page. Cert fee- $1.50 per page includes copy fee. Payee- Butler County Clerk. **Other phones:** Treasurer- 402-367-7450; Elections- 402-367-7430; Vital Records- 402-471-2871. **Property tax/Assessing**- 451 N 5th St, David City, NE 68632; 402-367-7420, assessor fax- 402-367-3329. **Online access**- Search assessor property data on the GIS site free at http://butler.gisworkshop.com/ButlerIMS/.

Cass County Clerk

County Clerk, 346 Main St, Rm 202; Courthouse, Plattsmouth, NE 68048-1964. 402-296-9300; fax-402-296-9332; 8AM-5PM (CST)
Index: All in one. Records indexed on a public use terminal back to 2002. Office will perform a UCC search but public must search other records themselves. No fee for search. Copy fee $.50 per page.Real estate record copy- $1.50 per page. Cert fee- $5.00 per cert plus copy fee. Payee- Cass County Clerk. **Other phones:** Treasurer- 402-296-9320; Elections- 402-296-9309.

Cass County Register of Deeds

Register of Deeds, 346 Main St; County Courthouse, Plattsmouth, NE 68048-1964. 402-296-9330; fax-402-296-9331; 8AM-5PM (CST) www.cassne.org
Office will look at records when asked if request is not too involved or they have the time. Index: All in one. Records indexed on a public use terminal back to 2001. Office will perform a UCC search, but public must search other records themselves. Search fee $1.50 per name. Office will not search real estate records. Copy fee $.50 per page. Cert fee- $1.50 per page includes copy fee. Payee- Register of Deeds. **Other phones:** Treasurer- 402-296-9320; Elections- 402-296-9306. **Property tax/Assessing**- 346 Main St, Plattsmouth, NE 68048; 402-296-9310, assessor fax- 402-296-9319. (Appraiser/Auditor- 402-296-9310) www.cassne.org/assessor.html **Online access**- Access GIS and Assessor data free at www.gis-srv.cassne.org/CassIMSPublic/index.html. Also, access property data free at www.nebraskataxesonline.us/taxcollpage1.aspx?county=Cass.

Cedar County

County Clerk, PO Box 47, Hartington, NE 68739. Recording, R/E phone-402-254-7411, UCC recording phone-402-471-2554; fax-402-254-7410; 8AM-5PM. www.co.cedar.ne.us
Index: All in one. Records indexed on a public use terminal back to 010100. Office will perform a UCC search but public must search other records themselves. Search fee $4.50. Office will search very limited real estate records. Copy fee $.50 per page. Cert fee- $1.50 per doc plus copy fee. Payee- County Clerk. **Other phones:** Treasurer- 402-254-7421; Elections- 402-254-7411; Vital Records- 402-254-7411. **Property tax/Assessing**- PO Box 668, 101 S Broadway, Hartington, NE 68739; 402-254-7431. www.co.cedar.ne.us/webpages/assessor/assessor.htm

Chase County

County Clerk, PO Box 1299, Imperial, NE 69033-1299. 308-882-7500; fax-308-882-7552; 8AM-4PM (MST) www.co.chase.ne.us
Index: Separate indices to search include deeds, mortgages, miscellaneous, oil & gas, incorporations, federal and state tax liens. Record index not computerized. Only the public may search. Office will search last deed records, with disclaimer. Copy fee $.25 per page. Cert fee- $1.50 per cert page plus copy fee. Payee- Chase County. **Other phones:** Treasurer- 308-882-7510; Elections- 308-882-7500; Vital Records- 402-471-2871 (state). **Property tax/Assessing**- PO Box 1299, 921 Broadway, Imperial, NE 69033; 308-882-7506, assessor fax- 308-882-7556. www.co.chase.ne.us/assessor.html **Online access**- Access real estate or personal property data free at www.nebraskataxesonline.us/taxcollpage1.aspx?county=Chase.

Cherry County

County Clerk, PO Box 120, Valentine, NE 69201-0120. 402-376-2771; fax-402-376-3095; 8:30AM-N, 1-4:30PM. www.co.cherry.ne.us/
Index: Separate indices to search include deeds, mtgs, misc. Record index not computerized. Only the public may search. Copy fee $.25 per page. Cert fee- $1.75 per page plus copy fee. Payee- Cherry County Clerk. **Other phones:** Treasurer- 402-376-1580; Elections- 402-376-2771; Vitals- 402-471-2871. **Property tax/Assessing**- 365 N Main St, Valentine, NE 69201; 402-376-1630, assessor fax- 402-376-3095. 8:30AM-4:30PM www.co.cherry.ne.us/assessor.html

Cheyenne County

County Clerk, PO Box 217, Sidney, NE 69162-0217. 308-254-2141; fax-308-254-5049; 8AM-5PM (MST) www.co.cheyenne.ne.us
Index: All in one numerical index. Record index not computerized. Only the public may search. Copy fee $1.00 per page mailed; $2.00 per page faxed, prepaid. Cert fee- $1.50 per page includes copy fee. Payee- Cheyenne County Clerk. **Other phones:** Treasurer- 308-254-2733; Elections- 308-254-2141; Vital Records- 308-254-2141. **Property tax/Assessing**- PO Box 217, 1000 10th Ave, Sidney, NE 69162; 308-254-2633. www.co.cheyenne.ne.us/assessor.html

Clay County

County Clerk, PO Box 67, Clay Center, NE 68933-0067. 402-762-3463; fax-402-762-3506; 8:30AM-5PM (CST) www.claycounty.ne.gov
Index: Separate indices to search include deeds, mortgages, misc. Not all other record indexes are computerized. Only the public may search. Will not search UCC records. Copy fee $1.00 per page. Cert fee- $1.50 per page includes copy fee. Payee- County Clerk. **Other phones:** Treasurer- 402-762-3505; Elections- 402-762-3463. **Property tax/Assessing**- 111 W Fairfield St, Clay Center, NE 68933; 402-762-3792, assessor fax- 402-762-3506. www.claycounty.ne.gov/assessor.html

Colfax County

County Clerk, 411 E 11th St, Schuyler, NE 68661. 402-352-8504; fax-402-352-8515; 8:30AM-4:30PM (CST) www.colfaxcounty.ne.gov/clerk.html
Index: Separate indices to search include deeds, Mortgages, miscellaneous. Records indexed on a public use terminal back to 1/2006. Only the public may search. Copy fee $.25 per page; $1.00 per page if mail return, $2.00 by fax. Cert fee- $1.50 per page plus copy fee. Payee- Colfax County Clerk. Bulk data available for purchaseas monthly CDs, $100 per month, contact Lisa. **Other phones:** Treasurer- 402-352-8519; Elections- 402-352-8504; Vital Records- 402-471-2871. **Property tax/Assessing**- 411 E 11th St, Schuyler, NE 68661; 402-352-8500, assessor fax- 402-352-8515. (Appraiser/Auditor- 402-352-8500) www.colfaxcounty.ne.gov/assessor.html **Online access**- Access real estate or personal property data free at www.nebraskataxesonline.us.

Cuming County

County Clerk, PO Box 290, West Point, NE 68788. 402-372-6002; fax-402-372-6013; 8:30AM-4:30PM. www.co.cuming.ne.us
Index: Separate indices to search include deeds, mortgages, miscellaneous, wills, mechanics liens, corporations. Record index not computerized, but documents can be found on public access terminal. Only the public may search. Copy fee $.25 per page. Cert fee- $3.00 per doc plus copy fee. Payee- Cuming Co. Clerk. Index tract book and most county docs available in bulk. **Other phones:** Treasurer- 402-372-6011; Elections- 402-372-6002. **Property tax/Assessing**- 200 S Lincoln St, Rm 101, West Point, NE 68788; 402-372-6000, assessor fax- 402-372-6013. www.co.cuming.ne.us/assessor.html **Online access**- Access real estate or personal property data free at www.nebraskataxesonline.us/taxcollpage1.aspx?county=Cuming.

Custer County

Register of Deeds, 431 S 10th, Broken Bow, NE 68822. 308-872-2221; fax-308-872-6139; 9AM-5PM (CST) www.co.custer.ne.us/content/content/deeds_content
Recording officer is now the Register of Deeds. Index: Separate indices to search. Records indexed on computer. Office personnel or visitors may perform searches. Search fee $3.00 per name. Office will search real estate records. Limited. Office will not search UCC records. Copy fee $.25 per page. Cert fee- $1.50 per page. Payee- Register of Deeds. **Other phones:** Treasurer- 308-872-2921; Elections- 308-872-5701; Vital Records- 308-872-2571. **Property tax/Assessing**- 431 S 10th, Broken Bow, NE 68822; 308-872-2981, assessor fax- 308-872-6139. www.co.custer.ne.us/content/content/assessor_content

Dakota County Clerk

County Clerk, PO Box 39, Dakota City, NE 68731. 402-987-2126, R/E recording phone-402-987-0264; fax-402-494-9234; 8AM-4:30PM (CST) www.dakotacountyne.org

Has marriage records only. Shares fax with treasurer office. Index: All in one back to 1800s. Records indexed on computer back to 2002. Only the public may search. Copy fee $.25 per page. Cert fee- $2.50 per doc includes copy fee. Payee- Dakota County Clerk. **Other phones:** Treasurer- 402-987-2133. **Property tax/Assessing**- 1601 Broadway, Courthouse, Dakota City, NE 68731; 402-987-0264. **Online access**- Access to property search for free go to http://dakota.pat.gisworkshop.com/

Dakota County Register of Deeds

County Register of Deeds, PO Box 511, Dakota City, NE 68731. Recording, R/E phone-402-987-2166, UCC phone-402-987-2126; 8AM-4:30PM (CST)

See county clerk for marriage records. Index: All in one. Records indexed on computer back to 1998. Only title companies may search. Office will not search real estate records. Office will not search UCC records. Copy fee $1.00 per page. Cert fee- $2.50 per cert plus copy fee. Payee- Dakota County Register of Deeds. Data recorded monthly is available for purchase on CD for $110.00. **Other phones:** Treasurer- 402-987-2131; Elections- 402-987-2126; Vital Records- 402-471-2871. **Property tax/Assessing**- PO Box 9, 1601 Broadway, Dakota City, NE 68731; 402-987-0264. **Online** - Access assessor records- http://dakota.pat.gisworkshop.com/.

Dawes County

County Clerk, 451 Main St; Courthouse, Chadron, NE 69337-2698. Recording, R/E & UCC phone-308-432-0100; fax-308-432-5179; 8:30AM-4:30PM (MST) www.co.dawes.ne.us

Index: Separate indices to search include each range has its own index, town has its own index. Record index not computerized. Only the public may search. General copy fee $1.00 per page.Real estate record copy- $.50 per page. Cert fee- $1.50 cert fee plus copy fee. Payee- Dawes County Clerk. **Other phones:** Treasurer- 308-432-0105; Elections- 308-432-0100; Vitals- 308-432-0100. **Property tax/Assessing**- 451 Main St, Chadron, NE 69337; 308-432-0103. www.assessor.dawes.com/ **Online**- Access real estate or personal property data free at www.nebraskataxesonline.us/taxcollpage1.aspx?county=Dawes.

Dawson County Clerk

County Clerk, 700 N Washington St, Rm D, Lexington, NE 68850-0370. 308-324-4271; fax-308-324-6106; 8AM-5PM.

See Register of Deeds for real estate records. Index: All in one. Record index not computerized. Only the public may search. Copy fee $.50 per page. Cert fee- $5.00 per form includes copy fees. Payee- Dawson County Clerk. **Other phones:** Treasurer- 308-324-3241; Elections-308-324-6106; Vitals-308-324-2127.

Dawson County Register of Deeds

County Register of Deeds, 700 N Washington; County Courthouse, Lexington, NE 68850. 308-324-4271; 8AM-N, 1-5PM (CST)

Index: All in one. Records indexed on a public use terminal back to 0699. Will search UCC records. Copy fee $1.00 per page. Cert fee- $1.50 per page includes copy fee. Payee- Dawson County Register of Deeds. **Other phones:** Treasurer- 308-324-3241. **Property tax/Assessing**- 700 N Washington St, Lexington, NE 68850; 308-324-3471, assessor fax- 308-324-5614. (Appraiser/Auditor- 308-324-3471) **Online access**- Access property or personal property data free at www.nebraskataxesonline.us.

Deuel County

County Clerk, PO Box 327, Chappell, NE 69129. 308-874-3308; fax-308-874-3472; 8AM-4PM.

Index: Separate indices to search. Records indexed on a public use terminal back to 2000. Office personnel or visitors may perform searches. Search fee $4.50 per name. Office will not search real estate records. Copy fee $.50 per page. Cert fee- $1.50 1st page, $1.00 each add'l page plus copy fee. Payee- Deuel County Clerk. **Other phones:** Treasurer- 308-874-3307; Elections- 308-874-3308. **Property tax/Assessing**- PO Box 527, 718 3rd St, Chappell, NE 69129; 308-874-2608, assessor fax- 308-874-3472. No public access terminal. www.co.deuel.ne.us/assessor.html

Dixon County

County Clerk, PO Box 546, Ponca, NE 68770-0546. 402-755-5602; fax-402-755-5650; 8AM-4:30PM (CST) www.co.dixon.ne.us/deeds.html

Index: Separate indices to search. Record index not computerized. Office personnel or visitors may perform searches. Office will not search real estate records. Office will not search tax liens. UCC search per debtor name- $4.50. Copy fee $.50 per page. Cert fee- $1.50 per cert plus copy fee. Payee- Dixon County Clerk. **Other phones:** Treasurer- 402-755-5603; Vital Records- 402-471-2871. **Property tax/Assessing**- PO Box 369, 302 3rd St, Ponca, NE 68770; 402-755-5601, assessor fax- 402-755-5650. www.co.dixon.ne.us/assessor.html

Dodge County Clerk

County Clerk, 435 N Park, Rm 102; Courthouse, Fremont, NE 68025-4967. 402-727-2767, R/E recording phone-402-727-2735, UCC recording phone-402-471-4080; fax-402-727-2764; 8:30AM-4:30PM (CST) www.dodgecounty.ne.gov/deeds.html

See Register of Deeds for real estate records. Index: All in one. Records indexed on a public use terminal back to 1997. Only the public may search. Copy fee $1.00 per page. Cert fee- $10.00 per page plus copy fee. **Other phones:** Treasurer- 402-727-2750; Elections- 402-727-2767; Vital Records- 402-471-2871; UCC Searches-County Level- 402-727-2767.

Dodge County Register of Deeds

Register of Deeds, 435 N Park, Rm 201, Fremont, NE 68025. 402-727-2735; fax-402-727-2734; 8:30AM-4:30PM (CST) www.registerofdeeds.com

Index: Separate indices to search include alpha grantor/grantee, legal description. Records indexed on a public use terminal back to 1998. Only the public may search. Office will only lookup specific files. Office will not name search real estate records. Copy fee $1.00 per page. Cert fee- $1.50 per cert includes copy fee. Payee- Dodge County Register of Deeds. **Online access to Real Estate, Deed, Mortgage records:** Access to Register of Deeds mortgages database site is under development. Registration will be required. Also, search legal descriptions lists free at www.registerofdeeds.com/Legal%20Index.htm. **Other phones:** Treasurer- 402-727-2750. **Property tax/Assessing**- 435 N Park Ave, Rm 202, Fremont, 68025; 402-727-3918. www.dodgecounty.ne.gov/assessor.html **Online access**- Access assessor records free at http://dodge.pat.gisworkshop.com/.

Douglas County Clerk

County Clerk, 1819 Farnam St, Rm H08, Omaha, NE 68183-0008. 402-444-6767; fax-402-444-6456; 8AM-4:30PM. www.douglascountyclerk.org/

See Register of Deeds for real estate records. Index: All in one. Records indexed on a public use terminal back to 1990. Office will perform a UCC search but public must search other records themselves. UCC search per debtor name- $5.00. General copy fee $.50 per page off microfilm, $0.00 for computer. Cert fee- $5.00 per copy. Payee- Douglas County Clerk. **Other phones:** Treasurer- 402-444-7103 Info; Elections- 402-444-8683; Treasurer- 402-444-7082. **Property tax/Assessing**- 1819 Farnam St, Rm H04, Omaha/Douglas Civic Ctr, Omaha, NE 68183; 402-444-6387 RE, 444-7060 PP, assessor fax- n/a. (Appraiser/Auditor- n/a) hours- Roger F Morrissey-Assessor www.dcassessor.org/index.php **Online access**- Records on the county Assessor Property Information Search database are free at www.dcassessor.org/disclaimer.php and also. Search property tax online payments database free at http://webapps.dotcomm.org:8080/TreasTax/ but no name searching.

Douglas County Register of Deeds

Register of Deeds, 1819 Farnam, Rm H09, Omaha, NE 68183. 402-444-7194; fax-402-444-6693; 8AM-4:30PM. www.co.douglas.ne.us

Index: All in one. Records indexed on a public use terminal back to 1987. Only the public may search. Copy fee $.75 per page. Cert fee- $1.50 per page includes copy fee. Payee- Register of Deeds. **Online Marriage records:** Search the clerk/comptroller marriage data at www.douglascountyclerk.org/marriage-licenses/marriagelicensesearch. **Other phones:** Treasurer- 402-444-7272; Elections- 402-444-7200; Clerk- 402-444-7147. **Property tax/Assessing**- 1819 Farnam St, Rm H04, Omaha, NE 68183; 402-444-7060, assessor fax- 402-444-6710. Office physically located at 11422 Miracle Hills Dr.; a public access terminal is available. www.dcassessor.org/ **Online access**- Assessor to the county assessor property valuation lookup is free at http://douglasne.mapping-online.com/DouglasCoNe/static/valuation.jsp. Also search the treasurer's property tax data free at http://webapps.dotcomm.org:8080/TreasTax/ but no name searching.

Dundy County

County Clerk, PO Box 506, Benkelman, NE 69021-0506. 308-423-2058, R/E recording phone-402-471-4429 Fax# 402-471-4429; 8AM-4PM (MST)

Index: Separate indices to search include separate books. Record index not computerized. Only the public may search. Copy fee $1.00 per page. Cert fee- $1.50 per cert plus copy fee. Payee- Dundy County Clerk. **Other phones:** Treasurer- 308-423-2346; Vital Records- 402-471-2871. **Property tax/Assessing**- PO Box 487, 102 7th Ave W, Benkelman, NE 69021; 308-423-2821. www.co.dundy.ne.us/assessor.html **Online access**- Access real estate or personal property data free at www.nebraskataxesonline.us/taxcollpage1.aspx?county=Dundy.

Fillmore County

Register of Deeds, PO Box 307, Geneva, NE 68361-0307. Recording, R/E & UCC phone-402-759-4931, UCC recording phone-402-471-4080; fax-402-759-4307; 8AM-4:30PM. www.fillmorecounty.org/

Recording officers are County Clerk (Federal and state tax liens) and Register of Deeds (real estate and most tax liens). Index: All in one. Records indexed on a public use terminal back to 0701/2005. Office personnel (time permitting) or visitors may perform searches. Search fee $4.50 per name. Office will search real estate records. Copy fee $1.00 per page. Cert fee- $1.50 per page includes copy fee. Payee- Fillmore County Clerk. Contact Amy Nelson, Election Commission. **Other phones:** Treasurer- 402-759-3812; Elections- 402-759-4931; Vital Records- 402-471-2871. **Property tax/Assessing**- PO Box 351, 900 G St, Geneva, NE 68361; 402-759-3613, assessor fax- 402-759-3415. www.fillmorecounty.org/webpages/assessor/assessor.htm **Online access**- Access to GIS/mapping for free go to http://fillmore.assessor.gisworkshop.com/

Franklin County

County Clerk, PO Box 146, Franklin, NE 68939. 308-425-6202; fax-308-425-6093; 8:30AM-4:30PM (CST) http://co.franklin.ne.us

Index: Separate indices to search include alphabetical, numerical. Record index not computerized. Only the public may search. Copy fee $1.00 per page. Cert fee- $1.50 per page for Real Estate records. Payee- Franklin County Clerk. **Other phones:** Treasurer- 308-425-6265; Elections- 308-425-6202. **Property tax/Assessing**- PO Box 183, 405 15th Ave, Franklin, NE 68939; 308-425-6229, assessor fax- 308-425-6319. www.co.franklin.ne.us/assessor.html

Frontier County

County Clerk, PO Box 40, Stockville, NE 69042-0040. 308-367-8641; fax-308-367-8730; 8:30AM-N, 1-5PM (CST) www.co.frontier.ne.us
Index: All in one. Records indexed on computer from 7/1/06 to present. Office personnel or visitors may perform searches. Real estate owner, mortgage, and property transfer searches available. Tax liens not included in UCC search. UCC search per debtor name- $4.50. Copy fee $1.00 per page. Cert fee- Certified copies $5.00. Payee- Frontier County Register of Deeds. **Other phones:** Treasurer- 308-367-8631; Elections- 308-367-8641; Vital Records- 308-367-8641. **Property tax/Assessing-** PO Box 9, #1 Wellington St, Stockville, NE 69042; 308-367-8637. (Appraiser/Auditor- 308-367-8637) www.co.frontier.ne.us/assessor.html **Online access-** Access to basic property assessor data is available free at http://frontier.gisworkshop.com. A subscription is required for full data including sales, photos, history, buildings for $200 per year. Also, access real estate or personal property data free at www.nebraskataxesonline.us/taxcollpage1.aspx?county=Frontier.

Furnas County

County Clerk, PO Box 387, Beaver City, NE 68926. 308-268-4145; fax-308-268-3205; 8AM-4PM (CST)
Index: All in one. Record index not computerized. Only the public may search. Copy fee $.25 per page. Cert fee- $1.50 per cert plus copy fee. Payee- Furnas County Clerk. **Other phones:** Treasurer- 308-268-2195; Elections- 308-268-4145; Vital Records- 402-471-2871. **Property tax/Assessing-** PO Box 368, 912 R St, Beaver City, NE 68926; 308-268-3145.

Gage County Clerk

County Clerk, PO Box 429, Beatrice, NE 68310-0429. 402-223-1300, R/E phone-402-223-1361; fax-402-223-1371; 8-5PM. www.co.gage.ne.us/clerk.html
See Register of Deeds for real estate records. Index: All in one. Records indexed on a public use terminal back to 1997. Only the public may search on computer. Office will not search UCC records. General copy fee-$.50 per page, $1.00 if mailed. Certified marriage certificate- $5.00.Payee- Gage County Clerk. **Other phones:** Treasurer- 402-223-1315; Elections- 402-223-1300; Marriage Licenses- 402-223-1300. **Property tax/Assessing-** 612 Grant St, Rm 8, Beatrice, 68310; 402-223-1308, assessor fax- 402-228-2694. www.co.gage.ne.us/assessor.html **Online access-** Access assessor property data free at http://gage.assessor.gisworkshop.com/.

Gage County Register of Deeds

Register of Deeds, PO Box 337, Beatrice, NE 68310. 402-223-1361; fax-n/a; 8AM-4:30PM (CST)
Index: All in one. Records indexed on a public use terminal back to 1997. Office will not search real estate records. Will not search UCC records. UCC search per debtor name- $4.50. Copy fee $.50 per page plus $1.00 for postage & handling when mailed. Cert fee- $1.50 per page plus copy fee. Payee- Gage County Register of Deeds. **Other phones:** Treasurer- 402-223-1315. **Property tax/Assessing-** 612 Grant St, Beatrice, NE 68310; 402-223-1308, assessor fax- 402-228-2694. www.co.gage.ne.us/assessor.html **Online access-** Access real estate or personal property data free at www.nebraskataxesonline.us/taxcollpage1.aspx?county=Gage. Also, access property data via the county Assessor GIS service free at http://gage.assessor.gisworkshop.com/

Garden County

County Clerk, PO Box 486, Oshkosh, NE 69154. Recording, R/E & UCC phone-308-772-3924; fax-308-772-0124; 8AM-4PM (MST)
Index: Separate indices to search include deeds, mortgages, misc, or legal descriptions. Record index not computerized. Office will perform a UCC search but public must search other records themselves. Search fee-$5.00 per name. Copy fee $.50 per page. Cert fee- $1.50 1st page plus copy fee. Payee- County Clerk. **Other phones:** Treasurer- 308-772-3622; Elections- 308-772-3924; Vital Records- 402-471-2871. **Property tax/Assessing-** PO Box 468, 611 Main St, Oshkosh, NE 69154; 308-772-4464. www.co.garden.ne.us/assessor.html

Garfield County

County Clerk, PO Box 218, Burwell, NE 68823. 308-346-4161; 9AM-N, 1-5PM (CST)
Index: Separate indices to search. Record index not computerized. Office personnel or visitors may perform searches. Search fee $4.50 per name. Office will search real estate records. Copy fee $1.00 per page. Cert fee- $1.50 per cert plus copy fee. Payee- Garfield County Clerk. **Other phones:** Treasurer- 308-346-4125; Elections- 308-346-4161. **Property tax/Assessing-** PO Box 411, 250 S 8th St, Burwell, NE 68823; 308-346-4045, assessor fax- 308-346-5536. (Appraiser/Auditor- 308-346-4542) hours- 8AM-5PM www.garfieldcounty.ne.gov/assessor.html **Online access-** Access parcel records free at http://garfield.pat.gisworkshop.com/.

Gosper County

County Clerk, PO Box 136, Elwood, NE 68937-0136. Recording, R/E & UCC phone-308-785-2611; fax-308-785-2300; 8:30AM-4:30PM (CST) www.co.gosper.ne.us
Index: Separate indices to search include deeds, mortgages & misc. Court records indexed on a public use terminal back to 1997. Office personnel or visitors may perform searches. Office will not search real estate records. UCC search includes tax liens if requested. UCC search per debtor name- $4.50. Combined federal/state combined tax lien search- $3.00 per debtor. Copy fee $.25 per 8 1/2 x 11 page, $.50 per 8 1/2 x 14 page. Fax fees are $2.00 per page. Cert fee- $1.00 per doc plus copy fee. Payee- Gosper County Clerk. **Other phones:** Treasurer- 308-785-2450; Elections- 308-785-2611; Vital Records- 308-785-2611 (Marriage and Probate). **Property tax/Assessing-** PO Box 52, 507 Smith Ave, Elwood, NE 68937; 308-785-2250, assessor fax- 308-785-2300. (Appraiser/Auditor- 308-785-2250) www.co.gosper.ne.us/webpages/assessor/assessor.htm

Grant County

County Clerk, PO Box 139, Hyannis, NE 69350-0139. Recording, R/E & UCC phone-308-458-2488; fax-308-458-2780; 8AM-4PM (MST)
Index: All in one. Record index not computerized. Office personnel or visitors may perform searches. Search fee- $1.00 per name. Office will search real estate records. Office will not search UCC records. Copy fee $.50 per page. Cert fee- $1.50 per instrument plus copy fee. Payee- Grant County Clerk. Whatever you want we will try to give it to you and it will be $0.50 per copy. **Other phones:** Treasurer- 308-458-2422; Elections- 308-458-2488; Vital Records- 308-458-2488; Marriages -308-458-2488. **Property tax/Assessing-** PO Box 139, Hyannis, NE 69350-0139; 308-458-2488, assessor fax- 308-458-2780. (Appraiser - 308-762-2474);

Greeley County

County Clerk, PO Box 287, Greeley, NE 68842. 308-428-3625; fax-308-428-3022; 8AM-4PM. http://greeleycounty.nol.org
Index: All in one. Records indexed on a public use terminal back to 1990. Office personnel or visitors may perform searches. Office will search real estate records. General copy fee $.25 per page, mailed is $1.50. Cert fee- $5.00 per page plus copy fee. Payee- Greeley County Recorder. **Other phones:** Treasurer- 308-428-3535; Elections- 402-428-3625; Vital Records- 402-471-2871. **Property tax/Assessing-** PO Box 247, 28th & Kildare, Greeley, NE 68842; 308-428-5310, assessor fax- 308-428-5020. **Online access-** Access real estate or personal property data free at www.nebraskataxesonline.us/taxcollpage1.aspx?county=Greeley also access parcel records free at http://greeley.pat.gisworkshop.com/.

Hall County Clerk

County Clerk, 121 S Pine, Grand Island, NE 68801. 308-385-5080, R/E recording phone-308-385-5040, 8:30AM-5PM. www.hcgi.org
Index: All in one. Record index not computerized. There is a map program. Office will perform a UCC search but public must search other records themselves. Search fee $4.50. Copy fee $3.50 per name. Cert fee- $1.50 per page plus copy fee. Payee- Hall County Clerk. **Online access to Real Estate, Grantor/Grantee, Deed records:** Access register of deeds real estate data free at http://deeds.hallcountyne.gov/fSearch.aspx. **Other phones:** Treasurer- 308-385-5025; Elections- 308-385-5085; Vital Records- 402-471-2871.

Hall County Register of Deeds

Register of Deeds, PO Box 1692, Grand Island, NE 68802-1692. 308-385-5040; fax-308-385-5107; 8:30AM-5PM (CST) www.hallcountyne.gov/
Index: All in one. Records indexed on a public use terminal back to 1989. Only the public may search. Copy fee $.20 per page self serve; $2.00 each if mailed back. Fee to fax doc- $1.00 per page. Computer printouts- $1.00 per page. Cert fee- $1.50 per page includes copy fee. Payee- Hall County Register of Deeds. **Online access to Real Estate, Grantor/Grantee, Deed, Lien, Judgment records:** Access to the county Register of Deeds Document Search is free at http://deeds.hallcountyne.gov. **Other phones:** Treasurer- 308-385-5025. **Property tax/Assessing-** 121 S Pine St, Grand Island, NE 68801; 308-385-5050, assessor fax- 308-385-5059. **Online access-** Access property data free at http://gis.grand-island.com/mapsifter/landinfofront/. Also, access parcels and sales free at http://gis.grand-island.com/taxsifter/T-Parcelsearch.asp.

Hamilton County

County Clerk/Register of Deeds, 1111 13th St, #1; Courthouse, Aurora, NE 68818-2017. Recording, R/E phone-402-694-3443, UCC recording phone-402-471-2554; fax-402-694-2396; hours- 8AM-5PM. www.co.hamilton.ne.us
Index: Separate indices to search include federal and state tax liens. Records indexed on computer back to July, 2004. Office will perform a UCC search but public must search other records themselves. Copy fee $.25 per page. Cert fee- $1.50 plus $1.50 per page includes copy fee. Payee- Hamilton Co. Clerk. **Other phones:** Treasurer- 402-694-2291; Elections- 402-694-3443; Vital Records- 402-471-2871. **Property tax/Assessing-** 1111 13th St, #5, Aurora, NE 68818; 402-694-2757, assessor fax- 402-694-3755. www.co.hamilton.ne.us/assessor.html **Online access-** Access real estate or personal property data free at www.nebraskataxesonline.us. Also, access parcel records free at http://hamilton.gisworkshop.com/.

Harlan County

County Clerk, PO Box 698, Alma, NE 68920-0698. 308-928-2173; fax-308-928-2079; 8:30-4:30 (CST)
Index: Separate indices to search include numerical index (legal description), general index (name). Record index not computerized. Only the public may search. Copy fee $.25 per page. Cert fee- $1.00 1st pg; $.25 each add'l page plus copy fee. Payee- Harlan County Clerk. **Other phones:** Treasurer- 308-928-2171; Elections- 308-928-2173; Vital Records- 402-471-2871. **Property tax/Assessing-** PO Box 758, 706 W 2nd St, Alma, NE 68920; 308-928-2177, assessor fax- 308-928-9943. (Appraiser - 308-928-2178) hours- 7:30AM-4:30PM A public access terminal is available. http://harlan.pat.gisworkshop.com **Online access-** Access parcel records free at http://harlan.pat.gisworkshop.com/.

Hayes County

County Clerk, PO Box 370, Hayes Center, NE 69032-0370. 308-286-3413; 8AM-4PM (CST) www.hayescounty.ne.gov/index_html?page=content/clerk.html
The County Clerk is the ex officio Register of Deeds. Index: Separate indices to search include real estate,

mortgage, liens, deeds, misc. Record index not computerized. Office personnel or visitors may perform searches. Search fee $4.50 per name. Copy fee $1.00 per page. Cert fee- $4.00 per cert includes copy fee. Payee- Hayes County Clerk. **Other phones:** Treasurer- 308-286-3214. **Property tax/Assessing-** PO Box 370, Hayes Center, NE 69032; 308-286-3413, assessor fax- 308-286-3208.

Hitchcock County

County Clerk, PO Box 248, Trenton, NE 69044. 308-334-5646; fax-308-334-5398; 8:30AM-4PM (CST) www.co.hitchcock.ne.us

Index: Separate indices to search include deeds, mtg, misc. Office will perform a UCC search but public must search other records themselves. Copy fee $.50 per page. Cert fee- $1.50 per page includes copy fee. Payee- Hitchcock County Clerk. **Other phones:** Treasurer- 308-334-5544; Elections- 308-334-5646; Vital Records- 308-334-5646- Marriage Only. **Property tax/Assessing-** PO Box 446, 229 East D St, Trenton, NE 69044; 308-334-5219, assessor fax- 308-334-5784. (Appraiser/Auditor- 308-334-5219) hours- 8AM-5PM www.co.hitchcock.ne.us/assessor.html **Online-** Access real estate or personal property data free at www.nebraskataxesonline.us and also access parcel records free at http://hitchcock.pat.gisworkshop.com/.

Holt County

County Clerk, PO Box 329, O'Neill, NE 68763-0329. 402-336-2250; fax-402-336-1762; 8AM-4:30PM.

Index: Separate indices to search include section-township-range and cities and villages. Record index not computerized. Office will perform a UCC search but public must search other records themselves. Copy fee $.25 per page. Cert fee- $1.50 per page plus copy fee. Payee- Register of Deeds. **Other phones:** Treasurer- 402-336-1291; Elections- 402-336-1762. **Property tax/Assessing-** PO Box 487, 204 N 4th St, O'Neill, NE 68763; 402-336-1624, assessor fax- 402-336-1624. www.co.holt.ne.us/assessor.html

Hooker County

County Clerk, PO Box 184, Mullen, NE 69152. Recording, R/E & UCC phone-308-546-2244; fax-308-546-2490; 8:30AM-N, 1PM-4:30PM (MST)

Index: Separate indices to search include misc, deed, mtg. Record index not computerized. Only the public may search. Copy fee $1.00 per page. Cert fee- $10.00 per page plus copy fee. Payee- Hooker County Clerk. **Other phones:** Treasurer- 308-546-2245; Elections- 308-546-2244; Vital Records- 308-546-2244. **Property tax/Assessing-** PO Box 184, 303 NW 1st St, Mullen, 69152; 308-546-2244, fax- 308-546-2490. www.co.hooker.ne.us/assessor.html

Howard County

County Clerk, PO Box 25, St. Paul, NE 68873. 308-754-4343; fax-308-754-4125; 8AM-5PM (CST)

Index: All in one. Record index not computerized. Only the public may search. Copy fee $.25 per page. Cert fee- $5.00 per cert includes copy fee. Payee- Howard County Clerk. Treasurer- 308-754-4852; Elections- 308-754-4343. **Property tax/Assessing-** 612 Indian St, #10, St. Paul, NE 68873; 308-754-4261, fax- 308-754-4125. A public access terminal is available. www.howardcounty.ne.gov/assessor.html

Jefferson County

County Clerk, 411 4th St; Courthouse, Fairbury, NE 68352-1619. Recording, R/E phone-402-729-6819, UCC phone-402-471-2554; fax-402-729-6806; 9AM-N, 1-5PM (CST) www.co.jefferson.ne.us/clerk.html

Recording officers are County Clerk (some state tax liens) and Register of Deeds (real estate and most tax liens). Index: Separate indices to search include deeds, mortgage, misc., also numerical by description. Records indexed on a public use terminal back 1 1/2 years. Office will do name lookups, but cannot guarantee searches. Office will search real estate records. Office will search UCC records. Copy fee $.50 per page. Cert fee- $1.50 per page plus copy fee. Payee- County Register of Deeds. **Other phones:** Treasurer- 402-729-6827; Elections- 402-729-6818; Vitals- 402-471-2872. **Property tax/Assessing-** 411 4th St, Fairbury, NE 68352; 402-729-6835, assessor fax- 402-729-6834. hours- 8AM-5PM www.co.jefferson.ne.us/assessor.html **Online-** Access real estate or personal property data free at www.nebraskataxesonline.us/taxcollpage1.aspx?county=Jefferso.

Johnson County

County Clerk, PO Box 416, Tecumseh, NE 68450. Recording, R/E & UCC phone-402-335-6300; fax-402-335-6311; 8AM-12:30PM, 1PM-4:30PM (CST) www.co.johnson.ne.us/clerk.html

Index: All in one. Record index not computerized. Office will perform a UCC search but public must search other records themselves. Copy fee $1.00 per page. Cert fee- $1.50 per page includes copy fee. Payee- Johnson County Clerk. **Other phones:** Treasurer- 402-335-6310; Elections- 402-335-6300. **Property tax/Assessing-** PO Box 356, 301 Broadway, Tecumseh, NE 68450; 402-335-6303. www.co.johnson.ne.us/assessor.html **Online access-** Access property data free at http://johnsonne.taxsifter.com/taxsifter/disclaimer.asp. Also, access parcel or personal property data free at www.nebraskataxesonline.us/taxcollpage1.aspx?county=Johnson.

Kearney County

County Clerk, PO Box 339, Minden, NE 68959-0339. 308-832-2723; fax-308-832-2729; 8:30AM-5PM. www.kearneycounty.ne.gov/index_html?page=content/clerk.html

Index: All in one. Record index not computerized. Only the public may search. Copy fee $.50 per page; fax copy $1.50 per page. Cert fee- $3.00 per cert plus copy fee. Payee- Kearney County Clerk. **Other phones:** Treasurer- 308-832-2730. **Property tax/Assessing-** PO Box 207, 424 N Colorado Ave, Minden, NE 68959; 308-832-2625, assessor fax- 308-832-2645. www.kearneycounty.ne.gov/ **Online access-** Access property data and parcel records free at http://kearney.gisworkshop.com/KearneyIMS/ or at http://kearney.gisworkshop.com/

Keith County

County Clerk, 511 N Spruce, #102, Ogallala, NE 69153. 308-284-4726; fax-308-284-6277; 8AM-4PM. www.keithcountyne.gov

Records indexed on a public use terminal back to 2005. Only the public may search. Tax liens are searched no charge. Copy fee $.50 per page. Cert fee- $1.50 per page. Payee- Keith County Clerk. **Other phones:** Treasurer- 308-284-3231; Elections- 308-284-4726. **Property tax/Assessing-** 511 N Spruce, #200, Ogallala, NE 69153; 308-284-8045, assessor fax- 308-284-8047. www.co.keith.ne.us/assessor.html **Online access-** Access real estate or personal property data free at www.nebraskataxesonline.us/taxcollpage1.aspx?county=Keith and also access parcel records free at http://keith.pat.gisworkshop.com/.

Keya Paha County

County Clerk, PO Box 349, Springview, NE 68778. phone-402-497-3791; fax-402-497-3799; 8AM-N,1-5PM (CST) www.co.keya-paha.ne.us/

Index: Separate indices to search include deeds, mortgages, miscellaneous, District Court index. Office personnel or visitors may perform searches. Search fee $4.00 per name. Copy fee $.25 per page. Cert fee- $4.00 per cert includes copy fee. Payee- Keya Paha County Clerk. **Other phones:** Treasurer- 402-497-3891; Elections- 402-497-3791. **Property tax/Assessing-** PO Box 349, 310 Courthouse Dr, Springview; 402-497-3791, assessor fax- 402-497-3799. www.co.keya-paha.ne.us/assessor.html

Kimball County

County Clerk, 114 E 3rd St, Ste 6, Kimball, NE 69145-1296. 308-235-2241; fax-308-235-3654; 8AM-5PM M-Th, 8AM-4PM F. (MST) www.co.kimball.ne.us

Index: Separate indices to search include numerical and alphabetical. Record index not computerized. Office will perform a UCC search but public must search other records themselves. Search fee $4.50. Office will not search real estate records. Copy fee $1.00 per page. Cert fee- $1.50 per page plus copy fee. Payee- Kimball County Clerk. **Other phones:** Treasurer- 308-235-2242; Elections- 308-235-2241; Vitals- 402-471-2871. **Property tax/Assessing-** 114 E 3rd St, Kimball, NE 69145; 308-235-2362, assessor fax- 308-235-2362. www.co.kimball.ne.us/content/assessor_content **Online access-** Access real estate or personal property data free at www.nebraskataxesonline.us/taxcollpage1.aspx?county=Kimball.

Knox County Clerk

County Clerk, PO Box 166, Center, NE 68724-0166. 402-288-5604, R/E recording phone-402-288-5613, UCC recording phone-402-288-5604; fax-402-288-5605; 8:30AM-4:30PM. www.co.knox.ne.us

Index: All in one. Records indexed on computer back to 2004, but not available to public. Only the public may search. Will not search UCC records. Copy fee $1.00 per page. Cert fee- $.50 per page plus copy fee. Payee- Knox County Register of Deeds. **Other phones:** Treasurer- 402-288-5615; Elections- 402-288-5604. **Property tax/Assessing-** PO Box 87, Center, NE 68724-0087; 402-288-5601, assessor fax- 402-288-5602. (Appraiser/Auditor- 402-288-5601) www.co.knox.ne.us/assessor.html

Lancaster County Clerk

County Clerk, 555 S 10th St; County-City Bldg, Lincoln, NE 68508-2867. 402-441-7482, R/E recording phone-402-441-7577; fax-402-441-8728; 7:30-4:30PM (CST) http://interlinc.ci.lincoln.ne.us

See Register of Deeds for real estate records. Index: Separate indices to search include books by year. Record index not computerized. Only the public may search. Copy fee- $1.00 per page. Cert fee- $1.50 per cert plus copy fee. Payee- Lancaster County Clerk. **Online Marriage, Building Permit records:** Search Lincoln Document Management records site free at www.lincoln.ne.gov/asp/city/clerk/docman.asp. See also Register of Deeds. Search county marriages at www.lincoln.ne.gov/cnty/clerk/marrsrch.htm; building permits- www.lincoln.ne.gov/city/build/bldgsrv/permits.htm. **Other phones:** Treasurer- 402-441-7425; Elections- 402-441-7311; Vital Records- 402-471-2872. **Property tax/Assessing-** PO Box 45, 555 S 10th St, Rm 102, Lincoln, NE 68508; 402-441-7463, fax- 402-441-8759. (Appraiser/Auditor- 402-441-7463) www.lincoln.ne.gov/cnty/assess/index.htm **Online access-** Access parcel records at http://orion.lancaster.ne.gov/Appraisal/PublicAccess/. Also, search treasurer' property info at www.lincoln.ne.gov/cnty/treas/property.htm.

Lancaster County Register of Deeds

Register of Deeds, 555 S 10th St, Lincoln, NE 68508. 402-441-7577; fax-402-441-7012; 7:30AM-4:30PM. http://deeds.lincoln.ne.gov/recorder/web/login.jsp

Index: All in one. Records indexed on a public use terminal back to 1867. Only the public may search. Copy fee $1.00 per page; $2.00 per page if clerk returns by mail. Cert fee- $1.50 per page. Payee- Register of Deeds. **Online access to Real Estate, Deed, Grantor/Grantee, Lien, Judgment records:** Search register of deeds Grantor/Grantee index free at http://deeds.lincoln.ne.gov/recorder/web/login.jsp. Use Public Login or you may register. See also County Clerk for other databases online. Treasurer- 402-441-7425; Vital Records- 402-441-2871.

Lincoln County Clerk

County Clerk, 301 N Jeffers, Rm 101, North Platte, NE 69101. 308-534-4350; fax-308-535-3522; 9AM-5PM (CST) www.co.lincoln.ne.us
See Register of Deeds for real estate records. Index: Separate indices to search include marriages, corps, misc., election, by department. Record index not computerized. Only the office personnel may search. Search fee-$4.50 per name. Copy fee $.50 per page. Cert fee- $5.00 per page plus copy fee. Payee- Lincoln County Clerk. Treasurer- 308-534-4350; Elections-308-534-4350. **Property tax/Assessing-** 301 N Jeffers Rm 110A, North Platte, 69101; 308-534-4350.

Lincoln County Register of Deeds

Register of Deeds, 301 N Jeffers, Rm 103, North Platte, NE 69101-3931. 308-534-4350, R/E recording phone-308-534-4350 x 192; fax-308-535-3524; 9AM-5PM. www.co.lincoln.ne.us/
Index: Separate indices to search include grantor/grantee, Deeds, Mtgs, Misc, numerical index. Records indexed on a public use terminal back to 2000. Office will perform a UCC search but public must search other records themselves. Copy fee $.25 per page;if mailed, $1.00 1st page, $.25 each add'l; if faxed, $2.00 1st page, $1.00 each add'l. UCC copy fee- $.50 per page. Cert fee- $1.50 per page includes copy fee. Payee- Lincoln County Register of Deeds. Treasurer- 308-534-4350. **Property tax/Assessing-** 301 N Jeffers, Rm 110A, North Platte, NE 69101; 308-534-4350. www.co.lincoln.ne.us/assessor.html **Online** - Access real estate or personal property data free at www.nebraskataxesonline.us/taxcollpage1.aspx?county=Lincoln.

Logan County

County Clerk, PO Box 8, Stapleton, NE 69163. 308-636-2311; fax-308-636-2333; 8:30AM-4:30PM M,T,W,Th; 8:30AM-4PM F. (CST)
Index: Separate indices to search include books by year. Record index not computerized. Office personnel or visitors may perform searches. Search fee $4.50 per name. Office will not search real estate or UCC records. Copy fee $.25 per page. Cert fee-$1.50 per cert plus copy fee. Payee- Logan County Clerk. **Other phones:** Treasurer- 308-636-2441. **Property tax/Assessing-** PO Box 8, 317 Main St, Stapleton, NE 69163; 308-636-2311.

Loup County

County Clerk, PO Box 187, Taylor, NE 68879-0187. 308-942-3135; fax-308-942-6015; 8:30AM-N, 1-5PM M,T,W,Th; 8:30AM-N Fri. (CST)
Index: Separate indices. Record index not computerized. Office personnel or visitors may perform searches. Search fee $4.00 per name. Office will not search real estate records. Copy fee $.50 per page. Cert fee- $1.00 per page. Payee- Loup County Clerk. **Other phones:** Treasurer- 308-942-3115. **Property tax/Assessing-** PO Box 187, 408 4th St, Taylor, NE 68879; 308-942-3135, assessor fax- 308-942-3103. www.co.loup.ne.us/assessor.html

Madison County Clerk

County Clerk, PO Box 290, Madison, NE 68748-0290. 402-454-3311 x137, R/E recording phone-402-454-3311 x124, UCC recording phone-402-454-3311 x136; fax-402-454-6682; hours- 8:30AM-5PM. http://co.madison.ne.us/clerk.htm
See Register of Deeds for real estate records. Index: All in one. Records indexed on computer. No public access terminal available. Only office personnel may search. Search fee $4.50 per name. Office will search UCC records via the SOS office. Copy fee $.25 per page. Cert fee- $1.50 per page. Payee- County Clerk. **Other phones:** Treasurer- 402-454-3311 x133; Elections- 402-454-3311 x136; Vital Records- 402-471-2871. **Property tax/Assessing-** PO Box 250, Madison, NE 68748; 402-454-3311 x179, http://co.madison.ne.us/assessor.htm **Online access-** Access county taxes online free at www.nebraskataxesonline.us/taxcollpage1.aspx?county=Madison.

Madison County Register of Deeds

Register of Deeds, PO Box 229, Madison, NE 68748. 402-454-3311, R/E recording phone-402-454-3311 x124; fax-402-454-6682; 8:30AM-5PM (CST)
Index: All in one. Records indexed on computer back to April 1, 2004. Only the public may search. Copy fee $.50 per page if mailed, $.25 per page in office. Cert fee- $1.50 per page includes copy fee. Payee-Madison County Register of Deeds. Bulk data available for purchase on CD with images. **Other phones:** Treasurer- 402-454-3311 x133; Elections-402-454-3311 x136; Vital Records- 402-471-2871. **Property tax/Assessing-** PO Box 250, 1313 N Main St, Madison, NE 68748; 402-454-3311 x178, assessor fax- 402-454-2441. (Appraiser/Auditor- 402-454-3311) http://co.madison.ne.us/assessor.htm **Online access-** Access real estate or personal property data free at www.nebraskataxesonline.us and also access assessor records at http://madison.gisworkshop.com/.

McPherson County

County Clerk, PO Box 122, Tryon, NE 69167-0122. 308-587-2363; fax-308-587-2363; 8:30AM-4:30PM (CST)
Index: Separate indices to search include mortgages, deeds or misc. Record index not computerized. Only the public may search. Copy fee $.50 per page. Cert fee- $1.50 per page plus copy fee. Payee- McPherson County Clerk. **Other phones:** Treasurer- 308-587-2442; Elections- 308-587-2363. **Property tax/Assessing-** PO Box 122, 500 Anderson St, Tryon, NE 69167; 308-587-2363, assessor fax- 308-587-2363. hours- 8:30AM-N, 1PM-4:30PM

Merrick County

County Clerk, PO Box 27, Central City, NE 68826. Recording, R/E & UCC phone-308-946-2881, UCC recording phone-The Secretary of State; fax-308-946-2332; 8AM-5PM (CST)
Index: Separate indices to search include deeds, mortgages, miscellaneous, liens, associations. Record index not computerized. Office will perform a pre-1999 UCC search but public must search other records themselves. General search fee $2.00 per name. Office will not search real estate records. UCC search per debtor name- $4.50 per page (includes copy fee). Copy fee $.50 per page. Cert fee- $5.00 per cert includes copy fee. Payee- Merrick County Clerk. **Other phones:** Treasurer- 308-946-2171; Elections-308-946-2881; Vitals- 402-471-2871. **Property tax/Assessing-** PO Box 27, 1510 18th St, Central City, NE 68826; 308-946-2443, fax- 308-946-2332. (Appraiser- do not have on staff; call Assessor's Office) www.merrickcounty.ne.gov/assessor.html

Morrill County

County Clerk, PO Box 610, Bridgeport, NE 69336. 308-262-0860; fax-308-262-1469; 8AM-4:30PM (MST) www.morrillcounty.ne.gov
Only the public may search. Copy fee $.50 per page in office; $1.00 per page mailed or faxed. Cert fee-$1.50per page. Payee- Morrill County Clerk. **Other phones:** Treasurer- 308-262-1177; Elections- 308-262-0860. **Property tax/Assessing-** PO Box 868, 6th & Main, Bridgeport, 69336; 308-262-1534, fax- 308-262-1469. www.morrillcounty.ne.gov/assessor.html

Nance County

County Clerk, PO Box 338, Fullerton, NE 68638. 308-536-2331; fax-308-536-2742; 8AM-5PM (CST)
Record index not computerized. Office will perform a UCC search but public must search other records themselves. Search fee $5.00 per name. Office will not search real estate records. Copy fee $1.00 per page. Cert fee- $1.50 per page. Payee- County Clerk. **Other phones:** Treasurer- 308-536-2165; Elections-308-536-2331. **Property tax/Assessing-** PO Box 338, 209 Esther St, Fullerton, NE 68638; 308-536-2653, assessor fax- 308-536-2653. hours- 8:30AM-4:30PM www.co.nance.ne.us/webpages/assessor/assessor.htm **Online access-** Access tax data free at www.nebraskataxesonline.us/

Nemaha County

County Clerk, 1824 N St, #201; Courthouse, Auburn, NE 68305-2399. Recording, R/E & UCC phone-402-274-4213; fax-402-274-4389; 8AM-5PM (CST) www.nemahacounty.ne.gov
Index: Separate indices to search. Records indexed on computer. Office will perform a UCC search but public must search other records themselves. Search fee-$4.50 per name. Copy fee $.25 per page. Cert fee-$1.50 per page plus copy fee. Payee- Nemaha County Clerk. **Other phones:** Treasurer- 402-274-3319; Elections- 402-274-4213. **Property tax/Assessing-** 1824 N St, Ste 205, Auburn, NE 68305; 402-274-3820, assessor fax- 402-274-4389. www.nemahacounty.ne.gov/assessor.html **Online-** Access real estate or personal property data free at www.nebraskataxesonline.us/taxcollpage1.aspx?county=Nemaha.

Nuckolls County

County Clerk, PO Box 366, Nelson, NE 68961-0366. 402-225-4361; fax-402-225-4301; 8:30AM-4:30PM. www.nuckollscounty.ne.gov
Index: Separate indices to search include deed, mortgage, misc, liens, veteran records. Record index not computerized. Office personnel or visitors may perform searches. General search fee- call for information. Office will search real estate records as time allows. Will search UCC records. Copy fee $1.00 per page.Real estate record copy- $.25 per page. If mailed $.75 for 1st page; $.25 each add'l page. Cert fee- $1.50 per page plus copy fee. UCC certification fee is $10.00 plus copy fee. Payee- Nuckolls County Clerk. **Other phones:** Treasurer- 402-225-4351; Elections- 402-225-4361; Vital Records- 402-225-4361. **Property tax/Assessing-** PO Box 371, 150 S Main, Nelson, 68961-0371; 402-225-2401, fax- 402-225-4301. www.nuckollscounty.ne.gov/assessor.html

Otoe County Clerk

County Clerk, PO Box 249, Nebraska City, NE 68410. 402-873-9505, R/E recording phone-402-873-9530; fax-402-873-9506; 8AM-5PM (CST) www.co.otoe.ne.us/clerk.html
Has marriage records only. Record index not computerized. Only the public may search. Will not search UCC records. Copy fee $1.00 per doc. Cert fee- $5.00 per doc (marriage records) includes copy fee. All other copies are $0.25 per page. Payee- Otoe County Clerk. **Other phones:** Treasurer- 402-873-9510; Elections- 402-873-9501. **Property tax/Assessing-** 1021 Central Ave, Rm 105, Nebraska City, NE 68410; 402-873-9520.

Otoe County Register of Deeds

Register of Deeds, 1021 Central Ave, Rm 203, Nebraska City, NE 68410. Recording, R/E & UCC phone-402-873-9530, UCC recording phone-402-873-9505; fax-402-873-9507; 8AM-4:30PM (CST) www.co.otoe.ne.us/deeds.html
See county clerk for marriage records. Index: Separate indices to search include records prior to 5/2002 in index books, deed books, and mortgage books. Records indexed on a public use terminal back to 5/02. Only the public may search. Copy fee $.50 per page. Cert fee- $1.50 per page includes copy fee. Payee- Otoe County Register of Deeds. **Other phones:** Treasurer- 402-873-9510; Elections- 402-873-9505; Vital Records- 402-471-2872. **Property tax/Assessing-** 1021 Central Ave, Rm 104, Nebraska City, NE 68410; 402-873-9520, assessor fax- 402-873-9523. (Appraiser/Auditor- 402-873-9522) www.co.otoe.ne.us/assessor.html **Online-** Access real estate or personal property data free at www.nebraskataxesonline.us/taxcollpage1.aspx?county=Otoe.

Pawnee County

County Clerk, PO Box 431, Pawnee City, NE 68420. 402-852-2962; fax-402-852-2963; 8AM-4PM (CST)
Index: Separate indices to search include alphabetical and numerical. Records indexed on a public use terminal back to 1/2005. Only the public may search. Copy fee $.25 per page. Marriage license copy- $5.00. Cert fee- $1.00 per cert plus copy fee. Payee- Pawnee

County Clerk. **Other phones:** Treasurer- 402-852-2380. **Property tax/Assessing**- PO Box 467, 625 6th St, Pawnee City, NE 68420; 402-852-2292, fax- 402-852-2298. www.co.pawnee.ne.us/assessor.html#Top **Online** - real estate or personal property data free at www.nebraskataxesonline.us/taxcollpage1.aspx?county=Pawnee.

Perkins County

County Clerk, PO Box 156, Grant, NE 69140-0156. Recording, R/E & UCC phone-308-352-4643; fax-308-352-2455; 8AM-4PM (MST)
Index: All in one. Records indexed on computer. Only the public may search. Office will search if you provide case number. Will not search UCC records. Copy fee $.50 per page. Cert fee- $1.75 per cert plus copy fee. Payee- Perkins County Clerk. **Other phones:** Treasurer- 308-352-4542; Elections- 308-352-4643. **Property tax/Assessing**- PO Box 248, 200 Lincoln Ave, Grant, NE 69140; 308-352-4938. www.co.perkins.ne.us/assessor.html **Online access**- Access to property searches for free go to www.perkins.gisworkshop.com/

Phelps County

County Clerk, PO Box 404, Holdrege, NE 68949-0404. 308-995-4469; fax-308-995-4368; 9AM-5PM (CST) www.phelpsgov.org
Index: Separate indices to search include deeds, Mortgages, real estate by legal description. Records indexed on a public use terminal back to 3/7/05. Office prefers public do their own searches. Search fee $.50 per name. Office will search real estate records only from legal description. Office will search UCC records, but not tax liens. UCC search per debtor name- $4.50. Copy fee $.50 per page. Cert fee- $1.50 per page includes copy fee. Payee- Phelps County Clerk. **Other phones:** Treasurer- 308-995-6115; Elections- 308-995-4469; Vital Records- 308-995-4469. **Property tax/Assessing**- 715 5th Ave, Holdrege, NE 68949; 308-995-4061, assessor fax-308-995-4368. http://phelpsgov.org/gov/assessor/ **Online** - real estate or personal property data free at www.nebraskataxesonline.us/taxcollpage1.aspx?county=Phelps. Also, search property records free on the GIS mapping site at www.phelps.gisworkshop.com.

Pierce County

County Clerk, 111 W Court, Rm 1; Courthouse, Pierce, NE 68767-1224. Recording, R/E & UCC phone-402-329-4225; fax-402-329-6439; 8:30AM-4:30PM (CST) www.co.pierce.ne.us
Index: Separate indices to search. Records indexed on a public use terminal back to 2005. Office personnel or visitors may perform searches. Search fee $5.00 per name. Office will search real estate records. Copy fee $1.00 per page. Marriage license copy- $5.00 each. Cert fee- $1.50 per cert plus copy fee. Payee- Pierce County Clerk. **Other phones:** Treasurer- 402-329-6335; Elections- 402-329-4225. **Property tax/Assessing**- 111 W Court St, #5, Pierce, NE 68767; 402-329-4215, assessor fax- 402-329-6413. www.co.pierce.ne.us/assessor.html

Platte County Clerk

County Clerk, 2610 14th St, Columbus, NE 68601. 402-563-4904, R/E recording phone-402-563-4911, UCC recording phone-402-563-4904; fax-402-564-4164; 8AM-5PM. www.plattecounty.net
See Register of Deeds for real estate records. Records indexed on a public use terminal back to 1988. Office personnel or visitors may perform searches. Search fee-$3.50 per name. Office will not search UCC records or tax liens. Copy fee $.50 per page. Cert fee-$4.50 per doc plus copy fee. **Other phones:** Treasurer- 402-563-4913; Elections- 402-563-4908.

Platte County Register of Deeds

Register of Deeds, 2610 14th St, Columbus, NE 68601. Recording, R/E phone-402-563-4911, UCC recording phone-402-563-4904; fax-402-563-9173; 8AM-5PM (CST) www.plattecounty.net/deeds.htm
Index: Separate indices to search include deeds, mtgs, UCCs, state/federal liens. Records indexed on computer back to 2/05. Office will perform a UCC search but public must search other records themselves. Copy fee $1.00 per page. Cert fee- $1.50 per page. Payee- Platte County Register of Deeds. **Other phones:** Treasurer- 402-563-4913; Elections-402-563-4908. **Property tax/Assessing**- 2610 14th St, Columbus, NE 68601; 402-563-4902, assessor fax- 402-562-6965. (Appraiser/Auditor- 402-563-4928) www.plattecounty.net/assessor.htm **Online access**- Access the assessor index at http://platte.gisworkshop.com/PlatteIMS/. Access real estate or personal property data free at www.nebraskataxesonline.us/taxcollpage1.aspx?county=Platte.

Polk County

County Clerk, PO Box 276, Osceola, NE 68651-0276. 402-747-5431; fax-402-747-2656; 8AM-5PM (CST) www.polkcounty.ne.gov/clerk.html
Index: Separate indices to search include numerical (legal description) and general (alphabetical). Record index not computerized. Office will perform a UCC search but public must search other records themselves. Search fee $4.50 per name, UCC only. Copy fee $.50 per page. Cert fee- $1.50 per page includes copy fee. Payee- Polk County Clerk. **Other phones:** Treasurer- 402-747-5441; Elections- 402-747-5431; Vital Records- 402-471-2871. **Property tax/Assessing**- PO Box 375, Osceola, NE 68651; 402-747-4491, assessor fax- 402-747-2656. www.polkcounty.ne.gov/assessor.html **Online access**- Search property and mapping free at http://polk.gisworkshop.com/. Access the treasurer county tax record search free at http://polktreasurer.gisworkshop.com/.

Red Willow County

County Clerk, 502 Norris Ave, McCook, NE 69001. Recording, R/E & UCC phone-308-345-1552, UCC recording phone-(State Office 402-471-4080); fax-308-345-4460; 8AM-4PM (CST) www.co.red-willow.ne.us/clerk.html
Index: Separate indices to search include legal description and grantor/grantee. Records indexed on a public use terminal back to 0101/2006. Office will perform a UCC search but public must search other records themselves. Copy fee $.25 in-office researched by customer, faxed copies $1.00 per page. Cert fee- $1.50 per page plus copy fee. Payee- Red Willow County Clerk. Bulk data available for purchase, contact Pauletta Gerver. $50.00 per month for electronic instruments-no indexing, requestor provides CD's and postage. **Other phones:** Treasurer-308-345-6515; Elections- 308-345-1552; Vital Records- State Office 402-471-2306); Property Tax Administrator- 402-471-5919. **Property tax/Assessing**- 502 Norris Ave, McCook, NE 69001; 308-345-4388, assessor fax- 308-345-6944. www.co.red-willow.ne.us/assessor.html **Online**- Search auditor's county property data on gis-mapping site free at http://redwillow.gisworkshop.com.

Richardson County

County Clerk, 1700 Stone St; Courthouse, Falls City, NE 68355. 402-245-2911; fax-402-245-2946; 8:30AM-5PM (CST)
www.co.richardson.ne.us/clerk.html
No tax liens filed here. Index: All in one. Record index not computerized. Only the public may search. Copy fee $.50 per page. Cert fee- $5.00 per page. Payee- Richardson County Clerk. **Other phones:** Treasurer- 402-245-3511; Elections- 402-245-2911; Vitals- 402-245-2535. **Property tax/Assessing**- 1700 Stone St, Falls City, NE 68355; 402-245-4012. www.co.richardson.ne.us/assessor.html

Rock County

County Clerk, PO Box 367, Bassett, NE 68714. 402-684-3933; fax-402-684-2741; 9AM-N, 1-5PM (CST)
Index: Separate indices to search include deeds, mortgages, miscellaneous. Record index not computerized. Office will perform a UCC search time permitting but public must search other records themselves. General search fee- charge by page found. UCC search per debtor name- $4.50. Copy fee $.25 per page. Cert fee- $4.50 per cert includes copy fee. Payee- Rock County Clerk. **Other phones:** Treasurer- 402-684-3515. **Property tax/Assessing**- PO Box 446, 400 State St, Bassett, NE 68714; 402-684-3831, assessor fax- 402-684-2741. 9AM-5PM

Saline County

County Clerk, Real Estate, PO Box 865, Wilber, NE 68465. Recording, R/E phone-402-821-2374, UCC recording phone-402-471-4080; fax-402-821-3381; 8AM-5PM (CST) www.co.saline.ne.us
Index: All in one. Record index not computerized. Office will perform a UCC search but public must search other records themselves. Office will not search real estate records. UCC searches performed only if filling numbers are known. Copy fee $.50 per page. Cert fee- $2.00 per cert plus $1.50 each add'l page copied. Payee- Saline County Clerk. **Other phones:** Treasurer- 402-821-2375; Elections- 402-821-2374; Vital Records- 402-471-2872 (State Bureau of Vital Statistics). **Property tax/Assessing**- PO Box 865, 215 S Court, Wilber, NE 68465; 402-821-2588, assessor fax- 402-821-3319. www.co.saline.ne.us/webpages/assessor/assessor.htm **Online access**- Access property data free at http://saline.assessor.gisworkshop.com/. Also, real estate or personal property data free at www.nebraskataxesonline.us/taxcollpage1.aspx?county=Saline.

Sarpy County Clerk

County Clerk, 1210 Golden Gate Dr, #1118, Papillion, NE 68046-2895. 402-593-2114; fax-402-593-4360; 8AM-4:45PM; til 6PM Wed. (CST) www.sarpy.com Index: All in one; marriages, trade names. Records indexed on a public use terminal back to 1987. Office personnel or visitors may perform searches. Search fee-$4.50 per name. copy fee- $.75 1st page, $.25 each add'l. Cert fee- $5.00 per page plus copy fee. Payee- Sarpy County Clerk. Bulk data available for purchase.

Sarpy County Register of Deeds

Register of Deeds, 1210 Golden Gate Dr, #1109, Papillion, NE 68046. 402-593-2107; fax-402-593-4360; 8AM-4:45PM. www.sarpy.com
Index: All in one. Records indexed on a public use terminal back to 1990's. Office personnel or visitors may perform searches. Search fee $4.50 per name. Office will not search real estate records. Copy fee $.50 per page. Cert fee- $1.50 per page. Payee- Sarpy County Register of Deeds. **Online access to Real Estate, Grantor/Grantee, Deed, Lien records:** Search the historical grantor/grantee index 1857-1990 free at www.sarpy.com/rodggi/. **Other phones:** Treasurer- 402-593-2188. **Property tax/Assessing**- 1210 Golden Gate Dr, Ste 1122, Papillion, NE 68046; 402-593-2122. A public access terminal is available. www.sarpy.com/assessor/ **Online** - A simple property search is free at www.sarpy.com/sarpyproperty/ but no name searching. A premium subscription service built based on your needs is available starting at $240 per year and goes higher. see contract at www.sarpy.com/oldterra/SarpyContract.pdf. Also, register to accept tax sales lists at www.sarpy.com/taxsale/.

Saunders County Clerk

County Clerk, PO Box 184, Wahoo, NE 68066-0187. 402-443-8101; fax-402-443-5010; 8AM-5PM (CST)
See Register of Deeds for real estate records. Index: Separate indices to search for marriages. Marriages indexed on a public use terminal back to 2001. Office personnel or visitors may perform searches. Copy fee $1.00 per page. Cert fee- $5.00 per cert. Payee-Saunders County Clerk.

Saunders County Register of Deeds

Register of Deeds, PO Box 184, Wahoo, NE 68066. Recording, R/E & UCC phone-402-443-8111; fax-402-443-5010; 8AM-5PM.

Index: All in one. Record index not computerized. Only the public may search. Copy fee $1.00 per page. Cert fee- $1.50 per page includes copy fee. Payee- Register of Deeds. **Other phones:** Treasurer- 402-443-8129; Elections- 402-443-8100. **Property tax/Assessing**- 433 N Chestnut St, #202, Wahoo, NE 68066; 402-443-5703, assessor fax- 402-443-5708. www.saunderscounty.ne.gov/webpages/assessor/assessor.htm **Online** - Access assessment data on the GIS-site free at www.saunders.pat.gisworkshop.com/. Also, access real estate or personal property data free www.nebraskataxesonline.us/taxcollpage1.aspx?county=Saunders.

Scotts Bluff County Clerk

Register of Deeds, 1825 10th St; Gering, NE 69341. 308-436-6601; fax-308-436-3178; 8AM-4:30PM (MST) www.scottsbluffcounty.org/deeds/deeds.htm
Index: Separate indices to search include books back to 1898, marriages. Records indexed on a public use terminal back to 1883. Only the public may search. UCCs can be searched by staff in a separate office. Office will not search real estate records. Copy fee $.50 per page. Cert fee- $5.00 per doc plus copy fee. Payee- Scotts Bluff County Clerk. **Online Real Estate, Deed, Lien records:** View and download recorded docs free after registration; instructions at www.scottsbluffcounty.org/deedsonline/Browse.aspx or from jbauer@scottsbluffcounty.org. Login page at www.scottsbluffcounty.org/deedsonline/. **Other phones:** Treasurer- 308-436-6617; Elections- 308-436-6653. **Property tax/Assessing**- Scb Co Clerk, c/0 Vera Dulaney, 1825 10th St, Gering, 69341; 308-436-6627, fax- 308-436-6699. (appraiser-308-436-6627) www.scottsbluffcounty.org/Assessor/assessor.htm **Online access**- Search the TaxSifter Parcel Search database for property data free at http://scottsbluffne.taxsifter.com/taxsifter/T-Parcelsearch.asp. Also, access real estate or personal property data free at www.nebraskataxesonline.us/taxcollpage1.aspx?county=Scotts.

Scotts Bluff Register of Deeds

Register of Deeds, 1825 10th St; Admin Office Bldg, Gering, NE 69341. Recording, R/E & UCC phone-308-436-6607; fax-308-436-6609; 8AM-4:30PM (MST) www.scottsbluffcounty.org
Index: All in one. Records indexed on a public use terminal back to 1989. Only the public may search. Copy fee $.50 per page; UCC copy- $1.00 per page. Cert fee- $1.50 per page plus copy fee. Payee- Scotts Bluff County Register of Deeds. **Other phones:** Treasurer- 308-436-6621.

Seward County

County Clerk, PO Box 190, Seward, NE 68434-0190. 402-643-2883; fax-402-643-9243; 8AM-5PM.
Index: All in one. Record index not computerized. Office will perform a UCC search but public must search other records themselves. Office will not search real estate records. Copy fee $.25 per page. Cert fee- $1.50 per page includes copy fee. Payee- Seward County Clerk. **Other phones:** Treasurer- 402-643-4574; Elections- 402-643-2883; Land or Marriage records- 402-643-2883. **Property tax/Assessing**- 529 Seward St, Rm 206, Seward, NE 68434; 402-643-3311, assessor fax- 402-643-9243. A public access terminal is available. http://connectseward.org/cgov/assessor.htm **Online access**- Access real estate or personal property data free at www.nebraskataxesonline.us. Also, search parcel records free at http://seward.gisworkshop.com/.

Sheridan County

County Clerk, PO Box 39, Rushville, NE 69360. 308-327-5650; fax-308-327-5624; 8:30-4:30PM (MST)
Index: Separate indices to search include general alpha and numeric by legal description. Record index not computerized. Office personnel or visitors may perform searches. Office will not search real estate records. UCC search includes tax liens if requested. UCC search per debtor name- $4.50. Copy fee $1.00 per page. Cert fee- $1.50 per cert includes copy fee. Payee- Sheridan County Clerk. **Other phones:** Treasurer- 308-327-5651. **Property tax/Assessing**- PO Box 391, 301 E 2nd St, Rushville, NE 69360; 308-327-5652. No public access terminal.

Sherman County

County Clerk, PO Box 456, Loup City, NE 68853-0456. 308-745-1513 x103, R/E recording phone-308-745-1513 x100; fax-308-745-0297; 8:30AM-4:30PM. www.co.sherman.ne.us/court.html
Index: Separate indices to search include mortgages, deeds, miscellaneous. Record index not computerized. Only the public may search. Copy fee $.50 per page plus $3.00 pull charge. Cert fee- $1.50 per page. Payee- Sherman County Clerk. **Other phones:** Treasurer- 308-745-1513 x101; Elections- 308-745-1513 x100; Vital Records- 308-471-2871. **Property tax/Assessing**- PO Box 652, 630 O St, Loup City, NE 68853; 308-745-0113, assessor fax- 308-745-0129. www.co.sherman.ne.us/assessor.html **Online**- parcel records free at http://sherman.pat.gisworkshop.com/.

Sioux County

County Clerk, PO Box 158, Harrison, NE 69346. 308-668-2443; fax-308-668-2443; 8AM-4:30PM.
Index: Separate indices to search include books by year. Record index not computerized. Only the public may search. Will not search UCC records. Copy fee $1.00 per page. Cert fee- $1.50 per page, $1.00 each add'l. Payee- Sioux County Clerk. **Other phones:** Treasurer- 308-668-2422. **Property tax/Assessing**- PO Box 158, 325 Main St, Harrison, NE 69346; 308-668-2401. www.co.sioux.ne.us/assessor.html

Stanton County

Register of Deeds, PO Box 347, Stanton, NE 68779-0347. Recording, R/E & UCC phone-402-439-2222; fax-402-439-2200; 8:30AM-4:30PM (CST) www.co.stanton.ne.us
Index: All in one. Records indexed on a public use terminal back to 12/2003. Only the public may search. Copy fee $.25 per page. UCC copy fee- $.50 per page. Cert fee- $1.50 per instrument plus copy fee. Payee- County Clerk. **Other phones:** Treasurer- 402-439-2223; Elections- 402-439-2222. **Property tax/Assessing**- PO Box 895, 804 Ivy St, Stanton, NE 68779; 402-439-2210, assessor fax- 402-439-2262. www.co.stanton.ne.us/assessor.html **Online**- Access real estate or personal property data free at www.nebraskataxesonline.us/taxcollpage1.aspx?county=Stanton.

Thayer County

County Clerk, 225 N 4th St, Rm 201, Hebron, NE 68370-1517. 402-768-6126; fax-402-768-2129; 8AM-4:30PM (CST) www.thayercounty.ne.gov/
Index: All in one. Records indexed on computer back to 5/01. Office personnel or visitors may perform searches. No fee for search. Office will search real estate records. Office will not search UCCs. Federal/state combined tax lien search- $4.00 per debtor. Copy fee $.25 per page. UCC copy $1.00 per page. Cert fee- $5.00 per cert includes copy fee. Payee- Thayer County Clerk. **Other phones:** Treasurer- 402-768-6227; Elections- 402-768-6126. **Property tax/Assessing**- 225 N 4th St, Rm 202, Hebron, NE 68370; 402-768-6417. (Appraiser/Auditor- 402-768-6417) www.thayercounty.ne.gov/index_html?page=content/assessor.html **Online**- Access real estate or personal property data free at www.nebraskataxesonline.us/taxcollpage1.aspx?county=Thayer.

Thomas County

County Clerk, PO Box 226, Thedford, NE 69166-0226. 308-645-2261; fax-308-645-2623; 8AM-N, 1-4PM M-Th; 8AM-N, 1-3PM F. (CST)
Index: Separate indices to search include deeds, Mtgs and misc. Records indexed on a public use terminal back to 98. Office personnel or visitors may perform searches. Search fee $5.00. Office will not search UCC records. Copy fee $1.00 per page.Real estate or tax lien copy- $.50 per copy. Cert fee- $5.00 per page plus copy fee. Payee- Thomas County Clerk. **Other phones:** Treasurer- 308-645-2262. **Property tax/Assessing**- PO Box 226, 503 Main St, Thedford, NE 69166; 308-645-2261.

Thurston County

County Clerk, PO Box G, Pender, NE 68047. 402-385-2343; fax-402-385-3544; 8:30AM-5PM (CST)
Index: All in one, arranged by legal description. Records indexed on computer back to 2003. Public access terminal available. Office will perform a UCC search but public must search other records themselves. Copy fee $.50 per page. Cert fee- $1.50 per page includes copy fee. Payee- County Clerk. **Other phones:** Treasurer- 402-385-3058; Elections- 402-385-2343. **Property tax/Assessing**- PO Box I, 106 S 5th St, Pender, NE 68047; 402-385-2251, assessor fax- 402-385-3544.

Valley County

County Clerk, 125 S 15th St, Ord, NE 68862-1499. 308-728-3700; fax-308-728-7725; 8AM-5PM (CST) www.co.valley.ne.us
Index: Separate indices to search include alpha and numerical. Record index not computerized. Only the public may search, as a general rule. Office can only assist with searches. General index search fee $5.00 per hour. Office will search specific/limited real estate records. Office will not search UCC records. Copy fee self serve $.10 per page letter size; $.15 per page legal. Cert fee- $1.50 per page includes copy fee. Payee- Valley County Clerk. **Other phones:** Treasurer- 308-728-5606. **Property tax/Assessing**- 125 S 15th St, Ord, NE 68862; 308-728-5081, assessor fax- 308-728-7725. www.co.valley.ne.us/assessor.html

Washington County

County Clerk, PO Box 466, Blair, NE 68008. 402-426-6822, R/E phone-402-426-6824, UCC phone-402-472-2554; fax-402-426-6825; 8AM-4:30PM (CST) www.co.washington.ne.us/clerk.html
We do not have UCC Records. UCC records are kept at the Nebraska Secretary of State's Office. Index: Separate indices to search include numerical indexes by legal description. Record index not computerized. Only the public may search. Copy fee $.25 per page. Cert fee- $1.50 per page included copy fee. Payee- Washington County Register of Deeds. **Other phones:** Treasurer- 402-426-6888; Elections- 402-426-6822; Vital Records- 402-471-2871. **Property tax/Assessing**- 1555 Colfax St, Blair, NE 68008; 402-426-6800. www.co.washington.ne.us/assessor.html

Wayne County

County Clerk, PO Box 248, Wayne, NE 68787-0248. 402-375-2288; fax-402-375-4137; 8:30AM-5PM (CST) http://county.waynene.org
Index: All in one. Records indexed on a public use terminal back to 10/2003. Office personnel or visitors may perform searches. Office will not search real estate records. Office will search UCC records as time permits. UCC search per debtor name- $4.50. Copy fee $1.00 per page. Cert fee- $1.50 per page includes copy fee. Payee- Wayne County Clerk. **Other phones:** Treasurer- 402-375-3885; Elections- 402-375-2288. **Property tax/Assessing**- 510 Pearl St, Wayne, NE 68787; 402-375-1979, assessor fax- 402-375-3702. http://county.waynene.org/County_Offices/Assessor/ **Online access**- Access real estate or personal property data free at www.nebraskataxesonline.us/taxcollpage1.aspx?county=Wayne. Search the sheriff's sales list free at http://county.waynene.org/County_Offices/Sheriff/.

Webster County

County Clerk, PO Box 250; County Clerk Office, Red Cloud, NE 68970. 402-746-2716; fax-402-746-2710; 8:30AM-4:30PM (CST) www.co.webster.ne.us
Index: Computer, mtg, deed and misc index. Records indexed on a public use terminal back to 1100. Only the public may search. Copy fee $.25 per page for photo copier, $1.00 per page off microfilm. Cert fee- $1.50 per page plus copy fee. Payee- Webster County

Clerk. **Other phones:** Treasurer- 402-746-2877; Elections- 402-746-2716; Vital Records- 402-471-2871. **Property tax/Assessing**- 621 N Cedar St, Red Cloud, NE 68970; 402-746-2717, assessor fax- 402-746-2717. www.co.webster.ne.us/assessor.html **Online** - Access real estate or personal property data free at www.nebraskataxesonline.us/taxcollpage1.aspx?county=Webster. Access to parcels for free at http://websterne.taxsifter.com/taxsifter/disclaimer.asp.

Wheeler County

County Clerk, PO Box 127, Bartlett, NE 68622. 308-654-3235; fax-308-654-3470; 9AM-N, 1-5PM.
Index: Separate indices to search include books by year. Record index not computerized. Office personnel or visitors may perform searches. Search fee $4.50 per name. Copy fee $.50 per page. Cert fee- $7.00 per doc plus copy fee. Payee- Wheeler County Clerk. **Other phones:** Treasurer- 308-654-3236. **Property tax/Assessing**- PO Box 127, 3rd & Main, Bartlett, NE 68622; 308-654-3235.

York County

County Clerk, 510 Lincoln Ave; Courthouse, York, NE 68467. 402-362-7759; fax-402-362-7558; 8:30AM-5PM.
Index: Separate indices to search. Records indexed on computer back to 7/1/03. Public access terminal available. Only the public may search. Will not search UCC records. Copy fee $1.00 per page. Fax $.25 per page if copied in office. Cert fee- $1.50 per page. Payee- York County Clerk- Register of Deeds. **Other phones:** Treasurer- 402-362-4949; Elections- 402-362-7759. **Property tax/Assessing**- 510 Lincoln Ave, York, NE 68467; 402-362-4926, assessor fax- 402-362-4735. **Online access**- Access parcel records free at http://yorkne.taxsifter.com/taxsifter/disclaimer.asp, but no name searching.

Nebraska County Locator

You will usually be able to find the city name in the City/County Cross Reference below. In that case, it is a simple matter to determine the county from the cross reference. However, only the official US Postal Service city names are included in this index. There are an additional 40,000 place names that people use in their addresses. Therefore, we have also included a ZIP/City Cross Reference immediately following the City/County Cross Reference.

If you know the ZIP Code but the city name does not appear in the City/County Cross Reference index, look up the ZIP Code in the ZIP/City Cross Reference, find the city name, then look up the city name in the City/County Cross Reference. For example, you want to know the county for an address of Menands, NY 12204. There is no "Menands" in the City/County Cross Reference. The ZIP/City Cross Reference shows that ZIP Codes 12201-12288 are for the city of Albany. Looking back in the City/County Cross Reference, Albany is in Albany County.

Nebraska City/County Cross Reference

ABIE Butler
ADAMS (68301) Gage(71), Lancaster(22), Otoe(5)
AINSWORTH Brown
ALBION Boone
ALDA Hall
ALEXANDRIA (68303) Thayer(97), Jefferson(2)
ALLEN Dixon
ALLIANCE (69301) Box Butte(97), Sioux(1)
ALMA Harlan
ALVO Cass
AMELIA Holt
AMES Dodge
AMHERST Buffalo
ANGORA Morrill
ANSELMO (68813) Custer(83), Blaine(10), Loup(6)
ANSLEY Custer
ARAPAHOE (68922) Furnas(80), Gosper(19)
ARCADIA (68815) Valley(63), Custer(18), Sherman(17)
ARCHER Merrick
ARLINGTON Washington
ARNOLD (69120) Custer(73), Lincoln(16), Logan(9)
ARTHUR Arthur
ASHBY (69333) Grant(89), Garden(10)
ASHLAND (68003) Saunders(74), Cass(24)
ASHTON (68817) Sherman(91), Howard(8)
ATKINSON Holt
ATLANTA Phelps
AUBURN Nemaha
AURORA (68818) Hamilton(98), Clay(1)
AVOCA (68307) Cass(85), Otoe(15)
AXTELL (68924) Kearney(94), Phelps(5)
AYR Adams
BANCROFT (68004) Cuming(98), Burt(1)
BARNESTON Gage
BARTLETT Wheeler
BARTLEY Red Willow
BASSETT (68714) Rock(71), Holt(25), Brown(1)
BATTLE CREEK Madison
BAYARD (69334) Morrill(63), Scotts Bluff(34), Banner(2)
BEATRICE Gage
BEAVER CITY Furnas
BEAVER CROSSING (68313) Seward(98), York(1)
BEE (68314) Seward(88), Butler(11)
BEEMER Cuming
BELDEN Cedar
BELGRADE (68623) Nance(90), Boone(9)
BELLEVUE (68147) Sarpy(97), Douglas(2)
BELLEVUE Sarpy
BELLWOOD Butler
BELVIDERE Thayer
BENEDICT (68316) York(91), Polk(8)
BENKELMAN Dundy
BENNET (68317) Lancaster(95), Otoe(4)
BENNINGTON (68007) Douglas(92), Washington(7)
BERTRAND (68927) Phelps(78), Gosper(21)
BERWYN Custer
BIG SPRINGS (69122) Deuel(85), Keith(6), Perkins(4), Garden(2)
BINGHAM (69335) Garden(73), Sheridan(26)
BLADEN (68928) Webster(79), Adams(20)
BLAIR Washington
BLOOMFIELD Knox
BLOOMINGTON Franklin
BLUE HILL (68930) Webster(80), Adams(19)
BLUE SPRINGS Gage
BOELUS Howard
BOYS TOWN Douglas
BRADSHAW (68319) York(95), Hamilton(4)
BRADY Lincoln
BRAINARD (68626) Butler(98), Saunders(1)
BREWSTER Blaine
BRIDGEPORT (69336) Morrill(97), Banner(2)
BRISTOW Boyd
BROADWATER Morrill
BROCK Nemaha
BROKEN BOW Custer
BROWNVILLE Nemaha
BRULE (69127) Keith(97), Perkins(2)
BRUNING (68322) Thayer(71), Fillmore(28)
BRUNO (68014) Butler(74), Saunders(25)
BRUNSWICK Antelope
BURCHARD (68323) Pawnee(98), Gage(1)
BURR (68324) Otoe(98), Johnson(1)
BURWELL (68823) Garfield(66), Loup(17), Valley(10), Rock(3)
BUSHNELL Kimball
BUTTE Boyd
BYRON Thayer
CAIRO (68824) Hall(96), Howard(3)
CALLAWAY Custer
CAMBRIDGE (69022) Furnas(73), Frontier(13), Red Willow(10), Gosper(2)
CAMPBELL (68932) Franklin(56), Adams(18), Kearney(15), Webster(9)
CARLETON Thayer
CARROLL Wayne
CEDAR BLUFFS Saunders
CEDAR CREEK Cass
CEDAR RAPIDS (68627) Boone(95), Nance(4)
CENTER Knox
CENTRAL CITY Merrick
CERESCO (68017) Saunders(53), Lancaster(46)
CHADRON Dawes
CHAMBERS (68725) Holt(96), Wheeler(2), Garfield(1)
CHAMPION Chase
CHAPMAN Merrick
CHAPPELL (69129) Deuel(87), Garden(12)
CHESTER Thayer
CLARKS (68628) Merrick(78), Polk(12), Hamilton(9)
CLARKSON (68629) Colfax(73), Stanton(26)
CLATONIA Gage
CLAY CENTER Clay
CLEARWATER (68726) Antelope(94), Holt(5)
CODY Cherry
COLERIDGE Cedar
COLON Saunders
COLUMBUS (68601) Platte(94), Polk(2), Butler(1), Colfax(1)
COLUMBUS Platte
COMSTOCK (68828) Custer(68), Valley(31)
CONCORD Dixon
COOK (68329) Otoe(51), Johnson(47), Nemaha(1)
CORDOVA Seward
CORNLEA Platte
CORTLAND Gage
COTESFIELD (68829) Howard(89), Greeley(10)
COZAD Dawson
CRAB ORCHARD (68332) Johnson(92), Gage(7)
CRAIG (68019) Burt(95), Washington(3), Dodge(1)
CRAWFORD Dawes
CREIGHTON (68729) Knox(89), Antelope(9)
CRESTON (68631) Platte(90), Stanton(10)
CRETE (68333) Saline(90), Lancaster(9)
CROFTON (68730) Knox(76), Cedar(23)
CROOKSTON Cherry
CULBERTSON (69024) Hitchcock(82), Hayes(11), Red Willow(6)
CURTIS (69025) Frontier(83), Lincoln(14), Hitchcock(1)
DAKOTA CITY Dakota
DALTON Cheyenne
DANBURY Red Willow
DANNEBROG (68831) Howard(98), Hall(1)
DAVENPORT (68335) Thayer(68), Nuckolls(24), Fillmore(6)
DAVEY Lancaster
DAVID CITY Butler
DAWSON Richardson
DAYKIN (68338) Jefferson(96), Saline(3)
DE WITT (68341) Saline(58), Gage(41)
DECATUR (68020) Burt(92), Thurston(7)
DENTON (68339) Lancaster(59), Seward(39), Saline(1)
DESHLER Thayer
DEWEESE (68934) Clay(72), Nuckolls(27)
DICKENS Lincoln
DILLER (68342) Jefferson(77), Gage(22)
DIX (69133) Kimball(98), Cheyenne(1)
DIXON (68732) Dixon(98), Cedar(1)
DODGE (68633) Dodge(66), Cuming(20), Colfax(12)
DONIPHAN (68832) Hall(66), Hamilton(33)
DORCHESTER (68343) Saline(78), Seward(21)
DOUGLAS Otoe
DU BOIS (68345) Pawnee(75), Richardson(24)
DUNBAR Otoe
DUNCAN Platte
DUNNING (68833) Blaine(79), Logan(13), Custer(6)
DWIGHT Butler
EAGLE (68347) Cass(71), Otoe(27)
EDDYVILLE (68834) Dawson(83), Custer(16)
EDGAR (68935) Clay(82), Nuckolls(17)
EDISON (68936) Furnas(74), Gosper(14), Greeley(11)
ELBA (68835) Howard(96), Greeley(3)
ELGIN (68636) Antelope(97), Wheeler(1), Boone(1)
ELK CREEK (68348) Johnson(71), Nemaha(19), Pawnee(8)
ELKHORN Douglas
ELLSWORTH (69340) Sheridan(91), Garden(8)
ELM CREEK (68836) Buffalo(79), Phelps(14), Dawson(6)
ELMWOOD Cass
ELSIE (69134) Perkins(92), Chase(6)
ELSMERE (69135) Cherry(52), Brown(47)
ELWOOD (68937) Gosper(83), Dawson(16)
ELYRIA Valley
EMERSON (68733) Dakota(44), Dixon(34), Thurston(20)
EMMET Holt
ENDERS (69027) Chase(96), Dundy(3)
ENDICOTT Jefferson
ERICSON (68637) Wheeler(78), Garfield(22)
EUSTIS (69028) Frontier(63), Dawson(27), Gosper(8)
EWING (68735) Holt(75), Antelope(15), Wheeler(9)
EXETER (68351) Fillmore(81), York(18)
FAIRBURY Jefferson
FAIRFIELD Clay
FAIRMONT (68354) Fillmore(91), York(8)
FALLS CITY Richardson
FARNAM (69029) Dawson(82), Lincoln(17)
FARWELL Howard
FILLEY (68357) Gage(98), Johnson(1)
FIRTH (68358) Lancaster(68), Gage(31)
FORDYCE Cedar
FORT CALHOUN Washington
FOSTER Pierce
FREMONT (68025) Dodge(95), Saunders(4)
FREMONT Dodge
FRIEND (68359) Saline(95), Seward(4)
FULLERTON (68638) Nance(97), Merrick(1)
FUNK Phelps
GARLAND Seward
GENEVA Fillmore
GENOA (68640) Nance(63), Platte(33), Merrick(3)
GERING Scotts Bluff
GIBBON (68840) Buffalo(94), Kearney(5)

GILEAD Thayer
GILTNER Hamilton
GLENVIL (68941) Clay(55), Adams(44)
GOEHNER Seward
GORDON (69343) Sheridan(93), Cherry(6)
GOTHENBURG (69138) Dawson(93), Lincoln(4), Custer(2)
GRAFTON (68365) Fillmore(95), York(4)
GRAND ISLAND (68801) Hall(97), Merrick(2)
GRAND ISLAND Hall
GRANT Perkins
GREELEY Greeley
GREENWOOD (68366) Cass(94), Lancaster(3), Saunders(1)
GRESHAM (68367) York(45), Polk(32), Seward(20), Butler(1)
GRETNA (68028) Sarpy(98), Douglas(1)
GUIDE ROCK (68942) Webster(80), Nuckolls(19)
GURLEY Cheyenne
HADAR Pierce
HAIGLER (69030) Dundy(92), Chase(7)
HALLAM (68368) Lancaster(93), Gage(6)
HALSEY Thomas
HAMLET Hayes
HAMPTON (68843) Hamilton(97), York(2)
HARDY (68943) Nuckolls(99), Thayer(1)
HARRISBURG Banner
HARRISON Sioux
HARTINGTON Cedar
HARVARD (68944) Hamilton(53), Clay(46)
HASTINGS Adams
HAY SPRINGS (69347) Sheridan(65), Dawes(34)
HAYES CENTER Hayes
HAZARD Sherman
HEARTWELL Kearney
HEBRON Thayer
HEMINGFORD (69348) Box Butte(67), Dawes(32)
HENDERSON (68371) York(73), Hamilton(26)
HENDLEY Furnas
HENRY (69349) Scotts Bluff(84), Sioux(15)
HERMAN (68029) Washington(90), Burt(9)
HERSHEY Lincoln
HICKMAN Lancaster
HILDRETH (68947) Franklin(78), Kearney(21)
HOLBROOK (68948) Furnas(71), Gosper(24), Frontier(3)
HOLDREGE (68949) Phelps(98), Harlan(1)
HOLMESVILLE Gage
HOLSTEIN Adams
HOMER Dakota
HOOPER (68031) Dodge(91), Washington(6), Cuming(1)
HORDVILLE Hamilton
HOSKINS (68740) Wayne(89), Stanton(10)
HOWELLS (68641) Colfax(47), Cuming(32), Stanton(20)
HUBBARD Dakota
HUBBELL Thayer
HUMBOLDT (68376) Richardson(86), Nemaha(11), Pawnee(1)
HUMPHREY (68642) Platte(89), Madison(10)
HUNTLEY Harlan
HYANNIS Grant
IMPERIAL (69033) Chase(97), Perkins(2)
INAVALE Webster
INDIANOLA (69034) Red Willow(93), Frontier(6)
INLAND Clay
INMAN Holt
ITHACA Saunders
JACKSON Dakota
JANSEN Jefferson
JOHNSON (68378) Nemaha(92), Johnson(4), Otoe(3)
JOHNSTOWN (69214) Brown(98), Cherry(1)
JULIAN Nemaha
JUNIATA Adams
KEARNEY Buffalo
KENESAW (68956) Adams(80), Buffalo(11), Hall(7)
KENNARD Washington
KEYSTONE (69144) Keith(97), Arthur(2)
KILGORE Cherry
KIMBALL (69145) Kimball(96), Banner(3)
LAKESIDE Sheridan
LAMAR Chase
LAUREL (68745) Cedar(95), Wayne(2), Dixon(1)
LAVISTA (68128) Sarpy(98), Douglas(1)
LAWRENCE (68957) Nuckolls(57), Webster(33), Adams(7), Clay(2)
LEBANON Red Willow
LEIGH (68643) Colfax(47), Platte(35), Stanton(16)
LEMOYNE (69146) Keith(95), Arthur(4)
LESHARA Saunders
LEWELLEN (69147) Keith(61), Garden(37)
LEWISTON Pawnee
LEXINGTON Dawson
LIBERTY (68381) Gage(88), Pawnee(11)
LINCOLN Lancaster
LINDSAY (68644) Platte(83), Madison(16)
LINWOOD (68036) Butler(80), Saunders(19)
LISCO (69148) Garden(85), Morrill(14)
LITCHFIELD (68852) Sherman(90), Custer(9)
LODGEPOLE (69149) Cheyenne(82), Garden(14), Deuel(2)
LONG PINE Brown
LOOMIS Phelps
LORTON Otoe
LOUISVILLE Cass
LOUP CITY Sherman
LYMAN Scotts Bluff
LYNCH (68746) Boyd(84), Holt(15)
LYONS (68038) Burt(93), Cuming(6)
MACY Thurston
MADISON (68748) Madison(93), Stanton(6)
MADRID Perkins
MAGNET Cedar
MALCOLM Lancaster
MALMO Saunders
MANLEY Cass
MARQUETTE Hamilton
MARSLAND Dawes
MARTELL Lancaster
MASKELL Dixon
MASON CITY Custer
MAX Dundy
MAXWELL Lincoln
MAYWOOD (69038) Frontier(85), Lincoln(14)
MC COOK (69001) Red Willow(97), Frontier(1)
MC COOL JUNCTION (68401) York(98), Fillmore(1)
MCGREW Scotts Bluff
MCLEAN Pierce
MEAD Saunders
MEADOW GROVE (68752) Madison(92), Pierce(7)
MELBETA Scotts Bluff
MEMPHIS Saunders
MERNA Custer
MERRIMAN Cherry
MILFORD Seward
MILLER (68858) Buffalo(97), Custer(2)
MILLIGAN Fillmore
MILLS Keya Paha
MINATARE Scotts Bluff
MINDEN Kearney
MITCHELL (69357) Scotts Bluff(95), Sioux(4)
MONROE Platte
MOOREFIELD (69039) Frontier(63), Lincoln(36)
MORRILL (69358) Scotts Bluff(80), Sioux(19)
MORSE BLUFF Saunders
MULLEN Hooker
MURDOCK Cass
MURRAY Cass
NAPER Boyd
NAPONEE (68960) Franklin(78), Harlan(21)
NEBRASKA CITY Otoe
NEHAWKA (68413) Cass(97), Otoe(2)
NELIGH Antelope
NELSON Nuckolls
NEMAHA Nemaha
NENZEL Cherry
NEWCASTLE (68757) Dixon(88), Cedar(11)
NEWMAN GROVE (68758) Madison(64), Platte(21), Boone(13)
NEWPORT (68759) Rock(68), Keya Paha(31)
NICKERSON (68044) Washington(57), Dodge(42)
NIOBRARA Knox
NORFOLK (68701) Madison(95), Stanton(4)
NORFOLK Madison
NORMAN Kearney
NORTH BEND Dodge
NORTH LOUP (68859) Valley(94), Greeley(3), Sherman(1)
NORTH PLATTE Lincoln
OAK (68964) Nuckolls(94), Thayer(5)
OAKDALE Antelope
OAKLAND (68045) Burt(94), Cuming(4)
OBERT Cedar
OCONTO (68860) Custer(94), Dawson(5)
OCTAVIA Butler
ODELL Gage
ODESSA Buffalo
OFFUTT A F B Sarpy
OGALLALA (69153) Keith(97), Perkins(2)
OHIOWA (68416) Fillmore(94), Thayer(5)
OMAHA (68152) Douglas(84), Washington(15)
OMAHA (68157) Sarpy(97), Douglas(2)
OMAHA Douglas
OMAHA Sarpy
ONEILL Holt
ONG (68452) Clay(76), Fillmore(24)
ORCHARD (68764) Antelope(65), Knox(27), Holt(7)
ORD Valley
ORLEANS Harlan
OSCEOLA Polk
OSHKOSH Garden
OSMOND Pierce
OTOE Otoe
OVERTON (68863) Dawson(89), Phelps(10)
OXFORD (68967) Furnas(62), Harlan(37)
PAGE Holt
PALISADE (69040) Hayes(63), Hitchcock(36)
PALMER (68864) Merrick(77), Nance(21)
PALMYRA (68418) Otoe(96), Cass(3)
PANAMA Lancaster
PAPILLION Sarpy
PARKS Dundy
PAWNEE CITY Pawnee
PAXTON (69155) Keith(96), Perkins(2)
PENDER (68047) Thurston(72), Cuming(18), Wayne(9)
PERU (68421) Nemaha(92), Otoe(7)
PETERSBURG (68652) Boone(69), Antelope(30)
PHILLIPS (68865) Hamilton(98), Hall(1)
PICKRELL Gage
PIERCE Pierce
PILGER (68768) Stanton(91), Cuming(4), Wayne(3)
PLAINVIEW (68769) Pierce(79), Antelope(19), Knox(1)
PLATTE CENTER Platte
PLATTSMOUTH Cass
PLEASANT DALE (68423) Seward(82), Lancaster(17)
PLEASANTON (68866) Buffalo(98), Custer(1)
PLYMOUTH (68424) Jefferson(98), Gage(1)
POLK (68654) Polk(66), York(20), Hamilton(12)
PONCA (68770) Dixon(55), Dakota(44)
POTTER (69156) Cheyenne(82), Banner(12), Kimball(4)
PRAGUE Saunders
PRIMROSE (68655) Boone(96), Greeley(3)
PROSSER Adams
PURDUM (69157) Blaine(47), Cherry(34), Thomas(13), Brown(4)
RAGAN Harlan
RANDOLPH (68771) Cedar(57), Pierce(25), Wayne(16)
RAVENNA (68869) Buffalo(94), Sherman(5)
RAYMOND (68428) Lancaster(97), Seward(2)
RED CLOUD Webster
REPUBLICAN CITY Harlan
REYNOLDS Thayer
RICHFIELD Sarpy
RISING CITY Butler
RIVERDALE Buffalo
RIVERTON Franklin
ROCA Lancaster
ROCKVILLE Sherman
ROGERS Colfax
ROSALIE (68055) Thurston(74), Cuming(25)
ROSE (68772) Rock(90), Loup(9)
ROSELAND Adams
ROYAL (68773) Antelope(97), Brown(2)
RULO Richardson
RUSHVILLE Sheridan
RUSKIN (68974) Nuckolls(90), Thayer(9)
SAINT EDWARD (68660) Boone(72), Platte(23), Nance(3)
SAINT HELENA Cedar
SAINT LIBORY (68872) Howard(82), Merrick(17)
SAINT MARY Johnson
SAINT PAUL Howard
SALEM Richardson
SARGENT (68874) Custer(95), Loup(2), Hall(1)
SARONVILLE (68975) Fillmore(55), Clay(44)
SCHUYLER Colfax
SCOTIA (68875) Greeley(95), Howard(4)
SCOTTSBLUFF Scotts Bluff
SCRIBNER Dodge
SENECA (69161) Thomas(63), Cherry(36)
SEWARD Seward
SHELBY (68662) Polk(96), Butler(3)
SHELTON (68876) Buffalo(86), Hall(13)
SHICKLEY (68436) Fillmore(98), Clay(1)
SHUBERT (68437) Richardson(80), Nemaha(19)
SIDNEY Cheyenne
SILVER CREEK (68663) Merrick(41), Polk(39), Nance(17), Platte(1)
SMITHFIELD Gosper
SNYDER Dodge
SOUTH BEND Cass
SOUTH SIOUX CITY Dakota
SPALDING (68665) Greeley(78), Wheeler(21)
SPARKS Cherry
SPENCER (68777) Boyd(86), Holt(13)
SPRAGUE Lancaster

SPRINGFIELD Sarpy
SPRINGVIEW Keya Paha
ST COLUMBANS Sarpy
ST MARY Johnson
STAMFORD (68977) Harlan(68), Furnas(31)
STANTON Stanton
STAPLEHURST Seward
STAPLETON (69163) Logan(72), Lincoln(27)
STEELE CITY Jefferson
STEINAUER (68441) Pawnee(98), Johnson(1)
STELLA (68442) Richardson(83), Nemaha(16)
STERLING (68443) Johnson(92), Otoe(7)
STOCKVILLE Frontier
STRANG Fillmore
STRATTON (69043) Hitchcock(96), Dundy(3)
STROMSBURG (68666) Polk(98), York(1)
STUART Holt
SUMNER (68878) Dawson(94), Custer(5)
SUPERIOR Nuckolls
SURPRISE Butler
SUTHERLAND (69165) Lincoln(84), McPherson(7), Keith(4), Arthur(3)
SUTTON (68979) Clay(87), Fillmore(7), Hamilton(3)
SWANTON Saline
SYRACUSE Otoe
TABLE ROCK (68447) Pawnee(93), Nemaha(4), Johnson(2)
TALMAGE (68448) Otoe(82), Nemaha(10), Johnson(6)
TAYLOR Loup
TECUMSEH Johnson
TEKAMAH Burt
THEDFORD Thomas
THURSTON Thurston
TILDEN (68781) Madison(66), Antelope(26), Pierce(3), Boone(2)
TOBIAS (68453) Saline(88), Jefferson(7), Thayer(3), Fillmore(1)
TRENTON Hitchcock
TRUMBULL (68980) Clay(53), Adams(28), Hamilton(13), Hall(4)
TRYON McPherson
UEHLING Dodge
ULYSSES (68669) Butler(85), Seward(14)
UNADILLA (68454) Otoe(98), Cass(1)
UNION (68455) Cass(98), Otoe(1)
UPLAND (68981) Franklin(85), Kearney(14)
UTICA Seward
VALENTINE (69201) Cherry(98), Merrick(1)
VALLEY (68064) Douglas(93), Saunders(5), Dodge(1)
VALPARAISO (68065) Saunders(53), Lancaster(39), Seward(4), Butler(2)
VENANGO (69168) Perkins(75), Chase(25)
VERDIGRE Knox
VERDON Richardson
VIRGINIA (68458) Gage(89), Pawnee(6), Johnson(3)
WACO (68460) York(98), Seward(1)
WAHOO Saunders
WAKEFIELD (68784) Dixon(60), Wayne(38)
WALLACE (69169) Lincoln(73), Perkins(21), Hayes(4)
WALTHILL Thurston
WALTON (68461) Lancaster(97), Cass(1)
WATERBURY (68785) Dixon(77), Dakota(22)
WATERLOO (68069) Douglas(96), Sarpy(3)
WAUNETA (69045) Chase(47), Dundy(25), Hayes(24), Hitchcock(2)
WAUSA (68786) Knox(92), Cedar(4), Pierce(2)
WAVERLY (68462) Lancaster(98), Cass(1)
WAYNE (68787) Wayne(98), Dixon(1)
WEEPING WATER Cass
WEISSERT Custer
WELLFLEET Lincoln
WEST POINT Cuming
WESTERN (68464) Saline(95), Jefferson(4)
WESTERVILLE Custer
WESTON Saunders
WHITECLAY Sheridan
WHITMAN Grant
WHITNEY Dawes
WILBER (68465) Saline(93), Gage(4), Lancaster(1)
WILCOX (68982) Harlan(31), Kearney(31), Franklin(22), Phelps(14)
WILLOW ISLAND Dawson
WILSONVILLE (69046) Furnas(93), Red Willow(6)
WINNEBAGO Thurston
WINNETOON Knox
WINSIDE Wayne
WINSLOW Dodge
WISNER (68791) Cuming(94), Wayne(4)
WOLBACH (68882) Greeley(50), Howard(39), Nance(8), Boone(2)
WOOD LAKE Cherry
WOOD RIVER Hall
WYMORE Gage
WYNOT (68792) Cedar(97), Dixon(2)
YUTAN Saunders

Nebraska ZIP/City Cross Reference

68001-68001 ABIE
68002-68002 ARLINGTON
68003-68003 ASHLAND
68004-68004 BANCROFT
68005-68005 BELLEVUE
68007-68007 BENNINGTON
68008-68009 BLAIR
68010-68010 BOYS TOWN
68014-68014 BRUNO
68015-68015 CEDAR BLUFFS
68016-68016 CEDAR CREEK
68017-68017 CERESCO
68018-68018 COLON
68019-68019 CRAIG
68020-68020 DECATUR
68022-68022 ELKHORN
68023-68023 FORT CALHOUN
68025-68026 FREMONT
68028-68028 GRETNA
68029-68029 HERMAN
68030-68030 HOMER
68031-68031 HOOPER
68033-68033 ITHACA
68034-68034 KENNARD
68035-68035 LESHARA
68036-68036 LINWOOD
68037-68037 LOUISVILLE
68038-68038 LYONS
68039-68039 MACY
68040-68040 MALMO
68041-68041 MEAD
68042-68042 MEMPHIS
68044-68044 NICKERSON
68045-68045 OAKLAND
68046-68046 PAPILLION
68047-68047 PENDER
68048-68048 PLATTSMOUTH
68050-68050 PRAGUE
68054-68054 RICHFIELD
68055-68055 ROSALIE
68056-68056 ST COLUMBANS
68057-68057 SCRIBNER
68058-68058 SOUTH BEND
68059-68059 SPRINGFIELD
68061-68061 TEKAMAH
68062-68062 THURSTON
68063-68063 UEHLING
68064-68064 VALLEY
68065-68065 VALPARAISO
68066-68066 WAHOO
68067-68067 WALTHILL
68068-68068 WASHINGTON
68069-68069 WATERLOO
68070-68070 WESTON
68071-68071 WINNEBAGO
68072-68072 WINSLOW
68073-68073 YUTAN
68100-68112 OMAHA
68113-68113 OFFUTT A F B
68114-68122 OMAHA
68123-68123 BELLEVUE
68124-68127 OMAHA
68128-68128 LAVISTA
68130-68132 OMAHA
68133-68133 PAPILLION
68134-68145 OMAHA
68147-68147 BELLEVUE
68152-68198 OMAHA
68301-68301 ADAMS
68303-68303 ALEXANDRIA
68304-68304 ALVO
68305-68305 AUBURN
68307-68307 AVOCA
68309-68309 BARNESTON
68310-68310 BEATRICE
68313-68313 BEAVER CROSSING
68314-68314 BEE
68315-68315 BELVIDERE
68316-68316 BENEDICT
68317-68317 BENNET
68318-68318 BLUE SPRINGS
68319-68319 BRADSHAW
68320-68320 BROCK
68321-68321 BROWNVILLE
68322-68322 BRUNING
68323-68323 BURCHARD
68324-68324 BURR
68325-68325 BYRON
68326-68326 CARLETON
68327-68327 CHESTER
68328-68328 CLATONIA
68329-68329 COOK
68330-68330 CORDOVA
68331-68331 CORTLAND
68332-68332 CRAB ORCHARD
68333-68333 CRETE
68335-68335 DAVENPORT
68336-68336 DAVEY
68337-68337 DAWSON
68338-68338 DAYKIN
68339-68339 DENTON
68340-68340 DESHLER
68341-68341 DE WITT
68342-68342 DILLER
68343-68343 DORCHESTER
68344-68344 DOUGLAS
68345-68345 DU BOIS
68346-68346 DUNBAR
68347-68347 EAGLE
68348-68348 ELK CREEK
68349-68349 ELMWOOD
68350-68350 ENDICOTT
68351-68351 EXETER
68352-68352 FAIRBURY
68354-68354 FAIRMONT
68355-68355 FALLS CITY
68357-68357 FILLEY
68358-68358 FIRTH
68359-68359 FRIEND
68360-68360 GARLAND
68361-68361 GENEVA
68362-68362 GILEAD
68364-68364 GOEHNER
68365-68365 GRAFTON
68366-68366 GREENWOOD
68367-68367 GRESHAM
68368-68368 HALLAM
68370-68370 HEBRON
68371-68371 HENDERSON
68372-68372 HICKMAN
68374-68374 HOLMESVILLE
68375-68375 HUBBELL
68376-68376 HUMBOLDT
68377-68377 JANSEN
68378-68378 JOHNSON
68379-68379 JULIAN
68380-68380 LEWISTON
68381-68381 LIBERTY
68382-68382 LORTON
68401-68401 MC COOL JUNCTION
68402-68402 MALCOLM
68403-68403 MANLEY
68404-68404 MARTELL
68405-68405 MILFORD
68406-68406 MILLIGAN
68407-68407 MURDOCK
68409-68409 MURRAY
68410-68410 NEBRASKA CITY
68413-68413 NEHAWKA
68414-68414 NEMAHA
68415-68415 ODELL
68416-68416 OHIOWA
68417-68417 OTOE
68418-68418 PALMYRA
68419-68419 PANAMA
68420-68420 PAWNEE CITY
68421-68421 PERU
68422-68422 PICKRELL
68423-68423 PLEASANT DALE
68424-68424 PLYMOUTH
68428-68428 RAYMOND
68429-68429 REYNOLDS
68430-68430 ROCA
68431-68431 RULO
68432-68432 SAINT MARY
68432-68432 ST MARY
68433-68433 SALEM
68434-68434 SEWARD
68436-68436 SHICKLEY
68437-68437 SHUBERT
68438-68438 SPRAGUE
68439-68439 STAPLEHURST
68440-68440 STEELE CITY
68441-68441 STEINAUER
68442-68442 STELLA
68443-68443 STERLING
68444-68444 STRANG
68445-68445 SWANTON
68446-68446 SYRACUSE
68447-68447 TABLE ROCK
68448-68448 TALMAGE
68450-68450 TECUMSEH
68452-68452 ONG
68453-68453 TOBIAS
68454-68454 UNADILLA
68455-68455 UNION
68456-68456 UTICA
68457-68457 VERDON
68458-68458 VIRGINIA
68460-68460 WACO
68461-68461 WALTON
68462-68462 WAVERLY
68463-68463 WEEPING WATER
68464-68464 WESTERN
68465-68465 WILBER
68466-68466 WYMORE
68467-68467 YORK
68500-68588 LINCOLN
68601-68602 COLUMBUS
68620-68620 ALBION
68621-68621 AMES
68622-68622 BARTLETT
68623-68623 BELGRADE
68624-68624 BELLWOOD
68625-68625 BOONE
68626-68626 BRAINARD
68627-68627 CEDAR RAPIDS
68628-68628 CLARKS
68629-68629 CLARKSON
68630-68630 CORNLEA
68631-68631 CRESTON
68632-68632 DAVID CITY

ZIP Range	City
68633-68633	DODGE
68634-68634	DUNCAN
68635-68635	DWIGHT
68636-68636	ELGIN
68637-68637	ERICSON
68638-68638	FULLERTON
68640-68640	GENOA
68641-68641	HOWELLS
68642-68642	HUMPHREY
68643-68643	LEIGH
68644-68644	LINDSAY
68647-68647	MONROE
68648-68648	MORSE BLUFF
68649-68649	NORTH BEND
68650-68650	OCTAVIA
68651-68651	OSCEOLA
68652-68652	PETERSBURG
68653-68653	PLATTE CENTER
68654-68654	POLK
68655-68655	PRIMROSE
68658-68658	RISING CITY
68659-68659	ROGERS
68660-68660	SAINT EDWARD
68661-68661	SCHUYLER
68662-68662	SHELBY
68663-68663	SILVER CREEK
68664-68664	SNYDER
68665-68665	SPALDING
68666-68666	STROMSBURG
68667-68667	SURPRISE
68669-68669	ULYSSES
68701-68702	NORFOLK
68710-68710	ALLEN
68711-68711	AMELIA
68713-68713	ATKINSON
68714-68714	BASSETT
68715-68715	BATTLE CREEK
68716-68716	BEEMER
68717-68717	BELDEN
68718-68718	BLOOMFIELD
68719-68719	BRISTOW
68720-68720	BRUNSWICK
68722-68722	BUTTE
68723-68723	CARROLL
68724-68724	CENTER
68725-68725	CHAMBERS
68726-68726	CLEARWATER
68727-68727	COLERIDGE
68728-68728	CONCORD
68729-68729	CREIGHTON
68730-68730	CROFTON
68731-68731	DAKOTA CITY
68732-68732	DIXON
68733-68733	EMERSON
68734-68734	EMMET
68735-68735	EWING
68736-68736	FORDYCE
68737-68737	FOSTER
68738-68738	HADAR
68739-68739	HARTINGTON
68740-68740	HOSKINS
68741-68741	HUBBARD
68742-68742	INMAN
68743-68743	JACKSON
68745-68745	LAUREL
68746-68746	LYNCH
68747-68747	MCLEAN
68748-68748	MADISON
68749-68749	MAGNET
68751-68751	MASKELL
68752-68752	MEADOW GROVE
68753-68753	MILLS
68755-68755	NAPER
68756-68756	NELIGH
68757-68757	NEWCASTLE
68758-68758	NEWMAN GROVE
68759-68759	NEWPORT
68760-68760	NIOBRARA
68761-68761	OAKDALE
68762-68762	OBERT
68763-68763	ONEILL
68764-68764	ORCHARD
68765-68765	OSMOND
68766-68766	PAGE
68767-68767	PIERCE
68768-68768	PILGER
68769-68769	PLAINVIEW
68770-68770	PONCA
68771-68771	RANDOLPH
68772-68772	ROSE
68773-68773	ROYAL
68774-68774	SAINT HELENA
68776-68776	SOUTH SIOUX CITY
68777-68777	SPENCER
68778-68778	SPRINGVIEW
68779-68779	STANTON
68780-68780	STUART
68781-68781	TILDEN
68783-68783	VERDIGRE
68784-68784	WAKEFIELD
68785-68785	WATERBURY
68786-68786	WAUSA
68787-68787	WAYNE
68788-68788	WEST POINT
68789-68789	WINNETOON
68790-68790	WINSIDE
68791-68791	WISNER
68792-68792	WYNOT
68801-68803	GRAND ISLAND
68810-68810	ALDA
68812-68812	AMHERST
68813-68813	ANSELMO
68814-68814	ANSLEY
68815-68815	ARCADIA
68816-68816	ARCHER
68817-68817	ASHTON
68818-68818	AURORA
68819-68819	BERWYN
68820-68820	BOELUS
68821-68821	BREWSTER
68822-68822	BROKEN BOW
68823-68823	BURWELL
68824-68824	CAIRO
68825-68825	CALLAWAY
68826-68826	CENTRAL CITY
68827-68827	CHAPMAN
68828-68828	COMSTOCK
68829-68829	COTESFIELD
68831-68831	DANNEBROG
68832-68832	DONIPHAN
68833-68833	DUNNING
68834-68834	EDDYVILLE
68835-68835	ELBA
68836-68836	ELM CREEK
68837-68837	ELYRIA
68838-68838	FARWELL
68840-68840	GIBBON
68841-68841	GILTNER
68842-68842	GREELEY
68843-68843	HAMPTON
68844-68844	HAZARD
68845-68845	KEARNEY
68846-68846	HORDVILLE
68847-68849	KEARNEY
68850-68850	LEXINGTON
68852-68852	LITCHFIELD
68853-68853	LOUP CITY
68854-68854	MARQUETTE
68855-68855	MASON CITY
68856-68856	MERNA
68858-68858	MILLER
68859-68859	NORTH LOUP
68860-68860	OCONTO
68861-68861	ODESSA
68862-68862	ORD
68863-68863	OVERTON
68864-68864	PALMER
68865-68865	PHILLIPS
68866-68866	PLEASANTON
68868-68868	PROSSER
68869-68869	RAVENNA
68870-68870	RIVERDALE
68871-68871	ROCKVILLE
68872-68872	SAINT LIBORY
68873-68873	SAINT PAUL
68874-68874	SARGENT
68875-68875	SCOTIA
68876-68876	SHELTON
68878-68878	SUMNER
68879-68879	TAYLOR
68880-68880	WEISSERT
68881-68881	WESTERVILLE
68882-68882	WOLBACH
68883-68883	WOOD RIVER
68901-68902	HASTINGS
68920-68920	ALMA
68922-68922	ARAPAHOE
68923-68923	ATLANTA
68924-68924	AXTELL
68925-68925	AYR
68926-68926	BEAVER CITY
68927-68927	BERTRAND
68928-68928	BLADEN
68929-68929	BLOOMINGTON
68930-68930	BLUE HILL
68932-68932	CAMPBELL
68933-68933	CLAY CENTER
68934-68934	DEWEESE
68935-68935	EDGAR
68936-68936	EDISON
68937-68937	ELWOOD
68938-68938	FAIRFIELD
68939-68939	FRANKLIN
68940-68940	FUNK
68941-68941	GLENVIL
68942-68942	GUIDE ROCK
68943-68943	HARDY
68944-68944	HARVARD
68945-68945	HEARTWELL
68946-68946	HENDLEY
68947-68947	HILDRETH
68948-68948	HOLBROOK
68949-68949	HOLDREGE
68950-68950	HOLSTEIN
68951-68951	HUNTLEY
68952-68952	INAVALE
68954-68954	INLAND
68955-68955	JUNIATA
68956-68956	KENESAW
68957-68957	LAWRENCE
68958-68958	LOOMIS
68959-68959	MINDEN
68960-68960	NAPONEE
68961-68961	NELSON
68963-68963	NORMAN
68964-68964	OAK
68966-68966	ORLEANS
68967-68967	OXFORD
68969-68969	RAGAN
68970-68970	RED CLOUD
68971-68971	REPUBLICAN CITY
68972-68972	RIVERTON
68973-68973	ROSELAND
68974-68974	RUSKIN
68975-68975	SARONVILLE
68976-68976	SMITHFIELD
68977-68977	STAMFORD
68978-68978	SUPERIOR
68979-68979	SUTTON
68980-68980	TRUMBULL
68981-68981	UPLAND
68982-68982	WILCOX
69001-69001	MC COOK
69020-69020	BARTLEY
69021-69021	BENKELMAN
69022-69022	CAMBRIDGE
69023-69023	CHAMPION
69024-69024	CULBERTSON
69025-69025	CURTIS
69026-69026	DANBURY
69027-69027	ENDERS
69028-69028	EUSTIS
69029-69029	FARNAM
69030-69030	HAIGLER
69031-69031	HAMLET
69032-69032	HAYES CENTER
69033-69033	IMPERIAL
69034-69034	INDIANOLA
69035-69035	LAMAR
69036-69036	LEBANON
69037-69037	MAX
69038-69038	MAYWOOD
69039-69039	MOOREFIELD
69040-69040	PALISADE
69041-69041	PARKS
69042-69042	STOCKVILLE
69043-69043	STRATTON
69044-69044	TRENTON
69045-69045	WAUNETA
69046-69046	WILSONVILLE
69101-69103	NORTH PLATTE
69120-69120	ARNOLD
69121-69121	ARTHUR
69122-69122	BIG SPRINGS
69123-69123	BRADY
69125-69125	BROADWATER
69127-69127	BRULE
69128-69128	BUSHNELL
69129-69129	CHAPPELL
69130-69130	COZAD
69131-69131	DALTON
69132-69132	DICKENS
69133-69133	DIX
69134-69134	ELSIE
69135-69135	ELSMERE
69138-69138	GOTHENBURG
69140-69140	GRANT
69141-69141	GURLEY
69142-69142	HALSEY
69143-69143	HERSHEY
69144-69144	KEYSTONE
69145-69145	KIMBALL
69146-69146	LEMOYNE
69147-69147	LEWELLEN
69148-69148	LISCO
69149-69149	LODGEPOLE
69150-69150	MADRID
69151-69151	MAXWELL
69152-69152	MULLEN
69153-69153	OGALLALA
69154-69154	OSHKOSH
69155-69155	PAXTON
69156-69156	POTTER
69157-69157	PURDUM
69160-69160	SIDNEY
69161-69161	SENECA
69162-69162	SIDNEY
69163-69163	STAPLETON
69165-69165	SUTHERLAND
69166-69166	THEDFORD
69167-69167	TRYON
69168-69168	VENANGO
69169-69169	WALLACE
69170-69170	WELLFLEET
69171-69171	WILLOW ISLAND
69190-69190	OSHKOSH
69201-69201	VALENTINE
69210-69210	AINSWORTH
69211-69211	CODY
69212-69212	CROOKSTON
69214-69214	JOHNSTOWN
69216-69216	KILGORE
69217-69217	LONG PINE
69218-69218	MERRIMAN
69219-69219	NENZEL
69220-69220	SPARKS
69221-69221	WOOD LAKE
69301-69301	ALLIANCE
69331-69331	ANGORA
69333-69333	ASHBY
69334-69334	BAYARD
69335-69335	BINGHAM
69336-69336	BRIDGEPORT
69337-69337	CHADRON
69339-69339	CRAWFORD
69340-69340	ELLSWORTH
69341-69341	GERING
69343-69343	GORDON
69345-69345	HARRISBURG
69346-69346	HARRISON
69347-69347	HAY SPRINGS
69348-69348	HEMINGFORD
69349-69349	HENRY
69350-69350	HYANNIS
69351-69351	LAKESIDE
69352-69352	LYMAN
69353-69353	MCGREW
69354-69354	MARSLAND
69355-69355	MELBETA
69356-69356	MINATARE
69357-69357	MITCHELL
69358-69358	MORRILL
69360-69360	RUSHVILLE
69361-69363	SCOTTSBLUFF
69365-69365	WHITECLAY
69366-69366	WHITMAN
69367-69367	WHITNEY

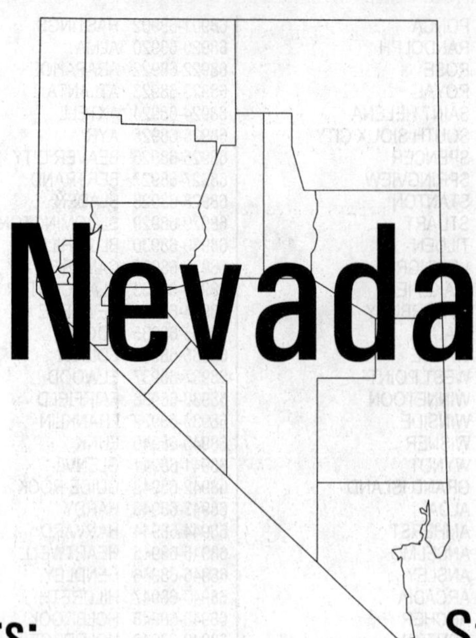

Nevada

General Help Numbers:

Governor's Office
Capitol Building 775-684-5670
Carson City, NV 89701 Fax 775-684-5683
http://gov.state.nv.us 8AM-5PM

Attorney General's Office
100 N Carson St 775-684-1100
Carson City, NV 89701 Fax 775-684-1108
http://ag.state.nv.us 8AM-5PM

Legislative Records
Nevada Legislature 775-684-6827 (Bill Status)
401 S Carson St 775-684-6800
Carson City, NV 89701-4747 Fax 775-684-6663
www.leg.state.nv.us 8AM-5PM

State Archives
100 N Stewart St 775-684-3360
Carson City, NV 89701-4285 Fax 775-684-3330
http://nevadaculture.org/nsla/index.php 8AM-5PM

State Specifics:

Capital: Carson City
Carson City County

Time Zone: PST

Number of Counties: 17

Number of Filing Locations: 17

Population: 2,600,167

Web Site: www.nv.gov

State Agencies

Criminal Records

DPS-Records & Technology Div, Records Bureau, 333 W Nye Lane, #100, Carson City, NV 89706; 775-684-6262, Fax- 775-684-6265; 8AM-5PM.

www.nvrepository.state.nv.us

Records are available if you provide fingerprints and consent of subject. Otherwise, this agency suggests a court record search instead.

Indexing & Storage: Records available from 1987 and are on computer. Records are maintained indefinitely, unless sealed due to court order or on the death or 100th birthday of the individual. New records available for inquiry in 2-3 weeks. According to a U.S. DOJ study in 2003 37% of all arrests in database have final dispositions recorded, approximately 30% for those arrests within last 5 years.

Searching: This repository maintains all retainable criminal charges as defined by state statute including DUI and domestic violence. 100% of arrest records are fingerprint supported. Include in request- set of fingerprints, signed release, full name, DOB, SSN, sex and race. This data not released- sealed records or juvenile records. Records without dispositions are released.

Access by: mail, in person.

Fee & Payment: The fingerprint search fee is $21.00 per individual. If the search requires an FBI fingerprint check (for record checks on occupations concerning children or the elderly, per state statute), the fee is $30.25 manual, or $19.25 live scan. Fee payee- Nevada Department of Public Safety Prepayment required. money order or cashier's check required. No credit cards, personal checks, or cash accepted.

Mail search: Turnaround time- 30 days. SASE not required.

In person: Records are still returned by mail.

Statewide Court Records

Supreme Court of Nevada, Administrative Office of the Courts, 201 S Carson St, #250, Carson City, NV 89701-4702; 775-684-1700, Fax- 775-684-1723; 8AM-5PM.

www.nvsupremecourt.us/index.php

Except for certain online research capabilities, all court record access must be done at the local level. The state does not have a unified court system database.

Online search: The Supreme Court website gives access to opinions and decisions. Some Nevada Courts have internal online computer systems, but only Clark and Washoe counties offer online access of a record index to the public. A statewide court automation system is being implemented.

Sexual Offender Registry

Records and Identification Bureau, Sex Offender Registry, 333 W Nye Lane, #100, Carson City, NV 89706; 775-684-6256, Fax- 775-684-6266; 8AM-5PM. www.nvsexoffenders.gov

In 1997, the Community Notification of Sex Offenders law was passed (NRS Chapter 179D). There are over 12,000 offenders registered in the state.

Indexing & Storage: Records available from 1997 forward on computer, from 1987 on paper. New records available for inquiry in 60-90 days.

Searching: Email questions to sorhelp@dps.state.nv.us. Include in search request- name, DOB, DL or SSN.

Access by: mail, phone, fax, in person, online.

Fee & Payment: There is no fee.

Mail search: Turnaround time- 1 day. SASE not required.

Phone search: Requests can be made.

Fax search: Searching by fax permitted.

In person: Records are still returned by mail.

Online search: Information available on the website is extensive, including aliases, photograph (where available), injury and conviction information, and latest registered address. Information is provided for sex offenders with a risk assessment score of a TIER Level 3 or TIER Level 2. Search by name, ZIP Code, or license plate number.

Incarceration Records

Nevada Department of Corrections, ATTN: Family & Community Services, PO Box 7011, Carson City, NV 89702 (Courier address- 5500 Snyder Ave, Bldg 89, Carson City, NV 89701); 775-887-3367, Fax- 775-887-3381; 8AM-5PM.

www.doc.nv.gov

For questions about offender records, contact Offender Management at info@doc.nv.gov.

Indexing & Storage: Records available on current and former inmates. New records available for inquiry in 1 to 3 days.

Searching: Records are not destroyed, but are archived after one year. Paper records are kept for 25 years after the release. Include in request- full name; DOC number helpful. Location, conviction and sentencing information, case number, and release dates are released. Searches can be done back to 1864, with varying results. This data not released- medical and mental health data, disciplinarians, correspondence, chronos.

Access by: mail, phone, online.

Fee & Payment: There is a $.25 fee per page. Fee payee- Department of Corrections Prepayment required. Personal checks accepted.

Mail search: Turnaround time- 30 days. SASE not required.

Phone search: Limited name searching available.

Online search: Offender Tracking System searchable at www.doc.nv.gov/notis/search.php. Click on Download Information to obtain electronic files of all the information available. Many options are provided. This system contains information about current inmates and those discharged in the past 18 months.

Corporation, LP, LLC

Secretary of State, Records, 202 N Carson City, Carson City, NV 89701-4707; 775-684-5708, Fax-775-684-5645; 8AM-5PM.

www.nvsos.gov

Fax given above is for copies division; for administration and mail room, use fax 775-684-5725.

Indexing & Storage: Records available since inception of laws (1912). Old, inactive records are purged from computer and archived. Most can still be accessed manually by request. New records available for inquiry in current (but 7-10 days if filed manually).

Searching: Search requests must be on letterhead or use this agency's form, which is preferred. Download forms at www.nvsos.gov/business/forms/index.asp. Agency suggest to search online first. Include in request- full name of business, corporation file number. Credit card payment info can be included on request form. In addition to the articles of organization, business entity records available include: Annual Lists of Officers & Directors, Prior (merged) names, Inactive and Reserved names, and Resident Agent names. This data not released- payment and fee data, correspondences.

Access by: mail, phone, fax, in person, online.

Fee & Payment: The search fee is $50.00. The certification fee is $30.00. Copy fees are $2.00 per page. A certificate of Good Standing is $50.00. Fee payee- Secretary of State. Prepayment required. Trust accounts can be established especially for phone requesters. Personal checks accepted. Major credit cards accepted.

Mail search: Turnaround time- 1 to 2 weeks. SASE not required.

Phone search: Staff will give status for corporations and partnerships, corporate officer names, and trademark information.

Fax search: One may request searches and copies by fax. Fax to use for status request-775-684-7123.

In person: Public Access Terminal is the same as the web. Information requests are available.

Online search: Online access is offered on the Internet site for no charge. You can search by corporate name, resident agent, corporate officers, or by file number. Also, good standing certificates can be ordered online - no add'l search fee. Email search requests encouraged, copies@sos.nv.gov.

Other access: Reports and data downloads available - Foreign Corporation lists, Non-Profits, for example - under the Online Services tab at the website; fees vary.

Expedited service: Expedited service is available for mail, fax, phone and in person searches. The expedite search fee is $25.00. Fed Ex overnight return for $25.00. There is an additional $75.00 fee for overnight service of copies or certificates if 1 to 10 pages, and $125.00 if over 10 pages.

Assumed Name, Fictitious Name

Records not maintained by a state level agency.

Records are at the county level.

Trademarks/Servicemarks

Secretary of State, Corporate Expedite Office, 555 E. Washington Ave, #4000, Las Vegas, NV 89101; 702-486-2880, Fax- 702-486-2888; 8AM-5PM.

http://secretaryofstate.biz/business/trademarks/faq.asp

Trademark files are kept here and copies of document must be requested from this office. The SOS office in Carson City can look records on computer, but cannot make copies of actual documents in files.

Indexing & Storage: Records available since inception.

Searching: The same search requirements apply here as in Carson City.

Access by: mail, phone, in person, online.

Fee & Payment: The search fee is $50.00. Copies are $2.00 per page and $30.00 for certification per document. Fee payee- NV Secretary of State. Prepayment required. Personal checks and major credit cards accepted.

Mail search: Turnaround time- 1 to 2 weeks.

Phone search: Limited information is offered over the phone.

In person: Turnaround immediate, time permitting.

Online search: Search marks at https://esos.state.nv.us/SOSServices/AnonymousAccess/CorpSearch/CorpSearch.aspx. While this may look like a business entity search, it will bring up marks. Look on the document number; SM is servicemark; TM is trademark.

Expedited service: 24-Hour Expedite 1 to 10 pages $75.00; 24- Hour Expedite 11 or more pages $125; 2-Hour Expedite $500.00; 1-Hour Expedite $1000.

Uniform Commercial Code, Federal & State Tax Liens

UCC Division, Secretary of State, 200 N Carson St, Carson City, NV 89701-4069; 775-684-7100, Fax- 775-684-5630; 8AM-5PM.

www.sos.state.nv.us/business/ucc/faq.asp

Federal tax lien search must be requested separately and only contains data on businesses. Tax liens on individuals are filed at the county level. There is no state income tax, thus no recorded state tax liens.

Indexing & Storage: Records available from 1967 on both computer and microfilm. New records available for inquiry in 1-2 days.

Searching: Use search request form UCC-11. Include in request- debtor name.

Access by: mail, fax, in person, online.

Fee & Payment: The fee for written request to search a debtor name is $40.00, via the Internet is $20.00. Copies cost $2.00 per page. Remember a tax lien search is a separate fee. Fee payee- Secretary of State. Prepayment required. Personal checks and major credit cards accepted.

Mail search: Turnaround time- 1 to 3 days. A SASE is not requested.

Fax search: See expedited service.

In person: Counter service available.

Online search: After registration, search available at https://esos.state.nv.us/NVUCC/user/login.asp. To receive documents the fee is $20.00, an order form may be downloaded. A full commercial system is also available.

Other access: Bulk purchase services available. Got to https://esos.state.nv.us/sosservices/ and click on fee schedule.

Expedited service: Expedited service is available for mail and fax request searches. Searches will not be returned by fax. Turnaround time- 2 to 24 hours. For 24 hour service, add $75.00. For 2 hour service, add $500 if for 1 to 10 copies, $1000 if 11 or more copies.

Sales Tax Registrations

State does not impose sales tax.

Birth Certificates

Nevada Department of Health, Office of Vital Statistics, 4150 Technology Way, #104, Carson City, NV 89706; 775-684-4242, 775-684-4280 (Message Phone), 877-456-5410 (Orders), Fax- 775-684-4156; 8AM-5PM. www.health.nv.gov/

Indexing & Storage: Records available from 1911 to present. New records available for inquiry in 30 days of filing.

Searching: Birth and death records are considered confidential and not open to the general public. Include in request- full name, names of parents, mother's maiden name, date of birth, place of birth, relationship to person of record, reason for information request. Parents' names are a must to get record.

Access by: mail, phone, fax, in person, online.

Fee & Payment: For a certified copy the fee is $13.00. The fee for a verification only or for a no record found the fee is $8.00. If you wish to purchase using a credit card, see expedited service. Fee payee- Office of Vital Statistics. Prepayment required. Personal checks accepted. Major credit cards accepted by vendor.

Mail search: Turnaround time- 10 to 15 days. SASE not required.

Phone search: See expedited service.

Fax search: See expedited service.

In person: Turnaround time 20 minutes.

Online search: Online ordering available from state designated vendor at www.vitalchek.com.

Expedited service: Expedited service is available for online, phone and fax requests from VitalChek. Add vendor fee of $10.95 plus express delivery fee is desired. A credit card is required.

Death Records

Nevada Department of Health, Office of Vital Statistics, 4150 Technology Way, #104, Carson City, NV 89706; 775-684-4242, 775-684-4280 (Message Phone), 877-456-5410 (Orders), Fax- 775-684-4156; 8AM-5PM. www.health.nv.gov/

Indexing & Storage: Records available from 1911 on. New records available for inquiry in 30 days of filing.

Searching: Records are considered confidential, need to state relationship. However, a verification printout with name, date, and location is available to the public. Include in request- full name, date of death, place of death, relationship to person of record, reason for information request.

Access by: mail, phone, fax, in person, online.

Fee & Payment: A certified copy is $10.00 for deaths occurring in all counties except Clark, Douglas, Mineral, and Washoe where the fee is $11.00. The fee for a verification only or if no record found is $8.00. Fee payee- Office of Vital Statistics. Prepayment required. Personal checks accepted. Major credit cards accepted by vendor.

Mail search: Turnaround time- 10-12 working days. SASE not required.

Phone search: See expedited service.

Fax search: See expedited service.

In person: Turnaround time is 20 minutes.

Online search: Expedited service available from state designated vendor at www.vitalchek.com.

Expedited service: Expedited service is available for online, phone and fax requests from VitalChek. Add vendor fee of $10.95 plus express delivery fee is desired. A credit card is required.

Marriage Certificates, Divorce Records

Access to Records is Restricted.

Nevada Department of Health, Office of Vital Statistics, 4150 Technology Way, #104, Carson City, NV 89706; 775-684-4481.

www.health.nv.gov/

Marriage and divorce records are found at county recorder office of issue and not here. However, this agency has a list each county agency at the webpage at http://health2k.state.nv.us/forms/formtypes/stateindex.pdf. Agency will sometimes be able to verify if record exists with an index search.

Workers' Compensation Records

Access to Records is Restricted.

Davison of Industrial Relations, Workers' Compensation Section, 400 West King Street, Suite 400, Carson City, NV 89703; 775-684-7260, Fax- 775-687-6305; 8AM-5PM.

http://dirweb.state.nv.us/WCS/wcs.htm

Since 1/1/00, Nevada privatized the business of workers' compensation insurance. This agency holds an index of statewide records. Only those entities that contribute to the index may search the index. The index is not available to employers for post-hire research.

Driver Records

Department of Motor Vehicles, Records Section, 555 Wright Way, Carson City, NV 89711-0250; 775-684-4590, 877-368-7828 (In-state), Fax- 775-684-4899; 8AM-5PM. www.dmvnv.com/

Copies of citations may be obtained at the same address. There is no fee when requesting your own citation, otherwise the fee is $8.00.

Indexing & Storage: Records available for 3 yrs. Non-moving violations not listed on the driving record for non-CDL drivers. Nevada complies with the Driver's Privacy Protection Act, so personal data is available only to specific users. Records are computer indexed since 1980.

Searching: Authorized users may establish an account by completing the appropriate application. Call 775-684-4590 to request an application. Casual requesters without written consent of subject receive records without personal information. The driver's license number, or name and DOB are needed for a request. The SSN is helpful for searching, but is only released on the record to government agencies. Accidents do not appear on the record.

Access by: mail, phone, fax, in person, online.

Fee & Payment: The fee is $7.00 per driving record or $5.00 for license information. Add $4.00 for certification. Three record types are available (except online): three-year, ten-year, and school bus records. Fee payee- Nevada Department of Motor Vehicles. Prepayment required. Personal checks and credit cards accepted.

Mail search: Turnaround time- 10 days. Request must be on department approved forms. SASE not required.

Phone search: phone-in requesters must be pre-approved, are assigned a 5-digit account number and can request up to 5 records at one time over the phone. Call 775-684-4590 for information.

Fax search: Pre-approved accounts may fax in requests.

In person: Drivers may obtain their own record from any DMV office, but the address above is the only location that provides certified records.

Online search: The state has an FTP type online system available for high volume users. All files received by 5:30 PM are processed and returned at 6:30 PM. Fee is $7.00 per record. Call 775-684-4702 for details. Also, a batch processing system has recently be added for higher volume accounts. Only three-year histories are available online. A person may order his or her own record at online. Go to https://dmvapp.state.nv.us/OL_DH/Drvr_Usr_Info.aspx. The fee is $7.00.

Vehicle Ownership & Registration

Department of Motor Vehicles, Motor Vehicle Record Section, 555 Wright Way, Carson City, NV 89711-0250; 775-684-4590, Fax- 775-684-4740; 8AM-5PM. www.dmvnv.com

Indexing & Storage: Records available for the present on computer; on microfilm back to 1980.

Searching: SSNs, withdrawal action, accidents, and information connected to a license plate are not released to the general public. Requests form insurance companies must include the NAIC number. Nevada complies with DPPA and restricts access of records with personal information to permissible users. Requesters must show a legal right to the information or provide written consent or records are released with no personal data.

Access by: mail, phone, online.

Fee & Payment: The cost is $5.00 per record for current vehicle title or for registration information. A vehicle history is $7.00, a title verification letter is also $7.00. Certification is an additional $4.00. Photo copies are $3.00 each. Fee payee- Nevada Department of Motor Vehicles. Prepayment required. Personal checks accepted, credit cards are not.

Mail search: Turnaround time- 10 days. Be sure to give as much specific information as possible. Your request must be on department-approved forms. SASE not required.

Phone search: phone-in requesters must be pre-approved, are assigned a five-digit account number and can request up to 5 records at one time over the phone. Call 775-684-4590 for more information.

Online search: A registration status inquiry is at https://dmvapp.state.nv.us/dmv/vr/vr_reg/vr_reg_default.aspx. The license plate number and last four digits of the VIN are required to display the registration information. There is no fee.

Other access: Database is available for sale to permissible users under DPPA at costs varying from $500 to $2,500.

Accident Reports

Department of Public Safety, Nevada Highway Patrol, 555 Wright Way, Carson City, NV 89711; 775-687-5300 (HQ), 775-684-7381 (Substation), Fax- 775-684-4879; 8AM-5PM.

http://nhp.nv.gov/index.shtml

Indexing & Storage: New records available for inquiry in 7-10 working days.

Searching: Requests must be in writing. Include in request- full name, date of accident, location of accident, report number. Reports may also be ordered from a regional office (Las Vegas 702-486-4100; Reno 775-688-2500; or Elko 775-753-1111). Same fee applies.

Access by: mail, fax, in person.

Fee & Payment: The fee is $6.00 per report, and report(s) will not be mailed until payment has been received. Fee payee- Nevada Highway Patrol. Prepayment required. Personal checks accepted, credit cards are not.

Mail search: Turnaround time- 1 week. A SASE is requested.

Fax search: Fax searching available, but only if pre-paid.

In person: Turnaround time is immediate if the record is on file.

Vessel Ownership & Registration

Department of Wildlife Headquarters, Boat Registration, 4600 Kietzke Ln, D-135, Reno, NV 89502; 775-688-1983, 775-688-1507, Fax- 775-688-1509; 8AM-5PM M-F.

www.ndow.org

Indexing & Storage: Records available from 1972 to the present and are indexed on computer and microfiche. All boats must be registered and titled. New records available for inquiry in less than 1 day.

Searching: To search, one of the following is required: hull ID #, boat #, or name, plus name and address of requester. This data not released- SSNs, phone numbers, email addresses.

Access by: mail, in person.

Fee & Payment: The fee is $5.00 per boat, which includes 1 computer print-out. Photocopies cost $.50 per page. Fee payee- NDOW. Prepayment required. Cash is accepted from in person searchers only. Out-of-state No personal checks or credit cards accepted.

Mail search: Turnaround time- 4 days. SASE not required.

In person: Turnaround time can be immediate if search is not lengthy.

Other access: Information is available on disk, fee is $1000.

Legislation Records

Nevada Legislature, Legislative Counsel Bureau, 401 S Carson St, Carson City, NV 89701-4747; 775-684-6827 (Bill Status Only), 775-684-6800 (Main Number), 775-684-6835 (Publications), Fax- 775-684-6663; 8AM-5PM.

www.leg.state.nv.us

To order copies, call the research number.

Indexing & Storage: Records available from late 1800's. Records are computer indexed from 1985 to present, and on microfiche from 1967 to present.

Searching: Include in request- bill number, year.

Access by: mail, phone, fax, in person, online.

Fee & Payment: No charge for one or two bills. If you request more than two, the fee varies by page numbers requested. You may request any search by mail or telephone. The agency will determine fee, but will not release copies until paid. Fee payee- Legislative Counsel Bureau. Prepayment required. Personal checks, Visa, and MasterCard accepted.

Mail search: Turnaround time- 1 to 2 days. Information requests are available. SASE not required.

Phone search: You may request bills by phone.

Fax search: Turnaround time is generally in 1 to 2 days.

In person: You may request bills in person.

Online search: Bills and bill status information is available via this agency's web, as well as the Revised Statutes. Legislative session information is searchable online since 1993.

Expedited service: Expedited service is available for mail and phone searches. You must provide an account number with a shipper.

Voter Registration

Secretary of State, Elections Division, 101 N Carson Street #3, Carson City, NV 89701; 775-684-5705, Fax- 775-684-5718; 8AM-5PM.

http://nvsos.gov/elections/

The statewide database (NevVoter) is open to the public either hardcopy of electronic format; however, the SOS Office retains full authority in granting or denying access.

Searching: Lists may be requested from the individual counties. This data not released- SSN.

Access by: mail, fax, online.

Mail search: Turnaround time- 7 days. Use the state's Official Request for List of Registered Voter's Form. Records may be requested by mail.

Fax search: See mail search criteria.

Online search: A names search, single inquiry is offered. Either the last four digits of the SSN or the DL number of the subject must be entered. Requesting access to the statewide list is also available online. First, submit the Official Request for List of Registered Voters form (found on the web). This submission must be made by made, fax or in person. Upon acceptance (which can take 7 days), the requester is notified by email. Then the approved requester may download online.

Other access: Bulk access is available for purchase in electronic format. See the web page listed above for details.

GED Transcripts

Department of Education, State GED Administrator, 755 N Roop St, #201, Carson City, NV 89701; 775-687-7294, Fax- 775-687-8636; 8AM-5PM. www.literacynet.org/nvadulted/

These records are not public records and require written consent of the examinee.

Indexing & Storage: Records available from 1948 to present. This agency holds many limited GED records on individuals tested in the military, federal prison, etc. New records available for inquiry in 2 to 4 weeks.

Searching: Only "passing scores" were kept from 1948 through 2001. Include in request- name used when tested, year and location of test, signed release, date of birth, SSN, information about and signature of requester.

Access by: mail, fax, in person.

Fee & Payment: There is no fee.

Mail search: Turnaround time- 7 to 10 days. SASE is not required.

Fax search: Same criteria as mail searching.

In person: Turnaround immediate, if request not lengthy. The agency suggests to first make an appointment.

Hunting & Fishing License Information

Department of Wildlife, Licensing Office, 4600 Kietzke LN, D135, Reno, NV 89502; 775-688-1507, Fax- 775-688-1509; 8AM-5PM.

www.ndow.org

Indexing & Storage: Records available from 1976 to present on microfiche. New records available for inquiry in 3-6 months.

Searching: Include in request- full name, date of birth, SSN. This data not released- SSN, DOB, or telephone number.

Access by: mail.

Fee & Payment: The fee is $5.00 per name per year searched. Fee payee- NDOW Prepayment required with guaranteed funds. No personal checks or credit cards accepted.

Mail search: Turnaround time- 3 to 5 working days. It will help to use their record request form, which you can request by phone. SASE not required.

Other access: The Department offers electronic records of hunting and fishing license holders for fees ranging from $500 to $1750.

Nevada State Licensing Agencies

For details about the agency responsible for licensing/certifying/registering an item below or in the Agency Quick Finder section, match an item's number with the number of the agency in the *Licensing Agency Information* section.

Nevada Licenses Searchable Online

Advanced Nurse Practitioner #13	www.nursingboard.state.nv.us/Verification/formLicense.html
Ambulatory Surgery Ctr (Pharm) #16	http://64.42.58.74/datamart/mainMenu.do
Animal Technician #21	https://www.nvvetboard.us/renewal/glsweb/homeframe.aspx
Architect #2	http://nsbaidrd.state.nv.us/directory.htm
Attorney #44	www.nvbar.org/findalawyer.asp
Audiologist #31	http://speech_pathology.state.nv.us/LicenseVerification.htm
Auditor, Accountancy #1	www.nvaccountancy.com/search.fx
Automobile/Vehicle Garage #25	https://dmvapp.state.nv.us/DMV/OBL/Business_Reports/Pages/BusinessLicenses.aspx
Automobile/Vehicle Mfg'r #25	https://dmvapp.state.nv.us/DMV/OBL/Business_Reports/Pages/BusinessLicenses.aspx
Automobile/Vehicle Rebuilder #25	https://dmvapp.state.nv.us/DMV/OBL/Business_Reports/Pages/BusinessLicenses.aspx
Automobile/Vehicle Transporter #25	https://dmvapp.state.nv.us/DMV/OBL/Business_Reports/Pages/BusinessLicenses.aspx
Automobile/Vehicle Wrecker/Salvage #25	https://dmvapp.state.nv.us/DMV/OBL/Business_Reports/Pages/BusinessLicenses.aspx
Bank #29	http://fid.state.nv.us/New_LicenseeMenu.htm
Body Shop #25	https://dmvapp.state.nv.us/DMV/OBL/Business_Reports/Pages/BusinessLicenses.aspx
Building Mover #46	www.nvcontractorsboard.com
Carpentry Contractor #46	www.nvcontractorsboard.com
Check Casher #29	http://fid.state.nv.us/New_LicenseeMenu.htm
Chiropractor #3	http://chirobd.nv.gov/query_licensee2.asp
Collection Agency #29	http://fid.state.nv.us/New_LicenseeMenu.htm
Concrete Contractor #46	www.nvcontractorsboard.com
Contractor, General #46	www.nvcontractorsboard.com
Credit Union #29	http://fid.state.nv.us/New_LicenseeMenu.htm
Debt Adjuster #29	http://fid.state.nv.us/New_LicenseeMenu.htm
Deferred Deposit Company #29	http://fid.state.nv.us/New_LicenseeMenu.htm
Denied/Unsuitable Gaming Person #36	http://gaming.nv.gov/unsuitable.htm
Dental Hygienist #4	www.nvdentalboard.nv.gov/Vertification.htm
Dentist #4	www.nvdentalboard.nv.gov/Vertification.htm
Doctor #11	http://medboard.nv.gov/default.asp
Doctor, Disciplinary Action #11	http://medboard.nv.gov/Disciplinary%20Actions/disciplinary_list.htm
Driving School #25	https://dmvapp.state.nv.us/DMV/OBL/Business_Reports/Pages/BusinessLicenses.aspx
Drug Wholesaler/Dist./Mfg. #16	http://64.42.58.74/datamart/mainMenu.do
DUI School #25	https://dmvapp.state.nv.us/DMV/OBL/Business_Reports/Pages/BusinessLicenses.aspx
Electrical Contractor #46	www.nvcontractorsboard.com
Elevator/Conveyor #46	www.nvcontractorsboard.com
Emergency Medical Service Nurse #13	www.nursingboard.state.nv.us/Verification/formLicense.html
Engineer #19	http://boe.state.nv.us/ROST_HOME.HTM
Engineering, General #46	www.nvcontractorsboard.com
Euthanasia Technician #21	https://www.nvvetboard.us/Renewal/glsweb/homeframe.aspx
Euthanasia Technician (Animal) #16	http://64.42.58.74/datamart/mainMenu.do
Fencing #46	www.nvcontractorsboard.com
Financial Advisor (Investments) #40	www.sos.state.nv.us/securities/
Fire Protection Contractor #46	www.nvcontractorsboard.com
Fishing Guide #26	www.ndow.org/law/licensed/
Floor/Tile/Carpet Layer #46	www.nvcontractorsboard.com
Fur Dealer #26	www.ndow.org/law/licensed/
Garage, Registered #25	https://dmvapp.state.nv.us/DMV/OBL/Business_Reports/Pages/BusinessLicenses.aspx
Gas Fitter #46	www.nvcontractorsboard.com
GCB Most-Wanted & Banned List #36	http://gaming.nv.gov/unsuitable.htm
Glazier Contractor #46	www.nvcontractorsboard.com
Guard Dog Handler #39	http://nevadapilb.glsuite.us/
Heating/Air Conditioning Mechanic #46	www.nvcontractorsboard.com
Hospital Pharmacy, Institutional #16	http://64.42.58.74/datamart/mainMenu.do
Installment Loan Company #29	http://fid.state.nv.us/New_LicenseeMenu.htm
Insulation Installer Contractor #46	www.nvcontractorsboard.com
Interior Designer #2	http://nsbaidrd.state.nv.us/directory.htm
Investment Advisor #40	www.sos.state.nv.us/securities/
Landscape Architect #10	http://nsbla.state.nv.us/Licensed.htm

Landscape Contractor #46 .... www.nvcontractorsboard.com
Mason #46 .... www.nvcontractorsboard.com
Medical Device, Equipment or Gas #16 ..... http://64.42.58.74/datamart/mainMenu.do
Medical Doctor #11 .... http://medboard.nv.gov/default.asp
Money Transmitter Agent/Firm #29 .... http://fid.state.nv.us/New_LicenseeMenu.htm
Narcotic Treatment Center #16 .... http://64.42.58.74/datamart/mainMenu.do
Nurse Aide, CAN #13 .... www.nursingboard.state.nv.us/Verification/formLicense.html
Nurse Anesthetist #13 .... www.nursingboard.state.nv.us/Verification/formLicense.html
Nurse, Adv'd Practitioner (Pharm) #16 .... http://64.42.58.74/datamart/mainMenu.do
Nurse, Adverse Action Report #13 .... www.nursingboard.state.nv.us/dactions/
Nurse, RN/LPN/Advanced Practice #13 ..... www.nursingboard.state.nv.us/Verification/formLicense.html
Occupational Therapist/Assistant #12 .... www.nvot.org/index.php?click=search
Optometrist #50 .... http://optometry.nv.gov/Qry-LicenseeInfoForm1.asp
Oriental Medical Doctor (OMD) #14 .... www.oriental.nv.gov/qry-licensees_name.asp
Osteopathic Physician #15 .... http://license.k3systems.com/LicensingPublic/app?page=licenseeSearch&service=page
Osteopathic Physician Assistant #15.......... http://license.k3systems.com/LicensingPublic/app?page=licenseeSearch&service=page
Painter/Paper Hanger #46 .... www.nvcontractorsboard.com
Patrol Company/Man, Private #39 .... http://nevadapilb.glsuite.us/
Pharmacist/Pharmaceutical Tech #16 .... http://64.42.58.74/datamart/mainMenu.do
Pharmacy/Pharmacy Practitioner #16 .... http://64.42.58.74/datamart/mainMenu.do
Physical Therapist #17 .... http://ptboard.nv.gov/PT-verif-index.htm
Physical Therapist Assistant #17............... http://ptboard.nv.gov/PT-verif-index.htm
Physician Assistant #11 .... http://medboard.nv.gov/default.asp
Physician Assistant (Pharm) #16............... http://64.42.58.74/datamart/mainMenu.do
Plaster/Lather #46 .... www.nvcontractorsboard.com
Plasterer/Drywall Installer #46 .... www.nvcontractorsboard.com
Playground Builder #46 .... www.nvcontractorsboard.com
Plumber #46 .... www.nvcontractorsboard.com
Podiatrist #18 .... http://podiatry.state.nv.us/qry-Licenses.asp
Polygraph Examiner #39 .... http://nevadapilb.glsuite.us/
Prison Pharmacy #16 .... http://64.42.58.74/datamart/mainMenu.do
Private Investigator #39 .... http://nevadapilb.glsuite.us/
Process Server #39 .... http://nevadapilb.glsuite.us/
Public Accountant-CPA #1 .... www.nvaccountancy.com/search.fx
Pump Installer #46........................ www.nvcontractorsboard.com
Referee/Judge/Timekeeper #35 .... http://boxing.nv.gov/New_ROfficInsp.htm
Refractory/Firebrick Contractor #46.......... www.nvcontractorsboard.com
Repossessor #39........................ http://nevadapilb.glsuite.us/
Residential Designer #2........................ http://nsbaidrd.state.nv.us/directory.htm
Respiratory Care Practitioner #11 .... http://medboard.nv.gov/default.asp
Roofer #46........................ www.nvcontractorsboard.com
Savings & Loan #29........................ http://fid.state.nv.us/New_LicenseeMenu.htm
Scientific Collector #26 .... www.ndow.org/law/licensed/
Securities Broker/Dealer #40..................... www.sos.state.nv.us/securities/
Sewerage Contractor #46........................ www.nvcontractorsboard.com
Sheet Metal Fabricator #46 .... www.nvcontractorsboard.com
Siding Installer #46 .... www.nvcontractorsboard.com
Sign Erector #46........................ www.nvcontractorsboard.com
Social Worker #6 .... www.socwork.nv.gov/
Solar Contractor #46........................ www.nvcontractorsboard.com
Speech Pathologist #31........................ http://speech_pathology.state.nv.us/LicenseVerification.htm
Steel Contractor #46........................ www.nvcontractorsboard.com
Surveyor, Land #19 .... http://boe.state.nv.us/pls.htm
Tank Installer, Pressure/Storage #46 .... www.nvcontractorsboard.com
Taxicab Authority #48........................ www.taxi.state.nv.us
Thrift Company #29 .... http://fid.state.nv.us/New_LicenseeMenu.htm
Traffic Safety School #25........................ https://dmvapp.state.nv.us/DMV/OBL/Business_Reports/Pages/BusinessLicenses.aspx
Transporter, Vehicle #25 .... https://dmvapp.state.nv.us/DMV/OBL/Business_Reports/Pages/BusinessLicenses.aspx
Trust Company #29 .... http://fid.state.nv.us/New_LicenseeMenu.htm
Vehicle Broker/Dealer #25........................ https://dmvapp.state.nv.us/DMV/OBL/Business_Reports/Pages/BusinessLicenses.aspx
Veterinarian/Veterinary Facility #21............ https://www.nvvetboard.us/Renewal/glsweb/homeframe.aspx
Well Driller #46 .... www.nvcontractorsboard.com
Well Driller/Monitor #30 .... http://water.nv.gov/Engineering/wd/wd_queries.cfm
Wrecker #25 .... https://dmvapp.state.nv.us/DMV/OBL/Business_Reports/Pages/BusinessLicenses.aspx
Wrecker/Demolisher #46 .... www.nvcontractorsboard.com

Nevada Licensing Quick Finder

Adult Day Care #22	775-687-4475
Adult Group Care #22	775-687-4475
Advanced Nurse Practitioner #13	888-590-6726
Aesthetician #38	702-486-6542
Alcohol & Drug Abuse Center #22	775-687-4475
Alcohol/Drug Abuse Counselor #22	775-687-4475
Ambulance Attendant #22	775-687-4475
Ambulance Permit #22	775-687-4475
Ambulatory Surgery Ctr (Pharm) #16	775-850-1440
Animal Technician #21	775-688-1788
Announcer, Athletic Event/Ring #35	702-486-2575
Appraiser (MVD) #24	702-486-4009
Architect #2	702-486-7300
Athletic Promoter, Prof/Amateur #35	702-486-2575
Attorney #44	702-382-2200
Audiologist #31	775-857-3500
Auditor, Accountancy #1	775-786-0231
Automobile/Vehicle Garage #25	775-684-4590
Automobile/Vehicle Mfg'r #25	775-684-4590
Automobile/Vehicle Rebuilder #25	775-684-4590
Automobile/Vehicle Transporter #25	775-684-4590
Automobile/Vehicle Wrecker/Salv. #25	775-684-4590
Bank #29	775-684-1830
Barber #45	702-456-4769
Blood Gas Tech./Technologist #22	775-687-4475
Body Shop #25	775-684-4590
Boxer #35	702-486-2575
Boxing Gym #35	702-486-2575
Boxing Organization #35	702-486-2575
Building Mover #46	702-486-1100
Bus Driver #25	775-684-4590
Carpentry Contractor #46	702-486-1100
Casino General Manager #36	775-684-7770
Cemetery #7	702-290-5366
Check Casher #29	775-684-1830
Chiropractor #3	775-688-1921
Claims Adjuster #24	702-486-4009
Clinical Laboratory Technologist #22	775-687-4475
Coach Dealer, Commercial #34	702-486-4590
Collection Agency #29	775-684-1830
Collection Manager #29	775-684-1830
Concrete Contractor #46	702-486-1100
Contractor, General #46	702-486-1100
Cosmetologist #38	702-486-6542
Court Reporter, Certified #23	702-448-8140
Credit Union #29	775-684-1830
Crematorium #7	702-290-5366
Debt Adjuster #29	775-684-1830
Deferred Deposit Company #29	775-684-1830
Denied/Unsuitable Gaming Person #36	775-684-7770
Dental Hygienist #4	702-486-7044
Dentist #4	702-486-7044
Director (Medical Laboratory) #22	775-687-4475
Doctor #11	775-688-2559
Doctor, Disciplinary Action #11	775-688-2559
Driving School #25	775-684-4590
Drug Wholesaler/Dist./Mfg. #16	775-850-1440
DUI School #25	775-684-4590
Electrical Contractor #46	702-486-1100
Electrologist #38	702-486-6542
Elevator/Conveyor #46	702-486-1100
Embalmer #7	702-290-5366
Emerg'cy Care Ctr, Independent #22	775-687-4475
Emergency Medical Service Nurse #13	888-590-6726
Emergency Medical Technician #22	775-687-4475
Engineer #19	775-688-1231
Engineering, General #46	702-486-1100
Environment'l Health Div. Director #42	775-328-2489
ESRD #22	775-687-4475
Euthanasia Technician #21	775-688-1788
Euthanasia Technician (Animal) #16	775-850-1440
Exempt Laboratory #22	775-687-4475
Fencing #46	702-486-1100
Financial Advisor (Investment Advisor) #40	702-486-2440
Financial Development Company #29	775-684-1830
Fire Protection Contractor #46	702-486-1100
First Responder EMT #22	775-687-4475
Fishing Guide #26	775-688-1512
Floor/Tile/Carpet Layer #46	702-486-1100
Funeral Director #7	702-290-5366
Fur Dealer #26	775-688-1512
Gaming #36	775-684-7770
Gaming Device Mfg./Dist. #36	775-684-7770
Gaming License Company #36	775-684-7770
Garage, Registered #25	775-684-4590
Gas Fitter #46	702-486-1100
GCB Most-Wanted & Banned List #36	775-684-7770
Glazier Contractor #46	702-486-1100
Groundskeeper/Gardener #28	775-688-1182 x243
Guard Dog Handler #39	775-687-3223
Hair Stylist (Designer) #38	702-486-6542
Health Clinic, Rural #22	775-687-4475
Hearing Aid Specialist #8	702-571-9000
Heating & Air Conditi'ng Mechanic #46	702-486-1100
Histologic Technician #22	775-687-4475
Histotechnologist #22	775-687-4475
Home Health Agency #22	775-687-4475
Homeopathic Physician/Assistant #9	702-451-3332
Homeopathic Practitioner, Adv'd #9	702-451-3332
Hospice #22	775-687-4475
Hospital #22	775-687-4475
Hospital Pharmacy, Institutional #16	775-850-1440
IC Emergency Center #22	775-687-4475
Installment Loan Company #29	775-684-1830
Instructor #38	702-986-6542
Insulation Installer Contractor #46	702-486-1100
Insurance Agent #24	702-486-4009
Interior Designer #2	702-486-7300
Intermediate Care Facility (Ret'd) #22	775-687-4475
Intermedical Care Facility #22	775-687-4475
Investment Advisor #40	702-486-2440
Kickboxer #35	702-486-2575
Laboratory Assist./Blood Gas Asst. #22	775-687-4475
Laboratory Certification #22	775-687-4475
Laboratory Office Assistant #22	775-687-4475
Laboratory, Medical #22	775-687-4475
Landscape Architect #10	775-530-4602
Landscape Contractor #46	702-486-1100
Lobbyist #27	775-684-6800
LPG Gas Distributor/Technician #33	775-687-4890
Manicurist #38	702-486-6542
Marriage & Family Therapist #32	702-486-7388
Mason #46	702-486-1100
Medical Device, Equipment or Gas #16	775-850-1440
Medical Doctor #11	775-688-2559
Medical Technician #22	775-687-4475
Mixed Martial Arts #35	702-486-2575
Mobile Home Dealer/Ltd. Dealer #34	702-486-4590
Mobile Home Installer/Mfg. #34	702-486-4590
Mobile Home Salesman #34	702-486-4590
Mobile Home Serviceman #34	702-486-4590
Mobile/Manufactur'd Home Rebuilder #34	702-486-4590
Mobile/Manufactured Home RME #34	702-486-4590
Money Transmitter Agent/Firm #29	775-684-1830
Narcotic Treatment Center #16	775-850-1440
Notary Public #41	775-684-5729
Nurse Aide, CAN #13	888-590-6726
Nurse Anesthetist #13	888-590-6726
Nurse, Adv'd Practitioner (Pharm) #16	775-850-1440
Nurse, Adverse Action Report #13	888-590-6726
Nurse, RN/LPN/Advanced Practice #13	888-590-6726
Nursing Care (Skilled) Facility #22	775-687-4475
Nursing Facility #22	775-687-4475
Nursing Home Administrator #49	702-486-5445
Nursing Pool Operator #22	775-687-4475
Occupational Therapist/Assistant #12	775-857-1700
Optician #5	775-853-1421
Optician Apprentice #5	775-853-1421
Optometrist #50	775-883-8367
Oriental Medical Doctor (OMD) #14	702-837-8921
Osteopathic Physician #15	702-732-2147
Osteopathic Physician Assistant #15	702-732-2147
Painter #46	702-486-1100
Painter/Paper Hanger #46	702-486-1100
Pathologist Assistant #22	775-687-4475
Patrol Company/Man, Private #39	775-687-3223
Pest Control Applicator/Company #28	775-688-1182 x252
Pesticide, Restricted Use #28	775-688-1182 x251
Pharmacist/Pharmaceutical Tech #16	775-850-1440
Pharmacy/Pharmacy Practitioner #16	775-850-1440
Physical Therapist #17	702-876-5535
Physical Therapist Assistant #17	702-876-5535
Physician Assistant #11	775-688-2559
Physician Assistant (Pharm) #16	775-850-1440
Plaster/Lather #46	702-486-1100
Plasterer/Drywall Installer #46	702-486-1100
Playground Builder #46	702-486-1100
Plumber #46	702-486-1100
Podiatrist #18	775-789-2605
Polygraph Examiner #39	775-687-3223
Prison Pharmacy #16	775-850-1440
Private Investigator #39	775-687-3223
Process Server #39	775-687-3223
Psychologist #20	775-688-1268
Public Accountant-CPA #1	775-786-0231
Pump Installer #46	702-486-1100
Racing (Horse) Owner/Trainer #37	775-684-7900
Real Estate Agent/Seller/Broker #43	702-486-4033
Referee/Judge/Timekeeper #35	702-486-2575
Refractory/Firebrick Contractor #46	702-486-1100
Rehabilitation Service #22	775-687-4475
Repossessor #39	775-687-3223
Residential Designer #2	702-486-7300
Respiratory Care Practitioner #11	775-688-2559
Roofer #46	702-486-1100
Savings & Loan #29	775-684-1830
School Administrator #47	702-486-6458
School Counselor/Librarian #47	702-486-6458
Scientific Collector #26	775-688-1512
Securities Branch Office #40	702-486-2440
Securities Broker/Dealer #40	702-486-2440
Securities Registration #40	702-486-2440
Securities Sales Representative #40	702-486-2440
Sewerage Contractor #46	702-486-1100
Sheet Metal Fabricator #46	702-486-1100
Siding Installer #46	702-486-1100
Sign Erector #46	702-486-1100
Slot Route Operator #36	775-684-7770
Social Worker #6	775-688-2555
Solar Contractor #46	702-486-1100
Speech Pathologist #31	775-857-3500
Steel Contractor #46	702-486-1100
Supvr. Medical Techn'l'gy, General #22	775-687-4475
Surgical Center, Ambulatory #22	775-687-4475
Surveyor, Land #19	775-688-1231
Tank Installer, Pressure/Storage #46	702-486-1100
Taxi Cab Company (Clark County) #48	702-486-6532
Taxi Driver #48	702-486-6532
Taxicab Authority #48	702-486-6532
Teacher #47	702-486-6458
Thrift Company #29	775-684-1830
Traffic Safety School #25	775-684-4590
Transporter, Vehicle #25	775-684-4590
Trust Company #29	775-684-1830
Vehicle Broker/Dealer #25	775-684-4590
Veterinarian/Veterinary Facility #21	775-688-1788
Water Well Driller #46	702-486-1100
Well Driller/Monitor #30	775-684-2800
Wrecker #25	775-684-4590
Wrecker/Demolisher #46	702-486-1100
Wrestler #35	702-486-2575

Nevada Licensing Agency Information

#1 Board of Accountancy, 1325 Airmotive Way, #220, Reno, NV 89502-3240; 775-786-0231, Fax- 775-786-0234. www.nvaccountancy.com Search data at- www.nvaccountancy.com/search.fx

#2 Interior & Residential Design, Board of Interior & Residential Design, 2080 E Flamingo Rd, #120, Las Vegas, NV 89119; 702-486-7300, Fax- 702-486-7304. http://nsbaidrd.state.nv.us Search data at- http://nsbaidrd.state.nv.us/directory.htm Phone 702-486-7300 for information on disciplinary actions.

#3 Board of Chiropractic Examiners, 4600 Kietzke Ln, Bldg M, #245, Reno, NV 89502; 775-688-1921, Fax- 775-688-1920. http://chirobd.nv.gov

#4 Board of Dental Examiners, 6010 S Rainbow Blvd, #A-1, Las Vegas, NV 89118; 800-337-3926 or 702-486-7044, Fax- 702-486-7046. 8AM-5PM. www.nvdentalboard.nv.gov/ Search data at- www.nvdentalboard.nv.gov/Vertification.htm

#5 Board of Dispensing Opticians, PO Box 19625, Reno, NV 89511-0868; 775-853-1421, Fax- 775-853-1408. Hours- 9AM-5PM. http://nvbdo.state.nv.us Complete list is available by mail from the board for a minimal fee.

#6 Board of Examiners for Social Workers, 4600 Kietzke Ln, Bldg C, Rm 121, Reno, NV 89502; 775-688-2555, Fax- 775-688-2557. Hours- 8AM-5PM. www.socwork.nv.gov

#7 Board of Funeral Directors & Embalmers, 4894 Lone Mt Rd PMB186, Las Vegas, NV 89130; 702-290-5366, Fax- 702-648-5100. http://funeral.state.nv.us

#8 Board of Hearing Aid Specialists, PO Box 190, Carson City, NV 89702; 702-571-9000, Fax- 775-267-9374. http://hearingaidboard.nv.gov

#9 Board of Homeopathic Medical Examiners, 435 Court St, Reno, NV 89501; 775-324-3353, Fax- 775-324-3353. Hours- 1PM-5PM. www.nvbhme.com

#10 Board of Landscape Architecture, PO Box 17039, Reno, NV 89511; 775-530-4602, Fax- 775-688-1317. http://nsbla.state.nv.us Search data at- http://nsbla.state.nv.us/Licensed.htm Complete list is available for $5.00 from the Board.

#11 Board of Medical Examiners, PO Box 7238 (1105 Terminal Way, #301), Reno, NV 89510; 775-688-2559, Fax- 775-688-2321. http://medboard.nv.gov Search data at- http://medboard.nv.gov/default.asp

#12 Board of Occupational Therapy, PO Box 34779, Reno, NV 89533-4779; 800-431-2659 or 775-746-4101, Fax- 775-746-4105. 8AM-4:30PM. www.nvot.org

#13 State Board of Nursing, 2500 W Sahara Ave, #207, Las Vegas, NV 89102-4392; 888-590-6726 or 702-486-5800, Fax- 702-486-5803. Hours- 8AM-5PM. www.nursingboard.state.nv.us Search data at- www.nursingboard.state.nv.us/Verification/formLicense.html Disciplinary actions and investigations are handled by the Reno office, 5011 Meadowood Mall Way #201, 89502, 888-590-6726. They now have batch verification available through their website, many names or license numbers can be entered at one time.

#14 Board of Oriental Medicine, 9775 S Maryland Pkwy, #F-280, Las Vegas, NV 89183; 702-837-8921, Fax- 702-914-8921. www.oriental.nv.gov Search data at- www.oriental.nv.gov/qry-licensees_name.asp

#15 Board of Osteopathic Medicine, 2860 E Flamingo Rd, #D, Las Vegas, NV 89121; 702-732-2147, Fax- 702-732-2079. http://license.k3systems.com/LicensingPublic/app?page=main&service=page Search data at- http://license.k3systems.com/LicensingPublic/app?page=licenseeSearch&service=page

#16 Board of Pharmacy, 431 W Plumb Ln, Reno, NV 89509; 775-850-1440, 800-364-2081, Fax- 775-850-1444. http://bop.nv.gov Search data at- http://64.42.58.74/datamart/mainMenu.do

#17 Physical Therapy Examiners Board, 810 S Durango Dr #109, Las Vegas, NV 89145; 702-876-5535, Fax- 702-876-2097. Hours- 9AM-4PM. http://ptboard.nv.gov Search data at- http://ptboard.nv.gov/PT-verif-index.htm

#18 Board of Podiatry, PO Box 12215 (1105 Terminal Way, #202), Reno, NV 89510-2215; 775-789-2605, Fax- 775-786-7188. Hours- 9AM-5PM. http://podiatry.state.nv.us

#19 Board of Professional Engineers & Land Surveyors, 1755 E Plumb Ln, #135, Reno, NV 89502; 775-688-1231, Fax- 775-688-2991. http://boe.state.nv.us

#20 Board of Psychological Examiners, 4600 Kietzke Ln, Bldg E-141, Reno, NV 89505-2286; 775-688-1268, Fax- 775-688-1272. Hours- 9Am-5PM. http://psyexam.state.nv.us Email verifications & lists are free. Fax or mailed verifications $15.00 per person. List of Psychologists mailed $10.00, includes effective date, expiration date and license number.

#21 Board of Veterinary Medical Examiners, 4600 Kietzke Ln, Bldg O-265, Reno, NV 89502; 775-688-1788, Fax- 775-688-1808. 7:30AM-4:30PM. https://www.nvvetboard.us/Renewal/glsweb/homeframe.aspx Search data at- https://www.nvvetboard.us/renewal/glsweb/homeframe.aspx

#22 Bureau of Health Care Quality and Compliance, Medical Laboratory Services, 1550 College Parkway #158, Carson City, NV 89710; 775-687-4475, Fax- 775-687-6588. http://health.nv.gov/index.php?option=com_content&task=view&id=31&Itemid=68

#23 Certified Court Reporters Board, 500 N Rainbow Blvd #300, Las Vegas, NV 89107; 702-448-8140, Fax- 702-448-8141. http://crptr.state.nv.us

#24 Department of Business & Industry, Insurance Division, 2501 E Sahara Ave, #302, Las Vegas, NV 89104; 702-486-4009, Fax- 702-486-4007. www.doi.state.nv.us

#25 Department of Motor Vehicles & Public Safety, Records Section, 555 Wright Way, Carson City, NV 89711-0250; 775-684-4590, Fax- 775-684-4740. http://nevadadmv.state.nv.us Search at- https://dmvapp.state.nv.us/DMV/OBL/Business_Reports/Pages/BusinessLicenses.aspx

#26 Department of Wildlife, Licensed Wildlife Services, 1100 Valley Rd, Reno, NV 89512; 775-688-1500, Fax- 775-688-1551. www.ndow.org Search data at- www.ndow.org/law/licensed/

#27 Director of Legislative Counsel Bureau, 401 S Carson St, Carson City, NV 89701-4747; 775-684-6800, Fax- 775-684-6600. www.leg.state.nv.us/lcb/admin/lobbyist.htm

#28 Department of Agriculture, Pest Control Licensing Division, 350 Capitol Hill, Reno, NV 89502-2923; 775-688-1180, Fax- 775-688-1178. http://agri.state.nv.us

#29 Department of Business & Industry, Division of Financial Institutions, 1179 Fairview Dr #201, Carson City, NV 89701; 775-687-5522; 702-486-4120-Las Vegas, Fax- 775-687-5523. Hours-8AM-5PM. http://fid.state.nv.us Search data at- http://fid.state.nv.us/New_LicenseeMenu.htm Las Vegas office located at 2785 E Desert Inn Rd., #180, 89121; 702-486-4120, fax 702-486-4563.

#30 Division of Water Resources, Well Drillers' Advisory Board, 901 S Stewart St, #2002, Carson City, NV 89701; 775-684-2800, F-775-684-2811. http://ndwr.state.nv.us Search data at- http://water.nv.gov/Engineering/wd/wd_queries.cfm

#31 Board of Examiners for Audiology & Speech Pathology, PO Box 70550, Reno, NV 89570; 775-857-3500, Fax- 775-857-2121. http://speech_pathology.state.nv.us

#32 Board of Examiners of Marriage & Family Therapists, PO Box 370130, Las Vegas, NV 89134-0130; 702-486-7388, Fax- 702-486-7258. http://marriage.state.nv.us

#33 Liquefied Petroleum Gas Regulation Board, PO Box 338 (106 E Adams St, Rm 216), Carson City, NV 89702; 775-687-4890, Fax- 775-687-3956. http://lpg.nv.gov

#34 Attn: Gisele Jordan, Licensing Officer, Manufactured Housing Division, 2501 E Sahara Ave, #204, Las Vegas, NV 89104; 702-486-4135, Fax- 702-486-4309. http://mhd.state.nv.us/ Other office: 788 Fairview Dr #100, Carson City, NV 89701, 775-687-5500, 775-687-5521-Fax.

#35 Athletic Commission, 555 E Washington Ave, #3200, Las Vegas, NV 89101; 702-486-2575, Fax- 702-486-2577. www.boxing.nv.gov

#36 Tax & License Division, Gaming Control Board, PO Box 8003 (1919 E College Pky), Carson City, NV 89702-8003; 775-684-7770, Fax- 775-684-7787. http://gaming.nv.gov

#37 Gaming Control Board, Enforcement Division, PO Box 8003 (1919 College Pky), Carson City, NV 89702; 775-684-7900, Fax- 775-687-5362. http://gaming.nv.gov

#38 Board of Cosmetology, 1785 E Sahara Ave, #255, Las Vegas, NV 89104; 702-486-6542, Fax- 702-369-8064. www.cosmetology.nv.gov

#39 Office of the Attorney General, Private Investigators Licensing Board, 3476 Executive Pointe Way, #14, Carson City, NV 89706; 775-687-3223, Fax- 775-687-3226. Hours- 8AM-5PM. http://nevadapilb.glsuite.us Lists only those who want to be listed.

#40 Office of the Secretary of State, Securities Division, 555 E Washington Ave, #5200, Las Vegas, NV 89101; 702-486-2440, Fax- 702-486-2452. www.sos.state.nv.us/securities/

#41 Office of the Secretary of State, Notary Division, 101 N Carson St, #3, Carson City, NV 89701-3714; 775-684-5708, Fax- 775-684-5725. http://sos.state.nv.us/licensing/notary/generalinfo.asp

#42 Environmental Health Services Division, Washoe County District Health Department, PO Box 11130 (1001 E 9th St), Reno, NV 89520; 775-328-2434, Fax- 775-328-6176. Hours- 8AM-5PM. www.co.washoe.nv.us/health/ehs/regulations.html

#43 Department of Business & Industry, Real Estate Division, 2501 E Sahara Ave, #102, Las Vegas, NV 89104-4137; 702-486-4033, Fax- 702-486-4275. www.red.state.nv.us Carson City Office; 788 Fairview Dr #200, Carson City, NV 89701-5453; 775-687-4280; 775-687-4868 Fax.

#44 State Bar of Nevada, 600 E Charleston Blvd, Las Vegas, NV 89104; 702-382-2200, Fax- 702-385-2878. www.nvbar.org Search data at- www.nvbar.org/findalawyer.asp

#45 Barbers' Health & Sanitation Board, 4710 E Flamingo Rd, Las Vegas, NV 89121; 702-456-4769 LV (775-688-1988 Reno), Fax- 702-456-1948. http://barber.state.nv.us

#46 Contractors' Board, 9670 Gateway Dr, #100, Reno, NV 89521; 775-688-1141-Reno, Fax- 775-688-1271. Hours- 8AM-5PM. www.nvcontractorsboard.com Phone for the Henderson office 702-486-1100; fax- 702-486-1190; address- 2310 Corporate Circle #200.

#47 Department of Education, Teacher Licensure, 1820 E Sahara, #205, Las Vegas, NV 89104; 702-486-6458, Fax- 702-486-6450. Hours- 8AM-5PM. www.doe.nv.gov

#48 Taxicab Authority, 1785 E Sahara Ave, #200, Las Vegas, NV 89104; 702-668-4000, Fax- 702-668-4001. 7AM-5PM. www.taxi.state.nv.us

#49 Board of Examiners for Long Term Care Administrators, 3157 N Rainbow Blvd, #313, Las Vegas, NV 89108; 702-486-5445, Fax- 702-486-5434. Hours- 8AM-5PM. http://beltca.nevada.gov

#50 Board of Optometry, PO Box 1824, Carson City, NV 89702; 775-883-8367, Fax- 775-883-1938. http://optometry.nv.gov Search data at- http://optometry.nv.gov/Qry-LicenseeInfoForm1.asp

Nevada Federal Courts

The following list indicates the district and division name for each county in the state. If the bankruptcy court location is different from the district court, then the location of the bankruptcy court appears in parentheses.

Nevada County/Court Cross Reference

County	Court	County	Court
Carson City	Reno	Lincoln	Las Vegas
Churchill	Reno	Lyon	Reno
Clark	Las Vegas	Mineral	Reno
Douglas	Reno	Nye	Las Vegas
Elko	Reno	Pershing	Reno
Esmeralda	Las Vegas	Storey	Reno
Eureka	Reno	Washoe	Reno
Humboldt	Reno	White Pine	Reno
Lander	Reno		

US District Court

Las Vegas Division Court Clerk, 333 Las Vegas Blvd S, Rm 4425, Las Vegas, NV 89101, 702-464-5400; records- 702-464-5408. Hours- 9AM-4PM. www.nvd.uscourts.gov

Counties/Note: Clark, Esmeralda, Lincoln, Nye.

Searches/Indexing: Only full name required in search request. Results do not include SSN or DOB. New cases are in the index same day after filing date. Computer index maintained back to 1999. Records available electronically only. **Search Access:** Only docket info available by phone. **Mail:** Search usually completed- 1-2 days. SASE not required. **In person:** Public access terminal provides statewide access; records here go back to 2000. No self-serve copier.

Payment: Pay by money order, cashier's or personal check. Payee: Clerk, US District Court.

E-Services: PACER now on ECF. Document images available. ECF at https://ecf.nvd.uscourts.gov. Search cases free at www.nvd.uscourts.gov/IndexCases/applicationroot.asp.

Reno Division Court Clerk, 400 S Virginia St, Rm 301, Reno, NV 89501, 775-686-5800; records- 775-686-5909; crim dockets- 775-686-5844; civil dockets- 775-686-5845; Fax- 775-686-5851. Hours-9AM-4PM. www.nvd.uscourts.gov

Counties/Note: Carson City, Churchill, Douglas, Elko, Eureka, Humboldt, Lander, Lyon, Mineral, Pershing, Storey, Washoe, White Pine.

Searches/Indexing: Only full name required in search request. Results do not include SSN or DOB. New cases are in the index 1-2 days after filing date. Computer index maintained back to 1999. Case files sent to archives yearly, however electronic cases not purged. **Search Access:** Only docket info available by phone. **Mail:** Search usually completed- within 1 week. SASE not required. **In person:** 1 public terminal provides statewide access; records here go back to 2000. No self-serve copier.

Payment: Pay by Visa/MC, money order, cashier's or personal check. Payee: Clerk, US District Court.

E-Services: PACER now on ECF. Document images available. PACER records go back to 1992. ECF at https://ecf.nvd.uscourts.gov. Search cases free at www.nvd.uscourts.gov/IndexCases/applicationroot.asp.

US Bankruptcy Court

Las Vegas Division Court Clerk, 300 Las Vegas Blvd South, #8112, Lloyd D George Federal Bldg, Las Vegas, NV 89101 (In person: Clerk's Office, 1st Fl, Lloyd D George Federal Bldg, 300 Las Vegas Blvd South, Las Vegas), 702-388-6257. Hours- 9AM - 4PM. www.nvb.uscourts.gov

Counties/Note: Clark, Esmeralda, Lincoln, Nye.

Searches/Indexing: Include current and maiden names and alias and SSN in search request. Results do not include SSN or DOB. Will not fax back documents. New cases are in the index 24 hours after filing date. Both computer and card indexes maintained. All cases stored electronically, kept indefinitely.

Search Access: Voice Case Information Service available, call VCIS at 800-294-6920 or 702-388-6708. **Mail:** Search usually completed- 1 day. Include SASE for return. **In person:** 3 public terminals available. Copies printed from public terminal- $.10 each.

Payment: Pay by money order, cashier's or personal checks. No debtor checks/credit cards. Payee: Clerk, US Bankruptcy Court.

E-Services: PACER records go back to 9/1993. New records online after 1 day. ECF at https://ecf.nvb.uscourts.gov. **Opinions Online:** www.nvb.uscourts.gov/Opinions/Opinions_Home.htm. Opinions are also found under individual judge's names; Latest Opinions featured on this Judicial Opinions page. **Note:** Court calendars and Judge preferences available at the court website.

Reno Division Court Clerk, 300 Booth St, Rm 1109, Reno, NV 89509, 775-784-5559. Hours- 9AM-4PM. www.nvb.uscourts.gov

Counties/Note: Carson City, Churchill, Douglas, Elko, Eureka, Humboldt, Lander, Lyon, Mineral, Pershing, Storey, Washoe, White Pine.

Searches/Indexing: Include current and maiden names and alias and SSN in search request. Results do not include SSN or DOB. Will not fax back documents. New cases are in the index immediately after filing date. Closed case files sent to archives quarterly.

Search Access: Voice Case Information Service available, call VCIS at 800-294-6920 or 702-388-6708. **Mail:** Search usually completed- 3 days. Include SASE for return. **In person:** 2 public terminals available. No self-serve copier available. A copy service available.

Payment: Pay by money order, cashier's or personal checks. No debtor checks/credit cards. Payee: Clerk, US Bankruptcy Court.

E-Services: PACER records go back to 9/1993. New records online after 1 day. ECF at https://ecf.nvb.uscourts.gov. **Opinions Online:** www.nvb.uscourts.gov/Opinions/Opinions_Home.htm. Opinions are also found under individual judge's names; Latest Opinions featured on this Judicial Opinions page. **Note:** Court calendars and Judge preferences available at the court website.

Standards for Federal Courts: Fees are standard unless noted in profile. Search fee is $26.00 per item (one party name or case number). Copy fee is $.50 per page. Certification fee is $9.00 per document, double for exemplification, if available. Most courts require prepayment. Mail requests should enclose a SASE unless otherwise noted. Before releasing records, all courts require prepayment, unless noted.

District courts index by defendant and plaintiff and by case number. Bankruptcy courts usually index by debtor and case number. While most courts now have their indexes on computer, many may still maintain index card files as well. Courts will archive closed case files at different times.

There are numerous public access programs available to online subscribers. Search the U.S. Party/Case Index to find party names and case numbers among all courts. Individual case data is provided on PACER. A search of CM/ECF provides copies of cases filed electronically. For details about PACER, the US Party/Case Index, and CM/ECF see the Appendix or go to http://pacer.psc.uscourts.gov or call 800-676-6856.

Nevada County Courts

Court	Jurisdiction	No. of Courts	How Organized
District Courts*	General	17	9 Districts
Justice Courts*	Limited	46	Townships
Municipal Courts	Municipal	17	19 Incorporated Cities/Towns

* Profiled in this Sourcebook.

Court	CIVIL Tort	Contract	Real Estate	Min. Claim	Max. Claim	Small Claims	Estate	Eviction	Domestic Relations
District Courts*	X	X	X	10,000	No Max		X		X
Justice Courts*	X	X	X	$0	$10,000	$3500		X	
Municipal Courts	X	X	X	$0	$3500	$3500			

Court	CRIMINAL Felony	Misdemeanor	DWI/DUI	Preliminary Hearing	Juvenile
District Courts*	X		X		X
Justice Courts*		X	X	X	
Municipal Courts		X			

Administration

Supreme Court of Nevada, Administrative Office of the Courts, Capitol Complex, 201 S Carson Street #250, Carson City, Nevada, 89701; 775-684-1700, Fax: 775-684-1723. (PST) www.nvsupremecourt.us/index.php

Court Structure

The District Courts are the courts of general jurisdiction. Probate is handled by the District Courts, as are divorce records. The minimum civil limit raised from $7,500 to $10,000 on Jan 1, 2005. The judges also hear appeals from Justice and Municipal Court cases. The Justice Courts are named for the township of jurisdiction. Due to their small populations, some townships no longer have Justice Courts. The Justice Courts handle misdemeanor crime and traffic matters, small claims disputes, evictions, and other civil matters less than $10,000. The Justices of the Peace also preside over felony and gross misdemeanor arraignments and conduct preliminary hearings to determine if sufficient evidence exists to hold criminals for trial at District Court. The Municipal Courts manage cases involving violations of traffic and misdemeanor ordinances that occur within the city limits of incorporated municipalities.

Online Access

Some Nevada courts have internal online computer systems, but only Clark and Washoe counties offer online access to the public. A statewide court automation system is being implemented. The Supreme Court website gives access to opinions.

Searching Tips, Fees, and Other Guidelines

Many Nevada Justice Courts are small and have very few records. Their hours of operation vary widely and contact is difficult. It is recommended that requesters call ahead for information prior to submitting a written request or attempting an in person retrieval. Fees will vary; many Justice Courts charge $1.00 per name per year to do a name search.

Carson City

1st Judicial District Court 885 E Musser St, #3031, Carson City, NV 89701-4775; 775-887-2082; fax: 775-887-2177; 9AM-5PM (PST). ***Felony, Gross Misdemeanor, Civil Actions over $10,000, Probate.***

www.carson-city.nv.us/Index.aspx?page=240

The Justice Courts retain records for minor misdemeanors.

Civil Records: Access: Mail, in person. Only the court performs in person searches; visitors may not. Search fee: $1.00 per name per year. Required to search: name, years to search. Civil cases indexed by defendant, plaintiff; index on computer from 1987, on microfiche and archives from 1861. Mail turnaround time 2-3 days.

Criminal Records: Access: Mail, in person. Only the court performs in person searches; visitors may not. Search fee: $1.00 per name per year. Required to search: name, years to search. Criminal records computerized from 1987, on microfiche and archives from 1861. Mail turnaround time 2-3 days.

General Information: No sealed or juvenile records released. Will fax documents to local or toll free line. Court makes copy: $1.00 per page. Certification fee: $5.00 if copy is presented to this office, $3.00 if they make the copies. Payee: Carson City. Personal check accepted with check guarantee card only. No credit cards accepted. Prepayment required. Mail requests: SASE required.

Justice & Municipal Court 885 E Musser St, #2007, Carson City, NV 89701-4775; 775-887-2121; fax: 775-887-2297; 8AM-5PM (PST). ***Misdemeanor, Civil Actions under $10,000, Eviction, Small Claims.***

www.carson-city.nv.us/Index.aspx?page=413

Civil Records: Access: Mail, in person. Only the court performs in person searches; visitors may not. Search fee: $1.00 per name per year. Required to search: name, years to search. Criminal records on computer alpha index from 1991. Mail turnaround time 1 week.

Criminal Records: Access: Mail, in person. Only the court performs in person searches; visitors may not. Search fee: $1.00 per name per year. Required to search: name, years to search. Criminal records on computer alpha index from 1991. Note: In person is not while you wait. Mail turnaround time 1 week.

General Information: No sealed, sexual victims, juvenile records released. Will fax documents to local or toll free line. Court makes copy: $.30 per page. Certification fee: $3.00 per doc. Payee: Carson City. Personal checks accepted. Visa/MC accepted inperson only. Prepayment required. Mail requests: SASE required.

Churchill County

3rd Judicial District Court 73 N Maine St, #B, Fallon, NV 89406; 775-423-6080; fax: 775-423-8578; 8AM-N, 1-5PM (PST). ***Felony, Gross Misdemeanor, Civil Actions over $10,000, Probate.***
www.churchillcounty.org/dcourt
Probate fax is same as main fax number.
Civil Records: Access: Fax, mail, in person. Only the court performs in person searches; visitors may not. Search fee: $1.00 per name per year. Required to search: name, years to search. Civil cases indexed by defendant, plaintiff; index on computer from 1990, prior on books, microfiche. Mail turnaround time 1-2 days.
Criminal Records: Access: Fax, mail, in person. Only the court performs in person searches; visitors may not. Search fee: $1.00 per name per year. Required to search: name, years to search, DOB; also helpful: SSN. Criminal records computerized from 1990, prior on books, microfiche to 1910. Mail turnaround time 1-2 days.
General Information: No juvenile, adoption or sealed records released. No fee to fax documents to local or toll free numbers only. Court makes copy: $1.00 per page. Certification fee: $5.00 per document. Payee: Office of Court Clerk. Business checks accepted; no personal checks. No credit cards accepted. Prepayment required. Mail requests: SASE required.

New River Justice Court 71 N Maine St, Fallon, NV 89406; 775-423-2845; fax: 775-423-0472; 8AM-5PM (PST). ***Misdemeanor, Civil Actions under $10,000, Eviction, Small Claims.***
www.churchillcounty.org/jcourt
Fax search requests must be prepaid; use credit card. Use fax number 775-423-3202 for search request, and include credit card for payment.
Civil Records: Access: Mail, fax, in person. Both court and visitors may perform in person searches. Search fee: $1.00 per name per year. Required to search: name, years to search. Civil cases indexed by defendant, plaintiff; index on computer from 1987, prior on microfiche back to 1980. Mail turnaround time 1 day.
Criminal Records: Access: Mail, fax, in person. Both court and visitors may perform in person searches. Search fee: $1.00 per name per year. Required to search: name, years to search, DOB. Criminal records computerized from 1987, prior on microfiche back to 1980. Mail turnaround time 1 day.
General Information: No sealed records released. Will fax search results to toll-free line. Court makes copy: $.30 per page. Certification fee: $3.00 per doc; Exemplification- $6.00 per doc. Payee: Justice Court. Personal checks accepted. Visa/MC accepted. Prepayment required.

Clark County

8th Judicial District Court 200 Lewis Ave, 3rd Fl, Records Dept, Las Vegas, NV 89155; 702-671-4554; criminal phone: 702-671-0501; civil phone: 702-671-0530; probate phone: 702-455-2373 family ct; fax: 702-474-2434; 8AM-5PM (PST). ***Felony, Gross Misdemeanor, Civil Actions over $10,000, Probate.***
www.clarkcountycourts.us/
Records Dept is on the 3rd Fl. Records Dept does have microfilm of probate records, though actual probate records are managed by the family court.
Civil Records: Access: Mail, in person, online. Both court and visitors may perform in person searches. Search fee: $1.00 per name per year. Fee is per case type. Required to search: name, years to search. Civil cases indexed by defendant, plaintiff; index on computer back to 11/90, prior records on microfilm to 1909. Note: Clerks will search several names in person but if 5 or more names presented, wait is 1-2 days. Mail turnaround time 10 working days. Civil PAT goes back to 1/1990. PAT results show name only. Records from 1990 to present are searchable free at http://courtgate.coca.co.clark.nv.us:8490. Search by case number or party name. A wealth of data is available including calendars, but few personal identifiers. Probate records also online.
Criminal Records: Access: Mail, in person, online. Both court and visitors may perform in person searches. Search fee: $1.00 per name per year. Fee is per case type, i.e.: crim, civil. Required to search: name, years to search, DOB, alias, charges. Criminal records computerized from 11/90, prior records on microfilm to 1909. Note: Clerks will search 1 to 2 names in person but if a list is presented, expect to wait 24-48 hours for results. Personal identifiers most likely found in case pleadings and in police reports. Mail turnaround time 10 working days. Criminal PAT goes back to 1/1991. PAT results show middle initial, DOB. Online access to criminal records is the same as civil. Online results show name only.
General Information: No sealed records released. Will not fax out documents. Court makes copy: $1.00 per page. Self serve: $.10 per page but cannot be used to copy from files. Certification fee: $3.00 to Certify or $6.00 to Exemplify when copies supplied by court. If own copies, $5.00 to Cert, $9.00 to Exemp. Payee: 8th Judicial District Court. Personal checks accepted if pre-printed. No credit cards accepted. Prepayment required. Mail requests: SASE required.

Boulder Township Justice Court 505 Ave G, Boulder City, NV 89005; 702-455-8000; fax: 702-455-8003; 7:30AM-5PM M-TH (PST). ***Misdemeanor, Civil Actions under $10,000, Eviction, Small Claims.***
www.lasvegascourts.org/
Civil Records: Access: Fax, mail, in person, online. Both court and visitors may perform in person searches. Search fee: $1.00 per name per year. Required to search: name, years to search; also helpful: address. Civil cases indexed by defendant. Civil records on microfiche varies depending on subject. Mail turnaround time 1 week. Access civil cases at http://cvpublicaccess.co.clark.nv.us/pa/. Search calendars free at http://redrock.co.clark.nv.us/jcCalendar/CalendarSearch.aspx.
Criminal Records: Access: Fax, mail, in person, online. Only the court performs in person searches; visitors may not. Search fee: $1.00 per name per year. Required to search: name, years to search, DOB, date of offense; also helpful: SSN. Criminal records on microfiche varies depending on subject. Mail turnaround time 1 week. Access to Misdemeanor cases online is same as civil, see above. Online results show middle initial, DOB.
General Information: No financial records released. Will not fax documents. Court makes copy: $.30 per page. Certification fee: $3.00. Payee: Justice Court. Personal checks accepted. Visa/MC accepted. Prepayment required. Mail requests: SASE required.

Bunkerville Justice Court 190 W Virgin St, PO Box 7185, Bunkerville, NV 89007; 702-346-5711; fax: 702-346-7212; 7AM-4PM M-TH (PST). ***Misdemeanor, Civil Actions under $10,000, Eviction, Small Claims.***
www.lasvegascourts.org/
Civil Records: Access: Mail, in person, online. Only the court performs in person searches; visitors may not. Search fee: $1.00 per name per year. Required to search: name, years to search. Civil cases indexed by case number. Civil records (citations) on computer from 1991, on docket books. Mail turnaround time 2 weeks. Access civil cases at http://cvpublicaccess.co.clark.nv.us/pa/. Search calendars free at http://redrock.co.clark.nv.us/jcCalendar/CalendarSearch.aspx.
Criminal Records: Access: Mail, in person, online. Only the court performs in person searches; visitors may not. Search fee: $1.00 per name per year. Required to search: name, years to search, DOB; also helpful: SSN. Criminal records (citations) on computer from 1997, on docket books. Mail turnaround time 2 weeks. Access to Misdemeanor cases online is same as civil, see above. Online results show middle initial, DOB.
General Information: No sealed or confidential records released. Will fax documents. Court makes copy: $.30 per page. Certification fee: $3.00 per cert. Payee: Bunkerville Justice Court. No personal checks accepted. Visa/MC accepted. Prepayment required.

Goodsprings Township Jean Justice Ct PO Box 19155, 23120 Las Vegas Blvd South, Jean, NV 89019; 702-874-1405; fax: 702-874-1612; 7AM-4PM M-TH (PST). ***Misdemeanor, Civil Actions under $10,000, Eviction, Small Claims.***
www.lasvegascourts.org/
Civil Records: Access: Fax, mail, in person, online. Only the court performs in person searches; visitors may not. Search fee: $1.00 per name per year. Required to search: name, years to search, case number. Civil cases indexed by defendant, plaintiff; index on computer for 6 months, file reports from 1990. Mail turnaround time within 2 weeks. Court cases and calendars may be available free at www.accessclarkcounty.com/depts/clark_county/pages/justicecourt_index.aspx.
Criminal Records: Access: Fax, mail, in person, online. Only the court performs in person searches; visitors may not. Search fee: $1.00 per name per year. Required to search: name, years to search, DOB, case number; also helpful: SSN. Criminal records on computer for 6 months, file reports from 1990. Mail turnaround time within 2 weeks. Court cases and calendars may be available free at www.accessclarkcounty.com/depts/clark_county/pages/justicecourt_index.aspx. Access to Misdemeanor cases online is same as civil, see above. Online results show middle initial, DOB.
General Information: No sealed records released. Will not fax documents. Court makes copy: $.25 per page. Certification fee: $2.00 per doc. Payee: Goodsprings Justice Court. Business checks accepted. Visa/MC accepted. Prepayment required. Mail requests: SASE required.

Henderson Township Justice 243 S Water St, Henderson, NV 89015; 702-455-7930; criminal phone: 702-455-7929; civil phone: 702-455-7978; fax: 702-455-7977; 7AM-5:30PM M-TH (PST). ***Misdemeanor, Civil Actions under $10,000, Eviction, Small Claims, Felony Prelim.***
www.lasvegascourts.org/
Traffic can be reached at 702-455-7980.
Civil Records: Access: Mail, in person, online. Only the court performs in person searches; visitors may not. Search fee: $1.00 per name per year. Required to search: name, years to search, DOB, SSN. Civil cases indexed by defendant. Civil index on cards and docket books. Evictions kept for 2-6 years; civil and small claims for 6 years. Mail turnaround time 2 weeks. Access civil cases at http://cvpublicaccess.co.clark.nv.us/pa/. Search calendars free at http://redrock.co.clark.nv.us/jcCalendar/CalendarSearch.aspx.
Criminal Records: Access: Mail, in person, online. Only the court performs in person searches; visitors may not. Search fee: $1.00 per name per year. Required to search: name, years to search, DOB; also helpful: SSN. Criminal records go back 10 years. Mail turnaround time 2 weeks. Access to Misdemeanor cases online is same as civil, see above. Online results show middle initial, DOB.
General Information: Will not fax documents. Court makes copy: $.30 per page. Certification fee: $3.00. Payee: Henderson Justice Court. Personal checks accepted. Visa/MC accepted. Prepayment required. Mail requests: SASE required.

Las Vegas Township Justice PO Box 552511, 200 Lewis Ave, Regional Justice Center, Las Vegas, NV 89155; 702-671-3116; fax: 702-671-3175; 8AM-5PM (PST). ***Misdemeanor, Civil Actions under $10,000, Eviction, Small Claims, Traffic.***
www.clarkcountycourts.us/lvjc/index.html
Payment System phone- 877-455-1289.
Civil Records: Access: Phone, fax, mail, in person, online. Both court and visitors may perform in person searches. Search fee: $1.00 per name per year. Required to search: name, years to search. Civil cases indexed by defendant, plaintiff. Civil records go back 8 years. Note: Court will search up to 5 names in person but if more, expect a multi-day turnaround time. Mail turnaround time 3 weeks. Search calendars ONLY free at http://redrock.co.clark.nv.us/jcCalendar/CalendarSearch.aspx. Also, name or case number search at https://www.clarkcountycourts.us/Anonymous/default.aspx for traffic citations, family court.

Criminal Records: Access: Phone, fax, mail, in person. Only the court performs in person searches; visitors may not. Search fee: $1.00 per name per year. Required to search: name, years to search, DOB; also helpful: SSN. Criminal records go back 10 years. Note: Court will search up to 5 names in person but if more, expect a multi-day turnaround time. Also, Court says for background checks- call the Metro Police, 702-229-3271. Mail turnaround time 3 weeks. Access to misdemeanor traffic records and schedules is same as civil, see above. Online results show middle initial, DOB.
General Information: No sealed, confidential or judge's notes records released. Will fax documents to local or toll free line. Court makes copy: $.30 per page. Certification fee: $3.00 per doc. Payee: Justice Court, Las Vegas Township. Personal checks accepted. Prepayment required. Mail requests: SASE requested.

Laughlin Township Justice Court 101 Civic Way, #2, Laughlin, NV 89029; 702-298-4622; criminal phone: same; civil phone: 702-298-6130; fax: 702-298-7508; 8AM-4PM T-TH, closed F (PST). ***Misdemeanor, Civil Actions under $10,000, Eviction, Small Claims.***
www.lasvegascourts.org/
Civil Records: Access: Fax, mail, in person, online. Both court and visitors may perform in person searches. Search fee: $1.00 per name per year. Required to search: name, years to search. Civil cases indexed by defendant, plaintiff; index on docket book by name and case number. Note: All closed files are shredded 10 years from closed date. Mail turnaround time 2 weeks. Access civil cases at http://cvpublicaccess.co.clark.nv.us/pa/. Search calendars free at http://redrock.co.clark.nv.us/jcCalendar/CalendarSearch.aspx.
Criminal Records: Access: Fax, mail, in person, online. Only the court performs in person searches; visitors may not. Search fee: $1.00 per name per year. Required to search: name, years to search, DOB. Criminal records computerized from 1990, prior in files and must be cross referenced. Note: All closed files are shredded 10 years from closed date. Mail turnaround time 2 weeks. Access to Misdemeanor cases online is same as civil, see above. Online results show middle initial, DOB.
General Information: No sealed records released. Will fax documents to local or toll free line. Court makes copy: $1.00 per page. Certification fee: $3.00 per cert. Payee: Laughlin Justice Court. No checks accepted. Visa/MC cards accepted; $15.00 minimum. Prepayment required. Mail requests: SASE required.

Mesquite Township Justice Court 500 Hillside Dr, Mesquite, NV 89027-3116; 702-346-5298; fax: 702-346-7319; 7:30AM-4:30PM M-TH (PST). ***Felony, Misdemeanor, Civil Actions under $10,000, Eviction, Small Claims.***
www.lasvegascourts.org/
Civil Records: Access: Fax, mail, in person, online. Only the court performs in person searches; visitors may not. Search fee: $1.00 per name per year. Required to search: name, years to search. Civil cases indexed by defendant. Criminal records on computer back to 1998. Mail turnaround time approx. 1-2 weeks. Access civil cases at http://cvpublicaccess.co.clark.nv.us/pa/. Search calendars free at http://redrock.co.clark.nv.us/jcCalendar/CalendarSearch.aspx.
Criminal Records: Access: Phone, fax, mail, in person, online. Only the court performs in person searches; visitors may not. Search fee: $1.00 per name per year. Required to search: name, years to search, DOB; also helpful: SSN. Criminal records computerized from 1998. Mail turnaround time approx. 1-2 weeks. Access to Misdemeanor cases online is same as civil, see above. Online results show middle initial, DOB.
General Information: No sealed records released. Will fax documents $1.00 each. Court makes copy: $1.00 per page. Certification fee: $3.00. Payee: Mesquite Justice Court. Only cashiers checks and money orders accepted. No credit cards accepted. Prepayment required. Mail requests: SASE required.

Moapa Township Justice Court PO Box 280, 1340 E Hwy 168, Moapa, NV 89025; 702-864-2333; fax: 702-864-2585; 7:30AM-5:30PM (PST). ***Misdemeanor, Civil Actions under $10,000, Eviction, Small Claims.***
www.lasvegascourts.org/
Email the court at moapajusticecourt@co.clark.nv.us
Civil Records: Access: Fax, mail, in person, online. Only the court performs in person searches; visitors may not. Search fee: $1.00 per name per year. Required to search: name, years to search. Civil cases indexed by defendant, plaintiff; index on computer from 10/90, prior records on index cards and docket books. Archives flooded in 1980s. Mail turnaround time 1-5 days. Access civil cases at http://cvpublicaccess.co.clark.nv.us/pa/. Search calendars free at http://redrock.co.clark.nv.us/jcCalendar/CalendarSearch.aspx.
Criminal Records: Access: Fax, mail, in person, online. Only the court performs in person searches; visitors may not. Search fee: $1.00 per name per year. Required to search: name, years to search; also helpful: DOB, SSN. Criminal records computerized from 10/90, prior records on index cards and docket books. Archives flooded in 1980s. Mail turnaround time 1-5 days. Access to Misdemeanor cases online is same as civil, see above. Online results show middle initial, DOB.
General Information: No sealed records released. No fee to fax documents. Court makes copy: $.30 per page. Certification fee: $3.00 per cert. Payee: Moapa Township Justice Court. Personal checks and credit cards accepted. Prepayment required. Mail requests: SASE required.

Moapa Valley Township Justice Court 320 N Moapa Valley Blvd, PO Box 337, Overton, NV 89040; 702-397-2840; fax: 702-397-2842; 7:30AM-4:30PM M-TH (PST). ***Misdemeanor, Civil Actions under $10,000, Eviction, Small Claims, Traffic.***
www.lasvegascourts.org/
Civil Records: Access: Mail, in person, online. Only the court performs in person searches; visitors may not. Search fee: $1.00 per name per year. Required to search: name, years to search. Civil cases indexed by defendant, plaintiff; index on computer from 1991, prior on docket books. Mail turnaround time approx. 1-2 weeks. Access civil cases at http://cvpublicaccess.co.clark.nv.us/pa/. Search calendars free at http://redrock.co.clark.nv.us/jcCalendar/CalendarSearch.aspx.
Criminal Records: Access: Mail, in person, online. Only the court performs in person searches; visitors may not. Search fee: $1.00 per name per year. Required to search: name, years to search, DOB; also helpful: SSN. Criminal records computerized from 1991, prior on docket books. Mail turnaround time approx. 1-2 weeks. Access to Misdemeanor cases online is same as civil, see above. Online results show middle initial, DOB.
General Information: No sealed records released. Will fax documents $1.00 per page. Court makes copy: $.30 per page. Certification fee: $3.00. Payee: Moapa Valley Justice Court. Personal checks accepted. Visa/MC accepted. Prepayment required. Mail requests: SASE required.

North Las Vegas Township Justice 2428 N Martin L King Blvd, N Las Vegas, NV 89032-3700; 702-455-7802; civil phone: 702-455-7801; fax: 702-455-7832; 7:15AM-5:45PM (PST). ***Misdemeanor, Civil Actions under $10,000, Eviction, Small Claims.***
www.accessclarkcounty.com/depts/justicecourt_nlv/Pages/index.aspx
Judge must approve all search requests.
Civil Records: Access: Mail, in person, online. Only the court performs in person searches; visitors may not. Search fee: $1.00 per name per year. Required to search: name, years to search. Civil cases indexed by defendant, plaintiff. Civil index on docket books. Mail turnaround time 2 weeks. Access civil cases at http://cvpublicaccess.co.clark.nv.us/pa/. Search calendars free at http://redrock.co.clark.nv.us/jcCalendar/CalendarSearch.aspx.
Criminal Records: Access: Mail, in person, online. Only the court performs in person searches; visitors may not. Search fee: $1.00 per name per year. Required to search: name, years to search, DOB, SSN. Criminal docket on books, microfilm. Mail turnaround time 1-10 days. Access to Misdemeanor cases online is same as civil, see above. Online results show middle initial but DOB does not always appear in index search results.
General Information: Will not fax documents. Court makes copy: $.30 per page. Certification fee: $3.00 per document. Payee: North Las Vegas Justice Court. Personal check accepted with bankcard. Visa/MC credit cards accepted. Prepayment required. Mail requests: SASE required.

Searchlight Township Justice PO Box 815, 1090 Cottonwood Cove Rd, Searchlight, NV 89046; 702-297-1252; fax: 702-297-1022; 7AM-5PM M-TH (PST). ***Misdemeanor, Civil Actions under $10,000, Eviction, Small Claims.***
www.lasvegascourts.org/
Civil Records: Access: Fax, mail, in person, online. Only the court performs in person searches; visitors may not. Search fee: $1.00 per name per year. Required to search: name, years to search. Civil cases indexed by defendant, plaintiff; index on computer from 1988, prior to 1988 filed by case number. Mail turnaround time 1-2 weeks. Access civil cases at http://cvpublicaccess.co.clark.nv.us/pa/. Search calendars free at http://redrock.co.clark.nv.us/jcCalendar/CalendarSearch.aspx.
Criminal Records: Access: Fax, mail, in person, online. Only the court performs in person searches; visitors may not. Search fee: $1.00 per name per year. Required to search: name, years to search, DOB; also helpful: SSN. Criminal records computerized from 1988, prior to 1988 filed by case number. Mail turnaround time 1-2 weeks. Access to Misdemeanor cases online is same as civil, see above. Online results show middle initial, DOB.
General Information: No sealed records released. Will not fax documents. Court makes copy: $1.00 per page. Certification fee: $2.00 per cert. Payee: Searchlight Justice Court. No personal checks accepted. Visa/MC accepted. Prepayment required. Mail requests: SASE required.

Douglas County

9th Judicial District Court PO Box 218, Minden, NV 89423; 775-782-9820; fax: 775-782-9954; 8AM-5PM (PST). ***Felony, Gross Misdemeanor, Civil Actions over $10,000, Probate.***
http://cltr.co.douglas.nv.us/CourtClerk/courtideas/courtclerkhome.htm
Misdemeanors are handled by the East Fork Justice Court and Tahoe Township Justice Court. Probate fax is same as main fax number.
Civil Records: Access: Mail, in person. Only the court performs in person searches; visitors may not. Search fee: $1.00 per name per year. Required to search: name, years to search. Civil cases indexed by defendant, plaintiff. Civil index on cards from 1962, docket books prior to 1962, archived from mid-1850s. On computer back to 1996. Mail turnaround time 2 days.
Criminal Records: Access: Mail, in person. Only the court performs in person searches; visitors may not. Search fee: $1.00 per name per year. Required to search: name, years to search, DOB. Criminal records indexed on cards from 1962, docket books prior to 1962, archived from mid-1850s. On computer back to 1996. Mail turnaround time 2 days.
General Information: No sealed records released. Will fax documents after all payments received. Court makes copy: $1.00 per page. Certification fee: $3.00 per document. If document is presented to clerk for certification (no reproduction needed) fee is $5.00. Payee: Douglas County Court Clerk. Business checks accepted. No credit cards accepted. Prepayment required. Mail requests: SASE required.

East Fork Justice Court PO Box 218, Minden, NV 89423; 775-782-9955; fax: 775-782-9947; 8AM-5PM (PST). ***Misdemeanor, Civil Actions under $10,000, Eviction, Small Claims.***
www.douglascountynv.gov/sites/EFJC/Contact_Us_EFJC.cfm
Civil Records: Access: Mail, in person. Only the court performs in person searches; visitors may not. Search fee: $1.00 per name per year. Required to

search: name, years to search, DOB or SSN. Civil cases indexed by defendant, plaintiff. Computerized records from 1996. Mail turnaround time 5-7 days.
Criminal Records: Access: Mail, in person. Only the court performs in person searches; visitors may not. Search fee: $1.00 per name per year. Required to search: name, years to search, DOB or SSN. Computerized records from 1996. Mail turnaround time 5-7 days.
General Information: No sealed records released. Will fax out docs if prepaid. Court makes copy: $.30 per page. Certification fee: $3.00; Exemplification fee, $6.00. Payee: East Fork Justice Court. Local personal or business checks accepted. Credit cards accepted in person only. Prepayment required. Mail requests: SASE required.

Tahoe Justice Court PO Box 7169, 175 US Hwy 50, Stateline, NV 89449; 775-586-7200; fax: 775-586-7203; 9AM-5PM (PST). ***Misdemeanor, Civil Actions under $10,000, Eviction, Small Claims.***
www.douglascountynv.gov/sites/main/
Civil Records: Access: Phone, mail, in person. Only the court performs in person searches; visitors may not. Search fee: $1.00 per name per year per case. Required to search: name or case number, years to search. Civil cases indexed by defendant, plaintiff. Civil index on cards from 1985-1995; 1995-present on computer. Prior to 1985 some records in docket books, some on microfilm. Mail turnaround time 2 weeks or less.
Criminal Records: Access: Phone, mail, in person. Only the court performs in person searches; visitors may not. Search fee: $1.00 per name per year per case. Required to search: name or case number, years to search, DOB. Criminal records on docket cards 1985-1995; 1995 to present on computer. Pre-1985 records on books and microfilm. Mail turnaround time 2 weeks.
General Information: No sealed records released. Will not fax documents. Court makes copy: $.30 per page. Certification fee: $3.00 per page. Payee: Tahoe Justice Court. Local personal checks accepted. Visa/MC accepted. Prepayment required. Mail requests: SASE required.

Elko County

4th Judicial District Court 571 Idaho St, 3rd Fl, Elko, NV 89801; 775-753-4600; fax: 775-753-4610; 9AM-5PM (PST). ***Felony, Gross Misdemeanor, Civil Actions over $10,000, Probate.***
www.elkonv.com/%7Efourjdc1/
Probate fax is same as main fax number.
Civil Records: Access: Phone, mail, in person, email. Both court and visitors may perform in person searches. Search fee: $1.00 per name per year. Fee is for years prior to 10/01/91. Required to search: name, years to search. Civil cases indexed by defendant, plaintiff; index on computer back to 1970; prior on index cards. Note: Direct email requests to clerk@elkocountynv.net. Mail turnaround time 1 day. Civil PAT goes back to 1970s.
Criminal Records: Access: Phone, mail, in person. Both court and visitors may perform in person searches. Search fee: $1.00 per name per year. Fee is for years prior to 1980. Required to search: name, years to search. Criminal records computerized from 1970; prior on index cards. Mail turnaround time 1 day. Criminal PAT goes back to same as civil.
General Information: No sealed records released. Fee to fax out file $1.00 per page. Court makes copy: $1.00 per page. Self serve: $.50 per page.Exemplified copies are $6.00 Certification fee: $3.00 for cert plus copy fee if court prepares copies; $5.00 cert if you prepare copies. Payee: Elko County Clerk. Personal checks accepted. Visa/MC accepted. Prepayment required. Mail requests: SASE required.

Carlin Justice Court PO Box 789, Carlin, NV 89822; 775-754-6321; fax: 775-754-6893; 8AM-5PM (PST). ***Misdemeanor, Civil Actions under $10,000, Eviction, Small Claims.***
Civil Records: Access: Mail, in person. Both court and visitors may perform in person searches. Search fee: $1.00 per name per year. Required to search: name, years to search. Civil cases indexed by defendant, plaintiff; index on computer starting in 1994, prior are in books. Mail turnaround time 1 week.
Criminal Records: Access: Mail, in person. Only the court performs in person searches; visitors may not. Search fee: $1.00 per name per year. Required to search: name, years to search, DOB, SSN. Criminal records on computer starting in 1994, prior are in books. Mail turnaround time 1 week.
General Information: Will fax documents to local or toll-free number. Court makes copy: $.30 per page. Self serve: same. Certification fee: $3.00 per document. Payee: Carlin Court. Personal checks and major credit cards accepted. Prepayment required. Mail requests: SASE required.

Eastline Justice Court PO Box 2300, West Wendover, NV 89883; 775-664-2305; fax: 775-664-2979; 8AM-5PM (MST). ***Misdemeanor, Civil Actions under $10,000, Eviction, Small Claims.***
Has a sister court named West Wendover Municipal. Fee for 7 years search is $14.00 for one name; this would cover BOTH courts. If you only want one court you must be specific.
Civil Records: Access: Mail, in person. Only the court performs in person searches; visitors may not. Search fee: $1.00 per name per year per court. Fee for 7 years search is $14.00 for one name. This would cover BOTH courts. If you only want one court you must be spe. Required to search: name, years to search. Civil cases indexed by defendant. Civil records on computer from 1992, prior on index, docket book. Mail turnaround time 1 week.
Criminal Records: Access: Mail, in person. Only the court performs in person searches; visitors may not. Search fee: $1.00 per name per year per court. Fee for 7 years search is $14.00 for one name. This would cover BOTH courts. If you only want one court you must be spe. Required to search: name, years to search; also helpful: DOB. Criminal records computerized from 1992, prior on index, docket book. Mail turnaround time 1 week.
General Information: No open case records released. Will fax documents to local or toll-free number. Court makes copy: $.30 per page. Certification fee: $3.00. Payee: Eastline Justice Court. Personal checks accepted. Prepayment required. Mail requests: SASE required.

Elko Justice Court PO Box 176, Elko, NV 89803; 775-738-8403; fax: 775-738-8416; 8AM-5PM (PST). ***Misdemeanor, Civil Actions under $10,000, Eviction, Small Claims.***
Civil Records: Access: Fax, mail, in person. Both court and visitors may perform in person searches. Search fee: $1.00 per name per year. Fee is per court. Required to search: name, years to search. Civil cases indexed by defendant, plaintiff; index on computer after 1994, on docket books after 1980s, prior in county archives. Mail turnaround time 7-10 days.
Criminal Records: Access: Mail, in person. Both court and visitors may perform in person searches. Search fee: $1.00 per name per year. Fee is per court. Required to search: name, years to search; DOB or SSN also required. Criminal records on computer after 1994, on docket books after 1980s, prior in county archives. Mail turnaround time 7-10 days.
General Information: No confidential evaluations or sealed records released. Will fax documents to local or toll-free number. Court makes copy: $1.00 per page. Certification fee: $3.00; exemplification fee-$5.00. Payee: Elko Justice Court. Personal checks accepted; credit cards are not. Prepayment required. Mail requests: SASE required.

Jackpot Justice Court PO Box 229, Jackpot, NV 89825; 775-755-2456; fax: 775-755-2455; 9AM-N, 1-5PM (PST). ***Misdemeanor, Civil Actions under $10,000, Eviction, Small Claims.***
Civil Records: Access: Mail, in person. Only the court performs in person searches; visitors may not. Search fee: $7.00 per name per year. Required to search: name, years to search. Civil cases indexed by defendant. Civil index on docket books per year since 1988; on computer back to 1995. Mail turnaround time 1 week.
Criminal Records: Access: Fax, mail, in person. Only the court performs in person searches; visitors may not. Search fee: $7.00 per name per year. Required to search: name, years to search, DOB. Criminal docket on books per year since 1988; on computer back to 1995. Mail turnaround time 1 week.
General Information: No fee to fax documents. Court makes copy: $.25 per page. Certification fee: $3.00. Payee: Jackpot Justice Court. Business checks accepted. No credit cards accepted. Prepayment required. Mail requests: SASE required.

Wells Justice Municipal Court PO Box 297, Wells, NV 89835; 775-752-3726; fax: 775-752-3363; 9AM-N,1-5PM (PST). ***Misdemeanor, Civil Actions under $10,000, Eviction, Small Claims.***
Civil Records: Access: Mail, in person. Only the court performs in person searches; visitors may not. Search fee: $1.00 per name per year. Required to search: name, years to search. Civil cases indexed by defendant, plaintiff; index on computer from 1989, prior on docket books. Note: In person access may require fee for clerical assistance. Mail turnaround time 2 weeks.
Criminal Records: Access: Mail, in person. Only the court performs in person searches; visitors may not. Search fee: $1.00 per name per year. Required to search: name, years to search; also DOB or SSN. Criminal records computerized from 1989, prior on docket books. Note: In person access may require fee for clerical assistance. Mail turnaround time 2 weeks.
General Information: No pending, confidential records released. Will not fax documents. Court makes copy: $.30 per page. Certification fee: $3.00. Payee: Wells Justice Court. Personal checks accepted; credit cards are not. Prepayment required. Mail requests: SASE required.

Jarbidge Justice Court, NV.
This is an "unincorporated ghost town." No criminal or civil cases in more than 20 years. Mostly marriages, fish and game violations. Only 40 year round residents. All records at the Elko Justice Court.

Mountain City Justice Court, NV.
Closed. Records held in Elko Justice Court, 775-738-8403.

Esmeralda County

5th Judicial District Court PO Box 547, Goldfield, NV 89013; 775-485-6309; probate phone: same; fax: 775-485-6376; 8AM-5PM; Closed 12-1PM (PST). ***Felony, Gross Misdemeanor, Civil Actions over $10,000, Probate.***
www.accessesmeralda.com/Court.htm
Civil Records: Access: Fax, mail, in person. Both court and visitors may perform in person searches. Search fee: $1.00 per name per year. Required to search: name, years to search. Civil cases indexed by defendant, plaintiff. Civil index in docket books from 1800s. Mail turnaround time 2 weeks.
Criminal Records: Access: Fax, mail, in person. Both court and visitors may perform in person searches. Search fee: $1.00. Required to search: name, years to search. Criminal docket on books from 1800s. Mail turnaround time 2 weeks.
General Information: No juvenile or pre-sentence records released. Fee to fax out file $1.00 per page. Court makes copy: $1.00 per page. Certification fee: $3.00. Payee: Esmeralda County Clerk. Personal checks and credit cards accepted. Prepayment required. Mail requests: SASE required.

Esmeralda Justice Court PO Box 370, Goldfield, NV 89013; 775-485-6359; fax: 775-485-3462; 8AM-5PM (PST). ***Misdemeanor, Civil Actions under $10,000, Eviction, Small Claims.***
Civil Records: Access: Phone, fax, mail, in person. Only the court performs in person searches; visitors may not. Search fee: $1.00 per name per year. Required to search: name, years to search. Civil cases indexed by plaintiff. Civil index on docket books since 1987. Mail turnaround time 1 day.
Criminal Records: Access: Phone, fax, mail, in person. Only the court performs in person searches; visitors may not. Search fee: $1.00 per name per year. Required to search: name, years to search. Criminal docket on books since 1987. Mail turnaround time 1 day.
General Information: No sealed records released. Will fax documents $1.00 per page. Court makes

copy: $.30 per page. Certification fee: $3.00. Payee: Justice Court. Only cashiers checks and money orders accepted. No credit cards accepted. Prepayment required. Mail requests: SASE required.

Eureka County

7th Judicial District Court PO Box 677, Eureka, NV 89316; 775-237-5262; fax: 775-237-6015; 8AM-N, 1-5PM (PST). ***Felony, Gross Misdemeanor, Civil Actions over $10,000, Probate.***

Civil Records: Access: Phone, fax, mail, in person. Both court and visitors may perform in person searches. Search fee: $1.00 per name per year. Required to search: name, years to search. Civil cases indexed by defendant, plaintiff. Civil records archived from 1873. Note: Public can search docket books. Mail turnaround time 1 day.

Criminal Records: Access: Phone, fax, mail, in person. Both court and visitors may perform in person searches. Search fee: $1.00 per name per year. Required to search: name, years to search. Criminal records archived from 1873. Note: Public can search docket books. Mail turnaround time 1 day.

General Information: No juvenile, sealed records released. Will fax to toll-free number. Court makes copy: $1.00 per page. Certification fee: $5.00 per document. Payee: Eureka County Clerk. Personal checks accepted. Visa/MC accepted. Prepayment required. Mail requests: SASE required.

Beowawe Justice Court PO Box 211338, Crescent Valley, NV 89821; 775-468-0244; fax: 775-468-0323; 8AM-N, 12:30PM-4:30PM (PST). ***Misdemeanor, Civil Actions under $10,000, Eviction, Small Claims.***

www.co.eureka.nv.us/court/beowawe.htm

Civil Records: Access: Mail, in person. Only the court performs in person searches; visitors may not. Search fee: $1.00 per name per year. Required to search: name, years to search. Civil cases indexed by plaintiff. Civil records go back to 2/1994; computerized records go back to 1997. Mail turnaround time 5 days.

Criminal Records: Access: Mail, in person. Only the court performs in person searches; visitors may not. Search fee: $1.00 per name per year. Required to search: name, years to search. Criminal records go back to 11/1993; computerized records go back to 1997. Mail turnaround time 5 days.

General Information: Will fax documents to local or toll-free number. Court makes copy: $.30 per page. Certification fee: $3.00. Payee: Beowawe Justice Court. Only cashiers checks and money orders accepted. Visa/MC accepted. Prepayment required. Mail requests: SASE required.

Eureka Justice Court PO Box 496, Eureka, NV 89316; 775-237-5540; fax: 775-237-6016; 8AM-N,1-5PM (PST). ***Misdemeanor, Civil Actions under $10,000, Eviction, Small Claims.***

Civil Records: Access: Phone, mail, in person. Only the court performs in person searches; visitors may not. No search fee. Required to search: name, years to search. Civil cases indexed by defendant, plaintiff; index on computer since 1995; on docket books, archived from 1940. Mail turnaround time 2 days.

Criminal Records: Access: Phone, mail, in person. Only the court performs in person searches; visitors may not. No search fee. Required to search: name, years to search. Criminal records on computer since 1995; on docket books, archived from 1940. Mail turnaround time 2 days.

General Information: Will fax documents $1.00 per page. Court makes copy: $.25 per page for 1-10 pages, $.20 per page for 11-50, $.15 per page for over 50 pages. Certification fee: $3.00. Payee: Eureka Justice Court. Cashiers checks and money orders accepted. Major credit cards accepted. Prepayment required. Mail requests: SASE required.

Humboldt County

6th Judicial District Court 50 W 5th St, Winnemucca, NV 89445; 775-623-6343; fax: 775-623-6309; 8AM-5PM (PST). ***Felony, Gross Misdemeanor, Civil Actions over $10,000, Probate.***

Public access terminals to be available soon, but results will not include all personal identifiers. Personal identifiers only go back 10 years on the court's inhouse computer system.

Civil Records: Access: Phone, fax, mail, in person. Only the court performs in person searches; visitors may not. Search fee: No search fee unless old record: $1.00 per name per year if over 22 years ago. Required to search: name, years to search; also helpful- any personal identifiers- DOB, etc. Civil cases indexed by defendant, plaintiff; index on computer from 1984, on microfiche from 1900. Mail turnaround time 1 day. Older records - over 10 years old - may not contain DOB.

Criminal Records: Access: Phone, fax, mail, in person. Both court and visitors may perform in person searches. Search fee: No search fee. $1.00 per name per year if over 22 years ago. Required to search: name, years to search; also helpful- any personal identifiers- DOB, etc. Criminal records computerized from 1984, on microfiche from 1900. Mail turnaround time 1 day, immediate if phone request aand record on computer. Older records - over 10 years old - may not contain DOB.

General Information: No adoption, sealed records released. Will fax documents $1.00 per page, prepaid only. Court makes copy: $1.00 per page. Certification fee: $3.00 per cert. Payee: Humboldt County Clerk. Personal checks accepted; credit cards are not. Prepayment required.

Union Justice Court PO Box 1218, Winnemucca, NV 89446; 775-623-6059; civil phone: 775-623-6379; fax: 775-623-6458; 8AM-5PM (PST). ***Misdemeanor, Civil Actions under $10,000, Eviction, Small Claims.***

www.hcnv.us/justice/justice_home.htm

Civil Records: Access: Fax, mail, in person. Only the court performs in person searches; visitors may not. Search fee: $1.00 per name per year; minimum of $7.00. Required to search: name, years to search; also helpful: address. Civil cases indexed by defendant, plaintiff; index on computer from 1988, prior on docket books. Mail turnaround time 1-2 days.

Criminal Records: Access: Fax, mail, in person. Only the court performs in person searches; visitors may not. Search fee: $1.00 per name per year; minimum of $7.00. Required to search: name, years to search, DOB; also helpful: address, SSN. Criminal records computerized from 1988. Mail turnaround time 1-2 days.

General Information: No fee to fax documents. Court makes copy: $.30 per page. Certification fee: $3.00 per cert plus copy fee; exemplified- $9.00. Payee: Justice Court. Personal checks accepted. Add a $3.00 preocessing fee if you pay via credit card. Prepayment required. Mail requests: SASE required.

McDermitt Justice Court, NV. ***Misdemeanor, Civil Actions under $10,000, Eviction, Small Claims.***

Closed case records are at the Union Justice Court.

Paradise Valley Justice Court, NV. ***Misdemeanor, Civil Actions under $10,000, Eviction, Small Claims.***

Closed case records are at the Union Justice Court.

Lander County

6th Judicial District Court 315 S Humboldt, Battle Mountain, NV 89820; 775-635-5738; fax: 775-635-5761; 8AM-5PM (PST). ***Felony, Gross Misdemeanor, Civil Actions over $10,000, Probate.***

www.landercounty.org/county/clerk.htm

Probate fax is same as main fax number.

Civil Records: Access: Phone, fax, mail, in person. Only the court performs in person searches; visitors may not. No search fee. Required to search: name, years to search. Civil cases indexed by defendant, plaintiff; index on computer from 1990, on index from 1986-1990, on microfiche until 1985, prior records on docket books. Mail turnaround time 7 days.

Criminal Records: Access: Phone, fax, mail, in person. Only the court performs in person searches; visitors may not. No search fee. Required to search: name, years to search. Criminal records computerized from 1990, on index from 1986-1990, on microfiche until 1985, prior records on docket books. Mail turnaround time 7 days.

General Information: No juvenile, sealed records released. Fee to fax out file $1.00 per page. Court makes copy: $1.00 per page. Certification fee: $3.00 per document. Payee: Lander County Clerk. Personal checks accepted; credit cards are not. Prepayment required. Mail requests: SASE required.

Argenta Justice Court 315 S Humboldt, Battle Mountain, NV 89820; 775-635-5151; fax: 775-635-0604; 8AM-5PM (PST). ***Misdemeanor, Civil Actions under $10,000, Eviction, Small Claims.***

Civil Records: Access: Phone, mail, in person. Only the court performs in person searches; visitors may not. Search fee: $1.00 per name per year. Required to search: name, years to search. Civil cases indexed by defendant, plaintiff; index on computer from 1988, prior on docket books. Mail turnaround time 1 day.

Criminal Records: Access: Phone, mail, in person. Only the court performs in person searches; visitors may not. Search fee: $1.00 per name per year. Required to search: name, years to search; also helpful: DOB, SSN. Criminal records computerized from 1988, prior on docket books. Mail turnaround time 1 day.

General Information: No unserved search warrant records released. Fee to fax out file $1.00 per page. Court makes copy: $.50 per page. Certification fee: $1.00 per page. Payee: Argenta Justice Court. Only cashiers checks and money orders accepted. No credit cards accepted. Prepayment required. Mail requests: SASE required.

Austin Justice Court PO Box 100, Austin, NV 89310; 775-964-2380; fax: 775-964-2327; 8AM-4PM M, 8AM-N T-TH (PST). ***Misdemeanor, Civil Actions under $10,000, Eviction, Small Claims.***

No fees for requests from government agencies.

Civil Records: Access: Phone, mail, fax, in person. Only the court performs in person searches; visitors may not. No search fee. Required to search: name, years to search. Civil cases indexed by plaintiff and defendant. Civil index on docket books, computerized since 1988. Mail turnaround time 1 week.

Criminal Records: Access: Phone, mail, fax, in person. Only the court performs in person searches; visitors may not. No search fee. Required to search: name, years to search. Criminal records computerized from 1988, easily available since 1976. Mail turnaround time 1 week.

General Information: Will fax documents to local or toll free line. Court makes copy: $.25 per page. Self serve: same. No certification fee. Payee: Austin Justice Court. Personal checks accepted; credit cards are not. Mail requests: SASE required.

Lincoln County

7th Judicial District Court PO Box 90, Pioche, NV 89043; 775-962-5390; fax: 775-962-5180; 9AM-5PM (PST). ***Felony, Gross Misdemeanor, Civil Actions over $10,000, Probate.***

Civil Records: Access: Mail, in person. Both court and visitors may perform in person searches. Search fee: $1.00 per name per year. Required to search: name, years to search. Civil cases indexed by defendant, plaintiff. Civil index in docket books from 1876. Records are computerized since 2001. Mail turnaround time 1-2 days.

Criminal Records: Access: Mail, in person. Both court and visitors may perform in person searches. Search fee: $1.00 per name per year. Required to search: name, years to search. Criminal docket on books from 1876. Records are computerized since 2001. Mail turnaround time 1-2 days.

General Information: No juvenile, sealed records released. Fee to fax out file $1.00 per page. Court makes copy: $1.00 per page. Self serve: same. Certification fee: $5.00. Payee: Lincoln County Clerk. Personal checks accepted; credit cards are not. Prepayment required. Mail requests: SASE required.

Meadow Valley Justice Court PO Box 36, Pioche, NV 89043; 775-962-5140; criminal fax: 775-962-5559; civil fax: same; 9AM-4PM (PST). ***Misdemeanor, Civil Actions under $10,000, Eviction, Small Claims.***

Civil Records: Access: Phone, fax, mail, in person. Only the court performs in person searches; visitors may not. No search fee. Required to search:

name, years to search. Civil cases indexed by defendant, plaintiff. Civil records archived from 1982 on docket books. Mail turnaround time 1-5 days.
Criminal Records: Access: Phone, fax, mail, in person. Only the court performs in person searches; visitors may not. No search fee. Required to search: name, years to search. Criminal records are all originals; they go back to 1982; on computer back to 2000. Mail turnaround time 1-5 days.
General Information: Juvenile records are not released. Will fax documents to local or toll-free number. Court makes copy for no fee. Self serve: same. No certification fee. Payee: Meadow Valley Justice Court. Personal checks accepted. Visa/MC accepted. Prepayment required. Mail requests: SASE required.

Pahranagat Valley Justice Court PO Box 449, Alamo, NV 89001; 775-725-3357; fax: 775-725-3566; 8AM-5PM (PST). ***Misdemeanor, Civil Actions under $10,000, Eviction, Small Claims.***
Civil Records: Access: Fax, mail, in person. Only the court performs in person searches; visitors may not. Search fee: $1.00 per name per year. Required to search: name, years to search. Civil cases indexed by defendant. Civil index on docket books to 1980; on computer back to 1997. Mail turnaround time 1-3 days.
Criminal Records: Access: Fax, mail, in person. Only the court performs in person searches; visitors may not. Search fee: $1.00 per name per year. Required to search: name, years to search, DOB; also helpful: SSN, signed release. Criminal docket on books to 1980; on computer back to 1997. Mail turnaround time 1-3 days.
General Information: No personal notes released. Will fax out documents $1.00 per page. Court makes copy: $.30 per page. Certification fee: $3.00 per page. Payee: Pahranagat Valley Justice Court. Personal checks accepted. Visa/MC accepted. Prepayment required. Mail requests: SASE required.

Lyon County

3rd Judicial District Court 27 S Main St, Yerington, NV 89447; 775-463-6503; criminal fax: 775-463-3643; civil fax: same; 8AM-5PM (PST). ***Felony, Gross Misdemeanor, Civil Actions over $10,000, Probate.***
www.lyon-county.org/index.asp?nid=675
Civil Records: Access: Phone, mail, in person. Only the court performs in person searches; visitors may not. Search fee: $1.00 per name per year. Required to search: name, years to search. Civil cases indexed by defendant, plaintiff; index on computer back to 1989. Mail turnaround time 1 week for mail requests, immediate by phone if on computer.
Criminal Records: Access: Phone, mail, in person. Only the court performs in person searches; visitors may not. Search fee: $1.00 per name per year. Required to search: name, years to search. Criminal records computerized from 1985. Mail turnaround time 1 week for mail requests, immediate for phone request if on computer.
General Information: No adoption, juvenile or sealed records released. Will fax documents $3.00 per page. Court makes copy: $.25 per page. Certification fee: $3.00 per document. Payee: Lyon County Clerk. Personal checks and major credit cards accepted. Prepayment required. Mail requests: SASE required.

Dayton Township Justice Court 235 Main St, Dayton, NV 89403; 775-246-6233; fax: 775-246-6203; 8AM-5PM (PST). ***Misdemeanor, Civil Actions under $10,000, Eviction, Small Claims.***
www.lyon-county.org/index.asp?nid=230
Civil Records: Access: Phone, fax, mail, in person. Only the court performs in person searches; visitors may not. Search fee: $1.00 per name per year. Required to search: name, years to search. Civil cases indexed by defendant, plaintiff; index on computer from 1991, prior on docket books by year. Mail turnaround time within 1 week.
Criminal Records: Access: Phone, fax, mail, in person. Only the court performs in person searches; visitors may not. Search fee: $1.00 per name per year, back 7 years. Required to search: name, years to search. Criminal records computerized from 1991, prior on docket books by year. Mail turnaround time within 1 week.
General Information: No sealed records released. Will fax back documents for no fee. Court makes copy: $.30 per page. Certification fee: $3.00 per certification. Payee: Dayton Township Justice Court. Personal checks accepted. Visa/MC accepted. Prepayment required. Mail requests: SASE required.

Fernley Justice Court 565 E Main St, Fernley, NV 89408; 775-575-3355; fax: 775-575-3359; 8AM-5PM (PST). ***Misdemeanor, Civil Actions under $10,000, Eviction, Small Claims.***
www.lyon-county.org/index.asp?nid=235
Civil Records: Access: Phone, mail, in person. Only the court performs in person searches; visitors may not. Search fee: $1.00 per name per year. Required to search: name, years to search. Civil cases indexed by defendant, plaintiff; index on computer from 1992, prior on docket books. Mail turnaround time 1 week.
Criminal Records: Access: Phone, mail, in person. Only the court performs in person searches; visitors may not. Search fee: $1.00 per name per year. Required to search: name, years to search; also helpful: SSN. Criminal records computerized from 1992, prior on docket books. Mail turnaround time 1 week.
General Information: No police reports or sealed records released. Will fax documents $3.00 per page. Court makes copy: $.30 per page. Certification fee: $3.00 per cert. Payee: Fernley Justice Court. Personal checks accepted. Out of state checks not accepted. Visa/MC accepted. Prepayment required. Mail requests: SASE required.

Walker River Justice Court 30 Nevin Way, Yerington, NV 89447; 775-463-6639; fax: 775-463-6638; 8AM-5PM (PST). ***Misdemeanor, Civil Actions under $10,000, Eviction, Small Claims.***
www.lyon-county.org/index.asp?nid=240
Effective July 1, 2006 the Smith Valley Justice Court and the Mason Valley Justice Court merged to form the Walker River Justice Court in Yerington. Records are being consolidated, but a separate index search is suggested.
Civil Records: Access: Phone, mail, in person. Only the court performs in person searches; visitors may not. Search fee: $1.00 per name per year. Required to search: name, years to search. Civil cases indexed by defendant, plaintiff; index on computer from 1992, archives from 1900s. Mail turnaround time 3 days, immediate for phone requests.
Criminal Records: Access: Phone, mail, in person. Only the court performs in person searches; visitors may not. Search fee: $1.00 per name per year. Required to search: name, years to search; also helpful: DOB, SSN. Criminal records computerized from 1992, archives from 1900s. Note: Phone requests are limited to 3 names only. Mail turnaround time 3 days, immediate for phone requests.
General Information: No police, sheriff reports released. Will fax documents $1.00 per page. Court makes copy: $.25 per page. Certification fee: $3.00. Payee: Walker River Justice Court. No personal checks. Major credit cards accepted. Prepayment required. Mail requests: SASE required.

Mineral County

5th Judicial District Court PO Box 1450, Hawthorne, NV 89415; 775-945-2446; criminal fax: 775-945-0706; civil fax: same; 8AM-5PM (PST). ***Felony, Gross Misdemeanor, Civil Actions over $10,000, Probate.***
Probate fax is same as main fax number.
Civil Records: Access: Phone, fax, mail, in person. Both court and visitors may perform in person searches. Search fee: $1.00 per name per year. Required to search: name, years to search. Civil cases indexed by defendant, plaintiff. Civil records go back to 1911; computerized records since 1993. Mail turnaround time 1 day.
Criminal Records: Access: Phone, fax, mail, in person. Both court and visitors may perform in person searches. Search fee: $1.00 per name per year. Required to search: name, years to search. Criminal records go back to 1911; computerized records since 1993. Mail turnaround time 1 day.
General Information: No juvenile records released. Will fax documents $1.50 per page. Court makes copy: $1.00 per page. Self serve: same. Certification fee: $3.00 per certification. Payee: Mineral County Clerk. Personal checks accepted; credit cards are not. Prepayment required.

Hawthorne Justice Court PO Box 1660, Hawthorne, NV 89415; 775-945-3859; fax: 775-945-0700; 8AM-5PM (PST). ***Misdemeanor, Civil Actions under $10,000, Eviction, Small Claims.***
This court holds records from Schurz Justice Court.
Civil Records: Access: Phone, mail, in person. Both court and visitors may perform in person searches. No search fee. Required to search: name, years to search. Civil cases indexed by defendant. Civil records on computer from 1994, prior on docket books. Mail turnaround time 1-5 days.
Criminal Records: Access: Phone, mail, in person, fax. Both court and visitors may perform in person searches. No search fee. Required to search: name, years to search. Criminal records computerized from 1992. Mail turnaround time 1-5 days.
General Information: No pending case or sealed records released. Will fax documents to local or toll-free number. Court makes copy: $.25 per page. Legal size- $1.00 per page. No certification fee. Payee: Hawthorne Justice Court. Personal checks accepted; credit cards are not. Prepayment required. Mail requests: SASE required.

Mina Justice Court, NV.
Court has been closed. All records at the Hawthorne Justice Court.

Schurz Justice Court c/o Hawthorne Justice Ct, PO Box 1660, 160 E St, Hawthorne, NV 89415; 775-945-3859; fax: 775-945-0700; 8AM-5PM (PST). ***Misdemeanor.***
Schurz court closed 1/1/2001; records now housed at Hawthorne Justice Court, address and phone given above.

Nye County

5th Judicial District Court PO Box 1031, Tonopah, NV 89049; 775-482-8131; probate phone: 775-482-8127; fax: 775-482-8133; 8AM-5PM (PST). ***Felony, Gross Misdemeanor, Civil Actions over $10,000, Probate.***
www.nyecounty.net/index.asp?NID=92
Probate fax- 775-482-8133
Civil Records: Access: Phone, fax, mail, in person. Only the court performs in person searches; visitors may not. Search fee: $1.00 per name. Required to search: name, years to search. Civil records on computer from 1991, on docket books from 1864, many are microfilmed. Mail turnaround time 1 day.
Criminal Records: Access: Phone, fax, mail, in person. Only the court performs in person searches; visitors may not. Search fee: $1.00 per name. Required to search: name, years to search. Criminal records computerized from 1991, on docket books from 1800s, many are microfilmed. Mail turnaround time 1 day.
General Information: No adoption or juvenile records released. Will fax documents $2.00 1st page, $1.00 each add'l. Court makes copy: $1.00 per page. Self serve: same. Certification fee: $3.00. Payee: Nye County Clerk. Business checks or in state personal checks accepted. No credit cards accepted. Prepayment required. Mail requests: SASE required.

Beatty Justice Court PO Box 805, Beatty, NV 89003; 775-553-2951; criminal fax: 775-553-2136; civil fax: same; 8AM-5PM (PST). ***Misdemeanor, Civil Actions up to $10.000, Eviction, Small Claims.***
Civil Records: Access: Phone, mail, in person. Only the court performs in person searches; visitors may not. Search fee: $1.00 per name per year. Computer printouts on all civil actions (no way to segregate small claims or evictions) is $0.016 per page. Required to search: name, years to search. Civil cases indexed by defendant, plaintiff; index on computer from 1989, archived from 1950s, some on docket books. Mail turnaround time 1 week for mail requests, same day for phone requests when possible.

Criminal Records: Access: Phone, mail, in person. Only the court performs in person searches; visitors may not. Search fee: $1.00 per name per year. Required to search: name, years to search, DOB. Criminal records computerized from 1989. Mail turnaround time 1 week for mail requests, same day for phone request, when possible.
General Information: No sealed, confidential records released. Will fax documents if all fees paid; fax copies are $0.019 per page (no charge to fax original). If project more than 15 minutes, add'l fees may apply. Court makes copy: $.30 per page. Self serve: same. Certification fee: $3.00 per document. Payee: Beatty Justice Court. Personal checks accepted. Visa/MC accepted. Prepayment required. Mail requests: SASE required.

Tonopah Justice Court PO Box 1151, Tonopah, NV 89049; 775-482-8155; fax: 775-482-7349; 8AM-N, 1-5PM (PST). ***Misdemeanor, Civil Actions under $10,000, Eviction, Small Claims.***
Civil Records: Access: Phone, mail, in person. Only the court performs in person searches; visitors may not. Search fee: $1.00 per name per year. Required to search: name, years to search. Civil cases indexed by plaintiff. Civil records on computer from 1992, on archives from 1950s, some on docket books. Mail turnaround time 1-2 weeks.
Criminal Records: Access: Phone, mail, in person. Only the court performs in person searches; visitors may not. Search fee: $1.00 per name per year. Required to search: name, years to search, offense, date of offense; also helpful: DOB, SSN. Criminal records computerized from 1992, on docket books from 1943. Mail turnaround time 1-2 weeks.
General Information: Will fax documents to local or toll free line. Court makes copy: $.30 per page. Certification fee: $3.00 per cert. Payee: Tonopah Justice Court. Business checks accepted. Major credit cards accepted. Prepayment required. Mail requests: SASE required.

Gabbs Justice Court, NV.
This court is closed; any records are now at Tonopah 775-482-8155.

Pershing County

6th Judicial District Court PO Box 820, Lovelock, NV 89419; 775-273-2410; probate phone: same; fax: 775-273-2434; 9AM-5PM (PST). ***Felony, Civil Actions over $10,000, Probate.***
Misdemeanors are handled by the Lake Township Justice Court.
Civil Records: Access: Phone, fax (3 names or less), mail, in person. Only the court performs in person searches; visitors may not. Search fee: $1.00 per year per name. Required to search: name, years to search. Civil cases indexed by defendant, plaintiff; index on computer from 1992, microfilmed from 1919-1938, books from 1919. Note: Court will do up to 3 or more searches by phone Mail Turnaround time 1-3 days.
Criminal Records: Access: Phone, fax (3 names or less), mail, in person. Only the court performs in person searches; visitors may not. Search fee: $1.00 per year per name. Required to search: name, years to search. Criminal records computerized from 1992, microfilmed from 1919-1938, books from 1919. Note: Court will do up to 3 or more searches by phone. Mail turnaround time 1-3 days.
General Information: No adoption, juvenile or sealed records released. No fee to fax documents. Court makes copy: $1.00 per page. Self serve: same. Certification fee: $3.00 per doc; exemplification-$6.00. Payee: Pershing County District Court. Personal checks accepted; credit cards are not. Prepayment required. Mail requests: SASE required.

Lake Township Justice Court PO Box 8, Lovelock, NV 89419; 775-273-2753; fax: 775-273-0416; 8AM-5PM (PST). ***Misdemeanor, Civil Actions under $10,000, Eviction, Small Claims.***
www.pershingcounty.net/
Civil Records: Access: Phone, mail, in person. Visitors must perform in person searches themselves. Search fee: $1.00 per name per year. Required to search: name, years to search; also helpful: address. Civil cases indexed by defendant, plaintiff; index on computer from 1988, on docket books prior. Mail turnaround time 2 days. Civil PAT goes back to 1988.
Criminal Records: Access: Phone, mail, in person. Visitors must perform in person searches themselves. Search fee: $1.00 per name per year. Required to search: name, years to search; also helpful: DOB. Criminal records computerized from 1988, on docket books prior. Mail turnaround time 2 days, 30 minutes for phone requests for records prior to 1988. Criminal PAT goes back to same as civil.
General Information: No sealed, driver's history or highway patrol records released. Will fax documents to local or toll-free number. Court makes copy: $.30 per page. Certification fee: $3.00. Payee: Lake Township Justice Court. Personal checks accepted; ID required. No credit cards accepted. Prepayment required. Mail requests: SASE required.

Storey County

1st Judicial District Court PO Drawer D, Virginia City, NV 89440; 775-847-0969; fax: 775-847-0921; 9AM-5PM (PST). ***Felony, Gross Misdemeanor, Civil Actions over $10,000, Probate.***
Civil Records: Access: Phone, mail, fax, in person. Both court and visitors may perform in person searches. Search fee: $1.00 per name per year. Required to search: name, years to search. Civil cases indexed by defendant, plaintiff; index on computer since 1997; prior years on books. Note: Accepts phone search requests only if paid in advance. Mail turnaround time 1 week; 1 day by fax; 5 minutes for phone requests when possible.
Criminal Records: Access: Phone, mail, fax, in person. Both court and visitors may perform in person searches. Search fee: $1.00 per name per year. Required to search: name, years to search, signed release; also helpful: DOB, SSN. Criminal records on computer since 1997; prior years on books. Note: Search by phone only if pre-paid. Mail turnaround time 1 week; 1 day by fax; 5 minutes for phone requests when possible.
General Information: No juvenile or sealed records released. Will fax documents to local or toll free line, will fax long distance with copy of check. Court makes copy: $1.00 per page. Self serve: same. Certification fee: $6.00 per document. Payee: Storey County Clerk. Personal checks accepted. Visa/MC accepted. Prepayment required. Mail requests: SASE required.

Virginia Township Justice Court PO Box 674, Virginia City, NV 89440; 775-847-0962; fax: 775-847-0915; 9AM-5PM (PST). ***Misdemeanor, Civil Actions under $10,000, Eviction, Small Claims.***
Civil Records: Access: Phone, mail, in person. Only the court performs in person searches; visitors may not. Search fee: $1.00 per name per year. Required to search: name, years to search. Civil cases indexed by defendant, plaintiff. Civil records retained for 7 years, some on docket books. Mail turnaround time 1 week.
Criminal Records: Access: Phone, mail, in person. Only the court performs in person searches; visitors may not. Search fee: $1.00 per name per year. Required to search: name, years to search, DOB; also helpful: SSN. Criminal records on computer since 1988. Mail turnaround time 1 week.
General Information: Will fax documents to local or toll free line. Court makes copy: $.30 per page. Certification fee: $3.00. Payee: Justice Court. Personal checks accepted. Visa/MC accepted. Debit cards also accepted. Prepayment required. Mail requests: SASE required.

Washoe County

2nd Judicial District Court PO Box 30083, 75 Court St, Reno, NV 89501; 775-328-3110; fax: 775-325-6658; 8AM-5PM (PST). ***Felony, Gross Misdemeanor, Civil Actions over $10,000, Probate.***
www.washoecourts.com
From 1985 to 1999 need to do self search because computer crashed and cannot be recovered for those years.
Civil Records: Access: Phone, mail, online, in person. Both court and visitors may perform in person searches. Search fee: $1.00 per name per year. Required to search: name, years to search. Civil cases indexed by defendant, plaintiff; index on computer back to 1984, microfiche from 1983, archives from 1920. Note: Phone access limited to computer records. Mail turnaround time 2-4 weeks. Civil PAT goes back to 2000. PAT civil results show middle initial. CourtConnect online access is at the website. Case data in CourtConnect only limited to cases filed after 1/2000. Calendars also free at website.
Criminal Records: Access: Phone, online, mail, in person. Both court and visitors may perform in person searches. Search fee: $1.00 per name per year. Required to search: name, years to search. Criminal records computerized from 1984, microfiche from 1983, archives from 1920. Note: Phone access limited to computer records. Mail turnaround time 2-4 weeks. Criminal PAT goes back to same as civil. PAT criminal results show middle initial. CourtConnect online access is at the website. Case data in CourtConnect only limited to cases filed after 1/2000. Calendars also free at website.
General Information: No sealed or juvenile records released. Will not fax documents. Court makes copy: $1.00 per page. Certification fee: $3.00 per page. Payee: Washoe County District Court, or WCDC. Business checks, cashiers checks and money orders accepted. No credit cards accepted. Prepayment required. Mail requests: SASE required.

Incline Village Justice Court 865 Tahoe Blvd, #301, Incline Village, NV 89451; 775-832-4100; fax: 775-832-4162; 9AM-5PM (PST). ***Misdemeanor, Civil Actions under $10,000, Eviction, Small Claims.***
www.co.washoe.nv.us/ijc
The court records are not computerized for searching. Paper records must be searched in binders.
Civil Records: Access: Mail, in person. Both court and visitors may perform in person searches. Search fee: $2.00 per name per year. Required to search: name, years to search. Civil cases indexed by defendant, plaintiff; index on dockets to 1980's. Mail turnaround time 1-3 days.
Criminal Records: Access: Mail, in person. Both court and visitors may perform in person searches. Search fee: $2.00 per name per year. Required to search: name, years to search; also helpful: DOB, SSN. Full dockets of criminal records searchable for 6-7 years, docket sheets available from 1980 to present. Mail turnaround time 1-3 days.
General Information: Will fax documents if prepaid. Court makes copy: $.30 per page. Certification fee: $3.00. Payee: Justice Court. Personal checks accepted; check guarantee card required. No credit cards accepted. Prepayment required. Mail requests: SASE required.

Reno Justice Court PO Box 30083, Reno, NV 89520; 775-325-6501; criminal phone: 775-325-6500; criminal fax: 775-325-6510; civil fax: 775-325-6715; 8AM-5PM (PST). ***Misdemeanor, Civil Actions under $10,000, Eviction, Small Claims.***
Also hold records for Verdi Justice Court which closed 05/2005.
Civil Records: Access: Mail, in person. Both court and visitors may perform in person searches. Search fee: $2.00 per name per year. If search requires offsite to storage, additional fees of $25.00 for 1st trip, $5.00 a file, apply. Required to search: name, years to search. Civil cases indexed by plaintiff and defendant. Civil records archived from 1997, on docket book; computerized records since 1997. Note: For mail access call first. Court will send form (also found on website) to be filled out & returned with payment. Mail turnaround time 2-5 days depending on workload.
Criminal Records: Access: Mail, in person. Only the court performs in person searches; visitors may not. Search fee: $2.00 per name per year. Required to search: name, years to search; also helpful: DOB, SSN, aliases. Criminal records archived from 1982, on docket books; computerized records since 1980. Note: For mail access call first. Court will send form to be filled out and returned with payment. Mail turnaround time 2-5 days depending on workload.

General Information: No sealed records released. Will fax documents to local or toll-free number. Court makes copy: $.30 per page. Certification fee: $3.00 per page. Payee: Reno Justice Court. Only cashiers checks and money orders accepted. Prepayment required. Mail requests: SASE required.

Sparks Justice Court 630 Greenbrae Dr, Sparks, NV 89431; 775-352-7600; fax: 775-352-3004; 8AM-5PM (PST). ***Misdemeanor, Civil Actions under $10,000, Eviction, Small Claims.***
www.co.washoe.nv.us/sjc
Civil Records: Access: Phone, mail, in person. Both court and visitors may perform in person searches. Search fee: $1.00 per name per year. Required to search: name, years to search. Civil cases indexed by defendant, plaintiff; index on computer 1990 to present, prior in books and on cards. Note: Case number required to search pre-1990 records. Mail turnaround time 1-3 days. Civil PAT goes back to 1990. PAT civil results show middle initial.
Criminal Records: Access: Phone, mail, in person. Both court and visitors may perform in person searches. Search fee: $1.00 per name per year. Required to search: name, years to search; also helpful: DOB, SSN. Full dockets of criminal records on computer last 10 years, 1990-1996 partially on computer, prior in books and on cards. Note: Case number required to search pre-1990 records. Traffic record search fees are same. Mail turnaround time 1-3 days. Criminal PAT goes back to 1993. PAT results show middle initial, DOB.
General Information: Will fax documents if prepaid. Court makes copy: $.30 per page. Certification fee: $3.00. Payee: Justice Court. Personal checks accepted; check guarantee card required. No credit cards accepted. Prepayment required.

Wadsworth Justice Court PO Box 68, Wadsworth, NV 89442; 775-575-4585; criminal fax: 775-575-0253; civil fax: same; 8AM-5PM T,W,TH only (PST). ***Misdemeanor, Civil Actions under $10,000, Eviction, Small Claims.***
Civil Records: Access: Mail, in person. Both court and visitors may perform in person searches. Search fee: $1.00 per name. Required to search: name, years to search. Civil cases indexed by defendant, plaintiff. Civil records go back to 1998. Mail turnaround time 5-10 days.
Criminal Records: Access: Mail, in person. Both court and visitors may perform in person searches. Search fee: $1.00 per name. Required to search: name, years to search; also helpful: DOB. Criminal records go back to 1998. Mail turnaround time 5-10 days.
General Information: Will fax documents if prepaid. Court makes copy: $.30 per page. Certification fee: $3.00 per page. Payee: Justice Court. Personal checks accepted; check guarantee card required. No credit cards accepted. Prepayment required.

White Pine County

7th Judicial District Court 801 Clark St, Court Clerk, #4, Ely, NV 89301; 775-289-2341; fax: 775-289-2544; 8AM-5PM (PST). ***Felony, Gross Misdemeanor, Civil Actions over $10,000, Probate.***
Civil Records: Access: Mail, fax, in person. Both court and visitors may perform in person searches. Search fee: 1st name free; $1.00 per name per year per add'l name. Required to search: Name, years to search. Civil cases indexed by defendant, plaintiff; index on computer back to 1991; older records go back to the beginning. Mail turnaround time 1 day.
Criminal Records: Access: Mail, fax, in person. Search fee: 1st name free; $1.00 per name per year per add'l name. Required to search: Name, years to search. Criminal records computerized from 1991; older records go back to the beginning. Mail turnaround time 1 day.
General Information: No sealed or juvenile records released. Will fax out documents no add'l fee. Court makes copy: $1.00 per page. Certification fee: $6.00 per doc. Payee: Office of Court Clerk. Will accept personal checks. No credit cards accepted. They prefer prepayment, but will sent without it if they know and trust you. Mail requests: SASE required.

Ely Justice Court 801 Clark St, #6, Ely, NV 89301; 775-289-2678; criminal fax: 775-289-3392; civil fax: same; 9AM-5PM (PST). ***Misdemeanor, Civil Actions under $10,000, Eviction, Small Claims.***
Civil Records: Access: Phone, fax, mail, in person. Only the court performs in person searches; visitors may not. Search fee: $1.00 per name per year. Required to search: name, case number, years to search. Civil cases indexed by defendant, plaintiff; index on computer from 1988, archived from 1899. Mail turnaround time 1-5 days.
Criminal Records: Access: Phone, fax, mail, in person. Only the court performs in person searches; visitors may not. Search fee: $1.00 per name per year. Required to search: name, case number, years to search; also helpful: DOB, SSN. Criminal records computerized from 1988, archived from 1899. Mail turnaround time 1-5 days.
General Information: No sealed records released. Will fax documents to toll-free number. Court makes copy: $.30 per page. Certification fee: $3.00. Payee: Ely Justice Court. Only cashiers checks and money orders accepted. Accepts any credit card accepted by Western Union Quick Collect Svc. Prepayment required. Mail requests: SASE required.

Lund Justice Court PO Box 87, Lund, NV 89317; 775-238-5400; fax: 775-238-5400; 10AM-2:30PM M,W,F (PST). ***Misdemeanor, Civil Actions under $10,000, Eviction, Small Claims.***
Civil Records: Access: Mail only. Only the court performs in person searches; visitors may not. Search fee: $1.00 per name per year. Required to search: name, years to search. Civil records only kept in files, archives from 1899. Mail turnaround time 3 days.
Criminal Records: Access: Mail only. Only the court performs in person searches; visitors may not. Search fee: $1.00 per name per year. Required to search: name, years to search, DOB; also helpful: SSN. Criminal records only kept in files, archives from 1899. Mail turnaround time 2 days.
General Information: Will not fax documents. Court makes copy: $1.00 per page. Certification fee: $2.00. Payee: Lund Justice Court. No personal checks accepted. Money orders required. No credit cards accepted. Prepayment required. Mail requests: SASE required.

Baker Justice Court 801 Clark St #6, Ely, NV 89301; 775-289-2678; fax: 775-289-3392; 9AM-5PM (PST). ***Misdemeanor, Civil Actions under $10,000, Eviction, Small Claims.***
Baker court is now closed; cases heard at Ely Justice Court in Ely, phone, fax and address given above; records also located there.

Nevada Recording Offices

ORGANIZATION: 16 counties and one independent city; 17 recording offices. The recording officer is the County Recorder. Carson City has a separate filing office. Nevada is entirely in the Pacific Time Zone (PST).

REAL ESTATE RECORDS: Most counties will not provide real estate searches. Real estate related copies cost $1.00 per page and certification fee is $4.00 per document.

UCC RECORDS: Financing statements are filed at the state level except for real estate related collateral which are filed with the County Recorder. However, prior to July, 2001, consumer goods and farm collateral were also filed at the County Recorder and these older records can be searched there, and most offices will still perform the search, usually $40.00 per debtor.

TAX LIEN RECORDS: Federal tax liens on personal property of businesses are filed with the Secretary of State. Federal tax liens on personal property of individuals are filed with the County Recorder. Although not called state tax liens, employment withholding judgments have the same effect and are filed with the County Recorder. Some, not all, counties provide tax lien searches.

OTHER LIENS: Mechanics.

ONLINE ACCESS: A number of counties have searchable databases online. A private company, GoverNet, offers online access to Assessor, Treasurer, Recorder and other county databases for Churchill, Clark, Esmeralda, and Pershing. Registration is required; sliding monthly and per-hit fees apply. System includes access to Secretary of State's Corporation, Partnership, UCC, Fictitious Name, and Federal Tax Lien records. For more information, call 208-522-1225. Also, after registration, search UCCs free at https://esos.state.nv.us/NVUCC/user/login.asp. To receive documents the fee is $20.00.

Carson City

City Recorder, 885 E Musser St, #1028, Carson City, NV 89701-4775. Recording, R/E & UCC phone-775-887-2260, UCC recording phone-775-887-2260 city level or 775-687-4280 St level; fax-775-887-2146; 8AM-5PM) www.carson-city.nv.us/

Index: All in one. Records indexed on a public use terminal back to 1985. Office will perform a UCC or federal tax lien search but public must search other records themselves. Search fee $40.00. Copy fee $2.00, if tax lien or real estate $1.00 per page. Cert fee- $4.00 per seal. Payee- Carson City Recorder. CDs of bulk information are available for purchase; contact Robin Houston. **Online access to Real Estate, Deed, Marriage, Vital Statistic records:** Most all recordings are indexed online at www.carson-city.nv.us/Index.aspx?page=155 but no images. Use the pull-down menu. Search issued marriage licenses free at www.ccapps.org/cgi-bin/dmw200. **Other phones:** Treasurer- 775-887-2092; Elections- 775-887-2087; Vital Records- 775-684-4242. **Property tax/Assessing-** 201 N Carson St, #6, Carson City, NV 89701; 775-887-2130, assessor fax- 775-887-2139. **Online access-** Access assessor data of parcels and secured property free at www.ccapps.org/cgi-bin/asw100. Access secured property data free at www.ccapps.org/cgi-bin/tcw100. Find Carson city parcel maps by parcel number at www.carson-city.nv.us/Index.aspx?page=59.

Churchill County

County Recorder, 155 N Taylor, #131, Fallon, NV 89406-2748. Recording, R/E & UCC phone-775-423-6001; fax-775-423-8933; 8AM-5PM) www.churchillcounty.org/recorder/

Index: Separate indices to search include regular, commercial. Records indexed on a public use terminal back to 1983. Office will perform a UCC or tax lien search but public must search other records themselves. UCC search fee $40.00 for 5 years. Office will not search real estate records. Copy fee $1.00 per page; UCC copy $2.00 per page. Cert fee- $4.00 per cert plus copy fee. Payee- Churchill County Recorder. **Online access to Real Estate, Grantor/Grantee, Deed, Judgment, UCC, Lien records:** Access recorder records at www.churchillcounty.org/recorder/. Documents 2005 and forward can be viewed, all maps can be viewed. **Other phones:** Treasurer- 775-423-6028; Elections- 775-423-6028; Vital Records- 775-684-4280 (Birth/Death). **Property tax/Assessing-** 155 N Taylor St, #200, Fallon, NV 89406; 775-423-6584, assessor fax- 775-423-2429. (Appraiser/Auditor- 775-423-6584) www.churchillcounty.org **Online access-** Access assessor property records free at www.churchillcounty.org/assessor/.

Clark County

County Recorder, Box 551510, Las Vegas, NV 89155-1510. 702-455-4336; fax-702-455-5644; 8AM-5PM) www.accessclarkcounty.com/recorder

Index: Separate indices to search include old records on microfilm back to 1909, computer. Records indexed on public access terminal back to 1988. Only the public may search. Copy fee $1.00 per page. Cert fee- $4.00 per doc plus copy fee. Payee- Clark County Recorder. Recorded document data available for purchase weekly, monthly, daily ($11.00 per day) on CD; custom orders also accepted-702-455-4336. **Online Real Estate, Deed, Lien, UCC, Marriage, Fictitious Name, Business License, Voter Registration records:** Recorder's real estate, UCC and vital records free at www.accessclarkcounty.com/recorder but no images. UCCs go back to 1986; liens to '84. Search county fictitious names at http://sandgate.co.clark.nv.us:8498/clarkcounty/clerk/clerkSearch.html. Marriages- http://redrock.co.clark.nv.us/RecSearch/MarriageSearchMain.aspx. Business license- http://sandgate.co.clark.nv.us/businessLicense/businessSearch/blindex.asp. Voter Registration- www.accessclarkcounty.com/depts/election/english/Pages/home.aspx. **Other phones:** Treasurer- 702-455-4323; Elections- 702-455-8683; Health District- 702-759-1010. **Property tax/Assessing-** 500 S Grand Central Pky, 2nd Fl, Las Vegas, NV 89155; 702-455-3882. **Online access-** Property records, assessor maps, manufactured housing, road documents, and business personal property on the county Assessor database are free at www.accessclarkcounty.com/depts/assessor/pages/Disclaim.aspx. Property-GIS at http://gisgate.co.clark.nv.us.

Douglas County

County Recorder, PO Box 218, Minden, NV 89423. 775-782-9025; fax-775-783-6413; 9AM-5PM. www.douglascountynv.gov/sites/recorder/

Index: All in one. Records indexed on a public use terminal back to 1/1/1983. Office will perform a UCC search for a fee, but public must search other records themselves. Copy fee $1.00 per page. Cert fee- $4.00 per doc plus copy fee. Payee- Douglas County Recorder. Office does sell bulk data on CD's, contact Erin Inman at 775-782-9026. **Online access to Real Estate, Deed, Mortgage, Lien, Judgment, Voter Registration, Building Permit records:** Access recorded documents index back thru 1983 free at www.douglascountynv.gov/sites/recorder/database/default.asp (index only, images not online). Also, search voter rolls free at http://cltr.co.douglas.nv.us/elections/vripri-general.cfm with birthdate required. Also, building permits free at www.douglascountynv.gov/sites/cd-building/index.cfml. **Other phones:** Treasurer- 775-782-9017; Vital Records- 775-782-9028. **Property tax/Assessing-** PO Box 218, Minden, NV 89423; 775-782-9830, assessor fax- 775-782-9884. http://assessor.co.douglas.nv.us **Online access-** Parcel records on the Assessor's database are free at http://assessor.co.douglas.nv.us/database/2008/parcel/index.asp. Also, download maps at http://assessor.co.douglas.nv.us/database/. Also, the clerk/treasurer property tax database is free at http://cltr.co.douglas.nv.us/database/treasurers/.

Elko County

County Recorder, 571 Idaho St, Rm 103, Elko, NV 89801-3770. 775-738-6526; fax-775-738-3299; 9AM-5PM) www.elkocountynv.net

Index: Separate indices to search include marriage records, maps, and general. Records indexed on a public use terminal back to 1/1984, marriages to 1/1960, maps to 1869. Office will perform a UCC search but public must search other records themselves. Search fee $40.00 for UCC's. Copy fee $1.00 per page. Cert fee- $4.00 per doc plus copy fee. Payee- Elko County Recorder. Bulk data available for purchase in various formats. **Online access to Real Estate, Deed, Marriage records:** Access to the recorder database including marriages is free at www.elkocountynv.net/recorder.htm. Recording records go back to 1984. Most documents back to 2000 are viewable and/or printable. **Other phones:** Treasurer- 775-738-5694; Elections- 775-753-4600; Vital Records- 775-684-4242; County Clerk- 775-753-4600; Marriages -775-738-6526. **Property tax/Assessing**- 571 Idaho St, PO Box 8, Elko, NV 89801-3370; 775-738-5217 x21, assessor fax- 775-778-6795. (Appraiser/Auditor- 775-738-5217 x33) hours- 8AM-5PM http://elkocountynv.net **Online-** Access to the assessor database including personal property free at www.elkocountynv.net/assessor.htm.

Esmeralda County

County Recorder, PO Box 458, Goldfield, NV 89013. Recording, R/E & UCC phone-775-485-6337; fax-775-485-3524; 8AM-Noon, 1PM-5PM)

Index: Separate indices to search include books. Record index not computerized. Office personnel or visitors may perform searches. Search fee $15.00 per name. Copy fee $1.00 per page. Cert fee- $4.00 per seal. Payee- Esmeralda County Recorder. **Other phones:** Treasurer- 775-485-6367; Elections- 775-485-6367. **Property tax/Assessing**- PO Box 471, 233 Crook St, Goldfield, NV 89013; 775-485-6380, assessor fax- 775-485-3450. (Appraiser/Auditor- 775-485-6380) **Online access**- Access the assessment roll free at www.accessesmeralda.com/Assessor.htm. Click on Assessment Roll.

Eureka County

County Recorder, PO Box 556, Eureka, NV 89316. 775-237-5263; fax-775-237-5614; 8AM-N, 1-5PM. www.co.eureka.nv.us

Index: All in one. Records indexed on a public use terminal back to 1988. Office will perform a UCC search but public must search other records themselves. Copy fee $1.00 per page. Cert fee- $4.00 per doc plus copy fee. Payee- Eureka County Recorder. Bulk data available for purchase, new books on CD and $.05 per image, contact the Recorders Office. **Other phones:** Treasurer- 775-237-5262; Elections- 775-237-5262. **Property tax/Assessing**- PO Box 88, 20 S Main, Eureka, NV 89316; 775-237-5270, assessor fax- 775-237-5614. (Appraiser/Auditor- 775-237-5270) A public access terminal is available. **Online**- Search the assessor property data at http://eurekacounty.net:1401/cgi-bin/asw100. Search treasurer's secured property tax roll at http://eurekacounty.net:1401/cgi-bin/tcw100.

Humboldt County

County Recorder, 25 W 4th St, Winnemucca, NV 89445. Recording, R/E & UCC phone-775-623-6414, UCC recording phone-775-623-6412; fax-775-623-6337; 8AM-5PM) www.hcnv.us

Index: Separate indices to search include various books 1860's to 1983; Computer- grantor/grantee, 1983 forward Official Records- deeds, deeds of trust, contracts of sales, misc, probate, etc. Records indexed on a public use terminal back to 1983. Office will perform a UCC search but public must search other records themselves. Search fee $40.00 for UCC. Copy fee $1.00 per page. Cert fee- $4.00 per cert plus copy fee. Payee- Humboldt County Recorder. Treasurer-775-623-6444; Elections- 775-623-6343; Vital Records- 775-623-6412; 775-623-6414. **Property tax/Assessing**- 50 W 5th St, Winnemucca, NV 89445; 775-623-6310, assessor fax- 775-623-6311. (Appraiser - 775-623-6310) A public terminal is available. www.hcnv.us/assessor/assessor.htm **Online access**- Online access to assessor records is available at www.humboldtcountynv.org:1401/cgi-bin/asw100. Treasurers secured tax inquiry is at www.humboldtcountynv.org:1401/cgi-bin/tcw100.

Lander County

County Recorder, 315 S Humboldt, Battle Mountain, NV 89820. Recording, R/E & UCC phone-775-635-5173; fax-775-635-8272; 8AM-5PM)

Index: All in one. Records indexed on a public use terminal back to 1963. Office will perform a UCC and Tax lien search but public must search other records themselves. Search fee $40.00. Copy fee $1.00 per page. Marriage certificate $10.00. Cert fee- $4.00 per cert plus copy fee. Payee- Lander County Recorder. Bulk data available in microfilm and CD format. Treasurer- 775-635-5127; Elections- 775-635-5738. **Property tax/Assessing**- 315 Humboldt, Battle Mountain, 89820; 775-635-2610, fax- 775-635-5520. www.landercounty.org/official/AssessorInfo.htm **Online access**- Access real property tax, personal property, and sales free at www.landercounty.org:1401/cgi-bin/asw100.

Lincoln County

County Recorder, PO Box 218, Pioche, NV 89043. 775-962-5495; fax-775-962-5180; 9AM-5PM)

Index: All in one. Records indexed on a public use terminal back to 1972. Office personnel or visitors may perform searches. Office will not search real estate records. UCC search per debtor name- $40.00. Copy fee $1.00 per page. Cert fee- $4.00 per doc plus copy fee. Payee- Lincon County Recorder. **Other phones:** Treasurer- 775-962-5805. **Property tax/Assessing**- PO Box 420, Pioche, NV 89043; 775-962-5890, assessor fax- 775-962-5892.

Lyon County

County Recorder, 27 S Main St, Yerington, NV 89447-0927. 775-463-6581; fax-775-463-6585; 8AM-5PM www.lyon-county.org/index.asp

Index: All in one. Records indexed on a public use terminal back to 1/1/1984. Office will perform a UCC search but public must search other records themselves. Search fee $40.00. Office will not search real estate records. Copy fee $1.00 per page. UCC copy $2.00 per page. Cert fee- $4.00 per doc plus copy fee. Payee- County Recorder. Bulk documents and map images available on CD; contact Margie Kassebaum 775-463-6581 x293. **Online access to Real Estate, Deed, UCC, Map records:** Access recorder records free at www.lyon-county.org/index.asp?nid=110; images go back to 1/2006. **Other phones:** Treasurer- 775-463-6502; Elections- 775-463-6502; Vital Records- 775-463-6581. **Property tax/Assessing**- 27 S Main St, Yerington, NV 89447; 775-463-6524, assessor fax-775-463-6599. (Appraiser/Auditor- 775-463-6524) **Online** - Search assessor data at www.lyon-county.org/index.asp?nid=55 and click on On-Line Data.

Mineral County

Recorder, PO Box 1447, Hawthorne, NV 89415-1447. 775-945-3676; fax-775-945-1749; 8AM-5PM)

Index: Books, computer. Records indexed on a public use terminal back to 1985. Only the public may search. Copy fee $1.00 per page. Cert fee- $4.00 per page plus copy fee. Payee- Mineral County Recorder. Bulk data available for purchase, contact Gloria Hughes. **Other phones:** Treasurer- 775-945-2446; Elections- 775-945-2446. **Property tax/Assessing**- PO Box 400, Hawthorne, 89415; 775-945-3684, fax-775-945-0717. A public access terminal is available.

Nye County

County Recorder, PO Box 1111, Tonopah, NV 89049-1111. 775-482-8116; fax-775-482-8111; 8AM-5PM. www.nyecounty.net/

Index: All in one. Records indexed on a public use terminal back to 1986. Only the public may search. Copy fee $1.00 per page. Cert fee- $4.00per cert plus copy fee. Payee- Nye County Recorder. **Other phones:** Treasurer- 775-482-8194. **Property tax/Assessing**- PO Box 271, Tonapah, NV 89049; 775-482-8174. hours- 8AM-N, 1-5PM www.nyecounty.net/index.asp?NID=267 **Online access**- Search property assessor data free at http://asdb.co.nye.nv.us:1401/cgi-bin/asw100. Access secured tax data sheets free at www.nyecounty.net/.

Pershing County

County Recorder, PO Box 736, Lovelock, NV 89419-0736. 775-273-2408; fax-775-273-1039; 8AM-5PM) www.pershingcounty.net/recorderauditor.htm

Index: All in one. Records indexed on a public use terminal back to 1986. Full documents scanned since 08/03. Books with index's from 1919 to 1985. Office will perform a UCC or tax lien search but public must search other records themselves. Search fee-$40.00 per name. Copy fee $1.00 per page. Cert fee- $4.00 per cert plus copy fee. Payee- Pershing County Recorder. Bulk data available for purchase, contact Dixie or Pam. **Other phones:** Treasurer- 775-273-2208; Elections- 775-273-2208; Vital Records- 775-273-2408 (marriage only). **Property tax/Assessing**- PO Box 89, 398 Main St, Lovelock, NV 89419; 775-273-2369, assessor fax- 775-273-5037. (Appraiser/Auditor- 775-273-2369) A public access terminal is available.

Storey County

County Recorder, PO Box 493, Virginia City, NV 89440. 775-847-0967; fax-775-847-1009; 9AM-5PM) www.storeycounty.org

Index: All in one. Records indexed on a public use terminal back to 1985. Office personnel or visitors may perform searches. Office will not search real estate records. Office will search UCC records, but not tax liens. UCC search per debtor name- $20.00. Copy fee $1.00 per page. Copy from computer- $.50 each. Cert fee- $4.00 per cert plus copy fee. Payee- Storey County Recorder. Office will sell books on CD-rom, also yearly grantor/grantee index on Microfiche; call assessors office. **Other phones:** Treasurer- 775-847-0969; Elections- 775-847-0969; Vital Records- 775-847-0969. **Property tax/Assessing**- PO Box 494, 26 S " B" St, Virginia City, NV 89440; 775-847-0961, assessor fax- 775-847-0904. A public access terminal is available for searches in the Recorders office. www.storeycounty.org **Online access**- Search assessor's assessment roll free at www.storeycounty.org/assessor/search_new.asp.

Washoe County

County Recorder, PO Box 11130, Reno, NV 89520-0027. 775-328-3661, R/E recording phone-775-328-2230; fax-775-325-8010; hours- 8AM-5PM) www.co.washoe.nv.us/recorder

Index: All in one. Records indexed on a public use terminal back to 1991. Only the public may search. Copy fee $2.00, if tax lien or real estate $1.00 per page. Cert fee- $4.00 per cert plus copy fee. Payee-Washoe County Recorder. Bulk data available for purchase, contact Goug Dufva. **Online Real Estate, Grantor/Grantee, Deed, Voter Regist. records:** Access grantor/grantee index free at www.co.washoe.nv.us/recorder/icris.washoecounty.us; a $1.00 per page fee for docs. Search voter registration roll at www.co.washoe.nv.us/voters/regsearch.php~color=grey&text_version=. **Other phones:** Treasurer- 775-328-2510. **Property tax/Assessing**- 1001 E 9th St, Reno, NV 89512; 775-328-2277, assessor fax- 775-328-3641. A public access terminal is available. **Online access**- Access property tax data at www.co.washoe.nv.us/assessor/cama/search.php. Download property sales 2003-2005 data free at www.co.washoe.nv.us/assessor/SalesRpt.htm. Also, search aircraft, business property, mobile home data free at www.co.washoe.nv.us/assessor/index.htm.

White Pine County

County Recorder, 801 Clark St, #1, Ely, NV 89301. Recording, R/E & UCC phone-775-289-4567; fax-775-289-1566; 8AM-5PM.

Index: Separate indices to search include grantor/grantee on computer and old books. Records indexed on a public use terminal back to 1985. Office will do a quick search if you provide name and approximate date, otherwise searchers must search for themselves. Search UCC fee $40.00 per name. Office will search minimal real estate records. Copy fee $1.00 per page. Cert fee- $4.00 per cert plus copy fee. Exemplification- $10.00. Payee- White Pine County Recorder. **Other phones:** Treasurer- 775-289-4783; Elections- 775-289-2341. **Property tax/Assessing**- 995 Campton, Ely, NV 89301; 775-289-3016, assessor fax- 775-289-8842.

Nevada County Locator

You will usually be able to find the city name in the City/County Cross Reference below. In that case, it is a simple matter to determine the county from the cross reference. However, only the official US Postal Service city names are included in this index. There are an additional 40,000 place names that people use in their addresses. Therefore, we have also included a ZIP/City Cross Reference immediately following the City/County Cross Reference.

If you know the ZIP Code but the city name does not appear in the City/County Cross Reference index, look up the ZIP Code in the ZIP/City Cross Reference, find the city name, then look up the city name in the City/County Cross Reference. For example, you want to know the county for an address of Menands, NY 12204. There is no "Menands" in the City/County Cross Reference. The ZIP/City Cross Reference shows that ZIP Codes 12201-12288 are for the city of Albany. Looking back in the City/County Cross Reference, Albany is in Albany County.

Nevada City/County Cross Reference

ALAMO Lincoln
AMARGOSA VALLEY Nye
AUSTIN Lander
BAKER White Pine
BATTLE MOUNTAIN Lander
BEATTY Nye
BLUE DIAMOND Clark
BOULDER CITY Clark
BUNKERVILLE Clark
CAL NEV ARI Clark
CALIENTE Lincoln
CARLIN Elko
CARSON CITY (89706) Carson City(87), Lyon(12)
CARSON CITY Carson City
CARSON CITY Douglas
CRESCENT VALLEY Eureka
CRYSTAL BAY Washoe
DAYTON (89403) Lyon(93), Storey(6)
DEETH Elko
DENIO Humboldt
DUCKWATER White Pine
DYER Esmeralda
EAST ELY White Pine
ELKO Elko
ELY White Pine
EMPIRE Washoe
EUREKA Eureka
FALLON Churchill
FERNLEY (89408) Lyon(97), Churchill(2)
GABBS Nye
GARDNERVILLE Douglas
GENOA Douglas
GERLACH Washoe
GLENBROOK Douglas
GOLCONDA Humboldt
GOLDFIELD Esmeralda
HALLECK Elko
HAWTHORNE Mineral
HENDERSON Clark
HIKO Lincoln
IMLAY Pershing
INCLINE VILLAGE Washoe
INDIAN SPRINGS Clark
JACKPOT Elko
JARBIDGE Elko
JEAN Clark
LAMOILLE Elko
LAS VEGAS Clark
LAUGHLIN Clark
LOGANDALE Clark
LOVELOCK Pershing
LUND White Pine
LUNING Mineral
MANHATTAN Nye
MC DERMITT Humboldt
MC GILL White Pine
MERCURY Nye
MESQUITE Clark
MINA Mineral
MINDEN Douglas
MOAPA Clark
MONTELLO Elko
MOUNTAIN CITY Elko
NELLIS AFB Clark
NIXON Washoe
NORTH LAS VEGAS Clark
OROVADA Humboldt
OVERTON Clark
OWYHEE Elko
PAHRUMP Nye
PANACA Lincoln
PARADISE VALLEY Humboldt
PIOCHE Lincoln
RENO (89521) Washoe(84), Storey(15)
RENO Washoe
ROUND MOUNTAIN Nye
RUBY VALLEY Elko
RUTH White Pine
SCHURZ Mineral
SEARCHLIGHT Clark
SILVER CITY Lyon
SILVER SPRINGS Lyon
SILVERPEAK Esmeralda
SMITH Lyon
SPARKS (89434) Washoe(94), Storey(5)
SPARKS Washoe
SPRING CREEK Elko
STATELINE Douglas
SUN VALLEY Washoe
THE LAKES Clark
TONOPAH Nye
TUSCARORA Elko
VALMY Humboldt
VERDI Washoe
VIRGINIA CITY Storey
WADSWORTH Washoe
WASHOE VALLEY Washoe
WELLINGTON (89444) Lyon(52), Douglas(47)
WELLS Elko
WEST WENDOVER Elko
WINNEMUCCA (89445) Humboldt(91), Pershing(8)
WINNEMUCCA Humboldt
YERINGTON Lyon
ZEPHYR COVE Douglas

Nevada ZIP/City Cross Reference

88901-88901 THE LAKES
88902-88904 LAS VEGAS
88905-88905 THE LAKES
89001-89001 ALAMO
89003-89003 BEATTY
89004-89004 BLUE DIAMOND
89005-89006 BOULDER CITY
89007-89007 BUNKERVILLE
89008-89008 CALIENTE
89009-89009 HENDERSON
89010-89010 DYER
89011-89012 HENDERSON
89013-89013 GOLDFIELD
89014-89016 HENDERSON
89017-89017 HIKO
89018-89018 INDIAN SPRINGS
89019-89019 JEAN
89020-89020 AMARGOSA VALLEY
89021-89021 LOGANDALE
89022-89022 MANHATTAN
89023-89023 MERCURY
89024-89024 MESQUITE
89025-89025 MOAPA
89026-89026 JEAN
89027-89027 MESQUITE
89028-89029 LAUGHLIN
89030-89036 NORTH LAS VEGAS
89039-89039 CAL NEV ARI
89040-89040 OVERTON
89041-89041 PAHRUMP
89042-89042 PANACA
89043-89043 PIOCHE
89044-89044 HENDERSON
89045-89045 ROUND MOUNTAIN
89046-89046 SEARCHLIGHT
89047-89047 SILVERPEAK
89048-89048 PAHRUMP
89049-89049 TONOPAH
89052-89053 HENDERSON
89060-89061 PAHRUMP
89070-89070 INDIAN SPRINGS
89074-89077 HENDERSON
89081-89087 NORTH LAS VEGAS
89101-89162 LAS VEGAS
89163-89163 THE LAKES
89164-89185 LAS VEGAS
89191-89191 NELLIS AFB
89193-89199 LAS VEGAS
89301-89301 ELY
89310-89310 AUSTIN
89311-89311 BAKER
89314-89314 DUCKWATER
89315-89315 EAST ELY
89315-89315 ELY
89316-89316 EUREKA
89317-89317 LUND
89318-89318 MC GILL
89319-89319 RUTH
89402-89402 CRYSTAL BAY
89403-89403 DAYTON
89404-89404 DENIO
89405-89405 EMPIRE
89406-89407 FALLON
89408-89408 FERNLEY
89409-89409 GABBS
89410-89410 GARDNERVILLE
89411-89411 GENOA
89412-89412 GERLACH
89413-89413 GLENBROOK
89414-89414 GOLCONDA
89415-89416 HAWTHORNE
89418-89418 IMLAY
89419-89419 LOVELOCK
89420-89420 LUNING
89421-89421 MC DERMITT
89422-89422 MINA
89423-89423 MINDEN
89424-89424 NIXON
89425-89425 OROVADA
89426-89426 PARADISE VALLEY
89427-89427 SCHURZ
89428-89428 SILVER CITY
89429-89429 SILVER SPRINGS
89430-89430 SMITH
89431-89432 SPARKS
89433-89433 SUN VALLEY
89434-89436 SPARKS
89438-89438 VALMY
89439-89439 VERDI
89440-89440 VIRGINIA CITY
89442-89442 WADSWORTH
89444-89444 WELLINGTON
89445-89446 WINNEMUCCA
89447-89447 YERINGTON
89448-89448 ZEPHYR COVE
89449-89449 STATELINE
89450-89452 INCLINE VILLAGE
89460-89460 GARDNERVILLE
89496-89496 FALLON
89500-89599 RENO
89701-89703 CARSON CITY
89704-89704 WASHOE VALLEY
89705-89721 CARSON CITY
89801-89803 ELKO
89815-89815 SPRING CREEK
89820-89820 BATTLE MOUNTAIN
89821-89821 CRESCENT VALLEY
89822-89822 CARLIN
89823-89823 DEETH
89824-89824 HALLECK
89825-89825 JACKPOT
89826-89826 JARBIDGE
89828-89828 LAMOILLE
89830-89830 MONTELLO
89831-89831 MOUNTAIN CITY
89832-89832 OWYHEE
89833-89833 RUBY VALLEY
89834-89834 TUSCARORA
89835-89835 WELLS
89883-89883 WEST WENDOVER

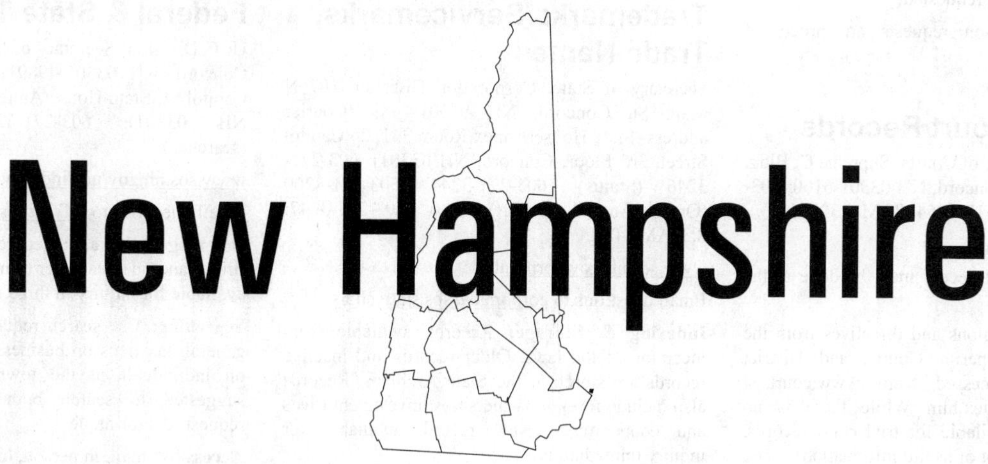

New Hampshire

General Help Numbers:

Governor's Office
State House
25 Capitol St.
Concord, NH 03301-4990
www.governor.nh.gov/
603-271-2121
Fax 603-271-7680
8AM-5PM

Attorney General's Office
33 Capitol St
Concord, NH 03301-6397
http://doj.nh.gov
603-271-3658
Fax 603-271-2110
8AM-5PM

Legislative Records
New Hampshire State Library
20 Part St
Concord, NH 03301
http://gencourt.state.nh.us/ie
603-271-2239
Fax 603-271-2205
8AM-4:30PM

State Archives
Division of Records Management & Archives
71 S Fruit St
Concord, NH 03301
http://www.sos.nh.gov/archives/
603-271-2236
Fax 603-271-2272
8AM-4:30PM

State Specifics:

Capital:	Concord Merrimack County
Time Zone:	EST
Number of Counties:	10
Population:	1,315,809
Web Site:	www.nh.gov/

State Agencies

Criminal Records

State Police Headquarters, Criminal Records, James H. Hayes Bldg,, 33 Hazen Dr, Concord, NH 03305; 603-271-2538, Fax- 603-271-2339; 8:15AM-4:15PM.

www.nh.gov/safety/divisions/nhsp/ssb/crimrecords/index.html

The web page does a nice job of outlining who can obtain records and for what reason. In general, records are not available to the public unless written authorization by the subject is provided.

Indexing & Storage: Records available from circa 1900. New records available for inquiry in 1 day. 80% of all arrests in database have final dispositions recorded, 87% for those arrests within last 5 years.

Searching: Requester must have "authorization in writing, duly signed and notarized, explicitly allowing the requester to receive such information." Also specify exactly what information is needed. Statutorily-required fingerprint searches include FBI check. Include in request- notarized release, full name, date of birth, any aliases, sex, race. Fingerprint searches are required for certain occupations (i.e. teachers) per state statute. 75% of the records are fingerprint supported. This data not released- records without convictions

Access by: mail, in person.

Fee & Payment: The search fee is $15.00 per name. When required, FBI fingerprint searches are an additional fee depending on reason and type of submittal. Fee payee- NH State Police. Prepayment required. Personal checks accepted, credit cards are not.

Mail search: Turnaround time- 1 week. A self addressed envelope is requested.

In person: in person requests are processed immediately.

Statewide Court Records

Administrative Office of Courts, Supreme Ct Bldg, 2 Charles Doe Dr, Concord, NH 03301-6160; 603-271-2521, Fax- 603-513-5454; 8AM-4:30PM.

www.courts.state.nh.us

All trial court record access must be done at the local level.

Online search: Opinions and directives from the Supreme Court, Superior Courts, and District Courts can be accessed from www.courts.state.nh.us/supreme/index.htm While there is no statewide access available for trial court records, the web page has a lot of useful information.

Sexual Offender Registry

State Police Headquarters, Special Investigations Unit-SOR, James H. Hayes Bldg, 33 Hazen Dr, Concord, NH 03305; 603-271-6344; 8:15AM-4:15PM. www.egov.nh.gov/nsor/

Indexing & Storage: New records available for inquiry in weekly (on the web).

Searching: The agency prefers requesters go to the local police departments if the requester does not have Internet access.

Fee & Payment: There is no search fee.

Online search: For web access, click on the Offenders Against Children link. This list only contains certain information about registered offenders who have committed certain criminal offenses against children. The list also contains outstanding arrest warrants for any sexual offender or offender against children who did not register.

Incarceration Records

New Hampshire Department of Corrections, Offender Records Office, PO Box 14, Concord, NH 03302; 603-271-1825, Fax- 603-271-1867; 8AM-4PM. www.nh.gov/nhdoc/

Indexing & Storage: Records available on current and former inmates. New records available for inquiry in up to 3 days.

Searching: Include in request- full name, DOB. Computerized records go back to 1995.

Access by: mail, phone, fax, in person, online.

Fee & Payment: There is no search fee for a single record search. If a list is present, the fee is $10.00 total for up to 10 names and $25.00 total if over 10 names. Fee payee- Treasurer, State of New Hampshire Prepayment required. Personal checks not accepted.

Mail search: Turnaround time- 1-2 weeks.

Phone search: Call the number above for a phone name search.

Fax search: Requests may be faxed.

In person: Searchers must present ID and release info.

Online search: An inmate locator is available on their web page. The inmate locator displays the offender's current controlling sentence and does not show concurrent sentences also being served or consecutive sentences that have yet to be served.

Corporation, LP, LLP, LLC, Trademarks/Servicemarks, Trade Names

Secretary of State, Corporation Division, 107 N Main St, Concord, NH 03301-4989 (Courier address- State House Annex Room 341, 25 Capitol Street, 3rd Floor, Concord, NH 03301); 603-271-3246 (Status), 603-271-3244, 603-271-8200 (Order Annual Report), Fax- 603-271-3247; 8:30AM-4PM.

www.sos.nh.gov/corporate/

Email questions to corporate@sos.state.nh.us.

Indexing & Storage: Records available from inception of the laws. Older records and inactive records are stored at the State Archives. Records also include foreign partnerships, investment trusts and cooperatives. New records available for inquiry immediately.

Searching: Retrieval of records from storage at Archives takes one week Include in request- full name of business, specific records needed. In addition to the articles of organization, business entity records available include: Annual Reports, Officers, Directors, Prior (merged) names, Inactive and Reserved names. This data not released- old addendums/SRA forms and correspondence or letters submitted by filer.

Access by: mail, phone, in person, online.

Fee & Payment: No copy fee for 20 pages, over 20 pages is $.50 per page. A Good Standing is $5.00. An ACH account can be established for ongoing requesters. Fee payee- Secretary of State. They will invoice for copy fees, but you must pay in advance for certificates of good standing. Personal checks accepted, cash accepted in person but must be exact: no change given. No credit cards accepted.

Mail search: Turnaround time- 1 to 2 days. A SASE is requested.

Phone search: No fee for telephone request. Call between 8:30AM-4PM to obtain name, address, incorporation date, and registered agent, check name availability, and request document copies.

In person: You may request information in person, the agency does the copying. The counter closes at 3:30PM.

Online search: A free business name lookup is available at the website. Results include a wealth of information including registered agent. Documents filed after 12/2004 and some older documents have been imaged and are also available in the entity's Filed Documents.

Other access: Monthly lists of corporations, LLCs, or trade names are $50 per month or $500 for last 12 months. ; A list of all non-profits on file is available for $250.00.

Expedited service: You may fax requests for same day service (if received by 2 PM) for information on company status, details, annual reports (current and past 2 years only), and name availability. You may request 2 names or items per fax. Turnaround time- 1-2 days. Certified copies in person considered expedited, as are in-person requests for Good Standing. Copies are $1.00 per page plus $5.00 for certification plus $25.00 expedite fee.

Uniform Commercial Code, Federal & State Tax Liens

UCC Division, Secretary of State, 107 N Main St, Concord, NH 03301-4989 (Courier address- 25 Capitol St, State House Annex, Rm 313, Concord, NH 03301); 603-271-3276; 9AM-3:30PM (searches).

www.sos.nh.gov/ucc/index.html

Email questions to UCC@sos.state.nh.us.

Indexing & Storage: Records available for active filings and one year after termination. New records available for inquiry in three months or less.

Searching: Use search request form UCC-11. In general, tax liens on businesses are filed here and on individuals at the town/county level. It is suggested to search both places. Include in request- debtor name.

Access by: mail, in person, online.

Fee & Payment: Fees is $10.00 per name, copies $1.00 per page. Online or expedited service is more, see below. Fee payee- Secretary of State. Prepayment required. Search requests and filings must be prepaid, they will invoice for copies. Personal checks accepted. No credit cards accepted, except if online.

Mail search: Turnaround time- 2 weeks. A SASE is requested.

In person: See expedited service.

Online search: Visit https://www.sos.nh.gov/uccegov/ for commercial online access to records. Accounts may be established using either automated clearing house (ACH) debit account or credit card. The fee is $27.00 per debtor name on a pay as you go basis, or for a $5,000 subscription fee receive unlimited online searches for one full year. Users can apply for an ACH (Automated Clearing House) account to be used as a payment option for filings or search.

Expedited service: For in person requests. Same day service is $35.00, 24-hour service is $25.00.

Sales Tax Registrations

State does not impose sales tax.

Birth Certificates

Department of State, Bureau of Vital Records, 71 South Fruit St, Concord, NH 03301-2410; 603-271-4650, 877-878-8007 (Orders), Fax- 603-271-3447; 8:30AM-3:30PM.

www.sos.nh.gov/vitalrecords/index.html

For genealogical purposes, birth records prior less than 100 years old may be released without restriction.

Indexing & Storage: Records available from 1640 to present. Records are on computer since 1990, indexed since 1948.

Searching: Must have a signed release from person of record or immediate family member or show proof of "tangible interest." Order forms are available at the website. Include in request- full name, names of parents, mother's maiden name, date of birth, place of birth, relationship to person of record, reason for information request. Include valid photo ID of requester.

Access by: mail, phone, in person, online.

Fee & Payment: The search fee is $12.00 per record and $8.00 for each additional copy of the same record. Fee payee- Treasurer of State of New

Hampshire. Prepayment required. Credit cards accepted for expedited service only. Personal checks accepted. Major credit cards accepted.

Mail search: Turnaround time- 4 weeks. A SASE is requested.

Phone search: Must use credit card for additional $7.00 fee.

In person: Turnaround time while you wait.

Online search: Records may be ordered online from www.vitalchek.com (see expedited services).

Expedited service: Expedited service is available for phone and online orders. Turnaround time- 7 to 10 days. Call to hear delivery options and costs, add credit card fee.

Death Records

Department of State, Division of Vital Records Admin, 71 South Fruit St, Concord, NH 03301-2410; 603-271-4650, 877-878-8007 (Orders), Fax-603-271-3447; 8:30AM-3:30PM.

www.sos.nh.gov/vitalrecords/index.html

For genealogical purposes, death records older than 50 years may be released without restriction.

Indexing & Storage: Records available from 1640 to present. Records are computerized since 1990, indexed on computer since 1948.

Searching: Must have a signed release from immediate family member. Include in request- full name, date of death, place of death, parents' names, relationship to person of record, reason for information request. Include valid photo ID of requester. This data not released- cause of death.

Access by: mail, phone, in person, online.

Fee & Payment: The search fee is $12.00 per record, additional copies are $8.00 each. Fee payee- Treasurer of State of New Hampshire. Prepayment required. Credit cards accepted for expedited service only. Personal checks accepted. Major credit cards accepted.

Mail search: Turnaround time- up to 4 weeks. A SASE is requested.

Phone search: Must use a credit card for an additional $7.00 fee.

In person: Turnaround time while you wait.

Online search: Records may be ordered online from www.vitalchek.com (see expedited services).

Expedited service: Expedited service is available for phone and online orders. Turnaround time- 7 to 10 days. Call to hear delivery options and costs, add credit card fee.

Marriage Certificates

Department of State, Division of Vital Records Admin, 71 South Fruit St, Concord, NH 03301-2410; 603-271-4650, 877-878-8007 (Orders), Fax-603-271-3447; 8:30AM-3:30PM.

www.sos.nh.gov/vitalrecords/index.html

Indexing & Storage: Records available from 1640 to present. Records are computerized from 1990, indexed on computer since 1948.

Searching: Must have a signed release from persons of record or immediate family member. Include in request- names of husband and wife, date of marriage, place or county of marriage, relationship to person of record, reason for information request, wife's maiden name. Include valid photo ID of requester.

Access by: mail, phone, in person, online.

Fee & Payment: The search fee is $12.00 per record, each additional copy is $8.00. Fee payee- Treasurer of State of New Hampshire. Prepayment required. Credit cards accepted for expedited service only. Personal checks accepted. Major credit cards accepted.

Mail search: Turnaround time- up to 4 weeks. A SASE is requested.

Phone search: Must use a credit card for an additional $7.00 fee.

In person: Turnaround time while you wait.

Online search: Records may be ordered online from www.vitalchek.com (see expedited services).

Expedited service: Expedited service is available for phone and online orders. Turnaround time- 7 to 10 days. Call to hear delivery options and costs, add credit card fee.

Divorce Records

Department of State, Division of Vital Records Admin, 71 South Fruit St, Concord, NH 03301-2410; 603-271-4650, 877-878-8007 (Orders), Fax-603-271-3447; 8:30AM-3:30PM.

www.sos.nh.gov/vitalrecords/index.html

Indexing & Storage: Records available from 1640 to present. Records are computerized since 1990, indexed on computer since 1948.

Searching: Must have a signed release from person of record or immediate family member. Include in request- names of husband and wife, date of divorce, year divorce case began, city or town, case number (if known), relationship to person of record, reason for information request. Include valid photo ID of requester.

Access by: mail, phone, in person, online.

Fee & Payment: The search fee is $12.00 per record, additional copies are $8.00 each. Fee payee- Treasurer of State of New Hampshire. Prepayment required. Credit cards accepted for expedited service only. Personal checks accepted. Major credit cards accepted.

Mail search: Turnaround time- up to 4 weeks. A SASE is requested.

Phone search: Must use a credit card for an additional $7.00 fee.

In person: Turnaround time while you wait.

Online search: Records may be ordered online from www.vitalchek.com (see expedited services).

Expedited service: Expedited service is available for phone and online orders. Turnaround time- 7 to 10 days. Call to hear delivery options and costs, add credit card fee.

Workers' Compensation Records

Labor Department, Workers Compensation Division, 95 Pleasant St, Concord, NH 03301; 603-271-3174, Fax- 603-271-6149; 8AM-4:30PM.

Indexing & Storage: Records available from 1996 to present on microfilm. Records prior to 1996 are kept at the State Archives. However, one must go through this office for records. New records available for inquiry in 1-2 weeks.

Searching: Must have an authorized release from claimant. Include in request- claimant name, SSN, date of accident, place of employment at time of accident.

Access by: mail, fax.

Fee & Payment: There is no search fee, copy fee is $.35 per page. Fee payee- State of NH Prepayment required. Personal checks accepted, credit cards are not.

Mail search: Turnaround time- 2 to 3 weeks. A SASE is requested.

Fax search: Same as mail request.

Driver Records

Department of Motor Vehicles, Driving Records, 23 Hazen Dr, Concord, NH 03305; 603-271-2322, Fax- 603-271-1555; 8:15AM-4:15PM.

www.nh.gov/safety/divisions/dmv/

New Hampshire recommends going to the local courts for copies of tickets or to state Financial Responsibility agency.

Indexing & Storage: Records available for 7 years for moving violations and 10 for DWIs. Surrendered license information remains on the system at least 5 years after the expiration date. The driver's address is on manually processed records, but not on electronic records. New records available for inquiry in 2 to 3 weeks normally.

Searching: Use of DSMV Form 505 is required. Frequent requesters should establish an account with the state. Include in request- full name, date of birth. Casual (non-permissible use) requesters are required to submit the subject's notarized signature on the Form 505. The license number is not required for a search, but is suggested. This data not released- a person's photograph, computerized image and SSN;

Access by: mail, in person, online.

Fee & Payment: Records are $8.00. If you wish the record certified the fee is $10.00. The $8.00 record is referred to as the insurance record and goes back 5 years. Legislation may raise fee to $15.00 in 2009. Fee payee- Department of Safety. Prepayment required. Personal checks and major credit cards accepted.

Mail search: Turnaround time- 7-10 days. Mail in requests must include requester's name and address. A SASE is requested.

In person: Five requests can be processed while you wait.

Online search: Online access and FTP (file transfer protocol) is offered for approved commercial accounts. Searches are by license number or by name and DOB. Fee is $8.00 per record. For more information, call the Director's Office and ask for Kirsten Provost. Fee may increase to $14.00 in 2009, per legislation introduced ($1.00 less than manual search).

Vehicle Registration

Department of Safety, DMV, Bureau of Titles, 23 Hazen Dr, Concord, NH 03305; 603-271-3111 (Bureau of Title), 603-271-2251 (Registration), Fax- 603-271-0369; 8:15AM-4:15PM.

www.nh.gov/safety/divisions/dmv/registration/index.html

Requests for registration information should be directed to the Registration Unit (not to the Titles Unit). The fax for this unit is 603-271-1061.

Indexing & Storage: Records available for 15 years to present. New records available for inquiry in 2 weeks.

Searching: The agency will only release to requesters authorized by statute or requester with a signed release from subject. Include in request- Form DSMV 505, which requires notarized signature of the requester. This data not released- SSN, photo

Access by: mail, in person.

Fee & Payment: The fee is $20.00 for a title and lien history. The fee for a registration listing is $5.00 and $10.00 if certified. Fee payee- Department of Safety, DMV. Prepayment required. Personal checks and major credit cards accepted.

Mail search: Turnaround time- 5 days.

In person: Turnaround time while you wait, depending on workload of personnel. Note there are two different counter locations; one for Titles and one for Registration.

Other access: Bulk information is available to approved venders per DPPA. Call 603-271-2314 for information.

Vessel Registration

Department of Safety, Bureau of Registration, Boat Desk, 23 Hazen Dr, Concord, NH 03305; 603-271-3333, 603-271-3242 (Liens), Fax- 603-271-1061; 8:15AM-4:15PM.

www.nh.gov/safety/divisions/dmv/registration/index.html

Indexing & Storage: Records available for current and expired registration records. All motorized boats and all sailboats over 12 ft must be registered. Boats are not titled and liens on boats are found at the Secretary of State - 603-271-3242.

Searching: Records are restricted to those authorized by statute. Authorization is stricter than the DPPA requirements. Include in request- owner's name, plate number or VIN is required to search.

Access by: mail, in person.

Fee & Payment: The fee is $5.00 for current year only; add $5.00 for certification. Fee payee- State of New Hampshire. Prepayment required. Personal checks accepted. Visa. MC, AmEx accepted.

Mail search: Turnaround time- timely manner.

In person: Turnaround time is immediate.

Accident Reports

Department of Safety, DMV, Crash Section, Bur. of Financial Resp, 23 Hazen Dr, Concord, NH 03305; 603-271-2128, 603-271-2322, Fax- 603-271-1555; 8:15AM-4:15PM.

Indexing & Storage: Records available for 5 years. Records are indexed on computer. New records available for inquiry in 3 to 4 weeks.

Searching: Access is not open to the public due to Privacy Act, Chapter 260:14. This law requires a notarized DSMV 505 Form to be filled out by the subject involved or by an insurance representative licensed to write auto policies in this state. Include in request- full driver name, date of birth, date of accident, location of accident (city and street). It is suggested to include both operators' names in the request.

Access by: mail, in person.

Fee & Payment: The fee is $1.00 per page with a $5.00 minimum. There is no charge for a "no record found." Requesters are notified of the fee for reports after the report has become available. Fee payee- Department of Safety. Prepayment required. Personal checks and credit cards accepted.

Mail search: Turnaround time- 3 to 4 weeks. A SASE is requested.

In person: Over the counter requests are available.

Legislation Records

New Hampshire State Library, Reference and Information Services, 20 Park St, Concord, NH 03301; 603-271-2239, 603-271-2144, Fax- 603-271-2205; 8AM-4:30PM.

http://gencourt.state.nh.us/ie/

Visit http://gencourt.state.nh.us/rsa/html/indexes/default.html for the state statutes.

Indexing & Storage: Records available from 1989 to present on computer. There are also bound House and Senate Journals from 1800's to present.

Searching: Bill number or key word required to search.

Access by: mail, phone, fax, in person, online.

Fee & Payment: There is no search fee, but there is a copy fee of $.20 per page, minimum $1.00. Fee payee- New Hampshire State Library. Personal checks accepted, credit cards are not.

Mail search: Turnaround time- 1 day. SASE not required.

Phone search: Will invoice.

Fax search: Fax charge is $.35 per page, minimum $1.00.

In person: Simple requests may be processed while you wait.

Online search: A Myriad of information can be viewed from the web. Search back to 1989. The Revised Statutes are found at http://gencourt.state.nh.us/rsa/html/indexes/default.html.

Voter Registration

Access to Records is Restricted.

Secretary of State, Election Division, 107 N. Main Street - State House Rm 204, Concord, NH 03301; 603-271-3242, Fax- 603-271-6316; 8AM-4:30PM.

www.sos.nh.gov/elections.htm

The statewide system DB is only open to political candidates. All records kept by Town Clerks are open to view or for purchase with no restrictions at the local level.

GED Certificates

Adult Education - Dept of Education, GED Testing, 21 S Fruit Street #20, Concord, NH 03301; 603-271-6699, Fax- 603-271-3454; 8AM-4:30PM.

www.ed.state.nh.us/education/index.htm

Indexing & Storage: Records available from 1937. New records available for inquiry in one month.

Searching: Include in request- SSN, date of birth, year of issue, name at the time, and a signed release. The date is needed since records are filed by year. The signed release is needed for either a verification or transcript. Mention GED specifically in the request.

Access by: mail, fax.

Fee & Payment: The fee is $5.00 for a transcript, there is no fee for a verification. Fee payee- State of New Hampshire. Prepayment required. Personal checks accepted, credit cards are not.

Mail search: Turnaround time- 2 days. SASE not required.

Fax search: You may request verifications by fax.

Hunting & Fishing License Information

Fish & Game Department, Licensing Department, 11 Hazen Dr, Concord, NH 03301; 603-271-3421, 603-271-3422, Fax- 603-271-5829; 8:15AM-4:15PM.

www.wildlife.state.nh.us

Indexing & Storage: Records available for 3 years back to present. Records are indexed on computer. New records available for inquiry in 2 to 4 months.

Searching: Requests must be in writing using their form. Include in request- full name, date of birth. This data not released- financial information.

Access by: mail, fax, in person.

Fee & Payment: There may be a charge of $.10 per page. Fee payee- NH Fish & Game. Prepayment required. Personal checks, Visa/MC accepted.

Mail search: Turnaround time- 3-5 days. Request must be in writing with payment in advance. A SASE is required.

Fax search: Search requests accepted by fax.

In person: Written request is require with payment in advance.

Other access: Mailing labels are available at a cost of $25.00 plus $.10 per label.

New Hampshire State Licensing Agencies

For details about the agency responsible for licensing/certifying/registering an item below or in the Agency Quick Finder section, match an item's number with the number of the agency in the *Licensing Agency Information* section.

New Hampshire Licenses Searchable Online

Architect #34 .... https://nhlicenses2.nh.gov/cgi-bin/professional/nhprof/search.pl
Attorney #43 .... www.courts.state.nh.us/nhbar/barexamresultjuly08.pdf
Bank #1 .... www.nh.gov/banking/banking.html
Bank Holding Company #1 .... www.nh.gov/banking/banking.html
Bank, Cooperative #1 .... www.nh.gov/banking/banking.html
Banking Service Unit #1 .... www.nh.gov/banking/banking.html
Cash Dispenser Machine, Non-bank #1 .... www.nh.gov/banking/machines.html
Child Care Facility #21 .... www.dhhs.nh.gov/DHHS/CDB/licensedplus-providers.htm
Court Reporter #37 .... https://nhlicenses2.nh.gov/cgi-bin/professional/nhprof/search.pl
Credit Union #1 .... www.nh.gov/banking/banking.html
Debt Adjuster #1 .... www.nh.gov/banking/consumer.html
Drug Wholesaler/Manufacturer #27 .... www.nh.gov/pharmacy/database.html
Engineer #34 .... https://nhlicenses2.nh.gov/cgi-bin/professional/nhprof/search.pl
Forester #34 .... https://nhlicenses2.nh.gov/cgi-bin/professional/nhprof/search.pl
Geologist #34 .... https://nhlicenses2.nh.gov/cgi-bin/professional/nhprof/search.pl
Insurance Agent/Broker #33 .... https://sbs-nh.naic.org/Lion-Web/jsp/sbsreports/AgentLookup.jsp
Leadworker #46 .... www.dhhs.state.nh.us/DHHS/CLPPP/LIBRARY/Fact+Sheet/lead-contractors.htm
Liquor Keg Shipper, Direct #35 .... www.nh.gov/liquor/direct_shippers.shtml
Liquor Product #35 .... www.nh.gov/liquor/pllicen.shtml
Liquor Store #35 .... www.nh.gov/liquor/stores.shtml
Lobbyist #42 .... www.sos.nh.gov/lobbyist%20information.htm
Marital Mediator #36 .... www.nh.gov/marital/mediators.htm
Marriage & Family Therapist #26 .... http://nhlicenses.nh.gov/WebLookUp/
Mental Health Counselor, Clinical #26 .... http://nhlicenses.nh.gov/WebLookUp/
Midwife #24 .... www.acnm.org/find.cfm
Mortgage Banker #1 .... www.nh.gov/banking/consumer.html
Mortgage Broker/Mortgage Servicer #1 .... www.nh.gov/banking/consumer.html
Motor Vehicle Retailer #1 .... www.nh.gov/banking/consumer.html
Motor Vehicle Sales Finance #1 .... www.nh.gov/banking/consumer.html
Nurse, LPN/Practical/Advanced #18 .... https://nhlicenses.nh.gov/WebLookUp/
Nursing Assistant #18 .... https://nhlicenses.nh.gov/WebLookUp/
Optometrist #23 .... www.arbo.org/index.php?action=findanoptometrist
Pastoral Psychotherapist #26 .... http://nhlicenses.nh.gov/WebLookUp/
Pharmacist / Pharmacy #27 .... www.nh.gov/pharmacy/database.html
Pharmacy Technician #27 .... www.nh.gov/pharmacy/database.html
Pharmacy, Mail Order #27 .... www.nh.gov/pharmacy/database.html
Physician #19 .... http://www4.egov.nh.gov/medicineboard/
Physician Assistant #19 .... http://www4.egov.nh.gov/medicineboard/
Psychologist #26 .... http://nhlicenses.nh.gov/WebLookUp/
Public Health Clinic #27 .... www.nh.gov/pharmacy/database.html
Real Estate Agent/Seller/Firm/Broker #32 .... www.nhlicenses.nh.gov/WebLookUp/
Real Estate Appraiser #31 .... www.asc.gov/content/category1/nr_intro.aspx?id=10
Savings Bank #1 .... www.nh.gov/banking/banking.html
Scientist, Natural #34 .... https://nhlicenses2.nh.gov/cgi-bin/professional/nhprof/search.pl
Scientist, Wetlands #34 .... https://nhlicenses2.nh.gov/cgi-bin/professional/nhprof/search.pl
Small Loan Lender #1 .... www.nh.gov/banking/consumer.html
Social Worker, Clinical #26 .... http://nhlicenses.nh.gov/WebLookUp/
Surveyor, Land #34 .... https://nhlicenses2.nh.gov/cgi-bin/professional/nhprof/search.pl
Trust Company #1 .... www.nh.gov/banking/banking.html
Verbatim Court Reporter #37 .... https://nhlicenses2.nh.gov/cgi-bin/professional/nhprof/search.pl

New Hampshire Licensing Quick Finder

Accessibility Lift Mechanic #28............603-271-2585
Acupuncturist #10..............................603-335-1425
Alcohol/Drug Counselor #41................603-271-4936
Ambulance Attendant/Svc #22.............603-271-7048
Architect #34......................................603-271-2219
Asbestos Worker #46..........................603-271-4609
Athletic Trainer #45.............................603-271-8389
Attorney #43..603-271-2646
Auctioneer #3......................................603-271-3242
Audiologist #25....................................603-433-7512
Bail Bondsman #11..............................603-271-1463
Bail Recovery Agent #11......................603-271-1463
Bank #1..603-271-3561
Bank Holding Company #1...................603-271-3561
Banking Service Unit #1......................603-271-3561
Barber #4...603-271-3608
Betting Location #47............................603-271-2158
Bingo/Lottery Operation #44................603-271-3391
Boiler Inspector #28..... 603-271-2584/ 603-271-7599
Boxing/Wrest'g Referee/2nd/Timekee'r #30
....603- 271-2341
Boxing/Wrestling Contestant #30........603- 271-2341
Boxing/Wrestling Mgr/Promoter #30...603- 271-2341
Canadian Broker/Dealer #11...............603-271-1463
Cash Dispenser Machine, non-bank #1 603-271-8675
Child Care Facility #21........................603-271-4624
Child Placing Agency #10....................800-852-3345
Chiropractor #14..................................603-271-4560
Concealed Weapons Lic., non-resi #39 603-271-3575
Corrections Officer #20........................603-271-2133
Cosmetologist #4.................................603-271-3608
Court Reporter #37...............................603-271-2030
Credit Union #1....................................603-271-3561
Debt Adjuster #1..................................603-271-8675
Dental Hygienist #15............................603-271-4561
Dentist #15...603-271-4561
Dietitian #10...800-852-3345
Dog Trainer #47....................................603-271-2158
Drug Wholesaler/Manufacturer #27.....603-271-2362
Electrician Apprentice #29...................603-223-4289
Electrician, Master/Journeyman #29....603-223-4289
Electrologist #12..................................603-271-4814
Elevator Inspector/ Mechanic #28........603-271-2585
Embalmer #17.......................................603-271-4648
Energy Facility Site/Construct'n #8......603-271-3503
Engineer #34..603-271-2219
Esthetician #4.......................................603-271-3608
Explosive Storage License #39...........603-271-3575
Explosives Competency License #39..603-271-3575
Fire Inspector #38................................603-271-2661
Firefighter #38......................................603-271-2661
Fireworks Competency License #39....603-271-3575
Forester #34...603-271-2219
Foster Family Home #10.......................800-852-3345
Funeral Director #17.............................603-271-4648
Geologist #34..603-271-2219
Hearing Aid Dispenser/Fitter #25.........603-433-7512
High/Medium Volt Electrician/Trainee #29
....603-223-4289
Horse Trainer #47..................................603-271-2158
Insurance Adjuster #33.........................603-271-2261
Insurance Advisor/Consultant #33.......603-271-2261
Insurance Agent/Broker #33.................603-271-2261
Insurance Company #33.......................603-271-2261
Investment Advisor #11........................603-271-1463
Jockey #47..603-271-2158
Leadworker #46.....................................603-271-4609
Liquor Keg Shipper, Direct #35...........603-271-3523
Liquor License #35...............................603-271-3523
Liquor Product #35...............................603-271-3523
Liquor Store #35....................................603-271-3523
Loan Production Office #1....................603-271-3561
Lobbyist #42..603-271-3242
Manicurist #4..603-271-3608
Marital Mediator #36.............................603-271-6593
Marriage & Family Therapist #26........603-271-6762
Mental Health Counselor, Clinical #26.603-271-6762
Midwife #24...603-224-0049
Mortgage Banker #1.............................603-271-8675
Mortgage Broker #1..............................603-271-8675
Mortgage Servicer #1...........................603-271-8675
Motor Vehicle Financer #1...................603-271-8675
Motor Vehicle Retailer #1.....................603-271-8675
Motor Vehicle Sales Finance #1..........603-271-8675
Naturopath #10.....................................603-271-4814
Notary Public #42..................................603-271-3242
Nurse, LPN/Practical/Advanced #18....603-271-2323
Nursing Assistant #18..........................603-271-2323
Nursing Home Administrator #16.........603-271-6936
Occupational Therapist #45.................603-271-8389
Occupational Therapy Assistant #45...603-271-8389
Ophthalmic Dispenser #10...................603-271-5127
Optometrist #23....................................603-271-6936
Pastoral Psychotherapist #26..............603-271-6762
Pesticide Dealer/Seller/User #6...........603-271-3550
Pesticide Disposal/Labeling #6............603-271-3550
Pharmacist #27.....................................603-271-2362
Pharmacy #27..603-271-2362
Pharmacy Technician #27....................603-271-2362
Pharmacy, Mail Order #27....................603-271-2362
Physical Therapist #45.........................603-271-8389
Physical Therapist Assistant #45.........603-271-8389
Physician #19..603-271-6936
Physician Assistant #19.......................603-271-6936
Plumber #9..603-271-3267
Podiatrist #19..603-271-6936
Police Officer/Detective #20.................603-271-2133
Private Detective #39............................603-271-3575
Psychologist #26...................................603-271-6762
Public Accountant-CPA #2....................603-271-3286
Public Health Clinic #27........................603-271-2362
Pump Installer #40................................603-271-3503
Racing Owner #47.................................603-271-2158
Racing Professional #47.......................603-271-2158
Real Estate Agent/Seller #32................603-271-6658
Real Estate Appraiser #31....................603-271-6186
Real Estate Broker/RE Firm #32...........603-271-2702
Residential Care Facility, Children #21 603-271-4624
Respiratory Care Practitioner #45........603-271-8389
Savings Bank #1...................................603-271-3561
School Administrator #7.......................603-271-3871
Scientist, Natural #34..........................603-271-2219
Scientist, Wetlands #34........................603-271-2219
Securities Broker/Dealer/Agent #11.....603-271-1463
Securities Salesperson #11.................603-271-1463
Security Guard #39...............................603-271-3575
Shorthand Reporter #37.......................603-271-2030
Small Loan Lender #1...........................603-271-8675
Social Worker, Clinical #26...................603-271-6762
Speech-Language Pathologist #45......603-273-8389
Surveyor, Land #34..............................603-271-2219
Tanning #4..603-271-3608
Tattoo Establishment/Practitioner #13.603-271-4592
Teacher #7..603-271-3871
Tobacco Law Enforcement #35............603-271-8531
Trust Company #1................................603-271-3561
Vendor, Itinerant #30............................603- 271-2341
Verbatim Court Reporter #37................603-271-2030
Veterinary Medicine #5.........................603-271-3706
Vocational Rehabilitation Provider #28.603-271-3328
Waste Water Treatment Plant Operator #40
....603-271-3503
Water Distribution System Operat'r #40 603-271-3503
Water Well Contractor #40....................603-271-3503

New Hampshire Licensing Agency Information

#1 Banking Department, 53 Regional Dr #200, Concord, NH 03301; 603-271-3561, Fax- 603-271-1090 or 0750. Hours- 8AM-4:30PM. www.nh.gov/banking/ 603-271-8675 is the direct phone # for Consumer Credit Division, Licenses Verification and the direct fax is 603-271-0750.

#2 Department of State, Board of Accountancy, 78 Regional Dr, Bldg #2, Concord, NH 03301; 603-271-3286, Fax- 603-271-8702. www.nh.gov/accountancy/

#3 Office of Secretary of State, Board of Auctioneers, 107 N Main St, State House, Rm 204, Concord, NH 03301; 603-271-3242, Fax- 603-271-6316. www.sos.nh.gov/auctioneers/

#4 Board of Barbering, Cosmetology & Esthetics, 2 Industrial Park Dr, Concord, NH 03301; 603-271-3608, Fax- 603-271-8889. Hours- 8AM-4PM. www.nh.gov/cosmet/

#5 Board of Veterinary Medicine, PO Box 2042 (25 Capitol St), Concord, NH 03302-2042; 603-271-3706, Fax- 604-271-1109. www.nh.gov/veterinary/ Lists of currently licensed veterinarians are available for $4.00 on diskette or by email. Lists on paper $.25 per page + postage.

#6 Department of Agriculture, 25 Capitol St 2nd Fl, Concord, NH 03301-2042; 603-271-3550, Fax- 603-271-1109. http://agriculture.nh.gov/constants/contact.htm

#7 Department of Education, Division of Educational Improvement, 101 Pleasant St, State Office Park S, Concord, NH 03301-3860; 603-271-3494, Fax- 603-271-1953. www.ed.state.nh.us/education/

#8 Department of Environmental Services, Energy Services Division, PO Box 95, 29 Hazen Dr, Concord, NH 03302; 603-271-3503, Fax- 603-271-8013. Hours- 8AM-4PM. http://des.nh.gov/

#9 Plumbing Licensing Board, 21 S Fruit St, #24, Concord, NH 03301-2452; 603-271-3267, Fax- 603-271-6656. www.nh.gov/plumbing/

#10 Department of Health & Human Svcs, Licensing & Regulative Services, 129 Pleasant St, Concord, NH 03301; 800-852-3345, Fax- 603-271-5590. Hours- 8AM-4:30PM. www.dhhs.state.nh.us/DHHS/LRS/default.htm

#11 Department of State, Bureau of Securities Regulation, 107 N. Main St, #204, Concord, NH 03301; 603-271-1463, Fax- 603-271-7933. Hours- 8AM-4:30PM. www.sos.nh.gov/securities/

#12 Department of Health & Human Svcs, Advisory Board of Electrologists, 129 Pleasant St, Concord, NH 03301; 603-271-0853, Fax- 603-271-5590. Hours- 8AM-4:30PM. www.dhhs.nh.gov/DHHS/LRS/ELIGIBILITY/electrologist-license.htm Licensed electrologists list can be emailed or mailed.

#13 Department of Health & Human Svcs, Advisory Board of Massage Practitioners, 129 Pleasant St, Concord, NH 03301; 603-271-4592, Fax- 603-271-4968. www.dhhs.state.nh.us/DHHS/LRS/CONTACT+INFO/default.htm

#14 Department of Health & Human Svcs, Board of Chiropractic Examiners, 29 Hazen Dr, Concord, NH 03301-6504; 603-271-4560, Fax- 603-271-0597. Hours- 8AM-4PM. www.sos.nh.gov/redbook/first%20section.htm#iropractic

#15 Department of Health & Human Svcs, Board of Dental Examiners, 2 Industrial Park Dr, Concord, NH 03301-8520; 603-271-4561, Fax- 603-271-6702. Hours- 8AM-4PM. www.nh.gov/dental/

#16 Board of Examiners of Nursing Home Administrators, 2 Industrial Park Dr #8, Concord, NH 03301; 603-271-4728, Fax- 603-271-6702. Hours- 8AM-4PM. www.nh.gov/nha/

#17 Department of Health & Human Svcs, Board of Funeral Directors & Embalmers, 6 Hazen Dr, Concord, NH 03301-6507; 603-271-4648, Fax- 603-271-3447. www.nh.gov/funeral/

#18 Department of Health & Human Svcs, Board of Nursing, 21 S Fruit St #16, Concord, NH 03301-2431; 603-271-2323, Fax- 603-271-6605. Hours- 8AM-4PM. www.nh.gov/nursing/ Search data at- https://nhlicenses.nh.gov/WebLookUp/ Will sell/provide lists; contact Kathy Crumb at 603-271-2323.

#19 Board of Medicine, 2 Industrial Park Dr, #8, Concord, NH 03301; 603-271-1203, Fax- 603-271-6702. Hours- 8AM-4PM. www.nh.gov/medicine/index.htm Search data at- http://www4.egov.nh.gov/medicineboard/

#20 Police Standards & Training Council, 17 Institute Dr, Concord, NH 03301-7413; 603-271-2133, Fax- 603-271-1785. Hours- 8:30AM-4:30PM. www.pstc.nh.gov/mission.htm

#21 Department of Health & Human Svcs, Bureau of Child Care Licensing, 129 Pleasant St, Brown Bldg, Concord, NH 03301-3857; 603-271-4624, Fax- 603-271-4782. Hours- 8AM-4:30PM. www.dhhs.state.nh.us/DHHS/BCCL/default.htm Search data at- www.childcaresearch.dhhs.nh.gov For a $50.00 fee you can receive their area list on disk.

#22 Department of Safety, Division of Emergency Medical Services, 33 Hazen Dr, Concord, NH 03305-0003; 603-271-4568, Fax- 603-271-4567. Hours- 8:15AM-4:15PM. www.nh.gov/safety/divisions/fstems/ems/index.html

#23 Board of Registration in Optometry, 2 Industrial Park Dr #8, Concord, NH 03301; 603-271-2428, Fax- 603-271-6702. Hours- 8AM-4PM. www.nh.gov/optometry/ Search data at- www.arbo.org/index.php?action=findanoptometrist

#24 Department of Health & Human Svcs, New Hampshire Midwifery Council, 124 Winona Rd, Meredith, NH 03253; 603-224-0049. http://cfmidwifery.org/states/states.aspx?ST=NH

#25 Board of Hearing Care Providers, PO Box 446, Greenland, NH 03840; 603-433-7512. www.nh.gov/nhes/elmi/licertoccs/hearnaid.htm

#26 Board of Mental Health Practices, 117 Pleasant St Dolloff Bldg, Concord, NH 03301; 603-271-6762, Fax- 603-271-3950. 7:30AM-4PM. www.nh.gov/mhpb/ Search data at- http://nhlicenses.nh.gov/WebLookUp/ Will do phone verifications.

#27 State of New Hampshire, Board of Pharmacy, 57 Regional Dr, Concord, NH 03301-8518; 603-271-2350, Fax- 603-271-2856. Hours- 8AM-4PM. www.nh.gov/pharmacy/ Search data at- www.nh.gov/pharmacy/database.html

#28 Department of Labor, 95 Pleasant St, State Office Park S, Concord, NH 03301-3836; 603-271-3176, Fax- 603-271-2668. 8AM-4:30PM. www.labor.state.nh.us

#29 Electricians' Licensing Board, 33 Harbor Dr (2 Industrial Park Dr), Concord, NH 03305; 603-223-4289, Fax- 603-223-4295. 8:15AM-4:14PM. www.nh.gov/nhes/elmi/licertoccs/electjou.htm

#30 Department of State, Boxing & Wrestling Commission, 234 Webster St, Manchester, NH 03109; 603- 271-2341, Fax- 603-271-6784. Hours- 7AM-5PM. www.nh.gov/boxing/

#31 Real Estate Appraiser Board, 25 Capitol St, Rm 426, Concord, NH 03301-6312; 603-271-6186, Fax- 603-271-6513. www.nh.gov/nhreab/ Complete lists - $50.00. Individual towns - free, call 603-371-6186.

#32 Department of State, Real Estate Commission, 25 Capitol St, Rm 434, Concord, NH 03301; 603-271-2701, Fax- 603-271-1039. www.nh.gov/nhrec/ Search data at- www.nhlicenses.nh.gov/WebLookUp/ Purchase lists of salespersons, brokers, and or firms by contacting the commission at 603-271-2701.

#33 Insurance Department, Division of Licensing, 21 S Fruit St #14, Concord, NH 03301; 603-271-2261, Fax- 603-271-1406. Hours- 8AM-4:30PM. www.nh.gov/insurance/

#34 Joint Board of Licensure & Certification, 57 Regional Dr, Concord, NH 03301; 603-271-2219, Fax- 603-271-6990. www.nh.gov/jtboard/home.htm Search data at- https://nhlicenses2.nh.gov/cgi-bin/professional/nhprof/search.pl

#35 Licensing & Enforcement, Liquor Commission, 10 Commercial St, Concord, NH 03301; 603-271-3521, Fax- 603-271-3758. www.nh.gov/liquor/laws_licensing.shtml

#36 c/o Judicial Council, Marital Mediator Certification Board, 25 Capitol St, Rm 424, Concord, NH 03301; 603-271-6593, Fax- 603-271-1112. www.nh.gov/marital/ Search data at- www.nh.gov/marital/mediators.htm

#37 Board of Court Reporters, 57 Regional Dr, Concord, NH 03301; 603-271-2030, Fax- 603-271-2080. Hours- 8AM-4:30PM. www.nh.gov/jtboard/ctrpt.htm

#38 Department of Safety, Division of Fire Standards & Training, 33 Hazen Dr, Concord, NH 03305-0001; 603-271-2661, Fax- 603-271-1091. Hours- 8:15AM-4:15PM. www.nh.gov/safety/divisions/fstems/

#39 State Police, Permits and License Unit, 33 Hazen Dr, Concord, NH 03305; 603-271-3575, Fax- 603-271-0306. Hours- 8:15AM-4:15PM. www.nh.gov/safety/divisions/nhsp/

#40 Department of Environmental Services, Water Division, PO Box 95, 29 Hazen Dr, Concord, NH 03302-0095; 603-271-3503, Fax- 603-271-2867. http://des.nh.gov/organization/divisions/water/index.htm

#41 Board of Licensing, Alcohol & Other Drug Use Treatment, 29 Hazen Dr, Concord, NH 03301; 603-271-4936. Hours- 8AM-4PM. By phone only, will verify license and give expiration date.

#42 Office of Secretary of State, 107 N Main St, State House, Rm 204, Concord, NH 03301-4989; 603-271-3242, Fax- 603-271-6316. Hours- 8AM-4:30PM. www.sos.nh.gov

#43 Supreme Court, Attn: Attorney Registration, 1 Noble Dr, Concord, NH 03301; 603-271-2646, Fax- 603-271-6630. www.courts.state.nh.us

#44 New Hampshire Lottery, Bingo/Lucky 7 Division, Sweepstakes Commission, PO Box 1208 (14 Integra Dr), Concord, NH 03302; 603-271-3391, Fax- 603-271-1160. Hours- 8AM-4PM. www.nhlottery.org

#45 Department of Health & Human Svcs, Office of Allied Health Professions, 2 Industrial Park Dr, Concord, NH 03301-8520; 603-271-8389, Fax- 603-271-6702. Hours- 8AM-4PM. www.nh.gov/alliedhealth/

#46 Department of Health & Human Svcs, Bureau of Health Risk Assessment, 29 Hazen Dr, Concord, NH 03301-6527; 603-271-4609, Fax- 603-271-2667. www.contractors-license.org/nh/nh.htm

#47 Pari-Mutuel Commission, 78 Regional Dr #3, Concord, NH 03301; 603-271-2158, Fax- 603-271-3381. Hours- 8AM-4PM. www.racing.nh.gov For horse info- www.gencourt.state.nh.us/rules/pari600.html

New Hampshire Federal Courts

The following list indicates the district and division name for each county in the state. If the bankruptcy court location is different from the district court, then the location of the bankruptcy court appears in parentheses.

New Hampshire County/Court Cross Reference

County	Court	County	Court
Belknap	Concord (Manchester)	Hillsborough	Concord (Manchester)
Carroll	Concord (Manchester)	Merrimack	Concord (Manchester)
Cheshire	Concord (Manchester)	Rockingham	Concord (Manchester)
Coos	Concord (Manchester)	Strafford	Concord (Manchester)
Grafton	Concord (Manchester)	Sullivan	Concord (Manchester)

US District Court

Concord Division Court Clerk, 55 Pleasant St, #110, Warren B Rudman Courthouse, Concord, NH 03301, 603-225-1423. Hours-8:30AM-4PM. www.nhd.uscourts.gov

Counties/Note: Belknap, Carroll, Cheshire, Coos, Grafton, Hillsborough, Merrimack, Rockingham, Strafford, Sullivan.

Searches/Indexing: Search request requires name only. Results do not include SSN or DOB. Will not fax back documents. New cases are in the index 24 hours after filing date. Paper case files sent to archives 1 years after closed; electronic maintained indefinitely

Search Access: Only docket info is available by phone. **Mail:** Search usually completed- within 7 days. SASE not required. **In person:** 3 public terminals available. Self-serve copies from computer- $.10 each.

Payment: Pay by Visa/MC, money order, cashier's check, business check. No personal checks. Payee: Clerk, US District Court.

E-Services: PACER records go back to 1980. New records online after 1 day. ECF at https://ecf.nhd.uscourts.gov. **Opinions Online:** www.nhd.uscourts.gov/oo/default.asp. Includes orders and standing orders as well.

US Bankruptcy Court

Manchester Division Court Clerk, 1000 Elm St, Ste 1001, Manchester, NH 03101, 603-222-2600; Fax- 603-222-2697. Hours- 8:30AM-4:30PM. www.nhb.uscourts.gov

Counties/Note: Belknap, Carroll, Cheshire, Coos, Grafton, Hillsborough, Merrimack, Rockingham, Strafford, Sullivan.

Searches/Indexing: In request include the full name in search request; SSN is helpful. Results include last 4 SSN digits. Will not fax back documents. New cases are in the index immediately after filing date. Both computer and card indexes maintained. Case files sent to archives 1 year after closed.

Search Access: Only case number, name, trustee, debtor's attorney and deadlines is released. Voice Case Information Service available, call VCIS at 800-851-8954 or 603-222-2626. **Mail:** Search usually completed- 2 weeks. SASE not required. **In person:** 2 public terminals available; index goes back to 1988. Self-serve copies from computer- $.10 each.

Payment: Pay by Visa/MC, money order, cashier's or personal check. No debtor checks/credit cards accepted. Payee: Clerk, US Bankruptcy Court.

E-Services: PACER records go back to 1989. New records online immediately. ECF at https://ecf.nhb.uscourts.gov. **Opinions Online:** www.nhb.uscourts.gov/Court_Opinions/court_opinions.html.

Standards for Federal Courts: Fees are standard unless noted in profile. Search fee is $26.00 per item (one party name or case number). Copy fee is $.50 per page. Certification fee is $9.00 per document, double for exemplification, if available. Most courts require prepayment. Mail requests should enclose a SASE unless otherwise noted. Before releasing records, all courts require prepayment, unless noted.

District courts index by defendant and plaintiff and by case number. Bankruptcy courts usually index by debtor and case number. While most courts now have their indexes on computer, many may still maintain index card files as well. Courts will archive closed case files at different times.

There are numerous public access programs available to online subscribers. Search the U.S. Party/Case Index to find party names and case numbers among all courts. Individual case data is provided on PACER. A search of CM/ECF provides copies of cases filed electronically. For details about PACER, the US Party/Case Index, and CM/ECF see the Appendix or go to http://pacer.psc.uscourts.gov or call 800-676-6856.

New Hampshire County Courts

Court	Jurisdiction	No. of Courts	How Organized
Superior Courts*	General	11	10 Counties
District Courts*	Limited	36	40 Districts
Probate Courts*	Probate	10	10 Counties
Family Court	Special	8	

* Profiled in this Sourcebook.

Court	CIVIL								
	Tort	Contract	Real Estate	Min. Claim	Max. Claim	Small Claims	Estate	Eviction	Domestic Relations
Circuit Courts*	X	X	X	$1500	No Max				
District Courts*	X	X	X	$0	$25,000	$5000		X	
Probate Courts*							X		
Family Courts									X

Court	CRIMINAL				
	Felony	Misdemeanor	DWI/DUI	Preliminary Hearing	Juvenile
Circuit Courts*	X	some			
District Courts*		X	X	X	X
Probate Courts*					
Family Courts					X

Administration

Administrative Office of the Courts, Supreme Court Bldg, 2 Charles Doe, Concord, NH, 03301; (EST) Telephone: 603-271-2521, Fax: 603-271-3977. www.courts.state.nh.us

Court Structure

The Superior Court is the court of General Jurisdiction and has jurisdiction over a wide variety of cases, including criminal, domestic relations, and civil cases, and provides the only forum in this state for trial by jury. Felony cases include Class A misdemeanors. The District Court involve families, juveniles, small claims ($5,000), landlord tenant matters, minor crimes and violations and civil cases in which the disputed amount does not exceed $25,000. Divorces prior to 4/2004 are at the Superior Court. After that date, at Family Division of the local district court where divorce occurred; there are multiple district courts in each county. The Superior Court and the District Court share jurisdiction over domestic violence cases. In Grafton and Rockingham Counties, the Family Division Pilot Project has jurisdiction over divorce, custody/support and domestic violence cases

Filing a civil case in the monetary “overlap area” between the Superior Court minimum and the District Court maximum is at the discretion of the filer. Older Municipal Courts have all been closed, the caseload and records were absorbed by the nearest District Court.

Online Access

While there is no statewide access available for trial court records,the home page has useful information including opinions and directives from the Supreme Court, Superior Courts, and District Courts; search at www.courts.state.nh.us/search/index.htm.

Searching Tips, Fees, and Other Guidelines

Since District Courts are organized by town and not by county, the District Court in each county maintains its own database of records. For example, a search of misdemeanor records in a county would require a search at each of the District Courts in that county. Fees for searching, copies, and certification are set by the New Hampshire Supreme Court. The fee structure is as follows: computer search - $10.00 for up to 9 names in one request; $25.00 for 10 or more names in one request; $25.00 per manual search, usually when archived or paper records are included. Most courts follow this fee schedule. Copies are usually $.50 per page and certification $5.00. All courts are on Eastern Standard Time. No public access terminals are found at NH courts.

Belknap County

Superior Court 64 Court St, Laconia, NH 03246; 603-524-3570; 8AM-4:30PM (EST). ***Felony, Civil Actions over $1,500, Equity.***

Search fee includes all indexes, if asked.

Civil Records: Access: Mail, in person. Only the court performs in person searches; visitors may not. Search fee: $10 for up to 9 names; 10 or more names- $25.00. Required to search: name, years to search. Civil cases indexed by defendant, plaintiff; index on computer from 1/86, index cards from 1950, docket books from 1900. Mail turnaround time 1 week.

Criminal Records: Access: Phone, mail, in person. Only the court performs in person searches; visitors may not. Search fee: $10.00 up to 9 names; 10 or more names- $25.00. Required to search: name, years to search; also helpful: DOB, SSN. Criminal records computerized from 1/82, index cards from 1950, docket books from 1900. Mail turnaround time 1 week.

General Information: No adoption, sealed, juvenile, mental health, expunged, or dismissed records released. Will not fax documents. Court makes copy: $.50 per page. Certification fee: $5.00 per doc. Payee: Belknap County Superior Court. Business checks accepted. Major credit cards accepted. Prepayment required.

Laconia District Court PO Box 1010 (26 Academy St), Laconia, NH 03247; 603-524-4128; fax: 602-524-7573; 8AM-4PM (EST).

Misdemeanor, Violations, Civil Actions under $25,000, Eviction, Small Claims.
Court temporarily located at 171 Fair St. Includes City of Laconia and the towns of Meredith, New Hampton, Gilford, Belmont, Alton, Gilmanton, Center Harbor, and Barnstead. Search fee includes all 4 indexes, if asked.
Civil Records: Access: Mail, in person. Only the court performs in person searches; visitors may not. Search fee: $10.00 up to 9 names; 10 or more names or pre-5/1992- $25.00. Required to search: name, years to search. Civil cases indexed by defendant, plaintiff; index on computer from 5/1992, index cards from 7/1964. Mail turnaround time 2 weeks.
Criminal Records: Access: Mail, in person. Only the court performs in person searches; visitors may not. Search fee: $10 for up to 9 names; 10 or more names or pre-5/1992- $25.00. Required to search: name, years to search, DOB. Criminal records computerized from 1992, index cards from 7/1964. Mail turnaround time 2 weeks.
General Information: No sealed, juvenile, mental health, expunged or dismissed records released. Will not fax documents. Court makes copy: $.50 per page. Certification fee: $5.00 per doc. Payee: Laconia District Court. Personal checks and credit cards accepted. Prepayment required.

Probate Court 64 Court St, PO Box 1343, Laconia, NH 03247-1343; 603-524-0903; 8AM-4PM (EST). ***Probate.***

Carroll County

Superior Court 96 Water Village Rd - Box 3, Ossipee, NH 03864-7267; 603-539-2201; 8AM-4PM (EST). ***Felony, Civil Actions over $1,500.***
www.courts.state.nh.us/courtlocations/carrsupedir.htm
Search fee includes all indexes, if asked.
Civil Records: Access: Mail, in person. Only the court performs in person searches; visitors may not. Search fee: $10 for up to 9 names; 10 or more names- $25.00. Required to search: name, years to search. Civil cases indexed by defendant, plaintiff. Civil index on cards from 1960, index books from 1840. Mail turnaround time- up to 1 week.
Criminal Records: Access: Mail, in person. Only the court performs in person searches; visitors may not. Search fee: $10 for up to 9 names; over 10 names- $25.00. Required to search: name, years to search; also helpful: DOB, SSN. Criminal records indexed on cards from 1960, index books from 1840. Mail turnaround time same day.
General Information: No adoption, sealed, juvenile, mental health, expunged or dismissed records released. Will not fax documents. Court makes copy: $.50 per page. Self serve: $.25 per page. Certification fee: $5.00 per doc. Payee: Carroll County Superior Ct. Personal checks accepted; credit cards are not. Prepayment required. Mail requests: SASE required.

Northern Carroll County District Court PO Box 940, Conway, NH 03818; 603-356-7710; 8AM-4PM (EST). ***Misdemeanor, Civil Actions under $25,000, Eviction, Small Claims.***
Includes Towns of Conway, Bartlett, Jackson, Eaton, Chatham, Hart's Location, Albany, Madison and places of Hale's Location, Cutt's Grant, Hadley's Purchase, and portions of Livermore and Waterville. Search fee includes all 4 indexes, if asked.
Civil Records: Access: Mail, in person. Both court and visitors may perform in person searches. Search fee: $10.00 up to 9 names; 10 or more names or pre-10/1992- $25.00. Required to search: name, years to search. Civil cases indexed by defendant, plaintiff; index on computer from 1993, on index cards from 1980, on index books from 1954. Mail turnaround time 1 week.
Criminal Records: Access: Mail, in person. Only the court performs in person searches; visitors may not. Search fee: $10.00 up to 9 names; 10 or more names- $25.00. Required to search: name, years to search; also helpful: DOB. Criminal records computerized from 1993, on index cards from 1980, on index books from 1954. Mail turnaround time 1 week.
General Information: No adoption, sealed, juvenile, mental health, expunged or dismissed records released. Will not fax documents. Court makes copy: $.50 per page. Certification fee: $5.00 per page. Payee: District Court for Northern Carroll County. Personal checks accepted. Prepayment required.

Southern Carroll County District Court 96 Water Village Rd #2, Ossipee, NH 03864; 603-539-4561; criminal phone: 603-539-4561; civil phone: 603-539-5993; fax: 603-539-3751; 8AM-4PM (EST). ***Misdemeanor, Civil Actions under $25,000, Eviction, Small Claims.***
www.courts.state.nh.us/courtlocations/carrdistdir.htm#south_carroll
The former Wolfeboro District Court has been combined with this court. Includes Towns of Ossipee, Tamworth, Freedom, Effingham, Wakefield, Wolfeboro, Brookfield, Tuftonboro, Moultonborough, and Sandwich. Search fee includes all 4 indexes, if asked.
Civil Records: Access: Mail, in person. Only the court performs in person searches; visitors may not. Search fee: $10.00 up to 9 names. 10 or more names or manual search of pre-1991 non-computerized records- $25.00. Required to search: name, years to search. Civil cases indexed by defendant, plaintiff; index on computer from 1992, on index cards from 1989. Mail turnaround time 2-3 days.
Criminal Records: Access: Mail, in person. Only the court performs in person searches; visitors may not. Search fee: $10.00 up to 9 names. 10 or more names or manual search of pre-1991 non-computerized records is $25.00. Required to search: name, years to search; also helpful: DOB, SSN. Criminal records computerized from 1992, on index cards from 1989. Mail turnaround time 2-3 days.
General Information: No sealed, juvenile, mental health, expunged or dismissed records released. Will not fax documents. Court makes copy: $.50 per page. Self serve: same. Certification fee: $5.00. Payee: South Carroll County District Court. Only cashiers checks and money orders accepted. Visa/MC, Discover accepted. Prepayment required. Mail requests: SASE required.

Probate Court 96 Water Village Rd, Box 1, Ossipee, NH 03864; 603-539-4123; fax: 603-539-4761; 8AM-4PM (EST). ***Probate.***

Cheshire County

Superior Court 12 Court St, Keene, NH 03431; 603-352-6902; 8:30AM-4PM (EST). ***Felony, Civil Actions over $1,500, Family Law, Equity.***
www.courts.state.nh.us/superior/index.htm
Search fee includes all 4 indexes, if asked. Probate is a separate office at this same address.
Civil Records: Access: Mail, in person. Only the court performs in person searches; visitors may not. Search fee: $10.00 up to 9 names. Required to search: name, years to search. Civil cases indexed by defendant, plaintiff; index on computer from 1992, on index cards from 1920; records prior to 1918 difficult to access; organized 1769. Mail turnaround time 48 hours.
Criminal Records: Access: Mail, in person. Only the court performs in person searches; visitors may not. Search fee: $10.00 up to 9 names; $25.00 for 10 or more; $25.00 per hour for manual search. Required to search: name, years to search, DOB. Criminal records computerized from 1950, criminal records go back to 1900. Mail turnaround time 48 hours.
General Information: No sealed, juvenile or expunged records released. Court makes copy: $.50 per page. Self serve: $.15 per page. Certification fee: $5.00 per doc. Payee: Cheshire Superior Court. No personal checks. Credit cards accepted. Prepayment required. Mail requests: SASE required.

Jaffrey-Peterborough District Court PO Box 39, 84 Peterborough St, Jaffrey, NH 03452-0039; 603-532-8698; 8AM-4PM (EST). ***Misdemeanor, Civil Actions under $25,000, Eviction, Small Claims.***
Includes towns of Peterborough, Hancock, Greenville, Greenfield, New Ipswich, Temple, Sharon, Jaffrey, Dublin, Fitzwilliam, and Rindge. Search fee includes all 4 indexes, if asked.
Civil Records: Access: Mail, in person. Only the court performs in person searches; visitors may not. Search fee: $10.00 up to 9 names; 10 or more names or pre-1993- $25.00. Required to search: name, years to search. Civil cases indexed by defendant, plaintiff; index on computer back to 1993, on index cards from 1980, index books in back room. Mail turnaround time 3-4 weeks.
Criminal Records: Access: Mail, in person. Only the court performs in person searches; visitors may not. Search fee: $10 for up to 9 names; 10 or more names or pre-1993- $25.00. Required to search: name, years to search, DOB; also helpful: SSN. Criminal records computerized from 4/1993, on index cards from 1980, index books stored. Mail turnaround time 3-4 weeks. Public use terminal has crim records back to 1990s. PAT results show name, DOB, SSN.
General Information: No sealed, juvenile, mental health records released. Will fax documents of specific cases only. Court makes copy: $.50 per page. Certification fee: $5.00 per cert. Payee: Jaffrey-Peterborough District Court. Personal checks accepted. Visa/MC accepted. Prepayment required. Mail requests: SASE required.

Keene District Court PO Box 364, 3 Washington St, Keene, NH 03431; 603-352-2559; 8AM-4PM (EST). ***Misdemeanor, Civil Actions under $25,000, Eviction, Small Claims.***
Search fee includes all 4 indexes, if asked. Includes Keene and towns of Stoddard, Westmoreland, Surry, Gilsum, Sullivan, Nelson, Roxbury, Marlow, Swanzey, Marlborough, Winchester, Richmond, Hinsdale, Harrisville, Walpole, Alstead, Troy, Chesterfield.
Civil Records: Access: Mail, in person. Only the court performs in person searches; visitors may not. Search fee: $10.00 up to 9 names; 10 or more names- $25.00. Required to search: name, years to search. Civil cases indexed by defendant, plaintiff; index on computer from 7/92, on index cards from 1980, docket books from 1968 to 1979. Mail turnaround time 5-10 days.
Criminal Records: Access: Mail, in person. Only the court performs in person searches; visitors may not. Search fee: $10.00 up to 9 names; 10 or more names- $25.00. Required to search: name, DOB, years to search; also helpful: SSN. Criminal records computerized from 7/92, on index cards from 1980, docket books from 1968 to 1979. Mail turnaround time 5-10 days.
General Information: No sealed, juvenile, mental health or expunged records released. Will not fax documents. Court makes copy: $.50 per page. No copy fee if document is certified. Certification fee: $5.00 per doc includes copies. Payee: Keene District Court. Personal checks accepted. Visa/MC accepted. Prepayment required.

Probate Court 12 Court St, Keene, NH 03431; 603-357-7786; 8AM-4:00PM (EST). ***Probate.***

Coos County

Superior Court 55 School St #301, Lancaster, NH 03584; 603-788-4702; 8AM-4PM (EST). ***Felony, Civil Actions over $1,500, Equity Actions.***
Search fee includes all indexes, if asked.
Civil Records: Access: Mail, in person. Only the court performs in person searches; visitors may not. Search fee: $10.00 for up to 9 names; 10 or more names- $25.00. Required to search: name, years to search. Civil cases indexed by defendant, plaintiff; index on computer from 1960; index books from 1887; courthouse burned in 1887, prior records lost (organized 1803). Mail turnaround time 1 day.
Criminal Records: Access: Mail, in person. Only the court performs in person searches; visitors may not. Search fee: $10.00 up to 9 names; 10 or more names- $25.00. Required to search: name, years to search, DOB. Criminal records computerized from 1960; index books from 1887. Mail turnaround time 1 day.
General Information: No adoption, sealed, juvenile, mental health, expunged or dismissed records released. Will not fax documents. Court makes copy: $.50 per page. Self serve: $.25 per page. Certification fee: $5.00 per cert. Payee: Coos Superior Court.

Personal checks accepted. Visa/MC accepted. Prepayment required. Mail requests: SASE required.

Berlin District Court 220 Main St, Berlin, NH 03570; 603-752-3160; 8AM-4PM (EST). ***Misdemeanor, Civil Actions under $25,000, Eviction, Small Claims.***

Includes towns of Berlin, Dummer, Milan and places of Cambridge and Success. This Berlin Court absorbed in the Gorham District Court in mid 2006, including Shelburne, Gorham, Randolph. Search fee includes all 4 indexes, if asked.

Civil Records: Access: Mail, in person. Only the court performs in person searches; visitors may not. Search fee: $10.00 up to 9 names; 10 or more names or pre-1993-$25.00. Required to search: name, years to search. Civil cases indexed by defendant, plaintiff. Computerized records from 1993, civil records on index cards from 1980, index books from 1970, prior to 1970 archived in basement. Note: A separate search is required for records from the Gorham District. Records are not co-mingled prior to March 15, 2006. Mail turnaround time 1 week.

Criminal Records: Access: Mail, in person. Only the court performs in person searches; visitors may not. Search fee: $10.00 up to 9 names; 10 or more names or pre-1993- $25.00. Required to search: name, years to search, DOB, SSN. Criminal records computerized since 1993, on index cards from 1980, index books from 1970, prior to 1970 archived in basement. Note: A separate search is required for records from the Gorham District. Records are not co-mingled prior to 3/15/2006. Mail turnaround time 1 week.

General Information: No sealed, juvenile, mental health, expunged or dismissed records released. Will not fax documents. Court makes copy: $.50 per page. Certification fee: $5.00 per cert. Payee: Berlin District Court. Personal checks and credit cards accepted. Prepayment required.

Colebrook District Court PO Box 5, 17 Bridge St, Colebrook, NH 03576; 603-237-4229; 8AM-N,1-4PM (EST). ***Misdemeanor, Civil Actions under $25,000, Eviction, Small Claims.***

Includes Colebrook, Pittsburg, Clarksville, Wentworth's, Errol, Millsfield, Columbia, Stewartstown, Stratford, Dix's Grant, Atkinson & Gilmanton Grant, 2nd College, Grant, Dixville, Erving's Location, Odell. Search fee includes all 4 indexes, if asked.

Civil Records: Access: Mail, in person. Only the court performs in person searches; visitors may not. Search fee: $10.00 up to 9 names; 10 or more names or pre-1993- $25.00. Required to search: name, years to search. Civil cases indexed by defendant, plaintiff. Civil index on cards from 1979, index books from 1964. Mail turnaround time same day.

Criminal Records: Access: Mail, in person. Only the court performs in person searches; visitors may not. Search fee: $10.00 up to 9 names; 10 or more names or pre-1993- $25.00. Required to search: name, years to search, DOB. Criminal records indexed on cards from 1979, index books from 1964. Note: Search requests include both the civil and criminal indexes. Mail turnaround time same day.

General Information: No sealed, juvenile, mental health or expunged records released. Will not fax documents. Court makes copy: $.50 per page. Certification fee: $5.00 per page includes copies. Payee: Colebrook District Court. Personal checks and credit cards accepted. Prepayment required. Mail requests: SASE required.

Gorham District Court (former) 220 Main St, Berlin, NH 03570; 603-752-3160; 8AM-4PM (EST). ***Misdemeanor, Civil Actions under $25,000, Eviction, Small Claims.***

Co-located with Berlin Court in 2006. Includes Gorham, Shelburne, Randolph and unincorporated places of Bean's Purchase, Martin's Location, Green's or Pinkham's Grant, and more.

Lancaster District Court 55 School St, #201, Lancaster, NH 03584; 603-788-4485; fax: 603-788-2005; 8:30AM-4PM (EST). ***Misdemeanor, Civil Actions under $25,000, Eviction, Small Claims.***

Includes Lancaster, Whitefield, Northumberland, Stark, Jefferson, Carroll, Kilkenny, Bean's Grant, Chandler's Purchase and Crawford's Purchase. Search fee includes all 4 indexes, if asked.

Civil Records: Access: Mail, in person. Only the court performs in person searches; visitors may not. Search fee: $10 for up to 9 names; 10 or more names- $25.00. Required to search: name, years to search; also helpful: DOB, address. Civil cases indexed by defendant, plaintiff. Civil index on cards from 1981, index books for public review only, computerized since 1993. Mail turnaround time 1 week.

Criminal Records: Access: Mail, in person. Only the court performs in person searches; visitors may not. Search fee: $10.00 up to 9 names; 10 or more names- $25.00. Required to search: name, years to search, DOB; also helpful: address. Criminal records indexed on cards from 1980, index books for public review only, computerized since 1993. Mail turnaround time 1 week.

General Information: No adoption, sealed, juvenile, mental health, expunged or dismissed records released. Will not fax documents. Court makes copy: $.50 per page. Certification fee: $5.00 per page. Payee: Lancaster District Court. Personal checks and major credit cards accepted. Prepayment required. Mail requests: SASE required.

Probate Court 55 School St #104, Lancaster, NH 03584; 603-788-2001; fax: 603-788-4345; 8AM-4PM (EST). ***Probate.***

Grafton County

Superior Court 3785 Dartmouth College Hwy, North Haverhill, NH 03774; 603-787-6961; 8AM-4PM (EST). ***Felony, Civil Actions over $1,500.***

Search fee includes all indexes, if asked.

Civil Records: Access: Mail, in person. Only the court performs in person searches; visitors may not. Search fee: $10.00 up to 9 names; $25.00 if over 10 names or if searched manually. Required to search: name, years to search. Civil cases indexed by defendant, plaintiff; index on computer back to 1995; on index cards from 1900, index books from 1950. Mail turnaround time 10 days.

Criminal Records: Access: Mail, in person. Only the court performs in person searches; visitors may not. Search fee: $10.00 up to 9 names; $25.00 if 10 names or more. $25.00 per hour for manual search. Required to search: name, years to search; also helpful: DOB, SSN. Criminal records computerized from 1995; on index cards from 1900. Mail turnaround time 10 days.

General Information: No sealed records released. Will not fax documents. Court makes copy: $.50 per page. Certification fee: $5.00 per cert. Payee: Grafton County Superior Court. Personal checks accepted; credit cards are not. Prepayment required. Mail requests: SASE required.

Haverhill District Court Grafton County Courthouse, 3785 Dartmouth College Highway - Box 10, North Haverhill, NH 03774; 603-787-6626; 8AM-4:30PM (EST). ***Misdemeanor, Civil Actions under $25,000, Eviction, Small Claims.***

Includes towns of Haverhill, Bath, Landaff, Benton, Piermont, and Warren. Search fee includes all 4 indexes, if asked.

Civil Records: Access: Mail, in person. Only the court performs in person searches; visitors may not. Search fee: Electronic records search fee- $10.00 up to 9 names; 10 or more names- $25.00. Manual search fee $25.00 per hour. The fee may change to $25.00 per name shortly. Required to search: name, years to search. Civil cases indexed by defendant, plaintiff; index on computer from 1993, on index cards from 1980, index books from 1950s. Mail turnaround time 1-2 days.

Criminal Records: Access: Mail, in person. Only the court performs in person searches; visitors may not. Search fee: $10.00 up to 9 names; 10 or more names- $25.00. Required to search: name, years to search, DOB. Criminal records computerized from 1993, on index cards from 1980, index books from 1950s. Mail turnaround time 1-2 days.

General Information: No adoption, sealed, juvenile, mental health, expunged or dismissed records released. Will fax documents to toll-free number. Court makes copy: $.50 per page. Certification fee: $5.00 per cert includes copy fee. Payee: Haverhill District Court. Personal checks and credit cards accepted. Prepayment required. Mail requests: SASE required.

Lebanon District Court 38 Centerra Parkway, Lebanon, NH 03766; 603-643-3555; fax: 603-643-1346; 8AM-4PM (EST). ***Misdemeanor, Civil Actions under $25,000, Eviction, Small Claims.***

Includes towns of Lebanon, Enfield, Canaan, Grafton, Orange, Hanover, Orford, and Lyme. Search fee includes all 4 indexes, if asked.

Civil Records: Access: Mail, in person. Only the court performs in person searches; visitors may not. Search fee: $10:00 up to 9 names; 10 or more names or pre-1993- $25.00. Required to search: name, years to search. Civil cases indexed by defendant, plaintiff; index on computer from 1993, on index cards from 1986, index books from 1960s. Mail turnaround time 5 business days.

Criminal Records: Access: Mail, in person. Only the court performs in person searches; visitors may not. Search fee: $10 for up to 9 names; 10 or more names or pre-1993- $25.00. Required to search: name, years to search, DOB. Criminal records computerized from 1993, on index cards from 1986, index books from 1960s. Mail turnaround time 5 business days.

General Information: No sealed, juvenile, mental health or expunged records released. Will fax back documents. Court makes copy: $.50 per page. Certification fee: $5.00 per cert. Payee: Lebanon District Court. Personal checks and major credit cards accepted. Prepayment required. Mail requests: SASE required.

Littleton District Court 134 Main St, Littleton, NH 03561; 603-444-7750; 8AM-4PM (EST). ***Misdemeanor, Civil Actions under $25,000, Eviction, Small Claims.***

Includes towns of Littleton, Monroe, Lyman, Lisbon, Franconia, Bethlehem, Sugar Hill, and Easton. Search fee includes all 4 indexes, if asked.

Civil Records: Access: Mail, in person. Only the court performs in person searches; visitors may not. Search fee: $10.00 up to 9 names; 10 or more names or pre-1993- $25.00. Required to search: name, years to search. Civil cases indexed by defendant, plaintiff; index on computer from 1993, index cards from 1985, index books from 1950. Mail turnaround time 3 weeks.

Criminal Records: Access: Mail, in person. Only the court performs in person searches; visitors may not. Search fee: $10.00 up to 9 names; 10 or more names or pre-1993- $25.00. Required to search: name, years to search; also helpful: DOB, SSN. Criminal records computerized from 1993, index cards from 1985, index books from 1950. Mail turnaround time 3 weeks.

General Information: No adoption, sealed, juvenile, mental health, domestic violence, expunged or dismissed records released. Will not fax documents. Court makes copy: $.50 per page. Certification fee: $5.00 per cert. Payee: Littleton District Court. Personal checks accepted. Visa/MC accepted. Prepayment required. Mail requests: SASE required.

Plymouth District Court 26 Green St, Plymouth, NH 03264; 603-536-3326; 8AM-4PM (EST). ***Misdemeanor, Civil Actions under $25,000, Eviction, Small Claims.***

www.courts.state.nh.us/courtlocations/grafdistdir.htm#Plymout

Includes towns of Plymouth, Bristol, Groton, Wentworth, Rumney, Ellsworth, Thornton, Campton, Ashland, Hebron, Holderness, Bridgewater, Alexandria, Lincoln, Woodstock, and portions of Livermore and Waterville. Search fee includes all 4 indexes, if asked.

Civil Records: Access: Mail, in person. Only the court performs in person searches; visitors may not. Search fee: $10.00 up to 9 names back to 1991; 10 or more names or complete search back to 1981- $25.00. Required to search: name, years to search. Civil cases indexed by defendant, plaintiff; index on computer from 1991, index cards from 1981. Note: Request for an appointment must be made two weeks prior to in person searching. Mail turnaround time 1 week.

Criminal Records: Access: Mail, in person. Only the court performs in person searches; visitors may not. Search fee: $10.00 up to 9 names back to 1991; 10 or more names or a complete search back to 1981- $25.00. Required to search: name, years to search; also helpful: DOB, SSN. Criminal records computerized from 1991, index cards from 1981. Note: Request for an appointment must be made two weeks prior to in person searching. Mail turnaround time 1 week.
General Information: No sealed, mental health, expunged or dismissed records released. Will not fax documents. Court makes copy: $.50 per page. Certification fee: $5.00 per cert. Payee: Plymouth District Court. Personal checks accepted. Visa/MC accepted. Prepayment required. Mail requests: SASE required.

Probate Court 3785 Dartmouth College Hwy, Box 3, North Haverhill, NH 03774-4936; 603-787-6931; 8AM-4PM (EST). ***Probate.***

Hillsborough County

Superior Court - North District 300 Chestnut St Rm 127, Manchester, NH 03101; 603-669-7410; 8AM-4PM (EST). ***Felony, Civil Actions over $1,500.***
Search fee includes all indexes, if asked.
Civil Records: Access: Mail, in person. Only the court performs in person searches; visitors may not. Search fee: $25.00 per hour. Electronic searches are $10 for less than 10 names, $25 for 10-25 names, then hourly rate. Required to search: name, years to search. Civil cases indexed by defendant, plaintiff; index on computer from 5/85, index cards from 1980s, index books from 1900s; organized 1769. Mail turnaround time 3 days.
Criminal Records: Access: Mail, in person. Only the court performs in person searches; visitors may not. Search fee: $25.00 per hour for manual search. Electronic searches are $10 up to 9 names, $25 for 10-25 names, then the hourly kicks in. Required to search: name, years to search, DOB. Criminal records computerized from 5/85, index cards from 1980s, index books from 1900s; organized 1769. Mail turnaround time 3 days.
General Information: No sealed, juvenile, mental health records released. Will not fax documents. Court makes copy: $.50 per page. Self serve: $.25 per page. Certification fee: $5.00 per cert. Payee: Hillsborough Superior Court-Northern District. Personal checks and major credit cards accepted. Prepayment required. Mail requests: SASE required.

Superior Court - Southern District 30 Spring St, Nashua, NH 03061; 603-883-6461; 8AM-4PM (EST). ***Felony, Civil Actions over $1,500.***
Search fee includes all indexes, if asked.
Civil Records: Access: Mail, in person. Only the court performs in person searches; visitors may not. Search fee: $10.00 up to 9 names; 10 or more names- $25.00. Required to search: name, years to search. Civil cases indexed by defendant, plaintiff; index on computer back to 3/92; overall records go back to 1992. Mail turnaround time 2-3 days.
Criminal Records: Access: Mail, in person. Only the court performs in person searches; visitors may not. Search fee: $10.00 up to 9 names; 10 or more names- $25.00. Required to search: name, years to search; also helpful: DOB. Criminal records computerized from 3/92; overall records go back to 1992. Mail turnaround time 2-3 days.
General Information: No sealed, juvenile or annulled records released. Will not fax documents. Court makes copy: $.50 per page. Self serve: $.05 per page. Certification fee: $5.00 per doc. Payee: Superior Court. Personal checks and credit cards accepted. Prepayment required.

Goffstown District Court PO Box 129, 16 Main St, Goffstown, NH 03045; 603-497-2597; 8AM-4PM (EST). ***Misdemeanor, Civil Actions under $25,000, Eviction, Small Claims.***
Includes towns of Goffstown, Weare, New Boston, and Francestown. Search fee includes all 4 indexes, if asked.
Civil Records: Access: Mail, in person. Only the court performs in person searches; visitors may not. Search fee: $10.00 up to 9 names; 10 or more names- $25.00. Required to search: name, years to search. Civil cases indexed by defendant, plaintiff; index on computer from 3/92, kept in files prior. Mail turnaround time 2 weeks.
Criminal Records: Access: Mail, in person. Only the court performs in person searches; visitors may not. Search fee: $10.00 up to 9 names; 10 or more names- $25.00. Required to search: name, years to search, DOB; also helpful: SSN. Criminal records computerized from 3/92, kept in files prior. Mail turnaround time 2 weeks.
General Information: No sealed, juvenile, mental health, expunged or dismissed records released. Court makes copy: $.50 per page. Certification fee: $5.00 per cert. Payee: Goffstown District Court. Personal checks accepted; credit cards are not. Prepayment required. Mail requests: SASE helpful.

Henniker District Court PO Box 763, Hillsborough, NH 03244; 603-464-5811; 8AM-4PM (EST). ***Misdemeanor, Civil Actions under $25,000, Eviction, Small Claims.***
Formerly known as Hillsborough District Court. Includes towns of Hillsborough, Deering, Windsor, Antrim, and Bennington. Search fee includes all 4 indexes, if asked.
Civil Records: Access: Mail, in person. Both court and visitors may perform in person searches. Search fee: $10.00 up to 9 names; 10 or more names or pre-1992- $25.00. Required to search: name, years to search. Civil cases indexed by defendant, plaintiff; index on computer from 1992, on index cards from 1980, index books from 1960. Note: Appointment required for in person searching. Mail turnaround time 1 week.
Criminal Records: Access: Mail, in person. Both court and visitors may perform in person searches. Search fee: $10.00 up to 9 names; 10 or more names or pre-1992- $25.00. Required to search: name, years to search, DOB; also helpful: SSN. Criminal records computerized from 1992, on index cards from 1980, index books from 1960. Mail turnaround time 1 week.
General Information: No adoption, sealed, juvenile, mental health, expunged or dismissed records released. Will not fax documents. Court makes copy: $.50 per page. Certification fee: $5.00 per cert. Payee: Hillsborough District Court. Personal checks accepted; credit cards are not. Prepayment required. Mail requests: SASE required.

Manchester District Court PO Box 456, Manchester, NH 03105; 603-624-6510; 8AM-4PM (EST). ***Misdemeanor, Civil Actions under $25,000, Eviction, Small Claims.***
www.courts.state.nh.us
Includes city of Manchester. They have a Records Research & Report Form to use for search requests. Search fee includes all 4 indexes, if asked.
Civil Records: Access: Mail, in person. Only the court performs in person searches; visitors may not. Search fee: $10.00 for less than 10 names (back to 6/15/1992 only), $25.00 for 10 or more names; manual searches (1-1980 to 6/14/1992) per name- $25.00 per hour or portion of. Required to search: name, years to search, DOB. Civil cases indexed by defendant, plaintiff; index on computer from 6//15/1992, on index cards from 1960. Note: All requests must be in writing. Mail turnaround time 2-3 weeks.
Criminal Records: Access: Mail, in person. Only the court performs in person searches; visitors may not. Search fee: $10.00 up to 9 names back to 6/15/1992 only; $25.00 for 10 or more names; manual searches (1-1980 to 6/14/1992) per name- $25.00 per hour or portion of. Required to search: name, years to search, DOB. Criminal records computerized from 6/15/1992, on index cards from 1960. Note: All requests must be in writing. Manual criminal record searches would be searches back to 1980, unless otherwise specified. Mail turnaround time 2-3 weeks.
General Information: No adoption, sealed, juvenile, mental health, expunged or dismissed records released. Will fax documents to local or toll-free number. Court makes copy: $.50 per page. Certification fee: $5.00 per page; exemplification- $25.00. Payee: Manchester District Court. Personal checks and major credit cards accepted. Prepayment required. Mail requests: SASE required.

Merrimack District Court PO Box 324, Merrimack, NH 03054-0324; 603-424-9916; 8AM-4PM (EST). ***Misdemeanor, Civil Actions under $25,000, Eviction, Small Claims.***
Includes towns of Merrimack, Litchfield, and Bedford. Search fee includes all 4 indexes, if asked.
Civil Records: Access: Mail, in person. Only the court performs in person searches; visitors may not. Search fee: $25 per hour for manual searches; electronic- $10 for up to first 9 names, $25 for 10-25 names, then hour rate. Required to search: name, years to search. Civil cases indexed by defendant, plaintiff; index on computer from 7/92, on index cards from 1972, index books in archives at Concord. Note: All requests must be in writing. Mail turnaround time 1-2 days.
Criminal Records: Access: Mail, in person. Both court and visitors may perform in person searches. Search fee: $10.00 up to 9 names; 10 or more names- $25.00. Required to search: name, years to search; also helpful: DOB. Criminal records computerized from 7/92, on index cards from 1972, index books in archives at Concord. Note: Requests must be in writing. Mail turnaround time 1-2 days.
General Information: No adoption, sealed, juvenile, mental health, expunged or dismissed records released. Will not fax documents. Court makes copy: $.50 per page. Certification fee: $5.00 per doc. Payee: Merrimack District Court. Personal checks and major credit cards accepted. Prepayment required. Mail requests: SASE required.

Milford District Court PO Box 943, 180 Elm St, Milford, NH 03055-0943; 603-673-2900; 8AM-4PM (EST). ***Misdemeanor, Civil Actions under $25,000, Eviction, Small Claims.***
Includes towns of Milford, Brookline, Amherst, Mason, Wilton, Lyndeborough, and Mont Vernon. Search fee includes all 4 indexes, if asked.
Civil Records: Access: Mail, in person. Only the court performs in person searches; visitors may not. Search fee: $10.00 up to 9 names; 10 or more names or pre-8/1992- $25.00. Required to search: name, years to search. Civil cases indexed by defendant, plaintiff; index on computer from 8/92, on index cards from 1950s, prior records may or may not be at old courthouse. Mail turnaround time 7 days.
Criminal Records: Access: Mail, in person. Only the court performs in person searches; visitors may not. Search fee: $10.00 up to 9 names; 10 or more names or pre-8/1992- $25.00. Required to search: name, years to search; also helpful: DOB, SSN. Criminal records computerized from 8/92, on index cards from 1950s, prior records may or may not be at old courthouse. Mail turnaround time 14 days.
General Information: No adoption, sealed, juvenile, mental health, expunged or dismissed records released. Will not fax documents. Court makes copy: $.50 per page. Certification fee: $5.00 per cert. Payee: Milford District Court. Personal checks and major credit cards accepted. Prepayment required. Mail requests: SASE required.

Nashua District Court PO Box 310, Nashua, NH 03061-0310; 603-880-3333; 8AM-4PM (EST). ***Misdemeanor, Civil Actions under $25,000, Eviction, Small Claims.***
Includes city of Nashua and the towns of Hudson and Hollis. Search fee includes all 4 indexes, if asked.
Civil Records: Access: Mail, in person. Only the court performs in person searches; visitors may not. Search fee: $10.00 up to 9 names; 10 or more names or pre-8/1992- $25.00. Required to search: name, years to search. Civil cases indexed by defendant, plaintiff; index on computer from 1993, index cards from 1982. Note: All requests must be in writing. Mail turnaround time 5 days.
Criminal Records: Access: Mail, in person. Only the court performs in person searches; visitors may not. Search fee: $10.00 up to 9 names; 10 or more names or pre-8/1992- $25.00. Required to search: name, years to search; also helpful: DOB, SSN. Criminal records computerized from 8/1992, index cards from 1982. Note: All requests must be in writing. Mail turnaround time 5 days.

General Information: No adoption, sealed, juvenile, mental health, expunged records released. Will not fax documents. Court makes copy: $.50 per page. Certification fee: $5.00 per cert. Payee: Nashua District Court. Personal checks accepted; credit cards are not. Prepayment required. Mail requests: SASE required.

Probate Court PO Box 387, 30 Spring St, Nashua, NH 03061-0387; 603-882-1231; fax: 603-882-1620; 8AM-4PM (EST). ***Probate.***

Merrimack County

Superior Court PO Box 2880, Concord, NH 03302-2880; 603-225-5501; 8AM-4PM (EST). ***Felony, Civil Actions over $1,500.***
Actual records kept off site - files prior to 1983 are at State Archives. Files more than 5 years old but not prior to 1983 are retrieved by courier with 3-5 day wait. Search fee includes all indexes, if asked.
Civil Records: Access: Mail, in person. Only the court performs in person searches; visitors may not. Search fee: $10.00 up to 9 names; 10 or more names or pre-1984- $25.00. Required to search: name, years to search. Civil cases indexed by defendant, plaintiff; index on computer from 1983, index cards from 1950, index books from 1800s; organized 1823. Mail turnaround time 2-3 weeks.
Criminal Records: Access: Phone, mail, in person. Only the court performs in person searches; visitors may not. Search fee: $10.00 up to 9 names; 10 or more names or pre-1984- $25.00. Required to search: name, years to search, DOB; also helpful: SSN. Criminal records on computer since 1984. Mail turnaround time 2-3 weeks.
General Information: No adoption, sealed, juvenile, mental health, expunged or dismissed records released. Will not fax documents. Court makes copy: $.50 per page. Self serve: $.15 per page. Certification fee: $7.00 per cert includes copy fee. Payee: Merrimack Superior Court. Personal checks and major credit cards accepted. Prepayment required. Mail requests: SASE required.

Concord District Court PO Box 3420, 32 Clinton St, Concord, NH 03302-3420; 603-271-6400; criminal phone: x3; civil phone: x4; 8AM-4PM (EST). ***Misdemeanor, Civil Actions under $25,000, Eviction, Small Claims, Traffic.***
Search fee includes all 4 indexes, if asked. The former Pittsfield District Court has been combined with this court. Includes city of Concord, and the towns of Loudon, Canterbury, Dunbarton, Bow, Hopkinton, Pittsfield, Chichester, and Epsom.
Civil Records: Access: Mail, in person. Only the court performs in person searches; visitors may not. Search fee: $10.00 up to 9 names; 10 or more names or pre-1989- $25.00. Required to search: name, years to search. Civil cases indexed by defendant, plaintiff; index on computer from 1989, index cards from 1978, docket books from 1800. Mail turnaround time 10 days.
Criminal Records: Access: Mail, in person. Only the court performs in person searches; visitors may not. Search fee: $10.00 up to 9 names; 10 or more names or pre-1989- $25.00. Required to search: name, years to search, DOB. Criminal records computerized from 1989, index cards from 1978, docket books from 1800. Note: In person search requests are not same day; they're treated same as a mail request. Mail turnaround time 10 days.
General Information: No sealed, juvenile, mental health, expunged or dismissed records released. Will not fax documents. Court makes copy: $.50 per page. Self serve: $.15 per page. Certification fee: $5.00 per cert. Payee: Concord District Court. Personal checks and major credit cards accepted. Prepayment required. Mail requests: SASE requested.

Franklin District Court 7 Hancock Terrace, Franklin, NH 03235; 603-934-3290; 8AM-4PM (EST). ***Misdemeanor, Civil Actions under $25,000, Eviction, Small Claims.***
Search fee includes all 4 indexes, if asked. Includes city of Franklin and the towns of Northfield, Danbury, Andover, Boscawen, Salisbury, Hill, Webster, Sanbornton, and Tilton.
Civil Records: Access: Mail, in person. Only the court performs in person searches; visitors may not. Search fee: $10.00 up to 9 names; 10 or more names- $25.00. Required to search: name, years to search. Civil cases indexed by plaintiff. Civil records on computer from 1/91, index cards from 1/80, index books from 1960s. Mail turnaround time 2-3 days.
Criminal Records: Access: Mail, in person. Only the court performs in person searches; visitors may not. Search fee: $10.00 up to 9 names, 10 or more names- $25.00. Required to search: name, years to search; also helpful: DOB, SSN. Criminal records computerized from 1/91, index cards from 1/80, index books from 1960s. Mail turnaround time 2-3 days.
General Information: No adoption, sealed, juvenile, mental health, expunged or dismissed records released. Will not fax documents. Court makes copy: $.50 per page. Certification fee: $5.00 per doc. Payee: Franklin District Court. Personal checks accepted. Visa/MC accepted. Prepayment required. Mail requests: SASE required.

Henniker District Court 41 Liberty Hill Rd, Bldg #2, Suite 110, Henniker, NH 03242; 603-428-3214; 8AM-4PM (EST). ***Misdemeanor, Civil Actions under $25,000, Eviction, Small Claims.***
Includes towns of Henniker, Warner, and Bradford. Search fee includes all 4 indexes, if asked.
Civil Records: Access: Mail, in person. Only the court performs in person searches; visitors may not. Search fee: $10.00 up to 9 names; 10 or more names- $25.00. Required to search: name, years to search. Civil cases indexed by defendant, plaintiff. Civil index on cards from 1988, index books from 1960s; on computer back to 1992. Mail turnaround time can take as long as 6 weeks.
Criminal Records: Access: Mail, in person. Only the court performs in person searches; visitors may not. Search fee: $10.00 up to 9 names; 10 or more names- $25.00. Required to search: name, years to search, DOB; also helpful: SSN. Criminal records indexed on cards from 1988, index books from 1960s; on computer back to 1992. Mail turnaround time can take as long as 6 weeks.
General Information: No adoption, sealed, juvenile, mental health, expunged or dismissed records released. Will not fax documents. Court makes copy: $.50 per page. Certification fee: $5.00 per cert. Payee: Henniker District Court. Personal checks accepted; credit cards are not. Prepayment required. Mail requests: SASE required.

Hooksett District Court 101 Merrimack, Hooksett, NH 03106; 603-485-9901; 8AM-4PM (EST). ***Misdemeanor, Civil Actions under $25,000, Eviction, Small Claims.***
Includes towns of Allenstown, Pembroke, and Hooksett. Search fee includes all 4 indexes, if asked.
Civil Records: Access: Mail, in person. Only the court performs in person searches; visitors may not. Search fee: Electronic search- $10.00 up to 9 names; if over 9 names- $25.00; manual research is $25.00 per hour. Required to search: name, years to search. Civil cases indexed by defendant, plaintiff; index on computer from 1993, on index cards from 1980, index books from 1975. Note: All requests must be in writing. Mail turnaround time 1-2 months.
Criminal Records: Access: Mail, in person. Only the court performs in person searches; visitors may not. Search fee: $10.00 up to 9 names; 10 or more names- $25.00. Required to search: name, years to search; also helpful: DOB, SSN. Criminal records computerized from 1993, on index cards from 1980, index books from 1975. Mail turnaround time 1-2 months.
General Information: No sealed, juvenile, mental health, expunged or dismissed records released. Will not fax documents. Court makes copy: $.50 per page. Certification fee: $5.00 per page. Cert fee includes copies. Payee: Hooksett District Court. Personal checks and major credit cards accepted. Prepayment required. Mail requests: SASE required.

New London District Court PO Box 1966, New London, NH 03257; 603-526-6519; 8:30AM-4PM (EST). ***Misdemeanor, Civil Actions under $25,000, Eviction, Small Claims.***
Includes towns of New London, Wilmot, Newbury, and Sutton. Search fee includes all 4 indexes, if asked.
Civil Records: Access: Mail, in person. Only the court performs in person searches; visitors may not. Search fee: $10.00 up to 9 names; 10 or more names or pre-1993- $25.00. Required to search: name, years to search. Civil cases indexed by defendant, plaintiff; index on computer from 1993, on index cards from 1980, index books from 1970. Note: An appointment is necessary before performing an in person search. Mail turnaround time 1-2 days.
Criminal Records: Access: Mail, in person. Only the court performs in person searches; visitors may not. Search fee: $10.00 up to 9 names; 10 or more names or pre-1993- $25.00. Required to search: name, years to search; also helpful: DOB, SSN. Criminal records computerized from 1993, on index cards from 1980, index books from 1970. Note: An appointment is necessary before performing an in person search. Mail turnaround time 1-2 days.
General Information: No adoption, sealed, juvenile, mental health, expunged or dismissed records released. Will not fax documents. Court makes copy: $.50 per page. Certification fee: $5.00 per page. Payee: New London District Court. Personal checks accepted; credit cards are not. Prepayment required. Mail requests: SASE required.

Probate Court 163 N Main St, Concord, NH 03301; 603-224-9589; fax: 603-225-0179; 8AM-4PM (EST). ***Probate.***

Rockingham County

Superior Court PO Box 1258, Kingston, NH 03848-1258; 603-642-5256; 8AM-4PM (EST). ***Felony, Civil Actions over $1,500.***
Search fee includes all indexes, if asked.
Civil Records: Access: Mail, in person. Only the court performs in person searches; visitors may not. Search fee: $10.00 up to 9 names; 10 or more names- $25.00. $25.00 per hour for manual searches. Required to search: name, years to search. Civil cases indexed by defendant, plaintiff; index on computer from 1988, index cards from 1920, organized 1769.
Criminal Records: Access: Mail, in person. Only the court performs in person searches; visitors may not. Search fee: $10.00 up to 9 names; 10 or more names- $25.00. $25.00 per hour for manual searches. Required to search: name, years to search; also helpful: DOB. Criminal records computerized from 1988, index cards from 1920, organized 1769.
General Information: No sealed, juvenile, mental health, expunged, annulled records released. Will not fax documents. Court makes copy: $.50 per page. Self serve: $.25 per page. Certification fee: $5.00 per cert. Payee: Clerk Superior Court. Personal checks and credit cards accepted. Prepayment required.

Auburn District Court 110 Raymond Rd, Candia, NH 03034; 603-483-2789; 8AM-4PM (EST). ***Misdemeanor, Civil Actions under $25,000, Eviction, Small Claims.***
Includes towns of Auburn, Candia, Deerfield, Northwood, Nottingham, and Raymond. This court was formerly located in Auburn, NH. Search fee includes all 4 indexes, if asked.
Civil Records: Access: Mail, in person. Only the court performs in person searches; visitors may not. Search fee: $10.00 up to 9 names; 10 or over- $25.00; if pre-1993 or manual searches- $25.00. Required to search: name, years to search; also helpful: address. Civil cases indexed by defendant, plaintiff; index on computer from 5/92, index cards from 1980, index books from 1968. Mail turnaround time 10 days.
Criminal Records: Access: Mail, in person. Only the court performs in person searches; visitors may not. Search fee: $10.00 up to 9 names; 10 or more names or pre-1993 or manual searches- $25.00. Required to search: name, years to search, DOB, signed release. Criminal records computerized from 5/92, index cards from 1980, index books from 1968. Mail turnaround time 10 days.
General Information: No adoption, sealed, juvenile, mental health, expunged or dismissed records released. Will not fax documents. Court makes copy: $.50 per page. Certification fee: $5.00 per cert. Payee: Auburn District Court. Personal checks accepted; credit cards are not. Prepayment required. Mail requests: SASE required.

Derry District Court 10 Manning St, Derry, NH 03038; 603-434-4676; 8AM-4PM (EST). ***Misdemeanor, Civil Actions under $25,000, Eviction, Small Claims.***

Includes towns of Derry, Londonderry, Chester, and Sandown. Search fee includes all 4 indexes, if asked.

Civil Records: Access: Phone, mail, in person. Only the court performs in person searches; visitors may not. Search fee: $10.00 up to 9 names; 10 or more names or pre-1992- $25.00. Required to search: name, years to search. Civil cases indexed by defendant, plaintiff; index on computer from 10/92, on index cards prior. Mail turnaround time 1 week.

Criminal Records: Access: Phone, mail, in person. Only the court performs in person searches; visitors may not. Search fee: $10.00 up to 9 names; 10 or more names or pre-1992- $25.00. Required to search: name, years to search; also helpful: DOB, SSN. Criminal records computerized from 10/92, on index cards prior. Mail turnaround time 1 week.

General Information: No adoption, sealed, juvenile, mental health, expunged, dismissed or annulment records released. Will not fax documents. Court makes copy: $.50 per page. Certification fee: $5.00 per cert. Payee: Derry District Court. Personal checks and major credit cards accepted. Prepayment required. Mail requests: SASE required.

Exeter District Court PO Box 1149, Kingston, NH 03848; 603-642-9173, 642-9145; 8AM-4PM (EST). ***Misdemeanor, Civil Actions under $25,000, Eviction, Small Claims.***

Relocated to Kingston from Exeter in 2004. Jurisdiction includes towns of Exeter, Newmarket, Stratham, Newfields, Fremont, East Kingston, Kensington, Epping, and Brentwood. Search fee includes all 4 indexes, if asked.

Civil Records: Access: Mail, in person. Only the court performs in person searches; visitors may not. Search fee: $10.00 up to 9 names; 10 or more names- $25.00. Required to search: name, years to search; also helpful: address. Civil cases indexed by defendant, plaintiff; index on computer back to 1991. Mail turnaround time 3 days.

Criminal Records: Access: Mail, in person. Both court and visitors may perform in person searches. Search fee: $10.00 up to 9 names, 10 or more names- $25.00. Required to search: name, years to search, DOB. Criminal records computerized from 1991. Mail turnaround time 3 days.

General Information: No adoption, sealed, juvenile, mental health, expunged or dismissed records released. Will fax documents to local or toll-free number, all fees prepaid. Court makes copy: $.50 per page. Certification fee: $5.00 per cert. Payee: Exeter District Court. Personal checks and major credit cards accepted. Prepayment required.

Hampton District Court 130 Ledge Rd, Seabrook, NH 03874-4322; 603-474-2637; 8AM-4PM (EST). ***Misdemeanor, Civil Actions under $25,000, Eviction, Small Claims.***

Search fee includes all 4 indexes, if asked. Jurisdiction includes towns of Hampton, Hampton Falls, North Hampton, South Hampton, and Seabrook.

Civil Records: Access: Mail, in person. Only the court performs in person searches; visitors may not. Search fee: $10.00 up to 9 names; 10 or more names or pre-1991- $25.00. Required to search: name, years to search. Civil cases indexed by defendant. Civil records on computer from 4/91, index cards from 1979, index books from 1900s. Mail turnaround time 1 week.

Criminal Records: Access: Mail, in person. Only the court performs in person searches; visitors may not. Search fee: $10.00 up to 9 names; 10 or more names or pre-1991- $25.00. Required to search: name, years to search; also helpful: DOB, SSN. Criminal records computerized from 4/91, index cards from 1979, index books from 1900s. Mail turnaround time 1 week.

General Information: No adoption, sealed, juvenile, mental health, expunged or dismissed records released. Will fax documents to local or toll-free number. Court makes copy: $.50 per page. Certification fee: $5.00 per cert. Payee: Hampton District Court. Personal checks accepted. Visa/MC accepted. Prepayment required. Mail requests: SASE required.

Plaistow District Court PO Box 129, 14 Elm St, Plaistow, NH 03865; 603-382-4651; fax: 603-382-4952; 8AM-4PM (EST). ***Misdemeanor, Civil Actions under $25,000, Eviction, Small Claims.***

Includes towns of Plaistow, Hampstead, Kingston, Newton, Atkinson, and Danville. Search fee includes all 4 indexes, if asked.

Civil Records: Access: Mail, in person. Only the court performs in person searches; visitors may not. Search fee: $10.00 up to 9 names; $25.00 for over 9 names. $25.00 per hour manual search fee. Required to search: name, years to search. Civil cases indexed by defendant, plaintiff; index on computer from 7/91, index cards from 1980, index books from 1960s. Mail turnaround time 2-3 days.

Criminal Records: Access: Mail, in person. Only the court performs in person searches; visitors may not. Search fee: $10.00 up to 9 names; 10 or more names- $25.00. Required to search: name, years to search, DOB. Criminal records computerized from 7/91, index cards from 1980, index books from 1960s. Mail turnaround time 2-3 days.

General Information: No adoption, sealed, juvenile, mental health, expunged or dismissed records released. Will not fax documents. Court makes copy: $.50 per page. Certification fee: $5.00 per cert. Payee: Plaistow District Court. Personal checks and major credit cards accepted. Prepayment required. Mail requests: SASE required.

Portsmouth District Court 111 Parrott Ave, Portsmouth, NH 03801; 603-431-2192; 8AM-4PM (EST). ***Misdemeanor, Civil Actions under $25,000, Eviction, Small Claims.***

Includes city of Portsmouth and the towns of Newington, Greenland, Rye, and New Castle. Search fee includes all 4 indexes, if asked.

Civil Records: Access: Mail, in person. Only the court performs in person searches; visitors may not. Search fee: $10.00 up to 9 names; 10 or more names or pre-1992- $25.00. Required to search: name, years to search. Civil cases indexed by defendant, plaintiff; index on computer from 4/92, docket cards from 1980, index books from 1960s. Mail turnaround time 2-3 days.

Criminal Records: Access: Mail, in person. Only the court performs in person searches; visitors may not. Search fee: $10.00 up to 9 names; 10 or more names or pre-1992- $25.00. Required to search: name, years to search; also helpful: DOB, SSN. Criminal records computerized from 4/92, docket cards from 1980, index books from 1960s. Mail turnaround time 2-3 days.

General Information: No adoption, sealed, juvenile, mental health, expunged or dismissed records released. Will not fax documents. Court makes copy: $.50 per page. Certification fee: $1.00 per page included in search fee plus $.30 per page after first. Payee: Portsmouth District Court. Personal checks accepted; credit cards are not. Prepayment required. Mail requests: SASE required.

Salem District Court 35 Geremonty Dr, Salem, NH 03079; 603-893-4483; 8AM-4PM (EST). ***Misdemeanor, Civil Actions under $25,000, Eviction, Small Claims.***

Includes towns of Salem, Windham, and Pelham. Search fee includes all 4 indexes, if asked.

Civil Records: Access: Mail, in person. Only the court performs in person searches; visitors may not. Search fee: $10.00 up to 9 names; 10 or more names or pre-1993- $25.00. Required to search: name, years to search, DOB. Civil cases indexed by defendant, plaintiff; index on computer from 4/92, docket cards from 1980, docket books from 1950. Note: An appointment is necessary before performing an in person search. Mail turnaround time 2-3 weeks.

Criminal Records: Access: Mail, in person. Only the court performs in person searches; visitors may not. Search fee: $10.00 up to 9 names; 10 or more names or pre-1993- $25.00. Required to search: name, years to search, DOB. Criminal records computerized from 4/92, docket cards from 1980, docket books from 1950. Mail turnaround time 2-3 weeks.

General Information: No adoption, sealed, juvenile, mental health, expunged or dismissed records released. Will fax documents $3.00. Court makes copy: $.50 per page. Certification fee: $5.00 per cert. Payee: Salem District Court. Personal checks accepted; credit cards are not. Prepayment required. Mail requests: SASE required.

Probate Court PO Box 789, (#10 Rt 125, Brentwood), Kingston, NH 03848; 603-642-7117; 8AM-4PM (EST). ***Probate.***

Strafford County

Superior Court PO Box 799, Dover, NH 03821-0799; 603-742-3065; criminal phone: x305; civil phone: x350; probate phone: 603-742-2550; 8AM-4PM (EST). ***Felony, Civil Actions over $1,500, DR.***

Search fee includes all indexes, if asked.

Civil Records: Access: Mail, in person. Only the court performs in person searches; visitors may not. Search fee: $10.00 up to 9 names; $25.00 over 10 names. Required to search: name, years to search. Civil cases indexed by defendant, plaintiff; index on computer from 3/89, index cards from 1970, index books from 1900s, organized 1769. Mail turnaround time 1 week.

Criminal Records: Access: Mail, in person. Only the court performs in person searches; visitors may not. Search fee: $10.00 up tp 9 names; 10 or more names- $25.00. Required to search: name, years to search; also helpful: DOB, SSN. Criminal records computerized from 3/89, index cards from 1970, index books from 1900s, organized 1769. Mail turnaround time 1 week.

General Information: No sealed, juvenile, mental health, expunged or dismissed records released. Will not fax documents. Court makes copy: $.50 per page. Self serve: $.25 per page. Certification fee: $5.00 per cert. Cert fee includes copies. Payee: Strafford Superior Court. Personal checks and credit cards accepted. Prepayment required.

Dover District Court 25 St Thomas St, Dover, NH 03820; 603-742-7202; fax: 603-742-5956; 8AM-4PM (EST). ***Misdemeanor, Civil Actions under $20,000, Eviction, Small Claims.***

Includes City of Dover, Somersworth, and Rollinsford. Search fee includes all 4 indexes, if asked.

Civil Records: Access: Mail, in person. Only the court performs in person searches; visitors may not. Search fee: $10 for up to 9 names; 10 or more names- $25.00. Required to search: name, years to search. Civil cases indexed by defendant, plaintiff; index on computer from 1993, on index cards from 1980, index books from 1970. Mail turnaround time 1-2 days.

Criminal Records: Access: Mail, in person. Only the court performs in person searches; visitors may not. Search fee: $10.00 up to 9 names; 10 or more names- $25.00. Required to search: name, years to search, DOB. Criminal records computerized from 1993, on index cards from 1980, index books from 1970. Mail turnaround time 1-2 days.

General Information: No adoption, sealed, juvenile, mental health, expunged or dismissed records released. May fax documents if not busy. Court makes copy: $.50 per page. Certification fee: $5.00 per doc. Payee: Dover District Court. Personal checks and major credit cards accepted. Prepayment required. Mail requests: SASE required.

Durham District Court 1 Main St, Durham, NH 03824; 603-868-2323; fax: 603-868-2024; 8:30AM-4PM (EST). ***Misdemeanor, Civil Actions under $25,000, Eviction, Small Claims.***

Includes towns of Durham, Lee, and Madbury. Search fee includes all 4 indexes, if asked.

Civil Records: Access: Mail, in person. Only the court performs in person searches; visitors may not. Search fee: $10.00 up to 9 names; 10 or more names or pre-1990- $25.00. Required to search: name, years to search. Civil cases indexed by defendant, plaintiff; index on computer back to 1990; index cards from 1980, index books from 1945. Mail turnaround time 4 days.

Criminal Records: Access: Mail, in person. Only the court performs in person searches; visitors may not. Search fee: $10.00 up to 9 names; 10 or more names or pre-1990- $25.00. Required to search: name, years to search, DOB; also helpful: SSN. Criminal records computerized from 1990; index cards from

1980, index books from 1948. Mail turnaround time 4 days.
General Information: No adoption, sealed, juvenile, mental health, expunged or dismissed records released. Will not fax documents. Court makes copy: $.50 per page. Certification fee: $5.00 per cert. Payee: Durham District Court. Personal checks and major credit cards accepted. Prepayment required. Mail requests: SASE required.

Rochester District Court 76 N Main St, Rochester, NH 03867; 603-332-3516; 8AM-4PM (EST). ***Misdemeanor, Civil Actions under $25,000, Eviction, Small Claims.***
Includes city of Rochester and the towns of Barrington, Milton, New Durham, Farmington, Strafford, and Middleton. Search fee includes all 4 indexes, if asked.
Civil Records: Access: Mail, in person. Only the court performs in person searches; visitors may not. Search fee: $10.00 up to 9 names; 10 or more names or pre-1990- $25.00. Required to search: name, years to search; also helpful DOB. Civil cases indexed by defendant, plaintiff; index on computer from 1989, index cards from 7/80, index books from 1960s. Note: Requests must be in writing. Mail turnaround time 1 week.
Criminal Records: Access: Mail, in person. Only the court performs in person searches; visitors may not. Search fee: $10.00 up to 9 names; 10 or more names or pre-1990- $25.00. Required to search: name, years to search; also helpful: DOB. Criminal records computerized from 1989, index cards from 7/80, index books from 1960s. Note: Requests must be in writing. Mail turnaround time 1 week.
General Information: No sealed, juvenile, mental health, expunged records released. Will fax documents to local or toll-free number. Court makes copy: $.50 per page. Certification fee: $5.00 per page. Payee: Rochester District Court. Personal checks accepted. Visa/MC and Discover accepted. Prepayment required. Mail requests: SASE required.

Somersworth District Court, NH. ***Misdemeanor, Civil Actions under $25,000, Eviction, Small Claims.***
This court combined with the Dover District Court on 11/1/02.

Probate Court PO Box 799, 259 County Farm Rd, Dover, NH 03820; 603-742-2550; 8AM-4PM (EST). ***Probate.***
www.courts.state.nh.us/courtlocations/straffprobdir.htm

Sullivan County

Superior Court 22 Main St, Newport, NH 03773; 603-863-3450; 8AM-4:00PM (EST). ***Felony, Civil Actions over $1,500.***
Search fee includes all indexes, if asked.
Civil Records: Access: Mail, in person. Only the court performs in person searches; visitors may not. Search fee: $25.00 per hour pro-rated manual search; $10.00 for computer search for up to 9 names; $25.00 if over 9 names. Required to search: name, years to search, DOB. Civil cases indexed by defendant, plaintiff; index on computer from 1992, on index cards from 1980s, index books from 1800s. Mail turnaround time 1 week.
Criminal Records: Access: Mail, in person. Only the court performs in person searches; visitors may not. Search fee: $25.00 per hour pro-rated manual search; $10.00 for computer search for up to 9 names; $25.00 if over 10 names. Required to search: name, years to search, DOB. Criminal records computerized from 1992, on index cards from 1980s, index books from 1800s. Mail turnaround time 1 week.
General Information: No adoption, sealed, juvenile, mental health, expunged or dismissed records released. Will not fax documents. Court makes copy: $.50 per page. Self serve: $.25 per page. Certification fee: $5.00 for attestation; copies included. Payee: Sullivan County Superior Court. Personal checks accepted. Prepayment required. Mail requests: SASE required.

Claremont District Court 1 Police Court, Claremont, NH 03743; 603-542-6064; 8AM-4PM (EST). ***Misdemeanor, Civil Actions under $25,000, Eviction, Small Claims.***
Search fee includes all 4 indexes, if asked. Jurisdiction area includes city of Claremont and the towns of Cornish, Unity, Charlestown, Acworth, Langdon, and Plainfield.
Civil Records: Access: Phone, mail, in person. Only the court performs in person searches; visitors may not. Search fee: $10.00 up to 9 names; 10 or more names or pre-1992- $25.00. Required to search: name, years to search, DOB. Civil cases indexed by defendant, plaintiff; index on computer from 10/92, on index cards from 1980, index books from 1960. Mail turnaround time 1 week.
Criminal Records: Access: Phone, mail, in person. Only the court performs in person searches; visitors may not. Search fee: $10.00 up to 9 names; 10 or more names or pre-1992- $25.00. Required to search: name, years to search, DOB. Criminal records computerized from 10/92, on index cards from 1980, index books from 1960. Mail turnaround time 1 week.
General Information: No adoption, sealed, juvenile, mental health, expunged or dismissed records released. Will fax documents to local or toll-free number. Court makes copy: $.50 per page. Certification fee: $5.00 per cert. Payee: Claremont District Court. Personal checks accepted. Visa/MC accepted. Prepayment required. Mail requests: SASE required.

Newport District Court 55 Main St, Newport, NH 03773; 603-863-1832; 8AM-4PM (EST). ***Misdemeanor, Civil Actions under $25,000, Eviction, Small Claims.***
Search fee includes all 4 indexes, if asked. Jurisdiction includes towns of Newport, Grantham, Croydon, Springfield, Sunapee, Goshen, Lempster, and Washington.
Civil Records: Access: Mail, in person. Only the court performs in person searches; visitors may not. Search fee: $10.00 up to 9 names; 10 or more names or pre-1993- $25.00. Required to search: name, years to search. Civil cases indexed by defendant, plaintiff; index on computer from 1993, on index cards from 1980, index books from 1960s. Note: All requests must be in writing. Mail turnaround time 2-3 days.
Criminal Records: Access: Mail, in person. Only the court performs in person searches; visitors may not. Search fee: $10.00 up to 9 names; 10 or more names or pre-1993- $25.00. Required to search: name, years to search, DOB. Criminal records computerized from 1993, on index cards from 1980, index books from 1960s. Note: Requests must be in writing. Mail turnaround time 2-3 days.
General Information: No adoption, sealed, juvenile, mental health, expunged or dismissed records released. Will fax documents by special request. Court makes copy: $.50 per page. Certification fee: $1.00 per cert. Payee: Newport District Court. Personal checks accepted. Visa/MC accepted. Prepayment required. Mail requests: SASE required.

Probate Court PO Box 417, 14 Main St, Newport, NH 03773; 603-863-3150; 8AM-4PM (EST). ***Probate.***

New Hampshire Recording Offices

ORGANIZATION: New Hampshire has 10 recording offices. There are 233 cities/town which previously handled the filing of UCCs. The recording officers are Register of Deeds (for real estate only) and Town/City Clerk (for UCCs). Be careful to distinguish the following names that are identical for both a town/city and a county - Grafton, Hillsborough, Merrimack, Strafford, and Sullivan. The following unincorporated towns do not have a Town Clerk, so all liens are located at the corresponding county: Cambridge (Coos), Dicksville (Coos), Green's Grant (Coos), Hale's Location (Carroll), Millsfield (Coos), and Wentworth's Location (Coos). New Hampshire is in the Eastern Time Zone (EST).

REAL ESTATE RECORDS: Real estate transactions are recorded at the county level, and property taxes are handled at the town/city level. Local town real estate ownership and assessment records are usually located at the Selectman's Office. Most New Hampshire counties will not perform real estate searches. Copy fees vary, usually $1.00 per page. Certification fee generally is $2.00 per document.

UCC RECORDS: This was a dual filing state until Revised Article 9. Previously, financing statements were filed at the state level and with the Town/City Clerk, except for consumer goods and farm related collateral which were filed only with the Town/City Clerk, and for real estate related collateral which was and still is filed with the county Register of Deeds. Most recording offices will perform UCC searches. Use search request form UCC-11. UCC search fees range from $5.00 to $10.00 per debtor name. Use standard UCC-11 request form. Copy fee is usually $1.00 per page.

TAX LIEN RECORDS: Federal and state tax liens on personal property of businesses are filed with the Secretary of State. Other federal and state tax liens on personal property are filed with the Town/City Clerk. Federal and state tax liens on real property are filed with the county Register of Deeds. There is wide variations in indexing and searching practices among the recording offices.

OTHER LIENS: Condominium, town tax, mechanics, welfare.

ONLINE ACCESS: The New Hampshire Counties Registry of Deeds website at www.nhdeeds.com allows free searching of real estate related records for Belknap, Cheshire, Coos, Hillsborough, Rockingham, Strafford and Sullivan counties. Also, a private vendor has placed assessor records from a number of towns on the internet, visit www.visionappraisal.com/databases/. Another vendor offers Property Card data for 75+ NH Towns, see www.avitarofneinc.com. Fees apply.

Belknap County

Register of Deeds, PO Box 1343, Laconia, NH 03247-1343. Recording, R/E & UCC phone-603-527-5420; fax-603-527-5429; 8AM-4PM www.nhdeeds.com Index: All in one. Records indexed on a public use terminal back to 1765. Only the public may search. Copy fee $1.00 per page. Cert fee- $2.00 per doc plus copy fee. Payee- Belknap County Registry of Deeds. **Online Real Estate, Grantor/Grantee, Deed, Mortgage, Lien records:** Access to county register of deeds data is free at www.nhdeeds.com/belk/web/BeDisclaimer.html. Online records go back to 1765. To establish an account for copies of documents from the internet, go to www.nhdeeds.com/belk/web/BeSearchWeb.html. **Property tax/Assessing**- Beacon St E, Laconia City Assessor, Laconia, NH 03246; 603-527-1268. hours-8:30AM-4:30PM

Alton Town, PO Box 637, Alton, NH 03809, (1 Monument Sq, Town Hall, Alton, NH 03809) 603-875-2101, fax-603-875-3894; 8:30AM-4:30PM Public access computer in office. **Online-** assessor database at http://data.visionappraisal.com/AltonNH/.

Barnstead Town, PO Box 11, Center Barnstead, NH 03225, (108 S Barnstead Rd, Town Hall, Center Barnstead, NH 03225) 603-269-4631, fax-603-269-4072; 9AM-4:30PM M,W,Th,F; 9AM-7PM Tues. No public terminal available. www.barnstead.org

Belmont Town, PO Box 310, Belmont, NH 03220, (143 Main St, Town Hall, Belmont, NH 03220) 603-267-8302, fax-603-267-8305; 7:30AM-4PM Public access computer in office. **Online-** Access to property assessor data is at http://data.visionappraisal.com/BelmontNH/.

Center Harbor Town, PO Box 140, Center Harbor, NH 03226, (36 Main St) 603-253-4561, fax-603-253-8420; 9AM-3PM

Gilford Town, 47 Cherry Valley Rd, Town Hall, Gilford, NH 03249, 603-527-4713, fax-603-527-4719; 8AM-5PM M-F, 5PM-7PM Th Evenings. A public access terminalis available. www.gilfordnh.org **Online-** Access assessor and other town online documents free at www.gilfordnh.org/Public_Documents/GilfordNH_BBoard/Document%20Index. Click on Alpha with Addresses.

Gilmanton Town, PO Box 550, Gilmanton, NH 03237-0550, (503 Province Rd, Academy Bldg, Gilmanton, NH 03237) 603-267-6726, fax-603-267-6704; 9AM-N, 7-8:30PM M; 9AM-4PM W F; 9AM-N, 6-8PM Th

Laconia City, PO Box 489, Laconia, NH 03247, (45 Beacon St E, 1st Fl, City Hall) 603-527-1265, fax-603-524-1766; 8:30AM-4:30PM www.city.laconia.nh.us/ **Online-** Records on the town assessor database at http://data.visionappraisal.com/LaconiaNH/DEFAULT.asp.

Meredith Town, 41 Main St, Meredith, NH 03253-9704, 603-279-4538, fax-603-279-1042; 8AM-5PM A public access terminal is available. http://meredithnh.org/ase.php **Online-** Access to Belknap County Registry of Deeds records is at www.nhdeeds.com. Also, search town assessor data free at http://data.visionappraisal.com/MeredithNH/.

New Hampton Town, PO Box 538, New Hampton, NH 03256, (6 Pinnacle Hill Rd) 603-744-8454, fax-603-744-5106; 7:30AM-11:45PM, 12:30PM-4PM M,T,W,F; 1PM-7PM TH www.new-hampton.nh.us/newhampton/depts_assessing.asp **Online-** Access assessment lists free at www.new-hampton.nh.us/newhampton/ and click on Assessment Lists and choose to view by owner. Also, access assessor property data free at http://data.visionappraisal.com coming soon.

Sanbornton Town, PO Box 124, Sanbornton, NH 03269, (573 Sanborn Rd, Town Office Bldg) 603-286-4034, fax-603-286-9544; 8AM-7:30 M; 8AM-4PM T,TH,F; 8AM-N Wed **Online-** Access assessor property data is at http://data.visionappraisal.com/SanborntonNH/. Free registration for full data.

Tilton Town, 257 Main St, Tilton, NH 03276-1207, 603-286-4425, fax-603-286-3519; 8:30AM-4:15PM **Online-** Search the assessor database at http://data.visionappraisal.com/TiltonNH/, no charge.

Carroll County

Register of Deeds, PO Box 163, Ossipee, NH 03864-0163. 603-539-4872; fax-603-539-5239; 9AM-5PM. Index: All in one. Records indexed on a public use terminal back to 1962. Only the public may search. Copy fee $1.00 per page. Fee for Glans $5.00. Cert fee- $1.00 per doc plus copy fee. Payee- Carroll County Register of Deeds.

Albany Town, 1972 NH Rte 16, #B, Albany, NH 03818, (Town Hall) 603-447-2877, fax-603-447-2877; 8AM-N M; 4PM-7PM W; 9AM-N Sat No public access terminal. www.albanynh.org **Online-** Access assessor property card data by subscription at www.avitarofneinc.com or call 603-798-4419. Annual subscription fee is $150 per Town.

Bartlett Town, RR 1 Box 50, Town Hall Rd, Intervale, NH 03845, 603-356-2300, fax-603-356-2300; 8AM-4PM M,T W, F; 8-11AM Sat

Brookfield Town, PO Box 756, Sanbornville, NH 03872, (2 Piney Rd, Cedar Park, Brookfield, NH 03872) 603-522-3231, fax-603-522-6245; 1-8PM Mon; 8:30AM-1PM Tues www.brookfieldnh.org

Chatham Town, 1681 Main Rd, Chatham, NH 03813, (Rte 113 North Chatham) 603-694-2043, fax-same; 5PM-7PM T

Conway Town, 1634 E Main St, Center Conway, NH 03813, 603-447-3822, fax-603-447-1348; 9AM-5PM

Eaton Town, Box 118, Eaton Center, NH 03832, (Rte 153) 603-447-2840, fax-603-447-2560; 9AM-11AM M; 7-9PM Tue or by appointment

Effingham Town, PO Box 117, Effingham, NH 03882, (68 School St) 603-539-7551, fax-603-539-7637; 8AM-5PM T & TH; 8AM-N Sat **Online-** Access assessor property card data by subscription at www.avitarofneinc.com or call 603-798-4419. Annual subscription fee is $150 per Town.

Freedom Town, PO Box 457, Freedom, NH 03836, (33 Old Portland Rd) 603-539-8269, fax-603-539-8270; 6:30-8PM Mon & Wed; 9-N Sat.

Hart's Location Town, 5 Forest Rd, Hart's Location, NH 03812, 603-374-2436; by appointment **Online-** The town is intending on posting property data on the internet in the future.

Jackson Town, PO Box 336, Jackson, NH 03846-0336, (54 Main St, Town Hall, Jackson, NH 03846) 603-383-6248, fax-603-383-6248; 3PM-7PM M, 8:30AM-12:30PM T,W,TH **Online-** Access assessor property card data by subscription at www.avitarofneinc.com or call 603-798-4419. Annual subscription fee is $150 per Town.

Madison Town, PO Box 248, Madison, NH 03849, (1923 Village Rd) 603-367-9931 x5, fax-603-367-4547; 8AM-4PM M,T,W,F A public access terminal is available. **Online-** Access assessor property card data by subscription at www.avitarofneinc.com or call 603-798-4419. Annual subscription fee is $150 per Town.

Moultonborough Town, PO Box 15, Moultonborough, NH 03254, (36 Holland St., Town Hall) 603-476-2347, fax-603-476-5835; 9AM-N 1-4PM M W F; 9AM-1PM Tu; closed Th A public access terminal is available. www.moultonborough.org/ **Online-** town assessor data at http://data.visionappraisal.com/MoultonboroughNH/. Free registration for full data.

Ossipee Town, PO Box 67, Center Ossipee, NH 03814, (55 Main St) 603-539-2008, fax-603-539-2856; 8:30AM-4:30PM

Sandwich Town, PO Box 194, Center Sandwich, NH 03227, (8 Maple St, Town Hall) 603-284-7113, fax-603-284-6819; 7-9PM M evening; 8AM-4PM T,Th **Online-** Access assessor property card data formerly by subscription at www.avitarofneinc.com or call 603-798-4419.

Tamworth Town, 84 Main St, Tamworth, NH 03886, 603-323-7971, fax-603-323-2347; 8AM-N, 1-4:30PM T-F

Tuftonboro Town, PO Box 98, Center Tuftonboro, NH 03816, (Town Hall) 603-569-4539 x11, fax-603-569-4328; 9AM-4PM M,F, 6-8PM T; 9AM-6PM W; closed Th **Online-** Access assessor property card data by subscription at www.avitarofneinc.com or call 603-798-4419. Annual subscription fee is $150 per Town.

Wakefield Town, 2 High St, Sanbornville, NH 03872, 603-522-6205 x306, fax-603-522-6794; 8:30AM-4AM T,TH,F; 8:30-12 W, 8:30-12:30 M,Sat **Online-** Access assessor property card data by subscription at www.avitarofneinc.com or call 603-798-4419. Annual subscription fee is $150 per Town.

Wolfeboro Town, Box 1207, Wolfeboro, NH 03894, (88 S Main St) 603-569-5328, fax-603-569-5328; 8AM-1PM, 2-4PM **Online-** Access to assessor property data is at http://data.visionappraisal.com/wolfeboroNH/. Free registration for full data. Also, access assessor property card data back to 11/07 by subscription at www.avitarofneinc.com or call 603-798-4419. Annual sub fee $150 per Town; free index searching.

Cheshire County

Register of Deeds, PO Box 584, Keene, NH 03431. 603-352-0403; fax-603-352-7678; 8:30AM-4:30PM. http://nhdeeds.com

Index: Separate indices to search include grantor/grantee. Records indexed on a public use terminal back to 1975. Only the public may search. Copy fee $2.00 1st page; $1.00 each add'l page. Cert fee- $2.00 per doc plus copy fee. Payee- Registry of deeds. **Online Real Estate, Deed, Mortgage, Lien records:** Access to register of deeds data is free at www.nhdeeds.com/chsr/web/ChDisclaimer.html . Online records go back to 1980.

Alstead Town, PO Box 65, Alstead, NH 03602, (15 Mechanic St) 603-835-2242, fax-603-835-2178; 8AM-4PM M-W; 8AM-6PM TH; Closed F

Chesterfield Town, PO Box 64, Chesterfield, NH 03443-0064, (504 Rte 63) 603-363-8071, fax-603-363-8047; 9-10AM, 5-8PM M-Th; 9-10AM, 2-5PM W

Dublin Town, Box 62, Dublin, NH 03444, (Main St, Town Hall) 603-563-8859, fax-603-563-9221; 9AM-4PM, 6-9PM M; 9AM-4PM T,TH; 9-5 Wed **Online-** Access assessor property card data by subscription at www.avitarofneinc.com or call 603-798-4419. Annual subscription fee is $150 per Town.

Fitzwilliam Town, PO Box 504, Fitzwilliam, NH 03447-0504, (13 Templeton Tnpk, Town Hall, Fitzwilliam, NH 03447) 603-585-7791, fax-603-585-7744; 8:30AM-12:30PM M,W; 1-5PM Thurs; Wed Eve-6-9PM **Online-** Search assessor database at http://data.visionappraisal.com/FitzwilliamNH/. Also search free after registration at www.avitarofneinc.com/listoftowns.asp.

Gilsum Town, PO Box 67, Gilsum, NH 03448, (650 Rte 10) 603-357-0320, fax-603-352-0845; 6PM-8PM T; 8AM-Noon Wed. **Online-** Access assessor property card data by subscription at www.avitarofneinc.com or call 603-798-4419. Annual subscription fee is $150 per Town.

Harrisville Town, PO Box 284, Harrisville, NH 03450, (705 Chesham Rd, Town Clerk) 603-827-5546, fax-603-827-2917; 2-7PM, T; 4-6:30PM, W; 9-11:30AM Th. **Online-** Access assessor property card data by subscription at www.avitarofneinc.com or call 603-798-4419. Annual sub fee $150 per Town.

Hinsdale Town, PO Box 31, Hinsdale, NH 03451, 603-336-5719, fax-603-336-5711; 8-N, 1-4 M-Th; till 6:30PM Th; 8-N Fri; 1st/3rd Sat 8-N

Jaffrey Town, 10 Goodnow St, Jaffrey, NH 03452, 603-532-7861, fax-603-532-7862; 8:30AM-3:30PM M-TH; 6-8PH Th; 8:30-N Fri **Online-** Search town assessor database at http://data.visionappraisal.com/JaffreyNH/.

Keene City, 3 Washington St, Keene, NH 03431, 603-352-0133, fax-603-357-9884; 8AM-5PM www.ci.keene.nh.us **Online-**access to property values at www.ci.keene.nh.us/onlineservices/index.htm.

Marlborough Town, PO Box 487, Marlborough, NH 03455-0487, (236 E Main St, Town Hall, Marlborough, NH 03455) 603-876-4529, fax-603-876-4703; 9AM-4:30PM M,T,TH; 9AM-Noon W; 9AM-2PM Fri www.marlboroughnh.org/

Marlow Town, PO Box 184, Marlow, NH 03456, (Town Hall) 603-446-2245 x3, fax-603-446-3806; 4:30-7PM W-Th

Nelson Town, 7 Nelson Common Rd, Nelson, NH 03457, (Nelson Village, Old Brick Schoolhouse) 603-847-9043, fax-603-847-3197; 9AM-N Tu.; 5-8PM W; 9AM-N Th

Richmond Town, 105 Old Homestead Hwy, Richmond, NH 03470, 603-239-6202, fax-603-239-6202; 9AM-N, 1-4PM, 6-8PM M; 9AM-N T,Th; 9AM-N, 1-4 W

Rindge Town, PO Box 11, Rindge, NH 03461, (30 Payson Hill Rd, Town Office) 603-899-5181 x107, fax-603-899-2101; 9AM-1PM 2PM-4PM M-Th; 6-8PM Th Eve; 9AM-1PM Fri. **Online-** Search town assessor database at http://data.visionappraisal.com/RindgeNH/.

Roxbury Town, 404 Branch Rd, Roxbury, NH 03431, 603-352-4903; 7-8PM M **Online-** Access assessor property card data by subscription at www.avitarofneinc.com or call 603-798-4419. Annual subscription fee is $150 per Town.

Stoddard Town, 2175 Rte 9, Stoddard, NH 03464, 603-446-2214, fax-603-446-2214; 9AM-2PM 4PM-6PM T TH

Sullivan Town, PO Box 110, Sullivan, NH 03445-0110, (522 South Rd) 603-352-1495; 8AM-9AM **Online-** Access assessor property card data by subscription at www.avitarofneinc.com or call 603-798-4419. Annual subscription fee is $150 per Town.

Surry Town, 1 Village Rd, Surry, NH 03431, 603-352-3075, fax-603-357-4890; 1st and 3rd Thursday eves **Online-** Access assessor property card data by subscription at www.avitarofneinc.com or call 603-798-4419. Annual sub fee $150 per Town.

Swanzey Town, PO Box 10009, Swanzey, NH 03446, (620 Old Homestead) 603-352-7411, fax-603-352-6250; 9AM-5PM **Online-** Access assessor data at http://data.visionappraisal.com/SwanzeyNH/. Free registration for full data.

Troy Town, PO Box 249, Troy, NH 03465-0249, (16 Central Sq, Town Hall, Troy, NH 03465) 603-242-3845, fax-603-242-3430; 9AM-4:30PM M-W; 1-7PM Th; 9AM-1:30PM Fri

Walpole Town, PO Box 756, Walpole, NH 03608, (T34 Elm St, Town Hall, Walpole, NH 03608) 603-756-3514, fax-603-756-4153; 7AM-4PM M-Th; 6-7PM W; closed F **Online-** Access assessor property card data by subscription at www.avitarofneinc.com or call 603-798-4419. Annual subscription fee is $150 per Town.

Westmoreland Town, PO Box 111, Westmoreland, NH 03467, (108 Pierce Ln) 603-399-7211, fax-603-399-7211; 7-8:30PM M,W; 7:30AM-2PM M **Online-** Access assessor property card data by subscription at www.avitarofneinc.com or call 603-798-4419. Annual sub fee $150 per Town.

Winchester Town, 1 Richmond Rd, Winchester, NH 03470, 603-239-6233 x102, fax-603-239-4146; 8AM-5PM **Online-** Access assessor property card data by subscription at www.avitarofneinc.com or call 603-798-4419. Annual sub fee $150 per Town.

Coos County

Register of Deeds, 55 School St, #103; Registry of Deeds, Lancaster, NH 03584. Recording, R/E & UCC phone-603-788-2392; fax-603-788-4291; 8AM-4PM www.nhdeeds.com/coos/web/start.htm

County Register of Deeds records real estate and Real Estate/UCC transactions; Town/City Clerk records UCC filings. Index: All in one. Records indexed on a public use terminal back to 1982. Only the public may search. Copy fee $2.00 per page. Cert fee- $2.00 per doc plus copy fee. Payee- County Registry of Deeds. **Online access to Real Estate, Deed, Mortgage, Lien records:** Access to county register of deeds data is free at www.nhdeeds.com/coos/web/start.htm. Subscription required to print images.

Berlin City, 168 Main St, City Hall, Berlin, NH 03570, 603-752-2340, fax-603-752-1654; 8:30-N, 1-4:30PM www.berlinnh.gov/Pages/BerlinNH_Assessor/index **Online-** Access assessor property card data by subscription at www.avitarofneinc.com or call 603-798-4419. Annual subscription fee is $150 per Town. Free information and searching available at www.mapsonline.net/berlinnh/

Carroll Town, PO Box 88, Twin Mountain, NH 03595-0088, (School Rd) 603-846-5494, fax-603-846-5713; 8:30AM-3PM M,T,W,Th

Clarksville Town, 408 NH Rte 145, Clarksville, NH 03592, 603-246-7751, fax-603-246-3480; 1-5PM M; 9AM-4PM T,Th; 12:30-6:30PM W; 9AM-Noon F

Colebrook Town, 17 Bridge St, Colebrook, NH 03576, 603-237-5200, fax-603-237-5069; 8AM-5PM M; 8AM-3:30PM T,TH,F; 1-3:30PM Wed **Online-** Access assessor property card data by subscription at www.avitarofneinc.com or call 603-798-4419. Annual subscription fee is $150 per Town.

Columbia Town, PO Box 157, Colebrook, NH 03576, (1679 US Rte 3) 603-237-5255, fax-603-237-8270; 10AM-5PM, M,W; 8AM-3PM, T,F **Online-** Access assessor property card data by subscription at www.avitarofneinc.com or call 603-798-4419. Annual subscription fee is $150 per Town.

Dalton Town, 741 Dalton Rd, Dalton, NH 03598, 603-837-2096, fax-603-837-9642; 11AM-5:45PM Mon; 7AM-5PM T,W,Th

Dummer Town, 75 Hill Rd, Dummer, NH 03588, 603-449-2006, fax-603-449-3349; 9AM-2PM M; 5:30PM-6:30PM T-TH; 8AM-N F **Online-** Access assessor property card data by subscription at www.avitarofneinc.com or call 603-798-4419. Annual subscription fee is $150 per Town.

Errol Town, PO Box 100, Errol, NH 03579, (Town Hall) 603-482-3351, fax-603-482-3804; 9AM-11AM M; 5PM-7:30PM, T; 8:30-11AM, TH

Gorham Town, 20 Park St, Gorham, NH 03581-1694, 603-466-2744, fax-603-466-2744; 8:30AM-4:30PM

Jefferson Town, 84 Stag Hollow Rd, Jefferson, NH 03583, (Main St, Town Hall) 603-586-4553, fax-603-586-4553

Lancaster Town, 25 Main St, Lancaster, NH 03584, 603-788-2306, fax-603-788-2114; 8:30AM-5PM M-TH; 8:30AM-4:30PM F

Milan Town, PO Box 158, Milan, NH 03588, (20 Bridge St) 603-449-3461, fax-603-449-2624; 9AM-N, 1-5PM M; 9AM-N, 1-4PM, 6-8PM T,W,Th **Online-** Access assessor property card data by subscription at www.avitarofneinc.com or call 603-798-4419. Annual sub fee is $150 per Town.

Northumberland Town, 3 State St, Groveton, NH 03582, 603-636-1451, fax-603-636-6098; 8:30AM-4PM **Online-** Access assessor property data free at http://data.visionappraisal.com coming soon.

Pittsburg Town, 1526 Main St, Pittsburg, NH 03592, 603-538-6699, fax-603-538-6697; Noon-4PM T; 2-7PM W; 8AM-2PM Th; 8AM-Noon Fri; closed M **Online-** Access assessor property card data by subscription at www.avitarofneinc.com or call 603-798-4419. Annual sub fee is $150 per Town.

Randolph Town, 130 Durand Rd, Randolph, NH 03593, 603-466-5771, fax-603-466-9856; 9-11AM M; 7-9PM W

Shelburne Town, 74 Town Hall, Village Rd, Shelburne, NH 03581, 603-466-2262, fax-603-466-5271; 11AM-3PM T; 3-6PM TH

Stark Town, 1189 Stark Hwy, Stark, NH 03582, 603-636-2118, fax-603-636-6199; 10AM-4PM T,Th **Online-** Access assessor property card data by subscription at www.avitarofneinc.com or call 603-798-4419. Annual subscription fee is $150 per Town.

Stewartstown Town, PO Box 119, West Stewartstown, NH 03597-0035, (888 Washington St) 603-246-3329, fax-603-246-3329; 9:30AM-2PM Tu.; 9AM-4PM M,W, F **Online-** Access assessor property card data by subscription at www.avitarofneinc.com or call 603-798-4419. Annual subscription fee is $150 per Town.

Stratford Town, PO Box 366, North Stratford, NH 03590, (Fire Station) 603-922-5598, fax-603-922-3317; 4PM-7PM, M; 4PM-7PM, W

Whitefield Town, 7 Jefferson Rd, Whitefield, NH 03598, 603-837-9871, fax-603-837-3148; 9AM-4PM M, W, Th; 9AM-6PM Tu

Grafton County

Register of Deeds, 3855 Dartmouth College Hwy, Box 4, North Haverhill, NH 03774-9700. Recording, R/E & UCC phone-603-787-6921; fax-603-787-2363; 7:30AM-4:30PM(Research) 8AM-3:45(Recording). www.nhdeeds.com/gftn/web/GfHome.html

Index: All in one. Records indexed on a public use terminal back to 1960. Only the public may search. Copy fee $1.00 per page; self serve same. Cert fee-$2.00 per doc plus copy fee. Payee- Grafton County Registry of Deeds. **Online Real Estate, Deed, Lien, Mortgage records:** Access to county register of deeds data is free at www.nhdeeds.com/gftn/web/GfHome.html. A subscription is required to print images. Access to the County dial-up service requires a $50.00 set up fee and $1.00 per page charge. Lending agency data is available. A fax-back service is available, need to have payment before they fax out whether in or out of state. For info, call 603-787-6921. **Other phones:** Treasurer- 603-787-6941; Elections-603-787-6941.

Alexandria Town, 45 A Washburn Rd, Alexandria, NH 03222, 603-744-3288, fax-603-744-8577; 9AM-4PM M,T,F; 9AM-7PM Th; Closed Wed **Online-** Access assessor property card data by subscription at www.avitarofneinc.com or call 603-798-4419. Annual sub fee is $150 per Town.

Ashland Town, PO Box 517, Ashland, NH 03217, (20 Highland St) 603-968-4432, fax-603-968-3776; 8AM-4PM

Bath Town, PO Box 165, Bath, NH 03740, (West Bath Rd, Town Hall, Bath, NH 03740) 603-747-2454, fax-603-747-0497; 8AM-N, 1PM-4PM M-Th; 8AM-N Fri

Benton Town, 221 Coventry Rd, Benton, NH 03785-6402, 603-787-6541, fax-none; 6:30-8:30PM Monday night

Bethlehem Town, PO Box 189, Bethlehem, NH 03574, (2155 Main St, Town Bldg, Bethlehem, NH 03574) 603-869-2293 x15, fax-603-869-2280; 4:30-7PM M,T,W; 9-11AM Sat; closed Th-F

Bridgewater Town, PO Box 419, Plymouth, NH 03264, (1052 River Rd) 603-968-7911, fax-603-968-3506; 6PM-8:30PM T- W; 8:30AM-10AM 3rd Sat, Closed TH,F **Online-** town assessor data at http://data.visionappraisal.com/BridgewaterNH/.

Bristol Town, 230 Lake St, Bristol, NH 03222-1120, 603-744-8478, fax-603-744-2521; 8:30AM-4PM - M,T,W,F; 8AM-7PM - Th www.townofbristolnh.org/

Campton Town, 1307 NH Rte 175, Campton, NH 03223, 603-726-3223, fax-603-726-9817; 9AM-3:30PM M W TH F; 11AM-6PM T

Canaan Town, PO Box 38, Canaan, NH 03741-0038, (1169 US Rte 4) 603-523-7106, fax-603-523-4526; 9AM-12 1PM-4PM M,W,F; 9AM-12 T TH; 9-N Sat www.townofcanaannh.us/stories/storyReader$45 **Online-** Access assessor property card data by subscription at www.avitarofneinc.com or call 603-798-4419. Annual subscription fee is $150 per Town. Yearly assessor data available at www.townofcanaannh.us/stories/storyReader$45

Dorchester Town, 368 N Dorchester Rd, #2, Dorchester, NH 03266, 603-523-7119, fax-603-523-8860; 9-11AM M; 3-6PM W; 9-11AM last Sat. **Online-** Access assessor property card data by subscription at www.avitarofneinc.com or call 603-798-4419. Annual subscription fee is $150 per Town.

Easton Town, 418 Easton Valley Rd, Easton, NH 03580, 603-823-8017, fax-603-823-7780; 1-6PM Th **Online-** Access assessor property data free at http://data.visionappraisal.com coming soon.

Ellsworth Town, 12 Ellsworth Pond Rd, c/o Donna O'Brien, Plymouth, NH 03223, 603-726-3551, fax-603-726-8994; by appointment **Online-** Access assessor property card data by subscription at www.avitarofneinc.com or call 603-798-4419. Annual subscription fee is $150 per Town.

Enfield Town, PO Box 373, Enfield, NH 03748-0373, (23 Main St) 603-632-5001, fax-603-632-5182; 8:30AM-3:30PM M,W,F; 9:30AM-4:30PM T; 11AM-7PM TH **Online-** Assessor data is free at www.visionappraisal.com/databases/nh/.

Franconia Town, PO Box 900, Franconia, NH 03580, (421 Main St, Town Hall, Franconia, NH 03580) 603-823-5237, fax-603-823-5581; 8AM-1PM, 5-7PM Tues.; 8AM-1PM Th **Online-** Access assessor property card data by subscription at www.avitarofneinc.com or call 603-798-4419. Annual subscription fee is $150 per Town.

Grafton Town, PO Box 297, Grafton, NH 03240, (Library Rd) 603-523-7270, fax-603-523-4397; 6-8PM M; 9AM-N W; 5PM-7PM Th; 9AM-Noon Last Sat of month.

Groton Town, 754-A Groton Rd, Groton, NH 03241, 603-744-8849; 10AM-6PM M,F;11AM-4PM,W; 10AM-2PM 1st & last Sat **Online-** Access assessor property card data by subscription at www.avitarofneinc.com or call 603-798-4419. Annual subscription fee is $150 per Town.

Hanover Town, PO Box 483, Hanover, NH 03755-0483, (41 S Main St) 603-643-0701, fax-603-643-1720; 8:30AM-4:30PM **Online-** Access current assessment data free by owner name or locations at www.hanovernh.org/assessing. Click on Current Assessment Information.

Haverhill Town, 2975 Dartmouth College Hwy, N. Haverhill, NH 03774, 603-787-6200, fax-603-787-2226; 9AM-4:30PM

Hebron Town, PO Box 55, East Hebron, NH 03241, (Church Ln, Town Hall) 603-744-7999, fax-603-744-7999; 3-8PM T; 9:30-11:30AM Sat. **Online-** Access assessor property card data by subscription at www.avitarofneinc.com or call 603-798-4419. Annual subscription fee is $150 per Town.

Holderness Town, PO Box 203, Holderness, NH 03245, (1089 US Rte 3, Town Hall) 603-968-7536, fax-603-968-9954; 8:30AM-4PM www.holderness-nh.gov/ **Online-** assessment data at www.holderness-nh.gov/Public_Documents/HoldernessNH_Assessor/assessments

Landaff Town, PO Box 125, Landaff, NH 03585, (23 Jim Noyes Hill Rd) 603-838-6220, fax-603-838-5225; 9AM-11AM & 5PM-7PM Tues

Lebanon City, 51 N Park St, Lebanon, NH 03766, 603-448-3054, fax-603-448-4891; 8AM-5PM A public access terminal is available. www.lebcity.com/Public_Documents/LebanonNH_Assessors/index **Online-** current assessment pages free on website. Also, records from city assessor data free at http://data.visionappraisal.com/LEBANONNH/. Free registration is required to view full data. Search interactive GIS maps free at http://ims.lebcity.com/.

Lincoln Town, PO Box 39, Lincoln, NH 03251, (148 Main St) 603-745-8971, fax-603-745-6743; 8AM-4PM A public access terminal is available. www.lincolnnh.org/

Lisbon Town, 46 School St, Lisbon, NH 03585, 603-838-2862, fax-603-838-6790; 9AM-N,1-4:30

Littleton Town, 125 Main St, #202, Littleton, NH 03561, 603-444-3995 x20, fax-603-444-0735; 8:00AM-12:30PM, 1-4PM, M,T,Th; 8-5PM W; 7AM-12:30 F **Online-** Search town assessor database at http://data.visionappraisal.com/LittletonNH/.

Lyman Town, 65 Parker Hill Rd, Lyman, NH 03585, 603-838-6113, fax-603-838-6818; 8AM-3:30AM M,W; 8AM-1:30PM TH; Closed F **Online-** Access assessor property card data by subscription at www.avitarofneinc.com or call 603-798-4419. Annual subscription fee is $150 per Town.

Lyme Town, PO Box 342, Lyme, NH 03768, (38 Union St) 603-795-2535, fax-603-795-4637; 8AM-2PM M,W,F,

Monroe Town, PO Box 63, Monroe, NH 03771-0063, (50 Main St, Town Hall, Monroe, NH 03771) 603-638-2644, fax-603-638-2021

Orford Town, 59 Archertown Rd, Clerk's Office, Orford, NH 03777, 603-353-4404, fax-603-353-4889; 2-7PM T; 6-8PM W; 8-11AM Th **Online-** Access assessor property card data by subscription at www.avitarofneinc.com or call 603-798-4419. Annual subscription fee is $150 per Town.

Piermont Town, PO Box 27, Piermont, NH 03779, (573 Rte 25C) 603-272-4840, fax-603-272-4947; 1-7PM T,W

Plymouth Town, 6 Post Office Sq, Town Hall, Plymouth, NH 03264, (Town Hall) 603-536-1732, fax-603-536-0036; 8:30AM-4:30PM

Rumney Town, PO Box 275, Rumney, NH 03266, (79 Depot St) 603-786-2237, fax-603-786-2237; 4PM-8PM M; 9AM-2PM, T, W, TH, F

Sugar Hill Town, Box 574, Sugar Hill, NH 03586, (1411 Rte 117, Town Hall) 603-823-8516, fax-603-823-8446; 4PM-6PM M; 9AM-1PM T TH **Online-** Access assessor property data free at http://data.visionappraisal.com coming soon.

Thornton Town, 16 Merrill Access Rd, Thornton, NH 03285, 603-726-4232, fax-603-726-2078; 9AM-4PM M,W,Th; 11AM-6PM T; 9AM-3:30PM F **Online-** Access assessor property card data by subscription at www.avitarofneinc.com or call 603-798-4419. Annual sub fee is $150 per Town.

Warren Town, PO Box 40, Warren, NH 03279, (8 Water St) 603-764-5780, fax-603-764-9296; 4PM-8PM M; 6PM-8PM W; 1-3PM F

Waterville Valley Town, Box 500, Waterville Valley, NH 03215, (Rust Municipal Bldg) 603-236-4730, fax-603-236-2056; 8AM-4PM

Wentworth Town, PO Box 2, Wentworth, NH 03282, (7 Atwell Hill Rd) 603-764-5244, fax-603-764-9362; 12-7PM T; 8:30AM-3PM W,Th.

Woodstock Town, PO Box 156, North Woodstock, NH 03262, (165 Lost River Rd, Clerk's Office) 603-745-8752, fax-603-745-2393; 8:30AM-12:30PM T-Th

Hillsborough County

Registry of Deeds, PO Box 370, Nashua, NH 03061-0370. 603-882-6933, R/E recording phone-603-882-6933 x115; fax-603-882-7527; 8AM-3:45PM www.nhdeeds.com/hils/web/HiHome.html
Index: All in one. Records indexed on a public use terminal back to 1966. Office will perform a UCC search but public must search other records themselves. Copy fee $1.00 per page. Cert fee- $2.00 per doc plus copy fee. Payee- Hillsborough County Treasurer. **Online access to Real Estate, Grantor/Grantee, Deed, Mortgage, Lien records:** Access to county register of deeds data is free at www.nhdeeds.com/hils/web/HiDisclaimer.html. Online records go back to 1966. **Property tax/Assessing-** 29 School St, PO Box 7, Hillsborough, NH 03244-0007; 603-464-3877 x221, assessor fax- 603-464-4270. hours- 8:30AM-5PM

Amherst Town, PO Box 960, Amherst, NH 03031, (2 Main St, Town Hall, Amherst, NH 03031) 603-673-6041 x203, fax-603-673-4138; 9AM-3PM M-F; 4:40-6:30PM Tues www.amherstnh.gov/Assessor/index.html **Online-** Records on the town assessor database are free at http://data.visionappraisal.com/AmherstNH/.

Antrim Town, PO Box 517, Antrim, NH 03440, (66 Main St) 603-588-6785 x223, fax-603-588-2969; 8AM-N M-Th; 5PM-7PM M; 1PM-4PM Th **Online-** Name search the map page free at www.mapsonline.net/antrimnh/.

Bedford Town, 24 N Amherst Rd, Bedford, NH 03110, 603-472-3550, fax-603-472-4573; 8AM-4:30PM M,W,Th,F; 7AM-4:30PM Tu. Public computer in office. **Online-** Access assessor data at http://data.visionappraisal.com/BedfordNH/DEFAULT.asp. Free registration for full data.

Bennington Town, 7 School St, #101, Bennington, NH 03442, 603-588-2189, fax-603-588-8005; 9AM-N M & Sat; 8:30AM-12:30PM T; 4:30-8:30PM Th

Brookline Town, PO Box 336, Brookline, NH 03033, (Main St, Town Hall, Brookline, NH 03033) 603-673-8855 x218, fax-603-673-8136; 8AM-2PM M-F, 5-8 PM W, 9AM-N last Sat.

Deering Town, 762 Deering Ctr Rd, Deering, NH 03244, 603-464-3224, fax-603-464-3804; 8:30PM-3PM M; 8:30AM-5PM W; 3PM-7PM Th **Online-** Access assessor property card data by subscription at www.avitarofneinc.com or call 603-798-4419. Annual subscription fee is $150 per Town.

Francestown Town, PO Box 67, Francestown, NH 03043-0067, (27 Main St) 603-547-6251, fax-603-547-2622; 8AM-N M-Th; 6-8PM M **Online-** Access assessor property card data by subscription at www.avitarofneinc.com or call 603-798-4419. Annual subscription fee is $150 per Town.

Goffstown Town, 16 Main St, Goffstown, NH 03045, 603-497-8990, fax-603-497-8993; 8:30AM-4:30PM M,T,F; 8:30AM-N W; 8:30AM-6PM Th

Greenfield Town, PO Box 256, Greenfield, NH 03047, (7 Sawmill Rd) 603-547-2782, fax-603-547-2782; 6-7:30PM Th; 9AM-N Th; 1st & 3rd Sat 9AM-Noon www.greenfield-nh.gov/Public_Documents/GreenfieldNH_Assessor/index **Online-** Access assessor property card data by subscription at www.avitarofneinc.com or call 603-798-4419. Annual subscription fee is $150 per Town.

Greenville Town, PO Box 354, Greenville, NH 03048-0354, (46 Main St) 603-878-4155, fax-603-878-4951; 10AM-Noon, 1PM-4PM T Th; 10AM-Noon, 1PM-3PM & 7PM-9PM W **Online-** Access assessor property card data by subscription at www.avitarofneinc.com or call 603-798-4419. Annual subscription fee is $150 per Town.

Hancock Town, PO Box 6, Hancock, NH 03449, (50 Main St) 603-525-4441, fax-603-525-4427; 9AM-4PM

Hillsborough Town, PO Box 1699, Hillsborough, NH 03244, (29 School St) 603-464-3877 x224, fax-603-464-4270; 9AM-4:45PM A public access terminal is available. www.town.hillsborough.nh.us/ **Online-** Access assessor data and property cards by subscription from private company at www.avitarofneinc.com/online.html.

Hollis Town, 7 Monument Sq, Hollis, NH 03049-6568, (3G Marketplace) 603-465-2064, fax-603-465-2964; 8AM-1PM M-W-F ; Mon Eve. 7-9PM; 1st Sat. 8-11AM **Online-** Access assessor data free at http://data.visionappraisal.com/HollisNH/.

Hudson Town, 12 School St, Hudson, NH 03051-4294, 603-886-6003, fax-603-598-6481; 8:30AM-4:30PM A public access terminal is available. www.ci.hudson.nh.us/ **Online-** Access property data free at http://hudsonnh.patriotproperties.com.

Litchfield Town, 2 Liberty Way, #3, Litchfield, NH 03052, 603-424-4045, fax-603-424-8154; 10AM-6PM, M; 7:30AM-3PM, T-F **Online-** Access assessor property card data by subscription at www.avitarofneinc.com or call 603-798-4419. Annual subscription fee is $150 per Town.

Lyndeborough Town, PO Box 6, Lyndeborough, NH 03082, (9 Citizens Hall Rd, Clerk's Office, Lyndeborough, NH 03082) 603-654-9653 x2, fax-603-654-5777; 8AM-1PM, 2-7PM M; 8AM-1PM T; 8AM-4PM W,Th www.lyndeboroughnh.us/

Manchester City, One City Hall Plaza, Manchester, NH 03101, 603-624-6455, fax-603-624-6481; 8AM-5PM www.manchesternh.gov/website/ **Online-** Search Property data on GIS-mapping site free at http://216.204.202.123/pubgis/default.htm but no name searching. Also, Tax Collector accounts at http://216.204.202.85/Click2GovTX/entry.html but no name searching. Also, city assessor database free at http://data.visionappraisal.com/ManchesterNH/.

Mason Town, 16 Darling Hill Rd, Mason, NH 03048-4717, 603-878-3768, fax-603-878-4892; 1-4PM T; 6:30-8PM W; 9AM-N Th; 10-N last Sat.

Milford Town, 1 Union Sq, Milford, NH 03055, 603-673-3514, 673-3403, fax-603-673-2273; 8AM-3PM A public access terminal is available. **Online-** Search town assessor database free at http://data.visionappraisal.com/MilfordNH/.

Mont Vernon Town, PO Box 417, Mont Vernon, NH 03057, (2 Main St, McCollom Bldg, Clerk's Office) 603-673-9126, fax-603-673-0914; 5-8PM M & W; 9AM-N T & Th

Nashua City, PO Box 2019, Nashua, NH 03061, (229 Main St) 603-589-3010, fax-603-589-3029; 8AM-5PM **Online-** Search City Assessor database of property, GIS-mapping, sales histories for free at www.ci.nashua.nh.us/CityGovernment/Departments/Assessing/tabid/440/Default.aspx

New Boston Town, PO Box 250, New Boston, NH 03070-0250, (7 Meeting House Hill) 603-487-5504 x106, fax-603-487-2975; 9AM-4PM M,W,F; 4PM-8PM TH A public access terminal is available. http://www2.new-boston.nh.us/ **Online-** Access assessor property card data by subscription at www.avitarofneinc.com or call 603-798-4419. Annual subscription fee is $150 per Town. This data is accessible free through the town website.

New Ipswich Town, 661 Turnpike Rd, New Ipswich, NH 03071, 603-878-3567, fax-603-878-3855; 9AM-12:30, 1:30-4PM M,W,Th; 1-7PM Tues www.townofnewipswich.org/boa/index.asp **Online-** Access assessor property card data by subscription at www.avitarofneinc.com or call 603-798-4419. Annual subscription fee is $150 per Town.

Pelham Town, 6 Village Green, Pelham, NH 03076, 603-635-2040, fax-603-508-3096; 8AM-4PM M,W,Th.,F; 8AM-7PM Tu. **Online-** Search town assessor database at http://data.visionappraisal.com/PelhamNH/.

Peterborough Town, 1 Grove St, Peterborough, NH 03458, 603-924-8000 x105, fax-603-924-8001; 8AM-4:15 M-F; 5-7PM Th.

Sharon Town, 432 Rte 123, Sharon, NH 03458, 603-924-9250, fax-same; 6-8PM T **Online-** Access assessor property card data by subscription at www.avitarofneinc.com or call 603-798-4419. Annual subscription fee is $150 per Town.

Temple Town, Box 69, Temple, NH 03084, (423 NH Rte 45) 603-878-3873, fax-603-878-5067; 9AM-2PM- T,W,Th. **Online-** Access assessor property card data by subscription at www.avitarofneinc.com or call 603-798-4419. Annual subscription fee is $150 per Town.

Weare Town, PO Box 190, Weare, NH 03281-0190, (15 Flanders Memorial Dr, Town Office Bldg, Weare, NH 03281) 603-529-7575, fax-603-529-7571; 8AM-4PM M, T, Th, F; 8AM-7PM W

Wilton Town, PO Box 83, Wilton, NH 03086, (42 Main St) 603-654-9451, fax-603-654-6663; 9AM-4PM,M,T,F; 9-7PM Th; closed Wed

Windsor Town, 14 White Pond Rd, Windsor, NH 03244, 603-478-3292, fax-603-478-3293; 3:30PM-7PM Wed; 9-11AM last Sat. **Online-** Access assessor property card data by subscription at www.avitarofneinc.com or call 603-798-4419. Annual subscription fee is $150 per Town.

Merrimack County

Register of Deeds, PO Box 248, Concord, NH 03302-0248. Recording, R/E phone-603-228-0101, UCC recording phone-603-271-3242; fax-603-226-0868; 8AM-4PM www.merrimackcounty.nh.us.landata.com
Index: All in one. Records indexed on a public use terminal back to 1920. Only the public may search. Copy fee $1.00 per page. Plans copies are $7.00. Cert fee- $2.00 per doc plus copy fee. Payee- Register of Deeds. **Online access to Real Estate, Grantor/Grantee, Deed records:** Access records on the county Registry of Deeds index for free after registration; images require subscription at www.merrimackcounty.nh.us.landata.com. Indexes are 1920-present, document images, 1945-present. **Other phones:** Treasurer- 603-228-0331.

Allenstown Town, 16 School St, Allenstown, NH 03275, 603-485-4276, fax-603-485-8669; 8:30AM-1PM & 3-7PM Mon; T/W 8:30-1 & 3-5; Th 8:30-3; No F. No public access terminal.

Andover Town, PO Box 61, Andover, NH 03216, (31 School St) 603-735-5332, fax-603-735-6975; 10AM-1PM T Th, 6:30PM-8:30PM W, 9AM-N Sat **Online-** Access assessor property card data by subscription at www.avitarofneinc.com or call 603-798-4419. Annual subscription fee is $150 per Town.

Boscawen Town, 116 N Main St, Boscawen, NH 03303, 603-753-9188, fax-603-753-9184; 8-11AM, 12-4:30 M,Th; T & W 8-11AM; 12-6:30PM Public access computer in office. **Online-** Access assessor property card data by subscription at www.avitarofneinc.com or call 603-798-4419. Annual subscription fee is $150 for 1st Town, $50.00 for each add'l town, or $500 for all 70+ Towns.

Bow Town, 10 Grandview Rd, Bow, NH 03304-3410, 603-225-2683, fax-603-225-5428; 7:30AM-4PM **Online-** Records on the town assessor database are free at http://data.visionappraisal.com/BowNH/. Registration required to view full data. Property data available free at www.mapsonline.net/bownh/

Bradford Town, PO Box 607, Bradford, NH 03221-0607, (75 Main St, Town Hall, Bradford, NH 03221) 603-938-2288, fax-603-938-5694; Noon-7PM Mon.; 7AM-5PM Tues; 8AM-5PM Fri. Public access computer in office. **Online-** Access assessor property card data by subscription at www.avitarofneinc.com or call 603-798-4419. Annual subscription fee is $150 per Town.

Canterbury Town, PO Box 500, Canterbury, NH 03224, (10 Hackleboro Rd) 603-783-9955, fax-603-783-0501; 10AM-2PM M; 11AM-6PM T; 5-8:30PM Th **Online-** Access assessor property card data by subscription at www.avitarofneinc.com or call 603-798-4419. Annual sub fee is $150 per Town.

Chichester Town, 54 Main St, Chichester, NH 03258, 603-798-5808, fax-603-798-3170; 8:30AM-4PM M; 8:30AM-2PM T, also 4-7PM, 8:30-2PM W-Th **Online-** Access assessor property card data by subscription at www.avitarofneinc.com or call 603-798-4419. Annual sub fee $150 per Town.

Concord City, 41 Green St, Concord, NH 03301-4255, 603-225-8500, fax-603-225-8592; 8AM-4:30PM **Online-** Records on city assessor database free at http://data.visionappraisal.com/ConcordNH/.

Danbury Town, 23 High St, Danbury, NH 03230, 603-768-5448, fax-603-768-3100; 9AM-6PM M,T,TH; 1-6PM W; 3rd Sat 8-11AM

Dunbarton Town, 1011 School St, Dunbarton, NH 03045, 603-774-3547 x107, fax-603-774-5541; 7:30AM-3:30PM M,W; 11AM-7PM T,Th

Online- Search town assessor database at http://data.visionappraisal.com/DunbartonNH/.

Epsom Town, PO Box 10, Epsom, NH 03234, (27 Black Hall Rd) 603-736-4825, fax-603-736-8539; 8-1PM;4:30-6:30PM, M;10-3PM T; 8-3PM TH;8-3PM F www.epsomnh.org **Online-** Access assessor property card data by subscription at www.avitarofneinc.com or call 603-798-4419. Annual subscription fee is $150 per Town.

Franklin City, 316 Central St, Franklin, NH 03235, 603-934-3109, fax-603-934-7413; 8AM-4:30PM www.franklinnh.org

Henniker Town, 18 Depot Hill Rd, Henniker, NH 03242, 603-428-3240, fax-603-428-4366; 8AM-5:30PM M; 8AM-4:30PM T,W,F; closed Th www.henniker.org

Hill Town, PO Box 251, Hill, NH 03243, (30 Crescent St) 603-934-3951, fax-603-934-2174; 6-8:30PM Tues; 9AM-1PM W; 9AM-5PM Th-F

Hooksett Town, 16 Main St, Hooksett, NH 03106, 603-485-9534, fax-603-485-4423; 8AM-4:30PM; 8AM-6:30PM W

Hopkinton Town, PO Box 446, Contoocook, NH 03229-0446, (846 Main St) 603-746-3180, fax-603-746-4011; 8AM-4:30PM. No public terminal. www.hopkinton-nh.gov/Pages/HopkintonNH_Assessor/index

Loudon Town, PO Box 7837, Loudon, NH 03301, (29 S Village Rd) 603-798-4542, fax-603-798-3539; 8AM-2PM Mon; 3-9PM Tues; 9AM-4PM Wed **Online-** Access assessor property card data by subscription at www.avitarofneinc.com or call 603-798-4419. Annual sub fee is $150 per Town.

Merrimack Town, 6 Baboosic Lk Rd, Merrimack, NH 03054, 603-424-3651, fax-603-424-0461; 8:30AM-4:30PM **Online-** Access assessor property data free at http://merrimacknh.patriotproperties.com/default.asp.

New London Town, 375 Main St, New London, NH 03257-0314, 603-526-4046, fax-603-526-9494; 8AM-4PM A public terminal is available. www.nl-nh.com/ **Online-** Search assessor data at http://data.visionappraisal.com/NEWLONDONNH/.

Newbury Town, PO Box 253, Newbury, NH 03255, (#937 Rte 103, Old Newbury School, Newbury, NH 03255) 603-763-5326, fax-603-763-5298; 1-7PM Mon; 8AM-N, 1-4PM T-F www.newburynh.org/Public_Documents/NewburyNH_Assessor **Online-** Access property assessor data at http://data.visionappraisal.com/NewburyNH/DEFAULT.asp.

Northfield Town, 21 Summer St, Northfield, NH 03276, 603-286-4482, fax-603-286-3328; 8:30AM-5PM, 8:30AM-7PM Tues; 8:30-12:30 Weds **Online-** Access assessor property card data by subscription at www.avitarofneinc.com or call 603-798-4419. Annual subscription fee is $150 per Town.

Pembroke Town, 311 Pembroke St, Pembroke, NH 03275, 603-485-4747, fax-603-485-3967; 8AM-4PM, Wed 5-7PM **Online-** Assessor data free at http://data.visionappraisal.com/PembrokeNH/.

Pittsfield Town, Box 98, Pittsfield, NH 03263-0098, (85 Main St) 603-435-6773, fax-603-435-7922; 11AM-7PM M; 8AM-4PM T,W,TH,F

Salisbury Town, Box 180, Salisbury, NH 03268-0180, (70 Franklin Rd) 603-648-2473, fax-603-648-6658; 8:30AM-N, 4:30-8:30PM T; 1-4PM W

Sutton Town, PO Box 487, North Sutton, NH 03260-0487, (93 Main St) 603-927-4575, fax-603-927-4631; Noon-6PM M; 8AM-N T; 8AM-4PM W-Th; 9AM-N last Sat

Warner Town, PO Box 265, Warner, NH 03278-0265, (Main St) 603-456-3362 x2, fax-603-456-3576; 8AM-3PM M-TH; 5-7PM T; Closed F

Webster Town, 945 Battle St, Rte 127, Webster, NH 03303, 603-648-2538, fax-603-648-6055; 9AM-N, 1-4PM M, W; 6-8PM Mon

Wilmot Town, PO Box 94, Wilmot, NH 03287, (9 Kearsarge Valley Rd, Town Clerk's Office) 603-526-9639, fax-603-526-2523; 8:30AM-1:30PM T,Th; 4-7PM W, 8AM-N 1st & last Sat.

Rockingham County

Register of Deeds, PO Box 896, Kingston, NH 03848. 603-642-5526; fax-603-642-8548/642-5930; 8AM-4PM. www.nhdeeds.com/rock/web/RoHome.html For Assessor data, contact Tax Assessor for each town within county. Index: All in one. Records indexed on a public use terminal back to 1980s; older records go back to 1643. Only the public may search. Copy fee $1.00 per page; Plans- $1.50 per sheet. Cert fee- $1.00 per page plus copy fee. Payee-Rockingham County Recorder of Deeds. **Online access to Real Estate, Grantor/Grantee, Deed, Lien records:** Access to the register of deeds database is free at www.nhdeeds.com/rock/web/RoHome.html. Index goes back to 1980; search by book and page numbers. **Property tax/Assessing-** Lower Level, Town Hall, Selectmen's Office, Kingston, NH 03848; 603-642-3342 x105, assessor fax- 603-642-4108. hours- 9AM-4PM M,T,TH,F www.kingstonnh.org/departments/Assesors/index.htm

Atkinson Town, 21 Academy Ave, Town Hall, Atkinson, NH 03811-2204, 603-362-4920, fax-603-362-5305; 8:30AM-6:30PM M; 8:30AM-4PM T-F Public access computer in office. **Online-** Access town property values for free at www.town-atkinsonnh.com/values.htm. Also, access assessor property card data by subscription at www.avitarofneinc.com or call 603-798-4419. Annual subscription fee is $150 for 1st Town, $50.00 for each add'l town, or $500 for all 70+ Towns.

Auburn Town, PO Box 309, Auburn, NH 03032-0309, (47 Chester Rd, Town Hall, Auburn, NH 03032) 603-483-2281 (1), fax-603-483-0518; 8AM-2PM, M,W,TH; 8AM-12PM, F; 6PM-8PM, M Evening **Online-** Access assessor property card data by subscription at www.avitarofneinc.com or call 603-798-4419. Annual sub fee is $150 per Town.

Brentwood Town, 1 Dalton Rd, Brentwood, NH 03833, 603-642-6400 x14, fax-603-642-6310; 9AM-4:30PM M-F; 7-9PM T; 9AM-N Sat Sept-May Public access computer in office.

Candia Town, 74 High St, Town Hall, Candia, NH 03034-2713, 603-483-5573, fax-603-483-0252; 8:30AM-11AM Mon; 5PM-8PM T,TH; 9AM-1PM W,F. A public access terminal is in the office. www.candianh.org/taxcollector.php **Online-** data at http://data.visionappraisal.com/CandiaNH/. Free registration for full data.

Chester Town, 84 Chester St, Chester, NH 03036, 603-887-3636, fax-603-887-4334; 8AM-12:30PM M,T,TH,F; 8AM-4PM Wed. **Online-** assessor data free at http://data.visionappraisal.com/ChesterNH/.

Danville Town, PO Box 11, Danville, NH 03819, (210 Main St) 603-382-8253, fax-603-382-3363; 8AM-1PM M; 3-8PM T&Th; 8AM-2:30PM W

Deerfield Town, PO Box 159, Deerfield, NH 03037, (8 Raymond Rd) 603-463-8811, fax-603-463-2820; 8AM-2:30PM T-F; 8AM-7PM M **Online-** Access assessor property card data by subscription at www.avitarofneinc.com or call 603-798-4419. Annual subscription fee is $150 per Town, but search is free.

Derry Town, 14 Manning St, Derry, NH 03038, 603-432-6105, fax-603-432-8176; 7AM-4PM M-F; 10AM-7PM W **Online-** assessor database free at http://data.visionappraisal.com/DerryNH/.

East Kingston Town, PO Box 249, East Kingston, NH 03827-0249, (24 Depot Rd) 603-642-8794, fax-same; 8AM-2:30PM M, T, Th, F; open again 6-8PM M, closed W **Online-** Access assessor property card data by subscription at www.avitarofneinc.com or call 603-798-4419. Annual subscription fee is $150 per Town.

Epping Town, 157 Main St, Epping, NH 03042, 603-679-8288, fax-603-679-3002; Noon-8PM M; 9AM-6PM W; 9AM-3PM F www.ci.epping.nh.us/ **Online-** Search the assessor database at http://data.visionappraisal.com/EppingNH/.

Exeter Town, 10 Front St, Exeter, NH 03833-2792, 603-778-0591, fax-603-772-4709; 8:30AM-3:30PM **Online-** Access assessor property data free at www.visionappraisal.com/databases/.

Fremont Town, PO Box 120, Fremont, NH 03044, (295 Main St) 603-895-8693, fax-603-895-3149; 8:30AM-N M,F; 8:30AM-4PM T,W; 11AM-8PM Th A public access terminal is available. **Online-** Search town assessor database at http://data.visionappraisal.com/FremontNH/.

Greenland Town, PO Box 100, Greenland, NH 03840-0100, (575 Portsmouth Ave) 603-431-7111, fax-603-430-3761; 9AM-4:30PM; closed Thursday in July/Aug **Online-** Access at http://data.visionappraisal.com/GreenlandNH/. Free registration is required to view full data.

Hampstead Town, PO Box 298, Hampstead, NH 03841, (11 Main St, Town Office Bldg) 603-329-4100, fax-603-329-7174; 8AM-7PM, M; 8AM-4PM, T,W,TH; 8AM-12PM F ri.

Hampton Falls Town, 1 Drinkwater Rd, Town Hall, Hampton Falls, NH 03844, 603-926-4618; 9AM-N, 1-4PM M,T,Th

Hampton Town, 100 Winnacunnet Rd, Hampton, NH 03842, 603-926-0406, fax-603-929-5917; 9AM-4:30PM **Online-** assessor database free at www.town.hampton.nh.us/assessing/Assessing_database.html.

Kensington Town, 95 Amesbury Rd, Rte 150, Town Hall, Kensington, NH 03833, 603-772-5423, fax-603-772-6841; 8:30AM-N M,T,TH; 6-8PM T-W

Kingston Town, PO Box 657, Kingston, NH 03848-0657, (163 Main St) 603-642-3112, fax-603-642-3204; 8:30AM-N 1-4 M-F; 7-9PM M, T

Londonderry Town, 268B Mammoth Rd, Londonderry, NH 03053, 603-432-1100 x195, fax-603-421-9617; 8:30AM-5PM A public access terminal available. **Online-** property data free at http://londonderrynh.patriotproperties.com/default.asp

New Castle Town, PO Box 367, New Castle, NH 03854-0367, (49 Main St., Town Hall, New Castle, NH 03854) 603-431-6710, fax-603-433-6198; 9AM-1PM M W; 11AM-3PM Th **Online-** Access assessor property card data by subscription at www.avitarofneinc.com or call 603-798-4419. Annual subscription fee is $150 per Town.

Newfields Town, 65 Main St, Newfields, NH 03856-0300, 603-772-5070, fax-603-772-9004; 8:30AM-2:30PM

Newington Town, 205 Nimble Hill Rd, Town Offices, Newington, NH 03801, 603-436-7640 x14, fax-603-436-7188; 10AM-3PM T,W,Th; closed M,F

Newmarket Town, 186 Main St, Town Hall, Newmarket, NH 03857, 603-659-3073, fax-603-659-3441; 7-7 M; 8-4:30PM T,W,Th; 8AM-N F www.newmarketnh.gov/content/view/155/262/ **Online-** Access is free via a private company at http://data.visionappraisal.com/NewmarketNH/DEFAULT.asp.

Newton Town, PO Box 375, Newton, NH 03858-0375, (2 Town Hall Rd, Town Hall, Newton, NH 03858) 603-382-4096, fax-603-382-2596; 8AM-4PM M-W; Noon-8PM Th A public access terminal is available. **Online-** Access assessor property card data by subscription at www.avitarofneinc.com or call 603-798-4419. Annual sub fee is $150 per Town.

North Hampton Town, PO Box 141, North Hampton, NH 03862-0141, (237 Atlantic Ave) 603-964-6029, fax-603-964-2906; 8:30AM-7PM M; 8:30-3PM T-F A public access terminal is available. **Online-** Access to property assessor data is at http://data.visionappraisal.com/NorthHamptonNH/.

Northwood Town, 818 1st NH Turnpike, Northwood, NH 03261-0314, 603-942-5586 x201, fax-603-942-9107; 8AM-10AM 4PM-7PM M; 8AM-4PM T-F; 9AM-N Last Sat **Online-** Access assessor property card data by subscription at www.avitarofneinc.com or call 603-798-4419. Annual subscription fee is $150 per Town.

Nottingham Town, PO Box 114, Nottingham, NH 03290, (139 Stage Rd, Town Hall, Nottingham, NH 03290) 603-679-9598, fax-603-679-9598; 3-7PM M,W; 1-5PM T; 9AM-1PM Th Last Sat of Month **Online-** Access assessor property card data by subscription at www.avitarofneinc.com or call 603-798-4419. Annual subscription fee is $150 per Town.

Plaistow Town, 145 Main St, #2, Town Hall, Plaistow, NH 03865, 603-382-8129, fax-603-382-0006; 8AM-7PM M, 8AM-4:30PM T-TH; 7AM-N

Fri. **Online-** Property owner list free at www.plaistow.com/Pages/PlaistowNH_Assessor/index and click on Current Year Property Owner List. Mapping and property interface being developed; www.plaistow.com/Pages/PlaistowNH_WebDocs/maps.

Portsmouth City, 1 Junkins Ave, Portsmouth, NH 03801, 603-610-7207, fax-603-427-1579; 8AM-4:30PM **Online-** Search the Portsmouth Assessed Property Values database free at www.portsmouthnh.com/realestate//

Raymond Town, 4 Epping St, Town Office Bldg, Raymond, NH 03077, 603-895-4735 x110, fax-603-895-0903; 8AM-7PM M; 8AM-4:30PM T-F **Online-** Search the town assessor database at http://data.visionappraisal.com/RaymondNH/.

Rye Town, 10 Central Rd, Rye, NH 03870, 603-964-8562, fax-603-964-4132; 8AM-4:30PM **Online-** Access is via a private company at http://data.visionappraisal.com/RyeNH/DEFAULT.asp. Free registration is required to view full data.

Salem Town, 33 Geremonty Dr, Municipal Bldg, Salem, NH 03079-3390, 603-890-2110, fax-603-898-1223; 8:30AM-5PM **Online-** Records from the town database are free at http://data.visionappraisal.com/SalemNH/.

Sandown Town, 320 Main St, Town Hall, PO Box 583, Sandown, NH 03873-2627, 603-887-4870, fax-603-887-5163; 8-12PM/2-8PM Mon; T-Th 8-12PM/12:30-3PM; F 8-12PM

Seabrook Town, PO Box 476, Seabrook, NH 03874, (99 Lafayette Rd) 603-474-3152, fax-603-474-8007; 9AM-4PM

South Hampton Town, 3 Hilldale Ave, South Hampton, NH 03827, (190 Hilldale) 603-394-7696, fax-603-394-7696; 7-8:30PM M,T; 12:30-2PM W; 9:30-11:30AM F

Stratham Town, 10 Bunker Hill Ave, Stratham, NH 03885, 603-772-4741, fax-603-775-0517; 8:30AM-4PM **Online-** Access assessor property card data by subscription at www.avitarofneinc.com or call 603-798-4419. Annual sub fee is $150 per Town.

Windham Town, PO Box 120, Windham, NH 03087, (3 N Lowell Rd) 603-434-5075, fax-603-425-6582; 8AM-7PM M, 8AM-4PM T W Th F **Online-** Access lists of parcels and sales data free at http://windhamnewhampshire.com/depts/assess(3).htm.

Strafford County

Register of Deeds, PO Box 799, Dover, NH 03821-0799. 603-742-1741; fax-603-749-5130; 8:30AM-4:30PM www.nhdeeds.com/stfd/web/start.htm

Index: Separate indices to search include grantor/grantee. Records indexed on a public use terminal back to 1970. Only the public may search. Copy fee $1.00 per page. Cert fee- $1.00 per cert plus copy fee. Payee- Strafford County Registry of Deeds. **Online access to Real Estate, Grantor/Grantee, Deed, Mortgage, Lien records:** Access to county register of deeds data is free at www.nhdeeds.com/stfd/web/agree3.htm. Online records go back to 1931. **Other phones:** Treasurer-603-742-1458. **Property tax/Assessing-** 603-743-6014.

Barrington Town, 41 Province Ln, Barrington, NH 03825, 603-664-5476, fax-603-664-0177; 8AM-4:15PM M T; 4-6PM W; 8AM-4:15PM Th; 8AM-Noon F No public access computer in office. **Online-** Search by address, owner name, parcel number, parcel ID, or distance for property data free at www.mapsonline.net/barringtonnh/

Dover City, 288 Central Ave, City Hall, Dover, NH 03820, 603-743-6021, fax-603-516-6666; 8AM-4PM; Till 6PM Wed

Durham Town, 15 Newmarket Rd, Town Hall, Durham, NH 03824-2898, 603-868-5577, fax-603-868-8033; 8AM-5PM www.ci.durham.nh.us/ (Click on Departments,click Assessor office.) **Online-** Search assessor data for free at http://data.visionappraisal.com/DurhamNH/.

Farmington Town, 356 Main St, Town Hall, Farmington, NH 03835, 603-755-3657, fax-603-755-9128; 8:30AM-5PM M-W, 8:30AM-7PM TH, 8:30AM-12:30 PM F www.farmington.nh.us/Public_Documents/FarmingtonNH_Assessing/index

Lee Town, 7 Mast Rd, Town Hall, Lee, NH 03824, 603-659-2964, fax-603-659-7202; 8AM-6PM Wed, Fri www.leenh.org **Online-** Access assessor property card data by subscription at www.avitarofneinc.com or call 603-798-4419. Annual subscription fee is $150 for 1st Town, $50.00 for each add'l town, or $500 for all 70+ Towns.

Madbury Town, 13 Town Hall Rd, Madbury, NH 03823, 603-742-5131, fax-603-742-2505; 8AM-1PM M W TH http://lefh.net/madbury/ **Online-** Assessor property card data by subscription at www.avitarofneinc.com or call 603-798-4419. Annual subscription fee is $150 for 1st Town, $50.00 for each add'l town, or $500 for all 70+ Towns.

Middleton Town, 182 Kings Hwy, Middleton Town Offices, Middleton, NH 03887, 603-473-2134, fax-603-473-2577; 8AM-7PM M T **Online-** Access assessor property card data by subscription at www.avitarofneinc.com or call 603-798-4419. Annual subscription fee is $150 for 1st Town, $50.00 for each add'l town, or $500 for all 70+ Towns.

Milton Town, PO Box 180, Milton, NH 03851-0180, (424 White Mountain Hwy, Town Office, Milton, NH 03851) 603-652-9414, fax-603-652-4120; 8AM-12:30PM 1:30-4:30PM MTF; 8AM-Noon 2PM-7PM Th **Online-** Access assessor property card data by subscription at www.avitarofneinc.com or call 603-798-4419. Annual subscription fee is $150 for 1st Town, $50.00 for each add'l town, or $500 for all 70+ Towns.

New Durham Town, PO Box 207, New Durham, NH 03855, (4 Main St) 603-859-2091, fax-603-859-6644; 9AM-4PM, **Online-** assessor data free at http://data.visionappraisal.com/NewDurhamNH/.

Rochester City, 31 Wakefield St, City Hall, Rochester, NH 03867-1917, 603-332-2130, fax-603-335-7565; 8AM-5PM **Online-** Access property data free at http://rochesternh.patriotproperties.com/default.asp.

Rollinsford Town, PO Box 309, Rollinsford, NH 03869, (667 Main St) 603-742-2510, fax-603-740-0254; 9AM-1PM M,T,W,F; 3-7PM Th **Online-** Access assessor property card data by subscription at www.avitarofneinc.com or call 603-798-4419. Annual subscription fee is $150 for 1st Town, $50.00 for each add'l town, or $500 for all 70+ Towns.

Somersworth City, 1 Government Way, Somersworth, NH 03878, 603-692-4262, fax-603-692-9574; 9AM-5PM M,W,F; 8AM-5PM T,Th

Strafford Town, PO Box 169, Strafford, NH 03884-0169, (22 Roller Coaster Rd) 603-664-2192 x14, fax-603-664-7276; 9AM-1PM, 4-7PM Mon; 9AM-2:30 T-Wed.; 9AM-N Th **Online-** property data at http://data.visionappraisal.com/StraffordNH/

Sullivan County

Register of Deeds, PO Box 448, Newport, NH 03773. Recording, R/E & UCC phone-603-863-2110; fax-603-863-0013; 8AM-3PM (copy request hrs-8AM-3:30PM).

Office will not research records for any reason. Records go back to 1827. In NH each town has their own assessors, tax collectors, etc. If you want tax information you must call the town in which the property is located. Index: Separate indices to search include grantor/grantee, Plan index. Records indexed on a public use terminal back to 1827. Only the public may search. Copy fee $1.00. per page. Plans and plats usually $7.00 (full size p/sheet). Cert fee- $2.00 per doc plus copy fee. Payee- Register of Deeds. **Online access to Real Estate, Grantor/Grantee, Deed, Lien records:** Access to the county Register of Deeds database is free at www.nhdeeds.com/slvn/web/agree7.htm.

Acworth Town, PO Box 37, Town Clerk, Acworth, NH 03601, (Town Hall) 603-835-6879, fax-603-835-7901; 6:30-8PM M-W; 9-11AM Sat **Online-** Access assessor property data free at http://data.visionappraisal.com/AcworthNH/DEFAULT.asp.

Charlestown Town, PO Box 834, Charlestown, NH 03603, (26 Railroad St) 603-826-5821, fax-603-826-5181; 8AM-1PM, 1:30-6PM M; 8AM-1PM, 1:30-4PM T-F No public access computer available. **Online-** Search town assessor database free at http://data.visionappraisal.com/CharlestownNH/.

Claremont City, 58 Opera House Sq, City Hall, Claremont, NH 03743, 603-542-7003, fax-603-542-7014; hours - 9AM-12:30PM, 1:30-5PM www.claremontnh.com/

Cornish Town, PO Box 183, Cornish Flat, NH 03746, (488 Townhouse Rd) 603-675-5207, fax-603-675-5605; 9AM-N M-Th; 4:30PM-7PM M-Th; Closed Fri

Croydon Town, 879 NH Rte 10, Croydon, NH 03773, 603-863-7830, fax-603-863-2601; 9AM-1PM M-Th; 5PM-7PM W & Th

Goshen Town, PO Box 58, Goshen, NH 03752, (54 Mill Village Rd N) 603-863-5655, fax-603-863-6139; 8:30AM-N, 1-5PM M,W,F; Last Sat of each month

Grantham Town, PO Box 135, Grantham, NH 03753-0135, (300 Rte 10 S) 603-863-5608, fax-603-863-4499; 7:30AM-4:30PM M-Th; 7-9PM T-W **Online-** Search town assessor database free at http://data.visionappraisal.com/GranthamNH/.

Langdon Town, 122 Rte 12A, Baker Bldg, Langdon, NH 03602, (112 Rte 12A, Baker Bldg, Langdon, NH 03602) 603-835-2389, fax-603-835-6055; 10AM-N, 3-6PM M

Lempster Town, PO Box 33, Lempster, NH 03605-0033, (856 US Rte 10) 603-863-3213, fax-603-863-8105; 8AM-1PM, 4-7PM M,W; 2-7PM Th; 8AM-1PM F; 8AM-N Sat **Online-** Access assessor property card data by subscription at www.avitarofneinc.com or call 603-798-4419. Annual subscription fee is $150 per Town.

Newport Town, 15 Sunapee St, Newport, NH 03773, 603-863-2224, fax-603-863-8008; 8AM-4:30PM A public access terminal is available. www.newportnh.net/ **Online-** Access assessor property card data by subscription at www.avitarofneinc.com.

Plainfield Town, Box 380, Town Clerk's Office, Meriden, NH 03770, (Town Clerk's Office) 603-469-3201, fax-603-469-3642; 8AM-4PM M-Th, closed F ri

Springfield Town, PO Box 22, Springfield, NH 03284, (759 Main St) 603-763-4805, fax-603-763-3336; 9AM-N 1-4PM M-W; till 8PM Th; closed Fri **Online-** Access assessor property card data by subscription at www.avitarofneinc.com or call 603-798-4419. Annual subscription fee is $150 per Town.

Sunapee Town, PO Box 303, Sunapee, NH 03782-0303, (23 Edgemont Rd) 603-763-2449 x18; 8AM-5PM M.T,Th,F; 8AM-1PM W; 8-N 2nd/4th Sat A public assess terminal is available. www.town.sunapee.nh.us/Pages/SunapeeNH_Assessing/index2 **Online-** property tax and parcel data free at http://data.visionappraisal.com/SunapeeNH/default.asp

Unity Town, 13 Center Rd, Unit 1, Unity, NH 03603, 603-542-9665, fax-603-542-9736; 9AM-5PM M-Tu; Wed 9AM-6PM; Th 8AM-N

Washington Town, 7 Halfmoon Pond Rd, Washington, NH 03280, 603-495-3667, fax-603-495-3299; 9AM-3PM F **Online-** Access assessor property card data by subscription at www.avitarofneinc.com or call 603-798-4419. Annual subscription fee is $150 per Town.

New Hampshire County Locator

You will usually be able to find the city name in the City/County Cross Reference below. In that case, it is a simple matter to determine the county from the cross reference. However, only the official US Postal Service city names are included in this index. There are an additional 40,000 place names that people use in their addresses. Therefore, we have also included a ZIP/City Cross Reference immediately following the City/County Cross Reference.

If you know the ZIP Code but the city name does not appear in the City/County Cross Reference index, look up the ZIP Code in the ZIP/City Cross Reference, find the city name, then look up the city name in the City/County Cross Reference.

New Hampshire City/County Cross Reference

ACWORTH Sullivan
ALSTEAD Cheshire
ALTON Belknap
ALTON BAY Belknap
AMHERST Hillsborough
ANDOVER Merrimack
ANTRIM Hillsborough
ASHLAND Grafton
ASHUELOT Cheshire
ATKINSON Rockingham
AUBURN Rockingham
BARNSTEAD (03218) Belknap(97), Strafford(2)
BARRINGTON Strafford
BARTLETT Carroll
BATH Grafton
BEDFORD Hillsborough
BELMONT (03220) Belknap(98), Merrimack(1)
BENNINGTON Hillsborough
BERLIN Coos
BETHLEHEM (03574) Grafton(98), Coos(1)
BOW Merrimack
BRADFORD Merrimack
BRETTON WOODS Coos
BRISTOL Grafton
BROOKLINE Hillsborough
CAMPTON Grafton
CANAAN Grafton
CANDIA Rockingham
CANTERBURY Merrimack
CENTER BARNSTEAD (03225) Belknap(97), Strafford(2)
CENTER CONWAY Carroll
CENTER HARBOR (03226) Belknap(76), Carroll(22)
CENTER OSSIPEE Carroll
CENTER SANDWICH Carroll
CENTER STRAFFORD Strafford
CENTER TUFTONBORO Carroll
CHARLESTOWN Sullivan
CHESTER Rockingham
CHESTERFIELD Cheshire
CHICHESTER Merrimack
CHOCORUA Carroll
CLAREMONT Sullivan
COLEBROOK Coos
CONCORD Merrimack
CONTOOCOOK Merrimack
CONWAY Carroll
CORNISH Sullivan
CORNISH FLAT Sullivan
DANBURY Merrimack
DANVILLE Rockingham
DEERFIELD Rockingham
DERRY Rockingham
DOVER Strafford
DREWSVILLE Cheshire
DUBLIN Cheshire
DUNBARTON Merrimack
DURHAM Strafford
EAST ANDOVER Merrimack
EAST CANDIA Rockingham
EAST DERRY Rockingham
EAST HAMPSTEAD Rockingham
EAST HEBRON Grafton
EAST KINGSTON Rockingham
EAST WAKEFIELD Carroll
EATON CENTER Carroll
ELKINS Merrimack
ENFIELD (03748) Grafton(95), Sullivan(4)
ENFIELD CENTER Grafton
EPPING Rockingham
EPSOM Merrimack
ERROL Coos
ETNA Grafton
EXETER Rockingham
FARMINGTON Strafford
FITZWILLIAM Cheshire
FRANCESTOWN Hillsborough
FRANCONIA Grafton
FRANKLIN Merrimack
FREEDOM Carroll
FREMONT Rockingham
GEORGES MILLS Sullivan
GILFORD Belknap
GILMANTON Belknap
GILMANTON IRON WORKS Belknap
GILSUM Cheshire
GLEN Carroll
GLENCLIFF Grafton
GOFFSTOWN Hillsborough
GORHAM Coos
GOSHEN Sullivan
GRAFTON Grafton
GRANTHAM Sullivan
GREENFIELD Hillsborough
GREENLAND Rockingham
GREENVILLE Hillsborough
GROVETON Coos
GUILD Sullivan
HAMPSTEAD Rockingham
HAMPTON Rockingham
HAMPTON FALLS Rockingham
HANCOCK Hillsborough
HANOVER Grafton
HARRISVILLE Cheshire
HAVERHILL Grafton
HEBRON Grafton
HENNIKER Merrimack
HILL Merrimack
HILLSBORO (03244) Hillsborough(98), Sullivan(1)
HINSDALE Cheshire
HOLDERNESS Grafton
HOLLIS Hillsborough
HOOKSETT Merrimack
HUDSON Hillsborough
INTERVALE Carroll
JACKSON Carroll
JAFFREY Cheshire
JEFFERSON Coos
KEARSARGE Carroll
KEENE Cheshire
KINGSTON Rockingham
LACONIA Belknap
LANCASTER Coos
LEBANON Grafton
LEMPSTER Sullivan
LINCOLN Grafton
LISBON Grafton
LITCHFIELD Hillsborough
LITTLETON Grafton
LOCHMERE Belknap
LONDONDERRY Rockingham
LOUDON Merrimack
LYME Grafton
LYME CENTER Grafton
LYNDEBOROUGH Hillsborough
MADBURY Strafford
MADISON Carroll
MANCHESTER Hillsborough
MARLBOROUGH Cheshire
MARLOW Cheshire
MEADOWS Coos
MELVIN VILLAGE Carroll
MEREDITH Belknap
MERIDEN Sullivan
MERRIMACK Hillsborough
MILAN Coos
MILFORD Hillsborough
MILTON Strafford
MILTON MILLS Strafford
MIRROR LAKE Carroll
MONROE Grafton
MONT VERNON Hillsborough
MOULTONBOROUGH Carroll
MOUNT SUNAPEE Merrimack
MOUNT WASHINGTON Coos
MUNSONVILLE Cheshire
NASHUA Hillsborough
NEW BOSTON Hillsborough
NEW CASTLE Rockingham
NEW DURHAM Strafford
NEW HAMPTON Belknap
NEW IPSWICH Hillsborough
NEW LONDON (03257) Merrimack(98), Sullivan(1)
NEWBURY Merrimack
NEWFIELDS Rockingham
NEWMARKET Rockingham
NEWPORT Sullivan
NEWTON Rockingham
NEWTON JUNCTION Rockingham
NORTH CONWAY Carroll
NORTH HAMPTON Rockingham
NORTH HAVERHILL Grafton
NORTH SALEM Rockingham
NORTH SANDWICH Carroll
NORTH STRATFORD Coos
NORTH SUTTON Merrimack
NORTH WALPOLE Cheshire
NORTH WOODSTOCK Grafton
NORTHWOOD Rockingham
NOTTINGHAM Rockingham
ORFORD Grafton
OSSIPEE Carroll
PELHAM Hillsborough
PETERBOROUGH (03458) Hillsborough(96), Cheshire(3)
PETERBOROUGH Hillsborough
PIERMONT Grafton
PIKE Grafton
PITTSBURG Coos
PITTSFIELD Merrimack
PLAINFIELD Sullivan
PLAISTOW Rockingham
PLYMOUTH Grafton
PORTSMOUTH Rockingham
RANDOLPH Coos
RAYMOND Rockingham
RINDGE Cheshire
ROCHESTER Strafford
ROLLINSFORD Strafford
RUMNEY Grafton
RYE Rockingham
RYE BEACH Rockingham
SALEM Rockingham
SALISBURY Merrimack
SANBORNTON Belknap
SANBORNVILLE Carroll
SANDOWN Rockingham
SEABROOK Rockingham
SILVER LAKE Carroll
SOMERSWORTH Strafford
SOUTH ACWORTH Sullivan
SOUTH EFFINGHAM Carroll
SOUTH NEWBURY Merrimack
SOUTH SUTTON Merrimack
SOUTH TAMWORTH Carroll
SPOFFORD Cheshire
SPRINGFIELD Sullivan
STINSON LAKE Grafton
STODDARD Cheshire
STRAFFORD Strafford
STRATHAM Rockingham
SUGAR HILL Grafton
SULLIVAN Cheshire
SUNAPEE Sullivan
SUNCOOK Merrimack
SWANZEY Cheshire
TAMWORTH Carroll
TEMPLE Hillsborough
TILTON (03276) Belknap(55), Merrimack(44)
TILTON Belknap
TROY Cheshire
TWIN MOUNTAIN Coos
UNION (03887) Strafford(70), Carroll(29)
WALPOLE Cheshire
WARNER Merrimack
WARREN Grafton
WASHINGTON Sullivan
WATERVILLE VALLEY Grafton
WEARE Hillsborough
WENTWORTH Grafton
WEST CHESTERFIELD Cheshire
WEST LEBANON Grafton
WEST NOTTINGHAM Rockingham
WEST OSSIPEE Carroll
WEST PETERBOROUGH Hillsborough
WEST STEWARTSTOWN Coos
WEST SWANZEY Cheshire
WESTMORELAND Cheshire
WHITEFIELD Coos
WILMOT Merrimack
WILTON Hillsborough
WINCHESTER Cheshire
WINDHAM Rockingham
WINNISQUAM Belknap
WOLFEBORO Carroll
WOLFEBORO FALLS Carroll
WONALANCET Carroll
WOODSTOCK Grafton
WOODSVILLE Grafton

New Hampshire ZIP/City Cross Reference

00210-00215	PORTSMOUTH
03031-03031	AMHERST
03032-03032	AUBURN
03033-03033	BROOKLINE
03034-03034	CANDIA
03036-03036	CHESTER
03037-03037	DEERFIELD
03038-03038	DERRY
03040-03040	EAST CANDIA
03041-03041	EAST DERRY
03042-03042	EPPING
03043-03043	FRANCESTOWN
03044-03044	FREMONT
03045-03045	GOFFSTOWN
03046-03046	DUNBARTON
03047-03047	GREENFIELD
03048-03048	GREENVILLE
03049-03049	HOLLIS
03051-03051	HUDSON
03052-03052	LITCHFIELD
03053-03053	LONDONDERRY
03054-03054	MERRIMACK
03055-03055	MILFORD
03057-03057	MONT VERNON
03060-03064	NASHUA
03070-03070	NEW BOSTON
03071-03071	NEW IPSWICH
03073-03073	NORTH SALEM
03076-03076	PELHAM
03077-03077	RAYMOND
03079-03079	SALEM
03082-03082	LYNDEBOROUGH
03084-03084	TEMPLE
03086-03086	WILTON
03087-03087	WINDHAM
03100-03105	MANCHESTER
03106-03106	HOOKSETT
03107-03109	MANCHESTER
03110-03110	BEDFORD
03111-03111	MANCHESTER
03215-03215	WATERVILLE VALLEY
03216-03216	ANDOVER
03217-03217	ASHLAND
03218-03218	BARNSTEAD
03220-03220	BELMONT
03221-03221	BRADFORD
03222-03222	BRISTOL
03223-03223	CAMPTON
03224-03224	CANTERBURY
03225-03225	CENTER BARNSTEAD
03226-03226	CENTER HARBOR
03227-03227	CENTER SANDWICH
03229-03229	CONTOOCOOK
03230-03230	DANBURY
03231-03231	EAST ANDOVER
03232-03232	EAST HEBRON
03233-03233	ELKINS
03234-03234	EPSOM
03235-03235	FRANKLIN
03237-03237	GILMANTON
03238-03238	GLENCLIFF
03240-03240	GRAFTON
03241-03241	HEBRON
03242-03242	HENNIKER
03243-03243	HILL
03244-03244	HILLSBORO
03245-03245	HOLDERNESS
03246-03247	LACONIA
03249-03249	GILFORD
03251-03251	LINCOLN
03252-03252	LOCHMERE
03253-03253	MEREDITH
03254-03254	MOULTONBOROUGH
03255-03255	NEWBURY
03256-03256	NEW HAMPTON
03257-03257	NEW LONDON
03258-03258	CHICHESTER
03259-03259	NORTH SANDWICH
03260-03260	NORTH SUTTON
03261-03261	NORTHWOOD
03262-03262	NORTH WOODSTOCK
03263-03263	PITTSFIELD
03264-03264	PLYMOUTH
03265-03265	ANDOVER
03266-03266	RUMNEY
03268-03268	SALISBURY
03269-03269	SANBORNTON
03272-03272	SOUTH NEWBURY
03273-03273	SOUTH SUTTON
03274-03274	STINSON LAKE
03275-03275	SUNCOOK
03276-03276	TILTON
03278-03278	WARNER
03279-03279	WARREN
03280-03280	WASHINGTON
03281-03281	WEARE
03282-03282	WENTWORTH
03284-03284	SPRINGFIELD
03285-03285	CAMPTON
03287-03287	WILMOT
03289-03289	WINNISQUAM
03290-03290	NOTTINGHAM
03291-03291	WEST NOTTINGHAM
03293-03293	WOODSTOCK
03298-03299	TILTON
03300-03303	CONCORD
03304-03304	BOW
03305-03306	CONCORD
03307-03307	LOUDON
03431-03435	KEENE
03440-03440	ANTRIM
03441-03441	ASHUELOT
03442-03442	BENNINGTON
03443-03443	CHESTERFIELD
03444-03444	DUBLIN
03445-03445	SULLIVAN
03446-03446	SWANZEY
03447-03447	FITZWILLIAM
03448-03448	GILSUM
03449-03449	HANCOCK
03450-03450	HARRISVILLE
03451-03451	HINSDALE
03452-03452	JAFFREY
03455-03455	MARLBOROUGH
03456-03456	MARLOW
03457-03457	MUNSONVILLE
03458-03460	PETERBOROUGH
03461-03461	RINDGE
03462-03462	SPOFFORD
03464-03464	STODDARD
03465-03465	TROY
03466-03466	WEST CHESTERFIELD
03467-03467	WESTMORELAND
03468-03468	WEST PETERBOROUGH
03469-03469	WEST SWANZEY
03470-03470	WINCHESTER
03561-03561	LITTLETON
03570-03570	BERLIN
03574-03574	BETHLEHEM
03575-03575	BRETTON WOODS
03576-03576	COLEBROOK
03579-03579	ERROL
03580-03580	FRANCONIA
03581-03581	GORHAM
03582-03582	GROVETON
03583-03583	JEFFERSON
03584-03584	LANCASTER
03585-03585	LISBON
03586-03586	SUGAR HILL
03587-03587	MEADOWS
03588-03588	MILAN
03589-03589	MOUNT WASHINGTON
03590-03590	NORTH STRATFORD
03592-03592	PITTSBURG
03593-03593	RANDOLPH
03595-03595	TWIN MOUNTAIN
03597-03597	WEST STEWARTSTOWN
03598-03598	WHITEFIELD
03601-03601	ACWORTH
03602-03602	ALSTEAD
03603-03603	CHARLESTOWN
03604-03604	DREWSVILLE
03605-03606	LEMPSTER
03607-03607	SOUTH ACWORTH
03608-03608	WALPOLE
03609-03609	NORTH WALPOLE
03740-03740	BATH
03741-03741	CANAAN
03743-03743	CLAREMONT
03745-03745	CORNISH
03746-03746	CORNISH FLAT
03748-03748	ENFIELD
03749-03749	ENFIELD CENTER
03750-03750	ETNA
03751-03751	GEORGES MILLS
03752-03752	GOSHEN
03753-03753	GRANTHAM
03754-03754	GUILD
03755-03755	HANOVER
03756-03756	LEBANON
03765-03765	HAVERHILL
03766-03766	LEBANON
03768-03768	LYME
03769-03769	LYME CENTER
03770-03770	MERIDEN
03771-03771	MONROE
03772-03772	MOUNT SUNAPEE
03773-03773	NEWPORT
03774-03774	NORTH HAVERHILL
03777-03777	ORFORD
03779-03779	PIERMONT
03780-03780	PIKE
03781-03781	PLAINFIELD
03782-03782	SUNAPEE
03784-03784	WEST LEBANON
03785-03785	WOODSVILLE
03801-03804	PORTSMOUTH
03805-03805	ROLLINSFORD
03809-03809	ALTON
03810-03810	ALTON BAY
03811-03811	ATKINSON
03812-03812	BARTLETT
03813-03813	CENTER CONWAY
03814-03814	CENTER OSSIPEE
03815-03815	CENTER STRAFFORD
03816-03816	CENTER TUFTONBORO
03817-03817	CHOCORUA
03818-03818	CONWAY
03819-03819	DANVILLE
03820-03822	DOVER
03823-03823	MADBURY
03824-03824	DURHAM
03825-03825	BARRINGTON
03826-03826	EAST HAMPSTEAD
03827-03827	EAST KINGSTON
03830-03830	EAST WAKEFIELD
03832-03832	EATON CENTER
03833-03833	EXETER
03835-03835	FARMINGTON
03836-03836	FREEDOM
03837-03837	GILMANTON IRON WORKS
03838-03838	GLEN
03839-03839	ROCHESTER
03840-03840	GREENLAND
03841-03841	HAMPSTEAD
03842-03843	HAMPTON
03844-03844	HAMPTON FALLS
03845-03845	INTERVALE
03846-03846	JACKSON
03847-03847	KEARSARGE
03848-03848	KINGSTON
03849-03849	MADISON
03850-03850	MELVIN VILLAGE
03851-03851	MILTON
03852-03852	MILTON MILLS
03853-03853	MIRROR LAKE
03854-03854	NEW CASTLE
03855-03855	NEW DURHAM
03856-03856	NEWFIELDS
03857-03857	NEWMARKET
03858-03858	NEWTON
03859-03859	NEWTON JUNCTION
03860-03860	NORTH CONWAY
03862-03862	NORTH HAMPTON
03864-03864	OSSIPEE
03865-03865	PLAISTOW
03866-03868	ROCHESTER
03869-03869	ROLLINSFORD
03870-03870	RYE
03871-03871	RYE BEACH
03872-03872	SANBORNVILLE
03873-03873	SANDOWN
03874-03874	SEABROOK
03875-03875	SILVER LAKE
03878-03878	SOMERSWORTH
03882-03882	SOUTH EFFINGHAM
03883-03883	SOUTH TAMWORTH
03884-03884	STRAFFORD
03885-03885	STRATHAM
03886-03886	TAMWORTH
03887-03887	UNION
03890-03890	WEST OSSIPEE
03894-03894	WOLFEBORO
03896-03896	WOLFEBORO FALLS
03897-03897	WONALANCET

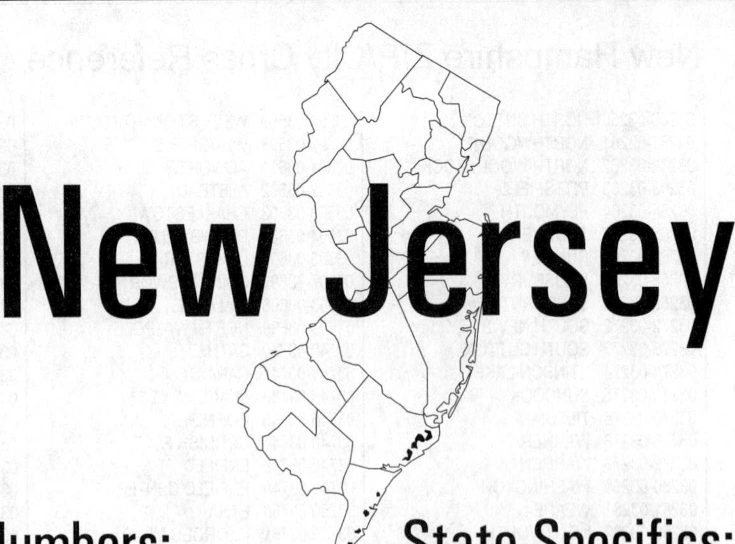

New Jersey

General Help Numbers:

Governor's Office

PO Box 001, 125 W State St — 609-292-6000
Trenton, NJ 08625-0001 — Fax 609-292-3454
www.state.nj.us/governor — 8:30AM-4:30PM

Attorney General's Office

Law & Public Safety Department — 609-292-8740
PO Box 080, 25 Market St — Fax 609-292-3508
Trenton, NJ 08625-0080 — 8:30AM-5PM
www.state.nj.us/lps

Legislative Records

State House Annex, Room B01 — 609-292-4840
PO Box 068 — Fax 609-777-2440
Trenton, NJ 08625-0068 — 8:30AM-5PM
www.njleg.state.nj.us

State Archives

PO Box 307, 225 W. State Street, L2 — 609-292-6260
Trenton, NJ 08625-0307 — Fax 609-396-2454
www.state.nj.us/state/darm/index.html
8:30AM-4:30PM T-F

State Specifics:

Capital: Trenton, Mercer County

Time Zone: EST

Number of Counties: 21

Population: 8,682,661

Web Site: www.state.nj.us

State Agencies

Criminal Records

Division of State Police, Records and Identification Section, PO Box 7068, West Trenton, NJ 08628-0068; 609-882-2000 x2991, 609-882-2000 x2918 (Crim Info Unit), Fax- 609-530-5780; 9AM-5PM.

www.njsp.org/about/serv_chrc.html

Indexing & Storage: Records available from 1951 forward. Records destroyed upon verification that subject is no longer alive. New records available for inquiry in 1 to 5 days. 84% of all arrests in database have final dispositions recorded, 72% for those arrests within last 5 years.

Searching: Record access is limited to attorney firms, employers, private investigators, and the subject. Records may be ordered with or without fingerprints, except if ordered by the subject then fingerprints are required. Include in request- date of birth, SSN. Requesters must use form 212B. Attorney firms may submit a subpoena instead of the form. The name must match exactly. 100% of the records are fingerprint supported. Fingerprints are required with a request made by the subject. This data not released- juvenile records. Dismissals, acquittals, not-guilty verdicts are excluded to PIs and employers. Only convictions and naked arrests are provided, unless the request is fingerprint-based and then the entire criminal history is provided.

Access by: mail.

Fee & Payment: The fee is $18.00 for a name check, $30.00 for a full check, $41.00 with fingerprints. Will not do FBI fingerprint checks. Fee payee- Division of State Police-SBI. Prepayment required. No personal checks or credit cards accepted.

Mail search turnaround time- 5-10 working days.

Statewide Court Records

Administrative Office of Courts, RJH Justice Complex, 7th Fl, PO Box 037, Trenton, NJ 08625; 609-984-0275, Fax- 609-984-6968; 8:30AM-4:30PM. www.judiciary.state.nj.us/admin.htm

Supreme and Appellate opinions and current calendars are available at the website. The state has several automated case tracking systems, including case histories. However, this is not accessible directly by the public.

Access by: phone, online.

Phone search: The Judgment Unit at 609-292-4804 will confirm if a case is still open or closed; requester must submit docket number.

Online search: Supreme and Appellate case data is found at www.judiciary.state.nj.us/opinions/index.htm. Restricted online access to all civil records is available through the ACMS, AMIS, and FACTS systems. The fee is $1.00 per minute of use. For more information, contact the Superior Court Clerk's Office, Electronic Access Program. Write to 25 Market St, CN971, Trenton NJ 08625, or fax 609-292-6564, or call 609-292-4987. Ask for the Inquiry System Guidebook containing hardware and software requirements and an enrollment form. A Superior Court Civil Motion Calendar is at www.judiciary.state.nj.us/calendars.htm. A useful site is found at http://lawlibrary.rutgers.edu/search.shtml.

Sexual Offender Registry

Division of State Police, Sexual Offender Registry, PO Box 7068, West Trenton, NJ 08628-0068; 609-882-2000 x2886, Fax- 609-538-0544; 9AM-5PM.

www.njsp.org

Local law enforcement will assist with localized searches. The agency will only provide access to records online.

Indexing & Storage: New records available for inquiry in 1 to 5 days.

Online search: Data can be searched online at the website. Click on NJ Sex Offender Registry. There are a variety of searches available including geographic, individual, advanced, and fugitives,

Incarceration Records

New Jersey Department of Corrections, Central Reception & Assignment Facility, PO Box 7450, Trenton, NJ 08628; 609-777-5753, 609-984-2695, Fax- 609-777-8369; 8AM-5PM.

www.state.nj.us/corrections/index.shtml

There are three possible locations for records. Processing can take longer if records must be obtained at one of the other 2 locations.

Indexing & Storage: Records available on current and former inmates. New records available for inquiry in 1 day.

Searching: Location, DOC number, physical identifiers, conviction information, and release dates are released. Include in request- full name, DOB and SSN helpful. This data not released- certain medical records

Access by: mail, phone, fax, online.

Fee & Payment: Some fees may be involved, depending on extent of research involved. This is decided on a case-by-case basis.

Mail search: Turnaround time- 5 working days. SASE not required.

Phone search: Limited telephone verification services available. **Fax search:** Fax requests can be used in place of phone requests if you have four or more names to search.

Online search: Extensive search capabilities are offered from the website; click on "Offender Search" or visit https://www6.state.nj.us/DOC_Inmate/inmatefinder?i=I. Offenders on Work Release, Furlough, or in a Halfway House are not necessarily reflected as such in their profile. Also, search offenders and inmates on private site free at https://www.vinelink.com/vinelink/siteInfoAction.do?siteId=29017.

Corporation, LLC, LP, Fictitious Name

Division of Revenue, Records Unit, PO 450, Trenton, NJ 08646 (Courier address- 225 W State St, 3rd Fl, Trenton, NJ 08608); 609-292-9292, Fax- 609-984-6855; 8:30AM-4:30PM.

www.state.nj.us/treasury/revenue/certcomm.htm

Indexing & Storage: Records available from inception of laws. New records available for inquiry immediately.

Searching: Include in request- full name of business. In addition to the articles of organization, business entity records available include: Annual Reports, Amendments, Alternative names, Officers, Directors, Prior (merged) names, and Inactive names. Trade names filed at county level.

Access by: mail, phone, fax, in person, online.

Fee & Payment: A status report is $5.00. Copies are $1.00 per page (except LLC, then $10.00 first and $2.00 each additional). There is a $25.00 ($15.00 if non-profit) fee to certify a document. A Good Standing is $25.00. Fee payee- Treasurer, State of NJ. Prepayment required. Ongoing requesters may set up a pre-paid account. Call 609-633-8255 for more information. Personal checks accepted. Major credit cards accepted

Mail search: Turnaround time- 2 to 3 weeks.

Phone search is considered expedited service.

Fax search: This is considered expedited service.

In person: You can look at 3 records per day for no fee. Copies can be provided. The turnaround time is over 1 week.

Online search: Business entities may be searched at https://accessnet.state.nj.us/home.asp. Records are available from the New Jersey Business Gateway Service (NJBGS) website at www.state.nj.us/njbgs/. There is no fee to browse the site to locate a name; however fees are involved for copies or status reports. There is also a business list search function at www.state.nj.us/treasury/revenue/searchfile.htm. Also, search securities agency enforcement actions at www.njsecurities.gov/bosdisc.htm.

Expedited service: Expedited service is available for phone, fax, and in person searches. Turnaround time- 8.5 business hours. Add $15.00 per transaction for corporations, non-profits and LPs and $25.00 per filing for LLCs and LLP. Records may be picked up the next day.

Trademarks/Servicemarks

Department of Treasury, Trademark Division, PO Box 453, Trenton, NJ 08625-0453 (Courier address- 225 W State St, 3rd Floor, Trenton, NJ 08608); 609-292-9292 x3, Fax- 609-984-6681; 8:30AM-5PM.

www.state.nj.us/treasury/revenue/regmark.htm

Indexing & Storage: Records available from the inception of the Division. Records are registered for a five year period. New records available for inquiry in less than 1 day.

Searching: Include in request- trademark/servicemark name, name of owner, date of application. Information returned includes name and address of owner and date of filing.

Access by: mail, in person, online.

Fee & Payment: Search fee is $25.00 for up to 3 names (for name availability). Copies are $1.00 per page. A status is $5.00 per name searched. Fee payee- NJ State Treasurer. Prepayment required. Personal checks and major credit cards accepted.

Mail search: Turnaround time- 1 week. SASE is appreciated.

In person: You can take the request in person, but they return the records by mail unless expedited service is requested.

Online search: Search the trademark database at https://accessnet.state.nj.us/home.asp.

Expedited service: Add $15.00 per document. Turnaround time- next day service.

Uniform Commercial Code

UCC Section, Certification and Status Unit, PO Box 303, Trenton, NJ 08646 (Courier address- 33 West State Street, 5th Fl, Trenton, NJ 08608); 609-292-9292, Fax- 609-984-6883; 8AM-5PM.

www.state.nj.us/njbgs/

Indexing & Storage: New records available for inquiry in 2 weeks.

Searching: Use search request form UCC-11. Federal tax liens are filed at the county level. State tax liens follow two rules: certificates of debt are filed in Superior Court at Trenton; a warrant of execution is filed at the county level. Include in request- debtor name.

Access by: mail, fax, in person, online.

Fee & Payment: The fee is $25.00 for a search certificate per debtor name, $5.00 for non-certified computer printout of any document, copies are $1.00 per page. Fee payee- Treasurer, State of NJ Prepayment required. Regular requesters can set up a pre-paid account. Personal checks, Visa, and MasterCard accepted.

Mail search: Turnaround time- 2 weeks. A SASE is requested.

Fax search: You can order using a credit card; however, results will be mailed or available for pickup by a courier.

In person: Information is mailed, unless you pay the $15.00 expedite fee for quicker service, or pickup later by courier.

Online search: Go to https://www.state.nj.us/treasury/revenue/dcr/filing/ucc_lead.htm to search the UCC index. Go to https://accessnet.state.nj.us/home.asp to find a business entity, UCC debtor, or other business name without accruing a service charge with the Division of Revenue. However, if you wish to receive status reports or other information services, you will need to pay the applicable statutory fee.

Expedited service: Expedited services is available, upon requested, by mail, fax or in person. Turnaround time- 8 1/2 hours. The fee is $15.00 per transaction and is in addition to other charges.

Federal & State Tax Liens

Records not maintained by a state level agency.

Federal tax liens are filed with the county clerk or register of deeds. All state "docket judgment" liens are filed at the Superior Court in Trenton. "Certificates of Debt" are filed at the respective county superior court.

Sales Tax Registrations

Access to Records is Restricted.

Department of Revenue, Sales Tax Licensing, PO Box 252, Trenton, NJ 08646-0252 (Courier address- 847 Roebling Ave, Trenton, NJ 08611); 609-292-1730, Fax- 609-292-4291; 8:30AM-4:30PM. www.state.nj.us/treasury/taxation/

Sales tax information is considered confidential. Order forms and information about publications are available on this agency's website.

Birth Certificates

Department of Health & Senior Svcs, Bureau of Vital Statistics, PO Box 370, Trenton, NJ 08625-0370 (Courier address- S Warren St, Room 504, Health & Agriculture Building, Trenton, NJ 08625); 609-292-4087, 866-649-8726, 877-622-7549 (Credit Card Requests), Fax- 609-392-4292; 8:30AM-4PM.

www.state.nj.us/health/vital/index.shtml

For copies of vital records from 1848 to 1877, please contact New Jersey Dept. of State, Division of Archives and Records Management at P.O. Box 307, Trenton NJ 08625, or call 609-292-6260.

Indexing & Storage: Records available from 1878 to present. New records available for inquiry in 30 days.

Searching: Include in request- full name, names of parents, mother's maiden name, date of birth, place of birth. Requester must submit photo ID and proof of relationship to subject.

Access by: mail, phone, fax, in person.

Fee & Payment: The fee is $25.00 per record. Add $2.00 per copy for additional copies. Add $1.00 per year for each additional year searched if event occurred over 80 years ago. Fee payee- New Jersey Department of Health & Senior Services. Prepayment required. Personal checks accepted. Major credit cards only accepted by VitalChek.

Mail search: Turnaround time- 12 to 14 weeks. 14-16 weeks for genealogy requests. No SASE is required.

Phone search: Must use a credit card.

Fax search: Same criteria as phone searching.

In person: Turnaround time 2 hours or less, except for genealogy requests.

Expedited service: Expedited service is available for fax or phone requests via www.vitalchek.com and not through this agency. Turnaround time- 3 to 25 days. The vendor requires added $14.75 carrier fee if overnight shipping and a $10.95 credit card/handling fee.

Death Records

Department of Health & Senior Svcs, Bureau of Vital Statistics, PO Box 370, Trenton, NJ 08625-0370 (Courier address- S Warren St, Room 504, Health & Agriculture Building, Trenton, NJ 08625); 609-292-4087, 866-649-8726, 877-622-7549 (Credit Card Requests), Fax- 609-392-4292; 8:30AM-4PM.

www.state.nj.us/health/vital/index.shtml

For copies of vital records from 1848 to 1877, please contact New Jersey Dept. of State, Division of Archives and Records Management at P.O. Box 307, Trenton NJ 08625, or call 609-292-6260.

Indexing & Storage: Records available from 1878 to present. New records available for inquiry in 30 days.

Searching: Cause of death, unless immediate family, is not released. Immediate family and those with a legal interest may obtain a record, unless death occurred over 40 years ago (then considered a genealogical search). Include in request- full name, date of death, place of death, parents names, mother's maiden name if possible. Submit photo ID and proof of relationship. If event is more than 40 years old, requester may provide the year of event and county of occurrence instead of exact information, parent names are preferred but not required.

Access by: mail, phone, fax, in person.

Fee & Payment: The fee is $25.00 per record. Add $2.00 per copy for additional copies. Add $1.00 per year for each additional year searched if event occurred over 80 years ago. Add $10.95 if credit card is used. Fee payee- NJ Department of Health and Senior Services. Prepayment required. Personal checks accepted. Major credit cards only accepted by VitalChek.

Mail search: Turnaround time- 12 to 14 weeks. 14-16 weeks for genealogy requests. No SASE is required.

Phone search: Must use a credit card, open 24 hours. **Fax search:** Same criteria as phone, turnaround time is 5-12 days.

In person: Turnaround time 2 hours or less, except for genealogy requests.

Expedited service: Expedited service is available for fax or phone requests via www.vitalchek.com and not through this agency. Turnaround time- 3 to 25 days. The vendor requires added $14.75 carrier fee if overnight shipping and a $10.95 credit card/handling fee.

Marriage, Civil Union, and Domestic Partnership Certificates

Department of Health & Senior Svcs, Bureau of Vital Statistics, PO Box 370, Trenton, NJ 08625 (Courier address- S Warren St, Room 504, Health & Ag. Building, Trenton, 08625); 609-292-4087, 866-649-8726, 877-622-7549 (Credit Card Requests), Fax- 609-392-4292; 8:30AM-4PM.

www.state.nj.us/health/vital/index.shtml

For copies of vital records from 1848 to 1877, please contact New Jersey Dept. of State, Division of Archives and Records Management at P.O. Box 307, Trenton NJ 08625, or call 609-292-6260.

Indexing & Storage: Records available from 1878 to present for marriage, 2004 to present for domestic partnership, 2007 to present civil union. New records available for inquiry in 30 days.

Searching: Include in request- names of husband and wife, date of marriage, place or county of marriage. Also submit photo ID and proof of relationship to the subject. If event is more than 50 years old, requester may provide year of event and county of occurrence instead of exact information.

Access by: mail, phone, fax, in person, online.

Fee & Payment: The fee is $25.00 per record. Add $2.00 per copy for additional copies. Add $1.00 per year for each additional year searched if event occurred over 80 years ago. The fee to use a credit card is $10.95. Fee payee- New Jersey Department of Health. Prepayment required. Personal checks accepted. Major credit cards only accepted by VitalChek.

Mail search: Turnaround time- 12 to 14 weeks. 14-16 weeks for genealogy requests. No SASE is required. **Phone search:** Must use a credit card. Open 24 hours. **Fax search:** Same criteria as phone searches. **In person:** Turnaround time 2 hours or less, except for genealogy requests.

Online search: See expedited service.

Expedited service: Expedited service is available for fax or phone requests via www.vitalchek.com and not through this agency. Turnaround time- 3 to 25 days. The vendor requires added $14.75 carrier fee if overnight shipping and a $10.95 credit card/handling fee.

Divorce Records

Clerk of Superior Court, Records Center, PO Box 967, Trenton, NJ 08625-0967 (Courier address- 171 Jersey St, Bldg 2, Corner of Jersey & Tremont, Trenton, NJ 08611); 609-777-0092, Fax- 609-777-0094; 8:30AM-3:30PM.

www.judiciary.state.nj.us

For copies of vital records from 1848 to 1886, please contact New Jersey Dept. of State, Division of Archives and Records Management at P.O. Box 307, Trenton NJ 08625, or call 609-292-6260.

Indexing: Records available from 1886 to present.

Searching: Also provide married name, unless maiden name was used during the marriage. Information on cases that are impounded is not released. Include in request- names of husband and wife, date of divorce, year divorce case began, docket number (if known). No copies are made and no records are retrieved after 3:30PM. This data not released- adoption, impound cases.

Access by: mail, fax, in person.

Fee & Payment: There is no search fee, but there is a $10.00 certification fee. Fee payee- Treasurer, State of New Jersey Prepayment required. If you are not sure how many pages the results or your request will be, you may send a blank check with "Not to exceed $25.00" written in the memo. Personal checks accepted, credit cards are not.

Mail search: Turnaround time- 2 to 3 weeks. Mail is the preferred request method. A SASE is requested. **Fax search:** Requesters must be pre-approved to fax, and only written information is faxed back. Attorneys with charge accounts with the Superior Court can receive copies, without the seal of the court, via fax.

In person: Turnaround time while you wait. The Clerk's Office recommends that you not come to the office in person except for emergency requests.

Workers' Compensation

Labor Department, Division of Workers Compensation, PO Box 381, Trenton, NJ 08625-0381 (Courier address- Labor Building, 6th Floor, John Fitch Plaza, Trenton, 08625); 609-292-6026, 609-292-2515 (Hotline), Fax- 609-984-2515; 8:30-4:30PM. www.nj.gov/labor/wc/wcindex.html

Indexing & Storage: Records available for 45 years, then are purged. New records available for inquiry immediately.

Searching: Records are subject to NJSA 34:15-128 which prohibits the copying of records to all persons not a party to a current related case. Use WC-147 if you want copies of a case. Include in request- claimant name, SSN, date of accident. Use the agency's record request form found at www.nj.gov/labor/wc/forms/wc-147(r7-04).pdf. Data not released- first report of injury-accident.

Access by: mail, in person, online.

Fee & Payment: There is no search fee. The certified copy fee is $.75 each for first 10 pages; $.50 each for next 10; and $.25 per page over 20, plus any postage costs. Fee payee- Division of Workers' Compensation. Copies can be billed Personal checks accepted, credit cards are not.

Mail search: Turnaround time- 1 to 3 weeks. If request is just to know if the person has a claim,; turnaround time is same day. SASE is requested. Otherwise postage is added to copy fees.

In person: Turnaround time is same day.

Online search: COURTS on-line is a secure Internet website that provides authorized subscribers access to the Division's database. Possible subscribers include: Insurance Carrier/Law Firms; Court Reporting Firms; and WC Forensic Experts (Physicians).

Driver Records

Motor Vehicle Commission, Driver History Abstract Unit, PO Box 142, Trenton, NJ 08666; 609-984-7771, 609-292-6500 (Forms request), 609-292-7500 (Suspensions); 8AM-4:30PM.

www.state.nj.us/mvc/ Copies of tickets are not kept on file and must be obtained from the municipal courts.

Indexing & Storage: Records available for 5 yrs for the public (complete history for attorneys). Non-moving violations are not reported on the record. Accidents in excess of $500 are reported, but fault is not shown. Driver's address is provided on the record.

Searching: Access of driving records is strict, release to casual requesters is prohibited unless Form DO-21A contains notarized authority from subject. Permissible use requesters should use Form ISM-21. Include in request- full name, DOB and DL. Sex, and eye color are also helpful for manual requests. The driver's license number should be submitted with all requests including the full name and DOB. This data not released- SSNs or medical records.

Access by: mail, in person, online.

Fee & Payment: The current fee is $10.00 for certified mail-in or walk-in requests, or for electronic access. Fee payee- Motor Vehicle Commission Prepayment required. Personal checks accepted; credit cards accepted only online.

Mail search: Turnaround time- 2 weeks. A SASE is requested. **In person:** Driving records can obtained at any one of 4 Regional Service Centers - West Deptford, Wayne, Eatontown, and Trenton.

Online search: The commercial access system is called CAIR. Fee is $10.00 per record. Access is limited to approved vendors entities per DPPA. For more information, visit www.state.nj.us/mvc/Licenses/CustomerAbstract.htm or call 609-292-4572. NJ drivers may order their own record online at www.state.nj.us/mvc/Licenses/DriverHistory.htm. A user ID number must be obtained first. The fee is $10.00 per record.

Vehicle, Vessel Ownership & Registration

Motor Vehicle Commission, Office of Communication, PO Box 176, Trenton, NJ 08666; 609-292-6500, 888-486-3339 (In-state); 8:30AM-4:30PM. www.state.nj.us/mvc/Vehicle/index.htm

Ownership and lien records must be ordered from Motor Vehicle Commission, Special Titles, PO Box 017 (Zip is 08666-0017). Lien searches are on current record or particular requests, also can be purchased at $5.00 for each lien history search.

Indexing & Storage: Records available for 3 years (registration) and 8 years (title). All boats over 12 feet must be titled and registered. Also, this agency maintains records on mobile homes. New records available for inquiry in 3 to 4 months.

Searching: Non-permissible use requesters cannot obtain records. Include in request- dob, address. A special request form is required for most searches as follows: DO-22A for title search, DO-22 for lien search, and DO-11A for vehicle registration application search. This data not released- SSN, medical information, address, DL#, DOB.

Access by: mail, in person, online.

Fee & Payment: For registration records fee is $8.00 non-certified, $10.00 certified and will take 6-8 weeks to process. A lien history search is $5.00 for each lien. A complete title history costs $10.50 and can take as long as 6 weeks to obtain. Fee payee- Motor Vehicle Commission Prepayment required. Personal checks and money orders accepted. Credit cards accepted if in-person.

Mail search: Turnaround time- 4 to 6 weeks. Requests must be submitted on Forms mentioned above. **In person:** Record requests are accepted, but only for title histories and lien searches.

Online search: Limited online access is available for approved commercial, public and non-profit organizations. Fees are $4.00 per request for registration and title records, and $8.00 for ownership history. Call 609-292-4572 or visit the web for further details.

Accident Reports

New Jersey State Police, CJRB - Traffic, PO Box 7068, West Trenton, NJ 08628-0068; 609-882-2000 x2280; 8AM-5PM. www.njsp.org

This profile is only for accidents investigated by the State Police. If investigated by local police, copies must be obtained either from the local PD unit or from the MVC Abstract Unit at PO Box 142, Trenton, NJ 08666. Fee-$10.00 from MVC.

Indexing & Storage: Records available for 6 years. Records are computer indexed by driver name and case number. New records available for inquiry in 2-3 weeks.

Searching: Only the basics of fatal accident reports are available until the full report has been released from the County Prosecutor. While the report is pending, no statements, evidence or photographs can be released without the written consent of the prosecutor. Include in request- location of accident, date of accident, driver's full name. in person requests can be processed at stations, but not at this location. If incident occurred on a toll-road, then contact the NJ Turnpike Authority (732-442-8600 x2908) or Garden State Pky (ext.2419), or Atlantic City Expressway (609-965-7200 x108).

Fee & Payment: A report consisting of 1 to 5 pages is $10.00. 6 or more pages is $16.00. Photographs are $5.00 each, if over 10 are needed each additional is $3.00. Fee payee- New Jersey State Police Department. Prepayment required. No personal checks or credit cards accepted.

Mail search: Turnaround time- 3 to 4 weeks. A SASE is requested.

Expedited service: If the report is available in the agency office, request can be sent overnight delivery if prepaid and record fee is paid with certified funds.

Legislation Records

New Jersey State Legislature, State House Annex, PO Box 068, Room B01, Trenton, NJ 08625-0068; 609-292-4840, 609-292-6395 (Copies of Bills Room), 800-792-8630 (In State Only), Fax- 609-777-2440; 8:30AM-5PM. www.njleg.state.nj.us

Records available from 1988 to present. New records available for inquiry immediately. Older bills may be found at the State Law Library. This agency prefers not to publish its fax number.

Voter Registration

Access to Records is Restricted.

Dept of Law and Public Safety, Division of Elections, PO Box 304, Trenton, NJ 08625 (Courier address- 225 W State Street, 3rd Fl,); 609-292-3760, 877-NJVOTER (24-hr Assistance), 800-292-0039 (TTD/TTY), Fax- 609-777-1280; 8:30AM-5PM. www.njelections.org

Individual records must be searched at the county level. This agency will sell the database names only for political purposes. Write to Justin Zimmerman, Dir. Of Intergovernmental Affairs, Dept of State, PO Box 300, Trenton NJ 08625-0300. Since September 2006, bulk purchase is available for political purposes.

GED Certificates

GED Testing Program, Dept. of Education - Bureau Adult Ed. & Literacy, PO Box 500, Trenton, NJ 08625-0500; 609-777-1050, Fax- 609-984-0573; 9AM-4PM.

www.state.nj.us/education/students/ged/

Email questions to GED_INFO@doe.state.nj.us.

Indexing & Storage: Records go back to 1959. New records available for inquiry in 2 to 4 weeks.

Searching: GED Information Request Form is required. Obtain one by calling 609-777-1050 or at www.state.nj.us/education/students/ged/transreq.pdf. Include in request- a signed release, name, date/year of test, SSN, and city of test. The web has a request form to download. Records are not maintained for persons tested at federal correctional institutions.

Access by: mail, online.

Fee & Payment: The fee is $5.00 for a verification or a copy of the transcript. Fee payee- Treasurer, State of NJ Prepayment required. Money orders and business checks are accepted. No personal checks or credit cards accepted.

Mail search: Turnaround time- up to 2 weeks. SASE is not required. **Online search:** Electronic transcript capability provided for the $5.00 fee, but only for record holder.

Hunting & Fishing License Information

Records not maintained by a state level agency.

They do not have a central database. You must contact the vendor where the license was purchased. Plans are underway to implement a computerized database.

New Jersey State Licensing Agencies

For details about the agency responsible for licensing/certifying/registering an item below or in the Agency Quick Finder section, match an item's number with the number of the agency in the *Licensing Agency Information* section.

New Jersey Licenses Searchable Online

Acupuncturist #1 .... www.state.nj.us/cgi-bin/consumeraffairs/search/searchentry.pl?searchprofession=3251
Alcohol/Drug Counselor #13 .... www.state.nj.us/cgi-bin/consumeraffairs/search/searchentry.pl?searchprofession=3703
Appraiser, General/Residential #23 .... www.state.nj.us/cgi-bin/consumeraffairs/search/searchentry.pl?searchprofession=4202
Architect #6 .... www.state.nj.us/cgi-bin/consumeraffairs/search/searchentry.pl?searchprofession=210
Athletic Trainer #14 .... www.state.nj.us/cgi-bin/consumeraffairs/search/searchentry.pl
Audiologist #7 .... www.state.nj.us/cgi-bin/consumeraffairs/search/searchentry.pl?searchprofession=4101
Barber / Barber Shop #9 .... www.state.nj.us/lps/ca/nonmedical/coshair.htm
Beautician #9 .... www.state.nj.us/lps/ca/nonmedical/coshair.htm
Candidate Report #43 .... www.elec.state.nj.us/publicinformation.htm
Cemetery #46 .... www.state.nj.us/cgi-bin/consumeraffairs/search/searchentry.pl?searchprofession=4701
Cemetery Salesperson #46 .... www.state.nj.us/cgi-bin/consumeraffairs/search/searchentry.pl?searchprofession=4701
Certificate of Authorization #6 .... www.state.nj.us/cgi-bin/consumeraffairs/search/searchentry.pl?searchprofession=210
Charity #3 .... www.njconsumeraffairs.gov/charity/chardir.htm
Check Casher/Seller #38 .... https://www6.state.nj.us/DOBI_LicSearch/Jsp/bnkSearch.jsp
Chiropractor #8 .... www.state.nj.us/cgi-bin/consumeraffairs/search/searchentry.pl?searchprofession=3801
Contributor, Political #43 .... www.elec.state.nj.us/publicinformation.htm
Cosmetologist/Hairstylist #9 .... www.state.nj.us/lps/ca/nonmedical/coshair.htm
Cosmetology/Manicurist Shop #9 .... www.state.nj.us/lps/ca/nonmedical/coshair.htm
Counselor, Professional #13 .... www.state.nj.us/cgi-bin/consumeraffairs/search/searchentry.pl
Court Reporter #24 .... www.state.nj.us/cgi-bin/consumeraffairs/search/searchentry.pl?searchprofession=3000
CPA/Public Accountant #5 .... www.state.nj.us/cgi-bin/consumeraffairs/search/searchentry.pl?searchprofession=2000
Dental Assistant #10 .... www.state.nj.us/cgi-bin/consumeraffairs/search/searchentry.pl
Dental Hygienist #10 .... www.state.nj.us/cgi-bin/consumeraffairs/search/searchentry.pl
Dentist #10 .... www.state.nj.us/cgi-bin/consumeraffairs/search/searchentry.pl
Electrical Contractor #11 .... www.state.nj.us/cgi-bin/consumeraffairs/search/searchentry.pl?searchprofession=3400
Embalmer #15 .... www.state.nj.us/cgi-bin/consumeraffairs/search/searchentry.pl?searchprofession=2
Emergency Medical Svc Provider #32 .... www.state.nj.us/health/ems/documents/providers.pdf
Engineer #20 .... www.njconsumeraffairs.com/nonmedical/pels.htm
Engineer/Survey Company #20 .... www.njconsumeraffairs.com/nonmedical/pels.htm
Funeral Home #15 .... www.state.nj.us/cgi-bin/consumeraffairs/search/searchentry.pl
Funeral Practitioner #15 .... www.state.nj.us/cgi-bin/consumeraffairs/search/searchentry.pl?searchprofession=2
Hearing Aid Dispenser/Fitter #44 .... www.state.nj.us/cgi-bin/consumeraffairs/search/searchentry.pl?searchprofession=2253
Home Health Aide #16 .... www.state.nj.us/lps/ca/medical/nursing.htm
Home Repair Contractor/Seller #39 .... www.state.nj.us/cgi-bin/consumeraffairs/search/searchentry.pl?searchprofession=1301
Insurance Agent #41 .... https://www6.state.nj.us/DOBI_LicSearch/Jsp/index.jsp
Insurance Public Adjuster #41 .... https://www6.state.nj.us/DOBI_LicSearch/Jsp/index.jsp
Interior Design #6 .... www.state.nj.us/cgi-bin/consumeraffairs/search/searchentry.pl?searchprofession=210
Lab Director, Bio-Analytical #14 .... www.state.nj.us/cgi-bin/consumeraffairs/search/searchentry.pl?searchprofession=2505
Landfill #4 .... www.nj.gov/dep/dshw/
Landscape Architect #6 .... www.state.nj.us/cgi-bin/consumeraffairs/search/searchentry.pl?searchprofession=210
Lender, Consumer #39 .... https://www6.state.nj.us/DOBI_LicSearch/Jsp/index.jsp
Lobbyist #43 .... www.elec.state.nj.us/PublicInformation/GAA_Annual.htm
Manicurist/Manicurist Shop #9 .... www.state.nj.us/lps/ca/nonmedical/coshair.htm
Marriage & Family Counselor #13 .... www.state.nj.us/cgi-bin/consumeraffairs/search/searchentry.pl?searchprofession=3703
Marriage Counselor #13 .... www.state.nj.us/cgi-bin/consumeraffairs/search/searchentry.pl?searchprofession=3703
Medical Doctor #14 .... www.state.nj.us/cgi-bin/consumeraffairs/search/searchentry.pl?searchprofession=2501
Medical Waste Generator #4 .... www.nj.gov/dep/dshw/
Midwife #14 .... www.state.nj.us/cgi-bin/consumeraffairs/search/searchentry.pl?searchprofession=2510
Mortgage (2nd) Lender #39 .... https://www6.state.nj.us/DOBI_LicSearch/Jsp/index.jsp
Mortician #15 .... www.state.nj.us/cgi-bin/consumeraffairs/search/searchentry.pl?searchprofession=2
Nuclear Medicine Technologist #60
.... http://datamine2.state.nj.us/DEP_OPRA/OpraMain/categories?category=Radiologic%20Technologists
Nurse-Advanced/LPN/RN #16 .... www.state.nj.us/lps/ca/medical/nursing.htm
Nursing Home Administrator #50 .... http://nj.gov/health/healthfacilities/ltclicensure.shtml
Occupational Therapist #57 .... www.state.nj.us/cgi-bin/consumeraffairs/search/searchentry.pl?searchprofession=4601
Occupational Therapy Assistant #57 .... www.state.nj.us/cgi-bin/consumeraffairs/search/searchentry.pl?searchprofession=4603
Ophthalmic Dispenser #51 .... www.state.nj.us/cgi-bin/consumeraffairs/search/searchentry.pl
Optician/Ophthalmic Technician #51 .... www.state.nj.us/cgi-bin/consumeraffairs/search/searchentry.pl?searchprofession=3102

Optometrist #17 .... www.state.nj.us/cgi-bin/consumeraffairs/search/searchentry.pl
Orthopedist #14 .... www.state.nj.us/cgi-bin/consumeraffairs/search/searchentry.pl
Orthotist/Prosthetist #52 .... www.state.nj.us/cgi-bin/consumeraffairs/search/searchentry.pl
Pharmacist #18 .... www.state.nj.us/cgi-bin/consumeraffairs/search/searchentry.pl?searchprofession=2801
Physical Therapist/Assistant #19 .... www.state.nj.us/cgi-bin/consumeraffairs/search/searchentry.pl?searchprofession=4001
Physician #14 .... www.state.nj.us/cgi-bin/consumeraffairs/search/searchentry.pl?searchprofession=2501
Physician Assistant #14 .... www.state.nj.us/cgi-bin/consumeraffairs/search/searchentry.pl
Planner, Professional #21 .... www.state.nj.us/cgi-bin/consumeraffairs/search/searchentry.pl?searchprofession=3300
Plumber/Master Plumber #12 .... www.state.nj.us/cgi-bin/consumeraffairs/search/searchentry.pl?searchprofession=3601
Podiatrist #14 .... www.state.nj.us/cgi-bin/consumeraffairs/search/searchentry.pl?searchprofession=2507
Psychologist #22 .... www.state.nj.us/cgi-bin/consumeraffairs/search/searchentry.pl?searchprofession=3
Radiation Technologists / Therapists / Machine Registration #60
... ... http://datamine2.state.nj.us/DEP_OPRA/OpraMain/categories?category=Radiologic%20Technologists
Radon Tester #60 .... www.nj.gov/dep/rpp/radon/CERTMES2.HTM
Real Estate Agent/Broker/Seller #48 .... https://www6.state.nj.us/DOBI_LicSearch/Jsp/recSearch.jsp
Real Estate Appraiser/Apprentice #23 .... www.state.nj.us/cgi-bin/consumeraffairs/search/searchentry.pl?searchprofession=4202
Real Estate School/ Instructor #48 .... www.state.nj.us/cgi-bin/dobi/urs/schlist.pl
Recycle Coordinator #4 .... www.nj.gov/dep/dshw/
Recycling Facility #4 .... www.nj.gov/dep/dshw/
Respiratory Therapist #54 .... www.state.nj.us/cgi-bin/consumeraffairs/search/searchentry.pl
Skin Care Specialist/Shop #9 .... www.state.nj.us/lps/ca/nonmedical/coshair.htm
Social Worker #25 .... www.state.nj.us/cgi-bin/consumeraffairs/search/searchentry.pl?searchprofession=4401
Speech-Language Pathologist #7 .... www.state.nj.us/cgi-bin/consumeraffairs/search/searchentry.pl?searchprofession=4101
Surveyor, Land #20 .... www.njconsumeraffairs.com/nonmedical/pels.htm
Tree Expert #55 .... www.state.nj.us/dep/parksandforests/forest/community/cte.html
Veterinarian #26 .... www.state.nj.us/cgi-bin/consumeraffairs/search/searchentry.pl?searchprofession=2901
Viatical Settlement Broker #41 .... https://www6.state.nj.us/DOBI_LicSearch/Jsp/index.jsp
Waste Company #4 .... www.nj.gov/dep/dshw/
X-Ray Equipment #60
... ... http://datamine2.state.nj.us/DEP_OPRA/OpraMain/categories?category=Radiologic%20Technologists

New Jersey Licensing Quick Finder

Accountant, Municipal #5 973-504-6380
Accounting Firm #5 973-504-6380
Acupuncturist #1 973-273-8092
Alcohol/Drug Counselor #13 973-504-6582
Amusement Ride Inspector #45 609-984-7834
Animal Control Officer #59 609-588-3121
Appraiser, General/Residential #23 973-504-6480
Architect #6 973-504-6385
Asbestos Employee/Employer #33 609-633-3760
Asbestos Permit #33 609-633-3760
Athletic Booking Agency #40 973-504-6370
Athletic Trainer #14 973-504-6414
Attorney #49 609-292-8079
Audiologist #7 973-504-6390
Automobile Dealer #42 609-292-4517
Barber #9 973-504-6400
Barber Shop #9 973-504-6400
Beautician #9 973-504-6400
Boiler Operator #34 609-292-2921
Boiler/Pressure Ves'l/Refrig'n Inspector #45
.... 609-984-7834
Boxer #53 609-292-0317
Boxing Manager #28 609-292-0317
Building Inspector #45 609-984-7834
Candidate Report #43 609-292-8700
Career Counselor #40 973-504-6370
Casino #28 609-441-3555
Casino Employee #28 609-441-3015
Cemetery #46 973-504-6553
Cemetery Salesperson #46 973-504-6553
Certificate of Authorization #6 973-504-6385
Charity #3 973-504-6215
Check Casher/Seller #38 609-292-5340
Chiropractor #8 973-504-6395
Club/Cabaret #37 609-984-2830
Collection Agency Bond #36 609-292-9292
Computer Job-Matching Service #40 973-504-6370

Construction Code Official #45 609-984-7834
Contributor, Political #43 609-292-8700
Cosmetologist/Hairstylist #9 973-504-6400
Cosmetology/Manicurist Shop #9 973-504-6400
Counselor, Professional #13 973-504-6582
Court Reporter #24 973-504-6490
CPA/Public Accountant #5 973-504-6380
CPE Sponsor #5 973-504-6380
Crane Operator #34 609-292-5626
Dental Assistant #10 973-504-6405
Dental Hygienist #10 973-504-6405
Dental Radiation Technologist #60 609-984-5890
Dentist #10 973-504-6405
Education'l Media Specialist/Librarian #29
.... 609-292-2070
Electrical Contractor #11 973-504-6410
Electrical Inspector #45 609-984-7834
Elevator Inspector #45 609-984-7834
Embalmer #15 973-504-6425
Emergency Medical Svc Provider #32 609-633-7777
Emergency Medical Technician #32 609-633-7777
Employment Agency #40 973-504-6370
Engineer #20 973-504-6460
Engineer/Survey Company #20 973-504-6460
Fire Protection Inspector #45 609-984-7834
Firefighter #58 609-633-6106
Funeral Home /Practitioner #15 973-504-6425
Health Care Service Agency #40 973-504-6370
Health Spa #40 973-504-6370
Hearing Aid Dispenser/Fitter #44 973-504-6331
Home Health Aide #16 973-504-6504
Home Repair Contractor/Seller #39 888-656-6225
Hotel/Motel #37 609-984-2830
Housing Code Official #45 609-984-7834
Inplant Inspector #45 609-984-7834
Inspector of Hotels/Multiple Dwellings #45
.... 609-984-7834

Insurance Agent #41 609-292-4337
Insurance Public Adjuster #41 609-292-4337
Interior Design #6 973-504-6385
Investment Advisor/Representative #27973-504-3600
Job Listing Service #40 973-504-6370
Lab Director, Bio-Analytical #14 609-292-4843
Landfill #4 609-984-6880
Landscape Architect #6 973-504-6385
Lender, Consumer #39 609-292-5340
Librarian #29 609-292-2070
Liquor Control #37 609-984-2830
Liquor Distribution, Retail, Plenary/Ltd #37
.... 609-984-2830
Liquor Rectifier/Blender #37 609-984-2830
Liquor Retail, Plenary/Seasonal #37 609-984-2830
Liquor Sales, Retail/Ltd/Plenary #37 609-984-2830
Liquor Transit, Plenary Retail #37 609-984-2830
Liquor Wholesale, Limited/Plenary #37 609-984-2830
Lobbyist #43 609-292-8700
Manicurist/Manicurist Shop #9 973-504-6400
Marriage & Family Counselor #13 973-504-6582
Marriage Counselor #13 973-504-6582
Mechanical Inspector 1 & 2 Family #45 609-984-7834
Medical Doctor #14 609-292-4843
Medical Waste Generator #4 609-984-6880
Midwife #14 973-273-8900
Modeling & Talent Agency #40 973-504-6370
Mortgage (2nd) Lender #39 609-292-5340
Mortician #15 973-504-6425
Mover #2 973-504-6512
Notary Public #36 609-292-9292
Nuclear Medicine Technologist #60 609-984-5890
Nurse, Advance Practice #16 973-504-6504
Nurse-LPN/RN #16 973-504-6504
Nursing Home Administrator #50 609-633-9706
Nursing Registry Svc #40 973-504-6370
Occupational Therapist #57 973-504-6570

Occupational Therapy Assistant #57....973-504-6570
Ophthalmic Dispenser #51....................973-504-6435
Optician/Ophthalmic Technician #51....973-504-6435
Optometrist #17....................................973-504-6440
Orthodontic Assistant #10....................973-504-6405
Orthopedist #14....................................609-292-4843
Orthotist/Prosthetist #52.......................973-504-6445
Paramedic #32.......................................609-633-7777
Pesticide Appl./Operator/Dealer #31....609-530-4070
Pharmacist #18.....................................973-504-6450
Pharmacy #18.......................................973-504-6450
Physical Therapist/Assistant #19.........973-504-6455
Physician #14..609-292-4843
Physician Assistant #14........................973-504-6580
Planner, Professional #21....................973-504-6465
Plumber/Master Plumber #12..............973-504-6420
Plumbing Inspector #45........................609-984-7834
Podiatrist #14..609-292-4843
Private Detective #56...... 609-341-3426 or 633-9352
Psychologist #22...................................973-504-6470
Pump Installer #30................................609-984-6831
Race Horse #47.....................................609-984-1554
Race Horse Owner/Trainer #47...........609-984-1554
Radiation Machine Registration #60....609-984-5370
Radiation Report #60...........................609-984-5890
Radiation Technologist #60.................609-984-5890
Radiation Therapist #60.......................609-984-5890
Radon Tester #60........ 800-648-0394, 609-984-5425
Real Estate Agent/Broker/Seller #48....609-292-8280
Real Estate Appraiser/Apprentice #23..973-504-6480
Real Estate School/ Instructor #48.......609-292-8280
Recycle Coordinator/Facility #4...........609-984-6880
Refrigeration Technician #34...............609-984-3001
Respiratory Therapist #54....................973-504-6485
Resume Service #40.............................973-504-6370
School Accountant #5...........................973-504-6380
School Counselor #29...........................609-292-2070
School Principal/Admin./Superv'r #29..609-292-2070
School, Accredited #29.........................609-292-2070
Securities Agent #27............................973-504-3600
Securities Broker/Dealer #27...............973-504-3600
Securities Issuer #27............................973-504-3600
Shorthand Reporter #24.......................973-504-6490
Skin Care Specialist/Shop #9...............973-504-6400
Social Worker #25.................................973-504-6495
Speech-Language Pathologist #7........973-504-6390
Stable Mate #47....................................609-984-1554
Student Personnel Svc Director #29....609-292-2070
Surveyor, Land #20...............................973-504-6460
Teacher #29..609-292-2070
Temporary Help Agency #40................973-504-6370
Theater #37...609-984-2830
Ticket Reseller #40...............................973-504-6370
Trademark #36......................................609-292-9292
Tree Expert #55.....................................609-292-2532
Veterinarian #26....................................973-504-6500
Viatical Settlement Broker #41............609-292-4337
Warehouseman #2................................973-504-6512
Waste Company #4...............................609-984-6880
Waste Water System Operator #61.....609-777-1013
Weighmaster #35..................................732-815-4840
Weights & Measures Mechanic #35....732-815-4840
Well Driller #30.....................................609-984-6831
Wine Wholesaler/Winery #37..............609-984-2830
X-Ray Equipment #60..........................609-984-5370

New Jersey Licensing Agency Information

#1 Board of Medical Examiners, Acupuncture Examining Board, PO Box 46021, Newark, NJ 07101; 973-273-8092, Fax- 973-273-8075. 9AM-5PM. www.nj.gov/lps/ca/medical/acupuncture.htm Search data at- www.state.nj.us/lps/ca/bme/acupdir.htm

#2 Division of Consumer Affairs, Regulated Business Section, PO Box 45025 (124 Halsey St), Newark, NJ 07101; 973-504-6442, Fax- 973-648-2807. www.state.nj.us/lps/ca/brief/mover.pdf

#3 Charities Registration Section, Consumer Affairs, PO Box 45021 (124 Halsey St), Newark, NJ 07101; 973-504-6215, Fax- 973-273-8035. www.njconsumeraffairs.gov/charity/chardir.htm

#4 Department of Environmental Protection, Division of Solid & Hazardous Waste, PO Box 414 (401 E State St), Trenton, NJ 08625; 609-633-1418, Fax- 609-777-0769. www.nj.gov/dep/dshw/

#5 Board of Accountancy, PO Box 45000, Newark, NJ 07101; 973-504-6380, Fax- 973-648-2855. www.state.nj.us/lps/ca/accountancy/index.htm

#6 Board of Architects, Division of Consumer Affairs, PO Box 45001, Newark, NJ 07101; 973-504-6385, Fax- 973-504-6458. www.state.nj.us/lps/ca/nonmedical/architects.htm Search data at- www.state.nj.us/cgi-bin/consumeraffairs/search/searchentry.pl?searchprofession=210

#7 Board of Audiology & Speech Language Pathology, Division of Consumer Affairs, PO Box 45002 (124 Halsey St), Newark, NJ 07101; 973-504-6390, Fax- 973-648-3355. www.state.nj.us/lps/ca/medical/audiology.htm Search data at- www.state.nj.us/cgi-bin/consumeraffairs/search/searchentry.pl?searchprofession=4101

#8 Board of Chiropractic Examiners, Division of Consumer Affairs, PO Box 45004, Newark, NJ 07101; 973-504-6395, Fax- 973-648-3538. www.state.nj.us/lps/ca/medical/chiropractic.htm Search data at- www.state.nj.us/cgi-bin/consumeraffairs/search/searchentry.pl?searchprofession=3801

#9 Board of Cosmetology & Hairstyling, PO Box 45003, Newark, NJ 07101; 973-504-6400, Fax- 973-648-3536. www.state.nj.us/lps/ca/nonmedical/coshair.htm Search data at- www.state.nj.us/lps/ca/nonmedical/coshair.htm

#10 Board of Dentistry, PO Box 45005 (124 Halsey St), Newark, NJ 07101; 973-504-6405, Fax- 973-273-8075. Hours- 9AM-5PM. www.state.nj.us/lps/ca/medical/dentistry.htm Search data at- www.state.nj.us/cgi-bin/consumeraffairs/search/searchentry.pl?searchprofession=2201 Has an automated license verification line (need license number) 973-273-8090 with fax back capability for written verifications.

#11 Board of Examiners of Electrical Contractors, Division of Consumer Affairs, PO Box 45006 (124 Halsey St), Newark, NJ 07101; 973-504-6410, Fax- 973-648-3355. www.state.nj.us/lps/ca/nonmedical/electrical.htm Search data at- www.state.nj.us/cgi-bin/consumeraffairs/search/searchentry.pl?searchprofession=3400

#12 Board of Examiners of Master Plumbers, PO Box 45008 (124 Halsey St), Newark, NJ 07101; 973-504-6420. Hours- 9AM-4:30PM. www.state.nj.us/lps/ca/nonmedical/plumbers.htm Search data at- www.state.nj.us/cgi-bin/consumeraffairs/search/searchentry.pl?searchprofession=3601

#13 Board of Marriage & Family Therapy Examiners, PO Box 45007 (124 Halsey St, 6th Fl), Newark, NJ 07101; 973-504-6415 or 504-6582. www.state.nj.us/lps/ca/medical/familytherapy.htm Search data at- www.state.nj.us/lps/ca/marriage/pcdir.htm

#14 Board of Medical Examiners, PO Box 183 (140 E Front St), Trenton, NJ 08625-0183; 609-826-7100, Fax- 609-826-7117. www.state.nj.us/lps/ca/bme/index.html Search data at- www.state.nj.us/cgi-bin/consumeraffairs/search/searchentry.pl

#15 Board of Mortuary Science, Division of Consumer Affairs, P.O. Box 45009 (124 Halsey St), Newark, NJ 07101; 973-504-6425, Fax- 973-648-2855. Hours- 8:30AM-4:30PM. www.state.nj.us/lps/ca/nonmedical/mortuary.htm Search data at- www.state.nj.us/lps/ca/mort/mortdir.htm

#16 Board of Nursing, PO Box 45010 (124 Halsey St), Newark, NJ 07101; 973-504-6430, Fax- 973-648-3481. www.state.nj.us/lps/ca/medical/nursing.htm Search data at- www.state.nj.us/lps/ca/medical/nursing.htm

#17 Board of Optometrists, Division of Consumer Affairs, PO Box 45012, Newark, NJ 07101; 973-504-6440, Fax- 973-648-3536. www.state.nj.us/lps/ca/medical/optometrist.htm Search data at- www.state.nj.us/cgi-bin/consumeraffairs/search/searchentry.pl

#18 Board of Pharmacy, PO Box 45013 (124 Halsey St), Newark, NJ 07101; 973-504-6450, Fax- 973-648-3355. www.state.nj.us/lps/ca/medical/pharmacy.htm Search data at- www.state.nj.us/lps/ca/pharm/pharmdir.htm

#19 Board of Physical Therapists, PO Box 45014 (124 Halsey St), Newark, NJ 07101; 973-504-6455, Fax- 973-648-3536. www.nj.gov/lps/ca/medical/pt.htm Search data- www.state.nj.us/cgi-bin/consumeraffairs/search/searchentry.pl?searchprofession=4001

#20 Board of Professional Engineers & Land Surveyors, PO Box 45015 (124 Halsey St, 3rd Fl), Newark, NJ 07101; 973-504-6460, Fax- 973-273-8020. www.njconsumeraffairs.com/nonmedical/pels.htm Search data at- www.njconsumeraffairs.com/nonmedical/pels.htm

#21 Board of Professional Planners, PO Box 45016 (124 Halsey St), Newark, NJ 07101; 973-504-6465, Fax- 973-648-2855. www.state.nj.us/lps/ca/plan/planner.htm Search data at- www.state.nj.us/lps/ca/plan/plandir.htm

#22 Board of Psychological Examiners, Division of Consumer Affairs, PO Box 45017 (124 Halsey St), Newark, NJ 07101; 973-504-6470, Fax- 973-648-3536. Hours- 9AM-5PM. www.state.nj.us/lps/ca/medical/psycho.htm Search data at- www.state.nj.us/lps/ca/psy/psydir.htm

#23 Board of Real Estate Appraisers, Division of Consumer Affairs, PO Box 45032 (124 Halsey St, 07102), Newark, NJ 07101; 973-504-6480, Fax-973-648-3536. www.state.nj.us/lps/ca/nonmedical/reappraisers.htm Search data at- www.state.nj.us/lps/ca/real/realdir.htm

#24 Board of Shorthand Reporting, PO Box 45019, Newark, NJ 07101; 973-504-6490. www.state.nj.us/lps/ca/nonmedical/reporter.htm

#25 Board of Social Work Examiners, PO Box 45033, Newark, NJ 07101; 973-504-6495, Fax- 973-273-8067. www.state.nj.us/lps/ca/medical/socialwork.htm Search data at- www.state.nj.us/lps/ca/social/socdir.htm

#26 Board of Veterinary Medical Examiners, PO Box 45020, Newark, NJ 07101; 973-504-6500, Fax- 973-648-3355. www.state.nj.us/lps/ca/medical/veterinary.htm Search data at- www.state.nj.us/lps/ca/vetmed/vetdir.htm

#27 Bureau of Securities, PO Box 47029 (153 Halsey St, 6th Fl), Newark, NJ 07101; 973-504-3600, Fax- 973-504-3601. www.state.nj.us/lps/ca/bos.htm

#28 Casino Control Commission, Tennessee Ave & Boardwalk, Arcade Bldg, Atlantic City, NJ 08401; 609-441-3799, Fax- 609-441-3752. www.state.nj.us/casinos/

#29 Department of Education, Licensing and Credentials, PO Box 500, 100 Riverview Plaza, Trenton, NJ 08625-0500; 609-292-2070, Fax- 609-292-3768. www.state.nj.us/education/educators/license/

#30 Department of Environmental Protection, Bureau of Water Systems & Well Permitting, PO Box 426 (401 E State St), Trenton, NJ 08628; 609-984-6831. www.state.nj.us/dep/watersupply/advisoryboard.htm Can provide free lists of licensed well drillers & pump installers.

#31 Department of Environmental Protection, Pesticide Control Program, PO Box 411 (401 E State St), Trenton, NJ 08625-0411; 609-530-4070, Fax- 609-984-6555. Hours- 8AM-5PM. www.pcpnj.org

#32 Office of Emergency Medical Svcs, Department of Health, [500-599] John Fitch Way, Market & Warren Sts, Trenton, NJ 08611; 609-633-7777, Fax- 609-633-7954. 8:30AM-4:30PM. www.state.nj.us/health/ems/ Only disciplinary actions, fines, and enforcement actions are online.

#33 Asbestos Control and Licensing, Department of Workforce Dev.; Occupational Safety & Health, PO Box 949 (1 John Fitch Plaza, 3rd Fl), Trenton, NJ 08625-0949; 609-633-3760, Fax- 609-633-0664. http://lwd.dol.state.nj.us/labor/lsse/employee/asbestos_control_and_licensing.html

#34 Bureau of Boiler & Pressure Vessel Compliance, Department of Community Affairs, PO Box 392 (1 John Fitch Plaza), Trenton, NJ 08625; 609-292-2921, Fax- 609-984-1577.

#35 Department of Law & Public Safety, Office of Weights & Measures, 1261 Routes 1 & 9 South, Avenel, NJ 07001; 732-815-4840, Fax- 732-382-5298. www.state.nj.us/lps/ca/owm.htm

#36 Dept. of Treasury, Division of Revenue, Notary Section, PO Box 452, West Trenton, NJ 08625; 609-292-9292, Fax- 609-984-6681. www.state.nj.us/treasury/revenue/dcr/programs/notary.html

#37 Division of Alcoholic Beverage Control, 140 E Front St, CN087, Trenton, NJ 08625-0087; 609-984-3230, Fax- 609-633-6078. Hours- 8:30AM-4:30PM. www.state.nj.us/lps/abc/index.html

#38 Division of Banking, Consumer Credit Bureau, PO Box 473 (20 W State St, CN-040), Trenton, NJ 08625; 609-292-5340, Fax- 609-633-0822. Hours- 8:30AM-5PM. www.state.nj.us/dobi/bankmnu.shtml

#39 Division of Banking, Office of Consumer Finance, 20 W State St, CN-040, Trenton, NJ 08625; 609-292-7659, Fax- 609-292-5461. Hours- 8:30AM-5PM. www.state.nj.us/dobi/ Search at- https://www6.state.nj.us/DOBI_LicSearch/Jsp/index.jsp

#40 Regulated Business Section, Division of Consumer Affairs, PO Box 45028 (124 Halsey St), Newark, NJ 07101; 973-504-6370, Fax- 973-648-2807.

#41 Division of Insurance, License Processing, PO Box 327 (20 W State St), Trenton, NJ 08625-0327; 609-292-4337, Fax- 609-984-0092. www.njdobi.org/insmnu.shtml Search data at- https://www6.state.nj.us/DOBI_LicSearch/Jsp/index.jsp

#42 Division of Motor Vehicles, Dealer Licensing Section, PO Box 171 (225 E State St), Trenton, NJ 08666; 609-292-4517, Fax- 609-292-5153. www.state.nj.us/mvc/

#43 Election Law Enforcement Commission, PO Box 185, Trenton, NJ 08625-0185; 609-292-8700, Fax- 609-777-1457. Hours- 9AM-5PM. www.elec.state.nj.us

#44 Hearing Aid Dispensers Examining Committee, PO Box 45038, Newark, NJ 07101; 973-504-6331, Fax- 973-648-3355. www.state.nj.us/lps/ca/medical/hearingaid.htm Search at- www.state.nj.us/lps/ca/hear/heardir.htm

#45 Department of Community Affairs, Bureau of Code Services, Attn: Licensing Unit, PO Box 816, Trenton, NJ 08625-0816; 609-984-7834, Fax- 609-984-7952. www.state.nj.us/dca/codes/

#46 Cemetery Board, PO Box 45036, Newark, NJ 07101; 973-504-6553, Fax- 973-648-3536. www.state.nj.us/lps/ca/nonmedical/cemetery.htm Search data at- www.state.nj.us/lps/ca/director.htm

#47 Racing Commission, POB 088 (140 E Front St, 4th Fl), Trenton, NJ 08625-0080; 609-984-1554, Fax- 609-599-1785. Hours- 8:30AM-5PM. www.njrconline.org

#48 Department of Banking & Insurance, Real Estate Commission, PO Box 328 (20 W State St), Trenton, NJ 08625-0328; 609-292-7272, Fax- 609-292-0944. www.state.nj.us/dobi/remnu.htm Search data at- https://www6.state.nj.us/DOBI_LicSearch/Jsp/recSearch.jsp

#49 Supreme Court, New Jersey Lawyers Fund, PO Box 961, Trenton, NJ 08625; 609-292-8079, Fax- 609-394-3637. www.judiciary.state.nj.us/cpf/

#50 Nursing Home Administrators Licensing Board, PO Box 367, Trenton, NJ 08625-0367; 609-633-9706, Fax- 609-633-9087. http://nj.gov/health/healthfacilities/ltclicensure.shtml

#51 Ophthalmic Dispensers & Ophthalmic Technicians Board, Division of Consumer Affairs, PO Box 45011 (124 Halsey St), Newark, NJ 07101; 973-504-6435. www.state.nj.us/lps/ca/medical/ophthalmic.htm Search data at- www.state.nj.us/lps/ca/director.htm

#52 Orthotics & Prosthetics Board of Examiners, Division of Consumer Affairs, PO Box 45034 (124 Halsey St), Newark, NJ 07101; 973-504-6445, Fax- 973-648-3536. www.state.nj.us/lps/ca/medical/orthotic.htm Search data at- www.state.nj.us/cgi-bin/consumeraffairs/search/searchentry.pl

#53 Athletic Control Board, PO Box 180 (25 Market St, 3rd Fl, W Wing), Trenton, NJ 08625; 609-292-0317, Fax- 609-292-3756. www.state.nj.us/lps/sacb/

#54 Board of Respiratory Care, PO Box 45031 (122 Halsey St), Newark, NJ 07101; 973-504-6485, Fax- 973-648-3355. www.state.nj.us/lps/ca/medical/respcare.htm Search data at- www.state.nj.us/cgi-bin/consumeraffairs/search/searchentry.pl

#55 Forestry Service, 501 E State St, CN-404, Trenton, NJ 08625-0404; 609-292-2532, Fax- 609-984-0378. www.state.nj.us/dep/parksandforests/forest/community/ Search data at- www.state.nj.us/dep/parksandforests/forest/community/cte.html

#56 State Police Department, Private Detective Division, NJSP Technical Complex, PO Box 7068, West Trenton, NJ 08628; 609-341-3426 or 633-9352. www.njsp.org/about/private-detective.html

#57 Occupational Therapy Advisory Council, Division of Consumer Affairs, PO Box 45037 (124 Halsey St), Newark, NJ 07101; 973-504-6570. www.state.nj.us/lps/ca/medical/occuptherapy.htm

#58 Department of Community Affairs, Division of Fire Safety, PO Box 809, Trenton, NJ 08625-0809; 609-633-6106, Fax- 609-633-6134. www.state.nj.us/dca/dfs/

#59 Department of Health & Senior Svcs, Office of Animal Welfare, PO Box 360, Trenton, NJ 08625-0360; 609-588-3121, Fax- 609-588-3894. www.state.nj.us/health/animalwelfare/animalcontrol.shtml

#60 Department of Environmental Protection, Radiation Protection and Release Prevention, PO Box 415 (25 Arctic Pky), Trenton, NJ 08625-0415; 609-984-5636, Fax- 609-633-2210. Hours- 8AM-5PM. www.nj.gov/dep/rpp/

#61 Department of Environmental Protection, Contract & Admin. Open Examination & Licensing Unit, PO Box 441, Trenton, NJ 98625; 609-777-1013. www.state.nj.us/dep/

New Jersey Federal Courts

The following list indicates the district and division name for each county in the state. If the bankruptcy court location is different from the district court, then the location of the bankruptcy court appears in parentheses. **For information about the standards of fees and electronic access at Federal Courts, see the Appendix.**

County/Court Cross Reference

Atlantic ....Camden
Bergen ....Newark
Burlington ....Camden (Camden/Trenton)
Camden ....Camden
Cape May.........Camden
Cumberland..... Camden
Essex .... Newark
Gloucester........ Camden
Hudson............ Newark
Hunterdon........ Trenton
Mercer............ Trenton
Middlesex ....Newark (Trenton/Camden)
Monmouth ...... Newark (Trenton)
Morris............... Newark
Ocean .... Trenton
Passaic............. Newark
Salem..............Camden
Somerset..........Trenton
Sussex.............Newark
Union...............Newark
Warren.............Trenton

US District Court

Camden Division Clerk of Court, PO Box 2797, Camden, NJ 08101 (In person: 4th and Cooper Sts, Rm 1050, Camden), 856-757-5021; Fax- 856-757-5370. Hours- 9AM-4PM. www.njd.uscourts.gov

Counties/Note: Atlantic, Burlington, Camden, Cape May, Cumberland, Gloucester, Salem.

Searches/Indexing: Include name and DOB, SSN, and/or address in search request. Court will examine identifiers for possible match. Results do not include SSN or DOB. Will not fax back documents. New cases in the index 2 days after filing. Computer and microfiche indexes maintained; computer back to 1990. District-wide searches available here. Searchers can print dockets from the computer. Closed case files sent to archives irregularly.

Search Access: Only docket info is available by phone. **Mail:** Search usually completed- 3-4 working days. Include SASE for return. **In person:** 1 public terminal available..

Payment: Pay by Visa/MC/AmEx/Discover, money order, cashier's or personal check. Payee: Clerk, US District Court.

E-Svcs: PACER- http://pacer.njd.uscourts.gov. PACER records go back to 5/1991. New records online after 1 day. ECF at https://ecf.njd.uscourts.gov. **Opinions Online:** http://lawlibrary.rutgers.edu/fed/search.html.

Newark Division Court Clerk, ML King, Jr Federal Bldg & US Courthouse, 50 Walnut St, Rm 4015, Newark, NJ 07101, 973-645-3730; records- 973-645-4565. Hours- 9AM-4PM. www.njd.uscourts.gov

Counties/Note: Bergen, Essex, Hudson, Middlesex, Morris, Passaic, Sussex, Union. Monmouth County cases at Newark from late 1997-200?; Pre-1997 closed cases in Trenton.

Searches/Indexing: Include name and DOB, SSN, and/or address in search request. Court will examine identifiers for possible match. Results do not include SSN or DOB. Will not fax back documents. New cases are in the index 2 days after filing date. Computer and microfiche indexes maintained; computer back to 1990. District-wide searches available here. Closed case files sent to archives irregularly. **Search Access:** Only docket info available by phone. **Mail:** Search usually completed- 1 week. Include SASE for return. **In person:** 2 public terminals available.

Payment: Pay by Visa/MC/AmEx/Discover, money order, cashier's or personal check. Payee: Clerk, US District Court.

E-Svcs: PACER- http://pacer.njd.uscourts.gov. PACER records go back to 5/1991. New records online after 1 day. ECF at https://ecf.njd.uscourts.gov. **Online Opinions:** http://lawlibrary.rutgers.edu/fed/search.html.

Trenton Division Court Clerk, 402 E State St, Rm 2020, Trenton, NJ 08608, 609-989-2065. Hours-9AM-4PM. www.njd.uscourts.gov

Counties/Note: Hunterdon, Mercer, Monmouth, Ocean, Somerset, Warren. 1997-200? Monmouth County may be found at Newark Division. Pre-1997 closed Monmouth cases remain in Trenton.

Searches/Indexing: Include name and DOB, SSN, and/or address in search request. Court will examine identifiers for possible match. Results do not include SSN or DOB. Will not fax back documents. New cases are in the index 2 days after filing date. Computer and microfiche indexes maintained; computer back to 1990. District-wide searches available; Trenton records go back 1920; closed files for Newark division here up to 1997. Closed case files sent to archives irregularly.

Search Access: Only docket info available by phone. **Mail:** Search usually completed- 2 days. SASE not required. **In person:** Public terminal available. No self-serve copier.

Payment: Pay by Visa/MC/AmEx/Discover, money order, cashier's or personal check. Payee: Clerk, US District Court.

E-Svcs: PACER- http://pacer.njd.uscourts.gov. PACER records go back to 5/1991. New records online after 1 day. ECF at https://ecf.njd.uscourts.gov. **Opinions Online:** http://lawlibrary.rutgers.edu/fed/search.html.

US Bankruptcy Court

Camden Division Court Clerk, PO Box 2067, Camden, NJ 08101 (In person: 401 Market St, 2nd Fl, Camden, NJ 08101), 856-757-5485; records- 856-757-5485 x360; Fax- 856-757-5425. Hours- 8:30AM-4PM. www.njb.uscourts.gov

Counties/Note: Atlantic, Burlington (partial), Camden, Cape May, Cumberland, Gloucester, Salem. See Trenton Division for remainder of Burlington County.

Searches/Indexing: Include SSN and full name in request. Results include last 4 SSN digits. Will not fax back documents. New cases are in the index immediately after filing date. **Search Access:** Only docket info available by phone. Voice Case Information Service available, call VCIS at 877-239-2547 or 973-645-6044. **Mail:** Search usually completed- 2-5 days. Include SASE for return. **In person:** 3 public terminals available.

Payment: Pay by money order, cashier's check, business check. No personal checks. Attorney credit cards accepted. Payee: Clerk, US Bankruptcy Court.

E-Services: Document images available. PACER records go back to 1991. New records online after 1-2 days. ECF at https://ecf.njb.uscourts.gov. **Online Note:** Calendars free at www.njb.uscourts.gov/hearingdate/index.pl.

Newark Division Court Clerk, PO Box 1352, Newark, NJ 07101-1352 (In person: ML King Jr Federal Bldg, 50 Walnut St, 3rd Fl, Newark), 973-645-4764. 8:30-4PM. www.njb.uscourts.gov

Counties/Note: Bergen, Essex, Hudson, Morris, Passaic, Sussex, Union.

Searches/Indexing: Include SSN and full name in request. Results include last 4 SSN digits. Will not fax back documents. New cases are in the index immediately after filing date. Case files sent to archives 6 months after closed. **Search Access:** Voice Case Information Service available, call VCIS at 877-239-2547 or 973-645-6044. **Mail:** Search usually completed- 2-5 days. Include SASE for return. **In person:** 2 public terminals available.

Payment: Pay by money order, cashier's check, business check. No personal checks. Attorney credit cards accepted. Payee: Clerk, US Bankruptcy Court.

E-Services: Document images available. PACER records go back to 1991. New records online after 1-2 days. ECF at https://ecf.njb.uscourts.gov. **Online Note:** Calendars free at www.njb.uscourts.gov/hearingdate/index.pl.

Trenton Division Clerk of Court, US Courthouse, 402 E State St, 1st Fl, Trenton, NJ 08608, 609-989-2129; Fax- 609-989-0580. Hours- 8:30AM-4PM. www.njb.uscourts.gov

Counties/Note: Burlington (partial), Hunterdon, Mercer, Middlesex, Monmouth, Ocean, Somerset, Warren. See Camden Division for remainder of Burlington County.

Searches/Indexing: Include SSN and full name in request. Results do not include SSN or DOB. Will not fax back documents. New cases are in the index immediately after filing. To date, electronic files continue to be maintained at this court.

Search Access: Voice Case Information Service available, call VCIS at 877-239-2547 or 973-645-6044. **Mail:** Search usually completed- 1-2 days. Include SASE for return. **In person:** 2 public terminals available. No self-serve copier.

Payment: Pay by money order, cashier's check, business check. No personal checks. Attorney credit cards accepted. Payee: Clerk, US Bankruptcy Court.

E-Services: Document images available. PACER records go back to 1991. New records online after 1-2 days. ECF at https://ecf.njb.uscourts.gov. **Online Note:** Calendars free at www.njb.uscourts.gov/hearingdate/index.pl.

New Jersey County Courts

Court	Jurisdiction	No. of Courts	How Organized
Superior Courts*	General	21	21 Counties/15 Vicinages
Special Civil Part*	Limited	21	21 Counties
Municipal Courts	Municipal	535	
Tax Court	Special	1	

* Profiled in this Sourcebook.

Court	CIVIL								
	Tort	Contract	Real Estate	Min. Claim	Max. Claim	Small Claims	Estate	Eviction	Domestic Relations
Superior Courts*	X	X	X	$15,000	No Max		X		X
Special Civil Part*	X	X	X	$0	$15,000	$3000		X	
Municipal Courts									
Tax Court									

Court	CRIMINAL				
	Felony	Misdemeanor	DWI/DUI	Preliminary Hearing	Juvenile
Superior Courts*	X				X
Special Civil Part*					
Municipal Courts		X	X		

Administration

Administrative Office of the Courts, RJH Justice Complex, Courts Bldg 7th Fl, PO Box 037, Trenton, NJ, 08625; (EST) 609-984-0275, Fax: 609-984-6968. All courts are Eastern Standard Time. www.judiciary.state.nj.us

Court Structure

Each Superior Court has 3 divisions; Civil, Criminal, and Family. Search requests should be addressed separately to each division. Criminal cases are those in which a defendant stands accused of a serious crime, such as assault, theft, robbery, fraud, or murder. Civil cases in which the amount in controversy exceeds $15,000 are heard in the Civil Division of Superior Court. Cases in which the amounts in controversy are between $3,000 and $15,000 are heard in the Special Civil Part of the Civil Division. Those in which the amounts in controversy are less than $3,000 also are heard in the Special Civil Part and are known as Small Claims cases. Family related cases, such as those involving divorce, domestic violence, juvenile delinquency, child support, foster-care placements and termination of parental rights, are heard by the Family Division. Probate is handled by Surrogates.

The Municipal Courts are courts of limited jurisdiction with responsibility for motor vehicle and parking tickets, minor criminal-type offenses (simple assault and bad checks), municipal ordinance offenses, and other offenses, such as fish and game violations.

Online Access

The Judiciary's civil motion calendar and schedule is searchable at www.judiciary.state.nj.us/calendars.htm. The database includes all Superior Court Motion calendars for the Civil Division (Law-Civil Part, Special CivilPart and Chancery-General Equity), and proceeding information for a six-week period (two weeks prior to the current date and four weeks following the current date). Another useful website giving decisions is maintained by the Rutgers Law School at http://lawlibrary.rutgers.edu/search.shtml. Supreme and Appellate case data is found at www.judiciary.state.nj.us/opinions/index.htm.

Restricted online access to all civil records is available through the ACMS, AMIS, and FACTS systems. The fee is $1.00 per minute of use. For more information, contact the Superior Court Clerk's Office, Electronic Access Program. Write to 25 Market St, CN971, Trenton NJ 08625, or fax 609-292-6564, or call 609-292-4987. Ask for the Inquiry System Guidebook containing hardware and software requirements and an enrollment form.

Searching Tips, Fees, and Other Guidelines

The Judgment Unit at 609-292-4804 will confirm if a case is still open or closed; requester must submit docket number. Criminal searches may be done in person at the courts on their public access terminals, but the Superior Court now directs non-in person searches to the New Jersey State Police Records and ID Section at 609-882-2000, x2991 or x2918. State Police records are fingerprint-based searches.

Originally developed for county prosecutors, the Promis/Gavel is an automated criminal case tracking system that provides the function of docketing, indexing, noticing, calendaring, statistical reporting, and case management reporting, etc. Promis/Gavel is interactive with the courts as well as with the NJSP. But rules do not allow the public to access the complete Promis/Gavel system—only a filtered Promis/Gavel Public Access (PGPA) system is available to the public on the public access terminals in the courts. Also, the PGPA does not include contain offenses or petty offenses recorded in 530+ municipal courts, unless they are filed with indictables. The more serious of these petty offenses include drug offenses, violence, theft, sexual assault, and pedophilia. An AOC press release about the PGPA states, "The court records obtained from Promis/Gavel do not constitute a criminal history records check, which must be obtained through law enforcement." However, because of the simplicity of access and cost, the PGPA is the system of choice for most screening companies.

Note that Cape May County offices are located in City of "Cape May Court House," and not in "City of Cape May."

Atlantic County

Superior Court - Criminal Criminal Courthouse, 4997 Unami Blvd, Mays Landing, NJ 08330; criminal phone: 609-909-8154; fax: 609-909-8190; 8:30AM-4:30PM (EST). ***Felony.***
www.judiciary.state.nj.us/atlantic/index.htm
Criminal Records: Access: In person only. Visitors must perform in person searches themselves. Required to search: name, years to search, DOB; SSN helpful. Criminal records computerized from 1985, prior on docket books and index cards back to 1940. Public use terminal has crim records back to 1985. PAT results show middle initial, DOB. Aliases also shown in results.
General Information: No sealed, expunged, judges notes, PSI's, or mental illness records released. Will not fax documents. Court makes copy: $.75 per page. Certification fee: $5.00. Payee: Treasurer, State of NJ. Personal checks accepted; credit cards are not. Prepayment required.

Superior Court - Civil 1201 Bacharach Blvd., Atlantic City, NJ 08401; 609-345-6700; fax: 609-343-2326; 8:30AM-4:30PM (EST). ***Civil Actions over $15,000, Probate.***
www.judiciary.state.nj.us/atlantic/index.htm
Civil Records: Access: Mail, in person. Both court and visitors may perform in person searches. No search fee. Required to search: name, years to search. Civil cases indexed by defendant, plaintiff; index on computer from 9/84, on dockets from 1960, prior to 1960 archived. Prior to 1960 records are for public review only (in large books, d. Mail turnaround time 1 day. Public use terminal has civil records back to 1985. PAT civil results show middle initial.
General Information: No sealed, expunged, judges notes, PSI's, or mental illness records released. Will not fax documents. Court makes copy: $.75 per page 1st 10 pages; $.50 per page next 10; each add'l $.25. Self serve: $.15 per page. Certification fee: $10.00 per page. Payee: Clerk of Special Civil Ct. Personal checks accepted; credit cards are not. Prepayment required. Mail requests: SASE required.

Superior Court Special Civil Part 1201 Bacharach Blvd., Atlantic City, NJ 08401; 609-345-6700 X3347; fax: 609-343-2326; 8:30AM-4:30PM (EST). ***Civil Actions under $15,000, Eviction, Small Claims.***
www.judiciary.state.nj.us/atlantic/index.htm
Civil Records: Access: Mail, in person, fax. Both court and visitors may perform in person searches. No search fee. Required to search: name, years to search. Civil cases indexed by defendant, plaintiff; index on computer from 1985 (some from 1987), prior on index books. In order to review index books, call in advance for an appointment. Mail turnaround time 1 week. Public use terminal has civil records back to 1987.
General Information: No adoption, sealed, juvenile, expunged, dismissed, or mental health records released. Will not fax documents. Court makes copy: $.75 per page. Self serve: $.15 per page. Certification fee: $5.00. Payee: Clerk, Special Civil Part. Personal checks accepted; credit cards are not. Prepayment required. Mail requests: SASE required.

Bergen County

Superior Court - Criminal 10 Main St, Rm 124, Justice Ctr, Hackensack, NJ 07601; 201-527-2445; criminal phone: x3; fax: 201-371-1118; 8:30AM-4:30PM (EST). ***Felony.***
www.judiciary.state.nj.us/bergen/index.htm
Criminal Records: Access: In person only. Both court and visitors may perform in person searches. No search fee. Required to search: name, years to search. Criminal records computerized from 1995. Public use terminal has crim records. Public record terminal located in the Library.
General Information: No sealed, expunged, dismissed, judges notes, PSI's, or discovery packets records released. Will not fax documents. Court makes copy: $.50. No charge for single copy of criminal record. Certification fee: $5.00 per doc. Payee: Bergen County Clerk. Personal checks accepted; credit cards are not. Prepayment required.

Superior Court - Civil 10 Main St. Rm 111, Justice Ctr, Hackensack, NJ 07601; 201-527-2700; civil phone: x2601; probate phone: 201-646-2252; 8:30AM-4:30PM (EST). ***Civil Actions over $15,000, Probate.***
www.judiciary.state.nj.us/bergen/index.htm
Probate records managed by Surrogate's Court.
Civil Records: Access: Mail, in person. Only the court performs in person searches; visitors may not. Required to search: name, years to search. Civil cases indexed by defendant, plaintiff; index on computer for 2-5 years, on dockets from 1900s. Mail turnaround time 1 week. Public use terminal has civil records back to 2-5 years. PAT results show name only. Public terminals in law library.
General Information: No sealed, expunged, dismissed, judges notes, PSI's, or discovery packets records released. Will not fax documents. Court makes copy: $.75 per page. Self serve: $.25 per page. Certification fee: $5.00. Payee: Bergen County Clerk. Personal checks accepted; credit cards are not. Prepayment required. Mail requests: SASE required for civil.

Superior Court Special Civil Part 10 Main St, Rm 427, Justice Ctr, Hackensack, NJ 07601; 201-527-2700; civil phone: x2; 8:30AM-4:30PM (EST). ***Civil Actions under $15,000, Eviction, Small Claims.***
www.judiciary.state.nj.us/bergen/index.htm
Civil Records: Access: In person, phone. Both court and visitors may perform in person searches. No search fee. Required to search: name, years to search, case identifiers. Civil cases indexed by defendant, plaintiff; index on computer from 1990, prior on index cards. Note: Due to identity matchings problems, this Special Civil Parts prefer not to perform name searches; please provide a case or docket number. Public use terminal has civil records. PAT results show name only. Public terminal is located in the law library.
General Information: No adoption, sealed, juvenile, expunged, dismissed, or mental illness records released. Will not fax documents. Court makes copy: $.75 per page 1st 10 pgs; $.50 each add'l. Certification fee: $5.00. Payee: Bergen County Special Civil Part. Personal checks accepted; credit cards are not. Prepayment required. Mail requests: SASE required.

Burlington County

Superior Court - Criminal 49 Rancocas Rd, Mount Holly, NJ 08060; 609-518-2560; 8AM-5PM (EST). ***Felony.***
www.judiciary.state.nj.us/burlington/index.htm
Criminal Records: Access: In person only. Visitors must perform in person searches themselves. Required to search: name, years to search; also helpful: DOB, SSN. Criminal records computerized from 1986, on docket books from 1954, archived from early 1900s. Public use terminal has crim records.PAT results show name, DOB.
General Information: No sealed, expunged, judges notes, PSI's, or discovery packets released. Will not fax documents. Court makes copy: $.75 per page for 1st 10 pages; $.50 per page next 10; each add'l $.25. Certification fee: $5.00. Payee: State of New Jersey Treasurer. Personal checks accepted; credit cards are not. Prepayment required.

Superior Court - Civil 49 Rancocas Rd, Mount Holly, NJ 08060; 609-518-2815; fax: 609-518-2826; 8AM-4:30PM (EST). ***Civil Actions over $15,000, Probate.***
www.judiciary.state.nj.us/burlington/index.htm
Civil Records: Access: Mail, in person. Both court and visitors may perform in person searches. No search fee. Required to search: name, years to search. Civil cases indexed by defendant, plaintiff. Local judgment records on computer since 1989, all others from 1954 to present. Mail turnaround time 10 days. Public use terminal has civil records back to 1989. PAT results show name only.
General Information: No sealed, expunged, judges notes, PSI's, or discovery packets released. Court makes copy: $.75 per page 1st 10 pages; $.50 per page next 10; each add'l $.25. Certification fee: $5.00 per doc. Payee: State of New Jersey Treasurer. Personal checks accepted; credit cards are not. Prepayment required. Mail requests: SASE required for civil.

Superior Court Special Civil Part 49 Rancocas Rd., Mount Holly, NJ 08060; 609-518-2865; fax: 609-518-2872; 8:30AM-4:30PM (EST). ***Civil Actions under $15,000, Eviction, Small Claims.***
www.njcourtsonline.com
Civil Records: Access: Phone, fax, mail, in person. Both court and visitors may perform in person searches. No search fee. Required to search: name, years to search. Civil cases indexed by defendant, plaintiff; index on computer from 1995, microfilm from 1984, prior on index books by docket number. Mail turnaround time 1-2 weeks. Public use terminal has civil records back to 1995. PAT results show name only.
General Information: This court does not handle criminal matters in the Special Civil Part. No fee to fax documents. Court makes copy: $.75 per page 1st 10 pages; $.50 per page next 10; each add'l $.25. Certification fee: $5.00 per doc. Payee: Treasurer, State of NJ. Personal checks accepted; credit cards are not. Prepayment required. Mail requests: SASE required.

Camden County

Superior Court - Criminal Hall of Justice, 101 S 5th St, Camden, NJ 08103; 856-379-2200; criminal phone: x3343; fax: 856-379-2255; 8AM-4PM (EST). ***Felony.***
www.judiciary.state.nj.us/camden/index.htm
Criminal Records: Access: Mail, fax, in person. Both court and visitors may perform in person searches. No search fee, but a fee is to be implemented soon. Required to search: name, years to search, DOB, SSN. Criminal records computerized from 1986, on docket books from 1940. Mail turnaround time 3 days. Public use terminal has crim records back to 1986. PAT results show name only.
General Information: No sealed, expunged, dismissed, judges notes, PSI's or discovery packets records released. Will not fax documents. Court makes copy: $.75 ea up to 10 pages, then $.50 ea next 10. If over 20 pages then $.25 ea. Certification fee: $5.00. Payee: NJ State Treasurer. Cash, money orders or personal checks accepted. No credit cards accepted. Prepayment required. Mail requests: SASE required.

Superior Court - Civil Hall of Justice, #150, 101 S 5th St, Camden, NJ 08103; 856-379-2200; civil phone: 856-379-2202; fax: 856-379-2255; 8:30AM-4:30PM (EST). ***Civil Actions over $15,000, Probate.***
www.judiciary.state.nj.us/camden/index.htm
Civil Records: Access: Mail, in person. Both court and visitors may perform in person searches. No search fee. Required to search: name, years to search. Civil cases indexed by defendant, plaintiff; index on computer from 1987. Note: Also, mail or in person judgment searches are directed to Trenton. Mail turnaround time 5 days. Public use terminal has civil records back to 1987.
General Information: No sealed, dismissed, judges notes, or discovery packets records released. Will not fax documents. Court makes copy for no fee. Certification fee: $5.00. Payee: Clerk of Superior Court. Personal checks accepted; credit cards are not. Prepayment required. Mail requests: SASE required.

Superior Court Special Civil Part Hall of Justice Complex, 101 S. 5th St., Camden, NJ 08103; 856-379-2202; fax: 856-379-2252; 8:30AM-4:30PM (EST). ***Civil Actions under $15,000, Eviction, Small Claims.***
www.judiciary.state.nj.us/camden/index.htm
Alternate fax number- 856-379-2253.
Civil Records: Access: Mail, in person. Both court and visitors may perform in person searches. No search fee. Required to search: name, years to search. Civil cases indexed by defendant, plaintiff; index on computer from 1988. Prior records on docket books. Note: In person access is limited to one name. Mail turnaround time varies; larger orders take longer. Public use terminal has civil records back to 1988.
General Information: No adoption, sealed, juvenile, expunged, restricted, or mental health records released. Will not fax documents. Court makes copy: $.75 per page 1st 10 pages; $.50 per page next 10; each add'l $.25. Certification fee: $5.00. Payee: Treasurer, State of NJ. Personal checks accepted; credit cards are not. Prepayment required. Mail requests: SASE required for mail return of any copies.

Cape May County

Superior Court - Criminal 9 N Main St, Superior Court, Cape May Court House, NJ 08210; 609-463-6550; criminal phone: 609-463-6500; fax: 609-463-6458; 8:30AM-4:30PM (EST). ***Felony.***
www.judiciary.state.nj.us/atlantic/index.htm
Criminal Records: Access: In person only. Visitors must perform in person searches themselves. Required to search: name, years to search, DOB; SSN helpful. Criminal records computerized from 1985; on index books back to 1950. Public use terminal has crim records back to 1985.
General Information: No sealed, expunged, dismissed, judges notes, PSI's, or discovery packets records released. Court makes copy: $.75 per page. Certification fee: $5.00 per doc. Payee: State of New Jersey Treasurer. Personal checks accepted; credit cards are not. Prepayment required.

Superior Court - Civil Civil/Equity Division-Law, DN-203, 9 N Main St, Cape May Court House, NJ 08210; 609-463-6514; fax: 609-463-6465; 8:30AM-4:30PM (EST). ***Civil Actions over $15,000, Probate.***
www.judiciary.state.nj.us/atlantic/index.htm
Civil Records: Access: In person only. Visitors must perform in person searches themselves. Required to search: name, years to search. Civil cases indexed by defendant, plaintiff; index on computer from 4/91, on index books and archived from 1900s. Public use terminal has civil records back to 1991. PAT results show name only.
General Information: No sealed records released. Will not fax documents. Court makes copy: $.75 per page 1st 10 pages; $.50 per page next 10; each add'l $.25. Certification fee: $5.00 per doc. Payee: Treasurer, State of NJ. Personal checks accepted; credit cards are not. Prepayment required.

Superior Court Special Civil Part DN-203, 9 N. Main St, Cape May Court House, NJ 08210; 609-463-6522; fax: 609-463-6465; 8:30AM-4:30PM (EST). ***Civil Actions under $15,000, Eviction, Small Claims.***
www.judiciary.state.nj.us/atlantic/index.htm
Civil Records: Access: In person only. Visitors must perform in person searches themselves. Required to search: name, years to search; also helpful: address. Civil cases indexed by defendant, plaintiff; index on computer from 4/1991, on index from 1973. Public use terminal has civil records. PAT civil results show middle initial.
General Information: No sealed records released. Will not fax documents. Court makes copy: $.75 per page 1st 10 pages; $.50 per page next 10; each add'l $.25. Certification fee: $5.00 if not a party to the action; no cert fee is a party. Payee: Treasurer, State of NJ. Personal checks accepted; credit cards are not. Prepayment required.

Cumberland County

Superior Court - Criminal PO Box 757, Courthouse, Broad/Fayette Strs, Bridgeton, NJ 08302; 856-453-4300; fax: 856-451-7152; 8:30AM-4:30PM (EST). ***Felony.***
www.judiciary.state.nj.us/gloucester/cum/index.htm
NJ State Police Search, PO Box 7068, West Trenton, NJ 08625. Phone number is 609-882-2000.
Criminal Records: Access: Mail, in person. Both court and visitors may perform in person searches. Search fee: $4.00 per name. Required to search: name, years to search, DOB, SSN, signed release; also helpful: address. Criminal records computerized from 1986, on index from 1900. Mail turnaround time 1 week. Public use terminal has crim records back to 1986. PAT results show middle initial, DOB. Public access terminal in Law Library.
General Information: No sealed, expunged, dismissed, judges notes, PSI's, or discovery packets records released. Will not fax documents. Court makes copy: $.75 each 1st 10, $.50 each 11-20, $25 21+. Certification fee: $5.00 per doc. Payee: State of New Jersey, Misc Fund. Personal checks accepted; credit cards are not. Prepayment required. Mail requests: SASE required.

Superior Court - Civil PO Box 10, Broad & Sayfayette Sts., Bridgeton, NJ 08302; 856-453-4330; civil phone: 856-453-4350; fax: 856-453-4349; 8:30AM-4:30PM (EST). ***Civil Actions over $15,000, Probate.***
www.judiciary.state.nj.us/gloucester/cum/index.htm
Civil Records: Access: Mail, in person. Only the court performs in person searches; visitors may not. Search fee: $4.00 per name. Required to search: name, years to search. Civil records on computer from 1986, on index from 1900. Mail turnaround time 1 week.
General Information: No sealed, expunged, dismissed, judges notes, PSI's, or discovery packets records released. Court makes copy: $.25 per page. Certification fee: $5.00 per doc. Payee: State of New Jersey, Misc Fund. Personal checks accepted; credit cards are not. Prepayment required. Mail requests: SASE required.

Superior Court Special Civil Part PO Box 10, 60 W Broad, Bridgeton, NJ 08302; 856-453-4350; fax: 856-453-4349; 8:30AM-4:30PM (EST). ***Civil Actions under $15,000, Eviction, Small Claims.***
www.judiciary.state.nj.us/gloucester/cum/index.htm
Judgment Unit Information phone number is 609-292-4481.
Civil Records: Access: Phone, mail, in person. Only the court performs in person searches; visitors may not. No search fee. Required to search: name, years to search. Civil cases indexed by defendant, plaintiff; index on computer from 12/89, on docket books from 1949 to 11/89. Note: Phone access is limited to 1 or 2 searches. Mail turnaround time 1 week.
General Information: No adoption, sealed, juvenile, expunged, dismissed, or mental illness records released. Court makes copy: $.75 per page 1st 10 pages; $.50 per page next 10; each add'l $.25. Certification fee: $5.00. Payee: Clerk, Special Civil Part. Personal checks accepted; credit cards are not. Prepayment required. Mail requests: SASE requested.

Essex County

Superior Court - Criminal 50 W Market St, Rm 912 & 1012, County Court Bldg, Veterans Ct, Newark, NJ 07102-1681; 973-693-5965, 973-693-5700 (switchboard); 8:30AM-4:30PM (EST). ***Felony.***
www.judiciary.state.nj.us/essex/index.htm
Criminal Records: Access: Mail, in person. Both court and visitors may perform in person searches. Search fee: $5.00 per indictment. Required to search: name, years to search, DOB, SSN. Criminal records computerized from 1985. Note: All records requests must be mailed with pre-payment. Mail turnaround time 1 week. Public use terminal has crim records back to 1985.
General Information: No sealed, expunged, dismissed, judges notes, PSI's, or discovery packets records released. Will fax documents to local or toll free line. Court makes copy: $.75 per page. Certification fee: $5.00. Payee: State of New Jersey Treasurer. Only cashiers checks and money orders accepted. No credit cards accepted. Prepayment required. Mail requests: SASE required.

Superior Court - Civil 465 Dr. Martin Luther King Blvd, Newark, NJ 07102-1681; 973-693-6460; fax: 973-424-2426; 8:30AM-4:30PM (EST). ***Civil Actions, Law, Probate.***
www.judiciary.state.nj.us/essex/index.htm
Civil Records: Access: In person only. Only the court performs in person searches; visitors may not. No search fee. Required to search: name, years to search. Civil cases indexed by defendant, plaintiff; index on computer from 1984, on index from 1930. Note: Visitors may perform their own searches at the Omsbudsman Office, Rm 132, 50 W Market St, Newark.
General Information: No sealed, expunged, dismissed, judges notes, PSI's, or discovery packets records released. Will fax documents $3.00 per page. Court makes copy: $.75 per page; 11-20 copies- $.50 per page; 21 or more- $.25 per page. Self serve: $.10 per copy; machince accepts upt to $5.00 bills. Certification fee: $5.00 per doc. Payee: State of New Jersey Treasurer. Business checks accepted. No credit cards accepted. Prepayment required. Mail requests: SASE required.

Superior Court Special Civil Part 465 Martin Luther King Blvd, Rm 240, Hall of Records, Newark, NJ 07102; 973-693-6494; 693-6460- recs; fax: 973-424-2426; 8:30AM-4:30PM (EST). ***Civil Actions under $15,000, Eviction, Small Claims.***
www.judiciary.state.nj.us/essex/index.htm
Civil Records: Access: Mail, fax, in person. Both court and visitors may perform in person searches. No search fee. Required to search: name, years to search. Civil cases indexed by defendant, plaintiff; index on computer from 1986 and archived 1982-2004. Note: Pre- 2005 records are in storage and will take longer to process. Mail turnaround time 7-10 days. Public use terminal has civil records back to 1990's. PAT results show name, DOB. Search PAT index free in Rm 132 only.
General Information: No adoption, sealed, juvenile, expunged, dismissed, or mental illness records released. Will not fax out documents. Court makes copy: $.75 per page. Certification fee: $5.00 per cover page. Payee: Essex County Special Civil Part. Personal checks accepted; credit cards are not. Prepayment required. Mail requests: SASE helpful.

Gloucester County

Superior Court - Criminal PO Box 187, 70 Hunter St, Woodbury, NJ 08096; 856-853-3531; fax: 856-853-3735; 8:30AM-4:30PM (EST). ***Felony.***
www.judiciary.state.nj.us/gloucester/glo/index.htm
Criminal Records: Access: Mail, in person. Visitors must perform in person searches themselves. Search fee: $4.00 per name. Required to search: name, years to search, DOB, SSN, signed release. Criminal records computerized from 1982, on index from 1955. Mail turnaround time 1-3 days. Public use terminal has crim records back to 1982. Law library computer available in building complex.
General Information: No sealed, expunged, dismissed, judges notes, PSI's, or discovery packets records released. Will not fax documents. Court makes copy: $1.00 per page. Certification fee: $5.00 per doc. Payee: State of New Jersey, Miscellaneous. Personal checks accepted; credit cards are not. Prepayment required. Mail requests: SASE required.

Superior Court - Civil 1 N Broad St, Woodbury, NJ 08096; 856-853-3232; civil phone: 856-853-3392; fax: 856-853-3429; 8:30AM-4:30PM (EST). ***Civil Actions, Probate.***
www.judiciary.state.nj.us/gloucester/glo/index.htm
Civil Records: Access: Mail, in person, online. Only the court performs in person searches; visitors may not. No search fee. Required to search: name, years to search. Civil cases indexed by defendant, plaintiff; index on computer from 1988, prior records on county books. Mail turnaround time ASAP. Search the Motion Calendar free at www.judiciary.state.nj.us/acms/MOTN/CV0390W0E.ASP. Calendar limited to about 6 weeks.

General Information: No sealed, expunged, dismissed, judges notes, PSI's, or discovery packets records released. Will not fax documents. Court makes copy: $.75 per page 1st 10 pages; $.50 per page next 10; each add'l $.25. Certification fee: $1.50. Payee: Treasurer State of New Jersey. Personal checks accepted; credit cards are not. Prepayment required. Mail requests: SASE required.

Superior Court Special Civil Part 1 N Broad St., Woodbury, NJ 08096; 856-853-3392; fax: 856-853-3416; 8:30AM-4:30PM (EST). ***Civil Actions under $15,000, Eviction, Small Claims.***
www.judiciary.state.nj.us/gloucester/glo/index.htm
Civil Records: Access: Mail, in person, online. Only the court performs in person searches; visitors may not. No search fee. Required to search: name, years to search. Civil cases indexed by defendant, plaintiff; index on computer from 8/89, on index books from 1900. Search the Motion Calendar free at www.judiciary.state.nj.us/acms/MOTN/CV0390W0E.ASP. Calendar limited to about 6 weeks.
General Information: Court makes copy: $.75 per page 1st 10 pages; $.50 per page next 10; each add'l $.25. Certification fee: $5.00 per doc. Payee: Clerk, Superior Court of NJ. Personal checks accepted. Prepayment required. Mail requests: SASE required.

Hudson County

Superior Court - Criminal 595 Newark Ave, Rm 104, Jersey City, NJ 07306; 201-795-6704; fax: 201-795-6705; 8:30AM-4:30PM (EST). ***Felony.***
www.judiciary.state.nj.us/hudson/index.htm
Criminal Records: Access: Mail, in person. Visitors must perform in person searches themselves. No search fee. Required to search: name, years to search, DOB, SSN. Criminal records computerized from 1985, on index books from 1900. Note: Court suggests access for a fee via www.state.nj.us/lps/njsp/about/serv_chrc.html - the NJ State Police. Mail turnaround time 1 week. Public use terminal has crim records back to 1985.
General Information: No sealed, expunged, dismissed, judges notes, PSI's, or discovery packets records released. Will not fax documents. Court makes copy: $.75 per page for 1st 10 pages; $.50 per page next 10; each add'l $.25. Certification fee: $5.00. Uncertified copy of a judgment of conviction-$1.50. Payee: Treasurer, State of NJ. Personal checks accepted; credit cards are not. Prepayment required.

Superior Court - Civil 583 Newark Ave, Jersey City, NJ 07306; 201-217-5162; 201-217-5163 (Records Rm); fax: 201-217-5241; 8:30AM-4:30PM (EST). ***Civil Actions over $15,000, Probate.***
www.judiciary.state.nj.us/hudson/index.htm
Civil Records: Access: In person only. Both court and visitors may perform in person searches. No search fee. Required to search: name, years to search. Civil cases indexed by defendant, plaintiff; index on computer for 18 months after disposition. Public use terminal has civil records back to 1992. PAT civil results show middle initial.
General Information: No sealed, expunged, dismissed, judges notes, PSI's, or discovery packets records released. Will not fax documents. Court makes copy: $.75 per page 1st 10 pages; $.50 per page next 10; each add'l $.25. Certification fee: $5.00 per cert. Payee: Treasurer, State of NJ. Personal checks accepted; credit cards are not. Prepayment required.

Superior Court Special Civil Part 595 Newark Ave, Rm G-9, Jersey City, NJ 07306; 201-795-6680; fax: 201-795-6053; 8:30AM-4:30PM (EST). ***Civil Actions under $15,000, Eviction, Small Claims.***
www.judiciary.state.nj.us/hudson/index.htm
Civil Records: Access: In person only. Visitors must perform in person searches themselves. Required to search: name, years to search, address. Civil cases indexed by defendant, plaintiff. Civil index on cards from 1993, prior on docket books. Public use terminal has civil records back to 1995.
General Information: No adoption, sealed, juvenile, expunged, dismissed, or mental illness released. Court makes copy: $.75 per page 1st 10 pages; $.50 per page next 10; each add'l $.25. Self serve: Self serve copier in 5th Fl Library. Certification fee: $5.00 per doc. Payee: Treasurer, State of NJ. Personal checks accepted; credit cards are not. Prepayment required.

Hunterdon County

Superior Court - Criminal 65 Park Ave, Flemington, NJ 08822; 908-237-5840; fax: 908-237-5841; 8:30AM-4:30PM (EST). ***Felony.***
www.judiciary.state.nj.us/somerset/index.htm
Criminal Records: Access: Fax, mail, in person. Visitors must perform in person searches themselves. Search fee: $6.00 per name. Required to search: name, years to search, DOB; also helpful: SSN. Criminal records computerized from 1987, prior on index books. Mail turnaround time 1-3 weeks. Public use terminal has crim records back to 1987.
General Information: No sealed, expunged, dismissed, judges notes, PSI's, or discovery packets records released. Will fax documents, no charge. Court makes copy: $.75 per page. Certification fee: $5.00 per doc. Payee: Treasurer, State of New Jersey. Personal checks accepted; credit cards are not. Prepayment required. Mail requests: SASE required.

Superior Court - Civil Hunterdon County Justice Ctr, 65 Park Ave, Flemington, NJ 08822; 908-237-5820; probate phone: 908-788-1156; fax: 908-237-5821; 8:30AM-4:30PM (EST). ***Civil Actions over $15,000, Probate.***
www.judiciary.state.nj.us/somerset/index.htm
Probate records are indexed separately and are located on the 2nd Fl Surrogate/Probate office.
Civil Records: Access: Mail, in person, phone. Both court and visitors may perform in person searches. No search fee. Required to search: name, years to search. Civil cases indexed by defendant, plaintiff; index on computer since 1990, on index from 1950. Mail turnaround time 1-2 weeks. Public use terminal has civil records back to 1990. PAT results show name only.
General Information: No sealed, expunged, dismissed, judges notes, PSI's, or discovery packets records released. Will not fax documents. Court makes copy: $.75 per page 1st 10 pages; $.50 per page next 10; each add'l $.25. Certification fee: $5.00 per doc. Payee: Treasurer State of New Jersey. Personal checks accepted; credit cards are not. Prepayment required. Mail requests: SASE required.

Superior Court Special Civil Part Hunterdon County Justice Ctr, 65 Park Ave, 2nd Fl, Flemington, NJ 08822; 908-237-5820; fax: 908-237-5821; 8:30AM-4:30PM (EST). ***Civil Actions under $15,000, Eviction, Small Claims.***
www.judiciary.state.nj.us/somerset/index.htm
Civil Records: Access: Phone, mail, in person. Both court and visitors may perform in person searches. No search fee. Required to search: name, years to search. Civil cases indexed by plaintiff, defendant. Civil records on computer from 1991, on index books from 1900. Mail turnaround time 1 week. Public use terminal has civil records back to 1991. PAT civil results show middle initial.
General Information: No protective order files records released. Will not fax documents. Court makes copy: $.75 per page 1st 10 pages; $.50 per page next 10; each add'l $.25. Self serve: $.15 per page. Certification fee: $5.00 per doc. Payee: Treasurer, State of NJ. Money orders, cash or personal checks accepted. No credit cards accepted. Prepayment required. Mail requests: SASE required.

Mercer County

Superior Court - Criminal 209 S. Broad, PO Box 8068, Trenton, NJ 08650-0068; 609-571-4000 x4; 8:30AM-4:30PM; Search hrs: 9AM-3:30PM (EST). ***Felony.***
www.judiciary.state.nj.us/mercer/index.htm
Criminal Records: Access: In person only. Visitors must perform in person searches themselves. Required to search: name, years to search, DOB, SSN. Criminal records computerized from 1985, on docket books from 1900s. Public use terminal has crim records back to 1985. PAT results show middle initial, DOB.
General Information: No sealed, expunged, judges notes, PSI's, or discovery packets records released. Will not fax documents. Court makes copy: $.75 per page. $5.00 minimum. Fee less after 10 pages. Certification fee: $5.00. Payee: Treasurer, State of NJ. Personal checks accepted; credit cards are not. Prepayment required.

Superior Court - Civil 175 S Broad, PO Box 8068, Trenton, NJ 08650-0068; 609-571-4490; fax: 609-571-4473; 8:30AM-4:30PM (EST). ***Civil Actions over $15,000, Probate.***
www.judiciary.state.nj.us/mercer/index.htm
Civil Records: Access: Fax, mail, in person. Only the court performs in person searches; visitors may not. No search fee. Required to search: name, years to search. Civil cases indexed by defendant, plaintiff; index on computer since 1995, archived from 1972, on microfiche from 1965, prior indexed from 1894. Mail turnaround time up to 2 weeks.
General Information: No sealed, expunged, dismissed, judges notes, PSI's, or discovery packets records released. Will not fax documents. Court makes copy: $.75 per page 1st 10 pages; $.50 per page next 10; each add'l $.25. Certification fee: $5.00 per doc. Payee: Treasurer, State of NJ. Personal checks accepted; credit cards are not. Prepayment required. Mail requests: SASE required for Civil.

Superior Court Special Civil Part Box 8068, 175 S Broad St, 1st Fl, Trenton, NJ 08650; 609-571-4490 x1; civil phone: 609-571-4484; fax: 609-571-4489; 8:30AM-4:30PM (EST). ***Civil Actions under $15,000, Eviction, Small Claims.***
www.judiciary.state.nj.us/mercer/index.htm
Record index on a public access terminal at Hughes Justice Ctr, 25 Market St.
Civil Records: Access: In person only. Visitors must perform in person searches themselves. Required to search: name, years to search. Civil cases indexed by defendant, plaintiff; index on computer from 1989, on index from 1984. Public use terminal has civil records back to 1989. PAT results show name only.
General Information: No adoption, sealed, juvenile, expunged, dismissed, or mental illness records released. Will not fax documents. Court makes copy: $.75 per page 1st 10 pages; $.50 per page next 10; each add'l $.25. Self serve: $.50 per page. No certification fee. Payee: State of New Jersey. Only cashiers checks and money orders accepted. No credit cards accepted. Prepayment required.

Middlesex County

Superior Court - Criminal PO Box 964 (1 JFK Sq), New Brunswick, NJ 08903; 732-519-3853; 8:30AM-4:30PM (EST). ***Felony.***
www.judiciary.state.nj.us/middlesex/index.htm
Criminal Records: Access: Mail, in person. Visitors must perform in person searches themselves. No search fee. Required to search: name and DOB. Criminal records computerized from 1981, prior on index books back to 1956. Note: Court will only search if provided with arrest date, summons, complaint or indictment number; no name searches performed. Mail turnaround time up to 2 weeks. Public use terminal has crim records back to 1981. PAT results show middle initial, DOB.
General Information: No sealed, expunged, dismissed, judges notes, PSI's, on discovery packets records released. Will fax documents $.75 per page. Court makes copy: $.75 per page for 1st 10 pages; $.50 per page next 10; each add'l $.25. Self serve: $.15 per page. Certification fee: $5.00 per page. Payee: State of New Jersey Treasurer. Cash, personal checks, or money order accepted. No credit cards accepted. Prepayment required. Mail requests: SASE required.

Superior Court - Civil PO Box 2633, 56 Patterson St, 1 JFK Sq, 2nd Fl Tower, New Brunswick, NJ 08903; 732-981-2464, 519-3737, 519-3678; probate phone: 732-745-3055; 8:30AM-4:30PM (EST). ***Civil Actions over $15,000, Probate.***
www.judiciary.state.nj.us/middlesex/index.htm
Probate is located at 75 Bayard St.
Civil Records: Access: Mail, in person. Both court and visitors may perform in person searches. No search fee. Required to search: name, years to search, if copies needed place request in writing. Civil cases indexed by defendant, plaintiff; index on computer

from 1992, on docket books from 1940. Mail turnaround time up to 3 weeks. Public use terminal has civil records back to 1992. PAT results show name only.
General Information: No sealed, expunged, dismissed, judges notes, PSI's, on discovery packets records released. Will not fax documents. Court makes copy: $.75 per page 1st 10 pages; $.50 per page next 10; each add'l $.25. Certification fee: $5.00 per doc. Payee: Treasurer of New Jersey. Personal checks accepted; credit cards are not. Prepayment required. Mail requests: SASE required.

Superior Court Special Civil Part PO Box 1146, 1 JKF Sq, 3rd Fl Tower, New Brunswick, NJ 08903; 732-981-2044; civil phone: x3301; 8:30AM-4:30PM (EST). ***Civil Actions under $15,000, Eviction, Small Claims.***
www.judiciary.state.nj.us/middlesex/index.htm
Civil Records: Access: Mail, in person. Both court and visitors may perform in person searches. No search fee. Required to search: name, years to search. Civil cases indexed by defendant, plaintiff; index on computer from 1985, on docket books from 1960. Mail turnaround time 30 days. Public use terminal has civil records back to 1985.
General Information: No adoption, sealed, juvenile, expunged, dismissed, or mental health records released. Will not fax documents. Court makes copy: $.75 per page 1st 10 pages; $.50 per page next 10; each add'l $.25. Certification fee: $5.00 for seal. Payee: Middlesex Special Civil Part. Personal checks accepted; credit cards are not. Prepayment required.

Monmouth County

Superior Court - Criminal 71 Monument Park, Rm 149, 1st Fl, E Wing, PO Box 1271, Freehold, NJ 07728-1271; 732-677-4300; 8:30AM-4:30PM (EST). ***Felony.***
www.judiciary.state.nj.us/monmouth/index.htm
Criminal Records: Access: In person only. Visitors must perform in person searches themselves. Required to search: name, years to search. Criminal records computerized from 1990, on index books from 1956. Public use terminal has crim records back to 1986.
General Information: No sealed or expunged, judges notes, PSI's, or discovery packets records released. Will not fax documents. Court makes copy: $.75 per page for 1st 10 pages; $.50 per page next 10; each add'l $.25. Certification fee: $5.00. Cert fee includes copies. Payee: State of New Jersey Treasurer. Personal checks accepted; ID required. Prepayment required.

Superior Court - Civil PO Box 1269, 71 Monument Pk, Freehold, NJ 07728-1255; 732-677-4298; civil phone: 732-677-4240; Special civil- 732-677-4270; Sm Claims- 732-677-4292; fax: 732-677-4369; 8:30AM-4:30PM (EST). ***Civil Actions over $15,000; Special Civil.***
www.judiciary.state.nj.us/monmouth/index.htm
Direct civil search questions to Jennifer Oliver at 732-677-4257.
Civil Records: Access: Mail, fax, in person. Visitors must perform in person searches themselves. Search fee: Fee depends on nature of job. Clerk will call back with cost. Accounts available. Required to search: name, years to search. Civil cases indexed by defendant, plaintiff; index on computer from 1990, on index books from 1956. Mail turnaround time 48 hours. Public use terminal has civil records back to 1990.
General Information: No sealed, expunged, dismissed, judges notes, PSI's, or discovery packets records released. Court makes copy: $.75 per page 1st 10 pages; $.50 each pages 11-20; $.25 each over 20. Certification fee: $5.00 per doc; Exemplification-$10.00. Payee: Treasurer State of New Jersey. Personal checks accepted; credit cards are not. Prepayment required. Mail requests: SASE required.

Superior Court Special Civil Part Courthouse, 71 Monument Pk., PO Box 1270, Freehold, NJ 07728; 732-677-4223; civil phone: 732-677-4290 Small Claims; fax: 732-677-4362; 8:30AM-4:30PM (EST). ***Civil Actions under $15,000, Eviction, Small Claims.***
www.judiciary.state.nj.us/monmouth/index.htm
Civil Records: Access: Mail, in person. Both court and visitors may perform in person searches. No search fee. Required to search: name, years to search. Civil cases indexed by defendant, plaintiff; index on computer from 1996, on index books from 1985, prior in archives. Mail turnaround time 1 day to weeks; longer if archived. Public use terminal has civil records back to 1985. PAT results show name only.
General Information: Will not fax documents. Court makes copy: $.75 per page 1st 10 pages; $.50 per page next 10; each add'l $.25. Self serve: Self serve copier located in Rm 143 East Central. There is a charge. Certification fee: $5.00 per doc. Payee: Treasurer State of New Jersey. Personal checks accepted; credit cards are not. Prepayment required. Mail requests: SASE required.

Morris County

Superior Court - Criminal PO Box 910, Washington & Court St, Morristown, NJ 07963-0910; 973-656-4115; criminal phone: 973-656-6963; fax: 973-656-4123; 8:30AM-4:30PM (EST). ***Felony.***
www.judiciary.state.nj.us/morris/index.htm
Criminal Records: Access: Fax, mail, in person. Both court and visitors may perform in person searches. No search fee. Required to search: name, years to search, DOB, SSN, signed release. Criminal records computerized from 1984, on index books from 1966. Mail turnaround time 1 week.
General Information: No sealed, expunged, dismissed, judges notes, PSI's, or discovery packets records released. Will not fax documents. Court makes copy: $.75 per page for 1st 10 pages; $.50 per page next 10; each add'l $.25. Certification fee: $5.00 per doc. Payee: State of New Jersey Treasurer. Personal checks accepted; credit cards are not. Prepayment required. Mail requests: SASE required.

Superior Court - Civil PO Box 910, Washington St Courthouse, 2nd Fl, Morristown, NJ 07963-0910; 973-656-4115; fax: 973-656-4123; 8:30AM-4:30PM (EST). ***Civil Actions over $15,000, Probate.***
www.judiciary.state.nj.us/morris/index.htm
Civil Records: Access: In person only. Visitors must perform in person searches themselves. Required to search: name, years to search; also helpful: address. Civil cases indexed by defendant, plaintiff; index on computer from 1984, on index books from 1966. Public use terminal has civil records back to 1990. PAT civil results show middle initial.
General Information: No sealed, expunged, dismissed, judges notes, PSI's, or discovery packets records released. Will fax documents for $.75 per page fee. Court makes copy: $.25 per page. Self serve: $.25 per page. Certification fee: $5.00 per doc. Payee: State of New Jersey Treasurer. No personal checks or credit cards accepted. Prepayment required.

Superior Court Special Civil Part PO Box 910, Court and Washington Sts, Morristown, NJ 07963-0910; 973-656-4125; fax: 973-656-4123; 8:30AM-4:30PM (EST). ***Civil Actions under $15,000, Eviction, Small Claims.***
Civil Records: Access: Mail, in person. Visitors must perform in person searches themselves. No search fee. Required to search: name, years to search. Civil cases indexed by defendant, plaintiff; index on computer from 8/1988, on index books from 1979. Mail turnaround time 1 week. Public use terminal has civil records back to 8/1988. PAT results show middle initial, DOB.
General Information: No adoption, sealed, juvenile, expunged, dismissed, or mental illness records released. Will not fax documents. Court makes copy: $.75 per page 1st 10 pages; $.50 per page next 10; each add'l $.25. Self serve: $.25 per page. Certification fee: $5.00 per doc. Payee: State of New Jersey Treasurer. Personal checks accepted; credit cards are not. Prepayment required. Mail requests: SASE required.

Ocean County

Superior Court - Criminal PO Box 2191, 120 Hooper Ave, Justice Complex, Rm 220, Toms River, NJ 08754-2191; 732-929-2009; fax: 732-506-5067; 8:30AM-4:30PM (EST). ***Felony.***
www.judiciary.state.nj.us/ocean/index.htm
Criminal Records: Access: In person only. Both court and visitors may perform in person searches. No search fee. Required to search: name, years to search; also helpful: address, DOB, SSN. Criminal records computerized from 1990, on index books from 1920. Public use terminal has crim records back to 1990. Public access terminal allows you to search statewide.
General Information: No sealed, expunged, judges notes, PSI's, or discovery packets records released. Will fax reply if no record found. Court makes copy: $.75 per page for 1st 10 pages; $.50 per page next 10; each add'l $.25. Certification fee: $5.00. Payee: NJ State Treasurer. Personal checks accepted; credit cards are not. Prepayment required.

Superior Court - Civil 118 Washington #121, Toms River, NJ 08753; 732-929-2016; fax: 732-506-5398; 8:30AM-4:30PM (EST). ***Civil Actions over $15,000, Probate.***
www.judiciary.state.nj.us/ocean/index.htm
Civil Records: Access: In person only. Visitors must perform in person searches themselves. Search fee: Court charges no fee if and when they assist you with search. Required to search: name, years to search. Civil cases indexed by defendant, plaintiff; index on computer from 1989, on index books from 1920. Public use terminal has civil records back to 1989. PAT results show name only. A subscription online service is available to attorneys only.
General Information: Will not fax documents. Court makes copy: $.75 per page 1st 10 pages, 11-20 pgs $.50 each; 21 and over $.25 each. No certification fee. Payee: Treasurer, State of NJ. Personal checks accepted; credit cards are not. Prepayment required.

Superior Court Special Civil Part 118 Washington St, Rm 121, Toms River, NJ 08753; 732-929-2016; fax: 732-506-5398; 8:30AM-4:30PM (EST). ***Civil Actions under $15,000, Eviction, Small Claims.***
www.judiciary.state.nj.us/ocean/index.htm
Civil Records: Access: In person only. Both court and visitors may perform in person searches. No search fee. Required to search: name, years to search. Civil cases indexed by defendant, plaintiff; index on computer from 1985, on index books from 1972, on microfilm prior. Public use terminal has civil records back to 1985.
General Information: No adoption, sealed, juvenile, expunged, dismissed, or mental illness records released. Will not fax documents. Court makes copy: $.75 per page. Certification fee: $5.00 per doc. Payee: Treasurer, State of NJ. Personal checks accepted; credit cards are not. Prepayment required. Mail requests: SASE requested.

Passaic County

Superior Court - Criminal 77 Hamilton St. 2nd Fl, Paterson, NJ 07505-2108; 973-247-8402; fax: 973-247-8401; 8:30AM-4:30PM (EST). ***Felony.***
www.judiciary.state.nj.us/passaic/index.htm
Criminal Records: Access: In person only. Visitors must perform in person searches themselves. Required to search: name; also helpful: DOB. Criminal records computerized from 1986, on microfiche prior. Note: Court will only retrieve a record if you provide an indictment or assumption or complaint number, which can be garnered from state police or the public access terminal. Public use terminal has crim records back to 1986. PAT results show middle initial, DOB.
General Information: No sealed, expunged, judges notes, PSI's, or discovery packets records released. Will fax documents. Court makes copy: $.75 per page for 1st 10 pages; $.50 per page next 10; each add'l $.25. Self serve: $.25 per page. Certification fee: $5.00 per doc. Payee: Treasurer, State of New Jersey.

Personal checks accepted; credit cards are not. Prepayment required.

Superior Court - Civil 77 Hamilton St, Ist Fl, Paterson, NJ 07505-2108; 973-247-8000; civil phone: 973-247-8227; probate phone: 973-881-4760; fax: 973-247-8186; 8:30AM-4:30PM (EST). ***Civil Actions over $15,000, Probate.***
www.judiciary.state.nj.us/passaic/index.htm
Civil records and Civil Special Part records are now co-located in the same area. Probate is located on the 2nd Fl
Civil Records: Access: Phone, mail, in person. Both court and visitors may perform in person searches. No search fee. Required to search: name, years to search. Civil cases indexed by defendant, plaintiff; index on computer from 1986, on index books from 1979. Note: Phone access limited to short searches. Mail turnaround time up to 1 week. Public use terminal has civil records back to 1993. Public terminal results may show address, sometime DOB and other identifiers.
General Information: No sealed, expunged, dismissed, judges notes, PSI's, or discovery packets records released. Will fax documents for fee same as copy fee. Court makes copy: $.75 per page 1st 10 pages; $.50 per page next 10; each add'l $.25. Certification fee: $5.00 per doc. Payee: Treasurer State of New Jersey. Personal checks accepted; credit cards are not. Prepayment required.

Superior Court Special Civil Part 77 Hamilton St., Old Courthouse, 1st Fl, Paterson, NJ 07505; 973-247-8000, 973-247-3259; 8:30AM-4:30PM (EST). ***Civil Actions under $15,000, Eviction, Small Claims.***
www.judiciary.state.nj.us/passaic/index.htm
Civil records and Civil Special Part records are now co-located in the same area.
Civil Records: Access: Mail, in person. Both court and visitors may perform in person searches. No search fee. Required to search: name, years to search. Civil cases indexed by defendant, plaintiff; index on computer from 1993, on index from 1980, prior archived. Note: Include your phone number with written requests. It may take up to 2 days for court to retrieve case files. Mail turnaround time 2-3 days. Public use terminal has civil records back to 1993. Public terminal results may show address, sometime DOB and other identifiers.
General Information: No adoption, sealed, juvenile, expunged, dismissed, or mental illness records released. Will fax documents for fee same as copy fee. Court makes copy: $.75 per page 1st 10 pages; $.50 per page next 10; each add'l $.25. Certification fee: $5.00 per doc. Payee: Passaic County Special Civil Part. Personal checks accepted; credit cards are not. Prepayment required.

Salem County

Superior Court - Criminal PO Box 78, 92 Market St, Salem, NJ 08079-1913; 856-935-7510 x8276; fax: 856-935-8291; 8:30AM-4:30PM (EST). ***Felony.***
www.judiciary.state.nj.us/gloucester/sal/index.htm
Criminal Records: Access: In person only. Visitors must perform in person searches themselves. Required to search: name, years to search, DOB, SSN; indictment number helpful. Criminal records computerized from 1989; indexed from 1957. Public use terminal has crim records back to 1989.PAT results show name, DOB.
General Information: No sealed, expunged, dismissed, judges notes, PSI's, or discovery packets records released. Will not fax documents. Court makes copy: $.75 per page. Certification fee: $5.00. Payee: State of New Jersey Treasurer. Personal checks accepted; credit cards are not. Prepayment required. Mail requests: SASE required for civil.

Superior Court - Civil PO Box 29, 92 Market St, Salem, NJ 08079-1913; 856-935-7510 x8211, x8214; probate phone: 856-935-7510 x8322; fax: 856-935-6551; 8:30AM-4:30PM (EST). ***Civil Actions over $15,000, Probate.***
www.judiciary.state.nj.us/gloucester/sal/index.htm
Probate located at the County Surrogate's office at this 92 Market St address.
Civil Records: Access: In person only. Both court and visitors may perform in person searches. No search fee. Required to search: name, years to search. Civil cases indexed by defendant, plaintiff; index on computer from 1987, indexed from 1953. Public use terminal has civil records back to 1987.
General Information: No sealed, expunged, dismissed, judges notes, PSI's, or discovery packets records released. Will fax documents if fees prepaid. Court makes copy: $.25 per page. Certification fee: $5.00 per doc. Payee: Superior Court of NJ. Personal checks accepted. Prepayment required.

Superior Court Special Civil Part PO Box 29, 92 Market St, Salem, NJ 08079; 856-935-7510 x8214; fax: 856-935-6551; 8:30AM-4:30PM (EST). ***Civil Actions under $15,000, Eviction, Small Claims.***
www.judiciary.state.nj.us/gloucester/sal/index.htm
Civil Records: Access: Phone, fax, mail, in person. Both court and visitors may perform in person searches. No search fee. Required to search: name, years to search. Civil cases indexed by defendant, plaintiff; index on computer from 1990, on index from 1953. Mail turnaround time 1-2 days. Public use terminal has civil records back to 1990.
General Information: No adoption, sealed, juvenile, expunged, dismissed, or mental illness records released. Court makes copy: $.25 per page. Certification fee: $5.00 per doc. Payee: Special Civil Part. Personal checks accepted. Prepayment required.

Somerset County

Superior Court - Criminal PO Box 3000 (20 N Bridge St, 2nd Fl), Somerville, NJ 08876-1262; 908-231-7600; fax: 908-231-9276; 8:30AM-4:30PM (EST). ***Felony.***
www.judiciary.state.nj.us/somerset/index.htm
Criminal Records: Access: Phone, fax, mail, in person. Both court and visitors may perform in person searches. Search fee: $6.00 per name. Required to search: name, years to search, DOB; also helpful: SSN. Criminal records computerized from 1981, prior on index books. Mail turnaround time 2-3 days. Public use terminal has crim records back to 1981.
General Information: No sealed, expunged, judges notes, PSI's, or discovery packets records released. Will not fax documents. Court makes copy: $.75 per page for 1st 10 pages; $.50 per page next 10; each add'l $.25. Certification fee: $5.00. Payee: State of New Jersey Treasurer. Personal checks accepted; credit cards are not. Prepayment required. Mail requests: SASE required.

Superior Court - Civil PO Box 3000, Civil Division, 20 N Bridge St, County Courthouse, Somerville, NJ 08876-1262; 908-231-7054; fax: 908-231-7167; 8:30AM-4:30PM (EST). ***Civil Actions, Probate, Equity.***
www.judiciary.state.nj.us/somerset/index.htm
Civil Records: Access: Phone, mail, in person. Both court and visitors may perform in person searches. No search fee. Required to search: name; also helpful: years to search. Civil cases indexed by defendant, plaintiff; index on computer from 1990. Note: Civil cases are archived 18 months after their last activity. Mail turnaround time 1-2 days. Public use terminal has civil records back to 1990. Terminal located at 40 N Brady St.
General Information: No sealed, expunged, dismissed, judges notes, PSI's, or discovery packets records released. Will not fax documents. Court makes copy: $.75 per page 1st 10 pages; $.50 per page next 10; each add'l $.25. Certification fee: $5.00 per page. Payee: Treasurer, State of NJ. Personal checks accepted; credit cards are not. Prepayment required. Mail requests: SASE required.

Superior Court Special Civil Part PO Box 3000, County Courthouse, Bridge & Main St, Somerville, NJ 08876-1262; 908-231-7014/7015; 8:30AM-4:30PM (EST). ***Civil Actions under $15,000, Eviction, Small Claims.***
www.judiciary.state.nj.us/somerset/index.htm
Civil Records: Access: Mail, in person. Visitors must perform in person searches themselves. No search fee. Required to search: name, years to search. Civil cases indexed by defendant, plaintiff; index on computer from 1990, prior on index books. Note: In person access requires an appointment. Mail turnaround time 1-2 days. Public use terminal has civil records back to 1995. Public terminal at counter provides visitor with book lookup help only.
General Information: No adoption, sealed, juvenile, expunged, dismissed, or mental illness records released. Will not fax documents. Court makes copy: $.75 per page 1st 10 pages; $.50 per page next 10; each add'l $.25. No certification fee. Payee: Treasurer, State of NJ. Personal checks accepted; credit cards are not. Prepayment required. Mail requests: SASE required.

Sussex County

Superior Court - Criminal 43-47 High St, Sussex Judicial Ctr, Newton, NJ 07860; 973-579-0696; fax: 973-579-0767; 8:30AM-4:30PM (EST). ***Felony.***
www.judiciary.state.nj.us/morris/index.htm
Criminal Records: Access: In person only. Only the court performs in person searches; visitors may not. No search fee; copy fee only. Required to search: name, years to search, DOB; the court prefers that you provide the case number, complaint number, arrest date, etc; get that info off public access terminal. Criminal records computerized from 1986, on docket books to 1950s. Public use terminal has crim records back to 1956 apx. PAT results show name, DOB, SSN.
General Information: No sealed, expunged, dismissed, judges notes, PSI's, or discovery packets records released. Will not fax out documents. Court makes copy: $.75 per page for 1st 10 pages; $.50 per page next 10; each add'l $.25.If file copy is extensive, minimum fee is $5.00 for copies. Certification fee: $5.00. Payee: Treasurer, State of NJ. Only cashiers checks and money orders accepted. No credit cards accepted. Prepayment required.

Superior Court - Civil 43-47 High St, Sussex Judicial Ctr, Newton, NJ 07860; 973-579-0914/0915; fax: 973-579-0736; 8:30AM-4:30PM (EST). ***Special Civil Actions, Eviction, Probate.***
www.judiciary.state.nj.us/morris/index.htm
Civil Records: Access: Phone, mail, in person. Only the court performs in person searches; visitors may not. No search fee. Required to search: name, years to search. Civil cases indexed by defendant, plaintiff; index on computer from 1989, on microfiche by plaintiff prior to 1989, closed cases archived yearly and sent to Trenton. Mail turnaround time up to 1 week. Public use terminal has civil records. Public access terminal located in Law Library.
General Information: No sealed, expunged, dismissed, judges notes, PSI's, or discovery packets records released. Will fax documents if prepaid. Court makes copy: $.75 per page 1st 10 pages; $.50 per page next 10; each add'l $.25. Certification fee: $5.00 per doc. Payee: Treasurer State of New Jersey. Personal checks accepted; credit cards are not. Prepayment required.

Superior Court Special Civil Part 43-47 High St., Newton, NJ 07860; 973-579-0918; fax: 973-579-0736; 8:30AM-4:30PM (EST). ***Civil Actions under $15,000, Eviction, Small Claims.***
www.judiciary.state.nj.us/morris/index.htm
Civil Records: Access: Phone, fax, mail, in person. Both court and visitors may perform in person searches. No search fee. Required to search: name, years to search. Civil cases indexed by defendant, plaintiff; index on computer from mid 1989, on index books from 1940. Note: Court will accept name phone and fax search requests for up to 3 names. Mail turnaround time up to 2 weeks. Public use terminal has civil records. Public access terminal located in law library.
General Information: No adoption, sealed, juvenile, expunged, dismissed, or mental illness records released. Will not fax documents. Court makes copy: $.75 per page 1st 10 pages; $.50 per page next 10; each add'l $.25. Certification fee: $5.00 per doc. Payee: State of New Jersey Treasurer. Personal checks accepted; credit cards are not. Prepayment required.

Union County

Superior Court - Criminal County Courthouse, 2 Broad St - Tower Bldg 5th Fl, Elizabeth, NJ 07207; 908-659-4690; 8:30AM-4:30PM (EST). ***Felony.***
www.judiciary.state.nj.us/union/index.htm

Criminal Records: Access: In person only. Visitors must perform in person searches themselves. Required to search: name, years to search; also helpful: DOB, SSN. Criminal records computerized from 1985-prior with name and indictment # from 1967. Note: In person access 9AM-3:30PM. For any requests regarding records prior to 1985, contact the NJ State Police for a criminal history sheet, and from the IND/ACC# this court can quickly find the reference in their records. Public use terminal has crim records back to 1985. PAT results show middle initial, DOB.

General Information: No sealed, expunged, dismissed, judges notes, PSI's, warrants, or discovery packets records released. Will not fax documents. Court makes copy: $.75 per page for 1st 10 pages; $.50 per page next 10; each add'l $.25. Self serve: $.75 per page. Certification fee: $5.00 per doc. Payee: Treasurer, State of NJ. Business checks and money orders accepted. No credit cards accepted. Prepayment required.

Superior Court - Civil 2 Broad St, Elizabeth, NJ 07207; 908-659-3844; probate phone: 908-527-4270; fax: 908-659-4185; 8:30AM-4:30PM (EST). ***Civil Actions over $15,000, Probate.***
www.judiciary.state.nj.us/union/index.htm
The probate phone is for the Surrogate Div who holds probate court records; located at same address.

Civil Records: Access: Phone, mail, in person. Visitors must perform in person searches themselves. No search fee. Required to search: name, years to search, or docket number. Civil cases indexed by defendant, plaintiff; index on computer from 1984, prior records archived in Trenton. Mail turnaround time 1-2 days. Public use terminal has civil records back to 1984. PAT results show name only.

General Information: No sealed, expunged, dismissed, judges notes, PSI's, or discovery packets records released. Will not fax documents. Court makes copy: $.75 per page 1st 10 pages; $.50 per page next 10; each add'l $.25. Certification fee: $5.00. Payee: Treasurer, State of NJ. Personal checks accepted; credit cards are not. Prepayment required.

Superior Court Special Civil Part 2 Broad St, Elizabeth, NJ 07207; 908-659-3637/8; 8:30AM-4:30PM (EST). ***Civil Actions under $15,000, Eviction, Small Claims.***
www.judiciary.state.nj.us/union/index.htm

Civil Records: Access: Phone, mail, in person. Both court and visitors may perform in person searches. No search fee. Required to search: name, years to search. Civil cases indexed by defendant, plaintiff; index on computer from 1993, on index books 1965, prior archived. Note: Phone access limited to info after 11/93. Mail turnaround time varies. Public use terminal has civil records.

General Information: No adoption, sealed, juvenile, expunged, dismissed, or mental illness records released. Will not fax documents. Court makes copy: $.75 per page 1st 10 pages; $.50 per page next 10; each add'l $.25. No certification fee. Payee: Treasurer, State of NJ. Personal checks accepted; credit cards are not. Prepayment required.

Warren County

Warren County Superior Court Criminal Case Management Division, PO Box 900, Belvidere, NJ 07823; 908-475-6990; criminal phone: 908-475-6990; fax: 908-475-6982; 8:30AM-4:30PM (EST). ***Felony.***
www.judiciary.state.nj.us/somerset/index.htm

Criminal Records: Access: Phone, mail, fax, in person. Both court and visitors may perform in person searches. Search fee: $6.00 per name. Required to search: name, years to search, DOB; also helpful: signed release. Criminal records computerized from 1985; prior on index cards to 1927. Mail turnaround time 2-5 days. Public use terminal has crim records back to 1985.PAT results show name, DOB.

General Information: No sealed, expunged, dismissed, judges notes, PSI's, or discovery packets records released. Will fax documents to local or toll free line. Court makes copy: $.75 each up to 10 pages; $.50 11-20th pages; $.25 each add'l. Certification fee: $5.00. Payee: State of New Jersey Treasurer. Personal checks accepted; credit cards are not. Prepayment required.

Superior Court - Civil PO Box 900, 413 2nd St, Belvidere, NJ 07823; 908-475-6140; probate phone: 908-475-6223; 8:30AM-4:30PM (EST). ***Civil Actions over $15,000, Probate.***
www.judiciary.state.nj.us/somerset/index.htm
Surrogates/Probate court is located at 413 2nd St in the courthouse. Probate fax- 908-475-6319

Civil Records: Access: Mail, in person. Only the court performs in person searches; visitors may not. No search fee. Court will perform one search no fee. Required to search: name, years to search. Civil cases indexed by defendant, plaintiff; index on computer from 1991, prior on index books from 1951. Note: In person access requires an appointment. Mail turnaround time 2 days. Public use terminal has civil records back to - closed cases in last 18 months.

General Information: No sealed, expunged, or dismissed records released. Will not fax documents. Court makes copy: $.75 per page 1st 10 pages; $.50 per page next 10; each add'l $.10. Certification fee: 1st page free; $5.00 for next 5 pages; add'l pg- $.75. Payee: Treasurer, State of NJ. Personal checks accepted; credit cards are not. Prepayment required.

Superior Court Special Civil Part PO Box 900, 413 2nd St, Belvidere, NJ 07823; 908-475-6140; 8:30AM-4:30PM (EST). ***Civil Actions under $15,000, Eviction, Small Claims.***
www.judiciary.state.nj.us/somerset/index.htm

Civil Records: Access: Mail, in person. Only the court performs in person searches; visitors may not. No search fee. Court will do one search no fee. Required to search: name, years to search. Civil cases indexed by defendant, plaintiff; index on computer from 10/91, prior on index books from 1951. Note: In person access requires an appointment. Mail turnaround time 2-3 days. Public use terminal has civil records.

General Information: No adoption, sealed, juvenile, expunged, dismissed, or mental illness records released. Will not fax documents. Court makes copy: $.75 per page 1st 10 pages; $.50 per page next 10; each add'l $.25. No certification fee. Payee: Treasurer, State of NJ. Personal checks accepted; credit cards are not. Prepayment required. Mail requests: SASE required.

New Jersey Recording Offices

ORGANIZATION: 21 counties, 21 recording offices. The recording officer title varies depending upon the county, either the Register of Deeds or the County Clerk. The Clerk of Circuit Court records the equivalent of some state's tax liens. New Jersey is in the Eastern Time Zone (EST).

REAL ESTATE RECORDS: No counties will provide real estate searches. Copy and certification fees vary. Assessment and tax offices are at the municipal level.

UCC RECORDS: Financing statements are filed at the state level, except for real estate related collateral, which are filed with the County Clerk. However, prior to 07/2001, consumer goods and farm collateral were also filed at the County Clerk and these older records can be searched there. Less than half of the recording offices will perform UCC searches. Use search request form UCC-11. UCC search fee is usually $25.00 per debtor name.

TAX LIEN RECORDS: All federal tax liens are filed with the County Clerk/Register of Deeds and are indexed separately from all other liens. State tax liens comprise two categories - Certificates of Debt are filed with the Clerk of Superior Court (some, called docketed judgments are filed specifically with the Trenton court), and Warrants of Execution are filed with the County Clerk/Register of Deeds. Few counties provide tax lien searches.

OTHER LIENS: Judgment, mechanics, bail bond.

ONLINE ACCESS: A statewide database of property tax records can be accessed at http://taxrecords.com. The site is operated by a private company; register for the free or the fee services at http://imac.taxrecords.com/login/signup.html?url=www.taxrecords.com. You may also search property data for New Jersey counties free at http://tax1.co.monmouth.nj.us/cgi-bin/prc6.cgi?menu=index&ms_user=glou&passwd=. This is a backdoor URL for a free search. Go to https://www.state.nj.us/treasury/revenue/dcr/filing/ucc_lead.htm to search the statewide UCC index.

Atlantic County

County Clerk, 5901 Main St, CN 2005; Courthouse, Mays Landing, NJ 08330-1797. 609-625-4011; fax-609-625-4738; 8:30AM-6 PM M W; 8:30AM-4:30PM T TH F. www.atlanticcountyclerk.org

Index: All in one since 2000. Records indexed on a public use terminal back to 1972. UCCs only back to 9/95. Office will perform a UCC search (6 year) but public must search other records themselves. Search fee $25.00 for UCC search only. Office will search real estate records for specific documents only. Copy fee $2.00 per page by mail, in person $.15 per page. Cert fee- $5.00 per cert plus copy fee. Payee- Atlantic County Clerk. Bulk data available for purchase, contact Art Locchesi at 609-625-4011 x5243 for all scanned documents. **Online access to Real Estate, Deed records:** Access to public record index for free go to www.atlanticcountyclerk.org/onlinesearch.htm. **Other Online Records-** Access property data free at http://tax1.co.monmouth.nj.us/cgi-bin/prc6.cgi?menu=index&ms_user=glou&passwd=. This is a backdoor and may be closed. Also, see online notes in state summary.

Bergen County

County Clerk, One Bergen County Plaza, Rm 110, Hackensack, NJ 07601. 201-336-7007; fax-201-336-7010; 9AM-4PM

Index: Separate indices to search. Records indexed on a public use terminal back to 1920s. Only the public may search. Copy fee $.25 per page. Cert fee- $10.00 per page. Payee- Bergen County Clerk. **Other phones:** Treasurer- 201-336-6000; Elections- 201-336-7000. **Property tax/Assessing-** Board of Taxation, One Bergen County Plza, Rm 370, Hackensack, NJ 07601; 201-336-6300, assessor fax-201-336-6310. hours- 8:30AM-4:30PM A public access terminal is available. www.co.bergen.nj.us/taxboard/index.html **Online access-** Access property data free at http://tax1.co.monmouth.nj.us/cgi-bin/prc6.cgi?menu=index&ms_user=glou&passwd=. This is a backdoor and may be closed. Also, see online notes in state summary.

Burlington County

County Clerk, PO Box 6000, Mount Holly, NJ 08060. 609-265-5122; fax-609-265-0696; 8AM-7PM M; 8AM-4PM T-F. www.co.burlington.nj.us/departments/countyclerk/index.htm

Index: Separate indices to search include pre 1965 indexes in book form, UCCs separate index. Records indexed on a public use terminal back to 1965. Only the public may search. Copy fee $2.00 per page. Cert fee- $10.00 per doc plus copy fee. Payee- Burlington County Clerk. **Other phones:** Treasurer- 609-265-5018. **Property tax/Assessing-** 49 Cancosa Rd, #105, Mount Holly, NJ 08060; 609-265-5056, assessor fax-609-265-8074. **Online access-** Access property data free at http://tax1.co.monmouth.nj.us/cgi-bin/prc6.cgi?menu=index&ms_user=glou&passwd=. This is a backdoor and may be closed. Att http://tax1.co.monmouth.nj.us use username "monm" and password "data" then select county. Also, see online notes in state summary.

Camden County

County Clerk, 520 Market St, Rm 102; Courthouse, Camden, NJ 08102-1375. Recording, R/E & UCC phone-856-225-5300; fax-856-225-7100; 8AM-4PM www.camdencounty.com

Index: Separate indices to search include name, year. Records indexed on computer back to 1988. Office will perform a UCC search but public must search other records themselves. Search fee-$10.00 per name. Computer index available for all real estate transactions after 8/1988. Copy fee $2.00 per page; self serve $.10 each. Cert fee- $2.00 per cert plus copy fee. Payee- Camden County Clerk. **Other phones:** Treasurer- 856-225-5383; Elections- 856-661-3600. **Property tax/Assessing-** Board of Taxation, 520 Market St, 7th Fl, City Hall, Camden, NJ 08102; 856-225-5238, assessor fax- 856-225-5242. hours- 9AM-4PM **Online access-** Access property data free at http://tax1.co.monmouth.nj.us/cgi-bin/prc6.cgi?menu=index&ms_user=glou&passwd=. This is a backdoor and may be closed. Also, see online notes in summary.

Cape May County

County Clerk, PO Box 5000, Cape May Court House, NJ 08210-5000. Recording, R/E & UCC phone-609-465-1010; fax-609-465-8625; 8:30AM-4:30PM www.capemaycountygov.net

Index: All in one. Records indexed on computer back to 1996. Only the public may search. Office will search real estate records but will not do title searches. Copy fee $2.00 per page. Cert fee- $10.00 per cert plus $1.00 per page. Payee- Cape May County Clerk. **Online Real Estate, Deed, Lien records:** Property records for Cape May county are free to view online at http://209.204.84.120/ALIS/WW400R.PGM. To print, registration and login is required. $1.00 per page copy and/or $10.00 certification fees apply to documents. Online documents go back to 1996, images to 2000. For assistance, telephone 609-465-1010. Also, see online notes in state summary at beginning of section. **Other phones:** Treasurer- 609-465-1170; Elections- 609-465-1013; Record Room-609-465-1023. **Property tax/Assessing-** 7 N Main St, Cape May Court House, NJ 08210; 609-465-1030. **Online access-** Access property data free at http://tax1.co.monmouth.nj.us/cgi-bin/prc6.cgi?menu=index&ms_user=glou&passwd=. Also, see online notes in state summary.

Cumberland County

County Clerk, 60 W Broad St, Rm A137; Courthouse, Bridgeton, NJ 08302. 856-453-4864, R/E recording phone-856-453-4860; fax-856-455-1410; 8:30-4PM www.co.cumberland.nj.us/content/173/2133/2190.aspx

Index: All in one. Records indexed on a public use terminal back to 1989. Only the public may search; office personnel will assist. Office will not name search real estate records. Copy fee $2.00 per page. Self Serve- $.15 per page. Cert fee- $10.00 per doc plus copy fee. Payee- Cumberland County Clerk. **Other phones:** Elections- 856-453-4850. **Property tax/Assessing-** 60 W Broad St, Courthouse, Bridgeton, NJ 08302; see above. **Online access-** Access property data free at http://tax1.co.monmouth.nj.us/cgi-bin/prc6.cgi?men

u=index&ms_user=glou&passwd=. This is a backdoor and may be closed. Also, see online notes in state summary.

Essex County

Register of Deeds, 465 Martin Luther King Jr Blvd, Rm 130; Hall of Records, Newark, NJ 07102. 973-621-4960, R/E recording phone-973-621-4960 x228, UCC recording phone-973-621-4960 x225; fax-973-621-2590; 9AM-4PM www.essexregister.com

Index: Separate indices to search include each document type. Records indexed on a public use terminal back to 1988. Only the public may search. Will not search UCC records. Copy fee $.25 per page. Cert fee- $4.00 1st page, $2.00 each add'l, includes copies. Payee- Essex County Register. **Other phones:** Treasurer- 973-621-4997; Elections- 973-621-4921. **Property tax/Assessing**- 50 S Clinton St, #5200, Board of Taxation, East Orange, NJ 07017; 973-395-8525, assessor fax- 973-395-8481. hours- 8:30AM-4:30PM Public access terminal available. **Online access**- Access property data free at http://tax1.co.monmouth.nj.us/cgi-bin/prc6.cgi?menu=index&ms_user=glou&passwd=. This is a backdoor and may be closed. Also, see online notes in state summary.

Gloucester County

County Clerk, PO Box 129, Woodbury, NJ 08096-0129. 856-853-3237; fax-856-853-3327; 8:30AM-4PM www.co.gloucester.nj.us

Index: Separate indices to search include mortgage, grantor/grantee. Records indexed on computer, printed indexes separate. Only the public may search. Copy fee $.10 per page. Cert fee- $2.00 per cert plus copy fee. Payee- Gloucester County Clerk. **Online access to Real Estate, Deed, Lien, UCC, Mortgage, Trade Name records:** recording office land records at https://www.landaccess.com/sites/nj/gloucester/. For more recording sources, see online notes in state summary at top of section. A variety of online svcs at www.co.gloucester.nj.us/OnlineSrv/onlinesrv.cfm. **Other phones:** Treasurer- 856-853-3353; Elections- 856-384-4501; Tax Collector- 856-853-6945. **Property tax/Assessing**- Budd Blvd, PO Box 180, Woodbury, NJ 08096; 856-845-1300, assessor fax- 856-845-1309. **Online access**- Access property data free at http://tax1.co.monmouth.nj.us/cgi-bin/prc6.cgi?menu=index&ms_user=glou&passwd=. This is a backdoor and may be closed. Also, see online notes in state summary.

Hudson County

Register of Deeds, 595 Newark Ave, Rm 105, Jersey City, NJ 07306. 201-795-6577, R/E recording phone-201-795-6574; fax-201-795-5179; 9AM-5PM

Index: All in one. Records indexed on computer back to 1985. Office will perform a UCC search but public must search other records themselves. Search fee $25.00 for UCC. Office will assist with searches. Copy fee $.25 per page. Cert fee- $10.50 per page $1.50 add'l, includes copy fee. Payee- Hudson County Register. **Other phones:** Elections- 201-795-6125. **Online**- Access property data free at http://tax1.co.monmouth.nj.us/cgi-bin/prc6.cgi?menu=index&ms_user=glou&passwd=. Also, see online notes in state summary.

Hunterdon County

County Clerk, 71 Main St; Hall of Records, Flemington, NJ 08822. 908-788-1221, R/E recording phone-908-788-1223; fax-908-782-4068; 8:30AM-4PM. www.co.hunterdon.nj.us

Index: All in one index except mortgage data which is in 3 separate indexes. Records indexed on a public use terminal back to 1997. Office personnel or visitors may perform searches. Search fee $25.00 per name. Office will not search real estate or tax lien records. Copy fee $.25 per page, mailed copies are $1.00 per page. Cert fee- $5.00 per cert plus $2.00 per page includes copy fee. Payee- Hunterdon County Clerk. Unindexed images available on CD; contact Karla Lamenalola 908-788-1217. **Other phones:** Treasurer- 908-806-3721; Elections- 908-788-1190. **Property tax/Assessing**- Rte 12, County Complex, Bldg 5A, Flemington, NJ 08822; 908-788-1173, assessor fax-908-806-4686. **Online access**- Access property data free at http://tax1.co.monmouth.nj.us/cgi-bin/prc6.cgi?menu=index&ms_user=glou&passwd=. This is a backdoor and may be closed. Also, see online notes in state summary.

Mercer County

County Clerk, 209 S Broad St, Rm 100; Courthouse, Trenton, NJ 08650. 609-989-6466, R/E recording phone-609-989-6476, UCC recording phone-609-989-6487; fax-609-989-1111; 8:30AM-4:30PM. http://nj.gov/counties/mercer/

Index: Separate indices to search. Records indexed on a public use terminal back to 8/24/97. Only the public may search. Copy fee $2.00 per page for mail in. Self serve copies- $.10 each. Cert fee- $10.00 1st page; $1.50 each add'l page includes copy fee. Payee- Mercer County Clerk. Bulk data available for purchase through the Indexing Department, please call 609-989-6475 for info. **Other phones:** Treasurer- 609-989-6694; Elections- 609-989-6495; Vital Records- 609-292-2718. **Property tax/Assessing**- 640 S Broad St, Trenton, NJ 08650; 609-989-6704. **Online access**- Access property data free at http://tax1.co.monmouth.nj.us/cgi-bin/prc6.cgi?menu=index&ms_user=glou&passwd=. This is a backdoor and may be closed. Also, see online notes in state summary.

Middlesex County

County Clerk, PO Box 1110, New Brunswick, NJ 08903. 732-745-3364, 732-745-3204; fax-732-745-5921; 8:30-4 www.co.middlesex.nj.us/countyclerk/

Index: Separate indices to search. Records indexed on a public use terminal back to 1998. Only the public may search. Copy fee $2.00 per page. Cert fee- $10.00 per cert includes copy fee. Payee- Middlesex County Clerk. **Online access to Real Estate, Deed, Lien, Mortgage records:** Access the county public access system index free at https://mcrecords.co.middlesex.nj.us/records/index.jsp. For full images there is a sign up fee plus $.25 per page fee. Also, see online notes in state summary at beginning of section. **Other phones:** Treasurer- 732-754-3482. **Property tax/Assessing**- 732-745-3000. **Online access**- Access property data free at http://tax1.co.monmouth.nj.us/cgi-bin/prc6.cgi?menu=index&ms_user=glou&passwd=. A backdoor and may be closed. See online notes in state summary.

Monmouth County

County Clerk, 33 Mechanic St; Market Yard, Freehold, NJ 07728. 732-431-7324, R/E recording phone-732-431-7321; fax-732-761-9371; 8:30-4:30 http://co.monmouth.nj.us/page.asp?agency=8&Section=125&ID=125

Index: All in one. Records indexed on a public use terminal back to 1930. Office will perform a UCC search but public must search other records themselves. UCC search per debtor name- $25.00. Copy fee $2.00 per page by mail; $.25 per page in person. Cert fee- $10.00 per cert plus $1.50 per page includes copy fee. Payee- Monmouth County Clerk. **Online access to Real Estate, Grantor/Grantee, Deed, Mortgage records:** Access county clerk deed and mortgage data free at http://oprs.co.monmouth.nj.us/Oprs/clerk/ClerkHome.aspx?op=basic. Records go back to 10/1996. Go to http://www1.njcountyrecording.com/njcr/home.aspx for NJ Electronic Recordation. Also, see online notes in state summary at beginning of section. Access the recorder index via www.landex.com/webstore/jsp/cart/DocumentSearch.jsp. Full access to Recorder of Deeds is by subscription at www.landex.com/remote/. Index goes back to 1930; images to 10/1996. **Other phones:** Treasurer- 732-431-7391; Elections- 732-431-7780. **Property tax/Assessing**- 1 E Main St, Freehold, NJ 07728; 732-431-7404. (Appraiser/Auditor- 732-431-7404) http://co.monmouth.nj.us/page.asp?agency=18&ID=134 **Online**- Search Tax list by owner free at http://oprs.co.monmouth.nj.us/Oprs/taxboard/tbindex.aspx?idx=own or Taxation Board free at http://oprs.co.monmouth.nj.us/Oprs/taxboard/HeadFrame.aspx?idx=mod. Access property data free at http://tax1.co.monmouth.nj.us/cgi-bin/prc6.cgi?menu=index&ms_user=glou&passwd=. Also search GIS Taxview free at http://oprs.co.monmouth.nj.us/Oprs/Clerk/Gis.aspx.

Morris County

County Clerk, PO Box 315, Morristown, NJ 07963-0315. 973-285-6059, R/E recording phone-973-285-6130/6144, UCC recording phone-973-285-6130; fax-973-285-5231; 8AM-4PM; record vault- 8AM-6PM W. www.morriscountyclerk.com/

Index: Separate indices to search include deeds, mortgage, liens. Records indexed on a public use terminal back to 1968. Only the public may search. Copy fee $.25 per page. Cert fee- $10.00 per doc plus $1.00 per page includes copy fee. Payee- Morris County Clerk. **Online access to Real Estate, Deed, Lien, Judgment, Will records:** Access the county clerk's access site free at http://mcclerkweb.co.morris.nj.us/or_wb1/or_sch_1.asp. **Other phones:** Elections- 973-285-6126. **Property tax/Assessing**- 200 South St, PO Box 914, Morristown, NJ 07963; 973-292-6667. **Online access**- Access property data free at http://tax1.co.monmouth.nj.us/cgi-bin/prc6.cgi?menu=index&ms_user=glou&passwd=. Also, search assessor/treasurer property tax data free at http://mcweb1.co.morris.nj.us/TaxBoard/SearchTR.jsp. Also, see online notes in state summary.

Ocean County

County Clerk, PO Box 2191, Toms River, NJ 08754. 732-929-2018; fax-732-349-4336; 8:30AM-4PM www.oceancountyclerk.com

Index: All in one. Records indexed on computer back to 1974. Office will perform a UCC search but public must search other records themselves. Copy fee $.15 per page. Cert fee- $2.00 per doc plus copy fee. Payee- Ocean County Clerk. **Online access to Real Estate, Deed, Lien, Mortgage, UCC records:** Land records on the County Clerk database are free at www.oceancountyclerk.com/search.htm. Search by parties, document or instrument type, or township. Also, see online notes at beginning of section. **Other phones:** Elections- 732-929-2153. **Property tax/Assessing**- 118 Washington St Rm 215, Toms River, NJ 08753; 732-929-2008, assessor fax- 732-506-5197. **Online access**- County tax records available from a private company at http://imac.taxrecords.com/login/signup.html?url=www1.taxrecords.com. Free index search, but fees for deeper info. Search by name, address, or property description. Also, access property data free at http://tax1.co.monmouth.nj.us/cgi-bin/prc6.cgi?menu=index&ms_user=glou&passwd=. A backdoor and may be closed. See online notes in state summary.

Passaic County

County Clerk Registry Division, 401 Grant St, Rm 113, Paterson, NJ 07505. 973-881-4777; fax-973-357-1046; 8:30AM-4:30PM; Vault Hours: 7:45AM-5:45PM www.passaiccountyNJ.org

Index: All in one. Records indexed on computer from 1989 to present, paper index from 1837-1989. Only the public may search. Will not search UCC records. Copy fee $2.00 per page; self serve- $.25 each. Cert fee- $10.00 1st page plus copy fee add'l pages. Payee- Passaic County Clerk. **Online Real Estate, Deed, Mortgage records:** Access the county clerk index at www.landex.com/webstore/jsp/cart/DocumentSearch.jsp. Full access is by subscription at www.landex.com/remote/. Index goes back to 8/1998, images to 12/2000. **Property tax/Assessing**- 435 Hamburg Turnpike, Wayne, NJ 07470; 973-720-7399, assessor fax- 973-720-6846. hours- 8:30AM-4:30PM **Online access**- Access property data free at http://tax1.co.monmouth.nj.us/cgi-bin/prc6.cgi?menu

=index&ms_user=glou&passwd=. This is a backdoor and may be closed. See online notes in state summary.

Salem County

County Clerk, 92 Market St, Salem, NJ 08079-1911. Recording, R/E phone-856-935-7510 x8206, UCC recording phone- x8218; fax-856-935-8882; 8:30AM-4:30PM www.salemcountyclerk.org

Index: Separate indices to search include books, computer. Records indexed on a public use terminal back to 1990. Only the public may search. Search fee- $25.00 for each 1/2 hour for historic records only. Copy fee $2.00 per page; self serve $.25. Cert fee- $5.00 per cert plus copy fee. Payee- Salem County Clerk. **Other phones:** Treasurer- 856-935--9036; Elections- 856-935-7510 x8610. **Other Online Records-** Access property data free at http://tax1.co.monmouth.nj.us/cgi-bin/prc6.cgi?menu=index&ms_user=glou&passwd=. This is a backdoor and may be closed. Also, see online notes in state summary.

Somerset County

County Clerk, PO Box 3000, Somerville, NJ 08876. Recording, R/E & UCC phone-908-231-7006; fax-908-253-8853; 8:15AM-4PM www.co.somerset.nj.us

Index: All in one. From 0101/93 to present computerized, prior in separate indices. Only the public may search. Copy fee $.05 per page for most docs after 1987, $.15 per page for older docs, $2.00 per page if mailed. Cert fee- $2.00 per cert plus copy fee. Payee- Somerset County Clerk. Bulk data available for purchase; contact Marsha Bethke at office for details. **Online access to Real Estate, Deed, Lien, Judgment records:** Access to the County Clerk's recordings database is free at http://64.206.95.6/. Free index of deeds, mortgages, federal liens, trade names, assignments, releases, discharges-perm indexes; images from 7/1/87 to 6/11/01. All maps from 1800. Also, see online notes in state summary at beginning of section. **Other phones:** Treasurer- 908-231-7000 x7631; Elections- 908-231-7084; Board of Taxation- 908-541-5701. **Property tax/Assessing-** 925 E Main St, Somerville, NJ 08876; see above. **Online access-** Access property data free at http://tax1.co.monmouth.nj.us/cgi-bin/prc6.cgi?menu=index&ms_user=glou&passwd=. This is a backdoor and may be closed. Also, see online notes in state summary.

Sussex County

County Clerk, 83 Spring St, #304; Hall of Records, Newton, NJ 07860-1795. Recording, R/E & UCC phone-973-579-0900; fax-973-383-7493; 8:30AM-4PM, till 6PM Mon. www.sussexcountyclerk.com

Index: Separate indices to search include liens, deeds, mtgs. Records indexed on a public use terminal back to 1964. Only the public may search. Copy fee $2.00 per page. Cert fee- $5.00 per page plus copy fee. Payee- Sussex County Clerk. Deeds and mortgages in bulk available in microfilm; call AMCAD at 800-800-7009. **Online access to Real Estate, Deed, Lien, Judgment, Miscellaneous records:** Access recorder records back to 1/1964 free at http://sussex.landrecordsonline.com/. Also, see online notes in state summary at beginning of section. **Other phones:** Treasurer- 973-579-0200; Elections- 973-579-0950; Administrator- 973-579-0200. **Property tax/Assessing-** 83 Spring St, #301, Newton, NJ 07860; 973-579-0970, assessor fax- 973-579-0977. hours- 8AM-4PM **Online access-** Access property data free at http://tax1.co.monmouth.nj.us/cgi-bin/prc6.cgi?menu=index&ms_user=glou&passwd=. This is a backdoor and may be closed. Also, see online notes in state summary.

Union County

County Clerk, 2 Broad St, Rm 115; Courthouse, Elizabeth, NJ 07207. 908-527-4794, R/E recording phone-908-527-4787, UCC recording phone-908-527-4794; fax-908-558-2589; 8:30AM-4:30PM http://clerk.ucnj.org

Index: Separate indices to search include real estate, corporations/UCC. Records indexed on a public use terminal back to 1991 for real estate, 1994 for UCCs. Only the public may search. Copy fee $2.00 per page; self serve $.25 each. Cert fee- $8.00 1st page plus copy fee. Payee- Union County Clerk. **Online access to Real Estate, Grantor/Grantee, Deed, Lien, Mortgage, UCC records:** Search recorded real estate related docs at http://clerk.ucnj.org/UCPA/DocIndex. **Other phones:** Elections- 908-527-4996. **Other Online Records-** Access property data free at http://tax1.co.monmouth.nj.us/cgi-bin/prc6.cgi?menu=index&ms_user=glou&passwd=. This is a backdoor and may be closed. Also, see online notes in state summary.

Warren County

County Clerk, 413 2nd St; Courthouse, Belvidere, NJ 07823-1500. Recording, R/E & UCC phone-908-475-6211; fax-908-475-6208; 8:30AM-4PM

Index: Separate indices to search before 7/12/04 include deeds, mtgs, liens. Index all in one since 7/12/04. Records indexed on a public use terminal back to 1982 and 1966 to 1825. Office will perform a UCC search but public must search other records themselves. Copy fee $2.00 per page. Self serve $.10. Cert fee- $5.00 per doc plus copy fee. Payee- Warren County Clerk. Bulk scanned images available to purchase on CD-rom. **Other phones:** Treasurer- 908-475-6542; Elections- 908-475-6211. **Property tax/Assessing-** 908-475-6229. **Online-** Access property data free at http://tax1.co.monmouth.nj.us/cgi-bin/prc6.cgi?menu=index&ms_user=glou&passwd=. This is a backdoor and may be closed. Also, see online notes in state summary.

New Jersey County Locator

You will usually be able to find the city name in the City/County Cross Reference below. In that case, it is a simple matter to determine the county from the cross reference. However, only the official US Postal Service city names are included in this index. We have also included a ZIP/City Cross Reference immediately following the City/County Cross Reference.

If you know the ZIP Code but the city name does not appear in the City/County Cross Reference index, look up the ZIP Code in the ZIP/City Cross Reference, find the city name, then look up the city name in the City/County Cross Reference.

New Jersey City/County Cross Reference

ABSECON Atlantic
ADELPHIA Monmouth
ALLAMUCHY Warren
ALLENDALE Bergen
ALLENHURST Monmouth
ALLENTOWN (08501) Monmouth(82), Burlington(10), Mercer(7)
ALLENWOOD Monmouth
ALLOWAY Salem
ALPINE Bergen
ANDOVER Sussex
ANNANDALE Hunterdon
ASBURY (08802) Hunterdon(67), Warren(32)
ASBURY PARK Monmouth
ATCO (08004) Camden(98), Burlington(1)
ATLANTIC CITY Atlantic
ATLANTIC HIGHLANDS Monmouth
AUDUBON Camden
AUGUSTA Sussex
AVALON Cape May
AVENEL Middlesex
AVON BY THE SEA Monmouth
BAPTISTOWN Hunterdon
BARNEGAT Ocean
BARNEGAT LIGHT Ocean
BARRINGTON Camden
BASKING RIDGE (07920) Somerset(98), Morris(1)
BAYONNE Hudson
BAYVILLE Ocean
BEACH HAVEN Ocean
BEACHWOOD Ocean
BEDMINSTER Somerset
BELFORD Monmouth
BELLE MEAD Somerset
BELLEVILLE Essex
BELLMAWR Camden
BELMAR Monmouth
BELVIDERE Warren
BERGENFIELD Bergen
BERKELEY HEIGHTS Union
BERLIN Camden
BERNARDSVILLE Somerset
BEVERLY Burlington
BIRMINGHAM Burlington
BLACKWOOD (08012) Camden(55), Gloucester(44)
BLAIRSTOWN Warren
BLAWENBURG Somerset
BLOOMFIELD Essex
BLOOMINGDALE Passaic
BLOOMSBURY (08804) Hunterdon(70), Warren(29)
BOGOTA Bergen
BOONTON Morris
BORDENTOWN Burlington
BOUND BROOK Somerset
BRADLEY BEACH Monmouth
BRANCHVILLE Sussex
BRICK Ocean
BRIDGEPORT Gloucester
BRIDGETON (08302) Cumberland(93), Salem(6)
BRIDGEWATER Somerset
BRIELLE Monmouth
BRIGANTINE Atlantic
BROADWAY Warren
BROOKSIDE Morris
BROWNS MILLS Burlington
BUDD LAKE Morris
BUENA Atlantic
BURLINGTON Burlington
BUTLER Morris
BUTTZVILLE Warren
CALDWELL Essex
CALIFON (07830) Hunterdon(88), Morris(11)
CAPE MAY Cape May
CAPE MAY COURT HOUSE Cape May
CAPE MAY POINT Cape May
CARLSTADT Bergen
CARTERET Middlesex
CEDAR BROOK Camden
CEDAR GROVE Essex
CEDAR KNOLLS Morris
CEDARVILLE Cumberland
CHANGEWATER Warren
CHATHAM Morris
CHATSWORTH Burlington
CHERRY HILL Camden
CHESTER Morris
CLARK Union
CLARKSBORO Gloucester
CLARKSBURG Monmouth
CLAYTON Gloucester
CLEMENTON Camden
CLIFFSIDE PARK Bergen
CLIFFWOOD Monmouth
CLIFTON Passaic
CLINTON Hunterdon
CLOSTER Bergen
COLLINGSWOOD Camden
COLOGNE Atlantic
COLONIA Middlesex
COLTS NECK Monmouth
COLUMBIA Warren
COLUMBUS Burlington
COOKSTOWN Burlington
CRANBURY (08512) Middlesex(68), Mercer(31)
CRANBURY Middlesex
CRANFORD Union
CREAM RIDGE (08514) Monmouth(70), Ocean(29)
CREAMRIDGE (08514) Monmouth(70), Ocean(29)
CRESSKILL Bergen
CROSSWICKS Burlington
DAYTON Middlesex
DEAL Monmouth
DEEPWATER Salem
DEERFIELD STREET Cumberland
DELAWARE Warren
DELMONT Cumberland
DEMAREST Bergen
DENNISVILLE Cape May
DENVILLE Morris
DIVIDING CREEK Cumberland
DORCHESTER Cumberland
DOROTHY Atlantic
DOVER Morris
DUMONT Bergen
DUNELLEN (08812) Somerset(51), Middlesex(48)
EAST BRUNSWICK Middlesex
EAST HANOVER Morris
EAST ORANGE Essex
EAST RUTHERFORD Bergen
EATONTOWN Monmouth
EDGEWATER Bergen
EDISON Middlesex
EGG HARBOR CITY (08215) Atlantic(94), Burlington(5)
EGG HARBOR TOWNSHIP Atlantic
ELIZABETH Union
ELMER Salem
ELMWOOD PARK Bergen
ELWOOD Atlantic
EMERSON Bergen
ENGLEWOOD Bergen
ENGLEWOOD CLIFFS Bergen
ENGLISHTOWN Monmouth
ESSEX FELLS Essex
ESTELL MANOR Atlantic
EWAN Gloucester
FAIR HAVEN Monmouth
FAIR LAWN Bergen
FAIRFIELD Essex
FAIRTON Cumberland
FAIRVIEW Bergen
FANWOOD Union
FAR HILLS Somerset
FARMINGDALE Monmouth
FLAGTOWN Somerset
FLANDERS Morris
FLEMINGTON Hunterdon
FLORENCE Burlington
FLORHAM PARK Morris
FORDS Middlesex
FORKED RIVER Ocean
FORT LEE Bergen
FORT MONMOUTH Monmouth
FORTESCUE Cumberland
FRANKLIN Sussex
FRANKLIN LAKES Bergen
FRANKLIN PARK Somerset
FRANKLINVILLE Gloucester
FREEHOLD Monmouth
FRENCHTOWN Hunterdon
GARFIELD Bergen
GARWOOD Union
GIBBSBORO Camden
GIBBSTOWN Gloucester
GILLETTE Morris
GLADSTONE Somerset
GLASSBORO Gloucester
GLASSER Sussex
GLEN GARDNER Hunterdon
GLEN RIDGE Essex
GLEN ROCK Bergen
GLENDORA Camden
GLENWOOD Sussex
GLOUCESTER CITY Camden
GOSHEN Cape May
GREAT MEADOWS Warren
GREEN CREEK Cape May
GREEN VILLAGE Morris
GREENDELL Sussex
GREENWICH Cumberland
GRENLOCH Gloucester
HACKENSACK Bergen
HACKETTSTOWN (07840) Warren(82), Morris(17)
HADDON HEIGHTS Camden
HADDONFIELD Camden
HAINESPORT Burlington
HALEDON Passaic
HAMBURG Sussex
HAMMONTON (08037) Atlantic(81), Camden(18)
HAMPTON (08827) Hunterdon(93), Warren(6)
HANCOCKS BRIDGE Salem
HARRINGTON PARK Bergen
HARRISON Hudson
HARRISONVILLE Gloucester
HASBROUCK HEIGHTS Bergen
HASKELL Passaic
HAWORTH Bergen
HAWTHORNE Passaic
HAZLET Monmouth
HEISLERVILLE Cumberland
HELMETTA Middlesex
HEWITT (07421) Passaic(98), Sussex(1)
HIBERNIA Morris
HIGH BRIDGE Hunterdon
HIGHLAND LAKES Sussex
HIGHLAND PARK Middlesex
HIGHLANDS Monmouth
HIGHTSTOWN Mercer
HILLSBOROUGH Somerset
HILLSDALE Bergen
HILLSIDE Union
HO HO KUS Bergen
HOBOKEN Hudson
HOLMDEL Monmouth
HOPATCONG Sussex
HOPE Warren
HOPEWELL (08525) Mercer(92), Hunterdon(6)
HOWELL Monmouth
IMLAYSTOWN Monmouth
IRONIA Morris
IRVINGTON Essex
ISELIN Middlesex
ISLAND HEIGHTS Ocean
JACKSON Ocean
JAMESBURG Middlesex
JERSEY CITY Hudson
JOBSTOWN Burlington
JOHNSONBURG Warren
JULIUSTOWN Burlington
KEANSBURG Monmouth
KEARNY Hudson
KEASBEY Middlesex
KENDALL PARK Middlesex
KENILWORTH Union
KENVIL Morris
KEYPORT (07735) Monmouth(92), Middlesex(7)
KINGSTON Somerset
KIRKWOOD VOORHEES Camden
LAFAYETTE Sussex
LAKE HIAWATHA Morris
LAKE HOPATCONG Morris
LAKEHURST Ocean
LAKEWOOD Ocean
LAMBERTVILLE (08530) Hunterdon(96), Mercer(3)
LANDING Morris
LANDISVILLE Atlantic
LANOKA HARBOR Ocean
LAVALLETTE Ocean
LAWNSIDE Camden
LAYTON Sussex

LEBANON Hunterdon
LEDGEWOOD Morris
LEEDS POINT Atlantic
LEESBURG Cumberland
LEONARDO Monmouth
LEONIA Bergen
LIBERTY CORNER Somerset
LINCOLN PARK Morris
LINCROFT Monmouth
LINDEN Union
LINWOOD Atlantic
LITTLE FALLS Passaic
LITTLE FERRY Bergen
LITTLE SILVER Monmouth
LITTLE YORK Hunterdon
LIVINGSTON Essex
LODI Bergen
LONG BRANCH Monmouth
LONG VALLEY Morris
LONGPORT Atlantic
LUMBERTON Burlington
LYNDHURST Bergen
LYONS Somerset
MADISON Morris
MAGNOLIA Camden
MAHWAH Bergen
MALAGA Gloucester
MANAHAWKIN Ocean
MANASQUAN Monmouth
MANTOLOKING Ocean
MANTUA Gloucester
MANVILLE Somerset
MAPLE SHADE Burlington
MAPLEWOOD Essex
MARGATE CITY Atlantic
MARLBORO Monmouth
MARLTON Burlington
MARMORA Cape May
MARTINSVILLE Somerset
MATAWAN (07747) Monmouth(65), Middlesex(34)
MAURICETOWN Cumberland
MAYS LANDING Atlantic
MAYWOOD Bergen
MC AFEE Sussex
MEDFORD Burlington
MENDHAM Morris
MERCHANTVILLE Camden
METUCHEN Middlesex
MICKLETON Gloucester
MIDDLESEX Middlesex
MIDDLETOWN Monmouth
MIDDLEVILLE Sussex
MIDLAND PARK Bergen
MILFORD Hunterdon
MILLBURN Essex
MILLINGTON Morris
MILLTOWN Middlesex
MILLVILLE Cumberland
MILMAY Atlantic
MINE HILL Morris
MINOTOLA Atlantic
MIZPAH Atlantic
MONMOUTH BEACH Monmouth
MONMOUTH JUNCTION Middlesex
MONROE TOWNSHIP Middlesex
MONROEVILLE (08343) Gloucester(58), Salem(41)
MONTAGUE Sussex
MONTCLAIR (07043) Essex(96), Passaic(3)
MONTCLAIR Essex
MONTVALE Bergen
MONTVILLE Morris
MOONACHIE Bergen
MOORESTOWN Burlington
MORGANVILLE Monmouth
MORRIS PLAINS Morris
MORRISTOWN Morris
MOUNT ARLINGTON Morris
MOUNT EPHRAIM Camden
MOUNT FREEDOM Morris
MOUNT HOLLY Burlington
MOUNT LAUREL Burlington
MOUNT ROYAL Gloucester
MOUNT TABOR Morris
MOUNTAIN LAKES Morris
MOUNTAINSIDE Union
MULLICA HILL Gloucester
MUSICAL HERITAGE Monmouth
NATIONAL PARK Gloucester
NAVESINK Monmouth
NEPTUNE Monmouth
NESHANIC STATION (08853) Somerset(86), Hunterdon(13)
NETCONG Morris
NEW BRUNSWICK Middlesex
NEW EGYPT (08533) Ocean(98), Burlington(1)
NEW GRETNA Burlington
NEW LISBON Burlington
NEW MILFORD Bergen
NEW PROVIDENCE Union
NEW VERNON Morris
NEWARK Essex
NEWFIELD (08344) Gloucester(65), Cumberland(24), Atlantic(6), Salem(3)
NEWFOUNDLAND Passaic
NEWPORT Cumberland
NEWTON Sussex
NEWTONVILLE Atlantic
NORMA Salem
NORMANDY BEACH Ocean
NORTH ARLINGTON Bergen
NORTH BERGEN Hudson
NORTH BRUNSWICK Middlesex
NORTHFIELD Atlantic
NORTHVALE Bergen
NORWOOD Bergen
NUTLEY Essex
OAK RIDGE (07438) Passaic(78), Morris(21)
OAKHURST Monmouth
OAKLAND Bergen
OAKLYN Camden
OCEAN CITY Cape May
OCEAN GATE Ocean
OCEAN GROVE Monmouth
OCEAN VIEW Cape May
OCEANPORT Monmouth
OCEANVILLE Atlantic
OGDENSBURG Sussex
OLD BRIDGE Middlesex
OLDWICK Hunterdon
ORADELL Bergen
ORANGE Essex
OSGLI Essex
OXFORD Warren
PALISADES PARK Bergen
PALMYRA Burlington
PARAMUS Bergen
PARK RIDGE Bergen
PARLIN Middlesex
PARSIPPANY Morris
PASSAIC Passaic
PATERSON Passaic
PAULSBORO Gloucester
PEAPACK Somerset
PEDRICKTOWN Salem
PEMBERTON Burlington
PENNINGTON Mercer
PENNS GROVE Salem
PENNSAUKEN Camden
PENNSVILLE Salem
PEQUANNOCK Morris
PERRINEVILLE Monmouth
PERTH AMBOY Middlesex
PHILLIPSBURG Warren
PICATINNY ARSENAL Morris
PINE BEACH Ocean
PINE BROOK Morris
PISCATAWAY Middlesex
PITMAN Gloucester
PITTSTOWN Hunterdon
PLAINFIELD (07063) Union(72), Somerset(27)
PLAINFIELD Union
PLAINSBORO Middlesex
PLEASANTVILLE Atlantic
PLUCKEMIN Somerset
POINT PLEASANT BEACH Ocean
POMONA Atlantic
POMPTON LAKES Passaic
POMPTON PLAINS Morris
PORT ELIZABETH Cumberland
PORT MONMOUTH Monmouth
PORT MURRAY Warren
PORT NORRIS Cumberland
PORT READING Middlesex
PORT REPUBLIC Atlantic
POTTERSVILLE Hunterdon
PRINCETON (08540) Mercer(72), Middlesex(15), Somerset(12)
PRINCETON JUNCTION Mercer
QUAKERTOWN Hunterdon
QUINTON Salem
RAHWAY Union
RAMSEY Bergen
RANCOCAS Burlington
RANDOLPH Morris
RARITAN Somerset
READINGTON Hunterdon
RED BANK Monmouth
RICHLAND Atlantic
RICHWOOD Gloucester
RIDGEFIELD Bergen
RIDGEFIELD PARK Bergen
RIDGEWOOD Bergen
RINGOES Hunterdon
RINGWOOD Passaic
RIO GRANDE Cape May
RIVER EDGE Bergen
RIVERDALE Morris
RIVERSIDE Burlington
RIVERTON Burlington
ROCHELLE PARK Bergen
ROCKAWAY Morris
ROCKY HILL Somerset
ROEBLING Burlington
ROOSEVELT Monmouth
ROSELAND Essex
ROSELLE Union
ROSELLE PARK Union
ROSEMONT Hunterdon
ROSENHAYN Cumberland
RUMSON Monmouth
RUNNEMEDE Camden
RUTHERFORD Bergen
SADDLE BROOK Bergen
SADDLE RIVER Bergen
SALEM Salem
SAYREVILLE Middlesex
SCHOOLEYS MOUNTAIN Morris
SCOTCH PLAINS Union
SEA GIRT Monmouth
SEA ISLE CITY Cape May
SEASIDE HEIGHTS Ocean
SEASIDE PARK Ocean
SECAUCUS Hudson
SERGEANTSVILLE Hunterdon
SEWAREN Middlesex
SEWELL Gloucester
SHILOH Cumberland
SHORT HILLS Essex
SHREWSBURY Monmouth
SICKLERVILLE (08081) Camden(96), Gloucester(3)
SKILLMAN (08558) Somerset(98), Mercer(1)
SOMERDALE Camden
SOMERS POINT Atlantic
SOMERSET Somerset
SOMERVILLE (08876) Somerset(98), Hunterdon(1)
SOUTH AMBOY Middlesex
SOUTH BOUND BROOK Somerset
SOUTH DENNIS Cape May
SOUTH HACKENSACK Bergen
SOUTH ORANGE Essex
SOUTH PLAINFIELD Middlesex
SOUTH RIVER Middlesex
SOUTH SEAVILLE Cape May
SPARTA Sussex
SPOTSWOOD Middlesex
SPRING LAKE Monmouth
SPRINGFIELD Union
STANHOPE Sussex
STANTON Hunterdon
STEWARTSVILLE Warren
STILLWATER Sussex
STIRLING Morris
STOCKHOLM (07460) Sussex(96), Morris(2)
STOCKTON Hunterdon
STONE HARBOR Cape May
STRATFORD Camden
STRATHMERE Cape May
SUCCASUNNA Morris
SUMMIT Union
SUSSEX Sussex
SWARTSWOOD Sussex
SWEDESBORO Gloucester
TEANECK Bergen
TENAFLY Bergen
TENNENT Monmouth
TETERBORO Bergen
THOROFARE Gloucester
THREE BRIDGES Hunterdon
TITUSVILLE Mercer
TOMS RIVER Ocean
TOTOWA Passaic
TOWACO Morris
TOWNSHIP OF WASHINGTON Bergen
TRANQUILITY Sussex
TRENTON (08620) Mercer(85), Burlington(14)
TRENTON (08691) Mercer(95), Monmouth(4)
TRENTON Burlington
TRENTON Mercer
TUCKAHOE Cape May
TUCKERTON (08087) Ocean(94), Burlington(5)
UNION Union
UNION CITY Hudson
VAUXHALL Union
VENTNOR CITY Atlantic
VERNON Sussex
VERONA Essex
VIENNA Warren
VILLAS Cape May
VINCENTOWN Burlington
VINELAND (08360) Cumberland(90), Atlantic(5), Gloucester(3)
VINELAND Cumberland
VOORHEES Camden
WALDWICK Bergen
WALLINGTON Bergen
WALLPACK CENTER Sussex
WANAQUE Passaic
WARETOWN Ocean
WARREN Somerset
WASHINGTON Warren
WATCHUNG Somerset
WATERFORD WORKS Camden
WAYNE Passaic
WEEHAWKEN Hudson
WENONAH Gloucester
WEST BERLIN Camden
WEST CREEK Ocean
WEST LONG BRANCH Monmouth
WEST MILFORD Passaic
WEST NEW YORK Hudson
WEST ORANGE Essex
WESTFIELD Union
WESTVILLE Gloucester
WESTWOOD Bergen
WHARTON Morris

WHIPPANY Morris
WHITEHOUSE Hunterdon
WHITEHOUSE STATION Hunterdon
WHITESBORO Cape May
WHITING Ocean
WICKATUNK Monmouth
WILDWOOD Cape May
WILLIAMSTOWN (08094) Gloucester(90), Atlantic(9)
WILLINGBORO Burlington
WINDSOR Mercer
WINSLOW Camden
WOOD RIDGE Bergen
WOODBINE (08270) Cape May(89), Atlantic(10)
WOODBRIDGE Middlesex
WOODBURY Gloucester
WOODBURY HEIGHTS Gloucester
WOODCLIFF LAKE Bergen
WOODSTOWN Salem
WRIGHTSTOWN Burlington
WYCKOFF Bergen
ZAREPHATH Somerset

New Jersey ZIP/City Cross Reference

07001-07001 AVENEL
07002-07002 BAYONNE
07003-07003 BLOOMFIELD
07004-07004 FAIRFIELD
07005-07005 BOONTON
07006-07007 CALDWELL
07008-07008 CARTERET
07009-07009 CEDAR GROVE
07010-07010 CLIFFSIDE PARK
07011-07015 CLIFTON
07016-07016 CRANFORD
07017-07019 EAST ORANGE
07020-07020 EDGEWATER
07021-07021 ESSEX FELLS
07022-07022 FAIRVIEW
07023-07023 FANWOOD
07024-07024 FORT LEE
07026-07026 GARFIELD
07027-07027 GARWOOD
07028-07028 GLEN RIDGE
07029-07029 HARRISON
07030-07030 HOBOKEN
07031-07031 NORTH ARLINGTON
07032-07032 KEARNY
07033-07033 KENILWORTH
07034-07034 LAKE HIAWATHA
07035-07035 LINCOLN PARK
07036-07036 LINDEN
07039-07039 LIVINGSTON
07040-07040 MAPLEWOOD
07041-07041 MILLBURN
07042-07043 MONTCLAIR
07044-07044 VERONA
07045-07045 MONTVILLE
07046-07046 MOUNTAIN LAKES
07047-07047 NORTH BERGEN
07050-07051 ORANGE
07052-07052 WEST ORANGE
07054-07054 PARSIPPANY
07055-07055 PASSAIC
07057-07057 WALLINGTON
07058-07058 PINE BROOK
07059-07059 WARREN
07060-07063 PLAINFIELD
07064-07064 PORT READING
07065-07065 RAHWAY
07066-07066 CLARK
07067-07067 COLONIA
07068-07068 ROSELAND
07069-07069 WATCHUNG
07070-07070 RUTHERFORD
07071-07071 LYNDHURST
07072-07072 CARLSTADT
07073-07073 EAST RUTHERFORD
07074-07074 MOONACHIE
07075-07075 WOOD RIDGE
07076-07076 SCOTCH PLAINS
07077-07077 SEWAREN
07078-07078 SHORT HILLS
07079-07079 SOUTH ORANGE
07080-07080 SOUTH PLAINFIELD
07081-07081 SPRINGFIELD
07082-07082 TOWACO
07083-07083 UNION
07086-07086 WEEHAWKEN
07087-07087 UNION CITY
07088-07088 VAUXHALL
07090-07091 WESTFIELD
07092-07092 MOUNTAINSIDE
07093-07093 WEST NEW YORK
07094-07094 SECAUCUS
07095-07095 WOODBRIDGE
07096-07096 SECAUCUS
07097-07097 JERSEY CITY
07098-07098 AVENEL
07099-07099 KEARNY
07100-07108 NEWARK
07109-07109 BELLEVILLE
07110-07110 NUTLEY
07111-07111 IRVINGTON
07112-07187 NEWARK
07187-07187 OSGLI
07188-07199 NEWARK
07200-07202 ELIZABETH
07203-07203 ROSELLE
07204-07204 ROSELLE PARK
07205-07205 HILLSIDE
07206-07216 ELIZABETH
07300-07399 JERSEY CITY
07401-07401 ALLENDALE
07403-07403 BLOOMINGDALE
07405-07405 BUTLER
07407-07407 ELMWOOD PARK
07410-07410 FAIR LAWN
07416-07416 FRANKLIN
07417-07417 FRANKLIN LAKES
07418-07418 GLENWOOD
07419-07419 HAMBURG
07420-07420 HASKELL
07421-07421 HEWITT
07422-07422 HIGHLAND LAKES
07423-07423 HO HO KUS
07424-07424 LITTLE FALLS
07428-07428 MC AFEE
07430-07430 MAHWAH
07432-07432 MIDLAND PARK
07435-07435 NEWFOUNDLAND
07436-07436 OAKLAND
07438-07438 OAK RIDGE
07439-07439 OGDENSBURG
07440-07440 PEQUANNOCK
07442-07442 POMPTON LAKES
07444-07444 POMPTON PLAINS
07446-07446 RAMSEY
07450-07451 RIDGEWOOD
07452-07452 GLEN ROCK
07456-07456 RINGWOOD
07457-07457 RIVERDALE
07458-07458 SADDLE RIVER
07460-07460 STOCKHOLM
07461-07461 SUSSEX
07462-07462 VERNON
07463-07463 WALDWICK
07465-07465 WANAQUE
07470-07477 WAYNE
07480-07480 WEST MILFORD
07481-07481 WYCKOFF
07495-07498 MAHWAH
07501-07505 PATERSON
07506-07507 HAWTHORNE
07508-07508 HALEDON
07509-07510 PATERSON
07511-07512 TOTOWA
07513-07533 PATERSON
07538-07538 HALEDON
07543-07544 PATERSON
07601-07602 HACKENSACK
07603-07603 BOGOTA
07604-07604 HASBROUCK HEIGHTS
07605-07605 LEONIA
07606-07606 SOUTH HACKENSACK
07607-07607 MAYWOOD
07608-07608 TETERBORO
07620-07620 ALPINE
07621-07621 BERGENFIELD
07624-07624 CLOSTER
07626-07626 CRESSKILL
07627-07627 DEMAREST
07628-07628 DUMONT
07630-07630 EMERSON
07631-07631 ENGLEWOOD
07632-07632 ENGLEWOOD CLIFFS
07640-07640 HARRINGTON PARK
07641-07641 HAWORTH
07642-07642 HILLSDALE
07643-07643 LITTLE FERRY
07644-07644 LODI
07645-07645 MONTVALE
07646-07646 NEW MILFORD
07647-07647 NORTHVALE
07648-07648 NORWOOD
07649-07649 ORADELL
07650-07650 PALISADES PARK
07652-07653 PARAMUS
07656-07656 PARK RIDGE
07657-07657 RIDGEFIELD
07660-07660 RIDGEFIELD PARK
07661-07661 RIVER EDGE
07662-07662 ROCHELLE PARK
07663-07663 SADDLE BROOK
07666-07666 TEANECK
07670-07670 TENAFLY
07675-07675 WESTWOOD
07676-07676 TOWNSHIP OF WASHINGTON
07677-07677 WOODCLIFF LAKE
07688-07688 TEANECK
07699-07699 TETERBORO
07701-07701 RED BANK
07702-07702 SHREWSBURY
07703-07703 FORT MONMOUTH
07704-07704 FAIR HAVEN
07709-07709 ALLENHURST
07710-07710 ADELPHIA
07711-07711 ALLENHURST
07712-07712 ASBURY PARK
07713-07713 MUSICAL HERITAGE
07715-07715 BELMAR
07716-07716 ATLANTIC HIGHLANDS
07717-07717 AVON BY THE SEA
07718-07718 BELFORD
07719-07719 BELMAR
07720-07720 BRADLEY BEACH
07721-07721 CLIFFWOOD
07722-07722 COLTS NECK
07723-07723 DEAL
07724-07724 EATONTOWN
07726-07726 ENGLISHTOWN
07727-07727 FARMINGDALE
07728-07728 FREEHOLD
07730-07730 HAZLET
07731-07731 HOWELL
07732-07732 HIGHLANDS
07733-07733 HOLMDEL
07734-07734 KEANSBURG
07735-07735 KEYPORT
07737-07737 LEONARDO
07738-07738 LINCROFT
07739-07739 LITTLE SILVER
07740-07740 LONG BRANCH
07746-07746 MARLBORO
07747-07747 MATAWAN
07748-07748 MIDDLETOWN
07750-07750 MONMOUTH BEACH
07751-07751 MORGANVILLE
07752-07752 NAVESINK
07753-07754 NEPTUNE
07755-07755 OAKHURST
07756-07756 OCEAN GROVE
07757-07757 OCEANPORT
07758-07758 PORT MONMOUTH
07760-07760 RUMSON
07762-07762 SPRING LAKE
07763-07763 TENNENT
07764-07764 WEST LONG BRANCH
07765-07765 WICKATUNK
07777-07777 HOLMDEL
07799-07799 EATONTOWN
07801-07802 DOVER
07803-07803 MINE HILL
07806-07806 PICATINNY ARSENAL
07820-07820 ALLAMUCHY
07821-07821 ANDOVER
07822-07822 AUGUSTA
07823-07823 BELVIDERE
07825-07825 BLAIRSTOWN
07826-07826 BRANCHVILLE
07827-07827 MONTAGUE
07828-07828 BUDD LAKE
07829-07829 BUTTZVILLE
07830-07830 CALIFON
07831-07831 CHANGEWATER
07832-07832 COLUMBIA
07833-07833 DELAWARE
07834-07834 DENVILLE
07836-07836 FLANDERS
07837-07837 GLASSER
07838-07838 GREAT MEADOWS
07839-07839 GREENDELL
07840-07840 HACKETTSTOWN
07842-07842 HIBERNIA
07843-07843 HOPATCONG
07844-07844 HOPE
07845-07845 IRONIA
07846-07846 JOHNSONBURG
07847-07847 KENVIL
07848-07848 LAFAYETTE
07849-07849 LAKE HOPATCONG
07850-07850 LANDING
07851-07851 LAYTON
07852-07852 LEDGEWOOD
07853-07853 LONG VALLEY
07855-07855 MIDDLEVILLE
07856-07856 MOUNT ARLINGTON
07857-07857 NETCONG
07860-07860 NEWTON
07863-07863 OXFORD
07865-07865 PORT MURRAY
07866-07866 ROCKAWAY
07869-07869 RANDOLPH
07870-07870 SCHOOLEYS MOUNTAIN
07871-07871 SPARTA
07874-07874 STANHOPE
07875-07875 STILLWATER
07876-07876 SUCCASUNNA
07877-07877 SWARTSWOOD
07878-07878 MOUNT TABOR
07879-07879 TRANQUILITY
07880-07880 VIENNA
07881-07881 WALLPACK CENTER
07882-07882 WASHINGTON
07885-07885 WHARTON
07890-07890 BRANCHVILLE
07901-07902 SUMMIT
07920-07920 BASKING RIDGE
07921-07921 BEDMINSTER
07922-07922 BERKELEY HEIGHTS
07924-07924 BERNARDSVILLE
07926-07926 BROOKSIDE
07927-07927 CEDAR KNOLLS
07928-07928 CHATHAM
07930-07930 CHESTER

07931-07931	FAR HILLS
07932-07932	FLORHAM PARK
07933-07933	GILLETTE
07934-07934	GLADSTONE
07935-07935	GREEN VILLAGE
07936-07936	EAST HANOVER
07938-07938	LIBERTY CORNER
07939-07939	LYONS
07940-07940	MADISON
07945-07945	MENDHAM
07946-07946	MILLINGTON
07950-07950	MORRIS PLAINS
07960-07963	MORRISTOWN
07970-07970	MOUNT FREEDOM
07974-07974	NEW PROVIDENCE
07976-07976	NEW VERNON
07977-07977	PEAPACK
07978-07978	PLUCKEMIN
07979-07979	POTTERSVILLE
07980-07980	STIRLING
07981-07999	WHIPPANY
08001-08001	ALLOWAY
08002-08003	CHERRY HILL
08004-08004	ATCO
08005-08005	BARNEGAT
08006-08006	BARNEGAT LIGHT
08007-08007	BARRINGTON
08008-08008	BEACH HAVEN
08009-08009	BERLIN
08010-08010	BEVERLY
08011-08011	BIRMINGHAM
08012-08012	BLACKWOOD
08014-08014	BRIDGEPORT
08015-08015	BROWNS MILLS
08016-08016	BURLINGTON
08018-08018	CEDAR BROOK
08019-08019	CHATSWORTH
08020-08020	CLARKSBORO
08021-08021	CLEMENTON
08022-08022	COLUMBUS
08023-08023	DEEPWATER
08025-08025	EWAN
08026-08026	GIBBSBORO
08027-08027	GIBBSTOWN
08028-08028	GLASSBORO
08029-08029	GLENDORA
08030-08030	GLOUCESTER CITY
08031-08031	BELLMAWR
08032-08032	GRENLOCH
08033-08033	HADDONFIELD
08034-08034	CHERRY HILL
08035-08035	HADDON HEIGHTS
08036-08036	HAINESPORT
08037-08037	HAMMONTON
08038-08038	HANCOCKS BRIDGE
08039-08039	HARRISONVILLE
08040-08040	KIRKWOOD VOORHEES
08041-08041	JOBSTOWN
08042-08042	JULIUSTOWN
08043-08043	VOORHEES
08045-08045	LAWNSIDE
08046-08046	WILLINGBORO
08048-08048	LUMBERTON
08049-08049	MAGNOLIA
08050-08050	MANAHAWKIN
08051-08051	MANTUA
08052-08052	MAPLE SHADE
08053-08053	MARLTON
08054-08054	MOUNT LAUREL
08055-08055	MEDFORD
08056-08056	MICKLETON
08057-08057	MOORESTOWN
08059-08059	MOUNT EPHRAIM
08060-08060	MOUNT HOLLY
08061-08061	MOUNT ROYAL
08062-08062	MULLICA HILL
08063-08063	NATIONAL PARK
08064-08064	NEW LISBON
08065-08065	PALMYRA
08066-08066	PAULSBORO
08067-08067	PEDRICKTOWN
08068-08068	PEMBERTON
08069-08069	PENNS GROVE
08070-08070	PENNSVILLE
08071-08071	PITMAN
08072-08072	QUINTON
08073-08073	RANCOCAS
08074-08074	RICHWOOD
08075-08075	RIVERSIDE
08076-08077	RIVERTON
08078-08078	RUNNEMEDE
08079-08079	SALEM
08080-08080	SEWELL
08081-08081	SICKLERVILLE
08083-08083	SOMERDALE
08084-08084	STRATFORD
08085-08085	SWEDESBORO
08086-08086	THOROFARE
08087-08087	TUCKERTON
08088-08088	VINCENTOWN
08089-08089	WATERFORD WORKS
08090-08090	WENONAH
08091-08091	WEST BERLIN
08092-08092	WEST CREEK
08093-08093	WESTVILLE
08094-08094	WILLIAMSTOWN
08095-08095	WINSLOW
08096-08096	WOODBURY
08097-08097	WOODBURY HEIGHTS
08098-08098	WOODSTOWN
08099-08099	BELLMAWR
08100-08105	CAMDEN
08106-08106	AUDUBON
08107-08107	OAKLYN
08108-08108	COLLINGSWOOD
08109-08109	MERCHANTVILLE
08110-08110	PENNSAUKEN
08201-08201	ABSECON
08202-08202	AVALON
08203-08203	BRIGANTINE
08204-08204	CAPE MAY
08205-08205	ABSECON
08210-08210	CAPE MAY COURT HOUSE
08212-08212	CAPE MAY POINT
08213-08213	COLOGNE
08214-08214	DENNISVILLE
08215-08215	EGG HARBOR CITY
08217-08217	ELWOOD
08218-08218	GOSHEN
08219-08219	GREEN CREEK
08220-08220	LEEDS POINT
08221-08222	LINWOOD
08223-08223	MARMORA
08224-08224	NEW GRETNA
08225-08225	NORTHFIELD
08226-08226	OCEAN CITY
08227-08227	LINWOOD
08230-08230	OCEAN VIEW
08231-08231	OCEANVILLE
08232-08233	PLEASANTVILLE
08234-08234	EGG HARBOR TOWNSHIP
08240-08240	POMONA
08241-08241	PORT REPUBLIC
08242-08242	RIO GRANDE
08243-08243	SEA ISLE CITY
08244-08244	SOMERS POINT
08245-08245	SOUTH DENNIS
08246-08246	SOUTH SEAVILLE
08247-08247	STONE HARBOR
08248-08248	STRATHMERE
08250-08250	TUCKAHOE
08251-08251	VILLAS
08252-08252	WHITESBORO
08260-08260	WILDWOOD
08270-08270	WOODBINE
08302-08302	BRIDGETON
08310-08310	BUENA
08311-08311	CEDARVILLE
08312-08312	CLAYTON
08313-08313	DEERFIELD STREET
08314-08314	DELMONT
08315-08315	DIVIDING CREEK
08316-08316	DORCHESTER
08317-08317	DOROTHY
08318-08318	ELMER
08319-08319	ESTELL MANOR
08320-08320	FAIRTON
08321-08321	FORTESCUE
08322-08322	FRANKLINVILLE
08323-08323	GREENWICH
08324-08324	HEISLERVILLE
08326-08326	LANDISVILLE
08327-08327	LEESBURG
08328-08328	MALAGA
08329-08329	MAURICETOWN
08330-08330	MAYS LANDING
08332-08332	MILLVILLE
08340-08340	MILMAY
08341-08341	MINOTOLA
08342-08342	MIZPAH
08343-08343	MONROEVILLE
08344-08344	NEWFIELD
08345-08345	NEWPORT
08346-08346	NEWTONVILLE
08347-08347	NORMA
08348-08348	PORT ELIZABETH
08349-08349	PORT NORRIS
08350-08350	RICHLAND
08352-08352	ROSENHAYN
08353-08353	SHILOH
08358-08358	CHERRY HILL
08360-08362	VINELAND
08370-08370	RIVERSIDE
08400-08401	ATLANTIC CITY
08402-08402	MARGATE CITY
08403-08403	LONGPORT
08404-08405	ATLANTIC CITY
08406-08406	VENTNOR CITY
08411-08411	ATLANTIC CITY
08501-08501	ALLENTOWN
08502-08502	BELLE MEAD
08504-08504	BLAWENBURG
08505-08505	BORDENTOWN
08510-08510	CLARKSBURG
08511-08511	COOKSTOWN
08512-08512	CRANBURY
08514-08514	CREAMRIDGE
08514-08514	CREAM RIDGE
08515-08515	CROSSWICKS
08518-08518	FLORENCE
08520-08520	HIGHTSTOWN
08525-08525	HOPEWELL
08526-08526	IMLAYSTOWN
08527-08527	JACKSON
08528-08528	KINGSTON
08530-08530	LAMBERTVILLE
08533-08533	NEW EGYPT
08534-08534	PENNINGTON
08535-08535	PERRINEVILLE
08536-08536	PLAINSBORO
08540-08544	PRINCETON
08550-08550	PRINCETON JUNCTION
08551-08551	RINGOES
08553-08553	ROCKY HILL
08554-08554	ROEBLING
08555-08555	ROOSEVELT
08556-08556	ROSEMONT
08557-08557	SERGEANTSVILLE
08558-08558	SKILLMAN
08559-08559	STOCKTON
08560-08560	TITUSVILLE
08561-08561	WINDSOR
08562-08562	WRIGHTSTOWN
08570-08570	CRANBURY
08600-08695	TRENTON
08701-08701	LAKEWOOD
08720-08720	ALLENWOOD
08721-08721	BAYVILLE
08722-08722	BEACHWOOD
08723-08723	BRICK
08730-08730	BRIELLE
08731-08731	FORKED RIVER
08732-08732	ISLAND HEIGHTS
08733-08733	LAKEHURST
08734-08734	LANOKA HARBOR
08735-08735	LAVALLETTE
08736-08736	MANASQUAN
08738-08738	MANTOLOKING
08739-08739	NORMANDY BEACH
08740-08740	OCEAN GATE
08741-08741	PINE BEACH
08742-08742	POINT PLEASANT BEACH
08750-08750	SEA GIRT
08751-08751	SEASIDE HEIGHTS
08752-08752	SEASIDE PARK
08753-08757	TOMS RIVER
08758-08758	WARETOWN
08759-08759	WHITING
08801-08801	ANNANDALE
08802-08802	ASBURY
08803-08803	BAPTISTOWN
08804-08804	BLOOMSBURY
08805-08805	BOUND BROOK
08807-08807	BRIDGEWATER
08808-08808	BROADWAY
08809-08809	CLINTON
08810-08810	DAYTON
08812-08812	DUNELLEN
08816-08816	EAST BRUNSWICK
08817-08820	EDISON
08821-08821	FLAGTOWN
08822-08822	FLEMINGTON
08823-08823	FRANKLIN PARK
08824-08824	KENDALL PARK
08825-08825	FRENCHTOWN
08826-08826	GLEN GARDNER
08827-08827	HAMPTON
08828-08828	HELMETTA
08829-08829	HIGH BRIDGE
08830-08830	ISELIN
08831-08831	JAMESBURG
08831-08831	MONROE TOWNSHIP
08832-08832	KEASBEY
08833-08833	LEBANON
08834-08834	LITTLE YORK
08835-08835	MANVILLE
08836-08836	MARTINSVILLE
08837-08837	EDISON
08840-08840	METUCHEN
08844-08844	HILLSBOROUGH
08846-08846	MIDDLESEX
08848-08848	MILFORD
08850-08850	MILLTOWN
08852-08852	MONMOUTH JUNCTION
08853-08853	NESHANIC STATION
08854-08855	PISCATAWAY
08857-08857	OLD BRIDGE
08858-08858	OLDWICK
08859-08859	PARLIN
08861-08862	PERTH AMBOY
08863-08863	FORDS
08865-08865	PHILLIPSBURG
08867-08867	PITTSTOWN
08868-08868	QUAKERTOWN
08869-08869	RARITAN
08870-08870	READINGTON
08871-08872	SAYREVILLE
08873-08875	SOMERSET
08876-08876	SOMERVILLE
08877-08877	SOUTH RIVER
08878-08879	SOUTH AMBOY
08880-08880	SOUTH BOUND BROOK
08882-08882	SOUTH RIVER
08884-08884	SPOTSWOOD
08885-08885	STANTON
08886-08886	STEWARTSVILLE
08887-08887	THREE BRIDGES
08888-08888	WHITEHOUSE
08889-08889	WHITEHOUSE STATION
08890-08890	ZAREPHATH
08896-08896	RARITAN
08899-08899	EDISON
08901-08901	NEW BRUNSWICK
08902-08902	NORTH BRUNSWICK
08903-08903	NEW BRUNSWICK
08904-08904	HIGHLAND PARK
08905-08989	NEW BRUNSWICK

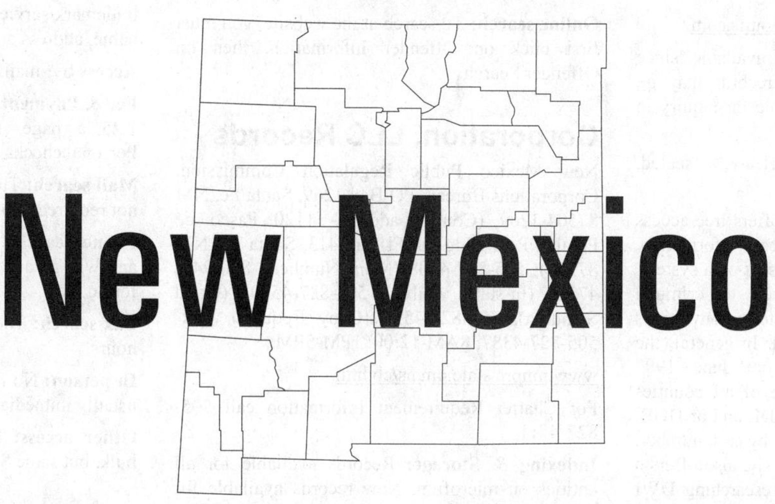

New Mexico

General Help Numbers:

Governor's Office
State Capitol, Room 400
Santa Fe, NM 87503
www.governor.state.nm.us
505-476-2200
Fax 505-676-2226
8AM-5PM

Attorney General's Office
PO Drawer 1508
Santa Fe, NM 87504-1508
www.nmag.gov/
505-827-6000
Fax 505-827-5826
8AM-5PM

Legislative Records
Legislative Council Service
State Capitol Bldg, Room 411
Santa Fe, NM 87501
http://legis.state.nm.us/lcs/
505-986-4600
Fax 505-986-4610
8AM-5PM

State Archives
1205 Camino Carlos Rey
Santa Fe, NM 87505
www.nmcpr.state.nm.us/
505-476-7902
Fax 505-476-7901
8AM-5PM

State Specifics:

Capital:	Santa Fe Santa Fe County
Time Zone:	MST
Number of Counties:	33
Population:	1,984,356
Web Site:	www.newmexico.gov/

State Agencies

Criminal Records

Department of Public Safety, Criminal Records Bureau, PO Box 1628, Santa Fe, NM 87504-1628 (Courier- 4491 Cerrillos Rd, Santa Fe, 87504); 505-827-9181, Fax- 505-827-3388; 8AM-5PM.

www.dps.nm.org

Indexing & Storage: Records available from 1935 on. New records available for inquiry in 2 to 4 weeks. 32% of all arrests in database have final dispositions recorded, 35% for those arrests within last 5 years.

Searching: Fingerprint search requests are not available except for checks for children or elderly-related occupations mandated by state statute, and an FBI search can be done for those groups. The state's records are 100% fingerprint-supported. Include in request- date of birth, SSN, full name, DPS notarized signed release by subject. Download the release form at the web page. This data not released- juvenile records All records are released, including those without dispositions. This includes arrest record information on persons arrested in New Mexico for felony, misdemeanor (offenses punishable by 6 months or more imprisonment) and DWI offenses.

Access by: mail, in person.

Fee & Payment: The fee is $10.00 per individual. Fee payee- Department of Public Safety. Prepayment required. Must use cashiers check or money order. No credit cards accepted.

Mail search: Turnaround time- 1 to 3 weeks. Turnaround time is for "no record found." If records exist, turnaround time may be 3 to 4 weeks. A SASE is requested.

In person: If records are found, they may be available in 5 to 7 working days.

Statewide Court Records

Administrative Office of the Courts, Judicial Information Division, 2905 Rodeo Park Dr East, Bldg #5, Santa Fe, NM 87505; 505-476-6900, Fax- 505-476-6952; 8AM-5PM.

www.nmcourts.gov/

Direct questions to webmstr@nmcourts.com.

Indexing & Storage: Records available since 1997, in general. Some county records may go back farther. New records available for inquiry in 48 hours.

Searching: This data not released- sealed, restricted, or party information.

Online search: The home page offers free access to District and Magistrate Court case information, except Bernalillo Metro which has its own system. Municipal court data is limited to criminal Domestic Violence and DWI historic convictions from September 1, 1991 forward. In general, the other records are available from June 1997 forward. The search is inclusive of all counties participating. Search by name & DL and/or DOB, and by county and type of case or by case number. DOB is shown 75% of time. The site also offers a DWI Offender History tool for researching DWI history. Search by name. Supreme Court opinions may be researched at www.supremecourt.nm.org/.

Sexual Offender Registry

Department of Public Safety, Records Bureau, PO Box 1628, Santa Fe, NM 87504-1628 (Courier address- 4491 Cerrillos Rd, Santa Fe, NM 87504); 505-827-9297, 505-827-9193, Fax- 505-827-3399; 8AM-5PM. www.nmsexoffender.dps.state.nm.us

Indexing & Storage: Records available from 07/95. New records available for inquiry in 2 to 4 weeks.

Searching: Email questions to dps.sorna@state.nm.us. Include in request- name, DOB. The work address belonging to a sex offender is released if he/she will come into direct contact with children. This data not released- SSN

Access by: mail, phone, online.

Fee & Payment: There is no fee. Copies are $1.00 first page, $.25 ea add'l.

Mail search: Turnaround time- 1 to 2 weeks. A SASE is requested.

Phone search: Name searching available.

Online search: The website offers a variety of search methods including by name, county, city, and ZIP Code. The site also offers a complete state list, also an absconder list.

Incarceration Records

New Mexico Corrections Department, Central Records Unit, PO Box 27116, Santa Fe, NM 87502; 505-827-8674, Fax- 505-827-8821; 7AM-4PM. http://corrections.state.nm.us

Indexing & Storage: Records available on current and former inmates. New records available for inquiry in 1-3 days.

Searching: Include in request- name; DOB and SSN are helpful. Location, conviction and sentencing information, behavior, release dates are provided. This data not released- NCIC, police reports, pre-sentence, discipline reports, parole data.

Access by: mail, phone, online.

Fee & Payment: Fee is $.50 per copy. Fee payee- NM Department of Corrections Prepayment required. Personal checks and credit cards not accepted.

Mail search: Turnaround time- 7 to 10 days. A SASE is not required.

Phone search: Limited name searching available.

Online search: To search at the website, you must first click on Offender Information, then on Offender Search.

Corporation, LLC Records

New Mexico Public Regulation Commission, Corporations Bureau, PO Box 1269, Santa Fe, NM 87504-1269 (Courier address- 1120 Paseo de Peralta, Pera Bldg 4th Fl, Rm 413, Santa Fe, NM 87501); 505-827-4508 (Main Number), 800-947-4722 (In-state Only), 505-827-4510 (Good Standing), 505-827-4513 (Copy Request), Fax- 505-827-4387; 8AM-12:00: 1PM-5PM.

www.nmprc.state.nm.us/cb.htm

For Charter Requirement Information call 505-827-4511.

Indexing & Storage: Records available for all entities on microfilm. New records available for inquiry in 1-2 days.

Searching: Include in request- full name of business. In addition to the articles of organization, business entity records available include: Annual Reports, Officers, Directors, Prior (merged) names, Inactive, Registered and Reserved names. This data not released- financial information.

Access by: mail, phone, fax, in person, online.

Fee & Payment: There is no charge for a computer printout. Copies are $1.00 per page with minimum fee of $10.00 for for-profit companies or domestic LLCs and $5.00 for non-profit companies. Certification fee is $25.00, except for non-profits which is $10.00. Fee payee- Public Regulation Commission. Prepayment required. Personal checks and money orders accepted. No credit cards or cash accepted.

Mail search: Turnaround time- 4-10 days. A SASE is requested.

Phone search: Limited information is given over the phone.

Fax search: Information can be requested by fax, but is not returned until payment received.

In person: Search requests can be made in person, timeframe of results depends on how extensive research is.

Online search: There is no charge to view records at Internet site, www.nmprc.state.nm.us/cii.htm. Records can be searched by company name or by director name.

Other access: This agency makes the database available on electronic format using a 3480 tape cartridge. Fee is $3,600, monthly updates available for $600.

Expedited service: Expedited service is available, but only with supervisor approval.

Trademarks/Servicemarks, Trade Names

Secretary of State, Trademarks Division, 325 Don Gaspar, #301, Santa Fe, NM 87503; 505-827-3609, Fax- 505-827-3611; 8AM-5PM.

www.sos.state.nm.us/sos-Trademarks.html

Since July 1, 1997, New Mexico no longer registers trade names. However, the agency will do searches for records on file.

Indexing & Storage: Records available from 1980 to present. New records available for inquiry in 1 to 2 days.

Searching: Include in request- trademark/servicemark name. Include your full name, address and telephone number.

Access by: mail, phone, fax, in person.

Fee & Payment: There is no search fee, copies are $.25 a page. Fee payee- Secretary of State. Personal checks accepted. Credit cards are not.

Mail search: Turnaround time- 2 to 3 days. SASE not required. No fee for mail request.

Phone search: They will do a computer search and will give you the information over the phone for no fee.

Fax search: There is no fee. Turnaround time: 24 hours.

In person: No fee for request. Turnaround time is usually immediate.

Other access: File copies may be purchased in bulk, but same $.25 per copy fee applies.

Uniform Commercial Code

UCC Division, Secretary of State, 325 Don Gaspar, St #301, Santa Fe, NM 87503; 505-827-3615, 505-827-3608, Fax- 505-827-3611; 8AM-5PM.

http://secure.sos.state.nm.us/ucc/default.asp

This agency will not conduct searches. You must hire a local search company or conduct your search via the agency website.

Indexing & Storage: Records available from 1965, but most available records are from 1998 forward. New records available for inquiry in 24 hours.

Searching: Please note that all tax liens are filed at the county level. The system does not permit a search by collateral. Searching is not permitted by mail, phone or fax, but the agency will look up an image if a specific file number is given. This data not released- SSN or tax IDs.

Access by: mail, fax, in person, online.

Fee & Payment: Copies are $1.00 per page, plus $3.00 if certification requested. Fee payee- Secretary of State. Prepayment required. Personal checks accepted, credit cards are not.

Mail search: Turnaround time- 3 days. No name requests by mail, you must give specific document number.

Fax search: Fax requests accepted if file number provided; search requests by name not accepted.

In person: A public access terminal is available. You may view documents for free.

Online search: The website permits searching and provides a form to use to order copies of filings.

Other access: Microfilm and images (from 7/99) on disk may be purchased.

Federal & State Tax Liens

Records not maintained by a state level agency.

Records are filed with the Clerk at the county level.

Gross Receipts Tax Registrations

Taxation & Revenue Department, Tax Administrative Services Division, PO Box 630, Santa Fe, NM 87504; 505-827-0700, Fax- 505-827-0614; 8AM-5PM. www.tax.state.nm.us/

New Mexico does not have a sales tax. It has a gross receipts tax instead.

Indexing & Storage: Records available from 1996. New records available for inquiry in 1 week.

Searching: This agency will only confirm that a business is registered and active. They will provide no other information. Include in request- company name or ID#. The business name is required, the permit number and federal ID are optional. There is no search fee, no copy fee.

Access by: mail, in person.

Mail search: Turnaround time- 6 to 12 weeks. A SASE is requested.

In person: Simple requests processed immediately.

Expedited service: no expedited service available.

Birth Certificates

Department of Health, Bureau of Vital Records, PO Box 26110, Santa Fe, NM 87502 (Courier address- 1105 South St Francis Dr, Santa Fe, NM 87502); 505-827-0121, 505-827-2338 (Information), 877-284-0963 (Phone Order), 505-841-4185 (Albuquerque), Fax- 505-984-1048; 8AM-5:00PM (Counter Service: 8:30AM-4PM).

www.health.state.nm.us

All requesters must sign and date the request. It is a felony to obtain a record fraudulently.

Indexing & Storage: Records available from 1920 on. New records available for inquiry immediately.

Searching: Records available only to immediate family members or those demonstrating legal tangible interest in the desired record. Sealed records (e.g. adoptions and paternity) are unavailable. Include in request- full name, names of parents, mother's maiden name, date of birth, place of birth, relationship to person of record, reason for information request. Signature of requester and physical & mailing addresses are required.

Access by: mail, phone, fax, in person, online.

Fee & Payment: The search fee is $10.00 per record. Fee payee- NM Vital Records. Prepayment required. Personal checks accepted. Major Credit cards accepted only by VitalChek.

Mail search: Turnaround time- 3-4 weeks. SASE not required.

Phone search: From VitalChek, see expedited services. Phone is 877-284-0963.

Fax search: From VitalChek, see expedited services. Fax is 877-284-1066

In person: Turnaround time is usually less than 1/2 hour. Also, counter service for requesting birth certificates through the Albuquerque Stanford Public Health Office is available Monday through Friday from 9:00 a.m. until 4:00 p.m. The Albuquerque Office is housed at the Stanford Public Health Office at 1111 Stanford NE. The telephone number is 505-841-4185.

Online search: Records can be ordered at www.vitalchek.com, a state designated vendor.

Expedited service: Expedited service is available for online, phone and fax requests from www.vitalchek. Add $16.00 for a vendor fee and use of credit card, plus cost of express service is desired.

Death Records

Department of Health, Bureau of Vital Records, PO Box 26110, Santa Fe, NM 87502 (Courier address- 1105 South St Francis Dr, Santa Fe, NM 87502); 505-827-0121, 505-827-2338 (Information), 877-284-0963 (Phone Order), 505-841-4185 (Albuquerque), Fax- 505-984-1048; 8AM-5PM (Counter Service: 8:30AM-4PM).

www.health.state.nm.us

Indexing & Storage: Records available from 1920 to present. New records available for inquiry immediately.

Searching: Only immediate family member or a person with tangible interest can receive record. Include in request- full name, date of death, place of death, SSN, relationship to person of record, reason for information request. Age at death and name of mortuary must also be included for search.

Access by: mail, phone, fax, in person, online.

Fee & Payment: The fee is $5.00 per record. An additional fee may be charged if required information is not submitted. Use of credit card is an additional $15.00 (thru VitalChek). Fee payee- NM Vital Records. Prepayment required. Personal checks accepted. Major Credit cards accepted only by VitalChek.

Mail search: Turnaround time- 3 to 4 weeks. SASE not required.

Phone search: From VitalChek, see expedited services. Phone is 877-284-0963.

Fax search: From VitalChek, see expedited services. Fax is 877-284-1066

In person: Turnaround time is usually 1 hour or less. The Albuquerque Office is housed at the Stanford Public Health Office at 1111 Stanford NE. The telephone number is (505) 841-4185.

Online search: A free lookup is available at www.usgwarchives.org/nm/nmdi.htm. Records date from 1899 to 1949. Expedited records can be ordered at www.vitalchek.com, a state designated vendor.

Expedited service: Expedited service is available for online, phone and fax requests from www.vitalchek. Add $16.00 for a vendor fee and use of credit card, plus cost of express service is desired.

Marriage Certificates, Divorce Records

Records not maintained by a state level agency.

Marriage and divorce records are found at county of issue.

Workers' Compensation Records

Access to Records is Restricted.

Workers Compensation Administration, PO Box 27198, Albuquerque, NM 87125-7198 (Courier address- 2410 Centre Ave, SE, Albuquerque, NM 87106); 505-841-6000, 800-255-7965 (In-State Toll Free), Fax- 505-841-6060; 8AM-5PM.

www.workerscomp.state.nm.us/

The subject must write the agency, provide proof of ID with a driver's license, and request the record, and pay a copy fee of $.25 per page. Most records are confidential but access is permitted for all parties to a case and other cases involving the same worker. Only upon filing of rejection of a recommended resolution shall records be open to the public.

Driver Records

Motor Vehicle Division, Driver Services Bureau, PO Box 1028, Santa Fe, NM 87504-1028 (Courier address- Joseph M. Montoya Bldg, 1100 S St. Francis Dr, 2nd Floor, Santa Fe, NM 87504); 505-827-2241, 888-683-4636 (Toll Free-Automated), 505-827-4636 (Local-Automated), Fax- 505-827-2792; 8AM-5PM. www.tax.state.nm.us/mvd/

Copies of tickets may be obtained from the same address. There is no fee.

Indexing & Storage: Records available for 3 years for moving violations; 25 years DWIs. Accidents are not reported on the record and neither are violations less than 10 mph over the limit in 55 or 65 zones. The driver's address is included on the record. New records available for inquiry in 30 to 40 days.

Searching: State law lists 9 permissible user groups and permits release of records with written consent. Purchasers may not use the information for direct mail solicitation or resell the reports after usage. The full name, DOB and either the license number or SSN is required when ordering. Casual requesters must have signed, notarized consent from subject. This data not released- SSN, address, and date of birth.

Access by: mail, phone, in person, online.

Fee & Payment: There is no fee for mail or walk-in requests, as long as requester qualifies. Fee payee- Motor Vehicle Division. Prepayment required. Personal checks accepted, credit cards are not.

Mail search: Turnaround time- 5 to 7 days. No fee for manual search. A SASE is requested.

Phone search: Use the toll-free line listed above.

In person: No fee for manual search. Up to 10 requests can be processed while you wait, the rest must be in writing and left overnight.

Online search: Visit www.nmcourts.gov/dwi.html for a free DUI Offender History search. This is not an official record and may not contain all court records. A 2nd DUI search option is www.dwiresourcecenter.org/datacenter/statedata.shtml. Records are available, for authorized users, from the state's designated vendors - Oso Grande (505-343-7639) www.osogrande.com and Samba (888-94-samba) www.samba.biz. In general, subscription fees are $1.49 to $3.50 depending on the type of record ordered, plus possible network or access fees. The systems are open 24 hours a day, batch requesters must wait 24 hours.

Vehicle, Vessel Ownership & Registration

Motor Vehicle Division, Vehicle Services Bureau, PO Box 1028, Santa Fe, NM 87504-1028 (Courier address- Joseph M. Montoya Bldg, 1100 S St. Francis Dr, 2nd Floor, Santa Fe, NM 87504); 505-827-4636, 888-683-4636, Fax- 505-827-0395; 8AM-5PM. www.tax.state.nm.us/mvd/

Indexing & Storage: Records available for a minimum of 3 years on boats and 6 years on vehicles. All motorized boats, sailboats, and jet skis must be both titled and registered if over 10 ft, and only registered if 10 ft or less. New records available for inquiry in 30 days.

Searching: Authorized requesters are restricted to 9 user groups and must sign a contract that states purpose of request and subsequent use. Requesters may not use ownership and vehicle information to create a resalable database. Liens on vehicles show the title records. Liens on vessels are filed at the Sec. of State's office. This data not released- addresses, SSNs or date of birth.

Access by: mail, in person, online.

Fee & Payment: There are no fees for mail or in person requests. A vehicle history search (microfilm) goes back 4 years. Fee payee- Department of Motor Vehicles. Prepayment required. Personal checks accepted, credit cards are not.

Mail search: Turnaround time- 4 to 6 weeks. A SASE is requested.

In person: Up to ten requests will be processed while you wait for information only. If copies are needed, records will be returned by mail in 4 to 6 weeks.

Online search: Records are available, for authorized users, from either of the state's designated vendors. Oso Grande offers XML interface as well as interactive searching. Call them at 505-343-7639. SAMBA offers interactive and operates a title and registration program for car dealers and banks. Call SAMBA at 505-797-2622 x3. Authorization to work with either vendor must first come from the state agency.

Other access: Bulk requests for vehicle or ownership information must be approved by the Director's office. Once a sale is made, further resale is prohibited.

Accident Reports

Department of Public Safety, Attn: Records, PO Box 1628, Santa Fe, NM 87504-1628 (Courier address- New Mexico State Police Complex, 4491 Cerrillos Rd, Santa Fe, 87504); 505-827-9181, 505-827-9182, Fax- 505-827-9189; 8AM-5PM.

www.dps.nm.org/

Indexing & Storage: Records available up to 20 years to present in-house (on computer) and up to 25 years for fatalities. New records available for inquiry in up to 15 days.

Searching: Arrest information is not released. Include in request- full name, date of accident, county location of accident.

Access by: mail, phone, in person.

Fee & Payment: The fee is $1.00 per page plus $.25 each individual page. There is no fee for a no record found. There is no fee charged for persons directly involved in the accident. Fee payee- Department of Public Safety. Prepayment required. Personal checks accepted.

Mail search: Turnaround time- 2 weeks. A SASE is requested.

Phone search: No fee for telephone request.

In person: Turnaround time is immediate if incident one year or less old.

Legislation Records

Legislative Council Service, State Capitol Bldg, Room 411, Santa Fe, NM 87501; 505-986-4600 (Information Systems), 505-986-4350 (Bill Room During Session Only), 505-986-4667 (Library), Fax- 505-986-4610; 8AM-5PM.

http://legis.state.nm.us/lcs/

Signed laws of the current year can be obtained from the Secretary of State's Office at 505-827-3600. Searchers are encouraged to use the web.

Indexing & Storage: Records available from 1973, 1996 to present online. The current session meets starting the third Tuesday in January. Sessions are 60 days in odd-numbered years and 30 days in even-numbered years. New records available for inquiry in 24 hours or less.

Searching: The LCS operates a legislative library that is available to members of the Legislature, legislative staff, other state agencies and the public. Submit bill number or topic to search with session or year. Records on computer.

Access by: mail, phone, in person, online.

Fee & Payment: Depending on the extent of the search, the agency may charge for copies. There is no search fee. Fee payee- New Mexico State Legislature. Personal checks accepted, credit cards are not.

Mail search: Turnaround time- variable. SASE not required.

Phone search: Limited searching is available during session.

In person: You may request bills in person.

Online search: The Internet site is a complete source of information about bills and legislators. There are also links to other NM state agencies and NM statutes. Bill Finder- http://nmlegis.gov/lcs/BillFinder.aspx.

Other access: Subscription purchase for the complete file of current session is available. However, you must request your subscription by mid-session.

Voter Registration

Secretary of State, Bureau of Elections, 325 Don Gaspar, #300, Santa Fe, NM 87503; 505-827-3621, 800-477-3632, Fax- 505-827-8403; 8AM-5PM.

www.sos.state.nm.us/sos-elections.html

This agency maintains a statewide database and complies with HAVA. The agency does sell statewide lists but only for restricted (political) purposes and not for commercial purposes.

Searching: Individual look-ups must be done at the county clerk level or via the online look-up. Email question to daniel.miera@state.nm.us.

Access by: mail, online.

Mail search:

Online search: A registrant verification is provided at https://voterview.state.nm.us/. Results give zip code of registrant and polling place.

GED Certificates

Department of Education, GED Testing Program, 300 Don Gaspar, Rm 122, Santa Fe, NM 87501-2786; 505-827-6702, Fax- 505-827-6616; 8AM-5PM.

http://sde.state.nm.us/AssessmentAccountability/GED/index.html

Request forms may be downloaded from the website. Unless ordered by the subject, transcripts are mailed directly to institutions or employers only.

Indexing & Storage: Records available from 1943 to present, 80 years on paper. New records available for inquiry in 45 days.

Searching: Include in request- name, DOB, SSN, date of test, and signed release (for either a verification or transcript).

Access by: mail, fax, in person.

Fee & Payment: There are no fees.

Mail search: Turnaround time- 2 weeks. SASE not required.

Fax search: Same criteria as mail searching, 2 weeks turnaround time.

In person: Simple requests may be processed while you wait.

Hunting & Fishing License Information

Public Information & Outreach, NM Dept of Game & Fish, PO Box 25112, Santa Fe, NM 87504 (Courier address- #1 Wildlife Way, Santa Fe, NM 87507); 505-476-8000, 800-862-931-, Fax- 505-476-8116; 8AM-5PM.

www.wildlife.state.nm.us

Indexing & Storage: Records available for last season only. New records available for inquiry in 6 weeks for drawing results.

Searching: Include in request- name, contact information. This data not released- phone number, email address, personal information.

Access by: mail, fax, in person.

Fee & Payment: Fee is $60 per hour for computer access, $.50 per copy. Fee payee- NM Dept of Fish & Game. Prepayment not required. Personal checks accepted.

Mail search: Turnaround time- 1 month. SASE not required.

Fax search: Requests accepted.

In person: You may do the search yourself for no fee.

Other access: CD of data is available for purchase.

New Mexico State Licensing Agencies

For details about the agency responsible for licensing/certifying/registering an item below or in the Agency Quick Finder section, match an item's number with the number of the agency in the *Licensing Agency Information* section.

New Mexico Licenses Searchable Online

Acupuncturist #26 .... http://164.64.87.25/MyLicenseVerification/
Alcohol Server #14 .... http://164.64.87.25/MyLicenseVerification/
Announcer, Athletic Event/Ring #39 .... http://164.64.87.25/MyLicenseVerification/
Architect #17 .... www.nmbea.org/People/Aroster.htm
Armored Car Company #9 .... http://164.64.87.25/MyLicenseVerification/
Art Therapist #15 .... http://164.64.87.25/MyLicenseVerification/
Athletic Promoter/Matchmaker #39 .... http://164.64.87.25/MyLicenseVerification/
Athletic Trainer #1 .... http://164.64.87.25/MyLicenseVerification/
Audiologist #11 .... http://164.64.87.25/MyLicenseVerification/
Bank #48 .... http://164.64.87.25/MyLicenseVerification/Search.aspx?facility=Y
Barber #2 .... http://164.64.87.25/MyLicenseVerification/
Bingo/Raffle, Non-profit #14 .... http://164.64.87.25/MyLicenseVerification/
Booking Agent #39 .... http://164.64.87.25/MyLicenseVerification/
Boxer #39 .... http://164.64.87.25/MyLicenseVerification/
Boxer Manager #39 .... http://164.64.87.25/MyLicenseVerification/
Boxing Judge/Timekeeper #39 .... http://164.64.87.25/MyLicenseVerification/
Cemetery, Endow'd/Perpet'l Care #48 .... http://164.64.87.25/MyLicenseVerification/Search.aspx?facility=Y
Certified Court Reporter #16 .... www.imagehost.net/ccrboard/courtreporterslist.html
Chiropractor #3 .... http://164.64.87.25/MyLicenseVerification/
Clinical Nurse Specialist #19 .... https://www.state.nm.us/bon/lookup.html
Collection Agency/Manager #48 .... http://164.64.87.25/MyLicenseVerification/Search.aspx?facility=Y
Consumer Credit Grantor/Loaner #48 .... http://164.64.87.25/MyLicenseVerification/Search.aspx?facility=Y
Contractor #13 .... http://public.psiexams.com/index_login.jsp
Cosmetologist #2 .... http://164.64.87.25/MyLicenseVerification/
Counseling/Therapy Practice #15 .... http://164.64.87.25/MyLicenseVerification/
Credit Union #48 .... http://164.64.87.25/MyLicenseVerification/Search.aspx?facility=Y
Crematory #12 .... www.rld.state.nm.us/b&c/thanato/Licensee%20Search/licensee_search_index.asp
Dental Assistant #4 .... http://164.64.87.25/MyLicenseVerification/
Dental Hygienist #4 .... http://164.64.87.25/MyLicenseVerification/
Dentist #4 .... http://164.64.87.25/MyLicenseVerification/
Dietitian/Nutritionist #8 .... http://164.64.87.25/MyLicenseVerification/
Direct Disposer (Funerary) #12 .... www.rld.state.nm.us/b&c/thanato/Licensee%20Search/licensee_search_index.asp
Dispens'g Physician Cont'd Substance #41 .... http://164.64.87.25/MyLicenseVerification/
Electrologist #2 .... http://164.64.87.25/MyLicenseVerification/
Electrophysician #2 .... http://164.64.87.25/MyLicenseVerification/
Emergency Medical Technician #22 .... www.nmems.org/License%20varification.htm
Engineer #44 .... www.sblpes.state.nm.us/PEPSBoard/PEPSBoard.jsp
Escrow Company #48 .... http://164.64.87.25/MyLicenseVerification/Search.aspx?facility=Y
Esthetician #2 .... http://164.64.87.25/MyLicenseVerification/
FSI (Funerary) #12 .... www.rld.state.nm.us/b&c/thanato/Licensee%20Search/licensee_search_index.asp
Funeral Director/Practitioner #12 .... www.rld.state.nm.us/b&c/thanato/Licensee%20Search/licensee_search_index.asp
Funeral Home #12 .... www.rld.state.nm.us/b&c/thanato/Licensee%20Search/licensee_search_index.asp
Funeral Service Intern #12 .... www.rld.state.nm.us/b&c/thanato/Licensee%20Search/licensee_search_index.asp
Gambling, Non-Profit #14 .... http://164.64.87.25/MyLicenseVerification/
Hearing Aid Specialist #11 .... http://164.64.87.25/MyLicenseVerification/
Hemodialysis Technician #19 .... https://www.state.nm.us/bon/lookup.html
Interior Designer #25 .... http://164.64.87.25/MyLicenseVerification/
Journeyman Contractor #13 .... http://public.psiexams.com/index_login.jsp
Landscape Architect #18 .... http://164.64.87.25/MyLicenseVerification/
Liquor Distributor #14 .... http://164.64.87.25/MyLicenseVerification/
Loan Company, Small #48 .... http://164.64.87.25/MyLicenseVerification/Search.aspx?facility=Y
Lobbying Organization #32 .... http://ethics.sos.state.nm.us/LOBBY/ORG.htm
Lobbyist #32 .... http://ethics.sos.state.nm.us/LOBBY/LOB.htm
LPG Gas License #13 .... http://public.psiexams.com/index_login.jsp
Manicurist #2 .... http://164.64.87.25/MyLicenseVerification/
Manufactur'd Housing Dealer/Broker #47 .... http://164.64.87.25/MyLicenseVerification/
Manufactur'd Housing Install/Repair #47 .... http://164.64.87.25/MyLicenseVerification/

Manufactured Housing Manufacturer #47	http://164.64.87.25/MyLicenseVerification/
Manufactured Housing Salesperson #47	http://164.64.87.25/MyLicenseVerification/
Marriage & Family Therapist #15	http://164.64.87.25/MyLicenseVerification/
Martial Arts Contest #39	http://164.64.87.25/MyLicenseVerification/
Massage Instr./Practitioner #5	http://164.64.87.25/MyLicenseVerification/
Massage Therapist #5	http://164.64.87.25/MyLicenseVerification/
Massage Therapy School #5	www.rld.state.nm.us/massage/schools.html
Medical Doctor #36	www.docboard.org/nm/
Medical Researcher/ Facility #41	http://164.64.87.25/MyLicenseVerification/
Medical Wholesale Company #41	http://164.64.87.25/MyLicenseVerification/
Medication Aide #19	https://www.state.nm.us/bon/lookup.html
Mental Health Counselor #15	http://164.64.87.25/MyLicenseVerification/
Midwife, Certified Nurse-Midwife #34	www.health.state.nm.us/midwife-roster.html
Midwife, Licensed #34	www.health.state.nm.us/midwife-roster.html
Money Order Agent/Firm/Exempts #48	http://164.64.87.25/MyLicenseVerification/Search.aspx?facility=Y
Mortgage Firm/Loan Broker/Branch #48	http://164.64.87.25/MyLicenseVerification/Search.aspx?facility=Y
Motor Vehicle Sales Financer #48	http://164.64.87.25/MyLicenseVerification/Search.aspx?facility=Y
Nuclear Medicine Technologist #38	www.nmenv.state.nm.us/nmrcb/radtech.html
Nurse Anesthetist #19	https://www.state.nm.us/bon/lookup.html
Nurse Practitioner #19	https://www.state.nm.us/bon/lookup.html
Nurse-LPN, RN #19	https://www.state.nm.us/bon/lookup.html
Nursing Home Administrator #6	http://164.64.87.25/MyLicenseVerification/
Occupational Therapist/Assistant #28	http://164.64.87.25/MyLicenseVerification/
Optometrist #40	http://164.64.87.25/MyLicenseVerification/
Oriental Medicine Doctor #26	http://164.64.87.25/MyLicenseVerification/
Osteopathic Physician #7	http://164.64.87.25/MyLicenseVerification/
Osteopathic Physician Assistant #7	http://164.64.87.25/MyLicenseVerification/
Patrol Operator, Private #9	http://164.64.87.25/MyLicenseVerification/
Pharmacist #41	http://164.64.87.25/MyLicenseVerification/
Pharmacy, Non-Residential #41	http://164.64.87.25/MyLicenseVerification/
Physical Therapist/Assistant #28	http://164.64.87.25/MyLicenseVerification/
Physician Assistant #36	www.docboard.org/nm/
Podiatrist #42	http://164.64.87.25/MyLicenseVerification/
Polygraph Examiner #9	http://164.64.87.25/MyLicenseVerification/
Private Investigator #9	http://164.64.87.25/MyLicenseVerification/
Psychologist #37	http://164.64.87.25/MyLicenseVerification/
Psychologist Associate #37	http://164.64.87.25/MyLicenseVerification/
Public Accountant-CPA #35	http://164.64.87.25/MyLicenseVerification/
Radiation Therapy Technologist #38	www.nmenv.state.nm.us/nmrcb/radtech.html
Radiologic Technologist #38	www.nmenv.state.nm.us/nmrcb/NM_Radtech_Registrations.xls
Real Estate Agent/Seller #46	http://164.64.87.25/MyLicenseVerification/
Real Estate Appraiser #27	http://164.64.87.25/MyLicenseVerification/
Real Estate Broker #46	http://164.64.87.25/MyLicenseVerification/
Referee #39	http://164.64.87.25/MyLicenseVerification/
Respiratory Care Therapist #29	http://164.64.87.25/MyLicenseVerification/
Savings & Loan #48	http://164.64.87.25/MyLicenseVerification/Search.aspx?facility=Y
Security Dog Company #9	http://164.64.87.25/MyLicenseVerification/
Security Guard/Company #9	http://164.64.87.25/MyLicenseVerification/
Social Worker (LBSW, LI, LM, Prov) #10	http://164.64.87.25/MyLicenseVerification/
Speech-Language Pathologist #11	http://164.64.87.25/MyLicenseVerification/
Substance Abuse Counselor/Intern #15	http://164.64.87.25/MyLicenseVerification/
Surveyor, Land #44	www.sblpes.state.nm.us/PEPSBoard/PEPSBoard.jsp
Trust Company #48	http://164.64.87.25/MyLicenseVerification/Search.aspx?facility=Y
Wrestler #39	http://164.64.87.25/MyLicenseVerification/

New Mexico Licensing Quick Finder

Acupuncturist #26	505-476-4630
Alcohol Server #14	505-476-4875
Animal Pregnancy Diagnosis #30	505-841-9112
Announcer, Athletic Event/Ring #39	505-222-9860
Architect #17	505-827-6375
Armored Car Company #9	505-476-4650
Art Therapist #15	505-476-4610
Artificial Inseminator #30	505-841-9112
Athletic Promoter/Matchmaker #39	505-222-9860
Athletic Trainer #1	505-476-7098
Attorney #20	505-271-9706
Audiologist #11	505-476-4640
Bank #48	505-476-4885
Barber #2	505-476-4690
Barber Shop/School #2	505-476-4690
Bingo/Raffle, Non-profit #14	505-476-4875
Boiler Operator Journeyman #33	505-452-8311
Booking Agent #39	505-222-9860
Boxer #39	505-222-9860
Boxer Manager #39	505-222-9860
Boxing Judge/Timekeeper #39	505-222-9860
Cemetery, Endow'd/Perpet'l Care #48	505-476-4885
Certified Court Monitor #16	505 821-1440
Certified Court Reporter #16	505-821-1440
Chiropractor #3	505-476-4695
Clinical Nurse Specialist #19	505-841-8340
Collection Agency/Manager #48	505-476-4885

Consumer Credit Grantor/Loaner #48 .. 505-476-4885
Contractor #13 505-467-4700
Cosmetologist #2 505-476-4690
Cosmetology Shop/School #2 505-476-4690
Counseling/Therapy Practice #15 505-476-4610
Credit Union #48 505-476-4885
Crematory #12 505-476-4870
Dental Assistant #4 505-476-4680
Dental Hygienist #4 505-476-4680
Dentist #4 505-476-4680
Dietitian/Nutritionist #8 505-476-7053
Direct Disposer (Funerary) #12 505-476-4870
Dispens'g Physician Cont'd Substance #41 505-222-9830
Electrologist #2 505-827-7550
Electrophysician #2 505-476-4690
Emergency Medical Technician #22 505-476-7701
Engineer #44 505-827-7561
Escrow Company #48 505-476-4885
Esthetician #2 505-476-4690
Fireworks Distributor Class C or B #31 . 505-827-3761
Fireworks Manufacturer 1.4G #31 505-827-3761
Fireworks Vendor (Retail, Wholesale) #31 505-827-3761
FSI (Funerary) #12 505-476-4870
Funeral Director/Practitioner #12 505-476-4870
Funeral Home #12 505-476-4870
Funeral Service Intern #12 505-476-4870
Gambling, Non-Profit #14 505-476-4875
Hearing Aid Specialist #11 505-476-4640
Hemodialysis Technician #19 505-841-8340
Insurance Agent #23 505-827-4637
Interior Designer #25 505-476-4865
Investment Advisor/Represent've #32 .. 505-476-4580
Journeyman Contractor #13 505-467-4700
Landscape Architect #18 505-476-4625
Liquor Distributor #14 505-476-4875
Loan Company, Small #48 505-476-4885
Lobbying Organization #32 505-476-4580
Lobbyist #32 505-476-4580
LPG Gas License #13 505-467-4700
Manicurist #2 505-476-4690
Manufactured Housing Dealer/Broker #47 505-476-4770
Manufactured Housing Installer/Repair #47 505-476-4770
Manufactured Housing Mfg'r #47 505-476-4770
Manufactured Housing Seller #47 505-476-4770
Marriage & Family Therapist #15 505-476-4610
Martial Arts Contest #39 505-222-9860
Massage Instr./Practitioner #5 505-476-4870
Massage Therapist #5 505-476-4870
Massage Therapy School #5 505-476-4870
Medical Doctor #36 505-476-7220
Medical Researcher/ Facility #41 505-222-9830
Medical Wholesale Company #41 505-222-9830
Medication Aide #19 505-841-8340
Mental Health Counselor #15 505-476-4610
Midwife, Certified Nurse-Midwife #34 ... 505-476-8908
Midwife, Licensed #34 505-476-8908
Money Order Agent/Firm/Exempts #48 505-476-4885
Mortgage Firm/Loan Brok'r/Branch #48 505-476-4885
Motor Vehicle Sales Financer #48 505-476-4885
Notary Public #43 505-827-3605
Nuclear Medicine Technologist #38 505-476-3264
Nurse Anesthetist #19 505-841-8340
Nurse Practitioner #19 505-841-8340
Nurse-LPN, RN #19 505-841-8340
Nursing Home Administrator #6 505-476-4660
Occupational Therapist/Assistant #28 .. 505-476-4940
Optometrist #40 505-476-4660
Oriental Medicine Doctor #26 505-476-4630
Osteopathic Physician #7 505-476-4695
Osteopathic Physician Assistant #7 505-476-4695
Patrol Operator, Private #9 505-476-4650
Pest Management Consultant #21 575-646-2133
Pesticide Applicator/Operator #21 575-646-2133
Pesticide Dealer #21 575-646-2133
Pharmacist #41 505-222-9830
Pharmacy, Non-Residential #41 505-222-9830
Physical Therapist/Assistant #28 505-476-4880
Physician Assistant #36 505-476-7220
Podiatrist #42 505-476-4695
Polygraph Examiner #9 505-476-4650
Private Investigator #9 505-476-4650
Psychologist #37 505-476-4607
Psychologist Associate #37 505-476-4607
Public Accountant-CPA #35 505-222-9850
Racing #45 505-841-6400
Radiation Therapy Technologist #38 ... 505-476-3264
Radiologic Technologist #38 505-476-3264
Real Estate Agent/Seller #46 505-476-4512
Real Estate Appraiser #27 505-476-4611
Real Estate Broker #46 505-476-4512
Referee #39 505-222-9860
Respiratory Care Therapist #29 505-476-4660
Savings & Loan #48 505-476-4885
School Administrator #24 505-827-6587
School Counselor #24 505-827-6587
Securities Broker/Dealer #32 505-476-4580
Securities Division Agent #32 505-476-4580
Securities Sales Representative #32 ... 505-476-4580
Security Dog Company #9 505-476-4650
Security Guard/Company #9 505-476-4650
Social Worker (LBSW, LI, LM) #10 505-476-4890
Social Worker, Provisional #10 505-476-4890
Speech-Language Pathologist #11 505-476-4640
Substance Abuse Counsel'r/Intern #15 505-476-4610
Surveyor, Land #44 505-827-7561
Teacher #24 505-827-6587
Trust Company #48 505-476-4885
Veterinarian/Veterinary Technician #30 505-841-9112
Veterinary Facility #30 505-841-9112
Wrestler #39 505-222-9860

New Mexico Licensing Agency Information

#1 Regulation & Licensing Dept., Athletic Trainers Board, 2550 Cerrillos Rd 2nd Fl, Santa Fe, NM 87505; 505-476-4925, F- 505-476-4633. www.rld.state.nm.us/AthleticTrainers/index.html Search data at- http://164.64.87.25/MyLicenseVerification/

#2 Regulation & Licensing Dept., Board of Barbers & Cosmetologists, PO Box 25101 (2550 Cerrillos Rd), Santa Fe, NM 87504; 505-476-4690, Fax- 505-476-4645. www.rld.state.nm.us/BarbersCosmetologists/index.html Search data at- http://164.64.87.25/MyLicenseVerification/

#3 Regulation & Licensing Dept., Board of Chiropractic Examiners, 2550 Cerrillos Rd 2nd Fl, Santa Fe, NM 87504; 505-476-4695, Fax- 505-476-4645. www.rld.state.nm.us/chiropractic/index.html Search data at- http://164.64.87.25/MyLicenseVerification/ Lists provided online do not include sanctions.

#4 Regulation & Licensing Dept., Board of Dental Health Care, 2550 Cerrillos Rd, Toney Anaya Bldg, Santa Fe, NM 87504-5101; 505-476-4680, Fax- 505-476-4545. Hours- 8AM-5PM. www.rld.state.nm.us/Dental/index.html Search data at- http://164.64.87.25/MyLicenseVerification/

#5 Regulation & Licensing Dept., Massage Therapy Board, 2550 Cerrillos Rd, Toney Anaya Bldg, Santa Fe, NM 87505; 505-476-4870, Fax- 505-476-7095. Hours- 8AM-5PM. www.rld.state.nm.us/massage/index.html Search data at- http://164.64.87.25/MyLicenseVerification/

#6 Regulation & Licensing Dept., Nursing Home Administrators Board, 2550 Cerrillos Rd, Santa Fe, NM 87505-3260; 505-476-4660, Fax- 505-476-4660. Hours- 8AM-5PM. www.rld.state.nm.us/NursingHomeAdministrators/index.html Search data at- http://164.64.87.25/MyLicenseVerification/

#7 Regulation & Licensing Dept., Board of Osteopathic Medical Examiners, 2550 Cerrillos Rd 2nd Fl, Santa Fe, NM 87505-3260; 505-476-4654, Fax- 505-476-4645. www.rld.state.nm.us/Osteopathy/index.html Search data at- http://164.64.87.25/MyLicenseVerification/

#8 Regulation & Licensing Dept., Nutrition & Dietetics Practice Board, 2550 Cerrillos Rd, Santa Fe, NM 87505; 505-476-4935, Fax- 505-476-4665. www.rld.state.nm.us/Nutrition/index.html Search data at- http://164.64.87.25/MyLicenseVerification/

#9 Regulation & Licensing Dept., Private Investigators & Polygraph Board, PO Box 25101 (2550 Cerrillos Rd), Santa Fe, NM 87504; 505-476-4664, Fax- 505-476-4615. www.rld.state.nm.us/PrivateInvestigations/index.html Search data at- http://164.64.87.25/MyLicenseVerification/

#10 Regulation & Licensing Dept., Social Work Examiners Board, 2550 Cerrillos Rd, Santa Fe, NM 87504; 505-476-4890, Fax- 505-476-4620. www.rld.state.nm.us/SocialWork/index.html Search data at- http://164.64.87.25/MyLicenseVerification/

#11 Regulation & Licensing Dept., Speech, Language, Audiology, & Hearing Aid Board, 2550 Cerrillos Rd 2nd Fl, Santa Fe, NM 87505-3260; 505-476-4640, Fax- 505-476-4620. www.rld.state.nm.us/b&c/speech/ Search data at- http://164.64.87.25/MyLicenseVerification/

#12 Regulation & Licensing Dept., Thanatopractice Board, 2550 Cerrillos Rd 2nd Fl, Santa Fe, NM 87505-3260; 505-476-4970, Fax- 505-476-4665. www.rld.state.nm.us/thanatopractice/index.html Search data at- www.rld.state.nm.us/b&c/thanato/Licensee%20Search/licensee_search_index.asp

#13 Regulation & Licensing Dept., Construction Industries Division, 2550 Cerrillos Rd, Santa Fe, NM 87505-3260; 505-467-4700, Fax- 505-765-5670. www.rld.state.nm.us/cid/ Search data at- http://public.psiexams.com/index_login.jsp

#14 Regulation & Licensing Dept., Alcohol & Gaming Division, 2550 Cerrillos Rd, Toney Anaya Bldg, Santa Fe, NM 87505-3260; 505-476-4875, Fax- 505-476-4595. www.rld.state.nm.us/AGD/index.html

#15 Regulation & Licensing Dept., Counseling & Therapy Practice Board, 2550 Cerrillos Rd, Santa Fe, NM 87505-3260; 505-476-4610, Fax- 505-476-4633.

www.rld.state.nm.us/Counseling/index.html Search data at- http://164.64.87.25/MyLicenseVerification/

#16 Board Governing Recording of Judicial Proceedings, PO Box 92648, Albuquerque, NM 87199-2648; 505-821-1440, Fax- 505-821-2940. Hours- 8AM-5PM. www.ccrboard.com

#17 Board of Examiners for Architects, PO Box 509 (491 Old Santa Fe Tr, Lamy Bldg, 2nd Fl N, 87501), Santa Fe, NM 87504; 505-827-6375, Fax- 505-827-6373. Hours- 8AM-N, 1PM-5PM. www.nmbea.org Search data at- www.nmbea.org/People/Aroster.htm

#18 Board of Landscape Architects, 2550 Cerrillos Rd, Toney Anaya Bldg, Santa Fe, NM 87505-3260; 505-476-4930, Fax- 505-476-4645. Hours- 8AM-5PM. www.rld.state.nm.us/landscape/index.html Search data at- http://164.64.87.25/MyLicenseVerification/

#19 Board of Nursing, 6301 Indian School NE #710, Albuquerque, NM 87110; 505-841-8340, Fax- 505-841-8347. Hours- 8AM-N 1PM-5PM. www.bon.state.nm.us/ Search data at- https://www.state.nm.us/bon/lookup.html Credentials verification for Employers/Professional Firms at https://www.nursys.com/Common.asp?pt=LICENSEVERIFICATION. They sell lists. Other verifications through NURSYS at www.nursys.com for RN/LPN.

#20 Board of Bar Examiners, 9420 Indian School NE, Albuquerque, NM 87112; 505-271-9706, Fax- 505-271-9768. www.nmexam.org Exam results are found at www.nmexam.org/exam_results.html.

#21 Department of Agriculture, Pesticide Management Bureau, MSC 3AQ, PO Box 30005, MSC 3AQ, Las Cruces, NM 88003-8005; 575-646-2134, Fax- 575-646-5977. http://nmdaweb.nmsu.edu/pesticides

#22 Department of Health, Injury Prevention & EMS Bureau, 1301 Siler Rd, Bldg F, Santa Fe, NM 87507; 505-476-8200, Fax- 505-476-8201. www.nmems.org/ Search data at- www.nmems.org/License%20varification.htm

#23 Department of Insurance, Insurance Licensing Division, PO Box 1269, Santa Fe, NM 87504; 505-827-4637, Fax- 505-827-4734. www.nmprc.state.nm.us/id.htm

#24 Education Department, Professional Licensure, 300 Don Gaspar, Education Bldg, Santa Fe, NM 87501-2786; 505-827-6587 option 1, Fax- 505-827-6696. www.sde.state.nm.us

#25 Regulation & Licensing Dept., Board of Interior Design, 2550 Cerrillos Rd 2nd Fl, Santa Fe, NM 87505-3260; 505-476-4762, Fax- 505-476-4865. www.rld.state.nm.us/interior/index.html Search data at- http://164.64.87.25/MyLicenseVerification/

#26 Regulation & Licensing Dept., Acupuncture & Oriental Medicine Board, 2550 Cerrillos Rd (PO Box 25101, 87504), Santa Fe, NM 87505-3260; 505-476-4630, Fax- 505-476-4620. www.rld.state.nm.us/acupuncture/index.html Search data at- http://164.64.87.25/MyLicenseVerification/

#27 Regulation & Licensing Dept., Real Estate Appraisers Board, 2550 Cerrillos Rd 2nd Fl, Toney Anaya Bldg, Santa Fe, NM 87505-3260; 505-476-4860, Fax- 505-476-4645. www.rld.state.nm.us/RealEstateAppraisers/index.html Search data at- http://164.64.87.25/MyLicenseVerification/

#28 Regulation & Licensing Dept., Physical Therapy / Occupational Therapy Boards, 2550 Cerrillos Rd 2nd Fl, Santa Fe, NM 87505; 505-476-4880 or 476-4940, Fax- 505-476-4645. www.rld.state.nm.us/OccupationalTherapy/index.html Search data at- http://164.64.87.25/MyLicenseVerification/

#29 Regulation & Licensing Dept., Respiratory Care Advisory Board, 2550 Cerrillos Rd, Santa Fe, NM 87505; 505-476-4965, Fax- 505-476-4645. Hours- 8AM-5PM. www.rld.state.nm.us/RespiratoryCare/index.html Search data at- http://164.64.87.25/MyLicenseVerification/

#30 Board of Veterinary Medicine, 7301 Jefferson St NE #H, Albuquerque, NM 87109-4363; 505-841-9112, Fax- 505-841-9127. www.newmexicoveterinaryboard.us To search website, click on "license verification.".

#31 State Fire Marshal, Public Regulation Commission, 604 West San Mateo (PO Box 1269), Santa Fe, NM 87504; 505-827-3761, Fax- 505-827-3778. www.nmprc.state.nm.us/sfm.htm

#32 Securities Division, Regulation and Licensing Dept., 2550 Cerrillos Rd, Santa Fe, NM 87505-3260; 505-476-4580, 800-704-5533 in N.M., Fax- 505-476-4511. www.rld.state.nm.us/Securities/feesandforms.html

#33 Boiler Operator Journeyman Licensing Board, c/o Contractor Licensing Services, 3211 Coors Blvd SW #A3, Albuquerque, NM 87121; 505-452-8311, Fax- 505-452-8310. www.constructionbook.com/contractor-license/new-mexico/index.asp

#34 Maternal Health Program, Public Health, PO Box 26110, Santa Fe, NM 87502; 505-476-8908, Fax- 505-476-8941. Hours- 8AM-5PM. www.health.state.nm.us Search data at- www.health.state.nm.us/midwife-roster.html

#35 Regulation & Licensing Dept., Accountancy Board, 5200 Oakland NE, Suite D, Albuquerque, NM 87113; 505-222-9850, Fax- 505-222-9855. Hours- 8AM-5PM. www.rld.state.nm.us/accountancy/index.html Search data at- http://164.64.87.25/MyLicenseVerification/

#36 Board of Medical Examiners, 2055 S Pacheco St, Bldg 400, Santa Fe, NM 87505; 505-476-7220, Fax- 505-476-7237. Hours- 8AM-5PM. www.nmmb.state.nm.us Search data at- www.docboard.org/nm/ 2007 Official List at www.nmmb.state.nm.us/pdffiles/2007Roster.pdf.

#37 Regulation & Licensing Dept., Board of Psychologist Examiners, 2550 Cerrillos Rd 2nd Fl, Santa Fe, NM 87505; 505-476-4960, Fax- 505-827-7017. www.rld.state.nm.us/Psychology/index.html Search data at- http://164.64.87.25/MyLicenseVerification/

#38 Environment Department, Radiation Control Bureau, PO Box 26110 (1190 St Francis Dr, Rm S2100), Santa Fe, NM 87502; 505-476-3264, Fax- 505-476-3015. Hours- 8AM-5PM. www.nmenv.state.nm.us/nmrcb/radtech.html

#39 Regulation & Licensing Dept., Athletic Commission, 5200 Oakland Ave NE #C, Albuquerque, NM 87113; 505-222-9860, Fax- 505-222-9865. www.rld.state.nm.us/AthleticCommission/index.html Search data at- http://164.64.87.25/MyLicenseVerification/

#40 Regulation & Licensing Dept., Board of Examiners in Optometry, 2550 Cerrillos Rd 2nd Fl, Santa Fe, NM 87505-3260; 505-476-4945, Fax- 505-476-4620 or 4645. www.rld.state.nm.us/Optometry/index.html Search data at- http://164.64.87.25/MyLicenseVerification/

#41 Regulation & Licensing Dept., Pharmacy Board, 5200 Oakland NE, Ste A, Albuquerque, NM 87113; 505-222-9830, Fax- 505-222-9845. Hours- 8AM-5PM. www.rld.state.nm.us/Pharmacy/ Search data at- http://164.64.87.25/MyLicenseVerification/

#42 Regulation & Licensing Dept., Podiatry Board, 2550 Cerrillos Rd 2nd Fl, Santa Fe, NM 87505-3260; 505-476-4655, Fax- 505-476-4645. www.rld.state.nm.us/Podiatry/index.html Search data at- http://164.64.87.25/MyLicenseVerification/

#43 Secretary of State, Notary Public Section, 325 Don Gaspar #300, Santa Fe, NM 87503; 505-827-3600 or 800-477-3632, Fax- 505-827-3634. www.sos.state.nm.us

#44 Professional Engineers & Surveyors Board, 4001 Office Court Dr, #903, Santa Fe, NM 87507-4962; 505-827-7561, Fax- 505-827-7566. www.sblpes.state.nm.us/ Search data at- www.sblpes.state.nm.us/PEPSBoard/PEPSBoard.jsp

#45 Racing Commission, 4900 Alameda NE #A, Albuquerque, NM 87113; 505-222-0700, Fax- 505-222-0713. http://nmrc.state.nm.us

#46 Regulation & Licensing Dept., Real Estate Commission, 5200 Oakland Ave. NE #B, Albuquerque, NM 87113; 505-222-9820, 800-801-7505, Fax- 505-222-9886. www.rld.state.nm.us/RealEstateCommission/index.html Search data at- http://164.64.87.25/MyLicenseVerification/

#47 Regulation & Licensing Dept., Manufactured Housing Division, 2550 Cerrillos Rd, Santa Fe, NM 87505-3260; 505-476-4770, Fax- 505-827-7074. www.rld.state.nm.us/mhd/ Search data at- http://164.64.87.25/MyLicenseVerification/

#48 Regulation & Licensing Dept., Financial Institutions Division, 2550 Cerrillos Rd, 3rd Fl, Santa Fe, NM 87505-3260; 505-476-4885, Fax- 505-476-4670. www.rld.state.nm.us/fid/ Search data at- http://164.64.87.25/MyLicenseVerification/Search.aspx?facility=Y

New Mexico Federal Courts

The following list indicates the district and division name for each county in the state.

New Mexico County/Court Cross Reference

County	Division
Bernalillo	Albuquerque
Catron	Albuquerque
Chaves	Albuquerque
Cibola	Albuquerque
Colfax	Albuquerque
Curry	Albuquerque
De Baca	Albuquerque
Dona Ana	Albuquerque
Eddy	Albuquerque
Grant	Albuquerque
Guadalupe	Albuquerque
Harding	Albuquerque
Hidalgo	Albuquerque
Lea	Albuquerque
Lincoln	Albuquerque
Los Alamos	Albuquerque
Luna	Albuquerque
McKinley	Albuquerque
Mora	Albuquerque
Otero	Albuquerque
Quay	Albuquerque
Rio Arriba	Albuquerque
Roosevelt	Albuquerque
San Juan	Albuquerque
San Miguel	Albuquerque
Sandoval	Albuquerque
Santa Fe	Albuquerque
Sierra	Albuquerque
Socorro	Albuquerque
Taos	Albuquerque
Torrance	Albuquerque
Union	Albuquerque
Valencia	Albuquerque

US District Court

Albuquerque Division Court Clerk, 333 Lomas Blvd NW #270, Albuquerque, NM 87102-2274, 505-348-2000; records- 505-348-2020; Fax-505-348-2028. Hours-8:30AM-N, 1-4:30PM. www.nmcourt.fed.us/web/DCDOCS/dcindex.html

Jurisdiction: All counties in New Mexico. Cases may be assigned to any of 3 divisions - Santa Fe (505-988-6481), Las Cruces (505-528-1400), and Roswell (505-625-2388). Santa Fe and Las Cruces have searchable records; Roswell does not.

Searches/Indexing: Requester's phone number and years to search required. Search records 1990 to present by plaintiff name. Search prior records by defendant or case number. Results do not include SSN or DOB on civil; older criminal cases may include last 4 SSN digits. New cases are in the index 2 days after filing date. Computer index maintained back to 1992. Case files sent to archives 6 months after closed.

Search Access: Only docket info available by phone. **Mail:** Search usually completed- 24 hours. SASE not required. **Fax:** Fax search requests accepted. **In person:** 2 public terminals available back to 1990. No self-serve copier. Court can recommend an outside vendor to make copies.

Payment: Pay by Visa/MC, money order, cashier's or personal check. Payee: Clerk, US District Court.

E-Services: Court started CM/ECF 9/2006 and PACER for 2007. The courts' ACE system and other electronic public record access has been retired. PACER records go back to 1990. New records online after 1 day. ECF at www.nmcourt.fed.us/web/DCDOCS/dcindex.html. **Opinions Online:** www.nmcourt.fed.us/Drs-Web/input. Opinions may go as far back as 1989. **Online Note:** Does not participate in the US. Party Case Index.

US Bankruptcy Court

Albuquerque Division Court Clerk, PO Box 546, Albuquerque, NM 87103-0546 (In person: 500 Gold Ave SW, 10th Fl, Albuquerque, NM 87102), 505-348-2500; Fax- 505-348-2473. Hours-8:30AM-4:30PM. www.nmcourt.fed.us/usbc/

Jurisdiction: All counties in New Mexico. Judges do travel to Las Cruces and Roswell, however, bankruptcy records are not searchable at those courthouses.

Searches/Indexing: Include full name and SSN or EIN in search request. Results include last 4 SSN digits. Will fax back documents no fee up to 10 pages. New cases are in the index 24 hours after filing date. Both computer and card indexes maintained; computer back to 5/26/1987. Case files sent to archives 5 years after closed.

Search Access: Index, docket and claim info is released via phone. Voice Case Information Service available, call VCIS at 888-435-7822 or 505-348-2444. **Mail:** Search usually completed- 8 business days. Fee is charged only when a case file search is required. Include SASE for return. **Fax:** Fax search requests accepted, prepaid. **In person:** 3 public terminals available. No self-serve copier. Court can recommend an outside vendor to so searches and copies.

Payment: Pay by Visa/MC/AmEx, debit card, money order, cashier's or personal check. No debtor checks accepted. Payee: Clerk, US Bankruptcy Court.

E-Services: PACER now on ECF. PACER records go back to 7/1991. New records online after 1 day. ECF at https://ecf.nmb.uscourts.gov/. **Opinions:** www.nmcourt.fed.us/usbc/judges. Find select judges opinions, or find full opinions on the new subscription PACER access.

Standards for Federal Courts: Fees are standard unless noted in profile. Search fee is $26.00 per item (one party name or case number). Copy fee is $.50 per page. Certification fee is $9.00 per document, double for exemplification, if available. Most courts require prepayment. Mail requests should enclose a SASE unless otherwise noted. Before releasing records, all courts require prepayment, unless noted.

District courts index by defendant and plaintiff and by case number. Bankruptcy courts usually index by debtor and case number. While most courts now have their indexes on computer, many may still maintain index card files as well. Courts will archive closed case files at different times.

There are numerous public access programs available to online subscribers. Search the U.S. Party/Case Index to find party names and case numbers among all courts. Individual case data is provided on PACER. A search of CM/ECF provides copies of cases filed electronically. For details about PACER, the US Party/Case Index, and CM/ECF see the Appendix or go to http://pacer.psc.uscourts.gov or call 800-676-6856.

New Mexico County Courts

Court	Jurisdiction	No. of Courts	How Organized
District Courts*	General	30	13 Districts
Magistrate Courts*	Limited	54	32 Magistrate Districts
Metropolitan Court of Bernalillo County*	Municipal	1	
Municipal Courts	Municipal	80	
Probate Courts	Probate	30	33 Counties

* Profiled in this Sourcebook.

Court	CIVIL								
	Tort	Contract	Real Estate	Min. Claim	Max. Claim	Small Claims	Estate	Eviction	Domestic Relations
District Courts*	X	X	X	$0	No Max		X		X
Magistrate Courts*	X	X	X	$0	$10000	$10000		X	
Metropolitan Court of Bernalillo County*	X	X	X	$0	$10000	$10000			
Municipal Courts									
Probate Courts*							X		

Court	CRIMINAL				
	Felony	Misdemeanor	DWI/DUI	Preliminary Hearing	Juvenile
District Courts*	X				X
Magistrate Courts*		X	X	X	
Metropolitan Court of Bernalillo County*		X	X	X	
Municipal Courts		Petty	X		

Administration

Administrative Office of the Courts, Judicial Information Division, 2905 Rodeo Park Dr East, Bldg #5, Santa Fe, NM, 87505; 505-476-6900, Fax: 505-476-6952. www.nmcourts.com

Court Structure

The 30 District Courts in 13 districts are the courts of general jurisdiction. The Magistrate Courts handle tort, contract, landlord/tenant rights, small claims ($0-10,000); felony preliminary hearings; misdemeanor, DWI/DUI and other traffic violations. Municipal Courts handle petty misdemeanors, DWI/DUI, traffic violations, and other municipal ordinance violations. The Bernalillo Metropolitan Court has jurisdiction in cases up to $10,000.

County Clerks handle "informal" (uncontested) probate cases, and the District Courts handle "formal" (contested) probate cases.

Online Access

The home page offers free access to District Courts and Magistrate Courts case information (except Bernalillo Metropolitan Court, see below). Municipal court data is limited to criminal Domestic Violence and DWI historic convictions from September 1, 1991 forward. In general, the other records are available from June 1997 forward. The search is inclusive of all counties participating. Search by name & DL and/or DOB, and by county and type of case or by case number. DOB is shown 75% of time. The site also offers a DWI Offender History tool for researching DWI history; search by name.

A commercial online service is available for the Metropolitan Court of Bernalillo County, via a vendor. There is a $35.00 set up fee, a connect time fee based on usage. The system is available 24 hours daily. Call 505-345-6555 for more information.

Supreme Court opinions may be researched at www.supremecourt.nm.org.

Searching Tips, Fees, and Other Guidelines

There are some "shared courts" in low-populated counties in New Mexico, with one county handling cases arising in another. Records are held at the locations indicated in the text. Most District Courts charge $.35 per copy and Magistrate Courts $.50 per copy. Prepayment required unless otherwise noted.

Bernalillo County

2nd Judicial District Court PO Box 488, Albuquerque, NM 87103; 505-841-7425 (Administration); criminal phone: 505-841-7542; civil phone: 505-841-7451; criminal fax: 505-841-7463; civil fax: 505-841-7446; 8AM-5PM (MST). ***Felony, Civil.*** www.seconddistrictcourt.com

Civil Records: Access: Mail, in person, online. Both court and visitors may perform in person searches. Search fee: $1.50 per name. Required to search: name, years to search. Civil cases indexed by defendant, plaintiff; index on computer from 1984, prior on docket books/microfiche. Mail turnaround time up to 10 days. Civil PAT goes back to 1984. PAT civil results show middle initial. Online access is free at www.nmcourts.gov Most data goes back to 6/1985.

Criminal Records: Access: Mail, online, in person. Both court and visitors may perform in person searches. Search fee: $1.50 per name. Required to search: name, years to search; also helpful: DOB, SSN. Criminal records computerized from 1979, prior on docket books/microfiche. Mail turnaround time up to 10 days. Criminal PAT goes back to 1979. Terminal results may or may not have complete name or a DOB. Online access to criminal records is free at www.nmcourts.gov. Most data goes back to 6/1979. Most but not all online results show middle initial and/or DOB.

General Information: Online identifiers in results same as on public terminal. No sequestered or juvenile records released. Will not fax documents. Court makes copy: $.35 per page. Certification fee: $1.50, Exemplification fee: $4.50. Payee: Clerk of the Court. Cashiers checks and money orders accepted. No credit card. Mail requests: SASE requested.

Metropolitan Court 401 Lomas NW, Albuquerque, NM 87102; 505-841-8151; fax: 505-222-4831; 7AM-5PM (MST). ***Misdemeanor, Civil Actions under $10,000, Eviction, Small Claims.*** www.metrocourt.state.nm.us

Records phone is 505-841-8230.

Civil Records: Access: Phone, fax, mail, online, in person. Both court and visitors may perform in person searches. Search fee: $1.00 per page found. Required to search: name, years to search; you give identifiers to help court match the results to the person. Civil cases indexed by defendant, plaintiff; index on computer from 1987. Max. 5 years back except uncollected judgments which stay open 14 years from date of judgment. Note: Visit the viewing room to examine current cases and cases back to 1989. Mail turnaround time 3-5 days. Civil PAT goes back to 1987. PAT results show name only. Access Metropolitan court civil records online at www.metrocourt.state.nm.us.

Criminal Records: Access: Phone, fax, mail, online, in person. Both court and visitors may perform in person searches. Search fee: $1.00 per page found. Required to search: name, SSN, DOB; you give identifiers to help court match the results to the person. Criminal records computerized from 1983. Note: Visit the viewing room to examine current cases and cases back to 1989. Mail turnaround time 3-5 days. Criminal PAT goes back to same as civil. Terminal results may or may not have complete name or a DOB. Search Metro Court criminal case records free at www.metrocourt.state.nm.us. Online results show middle initial, DOB.

General Information: Online identifiers in results same as on public terminal. No pre-sentence reports, psychological evaluations, confidential records released. Will fax out documents. Court makes copy: $1.00 per page. Computer printout $.50 per page. Certification fee: $1.50 per cert. Payee: Metro Court. Personal checks accepted. Visa/MC accepted.

County Clerk #1 Civic Plaza NW, 6th Fl, Albuquerque, NM 87102; 505-468-1233; fax: 505-768-5180; 8AM-4:30PM (MST). ***Probate.*** www.bernco.gov/live/departments.asp?dept=2317

Access county probate cases free at www.bernco.gov/probate_lookup/.

Catron County

7th Judicial District Court PO Drawer 1129, Socorro, NM 87801; 575-835-0050 x10; fax: 575-838-5217; 8AM-4PM (MST). ***Felony, Civil Actions over $7,500, Probate.***

Socorro and Catron Counties share this court clerk. All Catron civil and criminal case files are housed at the Socorro County District Court at the address above. Court physical address is 200 Church, Socorro. Index at www.nmcourts.gov/caselookup/.

Quemado Magistrate Court PO Box 283, Quemado, NM 87829; 575-773-4604; fax: 575-773-4688; 8AM-5PM (MST). ***Misdemeanor, Civil Actions under $10,000, Eviction, Small Claims.***

Civil Records: Access: Mail, fax, in person, online. Only the court performs in person searches; visitors may not. No search fee. Required to search: name, years to search; also helpful-DOB, SSN, address. Civil cases indexed by defendant, plaintiff and docket number. Records computerized since 1997. Mail turnaround time 1-2 weeks. Civil PAT goes back to 1996. Case lookup from 1997 forward is free at www.nmcourts.gov.

Criminal Records: Access: Mail, fax, in person, online. Only the court performs in person searches; visitors may not. No search fee. Required to search: name, years to search, DOB; also helpful: SSN. Records computerized since 1997. Mail turnaround time 1-2 weeks. Criminal PAT goes back to 1996. Terminal results may or may not have complete name or a DOB. Online access to criminal records is free at www.nmcourts.gov. Most but not all online results show middle initial and/or DOB.

General Information: Online identifiers in results same as on public terminal. Fee to fax out file $1.00 per page. Court makes copy: $.10 per page. Certification fee: $.50 per page includes copy fee. Payee: Magistrate Court. Personal checks accepted; credit cards are not.

Reserve Magistrate Court PO Box 447, Reserve, NM 87830; 575-533-6474; fax: 575-533-6623; 8AM-5PM (MST). ***Misdemeanor, Civil Actions under $10,000, Eviction, Small Claims.***

Civil Records: Access: Mail, fax, in person, online. Both court and visitors may perform in person searches. No search fee. Required to search: name, years to search, address, other names used. Records computerized since 1996. Mail turnaround time 1 week. Civil PAT goes back to 1996. Case lookup from 1997 forward is free at www.nmcourts.gov.

Criminal Records: Access: Mail, fax, in person, online. Both court and visitors may perform in person searches. No search fee. Required to search: name, years to search; also helpful: DOB, SSN. Records computerized since 1996. Mail turnaround time 1 week. Criminal PAT goes back to same as civil. Terminal results may or may not have complete name or a DOB. Online access to criminal records is free at www.nmcourts.gov. Most but not all online results show middle initial and/or DOB.

General Information: Online identifiers in results same as on public terminal. Will fax $.50 per page. Court makes copy: $.50 per page. Self serve: same. Certification fee: $1.00 per page includes copy fee. Payee: Magistrate Court. Personal checks accepted; credit cards are not.

County Clerk PO Box I97, 100 N main St, Reserve, NM 87830; 575-533-6400; fax: 575-533-6400; 8AM-4:30PM (MST). ***Probate.***

Local Probate Judge-575-533-6247, PO Box 663, Reserve NM, 87830 by appointment.

Chaves County

5th Judicial District Court Box 1776, Roswell, NM 88202; 575-622-2212; criminal phone: x114 & x119; civil phone: x143 & x110; fax: 575-624-9510; 8AM-N,1-5PM (MST). ***Felony, Civil.*** www.fifthdistrictcourt.com

Civil Records: Access: Online, in person. Visitors must perform in person searches themselves. Required to search: name, years to search. Civil cases indexed by defendant, plaintiff; index on computer from 1996, on microfiche and archived from 1891. Civil PAT goes back to 1996. Case lookup from 1997 forward is free at www.nmcourts.gov.

Criminal Records: Access: Online, in person. Visitors must perform in person searches themselves. Required to search: name, years to search, DOB, aliases. Criminal records computerized from 1996, on microfiche and archived from 1891. Criminal PAT goes back to same as civil. Terminal results may or may not have complete name or a DOB. Online access to criminal records is free at www.nmcourts.gov. Most but not all online results show middle initial and/or DOB.

General Information: Online identifiers in results same as on public terminal. No sequestered records released. Will fax documents, sometimes. Court makes copy: $.35 per page. Self serve: same. Certification fee: $1.50 per document. Payee: District Court Clerk. Only cashiers checks and money orders accepted. No credit cards accepted. Mail requests: SASE required for mail return of any copies.

Magistrate Court 400 N Virginia St, # G-1, Roswell, NM 88201; 575-624-6088; fax: 575-624-6092; 8AM-4PM M,T,TH,F; 9AM-4PM W (MST). ***Misdemeanor, Civil Actions under $10,000, Eviction, Small Claims.***

Civil Records: Access: Online, in person. Both court and visitors may perform in person searches. No search fee. Civil cases indexed by defendant. Civil PAT goes back to 1997. Case lookup from 1997 forward is free at www.nmcourts.gov.

Criminal Records: Access: Online, in person. Both court and visitors may perform in person searches. No search fee. Required to search: name, years to search, DOB; also helpful: SSN. Criminal records are keep 2 years (except DUIs and domestic) before being destroyed. Criminal PAT goes back to same as civil. Terminal results may or may not have complete name or a DOB. Online access to criminal records is free at www.nmcourts.gov. Most but not all online results show middle initial and/or DOB.

General Information: Online identifiers in results same as on public terminal. Will fax documents to local or toll-free number. Court makes copy: $.50 per page. Cert fee: $.50 per page. Payee: Magistrate Court. Personal checks accepted; credit cards are not.

County Clerk Box 580, #1 St Mary's Pl #110, 88203, Roswell, NM 88202; 575-624-6614; fax: 575-624-6523; 8AM-5PM (MST). ***Probate.***

Cibola County

13th Judicial District Court Box 758, Grants, NM 87020; 505-287-8831; fax: 505-285-5755; 8AM-5PM (MST). ***Felony, Civil, Probate.*** www.13districtcourt.com

Probate fax is same as main fax number.

Civil Records: Access: Fax, mail, online, in person. Both court and visitors may perform in person searches. Search fee: $5.00 per name. Required to search: name, years to search. Civil cases indexed by defendant, plaintiff; index on microfiche from 1981; prior to 1981 belong to Valencia County. Mail turnaround time 2-3 days. Case lookup from 1997 forward is free at www.nmcourts.gov. Also, view all civil jury verdicts in the 13th Judicial District Court free back to 1995 at www.13districtcourt.com/verdict/jury_verdict_intro.php.

Criminal Records: Access: Fax, mail, online, in person. Only the court performs in person searches; visitors may not. Search fee: $5.00 per name. Required to search: name, years to search. Criminal records on microfiche from 1981; prior to 1981 belong to Valencia County. Mail turnaround time 2-3 days. Online access to criminal records is free at www.nmcourts.gov. Most but not all online results show middle initial and/or DOB.

General Information: Online identifiers in results same as on public terminal. No sequestered records released. Will fax documents; unless toll-free number provided, fee is $2.50 in-state; $5.00 out-of-state. Court makes copy: $.35 per page. Self serve: same. Cert fee: $1.50 per page. Payee: District Court Clerk. Cashier checks or money orders. No credit cards.

Magistrate Court 515 W High, Grants, NM 87020; 505-285-4605; fax: 505-285-6485; 8AM-

4PM (MST). ***Misdemeanor, Civil Actions under $10,000, Eviction, Small Claims.***

Civil Records: Access: Fax, mail, in person, online. Only the court performs in person searches; visitors may not. Mail turnaround time up to 2 weeks. Case lookup from 1997 forward is free at www.nmcourts.gov.

Criminal Records: Access: Fax, mail, in person, online. Only the court performs in person searches; visitors may not. No search fee. Required to search: name, years to search. Mail turnaround time up to 2 weeks. Online access to criminal records is free at www.nmcourts.gov. Most but not all online results show middle initial and/or DOB.

General Information: Online identifiers in results same as on public terminal. Will fax documents $1.00 per page. Court makes copy: $.50 per page. No certification fee. Payee: Magistrate Court. No credit cards accepted. Mail requests: SASE required.

County Clerk PO Box 190, 515 W. High St, Grants, NM 87020; 505-285-2535; fax: 505-285-2562; 8AM-5PM (MST). ***Probate.***

Colfax County

8th Judicial District Court Box 160, Raton, NM 87740; 575-445-5585; fax: 575-445-2626; 8AM-4PM (MST). ***Felony, Civil.***

Civil Records: Access: Phone, mail, online, in person. Both court and visitors may perform in person searches. No search fee. Required to search: name, years to search. Civil cases indexed by defendant, plaintiff. Civil records archived from 1912. Mail turnaround time 1 week. Civil PAT goes back to 1997. Case lookup from 1997 forward is free at www.nmcourts.gov Pleadings are unavailable.

Criminal Records: Access: Phone, mail, online, in person. Both court and visitors may perform in person searches. No search fee. Required to search: name, years to search; also helpful: DOB, SSN. Criminal records archived from 1912; computerized records go back to 1996/97. Mail turnaround time 1 week. Criminal PAT goes back to same as civil. Terminal results may or may not have complete name or a DOB. Online access to criminal records is free at www.nmcourts.gov. Pleadings are unavailable. Most but not all online results show middle initial and/or DOB.

General Information: Online identifiers in results same as on public terminal. No adoption, mental, guardianship, children's cases (neglect & child in need of supervision) records released. Fee to fax out file $2.00 per page. Court makes copy: $.35 per page. Self serve: same. Certification fee: $1.50. Payee: District Court. Business checks accepted. No credit cards accepted. Mail requests: SASE required.

Cimarron Magistrate Court PO Drawer 367, Highway 21, Cimarron, NM 87714; 575-376-2634; 8:30AM-N alternating W only (MST). ***Misdemeanor, Civil Actions under $10,000, Eviction, Small Claims.*** On days when this court is not in session, you may call the Springer Magistrate Court at 505-483-2417.

Civil Records: Access: In person, mail, online. Visitors must perform in person searches themselves. No search fee. Required to search: Name, years to search; also helpful: DOB. Civil cases indexed by defendant, plaintiff. Records searchable from 3/97 on computer. Mail turnaround time 10 days. Case lookup from 1997 forward is free at www.nmcourts.gov.

Criminal Records: Access: In person, mail, online. Visitors must perform in person searches themselves. No search fee. Required to search: name, years to search; also helpful: DOB. Records searchable from 3/97 on computer, except DUI. Mail turnaround time 10 days. Online access to criminal records is free at www.nmcourts.gov. Online results show middle initial, DOB, usually.

General Information: Online identifiers in results same as on public terminal. Will fax out documents. Court makes copy for no fee. No certification fee. Payee: Magistrate Court. Personal checks accepted; credit cards are not.

Raton Magistrate Court PO Box 68, Raton, NM 87740; 575-445-2220; fax: 575-445-8966; 8AM-4PM (MST). ***Misdemeanor, Civil Actions under $10,000, Eviction, Small Claims.***

Civil Records: Access: Phone, mail, fax, in person, online. Only the court performs in person searches; visitors may not. No search fee. Required to search: name, years to search; also helpful: DOB, SSN. Records held for 14 years. Mail turnaround time within 1 week. Case lookup from 1997 forward is free at www.nmcourts.gov.

Criminal Records: Access: Phone, mail, fax, in person, online. Only the court performs in person searches; visitors may not. No search fee. Required to search: name, years to search; also helpful: DOB, SSN. Hard copies are kept on file for one year. Mail turnaround time within 1 week. Online access to criminal records is free at www.nmcourts.gov. Most but not all online results show middle initial and/or DOB.

General Information: Online identifiers in results same as on public terminal. Will fax documents $1.00 per page. Court makes copy: $.50 per page. No certification fee. Payee: Magistrate Court. Personal checks accepted; credit cards are not.

Springer Magistrate Court 300 Colbert Ave. PO Box 760, Springer, NM 87747; 575-483-2417; fax: 575-483-0127; 8AM-4PM (MST). ***Misdemeanor, Civil Actions under $10,000, Eviction, Small Claims.***

Civil Records: Access: Online, in person. Both court and visitors may perform in person searches. No search fee. Required to search: name, years to search; also helpful: DOB. Records indexed by plaintiff and defendant. On computer back to 3/1997. Case lookup from 1997 forward is free at www.nmcourts.gov.

Criminal Records: Access: Online, in person. Both court and visitors may perform in person searches. No search fee. Required to search: name, years to search; also helpful: DOB, SSN. On computer back to 3/1997, DUI kept longer. Online access to criminal records is free at www.nmcourts.gov. Most but not all online results show middle initial and/or DOB.

General Information: Online identifiers in results same as on public terminal. Will fax documents. Court makes copy for no fee. Certification fee: No charge. Payee: Magistrate Court. Personal checks accepted; credit cards are not.

County Clerk PO Box 159, 230 N 3rd St, Raton, NM 87740; 575-445-5551; fax: 575-445-4031; 8AM-N, 1-5PM (MST). ***Probate.***

Curry County

9th Judicial District Court Curry County Courthouse, 700 N Main, #11, Clovis, NM 88101; 575-762-9148; fax: 575-763-5160; 8AM-4PM (MST). ***Felony, Civil.*** www.nmcourts9thjdc.com

Civil Records: Access: Online, in person. Visitors must perform in person searches themselves. Required to search: name, years to search, address. Civil cases indexed by defendant, plaintiff; index on computer from 1997, on microfiche and archived from 1910. Civil PAT goes back to 1997. Case lookup 1997 forward is free at www.nmcourts.gov.

Criminal Records: Access: Online, in person. Visitors must perform in person searches themselves. Required to search: name, years to search; also helpful: SSN. Criminal records computerized from 1997, on microfiche and archived from 1910. Criminal PAT goes back to same as civil. Terminal results may or may not have complete name or a DOB. Online access to criminal records is free at www.nmcourts.gov. Most but not all online results show middle initial and/or DOB.

General Information: Online identifiers in results same as on public terminal. No adoption, insanity, sequestered, neglect or abuse released. Court makes copy: $.35 per page. Certification fee: $1.50. Payee: 9th Judicial District Court. Only cashiers checks and money orders accepted. No credit cards accepted. Mail requests: SASE required for mail return of any copies.

Magistrate Court 221 Pile, Clovis, NM 88101; 575-762-3766; fax: 575-769-1437; 8AM-4PM (MST). ***Misdemeanor, Civil Actions under $10,000, Eviction, Small Claims.***

Civil Records: Access: Phone, mail, fax, online, in person. Only the court performs in person searches; visitors may not. No search fee. Required to search: name, years to search. Civil cases indexed by plaintiff and defendant. Mail turnaround time 1 week. Civil PAT goes back to 1/1995. Case lookup from 1997 forward is free at www.nmcourts.gov.

Criminal Records: Access: Phone, mail, fax, online, in person. Only the court performs in person searches; visitors may not. No search fee. Required to search: name, years to search; also helpful: DOB, SSN. Mail turnaround time 1 week. Criminal PAT goes back to 1/1995. Terminal results may or may not have complete name or a DOB. Online access to criminal records is free at www.nmcourts.gov. Most but not all online results show middle initial and/or DOB.

General Information: Online identifiers in results same as on public terminal. Will fax documents for fee of $1.00 per page. Court makes copy: $.50 per page. Cert fee: $.50 per page. Payee: Magistrate Court. Cshiers checks and money orders accepted. No credit cards. Mail requests: SASE required.

De Baca County

10th Judicial District Court Box 910, Ft. Sumner, NM 88119; 575-355-2896; fax: 575-355-2899; 8AM-4:30PM (MST). ***Felony, Civil.***

Civil Records: Access: Phone, mail, online, in person. Only the court performs in person searches; visitors may not. No search fee. Required to search: name, years to search. Civil cases indexed by defendant, plaintiff. Civil index on cards and docket books archived from 1917; on computer since 1997. Mail turnaround time 2 days. Case lookup from 1997 forward is free at www.nmcourts.gov.

Criminal Records: Access: Phone, mail, online, in person. Only the court performs in person searches; visitors may not. No search fee. Required to search: name, years to search. Criminal records indexed on cards and docket books archived from 1917; on computer since 1997. Mail turnaround time 2 days. Online access to criminal records is free at www.nmcourts.gov. Most but not all online results show middle initial and/or DOB.

General Information: Online identifiers in results same as on public terminal. No mental, adoptions, or juvenile released. Fee to fax out file $1.00 per page. Court makes copy: $.35 per page. Self serve: same. Certification fee: $1.50 per cert. Payee: District Court. Only cashiers checks and money orders accepted. No credit cards accepted. Mail requests: SASE required.

Magistrate Court Box 24, Ft Sumner, NM 88119; 575-355-7371; fax: 575-355-7149; 8AM-5PM (MST). ***Misdemeanor, Civil Actions under $10,000, Eviction, Small Claims.*** www.nmsc.state.nm.us/directory/program.php?program_id=521

Civil Records: Access: In person, mail, online. Both court and visitors may perform in person searches. No search fee. Required to search: name, COB; SSN is helpful. Civil cases indexed by defendant, plaintiff. Online records go back to 1997. Mail turnaround time 1 week. Civil PAT goes back to 1997. PAT civil results show middle initial. Case lookup from 1997 forward is free at www.nmcourts.gov.

Criminal Records: Access: In person, mail, online. Both court and visitors may perform in person searches. No search fee. Required to search: name, years to search, DOB, SSN. Online records go back to 1997. Mail turnaround time 1 week. Criminal PAT goes back to same as civil. Terminal results may or may not have complete name or a DOB. Online access to criminal records is free at www.nmcourts.gov. Most but not all online results show middle initial and/or DOB.

General Information: Online identifiers in results same as on public terminal. Will fax documents. Court makes copy: $.50 per page. Certification fee: $.50 per page. Payee: Magistrate Court. No personal checks or credit cards accepted.

County Clerk PO Box 347, 218 E Ave C, Ft. Sumner, NM 88119; 575-355-2601; fax: 575-355-2441; 8AM-N, 1-4:30PM (MST). ***Probate.***

Dona Ana County

3rd Judicial District Court 201 W Picacho, Ste A, Las Cruces, NM 88005; 575-523-8200; civil phone: 575-523-8255; fax: 575-523-8290; 8AM-N, 1-5PM ***Felony, Civil.*** www.thirddistrictcourt.com

Civil Records: Access: Mail, fax, online, in person. Both court and visitors may perform in person searches. Search fee: $1.50 per name. Required to search: name, years to search. Civil cases indexed by defendant, plaintiff; index on computer from 1986 (clerk's index 1986 to 9/96), on microfiche and archived from 1912. Mail turnaround time 2-3 days. Civil PAT goes back to 9/1996. PAT results show name only. Access to court records back to 9/1996 is free at www.nmcourts.gov.

Criminal Records: Access: Mail, fax, online, in person. Both court and visitors may perform in person searches. Search fee: $1.50 per name. Required to search: name, years to search; also helpful: DOB, SSN. Criminal records computerized from 1986 (clerk's index 1977 to 9/96), on microfiche and archived from 1912. Mail turnaround time 2-3 days. Criminal PAT goes back to same as civil. Terminal results may or may not have complete name or a DOB. Online access to criminal records back to 9/1996 is free at www.nmcourts.gov. Most but not all online results show middle initial and/or DOB.

General Information: Online identifiers in results same as on public terminal. No adoption, mental health, or juvenile released. Court makes copy: $.35 per page. Self serve: same. Cert fee: $1.50. Payee: 3rd Judicial District. Only cashiers checks and money orders accepted. Mail requests: SASE required.

Anthony Magistrate Court PO Box 1259, 935 Anthony Dr, Anthony, NM 88021; 575-233-3147; fax: 575-882-0113; 8AM-4PM M,T,TH,F; 8AM-3PM Wed (MST). ***Misdemeanor, Civil Actions under $10,000, Eviction, Small Claims.***

Civil Records: Access: Online, mail, in person. Only the court performs in person searches; visitors may not. No search fee. Civil cases indexed by plaintiff & defendant. Civil records go back to 1999. Mail turnaround time 3 days Case lookup from 1997 forward is free at www.nmcourts.gov.

Criminal Records: Access: Mail, in person, online. Only the court performs in person searches; visitors may not. No search fee. Required to search: name, years to search, DOB, SSN. Criminal records go back to 1999. Mail turnaround time is 3 days. Online access to criminal records is free at www.nmcourts.gov. Most but not all online results show middle initial and/or DOB.

General Information: Online identifiers in results same as on public terminal. Will not fax documents. Court makes copy: $.50 per page. No certification fee. Payee: Anthony Magistrate Court. Personal checks accepted; credit cards are not.

Hatch Magistrate Court PO Box 896, Hatch, NM 87937; 575-267-5202; fax: 575-267-5088; 9AM-Noon 2nd & 4th Mondays (MST). ***Misdemeanor, Civil Actions under $10,000, Eviction, Small Claims.***

Note that this court is only open on Mondays.

Civil Records: Access: Mail, in person, online. Only the court performs in person searches; visitors may not. No search fee. Records go back 1-14 years. Mail turnaround time 1 week. Case lookup from 1997 forward is free at www.nmcourts.gov.

Criminal Records: Access: Mail, in person, online. Only the court performs in person searches; visitors may not. No search fee. Required to search: name, years to search, DOB, SSN. Mail turnaround time 1 week. Online access to criminal records is free at www.nmcourts.gov. Most but not all online results show middle initial and/or DOB.

General Information: Online identifiers in results same as on public terminal. Will fax documents to local or toll-free number. Court makes copy: $.50 per page. No certification fee. Payee: Magistrate Court. Only cashiers checks and money orders accepted. No credit cards accepted. Mail requests: SASE required.

Las Cruces Magistrate Court 151 N Church, Las Cruces, NM 88001; 575-524-2814; civil phone: 575-647-3816; fax: 575-525-2951; 8AM-4PM (MST). ***Misdemeanor, Civil Actions under $10,000, Eviction, Small Claims.***

Civil Records: Access: Fax, mail, in person, online. Both court and visitors may perform in person searches. No search fee. Required to search: Civil cases indexed by defendant, plaintiff. Civil records go back 14 years. Mail turnaround time 48 hours. Civil PAT goes back to 1997. Case lookup from 1997 forward is free at www.nmcourts.gov.

Criminal Records: Access: Fax, mail, in person, online. Both court and visitors may perform in person searches. No search fee. Required to search: name, years to search; also helpful: DOB, SSN. Petty misdemeanor and traffic records go back 1 year. DUIs and domestic go back to 1980s. Mail turnaround time 48 hours. Criminal PAT goes back to same as civil. Terminal results may or may not have complete name or a DOB. Online access to criminal records is free at www.nmcourts.gov. Most but not all online results show middle initial and/or DOB.

General Information: Online identifiers in results same as on public terminal. Will fax out docs no add'l fee. Court makes copy: $.50 by copy machine; free from computer. No certification fee. Payee: Magistrate Court. Personal checks and Western Union accepted. No credit cards accepted.

Probate Court Clerk c/o Third Judicial District, 201 W Picacho, Las Cruces, NM 88005; 575-523-8200; fax: 575-523-8290; 8AM-N, 1-5PM (MST). ***Probate.*** Probate is now handled by the District Court Clerk, not the county clerk,

Eddy County

5th Judicial District Court 102 N Canal St #240, Carlsbad, NM 88220; 575-885-4740; criminal phone: x120; civil phone: x123; fax: 575-887-7095; 8AM-N, 1-5PM (MST). ***Felony, Civil.*** www.fifthdistrictcourt.com

Civil Records: Access: In person, online. Visitors must perform in person searches themselves. Required to search: name, years to search. Civil cases indexed by defendant. Civil records on computer from 1986, microfiche from 1891. Public use terminal has civil records back to 1996. Terminal results may or may not have complete name or a DOB. Case lookup from 1997 forward is free at www.nmcourts.gov, or via the court website above. All searching referred to record retrievers.

Criminal Records: Access: In person, online. Only the court performs in person searches; visitors may not. Required to search: name, years to search, SSN or DOB. Criminal records computerized from 1986, microfiche from 1900s. Online access to criminal records from 1997 forward is free at www.nmcourts.gov. Most but not all online results show middle initial and/or DOB.

General Information: Online identifiers in results same as on public terminal. No adoption, SS case w/children, or guardianship released. Will fax out specific case files if urgent for $1.00 per page. Court makes copy: $.35 per page. Certification fee: $1.50 per pleading. Payee: District Court Clerk. Only cashiers checks, money orders and law firm checks accepted. No credit cards accepted.

Artesia Magistrate Court 109 N 15th St, Artesia, NM 88210; 575-746-2481; fax: 575-746-6763; 8AM-4PM (MST). ***Misdemeanor, Civil Actions under $10,000, Eviction, Small Claims.***

This court also handles preliminary felonies, traffic, and DUI cases.

Civil Records: Access: Phone, mail, online. Only the court performs in person searches; visitors may not. No search fee. Required to search: name, and DOB or SSN. Civil cases indexed by defendant, plaintiff. Records available from 1992, computerized since 1996. Mail turnaround time 1-2 days. Case lookup from 1997 forward is free at www.nmcourts.gov.

Criminal Records: Access: Phone, mail, online. Only the court performs in person searches; visitors may not. No search fee. Required to search: name, years to search; also helpful: DOB, SSN. Records computerized since 1996. Mail turnaround time 1-2 days. Online access to criminal records is free at www.nmcourts.gov. Most but not all online results show middle initial and/or DOB.

General Information: Online identifiers in results same as on public terminal. Will fax out documents $1.00 per page. Court makes copy: $.50 per page. Certification fee: $.50 per page. Payee: Magistrate Court. Personal checks accepted; credit cards are not. Mail requests: SASE required for mail return of any copies.

Carlsbad Magistrate Court 1949 S Canal St, Carlsbad, NM 88220; 575-885-3218; fax: 575-887-3460; 8AM-4PM (MST). ***Misdemeanor, Civil Actions under $10,000, Eviction, Small Claims.***

Civil Records: Access: Phone, mail, fax, in person, online. Only the court performs in person searches; visitors may not. No search fee. Required to search: name, DOB, SSN, address, other names used. Civil cases indexed by defendant, plaintiff. Records held 14 years, computerized since 1996. Mail turnaround time 1-4 days. Case lookup from 1997 forward is free at www.nmcourts.gov.

Criminal Records: Access: Online, mail, in person. Only the court performs in person searches; visitors may not. No search fee. Required to search: name, years to search, DOB, SSN, other names used. Records held 3 years, computerized since 1996. Mail turnaround time 1-5 days. Online access to criminal records is free at www.nmcourts.gov. Most but not all online results show middle initial and/or DOB.

General Information: Online identifiers in results same as on public terminal. Will fax documents $.50 per page. Court makes copy: $.50 per page. Certification fee: $.50 per page. Payee: Magistrate Court. No personal checks or credit cards accepted.

County Clerk Eddy County Probate, 101 W. Greene St, #312, Carlsbad, NM 88220; 575-885-3383; fax: 575-234-1793; 8-5PM (MST). ***Probate.***

Grant County

6th Judicial District Court Box 2339, Silver City, NM 88062; 575-538-3250; fax: 575-388-5439; 8AM-N, 1-5PM (MST). ***Felony, Civil.***

Civil Records: Access: Fax, mail, online, in person. Only the court performs in person searches; visitors may not. No search fee. Required to search: name, years to search. Civil cases indexed by defendant, plaintiff; index on microfiche from 1942-1987, on books from 1987; on computer back to 1996. Mail turnaround time 2 weeks. Civil PAT goes back to 1996. PAT civil results show middle initial. Case lookup from 1997 forward is free at www.nmcourts.gov.

Criminal Records: Access: Fax, mail, online, in person. Only the court performs in person searches; visitors may not. No search fee. Required to search: name, years to search. Criminal records on microfiche from 1942-1987, on books from 1987; on computer back to 1996. Mail turnaround time 2 weeks. Criminal PAT goes back to 1996. Terminal results may or may not have complete name or a DOB. Online access to criminal records is free at www.nmcourts.gov. Most but not all online results show middle initial and/or DOB.

General Information: Online identifiers in results same as on public terminal. No adoption, guardianship or abuse records released. Will fax documents $2.50 per page. Court makes copy: $.35 per page. Certification fee: $1.50. Payee: District Court Clerk. Only cashiers checks and money orders accepted. No credit cards accepted. Mail requests: SASE required.

Bayard Magistrate Court 701 Central Ave, Bayard, NM 88023; 575-537-3042; fax: 575-537-7365; 8AM-4PM (MST). ***Misdemeanor, Civil Actions under $10,000, Eviction, Small Claims.***

Civil Records: Access: Mail, fax, in person, online. Only the court performs in person searches; visitors may not. No search fee. Civil cases indexed by plaintiff & defendant. Civil records go back to 1992. Mail turnaround time 3 days. Case lookup from 1997 forward is free at www.nmcourts.gov.

Criminal Records: Access: Mail, fax, in person, online. Only the court performs in person searches; visitors may not. No search fee. Required to search: name, years to search. Criminal records go back to 1999. Mail turnaround time is 3 days. Online access to criminal records is free at www.nmcourts.gov.

Most but not all online results show middle initial and/or DOB.
General Information: Online identifiers in results same as on public terminal. Will not fax documents. Court makes copy: $.50 per page. Certification fee: $1.00. Payee: Baynard Magistrate Court. Local personal checks accepted. No credit cards accepted. Mail requests: SASE required.

Silver City Magistrate Court 1620 E Pine St, Silver City, NM 88061; 575-538-3811; fax: 575-538-8079; 8AM-4PM (MST). ***Misdemeanor, Civil Actions under $10,000, Eviction, Small Claims.***
Civil Records: Access: Mail, fax, in person, online. Only the court performs in person searches; visitors may not. No search fee. Required to search: name, years to search, DOB, SSN. Records computerized since 1995. Mail turnaround time 2 days. Case lookup from 1997 forward is free at www.nmcourts.gov.
Criminal Records: Access: Mail, fax, in person, online. Only the court performs in person searches; visitors may not. No search fee. Required to search: name, years to search, DOB; also helpful: SSN. Records held here from 1988, computerized since 6/16/95. Mail turnaround time 2 days. Online access to criminal records is free at www.nmcourts.gov. Most but not all online results show middle initial and/or DOB.
General Information: Online identifiers in results same as on public terminal. Will fax back $1.00 per page. Court makes copy: $.50 per page. No certification fee. Payee: Magistrate Court. Personal checks accepted; credit cards are not.

County Clerk PO Box 898, 1400 Hwy 180 E, Silver City, NM 88062; 575-574-0042; 8AM-5PM (MST). ***Probate.***

Guadalupe County

4th Judicial District Court 420 Parker Ave #5, County Courthouse, Santa Rosa, NM 88435; 575-472-3888; fax: 575-472-4451; 8AM-N, 1PM-4PM (MST). ***Felony, Civil, Probate, Domestic.***
Reequests must be on search/copy request form.
Civil Records: Access: Fax, mail, in person, online. Only the court performs in person searches; visitors may not. Required to search: name, years to search, DOB. Civil cases indexed by Defendant, Plaintiff. Civil index in docket books from 1912. Mail turnaround time 3 days. Access to court records from 1997 to present is free at www.nmcourts.gov
Criminal Records: Access: Fax, mail, in person, online. Only the court performs in person searches; visitors may not. Required to search: name, years to search, DOB; also helpful: SSN. Criminal docket on books from 1912. Mail turnaround time 3 days. Online access to criminal records is free at www.nmcourts.gov. Most but not all online results show middle initial and/or DOB.
General Information: Online identifiers in results same as on public terminal. No adoption, insanity, guardianship records released. Will fax documents to local number for $2.00 1st page and $1.00 ea add'l page fee. Will fax out-of-state for $2.00 per page. Court makes copy: $.35 per page. Self serve: same. Certification fee: $1.50 per seal. Payee: District Court Clerk Office. Cashiers check, money order, or exact cash accepted. No credit cards accepted.

Santa Rosa Magistrate Court 603 Parker Ave, Santa Rosa, NM 88435; 575-472-3237; fax: 575-472-3592; 8AM-4PM (MST). ***Misdemeanor, Civil Actions under $10,000, Eviction, Small Claims.***
Now holds records for the Vaughn Magistrate Court, which closed 2008.
Civil Records: Access: Online, mail, in person. Only the court performs in person searches; visitors may not. No search fee. Civil cases indexed by both plaintiff and defendant. Mail turnaround time 3 days. Case lookup 1997 forward at www.nmcourts.gov.
Criminal Records: Access: Online, mail, in person. Only the court performs in person searches; visitors may not. No search fee. Required to search: name, years to search, DOB, offense, date of offense; also helpful: SSN. Mail turnaround time 3 days. Online access to criminal records is free at www.nmcourts.gov. Most but not all online results show middle initial and/or DOB.
General Information: Online identifiers in results same as on public terminal. Will fax documents $10.00 each. Court makes copy: $.50 per page. No certification fee. Payee: Santa Rosa Magistrate Court. No personal checks or credit cards accepted. Mail requests: SASE required.

Vaughn Magistrate Court c/o Santa Rosa Justice Court, 603 Parker Av, Santa Rosa, NM 88435; 575-472-3237; fax: 575-472-3592; 8AM-4PM (MST). ***Misdemeanor, Civil Actions under $10,000, Eviction, Small Claims.*** The Vaughn court has been closed. Records at Santa Rosa - phone # given here.

County Clerk 420 Parker Ave, #1, Courthouse, 1448 Historic Route 66, Santa Rosa, NM 88435; 575-472-3791; fax: 575-472-4791; 8AM-N, 1-5PM (MST). ***Probate.***

Harding County

10th Judicial District Court Box 1002, Mosquero, NM 87733; 575-673-2252; fax: 575-673-0333; 9AM-1PM (MST). ***Felony, Civil.***
Civil Records: Access: Phone, fax, mail, online, in person. Only the court performs in person searches; visitors may not. No search fee. Required to search: name; also helpful: years to search. Civil cases indexed by defendant, plaintiff; index on books from 1927. Computerized records go back to 1997. Mail turnaround time 1 week. Case lookup from 1997 forward is free at www.nmcourts.gov.
Criminal Records: Access: Phone, fax, mail, online, in person. Only the court performs in person searches; visitors may not. No search fee. Required to search: name, DOB, SSN; also helpful: years to search. Criminal docket on books from 1927. Computerized records go back to 1997. Mail turnaround time 1 week. Online access to criminal records is free at www.nmcourts.gov. Most but not all online results show middle initial and/or DOB.
General Information: Online identifiers in results same as on public terminal. No adoption records released. Will fax documents $1.00 per page. Court makes copy: $.35 per page. Self serve: same. Certification fee: $1.50. Payee: District Court Clerk. Business checks accepted from attorneys only. No personal checks, no cash accepted. No credit cards accepted. Mail requests: SASE required.

Magistrate Court Box 9, Roy, NM 87743; 575-485-2549; fax: 575-485-2407; 8AM-4PM (MST). ***Misdemeanor, Civil Actions under $10,000, Eviction, Small Claims.***
Civil Records: Access: Mail, phone, in person, fax, online. Both court and visitors may perform in person searches. No search fee. Required to search: name, DOB, years to search, other names used; also helpful-SSN, address. Records indexed by plaintiff and defendant. Records computerized since 1996. Mail turnaround time 2 days. Civil PAT goes back to 1997. PAT results show middle initial, DOB. Case lookup 1997 forward at www.nmcourts.gov.
Criminal Records: Access: Mail, phone, in person, fax, online. Both court and visitors may perform in person searches. No search fee. Required to search: name, years to search, DOB; also helpful: address, SSN. Records computerized since 1996. Mail turnaround time 2 days. Criminal PAT goes back to same as civil. Terminal results may or may not have complete name or a DOB. Online access to criminal records is free at www.nmcourts.gov. Most but not all online results show middle initial and/or DOB.
General Information: Online identifiers in results same as on public terminal. Will fax documents. Court makes copy: $.50 per page. No certification fee. Payee: Magistrate Court. Personal checks accepted; credit cards are not.

County Clerk PO Box 1002, County Clerk, 35 Pine St, Mosquero, NM 87733; 575-673-2301; fax: 575-673-2922; 8AM-4PM (MST). ***Probate.***

Hidalgo County

6th Judicial District Court PO Box 608, Lordsburg, NM 88045; 575-542-3411; fax: 575-542-3481; 8AM-N, 1-5PM (MST). ***Felony, Civil.***
Civil Records: Access: Phone, fax, mail, online, in person. Only the court performs in person searches; visitors may not. No search fee. Required to search: name, years to search. Civil cases indexed by defendant, plaintiff; index on microfiche and archived from 1920. Mail turnaround 3-5 days. Case lookup from 1997 forward is free at www.nmcourts.gov.
Criminal Records: Access: Phone, fax, mail, online, in person. Only the court performs in person searches; visitors may not. No search fee. Required to search: name, years to search; also helpful: alias. Criminal records on microfiche and archived from 1920. Mail turnaround time 3-5 days. Online access to criminal records is free at www.nmcourts.gov. Most but not all online results show middle initial and/or DOB.
General Information: Online identifiers in results same as on public terminal. No juvenile or adoption records released. Fee to fax out file $5.00 each; will not fax search results to toll-free numbers. Court makes copy: $.35 per page. Certification fee: $1.50. Payee: District Court Clerk. Business checks accepted. No personal checks or credit cards accepted. Mail requests: SASE required.

Magistrate Court 420 Wabash Ave, Lordsburg, NM 88045; 575-542-3582; fax: 575-542-3596; 8AM-4PM (MST). ***Misdemeanor, Civil Actions under $10,000, Eviction, Small Claims.***
Civil Records: Access: Online, mail, in person. Only the court performs in person searches; visitors may not. No search fee. Civil cases indexed by Defendant, Plaintiff. Mail turnaround time 1 week. Case lookup from 1997 forward is free at www.nmcourts.gov.
Criminal Records: Access: Mail, in person, fax, online. Only the court performs in person searches; visitors may not. No search fee. Required to search: name, years to search; also helpful: DOB, SSN. Mail turnaround time 1 week. Online access to criminal records is free at www.nmcourts.gov. Most but not all online results show middle initial and/or DOB.
General Information: Online identifiers in results same as on public terminal. Fee to fax out file $1.00 per page. Court makes copy: $.50 per page. No certification fee. Payee: Magistrate Court. Only cashiers checks and money orders accepted. No credit cards accepted. Mail requests: SASE required.

County Clerk 300 S Shakespeare, Lordsburg, NM 88045; 575-542-9213; fax: 575-542-3193; 8AM-5PM (MST). ***Probate.***

Lea County

5th Judicial District Court Box #6-C, 100 N. Main, Lovington, NM 88260; 575-396-8571; fax: 575-396-2428; 8AM-5PM (MST). ***Felony, Civil.*** www.fifthdistrictcourt.com
Civil Records: Access: Online, in person. Both court and visitors may perform in person searches. No search fee. Required to search: name, years to search. Civil cases indexed by defendant, plaintiff; index on computer from 1990, on microfiche from 1912. Civil PAT goes back to 1990. PAT civil results show middle initial. Case lookup from 1997 forward is free at www.nmcourts.gov.
Criminal Records: Access: Online, in person. Both court and visitors may perform in person searches. No search fee. Required to search: name, years to search. Criminal records computerized from 1997, on microfiche from 1912. Criminal PAT goes back to same as civil. Terminal results may or may not have complete name or a DOB. Online access to criminal records is free at www.nmcourts.gov. Most but not all online results show middle initial and/or DOB.
General Information: Online identifiers in results same as on public terminal. No adoption, mental, abuse records released. Will not fax documents. Court makes copy: $.35 per page. Self serve: same. Certification fee: $1.50 per cert. Payee: District Court Clerk. Only cashiers checks and money orders accepted. No credit cards accepted.

Eunice Magistrate Court PO Box 240, 2200 W Avenue "O", Eunice, NM 88231; 575-394-3368; fax: 575-394-3335; 8AM-4PM M,W,F; N-4PM T,Th (MST). ***Misdemeanor, Civil Actions under $10,000, Eviction, Small Claims.***

Civil Records: Access: Online, mail, fax, in person. Only the court performs in person searches; visitors may not. No search fee. Required to search: name only. Civil cases indexed by both plaintiff & defendant. Mail turnaround 3 days. Case lookup from 1997 forward is free at www.nmcourts.gov.

Criminal Records: Access: Online, mail, fax, in person. Only the court performs in person searches; visitors may not. No search fee. Required to search: name, years to search, DOB; also helpful: SSN. Criminal records go back 10 years. Mail turnaround time 3 days. Online access to criminal records is free at www.nmcourts.gov. Most but not all online results show middle initial and/or DOB.

General Information: Online identifiers in results same as on public terminal. Will fax back documents. Court makes copy: $.50 per page. Certification fee: $.50 per page. Payee: Eunice Magistrate Court. No personal or business checks or. credit cards accepted. Mail requests: SASE required.

Hobbs Magistrate Court 2110 N Alto Dr, Hobbs, NM 88240-3455; 575-397-3621; fax: 575-393-9121; 8AM-4PM (MST). ***Misdemeanor, Civil Actions under $10,000, Eviction, Small Claims.***

Civil Records: Access: Online, mail, in person. Only the court performs in person searches; visitors may not. No search fee. Required to search: name, years to search, signed release, address, other names used; DOB, SSN helpful. Civil cases indexed by defendant, plaintiff. Civil records held 14 years, computerized since July, 1996. Mail turnaround time seven days for mail; 3 days for fax. Case lookup from 1997 forward is free at www.nmcourts.gov.

Criminal Records: Access: Online, mail, in person. Only the court performs in person searches; visitors may not. No search fee. Required to search: name, years to search, DOB; SSN and signed release helpful. Criminal records held 1 year after disposition; computerized since July, 1996. Mail turnaround time 3-5 days. Online access to criminal records is free at www.nmcourts.gov. Most but not all online results show middle initial and/or DOB.

General Information: Online identifiers in results same as on public terminal. Will fax documents to local or toll free line. Court makes copy: $.50 per page. Self serve: same. No certification fee Certification included in copy fee. Payee: Magistrate Court. No personal checks or credit cards accepted. Mail requests: SASE required.

Jal Magistrate Court PO Box 507, Jal, NM 88252; 575-395-2740; fax: 575-395-2595; 8AM-4PM T,TH (MST). ***Misdemeanor, Civil Actions under $10,000, Eviction, Small Claims.***

All record requests must be in writing.

Civil Records: Access: Mail, in person, online. Only the court performs in person searches; visitors may not. No search fee. Civil cases indexed by both plaintiff & defendant. Mail turnaround 3 days. Case lookup from 1997 forward at www.nmcourts.gov.

Criminal Records: Access: Mail, in person, online. Only the court performs in person searches; visitors may not. No search fee. Required to search: name, years to search, DOB; also helpful: SSN. Mail turnaround time 3 days. Online access to criminal records is free at www.nmcourts.gov. Most but not all online results show middle initial and/or DOB.

General Information: Online identifiers in results same as on public terminal. Will not fax documents. Court makes copy: $.50 per page. Certification fee: $.50 per page. Payee: Jal Magistrate Court. Mail requests: SASE required.

Lovington Magistrate Court 100 W Central St, #D, Lovington, NM 88260; 575-396-6677; fax: 575-396-6163; 8AM-4PM; 1st & 3rd M to 3:30PM (MST). ***Misdemeanor, Civil Actions under $10,000, Eviction, Small Claims.***

Civil Records: Access: Phone, fax, mail, in person, online. Both court and visitors may perform in person searches. No search fee. Required to search: name, years to search. Civil cases indexed by defendant, plaintiff. Mail turnaround time 3 days. Public use terminal available. PAT results show name only. Case lookup from 1997 forward is free at www.nmcourts.gov.

Criminal Records: Access: Phone, fax, mail, in person, online. Both court and visitors may perform in person searches. No search fee. Required to search: name, years to search, DOB. Mail turnaround time 3 days. Public use terminal available. Terminal results may or may not have complete name or a DOB. Online access to criminal records is free at www.nmcourts.gov. Court warns to be cautious to match the name to the right record. Most but not all online results show middle initial and/or DOB.

General Information: Online identifiers in results same as on public terminal. Will fax documents per arrangement. Court makes copy: $.50 per page. Certification fee: $.50 per page. Payee: Magistrate Court. Business checks accepted. Mail requests: SASE required.

Tatum Magistrate Court PO Box 918, Tatum, NM 88267; 575-398-5300; fax: 575-398-5310; 8AM-4PM (MST). ***Misdemeanor, Civil Actions under $10,000, Eviction, Small Claims.***

Civil Records: Access: Phone, mail, fax, in person, online. Both court and visitors may perform in person searches. No search fee. Required to search: name, signed release, address, other names used. Civil records indexed by case number. Records searchable seven years, with add'l seven years available. Mail turnaround time 5 days. Case lookup from 1997 forward is free at www.nmcourts.gov.

Criminal Records: Access: Phone, mail, fax, in person, online. Both court and visitors may perform in person searches. No search fee. Required to search: name, years to search, DOB, SSN, signed release; also helpful: address. Criminal records go back to 1996. All DWI case are on file forever. Note: Phone access only on cases with final disposition. Mail turnaround time 5 days. Online access to criminal records is free at www.nmcourts.gov. Most but not all online results show middle initial and/or DOB.

General Information: Online identifiers in results same as on public terminal. Will not fax documents. Court makes copy: $.50 per page. Certification fee: $2.00 per document. Payee: Magistrate Court. No personal checks or credit cards accepted. Mail requests: SASE required.

County Clerk Box 1507, 100 N Main St, Lovington, NM 88260; 575-396-8614; fax: 575-396-3293; 8AM-5PM (MST). ***Probate, Ordinance.*** www.leacounty.net/Clerk.htm

Lincoln County

12th Judicial District Court Box 725, Carrizozo, NM 88301; 575-648-2432; fax: 575-648-2581; 8AM-5PM (MST). ***Felony, Civil.*** www.12thdistrict.net

Civil Records: Access: Online, mail, in person. Both court and visitors may perform in person searches. No search fee. Required to search: name, years to search. Civil cases indexed by defendant, plaintiff; index on computer from 1991, docket books from 1960, microfiche to 1960. Civil PAT goes back to 1991. Case lookup from 1997 forward is free at www.nmcourts.gov.

Criminal Records: Access: Online, in person. Both court and visitors may perform in person searches. No search fee. Required to search: name, years to search. Criminal records computerized from 1991, docket books from 1960, microfiche to 1960. Criminal PAT goes back to same as civil. Terminal results may or may not have complete name or a DOB. Online access to criminal records is free at www.nmcourts.gov. Most but not all online results show middle initial and/or DOB.

General Information: Online identifiers in results same as on public terminal. No juvenile, adoption, or mental records released. Will fax documents to toll free number. Court makes copy: $.35 per page. Certification fee: $1.50 per stamp. Payee: District Court Clerk. No personal checks accepted. Money orders or cashier's checks accepted. No credit cards accepted. Mail requests: SASE required.

Carrizozo Magistrate Court 310 11th St, PO Box 488, Carrizozo, NM 88301; 575-648-2380; fax: 575-648-2695; 8AM-Noon; 1-5PM (MST). ***Misdemeanor, Civil Actions under $10,000, Eviction, Small Claims.***

Civil Records: Access: Mail, in person, online. Both court and visitors may perform in person searches. No search fee. Civil cases indexed by both plaintiff & defendant. Mail turnaround 3 days. Case lookup from 1997 forward is free at www.nmcourts.gov.

Criminal Records: Access: Fax, in person, mail, online. Visitors must perform in person searches themselves. Search fee: $7.00 per name, if more than 1 name. Required to search: name, years to search; also helpful: DOB, SSN. Mail turnaround time 3 days. Online access to criminal records for past 10 years is free at www.nmcourts.gov. Most but not all online results show middle initial and/or DOB.

General Information: Online identifiers in results same as on public terminal. Will not fax documents. Court makes copy: $.50 per page. No certification fee. Payee: Carrizozo Magistrate Court. No personal checks or credit cards accepted. Mail requests: SASE required.

Ruidoso Magistrate Court 301 W Highway 70 #2, Ruidoso, NM 88345; 575-378-7022; fax: 575-378-8508; 8AM-4PM (MST). ***Misdemeanor, Civil Actions under $10,000, Eviction, Small Claims.***

Civil Records: Access: Online, mail, in person. Both court and visitors may perform in person searches. No search fee. Civil cases indexed by both plaintiff & defendant. Mail turnaround time 3 days. Case lookup from 1997 forward is free at www.nmcourts.gov.

Criminal Records: Access: Online, mail, in person. Visitors must perform in person searches themselves. No search fee. Required to search: name, years to search; also helpful: DOB, SSN. Mail turnaround time 3 days. Online access to criminal records is free at www.nmcourts.gov. Most but not all online results show middle initial and/or DOB.

General Information: Online identifiers in results same as on public terminal. Will not fax documents. Court makes copy: $.50 per page. Certification fee: $1.00 per cert. Payee: Ruidoso Magistrate Court. No personal checks or credit cards accepted.

County Clerk PO Box 338, 300 Central Ave, Carrizozo, NM 88301; 575-648-2394; fax: 575-648-2576; 8AM-5PM (MST). ***Probate.***

This court will do uncertified searches.

Los Alamos County

1st Judicial District Court c/o Santa Fe 1st District Court, PO Box 2268, Santa Fe, NM 87504. http://firstdistrictcourt.com All civil and criminal cases now handled by Santa Fe District Court.

Magistrate Court 1319 Trinity Dr, Los Alamos, NM 87544; 505-662-2727; fax: 505-661-6258; 8AM-4PM (MST). ***Misdemeanor, Civil Actions under $10,000, Eviction, Small Claims.***

Civil Records: Access: Online, in person. Only the court performs in person searches; visitors may not. No search fee. Required to search: name, years to search, address, other names used, signed release. 1997 records forward are on database. Case lookup from 1997 forward is free at www.nmcourts.gov.

Criminal Records: Access: Online, in person. Only the court performs in person searches; visitors may not. No search fee. Required to search: name, years to search, address, DOB, signed release; also helpful: SSN. Normally destroyed after 1 years from closure; except DWIs. Online access to criminal records is free at www.nmcourts.gov. Most but not all online results show middle initial and/or DOB.

General Information: Online identifiers in results same as on public terminal. Will fax documents $1.00 per page. Court makes copy: $.50 per page. No certification fee. Payee: Los Alamos Magistrate Court. Personal checks accepted; credit cards are not. Mail requests: SASE required for mail return of any copies.

County Clerk-Probate PO Box 30, 2451 Central Ave, #D, Los Alamos, NM 87544; 505-662-8013, 8010; fax: 505-662-8008; 8AM-5PM (MST).

Luna County

6th Judicial District Court Luna County Courthouse, Rm 40, Deming, NM 88030; 575-546-9611; fax: 575-546-0971; 8AM-N, 1-5PM (MST). ***Felony, Civil.***

Civil Records: Access: Mail, in person, online. Both court and visitors may perform in person searches. No search fee. Required to search: name, years to search. Civil cases indexed by defendant, plaintiff; index on microfiche from 1911; on computer back to 1997. Mail turnaround time 5 days. Civil PAT goes back to 1997. Case lookup from 1997 forward is free at www.nmcourts.gov.

Criminal Records: Access: Mail, online, in person. Both court and visitors may perform in person searches. No search fee. Required to search: name, years to search. Criminal records on microfiche from 1911; on computer back to 1997. Mail turnaround time 5 days. Criminal PAT goes back to same as civil. Terminal results may or may not have complete name or a DOB. Online access to criminal records is free at www.nmcourts.gov. Most but not all online results show middle initial and/or DOB.

General Information: Online identifiers in results same as on public terminal. No adoption, mental, sequestered or juvenile records released. Will fax documents $.35 per page. Court makes copy: $.35 per page. Self serve: same. Certification fee: $1.50 per document. Payee: District Court Clerk. Only cashiers checks and money orders accepted. No credit cards accepted. Mail requests: SASE required.

Magistrate Court 912 S Silver St, Deming, NM 88030; 575-546-9321; fax: 575-546-4896; 8AM-N, 1-5PM (MST). ***Misdemeanor, Civil Actions under $10,000, Eviction, Small Claims.***

Civil Records: Access: Mail, in person, online. Only the court performs in person searches; visitors may not. No search fee. Required to search: name, years to search, if judgment was rendered. Civil records go back 14 years. Mail turnaround time 2-3 days. Case lookup from 1997 forward at www.nmcourts.gov.

Criminal Records: Access: Mail, in person, online. Only the court performs in person searches; visitors may not. No search fee. Required to search: name, years to search. Criminal records computerized from 1/1996. Physical files are maintained for 1 fiscal year. Mail turnaround time 2-3 days. Online access to criminal records is free at www.nmcourts.gov. Most but not all online results show middle initial and/or DOB.

General Information: Online identifiers in results same as on public terminal. Will fax documents $1.00 per page. Court makes copy: $.50 per page includes certification. No certification fee. Payee: Luna Magistrate Court. Personal checks are accepted. No credit cards. Mail requests: SASE required.

County Clerk PO Box 1838, 700 S Silver, Deming, NM 88031; 575-546-0491; fax: 575-542-6617; 8AM-5PM (MST). ***Probate.***

There can be some probate cases (those in dispute) at the District Court level.

McKinley County

11th Judicial District Court 201 W. Hill, Rm 4, Gallup, NM 87301; 505-863-6816; fax: 505-722-3401; 8AM-N, 1-5PM (MST). ***Felony, Civil.***

Civil Records: Access: Phone, mail, online, in person. Both court and visitors may perform in person searches. No search fee. Required to search: name, years to search. Civil cases indexed by defendant, plaintiff; index on computer from 1989, on microfiche from 1923. Note: One name only by phone. Mail turnaround time 3-5 days. Civil PAT goes back to 1988. Case lookup from 1997 forward is free at www.nmcourts.gov.

Criminal Records: Access: Phone, mail, online, in person. Both court and visitors may perform in person searches. No search fee. Required to search: name, years to search, DOB; also helpful: SSN. Criminal records computerized from 1989, on microfiche from 1923. Note: Will search one name only by phone. Mail turnaround time 3-5 days. Criminal PAT goes back to same as civil. Terminal results may or may not have complete name or a DOB. Online access to criminal records is free at www.nmcourts.gov. Most but not all online results show middle initial and/or DOB.

General Information: Online identifiers in results same as on public terminal. No adoption or juvenile records released. Fee to fax out file $5.00 per call. Court makes copy: $.35 per page. Self serve: same. Certification fee: $1.50. Payee: McKinley County District Court. No personal checks or credit cards accepted. Mail requests: SASE required.

Magistrate Court 285 Boardman Dr, Gallup, NM 87301; 505-722-6636; fax: 505-863-3510; 8AM-4PM (MST). ***Misdemeanor, Civil Actions under $10,000, Eviction, Small Claims.***

Felony preliminary hearings held here.

Civil Records: Access: Online, in person. Only the court performs in person searches; visitors may not. Civil cases indexed by Defendant, Plaintiff. Case lookup from 1997 forward at www.nmcourts.gov.

Criminal Records: Access: Online, in person. Only the court performs in person searches; visitors may not. No search fee. Required to search: name, years to search, DOB; also helpful: SSN. Online access to criminal records is free at www.nmcourts.gov. Most but not all online results show middle initial and/or DOB, may also show only the last 4 digits of the SSN, if available.

General Information: Online identifiers in results same as on public terminal. Will not fax documents. Court makes copy: $.50 per page. No certification fee. Payee: Magistrate Court. Personal checks accepted. Major credit cards accepted in person only.

Thoreau Magistrate Court, Thoreau, NM 87323. ***Misdemeanor, Civil Actions under $10,000, Eviction, Small Claims.***

See Gallup Magistrate clerk; ask for Deloria. Index at www.nmcourts.gov/caselookup/.

County Clerk PO Box 1268, 207 W Hill, Gallup, NM 87305; 505-863-6866; fax: 505-863-1419; 8AM-5PM (MST). ***Probate, Ordinance.***

Mora County

4th Judicial District Court PO Box 1540, Las Vegas, NM 87701; 505-425-7281; criminal phone: x40; civil phone: x40; fax: 505-454-8611; 8AM-4PM (MST). ***Felony, Civil.***

All records requests must be submitted in writing. Mora District Court records maintained in Las Vegas.

Civil Records: Access: Fax, mail, in person, online. Only the court performs in person searches; visitors may not. Required to search: name, years to search, DOB, County. Civil cases indexed by Defendant, Plaintiff. Civil records available back to 1912. Mail turnaround time 3 days; results not sent until payment received. Access court case information back to 1997 free at www.nmcourts.gov under Case Look-up option.

Criminal Records: Access: Fax, mail, in person, online. Both court and visitors may perform in person searches. No search fee. Required to search: name, years to search, DOB, County; also helpful: SSN. Criminal records available back to 1918. Mail turnaround time 3 days with pre-payment. Access criminal case information back to 1997 free at www.nmcourts.gov under Case Look-up option. Most but not all online results show middle initial and/or DOB.

General Information: Online identifiers in results same as on public terminal. No adoption, insanity, guardianship records released without court approval. Will fax documents to local number $1.00 per page; long-distance numbers $2.00 per page. Court makes copy: $.35 per page. Self serve: same. Certification fee: $1.50 per doc. Payee: Fourth Judicial District Court. Cashiers check, money order, or exact cash accepted. No personal checks or credit cards accepted. Mail requests: SASE not required, but postage fee based on weigh applies.

Magistrate Court PO Box 131, Mora, NM 87732; 575-387-2937 x3; fax: 575-387-9081; 8AM-4PM (MST). ***Misdemeanor, Civil Actions under $10,000, Eviction, Small Claims.***

Civil Records: Access: In person, online. Both court and visitors may perform in person searches. No search fee. Civil cases indexed by defendant, plaintiff. Records maintained for 16 years. Case lookup from 1997 forward is free at www.nmcourts.gov.

Criminal Records: Access: In person, online. Both court and visitors may perform in person searches. No search fee. Required to search: name, years to search. File copies kept here for 3 years only. Online access to criminal records is free at www.nmcourts.gov. Most but not all online results show middle initial and/or DOB.

General Information: Online identifiers in results same as on public terminal. Will fax documents to local or toll-free number. Court makes copy: $.50 per page. No certification fee. Payee: Magistrate Court. Only cashiers checks and money orders accepted. Major credit cards accepted.

Probate Court PO Box 580, Hwy 518 Main St, Mora, NM 87732; 575-387-5014; fax: 575-387-9022; 9:30AM-4:30PM M (MST). ***Probate.***

Otero County

12th Judicial District Court 1000 New York Ave, Rm 209, Alamogordo, NM 88310-6940; 575-437-7310; fax: 575-434-8886; 8AM-5PM (MST). ***Felony, Civil.*** www.12thdistrict.net

Civil Records: Access: Online, mail, in person. Visitors must perform in person searches themselves. No search fee. Required to search: name, years to search. Civil cases indexed by defendant, plaintiff; index on computer from 1991, on microfiche from 1926. Note: Phone & mail access limited to 5 names each. Civil PAT goes back to 1992. PAT results show name, DOB. Case lookup from 1997 forward is free at www.nmcourts.gov Also, current court dockets are at the court website.

Criminal Records: Access: Online, mail, in person. Both court and visitors may perform in person searches. No search fee. Required to search: name, years to search. Criminal records computerized from 1991, on microfiche from 1926. Note: Only court performs searches prior to March 1986. Mail turnaround time 48 hours. Criminal PAT goes back to same as civil. Driver License number may also appear on terminal result. Terminal results may or may not have complete name or a DOB. Online access to criminal records is free at www.nmcourts.gov. Most but not all online results show middle initial and/or DOB.

General Information: Online identifiers in results same as on public terminal. No sealed, adoption records released. Will not fax documents. Court makes copy: $.35 per page. Self serve: same. Certification fee: $1.50; exemplification- $4.50. Payee: District Court. Only cashiers checks, cash or money orders accepted. No credit cards accepted.

Magistrate Court 263 Robert H Bradley Dr, Alamogordo, NM 88310-8288; 575-437-9000 x256; fax: 575-439-1365; 8AM-4PM (MST). ***Misdemeanor, Civil Actions under $10,000, Eviction, Small Claims.***

Civil Records: Access: Online, mail, in person. Only the court performs in person searches; visitors may not. No search fee. Civil cases indexed by both plaintiff & defendant. Records placed in storage after one year. Mail turnaround time 3 days. Case lookup from 1997 forward is free at www.nmcourts.gov.

Criminal Records: Access: Online, mail, in person. Only the court performs in person searches; visitors may not. No search fee. Required to search: name, years to search, DOB; also helpful: SSN. Records placed in storage after one year. Mail turnaround time 3 days. Online access to criminal records is free at www.nmcourts.gov. Most but not all online results show middle initial and/or DOB.

General Information: Online identifiers in results same as on public terminal. Will not fax documents. Court makes copy: $.50 per page. Cert fee: $1.00 per page. Payee: Magistrate Ct. Personal checks accepted; credit cards are not. Mail requests: SASE required.

County Clerk 1000 New York Ave, Rm 108, Alamogordo, NM 88310-6932; 575-437-4942; fax: 575-443-2922; 7:30AM-6PM (MST). ***Probate.***

Quay County

10th Judicial District Court Box 1067, Tucumcari, NM 88401; 575-461-2764; fax: 575-461-4498; 8AM-Noon, 1PM-4PM (MST). ***Felony, Civil.***

Civil Records: Access: Phone, fax, mail, online, in person. Only the court performs in person searches; visitors may not. No search fee. Required to search: name, years to search. Civil cases indexed by defendant, plaintiff; index on hard copy file from 1995 to present, microfiche 1912 to 1994, archived from 1911, on computer back to 1997. Mail turnaround time same day. Civil PAT goes back to 1912. Case lookup from 1997 forward is free at www.nmcourts.gov.

Criminal Records: Access: Phone, fax, mail, online, in person. Only the court performs in person searches; visitors may not. No search fee. Required to search: name; also helpful: years to search, DOB, SSN. Criminal records on hard copy file from 1995 to present, microfiche 1912 to 1994, archived from 1911, on computer back to 1997. Mail turnaround time same day. Criminal PAT available. Terminal results may or may not have complete name or a DOB. Online access to criminal records is free at www.nmcourts.gov. Most but not all online results show middle initial and/or DOB.

General Information: Online identifiers in results same as on public terminal. No adoption, juvenile, insanity records released. Will fax documents $2.00 1st page, $1.00 each add'l. Court makes copy: $.35 per page. Certification fee: $1.50. Payee: District Court Clerk. No personal checks or credit cards accepted. Mail requests: SASE required.

Tucumcari Magistrate Court PO Box 1301, Tucumcari, NM 88401; 575-461-1700; fax: 575-461-4522; 8AM-4PM; 9AM-5PM T (MST). ***Misdemeanor, Civil Actions under $10,000, Eviction, Small Claims.***

San Jon Magistrate Court (closed) records are here.

Civil Records: Access: Online, in person. Only the court performs in person searches; visitors may not. Civil cases indexed by defendant, plaintiff. Case lookup from 1997 forward at www.nmcourts.gov.

Criminal Records: Access: Online, in person. Only the court performs in person searches; visitors may not. No search fee. Required to search: name, years to search, DOB, SSN. Online access to criminal records is free at www.nmcourts.gov. Most but not all online results show middle initial and/or DOB.

General Information: Online identifiers in results same as on public terminal. Will fax documents $1.00 per page. Court makes copy: $.50 per page. Cert fee: $1.00 per page. Payee: Quay Magistrate Court. Personal checks accepted; credit cards are not.

County Clerk 300 S 3rd St, PO Box 1225, Tucumcari, NM 88401; 575-461-0510; fax: 575-461-0513; 8AM-N, 1-5PM (MST). ***Probate.***

Rio Arriba County

1st Judicial District Court PO Drawer 40, Tierra Amarilla, NM 87575; 575-588-0058; fax: 575-588-9898; 8AM-N, 1-4PM (MST). ***Felony, Misdemeanor, Civil, Probate.***
http://firstdistrictcourt.com

Civil Records: Access: Phone, mail, fax, in person, online. Only the court performs in person searches; visitors may not. No search fee. Required to search: Name, years to search, SSN, DOB. Records on computer back to 1997. Case lookup from 1997 forward is free at www.nmcourts.gov.

Criminal Records: Access: Phone, mail, fax, in person, online. Only the court performs in person searches; visitors may not. No search fee. Required to search: name, years to search. Records on computer back to 1997. Access to court records from 1997 forward is free at www.nmcourts.gov. Most but not all online results show middle initial and/or DOB.

General Information: Online identifiers in results same as on public terminal. Will not fax documents. Court makes copy: $.35 per page. Certification fee: $1.50 per page. Payee: 1st Judicial District Court. No personal checks or credit cards accepted. Mail requests: SASE required.

Rio Arriba Magistrate Court - Division 1 PO Box 538, 2332 Hwy 17, Chama, NM 87520; 575-756-2278; fax: 575-756-2477; 8AM-N, 1-4PM (MST). ***Misdemeanor, Civil Actions under $10,000, Eviction, Small Claims.***

Civil Records: Access: Mail, fax, in person, online. Both court and visitors may perform in person searches. No search fee. Required to search: name, years to search. On computer back to 1997. Mail turnaround time 1 week. Case lookup from 1997 forward is free at www.nmcourts.gov.

Criminal Records: Access: Mail, fax, in person, online. Only the court performs in person searches; visitors may not. No search fee. Required to search: name, years to search. On computer back to 1997. Mail turnaround time 1 week. Online access to criminal records is free at www.nmcourts.gov. Most but not all online results show middle initial and/or DOB.

General Information: Online identifiers in results same as on public terminal. Will not fax documents. Court makes copy: $.50 per page. No certification fee. Payee: Rio Arriba Magistrate Ct. Personal checks accepted; credit cards are not. Mail requests: SASE required.

Rio Arriba Magistrate Court - Division 2 410 Paseo de Onate, Espanola, NM 87532; 505-753-2532; fax: 505-753-4802; 8AM-4PM (MST). ***Misdemeanor, Civil Actions under $10,000, Eviction, Small Claims.***
www.nmsc.state.nm.us/directory/program.php?program_id=557

Civil Records: Access: Mail, in person, online. Only the court performs in person searches; visitors may not. No search fee. Civil cases indexed by defendant, plaintiff. Case records available from 1990. Mail turnaround time 3 days. Case lookup from 1997 forward is free at www.nmcourts.gov.

Criminal Records: Access: Mail, in person, online. Only the court performs in person searches; visitors may not. No search fee. Required to search: name, years to search. Case records available from 1997. Mail turnaround time within 1 week. Online access to criminal records is free at www.nmcourts.gov. Most but not all online results show middle initial and/or DOB.

General Information: Online identifiers in results same as on public terminal. Will fax documents. Court makes copy: $.50 per page. Self serve: same. Certification fee: $.50 per copy. Payee: RA Magistrate Court. Personal checks accepted; credit cards are not.

County Clerk PO Box 158, 7 Main St, Tierra Amarilla, NM 87575; 575-588-7724; fax: 575-588-7418; 8AM-5PM (MST). ***Probate.***

Roosevelt County

9th Judicial District Court 109 W 1st St, #207, Portales, NM 88130; 575-356-4463; fax: 575-359-2140; 8AM-4PM (MST). ***Felony, Civil.***
www.nmcourts9thjdc.com

Civil Records: Access: Online, in person. Visitors must perform in person searches themselves. Required to search: name, years to search. Civil cases indexed by defendant, plaintiff; index on microfiche from 1912, archived before 1912. Civil PAT goes back to 1997. PAT results show name, DOB. Case lookup from 1997 forward is free at www.nmcourts.gov.

Criminal Records: Access: Online, in person. Visitors must perform in person searches themselves. Required to search: name, years to search. Criminal records on microfiche from 1912, archived before 1912. Criminal PAT goes back to 1997. Terminal results may or may not have complete name or a DOB. Online access to criminal records is free at www.nmcourts.gov. Most but not all online results show middle initial and/or DOB.

General Information: Online identifiers in results same as on public terminal. No adoption, guardianship, insanity records released. Will fax documents $2.00 1st page, $1.00 each add'l page. Court makes copy: $.35 per page. Self serve: same. Certification fee: $1.50; Exemplification fee- $4.50. Payee: 9th Judicial District Court. Only cashiers checks and money orders accepted. No credit cards accepted. Mail requests: SASE required for mail return of any copies.

Magistrate Court 42427 US Hwy 70, Portales, NM 88130; 575-356-8569; fax: 575-359-6883; 8AM-4PM (MST). ***Misdemeanor, Civil under $10,000, Eviction, Small Claims, Felony Prelim.***

Civil Records: Access: Phone, mail, fax, in person, online. Only the court performs in person searches; visitors may not. Civil cases indexed by defendant, plaintiff. Records computerized since 1995. Mail turnaround time 5 days. Case lookup from 1997 forward is free at www.nmcourts.gov.

Criminal Records: Access: Phone, mail, fax, in person, online. Only the court performs in person searches; visitors may not. No search fee. Required to search: name, DOB; also helpful: SSN. Records computerized since 1995. Mail turnaround time 5 days. Online access to criminal records is free at www.nmcourts.gov. Most but not all online results show middle initial and/or DOB.

General Information: Online identifiers in results same as on public terminal. Will fax documents $1.00 per page. Court makes copy: $.50 per page. Certification fee: $1.00. Payee: Magistrate Court. Personal checks accepted; credit cards are not. Mail requests: SASE required.

County Clerk Lobby Box 4, County Courthouse, 109 W 1st, Portales, NM 88130; 575-356-8562; fax: 575-356-3560; 8AM-5PM (MST). ***Probate.***

San Juan County

11th Judicial District Court 103 S Oliver, Aztec, NM 87410; 505-334-6151; fax: 505-334-1940; 8AM-N, 1-5PM (MST). ***Felony, Civil.***

Civil Records: Access: Online, in person. Visitors must perform in person searches themselves. Required to search: name, years to search; also helpful: address. Civil cases indexed by defendant, plaintiff; index on computer from 1986, on microfiche from 1925; card file from 1912. Civil PAT goes back to 1986. Case lookup from 1997 forward is free at www.nmcourts.gov.

Criminal Records: Access: Online, in person, mail, fax. Both court and visitors may perform in person searches. Required to search: name, years to search, DOB; also helpful: address, SSN. Criminal records computerized from 1986, on microfiche from 1925; card file from 1912. Note: Court will not perform search before 1986. Mail turnaround time 3 days. Criminal PAT goes back to same as civil. Terminal results may or may not have complete name or a DOB. Online access to criminal records is free at www.nmcourts.gov. Most but not all online results show middle initial and/or DOB.

General Information: Online identifiers in results same as on public terminal. No adoption, insanity, sealed, expunged records released. Will fax documents $5.00 plus $.70 per page. Court makes copy: $.35 per page. Self serve: same. Certification fee: $1.50 per page. Payee: Eleventh District Court. No personal or out-of-state checks accepted. No credit cards accepted. Mail requests: SASE required for criminal.

Aztec Magistrate Court 200 Gossett, Aztec, NM 87410; 505-334-9479; fax: 505-334-2178; 8AM-4PM (MST). ***Misdemeanor, Civil Actions under $10,000, Eviction, Small Claims.***

Civil Records: Access: Online, in person. Both court and visitors may perform in person searches. No search fee. Civil cases indexed by both plaintiff & defendant. PAT civil results show middle initial. Case lookup from 1997 forward is free at www.nmcourts.gov.

Criminal Records: Access: Online, in person. Both court and visitors may perform in person searches. No search fee. Required to search: name, years to search; also helpful: DOB, SSN. Online access to criminal records is free at www.nmcourts.gov. Most but not all online results show middle initial and/or DOB.

General Information: Online identifiers in results same as on public terminal. Will not fax documents. Court makes copy: $.50 per page. No certification fee. Payee: Aztec Magistrate Court. Personal checks accepted; credit cards are not.

Farmington Magistrate Court 950 W Apache St, Farmington, NM 87401; 505-326-4338; criminal phone: 2017; civil phone: 2010; criminal fax: 505-325-2618; civil fax: 505-326-4623; 8AM-4PM (MST). ***Misdemeanor, Civil Actions under $10,000, Eviction, Small Claims.***

Civil Records: Access: Online, in person. Both court and visitors may perform in person searches. No search fee. Required to search: name; also helpful-years to search, other names used, address. Civil records go back 14 years for open cases. Closed case records go back to 6-30-05. Access to court records are free at www.nmcourts.gov. Records are removed from display according to retention schedule. Civil cases that have a satisfaction of judgments or dismissal filed can only be viewed online for one year after closing document is filed.

Criminal Records: Access: Online, in person. Both court and visitors may perform in person searches. No search fee. Required to search: name, years to search, DOB; also helpful: SSN. Criminal records go back to 6-30-05; DWI's 1986. Online access to criminal records is free at www.nmcourts.gov. Most but not all online results show middle initial and/or DOB.

General Information: Online identifiers in results same as on public terminal. Will fax documents $1.00 per page. Court makes copy: $.50 per page; $1.00 per page if computer generated. No certification fee. Payee: Magistrate Court. Personal checks accepted; credit cards are not.

County Clerk PO Box 550, 100 S Oliver, #200, Aztec, NM 87410; 505-334-9471; fax: 505-334-3635; 7AM-5:30PM (MST). ***Probate.***
www.sjcounty.net/Dpt/Clerk/Index.aspx

San Miguel County

4th Judicial District Court PO Box 1540, Las Vegas, NM 87701; 505-425-7281 x40; probate phone: same; fax: 505-454-8611; 8AM-4PM (MST). ***Felony, Civil, Probate.***

Also handles cases for Mora County. All records requests must be submitted in writing.

Civil Records: Access: Mail, in person, online, fax. Only the court performs in person searches; visitors may not. No search fee. Required to search: name, years to search, DOB, County. Civil cases indexed by Defendant, Plaintiff. Civil records available back to 1912. Note: All requests to the court must be in writing. Mail turnaround time 3 days. Access civil court case information from 1997 to present is free at www.nmcourts.gov under the case-lookup option.

Criminal Records: Access: Fax, mail, in person, online. Only the court performs in person searches; visitors may not. No search fee. Required to search: name, years to search, DOB, County; also helpful: SSN. Criminal records available back to 1918. Mail turnaround time 3 days. Online access to criminal case information is free at www.nmcourts.gov, see civil above. Most but not all online results show middle initial and/or DOB.

General Information: Online identifiers in results same as on public terminal. No adoption, insanity, guardianship records released without court approval. Will fax docs to local or toll free number- $1.00 per page; long-distance fax $2.00 per page. Court makes copy: $.35 per page. Certification fee: $1.50 per doc. Payee: Fourth Judicial District Court Clerk. Cashiers check, money order, or exact cash accepted. No personal checks or credit cards accepted.

Magistrate Court 1927 7th St, Las Vegas, NM 87701-4957; 505-425-5204; fax: 505-425-0422; 8AM-4PM (MST). ***Misdemeanor, Civil Actions under $10,000, Eviction, Small Claims.***

Civil Records: Access: Fax, online, in person. Only the court performs in person searches; visitors may not. No search fee. Required to search: name, years to search. Civil cases indexed by both plaintiff & defendant. Physical records kept for 2 years then purged. Case lookup from 1997 forward is free at www.nmcourts.gov.

Criminal Records: Access: Fax, online, in person. Only the court performs in person searches; visitors may not. No search fee. Required to search: name, years to search, DOB; also helpful: address, SSN. Physical records kept for 2 years then purged. Online access to criminal records is free at www.nmcourts.gov. Most but not all online results show middle initial and/or DOB.

General Information: Online identifiers in results same as on public terminal. Will not fax documents. Court makes copy: $.50 per page. No certification fee. Payee: Magistrate Court. No personal checks or credit cards accepted.

County Clerk San Miguel County Clerk, 500 W National Ave, #113, Las Vegas, NM 87701; 505-425-9331; fax: 505-454-1799; 8AM-N, 1-5PM, M-TH, 8AM-4PM, F (MST). ***Probate.***

Sandoval County

13th Judicial District Court PO Box 600, 1500 Idalia, Bldg A, Bernalillo, NM 87004; 505-867-2376; fax: 505-867-5161; 8AM-N, 1-5PM (MST). ***Felony, Civil, Probate, Domestic.***
www.13districtcourt.com

Civil Records: Access: Fax, mail, online, in person. Both court and visitors may perform in person searches. Search fee: $5.00 search fee. Required to search: name, years to search. Civil cases indexed by defendant, plaintiff; index on computer back to 11/96; prior on microfiche. Mail turnaround time 3-5 days. Case lookup from 1997 forward is free at www.nmcourts.gov. Also, view all civil jury verdicts in the 13th Judicial District Court free back to 1995 at www.13districtcourt.com/verdict/jury_verdict_intro.php.

Criminal Records: Access: Fax, mail, online, in person. Both court and visitors may perform in person searches. Search fee: $5.00 per name. Required to search: name, years to search. Criminal records computerized from 11/96. Mail turnaround time 3-5 days. Online access to criminal records is free at www.nmcourts.gov. Most but not all online results show middle initial and/or DOB.

General Information: Online identifiers in results same as on public terminal. No adoption, neglect and abuse records released. Fee to fax out file $2.50 per page; out of state $5.00 per page. Court makes copy: $.35 per page. Microfilm copies $.50 per page 1991 and prior. Certification fee: $1.50 per page. Payee: 13th Judicial District Court. Business checks accepted. No personal checks or credit cards accepted.

Bernalillo Magistrate Court 1000 Montoya Rd, Bernalillo, NM 87004; 505-867-5202 x2-6; fax: 505-867-0970; 8AM-4PM (MST). ***Misdemeanor, Civil Actions under $10,000, Eviction, Small Claims.***
www.13districtcourt.com/court-info-magistrate-sandoval.htm

Civil Records: Access: Mail, fax, in person, online. Both court and visitors may perform in person searches. No search fee. Civil records go back to 12/1996; prior destroyed. Mail turnaround time 1-2 weeks. Civil PAT goes back to 12/1996. Case lookup from 1997 forward is free at www.nmcourts.gov.

Criminal Records: Access: Online, mail, in person. Visitors must perform in person searches themselves. No search fee. Required to search: name, years to search. Criminal records go back to 12/1996; prior destroyed. Mail turnaround time 1-2 weeks. Criminal PAT goes back to 12/1996. Terminal results may or may not have complete name or a DOB. Online access to criminal records is free at www.nmcourts.gov. Most but not all online results show middle initial and/or DOB.

General Information: Online identifiers in results same as on public terminal. Will not fax documents. Court makes copy: $.50 per page. Self serve: same. Certification fee: $.50 per page. Payee: Magistrate Court. Personal checks accepted. Visa/MC accepted.

Cuba Magistrate Court PO Box 1497, Cuba, NM 87013; 575-289-3519; fax: 575-289-3013; 8AM-4PM (MST). ***Misdemeanor, Civil Actions under $10,000, Eviction, Small Claims.***

Civil Records: Access: Online, in person. Visitors must perform in person searches themselves. Civil cases indexed by defendant, plaintiff. Civil PAT goes back to 14 years. Case lookup from 1997 forward is free at www.nmcourts.gov.

Criminal Records: Access: Online, in person. Visitors must perform in person searches themselves. Required to search: name, years to search. Criminal PAT goes back to 3 years. Terminal results may or may not have complete name or a DOB. Online access to criminal records is free at www.nmcourts.gov. Most but not all online results show middle initial and/or DOB.

General Information: Online identifiers in results same as on public terminal. Will fax documents to local or toll-free number. Court makes copy: $.50 per page. Self serve: same. No personal checks or credit cards accepted.

Probate Court PO Box 40, 711 Camino del Pueblo, Bernalillo, NM 87004; 505-867-7647; civil phone: 505-867-7645; fax: 505-771-7184; 8AM-4PM (MST). ***Probate.***
www.sandovalcounty.com

Santa Fe County

First Judicial District Court Box 2268, Santa Fe, NM 87504; 505-476-0189; fax: 505-827-5055; 8AM-4PM (MST). ***Felony, Civil.***
http://firstdistrictcourt.com

Because this court also handles the counties of Los Alamos and Rio Arriba, you must indicate which county you are searching.

Civil Records: Access: Phone, mail, online, in person. Both court and visitors may perform in person searches. No search fee. Required to search: name, years to search. Civil cases indexed by defendant, plaintiff; index on computer from 1984, older records on docket books. Note: Requests to court must be in writing. Mail turnaround time 2 days. Civil PAT goes back to 1995. PAT results show name only. Access to index of court records from 1997 forward is free at www.nmcourts.gov

Criminal Records: Access: Phone, mail, online, in person. Both court and visitors may perform in person searches. No search fee. Required to search: name, years to search; also helpful: DOB, SSN. Criminal records computerized from 1984, older records on docket books. Mail turnaround time 2 days. Criminal PAT goes back to same as civil. Terminal results may or may not have complete name or a DOB. Online access to index of criminal records is free at www.nmcourts.gov. Most but not all online results show middle initial and/or DOB.

General Information: Online identifiers in results same as on public terminal. No adoption, juvenile, mental or abuse records released. Will not fax documents. Court makes copy: $.35 per page. Certification fee: $1.50 per seal. Payee: First Judicial District Court. Business checks accepted from law firms. No credit cards accepted. Mail requests: SASE required.

Pojoaque Magistrate Court, NM; 575-498-9914; 8AM-N,1-5PM (MST). ***Misdemeanor, Civil Actions under $10,000, Eviction, Small Claims.***

The Court In Pojoaque is often closed; the clerk can be contacted at the Santa Fe Magistrate Court.

Santa Fe Magistrate Court 2056 Galisteo St, Santa Fe, NM 87505; 505-984-9914; fax: 505-986-5866; 8AM-4PM M,W,F; 8AM-3PM T,TH (MST). ***Misdemeanor, Civil Actions under $10,000, Eviction, Small Claims.***

Also, the clerk for the Pojoaque Magistrate Court may be contacted here.

Civil Records: Access: Fax, mail, in person, online. Both court and visitors may perform in person searches. No search fee. Required to search: Name, years to search. Civil records on computer back to 1997. Mail turnaround time 2 weeks. Case lookup from 1997 forward is free at www.nmcourts.gov

Criminal Records: Access: Fax, mail, in person, online. Both court and visitors may perform in person searches. No search fee. Required to search: name, years to search, DOB; also helpful: SSN. Criminal records computerized from 1997. Mail turnaround time 2 weeks. Online access to criminal records is free at www.nmcourts.gov. Most but not all online results show middle initial and/or DOB.

General Information: Online identifiers in results same as on public terminal. Will fax documents for no fee. Court makes copy: $1.00 per page. No certification fee. Payee: Santa Fe Magistrate Court. Personal checks and major credit cards accepted.

County Clerk PO Box 195, 102 Grant Ave, Santa Fe, NM 87504-0276; 505-992-1636; fax: 505-995-2767; 8AM-5PM (MST). ***Probate.***
When faxing, send to the attention of "Probate."

Sierra County

7th Judicial District Court PO Box 3009, 311 N Date, Truth or Consequences, NM 87901; 575-894-7167; fax: 575-894-7168; 8AM-4PM (MST). ***Felony, Civil.***
Civil Records: Access: Fax, mail, online, in person. Only the court performs in person searches; visitors may not. No search fee. Required to search: name, years to search, address. Civil cases indexed by defendant, plaintiff; index on microfiche from 1920, archived before 1920. Mail turnaround time 2 days. Civil PAT goes back to 1997. PAT results show name, DOB. Case lookup from 1997 forward is free at www.nmcourts.gov.
Criminal Records: Access: Fax, mail, online, in person. Only the court performs in person searches; visitors may not. No search fee. Required to search: name, years to search, address, SSN. Criminal records on microfiche from 1920, archived before 1920. Mail turnaround time 2 days. Criminal PAT goes back to same as civil. Terminal results may or may not have complete name or a DOB. Online access to criminal records is free at www.nmcourts.gov. Most but not all online results show middle initial and/or DOB.
General Information: Online identifiers in results same as on public terminal. No adoption, insanity, juvenile, guardianship records released. Court makes copy: $.35 per page. Certification fee: $1.50. Payee: Sierra County District Court. Only cashiers checks and money orders accepted. No credit cards accepted. Mail requests: SASE required.

Magistrate Court 155 W Barton, Truth or Consequences, NM 87901; 575-894-3051; fax: 575-894-0476; 8AM-4PM (MST). ***Misdemeanor, Civil Actions under $10,000, Eviction, Small Claims.***
Civil Records: Access: Online, in person. Both court and visitors may perform in person searches. No search fee. Physical records kept for 2 years then purged. Case lookup from 1997 forward is free at www.nmcourts.gov.
Criminal Records: Access: Online, in person. Both court and visitors may perform in person searches. No search fee. Required to search: name, years to search. Physical records kept for 2 years then purged. Online access to criminal records is free at www.nmcourts.gov. Most but not all online results show middle initial and/or DOB.
General Information: Online identifiers in results same as on public terminal. Will fax documents $.50 per page. Court makes copy: $.50 per page. No certification fee. Payee: Magistrate Court. Personal checks accepted; credit cards are not. Mail requests: SASE required for mail return of any copies.

County Clerk 100 N Date St, Probate Records, Truth or Consequences, NM 87901; 575-894-2840; fax: 575-894-2516; 8AM-5PM (MST). ***Probate.***

Socorro County

7th Judicial District Court PO Drawer 1129, Socorro, NM 87801; 575-835-0050 x10; fax: 575-838-5217; 8AM-4PM (MST). ***Felony, Civil.***
This court is also responsible for Socorro County.
Civil Records: Access: Phone, fax, mail, online, in person. Both court and visitors may perform in person searches. No search fee. Required to search: name, years to search. Civil cases indexed by defendant, plaintiff; index on microfiche and hard copies from 1925; on computer back to 1997. Mail turnaround time 1 day. Civil PAT goes back to 1997. PAT results show middle initial, DOB. Results include case type. Case lookup from 1997 forward is free at www.nmcourts.gov.
Criminal Records: Access: Phone, fax, mail, online, in person. Both court and visitors may perform in person searches. No search fee. Required to search: name, years to search, DOB; also helpful-SSN, signed release. Criminal records on microfiche and hard copies from 1925; on computer back to 1997. Mail turnaround time 1 day. Criminal PAT goes back to 1997. Terminal results may or may not have complete name or a DOB. Online access to criminal records is free at www.nmcourts.gov. Results include case type. Most but not all online results show middle initial and/or DOB.
General Information: Online identifiers in results same as on public terminal. No sequestered records released. Will fax documents to local or toll free line. Court makes copy: $.35 per page. Certification fee: $1.50 per cert. Payee: District Court Clerk. Only business checks accepted. No credit cards accepted. Mail requests: SASE required.

Magistrate Court 102 Winkler St, Socorro, NM 87801; 575-835-2500; fax: 575-838-0428; 8AM-4PM (MST). ***Misdemeanor, Civil Actions under $10,000, Eviction, Small Claims.***
Civil Records: Access: Mail, in person, online. Only the court performs in person searches; visitors may not. No search fee. Required to search: name, years to search, address, other names used. Civil cases indexed by defendant, plaintiff; index on computer back to 1997; judgments back 14 years or until satisfied. Mail turnaround time 1-5 days. Case lookup from 1997 forward is free at www.nmcourts.gov.
Criminal Records: Access: Mail, in person, online. Only the court performs in person searches; visitors may not. No search fee. Required to search: name, years to search, other names used; also helpful-DOB, SSN. Criminal records computerized from 1997; files destroyed 2 years after closure. Mail turnaround time 1-5 days. Online access to criminal records is free at www.nmcourts.gov. Most but not all online results show middle initial and/or DOB.
General Information: Online identifiers in results same as on public terminal. Will fax back to gov't agencies only. Court makes copy: $.50 per page. Certification fee: $1.00. Payee: Magistrate Court. Personal checks accepted; credit cards are not. Mail requests: SASE required.

County Clerk PO Box I, 200 Church St, Socorro, NM 87801; 575-835-0423; fax: 575-835-1043; 8AM-5PM (MST). ***Probate.***

Taos County

8th Judicial District Court 105 Albright St, #H, Taos, NM 87571; 575-758-3173 x1; fax: 575-751-1281; 8AM-4PM (MST). ***Felony, Civil.***
Civil Records: Access: In person, online. Visitors must perform in person searches themselves. Required to search: name, years to search. Civil cases indexed by defendant, plaintiff; index on computer since 1993, books since 1912, microfiche from 1912-1980. Access to court records from 1993 forward is free at www.nmcourts.gov.
Criminal Records: Access: In person, online. Visitors must perform in person searches themselves. Required to search: name, years to search, DOB; also helpful: signed release, SSN. Criminal records on computer since 1993, books since 1912, microfiche from 1912-1950. Online access to criminal records is free at www.nmcourts.gov. Most but not all online results show middle initial and/or DOB.
General Information: Online identifiers in results same as on public terminal. No adoption, juvenile, abuse or sequestered case records released. Will fax documents $2.00 per page. Court makes copy: $.35 per page. Self serve: same. Certification fee: $1.50 per doc. Payee: District Court. Only cashiers checks and money orders accepted.

Questa Magistrate Court PO Box 586, State Rd 522 and Hwy 230, Questa, NM 87556; 575-586-0761; fax: 575-586-0428; 8AM-4PM M,W; 8AM-N, 1PM-4PM T,TH; F closed (MST). ***Misdemeanor, Civil Actions under $10,000, Eviction, Small Claims.***
Civil Records: Access: Mail, in person, online. Both court and visitors may perform in person searches. No search fee. Required to search: name, signed release, address. Civil cases indexed by Defendant, Plaintiff. Civil records go back to 1984. Mail turnaround time 23 days. Civil PAT goes back to 1984. Results include case number. Case lookup from 1997 forward is free at www.nmcourts.gov.
Criminal Records: Access: Mail, in person, online. Both court and visitors may perform in person searches. No search fee. Required to search: name, years to search; also helpful: DOB, SSN. Criminal records go back to 1998. Note: Results include case number. Mail turnaround time 23 days. Criminal PAT goes back to 1999. Terminal results may or may not have complete name or a DOB. Online access to criminal records is free at www.nmcourts.gov. Most but not all online results show middle initial and/or DOB.
General Information: Online identifiers in results same as on public terminal. Fee to fax out file $1.00 per page. Court makes copy: $.50 per page. Certification fee: $3.00 per copy. Payee: Taos Circuit Court. Personal checks accepted; credit cards are not. Mail requests: SASE required.

Taos Magistrate Court 920 Salazar Rd, #B, Taos, NM 87571; 575-758-4030; fax: 575-751-0983; 8AM-4PM (MST). ***Misdemeanor, Civil Actions under $10,000, Eviction, Small Claims.***
Civil Records: Access: Online, in person. Both court and visitors may perform in person searches. No search fee. Civil cases indexed by both plaintiff & defendant. Civil records go back to 1997. Case lookup from 1997 forward is free at www.nmcourts.gov.
Criminal Records: Access: Online, in person. Both court and visitors may perform in person searches. No search fee. Required to search: name, years to search, DOB; also helpful: SSN. Criminal records go back to 1997. Online access to criminal records is free at www.nmcourts.gov. Most but not all online results show middle initial and/or DOB.
General Information: Online identifiers in results same as on public terminal. Will not fax documents. Court makes copy: $.50 per page. Certification fee: $.50 per page. Payee: Taos Magistrate Court. No personal checks or credit cards accepted.

County Clerk 105 Albright, #D, Taos, NM 87571; 575-737-6391; fax: 575-737-6390; 8AM-N, 1-4PM M (MST). ***Probate.***

Torrance County

7th Judicial District Court Neil Mertz Judicial Complex, PO Box 78, Estancia, NM 87016; 505-384-2974; fax: 505-384-2229; 8AM-4PM (MST). ***Felony, Civil.***
Civil Records: Access: Mail, in person, online. Both court and visitors may perform in person searches. No search fee. Required to search: name, years to search. Civil cases indexed by defendant, plaintiff; index on hard copy until filmed, microfiche from 1912; on computer back to 1997. Mail turnaround time 1 week. Civil PAT goes back to 1997. Case lookup from 1997 forward is free at www.nmcourts.gov.
Criminal Records: Access: Mail, online, in person. Both court and visitors may perform in person searches. No search fee. Required to search: name, years to search; also helpful: SSN, DOB. Criminal records on hard copy until filmed, microfiche from 1912; on computer back to 1997. Mail turnaround time 1 week. Criminal PAT goes back to same as civil. Terminal results may or may not have complete name or a DOB. Online access to criminal records is free at www.nmcourts.gov. Most but not all online results show middle initial and/or DOB.
General Information: Online identifiers in results same as on public terminal. No juvenile, neglect, adoption, mental health records released. Will fax out civil file to local or toll free line if request received by fax. Will not fax out criminal records. Court makes copy: $.35 per page. Self serve: same. Certification fee: $1.50 per cert. Payee: Seventh Judicial District Court. Only cashiers checks, money orders, and exact change accepted. No credit cards accepted. Mail requests: SASE required.

Estancia Magistrate Court Neil Mertz Judicial Complex, 903 N 5th St, PO Box 274, Estancia, NM 87016; 505-384-2926; fax: 505-384-3157; 8AM-4PM W-F (MST). ***Misdemeanor, Civil Actions under $10,000, Eviction, Small Claims.***
All record requests must be in writing.

Civil Records: Access: Mail, fax, in person, online. Both court and visitors may perform in person searches. No search fee. Closed case files maintained 1 year then archived, record index on computer since 1997. Mail turnaround time 3-5 days. PAT results show name only. Case lookup from 1997 forward is free at www.nmcourts.gov.
Criminal Records: Access: Mail, fax, in person, online. Both court and visitors may perform in person searches. No search fee. Required to search: name, years to search; also helpful: DOB, SSN. Closed case files maintained 1 years then destroyed 1 year from date of closure; record index on computer since 1997 (DWI and VR {domestic cases retained}). Mail turnaround time up to 3 days. Online access to criminal records is free at www.nmcourts.gov. Most but not all online results show middle initial and/or DOB.
General Information: Online identifiers in results same as on public terminal. Will fax documents $1.00 per page. Court makes copy: $.50 per page. Certification fee: $.50. Payee: Magistrate court. No personal checks or credit cards accepted. Mail requests: SASE required.

Moriarty Magistrate Court PO Box 2027, Moriarty, NM 87035; 505-832-4476; fax: 505-832-1563; 8AM-4PM (MST). ***Misdemeanor, Civil Actions under $10,000, Eviction, Small Claims.***
Civil Records: Access: Mail, fax, mail, in person, online. Both court and visitors may perform in person searches. No search fee. Required to search: name, DOB, SSN, years to search. Closed case files maintained 1 year, record index on computer since 1997. Judgments held for 14 years. Mail turnaround time up to 3 days. Civil PAT goes back to 2/1997. PAT results show middle initial, DOB. Case lookup from 1997 forward is free at www.nmcourts.gov.
Criminal Records: Access: Online, mail, in person. Both court and visitors may perform in person searches. No search fee. Required to search: name, years to search; also helpful: DOB, SSN. Closed case files maintained 1 year, record index on computer since 1997. Mail turnaround time up to 3 days. Criminal PAT goes back to same as civil. Terminal results may or may not have complete name or a DOB. Online access to criminal records is free at www.nmcourts.gov. Most but not all online results show middle initial and/or DOB.
General Information: Online identifiers in results same as on public terminal. Will fax documents $1.00 per page. Court makes copy: $.50 per page. No certification fee. Payee: Magistrate Court. No personal checks or credit cards accepted. Mail requests: SASE required.

County Clerk PO Box 767, 205 9th St and Allen, Estancia, NM 87016; 505-246-4735; fax: 505-384-4080; 8AM-5PM (MST). ***Probate.***

Union County

8th Judicial District Court Box 310, Clayton, NM 88415; 575-374-9577; fax: 575-374-2089; 8AM-N, 1-5PM (MST). ***Felony, Civil.***
Civil Records: Access: Mail, in person, online. Both court and visitors may perform in person searches. No search fee. Required to search: name, years to search. Civil cases indexed by defendant, plaintiff; index on cards from 1981. Computerized records start from 1997. Mail turnaround time 1-2 days. Civil PAT goes back to 1997. Case lookup from 1997 forward is free at www.nmcourts.gov.
Criminal Records: Access: Mail, online, in person. Both court and visitors may perform in person searches. No search fee. Required to search: name, years to search. Criminal records on docket sheets from 1981. Computerized records start from 1997. Mail turnaround time 1-2 days. Criminal PAT goes back to same as civil. Terminal results may or may not have complete name or a DOB. Online access to criminal records is free at www.nmcourts.gov. Most but not all online results show middle initial and/or DOB.
General Information: Online identifiers in results same as on public terminal. No adoption, juvenile records released. Will fax documents $.35 per page. Court makes copy: $.35 per page. Self serve: same. Certification fee: $1.50 per cert. Payee: Clerk of District Court. Only cashiers checks and money orders accepted. No credit cards accepted. Mail requests: SASE required.

Magistrate Court 836 Main St, Clayton, NM 88415; 575-374-9472; fax: 575-374-9368; 8AM-N, 12:30-4:30PM (MST). ***Misdemeanor, Civil Actions under $10,000, Eviction, Small Claims.***
The court also handles preliminary felony hearings and felony probable cause.
Civil Records: Access: Mail, in person, online. Only the court performs in person searches; visitors may not. No search fee. Civil cases indexed by defendant, plaintiff. Records available since 6/30/92, computerized since 3/13/97. Mail turnaround time 3 days. Access to court records from 3/13/1997 forward is free at www.nmcourts.gov
Criminal Records: Access: Mail, in person, online. Only the court performs in person searches; visitors may not. No search fee. Required to search: name, years to search; also helpful: address, DOB, SSN. Records computerized since 1/1/03. Mail turnaround time 3 days. Online access to criminal records is free at www.nmcourts.gov. Most but not all online results show middle initial and/or DOB.
General Information: Online identifiers in results same as on public terminal. Will fax documents $1.00 per page. Court makes copy: $.50 per page. Payee: Magistrate Court. No personal checks or credit cards accepted. Mail requests: SASE required.

County Clerk PO Box 430, 200 Court St, Clayton, NM 88415; 575-374-9491; fax: 575-374-9591; 9AM-N, 1-5PM (MST). ***Probate.***

Valencia County

13th Judicial District Court Box 1089, Los Lunas, NM 87031; 505-865-4291; fax: 505-865-8801; 8AM-5PM (MST). ***Felony, Civil.***
www.13districtcourt.com
Civil Records: Access: Fax, mail, online, in person. Both court and visitors may perform in person searches. Search fee: $2.50 per name; 5.00 for 2, $10.00 for 3-10 names. Required to search: name, years to search. Civil cases indexed by defendant, plaintiff; index on microfiche from 1915. Mail turnaround time 10 days. Civil PAT goes back to 1996. Access to court records from 1996 forward is free at www.nmcourts.gov. Also, view all civil jury verdicts in the 13th Judicial District Court free back to 1995 at www.13districtcourt.com/verdict/jury_verdict_intro.php.
Criminal Records: Access: Mail, online, in person. Both court and visitors may perform in person searches. Search fee: $2.50 per name; 5.00 for 2, $10.00 for 3-10 names. Required to search: name, years to search. Criminal records on microfiche from 1915. Mail turnaround time 2-10 days. Criminal PAT goes back to 1996. Terminal results may or may not have complete name or a DOB. Online access to criminal records is free at www.nmcourts.gov. Most but not all online results show middle initial and/or DOB.
General Information: Online identifiers in results same as on public terminal. No adoption or juvenile records released. Will fax documents $2.50 in-state; $5.00 out-of-state. Court makes copy: $.35 per page; $.50 from microfilm. Found copy- $2.50 in-state; $5.00 out of state. Self serve: same. Certification fee: $1.50 per cert. Payee: 13th Judicial District Court. Only cashiers checks and money orders accepted. No credit cards accepted. Mail requests: SASE required.

Belen Magistrate Court 901 W Castillo, Belen, NM 87002; 505-864-7509; fax: 505-864-9532; 8AM-4PM (MST). ***Misdemeanor, Civil Actions under $10,000, Eviction, Small Claims.***
Civil Records: Access: Online, mail, in person. Only the court performs in person searches; visitors may not. No search fee. Civil cases indexed by defendant, plaintiff. Physical records held 1 year, domestic violence 2 years. Mail turnaround time 1 day. Case lookup from 1997 forward is free at www.nmcourts.gov.
Criminal Records: Access: Online, mail, in person. Only the court performs in person searches; visitors may not. No search fee. Required to search: name, years to search, DOB, date of offense; also helpful: address, SSN. Physical records held 2 years, DUI held since 1997. Mail turnaround time 2 days. Online access to criminal records is free at www.nmcourts.gov. Most but not all online results show middle initial and/or DOB.
General Information: Online identifiers in results same as on public terminal. Will fax documents to local or toll-free number. Court makes copy: $.50 per page. No certification fee. No personal checks or credit cards accepted. Mail requests: SASE required.

Los Lunas Magistrate Court 1206 Main St, Los Lunas, NM 87031; 505-865-4637; fax: 505-865-0639; 8AM-4PM (MST). ***Misdemeanor, Civil Actions under $10,000, Eviction, Small Claims.***
Civil Records: Access: Online, mail, in person. Only the court performs in person searches; visitors may not. No search fee. Civil cases indexed by both plaintiff & defendant. Mail turnaround time 3 days. Case lookup from 1997 forward is free at www.nmcourts.gov.
Criminal Records: Access: Online, mail, in person. Only the court performs in person searches; visitors may not. No search fee. Required to search: name, years to search, DOB; also helpful: SSN. Mail turnaround time 3 days. Online access to criminal records is free at www.nmcourts.gov. Most but not all online results show middle initial and/or DOB.
General Information: Online identifiers in results same as on public terminal. Will not fax documents. Court makes copy: $.50 per page. Certification fee: $1.00 per copy. Payee: Los Lunas Magistrate Court. Personal checks accepted; credit cards are not.

County Clerk PO Box 969, 444 Luna Ave, Los Lunas, NM 87031; 505-866-2073; fax: 505-866-2023; 8AM-4:30PM (MST). ***Probate.***
www.co.valencia.nm.us/Clerk.htm

New Mexico Recording Offices

ORGANIZATION: 33 counties, 33 recording offices. The recording officer is the County Clerk. Most New Mexico counties maintain both a grantor/grantee index and a miscellaneous index. New Mexico is entirely in the Mountain Time Zone (MST).

REAL ESTATE RECORDS: Most counties will not perform real estate searches. Copy and certification fees vary.

UCC RECORDS: Financing statements are filed at the state level except for real estate related collateral which are filed with the County Clerk. However, prior to July, 2001, consumer goods and farm collateral were also filed at the County Clerk and these older records can be searched there. Only a few recording offices will perform UCC searches. Use search request form UCC-11.

TAX LIEN RECORDS: All federal and state tax liens are filed with the County Clerk. Most counties will not provide tax lien searches.

OTHER LIENS: Judgment, mechanics, lis pendens, contractors, hospital.

ONLINE ACCESS: A growing number of counties offer online access. Access UCCs on the statewide system free at http://secure.sos.state.nm.us/ucc/default.asp.

Bernalillo County

County Clerk, PO Box 542, Albuquerque, NM 87103-0542. 505-468-1290, R/E recording phone-505-768-4268; fax-505-768-4190; 8AM-5PM (MST) www.bernco.gov/live/departments.asp?dept=2315

Index: Separate indices to search include computer back to 1978, microfiche pre-1978. Records indexed on 7 public use terminals back to 1978. Office personnel or visitors may perform searches, but office search is limited to current owner and other simple data 1978 to present. No fee for search. Copy fee $1.00 per page. Cert fee- $1.00 per doc plus copy fee. Payee- Bernalillo County. Bulk data available for purchase on microfilm, contact Denene at 505-468-1237. **Online access to Real Estate, Deed, Lien, Judgment, Death, Marriage, UCC records:** Search recorders data and Grantor/Grantee index free at www.bernco.gov/live/departments.asp?dept=2315 . Free registration but small charge for copies of images. **Other phones:** Treasurer- 505-768-4031; Elections- 505-468-1290; Vital Records- 505-841-4185; Maps/Plats- 505-222-3700 x5; Alt Customer Svc -505-468-1238. **Property tax/Assessing-** PO Box 27108, 501 Tujeras NW (87102), Albuquerque, NM 87125; 505-222-3700, assessor fax- 505-222-3770. **Online access-** Search assessor records at www.bernco.gov/property/default.asp?qpaction=search_form&type=situs.

Catron County

County Clerk, PO Box 197, Reserve, NM 87830-0197. Recording, R/E & UCC phone-575-533-6400; fax-575-533-6400; 8AM-4:30PM (MST)

May provide unofficial searches as a courtesy, and if mail and copy fees prepaid. Index: All in one. Records indexed on a public use terminal back to 1921. Office will perform a UCC search but public must search other records themselves. Copy fee $1.00 per page if mailed. Cert fee- $1.00 per doc plus copy fee. Payee- Catron County Clerk. **Other phones:** Treasurer- 575-533-6384; Elections- 575-533-6400. **Property tax/Assessing-** PO Box 416, Reserve, NM 87830; 575-533-6577, assessor fax- 575-533-6556.

Chaves County

County Clerk, PO Box 580, Roswell, NM 88202-0580. Recording, R/E & UCC phone-575-624-6614; fax-575-624-6523; 8AM-5PM (MST) http://co.chaves.nm.us/clerk.htm

Index: Separate indices to search include computer and old records in books. Records indexed on a public use terminal back to 1987, some to 1983. Only the public may search. Search fee for older records- $5.00 per name. General copy fee $1.00 per page. Will fax back doc for $5.00 each.Real estate or tax lien copy- $.25 per page. Cert fee- $1.00 per doc plus copy fee. Payee- Chaves County Clerk. Bulk data available for purchase by the book on CD; contact Marina. **Other phones:** Treasurer- 575-624-6618; Elections- 575-624-6614; Vital Records- 575-827-0121. **Property tax/Assessing-** #1 St Mary Pl #130, Roswell, NM 88203; 575-624-6603, assessor fax- 575-624-6647. (Appraiser/Auditor- 575-624-6603) A public access terminal is available. http://co.chaves.nm.us/assessor/

Cibola County

County Clerk, PO Box 190, Grants, NM 87020. 505-287-2539, R/E recording phone-505-285-2539; fax-505-285-2562; 8AM-5PM.

Index: All in one. Records indexed on computer. Office will perform a real estate search but public must search other records themselves. Copy fee $1.00 per page. Cert fee- $2.00 per doc includes copy fee. Payee- Cibola County Clerk. **Other phones:** Treasurer- 505-285-2520; Elections- 505-285-2540. **Property tax/Assessing-** 515 W High St, Grants, NM 87020; 505-285-2527, assessor fax- 505-285-2561.

Colfax County

County Clerk, PO Box 159, Raton, NM 87740-0159. Recording, R/E & UCC phone-575-445-5551; fax-575-445-4031; 8AM-5PM (MST)

Index: All in one. Records indexed on a public use terminal back to 1985. Only the public may search. Will not search UCC records. Copy fee $.35 per page. Plats/surveys- $3.50 small, $7.00 large. Cert fee- $1.00 per doc plus copy fee. Payee- Colfax County Clerk. **Other phones:** Treasurer- 575-445-3171; Elections- 575-445-5551; Vital Records- 866-534-0051. **Property tax/Assessing-** PO Box 427, Raton, NM 87740; 575-445-2314, assessor fax- 575-445-2207. hours- 7AM-3:30PM (summer hours) 8AM-N 1PM-5PM Public access terminal available.

Curry County

County Clerk, PO Box 1168, Clovis, NM 88102-1168. Recording, R/E & UCC phone-575-763-5591; fax-575-763-4232; 8AM-5PM (MST)

Index: All in one. Records indexed on a public use terminal back to 00. Only the public may search. Copy fee $.25 per page, $1.00 per page for UCC. Cert fee- $1.00 per doc plus copy fee. Payee- Curry County Clerk. **Other phones:** Treasurer- 575-763-3931; Elections- 575-763-5591; Vital Records- 505-827-0121. **Property tax/Assessing-** 700 N Main St, #6, Clovis, NM 88101; 575-763-5731 x149, assessor fax- 575-763-8097. (Appraiser/Auditor- 575-763-6581) A public access terminal is available.

De Baca County

County Clerk, PO Box 347, Fort Sumner, NM 88119. Recording, R/E & UCC phone-575-355-2601; fax-575-355-2441; 8AM-N, 1-4:30PM (MST)

Index: All in one. Record index not computerized. Only the public may search. Copy fee $.50 per page. Cert fee- $1.50 per doc plus copy fee. Payee- De Baca County Clerk. **Other phones:** Treasurer- 575-355-7395; Elections- 575-355-2601. **Property tax/Assessing-** 248 Ave C, Courthouse Sq, Fort Sumner, NM 88119; 575-355-7448. (Appraiser/Auditor- 575-355-7448)

Dona Ana County

County Clerk, 845 N Motel Blvd, #1-200, Las Cruces, NM 88005-2893. 575-525-6135; fax-575-525-6159; 8AM-5PM (MST) www.donaanacounty.org

Index: All in one. Records indexed on a public use terminal back to 1979. Only the public may search. Copy fee $.50 per page. Cert fee- $1.50 per doc plus copy fee. Payee- Dona Ana County Clerk. **Other phones:** Treasurer- 575-525-5931; Elections- 575-525-6147; Vital Records- 575-827-0121. **Property tax/Assessing-** 845 N Motel Blvd, Las Cruces, NM 88005; 575-647-7400, assessor fax- 575-525-5538. (Appraiser/Auditor- 575-525-5500) **Online access-** Access county real property index free at www.donaanacounty.org/clerk/docs/. Index search free; Login and password is required to view documents; contact the office of the assessor for an access agreement. Access property data free on the GIS-mapping site at http://gis.co.dona-ana.nm.us/advparcels/viewer.htm. No name searching. Use the black circle with the 'I' in it to show parcel data.

Eddy County

County Clerk, 101 W Greene St, Rm 312, Carlsbad, NM 88220. Recording, R/E & UCC phone-575-885-3383; fax-575-234-1793; 8AM-5PM.

Index: All in one. Records indexed on a public use terminal back to 1980. Only the public may search. Will help look up UCC records. Copy fee $.50 per page. Cert fee- $1.00 per doc plus copy fee. Payee- Eddy County Clerk. Bulk data available for purchase, contact Robin Van Natta. **Other phones:** Treasurer- 575-885-3913; Elections- 575-885-3383; Vital Records- 505-827-0121. **Property tax/Assessing-** 101 W Greene St, Rm 319, Carlsbad, NM 88220; 575-885-3813, assessor fax- 575-887-3331. (Appraiser/Auditor- 575-885-3813) Public access terminal available.

Grant County

County Clerk, PO Box 898, Silver City, NM 88062. Recording, R/E & UCC phone-575-574-0042; fax-575-574-0076; 8AM-5PM.

Index: All in one. Records indexed on a public use terminal back to 1978. Office will perform a UCC search but public must search other records themselves. Copy fee $.25 per page. Cert fee- $1.00 per page plus copy fee. Payee- Grant County Clerk. **Other phones:** Treasurer- 575-574-0055; Elections- 575-574-0042. **Property tax/Assessing-** PO Box 972, 1400 Hwy 180 E, Silver City, NM 88062; 575-574-

0030, assessor fax- 575-574-0074. (Appraiser/Auditor- 575-574-0030) A public access terminal is available.

Guadalupe County

County Clerk, 420 Parker Ave, #1; Courthouse, Santa Rosa, NM 88435. Recording, R/E & UCC phone-575-472-3791; fax-575-472-4791; 8AM-N, 1PM-5PM.
Index: Separate indices to search include deeds, misc, mortgages, judgments, marriage licenses. Records indexed on a public use terminal back to 1983. Only the public may search. Copy fee $1.00 per page if mailed back; $.50 in person. Cert fee- $3.00 per doc plus copy fee. Payee- Guadalupe Co.Clerk. **Other phones:** Treasurer- 575-472-3133; Elections- 575-472-3741; Vital Records- 575-472-3211. **Property tax/Assessing**- 1448 Historic Rte 66, #3, Santa Rosa, NM 88435; 575-472-3738, assessor fax- 575-472-3735. (Appraiser/Auditor- 575-472-3738) hours- 8AM-5PM A public access terminal is available.

Harding County

County Clerk, PO Box 1002, Mosquero, NM 87733-1002. Recording, R/E & UCC phone-575-673-2301; fax-575-673-2922; 8AM-4PM (MST) www.hardingcounty.org
No vital statistic records - see state records section.
Index: Separate indices to search include mortgage, oil & gas, quit claim deeds, plats, patents, warranty deed all in real estate and miscellaneous. Records indexed on computer from 1998. Only the public may search. General copy fee $.50 per page.R/E record copy-$.25 if from book; $.50 if from microfiche. Cert fee- $1.00 per doc plus copy fee. Payee- Harding County Clerk. **Other phones:** Treasurer- 575-673-2928; Elections- 575-673-2301; Vital Records- 505-827-0121 (Info-505-827-2338). **Property tax/Assessing**- PO Box 1002, 35 Pine St, Mosquero, NM 87733; 575-673-2926. (Appraiser/Auditor- 575-673-2926) Public access terminal available.

Hidalgo County

County Clerk, 300 Shakespeare St, Lordsburg, NM 88045. 575-542-9213; fax-575-542-3193; 9AM-5PM (MST)
Index: All in one. Records indexed on computer back to 9/95. Only the public may search. Copy fee $.25 per page. Cert fee- $1.25 per cert includes copy fee. Payee- Hidalgo County Clerk. **Other phones:** Treasurer- 575-542-9313. **Property tax/Assessing**- 300 Shakespeare St, Lordsburg, NM 88045; 575-542-3433, fax- 575-542-3193. No public terminal here.

Lea County

County Clerk, PO Box 1507, Lovington, NM 88260. Recording, R/E & UCC phone-575-396-8614, UCC recording phone-575-396-8638; fax-575-396-3293; 8AM-5PM. www.leacounty.net/Clerk.htm
Index: All in one. Records indexed on a public use terminal back to 1982. Office personnel or visitors may perform searches. Office will not search real estate records. Office will perform very limited searches; office is not bonded. Copy fee none 1st 5 pages, $.50 per page each add'l. Cert fee- No certification fee. Payee- Lea County Clerk. **Other phones:** Treasurer- 575-396-8643; Elections- 575-396-8624; Vital Records- 505-827-0121. **Property tax/Assessing**- 100 N Main, #2, Lovington, NM 88260; 575-396-8626, assessor fax- 575-396-8529. Public access terminal available.

Lincoln County

County Clerk, PO Box 338, Carrizozo, NM 88301. Recording, R/E & UCC phone-575-648-2394; fax-575-648-2576; 8AM-5PM (MST) www.lincolncountynm.net
Index: All in one. Records indexed on a public use terminal back to 1983, and back to 1970 for deeds. Office personnel (will look-up by name only) or visitors may perform searches. Office will search for brief real estate records. Will search UCC records (name only). Copy fee $.25 per page. Cert fee- $1.50 plus copy fee. Payee- Lincoln County Clerk. CDs of bulk data available; contact Diane Shoemaker. **Other phones:** Treasurer- 575-648-2397; Elections- 575-648-2331; Vital Records- 575-648-2394; Manager-575-648-2385. **Property tax/Assessing**- PO Box 38, Carrizozo, NM 88301; 575-648-2306 X5, assessor fax- 575-648-2390. (Appraiser/Auditor- 575-648-2306) Public access terminal available. **Online-** Access to the assessor property records is free at www.lincolncountynm.net/ACCESS[1].htm. Registration, software, username and password is required. Follow prompts at website.

Los Alamos County

County Clerk, PO Box 30, Los Alamos, NM 87544. 505-662-8010; fax-505-662-8008; 8AM-5PM (MST) www.losalamosnm.us/clerk/Pages/default.aspx
Index: Separate indices to search. Records indexed on a public use terminal back to 2000. Office will perform a UCC search but public must search other records themselves. Copy fee $1.00 per page. Cert fee- $1.00 per cert plus copy fee. Payee- Los Alamos County Clerk. Bulk data available for purchase, contact County Clerk office. **Online Real Estate, Deed, Lien records:** Access to recorded data at http://counties.recordfusion.com/countyweb/login.jsp?countyname=LosAlamos - username/password required or logon free at Guest. **Other phones:** Treasurer- 505-662-8070; Elections- 505-662-8011; Vital Records- 505-827-2338. **Property tax/Assessing**- PO Box 30, 2451 Central Ave, #C, Los Alamos, NM 87544; 505-662-8030, assessor fax-505-663-1764. No public terminal available.

Luna County

County Clerk, PO Box 1838, Deming, NM 88031-1838. Recording, R/E & UCC phone-575-546-0491; 8AM-5PM (MST)
Index: All in one. Records indexed on a public use terminal back to 1977. Only the public may search. Copy fee $.50 per page. Will fax back for $1.00 per page. Cert fee- $1.00 per page plus copy fee. Payee- Luna County Clerk. **Other phones:** Treasurer- 575-546-0401; Elections- 575-546-0491; Vital Records-505-827-0121- Santa Fe. **Property tax/Assessing**- 700 S Silver, Deming, NM 88030; 575-546-0404, assessor fax- 575-546-4187.

McKinley County

County Clerk, PO Box 1268, Gallup, NM 87301. 505-863-6866; fax-505-863-1419; 8AM-5PM (MST) www.co.mckinley.nm.us
Index: Separate indices to search include grantor/grantee, books, Microfiche. Records indexed on a public use terminal back to 8/1/89. Only the public may search but office will perform a limited search of computer data only. Office will not search UCC records. General copy fee $.50 per page. Will fax back for $1.50. Cert fee- $2.00 per cert plus copy fee. Payee- McKinley County Clerk. **Other phones:** Treasurer- 505-722-4459; Elections- 505-722-4469; Vitals- 505-821-0121. **Property tax/ Assessing**- 207 W Hill Ave, #102, Gallup, NM 87301; 505-863-3032, assessor fax- 505-863-6517. (Appraiser/Auditor- 505-863-3032) Public access terminal available.

Mora County

County Clerk, PO Box 360, Mora, NM 87732-0360. Recording, R/E & UCC phone-575-387-2448; fax-575-387-9023; 8AM-4:30PM (MST)
Index: Separate indices to search include grantor/grantee. Records indexed on computer back to 2007. Prior on books. Office personnel or visitors may perform searches. General index search fee $10.00 per name per 10 years. Office will search real estate records. Will search UCC records. Copy fee $1.00 per page. Cert fee- $2.00 per doc includes copy fee. Payee- Mora County Clerk. **Other phones:** Treasurer- 575-387-2756; Elections- 575-387-2448. **Property tax/Assessing**- PO Box 609, Mora, NM 87732; 575-387-5289, assessor fax- 575-387-9040. (Appraiser/Auditor- 575-387-5289);

Otero County

County Clerk, 1000 New York Ave, Rm 108, Alamogordo, NM 88310-6932. Recording, R/E & UCC phone-575-437-4942; fax-575-443-2922; 7:30AM-6PM (MST) www.co.otero.nm.us
Index: All in one. Records indexed on computer back to 1985. Office will perform a UCC search but public must search other records themselves. Copy fee $.25 per page. Cert fee- $1.00 per page plus copy fee. Payee- Otero County Clerk. **Other phones:** Treasurer- 575-437-2030; Elections- 575-437-4942; Vitals- 575-437-0121. **Property tax/Assessing**- 1000 New York Ave, Rm 109, Alamogordo, NM 88310; 575-437-5310, assessor fax- 575-443-2918. www.co.otero.nm.us **Online access**- Search the treasurer's tax data inquiry site free at http://ocwebserver2.co.otero.nm.us:81/webtaxinq/default.asp?action=taxdatainq.

Quay County

County Clerk, PO Box 1225, Tucumcari, NM 88401-1225. Recording, R/E & UCC phone-575-461-0510; fax-575-461-0513; 8AM-5PM (MST)
Index: All in one. Records indexed on a public use terminal back to 1980. Office personnel or visitors may perform searches. Copy fee $.50 per page. Cert fee- $1.00 per page plus copy fee. Payee- Quay County Clerk. Bulk data available for purchase, contact County Clerk. **Other phones:** Treasurer- 575-461-0470; Elections- 575-461-0510; Vital Records-575-827-2532. **Property tax/Assessing**- PO Box 1227, Tucumcari, NM 88401; 575-461-1760, assessor fax- 575-461-8465. (Appraiser/Auditor- 575-461-1760) No public terminal available.

Rio Arriba County

County Clerk, PO Box 158, Tierra Amarilla, NM 87575. 575-588-7724; fax-575-588-7418; 8AM-5PM
Index: All in one. Records indexed on a public use terminal back to 1997; computer located in Assessor's office next door. Only the public may search. Copy fee $.50 per page. Cert fee- $1.00 per cert plus copy fee. Payee- Rio Arriba County Clerk. **Other phones:** Treasurer- 505-588-7727. **Property tax/Assessing**- 7 Main St, Courthouse, Tierra Amarilla, NM 87575; 575-588-7726.

Roosevelt County

County Clerk, 109 W 1st Lobby Box 4, Portales, NM 88130. 575-356-8562; fax-575-356-3560; 8AM-5PM. www.rooseveltcounty.com
Index: Separate indices to search include real property, mortgage deeds, oil & gas, mineral deed, warranty deeds, miscellaneous records, plats, surveys, marriage license. Records indexed on computer back to 1986. Only the public may search. Copy fee $.15 for 8 1/2 x 11; $.25 for 8 1/2 x 14; $.50 for 11 x 17.Real estate or tax lien copy- $.50 per page. Cert fee- $.50 per page plus copy fee. Payee- Roosevelt County Clerk. Bulk data available for purchase. **Other phones:** Treasurer- 575-356-4081. **Property tax/Assessing**- 109 W 1st, Portales, NM 88130; 575-356-6971. Public access terminal in clerk's office.

San Juan County

County Clerk, PO Box 550, Aztec, NM 87410. 505-334-9471; fax-505-334-3635; 7AM-5:30PM. www.sjcounty.net/Dpt/Clerk/Index.aspx
Index: All in one. Records indexed on a public use terminal back to 1983. Only the public may search. Copy fee $.50 per page. Cert fee- $1.00 per cert plus copy fee. Payee- County Clerks Office. **Other phones:** Treasurer- 505-334-9421; Elections- 505-334-9471. **Property tax/Assessing**- 100 S Oliver Dr, #400, Aztec, NM 87410; 505-334-6157, assessor fax-505-334-1669. (Appraiser/Auditor- 505-334-6157) www.sjcassessor.net/ **Online access**- Access to county property tax data is free at www.sjcassessor.net/search.asp.

San Miguel County

County Clerk, 500 W National Ave, #113, Las Vegas, NM 87701. Recording, R/E & UCC phone-505-425-9331; fax-505-454-1799; 8AM-5PM (MST)
Index: All in one. Records indexed on computer back to 1999. Only the public may search. Copy fee $.50 per copy. Cert fee- $2.00 per doc plus copy fee. Payee- San Miguel County. **Other phones:** Treasurer- 505-425-9736; Elections- 505-425-9331; Vital Records- 505-425-9368. **Property tax/Assessing**- 500 W National, #105, Las Vegas, NM 87701; 505-454-1439, assessor fax- 505-454-9625. hours- 8AM-N, 1-5PM M-TH; 8AM-4PM F

Sandoval County

County Clerk, PO Box 40, Bernalillo, NM 87004. 505-867-7572; fax-505-771-8610; 8AM-5PM. www.sandovalcounty.com
Index: All in one. Records indexed on a public use terminal back to 1985. Office will perform a UCC search but public must search other records themselves. If search is pre-1985, index search fee is $5.00 per 5 years searched. Copy fee $1.00 per page. Cert fee- $.75 per doc plus copy fee. Payee- Sandoval County Clerk. **Other phones:** Treasurer- 505-867-7581; Elections- 505-867-7577; Vital Records- 505-841-4185. **Property tax/Assessing**- 711 Camino Del Pueblo, Bernalillo, NM 87004; 505-867-7562, assessor fax-505-867-7596. Appraiser- 505-867-7503. www.sandovalcounty.com/images/assessor/index.htm **Online access**- Access assessor property data free at www.sandovalcounty.com/images/assessor/disclaimer.htm

Santa Fe County

County Clerk, PO Box 1985, Santa Fe, NM 87504-1985. 505-986-6280; fax-505-995-2767; 8AM-5PM (MST) www.santafecounty.org/
Index: All in one. Records indexed on a public use terminal back to 1991. Office personnel or visitors may perform searches. Office will do phone search from 1991-present. No search fee if found on computer. Office will search real estate and UCC records after 1991. Copy fee $.50 per page; $.75 if from microfilm. Cert fee- $1.50 per doc plus $.50 per page, plus copy fee. Payee- Santa Fe County Clerk. Bulk data available for purchase, contact Susan Montoya at 505-995-2763. **Online access to Real Estate, Grantor/Grantee, Deed records:** Access to recorder's grantor/grantee index available by subscription on the WEBXtender Document Imaging System; call Melanie at 505-986-6375. $30.00 setup fee and $25.00 monthly and $7.00 per hour usage fee. **Other phones:** Treasurer- 505-986-6245; Elections- 505-986-6287; Vital Records- 505-827-0121. **Property tax/Assessing**- PO Box 126, 102 Grant Ave, Santa Fe, NM 87504; 505-986-6309, assessor fax- 505-986-6316. (Appraiser/Auditor- 505-986-6300) www.santafecounty.org/ **Online access**- Access to county property data is at www.santafecounty.org/find/appraisal_tax_information.php but registration and account number may be required. Also, for appraisal and tax information for free go to www.santafecounty.org/assessor/appraisal_tax_information.php.

Sierra County

County Clerk, 100 Date St, Truth or Consequences, NM 87901. Recording, R/E & UCC phone-575-894-2840; fax-575-894-2516; 8AM-5PM (MST)
If asked, agency will do computer lookup for you but they are not bonded to do searches. Index: All in one. Records indexed on a public use terminal back to the mid 1980's. Office personnel or visitors may perform searches. Office will not search UCC or real estate records. Copy fee $.50 per copy. Cert fee- $1.00 per cert plus copy fee. Payee- Sierra County Clerk. **Other phones:** Treasurer- 575-894-3524; Elections- 575-894-2840; Vital Records- 575-827-2338. **Property tax/Assessing**- 100 Date St, #15, Truth or Consequences, NM 87901; 575-894-2589, assessor fax- 575-894-2829. No public terminal available.

Socorro County

County Clerk, PO Box I, Socorro, NM 87801. 575-835-3263, R/E recording phone-575-835-0423; fax-575-835-1043; 8AM-5PM (MST)
Index: All in one. Records indexed on a public use terminal back to 1989. Only the public may search. Copy fee $.25 per page, $12.00 for plats. Cert fee- $1.50 per page plus copy fee. Payee- Socorro County. **Other phones:** Treasurer- 575-835-1701; Elections- 575-835-0423; Vital Records- 575-835-0423. **Property tax/Assessing**- PO Box J, 200 Church St, Socorro, NM 87801; 575-835-0714, assessor fax-575-835-0940. (Appraiser/Auditor- 575-835-0714)

Taos County

County Clerk, 105 Albright St, #D, Taos, NM 87571. Recording, R/E & UCC phone-575-737-6380; fax-575-737-6390; 8AM-5PM (MST)
Index: All in one. Records indexed on a public use terminal back to 1980. Only the public may search. Copy fee $.50 per page. Cert fee- $1.50 per cert plus copy fee. Payee- Taos County Clerk. **Other phones:** Treasurer- 575-737-6340; Elections- 575-737-6400; Tax Collector- 575-737-6340. **Property tax/Assessing**- 105 Albright St, #F, Taos, NM 87571; 575-737-6360, fax- 575-737-6379. (Appraiser - 575-737-6360) www.taoscounty.org/index.asp?nid=93

Torrance County

County Clerk, PO Box 48, Estancia, NM 87016. 505-246-4735; fax-505-384-4080; 8AM-5PM (MST)
Index: All in one. Records indexed on a public use terminal back to 1985. Only the public may search. Copy fee $1.00 per page. Cert fee- $1.00 per doc plus copy fee. Payee- Torrance County Clerk. **Other phones:** Treasurer- 505-246-4787. **Property tax/Assessing**- PO Box 58, Estancia, NM 87016; 505-246-4727, assessor fax- 505-384-4362. Public access terminal available.

Union County

County Clerk, PO Box 430, Clayton, NM 88415. Recording, R/E & UCC phone-575-374-9491; fax-575-374-9591; 9AM-5PM (MST)
Index: All in one. Records indexed on a public use terminal back to 1987. Only the public may search. General copy fee $.50 per page. UCC copy fee- $1.00 per page. Cert fee- $1.00 per page plus copy fee. Payee- Union County Clerk. **Other phones:** Treasurer- 575-374-2331; Elections- 575-374-9491. **Property tax/Assessing**- PO Box 430, Clayton, NM 88415; 575-374-9441, assessor fax- 575-374-9442. (Appraiser/Auditor- 575-374-9441) Public use computer available.

Valencia County

County Clerk, PO Box 969, Los Lunas, NM 87031. 505-866-2073; fax-505-866-2023; 8AM-4:30PM. www.co.valencia.nm.us/County%20Clerk/County_Clerk.html
Index: All in one. Records indexed on computer back to 1989, prior in indexes by date and letter. Only the public may search. General copy fee $.50 if in person, $1.00 if mail request. Cert fee- $2.50 per cert plus copy fee. Payee- County Clerk. **Other phones:** Treasurer- 505-866-2090; Elections- 505-866-2080; Vital Records- 505-841-4100. **Property tax/Assessing**- PO Box 909, 444 Luna Ave, Los Lunas, NM 87031; 505-866-2065, assessor fax- 505-866-2025. 8AM-5PM. Public terminal is available. www.co.valencia.nm.us/County%20Assesor/County_Assessor.html **Online access**- Access to GIS/mapping for free go to www.co.valencia.nm.us/GIS/GIS.html.

New Mexico County Locator

You will usually be able to find the city name in the City/County Cross Reference below. In that case, it is a simple matter to determine the county from the cross reference. However, only the official US Postal Service city names are included in this index. There are an additional 40,000 place names that people use in their addresses. Therefore, we have also included a ZIP/City Cross Reference immediately following the City/County Cross Reference.

If you know the ZIP Code but the city name does not appear in the City/County Cross Reference index, look up the ZIP Code in the ZIP/City Cross Reference, find the city name, then look up the city name in the City/County Cross Reference. For example, you want to know the county for an address of Menands, NY 12204. There is no "Menands" in the City/County Cross Reference. The ZIP/City Cross Reference shows that ZIP Codes 12201-12288 are for the city of Albany. Looking back in the City/County Cross Reference, Albany is in Albany County.

New Mexico City/County Cross Reference

ABIQUIU Rio Arriba
ALAMOGORDO Otero
ALBUQUERQUE Bernalillo
ALBUQUERQUE Sierra
ALCALDE Rio Arriba
ALGODONES Sandoval
ALTO Lincoln
AMALIA Taos
AMISTAD Union
ANGEL FIRE Colfax
ANIMAS Hidalgo
ANTHONY (88021) Dona Ana(98), Otero(1)
ANTON CHICO Guadalupe
ARAGON Catron
ARENAS VALLEY Grant
ARREY Sierra
ARROYO HONDO Taos
ARROYO SECO Taos
ARTESIA Eddy
AZTEC San Juan
BARD Quay
BAYARD Grant
BELEN Valencia
BELL RANCH San Miguel
BELLVIEW Curry
BENT Otero
BERINO Dona Ana
BERNALILLO Sandoval
BINGHAM Socorro
BLANCO San Juan
BLOOMFIELD San Juan
BLUEWATER Cibola
BOSQUE (87006) Socorro(83), Valencia(16)
BOSQUE FARMS Valencia
BRIMHALL McKinley
BROADVIEW (88112) Quay(60), Curry(39)
BUCKHORN Grant
BUENA VISTA Mora
BUEYEROS Harding
CABALLO Sierra
CANJILON Rio Arriba
CANNON AFB Curry
CANONES Rio Arriba
CAPITAN Lincoln
CAPROCK Lea
CAPULIN Union
CARLSBAD Eddy
CARRIZOZO (88301) Lincoln(80), Torrance(20)
CARSON Taos
CASA BLANCA Cibola
CAUSEY Roosevelt
CEBOLLA Rio Arriba
CEDAR CREST Bernalillo
CEDARVALE Torrance
CERRILLOS Santa Fe
CERRO Taos
CHACON Mora
CHAMA Rio Arriba
CHAMBERINO Dona Ana
CHAMISAL Taos
CHAPARRAL (88081) Dona Ana(74), Otero(25)
CHIMAYO Rio Arriba
CHURCH ROCK McKinley
CIMARRON Colfax
CLAUNCH Socorro
CLAYTON Union
CLEVELAND Mora
CLIFF Grant
CLINES CORNERS Torrance
CLOUDCROFT Otero
CLOVIS Curry
COCHITI LAKE Sandoval
COCHITI PUEBLO Sandoval
COLUMBUS Luna
CONCHAS DAM San Miguel
CONTINENTAL DIVIDE McKinley
CORDOVA Rio Arriba
CORONA Lincoln
CORRALES (87048) Sandoval(85), Bernalillo(14)
COSTILLA Taos
COUNSELOR Sandoval
COYOTE Rio Arriba
CROSSROADS Lea
CROWNPOINT McKinley
CUBA Sandoval
CUBERO Cibola
CUCHILLO Sierra
CUERVO Guadalupe
DATIL Catron
DEMING Luna
DERRY Sierra
DES MOINES Union
DEXTER Chaves
DIXON Rio Arriba
DONA ANA Dona Ana
DORA Roosevelt
DULCE Rio Arriba
DURAN Torrance
EAGLE NEST Colfax
EDGEWOOD (87015) Santa Fe(69), Torrance(17), Bernalillo(12)
EL PRADO Taos
EL RITO Rio Arriba
ELEPHANT BUTTE Sierra
ELIDA (88116) Roosevelt(94), Chaves(5)
EMBUDO Rio Arriba
ENCINO (88321) Torrance(70), Guadalupe(29)
ESPANOLA Rio Arriba
ESTANCIA Torrance
EUNICE Lea
FAIRACRES Dona Ana
FARMINGTON San Juan
FAYWOOD Grant
FENCE LAKE Cibola
FLORA VISTA San Juan
FLOYD (88118) Roosevelt(94), Curry(5)
FLYING H Chaves
FOLSOM Union
FORT BAYARD Grant
FORT STANTON Lincoln
FORT SUMNER De Baca
FORT WINGATE McKinley
FRUITLAND San Juan
GALLINA Rio Arriba
GALLUP McKinley
GALLUP San Juan
GAMERCO McKinley
GARFIELD Dona Ana
GARITA San Miguel
GILA Grant
GLADSTONE Union
GLENCOE Lincoln
GLENRIO Quay
GLENWOOD Catron
GLORIETA Santa Fe
GONZALES RANCH San Miguel
GRADY (88120) Quay(57), Curry(42)
GRANTS Cibola
GRENVILLE Union
GUADALUPITA Mora
HACHITA Grant
HAGERMAN Chaves
HANOVER Grant
HATCH Dona Ana
HERNANDEZ Rio Arriba
HIGH ROLLS MOUNTAIN PARK Otero
HILLSBORO Sierra
HOBBS Lea
HOLLOMAN AIR FORCE BASE Otero
HOLMAN Mora
HONDO Lincoln
HOPE (88250) Chaves(62), Eddy(37)
HOUSE Quay
HURLEY Grant
ILFELD San Miguel
ISLETA Bernalillo
JAL Lea
JAMESTOWN McKinley
JARALES Valencia
JEMEZ PUEBLO Sandoval
JEMEZ SPRINGS Sandoval
KENNA Roosevelt
KIRTLAND San Juan
KIRTLAND AFB Bernalillo
LA JARA Sandoval
LA JOYA Socorro
LA LOMA Guadalupe
LA LUZ Otero
LA MADERA Rio Arriba
LA MESA Dona Ana
LA PLATA San Juan
LAGUNA Cibola
LAKE ARTHUR (88253) Chaves(96), Eddy(3)
LAKEWOOD Eddy
LAMY Santa Fe
LAS CRUCES Dona Ana
LAS TABLAS Rio Arriba
LAS VEGAS San Miguel
LEDOUX Mora
LEMITAR Socorro
LINDRITH Rio Arriba
LINGO Roosevelt
LLANO Taos
LOCO HILLS Eddy
LOGAN Quay
LORDSBURG Hidalgo
LOS ALAMOS Los Alamos
LOS LUNAS Valencia
LOS OJOS Rio Arriba
LOVING Eddy
LOVINGTON Lea
LUMBERTON Rio Arriba
LUNA Catron
MAGDALENA Socorro
MALAGA Eddy
MALJAMAR Lea
MAXWELL Colfax
MAYHILL (88339) Otero(77), Chaves(22)
MC ALISTER Quay
MC DONALD Lea
MC INTOSH Torrance
MEDANALES Rio Arriba
MELROSE (88124) Curry(83), Quay(11), Roosevelt(5)
MENTMORE McKinley
MESCALERO Otero
MESILLA Dona Ana
MESILLA PARK Dona Ana
MESQUITE Dona Ana
MEXICAN SPRINGS McKinley
MIAMI Colfax
MILAN Cibola
MILLS Harding
MILNESAND Roosevelt
MIMBRES Grant
MONTEZUMA San Miguel
MONTICELLO Sierra
MONUMENT Lea
MORA Mora
MORIARTY Torrance
MOSQUERO Harding
MOUNT DORA Union
MOUNTAINAIR Torrance
MULE CREEK Grant
NAGEEZI San Juan
NARA VISA Quay
NAVAJO (87328) McKinley(87), San Juan(12)
NAVAJO DAM San Juan
NEW LAGUNA Cibola
NEWCOMB San Juan
NEWKIRK Guadalupe
NOGAL Lincoln
OCATE Mora
OIL CENTER Lea
OJO CALIENTE Taos
OJO FELIZ Mora
OJO SARCO Rio Arriba
ORGAN Dona Ana
OROGRANDE Otero
PAGUATE Cibola
PECOS San Miguel
PENA BLANCA Sandoval
PENASCO Taos
PEP Roosevelt

PERALTA Valencia
PETACA Rio Arriba
PICACHO Lincoln
PIE TOWN Catron
PINEHILL Cibola
PINON (88344) Chaves(84), Otero(15)
PINOS ALTOS Grant
PLACITAS Sandoval
PLAYAS Hidalgo
POLVADERA Socorro
PONDEROSA Sandoval
PORTALES Roosevelt
PREWITT (87045) McKinley(78), Cibola(22)
PUEBLO OF ACOMA Valencia
QUAY Quay
QUEMADO Catron
QUESTA Taos
RADIUM SPRINGS Dona Ana
RAINSVILLE Mora
RAMAH (87321) Cibola(57), McKinley(42)
RANCHOS DE TAOS Taos
RATON Colfax
RED RIVER Taos
REDROCK Grant
REGINA Sandoval
REHOBOTH McKinley
RESERVE Catron
RIBERA San Miguel
RINCON Dona Ana
RIO RANCHO Sandoval
ROCIADA (87742) Mora(68), San Miguel(31)
RODARTE Taos
RODEO Hidalgo
ROGERS Roosevelt
ROSWELL Chaves
ROWE San Miguel
ROY Harding
RUIDOSO Lincoln
RUIDOSO DOWNS Lincoln
RUTHERON Rio Arriba
SACRAMENTO Otero
SAINT VRAIN Curry
SALEM Dona Ana
SAN ACACIA Socorro
SAN ANTONIO Socorro
SAN CRISTOBAL Taos
SAN FIDEL Cibola
SAN JON Quay
SAN JOSE San Miguel
SAN JUAN PUEBLO Rio Arriba
SAN MATEO Cibola
SAN MIGUEL Dona Ana
SAN PATRICIO Lincoln
SAN RAFAEL Cibola
SAN YSIDRO Sandoval
SANDIA PARK (87047) Bernalillo(70), Sandoval(18), Santa Fe(11)
SANOSTEE San Juan
SANTA CLARA Grant
SANTA CRUZ Santa Fe
SANTA FE Santa Fe
SANTA ROSA Guadalupe
SANTA TERESA Dona Ana
SANTO DOMINGO PUEBLO Sandoval
SAPELLO San Miguel
SEBOYETA Cibola
SEDAN Union
SENA San Miguel
SENECA Union
SERAFINA San Miguel
SHEEP SPRINGS San Juan
SHIPROCK San Juan
SILVER CITY Grant
SMITH LAKE McKinley
SOCORRO Socorro
SOLANO Harding
SPRINGER Colfax
STANLEY Santa Fe
STEAD Union
SUNLAND PARK Dona Ana
SUNSPOT Otero
TAIBAN (88134) De Baca(72), Roosevelt(20), Quay(8)
TAJIQUE Torrance
TAOS Taos
TAOS SKI VALLEY Taos
TATUM Lea
TERERRO San Miguel
TESUQUE Santa Fe
TEXICO Curry
THOREAU McKinley
TIERRA AMARILLA Rio Arriba
TIJERAS Bernalillo
TIMBERON Otero
TINNIE Lincoln
TOHATCHI McKinley
TOME Valencia
TORREON Torrance
TRAMPAS Taos
TREMENTINA San Miguel
TRES PIEDRAS Taos
TRUCHAS Rio Arriba
TRUTH OR CONSEQUENCES Sierra
TUCUMCARI Quay
TULAROSA Otero
TYRONE Grant
UTE PARK Colfax
VADITO Taos
VADO Dona Ana
VALDEZ Taos
VALLECITOS Rio Arriba
VALMORA Mora
VANADIUM Grant
VANDERWAGEN McKinley
VAUGHN Guadalupe
VEGUITA Socorro
VELARDE Rio Arriba
VILLANUEVA San Miguel
WAGON MOUND Mora
WATERFLOW San Juan
WATROUS Mora
WEED Otero
WHITE SANDS MISSILE RANGE Dona Ana
WHITES CITY Eddy
WILLARD Torrance
WILLIAMSBURG Sierra
WINSTON Sierra
YATAHEY McKinley
YESO De Baca
YOUNGSVILLE Rio Arriba
ZUNI McKinley

New Mexico ZIP/City Cross Reference

87001-87001 ALGODONES
87002-87002 BELEN
87004-87004 BERNALILLO
87005-87005 BLUEWATER
87006-87006 BOSQUE
87007-87007 CASA BLANCA
87008-87008 CEDAR CREST
87009-87009 CEDARVALE
87010-87010 CERRILLOS
87011-87011 CLAUNCH
87012-87012 COYOTE
87013-87013 CUBA
87014-87014 CUBERO
87015-87015 EDGEWOOD
87016-87016 ESTANCIA
87017-87017 GALLINA
87018-87018 COUNSELOR
87020-87020 GRANTS
87021-87021 MILAN
87022-87022 ISLETA
87023-87023 JARALES
87024-87024 JEMEZ PUEBLO
87025-87025 JEMEZ SPRINGS
87026-87026 LAGUNA
87027-87027 LA JARA
87028-87028 LA JOYA
87029-87029 LINDRITH
87031-87031 LOS LUNAS
87032-87032 MC INTOSH
87034-87034 PUEBLO OF ACOMA
87035-87035 MORIARTY
87036-87036 MOUNTAINAIR
87037-87037 NAGEEZI
87038-87038 NEW LAGUNA
87040-87040 PAGUATE
87041-87041 PENA BLANCA
87042-87042 PERALTA
87043-87043 PLACITAS
87044-87044 PONDEROSA
87045-87045 PREWITT
87046-87046 REGINA
87047-87047 SANDIA PARK
87048-87048 CORRALES
87049-87049 SAN FIDEL
87050-87050 SAN MATEO
87051-87051 SAN RAFAEL
87052-87052 SANTO DOMINGO PUEBLO
87053-87053 SAN YSIDRO
87055-87055 SEBOYETA
87056-87056 STANLEY
87057-87057 TAJIQUE
87059-87059 TIJERAS
87060-87060 TOME
87061-87061 TORREON
87062-87062 VEGUITA
87063-87063 WILLARD
87064-87064 YOUNGSVILLE
87068-87068 BOSQUE FARMS
87070-87070 CLINES CORNERS
87072-87072 COCHITI PUEBLO
87083-87083 COCHITI LAKE
87100-87116 ALBUQUERQUE
87117-87117 KIRTLAND AFB
87118-87123 ALBUQUERQUE
87124-87124 RIO RANCHO
87125-87140 ALBUQUERQUE
87144-87144 RIO RANCHO
87151-87158 ALBUQUERQUE
87174-87174 RIO RANCHO
87176-87201 ALBUQUERQUE
87300-87305 GALLUP
87310-87310 BRIMHALL
87311-87311 CHURCH ROCK
87312-87312 CONTINENTAL DIVIDE
87313-87313 CROWNPOINT
87315-87315 FENCE LAKE
87316-87316 FORT WINGATE
87317-87317 GAMERCO
87319-87319 MENTMORE
87320-87320 MEXICAN SPRINGS
87321-87321 RAMAH
87322-87322 REHOBOTH
87323-87323 THOREAU
87324-87324 GALLUP
87325-87325 TOHATCHI
87326-87326 VANDERWAGEN
87327-87327 ZUNI
87328-87328 NAVAJO
87347-87347 JAMESTOWN
87357-87357 PINEHILL
87364-87364 SHEEP SPRINGS
87365-87365 SMITH LAKE
87375-87375 YATAHEY
87401-87402 FARMINGTON
87410-87410 AZTEC
87412-87412 BLANCO
87413-87413 BLOOMFIELD
87415-87415 FLORA VISTA
87416-87416 FRUITLAND
87417-87417 KIRTLAND
87418-87418 LA PLATA
87419-87419 NAVAJO DAM
87420-87420 SHIPROCK
87421-87421 WATERFLOW
87455-87455 NEWCOMB
87461-87461 SANOSTEE
87499-87499 FARMINGTON
87500-87509 SANTA FE
87510-87510 ABIQUIU
87511-87511 ALCALDE
87512-87512 AMALIA
87513-87513 ARROYO HONDO
87514-87514 ARROYO SECO
87515-87515 CANJILON
87516-87516 CANONES
87517-87517 CARSON
87518-87518 CEBOLLA
87519-87519 CERRO
87520-87520 CHAMA
87521-87521 CHAMISAL
87522-87522 CHIMAYO
87523-87523 CORDOVA
87524-87524 COSTILLA
87525-87525 TAOS SKI VALLEY
87527-87527 DIXON
87528-87528 DULCE
87529-87529 EL PRADO
87530-87530 EL RITO
87531-87531 EMBUDO
87532-87533 ESPANOLA
87535-87535 GLORIETA
87536-87536 GONZALES RANCH
87537-87537 HERNANDEZ
87538-87538 ILFELD
87539-87539 LA MADERA
87540-87540 LAMY
87541-87541 LAS TABLAS
87543-87543 LLANO
87544-87545 LOS ALAMOS
87547-87547 LUMBERTON
87548-87548 MEDANALES
87549-87549 OJO CALIENTE
87550-87550 OJO SARCO
87551-87551 LOS OJOS
87552-87552 PECOS
87553-87553 PENASCO
87554-87554 PETACA
87556-87556 QUESTA
87557-87557 RANCHOS DE TAOS
87558-87558 RED RIVER
87560-87560 RIBERA
87561-87561 RODARTE
87562-87562 ROWE
87563-87563 RUTHERON
87564-87564 SAN CRISTOBAL
87565-87565 SAN JOSE
87566-87566 SAN JUAN PUEBLO
87567-87567 SANTA CRUZ
87568-87568 SENA
87569-87569 SERAFINA
87571-87571 TAOS
87573-87573 TERERRO
87574-87574 TESUQUE
87575-87575 TIERRA AMARILLA
87576-87576 TRAMPAS
87577-87577 TRES PIEDRAS
87578-87578 TRUCHAS
87579-87579 VADITO
87580-87580 VALDEZ
87581-87581 VALLECITOS
87582-87582 VELARDE
87583-87583 VILLANUEVA

87592-87594 SANTA FE
87701-87701 LAS VEGAS
87710-87710 ANGEL FIRE
87711-87711 ANTON CHICO
87712-87712 BUENA VISTA
87713-87713 CHACON
87714-87714 CIMARRON
87715-87715 CLEVELAND
87718-87718 EAGLE NEST
87722-87722 GUADALUPITA
87723-87723 HOLMAN
87724-87724 LA LOMA
87725-87725 LEDOUX
87728-87728 MAXWELL
87729-87729 MIAMI
87730-87730 MILLS
87731-87731 MONTEZUMA
87732-87732 MORA
87733-87733 MOSQUERO
87734-87734 OCATE
87735-87735 OJO FELIZ
87736-87736 RAINSVILLE
87740-87740 RATON
87742-87742 ROCIADA
87743-87743 ROY
87745-87745 SAPELLO
87746-87746 SOLANO
87747-87747 SPRINGER
87749-87749 UTE PARK
87750-87750 VALMORA
87752-87752 WAGON MOUND
87753-87753 WATROUS
87801-87801 SOCORRO
87815-87815 BINGHAM
87820-87820 ARAGON
87821-87821 DATIL
87823-87823 LEMITAR
87824-87824 LUNA
87825-87825 MAGDALENA
87827-87827 PIE TOWN
87828-87828 POLVADERA
87829-87829 QUEMADO
87830-87830 RESERVE
87831-87831 SAN ACACIA
87832-87832 SAN ANTONIO
87901-87901 TRUTH OR CONSEQUENCES
87910-87910 ALBUQUERQUE
87930-87930 ARREY
87931-87931 CABALLO
87932-87932 CUCHILLO
87933-87933 DERRY
87935-87935 ELEPHANT BUTTE
87936-87936 GARFIELD
87937-87937 HATCH
87939-87939 MONTICELLO
87940-87940 RINCON
87941-87941 SALEM
87942-87942 WILLIAMSBURG
87943-87943 WINSTON
88000-88001 LAS CRUCES
88002-88002 WHITE SANDS MISSILE RANGE
88003-88007 LAS CRUCES
88008-88008 SANTA TERESA
88009-88009 PLAYAS
88011-88012 LAS CRUCES
88020-88020 ANIMAS
88021-88021 ANTHONY
88022-88022 ARENAS VALLEY
88023-88023 BAYARD
88024-88024 BERINO
88025-88025 BUCKHORN
88026-88026 SANTA CLARA
88027-88027 CHAMBERINO
88028-88028 CLIFF
88029-88029 COLUMBUS
88030-88031 DEMING
88032-88032 DONA ANA
88033-88033 FAIRACRES
88034-88034 FAYWOOD
88036-88036 FORT BAYARD
88038-88038 GILA
88039-88039 GLENWOOD
88040-88040 HACHITA
88041-88041 HANOVER
88042-88042 HILLSBORO
88043-88043 HURLEY
88044-88044 LA MESA
88045-88045 LORDSBURG
88046-88046 MESILLA
88047-88047 MESILLA PARK
88048-88048 MESQUITE
88049-88049 MIMBRES
88051-88051 MULE CREEK
88052-88052 ORGAN
88053-88053 PINOS ALTOS
88054-88054 RADIUM SPRINGS
88055-88055 REDROCK
88056-88056 RODEO
88058-88058 SAN MIGUEL
88061-88062 SILVER CITY
88063-88063 SUNLAND PARK
88065-88065 TYRONE
88072-88072 VADO
88073-88073 VANADIUM
88081-88081 CHAPARRAL
88101-88102 CLOVIS
88103-88103 CANNON AFB
88111-88111 BELLVIEW
88112-88112 BROADVIEW
88113-88113 CAUSEY
88114-88114 CROSSROADS
88115-88115 DORA
88116-88116 ELIDA
88118-88118 FLOYD
88119-88119 FORT SUMNER
88120-88120 GRADY
88121-88121 HOUSE
88122-88122 KENNA
88123-88123 LINGO
88124-88124 MELROSE
88125-88125 MILNESAND
88126-88126 PEP
88130-88130 PORTALES
88132-88132 ROGERS
88133-88133 SAINT VRAIN
88134-88134 TAIBAN
88135-88135 TEXICO
88136-88136 YESO
88201-88203 ROSWELL
88210-88211 ARTESIA
88213-88213 CAPROCK
88220-88221 CARLSBAD
88230-88230 DEXTER
88231-88231 EUNICE
88232-88232 HAGERMAN
88240-88244 HOBBS
88250-88250 HOPE
88252-88252 JAL
88253-88253 LAKE ARTHUR
88254-88254 LAKEWOOD
88255-88255 LOCO HILLS
88256-88256 LOVING
88260-88260 LOVINGTON
88262-88262 MC DONALD
88263-88263 MALAGA
88264-88264 MALJAMAR
88265-88265 MONUMENT
88266-88266 OIL CENTER
88267-88267 TATUM
88268-88268 WHITES CITY
88301-88301 CARRIZOZO
88310-88311 ALAMOGORDO
88312-88312 ALTO
88314-88314 BENT
88316-88316 CAPITAN
88317-88317 CLOUDCROFT
88318-88318 CORONA
88319-88319 DURAN
88321-88321 ENCINO
88322-88322 FLYING H
88323-88323 FORT STANTON
88324-88324 GLENCOE
88325-88325 HIGH ROLLS MOUNTAIN PARK
88330-88330 HOLLOMAN AIR FORCE BASE
88336-88336 HONDO
88337-88337 LA LUZ
88338-88338 LINCOLN
88339-88339 MAYHILL
88340-88340 MESCALERO
88341-88341 NOGAL
88342-88342 OROGRANDE
88343-88343 PICACHO
88344-88344 PINON
88345-88345 RUIDOSO
88346-88346 RUIDOSO DOWNS
88347-88347 SACRAMENTO
88348-88348 SAN PATRICIO
88349-88349 SUNSPOT
88350-88350 TIMBERON
88351-88351 TINNIE
88352-88352 TULAROSA
88353-88353 VAUGHN
88354-88354 WEED
88355-88355 RUIDOSO
88401-88401 TUCUMCARI
88410-88410 AMISTAD
88411-88411 BARD
88412-88412 BUEYEROS
88414-88414 CAPULIN
88415-88415 CLAYTON
88416-88416 CONCHAS DAM
88417-88417 CUERVO
88418-88418 DES MOINES
88419-88419 FOLSOM
88421-88421 GARITA
88422-88422 GLADSTONE
88423-88423 GLENRIO
88424-88424 GRENVILLE
88426-88426 LOGAN
88427-88427 MC ALISTER
88429-88429 MOUNT DORA
88430-88430 NARA VISA
88431-88431 NEWKIRK
88432-88432 SANTA ROSA
88433-88433 QUAY
88434-88434 SAN JON
88435-88435 SANTA ROSA
88436-88436 SEDAN
88437-88437 SENECA
88438-88438 STEAD
88439-88439 TREMENTINA
88441-88441 BELL RANCH

New York

General Help Numbers:

Governor's Office

Executive Chamber, State Capitol — 518-474-8390
Albany, NY 12224 — Fax 518-474-1513
www.ny.gov/governor/ — 9AM-5PM

Attorney General's Office

State Capitol — 518-474-7330
Albany, NY 12224-0341 — Fax 518-473-9909
www.oag.state.ny.us — 9AM-5:30PM

Legislative Records

State Capitol — 518-455-2312
State Street Rm 317 — Fax 518-426-6841
Albany, NY 12247 — 9AM-5PM
http://public.lcginfo.state.ny.us/menuf.cgi

State Archives

Empire State Plaza — 518-474-8955
Cultural Education Center, 11D40 — Fax 518-473-9985
Albany, NY 12230 — 9AM-5PM
http://www.nysarchives.org/gindex.shtml

State Specifics:

Capital:	Albany Albany County
Time Zone:	EST
Number of Counties:	62
Population:	19,490,297
Web Site:	www.ny.gov

State Agencies

Criminal Records

Access to Records is Restricted.

Division of Criminal Justice Services, Record Review Unit, 4 Tower Place, Stuyvesant Plaza, Albany, NY 12203; 518-457-6043, 518-485-7675, Fax- 518-457-6550; 8AM-5PM.

www.criminaljustice.state.ny.us

Email questions- RecordReview@dcjs.state.ny.us. Records are only released pursuant to court order, subpoena, to entities authorized by statute, or to person of record. The public must search at the county court level and via the state OCA system. One may obtain their own personal criminal history record review by requesting a Record Review Packet from DCJS, and following the directions for the completion and submission of a fingerprint card to DCJS, along with a fee of $50.

Statewide Court Records

NY State Office of Court Administration, Office History Record Search, 25 Beaver St, Rm 840, New York, NY 10004; 212-428-2100, 212-428-2990, 212-428-2493 (Search Unit), Fax- 212-428-2190; 9AM-5PM. www.courts.state.ny.us

The details below primarily refer to criminal court cases. The OCA mandates that all criminal record requests made to county Supreme Court Clerks and City Courts be forwarded to this office for processing. Direct questions to question@courts.state.ny.us.

Indexing & Storage: New records available for inquiry in 24 hours in NYC; 7 days rest of state.

Searching: Most counties provide felony case information back to 1981. Notable exceptions are New York (1987), Richmond (1987), and Kings (1987). NYS town and village court criminal disposition data contains approx. 20% of cases since 2003. Include in request- name, DOB, and SASE. Conviction and "pending" records are reported. This data not released- misdemeanor records prior to 2003.

Access by: mail, phone, in person, online. **Fee & Payment:** The fee for a statewide search is $55.00. Fee payee- NYS Office of Court Administration Prepayment or pre-approved account required. Personal checks accepted. Credit cards are not.

Mail search: Turnaround time- 2 days or more. The search is a statewide search. **Phone search:** The Search Unit is available from 10 AM to 4 PM.

In person: Records may be requested at this office and picked up the next day.

Online search: The OCA offers online or email access to criminal case records for approved requesters. Call the OCA to set up an account. The fee is $55.00 per record. Criminal History Record Search Unit can be reached at 212-428-2943 or www.nycourts.gov/apps/chrs/. Visit http://iapps.courts.state.ny.us/webcivil/ecourtsMain. This site provides access to a number of records, including WebCrims to criminal case dockets with future appearance dates in 13 counties. Also from here access or monitor Supreme Court and Family Court case information on open cases for all 62 counties, open landlord tenant cases from NYC, and open family court cases from all 62 counties.

Sexual Offender Registry

Division of Criminal Justice Svcs, Sexual Offender Registry, 4 Tower Place, Rm 604, Albany, NY 12203; 518-457-3167 (Main Number), 800-262-3257 (Search), Fax- 518-485-5805; 8AM-5PM.

www.criminaljustice.state.ny.us/nsor/index.htm

There are over 25,000 sex offenders registered in the state.

Indexing & Storage: Records available back to 01/22/96. New records available for inquiry in 1 day.

Searching: Local law enforcement is required to maintain the database for the public to view upon request. Include in request- name, and one of following if by mail, fax or phone: SSN, DOB, DL# or exact address. Email questions to infodcjs@dcjs.state.ny.us.

Access by: mail, phone, fax, online.

Fee & Payment: There is no fee to use the 800 telephone.

Mail search: Turnaround time- 1 week.

Phone search: Search requests can be done over the phone. Lengthy lists should be mailed or faxed.

Fax search: Will respond to a toll free or local fax line.

Online search: The sex offender registry of level 2 and 3 can be searched at the website. Search by last name, ZIP or by county.

Incarceration Records

New York Department of Correctional Services, Building 2 - Central Files, 1220 Washington Ave, Albany, NY 12226-2050; 518-457-5000, 518-457-8126 (Contact phone), Fax- 518-457-4966; 8AM-4PM. www.docs.state.ny.us

Written requests should be directed to FOIA Unit.

Indexing & Storage: Records available on current and former inmates. New records available for inquiry in 1 to 20 days.

Searching: Include in request- full name; the DOB, SSN, and DIN (inmate number) are helpful. Location, DIN number, conviction and sentencing information, and release dates are provided.

Access by: mail, phone, fax, online.

Fee & Payment: There is no search fee. Copy fee is $.25 per page.

Mail search: Turnaround time- 7 to 10 days. A SASE is requested.

Phone search: Limited name searching by phone is available from the agency. For information on the location of a NYS prison inmate, call 518-457-5000 during normal business hours.

Fax search: Requests accepted via fax

Online search: Computerized inmate information is available from the Inmate Lookup at http://nysdocslookup.docs.state.ny.us/kinqw00 or follow "inmate lookup" link at main site. Records go back to early 1970s. To acquire inmate DIN number, you may call 518-457-5000. The site is open, in general, from Mon. thru Sat. 2:00 a.m.-11:00 p.m. & Sun. 4:00 a.m. thru 11:00 p.m. which has state DOC data but not data from all counties.

Corporation, LP, LLC, LLP

Division of Corporations, Sec. of State, One Commerce Plaza, 99 Washington Avenue, #600, Albany, NY 12231; 518-473-2492 (General Info), Fax- 518-473-1654; 8:30AM-4:30PM.

www.dos.state.ny.us

Assumed name certificates are filed directly with the county clerk in each county in which the entity conducts or transacts business, unless the entity is a corporation, LLC or LP and wishes to file here.

Indexing & Storage: Records available from inception (1811). Information on active entities is automated. Records on entities inactive prior to 1978 are not automated and require additional research. New records available for inquiry immediately.

Searching: Information available includes date of incorporation, subsequent filings, status, principle business location, registered agent, service of process address, number and type of stock shares entitled to issue, and executive officers. Include in request- full name of business. Record requests may be emailed to corporations@dos.state.ny.us. Searches of records of assumed names used by corporations, limited liability companies and limited partnerships must be made by a written, faxed or e-mail request to the Division

Access by: mail, phone, fax, in person, online.

Fee & Payment: There is no fee for basic information up to 5 names. Over 5 names, the fee is $5.00 per name. For documents, the certification fee is $10.00, $25.00 if SOS seal is required. The fee is $5.00 for every name availability checked. Fee payee- New York Department of State. prepayment required. Payments must be by check, money order, credit card or draw down account. If amount is over $500, funds must be certified. Major credit cards accepted.

Mail search: Turnaround time- 1 week. A SASE is requested.

Phone search: Information on a maximum of five entities during a single telephone call is provided free of charge. **Fax search:** Fax requests accepted.

In person: The general public may obtain copies of documents and certificates under seal while they wait ONLY if expedited fees are paid.

Online search: A commercial account can be set up for direct access. Fee is $.75 per transaction through a draw down account. There is an extensive amount of information available including historical information. Also, the Division's corporate and business entity database may be accessed via the Internet without charge. The direct link is http://appsext8.dos.state.ny.us/corp_public/corpsearch.entity_search_entry. The web has not-for-profit corporations, limited partnerships, limited liability companies and limited liability partnerships as well.

Other access: One may submit an email search request to corporations@dos.state.ny.us.

Expedited service: Expedited service is available for in person, mail and fax for filing and other services. Fees are $150 for 2-hour service; $75 for same day service and $25 for 24-hour service.

Trademarks/Service Marks

Department of State, Miscellaneous Records Unit, 99 Washington Avenue, #600, Albany, NY 12231; 518-474-4770, Fax- 518-473-0730; 8AM-4:30PM.

http://dos.state.ny.us

Indexing & Storage: Records available for past 10 years. New records available for inquiry in 1 to 2 weeks.

Searching: Searches are only done on registered marks, not on pending marks. Must provide written description of design or features of mark.

Access by: mail, phone, fax, in person.

Fee & Payment: The first two requests by mail, fax, or phone are free. Additional requests cost $5.00 per search. Fee payee- New York Department of State. Prepayment required. Payments of more than $500.00 must be certified check or money order; personal checks accepted for amounts less than $500.00. Personal checks accepted, credit cards are not.

Mail search: Turnaround time- 2 to 3 days. A SASE is requested.

Phone search: Limited verification information is available. **Fax search:** Turnaround time is 2-3 days. There is a $.50 fee per page to return results by fax.

In person: No fee for request. You can request 1 search in person.

Other access: New marks can be photocopied and sent out on a regular monthly basis. Fees are same as above.

Uniform Commercial Code, Federal & State Tax Liens

Department of State, UCC Unit - Records, 99 Washington Avenue, #600, Albany, NY 12231; 518-474-4763, 518-474-5418, Fax- 518-474-4478; 8AM-4:30PM.

www.dos.state.ny.us/corp/ucc.html

Indexing & Storage: Records available from 1964. Records are computerized from 1/96.

Searching: Use search request form UCC-11. Federal tax liens on businesses will be included. Lists of state tax liens (warrants) are available, but must be searched separately on premises. Federal tax liens on individuals are filed at the county level. Include in request- debtor name. It is suggested for written requests that the form be 5" x 8" or use the UCC-11.

Access by: mail, in person, online.

Fee & Payment: UCC search is $25.00 per debtor name, one name per UCC-11 form. Individual debtor names should list addresses. The copy fee is $5.00 per file number, add $5.00 to certify. You can search state tax liens, in person, at no charge. Fee payee- Department of State. Prepayment required. All checks over $500.00 must be certified. The department will certify search listings for an additional $25.00. Visa and MasterCard accepted.

Mail search: Turnaround time- 2 days. SASE not required.

In person: Counter service available.

Online search: Free access is available at http://appsext8.dos.state.ny.us/pls/ucc_public/web_search.main_frame. Search financing statements and federal tax lien notices by debtor name, or secured party name, or by filing number and date. Document images are no longer provided until further notice. There are two other searchable databases from this site, the State Child Support Enforcement Warrant Notice System and the State Tax Warrant Notice System.

Other access: This agency offers its database for sale on microfilm.

Expedited service: Turnaround time- same day. There is a $75.00 charge.

Sales Tax Registrations

NY Dept of Taxation & Finance, Records Access - WA Harriman Campus, Building 8, Rm 100, Albany, NY 12227; 518-457-2070 (FOIA Requests), Fax- 518-435-2974; 7AM-5PM.

www.nystax.gov

Direct written requests to the legal division which handles FOIA requests. Legal Dept contact is Christina Siefert.

Indexing & Storage: Records available for current records only. Records are computerized since 1970. New records available for inquiry in 20 days.

Searching: This agency will confirm that a business is registered and release the legal name. Include in request- business name. They will also search by tax permit number or federal tax number.

Access by: mail, phone, fax, in person.

Fee & Payment: There is a copy of $.25 per page.

Mail search: Turnaround time- 2 to 3 weeks. A SASE is requested. No fee for mail request.

Phone search: No fee for telephone request.

Fax search: Fax searching available.

In person: No fee for request.

Birth Certificates

Vital Records Section, Certification Unit, 800 N Pearl St, Menands, NY 12204; 518-474-3038, 518-474-3077, 877-854-4481 (Searching), Fax- 877-854-4607; 8:30AM-4:30PM.

www.health.state.ny.us/vital_records/

For records from New York City information, see that profile. Records may be ordered online from a vendor website www.vitalchek.com.

Indexing & Storage: Records available from 1881 on. New records available for inquiry immediately.

Searching: May only obtain your own or a dependent child's records, without notarized release. They will not return records to a PO Box or an "in care of." Include in request- full name, names of parents, mother's maiden name, date of birth, place of birth, relationship to person of record, reason for information request. Requester must show or include valid identification or 2 items showing proof of address (utility or telephone bill, etc.)

Access by: mail, phone, fax, in person.

Fee & Payment: The fee is $30.00 for searching and additional $15.00 if priority handling requested. Add $11.95 if credit card used (phone and Internet searching only). Fee payee- New York State Department of Health. Prepayment required. Personal checks and major credit cards accepted.

Mail search: Turnaround time- 1 month. Turnaround time will be 2 weeks if you send your request by Express Mail, or if you pay an additional $15.00 for priority handling. A SASE is requested.

Phone search: See expedited service. **Fax search:** See expedited service, use 518-432-6286.

In person: Turnaround time is 2 weeks, unless an add'l $15.00 fee is paid for immediate service.

Expedited service: Expedited service is available for phone and fax searches. Turnaround time- 1 week. Add $15.00 for priority handling and $11.95 for use of credit card.

Death Records

Vital Records Section, Certification Unit, 800 N Pearl St, Menands, NY 12204 (Courier address- PO Box 2602, Albany, NY 12220-2602); 518-474-3038, 518-474-3077, Fax- 518-474-9168; 8:30AM-4:30PM.

www.health.state.ny.us/vital_records/

For New York City, see separate entry. Records may be ordered online from web via VitalChek.

Indexing & Storage: Records available from 1881 on. New records available for inquiry immediately.

Searching: One must show cause why record is needed on letterhead, if not member of the immediate family. Include in request- full name, date of death, place of death, relationship to person of record, reason for information request, and telephone number. Requester must show or include valid identification or 2 items showing proof of address (utility or telephone bill, etc.)

Access by: mail, phone, fax, in person, online.

Fee & Payment: The fee is $30.00 for searching and additional $15.00 if priority handling requested. Add $11.95 if credit card used (phone and Internet searching only). Fee payee- New York State Department of Health. Prepayment required. Personal checks and major credit cards accepted.

Mail search: Turnaround time- 1 month. Turnaround time will be 2 weeks if you send your request by Express Mail, or if you pay an additional $15.00 for priority handling. A SASE is requested. **Phone or Fax search:** See expedited service, use fax 518-432-6286.

In person: Turnaround time is 2 weeks, unless an add'l $15.00 fee is paid for immediate service.

Online search: Online ordering is available via an approved third party vendor, go to www.vitalchek.com.

Expedited service: Expedited service is available for mail, phone and fax searches. Turnaround time- 1 week. Add priority and credit card fees.

Marriage Certificates

Vital Records Section, Certification Unit, 800 N Pearl St, Menands, NY 12204 (Courier address- PO Box 2602, Albany, NY 12220-2602); 518-474-3038, 518-474-3077, Fax- 518-474-9168; 8:30AM-4:30PM.

www.health.state.ny.us/vital_records/

For New York City information, see the separate entry. Records may be ordered online from website via VitalChek.

Indexing & Storage: Records available from 1881 on. New records available for inquiry immediately.

Searching: Must have a notarized release from persons of record or immediate family member for investigative purposes. Include in request- names of husband and wife, date of marriage, place or county of marriage, relationship to person of record, reason for information request, wife's maiden name. Requester must show or include valid identification or 2 items showing proof of address (utility or telephone bill, etc.)

Access by: mail, phone, fax, in person, online.

Fee & Payment: The fee is $30.00 for searching and additional $15.00 if priority handling requested. Add $11.95 if credit card used (phone and Internet searching only). Fee payee- New York State Department of Health. Prepayment required. Personal checks and major credit cards accepted.

Mail search: Turnaround time- 1 month. Turnaround time will be 2 weeks if you send your request by Express Mail, or if you pay an additional $15.00 for priority handling. A SASE is requested.

Phone search: See expedited service. **Fax search:** See expedited service, use 518-432-6286.

In person: Turnaround time is 2 weeks, unless an add'l $15.00 fee is paid for immediate service.

Online search: Online ordering is available via an approved third party vendor, go to www.vitalchek.com.

Expedited service: Expedited service is available for mail, phone and fax searches. Turnaround time- 1 week. Add priority and credit card fees.

Divorce Records

Vital Records Section, Certification Unit, 800 N Pearl St, Menands, NY 12204 (Courier address- PO Box 2602, Albany, NY 12220-2602); 518-474-3038, 518-474-3077, Fax- 518-474-9168; 8:30AM-4:30PM.

www.health.state.ny.us/vital_records/

To obtain a copy of a divorce decree prior to 1963, visit county court where the document was filed.

Indexing & Storage: Records available from 1963 on. New records available for inquiry immediately.

Searching: If you are not a party to the divorce you must have a court order to obtain records or show legal cause. Include in request- names of husband and wife, date of divorce, place of divorce, relationship to person of record, reason for information request, and your telephone number. Requester must show or include valid identification or 2 items showing proof of address (utility or telephone bill, etc.)

Access by: mail, phone, fax, in person, online.

Fee & Payment: The fee is $30.00 for searching and additional $15.00 if priority handling requested. Add $11.95 if credit card used (phone and Internet searching only). Fee payee- New York State Department of Health. Prepayment required. Personal checks and major credit cards accepted.

Mail search: Turnaround time- 1 month. Turnaround time will be 2 weeks if you send your request by Express Mail, or if you pay an additional $15.00 for priority handling. A SASE is requested.

Phone search: See expedited service. **Fax search:** See expedited service, use 518-432-6286.

In person: Turnaround time is 2 weeks, unless an add'l $15.00 fee is paid for immediate service.

Online search: Online ordering is available via an approved third party vendor, go to www.vitalchek.com.

Expedited service: Expedited service is available for mail, phone and fax searches. Turnaround time- 1 week. Add priority and credit card fees.

Birth Certificate-New York City, Death Records-New York City

Department of Health, Bureau of Vital Records, 125 Worth St, Box 4, Rm 133, New York, NY 10013; 212-788-4520 (Order), 212-442-1999, Fax-212-962-6105; 9AM-4PM.

www.nyc.gov/html/doh/html/vr/vr.shtml

Records may be ordered online from an approved vendor at www.vitalchek.com. The fax number if calling outside NYC is 800-908-9146.

Indexing & Storage: Records available from 1910 to present for birth and from 1949 forward for death. For prior records call Municipal Archives at 212-788-8580. New records available for inquiry in 2 months.

Searching: To request a birth certificate for any other person, including any child where your name does not appear on the birth certificate, you must order in person or by mail. Include in request- full name, date of birth, date of death, place of birth, place of death, reason for information request, name of the hospital, and signed release if necessary. Parents' names are also required, mother's maiden name for birth.

Access by: mail, phone, fax, in person, online.

Fee & Payment: The fee is $15.00 per record plus $5.50 if using a credit card. Only those parties appearing on the birth record may order via a credit card. All other parties must order by mail or in-person and show cause or reason for the request. Fee payee- Department of Health. Prepayment required. Personal checks and major credit cards accepted.

Mail search: Allow 3-4 weeks for a birth record and 8-10 weeks for a death record. A SASE is requested.

Phone search: Online ordering is thru a message system. Use of a credit card is required. The automated voice ordering system is available 24 hours a day, seven days a week. **Fax search:** Same criteria as phone searching.

In person turnaround time usually while you wait.

Online search: Records may be requested via www.vitalchek.com. Use of credit card is required.

Expedited service: Expedited service is available for phone, fax searches. Turnaround time- 1 to 2 days. Add $12.50 for overnight delivery service.

Marriage Certificates-New York City

Office of the City Clerk, Municipal Building, 1 Centre St, Rm 252 South, New York, NY 10007; 212-669-8090; 9AM-4:30PM (till 1PM on F).

www.cityclerk.nyc.gov/html/home/home.shtml

Indexing & Storage: Records available from 1930 to present. In person requests from 1996 to present.

Searching: Current records (50 years or less) are not public information and are only available to the parties involved or their authorization or to legal representatives for litigation purposes. Otherwise, records are open. Include in request-names and DOBs of parties, date of marriage, relationship of requester to involved parties, government issued photo ID of requester. Use of their form is required. The form may be downloaded form the web page or call to have one mailed.

Access by: mail, in person.

Fee & Payment: There is a $15.00 search fee for the first year searched, then $2.00 add'l for each add'l year searched. Certification is another $10.00. More fees are incurred if needed for foreign use. Fee payee- City Clerk of New York Prepayment required. No personal checks accepted, except attorneys.

Mail search: Turnaround time- 6-8 weeks. Requesters must use the agency form. Call to have a copy mailed or download from the web.

In person: Simple requests may be processed while you wait.

Workers' Compensation Records

NY Workers' Compensation Board, Office of General Counsel, 20 Park Street # 401, Albany, NY 12207; 877-632-4996; 9AM-5PM.

www.wcb.state.ny.us

The Board maintains eleven district offices located in Albany, Binghamton, Brooklyn, Buffalo, Hauppauge, Hempstead, Manhattan, Peekskill, Queens, Rochester and Syracuse. Record requests should be made to these offices; see web for contact data.

Indexing & Storage: Records available from www.wcb.state.ny.us/content/main/forms/oc110a.pdf. New records available for inquiry immediately.

Searching: Must have a original signed Form OC-110A see www.wcb.state.ny.us/content/main/forms/oc110a.pdf or original notarized authorization from claimant naming requesting party. Include in request- claimant name, SSN, claim number, date of accident in order to reasonably identify the claimant. Again, requests must be made to the individual offices. The information in this profile pertains to searching at these offices. The web page contains the phone numbers (too lengthy to print here).

Access by: mail, in person.

Fee & Payment: Copies are $.25 each. Fee payee-Workers' Compensation Board. Prepayment required. Personal checks accepted, credit cards are not.

Mail search: Turnaround time- varies. SASE not required. Include proper authorization and identification.

In person: Visitors may make in person requests with proper authorization and identification. Turnaround time varies.

Driver Records

Department of Motor Vehicles, MV-15 Processing, 6 Empire State Plaza, Albany, NY 12228; 518-473-5595, 800-225-5368 (In-state), Fax- 518-474-0718; 8AM-4PM.

www.nysdmv.com/

Indexing & Storage: Records available for 3 years in addition to the current year for moving violations, 10 years for DWIs, and indefinitely for open (4 years for closed) suspensions. Most non-moving violations are not shown on record. New records available for inquiry in a few days after conviction.

Searching: New York restricts the release of personal information on driving records to casual requesters. However, they will provide a "masked" abstract that contains no address. It will contain the DL# or name plus DOB as identifier. Use Form MV-15 to request. Include in request- DL# or ID#, name, and DOB. Use Form MV-15, if notarized consent of driver is needed use Form MV-15GC. The forms can be downloaded from the web (forms section). This data not released- SSN, medical information, photographs.

Access by: mail, phone, fax, in person, online.

Fee & Payment: The fee is $10.00 per record, $7.00 if returned online, $15.00 by telephone. The Form MV-15 lists all fees. Fee payee-Commissioner of Motor Vehicles. Prepayment required. Escrow accounts can be set up for high volume users. Personal checks accepted. Credit cards accepted for phone and online orders only.

Mail search: Turnaround time- within 2 weeks. Form MV-15 is required when ordering. A SASE is not requested.

Phone search: Drivers wishing to obtain their own record or account holders may call. The DL# or name and DOB are required when ordered. Payment by a credit card is required and an additional $5.00 is charged.

Fax search: Fax requests are available to customers with escrow accounts. The MV-15 fax is 518-474-0718.

In person: Records can be ordered from most any county-operated motor vehicle office and at the state offices in Albany. A photo ID of the requester and use of Form MV-15C is required.

Online search: NY has implemented a "Dial-In Display" system which enables customers to obtain data online 24 hours a day. An application and pre-paid escrow account are required. The fee is $7.00 per record. For more information, visit www.nysdmv.com/dialin.htm. Also, drivers may request their own DMV records at www.nydmv.state.ny.us/driverabstract/default.html; however, records are returned by mail and the fee is $10.00.

Other access: This agency offers a program to employers whereby the agency will notify the employers when a change posts to an employee's record. To find out about the "LENS" program, visit www.nysdmv.com/lens.htm.

Vehicle, Vessel Ownership & Registration

Department of Motor Vehicles, MV-15 processing, 6 Empire State Plaza, Room 430, Albany, NY 12228; 518-474-0710, 518-474-8510; 8AM-4PM. www.nysdmv.com/

Indexing & Storage: Records available for a minimum of 4 years on computer. All motorized vessels must be registered. Titles on boats are issued for model year 1987 and newer, if boat is at least 14 ft long. New records available for inquiry immediately.

Searching: Generally, vehicle and ownership information is available. However, accessed is restricted in adherence to the Drivers' Privacy Protection Act and casual requesters cannot obtain records without consent. Use of Form MV-15 required. If consent is needed, use MV-15GC, consent must be notarized. The forms are downloadable from the website.

Access by: mail, fax, in person, online.

Fee & Payment: Search requests are $10.00 per record, Dial-in Display is $7.00. A complete price list is on Form MV-15. Fee payee- Commissioner of Motor Vehicles. Prepayment required. For information regarding deposit accounts, call 518-474-4293. Personal checks accepted, credit cards are not.

Mail search: Turnaround time- 2 to 4 weeks. Include copy of requester's ID. Mail to MV-15 Form Processing for fastest turnaround time. A SASE is not requested.

Fax search: This method is available for customers with escrow accounts. The MV-15 fax line is 518-474-0718.

In person: Documents may be requested at the counter, but cannot be picked up (or mailed) until the next day. Use of the same form is required.

Online search: New York offers plate, VIN and ownership data through the same network discussed in the Driving Records Section. The system is interactive and open 24 hours a day. The fee is $7.00 per record. All accounts must be approved, requesters must follow DPPA guidelines. Call 518-474-4293 or visit www.nysdmv.com/dialin.htm for more information. A free title/lien status check is offered at www.nydmv.state.ny.us/titlestat/default.html. The VIN is needed, this is not a name search. A free insurance status check is at www.nysdmv.com/insStatus/default.html, but a control number is needed.

Other access: Vehicle owners and drivers may order their own title abstract by phone at 518-473-5595.

Accident Reports

DMV Certified Document Center, MV-198C Accident Report Section, PO Box 2086, Albany, NY 12228-2086; 518-474-0710; 8AM-4:15PM.

www.nysdmv.com/dmvfaqs.htm

The DMV has copies of accident reports, but requester may also call or visit the local police agency or precinct where the accident occurred, or the State Police troop headquarters where the accident was reported

Indexing & Storage: Records available for 4 years to present. New records available for inquiry in 180 days after date of accident.

Searching: Use of Form MV-198C is strongly suggested, downloadable from web under forms. Include in request- date of accident, location of accident, full name. Provide driver's address, if known. Available accident reports filed by a police agency are available to all requesters. Reports filed by those involved are governed by DPPA.

Access by: mail, phone, fax, online.

Fee & Payment: Fees include $10.00 ($7.00 if online) per search if name search needed, plus a fee of $15.00 per copy of accident report. Fee payee- Commissioner of Motor Vehicles. Prepayment required. Personal checks accepted. No credit cards accepted except online.

Mail search: Turnaround time- 2 to 3 weeks. SASE not required. Express mail is given priority.

Phone search: There is an additional $5.00 fee if processed by phone.

Fax search: Fax requests accepted from ongoing accounts.

Online search: Online access is available to eligible requesters. There is a $7.00 search fee and a $15.00 report fee. Available records go back 4 years. Reports can be viewed and printed. Visit www.nysdmv.com/AIS/default.html.

Legislation Records

NY Senate Document Room, State Capitol, State Street Rm 317, Albany, NY 12247; 518-455-2312 (Senate Document Room), 518-455-3216 (Legislative Assistance), Fax- 518-426-6841; 9AM-5PM.

http://public.leginfo.state.ny.us/menuf.cgi

Prior session bills may be found at the State Library, 518-474-5355.

Indexing & Storage: Records available for current session and beyond.

Searching: Include in request- bill number. The law section number or description can be helpful.

Access by: mail, phone, fax, in person, online.

Fee & Payment: There is no search fee.

Mail search: Turnaround time- same day. SASE not required.

Phone search: Records are available by phone.

Fax search: Fax requests are accepted.

In person: research materials are available if bill number is not known.

Online search: Both the Senate - www.senate.state.ny.us - and the Assembly - www.assembly.state.ny.us - have websites to search for a bill or specific bill text. An excellent free site is http://public.leginfo.state.ny.us/menuf.cgi. A much more complete system is the LRS online system. This offers complete state statutes, agency rules and regulations, bill text, bill status, summaries, and more. For more information, call Barbara Lett at 800-356-6566.

Expedited service: Overnight express can be arranged. However, requester must pay the charges involved.

Voter Registration

Access to Records is Restricted.

State Board of Elections, Public Information Officer, 40 Steuben Street, Albany, NY 12207-2108; 518-474-6220, 518-474-1953, Fax- 518-486-4068; 9AM-5PM.

www.elections.state.ny.us

Records access from this agency is for election purposes only. Individual records must be researched at the county level. Qualifying entities pay no fees. Look at the web page under FOIL requests.

GED Certificates

NY State Education Dept, GED Testing, PO Box 7348, Albany, NY 12224-0348; 518-474-5906, Fax- 518-474-3041; 8AM-4:30PM.

www.emsc.nysed.gov/ged/

The web page at www.emsc.nysed.gov/ged/otherserv.shtml gives detailed instruction and forms needed to obtain test results.

Indexing & Storage: Records available from 1985 to present. New records available for inquiry in 4 to 6 weeks, if paper.

Searching: Include in request- full name when tested, data and location of test, SSN, DOB. Signature of the testee for a copy of transcript or diploma.

Access by: mail, phone, in person.

Fee & Payment: There is no fee for verification. Copies of transcripts are $4.00 each. A duplicate diploma with a transcript is $10.00. Fee payee- NY State Education Dept. Prepayment required. Money orders are accepted. No personal checks or credit cards accepted.

Mail search: Turnaround time- 3 to 4 weeks. SASE not required. Use "Attachment G" found on the web page.

Phone search: Phone verification service is provided if the transcript ID number or SSN is provided.

In person: The hours of operation are Monday through Friday, 1:00 pm through 3:00 pm. The window is located in the New York State Education Building Annex, 89 Washington Avenue in Albany, at the Hawk Street entrance.

Expedited service: Will expedite if you provide a prepaid express envelope.

Hunting & Fishing License Information

DEC - Fish & Wildlife Division, Records Access Officer, 625 Broadway, 14th Fl, Albany, NY 12233-1016; 518-402-8000, Fax- 518-402-2209; 8:30AM-4:45PM. www.dec.ny.gov/

Indexing & Storage: Records available since 2002. New records available for inquiry immediately.

Searching: Include in request- correct spelling of 1st and last name plus DOB. Also, email requests to foil@gw.dec.state.ny.us This data not released- personal information on the license.

Access by: mail, fax, in person.

Fee & Payment: There is no search fee, copies are $.25 per page. Fee payee- DEC Prepayment required. Personal checks accepted.

Mail search: Turnaround time- 1-2 days. SASE is not required.

Fax search: Requests accepted by fax.

In person: Counter service does not mean instant access. Depending on personnel and extent of research, records may need to be picked up later or returned by mail.

New York State Licensing Agencies

For details about the agency responsible for licensing/certifying/registering an item below or in the Agency Quick Finder section, match an item's number with the number of the agency in the *Licensing Agency Information* section.

New York Licenses Searchable Online

Accountant, CPA/Public #19 .... www.op.nysed.gov/opsearches.htm#nme
Acupuncturist/Acupuncture Assis't #19 .... www.op.nysed.gov/opsearches.htm#nme
Addiction Counselor #31 .... www.oasas.state.ny.us/credentialingVerification/verification/home.cfm
Addiction Treatment Center #31 .... www.oasas.state.ny.us/credentialingVerification/verification/home.cfm
Adult Care Medical Facility #38 .... www.health.state.ny.us/facilities/adult_care/
Adult Care Suspended List #38 .... www.health.state.ny.us/facilities/adult_care/memorandum.htm
Alarm Installer #10 .... http://appsext8.dos.state.ny.us/lcns_public/chk_load
Alcohol Abuse Provider #31 .... www.oasas.state.ny.us/credentialingVerification/verification/home.cfm
Alcohol/Substance Abuse Counselor #31 .... www.oasas.state.ny.us/credentialingVerification/verification/home.cfm
Apartment Info Vendor #10 .... http://appsext8.dos.state.ny.us/lcns_public/chk_load
Apartment Mgr/Vendor/Agent #10 .... http://appsext8.dos.state.ny.us/lcns_public/chk_load
Apartment Sharing Manager #10 .... http://appsext8.dos.state.ny.us/lcns_public/chk_load
Appearance Enhancement Firm #10 .... http://appsext8.dos.state.ny.us/lcns_public/chk_load
Appearance Enhancement Prof. #10 .... http://appsext8.dos.state.ny.us/lcns_public/chk_load
Architect #19 .... www.op.nysed.gov/opsearches.htm#nme
Armored Car/Car Carrier #10 .... http://appsext8.dos.state.ny.us/lcns_public/chk_load
Athlete Agent #10 .... http://appsext8.dos.state.ny.us/lcns_public/chk_load
Athletic Trainer #19 .... www.op.nysed.gov/opsearches.htm#nme
Attorney #18 .... www.nycourts.gov/attorneys/registration/index.shtml
Audiologist #19 .... www.op.nysed.gov/opsearches.htm#nme
Backflow Prev't'n Device Tester #13 .... www.health.state.ny.us/environmental/water/drinking/cross/cross.htm
Bail Enforcement Agent #10 .... http://appsext8.dos.state.ny.us/lcns_public/chk_load
Bank Branch, Foreign #23 .... www.banking.state.ny.us/sifbranc.htm
Bank Rep. Office, Foreign #23 .... www.banking.state.ny.us/silicrepo.htm
Bank, Domestic #23 .... www.banking.state.ny.us/sibank.htm
Bank, Foreign #23 .... www.banking.state.ny.us/sifagen.htm
Banker, Private #23 .... www.banking.state.ny.us/siprivat.htm
Banking Regulatory Action #23 .... www.banking.state.ny.us/ea.htm
Barber Apprentice #10 .... http://appsext8.dos.state.ny.us/lcns_public/chk_load
Barber/Barber Shop #10 .... http://appsext8.dos.state.ny.us/lcns_public/chk_load
Bedding Manufacturing #10 .... http://appsext8.dos.state.ny.us/lcns_public/chk_load
Boat Launch Site #50 .... www.nysparks.com/boating/resource.asp
Budget Planner, Banking-related #23 .... www.banking.state.ny.us/sibudget.htm
Casino Employee #15 .... www.racing.state.ny.us/racing/licsrch/searchlicense.php
Charitable Gaming #15 .... www.racing.state.ny.us/racing/licsrch/searchlicense.php
Check Casher #23 .... www.banking.state.ny.us/sicheckc.htm
Chemical Dependence Operation #31 .... www.oasas.state.ny.us/credentialingVerification/verification/home.cfm
Chiropractor #19 .... www.op.nysed.gov/opsearches.htm#nme
Cigarette/Tobacco Tax Agent #52 .... http://www7.nystax.gov/CGTX/cgtxHome
Cigarette/Tobacco Whlse/Retailer #52 .... http://www7.nystax.gov/CGTX/cgtxHome
Cosmetologist #10 .... http://appsext8.dos.state.ny.us/lcns_public/chk_load
Credit Union #23 .... www.banking.state.ny.us/sicredit.htm
Day Care, Farm Worker (ABCD) #29 .... www.agmkt.state.ny.us/programs/childdev.html
DEC Permit Application #11 .... www.dec.ny.gov/
Dental Hygienist #19 .... www.op.nysed.gov/opsearches.htm#nme
Dentist/Dental Assistant #19 .... www.op.nysed.gov/opsearches.htm#nme
Dietitian #19 .... www.op.nysed.gov/opsearches.htm#nme
Dispatch Facility- Alarm/Sec./Fire #10 .... http://appsext8.dos.state.ny.us/lcns_public/chk_load
Dog License #27 .... www.agmkt.state.ny.us/AI/doglic.html
Emergency Medical Technician #7 .... www.health.state.ny.us/nysdoh/ems/charta.htm
Engineer #19 .... www.op.nysed.gov/opsearches.htm#nme
Environmental Permit #11 .... www.dec.ny.gov/
Esthetics Specialist #10 .... http://appsext8.dos.state.ny.us/lcns_public/chk_load
Farm Products Dealer #26 .... www.agmkt.state.ny.us/AP/LicFarmProdDealersList.asp
Foreign Banking Agency #23 .... www.banking.state.ny.us/sifagen.htm
Greenhouse #26 .... www.agmkt.state.ny.us/PI/PlantGrower.asp

Guard Dog Agency #10 .... http://appsext8.dos.state.ny.us/lcns_public/chk_load
Guard/Patrol Agency #10 .... http://appsext8.dos.state.ny.us/lcns_public/chk_load
Hair Styling, Natural #10 .... http://appsext8.dos.state.ny.us/lcns_public/chk_load
Hearing Aid Dealer #10 .... http://appsext8.dos.state.ny.us/lcns_public/chk_load
HMO (Insurance) #12 .... www.ins.state.ny.us/tocol4.htm
Holding Company #23 .... www.banking.state.ny.us/siholdmu.htm
Hospital #38 .... www.health.state.ny.us/nysdoh/hospital/index.htm
Insurance Company #12 .... www.ins.state.ny.us/tocol4.htm
Interior Designer #19 .... www.op.nysed.gov/opsearches.htm#nme
Investment Company Article XII #23 .... www.banking.state.ny.us/siinvest.htm
Kosher Food #30 .... www.agmkt.state.ny.us/kosher/search.aspx
Landscape Architect #19 .... www.op.nysed.gov/opsearches.htm#nme
Lender, Licensed #23 .... www.banking.state.ny.us/silicend.htm
Lobbyist/Client/Public Corporation #16 .... www.nyintegrity.org/public/lobby_data.html
Mammography Facility #38 .... www.accessdata.fda.gov/scripts/cdrh/cfdocs/cfMQSA/mqsa.cfm
Massage Therapist #19 .... www.op.nysed.gov/opsearches.htm#nme
Medicaid Long-Term Care Service #43 .... www.health.state.ny.us/health_care/managed_care/mltc/mltcplans.htm
Medical Doctor #19 .... www.op.nysed.gov/opsearches.htm#nme
Medical Examiner, Independent #57 .... www.wcb.state.ny.us/content/main/hcpp/ListofAuthIME.jsp
Mentally Retarded Facility/Service #49 .... www.omr.state.ny.us/ws/servlets/WsAdminServlet
Midwife #19 .... www.op.nysed.gov/opsearches.htm#nme
Minority/Woman-owned Business #35 .... http://205.232.252.35/
Money Transmitter #23 .... www.banking.state.ny.us/simoneyt.htm
Mortgage Banker #23 .... www.banking.state.ny.us/simbanke.htm
Mortgage Broker #23 .... www.banking.state.ny.us/simbroke.htm
Nail Technologist #10 .... http://appsext8.dos.state.ny.us/lcns_public/chk_load
Notary Public #10 .... http://appsext8.dos.state.ny.us/lcns_public/chk_load
Nurse-LPN/RPN #19 .... www.op.nysed.gov/opsearches.htm#nme
Nursery, Plant #26 .... www.agmkt.state.ny.us/PI/PlantGrower.asp
Nurses' Aide #5 .... https://nynar.chauncey.com/registry/public/
Nursing Home #38 .... www.health.state.ny.us/facilities/nursing/
Nursing Home Administrator #5 .... www.health.state.ny.us/professionals/nursing_home_administrator/
Nutritionist #19 .... www.op.nysed.gov/opsearches.htm#nme
Occupational Therapist/Assistant #19 .... www.op.nysed.gov/opsearches.htm#nme
Off-Track Betting #15 .... www.racing.state.ny.us/racing/licsrch/searchlicense.php
Ophthalmic Dispenser #19 .... www.op.nysed.gov/opsearches.htm#nme
Optometrist #19 .... www.op.nysed.gov/opsearches.htm#nme
Out-of-state Bank Representative Ofc.#23 .... www.banking.state.ny.us/sioosrep.htm
Pesticide Business #2 .... www.dec.ny.gov/docs/materials_minerals_pdf/busweb.pdf
Pesticide/Commercial Applicator #2 .... www.dec.ny.gov/docs/materials_minerals_pdf/appweb.pdf
Pet Dealer #27 .... www.agmkt.state.ny.us/petdealer/petdealerextract.asp
Pharmacist #19 .... www.op.nysed.gov/opsearches.htm#nme
Physical Therapist/Assistant #19 .... www.op.nysed.gov/opsearches.htm#nme
Physician #19 .... www.op.nysed.gov/opsearches.htm#nme
Physician Assistant #19 .... www.op.nysed.gov/opsearches.htm#nme
Physicians Specialist Assistant #19 .... www.op.nysed.gov/opsearches.htm#nme
Plant Dealer #26 .... www.agmkt.state.ny.us/PI/PlantDealer.asp
Podiatrist #19 .... www.op.nysed.gov/opsearches.htm#nme
Premium Finance Company #23 .... www.banking.state.ny.us/sipremfi.htm
Private Investigator #10 .... http://appsext8.dos.state.ny.us/lcns_public/chk_load
Psychologist #19 .... www.op.nysed.gov/opsearches.htm#nme
Public Accountant-CPA #19 .... www.op.nysed.gov/opsearches.htm#nme
Racetrack #15 .... www.racing.state.ny.us/racing/licsrch/searchlicense.php
Racing Occupation #15 .... www.racing.state.ny.us/racing/licsrch/searchlicense.php
Radiologic Technologist #14 .... www.health.state.ny.us/professionals/doctors/radiological/
Radiologic Technology School #14 .... www.health.state.ny.us/professionals/doctors/radiological/schlist2.htm
Radon Testing Lab #14 .... www.wadsworth.org/labcert/elap/radon.html
Real Estate Agent/Broker/Office #10 .... http://appsext8.dos.state.ny.us/lcns_public/id_search_frm
Real Estate Appraiser #10 .... http://appsext8.dos.state.ny.us/lcns_public/chk_load
Respiratory Therapist/Therapy Tech. #19 .... www.op.nysed.gov/opsearches.htm#nme
Safe Deposit Company #23 .... www.banking.state.ny.us/sisafede.htm
Sales Finance Company #23 .... www.banking.state.ny.us/sisalesf.htm
Savings & Loan #23 .... www.banking.state.ny.us/sisavloa.htm
Savings Bank #23 .... www.banking.state.ny.us/sisaving.htm
School, Non-Degree Proprietary #34 .... www.highered.nysed.gov/bpss/directory_main_page.htm

Security & Fire Alarm Installer #10 ... http://appsext8.dos.state.ny.us/lcns_public/chk_load
Security Guard #10 ... http://appsext8.dos.state.ny.us/lcns_public/chk_load
Social Worker #19 ... www.op.nysed.gov/opsearches.htm#nme
Speech Pathologist/Audiologist #19 ... www.op.nysed.gov/opsearches.htm#nme
State Telecommunication Contractor #37 ... www.ogs.state.ny.us/purchase/telecomContracts.asp
Substance Abuse Provider #31 ... www.oasas.state.ny.us/credentialingVerification/verification/home.cfm
Summer Camp for Mental Retarded #49 ... www.omr.state.ny.us//hp_camp_directory.jsp
Surveyor, Land #19 ... www.op.nysed.gov/opsearches.htm#nme
Teacher #17 ... http://eservices.nysed.gov/teach/certhelp/CpPersonSearchExternal.jsp?trgAction=INQUIRY
Telemarketer Business #10 ... http://appsext8.dos.state.ny.us/lcns_public/chk_load
Trust Company #23 ... www.banking.state.ny.us/sibank.htm
Uniform Procedures Act Permit #11 ... www.dec.ny.gov/
Upholster & Bedding Industry #10 ... http://appsext8.dos.state.ny.us/lcns_public/chk_load
Vendor, New York City #58 ... http://slnx-prd-web.nyc.gov/cfb/
Veteran Home- Skill'd Nursing Home #38 ... www.nysvets.org/
Veterinarian/Veterinary Technician #19 ... www.op.nysed.gov/opsearches.htm#nme
Water Processing Facility, Bulk #13 ... www.health.state.ny.us/environmental/water/drinking/bulk_bottle/bulkwter.htm
Water Supply Permit #11 ... www.dec.ny.gov/
Water Treatment Plant Operator #13 ... www.health.state.ny.us/environmental/water/drinking/operate/operate.htm
Waxing Establishment/Operator/Tech #10 ... http://appsext8.dos.state.ny.us/lcns_public/chk_load
Workers Comp Health Provid'r #57 ... www.wcb.state.ny.us/hps/HPSearch.jsp

New York Licensing Quick Finder

Accident & Health Insurer #12 ... 518-474-6623
Accountant, CPA/Public #19 ... 518-474-3817
Acupuncturist/Acupuncture Assis't #19 518-474-3817
Addict'n Counselor #31 800-482-9564, 518-485-2057
Addiction Treatment Center #31 ... 518-457-4384
Adoption Agency #24 ... 800-345-5437
Adult Care Medical Facility #38 ... 518-408-1264
Adult Care Suspended List #38 ... 518-408-1133
Adult Family Home #24 ... 518-474-7112
Aircraft Thruway Take-off Permit #55 ... 518-436-3079
Alarm Installer #10 ... 518-474-4429
Alcohol Abuse Provider #31 ... 518-457-4384
Alcohol Beverage Bond Firm #46 ... 212-961-8385
Alcohol Distiller/Whlse/Mfg #46 ... 212-961-8385
Alcohol Service Permit #46 ... 212-961-8385
Alcohol Svc Establishment #46 ... 212-961-8385
Alcohol/Substance Abuse Counselor #31 ... 800-482-9564, 518-485-2057
Alcoholic Beverage Distributor #52 ... 800-225-5829
Alternative Fueling Site #37 ... 518-862-1090
Ambulance Service #7 ... 518-402-0996
Ambulatory Svc, Mentally Retr'd #49 ... 518-473-9689
Amusement Device #9 ... 518-457-2735
Animal Disposal Plant/Transport #27 ... 518-457-5459
Animal Lab Permit #41 ... 518-485-5378
Apartment Info Vendor #10 ... 518-474-4429
Apartment Mgr/Vendor/Agent #10 ... 518-474-4429
Apiary #26 ... 518-457-2087
Apparel Industry Manufacturer #9 ... 518-457-1942
Appearance Enhancement Firm #10 ... 518-474-4429
Appearance Enhancement Prof. #10 ... 518-474-4429
Aquaculture-related Permit #11 ... 631-444-0483
Architect #19 ... 518-474-3817
Armored Car/Car Carrier #10 ... 518-474-4429
Asbestos Handler #9 ... 518-457-2735
Asbestos Safety Trainer #39 ... 518-402-7940
Athlete Agent #10 ... 518-474-4429
Athletic Trainer #19 ... 518-474-3817
ATM Machine #23 ... 877-BANK-NYS, 212-709-1511
Attorney #18 ... 212-428-2800
Audiologist #19 ... 518-474-3817
Backflow Prev't'n Device Tester #13 ... 518-402-7712
Bail Bond Agent #12 ... 518-474-6630
Bail Enforcement Agent #10 ... 518-474-4429
Bank Branch, Foreign #23 ... 877-BANK-NYS, 212-709-1559
Bank Rep. Office, Foreign #23 ... 877-BANK-NYS, 212-709-1559
Bank, Domestic #23 . 877-BANK-NYS, 212-709-1503
Bank, Foreign #23 ... 877-BANK-NYS, 212-709-1559
Banker, Private #23 .. 877-BANK-NYS, 212-709-1503
Banking Regulatory Action #23 ... 877-BANK-NYS
Barber Apprentice #10 ... 518-474-4429
Barber/Barber Shop #10 ... 518-474-4429
Bathing Beach #40 ... 518-402-7600
Bedding Manufacturing #10 ... 518-474-4429
Beer/Malt Beverage Distributor #52 ... 800-225-5829
Blaster #9 ... 518-457-2735
Blood Alcohol Analyzer #41 ... 518-474-0005
Blood Bank #41 ... 518-485-5378
Boat Launch Site #50 ... 518-474-0445
Boating Permit, State Park #50 ... 518-474-0456
Boiler Inspector #8 ... 518-457-2722
Boxer #21 ... 212-417-5700
Boxing/Wrestling-related Professional #21 ... 212-417-5700
Breath Analysis Operator #41 ... 518-474-2821
Brewer #46 ... 212-961-8385
Budget Planner, Banking-related #23 ... 877-BANK-NYS, 212-709-5498
Building Permit #10 ... 518-474-4429
Bulk Milk Permit (Thruway) #55 ... 518-436-3079
Business School Agent/Teacher #34 ... 518-474-3969
Canal Recreational Vessel Permit #32 518-436-2894
Care Facility, Family Board-sponsored #25 ... 518-473-4630
Casino Employee #15 ... 518-453-8460 x2
Charitable Annuity #12 ... 212-480-4778
Charitable Gaming #15 ... 518-453-8460 x2
Charity, Registered #44 ... 212-416-8430
Check Casher #23 ... 877-BANK-NYS, 212-709-5494
Chemical Dependence Operation #31 . 518-457-4384
Children's Overnight Camp #40 ... 518-402-7600
Chiropractor #19 ... 518-474-3817
Cigarette/Tobacco Tax Agent #52 ... 800-225-5829
Cigarette/Tobacco Whlse/Retailer #52 800-225-5829
Clinical Lab Director/Assistant #41 ... 518-485-5378
Clinical Lab/Blood Bank #41 ... 518-485-5378
Coastal/Marine-related Permit #11 ... 631-444-0470
Coin Processor #10 ... 518-474-4429
Commercial Vessel (Canal) #32 ... 518-471-5010
Commodity Investment Advisor #1 ... 212-416-8222
Community Residence, Ment'l Health #48 ... 518-474-5570
Condominium #45 ... 212-416-8122
Construction Permit #36 ... 518-474-1314
Construction Plans Purchased #36 ... 518-474-1314
Control'd Substance Mfg/Dist/Exporter #42 ... 518-402-0707
Controlled Substance Dispenser #42 .. 518-402-0707
Controlled Substance Lab/Import #42 .. 518-402-0707
Controlled Substance Researcher #42 . 518-402-0707
Cooperative Insurance Firm, Adv/Prem. #12 ... 212-480-5565
Cooperative, Housing #45 ... 212-416-8122
Cosmetologist #10 ... 518-474-4429
Crane Operator #9 ... 518-457-2735
Credit Union #23 ... 877-BANK-NYS, 212-709-1511
Cytotechnologist #41 ... 518-485-5378
Day Care Center #24 ... 518-474-7112
Day Care, Farm Worker (ABCD) #29 .. 518-457-7076
Day Service Program #24 ... 518-474-7112
DEC Permit Application #11 ... 518-402-8985
Dental Hygienist #19 ... 518-474-3817
Dentist/Dental Assistant #19 ... 518-474-3817
Diagnostic/Treatment Ctr/Clinic #22 ... 518-402-0911
Dietitian #19 ... 518-474-3817
Dispatch Facility- Alarm/Sec./Fire #10. 518-474-4429
Dog License #27 ... 519-457-2728
Dog/Cat Breeder #27 ... 518-457-2728
Domestic Violence Facility #24 ... 518-474-7112
Drugs/Pharm. Device, Mfg/Whsl/Dist. #19 ... 518-474-3817
Electrician, Master #10 ... 518-474-4429
Emergency Medical Technician #7 ... 518-402-0996
Employment Agency/Manager #9 ... 518-4[illegible]-1942
Engineer #19 ... 518-474-3817
Engineering Corporation #19 ... 518-474-3817
English as a 2nd Language School #34518-474-3969
Environmental Permit #11 ... 518-402-8985
Esthetics Specialist #10 ... 518-474-4429
Euthanasia Dogs/Cats #42 ... 518-402-0707
Excavate/Remove/Dispose of Material #37 ... 518-474-2195
Excess Line Broker #12 ... 518-474-6630
Explosive Registration/Handling #9 ... 518-457-2735
Explosives Transportation #55 ... 518-436-3079
Falconer #11 ... 518-402-8843
Family Program, Interim #24 ... 518-474-7112

Family/Group Day Care #24 ... 518-474-7112
Farm Camp/Commissary/Store #9 ... 518-457-1942
Farm Products Dealer #26 ... 518-457-1954
Farmworker Specialty Certification #29. 518-457-7076
Feed Facility #29 ... 519-457-5457
Fertilizer Distributor #26 ... 518-457-2087
Firearms Manufacturer #51 ... 518-457-2627
First Responder #7 ... 518-402-0996
Fish Processor #29 ... 518-457-5459
Fishing Guide #3 ... 518-402-8838
Flat Glass Permit (Thruway) #55 ... 518-436-3079
Food Inspector #29 ... 518-457-5459
Food Processor #29 ... 518-457-7139
Food Salvager #29 ... 518-457-1215
Food Service Establishment #40 ... 518-402-7630
Food Store, Retail #29 ... 518-457-1215
Foreign Banking Agency #23 ... 877-BANK-NYS, 212-709-1559
Foster Care #24 ... 518-474-7112
Franchise Sales #1 ... 212-416-8222
Franchise, Approved #1 ... 212-416-8222
Fraternal Benefit Society #12 ... 212-480-5027
Freshwater Fish Related #11 ... 518-402-8985
Fund Raider, Professional #44 ... 518-486-9797
Fund Raising Counsel #44 ... 518-473-2374
Funeral Home/Director #6 ... 518-402-0785
Game Bird Breeder #11 ... 518-402-8985
Games of Chance Registration #10 ... 518-474-4429
Greenhouse #26 ... 518-457-2087
Guard Dog Agency #10 ... 518-474-4429
Guard/Patrol Agency #10 ... 518-474-4429
Guide, Camp/Fishing/Hiking/Hunt #3 ... 518-402-8838
Guide, Rock/Ice Climbing #3 ... 518-402-8838
Hair Styling, Natural #10 ... 518-474-4429
Hatchery/Fish Farm #11 ... 518-402-8985
Hauling Permit, Specialty #55 ... 518-436-2793
Health Care Plan, Prepaid #43 ... 518-473-4842
Health Club #10 ... 518-474-4429
Hearing Aid Dealer #10 ... 518-474-4429
Heating Oil Seller #53 ... 800-972-1233
Highway Use Tax Registration #53 ... 800-972-1233
Hiking Guide #3 ... 518-402-8838
HMO (Insurance) #12 ... 518-474-6630
HMO (Medical Operation) #43 ... 518-473-4842
Holding Company#23 877-BANK-NYS, 212-709-1503
Home Care Service #38 ... 518-408-1629
Home Health Agency/Trainer #38 ... 518-408-1629
Homeworker Industrial Distributor #9 ... 518-457-1942
Hospice #38 ... 518-408-1629
Hospital #38 ... 518-402-1004
Hotel/Motel Name Certificate #10 ... 518-474-4429
Hunting Guide #3 ... 518-402-8838
Insurance Adjuster #12 ... 518-474-6630
Insurance Agent/Consultant/Broker #12 518-474-6630
Insurance Appraiser #12 ... 518-474-6630
Insurance Company #12 ... 518-474-6630
Insurance Cont. Educ. Provider #12 ... 518-474-6630
Interior Designer #19 ... 518-474-3817
Investment Advisor #1 ... 212-416-8222
Investment Company Article XII #23 ... 877-BANK-NYS, 212-709-1503
Juvenile Detention Facility #25 ... 518-473-4630
Kosher Food #30 ... 718-722-2852
Landscape Architect #19 ... 518-474-3817
Laser Operator, Mobile #9 ... 518-457-1942
Lender, Licens'd #23 . 877-BANK-NYS, 212-709-5496
Loan Broker #33 ... 518-270-2200
Lobbyist/Client/Public Corporation #16 . 518-474-7126
Lottery Agent/Ticket Seller #47 ... 518-388-3300
Lottery Claim Center #47 ... 518-388-3300
LPG-related #53 ... 800-972-1233
Mammography Facility #38 ... 518-402-1004
Mass Gathering #40 ... 518-402-7600
Massage Therapist #19 ... 518-474-3817
Medicaid Long-Term Care Svc #43 ... 518-473-4842
Medical Delivery System, Integrated #43 ... 518-473-4842

Medical Disciplinary Action #22 ... 800-663-6114
Medical Doctor #19 ... 518-474-3817
Medical Examiner, Independent #57 ... 800-781-2362
Medical Personnel Profile #22 ... 888-338-6999
Med'l Facility, Worker's Comp App'vd #57 ... 800-781-2362
Mental Health Facility #48 ... 518-474-5570
Mentally Retarded Facility/Service #49. 518-473-9689
Midwife #19 ... 518-474-3817
Migrant Farmworker Facility #40 ... 518-402-7600
Milk Bacteriologist #27 ... 518-457-1772
Milk-related Dealer/Service #27 ... 518-457-5731
Mining/Exploration, State-Land #37 ... 518-473-1288
Minority/Woman-owned Business #35. 518-292-5250
Mobile Home Park #40 ... 518-402-7600
Money Transmitter #23 ... 877-BANK-NYS, 212-709-5494
Mortgage Banker #23 877-BANK-NYS, 212-709-5574
Mortgage Broker #23. 877-BANK-NYS, 212-709-5574
Mortgage Guaranty Insurance Agent #12 ... 518-474-6630
Mover #56 ... 518-457-6236
Municipal Health Benefit Plan #12 ... 212-480-5245
Nail Technologist #10 ... 518-474-4429
Notary Public #10 ... 518-474-4429
Nurse-LPN/RPN #19 ... 518-474-3817
Nursery, Plant #26 ... 518-457-2087
Nurses' Aide #5 ... 800-918-8818
Nursing Home #38 ... 518-408-1267
Nursing Home Administrator #5 ... 518-408-1297
Nutritionist #19 ... 518-474-3817
Occupational Therapist/Assistant #19.. 518-474-3817
Off-Track Betting #15 ... 518-453-8460 x2
Ophthalmic Dispenser #19 ... 518-474-3817
Optometrist #19 ... 518-474-3817
Out-of-state Bank Representative Ofc. #23 ... 877-BANK-NYS
Paramedic #7 ... 518-402-0996
Passenger Motor Carrier #56 ... 518-457-6503
Patient Service Center #41 ... 518-485-5378
Pesticide Business #2 ... 518-402-8748
Pesticide Distributor #2 ... 518-402-8748
Pesticide/Commercial Applicator #2 ... 518-402-8748
Pet Cemetery/Crematory #10 ... 518-474-4429
Pet Dealer #27 ... 518-457-7749
Pet Food Producer #29 ... 519-457-5457
Petroleum/Fuel Dealer/Handler #53 ... 800-972-1233
Pharmacist/Pharmacy #19 ... 518-474-3817
Physical Therapist/Assistant #19 ... 518-474-3817
Physician #19 ... 518-474-3817
Physician Assistant #19 ... 518-474-3817
Physicians Specialist Assistant #19 ... 518-474-3817
Phytosanitarian #26 ... 518-457-2087
Pistol Permit #51 ... 518-457-2627
Plant Dealer #26 ... 518-457-2087
Podiatrist #19 ... 518-474-3817
Premium Finance Company #23 ... 877-BANK-NYS, 212-709-5498
Private Investigator #10 ... 518-474-4429
Private School, Mentally Retarded #49. 518-473-9689
Promoter, Entertainment #54 ... 800-698-2909
Psychologist #19 ... 518-474-3817
Public Accountant-CPA #19 ... 518-474-3817
Public Vessel (State Waters) #50 ... 518-474-0445
Racetrack #15 ... 518-453-8460 x2
Racing Occupation #15 ... 518-453-8460 x2
Radiation Device, General-use #9 ... 518-457-1942
Radiation Materials Permit #14 ... 518-402-7590
Radiation Safety Officer #14 ... 518-402-7590
Radiation Therapy Technologist #14 ... 518-402-7580
Radiologic Technologist #14 ... 518-402-7580
Radiologic Technology School #14 ... 518-402-7580
Radon Testing Lab #14 ... 518-402-7556
Rafting Guide, Whitewater #3 ... 518-402-8838
Railroad/Steamboat Policeman #10 ... 518-457-1932
Real Estate Agent/Broker/Office #10 ... 518-474-4429
Real Estate Appraiser #10 ... 518-474-4429

Real Estate Investment Trust #45 ... 212-416-8122
Real Estate Offering, Registered #45 .. 212-416-8122
Real Estate Syndication #45 ... 212-416-8122
Regatta/Marina #50 ... 518-474-0445
Reinsurance Intermediary #12 ... 518-474-6630
Re-insurer #12 ... 518-474-6623
Renderer #29 ... 518-457-1215
Rental Agency, Limited #12 ... 518-474-6630
Residential Facility #24 ... 518-474-7112
Respiratory Therapist/Therapy Tech. #19 ... 518-474-3817
Restaurant Brewer #46 ... 212-961-8385
Rock and Ice Climbing Guide #3 ... 518-402-8838
Safe Deposit Company #23 ... 877-BANK-NYS, 212-709-1503
Sales Finance Company #23 ... 877-BANK-NYS, 212-709-5496
Sales Tax Permit #54 ... 800-698-2909
Savings & Loan #23 . 877-BANK-NYS, 212-709-1511
Savings Bank #23 ... 877-BANK-NYS, 212-709-1511
School Administrator/Supervisor #17 ... 518-474-3901
School Counselor #17 ... 518-474-3901
School Media Specialist #17 ... 518-474-3901
School, Non-Degree Proprietary #34 ... 518-474-3969
School, Private #34 ... 518-474-3969
School, Private, Dir./Teacher #34 ... 518-474-3969
Scientific Collection #11 ... 631-444-0483
Sealed Container (Thruway) #55 ... 518-436-3079
Securities Broker/Dealer #1 ... 212-416-8222
Securities Salesperson #1 ... 212-416-8222
Security & Fire Alarm Installer #10 ... 518-474-4429
Security Guard #10 ... 518-474-4429
Self-Insured Carrier Represent've#57 .. 800-664-2379
Shellfish-related Permit #11 ... 631-444-0483
Short Hand Reporter #19 ... 518-474-3817
Show, Permit to Operate #54 ... 800-698-2909
Ski Tow #9 ... 518-457-2131
Slaughterhouse #27 ... 518-457-5459
Snowmobile Event /Instructor #50 ... 518-474-0446
Social Worker #19 ... 518-474-3817
Solicitor (Fund Raising) #44 ... 518-486-9797
Special Event, Serving Alcohol #46 ... 212-961-8385
Specialty Food Producer #29 ... 519-457-1215
Speech Pathologist/Audiologist #19 ... 518-474-3817
Sporting License #11 ... 518-402-8843
Sportsman License, Lifetime #11 ... 518-402-8843
State Bid Result #36 ... 518-474-1314
State Telecommunicat'n Contract'r #37 518-473-2658
Steel Haulers Permit (Thruway) #55 ... 518-436-3079
Stevedore #20 ... 212-742-9280
Stock Life Insurer #12 ... 212-480-5038
Substance Abuse Provider #31 ... 518-457-4384
Summer Camp - Mental Retarded #49. 518-473-9689
Summer Day Camp #40 ... 518-402-7600
Surveyor, Land #19 ... 518-474-3817
Swimming Pool, Public/Group #40 ... 518-402-7600
Takeover Statement, Registration #1 .. 212-416-8222
Tandem Trailer Permit (Thruway) #55. 518-436-3150
Teacher #17 ... 518-474-3901
Teacher, Proprietary School #34 ... 518-474-3969
Telemarketer Business #10 ... 518-474-4429
Terminal Operator, Fuel #53 ... 800-972-1233
Theatrical Syndication #1 ... 212-416-8222
Ticket Distributor #1 ... 212-416-8222
Tour Vessel #32 ... 518-471-5010
Trading Stamp Registration #10 ... 518-474-4429
Tramway #9 ... 518-457-2131
Trapper #11 ... 518-402-8843
Traveling Summer Day Camp #40 ... 518-402-7600
Treatment Center/Clinic #22 ... 518-402-0911
Truck Safety/Compliance Bureau #56 .. 518-485-7770
Trust Company #23.. 877-BANK-NYS, 212-709-1503
Underwater Land Lease #37 ... 518-474-2195
Uniform Procedures Act Permit #11 ... 518-402-8985
Upholster & Bedding Industry #10 ... 518-474-4429
Utilization Mgmt. Registration #43 ... 518-473-4842
Vendor, New York City #58 ... 212-341-0933

Vessel Operator, Recreational/Touring #50 518-474-0445
Veteran Home- Skill'd Nursing Home #38 518-474-2772
Veterinarian/Veterinary Technician #19 518-474-3817
Viatical Settlement Broker #12 518-474-6630
Warehouse, Food #29 518-457-1215
Warehouse, Refrigerated #29 518-457-1215
Wastewater Treatm't Plant Operat'r #4 . 518-402-8177
Water Processing Facility, Bulk #13 518-402-7712
Water Supply Permit #11 518-402-8985
Waxing Establishment/Operator/Tech #10 518-474-4429
Weighmaster #28 518-457-3146
Wildlife Collector #11 518-402-8985
Wildlife Rehabilitator #11 518-402-8985
Window Cleaning Equipment #9 518-457-1536
Workers Comp Appr'v'd Health Provid'r #57 800-781-2362
Workers Comp Claim Rep. #57 800-664-2379
Workers Comp PPO Applicant #57 800-781-2362
Workers' Comp Preferred Provider #43 518-473-4842
Workplace Safety/loss Prev't'n Consult #9 518-457-2735
Wrestler #21 212-417-5700
Youth Shelter, Runaway/Homeless #24 518-474-7112

New York Licensing Agency Information

#1 Department of Law, Bureau of Investor Protection & Securities, 120 Broadway, 23rd Fl, New York, NY 10271; 212-416-8222, Fax- 212-416-8816. www.oag.state.ny.us

#2 Department of Environmental Conservation, Bureau of Pesticide Management, 625 Broadway, Albany, NY 12233-7254; 518-402-8788, Fax- 518-402-9024. www.dec.ny.gov/ Permits issued from various regional offices.

#3 Department of Environmental Conservation, Division of Forest Protection & Fire Mgmt., 625 Broadway, 8th Fl, Albany, NY 12233-2560; 518-402-8838, Fax- 518-485-8458. www.dec.ny.gov

#4 Department of Environmental Conservation, Division of Water, Bureau of Watershed Compliance, 625 Broadway, 9th Fl, Albany, NY 12233-3506; 518-402-8155, Fax- 518-402-8177. www.dec.ny.gov/chemical/292.html

#5 Board of Examiners of Nursing Home Administrators, Bureau of Professional Credentialing, 161 Delaware Ave, Delmar, NY 10254-1393; 518-408-1297, Fax- 518-408-1632. Hours- 8AM-5PM. www.nyhealth.gov

#6 Department of Health, Bureau of Funeral Directing, 433 River St, #303, Troy, NY 12180-2299; 518-402-0785, Fax- 518-402-0784.

#7 Department of Health, Emergency Medical Services, One Fulton St, Troy, NY 12180; 518-408-5318, Fax- 518-408-5392. www.health.state.ny.us/nysdoh/ems/main.htm

#8 Department of Labor, Boiler Safety Bureau, State Office Campus, Bldg 12, Rm 165, Albany, NY 12240-0102; 518-457-2722, Fax- 518-485-9077. www.labor.state.ny.us

#9 Department of Labor, Worker Protection Central Processing, State Office Bldg Campus 12, Rm 166, Albany, NY 12240; 518-457-7629, Fax- 518-485-6082. www.labor.state.ny.us

#10 Department of State, Division of Licensing Services, PO Box 22001 (80 S Swan St, 10th Fl), Albany, NY 12201-2201; 518-474-4429, Fax- 518-473-6648. Hours- 9AM-4:45PM. www.dos.state.ny.us/lcns/licensing.html Search data at- http://appsext8.dos.state.ny.us/lcns_public/chk_load

#11 Department of Environmental Conservation, Offices of Fish, Wildlife and Marine Resources, 625 Broadway, Albany, NY 12233-4750; 518-402-8924, Fax- 518-402-9027. www.dec.ny.gov/about/634.html

#12 Insurance Department, Licensing Bureau Agency, One Commerce Plaza, Albany, NY 12257; 518-474-6630. www.ins.state.ny.us

#13 Department of Health, Bureau of Water Supply Protection, 547 River St, Flanigan Sq, Rm 400, Troy, NY 12180; 518-402-7712, 800-458-1158 x27650, Fax- 518-402-7599. Hours-9AM-5PM. www.health.state.ny.us/environmental/water/drinking/operate/operate.htm

#14 Department of Health, Bureau of Environmental Radiation Protection, 547 River St, Flanigan Sq, Rm 530, Troy, NY 12180-2216; 518-402-7580, Fax- 518-402-7575. www.health.state.ny.us/professionals/doctors/radiological/ Information can be requested through FOIL.

#15 Racing & Wagering Board, 1 Broadway Center #600, Schenectady, NY 12305-2553; 518-395-5400, Fax- 518-347-1250. www.racing.state.ny.us

#16 Commission on Public Integrity, 540 Broadway, Albany, NY 12207; 518-408-3976, Fax- 518-473-6492. Hours- 8:30AM-5PM. www.nyintegrity.org/ Search data at- www.nyintegrity.org/

#17 State Education Department, Office of Teaching, 5N Education Bldg, Albany, NY 12234; 518-474-3901, Fax- 518-473-0271. www.highered.nysed.gov/tcert/ Search data at- http://eservices.nysed.gov/teach/certhelp/CpPersonSearchExternal.jsp?trgAction=INQUIRY

#18 Unified Court System, Attorney Registration Unit, 25 Beaver St, Rm 840, New York, NY 10008; 212-428-2800, Fax- 212-428-2804. 9AM-5PM. www.nycourts.gov/attorneys/ Search data at- www.nycourts.gov/attorneys/registration/index.shtml

#19 Education Department, Office of the Professions, 89 Washington Ave, State Education Bldg, 2nd Fl, Albany, NY 12234; 518-474-3817. www.op.nysed.gov Search data at- www.op.nysed.gov/opsearches.htm#e Other telephones- attendant available 9-11:45AM and 12:45-4:30PM EST. TDD 518-473-1426.

#20 Division of Licensing & EIC, Waterfront Commission of New York Harbor, 39 Broadway, 4th Fl, New York, NY 10006; 212-742-9280, Fax- 212-480-0587. www.wcnynj.org

#21 State Athletic Commission, Department of State, 123 Williams St, 20th Fl, New York, NY 10038; 212-417-5700, Fax- 212-417-4987. www.dos.state.ny.us/athletic/

#22 Department of Health, Office of Professional Medical Conduct, 433 River St, #303, Troy, NY 12180; 800-663-6114, 518-402-0836. Hours- 9AM-5PM. www.health.state.ny.us/nysdoh/opmc/main.htm Search data at- http://w3.health.state.ny.us/opmc/factions.nsf

#23 State Banking Department, Licensed Financial Services Division, One State St, 3rd Fl, New York, NY 10004-1417; 877-BANK-NYS, Fax- 212-709-3582. www.banking.state.ny.us Search data at- www.banking.state.ny.us/supinst.htm

#24 Office of Children and Family Services, Legal Division, 52 Washington St, Rensselaer, NY 12144; 518-474-7793, Fax- 518-486-7550. www.ocfs.state.ny.us/main/

#25 Office of Children and Family Services, Detention/Voluntary Agency Services Unit, 52 Washington St, Rensselaer, NY 12144-2796; 518-473-4630. www.ocfs.state.ny.us/main/

#26 Department of Agriculture and Markets, Division of Plant Industry, 10B Airline Dr, Albany, NY 12235; 800-554-4501. www.agmkt.state.ny.us

#27 Department of Agriculture and Markets, Division of Animal Industry, 10 B Airline Dr, Albany, NY 12235; 518-457-3880; 800-554-4501, Fax- 518-485-5816. www.agmkt.state.ny.us/AI/AIHome.html

#28 Department of Agriculture and Markets, Division of Weights and Measures, 10B Airline Dr, Albany, NY 12235-0001; 518-457-3146. www.agmkt.state.ny.us/WM/WMHome.html Local Offices 518-457- 3146 or www.agmkt.state.ny.us/WM/wmdirlst.html.

#29 Department of Agriculture and Markets, Division of Food Safety and Inspection, 10B Airline Dr, Albany, NY 12235; 518-457-5459, Fax- 518-457-8892. www.agmkt.state.ny.us/FS/FSHome.html

#30 Department of Agriculture and Markets, Division of Kosher Law Enforcement, 55 Hanson Pl, Brooklyn, NY 11217; 718-722-2852. www.agmkt.state.ny.us/KO/KOHome.html

#31 Office of Alcoholism and Substance Abuse Services, Bureau of Professional Development, 1450 Western Ave, Albany, NY 12203-3526; 518-473-3460. www.oasas.state.ny.us/index.cfm Search data at- www.oasas.state.ny.us/credentialingVerification/verification/home.cfm

#32 State Canal Corporation, Interchange 23, Rte 9W, Albany, NY 12209-2098; 518-436-2700. www.nyscanals.gov/

#33 Office of the State Comptroller, Office of Unclaimed Funds, 110 State St, 8th Fl, Albany, NY 12236; 518-270-2200, 800-221-9311. Hours- 7AM-5PM. www.osc.state.ny.us

#34 State Education Department, Bureau of Proprietary School Supervision, Education Building Addition, Rm 974, Albany, NY 12234; 518-474-3969, Fax- 518-473-3644. Hours- 8:30AM-5PM. www.highered.nysed.gov/bpss/

#35 Empire State Development, Division of Minority and Women's Business Development, 30 S Pearl St, Albany, NY 12245; 518-292-5250. www.empire.state.ny.us/pdf/htbcert.pdf Search data at- http://205.232.252.35/ A second office is at 633 3rd Av, NY, NY 10017, phone 212-803-2414.

#36 State Office of General Services, Design and Construction, Empire State Plza, Corning Tower, 35th Fl, Rm 3564, Albany, NY 12242; 518-474-0200, Fax- 518-486-1650. www.ogs.state.ny.us/dnc/defaultDandC.html

#37 State Office of General Services, Real Estate Development, 26th Fl, Corning Tower, Empire State Plaza, Albany, NY 12242; 518-474-2195, Fax- 518-474-0011. www.ogs.state.ny.us/default.asp

#38 Department of Health, Office of Health Systems Management, 161 Delaware Ave, Delmar, NY 12054; 518-408-1129. Search data at- www.health.state.ny.us/facilities/adult_care/

#39 State Department of Health, Bureau of Environmental Health, 547 River St, Rm 230, Flanigan Sq, Troy, NY 12180; 518-402-7940, Fax- 518-402-7949. Hours- 9AM-5PM. www.health.state.ny.us

#40 State Department of Health, Bureau of Community Environmental Health and Food Protection, 547 River St, Flanigan Sq, Rm 515, Troy, NY 12180; 518-402-7600, Fax- 518-402-7609. Hours- 8:30AM-4:45PM. www.health.state.ny.us/environmental/phone.htm

#41 State Department of Health, Wadsworth Center, Empire State Plaza, Concourse Level, Rm E324, Albany, NY 12201-0509; 518-474-0005. www.health.state.ny.us/

#42 Department of Health, Bureau of Narcotic Enforcement, 433 River St, #303, Troy, NY 12180-2299; 518-402-0707; 866-811-7957, Fax- 518-402-0709. www.health.state.ny.us/professionals/narcotic/

#43 State Department of Health, Bureau of Managed Care Certification & Surveillance, Corning Tower Bldg, Empire State Plaza, Rm 2001, Albany, NY 12237-0094; 518-473-4842. www.health.state.ny.us/health_care/managed_care/mltc/

#44 Office of the Attorney General, Charities Bureau, 120 Broadway, 3rd Fl, New York, NY 10271; 212-416-8400, Fax- 212-416-8393. www.oag.state.ny.us/bureaus/charities/pennies03/penintro.html 2nd office at the State Capitol in Albany in telephone area code 518.

#45 Office of the Attorney General, Bureau of Real Estate Finance, 120 Broadway, 23rd Fl, New York, NY 10271; 212-416-8122; 800-788-9898, Fax- 212-416-8179. www.oag.state.ny.us/bureaus/real_estate_finance/contact.html

#46 State Liquor Authority, Division of Alcoholic Beverage Control, 317 Lenox Ave, New York, NY 10027; 212-961-8385, Fax-212-961-8283. www.abc.state.ny.us Agency maintains three zone offices located in New York City, Albany (518-474-3114) and Buffalo (716-847-3035) and one satellite office in Syracuse (315-428-4198). Public Affairs office is 212-961-8300.

#47 New York Lottery, PO Box 7500 (1 Broadway Center), Schenectady, NY 12301-7500; 518-388-3300, Fax- 518-388-3403. www.nylottery.org

#48 State Office of Mental Health, Bureau of Inspection and Certification, 44 Holland Ave, Albany, NY 12229; 518-474-5570, Fax- 518-486-5587. www.omh.state.ny.us/omhweb/licensing/ Search data at- www.omh.state.ny.us/omhweb/licensing/

#49 Office of Mental Retardation and Developmental Disabilities, Developmental Disabilities Service Office, 30 Russell Rd, Albany, NY 12206; 518-486-1313, Fax- 518-457-3016. www.omr.state.ny.us Also a NYC Office at 75 Morton St, 212-229-3231.

#50 State Parks, Recreation and Historic Preservation, Bureau of Marine and Recreational Vehicles, Agency Building 1, 11th Fl, Empire State Plaza, Albany, NY 12238; 518-474-0456, Fax- 518-408-1030. Hours- 8AM-4:30PM. www.nysparks.com Snowmobiles must be registered with state DMV.

#51 State Police, BCI Section; Firearms Section, 1220 Washington Ave, Bldg 22, Albany, NY 12226-2252; 518-457-2627. www.troopers.state.ny.us

#52 Department of Taxation and Finance, Registration and Bonding Tax Unit, Building 8, Rm 855, State Campus, Albany, NY 12227; 800-225-5829, Fax- 518-457-9807. www.tax.state.ny.us/sbc/

#53 Department of Taxation & Finance, Taxpayer Contact Center, State Campus, Building 8, Rm 900, Albany, NY 12227; 800-972-1233. www.nystax.gov

#54 Department of Taxation & Finance, Sales Tax Registration Unit, State Campus, Building 8, Rm 431, Albany, NY 12201; 800-972-1233. Hours- 8AM-5PM. www.tax.state.ny.us

#55 State Thruway Authority, Department Traffic Management, PO Box 189 (200 Southern Blvd), Albany, NY 12201-0189; 518-436-2700. www.nysthruway.gov/commercial/

#56 State Department of Transportation, Passenger and Freight Safety Division, 50 Wolf Rd, Pod 53, Albany, NY 12205; 518-485-7770. Hours- 8AM-4:10PM. https://www.nysdot.gov/portal/page/portal/index

#57 State Workers' Compensation Board, Health Provider Administration, 100 Broadway-Menands, Albany, NY 12241; 866-750-5157, Fax- 518-473-9166. www.wcb.state.ny.us

#58 Vendor Enrollment Center, VENDEX, Mayor's Office of Contract Services, 253 Broadway, 9th Fl, New York, NY 10007; 212-341-0933, 212-857-1680, Fax- 212-855-1683. Hours- 9:30AM-5PM. www.nyc.gov/html/mocs/html/research/vendex.shtml Search data at- http://slnx-prd-web.nyc.gov/cfb/cfbSearch.nyc?method=search

New York Federal Courts

The following list indicates the district and division name for each county in the state. If the bankruptcy court location is different from the district court, then the location of the bankruptcy court appears in parentheses.

New York County/Court Cross Reference

County	District	Division
Albany	Northern	Albany
Allegany	Western	Buffalo
Bronx	Southern	New York City
Broome	Northern	Binghamton (Utica)
Cattaraugus	Western	Buffalo
Cayuga	Northern	Syracuse (Utica)
Chautauqua	Western	Buffalo
Chemung	Western	Rochester
Chenango	Northern	Binghamton (Utica)
Clinton	Northern	Albany-varies
Columbia	Northern (Southern)	Albany (Poughkeepsie)
Cortland	Northern	Syracuse (Utica)
Delaware	Northern	Binghamton (Utica)
Dutchess	Southern	White Plains (Poughkeepsie)
Erie	Western	Buffalo
Essex	Northern	Albany -varies
Franklin	Northern	Albany-varies (Albany)
Fulton	Northern	Utica (Albany)
Genesee	Western	Buffalo
Greene	Northern (Southern)	Albany (Poughkeepsie)
Hamilton	Northern	Utica
Herkimer	Northern	Utica
Jefferson	Northern	Albany-varies (Albany)
Kings	Eastern	Brooklyn
Lewis	Northern	Albany-varies (Utica)
Livingston	Western	Rochester
Madison	Northern	Syracuse (Utica)
Monroe	Western	Rochester
Montgomery	Northern	Utica (Albany)
Nassau	Eastern	Brooklyn (Westbury)
New York	Southern	New York City
Niagara	Western	Buffalo
Oneida	Northern	Utica
Onondaga	Northern	Syracuse (Utica)
Ontario	Western	Rochester
Orange	Southern	White Plains (Poughkeepsie)
Orleans	Western	Buffalo
Oswego	Northern	Syracuse (Utica)
Otsego	Northern	Binghamton (Utica)
Putnam	Southern	White Plains (Poughkeepsie)
Queens	Eastern	Brooklyn
Rensselaer	Northern	Albany
Richmond	Eastern	Brooklyn
Rockland	Southern	White Plains
Saratoga	Northern	Albany
Schenectady	Northern	Albany
Schoharie	Northern	Albany
Schuyler	Western	Rochester
Seneca	Western	Rochester
St. Lawrence	Northern	Albany-varies (Albany)
Steuben	Western	Rochester
Suffolk	Eastern	Central Islip
Sullivan	Southern	White Plains (Poughkeepsie)
Tioga	Northern	Binghamton (Utica)
Tompkins	Northern	Syracuse (Utica)
Ulster	Northern (Southern)	Albany (Poughkeepsie)
Warren	Northern	Albany
Washington	Northern	Albany
Wayne	Western	Rochester
Westchester	Southern	White Plains
Wyoming	Western	Buffalo
Yates	Western	Rochester

Standards for Federal Courts: Fees are standard unless noted in profile. Search fee is $26.00 per item (one party name or case number). Copy fee is $.50 per page. Certification fee is $9.00 per document, double for exemplification, if available. Most courts require prepayment. Mail requests should enclose a SASE unless otherwise noted. Before releasing records, all courts require prepayment, unless noted.

District courts index by defendant and plaintiff and by case number. Bankruptcy courts usually index by debtor and case number. While most courts now have their indexes on computer, many may still maintain index card files as well. Courts will archive closed case files at different times.

There are numerous public access programs available to online subscribers. Search the U.S. Party/Case Index to find party names and case numbers among all courts. Individual case data is provided on PACER. A search of CM/ECF provides copies of cases filed electronically. For details about PACER, the US Party/Case Index, and CM/ECF see the Appendix or go to http://pacer.psc.uscourts.gov or call 800-676-6856.

US District Court
New York Eastern District

Brooklyn Division Clerk of Court, 225 Cadman Plaza East, Brooklyn Courthouse, Brooklyn, NY 11201, 718-613-2600. Hours-8:30AM-5PM. www.nyed.uscourts.gov

Counties/Note: Kings, Queens, Richmond. Cases from Nassau and Suffolk may also be filed at Brooklyn (but paper records and cases are heard in Central Islip Div.), but all records are available electronically via PACER from Brooklyn Div.

Searches/Indexing: If civil search, include full name only; if criminal, SSN or DOB helpful. Results do not include SSN or DOB. Will not fax back documents. New cases are in the index 2 days after filing date. Computer index maintained back to 1982. Case records for Suffolk and Nassau counties are not physically located here - see Central Islip Division.

Search Access: Mail: Search usually completed-1-2 days. SASE not required. **In person:** 5 public terminals available. Self-serve copies $.25 each.

Payment: Pay by Visa/MC (in person only), money order, cashier's or personal check. Payee: Clerk, US District Court.

E-Services: PACER integrated with ECF. This system includes electronic records from Suffolk and Nassau Counties, Long Island. PACER records go back to 1/1990. New records online after 1 day. ECF at https://ecf.nyed.uscourts.gov.

Decisions of Interest and Cases of Interest at www.nyed.uscourts.gov/coi/cases_of_interest.html **Online Note:** Access to court calendars at www.nyed.uscourts.gov/cgi-bin/caldir.pl.

Central Islip Division Court Clerk, 100 Federal Plaza, Long Island Courthouse, Central Islip, NY 17722-4438, 631-712-6000; records-631-712-6032; Fax- 631-712-6043. Hours-8:30AM-5PM. www.nyed.uscourts.gov

Counties/Note: Nassau, Suffolk. Cases from these counties may be filed in Brooklyn Division, but heard in Central Islip. Central Islip cases can be found on Brooklyn's PACER system.

Searches/Indexing: If civil search, include full name only; if criminal, SSN or DOB helpful. Results do not include SSN or DOB. Will not fax back documents. New cases are in the index 2 days after filing date. Computer and card indexes maintained; computer index back to 1980, 1990.

Search Access: Limited docket info available by phone. **Mail:** Search usually completed- 1-2 days. Include SASE for return. **Fax:** Fax requests may only be made for a few names. **In person:** 5 public terminals available. Self-serve copies $.25 each.

Payment: Pay by Visa/MC (in person only), money order, cashier's or personal check. Payee: Clerk, US District Court.

E-Services: PACER records go back to 1/1990. New records online after 1 day. ECF at https://ecf.nyed.uscourts.gov. Decisions of Interest and Cases of Interest at www.nyed.uscourts.gov/coi/cases_of_interest.html **Online Note:** Access to court calendars at www.nyed.uscourts.gov/cgi-bin/caldir.pl.

US Bankruptcy Court New York Eastern District

Brooklyn Division Court Clerk, 271 Cadman Plaza East, Brooklyn, NY 11201, 347-394-1700. Hours-9AM-4:30PM. www.nyeb.uscourts.gov

Counties/Note: Kings, Queens, Richmond. Some Kings and Queens County Chapter 11 cases may also be assigned to Central Islip. Due to judge shortage, some Nassau County Chapter 11 cases may be assigned To Brooklyn.

Searches/Indexing: In search request include full name, SSN, date closed. Results do not include SSN or DOB; pre-2003 closed cases may include SSN. Will not fax back documents. New cases are in the index 1 day after filing date. Computer index maintained back to 2003, Chapter 11s to 2002. Older cases indexed on microfiche. District-wide searching on computer and public access terminal. Paper closed case files sent to archives 1 year after closed; computer records never purged.

Search Access: Only docket info is available by phone. Voice Case Information Service available, call VCIS at 347-394-1799 or 347-394-1790. **Mail:** Search usually completed- 1-2 weeks. SASE not required. **In person:** 6 public terminals available. Self-serve copy- $.25 per page; from computer terminal- $.10 each. **Payment:** Pay by money order, cashier's check. No personal or business checks. Attorney credit cards accepted. Payee: Clerk, US Bankruptcy Ct.

E-Services: PACER records go back to 1991. New records online after 1 day. ECF at https://ecf.nyeb.uscourts.gov. **Opinions Online:** www.nyeb.uscourts.gov/written_opinions.php. Opinions date back to 4/2004. **Online Note:** Access calendars free at www.nyeb.uscourts.gov/.

Central Islip Div. Court Clerk, 290 Federal Plaza, 2nd Fl, Long Island Federal Courthouse, Central Islip, NY 11722, 631-712-6200. Hours-9AM-4:30PM. www.nyeb.uscourts.gov

Counties/Note: Suffolk, Nassau. Some Kings and Queens County Chapter 11 cases may also be assigned to Central Islip. Due to judge shortage, some Nassau County Chapter 11 cases may be assigned to Brooklyn.

Searches/Indexing: In search request include full name, SSN, date closed. Results do not include SSN or DOB; pre-2003 closed cases may include SSN. Will not fax back documents. New cases are in the index 1-2 days after filing date. District-wide searching on computer and public access terminal. Paper case files sent to archives 1 year after closed; computer records never purged.

Search Access: Basic docket data only available by phone, call VCIS at 347-394-1799 or 347-394-1790. **Mail:** Search usually completed- 1 week. SASE not required. **In person:** Public terminal available. Self-serve copy- $.25 per page; from computer terminal- $.10 each. **Payment:** Pay by money order, cashier's check. No personal or business checks. Attorney credit cards accepted. Payee: Clerk, US Bankruptcy Court. Enclose a FedEx package for expedited return service.

E-Services: PACER records go back to 1991. New records online after 1 day. ECF at https://ecf.nyeb.uscourts.gov. **Opinions Online:** www.nyeb.uscourts.gov/written_opinions.php. Opinions date back to 4/2004. **Online Note:** Access calendars free at www.nyeb.uscourts.gov/.

US District Court New York Northern District

Albany Division Court Clerk, 445 Broadway, Rm 509, James T Foley Courthouse, Albany, NY 12207-2924, 518-257-1800; Fax- 518-257-1801. Hours-9AM-4PM. www.nynd.uscourts.gov

Counties/Note: Albany, Clinton, Columbia, Essex, Greene, Rensselaer, Saratoga, Schenectady, Schoharie, Ulster, Warren, Washington. This court provides the judges (and physical case records) for Plattsburgh Division - Clinton, Essex, Franklin counties - but cases are often assigned to Syracuse, Utica or Binghamton Divisions on occasion.

Searches/Indexing: Helpful to include SSN or DOB in criminal search requests; civil include full name only. Results include last 4 SSN digits, also birth year. Results do not include SSN or DOB if case after 2003. Will not fax back documents. New cases are in the index 1 day after filing date. Both computer and card indexes maintained. Case indexes on computer terminal in any Northern District Div. Files sent to archives after 1 year.

Search Access: Only docket info is available by phone. **Mail:** Search usually completed- 1-2 days. SASE not required. **Fax:** Fax search okay if directed to Syracuse Division. **In person:** 2 public terminals available. No self-serve copier. **Payment:** Pay by money order, cashier's or personal check. Attorney credit cards accepted. Payee: Clerk, US District Court.

E-Services: PACER records go back to 6/1991. New records online after 1 day. ECF at https://ecf.nynd.uscourts.gov

Binghamton Division Court Clerk, 15 Henry St, Binghamton, NY 13902, 607-773-2893; civil dockets- 607-773-2638. Hours- 9AM-4PM. www.nynd.uscourts.gov

Counties/Note: Broome, Chenango, Delaware, Jefferson, Lewis, Otsego, St. Lawrence, Tioga. This court provides the judges (and physical case records) for the Watertown Division - Jefferson, Lewis and St Lawrence counties - although cases are often assigned to Syracuse, Utica or especially Albany Divisions.

Searches/Indexing: Helpful to include SSN or DOB in criminal search requests; civil include full name only. Results include last 4 SSN digits, also birth year. Results do not include SSN or DOB if case after 2003. Will not fax back documents. New cases are in the index 1 day after filing date. Computer index maintained. Case indexes on computer terminal in any Northern District Division. Open records "may" be located at this court. Files sent to archives 1 year after closed.

Search Access: Only docket info is available by phone. **Mail:** Search usually completed- 1-2 days. Include SASE for return. **Fax:** Fax search okay if directed to Syracuse Division. **In person:** 1 public terminal available. No self-serve copier.

Payment: Pay by money order, cashier's or personal check. Attorney credit cards accepted. Payee: Clerk, US District Court.

E-Services: PACER records go back to 6/1991. New records online after 1 day. ECF at https://ecf.nynd.uscourts.gov

Syracuse Division Court Clerk, PO Box 7367, Syracuse, NY 13261-7367 (In person: 100 S Clinton St, Syracuse, NY 13261), 315-234-8500; records- 315-234-8544; Fax- 315-234-8501. Hours-9AM-4PM. www.nynd.uscourts.gov

Counties/Note: Cayuga, Cortland, Madison, Onondaga, Oswego, Tompkins. May also have some cases from Watertown Division - Jefferson, Lewis, or St Lawrence counties - and rarely from Clinton, Essex, Franklin counties.

Searches/Indexing: Helpful to include SSN or DOB in criminal search requests; civil include full name only. Results do not include SSN or DOB if case after 2003. Will not fax back documents. New cases are in the index 1 day after filing date. Computer index maintained; criminal goes back to 1994, civil to 1991. Case indexes on computer terminal in any Northern District Division. Clerk can search index back to 1953; microfiche back to 1979, current criminal to 2004 and civil to 1991. Case files sent to archives 1 year after closed.

Search Access: Only docket info is available by phone. **Mail:** Search usually completed- 1-2 days. Include SASE for return. **Fax:** Fax search requests accepted. **In person:** 2 public terminals available.

Payment: Pay by money order, cashier's or personal check. Attorney credit cards accepted. Payee: Clerk, US District Court.

E-Services: PACER records go back to 6/1991. New records online immediately. ECF at https://ecf.nynd.uscourts.gov

Utica Division Court Clerk, 10 Broad St, Alexander Pirnie Bldg, Utica, NY 13501, 315-793-8151; records- ext.8. Hours-9AM-4PM. www.nynd.uscourts.gov

Counties/Note: Fulton, Hamilton, Herkimer, Montgomery, Oneida. May also have some cases from Watertown Division - Jefferson, Lewis, or St Lawrence counties - and rarely from Clinton, Essex, Franklin counties. (As of 1995, Albany, Binghamton and Syracuse no longer send their physical records to Utica.) .

Searches/Indexing: Helpful to include SSN or DOB in criminal search requests; civil include full name only. Results do not include SSN or DOB if case after 2003. Will not fax back documents. New cases are in the index 1 day after filing date. Computer and card indexes available; computer back to 1996. Case indexes on computer terminal in any Northern District Division. Case files sent to archives 1 year after closed.

Search Access: Only computerized info back to 1991 is available by phone. **Mail:** Search usually completed- 1 week. SASE not required. **Fax:** Fax search okay if directed to Syracuse Division. **In person:** 1 public terminal available. No self-serve copier.

Payment: Pay by money order, cashier's, business or personal check. Attorney credit cards accepted. Payee: Clerk, US District Court.

E-Services: PACER records go back to 6/1991. New records online after 1 day. ECF at https://ecf.nynd.uscourts.gov

US Bankruptcy Court New York Northern District

Albany Div. Court Clerk Office, 445 Broadway #330, James T Foley Courthouse, Albany, NY 12207, 518-257-1661; records- 518-257-1650. Hours- 9AM-4PM. www.nynb.uscourts.gov

Counties/Note: Albany, Clinton, Columbia, Essex, Greene, Rensselaer, Saratoga, Schenectady, Schoharie, Ulster, Warren, Washington. Prior to 4/2006, this court included counties of Albany, Clinton, Columbia, Essex, Franklin, Fulton, Greene, Jefferson, Montgomery, Rensselaer, Saratoga, Schenectady, Schoharie, St. Lawrence, Ulster, Warren, Washington.

Searches/Indexing: Search request requires name only. Results include last 4 SSN digits. Will not fax back documents. New cases are in the index 24 hours after filing date. Both computer and card indexes maintained.

Search Access: Only docket info is available by phone. Voice Case Information Service available, call VCIS at 800-206-1952. **Mail:** Search usually completed- 1-2 days. If case number is not known, the turnaround time may be as long as 5 days. SASE required. **Fax:** Fax search requests accepted. **In person:** 3 public terminals available. No self-serve copier.

Payment: Pay by major credit cards, no business or personal checks accepted. No debtor checks/credit cards accepted. Payee: Clerk, US Bankruptcy Court.

E-Services: PACER records go back to 1992. New records online immediately. ECF at https://ecf.nynb.uscourts.gov. **Opinions Online:** www.nynb.uscourts.gov/decisions.htm. Access weekly calendars free at www.nynb.uscourts.gov/usbc/calendar/calendar.html.

Syracuse Div. Court Clerk Office, 100 S Salina St #310, The Atrium, Syracuse, NY 13202, 315-295-1600. 9-4PM. www.nynb.uscourts.gov

Counties/Note: Cayuga, Cortland, Jefferson, Onondaga, Oswego, Tioga, Tompkins. This court was organized about 4/2006.

Searches/Indexing: Search request requires name only. Results include last 4 SSN digits. Will not fax back documents. New cases are in the index 24 hours after filing date. Both computer and card indexes maintained.

Search Access: Only docket info is available by phone. Voice Case Information Service available, call VCIS at 800-206-1952. **Mail:** Search usually completed- 1-2 days. If case number is not known, the turnaround time may be as long as 5 days. SASE required. **In person:** 2 public terminals available. No self-serve copier. **Payment:** Pay by major credit cards, no business or personal checks accepted. No debtor checks/credit cards accepted. Payee: Clerk, US Bankruptcy Court.

E-Services: PACER records go back to 2006. New records online immediately. ECF at https://ecf.nynb.uscourts.gov. **Opinions Online:** www.nynb.uscourts.gov/decisions.htm. Access weekly calendars free at www.nynb.uscourts.gov/usbc/calendar/calendar.html.

Utica Division Court Clerk, 10 Broad St, Rm 230, Utica, NY 13502, 315-793-8101; records- 315-266-1150; Fax- 315-793-8128. 9AM-4PM. www.nynb.uscourts.gov

Counties/Note: Broome, Chenango, Delaware, Franklin, Fulton, Hamilton, Lewis, Madison, Montgomery, Oneida, Otsego, St Lawrence. Prior to 4/2006, this court included counties of Broome, Cayuga, Chenango, Cortland, Delaware, Hamilton, Herkimer, Lewis, Madison, Oneida, Onondaga, Otsego, Oswego, Tioga, Tompkins. When scheduling a motion, if debtor residence is in Broome, Chenango, Delaware, or Otsego County, use 15 Henry St, 1st Fl, Binghampton, in the Notice of Motion for a Binghamton motion return.

Searches/Indexing: Search request requires name only. Results include last 4 SSN digits. Will not fax back documents. New cases are in the index 24 hours after filing date. Both computer and card indexes maintained.

Search Access: Only docket info is available by phone. Voice Case Information Service available, call VCIS at 800-206-1952. **Mail:** Search usually completed- 5 days. Turnaround time may be as long as 5 days. SASE required. **Fax:** Fax search requests accepted. **In person:** 2 public terminals available. No self-serve copier.

Payment: Pay by major credit cards, money order, cashier's or personal check. No debtor checks/credit cards accepted. Payee: Clerk, US Bankruptcy Court.

E-Services: PACER records go back to 1992. ECF at https://ecf.nynb.uscourts.gov. **Opinions Online:** www.nynb.uscourts.gov/decisions.htm. Access weekly calendars free at www.nynb.uscourts.gov/usbc/calendar/calendar.html.

US District Court New York Southern District

New York City Div. Court Clerk, 500 Pearl St, 1st Fl, New York, NY 10007, 212-805-0136; records- Open recs- 212-805-0710; Closed recs- 212-805-0715. 8:30-5PM www.nysd.uscourts.gov

Counties/Note: Bronx, New York. A 2nd courthouse at 40 Centre St is under construction and will house the Appellate Div when it re-opens; search at Pearl St location. Some cases from counties in the White Plains Division are also assigned to this New York Division. This occurs because certain judges hear cases in both Divisions.

Searches/Indexing: Search request requires name, also other helpful identifiers- SSN, DOB, address. Results do not include SSN or DOB, though DOB may appear on records prior to 2004. Will not fax back documents. New cases are in the index 2 days after filing date. Records on computer back to 1989. District-wide searches available on computer and public access terminals. Case files sent to archives 5 years after closed, but due to construction, closed cases were recently purged.

Search Access: Only docket info available by phone, but no identifiers. **Mail:** Search usually completed- 1-2 weeks. Include SASE for return. **In person:** 4 public terminals available in lobby; 10 terminals available in record rm. Self-serve copies- $.25 per page. **Payment:** Pay by no business or personal checks accepted. Attorney checks/credit cards accepted. Payee: Clerk of Court, S.D.N.Y.

E-Services: PACER records go back to early 1990. New records online after 1 day. ECF at https://ecf.nysd.uscourts.gov. **Opinions:** www.nysd.uscourts.gov/courtweb/PubMain.htm. Search selected rulings online using CourtWeb. View Rulings of Special Interest free at court webpage.

White Plains Division Court Clerk, 300 Quarropas St, US Courthouse, White Plains, NY 10601, 914-390-4100; Fax- 914-390-4180. Hours- 8:30AM-5PM. www.nysd.uscourts.gov

Counties/Note: Dutchess, Orange, Putnam, Rockland, Sullivan, Westchester. Some cases may be assigned to New York Div. This occurs because certain judges hear cases in both Divisions.

Searches/Indexing: Search request requires name, also other helpful identifiers- SSN, DOB, address. Results do not include SSN or DOB, though DOB may appear on records prior to 2004. Will not fax back documents. New cases are in the index 2 days after filing date. Computer index maintained back to 1999. Indexes automated since 1983. District-wide searches available on computer and public access terminals. Case files sent to archives 5 years after closed.

Search Access: Only docket info available by phone, but no identifiers. **Mail:** Search usually completed- 1-2 days. Include SASE for return. **In person:** Self-serve copies- $.25 per page.

Payment: Pay by Visa/MC, no business or personal checks accepted. Attorney checks/credit cards accepted. Payee: Clerk of Court, S.D.N.Y.

E-Services: PACER records go back to early 1990. New records online after 1 day. ECF at https://ecf.nysd.uscourts.gov. **Opinions Online:** www.nysd.uscourts.gov/courtweb/PubMain.htm. Search selected rulings online using CourtWeb. View Rulings of Special Interest at court webpage.

US Bankruptcy Court New York Southern District

New York Div. Court Clerk, 1 Bowling Green, Rm 534, New York, NY 10004, 212-668-2870. Hours-8:30AM-5PM. www.nysb.uscourts.gov

Counties: Bronx, New York.

Searches/Indexing: Include name and SSN in search request. Results include last 4 SSN digits. Will not fax back documents. New cases are in the index immediately after filing date. Computer index maintained back to 1991. District-wide searches back to 1991 available on computer and public access terminals. Case files sent to archives approx. 2 years after closed.

Search Access: Court will give docket info by phone for 1 case only. They will also reveal whether a case is pending. Voice Case Information Service available, call VCIS at 212-668-2772 or 866-232-1268. **Mail:** Search usually completed- in

2-3 days. SASE not required. **In person:** 3 public terminals available. Copies from public terminal- $.10 each. Copy machine- $.50 each.

Payment: Pay by Visa/MC, money order, cashier's check, business check. No personal or debtor checks. Payee: Clerk, US Bankruptcy Court.

E-Services: PACER records go back to 6/1991. New records online after same day. ECF at https://ecf.nysb.uscourts.gov. ECF/PACER system has all cases, but cases closed before 3/15/2000 on ECF at https://ecf-closed.nysb.uscourts.gov/. Judges opinions available via main website. Also, browse MegaCases free at www.nysb.uscourts.gov/megacases.html. **Online Note:** Judges Bernstein, Gerber, Gonzales calendars at http://216.220.101.146/calendar/. All other judge calendars on ECF system and the main website.

Poughkeepsie Division Court Clerk, 355 Main St, 2nd Fl, Poughkeepsie, NY 12601, 845-452-4200; Fax- 845-452-8375. 8:30AM-5PM. www.nysb.uscourts.gov

Counties: Dutchess, Orange, Putnam, Sullivan.

Searches/Indexing: Include name and SSN in search request. Results include last 4 SSN digits. Will not fax back documents. New cases are in the index immediately after filing date. Both computer and card indexes maintained. District-wide searches back to 1991 available on computer and public access terminals. Case files sent to archives approx. 2 years after closed.

Search Access: Court will give docket info by phone for 1 case only. They will also reveal whether a case is pending. Voice Case Information Service available, call VCIS at 212-668-2772 or 866-232-1268. **Mail:** Search usually completed- 3 days. SASE not required. **In person:** 1 public terminal available. Self-serve copier available.

Payment: Pay by Visa/MC, money order, cashier's check, business check. No personal or debtor checks. Payee: Clerk, US Bankruptcy Court.

E-Services: PACER records go back to 6/1991. New records online after 1 day. ECF at https://ecf.nysb.uscourts.gov. ECF/PACER system has all cases, but cases closed before 3/15/2000 on ECF at https://ecf-closed.nysb.uscourts.gov/. Judges opinions available via main website. Also, browse MegaCases free at www.nysb.uscourts.gov/megacases.html. **Online Note:** Judges Bernstein, Gerber, Gonzales calendars at http://216.220.101.146/calendar/. All other judge calendars on ECF system and the main website.

White Plains Div. Court Clerk, 300 Quarropas St, White Plains, NY 10601, 914-390-4060. Hours-8:30AM-5PM. www.nysb.uscourts.gov

Counties: Rockland, Westchester.

Searches/Indexing: Include name and SSN in search request. Results include last 4 SSN digits. Will not fax back documents. New cases are in the index immediately after filing date. Computer index maintained back to 1991. District-wide searches back to 1991 available on computer and public access terminals. Case files sent to archives approx. 2 years after closed.

Search Access: Court will give docket info by phone for 1 case only. They will also reveal whether a case is pending. Voice Case Information Service available, call VCIS at 212-668-2772 or 866-232-1268. **Mail:** Search usually completed- 1-2 days. Include SASE for return. **In person:** 1 public terminal available. Self-serve copier available downstairs.

Payment: Pay by Visa/MC (in person only), money order, cashier's check, business check. No personal or debtor checks. Payee: Clerk, US Bankruptcy Court.

E-Services: PACER records go back to 6/1991. New records online after 1 day. ECF at https://ecf.nysb.uscourts.gov. ECF/PACER system has all cases, but cases closed before 3/15/2000 on ECF at https://ecf-closed.nysb.uscourts.gov/. Judges opinions available via main website. Also, browse MegaCases free at www.nysb.uscourts.gov/megacases.html. **Online Note:** Judges Bernstein, Gerber, Gonzales calendars at http://216.220.101.146/calendar/. All other judge calendars on ECF system and the main website.

US District Court New York Western District

Buffalo Division Court Clerk, 68 Court St, Rm 304, Buffalo, NY 14202, 716) 332-1700, 716-551-4211; Fax- 716-551-4850. Hours-9AM-5PM. www.nywd.uscourts.gov

Counties/Note: Allegany, Cattaraugus, Chautauqua, Erie, Genesee, Niagara, Orleans, Wyoming. Prior to 1982, this division included what is now the Rochester Division.

Searches/Indexing: Helpful to include identifiers in search requests of pre-2004 files. Results do not include SSN or DOB. Will not fax back documents. New cases are in the index 2 days after filing date. Computer index maintained; criminal back to 1990. Closed electronic cases not purged.

Search Access: Mail: Search usually completed- 1-2 days. SASE not required. **In person:** 1 public terminal available. No self-serve copier.

Payment: Pay by Visa/MC/AmEx (attorneys only), money order, cashier's check. Payee: Clerk, US District Court.

E-Services: PACER records go back to 1992. New records online after 1 day. ECF at https://ecf.nywd.uscourts.gov. **Opinions Online:** Judges opinions only available through PACER;. free after registration.

Rochester Div. Court Clerk, 100 State St, Rm 2120, Rochester, NY 14614, 585-613-4000; Fax- 585-613-4035. Hours- 9AM-5PM. www.nywd.uscourts.gov

Counties/Note: Chemung, Livingston, Monroe, Ontario, Schuyler, Seneca, Steuben, Wayne, Yates. Division established in 1981.

Searches/Indexing: Helpful to include identifiers in search requests of pre-2004 files. Results do not include SSN or DOB. Will fax back documents; call for instructions. New cases are in the index 1-2 days after filing date. Computer index maintained back to 1995. Cases closed back to 1996 also held here; earlier case records and indexes held in Buffalo Division, Erie County.

Search Access: Simple docket info available by phone. **Mail:** Search usually completed- 1-2 days. Mail searches including years prior to 1982 will be forwarded to the Buffalo Division. SASE not required. **Fax:** Fees for fax requests depend on the nature of the search; call for requirements. **In person:** 2 public terminals available back to 2004. No self-serve copier.

Payment: Pay by money order, cashier's or personal check. Will accept cash up to $50.00. Payee: Clerk, US District Court.

E-Services: PACER records go back to 1992. New records online after 1 day. ECF at https://ecf.nywd.uscourts.gov. **Opinions Online:** Judges opinions only available through PACER;. free after registration.

US Bankruptcy Court New York Western District

Buffalo Division Court Clerk, Olympic Towers, 300 Pearl St #250, Buffalo, NY 14202-2501, 716-551-4130, 716-362-3200. Hours-8AM-4:30PM. www.nywb.uscourts.gov

Counties/Note: Allegany, Cattaraugus, Chautauqua, Erie, Genesee, Niagara, Orleans, Wyoming. Unstaffed court locations at Batavia, Niagara Falls, Olean, Mayville, Watkins Glen.

Searches/Indexing: Include full name and SSN in search request. Results include last 4 SSN digits. New cases are in the index 24 hours after filing date. Both computer and card indexes maintained. Closed electronic cases not purged.

Search Access: Only docket info is available by phone. Voice Case Information Service available, call VCIS at 800-776-9578 or 716-551-5311. **Mail:** Search usually completed- 2-3 days. Include SASE for return. **In person:** 4 public terminals available. No self-serve copier.

Payment: Pay by Visa/MC, money order, cashier's check, business check. No personal checks. Payee: Clerk, US Bankruptcy Court.

E-Services: PACER records go back to 8/1987. New records online after 1 day. ECF at https://ecf.nywb.uscourts.gov. **Opinions Online:** www.nywb.uscourts.gov/decisions.php. Calendars free at www.nywb.uscourts.gov/calendars.php.

Rochester Div. Court Clerk, 100 State St, Rm 1220, Rochester, NY 14614, 585-613-4200. Hours-8AM-4:30PM. www.nywb.uscourts.gov

Counties Chemung, Livingston, Monroe, Ontario, Schuyler, Seneca, Steuben, Wayne, Yates.

Searches/Indexing: Include full name and SSN in search request. Results include last 4 SSN digits. New cases are in the index 24 hours after filing date. Computer and microfiche indexes maintained. District-wide searches available back to 9/1987. Closed electronic cases not purged.

Search Access: Only docket info is available by phone. Voice Case Information Service available, call VCIS at 800-776-9578 or 716-551-5311. **Mail:** Search usually completed- 1-2 days. Include SASE for return. **In person:** 2 public terminals available back to 1987. No self-serve copier.

Payment: Pay by Visa/MC, money order, cashier's check. No personal checks. Payee: Clerk, US Bankruptcy Court.

E-Services: PACER records go back to 8/1987. New records online after 1 day. ECF at https://ecf.nywb.uscourts.gov. **Opinions Online:** www.nywb.uscourts.gov/decisions.php. Calendars free at www.nywb.uscourts.gov/calendars.php.

New York County Courts

Court	Jurisdiction	No. of Courts	How Organized
Supreme Courts*	General	11	12 Districts
County Courts*	General	2	
Combined Supreme and County Courts*	General	57	57 Counties
City Courts*	Limited	72	61 Cities (outside of NYC)
District Courts*	Limited	10	Nassau, Suffolk Counties
Civil /Criminal Courts of the City of New York*	Municipal	6	Boroughs
Town and Village Justice Courts	Municipal	1485	(approximately)
Surrogates' Courts*	Probate	62	62 Counties and Boroughs
Court of Claims	Limited	1	
Family Courts	Special	62	62 Counties and Boroughs

* Profiled in this Sourcebook.

Court	CIVIL								
	Tort	Contract	Real Estate	Min. Claim	Max. Claim	Small Claims	Estate	Eviction	Domestic Relations
Supreme Courts*	X	X	X	$25,000	No Max				X
County Courts*	X	X	X	$0	$25,000				
City Courts*	X	X	X	$0	$15,000	$3000		X	
District Courts*	X	X	X	$0	$15,000	$3000		X	
Civil /Criminal Courts of the City of New York*	X	X	X	$0	$25,000	$5000		X	
Town and Village Justice Courts	X	X	X	$0	$3000	$3000			
Surrogates' Courts*							X		X
Court of Claims	X	X	X	$0	No Max				
Family Courts									X

Court	CRIMINAL				
	Felony	Misdemeanor	DWI/DUI	Preliminary Hearing	Juvenile
Supreme Courts*	X				
County Courts*				X	
City Courts*	X	X	X	X	
District Courts*		X	X	X	
Civil /Criminal Courts of the City of New York*		X	X	X	
Town and Village Justice Courts		X	X	X	
Family Courts					X

Administration

New York State Unified Court System, Office of Court Administration, 4 ESP, Suite 201, Empire State Plaza, Albany, NY 12223. There is also a New York City Office of Court Administration, 25 Beaver St, New York, NY 10004, 212-428-2700. www.courts.state.ny.us

Court Structure

"Supreme and County Courts" are the highest trial courts in the state, equivalent to what may be called circuit or district in other states. New York's Supreme and County Courts may be administered together or separately. When separate, there is a clerk for each. Supreme and/or County Courts are not appeals courts. Supreme Courts handle civil cases – usually civil cases over $25,000 – but there are many exceptions. The County Courts handle felony cases and, in many counties, these County Courts also handle misdemeanors. The New York City Courts are structed differently.

For non-NYC courts (called Upstate Courts), City Courts handle misdemeanors and civil case claims up to $15,000, small claims, and eviction cases. Not all counties have City Courts, thus cases there fall to the Supreme and County Courts for civil and criminal respectively, or, in a many counties, to the small Town and Village Courts, which can number in the dozens within a county. Probate is handled by Surrogate Courts. Surrogate Courts may also hear Domestic Relations cases in some counties.

In New York City, the Supreme Court is the trial court with unlimited jurisdiction. The Civil Court of the City of New York has jurisdiction on civil matters up to $25,000. The Criminla Court of the City of New York has jurisdiction over misdemenaors and minor violations. The Family Court hears matters involivng children and familes. Probate is handled by the Surrogate's Court.

About Upstate Courts - The staff at Upstate Superior, County, and City Courts are NY state employees. Records for Supreme and County Courts are maintained by the County Clerks, who are county employees. However, in some counties (usually less-populated counties), the clerk for Supreme and County Courts may also be the "County Clerk" - these duo-role clerks are employed partly by the county, and partly by the state, which at times creates a question of whose "directives" and rules do they follow in regard to court record search procedures. You will find separate entries for "County Clerks" for most NY counties in the court profiles since, while not "courts," they do hold court records. The methods for searching at the County Clerk office are far different from searching at the Courts themselves. In counties where the County Clerk and the Chief Court Clerk are one in the same, you will find only the standard Supreme & County Court listing. Note that in some NY counties the address for the County Clerk is the same as for the Supreme and County Courts. Exceptions are noted in the court profiles, and a separate profile is provided that lists the County Clerk and the "County rules" for a "countywide record search." Note also that, due to limitations in the receiving of records from the Chief Court Clerks, the County Clerk may only be able to do a civil record search, or, rarely, only a criminal record search.

In New York City - with its five boroughs - the courts records are administered directly by the state OCA – Office of Court Administration. Also, there are a small number of upstate counties where the Supreme Court OR County Court records are maintained by their court clerk (a state employee), and only an index list of cases and defendants is provided to the County Clerk (a county employee).

About City Courts - While all City Courts are administered by state employees, there are a few City Courts that will still do a city-only record check despite the edict to state employees that they must direct record searches to the OCA for the statewide record check. Records from City Courts do not go to the County Clerk -- records from City Courts go directly to the OCA.

In at least 20 New York Counties, misdemeanor records are only available at city, town, or village courts. This is also true of small claims and eviction records. Town and Village Courts are listed at the end of each county section.

Now you have an overview of the confusing array of NY courts. You may have concluded that record searching would be a daunting task if you did not have the individual court profiles, updated progressively, provided here to aid you. You may also conclude that an accurate search for misdemeanor records is nearly impossible as there are over 1400 Town and Village Courts in NY which may or may not be accurately reporting all their open and closed case records to the state OCA.

Access From the Office of Court Administration - OCA

OCA will perform an electronic search for criminal history information from a database of criminal case records from all boroughs and all counties, including Supreme Courts, County Courts, and City Courts. It is not clear that all Town, City, and Village Courts submit ALL misdemeanors to this database. The OCA search fee, payable by check, is $55.00 per name. The search is available by mail or in person (6 to 24-hour turnaround time), or high volume requesters may order online with email return (same day if ordered by 2:30 pm). The Criminal History Record Search Unit can be reached at 212-428-2943 or www.nycourts.gov/apps/chrs.

Direct mail and in person requests to:

Office of Court Administration (OCA), Criminal History Search, 25 Beaver St, 8th Floor, New York, NY 10004.

Please note that nearly all the NY City Courts no longer do criminal record searches. NYC City Courts send all misdemeanor record requesters to the OCA for the $55.00 statewide record search.

We have indicated the counties where the County Clerks (and a limited number of Supreme and County Court Clerks) continue to provide countywide criminal record searches. We have also indicated when the County Clerk or Chief Clerk instructs criminal record searchers to contact OCA. This information is subject to change, and does.

Online Access From the OCA and Others

In addition to the $55.00 statewide mail or in-person record search explained above, the OCA offers online access to "approved requesters" for criminal records. Requesters receive information back via email. Call the OCA for details on how to set up an account.

The site at https://iapps.courts.state.ny.us/caseTrac/jsp/ecourt.htm provides access to a number of records, including WebCrims to criminal case dockets with future appearance dates in 13 counties, open landlord tenant cases from NYC, and open family court cases from all 62 counties. Also, from here access or monitor Supreme Court and Family Court case information on open cases for all 62 New York counties. Appellate decisions are available at www.nycourts.gov/ctapps/latdec.htm.

Searching Tips, Fees, and Other Guidelines

In all but a few NY counties, the Supreme and County Court records are maintained in some format in the County Clerk's office, which (with the exception of New York City and its boroughs) may index Civil cases by defendant, whereas the courts themselves maintain only a plaintiff index. And, while most criminal courts in the state are indexed by defendant and plaintiff, many New York City courts are indexed by plaintiff only. All courts are Eastern Standard Time Zone (EST).

Almost all County Courts (felony records) will provide a Certificate of Disposition. This Certificate is a certified document from the court that indicates the disposition of a case. The fee for a Certificate of Disposition is either $5.00 or $6.00, depending upon the county. To obtain a Certificate of Disposition, you must prepay, you must include the name and an exact as possible date (either the disposition date or the arrest date - this requirement varies from county to county), or provide the case number. Some counties also ask for a signed release (this and other details will be noted in the individual court profiles).

Certification fees can vary depending on how the clerk office interprets the rules. Fortunately, most court clerk offices will simply apply a flat $5.00 per document certification fee, however, at some offices, if a document is more than 4 pages, then an add'l $1.25 per page is added for certification. If the certified document is to be mailed, the certification fee may be $6.00, the additional $1.00 of the certification fee going for no purpose if you have provided a SASE, and hopefully they will charge you only the $5.00 cert fee if you have provided that SASE. Prepayment is nearly always required; if it is not required, it is noted in the text.

Generally, a county search of the probate court index by mail for 25-year search is $30.00 fee. A full-county probate search of all years is usually $90.00.

Albany County

County Clerk 32 N Russell Rd, Albany, NY 12206; 518-487-5101; criminal phone: 518-487-5118; civil phone: same; fax: 518-487-5099; 9AM-4:45PM (recordings until 3PM). ***Felony, Civil.***
www.albanycounty.com/clerk
Countywide search requests made to the County Clerk are processed in the manner described below.
Civil Records: Access: Mail, in person, online. Both court and visitors may perform in person searches. Search fee: $5.00 per name. Fee is for each two years requested. Required to search: name, years to search. Civil cases indexed by defendant, plaintiff; index on computer from 1981, prior in books. Mail turnaround time 5-7 days, large files longer. Civil PAT goes back to 1980; results show middle initial. Historical records are not online, but access to current/pending Supreme Court civil cases is at http://iapps.courts.state.ny.us/webcivil/FCASMain
Criminal Records: Access: Mail, in person. Both court and visitors may perform in person searches. Search fee: $5.00 per name. Fee is per two years requested. Required to search: name, years to search, DOB. Criminal records computerized from 1981, prior in books. Mail turnaround time 5-7 days; large files longer. Criminal PAT goes back to same as civil. PAT criminal results show middle initial. This court does not participate in eCourt criminal records system at this time.
General Information: No sealed, expunged, adoption, sex offense, juvenile, mental health or divorce records released. Will not fax documents. Court makes copy: $.65 per page; minimum $1.30. Certification fee: $1.25 per page minimum of $5.00 for cert copy. Payee: County Clerk. Personal checks accepted; credit cards are not. Mail requests: SASE appreciated.

Supreme & County Court County Court, Courthouse, Rm 102, 16 Eagle St, Albany, NY 12207; 518-285-8777 county court (criminal); 518-285-8989 Supreme (civil): Crimnal fax: 518-487-5020; 9AM-5PM. ***Felony, Civil.***
Court-clerks direct record search requests to the OCA for a $55.00 statewide record check. For county only search requests, see the County Clerk in separate listing. Supreme court office located at #6 Lodge St. See County Clerk (above) for online civil access.

Albany City Court - Civil Part City Hall, Rm 209, Albany, NY 12207; 518-434-5115; fax: 518-434-5034; 8:30AM-5PM. ***Civil Actions under $15,000, Eviction, Small Claims, Commercial Claims Under $5000.***
Civil Records: Access: Mail, in person. Only the court performs in person searches; visitors may not. No search fee. Required to search: name, years to search, case type. Civil cases indexed by plaintiff, defendant. Civil records on computer from 1993, records go back 25 years. Mail turnaround time varies.
General Information: No code enforcement records released. Will fax documents. Court makes copy: $1.30 first page, $.65 each add'l. Certification fee: $6.00 per doc. Payee: Albany City Court. Business checks accepted. Visa/MC accepted. Mail requests: SASE required.

Albany City Court - Misdemeanors 1 Morton Ave, Albany, NY 12202; 518-462-6714; fax: 518-447-8778; 8:30-4:30PM. ***Misdemeanor.***
Criminal Records: Access: Mail, in person. Only the court performs in person searches; visitors may not. Search fee: $5.00 per name per certificate of disposition. Required to search: name, date of arrest, DOB. Criminal records on computer since mid-'93, on index cards prior. Court will search but you must provide the date of arrest; no name only searches. Mail turnaround time 1-5 days.
General Information: No sealed, expunged, adoption, sex offense, juvenile, or mental health records released without a signed release. Will not fax documents. Court makes copy: court says that they do not make copies; copy fee included in Cert of Dispostion. Certification fee: Cert fee include in Certificate of Disposition fee. Payee: Albany City Court Criminal Part. Business checks accepted. No credit cards accepted. Mail requests: SASE required.

Cohoes City Court PO Box 678, 97 Mohawk St, Cohoes, NY 12047-0678; 518-233-2133; criminal fax: 518-233-8202; civil fax: same; 8AM-4PM. ***Misdemeanor, Civil Actions under $15,000, Eviction, Small Claims.***
Criminal searches are done by: NYS Office of Court Administration, Office of Administrative Services, Criminal History Record Search, 25 Beaver St, Rm 840, NY, NY 10004. $55.00 statewide search fee.
Civil Records: Access: In person only. Only the court performs in person searches; visitors may not. No search fee. Required to search: name, years to search. Civil cases indexed by defendant, plaintiff; index on computer from 1/95, prior in books, on cards. When case number given, they will provide documents by mail within 5 days, longer if retrieved from storage. This court recommends searching for judgments through the County Clerk's office.
Criminal Records: Access: None. Criminal records computerized from 1/96, earlier in storage. Will not permit access to records. All name searches forwarded to OCA for $55.00 statewide search unless specific docket number given.
General Information: No sealed or expunged records released. Will not fax documents. Court makes copy: $.25 per page. Certification fee: $6.00, Court provides certificate of disposition or letter of disposition for $6.00 or free to defendant. Payee: Cohoes County Court. Only cashiers checks and money orders accepted. Visa/MC accepted.

Watervliet City Court 2 15th St, Watervliet, NY 12189; 518-270-3803; criminal fax: 518-270-3812; civil fax: same; 8AM-3PM. ***Misdemeanor, Civil Actions under $15,000, Eviction, Small Claims.***
www.nycourts.gov/courts/3jd/
Civil Records: Access: Phone, fax, mail, in person. Only the court performs in person searches; visitors may not. Search fee: $5.00 per name per 2 year period. Required to search: name, years to search. Civil cases indexed by plaintiff. Civil records on computer from 1991, prior on index cards back to 1975. Mail turnaround time 1-2 weeks.
Criminal Records: Access: Mail, in person. Only the court performs in person searches; visitors may not. Search fee: $5.00. Required to search: name, years to search, DOB. Criminal records computerized from 1991, prior on index cards back to 1975. All name searches forwarded to OCA for $55.00 statewide search, unless specific docket number given to this court. Mail turnaround 1-2 weeks.
General Information: No fee to fax out. Court makes copy: $.65 per page. Certification fee: $6.00 per document. Payee: City Court. Business checks accepted. Visa/MC accepted in person only. Mail requests: SASE required.

Surrogate's Court 30 Clinton Ave, Albany, NY 12207; 518-285-8585; 8:30AM-4PM ***Probate.***
A county search of the probate court index by mail for 25-year search is $30.00 fee. A full county probate search of all years is $90.00.

Albany Town/Village Courts- Altamont Village Court- 518-861-8554; Berne Town Court- 518-872-1448; Bethlehem Town Court- 518-439-9717; Coeymans Town Court- 518-756-8480; Colonie Town Court- 518-783-2714; Green Island Town Court- 518-273-0661; Guilderland Town Court- 518-356-1980; Knox Town Justice Court- 518-872-2551; Menands Village Court- 518-434-3992; New Scotland Town Court- 518-475-0493; Ravena Village Court- 518-756-2313; Rensselaerville Town Court- 518-239-4225; Voorheesville Village Court- 518-765-5524; Westerlo Town Court- 518-797-3239.

Allegany County

County Clerk 7 Court St, Belmont, NY 14813; 585-268-9270; fax: 585-268-9659; 9AM-N, 1-5PM ***Civil.***
www.alleganyco.com/default.asp?show=btn_county_clerk Felony records in Allegany County are managed by the County-Court Clerk (not the County Clerk) who directs search requests to OCA for $55.00 statewide search.
Civil Records: Access: In person, online. Visitors must perform in person searches themselves. Required to search: name, years to search. Civil cases prior to 1990 indexed by defendant only. Civil records on computer back to 1990; prior on docket books. Public use terminal has civil records back to 1990. PAT results show name only. Lookup current or pending Supreme Court civil cases at http://iapps.courts.state.ny.us/webcivil/FCASMain
General Information: No sealed records released. Will fax documents $3.00 per page, prepaid. Court makes copy: $.65 per page; $1.30 minimum. Certification fee: $5.00 per doc. Over 5 pgs, add $1.25 each add'l page. Payee: County Clerk. Personal checks accepted; credit cards are not.

Supreme & County Court 7 Court St, Belmont, NY 14813; 585-268-5813; fax: 585-268-7090; 9AM-5PM; 8:30AM-4PM Summer hours. ***Felony, Civil.***
Direct civil record requests to County Clerk, see separate listing. The County-Court directs criminal search requests to the OCA for a $55.00 statewide record check.

Surrogate's Court Courthouse, 7 Court St, Belmont, NY 14813; 585-268-5815; fax: 585-268-7090; 9AM-5PM Sept-May; 8:30AM-4PM June-Aug. ***Probate.***
A county search of the probate court index by mail for 25-year search is $30.00 fee. A full county probate search of all years is $90.00.

Allegany Town/Village Courts- Alfred Town Court- 607-587-9142; Alfred Village Court- 607-587-9142; Allen Town Court- 585-567-8320; Alma Town Court- 585-593-4021; Almond Town Court- 607-276-6650; Amity Town Court- 585-268-5305; Andover Town Court- 607-478-8446; Andover Village Court- 607-

478-8446; Angelica Town and Village Court- 585-466-7928; Belfast Town Court- 585-365-2623; Belmont Village Court- 585-268-5305; Birdsall Town Court- 607-545-6072; Bolivar Town Court- 585-928-1860; Bolivar Village Court- 585-928-2234; Burns Town Court- 607-545-6509; Caneadea Town Court- 585-365-8240; Centerville Town Court- 585-567-8424; Clarksville Town Court- 585-968-2031; Cuba Town Court- 585-968-1690; Friendship Town Court- 585-973-7566; Genesee Town Court- 585-928-2007; Granger Town Court- 585-567-8155; Grove Town Court- 607-545-8664; Hume Town Court- 585-567-2666; Independence Town Court- 607-356-3608; New Hudson Town Court- 585-968-2179; Richburg Village Court- 585-928-1370; Rushford Town Court- 585-437-2206; Scio Town Court- 585-593-5777; Ward Town Court- 585-593-7300; Wellsville Town Court- 585-593-1750; Wellsville Village Court- 585-593-5609; West Almond Town Court- 607-276-2629; Willing Town Court- 585-593-3210; Wirt Town Court- 585-928-1370.

Bronx County

Supreme Court - Civil Division 851 Grand Concourse, Mezzanine, Rm 118, Bronx, NY 10451; 718-618-3320; fax: 718-590-8122; 9AM-5PM. ***Civil Actions over $25,000.***
www.courts.state.ny.us/courts/12jd/
Civil Records: Access: In person, online. Both court and visitors may perform in person searches. No search fee. Required to search: name, years to search. Civil cases indexed by defendant, plaintiff; index on computer back to 1996; prior records on offsite archives. Public use terminal has civil records back to 1996. Terminal at County Clerk Office. Lookup current or pending Supreme Court civil cases at http://iapps.courts.state.ny.us/webcivil/FCASMain Also, access docket data free on law case search at www.bronxcountyclerkinfo.com/law/UI/Admin/login.aspx and sign in as guest.
General Information: No marriage or divorce records released. Will not fax documents. Court makes copy: $.25 per page. Self serve: $.15 per page. Certification fee: $8.00 per doc includes copy fee. Payee: Bronx County Clerk. Only cashiers checks and money orders accepted. No personal checks. Visa/MC accepted. Mail requests: SASE required for mail return of any copies.

Supreme Court - Criminal Division 851 Grand Concourse, Rm 123, Bronx, NY 10451; 718-618-3300; criminal phone: x7; 9AM-5PM. ***Felony.***
www.courts.state.ny.us/courts/12jd/
Criminal Records: Access: Mail, In person, online. Both court and visitors may perform in person searches. Search fee: $5.00 per name. Required to search: name, years to search, DOB. Criminal records computerized from 1977, prior on microfiche. Usually, this court directs criminal record name search requests to OCA for $55.00 statewide search. Public use terminal has crim records back to 1995. Subscribe or login as guest to search eCourts WebCrims future appearances system at http://iapps.courts.state.ny.us/webcrim_attorney/Login. Also, register and access docket data free on the law case search at www.bronxcountyclerkinfo.com/law/UI/Admin/login.aspx and sign in as guest.
General Information: No sealed, expunged, juvenile or sex offense records released. Will not fax documents. Court makes copy: $.75 per page. Self serve: $.15 per page.Search microfiche by appointment, call 718-590-4922. Certification fee: $10.00 per doc. Payee: Bronx County Clerk. Only cashiers checks and money orders accepted. Mail requests: SASE required.

Civil Court of the City of New York - Bronx Branch 851 Grand Concourse, Window 6, Basement, Bronx, NY 10451; 718-618-2500, Records-718-618-2563; 9AM-5PM. ***Civil Actions under $25,000, Eviction, Small Claims.***
www.courts.state.ny.us/courts/12jd/index.shtml
General civil dial-up info line- 212-791-6000. Small claims- 718-618-2518. Court holds records 3 years then sends to archives. Resi. Evictions/Housing phone- 718-466-3025 located at 1118 Grand Concourse at 166th St.
Civil Records: Access: Phone, in person. Visitors must perform in person searches themselves. No search fee. Required to search: name, years to search. Civil cases indexed by defendant, plaintiff. Small claims in docket books. Pre-1998 records archived in Queens; 1998 to present in Brooklyn. Civil records in books, file cards back to the 1970's; computerized records since 1998. Records archived after five years, requiring 4-8 weeks (four t. To view files, call ahead so that clerk can schedule a time and have files available. Please use their request form. Record requests via phone may be accepted in the Records Rm only. Public use terminal has civil records back to 1998. Public terminal has landlord/tenant, civil, and small claims.
General Information: Will not fax documents. Court makes copy: Court gives you file to copy. Self serve: $.25 per page.Copy machine located in B-125. Certification fee: $6.00 per doc. Payee: Clerk of the Court. Only money orders and cash accepted. No credit cards accepted.

Supreme Court - Criminal Div. - Misdemeanors Central Clerk's Office, 215 E 161st St, Bronx, NY 10451; 718-618-3100; 9AM-1PM, 2-4:30PM. ***Misdemeanor.***
www.courts.state.ny.us/courts/12jd/criminal.shtml
Criminal Records: Access: In person, online. Only the court performs in person searches; visitors may not. No search fee. Required to search: name, years to search, DOB. Some Criminal records computerized from 1976, prior on microfiche. Unless a specific docket number given, this court directs all criminal record name search requests to the OCA for statewide record search, $55.00 search fee. Subscribe or login as guest to search eCourts WebCrims future appearances system at http://iapps.courts.state.ny.us/webcrim_attorney/Login. Also, access docket data free on law search www.bronxcountyclerkinfo.com/law/UI/Admin/login.aspx. Sign in as guest. Also, access records on the statewide CHRS system; fee is $55.00 per statewide search per name; call 212-428-2943 for info/sign-up; www.courts.state.ny.us/apps/chrs/.
General Information: No sealed, expunged, juvenile or sex offense records released. Court makes copy: $10.00 per copy. Certification fee: $10.00 per doc. Payee: Bronx Supreme Court. Only cashiers checks and money orders accepted. Mail requests: SASE required for civil.

Surrogate's Court 851 Grand Concourse, Bronx, NY 10451; 718-590-4515; fax: 718-537-5158; 9AM-5PM. ***Probate.***
A county search of the probate court index by mail for 25-year search is $30.00 fee. A full county probate search of all years is $90.00.

Broome County

County Clerk PO Box 2062, Broome County Clerk, County Office Bldg, Binghamton, NY 13902; 607-778-2255; criminal fax: 607-778-2243; civil fax: same; 8AM-5PM; 7:30AM-4PM June-August. ***Felony, Civil.*** www.gobcclerk.com
Countywide search requests made to the County Clerk are processed in the manner described below.
Civil Records: Access: Fax, mail, in person, online. Both court and visitors may perform in person searches. Search fee: $5.00 per name. Fee is per 2 years searched, 10 years maximum. Required to search: name, years to search. Civil cases indexed by defendant, plaintiff; index on computer from 1987, prior in books. Mail turnaround time 5 days. Civil PAT goes back to 1986. PAT civil results show middle initial. Lookup current or pending Supreme Court civil cases at http://iapps.courts.state.ny.us/webcivil/FCASMain. Also, search clerk's court and judgment indexes free at www.gobcclerk.com/cgi/Official_Search_Types.html/input; records go back to 1987. Also, access to civil (judgment) records are available; for registration information on the county clerk online system, call Renny at 607-778-2377.
Criminal Records: Access: Fax, mail, in person, online. Both court and visitors may perform in person searches. Search fee: $5.00 per name. Fee is per 2 years searched, 10 year maximum. Required to search: name, years to search, DOB. Criminal records computerized from 1987, prior in books. Mail turnaround time 3-5 days. Criminal PAT goes back to same as civil. PAT criminal results show middle initial. Online access to criminal record index available; for online date and registration information on the county clerk online system, call Danielle at 607-778-2377. Also, search index for criminal actions include in civil actions 1987 to present free at www.gobcclerk.com/cgi/Official_Search_Types.html/input. Online results show middle initial.
General Information: No sealed or youthful offender records released. Will fax documents $1.00 per page. Court makes copy: $.65 per page, $1.30 minimum. Self serve: $.25 per page from book. Certification fee: $5.20 per 8-page document includes copy fee, then $.65 per page. Payee: Broome County Clerk. No personal checks over $1000.00. Visa/MC accepted. Mail requests: SASE requested.

Supreme & County Court PO Box 1766, 92 Court St, County Courthouse, Binghamton, NY 13902; 607-778-2448; fax: 607-778-6426; 9AM-5PM; 8AM-4PM June-August. ***Felony, Civil.***
The Supreme Court directs criminal record search requests to the OCA for processing. Countywide search requests can be made to the County Clerk, see separate listing.

Binghamton City Court Governmental Plaza, 38 Holley St, Binghamton, NY 13901; 607-772-7006; criminal fax: 607-772-7041; civil fax: same; 9AM-5PM; Summer- 8AM-4PM. ***Misdemeanor, Civil Actions under $15,000, Eviction, Small Claims.***
Civil Records: Access: Phone, mail, in person. Both court and visitors may perform in person searches. No search fee. Required to search: name, years to search. Civil cases indexed by defendant. Civil records on computer from 1990, prior in books, index cards. In person searching only for 04/21/99 forward. Mail turnaround time 1-2 weeks. Public use terminal has civil records back to 1996. PAT results show name only.
Criminal Records: Access: Mail, in person. Only the court performs in person searches; visitors may not. Required to search: notarized signature of requester (mail searches only), name, years to search, DOB. Criminal records computerized from 1990. Unless a specific docket number given, all criminal record name search requests are directed to the OCA for statewide record search, $55.00 search fee. Provide case number in mail request. Mail turnaround time 1-2 weeks.
General Information: No sealed records released. May fax documents; this is done irregularly. Court makes copy: $.65 per page; $1.30 minimum. Certification fee: $6.00 per cert civil; $5.00 if criminal. Payee: Binghamton City Court. Only cashiers checks and money orders accepted. Major credit cards accepted for criminal division fees only. Mail requests: SASE required.

Surrogate's Court PO Box 1766, 92 Court St, Binghamton, NY 13902; 607-778-2111; fax: 607-778-2308; 9AM-5PM; 8AM-4PM June-Sept. ***Probate.*** A county search of the probate court index by mail for 25-year search is $30.00 fee. A full county probate search of all years is $90.00.

Broome Town/Village Courts- Barker Town Court- 607-648-6961; Binghamton Town Court- 607-772-0357; Chenango Town Court- 607-648-4809; Colesville Town Court- 607-693-1172; Conklin Town Court- 607-775-5244; Deposit Village Court- 607-467-4240; Dickinson Town Court- 607-723-9403; Endicott Village Court- 607-757-2483; Fenton Town Court- 607-648-4801 x1; Johnson City Village Court- 607-798-0002; Kirkwood Town Court- 607-775-2653; Lisle Town Court- 607-849-4685; Maine Town Court- 607-862-3427; Nanticoke Town Court- 607-692-4041 x309; Sanford Town Court- 607-467-2516; Triangle Town Court- 607-692-7013; Union Town Court- 607-786-2965; Vestal Town Court- 607-748-1514; Windsor Town Court- 607-655-1973.

Cattaraugus County

County Clerk 303 Court St, Little Valley, NY 14755; 716-938-9111 x2297; probate phone: x2327; fax: 716-938-2773; 9AM-5PM. ***Felony, Civil.***
Countywide search requests made to the County Clerk are processed in the manner described below.

Civil Records: Access: Mail, in person, online. Both court and visitors may perform in person searches. Search fee: $5.00 per name. Fee is per 2 years searched. Required to search: name, years to search. Civil cases indexed by defendant, plaintiff; index on computer from 1987, prior in books, index cards from 1900. Mail turnaround time 2-3 days. Public use terminal has civil records back to 1995, judgments to 1987. PAT results show name only. Lookup current or pending Supreme Court civil cases at http://iapps.courts.state.ny.us/webcivil/FCASMain
Criminal Records: Access: Mail, in person. Both court and visitors may perform in person searches. Search fee: $5.00 per name. Fee is per 2 years searched. Required to search: name, years to search, DOB. Criminal records in books, index cards from 1900. Mail turnaround time 2-3 days.
General Information: No sealed or youthful offender records released. Will fax documents to local or toll free line for $3.00 add'l per page. Court makes copy: $1.00 per page. Certification fee: $5.00. Payee: County Clerk. Business checks accepted. No credit cards accepted. Mail requests: SASE required.

Supreme & County Court 303 Court St, Little Valley, NY 14755; 716-938-9111 x2378; fax: 716-938-6413; 9AM-5PM. ***Felony, Civil.***
Court-clerks direct search requests to the OCA for a $55.00 statewide record check. For a countywide search, see the County Clerk in separate listing. Historical records are not online, but access to current/pending Supreme Court civil cases is at http://iapps.courts.state.ny.us/webcivil/FCASMain.

Olean City Court PO Box 631, 101 E State St, Olean, NY 14760; 716-376-5620; fax: 716-376-5623; 8:30AM-4:30PM. ***Misdemeanor, Civil Actions under $15,000, Eviction, Small Claims, Traffic.***
Civil Records: Access: Mail, in person. Only the court performs in person searches; visitors may not. Search fee: $5.00 per name. Required to search: name, years to search, signed release; also helpful-case number. Civil cases indexed by defendant or docket number. Civil index on docket books. Mail turnaround time 1 week.
Criminal Records: Access: Mail, In person. Search fee: $5.00 for Certificate of Disposition; same fee if court agrees to perform a name search. Required to search: Name, years to search; also helpful- case number. Criminal records computerized from 1990, prior in books. With a few exceptions, unless a specific docket number given, all criminal record name search requests are directed to the OCA for statewide record search, $55.00 search fee.
General Information: No sealed or youthful offender records released. Will fax documents to local or toll free line, if prepaid. Court makes copy: $1.00 per page. Certification fee: $6.00. Payee: Olean City Court. Business checks accepted if in-state. Visa/MC accepted. Mail requests: SASE required.

Salamanca City Court Municipal Center, 225 Wildwood Ave, Salamanca, NY 14779; 716-945-4153; fax: 716-945-2362; 8-5PM. ***Misdemeanor, Civil Actions under $15,000, Eviction, Small Claims.***
Civil Records: Access: Mail, in person. Only the court performs in person searches; visitors may not. No search fee. Required to search: name, years to search. Civil cases indexed by defendant. Civil records on dockets from 1930s; on computer back to 1995. Mail turnaround time 1-2 weeks.
Criminal Records: Access: Mail, in person. Only the court performs in person searches; visitors may not. Search fee: A Certificate of Disposition is $5.00; signed release required. Required to search: name, years to search, DOB, case number. Criminal docket index from 1930s; on computer back to 1995. Unless a specific docket number given, all criminal record name search requests are directed to the OCA for a statewide record search. Mail turnaround time 1-2 weeks.
General Information: No sealed records released. Will fax documents. Court makes copy: $.50 per page. Self serve: same. Certification fee: $6.00 per doc. Payee: Salamanca City Court. No personal checks accepted. Visa/MC accepted. Mail requests: SASE required.

Surrogate's Court 303 Court St, Little Valley, NY 14755; 716-938-2327; fax: 716-938-6983; 9AM-5PM. ***Probate.***
Public can search, but if court has to search there is a fee. A county search of the probate court index by mail for 25-year search is $30.00 fee. A full county probate search of all years is $90.00.

Cattaraugus Town/Village Courts- Allegany Town Court- 716-373-3670; Allegany Village Court- 716-373-1460; Ashford Town Court- 716-942-6016; Carrollton Town Court- 716-925-7772; Coldspring Town Court- 716-354-5752; Conewango Town Court- 716-358-9321, 716-358-9152; Dayton Town Court- 716-532-3758; East Otto Town Court- 716-257-9071; Ellicottville Town Court- 716-699-2240; Ellicottville Village Court- 716-699-2900; Farmersville Town Court- 716-676-3030; Franklinville Town Court- 716-676-3077; Freedom Town Court- 716-492-5802; Great Valley Town Court- 716-945-4200; Hinsdale Town Court- 716-557-2478; Humphrey Town Court- 716-945-1010; Ischua Town Court- 716-557-8787; Leon Town Court- 716-296-8132; Little Valley Town Court- 716-938-6882; Lyndon Town Court- 716-676-9928; Machias Town Court- 716-353-8207; Mansfield Town Court- 716-257-9288; Napoli Town Court- 716-938-9492; New Albion Town Court- 716-257-5387; Olean Town Court- 716-373-0582; Otto Town Court- 716-257-9623; Perrysburg Town Court- 716-532-4090; Persia Town Court- 716-532-4042; Portville Town Court- 716-933-6432; Portville Village Court- 716-933-6288; Randolph Town Court- 716-358-4515; Red House Town Court- 716-354-5052; Salamanca Town Court- 716-945-4775; South Dayton Village Court- 716-988-3833; South Valley Town Court- 716-354-2005; Yorkshire Town Court- 716-492-1640.

Cayuga County

County Clerk 160 Genesee St, Attn: County Clerk, Auburn, NY 13021; 315-253-1271; civil phone: same; fax: 315-253-1653; 9AM-5PM Sept-June; 8AM-4PM July-Aug. ***Felony, Misdemeanor, Civil.***
This County Clerk will not do a felony record name search. Access to criminal records, including name searching, must be done at the OCA in New York City. The fees is $55.00 for a statewide search.
Civil Records: Access: Mail, in person, online. Both court and visitors may perform in person searches. Search fee: $5.00 per name per 5 years searched. Required to search: name, years to search. Civil cases indexed by defendant, plaintiff; index on computer from 1986, prior in books. Civil PAT goes back to 1987. Lookup Supreme Court civil cases at http://iapps.courts.state.ny.us/webcivil/FCASMain
Criminal Records: Access: In person (limited). Visitors must perform in person searches themselves. Required to search: name, years to search. Criminal PAT available. Other access to records must be performed at the OCA in New York City.
General Information: No sealed records released. Will not fax documents. Court makes copy: $.65 per page; $1.30 minimum. Certification fee: $5.00 per doc. Payee: County Clerk. Personal checks accepted; credit cards are not. Mail requests: SASE required.

Supreme & County Court 154 Genesee St, Auburn, NY 13021-3424; 315-255-4320; fax: 315-255-4322; 9AM-5PM Sept-June; 8AM-4PM July-Aug. ***Felony, Misdemeanor, Civil.***
The County Clerk provides county only record searches, see separate entry.

Auburn City Court 157 Genesee St, Auburn, NY 13021-3434; 315-253-1570; fax: 315-253-1085; 8AM-4PM; window- 8:15AM-3:45PM. ***Misdemeanor, Civil Actions under $15,000, Eviction, Small Claims.***
www.nycourts.gov/courts/7jd/Auburn/index.shtml
Civil Records: Access: Mail, fax, in person. Only the court performs in person searches; visitors may not. No search fee. Required to search: name, years to search. Civil cases indexed by defendant. Civil records on computer from 1986.
Criminal Records: Access: In person (limited). Search fee: Certificate of Disposition is $5.00. The court does not to permit access to records unless specific case file number or an arrest date is given. They direct searchers to the OCA statewide search.
General Information: No sealed, expunged, adoption, sex offense, juvenile or mental health records released. Will fax documents, no fee. Court makes copy: $.65 per page; $1.30 minimum. Certification fee: $6.00 per civil doc; $5.00 for criminal cert. Payee: City Court Clerk. No personal checks. Visa/MC accepted in person only.

Surrogate's Court Courthouse, 152 Genesee St, Auburn, NY 13021-3471; 315-255-4316; fax: 315-255-4324; 8:30AM-4:30PM. ***Probate.***
A county search of the probate court index by mail for 25-year search is $30.00 fee. A full county probate search of all years is $90.00.

Cayuga Town/Village Courts- Aurelius Town Court- 315-255-0065; Brutus Town Court- 315-834-6618; Cato Town Court- 315-626-6904; Conquest Town Court- 315-776-5703; Fleming Town Court- 315-255-8014; Genoa Town Court- 315-364-6722; Ira Town Court- 315-626-3500; Ledyard Town Court- 315-364-5708; Locke Town Court- 315-497-2605; Mentz Town Court- 315-776-8692; Meridian Village Court- 315-626-6904; Montezuma Town Court- 315-776-9163; Moravia Town Court- 315-497-0968; Moravia Village Court- 315-497-0968; Niles Town Court- 315-497-0066; Owasco Town Court- 315-255-0446; Port Byron Village Court- 315-776-9692; Scipio Town Court- 315-364-5325; Semperonius Town Court- 315-496-2376; Sennett Town Court- 315-253-7748; Springport Town Court- 315-889-5020; Sterling Town Court- 315-865-5508; Summerhill Town Court- 315-497-3496; Throop Town Court- 315-252-7373; Venice Town Court- 315-364-6875; Victory Town Court- 315-626-6817; Weedsport Village Court- 315-834-8634 X51.

Chautauqua County

County Clerk PO Box 170, 1 N Erie St, Courthouse, Mayville, NY 14757; 716-753-4331; probate phone: 716-753-4339; fax: 716-753-4293; 9AM-5PM/Summer 8:30AM-4:30PM. ***Felony, Civil.***
www.co.chautauqua.ny.us/clerk/clerkframe.htm
Non in-person felony record requests are managed by the Supreme Court clerk who directs searches to OCA for $55.00 statewide search.
Civil Records: Access: In person, online. Visitors must perform in person searches themselves. Required to search: name, years to search. Civil cases indexed by plaintiff and defendant. Civil PAT goes back to 8/1997. PAT results show name only. Lookup Supreme Court civil cases at http://iapps.courts.state.ny.us/webcivil/FCASMain
Criminal Records: Access: In person only. Visitors must perform in person searches themselves. Required to search: name, years to search, DOB. Criminal records on court's computer system from 8/1987; prior on docket books and cards. Court will not search felony records. A Certificate of Conviction can be ordered for $5.00. Criminal PAT goes back to same as civil. PAT results show name only.
General Information: No sealed records released. Will not fax documents. Court makes copy: $1.00 per page. No certification fee. Payee: County Clerk. Personal checks accepted; credit cards are not.

Supreme & County Court - Criminal PO Box 292, 1 N Erie St, Courthouse, Mayville, NY 14757; 716-753-4266; fax: 716-753-4993; 9AM-5P; Summer- 8:30AM-4:30PM. ***Felony.***
The County-court directs all search requests to the OCA for a $55.00 statewide record check.

Supreme & County Court - Civil PO Box 170, 1 N Erie St, Mayville, NY 14757; 716-753-4331; civil phone: 716-753-4976; fax: 716-753-4293; 9AM-5PM; Summer 8:30AM-4:30PM. ***Civil.***
www.co.chautauqua.ny.us/clerk/clerkframe.htm
Supreme Court Clerk phone is 716-753-4266 but they do not have the records.
Civil Records: Access: In person, online. Visitors must perform in person searches themselves. Required to search: name, years to search. Civil cases indexed by plaintiff. Civil records in docket books or cards; on computer back to 8/1/1997. Public use terminal has civil records back to 8/1997. PAT results show name only. Public terminal located in the county clerk office. Historical records are not

online, but access to Supreme Court civil cases at http://iapps.courts.state.ny.us/webcivil/FCASMain
General Information: No sealed records released. Will not fax documents. Court makes copy: $4.00 per doc; add $1.00 per page after first 4. Cert fee included in copy fee. Payee: Chautauqua County Clerk. Personal checks accepted; credit cards are not.

Dunkirk City Court City Hall, 342 Central Ave, Dunkirk, NY 14048; 716-366-2055; fax: 716-366-3622; 9AM-5PM. ***Misdemeanor, Civil Actions under $15,000, Eviction, Small Claims.***
Civil Records: Access: Mail, in person. Only the court performs in person searches; visitors may not. No search fee. Required to search: name, years to search. Civil cases indexed by defendant. Civil records on computer back to 1990, prior in books. Make appointment to search.
Criminal Records: Access: None. Only the court performs in person searches; visitors may not. Search fee: A Certificate of Disposition is $6.00. Required to search: name, DOB, arrest date (for Cert of Disposition). Criminal records go back to 1930s. Court refuses to permit access to records unless specific case file given. It suggests to send search requests to OCA for statewide search. Also, record checks from local Police- 716-366-2266.
General Information: No sealed, expunged, adoption, sex offense, juvenile or mental health records released. Will not fax documents. Court makes copy: $.65 per page; $1.30 minimum. Cert fee: $6.00 per doc. Payee: Dunkirk City Court. Only cashiers checks and money orders accepted. Visa/MC accepted. Mail requests: SASE required.

Jamestown City Court City Hall, Jamestown, NY 14701; 716-483-7561/7562; fax: 716-483-7519; 8:30AM-5PM. ***Misdemeanor, Civil Actions under $15,000, Eviction, Small Claims.***
Civil Records: Access: Fax, mail, in person. Only the court performs in person searches; visitors may not. No search fee. Required to search: name, years to search. Civil cases indexed by defendant. Civil records on computer back to 1989, prior in books.
Criminal Records: Access: None. Only the court performs in person searches; visitors may not. Search fee: $5.00 per name for each 2 year search, $5.00 fee for certification of conviction or disposition. Required to search: Name, DOB. Criminal records computerized from 1989, prior in books to 1965. The court refuses to permit access to records unless specific case file given. It is suggested to send requests to OCA for statewide search.
General Information: No sealed records released. Will fax documents to local or toll free line. Court makes copy: $.65 per page; $1.30 minimum. Certification fee: $6.00 per document. Payee: City Court. Business checks accepted. Visa/MC accepted. Mail requests: SASE required.

Surrogate's Court PO Box C, 3 N Erie St, Gerace Office Bldg, Mayville, NY 14757; 716-753-4339; fax: 716-753-4600; 9AM-5PM Summer; 8:30AM-4:30PM, July-Sept 3. ***Probate.***
A county search of the probate court index by mail for 25-year search is $30.00 fee. A full county probate search of all years is $90.00.

Chautauqua Town/Village Courts- Arkwright Town Court- 716-672-8672; Brocton Village Court- 716-792-4189; Busti Town Court- 716-763-4695; Carroll Town Court- 716-569-5365; Charlotte Town Court- 716-962-2004; Chautauqua Town Court- 716-753-5245; Cherry Creek Town Court- 716-296-8050; Clymer Town Court- 716-355-6331; Dunkirk Town Court- 716-366-3945; Ellery Town Court- 716-386-2521; Ellicott Town Court- 716-665-5319; Ellington Town Court- 716-287-2026; Fredonia Village Court- 716-679-2312; French Creek Town Court- 716-355-8801; Gerry Town Court- 716-985-5323; Hanover Town Court- 716-934-4770; Harmony Town Court- 716-488-1178; Kiantone Town Court- 716-488-0383; Mina Town Court- 716-769-7250; North Harmony Town Court- 716-789-3445 x1; Poland Town Court- 716-267-3809; Pomfret Town Court- 716-672-6867; Portland Town Court- 716-792-4111; Ripley Town Court- 716-736-7575; Sheridan Town Court- 716-672-2600; Sherman Town Court- 716-761-6770; Silver Creek Village Court- 716-934-3558; Stockton Town Court- 716-595-3192; Villenova Town Court- 716-988-3678; Westfield Town Court- 716-326-6255; Westfield Village Court- 716-326-6135.

Chemung County

Supreme & County Court - Criminal PO Box 588, Hazlett Bldg, 6th Fl, Elmira, NY 14902-0588; 607-737-2084; probate phone: 607-737-2873; fax: 607-732-8879; 9AM-5PM. ***Felony.***
See County Clerk for Supreme court civil case records.
Criminal Records: Access: Mail, in person. Only the court performs in person searches; visitors may not. Search fee: $5.00 for every 2 years searched or $20.00 for a seven year search. Searches with both maiden and married names are considered two searches. Required to search: name, years to search, DOB, SSN. Criminal records in docket books back to 1979. Mail turnaround time 4-6 weeks.
General Information: No sealed, divorce or adoption records released. Will fax documents to local or toll free line. Court makes copy: $.65 per page. Self serve: same. Certification fee: $5.00. Payee: County Clerk. Personal checks accepted; credit cards are not. Mail requests: SASE required.

County Clerk PO Box 588, 210 Lake St, Elmira, NY 14902; 607-737-2920; fax: 607-737-2897; 8:30AM-4:30PM. ***Civil.*** www.chemungcounty.com/
Search requests made to the County Clerk are processed in the manner described below.
Civil Records: Access: In person, online (limited). Both court and visitors may perform in person searches. Search fee: $5.00 per name. Fee is per 2 years searched. Required to search: name, years to search. Civil cases indexed by defendant, plaintiff; index on computer from 1994, prior in books to 1800s. Public use terminal has civil records. PAT civil results show middle initial. Public access terminal is in the Supreme & County Court clerk office. Access to WebCivil Supreme Court civil cases on the statewide system is at http://iapps.courts.state.ny.us/webcivil/FCASMain
General Information: No sealed, divorce or adoption records released. Will fax documents $1.00 per page. Court makes copy: $.65 per page, $1.30 minimum. Self serve: $.65 per page. Certification fee: $5.00 up to 4 pages, $1.25 each add'l page, includes copies. Payee: County Clerk. Personal checks accepted; credit cards are not. Mail requests: SASE required.

Elmira City Court 317 E Church St, Elmira, NY 14901; 607-737-5681; fax: 607-737-5820; 8AM-4PM. ***Misdemeanor, Civil Actions under $15,000, Eviction, Small Claims.***
Civil Records: Access: In person only. Visitors must perform in person searches themselves. Required to search: name, years to search. Civil cases indexed by defendant. Civil records on computer back to 1997; prior records on index cards. If searching for records prior to 1997, call office to make appointment to search. Public use terminal has civil records back to 1997. PAT results show name, case number, and address.
Criminal Records: Access: Mail, in person. Only the court performs in person searches; visitors may not. Search fee: A Certificate of Disposition is $5.00. Required to search: name, years to search, date of arrest (for Cert of Disposition). Criminal records computerized from 1987; prior on books. Court does not permit access to records unless specific case file given. Send search requests to OCA for statewide search.
General Information: No sealed records released. Will fax documents to local or toll free line. Court makes copy: $.65 per page; $1.30 minimum. Certification fee: $5.00 per doc. Payee: Elmira City Court. No personal checks accepted. Visa/MC accepted. Mail requests: SASE required for mail return of any copies.

Surrogate's Court PO Box 588, 224 Lake St, Elmira, NY 14902; 607-737-2946/2819; fax: 607-737-2874; 9AM-5PM; July 4 to Sept 3- 8:30AM-4:30PM. ***Probate.***
Public access terminal located in basement has complete index. A county search of the probate court index by mail for 25-year search is $30.00 fee. A full county probate search of all years is $90.00

Chemung Town/Village Courts- Ashland Town Court- 607-398-7119; Baldwin Town Court- 607-398-7208; Big Flats Town Court- 607-562-8443 x233; Catlin Town Court- 607-739-5598; Chemung Town Court- 607-529-3532 x2; Elmira Heights Village Court- 607-737-6750; Elmira Town Court- 607-734-5971; Erin Town Court- 607-739-3313 x2; Horseheads Town Court- 607-739-2113; Horseheads Village Court- 607-739-0158; Southport Town Court- 607-734-4446; Van Etten Town Court- 607-589-4925; Veteran Town Court- 607-739-3337; Wellsburg Village Court- 315-846-5222.

Chenango County

County Clerk County Office Bldg, 1st Fl, 5 Court St, Norwich, NY 13815-1676; 607-337-1450; fax: 607-337-1455; 8:30AM-5PM. ***Felony, Civil.*** www.co.chenango.ny.us
Countywide search requests made to the County Clerk are processed in the manner described below.
Civil Records: Access: Mail, in person, online. Both court and visitors may perform in person searches. Search fee: $5.00 per name. Fee is per 2 years searched. Required to search: name, years to search. Civil cases indexed by defendant, plaintiff; index on computer from 1994, prior in books since 1880. Mail turnaround time 1 week. Civil PAT goes back to 1994. Lookup Supreme Court civil cases at http://iapps.courts.state.ny.us/webcivil/FCASMain
Criminal Records: Access: Mail, in person. Both court and visitors may perform in person searches. Search fee: $5.00 per name. Fee is per 2 years searched. Required to search: name, years to search, DOB. Criminal records in docket books. Mail turnaround time 1 week. Criminal PAT goes back to 2004.
General Information: No sealed, expunged, adoption, sex offense, juvenile or mental health records released. Will fax documents $4.00 per page. Court makes copy: $.65 per page, $1.30 minimum. Certification fee: $1.25 per page, $5.00 minimum. Payee: County Clerk. Personal checks accepted; credit cards are not. Mail requests: SASE required.

Supreme & County Court County Office Bldg, 5 Court St, Norwich, NY 13815-1676; 607-337-1457; fax: 607-337-1835; 8:30AM-5PM. ***Felony, Civil.***
Direct all search requests to the County Clerk office, see separate listing. Historical records are not online, but access to Supreme Court civil cases is at http://iapps.courts.state.ny.us/webcivil/FCASMain.

Norwich City Court 1 Court Plaza, Norwich, NY 13815; 607-334-1224; fax: 607-334-8494; 8:30AM-4:30PM. ***Misdemeanor, Civil Actions under $15,000, Eviction, Small Claims, Traffic.***
Civil Records: Access: Fax, mail, in person. Only the court performs in person searches; visitors may not. No search fee. Required to search: name, years to search. Civil cases indexed by defendant. Civil records on computer from 1990, prior in books. Mail turnaround time 5-7 days.
Criminal Records: Access: Mail, in person. Only the court performs in person searches; visitors may not. Search fee: Clerk here will provide $6.00 Certificate of Disposition only. Criminal records go back to 1930's. Court directs criminal record searchers to OCA for $55.00 statewide search.
General Information: No sealed, expunged, adoption, sex offense, juvenile or mental health records released. Will fax documents to local or toll free line. Court makes copy: $.65 per page; minimum $1.30. Certification fee: $5.00 per doc. Payee: Norwich City Court. Business checks accepted. No personal check accepted. Visa/MC accepted. Mail requests: SASE required.

Surrogate's Court County Office Bldg, 5 Court St, Norwich, NY 13815; 607-337-1822/1827; fax: 607-337-1834; 8:30AM-4:30PM. ***Probate.***
A county search of the probate court index by mail for 25-year search is $30.00 fee. A full county probate search of all years is $90.00.

Chenango Town/Village Courts- Afton Town Court- 607-639-2505; Bainbridge Town & Village Court- 607-967-7465; Columbus Town Court- 607-847-6135; Coventry Town Court- 607-656-8602; Earlville Village Court- 315-691-6020; German Town Court-

No phone; Greene Town Court- 607-656-4333; Greene Village Court- 607-656-4544; Guilford Town Court- 607-895-6818; Lincklaen Town Court- 315-852-6128; New Berlin Town Court- 607-847-8962; New Berlin Village Court- 607-847-6249; North Norwich Town Court- 607-334-5994; Norwich Town Court- 607-337-2305; Otselic Town Court- 315-653-7201; Oxford Town & Village Court- 607-843-9772; Oxford Village Court- 607-843-9772; Pharsalia Town Court- 607-647-5081; Pitcher Town Court- 607-863-4929; Plymouth Town Court- no phone; Preston Town Court- 607-334-9334; Sherburne Town & Village Court- 607-674-4827; Smithville Town Court- 607-656-7969; Smyrna Town Court- no phone.

Clinton County

County Clerk County Government Ctr, 137 Margaret St, 1st Fl, Plattsburgh, NY 12901; 518-565-4701; civil phone: same; fax: 518-565-4718; 8AM-5PM. ***Civil.*** www.clintoncountygov.com

This County Clerk does not have a separate index of felony records; see the Supreme and County Court.

Civil Records: Access: In person, online. Visitors must perform in person searches themselves. Required to search: name, years to search. Civil cases indexed by defendant, plaintiff; by defendant only pre-May 2004. Civil records in docket books up to 2003; on computer 2003 to present. Public use terminal has civil records back to 2003. PAT results show name only. Online access to current/pending civil cases is free at http://iapps.courts.state.ny.us/webcivil/ecourtsMain.

General Information: No sealed or sex case records released. Will fax out specific case files to local or toll free line. Court makes copy: $.65 per page; $1.30 minimum. Certification fee: $1.25 per page, minimum $5.00. Payee: County Clerk. Personal checks accepted; credit cards are not.

Supreme & County Court County Government Ctr, 137 Margaret St, #311, Plattsburgh, NY 12901; 518-565-4715; fax: 518-565-4708; 9AM-5PM. ***Felony, Civil.***

The County Court directs criminal search requests to the OCA for a $55.00 statewide record check. Civil records are with the County Clerk, see separate listing.

Plattsburg City Court 24 US Oval, Plattsburgh, NY 12903; 518-563-7870; fax: 518-563-3124; 8AM-4PM. ***Misdemeanor, Civil Actions under $15,000, Eviction, Small Claims, Traffic.*** www.nycourts.gov/courts/4jd/plattsburgh_city/index.shtml

Civil Records: Access: Mail, in person. Only the court performs in person searches; visitors may not. No search fee. A Certificate of Disposition is $6.00 per name. Required to search: name, years to search. Civil cases indexed by defendant. Civil records on computer back to 1986, prior in books.

Criminal Records: Access: None. Only the court performs in person searches; visitors may not. Records available on computer since 1986, prior in books. The court will not support name searches unless specific case file given. Searchers must use OCA's statewide search.

General Information: No sealed records released. Court makes copy: $.65 per page. Certification fee: $5.00 per certificate. Payee: City Court. Only cashiers checks and money orders accepted. Visa/MC accepted. Mail requests: SASE required.

Surrogate's Court 137 Margaret St, #315, Plattsburgh, NY 12901-2933; 518-565-4630; fax: 518-565-4769; 8AM-5PM. ***Probate.***

A county search of the probate court index by mail for 25-year search is $30.00 fee. A full county probate search of all years is $90.00.

Clinton Town/Village Courts- Altona Town Court- 518-236-7035; Au Sable Town Court- 518-834-6095; Beekmantown Town Court- 518-563-9930; Black Brook Town Court- 518-647-5411 x25; Champlain Town Court- 518-298-8160 x207; Chazy Town Court- 518-846-8600; Clinton Town Court- 518-497-6133; Dannemora Town Court- 518-492-9751; Dannemora Village Court- 518-492-7000; Ellenburg Town Court- 518-594-7177; Keeseville Village Court- 518-834-9590; Mooers Town Court- 518-236-7927; Peru Town Court- 518-643-2745 x1; Plattsburgh Town Court- 518-562-6870; Rouses Point Village Court- 518-297-6648 x334; Saranac Town Court- 518-293-6666; Schuyler Falls Town Court- 518-563-1129.

Columbia County

County Clerk 560 Warren St, Hudson, NY 12534; 518-828-3339; fax: 518-828-5299; 9AM-5PM. ***Felony, Civil.***

Supreme and County courts are located at 401 Union in Hudson, but records for both courts are located at County Clerk's Office as listed above.

Civil Records: Access: Mail, in person, online. Both court and visitors may perform in person searches. Search fee: $5.00 per name. Fee is per 2 years searched. Required to search: name, years to search. Civil cases indexed by defendant. Civil records on computer from 1993, prior on cards to 1985. Mail turnaround time 1 week. Civil PAT goes back to 1993. PAT civil results show middle initial. Lookup current or pending Supreme Court civil cases at http://iapps.courts.state.ny.us/webcivil/FCASMain.

Criminal Records: Access: Mail, in person. Both court and visitors may perform in person searches. Search fee: $5.00 per name. Fee is for 10 years searched. Required to search: name, years to search. Criminal records computerized from 1993, prior on cards to 1985. Supreme and County courts are actually located at 401 Union in Hudson, but records for both courts are located at the County Clerk's Office as listed above. Mail turnaround time 3 weeks. Criminal PAT goes back to same as civil. PAT criminal results show middle initial.

General Information: No sealed records released. Will not fax documents. Court makes copy: $.65 per page. Self serve: $.25 per page. Certification fee: $5.00. Payee: Columbia County Clerk. Personal checks accepted if name imprinted. No credit cards accepted. Mail requests: SASE required.

Supreme & County Court 401 Union St, Hudson, NY 12534; 518-828-7858; fax: 518-828-1603; 9AM-5PM. ***Felony, Civil.***

Direct countywide search requests to the County Clerk, see separate listing.

Hudson City Court 427 Warren St, Hudson, NY 12534; 518-828-3100; fax: 518-828-3628; 8AM-3:45PM. ***Misdemeanor, Civil Actions under $15,000, Eviction, Small Claims.*** www.nycourts.gov/courts/3jd/

Civil Records: Access: Fax, mail, in person. Only the court performs in person searches; visitors may not. Search fee: $16.00 per name. Required to search: name, years to search; also helpful: address. Civil cases indexed by defendant, plaintiff; index on computer from 1991, prior in books. Mail turnaround time 5-7 days.

Criminal Records: Access: None. Criminal records computerized from 1991, prior in books. This court directs criminal records search requests to the OCA for a $55.00 statewide record check.

General Information: No sealed, expunged, adoption, sex offense, juvenile or mental health records released. Will fax documents to local or toll free line. Court makes copy: $.65 per page. Certification fee: $5.00. Payee: Hudson City Court. Business checks accepted. Major credit cards accepted. Mail requests: SASE required for civil.

Surrogate's Court Courthouse, 401 Union St, Hudson, NY 12534; 518-828-0414; fax: 518-828-1603; 9AM-5PM. ***Probate.***

A county search of the probate court index by mail for 25-year search is $30.00 fee. A full county probate search of all years is $90.00.

Columbia Town/Village Courts- Ancram Town Court- 518-329-6512; Austerlitz Town Court- 518-392-2777; Canaan Town Court- 518-781-3144 x2; Chatham Town Court- 518-392-5440; Chatham Village Court- 518-392-9476; Claverack Town Court- 518-672-4468; Clermont Town Court- 518-537-6868 x503/x505; Copake Town Court- 518-329-4042 x3; Gallatin Town Court- 518-398-7690; Germantown Town Court- 518-537-6687; Ghent Town Court- 518-392-4644; Greenport Town Court- 518-828-4656; Hillsdale Town Court- 518-325-5073; Kinderhook Town & Village Court- 518-784-2506; Livingston Town Court- 518-851-7210; New Lebanon Town Court- 518-794-9456; Philmont Village Court- 518-672-4886; Stockport Town Court- 518-822-8009; Stuyvesant Town Court- 518-758-6248; Taghkanic Town Court- 518-329-3030; Valatie Village Court- 518-758-9838.

Cortland County

County Clerk 46 Greenbush St, #105, Cortland, NY 13045; 607-753-5021; fax: 607-753-5378; 9PM-5PM. ***Felony, Civil.*** www.cortland-co.org/cc/index.htm

Countywide search requests made to the County Clerk are processed in the manner described below. The fax number is not for public use.

Civil Records: Access: Mail, in person, online. Both court and visitors may perform in person searches. Search fee: $10.00 per name per 10 year search. Required to search: name, years to search. Civil cases indexed by defendant, plaintiff; index on computer from 5/94, prior in books. Mail turnaround time 2 days. Public use terminal has civil records back to 1974. Online access at the home page gives judgments and other county clerk records. Online results show name only. Login using "public" as user name and password. A subscription service is also available Also, access to current/pending WebCivil Supreme Court civil cases is at http://iapps.courts.state.ny.us/webcivil/FCASMain

Criminal Records: Access: Mail, in person. Only the court performs in person searches; visitors may not. Search fee: $5.00 per name per 2 years. Required to search: name, years to search, DOB. Criminal records in books. Mail turnaround time 2 days.

General Information: No sealed or youthful offender records released. Will not fax documents. Court makes copy: $.65 per page. $1.30 minimum. Certification fee: $1.25 per page, $5.00 minimum. Payee: County Clerk. Personal checks and major credit cards accepted. Mail requests: SASE required.

Supreme & County Court 46 Greenbush St, #301, Cortland, NY 13045; 607-753-5013; fax: 607-756-3409; 9AM-5PM (in July/Aug 8:30AM-4:30PM). ***Felony, Civil.*** www.cortland-co.org/cc/index.htm

Direct record search requests to the County Clerk, see separate listing. Online access to current/pending Supreme Court civil cases is at http://iapps.courts.state.ny.us/webcivil/FCASMain. Criminal online access is via the state OCA statewide system.

Cortland City Court 25 Court St, Cortland, NY 13045; 607-753-1811; 8:30AM-4:30PM. ***Misdemeanor, Civil Actions under $15,000, Eviction, Small Claims.*** www.cortland.org/city/court.htm

Civil Records: Access: Mail, in person. Only the court performs in person searches; visitors may not. Search fee: $5.00 per name per 2 years. Required to search: name, years to search. Civil cases indexed by defendant. Civil records on computer from 1991, prior in books. Mail turnaround time 10 days.

Criminal Records: Access: Mail, in person. Only the court performs in person searches; visitors may not. Search fee: For violations only- $5.00 per name per 2 years. Certificate of Disposition- $5.00. Required to search: name, years to search, DOB. Criminal records computerized from 1991, prior in books. The court does not permit access to "fingerprint able records" unless specific case file given. You must send requests to OCA for $55.00 statewide search. Mail turnaround time 10 days.

General Information: No sealed records released. Will fax documents to local or toll free line. Court makes copy: $.65 per page; $1.65 minimum. Certification fee: $6.00 per doc; may be $5.00 if in person. Payee: Cortland City Court. No personal checks accepted. Visa/MC accepted. Mail requests: SASE required.

Surrogate's Court 46 Greenbush St, #301, Cortland, NY 13045; 607-753-5355; fax: 607-756-3409; 9AM-5PM; 8:30-4:30 July-Sept 3. ***Probate.*** www.courts.state.ny.us/6jd

A county search of the probate court index by mail for 25-year search is $30.00 fee. A full county probate search of all years is $90.00.

Cortland Town/Village Courts- Cincinnatus Town Court- 607-863-4220; Cortlandville Town Court- 607-756-2352; Cuyler Town Court- 607-836-6486; Freetown Town Court- 607-849-6372- Town Barn; Harford Town Court- 518-632-9151; Homer Town Court- 607-749-2326; Lapeer Town Court- 607-849-6198; Marathon Town Court- 607-849-6966; Preble Town Court- 607-749-2377; Scott Town Court- 607-749-2902; Solon Town Court- 607-836-6486; Taylor Town Court- 607-863-3556; Truxton Town Court- 607-842-6387; Virgil Town Court- 607-835-6587; Willet Town Court- 607-863-3261.

Delaware County

County Clerk PO Box 426, 3 Court St, Delhi, NY 13753; 607-746-2123; fax: 607-746-6924; 8:30AM-5PM. ***Felony, Civil.***

Countywide search requests made to the County Clerk are processed in the manner described below.

Civil Records: Access: In person, online. Visitors must perform in person searches themselves. Required to search: name, years to search. Civil cases indexed by defendant. Civil records in books. Civil PAT goes back to 2/2008. Lookup current or pending Supreme Court civil cases at http://iapps.courts.state.ny.us/webcivil/FCASMain

Criminal Records: Access: Mail, in person. Visitors must perform in person searches themselves. Search fee: $10.00 per name. Required to search: name, years to search, DOB. Criminal records in books. Misdemeanor records are maintained by city, town, and village courts. Mail turnaround time 2 days. Criminal PAT goes back to 2/2008.

General Information: No sealed records released. Will not fax documents. Court makes copy: $1.00 per page. Certification fee: $4.00 for judge's signature, then $1.00 per page. Payee: Delaware County Clerk. Personal checks accepted; credit cards are not. Mail requests: SASE required.

Supreme & County Court 3 Court St, Delhi, NY 13753; 607-746-2131; fax: 607-746-3253; 9AM-5PM. ***Felony, Civil.***

Direct record search requests to the County Clerk, see separate listing. Access to current/pending Supreme Court civil cases is at https://iapps.courts.state.ny.us/caseTrac/jsp/ecourt.htm

Surrogate's Court 3 Court St, Delhi, NY 13753; 607-746-2126; fax: 607-746-2288; 9AM-5PM. ***Probate.***

A county search of the probate court index by mail for 25-year search is $30.00 fee. A full county probate search of all years is $90.00.

Delaware Town/Village Courts- Andes Town Court- 845-676-3550; Bovina Town Court- 607-832-4500; Colchester Town Court- 607-363-7169; Davenport Town Court- 607-278-5105; Delhi Town Court- 607-746-7278; Deposit Town Court- 607-467-3233; Franklin Town Court- 607-829-3440; Hamden Town Court- 607-746-6660; Hancock Town Court- 607-637-3650; Hancock Village Court- 607-637-5789; Harpersfield Town Court- 607-652-5060; Kortright Town Court- 607-538-9319; Masonville Town Court- 607-265-9249; Meredith Town Court- 607-746-2431; Middletown Town Court- 845-586-2575; Roxbury Town Court- 607-588-7507; Sidney Town Court- 607-561-2309; Sidney Village Court- 607-561-2309; Stamford Town Court- 607-538-1825; Stamford Village Court- 607-652-2804; Tompkins Town Court- 607-865-4949; Walton Town Court- 607-865-5182; Walton Village Court- 607-865-6150.

Dutchess County

County Clerk 22 Market St, 2nd Fl, Poughkeepsie, NY 12601-3203; 845-486-2139- records; main- 845-486-2120; 9AM-5PM. ***Felony, Civil.***

www.dutchessny.gov/dcclerk.htm

Countywide search requests made to the County Clerk are processed in the manner described below. Civil search requests are considered separate for criminal searches.

Civil Records: Access: Mail, in person, online. Visitors must perform in person searches themselves. Search fee: $5.00 per name per year. Required to search: name, years to search. Civil cases indexed by defendant, plaintiff. Civil records in books back to 1847; on computer back to 1986. Mail turnaround time 1 week Public use terminal available, records go back to 1987. PAT results show name only. Access to current/pending WebCivil Supreme Court civil cases is free at http://iapps.courts.state.ny.us/webcivil/FCASMain. Also, access to civil, criminal and recording office records is to be available by subscription from the county. Fee will be $35.00 monthly; civil records back to 1986 and criminal back to 1987. Contact Andee Fountain (845-486-2397) for additional information.

Criminal Records: Access: Mail, in person, online. Both court and visitors may perform in person searches. Search fee: $5.00 per name per year. Required to search: name, years to search, aliases. Criminal records go back to 1847; on computer back to 1987. They will only create a certificate if their staff performs the search. Mail turnaround time 2 weeks. Public use terminal available, crim records go back to 1987. PAT results show name only. Online access is the same as civil; subscriber or login as guest to search eCourts WebCrims future appearances system at http://iapps.courts.state.ny.us/webcrim_attorney/Login.

General Information: No sealed or youthful offender records released. Will not fax documents. Court makes copy: $.65 per page; $1.65 minimum. Self serve: $.25 per page. Certification fee: $5.00 per doc for 4 pages ($11.00 if mailed); add $1.25 each add'l page. Payee: Dutchess County Clerk. Personal checks accepted; credit cards are not. Mail requests: SASE required.

Supreme & County Court 10 Market St, Poughkeepsie, NY 12601-3203; 845-486-2260; fax: 845-473-5403; 9AM-5PM. ***Felony, Civil.***

For countywide record search, see the County Clerk, otherwise this court recommends the $55.00 statewide search via the OCA. Current/pending Supreme Court civil cases are online at http://iapps.courts.state.ny.us/webcivil/FCASMain.

Beacon City Court One Municipal Plaza, #2, Beacon, NY 12508; 845-838-5030; fax: 845-838-5041; 8AM-4PM. ***Misdemeanor, Civil Actions under $15,000, Eviction, Small Claims.***

https://www.nycourts.gov/courts/9jd/dutchess/Beacon.shtml

Civil Records: Access: Mail, fax, in person. Both court and visitors may perform in person searches. No search fee. An electronic search is $16.00. Required to search: name, DOB, years to search; also helpful- address. Civil cases indexed by defendant, plaintiff; index on computer from 1996, prior in books and cards. Mail turnaround time 2 weeks Civil PAT goes back to 1996. Public terminal is in the County Clerk's office.

Criminal Records: Access: Mail, in person. No criminal searching at this court. Search fee: $5.00 per 2 years. A Certificate of Disposition is $5.00; signed release required. Searchers are usually asked to use the $55.00 statewide OCA search. Mail turnaround time is 2 weeks. Criminal PAT goes back to same as civil. Public terminal is in the County Clerk's office.

General Information: No sealed or youthful offender records released. Will fax documents to local or toll-free number. Court makes copy: $.65 per page; $1.30 minimum. Certification fee: $5.00 for criminal; $6.00 if civil. Payee: City Court of Beacon. Only cashiers checks and money orders accepted. Visa/MC accepted.

Poughkeepsie City Court Civic Center Plaza, PO Box 300, Poughkeepsie, NY 12602; 845-451-4091; fax: 845-485-6795; 8AM-4PM; counter until 3PM. ***Misdemeanor, Civil Actions under $15,000, Eviction, Small Claims.***

Civil Records: Access: Mail, in person. Both court and visitors may perform in person searches. Search fee: $5.00 per name per 2 years searched. $5.00 for certificate of disposition. Required to search: name, years to search. Civil cases indexed by defendant. Civil records on computer from 1993. Civil PAT goes back to 2000.

Criminal Records: Access: Mail, in person. Only the court performs in person searches; visitors may not. Search fee: $5.00 per name for Certificate of Disposition only. Required to search: Name, years to search. Criminal records computerized from 1990. Direct criminal records search requests to OCA for $55.00 statewide search. Mail turnaround time 2 weeks. Criminal PAT goes back to 2000.

General Information: No sealed, expunged, adoption, sex offense, juvenile or mental health records released. Will not fax documents. Court makes copy: $.65 per page, $1.30 minimum. Certification fee: $5.00. Payee: Poughkeepsie City Court. Cashiers checks and money orders accepted. Visa/MC accepted. Mail requests: SASE required.

Surrogate's Court 10 Market St, Poughkeepsie, NY 12601; 845-486-2235; fax: 845-486-2234; 9AM-5PM. ***Probate.***

A county search of the probate court index by mail for 25-year search is $30.00 fee. A full county probate search of all years is $90.00.

Dutchess Town/Village Courts- Amenia Town Court- 845-373-7017; Beekman Town Court- 845-724-5300 x3; Clinton Town Court- 845-266-5988; Dover Town Court- 845-832-3461; East Fishkill Town Court- 845-226-4229; Fishkill Town Court- 845-831-7860; Fishkill Village Court- 845-897-2103; Hyde Park Town Court- 845-229-5111 x106/107/108; La Grange Town Court- 845-452-1837; Milan Town Court- 845-758-6960; Millbrook Village Court- 845-677-8277; North East Town Justice Court- 518-789-3080; Pawling Town Court- 845-855-3516; Pawling Village Court- 845-855-5602; Pine Plains Town Court- 518-398-7194; Pleasant Valley Town Court- 845-635-2856; Poughkeepsie Town Court- 845-485-3690/3696; Red Hook Town Court- 845-758-4611/758-4609; Red Hook Village Court- 845-758-4113; Rhinebeck Town Court- 845-876-3858; Rhinebeck Village Court- 845-876-4119; Stanford Town Court- 845-868-2269; Tivoli Village Court- 845-757-3219; Union Vale Town Court- 845-724-3288/724-5600; Wappinger Town Court- 845-297-6070; Wappingers Falls Village Court- 845-297-6777; Washington Town Court- 845-677-6366.

Erie County

County Clerk 92 Franklin St, 1st Fl, Buffalo, NY 14202; 716-858-8865; criminal phone: 716-858-7877; civil phone: 716-858-7766; fax: 716-858-6550; 9AM-5PM. ***Felony, Civil.***

www.erie.gov/depts/government/clerk/civil_criminal.phtml

Countywide search requests made to the County Clerk are processed in the manner described below. Office now located near the 92 Franklin St entrance in old section of courthouse. No misdemeanor records located here.

Civil Records: Access: Mail, in person, online. Both court and visitors may perform in person searches. Search fee: $5.00 per name per 2 years. Required to search: name, years to search. Civil cases indexed by defendant. Civil records on computer from 1993, prior in books back to 1900's. Mail turnaround time 1 week. Public use terminal has civil records back to 1993. PAT civil results show middle initial. Online access to the county clerk's database of civil matters is free at http://ecclerk.erie.gov. Records go back to 01/93. Also, access to current/pending Supreme Court civil cases is at http://iapps.courts.state.ny.us/webcivil/ecourtsMain.

Criminal Records: Access: In person, online. Both court and visitors may perform in person searches. No search fee. Required to search: name, years to search, DOB. Criminal records in books back to 1900's. Mailed search requests directed to the OCA for $55.00 statewide record search, but Erie County clerk's office can provide a search of closed criminal records. District Attorney Offices will not supply County Clerk with conviction records. Subscribe or login as guest to search eCourts WebCrims future appearances system at http://iapps.courts.state.ny.us/webcrim_attorney/Login. Online results show middle initial.

General Information: Online identifiers in results same as on public terminal. No sealed records released. Will not fax documents. Court makes copy: $1.00 per page. Certification fee: $5.00 per doc. Payee: County Clerk. Personal checks accepted; credit cards are not. Mail requests: SASE required for civil.

Supreme & County Court 25 Delaware Ave, Ground Fl, Buffalo, NY 14202; 716-845-9301; fax: 716-851-3293; 9AM-5PM. ***Felony, Civil.***

www.erie.gov

Court directs search requests to county clerk or to OCA for $55.00 state record check. Access current/pending Supreme Ct cases at https://iapps.courts.state.ny.us/caseTrac/jsp/ecourt.htm and also search pending criminal appearances.

Buffalo City Court 50 Delaware Ave, Buffalo, NY 14202; 716-845-2689; criminal phone: 716-845-2661; civil phone: 716-845-2662; criminal fax: 716-847-8257; civil fax: 716-856-4670; 9AM-5PM. ***Misdemeanor, Civil Actions under $15,000, Eviction, Small Claims.***

Civil Records: Access: In person only. Visitors must perform in person searches themselves. Required to search: name, years to search. Civil cases indexed by defendant, plaintiff. Criminal records on computer back to 1983, prior in books back to 1974. Public use terminal has civil records back to 1996.

Criminal Records: Access: In person only. Only the court performs in person searches; visitors may not. Search fee: Clerk will do Certificate of Disposition for $5.00 per arrest. Required to search: name, DOB, date of offense. Criminal records computerized from 1983, prior in books back to 1974. No general searches are performed; criminal requests directed to OCA in NYC for $55.00 statewide search. Search future court appearances at http://iapps.courts.state.ny.us/webcrim_attorney/Login

General Information: No sealed or youthful offender records released. Will not fax documents. Court makes copy: $.65 per page; $1.30 minimum. Certification fee: $6.00 per cert. Payee: City Court. Business checks accepted. Visa/MC and debit cards accepted.

Lackawanna City Court 714 Ridge Rd, Rm 225, Lackawanna, NY 14218; 716-827-6486; criminal phone: 716-827-6487; civil phone: 716-827-6661; fax: 716-825-1874; 8:30AM-4:30PM. ***Misdemeanor, Civil Actions under $15,000, Eviction, Small Claims.***

Civil Records: Access: Mail, in person. Only the court performs in person searches; visitors may not. No search fee. Required to search: name; also helpful: years to search. Civil cases indexed by defendant. Civil records on computer from 1994, prior on docket books. Mail access available to government agencies only.

Criminal Records: Access: None. Criminal records computerized from 1994, prior on docket books. The court refuses to permit access to court records unless specific case file given; a Certificate of Disposition is $6.00. Court says to send search requests to OCA for $55.00 statewide search.

General Information: No sealed or youthful offender records released. Will not fax documents. Court makes copy: $.65 per page, $1.30 minimum. Certification fee: $6.00 per document. Payee: City Court. Only cash, cashiers checks and money orders accepted for court fees. Visa/MC accepted for traffic fees only. Mail requests: SASE required.

Tonawanda City Court 200 Niagara St, Tonawanda, NY 14150; 716-845-2160; fax: 716-693-1612; 9AM-4PM. ***Misdemeanor, Civil Actions under $15,000, Eviction, Small Claims.***

Civil Records: Access: Mail, in person. Only the court performs in person searches; visitors may not. No search fee. Required to search: name, years to search. Civil cases indexed by defendant, plaintiff; index on computer since 1996, prior on index cards, in books. Mail turnaround time 3-5 days.

Criminal Records: Access: Mail, in person. Only the court performs in person searches; visitors may not. Search fee: $5.00 per name each 2 years searched. A Certificate of Disposition is $5.00. Required to search: name, years to search (case number, arrest date if Cert of Disposition). Criminal records on computer since 1986, prior on index cards, in books. As a rule, the court will not permit access to its records unless specific case file given. It suggests to send requests to OCA for $55.00 statewide search. However, court will search older records for the fee listed below. Mail turnaround time 3-5 days.

General Information: No sealed records released. Will fax documents to local or toll-free number. Court makes copy: $.65 per page. $1.30 minimum. Certification fee: $5.00. Payee: City Court of Tonawanda. Business checks accepted. Visa/MC accepted. Mail requests: SASE required.

Surrogate's Court 92 Franklin St, Buffalo, NY 14202; 716-845-2560; fax: 716-858-7871; 9AM-5PM. ***Probate.*** www.courts.state.ny.us

Public access terminals located in records room and at main desk; index goes back to 1800s. A county search of the probate court index by mail for 25-year search is $30.00 fee. A full county probate search of all years is $90.00.

Erie Town/Village Courts- Akron Village Court- 716-542 9636 x3; Alden Town Court- 716-937-6969 x6; Alden Village Court- 716-937-9216 x14; Amherst Town Court- 716-689-4200; Angola Village Court- 716-549-4035; Aurora Town Court- 716-652-5275; Blasdell Village Court- 716-821-7908; Boston Town Court- 716-941-6115; Brant Town Court- 716-549-0300; Cheektowaga Town Court- 716-686-3436; Clarence Town Court- 716-741-8948; Colden Town Court- 716-941-6242; Collins Town Court- 716-532-4887; Concord Town Court- 716-592-9898; Depew Village Court- 716-683-0978; Eden Town Court- 716-992-3559; Elma Town Court- 716-652-1855; Evans Town Court- 716-549-3707; Grand Island Town Court- 716-773-9600 ext 650; Hamburg Town Court- 716-649-6111x2399; Hamburg Village Court- 716-649-7204; Holland Town Court- 716-537-2770; Kenmore Village Court- 716-873-4554; Lancaster Town Court- 716-683-1814; Lancaster Village Court- 716-683-6780; Marilla Town Court- 716-652-1213; Newstead Town Court- 716-542-4575; North Collins Town Court- 716-337-3712; Orchard Park Town & Village Court- 716-662-6415; Sardinia Town Court- 716-496-8900; Springville Village Court- 716-592-5360; Tonawanda Town Court- 716-876-5536; Wales Town Court- 716-652-3320; West Seneca Town Court- 716-674-5600 x246; Williamsville Village Court- 716-632-0450.

Essex County

County Clerk PO Box 247, 7559 Court St, Essex County Government Ctr, Elizabethtown, NY 12932; 518-873-3606; criminal phone: 518-873-3370; civil phone: 518-873-3600, 518-873-3601; criminal fax: 518-873-3376; civil fax: 518-873-3548; 8AM-5PM. ***Civil, Felony.***

County Clerk will not do felony record searches for County-Court felony records; clerk will only do civil. You may search felony books in person.

Civil Records: Access: Mail, in person, online. Both court and visitors may perform in person searches. No search fee. Required to search: name, years to search. Civil cases indexed by defendant, plaintiff; index on computer from 11/93, prior in books. Mail turnaround time 1 day. Public use terminal has civil records back to 1993. Lookup current or pending Supreme Court civil cases at http://iapps.courts.state.ny.us/webcivil/FCASMain

Criminal Records: Access: In person only. Visitors must perform in person searches themselves. Required to search: name, years to search, DOB. Criminal records computerized from 1950s, prior in books; you may search the books.

General Information: No sealed or youthful offender records released. Will not fax documents. Court makes copy: $.65 per page; $1.30 minimum. Self serve: $.65 per page. Certification fee: $1.00 per page; minimum $5.00. Payee: Essex County Clerk. Personal checks accepted; credit cards are not. Mail requests: SASE required for civil.

Supreme & County Court PO Box 217, 7559 Court St, Essex County Government Ctr, Elizabethtown, NY 12932; 518-873-3600; criminal phone: 518-873-3370; civil phone: 518-873-3370; fax: 518-873-3376; 8AM-5PM. ***Felony, Civil.***

County-court directs criminal searches to the OCA for $55.00 statewide record check. Countywide record checks can be made at County Clerk, see separate listing.

Surrogate's Court PO Box 217, 7559 Court St, Elizabethtown, NY 12932; 518-873-3384; fax: 518-873-3731; 9AM-5PM. ***Probate.***

A county search of the probate court index by mail for 25-year search is $30.00 fee. A full county probate search of all years is $90.00.

Essex Town/Village Courts- Chesterfield Town Court- 518-834-9211; Crown Point Town Court- 518-597-4144; Elizabethtown Town Court- 518-873-2047; Essex Town Court- 518-963-8016; Jay Town Court- 518-647-5574; Keene Town Court- 518-576-4556; Lake Placid Village Court- 518-523-2004; Lewis Town Court- 518-873-3204; Minerva Town Court- 518-251-2869; Moriah Town Court- 518-546-9955; Newcomb Town Court- 518-582-4255; North Elba Town Court- 518-523-2141; North Hudson Town Court- 518-532-0587; Schroon Town Court- 518-532-0569 or 7737, x16 or x17; St Armand Town Court- 518-891-3189; Ticonderoga Town Court- 518-585-7141; Westport Town Court- 518-962-4882; Willsboro Town Court- 518-963-4014; Wilmington Town Court- 518-946-2105.

Franklin County

County Clerk 355 W Main St, Attn: County Clerk, Malone, NY 12953-1817; 518-481-1681; fax: 518-483-9143; 8AM-4PM. ***Felony, Civil.***

Felony records are managed by the Supreme Court clerk who directs search requests to OCA for a $55.00 statewide search. However, felony record index is accessible in person here (at County Clerk Office) on the public access terminal.

Civil Records: Access: Mail, in person, online. Both court and visitors may perform in person searches. Search fee: $5.00 per name per 2 years. Required to search: name, years to search. Civil cases indexed by defendant. Civil index of dockets on computer from 1996, prior in file folders in Clerk's office. Mail turnaround time same day. Civil PAT goes back to 1966. Separate public terminals for criminal records and civil records. Lookup current or pending Supreme Court civil cases at http://iapps.courts.state.ny.us/webcivil/FCASMain

Criminal Records: Access: Mail, fax, in person. Visitors must perform in person searches themselves. Search fee: $5.00 per name per 2 years. Required to search: name, years to search, DOB. Criminal records computerized from 1962. Criminal PAT goes back to same as civil. Separate public terminals for criminal records and civil records.

General Information: No sealed or youthful offender records released. Will fax documents $2.60 per page. Court makes copy: $.65 per page. Self serve: same. Certification fee: $1.00 per page, $5.00 minimum fee. Payee: Franklin County Clerk. Personal checks accepted; credit cards are not. Mail requests: SASE required for civil.

Supreme & County Court 355 W Main St, #3223, Court Clerk, Malone, NY 12953-1817; 518-481-1748; criminal phone: 518-481-1749; fax: 518-481-5456; 9AM-5PM; 8AM-4PM Summer hours. ***Felony, Civil.***

Supreme court directs criminal search requests to the OCA for a $55.00 statewide record check but public terminals available to search felonies here. Or, search records at County Clerk, see separate listing. Fax for Surrogates court is 518-483-7583.

Civil Records: Access: In person, online. Visitors must perform in person searches themselves. Required to search: name, years to search. Civil cases indexed by defendant. Civil index of dockets on computer back to 1996, prior in file folders in Clerk's office. Current or pending Supreme Court civil case look-up is free at http://iapps.courts.state.ny.us/webcivil/FCASMain

Criminal Records: Access: In person only. Visitors must perform in person searches themselves. Required to search: name, years to search, DOB. Criminal records computerized from 1962. Unless you search here in person, all criminal record name search requests are directed to the OCA for $55.00 statewide record search. Public use terminal has crim records back to 1962. PAT results show middle initial, DOB. Two terminals are available for public searching; one at the Supreme court clerk and the other at the County Clerk office.

General Information: No sealed or youthful offender records released. Will fax out specific case files for $2.60 per page. Court makes copy: $.65 per page. Certification fee: $5.00 per doc. Payee: County Clerk. Personal checks accepted.

Surrogate's Court 355 W Main St, #3223, Malone, NY 12953-1817; 518-481-1736/1737; fax: 518-481-7583; 9AM-5PM Summer; 8:00-4PM June-Aug. ***Probate.***
www.nycourts.gov/courts/4jd/franklin/surrogates.shtml
A county search of the probate court index by mail for 25-year search is $30.00 fee. A full county probate search of all years is $90.00.

Franklin Town/Village Courts- Altamont Town Court- 518-359-9278; Bangor Town Court- 518-483-3754; Bellmont Town Court- 518-425-3349; Bombay Town Court- 518-358-9968; Brandon Town Court- 518-483-8043; Brighton Town Court- 518-327-3202; Burke Town Court- 518-483-5497; Chateaugay Town Court- 518-497-3429; Constable Town Court- 518-481-6113; Dickinson Town Court- 518-856-0201; Duane Town Court- 518-483-0386; Fort Covington Town Court- 518-358-2796; Franklin Town Court- 518-891-2189; Harrietstown Town Court- 518-891-4500; Malone Town Court- 518-481-6634; Malone Village Court- 518-483-5210; Moira Town Court- 518-529-2080; Santa Clara Town Court- 518-891-1919; Saranac Lake Village Court- 518-891-4423; Tupper Lake Village Court- 518-359-9161; Waverly Town Court- 518-856-9249; Westville Town Court- 518-358-2499, 518-358-3432.

Fulton County

Supreme & County Court 223 W Main St, County Bldg, Johnstown, NY 12095; 518-736-5539 (court) 518-736-5555 (county clerk); civil phone: 518-736-5555; fax: 518-762-5078; 9AM-5PM. ***Felony, Civil.***
Hamilton County Supreme Court cases are heard here. Supreme court clerk directs criminal search requests to the OCA for a $55.00 statewide record check, however the County Clerk office (same location) may permit in person criminal record search requests.
Civil Records: Access: Phone, mail, fax, in person, online. Both court and visitors may perform in person searches. Search fee: $16.00 per name. Required to search: name, years to search. Civil cases indexed by defendant, plaintiff. Civil records computerized since 1994. Mail turnaround time same day. No historical records online; current or pending only Supreme Court civil case look-up at http://iapps.courts.state.ny.us/webcivil/FCASMain
Criminal Records: Access: In person only. Only the court performs in person searches; visitors may not. Search fee: $5.00 if search done in archives. Required to search: name, years to search, DOB. Criminal records in file folders since 1915, computerized since 1977. While the court recommends the $55 statewide search, in person searchers may view court clerk's alpha list free.
General Information: No sealed, expunged, adoption, sex offense, juvenile or mental health records released. Will fax documents after payment received. Court makes copy: $1.00 per page. Self serve: $.50 per page. Certification fee: $5.00 per page. Payee: County Clerk. Business checks accepted. No credit cards accepted. Mail requests: SASE required for civil.

Gloversville City Court 3 Frontage Rd, City Hall, Gloversville, NY 12078; 518-773-4527; fax: 518-773-4599; 8AM-4PM; window closes at 3:30. ***Misdemeanor, Civil Actions under $15,000, Eviction, Small Claims.***
Civil Records: Access: Mail, in person. Only the court performs in person searches; visitors may not. No search fee. Required to search: name, years to search. Civil cases indexed by plaintiff. Civil records in books; on computer since. Mail turnaround time less than 1 week.
Criminal Records: Access: None. A Certificate of Disposition is $5.00. Required to search: name, years to search, charge, date of arrest or sentence. The court refuses to permit access to records unless specific case file given. Searchers must use the OCA $55.00 statewide search.
General Information: No sealed, youthful offender records released. Will not fax documents. Court makes copy: $.65 per page; $1.30 minimum. Certification fee: $5.00 per doc criminal; $6.00 if civil,. Payee: Gloversville City Court. No personal checks accepted. Visa/MC accepted. Mail requests: SASE required.

Johnstown City Court 33-41 E Main St, Johnstown, NY 12095; 518-762-0007; fax: 518-762-2720; 8AM-4PM. ***Misdemeanor, Civil Actions under $15,000, Eviction, Small Claims.***
Civil Records: Access: Mail, in person. Only the court performs in person searches; visitors may not. No search fee. Required to search: name, years to search. Civil cases indexed by plaintiff. Civil records in file folders, computerized since 1995.
Criminal Records: Access: None. Only the court performs in person searches; visitors may not. Criminal records computerized from 1990. The court does not permit access to court records unless specific case file number given. Requesters are directed to OCA for $55.00 statewide search.
General Information: No sealed or youthful offender records released. Will not fax documents. Court makes copy: $.65 per page, $1.30 minimum. Certification fee: $5.00 per document. Payee: Johnstown City Court. Only cashiers checks and money orders accepted. Visa/MC accepted. Mail requests: SASE required.

Surrogate's Court 223 W Main St, Johnstown, NY 12095; 518-736-5685; fax: 518-762-6372; 9AM-5PM (8AM-4PM July-August). ***Probate.***
A county search of the probate court index by mail for 25-year search is $30.00 fee. A full county probate search of all years is $90.00.

Fulton Town/Village Courts- Bleecker Town Court- 518-725-6897; Broadalbin Town & Village Court- 518-883-5131; Caroga Town Court- 518-835-4211; Ephratah Town Court- 518-568-7560; Johnstown Town Court- 518-762-6904; Mayfield Town Court- 518-661-5254; Oppenheim Town Court- 518-568-2837; Perth Town Court- 518-843-6977; Stratford Town Court- 315-429-8341.

Genesee County

County Clerk PO Box 379, Attn: County Clerk, 15 Main St, County Clerk, Batavia, NY 14021-0379; 585-344-2550; criminal phone: x2245; civil phone: x2242; fax: 585-344-8521; 8:30-5PM. ***Felony, Civil.***
www.co.genesee.ny.us/ Countywide criminal search requests made to the County Clerk are processed in the manner described below.
Civil Records: Access: Mail, in person, online. Both court and visitors may perform in person searches. Search fee: $10.00 per name per 5 year period. Required to search: name, years to search; also helpful: address. Civil cases indexed by defendant, plaintiff; indexed by defendant only prior to 1995. Civil records in books from 1802; on computer back to 1995. Mail turnaround time 1-3 days. Civil PAT goes back to 1/1995. PAT results show name only. Lookup current or pending Supreme Court civil cases at http://iapps.courts.state.ny.us/webcivil/FCASMain
Criminal Records: Access: Fax, mail, in person. Both court and visitors may perform in person searches. Search fee: $10.00 per name per 5 year period, $15.00 for 6-10 years, $20.00 for 11-20 years. Required to search: name, years to search, DOB. Criminal records in books from 1802; on computer back to 1995. With fax requests, include a photocopy of your fee payment check and they will entertain your search request and speed up the process. Mail turnaround time 1-3 days. Criminal PAT goes back to same as civil. PAT results show name only.
General Information: No sealed, expunged, adoption, sex offense, juvenile or mental health records released. Will fax out $5.00 per doc. Court makes copy: $.65 per page, $1.30 minimum. Certification fee: $5.00 per doc plus $1.25 per page after first 4. Exemplification fee- $10.00 plus copies. Payee: County Clerk. Personal checks accepted; credit cards are not. Mail requests: SASE required.

Supreme & County Court One W Main St, Batavia, NY 14020; 585-344-2550 x2239; fax: 585-344-8517; 9AM-5PM. ***Felony, Civil.***
The County Court directs criminal search requests to the OCA for a $55.00 statewide record check. See also County Clerk, see separate listing.

Batavia City Court Genesee County Courts Facility, 1 W Main St, Batavia, NY 14020; 585-344-2550 x2416, 2417, 2418, 2415; fax: 585-344-8556; 9AM-5PM. ***Misdemeanor, Civil Actions under $15,000, Eviction, Small Claims.***
www.nycourts.gov/courts/8jd/genesee/batavia.shtml
Civil Records: Access: Fax, mail, in person. Both court and visitors may perform in person searches. Search fee: A Certificate of Disposition is available for $6.00. Required to search: name, years to search. Civil cases indexed by plaintiff. Civil records on computer from 1990, in books from 1957. Mail turnaround time 1-3 days.
Criminal Records: Access: Mail, in person. Only the court performs in person searches; visitors may not. Search fee: A Certificate of Disposition is available for $6.00. Required to search: name, years to search, DOB. Criminal records computerized from 1993, in books from 1947. All criminal record name search requests are directed to the OCA for statewide record search, $55.00 search fee. Mail turnaround time 1-3 days.
General Information: No sealed, expunged, sex offense or mental health records released. Will fax documents to local or toll free line only. Court makes copy: $.65 per page. Certification fee: $6.00 per seal. Payee: Batavia City Court. Only cashiers checks and money orders accepted. Visa/MC accepted. Mail requests: SASE required.

Surrogate's Court 1 W Main St, Batavia, NY 14020; 585-344-2550 x2237; fax: 585-344-8517; 9AM-5PM. ***Probate.***
A county search of the probate court index by mail for 25-year search is $30.00 fee. A full county probate search of all years is $90.00.

Genesee Town/Village Courts- Alabama Town Court- no phone; Alexander Town Court- 585-591-8165; Batavia Town Court- 585-343-1729; Bergen Town Court- 585-494-1121; Bethany Town Court- 585-343-3325; Byron Town Court- 585-548-7123; Corfu Village Court- 585-599-3380; Darien Town Court- 585-547-2274 x21; Elba Town Court- 585-757-9200; Leroy Town & Village Court- 585-768-6910; Oakfield Town Court- 585-948-5835 x3; Pavilion Town Court- 585-584-2025; Pembroke Town Ct- 585-599-4817; Stafford Town Ct- 585-344-4020.

Greene County

Supreme & County Court County Clerk, Courthouse, 411 Main St, Catskill, NY 12414; 518-719-3255, (county clerk) 518-943-2230 (court clerk); fax: 518-719-3284; 9AM-5PM; 8:30AM-4:30PM June-Aug hours. ***Felony, Civil.***
Search requests are processed by the County Clerk office in the manner described below. Courts are located at 320 Main St. Fax to the County clerk office is 518-719-3284.
Civil Records: Access: In person, onine. Both court and visitors may perform in person searches. No search fee. Required to search: name, years to search. Civil cases indexed by defendant, plaintiff. Civil records in file folder, computerized since 6/13/97. Public use terminal has civil records back to 1999 for index. Historical records not online, but access to current/pending Supreme Court civil cases is at http://iapps.courts.state.ny.us/webcivil/FCASMain
Criminal Records: Access: In person. Only the court performs in person searches; visitors may not. Search fee: $17.50 per name for 7-20 years. May also do search for $5.00 per name for 2 years. Required to search: name, years to search, DOB. Criminal records indexed on cards.
General Information: No sealed or youthful offender records released. Will not fax documents. Court makes copy: $1.00 per page. Self serve: $.25 per page. Certification fee: $5.00 per doc. Payee: County Clerk. Personal checks accepted; credit cards are not.

Surrogate's Court Courthouse, 320 Main St, Catskill, NY 12414; 518-943-2484; fax: 518-943-1864; 9AM-5PM. ***Probate.***
A county search of the probate court index by mail for 25-year search is $30.00 fee. A full county probate search of all years is $90.00.

Greene Town/Village Courts- Ashland Town Court- 518-734-4760; Athens Town Court- 518-945-3360;

Athens Village Court- 518-945-3002; Cairo Town Court- 518-622-3388; Catskill Town Court- 518-943-2142; Catskill Village Court- 518-943-9544; Coxsackie Town Court- 518-731-6934; Durham Town Court- 518-239-8260; Greenville Town Court- 518-966-4873; Halcott Town Court- 845-254-6441; Hunter Town Court- 518-589-5882; Jewett Town Court- 518-263-4626; Lexington Town Court- 518-989-6303; New Baltimore Town Court- 518-756-2079; Prattsville Town Court- 518-299-3125; Windham Town Court- 518-734-3431.

Hamilton County

County Clerk & County Court Hamilton County Clerk, PO Box 204, Rte 8, Lake Pleasant, NY 12108; 518-548-7111; fax: 518-548-9740; 8:30AM-4:30PM. ***Felony, Civil.***
Countywide record search requests are processed in the manner described below. Civil cases are heard in Fulton County (518-736-5539, Patricia, for info). Once closed, civil case records are returned to Hamilton County clerk.
Civil Records: Access: Mail, phone, in person, online. Both court and visitors may perform in person searches. No search fee. Required to search: name, years to search. Civil cases indexed by defendant. Civil records in books, records go back to 1850's. Mail turnaround time 2-3 days. Lookup current or pending Supreme Court civil cases at http://iapps.courts.state.ny.us/webcivil/FCASMain
Criminal Records: Access: Mail, in person. Only the court performs in person searches; visitors may not. Search fee: $5.00 per name. Fee is per two years searched. Required to search: name, years to search, DOB. Criminal records go back to 1878; no computerized records. Record search request must be in writing. Mail turnaround time 2-3 days.
General Information: No sealed or youthful offender records released. Fee to fax document $1.00 each. Court makes copy: $.65 per page, $1.30 minimum. Certification fee: $1.25 per page; $5.00 minimum. Payee: Hamilton County Clerk. Personal checks accepted; credit cards are not. Mail requests: SASE required.

Supreme Court PO Box 204, County Clerk, Rte 8, Lake Pleasant, NY 12108; 518-548-7111 (Hamilton county clerk) 518-736-5539 (Fulton court clerk); fax: 518-548-9740; 8:30AM-4:30PM. ***Civil.***
Supreme court (civil cases) in Hamilton County are heard in Fulton County. Civil records eventually returned to Hamilton County Clerk once the case is completed in Fulton. Original filings made in Hamilton, but subsequent filings usually made at Fulton.
Civil Records: Access: Mail, fax, phone, in person, online. Both court and visitors may perform in person searches. No search fee. Required to search: name, years to search. Civil cases indexed by defendant. Civil records in books, records go back to 1850's. Mail turnaround time 2-3 days. Public use terminal has civil records. Hamilton County civil cases heard in Fulton County may be available on Fulton County civil records computer system. No public terminal in Hamilton County. Historical records are not online, but access to current/pending Supreme Court civil cases is at http://iapps.courts.state.ny.us/webcivil/FCASMain
General Information: No sealed or youthful offender records released. Fee to fax out is $1.00 per doc, Court makes copy: $.65 per page, $1.30 minimum. Certification fee: $1.00 per page; $5.00 minimum. Payee: Hamilton County Clerk. Personal checks accepted; credit cards are not.

Surrogate's Court PO Box 780, 79 White Birch Lane, Indian Lake, NY 12842; 518-648-5411; fax: 518-648-6286; 8:30AM-4:30PM. ***Probate.***
Court is located in Hamilton County Ofc. A county search of the probate court index by mail for 25-year search is $30.00 fee. A full county probate search of all years is $90.00.

Hamilton Town/Village Courts- Arietta Town Court- 518-548-6203; Benson Town Court- 518-221-6377; 518-863-6093 eves; Hope Town Court- 518-924-4302; Indian Lake Town Court- 518-648-6226; Inlet Town Court- 315-357-6121; Lake Pleasant Town Court- 518-548-3625; Long Lake Town Court- 518-624-3761; Morehouse Town Court- 315-826-7093; Wells Town Court- 518-924-7407.

Herkimer County

County Clerk 109 Mary St, #1111, County Office Bldg, Herkimer, NY 13350-1993; 315-867-1133; fax: 315-867-1349; 9AM-5PM Sept-May; 8:30AM-4PM June-Aug. ***Felony, Civil.***
Countywide search requests made to the County Clerk are processed in the manner described below.
Civil Records: Access: Mail, in person, online. Both court and visitors may perform in person searches. Search fee: $5.00 per name per 2 year period. Required to search: name, years to search. Civil cases indexed by defendant, plaintiff. Civil index on docket books since 1800s. Mail turnaround time varies- ASAP to days. Civil PAT goes back to mid-1990s. PAT results show name, DOB. Lookup current or pending Supreme Court civil cases at http://iapps.courts.state.ny.us/webcivil/FCASMain
Criminal Records: Access: mail, in person. Both court and visitors may perform in person searches. Search fee: $5.00 per name per 2 year period. Required to search: name, years to search, DOB. Criminal records indexed in books since 1800s. Mail turnaround time varies- ASAP to days. Criminal PAT goes back to 1800s; results show name, DOB.
General Information: No sealed, expunged, adoption, sex offense, juvenile or mental health records released. Will fax out documents, fax fee same as copy fee total. Court makes copy: $.65 per page, $1.30 minimum. Certification fee: 1-4 pages is $5.00; $1.25 each add'l page. Payee: County Clerk. Personal checks accepted; credit cards are not. Mail requests: SASE required.

Supreme & County Court 301 N Washington St, Herkimer, NY 13350-1993; criminal phone: 315-867-1282; civil phone: 315-867-1209; fax: 315-866-1802; 8:30AM-4:30PM; 8:30AM-4PM Summer hours. ***Felony, Civil.***
The County Court clerk directs felony requests to the OCA for a $55.00 statewide record check. See also separate listing for County Clerk. Access to current/pending Supreme Court civil cases is at http://iapps.courts.state.ny.us/webcivil/FCASMain.

Little Falls City Court 659 E Main St, Little Falls, NY 13365; 315-823-1690; fax: 315-823-1623; 8:30AM-4:30PM. ***Misdemeanor, Civil Actions under $15,000, Eviction, Small Claims.***
Civil Records: Access: Mail, fax, in person. Only the court performs in person searches; visitors may not. Search fee: $5.00 per name. Required to search: name, years to search. Civil cases indexed by defendant. Civil records go back to 1973; on computer back to 4/02. Mail turnaround time 1 week.
Criminal Records: Access: Mail, in person. Only the court performs in person searches; visitors may not. Search fee: $5.00 per name. Required to search: name, years to search, DOB, signed release. Criminal records go back to 1948; on computer back to 4/02. Mail turnaround time 1 week.
General Information: No sealed, expunged, adoption, sex offense, juvenile or mental health records released. Will fax documents to local or toll free line. Court makes copy: $.65 per page; minimum $1.30. Certification fee: $5.00 per document. Payee: City Court. Only cashiers checks and money orders accepted. Visa/MC accepted in person only. Mail requests: SASE required.

Surrogate's Court 301 N Washington St, #5550, Herkimer, NY 13350; 315-867-1170; fax: 315-866-1722; 8:30AM-4:30PM Sept-May; 8:00AM-4PM June-Aug. ***Probate.*** Access to limited (some, not all) 5th District Surrogate's Court records is free after registration at http://surrogate5th.courts.state.ny.us/Public/Login.aspx.

Herkimer Town/Village Courts- Cold Brook Village Court- 315-826-3432; Columbia Town Court- 315-866-1309; Danube Town Court- 315-823-4210; Fairfield Town Court- 315-823-2747; Frankfort Town Court- 315-895-7267; Frankfort Village Court- 315-894-8513; German Flatts Town Court- 315-866-3571; Herkimer Town Court- 315-866-1280; Herkimer Village Court- 315-866-0604; Ilion Village Court- 315-894-4175; Litchfield Town Court- no phone; Little Falls Town Court- 315-823-1202; Manheim Town Court- 315-429-9631; Middleville Village Court- 315-823-2747; Newport Town Court- 315-845-8060; Newport Village Court- 315-845-8938; Norway Town Court- 315-845-8272; Ohio Town Court- 315-826-3466; Poland Village Court- 315-826-3432; Russia Town Court- 315-826-3432; Salisbury Town Court- 315-429-8581; Schuyler Town Court- 315-733-1093; Stark Town Court- 315-858-2091; Warren Town Court- 315-858-2586; Webb Town Court- 315-369-3321; Winfield Town Court- 315-822-4555.

Jefferson County

Supreme & County Court Jefferson County Clerk's Office-Court Records, 175 Arsenal St, County Bldg, Watertown, NY 13601-3783; 315-785-3200 County Clerk; probate phone: 315-785-3019; fax: 315-785-5145; 9AM-5PM; 8:30AM-4PM July-Aug hours. ***Felony, Civil.***
www.co.jefferson.ny.us/Jefflive.nsf/cclerk
Countywide record search requests are processed in the manner described below by the County Clerk, phone above, or 785-3081.
Civil Records: Access: In person, online. Visitors must perform in person searches themselves. Required to search: name, years to search. Civil cases indexed by defendant, plaintiff; index on computer back to 1/1992; prior in books from 1805 by first defendant name only. Civil phone for Supreme Court clerk 315-785-7912. Civil PAT goes back to 1992; civil results show middle initial. Current or pending only Supreme Court civil case look-up at http://iapps.courts.state.ny.us/webcivil/FCASMain
Criminal Records: Access: Mail, in person. Both court and visitors may perform in person searches. Search fee: $5.00 per name. Fee is per 2 years searched. Required to search: name, years to search; also helpful: DOB, signed release. Criminal records computerized from 1/1992; prior in books from 1805 by first defendant name only. County court clerk is 315-785-3044. Mail turnaround time 1 week. Criminal PAT goes back to same as civil. PAT criminal results show middle initial.
General Information: No sealed, expunged, adoption, sex offense, juvenile or mental health records released. Will fax out specific case files. Court makes copy: $.65 per page; $1.30 minimum. Self serve: same. Certification fee: $1.25 per page, $5.00 minimum. with copies. Payee: County Clerk of Jefferson County. Personal checks accepted; credit cards are not. Mail requests: SASE required.

Watertown City Court 245 Washington St, Municipal Bldg, Watertown, NY 13601; 315-785-7785; fax: 315-785-7856; 8:30AM4:30PM. ***Misdemeanor, Civil Actions under $15,000, Eviction, Small Claims.***
Civil Records: Access: Mail, in person. Only the court performs in person searches; visitors may not. Search fee: $6.00 per name. Fee is per name & docket. Required to search: name, years to search. Civil cases indexed by defendant. Civil records in docket books. Mail turnaround time 1 day.
Criminal Records: Access: None. Only the court performs in person searches; visitors may not. Search fee: $16.00 per name. Criminal records in docket books. The court refuses to permit access to court records unless specific case file given. It is mandatory to send requests to OCA for $55.00 statewide search.
General Information: No sealed records released. Will fax documents to local or toll free line. Court makes copy: $.65 per page. Certification fee: $6.00. Payee: City Court. Only cashiers checks and money orders accepted. Visa/MC accepted. Mail requests: SASE required.

Surrogate's Court County Court Complex, 163 Arsenal St, 3rd Fl, Watertown, NY 13601-2562; 315-785-3019; fax: 315-785-5194; 8:30AM-4:30PM Sept-May; 8:30AM-4PM June-Aug. ***Probate.***
A county search of the probate court index by mail for 25-year search is $30.00 fee. A full county probate search of all years is $90.00.

Jefferson Town/Village Courts- Adams Town Court- 315-583-5085; Adams Village Court- 315-232-3849; Alexandria Bay Village Court- 315-482-4786; Alexandria Town Court- 315-482-9637; Antwerp

Town Court- 315-659-8989; Brownville Town Court- 315-639-6266; Brownville Village Court- 315-639-6266; Cape Vincent Town Court- 315-654-3883; Carthage Village Court- 315-493-2890; Champion Town Court- 315-493-2687; Clayton Town and Village Court- 315-686-2427; Ellisburg Town Court- 315-846-9216; Glen Park Village Court- 315-639-6266; Henderson Town Court- 315-938-5614; Hounsfield Town Court- 315-646-2767; LeRay Town Court- 315-629-0228; Lorraine Town Court- 315-232-2548; Lyme Town Court- 315-893-7544; Orleans Town Court- 315-658-2272; Pamelia Town Court- 315-785-9794; Philadelphia Town Court- 315-642-3421; Philadelphia Village Court- 315-642-3452; Rodman Town Court- 315-232-4029; Rutland Town Court- 315-788-1265; Theresa Town Court- 315-628-4148; Theresa Village Court- 315-628-4425; Watertown Town Court- 315-782-0412; West Carthage Village Court- 315-493-6345; Wilna Town Ct- 315-493-2771;

Kings County

Supreme Court - Civil Division 360 Adams St, #189, c/o County Clerk office, Brooklyn, NY 11201; 347-404-9772; 9AM-3PM for records. ***Civil Actions over $25,000.***
www.courts.state.ny.us/courts/2jd/kings.shtml
Supreme Ct civil records are managed by the County Clerk's office. Address and phone and searching methods at County Clerk are given here. In person search- see Window 6. See www.courts.state.ny.us/courts/2jd/kingsclerk/index.shtml for add'l info.
Civil Records: Access: In person, online. Visitors must perform in person searches themselves. Required to search: name, years to search; also requested by clerk- index number. Civil cases indexed by defendant. Civil records on computer back to 1993; in books, on microfiche back to 1900's. Picture ID required for in person searchers for matrimonial cases. Public use terminal has civil records back to 1993. PAT results show name and may also include address and attorney. Public terminal can be found in Law Library, Rm 349, 9AM-6PM, 347-296-1144. Access to current/pending Supreme Court civil cases is at http://iapps.courts.state.ny.us/webcivil/FCASMain
General Information: No sealed, expunged, adoption, juvenile or mental health records released. Will not fax documents. Court makes copy: $.65 per page; $1.30 minimum. Certification fee: $8.00 per doc. $25.00 for exemplification. Payee: County Clerk. Only cashiers checks and money orders accepted. Mail requests: SASE required for civil.

Supreme Court - Criminal 320 Jay St, Brooklyn, NY 11201; 347-296-1076; direct- 347-296-1122; criminal phone: x3 felony; x3 then x4 records rm; 9AM-5PM. ***Felony.***
www.courts.state.ny.us/courts/2jd/kings.shtml#sup
This court does not perform criminal searches; direct search requests to the OCA, 25 Beaver St, NYC, 212-428-2810. Also, search online for future court appearances and summons case info at http://iapps.courts.state.ny.us/webcrim_attorney/Login.

Criminal Court 120 Schermerhorn St, Brooklyn, NY 11201; 347-296-1076; criminal phone: x1 misd; fax: 718-643-7733; 9AM-5PM. ***Misdemeanor.***
www.courts.state.ny.us/courts/2jd/kings.shtml#sup
Court does not perform criminal searches; direct search requests to OCA, 25 Beaver St, NYC, 212-428-2810. Also, subscribe or login as guest to search eCourts WebCrims future appearances system at http://iapps.courts.state.ny.us/webcrim_attorney/Login.

Civil Court of the City of New York - Kings Branch, Brooklyn 141 Livingston St, #303, Brooklyn, NY 11201; 347-404-9123 Admin; civil phone: 347-404-9015 records rm; 9AM-5PM. ***Civil Actions under $25,000, Eviction, Small Claims.***
www.courts.state.ny.us/courts/2jd/kings.shtml
Searching performed in the basement record Rm-007 or on Civil Dept. public access terminal in #302. General civil dial-up info line- 212-791-6000. Sm Claims phone- 347-404-9020; housing ct- 347-404-9200; Admin- 347-404-9133.
Civil Records: Access: Phone, in person, online. Visitors must perform in person searches themselves. No search fee. Required to search: name, years to search. Civil cases indexed by plaintiff. Pre-1998 records archived in Queens; 1998 to present in Brooklyn. Civil records on computer from 1987 for small claims, 1990 for tenant/landlord, and from 1/1998 for civil. When not busy, the civil department is known to be able to do a computer lookup while you wait on the phone. Public use terminal has civil records back to 1997. Public terminal has Landlord/tenant, civil, and small claims. 1 PAT in basement, 3 on 3rd Fl. Access civil records free at http://iapps.courts.state.ny.us/webcivil/ecourtsMain. Landlord/Tenant index can also be found on the internet.
General Information: All records public. Will not fax documents. Court makes copy: Record Room gives you file to copy, once you present a case number. Self serve: $.15 per page. Certification fee: $6.00 per doc. Payee: NYC Civil Court. Only cashiers checks and money orders accepted. No credit cards.

Surrogate's Court 2 Johnson St, Brooklyn, NY 11201; 347-404-9700; fax: 718-643-6237; 9AM-5PM. ***Probate.*** A county search of the probate court index by mail for 25-year search is $30.00 fee. A full county probate search of all years is $90.00.

Lewis County

Supreme & County Court Courthouse, County Clerk, PO Box 232, Lowville, NY 13367; 315-376-5333 (County); 315-376-5380 (Supreme); fax: 315-376-3768; 8:30AM-4:30PM. ***Felony, Civil.***
Countywide search requests are processed in the manner described below.
Civil Records: Access: Mail, in person, online. Both court and visitors may perform in person searches. Search fee: $10.00 per name. Required to search: name, years to search. Civil cases indexed by defendant only. Civil index on cards from 1935. Mail turnaround time 2 days. Civil PAT goes back to 2002. Historical records are not online, but access to current/pending Supreme Court civil cases is at http://iapps.courts.state.ny.us/webcivil/FCASMain
Criminal Records: Access: Mail, in person. Both court and visitors may perform in person searches. Search fee: $10.00 per name. Required to search: name, years to search. Criminal records indexed on cards from 1935. Mail turnaround time 2 days. Criminal PAT goes back to same as civil.
General Information: No sealed, youthful offender or sex abuse case records released. Will fax documents $1.00 per page. Court makes copy: $.65 per page. Self serve same. Cert fee: $5.00 per doc. Payee: County Clerk. Personal checks accepted; credit cards are not. Mail requests: SASE required.

Surrogate's Court Courthouse, 7660 State St, Lowville, NY 13367; 315-376-5344; fax: 315-376-4145; 8:30AM-4:30PM; Jun-July-Aug 8:30-4PM. ***Probate.*** www.nycourts.gov/courts/5jd/lewis
Search Fee is $30 for under 25 years to $90 for over 70 years. Records available on Public Terminal in County Law Library, also free with registration at http://surrogate5th.courts.state.ny.us/Public/Login.aspx but records are not all inclusive.

Lewis Town/Village Courts- Croghan Town Court- 315-346-1272; Denmark Town Court- 315-493-1302; Diana Town Court- 315-543-2628; Greig Town Court- no phone; Harrisburg Town Court- 315-688-4193; Lewis Town Court- Leyden Town Court- 315-348-6215; Lowville Town Court- 315-376-8070; Lowville Village Court- 315-376-2834; Lyonsdale Town Court- 315-348-8666; Martinsburg Town Court- 315-376-2458; New Bremen Town Court- 315-376-3752; Osceola Town Court- 315-245-1610; Pinckney Town Court- no phone; Port Leyden Village Court- 315-348-6215; Turin Town Court- 315-348-6313; Watson Town Ct- 315-376-3866; West Turin Town Court- 315-397-2231.

Livingston County

County Clerk 6 Court St, Rm 201, Geneseo, NY 14454; 585-243-7010; fax: 585-243-7928; 8:30AM-4:30PM Oct-May; 8AM-4PM June-Sept. ***Felony, Civil.*** Countywide search requests made to the County Court Clerk are processed in the manner described below.
Civil Records: Access: Mail, fax, in person, online. Both court and visitors may perform in person searches. Search fee: $2.50 per name per year if a written request. Required to search: name, years to search. Civil cases indexed by defendant only. Civil records on computer since 1996. Plaintiff index available only on computer searches. Mail turnaround time same day. Civil PAT goes back to 1996. PAT results show name only. Lookup current or pending Supreme Court civil cases at http://iapps.courts.state.ny.us/webcivil/FCASMain
Criminal Records: Access: Mail, fax, in person. Both court and visitors may perform in person searches. Search fee: $2.50 per name per year if a written request. Required to search: name, years to search. Criminal records on computer since 1996. Plaintiff index available only on computer searches. Fax requests accepted with payment. Mail turnaround time same day. Criminal PAT goes back to same as civil. PAT results show middle initial, DOB.
General Information: No sealed or youthful offender records released. Will fax documents if prepaid or to toll-free number. Court makes copy: $.65 per page. Self serve: self serve available if you have a copy code or button, prefunded, prepaid. Certification fee: $5.00 up to 4 pages, $.65 each add'l page. Payee: County Clerk. Personal checks, money orders accepted. No credit cards accepted. Mail requests: SASE required.

Supreme & County Court 2 Court St, Geneseo, NY 14454; 585-243-7060; fax: 585-243-7067; 9AM-5PM. ***Felony, Civil.***
County-Court directs felony search requests to the OCA for a $55.00 statewide search fee. See also County Clerk in separate listing. Access current/pending Supreme Court civil cases is at http://iapps.courts.state.ny.us/webcivil/FCASMain.

Surrogate's Court 2 Court St, Geneseo, NY 14454; 585-243-7095; fax: 585-243-7583; 9AM-5PM. ***Probate.***
A county search of the probate court index by mail for 25-year search is $30.00 fee. A full county probate search of all years is $90.00.

Livingston Town/Village Courts- Avon Town Court- 585-226-2130; Avon Village Court- 585-226-3660; Caledonia Town Court- 585-538-4800; Caledonia Village Court- 585-538-4800; Conesus Town Court- 585-346-9240; Dansville Village Court- 585-335-2460; Geneseo Town & Village Court- 585-243-4530; Groveland Town Court- 585-243-3782; Leicester Town Court- 585-382-9419; Lima Town Court- 585-582-1011; Livonia Town Court- 585-346-0221; Mount Morris Town Court- 585-658-2333; Mount Morris Village Court- 585-658-3249; North Dansville Town Court- 585-335-2460; Nunda Village Court- 585-468-5558; Ossian Town Court- 585-335-8040; Portage Town Court- no phone; Sparta Town Court- 585-335-7045; Springwater Town Court- 585-669-2635; West Sparta Town Court- 585-335-2907; York Town Court- 585-243-0666.

Madison County

County Clerk County Office Bldg #4, PO Box 668, Wampsville, NY 13163-0668; 315-366-2261; probate phone: 315-366-2392; fax: 315-366-2615; 9AM-5PM. ***Felony, Civil.*** www.madisoncounty.org/
Countywide search requests made to the County Clerk are processed in the manner described below.
Civil Records: Access: Mail, in person, online (limited). Both court and visitors may perform in person searches. Search fee: $5.00 per name. Fee is per 5 years searched. Required to search: name, years to search. Civil cases indexed by defendant. Judgment records on computer from 1992, prior in books. Mail turnaround time 1 day. Public use terminal has civil records back to 1/1997. PAT results show name only. Lookup Supreme Court civil cases at http://iapps.courts.state.ny.us/webcivil/FCASMain
Criminal Records: Access: Mail, in person. Only the court performs in person searches; visitors may not. Search fee: $5.00 per name per 5 years. Required to search: name, years to search, DOB. Criminal records on computer to 1984, previous years in books. Mail turnaround time 2 days.
General Information: No sealed, expunged, adoption, sex offense, juvenile or mental health records released. Court makes copy: $1.00 per page. Certification fee: Minimum $5.00; $1.00 per page if over 4 pages. Payee: County Clerk. Personal checks

accepted; credit cards are not. Mail requests: SASE required.

Supreme & County Court PO Box 545, Wampsville, NY 13163; 315-366-2267; fax: 315-366-2539; 9AM-5PM. ***Felony, Civil.***
www.nycourts.gov/courts/6jd/madison/index.shtml
Direct countywide search requests to County Clerk, see separate listing.

Oneida City Court 109 N Main St, Oneida, NY 13421; 315-363-1310; criminal fax: 315-363-3230; civil fax: same; 8:30AM-4:30PM. ***Misdemeanor, Civil Actions under $15,000, Eviction, Small Claims.***
Civil Records: Access: Mail, in person. Only the court performs in person searches; visitors may not. Search fee: $5.00 per name per 2 years searched. Required to search: name, years to search. Civil cases indexed by plaintiff. Civil records on computer from 1990, prior in books back to 1950s. Mail turnaround time 1-2 days.
Criminal Records: Access: Mail, in person. Only the court performs in person searches; visitors may not. Search fee: $55.00 statewide search fee. Criminal records computerized from 1989; prior in books back to 1950s. All criminal record search requests made to the Court Clerk are forwarded to the OCA for processing (see Introduction). Mail turnaround time 1-2 days.
General Information: No sealed, expunged, sex offense, mental health or youthful offender records released. Will fax documents to local or toll free line. Court makes copy: $.65 per page. Certification fee: $6.00 per document; Exemplification fee $15.00. Payee: City Court. Personal checks accepted. Visa/MC accepted. Mail requests: SASE required.

Surrogate's Court PO Box 607, 138 N Court St, Wampsville, NY 13163; 315-366-2392; fax: 315-366-2539; 9AM-5PM. ***Probate.***
A county search of the probate court index by mail for 25-year search is $30.00 fee. A full county probate search of all years is $90.00.

Madison Town/Village Courts- Brookfield Town Court- 315-899-5856; Canastota Village Court- 315-697-9410; Cazenovia Town Court- 315-655-5631; Cazenovia Village Court- 315-655-4011; Chittenango Village Court- 315-687-3937; De Ruyter Town Court- 315-852-9650; Eaton Town Court- 315-684-9111; Fenner Town Court- 315-655-2705; Georgetown Town Court- 315-837-4795; Hamilton Town Court- 315-824-3508; Hamilton Village Court- 315-824-3508; Lebanon Town Court- 315-837-4844; Lenox Town Court- 315-697-9410; Lincoln Town Court- 315-363-6518; Madison Town Court- 315-893-7544; Morrisville Town Court- 315)-684-3154; Morrisville Village Court- 3150-684-3214; Nelson Town Court- 315-655-8582; Stockbridge Town Court- 315-495-6660; Sullivan Town Court- 315-687-3347; Wampsville Village Court- 315-363-5810.

Monroe County

County Clerk County Office Bldg, County Clerk Office, 39 W Main St #101, Rochester, NY 14614; 585-428-5151; fax: 585-428-4698; 9AM-5PM. ***Felony, Civil.***
www.monroecounty.gov/clerk-records.php
Countywide search requests made to the County Clerk are processed in the manner described below.
Civil Records: Access: Fax, mail, online, in person. Both court and visitors may perform in person searches. Search fee: $5.00 per name per 2 years. Required to search: name, years to search. Civil cases indexed by defendant only prior to 1993. Civil records on computer since 6/93, prior in books. Search judgments and other docs back to 6/9/1993 free w/ registration at www.monroe.ny.us.landata.com/. Mail turnaround time 2 weeks. Civil PAT goes back to 1993. PAT civil results show middle initial. Online access to felony, civil, and divorce records free online at www.clerk.co.monroe.ny.us. Records go back to 6/1993, and earlier film images are being added. Call 585-428-5151 for username, password, or more information. Also, access to WebCivil Supreme Court civil cases is at http://iapps.courts.state.ny.us/webcivil/FCASMain
Criminal Records: Access: Fax, mail, online, in person. Both court and visitors may perform in person searches. Search fee: $5.00 per name; fee is per 2 years searched. A $5.00 blanket index search is also available. Required to search: name, years to search, DOB. Criminal records on computer since 6/93, prior in books. Mail turnaround time 2 weeks. Criminal PAT goes back to same as civil. PAT criminal results show middle initial. Online access to criminal records is the same as civil. Online results show middle initial.
General Information: Online identifiers in results same as on public terminal. No sealed, divorce records, confidential files released. Will not fax documents. Court makes copy: $.65 per page, $1.30 minimum. Certification fee: $5.00 up to 4 pages, $1.25 each add'l page; includes copy fee. Payee: County Clerk. Personal checks accepted. Visa/MC accepted. Mail requests: SASE required.

Supreme & County Court 545 Hall of Justice, 99 Exchange Blvd, Rochester, NY 14614; 585-428-5001; fax: 585-428-2190; 9AM-5PM. ***Felony, Civil.***
www.monroecounty.gov/clerk-index.php
Direct countywide search requests to the County Clerk, see separate listing. With registration, access judgments, liens and other court docs online back to 1993 at www.monroe.ny.us.landata.com/.

Rochester City Court - Civil 99 Exchange Blvd, Rm 6, Hall of Justice, Rochester, NY 14614; 585-428-2444; fax: 585-428-2588; 9AM-5PM. ***Civil Actions under $15,000, Eviction, Small Claims.***
www.courts.state.ny.us/courts/7jd/rochester/index.shtml
Civil Records: Access: In person. Both court and visitors may perform in person searches. No search fee. Required to search: name, years to search. Civil cases indexed by defendant, plaintiff; index on computer from 1983, prior in books from 1973. Public use terminal has civil records back to 1983. PAT results show name, DOB.
General Information: Will not fax documents. Court makes copy: No copy fee but civil court has a $2.00 per case file retrieval fee. Self serve: same. Certification fee: $6.00 per document. Payee: Rochester City Court. Cashiers checks and money orders accepted. Visa/MC accepted.

Rochester City Court - Criminal 150 S Plymouth, Rm 123, Public Safety Bldg, Rochester, NY 14614; 585-428-2447; fax: 585-428-2732; 9AM-5PM. ***Misdemeanor.***
Criminal Records: Access: In person. Search fee: $5.00 per name for Certificate of Disposition. Required to search: Name, years to search, date, any exact details (for Certificate of Disposition). Criminal records on computer since 1986, prior on books from 1980. In person searches limited to pending and current cases on the public access terminal. The court directs name searches to the OCA for $55.00 statewide search, unless specific docket number given. Public use terminal has crim records back to 1986.PAT results show name, DOB.
General Information: No sealed, expunged, probation reports, adoption, sex offense, juvenile or mental health records released. Will fax back to attorneys only. Court makes copy: none for Certificate of Disposition. No certification fee. Payee: Rochester City Court. Only certified checks and money orders accepted. No credit cards accepted.

Surrogate's Court Hall of Justice, Rm 541, 99 Exchange Blvd, Rochester, NY 14614; 585-428-5200; fax: 585-428-2650; 9AM-5PM. ***Probate.***
A county search of the probate court index by mail for 25-year search is $30.00 fee. A full county probate search of all years is $90.00.

Monroe Town/Village Courts- Brighton Town Ct- 585-784-5152; Chili Town Court- 585-889-1999; Clarkson Town Court- 585-637-1134; East Rochester Town Court- 585-385-2576; Fairport Village Court- 585-223-0316; Gates Town Court- 585-247-6106; Greece Town Court- 585-227-3110; Hamlin Town Court- 585-964-8641; Henrietta Town Court- 585-359-2640; Honeoye Falls Village Court- 585-624-1711; Irondequoit Town Court- 585-336-6040; Mendon Town Court- 585-624-6064; Ogden Town Court- 585-352-2115; Parma Town Court- 585-392-9470; Penfield Town Court- 585-377-8623; Perinton Town Court- 585-223-0770; Pittsford Town Court- 585-248-6238; Riga Town Court- 585-293-3884; Rush Town Court- 585-533-1130; Sweden Town Court- 585-637-1070; Webster Town Ct- 585-872-7020/7022; Wheatland Town Ct- 585-889-3074.

Montgomery County

County Clerk PO Box 1500, 64 Broadway, County Office Bldg, Fonda, NY 12068; 518-853-8113; 8:30AM-4PM; summer- 9AM-5PM. ***Felony, Misdemeanor, Civil.***
Countywide civil search requests made to the County Clerk are processed in the manner described below.
Civil Records: Access: Mail, in person, online. Both court and visitors may perform in person searches. Search fee: $5.00 per name per 2 years. Required to search: name, years to search, address. Civil cases indexed by defendant, plaintiff. Civil records in books and on index cards back to 1965; on computer back to 1992. Mail turnaround time 3 days Public use terminal has civil records back to 1992. PAT results show name only. Lookup current or pending Supreme Court civil cases at http://iapps.courts.state.ny.us/webcivil/FCASMain
Criminal Records: Access: In person only. Visitors must perform in person searches themselves. Required to search: name, years to search, DOB. Criminal records computerized from 1992; file index back to 1965. County clerk directs criminal searches to OCA for $55.00 statewide search. See the County Clerk for an in person criminal search, call 518-853-4516.
General Information: No sealed or youthful offender records released. Will not fax documents. Court makes copy: $1.00 per page. Self serve: $.25 per page. Certification fee: $4.00 per doc. Payee: County Clerk. Personal checks accepted; credit cards are not. Mail requests: SASE required for civil.

Supreme & County Court PO Box 1500, 58 Broadway - County Courthouse, Fonda, NY 12068; 518-853-4516; fax: 518-853-3596; 9AM-5PM; 8AM-4PM May-Oct 5. ***Felony, Misdemeanor (limited), Civil.***
See County Clerk for civil search. See state OCA for $55.00 felony search. Court keeps its own Misdemeanor cases only, usually only drug cases; also search city, town, village courts for add'l misdemeanors.

Amsterdam City Court Public Safety Bldg, Rm 208, One Guy Park Ave Ext, Amsterdam, NY 12010; 518-842-9510; criminal fax: 518-843-8474; civil fax: same; 8AM-4PM. ***Misdemeanor, Civil Actions under $15,000, Eviction, Small Claims.***
Civil Records: Access: Mail, in person. Only the court performs in person searches; visitors may not. Search fee: $16.00 per name. Required to search: name, years to search. Civil cases indexed by defendant. Civil records on computer since 1995, prior on index cards. Mail turnaround time 1 week.
Criminal Records: Access: Mail, in person. Only the court performs in person searches; visitors may not. Search fee: A Certificate of Disposition from this court is $6.00. Required to search: name, DOB, years to search. Criminal records computerized from 11/93, prior on index cards. All criminal record name search requests are directed to the OCA for statewide record search, $55.00 search fee. This court does not have access to county records. Mail turnaround time 1 week.
General Information: No sealed, expunged, adoption, sex offense, juvenile or mental health records released. Will fax documents to local or toll free line. Court makes copy: $.65 per page. Certification fee: $10.00 per document. Payee: City Court. Cashiers checks and money orders accepted. Major credit cards accepted. Mail requests: SASE required.

Surrogate's Court New Court House, 58 Broadway, Rm 50, PO Box 1500, Fonda, NY 12068; 518-853-8108; fax: 518-853-8230; 9AM-5PM; 8AM-4PM summer hours. ***Probate.***
A county search of the probate court index by mail for 25-year search is $30.00 fee. A full county probate search of all years is $90.00.

Montgomery Town/Village Cts- Amsterdam Town Court- 518-842-7411; Canajoharie Town Court- 518-673-3013; Canajoharie Village Court- 518-673-5116; Charleston Town Court- 518-922-6279; Florida Town Court- 518-843-6468; Fultonville Village Court- 518-

853-3166; Glen Town Court- 518-853-4825; Minden Town Court- 518-568-2728 or 518-993-5180; Mohawk Town Court- 518-853-3031; Palatine Town Court- 518-673-1003; Root Town Court- 518-673-3549; St Johnsville Justice Ct- 518-568-2662; St Johnsville Village Ct- 518-568-5298.

Nassau County

County Clerk 240 Old Country Rd, Mineola, NY 11501; 516-571-2272; fax: 516-742-4099; 9AM-4:30PM. ***Felony, Civil Actions over $15,000.*** www.nassaucountyny.gov/

Holds records for Supreme Court and County Court. As a rule, this office directs felony record search requests to the OCA for the $55.00 statewide search, however, the records department can perform in person felony searches as described below.

Civil Records: Access: Mail, in person, online. Both court and visitors may perform in person searches. Search fee: $25.00 for judgment search. Required to search: name, years to search. Civil cases indexed by defendant, plaintiff; index on computer from 1992, prior in books. For answers to record search questions call Bob Grabel at County Clerk's office Rm 106 at 516-571-1448. Mail turnaround time 1-2 weeks. Public use terminal has civil records back to 1992. PAT results show name only. Search supreme court decisions for free from web page.

Criminal Records: Access: In person, online. Only the court performs in person searches; visitors may not. Required to search: name, DOB. The county clerk has felony case "minutes" from the County Court, but "minutes" data is only accessible by attorney's with a written letter of request. For full records, contact the County Court.

General Information: No sealed, expunged, adoption, sex offense, juvenile or mental health records released. Will not fax documents. Court makes copy: $.65 per page; $1.30 minimum. Self serve: $.25 per page. Certification fee: $5.00 per doc includes 4 copy pgs; $1.25 each add'l page. Includes copy fee. Payee: Nassau County Clerk's Office. Personal checks accepted; credit cards are not. Mail requests: SASE required for civil.

Supreme Court Supreme Court Bldg, 100 Supreme Court Dr, Mineola, NY 11501; civil phone: 516-571-2904; fax: 516-571-1575; 9AM-5PM. ***Civil Actions over $15,000.*** www.nassaucountyny.gov/

All physical records are maintained at the County Clerk's Office (see entry for County Clerk) 240 Old Country Rd, Mineola, 516-571-2272.

County Court 262 Old Country Rd, Mineola, NY 11501; 516-571-2800; fax: 516-571-2802; 9AM-4:40PM. ***Felony.*** www.nassaucountyny.gov/

The County Court clerk directs felony search requests to the OCA for a statewide record search. However, the court will search pre-1982 records (provide arrest date), which are on books only.

Criminal Records: Access: In person only. Only the court performs in person searches; visitors may not. Search fee: A Certifiacte of Disposition may be available from the court. Required to search: name, years to search, DOB. Criminal records computerized from 1982, prior in archives or on microfilm. Also, for "minutes," you may contact records section of the County Clerk office at 240 Old Country Rd, Mineola, NY, 11501, 516-571-2272. Minutes records are restricted to attorneys only. Public use terminal has crim records. Only registered attorneys may use public access terminal. Search future court appearances at http://iapps.courts.state.ny.us/webcrim_attorney/Login. Some records up to 1984 can be count on the state system as http://courts.state.ny.us.

General Information: No sealed, expunged, sex offense, juvenile, or mental health records released. Will not fax documents. Court makes copy: $.65 per page, $1.30 minimum. Cert fee: $5.20 per cert. Payee: Clerk of Court. No personal checks accepted. Major credit cards accepted but not over phone.

District Court - 1st, 2nd, 4th District 99 Main St, Hempstead, NY 11550; 516-572-2355; criminal phone: 516-572-2293; civil phone: 516-572-2266; fax: 516-572-2291; 9AM-5PM, transactions until 4:30PM. ***Civil Actions under $15,000, Eviction, Small Claims, Ordinance.***

Records for 2nd District are separate prior to 1980. 1st District handles misdemeanor cases. Sm Claims phone- 516-572-2261.

Civil Records: Access: Mail, fax, in person. Only the court performs in person searches; visitors may not. Search fee: $52.00 per name; Nassau County only, does not include Great Neck. Required to search: name, years to search. Civil cases indexed by defendant, plaintiff; index on computer back to 1990; prior in books. Mail turnaround time 1 week.

Criminal Records: Access: In person, online. Only the court performs in person searches; visitors may not. Search fee: $55.00 per name, statewide search. Required to search: name, DOB; also helpful: address. Criminal records computerized from 1980, prior on books back to 1960. Only minor misdemeanors found here. As a rule, the court directs requests to OCA for $55.00 statewide search. Online access is via the state OCA statewide system.

General Information: Will fax back documents if prepaid. Court makes copy: $1.30 each page; $.65 per page after first 2. Self serve: $.25 per page. Certification fee: $6.00; exemplification- $15.00. Payee: Clerk of District Court. No personal or business checks accepted. No credit cards accepted in person only. Mail requests: SASE required for civil.

District Court - 3rd District 435 Middle Neck Rd, Great Neck, NY 11023; 516-571-8400/8401; fax: 516-571-8403; 9AM-5PM; no transactions after 4:30PM. ***Civil Actions up to $15,000, Small Claims, Eviction, Ordinance.***

Court has records only for its district. Records include Town of North Hempstead ordinance violations. May take up to 3 days when specific case files are ordered.

Civil Records: Access: In person only. Only the court performs in person searches; visitors may not. No search fee. Required to search: name, years to search. Civil cases indexed by defendant, plaintiff; index on computer from 1989, prior in books.

Criminal Records: Access: Mail, in person (at county clerk). Only the court performs in person searches; visitors may not. Search fee: Only County Clerk will perform a Certificate of Disposition search for $6.00 per name. Required to search: name, years to search, DOB. Criminal records computerized from 1989, prior in books. Only minor misdemeanors found here. For a full criminal search, the court suggest the OCA for $55.00 statewide search.

General Information: No sealed, expunged, adoption, sex offense, juvenile or mental health records released. Will not fax documents. Court makes copy: $.65 per page, $1.30 minimum. Self serve: $.25 per page. Certification fee: $6.00 per doc. Payee: Clerk of Court. Only cashiers checks and money orders accepted. Visa/MC accepted. Mail requests: SASE required for mail return of any copies.

Glen Cove City Court 13 Glen St, Glen Cove, NY 11542; 516-676-0109; fax: 516-676-1570; 9AM-5PM. ***Misdemeanor, Civil Actions under $15,000, Eviction, Small Claims, Traffic.***

Civil Records: Access: Mail, fax, in person. Only the court performs in person searches; visitors may not. Search fee: $16.00 per name. Required to search: name, years to search. Civil records go back to 1970; on computer back to 1996.

Criminal Records: Access: None. Only the court performs in person searches; visitors may not. Required to search: DOB, years to search. Criminal records go back to 1966; on computer back to 1996. The court refuses to permit access to court records unless specific case file given. It is suggested to send requests to OCA for $55.00 statewide search.

General Information: No sealed, expunged, adoption, sex offense, juvenile or mental health records released. Will not fax documents. Court makes copy: $.65 per page; minimum $1.30. Certification fee: $6.00. Payee: Glen Cove City Court. No personal checks accepted. Visa/MC accepted. Mail requests: SASE required for civil.

Long Beach City Court 1 W Chester St, Long Beach, NY 11561; 516-431-1000; criminal phone: x261; civil phone: x261; fax: 516-889-3511; 9AM-5PM. ***Misdemeanor, Civil Actions under $15,000, Eviction, Small Claims, Traffic.***

Civil Records: Access: In person. Only the court performs in person searches; visitors may not. Search fee: Best to get Certificate of Disposition for $6.00, then get case numbers to make in person request. Required to search: name, years to search. Civil records are indexed by Plaintiff, Defendant. Civil records go back 25 years. Court recommends the $55.00 statewide search at the OCA.

Criminal Records: Access: In person. Search fee: $6.00 for Certificate of Disposition. Criminal records computerized from 1997. The court will not permit access to court records unless specific case file given. First, get Cert. of Disposition. Court suggests requests go to OCA for $55.00 search.

General Information: No sealed, expunged, adoption, sex offense, juvenile or mental health records released. Will not fax documents. Court makes copy: $.65 per page, $1.30 minimum. Self serve: $.65 per page. Certification fee: $5.00 per doc plus copy fee if criminal; $6.00 if civil. Payee: City Court of Long Beach. Only cashiers checks and money orders accepted. Visa/MC accepted.

Surrogate's Court 262 Old Country Rd, Mineola, NY 11501; 516-571-2082; fax: 516-571-3864; 9AM-4:45PM. ***Probate.***

Public access terminal available - index goes way back. A county search of the probate court index by mail for 25-year search is $30.00 fee.

Nassau Town/Village Courts- Atlantic Beach Village Court- 516-371-4552; Brookville Village Court-516-922-8191; Cove Neck Village Court- 516-624-7715x1; East Hills Village Court- 516-621-6117; East Rockaway Village Court- 516-887-6312; East Williston Village Court- 516-922-9154; Farmingdale Village Court- 516-293-2292; Flower Hill Village Court-516-627-8877; Garden City Village Court- 516-742-9886; Hempstead Village Court- 516-489-3400; Kings Point Village Court- 516-482-7872; Lake Success Village Court- 516-482-7430; Lattingtown Village Court- 516-681-9271; Lawrence Village Court-516-239-9166; Malverne Village Court- 516-599-1200; Manorhaven Village Court- 516- 883-7000; Massapequa Park Village Court- 516- 798-0244; Munsey Park Village Court- 516-365-7790; Muttontown Village Court- 516-364-2240; Old Brookville Village Court- 516-681-9271; Oyster Bay Cove Village Court- 516-681-9271; Plandome Heights Village Court- 516-627-1748; Plandome Manor Village Court- 516-627-3701; Plandome Village Court- 516-627-1748; Rockville Centre Village Court- 516-678-9233; Sea Cliff Village Court- 516-671-0328; South Floral Park Village Court- 516-353-8047; Stewart Manor Village Court- 516-354-1800; Upper Brookville Village Court- 516-624-7715; Valley Stream Village Court- 516- 825-4200; Westbury Village Court-516-334-1700 x116;

New York - Manhattan

Supreme Court - Civil Division County Clerk, 60 Centre St, Rm 103, New York City, NY 10007; 646-386-5955 x8; civil phone: 646-386-5942 records; 386-5940 (docket Section); 9AM-3PM county clerk; 9AM-5PM Supreme Ct Office. ***Civil Actions over $25,000.*** www.nycourts.gov/supctmanh

Record search requests are managed by the COUNTY CLERK office; information here is for that County Clerk office. The Supreme Ct clerk office phone is 636-386-3160 but they will refer you to the County Clerk Office.

Civil Records: Access: Mail, In person, online. Both court and visitors may perform in person searches. Search fee: $5.00 per 2 years per name. Also, in Rm 109B Docket Sect.: Statement of Satisfaction of Judgment- no fee. Certificate of Disposition- $8.00. Required to search: name, years to search. Civil cases indexed by defendant, plaintiff; index on computer from 1993, prior in books; records go back to 1971. Direct mail requests to the Mail Clerk, Rm 141B, certification phone 646-386-5935/or/5936 (Law & Equity) Mail Turnaround time 7-10 days Public use terminal has civil records back to 1993. PAT results show name only. Public terminal located in Rm 103B. Search the Sup. Ct Online records CCIS (back to 1986) or CCOP (back to 1972) free at http://iapps.courts.state.ny.us/iscroll/index.jsp. Click Advanced Search. $39.90 monthly sub; $19.95 base rate to purchase case file copy. Also, access to Supreme Court civil cases is at http://iapps.courts.state.ny.us/webcivil/FCASMain Opinions/decisions free at www.nycourts.gov/sup

ctmanh/Decisions_Online.htm. Online results show name only.
General Information: Will not fax documents. Court makes copy: $.25 per page. Self serve: $.25 per page. Certification fee: $8.00 per doc. Payee: County Clerk. Cashiers checks, attorney checks and money orders accepted; no personal checks. No credit cards accepted, except Visa/MC in person only.

Supreme Court - Criminal Division 100 Centre St, Rm 1000, New York, NY 10013; 646-386-4000; criminal phone: 646-386-3860 correspondence sec.; fax: 212-374-3177; 9AM-5PM. ***Felony, Misdemeanor.***
Court will only process mail or in person requests for specific documents or papers related to felony cases.
Criminal Records: Access: Mail, fax, in person, online. Visitors must perform in person searches themselves. Search fee: No search fee if in person. A Certificate of Disposition is $10.00. Required to search: name, years to search, DOB. Case number or other case identifiers are required for Certificate of Disposition; get case number from OCA or online search. Physical records back to 1999. Criminal records computerized from 1980s (less complete the further back), prior records archived. Written requests for name searches should be directed to OCA for $55.00 statewide search. With case number, the correspondence section will accept requests for specific document via fax, mail or phone. Mail turnaround time is 1 day; older records from archives- 1 week. Public use terminal has crim records back to 1980s. Docket or case number required for a terminal search; no name searching. Subscribe or login as guest to search eCourts WebCrims future appearances system at http://iapps.courts.state.ny.us/webcrim_attorney/Login.
General Information: No sealed, expunged, adoption, sex offense, juvenile or mental health records released. Will not fax documents. Self serve: $.15 per page. Certification fee: $8.00 per document; court must make cert copies; all court generated copies are certified. Payee: Office of Court Administration. No personal checks. No credit cards accepted. Mail requests: SASE requested.

Civil Court of the City of New York 111 Centre St, Rm 118, New York, NY 10013; 646-386-5600; 646-386-5700- info; 646-386-5730 Admin; fax: 212-374-8053; 9AM-5PM, open til 7PM TH. ***Civil Actions under $25,000, Eviction, Small Claims.***
www.courts.state.ny.us/courts/1jd/index.shtml
Fax number is for Admin ofc who distributes the faxes. Use 646-386-5500/5750 for landlord/tenant records. Small Claims- 646-386-5484/or/85. Archives phone- 646-386-5515. General NYC civil dial-up info line- 212-791-6000.
Civil Records: Access: Phone, in person, online. Visitors must perform in person searches themselves. No search fee. Required to search: name, years to search; also helpful: address. Civil cases indexed by plaintiff; computerized records since 1994. Pre-1998 records archived in Queens; 1998 to present in Brooklyn. Landlord/Tenant records on computer from 1984, civil from 1994, prior in books. Records are archived after 3 years. Clerk's office will do a name lookup to see if a case exists and its number. Public use terminal has civil records back to 1994. Results may include calendar number, partial address. Public terminal has Landlord/tenant, civil, small claims. Located on 1st Fl. Court decisions at http://decisions.courts.state.ny.us/search/query3.asp
General Information: no sealed records released. Will not fax documents. Court makes copy: $.65 per page. Self serve: $.25 per page. Certification fee: $6.00 per doc. Payee: Clerk of Civil Court. Only cashiers checks and money orders accepted. Attorney's checks accepted. No credit cards accepted. Mail requests: SASE required for civil.

Surrogate's Court 31 Chambers St, #402, New York City, NY 10007; 646-386-5000; 9AM-5PM. ***Probate*** www.courts.state.ny.us/courts/nyc/surrogates/index.shtml
Public terminal has index back to 1968. Mail search requests for past 25 years are $30.00; you may include your email address in your written request for fast reply. Make check to NY Surrogates Ct, but no personal checks accepted.

Niagara County

County Clerk 175 Hawley St, Lockport, NY 14094; 716-439-7030; civil phone: 716-439-7029; probate phone: 716-439-7135; criminal fax: 716-439-7066; civil fax: same; 9AM-5PM. ***Felony, Civil Actions over $25,000.*** www.niagaracounty.com
County Clerk maintains records for the Supreme Court (civil) and the County Court (felony).
Civil Records: Access: Mail, fax, in person, online. Both court and visitors may perform in person searches. Search fee: $5.00 per name per 2 years. Required to search: name, years to search. Civil cases indexed by defendant. Civil index in docket books from 1950, computerized since 1997. Will accept fax requests if payment arrangement is made in advance. Mail turnaround time 3-5 days. Civil PAT goes back to 1997. Lookup current or pending Supreme Court civil cases at http://iapps.courts.state.ny.us/webcivil/FCASMain
Criminal Records: Access: Mail, in person. Both court and visitors may perform in person searches. Search fee: $5.00 per name per 2 years. Required to search: name, years to search, DOB. Criminal records on computer since 1/97; prior records in books. The clerk now directs criminal search requests back to the court of jurisdiction, though the clerk here does not rule out searching here. Mail turnaround time 3-5 days. Criminal PAT goes back to 10/1997.
General Information: Online identifiers in results same as on public terminal. No sealed or youthful offender records released. Will fax documents for add'l $3.00 per name. Court makes copy: $1.00 per page. Certification fee: $5.00 minimum; up to 5 pages. Payee: County Clerk. Personal checks, money orders accepted. No credit cards accepted.

Supreme Court 775 3rd St, Niagara Falls, NY 14302; 716-278-1800; fax: 716-278-1809; 9AM-5PM; 8:30AM-4:30 Summer hours. ***Civil Actions over $25,000.*** All records are maintained at County Clerk office, 175 Hawley St, Lockport, NY 14094, 716-439-7030.
Civil Records: Access: In person, Online. Visitors must perform in person searches themselves. Civil cases indexed by defendant, plaintiff; index on computer since 1/96; prior records in books. Search civil in the County Clerk office. Public use terminal has civil records back to 1996. Current or pending only Supreme Court civil case look-up at http://iapps.courts.state.ny.us/webcivil/FCASMain

County Court Courthouse, 175 Hawley St, Lockport, NY 14094; 716-439-7022 (Cty Clerk); criminal phone: 716-439-7065; fax: 716-439-7066; 9AM-5PM. ***Felony, Civil Actions under $25,000.***
All records are maintained at County Clerk Office, 175 Hawley St, Lockport, NY 14094, 716-439-7030.
Criminal Records: Access: Mail, in person. Only the court performs in person searches; visitors may not. Search fee: Unless given very specific info such as case number, this court limits itself to issuing only Certificates of Disposition for $5.00. Required to search: Court will search if given a specific case file number or a complete name. Criminal records on computer since 1/96; prior records in books. Court suggests sending requests to OCA for $55.00 statewide search.
General Information: No sealed, youthful offender or sex abuse case records released. Will fax documents $3.00 per page. Court makes copy: $1.00 per page. Cert fee: $5.00 per cert. Payee: County Clerk. Business checks accepted. No credit cards accepted. Mail requests: SASE required for criminal.

Lockport City Court One Locks Plaza, Municipal Bldg, Lockport, NY 14094; criminal phone: 716-439-6671; civil phone: 716-439-6660; fax: 716-439-6684; 8AM-4:30PM. ***Misdemeanor, Civil Actions under $15,000, Eviction, Small Claims.***
Civil Records: Access: Phone, fax, mail, in person. Both court and visitors may perform in person searches. Search fee: $16.00 per name. Required to search: name, years to search. Civil cases indexed by defendant. Civil records on computer from 1988, prior in books from 1900s. Mail turnaround time 14 days.
Criminal Records: Access: None. Only the court performs in person searches; visitors may not. Criminal records in books from 1977 forward; computerized since 1988. The court is unable to search criminal records unless specific case file given. It is suggested to send requests to OCA for $55.00 statewide search.
General Information: No sealed, expunged, adoption, sex offense, juvenile or mental health records released. Will fax documents to local or toll free line. Court makes copy: $1.00 per page. Certification fee: $5.00. Payee: City Court of Lockport. Cashiers checks and money orders accepted. Major credit cards accepted. Mail requests: SASE required for civil.

Niagara Falls City Court 520 Hyde Park Blvd, Public Safety Bldg, Niagara Falls, NY 14301; 716-278-9800; criminal phone: 716-278-9800; civil phone: 716-278-9860; fax: 716-278-9809; 8:30AM-4:30PM. ***Misdemeanor, Civil Actions under $15,000, Eviction, Small Claims.***
Civil Records: Access: Mail, in person. Both court and visitors may perform in person searches. Search fee: $5.00 per name for 2 years; computer search is $16.00. Required to search: name, years to search. Civil cases indexed by defendant. Civil records on microfilm from 1985, in books since 1970. Mail turnaround time 7-10 working days.
Criminal Records: Access: Mail, in person. Only the court performs in person searches; visitors may not. Search fee: A certificate of Disposition is $5.00. Criminal records in books from 1970. The court refuses to permit access to criminal court records unless specific case file given. All criminal record name search requests are directed to the OCA for statewide record search. Mail turnaround time 7-10 working days.
General Information: No sealed, expunged, adoption, sex offense, juvenile or mental health records released. Will not fax documents. Court makes copy: $1.00 per page. Certification fee: $1.50 per page. Payee: City Court of Niagara Falls. No checks accepted. Visa/MC accepted.

North Tonawanda City Court 216 Payne Ave, City Hall, North Tonawanda, NY 14120; 716-693-1010; criminal phone: x504; civil phone: x501; fax: 716-743-1754; 8AM-4PM; 8AM-4PM Summer hrs. ***Misdemeanor, Civil Actions under $15,000, Eviction, Small Claims.***
Civil Records: Access: Mail, fax, in person. Only the court performs in person searches; visitors may not. Search fee: $6.00 for transcript. Required to search: name, years to search. Civil cases indexed by defendant. Civil records on computer from 1993, prior in books. Mail turnaround time 2-5 days.
Criminal Records: Access: Mail, fax, in person. Only the court performs in person searches; visitors may not. Search fee: $5.00 per name for Cert of Disposition only and date of arrest must be included. Required to search: Name, exact date of arrest, DOB. Criminal records computerized from 1986, prior in books back to late 1970s. No name searches here, instead the court suggests to send requests to OCA for $55.00 statewide search. Mail turnaround time 2-5 days.
General Information: No sealed, expunged, adoption, sex offense, juvenile or mental health records released. Will fax documents $5.00 fee. Court makes copy: $1.00 per page. Certification fee: $5.00 per document. Payee: City Court. Only cashiers checks and money orders accepted. Visa/MC accepted in person only or for traffic in person, fax, or mail only. Mail requests: SASE requested.

Surrogate's Court Niagara's County Courthouse, 175 Hawley St, Lockport, NY 14094; 716-439-7130/7131; fax: 716-439-7319; 9AM-5PM; 8:30AM-4:30 June 27-Sept 5. ***Probate.***
A county search of the probate court index by mail for 25-year search is $30.00 fee. A full county probate search of all years is $90.00.

Niagara Town/Village Courts- Cambria Town Court- 716-433-2468; Hartland Town Court- 716-735-7239; Lewiston Town Court- 716-754-8213; Lockport Town Court- 716-439-9528; Newfane Town Court- 716-778-9292; Niagara Town Court- 716-215-1480; Pendleton Town Court- 716-625-8833; Porter

Town Court- 716-745-7036 x6; Royalton Town Court- 716-772-2588; Somerset Town Court- 716-795-9193; Wheatfield Town Court- 716-694-6793; Wilson Town Court- 716-751-0549.

Oneida County

County Clerk 800 Park Ave, Utica, NY 13501; criminal phone: 315-798-5797; civil phone: 315-798-5797; fax: 315-798-6440; 8:30AM-5PM:8:30AM-4:30PM Summer hours. ***Felony, Civil.***
Countywide search requests made to the County Clerk are processed in the manner described below.
Civil Records: Access: Mail, fax, in person, online. Both court and visitors may perform in person searches. Search fee: $5.00 per name. Fee is for 2 year search. Required to search: name, years to search. Civil cases indexed by defendant, plaintiff; index on computer from 1992, prior in books by plaintiff only. Mail turnaround time 1 week. Civil PAT goes back to 1992. PAT civil results show middle initial. Lookup current or pending Supreme Court civil cases at http://iapps.courts.state.ny.us/webcivil/FCASMain.
Criminal Records: Access: Mail, fax, in person. Both court and visitors may perform in person searches. Search fee: $5.00 per name. Fee is for 2 years searched. Required to search: name, years to search, DOB, signed release. Criminal records computerized from 1992, prior in books by defendant only. Mail turnaround time 1 week. Criminal PAT goes back to 1992; results show middle initial.
General Information: Online identifiers in results same as on public terminal. No sealed, expunged, adoption, sex offense, juvenile or mental health records released. Will fax documents $1.00 per page. Court makes copy: $.65 per page, $5.00 minimum. Self serve: $.65 per page, $5.20 minimum. Certification fee: $5.00 includes copy fee. Payee: County Clerk. Personal checks accepted; credit cards are not. Mail requests: SASE required.

Supreme & County Court 200 Elizabeth St, Utica, NY 13501; 315-798-5890; fax: 315-798-6436; 8:30AM-4:30PM; 8:30AM-4PM Summer hours. ***Felony, Civil.***
Direct record search requests to the County Clerk, see separate listing. Access to current/pending Supreme Court civil cases is at https://iapps.courts.state.ny.us/caseTrac/jsp/ecourt.htm

Rome City Court 100 W Court St, Rome, NY 13440; 315-337-6440; fax: 315-338-0343; 8:30AM-4:30PM; 8:30AM-4PM Summer Hours. ***Misdemeanor, Civil Actions under $15,000, Eviction, Small Claims, Traffic.***
Civil Records: Access: In person only. Only the court performs in person searches; visitors may not. No search fee. Required to search: name, years to search. Civil cases indexed by defendant, plaintiff. Civil records in books and some on computer.
Criminal Records: Access: In person only. Only the court performs in person searches; visitors may not. Search fee: A Certificate of Disposition is $6.00. Required to search: name, years to search, (case number, arrest date for Cert. of Disposition). As a rule, this court does not permit access to court records unless specific case file given. It is suggested to send requests to OCA for $55.00 statewide search. Be aware that the state system does not include certain "violation" records, this court does allow an in person hand search.
General Information: No sealed or youthful offender records released. Will fax documents to local or toll free line. Court makes copy: $.65 per page, $1.30 minimum. Certification fee: $6.00 per doc. Exemplification fee $1.00. Payee: Rome City Court. Only cashiers checks and money orders accepted. Visa/MC accepted.

Sherrill City Court 373 Sherrill Rd, Sherrill, NY 13461; 315-363-0996; fax: 315-363-1176; 8:30AM-4:30PM. ***Misdemeanor, Civil Actions under $15,000, Eviction, Small Claims.***
Civil Records: Access: Mail, in person. Only the court performs in person searches; visitors may not. Search fee: $5.00 per name per 2 year period. Required to search: name, years to search. Civil cases indexed by defendant only. Civil records in books since 1988, rest archived. Mail turnaround 1-2 days.
Criminal Records: Access: Mail, in person. Only the court performs in person searches; visitors may not. Search fee: $5.00 per name per 2 year period. Also, a Certificate of Disposition is $6.00. Required to search: name, DOB, years to search. Criminal records in books since 1800s. Though the court will do a name search of their records, they suggest to send requests to OCA for $55.00 statewide search. Mail turnaround time 1-2 days.
General Information: No sealed, expunged, adoption, sex offense, juvenile or mental health records released. Will not fax documents. Court makes copy: $.65 per page. Certification fee: $6.00 per document. Payee: Sherrill City Court. Personal checks accepted; credit cards are not. Mail requests: SASE required.

Utica City Court 411 Oriskany St W, Utica, NY 13502; criminal phone: 315-724-8227 x2; civil phone: 315-724-8157; crim fax: 315-724-0762; civil fax: 315-792-8038; 8:30-4:30PM. ***Misdemeanor, Civil Actions under $15,000, Eviction, Small Claims.***
Civil Records: Access: In person only. Both court and visitors may perform in person searches. No search fee. Required to search: name, years to search, address. Civil cases indexed by defendant. Civil records in books from 1900s, computerized records back to 1980's. Civil PAT goes back to 1998.
Criminal Records: Access: In person. Both court and visitors may perform in person searches. Search fee: $6.00 for certificate of disposition. Required to search: name, years to search, address. Criminal records in books from 1900s, computerized records back to 1980's. The court refuses to permit access to court records unless specific case file given. It is suggested to send requests to OCA for statewide search. Criminal PAT goes back to 1998.
General Information: No sealed, expunged, adoption, sex offense, juvenile or mental health records released. Will not fax documents. Court makes copy: $.65 per page. $1.30 minimum. Certification fee: $5.00 per cert. Payee: City Court of Utica. Only cashiers checks and money orders accepted. Visa/MC accepted.

Surrogate's Court Oneida County Office Bldg 8th Fl, 800 Park Ave, Utica, NY 13501; 315-797-9230; fax: 315-797-9237; 8:30AM-4:30PM Sept-May; 8:30AM-4PM June-Aug. ***Probate, Adoption.***
Access to some, not all 5th District Surrogate's records is free after registration at http://surrogate5th.courts.state.ny.us/Public/Login.aspx. A county search of the probate court index by mail for 25-year search is $30.00 fee; all years $90.00.

Oneida Town/Village Courts- Annsville Town Court- 315-336-1295; Augusta Town Court- 315-821-3814; Ava Town Court- 315-942-5669; Boonville Town Court- 315-943-2071; Boonville Village Court- 315-943-2070; Bridgewater Town Court- 315-822-5909; Camden Town Court- 315-245-0817; Deerfield Town Court- 315-724-0413; Florence Town Court- no phone; Floyd Town Court- 315-865-4256; Forestport Town Court- 315-392-2801; Kirkland Town Court- 315-853-4538; Lee Town Court- 315-336-1585; Marcy Town Court- 315-768-1308; Marshall Town Court- 315-841-8525; New Hartford Town Court- 315-732-5924; New Hartford Village Court- 315-732-5924; New York Mills Village Court- 315-736-7811; Oriskany Village Court- 315-736-6349; Paris Town Court- 315-839-6208; Remsen Town Court- 315-831-8710; Sangerfield Town Court- 315-841-4108; Steuben Town Court- 315-865-5508; Sylvan Beach Village Court- 315-762-4246; Trenton Town Court- 315-896-4510; Vernon Town Court- 315-829-4481; Verona Town Court- 315-363-4394; Vienna Town Court- 315-245-2191; Waterville Village Court- 315-841-8007; Western Town Court- 315-827-4928; Westmoreland Town Court- 315-853-4333; Whitesboro Village Court- 315-736-4353; Whitestown Town Court- 315-736-1251

Onondaga County

County Clerk 401 Montgomery St, Rm 200, Syracuse, NY 13202; 315-435-2229; criminal phone: 315-435-2236; civil phone: 315-435-2234; fax: 315-435-3455; 8AM-4:30PM. ***Felony, Civil.***
Countywide search requests made to the County Clerk are processed in the manner described below. All requests must be in writing.
Civil Records: Access: Mail, in person, online. Both court and visitors may perform in person searches. Search fee: $2.50 per name per year. Required to search: name, years to search. Civil cases indexed by defendant, plaintiff; index on computer from 1989, prior in books but can only search by plaintiff name. Mail turnaround time 2-3 days. Civil PAT goes back to 1989. PAT results show name only. Lookup Supreme Court civil cases at http://iapps.courts.state.ny.us/webcivil/FCASMain Online results show name only.
Criminal Records: Access: Mail, in person. Both court and visitors may perform in person searches. Search fee: $2.50 per name per year. Required to search: name, years to search; also helpful: DOB. Criminal records computerized from 1990, prior in books. Mail turnaround time 2-3 days. Criminal PAT goes back to 1990; results show name only.
General Information: No sealed, divorce, judgment or sexual abuse records released. Will not fax documents. Court makes copy: $.65 per page, $1.30 minimum. Certification fee: $5.00 minimum; $1.25 per page over 4. Payee: County Clerk. Personal checks accepted; $60.00 limit. No credit cards accepted. Mail requests: SASE required.

Supreme Court 401 Montgomery St, 3rd Fl, Syracuse, NY 13202; 315-671-1030; fax: 315-671-1176; 8:30AM-4:30PM. ***Civil.***
Search requests to Supreme Court forwarded to the OCA for processing. Countywide only searches can be performed at the County Clerk, see separate listing. Access current/pending Supreme Court cases at http://iapps.courts.state.ny.us/webcivil/FCASMain.

County Court 505 S State St, Syracuse, NY 13202; 315-671-1020; fax: 315-671-1191; 8:30AM-4:30PM. ***Felony.***
Search requests made to County-Court are forwarded to the OCA for processing of $55.00 statewide record search. Countywide only searches can be performed at the County Clerk office, see separate listing.

Syracuse City Court 505 S State St, Rm 130, Syracuse, NY 13202-2104; 315-671-2742; criminal phone: 315-671-2760; civil phone: 315-671-2782; criminal fax: 315-671-2743; civil fax: 315-671-2741; 8:30AM-4:30PM; closes to public- 3:30PM. ***Misdemeanor, Civil Actions under $15,000, Eviction, Small Claims.***
www.nycourts.gov/courts/5jd/onondaga/syracuse/
Small claims phone is 315-671-3982; civil fax is 315-671-2741. Traffic phone- 315-671-2770.
Civil Records: Access: Mail, in person. Only the court performs in person searches; visitors may not. Search fee: $16.00 per name. Required to search: name, years to search; also helpful: address. Civil cases indexed by defendant, plaintiff or index number. Civil records on computer from 1993, from 1980-2000 on fiche or microfilm. Mail turnaround 1-2 wks.
Criminal Records: Access: Phone, fax, mail, in person. Only the court performs in person searches; visitors may not. Search fee: $5.00 for each 2 years searched. Required to search: name, years to search, DOB; also helpful: offense. Criminal records from 1960 to present are on either computer, dockets or manual books. If the case file is in electronic format, the court will direct searchers to the OCA statewide record search. Mail turnaround 1-2 wks.
General Information: No sealed, expunged, adoption, sex offense, juvenile or mental health records released. Will not fax documents. Court makes copy: $.65 per page. $1.30 minimum. Certification fee: $6.00 Civil cert fee; criminal records searched manually are certified as part of search fee. Payee: Syracuse City Court. Only cashiers checks, money orders and attorney checks accepted. Visa/MC accepted. Mail requests: SASE required.

Surrogate's Court Onondaga Courthouse, Rm 209, 401 Montgomery St, Syracuse, NY 13202; 315-671-2100; fax: 315-671-1162; 8:30AM-4:30PM. ***Probate.*** http://surrogate5th.courts.state.ny.us/public/
Access to some, not all 5th District Surrogate's records is free after registration at http://surrogate5th.courts.state.ny.us/Public/Login.aspx. A county search of the probate court index by mail for 25-year search- $30.00 fee; all years is $90.00.

Onondaga Town/Village Courts- Baldwinsville Village Court- 315-635-6355; Camillus Town Court- 315-487-7066; Cicero Town Court- 315-699-8478; Clay Town Court- 315-652-3800; De Witt Town Court- 315-446-9180; East Syracuse Village Court- 315-437-3541; Elbridge Town Court- 315-689-7380; Fabius Town Court- 315-683-9847 Com. Ctr; Fayetteville Village Court- 315-637-8070; Geddes Town Court- 315-468-3613; Jordan Village Court- 315-689-3483; La Fayette Town Court- 315-677-9350; Liverpool Village Court- 315-457-5379 x3; Lysander Town Court- 315-638-1308; Manlius Town Court- 315-637-3251; Manlius Village Court- 315-682-7245; Marcellus Town Court- 315-673-3269 x3; Minoa Village Court- 315-656-2203; North Syracuse Justice Court- 315-458-4695; Onondaga Town Court- 315-469-1674; Otisco Town Court- 315-696-6771; Pompey Town Court- 315-682-9877; Salina Town Court- 315-457 4252; Skaneateles Town Court- 315-685-5880; Solvay Village Court- 315-468-1608; Spafford Town Court- 315-673-0710; Tully Town Court- 315-696-5884; Van Buren Town Court- 315-635-3523;

Ontario County

County Clerk 20 Ontario St, Municipal Bldg, Canandaigua, NY 14424; 585-396-4251; criminal phone: 585-393-2953; civil phone: 585-396-4205; fax: 585-393-2951; 8:30AM-5PM. ***Felony, Civil.***
Felony search requests made to the County Court Clerk are processed by the County Clerk's office.
Civil Records: Access: Fax, mail, in person. Both court and visitors may perform in person searches. No search fee. Required to search: name, years to search. Civil cases indexed by defendant, plaintiff; index on computer from 1992, records go back to 1887. Mail turnaround time 1 week. Civil PAT goes back to 1992; civil results show middle initial.
Criminal Records: Access: Fax, mail, in person. Both court and visitors may perform in person searches. Search fee: $5.00 per name. Required to search: name, years to search; also helpful-DOB. Criminal records computerized from 1990, records go back to 1919. Mail turnaround time 1 week. Criminal PAT goes back to 1990. PAT results show middle initial, DOB.
General Information: No sealed, youthful offender, sex abuse, sex crime, divorce or sealed records released. Will fax civil search results for $1.50 1st page; $1.00 per add'l page. There is no fax fee to fax criminal search documents. Court makes copy: $.65 per page. $1.30 minimum. Self serve: same. Certification fee: $.65 per page with a $5.20 minimum if you prepare; $1.25 per page with $5.00 minimum if they prepare. Payee: County Clerk. Personal checks accepted; credit cards are not. Mail requests: SASE required.

Supreme & County Court 27 N Main St, Rm 130, Canandaigua, NY 14424-1447; 585-396-4239; criminal phone: 585-396-4025; fax: 585-396-4576; 9AM-5PM. ***Felony, Civil.***
www.nycourts.gov/courts/7jd/
Direct search requests to the County Clerk, see separate listing. Access to current/pending Supreme Court civil cases is at https://iapps.courts.state.ny.us/caseTrac/jsp/ecourt.htm

Canandaigua City Court 2 N Main St, City Hall, Canandaigua, NY 14424-1448; 585-396-5011; criminal fax: 585-396-5012; civil fax: same; 8AM-4PM. ***Misdemeanor, Civil Actions under $15,000, Eviction, Small Claims.***
www.canandaiguanewyork.gov/index.asp
Civil Records: Access: Mail, in person. Only the court performs in person searches; visitors may not. No search fee. Required to search: name, years to search. Civil cases indexed by defendant, plaintiff; index on computer from 1986, prior in books from 1960. Books are not kept on-site; as fee may apply to retrieve records from them.
Criminal Records: Access: In person. Only the court performs in person searches; visitors may not. Required to search: name, arrest/and/or conviction dates. Criminal records computerized from 1986, prior in books from 1960. Books not kept on-site. The court refuses to permit access to court records unless specific case file given. Without a case number, send requests to OCA for $55.00 statewide search.
General Information: No sealed, expunged, adoption, sex offense, juvenile or mental health records released. Will fax back documents. Court makes copy: $.65 per page; minimum $1.30. Certification fee: $5.00 per document includes copy fee. Payee: Canandaigua City Court. Only cashiers checks and money orders accepted. Visa/MC accepted. Mail requests: SASE required.

Geneva City Court 255 Exchange St, Public Safety Bldg, Geneva, NY 14456; 315-789-6560; fax: 315-781-2802; 8AM-4PM. ***Misdemeanor, Civil Actions under $15,000, Eviction, Small Claims.***
www.co.ontario.ny.us/index.html
Civil Records: Access: Mail, in person. Only the court performs in person searches; visitors may not. Search fee: $16.00 per name. Required to search: name, years to search. Civil cases indexed by plaintiff. Civil records on computer from 1992. Mail turnaround time 1 week.
Criminal Records: Access: None. Both court and visitors may perform in person searches. Criminal records computerized from 1992. The court refuses to permit access to court records unless specific case file given. Send requests to OCA for $55.00 statewide search.
General Information: No youthful offender records released. Will fax documents to local or toll free line. Court makes copy: $1.00 per page. Certification fee: $5.00 per doc. Payee: City Court. Only cashiers checks and money orders accepted. Visa/MC accepted. Mail requests: SASE required.

Surrogate's Court 27 N Main St, Canandaigua, NY 14424-1447; 585-396-4055; fax: 585-396-4576; 9AM-5PM. ***Probate.***
A county search of the probate court index by mail for 25-year search is $30.00 fee. A full county probate search of all years is $90.00.

Ontario Town/Village Courts- Bristol Town Court- 585-229-4523; Canadice Town Court- 585-367-3590; Canandaigua Town Court- 585-394-9040; Clifton Springs Village Court- 315-462-3048; East Bloomfield Town Court- 585-657-7248; Farmington Town Court- 315-986-3113 or 8195; Geneva Town Court- 315-789-1100; Gorham Town Court- 585-526-6298; Hopewell Town Court- 585-394-1963 x6; Manchester Town Court- 585-289-3010 x103 & x111; Naples Town Court- 585-374-2111; Phelps Town Court- 315-548-2090; Richmond Town Court- no phone; Seneca Town Court- 585-526-4780; South Bristol Town Court- 585-374-6355; Victor Town Court- 585-924-5775; West Bloomfield Town Court- 585-624-9860.

Orange County

County Clerk 255 Main St, Goshen, NY 10924; 845-291-3080; fax: 845-291-2691; 9AM-5PM. ***Felony, Civil.***
Search requests made to the County Clerk are processed in the manner described below.
Civil Records: Access: Mail, in person. Both court and visitors may perform in person searches. Search fee: $2.50 per name; $5.00 per 2 years. Required to search: name, years to search. Civil cases indexed by defendant, plaintiff; index on computer from 1993; prior indexed only by plaintiff. Mail turnaround time 2 weeks. Civil PAT goes back to 8/1993. PAT civil results show middle initial.
Criminal Records: Access: Mail, in person, online. Both court and visitors may perform in person searches. Search fee: $2.50 per name per year. Required to search: name, years to search, DOB. Criminal records on computer since 1993; prior on index Rolodex cards. Mail turnaround time 2 weeks. Criminal PAT goes back to same as civil. PAT results show middle initial, DOB. Also, subscribe or login as guest to search eCourts WebCrims future appearances system at http://iapps.courts.state.ny.us/webcrim_attorney/Login.
General Information: No sealed records released. Will not fax documents. Court makes copy: $.65 per page. Self serve: $.25 per page. Certification fee: $5.00 plus $1.25 per page after 1st 8 pgs. Payee: Orange County Clerk. Business checks accepted. No credit cards accepted. Mail requests: SASE required.

Supreme & County Court 255-285 Main St, Goshen, NY 10924; criminal phone: 845-291-3100; civil phone: 845-291-3111; fax: 845-291-2525; 9AM-5PM. ***Felony, Civil.***
Civil fax- 845-291-2595. Direct search requests to County Clerk; see separate listing. The County-Court (criminal court) is at 285 Main St., but records at County Clerk office.

Middletown City Court 2 James St, Middletown, NY 10940; 845-346-4050; fax: 845-343-5737; 8:30AM-4PM. ***Misdemeanor, Civil Actions under $15,000, Eviction, Small Claims.***
Civil Records: Access: Mail, in person. Only the court performs in person searches; visitors may not. No search fee. Required to search: name, years to search. Civil cases indexed by defendant, plaintiff; index on computer from 1994, prior on cards. Mail turnaround time 1 week.
Criminal Records: Access: None. Only the court performs in person searches; visitors may not. Criminal records computerized from 1986, prior on cards. The court refuses to permit access to court records unless specific case file given. It is suggested to send requests to OCA for $55.00 statewide search.
General Information: No sealed or youthful offender records released. Will not fax documents. Court makes copy: $.65 per page, $1.30 minimum. Certification fee: $5.00 per doc. Payee: City Court of Middletown. Only cashiers checks and money orders accepted. Mail requests: SASE required.

Newburgh City Court 57 Broadway, Newburgh, NY 12550; 845-565-3208; criminal phone: 845-565-3208; civil phone: 845-565-3074; fax: 845-565-1244; 8AM-4PM. ***Misdemeanor, Civil Actions up to $15,000, Eviction, Small Claims.***
Civil Records: Access: In person only. Only the court performs in person searches; visitors may not. Required to search: name, years to search; also helpful- case caption. Civil cases indexed by defendant. Civil records on computer from 1997, prior in docket books or on index cards. The court does not permit access to court records unless specific case file given.
Criminal Records: Access: None. Only the court performs in person searches; visitors may not. Criminal records computerized from 1986. The court does not permit access to court records unless specific case file given. Send search request to OCA for $55.00 statewide search.
General Information: No sealed, youthful offender or sex abuse victim records released. Will fax documents to local or toll free line. Court makes copy: $.65 per page. Certification fee: $6.00 per doc includes copy fee. Payee: Newburgh City Court. Only cashiers checks and money orders accepted. Visa/MC for fees and fines only.

Port Jervis City Court 20 Hammond St, Port Jervis, NY 12771-2495; 845-858-4034; fax: 845-858-9883; 9AM-5PM. ***Misdemeanor, Civil Actions under $15,000, Eviction, Small Claims.***
Civil Records: Access: Mail, in person. Both court and visitors may perform in person searches. No search fee. Required to search: name, years to search. Civil cases indexed by defendant. Civil records on dockets from 1978, computerized since 1996. Mail turnaround time 3 weeks.
Criminal Records: Access: Mail, in person. Search fee: $5.00 per name per 2 years for "violations" only, no misdemeanors. Required to search: Name, years to search. Criminal docket index from 1978, computerized since 1996. The court refuses to permit access to misdemeanor records unless specific case file given. It is suggested to send requests to OCA for $55.00 statewide search. Mail turnaround time 3 weeks.
General Information: No sealed, expunged, adoption, sex offense, juvenile or mental health records released. Will not fax documents. Court makes copy: $.65 per page, $1.30 minimum. Cert fee: $6.00. Payee: City Court of Port Jervis. Only cashiers checks and money orders accepted. Visa/MC accepted. Mail requests: SASE required.

Surrogate's Court 30 Park Pl, Surrogate's Courthouse, Goshen, NY 10924; 845-291-2193; fax: 845-291-2196; 9AM-5PM; Vault closes at 4PM. ***Probate.*** A county search of the probate court index by mail for 25-year search is $30.00 fee. A full county probate search of all years is $90.00.

Orange Town/Village Courts- Blooming Grove Town Court- 845-496-7631; Chester Town Court- 845-469-9541; Chester Village Court- 845-469-8584; Cornwall Town Court- 845-534-8717; Crawford Town Court- 845-744-2435; Deerpark Town Court- 845-856-2928; Florida Village Court- 845-651-4940; Goshen Town Court- 845-294-6477; Goshen Village Court- 845-294-5826; Greenville Town Court- 845-856-0564; Greenwood Lake Village Court- 845-477-9218; Hamptonburgh Town Court- 845-427-2424 x3; Harriman Village Court- 845-782-6853; Highlands Town Court- 845-446-8666; Maybrook Village Court- 845-427-2224; Minisink Town Court- 845-726-3700; Monroe Town Court- 845-783-9733; Montgomery Town Court- 845-457-2620; Montgomery Village Court- 845-457-9037; Mount Hope Town Court- 845-386-5303; New Windsor Town Court- 845-563-4682/845-563-4684; Newburgh Town Court- 845-564-7161; Otisville Village Court- 845-386-1004; Tuxedo Park Village Court- 845-928-2311; Tuxedo Town Court- 845-351-5655; Walden Village Court- 845-778-1632; Wallkill Town Court- 845-692-7822; Warwick Town Court- 845-986-1128; Warwick Village Court- 845-986-7044; Washingtonville Village Court- 845-496-9797; Wawayanda Town Court- 845-355-5706; Woodbury Justice Court- 845-928-2311.

Orleans County

County Clerk Courthouse, Attn: County Clerk, 3 S Main, Albion, NY 14411-9998; 585-589-5334; fax: 585-589-0181; 9AM-5PM; July/Aug is 8:30AM-4PM). ***Civil.*** www.orleansny.com/
For felony records see the County-Court clerk at the Supreme and County Court in separate listing.
Civil Records: Access: Mail, in person, online. Both court and visitors may perform in person searches. Search fee: $5.00 per name. Fee is for 2 year search. Required to search: name, years to search. Civil cases indexed by defendant. Civil records in books to 1940s; on computer back to 1998. Mail turnaround time 1 week. Public use terminal has civil records back to 1998. PAT results show name only. Lookup Supreme Court civil cases at http://iapps.courts.state.ny.us/webcivil/FCASMain
General Information: No sealed or divorce records released. Will fax documents if all fees prepaid. Court makes copy: $1.00 per page. Self serve: same. Certification fee: $4.00 plus $1.00 per page after first 4. Payee: County Clerk. Personal checks accepted; credit cards are not. Mail requests: SASE required.

Supreme & County Court Courthouse, 1 S Main, #3, Albion, NY 14411-9998; 585-589-5458; fax: 585-589-0632; 9AM-5PM. ***Felony, Civil.***
The court directs felony search requests to the OCA for a $55.00 statewide record search. Access civil records through the County Clerk, see separate entry.

Surrogate's Court 1 S Main St, #3, Albion, NY 14411; 585-589-4457; fax: 585-589-0632; 9AM-5PM. ***Probate.*** A county search of the probate court index by mail for 25-year search is $30.00 fee. A full county probate search of all years is $90.00.

Orleans Town/Village Courts- Albion Town Court- 585-589-7048 x18; Barre Town Court- 585-589-5100; Carlton Town Court- 585-682-4517; Clarendon Justice Court- 585-638-6371 x5; Gaines Town Court- 585-589-4592; Kendall Town Court- 716-659-2341; Medina Village Court- 585-798-4875; Murray Town Court- 585-638-7048; Ridgeway Town Court- 585-798-3282; Shelby Town Court- 585-798-3120 x309; Yates Town Court- 585-765-9603.

Oswego County

County Clerk 46 E Bridge St, Oswego, NY 13126; 315-349-8616; fax: 315-349-8692; 9AM-5PM. ***Felony, Civil.***
www.oswegocounty.com/clerk.shtml Countywide search requests made to the County Court Clerk are processed in the manner described below.
Civil Records: Access: In person, online. Visitors must perform in person searches themselves. Required to search: name, years to search. Civil cases indexed by defendant, plaintiff; index on computer from 1/90, prior in books from 1896. Public use terminal has civil records back to 1990. PAT results show name only. Lookup current or pending Supreme Court civil cases at http://iapps.courts.state.ny.us/webcivil/FCASMain
Criminal Records: Access: Mail, in person. Only the court performs in person searches; visitors may not. Search fee: $5.00 per name for every 2 years searched. Required to search: name, years to search, DOB. Criminal records computerized from 1973; prior in docket books from 1939. Mail turnaround time 2-3 days.
General Information: Online identifiers in results same as on public terminal. No sealed, youthful offender or divorce records released. Will not fax documents. Court makes copy: $.65 per page, $1.30 minimum. Certification fee: $5.00 minimum, includes 4 pages copies; $1.25 per page after 4. Payee: County Clerk. Personal checks accepted up to $250.00. No credit cards accepted. Mail requests: SASE required.

Supreme & County Court 25 E Oneida St, Oswego, NY 13126; 315-349-3280; civil phone: 315-349-3277; fax: 315-349-8513; 8:30AM-4:30PM. ***Felony, Civil.***
Direct search requests to the County Clerk, see separate listing. Access to current/pending Supreme Court civil cases is at https://iapps.courts.state.ny.us/caseTrac/jsp/ecourt.htm

Fulton City Court 141 S 1st St, Fulton, NY 13069; 315-593-8400; 8:30AM-4:30PM; Summer 8:30AM-4PM. ***Misdemeanor, Civil Actions under $15,000, Eviction, Small Claims.***
Civil Records: Access: Mail, in person. Only the court performs in person searches; visitors may not. No search fee. Required to search: name, years to search. Civil cases indexed by defendant. Civil records on dockets from 1991; computerized records since 1998. Mail turnaround time 2 weeks or less.
Criminal Records: Access: None. Only the court performs in person searches; visitors may not. Search fee: $6.00 for 2 year search. Required to search: name, DOB, charge. Criminal records go back to 1918, computerized records since 1997, criminal records on dockets from 1987. The court refuses to permit access to court records unless specific charge is given. They suggest to send requests to OCA for $55.00 statewide search.
General Information: No sealed, expunged, adoption, sex offense, juvenile or mental health records released. Will fax documents to local or toll free line. Court makes copy: $.65 per page; $1.30 minimum. Certification fee: $6.00 per doc. Payee: Fulton City Court. Only cashiers checks and money orders accepted. Visa/MC accepted. Mail requests: SASE requested for civil.

Oswego City Court Conway Municipal Bldg, 20 W Oneida St, Oswego, NY 13126; 315-343-0415; fax: 315-343-0531; 8:30-4:30PM. ***Misdemeanor, Civil Actions under $15,000, Eviction, Small Claims.***
Civil Records: Access: Mail, in person. Only the court performs in person searches; visitors may not. No search fee. Required to search: name, years to search. Civil cases indexed by defendant. Civil records on computer from 1987, prior in books.
Criminal Records: Access: None. Criminal records computerized from 1987, prior in books. The court refuses to permit access to court records unless specific case file given. It is suggested to send requests to OCA for $55.00 statewide search.
General Information: No sealed or youthful offender records released. Will fax documents to local or toll-free number. Court makes copy: $.65 per page; $1.30 minimum. Certification fee: $6.00 plus $.65 per page after first. Payee: Oswego City Court. Only cashiers checks and money orders accepted. Visa/MC accepted. Mail requests: SASE required.

Surrogate's Court Courthouse, 25 E Oneida St, Oswego, NY 13126; 315-349-3295; fax: 315-349-8514; 8:30AM-4:30PM Sept-May; 8:30AM-4PM June-Aug. ***Probate.***
A county search of the probate court index by mail for 25-year search is $30.00 fee. A full county probate search of all years is $90.00.

Oswego Town/Village Courts- Albion Town Court- 315-298-6325; Amboy Town Court- 315-964-7799; Boylston Town Court- 315-387-2320; Constantia Town Court- 315-623-7713; Granby Town Court- 315-598-2958; Hannibal Town Court- 315-564-6037; Hastings Town Court- 315-676-4317; Mexico Town Court- 315-963-3785; Minetto Town Court- 315-343-2393; New Haven Town Court- 315-963-8886; Orwell Town Court- 315-298-3236; Oswego Town Court- 315-343-7249; Palermo Town Court- 315-593-2333; Parish Town Court- 315-625-4592; Pulaski Village Court- 315-298-7431; Redfield Town Court- 315-599-7125; Richland Town Court- 315-298-5174; Sandy Creek Town Court- 315-387-5456; Schroeppel Town Court- 315-695-6177; Scriba Town Court- 315-343-3250; Volney Town Court- 315-598-7082; West Monroe Town Court- 315-676-3522; Williamstown Town Court- 315-964-2279.

Otsego County

County Clerk 197 Main St, Public Office Bldg, Cooperstown, NY 13326; 607-547-4276; fax: 607-547-7544; 9AM-5PM; 9AM-4PM Summer hours. ***Felony, Civil.*** www.otsegocounty.com
Countywide search requests made to the county clerk are processed in the manner described below.
Civil Records: Access: Mail, in person, online. Both court and visitors may perform in person searches. Search fee: $5.00 per name. Required to search: name, years to search. Civil cases indexed by defendant. Civil records on computer back to 1997; prior in books. Mail turnaround time 1-2 days. Public use terminal has civil records back to 5/1/1997. Lookup Supreme Court civil cases at http://iapps.courts.state.ny.us/webcivil/FCASMain
Criminal Records: Access: Mail, in person. Both court and visitors may perform in person searches. Search fee: $5.00 per name. Required to search: name, years to search, address, DOB. Criminal records computerized from 1997; prior in books. Misdemeanor records are maintained by city, town and village courts. In person criminal record searches should be performed over at the Supreme and County Court office at the courthouse. Mail turnaround time 1-2 days.
General Information: No sealed, expunged, adoption, sex offense, juvenile or mental health records released. Will fax documents on criminal cases. Court makes copy: $1.00 per page. Cert fee: $4.00. Payee: County Clerk. Business checks accepted. Mail requests: SASE required.

Supreme & County Court PO Box 710, 193 Main St, Cooperstown, NY 13326; 607-547-4364; criminal phone: 607-547-4388; civil phone: 607-547-4364; probate phone: 607-547-4213; fax: 607-547-7567; 9AM-5PM; 8AM-4PM Summer hours. ***Felony, Civil.***
www.nycourts.gov/courts/6jd/otsego/index.shtml
Probate/Family Court (Family- 607-547-6412) at 197 Main St. Probate fax- 607-547-7566. Direct search requests to County Clerk office, see separate listing. Access current/pending Supreme Ct civil cases at http://iapps.courts.state.ny.us/webcivil/FCASMain.

Oneonta City Court 81 Main St, Oneonta, NY 13820; 607-432-4480; fax: 607-432-2328; 8AM-3:30PM. ***Misdemeanor, Civil Actions under $15,000, Eviction, Small Claims.***
Civil Records: Access: Mail, in person. Only the court performs in person searches; visitors may not. Search fee: $5.00 per name per 2 years. Required to search: name, years to search. Civil cases indexed by defendant. Civil records on computer from 1987, prior in books. Mail turnaround 1 week from receipt.
Criminal Records: Access: None. Only the court performs in person searches; visitors may not. Search fee: A Certificate of Disposition is available for $5.00. Required to search: Name, case number, signed release. A release form is available from the clerk. Date of Birth required for accurate search. Most records go back 6 years; DWI 10 years. Court performs Certificate of Disposition searches only. Court does not have access to county records. To name search, requesters must use the OCA statewide search.
General Information: No sealed or youthful offender records released. Will fax documents to local or toll-free number. Court makes copy: $.65 per page, $1.30 minimum. Cert fee: $5.00 per page. Payee: Oneonta City Court. Required payment in certified funds only. No personal checks accepted. Visa/MC accepted. Mail requests: SASE required for civil.

Surrogate's Court Surrogate's Office, 197 Main St, Cooperstown, NY 13326; 607-547-4338; fax: 607-547-7566; 9AM-N, 1-5PM, Reg Hrs, 8AM-4PM July -Aug. ***Probate.***
A county search of the probate court index by mail for 25-year search is $30.00 fee. A full county probate search of all years is $90.00.

Otsego Town/Village Courts- Burlington Town Court- 607-965-8649; Butternuts Town Court- 607-783-2758; Cherry Valley Town Court- 607-264-8324; Cooperstown Village Court- 607-547-9597; Decatur Town Court- 607-397-8298, 397-7365; Edmeston Town Court- 607-965-9823; Exeter Town Court- 315-858-3905; Hartwick Town Court- 607-293-8133; Laurens Town Court & Village Court- 607-433-1053; Maryland Town Court- 607-638-9495; Middlefield Town Court- 607-547-2126; Milford Town Court- 607-286-7773; Morris Town Court & Village Court- 607-263-2224; New Lisbon Town Court- 607-965-8627; Oneonta Town Court- 607-432-0124; Otego Town Court- 607-988-2698; Otsego Town Court- 607-547-5689; Pittsfield Town Court- 607-847-6524; Plainfield Town Court- 315-855-7873; Richfield Springs Village Court- 315-858-2048; Richfield Town Court- 315-858-2830; Springfield Town Court- 315-858-1508; Unadilla Town Court- 607-369-7458; Westford Town Court- not known; Worcester Town Court- 607-397-8476.

Putnam County

County Clerk 40 Gleneida Ave, County Clerk Office, Carmel, NY 10512; 845-225-3641 x306; fax: 845-228-0231; 9AM-5PM; 8AM-4PM Summer hours. ***Felony, Civil.***
www.putnamcountyny.com/countyclerk/
Countywide search requests made to County Court Clerk are processed in the manner described below.
Civil Records: Access: Mail, in person, online. Both court and visitors may perform in person searches. Search fee: $5.00 per name. Fee is per 2 years searched. Required to search: name, years to search. Civil cases indexed by defendant, plaintiff; index on computer from 4/93, prior in books. Mail turnaround time 2 days. Civil PAT goes back to 1983. PAT results show name only. Lookup current or pending Supreme Court civil cases at http://iapps.courts.state.ny.us/webcivil/FCASMain Access to the clerk's records index (but not images except judgments) is via subscription service at http://www2.landaccess.com/cgibin/homepage?County=8002. Pay per use ($5.00 to view doc) or $100 per month plan available.
Criminal Records: Access: Mail, in person, online. Both court and visitors may perform in person searches. Search fee: $5.00 per name per certificate of search. Required to search: name, years to search, DOB. Criminal records computerized since 1983. Mail turnaround time 2 days. Criminal PAT goes back to 1983. PAT results show name only. Access to the clerk's records index but not images is via subscription service at http://www2.landaccess.com/cgibin/homepage?County=8002. Pay per use ($5.00 to view doc) or $100 per month plan available. Also, subscribe or login as guest to search eCourts WebCrims future appearances system at http://iapps.courts.state.ny.us/webcrim_attorney/Login.
General Information: No sealed or youthful offender records released. Will fax documents $1.00 per page. Court makes copy: $1.00 per page. Self serve: $.25 per page. Certification fee: $4.00 per doc; Exemplification fee- $10.00. Payee: County Clerk. Personal checks accepted; credit cards are not. Mail requests: SASE required.

Supreme & County Court 20 County Center, Supreme and County Court, Carmel, NY 10512; 845-208-7800 x4; 9AM-5PM. ***Felony, Civil.***
For a county only record search see the county clerk; see separate listing.

Surrogate's Court Historic Courthouse, 44 Gleneida Ave, Carmel, NY 10512; 845-208-7860; fax: 845-228-5761; 9AM-5PM. ***Probate.***
A county search of the probate court index by mail for 25-year search is $30.00 fee. A full county probate search of all years is $90.00.

Putnam Town/Village Courts- Brewster Village Court- 845-279-4020; Carmel Town Court- 845-628-1500; Cold Spring Village Court- 845-265-9070; Kent Town Court- 845-225-1606; Patterson Town Court- 845-878-1080; Philipstown Town Court- 845-265-2951; Putnam Valley Town Court- 845-526-3050; Southeast Town Court- 845-279-8939.

Queens County

Supreme Court - Civil Division 88-11 Sutphin Blvd, #106, County Clerk Records Rm, Jamaica, NY 11435; 718-298-0601, 718-298-0615 Records Rm; civil phone: 718-298-1073 Supreme Ct Clerk; fax: 718-520-4731; 9AM-5PM, no cashier transactions after 4:45PM. ***Civil over $25,000.***
www.courts.state.ny.us/courts/11jd/index.shtml
Records managed by County Clerk Office. The information here is for the County Clerk Records Rm. To identify a record, first search at the Search Dept, 718-298-0609; with a case number, go to records room who will pull record for you to copy.
Civil Records: Access: Mail, in person, online. Both court and visitors may perform in person searches. Search fee: $10.00 per name. Fee is for first two years; add $5.00 per add'l 2 years. Required to search: name, years to search, address. Civil cases indexed by plaintiff. Civil records on computer from 1992, prior in books back through 1980s. The records dept in basement has records on computer, PAT, and microfiche. Mail turnaround time 1 week. Public use terminal has civil records back to 1992. PAT results show name only. Public terminal in Search Dept, Rm #106. Access to current/pending Supreme Court civil cases is at http://iapps.courts.state.ny.us/webcivil/FCASMain
General Information: No marriage or incompetence records released. Identification required to review confidential matrimonial case records. Will not fax documents. Court makes copy: $.15 per page, self-serve. $.25 per page is scanned. Certification fee: $8.00 per doc. Payee: County Clerk. Only cashiers checks and money orders accepted. No credit cards accepted. Mail requests: SASE required.

Supreme Court - Criminal Term 125-01 Queens Blvd, Kew Gardens, NY 11415; 718-298-1400 records; fax: 718-520-2494; 9:30AM-4:30PM operating; 9AM-5PM public. ***Felony, Misdemeanor.***
www.courts.state.ny.us/courts/11jd/index.shtml
For Cert of Disposition, contact Correspondence Section, phone- 718-298-1319. For general into, Fiscal section phone- 718-298-1234. Or, with indictment number or arrest info you may search at the Queens County Clerk office, 718-298-0601.
Criminal Records: Access: In person, online. Only the court performs in person searches; visitors may not. No search fee in person, but there is an add'l fee for special orders retrieved from the archives. Required to search: name, DOB, years to search. Records Rm records go back to 2002. All criminal record search requests made to the Supreme Court Clerk are forwarded to the OCA for processing and $55.00 search fee. At the Correspondence section you may make an in person written search request, or a $10.00 Cert of Disposition request. Public use terminal has crim records back to 1980, but you need to be an attorney. Public terminal located in Rm 17. Subscribe or login as guest to eCourts WebCrims future appearances system at http://iapps.courts.state.ny.us/webcrim_attorney/Login.
General Information: Will fax documents to local or toll-free number. Court makes copy: $.15 per page. Certification fee: $10.00 for 1st page, $1.00 each add'l. Certification also available through the County Clerk Office. Payee: County Clerk. Personal checks accepted; credit cards are not. Mail requests: SASE required for civil.

Supreme Court - Long Is. City 25-10 Court Sq, Long Island City, NY 11101; 718-298-1616; fax: 718-520-2539; 9AM-5PM. ***Civil over $25,000.***
Trials only here, civil records available at Queens County Clerk, or at Jamaica Supreme Court.

Civil Court of the City of New York - Queens Branch 89-17 Sutphin Blvd, Jamaica, NY 11435; 718-262-7100; civil phone: 718-262-7300; fax: 718-262-7107; 9AM-5PM; small claims & housing open later on TH. ***Civil Actions under $25,000, Small Claims.***
www.courts.state.ny.us/courts/11jd/index.shtml
General housing court and eviction info phone- 646-386-5750. General civil dial-up info - 212-791-6000.
Civil Records: Access: In person, online. Visitors must perform in person searches themselves. Required to search: name, years to search; also helpful- case number. Civil cases indexed by plaintiff. Civil records indexed on computer. computer files keep 20 years then archived. Pre-1998 records archived in Queens; 1998 to present in Brooklyn. No searching unless specific case number given. If the case file is archived, it will take 3 weeks to retrieve. Only 2006 and 2007 and current case at court; remainder in archives. Public use terminal has civil records back to 1997; no judgments on terminal. Public terminal includes housing and civil records only. Sum Claims on separate system in Rm #116, 9AM-4:30PM. Access civil records free at http://iapps.courts.state.ny.us/webcivil/ecourtsMain.
General Information: Will not fax documents. Court makes copy: Court gives you file to copy. Self serve: $.15 per page. Certification fee: $6.00 per doc. Payee: Clerk of Civil Court. Only cashiers checks and money orders accepted. No credit cards accepted.

Surrogate's Court 88-11 Sutphin Blvd, 7th Fl, Jamaica, NY 11435; 718-298-0500; 9AM-1PM, 2-4:30PM (til 4:10PM Fri). ***Probate.***
Public access terminal is available. Mail requests accepted, fee $30,00 for index search back 25 years.

Rensselaer County

County Clerk 105 3rd St, Troy, NY 12180; 518-270-4080; fax: 518-271-7998; 8:30AM-5PM. ***Felony, Civil.*** www.rensco.com
Countywide record search requests made to the county clerk are processed in the manner described below. Civil and criminal divisions are separate and managed by separate clerks.
Civil Records: Access: Mail, in person, online. Visitors must perform in person searches themselves. Search fee: $10.00 per name. Required to search: name, years to search. Civil cases indexed by plaintiff pre-1996; by defendant & plaintiff after 1996. Civil records on computer back to 1997; prior in books to 1930s. Mail turnaround 1 week. Lookup current or pending Supreme Court civil cases at http://iapps.courts.state.ny.us/webcivil/FCASMain
Criminal Records: Access: Mail, in person. Only the court performs in person searches; visitors may not. Search fee: $5.00 per name per 2 years. Required to search: name, years to search; also helpful- DOB. Criminal records computerized from 1986; prior in books to 1976. An email search account can be set-up with this office. Mail turnaround time 1 week.
General Information: No sealed, open/pending cases, youthful offender records released. Will fax documents. Court makes copy: $1.00 per page. Self serve: $.50 per page. Certification fee: $4.00 per cert. Payee: County Clerk. Personal checks accepted; credit cards are not. Mail requests: SASE required.

Supreme & County Court 80 2nd St, Troy, NY 12180; 518-285-5025; fax: 518-270-3714; 8:30AM-5PM. ***Felony, Civil.*** Direct all search requests to the County Clerk office, see separate listing, or use the $55.00 statewide OCA search.

Rensselaer City Court 505 Broadway, Rensselaer, NY 12144; 518-462-6751; fax: 518-462-3307; 8AM-3:30PM. ***Misdemeanor, Civil Actions under $15,000, Eviction, Small Claims, Traffic.***
Civil Records: Access: Mail, in person. Only the court performs in person searches; visitors may not. Search fee: $6.00 per name. Required to search: name, years to search. Civil cases indexed by defendant. Civil records back 20 years. Mail turnaround time 72 hours.
Criminal Records: Access: Mail, in person. Only the court performs in person searches; visitors may not. Search fee: $6.00 for a Certificate of Disposition

only. Required to search: name, years to search, DOB, signed release. Criminal records back 20 years. Court will only confirm convictions with Certificate of Disposition. All criminal record name search requests are directed to the OCA for statewide record search, $55.00 search fee. Mail turnaround time 72 hours.
General Information: No sealed, expunged, adoption, sex offense, juvenile or mental health records released. Will not fax documents. Court makes copy: $.50 per page. Certification fee: $6.00. Payee: Rensselaer City Court. No personal checks accepted. Major credit cards accepted.

Troy City Court 51 State St, 2nd Fl, Troy, NY 12180; 518-271-1602; fax: 518-274-2816; 8:30AM-4PM. ***Misdemeanor.***
Criminal Records: Access: In person only. Only the court performs in person searches; visitors may not. Search fee: $5.00 per docket for certificate of disposition. Required to search: name, approx or exact date of arrest, DOB, aliases, offense. Criminal records computerized from 1989, prior in books. Court will only confirm convictions. Name search requests are directed to the state OCA for a $55.00 statewide record check.
General Information: No sealed records released. Will fax documents. Court makes copy: copies not made in court office. Certification fee: $5.00 per doc. Exemplification fee $15.00. Payee: Troy City Court. No personal checks accepted; credit cards are.

Surrogate's Court County Courthouse, 80 2nd St, Troy, NY 12180; 518-285-6100; fax: 518-272-5452; 9AM-5PM. ***Probate.***
A county search of the probate court index by mail for 25-year search is $30.00 fee. A full county probate search of all years is $90.00.

Rensselaer Town/Village Courts- Berlin Town Ct- 518-658-2020; Brunswick Town Court- 518-279-3461; Castleton-on-Hudson Village Court- 518-732-2211; East Greenbush Town Court- 518-477-5412; Grafton Town Court- 518-279-4385; Hoosick Falls Village Court- 518-686-4399; Hoosick Town Court- 518-686-3335; Nassau Town Court- 518-766-2343 x102; Nassau Village Court- 518-766-3044; North Greenbush Town Court- 518-283-2789 x28 or x29; Petersburgh Town Court- 518-658-3777; Pittstown Town Court- 518-753-4222 x 302; Poestenkill Town Court- 518-283-5100; Sand Lake Town Court- 518-674-3033; Schaghticoke Town Ct- 518-753-6915 x6, x7; Schodack Town Ct- 518-477-9390; Stephentown Town Court- 518-733-5636.

Richmond County

Supreme Court - Civil Division 130 Stuyvesant Pl, c/o Richmond County Clerk, Staten Island, NY 10301; 718-390-5389 Court Desk; 9AM-4:30PM; records rm-9AM-4PM. ***Civil Actions over $25,000.***
Civil Records: Access: Phone, in person, online. Visitors must perform in person searches themselves. Search fee: $5.00 per name per 2 years. Required to search: name, years to search. Civil cases indexed by plaintiff. Civil records on computer back to 1993. Public use terminal has civil records back to 1993. PAT results show name only. Also, access to Supreme Court civil cases is at http://iapps.courts.state.ny.us/webcivil/FCASMain
General Information: No matrimonial records released. Will not fax documents. Court makes copy: $.25 per page. Self serve: $.25 per page. Certification fee: $8.00 per doc includes copy fee. Payee: Richmond County Clerk. Only attorney's checks and money orders accepted. No credit cards accepted.

Supreme Court - Criminal Division 18 Richmond Terrace, Rm 110, Staten Island, NY 10301; criminal phone: 718-390-5280; 9AM-5PM. ***Felony, Misdemeanor.***
www.nycourts.gov/courts/2jd/richmond.shtml
Court no longer does any name searches. Must request all criminal record name searches from the OCA for statewide record search, $55.00 search fee.
Criminal Records: Access: Mail, in person. Visitors must perform in person searches themselves. Search fee: $10.00 fee for Certificate of Disposition. Required to search: name, DOB, years to search. Criminal records computerized from 1975, prior archived back to 1960. Access is for Certificate of Disposition only; this office does not allow in person or mail access to case files without a specific case number. All criminal record name search requests directed to the OCA for statewide record search, $55.00 search fee. Subscribe or login as guest to search eCourts WebCrims future appearances system at http://iapps.courts.state.ny.us/webcrim_attorney/Login.
General Information: No sealed or youthful offender records released unless to subject. Will not fax documents. Court makes copy: $.65 per page. Certification fee: $10.00 per doc. Payee: County Clerk, Richmond County. Only cashiers checks and money orders accepted. No credit cards accepted. Mail requests: SASE required.

Civil Court of the City of New York - Richmond Branch 927 Castleton Ave, Staten Island, NY 10310; 718-390-5417; fax: 718-390-8108; 9AM-5PM. ***Civil Actions under $25,000, Eviction, Small Claims.***
www.courts.state.ny.us/courts/2jd/richmond.shtml
General civil dial-up info line- 212-791-6000. Sm claims- 718-390-5421; Housing/Landlord/Tenant- 718-390-5420.
Civil Records: Access: In person, online. Visitors must perform in person searches themselves. Required to search: name. Civil cases indexed by plaintiff. Civil records on computer since 1999; prior on books Pre-1998 records archived in Queens; 1998 to present in Brooklyn. Public use terminal has civil records back to 1999. Public terminal has Landlord/tenant, civil, and small claims. Access schedules also civil records and landlord tenant cases free at http://iapps.courts.state.ny.us/webcivil/ecourtsMain.
General Information: No sealed records released. Will not fax documents. Court makes copy: Court gives you file to copy. Self serve: $.15 per page. Certification fee: $6.00 per doc includes copies. Payee: Clerk Civil Court. Only cashiers checks and money orders accepted. No credit cards accepted.

Surrogate's Court 18 Richmond Terrace, Rm 201, Staten Island, NY 10301; 718-390-5400; fax: 718-390-8741; 9AM-5PM. ***Probate, Adoption.***
A county search of the probate court index by mail for 25-year search is $30.00 fee. A full county probate search of all years is $90.00.

Rockland County

County Clerk 1 S. Main, Ste.100, New City, NY 10956; 845-638-5070; criminal phone: 845-638-5094; civil phone: 845-638-5094; fax: 845-638-5647; 7AM-6PM ***Felony, Misdemeanor, Civil.***
www.rocklandcountyclerk.com
Countywide search requests made to the county clerk are processed here. Misdemeanor records maintained by city, town, village courts, but this clerk may have a misdemeanor record if your provide an index number.
Civil Records: Access: Mail, in person, online. Both court and visitors may perform in person searches. Search fee: $5.00 per each 2 years. Required to search: name, years to search. Civil indexed by defendant, plaintiff. Civil records on computer from 1982. Mail turnaround time approx. 10 days. Civil PAT goes back to 1982. PAT results show name only. Online access to county clerk index is free at www.rocklandcountyclerk.com/court_records.html . Online includes civil judgments, real estate records, tax warrants. Call 845-638-5221 for info. Also, access to current Supreme court cases is at https://iapps.courts.state.ny.us/caseTrac/jsp/ecourt.htm.
Criminal Records: Access: Mail, online, in person. Both court and visitors may perform in person searches. Search fee: $5.00 each 2 years. Required to search: name, years to search. Criminal records computerized from 1982. Mail turnaround time approx. 10 days. Criminal PAT goes back to same as civil. PAT results show name only. Online access to county clerk INDEX is free at www.rocklandcountyclerk.com/court_records.html . Index includes criminal records back to 1982. Free registration required. Also, subscribe or login as guest to search eCourts WebCrims system at http://iapps.courts.state.ny.us/webcrim_attorney/Login. Also, access calendar of current Supreme court cases at https://iapps.courts.state.ny.us/caseTrac/jsp/ecourt.htm. Online results show name only.
General Information: Online identifiers in results same as on public terminal. No detention records release. Will not fax documents. Court makes copy: $1.00 per page. Self serve: $.25 per page. Certification fee: $1.25 per page, $5.00 minimum; exemplification- $15.00. Payee: Rockland County Clerk. Personal checks accepted; credit cards are not. Mail requests: SASE required.

Supreme & County Court 1 S Main St, #200, New City, NY 10956; criminal phone: 845-638-5363; civil phone: 845-638-5393; 9AM-5PM. ***Felony, Civil.***
www.rocklandcountyclerk.com/court_records.html
Direct all search requests to the County Clerk office, see separate listing. County-Court is located in #400. Search Civil Court record index back to 1971 free at http://12.25.92.131/resolution/search_menu.asp.

Surrogate's Court 1 S Main St, #270, New City, NY 10956; 845-638-5330; fax: 845-638-5632; 9AM-5PM. ***Probate.***
A county search of the probate court index by mail for 25-year search is $30.00 fee. A full county probate search of all years is $90.00.

Rockland Town/Village Courts- Chestnut Ridge Village Court- 845-425-3108; Clarkstown Town Court- 845-639-5960; Grand View-on-Hudson Court- 845-358-5078; Haverstraw Town Court- 845-947-0020; Haverstraw Village Justice Court- 845-947-4063; Hillburn Village Court- 845-357-2036; Nyack Village Court- 845-358-4464; Orangetown Town Court- 845-359-5100; Piermont Village Court- 845-359-0345; Ramapo Town Court- 845-357-5100; Sloatsburg Village Court- 845-753-2727; South Nyack Village Court- 845-358-5078; Spring Valley Village Court- 845-573-5820; Stony Point Town Court- 845-786-2506; Suffern Village Court- 845-357-6424; Upper Nyack Village Court- 845-358-0202; Wesley Hills Justice Court- 845-354-0404; West Haverstraw Village Court- 845-947-1013.

Saratoga County

County Clerk 40 McMaster St, Ballston Spa, NY 12020; 518-885-2213 X4410; civil phone: x4410; fax: 518-884-4726; 8AM-5PM. ***Felony, Civil.***
This County Clerk does not have a separate index of felony records; in person searching only, or contact the state OCA.
Civil Records: Access: Mail, in person, online. Both court and visitors may perform in person searches. Search fee: $5.00 per name per 2 years. Required to search: name, years to search; also helpful: address. Civil cases indexed by defendant, plaintiff; index on computer from 3/88, prior in books. Mail turnaround time 3-4 days. Public use terminal has civil records back to 1987. PAT civil results show middle initial. Lookup Supreme Court civil cases at http://iapps.courts.state.ny.us/webcivil/FCASMain
Criminal Records: Access: In person only. Both court and visitors may perform in person searches. No search fee. Required to search: name, years to search, DOB; also helpful: address. Criminal records not computerized here, on books. The clerk's office has the records but they will not search them.
General Information: No youthful offender or divorce records released. Will fax back documents. Court makes copy: $1.25 per page. Self serve: $.50 per page. Certification fee: $5.00 per cert includes 4 copy pages; $1.25 each add'l page; max $40.00. Payee: County Clerk. Only in-state personal checks with name/address and phone accepted. No credit cards accepted. Mail requests: SASE required.

Supreme & County Court 30 McMaster St, Ballston Spa, NY 12020; 518-885-2224; civil phone: 518-885-2213; 9AM-5PM. ***Felony, Civil.***
See the separate County Clerk entry for Supreme court civil case records. Access to current/pending Supreme Court civil cases is available at http://iapps.courts.state.ny.us/webcivil/FCASMain.

Mechanicville City Court 36 N Main St, Mechanicville, NY 12118; 518-664-9876; criminal fax: 518-664-8606; civil fax: same; 8AM-4PM. ***Misdemeanor, Civil Actions under $15,000, Eviction, Small Claims.***

Civil Records: Access: In person only. Both court and visitors may perform in person searches. No search fee. Required to search: name, years to search. Civil cases indexed by defendant. Civil records on computer since 1/94; records go back to 1900.
Criminal Records: Access: None. Only the court performs in person searches; visitors may not. No search fee. Criminal records computerized from 9/93; records go back to 1900. The court refuses to permit access to court records unless specific case file given. Court directs searchers to OCA for $55.00 statewide search.
General Information: No sealed, expunged, adoption, sex offense, juvenile or mental health records released. Will fax documents to local or toll free line. Court makes copy: $.65 per page; $1.30 minimum. Certification fee: $6.00 per doc. Payee: City Court. No personal checks accepted. Visa/MC accepted.

Saratoga Springs City Court City Hall, 474 Broadway, Ste #3, Saratoga Springs, NY 12866; 518-581-1797; fax: 518-584-3097; 8AM-4PM; ofc-9AM-3:45PM. ***Misdemeanor, Civil Actions under $15,000, Eviction, Small Claims, Traffic.***
Civil Records: Access: Mail, in person. Only the court performs in person searches; visitors may not. No search fee. Required to search: name, years to search. Civil cases indexed by defendant. Civil records on computer back to 10/94; prior records on index cards. Make search requests in writing. Mail turnaround time 1 week
Criminal Records: Access: In person only. Only the court performs in person searches; visitors may not. Search fee: Certificate of Disposition is $5.00 per name. Required to search: Name, years to search. Criminal records computerized from 8/93. This court directs record requests to OCA for the $55.00 statewide search.
General Information: Sealed files not released. Will not fax documents. Court makes copy: $1.30 1st page; $.65 each add'l. Certification fee: $5.00. Payee: City Court. Only cashiers checks and money orders accepted. Credit cards not accepted via phone. Mail requests: SASE required for civil.

Surrogate's Court 30 McMaster St, Bldg 3, Ballston Spa, NY 12020; 518-884-4722; fax: 518-884-4774; 9AM-5PM. ***Probate.***
Public access terminal goes back to 1990 and older records being added. A county search of the probate court index by mail for 25-year search is $30.00 fee. A full county probate search of all years is $90.00.

Saratoga Town/Village Courts- Ballston Spa Village Court- 518-885-6393; Ballston Town Court- 518-885-8559; Charlton Town Court- 518-384-0152 x201; Clifton Park Town Court- 518-371-6668; Corinth Town Court- 518-654-6991; Day Town Court- 518-696-3789; Galway Town Court- 518-882-6070; Galway Village Court- 518-882-6070; Greenfield Town Court- 518-893-7432 x310; Hadley Town Court- 518-696-4379 x8; Halfmoon Town Court- 518-371-7410; Malta Town Court- 518-899-6121; Milton Town Court- 518-885-9267; Moreau Town Court- 518-793-3188; Northumberland Town Court- 518-745-0178; Providence Town Court- Saratoga Town Court- 518-695-6887 x15; Stillwater Town Court- 518-664-6946; Waterford Town Court- 518-237-6788; Wilton Town Court- 518-587-1980.

Schenectady County

County Clerk 620 State St, 3rd Fl, Attn: County Clerk, Schenectady, NY 12305; 518-388-4220; fax: 518-388-4224; 9AM-5PM; July-Aug-9AM-4PM; file papers 1/2 hour before close. ***Civil.***
http://schenectadycounty.com/FullStory.aspx?m=47&amid=2070
For felony records see the County-Court clerk at the Supreme and County Court in separate listing.
Civil Records: Access: Mail, in person, online. Both court and visitors may perform in person searches. Search fee: $5.00 per name per 2 years. They can verify a no record found via the phone. Required to search: name, years to search. Civil cases indexed by plaintiff. Civil records on computer from 1989, prior on index cards. In person access is only here at the County Clerk, not the Supreme Court Clerk. Mail turnaround time 4 days. Will expedite requests if requested. Public use terminal has civil records back to 1988. PAT results show name and may also include other personal identifiers, depending on what data is originally entered. Online access to current/pending Supreme Court civil cases is at http://iapps.courts.state.ny.us/webcivil/ecourtsMain.
General Information: No sealed, youthful offenders, infant compromise or divorce records released. May fax documents if all fees prepaid, or to a toll-free number but usually won't. Court makes copy: $1.00 per page off computer. Self serve: $.50 per page. Certification fee: $5.00 includes copy fee for 4 pages; add $1.00 per add'l page; exemplification- add $10.00. Payee: County Clerk. Personal checks accepted; credit cards are not. Mail requests: SASE required.

Supreme & County Court 612 State St, Schenectady, NY 12305; 518-285-8401; civil phone: x1; fax: 518-388-4520; 9AM-5PM; 8:30-4:30 PM Summer hours. ***Felony, Civil.***
Direct civil record requests to County Clerk, see separate listing. Access to current/pending Supreme Court civil cases is available at https://iapps.courts.state.ny.us/caseTrac/jsp/ecourt.htm
Civil Records: Access: Mail, in person. Only the court performs in person searches; visitors may not. Search fee: $5.00 per name per 2 years searched, if searched at County Clerk office. Required to search: name, years to search. Civil cases indexed by plaintiff. Civil records on computer from 1989, prior on index cards.
Criminal Records: Access: Mail, in person. Only the court performs in person searches; visitors may not. Search fee: $5.00 per name per 2 years searched. Required to search: name, years to search, DOB; include indictment number for Cert of Disposition. Criminal records computerized from 1989, prior in index books. The County-Court Clerk now refers criminal record search requests to the OCA for $55.00 statewide search. Court will do a Certificate of Disposition for $5.00. Mail turnaround time 4 days.
General Information: No sealed, youthful offenders, infant compromise or divorce records released. Notarized, signed release required to access sealed records. Court makes copy: $.50 per page criminal; civil $1.00 per page if on computer. Self serve: No self serve criminal copier; Civil self serve- $.25 each. Certification fee: $5.00 per doc. Payee: County Clerk. Personal checks accepted; credit cards are not. Mail requests: SASE required.

Schenectady City Court - Civil Jay St, City Hall, #215, Schenectady, NY 12305; 518-382-5077; fax: 518-382-5080; 8AM-4PM. ***Civil Actions under $15,000, Eviction, Small Claims.***
Civil Records: Access: Mail, in person. Only the court performs in person searches; visitors may not. Search fee: $16.00 per name. Required to search: name, years to search. Civil cases indexed by docket #. Civil records on computer from 1998, prior in books. Mail turnaround time 2 weeks.
General Information: No sealed or youthful offender records released. Will fax documents. Court makes copy: $.65 per page. Certification fee: $6.00. Payee: City Court. Only cashiers checks and money orders accepted. Visa/MC accepted. Mail requests: SASE required.

Schenectady City Court - Criminal 531 Liberty St, Schenectady, NY 12305; 518-382-5239; fax: 518-382-5241; 8AM-4PM. ***Misdemeanor.***
Criminal Records: Access: None. Only the court performs in person searches; visitors may not. Search fee: A certificate of Disposition is $6.00. Required to search: Name, DOB, case number. Criminal records computerized from 1995, prior in books. The court directs name searches to the OCA for $55.00 statewide search, unless specific docket number given.
General Information: No sealed or youthful offender records released. Will not fax documents. Court makes copy: $.65 per page. Certification fee: $6.00. Payee: City Court. Only cashiers checks and money orders accepted. Visa/MC accepted. Mail requests: SASE required.

Surrogate's Court 612 State St, Judicial Bldg, Schenectady, NY 12305; 518-285-8455; fax: 518-377-6378; 9AM-5PM. ***Probate.***
A county search of the probate court index by mail for 25-year search is $30.00 fee. A full county probate search of all years is $90.00.

Schenectady Town/Village Courts- Duanesburg Town Court- 518-895-8922; Glenville Town Court- 518-688-1200 x409; Niskayuna Town Court- 518-386-4560; Princetown Town Court- 518-357-4047; Rotterdam Town Court- 518-355-7911; Scotia Village Court- 518-374-2099.

Schoharie County

Supreme & County Court PO Box 549, 284 Main St, Attn: County Clerk, Schoharie, NY 12157; 518-295-8316 (County Clerk); 518-295-8342 (Supreme); criminal fax: 518-295-8338; civil fax: same; 8:30AM-5PM; 8:30AM-7:00PM W. ***Felony, Civil, Misdemeanor, Eviction, Small Claims.***
www.schohariecounty-ny.gov
Direct search requests to the County Clerk who processes requests in the manner described below.
Civil Records: Access: Fax, mail, in person, online. Both court and visitors may perform in person searches. Search fee: $5.00 per name. Required to search: name, years to search. Civil cases indexed by defendant, plaintiff; index on computer from 1994, prior in books. Mail turnaround time 24-48 hours. Civil PAT goes back to 1994. PAT civil results show middle initial. Current or pending only Supreme Court civil case look-up is at http://iapps.courts.state.ny.us/webcivil/FCASMain
Criminal Records: Access: Fax, mail, in person. Both court and visitors may perform in person searches. Search fee: $5.00 per name. Required to search: name, years to search, DOB or SSN. Criminal records in books back to 1930; on computer back to 2000. Mail turnaround time 24-48 hours. Criminal PAT goes back to 2000. PAT results show middle initial, DOB. Terminal results include SSN.
General Information: No sealed criminal or divorce records released. Fee to fax out file $1.00 per page, free if you provide toll-free number. Court makes copy: $.50 per page. Self serve: same. Certification fee: $4.00. Payee: County Clerk. Personal checks accepted. Mail requests: SASE required.

Surrogate's Court Courthouse, 290 Main St, PO Box 669, Schoharie, NY 12157; 518-295-8387; fax: 518-295-8451; 9AM-5PM. ***Probate.***
A county search of the probate court index by mail for 25-year search is $30.00 fee. A full county probate search of all years is $90.00.

Schoharie Town/Village Cts- Blenheim Town Court- 518-827-6115; Broome Town Court- 518-827-5074; Carlisle Town Court- 518-234-3486; Cobleskill Town Court and Village Court- 518-234-7886; Conesville Town Court- 607-588-7211; Esperance Town Court- 518-875-6109; Fulton Town Court- 518-827-6695 (judge residence and court phone); Gilboa Town Court- 607-588-7604; Jefferson Town Court- 607-652-2109; Middleburgh Town Court- 518-827-7433; Middleburgh Village Court- 518-827-5143; Richmondville Town Court- 518-294-8851; Schoharie Town Court and Village Court- 518-295-6575; Seward Town Court- 518-234-3144, 234-2292; Sharon Town Court- 518-284-3419; Summit Town Court- 518-287-1194; Wright Town Court- 518-872-1705.

Schuyler County

County Clerk Courthouse, 105 9th St, Unit 8, Watkins Glen, NY 14891; 607-535-8133; 9AM-5PM. ***Felony, Civil.***
Countywide search requests made to the county clerk are processed in the manner described below. Winter 2008- clerk office temporarily located at 2 Montour St at the Rural-Urban Center in Montour Falls. Renovation to be completed 2009.
Civil Records: Access: Mail, in person, online. Both court and visitors may perform in person searches. Search fee: $5.00 per name. Required to search: name, years to search. Civil cases indexed by defendant. Civil records are indexed in books; on computer back to 1987. Mail turnaround time 2-3 days. Lookup Supreme Court civil cases at http://iapps.courts.state.ny.us/webcivil/FCASMain

Criminal Records: Access: Mail, in person. Only the court performs in person searches; visitors may not. Search fee: $5.00 per name. Required to search: name, years to search, DOB. Criminal records are indexed in books; on computer back to 1987. Misdemeanors go back to 1971. Mail turnaround time 2-3 days.
General Information: No sealed or youthful offender records released. Will not fax out documents. Court makes copy: $.65 per page. Certification fee: $5.00 per doc. Cert fee is for 1st 4 pages, add'l pages are $1.25 each, copies included. Payee: County Clerk. Personal checks accepted; credit cards are not. Mail requests: SASE required.

Supreme & County Court Courthouse, 105 9th St, Unit 35, Watkins Glen, NY 14891; criminal phone: 607-535-7015; civil phone: 607-535-7760; fax: 607-535-4918; 9AM-5PM. ***Felony, Civil.***
Court-clerks direct record search requests to the OCA for a $55.00 statewide record check. For county only search requests (including free), see the County Clerk in separate listing.

Surrogate's Court County Courthouse, 105 9th St, Unit 35, Watkins Glen, NY 14891; 607-535-7144; fax: 607-535-4918; 9AM-5PM (8:30AM-4:30 PM in Summer). ***Probate.***
A county search of the probate court index by mail for 25-year search is $30.00 fee. A full county probate search of all years is $90.00.

Schuyler Town/Village Courts- Catharine Town Court- 607-594-2273; Cayuta Town Court- 607-594-2507; Dix Town Court- 607-535-5103; Hector Town Court- 607-546-5286; Montour Falls Village Court- 607-535-7362; Montour Town Court- 607-535-2467; Odessa Village Court- 607-594-2273; Reading Town Court- No phone; Tyrone Town Court- no phone; Watkins Glen Village Court- 607-535-9717.

Seneca County

County Clerk 1 DiPronio Dr, County Office Bldg, Attn: Seneca County Clerk, Waterloo, NY 13165-1396; 315-539-1771; fax: 315-539-3789; 8:30AM-5PM. ***Felony, Civil.***
Countywide search requests made to the county clerk are processed in the manner described below.
Civil Records: Access: Mail, in person, online. Both court and visitors may perform in person searches. Search fee: $10.00 per name. Required to search: name, years to search. Civil cases indexed by defendant. Civil records on computer since 3/1997; prior records in books. Mail turnaround time 1 week. Civil PAT goes back to 3/1997. PAT civil results show middle initial. Lookup current or pending Supreme Court civil cases at http://iapps.courts.state.ny.us/webcivil/FCASMain
Criminal Records: Access: Mail, in person. Both court and visitors may perform in person searches. Search fee: $10.00 per name. Required to search: name, years to search, signed release. Criminal records on computer since 3/1997; prior records in books. Mail turnaround time 1 week. Criminal PAT goes back to same as civil. PAT criminal results show middle initial.
General Information: No divorce records released. Will fax documents to local or toll free line. Court makes copy: $.65 per page. Self serve: $.40 per page. Certification fee: $5.00. Payee: Seneca County Clerk. Personal checks accepted; credit cards are not. Mail requests: SASE required.

Supreme & County Court 48 W Williams St, Courthouse, Waterloo, NY 13165; 315-539-7021; fax: 315-539-7929; 9AM-5PM. ***Felony, Civil.***
Direct all search requests to the County Clerk office, see separate listing. Access to current/pending Supreme Court civil cases is available at https://iapps.courts.state.ny.us/caseTrac/jsp/ecourt.htm

Surrogate's Court 48 W Williams St, Waterloo, NY 13165; 315-539-7531; fax: 315-539-3267; 9AM-5PM. ***Probate.*** A county search of the probate court index by mail for 25-year search is $30.00 fee. A full county probate search of all years is $90.00.

Seneca Town/Village Courts- Covert Town Court- 607-387-3790; Fayette Town Court- 315-585-6282; Junius Town Court- 315-539-4667; Lodi Town Court- 607-582-7730; Ovid Town Court- 607-869-9845; Romulus Town Court- 607-869-9650; Seneca Falls Town Court- 315-568-9234; Tyre Town Court- 315-568-1221, 568-9417; Varick Town Court- 315-585-6018; Waterloo Town Court- 315-539-3213; Waterloo Village Court- 315-539-2512.

St. Lawrence County

Supreme & County Court 48 Court St, Canton, NY 13617-1169; 315-379-2237 (County Clerk); 315-379-2219 (Court Clerk); probate phone: 315-379-2217; fax: 315-379-2302; 8:30AM-4:30PM (Thurs til 7PM). ***Felony, Civil.***
Direct all search requests to the County Clerk office; information given here is for that County Clerk office.
Civil Records: Access: Fax, mail, in person, online. Both court and visitors may perform in person searches. Search fee: $5.00 per name. Required to search: name, years to search. Civil cases indexed by defendant, plaintiff. Civil records go back to 1986; on computer since 1990, prior in books. Mail turnaround time 2-3 days. Civil PAT goes back to 1986. PAT results show name only. Historical records are not online, but access to current/pending Supreme Court civil cases is at http://iapps.courts.state.ny.us/webcivil/FCASMain
Criminal Records: Access: Fax, mail, in person. Both court and visitors may perform in person searches. Search fee: $5.00 per name. Required to search: name, years to search, DOB. Criminal records on computer since 1985, prior in books. Mail turnaround time 2-3 days. Criminal PAT goes back to 1985. PAT results show name only.
General Information: No sealed or divorce records released. Will fax documents $4.00 each; no fee to toll-free numbers. Court makes copy: $.65 per page. Self serve: $.50 per page. Certification fee: $5.00. Payee: County Clerk. Personal checks accepted; credit cards are not. Mail requests: SASE required.

Ogdensburg City Court 330 Ford St, Ogdensburg, NY 13669; 315-393-3941; fax: 315-393-6839; 8AM-4PM. ***Misdemeanor, Civil Actions under $15,000, Eviction, Small Claims.***
Civil Records: Access: Mail, in person. Only the court performs in person searches; visitors may not. No search fee. Required to search: name, years to search. Civil cases indexed by defendant. Civil records on computer since 1995; prior records in books. Mail turnaround time 1 week.
Criminal Records: Access: None. Only the court performs in person searches; visitors may not. Computerized records go back to 1992; archives back to 19th Century. Requesters must use the $55.00 OCA statewide search.
General Information: No youthful offender records released. Will not fax documents. Court makes copy: $.65 per page. Certification fee: $5.00. Payee: City Court. Business checks accepted. Visa/MC accepted. Mail requests: SASE required.

Surrogate's Court 48 Court St, Courthouse, Canton, NY 13617; 315-379-2217/9427; fax: 315-379-2372; 9AM-5PM Sept-June; 8AM-4PM July-Aug. ***Probate.*** A county search of the probate court index by mail for 25-year search is $30.00 fee. A full county probate search of all years is $90.00.

St. Lawrence Town/Village Courts- Brasher Town Court- 315-389-4223 x5; Canton Town Court- 315-379-9844; Canton Village Court- 315-379-9844; Clare Town Court- 315-386-3084; Clifton Town Court- 315-848-5522; Colton Town Court- 315-262-2380; De Peyster Town Court- 315-344-7259; DeKalb Town Court- 315-347-2119 -clerk; 347-2071 -court; Depeyster Town Court- 315-344-7259; Edwards Town Court- 315-562-8113; Fine Town Court- 315-848-3413; Fowler Town Court- 315-287-9996; Gouverneur Town Court- 315-287-4623; Hammond Town Court- 315-324-5321; Hopkinton Town Court- 315-328-4187; Lawrence Town Court- 315-389-4487; Lisbon Town Court- 315-393-0489; Louisville Town Court- 315-764-1424; Macomb Town Court- 315-578-2212; Madrid Town Court- 315-328-3399; Massena Town Court and Village Court- 315-769-5431; Morristown Town Court- 315-375-4148; Norfolk Town Court- 315-384-4721; Oswegatchie Town Court- 315-344-7284; Parishville Town Court- 315-268-1722; Piercefield Town Court- 518-359-7544; Pierrepont Town Court- 315-379-0415; Pitcairn Town Court- 315-543-2111; Potsdam Town Court- 315-265-4318; Potsdam Village Court- 315-265-5890; Rossie Town Court- 315-324-5166; Russell Town Court- 315-347-4824; Stockholm Justice Court- 315-389-5171; Waddington Town Court- 315-388-5629.

Steuben County

Supreme & County Court 3 E Pulteney Sq - County Clerk, Bath, NY 14810; 607-776-9631 x3205; fax: 607-664-2157; 8:30AM-5PM. ***Felony, Civil.***
Direct all search requests to the County Clerk office; information given here is for that County Clerk office. The fax number given above is for the fax upstairs.
Civil Records: Access: Fax, mail, in person, online. Both court and visitors may perform in person searches. Search fee: $10.00 per name. Required to search: name, years to search. Civil cases indexed by defendant. Civil records on computer from 1965, in book from 1931, prior archived. Visitors are not allowed to search divorce files themselves. Mail turnaround time 1 day. Public use terminal has civil records back to 1960. PAT results show middle initial, DOB. Current or pending only Supreme Court civil case look-up is at http://iapps.courts.state.ny.us/webcivil/FCASMain
Criminal Records: Access: Fax, mail, in person. Only the court performs in person searches; visitors may not. Search fee: $10.00 per name. Required to search: name, years to search, DOB, SSN. Criminal records computerized from 1984, in book from 1931, prior archived. Mail turnaround time 1 day. PAT results show middle initial, DOB.
General Information: No sealed, expunged, adoption, sex offense, juvenile or mental health records released. Will fax documents $3.00 each plus $1.00 per page. Court makes copy: $.65 per page. $1.30 minimum. Self serve: same. Certification fee: $5.00. Payee: Steuben County Clerk. Personal checks accepted; credit cards are not. Mail requests: SASE required.

Corning City Court 12 Civic Center Plaza, Corning, NY 14830-2884; 607-936-4111; fax: 607-936-0519; 8AM-4PM. ***Misdemeanor, Civil Actions under $15,000, Eviction, Small Claims.***
www.nycourts.gov/courts/7jd/corning/
Civil Records: Access: Mail, in person. Only the court performs in person searches; visitors may not. Search fee: Fees subject to change; call for details. Required to search: name, years to search. Civil cases indexed by defendant. Civil records on computer from 1986, prior in books. Request must be in writing.
Criminal Records: Access: none. Criminal records computerized from 1986, prior in books. The court refuses to permit access to court records unless specific case file given. Requesters are directed to OCA for $55.00 statewide search.
General Information: No sealed or youthful offender records released. Will fax documents to local or toll free line. Court makes copy: $.65 per page; $1.30 minimum. Certification fee: $5.00. Payee: Corning City Court. No personal checks accepted. Visa/MC accepted. Mail requests: SASE required for civil.

Hornell City Court PO Box 627 (82 Main St), Hornell, NY 14843-0627; 607-324-7531; fax: 607-324-6325; 8AM-4PM. ***Misdemeanor, Civil Actions under $15,000, Eviction, Small Claims.***
www.nycourts.gov/courts/7jd/hornell/index.shtml
Civil Records: Access: Fax, mail, in person. Only the court performs in person searches; visitors may not. No search fee. Required to search: name, years to search. Civil cases indexed by defendant, plaintiff; index on computer from 1985, prior in books, folders and index cards go back 25 years. Mail turnaround time 5 days
Criminal Records: Access: None. Criminal records computerized from 1985, records go back 25 years. The court will not permit access to court records. The court directs requesters to OCA for $55.00 statewide search.
General Information: No sealed or sexual offense records released. Will fax documents to local or toll free line. Court makes copy: $.65 per page, minimum $1.30, maximum $30.00. Certification fee: $6.00. Payee: Hornell City Court. Cashiers checks and money orders accepted. Visa/MC accepted.

Surrogate's Court 3 E Pulteney Sq, Bath, NY 14810-1598; 607-776-7126; fax: 607-776-4987; 9AM-5PM. ***Probate.***
A county search of the probate court index by mail for 25-year search is $30.00 fee. A full county probate search of all years is $90.00.

Steuben Town/Village Courts- Addison Town Ct- 607-359-3615; Avoca Town Court Court- 607-566-2093; Bath Town Court and Village Court- 607-776-3192; Bradford Town Court- 607-583-4270, 607-776-6776; Cameron Town Court- 607-695-9022; Campbell Town Court- 607-527-8244; Canisteo Town Court- 607-698-2129; Caton Town Court- 607-524-6772; Cohocton Town Court- 585-534-5100; Corning Town Court- 607-936-9062; Dansville Town Court- 607-295-9917; Erwin Justice Court- 607-936-3122; Fremont Town Court- 607-324-0798; Greenwood Town Court- 607-225-4654 x3; Hartsville Town Court- 607-698-2305; Hornby Town Court- 607-962-0683; Hornellsville Town Court- 607-295-7768; Howard Town Court- 607-566-2058; Jasper Town Court- 607-792-3338; Lindley Town Court- 607-523-8816; Prattsburgh Town Court- 607-522-3761; Pulteney Town Court- 607-868-3931; Rathbone Town Court- 607-359-2258; Savona Village Court- 607-583-7618; Thurston Town Court- 607-527-4494; Troupsburg Town Court- 607-525-6403; Tuscarora Town Court- 607-359-2066; Urbana Town Court- 607-569-3738; Wayland Town Court and Village Court- 585-728-3504; Wayne Town Court- 607-292-6003; West Union Town Court- 607-225-4321, 225-4429; Wheeler Town Court- 607-776-7208; Woodhull Town Court- 607-458-5252.

Suffolk County

Supreme & County Court - Main 310 Centre Dr, Riverhead County Ctr, Attn: Court Actions, Riverhead, NY 11901; 631-852-2000/or/3793; criminal phone: 631-852-2000 x854; civil phone: 631-852-2000 x857; fax: 631-852-2004; 9AM-5PM; file rm- to 4:30PM only. ***Felony, Civil over $15,000.***
www.suffolkcountyny.gov/clerk and www.courts.state.ny.us/courts/10jd/suffolk/supreme.shtml
Records are managed by the County Clerk; information for County Clerk office is given here. Faxes accepted from gov't agencies only. Supreme Ct clerk info-631-852-2334; County Ct Clerk info-631-852-1462.
Civil Records: Access: Mail, in person, online. Both court and visitors may perform in person searches. Search fee: $5.00 per name per 2 years searched. $9.00 fee for Certificate of Search. Required to search: name, years to search. Civil cases indexed by defendant, plaintiff; index on computer back to 4/84; prior in books. Mail turnaround time 7-14 days. Civil PAT goes back to 1984. PAT results show name only. Access county clerk's civil court minutes data free at www.co.suffolk.ny.us/scco/web/. Judgments and Liens also found. Historical records are not online, but access to current/pending Supreme Court civil cases is at http://iapps.courts.state.ny.us/webcivil/FCASMain
Criminal Records: Access: Mail, in person, online. Both court and visitors may perform in person searches. Search fee: Felony- $9.00 per name (computer back to 1980s, paper back to '60s). $5.00 fee for Certificate of Disposition. $9.00 fee for Certificate of Search. Required to search: name, years to search, DOB. Criminal records computerized from 1984. Clerk may restrict searcher's number of records pulled to 10 per day. Clerk recommends $55.00 statewide record search through OCA for 1985 to present. Mail turnaround time 7-14 days. Criminal PAT goes back to 1984; records may not be on the terminal at this time. PAT results show name only. Also, subscribe or login as guest to search eCourts WebCrims future appearances system at http://iapps.courts.state.ny.us/webcrim_attorney/Login. Online results show name only.
General Information: No sealed or divorce records released. Clerk may fax back documents time permitting and if you're really sweet, no fee. Court makes copy: $1.25 per page. Self serve: $.25 per page. Certification fee: $5.00 per cert. Payee: County Clerk. Personal checks accepted with proper ID on check. No credit cards accepted. Mail requests: SASE required.

Supreme & County Court - Central Islip 400 Carleton Ave, Cohalan Court Complex, Central Islip, NY 11722; 631-853-5423, clerk- 631-853-5462; fax: 631-853-5835; 9AM-5PM. ***Felony, Civil.***
www.courts.state.ny.us/courts/10jd/suffolk/index.shtml
Records at Supreme Court in Riverhead only. Access county clerk's civil court minutes data at http://clerk.co.suffolk.ny.us/LisPendens/Web/. Judgments/liens also found. Search civil appearances at http://iapps.courts.state.ny.us/webcivil/FCASMain.

1st District Court - Criminal Dept 400 Carleton Ave, Central Islip, NY 11722; 631-853-5356/4562; 8:30AM-4:30PM. ***Misdemeanor.***
http://courts.state.ny.us/courts/10jd/suffolk/dist/
Criminal Records: Access: Mail (not always available), in person. Only the court performs in person searches; visitors may not. Search fee: $6.00 for Certificate of Disposition only. Required to search: Name, DOB, approx date of arrest and charge. Criminal records go back to 1971; on computer back to 3/2000. Court will pull record if docket number and proper identifiers are provided. Name search requesters are directed to send requests to OCA for $55.00 statewide search. Also, a Suffolk County only search is through the local Police Dept- 631-852-6015. Online access to active criminal court dates only listed by defendant or docket are free at http://iapps.courts.state.ny.us/webcrim_attorney/Login.
General Information: No sealed or youthful offender records released. Will not fax documents. Court makes copy: $.65 per page. Certification fee: $5.00 per doc. Payee: Clerk of the District Court. Personal checks accepted with proper ID. Credit cards accepted.

2nd District Court 30 E Hoffman Ave, Lindenhurst, NY 11757; 631-854-1121; fax: 631-854-1127; 9AM-1PM, 2-5PM; window closes at 12:30 and 4:30PM. ***Civil Actions under $15,000, Eviction, Small Claims, Ordinances, Traffic.***
http://courts.state.ny.us/courts/10jd/suffolk/
Very low misdemeanor cases were heard here; no felony or Misd. records here now. Also handles Babylon Town ordinance cases. Use your paid receipt for a civil search from any Suffolk District Court to search at any other Suffolk District courts for free.
Civil Records: Access: Mail, in person. Only the court performs in person searches; visitors may not. Search fee: $16.00 per name. Required to search: name, years to search. Civil cases indexed by plaintiff. Civil records on computer from 1996, prior in books, on cards. Mail turnaround time 2 weeks.
General Information: No sealed records released. Will not fax documents. Court makes copy: $.65 per page, $1.30 minimum. Certification fee: $6.00 per doc. Payee: Clerk of Court. Only cashiers checks and money orders accepted. Major credit cards accepted in person only. Mail requests: SASE required.

3rd District Court 1850 New York Ave, Huntington Station, NY 11746; 631-854-4545; fax: 631-854-4549; 9AM-12:30PM, 2-4:30PM. ***Misdemeanor, Civil Actions under $15,000, Eviction, Small Claims, Traffic.***
http://courts.state.ny.us/courts/10jd/suffolk/
Use your paid receipt for a civil search from any Suffolk District Court to search at any other Suffolk District courts for free.
Civil Records: Access: Mail, in person. Only the court performs in person searches; visitors may not. Search fee: $16.00 per name. Required to search: name, years to search. Civil cases indexed by defendant. Civil records on computer from 1988, prior in books, on microfilm. This court suggests a wider civil record search be performed at the County Clerk office. This court's civil records are indexed by key letters "HU" Currently adding public access terminals.
Criminal Records: Access: Mail (limited), in person. Only the court performs in person searches; visitors may not. Search fee: $6.00 for Certificate of Disposition only. Direct search requests to OCA for the $55.00 statewide record search for 1985 to present. Required to search: name, years to search, DOB, SSN. A signed release is necessary for a sealed case. Criminal records computerized from 1988, prior in books, on microfilm. Only minor misdemeanor records located here. Currently adding public access terminals.
General Information: No sealed records released. Will not fax documents. Court makes copy: $.65 per page. Certification fee: $6.00 per doc. Payee: Clerk of the Court. Business and personal checks accepted. Visa/MC accepted.

4th District Court North County Complex Bldg C158, Veteran's Memorial Highway, Hauppauge, NY 11787-4311; 631-853-5400; fax: 631-853-5951; 9AM-1PM; 2PM-5PM. ***Misdemeanor, Civil Actions under $15,000, Eviction, Small Claims.***
http://courts.state.ny.us/courts/10jd/suffolk/
Civil Records: Access: Mail, in person. Only the court performs in person searches; visitors may not. Search fee: $16.00 per name. Required to search: name, years to search. Civil cases indexed by defendant, plaintiff; index on computer from 1987, prior in books.
Criminal Records: Access: Mail (limited). Only the court performs in person searches; visitors may not. Search fee: $16.00 per name. $6.00 for Certificate of Disposition only. Required to search: name, years to search, DOB. Criminal records computerized from 1987, prior in books. Name searches for employment background checking are usually forwarded to OCA for $55.00 statewide search unless specific docket number given. Online access to criminal court dates only listed by defendant are free at http://iapps.courts.state.ny.us/webcrim_attorney/Login.
General Information: No sealed records released. Will not fax documents. Court makes copy: $.65 per page. Certification fee: $6.00 per cert; exemplification- $16.00. Payee: Clerk of Court. Personal checks accepted. Visa/MC accepted. Mail requests: SASE required.

6th District Court 150 W Main St, Patchogue, NY 11772; 631-854-1440; auto- 631-853-7500; fax: 631-854-1444; 9AM-1PM, 2-4:30PM; 5PM for civil. ***Misdemeanor, Civil Actions under $15,000, Eviction, Small Claims, Traffic.***
http://courts.state.ny.us/courts/10jd/suffolk/
Use your paid receipt for a civil search from any Suffolk District Court to search at any other Suffolk District courts for free. Misdemeanor records here cover only Brookhaven Town Ordinance violations.
Civil Records: Access: Mail, in person. Both court and visitors may perform in person searches. Search fee: $16.00 per name. Required to search: name, years to search. Civil records on computer from 1989, prior on microfilm. Public use terminal has civil records. Public terminals to be added.
Criminal Records: Access: Mail (limited), in person. Both court and visitors may perform in person searches. Search fee: $6.00 for Certificate of Disposition only. Court to search misdemeanor records- $52.00 per name. Criminal records computerized from 1992, prior on microfilm. Misdemeanor search limited to Brookhaven Town, or name search statewide via OCA for $55.00 search unless specific docket number given here. Mail turnaround time 3 days. Online access to criminal court dates only listed by defendant are free at http://iapps.courts.state.ny.us/webcrim_attorney/Login.
General Information: No sealed or youthful offender records released. Will not fax out documents. Court makes copy: $.65 per page. Certification fee: $6.00 per doc; exemplification- $15.00. Payee: Clerk of Court. Personal checks and major credit cards accepted. Mail requests: SASE required.

Suffolk District Courts 1 & 5 - Civil 3105-1 Veterans Memorial Hwy, Ronkonkoma, NY 11779-7614; 631-854-9676 (1st); 631-854-9673 (5th); fax: 631-854-9681; 9AM-1PM, 2-5PM. ***Civil Actions under $15,000, Eviction, Small Claims.***
http://courts.state.ny.us/courts/10jd/suffolk/
Use your paid receipt for a civil search from any Suffolk District Court to search at any other Suffolk District courts for free.
Civil Records: Access: Mail, in person. Only the court performs in person searches; visitors may not. Search fee: $16.00 per name. Required to search: name, years to search. Civil cases indexed by

defendant. Civil records on computer back to 1989, prior in books back to 1969. Mail turnaround 2 wks.
General Information: No sealed or youthful offender records released. Will fax documents for no fee. Court makes copy: $1.30 first page, $.65 each add'l. Certification fee: $6.00 per page includes copy fee. Exemplification fee- $15.00. Payee: Clerk of the Court. Cash, checks, or money orders accepted. Visa/MC accepted. Mail requests: SASE required.

Surrogate's Court 320 Centre Dr, Riverhead, NY 11901; 631-852-1745; fax: 631-852-1414; 9AM-5PM. ***Probate.*** A county search of the probate court index by mail for 25-year search is $30.00 fee. A full county probate search of all years is $90.00.

Suffolk Town/Village Courts- Asharoken Village Ct- 631-261-8677; Belle Terre Village Court- Bellport Village Court- 631-286-0327 x22; East Hampton Town Court- 631-324-4134; Greenport Village Court- 631-477-0248; Head of the Harbor Village Court- 631-584-5550; Islandia Village Court- 631-348-0470; Lake Grove Justice Court- 631-585-2008; Nissequogue Village Court- 631-862-8576; Ocean Beach Village Court- 631-583-0104; Old Field Village Court- 631-941-9416; Patchogue Village Court- 631-475-2753; Poquott Village Court- 631-331-0402; Port Jefferson Village Court- 631-802-2120; Quogue Village Justice Court- 631-653-9400; Riverhead Justice Court- 631-727-3200; Shelter Island Town Court- 631-749-8989; Shoreham Village Court- 631-821-0680; Southampton Town Court- 631-283-6017; Southampton Village Court- 631-204-2140; Southold Town Justice Court- 631-765-1852; West Hampton Dunes Village Court- 516-742-0800; Westhampton Beach Village Court- 631-288-3980;

Sullivan County

County Clerk 100 North St, Sullivan Gov't Ctr, Monticello, NY 12701; 845-794-3000 x5012; 9AM-5PM; 4:45PM computer closes. ***Felony, Civil.***
Countywide search requests made to the county clerk are processed in the manner described below. Supreme Court phone-845-794-4066. County Ct phone- 845-794-1248.
Civil Records: Access: Mail, in person, online. Both court and visitors may perform in person searches. Search fee: $5.00 per name on computer only. Required to search: name, years to search. Civil cases indexed by plaintiff. Civil records on computer from 1990, prior in books from 1800s. This office may search off the computer. Mail turnaround time 1-2 weeks. Public use terminal has civil records back to 1990. PAT results show name only. Lookup current or pending Supreme Court civil cases at http://iapps.courts.state.ny.us/webcivil/FCASMain
Criminal Records: Access: In person only. Only the court performs in person searches; visitors may not. Search fee: A Certificate of Disposition, by mail or in person, is $5.00. Criminal name search requests are directed to the OCA for a $55.00 statewide record check. Required to search: name, years to search, DOB. Criminal records go back to 1967; on computer back to 4/1990. For in person requests, first name search the County Clerk index for case numbers. To retrieve case records, take case numbers to the Supreme & County Court (see separate listing) County-Court clerk who will pull records for you.
General Information: No sealed, expunged, adoption, sex offense, juvenile or mental health records released. Will not fax documents. Court makes copy: $1.00 per page; $.25 if off computer. Self serve: $.25 per page. Certification fee: $5.20 if certification of prepared copy. Payee: County Clerk for civil; to Court Clerk for criminal. Personal checks accepted; credit cards are not.

Supreme & County Court County Courthouse, 414 Broadway, Monticello, NY 12701; 845-794-4066; probate phone: 845-794-3000 x3450; fax: 845-791-6170; 9AM-5PM. ***Felony, Civil, Misdemeanor.***
Civil records and criminal record index are maintained at County Clerk's office, see separate listing. However, actual felony records are located here at County-Court Clerk office.
Civil Records: Access: Mail, in person. Both court and visitors may perform in person searches. Search fee: $5.00 per civil case search. Required to search: name, years to search. Civil cases indexed by plaintiff. Civil records on computer from 1990, prior in books from 1800s. Perform civil searches at the Court Clerk office. Mail turnaround time 2-3 weeks. Public use terminal has civil records back to 4/1/1990. Current or pending only Supreme Court civil case look-up is at http://iapps.courts.state.ny.us/webcivil/FCASMain
Criminal Records: Access: Mail (limited), in person. Visitors must perform in person searches themselves. Search fee: $16.00 but you must provide case number. Required to search: name, years to search, DOB. Criminal records go back to 1967; on computer back to 4/1990. For mail request, County-Court directs search requests to OCA for $55.00 statewide check. In person search: 1st find case number by search at County Clerk office (see separate entry), then ask County-Court clerk office (address above) for case file. Mail turnaround time is 2-3 weeks.
General Information: No sealed, expunged, adoption, sex offense, juvenile or mental health records released. Court makes copy: $.65 per page, maximum- $40.00 per file. Certification fee: $5.00, Criminal Certificate of Disposition- $6.00, Divorce Judgments- $6.20. Payee: County Clerk for civil; to Court Clerk for criminal. Personal checks and credit cards accepted.

Surrogate's Court County Government Ctr, 100 North St, Monticello, NY 12701; 845-794-3000 X3450/3451; fax: 845-794-0310; 9AM-5PM may be closed for lunch N-1PM. ***Probate.***
A county search of the probate court index by mail for 25-year search is $30.00 fee. A full county probate search of all years is $90.00.

Sullivan Town/Village Courts- Bethel Town Court- 845-583-7420; Bloomingburg Justice Court- 845-733-1400; Callicoon Town Court- 845-482-5390 x301; Delaware Justice Court- 845-887-5849 x8; Fallsburg Town Court- 845-434-4574; Forestburgh Town Court- 845-794-0611 x 12; Fremont Town Court- 845-687-4883; Highland Town Court- 845-557-8132; Liberty Justice Court- 845-292-0290; Liberty Town Court- 845-292-6980; Lumberland Town Court- 845-858-8548; Mamakating Town Court- 845-888-3038; Monticello Village Court- 845-794-1222; Neversink Town Court- 845-985-7685 x311; Rockland Town Court- 607-498-4320; Thompson Town Court- 845-794-7130; Tusten Town Court- 845-252-7146.

Tioga County

County Clerk PO Box 307, 16 Court St, Owego, NY 13827; 607-687-8660; fax: 607-687-8686; 9AM-5PM. ***Civil.***
Countywide civil record search requests made to the county clerk are processed in the manner described below. County clerk has only a paper index list of felony proceedings. Felony records are managed by the County-Court Clerk, see separate listing.
Civil Records: Access: In person. Visitors must perform in person searches themselves. Required to search: name, years to search. Civil cases indexed by defendant. Civil records in books. Visitor can search in County Clerk's Office. Public use terminal has civil records back to 9/2003. PAT civil results show middle initial.
General Information: No sealed, expunged, adoption, sex offense, juvenile or mental health records released. Will not fax documents. Court makes copy: $.50 per page. Self serve: $.25 per page. Certification fee: $5.00 per doc includes copy fee. Payee: Tioga County Clerk. Personal checks accepted; credit cards are not. Mail requests: SASE required for mail return of any copies.

Supreme & County Court PO Box 307, 16 Court St, Owego, NY 13827; 607-687-0544; fax: 607-687-5680; 9AM-5PM. ***Felony.***
For civil records, see County Clerk. Historical civil records are not online, but access to current and pending Supreme Court civil cases is free at http://iapps.courts.state.ny.us/webcivil/FCASMain
Criminal Records: Access: In person only. Only the court performs in person searches; visitors may not. No search fee if in person search. Required to search: name, years to search, DOB. Criminal records in books since 1970s; earlier records stored off-site. Felony records are managed by the County-Court Clerk who directs search requests to OCA for $55.00 statewide search. You may also search County-court clerk felony files in person; details below.
General Information: No sealed, expunged, sex offense, or juvenile records released. Will not fax documents. Court makes copy: $.50 per page. Certification fee: $5.00. Payee: County Clerk. Personal checks accepted; credit cards are not.

Surrogate's Court PO Box 10, 20 Court St, Owego, NY 13827; 607-687-1303; fax: 607-687-3240; 9AM-5PM. ***Probate.***
Court is located in the County Court Annex Bldg. A county search of the probate court index by mail for 25-year search is $30.00 fee. A full county probate search of all years is $90.00.

Tioga Town/Village Courts- Barton Town Court- 607-565-8609; Berkshire Town Court- 607-657-8678; Candor Town Court and Village Court- 607-659-3175; Newark Valley Town Court- 607-642-5278; Nichols Town Court- 607-642-5278; Owego Town Court- 607-687-0123 x4; Owego Village Court- 607-687-2236; Richford Town Court- 607-539-7304; Spencer Town Court- 607-589-7342; Spencer Village Court- 607-589-4310; Tioga Town Court- 607-687-9577; Waverly Village Court- 607-565-4771.

Tompkins County

Supreme & County Court Tomkins County Clerk, 320 N Tioga St, Ithaca, NY 14850; 607-274-5431 (County Clerk); 607-272-0466 (Count Clerks); criminal phone: 607-274-5453; civil phone: 607-274-5453; criminal fax: 607-274-5445; civil fax: same; 9AM-5PM (Court Clerks have Summer hours-8:30AM-4:30PM). ***Felony, Civil.***
www.tompkins-co.org/cclerk/
Direct all search requests to the County Clerk office; information given here is for that County Clerk office.
Civil Records: Access: Fax, mail, in person, online. Both court and visitors may perform in person searches. Search fee: $5.00 per name if court does search. Fee is per 2 years searched. Required to search: name, years to search. Civil cases indexed by defendant, plaintiff. Civil records in books. Before faxing, you must first be approved with a credit account. Mail turnaround time 1-2 days. Public use terminal has civil records back to 7/7/1999. Historical records are not online, but access to current/pending Supreme Court civil cases is at http://iapps.courts.state.ny.us/webcivil/FCASMain
Criminal Records: Access: Fax, mail, in person. Only the court performs in person searches; visitors may not. Search fee: $5.00 per name if court does search. Fee is per 2 years searched. Required to search: name, years to search, signed release; also helpful: DOB. Felony records in books. Before faxing, you must first be approved with a credit account. Mail turnaround time 1-2 days.
General Information: No sealed, expunged, adoption, sex offense, juvenile or mental health records released. Will fax documents to local or toll free line. Court makes copy: $.65 per page, $1.30 minimum. Self serve: same. Certification fee: $5.00 per document. Payee: County Clerk. Personal checks accepted; credit cards are not. Mail requests: SASE required.

Ithaca City Court 118 E Clinton St, Ithaca, NY 14850; 607-273-2263; fax: 607-277-3702; 8AM-4PM. ***Misdemeanor, Civil Actions under $15,000, Eviction, Small Claims.***
www.nycourts.gov/ithaca/city
Local search is for violation level convictions only.
Civil Records: Access: Mail, in person. Only the court performs in person searches; visitors may not. Search fee: $5.00 per each 2 year period. Required to search: name, years to search. Civil cases indexed by defendant. Civil records on computer since 1996; prior records in books. Mail turnaround time 7-10 days.
Criminal Records: Access: Mail, in person. Search fee: $5.00 per each 2 year period. Required to search: name, years to search. Criminal records computerized from 1990, prior in books. Mail turnaround time 7-10 days.
General Information: No sealed, youthful offender records released. Will fax documents to local or toll free line. Court makes copy: $.65 per page; $1.30 minimum. Certification fee: $6.00 per cert. Payee: City Court. Only cashiers checks and money orders

accepted by mail; cash in person. Visa/MC accepted. Mail requests: SASE required.

Surrogate's Court P O Box 70, 320 N Tioga St, Ithaca, NY 14851; 607-277-0622; fax: 607-256-2572; 9AM-5PM, Reg Hrs, Summer 8:30AM-4:30PM July 5-Sept 5. ***Probate.***
A county search of the probate court index by mail for 25-year search is $30.00 fee. A full county probate search of all years is $90.00.

Tomkins Town/Village Courts- Caroline Town Court- 607-539-7796; Cayuga Heights Village Court- 607-257-3944; Danby Town Court- 607-277-4788; Dryden Town Court- 607-844-8888 x1; Enfield Town Court- 607-272-0363; Freeville Village Court- 607-844-8470; Groton Town Court- 607-898-5273; Ithaca Town Court- 607-273-1721; Lansing Town Court- 607-533-4776; Newfield Town Court- 607-564-9571; Ulysses Town Court- 607-387-5411.

Ulster County

County Clerk PO Box 1800, 244 Fair St, Kingston, NY 12401; 845-340-3288 (Clerk); 845-340-3000 (Switchboard); fax: 845-340-3299; 9AM-4:45PM. ***Felony, Civil.***
www.co.ulster.ny.us
Countywide search requests made to the County Clerk are processed in the manner described below.
Civil Records: Access: Phone, mail, in person, online. Both court and visitors may perform in person searches. Search fee: $5.00 per name per 2 years searched; county clerk may perform 1 search from 1987 forward for free over phone. Required to search: name, years to search. Civil cases indexed by defendant, plaintiff; index on computer from 1987, in books from 1920s, prior archived. Mail turnaround time 5 days. Civil PAT goes back to 1987. PAT civil results show middle initial. Access to current Supreme court cases is at http://iapps.courts.state.ny.us/webcivil/ecourtsMain.
Criminal Records: Access: Phone, mail, in person. Both court and visitors may perform in person searches. Search fee: $5.00 per name. Fee is per 2 years searched. Required to search: name, years to search. Criminal records computerized from 1987, in books from 1920s, prior archived. Mail turnaround time 5 days. Criminal PAT goes back to same as civil. PAT criminal results show middle initial.
General Information: No sealed, expunged, adoption, sex offense, juvenile or mental health records released. Will fax out documents for $2.00 per page. Court makes copy: $1.25 per page, minimum $5.00. Self serve: $.65 per page, 2 page minimum. Certification fee: $5.00. Payee: Ulster County Clerk. Personal checks accepted; credit cards are not. Mail requests: SASE required.

Supreme & County Court 285 Wall St, Kingston, NY 12401; 845-340-3377; fax: 845-340-3387; 9AM-5PM. ***Felony, Civil.***
The Court Clerk directs record search requests to the County Clerk, see separate listing.

Kingston City Court One Garraghan Dr, Kingston, NY 12401; 845-338-2974; fax: 845-338-1443; 8:30AM-4PM; Doors close 3:15-3:30PM. ***Misdemeanor, Civil Actions under $15,000, Eviction, Small Claims.***
Civil searches are treated separately from criminal searches; there is a fee for each. Generally, they will not search beyond 25 years back.
Civil Records: Access: Mail, in person. Only the court performs in person searches; visitors may not. Search fee: $5.00 per name per 2 years. If pre-1995, fee is $16.00. Required to search: name, years to search. Civil cases indexed by plaintiff. Civil records on computer from 1995. Overall records go back to 1983. Request must be in writing. Mail turnaround time 1-2 weeks.
Criminal Records: Access: Mail, in person. Only the court performs in person searches; visitors may not. Search fee: $5.00 per name per 2 years. If pre-1995, fee is $16.00. Required to search: Name, years to search, DOB. Criminal records computerized from 1995. Overall records go back to 1983. The court sometimes directs requesters to send requests to OCA for the statewide search. Mail turnaround time 1-2 weeks.
General Information: No sealed or youthful offender records released. Will not fax documents. Court makes copy: $1.00 per page. Certification fee: $5.00. Payee: City Court. No personal checks accepted. Visa/MC accepted. Mail requests: SASE required.

Surrogate's Court PO Box 1800, 240 Fair St, Kingston, NY 12402; 845-340-3348; fax: 845-340-3352; 9AM-5PM. ***Probate.***
A county search of the probate court index by mail for 25-year search is $30.00 fee. A full county probate search of all years is $90.00.

Ulster Town/Village Courts- Crawford Town Court- 845-744-2020; Denning Town Court- 845-985-2100; Ellenville Village Court- 845-647-7080; Esopus Town Court- 845-331-5776; Gardiner Town Court- 845-256-0017; Hurley Town Court- 845-331-9229; Kingston Town Court- 845-336-8853; Lloyd Town Court- 845-691-7544; Marbletown Town Court- 845-687-4328; Marlborough Town Court- 845-795-5100; New Paltz Town Court- 845-255-0041/0043; Olive Town Court- 845-657-2912; Plattekill Town Court- 845-883-5805; Rochester Town Court- 845-626-2522; Rosendale Town Court- 845-658-3686; Saugerties Town Court- 845-246-9989, 246-2800; Saugerties Village Court- 845-246-3958, 246-2321; Shandaken Town Court- 845-688-5005; Shawangunk Town Court- 845-895-2611; Ulster Town Court- 845-382-1737; Wawarsing Town Court- 845-647-4770; Woodstock Town Court- 845-679-6345.

Warren County

County Clerk 1340 State Route 9, Attn: County Clerk, Lake George, NY 12845; 518-761-6426; fax: 518-761-6551; 9AM-5PM. ***Civil, Felony.***
Countywide civil record search requests made to the county clerk are processed in the manner described below.
Civil Records: Access: Mail, in person, online. Both court and visitors may perform in person searches. Search fee: $5.00 per name for each 2 years. Required to search: name, years to search. Civil cases indexed by plaintiff & defendant. Civil records index on computer from 1917 to present. Mail turnaround time 1-2 days. Public use terminal has civil records back to 1900s. PAT results show name only. Get index numbers from PAT, then clerk will pull files. Lookup current or pending Supreme Court civil cases at http://iapps.courts.state.ny.us/webcivil/FCASMain
Criminal Records: Access: In person only. Both court and visitors may perform in person searches. No search fee. Required to search: name, years to search, DOB. Criminal records not on computer, on index from 1929. The clerk directs criminal search requests to the OCA for the $55.00 statewide search. Court clerk office will not do Certificate of Conviction reports. They may direct you to sheriff's office for record searches; first call sheriff's office-518-743-2500.
General Information: No adoption, juvenile or mental health records released. Will not fax documents. Court makes copy: $.65 per page, mailed copies $1.30 per page. Self serve: same. Certification fee: $5.00 for 1st four pages, $1.25 each add'l page. Payee: Warren County Clerk. Personal checks accepted; credit cards are not. Mail requests: SASE required for civil.

Supreme & County Court 1340 State Rte 9, Lake George, NY 12845; 518-761-6430/6431 county clerk; 9AM-5PM. ***Felony.***
Direct civil searches to County Clerk, see separate entry. A criminal record disposition index is maintained at County Clerk's office. Felony records are located here at Supreme & County Court Clerk office, though inaccessible unless case number given.

Glens Falls City Court 42 Ridge St, Glens Falls, NY 12801; 518-798-4714; fax: 518-798-0137; 8:30AM-4:30PM. ***Misdemeanor, Civil Actions under $15,000, Eviction, Small Claims.***
Civil Records: Access: None. Only the court performs in person searches; visitors may not. Required to search: name, years to search. Civil cases indexed by defendant, plaintiff. Civil records go back to 1975; on computer from 1987, prior on microfilm. This court will only provide record is a case number is provided. Because judgment releases are not always filed with this court, the court will not name search. This court will refer you to the County Clerk for civil searches.
Criminal Records: Access: None. Only the court performs in person searches; visitors may not. Criminal records go back to the late 1960's; on computer from 1990, prior on microfilm. The court does not permit access to court records unless specific case file given. Requesters are directed to OCA for $55.00 statewide search. Results include case number.
General Information: No sealed records released. Will fax documents to local or toll free line. Court makes copy: $.65 per page; $1.30 minimum. Certification fee: $6.00 per document plus copy fee for civil, $5.00 per document plus copy fee for all others. Payee: City Court. Only cashiers checks and money orders accepted.

Surrogate's Court 1340 State Rte 9, County Municipal Ctr, Lake George, NY 12845-9803; 518-761-6514; fax: 518-761-6511; 9AM-5PM. ***Probate.***
Public terminal available back to 1995 with older records being added. A county search of the probate court index by mail for 25-year search is $30.00 fee. A full county probate search of all years is $90.00.

Warren Town/Village Courts- Bolton Town Court- 518-644-2202; Chester Justice Court- 518-494-3133; Hague Town Court- 518-543-6161; Horicon Town Court- 518-494-7958; Johnsburg Town Court- 518-251-3011; Lake George Town Court- 518-668-5420; Lake Luzerne Town Court- 518-696-4294; Queensbury Town Court- 518-745-5571; Stony Creek Town Court- 518-696-3575; Thurman Town Court- 518-623-9660; Warrensburg Town Court- 518-623-9776.

Washington County

County Clerk 383 Broadway, Bldg A, Fort Edward, NY 12828; 518-746-2170; fax: 518-746-2177; 8:30AM-4:30PM. ***Civil.***
For felony records see the County-Court clerk at the Supreme and County Court in separate listing.
Civil Records: Access: Mail, in person, online (limited). Visitors must perform in person searches themselves. No search fee. Generally, court will answer mailed civil records requests but you must at least provide year to search. Required to search: name, years to search. Civil cases indexed by defendant. Civil records on books from 1800s. Mail turnaround time 1-2 days. Public use terminal has civil records. PAT results show name and index number only. Access to current/pending WebCivil Supreme Court civil cases may be at http://iapps.courts.state.ny.us/webcivil/FCASMain
General Information: No sealed or youthful offender records released. Will not fax documents. Court makes copy: $1.00 per page. Self serve: $.50 per page. Certification fee: $5.00 per doc. Payee: County Clerk. Business checks accepted. No credit cards accepted. Mail requests: SASE required.

Supreme & County Court 383 Broadway, Fort Edward, NY 12828; criminal phone: 518-746-2521; civil phone: 518-746-2520; fax: 518-746-2519; 8:30AM-4:30PM. ***Felony, Civil.***
Civil Records: Access: In person, online. For access to physical court records, direct civil record search requests to the County Clerk, see separate listing. Historical records are not online, but access to current/pending Supreme Court civil cases is at http://iapps.courts.state.ny.us/webcivil/FCASMain
Criminal Records: Access: In person only, mail. Only the court performs in person searches; visitors may not. Search fee: No fee if you search; $5.00 for Certificate of Disposition. Required to search: name, years to search. Criminal docket on books from 1800s, on computer back to late 1989. All criminal record name search requests are directed to the OCA for the $55.00 statewide record search. Visitors may not search the Book of Convictions. Public use terminal has crim records back to late 1989. PAT results show middle initial, DOB.
General Information: No sealed or youthful offender records released. Will not fax documents. Court makes copy: $1.00 per page. No cert fee at this court office. Payee: County Clerk. Business checks accepted at county clerk office. No credit cards accepted.

Surrogate's Court 383 Broadway, Fort Edward, NY 12828; 518-746-2546; fax: 518-746-2547; 8:30AM-4:30PM. ***Probate, Estate.***
A county search of the probate court index by mail for 25-year search is $30.00 fee. A full county probate search of all years is $90.00.

Washington Town/Village Courts- Argyle Town Court- 518-638-8681 x13; Cambridge Town Court- 518-677-2444; Cambridge Village Court- 518-677-8297; Dresden Town Court- 518-499-2040; Easton Town Court- 518-692-0027; Fort Ann Town Court- 518-639-4088; Fort Edward Town Court and Village Court- 518-747-2252; Granville Town Court- 518-642-9243; Granville Village Court- 518-642-9386; Greenwich Town Court- 518-692-7611; Greenwich Village Court- 518-692-2755; Hampton Town Court- 518-282-9830; Hartford Town Court- 518-632-5255; Hebron Town Court- 518-854-9300; Hudson Falls Village Court- 518-747-3292; Jackson Town Court- 518-677-8896; Kingsbury Town Court- 518-747-2188 x4; Putnam Town Court- 518-547-8317; Salem Town & Village Court- 518-854-9215; White Creek Town Court- 518-677-8545; Whitehall Town Court- 518-499-0772; Whitehall Village Court- 518-499-0772.

Wayne County

Supreme & County Court 9 Pearl St, PO Box 608, Lyons, NY 14489-0608; 315-946-7470; probate phone: 315-946-5430; criminal fax: 315-946-5978; civil fax: same; 9AM-5PM. ***Felony, Civil, Eviction, Small Claims.***
Direct all search requests to the County Clerk office; information given here is for that County Clerk office.
Civil Records: Access: Phone, fax, mail, in person. Both court and visitors may perform in person searches. Search fee: $5.00 per name per every 2 years. Required to search: name, years to search. Civil cases indexed by defendant, plaintiff; index on computer back to 1985, prior in books. Mail turnaround time 5-7 days. Civil PAT goes back to 1985. PAT civil results show middle initial. Current or pending only Supreme Court civil case look-up is at http://iapps.courts.state.ny.us/webcivil/FCASMain
Criminal Records: Access: Fax, mail, in person. Both court and visitors may perform in person searches. Search fee: $5.00 per name uncertified back to 1979. $5.00 per name for every 2 years certified search. Required to search: name, years to search, DOB; also helpful: gender. Criminal records computerized from 1979. Mail turnaround time 5-7 days. Criminal PAT goes back to 1979. PAT criminal results show middle initial.
General Information: No matrimonial records released. Fax out fee long distance within Wayne County $2.00 1st page, $1.00 each add'l page; long distance outside County $3.00 1st page, $1.00 each add'l page; no fax charge for 800 number. Court makes copy: $.65 per page; $1.30 minimum. Self serve: $.25 per page. Certification fee: $5.00 up to 4 pages, $1.25 each add'l page includes copy fee. Exemplification- $10.00. Payee: County Clerk. Personal checks accepted; credit cards are not. Mail requests: SASE requested.

Surrogate's Court 54 Broad St, Rm 106, Hall of Justice, Lyons, NY 14489; 315-946-5430; fax: 315-946-5433; 9AM-5PM. ***Probate.***
A county search of the probate court index by mail for 25-year search is $30.00 fee. A full county probate search of all years is $90.00.

Wayne Town/Village Courts- Arcadia Town C- 315-331-8020; Butler Town Court- 315-594-2719; Galen Town Court- 315-923-9375; Huron Town Court- 315-594-6511; Lyons Town Court- 315-946-4076; Lyons Village Court- 315-946-4565; Macedon Town Court- 315-986-5932; Macedon Village Court- 315-986-1597; Marion Town - 315-926-4461; Newark Village Court- 315-331-7666; Ontario Justice Court- 315-524-6511 x7; Palmyra Town Court- 315-597-5431; Rose Town Court- 315-587-4418; Savannah Town Court- 315-365-2811; Sodus Point Village Court- 315-483-9660; Sodus Town Court- 315-483-6807; Walworth Town Ct- 315-986-8544; Williamson Town Ct- 315-589-8250; Wolcott Town Ct- 315-594-8257; Wolcott Village Court- 315-594-6437.

Westchester County

County Clerk 110 Dr Martin L King Blvd, Rm 330, White Plains, NY 10601; 914-995-3070; fax: 914-995-3172; 8AM-5:30PM. ***Felony, Civil.***
www.westchesterclerk.com
Countywide search requests made to the County Clerk are processed in the manner described below. Fax number above is not for the public - do not use.
Civil Records: Access: Mail, in person, online. Both court and visitors may perform in person searches. Search fee: $5.00 per name per 2 years. Required to search: name, years to search. Civil cases indexed by defendant, plaintiff; index on computer from 1980, prior in books from 1847. Mail turnaround time 1 week. Civil PAT goes back to 1980. PAT results show name only. Access civil cases on the county clerk database search site back to 2002 at http://ccpv.westchesterclerk.com. Search is free, but registration and fees for images. Data includes liens, judgments, tax warrants, foreclosures, divorces. Also, access current/pending WebCivil Supreme Court civil cases at http://iapps.courts.state.ny.us/webcivil/FCASMain
Criminal Records: Access: Mail, in person, online. Both court and visitors may perform in person searches. Search fee: $5.00 per name per 2 years. Required to search: name, years to search. Criminal records computerized from 1980, prior in books from 1847. Mail turnaround time 1 week. Criminal PAT goes back to same as civil. PAT results show name only. Access criminal records on the county clerk database search site back to 2002 at http://ccpv.westchesterclerk.com. Search is free, but registration and fees for images. Also, subscribe or login as guest to search eCourts WebCrims future appearances system at http://iapps.courts.state.ny.us/webcrim_attorney/Login. Online results show middle initial.
General Information: No sealed, expunged, adoption, sex offense, juvenile or mental health records released. Will not fax documents. Court makes copy: $.65 per page, minimum $1.00. Self serve: $.25 per page. Certification fee: $5.00 per doc. Payee: County Clerk. Personal checks accepted. Visa/MC accepted. Mail requests: SASE required.

Supreme & County Court 111 Dr Martin L King Blvd, Rm 900, White Plains, NY 10601; criminal phone: 914-824-5400; civil phone: 914-9824-5300; 9AM-5PM. ***Felony, Civil.***
www.westchesterclerk.com and www.courts.state.ny.us/courts/9jd/Westchester/supremecounty.shtml
Direct search requests to the County Clerk, see separate listing, otherwise requests are directed to the OCA for the $55.00 statewide record search. Access judgments on the county clerk database search site at http://ccpv.westchesterclerk.com.

Mt Vernon City Court Ronald Blackwood Bldg, 2 Roosevelt Square, 2nd Fl, Mt Vernon, NY 10550-2019; 914-665-2400; criminal phone: 914-665-2409; fax: 914-699-1230; 9AM-5PM (payments to 4PM only). ***Misdemeanor, Civil Actions under $15,000, Eviction, Small Claims.***
Small claims: 665-2404; Landlord/Tenant: 665-2402; Traffic: 665-2405.
Civil Records: Access: Mail, in person. Only the court performs in person searches; visitors may not. No search fee. Required to search: name, years to search; also helpful: address. Civil cases indexed by defendant, plaintiff; index on computer since 1986, prior in books. Court holds records for 3 years and then send to archives Mail Turnaround 1 week.
Criminal Records: Access: In person only. Only the court performs in person searches; visitors may not. Criminal records on computer since 1986, prior in books.
General Information: No sealed records released. Will not fax documents. Court makes copy: $1.30 1st page, $.65 each add'l. Certification fee: $6.00. Payee: City Court. Cashiers checks and money orders accepted. Visa/MC accepted. Mail requests: SASE required for civil.

New Rochelle City Court 475 North Ave, New Rochelle, NY 10801; 914-654-2291; criminal phone: 914-654-2311; civil phone: 914-654-2299; fax: 914-654-0344; 9AM-5PM; entry gate closes at 4:30PM. ***Misdemeanor, Civil Actions under $15,000, Small Claims.***
www.courts.state.ny.us/courts/9jd/Westchester/NewRochelle.shtml Traffic phone- 914-654-2292.
Civil Records: Access: Mail, in person. Only the court performs in person searches; visitors may not. Search fee: $16.00 per name. Required to search: name, years to search. Civil records retained for 20 years.
Criminal Records: Access: Phone, mail, in person. Search fee: $16.00 per name. Certificate of Disposition- $10.00 with release. It has been found that this court may do short phone request lookups, but court may direct requesters to OCA for $55.00 statewide search.
General Information: No sealed records released. Will not fax documents. Court makes copy: $1.00 per page. Certification fee: $10.00 per doc for criminal, $6.00 civil. Payee: City Court of New Rochelle. No personal checks accepted. Visa/MC accepted if criminal division; not accepted for civil.

Peekskill City Court 2 Nelson Ave, Peekskill, NY 10566; 914-831-6480; fax: 914-736-1889; 9AM-4PM. ***Misdemeanor, Civil Actions under $15,000, Eviction, Small Claims.***
Civil Records: Access: In person only. Only the court performs in person searches; visitors may not. No search fee. Required to search: name, years to search. Civil cases indexed by plaintiff. Civil records on computer back to 1994, prior in books.
Criminal Records: Access: Mail, In person. Both court and visitors may perform in person searches. Search fee: Certificate of Disposition- $6.00 and you must supply specific case info. Required to search: name, years to search, DOB. Criminal records computerized from 1990, prior on cards. Search in person on computer or microfilm only on Fridays by appointment. Requesters usually directed to OCA for $55.00 statewide search. Mail turnaround time 1-5 days.
General Information: No sealed records released. Will not fax documents. Court makes copy: $.65 per page, $1.30 minimum. Certification fee: $6.00 per doc. Payee: Peekskill City Court. No personal or business checks accepted. Visa/MC accepted. Mail requests: SASE required for criminal.

Rye City Court 21 3rd St, Rye, NY 10580; 914-967-1599; 8:30AM-4:30PM. ***Misdemeanor, Civil Actions under $15,000, Eviction, Small Claims.***
Civil Records: Access: In person only. Only the court performs in person searches; visitors may not. No search fee. Required to search: name, years to search. Civil cases indexed by plaintiff. Civil records on computer from 1994, prior on index cards. Make an appointment to search in person.
Criminal Records: Access: In person only. Only the court performs in person searches; visitors may not. Search fee: Certificate of Disposition- $5.00 per name. Required to search: DOB, years to search. Criminal records computerized from 1986. The court will perform limited name searches. Court recommends search requests be sent to OCA for $55.00 statewide search.
General Information: No sealed records released. Court makes copy: $.65 per page; $1.30 minimum. Certification fee: $5.00 per cert. Payee: City Court. No personal checks accepted. Major credit cards accepted.

White Plains City Court 77 S Lexington Ave, Main Fl, White Plains, NY 10601; 914-824-5675; criminal phone: 914-824-5688; fax: 914-422-6058; 8:45AM-5PM; registers close- 4:45PM. ***Misdemeanor, Civil Actions under $15,000, Eviction, Small Claims.***
Civil Records: Access: Mail, fax, in person. Only the court performs in person searches; visitors may not. Search fee: $16.00 per name. Required to search: name, years to search. Civil cases indexed by defendant. Civil records on docket cards and computer. Mail turnaround time 1-2 days.
Criminal Records: Access: Mail, in person. Search fee: Certificate of Disposition- $5.00 per name.

Required to search: name, years to search, DOB. Criminal records computerized from 1988, prior on cards. Except for certificate of disposition, the court does not permit access to court records unless specific case file given. Requesters are directed to OCA for $55.00 statewide search. Mail turnaround time 1-2 days.
General Information: No sealed, youthful offender or sex case records released. Will fax documents no fee, all fees paid. Court makes copy: $1.00 1st page; $.50 each add'l. Certification fee: $6.00 per doc. Payee: City Court. Cashiers checks and money orders accepted. Visa/MC accepted in person only. Credit cards not accepted for Certificates of Disposition. Mail requests: SASE required.

Yonkers City Court 100 S Broadway, Yonkers, NY 10701; criminal phone: 914-377-6352; civil phone: 914-377-6376; fax: 914-377-6966; 9AM-5PM. ***Misdemeanor, Civil Actions under $15,000, Eviction, Small Claims.***
Civil Records: Access: Mail, in person. Only the court performs in person searches; visitors may not. Search fee: $16.00 per name. Required to search: name, years to search. Civil cases indexed by plaintiff. Civil records on computer since 1/95. Mail turnaround time 2-3 weeks.
Criminal Records: Access: Mail, in person. Only the court performs in person searches; visitors may not. Search fee: $16.00, if specific case # given. Criminal records on computer since 1993. The court does not permit access to court records unless specific case file given. Requesters are directed to the OCA for $55.00 statewide search. Mail turnaround time 2-3 weeks.
General Information: No sealed records released. Will not fax documents. Court makes copy: $.65 per page; $1.30 minimum. Certification fee: $6.00 per document. Payee: City Court. Cashiers checks and money orders accepted. Visa/MC accepted.

Surrogate's Court 111 Dr Martin Luther King Jr Blvd, 18th Fl, White Plains, NY 10601; 914-824-5656; fax: 914-995-3728; 9AM-5PM. ***Probate.***
A county search of the probate court index by mail for 25-year search is $30.00 fee. A full county probate search of all years is $90.00.

Westchester Town/Village Courts- Ardsley Village Court- 914-693-1703; Bedford Town Court- 914-666-6965; Briarcliff Manor Village Court- 914-944-2788; Bronxville Village Court- 914-337-2454; Buchanan Village Court- 914-737-1033; Cortlandt Town Court- 914-734-1090; Croton-on-Hudson Village Court- 914-271-6266; Dobbs Ferry Village Court- 914-693-6161; Eastchester Town Court- 914-771-3354; Elmsford Village Court- 914-592-8949; Greenburgh Town Court- 914-682-5365; Harrison Town Court- 914-670-3010; Hastings-on-Hudson Village Court- 914-478-3403; Irvington Village Court- 914-591-7095; Larchmont Village Court- 914-834-1826; Lewisboro Justice Court- 914-763-5417; Mamaroneck Town Court- 914-381-7875; Mamaroneck Village Court- 914-777-7710; Mount Kisco Town Court- 914-241-7033; Mount Pleasant Town Court- 914-742-2354; New Castle Justice Court- 914-238-4726; North Castle Justice Court- 914-273-8627; North Salem Town Court- 914-669-9691; Ossining Town Court- 914-762-8562; Ossining Village Court- 914-941-3067; Pelham Town Court- 914-738-7030; Pleasantville Village Court- 914-769-2027; Port Chester Justice Court- 914-939-8220; Pound Ridge Justice Court- 914-764-5511; Rye Town Court- 914-939-3305; Scarsdale Village Court- 914-722-1120/1123; Sleepy Hollow Village Court- 914-631-2783; Somers Town Ct- 914-277-8225; Tarrytown Village Ct- 914-631-5215; Tuckahoe Village Ct- 914-961-4787; Yorktown Justice Court- 914-962-6216.

Wyoming County

Supreme & County Court 147 N Main St, Warsaw, NY 14569; 585-786-8810-county clerk, 585-786-3148-court clerks); fax: 585-786-3703; 9AM-5PM. ***Felony, Civil.***
Direct all search requests to the County Clerk's office, 143 N Main St, #104; information given here is for the County Clerk's office.
Civil Records: Access: In person, online. Both court and visitors may perform in person searches. No search fee. Required to search: name, years to search. Civil cases indexed by defendant. Civil records on computer back to 2/14/2001; prior on books. Phone or fax searching allowed once you have an account setup with the county clerk office, contact them. Public use terminal has civil records back to 2001. PAT results show name only. Results often include address. Civil records available by subscription through ACS; contact Donna Hunt 800-800-7009 for info and registration. Historical records are not online, but access to current/pending Supreme Court civil cases is at http://iapps.courts.state.ny.us/webcivil/FCASMain
Criminal Records: Access: Phone, fax, mail, in person. Only the court performs in person searches; visitors may not. Search fee: $10.00 for 1-5 years searched per name; 6-10 years is $15.00; 11-20 years is $20.00. Required to search: name, years to search, DOB. Criminal records in books. Address requests to County Clerk. Phone or fax searching allowed once you have an account setup. Mail turnaround time 2-3 days.
General Information: No sealed, divorce or sexual abuse records released. Fee to fax out file $1.00 per page. Court makes copy: $.50 per page criminal; Civil- $1.00 per page mailed out. Self serve: No self serve criminal copier; Civil self serve- $.50 each. Certification fee: $5.00. Payee: County Clerk. Personal checks accepted. Mail requests: SASE required for mail return of any copies.

Surrogate's Court 147 N Main St, Warsaw, NY 14569; 585-786-3148; fax: 585-786-3800; 9AM-5PM. ***Probate.***
A county search of the probate court index by mail for 25-year search is $30.00 fee. A full county probate search of all years is $90.00.

Wyoming Town/Village Courts- Arcade Justice Court- 585-492-4479; Arcade Town Court- 585-492-4479; Attica Town Court- 585-591-4613; Attica Village Court- 585-591-2957; Bennington Town Court- 716-652-5585; Castile Town Court- 585-493-5875; Covington Town Court- 585-584-3565; Eagle Town Court- 585-322-7667; Gainesville Town Court- 585-493-3395; Genesee Falls Town Court- 585-468-5015; Java Town Court- 585-457-3233; Middlebury Town Court- 585-495-6300; Orangeville Town Court- 585-786-2883; Perry Town Court and Village Court- 585-237-2149; Pike Town Court- 585-493-5140; Sheldon Town Court- 585-535-0468; Silver Springs Village Court- 585-493-3395; Warsaw Town Court and Village Court- 585-786-3361; Wethersfield Town Court- 585-457-3384.

Yates County

County Clerk 417 Liberty St, #1107, Penn Yan, NY 14527; 315-536-5120; fax: 315-536-5545; 9AM-5PM; (8:30AM-4:30PM in July & Aug). ***Felony, Civil.***
www.yatescounty.org/display_page.asp?pID=78
Countywide search requests made to the County Clerk are processed in the manner described here, also see Supreme & County Court.
Civil Records: Access: In person, online. Both court and visitors may perform in person searches. Search fee: $10.00 per name. Required to search: name, years to search. Civil cases indexed by defendant, plaintiff. Civil record indices on computer back to 1/88, prior in books. Public use terminal has civil records back to 1/1988. PAT civil results show middle initial. Lookup Supreme Court civil cases at http://iapps.courts.state.ny.us/webcivil/FCASMain
Criminal Records: Access: Mail, fax, in person. Both court and visitors may perform in person searches. Search fee: $10.00 per name for 7 year search. Required to search: name, years to search. Criminal docket on books; not computerized. Mail turnaround time 2-3 days.
General Information: No divorce records outside parties involved, sealed records released. Will fax out specific case files for $.65 a page to non-toll-free number; add'l $2.00 for toll number. Court makes copy: $.65 per page, $1.30 minimum. Certification fee: $1.25 per page, $5.00 minimum includes cost of copies. Exemplification fee $10.00. Payee: Yates County Clerk. Personal checks accepted; credit cards are not.

Supreme & County Court 415 Liberty St, Penn Yan, NY 14527; 315-536-5126/5129; fax: 315-536-5190; 9AM-5PM; 8:30AM-4:30PM Summer Hours. ***Felony, Civil.***
Direct civil search requests to the County Clerk office. This court directs felony searches to OCA for a $55.00 statewide search, however, a countywide search can be made at the County Clerk office, see separate listing.

Surrogate's Court 415 Liberty St, Penn Yan, NY 14527; 315-536-5130; fax: 315-536-5190; 9AM-5PM. ***Probate.***
Hours are 8:30AM-4:30PM in July and August. A county search of the probate court index by mail for 25-year search is $30.00 fee. A full county probate search of all years is $90.00.

Yates Town/Village Courts- Barrington Town Ct- 607-243-8959; Benton Town Court- 315-536-2320; Dundee Village Court- 607-243-5551; Italy Town Court- 585-374-6194; Jerusalem Town Court- 315-595-6102; Middlesex Town Court- 585-554-3607; Milo Town Court- 315-531-8816; Penn Yan Village Court- 315-536-7243; Potter Town Court- 585-554-6758; Starkey Town Court- 607-243-5344; Torrey Town Court- 315-536-6376.

New York Recording Offices

ORGANIZATION: 62 counties, 62 recording offices. Recording officer is the County Clerk except in the counties of Bronx, Kings, New York, and Queens where the recording officer is the New York City Register. Note that Staten Island/Richmond County has a County Clerk.

The County Clerk also holds the papers for documents that have been filed through the courts, such as divorce cases. New York is in the Eastern Time Zone (EST)

REAL ESTATE RECORDS: Some counties will perform real estate searches. Certified copy fees are usually $1.00 per page, sometimes with a minimum. Certification fees are $5.00 per doc most locations. Tax records are located at the Treasurer's Office.

UCC RECORDS: Until July, 2001, New York was a dual filing state. Financing statements were filed both at the state level and with the County Clerk except for consumer goods, cooperatives, farm related and real estate related collateral which were filed only with the County Clerk. Effective July, 2001, only real estate related collateral is filed at the county, but searches may still be done on all the records prior to July, 2001. Most counties will perform UCC searches.

TAX LIEN RECORDS: Federal tax liens on personal property of businesses are filed with the Secretary of State. Other federal tax liens are filed with the County Clerk. State tax liens are filed with the County Clerk and placed on a master list - called State Tax Warrants - available at the Secretary of State's office. Federal tax liens are usually indexed with UCC records. State tax liens are usually indexed with other miscellaneous liens and judgments. Some counties include federal tax liens as part of a UCC search.

OTHER LIENS: Judgment, mechanics, welfare, hospital, matrimonial, wage assignment, lis pendens.

ONLINE ACCESS: Many counties and towns offer free internet access to assessor records and the number is growing. The New York City Register offers free access to all borough's real estate records (including Staten Island) at http://nyc.gov/html/dof/html/home/home.shtml. Search by address or legal description. A private company offers property assessment data for most New York Counties online at www.accuriz.com/index.aspx. Search financing statements and federal tax lien notices by debtor name, or secured party name, or by filing number and date free at http://appsext8.dos.state.ny.us/pls/ucc_public/web_search.main_frame.

Albany County

County Clerk, 32 N Russell Rd, Albany, NY 12206. 518-487-5120; fax-518-487-5099; 9AM-4:45PM www.albanycounty.com/clerk/

Index: All in one. Records indexed on a public use terminal back to 1980. Office personnel or visitors may perform searches. Accepts no telephone inquiries about real estate. General index search fee $5.00 per name per 2 years. UCC search fee- $25.00 per debtor. Copy fee $.65 per page; $1.30 minimum. Cert fee- $1.25 per page with minimum of $5.00. Payee- Albany County Clerk. **Online Real Estate, Deed, Mortgage records:** Access deeds and mortgages free at https://access.albanycounty.com/clerk/deedsandmortgages/. **Other phones:** Treasurer- 518-447-7070; Elections- 518-487-5060; Vital Records- 518-434-5045 (Albany City only). **Property tax/Assessing-** 32 N Russell Rd, Albany, NY 12206; 518-487-5290, assessor fax- 518-447-2503. hours- 8:30AM-4:30PM www.albanycounty.com/rptsa/ **Online access-** A private company offers property assessment data online at www.accuriz.com/index.aspx. Also search Town of Guilderland property data free at https://www.taxlookup.net.

Allegany County

County Clerk, 7 Court St; Courthouse, Belmont, NY 14813-0087. Recording, R/E & UCC phone-585-268-9270; fax-585-268-9659; 9AM-5PM (June-August 8:30AM-4PM). www.alleganyco.com

Index: All in one. Records indexed on a public use terminal back to 1992. Office will perform a UCC search but public must search other records themselves. UCC search on UCC 11 form per debtor name- $25.00. Copy fee $.65 per page, minimum $1.30 per doc. Cert fee- $5.00 per doc plus copy fee. Payee- Allegany County Clerk. **Other phones:** Treasurer- 585-268-9282; Elections- 585-268-9294; Vital Records- each town/village have their own vital records. **Property tax/Assessing-** 7 Court St, Courthouse, Belmont, NY 14813; 585-268-9381.

Bronx Borough

City Register, 1932 Arthur Ave, Bronx, NY 10457. 718-579-6825; 8:30AM-4:30PM

Index: Separate indices to search include block and lot real estate, UCCs. Records indexed on a public use terminal back to 1996. Only the public may search. Copy fee $1.00 per page. Rm 201 for copies. Cert fee- $4.00 per doc plus copy fee. Payee- NYC Dept. of Finance. **Online access to Real Estate, Deed, Lien, Judgment, UCC, Mortgage, Property, Assumed Name records:** Recording data from City Register is free at http://a836-acris.nyc.gov/scripts/docsearch.dll/index. Also, for deeper financial data back 10 years, subscribe to the NYC Dept of Finance dial-up system; fee-$250 monthly and $5.00 per item. Iinfo/signup- call Richard Reskin 718-935-6523. NYC's Dept of Finance offers daily downloads for borough-wide transactions of UCCs, Fed lien, deeds, real estate at http://nyc.gov/html/dof/html/home/home.shtml. Assumed names, court dockets at- www.bronxcountyclerksoffice.com/dynamic/user/create_profile.jsp. Free registration required. **Property tax/Assessing-** 1932 Arthur Ave, Rm #701, Bronx, NY 10457; 718-579-6879. hours- 9AM-5PM **Online access-** NYC's Dept of Finance Property Rolls free at http://nyc.gov/html/dof/html/home/home.shtml. No name searching. Also, a private company offers property assessment data online at www.uspdr.com/index.aspx.

Broome County

County Clerk, PO Box 2062, Binghamton, NY 13902-2062. 607-778-2451, R/E recording phone-607-778-2255; fax-607-778-2243; 9AM-4:45PM (Memorial Day to Labor Day-9AM-3:45PM). www.gobcclerk.com

Index: Separate indices to search include searches by name not particular documents. Records indexed on a public use terminal back to 1963. Office personnel or visitors may perform searches. General search fee $25.00 per 2 years. Office will not search real estate records. Copy fee $5.00 per UCC doc.Real estate or tax lien copy- $.65 per page. Cert fee- $5.20 per doc includes first 8 pages, add'l pages $.65 per page each. Payee- Broome County Clerk. **Online access to Real Estate, Deed, Mortgage, Real Estate, Lien, Judgment, Court Index records:** Search the clerk's indexes free at www.gobcclerk.com/cgi/Official_Search_Types.html/input. Online miscellaneous and lien records go back to 1989, deeds & mortgages go back to 1963, court records (civil and criminal) from 1985 to present. **Other phones:** Treasurer- 607-778-2161; Elections- 607-778-2172; Secretary- 607-778-2377. **Property tax/Assessing-** PO Box 1766, Binghamton, NY 13902-1766; 607-778-2169, assessor fax- 607-778-2359. hours- 8AM-5PM **Online access-** A private company offers property assessment data online at www.accuriz.com/index.aspx. Also search City of Binghampton and Towns of Chenango, Conklin, Dickinson, Fenton, Kirkwood, Maine, Union, Vestal, and Windsor property tax data free at https://www.taxlookup.net. City allows name searching; Town does not.

Cattaraugus County

County Clerk, 303 Court St, Little Valley, NY 14755. Recording, R/E & UCC phone-716-938-9111; fax-716-938-6009; 9AM-5PM. www.cattco.org

Index: Deeds, mtgs, civil actions, judgments, lis pendens, misc records, consolidated liens, fed. tax liens. Records indexed on computer. Office personnel or visitors may perform searches. Search fee $5.00 per 2 years. Office will not search real estate records. Office will not search UCC records. Real estate copy $1.00 per doc or $.50 per page whichever is more. UCC and tax lien copy fee- $5.00 per doc. Cert fee- $5.00 per doc plus copy fee. Payee- County Clerk. **Other phones:** Treasurer- 716-938-9111. **Property tax/Assessing-** 303 Court St, Little Valley, NY 14755; 716-938-9111, assessor fax- 716-938-9496. **Online-** property info on the interactive map at www.cattco.org/real_property/parcel_disclaimer.asp. To name search, select to search without the map. Also, a private company offers property assessment data at www.accuriz.com/index.aspx. Also, records on the City of Olean assessor database are free at www.cattco.org/real_property/ .

Cayuga County

County Clerk, 160 Genesee St, Auburn, NY 13021. Recording, R/E & UCC phone-315-253-1271; fax-315-253-1653; 8AM-4PM (July/August); 9AM-5PM (all other months). http://co.cayuga.ny.us/clerk/
Index: Separate indices to search include deeds, mortgages, assignments, discharges & releases. Records indexed on a public use terminal back to 1972. Office will perform a UCC search but public must search other records themselves. Search fee for UCC's- $25.00 per name. Office will not search real estate records. Copy fee $.65 per page, $1.30 minimum. Cert fee- $5.00 per doc includes copy fee up to 8 pages, then copy fee. Payee- Cayuga County Clerk. **Online Real Estate, Deed, Mortgage records:** mortgages and deeds at www.landaccess.com/proi/county.jsp?county=nycayuga. Subscription fee is $440 per year or $40 per month, $5.00 per image, plus a one time usage fee, credit cards accepted. Index goes back to 1972; images back to 1980. **Other phones:** Treasurer- 315-253-1211; Elections- 315-253-1285; Vital Records- 315-255-4100. **Property tax/Assessing**- 160 Genesee St, Auburn, NY 13021; 315-253-1270, assessor fax- 315-253-1517. hours- 9AM-5PM **Online access**- Search tax data, rolls, current sales, tax maps, final assessments free at www.cayugacounty.us/realproperty/index.htm. County-wide real estate/parcel/ property data required registration and password at http://12.177.200.161/imate/. Search property sales lists free at http://co.cayuga.ny.us/realproperty/sales/index.html.

Chautauqua County

County Clerk, PO Box 170, Mayville, NY 14757-0170. 716-753-4331; fax-716-753-4293; 9AM-5PM; Sum-8:30AM-4:30PM www.co.chautauqua.ny.us
Index: Separate indices to search include grantor/grantee. Records indexed on a public use terminal back to 1811. Only the public may search. Copy fee $1.00 per doc. $5.00 per marriage cert. Cert fee- none. Payee- Chautauqua County Clerk. **Other phones:** Treasurer- 716-661-7223. **Property tax/ Assessing**- 3 N Erie St, Courthouse, Mayville, NY 14757; 716-661-7223, assessor fax- 716-753-4394. **Online access**- Access property data free on the GIS-mapping site at www.chautauquagis.com. On the map page, click on Locate Parcel to search by name, address, etc.

Chemung County

County Clerk, PO Box 588, Elmira, NY 14902-0588. 607-737-2920; fax-607-737-2897; 8:30Am-4:30PM. www.chemungcounty.com/
Index: All in one. Records indexed on computer back to 1992. Office personnel or visitors may perform searches. Search fee $5.00 per 2 years. For UCC search $40.00. Real estate copy- $.65 per page; UCC and tax lien copy fee- $5.00 per doc. Cert fee- $5.00 per doc plus copy fee of $1.25 per page. Minimum charge $5.00. Payee- Chemung County Clerk. **Other phones:** Treasurer- 607-737-2927; Elections- 607-737-5475; Vital Records- 607-737-2018. **Property tax/Assessing**- 210 Lake St, Elmira, NY 14902; 607-737-2988. **Online access**- A private company offers property assessment data at www.accuriz.com/index.aspx. Also, search the treasurer's property tax data at http://chemung.sdgnys.com/index.aspx. Username and password is required for deeper data.

Chenango County

County Clerk, 5 Court St, Norwich, NY 13815. 607-337-1452, R/E recording phone-607-337-1450 (County Clerks Office); fax-607-337-1455; 8:30AM-5PM www.co.chenango.ny.us
No phone searches accepted. Index: All in one. Records indexed on a public use terminal back to 1990. Office personnel or visitors may perform searches. General search fee $5.00 per name per 2 years. Office will search real estate records (2 years). UCC records search includes federal tax liens if requested. UCC search per debtor name- $25.00. Separate Tax lien search- $25.00 per debtor. Real estate or tax lien copy- $.65 per page, $1.30 minimum. UCC copy fee $5.00 per doc. Cert fee- $5.00 per doc plus copy fee. Payee- Chenango County Clerk. **Other phones:** Treasurer- 607-337-1414; Elections- 607-337-1760; Vital Records- 607-337-1450. **Property tax/Assessing**- 5 Court St, Norwich, NY 13815; 607-337-1490. **Online access**- A private company offers property assessment data online at www.accuriz.com/index.aspx.

Clinton County

County Clerk, 137 Margaret St, #101; Government Ctr, Plattsburgh, NY 12901-2974. Recording, R/E & UCC phone-518-565-4700, UCC recording phone-518-565-4705; fax-518-565-4718; 8AM-5PM www.co.clinton.ny.us/Departments/CC/CCHome.htm
Index: Separate indices to search include deeds, mortgages, satisfactions, assignments. Records indexed on a public use terminal back to 1985. Office will perform a UCC search but public must search other records themselves. Search fee-$25.00 per name. Real estate copy- $.65 per page, $1.30 minimum. UCC Copy fee $5.00 per doc. Cert fee- $1.25 per page includes copy fee, $5.00 minimum. Payee- Clinton County Clerk. **Other phones:** Treasurer- 518-565-4730; Elections- 518-565-4740; Vital Records- 518-563-7702. **Property tax/Assessing**- 137 Margaret St, Real Property Office, Plattsburgh, NY 12901; 518-565-4760, assessor fax- 518-565-4616.

Columbia County

County Clerk, 560 Warren St, Hudson, NY 12534. 518-828-3339; fax-518-828-5299; 9AM-5PM www.columbiacountyny.com/
Index: All in one. Records indexed on a public use terminal back to 1973; some back to 1970. Office will perform a UCC search but public must search other records themselves. Copy fee $.65 per page, $.50 for images on computer, $.25 for photocopier. Cert fee- $5.00 per doc plus copy fee. Payee- Columbia County Clerk. Bulk data available for purchase. **Other phones:** Treasurer- 518-828-0513; Elections- 518-828-3115; Real Property Director- 518-828-7334. **Property tax/Assessing**- 518-828-7334.

Cortland County

County Clerk, 46 Greenbush St, #101, Cortland, NY 13045-3702. Recording, R/E & UCC phone-607-753-5021; fax-607-753-5378; 9AM-5PM; 8:30AM-4:30PM Summer hours. www.cortland-co.org/cc/
Index: All in one. Records indexed on a public use terminal back to 1986. Office personnel or visitors may perform searches. General index search fee $10.00 per name per 10 years; UCC search $25.00. Office will search real estate records. Will search UCC records. Copy fee $.65 per page. Cert fee- $1.25 per page plus copy fee, $5.00 minimum. Payee- Cortland County Clerk. Records are available for purchase in bulk; call Elizabeth Larkin county clerk for details. **Online Real Estate, Deed, Mortgage, Judgment, UCC, Lien, Fictitious Business Name records:** access free at http://72.43.24.100/cortland/login.aspx gives judgments and other county clerk records. Login using "public" as user name and password. **Other phones:** Treasurer- 607-753-5070; Elections- 607-753-5032; Vital Records- 607-756-6521. **Property tax/Assessing**- 60 Central Ave, Cortland, NY 13045; 607-756-3455, fax- 607-756-3492. www.cortland-co.org/Audit/index.html **Online access**- A private company offers property assessment data online at www.accuriz.com/index.aspx. Also, property data is available by $40 per month subscription at www.cortland-co.org/rpts/Imagemate.htm.

Delaware County

County Clerk, PO Box 426, Delhi, NY 13753. 607-746-2123; fax-607-746-6924; 8:30AM-5PM. www.co.delaware.ny.us/departments/clerk/clerk.htm
Index: Separate indices to search. Records indexed on a public use terminal back to 2/1/08. Office will perform a UCC search but public must search other records themselves. Real estate or tax lien copy- $.50 per page; UCC copy fee $5.00 per doc. Cert fee- $15.00 per doc plus copy fee. Payee- Delaware County Clerk. **Other phones:** Treasurer- 607-746-2121; Elections- 607-746-2315. **Property tax/Assessing**- 111 Main St, Delhi, NY 13753; 607-746-3747, assessor fax- 607-746-3742. **Online access**- A private company offers property assessment data at www.accuriz.com/index.aspx.

Dutchess County

County Clerk, 22 Market St, Poughkeepsie, NY 12601. 845-486-2120, R/E recording phone-845-486-2382, UCC recording phone-845-486-2139; fax-845-486-2138; 9AM-4:45PM www.dutchessny.gov
Index: Separate indices to search include grantor/grantee, mortgagee, judgment debtor, lis pendens, etc. Records indexed on a public use terminal back to 1986 for civil, 1997 for criminal cases, and 1989 for land records. Office will perform a UCC search but public must search other records themselves. General search fee $5.00 per 2 years. Office will search real estate records with fee. UCC search per debtor name- $25.00 per name per year. Copy fee $5.00 per doc for mail, $.65 per page for in person, $1.30 minimum. Cert fee- $6.00 per document by mail, in person-$5.00 for 1st 4 pages, $1.25 each add'l page, includes copy fee. Payee- Dutchess County Clerk. We can provide printouts of mainframe data, no images of documents. Speak to Andee at 845-486-2397. **Online access to Real Estate, Deed, Judgment records:** Subscription access to court records and recorder land data is to be available from the county in 2008. For information and registration, call Andee 845-486-2397. **Other phones:** Treasurer- 845-431-2025; Elections- 845-486-2477. **Property tax/Assessing**- 22 Market St, Poughkeepsie, NY 12601; 845-486-2140, assessor fax- 845-486-2093. **Online** - Search county tax roll at http://geoaccess.co.dutchess.ny.us/parcelaccess/. Search the Town of East Fishkill property tax roll data free at https://www.taxlookup.net.

Erie County

County Clerk, 92 Franklin St; County Hall, Buffalo, NY 14202. 716-858-8865, R/E recording phone-716-858-8785, UCC recording phone-716-858-6425; fax-716-858-6550; 9AM-5PM http://ecclerk.erie.gov
For search info, call 716-858-8785. Index: Separate old indices include manual mortgage, deed, judgment, releases, etc; newer records on computer. Records indexed on a public use terminal back to 1986 for deeds, other records back to 2/18/1994. Office personnel or visitors may perform searches. No phone searches. General index search fee $5.00 per 2 years per name. For UCC- $25.00 per name. Real estate or state tax lien copy- $1.00 per page; $5.00 per doc for UCC, Federal tax liens and court records. Cert fee- $4.00 per doc plus copy fee. Payee- Erie County Clerk. **Online Real Estate, Deed, Mortgage, UCC, Judgment records:** Access to the county clerk's database index and images is at http://ecclerk.erie.gov:9080/prod_public_view/login.jsp. Login as Guest. View index free. $5.00 fee to view full documents; a $250 initial escrow account required. **Property tax/Assessing**- 95 Franklin St, #100, Buffalo, NY 14202; 716-858-8333. **Online access**- Parcel data is free at http://erie-gis.co.erie.ny.us/website/erie_help/help.htm. To name search, click on Internet Mapping System, then "Locate property." Also, a company offers property assessments at www.accuriz.com/index.aspx. Also, a private company that sells county tax claim property, view list free at www.xspand.com/investors/realestate_sale/index.aspx.

Essex County

County Clerk, PO Box 247, Elizabethtown, NY 12932. 518-873-3601 & 873-3603, R/E recording phone-518-873-3601 or 873-3603, UCC recording phone-518-873-3601; fax-518-873-3548; 8AM-5PM www.co.essex.ny.us

Index: Separate indices to search include deeds, mortgages, APA's, assets & sats. Records indexed on a public use terminal back to early 1970s. Office personnel or visitors may perform searches. General search fee $5.00 per name. Office will do a basic search for real estate records. Will not do a title search. Office will search UCC records 5 years back only. UCC search per debtor name- $25.00. UCC search includes fed tax liens. General copy fee-$.65 per page. Cert fee- $5.00 per doc plus copy fee. Payee- Essex County Clerk. **Other phones:** Treasurer- 518-873-3310; Elections- 518-873-3474; Real Property- 518-873-3390. **Property tax/Assessing**- PO Box 217, 7551 Court St, Elizabethtown, NY 12932; 518-873-3390, assessor fax- 518-873-3400. hours- 8AM-4PM Each town has its own assessor. **Online access**- Parcel data available free at www.co.essex.ny.us/realproperty.asp. Also, a private company offers property assessment data online at www.accuriz.com/index.aspx. Also, assessor and property data available free at www.co.essex.ny.us/realproperty.asp.

Franklin County

County Clerk, PO Box 70, Malone, NY 12953. 518-481-1681; fax-518-483-9143; hours- 8AM-4PM. http://franklincony.org/content/Departments/View/4?

Index: Separate indices to search from 4/1/2000 to present. Records indexed on a public use terminal back to 1959 for deeds. Only the public may search. Copy fee $.65 per page, minimum $1.30. Include SASE for mail return. Cert fee- $1.00 per page, $5.00 minimum, includes copy fee. Exemplification fee- $10.00 plus copy fees. Payee- Franklin County Clerk. **Other phones:** Treasurer- 518-481-1516; Elections- 518-481-1662; Vital Records- 518-481-1671. **Property tax/ Assessing**- Real Property Tax Services, 355 W Main St, #251, Malone, NY 12953; 518-481-1610, assessor fax- 518-481-5995. http://franklincony.org/content/Departments/View/14? **Online access**- Access to real property and GIS/mapping for free go to http://208.125.110.170/franklinco/

Fulton County

County Clerk, PO Box 485, Johnstown, NY 12095. 518-736-5539, R/E recording phone-518-736-5555; fax-518-762-3839; 9AM-5PM.

Index: Separate indices to search include books, computer by name. Records indexed on a public use terminal back to 1983. Office personnel or visitors may perform searches. General search fee $5.00 per name. Office will not search real estate records. UCC search per debtor name- $25.00. Copy fee $5.00 per doc if mailed. $.50 a copy in person. Cert fee- $5.00 per doc plus copy fee. Payee- County Clerk. **Online access to Real Estate, Deed, UCC records:** Search recorder documents free at www.landaccess.com/sites/oh/disclaimer.php?county=ohfulton. **Other phones:** Treasurer- 518-736-5580; Elections- 518-736-5526; Vital Records- 518-736-5555. **Property tax/Assessing**- 223 W Main St, Johnstown, NY 12095; 518-736-5510.

Genesee County

County Clerk, PO Box 379, Batavia, NY 14021-0379. 585-344-2550 x2243, R/E recording phone-585-344-2550 x2242, UCC recording phone- x2243; fax-585-344-8521; 8:30AM-5PM. www.co.genesee.ny.us

Index: Separate indices to search include deeds, mortgages, misc. Records indexed on a public use terminal back to 1984 (deeds/mortgages). Office personnel or visitors may perform searches. General search fee $5.00 for 5 years per name. For UCC search-$25.00 per name. Office will not search real estate records. UCC search includes federal tax liens. Copy fee $.65 per page, $1.30 minimum. Cert fee- $5.00 minimum per doc plus copy fee. Exemplification- $15.00. Payee- Genesee County Clerk. DBA ($.20 per name) and mortgage lists (&75.00 per month) available to purchase, contact Patty at 334-2550 x2264. **Other phones:** Treasurer- 585-344-2550 x2210; Elections- 585-344-2550 x2206. **Property tax/Assessing**- 15 Main St, Batavia, NY 14020; 585-344-2550 x2218, assessor fax- 585-344-2442. **Online access**- A private company offers property assessment data online at www.accuriz.com/index.aspx.

Greene County

County Clerk, PO Box 446, Catskill, NY 12414. 518-719-3255; fax-518-719-3284; 9AM-5PM (July-Aug. 9AM-4:30PM). www.greenegovernment.com/department/clerk/index.htm

Index: Separate indices to search include land, judgments, lis pendens, civil action, UCC, Fed liens. Records indexed on a public use terminal back to 1992. Office will perform a UCC search but public must search other records themselves. Copy fee $1.00 per page or $5.00 per doc. Cert fee- $5.00 per doc plus copy fee. Payee- Greene County Clerk. **Other phones:** Treasurer- 518-719-3530; Elections- 518-719-3550. **Property tax/Assessing**- 411 Main St, 4th Fl, Catskill, NY 12414; 518-719-3525. **Online access**- Access to the Web Map for free go to http://gis.greenegovernment.com/giswebmap/. Also, access Town of Catskill GIS property data free at www.mapsonline.net/catskillny/.

Hamilton County

County Clerk, PO Box 204, Lake Pleasant, NY 12108. Recording, R/E & UCC phone-518-548-7111; fax-518-548-9740; 8:30AM-4:30PM

Index: Separate indices to search include deeds, mortgages, miscellaneous records, court orders, lis pendens, APA permits & judgments. Record index not computerized. Office will perform a UCC search but public must search other records themselves. Office will not search real estate records. UCC search request must be on form and prepaid. UCC search per debtor name- $25.00. Copy fee $5.00. Copy fee $.65 per page, minimum $1.30 per doc. Cert fee- $1.00 per page, minimum $5.00, includes copy fee. Payee- Hamilton County Clerk. **Other phones:** Treasurer- 518-548-7911; Elections- 518-548-4684. **Property tax/Assessing**- PO Box 168, Lake Pleasant, NY 12108; 518-548-5531, assessor fax- 518-548-7608. **Online access**- A private company offers property assessment data online at www.accuriz.com/index.aspx.

Herkimer County

County Clerk, 109 Mary St, #1111, Herkimer, NY 13350. 315-867-1137; fax-315-867-1349; 9AM-5PM; Summer- 8:30AM-4PM

Index: Pre-1991 records indexed by doc type; 1991 forward in global and real estate indices. Real estate records indexed on a public use terminal back to 1991. Office will perform a UCC or tax lien search but public must search other records themselves. UCC search per debtor name- $25.00. Copy fee $5.00 per UCC or tax lien per doc. Cert fee- $10.00 per exemplification plus copy fee. Payee- Herkimer County Clerk. **Other phones:** Treasurer- 315-867-1153; Elections- 315-867-1102. **Property tax/Assessing**- 108 Court St, #3200, Herkimer, NY 13350; 315-867-1153, assessor fax- 315-867-1561. **Online** - A company offers property assessment data online at www.accuriz.com/index.aspx. Also, search City of Little Falls property data free at https://www.taxlookup.net.

Jefferson County

County Clerk, 175 Arsenal St, Watertown, NY 13601-2555. Recording, R/E & UCC phone-315-785-3081; fax-315-785-5145; 9AM-5PM; 8:30AM-4PM July & August. www.co.jefferson.ny.us

Index: All in one. All judgments indexed from 10/2002, all other land records from 1/67. Office personnel or visitors may perform searches. Search fee $5.00 per 2 years per name. UCC search fee $25.00 per name. Office will search limited real estate records. Will search UCC records. Real estate $1.00 per page; UCC and tax lien copy fee $5.00. Cert fee- $4.00 per doc plus copy fee for real estate; $10.00 per doc plus copy fee for UCC/tax liens. Payee- Jefferson County Clerk. **Other phones:** Treasurer- 315-785-3055; Elections- 315-785-5119. **Property tax/Assessing**- 175 Arsenal St, Watertown, NY 13601; 315-785-3074, assessor fax- 315-785-3377. hours- 8AM-5PM **Online access**- A private company offers property assessment data online at www.accuriz.com/index.aspx. Also property assessment data offered online at www.co.jefferson.ny.us/rpstoweb.nsf/$$search.

Kings County

City Register, 210 Joralemon St, Rm 2, 1st Fl; Municipal Bldg, Brooklyn, NY 11201. 718-802-3589; fax-718-802-3745; 8:30AM-4:30PM

Index: Separate indices to search include block and lot, old paper indexes. Records indexed on a public use terminal back to 1982,. Only the public may search but office will assist. Copy fee $1.00 per page. Cert fee- $4.00 per doc plus copy fee. Payee- NYC Dept. of Finance. **Online access to Real Estate, Deed, Lien, Judgment, UCC, Mortgage records:** Recording data from the City Register free at http://a836-acris.nyc.gov/scripts/docsearch.dll/index. Also, for deeper financial data back 10 years, subscribe to the NYC Dept of Finance dial-up system; fee-$250 monthly and $5.00 per item. For info/signup, call Richard Reskin 718-935-6523. **Other phones:** Treasurer- 718-669-2746. **Property tax/Assessing**- 210 Joralemon St, Municipal Bldg, Rm 200, Brooklyn, NY 11201; 718-802-3560, assessor fax- 718-802-3953. hours- 9AM-5PM **Online** - Property assessment rolls from NYC's Dept. of Finance are free at http://nyc.gov/html/dof/html/home/home.shtml. No name searching. Also, a private company offers property assessment data online at www.accuriz.com/index.aspx.

Lewis County

County Clerk, PO Box 232, Lowville, NY 13367-0232. 315-376-5333; fax-315-376-3768; 8:30AM-4:30PM http://lewiscountyny.org/content/Departments/View/24?

Index: All in one. Records indexed on computer back to 1980. Deeds on computer back to 1800's. Office personnel or visitors may perform searches. General search fee $10.00. Office will not search real estate records. UCC search includes federal tax liens. UCC search per debtor name- $25.00. Real estate copy- $.65 per page. UCC and tax lien copy fee $5.00 per doc. Cert fee- $5.00 per doc plus copy fee. Exemplification fee- $10.00. Payee- Lewis County Clerk. **Other phones:** Treasurer- 315-376-5326; Elections- 315-376-5329. **Property tax/Assessing**- 7600 State St, Lowville, NY 13367; 315-376-5336, assessor fax- 315-376-5582. http://lewiscountyny.org/content/Assessment **Online access**- A private company offers property assessment data online at www.accuriz.com/index.aspx.

Livingston County

County Clerk, 6 Court St, Rm 201; Government Ctr, Geneseo, NY 14454-1043. 585-243-7010; fax-585-243-7928; 8:30AM-4:30PM Oct 1 to May 30; 8AM-4PM June 1 to Sept 30. www.co.livingston.state.n y.us/clerk.htm

Index: Separate indices to search include books, computer. Records indexed on a public use terminal back to 1994. Office will perform a UCC search but public must search other records themselves. UCC search per debtor name- $25.00. Copy fee $5.00 1st 4 pages. Cert fee- $5.00 per doc plus copy fee. Payee- Livingston County Clerk. **Online access to Real Estate, Deed records:** Access to recorded data at http://counties2.recordfusion.com/countyweb/login.jsp?countyname=Livingston. Username/password required or logon free at Guest. **Other phones:** Treasurer- 585-243-7050. **Property tax/Assessing**- 6

Court St, #302, Geneseo, NY 14454; 585-243-7192, assessor fax- 585-753-1192.

Madison County

County Clerk, PO Box 668, Wampsville, NY 13163. Recording, R/E & UCC phone-315-366-2261, UCC recording phone-315-366-2262; fax-315-366-2615; 9AM-4:45PM www.madisoncounty.org/
Index: All in one. Records indexed on computer back to 1966. Office personnel or visitors may perform searches. General index search fee $5.00 per name per 5 years. Copies $.65 per page, $1.30 minumum. Office will search real estate records. Will search UCC records. Cert fee- $5.00 includes copy fees. Exemplified copies- $15.00. Payee- Madison County Clerk. **Other phones:** Treasurer- 315-366-2371; Elections- 315-366-2231. **Property tax/Assessing-** County Office Bldg #4, PO Box 638, Wampsville, NY 13163; 315-366-2346, assessor fax- 315-366-2708. hours- 8AM-5PM **Online access-** A private company offers property assessment data online at www.accuriz.com/index.aspx. County tax data at www.madisoncounty.org/rpts/PROPERTYTAXINFO.htm. Search by town or village name.

Monroe County

County Clerk, 39 W Main St, Rm 101, Rochester, NY 14614. 585-753-1600, R/E recording phone-585-428-5151; fax-585-753-1624; hours - 9AM-5PM www.monroecounty.gov/clerk-index.php
Index: Separate indices to search include deeds, mortgages, judgments. Records indexed on a public use terminal back to 1982. Office personnel or visitors may perform searches. General search fee $5.00 for two years. UCC search per debtor name- $25.00. Copy fee $.65 per page. Cert fee- $5.00 1st page, $1.25 each add'l page. Payee- Monroe County Clerk. **Online Real Estate, Deed, Lien, Judgment, UCC, Voter Registration Roll records:** Access the county clerk database at www.monroe.ny.us.landata.com/. Includes mortgages, deeds, court records; free registration. Land records back to 1984. Liens, judgments, UCCs back to 5/1989. Also, access voter registration roll free at https://www.monroecounty.gov/apps/voterapp.php. DOB required to search. **Other phones:** Treasurer- 585-428-5290; Elections- 585-428-4550; Vital Records- 585-274-6141. **Property tax/Assessing-** 39 W Main St, Rochester, NY 14614; 585-428-5290, assessor fax- 585-753-1192. **Online-** Search County Real Property Portal at www.monroecounty.gov/apps/propertyapp.php. Also, a private company offers property assessment data online at www.accuriz.com/index.aspx. Also search Town of Penfield property data free at https://www.taxlookup.net.

Montgomery County

County Clerk, PO Box 1500, Fonda, NY 12068-1500. 518-853-8124, R/E recording phone-518-853-8111; 8:30AM-4PM (Summer hours- July-Aug 9AM-4PM). www.co.montgomery.ny.us
Index: Indices by instrument type. Records indexed on a public use terminal back to 1972. Office personnel or visitors may perform searches. General index search fee $5.00 per 2 years. Office will search real estate records if in writing. UCC search per debtor name- $25.00. Copy fee $1.00 per page. Cert fee- $5.00 per doc plus copy fee. Payee- Montgomery County Clerk. **Other phones:** Treasurer- 518-853-8175; Elections- 518-853-8181; Tax Service Agency- 518-853-3996. **Property tax/Assessing-** PO Box 1500, 20 Park St, County Annex Bldg, Fonda, NY 12068; see above, assessor fax- 518-853-8358. **Online access-** A private company offers property assessment data online at www.accuriz.com/index.aspx. Also, access property data via the GIS-mapping site free at www.co.montgomery.ny.us/mpv/frameset.asp. To name search, click on Search For Parcels.

Nassau County

County Clerk, 240 Old Country Rd, #105, Mineola, NY 11501. 516-571-1444; 571-2664 message; 9AM-4:45PM. www.nassaucountyny.gov/agencies/Clerk/index.html
Switchboard - 516-571-3000. Clerk's Records Dept located in basement, 516-571-3245. Research done in Rm #111. Index: Indexes arranged by doc type. Records indexed on a public use terminal back to 1992. Only the public may search. Copy fee $.65 per page, $1.30 minimum. Self serve copy- $.25 each. Cert fee- $5.00 minimum; add $1.25 each copy past 4th pg. Payee- Nassau County Clerk. **Other phones:** Treasurer- 516-571-5021. **Property tax/Assessing-** 24 Old Country Rd, 4th Fl, Mineola, NY 11501; 516-571-1500. **Online access-** Access to the county assessor tax data for free at www.nassaucountyny.gov/mynassauproperty/main.jsp. No name searching. Also, access to property reports is through a private company at www.courthousedirect.com. Fee for data.

New York County

City Register, 66 John St, Rm 202, New York, NY 10007. 212-361-7550; 8:30AM-4PM
Index: All in one. Records indexed on a public use terminal back to 1996. Only the public may search. Copy fee $5.00 per doc. Cert fee- $5.00 per doc plus copy fee. Payee- NYC Dept of Finance. **Online access to Real Estate, Deed, Lien, Judgment, UCC, Mortgage records:** Recording data from the City Register are free at http://a836-acris.nyc.gov/scripts/docsearch.dll/index. Also, for deeper financial data back 10 years, subscribe to the NYC Dept of Finance dial-up system; fee-$250 monthly and $5.00 per item. For info/signup, call Rich Reskin 718-935-6523. **Other phones:** Treasurer- 212-669-3913. **Property tax/Assessing-** 212-669-2387. **Online access-** Assessment roll searches are free at http://nycserv.nyc.gov/nycproperty/nynav/jsp/selectbbl.jsp; no name searching. Also, search assessments free at www.accuriz.com/index.aspx. Also, company sells county tax claim property, view list free at www.xspand.com/investors/realestate_sale/index.aspx.

Niagara County

County Clerk, PO Box 461, Lockport, NY 14095. 716-439-7022, R/E recording phone-716-439-7031, UCC recording phone-716-439-7307; fax-716-439-7066; 9AM-5PM (Summer 8:30AM-4:30PM). http://niagaracounty.com/
Index: Indices by instrument type. Records indexed on a public use terminal back to 1980's. Office personnel or visitors may perform searches. General search fee $5.00 per name per 2 year search. Office will search real estate records. UCC search per debtor name- $25.00. General copy fee- $1.00 per page. UCC copy fee- $5.00 per doc. Cert fee- $5.00 per doc includes copy fee if doc 5 pages or less. Payee- Niagara County Clerk. **Online access to Real Estate, Deed, Mortgage, Lien, Judgment records:** A private company offers access to recorder documents at http://72.43.24.100/. Username and password required. **Other phones:** Treasurer- 716-439-7007; Elections- 716-438-4040; Vital Records- 716-439-6676. **Property tax/Assessing-** 59 Park Ave, Lockport, NY 14094; 716-439-7077. **Online access-** Search Town of Wilson property data free at https://www.taxlookup.net but no name searching.

Oneida County

County Clerk, 800 Park Ave, Utica, NY 13501. 315-798-5792; fax-315-798-6440; hours- 8:30AM-5PM www.ocgov.net/oneidacty/gov/dept/countyclerk/clerkindex.htm
Index: All in one. Records indexed on office computer back to 1974. Office personnel or visitors may perform searches. General search fee $5.00 per name. Real estate record owner and mortgage searches available. UCC search includes federal tax liens if requested. UCC search per debtor name- $25.00. Copy fee $.65 per page; $1.30 minimum. Cert fee- $5.00 per doc plus copy fee. Payee- Oneida County Clerk. **Online access to Grantor/Grantee, Real Estate, Assumed Names records:** Access to public records for free go to www.ocgov.net/oneidacty/gov/dept/countyclerk/landrecordindex.htm . **Other phones:** Treasurer- 315-798-5750; Elections- 315-798-5763; Vital Records- 315-798-5833. **Property tax/Assessing-** 800 Park Ave, Utica, NY 13501; 315-798-5750. **Online access-** A private company offers property assessment data online at www.accuriz.com/index.aspx.

Onondaga County

County Clerk, 401 Montgomery St, Rm 200, Syracuse, NY 13202. 315-435-2226 or 2227, R/E recording phone-315-435-8250, UCC recording phone-315-435-8200; fax-315-435-3455; 8AM-5PM. www.ongov.net
Index: Separate indices to search include books, computer. Public terminals for deeds, mortgages back to 1950. Records indexed on a public use terminal. Office personnel or visitors may perform searches. Search fee $25.00 per name. Copy fee $5.00 per doc. Cert fee- $5.00 per doc plus copy fee. Payee- Onondaga County Clerk. Business Certs & Judgements available, contact Jackie Norfolk. **Other phones:** Treasurer- 315-435-2426; Elections- 315-435-3312; Vital Records- 315-435-3241. **Property tax/Assessing-** 201 E Washington St, Syracuse, NY 13202; 315-448-8280 (city), 315-435-2426 (outside city). **Online access-** property data free on the GIS-mapping page at www.maphost.com/syracuse%2Donondaga/main.asp. Click on "Query" and then "Find Tax Parcels". Access county property data free at www.ongov.net/Realproptax/taxinformation.html, includes access to City of Syracuse property data. Also, search Town of Tully tax roll free at www.taxlookup.net/tully/search_method.php.

Ontario County

County Clerk, 20 Ontario St; Ontario County Muni Bldg, Canandaigua, NY 14424. Recording, R/E & UCC phone-585-396-4200; fax-585-393-2951; 8:30AM-5PM www.co.ontario.ny.us
Index: All in one. Records indexed on a public use terminal back to 1973. Office will perform a UCC search but public must search other records themselves. Search fee-$25.00 per name for UCC's. Real estate copy- $.65 per page; $1.30 minimum UCC and tax lien copy fee $5.00 per doc. Cert fee- $5.00 per doc up to 4 pages, $1.25 each add'l page includes copy fee. Payee- Ontario County Clerk. Hard copies of monthly Deed recordings available for purchase, $.65 per page. **Other phones:** Treasurer- 585-396-4432; Elections- 585-396-4005. **Property tax/Assessing-** 20 Ontario St, Ontario County Muni Bldg, Canandaigua, NY 14424; 585-396-4382. **Online access-** A private company offers property assessment data online at www.accuriz.com/index.aspx. Also, City of Canandaigua property, assessment, and sales lists in pdf format available free via assessor link at. www.canandaiguanewyork.gov/index.asp.

Orange County

County Clerk, 255 Main St, Goshen, NY 10924. 845-291-2690, R/E recording phone-845-291-3074, UCC recording phone-845-291-3062; fax-845-291-2691; 9AM-5PM www.co.orange.ny.us/
Index: All in one. Records indexed on a public use terminal back to 1978 for land records, 1986 for judgments. Office personnel or visitors may perform searches. General search fee $2.50 per year per name. UCC search fee $25.00 per name (must have UCC form). Office will not search real estate records. Will search UCC records with UCC form. General copy fee $1.00 per page 1st 4 pages, $.50 each add'l page; UCC & Fed Tax Lien copy- $5.00 per doc. Cert fee- $1.25 per page with minimum of $5.00 plus copy fee. Payee- Orange County Clerk. **Other phones:** Treasurer- 845-291-2485; Elections- 845-291-2444. **Property tax/Assessing-** 124 Main St, #1887, Goshen, NY 10924; 845-291-2490, assessor fax- 845-

291-2499. (Appraiser - 845-291-2490) **Online access-** Real Property Tax Assessment data is free at http://propertydata.orangecountygov.com/imate/index.aspx. Registration and fees apply for fuller data. Also, search GIS-mapping site data at http://gis.orangecountygov.com/ after registration; password required. Click on GIS Products, then Online Data.

Orleans County

County Clerk, 3 S Main St; Courthouse Sq, Albion, NY 14411-1498. 585-589-5334; fax-585-589-0181; 8:30AM-4PM July-Aug; 9AM-5PM Sept-June. www.orleansny.com/default.aspx
Index: Pre-3/98 records in books. Records indexed on a public use terminal back to 3/98. Office personnel or visitors may perform searches. Search fee- $5.00 per 2 years. Office will lookup one or two real estate records only. Will search UCC records for $25.00 per name. Copy fee $1.00 per page. Cert fee- $4.00 per doc includes 4 copy pages. Payee- Orleans County Clerk. **Other phones:** Treasurer- 585-589-5353; Elections- 585-589-7004; Vital Records- In each township in the county. **Property tax/Assessing-** 3 S Main St, Courthouse Sq, Albion, NY 14411; 585-589-5400, assessor fax- 585-589-5505. **Online access-** A private company offers property assessment data online at www.accuriz.com/index.aspx.

Oswego County

County Clerk, 46 E Bridge St, Oswego, NY 13126. 315-349-8385; fax-315-349-8383; 9AM-5PM www.oswegocounty.com/clerk/index.html
Index: All in one. Records indexed on public access terminal back to 1963. Only the public may search. Copy fee $.65 per page, $1.30 minimum; UCCs and FTLs copy- $5.00 per doc. Cert fee- $5.00 per doc includes copy fee. Payee- Oswego County Clerk. **Online access to Real Estate, Deed records:** Access county clerk records 1963 to present at http://72.43.24.100/. Username and password required. You may email sales@InfoQuickSolutions.com for a free trial account or for info, or call Info Quick Solutions at 800-320-2617. **Other phones:** Treasurer- 315-349-8393; Elections- 315-349-8351; Vital Records- 315-342-8114. **Property tax/Assessing-** 46 E Bridge St, Oswego, NY 13126; 315-349-8621. **Online access-** Access tax roll data for Towns of Sandy Creek, Schroeppel, and Scriba free at www.taxlookup.net/#Oswego

Otsego County

County Clerk, PO Box 710, Cooperstown, NY 13326-0710. 607-547-4276, R/E recording phone-607-547-4277, UCC recording phone-607-547-4278; fax-607-547-7544; 9AM-5PM Sept-June; 9AM-4PM July-Aug. www.otsegocounty.com/depts/clk/
Index: All in one. Records indexed on a public use terminal back to 1997. Office personnel or visitors may perform searches. Search fee $25.00. Copy fee $5.00 per doc.Real estate record copy- $1.00 per page. Cert fee- $10.00 per doc includes copy fee. Payee- County Clerk. **Other phones:** Treasurer- 607-547-4235; Elections- 607-547-4247. **Property tax/Assessing-** 197 Main St, Cooperstown, NY 13326-0710; 607-547-4222, assessor fax- 607-547-7549. (Appraiser/Auditor- each town has own) **Online** - Search the county real property lookup free at www.otsegocounty.com/Public/Rpslookup/. A private company offers property assessment data online at www.accuriz.com/index.aspx. Search for property info on the GIS mapping site free at http://map.otsegocounty.com/Freeance/Client/PublicAccess1/index.html?appconfig=ParcelQuery.

Putnam County

County Clerk, 40 Gleneida Ave, Carmel, NY 10512. 845-225-3641, R/E recording phone-845-225-3641 x304, x305, UCC recording phone-845-225-3641 x300; fax-845-228-0231; 9AM-5PM (Summer 8AM-4PM). www.putnamcountyny.com
Application form to access public records at www.putnamcountyny.com/file/FOIL%20application.pdf. Inactive records at the Records Center and Micrographic Bureau at 69 Marvin Ave. Index: All in one. Records indexed on a public use terminal back to 1976. Office personnel or visitors may perform searches. General search fee $5.00 per 2 years. UCC search fee-$25.00 per UCC. Office will search real estate records. Will search UCC records. Copy fee $1.00 per page. Cert fee- $4.00 per doc plus copy fee. Payee- Putnam County Clerk. **Online access to Real Estate, Deed, UCC, Lien records:** Recorder records are accessible by subscription through a private online service at www.landaccess.com. Registration is required; pay per use or monthly plans available. **Other phones:** Treasurer- 845-225-3641 x321; Elections- 845-278-6970. **Property tax/Assessing-** 40 Gleneida Ave, Carmel, NY 10512; 845-225-3641 x310, assessor fax- 845-228-4030.

Queens Borough

City Register, 144-06 94th Ave, 1st Fl, Jamaica, NY 11435. 718-298-7200; 718-298-7000 message; fax-718-298-7153; 8:30AM-4:30PM www.queensbp.org/
Index: Separate indices to search include block and lot real estate, UCCs. Records indexed on a public use terminal back to 1966. Only the public may search. Copy fee $1.00 per page. A self serve copier may be available and working; fee not known. Cert fee- $4.00 per doc plus copy fee. Payee- New York City Department of Finance. **Online access to Real Estate, Deed, Lien, Judgment, UCC, Mortgage records:** Recording data from the City Register are free at www.nyc.gov/html/dof/html/jump/acris.shtml. Also, for deeper financial data back 10 years, subscribe to the NYC Dept of Finance dial-up system; fee-$250 monthly and $5.00 per item. For info/signup, call Richard Reskin 718-935-6523. **Property tax/Assessing-** 144-06 94th Ave, 3rd Fl, Jamaica, NY 11435; 718-298-7099, assessor fax- 718-298-7285. hours- 8AM-5PM; doors close at 4:30 Public access terminal at City Registrar ofc. Taxpayer Assistance Hotline- 718-935-6000. **Online access-** Property assessment rolls from NYC's Dept. of Finance are free at http://nyc.gov/html/dof/html/home/home.shtml. No name searching.

Rensselaer County

County Clerk, 105 3rd St; Troy, NY 12180. 518-270-4080; fax-518-271-7998; 8:30-5PM; 7PM on Th.. www.rensco.com/departments_countyclerk.asp
Index: All in one. Records indexed on a public use terminal back to 1995. Office will perform a UCC search but public must search other records themselves. Office will search deeds and mortgages with name and year. UCC search per debtor name-$40.00. General copy fee $1.00 per page; UCC copy-$5.00 per doc. Cert fee- $4.00 per doc plus copy fee. Payee- Rensselaer County Clerk. **Online access to Real Estate, Deed, Lien records:** Search real estate deeds and liens at www.nylandrecords.com. Click on Rensselaer. Registration required. Commercial users can subscribe for $25.00 per month and $.25 per search; Personal users can purchase documents for $5.00 each, no monthly fee. **Other phones:** Treasurer- 518-270-2751. **Property tax/Assessing-** 1600 7th Ave, Troy, NY 12180; 518-270-2755.

Richmond County

County Clerk, 130 Stuyvesant Pl, Staten Island, NY 10301. 718-390-5386, R/E recording phone-718-390-5387, UCC phone-718-390-5386; 9AM-5PM
Index: All in one. Records indexed on a public use terminal back to 1986 for real estate, UCCs to 1999. Office personnel or visitors may perform searches. UCC search per debtor name- $25.00. Copy fee $5.00 per doc. Cert fee- $5.00 per doc plus copy fee. Payee- Richmond County Clerk. **Online access to Real Estate, Deed, Lien, Judgment, UCC, Mortgage records:** Recording data from the City Register are free at http://a836-acris.nyc.gov/scripts/docsearch.dll/index. Also, for deeper financial data back 10 years, subscribe to the NYC Dept of Finance dial-up system; fee-$250 monthly and $5.00 per item. For info/signup, call Richard Reskin 718-935-6523. **Property tax/Assessing-** 350 St Marks Pl, Staten Island, NY 10301; 718-815-8511. **Online access-** Property assessment rolls from NYC's Dept. of Finance are free at http://nycserv.nyc.gov/nycproperty/nynav/jsp/selectbbl.jsp. No name searching.

Rockland County

County Clerk, 1 S Main St, #100, New City, NY 10956. 845-638-5070, R/E recording phone-845-638-5069, UCC recording phone-845-708-7180; fax-845-638-5647; 7AM-6PM www.rocklandcountyclerk.com
Index: All in one. Records indexed on a public use terminal back to 1932. Office personnel or visitors may perform searches. Search fee $5.00 per name per 10 years. Office will only perform simple real estate searches. Copy fee $1.25 per page, $5.00 minimum. Cert fee- $5.00 per doc minimum includes copy fee. Exemplification- $15.00. Payee- Rockland County Clerk. **Online access to Real Estate, Deed, Lien, Judgment, Court records:** Access is the county clerk's records index is free at www.rocklandcountyclerk.com/court_records.html. Includes criminal records back to 1982, civil judgments, real estate records, tax warrants. View images back to 6/96, and more are being added. Call Paul Pipearto at 845-638-5221 for more info. **Other phones:** Elections- 845-638-5712. **Property tax/Assessing-** 845-638-5131. **Online access-** A private company offers property assessment data online at www.accuriz.com/index.aspx.

Saratoga County

County Clerk, 40 McMaster St, Ballston Spa, NY 12020. 518-885-2213 ext 4412, R/E recording phone-518-885-2219; fax-518-884-4726; hours - 8AM-5PM www.saratogacountyny.gov/departments.asp?did=144
Index: Separate indices to search. Records indexed on a public use terminal back to 12/1987. Office personnel or visitors may perform searches. General search fee $5.00 per 2 years. Real Estate searches can only e requested mail or in person, but no title searches. Will search UCC records not yet terminated. UCC search per debtor name- $25.00 copies includes. Real estate copy fee $1.25 per page; UCC and tax lien copy fee $5.00. Cert fee- $5.00 includes 4 pages; $1.25 each add'l page. Exemplification of judgment-$15.00 each. Payee- Saratoga County Clerk. **Other phones:** Treasurer- 518-885-4724; Elections- 518-885-2249. **Property tax/Assessing-** Real Property Tax Service Agency, 35 W High St, Ballston Spa, NY 12020; 518)885-2219, assessor fax- 518)884-4744. 9AM-5PM www.saratogacountyny.gov/departments.asp?did=267 **Online access-** A private company offers property assessment data online at www.accuriz.com/index.aspx. Also, access the assessment database free at www.saratogacountyny.gov/subpage.asp?pageid=234

Schenectady County

County Clerk, 620 State St, Schenectady, NY 12305-2114. 518-388-4220; fax-518-388-4224; 9AM-4PM www.schenectadycountyclerk.com
Index: Separate indices to search include name, date. Records indexed on a public use terminal back to 1980. Office personnel or visitors may perform searches. General search fee $7.00 per name. UCC search per debtor name- $25.00 + $5.00 per doc. Copy fee $1.00 per page. Cert fee- $5.00 per doc plus copy fee. Payee- Schenectady County Clerk. **Online access to Real Estate, Deed, Mortgage, Lien, UCC records:** Access county land records back to 1996 free at http://landrecords.schenectadycounty.com. Also, access county clerk court and land indexes via www.landex.com/webstore/jsp/cart/DocumentSearch.jsp. Full access to records is by subscription at www.landex.com/remote/. The land records index goes back to 1984; courts indexes back to 1988. Images go back to 12/1999. **Other phones:** Treasurer- 518-388-4262. **Property tax/Assessing-** 620 State St, 3rd Fl, Schenectady, NY 12305-2114; 518-388-4246.

Schoharie County

County Clerk, PO Box 549, Schoharie, NY 12157. Recording, R/E & UCC phone-518-295-8316; fax-518-295-8338; 8:30AM-5PM M T TH F; 8:30AM-7PM Wed. www.schohariecountyny.gov/CountyWebSite/index.jsp

Index: Indices prior to 1/1/1994 in books. Records indexed on a public use terminal back to 1989, some indexes go back farther. Office personnel or visitors may perform searches. General index search fee $5.00 per name, $25.00 for a UCC search. Copy fee $.50 per page except maps. Cert fee- $4.00 per doc plus copy fee. Payee- Schoharie County Clerk. **Other phones:** Treasurer- 518-295-8386; Elections- 518-295-8326. **Property tax/Assessing**- PO Box 308, Real Property Tax Office, Schoharie, NY 12157; 518-295-8349, assessor fax- 518-295-8486. 8:30-5PM www.schohariecounty-ny.gov/CountyWebSite/RealProperty/realpropertyhome.jsp **Online access**- A private company offers property assessment data online at www.accuriz.com/index.aspx. Also, search property tax data free at www.schohariecounty-ny.gov/CountyWebSite/search.jsp.

Schuyler County

County Clerk, 105 Ninth St, Unit 8; County Office Bldg, Watkins Glen, NY 14891. phone-607-535-8133; 9AM-5PM www.schuylercounty.us/

Index: Separate indices to search include grantor/grantee, mortgage, assumed names, misc., maps. Record index not computerized. Only the public may search. Will search UCC records. Real estate or tax lien copy- $.65 per pae; UCC copy fee $5.00 per doc. Cert fee- $5.00 per doc includes copy fee; if over 4 pages, add $1.25 per add'l page. Payee- Schuyler County Clerk. **Other phones:** Treasurer- 607-535-8181. **Property tax/Assessing**- 105 9th St, Watkins Glen, NY 14891; 607-535-8118, assessor fax- 607-535-8124. **Online access**- A private company offers property assessment data online at www.accuriz.com/index.aspx.

Seneca County

County Clerk, 1 DiPronio Dr, Waterloo, NY 13165. 315-539-1771, R/E recording phone-315-539-1770, UCC recording phone-315-539-1772; fax-315-539-3789; 8:45AM-4:45PM. www.co.seneca.ny.us

Index: All in one. Records indexed on a public use terminal back to 1967. Office will perform a UCC and tax lien search but public must search other records themselves. Search fee-$20.00 per name. Office will not search real estate records. Copy fee $5.00 per doc. Cert fee- $5.00 per doc includes copy fee. Payee- Seneca County Clerk. **Other phones:** Treasurer- 315-539-1738; Elections- 315-539-1762. **Property tax/Assessing**- 1 DiPronio Dr, Waterloo, NY 13165; 315-539-1720. (Appraiser/Auditor- 315-539-1718) **Online access**- A private company offers property assessment data online at www.accuriz.com/index.aspx.

St. Lawrence County

County Clerk, 48 Court St, Canton, NY 13617-1198. Recording, R/E & UCC phone-315-379-2237; fax-315-379-2302; 8:30AM-4:30PM M,T,W,F; 8:30AM-7PM Th. www.co.st-lawrence.ny.us/CoTOC2.htm

Index: All in one. Records indexed on a public use terminal back to 1972. Office personnel or visitors may perform searches. General search fee $5.00 per name. UCCs- $25.00 each. Office may not search real estate records. Real estate or tax lien copy- $.65 per page; UCC copy $5.00 per doc. Cert fee- $5.00 per doc plus copy fee. Payee- St. Lawrence County Clerk. **Online access to Real Estate, Deed, Lien, Mortgage, Plat records:** Access real estate data after registration at http://72.43.24.100/ . **Other phones:** Treasurer- 315-379-2234; Elections- 315-379-2202. **Property tax/Assessing**- 48 Court St, #1, Canton, NY 13617; 315-379-2272, assessor fax- 315-379-0056. (Appraiser/Auditor- 315-379-2272) Also, search treasurer's delinquent tax records free at www.taxlookup.net/STLAWRENCE/. www.co.st-lawrence.ny.us/Real_Property/SLCRP.htm **Online access**- County assessor rolls available at www.co.st-lawrence.ny.us/Real_Property/SLCRP.htm. Search Towns of Brasher, Canton, Clare, Clifton, Colton, DeKalb, Depeyster, Edwards, Fine, Fowler, Gouverneur, Hammond, Hermon, Hopkinton, Lawrence, Lisbon, Louisville,. Macomb, Madrid, Massena, Morristown, Norfolk, Oswegatchie, Parishville, Piercefield, Pierrepont, Pitcairn, Potsdam, Rossie, Russell, Stockholm, Waddington property data free at https://www.taxlookup.net. 14 Villages also available.

Steuben County

County Clerk, 3 E Pulteney Sq; County Office Bldg, Bath, NY 14810. 607-776-9631 x3210, R/E recording phone-607-776-9631 x3203; fax-607-664-2157; 8:30AM-5PM www.steubencony.org

Index: Separate indices to search include deeds, judgments. Records indexed on a public use terminal back to 1986 for deeds, judgments to 1988. Office personnel or visitors may perform searches. Search fee $20.00 per name. Office will search real estate records. Real estate or tax lien copy- $.65 per page; UCC copy $5.00 per doc. Cert fee- $5.00 per doc plus copy fee. Payee- Steuben County Clerk. **Other phones:** Treasurer- 607-776-9631 x2488. **Property tax/Assessing**- 3 E Pulteney Sq, Bath, NY 14810; 607-776-9631x2373, assessor fax- 607-664-2168. **Online access**- Search Town of Erwin Real Property Assessment Roll free online at www.erwinny.org/ertxsrch.htm.

Suffolk County

County Clerk, 310 Center Dr, Riverhead, NY 11901-3392. 631-852-2000, R/E recording phone-631-852-2043, UCC phone-631-852-2038; fax-631-852-2004; 9AM-5PM www.suffolkcountyny.gov/departments/countyclerk.aspx

Index: Separate indices to search include real estate, judgments. Records indexed on public use terminal back to 1996 for real estate, 2000 for judgments. Office will perform a UCC search but public must search other records themselves. UCC search per debtor name- $25.00. Copy fee $.65 page, $1.30 minimum UCC copy fee $5.00 per doc. have copies made at the Print Station. Cert fee- $5.00 per doc real estate; UCC- $10.00 per doc includes copy fee. Payee- Suffolk County Clerk. **Online access to Real Estate, Grantor/Grantee, Deed, Mortgage, Lien, Judgment, Corporation, Business Name records:** Access county land records, business names, and limited civil court records free at www.co.suffolk.ny.us/scco/web/. Land records is index only. Search county corporation database free at http://clerk.co.suffolk.ny.us/buscerts/corpsearch.aspx. **Other phones:** Treasurer- 631-852-1500. **Property tax/Assessing**- 300 Center Dr, Riverhead, NY 11901; 631-852-1550, assessor fax- 631-852-1566. www.suffolkcountyny.gov/departments/tax.aspx **Online access**- County GIS-mapping site will have property data available at http://gis.co.suffolk.ny.us/.

Sullivan County

County Clerk, PO Box 5012, Monticello, NY 12701. 845-794-3000 x3150, R/E recording phone-x5020; fax-none; 9AM-5PM http://co.sullivan.ny.us/

Index: All in one. Records indexed on a public use terminal back to 1990. Office will perform a UCC search but public must search other records themselves. Search fee $5.00. UCC search $25.00. Office will not search real estate records. Tax liens not included in UCC search. Copy fee $1.00 per doc. Cert fee- $5.20 per doc plus copy fee. Payee- Sullivan County Clerk. **Other phones:** Treasurer- x5014; Elections- x5024. **Property tax/Assessing**- 845-794-3000 x5014. **Online access**- A private company offers property assessment data online at www.accuriz.com/index.aspx. Also search Towns of Bethel, Callicoon, Cocheeton, Delaware, Fallsburg, Fremont, Forestburgh, Highland, Liberty, Lumberland, Mamakating,. Neversink, Rockland, Thompson and Tusten property data free at https://www.taxlookup.net. Also includes Villages of Bloomingburg and Liberty.

Tioga County

County Clerk, PO Box 307, Owego, NY 13827. Recording, R/E & UCC phone-607-687-8660; fax-607-687-8686; 9AM-5PM. www.tiogacountyny.com/

Index: All in one. Records indexed on a public use terminal back to 9/03. Only the public may search. Office copy fee $5.00 per doc, include SASE. Self serve copy- $.50 per page. Cert fee- $5.00 per doc plus SASE. Payee- Tioga County Clerk. **Other phones:** Treasurer- 607-687-8670; Elections- 607-687-8261; Real Property Tax- 607-687-8661. **Property tax/Assessing**- 16 Court St, Owego, NY 13827; 607-687-8661, assessor fax- 607-223-7017. **Online**- Search Town of Owego property data free at https://www.taxlookup.net.

Tompkins County

County Clerk, 320 N Tioga St; Main Courthouse, Ithaca, NY 14850-4284. Recording, R/E & UCC phone-607-274-5431; fax-607-274-5445; 8:30AM-5PM www.tompkins-co.org

Index: All in one. Records indexed on a public use terminal back to 1968. Office personnel or visitors may perform searches. General search fee $5.00 per name per 2 years. Office will not search real estate records. UCC search includes federal tax liens. UCC search per debtor name- $25.00. Real estate record copy- $.65 per page $1.35 minimum. Cert fee- $5.00 per doc plus copy fee. Payee- Tompkins County Clerk. Bulk data available for purchase, call Maureen for details. **Other phones:** Treasurer- 607-274-5545; Elections- 607-274-5522; Vital Records- 607-274-6642. **Property tax/Assessing**- 128 E Buffalo St, Ithaca, Ny 14850; 607-274-5517. **Online access**- Access to property records on ImageMate system at www.tompkins-co.org/assessment/online.html has 2 levels: basic free and a registration/password fee-based full system. Free version has no name searching. Fee service is $20 monthly or $200 per year. For info or registration for the latter, email assessment@tompkins-co.org. Also, a private company offers property assessment data online at www.uspdr.com/consumer/ownersearch.asp.

Ulster County

County Clerk, PO Box 1800, Kingston, NY 12402-0800. 845-340-3288; fax-845-340-3299; 9AM-4:45PM www.co.ulster.ny.us

Index: All in one. Records indexed on a public use terminal back to 1984. Office personnel or visitors may perform searches. General index search fee $5.00 per 2 years. Real estate owner, mortgage, and property transfer searches available. Tax liens not included in UCC search. UCC search per debtor name- $25.00. Copy fee: real estate $.65 per page; UCC and tax lien copy fee $5.00 per doc. Cert fee- $5.00 per doc plus copy fee. Payee- Ulster County Clerk. **Online access to Real Estate, Deed, Lien, Mortgage, Voter Registration records:** Access to county online records requires a $33.33 (under 25 transactions) or $44.55 monthly fee; 12 month agreement required. Land Records date back to 1984. Includes county court records back to 7/1987. Lending agency data available. For info, contact Valerie Harris at 845-334-5367. **Other phones:** Treasurer- 845-340-3431; Elections- 845-340-5470. **Property tax/Assessing**- 244 Fair St, Kingston, NY 12401; 845-340-3490, assessor fax- 845-340-3499. **Online access**- A private company offers property assessment data at www.accuriz.com/index.aspx.

Warren County

County Clerk, 1340 State Rte 9; Municipal Ctr, Lake George, NY 12845. 518-761-6426, R/E recording phone-518-761-6464; fax-518-761-6551; 9AM-5PM www.co.warren.ny.us
Index: Separate indices to search before 5/10/2006. Records indexed on a public use terminal back to 1989. Office personnel or visitors may perform searches. General search fee $5.00 per name. Office will not search real estate records. UCC search per debtor name- $25.00. General copy fee $1.25 per page. Cert fee- $5.00 per doc up to 4 pages; add $1.25 each add'l, includes copy fee. Payee- Warren County Clerk. **Other phones:** Treasurer- 518-761-6375. **Property tax/Assessing**- 518-761-6464. **Online access**- A private company offers property assessment data online at www.accuriz.com/index.aspx.

Washington County

County Clerk, 383 Broadway, Bldg A, Fort Edward, NY 12828. Recording, R/E & UCC phone-518-746-2170, UCC phone-518-746-2176; fax-518-746-2177; 8:30AM-4:30PM www.co.washington.ny.us
Index: All in one. Records indexed on a public use terminal back to 3/00. Records back to 6/63 not verified. Office will perform a UCC search but public must search other records themselves. Search fee $25.00 per name. Copy fee $5.00 per doc. Cert fee- $1.00 per page includes copy fee. Payee- Washington County Clerk. **Other phones:** Treasurer- 518-746-2220; Elections- 518-746-2180. **Property tax/Assessing**- 518-746-2130 (Real Property Tax).

Wayne County

County Clerk, PO Box 608, Lyons, NY 14489-0608. Recording, R/E & UCC phone-315-946-7470; fax-315-946-5978; 9AM-5PM. www.co.wayne.ny.us
Index: All in one. Records indexed on a public use terminal back to 1979-criminal, back to 1985-civil, back to 1981-deeds, back to 1983-mortgages. Office personnel or visitors may perform searches. Search fee $5.00 per name; UCC information request- $25.00. Office will not search real estate records. Will search UCC records. General copy fee $.65 per page, minimum $1.30. For UCC's-$5.00 per page. Cert fee- $1.25 per page; $5.00 minimum per doc plus copy fee. Payee- Wayne County Clerk. **Other phones:** Treasurer- 315-946-7443; Elections- 315-946-7400. **Property tax/Assessing**- 16 William St, Lyons, NY 14489; 315-946-5916, assessor fax- 315-946-5930. **Online access**- Access tax property data free at www.co.wayne.ny.us/TaxSearch/. Also, search the real property tax data free at www.co.wayne.ny.us/RPT-TaxSearch/default.aspx

Westchester County

County Clerk, 110 Dr Martin Luther King Jr Blvd, White Plains, NY 10601. 914-995-3098, R/E recording phone-914-995-4030; fax-914-995-3172; 8AM-5:45PM. www.westchesterclerk.com/
Index: Separate indices to search. All records indexed on a public use terminal. Office personnel or visitors may perform searches. Search fee $25.00 per name. Office will not search real estate records. Copy fee $5.00 per doc. Cert fee- $10.00 per doc plus copy fee. Payee- Westchester County Clerk. **Online access to Real Estate, Deed, Land, Fictitious Name, Judgment, Lien, UCC records:** Access to the clerk's land record database is free at http://ccpv.westchesterclerk.com/WCCLogin.asp. There is also an advanced search that features images; registration is required. Data also includes corporations, foreclosures, divorces, civil courts. **Property tax/Assessing**- 110 Dr Martin Luther King Jr Blvd, #222, White Plains, NY 10601; 914-995-3080, assessor fax- 914-995-4030. **Online access**- Access Sleepy Hollow Village tax roll data free at www.taxlookup.net/ and click on Westchester County; no name searching.

Wyoming County

County Clerk, 143 N Main St, #104, Warsaw, NY 14569. Recording, R/E & UCC phone-585-786-8810; fax-585-786-3703; 9AM-5PM www.wyomingco.net
Index: All in one. Records indexed on a public use terminal back to 1997 for real estate, 1001 for judgments. Office personnel or visitors may perform searches. Search fee-$25.00 per name. Real estate or tax lien copy- $.50 per page; UCC copy fee $5.00 per doc. Cert fee- $5.00 per doc. Payee- Wyoming County Clerk. **Online access to Real Estate, Deed, Lien, Judgment records:** Recorder index is accessible free through a private online service at http://www2.landaccess.com/cgibin/homepage?County=8008. This is a subscription service, fees and registration may be required. **Other phones:** Treasurer- 585-786-8812; Elections- 585-786-8931; Records Center -585-493-3484. **Property tax/Assessing**- 585-786-8828, assessor fax- 585-786-8827. **Online access**- A private company offers property assessment data online at www.accuriz.com/index.aspx.

Yates County

County Clerk, 417 Liberty St, #1107, Penn Yan, NY 14527. Recording, R/E & UCC phone-315-536-5120; fax-315-536-5545; 9AM-5PM Sept-June; 8:30AM-4:30PM July-August. www.yatescounty.org
Index: Separate indices to search include land records (deed, mortgage, etc maintained in one index on computer); books separate index, miscellaneous, real estate transfer records all in separate indexes. Records indexed on a public use terminal back to 1988. Office will perform a UCC search but public must search other records themselves. UCC search per debtor name- $40.00. Real estate record copy- $.65 per page, minimum $1.30. UCC copy- $5.00 per doc. Cert fee- $1.25 per page, $5.00 minimum, plus copy fees ($.65 per page). Exemplified copies- $10.00 each. Payee- Yates County Clerk. **Other phones:** Treasurer- 315-536-5192; Elections- 315-536-5135. **Property tax/Assessing**- 417 Liberty St, #1093, Penn Yan, NY 14527; 315-536-5165, assessor fax- 315-531-3209. **Online** - A company offers property assessment data online at www.accuriz.com/index.aspx.

New York County Locator

You will usually be able to find the city name in the City/County Cross Reference below. In that case, it is a simple matter to determine the county from the cross reference. However, only the official US Postal Service city names are included in this index. There are an additional 40,000 place names that people use in their addresses. Therefore, we have also included a ZIP/City Cross Reference immediately following the City/County Cross Reference.

If you know the ZIP Code but the city name does not appear in the City/County Cross Reference index, look up the ZIP Code in the ZIP/City Cross Reference, find the city name, then look up the city name in the City/County Cross Reference. For example, you want to know the county for an address of Menands, NY 12204. There is no "Menands" in the City/County Cross Reference. The ZIP/City Cross Reference shows that ZIP Codes 12201-12288 are for the city of Albany. Looking back in the City/County Cross Reference, Albany is in Albany County.

New York City/County Cross Reference

ACCORD Ulster
ACRA Greene
ADAMS Jefferson
ADAMS BASIN Monroe
ADAMS CENTER Jefferson
ADDISON Steuben
ADIRONDACK Warren
AFTON (13730) Chenango(93), Broome(6)
AKRON (14001) Erie(92), Niagara(3), Genesee(3)
ALABAMA Genesee
ALBANY Albany
ALBERTSON Nassau
ALBION Orleans
ALCOVE Albany
ALDEN (14004) Erie(92), Wyoming(5), Genesee(2)
ALDER CREEK Oneida
ALEXANDER Genesee
ALEXANDRIA BAY Jefferson
ALFRED Allegany
ALFRED STATION (14803) Allegany(89), Steuben(10)
ALLEGANY Cattaraugus
ALLENTOWN Allegany
ALMA Allegany
ALMOND Allegany
ALPINE Schuyler
ALPLAUS Schenectady
ALTAMONT Albany
ALTMAR Oswego
ALTON Wayne
ALTONA Clinton
AMAGANSETT Suffolk
AMAWALK Westchester
AMENIA Dutchess
AMITYVILLE Suffolk
AMSTERDAM (12010) Montgomery(95), Schenectady(3), Fulton(1)
ANCRAM Columbia
ANCRAMDALE Columbia
ANDES Delaware
ANDOVER (14806) Allegany(83), Steuben(16)
ANGELICA Allegany
ANGOLA Erie
ANNANDALE ON HUDSON Dutchess
ANTWERP Jefferson
APALACHIN Tioga
APPLETON Niagara
APULIA STATION Onondaga
AQUEBOGUE Suffolk
ARCADE (14009) Wyoming(91), Cattaraugus(8)
ARDEN Orange
ARDSLEY Westchester
ARDSLEY ON HUDSON Westchester
ARGYLE Washington
ARKPORT (14807) Steuben(79), Allegany(20)
ARKVILLE (12406) Delaware(93), Ulster(6)
ARMONK Westchester
ASHLAND Greene
ASHVILLE Chautauqua
ATHENS Greene
ATHOL Warren
ATHOL SPRINGS Erie
ATLANTA Steuben
ATLANTIC BEACH Nassau
ATTICA (14011) Wyoming(91), Genesee(8)
AU SABLE FORKS (12912) Clinton(98), Essex(1)
AUBURN Cayuga
AURIESVILLE Montgomery
AURORA Cayuga
AUSTERLITZ Columbia
AVA Oneida
AVERILL PARK Rensselaer
AVOCA Steuben
AVON Livingston
BABYLON Suffolk
BAINBRIDGE (13733) Chenango(98), Delaware(1)
BAKERS MILLS Warren
BALDWIN Nassau
BALDWIN PLACE (10505) Westchester(83), Putnam(16)
BALDWINSVILLE Onondaga
BALLSTON LAKE Saratoga
BALLSTON SPA Saratoga
BALMAT St. Lawrence
BANGALL Dutchess
BANGOR Franklin
BARKER (14012) Niagara(95), Orleans(4)
BARNEVELD Oneida
BARRYTOWN Dutchess
BARRYVILLE Sullivan
BARTON Tioga
BASOM (14013) Genesee(98), Erie(1)
BATAVIA Genesee
BATH Steuben
BAY SHORE Suffolk
BAYPORT Suffolk
BAYSIDE Queens
BAYVILLE Nassau
BEACON Dutchess
BEAR MOUNTAIN Rockland
BEARSVILLE Ulster
BEAVER DAMS (14812) Schuyler(46), Chemung(30), Steuben(22)
BEAVER FALLS Lewis
BEDFORD Westchester
BEDFORD HILLS Westchester
BELFAST Allegany
BELLEVILLE Jefferson
BELLMORE Nassau
BELLONA Yates
BELLPORT Suffolk
BELLVALE Orange
BELMONT Allegany
BEMUS POINT Chautauqua
BERGEN (14416) Genesee(89), Monroe(9)
BERKSHIRE (13736) Tioga(94), Broome(4)
BERLIN Rensselaer
BERNE Albany
BERNHARDS BAY Oswego
BETHEL Sullivan
BETHPAGE Nassau
BIBLE SCHOOL PARK Broome
BIG FLATS (14814) Chemung(85), Steuben(14)
BIG INDIAN Ulster
BILLINGS Dutchess
BINGHAMTON Broome
BLACK CREEK Allegany
BLACK RIVER Jefferson
BLAUVELT Rockland
BLISS (14024) Wyoming(92), Allegany(7)
BLODGETT MILLS Cortland
BLOOMFIELD Ontario
BLOOMING GROVE Orange
BLOOMINGBURG (12721) Sullivan(93), Orange(6)
BLOOMINGDALE Essex
BLOOMINGTON Ulster
BLOOMVILLE Delaware
BLOSSVALE Oneida
BLUE MOUNTAIN LAKE Hamilton
BLUE POINT Suffolk
BOHEMIA Suffolk
BOICEVILLE Ulster
BOLIVAR Allegany
BOLTON LANDING Warren
BOMBAY Franklin
BOONVILLE Oneida
BOSTON Erie
BOUCKVILLE Madison
BOUQUET Essex
BOVINA CENTER Delaware
BOWMANSVILLE Erie
BRADFORD (14815) Schuyler(65), Steuben(34)
BRAINARD Rensselaer
BRAINARDSVILLE Franklin
BRANCHPORT (14418) Yates(90), Steuben(9)
BRANT Erie
BRANT LAKE Warren
BRANTINGHAM Lewis
BRASHER FALLS St. Lawrence
BREESPORT Chemung
BRENTWOOD Suffolk
BREWERTON Onondaga
BREWSTER Putnam
BRIARCLIFF MANOR Westchester
BRIDGEHAMPTON Suffolk
BRIDGEPORT (13030) Madison(56), Onondaga(43)
BRIDGEWATER Oneida
BRIER HILL St. Lawrence
BRIGHTWATERS Suffolk
BROADALBIN (12025) Fulton(84), Saratoga(15)
BROCKPORT Monroe
BROCTON Chautauqua
BRONX Bronx
BRONX New York
BRONXVILLE Westchester
BROOKFIELD Madison
BROOKHAVEN Suffolk
BROOKLYN Kings
BROOKTONDALE (14817) Tompkins(94), Tioga(5)
BROOKVIEW Rensselaer
BROWNVILLE Jefferson
BRUSHTON Franklin
BUCHANAN Westchester
BUFFALO Erie
BULLVILLE Orange
BURDETT Schuyler
BURKE Franklin
BURLINGHAM Sullivan
BURLINGTON FLATS Otsego
BURNT HILLS (12027) Saratoga(83), Schenectady(16)
BURT Niagara
BUSKIRK Rensselaer
BYRON (14422) Genesee(97), Orleans(2)
CADYVILLE Clinton
CAIRO Greene
CALCIUM Jefferson
CALEDONIA (14423) Livingston(98), Monroe(1)
CALLICOON Sullivan
CALLICOON CENTER Sullivan
CALVERTON Suffolk
CAMBRIA HEIGHTS Queens
CAMDEN Oneida
CAMERON Steuben
CAMERON MILLS Steuben
CAMILLUS Onondaga
CAMPBELL Steuben
CAMPBELL HALL Orange
CANAAN Columbia
CANAJOHARIE Montgomery
CANANDAIGUA Ontario
CANASERAGA (14822) Allegany(88), Livingston(11)
CANASTOTA Madison
CANDOR Tioga
CANEADEA Allegany
CANISTEO Steuben
CANTON St. Lawrence
CAPE VINCENT Jefferson
CARLE PLACE Nassau
CARLISLE Schoharie
CARMEL Putnam
CAROGA LAKE Fulton
CARTHAGE (13619) Lewis(97), St. Lawrence(2)
CASSADAGA Chautauqua
CASSVILLE Oneida
CASTILE Wyoming
CASTLE CREEK Broome
CASTLE POINT Dutchess
CASTLETON ON HUDSON Rensselaer
CASTORLAND Lewis
CATO (13033) Cayuga(96), Onondaga(2)
CATSKILL Greene
CATTARAUGUS Cattaraugus
CAYUGA Cayuga
CAYUTA (14824) Schuyler(72), Chemung(27)
CAZENOVIA (13035) Madison(96), Onondaga(3)

CEDARHURST Nassau
CELORON Chautauqua
CEMENTON Greene
CENTER MORICHES Suffolk
CENTEREACH Suffolk
CENTERPORT Suffolk
CENTERVILLE Allegany
CENTRAL BRIDGE Schoharie
CENTRAL ISLIP Suffolk
CENTRAL SQUARE Oswego
CENTRAL VALLEY Orange
CERES Allegany
CHADWICKS Oneida
CHAFFEE (14030) Erie(76), Cattaraugus(17), Wyoming(6)
CHAMPLAIN Clinton
CHAPPAQUA Westchester
CHARLOTTEVILLE Schoharie
CHASE MILLS St. Lawrence
CHATEAUGAY Franklin
CHATHAM Columbia
CHAUMONT Jefferson
CHAZY Clinton
CHELSEA Dutchess
CHEMUNG Chemung
CHENANGO BRIDGE Broome
CHENANGO FORKS Broome
CHERRY CREEK Chautauqua
CHERRY PLAIN Rensselaer
CHERRY VALLEY Otsego
CHESTER Orange
CHESTERTOWN Warren
CHICHESTER Ulster
CHILDWOLD St. Lawrence
CHIPPEWA BAY St. Lawrence
CHITTENANGO (13037) Madison(98), Onondaga(1)
CHURCHVILLE Monroe
CHURUBUSCO Clinton
CICERO Onondaga
CINCINNATUS Cortland
CIRCLEVILLE Orange
CLARENCE Erie
CLARENCE CENTER (14032) Erie(98), Niagara(1)
CLARENDON Orleans
CLARK MILLS Oneida
CLARKSON Monroe
CLARKSVILLE Albany
CLARYVILLE (12725) Sullivan(57), Ulster(42)
CLAVERACK Columbia
CLAY Onondaga
CLAYTON Jefferson
CLAYVILLE (13322) Herkimer(91), Oneida(8)
CLEMONS Washington
CLEVELAND (13042) Oswego(53), Oneida(46)
CLEVERDALE Warren
CLIFTON PARK Saratoga
CLIFTON SPRINGS Ontario
CLIMAX Greene
CLINTON Oneida
CLINTON CORNERS Dutchess
CLINTONDALE Ulster
CLOCKVILLE Madison
CLYDE (14433) Wayne(94), Seneca(5)
CLYMER Chautauqua
COBLESKILL Schoharie
COCHECTON Sullivan
COCHECTON CENTER Sullivan
COEYMANS Albany
COEYMANS HOLLOW (12046) Albany(90), Greene(9)
COHOCTON Steuben
COHOES Albany
COLD BROOK (13324) Herkimer(98), Hamilton(1)
COLD SPRING Putnam
COLD SPRING HARBOR Suffolk
COLDEN Erie
COLLIERSVILLE Otsego
COLLINS Erie
COLLINS CENTER Erie
COLTON St. Lawrence
COLUMBIAVILLE Columbia
COMMACK Suffolk
COMSTOCK Washington
CONESUS Livingston
CONEWANGO VALLEY (14726) Cattaraugus(90), Chautauqua(10)
CONGERS Rockland
CONKLIN Broome
CONNELLY Ulster
CONSTABLE Franklin
CONSTABLEVILLE Lewis
CONSTANTIA Oswego
COOPERS PLAINS Steuben
COOPERSTOWN Otsego
COPAKE Columbia
COPAKE FALLS Columbia
COPENHAGEN Lewis
COPIAGUE Suffolk
CORAM Suffolk
CORBETTSVILLE Broome
CORFU (14036) Genesee(97), Erie(2)
CORINTH Saratoga
CORNING (14830) Steuben(98), Chemung(1)
CORNING Steuben
CORNWALL Orange
CORNWALL ON HUDSON Orange
CORNWALLVILLE Greene
CORTLAND (13045) Cortland(91), Cayuga(6), Tompkins(1)
CORTLANDT MANOR Westchester
COSSAYUNA Washington
COTTEKILL Ulster
COWLESVILLE (14037) Wyoming(75), Erie(24)
COXSACKIE Greene
CRAGSMOOR Ulster
CRANBERRY LAKE St. Lawrence
CRARYVILLE Columbia
CRITTENDEN Erie
CROGHAN Lewis
CROMPOND Westchester
CROPSEYVILLE Rensselaer
CROSS RIVER Westchester
CROTON FALLS Westchester
CROTON ON HUDSON Westchester
CROWN POINT Essex
CUBA (14727) Allegany(79), Cattaraugus(20)
CUDDEBACKVILLE (12729) Orange(88), Sullivan(11)
CUTCHOGUE Suffolk
CUYLER (13050) Cortland(95), Onondaga(4)
DALE Wyoming
DALTON (14836) Livingston(57), Allegany(42)
DANNEMORA Clinton
DANSVILLE (14437) Livingston(90), Steuben(8)
DARIEN CENTER (14040) Genesee(87), Wyoming(12)
DAVENPORT (13750) Delaware(98), Otsego(1)
DAVENPORT CENTER Delaware
DAYTON Cattaraugus
DE KALB JUNCTION St. Lawrence
DE LANCEY Delaware
DE PEYSTER St. Lawrence
DE RUYTER (13052) Madison(52), Chenango(27), Cortland(18), Onondaga(1)
DEANSBORO Oneida
DEER PARK Suffolk
DEER RIVER Lewis
DEFERIET Jefferson
DELANSON (12053) Schenectady(86), Albany(13)
DELEVAN Cattaraugus
DELMAR Albany
DELPHI FALLS Onondaga
DENMARK Lewis
DENVER Delaware
DEPAUVILLE Jefferson
DEPEW Erie
DEPOSIT (13754) Broome(70), Delaware(29)
DERBY Erie
DEWITTVILLE Chautauqua
DEXTER Jefferson
DIAMOND POINT Warren
DICKINSON CENTER Franklin
DOBBS FERRY Westchester
DOLGEVILLE (13329) Herkimer(95), Fulton(4)
DORMANSVILLE Albany
DOVER PLAINS Dutchess
DOWNSVILLE Delaware
DRESDEN Yates
DRYDEN (13053) Tompkins(83), Cortland(16)
DUANESBURG Schenectady
DUNDEE (14837) Yates(74), Schuyler(20), Steuben(4)
DUNKIRK Chautauqua
DURHAM Greene
DURHAMVILLE Oneida
EAGLE BAY Herkimer
EAGLE BRIDGE Rensselaer
EAGLE HARBOR Orleans
EARLTON Greene
EARLVILLE (13332) Chenango(97), Madison(2)
EAST AMHERST Erie
EAST AURORA Erie
EAST BERNE Albany
EAST BETHANY (14054) Genesee(91), Wyoming(8)
EAST BLOOMFIELD Ontario
EAST BRANCH Delaware
EAST CHATHAM Columbia
EAST CONCORD Erie
EAST DURHAM Greene
EAST FREETOWN Cortland
EAST GREENBUSH Rensselaer
EAST GREENWICH Washington
EAST HAMPTON Suffolk
EAST HOMER Cortland
EAST ISLIP Suffolk
EAST JEWETT Greene
EAST MARION Suffolk
EAST MEADOW Nassau
EAST MEREDITH Delaware
EAST MORICHES Suffolk
EAST NASSAU (12062) Columbia(98), Rensselaer(1)
EAST NORTHPORT Suffolk
EAST NORWICH Nassau
EAST OTTO Cattaraugus
EAST PALMYRA Wayne
EAST PEMBROKE Genesee
EAST PHARSALIA Chenango
EAST QUOGUE Suffolk
EAST RANDOLPH Cattaraugus
EAST ROCHESTER Monroe
EAST ROCKAWAY Nassau
EAST SCHODACK Rensselaer
EAST SETAUKET Suffolk
EAST SPRINGFIELD Otsego
EAST SYRACUSE Onondaga
EAST WILLIAMSON Wayne
EAST WORCESTER Otsego
EASTCHESTER Westchester
EASTPORT Suffolk
EATON Madison
EDEN Erie
EDMESTON Otsego
EDWARDS St. Lawrence
ELBA (14058) Genesee(95), Orleans(4)
ELBRIDGE Onondaga
ELDRED Sullivan
ELIZABETHTOWN Essex
ELIZAVILLE Columbia
ELKA PARK Greene
ELLENBURG Clinton
ELLENBURG CENTER Clinton
ELLENBURG DEPOT Clinton
ELLENVILLE Ulster
ELLICOTTVILLE Cattaraugus
ELLINGTON Chautauqua
ELLISBURG Jefferson
ELMA Erie
ELMHURST Queens
ELMIRA Chemung
ELMONT Nassau
ELMSFORD Westchester
ENDICOTT (13760) Broome(90), Tioga(9)
ENDICOTT Broome
ENDWELL Broome
ERIEVILLE Madison
ERIN Chemung
ESOPUS Ulster
ESPERANCE Montgomery
ETNA Tompkins
EVANS MILLS Jefferson
FABIUS Onondaga
FAIR HAVEN (13064) Oswego(94), Onondaga(5)
FAIRFIELD Herkimer
FAIRPORT Monroe
FALCONER Chautauqua
FALLSBURG Sullivan
FANCHER Orleans
FAR ROCKAWAY Queens
FARMERSVILLE STATION (14060) Allegany(53), Cattaraugus(46)
FARMINGDALE (11735) Nassau(71), Suffolk(28)
FARMINGDALE Nassau
FARMINGTON Ontario
FARMINGVILLE Suffolk
FARNHAM Erie
FAYETTE Seneca
FAYETTEVILLE Onondaga
FELTS MILLS Jefferson
FERNDALE Sullivan
FEURA BUSH Albany
FILLMORE Allegany
FINDLEY LAKE Chautauqua
FINE St. Lawrence
FISHERS Ontario
FISHERS ISLAND Suffolk
FISHERS LANDING Jefferson
FISHKILL Dutchess
FISHS EDDY Delaware
FLEISCHMANNS (12430) Greene(59), Delaware(40)
FLORAL PARK (11001) Nassau(90), Queens(9)
FLORAL PARK Nassau
FLORAL PARK Queens
FLORIDA Orange
FLUSHING Queens
FLY CREEK Otsego
FONDA (12068) Montgomery(98), Fulton(1)
FORESTBURGH Sullivan
FORESTPORT Oneida
FORESTVILLE Chautauqua
FORT ANN Washington
FORT COVINGTON Franklin
FORT DRUM Jefferson
FORT EDWARD (12828) Washington(53), Saratoga(46)
FORT HUNTER Montgomery
FORT JACKSON St. Lawrence
FORT JOHNSON Montgomery
FORT MONTGOMERY Orange
FORT PLAIN (13339) Montgomery(73), Herkimer(15), Fulton(11)
FRANKFORT Herkimer
FRANKLIN Delaware
FRANKLIN SPRINGS Oneida

FRANKLIN SQUARE Nassau
FRANKLINVILLE (14737) Cattaraugus(98), Allegany(1)
FREDONIA Chautauqua
FREEDOM (14065) Cattaraugus(54), Allegany(45)
FREEHOLD Greene
FREEPORT Nassau
FREEVILLE Tompkins
FREMONT CENTER Sullivan
FREWSBURG (14738) Chautauqua(88), Cattaraugus(11)
FRIENDSHIP Allegany
FULTON Oswego
FULTONHAM Schoharie
FULTONVILLE Montgomery
GABRIELS Franklin
GAINESVILLE Wyoming
GALLUPVILLE Schoharie
GALWAY Saratoga
GANSEVOORT Saratoga
GARDEN CITY Nassau
GARDINER Ulster
GARNERVILLE Rockland
GARRATTSVILLE Otsego
GARRISON Putnam
GASPORT Niagara
GENESEO Livingston
GENEVA (14456) Ontario(92), Seneca(6)
GENOA Cayuga
GEORGETOWN (13072) Madison(96), Chenango(3)
GEORGETOWN Chenango
GERMANTOWN Columbia
GERRY Chautauqua
GETZVILLE Erie
GHENT Columbia
GILBERTSVILLE Otsego
GILBOA Schoharie
GLASCO Ulster
GLEN AUBREY Broome
GLEN COVE Nassau
GLEN HEAD Nassau
GLEN OAKS Queens
GLEN SPEY Sullivan
GLEN WILD Sullivan
GLENFIELD Lewis
GLENFORD Ulster
GLENHAM Dutchess
GLENMONT Albany
GLENS FALLS Warren
GLENWOOD Erie
GLENWOOD LANDING Nassau
GLOVERSVILLE Fulton
GODEFFROY Orange
GOLDENS BRIDGE Westchester
GORHAM Ontario
GOSHEN Orange
GOUVERNEUR St. Lawrence
GOWANDA (14070) Cattaraugus(57), Erie(42)
GRAFTON Rensselaer
GRAHAMSVILLE (12740) Sullivan(86), Ulster(13)
GRAND GORGE (12434) Delaware(92), Schoharie(7)
GRAND ISLAND Erie
GRANITE SPRINGS Westchester
GRANVILLE Washington
GREAT BEND Jefferson
GREAT NECK Nassau
GREAT RIVER Suffolk
GREAT VALLEY Cattaraugus
GREENE (13778) Chenango(66), Broome(33)
GREENFIELD CENTER Saratoga
GREENFIELD PARK Ulster
GREENHURST Chautauqua
GREENLAWN Suffolk
GREENPORT Suffolk
GREENVALE Nassau
GREENVILLE Greene
GREENWICH Washington
GREENWOOD Steuben
GREENWOOD LAKE Orange
GREIG Lewis
GROTON (13073) Tompkins(98), Cayuga(1)
GROVELAND Livingston
GUILDERLAND Albany
GUILDERLAND CENTER Albany
GUILFORD Chenango
HADLEY Saratoga
HAGAMAN Montgomery
HAGUE Warren
HAILESBORO St. Lawrence
HAINES FALLS Greene
HALCOTTSVILLE Delaware
HALL Ontario
HAMBURG Erie
HAMDEN Delaware
HAMILTON Madison
HAMLIN (14464) Monroe(97), Orleans(2)
HAMMOND St. Lawrence
HAMMONDSPORT (14840) Steuben(97), Schuyler(2)
HAMPTON Washington
HAMPTON BAYS Suffolk
HANCOCK Delaware
HANKINS Sullivan
HANNACROIX Greene
HANNAWA FALLS St. Lawrence
HANNIBAL Oswego
HARFORD Cortland
HARPERSFIELD Delaware
HARPURSVILLE Broome
HARRIMAN Orange
HARRIS Sullivan
HARRISON Westchester
HARRISVILLE (13648) St. Lawrence(84), Lewis(15)
HARTFORD Washington
HARTSDALE Westchester
HARTWICK Otsego
HARTWICK SEMINARY Otsego
HASTINGS Oswego
HASTINGS ON HUDSON Westchester
HAUPPAUGE Suffolk
HAVERSTRAW Rockland
HAWTHORNE Westchester
HECTOR Schuyler
HELENA St. Lawrence
HELMUTH Erie
HEMLOCK (14466) Ontario(58), Livingston(41)
HEMPSTEAD Nassau
HENDERSON Jefferson
HENDERSON HARBOR Jefferson
HENRIETTA Monroe
HENSONVILLE Greene
HERKIMER Herkimer
HERMON St. Lawrence
HEUVELTON St. Lawrence
HEWLETT Nassau
HICKSVILLE Nassau
HIGH FALLS Ulster
HIGHLAND Ulster
HIGHLAND FALLS Orange
HIGHLAND LAKE Sullivan
HIGHLAND MILLS Orange
HIGHMOUNT Ulster
HILLBURN Rockland
HILLSDALE Columbia
HILTON Monroe
HIMROD Yates
HINCKLEY Oneida
HINSDALE Cattaraugus
HOBART Delaware
HOFFMEISTER Hamilton
HOGANSBURG Franklin
HOLBROOK Suffolk
HOLLAND Erie
HOLLAND PATENT Oneida
HOLLEY (14470) Orleans(97), Monroe(2)
HOLLOWVILLE Columbia
HOLMES (12531) Dutchess(82), Putnam(17)
HOLTSVILLE Suffolk
HOMER (13077) Cortland(92), Onondaga(4), Cayuga(2)
HONEOYE Ontario
HONEOYE FALLS (14472) Monroe(90), Livingston(6), Ontario(2)
HOOSICK Rensselaer
HOOSICK FALLS Rensselaer
HOPEWELL JUNCTION (12533) Dutchess(98), Putnam(1)
HOPKINTON St. Lawrence
HORNELL Steuben
HORSEHEADS Chemung
HORTONVILLE Sullivan
HOUGHTON Allegany
HOWELLS Orange
HOWES CAVE Schoharie
HUBBARDSVILLE Madison
HUDSON Columbia
HUDSON FALLS Washington
HUGHSONVILLE Dutchess
HUGUENOT Orange
HULETTS LANDING Washington
HUME Allegany
HUNT (14846) Livingston(75), Allegany(24)
HUNTER Greene
HUNTINGTON Suffolk
HUNTINGTON STATION Suffolk
HURLEY Ulster
HURLEYVILLE Sullivan
HYDE PARK Dutchess
ILION Herkimer
INDIAN LAKE Hamilton
INDUSTRY Monroe
INLET Hamilton
INTERLAKEN Seneca
INWOOD Nassau
INWOOD Queens
IONIA (14475) Ontario(93), Monroe(6)
IRVING (14081) Chautauqua(50), Erie(47), Cattaraugus(2)
IRVINGTON Westchester
ISLAND PARK Nassau
ISLANDIA Suffolk
ISLIP Suffolk
ISLIP TERRACE Suffolk
ITHACA Tompkins
JACKSONVILLE Tompkins
JAMAICA Queens
JAMESPORT Suffolk
JAMESTOWN Chautauqua
JAMESVILLE Onondaga
JASPER Steuben
JAVA CENTER Wyoming
JAVA VILLAGE Wyoming
JAY Essex
JEFFERSON (12093) Schoharie(73), Delaware(26)
JEFFERSON VALLEY Westchester
JEFFERSONVILLE Sullivan
JERICHO Nassau
JEWETT Greene
JOHNSBURG Warren
JOHNSON Orange
JOHNSON CITY Broome
JOHNSONVILLE Rensselaer
JOHNSTOWN Fulton
JORDAN (13080) Onondaga(87), Cayuga(12)
JORDANVILLE Herkimer
KANONA Steuben
KATONAH Westchester
KATTSKILL BAY Warren
KAUNEONGA LAKE Sullivan
KEENE Essex
KEENE VALLEY Essex
KEESEVILLE (12944) Clinton(92), Essex(7)
KEESEVILLE Clinton
KENDALL (14476) Orleans(95), Monroe(4)
KENNEDY (14747) Chautauqua(90), Cattaraugus(9)
KENOZA LAKE Sullivan
KENT Orleans
KERHONKSON Ulster
KEUKA PARK Yates
KIAMESHA LAKE Sullivan
KILL BUCK Cattaraugus
KILLAWOG Broome
KINDERHOOK Columbia
KING FERRY Cayuga
KINGS PARK Suffolk
KINGSTON Ulster
KIRKVILLE (13082) Madison(57), Onondaga(42)
KIRKWOOD Broome
KNAPP CREEK Cattaraugus
KNOWLESVILLE Orleans
KNOX Albany
KNOXBORO Oneida
LA FARGEVILLE Jefferson
LA FAYETTE Onondaga
LACONA Oswego
LAGRANGEVILLE Dutchess
LAKE CLEAR Franklin
LAKE GEORGE Warren
LAKE GROVE Suffolk
LAKE HILL Ulster
LAKE HUNTINGTON Sullivan
LAKE KATRINE Ulster
LAKE LUZERNE Warren
LAKE PEEKSKILL Putnam
LAKE PLACID Essex
LAKE PLEASANT Hamilton
LAKE VIEW Erie
LAKEMONT Yates
LAKEVILLE Livingston
LAKEWOOD Chautauqua
LANCASTER Erie
LANESVILLE Greene
LANSING (14882) Tompkins(98), Cayuga(1)
LARCHMONT Westchester
LATHAM Albany
LAUREL Suffolk
LAURENS Otsego
LAWRENCE Nassau
LAWRENCEVILLE St. Lawrence
LAWTONS Erie
LAWYERSVILLE Schoharie
LE ROY (14482) Genesee(95), Livingston(3)
LEBANON Madison
LEBANON SPRINGS Columbia
LEE CENTER Oneida
LEEDS Greene
LEICESTER (14481) Livingston(98), Wyoming(1)
LEON Cattaraugus
LEONARDSVILLE Madison
LEVITTOWN Nassau
LEW BEACH (12753) Ulster(58), Sullivan(38), Delaware(4)
LEWIS Essex
LEWISTON Niagara
LEXINGTON Greene
LIBERTY Sullivan
LILY DALE Chautauqua
LIMA (14485) Livingston(93), Ontario(6)
LIMERICK Jefferson
LIMESTONE Cattaraugus
LINCOLNDALE Westchester
LINDENHURST Suffolk
LINDLEY Steuben
LINWOOD Genesee
LISBON St. Lawrence
LISLE Broome
LITTLE FALLS Herkimer
LITTLE GENESEE Allegany
LITTLE VALLEY Cattaraugus
LITTLE YORK Cortland

LIVERPOOL Onondaga
LIVINGSTON Columbia
LIVINGSTON MANOR (12758) Sullivan(91), Ulster(7)
LIVONIA (14487) Livingston(93), Ontario(6)
LIVONIA CENTER Livingston
LOCH SHELDRAKE Sullivan
LOCKE (13092) Tompkins(97), Cayuga(2)
LOCKPORT Niagara
LOCKWOOD (14859) Tioga(59), Chemung(40)
LOCUST VALLEY Nassau
LODI Seneca
LONG BEACH Nassau
LONG EDDY (12760) Delaware(67), Sullivan(32)
LONG ISLAND CITY Queens
LONG LAKE Hamilton
LORRAINE Jefferson
LOWMAN Chemung
LOWVILLE (13367) Lewis(94), Herkimer(5)
LYCOMING Oswego
LYNBROOK Nassau
LYNDONVILLE (14098) Orleans(98), Niagara(1)
LYON MOUNTAIN Clinton
LYONS (14489) Wayne(95), Ontario(2), Seneca(2)
LYONS FALLS Lewis
LYSANDER Onondaga
MACEDON (14502) Wayne(97), Monroe(2)
MACHIAS Cattaraugus
MADISON (13402) Madison(98), Oneida(1)
MADRID St. Lawrence
MAHOPAC (10541) Putnam(93), Westchester(6)
MAHOPAC FALLS Putnam
MAINE Broome
MALDEN BRIDGE Columbia
MALDEN ON HUDSON Ulster
MALLORY Oswego
MALONE Franklin
MALVERNE Nassau
MAMARONECK Westchester
MANCHESTER Ontario
MANHASSET Nassau
MANLIUS (13104) Onondaga(98), Madison(1)
MANNSVILLE Jefferson
MANORVILLE Suffolk
MAPLE SPRINGS Chautauqua
MAPLE VIEW Oswego
MAPLECREST Greene
MARATHON (13803) Cortland(94), Broome(5)
MARCELLUS Onondaga
MARCY Oneida
MARGARETVILLE (12455) Delaware(96), Ulster(3)
MARIETTA Onondaga
MARILLA Erie
MARION Wayne
MARLBORO (12542) Ulster(93), Orange(6)
MARTINSBURG Lewis
MARTVILLE (13111) Cayuga(87), Oswego(12)
MARYKNOLL Westchester
MARYLAND Otsego
MASONVILLE Delaware
MASSAPEQUA Nassau
MASSAPEQUA PARK Nassau
MASSENA St. Lawrence
MASTIC Suffolk
MASTIC BEACH Suffolk
MATTITUCK Suffolk
MATTYDALE Onondaga
MAYBROOK (12543) Orange(98), Dutchess(1)
MAYFIELD Fulton
MAYVILLE Chautauqua
MC CONNELLSVILLE Oneida
MC DONOUGH Chenango
MC GRAW Cortland
MC LEAN Tompkins
MECHANICVILLE (12118) Saratoga(98), Rensselaer(1)
MECKLENBURG Schuyler
MEDFORD Suffolk
MEDINA Orleans
MEDUSA Albany
MELLENVILLE Columbia
MELROSE Rensselaer
MELVILLE Suffolk
MEMPHIS Onondaga
MENDON Monroe
MERIDALE Delaware
MERIDIAN Cayuga
MERRICK Nassau
MEXICO Oswego
MID HUDSON Orange
MID ISLAND Suffolk
MIDDLE FALLS Washington
MIDDLE GRANVILLE Washington
MIDDLE GROVE Saratoga
MIDDLE ISLAND Suffolk
MIDDLE VILLAGE Queens
MIDDLEBURGH (12122) Albany(57), Schoharie(42)
MIDDLEPORT (14105) Niagara(94), Orleans(3), Genesee(1)
MIDDLESEX Yates
MIDDLETOWN (10940) Orange(98), Sullivan(1)
MIDDLETOWN Orange
MIDDLEVILLE Herkimer
MILFORD Otsego
MILL NECK Nassau
MILLBROOK Dutchess
MILLER PLACE Suffolk
MILLERTON (12546) Dutchess(96), Columbia(3)
MILLPORT (14864) Chemung(85), Schuyler(14)
MILLWOOD Westchester
MILTON Ulster
MINEOLA Nassau
MINERVA Essex
MINETTO Oswego
MINEVILLE Essex
MINOA Onondaga
MODEL CITY Niagara
MODENA Ulster
MOHAWK Herkimer
MOHEGAN LAKE Westchester
MOIRA Franklin
MONGAUP VALLEY Sullivan
MONROE Orange
MONSEY Rockland
MONTAUK Suffolk
MONTEZUMA Cayuga
MONTGOMERY Orange
MONTICELLO Sullivan
MONTOUR FALLS Schuyler
MONTROSE Westchester
MOOERS Clinton
MOOERS FORKS Clinton
MORAVIA Cayuga
MORIAH Essex
MORIAH CENTER Essex
MORICHES Suffolk
MORRIS Otsego
MORRISONVILLE Clinton
MORRISTOWN St. Lawrence
MORRISVILLE Madison
MORTON Orleans
MOTTVILLE Onondaga
MOUNT KISCO Westchester
MOUNT MARION Ulster
MOUNT MORRIS Livingston
MOUNT SINAI Suffolk
MOUNT TREMPER Ulster
MOUNT UPTON (13809) Chenango(66), Otsego(33)
MOUNT VERNON Westchester
MOUNT VISION Otsego
MOUNTAIN DALE Sullivan
MOUNTAINVILLE Orange
MUMFORD Monroe
MUNNSVILLE (13409) Madison(92), Oneida(7)
NANUET Rockland
NAPANOCH Ulster
NAPLES (14512) Ontario(75), Yates(19), Steuben(3)
NARROWSBURG Sullivan
NASSAU Rensselaer
NATURAL BRIDGE (13665) Jefferson(96), Lewis(3)
NEDROW Onondaga
NELLISTON Montgomery
NESCONSET Suffolk
NEVERSINK Sullivan
NEW BALTIMORE Greene
NEW BERLIN Chenango
NEW CITY Rockland
NEW HAMPTON Orange
NEW HARTFORD Oneida
NEW HAVEN Oswego
NEW HYDE PARK (11040) Nassau(96), Queens(3)
NEW HYDE PARK Nassau
NEW KINGSTON Delaware
NEW LEBANON Columbia
NEW LISBON Otsego
NEW MILFORD Orange
NEW PALTZ Ulster
NEW ROCHELLE Westchester
NEW RUSSIA Essex
NEW SUFFOLK Suffolk
NEW WINDSOR Orange
NEW WOODSTOCK (13122) Onondaga(65), Madison(34)
NEW YORK New York
NEW YORK MILLS Oneida
NEWARK (14513) Wayne(98), Ontario(1)
NEWARK VALLEY (13811) Tioga(93), Broome(6)
NEWBURGH Orange
NEWCOMB Essex
NEWFANE Niagara
NEWFIELD Tompkins
NEWPORT Herkimer
NEWTON FALLS St. Lawrence
NEWTONVILLE Albany
NIAGARA FALLS Niagara
NIAGARA UNIVERSITY Niagara
NICHOLS Tioga
NICHOLVILLE St. Lawrence
NINEVEH Broome
NIOBE Chautauqua
NIVERVILLE Columbia
NORFOLK St. Lawrence
NORTH BABYLON Suffolk
NORTH BANGOR Franklin
NORTH BAY Oneida
NORTH BLENHEIM Schoharie
NORTH BOSTON Erie
NORTH BRANCH Sullivan
NORTH BROOKFIELD Madison
NORTH CHATHAM Columbia
NORTH CHILI Monroe
NORTH CLYMER Chautauqua
NORTH COHOCTON Steuben
NORTH COLLINS Erie
NORTH CREEK Warren
NORTH EVANS Erie
NORTH GRANVILLE Washington
NORTH GREECE Monroe
NORTH HOOSICK Rensselaer
NORTH HUDSON Essex
NORTH JAVA Wyoming
NORTH LAWRENCE St. Lawrence
NORTH NORWICH Chenango
NORTH PITCHER Chenango
NORTH RIVER Warren
NORTH ROSE Wayne
NORTH SALEM Westchester
NORTH TONAWANDA Niagara
NORTHPORT Suffolk
NORTHVILLE Fulton
NORTON HILL Greene
NORWICH Chenango
NORWOOD St. Lawrence
NUNDA Livingston
NYACK Rockland
OAK HILL Greene
OAKDALE Suffolk
OAKFIELD Genesee
OAKS CORNERS Ontario
OBERNBURG Sullivan
OCEAN BEACH Suffolk
OCEANSIDE Nassau
ODESSA Schuyler
OGDENSBURG St. Lawrence
OLCOTT Niagara
OLD BETHPAGE Nassau
OLD CHATHAM Columbia
OLD FORGE Herkimer
OLD WESTBURY Nassau
OLEAN Cattaraugus
OLIVEBRIDGE Ulster
OLIVEREA Ulster
OLMSTEDVILLE Essex
ONCHIOTA Franklin
ONEIDA (13421) Madison(84), Oneida(15)
ONEONTA Otsego
ONTARIO (14519) Wayne(96), Monroe(3)
ONTARIO CENTER Wayne
ORAN Onondaga
ORANGEBURG Rockland
ORCHARD PARK Erie
ORIENT Suffolk
ORISKANY Oneida
ORISKANY FALLS (13425) Oneida(97), Madison(2)
ORWELL Oswego
OSSINING Westchester
OSWEGATCHIE St. Lawrence
OSWEGO Oswego
OTEGO (13825) Otsego(93), Delaware(6)
OTISVILLE (10963) Orange(97), Sullivan(2)
OTTO Cattaraugus
OUAQUAGA Broome
OVID Seneca
OWASCO Cayuga
OWEGO Tioga
OWLS HEAD Franklin
OXBOW Jefferson
OXFORD Chenango
OYSTER BAY Nassau
PAINTED POST (14870) Steuben(97), Schuyler(2)
PALATINE BRIDGE Montgomery
PALENVILLE Greene
PALISADES Rockland
PALMYRA (14522) Wayne(89), Ontario(10)
PANAMA Chautauqua
PARADOX Essex
PARIS Oneida
PARISH Oswego
PARISHVILLE St. Lawrence
PARKSVILLE Sullivan
PATCHOGUE Suffolk
PATTERSON Putnam
PATTERSONVILLE Schenectady
PAUL SMITHS Franklin
PAVILION (14525) Genesee(61), Wyoming(33), Livingston(5)
PAWLING Dutchess
PEARL RIVER Rockland
PECONIC Suffolk
PEEKSKILL Westchester
PELHAM Westchester
PENFIELD Monroe
PENN YAN Yates
PENNELLVILLE Oswego
PERKINSVILLE Steuben

PERRY Wyoming
PERRYSBURG Cattaraugus
PERRYVILLE Madison
PERU Clinton
PETERBORO Madison
PETERSBURG Rensselaer
PHELPS (14532) Ontario(94), Seneca(5)
PHILADELPHIA Jefferson
PHILLIPSPORT Sullivan
PHILMONT Columbia
PHOENICIA Ulster
PHOENIX (13135) Oswego(87), Onondaga(12)
PIERCEFIELD St. Lawrence
PIERMONT Rockland
PIERREPONT MANOR Jefferson
PIFFARD Livingston
PIKE Wyoming
PINE BUSH (12566) Ulster(58), Orange(37), Sullivan(3)
PINE CITY (14871) Chemung(83), Steuben(16)
PINE HILL Ulster
PINE ISLAND Orange
PINE PLAINS (12567) Dutchess(92), Columbia(7)
PINE VALLEY Chemung
PISECO Hamilton
PITCHER (13136) Chenango(96), Cortland(3)
PITTSFORD Monroe
PLAINVIEW Nassau
PLAINVILLE Onondaga
PLATTEKILL Ulster
PLATTSBURGH Clinton
PLEASANT VALLEY Dutchess
PLEASANTVILLE Westchester
PLESSIS Jefferson
PLYMOUTH Chenango
POESTENKILL Rensselaer
POINT LOOKOUT Nassau
POLAND (13431) Oneida(90), Herkimer(9)
POMONA Rockland
POMPEY Onondaga
POND EDDY Sullivan
POOLVILLE Madison
POPLAR RIDGE Cayuga
PORT BYRON Cayuga
PORT CHESTER Westchester
PORT CRANE Broome
PORT EWEN Ulster
PORT GIBSON Ontario
PORT HENRY Essex
PORT JEFFERSON Suffolk
PORT JEFFERSON STATION Suffolk
PORT JERVIS Orange
PORT KENT Essex
PORT LEYDEN Lewis
PORT WASHINGTON Nassau
PORTAGEVILLE (14536) Wyoming(74), Allegany(25)
PORTER CORNERS Saratoga
PORTLAND Chautauqua
PORTLANDVILLE Otsego
PORTVILLE (14770) Cattaraugus(75), Allegany(24)
POTSDAM St. Lawrence
POTTERSVILLE Warren
POUGHKEEPSIE Dutchess
POUGHQUAG Dutchess
POUND RIDGE Westchester
PRATTS HOLLOW Madison
PRATTSBURGH (14873) Steuben(98), Yates(1)
PRATTSVILLE (12468) Greene(95), Delaware(4)
PREBLE (13141) Cortland(63), Onondaga(36)
PRESTON HOLLOW (12469) Greene(95), Albany(4)
PROSPECT Oneida
PULASKI Oswego
PULTENEY Steuben
PULTNEYVILLE Wayne
PURCHASE Westchester
PURDYS Westchester
PURLING Greene
PUTNAM STATION Washington
PUTNAM VALLEY Putnam
PYRITES St. Lawrence
QUAKER STREET Schenectady
QUEENS VILLAGE Queens
QUEENSBURY Warren
QUOGUE Suffolk
RAINBOW LAKE Franklin
RANDOLPH Cattaraugus
RANSOMVILLE Niagara
RAQUETTE LAKE Hamilton
RAVENA Albany
RAY BROOK Essex
RAYMONDVILLE St. Lawrence
READING CENTER Schuyler
RED CREEK (13143) Wayne(98), Cayuga(1)
RED HOOK Dutchess
REDFIELD Oswego
REDFORD Clinton
REDWOOD Jefferson
REMSEN Oneida
REMSENBURG Suffolk
RENSSELAER Rensselaer
RENSSELAER FALLS St. Lawrence
RENSSELAERVILLE Albany
RETSOF Livingston
REXFORD (12148) Saratoga(96), Schenectady(3)
REXVILLE (14877) Steuben(98), Allegany(1)
RHINEBECK Dutchess
RHINECLIFF Dutchess
RICHBURG Allegany
RICHFIELD SPRINGS Otsego
RICHFORD (13835) Tioga(57), Broome(29), Cortland(12)
RICHLAND Oswego
RICHMOND HILL Queens
RICHMONDVILLE (12149) Schoharie(97), Otsego(2)
RICHVILLE St. Lawrence
RIDGE Suffolk
RIFTON Ulster
RIPARIUS Warren
RIPLEY Chautauqua
RIVERHEAD Suffolk
ROCHESTER Monroe
ROCK CITY FALLS Saratoga
ROCK HILL Sullivan
ROCK STREAM (14878) Schuyler(71), Yates(28)
ROCK TAVERN Orange
ROCKAWAY PARK Queens
ROCKLAND M P C Rockland
ROCKVILLE CENTRE Nassau
ROCKY POINT Suffolk
RODMAN Jefferson
RODMAN Lewis
ROME Oneida
ROMULUS Seneca
RONKONKOMA Suffolk
ROOSEVELT Nassau
ROOSEVELTOWN St. Lawrence
ROSCOE (12776) Sullivan(74), Delaware(25)
ROSE Wayne
ROSEBOOM Otsego
ROSENDALE Ulster
ROSLYN Nassau
ROSLYN HEIGHTS Nassau
ROSSBURG Allegany
ROTTERDAM JUNCTION Schenectady
ROUND LAKE Saratoga
ROUND TOP Greene
ROUSES POINT Clinton
ROXBURY Delaware
RUBY Ulster
RUSH Monroe
RUSHFORD Allegany
RUSHVILLE (14544) Yates(54), Ontario(45)
RUSSELL St. Lawrence
RYE Westchester
SABAEL Hamilton
SACKETS HARBOR Jefferson
SAG HARBOR Suffolk
SAGAPONACK Suffolk
SAINT BONAVENTURE Cattaraugus
SAINT JAMES Suffolk
SAINT JOHNSVILLE (13452) Montgomery(59), Fulton(40)
SAINT REGIS FALLS Franklin
SALAMANCA Cattaraugus
SALISBURY CENTER Herkimer
SALISBURY MILLS Orange
SALT POINT Dutchess
SANBORN Niagara
SAND LAKE Rensselaer
SANDUSKY Cattaraugus
SANDY CREEK Oswego
SANGERFIELD Oneida
SARANAC Clinton
SARANAC LAKE (12983) Franklin(82), Essex(17)
SARANAC LAKE Franklin
SARATOGA SPRINGS Saratoga
SARDINIA Erie
SAUGERTIES Ulster
SAUQUOIT (13456) Oneida(93), Herkimer(6)
SAVANNAH Wayne
SAVONA Steuben
SAYVILLE Suffolk
SCARSDALE Westchester
SCHAGHTICOKE Rensselaer
SCHENECTADY (12309) Schenectady(92), Albany(6)
SCHENECTADY Schenectady
SCHENEVUS Otsego
SCHODACK LANDING (12156) Rensselaer(91), Columbia(8)
SCHOHARIE Schoharie
SCHROON LAKE Essex
SCHUYLER FALLS Clinton
SCHUYLER LAKE Otsego
SCHUYLERVILLE Saratoga
SCIO Allegany
SCIPIO CENTER Cayuga
SCOTTSBURG Livingston
SCOTTSVILLE Monroe
SEA CLIFF Nassau
SEAFORD Nassau
SELDEN Suffolk
SELKIRK Albany
SENECA CASTLE Ontario
SENECA FALLS Seneca
SENNETT Cayuga
SEVERANCE Essex
SHANDAKEN (12480) Ulster(71), Greene(28)
SHARON SPRINGS (13459) Schoharie(94), Montgomery(5)
SHEDS Madison
SHELTER ISLAND Suffolk
SHELTER ISLAND HEIGHTS Suffolk
SHENOROCK Westchester
SHERBURNE (13460) Chenango(98), Madison(1)
SHERIDAN Chautauqua
SHERMAN Chautauqua
SHERRILL Oneida
SHINHOPPLE Delaware
SHIRLEY Suffolk
SHOKAN Ulster
SHOREHAM Suffolk
SHORTSVILLE Ontario
SHRUB OAK Westchester
SHUSHAN Washington
SIDNEY (13838) Delaware(94), Otsego(5)
SIDNEY CENTER Delaware
SILVER BAY Warren
SILVER CREEK Chautauqua
SILVER LAKE Wyoming
SILVER SPRINGS Wyoming
SINCLAIRVILLE Chautauqua
SKANEATELES (13152) Onondaga(92), Cayuga(7)
SKANEATELES FALLS Onondaga
SLATE HILL Orange
SLATERVILLE SPRINGS Tompkins
SLINGERLANDS Albany
SLOANSVILLE Schoharie
SLOATSBURG Rockland
SMALLWOOD Sullivan
SMITHBORO Tioga
SMITHS LANDING Greene
SMITHTOWN Suffolk
SMITHVILLE FLATS (13841) Cortland(80), Chenango(14), Broome(4)
SMYRNA Chenango
SODUS Wayne
SODUS CENTER Wayne
SODUS POINT Wayne
SOLSVILLE Madison
SOMERS Westchester
SONYEA Livingston
SOUND BEACH Suffolk
SOUTH BETHLEHEM Albany
SOUTH BUTLER Wayne
SOUTH BYRON Genesee
SOUTH CAIRO Greene
SOUTH COLTON St. Lawrence
SOUTH DAYTON (14138) Cattaraugus(65), Chautauqua(34)
SOUTH EDMESTON Otsego
SOUTH FALLSBURG Sullivan
SOUTH GLENS FALLS Saratoga
SOUTH JAMESPORT Suffolk
SOUTH KORTRIGHT Delaware
SOUTH LIMA Livingston
SOUTH NEW BERLIN Chenango
SOUTH OTSELIC Chenango
SOUTH PLYMOUTH Chenango
SOUTH RUTLAND Jefferson
SOUTH SALEM Westchester
SOUTH SCHODACK Rensselaer
SOUTH WALES Erie
SOUTH WESTERLO Albany
SOUTHAMPTON Suffolk
SOUTHFIELDS Orange
SOUTHOLD Suffolk
SPARKILL Rockland
SPARROW BUSH (12780) Orange(82), Sullivan(17)
SPECULATOR Hamilton
SPENCER (14883) Tioga(79), Tompkins(20)
SPENCERPORT Monroe
SPENCERTOWN Columbia
SPEONK Suffolk
SPRAKERS Montgomery
SPRING BROOK Erie
SPRING GLEN Ulster
SPRING VALLEY Rockland
SPRINGFIELD CENTER Otsego
SPRINGVILLE (14141) Erie(94), Cattaraugus(5)
SPRINGWATER (14560) Ontario(51), Livingston(49)
STAATSBURG Dutchess
STAFFORD Genesee
STAMFORD (12167) Delaware(76), Schoharie(23)
STANFORDVILLE Dutchess
STANLEY (14561) Ontario(94), Yates(5)
STAR LAKE St. Lawrence
STATEN ISLAND Richmond
STEAMBURG Cattaraugus
STELLA NIAGARA Niagara
STEPHENTOWN Rensselaer

STERLING Cayuga
STERLING FOREST Orange
STILLWATER Saratoga
STITTVILLE Oneida
STOCKTON Chautauqua
STONE RIDGE Ulster
STONY BROOK Suffolk
STONY CREEK Warren
STONY POINT Rockland
STORMVILLE Dutchess
STOTTVILLE Columbia
STOW Chautauqua
STRATFORD (13470) Fulton(77), Herkimer(22)
STRYKERSVILLE (14145) Wyoming(92), Erie(7)
STUYVESANT Columbia
STUYVESANT FALLS Columbia
SUFFERN Rockland
SUGAR LOAF Orange
SUGARBUSH Franklin
SUMMIT Schoharie
SUMMITVILLE Sullivan
SUNDOWN Ulster
SURPRISE Greene
SWAIN Allegany
SWAN LAKE Sullivan
SYLVAN BEACH Oneida
SYOSSET Nassau
SYRACUSE Onondaga
TABERG Oneida
TALLMAN Rockland
TANNERSVILLE Greene
TAPPAN Rockland
TARRYTOWN Westchester
THENDARA Herkimer
THERESA Jefferson
THIELLS Rockland
THOMPSON RIDGE Orange
THOMPSONVILLE Sullivan
THORNWOOD Westchester
THOUSAND ISLAND PARK Jefferson
THREE MILE BAY Jefferson
TICONDEROGA Essex
TILLSON Ulster
TIOGA CENTER Tioga
TIVOLI (12583) Dutchess(62), Columbia(37)
TOMKINS COVE Rockland
TONAWANDA Erie
TREADWELL Delaware
TRIBES HILL Montgomery
TROUPSBURG Steuben
TROUT CREEK Delaware
TROY Albany
TROY Rensselaer
TRUMANSBURG (14886) Tompkins(61), Schuyler(26), Seneca(12)
TRUXTON (13158) Cortland(97), Madison(2)
TUCKAHOE Westchester
TULLY (13159) Onondaga(82), Cortland(17)
TUNNEL Broome
TUPPER LAKE (12986) Franklin(94), St. Lawrence(5)
TURIN Lewis
TUXEDO PARK Orange
TYRONE Schuyler
ULSTER PARK Ulster
UNADILLA Otsego
UNION HILL Wayne
UNION SPRINGS Cayuga
UNIONDALE Nassau
UNIONVILLE Orange
UPPER JAY Essex
UPTON Suffolk
UTICA (13501) Oneida(97), Herkimer(2)
UTICA Oneida
VAILS GATE Orange
VALATIE Columbia
VALHALLA Westchester
VALLEY COTTAGE Rockland
VALLEY FALLS Rensselaer
VALLEY STREAM Nassau
VALOIS (14888) Schuyler(82), Seneca(17)
VAN BUREN POINT Chautauqua
VAN ETTEN (14889) Chemung(87), Schuyler(6), Tioga(5)
VAN HORNESVILLE (13475) Herkimer(82), Otsego(17)
VARYSBURG Wyoming
VERBANK Dutchess
VERMONTVILLE Franklin
VERNON Oneida
VERNON CENTER Oneida
VERONA Oneida
VERONA BEACH Oneida
VERPLANCK Westchester
VERSAILLES Cattaraugus
VESTAL Broome
VICTOR (14564) Ontario(97), Monroe(2)
VICTORY MILLS Saratoga
VOORHEESVILLE Albany
WACCABUC Westchester
WADDINGTON St. Lawrence
WADHAMS Essex
WADING RIVER Suffolk
WAINSCOTT Suffolk
WALDEN Orange
WALES CENTER Erie
WALKER VALLEY Ulster
WALLKILL (12589) Ulster(78), Orange(21)
WALTON Delaware
WALWORTH Wayne
WAMPSVILLE Madison
WANAKENA St. Lawrence
WANTAGH Nassau
WAPPINGERS FALLS Dutchess
WARNERS Onondaga
WARNERVILLE Schoharie
WARRENSBURG Warren
WARSAW Wyoming
WARWICK Orange
WASHINGTON MILLS Oneida
WASHINGTONVILLE Orange
WASSAIC Dutchess
WATER MILL Suffolk
WATERFORD Saratoga
WATERLOO Seneca
WATERPORT Orleans
WATERTOWN Jefferson
WATERVILLE (13480) Oneida(95), Madison(4)
WATERVLIET Albany
WATKINS GLEN Schuyler
WAVERLY (14892) Tioga(91), Chemung(8)
WAWARSING Ulster
WAYLAND (14572) Steuben(79), Livingston(20)
WAYNE Schuyler
WEBSTER Monroe
WEBSTER CROSSING Livingston
WEEDSPORT (13166) Cayuga(97), Onondaga(2)
WELLESLEY ISLAND Jefferson
WELLS Hamilton
WELLS BRIDGE Otsego
WELLSBURG Chemung
WELLSVILLE Allegany
WEST BABYLON Suffolk
WEST BLOOMFIELD Ontario
WEST BURLINGTON Otsego
WEST CAMP Ulster
WEST CHAZY Clinton
WEST CLARKSVILLE Allegany
WEST COPAKE Columbia
WEST COXSACKIE Greene
WEST DANBY Tompkins
WEST DAVENPORT Delaware
WEST EATON Madison
WEST EDMESTON (13485) Madison(74), Otsego(24)
WEST EXETER Otsego
WEST FALLS Erie
WEST FULTON Schoharie
WEST HARRISON Westchester
WEST HAVERSTRAW Rockland
WEST HEMPSTEAD Nassau
WEST HENRIETTA Monroe
WEST HURLEY Ulster
WEST ISLIP Suffolk
WEST KILL Greene
WEST LEBANON Columbia
WEST LEYDEN (13489) Lewis(98), Oneida(1)
WEST MONROE Oswego
WEST NYACK Rockland
WEST ONEONTA Otsego
WEST PARK Ulster
WEST POINT Orange
WEST SAND LAKE Rensselaer
WEST SAYVILLE Suffolk
WEST SHOKAN Ulster
WEST STOCKHOLM St. Lawrence
WEST VALLEY Cattaraugus
WEST WINFIELD (13491) Herkimer(90), Otsego(6), Oneida(2)
WESTBROOKVILLE Sullivan
WESTBURY Nassau
WESTDALE (13483) Oneida(97), Oswego(2)
WESTERLO Albany
WESTERN Oneida
WESTERNVILLE Oneida
WESTFIELD Chautauqua
WESTFORD Otsego
WESTHAMPTON Suffolk
WESTHAMPTON BEACH Suffolk
WESTMORELAND Oneida
WESTONS MILLS Cattaraugus
WESTPORT Essex
WESTTOWN Orange
WEVERTOWN Warren
WHALLONSBURG Essex
WHIPPLEVILLE Franklin
WHITE LAKE Sullivan
WHITE PLAINS Westchester
WHITE SULPHUR SPRINGS Sullivan
WHITEHALL Washington
WHITESBORO Oneida
WHITESVILLE (14897) Allegany(93), Steuben(6)
WHITNEY POINT Broome
WILLARD Seneca
WILLET (13863) Cortland(98), Broome(1)
WILLIAMSON Wayne
WILLIAMSTOWN Oswego
WILLISTON PARK Nassau
WILLOW Ulster
WILLSBORO Essex
WILLSEYVILLE (13864) Tioga(67), Tompkins(32)
WILMINGTON (12997) Saratoga(84), Essex(15)
WILSON Niagara
WINDHAM Greene
WINDSOR Broome
WINGDALE Dutchess
WINTHROP St. Lawrence
WITHERBEE Essex
WOLCOTT Wayne
WOODBOURNE (12788) Sullivan(97), Ulster(2)
WOODBURY Nassau
WOODGATE Oneida
WOODHULL Steuben
WOODMERE Nassau
WOODRIDGE Sullivan
WOODSTOCK Ulster
WOODVILLE Jefferson
WORCESTER Otsego
WURTSBORO Sullivan
WYANDANCH Suffolk
WYNANTSKILL Rensselaer
WYOMING (14591) Wyoming(87), Genesee(12)
YAPHANK Suffolk
YONKERS Westchester
YORK Livingston
YORKSHIRE Cattaraugus
YORKTOWN HEIGHTS Westchester
YORKVILLE Oneida
YOUNGSTOWN Niagara
YOUNGSVILLE Sullivan
YULAN Sullivan

New York ZIP/City Cross Reference

00401-00401 PLEASANTVILLE
00501-00544 HOLTSVILLE
06390-06390 FISHERS ISLAND
09002-09894 APO or FPO
10000-10292 NEW YORK
10300-10314 STATEN ISLAND
10400-10499 BRONX
10501-10501 AMAWALK
10502-10502 ARDSLEY
10503-10503 ARDSLEY ON HUDSON
10504-10504 ARMONK
10505-10505 BALDWIN PLACE
10506-10506 BEDFORD
10507-10507 BEDFORD HILLS
10509-10509 BREWSTER
10510-10510 BRIARCLIFF MANOR
10511-10511 BUCHANAN
10512-10512 CARMEL
10514-10514 CHAPPAQUA
10516-10516 COLD SPRING
10517-10517 CROMPOND
10518-10518 CROSS RIVER
10519-10519 CROTON FALLS
10520-10521 CROTON ON HUDSON
10522-10522 DOBBS FERRY
10523-10523 ELMSFORD
10524-10524 GARRISON
10526-10526 GOLDENS BRIDGE
10527-10527 GRANITE SPRINGS
10528-10528 HARRISON
10530-10530 HARTSDALE
10532-10532 HAWTHORNE
10533-10533 IRVINGTON
10535-10535 JEFFERSON VALLEY
10536-10536 KATONAH
10537-10537 LAKE PEEKSKILL
10538-10538 LARCHMONT
10540-10540 LINCOLNDALE
10541-10541 MAHOPAC
10542-10542 MAHOPAC FALLS
10543-10543 MAMARONECK
10545-10545 MARYKNOLL
10546-10546 MILLWOOD
10547-10547 MOHEGAN LAKE
10548-10548 MONTROSE
10549-10549 MOUNT KISCO
10550-10559 MOUNT VERNON
10560-10560 NORTH SALEM
10562-10562 OSSINING
10566-10566 PEEKSKILL
10567-10567 CORTLANDT MANOR
10570-10572 PLEASANTVILLE
10573-10573 PORT CHESTER
10576-10576 POUND RIDGE
10577-10577 PURCHASE
10578-10578 PURDYS

10579-10579 PUTNAM VALLEY
10580-10581 RYE
10583-10583 SCARSDALE
10587-10587 SHENOROCK
10588-10588 SHRUB OAK
10589-10589 SOMERS
10590-10590 SOUTH SALEM
10591-10592 TARRYTOWN
10594-10594 THORNWOOD
10595-10595 VALHALLA
10596-10596 VERPLANCK
10597-10597 WACCABUC
10598-10598 YORKTOWN HEIGHTS
10600-10603 WHITE PLAINS
10604-10604 WEST HARRISON
10605-10650 WHITE PLAINS
10700-10705 YONKERS
10706-10706 HASTINGS ON HUDSON
10707-10707 TUCKAHOE
10708-10708 BRONXVILLE
10709-10709 EASTCHESTER
10710-10710 YONKERS
10800-10802 NEW ROCHELLE
10803-10803 PELHAM
10804-10805 NEW ROCHELLE
10901-10901 SUFFERN
10910-10910 ARDEN
10911-10911 BEAR MOUNTAIN
10912-10912 BELLVALE
10913-10913 BLAUVELT
10914-10914 BLOOMING GROVE
10915-10915 BULLVILLE
10916-10916 CAMPBELL HALL
10917-10917 CENTRAL VALLEY
10918-10918 CHESTER
10919-10919 CIRCLEVILLE
10920-10920 CONGERS
10921-10921 FLORIDA
10922-10922 FORT MONTGOMERY
10923-10923 GARNERVILLE
10924-10924 GOSHEN
10925-10925 GREENWOOD LAKE
10926-10926 HARRIMAN
10927-10927 HAVERSTRAW
10928-10928 HIGHLAND FALLS
10930-10930 HIGHLAND MILLS
10931-10931 HILLBURN
10932-10932 HOWELLS
10933-10933 JOHNSON
10940-10943 MIDDLETOWN
10949-10950 MONROE
10951-10951 ROCKLAND M P C
10952-10952 MONSEY
10953-10953 MOUNTAINVILLE
10954-10954 NANUET
10956-10956 NEW CITY
10958-10958 NEW HAMPTON
10959-10959 NEW MILFORD
10960-10960 NYACK
10962-10962 ORANGEBURG
10963-10963 OTISVILLE
10964-10964 PALISADES
10965-10965 PEARL RIVER
10968-10968 PIERMONT
10969-10969 PINE ISLAND
10970-10970 POMONA
10973-10973 SLATE HILL
10974-10974 SLOATSBURG
10975-10975 SOUTHFIELDS
10976-10976 SPARKILL
10977-10977 SPRING VALLEY
10979-10979 STERLING FOREST
10980-10980 STONY POINT
10981-10981 SUGAR LOAF
10982-10982 TALLMAN
10983-10983 TAPPAN
10984-10984 THIELLS
10985-10985 THOMPSON RIDGE
10986-10986 TOMKINS COVE
10987-10987 TUXEDO PARK
10988-10988 UNIONVILLE
10989-10989 VALLEY COTTAGE
10990-10990 WARWICK
10992-10992 WASHINGTONVILLE
10993-10993 WEST HAVERSTRAW
10994-10995 WEST NYACK
10996-10997 WEST POINT
10998-10998 WESTTOWN
11001-11002 FLORAL PARK
11003-11003 ELMONT
11004-11004 GLEN OAKS
11005-11005 FLORAL PARK
11010-11010 FRANKLIN SQUARE
11020-11027 GREAT NECK
11030-11030 MANHASSET
11040-11044 NEW HYDE PARK
11050-11055 PORT WASHINGTON
11096-11096 INWOOD
11099-11099 NEW HYDE PARK
11100-11120 LONG ISLAND CITY
11200-11256 BROOKLYN
11300-11359 FLUSHING
11359-11359 BAYSIDE
11360-11379 FLUSHING
11379-11379 MIDDLE VILLAGE
11380-11380 FLUSHING
11380-11380 ELMHURST
11381-11390 FLUSHING
11400-11411 JAMAICA
11411-11411 CAMBRIA HEIGHTS
11412-11418 JAMAICA
11418-11418 RICHMOND HILL
11419-11427 JAMAICA
11427-11427 QUEENS VILLAGE
11428-11428 JAMAICA
11428-11428 QUEENS VILLAGE
11429-11499 JAMAICA
11501-11501 MINEOLA
11507-11507 ALBERTSON
11509-11509 ATLANTIC BEACH
11510-11510 BALDWIN
11514-11514 CARLE PLACE
11516-11516 CEDARHURST
11518-11518 EAST ROCKAWAY
11520-11520 FREEPORT
11530-11536 GARDEN CITY
11542-11542 GLEN COVE
11545-11545 GLEN HEAD
11547-11547 GLENWOOD LANDING
11548-11548 GREENVALE
11549-11551 HEMPSTEAD
11552-11552 WEST HEMPSTEAD
11553-11553 UNIONDALE
11554-11554 EAST MEADOW
11555-11556 UNIONDALE
11557-11557 HEWLETT
11558-11558 ISLAND PARK
11559-11559 LAWRENCE
11560-11560 LOCUST VALLEY
11561-11561 LONG BEACH
11563-11564 LYNBROOK
11565-11565 MALVERNE
11566-11566 MERRICK
11568-11568 OLD WESTBURY
11569-11569 POINT LOOKOUT
11570-11571 ROCKVILLE CENTRE
11572-11572 OCEANSIDE
11575-11575 ROOSEVELT
11576-11576 ROSLYN
11577-11577 ROSLYN HEIGHTS
11579-11579 SEA CLIFF
11580-11583 VALLEY STREAM
11588-11588 UNIONDALE
11590-11590 WESTBURY
11592-11592 ROCKVILLE CENTRE
11593-11595 WESTBURY
11596-11596 WILLISTON PARK
11597-11597 WESTBURY
11598-11598 WOODMERE
11599-11599 GARDEN CITY
11600-11694 FAR ROCKAWAY
11694-11694 ROCKAWAY PARK
11695-11695 FAR ROCKAWAY
11696-11696 INWOOD
11697-11697 FAR ROCKAWAY
11701-11701 AMITYVILLE
11702-11702 BABYLON
11703-11703 NORTH BABYLON
11704-11704 WEST BABYLON
11705-11705 BAYPORT
11706-11706 BAY SHORE
11707-11707 WEST BABYLON
11708-11708 AMITYVILLE
11709-11709 BAYVILLE
11710-11710 BELLMORE
11713-11713 BELLPORT
11714-11714 BETHPAGE
11715-11715 BLUE POINT
11716-11716 BOHEMIA
11717-11717 BRENTWOOD
11718-11718 BRIGHTWATERS
11719-11719 BROOKHAVEN
11720-11720 CENTEREACH
11721-11721 CENTERPORT
11722-11722 CENTRAL ISLIP
11724-11724 COLD SPRING HARBOR
11725-11725 COMMACK
11726-11726 COPIAGUE
11727-11727 CORAM
11729-11729 DEER PARK
11730-11730 EAST ISLIP
11731-11731 EAST NORTHPORT
11732-11732 EAST NORWICH
11733-11733 EAST SETAUKET
11735-11737 FARMINGDALE
11738-11738 FARMINGVILLE
11739-11739 GREAT RIVER
11740-11740 GREENLAWN
11741-11741 HOLBROOK
11742-11742 HOLTSVILLE
11743-11743 HUNTINGTON
11745-11745 SMITHTOWN
11746-11746 HUNTINGTON STATION
11747-11747 MELVILLE
11749-11749 FARMINGVILLE
11749-11749 ISLANDIA
11750-11750 HUNTINGTON STATION
11751-11751 ISLIP
11752-11752 ISLIP TERRACE
11753-11753 JERICHO
11754-11754 KINGS PARK
11755-11755 LAKE GROVE
11756-11756 LEVITTOWN
11757-11757 LINDENHURST
11758-11758 MASSAPEQUA
11760-11760 HAUPPAUGE
11760-11760 ISLANDIA
11762-11762 MASSAPEQUA PARK
11763-11763 MEDFORD
11764-11764 MILLER PLACE
11765-11765 MILL NECK
11766-11766 MOUNT SINAI
11767-11767 NESCONSET
11768-11768 NORTHPORT
11769-11769 OAKDALE
11770-11770 OCEAN BEACH
11771-11771 OYSTER BAY
11772-11772 PATCHOGUE
11773-11773 SYOSSET
11774-11774 FARMINGDALE
11775-11775 MELVILLE
11776-11776 PORT JEFFERSON STATION
11777-11777 PORT JEFFERSON
11778-11778 ROCKY POINT
11779-11779 RONKONKOMA
11780-11780 SAINT JAMES
11782-11782 SAYVILLE
11783-11783 SEAFORD
11784-11784 SELDEN
11786-11786 SHOREHAM
11787-11787 SMITHTOWN
11788-11788 HAUPPAUGE
11789-11789 SOUND BEACH
11790-11790 STONY BROOK
11791-11791 SYOSSET
11792-11792 WADING RIVER
11793-11793 WANTAGH
11794-11794 STONY BROOK
11795-11795 WEST ISLIP
11796-11796 WEST SAYVILLE
11797-11797 WOODBURY
11798-11798 WYANDANCH
11801-11802 HICKSVILLE
11803-11803 PLAINVIEW
11804-11804 OLD BETHPAGE
11805-11805 MID ISLAND
11815-11819 HICKSVILLE
11853-11853 JERICHO
11854-11855 HICKSVILLE
11901-11901 RIVERHEAD
11930-11930 AMAGANSETT
11931-11931 AQUEBOGUE
11932-11932 BRIDGEHAMPTON
11933-11933 CALVERTON
11934-11934 CENTER MORICHES
11935-11935 CUTCHOGUE
11937-11937 EAST HAMPTON
11939-11939 EAST MARION
11940-11940 EAST MORICHES
11941-11941 EASTPORT
11942-11942 EAST QUOGUE
11944-11944 GREENPORT
11946-11946 HAMPTON BAYS
11947-11947 JAMESPORT
11948-11948 LAUREL
11949-11949 MANORVILLE
11950-11950 MASTIC
11951-11951 MASTIC BEACH
11952-11952 MATTITUCK
11953-11953 MIDDLE ISLAND
11954-11954 MONTAUK
11955-11955 MORICHES
11956-11956 NEW SUFFOLK
11957-11957 ORIENT
11958-11958 PECONIC
11959-11959 QUOGUE
11960-11960 REMSENBURG
11961-11961 RIDGE
11962-11962 SAGAPONACK
11963-11963 SAG HARBOR
11964-11964 SHELTER ISLAND
11965-11965 SHELTER ISLAND HEIGHTS
11967-11967 SHIRLEY
11968-11969 SOUTHAMPTON
11970-11970 SOUTH JAMESPORT
11971-11971 SOUTHOLD
11972-11972 SPEONK
11973-11973 UPTON
11975-11975 WAINSCOTT
11976-11976 WATER MILL
11977-11977 WESTHAMPTON
11978-11978 WESTHAMPTON BEACH
11980-11980 YAPHANK
12007-12007 ALCOVE
12008-12008 ALPLAUS
12009-12009 ALTAMONT
12010-12010 AMSTERDAM
12015-12015 ATHENS
12016-12016 AURIESVILLE
12017-12017 AUSTERLITZ
12018-12018 AVERILL PARK
12019-12019 BALLSTON LAKE
12020-12020 BALLSTON SPA
12022-12022 BERLIN
12023-12023 BERNE
12024-12024 BRAINARD
12025-12025 BROADALBIN
12026-12026 BROOKVIEW
12027-12027 BURNT HILLS
12028-12028 BUSKIRK
12029-12029 CANAAN
12031-12031 CARLISLE
12032-12032 CAROGA LAKE
12033-12033 CASTLETON ON HUDSON
12035-12035 CENTRAL BRIDGE
12036-12036 CHARLOTTEVILLE
12037-12037 CHATHAM

12040-12040 CHERRY PLAIN
12041-12041 CLARKSVILLE
12042-12042 CLIMAX
12043-12043 COBLESKILL
12045-12045 COEYMANS
12046-12046 COEYMANS HOLLOW
12047-12047 COHOES
12050-12050 COLUMBIAVILLE
12051-12051 COXSACKIE
12052-12052 CROPSEYVILLE
12053-12053 DELANSON
12054-12054 DELMAR
12055-12055 DORMANSVILLE
12056-12056 DUANESBURG
12057-12057 EAGLE BRIDGE
12058-12058 EARLTON
12059-12059 EAST BERNE
12060-12060 EAST CHATHAM
12061-12061 EAST GREENBUSH
12062-12062 EAST NASSAU
12063-12063 EAST SCHODACK
12064-12064 EAST WORCESTER
12065-12065 CLIFTON PARK
12066-12066 ESPERANCE
12067-12067 FEURA BUSH
12068-12068 FONDA
12069-12069 FORT HUNTER
12070-12070 FORT JOHNSON
12071-12071 FULTONHAM
12072-12072 FULTONVILLE
12073-12073 GALLUPVILLE
12074-12074 GALWAY
12075-12075 GHENT
12076-12076 GILBOA
12077-12077 GLENMONT
12078-12078 GLOVERSVILLE
12082-12082 GRAFTON
12083-12083 GREENVILLE
12084-12084 GUILDERLAND
12085-12085 GUILDERLAND CENTER
12086-12086 HAGAMAN
12087-12087 HANNACROIX
12089-12089 HOOSICK
12090-12090 HOOSICK FALLS
12092-12092 HOWES CAVE
12093-12093 JEFFERSON
12094-12094 JOHNSONVILLE
12095-12095 JOHNSTOWN
12106-12106 KINDERHOOK
12107-12107 KNOX
12108-12108 LAKE PLEASANT
12110-12111 LATHAM
12113-12113 LAWYERSVILLE
12114-12114 LEBANON SPRINGS
12115-12115 MALDEN BRIDGE
12116-12116 MARYLAND
12117-12117 MAYFIELD
12118-12118 MECHANICVILLE
12120-12120 MEDUSA
12121-12121 MELROSE
12122-12122 MIDDLEBURGH
12123-12123 NASSAU
12124-12124 NEW BALTIMORE
12125-12125 NEW LEBANON
12128-12128 NEWTONVILLE
12130-12130 NIVERVILLE
12131-12131 NORTH BLENHEIM
12132-12132 NORTH CHATHAM
12133-12133 NORTH HOOSICK
12134-12134 NORTHVILLE
12135-12135 NORTON HILL
12136-12136 OLD CHATHAM
12137-12137 PATTERSONVILLE
12138-12138 PETERSBURG
12139-12139 PISECO
12140-12140 POESTENKILL
12141-12141 QUAKER STREET
12143-12143 RAVENA
12144-12144 RENSSELAER
12147-12147 RENSSELAERVILLE
12148-12148 REXFORD
12149-12149 RICHMONDVILLE
12150-12150 ROTTERDAM JUNCTION
12151-12151 ROUND LAKE
12153-12153 SAND LAKE
12154-12154 SCHAGHTICOKE
12155-12155 SCHENEVUS
12156-12156 SCHODACK LANDING
12157-12157 SCHOHARIE
12158-12158 SELKIRK
12159-12159 SLINGERLANDS
12160-12160 SLOANSVILLE
12161-12161 SOUTH BETHLEHEM
12162-12162 SOUTH SCHODACK
12163-12163 SOUTH WESTERLO
12164-12164 SPECULATOR
12165-12165 SPENCERTOWN
12166-12166 SPRAKERS
12167-12167 STAMFORD
12168-12169 STEPHENTOWN
12170-12170 STILLWATER
12172-12172 STOTTVILLE
12173-12173 STUYVESANT
12174-12174 STUYVESANT FALLS
12175-12175 SUMMIT
12176-12176 SURPRISE
12177-12177 TRIBES HILL
12179-12183 TROY
12184-12184 VALATIE
12185-12185 VALLEY FALLS
12186-12186 VOORHEESVILLE
12187-12187 WARNERVILLE
12188-12188 WATERFORD
12189-12189 WATERVLIET
12190-12190 WELLS
12192-12192 WEST COXSACKIE
12193-12193 WESTERLO
12194-12194 WEST FULTON
12195-12195 WEST LEBANON
12196-12196 WEST SAND LAKE
12197-12197 WORCESTER
12198-12198 WYNANTSKILL
12200-12288 ALBANY
12300-12345 SCHENECTADY
12401-12402 KINGSTON
12404-12404 ACCORD
12405-12405 ACRA
12406-12406 ARKVILLE
12407-12407 ASHLAND
12409-12409 BEARSVILLE
12410-12410 BIG INDIAN
12411-12411 BLOOMINGTON
12412-12412 BOICEVILLE
12413-12413 CAIRO
12414-12414 CATSKILL
12415-12415 CEMENTON
12415-12415 SMITHS LANDING
12416-12416 CHICHESTER
12417-12417 CONNELLY
12418-12418 CORNWALLVILLE
12419-12419 COTTEKILL
12420-12420 CRAGSMOOR
12421-12421 DENVER
12422-12422 DURHAM
12423-12423 EAST DURHAM
12424-12424 EAST JEWETT
12427-12427 ELKA PARK
12428-12428 ELLENVILLE
12429-12429 ESOPUS
12430-12430 FLEISCHMANNS
12431-12431 FREEHOLD
12432-12432 GLASCO
12433-12433 GLENFORD
12434-12434 GRAND GORGE
12435-12435 GREENFIELD PARK
12436-12436 HAINES FALLS
12438-12438 HALCOTTSVILLE
12439-12439 HENSONVILLE
12440-12440 HIGH FALLS
12441-12441 HIGHMOUNT
12442-12442 HUNTER
12443-12443 HURLEY
12444-12444 JEWETT
12446-12446 KERHONKSON
12448-12448 LAKE HILL
12449-12449 LAKE KATRINE
12450-12450 LANESVILLE
12451-12451 LEEDS
12452-12452 LEXINGTON
12453-12453 MALDEN ON HUDSON
12454-12454 MAPLECREST
12455-12455 MARGARETVILLE
12456-12456 MOUNT MARION
12457-12457 MOUNT TREMPER
12458-12458 NAPANOCH
12459-12459 NEW KINGSTON
12460-12460 OAK HILL
12461-12461 OLIVEBRIDGE
12462-12462 OLIVEREA
12463-12463 PALENVILLE
12464-12464 PHOENICIA
12465-12465 PINE HILL
12466-12466 PORT EWEN
12468-12468 PRATTSVILLE
12469-12469 PRESTON HOLLOW
12470-12470 PURLING
12471-12471 RIFTON
12472-12472 ROSENDALE
12473-12473 ROUND TOP
12474-12474 ROXBURY
12475-12475 RUBY
12477-12477 SAUGERTIES
12480-12480 SHANDAKEN
12481-12481 SHOKAN
12482-12482 SOUTH CAIRO
12483-12483 SPRING GLEN
12484-12484 STONE RIDGE
12485-12485 TANNERSVILLE
12486-12486 TILLSON
12487-12487 ULSTER PARK
12489-12489 WAWARSING
12490-12490 WEST CAMP
12491-12491 WEST HURLEY
12492-12492 WEST KILL
12493-12493 WEST PARK
12494-12494 WEST SHOKAN
12495-12495 WILLOW
12496-12496 WINDHAM
12498-12498 WOODSTOCK
12501-12501 AMENIA
12502-12502 ANCRAM
12503-12503 ANCRAMDALE
12504-12504 ANNANDALE ON HUDSON
12506-12506 BANGALL
12507-12507 BARRYTOWN
12508-12508 BEACON
12510-12510 BILLINGS
12511-12511 CASTLE POINT
12512-12512 CHELSEA
12513-12513 CLAVERACK
12514-12514 CLINTON CORNERS
12515-12515 CLINTONDALE
12516-12516 COPAKE
12517-12517 COPAKE FALLS
12518-12518 CORNWALL
12520-12520 CORNWALL ON HUDSON
12521-12521 CRARYVILLE
12522-12522 DOVER PLAINS
12523-12523 ELIZAVILLE
12524-12524 FISHKILL
12525-12525 GARDINER
12526-12526 GERMANTOWN
12527-12527 GLENHAM
12528-12528 HIGHLAND
12529-12529 HILLSDALE
12530-12530 HOLLOWVILLE
12531-12531 HOLMES
12533-12533 HOPEWELL JUNCTION
12534-12534 HUDSON
12537-12537 HUGHSONVILLE
12538-12538 HYDE PARK
12540-12540 LAGRANGEVILLE
12541-12541 LIVINGSTON
12542-12542 MARLBORO
12543-12543 MAYBROOK
12544-12544 MELLENVILLE
12545-12545 MILLBROOK
12546-12546 MILLERTON
12547-12547 MILTON
12548-12548 MODENA
12549-12549 MONTGOMERY
12550-12552 NEWBURGH
12553-12553 NEW WINDSOR
12555-12555 MID HUDSON
12561-12561 NEW PALTZ
12563-12563 PATTERSON
12564-12564 PAWLING
12565-12565 PHILMONT
12566-12566 PINE BUSH
12567-12567 PINE PLAINS
12568-12568 PLATTEKILL
12569-12569 PLEASANT VALLEY
12570-12570 POUGHQUAG
12571-12571 RED HOOK
12572-12572 RHINEBECK
12574-12574 RHINECLIFF
12575-12575 ROCK TAVERN
12577-12577 SALISBURY MILLS
12578-12578 SALT POINT
12580-12580 STAATSBURG
12581-12581 STANFORDVILLE
12582-12582 STORMVILLE
12583-12583 TIVOLI
12584-12584 VAILS GATE
12585-12585 VERBANK
12586-12586 WALDEN
12588-12588 WALKER VALLEY
12589-12589 WALLKILL
12590-12590 WAPPINGERS FALLS
12592-12592 WASSAIC
12593-12593 WEST COPAKE
12594-12594 WINGDALE
12600-12604 POUGHKEEPSIE
12701-12701 MONTICELLO
12719-12719 BARRYVILLE
12720-12720 BETHEL
12721-12721 BLOOMINGBURG
12722-12722 BURLINGHAM
12723-12723 CALLICOON
12724-12724 CALLICOON CENTER
12725-12725 CLARYVILLE
12726-12726 COCHECTON
12727-12727 COCHECTON CENTER
12729-12729 CUDDEBACKVILLE
12732-12732 ELDRED
12733-12733 FALLSBURG
12734-12734 FERNDALE
12736-12736 FREMONT CENTER
12737-12737 GLEN SPEY
12738-12738 GLEN WILD
12739-12739 GODEFFROY
12740-12740 GRAHAMSVILLE
12741-12741 HANKINS
12742-12742 HARRIS
12743-12743 HIGHLAND LAKE
12745-12745 HORTONVILLE
12746-12746 HUGUENOT
12747-12747 HURLEYVILLE
12748-12748 JEFFERSONVILLE
12749-12749 KAUNEONGA LAKE
12750-12750 KENOZA LAKE
12751-12751 KIAMESHA LAKE
12752-12752 LAKE HUNTINGTON
12753-12753 LEW BEACH
12754-12754 LIBERTY
12758-12758 LIVINGSTON MANOR
12759-12759 LOCH SHELDRAKE
12760-12760 LONG EDDY
12762-12762 MONGAUP VALLEY
12763-12763 MOUNTAIN DALE
12764-12764 NARROWSBURG
12765-12765 NEVERSINK
12766-12766 NORTH BRANCH
12767-12767 OBERNBURG
12768-12768 PARKSVILLE
12769-12769 PHILLIPSPORT
12770-12770 POND EDDY
12771-12771 PORT JERVIS

12775-12775 ROCK HILL
12776-12776 ROSCOE
12777-12777 FORESTBURGH
12778-12778 SMALLWOOD
12779-12779 SOUTH FALLSBURG
12780-12780 SPARROW BUSH
12781-12781 SUMMITVILLE
12782-12782 SUNDOWN
12783-12783 SWAN LAKE
12784-12784 THOMPSONVILLE
12785-12785 WESTBROOKVILLE
12786-12786 WHITE LAKE
12787-12787 WHITE SULPHUR SPRINGS
12788-12788 WOODBOURNE
12789-12789 WOODRIDGE
12790-12790 WURTSBORO
12791-12791 YOUNGSVILLE
12792-12792 YULAN
12801-12801 GLENS FALLS
12803-12803 SOUTH GLENS FALLS
12804-12804 QUEENSBURY
12808-12808 ADIRONDACK
12809-12809 ARGYLE
12810-12810 ATHOL
12811-12811 BAKERS MILLS
12812-12812 BLUE MOUNTAIN LAKE
12814-12814 BOLTON LANDING
12815-12815 BRANT LAKE
12816-12816 CAMBRIDGE
12817-12817 CHESTERTOWN
12819-12819 CLEMONS
12820-12820 CLEVERDALE
12821-12821 COMSTOCK
12822-12822 CORINTH
12823-12823 COSSAYUNA
12824-12824 DIAMOND POINT
12826-12826 EAST GREENWICH
12827-12827 FORT ANN
12828-12828 FORT EDWARD
12831-12831 GANSEVOORT
12832-12832 GRANVILLE
12833-12833 GREENFIELD CENTER
12834-12834 GREENWICH
12835-12835 HADLEY
12836-12836 HAGUE
12837-12837 HAMPTON
12838-12838 HARTFORD
12839-12839 HUDSON FALLS
12841-12841 HULETTS LANDING
12842-12842 INDIAN LAKE
12843-12843 JOHNSBURG
12844-12844 KATTSKILL BAY
12845-12845 LAKE GEORGE
12846-12846 LAKE LUZERNE
12847-12847 LONG LAKE
12848-12848 MIDDLE FALLS
12849-12849 MIDDLE GRANVILLE
12850-12850 MIDDLE GROVE
12851-12851 MINERVA
12852-12852 NEWCOMB
12853-12853 NORTH CREEK
12854-12854 NORTH GRANVILLE
12855-12855 NORTH HUDSON
12856-12856 NORTH RIVER
12857-12857 OLMSTEDVILLE
12858-12858 PARADOX
12859-12859 PORTER CORNERS
12860-12860 POTTERSVILLE
12861-12861 PUTNAM STATION
12862-12862 RIPARIUS
12863-12863 ROCK CITY FALLS
12864-12864 SABAEL
12865-12865 SALEM
12866-12866 SARATOGA SPRINGS
12870-12870 SCHROON LAKE
12871-12871 SCHUYLERVILLE
12872-12872 SEVERANCE
12873-12873 SHUSHAN
12874-12874 SILVER BAY
12878-12878 STONY CREEK
12879-12879 NEWCOMB
12883-12883 TICONDEROGA
12884-12884 VICTORY MILLS
12885-12885 WARRENSBURG
12886-12886 WEVERTOWN
12887-12887 WHITEHALL
12901-12903 PLATTSBURGH
12910-12910 ALTONA
12911-12911 KEESEVILLE
12912-12912 AU SABLE FORKS
12913-12913 BLOOMINGDALE
12914-12914 BOMBAY
12915-12915 BRAINARDSVILLE
12916-12916 BRUSHTON
12917-12917 BURKE
12918-12918 CADYVILLE
12919-12919 CHAMPLAIN
12920-12920 CHATEAUGAY
12921-12921 CHAZY
12922-12922 CHILDWOLD
12923-12923 CHURUBUSCO
12924-12924 KEESEVILLE
12926-12926 CONSTABLE
12927-12927 CRANBERRY LAKE
12928-12928 CROWN POINT
12929-12929 DANNEMORA
12930-12930 DICKINSON CENTER
12932-12932 ELIZABETHTOWN
12933-12933 ELLENBURG
12934-12934 ELLENBURG CENTER
12935-12935 ELLENBURG DEPOT
12936-12936 ESSEX
12937-12937 FORT COVINGTON
12938-12938 FORT JACKSON
12938-12938 NORTH LAWRENCE
12939-12939 GABRIELS
12940-12940 HOPKINTON
12941-12941 JAY
12942-12942 KEENE
12943-12943 KEENE VALLEY
12944-12944 KEESEVILLE
12945-12945 LAKE CLEAR
12946-12946 LAKE PLACID
12949-12949 LAWRENCEVILLE
12950-12950 LEWIS
12952-12952 LYON MOUNTAIN
12953-12953 MALONE
12955-12955 LYON MOUNTAIN
12956-12956 MINEVILLE
12957-12957 MOIRA
12958-12958 MOOERS
12959-12959 MOOERS FORKS
12960-12960 MORIAH
12961-12961 MORIAH CENTER
12962-12962 MORRISONVILLE
12964-12964 NEW RUSSIA
12965-12965 NICHOLVILLE
12966-12966 NORTH BANGOR
12967-12967 NORTH LAWRENCE
12968-12968 ONCHIOTA
12968-12968 SUGARBUSH
12968-12968 ONCHIOTA
12969-12969 OWLS HEAD
12970-12970 PAUL SMITHS
12972-12972 PERU
12973-12973 PIERCEFIELD
12974-12974 PORT HENRY
12975-12975 PORT KENT
12976-12976 RAINBOW LAKE
12977-12977 RAY BROOK
12978-12978 REDFORD
12979-12979 ROUSES POINT
12980-12980 SAINT REGIS FALLS
12981-12981 SARANAC
12982-12983 SARANAC LAKE
12985-12985 SCHUYLER FALLS
12986-12986 TUPPER LAKE
12987-12987 UPPER JAY
12989-12989 VERMONTVILLE
12990-12990 WADHAMS
12991-12991 BANGOR
12992-12992 WEST CHAZY
12993-12993 WESTPORT
12994-12994 BOUQUET
12994-12994 WHALLONSBURG
12995-12995 WHIPPLEVILLE
12996-12996 WILLSBORO
12997-12997 WILMINGTON
12998-12998 WITHERBEE
13020-13020 APULIA STATION
13021-13024 AUBURN
13026-13026 AURORA
13027-13027 BALDWINSVILLE
13028-13028 BERNHARDS BAY
13029-13029 BREWERTON
13030-13030 BRIDGEPORT
13031-13031 CAMILLUS
13032-13032 CANASTOTA
13033-13033 CATO
13034-13034 CAYUGA
13035-13035 CAZENOVIA
13036-13036 CENTRAL SQUARE
13037-13037 CHITTENANGO
13039-13039 CICERO
13040-13040 CINCINNATUS
13041-13041 CLAY
13042-13042 CLEVELAND
13043-13043 CLOCKVILLE
13044-13044 CONSTANTIA
13045-13045 CORTLAND
13050-13050 CUYLER
13051-13051 DELPHI FALLS
13052-13052 DE RUYTER
13053-13053 DRYDEN
13054-13054 DURHAMVILLE
13055-13055 EAST FREETOWN
13056-13056 EAST HOMER
13057-13057 EAST SYRACUSE
13060-13060 ELBRIDGE
13061-13061 ERIEVILLE
13062-13062 ETNA
13063-13063 FABIUS
13064-13064 FAIR HAVEN
13065-13065 FAYETTE
13066-13066 FAYETTEVILLE
13068-13068 FREEVILLE
13069-13069 FULTON
13071-13071 GENOA
13072-13072 GEORGETOWN
13073-13073 GROTON
13074-13074 HANNIBAL
13076-13076 HASTINGS
13077-13077 HOMER
13078-13078 JAMESVILLE
13080-13080 JORDAN
13081-13081 KING FERRY
13082-13082 KIRKVILLE
13083-13083 LACONA
13084-13084 LA FAYETTE
13085-13085 LEBANON
13087-13087 LITTLE YORK
13088-13090 LIVERPOOL
13092-13092 LOCKE
13093-13093 LYCOMING
13094-13094 LYSANDER
13101-13101 MC GRAW
13102-13102 MC LEAN
13103-13103 MALLORY
13104-13104 MANLIUS
13107-13107 MAPLE VIEW
13108-13108 MARCELLUS
13110-13110 MARIETTA
13111-13111 MARTVILLE
13112-13112 MEMPHIS
13113-13113 MERIDIAN
13114-13114 MEXICO
13115-13115 MINETTO
13116-13116 MINOA
13117-13117 MONTEZUMA
13118-13118 MORAVIA
13119-13119 MOTTVILLE
13120-13120 NEDROW
13121-13121 NEW HAVEN
13122-13122 NEW WOODSTOCK
13123-13123 NORTH BAY
13124-13124 NORTH PITCHER
13125-13125 ORAN
13126-13126 OSWEGO
13129-13129 GEORGETOWN
13130-13130 OWASCO
13131-13131 PARISH
13132-13132 PENNELLVILLE
13133-13133 PERRYVILLE
13134-13134 PETERBORO
13135-13135 PHOENIX
13136-13136 PITCHER
13137-13137 PLAINVILLE
13138-13138 POMPEY
13139-13139 POPLAR RIDGE
13140-13140 PORT BYRON
13141-13141 PREBLE
13142-13142 PULASKI
13143-13143 RED CREEK
13144-13144 RICHLAND
13145-13145 SANDY CREEK
13146-13146 SAVANNAH
13147-13147 SCIPIO CENTER
13148-13148 SENECA FALLS
13150-13150 SENNETT
13151-13151 SHEDS
13152-13152 SKANEATELES
13153-13153 SKANEATELES FALLS
13154-13154 SOUTH BUTLER
13155-13155 SOUTH OTSELIC
13156-13156 STERLING
13157-13157 SYLVAN BEACH
13158-13158 TRUXTON
13159-13159 TULLY
13160-13160 UNION SPRINGS
13162-13162 VERONA BEACH
13163-13163 WAMPSVILLE
13164-13164 WARNERS
13165-13165 WATERLOO
13166-13166 WEEDSPORT
13167-13167 WEST MONROE
13200-13210 SYRACUSE
13211-13211 MATTYDALE
13212-13290 SYRACUSE
13301-13301 ALDER CREEK
13302-13302 ALTMAR
13303-13303 AVA
13304-13304 BARNEVELD
13305-13305 BEAVER FALLS
13308-13308 BLOSSVALE
13309-13309 BOONVILLE
13310-13310 BOUCKVILLE
13312-13312 BRANTINGHAM
13313-13313 BRIDGEWATER
13314-13314 BROOKFIELD
13315-13315 BURLINGTON FLATS
13316-13316 CAMDEN
13317-13317 CANAJOHARIE
13318-13318 CASSVILLE
13319-13319 CHADWICKS
13320-13320 CHERRY VALLEY
13321-13321 CLARK MILLS
13322-13322 CLAYVILLE
13323-13323 CLINTON
13324-13324 COLD BROOK
13325-13325 CONSTABLEVILLE
13326-13326 COOPERSTOWN
13327-13327 CROGHAN
13328-13328 DEANSBORO
13329-13329 DOLGEVILLE
13331-13331 EAGLE BAY
13332-13332 EARLVILLE
13333-13333 EAST SPRINGFIELD
13334-13334 EATON
13335-13335 EDMESTON
13336-13336 FAIRFIELD
13337-13337 FLY CREEK
13338-13338 FORESTPORT
13339-13339 FORT PLAIN
13340-13340 FRANKFORT
13341-13341 FRANKLIN SPRINGS
13342-13342 GARRATTSVILLE
13343-13343 GLENFIELD
13345-13345 GREIG

13346-13346 HAMILTON
13348-13348 HARTWICK
13349-13349 HARTWICK SEMINARY
13350-13350 HERKIMER
13352-13352 HINCKLEY
13353-13353 HOFFMEISTER
13354-13354 HOLLAND PATENT
13355-13355 HUBBARDSVILLE
13357-13357 ILION
13360-13360 INLET
13361-13361 JORDANVILLE
13362-13362 KNOXBORO
13363-13363 LEE CENTER
13364-13364 LEONARDSVILLE
13365-13365 LITTLE FALLS
13367-13367 LOWVILLE
13368-13368 LYONS FALLS
13401-13401 MC CONNELLSVILLE
13402-13402 MADISON
13403-13403 MARCY
13404-13404 MARTINSBURG
13406-13406 MIDDLEVILLE
13407-13407 MOHAWK
13408-13408 MORRISVILLE
13409-13409 MUNNSVILLE
13410-13410 NELLISTON
13411-13411 NEW BERLIN
13413-13413 NEW HARTFORD
13415-13415 NEW LISBON
13416-13416 NEWPORT
13417-13417 NEW YORK MILLS
13418-13418 NORTH BROOKFIELD
13419-13419 WESTERN
13420-13420 OLD FORGE
13421-13421 ONEIDA
13424-13424 ORISKANY
13425-13425 ORISKANY FALLS
13426-13426 ORWELL
13428-13428 PALATINE BRIDGE
13429-13429 PARIS
13431-13431 POLAND
13432-13432 POOLVILLE
13433-13433 PORT LEYDEN
13434-13434 PRATTS HOLLOW
13435-13435 PROSPECT
13436-13436 RAQUETTE LAKE
13437-13437 REDFIELD
13438-13438 REMSEN
13439-13439 RICHFIELD SPRINGS
13440-13449 ROME
13450-13450 ROSEBOOM
13452-13452 SAINT JOHNSVILLE
13454-13454 SALISBURY CENTER
13455-13455 SANGERFIELD
13456-13456 SAUQUOIT
13457-13457 SCHUYLER LAKE
13459-13459 SHARON SPRINGS
13460-13460 SHERBURNE
13461-13461 SHERRILL
13464-13464 SMYRNA
13465-13465 SOLSVILLE
13466-13466 SOUTH EDMESTON
13468-13468 SPRINGFIELD CENTER
13469-13469 STITTVILLE
13470-13470 STRATFORD
13471-13471 TABERG
13472-13472 THENDARA
13473-13473 TURIN
13475-13475 VAN HORNESVILLE
13476-13476 VERNON
13477-13477 VERNON CENTER
13478-13478 VERONA
13479-13479 WASHINGTON MILLS
13480-13480 WATERVILLE
13482-13482 WEST BURLINGTON
13483-13483 WESTDALE
13484-13484 WEST EATON
13485-13485 WEST EDMESTON
13486-13486 WESTERNVILLE
13487-13487 WEST EXETER
13488-13488 WESTFORD
13489-13489 WEST LEYDEN
13490-13490 WESTMORELAND
13491-13491 WEST WINFIELD
13492-13492 WHITESBORO
13493-13493 WILLIAMSTOWN
13494-13494 WOODGATE
13495-13495 YORKVILLE
13500-13599 UTICA
13601-13601 WATERTOWN
13602-13602 FORT DRUM
13603-13603 WATERTOWN
13605-13605 ADAMS
13606-13606 ADAMS CENTER
13607-13607 ALEXANDRIA BAY
13608-13608 ANTWERP
13609-13609 BALMAT
13610-13610 RODMAN
13611-13611 BELLEVILLE
13612-13612 BLACK RIVER
13613-13613 BRASHER FALLS
13614-13614 BRIER HILL
13615-13615 BROWNVILLE
13616-13616 CALCIUM
13617-13617 CANTON
13618-13618 CAPE VINCENT
13619-13619 CARTHAGE
13620-13620 CASTORLAND
13621-13621 CHASE MILLS
13622-13622 CHAUMONT
13623-13623 CHIPPEWA BAY
13624-13624 CLAYTON
13625-13625 COLTON
13626-13626 COPENHAGEN
13627-13627 DEER RIVER
13628-13628 DEFERIET
13630-13630 DE KALB JUNCTION
13631-13631 DENMARK
13632-13632 DEPAUVILLE
13633-13633 DE PEYSTER
13634-13634 DEXTER
13635-13635 EDWARDS
13636-13636 ELLISBURG
13637-13637 EVANS MILLS
13638-13638 FELTS MILLS
13639-13639 FINE
13640-13640 WELLESLEY ISLAND
13641-13641 FISHERS LANDING
13642-13642 GOUVERNEUR
13643-13643 GREAT BEND
13645-13645 HAILESBORO
13646-13646 HAMMOND
13647-13647 HANNAWA FALLS
13648-13648 HARRISVILLE
13649-13649 HELENA
13650-13650 HENDERSON
13651-13651 HENDERSON HARBOR
13652-13652 HERMON
13654-13654 HEUVELTON
13655-13655 HOGANSBURG
13656-13656 LA FARGEVILLE
13657-13657 LIMERICK
13658-13658 LISBON
13659-13659 LORRAINE
13660-13660 MADRID
13661-13661 MANNSVILLE
13662-13662 MASSENA
13664-13664 MORRISTOWN
13665-13665 NATURAL BRIDGE
13666-13666 NEWTON FALLS
13667-13667 NORFOLK
13668-13668 NORWOOD
13669-13669 OGDENSBURG
13670-13670 OSWEGATCHIE
13671-13671 OXBOW
13672-13672 PARISHVILLE
13673-13673 PHILADELPHIA
13674-13674 PIERREPONT MANOR
13675-13675 PLESSIS
13676-13676 POTSDAM
13677-13677 PYRITES
13678-13678 RAYMONDVILLE
13679-13679 REDWOOD
13680-13680 RENSSELAER FALLS
13681-13681 RICHVILLE
13682-13682 RODMAN
13683-13683 ROOSEVELTOWN
13684-13684 RUSSELL
13685-13685 SACKETS HARBOR
13687-13687 SOUTH COLTON
13688-13688 SOUTH RUTLAND
13690-13690 STAR LAKE
13691-13691 THERESA
13692-13692 THOUSAND ISLAND PARK
13693-13693 THREE MILE BAY
13694-13694 WADDINGTON
13695-13695 WANAKENA
13696-13696 WEST STOCKHOLM
13697-13697 WINTHROP
13698-13698 WOODVILLE
13699-13699 POTSDAM
13730-13730 AFTON
13731-13731 ANDES
13732-13732 APALACHIN
13733-13733 BAINBRIDGE
13734-13734 BARTON
13736-13736 BERKSHIRE
13737-13737 BIBLE SCHOOL PARK
13738-13738 BLODGETT MILLS
13739-13739 BLOOMVILLE
13740-13740 BOVINA CENTER
13743-13743 CANDOR
13744-13744 CASTLE CREEK
13745-13745 CHENANGO BRIDGE
13746-13746 CHENANGO FORKS
13747-13747 COLLIERSVILLE
13748-13748 CONKLIN
13749-13749 CORBETTSVILLE
13750-13750 DAVENPORT
13751-13751 DAVENPORT CENTER
13752-13752 DE LANCEY
13753-13753 DELHI
13754-13754 DEPOSIT
13755-13755 DOWNSVILLE
13756-13756 EAST BRANCH
13757-13757 EAST MEREDITH
13758-13758 EAST PHARSALIA
13760-13761 ENDICOTT
13762-13762 ENDWELL
13763-13763 ENDICOTT
13774-13774 FISHS EDDY
13775-13775 FRANKLIN
13776-13776 GILBERTSVILLE
13777-13777 GLEN AUBREY
13778-13778 GREENE
13780-13780 GUILFORD
13782-13782 HAMDEN
13783-13783 HANCOCK
13784-13784 HARFORD
13786-13786 HARPERSFIELD
13787-13787 HARPURSVILLE
13788-13788 HOBART
13790-13790 JOHNSON CITY
13794-13794 KILLAWOG
13795-13795 KIRKWOOD
13796-13796 LAURENS
13797-13797 LISLE
13801-13801 MC DONOUGH
13802-13802 MAINE
13803-13803 MARATHON
13804-13804 MASONVILLE
13806-13806 MERIDALE
13807-13807 MILFORD
13808-13808 MORRIS
13809-13809 MOUNT UPTON
13810-13810 MOUNT VISION
13811-13811 NEWARK VALLEY
13812-13812 NICHOLS
13813-13813 NINEVEH
13814-13814 NORTH NORWICH
13815-13815 NORWICH
13820-13820 ONEONTA
13825-13825 OTEGO
13826-13826 OUAQUAGA
13827-13827 OWEGO
13830-13830 OXFORD
13832-13832 PLYMOUTH
13833-13833 PORT CRANE
13834-13834 PORTLANDVILLE
13835-13835 RICHFORD
13837-13837 SHINHOPPLE
13838-13838 SIDNEY
13839-13839 SIDNEY CENTER
13840-13840 SMITHBORO
13841-13841 SMITHVILLE FLATS
13842-13842 SOUTH KORTRIGHT
13843-13843 SOUTH NEW BERLIN
13844-13844 SOUTH PLYMOUTH
13845-13845 TIOGA CENTER
13846-13846 TREADWELL
13847-13847 TROUT CREEK
13848-13848 TUNNEL
13849-13849 UNADILLA
13850-13851 VESTAL
13856-13856 WALTON
13859-13859 WELLS BRIDGE
13860-13860 WEST DAVENPORT
13861-13861 WEST ONEONTA
13862-13862 WHITNEY POINT
13863-13863 WILLET
13864-13864 WILLSEYVILLE
13865-13865 WINDSOR
13900-13905 BINGHAMTON
14001-14001 AKRON
14003-14003 ALABAMA
14004-14004 ALDEN
14005-14005 ALEXANDER
14006-14006 ANGOLA
14008-14008 APPLETON
14009-14009 ARCADE
14010-14010 ATHOL SPRINGS
14011-14011 ATTICA
14012-14012 BARKER
14013-14013 BASOM
14020-14021 BATAVIA
14024-14024 BLISS
14025-14025 BOSTON
14026-14026 BOWMANSVILLE
14027-14027 BRANT
14028-14028 BURT
14029-14029 CENTERVILLE
14030-14030 CHAFFEE
14031-14031 CLARENCE
14032-14032 CLARENCE CENTER
14033-14033 COLDEN
14034-14034 COLLINS
14035-14035 COLLINS CENTER
14036-14036 CORFU
14037-14037 COWLESVILLE
14038-14038 CRITTENDEN
14039-14039 DALE
14040-14040 DARIEN CENTER
14041-14041 DAYTON
14042-14042 DELEVAN
14043-14043 DEPEW
14047-14047 DERBY
14048-14048 DUNKIRK
14051-14051 EAST AMHERST
14052-14052 EAST AURORA
14054-14054 EAST BETHANY
14055-14055 EAST CONCORD
14056-14056 EAST PEMBROKE
14057-14057 EDEN
14058-14058 ELBA
14059-14059 ELMA
14060-14060 FARMERSVILLE STATION
14061-14061 FARNHAM
14062-14062 FORESTVILLE
14063-14063 FREDONIA
14065-14065 FREEDOM
14066-14066 GAINESVILLE
14067-14067 GASPORT
14068-14068 GETZVILLE
14069-14069 GLENWOOD
14070-14070 GOWANDA
14072-14072 GRAND ISLAND
14075-14075 HAMBURG
14079-14079 HELMUTH

14080-14080 HOLLAND
14081-14081 IRVING
14082-14082 JAVA CENTER
14083-14083 JAVA VILLAGE
14085-14085 LAKE VIEW
14086-14086 LANCASTER
14091-14091 LAWTONS
14092-14092 LEWISTON
14094-14095 LOCKPORT
14098-14098 LYNDONVILLE
14101-14101 MACHIAS
14102-14102 MARILLA
14103-14103 MEDINA
14105-14105 MIDDLEPORT
14107-14107 MODEL CITY
14108-14108 NEWFANE
14109-14109 NIAGARA UNIVERSITY
14110-14110 NORTH BOSTON
14111-14111 NORTH COLLINS
14112-14112 NORTH EVANS
14113-14113 NORTH JAVA
14120-14120 NORTH TONAWANDA
14125-14125 OAKFIELD
14126-14126 OLCOTT
14127-14127 ORCHARD PARK
14129-14129 PERRYSBURG
14130-14130 PIKE
14131-14131 RANSOMVILLE
14132-14132 SANBORN
14133-14133 SANDUSKY
14134-14134 SARDINIA
14135-14135 SHERIDAN
14136-14136 SILVER CREEK
14138-14138 SOUTH DAYTON
14139-14139 SOUTH WALES
14140-14140 SPRING BROOK
14141-14141 SPRINGVILLE
14143-14143 STAFFORD
14144-14144 STELLA NIAGARA
14145-14145 STRYKERSVILLE
14150-14151 TONAWANDA
14166-14166 VAN BUREN POINT
14167-14167 VARYSBURG
14168-14168 VERSAILLES
14169-14169 WALES CENTER
14170-14170 WEST FALLS
14171-14171 WEST VALLEY
14172-14172 WILSON
14173-14173 YORKSHIRE
14174-14174 YOUNGSTOWN
14200-14280 BUFFALO
14300-14305 NIAGARA FALLS
14410-14410 ADAMS BASIN
14411-14411 ALBION
14413-14413 ALTON
14414-14414 AVON
14415-14415 BELLONA
14416-14416 BERGEN
14418-14418 BRANCHPORT
14420-14420 BROCKPORT
14422-14422 BYRON
14423-14423 CALEDONIA
14424-14424 CANANDAIGUA
14425-14425 FARMINGTON
14427-14427 CASTILE
14428-14428 CHURCHVILLE
14429-14429 CLARENDON
14430-14430 CLARKSON
14432-14432 CLIFTON SPRINGS
14433-14433 CLYDE
14435-14435 CONESUS
14437-14437 DANSVILLE
14441-14441 DRESDEN
14442-14442 EAGLE HARBOR
14443-14443 EAST BLOOMFIELD
14444-14444 EAST PALMYRA
14445-14445 EAST ROCHESTER
14449-14449 EAST WILLIAMSON
14450-14450 FAIRPORT
14452-14452 FANCHER
14453-14453 FISHERS
14454-14454 GENESEO
14456-14456 GENEVA
14461-14461 GORHAM
14462-14462 GROVELAND
14463-14463 HALL
14464-14464 HAMLIN
14466-14466 HEMLOCK
14467-14467 HENRIETTA
14468-14468 HILTON
14469-14469 BLOOMFIELD
14470-14470 HOLLEY
14471-14471 HONEOYE
14472-14472 HONEOYE FALLS
14474-14474 INDUSTRY
14475-14475 IONIA
14476-14476 KENDALL
14477-14477 KENT
14478-14478 KEUKA PARK
14479-14479 KNOWLESVILLE
14480-14480 LAKEVILLE
14481-14481 LEICESTER
14482-14482 LE ROY
14485-14485 LIMA
14486-14486 LINWOOD
14487-14487 LIVONIA
14488-14488 LIVONIA CENTER
14489-14489 LYONS
14502-14502 MACEDON
14504-14504 MANCHESTER
14505-14505 MARION
14506-14506 MENDON
14507-14507 MIDDLESEX
14508-14508 MORTON
14510-14510 MOUNT MORRIS
14511-14511 MUMFORD
14512-14512 NAPLES
14513-14513 NEWARK
14514-14514 NORTH CHILI
14515-14515 NORTH GREECE
14516-14516 NORTH ROSE
14517-14517 NUNDA
14518-14518 OAKS CORNERS
14519-14519 ONTARIO
14520-14520 ONTARIO CENTER
14521-14521 OVID
14522-14522 PALMYRA
14525-14525 PAVILION
14526-14526 PENFIELD
14527-14527 PENN YAN
14529-14529 PERKINSVILLE
14530-14530 PERRY
14532-14532 PHELPS
14533-14533 PIFFARD
14534-14534 PITTSFORD
14536-14536 PORTAGEVILLE
14537-14537 PORT GIBSON
14538-14538 PULTNEYVILLE
14539-14539 RETSOF
14541-14541 ROMULUS
14542-14542 ROSE
14543-14543 RUSH
14544-14544 RUSHVILLE
14545-14545 SCOTTSBURG
14546-14546 SCOTTSVILLE
14547-14547 SENECA CASTLE
14548-14548 SHORTSVILLE
14549-14549 SILVER LAKE
14550-14550 SILVER SPRINGS
14551-14551 SODUS
14554-14554 SODUS CENTER
14555-14555 SODUS POINT
14556-14556 SONYEA
14557-14557 SOUTH BYRON
14558-14558 SOUTH LIMA
14559-14559 SPENCERPORT
14560-14560 SPRINGWATER
14561-14561 STANLEY
14563-14563 UNION HILL
14564-14564 VICTOR
14568-14568 WALWORTH
14569-14569 WARSAW
14571-14571 WATERPORT
14572-14572 WAYLAND
14580-14580 WEBSTER
14584-14584 WEBSTER CROSSING
14585-14585 WEST BLOOMFIELD
14586-14586 WEST HENRIETTA
14588-14588 WILLARD
14589-14589 WILLIAMSON
14590-14590 WOLCOTT
14591-14591 WYOMING
14592-14592 YORK
14600-14694 ROCHESTER
14701-14704 JAMESTOWN
14706-14706 ALLEGANY
14707-14707 ALLENTOWN
14708-14708 ALMA
14709-14709 ANGELICA
14710-14710 ASHVILLE
14711-14711 BELFAST
14712-14712 BEMUS POINT
14714-14714 BLACK CREEK
14715-14715 BOLIVAR
14716-14716 BROCTON
14717-14717 CANEADEA
14718-14718 CASSADAGA
14719-14719 CATTARAUGUS
14720-14720 CELORON
14721-14721 CERES
14722-14722 CHAUTAUQUA
14723-14723 CHERRY CREEK
14724-14724 CLYMER
14726-14726 CONEWANGO VALLEY
14727-14727 CUBA
14728-14728 DEWITTVILLE
14729-14729 EAST OTTO
14730-14730 EAST RANDOLPH
14731-14731 ELLICOTTVILLE
14732-14732 ELLINGTON
14733-14733 FALCONER
14735-14735 FILLMORE
14736-14736 FINDLEY LAKE
14737-14737 FRANKLINVILLE
14738-14738 FREWSBURG
14739-14739 FRIENDSHIP
14740-14740 GERRY
14741-14741 GREAT VALLEY
14742-14742 GREENHURST
14743-14743 HINSDALE
14744-14744 HOUGHTON
14745-14745 HUME
14747-14747 KENNEDY
14748-14748 KILL BUCK
14749-14749 KNAPP CREEK
14750-14750 LAKEWOOD
14751-14751 LEON
14752-14752 LILY DALE
14753-14753 LIMESTONE
14754-14754 LITTLE GENESEE
14755-14755 LITTLE VALLEY
14756-14756 MAPLE SPRINGS
14757-14757 MAYVILLE
14758-14758 NIOBE
14759-14759 NORTH CLYMER
14760-14760 OLEAN
14766-14766 OTTO
14767-14767 PANAMA
14769-14769 PORTLAND
14770-14770 PORTVILLE
14772-14772 RANDOLPH
14774-14774 RICHBURG
14775-14775 RIPLEY
14776-14776 ROSSBURG
14777-14777 RUSHFORD
14778-14778 SAINT BONAVENTURE
14779-14779 SALAMANCA
14781-14781 SHERMAN
14782-14782 SINCLAIRVILLE
14783-14783 STEAMBURG
14784-14784 STOCKTON
14785-14785 STOW
14786-14786 WEST CLARKSVILLE
14787-14787 WESTFIELD
14788-14788 WESTONS MILLS
14801-14801 ADDISON
14802-14802 ALFRED
14803-14803 ALFRED STATION
14804-14804 ALMOND
14805-14805 ALPINE
14806-14806 ANDOVER
14807-14807 ARKPORT
14808-14808 ATLANTA
14809-14809 AVOCA
14810-14810 BATH
14812-14812 BEAVER DAMS
14813-14813 BELMONT
14814-14814 BIG FLATS
14815-14815 BRADFORD
14816-14816 BREESPORT
14817-14817 BROOKTONDALE
14818-14818 BURDETT
14819-14819 CAMERON
14820-14820 CAMERON MILLS
14821-14821 CAMPBELL
14822-14822 CANASERAGA
14823-14823 CANISTEO
14824-14824 CAYUTA
14825-14825 CHEMUNG
14826-14826 COHOCTON
14827-14827 COOPERS PLAINS
14830-14831 CORNING
14836-14836 DALTON
14837-14837 DUNDEE
14838-14838 ERIN
14839-14839 GREENWOOD
14840-14840 HAMMONDSPORT
14841-14841 HECTOR
14842-14842 HIMROD
14843-14843 HORNELL
14844-14845 HORSEHEADS
14846-14846 HUNT
14847-14847 INTERLAKEN
14850-14853 ITHACA
14854-14854 JACKSONVILLE
14855-14855 JASPER
14856-14856 KANONA
14857-14857 LAKEMONT
14858-14858 LINDLEY
14859-14859 LOCKWOOD
14860-14860 LODI
14861-14861 LOWMAN
14863-14863 MECKLENBURG
14864-14864 MILLPORT
14865-14865 MONTOUR FALLS
14867-14867 NEWFIELD
14868-14868 NORTH COHOCTON
14869-14869 ODESSA
14870-14870 PAINTED POST
14871-14871 PINE CITY
14872-14872 PINE VALLEY
14873-14873 PRATTSBURGH
14874-14874 PULTENEY
14876-14876 READING CENTER
14877-14877 REXVILLE
14878-14878 ROCK STREAM
14879-14879 SAVONA
14880-14880 SCIO
14881-14881 SLATERVILLE SPRINGS
14882-14882 LANSING
14883-14883 SPENCER
14884-14884 SWAIN
14885-14885 TROUPSBURG
14886-14886 TRUMANSBURG
14887-14887 TYRONE
14888-14888 VALOIS
14889-14889 VAN ETTEN
14891-14891 WATKINS GLEN
14892-14892 WAVERLY
14893-14893 WAYNE
14894-14894 WELLSBURG
14895-14895 WELLSVILLE
14896-14896 WEST DANBY
14897-14897 WHITESVILLE
14898-14898 WOODHULL
14900-14975 ELMIRA

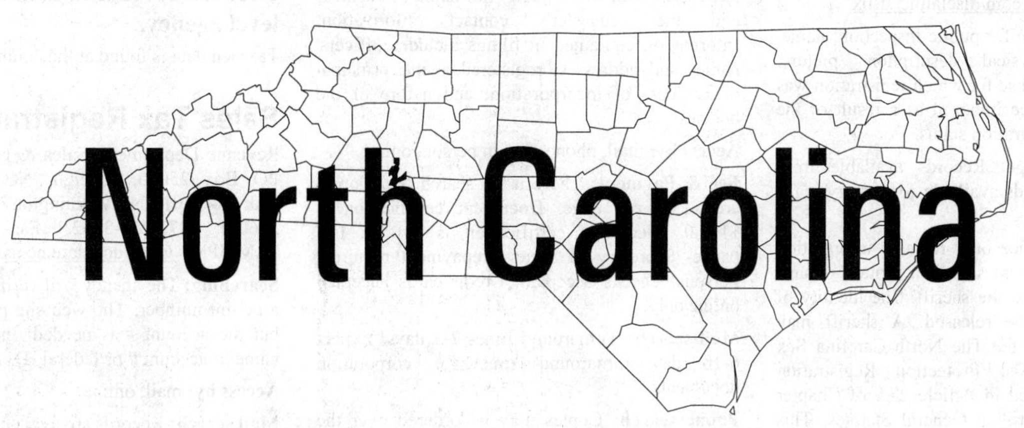

North Carolina

General Help Numbers:

Governor's Office
20301 Mail Service Center — 919-733-4240
Raleigh, NC 27699-0301 — Fax 919-715-3175
www.governor.state.nc.us — 8AM-6PM

Attorney General's Office
Justice Department — 919-716-6400
9001 Mail Service Center — Fax 919-716-6750
Raleigh, NC 27699-9001 — 8AM-5PM
www.ncdoj.com/default.jsp

Legislative Records
North Carolina General Assembly
16 W. Jones Street, Rm 2226 — 919-733-7779
Raleigh, NC 27603 — 919-733-7778
www.ncleg.net — 8:30AM-5:30PM

State Archives
Archives & History Division — 919-807-7280
109 E Jones St — Fax 919-733-8807
Raleigh, NC 27601-2807 — 8AM-5:30PM T-F, 9-5 SA
www.history.ncdcr.gov/

State Specifics:

Capital: Raleigh, Wake County

Time Zone: EST

Number of Counties: 100

Population: 9,222,414

Official State Website: www.ncgov.com

State Agencies

Criminal Records

Access to Records is Restricted.

State Bureau of Investigation, C.I.I.S., PO Box 29500, Raleigh, NC 27626 (Courier address- 3320 Garner Rd, Raleigh, NC 27626-0500); 919-662-4500, 919-662-4509 x6266 (Customer Svc Dept.), Fax- 919-662-4380; 8AM-5PM.
www.ncsbi.gov/default.jsp

Record access is limited to criminal justice and other government agencies authorized by law. Employers are denied access unless subject is in a business designated to receive records (i.e. health or child care). Contact agency for proper paperwork. This agency will direct you to the Admin. Office of the Courts (AOC) for online access to statewide Clerk of Court criminal records. Private companies offering NC criminal records are listed at www.nccourts.org/Citizens/GoToCourt/Default.asp?topic=1.

Statewide Court Records

Administrative Office of Courts, 901 Corporate Center Drive,, Raleigh, NC 27607-5045; 919-890-1000; 8AM-5PM. www.nccourts.org/Courts/

All trial court research for record copies must be done at the local level. The state AOC provides certain vendors with records on an ongoing basis pursuant to a licensing agreement. The data is available online, a list of the vendors is found at on the web. Search the District and Superior Court Query system for current criminal defendants, impaired driving, citations, and current civil and criminal calendars at http://www1.aoc.state.nc.us/www/calendars/CriminalQuery.html. Appellate & Supreme Court opinions are available www.aoc.state.nc.us/www/public/html/opinions.htm.

Sexual Offender Registry

State Bureau of Investigation, Criminal Information & Ident Sect - SOR Unit, PO Box 29500, Raleigh, NC 27626-0500 (Courier address-

3320 Garner Rd, Raleigh, NC 27626-0500); 919-662-4500, Fax- 919-661-6172; 8AM-5PM.

http://ncfindoffender.com/disclaimer.aspx

Records are available for public inspection; name, sex, address, physical description, picture, conviction date, offense for which registration was required, the sentence imposed as a result of the conviction, and registration status.

Indexing & Storage: Records available from 01/01/96. New records available for inquiry in 24 hours.

Searching: This office only releases information online. They suggest to submit a written request for the information to the sheriff. The identity of the victim cannot be released. A sheriff may charge a reasonable fee The North Carolina Sex Offender and Public Protection Registration Programs are codified in Article 27A of Chapter 14 of the North Carolina General Statutes. This data not released- victim information.

Online search: Search Level 3 records at the website. Search by name or geographic region.

Other access: Agency provides data on CD-Rom.

Incarceration Records

North Carolina Department of Corrections, Combined Records, 2020 Yonkers Road, 4226 MSC, Raleigh, NC 27699-4226; 919-716-3200, Fax- 919-716-3986; 8AM-4:30PM.

www.doc.state.nc.us

Indexing & Storage: Records available on current and former inmates. New records available for inquiry in up to 10 days.

Searching: Computer records go back to 1973. Probation records are maintained separately by the Division of Community Corrections at 919-716-3100 Include in request- full name. the DOB, SSN and DOC number are helpful. Location, conviction and sentencing information, and release dates are provided.

Access by: mail, phone, fax, in person, online.

Fee & Payment: The fee for copies is $1.00 for first page and $.25 each add'l. Fee payee- NC Dept of Corrections Personal checks are accepted.

Mail search: Turnaround time- 1 to 2 days. SASE not required.

Phone search: Name searching available. **Fax search:** Search requests accepted by fax.

In person: Walk-in requesters are serviced.

Online search: The web access allows searching by name or ID number for public information on inmates, probationers, or parolees since 1973. Go to http://webapps6.doc.state.nc.us/apps/offender/menu1.

Corporation, LP, LLC, Trademarks/Servicemarks

Secretary of State, Corporations Division, PO Box 29622, Raleigh, NC 27626-0622 (Courier address- 2 S Salisbury, Raleigh, NC 27601); 919-807-2225 (Corporations), 919-807-2162 (Trademarks), 888-246-7636, Fax- 919-807-2039; 8AM-5PM.

www.sosnc.com

DBAs, Fictitious Names and Assumed Name records found at county Register of Deeds offices.

Indexing & Storage: Records available from 1800's on. Most information is available on the computer database and on the agency's website. New records available for inquiry immediately.

Searching: Information is open to the public. Will only expedite the filing of documents, not for searches. Include in request- full name of business and the requester's contact information. Information contained in filings includes officers' names and addresses; registered agent; principal office; date of incorporation; and nature of the business.

Access by: mail, phone, fax, in person, online.

Fee & Payment: There is no search fee. Copies are $1.00 per page. Document certification is $15.00. Electronic certification is $10.00. Fee payee- Secretary of State. Prepayment required. Personal checks accepted. Credit cards accepted online only.

Mail search: Turnaround time- 2-3 days. Expect 6-10 day turnaround time for corporation documents.

Phone search: Copies may be ordered over the telephone. **Fax search:** They will invoice.

In person: Turnaround time is immediate. There is a public access terminal to view records.

Online search: The website offers a free search of status, corporate documents, and search by registered agent. The trademark database is not available online.

Other access: This agency makes database information available for purchase via an FTP site. Contact Bonnie Elek at 919-807-2196 for details.

Uniform Commercial Code, Federal Tax Liens

UCC Division, Secretary of State, PO Box 29626, Raleigh, NC 27626-0626 (Courier address- 2 S Salisbury St, Raleigh, NC 27602); 919-807-2111, 919-807-2219, Fax- 919-807-2120; 8AM-5PM.

www.secretary.state.nc.us/UCC/

Email questions to uccmail@sosnc.com.

Indexing & Storage: Records available from 1967. Records are computerized since 1985. New records available for inquiry in 72 hours.

Searching: Use search request form UCC-11. The search includes federal tax liens on businesses since 1985 if you request (add $5.00). You may search federal tax liens separately. Federal tax liens on individuals and all state tax liens are filed at Superior Courts. Include in request- debtor name. Name will be searched as submitted. This data not released- SSN

Access by: mail, in person, online.

Fee & Payment: The UCC search fee is $38.00 per debtor name. $2.00 per page for copies or $2.00 per specific page request. $6.25 for certification plus $2.00 ea add'l page. $.50 per reader printer copy reader printers. Tax lien search is $5.00, copy fee is $2.00. Fee payee- Secretary of State. Prepayment required. Underpayment requests will be rejected. Personal checks accepted, credit cards are not.

Mail search: Turnaround time- 3 days. A SASE is not requested.

In person: There is a $2.00 fee per page for requests turned in at front counter.

Online search: Free access is available at www.secretary.state.nc.us/ucc/. Click on "UCC research" or "Tax Liens." Search by ID number or debtor name.

Other access: The UCC or tax lien database can be purchased on an annual basis via an FTP site. For more information, call 919-807-2196.

State Tax Liens

Records not maintained by a state level agency.

Tax lien data is found at the county level.

Sales Tax Registrations

Revenue Department, Sales & Use Tax Division, PO Box 25000, Raleigh, NC 27640 (Courier address- 501 N Wilmington Street, Raleigh, 27604); 877-252-3052, Fax- 919-733-5750; 8AM-5PM. www.dor.state.nc.us

Searching: The agency will verify the existence of a permit number. The web site permits searching, but the account # is needed. Include in request- name or account # or federal ID.

Access by: mail, online.

Mail search: Records are available by mail.

Online search: Delinquent debtors shown on web at www.dor.state.nc.us/collect/delinquent.html.

Birth Certificates

Center for Health Statistics, Vital Records Branch, 1903 Mail Service Center, Raleigh, NC 27699-1903 (Courier address- 225 N McDowell St, Raleigh, NC 27603); 919-733-3526, 800-669-8310 (Credit Card Orders), Fax- 919-829-1359; 8AM-4PM.

http://vitalrecords.dhhs.state.nc.us/vr/index.html

Anyone can order an non-certified copy of a record with the exception of birth certificates for adopted persons. Only family members can order a certified copy. The fee is the same.

Indexing & Storage: Records available from 1913 to present. Prior to 1913, the state did not keep records of births. Recent records must be obtained at the county level. New records available for inquiry in 180 days after birth.

Searching: Investigative searches are permitted, but only non-certified copies are provided. Otherwise, requester must state relationship to subject and why record is needed. Include in request- full name, names of parents, mother's maiden name, date of birth, place of birth. Data not released- adoption records or medical records.

Access by: mail, phone, fax, in person, online.

Fee & Payment: Record fee is $15.00, includes per 5 years searched. Add $15.00 each add'l 5 years searched. Add $9.95 for using a credit card. Add $5.00 per copy for additional copies. Add $15.00 for in person requests serviced in 1 hour. Fee payee- North Carolina Vital Records. Prepayment required. Credit cards accepted for expedited service only. Personal checks accepted. Credit cards accepted only by VitalChek.

Mail search: Turnaround time- 2 weeks. SASE not required.

Phone search: See expedited service. **Fax search:** See expedited service.

In person: Walk-in services in the lobby is only for simple certificate requests. All other services (such as amending a certificate) will be conducted by appointment only. The walk-in service entails an additional $15.00 fee for immediate service or pick-up within 5 days.

Online search: Online ordering is available using a credit card via a state-designated vendor at www.vitalchek.com. Total fee is $55.45 and includes use of credit card and express delivery.

Expedited service: Online and in person ordering one hour service is considered expedited and fees are as outlined above.

Death Records

Dept of Environment, Health & Natural Resources, Vital Records Section, 1903 Mail Service Center, Raleigh, NC 27699-1903 (Courier address- 225 N McDowell St, Raleigh, NC 27603); 919-733-3526, 800-669-8310 (Credit card orders), Fax- 919-829-1359; 8AM-4PM.

http://vitalrecords.dhhs.state.nc.us/vr/index.html

Non-certified records may be obtained by the public; certified copies can only be purchased by family members. Fee is the same for either record.

Indexing & Storage: Records available from 1930 to present. Recent records must be obtained at the county level. New records available for inquiry in 180 days after death.

Searching: Investigative searches are permitted, but only non-certified copies are provided. Include in request- full name, date of death, date of birth, place of death. SSN is helpful.

Access by: mail, phone, fax, in person, online.

Fee & Payment: Record fee is $15.00, includes per 5 years searched. Add $15.00 each add'l 5 years searched. Add $9.95 for using a credit card. Add $5.00 per copy for additional copies. Add $15.00 for in person requests serviced in 1 hour. Fee payee- North Carolina Vital Records. Prepayment required. Credit cards accepted for phone service only. Personal checks accepted. Credit cards accepted only by VitalChek.

Mail search: Turnaround time- 2 weeks. SASE not required.

Phone or fax search: See expedited service.

In person: Walk-in services in the lobby is only for simple certificate requests. All other services (such as amending a certificate) will be conducted by appointment only. The walk-in service entails an additional $15.00 fee for immediate service or pick-up within 5 days.

Online search: Online ordering is available using a credit card via a state-designated vendor at www.vitalchek.com. Total fee is $55.45 and includes use of credit card and express delivery.

Expedited service: Online and in person ordering one hour service is considered expedited and fees are as outlined above.

Marriage Certificates

Dept of Environment, Health & Natural Resources, Vital Records Section, 1903 Mail Service Center, Raleigh, NC 27699-1903 (Courier address- 225 N McDowell St, Raleigh, NC 27603); 919-733-3526, 800-669-8310 (Credit card orders), Fax- 919-829-1359; 8AM-4PM.

http://vitalrecords.dhhs.state.nc.us/vr/index.html

Non-certified copies may be purchased by the public. Certified copies can be obtained by family members. The fee is the same for either report.

Indexing & Storage: Records available from 1962 to present. Recent records must be obtained at the county level. New records available for inquiry in 8 months.

Searching: Investigative searches are permitted, but only non-certified copies are provided. Include in request- names of husband and wife, date of marriage, place or county of marriage.

Access by: mail, phone, fax, in person, online.

Fee & Payment: Record fee is $15.00, includes per 5 years searched. Add $15.00 each add'l 5 years searched. Add $9.95 for using a credit card. Add $5.00 per copy for additional copies. Add $15.00 for in person requests serviced in 1 hour. Fee payee- North Carolina Vital Records. Prepayment required. Personal checks accepted. Credit cards accepted only by VitalChek.

Mail search: Turnaround time- 2 weeks. SASE not required.

Phone or fax search: See expedited service.

In person: Walk-in services in the lobby is only for simple certificate requests. All other services (such as amending a certificate) will be conducted by appointment only. The walk-in service entails an additional $15.00 fee for immediate service or pick-up within 5 days.

Online search: Online ordering is available using a credit card via a state-designated vendor at www.vitalchek.com. Total fee is $55.45 and includes use of credit card and express delivery.

Expedited service: Online and in person ordering one hour service is considered expedited and fees are as outlined above.

Divorce Records

Dept of Environment, Health & Natural Resources, Vital Records Section, 1903 Mail Service Center, Raleigh, NC 27699-1903 (Courier address- 225 N McDowell St, Raleigh, NC 27603); 919-733-3526, 800-669-8310 (Credit card orders), Fax- 919-829-1359; 8AM-4PM.

http://vitalrecords.dhhs.state.nc.us/vr/index.html

Non-certified copies are available to the public, certified copies to family members. The fee is the same for either report.

Indexing & Storage: Records available from 1958 to present. Recent records must be obtained at the county level. New records available for inquiry in up to 1 year.

Searching: Investigative searches are permitted, but only non-certified copies are provided. Include in request- names of husband and wife, date of divorce, place of divorce, case number (if known).

Access by: mail, phone, fax, in person, online.

Fee & Payment: Record fee is $15.00, includes per 5 years searched. Add $15.00 each add'l 5 years searched. Add $9.95 for using a credit card. Add $5.00 per copy for additional copies. Add $15.00 for in person requests serviced in 1 hour. Fee payee- North Carolina Vital Records. Prepayment required. Personal checks accepted. Credit cards accepted only by VitalChek.

Mail search: Turnaround time- 2 weeks. SASE not required.

Phone or fax search: See expedited service.

In person: Walk-in services in the lobby is only for simple certificate requests. All other services (such as amending a certificate) will be conducted by appointment only. The walk-in service entails an additional $15.00 fee for immediate service or pick-up within 5 days.

Online search: Online ordering is available using a credit card via a state-designated vendor at www.vitalchek.com. Total fee is $55.45 and includes use of credit card and express delivery.

Expedited service: Online and in person ordering one hour service is considered expedited and fees are as outlined above.

Workers' Compensation Records

NC Industrial Commission, Worker's Comp Records, 4340 Mail Service Center, Raleigh, NC 27699-4340; 919-807-2500, 800-688-8349 (Claims Questions), Fax- 919-715-0282; 8AM-5PM. www.comp.state.nc.us

One may search the Workers' Compensation Name Search System at the web to find the addresses of employers, insurance companies, third party administrators, and the parties responsible for workers' compensation coverage at the time of an accident.

Indexing & Storage: Records available from 1980 for files, from 1969 for coverage. From 1997 back records are stored in warehouse. New records available for inquiry in 24 hours.

Searching: Searches require a signed release or statement of purpose of request on letterhead. Only parties to claim will be allowed access. Per federal law, records may not be used for pre-employment screening.

Access by: mail, in person, online.

Fee & Payment: There is no search fee. There is no copy fee unless the file is over 20 pages, then the fee is $1.00 per page (over 20). Fee payee- NC Industrial Commission. Personal checks accepted, credit cards are not.

Mail search: Turnaround time- 2 to 3 days.

In person: Generally turnaround time is immediate, unless the case is closed and records must be researched.

Online search: Extensive information about employers and insurers may be searched online at www.comp.state.nc.us/iwcnss/. This site also gives access to court decisions involving worker's comp.

Driver Records

Division of Motor Vehicles, Driver License Records, 3113 MSC, Raleigh, NC 27699; 919-715-7000, Fax- 919-861-3919; 8AM-5PM.

www.ncdot.org/dmv/driver_services/

Records available include a limited three year (insurance purposes) and a seven year (employment purposes) record.

Indexing & Storage: Records available for 5 yrs or more for moving violations, 10 yrs or more for DWIs and suspensions. Surrendered license records are kept for 10 yr after the expiration date. New records available for inquiry in minutes.

Searching: Form DL-DPPA-1 is required. Casual requesters cannot obtain records without consent. Include in request- driver's license number, full name, SSN, date of birth. Search modes will look at the driver's license number first, then SSN, the name and DOB as a secondary search. This data not released- medical information.

Access by: mail, in person, online.

Fee & Payment: The current fee is $8.00 per record. Certified records are $11.00. Fee payee- NC Division of Motor Vehicles. Prepayment required. Personal checks accepted, no credit cards

Mail search: Turnaround time- 10business days. SASE not required.

In person: Requests will be processed immediately based on staffing and workload, and number of requests submitted.

Online search: To qualify for online availability, a client must be an insurance agent or insurance company support organization. The mode is interactive and is open from 7 AM to 10 PM. The DL# and name are needed when ordering. Records are $8.00 each. A minimum $500 security deposit is required. Call 919-861-3062 for details.

Vehicle Ownership & Registration

Division of Motor Vehicles, Registration/ Correspondence Unit, 1100 New Bern Ave, Rm 100, Raleigh, NC 27697-0001; 919-715-7000, Fax- 919-733-0126; 8AM-5PM.

www.ncdot.org/dmv/vehicle_services/

Indexing & Storage: Records available from their first records for title records (on microfilm). Computer records are purged periodically according to plate activity. Records are maintained for mobile homes and boat trailers, also. New records available for inquiry in 1 to 3 weeks, depending on record type.

Searching: The agency is in compliance with DPPA. Non-permissible requesters receive records without personal information. Include in request- vehicle description, name, and signed release of subject on Form MVR-605A if not an ongoing requester. The request form is at www.ncdot.org/dmv/forms/vehicleregistration/download/mvr605a.pdf.

Access by: mail, phone, in person.

Fee & Payment: The fee is $1.00 per record (includes lien data) or $10.00 for a certified record. Fee payee- Department of Motor Vehicles. Prepayment required. Personal checks accepted, credit cards are not.

Mail search: Turnaround time- 3 days. The use of Form MVR-605A is helpful. The request requires the requester's signature. A SASE is requested.

Phone search: Phone requester MUST be a subscriber who is pre-approved and assigned a User-Code by the DMV.

In person: Turnaround time is while you wait if you have the correct authorization.

Other access: North Carolina offers a bulk retrieval of ownership and registration information on magnetic tape. A written request specifying the purpose and details of the request is required. Request must comply with DPPA. For more information, call 919-861-3062

Accident Reports

Division of Motor Vehicles, Traffic Records Section, 3105 Mail Service Center, Raleigh, NC 27699-3105; 919-861-3098, Fax- 919-733-9605; 8AM-5PM.

www.ncdot.org/dmv/other_services/recordsstatistics/copyCrashReport.html

Release of records follows compliance of the DPPA, the information is not public record. If the requester does not have a permissible use then a signed release is needed for the affected individuals.

Indexing & Storage: Records available from 1986 to present on computer, from 1995 to present on microfiche. Hard copies are available from 2000. New records available for inquiry in 24 hours or less.

Searching: Records are not released on minor drivers. Using Form TR-67A, the requester should submit at least one of the names of the owner or driver, the county of occurrence, date of occurrence, and the exception under which he/she qualifies to receive personal information in accordance with DPPA.

Access by: mail, in person.

Fee & Payment: The fee is $5.00 for a certified copy or no cost for a non-certified copy. Fee payee- Division of Motor Vehicles. Prepayment required. Personal checks accepted, no credit cards

Mail search: Turnaround time- 5 days.

In person: Visit Traffic Records Section, Crash Reports Unit, NCDMV Headquarters Building, 1100 New Bern Avenue, Raleigh, NC 27697. Turnaround time is immediate if record available.

Other access: Bulk file purchase is available.

Vessel Ownership & Registration

North Carolina Wildlife Resources Commission, Transaction Management, 1709 Mail Service Center, Raleigh, NC 27699-1709 (Courier address- 1751 Varisty Dr, Raleigh, NC 27606); 800-628-3773, Fax- 919-707-0293; 8AM-5PM.

www.ncwildlife.org/

All motorized boats, including jet skis, and sailboats over 14 ft must be registered. Effective 01/07 titles are mandatory, previously optional. Lien information will show if the vessel is titled here. There are over 400 local agents statewide.

Indexing & Storage: Records available from 1970 and are computerized. Hard copies to 2003. New records available for inquiry immediately.

Searching: Although it is previously possible to record a vessel lien with a Uniform Commercial Code filing, most lenders choose to record it on the vessel's Title Certificate. Lien are now recorded here. Include in request- name and signed release if doing a name search. Otherwise submit registration number or hull number. This data not released- personal information. Lien holder information is restricted to only lienholder institute or by subpoena.

Access by: mail, fax.

Fee & Payment: The search fee is $20.00, if research is extensive, additional fees apply. Fee payee- NCWRC Personal Checks are accepted.

Mail search: Turnaround time- 1 to 2 weeks. SASE not required.

Fax search: Turnaround time is several days.

Legislation Records

North Carolina General Assembly, State Legislative Bldg - Library, 16 W. Jones Street, Rm 2226, Raleigh, NC 27603; 919-733-7778 (Bill Numbers or Status), 919-733-5648 (Printed Bills), 919-807-7310 (Archives), Fax- 919-733-2599; 8:30AM-5:30PM. www.ncleg.net

To obtain a copy of a bill, you must have a bill number first. Copies of bills usually come from the "Printed Bill" department.

Records available since 1971. Overall, records are computer indexed since 1985, and are indexed on microfiche from 1969 to 1984.

Voter Registration

State Board of Elections, PO Box 27255, Raleigh, NC 27611-7255; 919-733-7173, Fax- 919-715-0135; 8AM-5PM. www.sboe.state.nc.us

There is a statewide online system for record access. Records are open to the public, subject to certain legal limitations.

Indexing & Storage: Records available from early 1980's. New records available for inquiry immediately.

Searching: Include in request- sufficient data to define the records needed. This data not released- DOB.

Access by: mail, phone, fax, in person, online.

Fee & Payment: The only fees are for either specialized reports or for actual costs to reproduce the records in the desired format. Fee payee- State Board of Elections

Mail search: Turnaround time- 3-5 days. SASE is not requested.

Phone search: Records available by phone. **Fax search:** Records are available by fax, 3-5 days.

In person: Simple requests may be processed while you wait.

Online search: Online access to voter registration records available free at www.sboe.state.nc.us/votersearch/seimsvot.htm. A DOB is needed for best results.

Other access: Most records are sold in CD format, FTP or sent via email. The maximum fee is $25.00. Request forms are available at the webpage. This is the most prompt access to records, other than in person.

GED Certificates

NC Community College System, GED Office, 5016 Mail Service Center, Raleigh, NC 27699; 919-807-7138, Fax- 919-807-7172; 9AM-4PM.

www.nccommunitycolleges.edu/

Indexing & Storage: Records available from the 1944 to present, from 09/77 on microfilm. New records available for inquiry in 1-2 days.

Searching: There are no fees for verification or copies of transcripts. A request form is found at the web page. Include in request- SSN, date of birth, notarized signature of the subject. The year and place of the test is helpful.

Access by: mail, phone, fax, in person.

Mail search: Turnaround time- 1 week.

Phone search: No scores are given over the phone.

Fax search: Request form may be faxed. Proof of signature must be included (passport, ID, etc). Indicate if you merely need a "yes/no" answer.

In person: No fee for request.

Hunting & Fishing License Information

Access to Records is Restricted.

NCWRC, License Section, 1726 Mail Service Center, Raleigh, NC 27699-1726; 888-248-6834, 919-707-0391; 8AM-5PM. www.ncwildlife.org/

Lists of license holders are not available. Only counts are released. Email questions to licenses@ncwildlife.org.

North Carolina State Licensing Agencies

For details about the agency responsible for licensing/certifying/registering an item below or in the Agency Quick Finder section, match an item's number with the number of the agency in the *Licensing Agency Information* section.

North Carolina Licenses Searchable Online

Amusement Device #24 .... www.nclabor.com/elevator/elevator.htm
Anesthetist Nurse #8 .... https://www.ncbon.com/License/form1.asp
Architect #3 .... www.memberbase.com/ncbarch/public/lic/searchdb.asp
Architectural Firm #3 .... www.memberbase.com/ncbarch/public/firms/searchdb.asp
Athletic Trainer #38 .... www.ncbate.org/Licenses.pdf
Attorney #45 .... www.ncbar.com/discipline/
Auction Company #2 .... www.ncalb.org/search.cfm
Auctioneer Disciplinary Action #2 .... www.ncalb.org/discActions.cfm
Auctioneer/Auctioneer Appren. #2 .... www.ncalb.org/search.cfm
Bank #17 .... https://www.nccob.org/Online/brts/BanksAndTrusts.aspx
Bank Branch #17 .... https://www.nccob.org/Online/brts/BankBranchSearch.aspx
Barber Inspector/Instructor #4 .... www.ncbarbers.com/
Beauty Shop/Salon #54 ....
... ... https://www.member-base.net/NCCOSMORenew/login.aspx?ReturnUrl=/nccosmorenew/Welcome.aspx
Bodywork Therapist #56 .... www.bmbt.org/MTSEARCH.ASP
Boiler/Pressure Vessel Inspector #24 .... www.nclabor.com/boiler/boiler.htm
Building Inspector #23 .... www.ncdoi.com/OSFM/Engineering/COQB/engineering_coqb_inspectors.asp
Cemetery #19 .... http://www2.nccommerce.com/servicenter/blio/redbook/Licenselist.asp?DivID=42
Cemetery Salesperson #19 .... http://www2.nccommerce.com/servicenter/blio/redbook/Licenselist.asp?DivID=42
Charitable/Sponsor Organization #52 .... www.secretary.state.nc.us/csl/Search.aspx
Check Casher #17 .... https://www.nccob.org/Online/CCS/CompanyListing.aspx
Chiropractor #41 .... http://ncchiroboard.com/
Clinical Nurse Specialist #8 .... https://www.ncbon.com/License/form1.asp
Clinical Social Worker #15 .... www.ncswboard.org/
Consumer Financer #17 .... https://www.nccob.org/online/CFS/CFSCompanyListing.aspx
Contractor, General #32 .... www.nclbgc.org/lic_fr.html
Cosmetologist Instruct/Appretice/Practit'r #54....
... ... https://www.member-base.net/NCCOSMORenew/login.aspx?ReturnUrl=/nccosmorenew/Welcome.aspx
Cosmetology Disciplinary Action #54 ....
... ... https://www.member-base.net/NCCOSMORenew/login.aspx?ReturnUrl=/nccosmorenew/Welcome.aspx
Counselor, Professional #13 .... www.ncblpc.org/verify.php
Crematory #7 .... www.ncbfs.org/dir_crematoriesdb.htm
Dental Hygienist #42 .... www.ncdentalboard.org/ncdbe_search.asp
Dentist #42 .... www.ncdentalboard.org/ncdbe_search.asp
DME-Rx Device #11 .... www.ncbop.org/ncbop_verification.htm
Electrical Contractor/Inspector #6 .... http://lookup.ncbeec.org/
Electrologist #35 .... www.ncbee.com/electrologist_search.php
Electrology Instructor #35 .... www.ncbee.com/approved_schools.php
Elevator Inspector #24 .... www.nclabor.com/elevator/elevator.htm
Embalmer #7 .... www.ncbfs.org/dir_licenseedb.htm
Engineer #48 .... https://www.membersbase.com/ncbels-vs/public/searchdb.asp
Engineering/Surveying Firm #48 .... https://www.membersbase.com/ncbels-vs/public/searchdb.asp
Esthetician Instruc./Appren/Practition'r #54
... ... https://www.member-base.net/NCCOSMORenew/login.aspx?ReturnUrl=/nccosmorenew/Welcome.aspx
Family Therapist #33 .... www.nclmft.org/index.cfm?fuseaction=licenseVerify.home
Fire Sprinkler Contractor #31 .... www.nclicensing.org/OnlineReg.htm
Fire Sprinkler Inspection Contr. #31 .... www.nclicensing.org/OnlineReg.htm
Fire Sprinkler Inspection Technic'n #31 .... www.nclicensing.org/OnlineReg.htm
Fire Sprinkler Maintenance Tech. #31 .... www.nclicensing.org/OnlineReg.htm
Forester #53 .... www.ncbrf.org/list.htm
Fund Raiser Consultant/Solicitor #52 .... www.secretary.state.nc.us/csl/Search.aspx
Funeral Chapel #7 .... www.ncbfs.org/dir_chapeldb.htm
Funeral Director/Service #7 .... www.ncbfs.org/dir_licenseedb.htm
Funeral Home #7 .... www.ncbfs.org/dir_funeralhomedb.htm
Funeral Trainee #7 .... www.ncbfs.org/dir_traineesdb.htm
Geologist #46 .... www.ncblg.org/licensees.html
Hearing Aid Dispenser/Fitter #43 .... http://pop.nchalb.org/queryname.aspx

Heating Contractor #31 .... www.nclicensing.org/OnlineReg.htm
HMO #23 .... http://infoportal.ncdoi.net/cmp_lookup.jsp
Home Inspector #23 .... www.ncdoi.com/OSFM/Engineering/hilb/engineering_hilb_directories.asp
Insurance Agent #23 .... http://infoportal.ncdoi.net/agent_lookup.jsp
Insurance Company #23 .... http://infoportal.ncdoi.net/cmp_lookup.jsp
Insurer, Life/Health #23 .... http://infoportal.ncdoi.net/filelookup.jsp?divtype=3
Insurer, Property/Casualty #23 .... http://infoportal.ncdoi.net/filelookup.jsp?divtype=2
Landscape Architect #46 .... www.ncbola.org/licensees.htm
Lobbyist #51 .... www.secretary.state.nc.us/lobbyists/directory.aspx
Manicurist Instruct/Appren/Practitioner #54
... ... https://www.member-base.net/NCCOSMORenew/login.aspx?ReturnUrl=/nccosmorenew/Welcome.aspx
Manuf'd Housing Retailer/Mfg/Contr #23 .... www.ncdoi.com/osfm/manufacturedbuilding/licensees/mainmenu.asp
Manuf'd Housing Seller/Qualifier #23 .... www.ncdoi.com/osfm/manufacturedbuilding/licensees/mainmenu.asp
Marriage & Family Therapist #33 .... www.nclmft.org/index.cfm?fuseaction=licenseVerify.home
Massage Therapist #56 .... www.bmbt.org/MTSEARCH.ASP
Medical Doctor/Physician #47 .... www.ncmedboard.org/
Midwife Nurse #8 .... https://www.ncbon.com/License/form1.asp
Money Transmitter #17 .... https://www.nccob.org/Online/MTS/MTSCompanyListing.aspx
Nurse Practitioner #47 .... www.ncmedboard.org/
Nurse Practitioner #8 .... https://www.ncbon.com/License/form1.asp
Nurse-LPN #8 .... https://www.ncbon.com/License/form1.asp
Nursing Home Administrator #5 .... www.ncbenha.org/searchdb.asp
Occupat'l Therapist/Therapy Assist #9 .... www.ncbot.org/
Optometrist #18 .... www.ncoptometry.org/verify.aspx
Osteopathic Physician #47 .... www.ncmedboard.org/
Pesticide Applicator #16 .... www.ncagr.gov/SPCAP/pesticides/license.htm
Pesticide Dealer/Consultant #16 .... www.ncagr.gov/SPCAP/pesticides/license.htm
Pharmacist/Pharmacy Technician #11 .... www.ncbop.org/ncbop_verification.htm
Pharmacy/Physician Pharmacy #11 .... www.ncbop.org/ncbop_verification.htm
Physical Therapist #49 .... www.ncptboard2.org/OnlineServices/Secure/VerifyTherapist/VerifyTherapist.php
Physical Therapist Assistant #49 .... www.ncptboard2.org/OnlineServices/Secure/VerifyTherapist/VerifyTherapist.php
Physician Assistant #47 .... www.ncmedboard.org/
Plumber #31 .... www.nclicensing.org/OnlineReg.htm
Podiatrist #12 .... www.ncbpe.org/search.php
Psychologist/Psy. Associate #36 .... www.ncpsychologyboard.org/search.htm
Public Accountant-CPA #37 .... www.nccpaboard.gov/Clients/NCBOA/Public/Static/search_the_database.htm
RAL #17 .... https://www.nccob.org/online/RALS/RALSCompanyListing.aspx
Real Estate Agent/Broker/Dealer #39 .... www.members-base.com/ncrec/wwiz.asp?wwizmstr=LIC_SEARCH
Real Estate Firm #39 .... www.members-base.com/ncrec/wwiz.asp?wwizmstr=FIRM_SEARCH
Sanitarian #14 .... www.rsboard.com/rsweb/directory/directory.htm
Social Worker #15 .... www.ncswboard.org/
Social Worker Manager #15 .... www.ncswboard.org/
Soil Scientist #22 .... www.ncblss.org/director.html
Speech Pathologist/Audiologist #30 .... www.ncboeslpa.org/BOE.htm
Surveyor, Land #48 .... https://www.membersbase.com/ncbels-vs/public/searchdb.asp
Therapist, Bodywork-Massage #56 .... www.bmbt.org/MTSEARCH.ASP
Trust Company #17 .... https://www.nccob.org/Online/BRTS/TrustLicensees.aspx

North Carolina Licensing Quick Finder

Acupuncturist #40 919-773-0530
Alarm Installer #1 919-875-3611
Alarm System Business #1 919-875-3611
Alcoholic Beverage Control #20 919-779-0700
Ambulance Attendant #21 919-855-3750
Amusement Device #24 919-733-7166
Anesthetist Nurse #8 .... 919-782-3211 x245
Architect/Architectural Firm #3 919-733-9544
Armored Car #1 919-875-3611
Athletic Agent #51 919-733-0235
Athletic Trainer #38 919-821-4980
Attorney #45 919-828-4886
Auction Company #2 919-567-2844
Auctioneer Disciplinary Action #2 919-567-2844
Auctioneer/Auctioneer Appren. #2 919-567-2844
Bail Bond Runner #23 919-807-6800
Bank #27 919-508-5973
Bank / Bank Branch #17 919-733-3016
Barber Inspector/Instructor #4 919-981-5210
Barber/Barber Apprentice #4 919-981-5210
Beauty Shop/Salon #54 919-733-4117
Bodywork Therapist #56 919-546-0050
Boiler/Pressure Vessel Inspector #24 919-733-7166
Bondsman, Profession'l/Surety #23 919-807-6800
Building Inspector #23 919-661-5880
Cemetery #19 919-981-2536
Cemetery Salesperson #19 919-981-2536
Charitable/Sponsor Organization #52 919-807-2214
Check Casher #17 919-733-3016
Chiropractor #41 704-793-1342
Clinical Nurse Specialist #8 .... 919-782-3211 x244
Clinical Social Worker #15 336-625-1679
Consumer Financer #17 919-733-3016
Contractor, General #32 919-571-4183
Cosmetologist Instruct/Appren/Practit'r #54 919-733-4117
Cosmetology Disciplinary Action #54 919-733-4117
Counselor, Professional #13 919-661-0820
Counter Intelligence Service #1 919-875-3611
Courier Service #1 919-875-3611
Crematory #7 919-733-9380
Dental Hygienist #42 .... 919-678-8223 x1782
Dentist #42 .... 919-678-8223 x1782
Deputy Sheriff #55 919-716-6460
Detention Officer #55 919-716-6460
DME-Rx Device #11 919-246-1050
EDM #21 919-855-3750
Electrical Contractor/Inspector #6 919-733-9042
Electrologist #35 336-856-1010
Electrology Instructor #35 336-856-1010
Elevator Inspector #24 919-733-7166

Embalmer #7 919-733-9380
Emergency Medical Service #21 919-855-3750
Emergency Medical Technician #21 919-855-3750
Engineer #48 919-791-2000
Engineering/Surveying Firm #48 919-791-2000
Esthetician Instruc./Appren/Practitioner #54 919-733-4117
Family Therapist #33 919-772-6600
Fire Marshall #23 919-661-5880
Fire Sprinkler Contractor #31 919-875-3612
Fire Sprinkler Inspection Contr. #31 919-875-3612
Fire Sprinkler Inspection Technic'n #31 919-875-3612
Fire Sprinkler Maintenance Tech. #31 . 919-875-3612
Fire/Rescue Instructor #23 919-661-5880
Firearms Trainer #1 919-875-3611
Forester #53 919-847-5441
Fund Raiser Consultant/Solicitor #52 ... 919-807-2214
Funeral Chapel/Home/Director/Svc #7 .. 919-733-9380
Funeral Pre-Need Seller #7 919-733-9380
Fur Dealer #25 919-707-0010
Game Bird Propagator #25 919-707-0010
Geologist #46 919-850-9669
Guard Dog Service #1 919-875-3611
Hearing Aid Dispenser/Fitter #43 252-752-6382
Heating Contractor #31 919-875-3612
HMO #23 919-733-5060
Home Inspector #23 919-662-4480
Hospital #21 919-855-3750
Hunting Preserve Operator #25 919-707-0010
Insurance Agent #23 919-807-6800
Insurance Company #23 .... 919-733-2205 x276
Insurer, Life/Health #23 919-733-5060
Insurer, Property/Casualty #23 919-733-3368

Investment Represent've/Advisor #26 . 919-733-3924
Landscape Architect #46 919-850-9088
Librarian, Public #28 919-733-2570
Loan Officer #17 919-733-3016
Lobbyist #51 919-807-2005
Manicurist Instruct/Appren/Practitioner #54 919-733-4117
Manuf'd Housing Retail/Mfg/Contr. #23 919-661-5880
Marriage & Family Therapist #33 919-772-6600
Massage Therapist #56 919-546-0050
Medical Doctor/Physician #47 919-326-1100
Medical Program Director #21 919-855-3750
Medical Responder #21 919-855-3750
Midwife Nurse #8 .... 919-782-3211 x252
Money Transmitter #17 919-733-3016
Mortgage Lender/Broker #17 919-733-3016
Notary Public #44 919-807-2219
Nurse Practitioner #8 .... 919-782-3211 x252
Nurse Practitioner #47 919-326-1100
Nurse-LPN #8 919-782-3211
Nursing Home #21 919-855-4520
Nursing Home Administrator #5 919-571-4164
Occupational Therapist/Therapy Assist #9 919-832-1380
Optician #10 919-733-9321
Optometrist #18 910-285-3160
Osteopathic Physician #47 919-326-1100
Paramedic #21 919-855-3750
Pesticide Ap/Dealer/Consultant #16 919-733-3556
Pharmacist/Pharmacy Technician #11 . 919-246-1050
Pharmacy/Physician Pharmacy #11 919-246-1050
Physical Therapist #49 919-490-6393
Physical Therapist Assistant #49 919-490-6393

Physician Assistant #47 919-326-1100
Plumber #31 919-875-3612
Podiatrist #12 919-861-5583
Polygraph Examiner #1 919-875-3611
Private Investigator #1 919-875-3611
Psychological Associate #36 828-262-2258
Psychologist #36 828-262-2258
Public Accountant-CPA #37 919-733-4222
RAL #17 919-733-3016
Real Estate Ag'nt/Brok'r/Deal'r #39 .. 919-875-3700 x6
Real Estate Firm #39 .... 919-875-3700 x6
Sanitarian #14 910-608-0196
Securities Agent/Broker #26 919-733-3924
Security Guard & Patrol #1 919-875-3611
Security Guard, Armed/Unarmed #1 919-875-3611
Shorthand Reporter #29 919-733-2927
Social Worker #15 336-625-1679
Social Worker Manager #15 336-625-1679
Soil Scientist #22 919-851-8963
Solid Waste Facility Operator #34 919-733-0379
Speech Pathologist/Audiologist #30 336-272-1828
Surveyor, Land #48 919-791-2000
Taxidermist #25 919-707-0010
Teacher #57 919-807-3310
Telecommunication #55 919-716-6460
Therapist, Bodywork-Massage #56 919-546-0050
Trust Company #17 919-733-3016
Veterinarian #50 919-854-5601
Veterinary Technician #50 919-854-5601
Waste Water Treatm't Plant Operator #34 919-733-0379
Wildlife Collector #25 919-707-0010

North Carolina Licensing Agency Information

#1 Alarm Systems/Private Protective Svcs Board, Attorney General's Office, 1631 Midtown Pl, #104, Raleigh, NC 27609; 919-875-3611, Fax- 919-875-3609. www.ncdoj.com/law_enforcement/cle_pps.jsp

#2 Auctioneer Licensing Board, 602 Stellata Dr, Fuquay-Varina, NC 27526; 919-567-2844, Fax- 919-567-2865. www.ncalb.org Search data at- www.ncalb.org/search.cfm

#3 Board of Architecture, 127 Hargett St, #304, Raleigh, NC 27601; 919-733-9544, Fax- 919-733-1272. www.ncbarch.org Search data at- www.ncbarch.org/dbase.asp Mailing lists also available, see "Directory" section at main website.

#4 Board of Barber Examiners, 5809-102 Departure Dr, Raleigh, NC 27616; 919-981-5210, Fax- 919-981-5068. www.ncbarbers.com/

#5 Board of Examiners for Nursing Home Administrators, 3733 National Dr, #228, Raleigh, NC 27612; 919-571-4164, Fax- 919-571-4166. www.ncbenha.org Search data at- www.ncbenha.org/searchdb.asp

#6 State Board of Examiners of Electrical Contractors, PO Box 18727 (3101 Industrial Dr, #206), Raleigh, NC 27619; 919-733-9042, Fax- 919-733-6105. Hours- 8:30AM-5PM. www.ncbeec.org/modules/content/index.php?id=1 Search data at- http://lookup.ncbeec.org/

#7 Board of Funeral Service, 1033 Wade Avenue, #108, Raleigh, NC 27605-1158; 919-733-9380, Fax- 919-733-8271. http://ncbfs.org Search data at- www.ncbfs.org/directory.htm

#8 Board of Nursing, PO Box 2129 (3724 National Dr, #201), Raleigh, NC 27602; 919-782-3211, Fax- 919-781-9461. Hours- 8AM-5PM. www.ncbon.com Search data at- https://www.ncbon.com/License/form1.asp

#9 Board of Occupational Therapy, PO Box 2280, Raleigh, NC 27602; 919-832-1380, Fax- 919-833-1059. Search data at- www.ncbot.org/

#10 Board of Opticians, PO Box 25336, Raleigh, NC 27611-5336; 919-733-9321, Fax- 919-733-0040.

#11 Board of Pharmacy, PO Box 4560 (6015 Farrington Rd, #201), Chapel Hill, NC 27515-4560; 919-246-1050, Fax- 919-246-1056. www.ncbop.org Search data at- www.ncbop.org/ncbop_verification.htm

#12 Board of Podiatry Examiners, 1500 Sunday Dr #102, Raleigh, NC 27607-5151; 919-861-5583, Fax- 919-787-4916. www.ncbpe.org Search data at- www.ncbpe.org/search.php

#13 Board of Licensed Professional Counselors, PO Box 1369, Garner, NC 27529; 919-661-0820, Fax- 919-779-5642. www.ncblpc.org Search data at- www.ncblpc.org/verify.php $4.00 per name fee for verification request. Verifications are not given via phone.

#14 Board of Sanitarian Examiners, PO Box 610, Lumberton, NC 28359; 910-608-0196, Fax- 910-608-0448. www.rsboard.com Search data at- www.rsboard.com/rsweb/directory/directory.htm

#15 Social Work Certification & Licensure Board, PO Box 1043 (1207 S Cox St, #F), Asheboro, NC 27204; 336-625-1679; 800-550-7009, Fax- 336-625-4246. Hours- 9AM-5PM. Search data at- www.ncswboard.org/

#16 Department of Agriculture, Pesticide Section, 1090 Mail Service Ctr. (2109 Blue Ridge Rd), Raleigh, NC 27699-1090; 919-733-3556, Fax- 919-733-9796. www.ncagr.gov/SPCAP/pesticides/index.htm Search data at- www.ncagr.com/SPCAP/pesticides/license.htm

#17 Department of Commerce, Commission of Banks, 4309 Mail Service Center (316 W Edenton St), Raleigh, NC 27699; 919-733-3016, Fax- 919-733-6918. www.nccob.org/NCCOB/FinancialInstitutions/Banking/

#18 Board of Examiners in Optometry, 109 N Graham St, Wallace, NC 28466; 910-285-3160, Fax- 910-285-4546. Hours- 8AM-5PM. www.ncoptometry.org Search data at- www.ncoptometry.org/verify.aspx

#19 Department of Commerce, Cemetery Commission, 1001 Navaho Dr, #101, Raleigh, NC 27609; 919-981-2536, Fax- 919-981-2538. http://www2.nccommerce.com/servicenter/blio/redbook/Licenselist.asp?DivID=42

#20 Alcoholic Beverage Control Commission, PO Box 26687 (3322 Garner Rd), Raleigh, NC 27611-6687; 919-779-0700, Fax- 919-662-1946. www.ncabc.com

#21 Department of Health & Human Services, Division of Health Service Regulation, 2701 Mail Service Center, Raleigh, NC 27699-2701; 919-855-3750, Fax- 919-733-2757. http://facility-services.state.nc.us/

#22 Board For Licensing of Soil Scientists, 659 Cary Towne Blvd, PMB 281, Cary, NC 27511; 919-851-8963. www.ncblss.org

#23 Department of Insurance, 1201 Mail Service Center (430 N Salisbury St), Raleigh, NC 27699-1201; 919-807-6750. 8AM-5PM. www.ncdoi.com

#24 Department of Labor, 1101 Mail Service Center, Raleigh, NC 27699-1101; 919-807-2796. www.nclabor.com/index.htm

#25 Department of Natural Resources & Environment, Wildlife Resources Commission, 1751 Varsity Dr, NCSU Centennial Campus, Raleigh, NC 27606; 919-707-0010. www.ncwildlife.org/

#26 Securities Division, NC Secretary of State, PO Box 29622 (2 S Salisbury St), Raleigh, NC 27626; 919-733-3924, Fax- 919-821-0818. www.secretary.state.nc.us/sec/

#27 Department of State Treasurer, Investment & Banking Division, 325 N Salisbury St, Raleigh, NC 27603; 919-508-5176, Fax- 919-508-5167. www.nctreasurer.com/dsthome

#28 Division of State Library, Department of Cultural Resources, 109 E Jones St, MSC 4601, Raleigh, NC 27601-2807; 919-807-7385, Fax-919-733-1620. http://statelibrary.dcr.state.nc.us

#30 Examiners for Speech Pathologists & Audiologists, PO Box 16885, Greensboro, NC 27416-0885; 336-272-1828, Fax- 336-272-4353. www.ncboeslpa.org Search data at- www.ncboeslpa.org/BOE.htm

#31 Board of Examiners of Plumbing, Heating & Fire Sprinkler Contractors, 1109 Dresser Court, Raleigh, NC 27609; 919-875-3612, Fax- 919-875-3616. Hours- 8AM-5PM. www.nclicensing.org Search data at- www.nclicensing.org/OnlineReg.htm

#32 Licensing Board for General Contractors, PO Box 17187 (3739 National Dr, #225), Raleigh, NC 27619; 919-571-4183, Fax- 919-571-4703. www.nclbgc.net Search data at- www.nclbgc.org/lic_fr.html

#33 Marital & Family Therapy Licensure Board, PO Box 37669, Raleigh, NC 27627; 919-772-6600, Fax- 919-772-6007. Hours- 9AM-4PM. www.nclmft.org

#34 Water Treatment Facility Operators, Certification Board, 1635 Mail Service Center, Raleigh, NC 27699-1635; 919-733-0379, Fax- 919-715-2726. www.deh.enr.state.nc.us/oet/operator_cert/op_cert_main2.htm

#35 Board of Electrolysis Examiners, PO Box 34, 2 Centerview Dr, Pinehurst Bldg, Greensboro, NC 27407; 336-856-1010, Fax- 336-856-1010. Hours- 10AM-2PM T,TH. www.ncbee.com/

#36 Psychology Board, 895 State Farm Rd, #101, Boone, NC 28607; 828-262-2258, Fax- 828-265-8611. Hours- 8AM-5PM. www.ncpsychologyboard.org Search data at- www.ncpsychologyboard.org/search.htm

#37 Board of CPA Examiners, PO Box 12827 (1101 Oberlin Rd, #104), Raleigh, NC 27605-2827; 919-733-4222, Fax- 919-733-4209. www.nccpaboard.gov/Clients/NCBOA/Public/Static/index.html Search data at- www.nccpaboard.gov/Clients/NCBOA/Public/Static/search_the_database.htm

#38 Board of Athletic Trainer Examiners, PO Box 10769, Raleigh, NC 27605; 919-821-4980, Fax- 919-833-5743. www.ncbate.org Search data at- www.ncbate.org/Licenses.pdf

#39 Real Estate Commission, PO Box 17100 (1313 Navaho Dr), Raleigh, NC 27619-7100; 919-875-3700. www.ncrec.state.nc.us/default.html Search at- www.ncrec.state.nc.us/Licensees/licensees.html Online database contains only active licensees.

#40 Acupuncture Licensing Board, PO Box 10686, Raleigh, NC 27605; 919-773-0530, Fax-919-833-5743. http://ncaaom.org

#41 Board of Chiropractic Examiners, 174 Church St, Concord, NC 28025; 704-793-1342, Fax- 704-793-1385. Hours- 9AM-5PM. http://ncchiroboard.com

#42 Board of Dental Examiners, 507 Airport Blvd, #105, Morrisville, NC 27560; 919-678-8223, Fax- 919-678-8472. Hours- 8:30AM-5:30PM. www.ncdentalboard.org Search data at- www.ncdentalboard.org/ncdbe_search.asp Will sell lists of dentist and hygienists. More info available under "Publications" on website.

#43 Board of Hearing Aid Dealers & Fitters, 4030 Wake Forest Road #209 (PO Box 966, 27602), Raleigh, NC 27609; 919.834.3661, Fax- 919.834.3665. www.nchalb.org Search data at- http://pop.nchalb.org/queryname.aspx

#44 Secretary of State, Notary Public Section, PO Box 29626, Raleigh, NC 27626-0626; 919-807-2219, Fax- 919-807-2210. Hours- 8AM-5PM. www.secretary.state.nc.us/notary/

#45 North Carolina State Bar, Board of Law Examiners, PO Box 25908 (208 Fayetteville St Mall), Raleigh, NC 27611; 919-828-4620, Fax-919-821-9168. www.ncbar.com

#46 Landscape Architecture & Geologists Board, PO Box 41225 (3733 Benson Dr), Raleigh, NC 27629; 919-850-9088, Fax- 919-872-1598. www.ncbola.org Search data at- www.ncbola.org/licensees.htm

#47 Board of Medical Examiners, PO Box 20007 (1203 Front St, 27609), Raleigh, NC 27619; 919-326-1100; 919-326-1109, Fax- 919-326-0036. www.ncmedboard.org Search data at- www.ncmedboard.org/

#48 Board of Examiners for Prof Engineers & Land Surveyors, 4601 Six Forks Rd, # 310, Raleigh, NC 27609; 919-791-2000, Fax- 919-791-2012. www.ncbels.org Search data at- www.member-base.com/ncbels-vs/public/searchdb.asp

#49 Examining Board of Physical Therapy, 18 W Colony Pl, #140, Durham, NC 27705; 919-490-6393, Fax- 919-490-5106. 8AM-5PM. www.ncptboard2.org/ Search data at- www.ncptboard2.org/OnlineServices/Secure/VerifyTherapist/VerifyTherapist.php Licensure lists for PT & PTA may be obtained for $60.00 each as disk or labels.

#50 Veterinary Medical Board, PO Box 37549 (1611 Jones Franklin Rd, #106), Raleigh, NC 27627-7549; 919-854-5601, Fax- 919-854-5606. www.ncvmb.org

#51 Secretary of State, Lobbyist Registration, PO Box 29622, 2 N Salisbury St, Raleigh, NC 27626-0622; 919-807-2005, Fax- 919-807-2010. Hours- 8AM-5PM. www.secretary.state.nc.us/lobbyists/

#52 Secretary of State, Charitable Solicitation Licensing Section, PO Box 29622 (2 S Salisbury St), Raleigh, NC 27626-0622; 919-807-2214, Fax- 919-807-2220. Hours- 8AM-5PM. www.secretary.state.nc.us/csl/ Search at- www.secretary.state.nc.us/csl/Search.aspx

#53 Board of Registration of Foresters, PO Box 27393, Raleigh, NC 27611; 919-847-5441, Fax-919-847-5441. www.ncbrf.org/ Search data at- www.ncbrf.org/list.htm

#54 Board of Cosmetic Arts Examiners, 1201 Front St, #110, Raleigh, NC 27609; 919-733-4117, Fax- 919-733-4127. Hours- 8AM-5PM. www.nccosmeticarts.com Search data at- https://www.member-base.net/NCCOSMORenew/login.aspx?ReturnUrl=/nccosmorenew/Welcome.aspx License may be verified via email at a cost of $10.00.

#55 Department of Justice, Attorney General's Office, Sheriff's Standard Division, PO Drawer 629, Raleigh, NC 27602; 919-716-6460, Fax-919-716-6753. Hours- 8AM-5PM. www.ncdoj.com/law_enforcement/cle_sts_overview.jsp

#56 Board of Massage and Bodywork Therapy, PO Box 2539, 150 Fayetteville Street Mall #1900, Raleigh, NC 27602; 919-546-0050, Fax-919-833-1059. 9AM-4PM. www.bmbt.org Search data at- www.bmbt.org/MTSEARCH.ASP Purchase mailing labels, see www.bmbt.org/Mail_Labels.html; $75.00 fee.

#57 Department of Public Instruction, 301 N. Wilmington St, Raleigh, NC 27601; 919-807-3300, Fax- 919-807-3350. www.dpi.state.nc.us/

North Carolina Federal Courts

The following list indicates the district and division name for each county in the state. If the bankruptcy court location is different from the district court, then the location of the bankruptcy court appears in parentheses.

County/Court Cross Reference

County	District	Division
Alamance	Middle	Greensboro
Alexander	Western	Statesville (Charlotte)
Alleghany	Western	Statesville (Charlotte)
Anson	Western	Charlotte
Ashe	Western	Statesville (Charlotte)
Avery	Western	Asheville (Charlotte)
Beaufort	Eastern	Greenville-Eastern (Wilson)
Bertie	Eastern	Elizabeth City (Wilson)
Bladen	Eastern	Wilmington (Wilson)
Brunswick	Eastern	Wilmington (Wilson)
Buncombe	Western	Asheville (Charlotte)
Burke	Western	Asheville (Charlotte)
Cabarrus	Middle	Greensboro (Winston-Salem)
Caldwell	Western	Statesville (Charlotte)
Camden	Eastern	Elizabeth City (Wilson)
Carteret	Eastern	Greenville-Eastern (Wilson)
Caswell	Middle	Greensboro
Catawba	Western	Statesville (Charlotte)
Chatham	Middle	Greensboro
Cherokee	Western	Bryson City (Charlotte)
Chowan	Eastern	Elizabeth City (Wilson)
Clay	Western	Bryson City (Charlotte)
Cleveland	Western	Asheville (Charlotte)
Columbus	Eastern	Wilmington (Wilson)
Craven	Eastern	Greenville-Eastern (Wilson)
Cumberland	Eastern	Greenville-Eastern (Wilson)
Currituck	Eastern	Elizabeth City (Wilson)
Dare	Eastern	Elizabeth City (Wilson)
Davidson	Middle	Greensboro (Winston-Salem)
Davie	Middle	Greensboro (Winston-Salem)
Duplin	Eastern	Wilmington (Wilson)
Durham	Middle	Greensboro
Edgecombe	Eastern	Raleigh (Wilson)
Forsyth	Middle	Greensboro (Winston-Salem)
Franklin	Eastern	Raleigh
Gaston	Western	Charlotte
Gates	Eastern	Elizabeth City (Wilson)
Graham	Western	Bryson City (Charlotte)
Granville	Eastern	Raleigh
Greene	Eastern	Greenville-Eastern (Wilson)
Guilford	Middle	Greensboro
Halifax	Eastern	Greenville-Eastern (Wilson)
Harnett	Eastern	Raleigh
Haywood	Western	Asheville (Charlotte)
Henderson	Western	Asheville (Charlotte)
Hertford	Eastern	Elizabeth City (Wilson)
Hoke	Middle	Greensboro
Hyde	Eastern	Greenville-Eastern (Wilson)
Iredell	Western	Statesville (Charlotte)
Jackson	Western	Bryson City (Charlotte)
Johnston	Eastern	Raleigh
Jones	Eastern	Greenville-Eastern (Wilson)
Lee	Middle	Greensboro
Lenoir	Eastern	Greenville-Eastern (Wilson)
Lincoln	Western	Statesville (Charlotte)
Macon	Western	Bryson City (Charlotte)
Madison	Western	Asheville (Charlotte)
Martin	Eastern	Greenville-Eastern (Wilson)
McDowell	Western	Asheville (Charlotte)
Mecklenburg	Western	Charlotte
Mitchell	Western	Asheville (Charlotte)
Montgomery	Middle	Greensboro
Moore	Middle	Greensboro
Nash	Eastern	Raleigh (Wilson)
New Hanover	Eastern	Wilmington (Wilson)
Northampton	Eastern	Elizabeth City (Wilson)
Onslow	Eastern	Wilmington (Wilson)
Orange	Middle	Greensboro
Pamlico	Eastern	Greenville-Eastern (Wilson)
Pasquotank	Eastern	Elizabeth City (Wilson)
Pender	Eastern	Wilmington (Wilson)
Perquimans	Eastern	Elizabeth City (Wilson)
Person	Middle	Greensboro
Pitt	Eastern	Greenville-Eastern (Wilson)
Polk	Western	Asheville (Charlotte)
Randolph	Middle	Greensboro
Richmond	Middle	Greensboro
Robeson	Eastern	Wilmington (Wilson)
Rockingham	Middle	Greensboro
Rowan	Middle	Greensboro (Winston-Salem)
Rutherford	Western	Asheville (Charlotte)
Sampson	Eastern	Wilmington (Wilson)
Scotland	Middle	Greensboro
Stanly	Middle	Greensboro (Winston-Salem)
Stokes	Middle	Greensboro (Winston-Salem)
Surry	Middle	Greensboro (Winston-Salem)
Swain	Western	Bryson City (Charlotte)
Transylvania	Western	Asheville (Charlotte)
Tyrrell	Eastern	Elizabeth City (Wilson)
Union	Western	Charlotte
Vance	Eastern	Raleigh
Wake	Eastern	Raleigh
Warren	Eastern	Raleigh
Washington	Eastern	Elizabeth City (Wilson)
Watauga	Western	Statesville (Charlotte)
Wayne	Eastern	Raleigh (Wilson)
Wilkes	Western	Statesville (Charlotte)
Wilson	Eastern	Raleigh (Wilson)
Yadkin	Middle	Greensboro (Winston-Salem)
Yancey	Western	Asheville (Charlotte)

US District Court
North Carolina Eastern Dist.

Eastern Division Court Clerk, 201 S Evans St, Rm 209, Greenville, NC 27858-1137, 252-830-6009; Fax- 252-830-2793. 8:30AM-4:30PM. www.nced.uscourts.gov

Counties: Beaufort, Carteret, Craven, Edgecombe, Greene, Halifax, Hyde, Jones, Lenoir, Martin, Pamlico, Pitt.

Searches/Indexing: To search, include full name; SSN and DOB may be helpful. Results do not include SSN or DOB. Will fax back documents if prepaid. New cases are in the index 1 day after filing date. Both computer and card indexes maintained; computer back to 1993. Civil records retained 2 years. All criminal records after 1979 forwarded to Raleigh.

Search Access: Only docket info is available by phone. **Mail:** Search usually completed- 1 week. SASE not required. **Fax:** Fax search requests accepted if prepaid. **In person:** 1 public terminal available. Self-serve copies $.50 each.

Payment: Pay by Visa/MC, money order, cashier's or personal check. Payee: Clerk, US District Court.

E-Services: The old RACER and PACER systems have been replaced by the new CM/ECF system. PACER records go back to 1989. New records online after 3 days. ECF at https://ecf.nced.uscourts.gov. Opinions and Civil case openings also on CM/ECF. **Online Note:** Unofficial judge's calendars available free at www.nced.uscourts.gov/applications/calendars.asp

Standards for Federal Courts: *See the Appendix for information on Federal Court searching standards and fees.*

Northern Division c/o Raleigh Division, PO Box 25670, Raleigh, NC 27611 (In person: 310 New Bern Ave, Rm 574, Raleigh), 919-645-1700; Fax- 919-645-1750. Hours- 8:30AM-4:30PM. www.nced.uscourts.gov

Counties/Note: Bertie, Camden, Chowan, Currituck, Dare, Gates, Hertford, Northampton, Pasquotank, Perquimans, Tyrrell, Washington.

Searches/Indexing: To search, include full name; SSN and DOB may be helpful. Results include last 4 SSN digits, also birth year. Will fax back documents if prepaid. New cases are in the index 1 day after filing date. Both computer and card indexes maintained; computer back to 1993. Closed civil records retained 2 years.

Search Access: Mail: Search usually completed- 2 days. SASE not required. **Fax:** Fax search requests accepted if prepaid. **In person:** 1 public terminal available. No self-serve copier. **Payment:** Pay by Visa/MC, money order, cashier's or personal check.

E-Services: The old RACER and PACER systems have been replaced by the new CM/ECF system. PACER records go back to 1989. New records online after 3 days. ECF at https://ecf.nced.uscourts.gov. Opinions and Civil case openings also on CM/ECF. **Online Note:** Unofficial judge's calendars available free at www.nced.uscourts.gov/applications/calendars.asp

Southern Div. Court Clerk, 2 Princess St, Rm 239, Alton Lennon Federal Bldg, Wilmington, NC 28401, 910-815-4663; Fax- 910-815-4518. Hours- 8:30AM-4:30PM. www.nced.uscourts.gov

Counties: Bladen, Brunswick, Columbus, Duplin, New Hanover, Onslow, Pender, Robeson, Sampson.

Searches/Indexing: To search, include full name; SSN and DOB may be helpful. Results do not include SSN or DOB. Will fax back documents if prepaid. New cases are in the index 1 day after filing date. Both computer and card indexes maintained; computer back to 1993. Closed civil records retained 2 years.

Search Access: Phone searches available for info from 1992 to the present. **Mail:** Search usually completed- 10 days. SASE not required. **Fax:** Fax search requests accepted if prepaid. **In person:** 1 public terminal available. Self-serve copies $.50.

Payment: Pay by Visa/MC, money order, cashier's or personal check. Payee: Clerk, US District Court.

E-Services: The old RACER and PACER systems have been replaced by the new CM/ECF system. PACER records go back to 1989. New records online after 3 days. ECF at https://ecf.nced.uscourts.gov. Opinions and Civil case openings also on CM/ECF. **Online Note:** Unofficial judge's calendars available free at www.nced.uscourts.gov/applications/calendars.asp

Western Division Clerk's Office, PO Box 25670, Raleigh, NC 27611 (In person: 310 New Bern Ave, Rm 574, Raleigh), 919-645-1700; Fax- 919-645-1750. Hours- 8:30AM-4:30PM. www.nced.uscourts.gov

Counties/Note: Cumberland, Franklin, Granville, Harnett, Johnston, Nash, Vance, Wake, Warren, Wayne, Wilson. Records from Fayetteville, which handled Cumberland and Harnett counties, are maintained at Raleigh. District-wide searches available at Raleigh back to 1979 for crim records.

Searches/Indexing: To search, include full name; SSN and DOB may be helpful. Results include last 4 SSN digits, also birth year. Will fax back documents if prepaid. New cases are in the index 1 day after filing date. Both computer and card indexes maintained; computer back to 1993. Closed civil records retained 2 years.

Search Access: Only docket info is available by phone. **Mail:** Search usually completed- 2 days. SASE not required. **Fax:** Fax search requests accepted if prepaid. **In person:** 1 public terminal available. No self-serve copier.

Payment: Pay by Visa/MC, money order, cashier's or personal check. Payee: Clerk, US District Court.

E-Services: The old RACER and PACER systems have been replaced by the new CM/ECF system. PACER records go back to 1989. New records online after 3 days. ECF at https://ecf.nced.uscourts.gov. Opinions and Civil case openings also on CM/ECF. **Online Note:** Unofficial judge's calendars available free at www.nced.uscourts.gov/applications/calendars.asp

US Bankruptcy Court North Carolina Eastern Dist.

Raleigh Division Court Clerk, PO Box 1441, Raleigh, NC 27602 (In person: Century Station Bldg, Rm 209, 300 Fayetteville St Mall, Raleigh), 919-856-4752. Hours- 8:30AM - 4:30PM. www.nceb.uscourts.gov

Counties/Note: Franklin, Granville, Harnett, Johnston, Vance, Wake, Warren.

Searches/Indexing: Include SSN and full name in search requests. Results include last 4 SSN digits. Will not fax back documents. New cases are in the index immediately after filing date.

Search Access: Voice Case Information Service available, call VCIS at 888-847-9138 or 919-856-4618. **Mail:** Search usually completed- 2-3 days. Include SASE for return. **In person:** 2 public terminals available. Computer generated copies- $.10 each. **Payment:** Pay by Visa/MC (companies only), money order, cashier's check, business check. No personal checks. Payee: Clerk, US Bankruptcy Court.

E-Services: ECF at https://ecf.nceb.uscourts.gov. **Opinions:** www.nceb.uscourts.gov:8080/search/. Selected significant decisions back to 2000. Opinions also under Reports in CM-ECF. **Online Note:** Search calendars free at www.nceb.uscourts.gov/newcode/calendars.php.

Wilson Div. Court Clerk, 1760-A Parkwood Blvd Wet, Wilson, NC 27893-3564 (In person: Thomas Milton Moore Bldg), 252-237-0248. Hours-8:30AM-4:30PM. www.nceb.uscourts.gov

Counties/Note: Beaufort, Bertie, Bladen, Brunswick, Camden, Carteret, Chowan, Columbus, Craven, Cumberland, Currituck, Dare, Duplin, Edgecombe, Gates, Greene, Halifax, Hertford, Hyde, Jones, Lenoir, Martin, Nash, New Hanover, Northampton, Onslow, Pamlico, Pasquotank, Pender, Perquimans, Pitt, Robeson, Sampson, Tyrrell, Washington, Wayne, Wilson.

Searches/Indexing: Include SSN and full name in search requests. Results include last 4 SSN digits. Will not fax back documents. New cases are in the index immediately after filing date.

Search Access: Limited search; only major dates such as 341 date, discharge date and entry date is released. Voice Case Information Service available, call VCIS at 888-513-9765 or 252-234-7655. **Mail:** Search usually completed- 2-3 days. Include SASE for return. **In person:** 2 public terminals available. Computer generated copies- $.10 each.

Payment: Pay by Visa/MC, money order, cashier's check, business check. No personal checks. Payee: Clerk, US Bankruptcy Court.

E-Services: New records online immediately. ECF at https://ecf.nceb.uscourts.gov. **Opinions Online:** www.nceb.uscourts.gov:8080/search/. Selected significant decisions back to 2000. Opinions also under Reports in CM-ECF. **Note:** Search calendars at www.nceb.uscourts.gov/newcode/calendars.php.

US District Court North Carolina Middle District

Greensboro Division Clerk's Office, 324 W Market St, Rm 401, Greensboro, NC 27401, 336-332-6000; records- 336-332-6030; crim dockets- 336-332-6020; civil dockets- 336-332-6030. Hours-8AM-5PM. www.ncmd.uscourts.gov

Counties/Note: Alamance, Cabarrus, Caswell, Chatham, Davidson, Davie, Durham, Forsyth, Guilford, Hoke, Lee, Montgomery, Moore, Orange, Person, Randolph, Richmond, Rockingham, Rowan, Scotland, Stanly, Stokes, Surry, Yadkin. Winston-Salem and Durham Division clerk offices were abolished as of 7/1997. Winston-Salem Courthouse located at 251 N. Main St, 336-734-2516; the Durham Courthouse located at 323 E. Chapel Hill St, 919-541-5413.

Searches/Indexing: Search request requires name only. Results do not include SSN or DOB, only case numbers and cases found. Will not fax back documents. New cases are in the index 1 day after filing date. Both computer and card indexes maintained; computer goes back to 1990. Closed electronic cases not purged.

Search Access: Only docket info is available by case number via phone. **Mail:** Search usually completed- 7 days. SASE not required. **In person:** 2 public terminals available. No self-serve copier.

Payment: Pay by Visa/MC, money order, cashier's check. Payee: Clerk, US District Court.

E-Services: Document images available. PACER records go back to 9/1991. New records online after 1 day. ECF at https://ecf.ncmd.uscourts.gov. **Opinions Online:** www.ncmd.uscourts.gov. **Online Note:** Access court calendars at www.ncmd.uscourts.gov.

US Bankruptcy Court North Carolina Middle District

Greensboro Div. Court Clerk, POB 26100, Greensboro, NC 27420-6100 (In person: 101 S Edgeworth St, Greensboro, NC), 336-358-4000. Hours-8AM-5PM. www.ncmb.uscourts.gov

Counties/Notes: Durham Division records. Alamance, Caswell, Chatham, Durham, Guilford, Hoke, Lee, Montgomery, Moore, Orange, Person, Randolph, Richmond, Rockingham, Scotland.

Searches/Indexing: Include SSN and full name in search request. Results include full name and attorney. Will not fax back documents. New cases are in the index 1-2 days after filing date.

Search Access: Only basic docket info is available via phone. Voice Case Information Service available, call VCIS at 888-319-0455 or 336-358-4057. **Mail:** Search usually completed- 1-2 days. Include SASE for return. **In person:** 2 public terminals available. No self-serve copier.

Payment: Pay by money order, cashier's or personal check. No debtor checks/credit cards accepted. Payee: Clerk, US Bankruptcy Court.

E-Services: PACER records go back to 1992. New records online immediately. ECF at https://ecf.ncmb.uscourts.gov. ECF images go back to 1999. **Opinions Online:** http://www1.ncmb.uscourts.gov/opinions/search/Main.cfm. **Online Note:** Current calendars free at www.ncmb.uscourts.gov/cal.php.

Winston-Salem Division Court Clerk, 226 S Liberty St, Winston-Salem, NC 27101, 8AM-5PM. 336-397-7785. www.ncmb.uscourts.gov

Counties/Note: Cabarrus, Davidson, Davie, Forsyth, Rowan, Stanly, Stokes, Surry, Yadkin.

Searches/Indexing: Include SSN and full name in search request. Results include full name and attorney. Will not fax back documents. New cases are in the index 1-2 days after filing date. Both computer and card indexes maintained.

Search Access: Only basic docket info is available via phone. Voice Case Information Service available, call VCIS at 888-319-0455. **Mail:** Search usually completed- 1-2 days. Include SASE for return. **In person:** 2 public terminals available. No self-serve copier.

Payment: Pay by money order, cashier's or personal check. No debtor checks/credit cards accepted. Payee: Clerk, US Bankruptcy Court.

E-Services: Document images available back to 1999. PACER records go back to 1992. New records online immediately. ECF at https://ecf.ncmb.uscourts.gov. ECF images go back to 1999. **Opinions Online:** http://www1.ncmb.uscourts.gov/opinions/search/Main.cfm. **Online Note:** Current calendars free at www.ncmb.uscourts.gov/cal.php.

US District Court North Carolina Western Dist.

Asheville Division Clerk of the Court, Rm 309, US Courthouse Bldg, 100 Otis St, Asheville, NC 28801-2611, 828-771-7200; Fax- 828-271-4343. Hours- 8:30AM-12:30PM, 1:30-4PM. www.ncwd.uscourts.gov

Counties/Note: Avery, Buncombe, Burke, Cleveland, Haywood, Henderson, Madison, McDowell, Mitchell, Polk, Rutherford, Transylvania, Yancey. This Division now houses records from Shelby Division, which is closed. This division also holds Bryson City Div. records.

Searches/Indexing: Search request requires name only. Results do not include SSN or DOB. Will not fax back documents. New cases are in the index 1 day after filing date. Both computer and card indexes maintained; computer index back to 1993. Not all records are entered into the in house automated system. Closed cases sent to archives after 5 years.

Search Access: Only docket info is available by phone. **Mail:** Search usually completed- 7 days. SASE not required. **In person:** 1 public terminal available. Self-serve copies $.50 each.

Payment: Pay by money order, cashier's or personal check. No credit cards accepted. Attorney credit cards accepted in person only. Payee: Clerk, US District Court.

E-Services: WebPACER replaced by CM-ECF system. PACER records go back to 1991. New records online immediately. ECF at https://ecf.ncwd.uscourts.gov. **Opinions Online:** Opinions only available through PACER.. **Online Note:** Calendars free at www.ncwb.uscourts.gov/. Search pre-1992 cases free at www.ncwd.uscourts.gov/PICS/picsPublicQuery.asp.

Bryson City Division c/o Asheville Division, Clerk of the Court, Rm 309, US Courthouse, 100 Otis St, Asheville, NC 28801-2611, 828-771-7200; records room fax- 828-271-4343; fax record requests to- 828-271-4343. Hours- 8:30AM-12:30PM, 1:30-4PM. www.ncwd.uscourts.gov

Counties/Note: Cherokee, Clay, Graham, Jackson, Macon, Swain. Phone for Bryson City Office is 828-488-3783. Bryson Courthouse is only open on designated court days.

Searches/Indexing: Search request requires name only. Results do not include SSN or DOB. Will not fax back documents. New cases are in the index 2 days after filing date. Both computer and card indexes maintained; computer index back to 1993. Closed cases sent to archives after 5 years.

Search Access: Only docket info is available by phone. **Mail:** SASE not required. **In person:** One public terminal available. No self-serve copier.

Payment: Pay by no business or personal checks accepted. No credit cards accepted. Attorney credit cards accepted in person only. Payee: Clerk, US District Court.

E-Services: WebPACER replaced by CM-ECF system. PACER records go back to 1991. New records online immediately. ECF at https://ecf.ncwd.uscourts.gov. **Opinions Online:** Opinions only available through PACER.. **Online Note:** Calendars free at www.ncwb.uscourts.gov/. Search pre-1992 cases free at www.ncwd.uscourts.gov/PICS/picsPublicQuery.asp.

Charlotte Div. Clerk of Court, 401 W Trade St, Rm 210, Charlotte, NC 28202, 704-350-7400. 8:30-12:30, 1:30-4PM. www.ncwd.uscourts.gov

Counties: Anson, Gaston, Mecklenburg, Union.

Searches/Indexing: Search request requires name only. Results do not include SSN or DOB. Will not fax back documents. New cases are in the index immediately after filing date. Both computer and card indexes maintained; computer index back to 1993. District-wide searches available here back to 1950. Closed cases archived after 5 years.

Search Access: Only docket info is available by phone. **Mail:** Search usually completed- 7-10 days. SASE not required. **In person:** 2 public terminals available. No self-serve copier.

Payment: Pay by money order, cashier's or personal check. No credit cards accepted. Attorney credit cards accepted in person only. Payee: Clerk, US District Court.

E-Services: WebPACER replaced by CM-ECF system. PACER records go back to 1991. New records online immediately. ECF at https://ecf.ncwd.uscourts.gov. **Opinions Online:** Opinions only available through PACER.. **Online Note:** Calendars free at www.ncwb.uscourts.gov/. Search pre-1992 cases free at www.ncwd.uscourts.gov/PICS/picsPublicQuery.asp.

Statesville Division Court Clerk, 200 W Broad St #100, Statesville, NC 28677, 704-883-1000; Fax- 704-873-0903. Hours-8:30AM-12:30PM, 1:30-4PM. www.ncwd.uscourts.gov

Counties: Alexander, Alleghany, Ashe, Caldwell, Catawba, Iredell, Lincoln, Watauga, Wilkes.

Searches/Indexing: Search request requires name only. Results do not include SSN or DOB. Will not fax back documents. New cases are in the index 2 days after filing date. Both computer and card indexes maintained; computer index back to 1993. Closed cases sent to archives after 5 years.

Search Access: Only docket info is available by phone. **Mail:** Search usually completed- 2 days. SASE not required. **In person:** 1 public terminal available. Self-serve copier available.

Payment: Pay by money order, cashier's or personal check. No credit cards accepted. Attorney credit cards accepted in person only. Payee: Clerk, US District Court.

E-Services: WebPACER replaced by CM-ECF system. PACER records go back to 1991. New records online immediately. ECF at https://ecf.ncwd.uscourts.gov. **Opinions Online:** Opinions only available through PACER. **Note:** Calendars online at www.ncwb.uscourts.gov/. Search pre-1992 cases free at www.ncwd.uscourts.gov/PICS/picsPu blicQuery.asp.

US Bankruptcy Court North Carolina Western Dist.

Charlotte Division Court Clerk, PO Box 34189, Charlotte, NC 28234-4189 (In person: 401 W Trade St, Rm 111, Charlotte), 704-350-7500; Fax- 704-344-6403. Hours- 8:30AM-4:30PM. www.ncwb.uscourts.gov

Counties/Note: Alexander, Alleghany, Anson, Ashe, Avery, Buncombe, Burke, Caldwell, Catawba, Cherokee, Clay, Cleveland, Gaston, Graham, Haywood, Henderson, Iredell, Jackson, Lincoln, Macon, Madison, McDowell, Mecklenburg, Mitchell, Polk, Rutherford, Swain, Transylvania, Union, Watauga, Wilkes, Yancey. There are five offices within this division; records for all may be searched here at Charlotte or at Asheville: 100 Otis St #112, Asheville, NC 28801, 828-771-7300.

Searches/Indexing: Include name, address, SSN or Tax ID number. Results do not include SSN or DOB. Will not fax back documents. New cases are in the index 1-2 days after filing date. Case files sent to archives upon closing. Cases after 1/1997 are scanned and not retired.

Search Access: Only docket info available by phone. Voice Case Information Service available, call VCIS at 800-884-9868 or 704-350-7505. **Mail:** Search usually completed- 7-10 days. Include SASE for return. **In person:** 2 public terminals available. No self-serve copier.

Payment: Pay by money order, cashier's check, business check, attorney check or attorney MC/Visa/AmEx. No personal or debtor checks. Payee: Clerk, US Bankruptcy Court.

E-Services: PACER records go back to 1992. New records online after 1 day. ECF at https://ecf.ncwb.uscourts.gov. **Opinions Online:** www.ncwb.uscourts.gov/opinions/opinions.html. Select New Opinions or Miscellaneous Cases. **Online Note:** Calendars are free at www.ncwb.uscourts.gov. Browse unclaimed funds free at www.ncwb.uscourts.gov/!/index.html

North Carolina County Courts

Court	Jurisdiction	No. of Courts	How Organized
Superior Courts*	General	0	46 Districts
District Courts*	Limited	0	39 Districts
Combined Courts*		100	

* Profiled in this Sourcebook.

Court	CIVIL								
	Tort	Contract	Real Estate	Min. Claim	Max. Claim	Small Claim	Estate	Eviction	Domestic Relations
Superior Courts*	X	X	X	$10,000	No Max		X		
District Courts*	X	X	X	$0	$10,000	$5000		X	X

Court	CRIMINAL				
	Felony	Misdemeanor	DWI/DUI	Preliminary Hearing	Juvenile
Superior Courts*	X				
District Courts*		X	X	X	X

Administration

Administrative Office of the Courts, 901 Corporate Center Drive, Raleigh, NC 27607-5045; 919- 890-1000. (EST) www.nccourts.org

Court Structure

The Superior Court is the court of general jurisdiction; the District Court is limited jurisdiction. The counties combine the courts, thus searching is done through one court, not two, within the county. Small Claims Court is part of the District Court Division and handles civil cases where a plaintiff requests assignment to a magistrate and the amount in controversy is $5000 or less (raised from $4000 in Summer, 2005). The principal relief sought in Small Claims Court is money, the recovery of specific personal property, or summary ejectment (eviction).

Probate is handled by County Clerks.

Online Access

The state AOC provides certain vendors with electronic records on an ongoing basis pursuant to a licensing agreement. A list of the vendors is found at www.nccourts.org/Citizens/GoToCourt/Documents/WebsiteListing.pdf. Search for free the District and Superior Court Query system for current criminal defendants at http://www1.aoc.state.nc.us/www/calendars/CriminalQuery.html. There are also querys for Impaired Driving, Citations, and Current Civil and Criminal Calendars. Appellate and Supreme Court opinions are at www.aoc.state.nc.us/www/public/html/opinions.htm.

Searching Tips, Fees, and Other Guidelines

Many courts recommend that civil searches be done in person or by a retriever and that only criminal searches be requested in writing. A fee structure is in place that mandates copy fees to be $2.00 for the first page and $.25 each additional page, and $15.00 for a criminal record search, which includes certification in most jurisdictions. Most courts have adopted these rules. Many courts have archived their records prior to 1968 in the Raleigh State Archives, 919-807-7280.

Alamance County

Superior-District Court - Criminal 212 W Elm St, #105, Graham, NC 27253; 336-438-1001; fax: 336-570-6991; 8-5PM. ***Felony, Misdemeanor.***
www.nccourts.org/County/Alamance/Default.asp

Criminal Records: Access: Mail, in person. Both court and visitors may perform in person searches. Search fee: $15.00 per name, includes certification. Required to search: name, years to search, DOB; also helpful: address, SSN. Criminal records on computer since 1985, on index cards back to 1975. Mail turnaround time 1 week. Public use terminal has crim records back to 3/1985. Criminal calendars at www1.aoc.state.nc.us/www/calendars.html.

General Information: No sealed case records released. Will not fax documents. Court makes copy: $2.00 1st page, $.25 ea add'l. Self serve: $.25 per page. Cert fee: $3.00 per cert; exemplification-$10.00. Payee: Clerk of Superior Court. Only cashiers checks and money orders accepted. No credit cards accepted. Prepayment required.

Superior-District Court - Civil 1 Court Square, Graham, NC 27253; 336-438-1013; probate phone: 336-438-1008; fax: 336-570-6988; 8AM-5PM. ***Civil, Eviction, Small Claims, Probate.***
www.nccourts.org/County/Alamance/Default.asp

Civil Records: Access: Mail, in person. Visitors must perform in person searches themselves. No search fee. Required to search: name, years to search. Civil cases indexed by defendant, plaintiff. Civil records computerized since 1988, prior indexed on books. Public use terminal has civil records back to 1988. Search civil court calendars at www1.aoc.state.nc.us/www/calendars.html.

General Information: No adoption, sealed cases, juvenile, or mental records released. Will not fax documents. Court makes copy: $2.00 1st page, $.25 ea add'l page. Self serve: $.25 per page. Certification fee: $3.00. Payee: Clerk of Superior Court. No personal checks or credit cards accepted. Prepayment required.

Alexander County

Superior-District Court PO Box 100, Taylorsville, NC 28681; 828-632-2215; probate phone: same; fax: 828-632-3550; 8AM-5PM. ***Felony, Misdemeanor, Civil, Eviction, Small Claims, Probate.***
www.nccourts.org/County/Alexander/Default.asp

Search civil and criminal court calendars at www1.aoc.state.nc.us/www/calendars.html.

Civil Records: Access: Mail, in person. Both court and visitors may perform in person searches. No search fee. Required to search: name, years to search, address. Civil cases indexed by defendant, plaintiff; index on computer since 10/1989, prior on books to 1865. Mail turnaround time 1-3 days. Civil PAT goes back to 1989.

Criminal Records: Access: Mail, in person. Both court and visitors may perform in person searches. Search fee: $15.00 per name, includes certification. Required to search: name, years to search, address, DOB, SSN. Criminal records on computer since

10/1989, prior on books to 1865. Mail turnaround 1-3 days. Criminal PAT goes back to same as civil.
General Information: No adoption, sealed cases, juvenile, sex offenders, mental, expunged records released. Will not fax documents. Court makes copy: $2.00 1st page, $.25 ea add'l. Self serve: $.25 per page. Certification fee: None; $3.00 if you perform search in person. Payee: Clerk of Superior Court. Business checks accepted. No credit cards accepted. Prepayment required. Mail requests: SASE required.

Alleghany County

Superior-District Court PO Box 61, 12 N Main St, Sparta, NC 28675; 336-372-8949; fax: 336-372-4899; 8-5PM. ***Felony, Misdemeanor, Civil, Eviction, Small Claims, Probate.***
www.nccourts.org/County/Alleghany/Default.asp
Search civil and criminal court calendars at www1.aoc.state.nc.us/www/calendars.html.
Civil Records: Access: In person only. Visitors must perform in person searches themselves. Required to search: name, years to search; also helpful: address. Civil cases indexed by defendant, plaintiff; index on computer from 11/1988, index books prior. Civil PAT goes back to 1988.
Criminal Records: Access: Fax, mail, in person. Both court and visitors may perform in person searches. Search fee: $15.00 per name, includes certification. Required to search: name, years to search, DOB; also helpful: address, SSN. Criminal records computerized from 11/ 1988, index books prior. Mail turnaround time 2 days. Criminal PAT goes back to same as civil.
General Information: No adoption, sealed cases, juvenile, mental or expunged records released. Will not fax documents. Court makes copy: $2.00 1st page, $.25 ea add'l. Certification fee: $3.00 per doc. Payee: Clerk of Superior Court. Business checks accepted. Prepayment required. Mail requests: SASE required for criminal.

Anson County

Superior-District Court PO Box 1064 (114 N Greene St), Wadesboro, NC 28170; 704-694-2314; fax: 704-695-1161; 8:30AM-5PM. ***Felony, Misdemeanor, Civil, Eviction, Small Claims, Probate.***
www.nccourts.org/County/Anson/Default.asp
Search civil and criminal court calendars at www1.aoc.state.nc.us/www/calendars.html.
Civil Records: Access: In person only. Visitors must perform in person searches themselves. Required to search: name, years to search. Civil cases indexed by defendant, plaintiff; index on computer since 11/1989, in books prior. Public use terminal has civil records back to 1989. PAT civil results show middle initial. Public terminal has Estates/Special Proceedings. SSNs and middle initials do not appear on all records.
Criminal Records: Access: Mail, in person. Only the court performs in person searches; visitors may not. Search fee: $15.00 per name, includes certification. Required to search: name, years to search, DOB; also helpful: SSN. Criminal records on computer since 10/89, on microfilm 1982-89, in books prior. Mail turnaround time 2-5 days.
General Information: No adoption, sealed cases, juvenile, mental, or expunged records released. Will not fax documents. Court makes copy: $2.00 1st page, $.25 ea add'l. Certification fee: $3.00. Payee: Clerk of Superior Court. Business checks accepted. No personal checks. No credit cards accepted. Prepayment required. Mail requests: SASE required.

Ashe County

Superior-District Court 150 Government Circle #3100, Jefferson, NC 28640; 336-246-5641; fax: 336-246-4276; 8AM-5PM. ***Felony, Misdemeanor, Civil, Eviction, Small Claims, Probate.***
www.nccourts.org/County/Ashe/Default.asp
Search civil and criminal court calendars at www1.aoc.state.nc.us/www/calendars.html.
Civil Records: Access: Mail, in person. Both court and visitors may perform in person searches. Search fee: $15.00 per name. Required to search: name, years to search. Civil cases indexed by defendant, plaintiff; index on computer from 12/89, on index books back to 1900s. Mail turnaround time 1-3 days. Civil PAT goes back to 1989.
Criminal Records: Access: Mail, in person. Both court and visitors may perform in person searches. Search fee: $15.00 per name, includes certification. Required to search: name, years to search. Criminal records computerized from 12/89, on index books back to 1900s. Note: Court will search records after 1988; visitors or researchers must search themselves for records prior to 1988. Mail turnaround time 1-3 days. Criminal PAT goes back to 1988. PAT results show middle initial, DOB, SSN.
General Information: No adoption, sealed cases, juvenile, sex offenders, mental or expunged records released. Will fax out documents; fax fee varies from case to case. Court makes copy: $2.00 1st page, $.25 ea add'l. Self serve: $.25 per page. Certification fee: $3.00. Payee: Clerk of Superior Court. Only cashiers checks and money orders accepted. No credit cards accepted. Prepayment required.

Avery County

Superior-District Court PO Box 115, Newland, NC 28657; 828-733-2900; fax: 828-733-8410; 8AM-4:30PM. ***Felony, Misdemeanor, Civil, Eviction, Small Claims, Probate.***
www.nccourts.org/County/Avery/Default.asp
Search civil and criminal court calendars at www1.aoc.state.nc.us/www/calendars.html.
Civil Records: Access: In person only. Visitors must perform in person searches themselves. Required to search: name, years to search; also helpful: address. Civil cases indexed by defendant, plaintiff; index on computer since 1988, on index books to 1968. Civil PAT goes back to 10/1988. PAT results show name only.
Criminal Records: Access: Mail, in person. Both court and visitors may perform in person searches. Search fee: $15.00 per name, includes certification. Required to search: name, years to search; also helpful: address. Criminal records computerized from 11/88; on cards and books back to 1968. Mail turnaround time 2-3 days. Criminal PAT goes back to 11/1988. PAT results show name only.
General Information: No adoption, sealed cases, juvenile, sex offenders, mental or expunged records released. Will not fax documents. Court makes copy: $2.00 1st page, $.25 ea add'l. Self serve: $.25 per page. Certification fee: $3.00 if you perform search in person. Payee: Clerk of Superior Court. Only cashiers checks and money orders accepted. No credit cards accepted. Prepayment required. Will bill copy fees.

Beaufort County

Superior-District Court PO Box 1403, 112 W 2nd St, Washington, NC 27889; 252-946-5184; fax: 252-946-6448; 8-5PM. ***Felony, Misdemeanor, Civil, Eviction, Small Claims, Probate.***
www.nccourts.org/County/Beaufort/Default.asp
Search civil and criminal court calendars at www1.aoc.state.nc.us/www/calendars.html.
Civil Records: Access: In person only. Visitors must perform in person searches themselves. Required to search: name, years to search, address. Civil cases indexed by defendant, plaintiff; index on computer since 6/87, docket books to 1800s. Civil PAT goes back to 6/1987.
Criminal Records: Access: Mail, in person. Both court and visitors may perform in person searches. Search fee: $15.00 per name, includes certification. Required to search: name; also helpful: years to search, address, DOB, SSN. Criminal records on computer since 5/87, docket books to 1800s. Mail turnaround time 5 days. Criminal PAT goes back to 1987. PAT results show middle initial, DOB.
General Information: No adoption, sealed cases, juvenile, sex offenders, mental or expunged records released. Will not fax documents. Court makes copy: $2.00 1st page, $.25 ea add'l. Certification fee: $3.00 per doc. Payee: Clerk of Superior Court. Business checks accepted; no personal checks. No credit cards accepted. Prepayment required.

Bertie County

Superior-District Court PO Box 370, 108 Dundee St, Windsor, NC 27983; criminal phone: 252-794-3039; civil phone: 252-794-3030; fax: 252-794-2482; 8AM-5PM. ***Felony, Misdemeanor, Civil, Eviction, Small Claims, Probate.***
www.nccourts.org/County/Bertie/Default.asp
Search civil and criminal court calendars at www1.aoc.state.nc.us/www/calendars.html.
Civil Records: Access: In person only. Both court and visitors may perform in person searches. No search fee. Required to search: name, years to search. Civil cases indexed by defendant, plaintiff; index on computer from 11/96, prior on books to 1968. Note: Court will do a civil search if it is conjunction with a criminal search. Civil PAT goes back to 6/1989.
Criminal Records: Access: Mail, in person. Both court and visitors may perform in person searches. Search fee: $15.00 per name, includes certification. Required to search: name, years to search, DOB; also helpful: address, SSN. Criminal records computerized from 3/89, prior on books to 1968. Mail turnaround time 1-2 days. Criminal PAT goes back to 3/1989. PAT results show middle initial, DOB.
General Information: No adoption, sealed cases, juvenile, mental, expunged records released. Fee to fax document $1.00 1st page; $.25 each add'l. Court makes copy: $2.00 1st page, $.25 ea add'l. Certification fee: $3.00 per doc. Court will not certify any in person searches. Payee: Clerk of Superior Court. Only cashiers checks and money orders accepted. No credit cards accepted. Prepayment required. Mail requests: SASE requested for criminal.

Bladen County

Superior-District Court PO Box 2619, Elizabethtown, NC 28337; 910-872-7200; probate phone: 910-872-7202; fax: 910-872-7218; 8:30AM-5PM. ***Felony, Misdemeanor, Civil, Eviction, Small Claims, Probate.***
www.nccourts.org/County/Bladen/Default.asp
Search civil and criminal court calendars at www1.aoc.state.nc.us/www/calendars.html.
Civil Records: Access: In person only. Visitors must perform in person searches themselves. Required to search: name, years to search. Civil cases indexed by defendant, plaintiff; index on computer since 1989, prior on judgment books back to 1896 (fire). Civil PAT goes back to 1989. PAT results show middle initial, DOB.
Criminal Records: Access: Mail, in person. Both court and visitors may perform in person searches. Search fee: $15.00 per name, includes certification. Required to search: name, years to search, DOB. Criminal records computerized from 5/89, on books to 1968. Mail turnaround time 5 days. Criminal PAT goes back to 1988. PAT results show middle initial, DOB.
General Information: No adoption, sealed cases, juvenile, sex offenders, mental or expunged records released. Will not fax documents. Court makes copy: $2.00 1st page, $.25 ea add'l. Certification fee: None; $3.00 if you perform search in person. Only cashiers checks and money orders accepted. No credit cards accepted. Prepayment required.

Brunswick County

Superior-District Court 310 Goverment Ctr Dr, Unit 1, Attn: Clerk, Bolivia, NC 28422; criminal phone: 910-253-8512; civil phone: 910-253-8502; probate phone: 910-253-8505; fax: 910-253-8532; 8:30AM-5PM. ***Felony, Misdemeanor, Civil, Eviction, Small Claims, Probate.***
www.nccourts.org/County/Brunswick/Default.asp
Search civil and criminal court calendars at www1.aoc.state.nc.us/www/calendars.html.
Civil Records: Access: In person only. Visitors must perform in person searches themselves. Required to search: name, years to search. Civil cases indexed by defendant, plaintiff; index on computer since 1989, prior on books to 1968. Civil PAT goes back to 1989.
Criminal Records: Access: Mail, in person. Both court and visitors may perform in person searches. Search fee: $15.00 per name, includes certification. Required to search: name, years to search. Criminal

records on computer since 1989, prior on microfiche and books to 1968. Mail turnaround time 5 days. Criminal PAT goes back to same as civil.PAT results show name, DOB. Results include driver's license number.

General Information: No adoption, sealed cases, juvenile, mental or expunged records. Will fax documents $1.00 1st page, $.25 each add'l page to gov't agencies only. Court makes copy: $2.00 1st page, $.25 ea add'l. Certification fee: $3.00 per doc. Payee: Clerk of Court. Business checks accepted. No personal checks accepted. Prepayment required. Mail requests: SASE helpful.

Buncombe County

Superior-District Court 60 Court Plaza, Asheville, NC 28801; 828-232-2605; criminal phone: 828-232-2677; civil phone: 828-232-2636; probate phone: 828-232-2694; criminal fax: 828-251-6257; civil fax: 828-251-6257; 8:30AM-5PM. ***Felony, Misdemeanor, Civil, Eviction, Small Claims, Probate.***
www.nccourts.org/County/Buncombe/Default.asp
Search civil and criminal court calendars at www1.aoc.state.nc.us/www/calendars.html.

Civil Records: Access: Mail, fax, in person. Both court and visitors may perform in person searches. No search fee. Required to search: name, years to search. Civil cases indexed by defendant, plaintiff; index on computer since 1/88; on books or dockets to 1915; judgment books in archives. Mail turnaround time 1 week. Civil PAT goes back to 1988.

Criminal Records: Access: Mail, fax, in person. Both court and visitors may perform in person searches. Search fee: $15.00 per name, includes certification. Required to search: name, years to search, DOB. Criminal records on computer since 11/82; on books or dockets to 12/70. Mail turnaround time 1 week. Criminal PAT goes back to 12/82.

General Information: No adoption, sealed cases, juvenile, sex offenders, mental or expunged records required. Fee to fax document $1.00 1st page; $.25 each add'l. Court makes copy: $2.00 1st page, $.25 ea add'l. Certification fee: $3.00 per page. Payee: Clerk of Court. No personal checks accepted except for law firm filings. No credit cards accepted. Prepayment required. Prepayment required only for background checks. Mail requests: SASE required.

Burke County

Superior-District Court PO Box 796, Morganton, NC 28680; 828-432-2800; civil phone: 828-432-2805; fax: 828-438-5460; 8AM-5PM. ***Felony, Misdemeanor, Civil, Eviction, Small Claims, Probate.***
www.nccourts.org/County/Burke/Default.asp
Search civil and criminal court calendars at www1.aoc.state.nc.us/www/calendars.html.

Civil Records: Access: In person, mail. Visitors must perform in person searches themselves. No search fee. Required to search: name, years to search; also helpful: address. Civil cases indexed by defendant, plaintiff; index on computer since 10/1988, on index books to 1890s. Civil PAT goes back to 10/1988.

Criminal Records: Access: Mail, in person. Both court and visitors may perform in person searches. Search fee: $15.00 per name, includes certification. Required to search: name, years to search, DOB; also helpful: address, SSN. Criminal records on computer since 6/1986, on cards or books back to 1900s. Mail turnaround time 1-2 days. Criminal PAT goes back to 6/1986.

General Information: No adoption, sealed cases, juvenile, sex offenders, mental or expunged records released. Fee to fax out file $3.00 each. Court makes copy: $2.00 1st page, $.25 ea add'l. Certification fee: $10.00 per doc. Payee: Clerk of Court. Business checks accepted. Prepayment required. Mail requests: SASE required.

Cabarrus County

Superior-District Court PO Box 70, 77 Union St, Concord, NC 28026-0070; 704-786-4137 (Estates & Special Proceed); criminal phone: 704-786-4138 (Superior); 786-4211 (Dist.); civil phone: 704-786-4201; 8:30AM-5PM. ***Felony, Misdemeanor, Civil, Eviction, Small Claims, Probate.***
www.nccourts.org/County/Cabarrus/Default.asp
Search civil and criminal court calendars at www1.aoc.state.nc.us/www/calendars.html.

Civil Records: Access: In person only. Visitors must perform in person searches themselves. Required to search: name, years to search; also helpful: address. Civil cases indexed by defendant, plaintiff. Civil records go back to 1900s; on computer since 2/13/89. Civil PAT goes back to 1989. PAT civil results show middle initial.

Criminal Records: Access: Mail, in person. Both court and visitors may perform in person searches. Search fee: $15.00 per name, includes certification. Required to search: name, DOB; also helpful: address, SSN, maiden name. Criminal records go back to 12/70; on computer back to 1/85. Mail turnaround time 2-3 days. Criminal PAT goes back to 1985. PAT results show middle initial, DOB, SSN.

General Information: No adoption, sealed cases, juvenile, sex offenders, mental or expunged records released. Will not fax documents. Court makes copy: $2.00 1st page, $.25 ea add'l. Certification fee: $3.00 per doc. Payee: Clerk of Superior Court. Only cashiers checks, cash and money orders accepted. No credit cards accepted. Prepayment required.

Caldwell County

Superior-District Court PO Box 1376, Lenoir, NC 28645; criminal phone: 828-759-8402; civil phone: 828-759-8403; fax: 828-757-1479; 8AM-5PM. ***Felony, Misdemeanor, Civil, Eviction, Small Claims, Probate.***
www.nccourts.org/County/Caldwell/Default.asp
Search civil and criminal court calendars at www1.aoc.state.nc.us/www/calendars.html.

Civil Records: Access: In person only. Visitors must perform in person searches themselves. Required to search: name, years to search. Civil cases indexed by defendant, plaintiff; index on computer since 11/1988, prior on books to 1849. Civil PAT goes back to 11/1988.

Criminal Records: Access: Mail, in person. Both court and visitors may perform in person searches. Search fee: $15.00 per name, includes certification. Required to search: name. Criminal records computerized from 8/86, prior in books to 1966. Mail turnaround time 1-2 days. Criminal PAT goes back to 8/1986.

General Information: No adoption, sealed cases, juvenile, sex offenders, mental or expunged records released. Fee to fax out file $2.00 1st page; $.25 each add'l. Court makes copy: $2.00 1st page, $.25 ea add'l. Self serve: $.25 per page. Certification fee: $3.00. Payee: Clerk of Superior Court. Only cashiers checks and money orders accepted. No credit cards accepted. Prepayment required. Mail requests: SASE required.

Camden County

Superior-District Court PO Box 219, 117 Hwy 343 North, Camden, NC 27921; 252-331-4871; criminal phone: 252-331-4871 x270 (Superior), x269 (District); civil phone: 252-331-4871 x268 (District) 272 (Superior); probate phone: 252-331-4871 x273; fax: 252-331-4827; 8-5PM. ***Felony, Misdemeanor, Civil, Eviction, Small Claims, Probate.***
www.nccourts.org/County/Camden/Default.asp
Small Claims ext 274. Search civil and criminal court calendars at http://www1.aoc.state.nc.us/www/calendars.html.

Civil Records: Access: In person only. Visitors must perform in person searches themselves. Required to search: name, years to search. Civil cases indexed by defendant, plaintiff; index on computer since 11/27/1989, prior on index books to 12/05/1966. Civil PAT goes back to 1989.

Criminal Records: Access: Mail, fax, in person. Both court and visitors may perform in person searches. Search fee: $15.00 per name, includes certification. Required to search: name, years to search, DOB. Criminal record index on computer, on index books to 1966. Note: Fax search requests must be prepaid. Mail turnaround time 1-2 days. Criminal PAT goes back to 1990.

General Information: No adoption, sealed cases, juvenile, sex offenders, mental or expunged records released. Will fax documents for no fee. Court makes copy: $2.00 1st page, $.25 ea add'l. Self serve: $.25 per page with Hecon Key.You must acquire a HECON key to use self-serve copier. Certification fee: $3.00. Payee: Clerk of Superior Court. Business checks accepted. No credit cards accepted.

Carteret County

Superior-District Court - Carteret County Courthouse Square, Beaufort, NC 28516; 252-838-8140; fax: 252-838-8156; 8AM-5PM. ***Felony, Misdemeanor, Civil, Eviction, Small Claims, Probate.*** www.nccourts.org/County/Carteret/
Search civil and criminal court calendars at www.nccourts.org/County/Carteret/Calendars.asp.

Civil Records: Access: Mail, in person. Visitors must perform in person searches themselves. Search fee: $15.00 per name, includes certification. Required to search: name, years to search. Civil cases indexed by defendant, plaintiff; index on computer back to 1988, prior on books to 1800s. Mail turnaround time 1-2 days. Civil PAT goes back to 1988. PAT civil results show middle initial.

Criminal Records: Access: Mail, fax, in person. Both court and visitors may perform in person searches. Search fee: $15.00 per name, includes certification. Required to search: name, years to search; also helpful: address, DOB, SSN. Criminal records computerized from 1/87, prior on cards and books to 1800s. Mail turnaround time 1-2 days. Criminal PAT goes back to 1987. PAT results show middle initial, DOB.

General Information: No adoption, sealed cases, juvenile, sex offenders, mental or expunged records released. Will fax out docs no add'l fee. Court makes copy: $2.00 1st page, $.25 ea add'l. Certification fee: None; $3.00 if you perform search in person. Payee: Clerk of Superior Court. Attorney business checks accepted. No credit cards accepted. Prepayment required.

Caswell County

Superior-District Court PO Drawer 790, 139 E Church St, Yanceyville, NC 27379; 336-694-4171; fax: 336-694-7338; 8-5PM. ***Felony, Misdemeanor, Civil, Eviction, Small Claims, Probate.***
www.nccourts.org/County/Caswell/Default.asp
Search civil and criminal court calendars at www1.aoc.state.nc.us/www/calendars.html.

Civil Records: Access: In person only. Visitors must perform in person searches themselves. Required to search: name, years to search. Civil cases indexed by defendant, plaintiff; index on computer from 3/89 to present, on index books back to 1970, prior records in civil summons book. Civil PAT goes back to 3/1989.

Criminal Records: Access: Mail, in person. Both court and visitors may perform in person searches. Search fee: $15.00 per name, includes certification. Required to search: name, years to search, DOB; also helpful: address. Criminal records on computer since 5/88, prior on books and cards. Mail turnaround time 1-2 days. Criminal PAT goes back to 5/18/1988.

General Information: No adoption, sealed cases, juvenile, mental or expunged records released. Will fax documents $2.00 per page. Court makes copy: $2.00 1st page, $.25 ea add'l. Self serve: $.25 per page. Certification fee: $3.00 per doc. Payee: Clerk of Superior Court. Business checks accepted. No credit cards accepted. Prepayment required. Mail requests: SASE required for criminal.

Catawba County

Superior-District Court PO Box 790, Newton, NC 28658; 828-466-6100; criminal phone: 828-466-6106; civil phone: 828-466-6104; probate phone: 828-466-6103; fax: 828-465-8975; 8AM-5PM. ***Felony, Misdemeanor, Civil, Eviction, Small Claims, Probate.***
www.co.catawba.nc.us/state/clerk/clerklst.asp

Search civil and criminal court calendars at www1.aoc.state.nc.us/www/calendars.html.
Civil Records: Access: In person only. Visitors must perform in person searches themselves. Required to search: name, years to search. Civil cases indexed by defendant, plaintiff; index on computer since 3/1988, prior on books. Civil PAT goes back to 1988. PAT civil results show middle initial. Terminal results also show SSNs.
Criminal Records: Access: Mail, in person. Both court and visitors may perform in person searches. Search fee: $15.00 per name, includes certification. Required to search: name, years to search, DOB. Criminal records on computer since 4/85, on books to 1966, archived prior. Mail turnaround time 5 days. Criminal PAT goes back to 4/1985. PAT results show middle initial, DOB. Terminal results include SSN.
General Information: No adoption, sealed cases, juvenile, sex offenders, mental or expunged records released. Will not fax documents. Court makes copy: $2.00 1st page, $.25 ea add'l. Certification fee: $3.00 includes copies, but if over $3.00 worth of copies, add on add'l copy fee. Payee: Clerk of Court. Only cashiers checks and money orders accepted. No credit cards accepted. Prepayment required. Mail requests: SASE required for criminal.

Chatham County

Superior-District Court PO Box 369, 12 East St, Pittsboro, NC 27312; 919-542-3240; fax: 919-542-1402; 8AM-5PM. ***Felony, Misdemeanor, Civil, Eviction, Small Claims, Probate.***
www.nccourts.org/County/Chatham/Default.asp
Search civil and criminal court calendars at www1.aoc.state.nc.us/www/calendars.html.
Civil Records: Access: In person only. Both court and visitors may perform in person searches. No search fee. Required to search: name, years to search. Civil cases indexed by defendant, plaintiff; index on computer since 4/1989, prior on books, archived 1968 back in Raleigh. Civil PAT goes back to 4/1989. PAT results show name only.
Criminal Records: Access: Mail, in person. Both court and visitors may perform in person searches. Search fee: $15.00 per name, includes certification. Required to search: name, years to search; also helpful: address, DOB, SSN. Criminal records on computer since 7/1987, prior on books or cards to 1968. Mail turnaround time 1 day. Criminal PAT goes back to 7/1987. PAT results show name only.
General Information: No adoption, sealed cases, juvenile, sex offenders, mental or expunged records released. Will fax documents $1.00 1st page, $.25 each add'l page. Court makes copy: $2.00 1st page, $.25 ea add'l. Certification fee: $3.00. Will not certify civil. Payee: Clerk of Superior Court. No personal checks or credit cards accepted. Prepayment required. Mail requests: SASE required.

Cherokee County

Superior-District Court 75 Peachtree St, Rm 201, Murphy, NC 28906; 828-837-2522; fax: 828-837-8178; 8AM-5PM. ***Felony, Misdemeanor, Civil, Eviction, Small Claims, Probate.***
www.nccourts.org/County/Cherokee/Default.asp
Search civil and criminal court calendars at www1.aoc.state.nc.us/www/calendars.html.
Civil Records: Access: Phone, fax, mail, in person. Both court and visitors may perform in person searches. No search fee. Required to search: name, years to search, address. Civil cases indexed by defendant, plaintiff; index on computer since 5/89, on index books to 1867. Mail turnaround time 1-2 days. Public terminal has civil records back to 5/1989.
Criminal Records: Access: Mail, in person. Only the court performs in person searches; visitors may not. Search fee: $15.00 per name, includes certification. Required to search: name, years to search, DOB. Criminal records on computer since 5/89, index cards to 1985, index books to 1966. Note: Criminal calendars online at http://www1.aoc.state.nc.us/www/calendars/Contacts.html Mail Turnaround time 1-2 days.
General Information: No adoption, sealed cases, juvenile or mental records released. Fee to fax out file $2.00 1st page, $.25 each add'l. Will fax to toll-free number for no charge. Court makes copy: $2.00 1st page, $.25 ea add'l. No certification fee. Payee: Clerk of Superior Court. No personal checks or credit cards accepted. Prepayment required. Mail requests: SASE required.

Chowan County

Superior-District Court Clerk of Superior Ct; N.C. Courier Box 106319, PO Box 588, Edenton, NC 27932; 252-482-2323; criminal fax: 252-482-2190; civil fax: same; 9AM-5PM. ***Felony, Misdemeanor, Civil, Eviction, Small Claims, Probate.***
www.nccourts.org/County/Chowan/Default.asp
Search criminal court calendars at http://www1.aoc.state.nc.us/www/calendars.html.
Probate fax is same as main fax number.
Civil Records: Access: In person only. Visitors must perform in person searches themselves. Required to search: name, years to search; also helpful: address. Civil cases indexed by defendant, plaintiff; index on computer since 1990, prior on books to 1800s. Civil PAT goes back to 1990. PAT civil results show middle initial.
Criminal Records: Access: Mail, in person. Both court and visitors may perform in person searches. Search fee: $15.00 per name, includes certification. Required to search: name, years to search, DOB; also helpful: address, SSN. Criminal records computerized from 1/90, prior as civil. Mail turnaround time 3-5 days. Criminal PAT goes back to same as civil. PAT results show middle initial, DOB. Terminal results include SSN.
General Information: No adoption, sealed cases, juvenile, sex offenders, mental or expunged records released. Will not fax documents. Court makes copy: $2.00 1st page, $.25 ea add'l. Certification fee: $3.00; exemplification fee- $10.00. Payee: Clerk of Superior Court. Only cashiers checks and money orders accepted. No credit cards accepted. Prepayment required. Mail requests: SASE required for criminal.

Clay County

Superior-District Court PO Box 506, 25 Herbert St, Hayesville, NC 28904; 828-389-8334; fax: 828-389-3329; 8:30AM-5PM. ***Felony, Misdemeanor, Civil, Eviction, Small Claims, Probate.***
www.nccourts.org/County/Clay/Default.asp
Search civil and criminal court calendars, etc. at www1.aoc.state.nc.us/www/calendars.html.
Civil Records: Access: In person only. Visitors must perform in person searches themselves. Required to search: name, years to search; also helpful: address. Civil cases indexed by defendant, plaintiff; index on computer since 1989, on books since 1888. Public use terminal has civil records back to 1989.
Criminal Records: Access: Mail, in person. Only the court performs in person searches; visitors may not. Search fee: $15.00 per name, includes certification. Required to search: name, years to search, DOB; also helpful: address, SSN. Criminal records computerized from 1989, on books since 1888. Mail turnaround time 1 days.
General Information: No adoption, sealed cases, juvenile, sex offenders, mental or expunged records released. Fee to fax document $.25 per page. Court makes copy: $2.00 1st page, $.25 ea add'l. Self serve: $.25 per page. Certification fee: $3.00 per doc. Payee: Clerk of Court. Business checks accepted. No credit cards accepted. Prepayment required. Mail requests: SASE required for criminal.

Cleveland County

Superior-District Court 100 Justice Pl, Shelby, NC 28150; 704-484-4862; fax: 704-480-5487; 8:30AM-5PM. ***Felony, Misdemeanor, Civil, Eviction, Small Claims, Probate.***
www.nccourts.org/County/Cleveland/Default.asp
Search civil and criminal court calendars at www1.aoc.state.nc.us/www/calendars.html.
Civil Records: Access: In person only. Visitors must perform in person searches themselves. Required to search: name, years to search. Civil cases indexed by defendant, plaintiff; index on computer since 1988, books to 1968, archived prior. Civil PAT goes back to 1988.
Criminal Records: Access: Mail, in person. Both court and visitors may perform in person searches. Search fee: $15.00 per name, includes certification. Required to search: name, years to search, DOB; also helpful: address, SSN. Criminal records on computer since 6/86, on books to 1972, archived prior. Mail turnaround time 1-2 days. Criminal PAT goes back to 6/1988.
General Information: No adoption, sealed cases, juvenile, sex offenders, mental or expunged records released. Will fax documents $1.00 1st page, $.25 each add'l page. Court makes copy: $2.00 1st page, $.25 ea add'l. Certification fee: $3.00; Exemplification fee- $10.00. Payee: Clerk of Superior Court. No out-of-state checks accepted. Certified funds, money orders and bank checks accepted. No credit cards accepted. Prepayment required. Mail requests: SASE requested for criminal.

Columbus County

Superior-District Court PO Box 1587, Whiteville, NC 28472; criminal phone: 910-641-3020; civil phone: 910-641-3000; probate phone: 910-641-3010; fax: 910-641-3027; 8AM-5PM. ***Felony, Misdemeanor, Civil, Eviction, Small Claims, Probate.***
www.nccourts.org/County/Columbus/Default.asp
Search civil and criminal court calendars at www1.aoc.state.nc.us/www/calendars.html.
Civil Records: Access: Mail, fax, in person. Visitors must perform in person searches themselves. No search fee. Required to search: name, years to search; also helpful: address. Civil cases indexed by defendant, plaintiff; index on computer from 1989, prior on books to 1968. Civil PAT goes back to 5/1989.
Criminal Records: Access: Mail, fax, in person. Both court and visitors may perform in person searches. Search fee: $15.00 per name, includes certification. Required to search: name, years to search, DOB; also helpful: address, SSN. Criminal records computerized from 1987, prior on books or cards to 1968. Mail turnaround time 2-5 days. Criminal PAT goes back to 6/1987.
General Information: No adoption, sealed, juvenile, sex offender, mental, expunged or dismissed. Will not fax documents. Court makes copy: $2.00 per doc, $.25 ea add'l pg. Self serve: $.25 per page. Certification fee: $3.00. Payee: Clerk of Superior Court. Only cashiers checks and money orders accepted. No credit cards accepted. Prepayment required. Mail requests: SASE required.

Craven County

Superior-District Court PO Box 1187, New Bern, NC 28563; 252-639-9004; criminal phone: 252-639-9009; civil phone: 252-639-9003; fax: 252-514-4891; 8AM-5PM. ***Felony, Misdemeanor, Civil, Eviction, Small Claims, Probate.***
www.nccourts.org/County/Craven/Default.asp
Search civil and criminal court calendars at www1.aoc.state.nc.us/www/calendars.html.
Civil Records: Access: In person only. Visitors must perform in person searches themselves. Required to search: name, years to search; also helpful: address. Civil cases indexed by defendant, plaintiff; index on computer from 10/88, prior to 1968 are archived. Civil PAT goes back to 1997. PAT civil results show middle initial.
Criminal Records: Access: Mail, in person. Both court and visitors may perform in person searches. Search fee: $15.00 per name, includes certification. Required to search: name, years to search, DOB; also helpful: address, SSN. Criminal records on computer since 1/87, prior on books and cards to 1968. Mail turnaround time 1-2 days. Criminal PAT goes back to 1988. PAT results show middle initial, DOB. Terminal results include SSN.
General Information: No adoption, sealed cases, juvenile, sex offenders, mental, expunged, or dismissed. Will not fax documents. Court makes copy: $2.00 1st page, $.25 ea add'l. Self serve: $.25 per page. Certification fee: None; $3.00 if you perform search in person. Payee: Clerk of Superior Court. Only cashiers checks and money orders accepted. No credit cards accepted. Prepayment required. Mail requests: SASE required.

Cumberland County

Superior-District Court PO Box 363, 117 Dix St, Fayetteville, NC 28302; 910-678-2902; criminal phone: 910-678-2906; civil phone: 910-678-2909; probate phone: 910-678-2904; fax: 910-678-2936; 8AM-5PM. ***Felony, Misdemeanor, Civil, Eviction, Small Claims, Probate.***

www.aoc.state.nc.us/district12/

Search court calendars free at www1.aoc.state.nc.us/www/calendars.html.

Civil Records: Access: Mail, fax, in person. Both court and visitors may perform in person searches. No search fee. Required to search: name, years to search; also helpful: address. Civil cases indexed by defendant, plaintiff; index on computer since 1988, books back to 1956. Mail turnaround time 5-10 days. Civil PAT goes back to 7/1988.

Criminal Records: Access: Mail, fax, in person. Both court and visitors may perform in person searches. Search fee: $15.00 per name, includes certification. Required to search: name, years to search; also helpful: address, DOB, SSN. Criminal records on computer since 5/82, books and cards to 1920s. Mail turnaround time 2 weeks. Criminal PAT goes back to 1982. PAT results show name, DOB, SSN.

General Information: No adoption, sealed cases, juvenile, sex offenders, mental or expunged records released. Court makes copy: $2.00 1st page, $.25 ea add'l. Certification fee: $3.00 for 1st 5 pages. Cert fee includes copies. Payee: Clerk of Superior Court. No personal checks or credit cards accepted. Prepayment required.

Currituck County

Superior-District Court PO Box 175, Currituck, NC 27929; 252-232-2010; fax: 252-232-3722; 8AM-5PM. ***Felony, Misdemeanor, Civil, Eviction, Small Claims, Probate.***

www.nccourts.org/County/Currituck/Default.asp

Search criminal court calendars at www1.aoc.state.nc.us/www/calendars.html.

Civil Records: Access: In person only. Visitors must perform in person searches themselves. Required to search: name, years to search. Civil cases indexed by defendant, plaintiff; index on computer back to 1990, books to 1968, prior archived. Civil PAT goes back to 1990. PAT civil results show middle initial.

Criminal Records: Access: Mail, in person. Both court and visitors may perform in person searches. Search fee: $15.00 per name, includes certification. Required to search: name, years to search, DOB, signed release. Criminal records computerized from 11/27/89, books to 1968, prior archived. Note: Mail search requests must be on letterhead and include signed release. Mail turnaround time 1 day. Criminal PAT goes back to same as civil.

General Information: No adoption, sealed cases, juvenile, sex offenders, mental or expunged records released. Court makes copy: $2.00 1st page, $.25 ea add'l. Self serve: $.25 per page. Certification fee: $2.00. Payee: Clerk of Superior Court. Only cashiers checks and money orders accepted. No credit cards accepted. Prepayment required. Mail requests: SASE required.

Dare County

Superior-District Court PO Box 1849, 962 Marshall Collins Dr, Manteo, NC 27954; 252-475-9100; fax: 252-473-1620; 8AM-5PM. ***Felony, Misdemeanor, Civil, Eviction, Small Claims, Probate.***

www.nccourts.org/County/Dare/Default.asp

Search civil and criminal court calendars at www1.aoc.state.nc.us/www/calendars.html.

Civil Records: Access: In person only. Visitors must perform in person searches themselves. Required to search: name, years to search; also helpful: address, DOB. Civil cases indexed by defendant, plaintiff; index on computer since 1985, on books to 1966. Civil PAT goes back to 1987.

Criminal Records: Access: Mail, in person. Both court and visitors may perform in person searches. Search fee: $15.00 per name, includes certification. Required to search: name, years to search, DOB. Criminal records on computer since 1987, on books and cards to 1966. Mail turnaround time 2 days. Criminal PAT goes back to 1989.

General Information: No adoption, sealed cases, juvenile, sex offenders, mental or expunged records released. Fee to fax document $.25 per page. Court makes copy: $2.00 1st page, $.25 ea add'l. Self serve: $.25 per page. Certification fee: $3.00 per doc. Payee: Superior District Court. Business checks accepted. No personal checks accepted. Prepayment required.

Davidson County

Superior-District Court PO Box 1064, 110 W Center St, Lexington, NC 27293-1064; 336-242-6701; fax: 336-242-6759; 8AM-5PM. ***Felony, Misdemeanor, Civil, Eviction, Small Claims, Probate.***

www.nccourts.org/County/Davidson/Default.asp

Search civil and criminal court calendars at www1.aoc.state.nc.us/www/calendars.html. There is also a 2nd court location at 22 Randolph St in Thomasville, 336-474-3185 but records and mailing address here in Lexington.

Civil Records: Access: In person only. Visitors must perform in person searches themselves. Required to search: name, years to search; also helpful: address. Civil cases indexed by defendant, plaintiff; index on computer since 5/16/1988, prior on books. Civil PAT goes back to 1985.

Criminal Records: Access: Mail, in person. Both court and visitors may perform in person searches. Search fee: $15.00 per name, includes certification. Required to search: name, DOB, years to search; also helpful: address, SSN. Criminal records on computer since 10/1985, on books and cards to 1952. Mail turnaround time 2-3 days. Criminal PAT goes back to same as civil.

General Information: No adoption, sealed cases, juvenile, sex offenders, mental or expunged records released. Will not fax documents. Court makes copy: $2.00 1st page, $.25 ea add'l. Certification fee: $3.00. Payee: Clerk of Superior Court. Business checks accepted if on clerk's list. No credit cards accepted. Prepayment required. Mail requests: SASE requested for criminal.

Davie County

Superior-District Court 140 S Main St, Mocksville, NC 27028; 336-751-3507; criminal phone: 336-751-3508; probate phone: 336-751-3508; fax: 336-751-4720; 8:30AM-5PM. ***Felony, Misdemeanor, Civil, Eviction, Small Claims, Probate.***

www.nccourts.org/County/Davie/Default.asp

Search civil and criminal court calendars at www1.aoc.state.nc.us/www/calendars.html.

Civil Records: Access: In person only. Visitors must perform in person searches themselves. Required to search: name, years to search. Civil cases indexed by defendant, plaintiff; index on computer back to 10/89; on books to 1970. Civil PAT goes back to 11/1989.

Criminal Records: Access: Mail, in person. Both court and visitors may perform in person searches. Search fee: $15.00 per name, includes certification. Required to search: name, years to search, DOB, signed release. Criminal records computerized from 11/89. Mail turnaround time 5 days. Criminal PAT goes back to same as civil.

General Information: No adoption, sealed cases, juvenile, sex offenders, mental or expunged records released. Court makes copy: $2.00 1st page, $.25 ea add'l. Self serve: same. Certification fee: $3.00. Payee: Clerk of Superior Court. Personal checks accepted; credit cards are not. Prepayment required. Mail requests: SASE required for criminal.

Duplin County

Superior-District Court PO Box 189, 112 Duplin St, Kenansville, NC 28349; criminal phone: 910-296-2306; civil phone: 910-296-1686; fax: 910-296-2310; 8AM-5PM. ***Felony, Misdemeanor, Civil, Eviction, Small Claims, Probate.***

www.nccourts.org/County/Duplin/Default.asp

Search civil and criminal court calendars at www1.aoc.state.nc.us/www/calendars.html.

Civil Records: Access: In person only. Both court and visitors may perform in person searches. No search fee. Required to search: name, years to search. Civil cases indexed by defendant, plaintiff; index on computer since 1989, prior on books to early 1900s. Civil PAT goes back to 1989.

Criminal Records: Access: Mail, in person. Both court and visitors may perform in person searches. Search fee: $15.00 per name, includes certification. Required to search: name, years to search, DOB. Criminal records on computer since 5/1988, on cards and books to 1927. Mail turnaround time 2-5 days. Criminal PAT goes back to 5/1988.

General Information: No adoption, sealed cases, juvenile, sex offenders, mental or expunged records released. Will not fax documents. Court makes copy: $2.00 1st page, $.25 ea add'l. Self serve: $.25 per page. Certification fee: $3.00. Payee: Clerk of Superior Court. No personal checks. No credit cards accepted. Prepayment required. Mail requests: SASE required for criminal.

Durham County

Superior-District Court 201 E Main St, Durham, NC 27701; criminal phone: 919-564-7270; civil phone: 919-564-7050; fax: 919-560-3341; 8:30AM-5PM. ***Felony, Misdemeanor, Civil, Eviction, Small Claims, Probate.***

www.nccourts.org/County/Durham/Default.asp

Search civil and criminal court calendars at www1.aoc.state.nc.us/www/calendars.html.

Civil Records: Access: Mail, in person. Visitors must perform in person searches themselves. No search fee. Required to search: name, years to search; also helpful: address. Civil cases indexed by defendant, plaintiff; index on computer back 10 years, on books to late 1800s. Civil PAT available. PAT results show name only.

Criminal Records: Access: Mail, in person. Both court and visitors may perform in person searches. Search fee: $15.00 per name, includes certification. Required to search: name, years to search, DOB; also helpful: address. Criminal records on microfiche since 1982, prior on books to 1979. Mail turnaround time 3-4 days. Criminal PAT goes back to 1980s.PAT results show name, DOB.

General Information: No adoption, sealed cases, juvenile, sex offenders, mental or expunged records released. Will not fax documents. Court makes copy: $2.00 1st page, $.25 ea add'l. Certification fee: $3.00. Payee: Clerk of Superior Court. Only cashiers checks and money orders accepted. No credit cards accepted. Prepayment required. Mail requests: SASE required.

Edgecombe County

Superior-District Court PO Drawer 9, 301 St Andrews St, Tarboro, NC 27886; criminal phone: 252-823-2056; civil phone: 252-823-6161; fax: 252-823-1278; 8AM-5PM. ***Felony, Misdemeanor, Civil, Eviction, Small Claims, Probate.***

www.nccourts.org/County/Edgecombe/Default.asp

Search civil and criminal court calendars at www1.aoc.state.nc.us/www/calendars.html.

Civil Records: Access: In person only. Visitors must perform in person searches themselves. Required to search: name, years to search, address. Civil cases indexed by defendant, plaintiff; index on computer since 1988. Civil PAT goes back to 1988. PAT civil results show middle initial.

Criminal Records: Access: Mail, in person. Both court and visitors may perform in person searches. Search fee: $15.00 per name, includes certification. Required to search: name, DOB; also helpful: address, former names. Criminal records on computer since 4/87, on books and cards to 1900s. Mail turnaround time 1-2 days. Criminal PAT goes back to 1987. PAT results show middle initial, DOB.

General Information: No adoption, sealed cases, juvenile, sex offenders, mental or expunged records required. Court makes copy: $2.00 1st page, $.25 ea add'l. Certification fee: $3.00. Payee: Clerk of Superior Court. Only certified check or money order accepted. No credit cards accepted. Prepayment required. Mail requests: SASE helpful.

Forsyth County

Superior-District Court PO Box 20099, 200 N Main, Courthouse, Winston Salem, NC 27120-0099; 336-761-2250; criminal phone: 336-761-2366; civil phone: 336-761-2340; probate phone: 336-761-2470; criminal fax: 336-761-2120; civil fax: 336-761-2018; 8AM-5PM. ***Felony, Misdemeanor, Civil, Eviction, Small Claims, Probate.***
www.nccourts.org/County/Forsyth/Default.asp
Civil index is searched separately from the criminal index. Search civil and criminal court calendars at www1.aoc.state.nc.us/www/calendars.html.
Civil Records: Access: In person only. Only the court performs in person searches; visitors may not. Search fee: $15.00 per name, includes certification. Required to search: name, years to search. Civil cases indexed by defendant, plaintiff; index on computer since 4/1989, prior on books to 1968, on microfiche prior. Mail turnaround time 1-2 days. Civil PAT goes back to 4/1989. PAT results show name only.
Criminal Records: Access: Mail, in person. Only the court performs in person searches; visitors may not. Search fee: $15.00 per name, includes certification. Required to search: name, years to search, DOB. Criminal records on computer since 10/1983, prior on books to 1968, on microfiche prior. Mail turnaround time 1-2 days. Criminal PAT goes back to 10/1983. PAT results show middle initial, DOB.
General Information: No adoption, sealed cases, juvenile, sex offenders, mental or expunged records released. Will not fax documents. Court makes copy: $2.00 1st page, $.25 ea add'l. Certification fee: None; $3.00 if you perform search in person. Payee: Clerk of Superior Court. Business checks accepted. No credit cards accepted. Prepayment required. Mail requests: SASE required.

Franklin County

Superior-District Court 102 S Main St, Louisburg, NC 27549; 919-496-5104; fax: 919-496-0407; 8:30AM-5PM. ***Felony, Misdemeanor, Civil, Eviction, Small Claims, Probate.***
www.nccourts.org/County/Franklin/Default.asp
Search civil and criminal court calendars at www1.aoc.state.nc.us/www/calendars.html.
Civil Records: Access: Mail, in person. Visitors must perform in person searches themselves. No search fee. Required to search: name, years to search; also helpful: address. Civil cases indexed by defendant, plaintiff; index on computer since 6/1989, prior on books. Mail turnaround time 1-2 days. Civil PAT goes back to 1997. PAT results show name only.
Criminal Records: Access: Mail, in person. Both court and visitors may perform in person searches. Search fee: $15.00 per name, includes certification. Required to search: name, years to search, DOB; also helpful: address. Criminal records on computer since 1980, on index books back to 1968. Mail turnaround time 1-2 days. Criminal PAT goes back to 1980. PAT results show name only.
General Information: No adoption, sealed cases, juvenile, mental or expunged records released. Will not fax documents. Court makes copy: $2.00 1st page, $.25 ea add'l. Self serve: $.25 per page. Certification fee: $3.00; for exemplification fee $10.00. Payee: Clerk of Superior Court. No personal checks or credit cards accepted. Prepayment required. Mail requests: SASE requested.

Gaston County

Superior-District Court Gaston County Court House, 325 N Marietta St. #1004, Gastonia, NC 28052-2331; 704-852-3100; fax: 704-852-3267; 8:30AM-5PM. ***Felony, Misdemeanor, Civil, Eviction, Small Claims, Probate.***
www.nccourts.org/County/Gaston/Default.asp
Search civil and criminal court calendars at www1.aoc.state.nc.us/www/calendars.html.
Civil Records: Access: In person only. Visitors must perform in person searches themselves. Required to search: name, years to search; also helpful: address. Civil cases indexed by defendant, plaintiff; index on computer since 1988, prior on books to 1891. Civil PAT goes back to 1988.
Criminal Records: Access: Mail, in person. Both court and visitors may perform in person searches. Search fee: $15.00 per name, includes certification. Required to search: name, address, DOB; also helpful: years to search, SSN. Criminal records on criminal terminal from 1/83, on books and microfilm to 1973. Mail turnaround time 1-2 days. Criminal PAT goes back to 1983.
General Information: No adoption, sealed cases, juvenile, mental or expunged records released. Will not fax documents. Court makes copy: $2.00 1st page, $.25 ea add'l. Certification fee: $3.00. No out-of-state checks accepted. No credit cards accepted. Prepayment required. Mail requests: SASE required.

Gates County

Superior-District Court PO Box 31, Gatesville, NC 27938; 252-357-1365; fax: 252-357-1047; 8:30AM-5PM. ***Felony, Misdemeanor, Civil, Eviction, Small Claims, Probate.***
www.nccourts.org/County/Gates/Default.asp
Search civil and criminal court calendars at www1.aoc.state.nc.us/www/calendars.html.
Civil Records: Access: In person only. Visitors must perform in person searches themselves. Required to search: name, years to search; also helpful: address. Civil cases indexed by defendant, plaintiff; index on computer since 1990, prior on books to 1966. Civil PAT goes back to 1989.
Criminal Records: Access: Mail, in person. Both court and visitors may perform in person searches. Search fee: $15.00 per name, includes certification. Required to search: name, years to search, DOB; also helpful: address, SSN. Criminal records on computer since 1990, prior on books to 1966. Mail turnaround time 1-2 days. Criminal PAT goes back to 1990.
General Information: No adoption, sealed cases, juvenile, sex offenders, mental or expunged records released. Court makes copy: $2.00 1st page, $.25 ea add'l. Self serve: $.25 per page. Certification fee: $3.00 per doc. Payee: Clerk of Superior Court. Business checks accepted. No credit cards accepted. Prepayment required. Mail requests: SASE required for mail return of any copies.

Graham County

Superior-District Court PO Box 1179, Robbinsville, NC 28771; 828-479-7986; criminal phone: X7975; civil phone: X7973; fax: 828-479-6417; 8AM-5PM. ***Felony, Misdemeanor, Civil, Eviction, Small Claims, Probate.***
www.nccourts.org/County/Graham/Default.asp
Search civil and criminal court calendars at www1.aoc.state.nc.us/www/calendars.html.
Civil Records: Access: In person only. Visitors must perform in person searches themselves. Required to search: name, years to search. Civil cases indexed by defendant, plaintiff; index on computer since 1989, on books since 1920s. Civil PAT goes back to 1989.
Criminal Records: Access: Mail, in person. Only the court performs in person searches; visitors may not. Search fee: $15.00 per name, includes certification. Required to search: name, years to search; also helpful: address, DOB, SSN. Criminal records on computer since 1984, on books to 1920s. Mail turnaround time 3-5 days. Criminal PAT goes back to 1984.
General Information: No adoption, sealed cases, juvenile, sex offenders, mental or expunged records released. Will fax documents to local or toll-free number. Court makes copy: $2.00 1st page, $.25 ea add'l. Self serve: same. Certification fee: $3.00. Payee: Clerk of Superior Court. Only cashiers checks and money orders accepted. No credit cards accepted. Prepayment required. Mail requests: SASE required for criminal.

Granville County

Superior-District Court 101 Main St, Courthouse, Oxford, NC 27565; 919-693-2649; fax: 919-693-8944; 8:30AM-5PM. ***Felony, Misdemeanor, Civil, Eviction, Small Claims, Probate.***
www.nccourts.org/County/Granville/Default.asp
Search civil and criminal court calendars at www1.aoc.state.nc.us/www/calendars.html.
Civil Records: Access: In person only. Both court and visitors may perform in person searches. No search fee. Required to search: name, years to search; also helpful: address. Civil cases indexed by defendant, plaintiff; index on computer since 6/12/1989, on books to 1968, prior files destroyed. Civil PAT goes back to 6/1989.
Criminal Records: Access: Mail, in person. Both court and visitors may perform in person searches. Search fee: $15.00 per name, includes certification. Required to search: name, years to search, DOB; also helpful: address. Criminal records on computer since 2/29/1988, prior on books on cards to 1968. Mail turnaround time 1 day. Criminal PAT goes back to 3/1988.
General Information: No adoption, sealed cases, juvenile, mental or expunged records released. Will not fax documents. Court makes copy: $2.00 1st page, $.25 ea add'l. Certification fee: $3.00. Payee: Clerk of Superior Court. No personal checks. Money order or cash only. No credit cards accepted. Prepayment required. Mail requests: SASE helpful.

Greene County

Superior-District Court PO Box 675, Snow Hill, NC 28580; 252-747-3505; criminal fax: 252-747-2700; civil fax: same; 8AM-5PM. ***Felony, Misdemeanor, Civil, Eviction, Small Claims, Probate.***
www.nccourts.org/County/Greene/Default.asp
Search civil and criminal court calendars at www1.aoc.state.nc.us/www/calendars.html. Probate fax is same as main fax number.
Civil Records: Access: In person only. Visitors must perform in person searches themselves. Required to search: name, years to search; also helpful: address. Civil cases indexed by defendant, plaintiff; index on computer since 10/1989, prior on books to 1865. Civil PAT goes back to 1986. PAT results show middle initial, DOB.
Criminal Records: Access: Mail, in person. Both court and visitors may perform in person searches. Search fee: $15.00 per name, includes certification. Required to search: name, years to search; also helpful: address, DOB, SSN. Criminal records on computer since 10/1989, prior on books to 1865. Mail turnaround time 1-2 days. Criminal PAT goes back to 1989.
General Information: No adoption, sealed cases, juvenile, sex offenders, mental or expunged records released. Will fax documents if all fees prepaid. Court makes copy: $2.00 1st page, $.25 ea add'l. Self serve: $.25 per page. Certification fee: None; $3.00 if you perform search in person. Payee: Clerk of Superior Court. Business checks accepted. No credit cards accepted. Prepayment required.

Guilford County

Superior-District Court PO Box 3008, 201 S Eugene St, Greensboro, NC 27402; 336-412-7997; criminal phone: 336-412-7500; civil phone: 336-412-7400; fax: 336-412-7302; 8:30AM-5PM. ***Felony, Misdemeanor, Civil, Eviction, Small Claims, Probate.***
www.nccourts.org/County/Guilford/Default.asp
Search civil and criminal court calendars at www1.aoc.state.nc.us/www/calendars.html.
Civil Records: Access: In person only. Visitors must perform in person searches themselves. Required to search: name, years to search; also helpful: address. Civil cases indexed by defendant, plaintiff; index on computer since 9/88, on books to late 1800s. Civil PAT goes back to 9/1988. PAT results show name only.
Criminal Records: Access: Mail, in person. Both court and visitors may perform in person searches. Search fee: $15.00 per name, includes certification. Required to search: name, years to search, DOB; also helpful: address, full name. Criminal records on computer since 5/83, on cards and books to late 1800s. Mail turnaround time 1 week. Criminal PAT goes back to 5/1983. PAT results show name only.
General Information: No adoption, sealed cases, juvenile, sex offenders, mental or expunged records released. Will not fax documents. Court makes copy:

$2.00 1st page, $.25 ea add'l. Certification fee: $3.00; Exemplified copy $10.00. Payee: Clerk of Superior Court. Only cashiers checks and money orders accepted. No credit cards accepted. Prepayment required. Mail requests: SASE required for criminal.

Halifax County

Superior-District Court PO Box 66, Halifax, NC 27839; 252-583-5061; fax: 252-583-1005; 8:15AM-5:15PM crim; to 5PM civil. ***Felony, Misdemeanor, Civil, Eviction, Small Claims, Probate.***
www.nccourts.org/County/Halifax/Courthouse/Default.asp Search civil and criminal court calendars at www1.aoc.state.nc.us/www/calendars.html.
Civil Records: Access: in person only. Both court and visitors may perform in person searches. No search fee. Required to search: name, years to search; also helpful: address. Civil cases indexed by defendant, plaintiff; index on computer since 1988, on books to 1968, prior archived. Note: Visitors use only the public access terminal for civil searching. Civil PAT goes back to 1988. PAT results show middle initial, DOB, SSN.
Criminal Records: Access: Mail, in person. Only the court performs in person searches; visitors may not. Search fee: $15.00 per name, includes certification. Required to search: name, years to search; also helpful: address, DOB, SSN. Criminal records on computer since 9/1987, on books to 1968, prior archived. Mail turnaround time 1-2 days. Criminal PAT goes back to 9/1987. PAT results show name, DOB, SSN.
General Information: No adoption, sealed cases, juvenile, sex offenders, mental or expunged records released. Will fax documents $1.00 1st page, $.25 each add'l page. Court makes copy: $2.00 1st page, $.25 ea add'l. Self serve: $.25 per page from the public terminal, uncertified; public key required. Certification fee: $3.00 per doc; exemplification-$10.00. Payee: Clerk of Superior Court. No attorney checks accepted. No credit cards accepted. Prepayment required.

Harnett County

Superior-District Court 301 W Cornelius Blvd, Harnett Blvd, #100, Lillington, NC 27546; 910-814-4600; criminal phone: 910-814-4601; civil phone: 910-814-4602; probate phone: 910-814-4603; fax: 910-893-3683; 8:30AM-5PM. ***Felony, Misdemeanor, Civil, Eviction, Small Claims, Probate.***
www.nccourts.org/County/Harnett/Default.asp
Search civil and criminal court calendars at www.nccourts.org.
Civil Records: Access: In person only. Visitors must perform in person searches themselves. Required to search: name, years to search; also helpful: address. Civil cases indexed by defendant, plaintiff; index on computer since 4/17/1989, prior on books from 1938. Civil PAT goes back to 4/1989. Results include case name.
Criminal Records: Access: Mail, in person. Both court and visitors may perform in person searches. Search fee: $15.00 per name, includes certification. Required to search: name, years to search, address, DOB. Criminal records on computer since 5/87, on books from 1968. Mail turnaround time 1 week-10 days. Criminal PAT goes back to 5/1987. Results include case name.
General Information: No adoption, sealed cases, juvenile, mental or expunged records released. Will fax documents $2.00 1st page, $.25 each add'l. Court makes copy: $2.00 1st page, $.25 ea add'l. Certification fee: $3.00. Payee: Clerk of Superior Court. Only cashiers checks and money orders accepted. No credit cards accepted. Prepayment required. Mail requests: SASE required for mail returns of criminal results.

Haywood County

Superior-District Court 285 N. Main, Ste. 1500, Waynesville, NC 28786; 828-454-6501; criminal phone: 828-454-6347; civil phone: x5; fax: 828-456-4937; 8AM-5PM. ***Felony, Misdemeanor, Civil, Eviction, Small Claims, Probate.***
www.nccourts.org/County/Haywood/Default.asp
Search civil and criminal court calendars at www1.aoc.state.nc.us/www/calendars.html.
Civil Records: Access: Mail, in person. Both court and visitors may perform in person searches. Search fee: $15.00 per name. Required to search: name, years to search; also helpful: address. Civil cases indexed by defendant, plaintiff; index on computer since 10/13/1988, prior on books to 1955. Mail turnaround time 1-2 days. Civil PAT goes back to 10/1988.
Criminal Records: Access: Mail, in person. Both court and visitors may perform in person searches. Search fee: $15.00 per name, includes certification. Required to search: name, years to search, DOB; also helpful: address, SSN. Criminal records computerized from 5/87, on books or cards from 1800s. Mail turnaround time 1-2 days. Criminal PAT goes back to 10/1981.
General Information: No adoption, sealed cases, juvenile, sex offenders, mental or expunged records released. Will not fax documents. Court makes copy: $2.00 1st page, $.25 ea add'l. Certification fee: $3.00. Payee: Clerk of Superior Court. Only cashiers checks and money orders accepted. No credit cards accepted. Prepayment required. Mail requests: SASE required.

Henderson County

Superior-District Court PO Box 965, 200 N Grove St, #163, Hendersonville, NC 28793; 828-694-4100; probate phone: same; fax: 828-694-4107; 8AM-5PM. ***Felony, Misdemeanor, Civil, Eviction, Small Claims, Probate.***
www.nccourts.org/County/Henderson/Default.asp
Search civil and criminal court calendars at www1.aoc.state.nc.us/www/calendars.html.
Civil Records: Access: In person. Both court and visitors may perform in person searches. No search fee. Required to search: name, years to search; also helpful: address. Civil cases indexed by defendant, plaintiff; index on computer back to 1988, prior on books to 1968. Civil PAT goes back to 10/1988.
Criminal Records: Access: Mail, in person. Both court and visitors may perform in person searches. Search fee: $15.00 per name, includes certification. Required to search: full name; also helpful: address, DOB, SSN, years to search. Criminal records computerized from 9/86, prior on books to 1968. Mail turnaround time 1 week. Criminal PAT goes back to 9/1986.
General Information: No adoption, sealed cases, juvenile, sex offenders, mental or expunged records released. Will not fax documents. Court makes copy: $2.00 1st page, $.25 ea add'l. Certification fee: $3.00; Exemplified copy $10.00. Payee: Clerk of Superior Court. No personal checks or credit cards accepted. Prepayment required. Mail requests: SASE required.

Hertford County

Superior-District Court PO Box 86, 701 King St, Winton, NC 27986; 252-358-1711; 8AM-5PM. ***Felony, Misdemeanor, Civil, Eviction, Small Claims, Probate.***
www.nccourts.org/County/Hertford/Default.asp
Search civil and criminal court calendars at www1.aoc.state.nc.us/www/calendars.html.
Civil Records: Access: In person only. Visitors must perform in person searches themselves. Required to search: name, years to search; also helpful: address. Civil cases indexed by defendant, plaintiff; index on computer back to 4/1989, prior on index cards and judgment books to 1968. Civil PAT goes back to 1989.
Criminal Records: Access: Mail, in person. Both court and visitors may perform in person searches. Search fee: $15.00 per name, includes certification. Required to search: name, years to search, DOB; also helpful: address, SSN. Criminal records computerized from 4/1989, prior on index cards or judgment books to 1968. Mail turnaround time 1-2 days. Criminal PAT goes back to same as civil.
General Information: No adoption, sealed cases, juvenile, sex offenders, mental or expunged records released. Court makes copy: $2.00 1st page, $.25 ea add'l. Certification fee: $3.00; Exemplified copy $10.00. Payee: Clerk of Superior Court. Only cashiers checks and money orders accepted. No credit cards accepted. Prepayment required. Mail requests: SASE helpful.

Hoke County

Superior-District Court PO Drawer 1569, Raeford, NC 28376; 910-875-3728; fax: 910-904-1708; 8:30AM-5PM. ***Felony, Misdemeanor, Civil, Eviction, Small Claims, Probate.***
www.nccourts.org/County/Hoke/Default.asp
Search civil and criminal court calendars at www1.aoc.state.nc.us/www/calendars.html.
Civil Records: Access: In person only. Visitors must perform in person searches themselves. Required to search: name, years to search; also helpful: address. Civil cases indexed by defendant, plaintiff; index on computer since 10/89, on books to 1967. Civil PAT goes back to 10/1989.
Criminal Records: Access: Mail, in person. Both court and visitors may perform in person searches. Search fee: $15.00 per name, includes certification. Required to search: name, years to search, DOB; also helpful: address, SSN. Criminal records on computer since 10/89, on books to 1967. Mail turnaround time 1-2 days. Criminal PAT goes back to same as civil.
General Information: No adoption, sealed cases, juvenile, mental or expunged records released. Will not fax documents. Court makes copy: $2.00 1st page, $.25 ea add'l. Certification fee: None; $3.00 if you perform search in person. Payee: Clerk of Superior Court. Business checks accepted. No credit cards accepted. Prepayment required. Mail requests: SASE required for criminal.

Hyde County

Superior-District Court PO Box 337, 30 Oyster Creek St, Swanquarter, NC 27885; 252-926-4101; fax: 252-926-1002; 8AM-5PM. ***Felony, Misdemeanor, Civil, Eviction, Small Claims, Probate.***
www.nccourts.org/County/Hyde/Default.asp
Search civil and criminal court calendars at www1.aoc.state.nc.us/www/calendars.html.
Civil Records: Access: In person only. Visitors must perform in person searches themselves. Required to search: name, years to search. Civil cases indexed by defendant, plaintiff; index on computer since 7/89, on books to 1968; estate and special proceedings back to 1996. Civil PAT goes back to 1996. PAT results show name only.
Criminal Records: Access: Mail, in person. Visitors must perform in person searches themselves. Search fee: $15.00 per name, includes certification. Required to search: name, years to search, DOB; also helpful- signed release. Criminal records on computer since 7/89, on books to 1968. Note: Court refers to criminal searches as criminal background checks, not name searches. Criminal PAT goes back to 1989. PAT results show name only. Online results show name only.
General Information: No adoption, sealed cases, juvenile, sex offenders, mental, involuntary commitments, or expunged records released. Will fax documents if copy fee prepaid. Court makes copy: $2.00 1st page, $.25 ea add'l. Self serve: $.25 per page. Certification fee: $3.00 per page. Payee: Clerk of Superior Court. Only cashiers checks and money orders accepted. No credit cards accepted. Prepayment required. Mail requests: SASE required.

Iredell County

Superior-District Court 221 E Water St, Statesville, NC 28677; criminal phone: 704-878-4204; civil phone: 704-878-4306; probate phone: 704-878-4311; fax: 704-878-3261; 8:30AM-5PM. ***Felony, Misdemeanor, Civil, Eviction, Small Claims, Probate.***
www.nccourts.org/County/Iredell/Default.asp

Direct requests to Attention of Iredell County Clerk of Courts. Search civil and criminal court calendars at www1.aoc.state.nc.us/www/calendars.html.
Civil Records: Access: Mail, in person. Both court and visitors may perform in person searches. Search fee: $10.00 per name. Required to search: name, years to search. Civil cases indexed by defendant, plaintiff; index on computer since 07/88, in books since, 1786, on microfiche since 1971. Mail turnaround time 2 days. Civil PAT goes back to 1985. PAT civil results show middle initial.
Criminal Records: Access: Mail, in person. Both court and visitors may perform in person searches. Search fee: $15.00 per name, includes certification. Required to search: name, years to search, DOB. Criminal records on computer since 1985, prior on books and cards to 1970. Mail turnaround time 2 days. Criminal PAT goes back to same as civil. PAT results show middle initial, DOB.
General Information: No adoption, sealed cases, juvenile, sex offenders, mental or expunged records released. Will fax documents to local or toll free line, will not fax certified pages. Court makes copy: $2.00 1st page, $.25 ea add'l. Self serve: $.25 per page with copy button. Certification fee: $3.00 per page; exemplifications $10.00. Cert fee includes copy fee. Payee: Clerk of Superior Court. Only cashiers checks and money orders accepted. No credit cards accepted. Prepayment required. Mail requests: SASE required.

Jackson County

Superior-District Court 401 Grindstaff Cove Rd, Sylva, NC 28779; criminal phone: 828-586-7512; civil phone: 828-586-7512; criminal fax: 828-586-9009; civil fax: same; 8:30AM-5PM. ***Felony, Misdemeanor, Civil, Eviction, Small Claims, Probate.***
www.nccourts.org/County/Jackson/Default.asp
Search civil and criminal court calendars at www1.aoc.state.nc.us/www/calendars.html. Probate fax is same as main fax number.
Civil Records: Access: In person only. Visitors must perform in person searches themselves. Required to search: name, years to search; also helpful: address. Civil cases indexed by defendant, plaintiff; index on computer since 6/30/97, prior on books from 1966. Civil PAT goes back to 6/30/97. PAT results show name only.
Criminal Records: Access: Mail, in person. Both court and visitors may perform in person searches. Search fee: $15.00 per name, includes certification. Required to search: name, years to search, DOB; also helpful: address, SSN. Criminal records on computer since 5/01/1989, prior on books from 1966. Mail turnaround time 1-2 days. Criminal PAT goes back to 6/30/97. PAT results show name only.
General Information: No adoption, sealed cases, juvenile, mental or expunged records released. Will not fax documents. Court makes copy: $2.00 1st page, $.25 ea add'l. Self serve: $.25 per page. Certification fee: $10.00 per document includes copies. Payee: Clerk of Superior Court. Only cashiers checks and money orders accepted. No credit cards accepted. Prepayment required. Mail requests: SASE required for criminal.

Johnston County

Superior-District Court PO Box 297, Johnson and 2nd Strs, Smithfield, NC 27577; 919-209-5400; criminal fax: 919-934-5857; civil fax: same; 8AM-5PM. ***Felony, Misdemeanor, Civil, Eviction, Small Claims, Probate.***
www.nccourts.org/County/Johnston/Default.asp
Search civil and criminal court calendars at www1.aoc.state.nc.us/www/calendars.html. Probate is in a separate index at this courthouse. Probate fax is same as main fax number.
Civil Records: Access: Fax, mail, in person. Visitors must perform in person searches themselves. No search fee. Required to search: name, years to search; also helpful: address. Civil cases indexed by defendant, plaintiff; index on computer since 1989, prior on books to 1930s. Civil PAT goes back to 1982.
Criminal Records: Access: Fax, mail, in person. Both court and visitors may perform in person searches. Search fee: $15.00 per name, includes certification. Required to search: name, DOB; also helpful: years to search, address, SSN. Criminal records computerized from 5/86, prior on books and cards to 1968. Mail turnaround time 1-2 days. Criminal PAT goes back to same as civil.
General Information: No adoption, sealed cases, juvenile, sex offenders, mental or expunged records released. Will fax documents. Court makes copy: $2.00 1st page, $.25 ea add'l. Certification fee: $3.00 per document unless copy fee exceeds $3.00, then no cert fee. Payee: Clerk of Superior Court. Business checks accepted; no out-of-state checks accepted. No credit cards accepted. Prepayment required. Mail requests: SASE requested.

Jones County

Superior-District Court PO Box 280, Trenton, NC 28585; 252-448-7351; criminal phone: x1; civil phone: x3; fax: 252-448-1607; 8AM-5PM. ***Felony, Misdemeanor, Civil, Eviction, Small Claims, Probate.***
www.nccourts.org/County/Jones/Default.asp
Search civil and criminal court calendars at www1.aoc.state.nc.us/www/calendars.html.
Civil Records: Access: In person only. Visitors must perform in person searches themselves. Required to search: name, years to search. Civil cases indexed by defendant, plaintiff; index on computer since 1994, prior on microfilm. Civil PAT goes back to 1989.
Criminal Records: Access: Mail, in person. Both court and visitors may perform in person searches. Search fee: $15.00 per name, includes certification. Required to search: name, years to search; also helpful: DOB. Criminal records on computer since 1989, prior on microfilm. Mail turnaround time 5 days. Criminal PAT goes back to same as civil.
General Information: No adoption, sealed cases, juvenile, sex offenders, mental or expunged records released. Will not fax documents. Court makes copy: $2.00 1st page, $.25 ea add'l. Certification fee: $3.00. Payee: Clerk of Court. Only cashiers checks and money orders accepted. No credit cards accepted. Prepayment required. Mail requests: SASE required for criminal.

Lee County

Superior-District Court PO Box 4209, 1400 S Horner Blvd, Sanford, NC 27331; 919-708-4400; criminal phone: 919-708-4407 x1; civil phone: 919-708-4402 x4; probate phone: 919-708-4417; fax: 919-775-3483; 8AM-5PM. ***Felony, Misdemeanor, Civil, Eviction, Small Claims, Probate.***
www.nccourts.org/County/Lee/Default.asp
Search civil and criminal court calendars at www1.aoc.state.nc.us/www/calendars.html.
Civil Records: Access: In person only. Visitors must perform in person searches themselves. Required to search: name, years to search. Civil cases indexed by defendant, plaintiff; index on computer since 1989, prior on books to 1967, index to 1907. Civil PAT goes back to 1989. PAT results show name only.
Criminal Records: Access: Mail, in person. Both court and visitors may perform in person searches. Search fee: $15.00 per name, includes certification. Required to search: name, years to search, DOB. Criminal records on computer since 6/87, prior on books to 12/68, index to criminal actions books from 8/84 to 6/87. Mail turnaround time 1-3 days. Criminal PAT goes back to 6/1987. PAT results show name only.
General Information: No adoption, sealed cases, juvenile, sex offenders, mental or expunged records released. Will fax documents $2.00 1st page, $.25 ea add'l; prepaid. Court makes copy: $2.00 1st page, $.25 ea add'l. Self serve: same; or $.25 per page is you have purchased a copy key. Certification fee: $3.00. Payee: Clerk of Superior Court. Only cashiers checks and money orders accepted. No credit cards accepted. Prepayment required.

Lenoir County

Superior-District Court 130 S Queen St, Kinston, NC 28502-0068; 252-520-5300; fax: 252-520-5385; 8AM-5PM. ***Felony, Misdemeanor, Civil, Eviction, Small Claims, Probate.***
www.nccourts.org/County/Lenoir/Default.asp
Search civil and criminal court calendars at www1.aoc.state.nc.us/www/calendars.html.
Civil Records: Access: In person only. Both court and visitors may perform in person searches. No search fee. Required to search: name, years to search; also helpful: address. Civil cases indexed by defendant, plaintiff; index on computer since 10/24/1988, prior on books to 1900s, prior destroyed due to fire. Public use terminal has civil records back to 1988.
Criminal Records: Access: Mail, in person. Only the court performs in person searches; visitors may not. Search fee: $15.00 per name, includes certification. Required to search: name, years to search, DOB; also helpful: address. Criminal records on computer since 8/86, prior records on books and cards to 1925. Mail turnaround time 1-2 days.
General Information: No adoption, sealed cases, juvenile, sex offenders, mental or expunged records released. Will fax documents $1.00 1st page, $.25 each add'l page. Court makes copy: $2.00 1st page, $.25 ea add'l. Self serve: purchase $10.00 copy key. Certification fee: $3.00. Payee: Clerk of Superior Court. Only cashiers checks and money orders accepted. No credit cards accepted. Prepayment required. Mail requests: SASE required.

Lincoln County

Superior-District Court PO Box 8, Lincolnton, NC 28093; criminal phone: 704-736-8561 x3; civil phone: 704-736-8563 x4; probate: 704-736-8565; fax: 704-736-8718; 8:30AM-5PM. ***Felony, Misdemeanor, Civil, Eviction, Small Claims, Probate.***
www.nccourts.org/County/Lincoln/Default.asp
Search civil and criminal court calendars at www1.aoc.state.nc.us/www/calendars.html.
Civil Records: Access: In person only. Visitors must perform in person searches themselves. Required to search: name, years to search. Civil cases indexed by defendant, plaintiff; index on computer since 11-1-87, in books since mid-1800s, on microfiche from 1-1-68 to present. Civil PAT goes back to 11/1987. PAT results show name only.
Criminal Records: Access: Mail, in person. Both court and visitors may perform in person searches. Search fee: $15.00 per name, includes certification. Required to search: name, DOB; Also helpful: years to search. Criminal records on computer since 1987, prior on books and cards to 1968. Mail turnaround time 2 days to 1 week. Criminal PAT goes back to same as civil.
General Information: No adoption, sealed cases, juvenile, sex offenders, mental or expunged records released. Will fax documents $2.00 per page. Court makes copy: $2.00 1st page, $.25 ea add'l. Certification fee: None; $3.00 if you perform search in person. Payee: Clerk of Court. Business checks accepted. No personal checks or credit cards accepted. Prepayment required. Mail requests: SASE required for criminal.

Macon County

Superior-District Court 5 W Main St, Franklin, NC 28744; 828-349-2000; fax: 828-369-2515; 8AM-5PM. ***Felony, Misdemeanor, Civil, Eviction, Small Claims, Probate.***
www.nccourts.org/County/Macon/Default.asp
Search civil and criminal court calendars at www1.aoc.state.nc.us/www/calendars.html.
Civil Records: Access: In person only. Visitors must perform in person searches themselves. Required to search: name, years to search; also helpful: address. Civil cases indexed by defendant, plaintiff; index on computer since 5/1989, prior on books to 1968. Public use terminal has civil records back to 5/1989. PAT results show name only.
Criminal Records: Access: Mail, in person. Only the court performs in person searches; visitors may not. Search fee: $15.00 per name, includes certification. Required to search: name, DOB, years to search; also helpful- file number. Criminal records on computer since 5/1989, prior on books to 1968. Mail turnaround time 1-2 days.
General Information: No adoption, sealed cases, juvenile, sex offenders, mental or expunged records released. Will fax documents $1.00 1st page, $.25

each add'l page. Court makes copy: $2.00 1st page, $.25 ea add'l. Certification fee: $3.00 per cert. Payee: Clerk of Superior Court. No personal checks or credit cards accepted. Prepayment required. Mail requests: SASE required.

Madison County

Superior-District Court PO Box 217, 2 N Main St, Marshall, NC 28753; 828-649-2531; fax: 828-649-2829; 8AM-5PM. ***Felony, Misdemeanor, Civil, Eviction, Small Claims, Probate.***
www.nccourts.org/County/Madison/Default.asp
Search civil and criminal court calendars at www1.aoc.state.nc.us/www/calendars.html.
Civil Records: Access: In person only. Visitors must perform in person searches themselves. Required to search: name, years to search; also helpful: address. Civil cases indexed by defendant, plaintiff; index on computer back to 10/88, prior on books to 1968. Civil PAT goes back to 10/1988. PAT results show name only.
Criminal Records: Access: Mail, in person. Visitors must perform in person searches themselves. Search fee: $15.00 per name, includes certification. Required to search: name, DOB; also helpful: years to search. Criminal records on computer since 10/88, prior on books to 1968. Mail turnaround time 1-2 days. Criminal PAT goes back to same as civil.PAT results show name, DOB.
General Information: No adoption, sealed cases, juvenile, sex offenders, mental, expunged, or dismissed records released. Will fax documents $1.00 1st page, $.25 each add'l page. Court makes copy: $2.00 1st page, $.25 ea add'l. Certification fee: $3.00; Exemplified copy $10.00. Payee: Clerk of Superior Court. Only cashiers checks and money orders accepted. No credit cards accepted. Prepayment required.

Martin County

Superior-District Court PO Box 807, Williamston, NC 27892; 252-792-2515; fax: 252-792-6668; 8AM-5PM. ***Felony, Misdemeanor, Civil, Eviction, Small Claims, Probate.***
www.nccourts.org/County/Martin/Default.asp
Search criminal court calendars at http://www1.aoc.state.nc.us/www/calendars.html.
Civil Records: Access: In person. Both court and visitors may perform in person searches. No search fee. Required to search: name, years to search, address. Civil cases indexed by defendant, plaintiff. Civil records go back to 1800s, civil records on computer since 1989, in books since 1968. Public use terminal available. PAT civil results show middle initial.
Criminal Records: Access: Mail, in person. Both court and visitors may perform in person searches. Search fee: $15.00 per name, includes certification. Required to search: name, years to search, address, DOB; also helpful: SSN. Criminal records go back to 1800s criminal records on computer since 1996 in books since 1968. Mail turnaround time 1 week. Public use terminal available. PAT criminal results show middle initial.
General Information: No adoption, sealed cases, juvenile, mental or expunged records released. Will not fax documents. Court makes copy: $2.00 1st page, $.25 ea add'l. Certification fee: $3.00; Exemplified copy $10.00. Payee: Clerk of Court. Only cashiers checks and money orders accepted. No credit cards accepted. Prepayment required. Mail requests: SASE required for criminal.

McDowell County

Superior-District Court 21 S Main St, Marion, NC 28752; 828-652-7717 x201; criminal phone: x228; civil phone: x208; fax: 828-659-2641; 8:30AM-5PM. ***Felony, Misdemeanor, Civil, Eviction, Small Claims, Probate.***
www.nccourts.org/County/McDowell/Default.asp
Search civil and criminal court calendars at www1.aoc.state.nc.us/www/calendars.html.
Civil Records: Access: Mail, in person. Both court and visitors may perform in person searches. No search fee. Required to search: name, years to search; also helpful: address. Civil cases indexed by defendant, plaintiff; index on computer since 11/88, prior on books to 1930. Mail turnaround time 1-2 days. Public use terminal available.
Criminal Records: Access: Mail, in person. Both court and visitors may perform in person searches. Search fee: $15.00 per name, includes certification. Required to search: name, DOB; also helpful: years to search, address, SSN. Criminal records on computer since 10/1987, prior on books to 1968. Mail turnaround time 1-2 days. Public use terminal available.
General Information: No adoption, sealed cases, juvenile, sex offenders, mental or expunged records released. Court makes copy: $2.00 1st page, $.25 ea add'l. Certification fee: $3.00; Exemplified copy $10.00. Payee: Clerk of Superior Court. Business checks accepted. Prepayment required. Mail requests: SASE required.

Mecklenburg County

Superior-District Court PO Box 37971, 832 E 4th St, Charlotte, NC 28237; 704-686-0400 (info); criminal phone: 704-686-0600; civil phone: 704-686-0520; criminal fax: 704-686-0601; civil fax: 704-686-0501; 9AM-5PM. ***Felony, Misdemeanor, Civil, Eviction, Small Claims, Probate.***
www.nccourts.org/County/Mecklenburg/Staff/Clerk.asp
Search civil and criminal court calendars at www1.aoc.state.nc.us/www/calendars.html.
Civil Records: Access: In person only. Visitors must perform in person searches themselves. Required to search: name. Civil cases indexed by defendant, plaintiff; index on computer since 4/1988, prior on books to 1940s. Civil PAT goes back to 1988. PAT civil results show middle initial.
Criminal Records: Access: Mail, in person. Both court and visitors may perform in person searches. Search fee: $15.00 per name, includes certification. Required to search: name, years to search, address, DOB; also helpful: SSN. Criminal records computerized from 1/83, prior on cards and books to 1930s. Mail turnaround time 1-2 days. Criminal PAT goes back to 1983. PAT results show middle initial, DOB.
General Information: No adoption, sealed cases, juvenile, sex offenders, mental or expunged records released. Will not fax documents. Court makes copy: $2.00 1st page, $.25 ea add'l. Certification fee: $3.00 per doc. Payee: Clerk of Superior Court. Only cashiers checks and money orders accepted. No credit cards accepted. Prepayment required. Mail requests: SASE requested for criminal.

Mitchell County

Superior-District Court 328 Longview Dr, Bakersville, NC 28705; 828-688-2161; fax: 828-688-2168; 8:30AM-5PM M-TH; 8:30AM-4:30PM F. ***Felony, Misdemeanor, Civil, Eviction, Small Claims, Probate.***
www.nccourts.org/County/Mitchell/Default.asp
Search civil and criminal court calendars at www1.aoc.state.nc.us/www/calendars.html.
Civil Records: Access: In person only. Visitors must perform in person searches themselves. Required to search: name, years to search; also helpful: address. Civil cases indexed by defendant, plaintiff; index on computer since 1988, prior on books since 1968. Civil PAT goes back to 1988. PAT results show middle initial, DOB.
Criminal Records: Access: Mail, in person. Both court and visitors may perform in person searches. Search fee: $15.00 per name, includes certification. Required to search: name, years to search, DOB; also helpful- address. Criminal records on computer since 1988, prior on books since 1968; 1984-1988 on microfilm. Mail turnaround time 1-2 days. Criminal PAT goes back to same as civil. PAT results show middle initial, DOB.
General Information: No adoption, sealed cases, juvenile, sex offenders, mental or expunged records released. Will not fax documents. Court makes copy: $2.00 1st page, $.25 ea add'l. Certification fee: None; $3.00 if you perform search in person. Payee: Superior-District Court. No checks accepted, only certified checks or money orders. No credit cards accepted. Prepayment required. Mail requests: SASE required for criminal.

Montgomery County

Superior-District Court PO Box 527, Troy, NC 27371; 910-576-4211; fax: 910-576-5020; 8:30AM-5PM. ***Felony, Misdemeanor, Civil, Eviction, Small Claims, Probate.***
www.nccourts.org/County/Montgomery/Default.asp
Search civil and criminal court calendars at www1.aoc.state.nc.us/www/calendars.html. Address mail to Clerk of Superior Court.
Civil Records: Access: In person. Visitors must perform in person searches themselves. Required to search: name, years to search. Civil cases indexed by defendant, plaintiff; index on computer since 4/1989, on books to 170, archived in Raleigh to 1843, prior records destroyed in fire. Civil PAT available.
Criminal Records: Access: Phone, fax, mail, in person. Both court and visitors may perform in person searches. Search fee: $15.00 per name, includes certification. Required to search: name, years to search, address, DOB, signed release. Criminal records on computer since 4/1989, on books to 170, archived in Raleigh to 1843, prior records destroyed in fire. Mail turnaround time 1-2 days. Criminal PAT goes back to 1988.
General Information: No adoption, sealed cases, juvenile, sex offenders, mental or expunged records released. Will fax documents $2.00 per page. Court makes copy: $2.00 1st page, $.25 ea add'l. Self serve: $.25 per page. Certification fee: $3.00; Exemplification fee- $10.00 each. Payee: Clerk of Superior Court. Only cashiers checks and money orders accepted. No credit cards accepted. Prepayment required. Mail requests: SASE required for mail return of any copies.

Moore County

Superior-District Court PO Box 936, Carthage, NC 28327; 910-947-2396; fax: 910-947-1444; 8AM-5PM. ***Felony, Misdemeanor, Civil, Eviction, Small Claims, Probate.***
www.nccourts.org/County/Moore/Default.asp
Search civil and criminal court calendars at www1.aoc.state.nc.us/www/calendars.html.
Civil Records: Access: In person only. Both court and visitors may perform in person searches. No search fee. Required to search: name, DOB, years to search. Civil cases indexed by defendant, plaintiff; index on computer since 3/1989, prior on books, older records in basement. Civil PAT goes back to 1987. PAT results show middle initial, DOB.
Criminal Records: Access: Mail, in person. Both court and visitors may perform in person searches. Search fee: $15.00 per name, includes certification. Required to search: name, years to search, DOB, signed release; also helpful: address. Criminal records on computer since 3/1989, prior on books to 1968, older records in basement. Mail turnaround time 2-4 days. Criminal PAT goes back to 1989. PAT results show middle initial, DOB.
General Information: No adoption, sealed cases, juvenile, mental or expunged records released. Will not fax documents. Court makes copy: $2.00 1st page, $.25 ea add'l. Certification fee: $3.00 per cert. Payee: Clerk of Superior Court. Cashiers checks and money orders accepted. No credit cards accepted. Prepayment required. Mail requests: SASE required.

Nash County

Superior-District Court PO Box 759, 234 W Washington St, Nashville, NC 27856; 252-459-4081; criminal phone: 252-459-4085; fax: 252-459-6050; 8AM-5PM. ***Felony, Misdemeanor, Civil, Eviction, Small Claims, Probate.***
www.nccourts.org/County/Nash/Default.asp
Search civil and criminal court calendars at www1.aoc.state.nc.us/www/calendars.html.
Civil Records: Access: In person only. Both court and visitors may perform in person searches. No search fee. Required to search: name, years to search; also helpful: address. Civil cases indexed by defendant, plaintiff; index on computer since 6/1988, prior in books. Civil PAT goes back to 6/1988.
Criminal Records: Access: Mail, in person. Both court and visitors may perform in person searches.

Search fee: $15.00 per name, includes certification. Required to search: name, years to search, DOB; also helpful: address. Criminal records on computer since 5/1980, prior on books and cards dating back to late 1800s. Mail turnaround time 1 week. Criminal PAT goes back to 1980.
General Information: No adoption, sealed cases, juvenile, mental or expunged records released. Will not fax documents. Court makes copy: $2.00 1st page, $.25 ea add'l. Certification fee: $3.00; Exemplified copy $10.00. If certified copy exceeds 6 pages, then add $.25 for each add'l page. Payee: Clerk of Superior Court. Only cashiers checks and money orders accepted. No credit cards accepted. Prepayment required. Mail requests: SASE required for criminal.

New Hanover County

Superior-District Court PO Box 2023, 316 Princess St, Wilmington, NC 28402; 910-341-1111; criminal phone: 910-341-1301; civil phone: 910-341-1302; probate phone: 910-341-1304; criminal fax: 910-251-2676; civil fax: 910-341-1311; 8AM-5PM. ***Felony, Misdemeanor, Civil, Eviction, Small Claims, Probate.***
www.nccourts.org/County/NewHanover/Default.asp
Search civil and criminal court calendars at http://www1.aoc.state.nc.us/www/calendars.html.
Civil Records: Access: In person only. Visitors must perform in person searches themselves. Required to search: name, years to search; also helpful: address. Civil cases indexed by defendant, plaintiff; index on computer since 1988, on books to late 1800s. Public use terminal available.
Criminal Records: Access: Mail, in person. Both court and visitors may perform in person searches. Search fee: $15.00 per name, includes certification. Required to search: name, years to search, DOB; also helpful: address, SSN. Criminal records on computer since 11/83, prior on books and files to late 1800s. Mail turnaround time 1-2 days. Public use terminal available.
General Information: No adoption, sealed cases, juvenile, sex offenders, mental or expunged records released. Court makes copy: $2.00 1st page, $.25 ea add'l. Certification fee: $3.00 per doc. Payee: Clerk of Superior Court. Only cashiers checks and money orders accepted. Prepayment required. Mail requests: SASE required for criminal.

Northampton County

Superior-District Court PO Box 217, 102 W Jefferson St, Jackson, NC 27845; 252-534-1631; fax: 252-534-1308; 8:30AM-5PM. ***Felony, Misdemeanor, Civil, Eviction, Small Claims, Probate.***
www.nccourts.org/County/Northampton/Default.asp
Search civil and criminal court calendars at www1.aoc.state.nc.us/www/calendars.html.
Civil Records: Access: Mail, in person. Visitors must perform in person searches themselves. Search fee: $15.00 per name. Required to search: name, years to search; also helpful: address. Civil cases indexed by defendant, plaintiff; index on computer back to 1993, prior on books to 1968. Mail turnaround time 3-10 days Civil PAT goes back to 1989. PAT results show name only.
Criminal Records: Access: Mail, in person. Visitors must perform in person searches themselves. Search fee: $15.00 per name, includes certification. Required to search: name, years to search, DOB; also helpful: address, SSN. Criminal records computerized from 1989, prior on books to 1968. Mail turnaround time 3-10 days. Criminal PAT goes back to same as civil. PAT results show name only.
General Information: No adoption, sealed cases, juvenile, sex offenders, mental or expunged records released. Will not fax documents. Court makes copy: $2.00 1st page, $.25 ea add'l. Self serve: $.25 each copy with a purchase of a key at $10.00. Certification fee: $3.00 per doc. Payee: Clerk of Superior Court. Only cash or certified checks accepted. No personal checks or credit cards accepted. Prepayment required. Mail requests: SASE required.

Onslow County

Superior-District Court 625 Court St, Jacksonville, NC 28540; 910-455-4458; fax: 910-455-6285; 8AM-5PM. ***Felony, Misdemeanor, Civil, Eviction, Small Claims, Probate.***
www.nccourts.org/County/Onslow/Default.asp
Search civil and criminal court calendars at www1.aoc.state.nc.us/www/calendars.html.
Civil Records: Access: In person only. Visitors must perform in person searches themselves. Required to search: name, years to search; also helpful: address. Civil cases indexed by defendant, plaintiff; index on computer since 1988, prior on books to 1920s. Civil PAT goes back to 1988. PAT results show name only.
Criminal Records: Access: Mail, in person. Both court and visitors may perform in person searches. Search fee: $15.00 per name, includes certification. Required to search: name, years to search, DOB; also helpful: address, SSN. Criminal records on computer since 2/83, prior on books to 1920s. Mail turnaround time 1-2 days. Criminal PAT goes back to same as civil. PAT results show name only.
General Information: No adoption, sealed cases, juvenile, sex offenders, mental or expunged records released. Will fax documents $1.00 1st page, $.25 each add'l page. Court makes copy: $2.00 1st page, $.25 ea add'l.A copy key may be purchased from CSC & used in person only to make copies or print from public terminals, fee for photocopier key is $110.00 per key purchase, for printer key $60.00 per key purchase. Certification fee: $3.00; Exemplified copy $10.00. Payee: Clerk of Superior Court. Business checks accepted. No credit cards accepted. Prepayment required.

Orange County

Superior-District Court 106 E Margaret Lane, Hillsborough, NC 27278; criminal phone: 919-245-2200; civil phone: 919-245-2210; probate phone: 919-245-2214; fax: 919-644-3043; 8:30AM-5PM. ***Felony, Misdemeanor, Civil, Eviction, Small Claims, Probate.***
www.nccourts.org/County/Orange/Default.asp
Search civil and criminal court calendars at www1.aoc.state.nc.us/www/calendars.html.
Civil Records: Access: In person only. Visitors must perform in person searches themselves. Required to search: name, years to search; also helpful: address. Civil cases indexed by defendant, plaintiff; index on computer since 5/1989, prior on books to early 1800s. Civil PAT goes back to 1989. PAT results show name only.
Criminal Records: Access: Mail, in person. Both court and visitors may perform in person searches. Search fee: $15.00 per name, includes certification. Required to search: name, DOB; also helpful: address, SSN, race, sex. computer records go to 3/87. Mail turnaround time 4-5 days. Criminal PAT goes back to 1987.PAT results show name, DOB. Results include driver's license number.
General Information: No adoption, sealed cases, juvenile, sex offenders, mental or expunged records released. Will not fax documents. Court makes copy: $2.00 1st page, $.25 ea add'l. Certification fee: $3.00. Payee: Clerk of Superior Court. Only cashiers checks and money orders accepted. No credit cards accepted. Prepayment required. Mail requests: SASE required.

Pamlico County

Superior-District Court PO Box 38, Bayboro, NC 28515; criminal phone: 252-745-6001; civil phone: 252-745-6000; probate phone: 252-745-6003; criminal fax: 252-745-6018; civil fax: same; 8AM-5PM. ***Felony, Misdemeanor, Civil, Eviction, Small Claims, Probate.***
www.nccourts.org/County/Pamlico/Default.asp
Search civil and criminal court calendars at www1.aoc.state.nc.us/www/calendars.html. Probate fax is same as main fax number.
Civil Records: Access: In person only. Visitors must perform in person searches themselves. Required to search: name, years to search, address. Civil cases indexed by defendant, plaintiff. Civil records go back to 1988; criminal records on computer since 9/89, prior on books to 1968. Civil PAT goes back to 1989. PAT results show name only.
Criminal Records: Access: Mail, in person. Both court and visitors may perform in person searches. Search fee: $15.00 per name, includes certification. Required to search: name, years to search, DOB. Criminal records on computer since 9/84, prior on books to 1968. Mail turnaround time 1-2 days. Criminal PAT goes back to same as civil. PAT results show middle initial, DOB.
General Information: No adoption, sealed cases, juvenile, sex offenders, mental or expunged records released. Will fax documents $1.00 1st page, $.25 each add'l page. Court makes copy: $2.00 1st page, $.25 ea add'l. Certification fee: $3.00. Only cashiers checks and money orders accepted. No credit cards accepted. Prepayment required. Mail requests: SASE required for criminal.

Pasquotank County

Superior-District Court PO Box 449, Elizabeth City, NC 27907-0449; 252-331-4751; fax: 252-331-4826; 8AM-5PM. ***Felony, Misdemeanor, Civil, Eviction, Small Claims, Probate.***
www.nccourts.org/County/Pasquotank/Default.asp
Search civil and criminal court calendars at www1.aoc.state.nc.us/www/calendars.html.
Civil Records: Access: In person only. Visitors must perform in person searches themselves. Required to search: name, years to search; also helpful: address. Civil cases indexed by defendant, plaintiff; index on computer since 3/6/1989, books prior to 1800s (some in Raleigh). Civil PAT goes back to 1993. PAT results show name only.
Criminal Records: Access: Mail, in person. Both court and visitors may perform in person searches. Search fee: $15.00 per name, includes certification. Required to search: name, years to search, DOB; also helpful: address, SSN, race, sex. Criminal records on computer since 4/88, prior on books and microfiche. Mail turnaround time 2 days. Criminal PAT goes back to 1989. PAT results show middle initial, DOB.
General Information: No adoption, sealed cases, juvenile, sex offenders, mental or expunged records released. Will not fax documents. Court makes copy: $2.00 1st page, $.25 ea add'l. Self serve: same. Certification fee: None; $3.00 if you perform search in person. Payee: Clerk of Superior Court. Business checks accepted. No credit cards accepted. Prepayment required.

Pender County

Superior-District Court PO Box 310, Burgaw, NC 28425; 910-259-1229; probate phone: same; fax: 910-259-1292; 8:30AM-5PM. ***Felony, Misdemeanor, Civil, Eviction, Small Claims, Probate.***
www.nccourts.org/County/Pender/Default.asp
Search civil and criminal court calendars at www1.aoc.state.nc.us/www/calendars.html.
Civil Records: Access: In person only. Visitors must perform in person searches themselves. Required to search: name, years to search; also helpful: address. Civil cases indexed by defendant, plaintiff; index on computer since 1989, prior in books from 1875. Note: Civil search can be done statewide from any Clerk of Courts office. Civil PAT goes back to 1989.
Criminal Records: Access: Fax, mail, in person. Both court and visitors may perform in person searches. Search fee: $15.00 per name, includes certification. Required to search: name, years to search, DOB; also helpful: address, SSN. Criminal records on computer since 9/89, prior in books from 1968. Mail turnaround time 1 week. Criminal PAT goes back to 7/89.
General Information: No adoption, sealed cases, juvenile, sex offenders, mental or expunged records released. Will fax documents $2.00 1st page, $.25 each add'l. Court makes copy: $2.00 1st page, $.25 ea add'l. Self serve: same. Certification fee: $3.00. Exemplification fee- $10.00. Payee: Clerk of Superior Court. Business checks accepted. No credit cards accepted. Prepayment required. Mail requests: SASE required for mail return of any copies.

Perquimans County

Superior-District Court PO Box 33, 128 N Church St, Hertford, NC 27944; 252-426-1505; fax: 252-426-1901; 8-5PM. ***Felony, Misdemeanor, Civil, Eviction, Small Claims, Probate.*** www.nccourts.org/County/Perquimans/Default.asp Search civil and criminal court calendars at www1.aoc.state.nc.us/www/calendars.html.

Civil Records: Access: In person only. Visitors must perform in person searches themselves. Required to search: name, years to search. Civil cases indexed by defendant, plaintiff; index on computer since 1989, prior in books to 1966, rest archived and must be searched in person only. Civil PAT goes back to 10/23/89. PAT results show middle initial, DOB. Terminal results also show SSNs.

Criminal Records: Access: Mail, in person. Both court and visitors may perform in person searches. Search fee: $15.00 per name, includes certification. Required to search: name, years to search, DOB. Criminal records on computer since 1989, prior in books to 12/1966, rest archived and must be searched in person only. Mail turnaround time 1-2 days. Criminal PAT goes back to same as civil. PAT results show middle initial, DOB. Terminal results include SSN.

General Information: No adoption, sealed cases, juvenile, sex offenders, mental or expunged records released. Will not fax documents. Court makes copy: $2.00 1st page, $.25 ea add'l. Certification fee: None; $3.00 if you perform search in person. Payee: Clerk of Superior Court. Only cashiers checks and money orders accepted. No credit cards accepted. Prepayment required. Mail requests: SASE required.

Person County

Superior-District Court 105 S Main St, Roxboro, NC 27573; 336-503-5200; fax: 336-503-5229; 8AM-5PM. ***Felony, Misdemeanor, Civil, Eviction, Small Claims, Probate.*** www.nccourts.org/County/Person/Default.asp Search civil and criminal court calendars at www1.aoc.state.nc.us/www/calendars.html.

Civil Records: Access: In person only. Visitors must perform in person searches themselves. Required to search: name, years to search. Civil cases indexed by defendant, plaintiff; index on microfiche since 4/89, prior in index books to 1968. Civil PAT goes back to 4/1997.

Criminal Records: Access: Mail, in person. Visitors must perform in person searches themselves. Search fee: $15.00 per name, includes certification. Required to search: name, DOB; also helpful: years to search. Criminal records on computer since 3/88, index cards and books prior to 1968. Mail turnaround time 1-2 days. Criminal PAT goes back to 3/1988. PAT results show name only.

General Information: No adoption, sealed cases, juvenile, sex offenders, mental or expunged records released. Will fax documents $1.00 1st page, $.25 each add'l page. Court makes copy: $2.00 1st page, $.25 ea add'l. Certification fee: $3.00; Exemplified copy $10.00. Payee: Clerk of Superior Court. Business checks accepted. No credit cards accepted. Prepayment required. Mail requests: SASE required.

Pitt County

Superior - District Court PO Box 6067, 100 W Third St, Greenville, NC 27835; 252-695-7100; criminal phone: 252-695-7117; civil phone: 252-695-7150; fax: 252-695-7376; 8AM-5PM. ***Felony, Misdemeanor, Civil, Eviction, Small Claims, Probate.*** www.nccourts.org/County/Pitt/Default.asp Search civil and criminal court calendars at www1.aoc.state.nc.us/www/calendars.html.

Civil Records: Access: In person only. Visitors must perform in person searches themselves. Required to search: name, years to search; also helpful: address. Civil cases indexed by defendant, plaintiff; index on computer back to 1988, on books to 1968. Civil PAT goes back to 1988. PAT results show name, DOB.

Criminal Records: Access: Mail, in person. Both court and visitors may perform in person searches. Search fee: $15.00 per name, includes certification. Required to search: name, years to search, DOB; also helpful: address, SSN. Criminal records computerized from 2/85, on books and cards to early 1900s. Mail turnaround time 1-2 days. Criminal PAT goes back to 2/1985. PAT results show middle initial, DOB.

General Information: No adoption, sealed cases, juvenile, sex offenders, mental or expunged records released. Will not fax documents. Court makes copy: $2.00 1st page, $.25 ea add'l. Certification fee: $3.00. Payee: Clerk of Court. No personal checks or credit cards accepted. Prepayment required. Mail requests: SASE required.

Polk County

Superior-District Court PO Box 38, Columbus, NC 28722; 828-894-8231; probate phone: same; fax: 828-894-5752; 8AM-5PM. ***Felony, Misdemeanor, Civil, Eviction, Small Claims, Probate.*** www.nccourts.org/County/Polk/Default.asp Search civil and criminal court calendars at www1.aoc.state.nc.us/www/calendars.html.

Civil Records: Access: In person only. Visitors must perform in person searches themselves. Required to search: name, years to search. Civil cases indexed by defendant, plaintiff; index on computer since 5/89, prior on books to 1968. Civil PAT goes back to 1989.

Criminal Records: Access: Mail, in person. Both court and visitors may perform in person searches. Search fee: $15.00 per name, includes certification. Required to search: name, years to search, DOB. Criminal records on computer since 5/89, prior on books to 1968. Mail turnaround time 1-2 days. Criminal PAT goes back to same as civil. PAT results show middle initial, DOB.

General Information: No adoption, sealed cases, juvenile, sex offenders, mental, expunged or dismissed records released. Will fax documents $1.00 1st page, $.25 each add'l page. Court makes copy: $2.00 1st page, $.25 ea add'l. Certification fee: $3.00. Payee: Clerk of Superior Court. Business checks accepted. No credit cards accepted. Prepayment required. Mail requests: SASE required.

Randolph County

Superior-District Court 176 E Salisbury St #201, Asheboro, NC 27203; 336-328-3000; criminal phone: 336-328-3005; civil phone: 336-328-3004; fax: 336-328-3131; 8-5PM. ***Felony, Misdemeanor, Civil, Eviction, Small Claims, Probate.*** www.nccourts.org/County/Randolph/Default.asp Search civil and criminal court calendars at www1.aoc.state.nc.us/www/calendars.html.

Civil Records: Access: In person only. Visitors must perform in person searches themselves. Required to search: name, years to search. Civil cases indexed by defendant, plaintiff; index on computer since 2/89, prior on books to 1800s. Civil PAT available. PAT results show name only.

Criminal Records: Access: Mail, in person. Only the court performs in person searches; visitors may not. Search fee: $15.00 per name, includes certification. Required to search: name, years to search, address, DOB. Criminal records on computer since 6/85, prior on books and cards from 1970 to 1981. Microfilm from 1981 to 6/85. Mail turnaround time 1-2 days. Criminal PAT available. PAT results show name only.

General Information: No adoption, sealed cases, juvenile, sex offenders, mental or expunged records released. Will not fax documents. Court makes copy: $2.00 1st page, $.25 ea add'l. Certification fee: $3.00 per doc. Payee: Clerk of Superior Court. Only cashiers checks and money orders accepted. No credit cards accepted. Prepayment required. Mail requests: SASE required for criminal.

Richmond County

Superior-District Court 114 E Franklin St #103, Rockingham, NC 28379; criminal phone: 910-997-9101; civil phone: 910-997-9102; fax: 910-997-9126; 8AM-5PM. ***Felony, Misdemeanor, Civil, Eviction, Small Claims, Probate.*** www.nccourts.org/County/Richmond/Default.asp Search civil and criminal court calendars at www1.aoc.state.nc.us/www/calendars.html.

Civil Records: Access: In person only. Visitors must perform in person searches themselves. Required to search: name, years to search; also helpful- address. Civil cases indexed by defendant, plaintiff; index on computer since 4/89, prior on books since 1968. Civil PAT goes back to 1988.

Criminal Records: Access: Mail, in person. Both court and visitors may perform in person searches. Search fee: $15.00 per name, includes certification. Required to search: name, years to search, DOB; also helpful: address, SSN. Criminal records on computer since 1977, cards to 1977, books to 1940, prior archived. Mail turnaround time 1-2 days. Criminal PAT goes back to same as civil.

General Information: No adoption, sealed cases, juvenile, sex offenders, mental or expunged records released. Will not fax documents. Court makes copy: $3.00 per doc; divoces- $2.50 1st page, $.25 each add'l. Self serve: same. Certification fee: $3.00. Payee: Clerk of Superior Court. Business checks accepted. No credit cards accepted. Prepayment required. Mail requests: SASE required for criminal.

Robeson County

Superior-District Court PO Box 1084, Lumberton, NC 28359; 910-737-5035; criminal phone: 910-671-3395; civil phone: 910-671-3372; fax: 910-618-5598; 8:15AM-5:15PM. ***Felony, Misdemeanor, Civil, Eviction, Small Claims, Probate.*** www.nccourts.org/County/Robeson/Default.asp Search civil and criminal court calendars at www1.aoc.state.nc.us/www/calendars.html.

Civil Records: Access: In person only. Visitors must perform in person searches themselves. Required to search: name, years to search; also helpful: address. Civil cases indexed by defendant, plaintiff; index on computer since 1988, prior on books since 1966. Civil PAT goes back to 1988. PAT results show name only.

Criminal Records: Access: Mail, in person. Both court and visitors may perform in person searches. Search fee: $15.00 per name, includes certification. Required to search: name, years to search; also helpful: address, DOB. Criminal records on computer since 1983, index books prior. Mail turnaround time 1-2 days. Criminal PAT goes back to 1983. PAT results show middle initial, DOB.

General Information: Will not fax documents. Court makes copy: $2.00 1st page, $.25 ea add'l. Certification fee: $3.00 if you perform search; Exemplification is $10.00. Payee: Clerk of Superior Court. Business checks accepted. No credit cards accepted. Prepayment required. Mail requests: SASE required for criminal.

Rockingham County

Superior-District Court PO Box 127, 1086 NC Hwy 65, Wentworth, NC 27375; 336-342-8700; criminal phone: 336-342-8706; civil phone: 336-342-8722; probate phone: 336-342-8703; fax: 336-616-1991; 8AM-5PM. ***Felony, Misdemeanor, Civil, Eviction, Small Claims, Probate.*** www.nccourts.org/County/Rockingham/Default.asp Search civil and criminal court calendars at www1.aoc.state.nc.us/www/calendars.html.

Civil Records: Access: In person only. Both court and visitors may perform in person searches. No search fee. Required to search: name, years to search. Civil cases indexed by defendant, plaintiff; index on computer since 2/89, prior on books. Civil PAT goes back to 1989. PAT results show middle initial, DOB. Terminal results also show SSNs.

Criminal Records: Access: Mail, in person. Both court and visitors may perform in person searches. Search fee: $15.00 per name, includes certification. Required to search: name, years to search, DOB. Criminal records on computer since 5/85, prior on cards and books. Mail turnaround time 1-2 days. Criminal PAT goes back to 1985. PAT results show middle initial, DOB.

General Information: No adoption, sealed cases, juvenile, sex offenders, mental or expunged records released. Will not fax documents. Court makes copy: $2.00 1st page, $.25 ea add'l. Self serve: same. Certification fee: $3.00 per doc. Cert fee includes copies. Payee: Clerk of Superior Court. Only cashiers checks and money orders accepted. No credit cards accepted. Prepayment required. Mail requests: SASE required.

Rowan County

Superior-District Court PO Box 4599, 210 N Main St, Salisbury, NC 28145; 704-797-3001; criminal phone: 704-797-3016 (Supr), 3015 (Dist); civil phone: 704-797-3003; probate phone: 704-797-3005; fax: 704-797-3050; 8AM-5PM. ***Felony, Misdemeanor, Civil, Eviction, Small Claims, Probate.***

www.nccourts.org/County/Rowan/Default.asp

Search civil and criminal court calendars at http://www1.aoc.state.nc.us/www/calendars.html.

Civil Records: Access: Mail, in person. Both court and visitors may perform in person searches. No search fee. Required to search: name, years to search; also helpful: address. Civil cases indexed by defendant, plaintiff; index on computer since 1989, prior on books to 1800s. Mail turnaround time 1-3 days. Civil PAT goes back to 1987.

Criminal Records: Access: Mail, in person. Both court and visitors may perform in person searches. Search fee: $15.00 per name, includes certification. Required to search: name; also helpful: DOB, years to search, address, SSN. Criminal records computerized from 5/85, prior on books and cards to 1970. Mail turnaround time 1-3 days. Criminal PAT goes back to 1985.

General Information: No adoption, sealed cases, juvenile, sex offenders, mental or expunged records released. Will fax documents $2.00 1st page, $.25 each add'l. Court makes copy: $2.00 1st page, $.25 ea add'l. Certification fee: $3.00; Exemplified copy $10.00. Payee: Clerk of Superior Court. Local and some business checks accepted. No credit cards accepted. Prepayment required.

Rutherford County

Superior-District Court PO Box 630, 229 N Main St, Rutherfordton, NC 28139; 828-286-9136; criminal phone: 828-286-3243; civil phone: 828-286-9136; fax: 828-286-4322; 8AM-5PM. ***Felony, Misdemeanor, Civil, Eviction, Small Claims, Probate.***

www.nccourts.org/County/Rutherford/Default.asp

Search civil and criminal court calendars at www1.aoc.state.nc.us/www/calendars.html.

Civil Records: Access: In person only. Visitors must perform in person searches themselves. Required to search: name, years to search; also helpful: address. Civil cases indexed by defendant, plaintiff; index on computer 10/1988, prior on books, some records to 1700s. Civil PAT goes back to 10/1988.

Criminal Records: Access: Mail, in person. Both court and visitors may perform in person searches. Search fee: $15.00 per name, includes certification. Required to search: name, years to search, DOB; also helpful: address, SSN. Criminal records on computer since 6/87, prior on microfiche and books dating to 1800s. Mail turnaround time 1-2 days. Criminal PAT goes back to 6/1987.

General Information: No adoption, sealed cases, juvenile, sex offenders, mental or expunged records released. Will not fax documents. Court makes copy: $2.00 1st page, $.25 ea add'l. Certification fee: $3.00; Exemplified copy $10.00. Payee: Clerk of Superior Court. Business checks accepted. No credit cards accepted. Prepayment required. Mail requests: SASE required for criminal.

Sampson County

Superior-District Court County Courthouse, 101 E Main St, Clinton, NC 28328; 910-592-5191; criminal phone: 910-592-6981; probate phone: same; fax: 910-592-5502; 8-5PM. ***Felony, Misdemeanor, Civil, Eviction, Small Claims, Probate.***

www.sampsoncountyclerkofcourt.org

Search civil and criminal court calendars at www1.aoc.state.nc.us/www/calendars.html.

Civil Records: Access: In person only. Visitors must perform in person searches themselves. Required to search: name, years to search; also helpful: address. Civil cases indexed by defendant, plaintiff; index on computer since 1989, prior on books.

Criminal Records: Access: Mail, in person. Both court and visitors may perform in person searches. Search fee: $15.00 per name, includes certification. Required to search: name, years to search, DOB; also helpful: address, SSN. Criminal records on computer since 7/87, prior on books. Mail turnaround 1-2 days.

General Information: No adoption, sealed cases, juvenile, mental or expunged records released. Will fax documents. Court makes copy: $2.00 1st page, $.25 ea add'l. Certification fee: $3.00 per doc. Payee: Clerk of Superior Court. No personal checks or credit cards accepted. Prepayment required. Mail requests: SASE requested for criminal.

Scotland County

Superior-District Court PO Box 769, 212 Biggs St, Laurinburg, NC 28353; 910-266-4402; criminal phone: 910-266-4401; civil phone: 910-266-4403; criminal fax: 910-266-4466; civil fax: same; 8:30AM-5PM. ***Felony, Misdemeanor, Civil, Eviction, Small Claims, Probate.***

www.nccourts.org/County/Scotland/Default.asp

Search civil and criminal court calendars at http://www1.aoc.state.nc.us/www/calendars.html. Probate fax is same as main fax number.

Civil Records: Access: In person only. Visitors must perform in person searches themselves. Required to search: name, years to search. Civil cases indexed by defendant, plaintiff; index on computer since 1988, in books since 1966. Civil PAT goes back to 1989.

Criminal Records: Access: Mail, in person. Both court and visitors may perform in person searches. Search fee: $15.00 per name, includes certification. Required to search: name, years to search, DOB; SSN helpful. Criminal records on computer since 1988, in books 1966-1988, on microfiche 1984-1988. Mail turnaround time 1-2 days. Criminal PAT goes back to 1988.

General Information: No adoption, sealed cases, juvenile, sex offenders, mental or expunged records released. Will not fax documents. Court makes copy: $2.00 1st page, $.25 ea add'l. Certification fee: $3.00; Exemplified copy $10.00. Payee: Clerk of Court. Only cashiers checks and money orders accepted. No credit cards accepted. Prepayment required. Mail requests: SASE required.

Stanly County

Superior-District Court PO Box 668, 201 S 2nd St, Albemarle, NC 28002-0668; 704-982-2161; criminal phone: x176; probate phone: same; fax: 704-982-8107; 8:30AM-5PM. ***Felony, Misdemeanor, Civil, Eviction, Small Claims, Probate.***

www.nccourts.org/County/Stanly/Default.asp

Search civil and criminal court calendars at www1.aoc.state.nc.us/www/calendars.html.

Civil Records: Access: In person only. Visitors must perform in person searches themselves. Required to search: name, years to search; also helpful: address. Civil cases indexed by defendant, plaintiff; index on computer since 1989, books to 1968. Civil PAT goes back to 1989.

Criminal Records: Access: Mail, in person. Both court and visitors may perform in person searches. Search fee: $15.00 per name, includes certification. Required to search: name, years to search, DOB. Criminal records on computer since 1989; books from 1968 to May, 1983; microfilm from 1983 to Sept, 1989. Mail turnaround time 1-2 days. Criminal PAT goes back to same as civil.

General Information: No adoption, sealed cases, juvenile, sex offenders, mental or expunged records released. Court makes copy: $2.00 1st page, $.25 ea add'l. Certification fee: None; $3.00 if you perform search in person. Payee: Clerk of Superior Court. Only cashiers checks and money orders accepted. No credit cards accepted. Prepayment required. Mail requests: SASE required.

Stokes County

Superior-District Court PO Box 250, 1012 Main St, Danbury, NC 27016; 336-593-9173; probate phone: same; fax: 336-593-5459; 8AM-5PM. ***Felony, Misdemeanor, Civil, Eviction, Small Claims, Probate.***

www.nccourts.org/County/Stokes/Default.asp

Search civil and criminal court calendars at www1.aoc.state.nc.us/www/calendars.html.

Civil Records: Access: In person only. Visitors must perform in person searches themselves. Required to search: name, years to search; also helpful: address. Civil cases indexed by defendant, plaintiff; index on computer since 9/1988, prior on books to early 1900s. Note: Civil background checks not performed. Civil PAT goes back to 9/1988. PAT results show name only.

Criminal Records: Access: Mail, in person. Both court and visitors may perform in person searches. Search fee: $15.00 per name, includes certification. Required to search: name; also helpful: address, DOB. Criminal records on computer since 9/1988, prior on books to early 1900s. Mail turnaround time 1 week. Criminal PAT goes back to same as civil.PAT results show name, DOB.

General Information: No adoption, sealed cases, juvenile, sex offenders, mental or expunged records released. Will not fax documents. Court makes copy: $2.00 1st page, $.25 ea add'l. Certification fee: $3.00; exemplification- $20.00 per doc. Payee: Clerk of Superior Court. Only cashiers checks and money orders accepted. No credit cards accepted. Prepayment required. Mail requests: SASE required for criminal.

Surry County

Superior-District Court PO Box 345, 201 E. Kapp St, Dobson, NC 27017; 336-386-3700; fax: 336-386-9879; 8-5PM. ***Felony, Misdemeanor, Civil, Eviction, Small Claims, Probate.***

www.nccourts.org/County/Surry/Default.asp

Search civil and criminal court calendars at www1.aoc.state.nc.us/www/calendars.html.

Civil Records: Access: In person only. Visitors must perform in person searches themselves. Required to search: name, years to search, DOB; also helpful: address. Civil cases indexed by defendant, plaintiff; index on computer since 10/88, on books to 1970, must know township for earlier records. Civil PAT goes back to 1987.

Criminal Records: Access: Mail, in person. Both court and visitors may perform in person searches. Search fee: $15.00 per name, includes certification. Required to search: name, years to search, DOB. Criminal records on computer since 10/88, on books to 1970, must know township for earlier records. Mail turnaround time 1-2 days. Criminal PAT goes back to same as civil.

General Information: No adoption, sealed cases, juvenile, sex offenders, mental or expunged records released. Will fax documents $1.00 1st page, $.25 each add'l. Court makes copy: $2.00 1st page, $.25 ea add'l. Certification fee: $3.00; Exemplified copy $10.00. Payee: Clerk of Superior Court. Business checks accepted. No personal checks. No credit cards accepted. Prepayment required. Mail requests: SASE required for criminal.

Swain County

Superior-District Court PO Box 1397, Clerk of Superior Ct, 101 Mitchell St, Admin Bldg, Bryson City, NC 28713; 828-488-2288; probate phone: same; fax: 828-488-9360; 8:30AM-5PM. ***Felony, Misdemeanor, Civil, Eviction, Small Claims, Probate.***

www.nccourts.org/County/Swain/Default.asp

Search civil and criminal court calendars at www1.aoc.state.nc.us/www/calendars.html.

Civil Records: Access: Mail, in person. Both court and visitors may perform in person searches. Search fee: $15.00. Required to search: name, years to search. Civil cases indexed by defendant, plaintiff; index on computer since 5/1989, prior on books to 1920. Public use terminal has civil records back to 5/8/89. PAT results show middle initial, DOB.

Criminal Records: Access: Mail, in person. Both court and visitors may perform in person searches. Search fee: $15.00 per name, includes certification. Required to search: name, years to search, DOB; also helpful-signed release. Criminal records computerized from 8/1984, prior on books to 1969. PAT results show middle initial, DOB.

General Information: No adoption, sealed cases, juvenile, mental or expunged records released. Will fax specific case file $10.00 per page, prepaid. Court makes copy: $2.00 1st page, $.25 ea add'l. Self serve: $.25 per page. Cert fee: $3.00; Exemplified copy $10.00. Payee: Clerk of Superior Court. No personal checks or credit cards accepted. Prepayment required.

Transylvania County

Superior-District Court 12 E Main St, Brevard, NC 28712; 828-884-3120; criminal phone: 828-884-3128; civil phone: 828-884-3125; fax: 828-883-2161; 8AM-5PM. ***Felony, Misdemeanor, Civil, Eviction, Small Claims, Probate.***
www.nccourts.org/County/Transylvania/Default.asp
Search civil and criminal court calendars at www1.aoc.state.nc.us/www/calendars.html.
Civil Records: Access: In person only. Visitors must perform in person searches themselves. Required to search: name, years to search; also helpful: address. Civil cases indexed by defendant, plaintiff; index on computer from 11/99, on books from 1968. Civil PAT goes back to 11/1989.
Criminal Records: Access: Mail, in person. Both court and visitors may perform in person searches. Search fee: $15.00 per name, includes certification. Required to search: name, years to search, DOB; also helpful: address. Criminal records computerized from 6/89, on books 1968-1989. Mail turnaround time 1-3 days. Criminal PAT goes back to 6/1989. PAT results show middle initial, DOB.
General Information: No adoption, sealed cases, juvenile, mental or expunged records released. Will not fax documents. Court makes copy: $2.00 1st page, $.25 ea add'l. Certification fee: $3.00 plus $.25 each add'l page. Exemplification fee- $10.00. Payee: Clerk of Superior Court. In state personal checks accepted. No credit cards accepted. Prepayment required. Mail requests: SASE required for criminal.

Tyrrell County

Superior-District Court PO Box 406, 403 Main St, Columbia, NC 27925; 252-796-6281; fax: 252-796-0008; 8:30AM-5PM. ***Felony, Misdemeanor, Civil, Eviction, Small Claims, Probate.***
www.nccourts.org/County/Tyrrell/Default.asp
Search civil and criminal court calendars at www1.aoc.state.nc.us/www/calendars.html.
Civil Records: Access: In person only. Visitors must perform in person searches themselves. Required to search: name, years to search; also helpful: address. Civil cases indexed by defendant, plaintiff; index on computer since 10/89, prior on microfilm, books to 1968. Civil PAT goes back to 1996. PAT civil results show middle initial.
Criminal Records: Access: Mail, in person. Both court and visitors may perform in person searches. Search fee: $15.00 per name, includes certification. Required to search: name, years to search, DOB; also helpful: address, SSN. Criminal records on computer since 10/89, prior on books to 1968. Mail turnaround time 1-2 days. Criminal PAT goes back to 1990. PAT criminal results show middle initial.
General Information: No adoption, sealed cases, juvenile, sex offenders, mental records expunged. Will fax documents for no fee. Court makes copy: $2.00 1st page, $.25 ea add'l. Certification fee: $6.00 per doc. Payee: Clerk of Superior Court. Business checks accepted. No personal checks. No credit cards accepted. Prepayment required. Mail requests: SASE required.

Union County

Superior-District Court PO Box 5038, Monroe, NC 28111; 704-296-4600; criminal phone: 704-296-4602; civil phone: 704-296-4601; fax: 704-289-1283; 8:30AM-5PM. ***Felony, Misdemeanor, Civil, Eviction, Small Claims, Probate.***
www.nccourts.org/County/Union/Default.asp
Search civil and criminal court calendars at www1.aoc.state.nc.us/www/calendars.html.
Civil Records: Access: In person only. Visitors must perform in person searches themselves. Required to search: name, years to search; also helpful: address. Civil cases indexed by defendant, plaintiff; index on computer since 3/1989, prior on books to 1968. Civil PAT goes back to 1989. PAT results show middle initial, DOB, SSN.
Criminal Records: Access: Mail, in person. Both court and visitors may perform in person searches. Search fee: $15.00 per name, includes certification. Required to search: name, years to search; also helpful: address, DOB, SSN. Criminal record on computer since 1989; prior on books to 1968. Mail turnaround time 1-2 weeks. Criminal PAT goes back to 1989. PAT results show middle initial, DOB, SSN.
General Information: No adoption, sealed cases, juvenile, sex offenders, mental or expunged records released. Will not fax documents. Court makes copy: $2.00 1st page, $.25 ea add'l. Certification fee: None; $3.00 or copy fee if greater. Payee: Clerk of Superior Court. Will accept local business checks only for civil cases. No credit cards accepted. Prepayment required.

Vance County

Superior-District Court 156 Church St. #101, Henderson, NC 27536; 252-738-9000; criminal phone: x1; civil phone: x4; fax: 252-492-6666; 8:30AM-5PM. ***Felony, Misdemeanor, Civil, Eviction, Small Claims, Probate.***
www.nccourts.org/County/Vance/Default.asp
Search civil and criminal court calendars at www1.aoc.state.nc.us/www/calendars.html.
Civil Records: Access: In person only. Visitors must perform in person searches themselves. Required to search: name, years to search; also helpful: address. Civil cases indexed by defendant, plaintiff; index on computer since 1989, prior on books to 1881. Civil PAT goes back to 1979.
Criminal Records: Access: Mail, in person. Both court and visitors may perform in person searches. Search fee: $15.00 per name, includes certification. Required to search: name, years to search, address, DOB; also helpful: SSN. Criminal records on computer to 12/80, prior on books and cards to 1881. Mail turnaround time 1-2 days. Criminal PAT goes back to same as civil. PAT criminal results show middle initial.
General Information: No adoption, sealed cases, juvenile, sex offenders, mental or expunged records released. Will fax documents $1.00 1st page, $.25 each add'l page. Court makes copy: $2.00 1st page, $.25 ea add'l. Certification fee: $3.00. Payee: Clerk of Superior Court. Business checks accepted. No credit cards accepted. Prepayment required.

Wake County

Superior-District Court PO Box 351, 316 Fayetteville St Mall, Raleigh, NC 27602; 919-755-4105; criminal phone: 919-755-4112; civil phone: 919-755-4108; probate phone: 919-755-4116; criminal fax: 919-835-3039; civil fax: 919-755-4124; 8:30AM-5PM. ***Felony, Misdemeanor, Civil, Eviction, Small Claims, Probate.***
http://web.co.wake.nc.us/courts/
Search civil and criminal court calendars at www1.aoc.state.nc.us/www/calendars.html. Civil Div on 11th Fl; criminal on 1st.
Civil Records: Access: In person only. Visitors must perform in person searches themselves. Required to search: name, years to search. Civil cases indexed by defendant, plaintiff; index on computer since 1988, prior on books to 1920s. Civil PAT goes back to 2/1988. PAT civil results show middle initial.
Criminal Records: Access: Mail, in person. Both court and visitors may perform in person searches. Search fee: $15.00 per name, includes certification. Required to search: name, years to search. Criminal records computerized from 5/82, prior on books and cards from 1968. Mail turnaround time 3 days. Criminal PAT goes back to 1982. PAT results show middle initial, DOB.
General Information: Juvenile, judicial waivers, involuntary commitments are confidential. No sealed cases, juvenile, mental or expunged records released. Will not fax documents. Court makes copy: $2.00 1st page, $.25 ea add'l. Certification fee: $3.00 per doc. Payee: Clerk of Superior Court. Business checks accepted with prior registration. No personal checks or credit cards accepted. Prepayment required.

Warren County

Superior-District Court PO Box 709, Warrenton, NC 27589; 252-257-3261; criminal fax: 252-257-5529; civil fax: same; 8:30AM-5PM. ***Felony, Misdemeanor, Civil, Eviction, Small Claims, Probate.***
www.nccourts.org/County/Warren/Default.asp
Search civil and criminal court calendars at www1.aoc.state.nc.us/www/calendars.html. Probate fax is same as main fax number.
Civil Records: Access: In person only. Visitors must perform in person searches themselves. Required to search: name, years to search. Civil cases indexed by defendant, plaintiff; index on computer since 1989, prior on books to 1968. Civil PAT goes back to 1989. PAT results show name only.
Criminal Records: Access: Mail, in person. Both court and visitors may perform in person searches. Search fee: $15.00 per name, includes certification. Required to search: name, years to search, DOB. Criminal records computerized from 5/81, prior on books to 1968. Mail turnaround time 1-2 days. Criminal PAT goes back to 1981. PAT results show name only.
General Information: No adoption, sealed cases, juvenile, sex offenders, mental or expunged records released. Will fax documents $2.00 per page. Court makes copy: $2.00 1st page, $.25 ea add'l. Self serve: $.25 per page. Certification fee: $3.00 per copy; Exemplification fee- $10.00. Payee: Clerk of Superior Court. Business checks accepted; no personal checks. No credit cards accepted. Prepayment required. Mail requests: SASE required.

Washington County

Superior-District Court PO Box 901, Plymouth, NC 27962; 252-793-3013; fax: 252-793-1081; 8AM-5PM. ***Felony, Misdemeanor, Civil, Eviction, Small Claims, Probate.***
www.nccourts.org/County/Washington/Default.asp
Search civil and criminal court calendars at www1.aoc.state.nc.us/www/calendars.html.
Civil Records: Access: In person only. Visitors must perform in person searches themselves. Required to search: name, years to search. Civil cases indexed by defendant, plaintiff; index on computer back to 12/89, prior on books. Civil PAT goes back to 12/1989. PAT civil results show middle initial.
Criminal Records: Access: Mail, in person. Both court and visitors may perform in person searches. Search fee: $15.00 per name, includes certification. Required to search: name, years to search; also helpful: address, DOB, SSN. Criminal records computerized from 12/89, prior on books. Mail turnaround time 2-3 days. Criminal PAT goes back to same as civil. PAT results show middle initial, DOB.
General Information: No adoption, sealed, juvenile, mental health, expunged records released. Will not fax documents. Court makes copy: $2.00 1st page, $.25 ea add'l. Self serve: $.25 per page. Certification fee: $3.00. Payee: Clerk of Court. Business checks accepted. No personal checks or credit cards accepted. Prepayment required. Mail requests: SASE required for criminal.

Watauga County

Superior-District Court Courthouse #13, 842 W King St, Boone, NC 28607-3525; 828-265-5364; criminal phone: 828-265-5430; civil phone: 828-265-5432; probate phone: 828-265-5443; fax: 828-262-5753; 8AM-5PM. ***Felony, Misdemeanor, Civil, Eviction, Small Claims, Probate.***
www.nccourts.org/County/Watauga/Default.asp
Search civil and criminal court calendars at www1.aoc.state.nc.us/www/calendars.html.
Civil Records: Access: In person only. Visitors must perform in person searches themselves. Required to search: name, years to search. Civil cases indexed by defendant, plaintiff; index on computer since 12/5/88, on books to 1872, prior destroyed by fire. Civil PAT goes back to 1988. PAT civil results show middle initial.
Criminal Records: Access: Mail, in person. Both court and visitors may perform in person searches. Search fee: $15.00 per name, includes certification. Required to search: name, years to search, DOB, SSN. Criminal records computerized from 11/88, prior on cards and books to 1968. Mail turnaround time 1-2 days. Criminal PAT goes back to same as civil.PAT results show name, DOB.
General Information: No adoption, sealed, juvenile, sex offenders, mental, expunged or dismissed records released. Will not fax documents. Court makes copy:

$2.00 1st page, $.25 ea add'l. Self serve: $.25 per page. Certification fee: None; $3.00 if you perform search in person. Payee: Clerk of Court. Only cashiers checks and money orders accepted. No credit cards accepted. Prepayment required. Mail requests: SASE requested for criminal.

Wayne County

Superior-District Court 224 E Walnut St, Rm 230, Goldsboro, NC 27530; 919-731-7910; criminal phone: 919-731-7910; civil phone: 919-731-7919; probate phone: 919-731-7921; fax: 919-731-2037; 8AM-5PM. ***Felony, Misdemeanor, Civil, Eviction, Small Claims, Probate, Special Proceedings.***

www.nccourts.org/County/Wayne/Default.asp

Search civil and criminal court calendars at www1.aoc.state.nc.us/www/calendars.html. Reach Family Division at 919-731-7920.

Civil Records: Access: In person only. Visitors must perform in person searches themselves. Required to search: name, years to search; also helpful: address. Civil cases indexed by defendant, plaintiff; index on computer since 7-18-88, on books since 1968, open to public prior. Note: Court will not do a search unless book and page number or a year of judgment given. Civil PAT goes back to 1985. PAT civil results show middle initial.

Criminal Records: Access: Mail, in person. Both court and visitors may perform in person searches. Search fee: $15.00 per name, includes certification. Required to search: name, years to search, DOB; also helpful: address, aliases. Criminal records on computer since 7-18-88, on books since 1985, open to public prior. Mail turnaround time 1-2 days. Criminal PAT goes back to same as civil. PAT results show middle initial, DOB, SSN.

General Information: No adoption, sealed, juvenile, sex offenders, mental, expunged or dismissed. Will fax documents $2.00 1st page, $.25 each add'l. Court makes copy: $2.00 1st page, $.25 ea add'l. Add $1.00 to first copy of out of state. Self serve: $.25 per page. Certification fee: $3.00. Payee: Clerk of Superior Court. Business checks accepted. No credit cards accepted. Prepayment required. Mail requests: SASE requested for criminal.

Wilkes County

Superior-District Court 500 Courthouse Drive, #1115, Wilkesboro, NC 28697; criminal phone: 336-667-5266; civil phone: 336-667-1201; fax: 336-667-1985; 8AM-5PM. ***Felony, Misdemeanor, Civil, Eviction, Small Claims, Probate.***

www.nccourts.org/County/Wilkes

Search civil and criminal court calendars at www1.aoc.state.nc.us/www/calendars.html.

Civil Records: Access: In person only. Visitors must perform in person searches themselves. Required to search: name, years to search. Civil cases indexed by defendant, plaintiff; index on computer since 12/88, prior on books to early 1900s. Civil PAT goes back to 1987.

Criminal Records: Access: Mail, in person. Both court and visitors may perform in person searches. Search fee: $15.00 per name, includes certification. Required to search: name, years to search, DOB; also helpful: address. Criminal records on computer since 12/88, prior on books to early 1900s. Mail turnaround time 1-2 days. Criminal PAT goes back to same as civil.

General Information: No adoption, sealed cases, juvenile, sex offenders, mental or expunged records released. Will fax documents $1.00 1st page, $.25 each add'l page. Court makes copy: $2.00 1st page, $.25 ea add'l. Certification fee: $3.00. Payee: Clerk of Superior Court. Only cashiers checks and money orders accepted. No credit cards accepted. Prepayment required. Mail requests: SASE requested for criminal.

Wilson County

Superior-District Court PO Box 1608, 115 E Nash St, Wilson, NC 27894; 252-291-7500; civil phone: 252-291-7502; probate phone: 252-291-7502; criminal fax: 252-291-8049; civil fax: 252-291-8635; 8AM-5PM. ***Felony, Misdemeanor, Civil, Eviction, Small Claims, Probate.***

www.nccourts.org/County/Wilson/Default.asp

Search civil and criminal court calendars at www1.aoc.state.nc.us/www/calendars.html.

Civil Records: Access: In person only. Visitors must perform in person searches themselves. Required to search: name, years to search; also helpful: address. Civil cases indexed by defendant, plaintiff; index on computer since 8/88, prior on books to 1968, public viewing from 1915 to 1968. Civil PAT goes back to 10/1989. PAT results show middle initial, DOB.

Criminal Records: Access: Mail, fax, in person. Both court and visitors may perform in person searches. Search fee: $15.00 per name, includes certification. Required to search: name, years to search, DOB; also helpful: address, SSN. Criminal records on computer since 5/86, Index cards to 9/76, books to 1918. Mail turnaround time 2-4 days. Criminal PAT goes back to 5/1986. PAT results show middle initial, DOB.

General Information: No adoption, sealed cases, juvenile, sex offenders, mental, or expunged records released. Will not fax documents. Court makes copy: $2.00 1st page, $.25 ea add'l. Certification fee: $3.00; Exemplified copy $10.00. Payee: Clerk of Court. Only cashiers checks and money orders accepted. No credit cards accepted. Prepayment required. Mail requests: SASE requested for criminal.

Yadkin County

Superior-District Court PO Box 95, Yadkinville, NC 27055; 336-679-8838; fax: 336-679-4378; 8AM-5PM. ***Felony, Misdemeanor, Civil, Eviction, Small Claims, Probate.***

www.nccourts.org/County/Yadkin/Default.asp

Search civil and criminal court calendars at www1.aoc.state.nc.us/www/calendars.html.

Civil Records: Access: In person only. Visitors must perform in person searches themselves. Required to search: name, years to search; also helpful: address. Civil cases indexed by defendant, plaintiff; index on computer since 8/89, prior on books to 1970. Public use terminal available. PAT results show middle initial, DOB.

Criminal Records: Access: Mail, in person. Both court and visitors may perform in person searches. Search fee: $15.00 per name, includes certification. Required to search: name, years to search, DOB; also helpful: address. Criminal records on computer since 8/89, prior on books to 1970. Mail turnaround time 1-2 days. Public use terminal available. PAT results show middle initial, DOB.

General Information: No adoption, sealed cases, juvenile, sex offenders, mental or expunged records released. Will not fax documents. Court makes copy: $2.00 1st page, $.25 ea add'l. Certification fee: $3.00. Payee: Clerk of Superior Court. Business checks accepted. Prepayment required. Mail requests: SASE required for criminal.

Yancey County

Superior-District Court 110 Town Square, Rm 5, Burnsville, NC 28714; 828-682-2122; fax: 828-682-6296; 8AM-5PM. ***Felony, Misdemeanor, Civil, Eviction, Small Claims, Probate.***

www.nccourts.org/County/Yancey/Default.asp

Search civil and criminal court calendars at www1.aoc.state.nc.us/www/calendars.html.

Civil Records: Access: In person only. Visitors must perform in person searches themselves. Required to search: name, years to search; also helpful: address. Civil cases indexed by defendant, plaintiff; index on computer since 1988, prior on books. Civil PAT goes back to 1988.

Criminal Records: Access: Mail, in person. Only the court performs in person searches; visitors may not. Search fee: $15.00 per name, includes certification. Required to search: name, years to search, DOB; also helpful: address, SSN. Criminal records on computer since 1998, prior on books. Mail turnaround time depends on ease of access, can take up to 2 weeks. Criminal PAT available.

General Information: No adoption, sealed cases, juvenile, sex offenders, mental, expunged or dismissed records released. Will not fax documents. Court makes copy: $2.00 1st page, $.25 ea add'l. Certification fee: $3.00; Exemplified copy $10.00. Payee: Clerk of Superior Court. Business checks accepted. No personal checks. No credit cards accepted. Prepayment required.

North Carolina Recording Offices

ORGANIZATION: 100 counties, 100 recording offices. The recording officer is the Register of Deeds but for tax liens it is the Clerk of Superior Court. North Carolina is in the Eastern Time Zone (EST)

REAL ESTATE RECORDS: Counties will not perform real estate searches. Copy fee is usually $1.00 per page, often less. Certification fee is usually $5.00 for the first page and $2.00 for each add'l page of that document.

UCC RECORDS: This was a dual filing state. Financing statements were both at the state level and with the Register of Deeds, except for consumer goods, farm related and real estate related collateral. As of July 1, 2001, only real estate related collateral is filed at the county level. Many counties will perform UCC searches on records recorded prior to July, 2001. Use search request form UCC-11. UCC search fees vary - $30.00 or $38.00 per debtor name. UCC copy fee is usually $1.00 per page.

TAX LIEN RECORDS: Federal tax liens on personal property of businesses are filed with the Secretary of State. Other federal and all state tax liens are filed with the county Clerk of Superior Court. Oddly, even tax liens on real property are also filed with the Clerk of Superior Court, not with the Register of Deeds.

OTHER LIENS: Judgment, mechanics (all at Clerk of Superior Court)

ONLINE ACCESS: A growing number of counties offer free access to assessor and real estate records via the web. Free access available statewide at www.secretary.state.nc.us/ucc/. Click "UCC Research" or "Tax Liens."

Alamance County

Register of Deeds, PO Box 837, Graham, NC 27253. 336-570-6565; 8AM-5PM www.alamance-nc.com

No tax liens filed here. Index: All in one. Record index not computerized. Only the public may search. Copy fee $1.00 per page. Cert fee- $5.00 per cert plus copy fee. Payee- Alamance County Register of Deeds. **Online access to Real Estate, Deed, Lien, Birth, Death, Marriage, UCC records:** Access the recorded document database free at http://deeds.alamance-nc.com/. Vitals go back to 1984, UCCs back to 2001, real estate back to 1973. **Other phones:** Treasurer- 336-570-1318. **Property tax/Assessing**- 124 W Elm St, Graham, NC 27253; 336-228-1318. **Online** - Property tax and parcel data available free at www.alamance-nc.com/Alamance-NC/Online+Services/Real+Estate+Tax+System.htm but site is temporarily down. Also, search the GIS-mapping site for free parcel data at www.alamance-nc.com/alamancegis/.

Alexander County

Register of Deeds, 75 1st St SW, #1, Taylorsville, NC 28681-2504. 828-632-3152, R/E recording phone-704-632-3152; fax-828-632-1119; 8AM-5PM www.alexandercountync.gov/index/index.asp

No tax liens filed here. Index: All in one. Records indexed on a public use terminal back to 1/1/1993. Only the public may search. Copy fee $1.00 per page. Cert fee- $5.00 1st page, $2.00 each add'l page. Payee- Alexander County Register of Deeds. **Online access to Real Estate, Deed, Lien records:** Access recorder land records free at www.alexanderrod.com/view/disclaimer.html. Also, real property index and records available through 11/04/08 (Book 525) for free at www.alexandercountync.gov/index/online_services.php . **Property tax/ Assessing**- 75 1st St SW, #2, Taylorsville, NC 28681; 828-632-4346, assessor fax-828-632-1100. www.alexandercountync.gov/tax-office.php **Online access**- Access parcel data free on the GIS/mapping site at http://maps.co.alexander.nc.us/gomaps/index.cfm. Real property index and records through 11/4/08 (Book 525) free at www.alexandercountync.gov/index/online_services.php.

Alleghany County

Register of Deeds, PO Box 186, Sparta, NC 28675. 336-372-4342; fax-336-372-2061; 8AM-5PM www.alleghanycounty-nc.gov

Filing cut off time 4:30PM daily. No tax liens filed here. Index: All in one. Records indexed on a public use terminal back to 1989. Office will perform a UCC search but public must search other records themselves. Search fee $30.00. Copy fee $.05 per page. Large plat copy fee $2.00. Cert fee- $5.00 first page, $2.00 each add'l page thereafter. Payee- Alleghany County Register of Deeds. **Online access to Real Estate, Grantor/Grantee, Deed records:** Access to the Register of Deeds database is free at http://24.172.15.58/Opening.asp. All Deed images are online back thru 1859 to current. Real property indexes available 1/1/1989 to current. **Other phones:** Treasurer- 336-372-4179; Elections- 336-372-4557; Vital Records- 336-372-4342. **Property tax/Assessing**- PO Box 1027, Sparta, NC 28675; 336-372-8291. (Appraiser/Auditor- 336-372-8291) **Online** - Search for property data on a GIS mapping site at http://arcims.webgis.net/nc/Alleghany/default.asp. To name search click on Quick Search.

Anson County

Register of Deeds, PO Box 352, Wadesboro, NC 28170-0352. Recording, R/E phone-704-694-3212, UCCs-704-694-7594; fax-704-694-6135; 8:30-5PM www.co.anson.nc.us/content/index.php?services0

No tax liens filed here. Index: All in one index if recorded after 8/1/1989; prior records in a deed index or deed of trust index. Records indexed on a public use terminal back to 8/1/89. Office will perform a UCC search but public must search other records themselves. Search fee-$38.00 for UCC only. Copy fee $1.00 per page.Real estate record copy- $.25 per page. Cert fee- $5.00 1st page, $2.00 each add'l page, includes copy fee. Payee- Anson County Register of Deeds. **Other phones:** Treasurer- 704-694-6219; Elections- 704-694-3072; Vital Records- 704-694-7593. **Property tax/Assessing**- 210 Morgan St, Wadesboro, NC 28170; 704-694-2918. (Appraiser/Auditor- 704-694-2918) **Online access**- Search the county Online Tax Inquiry System free at www.co.anson.nc.us/pubcgi/taxinq/. Tax collections search at www.co.anson.nc.us/pubcgi/colinq/.

Ashe County

Register of Deeds, 150 Government Circle, #2300, Jefferson, NC 28640. 336-846-5580, R/E recording phone-336-219-2540; 8-4:30PM www.ashencrod.org

No tax liens filed here. Index: All in one. Records indexed on a public use terminal back to 07/1935. Office will perform a UCC search but public must search other records themselves. Search fee-$38.00 for UCC only. Copy fee $.05 per page. 18x24" Plat copy fee $.30 per page. Cert fee- $5.00 1st page, $2.00 each add'l plus copy fee. Payee- Ashe County Register of Deeds. **Online access to Real Estate, Grantor/Grantee, Deed records:** Access to the register of deeds real estate data is free at www.ashencrod.org/Opening.asp. Full index goes back to 1/1995; images to 1/1934. **Other phones:** Treasurer- 336-219-2560; Elections- 336-219-2570; Vital Records- 336-219-2540. **Property tax/Assessing**- 150 Government Circle, #2200, Jefferson, NC 28640; 336-219-2554, assessor fax-336-219-2564. (Appraiser/Auditor- 336-219-2554) www.ashecountygov.com/TaxAdmin/index.htm **Online access**- Access to records on the county Tax Parcel Information System is free at http://ashegis.ashecountygov.com/webgis/.

Avery County

Register of Deeds, PO Box 87, Newland, NC 28657. 828-733-8260; fax-828-733-8261; 8AM-4:30PM www.averydeeds.com/

No tax liens filed here. Index: All in one. Records indexed on a public use terminal back to 1995. Office will perform a UCC search but public must search other records themselves. Search fee $38.00. Office will perform a limited search of real estate records. Copy fee $1.00 per page.Real estate record copy- $.25 per page. Cert fee- $5.00 per cert plus $2.00 each add'l, includes copy fee. Payee- Avery County Register of Deeds. **Online access to Real Estate, Grantor/Grantee, Deed records:** Search the recorders database free at www.averyrod.com/view/disclaimer.html. **Other phones:** Elections-828-733-8282. **Property tax/Assessing**- PO Box 305, 200 Montezuma St, Newland, NC 28657; 828-733-8214, assessor fax- 828-733-8216. www.averycountync.gov/taxAssessor.htm **Online access**- Access to property data is free on the GIS mapping site at http://arcims.webgis.net/nc/avery/. To name search click Quick Search.

Beaufort County

Register of Deeds, PO Box 514, Washington, NC 27889. Recording, R/E & UCC phone-252-946-2323; 8:30AM-5PM

No tax liens filed here. Records indexed on a public use terminal back to 1995. Only the public may search. Copy fee $1.00 per page.Real estate record copy- $.25 per page. Cert fee- $5.00 1st page; $2.00 each add'l page plus copy fee. Payee- Beaufort County Register of Deeds. **Other phones:** Vital Records- 252-946-2323. **Property tax/Assessing**- 220 N Market St, Washington, NC 27889; 252-946-7981, assessor fax- 252-946-7981.

Bertie County

Register of Deeds, PO Box 340, Windsor, NC 27983. 252-794-5309; fax-252-794-5374; 8:30AM-5PM www.co.bertie.nc.us/Directory/departments/rod/rod.html

No tax liens filed here. Index: Separate indices to search. Records indexed on a public use terminal back to 1983. Office will perform a UCC search but public must search other records themselves. Real estate record copy fee $.20 per page. UCC record copy fee

$1.00 per page. Cert fee- $5.00 1st page, $2.00 each add'l page. Payee- Register of Deeds. **Online access to Real Estate, Deed, Lien records:** Access real property data back to 10/2001 free at http://bertie.gsaweb.com/web1.html . **Other phones:** Elections- 252-794-5306; Vital Records- 252-794-5309. **Property tax/Assessing-** PO Box 527, Windsor, NC 27983; 252-794-5310, assessor fax-252-794-5357. www.co.bertie.nc.us/Directory/departments/tax/tax.html **Online access-** Access property records through gis-mapping system free at www.co.bertie.nc.us/website/bertiegisweb/viewer.htm

Bladen County

Register of Deeds, PO Box 247, Elizabethtown, NC 28337. phone-910-862-6710; fax-910-862-6714; 8:30AM-5PM www.bladeninfo.org

No tax liens filed here. Index: All in one. Records indexed on a public use terminal from 1988-present. Only the public may search. Copy fee $.25 per page. Cert fee- $5.00 1st page; $2.00 each add'l page includes copy fee. Payee- Register of Deeds. **Online access to Real Estate, Grantor/Grantee, Deed, Lien, Mortgage records:** Access unofficial register of deeds site at www.withersravenel.com/deeds/; search comprehensive index or direct images. **Other phones:** Elections- 910-862-6951; Vital Records-910-862-6710. **Property tax/Assessing-** 910-862-6748. **Online** - Search GIS-mapping site for property info free at http://bladenrod.withersravenel.com/. Login as Guest and leave password blank.

Brunswick County

Register of Deeds, PO Box 87, Bolivia, NC 28422-0087. 877-625-9310, 910-253-2690, R/E recording phone-910-253-4371; fax-910-253-2703; 8:30AM-4:45PM http://rod.brunsco.net

No tax liens filed here. Index: All in one. Records indexed on a public use terminal back to 1953. Only the public may search. Copy fee $.25 per page. Mail request must include copy fee plus SASE. Cert fee- $5.00 1st page, $2.00 each add'l page. Payee-Register. **Online access to Real Estate, Deed, Mortgage records:** Access to the recorder database is free at http://rod.brunsco.net. Free registration, logon and password are required. Records are updated on the 10th, 20th, and 30th of the month. **Other phones:** Treasurer- 910-253-4331. **Property tax/Assessing-** 910-253-2829. **Online access-** Search the tax admin data for free at www.brunsconctax.org/.

Buncombe County

Register of Deeds, 60 Court Plaza, Rm 110, Asheville, NC 28801-3563. 828-250-4300, R/E recording phone-828-250-4302; fax-828-250-4338; 8AM-5PM www.buncombecounty.org

No tax liens filed here. Index: All in one. Records indexed on a public use terminal back to 1924. Office will perform a UCC search but public must search other records themselves. Search fee-$38.00 per name. Copy fee $.25 per page. Cert fee- $5.00 for 1st page, $2.00 each add'l, plus copy fee. Payee- Register of Deeds. **Online access to Real Estate, Deed, Mortgage, Fictitious Name records:** Access to county Register of Deeds records is free at http://registerofdeeds.buncombecounty.org/resolution/login.asp. Free registration is required; includes marriages, deaths, fictitious names, deeds. **Other phones:** Elections- 828-250-4200; Vital Records-828-250-4301. **Property tax/Assessing-** 60 Court Plazm, Rm 315, Asheville, NC 28801; 828-250-4940. (Appraiser/ - 828-250-4900) **Online access-** assessor tax records are free at www.buncombetax.org/Default.aspx. Also, GIS property search available at www.buncombecounty.org/governing/depts/GIS/disclaimer.htm. Also, search tax property sales free at www.buncombecounty.org/governing/citizens/prop4Sale.htm.

Burke County

Register of Deeds, PO Box 219, Morganton, NC 28680. Recording, R/E phone-828-438-5450, UCC recording phone-828-438-5456; fax-828-438-5463; 8AM-5PM http://co.burke.nc.us/departments/register-of-deeds/

No tax liens filed here. Index: Separate indices to search include computer and books. Records indexed on a public use terminal back to 1988. Only the public may search. Office will search limited real estate records. Office will not search UCC records. Copy fee $.15 per page. Cert fee- $5.00 per page plus $2.00 each add'l copy. Payee- Burke County Register of Deeds. **Online access to Grantor/Grantee, Real Estate, Marriage, Birth, Death, Assumed Names records:** Access to public records for free go to http://rod.co.burke.nc.us/ . **Other phones:** Treasurer-828-438-5446; Elections- 828-433-1703; Vital Records- 828-438-5453; Liens/Judgments- 828-432-2804. **Property tax/Assessing-** 110 N Green St, PO Box 219, Morganton, NC 28680; 828-438-5400, assessor fax- 828-438-5445. (Appraiser/Auditor- 828-438-5403) http://co.burke.nc.us/departments/tax-administration/ **Online access-** Access to property data is free on the GIS mapping site at http://arcims.webgis.net/nc/Burke/default.asp. Name search - click on Quick Search.

Cabarrus County

Register of Deeds, PO Box 707, Concord, NC 28025. 704-920-2112; fax-704-920-2898; 8AM-5PM www.cabarrusncrod.org/Opening.asp

No tax liens filed here. Index: All in one. Records indexed on a public use terminal back to 1983. Office will perform a UCC search but public must search other records themselves. Search fee-$38.00 for UCC only. Copy fee $.25 per page. Cert fee- $5.00 1st page, $2.00 each add'l page, includes copies. Payee-Register of Deeds. **Online access to Real Estate, Grantor/Grantee, Deed, Lien, UCC records:** Access to the recorder records is free at www.cabarrusncrod.org/Opening.asp by two methods: full system or image-only system. Land records go back to 1983; images to 1983. **Property tax/Assessing-** PO Box 707, 65 Church St SE, Concord, NC 28026; 704-920-2166, fax- 704-920-2250 www.cabarruscounty.us/taxpropertydeeds.html **Online** - Search tax appraisal cards by name free at http://onlineservices.cabarruscounty.us/Tax/TaxAppraisalCard/. Also, search tax bill scroll for free at www.co.cabarrus.nc.us/Tax/scrollsearch.html. Also, search land records of all kinds including GIS free on the ClaRIS system at www.co.cabarrus.nc.us/ClarisPC/Main.aspx.

Caldwell County

Register of Deeds, 905 West Ave NW; County Office Bldg, Lenoir, NC 28645. 828-757-1310, R/E recording phone-828-757-1311; fax-828-757-1294; 8AM-5PM. www.caldwellrod.org/

No tax liens filed here. Index: All in one. Records indexed on computer back to 1971. Scanned copy of older index books also online. Office will perform a UCC search but public must search other records themselves. Search fee-$38 per name, $2.00 per page for copy. Copy fee $1.00 per page. Cert fee- $5.00 1st page, $2.00 each add'l page includes copy fee. Payee-Register of Deeds. **Online access to Real Estate, Deed, Birth, Death, Marriage, Notary, Business Name records:** Access register of deeds recording data with images back to 1930 free at http://rod.co.caldwell.nc.us/resolution/. Choose advanced or simple search; online registration is required. **Other phones:** Vital Records- 828-757-1310. **Property tax/Assessing-** 828-757-1418. **Online access-** Property data is available free on the GIS map server site at http://maps.co.caldwell.nc.us. Click on "Start Spatial-data Explorer" then find query field at bottom of next page.

Camden County

Register of Deeds, PO Box 190, Camden, NC 27921. 252-338-1919; 8AM-5PM

No tax liens filed here. Index: All in one. Records indexed on a public use terminal back to 1998. Only the public may search. Copy fee $1.00 per page if mailed; standard fee- $.15 per page, $.35 for oversized. Cert fee- $5.00 per cert. Payee- Camden County Register of Deeds. **Online Real Estate, Grantor/Grantee, Deed, Lien, Mortgage records:** After registration and fee agreement, you may access recorders data at www.camdenrod.com/nfees.htm. **Other phones:** Treasurer- 252-338-1919; Elections-252-338-5530. **Property tax/Assessing-** PO Box 125, 117 North NC343, Camden, NC 27921; 252-338-1919, fax- 252-333-1603. (Appraiser - 252-338-1919) www.camdencountync.gov/government/taxdept.htm **Online access-** Search property records on the gis-mapping system free at www.camdencountync.gov/services/GIS.htm.

Carteret County

Register of Deeds, 302 Courthouse Sq, Beaufort, NC 28516-1898. Recording, R/E & UCC phone-252-728-8474; fax-252-728-7693; 8AM-5PM www.carteretcountygov.org/departments/register_deeds.asp

No tax liens filed here. Index: All in one. Records indexed on a public use terminal back to 1903. Grantor back to 1904/grantee back to 1976. Office will perform a UCC search (only by correct UCC request form), but public must search other records themselves. Copy fee set according to date of document, $.10,$.35 and $1.00 per page. Cert fee-$5.00 add'l $2.00 per page includes copy fee. Payee-Carteret County Register of Deeds. **Online Real Estate, Grantor/Grantee, Deed, Lien, Assumed Name records:** Access to Register of Deeds database for free at www.carteretcountygov.org/index.asp. These records are book 641 to present. **Other phones:** Vital Records- 252-728-8474. **Property tax/Assessing-** Tax Office, County Admin. Building 252-728-8490. www.carteretcountygov.org/departments/tax_office.asp **Online access-** Search tax parcel cards free at http://tax.carteretcountygov.org.

Caswell County

Register of Deeds, PO Box 98, Yanceyville, NC 27379. 336-694-4197; fax-336-694-7848; 8AM-5PM www.caswellrod.net/

Index: All in one. Records indexed on computer back to 1942. Only the public may search. Copy fee $1.00 per page.Real estate record copy- $.50 per page. Cert fee- $5.00 1st pg, $2.00 each add'l plus copy fee. Payee- Caswell County Register of Deeds. **Online access to Real Estate, Grantor/Grantee, Deed records:** Search recorded deeds at www.caswellrod.net/ and click Search Online. Images are shown. **Property tax/Assessing-** PO Box 204, Yanceyville, NC 27379; 336-694-4194, assessor fax-336-694-1405. www.caswellcountync.gov/county/depts/taxoffice.htm **Online access-** Access to property data is free on the GIS mapping site at http://arcims.webgis.net/nc/caswell/. To name search click on Quick Search.

Catawba County

Register of Deeds, PO Box 65, Newton, NC 28658-0065. 828-465-1573; fax-828-465-1911; 8AM-5PM www.catawbacountync.gov

No tax liens filed here. Index: All in one. Records indexed on a public use terminal back to 1984, images 1960. Office will perform a UCC search but public must search other records themselves. Copy fee $.50 per page; self serve $.25. Cert fee- $5.00 1st page, $2.00 each add'l page. Payee- Catawba County Register of Deeds. **Online access to Real Estate, Grantor/Grantee, Deed, Mortgage records:** Also, search Register of Deeds records free at www.catawbarod.org/Opening.asp. Land index goes back to 1984; images to 1/1/1960. **Other phones:** Elections- 828-464-2424. **Property tax/Assessing-** 828-465-8421. **Online access-** Search the Catawba County GIS Map Server database free at www.gis.catawba.nc.us/website/Parcel/parcel_main.asp. Search property tax bill data free at http://taxbill.catawbacountync.gov/ptsweb/main/billing/default.aspx. Also, access real estate reports at www.gis.catawba.nc.us/nomap/parcel_search.asp.

Chatham County

Register of Deeds, PO Box 756, Pittsboro, NC 27312. Recording, R/E & UCC phone-919-542-8235; 8AM-4:30PM www.chathamncrod.org/Opening.asp
No tax liens filed here. Index: Separate indices to search include grantor/grantee, index books. Records indexed on a public use terminal back to 1771. Office will perform a UCC search but public must search other records themselves. Search fee-$38.00 for UCC only. Office will not search real estate records. Will search UCC records. Copy fee $.25 per page, $1.00 per plat. Cert fee- $5.00 1st pg, $2.00 each add'l includes copy fee. Payee- Chatham County Register of Deeds. **Online access to Real Estate, Deed, Mortgage, UCC records:** Access land records free at www.chathamncrod.org/Opening.asp. Land Record Index Data back to 1771; UCC data goes back to 2008. **Other phones:** Treasurer- 919-542-8210; Elections- 919-542-8206; Vital Records- 919-542-8235; County Manager- 919-542-8200. **Property tax/Assessing**- PO Box 908, 12 East St, Pittsboro, NC 27312; 919-542-8250, assessor fax- 919-542-2963. (Appraiser/Auditor- 919-542-8287) hours- 8AM-5PM www.chathamnc.org/Index.aspx?page=133 **Online access**- Access property data and tax records free at http://ustaxdata.com/nc/chatham/Search.cfm.

Cherokee County

Register of Deeds, 53 Peachtree St, Murphy, NC 28906. 828-837-2613; fax-828-837-8414; 8AM-5PM www.cherokeencrod.org/
No tax liens filed here. Index: All in one. Records indexed on a public use terminal back to 1993. Only the public may search. Copy fee $.10 per page. Cert fee- $5.00 1st page, $2.00 each add'l page includes copy fee. Payee- Registrar. **Online access to Real Estate, Deed, Lien records:** Access to land records and imaging for free go to www.cherokeencrod.org/. Images go back to 07/1999, index back to 1993. **Other phones:** Elections- 828-837-6670. **Property tax/Assessing**- 75 Peachtree St, #108, Murphy, NC 28906; 828-837-6626, fax- 828-835-9228. www.cherokeecounty-nc.gov/departments/tax_assessor/ **Online** - Access to property data is free on the GIS mapping site at http://65.14.20.19/viewer.htm. Click on TaxWeb Online.

Chowan County

Register of Deeds, PO Box 487, Edenton, NC 27932-0487. 252-482-2619; fax-252-482-3062; 8AM-5PM www.chowancounty-nc.gov
No tax liens filed here. Index: All in one. Records indexed on a public use terminal back to 7/1/87. Only the public may search. Copy fee $.25 per page; $.50 if mailed. Cert fee- $5.00 1st pg, $2.00 each add'l, includes copy fee. Payee- Chowan County Register of Deeds. Bulk data available for purchase, contact IT Dept at 252-482-8257. **Online access to Real Estate, Deed records:** Access county property data free at http://208.27.112.94/paas/. You may also build customized data downloads. **Other phones:** Elections- 252-482-4010; Vital Records- 252-482-2619; Collections- 252-482-8486. **Property tax/Assessing**- PO Box 1030, 113 E King St, Edenton, NC 27932; 252-482-8487, assessor fax- 252-482-1528. www.chowancounty-nc.gov/index.asp? **Online access**- Access property tax records free at http://208.27.112.94/paas/. Double click on Parcels. Search property data on the GIS-mapping site free at http://www2.undersys.com/choweb/chowan.html and click on Property Search.

Clay County

Register of Deeds, PO Box 118, Hayesville, NC 28904. 828-389-0087; fax-828-389-1261; 8AM-5PM
No tax liens filed here. Index: All in one. Records indexed on a public use terminal back to 1995. Only the public may search. Copy fee $1.00 per page.Real estate record copy- $.25 per page. Cert fee- $5.00 1st pg, $2.00 each add'l includes copy fee. Payee- Clay County Register of Deeds. **Online access to Real Estate, Deed records:** Access to property and deeds indexes and images is via a private company at www.titlesearcher.com. Fee/registration required. Deeds go back to 1/1999; indices back to 1/1/94; images to 8/22/2003. **Property tax/Assessing**- Courthouse, Hayesville, NC 28904; 828-389-1266, assessor fax- 828-389-4070.

Cleveland County

Register of Deeds, PO Box 1210, Shelby, NC 28151-1210. 704-484-4834; fax-704-484-4909; 8AM-5PM www.clevelandrod.com
No tax liens filed here. Index: All in one. Records indexed on a public use terminal back to 1995. Only the public may search. Will not search UCC records. Copy fee minimum $1.00 per page (if by mail), $.10 per page from books, $.25 per page from microfilm. Cert fee- $5.00 per page, $2.00 each add'l. Payee- Cleveland County Register of Deeds. Bulk data available for purchase, contact Keith Parker-Lowe at Parker Lowe & Associates- keith@parker-lowe.net. **Online access to Real Estate, Grantor/Grantee, Deed records:** Access to register of deeds grantor/grantee index and property data is free at www.clevelandrod.com/view/disclaimer.html. **Other phones:** Treasurer- 704-484-4807; Elections- 704-484-4959; Vitals- 704-484-4834. **Property tax/Assessing**- PO Box 370, 311 E Marion St, Shelby, NC 28151-0370; 704-484-4847, fax- 704-484-4910. www.clevelandcounty.com/nav/county_departments.htm **Online access**- Access property records free on the GIS-mapping site at http://quicksearch.webgis.net/search.php?site=nc_cleveland_co.

Columbus County

Register of Deeds, PO Box 1086, Whiteville, NC 28472-1086. 910-640-6625; fax-910-640-2547; 8:30AM-5PM
No tax liens filed here. Index: Separate indices. Records indexed on a public use terminal back to 1995. Only the public may search. Copy fee $.25 per page. Cert fee- $5.00 per cert includes copy fee. Payee- Columbus County Register of Deeds. Bulk data available for purchase. **Online access to Real Estate, Deed, Assumed Name, Corporation, UCC records:** Access to the Recorder's database is free at www.columbusdeeds.com/ . **Property tax/Assessing**- PO Box 1468, 125A Washington St, Courthouse, Whiteville, NC 28472-1486; 910-640-6635, assessor fax- 910-640-3305. **Online** - Access property tax data free at http://webtax.columbusco.org/viewer.htm.

Craven County

Register of Deeds, 226 Pollock St, New Bern, NC 28560. 252-636-6617; fax-252-636-1937; 8AM-5PM www.co.craven.nc.us/departments/reg.cfm
No tax liens filed here. Index: All in one. Records indexed on a public use terminal back to 1995. Only the public may search. Copy fee $1.00 per page.Real estate record copy- $.25 per page. Cert fee- $5.00 per doc plus copy fee. Payee- Register of Deeds. **Online Real Estate, Grantor/Grantee, Deed, Boat, Birth, Death, Marriage, UCC, Corporation records:** Access to deeds on the county Public Inquiry System is free at http://deeds.cravencounty.com/resolution/ with many other databases available. Or, search register of deeds data free at www.co.craven.nc.us/departments/reg/regwwwdisclaimer.cfm. Real estate 1995-present; Corporations 2002-3/2007; Births/Deaths 1914-2007; UCCs 1999-2001; older real estate 1984-1994; marriages 1964-present. **Other phones:** Treasurer- 252-636-6603; Elections- 252-636-6610; Vital Records- 252-636-6617. **Property tax/Assessing**- PO Box 1128, 226 Pollock St, New Bern, NC 28560; 252-636-6604, assessor fax- 252-636-2569. (Appraiser/Auditor- 252-636-6640) www.co.craven.nc.us/departments/tax.cfm **Online** - Access to assessor and property data is free at http://gismaps.cravencounty.com/maps/map.asp. Access the tax database including foreclosures, mobiles, boats, parcel, appraisal and also deeds free at http://as400.cravencounty.com/

Cumberland County

Register of Deeds, PO Box 2039, Fayetteville, NC 28302-2039. 910-678-7775, R/E recording phone-910-678-7783, UCC recording phone-910-678-7718; fax-910-323-1456; 8AM-5PM www.ccrod.org
No tax liens filed here. Index: All in one. Records indexed on computer back to 1978. Only the public may search. Copy fee $.25 per page. Cert fee- $5.00 1st pg, $2.00 each add'l, includes copy fee. Payee- Cumberland County Register of Deeds. **Online access to Real Estate, Deed, UCC records:** Search two systems free at www.ccrodinternet.org. The land records index and images go back to 1978; images go back to 1/21/1972; UCCs are from 1995 to 6/29/2001. **Other phones:** Elections- 910-678-7733; Vital Records- 910-678-7767. **Property tax/Assessing**- 117 Dick St, Rm 530, PO Box 449, Fayetteville, NC 28302; 910-678-7507, assessor fax- 910-678-7582. (Appraiser - 910-678-7507) www.co.cumberland.nc.us/tax.asp **Online access**- Assessor real estate search is free at http://mainfr.co.cumberland.nc.us/. Also, search property data free on the GIS mapping site at http://152.31.99.8/. Click Search on the Parcel Viewer.

Currituck County

Register of Deeds, PO Box 71, Currituck, NC 27929. 252-232-3297; fax-252-232-3906; 8AM-5PM www.co.currituck.nc.us/Register-of-Deeds.cfm
No tax liens filed here. Index: Separate indices to search include computer, vital records books. Records indexed on computer back to 8/77. Office will perform a UCC search on records filed before 7/30/01, but public must search other records themselves. Search fee-$38.00 for UCC only. Copy fee $1.00 per page.Real estate record copy- $.25 per page. $1.00 per page to mail. Cert fee- $5.00 per cert, $2.00 per page, includes copy fee. Payee- Currituck County Register of Deeds. **Online access to Real Estate, Deed, Notary records:** Access to land recorded documents and notaries is free at https://currituckeoc.com/resolution/. **Property tax/Assessing**- PO Box 9, Currituck, NC 27929; 252-232-3005. **Online access**- Search property, sales, assessor data and more free at www.co.currituck.nc.us/Tax.cfm. Also, name search for parcel ownership data free on the GIS-mapping site at www.co.currituck.nc.us/Interactive-Online-MappingDup2.cfm.

Dare County

Register of Deeds, PO Box 70, Manteo, NC 27954. Recording, R/E & UCC phone-252-475-5970; 8:30AM-5PM www.co.dare.nc.us
No tax liens filed here. Index: All in one. Records indexed on a public use terminal back to 1976. Office personnel or visitors may perform searches. Search fee-$38.00 for UCC only. Office will not search real estate records. Office will search UCC records prior to 7/2001 and current fixture (land) files. Copy fee $.25 per page, map copies $2.00. Cert fee- $5.00 per cert plus copy fee. Payee- Dare County Register of Deeds. **Online Real Estate, Grantor/Grantee, Deed, Marriage, UCC records:** Recording office records free at http://eagleweb.darenc.com/recorder/eagleweb/docSearch.jsp. Real estate from 1976 forward, UCC from 1989 forward, and marriage from 1990 forward. Additionally, tax files can be downloaded from this site. Also, a land transfer search is free at www.darenc.com/public/LT/LTsearch.asp. **Other phones:** Treasurer- 252-475-5930; Elections- 252-475-5630; Vital Records- 252-475-5970. **Property tax/Assessing**- PO Box 1000, Manteo, NC 27954; 252-475-5952, assessor fax- 252-475-5949. (Appraiser/Auditor- 252-475-5940) Tax files may be downloaded at www.darenc.com/public/Tax_Files.htm. **Online access**- County assessor records free at www.co.dare.nc.us/public/TaxInquiry.htm. Search property data on the GIS-mapping site free at www.darenc.com/public/gis.htm but no name searching.

Davidson County

Register of Deeds, PO Box 464, Lexington, NC 27293-0464. 336-242-2150; fax-336-238-2318; 8AM-5PM. www.co.davidson.nc.us/
No tax liens filed here. Index: All in one. Records indexed on a public use terminal back to 1990. Only the public may search. Copy fee $1.00 per page. Cert fee- $5.00 per doc includes copy fee. Payee- Register of deeds. **Online access to Real Estate, Deed, Lien, Mortgage, Judgment, UCC, Assumed Name records:** Access recorders database free at http://davidsoncorod.org/. Registration for full subscription data also available. **Other phones:** Vital Records- 336-242-2150. **Other Online Records-** Records on the county Tax Dept database are free at www.co.davidson.nc.us/taxnet/. Search for property info on the GIS mapping site for free at http://arcims2.webgis.net/davidson/default.asp. To name search click on Quick Search.

Davie County

Register of Deeds, 123 S Main St, Mocksville, NC 27028. 336-751-2513, R/E recording phone-336-634-2513; 8:30AM-5PM www.co.davie.nc.us
No tax liens filed here. Index: All in one. Records indexed on a public use terminal back to 1993. Only the public may search. Copy fee $.25 per page. Cert fee- $5.00 1st pg, $2.00 each add'l. Payee- Davie County Register of Deeds. Bulk data available for purchase. **Property tax/Assessing-** 123 S Main St, Mocksville, NC 27028; 336-634-3416, assessor fax-336-751-0154. (Appraiser - 336-753-6120) hours- 8AM-5PM www.co.davie.nc.us/Departments/Tax%20Administration/taxadmin.htm **Online access-** Access to county property data on the GIS-mapping site is free at http://maps.co.davie.nc.us/website/mapviewer/GISviewerhome.htm.

Duplin County

Register of Deeds, PO Box 970, Kenansville, NC 28349. 910-296-2108; fax-910-296-2344; 8AM-5PM http://rod.duplincounty.org
No tax liens filed here. Index: All in one. Records indexed on a public use terminal back to 1982. Only the public may search. Copy fee $.70 1st page; $.25 each add'l page; self serve- $.25 each. Cert fee- $5.00 1st page; $2.00 each add'l page, includes copy fee. Payee- Register of Deeds. **Online access to Real Property, Deed, Mortgage, Marriage, Death, Notary, Military Discharge, GIS-mapping records:** Access to the Register's multiple databases is free at http://rod.duplincounty.org. Vital stats and discharges are index only. **Other phones:** Treasurer- 910-296-2104; Elections- 910-296-2170; Vital Records- 910-296-2108; Tax Collector- 910-296-2112. **Property tax/Assessing-** 118 Duplin St, Courthouse Annex, Rm 112, PO Box 968, Kenansville, NC 28349; 910-296-2110, assessor fax-910-296-2331. (Appraiser/Auditor- 910-296-2110) http://duplincountync.com/governmentOffices/taxOffice.html **Online access-** Access assessment data on real estate and personal property free at http://duplintax.duplincounty.org/

Durham County

Register of Deeds, PO Box 1107, Durham, NC 27702. 919-560-0480; fax-919-560-0497; 8:30AM-5PM. www.durhamcountync.gov/index.html
No tax liens filed here. Index: Separate indices to search since 1991, before 1991 corp docs separate file. Records indexed on a public use terminal back to 1962. Only the public may search. Copy fee $1.00 per page; from computer $.10. Cert fee- $5.00 1st page, $2.00 per add'l page includes copy fee. Payee- Register of Deeds. **Online Real Estate, Deed, Judgment, Voter Registration records:** Access the Register of Deeds database free at http://rodweb.co.durham.nc.us/. Also, search voter registration free at www.durhamcountync.gov/departments/elec/votersearch/index.cfm. **Other phones:** Elections- 919-560-0700; Vital Records- 919-560-0493 (births/deaths); Vital Records (Marriages) -919-560-0480. **Property tax/Assessing-** 200 E Main St, PO Box 3397, Durham, 27702; 919-560-0300, fax-919-560-0350. www.durhamcountync.gov/departments/txad/ **Online access-** Search property records and tax bills free at www.durhamcountync.gov/departments/txad/Tax_Record_Searches.html. Search property records from the GIS mapping site free at http://gisweb2.ci.durham.nc.us/sdx/imap_launch.html. Click on "Go Maps" to search.

Edgecombe County

Register of Deeds, PO Box 386, Tarboro, NC 27886. 252-641-7924; fax-252-641-1771; 7:30AM-5PM www.edgecombecountync.gov
No tax liens filed here. Index: All in one. Records indexed on computer back to 9/73. Office will perform a UCC search but public must search other records themselves. Search fee-$38.00 for UCC only. Office will not search real estate records. Copy fee $.10 per page.Real estate record copy- $1.00 2st page; $.10 each add'l page, more if to be mailed. Cert fee- $5.00 1st page; $2.00 each add'l page plus copy fee. Payee- Register of Deeds. **Online access to Real Estate, Deed, Lien, UCC records:** Access the recorder's database free at http://71.0.29.40/resolution/. RE index goes back to 1973, financing statements 1993 to 2005. Also, click on Deeds at http://206.107.103.195/paas/default.htm. **Other phones:** Treasurer- 252-641-7810; Elections- 252-641-7854; Vital Records- 252-641-7924. **Property tax/Assessing-** 201 St. Andrew St, PO Box 10, Tarboro, NC 27886; 252-641-7855, assessor fax-252-641-7864. (Appraiser/Auditor- 252-641-7860) hours- 8AM-5PM http://206.107.103.195/taxdepts/ **Online access-** Access to county property data is free at http://206.107.103.195/paas/default.htm. Access property data on the GIS-mapping site free at http://www2.undersys.com/edgecweb/edgecombe.html and click on Property Search.

Forsyth County

Register of Deeds, 201 N Chestnut St, 2nd Fl; County Gov't Ctr, Winston-Salem, NC 27101. 336-703-2700, info-336-703-2701, R/E recording phone-336-703-2700; fax-336-727-2341; hours- 8AM-5PM. www.co.forsyth.nc.us/ROD/
No tax liens filed here. Index: All in one. Records indexed on a public use terminal back to 1849. Office will perform a UCC search but public must search other records themselves. Copy fee $1.00 per page by mail or fax, $.35 per page in house. Cert fee- $5.00 for 1st page, $2.00 each add'l. Payee- Forsyth County Register of Deeds. Download maps and GIS data free for City of Winston-Salem. **Online access to Real Estate, Deed, Lien, Voter Registration records:** Access to property and deeds indexes and images is via a private company at www.titlesearcher.com. Fee/registration required; monthly and per day access available. Deeds and indices go back to 1849; images to 1973. Search voter registration records free at www.sboe.state.nc.us/votersearch/seimsvot.htm. **Other phones:** Treasurer- 336-727-2655; Vital Records- 336-703-2701; Tax Collector- 336-703-2300. **Property tax/Assessing-** PO Box 757, Winston-Salem, NC 27102; 336-703-2300, assessor fax- 336-727-2369. **Online access-** Access assessor records on Geo-Data free- www.co.forsyth.nc.us/Tax/geodata.aspx. Click "Launch Geo-Data Explorer." Also, search tax bills free at www.co.forsyth.nc.us/Tax/taxbilllookup/regular.aspx Tax Admin tax bill svc free at. www.co.forsyth.nc.us/tax/taxbill.aspx. View tax sale and auction lists at www.forsyth.cc/Tax/fcl_info.aspx. Also, assessment data for City of Winston-Salem available free at www.cwsonline.org/assessments/.

Franklin County

Register of Deeds, PO Box 545, Louisburg, NC 27549-0545. 919-496-3500; fax-919-496-1457; 8AM-5PM. www.co.franklin.nc.us
No tax liens filed here. Index: All in one. Records indexed on a public use terminal back to 1/1/79. Only the public may search. Copy fee $1.00 per page.Real estate record copy- $.25 per page. Cert fee- $2.00 per notary plus copy fee. Payee- Franklin County Register of Deeds. Office does not sell bulk data, but GIS-mapping dept does. **Online access to Real Estate, Grantor/Grantee, Deed, Line, UCC records:** Access to recording records index free at http://deeds.co.franklin.nc.us/resolution/. Real estate back to 1995, UCCs 1990 to 6/30/2001, Pre-1995 maps. Fee for deeper data. **Other phones:** Elections- 919-496-3710. **Property tax/Assessing-** 919-496-1497. **Online access-** Access to tax data on the county spatial data explorer database is free at www.co.franklin.nc.us/ROK/mapviewer/viewer.htm or at parcel search page at http://maps.roktech.net/Franklin/map/Index.cfm.

Gaston County

Register of Deeds, PO Box 1578, Gastonia, NC 28053. 704-862-7681; fax-704-862-7519; 8:30AM-5PM www.co.gaston.nc.us/registerofdeeds/
No tax liens filed here. Index: Separate indices to search include Corporations, Ordinances, and Vital Records. Records indexed on a public use terminal back to 1960 real estate. Only the public may search. Copy fee $.25 per page; large plats are $2.00. Cert fee- $5.00 for 1st pg., $2.00 each add'l pg, includes copy fee. Payee- Gaston County Register of Deeds. Bulk data available for purchase. **Online access to Real Estate, Deed, Lien, Corporation, Assumed Name, UCC records:** Access to recorded documents is free at http://207.235.60.108/resolution/ - registration and username are required. **Other phones:** Treasurer- 704-866-3034; Vital Records- 704-862-7687; Deed Room- 704-862-7683. **Property tax/Assessing-** PO Box 1578, 128 W Main Ave, Gastonia, NC 28053; 704-810-5851, assessor fax-704-866-3103. (Appraiser/Auditor- 704-810-5809) www.co.gaston.nc.us/TaxDept/index.HTM **Online access-** Access property data and tax records free at http://egov1.co.gaston.nc.us/website/ParcelDataSite/WelcomePage.html. Click on Search.

Gates County

Register of Deeds, PO Box 471, Gatesville, NC 27938-0471. 252-357-0850; fax-252-357-1568; 9AM-5PM www.gatesrod.com
No tax liens filed here. Index: All in one. Records indexed on a public use terminal back to 01. Only the public may search. General copy fee $.25 per page. UCC's copy fee- $1.00 per page. Cert fee- $5.00 per doc plus copy fee. **Online access to Real Estate, Grantor/Grantee, Deed records:** Real property records available free to residents at www.gatesrod.com. **Other phones:** Treasurer- 252-357-1240; Elections- 252-357-1780; Vital Records- 252-357-0850; Clerk of Court- 252-357-1365. **Property tax/Assessing-** PO Box 426, Gatesville, NC 27938; 252-357-1360, assessor fax- 252-357-0073. (Appraiser/Auditor- 252-357-1360) Public access terminal available.

Graham County

Register of Deeds, PO Box 406, Robbinsville, NC 28771. 828-479-7971; 8:30AM-5PM. www.grahamcounty.org/grahamcounty_departments_registrar.html
Index: All in one. Record index not computerized. Only the public may search. Copy fee $1.00 per page. Uncertified copies- $.25 per page. Fax fee is $1.00 per page. Cert fee- $5.00 per page plus $2.00 each add'l. Payee- Graham County Register of Deeds. **Online access to Real Estate, Deed, Mortgage records:** Access the consolidated real property database back to 1/1995 free at http://deeds.grahamncrod.com/. Also search pre-1995 real estate 7/1/1978 to 12/31/1994. **Other phones:** Treasurer- 828-479-7962; Elections- 828-479-7969; Vital Records- 828-479-7971. **Property tax/Assessing Dept.-** 828-479-7965. (Appraiser/Auditor- 828-479-7963)

Granville County

Register of Deeds, PO Box 427, Oxford, NC 27565. Recording, R/E. UCC phone-919-693-6314; 8:30-5PM www.granvillecountydeeds.org/resolution/

No tax liens filed here. Index: All in one. Records indexed on a public use terminal back to 1975. Only the public may search. Copy fee $1.00 per page, $.25 each add'l page. Cert fee- $5.00 1st page, $2.00 each add'l page includes copy fee. Payee- Register of Deeds. **Online access to Real Estate, Deed, Lien records:** Access recorders index free at www.granvillecountydeeds.org/resolution/. Registration, username and password required. **Other phones:** Treasurer- 919-603-1301 (Finance); Elections- 919-693-2515; Vital Records- 919-693-6314. **Property tax/Assessing**- 919-693-4181. **Online access**- Access to assessor property data is available for a one-time $250 fee, call Tax Assessor office a 919-693-4181 or visit www.granvillegis.org.

Greene County

Register of Deeds, PO Box 86, Snow Hill, NC 28580. 252-747-3620, R/E recording phone-919-747-3620; 8AM-5PM

No tax liens filed here. Index: All in one. Real estate records indexed back to 1993; other records not computerized. Office will perform a UCC search but public must search other records themselves. Office will not search real estate records. Copy fee $1.00 per page. Cert fee- $5.00 1st pg, $2.00 each add'l, plus copy fee. Payee- Greene County Register of Deeds. **Property tax/Assessing**- 229 Kinggold Blvd, County Complex, PO Box 482, Snow Hill, NC 28580; 252-747-3615, assessor fax- 252-747-5067. Public access terminal in lobby.

Guilford County

Register of Deeds, PO BOX 3427, Greensboro. NC 27402. 336-641-7556, R/E recording -336-845-6935; 8AM-5PM http://gcms0004.co.guilford.nc.us/departments/rod/index.php

No tax liens filed here. Index: All in one. Records indexed on a public use terminal back to 1982. Only the public may search. Copy fee $1.00 per page. Cert fee- $5.00 1st page, $2.00 each add'l plus copy fee. Payee- Guilford County Register of Deeds. **Online Real Estate, Deed, Lien, UCC, Vital Statistic records:** Access to county databases is free at http://gcms0004.co.guilford.nc.us/services/index.php. Vital statistic records after registration and login at http://66.162.203.229/vital/login.php. **Other phones:** Elections- 336-845-3836; Vital Records- 336-845-7931. **Property tax/Assessing**- Tax Department-PO Box 3138, 400 W Market St, Greensboro, NC 27402; 336-641-3362. (Appraiser/Auditor- 336-845-3330) http://gcms0004.co.guilford.nc.us/departments/tax/index.php **Online access**- Search for property data free on the GIS-mapping site at http://gisweb02.co.guilford.nc.us/guilford/default.htm. Also, name search tax data free at www.co.guilford.nc.us/Novation/taxpub.html. Add'l data may be available at www.co.guilford.nc.us/services/index.php.

Halifax County

Register of Deeds, PO Box 67, Halifax, NC 27839-0067. 252-583-2101; fax-252-583-1273; 8:30AM-5PM www.halifaxnc.com

No tax liens filed here. Index: Separate indices to search include real estate, grantor/grantee. Records indexed on a public use terminal back to 1976. Only the public may search. Will not search UCC records. Copy fee $.25 per page. Cert fee- $5.00 1st page, $2.00 each add'l page plus copy fee. Payee- Register of Deeds. **Online access to Real Estate, Deed, Lien, UCC, Map records:** Access to the Register's land records is at http://65.254.204.43/resolution/. Real Estate in two indexes back to 1976; UCCs from 1996 to 8/31/2001; maps are pre-1995. **Other phones:** Treasurer- 252-583-3771; Elections- 252-583-4391; Vital Records- 252-583-2101. **Property tax/Assessing**- PO Box 68, 357 Ferrell Ln, Halifax, NC 27839-0068; 252-583-2121, assessor fax- 252-583-9311. (Appraiser/Auditor- 252-583-2121) www.halifaxnc.com/taxadministration.cfm **Online access**- Search assessor property tax records free at http://gis.halifaxnc.com/Main/Home.aspx.

Harnett County

Register of Deeds, 305 W Cornelius Harnett Blvd, #200, Lillington, NC 27546. Recording, R/E & UCC phone-910-893-7540; fax-910-814-3841; 8AM-5PM http://rod.harnett.org

No tax liens filed here. Index: All in one. Records indexed on a public use terminal back to 1986. Office will perform a UCC search (with a specific date) but public must search other records themselves. Search fee-$38.00 for UCC only. Copy fee $1.00 per page.Real estate record copy- $.10 per page. Cert fee- $5.00 1st pg, $2.00 each add'l. Payee- Harnett County Register of Deeds. **Online access to Real Estate, Grantor/Grantee, Vital Statistic, UCC records:** County real estate and property tax data is free at http://rod.harnett.org. Search Births, Deaths, Marriages, UCCs and official public records. **Other phones:** Treasurer- 910-893-7557; Elections- 910-893-7553; Vital Records- 910-893-7542. **Property tax/Assessing**- 305 W Cornelius Harnett Blvd, #101, Lillington, NC 27546; 910-893-7520, assessor fax- 910-893-3801. www.harnett.org/tax/ **Online access**- Access property tax records free at http://tax.harnett.org/pws10/main/billing/default.aspx.

Haywood County

Register of Deeds, 215 N Main St; Courthouse, Waynesville, NC 28786. Recording, R/E & UCC phone-828-452-6635; fax-828-452-6762; 8AM-5PM http://rodweb.haywoodnc.net/

No tax liens filed here. Index: All in one. Records indexed on a public use terminal back to 1986. Only the public may search. Will not search UCC records. Copy fee $.25 per page. Cert fee- $5.00 per doc includes 1 copy; add copy fee for add'l pgs. Payee- Haywood County Register of Deeds. **Online access to Real Estate, Deed records:** Records on the Register of Deeds database are free at http://haywood.bisonline.com/sites/haywooddeeds.com/deedsearch/disclaimer.php. Real estate records go back to 1986. Also, search for deeds for free at http://rodweb.haywoodnc.net/ . **Other phones:** Vital Records- 828-452-6635. **Property tax/Assessing**- 215 N Main St, Courthouse, Rm 105, Waynesville, NC 28786; 828-452-6640, assessor fax- 828-356-2999. (Appraiser/Auditor- 828-452-6639) **Online access**- Access property tax records and GIS mapping free at http://public.haywoodnc.net/. Also, search for property data on the GIS-mapping site for free at http://maps.haywoodnc.net/.

Henderson County

Register of Deeds, 200 N Grove St, #129, Hendersonville, NC 28792. Recording, R/E & UCC phone-828-697-4901; 9AM-5PM

No tax liens filed here. Index: All in one. Records indexed on a public use terminal back to 1979. Only the public may search. Copy fee $.25 per page, $1.50 per page for Plat copies. Cert fee- $5.00 1st pg, $2.00 add'l. Payee- Henderson County Register of Deeds. **Other phones:** Vital Records- 828-697-4901. **Property tax/Assessing**- 200 N Grove St, #102, Hendersonville, NC 28792; 828-697-4870, assessor fax- 828-697-4578. www.hendersoncountync.org/ca/ **Online access**- Look-up tax bills free at www.hendersoncountync.org/ca/redirect.html. Access the GIS mapping system free at http://hendersoncountync.org/gis/. Also, search property data free at www.hendersoncountync.org/ca/realpropertydata.html.

Hertford County

Register of Deeds, PO Box 36, Winton, NC 27986. 252-358-7850; fax-252-358-7914; 8:30AM-5PM www.co.hertford.nc.us/rod.asp

No tax liens filed here. Index: All in one. Records indexed on a public use terminal back to 1984. Only the public may search. General copy fee $.25 per page. Cert fee- $5.00 per cert plus $2.00 each add'l page. Payee- Register of Deeds. **Online Real Estate, Deed records:** Access recorded land data free at http://216.27.81.171/hertfordnc/disclaimer.asp. **Other phones:** Treasurer- 252-358-7815; Elections- 252-358-7812; Vital Records- 252-358-7850. **Property tax/Assessing**- 704 N King St, Winton, NC 27986; 252-358-7810. www.co.hertford.nc.us/taxa.asp

Hoke County

Register of Deeds, 113 Campus Ave, Raeford, NC 28376. 910-875-2035; fax-910-875-9554; 8AM-5PM. www.hokencrod.org

No tax liens filed here. Index: All in one. Records indexed on computer back to late 1992. Only the public may search. Copy fee $1.00 per page.Real Estate record copy fee- $.25 per page; large maps- $5.00 each. Cert fee- $5.00 includes copy fee. Payee- Hoke County Register of Deeds. **Online access to Real Estate, Deed, Lien records:** Access recorder data for free at www.hokencrod.org/Opening.asp. Land records index goes back to 7/1992; images back to 12/1994. **Other phones:** Elections- 910-875-8751; Vital Records- 910-875-2035. **Property tax/Assessing**- 227 N Main St, PO Box 210, Raeford, NC 28376; 910-875-8751, fax- 910-875-9222. (Appraiser/ - 910-875-8751) www.hokecounty.org/taxoffice.htm **Online access**- Access property data on GIS mapping site free at http://gis.hokecounty.org/connectgis/hoke/welcome.htm.

Hyde County

Register of Deeds, PO Box 294, Swan Quarter, NC 27885. 252-926-4182; fax-252-926-3710; 8AM-5PM www.hyderod.com

No tax liens filed here. Index: Separate indices to search include real estate, vital records. Records indexed on a public use terminal back to 1991. Only the public may search. General copy fee $.10 per page. Will fax back for $2.00 per doc. Cert fee- $5.00 for 1st page, $1.00 each add'l page plus copy fee. Payee- Hyde County Register of Deeds. **Online access to Real Estate, Grantor/Grantee, Deed records:** Access to the Register of Deeds real property records is free at www.hyderod.com/. Non-resident may have to pay a fee. **Other phones:** Treasurer- 252-926-4192; Elections- 252-926-4400; Vital Records- 252-926-4182; Clerk of Court- 252-926-4101. **Property tax/Assessing**- PO Box 279, 30 Oyster Creek Rd, Swan Quarter, NC 27885; 252-926-4186/4187/4188, assessor fax- 252-926-3709. www.hydecounty.org/government/tax.asp

Iredell County

Register of Deeds, PO Box 904, Statesville, NC 28687. 704-872-7468; fax-704-878-3055; 8AM-5PM. www.co.iredell.nc.us

No tax liens filed here. Index: All in one. Records indexed on a public use terminal back to 1964. Office will perform a UCC search but public must search other records themselves. Search fee-$38.00 per name. Office will not search real estate records. Copy fee $1.00 per page. Cert fee- $5.00 1st page, $2.00 each add'l page. Payee- Iredell County Register of Deeds. Indexes available for purchase, contact Kay Matthew, Asst. **Online Real Estate, Deed, Vital Statistic, Pre-2001 UCC records:** Access recorder records at http://rodweb2.co.iredell.nc.us/resolution/. Registration required. **Other phones:** Elections- 704-878-3140. **Property tax/Assessing**- 135 E Water St, Statesville, NC 28687; 704-872-3021. **Online access**- Search property appraisal cards free at www.co.iredell.nc.us/apprcard/. Also, search property data free on the GI-mapping site at www.co.iredell.nc.us/Gismaps.asp. Once on the map page, click on the binoculars to text search.

Jackson County

Register of Deeds, 401 Grindstaff Cove Rd, #108, Sylva, NC 28779. 828-586-7530; fax-828-586-6879; 8AM-5PM. www.jacksonnc.org

No tax liens filed here. Index: Separate indices to search. Records indexed on a public use terminal back to 1991. Office will perform a UCC search but public must search other records themselves. Copy fee $2.00 per doc if mailed; self serve- $.30 per page.Real estate record copy- $3.00 per doc. Cert fee- $5.00 1st page; $2.00 each add'l, includes copy fee. Payee- Register of

Deeds. **Online Real Estate, Deed, UCC records:** Access data at http://deeds.jacksonnc.org/resolution/. Includes 2 real estate indexes back to 10/1991; Plats back to 1969; UCCs from 1992 to 2/2003. **Other phones:** Treasurer- 828-586-7550; Elections- 828-586-7538; Vital Records- 828-568-7530. **Property tax/Assessing**- 401 Grindstaff Cove Rd, #108, Sylva, NC 28779; 828-586-7540. (Appraiser/Auditor- 828-586-7542) gis@jacksonnc.org. www.jacksonnc.org **Online access**- Search assessor and property data free at http://maps.jacksonnc.org/gomaps/map/Index.cfm. This is a new site being tested and data is incomplete. Property cards to be available.

Johnston County

Register of Deeds, PO Box 118, Smithfield, NC 27577. Recording, R/E & UCC phone-919-989-5160; fax-919-989-5728; 8AM-5PM www.johnstonnc.com

No tax liens filed here. Index: All in one. Records indexed on a public use terminal back to 1940. Only the public may search. Copy fee $.10 per page. Cert fee- $5.00 1st pg, $2.00 each add'l. Payee- Johnston County Register of Deeds. **Online access to Real Estate, Deed, UCC records:** Access to Register's indexes is free at http://johnstonnc.com/deedsearch. Land records go back to 1972; UCCs back to 7/1997. **Other phones:** Elections- 919-989-5095; Vital Records- 919-989-5161; Deed Vault- 919-989-5165. **Property tax/Assessing**- PO Box 368, 207 E Johnston St, Smithfield, NC 27577; 919-989-5130, assessor fax- 919-989-5413. www.johnstonnc.com/mainpage.cfm?category_level_id=497 **Online access**- Access property records free at www.johnstonnc.com/mainpage.cfm?category_level_id=497&content_id=1127.

Jones County

Register of Deeds, PO Box 189, Trenton, NC 28585-0189. 252-448-2551; fax-252-448-1357; 8AM-5PM www.jonesrod.com

No tax liens filed here. Index: All in one. Records indexed on a public use terminal back to 1/2001. Only the public may search. UCC copy fee $1.00 per page.Real estate record copy- $.25 per page. Cert fee- $5.00 1st pg, $2.00 each add'l, includes copy fee. Payee- Jones County Register of Deeds. **Online access to Real Estate, Grantor/Grantee, Deed records:** Access recorded documents index at www.jonesrod.com/. Non-resident may have to pay a fee. **Other phones:** Vital Records- 252-448-2551. **Property tax/Assessing**- 252-448-2546.

Lee County

Register of Deeds, PO Box 2040, Sanford, NC 27331-2040. 919-718-4585; fax-919-718-4586; 8AM-5PM. www.leecountync.gov/

No tax liens filed here. Index: All in one. Records indexed on computer back to 1908. Only the public may search. Copy fee $.25 per page; $1.00 per plat page. Cert fee- $5.00 for 1st pg., $2.00 each add'l pg. Payee- Register of Deeds. **Online access to Real Estate, Grantor/Grantee, Deed, Mortgage records:** Access Register of Deeds index and images free at www.leencrod.org/Opening.asp. Land record index goes back to 1985; images to 1908-1984, and all plat images. **Other phones:** Elections- 919-776-0515; Vital Records- 919-718-4585. **Property tax/Assessing**- PO Box 1968, Sanford, NC 27331; 919-718-4600. (Appraiser - 919-718-4661) **Online access**- Access sales data and maps free at www.leecountync.gov/departments/StrategicServices/default.html.

Lenoir County

Register of Deeds, PO Box 3289, Kinston, NC 28502. Recording, R/E & UCC phone-252-559-6420; fax-252-523-6139; 8:30AM-5PM www.co.lenoir.nc.us

No tax liens filed here. Index: All in one. Record index not computerized. Only the public may search. Copy fee $1.00 per page. Cert fee- $5.00 1st page plus copy fee add'l pages. Payee- Register. **Online access to Real Estate, Deed, UCC records:** Access land records index back to 1995 at http://cottweb.co.lenoir.nc.us/resolution/ and financing statements 1976-1995. Older real estate 1976-1994 also available. **Other phones:** Treasurer- 252-527-7174; Vital Records- 252-559-6420. **Property tax/Assessing**- PO Box 3289, 101 N Queen St, Kinston, NC 28502; 252-527-7174, assessor fax- 252-527-4923. www.co.lenoir.nc.us/taxdept.html **Online access**- Access property records free at www.co.lenoir.nc.us/docs/disclaim.htm#. Click on Search.

Lincoln County

Register of Deeds, PO Box 218, Lincolnton, NC 28093-0218. 704-736-8530, R/E recording phone-704-736-8535, UCC phone-704-736-8533; fax-704-732-9049; 8AM-5PM. www.lincolncounty.org

No tax liens filed here. Index: All in one. Records indexed on a public use terminal back to 1993. Only the public may search. Copy fee $1.00 per page; large plats- $2.00. Cert fee- $5.00 per doc plus $2.00 add'l page. Payee- Register of Deeds. **Online access to Real Estate, Deed, Lien, Mapping, UCC, Comparable Sale records:** Access tax, property, and recording data for free at http://207.4.172.207/jw41c5/jwalkhtml2/default.asp. Grantor/Grantee indices go back to 1993. Images go back to Book 186. Search either of the 2 databases There is also a comparable properties search utility. **Other phones:** Treasurer- 704-736-8488; Elections- 704-736-8480; Vital Records- 704-736-8530. **Property tax/Assessing**- PO Box 938, Lincolnton, NC 28093-0218; 704-736-8540. **Online access**- Access to the county GIS Land System is free at http://207.4.172.206/website/lcproperty2/viewer.htm. At the website, under Data Tools, click on Search.

Macon County

Register of Deeds, 5 W Main St, Franklin, NC 28734. 828-349-2095; fax-828-349-2403; 8AM-5PM. www.maconnc.org

No tax liens filed here. Index: All in one. Records indexed on a public use terminal back to 1987. Only the public may search. General copy fee $.25 per page. Cert fee- $5.00 1st page, $2.00 each add'l page plus copy fee. Payee- Register. **Online access to Real Estate, Deed, UCC, Map records:** Access deed images back to book 6 free and selected other recording types free at www.maconncdeeds.com/sites/maconncdeeds/files/deedsearch/. Also, download property and map data free at http://216.119.24.38/website/macgis/download.htm. **Other phones:** Elections- 828-349-2034. **Property tax/Assessing**- 5 W Main St, Annex Bldg, Franklin, NC 28734; 828-349-2181, assessor fax- 828-349-2184. (Appraiser - 828-349-2143) **Online access**- Access property tax records free at http://216.119.24.38/pubaccess/macon.htm. Lookup Land records free at http://216.119.24.38/website/macgis/dbaccess/.

Madison County

Register of Deeds, PO Box 66, Marshall, NC 28753. Recording, R/E & UCC phone-828-649-3131; 8:30AM-5PM www.madisonrod.com

No tax liens filed here. Index: All in one. Records indexed on a public use terminal back to 1995. Office will perform a UCC search but public must search other records themselves. Search fee $30.00. General copy fee $3.00 1st page, $1.00 each add'l.Real estate record copy- $.25 per page. Cert fee- $5.00 1st pg, $2.00 each add'l. Payee- Madison County Register of Deeds. **Online Real Estate, Grantor/Grantee, Deed records:** Access real property records free at www.madisonrod.com/view/disclaimer.html. **Other phones:** Treasurer- 828-649-2521; Elections- 828-649-3731; Vital Records- 828-649-3131. **Property tax/Assessing**- 828-649-3014, assessor fax- 828-649-0615. (Appraiser/Auditor- 828-649-3014)

Martin County

Register of Deeds, PO Box 348, Williamston, NC 27892. Recording, R/E & UCC phone-252-789-4320; fax-252-789-4329; 8AM-5PM.

No tax liens filed here. Index: All in one. Records indexed on a public use terminal back to 1985. Only the public may search. Will not search UCC records. Copy fee $.25 per sheet. Cert fee- $5.00 1st page, $2.00 each add'l page plus copy fee. Payee- Martin County Register of Deeds. **Other phones:** Elections-252-789-4317; Vital Records- 252-789-4320; Collector- 252-789-4360; Finance -252-789-4330. **Property tax/Assessing**- 305 E Main St, PO Box 885, Williamston, NC 27892; 252-789-4350, assessor fax- 252-789-4359.

McDowell County

Register of Deeds, 21 S Main St, Ste A; Courthouse, Marion, NC 28752-3992. 828-652-4727; fax-828-652-1537; 8:30AM-5PM www.mcdowellgov.com

No tax liens filed here. Index: Separate indices to search include plats & highway right of ways, condo maps, real property. Records indexed on a public use terminal back to 1971. Only the public may search. Copy fee $.35 per page, $1.00 if mailed. Cert fee- $14.00 plus add'l $3.00 per page plus copy fee. Certified copies $12.00 first page, $3.00 each add'l page. Payee- McDowell County Register of Deeds. **Online access to Real Estate, Deed, GIS records:** Access to property and deeds indexes and images is via a private company at www.titlesearcher.com. Fee/registration required; see state introduction. Records go back to 1/1971. Also, access GIS data for free at http://gsri.mcdowellcountygis.com/. **Other phones:** Treasurer- 828-652-7121; Elections- 828-652-7121; Vital Records- 828-652-4727. **Property tax/Assessing**- 60 E Court St, Marion, NC 28752; 828-652-7121. hours- 8AM-5PM.

Mecklenburg County

Register of Deeds, 720 E 4th St, #103, Charlotte, NC 28202. 704-336-2443; fax-704-336-7699; 8:30AM-4:30PM http://meckrod.manatron.com/

Index: Separate indices to search include real estate, marriage-birth-death, notary, DD214 and UCC. Records indexed on a public use terminal from 1/1/90 forward. Only the public may search. Copy fee $1.00 per page. Vital statistic certified copies- $10.00 each. Cert fee- $5.00 1st pg, $2.00 each add'l. Payee- Mecklenburg County Register of Deeds. **Online access to Real Estate, Grantor/Grantee, Deed, Judgment, Lien, Mortgage, UCC, Vital Statistic records:** Access to birth, death, marriage, recordings, judgments, liens, and grantor/grantee indices are free at www.charmeck.org/eServices/home.htm. Also, access real estate from 1/1763 to 2/28/1990 for free at www.meckrodindex.com/gtgt/oldIndexes/index.php . **Property tax/Assessing**- 700 E Stonewall St, #300, Charlotte, NC 28202; 704-336-6367, assessor fax-704-336-6366. (Appraiser - 704-336-4600) hours-8AM-5PM www.charmeck.org/living/home.htm **Online access**- Access to the assessors records for real estate, personal property, and tax bills are free at www.charmeck.org/Departments/LUESA/Property+Assessment+and+Land+Records/home.htm . Also, a real estate lookup at http://meckcama.co.mecklenburg.nc.us/relookup/. Search property ownership and data free on the GIS site at http://polaris.mecklenburgcountync.gov/website/redesign/viewer.htm.

Mitchell County

Register of Deeds, 26 Crimson Laurel Cir, #4, Bakersville, NC 28705-9510. 828-688-2139, R/E recording phone-828-688-2139 x318; fax-828-688-3666; 8AM-5PM www.mitchellrod.com

No tax liens filed here. Index: All in one. Records indexed on a public use terminal back to 1994. Office personnel or visitors may perform searches. Search fee-$38.00 for UCC only. Office will not search real estate records. Office will search UCC records prior to 7/2001 and current fixture (land) files. Copy fee $1.00 per page. Cert fee- $5.00 for 1st page, $2 each add'l (includes copy fee). Payee- Mitchell County Register of Deeds. **Online access to Real Estate, Granter/Grantee, Deed records:** Search records free at www.mitchellrod.com/. Non-residents may have to pay a fee. **Other phones:** Treasurer- 828-688-2139 x325; Elections- 828-688-3101; Vital Records- 828-688-2139 x318. **Property tax/Assessing-** 828-688-2139 x315. (Appraiser/Auditor- 828-688-2139 x315)

Montgomery County

Register of Deeds, PO Box 695, Troy, NC 27371. 910-576-4271; fax-910-576-2209; 8AM-5PM www.montgomeryrod.net/

No tax liens filed here. Index: All in one. Records indexed on a public use terminal back to 99. Office will perform a UCC search but public must search other records themselves. Search fee $38.00. UCC copy fee $1.00 per page.Real estate record copy- $.25 per page. Cert fee- $5.00 1st pg, $3.00 each add'l, includes copy fee. Payee- Montgomery County Register of Deeds. **Online access to Real Estate, Grantor/Grantee, Deed, Lien records:** Access to recorders real estate data is free at www.montgomeryrod.net/. **Other phones:** Treasurer- 910-572-4221; Elections- 910-572-2024; Vital Records- 910-576-4271. **Property tax/Assessing-** PO Box 614, Troy, NC 27371; 910-576-4311, assessor fax- 910-576-2209. (Appraiser/Auditor- 910-576-4311) **Online access-** Search property records free on the GIS mapping site at http://arcims.webgis.net/nc/montgomery/.

Moore County

Register of Deeds, PO Box 1210, Carthage, NC 28327. 910-947-6370, R/E phone-910-947-6372; fax-910-947-6396; 8-5PM. http://rod.moorecountync.gov

No tax liens filed here. Index: All in one. Records indexed on a public use terminal back to 7/1/88. Office will perform a pre-7/2001 UCC search but public must search other records themselves. UCC search per debtor name $30.00. Copy fee $1.00 per copy. Cert fee- $5.00 1st page, $2.00 each add'l page, includes copy fee. Payee- Moore County Register of Deeds. **Online Real Estate, Grantor/Grantee, Deed, Lien, Birth, Death, UCC records:** Find a menu of search choices for recordings, land records at http://rod.moorecountync.gov. **Other phones:** Treasurer- 910-947-6310; Elections- 910-947-3868; Vital Records- 910-947-6370. **Other Online Records-** Access property and tax data free at www.moorecountync.gov/main/page.asp?rec=/pages/Taxapp/index.asp

Nash County

Register of Deeds, PO Box 974, Nashville, NC 27856. Recording, R/E & UCC phone-252-459-9836, UCC recording phone-252-459-9825; fax-252-459-9889; 8AM-5PM www.deeds.co.nash.nc.us

No tax liens filed here. Index: All in one. Records indexed on computer back to 1970. Only the public may search. Copy fee $1.00 per page. Cert fee- $5.00 1st page, $2.00 each add'l page. Payee- Register. **Online access to Real Estate, Grantor/Grantee, Deed, UCC records:** Search real estate and UCCs free back to 1970 free at www.deeds.co.nash.nc.us/resolution/. **Other phones:** Vital Records- 252-459-9839. **Property tax/Assessing-** 120 W Washington St, #2058, Nashville, NC 27856; 252-459-9824, assessor fax-252-462-0508. www.tax.co.nash.nc.us/ **Online access-** Access to tax records for free go to http://taxdata.nashcountync.gov/Main/Home.aspx

New Hanover County

Register of Deeds, 216 N 2nd St, Wilmington, NC 28401. 910-798-4530; fax-910-798-7751; 8AM-5PM. www.nhcgov.com/AgnAndDpt/RODS/Pages/RegisterofDeedsHome.aspx

Until further notice, real estate records are located at 216 N 2nd St. Index: All in one. Records indexed on a public use terminal back to 1954. Only the public may search. Copy fee $1.00 per page for UCC; other docs $.25 per page. Cert fee- $5.00 1st page; $2.00 each add'l page, includes copy fee. Payee- Register of Deeds. Bulk data available for purchase, contact Sina Vergen at 910-798-7740. **Online access to Real Estate, Grantor/Grantee, Deed, UCC, Marriage, Military Discharge, Birth, Death, Plat, Condo records:** Access to the Register of Deeds database is free at http://srvrodweb.nhcgov.com. Subscription svc also available. **Other phones:** Elections- 910-798-4060; Vital Records- 910-798-4547. **Property tax/Assessing-** 230 Market Place Dr, Wilmington, NC 28403; 910-798-7300. www.nhcgov.com/AgnAndDpt/TAXS/Pages/TaxAdministrationsHome.aspx **Online-** Access to the real estate tax database is free at http://etax.nhcgov.com/Search/Disclaimer2.aspx?. Also, access property data on GIS-mappings site at www.nhcgov.com/AgnAndDpt/INFO/GIS/Pages/GISMaps.aspx .

Northampton County

Register of Deeds, PO Box 128, Jackson, NC 27845. 252-534-2511; fax-252-534-1580; 8:30AM-5PM www.northamptonnc.com/register.asp

No tax liens filed here. Index: All in one. Records indexed on a public use terminal back to 1991. Only the public may search. Copy fee $1.00 per page.Real estate record copy- $.25 per page. Cert fee- $5.00 1st pg, $2.00 each add'l. Payee- Northampton County Register of Deeds. **Other phones:** Treasurer- 252-534-4461. **Property tax/Assessing-** PO Box 637, 104 Thomas Bragg Dr, Jackson, NC 27845; 252-534-4461, assessor fax- 252-534-1406. (Appraiser/Auditor- 252-534-4461) Public access terminal in Land Records office. www.northamptonnc.com/tax.asp **Online access-** Access to GIS/mapping for free go to http://gis.northamptonnc.com/

Onslow County

Register of Deeds, 109 Old Bridge St, Jacksonville, NC 28540. 910-347-3451; fax-910-347-3340; 8AM-5PM www.co.onslow.nc.us/

No tax liens filed here. Index: Separate indices to search include real estate, marriage, birth, death, UCC. Records indexed on computer back to 1977. Only the public may search. Copy fee $.10 per page. Cert fee- $5.00 1st page, $2 each add'l page, plus copy fee. Payee- County Register of Deeds. Bulk data available for purchase if you provide the CD. **Online access to Real Estate, Birth, Death, Marriage, UCC, Parcel, GIS-mapping records:** Access recorder office index data free at http://deeds.onslowcountync.gov. Real estate goes back to 1995, births 1980-2001, deaths 1983-2003, marriages 1962-1/2004, UCCs 1977-1994, conveyances 1977-1994. **Property tax/Assessing-** 79 Tallman St, Tax Admin/Collector, Jacksonville, NC 28540; 910-989-2200, assessor fax- 910-455-4579. **Online access-** Access to property data is free at http://maps.onslowcountync.gov/. Enter the site and name search using the advanced search in the Parcel Query box.

Orange County

Register of Deeds, PO Box 8181, Hillsborough, NC 27278-8181. 919-245-2675; fax-919-644-3018; 8AM-5PM. www.co.orange.nc.us/deeds/

No tax liens filed here. Index: Separate indices to search include vital and non-vitals. Records indexed on a public use terminal back to 1932 for non-vitals. Only the public may search. Copy fee $.50 per page. Cert fee- $5.00 1st 5 pages includes copy; copy fee applies after 5th page. **Other phones:** Elections- 919-245-2350; Vital Records- 919-245-2701. **Property tax/Assessing-** PO Box 8181, Hillsborough, NC 27278-8181; 919-245-2101. **Online access-** Access to property records on the GIS mapping site is free at http://gis.co.orange.nc.us/.

Pamlico County

Register of Deeds, PO Box 433, Bayboro, NC 28515. 252-745-4421; fax-252-745-7020; 8AM-5PM www.pamlicorod.com

No tax liens filed here. Index: Separate indices to search include grantor/grantee. Records indexed on a public use terminal back to 6/1/88. Only the public may search. Copy fee $1.00 per page (with postage), $.25 per page (if SASE included). Cert fee- $5.00 1st pg, $2.00 each add'l plus copy fee. Payee- Pamlico County Register of Deeds. **Online access to Real Estate, Grantor/Grantee, Deed records:** Access records for grantor/grantee and real property free at www.pamlicorod.com/. Images go back to 5/88. Non-residents may have to pay an access fee. **Other phones:** Elections- 252-745-4821; Vital Records-252-745-4421. **Property tax/Assessing-** PO Boc538, 151 Public Sq, Bayboro, NC 28515; 252-745-4125 x33, assessor fax- 252-745-4042. **Online access-** Search the GIS-mapping site for property data free at http://www2.undersys.com/pamweb/pamlicomain.html. Tax data to be available at www.pamlicorod.com/taxindex.html soon.

Pasquotank County

Register of Deeds, PO Box 154, Elizabeth City, NC 27907-0154. 252-335-4367; fax-252-335-5106; 8AM-5PM www.co.pasquotank.nc.us/departments/rod/default.htm

No tax liens filed here. Index: All in one. Records indexed on a public use terminal back to 1998. Only the public may search. General copy fee $.25 per page. Cert fee- $5.00 1st page, $2.00 each add'l page. Payee- Register. **Online access to Real Estate, Grantor/Grantee, Deed records:** Access recorder data free at http://pasquotankrod.com/ but non-residents may have to pay a fee. **Other phones:** Treasurer- 252-335-4580; Elections- 252-335-1739; Vital Records- 252-335-4367. **Property tax/Assessing-** PO Box 193, 206 E Main St, Elizabeth City, NC 27907; 252-338-5169, assessor fax- 252-338-6125. (Appraiser/Auditor- 252-338-5169) **Online access-** Search assessor database at www.co.pasquotank.nc.us/GIS/taxsearch.cfm.

Pender County

Register of Deeds, PO Box 43, Burgaw, NC 28425. 910-259-1225; fax-910-259-1299; 8AM-4:30PM www.pender-county.com/Departments/rod/

No tax liens filed here. Index: All in one. Records indexed on a public use terminal back to 1/1/1990. Only the public may search. Copy fee $1.00 per page. Cert fee- $5.00 1st page, $2.00 add'l includes copy fee. Payee- Pender County Register of Deeds. **Online access to Real Estate, Grantor/Grantee, Deed records:** Access recorder data free with registration at http://pender-rod.inttek.net/. **Other phones:** Elections- 910-259-1225; Vital Records- 910-259-1458. **Property tax/Assessing-** PO Box 67, Burgaw, NC 28425; 910-259-1221. **Online access-** GIS land records are available at www.pender-county.com/disclaimer.php but no name searching.

Perquimans County

Register of Deeds, PO Box 74, Hertford, NC 27944. Recording, R/E & UCC phone-252-426-5660; fax-252-426-7443; 8AM-5PM www.perquimansrod.com/

No tax liens filed here. Index: Separate indices to search. Records indexed on a public use terminal back to 1991. Only the public may search. Copy fee $1.00 per 1st page of UCC or tax lien; other recorded docs are $.25 each copy. Cert fee- $5.00 1st pg, $2.00 each add'l includes copy fee. Payee- Perquimans County Register of Deeds. **Online access to Real Estate, Deed, Lien records:** Access to county real property records is free at www.perquimansrod.com/ except non-residents must pay a fee. **Property tax/Assessing-** PO Box 7, 107 N Front St, Hertford, NC 27944; 252-426-7010, fax- 252-426-3624. www.co.perquimans.nc.us/index.php?page=departments&userid=8 **Online access-** Access property assessor, tax, property card and GIS data free at http://mapping.perquimanscountync.gov/perquimans/

Person County

Register of Deeds, Courthouse Sq, Roxboro, NC 27573. Recording, R/E & UCC phone-336-597-1733; 8:30AM-5PM www.personrod.net

No tax liens filed here. Index: All in one. Records indexed on a public use terminal back to 1900. Office will perform a UCC search but public must search other records themselves. Search fee-$38.00 for UCC only. Copy fee $1.00 per page if mailed. Cert fee-

$5.00 for 1st page; $2.00 each add'l, includes copy fees. Payee- Person County Register of Deeds. **Online access to Real Estate, Grantor/Grantee, Deed records:** Access to county real estate records is free at http://12.174.150.120/personnc/disclaimer.asp. Index goes back to 1/1/1995. **Other phones:** Elections- 336-597-1727; Vital Records- 336-597-1733; Deed Vault- 336-597-1729. **Property tax/Assessing**- PO Box 1701, Courthouse Sq, Rm 102, Roxboro, NC 27573; 336-597-1712, assessor fax- 336-597-2099.

Pitt County

Register of Deeds, PO Box 35, Greenville, NC 27835-0035. 252-902-1650, R/E recording phone-252-902-1660, UCC recording phone-252-902-1650; 8AM-5PM www.co.pitt.nc.us/depts/

No tax liens filed here. Index: Separate indices to search include books, computer. Records indexed on computer back to 1989. Only the public may search. Copy fee $1.00 per page. Cert fee- $5.00 1st pg, $2.00 each add'l, includes copies. Payee- Pitt County Register of Deeds. **Online access to Real Estate, Deed, Lien, UCC records:** Access recorder land data back to 1969 and UCCs from 1992 to 2001 free at http://regdeeds.pittcountync.gov/resolution/. **Property tax/Assessing**- PO Box 43, 110 S Evans St, Greenville, NC 27835; 252-902-3400, assessor fax- 252-830-0753. **Online** - access to property records at http://gis.pittcountync.gov/website/opis/. Also, view overdue tax accounts at http://tax.pittcountync.gov/ptsweb/main/billing/default.aspx.

Polk County

Register of Deeds, PO Box 308, Columbus, NC 28722. 828-894-8450; fax-828-894-5781; 8:30AM-5PM www.polkrod.com

No tax liens filed here. Index: All in one. Records indexed on a public use terminal back to 1994. Only the public may search. Copy fee $.25 per page. Cert fee- $5.00 1st page plus $2.00 each add'l includes copy fee. Payee- Polk County Register of Deeds. **Online access to Real Estate, Grantor/Grantee, Deed records:** Access the recorder land records free at www.polkrod.com/. Non-residents may have to pay a fee for access. **Other phones:** Treasurer- 828-894-8500. **Property tax/Assessing**- 828-894-8500.

Randolph County

Register of Deeds, PO Box 4458, Asheboro, NC 27204. Recording, R/E & UCC phone-336-318-6960; fax-336-318-6970; 8AM-5PM www.randrod.com

No tax liens filed here. Index: All in one. Records indexed. Office will perform a UCC search but public must search other records themselves. Search fee-$38.00 for UCC only. Office will not search real estate records. Copy fee $.50 per page. UCC copies-$1.00 per statement. Cert fee- $5.00 1st page, $2.00 each add'l includes copy fee. Payee- Randolph County Register of Deeds. Bulk data available for purchase. Call 336-318-6939 for information. **Online access to Real Estate, Deed, Plat records:** Real Estate records and plats at www.randrod.com/officialrecords.html after registration; index goes back to 1/1986, images to 4/1990. Registration required. **Other phones:** Elections- 336-318-6900; Vital Records- 336-318-6960. **Property tax/Assessing**- 725 McDowell Rd, Asheboro, NC 27204; 336-318-6500. **Online access**- Access to the county GIS database is free at www.co.randolph.nc.us/gis.htm. In the "Search functions" on the map page, click on "parcel owner". Access property owners/property data, liens, and foreclosure lists free at www.co.randolph.nc.us/tax/default.htm.

Richmond County

Register of Deeds, 114 E Franklin St, #101, Rockingham, NC 28379-3601. 910-997-8250; fax-910-997-8499; 8AM-5PM

No tax liens filed here. Index: All in one except military discharges and vital records. Records indexed on a public use terminal back to 1995. Office will perform a UCC search but public must search other records themselves. Copy fee $.35 per page. Will fax back for $1.00 per page. Cert fee- $5.00 1st page; $2.00 each add'l page includes copy fee. Payee- Register of Deeds. **Online access to Real Estate, Deed, Plat records:** With registration, username and password you may access Register of Deeds land records at http://216.27.81.170/login.asp. For login, use account ID "richmondnc" and password "richmondnc001". **Other phones:** Treasurer- 910-997-8220; Elections- 910-997-8254; Vital Records- 910 997-8251. **Property tax/Assessing**- PO Box 1644, Rockingham, NC 28379; 910-997-8274. **Online access**- Access property data on the GIS-mapping site at www.richmondnc.org/rc%5Fims/. Click on black dot with "i" to identify parcels or click on search to name search.

Robeson County

Register of Deeds, 500 N Elm St, Rm 102; Courthouse, Lumberton, NC 28358. 910-671-3046, R/E recording phone-910-671-3048, UCC recording phone-910-671-3049; fax-910-671-3041; 8:15AM-5:15PM http://rod.co.robeson.nc.us

No tax liens filed here. Index: UCCs in Real Estate Fixture Filings only after 7/1/2001; prior UCCs in separate file. Records indexed on a public use terminal back to 7/1/01. Only the public may search. Office will not search real estate records. Copy fee $.25 per page. Cert fee- $5.00 1st page, $2.00 each add'l page. Payee- Register. **Online access to Real Estate, Grantor/Grantee, Deed, Lien records:** Access to recorder data is free at http://rod.co.robeson.nc.us/search.php. Also, access to property and deeds indexes and images is via a private company at www.titlesearcher.com. Fee/registration required. Deeds and images go back to 1/12/1974; Indices back to 2/2/1974. **Other phones:** Treasurer- 910-671-3000; Elections- 910-671-3080; Vital Records- 910-671-3045; Deed Vault- 910-671-3049; Clerk of Court -910-671-3377. **Property tax/Assessing**- 500 N Elm St, #101, Lumberton, NC 28358; 910-671-3060, assessor fax- 910-671-6243. **Online** - Access assessor property records free at www.ustaxdata.com/nc/robeson/robesonsearch.cfm. Also, search parcels, sales, and subdivisions free at www.gis.co.robeson.nc.us/ConnectGISWeb/.

Rockingham County

Register of Deeds, PO Box 56, Wentworth, NC 27375-0056. Recording, R/E & UCC phone-336-342-8820; fax-336-342-6209; 8AM-5PM (recording cut off time 4:30PM). www.co.rockingham.nc.us/

No tax liens filed here. Index: All in one. Records indexed on a public use terminal back to 1996. Only the public may search. Copy fee $1.00 per page by mailed back, include SASE.Real estate record copy-$.25 per sheet. Cert fee- $5.00 1st pg, $2.00 each add'l includes copy fee. Payee- Rockingham County Register of Deeds. **Online access to Real Estate, Grantor/Grantee, Deed, Judgment records:** Access to Register of Deeds database is free at http://rod.co.rockingham.nc.us/oncoreweb/default.aspx. Land indexes 1996 to present; recorded images 1984 to present; plats 1907 to present. **Other phones:** Treasurer- 336-342-8120; Elections- 336-342-8107; Vital Records- 336-342-8820. **Property tax/Assessing**- County Government Center, Wentworth, NC 27375; 336-342-8280. (Appraiser/Auditor- 336-342-8280) **Online access**- Access to Tax Admin. property data (1996 forward) also tax bills are free at www.ustaxdata.com/nc/rockingham/RockinghamSearch.cfm. Also, search property data free at the GIS site at http://arcims.webgis.net/nc/rockingham/default.asp. To name search, click on Quick Search. Also, access to the tax sales property is at www.co.rockingham.nc.us/forecl.htm.

Rowan County

Register of Deeds, PO Box 2568, Salisbury, NC 28145. 704-216-8626; 8-5PM www.co.rowan.nc.us

No tax liens filed here. Index: All in one. Records indexed on a public use terminal back to 1975. Office will perform a UCC search but public must search other records themselves. Copy fee $1.00 per page.Real estate record copy- $.50 per page. Cert fee- $5.00 1st pg, $2.00 each add'l. Payee- Rowan County Register of Deeds. Land records available for purchase on CD. **Online access to Real Estate, Deed, UCC records:** Access to the Register of Deeds land records database is free after registration at www.co.rowan.nc.us. Records go back to 1975; financing statements back to 1993; deed images back to 1975. **Other phones:** Treasurer- 704-216-8544; Elections- 704-216-8140. **Property tax/Assessing**- 402 N Main St, Salisbury, NC 28144; 704-216-8558. **Online** - Access the county GIS mapping site free at http://arcims2.webgis.net/nc/Rowan/default.asp. To name search click on Quick Search. Also, there is a tax inquiry quick search at www.co.rowan.nc.us/taxinq/name/default.asp. More tax and property data may be available at www.rowancountync.gov/ONLINESERVICES/TaxAdministrationRecordSearch/tabid/947/Default.aspx.

Rutherford County

Register of Deeds, PO Box 551, Rutherfordton, NC 28139. 828-287-6155; fax-828-287-1229; 8:30AM-5PM www.rutherfordcountync.gov

No tax liens filed here. Index: All in one. Records indexed on a public use terminal back to 1974. Office will perform a UCC search but public must search other records themselves. Search fee-$38.00 for UCC only. Copy fee $1.00 per page. Cert fee- $5.00 1st page; $2.00 each add'l, plus copy fee. Payee- Rutherford County Register of Deeds. **Online access to Real Estate, Deed, Birth, Death, Marriage, UCC, Notary records:** Access property data free at www.rutherfordcountync.gov/dept/register_of_deeds/Main.php. UCCs 1995 to 2001; RE goes back to 1974; births 1991 to 2006; Deaths and marriages back t0 1994/1995. **Property tax/Assessing**- 828-287-6215.

Sampson County

Register of Deeds, Main St, Rm 109; Courthouse, Clinton, NC 28329. 910-592-8026; fax-910-592-1803; 8AM-5PM www.sampsonrod.org

No tax liens filed here. Index: All in one. Records indexed on a public use terminal back to 1962. Only the public may search. General copy $.25 per page. per page. Cert fee- $5.00 1st page; $2.00 each add'l page plus copy fee. Payee- Sampson County Register of Deeds. **Online access to Real Estate, Grantor/Grantee, Deed records:** Access to county Register of Deeds land data is free at www.sampsonrod.org/Opening.asp. Index goes back to 1962. **Other phones:** Treasurer- 910-592-6308; Vitals- 910-592-8026. **Property tax/Assessing**- 126 W Elizabeth St, Courthouse Annex, Clinton, NC 28328; 910-592-8146, assessor fax- 910-592-4865.

Scotland County

Register of Deeds, PO Box 769, Laurinburg, NC 28353. Recording, R/E & UCC phone-910-277-2575, UCC recording phone-910 277-2575; fax-910-277-3133; 8AM-5PM www.scotlandcounty.org

No tax liens filed here. Index: All in one. Records indexed on a public use terminal back to 1978; images back to 2003. Only the public may search. Copy fee $1.00 per copy.Real estate record copy- $.25 per page. Cert fee- $5.00 1st page; $2.00 each add'l, includes copy fee. Payee- Scotland County Register of Deeds. **Online Real Estate, Grantor/Grantee, Deed, Lien, UCC records:** Access ROD real estate records and also financing statements from 1999 to 2/2004 free at http://rod.scotlandcounty.org/resolution/. Also, search the tax payments page free at www.scotlandcountytaxes.com. **Other phones:** Treasurer- 910-277-2410; Elections- 910-277-2595; Vitals- 910-277-2575. **Property tax/Assessing**- 212 Biggs St, Courthouse, Laurinburg, NC 28352; 910-277-3270. (Appraiser/Auditor- 910-277-2566) **Online access**- Search property data free on the GIS site at http://65.254.200.14/ConnectGIS/Laurinburg/. Includes City of Laurinburg.

Stanly County

Register of Deeds, PO Box 97; 201 S 2nd St, Albemarle, NC 28002-0097. 704-986-3640; 8:30AM-5PM www.co.stanly.nc.us

No tax liens filed here. Index: All in one 1994 to present; Pre-1994 includes UCC separate; Pre-1985 includes mortgages separate. Records indexed on a public use terminal back to 1841. Only the public may search, except UCC. Search fee-$38.00 for UCC only. Office will search UCC records prior to 7/2001. Copy fee $.25 per page. Cert fee- $5.00 1st pg, $2.00 each add'l. Payee- Stanly County Register of Deeds. **Online Real Estate, Grantor/Grantee, Deed, Mortgage, Plat records:** Access Register of Deeds index back to 1841 at http://216.27.81.170/login.asp?password=stqn342&accountid=stanlyhome. Search deeds, plats by address or number free at www.stanlygis.net/website/public/DeedPlatSearch.htm. **Other phones:** Treasurer- 704-986-3618; Elections- 704-986-3647; Vital Records- 704-986-3640. **Property tax/Assessing**- 201 S 2nd St, Albemarle, NC 28001; 704-586-3626. (Appraiser - 704-986-3629) **Online access**- Access property data on the GIS search free at www.stanlygis.net/website/quicksearch/quicksearch.aspx.

Stokes County

Register of Deeds, PO Box 67, Danbury, NC 27016. Recording, R/E & UCC phone-336-593-2811; fax-336-593-9360; 8:30AM-5PM. www.stokescorod.org

No tax liens filed here. Index: All in one. Records indexed on a public use terminal back to 1993. Only the public may search. Real estate record copy $.50 per page by mail, $.25 in person, UCC copy fee $2.00 per page. Cert fee- $5.00 1st page, $2.00 each add'l page. **Online Real Estate, Grantor/Grantee, Deed, UCC records:** the Register of Deeds Remote Access site is free at www.stokescorod.org/Opening.asp. Land records go back to 1993, images to 2/1924; UCCs back to 1994. **Other phones:** Elections- 336-593-2811; Vital Records- 336-593-2811. **Property tax/Assessing**- PO Box 57, Danbury, NC 27053; 336-593-2811. (Appraiser - 336-593-2811) **Online access**- Access to property info on the GIS mapping site is free at http://arcims2.webgis.net/stokes/default.asp. To name search click on Quick Search.

Surry County

Register of Deeds, PO Box 303, Dobson, NC 27017-0303. 336-401-8150, R/E recording phone-336-386-9201; fax-336-401-8149; hours- 8:15AM-5PM www.co.surry.nc.us

No tax liens filed here. Index: Separate indices to search include real estate, vitals. Records indexed on a public use terminal back to 1980. Office will perform a UCC search but public must search other records themselves. Copy fee $.25 per page. Cert fee- $5.00 1st page, $2.00 each add'l. Bulk data available for purchase, contact Carolyn Comer. **Online Real Estate, Deed, Plat, UCC records:** Access recording index free at www.co.surry.nc.us/Departments/RegisterOfDeeds/RecordSearch.htm. Real property index goes back to 1/1995; financing statements 1989-6/30/2001; plats are 1/1980 to 12/21/1994. **Other phones:** Treasurer- 336-386-9230; Elections-336-401-8225; Clerk of Court- 336-386-3700. **Property tax/Assessing**- 201 E Kapp St, Dobson, NC 27017; 336-401-8100. **Online**- Access property data free at http://arcims.webgis.net/nc/surry/default.asp. Click on Quick search. Tax maps located at this site.

Swain County

Register of Deeds, PO Box 1183, Bryson City, NC 28713. 828-488-9273 x2205, R/E recording phone-828-488-9273 x205; fax-828-488-6947; 8:30AM-5PM www.swaincorod.org/

Index: All in one. Records indexed on a public use terminal back to 1995. Office will perform a UCC search but public must search other records themselves. Search fee-$38.00 for UCC only. Copy fee $1.00 per page. Cert fee- $5.00 per doc plus copy fee. Payee- Register of Deeds. **Online access to Real Estate, Grantor/Grantee, Deed records:** Access to recorder land data is free at www.swaincorod.org. There is a full system and an image only system. Land Record Indexing data goes back to 1/1995; images back to 8/1979. **Other phones:** Elections- 828-488-6177; Vital Records- 828-488-9273 x205. **Property tax/Assessing**- 101 Mitchell St, Admin Bldg, Bryson City, NC 28713; 828-488-9273 x249. hours- 8AM-5PM **Online access**- Access to parcel and land information for free go to www.qpublic.net/nc/swain/

Transylvania County

Register of Deeds, 7 E Main St; Courthouse, Brevard, NC 28712. Recording, R/E & UCC phone-828-884-3162; 8:30AM-5PM www.transylvaniacounty.org

No tax liens filed here. Index: All in one. Records indexed on a public use terminal back to 1973. Office personnel or visitors may perform searches. No search fee unless extensive research needed. $38.00 for UCC search only. Office will help public in document search; will not name search RE records if pertains to title work. Office will search UCC records prior to July 1, 2001. Copy fee $.25 per page. Copies of larger doc are $2.00 each. Vital records are $10.00 ea. Cert fee- $5.00 1st page, $2.00 each add'l includes copy fee. Payee- Transylvania County Register of Deeds. **Online access to Real Estate, Deed records:** Access real estate records at www.titlesearcher.com. Registration and username required. Images are viewable back to 12/30/2003; deeds and indices back to 1/3/1973. **Other phones:** Treasurer- 828-884-3104; Elections- 828-884-3114; Vital Records- 828-884-3162. **Property tax/Assessing**- 7 E Main St, Courthouse, Brevard, NC 28712; 828-884-3200. (Appraiser/Auditor- 828-884-3200) **Online access**- Access full or partial property data free on the GIS site at http://arcims.webgis.net/nc/transylvania/default.asp.

Tyrrell County

Register of Deeds, PO Box 449, Columbia, NC 27925. 252-796-2901; fax-252-796-0148; 9AM-5PM. www.tyrrellrod.com

No tax liens filed here. Index: All in one. Records indexed on a public use terminal back to 1997. Only the public may search. UCC copy fee $1.00 each.Real estate record copy- $.25 per page. Cert fee- $5.00 for 1st pg, $2.00 each add'l pg plus copy fee. Certified copies of Vital records $10.00 each. Payee- Register of Deeds. **Online access to Real Estate, Grantor/Grantee, Deed records:** Access to Register of Deeds real estate records is free at www.tyrrellrod.com/. Index goes back to 1997; images are from Book 137 forward. Non-residents may have to pay a fee for access. **Other phones:** Elections- 252-796-0775. **Property tax/Assessing**- 403 Main St, Columbia, NC 27925; 252-796-4964.

Union County

Register of Deeds, PO Box 248, Monroe, NC 28111-0248. 704-283-3727; fax-704-283-3569; 8AM-5PM www.unionconcrod.org

No tax liens filed here. Index: Separate indices to search include deeds and mortgages before 1990. Records indexed on a public use terminal back to 0101/1984. Office will perform a UCC search but public must search other records themselves. Search fee-$38.00 for UCC only. Office will not search real estate records. Will search UCC records. Copy fee $1.00 per page. Cert fee- $5.00 1st pg, $2.00 each add'l includes copy fee. Payee- Union County Register of Deeds. **Online access to Real Estate, Grantor/Grantee, Deed records:** Access to recorder land records is free at www.unionconcrod.org/Opening.asp; index go back to 6-15-2003; images to 6/3/2000. **Other phones:** Vital Records-704-283-3610; Land Records- 704-283-3728. **Property tax/ Assessing**- PO Box 97, 300 N Main St, Monroe, NC 28111; 704-283-3746.

Vance County

Register of Deeds, 122 Young St, #F; Courthouse, Henderson, NC 27536. 252-738-2110; 8:30AM-5PM

No tax liens filed here. Index: All in one. Records indexed on computer and paper back to 1993; 1881-1992 in one book. Only the public may search. Copy fee $.25 per page. Cert fee- $5.00 per cert for 1st page, $2.00 each add'l page includes copy fee. Payee- Vance County Register of Deeds. **Property tax/Assessing**- 122 Young St, Courthouse, Henderson, NC 27536; 252-738-2040.

Wake County

Register of Deeds, PO Box 1897, Raleigh, NC 27602. Recording, R/E & UCC phone-919-856-5460, UCC recording phone-919-856-5464; fax-919-856-5467; 8:30AM-5:15PM http://web.co.wake.nc.us/rdeeds/

No tax liens filed here. Index: All in one. Records indexed on a public use terminal back to 1900. Office will perform a UCC search but public must search other records themselves. Search fee $30.00 for UCC only. Copy fee $.15 per page; maps $1.00 per page. Cert fee- $5.00 1st page, $2.00 each add'l page. Payee- Wake County Register of Deeds. **Online access to Real Estate, Deed, Lien, Judgment, Voter Registration records:** Records from the County are available through the portal website at www.wakegov.com/tax/default.htm. Also, online access to the Register of Deeds database is free at http://rodweb01.co.wake.nc.us/books/genext/genextsearch.asp. Records go back to 1900. Registered voters data at http://msweb03.co.wake.nc.us/bordelec/Waves/WavesOptions.asp. **Other phones:** Treasurer-919-856-6600; Vital Records- 919-733-3526. **Property tax/Assessing**- 421 Fayetteville St #200, Raleigh, NC 27601; 919-856-5400. **Online access**- Free real estate property and tax bill search is at http://services.wakegov.com/realestate/search.asp. Also, access to Town of Cary property info on the map site for free at http://209.42.194.57/CaryMap/ViewMap.aspx?ItemID=11&PortalID=1. Also, download individual town property data free at www.wakegov.com/tax/downloads/default.htm.

Warren County

Register of Deeds, PO Box 506, Warrenton, NC 27589. Recording, R/E & UCC phone-252-257-3265; fax-252-257-7011; 8:30AM-5PM

No tax liens filed here. Index: All in one. Records indexed on a public use terminal back to 1989, images from 03/2003. Only the public may search. Copy fee $.25 per page. Cert fee- $5.00 per cert plus $2.00 per page. Payee- Warren County Register of Deeds. **Other phones:** Treasurer- 252-257-3337; 2nd Fax - 252-257-7011. **Property tax/Assessing**- 101 S Main St, Warrenton, NC 27589; 252-257-4158, assessor fax- 252-257-9369. www.warrencountync.com/taxadministrator.aspx

Washington County

Register of Deeds, PO Box 1007, Plymouth, NC 27962. 252-793-2325; fax-252-793-6982; 8:30AM-5PM www.washingtonrod.com/

No tax liens filed here. Index: All in one. Records indexed on a public use terminal back to 6/96. Only the public may search. Copy fee $.25 per page; $1.00 per page for UCC copy. Cert fee- $5.00 1st pg, $2.00 each add'l, includes copy fee. Payee- Washington County Register of Deeds. Bulk data can be purchased from Parker-Loew and Assoc, Ocracoke, NC, 252-928-7711. **Online access to Real Estate, Grantor/Grantee, Deed, Lien, Corporation records:** Access to recorder land records is available free at www.washingtonrod.com/. Non-residents may have to pay a fee for access. **Other phones:** Elections- 252-793-6017. **Property tax/Assessing**- Same address as recording office. 252-793-1176. **Online access**- Search assessor property record cards free at http://taxweb.washconc.org.

Watauga County

Register of Deeds, 842 W King St, #9, Boone, NC 28607-3585. Recording, R/E phone-828-265-8052, UCC phone-828-265-8056; fax-828-265-7632; 8AM-5PM www.wataugacounty.org/deeds/index.html

No tax liens filed here. Index: All in one. Records indexed on a public use terminal back to 2/00. Office will perform a real estate search but public must search other records themselves. Search fee $30.00 per name. Will not search UCC records. Copy fee $.50 per page. Plats copies- $1.00 per page. Cert fee- $5.00 1st page; $2.00 each add'l. Payee- Register of Deeds. Bulk indices and images on CD; contact JoAnn Townsend. **Online access to Real Estate, Grantor/Grantee, Deed, UCC records:** Access to register of deeds database is free at www.wataugacounty.org/deeds/disclaimer.shtml. **Other phones:** Elections- 828-265-8061; Vital Records- 828-265-8052. **Property tax/Assessing-** Courthouse, Boone, NC 28607; 828-265-8036. (Appraiser/Auditor- 828-265-8141) **Online access-** Access to county tax search data is free at www.wataugacounty.org/tax/search_tax.shtml. Also, search Town of Blowing Rock property info at http://arcims2.webgis.net/nc/blowingrock/ .

Wayne County

Register of Deeds, 224-226 E Walnut St, Goldsboro, NC 27530. 919-731-1449; fax-919-731-1441; 8AM-5PM www.waynegov.com/16581041015373230/site/default.asp

No tax liens filed here. Index: Separate indices to search include real estate, CRP, vitals, financing statements, military discharge. Records indexed on a public use terminal back to 1969. Only the public may search. Copy fee $.25 per page. Cert fee- $5.00 1st page + $2.00 each add'l page includes copy fee. Payee- Wayne County Register of Deeds. **Online Real Estate, Grantor/Grantee, Deed, UCC, Plat, Marriage, Death records:** Access to the registers CRP, financing statement, and real estate databases is free at http://rod.waynegov.com/resolution/. Real Estate includes records from 1969-1994; beginning 1995 all real estate records are indexed under CRP. Birth and Death records go back to 1995; marriages back to 1997. Financing statements go back to 1993. **Other phones:** Elections- 919-731-1411; Vitals- 919-733-3000. **Property tax/Assessing-** PO Box 1495, Goldsboro, NC 27533; 919-731-1461. **Online-** Access property records free at www.waynegov.com/16581041015290207/site/default.asp.

Wilkes County

Register of Deeds, 500 Courthouse Dr, #1000, Wilkesboro, NC 28697. Recording, R/E & UCC phone-336-651-7351; 8:30AM-5PM

No tax liens filed here. Index: All in one. Records indexed on a public use terminal back to 1992. Only the public may search. Office will not search real estate records. Will not search UCC records. Copy fee $1.00 per page.Real estate copy- $1.00 per page if mailed; $.25 per page otherwise. Cert fee- $5.00 1st pg, $2.00 each add'l plus copy fee. Payee- Wilkes County Register of Deeds. **Other phones:** Vital Records- 336-651-7351. **Property tax/Assessing-** . **Online access-** Access to property data is free on the GIS-mapping site at www.undersys.com/wilkesweb/wilkes.html.

Wilson County

Register of Deeds, PO Box 1728, Wilson, NC 27893. 252-399-2935; fax-252-399-2942; 8AM-5PM www.wilson-co.com/rod.html

No tax liens filed here. Index: All in one. Records indexed on a public use terminal back to 1974. Only the public may search. Copy fee $.25 per page, $1.00 per page for map copy. Cert fee- $5.00 1st page, $2.00 each add'l page. Payee- Register. **Online access to Real Estate, Deed records:** Access the Register of Deeds search site at www.wilson-co.com/wcjav_begin.html. If using property search function, username or password required; deeds section does not. **Other phones:** Treasurer- 252-399-2902; Elections- 252-399-2836; Vital Records- 252-399-2935. **Property tax/Assessing-** PO Box 1728, Wilson, NC 27894; 252-399-2901. **Online access-** Records on the county Geo-link property tax database are free at www.wilson-co.com/intro.html.

Yadkin County

Register of Deeds, PO Box 211, Yadkinville, NC 27055. 336-679-4225; fax-336-679-3239; 8AM-5PM www.yadkincountync.gov/content/view/19/327/

No tax liens filed here. Index: All in one. Records indexed on a public use terminal back to 1993. Only the public may search. Copy fee $1.00 per page.Real estate record copy- $.25 per page. Cert fee- $5.00 per cert plus $2.00 each add'l page. Payee- Yadkin County Register of Deeds. **Online access to Real Estate, Grantor/Grantee, Deed, Lien records:** Access recorder's land records free at www.yadkincorod.org/Opening.asp. Index goes back to 1/1/1993. Land Record Imaging Data back to Volume 0210 8/24/1978 through Volume 0790 page 76 6/20/2006. Search either the full system or the imaging system. **Other phones:** Treasurer- 336-679-4223; Elections- 336-679-4227; Vital Records- 336-679-4225. **Property tax/Assessing-** PO Box 1217, 101 S State St, Yadkinville, NC 27055; 336-679-4221, fax- 336-679-2703. (Appraiser- 336-679-2308) www.yadkincountync.gov/content/view/24/332/ **Online access-** Search property tax date free at www.ustaxdata.com/nc/yadkin/.

Yancey County

Register of Deeds, 110 Town Sq, Rm 4; Courthouse, Burnsville, NC 28714. 828-682-2174, R/E recording phone-704-682-2174; fax-828-682-4520; 8:30AM-5PM www.yanceyrod.com

No tax liens filed here. Index: All in one. Records indexed on a public use terminal back to 1995. Only the public may search. Copy fee $1.00 per page to copy and mail. Self serve- $.25 per page. Cert fee- $5.00 1st pg, $2.00 each add'l page, includes copy fee. Payee- Yancey County Register of Deeds. **Online access to Real Estate, Grantor/Grantee, Deed, Lien records:** Access to recording office records is free at www.yanceyrod.com/. Non-residents may have to pay a fee for access. **Property tax/Assessing-** 110 Town Sq, Burnsville, NC 28714; 828-682-2197, assessor fax- 828-682-4817.

North Carolina County Locator

You will usually be able to find the city name in the City/County Cross Reference below. In that case, it is a simple matter to determine the county from the cross reference. However, only the official US Postal Service city names are included in this index. There are an additional 40,000 place names that people use in their addresses. Therefore, we have also included a ZIP/City Cross Reference immediately following the City/County Cross Reference.

If you know the ZIP Code but the city name does not appear in the City/County Cross Reference index, look up the ZIP Code in the ZIP/City Cross Reference, find the city name, then look up the city name in the City/County Cross Reference. For example, you want to know the county for an address of Menands, NY 12204. There is no "Menands" in the City/County Cross Reference. The ZIP/City Cross Reference shows that ZIP Codes 12201-12288 are for the city of Albany. Looking back in the City/County Cross Reference, Albany is in Albany County.

North Carolina City/County Cross Reference

ABERDEEN (28315) Moore(76), Hoke(23)
ADVANCE Davie
AHOSKIE Hertford
ALAMANCE Alamance
ALBEMARLE Stanly
ALBERTSON Duplin
ALEXANDER Buncombe
ALEXIS Gaston
ALLIANCE Pamlico
ALMOND Swain
ALTAMAHAW Alamance
ANDREWS Cherokee
ANGIER (27501) Harnett(73), Johnston(25), Wake(1)
ANSONVILLE Anson
APEX (27523) Wake(66), Chatham(33)
APEX Wake
AQUONE Macon
ARAPAHOE Pamlico
ARARAT Surry
ARDEN (28704) Buncombe(91), Henderson(8)
ASH Brunswick
ASHEBORO Randolph
ASHEVILLE Buncombe
ATKINSON Pender
ATLANTIC Carteret
ATLANTIC BEACH Carteret
AULANDER (27805) Bertie(68), Hertford(31)
AURORA Beaufort
AUTRYVILLE (28318) Sampson(87), Cumberland(12)
AVON Dare
AYDEN (28513) Pitt(94), Greene(5)
AYDLETT Currituck
BADIN Stanly
BAHAMA Durham
BAILEY (27807) Nash(64), Wilson(35)
BAKERSVILLE Mitchell
BALSAM Jackson
BALSAM GROVE Transylvania
BANNER ELK (28604) Watauga(61), Avery(38)
BARBER Rowan
BARCO Currituck
BARIUM SPRINGS Iredell
BARNARDSVILLE Buncombe
BARNESVILLE Robeson
BAT CAVE Henderson
BATH Beaufort
BATTLEBORO (27809) Nash(53), Edgecombe(46)
BAYBORO Pamlico
BEAR CREEK Chatham
BEAUFORT Carteret
BELEWS CREEK Forsyth
BELHAVEN Beaufort
BELLARTHUR Pitt
BELMONT Gaston
BELVIDERE (27919) Perquimans(89), Chowan(6), Gates(3)
BENNETT (27208) Chatham(95), Moore(2), Randolph(1)
BENSON (27504) Johnston(97), Harnett(2)
BESSEMER CITY Gaston
BETHANIA Forsyth
BETHEL (27812) Pitt(95), Edgecombe(4)
BEULAVILLE (28518) Duplin(90), Onslow(9)
BISCOE (27209) Montgomery(81), Moore(18)
BLACK CREEK Wilson
BLACK MOUNTAIN Buncombe
BLADENBORO (28320) Bladen(91), Columbus(8)
BLANCH Caswell
BLOUNTS CREEK Beaufort
BLOWING ROCK Watauga
BOILING SPRINGS Cleveland
BOLIVIA Brunswick
BOLTON (28423) Columbus(95), Bladen(4)
BONLEE Chatham
BOOMER Wilkes
BOONE Watauga
BOONVILLE Yadkin
BOSTIC Rutherford
BRASSTOWN (28902) Clay(94), Cherokee(5)
BREVARD Transylvania
BRIDGETON Craven
BROADWAY (27505) Harnett(80), Lee(19)
BROWNS SUMMIT Guilford
BRUNSWICK Columbus
BRYSON CITY Swain
BUIES CREEK Harnett
BULLOCK (27507) Granville(93), Vance(6)
BUNN Franklin
BUNNLEVEL Harnett
BURGAW Pender
BURLINGTON (27217) Alamance(92), Caswell(7)
BURLINGTON Alamance
BURNSVILLE Yancey
BUTNER Granville
BUTTERS Bladen
BUXTON Dare
BYNUM Chatham
CALABASH Brunswick
CALYPSO Duplin
CAMDEN Camden
CAMERON (28326) Harnett(45), Moore(34), Lee(20)
CAMP LEJEUNE Onslow
CANDLER Buncombe
CANDOR Montgomery
CANTON Haywood
CAROLEEN Rutherford
CAROLINA BEACH New Hanover
CARRBORO Orange
CARTHAGE Moore
CARY (27519) Wake(97), Durham(1)
CARY Wake
CASAR (28020) Cleveland(85), Rutherford(14)
CASHIERS Jackson
CASTALIA (27816) Nash(76), Franklin(23)
CASTLE HAYNE New Hanover
CATAWBA Catawba
CEDAR FALLS Randolph
CEDAR GROVE Orange
CEDAR ISLAND Carteret
CEDAR MOUNTAIN Transylvania
CERRO GORDO Columbus
CHADBOURN Columbus
CHAPEL HILL (27517) Chatham(40), Orange(39), Durham(20)
CHAPEL HILL (27516) Orange(87), Chatham(12)
CHAPEL HILL Orange
CHARLOTTE (28215) Mecklenburg(94), Cabarrus(5)
CHARLOTTE Mecklenburg
CHEROKEE Swain
CHERRY POINT Craven
CHERRYVILLE (28021) Gaston(85), Lincoln(11), Cleveland(3)
CHIMNEY ROCK Rutherford
CHINA GROVE Rowan
CHINQUAPIN (28521) Duplin(95), Onslow(4)
CHOCOWINITY Beaufort
CLAREMONT Catawba
CLARENDON Columbus
CLARKTON (28433) Bladen(67), Columbus(32)
CLAYTON Johnston
CLEMMONS (27012) Forsyth(75), Davidson(24)
CLEVELAND (27013) Rowan(90), Iredell(9)
CLIFFSIDE Rutherford
CLIMAX (27233) Randolph(66), Guilford(33)
CLINTON Sampson
CLYDE Haywood
COATS Harnett
COFIELD Hertford
COINJOCK Currituck
COLERAIN Bertie
COLFAX Guilford
COLLETTSVILLE (28611) Caldwell(94), Avery(6)
COLUMBIA Tyrrell
COLUMBUS Polk
COMFORT Jones
COMO Hertford
CONCORD Cabarrus
CONETOE Edgecombe
CONNELLYS SPRINGS (28612) Burke(98), Catawba(1)
CONOVER Catawba
CONWAY Northampton
COOLEEMEE Davie
CORAPEAKE Gates
CORDOVA Richmond
CORNELIUS Mecklenburg
COROLLA Currituck
COUNCIL Bladen
COVE CITY Craven
CRAMERTON Gaston
CRANBERRY Avery
CREEDMOOR (27522) Granville(89), Wake(10)
CRESTON Ashe
CRESWELL (27928) Washington(96), Tyrrell(3)
CROSSNORE Avery
CROUSE (28033) Lincoln(90), Gaston(9)
CRUMPLER Ashe
CULBERSON Cherokee
CULLOWHEE Jackson
CUMBERLAND Cumberland
CUMNOCK Lee
CURRIE Pender
CURRITUCK Currituck
DALLAS Gaston
DANA Henderson
DANBURY Stokes
DAVIDSON (28036) Mecklenburg(73), Cabarrus(25), Iredell(1)
DAVIDSON Mecklenburg
DAVIS Carteret
DEEP GAP Watauga
DEEP RUN (28525) Lenoir(89), Duplin(10)
DELCO Columbus
DENTON (27239) Davidson(77), Randolph(22)
DENVER (28037) Lincoln(83), Catawba(16)
DILLSBORO Jackson
DOBSON Surry
DOVER (28526) Craven(83), Jones(13), Lenoir(2)
DREXEL Burke
DUBLIN Bladen
DUDLEY Wayne
DUNN (28334) Harnett(63), Sampson(28), Johnston(6), Cumberland(1)
DUNN Harnett
DURANTS NECK Perquimans
DURHAM (27707) Durham(98), Orange(1)
DURHAM (27713) Durham(98), Chatham(1)
DURHAM Durham
EAGLE ROCK (27523) Wake(66), Chatham(33)
EAGLE SPRINGS Moore
EARL Cleveland
EAST BEND Yadkin
EAST FLAT ROCK Henderson
EAST SPENCER Rowan
EDEN Rockingham
EDENTON Chowan
EDNEYVILLE Henderson
EDWARD Beaufort
EFLAND Orange
ELIZABETH CITY Pasquotank
ELIZABETHTOWN Bladen
ELK PARK Avery
ELKIN (28621) Surry(64), Wilkes(35)
ELLENBORO Rutherford
ELLERBE Richmond

ELM CITY (27822) Wilson(89), Nash(6), Edgecombe(3)
ELON COLLEGE (27244) Alamance(95), Guilford(4)
EMERALD ISLE Carteret
ENFIELD Halifax
ENGELHARD Hyde
ENKA Buncombe
ENNICE Alleghany
ERNUL Craven
ERWIN Harnett
ETHER Montgomery
ETOWAH Henderson
EURE Gates
EVERETTS Martin
EVERGREEN Columbus
FAIR BLUFF Columbus
FAIRFIELD (27826) Hyde(87), Tyrrell(12)
FAIRMONT Robeson
FAIRVIEW Buncombe
FAISON (28341) Sampson(77), Duplin(22)
FAITH Rowan
FALCON Cumberland
FALKLAND Pitt
FALLSTON Cleveland
FARMVILLE Pitt
FAYETTEVILLE (28304) Cumberland(98), Hoke(1)
FAYETTEVILLE (28312) Cumberland(91), Bladen(8)
FAYETTEVILLE Cumberland
FERGUSON Wilkes
FLAT ROCK Henderson
FLEETWOOD Ashe
FLETCHER (28732) Henderson(76), Buncombe(22)
FONTANA DAM Graham
FOREST CITY Rutherford
FORT BRAGG Cumberland
FOUNTAIN (27829) Wilson(72), Pitt(22), Edgecombe(5)
FOUR OAKS (27524) Johnston(97), Wayne(2)
FRANKLIN Macon
FRANKLINTON (27525) Franklin(74), Granville(25)
FRANKLINVILLE Randolph
FREMONT (27830) Wayne(95), Wilson(4)
FRISCO Dare
FUQUAY VARINA (27526) Wake(71), Harnett(28)
GARLAND (28441) Sampson(59), Bladen(39)
GARNER (27529) Wake(77), Johnston(22)
GARYSBURG Northampton
GASTON Northampton
GASTONIA Gaston
GATES Gates
GATESVILLE Gates
GERMANTON (27019) Stokes(74), Forsyth(25)
GERTON Henderson
GIBSON Scotland
GIBSONVILLE (27249) Guilford(63), Alamance(28), Caswell(5), Rockingham(2)
GLADE VALLEY Alleghany
GLEN ALPINE Burke
GLENDALE SPRINGS Ashe
GLENDON Moore
GLENVILLE Jackson
GLENWOOD McDowell
GLOUCESTER Carteret
GODWIN (28344) Sampson(80), Cumberland(19)
GOLD HILL (28071) Rowan(49), Cabarrus(29), Stanly(21)
GOLDSBORO Wayne
GOLDSTON Chatham
GRAHAM Alamance
GRANDY Currituck
GRANITE FALLS Caldwell
GRANITE QUARRY Rowan
GRANTSBORO Pamlico
GRASSY CREEK (28631) Ashe(98), Alleghany(1)
GRAYSON Ashe
GREEN MOUNTAIN Yancey
GREENMOUNTAIN Yancey
GREENSBORO Guilford
GREENVILLE Pitt
GRIFTON (28530) Pitt(46), Lenoir(26), Craven(23), Greene(3)
GRIMESLAND (27837) Pitt(94), Beaufort(5)
GROVER Cleveland
GULF Chatham
GUMBERRY Northampton
HALIFAX Halifax
HALLSBORO Columbus
HAMILTON Martin
HAMLET (28345) Richmond(98), Scotland(1)
HAMPSTEAD Pender
HAMPTONVILLE (27020) Yadkin(76), Wilkes(17), Iredell(6)
HARBINGER Currituck
HARKERS ISLAND Carteret
HARMONY (28634) Iredell(93), Davie(6)
HARRELLS (28444) Bladen(53), Sampson(44), Duplin(1)
HARRELLSVILLE Hertford
HARRIS Rutherford
HARRISBURG Cabarrus
HASSELL Martin
HATTERAS Dare
HAVELOCK Craven
HAW RIVER Alamance
HAYESVILLE Clay
HAYS Wilkes
HAZELWOOD Haywood
HENDERSON (27537) Vance(94), Franklin(3), Warren(1)
HENDERSON Vance
HENDERSONVILLE Henderson
HENRICO (27842) Northampton(97), Warren(2)
HENRIETTA Rutherford
HERTFORD Perquimans
HICKORY (28601) Catawba(96), Caldwell(2)
HICKORY (28602) Catawba(95), Burke(4)
HICKORY Catawba
HIDDENITE (28636) Alexander(96), Iredell(3)
HIGH POINT (27265) Guilford(76), Davidson(22), Forsyth(1)
HIGH POINT (27263) Randolph(59), Guilford(40)
HIGH POINT Guilford
HIGH SHOALS Gaston
HIGHFALLS Moore
HIGHLANDS Macon
HILDEBRAN (28637) Burke(98), Catawba(1)
HILLSBOROUGH (27278) Orange(96), Durham(3)
HOBBSVILLE (27946) Gates(97), Chowan(1)
HOBGOOD (27843) Halifax(90), Edgecombe(8)
HOBUCKEN Pamlico
HOFFMAN (28347) Richmond(92), Moore(7)
HOLLISTER Halifax
HOLLY RIDGE (28445) Onslow(57), Pender(42)
HOLLY SPRINGS (27540) Wake(89), Harnett(10)
HOOKERTON (28538) Greene(79), Lenoir(20)
HOPE MILLS Cumberland
HORSE SHOE Henderson
HOT SPRINGS Madison
HUBERT Onslow
HUDSON Caldwell
HUNTERSVILLE Mecklenburg
HURDLE MILLS (27541) Person(50), Orange(49)
HUSK Ashe
ICARD Burke
INDIAN TRAIL Union
INGOLD Sampson
IRON STATION (28080) Lincoln(98), Gaston(1)
IVANHOE (28447) Sampson(35), Pender(32), Bladen(31)
JACKSON Northampton
JACKSON SPRINGS (27281) Moore(58), Montgomery(35), Richmond(6)
JACKSONVILLE Onslow
JAMESTOWN Guilford
JAMESVILLE Martin
JARVISBURG Currituck
JEFFERSON (28640) Ashe(97), Wilkes(2)
JONAS RIDGE Burke
JONESVILLE (28642) Yadkin(93), Wilkes(6)
JULIAN (27283) Guilford(85), Randolph(14)
KANNAPOLIS (28083) Cabarrus(73), Rowan(26)
KANNAPOLIS Cabarrus
KELFORD Bertie
KELLY Bladen
KENANSVILLE Duplin
KENLY (27542) Wilson(50), Johnston(44), Wayne(5)
KERNERSVILLE (27284) Forsyth(93), Guilford(4), Davidson(2)
KERNERSVILLE Forsyth
KILL DEVIL HILLS Dare
KING (27021) Stokes(97), Forsyth(2)
KINGS MOUNTAIN Cleveland
KINSTON (28501) Lenoir(97), Jones(2)
KINSTON Lenoir
KIPLING Harnett
KITTRELL (27544) Vance(89), Granville(10)
KITTY HAWK Dare
KNIGHTDALE Wake
KNOTTS ISLAND Currituck
KURE BEACH New Hanover
LA GRANGE (28551) Lenoir(66), Wayne(26), Greene(6)
LAKE JUNALUSKA Haywood
LAKE LURE Rutherford
LAKE TOXAWAY Transylvania
LAKE WACCAMAW Columbus
LAKEVIEW Moore
LANDIS Rowan
LANSING Ashe
LASKER Northampton
LATTIMORE Cleveland
LAUREL HILL Scotland
LAUREL SPRINGS (28644) Alleghany(58), Ashe(38), Wilkes(2)
LAURINBURG Scotland
LAWNDALE (28090) Cleveland(90), Lincoln(8)
LAWSONVILLE Stokes
LEASBURG Caswell
LEICESTER Buncombe
LELAND Brunswick
LEMON SPRINGS Lee
LENOIR (28645) Caldwell(98), Wilkes(1)
LENOIR Caldwell
LEWISTON WOODVILLE Bertie
LEWISVILLE Forsyth
LEXINGTON Davidson
LIBERTY (27298) Randolph(59), Alamance(30), Guilford(8), Chatham(1)
LILESVILLE Anson
LILLINGTON Harnett
LINCOLNTON (28092) Lincoln(94), Gaston(4), Catawba(1)
LINCOLNTON Lincoln
LINDEN (28356) Cumberland(68), Harnett(31)
LINVILLE Avery
LINVILLE FALLS Burke
LINWOOD Davidson
LITTLE SWITZERLAND McDowell
LITTLETON (27850) Halifax(83), Warren(16)
LOCUST Stanly
LONGISLAND Catawba
LONGWOOD Brunswick
LOUISBURG Franklin
LOWELL Gaston
LOWGAP Surry
LOWLAND Pamlico
LUCAMA Wilson
LUMBER BRIDGE (28357) Robeson(54), Hoke(45)
LUMBERTON Robeson
LYNN Polk
MACCLESFIELD (27852) Wilson(81), Edgecombe(18)
MACON Warren
MADISON (27025) Rockingham(73), Stokes(26)
MAGGIE VALLEY Haywood
MAGNOLIA (28453) Duplin(73), Sampson(26)
MAIDEN Catawba
MAMERS Harnett
MANNS HARBOR Dare
MANSON (27553) Vance(65), Warren(34)
MANTEO Dare
MAPLE Currituck
MAPLE HILL (28454) Pender(77), Onslow(22)
MARBLE Cherokee
MARGARETTSVILLE Northampton
MARIETTA Robeson
MARION McDowell
MARS HILL (28754) Madison(88), Yancey(11)
MARSHALL Madison
MARSHALLBERG Carteret
MARSHVILLE (28103) Union(98), Anson(1)
MARSTON (28363) Scotland(57), Richmond(42)
MATTHEWS (28105) Mecklenburg(97), Union(2)
MATTHEWS (28104) Union(93), Mecklenburg(6)
MATTHEWS Mecklenburg
MAURY Greene
MAXTON (28364) Robeson(73), Scotland(26)
MAYODAN Rockingham
MAYSVILLE (28555) Onslow(75), Jones(24)
MC ADENVILLE Gaston
MC FARLAN Anson
MC GRADY Wilkes
MC LEANSVILLE Guilford
MCCAIN Hoke
MCCUTCHEON FIELD Onslow
MEBANE (27302) Alamance(60), Orange(26), Caswell(13)
MERRITT Pamlico
MERRY HILL Bertie
MICAVILLE Yancey
MICRO Johnston
MIDDLEBURG Vance
MIDDLESEX (27557) Johnston(51), Nash(46), Wilson(1)
MIDLAND (28107) Cabarrus(88), Mecklenburg(6), Stanly(3), Union(1)
MIDWAY PARK Onslow
MILL SPRING (28756) Polk(97), Rutherford(2)
MILLERS CREEK Wilkes
MILTON (27305) Caswell(98), Person(1)
MILWAUKEE Northampton
MINERAL SPRINGS Union

MINNEAPOLIS Avery
MISENHEIMER Stanly
MOCKSVILLE Davie
MONCURE Chatham
MONROE Union
MONTEZUMA Avery
MONTREAT Buncombe
MOORESBORO (28114) Rutherford(54), Cleveland(45)
MOORESVILLE (28115) Iredell(86), Rowan(13)
MOORESVILLE Iredell
MORAVIAN FALLS Wilkes
MOREHEAD CITY Carteret
MORGANTON Burke
MORRISVILLE (27560) Wake(94), Durham(5)
MORVEN Anson
MOUNT AIRY (27030) Surry(97), Stokes(2)
MOUNT GILEAD (27306) Richmond(59), Montgomery(40)
MOUNT HOLLY Gaston
MOUNT MOURNE Iredell
MOUNT OLIVE (28365) Wayne(65), Duplin(30), Sampson(4)
MOUNT PLEASANT Cabarrus
MOUNT ULLA (28125) Rowan(94), Iredell(5)
MOUNTAIN HOME Henderson
MOYOCK Currituck
MURFREESBORO (27855) Hertford(96), Northampton(3)
MURPHY Cherokee
NAGS HEAD Dare
NAKINA Columbus
NAPLES Henderson
NASHVILLE Nash
NEBO (28761) McDowell(83), Burke(16)
NEW BERN (28560) Craven(89), Pamlico(10)
NEW BERN (28562) Craven(96), Jones(3)
NEW BERN Craven
NEW HILL (27562) Wake(55), Chatham(43)
NEW LONDON (28127) Stanly(60), Montgomery(33), Davidson(5)
NEWELL Mecklenburg
NEWLAND (28657) Avery(88), Burke(11)
NEWPORT Carteret
NEWTON Catawba
NEWTON GROVE (28366) Sampson(81), Johnston(18)
NORLINA Warren
NORMAN Richmond
NORTH WILKESBORO Wilkes
NORTHSIDE Granville
NORWOOD Stanly
OAK CITY Martin
OAK ISLAND Brunswick
OAK RIDGE Guilford
OAKBORO Stanly
OCEAN ISLE BEACH Brunswick
OCRACOKE Hyde
OLD FORT McDowell
OLIN Iredell
OLIVIA Harnett
ORIENTAL Pamlico
ORRUM Robeson
OTTO Macon
OXFORD (27565) Granville(92), Vance(6), Person(1)
PALMYRA Halifax
PANTEGO Beaufort
PARKTON (28371) Robeson(83), Cumberland(16)
PARMELE Martin
PATTERSON Caldwell
PAW CREEK Mecklenburg
PEACHLAND (28133) Anson(90), Union(9)
PELHAM (27311) Caswell(93), Rockingham(6)
PEMBROKE Robeson
PENDLETON Northampton
PENLAND Mitchell
PENROSE (28766) Transylvania(78), Henderson(21)
PFAFFTOWN Forsyth
PIKEVILLE (27863) Wayne(70), Greene(29)
PILOT MOUNTAIN (27041) Surry(67), Stokes(32)
PINE HALL Stokes
PINE LEVEL Johnston
PINEBLUFF Moore
PINEHURST Moore
PINEOLA Avery
PINETOPS Edgecombe
PINETOWN Beaufort
PINEVILLE Mecklenburg
PINEY CREEK Alleghany
PINK HILL (28572) Duplin(55), Lenoir(36), Jones(7)
PINNACLE Stokes
PISGAH FOREST Transylvania
PITTSBORO Chatham
PLEASANT GARDEN (27313) Guilford(59), Randolph(40)
PLEASANT HILL Northampton
PLUMTREE Avery
PLYMOUTH Washington
POINT HARBOR Currituck
POLKTON Anson
POLKVILLE Cleveland
POLLOCKSVILLE (28573) Jones(98), Craven(1)
POPE A F B Cumberland
POPLAR BRANCH Currituck
POTECASI Northampton
POWELLS POINT Currituck
POWELLSVILLE Bertie
PRINCETON (27569) Johnston(88), Wayne(11)
PROCTORVILLE Robeson
PROSPECT HILL Caswell
PROVIDENCE Caswell
PURLEAR Wilkes
RAEFORD Hoke
RALEIGH (27603) Wake(98), Johnston(1)
RALEIGH (27613) Wake(97), Durham(2)
RALEIGH Wake
RAMSEUR Randolph
RANDLEMAN (27317) Randolph(98), Guilford(1)
RED OAK Nash
RED SPRINGS (28377) Robeson(62), Hoke(37)
REIDSVILLE (27320) Rockingham(90), Caswell(9)
REIDSVILLE Rockingham
REX Robeson
RHODHISS Caldwell
RICH SQUARE Northampton
RICHFIELD (28137) Rowan(50), Stanly(49)
RICHLANDS (28574) Onslow(94), Duplin(3), Jones(2)
RIDGECREST Buncombe
RIDGEWAY Warren
RIEGELWOOD (28456) Columbus(51), Bladen(42), Brunswick(6)
ROANOKE RAPIDS Halifax
ROARING GAP Alleghany
ROARING RIVER Wilkes
ROBBINS Moore
ROBBINSVILLE Graham
ROBERSONVILLE (27871) Pitt(83), Martin(16)
ROCKINGHAM Richmond
ROCKWELL (28138) Rowan(81), Cabarrus(18)
ROCKY MOUNT (27803) Nash(89), Wilson(10)
ROCKY MOUNT Edgecombe
ROCKY MOUNT Nash
ROCKY POINT Pender
RODANTHE Dare
RODUCO Gates
ROLESVILLE Wake
RONDA Wilkes
ROPER Washington
ROSE HILL (28458) Duplin(69), Sampson(30)
ROSEBORO (28382) Sampson(80), Cumberland(19)
ROSMAN Transylvania
ROUGEMONT (27572) Orange(40), Person(31), Durham(23), Granville(4)
ROWLAND Robeson
ROXBORO Person
ROXOBEL Bertie
RUFFIN (27326) Rockingham(60), Caswell(40)
RURAL HALL (27045) Forsyth(94), Stokes(5)
RURAL HALL Forsyth
RUTHERFORD COLLEGE Burke
RUTHERFORDTON Rutherford
SAINT PAULS (28384) Robeson(87), Bladen(11)
SALEMBURG Sampson
SALISBURY Rowan
SALTER PATH Carteret
SALUDA (28773) Polk(84), Henderson(15)
SALVO Dare
SANDY RIDGE Stokes
SANFORD (27330) Lee(91), Chatham(6)
SANFORD (27332) Lee(58), Harnett(41)
SANFORD Lee
SAPPHIRE (28774) Jackson(72), Transylvania(27)
SARATOGA Wilson
SAXAPAHAW Alamance
SCALY MOUNTAIN Macon
SCOTLAND NECK Halifax
SCOTTS Iredell
SCOTTVILLE Ashe
SCRANTON Hyde
SEABOARD (27876) Northampton(88), Pitt(11)
SEAGROVE (27341) Randolph(69), Moore(20), Montgomery(10)
SEALEVEL Carteret
SEDALIA Guilford
SELMA Johnston
SEMORA (27343) Person(67), Caswell(32)
SEVEN SPRINGS (28578) Wayne(69), Lenoir(17), Duplin(13)
SEVERN Northampton
SHALLOTTE Brunswick
SHANNON (28386) Robeson(61), Hoke(38)
SHARPSBURG Nash
SHAWBORO (27973) Camden(72), Currituck(27)
SHELBY Cleveland
SHERRILLS FORD (28673) Catawba(97), Lincoln(2)
SHILOH Camden
SILER CITY (27344) Chatham(98), Randolph(1)
SILOAM Surry
SIMPSON Pitt
SIMS (27880) Wilson(92), Nash(7)
SKYLAND Buncombe
SMITHFIELD Johnston
SMYRNA Carteret
SNEADS FERRY Onslow
SNOW CAMP (27349) Alamance(78), Chatham(21)
SNOW HILL Greene
SOPHIA Randolph
SOUTH BRUNSWICK Brunswick
SOUTH MILLS Camden
SOUTHERN PINES Moore
SOUTHMONT Davidson
SOUTHPORT Brunswick
SPARTA Alleghany
SPEED Edgecombe
SPENCER Rowan
SPINDALE Rutherford
SPRING HOPE Nash
SPRING LAKE (28390) Harnett(53), Cumberland(46)
SPRUCE PINE Mitchell
STACY Carteret
STALEY (27355) Randolph(71), Chatham(28)
STANFIELD Stanly
STANLEY (28164) Gaston(78), Lincoln(21)
STANTONSBURG (27883) Wilson(70), Wayne(18), Greene(11)
STAR (27356) Montgomery(85), Moore(14)
STATE ROAD (28676) Wilkes(95), Surry(4)
STATESVILLE Iredell
STEDMAN Cumberland
STELLA (28582) Onslow(63), Carteret(36)
STEM Granville
STOKES Pitt
STOKESDALE (27357) Rockingham(67), Guilford(32)
STONEVILLE Rockingham
STONEWALL Pamlico
STONY POINT Alexander
STOVALL Granville
STUMPY POINT Dare
SUGAR GROVE Watauga
SUMMERFIELD (27358) Guilford(67), Rockingham(32)
SUNBURY Gates
SUNSET BEACH Brunswick
SUPPLY Brunswick
SWANNANOA Buncombe
SWANQUARTER Hyde
SWANSBORO (28584) Carteret(60), Onslow(39)
SWEPSONVILLE Alamance
SYLVA Jackson
TABOR CITY Columbus
TAPOCO Graham
TAR HEEL Bladen
TARAWA TERRACE Onslow
TARBORO Edgecombe
TAYLORSVILLE Alexander
TEACHEY Duplin
TERRELL Catawba
THOMASVILLE (27360) Davidson(94), Randolph(5)
THOMASVILLE Davidson
THURMOND Wilkes
TILLERY Halifax
TIMBERLAKE (27583) Person(98), Orange(1)
TOAST Surry
TOBACCOVILLE (27050) Forsyth(85), Stokes(14)
TODD (28684) Ashe(53), Watauga(46)
TOPTON (28781) Macon(51), Cherokee(48)
TOWNSVILLE Vance
TRAPHILL Wilkes
TRENTON Jones
TRINITY Randolph
TRIPLETT Watauga
TROUTMAN Iredell
TROY (27371) Montgomery(86), Randolph(13)
TRYON Polk
TUCKASEGEE Jackson
TURKEY Sampson
TURNERSBURG Iredell
TUXEDO Henderson
TYNER Chowan
UNION GROVE Iredell
UNION MILLS Rutherford
VALDESE Burke
VALE (28168) Lincoln(55), Catawba(43)
VALLE CRUCIS Watauga
VANCEBORO (28586) Craven(87), Pitt(6), Beaufort(5)

VANDEMERE Pamlico
VASS Moore
VAUGHAN Warren
VILAS Watauga
WACO Cleveland
WADE Cumberland
WADESBORO Anson
WAGRAM Scotland
WAKE FOREST (27587) Wake(94), Granville(3), Franklin(2)
WAKE FOREST Wake
WAKULLA Robeson
WALKERTOWN Forsyth
WALLACE (28466) Duplin(78), Pender(20), Sampson(1)
WALLBURG Davidson
WALNUT COVE (27052) Stokes(89), Forsyth(10)
WALSTONBURG (27888) Wilson(51), Greene(45), Pitt(2)
WANCHESE Dare
WARNE Clay
WARRENSVILLE Ashe
WARRENTON (27589) Warren(97), Franklin(2)
WARSAW Duplin
WASHINGTON (27889) Beaufort(97), Pitt(2)
WATHA Pender
WAVES Dare
WAXHAW Union
WAYNESVILLE Haywood
WEAVERVILLE (28787) Buncombe(95), Madison(4)
WEBSTER Jackson
WELCOME Davidson
WELDON Halifax
WENDELL (27591) Wake(77), Johnston(22)
WENTWORTH Rockingham
WEST END Moore
WEST JEFFERSON Ashe
WESTFIELD Surry
WHITAKERS (27891) Nash(90), Edgecombe(8), Halifax(1)
WHITE OAK Bladen
WHITE PLAINS Surry
WHITEHEAD Alleghany
WHITEVILLE Columbus
WHITSETT Guilford
WHITTIER Jackson
WILBAR Wilkes
WILKESBORO Wilkes
WILLARD (28478) Pender(96), Sampson(3)
WILLIAMSTON Martin
WILLISTON Carteret
WILLOW SPRING (27592) Wake(52), Johnston(43), Harnett(3)
WILMINGTON (28411) New Hanover(88), Pender(11)
WILMINGTON Brunswick
WILMINGTON New Hanover
WILSON (27896) Wilson(84), Nash(15)
WILSON Wilson
WILSONS MILLS Johnston
WINDSOR Bertie
WINFALL Perquimans
WINGATE Union
WINNABOW Brunswick
WINSTON SALEM (27127) Forsyth(89), Davidson(10)
WINSTON SALEM Forsyth
WINSTON-SALEM Forsyth
WINTERVILLE Pitt
WINTON Hertford
WISE Warren
WOODLAND (27897) Northampton(92), Hertford(7)
WOODLEAF Rowan
WRIGHTSVILLE BEACH New Hanover
YADKINVILLE Yadkin
YANCEYVILLE Caswell
YOUNGSVILLE (27596) Franklin(87), Wake(8), Granville(3)
ZEBULON (27597) Wake(76), Franklin(14), Johnston(4), Nash(4)
ZIONVILLE (28698) Watauga(98), Ashe(1)
ZIRCONIA Henderson

North Carolina ZIP/City Cross Reference

27006-27006 ADVANCE
27007-27007 ARARAT
27008-27008 BARBER
27009-27009 BELEWS CREEK
27010-27010 BETHANIA
27011-27011 BOONVILLE
27012-27012 CLEMMONS
27013-27013 CLEVELAND
27014-27014 COOLEEMEE
27016-27016 DANBURY
27017-27017 DOBSON
27018-27018 EAST BEND
27019-27019 GERMANTON
27020-27020 HAMPTONVILLE
27021-27021 KING
27022-27022 LAWSONVILLE
27023-27023 LEWISVILLE
27024-27024 LOWGAP
27025-27025 MADISON
27027-27027 MAYODAN
27028-27028 MOCKSVILLE
27030-27030 MOUNT AIRY
27031-27031 WHITE PLAINS
27040-27040 PFAFFTOWN
27041-27041 PILOT MOUNTAIN
27042-27042 PINE HALL
27043-27043 PINNACLE
27045-27045 RURAL HALL
27046-27046 SANDY RIDGE
27047-27047 SILOAM
27048-27048 STONEVILLE
27049-27049 TOAST
27050-27050 TOBACCOVILLE
27051-27051 WALKERTOWN
27052-27052 WALNUT COVE
27053-27053 WESTFIELD
27054-27054 WOODLEAF
27055-27055 YADKINVILLE
27094-27099 RURAL HALL
27100-27100 WINSTON-SALEM
27100-27100 WINSTON SALEM
27100-27100 WINSTON-SALEM
27101-27199 WINSTON SALEM
27201-27201 ALAMANCE
27202-27202 ALTAMAHAW
27203-27205 ASHEBORO
27207-27207 BEAR CREEK
27208-27208 BENNETT
27209-27209 BISCOE
27212-27212 BLANCH
27213-27213 BONLEE
27214-27214 BROWNS SUMMIT
27215-27220 BURLINGTON
27228-27228 BYNUM
27229-27229 CANDOR
27230-27230 CEDAR FALLS
27231-27231 CEDAR GROVE
27233-27233 CLIMAX
27235-27235 COLFAX
27237-27237 CUMNOCK
27239-27239 DENTON
27242-27242 EAGLE SPRINGS
27243-27243 EFLAND
27244-27244 ELON COLLEGE
27247-27247 ETHER
27248-27248 FRANKLINVILLE
27249-27249 GIBSONVILLE
27251-27251 GLENDON
27252-27252 GOLDSTON
27253-27253 GRAHAM
27256-27256 GULF
27258-27258 HAW RIVER
27259-27259 HIGHFALLS
27260-27265 HIGH POINT
27278-27278 HILLSBOROUGH
27281-27281 JACKSON SPRINGS
27282-27282 JAMESTOWN
27283-27283 JULIAN
27284-27285 KERNERSVILLE
27288-27289 EDEN
27291-27291 LEASBURG
27292-27295 LEXINGTON
27298-27298 LIBERTY
27299-27299 LINWOOD
27301-27301 MC LEANSVILLE
27302-27302 MEBANE
27305-27305 MILTON
27306-27306 MOUNT GILEAD
27310-27310 OAK RIDGE
27311-27311 PELHAM
27312-27312 PITTSBORO
27313-27313 PLEASANT GARDEN
27314-27314 PROSPECT HILL
27315-27315 PROVIDENCE
27316-27316 RAMSEUR
27317-27317 RANDLEMAN
27320-27323 REIDSVILLE
27325-27325 ROBBINS
27326-27326 RUFFIN
27330-27332 SANFORD
27340-27340 SAXAPAHAW
27341-27341 SEAGROVE
27342-27342 SEDALIA
27343-27343 SEMORA
27344-27344 SILER CITY
27349-27349 SNOW CAMP
27350-27350 SOPHIA
27351-27351 SOUTHMONT
27355-27355 STALEY
27356-27356 STAR
27357-27357 STOKESDALE
27358-27358 SUMMERFIELD
27359-27359 SWEPSONVILLE
27360-27361 THOMASVILLE
27370-27370 TRINITY
27371-27371 TROY
27373-27373 WALLBURG
27374-27374 WELCOME
27375-27375 WENTWORTH
27376-27376 WEST END
27377-27377 WHITSETT
27379-27379 YANCEYVILLE
27395-27499 GREENSBORO
27501-27501 ANGIER
27502-27502 APEX
27503-27503 BAHAMA
27504-27504 BENSON
27505-27505 BROADWAY
27506-27506 BUIES CREEK
27507-27507 BULLOCK
27508-27508 BUNN
27509-27509 BUTNER
27510-27510 CARRBORO
27511-27513 CARY
27514-27517 CHAPEL HILL
27518-27519 CARY
27520-27520 CLAYTON
27521-27521 COATS
27522-27522 CREEDMOOR
27523-27523 EAGLE ROCK
27523-27523 APEX
27524-27524 FOUR OAKS
27525-27525 FRANKLINTON
27526-27526 FUQUAY VARINA
27527-27528 CLAYTON
27529-27529 GARNER
27530-27534 GOLDSBORO
27536-27537 HENDERSON
27539-27539 APEX
27540-27540 HOLLY SPRINGS
27541-27541 HURDLE MILLS
27542-27542 KENLY
27543-27543 KIPLING
27544-27544 KITTRELL
27545-27545 KNIGHTDALE
27546-27546 LILLINGTON
27549-27549 LOUISBURG
27551-27551 MACON
27552-27552 MAMERS
27553-27553 MANSON
27555-27555 MICRO
27556-27556 MIDDLEBURG
27557-27557 MIDDLESEX
27559-27559 MONCURE
27560-27560 MORRISVILLE
27562-27562 NEW HILL
27563-27563 NORLINA
27564-27564 NORTHSIDE
27565-27565 OXFORD
27568-27568 PINE LEVEL
27569-27569 PRINCETON
27570-27570 RIDGEWAY
27571-27571 ROLESVILLE
27572-27572 ROUGEMONT
27573-27574 ROXBORO
27576-27576 SELMA
27577-27577 SMITHFIELD
27581-27581 STEM
27582-27582 STOVALL
27583-27583 TIMBERLAKE
27584-27584 TOWNSVILLE
27586-27586 VAUGHAN
27587-27588 WAKE FOREST
27589-27589 WARRENTON
27591-27591 WENDELL
27592-27592 WILLOW SPRING
27593-27593 WILSONS MILLS
27594-27594 WISE
27596-27596 YOUNGSVILLE
27597-27597 ZEBULON
27599-27599 CHAPEL HILL
27600-27699 RALEIGH
27700-27722 DURHAM
27801-27804 ROCKY MOUNT
27805-27805 AULANDER
27806-27806 AURORA
27807-27807 BAILEY
27808-27808 BATH
27809-27809 BATTLEBORO
27810-27810 BELHAVEN
27811-27811 BELLARTHUR
27812-27812 BETHEL
27813-27813 BLACK CREEK
27814-27814 BLOUNTS CREEK
27816-27816 CASTALIA
27817-27817 CHOCOWINITY
27818-27818 COMO
27819-27819 CONETOE
27820-27820 CONWAY
27821-27821 EDWARD
27822-27822 ELM CITY
27823-27823 ENFIELD
27824-27824 ENGELHARD
27825-27825 EVERETTS
27826-27826 FAIRFIELD
27827-27827 FALKLAND

27828-27828	FARMVILLE
27829-27829	FOUNTAIN
27830-27830	FREMONT
27831-27831	GARYSBURG
27832-27832	GASTON
27833-27836	GREENVILLE
27837-27837	GRIMESLAND
27838-27838	GUMBERRY
27839-27839	HALIFAX
27840-27840	HAMILTON
27841-27841	HASSELL
27842-27842	HENRICO
27843-27843	HOBGOOD
27844-27844	HOLLISTER
27845-27845	JACKSON
27846-27846	JAMESVILLE
27847-27847	KELFORD
27848-27848	LASKER
27849-27849	LEWISTON WOODVILLE
27850-27850	LITTLETON
27851-27851	LUCAMA
27852-27852	MACCLESFIELD
27853-27853	MARGARETTSVILLE
27854-27854	MILWAUKEE
27855-27855	MURFREESBORO
27856-27856	NASHVILLE
27857-27857	OAK CITY
27858-27858	GREENVILLE
27859-27859	PALMYRA
27860-27860	PANTEGO
27861-27861	PARMELE
27862-27862	PENDLETON
27863-27863	PIKEVILLE
27864-27864	PINETOPS
27865-27865	PINETOWN
27866-27866	PLEASANT HILL
27867-27867	POTECASI
27868-27868	RED OAK
27869-27869	RICH SQUARE
27870-27870	ROANOKE RAPIDS
27871-27871	ROBERSONVILLE
27872-27872	ROXOBEL
27873-27873	SARATOGA
27874-27874	SCOTLAND NECK
27875-27875	SCRANTON
27876-27876	SEABOARD
27877-27877	SEVERN
27878-27878	SHARPSBURG
27879-27879	SIMPSON
27880-27880	SIMS
27881-27881	SPEED
27882-27882	SPRING HOPE
27883-27883	STANTONSBURG
27884-27884	STOKES
27885-27885	SWANQUARTER
27886-27886	TARBORO
27887-27887	TILLERY
27888-27888	WALSTONBURG
27889-27889	WASHINGTON
27890-27890	WELDON
27891-27891	WHITAKERS
27892-27892	WILLIAMSTON
27893-27896	WILSON
27897-27897	WOODLAND
27906-27909	ELIZABETH CITY
27910-27910	AHOSKIE
27915-27915	AVON
27916-27916	AYDLETT
27917-27917	BARCO
27919-27919	BELVIDERE
27920-27920	BUXTON
27921-27921	CAMDEN
27922-27922	COFIELD
27923-27923	COINJOCK
27924-27924	COLERAIN
27925-27925	COLUMBIA
27926-27926	CORAPEAKE
27927-27927	COROLLA
27928-27928	CRESWELL
27929-27929	CURRITUCK
27930-27930	DURANTS NECK
27932-27932	EDENTON
27935-27935	EURE
27936-27936	FRISCO
27937-27937	GATES
27938-27938	GATESVILLE
27939-27939	GRANDY
27941-27941	HARBINGER
27942-27942	HARRELLSVILLE
27943-27943	HATTERAS
27944-27944	HERTFORD
27946-27946	HOBBSVILLE
27947-27947	JARVISBURG
27948-27948	KILL DEVIL HILLS
27949-27949	KITTY HAWK
27950-27950	KNOTTS ISLAND
27953-27953	MANNS HARBOR
27954-27954	MANTEO
27956-27956	MAPLE
27957-27957	MERRY HILL
27958-27958	MOYOCK
27959-27959	NAGS HEAD
27960-27960	OCRACOKE
27962-27962	PLYMOUTH
27964-27964	POINT HARBOR
27965-27965	POPLAR BRANCH
27966-27966	POWELLS POINT
27967-27967	POWELLSVILLE
27968-27968	RODANTHE
27969-27969	RODUCO
27970-27970	ROPER
27972-27972	SALVO
27973-27973	SHAWBORO
27974-27974	SHILOH
27976-27976	SOUTH MILLS
27978-27978	STUMPY POINT
27979-27979	SUNBURY
27980-27980	TYNER
27981-27981	WANCHESE
27982-27982	WAVES
27983-27983	WINDSOR
27985-27985	WINFALL
27986-27986	WINTON
28001-28002	ALBEMARLE
28006-28006	ALEXIS
28007-28007	ANSONVILLE
28009-28009	BADIN
28010-28010	BARIUM SPRINGS
28012-28012	BELMONT
28016-28016	BESSEMER CITY
28017-28017	BOILING SPRINGS
28018-28018	BOSTIC
28019-28019	CAROLEEN
28020-28020	CASAR
28021-28021	CHERRYVILLE
28023-28023	CHINA GROVE
28024-28024	CLIFFSIDE
28025-28027	CONCORD
28031-28031	CORNELIUS
28032-28032	CRAMERTON
28033-28033	CROUSE
28034-28034	DALLAS
28035-28036	DAVIDSON
28037-28037	DENVER
28038-28038	EARL
28039-28039	EAST SPENCER
28040-28040	ELLENBORO
28041-28041	FAITH
28042-28042	FALLSTON
28043-28043	FOREST CITY
28051-28056	GASTONIA
28070-28070	HUNTERSVILLE
28071-28071	GOLD HILL
28072-28072	GRANITE QUARRY
28073-28073	GROVER
28074-28074	HARRIS
28075-28075	HARRISBURG
28076-28076	HENRIETTA
28077-28077	HIGH SHOALS
28078-28078	HUNTERSVILLE
28079-28079	INDIAN TRAIL
28080-28080	IRON STATION
28081-28083	KANNAPOLIS
28086-28086	KINGS MOUNTAIN
28088-28088	LANDIS
28089-28089	LATTIMORE
28090-28090	LAWNDALE
28091-28091	LILESVILLE
28092-28093	LINCOLNTON
28097-28097	LOCUST
28098-28098	LOWELL
28101-28101	MC ADENVILLE
28102-28102	MC FARLAN
28103-28103	MARSHVILLE
28104-28106	MATTHEWS
28107-28107	MIDLAND
28108-28108	MINERAL SPRINGS
28109-28109	MISENHEIMER
28110-28112	MONROE
28114-28114	MOORESBORO
28115-28117	MOORESVILLE
28119-28119	MORVEN
28120-28120	MOUNT HOLLY
28123-28123	MOUNT MOURNE
28124-28124	MOUNT PLEASANT
28125-28125	MOUNT ULLA
28126-28126	NEWELL
28127-28127	NEW LONDON
28128-28128	NORWOOD
28129-28129	OAKBORO
28130-28130	PAW CREEK
28133-28133	PEACHLAND
28134-28134	PINEVILLE
28135-28135	POLKTON
28136-28136	POLKVILLE
28137-28137	RICHFIELD
28138-28138	ROCKWELL
28139-28139	RUTHERFORDTON
28144-28147	SALISBURY
28150-28152	SHELBY
28159-28159	SPENCER
28160-28160	SPINDALE
28163-28163	STANFIELD
28164-28164	STANLEY
28166-28166	TROUTMAN
28167-28167	UNION MILLS
28168-28168	VALE
28169-28169	WACO
28170-28170	WADESBORO
28173-28173	WAXHAW
28174-28174	WINGATE
28200-28299	CHARLOTTE
28301-28306	FAYETTEVILLE
28307-28307	FORT BRAGG
28308-28308	POPE A F B
28309-28309	FAYETTEVILLE
28310-28310	FORT BRAGG
28311-28314	FAYETTEVILLE
28315-28315	ABERDEEN
28318-28318	AUTRYVILLE
28319-28319	BARNESVILLE
28320-28320	BLADENBORO
28323-28323	BUNNLEVEL
28324-28324	BUTTERS
28325-28325	CALYPSO
28326-28326	CAMERON
28327-28327	CARTHAGE
28328-28329	CLINTON
28330-28330	CORDOVA
28331-28331	CUMBERLAND
28332-28332	DUBLIN
28333-28333	DUDLEY
28334-28335	DUNN
28337-28337	ELIZABETHTOWN
28338-28338	ELLERBE
28339-28339	ERWIN
28340-28340	FAIRMONT
28341-28341	FAISON
28342-28342	FALCON
28343-28343	GIBSON
28344-28344	GODWIN
28345-28345	HAMLET
28347-28347	HOFFMAN
28348-28348	HOPE MILLS
28349-28349	KENANSVILLE
28350-28350	LAKEVIEW
28351-28351	LAUREL HILL
28352-28353	LAURINBURG
28355-28355	LEMON SPRINGS
28356-28356	LINDEN
28357-28357	LUMBER BRIDGE
28358-28360	LUMBERTON
28361-28361	MCCAIN
28362-28362	MARIETTA
28363-28363	MARSTON
28364-28364	MAXTON
28365-28365	MOUNT OLIVE
28366-28366	NEWTON GROVE
28367-28367	NORMAN
28368-28368	OLIVIA
28369-28369	ORRUM
28370-28370	PINEHURST
28371-28371	PARKTON
28372-28372	PEMBROKE
28373-28373	PINEBLUFF
28374-28374	PINEHURST
28375-28375	PROCTORVILLE
28376-28376	RAEFORD
28377-28377	RED SPRINGS
28378-28378	REX
28379-28380	ROCKINGHAM
28382-28382	ROSEBORO
28383-28383	ROWLAND
28384-28384	SAINT PAULS
28385-28385	SALEMBURG
28386-28386	SHANNON
28387-28388	SOUTHERN PINES
28390-28390	SPRING LAKE
28391-28391	STEDMAN
28392-28392	TAR HEEL
28393-28393	TURKEY
28394-28394	VASS
28395-28395	WADE
28396-28396	WAGRAM
28397-28397	WAKULLA
28398-28398	WARSAW
28399-28399	WHITE OAK
28401-28412	WILMINGTON
28420-28420	ASH
28421-28421	ATKINSON
28422-28422	BOLIVIA
28423-28423	BOLTON
28424-28424	BRUNSWICK
28425-28425	BURGAW
28428-28428	CAROLINA BEACH
28429-28429	CASTLE HAYNE
28430-28430	CERRO GORDO
28431-28431	CHADBOURN
28432-28432	CLARENDON
28433-28433	CLARKTON
28434-28434	COUNCIL
28435-28435	CURRIE
28436-28436	DELCO
28438-28438	EVERGREEN
28439-28439	FAIR BLUFF
28441-28441	GARLAND
28442-28442	HALLSBORO
28443-28443	HAMPSTEAD
28444-28444	HARRELLS
28445-28445	HOLLY RIDGE
28446-28446	INGOLD
28447-28447	IVANHOE
28448-28448	KELLY
28449-28449	KURE BEACH
28450-28450	LAKE WACCAMAW
28451-28451	LELAND
28452-28452	LONGWOOD
28453-28453	MAGNOLIA
28454-28454	MAPLE HILL
28455-28455	NAKINA
28456-28456	RIEGELWOOD
28457-28457	ROCKY POINT
28458-28458	ROSE HILL
28459-28459	SHALLOTTE
28460-28460	SNEADS FERRY
28461-28461	SOUTHPORT
28462-28462	SUPPLY
28463-28463	TABOR CITY

28464-28464 TEACHEY
28465-28465 OAK ISLAND
28466-28466 WALLACE
28467-28467 CALABASH
28468-28468 SUNSET BEACH
28469-28469 OCEAN ISLE BEACH
28470-28470 SOUTH BRUNSWICK
28471-28471 WATHA
28472-28472 WHITEVILLE
28478-28478 WILLARD
28479-28479 WINNABOW
28480-28480 WRIGHTSVILLE BEACH
28501-28504 KINSTON
28508-28508 ALBERTSON
28509-28509 ALLIANCE
28510-28510 ARAPAHOE
28511-28511 ATLANTIC
28512-28512 ATLANTIC BEACH
28513-28513 AYDEN
28515-28515 BAYBORO
28516-28516 BEAUFORT
28518-28518 BEULAVILLE
28519-28519 BRIDGETON
28520-28520 CEDAR ISLAND
28521-28521 CHINQUAPIN
28522-28522 COMFORT
28523-28523 COVE CITY
28524-28524 DAVIS
28525-28525 DEEP RUN
28526-28526 DOVER
28527-28527 ERNUL
28528-28528 GLOUCESTER
28529-28529 GRANTSBORO
28530-28530 GRIFTON
28531-28531 HARKERS ISLAND
28532-28532 HAVELOCK
28533-28533 CHERRY POINT
28537-28537 HOBUCKEN
28538-28538 HOOKERTON
28539-28539 HUBERT
28540-28541 JACKSONVILLE
28542-28542 CAMP LEJEUNE
28543-28543 TARAWA TERRACE
28544-28544 MIDWAY PARK
28545-28545 MCCUTCHEON FIELD
28546-28546 JACKSONVILLE
28547-28547 CAMP LEJEUNE
28551-28551 LA GRANGE
28552-28552 LOWLAND
28553-28553 MARSHALLBERG
28554-28554 MAURY
28555-28555 MAYSVILLE
28556-28556 MERRITT
28557-28557 MOREHEAD CITY
28560-28564 NEW BERN
28570-28570 NEWPORT
28571-28571 ORIENTAL
28572-28572 PINK HILL
28573-28573 POLLOCKSVILLE
28574-28574 RICHLANDS
28575-28575 SALTER PATH
28577-28577 SEALEVEL
28578-28578 SEVEN SPRINGS
28579-28579 SMYRNA
28580-28580 SNOW HILL
28581-28581 STACY
28582-28582 STELLA
28583-28583 STONEWALL
28584-28584 SWANSBORO
28585-28585 TRENTON
28586-28586 VANCEBORO
28587-28587 VANDEMERE
28589-28589 WILLISTON
28590-28590 WINTERVILLE
28594-28594 EMERALD ISLE
28601-28603 HICKORY
28604-28604 BANNER ELK
28605-28605 BLOWING ROCK
28606-28606 BOOMER
28607-28608 BOONE
28609-28609 CATAWBA
28610-28610 CLAREMONT
28611-28611 COLLETTSVILLE
28612-28612 CONNELLYS SPRINGS
28613-28613 CONOVER
28614-28614 CRANBERRY
28615-28615 CRESTON
28616-28616 CROSSNORE
28617-28617 CRUMPLER
28618-28618 DEEP GAP
28619-28619 DREXEL
28621-28621 ELKIN
28622-28622 ELK PARK
28623-28623 ENNICE
28624-28624 FERGUSON
28625-28625 STATESVILLE
28626-28626 FLEETWOOD
28627-28627 GLADE VALLEY
28628-28628 GLEN ALPINE
28629-28629 GLENDALE SPRINGS
28630-28630 GRANITE FALLS
28631-28631 GRASSY CREEK
28632-28632 GRAYSON
28633-28633 LENOIR
28634-28634 HARMONY
28635-28635 HAYS
28636-28636 HIDDENITE
28637-28637 HILDEBRAN
28638-28638 HUDSON
28639-28639 HUSK
28640-28640 JEFFERSON
28641-28641 JONAS RIDGE
28642-28642 JONESVILLE
28643-28643 LANSING
28644-28644 LAUREL SPRINGS
28645-28645 LENOIR
28646-28646 LINVILLE
28647-28647 LINVILLE FALLS
28648-28648 LONGISLAND
28649-28649 MC GRADY
28650-28650 MAIDEN
28651-28651 MILLERS CREEK
28652-28652 MINNEAPOLIS
28653-28653 MONTEZUMA
28654-28654 MORAVIAN FALLS
28655-28655 MORGANTON
28656-28656 NORTH WILKESBORO
28657-28657 NEWLAND
28658-28658 NEWTON
28659-28659 NORTH WILKESBORO
28660-28660 OLIN
28661-28661 PATTERSON
28662-28662 PINEOLA
28663-28663 PINEY CREEK
28664-28664 PLUMTREE
28665-28665 PURLEAR
28666-28666 ICARD
28667-28667 RHODHISS
28668-28668 ROARING GAP
28669-28669 ROARING RIVER
28670-28670 RONDA
28671-28671 RUTHERFORD COLLEGE
28672-28672 SCOTTVILLE
28673-28673 SHERRILLS FORD
28674-28674 NORTH WILKESBORO
28675-28675 SPARTA
28676-28676 STATE ROAD
28677-28677 STATESVILLE
28678-28678 STONY POINT
28679-28679 SUGAR GROVE
28680-28680 MORGANTON
28681-28681 TAYLORSVILLE
28682-28682 TERRELL
28683-28683 THURMOND
28684-28684 TODD
28685-28685 TRAPHILL
28686-28686 TRIPLETT
28687-28687 STATESVILLE
28688-28688 TURNERSBURG
28689-28689 UNION GROVE
28690-28690 VALDESE
28691-28691 VALLE CRUCIS
28692-28692 VILAS
28693-28693 WARRENSVILLE
28694-28694 WEST JEFFERSON
28695-28695 WHITEHEAD
28696-28696 WILBAR
28697-28697 WILKESBORO
28698-28698 ZIONVILLE
28699-28699 SCOTTS
28701-28701 ALEXANDER
28702-28702 ALMOND
28703-28703 AQUONE
28704-28704 ARDEN
28705-28705 BAKERSVILLE
28707-28707 BALSAM
28708-28708 BALSAM GROVE
28709-28709 BARNARDSVILLE
28710-28710 BAT CAVE
28711-28711 BLACK MOUNTAIN
28712-28712 BREVARD
28713-28713 BRYSON CITY
28714-28714 BURNSVILLE
28715-28715 CANDLER
28716-28716 CANTON
28717-28717 CASHIERS
28718-28718 CEDAR MOUNTAIN
28719-28719 CHEROKEE
28720-28720 CHIMNEY ROCK
28721-28721 CLYDE
28722-28722 COLUMBUS
28723-28723 CULLOWHEE
28724-28724 DANA
28725-28725 DILLSBORO
28726-28726 EAST FLAT ROCK
28727-28727 EDNEYVILLE
28728-28728 ENKA
28729-28729 ETOWAH
28730-28730 FAIRVIEW
28731-28731 FLAT ROCK
28732-28732 FLETCHER
28733-28733 FONTANA DAM
28734-28734 FRANKLIN
28735-28735 GERTON
28736-28736 GLENVILLE
28737-28737 GLENWOOD
28738-28738 HAZELWOOD
28739-28739 HENDERSONVILLE
28740-28740 GREENMOUNTAIN
28740-28740 GREEN MOUNTAIN
28741-28741 HIGHLANDS
28742-28742 HORSE SHOE
28743-28743 HOT SPRINGS
28744-28744 FRANKLIN
28745-28745 LAKE JUNALUSKA
28746-28746 LAKE LURE
28747-28747 LAKE TOXAWAY
28748-28748 LEICESTER
28749-28749 LITTLE SWITZERLAND
28750-28750 LYNN
28751-28751 MAGGIE VALLEY
28752-28752 MARION
28753-28753 MARSHALL
28754-28754 MARS HILL
28755-28755 MICAVILLE
28756-28756 MILL SPRING
28757-28757 MONTREAT
28758-28758 MOUNTAIN HOME
28760-28760 NAPLES
28761-28761 NEBO
28762-28762 OLD FORT
28763-28763 OTTO
28765-28765 PENLAND
28766-28766 PENROSE
28768-28768 PISGAH FOREST
28770-28770 RIDGECREST
28771-28771 ROBBINSVILLE
28772-28772 ROSMAN
28773-28773 SALUDA
28774-28774 SAPPHIRE
28775-28775 SCALY MOUNTAIN
28776-28776 SKYLAND
28777-28777 SPRUCE PINE
28778-28778 SWANNANOA
28779-28779 SYLVA
28780-28780 TAPOCO
28781-28781 TOPTON
28782-28782 TRYON
28783-28783 TUCKASEGEE
28784-28784 TUXEDO
28785-28786 WAYNESVILLE
28787-28787 WEAVERVILLE
28788-28788 WEBSTER
28789-28789 WHITTIER
28790-28790 ZIRCONIA
28791-28793 HENDERSONVILLE
28800-28816 ASHEVILLE
28901-28901 ANDREWS
28902-28902 BRASSTOWN
28903-28903 CULBERSON
28904-28904 HAYESVILLE
28905-28905 MARBLE
28906-28906 MURPHY
28909-28909 WARNE

North Dakota

General Help Numbers:

Governor's Office

State Capitol Dept.101 — 701-328-2200
600 E Boulevard Ave, 1st Floor — Fax 701-328-2205
Bismarck, ND 58505-0001 — 8AM-5PM
www.governor.state.nd.us

Attorney General's Office

State Capitol - Dept 125 — 701-328-2210
600 E Boulevard Ave — Fax 701-328-2226
Bismarck, ND 58505-0040 — 8AM-5PM
www.ag.state.nd.us

Legislative Records

North Dakota Legislative Council — 701-328-2916
600 E Blvd Ave — Fax 701-328-3615
Bismarck, ND 58505 — 8AM-5PM
www.legis.nd.gov/

State Archives

State Archives & — 701-328-2666
Historical Research Library — Fax 701-328-2650
N Dakota Heritage Center, 612 E Blvd Ave — 8AM-5PM
Bismarck, ND 58505-0830
www.nd.gov/hist/sal.htm

State Specifics:

Capital:	Bismarck Burleigh County
Time Zone:	CST
Number of Counties:	53
Population:	641,481
Web Site:	www.nd.gov/

State Agencies

Criminal Records

Bureau of Criminal Investigation, Criminal Records Section, PO Box 1054, Bismarck, ND 58502-1054 (Courier address- 4205 State St, Bismarck, ND 58501); 701-328-5500, Fax- 701-328-5510; 8AM-5PM.

www.ag.state.nd.us/BCI/CHR/CHR.html

Direct questions to bcinfo@state.nd.us.

Indexing & Storage: Records available from 1930 to present. New records available for inquiry in 6 to 10 days. 86% of all arrests in database have final dispositions recorded, including those arrests within last 5 years.

Searching: Subject will be notified of the request if a signed release is not submitted. A request form and an authorization form are both downloadable from the web. Include in request- either the signed release from subject or the address of subject, name, DOB, current address, SSN. Fingerprint searches are available to public. 100% of the records are fingerprint supported. This data not released- cases dismissed or scaled After three years, only records with convictions are released. Charges that are dismissed or sealed are not released as well as Jail or prison custody records that are more than three years old.

Access by: mail, in person.

Fee & Payment: The search fee is $15.00 per name. There is no extra fee for a fingerprint search, must be requested in writing. Fee payee- ND Attorney General. Prepayment required. Personal checks accepted, credit cards are not.

Mail search: Turnaround time- 3 to 5 days. SASE not required. **In person:** Turnaround time while you wait.

Statewide Court Records

Court Administrator, North Dakota Supreme Court, 600 E Blvd Ave, Dept 180, Bismarck, ND 58505-0530; 701-328-4216, Fax- 701-328-2092; 8AM-5PM. www.ndcourts.com

There is no statewide service for trial courts records. Except for certain online research capabilities, all court record access must be done at the local level at any court office.

Indexing & Storage: New records available for inquiry in 24 hours or less.

Online search: You may search ND Supreme Court dockets and opinions at the website. Search by docket number, party name, or anything else that may appear in the text. Records are from 1982 forward. Subscribe to receive e-mail notification when new Opinions are posted to the North Dakota Supreme Court website, and to be informed when Supreme Court Notices (of proposed or new rules, and the like) are posted.

Sexual Offender Registry

Bureau of Criminal Investigation, SOR Unit, PO Box 1054, Bismarck, ND 58502-1054 (Courier address- 4205 N State St, Bismarck, ND 58501); 701-328-5500, Fax- 701-328-5510; 8AM-5PM.

www.sexoffender.nd.gov/

The agency will not process search/name requests from this office. All searching must be performed at the web page.

Indexing & Storage: Records available from 1991. Paper records go back 10 years. New records available for inquiry in 6 to 10 days.

Searching: Offender information may be requested by city, county, or the entire state, and by type of risk. This data not released- juvenile record data.

Fee & Payment: There is no fee.

Online search: Access is available from the website. Information on all offenders with a registration requirement (including moderate and low risk offenders) can be downloaded. See 'Printable List of All Offenders' at www.sexoffender.nd.gov/PublicListing.aspx.

Incarceration Records

Department of Corrections and Rehabilitation, Records Clerk, PO Box 5521, Bismarck, ND 58506 (Courier address- 3100 E Railroad Ave, Bismarck, ND 58506); 701-328-6122, Fax- 701-328-6640; 8AM-5PM. www.nd.gov/docr/

Employees of the Prisons Division may not disclose inmate information except as granted in North Dakota Century Code 12-47-36.

Indexing & Storage: Records available on current and former inmates. New records available for inquiry in about 3 days.

Searching: Include in request- first and last name. DOB is helpful. Location, conviction and sentencing information, and release dates are provided. This data not released- treatment information, bulk data.

Access by: mail, phone, fax.

Fee & Payment: There is no fee.

Mail search: Turnaround time- 5 to 7 days. Requests in writing must be specific about information requested. A SASE is not requested.

Phone search: Searching available by telephone.

Fax search: May request via the fax.

Corporation, LLC, LP, LLP, Trademarks/Servicemarks, Fictitious/Assumed Name

Secretary of State, Business Information/ Registration, 600 E Boulevard Ave, Dept 108, Bismarck, ND 58505-0500; 701-328-4284, 800-352-0867, Fax- 701-328-2992; 8AM-5PM.

www.nd.gov/sos/businessserv/

Indexing & Storage: Records available from 1889. Records are computerized since 1989. Records inactive prior to 1989 are maintained by state archives; may take up to 2 weeks to search. New records available for inquiry immediately.

Searching: Include in request- full name of business. In addition to the articles of organization, business entity records available include: Annual Reports, Officers, Directors, DBAs, Prior (merged) names, Inactive names, and Reserved names. Data not released- financial information.

Access by: mail, phone, fax, in person, online.

Fee & Payment: There is a search fee of $5.00 if a written confirmation is required or if data must be retrieved from the archives. Copies cost $1.00 for each 4 pages or fraction thereof. Certification is an additional $15.00. Fee payee- Secretary of State. Prepayment required. Personal checks accepted. Visa/MC/Discover accepted.

Mail search: Turnaround time- 3 to 5 days. SASE not required.

Phone search: There is no fee for verbal confirmation on an active record, otherwise there is a $5.00 fee. **Fax search:** Same fees as phone searching. Turnaround time is 1-3 days if written confirmation required. Add $1.00 per page for fax results.

In person: No fee on active records, $5.00 fee on inactive records or if in archives. Turnaround time is usually while you wait.

Online search: The Secretary of State's registered business database may be viewed at the Internet for no charge. Documents are not available online. Records include corporations, limited liability companies, limited partnerships, limited liability partnerships, limited liability limited partnerships, partnership fictitious names, trade names, trademarks, and real estate investment trusts. The database includes all active records and records inactivated within past twelve months. Access by the first few words of a business name, a significant word in a business name, or by the record ID number assigned. If questions, email sosbir@nd.gov. Also, search securities industry professionals database free at www.ndsecurities.com/links/industry-professionals.asp.

Other access: This agency provides a database purchase program. Cost is $35.00 per database and processing fees vary for type of media.

Uniform Commercial Code, Federal & State Tax Liens

UCC Division, Secretary of State, 600 E Boulevard Ave Dept 108, Bismarck, ND 58505; 701-328-3662, Fax- 701-328-4214; 8AM-5PM.

www.nd.gov/sos/businessserv/centralindex/index.html

The state has a Central Indexing System which allows UCC and tax lien searches at this office or at any of the 53 County Recorders.

Indexing & Storage: Records available from 1966 or one year after lapse date. Records are computerized on index statewide since 1992. New records available for inquiry in less than 1 day.

Searching: Use search request form UCC-11. Include in request- debtor name. SSN and tax ID are optional and helpful.

Access by: mail, phone, fax, in person, online.

Fee & Payment: The search fee is $7.00 for the first 5 entries and $2.00 for each additional 5 entries or fraction thereof. A copy request with certificate is $7.00 for first 3 copies and $2.00 for each additional. All tax liens will show on the record request. Fee payee- Secretary of State. Will invoice, if requested. Monthly billing is offered to ongoing requesters. Personal checks accepted. Major credit cards accepted.

Mail search: Turnaround time- 1 day. A SASE is requested.

Phone search: General information is available without charge.

Fax search: There is an additional fee of $3.00 (maximum 20 pages) to return by fax. Please allow 20 minutes to 1 hour.

In person: Counter service available.

Online search: Access to the Central Indexing System provides both filing and online searching. There is an annual subscription $150 fee and a one-time $50.00 registration fee. The UCC-11 search fee (normally $7.00) applies, but documents will not be certified. Searches include UCC-11 information listing and farm product searches.

Other access: The agency offers bulk access on IBM cartridge or paper copy. Call for details.

Sales Tax Registrations

Office of State Tax Commissioner, Sales & Special Taxes Division, State Capitol, 600 E Boulevard Ave, Bismarck, ND 58505-0599; 701-328-3470, Fax- 701-328-0336; 8AM-5PM.

www.nd.gov/tax/salesanduse/

Indexing & Storage: Records available from 2000 to present, including inactive records. New records available for inquiry in hours.

Searching: This agency will only confirm if a business is registered and active. They will provide no other information as it is confidential. Include in request- business name. They will also search by tax permit number or owner name. This data not released- financial information, filing status.

Access by: mail, phone, fax, online.

Mail search: Turnaround time- 7 to 10 days. A SASE is requested. No fee for mail request.

Phone search: No fee for telephone request.

Fax search: There is no fee.

Online search: A permit number may be verified at www.nd.gov/tax/salesanduse/permitinquiry/. System indicates valid permit registered to company name.

Birth Certificates

ND Department of Health, Vital Records, State Capitol, 600 E Blvd, Dept 301, Bismarck, ND 58505-0200; 701-328-2360, Fax- 701-328-1850; 7:30AM-5PM. http://ndhealth.gov/vital/

Indexing & Storage: Records available from 1870 on. New records available for inquiry immediately.

Searching: Must have a signed release from person of record if it is an out-of-wedlock birth. If under 18, parent or legal guardian signature needed. Include in request- full name, names of parents, mother's maiden name, date of birth, place of birth, relationship to person of record, reason for information request.

Access by: mail, fax, in person, online.

Fee & Payment: The fee is $7.00 per name. Add $4.00 per name for second copies. Fee payee- North Dakota Department of Health. Prepayment required. Personal checks accepted. Visa/MC/Discover accepted.

Mail search: Turnaround time- 5 to 7 days. SASE not required.

Fax search: Use of credit card required. Turnaround time is same day if received by 10AM and request is marked for FedEx or UPS.

In person: Turnaround time is less than 15 minutes.

Online search: Records may be ordered online from the Internet site or from vitalchek.com. Records are not returned online.

Expedited service: Expedited service is available for fax or online searches. Turnaround time- overnight delivery. Expedited service options are available using a credit card and an additional $16.00 fee for shipping.

Death Records

ND Department of Health, Vital Records, State Capitol, 600 E Blvd, Dept 301, Bismarck, ND 58505-0200; 701-328-2360, Fax- 701-328-1850; 7:30AM-5PM. http://ndhealth.gov/vital/

Effective 01/01/2008, this agency will no longer issue certified copies of marriage records. These copies must be obtained from the county where the marriage took place.

Indexing & Storage: Records available from 1881 on. Early records are few. New records available for inquiry immediately.

Searching: Cause of death not shown on copy of Death Certificate if not a family member. Include in request- full name, date of death, place of death, relationship to person of record, reason for information request.

Access by: mail, fax, in person, online.

Fee & Payment: The fee is $5.00 per name. Add $2.00 per name for second copies. Fee payee- North Dakota Department of Health. Prepayment required. Personal checks accepted. Visa/MC/Discover accepted.

Mail search: Turnaround time- 5 to 7 days. A SASE is requested.

Fax search: This is considered expedited service. Turnaround time is same day if received by 10AM noon and request is marked for FedEx or UPS.

In person: Turnaround time is 10 to 15 minutes.

Online search: Search the Public Death Index free https://secure.apps.state.nd.us/doh/certificates/deathCertSearch.htm. Deaths within the past 12 months do not appear. Also, records may be ordered online from the Internet site or from vitalchek.com. Records are not returned online.

Expedited service: Expedited service is available for fax searches. Turnaround time- overnight delivery. Expedited service options are available using a credit card and an additional $16.00 fee for shipping.

Marriage Certificates

ND Department of Health, Vital Records, State Capitol, 600 E Blvd, Dept 301, Bismarck, ND 58505-0200; 701-328-2360, Fax- 701-328-1850; 7:30AM-5PM.

http://ndhealth.gov/vital/

Effective 01/01/2008, this agency will no longer issue certified copies of marriage records. These copies must be obtained from the county where the marriage took place.

Indexing & Storage: Records available from July 1, 1925 to present. New records available for inquiry immediately.

Searching: Include in request- names of husband and wife, date of marriage, place or county of marriage, relationship to person of record, reason for information request, wife's maiden name.

Access by: mail, fax, in person, online.

Fee & Payment: The fee is $5.00 per name. Add $2.00 per name for second copies. Fee payee- North Dakota Department of Health. Prepayment required. Personal checks and major credit cards accepted.

Mail search: Turnaround time- 5 to 7 days. SASE not required.

Fax search: Turnaround time is same day if received by 10 AM and request is being returned by FedEx or UPS.

In person: Turnaround time is 10 to 15 minutes.

Online search: Records may be ordered online from the Internet site or from vitalchek.com. Records are not returned online.

Expedited service: Expedited service is available for fax or online searches. Turnaround time- overnight delivery. Expedited service options are available using a credit card and an additional $16.00 fee for shipping.

Divorce Records

Access to Records is Restricted.

ND Department of Health, Vital Records, State Capitol, 600 E Blvd, Dept 301, Bismarck, ND 58505-0200; 701-328-2360, Fax- 701-328-1850; 7:30AM-5PM.

http://ndhealth.gov/vital/divorce.htm

Copies of divorce records can only be obtained from the county recorder in the county in which the divorce or annulment was decreed. This office will assist in determining what county to contact. Their index contains records from July 1, 1949 to present. Call or e-mail to vitalrec@state.nd.us.

Workers' Compensation Records

Workforce Safety & Insurance, Workers' Compensation Records, PO Box 5585, Bismarck ND 58506-5585 (Courier address- 1600 East Century Avenue, Suite 1, Bismarck, ND 58503-0644); 701-328-3800, 800-777-5033, Fax- 701-328-3750; 7:30AM-5PM.

www.workforcesafety.com

Indexing & Storage: Records available from 1919 but more reliable information is from 1975 on. New records available for inquiry in 24 hours.

Searching: Must have a signed release from person of record stating exactly what information is requested. Include in request- claimant name, SSN, date of birth. Also, a signed release by the subject is required, unless the requester is involved within the case.

Access by: mail.

Fee & Payment: Copies are $.35 per page. There is no search fee, unless file needs to be retrieved from off-site, then $5.00 is charged. Fee payee- Workforce Safety & Enforcement Prepayment required. Personal checks accepted.

Mail search: Turnaround time- 5 days. A SASE is requested.

Driver Records

Department of Transportation, Driver License & Traffic Safety Division, 608 E Boulevard Ave, Bismarck, ND 58505-0700; 701-328-2604, Fax- 701-328-2435; 8AM-5PM. www.dot.nd.gov

Copies of tickets must be obtained from the local courts.

Indexing & Storage: Records available for 3 yrs for moving violations, DWI and suspensions. Records available to the public show neither violations less than 2 points nor accidents. The record will not show driver's address to casual requesters without consent. New records available for inquiry in 1 day.

Searching: The Division sends an additional copy of the abstract to the driver whose record was requested, accompanied by a statement identifying the requester. Include in request- license number, name, and DOB are required when ordering, but "two out of three" may produce a "hit.". Written requests must also include reason for request.

Access by: mail, fax, in person, online.

Fee & Payment: The fee is $3.00 per record. Fee payee- Driver License & Traffic Safety. Prepayment required. Personal checks accepted. Visa/MC/Discover accepted.

Mail search: Turnaround time- 10 days.

Fax search: Use of a credit card is required, along with requester's phone and address.

In person: Up to five requests will be processed while you wait.

Online search: There are two systems. Ongoing, approved commercial accounts may request records with personal information via a commercial system. There is a minimum of 100 requests per month. For more information, call 701-328-4790. Also, from home page above one may view and print a limited record. The fee is $3.00 per record and a use of a credit card is required. The limited record does not include total points or convictions more than three years old, violations less than three points, or any crash information. No documents will be sent via mail. A free DL status check is found at https://secure.apps.state.nd.us/dot/dlts/dlos/requeststatus.htm, access by DL number.

Vehicle Ownership & Registration

Motor Vehicle Division, Business Operations, 608 E Boulevard Ave, Bismarck, ND 58505-0780; 701-328-2725, Fax- 701-328-1487; 8AM-4:50PM.

www.dot.nd.gov/public/licensing.htm

Records on mobile homes are also maintained by this agency.

Indexing & Storage: Records available from 1911 for license plate numbers. New records available for inquiry in 10 to 14 days.

Searching: Records are available with the prior authorization. Personal information is not released to casual requesters without consent. A written request or use of Form SFN-51269A is required and found at the web page. Requester must initial one of 12 categories. This data not released- SSNs or medical records.

Access by: mail, fax, in person.

Fee & Payment: The fee is $3.00 per vehicle per search or record. Liens are automatically shown with an ownership search. There is a fee for a no record found. Fee payee- Motor Vehicle Division. Prepayment required. Personal checks, Visa, and MasterCard accepted.

Mail search: Turnaround time- 3 to 5 days. A SASE is helpful.

Fax search: Fax requesting is available for pre-approved commercial accounts.

In person: The state may limit the number of requests processed immediately, if busy.

Other access: North Dakota offers bulk or batch retrieval of VIN or ownership information of vehicles. The requester must explain purpose and intent; however, there are no restrictions placed upon requests of a legal nature. Customized or special runs are available.

Accident Reports

Driver License & Traffic Safety Division, Traffic Records Section, 608 E Boulevard Ave, Bismarck, ND 58505-0780; 701-328-2604, 701-328-2601, Fax- 701-328-2435; 8AM-5PM.

www.dot.nd.gov/

Indexing & Storage: Records available from 1998. Records are computer indexed since 1998. New records available for inquiry in 1-2 months.

Searching: The front page which includes drivers, witnesses, and insurance information, can be ordered by anyone with a written request. The investigating officer's report is also only to parties involved or their legal representative or insurer. Include in request- date of accident, location of accident, full name of at least one driver, reason for information request. This data not released- SSN and DL#.

Access by: mail, in person.

Fee & Payment: Fee is $2.00 for front page record (drivers, witnesses, etc.). The investigating officer's opinion is $5.00 and both opinion and report is $7.00. Fee payee- Driver License & Traffic Safety Division. Prepayment required. Personal checks accepted. Major credit cards accepted

Mail search: Turnaround time- 5 days. A SASE is requested.

In person: Turnaround time while you wait.

Vessel Ownership & Registration

North Dakota Game & Fish Department, Boat Registration Records, 100 N Bismarck Expressway, Bismarck, ND 58501; 701-328-6335, Fax- 701-328-6374; 8AM-5PM.

http://gf.nd.gov

Liens are filed at same locations as UCCs. Owners of any watercraft propelled by motors must register their vessels with the Game and Fish Department. No titles are issued by this agency.

Indexing & Storage: Records available from 1975 to present on paper. Records are computer indexed for the last five years. New records available for inquiry in 2 weeks.

Searching: Include in request- one of the following is required: hull ID #, registration #, decal #, or name. The agency does NOT follow DPPA. All records are open to the public.

Access by: mail, phone, fax, in person, online.

Fee & Payment: There is no fee for searching 1-2 names.

Mail search: Turnaround time- 1 day. SASE not required.

Phone search: Records are available by phone.

Fax search: Results can be faxed, mailed, or phoned.

In person: Turnaround time is usually immediate.

Online search: There is a free public inquiry system at the web page. Click on "Register a Boat" then Find Watercraft Registration or visit https://secure.apps.state.nd.us/gnf/onlineservices/lic/public/online/main.htm. From this site one may also search watercraft safety cards, lottery hunting permit applications and hunter safety listings.

Other access: A printed list is available of all registered vessels.

Legislation Records

North Dakota Legislative Council, State Capitol, 600 E Boulevard Ave, Bismarck, ND 58505; 701-328-2916, Fax- 701-328-3615; 8AM-5PM.

www.legis.nd.gov/

The legislature meets every odd year.

Indexing & Storage: Records available from 1889 on. Records are on microfiche from 1959 to 2005, and all versions of bills are computerized from 1997 forward. New records available for inquiry in 1 day to 1 month.

Searching: Include in request- bill number, session, citation of code helpful. This data not released- any confidential draft files.

Access by: mail, phone, fax, in person, online.

Mail search: Turnaround time- 1 days. SASE not required.

Phone search: You may call for information.

Fax search: Fax requests are permitted.

In person: Counter service available.

Online search: Their Internet site offers an extensive array of legislative information at no charge, including proposed and enacted legislation since 1997. Also, one may email requests for information. Copies of "enrolled bills" are found online. The web also offers searching of the ND Century Code and the Administrative Rules. Standing committee minutes and exhibits are not available.

Other access: Bulk purchase on CD offered.

Voter Registration

Access to Records is Restricted.

Secretary of State, Elections Division, 600 E Boulevard Ave Dept 108, Bismarck ND 58505-0500; 701-328-4146, Fax- 701-328-2992; 8AM-5PM. www.nd.gov/sos/electvote/

Currently, records are maintained at the county level by the County Auditors in poll books. Records are open to the public. North Dakota does not have voter registration and is exempt from HAVA.

GED Certificates

Department of Public Instruction, GED Testing - CKEN-11, 600 E Blvd Ave, Bismarck, ND 58505; 701-328-2393, Fax- 701-328-4770; 8AM-4:30PM.

www.dpi.state.nd.us/adulted/index.shtm

Indexing & Storage: Records available for 50 years on paper.

Searching: A verification will only verify that a test was taken, but not if the subject passed the test. Include in request- name, signed release, SSN, date of birth.

Access by: mail, fax, in person, online.

Fee & Payment: There is no fee for a verification and a $2.00 fee for a copy of a transcript. Fee payee- Dept of Public Instruction. Prepayment required. Money orders and business checks accepted. No credit cards accepted.

Mail search: Turnaround time- 1 week. SASE not required.

Fax search: Used only for verification of a "yes or no" request.

In person: Picture ID required.

Online search: One may request records via email at JMarcellais@nd.gov. There is no fee, unless a transcript is ordered.

Hunting & Fishing License Information

ND Game & Fish Department, 100 N Bismarck Expressway, Bismarck, ND 58501-5095; 701-328-6300, 701-328-6335 (Licensing), Fax- 701-328-6352; 8AM-5PM. http://gf.nd.gov

Indexing & Storage: Records available from 1992 on computer. Big Game Lottery Permits are only available for the current season.

Searching: Include in request- full name, date of birth, SSN. This agency also registers boats.

Access by: mail, fax, in person.

Fee & Payment: There is no search fee.

Mail search: Turnaround time- 1 to 3 days. A SASE is requested.

Fax search: Same criteria as mail searches.

In person: You can go in and access their records. They also make the boat registrations available.

Other access: They sell mailing lists. Call Paul Schadewald at 701-328-6328 for more information.

North Dakota State Licensing Agencies

For details about the agency responsible for licensing/certifying/registering an item below or in the Agency Quick Finder section, match an item's number with the number of the agency in the *Licensing Agency Information* section.

Alcoholic Beverage Control #3 .... www.ag.nd.gov/Licensing/Beverage/Beverage.htm
Amusement Device, Coin-Op #3 .... www.ag.nd.gov/Licensing/Amusement/Amusement.htm
Architect #43 .... www.ndsba.net/?id=221&page=Active+License+Query
Asbestos Contractor #27 .... www.ndhealth.gov/AQ/IAQ/ASB/Asbestos%20Contractor%20List.pdf
Attorney #41 .... www.court.state.nd.us/court/lawyers/index/frameset.htm
Auction Clerk/Auctioneer #34 .... www.psc.state.nd.us/jurisdiction/auctioneers-entities.html
Bank, Commercial #20 .... www.nd.gov/dfi/regulate/reg/regulated.asp
Broker, Corporate #28 .... www.nd.gov/ndins/producer/details.asp?ID=303
Charitable Solicitation #39 .... www.nd.gov/sos/forms/pdf/charorg.pdf
Coal Mine, Surface #34 .... www.psc.state.nd.us/jurisdiction/reclamation.html
Collection Agency #20 .... www.nd.gov/dfi/regulate/reg/regulated.asp
Consumer Finance Company #20 .... www.nd.gov/dfi/regulate/reg/regulated.asp
Contractor/General Contractor #39 .... https://secure.apps.state.nd.us/sc/busnsrch/busnSearch.htm
Counselor, Professional #9 .... www.ndbce.org/PDFs/counselor-list.pdf
Credit Union #20 .... www.nd.gov/dfi/regulate/reg/regulated.asp
Debt Collector #20 .... www.nd.gov/dfi/regulate/reg/regulated.asp
Deferred Presentment Provider #20 .... www.nd.gov/dfi/regulate/reg/regulated.asp
Dentist / Dental Assistant #10 .... https://secure.ebigpicture.com/ndbode/renewals/verify.asp
Dental Hygienist #10 .... https://secure.ebigpicture.com/ndbode/renewals/verify.asp
Dietitian/Nutritionist #11 .... www.ndbodp.com/
Drug Mfg./Wholesaler #14 .... www.nodakpharmacy.com
Electrical Contractor #25 .... www.ndseb.com/findcontractor.asp
Fireworks, Wholesale #3 .... www.ag.nd.gov/Licensing/Fireworks/Fireworks.htm
Funeral Home #44 .... www.ndfda.org/joomla/index.php?option=com_sobi2&Itemid=20
Gaming #3 .... www.ag.nd.gov/Gaming/Gaming.htm
Gaming Distributor #3 .... www.ag.nd.gov/Licensing/LicenseHolders/LicGADist.pdf
Gaming Manufacturer #3 .... www.ag.nd.gov/Licensing/LicenseHolders/LicGAMan.pdf
Grain Buyer/Warehouse/Elevator #34 .... www.psc.state.nd.us/jurisdiction/grain-entities.html
Home Inspector #39 .... www.nd.gov/sos/forms/pdf/home-inspectors.pdf
Insurance Agency/Agent/Broker #28 .... www.nd.gov/ndins/producer/details.asp?ID=303
Investment Advisor #40 .... www.ndsecurities.com/links/industry-professionals.asp
Livestock Agent #19 .... www.agdepartment.com/Programs/Livestock/Agents.html
Livestock Auction Market #19 .... www.agdepartment.com/Programs/Livestock/markets.html
Livestock Dealer #19 .... www.agdepartment.com/Programs/Livestock/Dealers.html
Lobbyist #39 .... www.nd.gov/sos/lobbylegislate/lobbying/reg-mnu.html
Medical Doctor #47 .... www.ndbomex.com/SearchPage.asp
Medication Assistant #31 .... https://www.ndbon.org/verify_renew/verify_default.asp
Money Broker Firm #20 .... www.nd.gov/dfi/regulate/reg/regulated.asp
Nurse-LPN/RN / Nurse Assistant #31 .... https://www.ndbon.org/verify_renew/verify_default.asp
Nursing Home Administrator #13 .... www.ndnha.org/Admin%20List.pdf
Nutritionist #11 .... www.ndbodp.com/
Oil and Gas Broker #53 .... https://www.dmr.nd.gov/oilgas/findwellsvw.asp
Oil/gas Well #53 .... https://www.dmr.nd.gov/oilgas/confidential.asp
Optometrist #49 .... www.ndsbopt.org/directory.asp
Osteopathic Physician #47 .... www.ndbomex.com/SearchPage.asp
Pharmacist / Pharmacy #14 .... www.nodakpharmacy.com
Pharmacy Technician/Intern #14 .... www.nodakpharmacy.com
Physical Therapist/Assistant #51 .... https://secure.ndbpt.org/www/verify.asp
Physician Assistant #47 .... www.ndbomex.com/SearchPage.asp
Podiatrist #15 .... http://governor.state.nd.us/boards/bcpublicsearch.asp?searchtype=member
Polygraph Examiner #3 .... www.ag.nd.gov/Licensing/Polygraph/Polygraph.htm
Private Investigation Agency/PI #33 .... www.nd.gov/pisb/holders.html
Respiratory Care Practitioner #37 .... https://secure.ebigpicture.com/ndsbrc/renewals/verify.asp
Sale of Check #20 .... www.nd.gov/dfi/regulate/reg/regulated.asp
Securities Agent/Dealer #40 .... www.ndsecurities.com/links/industry-professionals.asp
Security Provider/Company #33 .... www.nd.gov/pisb/holders.html
Social Worker #18 .... http://secure.ebigpicture.com/ndbswe/live/public.asp
Soil Classifier #17 .... www.soilsci.ndsu.nodak.edu/soilclassifiers/roster.htm
Speech-Language Patholog't/Audiologist #12 .... http://governor.state.nd.us/boards/bcpublicsearch.asp?searchtype=member

Telecommunications Firm/Personnel #34 .... www.psc.state.nd.us/jurisdiction/telecom.html
Tobacco, Retail/Wholesale #3 .... www.ag.nd.gov/Licensing/Tobacco/Tobacco.htm
Transient Merchant #3 .... www.ag.nd.gov/Licensing/Transient/TransientMerchant.htm
Trust Company #20 .... www.nd.gov/dfi/regulate/reg/regulated.asp
Veterinarian / Veterinary Technician #29 .... www.ndbvme.org/
Water Well Driller #50 .... www.ndhealth.gov/wq/gw/wells.htm
Weighing Device Tester #34 .... www.psc.state.nd.us/jurisdiction/weights-list.html
Well Contractor, Monitoring #50 .... www.ndhealth.gov/wq/gw/wells.htm

North Dakota Licensing Quick Finder

Abstractor/Abstractor Company #1 701-947-2446
Adoption Service #22 701-328-4805
Aerial Applicator #30 701-328-9650
Aircraft Dealer #30 701-328-9650
Aircraft Registration #30 701-328-9650
Alcoholic Beverage Control #3 701-328-2329
Amusement Device, Coin-Op #3 701-328-2329
Architect #43 701-223-3540
Asbestos Landfill #27 701-328-5188
Asbestos-related Occupation #27 701-328-5188
Athletic Trainer #5 701-231-7779
Attorney #41 701-328-4201
Auction Clerk/Auctioneer #34 701-328-2400
Bank, Commercial #20 701-328-9933
Barber #6 701-223-5186
Barber Shop #6 701-255-3333
Boxer/Boxing Professional #38 701-328-2900
Broker, Corporate #28 .... 701-328-3548 x2
Charitable Solicitation #39 701-328-3665
Chiropractor #7 701-352-1690
Coal Mine, Surface #34 701-328-2400
Collection Agency #20 701-328-9933
Consumer Finance Company #20 701-328-9933
Contractor/General Contractor #39 701-328-3665
Cosmetologist/Cosmetol'g't Instr'ctr #8 701-224-9800
Counselor, Addiction #4 701-255-1439
Counselor, Professional #9 701-667-5969
Credit Union #20 701-328-9933
Crematorium #44 701-776-6222
Day Care Service #22 701-328-4809
Debt Collector #20 701-328-9933
Deferred Presentment Provider #20 701-328-9933
Dentist / Dental Assist / Hygenist #10 701-258-8600
Dietitian/Nutritionist #11 701-746-9171
Driver's Education Instructor #24 701-328-4563
Drug Mfg./Wholesaler #14 701-328-9535
Electrical Contractor #25 701-328-9522
Electrician/Electrician Apprentice #25 701-328-9522
Elementary Principal/Assistant #24 701-328-4571
Embalmer #44 701-776-6222
Employment Agency (Permanent) #23 701-328-2660
Engineer #36 701-258-0786
Esthetician #8 701-224-9800
Fireworks, Wholesale #3 701-328-2329
Fishing Guide #26 701-328-6300
Foster Care Program #22 701-328-4934
Fund Raiser, Professional #39 701-328-3665
Funeral Director /Funeral Home #44 701-776-6222
Gaming/Gaming Dist./Manuf't'r #3 701-328-2329
Grain Buyer #34 701-328-4097
Grain Warehouse/Elevator #34 701-328-4097
Hearing Aid Dealer/Fitter #45 701-237-9977
Home Inspector #39 701-328-2900
Hunting Guide/Fishing Guide #26 701-328-6300
Insurance Agncy/Agent/Broker #28 701-328-3548 x2
Investment Advisor #40 701-328-4698
Kickboxer #38 701-328-2900
Laboratory Clinician #52 701-530-0199
Land Surveyor #36 701-258-0786
Livestock Auction/Market/Agent/Dealer #19 701-328-4761
Lobbyist #39 701-328-3665
Manicurist #8 701-224-9800
Massage Therapist #46 701-872-4895
Medical Doctor #47 701-328-6500
Medication Assistant #31 701-328-9788
Money Broker Firm #20 701-328-9933
Mortician #44 701-776-6222
Notary Public #39 701-328-2901
Nurse-LPN/RN / Nurse Assistant #31 701-328-9788
Nursing Home Administrator #13 701-222-4867
Nutritionist #11 701-746-9171
Occupational Therapist #48 701-250-0847
Oil and Gas Broker/Welder #53 701-328-8020
Optometrist #49 701-225-9333
Osteopathic Physician #47 701-328-6500
Pharmacist / Pharmacy #14 701-328-9535
Pharmacy Technician/Intern #14 701-328-9535
Physical Therapist/Assistant #51 701-352-0125
Physician Assistant #47 701-328-6500
Plumber Journey'/Appren./Master #32 701-328-9977
Podiatrist #15 701-234-8770
Polygraph Examiner #3 701-328-2329
Private Investigation Agency/PI #33 701-222-3063
Psychologist #16 701-590-1754
Public Accountant-CPA #42 800-532-5904
Public Accounting Firm #42 800-532-5904
Real Estate Agent/Broker #35 701-328-9749
Respiratory Care Practitioner #37 701-222-1564
Sale of Check #20 701-328-9933
School Counselor #24 701-328-4571
School Library Media Specialist #24 701-328-4647
Schooling Aide/Paraprofessional #24 701-328-1876
Secondary Principal/Assistant #24 701-328-4571
Securities Agent/Dealer #40 701-328-4698
Security Employee #33 701-222-2063
Security Provider/Company #33 701-222-3063
Sewer/Water Contract'r/Installer/Appren. #32 701-328-9977
Social Worker #18 701-222-0255
Soil Classifier #17 701-530-2020
Special Ed. Teacher/Dir./Strateg'st #24 701-328-4571
Speech-Language Patholog't/Audiologist #12 701-777-4421
Superintendent/Assistant #24 701-328-4571
Taxidermist #26 701-328-6300
Teacher, Public School #54 701-328-9641
Telecommunications Company #34 701-328-4076
Telecommunications Personnel #34 701-328-4076
Title I Teacher/Counselor, Reading/Math #24 701-328-2170
Tobacco, Retail/Wholesale #3 701-328-2329
Transient Merchant #3 701-328-2329
Trust Company #20 701-328-9933
Veterinarian/Veterinary Tech'n #29 701-328-9540
Waste Water System Operator #21 701-328-5211
Water Condition'g Contr/Instal'r/Appren #32 701-328-9977
Water Distribution System Operat'r #21 701-328-5211
Water Well Driller #50 701-328-2754
Weather Modifier #2 701-328-2788
Weighing Device Firm/Tester #34 701-328-2400
Well Contractor, Monitoring #50 701-328-2754

North Dakota Licensing Agency Information

#1 Abstractors Board of Examiners, PO Box 551, New Rockford, ND 58356; 701-947-2446, F-701-947-2443. www.governor.nd.gov/boards/

#2 Atmospheric Resource Board, Water Commission, 900 E Boulevard Ave, Dept 770, Bismarck, ND 58505-0850; 701-328-2750, Fax- 701-328-3696. www.swc.state.nd.us/4dlink9/4dcgi/getcategoryrecord/atmospheric%20resources

#3 Office of Attorney General, Licensing Section, 600 E Boulevard Ave, Dept 125, Bismarck, ND 58505-0040; 701-328-2329, Fax 701-328-3535. 8AM-4:30PM. www.ag.nd.gov

#4 Board of Addiction Counseling Examiners, PO Box 975, Bismarck, ND 58502-0975; 701-255-1439, Fax- 701-224-9824. www.ndbace.org/ Board can sell lists for $20.00. Can be sent by email, labels or a list.

#5 Board of Athletic Trainers, 2834 S 33rd St, Fargo, ND 58103; 701-231-7779. www.governor.nd.gov/boards/

#6 Board of Barber Examiners, 1210 West Coulee Rd, Bismarck, ND 58501; 701-223-5186. Hours- 8AM-5:30PM T-TH. www.ndbarbers.org

#7 Board of Chiropractic Examiners, PO Box 185, Grafton, ND 58237; 701-352-1690, Fax-701-352-2258. Hours- 8AM-5PM.

#8 Board of Cosmetology, PO Box 2177 (1102 S Washington #200), Bismarck, ND 58502; 701-224-9800, Fax- 701-222-8756. 9AM-5PM. www.governor.nd.gov/boards/boards-query.asp?Board_ID=24

#9 Board of Counselor Examiners, 2112 10th Ave SE, Mandan, ND 58554-5066; 701-667-5969, Fax- 701-667-5969. http://www2.edutech.nodak.edu/ndbce/

#10 Board of Dental Examiners, PO Box 7246, Bismarck, ND 58507-7246; 701-258-8600, Fax- 701-224-9824. www.nddentalboard.org/ Search data at- https://secure.ebigpicture.com/ndbode/renewals/verify.asp

#11 Board of Dietetic Practice, PO Box 1524, Minot, ND 58702-1524; 701-838-2785, Fax-701-838-0199. www.ndbodp.com/

#12 Board of Examiners in Audiology/Speech Pathology, PO Box 7189 (231 Centennial Dr, #212), Grand Forks, ND 58202-7189; 701-777-4421, Fax- 701-777-4365. Hours- 8AM-1PM M-TH. www.governor.nd.gov/boards/boards-query.asp?Board_ID=14 Search data at- http://governor.state.nd.us/boards/bcpublicsearch.asp?searchtype=member

#13 Board of Examiners in Nursing Home Administrators, 1900 N 11th St, Bismarck, ND 58501-1914; 701-222-4867, Fax- 701-223-0977. www.ndnha.org/ Search data at- www.ndnha.org/Admin%20List.pdf

#14 Board of Pharmacy, PO Box 1354, Bismarck, ND 58502-1354; 701-328-9535, Fax- 701-258-9312. www.nodakpharmacy.com/ Search data at- www.nodakpharmacy.com/

#15 Board of Podiatric Medicine, 911 Elm Ave, Dickinson, ND 58601; 701-483-9165, Fax- 701-483-9165. http://governor.state.nd.us/boards/boards-query.asp?Board_ID=84

#16 Board of Psychologist Examiners, PO Box 661, Dickinson, ND 58602-0661; 701-590-1754, Fax- 701-225-6225. www.governor.nd.gov/boards/

#17 Board of Registry for Professional Soil Classifier, 820 10th Ave W, Dickinson, ND 58601; 701-225-0368. www.soilsci.ndsu.nodak.edu/soilclassifiers/pscand.htm

#18 Board of Social Worker Examiners, PO Box 914, Bismarck, ND 58502-0914; 701-222-0255, Fax- 701-224-9824. www.ndbswe.com/ Search data at- http://secure.ebigpicture.com/ndbswe/live/public.asp Also sell lists for $100.00 by email, disk list or labels - for continuing ed or research purposes only.

#19 Department of Agriculture, Livestock & Pesticide Programs, 600 E Boulevard Ave, Dept 602, Bismarck, ND 58505-0020; 701-328-2231, Fax- 701-328-4567. Search at- www.agdepartment.com/Programs/Livestock/Livestock.html

#20 Department of Financial Institutions, 2000 Schafer St, #G, Bismarck, ND 58501-1204; 701-328-9933, Fax- 701-328-9955. Hours- 8AM-5PM. www.nd.gov/dfi/ Search data at- www.nd.gov/dfi/regulate/reg/regulated.asp

#21 Department of Health, Municipal Facilities, 918 E Divide Ave, 4th Fl, Bismarck, ND 58501-1947; 701-328-5228, Fax- 701-328-5200. www.ndhealth.gov/WQ/

#22 Department of Human Services, Children & Family Services, 600 E Boulevard Ave, Dept 325, Bismarck, ND 58505-0250; 701-328-2316, Fax- 701-328-3538. Hours- 8AM-5PM. www.nd.gov/dhs/services/childfamily/

#23 Department of Labor, 600 E Blvd Ave, Dept 406, Bismarck, ND 58505-0340; 701-328-2660, Fax- 701-328-2031. www.nd.gov/labor/services/ea-licensing/

#24 Department of Public Instruction, 600 E Boulevard Ave, Dept 201, Bismarck, ND 58505-0440; 701-328-2260, Fax- 701-328-2461. Hours- 8AM-5PM. www.dpi.state.nd.us Actual public school teacher licensing is managed by the Edu. Standards and Practices Board, 701-328-9641 (Fax 701-328-9647).

#25 Electrical Board, PO Box 7335 (1929 N Washington St #A-1), Bismarck, ND 58507; 701-328-9522, Fax- 701-328-9524. www.ndseb.com/

#26 Game & Fish Department, 100 N Bismarck Exprwy, Bismarck, ND 58501-5095; 701-328-6300, Fax- 701-328-6352. http://gf.nd.gov

#27 Department of Health, Asbestos Control Program, 918 E Divide Ave, 2nd Fl, Bismarck, ND 58501-1947; 701-328-5188, Fax- 701-328-5200. 8AM-5PM. www.ndhealth.gov/AQ/IAQ/ASB/ Search data at- www.health.state.nd.us/AQ/IAQ/ASB/Asbestos%20Contractor%20List.pdf

#28 Insurance Department, Producer/Agent Information, 600 E Boulevard Ave, State Capitol-5th Fl-Dept. 401, Bismarck, ND 58505-0320; 701-328-3548, Fax- 701-328-4880. www.nd.gov/ndins/

#29 Board of Veterinary Medical Examiners, PO Box 5001, Bismarck, ND 58502-5001; 701-328-9540, Fax- 701-224-0435. Hours- 8:30AM-4PM. www.ndbvme.org/

#30 Aeronautics Commission, PO Box 5020 (2301 University Dr, Bldg 1652-22), Bismarck, ND 58502-5020; 701-328-9650, Fax- 701-328-9656. www.nd.gov/ndaero/

#31 Board of Nursing, 919 S 7th St, #504, Bismarck, ND 58504-5881; 701-328-9777, Fax- 701-328-9785. Hours- 8AM-5PM. www.ndbon.org/ Search data at- https://www.ndbon.org/verify_renew/verify_default.asp

#32 State Board of Plumbing, 1110 College Drive, Suite 210,, Bismarck, ND 58501; 701-328-9977, Fax- 701-328-9979. www.governor.nd.gov/boards/

#33 Private Investigation & Security Board, Private Investigators Licensing, 513 E Bismarck Expy, #5, Bismarck, ND 58504-6577; 701-222-3063, Fax- 701-222-3063. www.nd.gov/pisb/ Search data at- www.nd.gov/pisb/holders.html

#34 Public Service Commission, 600 E Boulevard Ave, Dept 408, Bismarck, ND 58505-0480; 701-328-2400, Fax- 701-328-2410. www.psc.state.nd.us

#35 Real Estate Commission, 200 E Main Ave #204 (PO Box 727), Bismarck, ND 58502-0727; 701-328-9749, Fax- 701-328-9750. Hours- 8:30AM-5PM. www.realestatend.org/

#36 Registration for Prof. Engineers & Land Surveyors, PO Box 1357 (723 W Memorial Hwy), Bismarck, ND 58502-1357; 701-258-0786, Fax- 701-258-7471. www.ndpelsboard.org

#37 Respiratory Care Examining Board, PO Box 2223, Bismarck, ND 58502; 701-222-1564, Fax- 701-224-9824. Hours- 8AM-N 1PM-5PM. www.ndsbrc.com/ Search data at- https://secure.ebigpicture.com/ndsbrc/renewals/verify.asp

#38 Secretary of State, Athletic Commissioner, Licensing Division, 600 East Blvd Ave, Dept 108, Bismarck, ND 58505-0040; 701-328-2900, Fax- 701-328-1690. Hours- 8AM-5PM. www.nd.gov/sos/athleticcommission/

#39 Secretary of State, Licensing Division, 600 E Boulevard Ave, Dept 108, Bismarck, ND 58505-0500; 701-328-3665, Fax- 701-328-1690. Hours- 8AM-5PM. www.nd.gov/sos/ Search data at- https://secure.apps.state.nd.us/sc/busnsrch/busnSearch.htm

#40 Securities Department, 600 E Blvd Ave, Dept 414, State Capitol, 5th Fl, Bismarck, ND 58505-0510; 701-328-2910, Fax- 701-328-2946. 8AM-5PM. www.ndsecurities.com/department-info/default.asp Search data at- www.ndsecurities.com/links/industry-professionals.asp

#41 State Board of Law Examiners, 600 E Boulevard Ave, Dept. 180, Bismarck, ND 58505-0530; 701-328-4201, Fax- 701-328-4480. www.ndcourts.com/lawyers/ Search at- www.court.state.nd.us/court/lawyers/index/frameset.htm

#42 Board of Accountancy, 2701 S Columbia Rd, Grand Forks, ND 58201-6029; 800-532-5904, Fax- 701-775-7430. www.nd.gov/ndsba/

#43 Board of Architecture, PO Box 7370, Bismarck, ND 58507-7370; 701-223-3540, Fax- 701-223-8154. www.ndsba.net/

#44 Board of Funeral Service, 213 2nd Ave SW, Rugby, ND 58368-0161; 701-776-6222. www.ndfda.org/joomla/

#45 Board of Hearing Instrument Specialists, 825 SW 25th St, Fargo, ND 58103; 701-237-9977, Fax- 701-237-6797. www.governor.nd.gov/boards/

#46 Board of Massage, PO Box 218, Beach, ND 58621; 701-872-4895, Fax- 701-872-4895. 10AM-5PM. www.ndboardofmassage.com/

#47 Board of Medical Examiners, 418 E Broadway Ave #12, Bismarck, ND 58501; 701-328-6500, Fax- 701-328-6505. 8AM-5PM. www.ndbomex.com/ Search data at- www.ndbomex.com/SearchPage.asp Order form needed. For bulk users, a $15.00 setup fee plus $.05 per name billed after order is filled.

#48 Board of Occupational Therapy Practice, PO Box 4005 (2900 E Broadway #1), Bismarck, ND 58502-4005; 701-250-0847, Fax- 701-224-9824. www.ndotboard.com

#49 Board of Optometry, 341 1st St E, Dickinson, ND 58601; 701-483-9141, Fax- 701-483-9501. www.ndsbopt.org/ Search data at- www.ndsbopt.org/directory.asp

#50 Board of Water Well Contractors, 900 E Boulevard Ave, Bismarck, ND 58505; 701-328-2754, Fax- 701-328-3696. www.governor.nd.gov/boards/

#51 Board of Physical Therapy, PO Box 69, Grafton, ND 58237; 701-352-0125, Fax- 701-352-3093. Hours- Voice Mail 24 hours. http://ndbpt.org/

#52 Board of Clinical Laboratory Practice, PO Box 4103, Bismarck, ND 58502-4103; 701-530-0199, Fax- 701-224-9824. www.ndclinlab.com/

#53 Department of Mineral Resources, Oil and Gas Division, 600 E Boulevard Ave, Dept 405, Bismarck, ND 58505; 701-328-8020, Fax- 701-328-8022. https://www.dmr.nd.gov/oilgas/

#54 Education Standards and Practices Board, 2718 Gateway Ave #303, Bismarck, ND 58503; 701-328-9641, Fax- 701-328-9647. 8AM-N, 1-5PM. www.nd.gov/espb/ Education specialties (admin, special ed, Title 1, etc) are administered by a separate agency- Dept of Public Instruction.

North Dakota Federal Courts

The following list indicates the district and division name for each county in the state. If the bankruptcy court location is different from the district court, then the location of the bankruptcy court appears in parentheses.

North Dakota County/Court Cross Reference

County	Court
Adams	Bismarck-Southwestern (Fargo)
Barnes	Fargo-Southeastern (Fargo)
Benson	Grand Forks-Northeastern (Fargo)
Billings	Bismarck-Southwestern (Fargo)
Bottineau	Minot-Northwestern (Fargo)
Bowman	Bismarck-Southwestern (Fargo)
Burke	Minot-Northwestern (Fargo)
Burleigh	Bismarck-Southwestern (Fargo)
Cass	Fargo-Southeastern (Fargo)
Cavalier	Grand Forks-Northeastern (Fargo)
Dickey	Fargo-Southeastern (Fargo)
Divide	Minot-Northwestern (Fargo)
Dunn	Bismarck-Southwestern (Fargo)
Eddy	Fargo-Southeastern (Fargo)
Emmons	Bismarck-Southwestern (Fargo)
Foster	Fargo-Southeastern (Fargo)
Golden Valley	Bismarck-Southwestern (Fargo)
Grand Forks	Grand Forks-Northeastern (Fargo)
Grant	Bismarck-Southwestern (Fargo)
Griggs	Fargo-Southeastern (Fargo)
Hettinger	Bismarck-Southwestern (Fargo)
Kidder	Bismarck-Southwestern (Fargo)
La Moure	Fargo-Southeastern (Fargo)
Logan	Bismarck-Southwestern (Fargo)
McHenry	Minot-Northwestern (Fargo)
McIntosh	Bismarck-Southwestern (Fargo)
McKenzie	Minot-Northwestern (Fargo)
McLean	Bismarck-Southwestern (Fargo)
Mercer	Bismarck-Southwestern (Fargo)
Morton	Bismarck-Southwestern (Fargo)
Mountrail	Minot-Northwestern (Fargo)
Nelson	Grand Forks-Northeastern (Fargo)
Oliver	Bismarck-Southwestern (Fargo)
Pembina	Grand Forks-Northeastern (Fargo)
Pierce	Minot-Northwestern (Fargo)
Ramsey	Grand Forks-Northeastern (Fargo)
Ransom	Fargo-Southeastern (Fargo)
Renville	Minot-Northwestern (Fargo)
Richland	Fargo-Southeastern (Fargo)
Rolette	Minot-Northwestern (Fargo)
Sargent	Fargo-Southeastern (Fargo)
Sheridan	Minot-Northwestern (Fargo)
Sioux	Bismarck-Southwestern (Fargo)
Slope	Bismarck-Southwestern (Fargo)
Stark	Bismarck-Southwestern (Fargo)
Steele	Fargo-Southeastern (Fargo)
Stutsman	Fargo-Southeastern (Fargo)
Towner	Grand Forks-Northeastern (Fargo)
Traill	Grand Forks-Northeastern (Fargo)
Walsh	Grand Forks-Northeastern (Fargo)
Ward	Minot-Northwestern (Fargo)
Wells	Minot-Northwestern (Fargo)
Williams	Minot-Northwestern (Fargo)

Standards for Federal Courts: Fees are standard unless noted in profile. Search fee is $26.00 per item (one party name or case number). Copy fee is $.50 per page. Certification fee is $9.00 per document, double for exemplification, if available. Most courts require prepayment. Mail requests should enclose a SASE unless otherwise noted. Before releasing records, all courts require prepayment, unless noted.

District courts index by defendant and plaintiff and by case number. Bankruptcy courts usually index by debtor and case number. While most courts now have their indexes on computer, many may still maintain index card files as well. Courts will archive closed case files at different times.

There are numerous public access programs available to online subscribers. Search the U.S. Party/Case Index to find party names and case numbers among all courts. Individual case data is provided on PACER. A search of CM/ECF provides copies of cases filed electronically. For details about PACER, the US Party/Case Index, and CM/ECF see the Appendix or go to http://pacer.psc.uscourts.gov or call 800-676-6856.

US District Court District of North Dakota

Bismarck-Southwestern Division Court Clerk, PO Box 1193, Bismarck, ND 58502 (In person: 220 E Rosser Ave #476, Bismarck, ND 58501), 701-530-2300; Fax- 701-530-2312. Hours-8AM-N, 1-5PM. www.ndd.uscourts.gov

Counties/Note: Adams, Billings, Bowman, Burleigh, Dunn, Emmons, Golden Valley, Grant, Hettinger, Kidder, Logan, McIntosh, McLean, Mercer, Morton, Oliver, Sioux, Slope, Stark.

Searches/Indexing: Indicate if you wish to obtain info by telephone or by Certificate of Search. Results do not include SSN or DOB. Will fax back documents $.50 per page. New cases are in the index 24 hours after filing date. Records on computer and also stored as hard copies. Records posted after 11/2005 are retained indefinitely.

Search Access: Only docket info is available by phone. **Mail:** Search usually completed- 1 week. SASE not required. **Fax:** Fax search requests accepted. **In person:** 1 public terminal available. No self-serve copier.

Payment: Pay by money order, cashier's check, in-state business or personal check. No credit cards accepted. Payee: Clerk, US District Court.

E-Services: PACER records go back to 10/1990. New records online after 1 day. ECF at www.ndd.uscourts.gov/cm_ecf.html. **Opinions:** www.ndd.uscourts.gov/opinions.html. Calendars free at www.ndd.uscourts.gov/calendar.html.

Fargo - Southeastern Division Court Clerk, PO Box 870, Fargo, ND 58107 (In person: 655 1st Ave N, #130, Fargo, ND 58102), 701-297-7000; Fax- 701-297-7005. Hours-8AM-N, 1-5PM. www.ndd.uscourts.gov

Counties/Note: Barnes, Cass, Dickey, Eddy, Foster, Griggs, La Moure, Ransom, Richland, Sargent, Steele, Stutsman. Rolette County cases prior to 1995 may be located at Fargo.

Searches/Indexing: Indicate if you wish to obtain info by telephone or by Certificate of Search. Results do not include SSN or DOB. Will fax back documents $.50 per page. New cases are in the index 1 day after filing date. Both computer and card indexes maintained; computer index back to 1992. Civil cases prior to 10/90 on index cards. All criminal records on cards. Records on computer and also stored as hard copies. Records posted after 11/2005 are retained indefinitely.

Search Access: Only docket info is available by phone. **Mail:** Search usually completed- 1 week. SASE not required. **Fax:** Fax search requests accepted, if prepaid. **In person:** 1 public terminal available. No self-serve copier.

Payment: Pay by money order, cashier's check, in-state business or personal check. No credit cards accepted. Payee: Clerk, US District Court.

E-Services: PACER records go back to 10/1990. New records online after 1 day. ECF at www.ndd.uscourts.gov/cm_ecf.html. **Opinions:** www.ndd.uscourts.gov/opinions.html. Calendars free at www.ndd.uscourts.gov/calendar.html.

Grand Forks - Northeastern Division c/o Fargo-Southeastern Division, PO Box 870, Fargo, ND 58102 (In person: 102 N 4th St, Grand Forks), 701-297-7000. Hours- 8AM-N, 1-5PM. www.ndd.uscourts.gov

Counties/Note: Benson, Cavalier, Grand Forks, Nelson, Pembina, Ramsey, Towner, Traill, Walsh. Grand Forks office now unstaffed.

Searches/Indexing: Indicate if you wish to obtain info by telephone or by Certificate of Search. Results do not include SSN or DOB. Will fax back documents $.50 per page. Records on computer and also stored as hard copies. Records posted after 11/2005 are retained indefinitely.

Search Access: Only docket info is available by phone. **Mail:** Search usually completed- 1 week. SASE not required. **Fax:** Fax search requests accepted. **In person:** 1 public terminal available. No self-serve copier.

Payment: Pay by money order, cashier's check, in-state business or personal check. No credit cards accepted. Payee: Clerk, US District Court.

E-Services: PACER records go back to 10/1990. New records online after 1 day. ECF at www.ndd.uscourts.gov/cm_ecf.html. **Opinions:** www.ndd.uscourts.gov/opinions.html. Calendars free at www.ndd.uscourts.gov/calendar.html.

Minot - Northwestern Div. c/o Bismarck Division, PO Box 1193, Bismarck, ND 58502 (In person: 100 1st Street SW, Minot, ND), 701-530-2300; Fax- 701-530-2312. Hours-8AM-N, 1-5PM. www.ndd.uscourts.gov

Counties: Bottineau, Burke, Divide, McHenry, McKenzie, Mountrail, Pierce, Renville, Rolette, Sheridan, Ward, Wells, Williams.

Searches/Indexing: Indicate if you wish to obtain info by telephone or by Certificate of Search. Results do not include SSN or DOB. Will fax back documents $.50 per page. New cases are in the index 1 day after filing date. Records on computer and also stored as hard copies. Records posted after 11/2005 are retained indefinitely.

Search Access: Only docket info is available by phone. **Mail:** Search usually completed- 1 week. SASE not required. **Fax:** Fax search requests accepted. **In person:** 1 public terminal available. No self-serve copier.

Payment: Pay by money order, cashier's, business or personal check. No credit cards accepted. Payee: US District Court. Prepayment required if copies are made.

E-Services: PACER records go back to 10/1990. New records online after 1 day. ECF at www.ndd.uscourts.gov/cm_ecf.html. **Opinions:** www.ndd.uscourts.gov/opinions.html. Calendars free at www.ndd.uscourts.gov/calendar.html.

US Bankruptcy Court District of North Dakota

Fargo Division Court Clerk, 655 1st Ave N, Rm 210, Fargo, ND 58102-4932, 701-297-7100; Fax- 701-297-7105. Hours- 8AM - 4:30PM. www.ndb.uscourts.gov

Counties/Note: All counties in North Dakota.

Searches/Indexing: Include name and SSN in search request. Results include last 4 SSN digits. Court will fax back in emergencies for $.50 per page. New cases in the index 1 day after filing.

Search Access: Only docket info available by phone. Voice Case Information Service available, call VCIS at 701-297-7166. **Mail:** Search usually completed- 1 day. SASE not required. **In person:** 1 public terminal available. No self-serve copier.

Payment: Pay by money order, cashier's check, business check. No personal checks or credit cards, except Visa/MC from attorneys. Payee: Clerk, US Bankruptcy Court.

E-Svcs: PACER- http://pacer.ndb.uscourts.gov. PACER records go back to 1991. New records online after one day. ECF at https://ecf.ndb.uscourts.gov. **Opinions Online:** www.ndb.uscourts.gov/court_decisions.html. Decisions back to 1993 are available. **Online Note:** RACER is no longer available, replaced by newer PACER system. Weekly court calendars available via main website.

North Dakota County Courts

Court	Jurisdiction	No. of Courts	How Organized
District Courts*	General	53	7 Judicial Districts
Municipal Courts	Municipal	76	80 Cities

* Profiled in this Sourcebook.

Court	CIVIL Tort	Contract	Real Estate	Min. Claim	Max. Claim	Small Claims	Estate	Eviction	Domestic Relations
District Courts*	X	X	X	$0	No Max	$5000	X	X	X
Municipal Courts									

Court	CRIMINAL Felony	Misdemeanor	DWI/DUI	Preliminary Hearing	Juvenile
District Courts*	X	X	X	X	X
Municipal Courts			X		

Administration

State Court Administrator, North Dakota Judiciary, 600 E Blvd, 1st Floor Judicial Wing, Dept. 180, Bismarck, ND, 58505-0530; 701-328-4216, Fax: 701-328-2092. www.ndcourts.com

Court Structure

The District Courts have general jurisdiction over criminal, civil, and juvenile matters. Municipal Courts in North Dakota have jurisdiction of all violations of traffic and municipal ordinances, with some exceptions. At one time there were County Courts, but these courts merged with the District Courts statewide in 1995. These older County Court records are held by the 53 District Court Clerks in the seven judicial districts.

Online Access

One may search North Dakota Supreme Court dockets and opinions at www.ndcourts.com. Search by docket number, party name, or anything else that may appear in the text. Records are from 1982 forward. Email notification of new opinions is also available. A statewide computer system for internal use only is in operation for most North Dakota counties.

Searching Tips, Fees, and Other Guidelines

Since 1997, the standardized search fee in District Courts is $10.00 per name and the certification fee is $10.00 per document. The standard copy fee is $.50 per page but most courts charge less. For search requests for records previous to 1995, it is recommended that you state "include all County Court cases" in the request. Prepayment of fees is required unless noted in profiles below.

Adams County

Southwest Judicial District Court PO Box 469, Attn- Clerk of Court, 602 Adams Ave, Hettinger, ND 58639; 701-567-2537; fax: 701-567-2910; 8:30AM-N; 1-5PM (MST). ***Felony, Misdemeanor, Civil, Eviction, Small Claims, Probate.***

Search requests must be in writing. Probate fax is same as main fax number.

Civil Records: Access: Fax, mail, in person, online. Both court and visitors may perform in person searches. Search fee: $10.00 per name. Required to search: name, years to search; also helpful: address. Civil cases indexed by defendant, plaintiff. Civil index on cards from 1990, on docket books in vault from 1900s. Mail turnaround time 1-2 days. Civil PAT goes back to 1/1995. Access civil index at www.ndcourts.gov/publicsearch/contactsearch.aspx. Index goes back to 12/2001.

Criminal Records: Access: Fax, mail, in person, online. Both court and visitors may perform in person searches. Search fee: $10.00 per name. Required to search: name, years to search, DOB; also helpful: address. Criminal records indexed on cards from 1990, on docket books in vault from 1900s. Mail turnaround time 1-2 days. Criminal PAT goes back to 1/1995. Access criminal index at www.ndcourts.gov/publicsearch/contactsearch.aspx. Index goes back to 12/2001. Online result may show city of residence.

General Information: No adoption, sealed, juvenile, mental health, expunged, DV or dismissed records released. Fee to fax out file $3.00 1st 2 pages, $.50 each add'l. Court makes copy: $.25 per page. Certification fee: $10.00 per document. Payee: Clerk of District Court. Personal checks accepted; credit cards are not. Mail requests: SASE required.

Barnes County

Southeast Judicial District Court PO Box 774, Valley City, ND 58072; 701-845-8512; fax: 701-845-1341; 8AM-5PM (CST). ***Felony, Misdemeanor, Civil, Eviction, Small Claims, Probate.***

Civil Records: Access: Fax, mail, in person, online. Both court and visitors may perform in person searches. Search fee: $10.00 per name. Required to search: name, years to search; also helpful: address. Civil cases indexed by defendant, plaintiff. Civil index on docket books from early 1900s; on computer back to March, 1997. Mail turnaround time 1-2 days. Civil PAT goes back to 1997. PAT civil results show middle initial. If civil money judgment, on computer back to the 1980's. Access civil index at www.ndcourts.gov/publicsearch/contactsearch.aspx. Index goes back to 3/1997.

Criminal Records: Access: Fax, mail, in person, online. Both court and visitors may perform in person searches. Search fee: $10.00 per name. Required to search: name, years to search; also helpful: address, DOB, SSN. Criminal records maintained here for 10 years, archived on index books from early 1900s; on computer back to March, 1997. Mail turnaround time 1-2 days. Criminal PAT goes back to same as civil. PAT criminal results show middle initial. Access criminal index at www.ndcourts.gov/publicsearch/contactsearch.aspx. Index goes back to 3/1997. Online results show name and may show city of residence.

General Information: No adoption, paternity, sealed, juvenile, mental health, expunged or dismissed records released. Will fax documents $10.00 per doc. Court makes copy: $.25 per page. Self serve: same. Cert fee: $10.00. $5.00 for second copy. Payee: Clerk of District Court. Personal checks accepted; credit cards are not. Mail requests: SASE required.

Benson County

Northeast Judicial District Court PO Box 213, Minnewaukan, ND 58351; 701-473-5345; fax: 701-473-5345; 8:30AM-4:30PM (CST). ***Felony, Misdemeanor, Civil, Eviction, Small Claims, Probate.***

Civil Records: Access: Fax, mail, in person, online. Only the court performs in person searches; visitors may not. Search fee: $10.00 per name. Required to search: name, years to search; also helpful: address. Civil cases indexed by defendant, plaintiff. Civil index on docket books and index books from early 1900s, on index cards from 6/10/91. Mail turnaround time 5 days. Online access to civil is same as criminal via the statewide court website.
Criminal Records: Access: Fax, mail, in person, online. Only the court performs in person searches; visitors may not. Search fee: $10.00 per name. Required to search: name, years to search, DOB, signed release; also helpful: address. Criminal docket on books and index books from early 1900s, on index cards from 6/10/91. Note: Signed release required for juvenile cases. Mail turnaround time 5 days. Access criminal index at www.ndcourts.gov/publicsearch/contactsearch.aspx. Index goes back to 4/1998. Online results show name and may show city of residence.
General Information: No adoption, sealed, juvenile, mental health, expunged or dismissed records released. Will fax documents $1.00 per page. Court makes copy: $.25 per page. Certification fee: $10.00 per doc includes copy fee. Payee: Benson County Court. Personal checks accepted; credit cards are not. Mail requests: SASE required.

Billings County

Southwest Judicial District Court PO Box 138, Medora, ND 58645; 701-623-4492; fax: 701-623-4896; 8AM-N, 4PM Labor to Mem Day; Summer- 8AM-5PM M,TH; 8AM-N F (MST). ***Felony, Misdemeanor, Civil, Eviction, Small Claims, Probate.***
Civil Records: Access: Fax, mail, in person, online. Both court and visitors may perform in person searches. Search fee: $10.00 per name. Required to search: name, years to search; also helpful: address. Civil cases indexed by defendant, plaintiff. Civil index on docket books from 1800s; on computer back to 1996. Mail turnaround 1 day. Access criminal index www.ndcourts.gov/publicsearch/contactsearch.aspx. Index goes back to 1/1996.
Criminal Records: Access: Fax, mail, in person, online. Both court and visitors may perform in person searches. Search fee: $10.00 per name. Required to search: name, years to search; also helpful: address, DOB, SSN. Criminal records in books. Mail turnaround 1 day. Access criminal index at www.ndcourts.gov/publicsearch/contactsearch.aspx. Index goes back to 1/1998. Online results show name and may show city of residence.
General Information: No adoption, sealed, juvenile, mental health, expunged or dismissed records released. Will fax documents $2.00 1st 4 pages, $.50 each add'l. Court makes copy: $1.00 per page. Self serve: $.25 per page. Certification fee: $10.00 plus $5.00 each add'l page. Payee: Clerk of District Court. No out-of-state checks accepted unless pre-approved; fax copy of check to clerk. No credit cards accepted. Copy of check maybe faxed to 701-623-4896. Mail requests: SASE required.

Bottineau County

Northeast Judicial District Court 314 W 5th St, #12, Bottineau, ND 58318; 701-228-3618; fax: 701-228-2336; 8:30AM-5PM (CST). ***Felony, Misdemeanor, Civil, Eviction, Small Claims, Probate.***
Civil Records: Access: Fax, mail, in person, online. Only the court performs in person searches; visitors may not. Search fee: $10.00 per name. Required to search: name, years to search; also helpful: address. Civil cases indexed by defendant, plaintiff. Civil index on cards from 1987, on docket books from 1972. Mail turnaround time 1 day. Online access to civil is same as criminal via the statewide court website.
Criminal Records: Access: Fax, mail, in person, online. Only the court performs in person searches; visitors may not. Search fee: $10.00 per name. Required to search: name, years to search; also helpful: address, DOB, SSN. Criminal docket on books from 1885. Mail turnaround time 1 day. Access criminal index at www.ndcourts.gov/publicsearch/contactsearch.aspx. Index goes back to 11/1997. Online results show name and may show city of residence.
General Information: No adoption, paternity, sealed, juvenile, mental health, expunged or dismissed records released. Will fax documents $4.00 1st page, $2.00 each add'l. Court makes copy: $.25 per page. Certification fee: $10.00 per doc. Payee: Clerk of the Court. Personal checks accepted; credit cards are not. Mail requests: SASE required.

Bowman County

Southwest Judicial District Court PO Box 379, Bowman, ND 58623; 701-523-3450; fax: 701-523-5443; 8AM-N, 1-4:30PM (MST). ***Felony, Misdemeanor, Civil, Eviction, Small Claims, Probate.*** Probate fax is same as main fax number.
Civil Records: Access: Mail, in person, phone, fax, online. Both court and visitors may perform in person searches. Search fee: $10.00 per name. Required to search: name, years to search; also helpful: address. Civil cases indexed by defendant, plaintiff; index on dockets from 1907; computerized records back to 1995. Mail turnaround time 1-2 days. Online access to civil is same as criminal via the statewide court website.
Criminal Records: Access: Mail, in person, online. Both court and visitors may perform in person searches. Search fee: $10.00 per name. Required to search: name, years to search, DOB; also helpful: address. Criminal records on microfiche from 1978, on dockets from 1907; computerized records back to 1995. Mail turnaround time 1-2 days. Access criminal index at www.ndcourts.gov/publicsearch/contactsearch.aspx. Index goes back to 12/1996. Online results show name and may show city of residence.
General Information: No adoption, sealed, juvenile, mental health, expunged or dismissed records released. Will fax documents to local or toll free line. Court makes copy: $.25 per page. Certification fee: $10.00 per document; add'l doc copies $5.00 each. Payee: Clerk of Court. Personal checks accepted; credit cards are not. Mail requests: SASE required.

Burke County

Northwest Judicial District Court PO Box 219, 103 Main St, Bowbells, ND 58721; 701-377-2718; fax: 701-377-2020; 8:30AM-N, 1-5 PM (CST). ***Felony, Misdemeanor, Civil, Eviction, Small Claims, Probate.***
Civil Records: Access: Fax, mail, in person, online. Both court and visitors may perform in person searches. Search fee: $10.00 if a written reply is required. Required to search: name, years to search; also helpful: address. Civil cases indexed by defendant, plaintiff. Civil records for county civil, probate, and district from 1910, county small claims from 1980. Mail turnaround time 1-3 days. Access civil index at www.ndcourts.gov/publicsearch/contactsearch.aspx. Index goes back to 4/2002.
Criminal Records: Access: Fax, mail, in person, online. Both court and visitors may perform in person searches. Search fee: $10.00 if a written reply is required. Required to search: name, years to search; also helpful: address, DOB, SSN. Criminal records for from 1910, county criminal from 1980. Mail turnaround time 1-3 days. Access criminal index at www.ndcourts.gov/publicsearch/contactsearch.aspx. Index goes back to 4/2002. Online results show name and may show city of residence.
General Information: No adoption, sealed, juvenile, mental health, expunged or dismissed records released. Will fax back docs for $2.00 per page. Court makes copy: $.50 per page. Certification fee: $10.00 per doc includes copies. Payee: Clerk of Court. Personal checks accepted; credit cards are not.

Burleigh County

South Central Judicial District Court PO Box 1055, Bismarck, ND 58502; 701-222-6690; probate phone: 701-222-6690; 8AM-5PM (CST). ***Felony, Misdemeanor, Civil, Eviction, Small Claims, Probate.*** Probate fax- 701-221-3756
Civil Records: Access: Mail, in person, online. Both court and visitors may perform in person searches. Search fee: $10.00 per name. Required to search: name; also helpful: years to search. Civil cases indexed by defendant, plaintiff; index on computer back to 1/91; in books from 1800s. Mail turnaround time 2 days. Civil PAT goes back to 1991. PAT results show DOB and middle initials but they do not always appear on results. Access criminal index at www.ndcourts.gov/publicsearch/contactsearch.aspx. Index goes back to 12/1990. Online includes Bismarck Muni Court.
Criminal Records: Access: Mail, in person, online. Both court and visitors may perform in person searches. Search fee: $10.00 per name. Required to search: name; also helpful: years to search, address, DOB, SSN. Criminal records computerized from 1/91; in books from early 1900s. Mail turnaround time 1-2 days. Criminal PAT goes back to same as civil. PAT results show DOB and middle initials but they do not always appear on results. Access criminal index at www.ndcourts.gov/publicsearch/contactsearch.aspx. Index goes back to 12/1990. Online includes Bismarck Muni Court. Online results show name and may show city of residence.
General Information: No adoption, sealed, juvenile, mental health, expunged or dismissed records released. Will fax documents to local or toll free line. Court makes copy: $.10 per page; $1.00 minimum. Certification fee: $10.00 plus $5.00 each add'l Cert copy. Payee: Clerk of Court. Personal checks accepted. Visa/MC accepted.

Cass County

East Central Judicial District Court PO Box 2806, 211 9th St, Fargo, ND 58108; criminal phone: 701-241-5660; civil phone: 701-241-5645; probate phone: 701-241-5655; fax: 701-241-5636; 8AM-5PM (CST). ***Felony, Misdemeanor, Civil, Eviction, Small Claims, Probate.***
Civil Records: Access: Mail, fax, in person, online. Both court and visitors may perform in person searches. Search fee: $10.00 per name. Required to search: name, years to search; also helpful: address. Civil cases indexed by defendant, plaintiff. Civil records index on computer from 1988, on index books from late 1800s. Mail turnaround time 3-5 days. Civil PAT goes back to 1988. Access civil index at www.ndcourts.gov/publicsearch/contactsearch.aspx. Index goes back to 1998. Online includes West Fargo Muni Court. Search probate records from the 1870s to 1944 online at www.lib.ndsu.nodak.edu/ndirs/databases/probate.php. There is no fee.
Criminal Records: Access: Mail, fax, in person, online. Both court and visitors may perform in person searches. Search fee: $10.00 per name. Required to search: name, DOB, years to search. Criminal records computerized from 1988, on index cards from 1980. Mail turnaround time 3-5 days. Criminal PAT goes back to same as civil. PAT results show name, DOB, and may include SSN. Access criminal index at www.ndcourts.gov/publicsearch/contactsearch.aspx. Index goes back to 1998. Online includes West Fargo Muni Court. Online results show name and may show city of residence.
General Information: No adoption, sealed, juvenile, mental health, expunged or dismissed records released. Court makes copy: $.10 per page, $1.00 minimum. Self serve: same. Certification fee: $10.00 per doc includes copy fee. Payee: Clerk of District Court. Personal checks and credit cards accepted. Mail requests: SASE required.

Cavalier County

Northeast Judicial District Court 901 Third St, Ste 1, Langdon, ND 58249; 701-256-2124; fax: 701-256-3468; 8:30AM-4:30PM (CST). ***Felony, Misdemeanor, Civil, Eviction, Small Claims, Probate.***
www.ndcourts.com/court/counties/cavalier.htm
Civil Records: Access: Fax, mail, in person, online. Both court and visitors may perform in person searches. Search fee: $10.00 per name. Required to search: name, years to search; also helpful: address. Civil cases indexed by defendant, plaintiff. Civil records going on computer, prior stored. Mail

turnaround time 1 week. Civil PAT goes back to 1997. PAT results show name only. Online access to civil is same as criminal via the statewide court website.
Criminal Records: Access: Fax, mail, in person, online. Both court and visitors may perform in person searches. Search fee: $10.00 per name. Required to search: name, years to search; also helpful: address, DOB, SSN. Criminal records for District Court on index books from 1937, for County Court on index books from 1983, prior stored. Mail turnaround time 1 week. Criminal PAT goes back to 1997. PAT results show name only. Access criminal index at www.ndcourts.gov/publicsearch/contactsearch.aspx. Index goes back to 11/1997. Online results show name and may show city of residence.
General Information: No adoption, sealed, juvenile, mental health, expunged or dismissed records released. No fee to fax documents. Court makes copy: $.25 per page. Certification fee: $10.00. Payee: Clerk of Court. Personal checks accepted; credit cards are not. Mail requests: SASE required.

Dickey County

Southeast Judicial District Court Clerk of Court, PO Box 336, Ellendale, ND 58436; 701-349-3249 X4; fax: 701-349-3560; 9AM-N, 1-4:30PM (CST). ***Felony, Misdemeanor, Civil, Eviction, Small Claims, Probate.***
Probate fax is same as main fax number.
Civil Records: Access: Mail, in person, online. Only the court performs in person searches; visitors may not. Search fee: $10.00 per name. Required to search: name, years to search; also helpful: address. Civil cases indexed by defendant, plaintiff. Civil index on docket books to 1983; 1997-present. Probate from 1800s. Old district court records have no index and are very hard to search. Mail turnaround time 1-2 days. Online access to civil is same as criminal via the statewide court website.
Criminal Records: Access: Mail, in person, online. Only the court performs in person searches; visitors may not. Search fee: $10.00 per name. Required to search: name, years to search, DOB; also helpful: address, SSN. Criminal records indexed in books to 1983, 1997- present. Old district court records have no index and are very hard to search. Mail turnaround time 1-2 days. Access criminal index at www.ndcourts.gov/publicsearch/contactsearch.aspx. Index goes back to 5/1997. Online results show name and may show city of residence.
General Information: No adoption, sealed, juvenile, mental health, expunged or dismissed-deferred records released. Will fax documents to local or toll free line. Court makes copy: $.25 per page. Cert fee: $10.00 per document. Payee: Clerk of Court. Personal checks accepted; credit cards are not.

Divide County

Northwest Judicial District Court PO Box 68, Crosby, ND 58730; 701-965-6831; fax: 701-965-6943; 8:30AM-N, 1-5PM (CST). ***Felony, Misdemeanor, Civil, Eviction, Small Claims, Probate.***
Civil Records: Access: Fax, mail, in person, online. Only the court performs in person searches; visitors may not. Search fee: $10.00 per name. Required to search: name, years to search; also helpful: address. Civil cases indexed by defendant, plaintiff. Civil index on docket books from 1910. Note: Visitor can check for judgments. Records for eviction, small claims and probate are an additional $10.00 if full certification needed. Mail turnaround time 1-2 days. Online access to civil is same as criminal via the statewide court website.
Criminal Records: Access: Fax, mail, in person, online. Only the court performs in person searches; visitors may not. Search fee: $10.00 per name. Required to search: name, years to search; also helpful: address, DOB, SSN. Criminal records indexed in books from 1910. Mail turnaround time 1-2 days. Access criminal index at www.ndcourts.gov/publicsearch/contactsearch.aspx. Index goes back to 4/2003. Online results show name and may show city of residence.
General Information: No adoption, sealed, juvenile, mental health, expunged or dismissed records released. Will fax documents $3.00 1st page, $1.00 each add'l. Also a $1.00 charge per incoming fax page. Court makes copy: $.25 per page, $1.00 minimum. Certification fee: $10.00 per doc. Payee: Clerk of District Court. Personal checks accepted; credit cards are not. Mail requests: SASE required.

Dunn County

District Court PO Box 136, Manning, ND 58642-0136; 701-573-4447; fax: 701-573-4444; 8AM-N,12:30-4:30PM (MST). ***Felony, Misdemeanor, Civil, Small Claims, Probate.***
Probate fax is same as main fax number.
Civil Records: Access: Fax, mail, in person, online. Both court and visitors may perform in person searches. Search fee: $10.00 per name. Required to search: name, years to search; also helpful: address. Civil cases indexed by defendant, plaintiff; index on plaintiff/defendant index cards from 1988, on docket books from 1900s, on computer since 1/97. Note: Fax requests must include copy of the check to be mailed. Mail turnaround time 2 days. Civil PAT goes back to 1/1997. Online access to civil is same as criminal via the statewide court website.
Criminal Records: Access: Fax, mail, in person, online. Both court and visitors may perform in person searches. Search fee: $10.00 per name. Required to search: name, years to search, DOB; also helpful: address, SSN. Criminal records on plaintiff/defendant index cards from 1988, on docket books from 1900s, on computer since 1/97. Note: Fax requesters must fax copy of the check, which can be mailed. Mail turnaround time 2 days. Criminal PAT goes back to same as civil. Access criminal index at www.ndcourts.gov/publicsearch/contactsearch.aspx. Index goes back to 1/1997. Online results show name and may show city of residence.
General Information: Adoptions, paternity, juvenile, mental health, deferred impositions, and termination of parental rights are restricted access files. Will fax documents $2.00 plus $1.00 per page. Court makes copy: $2.00 plus $1.00 each page mailed copies. Self serve: $.50 per page. Certification fee: $10.00 per document includes copy fee. Payee: Dunn County Clerk of Court. In state personal checks accepted. No credit cards accepted.

Eddy County

Southeast Judicial District Court 524 Central Ave, c/o Clerk of District Court, New Rockford, ND 58356; 701-947-2813 x2013; fax: 701-947-2067; 8AM-4PM (CST). ***Felony, Misdemeanor, Civil, Eviction, Small Claims, Probate.***
Civil Records: Access: Fax, mail, in person, online. Only the court performs in person searches; visitors may not. Search fee: $10.00 per name. Required to search: name, years to search; also helpful: address. Civil cases indexed by defendant, plaintiff. Civil index on cards from 4/92, on index books from early 1900s. Note: All requests must be in writing. Mail turnaround time 1-2 days. Online access to civil is same as criminal via the statewide court website.
Criminal Records: Access: Fax, mail, in person, online. Only the court performs in person searches; visitors may not. Search fee: $10.00 per name. Required to search: name, years to search; also helpful: address, DOB, SSN. Criminal records indexed on cards from 4/92, on index books from early 1900s. Note: All requests must be in writing. Mail turnaround time 1-2 days. Access criminal index at www.ndcourts.gov/publicsearch/contactsearch.aspx. Index goes back to 8/1997. Online results show name and may show city of residence.
General Information: No adoption, sealed, juvenile, mental health, expunged or dismissed records released. Fee to fax out file $4.00 1st 3 pages, $1.00 each add'l page. Court makes copy: $1.00 per document. Certification fee: $10.00. Payee: Eddy County District Court. Personal checks accepted; credit cards are not. Mail requests: SASE required.

Emmons County

South Central Judicial District Court PO Box 905, Linton, ND 58552; 701-254-4812; fax: 701-254-4012; 8:30AM-N, 1-5PM (CST). ***Felony, Misdemeanor, Civil, Eviction, Small Claims, Probate.*** Probate fax is same as main fax.
Civil Records: Access: Fax, mail, in person, online. Only the court performs in person searches; visitors may not. Search fee: $10.00 per name. Required to search: name, years to search; also helpful: address. Civil cases indexed by defendant, plaintiff. Civil index on cards from 1988, on index books from 1914, on computer back to 1995. Mail turnaround time 1-2 days. Online access to civil is same as criminal via the statewide court website.
Criminal Records: Access: Fax, mail, in person, online. Only the court performs in person searches; visitors may not. Search fee: $10.00 per name. Required to search: name, years to search, DOB; also helpful: address, SSN. Criminal records indexed in books back to 1983; on computer back to 1995. Mail turnaround time 1-2 days. Access criminal index at www.ndcourts.gov/publicsearch/contactsearch.aspx. Index goes back to 1/1996. Online results show name and may show city of residence.
General Information: No adoption, sealed, juvenile, mental health, expunged or dismissed records released. Fee to fax out file $3.00 1st page, $1.00 each add'l. Court makes copy: $.20 per page. Certification fee: $10.00 per document. Payee: Clerk of Courts. Personal checks accepted; credit cards are not. Mail requests: SASE required.

Foster County

Southeast Judicial District Court PO Box 257, Attn: Foster County Clerk of Court, Carrington, ND 58421; 701-652-1001; fax: 701-652-2173; 8:30AM-4:30PM (CST). ***Felony, Misdemeanor, Civil, Eviction, Small Claims, Probate.***
https://mylocalgov.com/FosterCountyND/index.asp
Civil Records: Access: Mail, in person, online. Both court and visitors may perform in person searches. Search fee: $10.00 per name if court performs search. Required to search: name, years to search; also helpful: address. Civil cases indexed by defendant, plaintiff. Civil index on docket books from early 1900s. Mail turnaround time 1-2 days. Civil PAT available. The public terminal connects to the statewide system. Access civil index at www.ndcourts.gov/publicsearch/contactsearch.aspx. Index goes back to 5/2000.
Criminal Records: Access: Mail, in person, online. Both court and visitors may perform in person searches. Search fee: $10.00 per name if court performs search. Required to search: name, years to search, DOB; also helpful: address. Felony records available for past 10 years, misdemeanors for 7, infractions for 3. Mail turnaround time 1-2 days. Criminal PAT available. The public terminal connects to the statewide system. Access criminal index at www.ndcourts.gov/publicsearch/contactsearch.aspx. Index goes back to 5/2000. Online results show name and may show city of residence.
General Information: No adoption, sealed, juvenile, mental health, expunged or dismissed records released. Will fax documents $3.00 each. Court makes copy: $1.00 per page. Self serve: same. Certification fee: $10.00. Payee: Clerk of Courts. Personal checks and credit cards accepted. Mail requests: SASE required.

Golden Valley County

Southwest Judicial District Court PO Box 9, Beach, ND 58621-0009; 701-872-3713; fax: 701-872-4383; 8AM-N, 1-4PM (MST). ***Felony, Misdemeanor, Civil, Eviction, Small Claims, Probate.***
Civil Records: Access: Fax, mail, in person, online. Only the court performs in person searches; visitors may not. Search fee: $10.00 per name. Required to search: name, years to search; also helpful: address. Civil cases indexed by defendant, plaintiff. Civil index on cards from 1987, on index books from 1913 to 1960. From 1960 to 1987, records are hard to find; there is no indexing. Note: Fax request must include copy of check. Mail

turnaround time 3-4 days. Online access to civil is same as criminal via the statewide court website.
Criminal Records: Access: Fax, mail, in person, online. Only the court performs in person searches; visitors may not. Search fee: $10.00 per name. Required to search: name, years to search, DOB; also helpful: address, SSN. Criminal records indexed on cards from 1987, on index books from 1913 to 1960. From 1960 to 1987, records are hard to find; there is no indexing. Note: Fax request must include copy of check. Statewide records on computer since 04/04/03. Mail turnaround time 3-4 days. Access criminal index at www.ndcourts.gov/publicsearch/contactsearch.aspx. Index goes back to 4/2003. Online results show name and may show city of residence.
General Information: No adoption, sealed, juvenile, mental health, expunged or dismissed records released. Will fax documents $1.00 per page. Court makes copy: $.50 per page. Self serve: same. Certification fee: $10.00. Payee: Clerk of Court. Personal checks accepted; credit cards are not. Mail requests: SASE required.

Grand Forks County

Northeast Central Judicial District Court PO Box 5939, Grand Forks, ND 58206-5939; criminal phone: 701-787-2700; civil phone: 701-787-2715; probate phone: 701-787-2715; criminal fax: 701-787-2701; civil fax: 701-787-2715; 8AM-5PM (CST). ***Felony, Misdemeanor, Civil, Eviction, Small Claims, Probate.***
Probate fax- 701-787-2716
Civil Records: Access: Mail, in person, online. Both court and visitors may perform in person searches. Search fee: $10.00 per name. Required to search: name, years to search; also helpful: address. Civil cases indexed by defendant, plaintiff; index on computer from 11/91, on index books from early 1900s. Mail turnaround time 1-2 days. Civil PAT goes back to 10/1991. Access criminal index at www.ndcourts.gov/publicsearch/contactsearch.aspx. Index goes back to 10/1991.
Criminal Records: Access: Mail, in person, online. Both court and visitors may perform in person searches. Search fee: $10.00 per name. Required to search: name, years to search, DOB, signed release; also helpful: address, SSN. Criminal records computerized from 10/91, on index books from early 1900s. Mail turnaround time 1-2 days. Criminal PAT goes back to same as civil. Access criminal index at www.ndcourts.gov/publicsearch/contactsearch.aspx. Index goes back to 10/1991. Online results show name and may show city of residence.
General Information: No adoption, sealed, juvenile, mental health, expunged or dismissed records released. Will fax documents for no fee. Court makes copy: $.10 per page; $1.00 minimum. Certification fee: $10.00. Payee: Clerk of District Court. Personal checks and major credit cards accepted.

Grant County

South Central Judicial District Court PO Box 258, 106 2nd Ave NE, Carson, ND 58529; 701-622-3615; fax: 701-622-3717; 8AM-N, 12:30-4PM (MST). ***Felony, Misdemeanor, Civil, Eviction, Small Claims, Probate.***
Civil Records: Access: Fax, mail, in person, online. Both court and visitors may perform in person searches. Search fee: $10.00 per name. Required to search: name, years to search; also helpful: address. Civil cases indexed by defendant, plaintiff. Civil index on cards from 1990, on docket books in vault from 1900s. Mail turnaround time 1 day. Online access to civil is same as criminal via the statewide court website.
Criminal Records: Access: Fax, mail, in person, online. Both court and visitors may perform in person searches. Search fee: $10.00 per name. Required to search: name, years to search; also helpful: address, DOB, SSN. Criminal records indexed on cards from 1990, on docket books in vault from 1900s. Mail turnaround time 1 day. Access criminal index at www.ndcourts.gov/publicsearch/contactsearch.aspx. Index goes back to 2/2003. Online results show name and may show city of residence.
General Information: No adoption, sealed, juvenile, mental health, expunged or dismissed records released. Will fax documents $3.00 each. Court makes copy: $.25 per page. Certification fee: $10.00 per doc includes copy fee. Payee: Clerk of Grant County Court. Personal checks accepted. Visa/MC accepted.

Griggs County

Southeast Judicial District Court PO Box 326, 808 Rollin, Cooperstown, ND 58425; 701-797-2772; probate phone: same; fax: 701-797-3587; 8AM-N, 1-4:30PM (CST). ***Felony, Misdemeanor, Civil, Eviction, Small Claims, Probate.***
Civil Records: Access: Fax, mail, in person, online. Both court and visitors may perform in person searches. Search fee: $10.00 per name. Required to search: name, years to search; also helpful: address. Civil cases indexed by defendant, plaintiff. Civil records in docket books from 1890 to 2001 and UCIS 2001 to present. Note: Phone access discouraged. Mail turnaround time 1-2 days. Online access to civil is same as criminal via the statewide court website.
Criminal Records: Access: Fax, mail, in person, online. Both court and visitors may perform in person searches. Search fee: $10.00 per name. Required to search: name, years to search; also helpful: address, DOB, SSN. Criminal docket on books from 1890 to 2001 and UCIS 2001 to present. Note: Phone access discouraged. Mail turnaround time 1-2 days. Access criminal index at www.ndcourts.gov/publicsearch/contactsearch.aspx. Index goes back to 1/2002. Online results show name and may show city of residence.
General Information: No adoption, sealed, juvenile, mental health, expunged or dismissed records released. Will fax documents $1.00 per page. Incoming fax- $1.00 per page; free for state attorneys. Court makes copy: $.25 per page, $1.00 minimum. Certification fee: $10.00. Payee: Clerk of Courts. Personal checks accepted; credit cards are not. Mail requests: SASE required.

Hettinger County

Southwest Judicial District Court PO Box 668, 336 Pacific Ave, Mott, ND 58646; 701-824-2645; fax: 701-824-2717; 8AM-N, 1-4:30PM (MST). ***Felony, Misdemeanor, Civil, Eviction, Small Claims, Probate.***
Civil Records: Access: Fax, mail, in person, online. Both court and visitors may perform in person searches. Search fee: $10.00 per name. Required to search: name, years to search; also helpful: address. Civil cases indexed by defendant, plaintiff. Civil index on cards from 1987, on index books from 1908. Mail turnaround time 1 day. Online access to civil is same as criminal via the statewide court website.
Criminal Records: Access: Fax, mail, in person, online. Both court and visitors may perform in person searches. Search fee: $10.00 per name. Required to search: name, years to search, DOB; also helpful: address. Criminal records indexed on cards from 1987, on index books from 1908. Mail turnaround time 1 day. Access criminal index at www.ndcourts.gov/publicsearch/contactsearch.aspx. Index goes back to 3/2003. Online results show name and may show city of residence.
General Information: No adoption, sealed, juvenile, mental health, expunged or dismissed records released. Will fax documents $3.00 per doc; fee is for up to 20 pages. Court makes copy: $1.00 per page. Cert fee: $10.00 per doc includes copies. Payee: Hettinger Court Clerk. Personal checks accepted; credit cards are not. Mail requests: SASE required.

Kidder County

District Court PO Box 66, Steele, ND 58482; 701-475-2632 x9224; fax: 701-475-2202; 9AM-5PM (CST). ***Felony, Misdemeanor, Civil, Eviction, Small Claims, Probate.***
Civil Records: Access: Fax, mail, in person, online. Both court and visitors may perform in person searches. Search fee: $10.00 per name. Required to search: name, years to search; also helpful: address. Civil cases indexed by defendant, plaintiff; index on index book from 1800s, on computer since 1990. Mail turnaround time 1-2 days. Civil PAT goes back to 1990. PAT results show middle initial, DOB. Online access to civil is same as criminal via the statewide court website.
Criminal Records: Access: Mail, in person, online. Both court and visitors may perform in person searches. Search fee: $10.00 per name. Required to search: name, years to search, DOB; also helpful: address. Records on index book from 1900s, on computer since 1990. Mail turnaround time 1-2 days. Criminal PAT goes back to same as civil. PAT results show middle initial, DOB. Access criminal index at www.ndcourts.gov/publicsearch/contactsearch.aspx. Index goes back to 1/2000. Online results show name and may show city of residence.
General Information: No adoption, sealed, juvenile, mental health, expunged or dismissed records released. Will fax documents $3.00 plus the copy fee. Court makes copy: $1.00 per document. Certification fee: $10.00. Payee: Clerk of Court. Personal checks accepted; credit cards are not. Mail requests: SASE required.

La Moure County

Southeast Judicial District Court PO Box 128, LaMoure, ND 58458; 701-883-5301; fax: 701-883-4240; 8:30AM-N, 1-4:30PM (CST). ***Felony, Misdemeanor, Civil, Eviction, Small Claims, Probate.*** Probate fax is same as main fax number.
Civil Records: Access: Fax, mail, in person, online. Only the court performs in person searches; visitors may not. Search fee: $10.00 per name. Required to search: name, years to search; also helpful: address, SSN, DOB. Civil cases indexed by defendant, plaintiff. Civil index in docket books from 1800s; on computer back to 2002. Mail turnaround time usually same day. Online access to civil is same as criminal via the statewide court website.
Criminal Records: Access: Fax, mail, in person, online. Only the court performs in person searches; visitors may not. Search fee: $10.00 per name. Required to search: name, years to search; also helpful: address, DOB. Felony records go back to 1987; misdemeanors back 15 years. Mail turnaround time 1 day. Access criminal index at www.ndcourts.gov/publicsearch/contactsearch.aspx. Index goes back to 2/2002. Online results show name and may show city of residence.
General Information: No adoption, sealed, juvenile, mental health, expunged or dismissed records released. Will not fax out docs without pre-payment or copy of payment check. Court makes copy: $.25 first page, $.10 each add'l. Self serve: same. Certification fee: $10.00. Payee: Clerk of Court. Personal checks accepted; credit cards are not. Mail requests: SASE required.

Logan County

South Central Judicial District Court PO Box 6, Napoleon, ND 58561; 701-754-2751; fax: 701-754-2270; 8:30-4:30PM (CST). ***Felony, Misdemeanor, Civil, Eviction, Small Claims, Probate.*** Probate fax is same as main fax.
Civil Records: Access: Fax, mail, in person, online. Both court and visitors may perform in person searches. Search fee: $10.00 per name. Required to search: name, years to search; also helpful: address, signed release. Civil cases indexed by defendant, plaintiff. Civil index on docket books from 1884. Mail turnaround time 1 day. Online access to civil is same as criminal via the statewide court website.
Criminal Records: Access: Fax, mail, in person, online. Only the court performs in person searches; visitors may not. Search fee: $10.00 per name. Required to search: name, years to search, DOB; also helpful: address, signed release. Criminal records indexed in books from 1890. Mail turnaround time 1 day. Access criminal index at www.ndcourts.gov/publicsearch/contactsearch.aspx. Index goes back to 5/2003. Online results show name and may show city of residence.
General Information: No adoption, sealed, juvenile, mental health, expunged or dismissed records released. Fee to fax out file $3.00 1st page, $1.00 each

add'l. Court makes copy: $1.00 per document. Self serve: same. Certification fee: $10.00 per document. Payee: Clerk of Court. Business checks accepted. No credit cards accepted. Mail requests: SASE requested.

McHenry County

Northeast Judicial District Court PO Box 117, Towner, ND 58788; 701-537-5729; fax: 701-537-5969; 8AM-4:30PM ***Felony, Misdemeanor, Civil, Eviction, Small Claims, Probate.***

Probate in a separate index at this same address. Probate fax is same as main fax number.

Civil Records: Access: Fax, mail, in person, online. Both court and visitors may perform in person searches. Search fee: $10.00 per name. Required to search: name, years to search; also helpful: address. Civil cases indexed by defendant, plaintiff. Civil index on cards from 1991, on index books from 1905. Mail turnaround time 1-2 days. Online access to civil is same as criminal via the statewide court website.

Criminal Records: Access: Fax, mail, in person, online. Both court and visitors may perform in person searches. Search fee: $10.00 per name. Required to search: name, years to search; also helpful: address, DOB, SSN. Criminal records indexed on cards from 1991, on index books from 1905. Mail turnaround time 1-2 days. Access criminal index at www.ndcourts.gov/publicsearch/contactsearch.aspx. Index goes back to 1/2000. Online results show name and may show city of residence; newer cases show DOB.

General Information: No adoption, sealed, juvenile, mental health, expunged or dismissed records released. Will fax documents $1.00 1st page, $.25 each add'l. Court makes copy: $.25 per page. Certification fee: $10.00 includes copies. Payee: Clerk of Courts. Personal checks accepted; credit cards are not. Mail requests: SASE required.

McIntosh County

South Central Judicial District Court PO Box 179, Ashley, ND 58413; 701-288-3450; fax: 701-288-3671; 8AM-4:30PM (CST). ***Felony, Misdemeanor, Civil, Eviction, Small Claims, Probate.***

Civil Records: Access: Phone, fax, mail, in person, online. Visitors must perform in person searches themselves. Search fee: $10.00 per name. Required to search: name, years to search; also helpful: address. Civil cases indexed by defendant, plaintiff. Civil index on cards from 1987, on index books from 1930s. Mail turnaround time 1-2 days. Civil PAT goes back to 1995. PAT civil results show middle initial. Online access to civil is same as criminal via the statewide court website.

Criminal Records: Access: Fax, mail, in person, online. Both court and visitors may perform in person searches. Search fee: $10.00 per name. Required to search: name, years to search, DOB; also helpful: address. Criminal records indexed on cards from 1987, on index books from 1930s. Mail turnaround time 1-2 days. Criminal PAT goes back to same as civil. PAT criminal results show middle initial. Access criminal index at www.ndcourts.gov/publicsearch/contactsearch.aspx. Index goes back to 4/2003. Online results show name and may show city of residence.

General Information: No adoption, sealed, juvenile, mental health, expunged or dismissed records released. Will fax documents to local or toll free line. Court makes copy: $.25 per page. Certification fee: $10.00 per doc. Payee: Clerk of Court. Only cashiers checks and money orders accepted. No credit cards accepted.

McKenzie County

Northwest Judicial District Court PO Box 524, Watford City, ND 58854; 701-444-3616 Dept 287; criminal phone: 701-444-3616 Dept 287; fax: 701-444-3916; 8AM-4PM (CST). ***Felony, Misdemeanor, Civil, Eviction, Small Claims, Probate, Traffic.***

Charge of $25.00 per hour will be assessed after the first hour of copying time.

Civil Records: Access: Mail, in person, online. Both court and visitors may perform in person searches. Search fee: $10.00 per name. Required to search: name, years to search; also helpful: address, SSN if available. Civil cases indexed by defendant, plaintiff; index on computer back to 1/96. Mail turnaround time 1-2 days. Online access to civil is same as criminal via the statewide court website. Calendars also available online.

Criminal Records: Access: Mail, in person, online. Only the court performs in person searches; visitors may not. Search fee: $10.00 per name. Required to search: name, years to search, DOB. Criminal records computerized from 12/87; on books back to 1908. Mail turnaround time 1-2 days. Access criminal index at www.ndcourts.gov/publicsearch/contactsearch.aspx. Index goes back to 1/2000. Online results show name and may show city of residence.

General Information: No adoption, juvenile, mental health, expunged or dismissed records released. Fee to fax out file $2.00 per page. Court makes copy: $.25 per page. Self serve: same. Certification fee: $10.00 per document. Payee: Clerk of Court, McKenzie County. Personal checks and credit cards accepted. Mail requests: SASE required.

McLean County

South Central Judicial District Court PO Box 1108, Washburn, ND 58577; 701-462-8541; fax: 701-462-8212; 8AM-N, 12:30-4:30PM (CST). ***Felony, Misdemeanor, Civil, Eviction, Small Claims, Probate.***

Probate fax is same as main fax number.

Civil Records: Access: Mail, in person, online. Both court and visitors may perform in person searches. Search fee: $10.00 per name. Required to search: name, years to search; also helpful: address. Civil cases indexed by defendant, plaintiff. Civil index on docket books from early 1900s; on computer back to 1996. Mail turnaround time 1-2 days. Civil PAT goes back to 1996. Online access to civil is same as criminal via the statewide court website.

Criminal Records: Access: Mail, in person, online. Both court and visitors may perform in person searches. Search fee: $10.00 per name. Required to search: name, years to search, DOB; also helpful: address, SSN. Criminal records indexed on cards from 1983, on index books from early 1900s; on computer back to 1996. Mail turnaround time 1-2 days. Criminal PAT goes back to same as civil. Access criminal index at www.ndcourts.gov/publicsearch/contactsearch.aspx. Index goes back to 8/1995. Online results show name and may show city of residence.

General Information: No adoption, sealed, juvenile, mental health, expunged or deferred imposition dismissed records released. Will fax documents to toll free line. Court makes copy: $.10 per page, $1.00 minimum. Self serve: $.10 per page. Certification fee: $10.00 per document. Payee: Clerk of Courts. Personal checks accepted; credit cards are not.

Mercer County

District Court PO Box 39, 1021 Arthur St, Stanton, ND 58571; 701-745-3262; fax: 701-745-3710; 8AM-4PM (CST). ***Felony, Misdemeanor, Civil, Eviction, Small Claims, Probate.***
www.mercercountynd.com/government.htm

Civil Records: Access: Fax, mail, in person, online. Both court and visitors may perform in person searches. Search fee: $10.00 per name. Required to search: name, years to search; also helpful: address. Civil cases indexed by defendant, plaintiff. Civil index on cards from 1979, on index books from 1889, computerized since 1990. Mail turnaround time 1-2 days. Civil PAT goes back to 1992. Online access to civil is same as criminal via the statewide court website.

Criminal Records: Access: Fax, mail, in person, online. Both court and visitors may perform in person searches. Search fee: $10.00 per name. Required to search: name, years to search, signed release; also helpful: address, DOB, SSN. Criminal records indexed on cards from 1979, on index books from 1889, computerized since 1990. Mail turnaround time 1-2 days. Criminal PAT goes back to same as civil. Access criminal index at www.ndcourts.gov/publicsearch/contactsearch.aspx. Index goes back to 3/1991. Online results show name and may show city of residence.

General Information: No adoption, sealed, juvenile, mental health, expunged or dismissed records released. Will fax documents $5.00 per doc. Court makes copy: $.25 per page. Self serve: $.25 per page. Certification fee: $10.00 per doc. Payee: Mercer County Clerk of Court. Personal checks accepted; credit cards are not. Mail requests: SASE required.

Morton County

South Central Judicial District Court 210 2nd Ave NW, Mandan, ND 58554; 701-667-3358; criminal phone: 701-667-3355; fax: 701-667-3474; 8AM-5PM (MST). ***Felony, Misdemeanor, Civil, Eviction, Small Claims, Probate.***

Civil Records: Access: Mail, in person, online. Both court and visitors may perform in person searches. Search fee: $10.00 per name. Fee is for written search request. Required to search: name, years to search; also helpful: address. Civil cases indexed by defendant, plaintiff; index on computer from 1990; on index books from 1985. Mail turnaround time 1-2 days. Civil PAT goes back to 1990. Online access to civil is same as criminal via the statewide court website.

Criminal Records: Access: Mail, in person, online. Both court and visitors may perform in person searches. Search fee: $10.00 per name. Fee is for written search request. Required to search: name, years to search, DOB; also helpful: address. Criminal records computerized from 1990, on index books from 1985. Mail turnaround time 1-2 days. Criminal PAT goes back to same as civil. Access criminal index at www.ndcourts.gov/publicsearch/contactsearch.aspx. Index goes back to 11/1993. Online includes Mandan Muni Court. Online results show name and may show city of residence.

General Information: No adoption, sealed, juvenile, mental health, expunged or dismissed records released. Will fax case files to local or toll free number. Court makes copy: $.10 per page. Certification fee: $10.00. Cert fee includes copies. Payee: Clerk of District Court. Personal checks accepted; credit cards are not. Mail requests: SASE helpful.

Mountrail County

Mountrail County District Court PO Box 69, Stanley, ND 58784; 701-628-2915; fax: 701-628-2276; 8:30AM-4:30PM (CST). ***Felony, Misdemeanor, Civil, Eviction, Small Claims, Probate.*** Probate is a separate index at this same address. Probate fax is same as main fax number.

Civil Records: Access: Mail, in person, fax, phone, online. Both court and visitors may perform in person searches. Search fee: $10.00 per name. Fee is for written search. Required to search: name, years to search; also helpful: address. Civil cases indexed by defendant, plaintiff. Civil index on docket books from 1909; on computer back to 1998. Mail turnaround time 1-2 days. Civil PAT goes back to 1998. PAT results show name only. Online access to civil is same as criminal via the statewide court website.

Criminal Records: Access: Mail, in person, online. Both court and visitors may perform in person searches. Search fee: $10.00 per name. Fee is for written search. Required to search: name, years to search, DOB. Criminal records indexed in books from 1909; on computer back to 1998. Mail turnaround time 1-2 days. Criminal PAT goes back to same as civil. PAT results show name only. Results include charges. Access criminal index at www.ndcourts.gov/publicsearch/contactsearch.aspx. Index goes back to 1/1998. Online results show name and may show city of residence.

General Information: No adoption, sealed, juvenile, mental health, expunged records released. No fee to fax documents. Court makes copy: $.25 per page. Certification fee: $10.00 per document includes copy fee. Payee: Clerk of District Court. Personal checks accepted; credit cards are not.

Nelson County

Northeast Central Judicial District Court Nelson County Recorder-Clerk of Court, 210 B Ave W, #203, Lakota, ND 58344-7410; 701-247-2462; fax: 701-247-2412; 8:30AM-N; 1-4:30PM (CST). ***Felony, Misdemeanor, Civil, Eviction, Small Claims, Probate.*** www.nelsonco.org/recorder.html

Probate fax is same as main fax number.

Civil Records: Access: Fax, mail, in person, email, online. Both court and visitors may perform in person searches. Search fee: $10.00 per name. Required to search: name, years to search; also helpful: address. Civil cases indexed by defendant, plaintiff. Civil index on docket books from 1883. Mail turnaround time 1-2 days. Civil PAT goes back to 10 years for judgments, 20 if renewed. PAT results show middle initial, DOB. Online access to civil is same as criminal via the statewide court website. Will accept email record requests at rstevens@nd.gov.

Criminal Records: Access: Fax, mail, in person, email, online. Both court and visitors may perform in person searches. Search fee: $10.00 per name. Required to search: name, years to search, DOB; also helpful: address, SSN. Criminal records indexed in books from 1883. Mail turnaround time 1-2 days. Criminal PAT goes back to 2002. PAT results show middle initial, DOB. Access criminal index www.ndcourts.gov/publicsearch/contactsearch.aspx. Index goes back to 3/2002. Court will accept email record requests at rstevens@nd.gov. Online results show name and may show city of residence.

General Information: No adoption, sealed, juvenile, mental health, expunged or dismissed records released. Will fax documents $3.00 each. Court makes copy: $1.00 per 4-page document; $.25 each add'l. Certification fee: $10.00 includes copies. Payee: Clerk of Courts. Personal checks accepted; credit cards are not. Mail requests: SASE required.

Oliver County

South Central Judicial District Court Box 125, Center, ND 58530; 701-794-8777; fax: 701-794-3476; 8AM-4PM (CST). ***Felony, Misdemeanor, Civil, Eviction, Small Claims, Probate.***

Civil Records: Access: Fax, mail, in person, online. Both court and visitors may perform in person searches. Search fee: $10.00 per name. Required to search: name, years to search; also helpful: address. Civil cases indexed by defendant. Civil index in docket books from 1920s. Mail turnaround time 1-2 days. Civil PAT goes back to 1995. Online access to civil is same as criminal via the statewide court website.

Criminal Records: Access: Fax, mail, in person, online. Both court and visitors may perform in person searches. Search fee: $10.00 per name. Required to search: name, years to search, DOB; also helpful: address. Criminal docket on books from 1920s. Mail turnaround time 1-2 days. Criminal PAT goes back to same as civil. Access criminal index at www.ndcourts.gov/publicsearch/contactsearch.aspx. Index goes back to 4/2003. Online results show name and may show city of residence.

General Information: No adoption, sealed, juvenile, mental health, expunged or dismissed records released. Will fax documents $1.00 1st page, $.50 each add'l. Court makes copy: $.25 per page. Certification fee: $10.00 per doc includes copies. Payee: Clerk of Court. Personal checks and major credit cards accepted. Mail requests: SASE required.

Pembina County

Pembina County District Court 301 Dakota St West #10, Cavalier, ND 58220-4100; 701-265-4373; fax: 701-265-4876; 8:30AM-4:30PM (CST). ***Felony, Misdemeanor, Civil, Eviction, Small Claims, Probate.*** Probate fax is same as main fax number.

Civil Records: Access: Fax, mail, in person, online. Both court and visitors may perform in person searches. Search fee: $10.00 per name. Required to search: name, years to search; also helpful: address, DOB, SSN. Civil cases indexed by defendant, plaintiff. Civil index on docket books from 1880s; computerized records go back to 1997. Mail turnaround time 1-2 days. Civil PAT goes back to 1997. PAT results show name only. Online access to civil is same as criminal via the statewide court website.

Criminal Records: Access: Fax, mail, in person, online. Both court and visitors may perform in person searches. Search fee: $10.00 per name. Required to search: name, years to search, DOB; also helpful: address, SSN. Felony records kept for 21 years, misdemeanor for 7 years; computerized records go back to 1997. Mail turnaround time 1-2 days. Criminal PAT goes back to 1997.PAT results show name, DOB. Access criminal index at www.ndcourts.gov/publicsearch/contactsearch.aspx. Index goes back to 10/1997. Online results show name and may show city of residence.

General Information: No adoption, sealed, juvenile, mental health, expunged or dismissed records released. Will fax documents to local or toll free line. Court makes copy: $.15 per page. Certification fee: $10.00 per document includes copy fee. Payee: Pembina County Clerk/Recorder. Personal checks accepted; credit cards are not.

Pierce County

Northeast Judicial District Court PO Box 258, 240 SE 2nd St, Rugby, ND 58368; 701-776-6161; fax: 701-776-5707; 9AM-5PM (CST). ***Felony, Misdemeanor, Civil, Eviction, Small Claims, Probate.***

Probate fax is same as main fax number.

Civil Records: Access: Fax, mail, in person, online. Both court and visitors may perform in person searches. Search fee: $10.00 per name. Required to search: name, years to search. Civil cases indexed by defendant, plaintiff; index on computer from 1996 (all civil money judgments are on computer), on index books and docket books from early 1900s. Mail turnaround time 1-2 days. Civil PAT goes back to 1996. PAT results show name, DOB, SSN. Online access to civil is same as criminal via the statewide court website.

Criminal Records: Access: Fax, mail, in person, online. Both court and visitors may perform in person searches. Search fee: $10.00 per name. Required to search: name, years to search, DOB; also helpful: SSN. Criminal records computerized from 1996, on index books and docket books from early 1900s. Note: Results include address. Mail turnaround time 1-2 days. Criminal PAT goes back to 1996. PAT results show name, DOB, SSN. Access criminal index at www.ndcourts.gov/publicsearch/contactsearch.aspx. Index goes back to 11/1997. Online results show name and may show city of residence.

General Information: Online identifiers in results same as on public terminal. No adoption, sealed, juvenile, mental health, expunged or dismissed records released. Court makes copy: $.10 per page. Certification fee: $10.00 per document; $5.00 for an add'l copy. Payee: Clerk of Courts. Personal checks accepted; credit cards are not. Mail requests: SASE helpful.

Ramsey County

District Court 524 4th Ave NE #4, Devils Lake, ND 58301; 701-662-1309; fax: 701-662-1303; 8AM-N; 1:00PM-5:00PM (CST). ***Felony, Misdemeanor, Civil, Eviction, Small Claims, Probate.***

Civil Records: Access: Mail, in person, online. Both court and visitors may perform in person searches. Search fee: $10.00 per name. Required to search: name; also helpful: years to search. Civil cases indexed by defendant, plaintiff. Civil index on cards from 1985, on index books from early 1900s. Mail turnaround time 1-2 days. Civil PAT goes back to 1997. PAT results show name, DOB. Online access to civil is same as criminal via the statewide court website.

Criminal Records: Access: Mail, in person, online. Both court and visitors may perform in person searches. Search fee: $10.00 per name. Required to search: name; also helpful: years to search, address, DOB, SSN. Criminal records indexed on cards from 1985, on index books from early 1900s. Mail turnaround time 1-2 days. Criminal PAT goes back to same as civil.PAT results show name, DOB. Access criminal index at www.ndcourts.gov/publicsearch/contactsearch.aspx. Index goes back to 10/1997. Online includes Devils Lake Muni Court. Online results show name and may show city of residence.

General Information: No adoption, sealed, juvenile, mental health, expunged or dismissed records released. No fee to fax documents; only available to businesses. Court makes copy: $.10 per page. Certification fee: $10.00 per doc includes copies. Payee: Clerk of Courts. Personal checks and credit cards accepted. Mail requests: SASE required.

Ransom County

Southeast Judicial District Court PO Box 626, Lisbon, ND 58054; 701-683-6120; criminal phone: 701-683-6142; fax: 701-683-5826; 8:30AM-5PM (CST). ***Felony, Misdemeanor, Civil, Eviction, Small Claims, Probate.***

Civil Records: Access: Fax, mail, in person, online. Only the court performs in person searches; visitors may not. Search fee: $10.00 per name. Required to search: name, years to search; also helpful: address. Civil cases indexed by defendant, plaintiff. Civil records computerized from 2000. Mail turnaround time 3-4 days. Online access to civil is same as criminal via the statewide court website.

Criminal Records: Access: Fax, mail, in person, online. Only the court performs in person searches; visitors may not. Search fee: $10.00 per name. Required to search: name, years to search, DOB; also helpful: address. Criminal records computerized from 2000. Mail turnaround time 3-4 days. Access criminal index at www.ndcourts.gov/publicsearch/contactsearch.aspx. Index goes back to 1/2000. Online results show name and may show city of residence.

General Information: No adoption, sealed, juvenile, mental health, expunged or dismissed records released. No fee to fax documents. Court makes copy: $.20 per page. Certification fee: $10.00. Payee: Clerk of Court. Personal checks accepted; credit cards are not. Mail requests: SASE required.

Renville County

Northeast Judicial District Court PO Box 68, Mohall, ND 58761; 701-756-6398; fax: 701-756-6494; 9AM-4:30PM (CST). ***Felony, Misdemeanor, Civil, Eviction, Small Claims, Probate.*** www.renvillecountynd.org/

Civil Records: Access: Fax, mail, in person, online. Both court and visitors may perform in person searches. Search fee: $10.00 per name. Required to search: name, years to search; also helpful: address. Civil cases indexed by defendant, plaintiff. Civil index on docket books from 1910. Mail turnaround time 1-2 days. Public use terminal has civil records. Online access to civil is same as criminal via the statewide court website.

Criminal Records: Access: Fax, mail, in person, online. Both court and visitors may perform in person searches. Search fee: $10.00 per name. Required to search: name, years to search, DOB; also helpful: address. Criminal records computerized from 1/88, on index books from 1910 but not reliable before 1940. Mail turnaround time 1-2 days. Access criminal index at www.ndcourts.gov/publicsearch/contactsearch.aspx. Index goes back to 1/2003. Online results show name and may show city of residence.

General Information: No adoption, sealed, juvenile, mental health, expunged or dismissed records released. Will fax documents $3.00 1st page, $1.00 each add'l. Court makes copy: $.25 per page. Certification fee: $10.00 per doc. Payee: Clerk of Courts. Personal checks accepted. Mail requests: SASE required.

Richland County

Southeast Judicial District Court 418 2nd Ave North, Wahpeton, ND 58074; 701-671-1524; fax: 701-671-4444; 8AM-5PM (CST). ***Felony, Misdemeanor, Civil, Eviction, Small Claims, Probate.***

Civil Records: Access: Mail, fax, in person, online. Visitors must perform in person searches

themselves. Search fee: $10.00 per name. Required to search: name, years to search, plaintiff and defendant names.; also helpful: address. Plaintiff and defendant names required to search. Civil records indexed in books and computer. Mail turnaround time 1-2 days. Civil PAT goes back to 1998. PAT results show name, DOB. Online access to civil is same as criminal via the statewide court website.
Criminal Records: Access: Mail, fax, in person, online. Visitors must perform in person searches themselves. Search fee: $10.00 per name. Required to search: name, years to search, DOB, SSN; also helpful: address. Criminal docket on books and computer. Mail turnaround time 1-2 days. Criminal PAT goes back to same as civil.PAT results show name, DOB. Access criminal index at www.ndcourts.gov/publicsearch/contactsearch.aspx. Index goes back to 1/1998. Online includes Wahpeton Muni Court. Online results show name and may show city of residence.
General Information: No adoption, sealed, juvenile, mental health, or expunged records released. Will fax documents to toll-free number, otherwise fax fee is $.25 per page, $1.00 minimum. Court makes copy: $.10 per page; $1.00 minimum. Certification fee: $10.00 per doc. Payee: Clerk of District Court. Personal checks and major credit cards accepted. Mail requests: SASE required.

Rolette County

Northeast Judicial District Court PO Box 460, 201 2nd St NE 2nd Fl, Rolla, ND 58367; 701-477-3816; fax: 701-477-8594; 8AM-5PM (CST). ***Felony, Misdemeanor, Civil, Eviction, Small Claims, Probate.***
Civil Records: Access: Fax, mail, in person, online. Both court and visitors may perform in person searches. Search fee: $10.00 per name. Required to search: name, years to search; also helpful: address. Civil cases indexed by defendant, plaintiff, stored since 1889; computerized since 1999. Mail turnaround time 1-2 days. Civil PAT goes back to 6/1999. PAT results show name only. Online access to civil is same as criminal via the statewide court website.
Criminal Records: Access: Fax, mail, in person, online. Both court and visitors may perform in person searches. Search fee: $10.00 per name. Required to search: name, years to search; also helpful: address, DOB, SSN. Criminal docket index from 1970, computerized since 2000. Prior to 1970, records hard to find and not very accurate. Mail turnaround time 1-2 days. Criminal PAT goes back to 6/1999. PAT results show name only. Access criminal index at www.ndcourts.gov/publicsearch/contactsearch.aspx. Index goes back to 6/1999. Online results show name and may show city of residence.
General Information: No adoption, sealed, juvenile, mental health, expunged or dismissed records released. Will fax documents $5.00 per doc. Court makes copy: $.10 per page; $1.00 mimimum. Self serve: same. Certification fee: $10.00. Payee: Clerk of Court. Business checks accepted. No credit cards accepted. Mail requests: SASE required.

Sargent County

Southeast Judicial District Court 355 Main St S #2, Forman, ND 58032-4149; 701-724-6241 X115 or 117; fax: 701-724-6244; 9AM-N, 12:30-4:30PM (CST). ***Felony, Misdemeanor, Civil, Eviction, Small Claims, Probate.***
Civil Records: Access: Fax, mail, in person, online. Both court and visitors may perform in person searches. Search fee: $10.00 per name. Required to search: name, years to search; also helpful: address. Civil cases indexed by defendant. Civil records on books from early 1800s. Mail turnaround time 1-2 days. Online access to civil is same as criminal via the statewide court website.
Criminal Records: Access: Fax, mail, in person, online. Both court and visitors may perform in person searches. Search fee: $10.00 per name. Required to search: name, years to search; also helpful-DOB. Criminal docket on books from early 1800s. Mail turnaround time 1-2 days. Access criminal index at www.ndcourts.gov/publicsearch/contactsearch.aspx. Index goes back to 1/2002. Online results show name and may show city of residence.
General Information: No adoption, sealed, juvenile, mental health, expunged or dismissed records released. Will fax documents $3.00 1st page, $1.00 each add'l. Court makes copy: $.10 per page. Self serve: same. Certification fee: $10.00. Payee: Clerk of Court. Personal checks accepted; credit cards are not.

Sheridan County

South Central Judicial District Court PO Box 409, 215 2nd St E, McClusky, ND 58463; 701-363-2207; fax: 701-363-2953; 9AM-N, 1-5PM (CST). ***Felony, Misdemeanor, Civil, Eviction, Small Claims, Probate.***
Civil Records: Access: Mail, in person, online. Both court and visitors may perform in person searches. Search fee: $10.00 per name. Required to search: name, years to search; also helpful: address. Civil cases indexed by defendant, plaintiff. Civil index on docket books from 1909. Mail turnaround time 1-2 days. Civil PAT goes back to 1909. Online access to civil is same as criminal via the statewide court website.
Criminal Records: Access: Mail, in person, online. Both court and visitors may perform in person searches. Search fee: $10.00 per name. Required to search: name, years to search, signed release; also helpful: address, DOB, SSN. Criminal records indexed in books from 1909. Mail turnaround time 1-2 days. Criminal PAT goes back to same as civil. Access criminal index at www.ndcourts.gov/publicsearch/contactsearch.aspx. Index goes back to 2/2003. Online results show name and may show city of residence.
General Information: No adoption, sealed, juvenile, mental health, expunged or dismissed records released. Will fax documents to local or toll-free number. Court makes copy: $.25 per page. Self serve: same. Certification fee: $10.00. Payee: Clerk of District Court. Business checks accepted. No credit cards accepted.

Sioux County

South Central Judicial District Court Box L, 303 2nd Ave, Fort Yates, ND 58538; 701-854-3853; fax: 701-854-3854; 8AM-4PM (CST). ***Felony, Misdemeanor, Civil, Eviction, Small Claims, Probate.***
Civil Records: Access: Mail, in person, online. Both court and visitors may perform in person searches. Search fee: $10.00 per name. Required to search: name, years to search; also helpful: address. Civil cases indexed by defendant, plaintiff. Civil index on docket books from 1914. Mail turnaround time 1-2 days. Online access to civil is same as criminal via the statewide court website.
Criminal Records: Access: Mail, in person, online. Both court and visitors may perform in person searches. Search fee: $10.00 per name. Required to search: name, years to search; also helpful: address, DOB, SSN. Criminal records indexed in books from 1914. Mail turnaround time 1-2 days. Access criminal index at www.ndcourts.gov/publicsearch/contactsearch.aspx. Index goes back to 3/2003. Online results show name and may show city of residence.
General Information: No adoption, sealed, juvenile, mental health, expunged or dismissed records released. Fee to fax out file $3.00 each. Court makes copy: $.50 per page. Certification fee: $10.00 per doc includes copies. Payee: Clerk of Court. Personal checks accepted; credit cards are not. Mail requests: SASE required.

Slope County

Southwest Judicial District Court PO Box JJ, 206 S Main, Amidon, ND 58620; 701-879-6275; fax: 701-879-6278; 8:30AM-4:30PM (MST). ***Felony, Misdemeanor, Civil, Eviction, Small Claims, Probate.***
Civil Records: Access: Fax, mail, in person, online. Only the court performs in person searches; visitors may not. Search fee: $10.00 per name. Required to search: name, years to search; also helpful: address. Civil cases indexed by defendant, plaintiff; index in books back to 1915. Mail turnaround time 1-2 days. Online access to civil is same as criminal via the statewide court website.
Criminal Records: Access: Fax, mail, in person, online. Only the court performs in person searches; visitors may not. Search fee: $10.00 per name. Required to search: name, years to search, DOB; also helpful: address. Criminal docket on books back to 1915. Mail turnaround time 1-2 days. Access criminal index at www.ndcourts.gov/publicsearch/contactsearch.aspx. Index goes back to 3/2003. Online results show name and may show city of residence.
General Information: No adoption, sealed, juvenile, mental health, expunged or dismissed records released. Will fax documents $3.00 each. Court makes copy: $.25 per page. Self serve: $.25 per page. Certification fee: $10.00. Payee: Clerk of Court. Personal checks accepted; credit cards are not. Mail requests: SASE required.

Stark County

District Court 51 Third St E #106, Dickinson, ND 58602; 701-227-3184; criminal phone: 701-227-3180; civil phone: 701-227-3182; probate phone: 701-227-3181; fax: 701-227-3185; 8AM-5PM (MST). ***Felony, Misdemeanor, Civil, Eviction, Small Claims, Probate.***
Civil Records: Access: Mail, in person, online. Both court and visitors may perform in person searches. Search fee: $10.00 per name. Required to search: name, years to search. Civil cases indexed by defendant, plaintiff; index on computer since 1/92, index cards or docket books since 1800s. Mail turnaround time 1-2 days. Civil PAT goes back to 1992. PAT civil results show middle initial. Online access to civil is same as criminal via the statewide court website.
Criminal Records: Access: Mail, in person, online. Both court and visitors may perform in person searches. Search fee: $10.00 per name. Required to search: name, years to search, DOB; also helpful: SSN. Criminal records on computer since 1/92, index cards or docket books since 1800s. Mail turnaround time 1-2 days. Criminal PAT goes back to same as civil. PAT criminal results show middle initial. Access criminal index at www.ndcourts.gov/publicsearch/contactsearch.aspx. Index goes back to 4/1992. Online includes Dickinson Muni Court. Online results show name and may show city of residence.
General Information: No adoption, sealed, juvenile, mental health, expunged or dismissed records. Will fax documents $.25 per page, $1.00 minimum. Court makes copy: $.10 per page; $1.00 minimum. Self serve: same. Certification fee: $10.00. Payee: Clerk of Court. Personal checks and major credit cards accepted. Mail requests: SASE required.

Steele County

East Central Judicial District Court PO Box 296, Finley, ND 58230; 701-524-2152; fax: 701-524-1325; 8AM-N; 1-4:30PM (CST). ***Felony, Misdemeanor, Civil, Eviction, Small Claims, Probate.***
Civil Records: Access: Mail, in person, online. Only the court performs in person searches; visitors may not. Search fee: $10.00 per name. Required to search: name, years to search; also helpful: address. Civil cases indexed by defendant, plaintiff. Civil index in docket books from approx 1894. Mail turnaround time 1-2 days. Online access to civil is same as criminal via the statewide court website.
Criminal Records: Access: Mail, in person, online. Only the court performs in person searches; visitors may not. Search fee: $10.00 per name. Required to search: name, years to search, DOB, signed release; also helpful: address. Criminal docket on books from approx 1894. Mail turnaround time 1-2 days. Access criminal index at www.ndcourts.gov/publicsearch/contactsearch.aspx. Index goes back to 12/2002. Online results show name and may show city of residence.
General Information: No adoption, sealed, juvenile, mental health, expunged or dismissed records released. Will fax documents $5.00 each. Court makes copy: $1.00 per page. Certification fee: $10.00.

Payee: Clerk of Court. Business checks accepted. No credit cards accepted. Mail requests: SASE required.

Stutsman County

Southeast Judicial District Court 511 2nd Ave SE, Jamestown, ND 58401; 701-252-9042; probate phone: 701-251-6331; fax: 701-251-6319; 8AM-5PM (CST). ***Felony, Misdemeanor, Civil, Eviction, Small Claims, Probate.***

Civil Records: Access: Mail, fax, in person, online. Both court and visitors may perform in person searches. Search fee: $10.00 per name. Required to search: name, years to search; also helpful: address. Civil records on computer back to 1/87, on index books from 1800s. Mail turnaround time 1-2 days. Civil PAT goes back to at least 1996. Online access to civil is same as criminal via the statewide court website.

Criminal Records: Access: Mail, fax, in person, online. Both court and visitors may perform in person searches. Search fee: $10.00 per name. Required to search: name, years to search, DOB; also helpful: address. Criminal records computerized from 1/96, on index books from 1800s. Mail turnaround time 1-2 days. Criminal PAT goes back to 1996. Access criminal index at www.ndcourts.gov/publicsearch/contactsearch.aspx. Index goes back to 9/1995. Online includes Jamestown Muni Court. Online results show name and may show city of residence.

General Information: No adoption, sealed, juvenile, mental health, expunged or dismissed records released. Will fax documents to local or toll free line. Court makes copy: $.10 per page, minimum charge $1.00. Certification fee: $10.00. Payee: Clerk of Court. Personal checks and major credit cards accepted. Mail requests: SASE required.

Towner County

Northeast Judicial District Court PO Box 517, 315 2nd St, Cando, ND 58324; 701-968-4340 x3; fax: 701-968-4344; 8:30AM-N; 1-5:00PM (CST). ***Felony, Misdemeanor, Civil, Eviction, Small Claims, Probate.***

www.court.state.nd.us/court/counties/dc_clerk/towner.htm

Civil Records: Access: Fax, mail, in person, online. Only the court performs in person searches; visitors may not. Search fee: $10.00 per name. Required to search: name, years to search; also helpful: address. Civil cases indexed by defendant, plaintiff. Civil index on docket books from 1800s, computerized since 1998. Mail turnaround time 1-2 days. Civil PAT goes back to 1998. PAT results show name, DOB. Online access to civil is same as criminal via the statewide court website.

Criminal Records: Access: Fax, mail, in person, online. Only the court performs in person searches; visitors may not. Search fee: $10.00 per name. Required to search: name, years to search; also helpful: address, DOB, SSN. Records computerized since 1998. Mail turnaround time 1-2 days. Criminal PAT goes back to 1998. Access criminal index at www.ndcourts.gov/publicsearch/contactsearch.aspx. Index goes back to 4/2002. Online results show name and may show city of residence.

General Information: Online identifiers in results same as on public terminal. No adoption, sealed, juvenile, mental health, expunged or dismissed records released. Will fax documents $10.00 each. Court makes copy: $1.00 per page. Certification fee: $10.00. Payee: Clerk of District Court. Personal checks accepted. Visa/MC accepted. Mail requests: SASE required.

Traill County

East Central Judicial District Court PO Box 805, Hillsboro, ND 58045; 701-636-4454; fax: 701-636-5124; 8AM-4:30PM (CST). ***Felony, Misdemeanor, Civil, Eviction, Small Claims, Probate.***

Civil Records: Access: Phone, fax, mail, in person, online. Only the court performs in person searches; visitors may not. Search fee: $10.00 per name. Required to search: name, years to search; also helpful: address. Civil cases indexed by defendant, plaintiff. Civil index on docket books from 1800s. Mail turnaround time 1-2 days. Public use terminal available, records go back to summer of 2002. PAT results show name, DOB. Online access to civil is same as criminal via the statewide court website.

Criminal Records: Access: Phone, fax, mail, in person, online. Only the court performs in person searches; visitors may not. Search fee: $10.00 per name. Required to search: name, years to search; also helpful: address, DOB, SSN. Criminal records indexed in books from 1800s. Mail turnaround time 1-2 days. Public use terminal available.PAT results show name, DOB. Access criminal index at www.ndcourts.gov/publicsearch/contactsearch.aspx. Index goes back to 5/2002. Online results show name, DOB. Online result may show city of residence.

General Information: No adoption, sealed, juvenile, mental health, expunged or dismissed records released. Will fax documents $1.00 per page. Court makes copy: $.10 per page criminal; civil- $.25 per page. Certification fee: $10.00 per doc includes copies. Payee: Clerk of Court. Personal checks accepted; credit cards are not. Mail requests: SASE required.

Walsh County

Northeast Judicial District Court Clerk of District Court, 600 Cooper Ave, Grafton, ND 58237; 701-352-0350; fax: 701-352-4466; 8:30AM-5PM (CST). ***Felony, Misdemeanor, Civil, Eviction, Small Claims, Probate.***

Civil Records: Access: Mail, in person, online. Both court and visitors may perform in person searches. Search fee: $10.00 per name. Required to search: name, years to search; also helpful: address, SSN. Civil cases indexed by defendant, plaintiff. Civil index on docket books from early 1900s; on computer from 11/97. Mail turnaround time 2-3 days. Civil PAT goes back to 11/1997. PAT results show name only. Online access to civil is same as criminal via the statewide court website.

Criminal Records: Access: Mail, in person, online. Both court and visitors may perform in person searches. Search fee: $10.00 per name. Required to search: name with middle initial, years to search, DOB; also helpful: address. Criminal records indexed in books from early 1900s; on computer from 11/97. Mail turnaround time 2-3 days. Criminal PAT goes back to same as civil. PAT results show name only. Access criminal index at www.ndcourts.gov/publicsearch/contactsearch.aspx. Index goes back to 11/1997. Online results show name and may show city of residence.

General Information: No adoption, sealed, juvenile, mental health, expunged or dismissed records released. Will fax documents to local or toll-free number. Court makes copy: $.10 per page; $1.00 minimum. Certification fee: $10.00, then $5.00 each add'l copy. Payee: Clerk of Court. Personal checks and major credit cards accepted. Mail requests: SASE required.

Ward County

Northwest Judicial District Court PO Box 5005, Minot, ND 58702-5005; criminal phone: 701-857-6600 x2; civil phone: 701-857-6600 x1; probate phone: 701-857-6600 x1; fax: 701-857-6623; 8AM-4:30PM (CST). ***Felony, Misdemeanor, Civil, Eviction, Small Claims, Probate.***

Civil Records: Access: Mail, in person, online. Both court and visitors may perform in person searches. Search fee: $10.00 per name. Required to search: name, years to search; also helpful: DOB, address. Civil cases indexed by defendant, plaintiff. Civil index on cards from 1990, on index books from late 1880s; computerized records go back to 1994. Mail turnaround time 5 days. Civil PAT goes back to 1994. PAT results show middle initial, DOB. Online access to civil is same as criminal via the statewide court website.

Criminal Records: Access: Mail, in person, online. Both court and visitors may perform in person searches. Search fee: $10.00 per name. Required to search: name, years to search; also helpful: address, DOB, SSN. Criminal records indexed on cards from 1990, on index books from late 1880s; computerized records go back to 1994. Mail turnaround time 5 days. Criminal PAT goes back to same as civil. PAT results show middle initial, DOB. Access criminal index at www.ndcourts.gov/publicsearch/contactsearch.aspx. Index goes back to 1994 but is incomplete back into 1993 back to 10/1992. Online includes recent Minot Muni Court. Online results show name and may show city of residence.

General Information: No adoption, sealed, juvenile, mental health, expunged or dismissed records released. Will not fax documents. Court makes copy: $.10 per page, $1.00 minimum. Certification fee: $10.00 for 1st doc; $5.00 each add'l doc. Payee: Clerk of District Court. Business checks accepted. Major credit cards accepted. Mail requests: SASE required.

Wells County

Southeast Judicial District Court PO Box 155, Fessenden, ND 58438; 701-547-3122; fax: 701-547-3840; 8AM-4PM (CST). ***Felony, Misdemeanor, Civil, Eviction, Small Claims, Probate.*** Probate fax is same as main fax.

Civil Records: Access: Mail, in person, online. Only the court performs in person searches; visitors may not. Search fee: $10.00 per name. Required to search: name, years to search; also helpful: address. Civil cases indexed by defendant, plaintiff. Civil index on docket books. Mail turnaround time same day. Online access to civil is same as criminal via the statewide court website.

Criminal Records: Access: Mail, in person, online. Only the court performs in person searches; visitors may not. Search fee: $10.00 per name. Required to search: name, years to search; also helpful: address, DOB, SSN. Criminal records indexed in books from 1980. Mail turnaround time 1-2 days. Access criminal index at www.ndcourts.gov/publicsearch/contactsearch.aspx. Index goes back to 2/2002. Online results show name and may show city of residence.

General Information: No adoption, sealed, juvenile, mental health, expunged or dismissed records released. Will fax documents to local or toll free line. Court makes copy: $1.00 per document. Certification fee: $10.00 per doc includes copies. Payee: District Court. Personal checks accepted; credit cards are not. Mail requests: SASE required.

Williams County

Northwest Judicial District Court PO Box 2047, Williston, ND 58802; 701-774-4374; criminal phone: 701-774-4377; fax: 701-774-4379; 8AM-5PM (CST). ***Felony, Misdemeanor, Civil, Eviction, Small Claims, Probate.***

Civil Records: Access: Mail, in person, online. Both court and visitors may perform in person searches. Search fee: $10.00 per name. Required to search: name, years to search; also helpful: address. Civil cases indexed by defendant, plaintiff. Civil records computerized since 1/98, on index cards from 1/92, on index books from 1899. Mail turnaround time 1-2 days. Civil PAT goes back to 1998. Online access to civil is same as criminal via the statewide court website.

Criminal Records: Access: Mail, in person, online. Both court and visitors may perform in person searches. Search fee: $10.00 per name. Required to search: name, years to search; also helpful: address, DOB, SSN. Criminal records computerized since 1/98, on index cards from 1/92, on index books from 1899. Mail turnaround time 1-2 days. Criminal PAT goes back to same as civil. Access criminal index at www.ndcourts.gov/publicsearch/contactsearch.aspx. Index goes back to 1/1998. Online includes Williston Muni Court. Online results show name and may show city of residence.

General Information: No adoption, sealed, juvenile, mental health, expunged or dismissed records released. Will fax documents. Court makes copy: $.10 per page; $1.00 minimum. Self serve: same. Certification fee: $10.00. Payee: Clerk of Court. Personal checks and major credit cards accepted. Mail requests: SASE required.

North Dakota Recording Offices

ORGANIZATION: 53 counties, 53 recording offices. The recording officer is the County Recorder, changed from Register of Deeds as of 8/2001. Most of North Dakota is in the Central Time Zone (CST). The Southwestern Counties (and most counties bordering on Montana except the northernmost) are in Mountain Standard Time (MST).

REAL ESTATE RECORDS: Some counties will perform real estate searches by name or by legal description. Real estate record copy fee is usually $1.00 per page. Certified copies are usually $5.00 for the first page and $2.00 for each additional page. Copies may be faxed back, often $3.00 per doc.

UCC RECORDS: Since July 1, 2001, all financing statements must be filed at the state level except for real estate related collateral which are filed only with the Recorder. Previously, the state was a dual filing state and UCC documents could be filed at either place. The good news is that all counties access a statewide computer database of filings and will perform UCC searches. Use search request form UCC-11. A UCC search with copies costs $7.00 per debtor name, including 3 pages of copies and $1.00 per additional page. UCC copies may be faxed for an additional $3.00 fee.

TAX LIEN RECORDS: Federal tax liens on personal property of businesses are filed with the Secretary of State. Other federal and all state tax liens are filed with the County Recorder. All counties will perform tax lien searches. Some counties automatically include business federal tax liens as part of a UCC search because they appear on the statewide database. However, be careful - federal tax liens on individuals may only be in the county lien books, and not on the statewide system. Separate tax lien searches are usually available at $5.00-$7.00 per name. Tax lien copy fees vary. Tax lien copies may be faxed.

OTHER LIENS: Mechanics, judgment, hospital, repair, egg cutter.

ONLINE ACCESS: The North Dakota Recorders Information Network (NDRIN) is a electronic central repository representing a number of North Dakota counties – all but 9 – and offering internet access to records, indices, and images. There is a $100 set-up fee a $25 monthly usage fee, and a $1.00 charge per image printed. Register or request information via the website at www.ndrin.com

Adams County

County Recorder, PO Box 469, Hettinger, ND 58639-0469. 701-567-2460; fax-701-567-2910; 8:30AM-N, 1-5PM (MST)
Index: All in one. Records indexed on a public use terminal back to 8/26/05. Office personnel or visitors may perform searches. Search fee $10.00 per name. Office will search real estate records. Will search UCC records. UCC copy request with certificate per debtor name- $7.00. Copy fee $1.00 up to a 4 page doc, over 4 pages $.25 per page. Digital copies- $.05 per image. Cert fee- $5.00 1st page; $2.00 each add'l. Payee- Adams County Recorder. **Other phones:** Treasurer- 701-567-4363; Elections- 701-567-4363; Vital Records- 701-328-2360 (Bismarck, ND). **Property tax/Assessing-** 602 Adams Ave, Courthouse, Hettinger, ND 58639; 701-567-4363, assessor fax- 701-567-2910.

Barnes County

County Recorder, 230 4th St NW, #201, Valley City, ND 58072. Recording, R/E & UCC phone-701-845-8506, UCC recording phone-701-845-8507; fax-701-845-8538; 8AM-5PM (CST) www.co.barnes.nd.us
Participates in the ND Recorders Information Network, www.ndrin.com. Index: Separate indices to search include land index, lots index. Records indexed on a public use terminal back to 2001. Office personnel or visitors may perform searches. Search fee $7.00+ per name. Office will search real estate records (1st 45 min free, $25.00 per hour after, at times available to recorders staff). Office will search old UCC records. Copy fee $1.00 per page. Cert fee- $5.00 per page, $2.00 each add'l, includes copy fee. Payee- Barnes County Recorder. Office does sell bulk data of monthly reports of images at $.10 per image, contact Kerstin Cochran. **Online access to Real Estate, Deed records:** Subscription access the recorder's land records via NDRIN's central repository at www.ndrin.com. See section introduction. **Other phones:** Treasurer- 701-845-8505; Elections- 701-845-8500; Vital Records- 701-845-8512. **Property tax/Assessing-** 230 4th St NW, Courthouse, Valley City, ND 58072; 701-845-8515, assessor fax- 701-845-8538. **Online access-** Tax lien sale list free at www.co.barnes.nd.us/dept/aud/. Link at bottom of page.

Benson County

County Recorder, PO Box 213, Minnewaukan, ND 58351. 701-473-5345, R/E recording phone-701-473-5332; fax-701-473-5345; 8:30AM-4:30PM.
Index: All in one. Records indexed on a public use terminal back 6 years. Only the public may search. Copy fee $1.00 per copy. Cert fee- $5.00 for 1st page, $2.each add'l. Payee- Benson County Recorder. **Online access to Real Estate, Deed records:** Subscription access the recorder's land records via NDRIN's central repository at www.ndrin.com. Registration and monthly fee applies. See section introduction. **Other phones:** Treasurer- 701-473-5458; Elections- 701-473-5340; Vital Records- 701-473-5345. **Property tax/Assessing-** PO Box 288, Minnewaukan, ND 58351; 701-473-5524, assessor fax- 701-473-5571.

Billings County

County Recorder, PO Box 138, Medora, ND 58645-0138. Recording, R/E & UCC phone-701-623-4491; fax-701-623-4896; 8AM-4PM (winter hrs); 8AM-5PM M-TH; 9AM-N F (summer hrs). (MST) www.billingscountynd.gov/recclerk.htm
Index: All in one. Records indexed on a public use terminal back to 2000. Office personnel or visitors may perform searches. Search fee $7.00 per name. Office will not search real estate records. Will search UCC records. Copy fee $1.00 per page; $.25 self serve. Cert fee- $5.00 for 1st pg, $2.00 each add'l pg, plus copy fee. Payee- Billings County Recorder. **Other phones:** Treasurer- 701-623-4484; Elections- 701-623-4377; Vitals- 701-623-4492. **Property tax/Assessing-** PO Box 247, Medora, ND 58645; 701-623-4810.

Bottineau County

County Recorder, 314 W 5th St, Bottineau, ND 58318-1265. 701-228-2786; fax-701-228-3658; 8:30AM-5PM.
Index: All in one. Records indexed on a public use terminal back to 7/97. Only the public may search. Copy fee $1.00 per doc. Cert fee- $7.00 1st pg; $2.00 each add'l page. Payee- Bottineau County Recorder. **Other phones:** Treasurer- 701-228-2035; Elections- 701-228-2225. **Property tax/Assessing-** 314 W 5th St, Bottineau, ND 58318; 701-228-2901.

Bowman County

County Recorder, 104 1st St NW, #3, Bowman, ND 58623. 701-523-3450; fax-701-523-5443; 8AM-4:30PM. www.ndcourts.gov/court/counties/reg_deed/bowman.htm
Index: All in one. Records indexed on a public use terminal back to 10/700. Office personnel or visitors may perform searches. Search fee $25.00; 1st hour free. Office will search real estate records. Will search UCC records back 5 years. Copy fee $.25 per page. Cert fee- $5.00 1st page; $2.00 each add'l page. Payee- County Recorder. **Online access to Real Estate, Deed, Death records:** Subscription access the recorder's land records via NDRIN's central repository at www.ndrin.com. Registration and monthly fee applies. See section introduction. Also, access to public death index for free go to https://secure.apps.state.nd.us/doh/certificates/deathCertSearch.htm . **Other phones:** Treasurer- 701-523-3665; Elections- 701-523-3130; Vital Records- 701-328-2360; Auditor- 701-523-3130; Clerk of Court - 701-523-3450. **Property tax/Assessing-** 104 1st St NW, #4, Bowman, ND 58623; 701-523-3129, assessor fax- 701-523-5443. (Appraiser/Auditor- 701-523-3129);

Burke County

County Recorder, PO Box 219, Bowbells, ND 58721-0219. Recording, R/E & UCC phone-701-377-2818; fax-701-377-2020; 8:30AM-5PM.
Index: Separate indices to search. Record index not computerized. Office personnel or visitors may perform searches. Search fee $7.00 per name. Office will search real estate records. Copy fee $1.00 per page.Real estate record copy- $.50 per page. Cert fee- $5.00 for 1st page; $2.00 each add'l plus copy fee. Payee- County Recorder. **Other phones:** Treasurer- 701-377-2917; Elections- 701-377-2861; Vital Records- 701-377-2718. **Property tax/Assessing**- 701-377-2661. (Appraiser/Auditor- 701-377-2661)

Burleigh County

County Recorder, PO Box 5518, Bismarck, ND 58506-5518. Recording, R/E & UCC phone-701-222-6749; fax-701-222-6717; 8AM-5PM (CST)
Index: All in one. Records indexed on computer back to 10/7/96. Office will perform a UCC search but public must search other records themselves. Search fee $7.00 per name minimum. Office can provide real estate data on current deed only. Copy fee $1.00 per page. Cert fee- $5.00 for 1st page, $2.00 each add'l includes copy fee. Payee- Burleigh County Recorder. **Online access to Real Estate, Deed records:** Subscription access the recorder's land records via NDRIN's central repository at www.ndrin.com. Registration and monthly fee applies. See section introduction. **Other phones:** Treasurer- 701-222-6696; Elections- 701-222-6718; Vital Records- 701-328-2360. **Property tax/Assessing**- 221 N 5th St, Bismarck, ND 58501; 701-222-6691. (Appraiser/Auditor- 701-222-6691) **Online access**- Access to treasurer and auditor property data is free at www.co.burleigh.nd.us/property-information/. No name searching.

Cass County

County Recorder, PO Box 2806, Fargo, ND 58108-2806. 701-241-5622, R/E recording phone-701-241-5620; fax-701-241-5621; 8AM-5PM.
Index: All in one. Records indexed on computer back to 1993. Office will perform a UCC search but public must search other records themselves. Search fee $7.00 per name. Copy fee $1.00 per page. Cert fee- $5.00 per cert plus copy fee. Payee- Cass County Recorder. **Online access to Real Estate, Deed records:** Subscription access the recorder's land records via NDRIN's central repository at www.ndrin.com. Registration and monthly fee applies. See section introduction. **Other phones:** Treasurer- 701-241-5611; Elections- 701-241-5601. **Property tax/Assessing**- Same address as recording office. 701-241-5611. **Online access**- Access the treasurer's property tax data free at https://cass.nd.ezgov.com/ezproperty/review_search.jsp but no name searching. Also, search data free at the Parcel Info site at http://apps.cityoffargo.com/parcel/ but no name searching.

Cavalier County

County Recorder, 901 3rd St, #13, Langdon, ND 58249. Recording, R/E & UCC phone-701-256-2136; fax-701-256-2566; 8:30AM-4:30PM.
Participates in the ND Recorders Information Network, www.ndrin.com. Index: All in one. Records indexed on a public use terminal back to 1988. Office personnel or visitors may perform searches. General search fee $3.00 per name. Office will not search real estate records. UCC copy request with certificate per debtor name- $7.00. Copy fee $1.00 per UCC. Cert fee- $7.00 per page plus copy fee. Payee- County Recorder. **Online access to Real Estate, Deed records:** Subscription access the recorder's land records via NDRIN's central repository at www.ndrin.com. Registration and monthly fee applies. See section introduction. **Other phones:** Treasurer- 701-256-2549; Elections- 701-256-2229; Vitals- 701-256-2124. **Property tax/Assessing**- 901 3rd St, Langdon, ND 58249; 701-256-2229.

Dickey County

County Recorder, PO Box 403, Ellendale, ND 58436. 701-349-3249 x5, R/E recording phone-701-349-3249; fax-701-349-4639; 8AM-4:30PM (CST)
Index: Separate indices to search include 6 index books. Records indexed on a public use terminal back 2 years. Office will perform a real estate search but public must search other records themselves. No fee for search. Copy fee $1.00 per page. Cert fee- $5.00 1st page, $2.00 each add'l page. Payee- Dickey County. **Other phones:** Elections- 701-349-3249. **Property tax/Assessing**- 309 N 2nd, Courthouse, Ellendale, ND 58436; 701-349-3218.

Divide County

County Recorder, PO Box 68, Crosby, ND 58730. 701-965-6661; fax-701-965-6943; 8:30-N, 1-5PM.
Index: Separate indices to search include deeds, misc in books. Office personnel or visitors may perform searches. Search fee $10.00 per name. Office will not search real estate records. Office will not search UCC records. Copy fee $2.00 per page. Cert fee- $5.00 per cert. Payee- Divide County Recorder. **Other phones:** Treasurer- 701-965-6312; Elections- 701-965-6351. **Property tax/Assessing**- Same address as recording office. 701-965-6351.

Dunn County

County Recorder, PO Box 106, Manning, ND 58642-0106. Recording, R/E & UCC phone-701-573-4443; fax-701-573-4444; 8AM-N, 12:30-4:30PM (MST)
Index: All in one. Records indexed on a public use terminal back to 1998. Only the public may search. Copy fee $1.00 per copy. Self serve- $.50 per page. Copy of indexes $1.00. Cert fee- $10.00 per cert plus copy fee. Payee- Dunn County Recorder. **Online access to Real Estate, Deed records:** Subscription access the recorder's land records via NDRIN's central repository at www.ndrin.com. Registration and monthly fee applies. See section introduction. **Other phones:** Treasurer- 701-573-4446; Elections- 701-573-4448 (Auditor); Vital Records- 701-328-2360. **Property tax/Assessing**- 701-573-4445, assessor fax-701-573-4444.

Eddy County

County Recorder, 524 Central Ave, New Rockford, ND 58356-1698. 701-947-2434, R/E recording phone-701-947-2813, UCC recording phone-701-947-2434 x2014; fax-701-947-2067; 8AM-N; 12:30-4:00PM (CST)
Index: All in one. Records indexed on computer back to 1999. Only office personnel may search. Search fee $10.00 per name. Office will not search real estate records. Copy fee $.25 per page. Call for UCC copy fee. Cert fee- $10.00 per cert plus copy fee. Payee- Eddy County. Deed and/or Mortgage Reports available in bulk; $10.00 per report per month; contact Recorder's office. **Other phones:** Treasurer- 701-947-5315; Elections- 701-947-2434; Vitals- 701-947-2434 x2013. **Property tax/Assessing**- 524 Central Ave, New Rockford, ND 58356; 701-947-5220.

Emmons County

County Recorder, PO Box 905, Linton, ND 58552. Recording, R/E & UCC phone-701-254-4812; fax-701-254-4012; 8:30AM-N, 1-5PM.
Index: 2 indices to search. Record index not computerized. Office personnel (minimal) or visitors may perform searches. Search fee varies depending on search type. Will not search UCC records. Copy fee $1.00 per doc. Cert fee- $10.00 per cert includes copy fee. Payee- Emmons County Recorder. Treasurer- 701-254-4802; Elections- 701-254-4807; Vitals- 701-328-2360. **Property tax/Assessing**- Courthouse, Linton, ND 58552; 701-254-4417.

Foster County

County Recorder, PO Box 76, Carrington, ND 58421. 701-652-2491; fax-701-652-2173; 8:30AM-4:30PM.
Index: Separate indices to search. Records indexed on computer. Only the public may search. General copy fee $1.00 per page. Cert fee- $5.00 for 1st page/$2.00 per add'l pages. Payee- Foster County Recorder. **Online access to Real Estate, Deed records:** Subscription access the recorder's land records via NDRIN's central repository at www.ndrin.com. Registration and monthly fee applies. See section introduction. **Other phones:** Treasurer- 701-652-2322; Elections- 701-652-2441. **Property tax/Assessing**- 701-652-2441.

Golden Valley County

County Recorder, PO Box 130, Beach, ND 58621-0130. Recording, R/E & UCC phone-701-872-3713; fax-701-872-4383; 8AM-N, 1PM-4PM (MST)
Index: Separate indexes to search include grantor/grantee, deeds, misc, mortgr/mortge, corner monument records. Records indexed on a public use terminal back to early 1980's. Only the public may search. Copy fee $.50 per page, printed off computer $.50 per page, $1.00 per page for fax. Cert fee- $5.00 1st page, $2.00 each add'l page includes copy fee. Payee- County Recorder. **Online access to Real Estate, Deed records:** Subscription access the recorder's land records via NDRIN's central repository at www.ndrin.com. Registration and monthly fee applies. See section introduction. **Other phones:** Treasurer- 701-872-4411; Elections- 701-872-4331; Vital Records- 701-328-2360; Auditor- 701-872-4331. **Property tax/Assessing**- PO Box 67, Beach, ND 58621; 701-872-4673, fax- 701-872-4383.

Grand Forks County

County Recorder, PO Box 5066, Grand Forks, ND 58206. Recording, R/E phone-701-780-8261, UCC recording phone-701-780-8247; fax-701-780-8212; 8-5PM. www.co.grand-forks.nd.us/homepage.htm
Index: All in one. Records indexed on a public use terminal back to 2002. Office will perform a UCC search but public must search other records themselves. UCC copy request with certificate per debtor name- $7.00. General copy fee $1.00 per page. Cert fee- $5.00 1st page, $2.00 each add'l page. Payee- County Recorder. **Online access to Real Estate, Grantor/Grantee, Deed, Death, Judgment, Lien records:** Access county property data free at www.co.grand-forks.nd.us/search.htm. Also, access the recorder's Grantor/Grantee database free at www.co.grand-forks.nd.us/recorders%20search.htm. **Other phones:** Treasurer- 701-780-8295; Elections- 701-780-8200; Vital Records- 701-780-8251. **Property tax/Assessing**- PO Box 5294, Grand Forks, ND 58206; 701-780-8259.

Grant County

County Recorder, PO Box 258, Carson, ND 58529. 701-622-3544; fax-701-622-3717; 8AM-4PM.
Record index not computerized. Office personnel or visitors may perform searches. Search fee $7.00 per name. Office will not search real estate records. Copy fee $1.00 per page. Cert fee- $10.00 per cert. Payee- Grant County Register of Deeds. **Other phones:** Treasurer- 701-622-3422; Elections- 701-622-3275. **Property tax/Assessing**- 701-622-3275.

Griggs County

County Recorder, PO Box 237, Cooperstown, ND 58425. 701-797-2771; fax-701-797-3587; 8AM-N, 1-4:30PM (CST)
Participates in the ND Recorders Information Network, www.ndrin.com. Index: Separate indices to search include deeds, mortgages. Records indexed on a public use terminal back to 1/1993; images back to 1/2003. Office personnel or visitors may perform searches. Search fee $11.00 per name. Office will not search real estate records. UCC search per debtor name- $7.00 per 5 entries. Copy fee $1.00 per page. Fax back fee- $3.00 (up to 20 pages) plus copy fee. Cert fee- $7.00 per cert plus copy fee. Payee- Griggs County Recorder. **Online access to Real Estate, Deed records:** Access the recorder's land records by subscription via NDRIN's central repository at www.ndrin.com. See section introduction. **Other phones:** Treasurer- 701-797-2411; Elections- 701-

797-3117. **Property tax/Assessing-** 808 Rollins Ave, Cooperstown, ND 58425; 701-797-3211.

Hettinger County

County Recorder, PO Box 668, Mott, ND 58646. 701-824-2545/2645, R/E recording phone-701-824-2545; fax-701-824-2717; 8AM-N, 1-4:30PM (MST) Index: All in one. Records indexed on a public use terminal back to 1800's. Office personnel or visitors may perform searches. Search fee $7.00 per name. Office will not search real estate records. Real estate record- $1.00 per copy. Cert fee- $7.00 1st pg; $2.00 each add'l page. Payee- Court Recorder. **Other phones:** Treasurer- 701-824-2655; Elections- 701-824-2515; Vital Records- 701-824-2545. **Property tax/Assessing-** 336 Pacific Ave, Courthouse, Mott, ND 58646; 701-824-2515. (Appraiser 701-824-2515)

Kidder County

County Recorder, PO Box 66, Steele, ND 58482. Recording, R/E & UCC phone-701-475-2632; fax-701-475-2202; 9AM-N; 1-5PM (CST) Index: All in one. Records indexed on computer back to 1992-93. Only the public may search. Office will only verify a real estate record; no name searching. Copy fee $1.00 per doc. Cert fee- $5.00 1st page; $2.00 each add'l page includes copy fee. Payee- County Recorder. **Online access to Real Estate, Deed records:** Subscription access the recorder's land records via NDRIN's central repository at www.ndrin.com. Registration and monthly fee applies. See section introduction. **Other phones:** Treasurer- 701-475-2632; Elections- 701-475-2632. **Property tax/Assessing-** PO Box 125, Steele, ND 58482; 701-475-2632, assessor fax- 701-475-2202.

La Moure County

County Recorder, PO Box 128, La Moure, ND 58458-0128. Recording, R/E & UCC phone-701-883-5301 x6; fax-701-883-4220; 8:30AM-N, 1-4:30PM (CST) http://lamoco.drtel.net/countyrecorder.html Index: All in one. Records indexed on a public use terminal back to 1994. Office personnel or visitors may perform searches. General index search fee $25.00 per hour, after 1st hour free. Office will search real estate records. UCC copy request with certificate per debtor name- $7.00 per 5 entries. Separate federal and/or state tax lien search- $7.00 per debtor per 5 entries. Copy fee $1.00 per doc up to 10 pages, $.10 per page after. Cert fee- $10.00 1st page, $3.00 each add'l page includes copy fee. Payee- County Recorder. **Online access to Real Estate, Deed records:** Subscription access the recorder's land records via NDRIN's central repository at www.ndrin.com. Registration and monthly fee applies. See section introduction. **Other phones:** Treasurer- 701-883-5101; Elections- 701-883-5301. **Property tax/Assessing-** 202 4th Ave NE, Courthouse, La Moure, ND 58458; 701-883-5301.

Logan County

County Recorder, PO Box 6, Napoleon, ND 58561-0006. Recording, R/E & UCC phone-701-754-2751; fax-701-754-2270; 8:30AM-N, 1-4:30PM (CST) Index: All in one. Record index not computerized. Only the office personnel may search. Search fee $7.00 per name. Office will search real estate records. Will search UCC records. Copy fee $1.00 per page. Cert fee- $5.00 1st page, $2.00 each add'l page. Payee- Logan County Recorder. **Other phones:** Treasurer- 701-754-2286; Elections- 701-754-2425; Vital Records- 701-754-2751. **Property tax/Assessing-** 301 Broadway, Napoleon, ND 58561; 701-754-2239, assessor fax- 701-754-2270.

McHenry County

County Recorder, 407 Main St S, Rm 206, Towner, ND 58788. Recording, R/E phone-701-537-5634; fax-701-537-5969; 8AM-N, 1PM-4:30PM (CST) Index: Separate indexes to search include computer and manually in books. Records indexed on a public use terminal back to 01/2002. Office personnel or visitors may perform searches. Search fee for UCC-$7.00 per name for 1st 5 filings; $2.00 each add'l page. Office will search real estate records; fee-$25.00 after 1st hour. All UCC records on computer; minimum search fee is $7.00. General copy fee $.50 per page. Cert fee- $5.00 1st page, $2.00 each add'l page for all records except UCC certifications. No extra fee for UCC certification. Payee- McHenry County Recorder. Bulk data available for purchase, contact Pam Kuk-Recorder. **Online access to Real Estate, Deed records:** Subscription access the recorder's land records via NDRIN's central repository at www.ndrin.com. Registration and monthly fee applies. See section introduction. **Other phones:** Treasurer- 701-537-5731; Elections- 701-537-5724; Vital Records- 701-537-5729. **Property tax/Assessing-** 407 Main St S, Rm 204, Towner, ND 58788; 701-537-5359, assessor fax- 701-537-5969.

McIntosh County

County Recorder, PO Box 179, Ashley, ND 58413. 701-288-3589/3450, R/E recording phone-701-288-3589; fax-701-288-3671; 8AM-4:30PM. Index: All in one. Records indexed on a public use terminal back to 2000. Office personnel or visitors may perform searches. Search fee $7.00. Office will search real estate records when provided with description. Copy fee $1.00 per page. Cert fee- $5.00 plus $2.00 each add'l page, includes copy fee. Payee- County Recorder. **Online access to Real Estate, Deed records:** Subscription access the recorder's land records via NDRIN's central repository at www.ndrin.com. Registration and monthly fee applies. See section introduction. **Other phones:** Treasurer- 701-288-3342; Elections- 701-288-3347. **Property tax/Assessing-** 701-288-3353.

McKenzie County

County Recorder, PO Box 523, Watford City, ND 58854. Recording, R/E & UCC phone-701-444-3453; fax-701-444-3902; 8AM-4:30PM. www.4eyes.net/McKenzieCounty/Default.aspx Index: All in one. Records indexed on a public use terminal. Office personnel or visitors may perform searches. Search fee $7.00. Office will search real estate records (search fee is 1st hour free, $25.00 per hour after). Will search UCC records. Copy fee $1.00 per page. Cert fee- $5.00 1st page plus $2.00 each add'l page. Payee- County Recorder. **Online access to Real Estate, Deed records:** Access the recorder's land records 5/1998 to present by subscription via NDRIN's central repository at www.ndrin.com. See section introduction. **Other phones:** Treasurer- 701-444-3457; Elections- 701-444-3616; Vital Records-701-444-3452. **Property tax/Assessing-** 201 W 5th St, Watford City, ND 58854; 701-444-6852. (Appraiser/Auditor- 701-444-6852);

McLean County

County Recorder, PO Box 1108, Washburn, ND 58577-1108. 701-462-8541 x226/5, R/E recording phone-701-462-8541 x226, x225, UCC recording phone-701-462-8541; fax-701-462-3633; 8AM-N, 12:30-4:30PM (CST) www.visitmcleancounty.com Index: All in one. Records indexed on a public use terminal back to 198. Office will search records depending on nature of request; prefers visitors do their own searches. Office will not search real estate records. Office will search UCC records including tax liens on the state system. UCC copy request with certificate per debtor name- $7.00 for 1st 5 entries; add' names $2.00 each. Copy fee $1.00 per page.Real estate record copy- $.50 per page plus postage. Cert fee- $5.00 per page plus $2.00 each add'l doc page. Payee- McLean County Recorder. **Online access to Real Estate, Deed records:** Subscription access the recorder's land records via NDRIN's central repository at www.ndrin.com. Registration and monthly fee applies. See section introduction. **Other phones:** Treasurer- 701-462-8541 x223; Elections- 701-462-8541 x216; Vital Records- 701-462-8541 x228. **Property tax/Assessing-** 712 5th Ave, Courthouse, Washburn, ND 58577; 701-462-8541 x220.

Mercer County

County Recorder, PO Box 39, Stanton, ND 58571. Recording, R/E & UCC phone-701-745-3272; fax-701-745-3364; 8AM-4PM. Index: Indices by instrument type. Record index not computerized. Office personnel or visitors may perform searches. Search fee $7.00 per name. Office will not search real estate records. Copy fee $2.00 per page. Will fax back- $3.00 per page. Cert fee- $2.00 per page plus copy fee. Payee- County Recorder. **Online access to Real Estate, Deed records:** Subscription access the recorder's land records via NDRIN's central repository at www.ndrin.com. Registration and monthly fee applies. See section introduction. **Other phones:** Treasurer- 701-745-3323; Elections- 701-745-3292. **Property tax/Assessing-** 1012 Arthur St, Stanton, ND 58571; 701-745-3294.

Morton County

County Recorder, 210 2nd Ave NW, Mandan, ND 58554. 701-667-3305; fax-701-667-3453; 8AM-5PM. Participates in the ND Recorders Information Network, www.ndrin.com. Index: All in one. Records indexed on a public use terminal back to 2003. Office personnel or visitors may perform searches. Search fee $7.00 per name. Office will not search real estate records. Will search UCC records with required UCC-11 form, office will search last deed of records only. General copy fee $1.00 per page. Cert fee- $5.00, $2.00 each page after 1st per cert plus copy fee. Payee- Morton County Recorder. **Online access to Real Estate, Deed records:** Subscription access the recorder's land records via NDRIN's central repository at www.ndrin.com. Registration and monthly fee applies. See section introduction. **Other phones:** Treasurer- 701-667-3310; Elections- 701-667-3300; Vital Records- 701-328-2360 (State Capitol); Auditor- 701-667-3300. **Property tax/Assessing-** 210 2nd Ave NW, Mandan, ND 58554; 701-667-3300.

Mountrail County

County Recorder, PO Box 69, Stanley, ND 58784. Recording, R/E & UCC phone-701-628-2945; fax-701-628-2276; 8AM-N, 12:30-4:30PM (CST) Index: Separate indexes to search. Records indexed on computer. Office will perform a UCC search but public must search other records themselves. UCC copy request with certificate per debtor name- $7.00. Copy fee $1.00 1st page; $.50 each add'l. Cert fee- $5.00 1st page plus $2.00 each add'l page, plus copy fee. Payee- Montrail County Recorder. **Other phones:** Treasurer- 701-628-2935; Elections- 701-628-2145. **Property tax/Assessing-** 701-826-2425.

Nelson County

County Recorder, 210 W "B" Ave, #203, Lakota, ND 58344. Recording, R/E & UCC phone-701-247-2433; fax-701-247-2412; 8AM-N, 1PM-4:30PM (CST) www.nelsonco.org Participates in the ND Recorders Information Network, www.ndrin.com. Index: Separate indices to search include deed/misc., mortgage. Records indexed on a public use terminal back to 1995. Office will perform a UCC search but public must search other records themselves. Copy fee $1.00 per page. Cert fee- $5.00 for 1st page, $2.00 each add'l, includes copy fee. Payee- Nelson County Recorder. Images and monthly Deed, Mortgage, and Satisfaction reports available for purchase on CD. Contact Ruth Stevens or Linda Vasicek. **Online access to Real Estate, Deed records:** Subscription access the recorder's land records via NDRIN's central repository at www.ndrin.com. Registration and monthly fee applies. See section introduction. **Other phones:** Treasurer- 701-247-2453; Elections- 701-247-2463; Vital Records- 701-247-2462. **Property tax/Assessing-** 210 W "B" Ave, #303, Lakota, ND 58344; 701-247-2840.

Oliver County

County Recorder, PO Box 125, Center, ND 58530-0125. 701-794-8777; fax-701-794-3476; 8AM-N, 1-4PM (CST)
Index: All in one. Records indexed on computer; no public use terminal available. Office personnel or visitors may perform searches. Search fee $10.00 per name. Office will search real estate records. Will search UCC records. Copy fee $1.00 per page.Real estate record copy- $.25 per page. Cert fee- $5.00 per cert. Payee- County Recorder. **Other phones:** Treasurer- 701-794-8737; Elections- 701-794-8721. **Property tax/Assessing**- Equalization Office, Center, ND 58530; 701-794-8721.

Pembina County

Clerk/Recorder, 301 Dakota St W, #10, Cavalier, ND 58220. 701-265-4373; fax-701-265-4876; 8AM-5PM (CST) www.pembinacountynd.gov
Index: All in one. Records indexed on a public use terminal back to 2002. Office personnel or visitors may perform searches. Search fee $7.00 per name. Office will not search real estate records. Will search UCC records. Copy fee $1.00 per doc. Cert fee- $5.00 1st page, $2.00 each add'l page includes copy fee. Payee- Pembina County. **Online access to Real Estate, Deed records:** Subscription access the recorder's land records via NDRIN's central repository at www.ndrin.com. Registration and monthly fee applies. See section introduction. **Other phones:** Treasurer- 701-265-4336; Elections- 701-265-4336; Vital Records- 701-328-2360. **Property tax/Assessing**- 301 Dakota St W, #4, Cavalier, ND 58220; 701-265-4697, assessor fax- 701-265-4876.

Pierce County

County Recorder, 240 SE 2nd St, Rugby, ND 58368. 701-776-5206 x4, R/E recording phone-701-776-5206; fax-701-776-5707; 9AM-5PM.
Index: Separate indices to search include deed and mortgage. Records indexed on a public use terminal back to 0300. Office personnel or visitors may perform searches. Search fee $7.00 per name. Office will search real estate records. Will search UCC records. Copy fee $.50 per page. Cert fee- $5.00 for 1st page, $2.00 for each add'l page. Payee- Pierce County Recorder. **Online access to Real Estate, Deed records:** Subscription access the recorder's land records via NDRIN's central repository at www.ndrin.com. Registration and monthly fee applies. See section introduction. **Other phones:** Treasurer- 701-776-6841; Elections- 701-776-5225. **Property tax/Assessing**- 701-776-5206.

Ramsey County

County Recorder, 524 4th Ave, #30, Devils Lake, ND 58301. Recording, R/E & UCC phone-701-662-7018; fax-701-662-7093; 8AM-5PM. www.co.ramsey.nd.us
Index: All in one. Records indexed on a public use terminal back to 1984. Office personnel or visitors may perform searches. Search fee $7.00 per name. Office will not search real estate records. Office will do UCC 11 search and if the filing is old and has had continuations filed it will show on the search. Done by name of SSN. Copy fee $1.00 per page. Cert fee- $5.00 for 1st page, $2.00 each add'l page. Payee- Ramsey County Recorder. **Online access to Real Estate, Deed records:** Subscription access the recorder's land records via NDRIN's central repository at www.ndrin.com. Registration and monthly fee applies. See section introduction. **Other phones:** Treasurer- 701-662-7021; Elections- 701-662-7007; Vitals- 701-662-7018. **Property tax/Assessing**- Same address as recording office. 701-662-7012.

Ransom County

County Recorder, PO Box 666, Lisbon, ND 58054-0666. 701-683-6115; fax-701-683-5827; 8:30AM-5PM (CST) www.ndaco.org
Participates in the ND Recorders Information Network, www.ndrin.com. Index: All in one. Records indexed on a public use terminal back to 2/02. Only the public may search. Will not search UCC records. Copy fee $1.00 per filing. Cert fee- $5.00 1st page, #2.00 each add'l. Payee- Ransom County Recorder. **Online access to Real Estate, Deed records:** Subscription access the recorder's land records via NDRIN's central repository at www.ndrin.com. Registration and monthly fee applies. See section introduction. **Other phones:** Treasurer- 701-683-6118; Elections- 701-683-6113; Vital Records- 701-683-6120. **Property tax/Assessing**- PO Box 830, Lisbon, ND 58054; 701-683-6111.

Renville County

County Recorder, PO Box 68, Mohall, ND 58761-0068. 701-756-6398; fax-701-756-6494; 9AM-4:30PM (CST) www.renvillecounty.org
Index: All in one. Record index not computerized. Office personnel or visitors may perform searches. Office will not search real estate records. UCC search includes federal tax liens. UCC copy request with certificate per debtor name- $7.00. Separate state tax lien search- $5.00 per debtor. Copy fee $1.00 per page. Cert fee- $7.00 1st pg, $3.00 each add'l, includes copies. Payee- Renville County Recorder. **Other phones:** Treasurer- 701-756-6304; Elections- 701-756-6301; Vital Records- 701-756-6398. **Property tax/Assessing**- PO Box 68, Mohall, ND 58761; 701-756-6304, assessor fax- 701-756-7158. (Appraiser/Auditor- 701-756-6304)

Richland County

County Recorder, 418 2nd Ave N; Courthouse, Wahpeton, ND 58075-4400. Recording, R/E & UCC phone-701-642-7800; fax-701-642-7820; 8AM-5PM
Index: All in one. Records indexed on a public use terminal back to 12/1993. Office personnel or visitors may perform searches. Search fee $25.00 per hour after the 1st hour. Office will search real estate records. UCC copy request with certificate per debtor name- $7.00 for 1st 5 entries. Copy fee $1.00 per page. Cert fee- $5.00 1st page; $2.00 each add'l page, includes copy fee. Payee- County Recorder. **Online access to Real Estate, Deed records:** Subscription access the recorder's land records via NDRIN's central repository at www.ndrin.com. Registration and monthly fee applies. See section introduction. **Other phones:** Treasurer- 701-642-7705; Elections- 701-642-7700; Vital Records- 701-642-7800. **Property tax/Assessing**- 418 2nd Ave N, Courthouse, Wahpeton, ND 58075; 701-642-7805, assessor fax- 701-642-7820.

Rolette County

County Recorder, PO Box 276, Rolla, ND 58367. 701-477-3166; fax-701-477-5770; 8:30AM-4:30PM (CST) www.rolettecounty.com
Index: Deed, mortgage/misc. Records indexed on computer back to 1999. Office personnel or visitors may perform searches. Search fee $7.00 per name. Office will search real estate records. Will search UCC records. Copy fee $1.00 per page. Cert fee- $7.00 per 1st page; $2.00 each add'l page includes copy fee. Payee- Recorder. Bulk data available for purchase. **Online access to Real Estate, Deed records:** Subscription access the recorder's land records via NDRIN's central repository at www.ndrin.com. Registration and monthly fee applies. See section introduction. **Other phones:** Treasurer- 701-477-3207; Elections- 701-477-5665; Vitals- 701-477-3166. **Property tax/Assessing**- PO Box 939, Rolla, ND 58367; 701-477-5665.

Sargent County

County Recorder, 355 Main St S, #2, Forman, ND 58032. 701-724-6241 x117; fax-701-724-6244; 9AM-4:30PM.
Index: All in one; on computer and tract index. Records indexed on a public use terminal back 5 years. Office personnel or visitors may perform searches. Search fee $7.00 1st 5, add'l 5 or fraction thereof $2.00. Copy fee $1.00 per page. Cert fee- $5.00 1st page, $2.00 each add'l page (includes copy fee). Exemplification fee- $10.00. Payee- County Recorder. **Online access to Real Estate, Deed records:** Subscription access the recorder's land records via NDRIN's central repository at www.ndrin.com. Registration and monthly fee applies. See section introduction. **Other phones:** Treasurer- 701-724-6241 x13,14; Elections- 701-724-6241. **Property tax/Assessing**- PO Box 177, Forman, ND 58032-0177; 701-724-6241 x15.

Sheridan County

County Recorder, PO Box 409, McClusky, ND 58463-0668. Recording, R/E & UCC phone-701-363-2207; fax-701-363-2953; 9AM-N, 1-5PM.
Index: All in one. Records indexed on computer back to 04/00. Office personnel or visitors may perform searches. Search fee $10.00 per name. Office will search real estate records. UCC search per debtor name- $7.00. Copy fee $1.00 per page. Cert fee- $5.00 1st page, $2.00 each add'l page includes copy fee. Payee- Sheridan County Recorder. **Other phones:** Treasurer- 701-363-2206; Elections- 701-363-2205; Vitals- 603-895-2207. **Property tax/Assessing**- PO Box 306, McClusky, ND 58463; 701-363-2201.

Sioux County

County Recorder, PO Box L, Fort Yates, ND 58538. 701-854-3853; fax-701-854-3854; 8AM-4:30PM
Index: All in one. Record index not computerized. Office personnel or visitors may perform searches. Search fee $7.50 per name. Office will search real estate records. Copy fee $2.00 per page. Cert fee- $5.00 per cert plus copy fee. Payee- Sioux County Recorder. **Other phones:** Treasurer- 701-854-3853; Elections- 701-854-3481; Vital Records- 701-854-3853. **Property tax/Assessing**- Same address as recording office. 701-854-3481.

Slope County

County Recorder, PO Box JJ, Amidon, ND 58620-0445. 701-879-6275; fax-701-879-6278; 8:30AM-4:30PM.
Index: Separate indices. Records indexed on computer back to 2003. Office personnel or visitors may perform searches. Search fee $10.00 per name. Office will search real estate records. Will search UCC records. General copy fee $.25 per page. Cert fee- $5.00 1st page, $2.00 each add'l page. Payee- County Recorder. **Online access to Real Estate, Deed records:** Subscription access the recorder's land records via NDRIN's central repository at www.ndrin.com. Registration and monthly fee applies. See section introduction. **Other phones:** Treasurer- 701-879-6272; Elections- 701-879-6276. **Property tax/Assessing**- 206 S Main, Amidon, ND 58620; 701-879-6370.

Stark County

County Recorder, 51 3rd St E, Dickinson, ND 58601. 701-456-7645; fax-701-456-7628; 8AM-5PM.
Index: Separate indices to search include computer and books. Records indexed on a public use terminal back to 1999. Office personnel or visitors may perform searches. Search fee $7.00 per name. Office will search real estate records (last deed of record). Office will search active UCC records. Copy fee $1.00 per page. Cert fee- $10.00 per page plus copy fee. Payee- Stark County Recorder. **Online access to Real Estate, Deed records:** Subscription access the recorder's land records via NDRIN's central repository at www.ndrin.com. Registration and monthly fee applies. See section introduction. **Other phones:** Treasurer- 701-456-7652; Elections- 701-456-7630; Vitals- 701-456-7645. **Property tax/Assessing**- 51 3rd St E, Dickinson, ND 58601; 701-456-7671.

Steele County

County Recorder, PO Box 296, Finley, ND 58230. 701-524-2152, R/E recording phone-701-524-2790; fax-701-524-1325; 8AM-N, 1-4:30PM.
Index: All in one. Record index not computerized. Only the public may search. Copy fee $1.00 per page. Cert fee- $10.00 1st page, $3.00 add'l pages plus copy fee. Payee- Steele County Recorder of Deeds. **Online access to Real Estate, Deed records:** Subscription

access the recorder's land records via NDRIN's central repository at www.ndrin.com. Registration and monthly fee applies. See section introduction. **Other phones:** Treasurer- 701-524-2890; Elections- 701-524-2110. **Property tax/Assessing**- 201 Washington St, Courthouse, Finley, ND 58230; 701-524-2110.

Stutsman County

County Recorder, 511 2nd Ave SE; Courthouse, Jamestown, ND 58401. Recording, R/E & UCC phone-701-252-9034; fax-701-251-1603; 8AM-5PM (CST) www.co.stutsman.nd.us
Participates in the ND Recorders Information Network, www.ndrin.com. Index: Separate indices to search include all documents with legal descriptions indexed in their tract books. Misc docs indexed in book "V", etc if they don't have a legal description on them. Records indexed on a public use terminal back to 11/1/1996 (for information only). All document scanned with image back to 06/30/1976. Office personnel or visitors may perform searches. Search fee $7.00 for computer general search. Office will search real estate records. If real estate search requires more than an hour, extra fees will be charged. Will search UCC records. Copy fee $1.00 per 4 pages; $3.00 to fax back. Cert fee- $5.00 per cert plus $2.00 per page after 1st includes copy fee. Payee- Stutsam County Recorder. **Online access to Real Estate, Deed records:** Subscription access the recorder's land records via NDRIN's central repository at www.ndrin.com. Registration and monthly fee applies. See section introduction. **Other phones:** Treasurer- 701-252-9036; Elections- 701-252-9035; Vitals- 701-252-9034. **Property tax/Assessing**- 511 2nd Ave SE, Courthouse, Jamestown, ND 58401; 701-252-9032, assessor fax- 701-251-6325.

Towner County

County Recorder, PO Box 517, Cando, ND 58324. 701-968-4343, R/E recording phone-701-968-4340 x5; fax-701-968-4344; 8:30AM-5PM.
Index: Indices by instrument type. Record index not computerized. Office personnel or visitors may perform searches. Search fee $7.00 per name. Office will not search real estate records. Office will not search UCC records. Copy fee $1.00 per page. Cert fee- $7.00 per doc; $1.00 each add'l page. Payee- County Recorder. **Online access to Real Estate, Deed records:** Subscription access the recorder's land records via NDRIN's central repository at www.ndrin.com. Registration and monthly fee applies. See section introduction. **Other phones:** Treasurer- 701-968-4347; Elections- 701-968-4340. **Property tax/Assessing**- 315 2nd St, Courthouse, Cando, ND 58324; 701-968-4352.

Traill County

County Recorder, PO Box 399, Hillsboro, ND 58045. Recording, R/E & UCC phone-701-636-4457; fax-701-636-2527; 8AM-N, 12:30-4:30PM.
Index: Separate indices to search include mortgages, deeds, corporation, misc. Record index not computerized. Office personnel or visitors may perform searches. Search fee $7.00 per name. Office will search real estate records. Will search UCC records. General copy fee $1.00 per page. Cert fee- $5.00 1st page, $2.00 each add'l page per cert. **Other phones:** Treasurer- 701-636-4459; Elections- 701-636-4458; Vital Records- 701-636-4454. **Property tax/Assessing**- PO Box 745, Hillsboro, ND 58045; 701-436-5950. hours- 8AM-4:30PM

Walsh County

County Recorder, 600 Cooper Ave; Courthouse, Grafton, ND 58237. 701-352-2380; fax-701-352-3340; 8AM-N, 12:30-4:30PM.
Index: Separate indices to search include deed, mortgage indexes where the legal descriptions eradicate property locations. Records indexed on computer back to 1997. Only the public may search. Office will fax real estate records. Copy fee $1.00 per page. Will fax out docs for $3.00 first page, $1.00 each add'l page. Cert fee- $5.00 1st page, $2.00 each add'l plus copy fee. Payee- Walsh County Recorder. **Online access to Real Estate, Deed records:** Subscription access the recorder's land records via NDRIN's central repository at www.ndrin.com. Registration and monthly fee applies. See section introduction. **Other phones:** Treasurer- 701-352-2541; Elections- 701-352-2851; Vital Records- 701-352-2380. **Property tax/Assessing**- 600 Cooper Ave, Courthouse, Grafton, ND 58237; 701-352-1077. hours- 8AM-5PM.

Ward County

County Recorder, PO Box 5005, Minot, ND 58705-5005. 701-857-6410, R/E recording phone-701-857-6420; fax-701-857-6414; 8AM-4:30PM. www.co.ward.nd.us/recorder/
Index: Separate indices. Records indexed on a public use terminal back to 1990. Only the public may search. Copy fee $1.00 per page. Cert fee- $7.00 per cert. Payee- Ward County Register of Deeds. **Online access to Real Estate, Deed records:** Subscription access the recorder's land records via NDRIN's central repository at www.ndrin.com. Registration and monthly fee applies. See section introduction. **Other phones:** Elections- 701-857-6420. **Property tax/Assessing**- 315 SE 3rd St, Courthouse, Minot, ND 58705; 701-857-6430.

Wells County

County Recorder, PO Box 125, Fessenden, ND 58438-0125. Recording, R/E & UCC phone-701-547-3141; fax-701-547-3719; 8AM-N, 12:30PM-4PM
Index: All in one. Records indexed on a public use terminal back to 8/95. Office personnel or visitors may perform searches. Name search and UCC search fee $7.00 for first 5 entries; $2.00 each add'l entry. Real estate record name search fee is free for 1st hour, then $25.00 per hour thereafter. Will search UCC records. Copy fee $1.00 per page. Cert fee- $7.00 for 1st page; $2.00 each add'l 5 entries. Payee- Wells County Recorder. **Online access to Real Estate, Deed records:** Subscription access the recorder's land records via NDRIN's central repository at www.ndrin.com. Registration and monthly fee applies. See section introduction. **Other phones:** Treasurer- 701-547-3161; Elections- 701-547-3521; Vital Records- 701-547-3141; State Vital Records - 701-328-2360. **Property tax/Assessing**- PO Box 37, 700 Railway St N, Fessenden, ND 58438-0037; 701-547-3521, assessor fax- 701-547-3719.

Williams County

County Recorder, PO Box 2047, Williston, ND 58802-2047. Recording, R/E & UCC phone-701-577-4540; fax-701-577-4535; 8AM-5PM (CST) www.williamsnd.com
Participates in the ND Recorders Information Network, www.ndrin.com. Index: All in one. Records indexed on a public use terminal back to 9/90. Office will perform a UCC search but public must search other records themselves. Search fee $7.00 per name. Office will not search real estate records. Copy fee $1.00 per page.Real estate record copy- $.50 per page. Cert fee- $5.00 1st page; $2.00 each add'l, plus copy fee. Payee- Williams County Recorder. **Online access to Real Estate, Deed records:** Also, subscription access to the recorder's land records via NDRIN's Central Repository available at www.ndrin.com. See section introduction. **Other phones:** Treasurer- 701-577-4530; Elections- 701-577-4500; Vital Records- 701-577-4580. **Property tax/Assessing**- PO Box 2047, Valuation/Equalization, Williston, ND 58802-2047; 701-577-4555. **Online**- Access to county tax data is free at www.williamsnd.com/tax/search/. Also, access to property tax records for free at www.williamsnd.com/Tax.aspx.

North Dakota County Locator

You will usually be able to find the city name in the City/County Cross Reference below. In that case, it is a simple matter to determine the county from the cross reference. However, only the official US Postal Service city names are included in this index. There are an additional 40,000 place names that people use in their addresses. Therefore, we have also included a ZIP/City Cross Reference immediately following the City/County Cross Reference. If you know the ZIP Code but the city name does not appear in the City/County Cross Reference index, look up the ZIP Code in the ZIP/City Cross Reference, find the city name, then look up the city name in the City/County Cross Reference.

North Dakota City/County Cross Reference

ABERCROMBIE Richland
ABSARAKA Cass
ADAMS Walsh
AGATE Rolette
ALAMO (58830) Williams(60), Divide(39)
ALEXANDER McKenzie
ALFRED La Moure
ALICE Cass
ALMONT (58520) Morton(73), Grant(26)
ALSEN Cavalier
AMBROSE Divide
AMENIA Cass
AMIDON (58620) Slope(97), Billings(2)
ANAMOOSE (58710) McHenry(61), Sheridan(22), Pierce(16)
ANETA (58212) Nelson(63), Griggs(25), Grand Forks(9), Steele(1)
ANTLER Bottineau
ARDOCH Walsh
ARENA (58412) Burleigh(98), Kidder(1)
ARGUSVILLE Cass
ARNEGARD McKenzie
ARTHUR Cass
ARVILLA Grand Forks
ASHLEY (58413) McIntosh(93), Dickey(6)
AYR Cass
BALDWIN Burleigh
BALFOUR McHenry
BALTA Pierce
BANTRY McHenry
BARNEY Richland
BARTON Pierce
BATHGATE Pembina
BEACH (58621) Golden Valley(96), McKenzie(2)
BELCOURT Rolette
BELFIELD (58622) Stark(72), Billings(27)
BENEDICT (58716) McLean(81), Ward(18)
BERLIN (58415) La Moure(98), Dickey(1)
BERTHOLD (58718) Ward(73), Mountrail(23), Renville(2)
BEULAH (58523) Mercer(94), Oliver(5)
BINFORD (58416) Griggs(97), Nelson(2)
BISBEE (58317) Towner(95), Rolette(3)
BISMARCK Burleigh
BLAISDELL Mountrail
BLANCHARD Traill
BOTTINEAU Bottineau
BOWBELLS (58721) Burke(96), Ward(3)
BOWBELLS Burke
BOWDON (58418) Wells(92), Kidder(7)
BOWMAN (58623) Bowman(91), Slope(8)
BRADDOCK (58524) Emmons(67), Kidder(21), Burleigh(10)
BREMEN Wells
BRINSMADE Benson
BROCKET (58321) Ramsey(50), Nelson(27), Walsh(21)
BUCHANAN Stutsman
BUFFALO Cass
BURLINGTON Ward
BUTTE (58723) Sheridan(44), McLean(44), McHenry(11)
BUXTON Traill
CALEDONIA Traill
CALVIN (58323) Cavalier(71), Towner(28)
CANDO Towner
CANNON BALL Sioux
CARPIO (58725) Renville(53), Ward(46)
CARRINGTON (58421) Foster(95), Stutsman(2), Wells(1)
CARSON Grant
CARTWRIGHT McKenzie
CASSELTON Cass
CATHAY Wells
CAVALIER Pembina
CAYUGA Sargent
CENTER Oliver
CHAFFEE Cass
CHASELEY (58423) Wells(84), Kidder(15)
CHRISTINE (58015) Richland(97), Cass(2)
CHURCHS FERRY (58325) Ramsey(61), Benson(38)
CLEVELAND Stutsman
CLIFFORD (58016) Traill(66), Steele(33)
COGSWELL Sargent
COLEHARBOR McLean
COLFAX Richland
COLUMBUS Burke
COOPERSTOWN Griggs
COURTENAY (58426) Stutsman(98), Foster(1)
CRARY Ramsey
CROSBY Divide
CRYSTAL Pembina
CRYSTAL SPRINGS Kidder
CUMMINGS Traill
DAHLEN (58224) Nelson(95), Walsh(4)
DAVENPORT Cass
DAWSON Kidder
DAZEY (58429) Barnes(97), Griggs(2)
DEERING (58731) McHenry(95), Ward(4)
DENHOFF Sheridan
DES LACS Ward
DEVILS LAKE Ramsey
DICKEY La Moure
DICKINSON (58601) Stark(96), Dunn(3)
DICKINSON Stark
DODGE (58625) Dunn(70), Mercer(29)
DONNYBROOK (58734) Ward(42), Mountrail(38), Renville(19)
DOUGLAS (58735) Ward(58), McLean(41)
DOYON Ramsey
DRAKE (58736) McHenry(88), Sheridan(11)
DRAYTON (58225) Pembina(87), Walsh(12)
DRISCOLL (58532) Burleigh(75), Kidder(24)
DUNN CENTER Dunn
DUNSEITH (58329) Rolette(83), Bottineau(16)
ECKELSON Barnes
EDGELEY (58433) La Moure(89), Dickey(10)
EDINBURG (58227) Walsh(62), Pembina(32), Cavalier(5)
EDMORE (58330) Ramsey(93), Walsh(4), Cavalier(2)
EGELAND Towner
ELGIN Grant
ELLENDALE Dickey
EMERADO Grand Forks
ENDERLIN (58027) Ransom(74), Cass(19), Barnes(5)
EPPING Williams
ERIE Cass
ESMOND (58332) Benson(87), Pierce(12)
FAIRDALE (58229) Walsh(75), Cavalier(20), Ramsey(3)
FAIRFIELD Billings
FAIRMOUNT Richland
FARGO Cass
FESSENDEN Wells
FINGAL (58031) Barnes(60), Cass(39)
FINLEY Steele
FLASHER (58535) Morton(78), Grant(21)
FLAXTON Burke
FORBES Dickey
FORDVILLE (58231) Walsh(73), Grand Forks(26)
FOREST RIVER (58233) Walsh(90), Grand Forks(9)
FORMAN Sargent
FORT RANSOM (58033) Ransom(98), La Moure(1)
FORT RICE Morton
FORT TOTTEN Benson
FORT YATES Sioux
FORTUNA Divide
FOXHOLM Ward
FREDONIA (58440) Logan(70), McIntosh(29)
FULLERTON Dickey
GACKLE (58442) Logan(85), Stutsman(14)
GALESBURG (58035) Traill(60), Cass(25), Steele(14)
GARDENA Bottineau
GARDNER Cass
GARRISON McLean
GILBY Grand Forks
GLADSTONE (58630) Stark(75), Dunn(24)
GLASSTON Pembina
GLEN ULLIN (58631) Morton(80), Grant(11), Mercer(7), Oliver(1)
GLENBURN (58740) Renville(70), Ward(25), Bottineau(1), McHenry(1)
GLENFIELD (58443) Foster(98), Griggs(1)
GOLDEN VALLEY Mercer
GOLVA Golden Valley
GOODRICH (58444) Sheridan(94), Burleigh(5)
GRACE CITY (58445) Foster(87), Eddy(12)
GRAFTON Walsh
GRAND FORKS Grand Forks
GRAND FORKS AFB Grand Forks
GRANDIN (58038) Cass(75), Traill(25)
GRANVILLE McHenry
GRASSY BUTTE (58634) McKenzie(92), Billings(7)
GREAT BEND Richland
GRENORA (58845) Williams(57), Divide(42)
GUELPH Dickey
GWINNER Sargent
HAGUE Emmons
HALLIDAY (58636) Dunn(97), Mercer(2)
HAMBERG Wells
HAMILTON Pembina
HAMPDEN (58338) Ramsey(54), Cavalier(45)
HANKINSON Richland
HANNAFORD (58448) Griggs(98), Barnes(1)
HANNAH Cavalier
HANSBORO Towner
HARVEY (58341) Wells(88), Pierce(9), Benson(1)
HARWOOD Cass
HATTON (58240) Traill(73), Steele(16), Grand Forks(10)
HAVANA Sargent
HAZELTON Emmons
HAZEN (58545) Mercer(94), Oliver(5)
HEATON (58450) Wells(86), Kidder(13)
HEBRON (58638) Morton(77), Mercer(9), Stark(8), Dunn(3)
HEIMDAL Wells
HENSEL Pembina
HENSLER Oliver
HETTINGER Adams
HILLSBORO Traill
HOOPLE (58243) Walsh(88), Pembina(12)
HOPE (58046) Steele(73), Barnes(23), Cass(3)
HORACE Cass
HUNTER (58048) Cass(95), Traill(4)
HURDSFIELD (58451) Wells(97), Sheridan(2)
INKSTER (58244) Grand Forks(96), Walsh(3)
JAMESTOWN Stutsman
JESSIE Griggs
JOLIETTE Pembina
JUD (58454) La Moure(80), Stutsman(19)
KARLSRUHE McHenry
KATHRYN (58049) Barnes(77), Ransom(16), La Moure(5)
KEENE McKenzie
KENMARE (58746) Ward(76), Renville(12), Burke(10)
KENSAL (58455) Stutsman(81), Foster(18)
KIEF (58747) Sheridan(70), McHenry(29)
KILLDEER (58640) Dunn(97), McKenzie(1)
KINDRED (58051) Cass(79), Richland(20)
KINTYRE (58549) Emmons(58), Logan(37), Kidder(3)
KNOX Benson
KRAMER (58748) Bottineau(96), McHenry(3)
KULM (58456) La Moure(77), Dickey(16), McIntosh(6)
LAKOTA (58344) Nelson(96), Ramsey(3)
LAMOURE (58458) La Moure(98), Dickey(1)
LANGDON Cavalier
LANKIN Walsh
LANSFORD (58750) Bottineau(64), Renville(35)
LARIMORE Grand Forks
LAWTON (58345) Ramsey(61), Walsh(38)
LEEDS (58346) Benson(92), Towner(7)
LEFOR Stark
LEHR (58460) McIntosh(55), Logan(44)
LEITH Grant
LEONARD (58052) Cass(80), Richland(15), Ransom(3)
LIDGERWOOD (58053) Richland(84), Sargent(15)
LIGNITE Burke
LINTON Emmons
LISBON Ransom
LITCHVILLE (58461) Barnes(74), La Moure(25)
LUVERNE (58056) Barnes(56), Steele(30), Griggs(12)
MADDOCK (58348) Benson(92), Wells(7)
MAIDA Cavalier

MAKOTI (58756) Ward(78), Mountrail(15), McLean(5)
MANDAN Morton
MANDAREE (58757) McKenzie(52), Dunn(47)
MANFRED Wells
MANNING (58642) Dunn(93), Billings(6)
MANTADOR Richland
MANVEL Grand Forks
MAPLETON Cass
MARION (58466) La Moure(77), Barnes(20), Stutsman(1)
MARMARTH (58643) Bowman(67), Slope(32)
MARSHALL Dunn
MARTIN (58758) Sheridan(66), Pierce(17), Wells(15)
MAX (58759) Ward(56), McLean(43)
MAXBASS Bottineau
MAYVILLE Traill
MCCANNA Grand Forks
MCCLUSKY Sheridan
MCGREGOR (58755) Williams(65), Divide(26), Burke(8)
MCHENRY (58464) Foster(52), Eddy(40), Griggs(7)
MCKENZIE Burleigh
MCLEOD (58057) Richland(72), Ransom(28)
MCVILLE Nelson
MEDINA (58467) Stutsman(94), Kidder(5)
MEDORA (58645) Billings(93), Golden Valley(6)
MEKINOCK Grand Forks
MENOKEN Burleigh
MERCER (58559) McLean(88), Sheridan(11)
MERRICOURT Dickey
MICHIGAN Nelson
MILNOR (58060) Sargent(80), Ransom(18)
MILTON (58260) Cavalier(93), Walsh(6)
MINNEWAUKAN (58351) Benson(95), Ramsey(4)
MINOT Ward
MINOT AFB Ward
MINTO (58261) Walsh(87), Grand Forks(12)
MOFFIT (58560) Burleigh(82), Emmons(17)
MOHALL (58761) Renville(72), Bottineau(27)
MONANGO Dickey
MONTPELIER (58472) Stutsman(69), La Moure(30)
MOORETON Richland
MOTT (58646) Hettinger(97), Adams(2)
MOUNTAIN (58262) Pembina(95), Cavalier(4)
MUNICH (58352) Cavalier(93), Towner(6)
MYLO Rolette
NAPOLEON Logan
NECHE Pembina
NEKOMA Cavalier
NEW ENGLAND (58647) Hettinger(66), Slope(26), Stark(7)
NEW LEIPZIG (58562) Grant(88), Hettinger(7), Adams(3)
NEW ROCKFORD (58356) Eddy(94), Wells(3), Foster(1)
NEW SALEM (58563) Morton(81), Oliver(17)
NEW TOWN (58763) Mountrail(77), McKenzie(22)
NEWBURG (58762) Bottineau(85), McHenry(14)
NIAGARA (58266) Grand Forks(82), Nelson(17)
NOME (58062) Barnes(80), Ransom(19)
NOONAN Divide
NORTHWOOD (58267) Grand Forks(98), Steele(1)
NORWICH (58768) McHenry(54), Ward(45)
OAKES (58474) Dickey(96), Sargent(3)
OBERON Benson
ORISKA Barnes
ORRIN Pierce
OSNABROCK Cavalier
OVERLY Bottineau
PAGE (58064) Cass(89), Barnes(8), Steele(1)
PALERMO Mountrail
PARK RIVER Walsh
PARSHALL (58770) Mountrail(82), McLean(17)
PEKIN Nelson
PEMBINA Pembina
PENN Ramsey
PERTH (58363) Towner(85), Rolette(14)
PETERSBURG Nelson
PETTIBONE (58475) Kidder(94), Stutsman(5)
PILLSBURY Barnes
PINGREE Stutsman
PISEK Walsh
PLAZA (58771) Mountrail(78), Ward(18), McLean(2)
PORTAL Burke
PORTLAND (58274) Traill(85), Steele(14)
POWERS LAKE (58773) Burke(73), Mountrail(26)
RALEIGH Grant
RAY Williams
REEDER (58649) Adams(85), Hettinger(7), Bowman(6)
REGAN Burleigh
REGENT (58650) Hettinger(94), Adams(5)
REYNOLDS (58275) Grand Forks(57), Traill(42)
RHAME (58651) Bowman(69), Slope(30)
RICHARDTON (58652) Stark(89), Dunn(10)
RIVERDALE McLean
ROBINSON Kidder
ROCKLAKE Towner
ROGERS Barnes
ROLETTE (58366) Rolette(97), Pierce(2)
ROLLA (58367) Rolette(91), Towner(8)
ROSEGLEN McLean
ROSS Mountrail
RUGBY (58368) Pierce(95), McHenry(2), Benson(2)
RUSO (58778) McLean(95), McHenry(4)
RUTLAND Sargent
RYDER (58779) McLean(54), Ward(45)
SAINT ANTHONY Morton
SAINT JOHN Rolette
SAINT MICHAEL Benson
SAINT THOMAS Pembina
SANBORN Barnes
SARLES (58372) Towner(51), Cavalier(48)
SAWYER Ward
SCRANTON (58653) Bowman(90), Slope(9)
SELFRIDGE Sioux
SELZ Pierce
SENTINEL BUTTE Golden Valley
SHARON Steele
SHELDON (58068) Ransom(98), Cass(1)
SHERWOOD (58782) Renville(95), Bottineau(4)
SHEYENNE (58374) Eddy(59), Benson(31), Wells(8)
SHIELDS Grant
SOLEN (58570) Morton(58), Sioux(41)
SOURIS Bottineau
SOUTH HEART Stark
SPIRITWOOD (58481) Stutsman(51), Barnes(48)
STANLEY (58784) Mountrail(95), Burke(4)
STANTON (58571) Mercer(76), Oliver(23)
STARKWEATHER (58377) Ramsey(81), Towner(11), Cavalier(7)
STEELE Kidder
STERLING Burleigh
STIRUM (58069) Sargent(95), Ransom(4)
STRASBURG Emmons
STREETER (58483) Stutsman(66), Logan(21), Kidder(12)
SURREY Ward
SUTTON (58484) Griggs(81), Foster(18)
SYKESTON (58486) Wells(92), Stutsman(7)
TAPPEN Kidder
TAYLOR (58656) Stark(83), Dunn(16)
THOMPSON Grand Forks
TIOGA (58852) Williams(91), Mountrail(8)
TOKIO Benson
TOLLEY (58787) Renville(96), Ward(3)
TOLNA (58380) Nelson(47), Eddy(43), Benson(8)
TOWER CITY (58071) Cass(80), Barnes(19)
TOWNER (58788) McHenry(95), Pierce(4)
TRENTON Williams
TROTTERS Golden Valley
TURTLE LAKE McLean
TUTTLE Kidder
UNDERWOOD McLean
UNION Cavalier
UPHAM (58789) McHenry(90), Bottineau(9)
VALLEY CITY Barnes
VELVA (58790) McHenry(92), Ward(7)
VENTURIA McIntosh
VERONA (58490) La Moure(86), Ransom(13)
VOLTAIRE McHenry
WAHPETON Richland
WALCOTT Richland
WALES Cavalier
WALHALLA (58282) Pembina(86), Cavalier(13)
WARWICK (58381) Benson(53), Eddy(46)
WASHBURN McLean
WATFORD CITY McKenzie
WEBSTER Ramsey
WEST FARGO Cass
WESTHOPE Bottineau
WHEATLAND Cass
WHITE EARTH (58794) Mountrail(98), Williams(1)
WILDROSE (58795) Divide(52), Williams(47)
WILLISTON Williams
WILLOW CITY (58384) Bottineau(65), Pierce(17), McHenry(11), Rolette(5)
WILTON (58579) McLean(51), Burleigh(48)
WIMBLEDON (58492) Barnes(78), Stutsman(12), Griggs(8)
WING Burleigh
WISHEK (58495) McIntosh(84), Logan(15)
WOLFORD (58385) Pierce(91), Rolette(8)
WOODWORTH Stutsman
WYNDMERE Richland
YORK (58386) Benson(74), Pierce(25)
YPSILANTI (58497) Stutsman(93), Barnes(6)
ZAHL (58856) Williams(65), Divide(34)
ZAP Mercer
ZEELAND McIntosh

North Dakota ZIP/City Cross Reference

58001-58001 ABERCROMBIE
58002-58002 ABSARAKA
58003-58003 ALICE
58004-58004 AMENIA
58005-58005 ARGUSVILLE
58006-58006 ARTHUR
58007-58007 AYR
58008-58008 BARNEY
58009-58009 BLANCHARD
58011-58011 BUFFALO
58012-58012 CASSELTON
58013-58013 CAYUGA
58014-58014 CHAFFEE
58015-58015 CHRISTINE
58016-58016 CLIFFORD
58017-58017 COGSWELL
58018-58018 COLFAX
58021-58021 DAVENPORT
58027-58027 ENDERLIN
58029-58029 ERIE
58030-58030 FAIRMOUNT
58031-58031 FINGAL
58032-58032 FORMAN
58033-58033 FORT RANSOM
58035-58035 GALESBURG
58036-58036 GARDNER
58038-58038 GRANDIN
58039-58039 GREAT BEND
58040-58040 GWINNER
58041-58041 HANKINSON
58042-58042 HARWOOD
58043-58043 HAVANA
58045-58045 HILLSBORO
58046-58046 HOPE
58047-58047 HORACE
58048-58048 HUNTER
58049-58049 KATHRYN
58051-58051 KINDRED
58052-58052 LEONARD
58053-58053 LIDGERWOOD
58054-58054 LISBON
58056-58056 LUVERNE
58057-58057 MCLEOD
58058-58058 MANTADOR
58059-58059 MAPLETON
58060-58060 MILNOR
58061-58061 MOORETON
58062-58062 NOME
58063-58063 ORISKA
58064-58064 PAGE
58065-58065 PILLSBURY
58067-58067 RUTLAND
58068-58068 SHELDON
58069-58069 STIRUM
58071-58071 TOWER CITY
58072-58072 VALLEY CITY
58074-58076 WAHPETON
58077-58077 WALCOTT
58078-58078 WEST FARGO
58079-58079 WHEATLAND
58081-58081 WYNDMERE
58102-58126 FARGO
58201-58203 GRAND FORKS
58204-58205 GRAND FORKS AFB
58206-58208 GRAND FORKS
58210-58210 ADAMS
58212-58212 ANETA
58213-58213 ARDOCH
58214-58214 ARVILLA
58216-58216 BATHGATE
58218-58218 BUXTON
58219-58219 CALEDONIA
58220-58220 CAVALIER
58222-58222 CRYSTAL
58223-58223 CUMMINGS
58224-58224 DAHLEN
58225-58225 DRAYTON
58227-58227 EDINBURG
58228-58228 EMERADO
58229-58229 FAIRDALE
58230-58230 FINLEY
58231-58231 FORDVILLE
58233-58233 FOREST RIVER
58235-58235 GILBY

58236-58236 GLASSTON
58237-58237 GRAFTON
58238-58238 HAMILTON
58239-58239 HANNAH
58240-58240 HATTON
58241-58241 HENSEL
58243-58243 HOOPLE
58244-58244 INKSTER
58246-58246 JOLIETTE
58249-58249 LANGDON
58250-58250 LANKIN
58251-58251 LARIMORE
58253-58253 MCCANNA
58254-58254 MCVILLE
58255-58255 MAIDA
58256-58256 MANVEL
58257-58257 MAYVILLE
58258-58258 MEKINOCK
58259-58259 MICHIGAN
58260-58260 MILTON
58261-58261 MINTO
58262-58262 MOUNTAIN
58265-58265 NECHE
58266-58266 NIAGARA
58267-58267 NORTHWOOD
58269-58269 OSNABROCK
58270-58270 PARK RIVER
58271-58271 PEMBINA
58272-58272 PETERSBURG
58273-58273 PISEK
58274-58274 PORTLAND
58275-58275 REYNOLDS
58276-58276 SAINT THOMAS
58277-58277 SHARON
58278-58278 THOMPSON
58279-58279 UNION
58281-58281 WALES
58282-58282 WALHALLA
58301-58301 DEVILS LAKE
58310-58310 AGATE
58311-58311 ALSEN
58313-58313 BALTA
58315-58315 BARTON
58316-58316 BELCOURT
58317-58317 BISBEE
58318-58318 BOTTINEAU
58319-58319 BREMEN
58320-58320 BRINSMADE
58321-58321 BROCKET
58323-58323 CALVIN
58324-58324 CANDO
58325-58325 CHURCHS FERRY
58327-58327 CRARY
58328-58328 DOYON
58329-58329 DUNSEITH
58330-58330 EDMORE
58331-58331 EGELAND
58332-58332 ESMOND
58335-58335 FORT TOTTEN
58337-58337 HAMBERG
58338-58338 HAMPDEN
58339-58339 HANSBORO
58341-58341 HARVEY
58342-58342 HEIMDAL
58343-58343 KNOX
58344-58344 LAKOTA
58345-58345 LAWTON
58346-58346 LEEDS
58348-58348 MADDOCK
58351-58351 MINNEWAUKAN
58352-58352 MUNICH
58353-58353 MYLO
58355-58355 NEKOMA
58356-58356 NEW ROCKFORD
58357-58357 OBERON
58359-58359 ORRIN
58360-58360 OVERLY
58361-58361 PEKIN
58362-58362 PENN
58363-58363 PERTH
58365-58365 ROCKLAKE
58366-58366 ROLETTE
58367-58367 ROLLA
58368-58368 RUGBY
58369-58369 SAINT JOHN
58370-58370 SAINT MICHAEL
58372-58372 SARLES
58373-58373 SELZ
58374-58374 SHEYENNE
58377-58377 STARKWEATHER
58379-58379 TOKIO
58380-58380 TOLNA
58381-58381 WARWICK
58382-58382 WEBSTER
58384-58384 WILLOW CITY
58385-58385 WOLFORD
58386-58386 YORK
58401-58405 JAMESTOWN
58411-58411 ALFRED
58412-58412 ARENA
58413-58413 ASHLEY
58415-58415 BERLIN
58416-58416 BINFORD
58418-58418 BOWDON
58420-58420 BUCHANAN
58421-58421 CARRINGTON
58422-58422 CATHAY
58423-58423 CHASELEY
58424-58424 CLEVELAND
58425-58425 COOPERSTOWN
58426-58426 COURTENAY
58427-58427 CRYSTAL SPRINGS
58428-58428 DAWSON
58429-58429 DAZEY
58430-58430 DENHOFF
58431-58431 DICKEY
58432-58432 ECKELSON
58433-58433 EDGELEY
58436-58436 ELLENDALE
58438-58438 FESSENDEN
58439-58439 FORBES
58440-58440 FREDONIA
58441-58441 FULLERTON
58442-58442 GACKLE
58443-58443 GLENFIELD
58444-58444 GOODRICH
58445-58445 GRACE CITY
58447-58447 GUELPH
58448-58448 HANNAFORD
58450-58450 HEATON
58451-58451 HURDSFIELD
58452-58452 JESSIE
58454-58454 JUD
58455-58455 KENSAL
58456-58456 KULM
58458-58458 LAMOURE
58460-58460 LEHR
58461-58461 LITCHVILLE
58463-58463 MCCLUSKY
58464-58464 MCHENRY
58465-58465 MANFRED
58466-58466 MARION
58467-58467 MEDINA
58469-58469 MERRICOURT
58471-58471 MONANGO
58472-58472 MONTPELIER
58474-58474 OAKES
58475-58475 PETTIBONE
58476-58476 PINGREE
58477-58477 REGAN
58478-58478 ROBINSON
58479-58479 ROGERS
58480-58480 SANBORN
58481-58481 SPIRITWOOD
58482-58482 STEELE
58483-58483 STREETER
58484-58484 SUTTON
58486-58486 SYKESTON
58487-58487 TAPPEN
58488-58488 TUTTLE
58489-58489 VENTURIA
58490-58490 VERONA
58492-58492 WIMBLEDON
58494-58494 WING
58495-58495 WISHEK
58496-58496 WOODWORTH
58497-58497 YPSILANTI
58501-58507 BISMARCK
58520-58520 ALMONT
58521-58521 BALDWIN
58523-58523 BEULAH
58524-58524 BRADDOCK
58528-58528 CANNON BALL
58529-58529 CARSON
58530-58530 CENTER
58531-58531 COLEHARBOR
58532-58532 DRISCOLL
58533-58533 ELGIN
58535-58535 FLASHER
58537-58537 FORT RICE
58538-58538 FORT YATES
58540-58540 GARRISON
58541-58541 GOLDEN VALLEY
58542-58542 HAGUE
58544-58544 HAZELTON
58545-58545 HAZEN
58547-58547 HENSLER
58549-58549 KINTYRE
58551-58551 LEITH
58552-58552 LINTON
58553-58553 MCKENZIE
58554-58554 MANDAN
58558-58558 MENOKEN
58559-58559 MERCER
58560-58560 MOFFIT
58561-58561 NAPOLEON
58562-58562 NEW LEIPZIG
58563-58563 NEW SALEM
58564-58564 RALEIGH
58565-58565 RIVERDALE
58566-58566 SAINT ANTHONY
58568-58568 SELFRIDGE
58569-58569 SHIELDS
58570-58570 SOLEN
58571-58571 STANTON
58572-58572 STERLING
58573-58573 STRASBURG
58575-58575 TURTLE LAKE
58576-58576 UNDERWOOD
58577-58577 WASHBURN
58579-58579 WILTON
58580-58580 ZAP
58581-58581 ZEELAND
58601-58602 DICKINSON
58620-58620 AMIDON
58621-58621 BEACH
58622-58622 BELFIELD
58623-58623 BOWMAN
58625-58625 DODGE
58626-58626 DUNN CENTER
58627-58627 FAIRFIELD
58630-58630 GLADSTONE
58631-58631 GLEN ULLIN
58632-58632 GOLVA
58634-58634 GRASSY BUTTE
58636-58636 HALLIDAY
58638-58638 HEBRON
58639-58639 HETTINGER
58640-58640 KILLDEER
58641-58641 LEFOR
58642-58642 MANNING
58643-58643 MARMARTH
58644-58644 MARSHALL
58645-58645 MEDORA
58646-58646 MOTT
58647-58647 NEW ENGLAND
58649-58649 REEDER
58650-58650 REGENT
58651-58651 RHAME
58652-58652 RICHARDTON
58653-58653 SCRANTON
58654-58654 SENTINEL BUTTE
58655-58655 SOUTH HEART
58656-58656 TAYLOR
58657-58657 TROTTERS
58701-58703 MINOT
58704-58705 MINOT AFB
58707-58707 MINOT
58710-58710 ANAMOOSE
58711-58711 ANTLER
58712-58712 BALFOUR
58713-58713 BANTRY
58716-58716 BENEDICT
58718-58718 BERTHOLD
58720-58720 BLAISDELL
58721-58721 BOWBELLS
58722-58722 BURLINGTON
58723-58723 BUTTE
58725-58725 CARPIO
58727-58727 COLUMBUS
58728-58728 BOWBELLS
58730-58730 CROSBY
58731-58731 DEERING
58733-58733 DES LACS
58734-58734 DONNYBROOK
58735-58735 DOUGLAS
58736-58736 DRAKE
58737-58737 FLAXTON
58738-58738 FOXHOLM
58739-58739 GARDENA
58740-58740 GLENBURN
58741-58741 GRANVILLE
58744-58744 KARLSRUHE
58746-58746 KENMARE
58747-58747 KIEF
58748-58748 KRAMER
58750-58750 LANSFORD
58752-58752 LIGNITE
58755-58755 MCGREGOR
58756-58756 MAKOTI
58757-58757 MANDAREE
58758-58758 MARTIN
58759-58759 MAX
58760-58760 MAXBASS
58761-58761 MOHALL
58762-58762 NEWBURG
58763-58763 NEW TOWN
58765-58765 NOONAN
58768-58768 NORWICH
58769-58769 PALERMO
58770-58770 PARSHALL
58771-58771 PLAZA
58772-58772 PORTAL
58773-58773 POWERS LAKE
58775-58775 ROSEGLEN
58776-58776 ROSS
58778-58778 RUSO
58779-58779 RYDER
58781-58781 SAWYER
58782-58782 SHERWOOD
58783-58783 SOURIS
58784-58784 STANLEY
58785-58785 SURREY
58787-58787 TOLLEY
58788-58788 TOWNER
58789-58789 UPHAM
58790-58790 VELVA
58792-58792 VOLTAIRE
58793-58793 WESTHOPE
58794-58794 WHITE EARTH
58795-58795 WILDROSE
58801-58802 WILLISTON
58830-58830 ALAMO
58831-58831 ALEXANDER
58833-58833 AMBROSE
58835-58835 ARNEGARD
58838-58838 CARTWRIGHT
58843-58843 EPPING
58844-58844 FORTUNA
58845-58845 GRENORA
58847-58847 KEENE
58849-58849 RAY
58852-58852 TIOGA
58853-58853 TRENTON
58854-58854 WATFORD CITY
58856-58856 ZAHL

Ohio

General Help Numbers:

Governor's Office

77 S High St, 30th Floor — 614-466-3555
Columbus, OH 43215 — Fax 614-466-9354
http://governor.ohio.gov — 8AM-5PM

Attorney General's Office

State Office Tower — 614-466-4320
30 E Broad St, 17th Floor — Fax 614-644-6135
Columbus, OH 43215-3428 — 8AM-5PM
www.ag.state.oh.us

Legislative Records

Ohio House of Representatives — 614-466-9745
77 S High Street — Fax 614-644-8744
Columbus, OH 43266 — 8:30AM-5PM
www.legislature.state.oh.us

State Archives

Archives/Library — 614-297-2300
1982 Velma Ave — Fax 614-297-2546
Columbus, OH 43211-2497 — 9AM-5PM TH-SA: 10-5 SU
www.ohiohistory.org/ar_tools.html

State Specifics:

Capital:	Columbus Franklin County
Time Zone:	EST
Number of Counties:	88
Population:	11,485,910
Web Site:	www.ohio.gov

State Agencies

Criminal Records

Ohio Bureau of Investigation, Civilian Background Section, PO Box 365, London, OH 43140 (Courier address- 1560 State Rte 56, London, OH 43140); 740-845-2000 (General Info), 740-845-2375 (Civilian Background Cks), Fax- 740-845-2633; 8AM-5PM.

www.ag.state.oh.us/business/fingerprint/index.asp

The state has an innovative system over the web for electronic transfer of fingerprints. See Online Access below.

Indexing & Storage: Records available from 1921 on. Records from 1960's on are computerized and the agency is in the process of computerizing older records. New records available for inquiry in 5 days, 15 with fingerprints. 65% of all arrests in database have final dispositions recorded, 85% for those arrests within last 5 years.

Searching: All out-of-state record requests must include a fingerprint card: name searches are not performed. In state requesters are access to use the web service, which also entails fingerprints. Include in request- witnessed signed release from subject, fingerprints, name DOB, SSN. 100% of the records are fingerprint supported. Records without dispositions are not released. Escalating misdemeanors are released; these are any offense classified as a misdemeanor on the 1st offense and felony on subsequent offense.

Access by: mail, online.

Fee & Payment: The search fee is $22.00 per record. Statutorily-required checks may include an FBI fingerprint check for an additional $24.00. Fee payee- Treasurer - State of Ohio. Prepayment required. No credit cards accepted.

Mail search: Turnaround time- up to 4 weeks. If request comes from out of state it can take 4 weeks. No SASE is required.

Online search: Civilian Background Checks (WebCheck) is a web-based system for all in-state record requests. Results are NOT returned via the

Internet. Agencies can send fingerprint images and other data via the Internet using a single digit fingerprint scanner and a driver's license magnetic strip reader. Hardware costs are involved.

Statewide Court Records

Administrative Director, Supreme Court of Ohio, 65 S Front Street, Columbus, OH 43215-3431; 614-387-9000, 800-826-9010, 614-387-9410 (Case Management), Fax- 614-387-9419; 8AM-5PM. www.supremecourtofohio.gov

This office does not provide access to county court records. Except for certain online research capabilities, all trial court record access must be done at the local level.

Online search: Appellate and Supreme Court opinions may be researched from the home page.

Sexual Offender Registry

Ohio Bureau of Investigation, Sexual Offender Registry, PO Box 365, London, OH 43140 (Courier address- 1560 State Rte 56 SW, London, OH 43140); 866-406-4534, Fax- 740-845-2021; 8AM-4:45PM.
www.esorn.ag.state.oh.us/Secured/p1.aspx

O.R.C. 2950.13 requires that the public eSORN database contain information on every person convicted as an adult and registered in the state registry of sex offenders and child-victim offenders.

Indexing & Storage: Records go back to 07/ 97. New records available for inquiry immediately.

Searching: The database that contains information regarding all registered sex offenders in the State of Ohio is known as eSORN. Include in request- name and DOB. The individual county sheriff's representatives are best situated to provide local sex offender and registration information. This data not released- most juvenile records.

Online search: Search online eSORN at www.esorn.ag.state.oh.us/Secured/p21_2.aspx. Users can search by offender name, zip code, county and / or school district. The site is linked to all 88 of Ohio's sheriff's offices.

Incarceration Records

Ohio Department of Rehabilitation and Correction, Bureau of Records Management, 978 Freeway Drive, N., Columbus, OH 43229; 614-752-1076, 614-752-1159 x3 (Inmate Records), Fax- 614-752-1086; 8AM-4:45PM. www.drc.state.oh.us

Indexing & Storage: Records available on current and former inmates, except online search only provides current inmates. New records available for inquiry in 1 to 5 days.

Searching: Include in request- first and last name or Offender Number. The DOB and SSN are helpful. Location, physical identifiers, conviction sentencing info, and release dates are provided.

Access by: mail, phone, fax, online.

Mail search: Turnaround time- 1 to 2 weeks. SASE not required.

Phone search: Record inquiry available by phone. To obtain information on offenders previously under the supervision of the Department, call 614-752-1159 and choose option 3. **Fax search:** Fax requests are accepted.

Online search: From the website, in the Select a Destination box, select Offender Search or see www.drc.state.oh.us/OffenderSearch/Search.aspx. You can search by name, geographic location, or inmate number. The Offender Search includes all offenders currently incarcerated or under some type of Department supervision (parole, post-release control, or transitional control).

Corporation, LLC, LP, Fictitious/Assumed Name, Trademarks/Servicemarks

Secretary of State, Corporate Records Access, PO Box 1329, Columbus, OH 43216 (Courier address- 30 E Broad Street, Level B-1, Columbus, OH 43215); 877-767-3453, 614-466-3910; 8AM-5PM.
www.sos.state.oh.us/SOS/businessServices.aspx

Information regarding officers is available from the Department of Taxation at 614-438-5339, but the requester must obtain the Charter # from this agency.

Indexing & Storage: Records available from the 1800's. New records available for inquiry immediately.

Searching: This agency also holds records for Real Estate Trusts, Business Trusts, Churches, and Nonprofits. Include in request- full name of business. Use the request form for certified documents (available from web). In addition to the articles of organization, business entity records available include: Annual Reports, Prior (merged) names, Inactive and Reserved names.

Access by: mail, phone, fax, in person, online.

Fee & Payment: There is no fee for a corporate printout of limited information or uncertified copies. The certification fee is $5.00, $10.00 if over 100 pages. A Good Standing is $5.00. Fee payee- Secretary of State. Prepayment required. Personal checks accepted. Credit cards accepted online for validations.

Mail search: Turnaround time- 2 days. SASE not required.

Phone search: They will release limited information over the phone. **Fax search:** No fee, turnaround time is 2 days. Do not fax for plain copy requests.

In person: There is no fee to look at records.

Online search: The agency provides free Internet searching for business and corporation records from the home page. A Good Standing can be ordered. Validation is available for $5.00. Also, search securities exemption filings (ERNIE) free at https://www.comapps.ohio.gov/secu/secu_apps/offering/offering.aspx. Search securities enforcement orders by year at https://www.comapps.ohio.gov/secu/secu_apps/FinalOrders/.

Other access: This agency makes the database available for purchase, call for details.

Uniform Commercial Code

UCC Records, Secretary of State, PO Box 669, Columbus, OH 43216 (Courier address- 180 E Broad St, Ground FL, Columbus, OH 43215); 877-767-3453, 614-466-3910, Fax- 614-466-2892; 8AM-5PM. www.sos.state.oh.us/SOS/Uniform%20Commercial%20Code.aspx

Indexing & Storage: Records available for only current or active filings. Lapsed records are available one year after lapse date. New records available for inquiry in 2 days.

Searching: Use search form UCC-11. All tax liens are filed at the county level. Include in request- debtor name. Be sure to include the words "any and all addresses" in your search request. This data not released- SSNs.

Access by: mail, phone, fax, in person, online.

Fee & Payment: The search fee is $20.00 per debtor name, copies included. A copy search with Finance Statement Number is $5.00 with a maximum of five numbers per request. Fee payee- Secretary of State. Prepayment required. Personal checks accepted, credit cards are not.

Mail search: Turnaround time- 2 days.

Phone search: Calls are limited to 10 filings, 3 debtor names per call. There is no charge for verbal information.

Fax search: Only available for prepaid accounts.

In person: Counter service is not offered.

Online search: The Internet site offers free online access to records. Search by debtor, secured party, or financing statement number.

Other access: The complete database is available on electronic media with weekly updates. Call for current pricing.

Federal & State Tax Liens

Records not maintained by a state level agency.

Records are not housed by a state agency. You must secure from the local county recorder offices.

Sales Tax Registrations

Taxation Department, Sale & Use Tax Division, PO Box 530, Columbus, OH 43216-0530 (Courier address- 30 E Broad St, 20th Floor, Columbus, OH 43215); 614-466-7351, 888-405-4039, Fax- 614-466-4977; 8AM-5PM. http://tax.ohio.gov

Indexing & Storage: New records available for inquiry in 2-14 days.

Searching: This agency will confirmation the existence of a sales tax license and will release the address. There is no fee. Include in request- business name, city of known. This data not released- financials

Access by: mail, phone, fax, in person.

Mail search: Turnaround time- 1-3 days.

Phone search: A simple confirmation is available.

Fax search: Will confirm by fax.

In person: Counter service is offered.

Birth Certificates

Ohio Department of Health, Bureau of Vital Statistics, PO Box 15098, Columbus, OH 43215-0098 (Courier address- 246 N High St, 1st Fl, Revenue Room, Columbus, OH 43215); 614-466-2531, 800-669-8313 (Vendor), Fax- 866-881-9699; 8AM-5PM. www.odh.ohio.gov

For faster service than by mail, the ODH suggests visiting the county agency when birth occurred or use the designated vendor for expedited service.

Indexing & Storage: Records available from 1908 to present. Records from 12/20/08 to 12/44 are at the Ohio Historical Society at 614-297-2510. New records available for inquiry in 3 months.

Searching: For questions, email VitalStat@odh.ohio.gov. Include in request- full name, names of parents including mother's maiden name, date of birth, city and county of birth.

Access by: mail, fax, in person, online.

Fee & Payment: A certified copy of $16.50. If year is not known the search fee is $3.00 for each 10 years searched per name spelling. Fee payee- Treasurer, State of Ohio Prepayment required. Personal checks accepted. Credit cards accepted only by VitalChek.

Mail search: Turnaround time- 4 to 6 weeks. SASE not required. **Fax search:** See expedited service below.

In person: Records are process within 20 minutes, usually. Counter open 8:30 to 4:30.

Online search: Records can be ordered from a state-designated vendor - see expedited service below.

Expedited service: For online, fax and phone requests. This is available from www.vitalchek.com. Turnaround time- 3 days to 2 weeks. Service fee is $9.95, using a credit card is required and extra fee for overnight or courier shipping.

Death Records

Ohio Department of Health, Bureau of Vital Statistics, PO Box 15098, Columbus, OH 43215-0098 (Courier address- 246 N High Street, 1st Fl, Revenue Room, Columbus, OH 43215); 614-466-2531, 800-669-8313 (Vendor), Fax- 866-881-9699; 8AM-5PM. www.odh.ohio.gov

For faster service than by mail, the ODH suggests visiting the county agency when death occurred or use the designated vendor for expedited service.

Indexing & Storage: Records available from 1954 to present. Death records from 1908 to 1953 are found at Ohio Historical Society, 1982 Velma Ave, Columbus, OH 43211. Records prior to 1908 are located at the county level. New records available for inquiry in approx. 3 months.

Searching: Requests must be in writing. For questions, email VitalStat@odh.ohio.gov. Include in request- full name, date of death, city and county of death.

Access by: mail, fax, in person, online.

Fee & Payment: A certified copy of $16.50. If year is not known the search fee is $3.00 for each 10 years searched per name spelling. Fee payee- Treasurer, State of Ohio. Prepayment required. Personal checks accepted. Credit cards accepted only by VitalChek.

Mail search: Turnaround time- 4 to 6 weeks. SASE not required. **Fax search:** See expedited service below.

In person: Records are process within 20 minutes, usually.

Online search: The Ohio Historical Society Death Certificate Index Searchable Database at http://ohsweb.ohiohistory.org/death// permits searching by name, county, index. Data is available from 1913 to 1944 only. Records can be ordered from a state-designated vendor - see expedited service below.

Expedited service: For fax, online and phone requests - available from www.vitalchek.com. Turnaround time- 3 days to 2 weeks. Service fee is $9.95, using a credit card is required and extra fee for overnight or courier shipping.

Marriage Certificates, Divorce Records

Ohio Department of Health, Bureau of Vital Statistics, PO Box 15098, Columbus, OH 43215-0098; 614-466-2531; 8AM-5PM.

www.odh.ohio.gov

Marriage and divorce records are found at county of issue. This agency will only do a search of the index from 1954 forward. Abstracts are brief forms that list limited information extracted from the original marriage licenses or divorce decrees.

Indexing & Storage: New records available for inquiry in 3 months.

Searching: For questions, email VitalStat@odh.ohio.gov. Include in request- names, date and location of the event. An abstract is not a marriage license or divorce decree.

Access by: mail, in person.

Fee & Payment: The search fee is $3.00 for each 10 years searched, if year not known. Fee payee- Treasurer, State of Ohio Personal checks accepted. Credit cards not accepted

Mail search: Turnaround time- 3 to 6 weeks. A search of the index is available by mail.

In person: Record index search may be requested in person, time permitting.

Workers' Compensation Records

Bureau of Workers Compensation, Customer Contact Center - Records Mgr, 30 W Spring St, 10th, Columbus, OH 43215-2241; 800-644-6292, 614-728-3210 (Records), Fax- 877-520-6446; 7:30AM-5:30PM.www.ohiobwc.com/Default.aspx

Indexing & Storage: Records available for the past 10 years.

Searching: All information is public except injured worker medical report and information pertaining to the employer's financial condition. Include in request- claimant name, SSN or claim number. Claim number is helpful. All requests must be in writing.

Access by: mail, phone, fax, in person, online.

Fee & Payment: There is no search fee, copy fee is $.05 per page. Fee payee- Ohio Bureau of Workers Compensation. Prepayment required. Personal checks accepted, credit cards are not.

Mail search: Turnaround time- 1 week. A SASE is requested.

Phone search: They will provide the information immediately unless file is lengthy or excessive.

Fax search: Service is available with a 24 hour turnaround time.

In person: Call for location of records before going in because there are 22 different office locations.

Online search: Injured workers, injured worker designees, representatives and managed care organizations (MCOs) can view a list of all claims associated with a given SSN, but are limited to viewing only the claims with which they are associated. Employers, their representatives or designees, and managed care organizations can view a list of all claims associated to their BWC policy number. Medical providers can view all claims associated with any given SSN. Access is through the website listed above.

Other access: Bulk data is released to approved accounts; however, the legal department must approve requesters. The agency has general information available on a website.

Driver Records

Department of Public Safety, Bureau of Motor Vehicles, 1970 W Broad St, Columbus, OH 43223-1102; 614-752-7600, Fax- 614-995-7946; 8AM-5:30PM M-F; till 2PM on Sat.

www.ohiobmv.com

Copies of tickets must be obtained from the local court or police.

Indexing & Storage: Records available for 3 years for moving violations, OVI's and suspensions. Records are purged from public view after 3 years; insurance laws require 36 months of availability. New records available for inquiry in 2 to 5 weeks.

Searching: Use Request Form BMV1173 (downloadable from Internet). If requester does not have permissible use per DPPA, Form BMV 5008 is also required, which requires notarized consent of subject. Include in request- driver's license number, full name, date of birth, SSN. Records with personal information are not released unless requester is DPPA qualified. Driver's address is included as part of the search report for permissible requesters, except for requests received from California. This data not released- mental health records, SSNs unless provided by requester (except government agency requesters).

Access by: mail, phone, fax, in person, online.

Fee & Payment: The fee is $2.00 per record. A license status check is available for $2.00. If a record is ordered in person at a regional office, the fee is $5.50 per record. Fee payee- Ohio Treasurer Prepayment required. Personal checks accepted, credit cards are not.

Mail search: Turnaround time- 5 to 7 days.

Phone search: Qualified, pre-approved accounts may order by phone. There is a $200.00 deposit.

Fax search: Qualified, pre-approved accounts may order by fax. There is a $200.00 deposit.

In person: Up to eight records will be processed by this location while you wait. There is an additional $3.50 service fee. Record requests are also processed at regional offices.

Online search: The Online Abstract System by FTP is suggested for requesters who order 100 or more motor vehicle reports per day in batch mode. The DL# or SSN and name are needed when ordering. Fee is $2.00 per record. For more information, call Fiscal Svrs at 614-752-2091. Also, Ohio drivers may view an unofficial copy of their record at https://www.dps.state.oh.us/netsys/netdb/ENGLISH/MMENW.asp. There is no fee.

Vehicle Ownership & Registration

Bureau of Motor Vehicles, Motor Vehicle Title Records, 1970 W Broad St, Columbus, OH 43223-1102; 614-752-7752, Fax- 614-752-7001; 8AM-6PM. www.ohiobmv.com

Indexing & Storage: Records available for the current year plus six. New records available for inquiry in 1 to 2 days normally.

Searching: Use Record Request Form 1173 (downloadable from Internet). If requester does not have permissible use per DPPA, Form BMV

5008 is also required, which requires notarized consent of subject. Records w/o personal information are not released to the public. Include in request- name, year, make VIN, license plate number if known. Lien information is not recorded on vehicle registration records in Ohio. This data not released- SSNs, unless included in request.

Access by: mail, phone, fax, in person, online.

Fee & Payment: The fee is $2.00 or each record searched. Fee payee- Treasurer, State of Ohio. Prepayment required. Personal checks accepted, credit cards are not.

Mail search: Turnaround time- 1 to 3 days. A SASE is requested.

Phone search: There is a pre-paid Search Account for addresses only. Call Fiscal Section at 614-752-2091 to establish an account. **Fax search:** Records are available only for pre-approved accounts with funds on file.

In person: There may be a limit on the number of requests processed immediately, most are not available until the next day.

Online search: Ohio offers online access through AAMVA. All requesters must comply with a contractual agreement prior to release of data, which complies with DPPA regulations. Fee is $2.00 per record. Call 614-752-7598 for more information. The web offers free access to title records for vehicles and watercraft. No personal information released. Search by title number or ID. Also search at https://www.dps.state.oh.us/atps/.

Other access: Bulk records are available for purchase, per DPPA guidelines.

Accident Reports

Department of Public Safety, OSHP Central Records, 1st Fl, PO Box 182074, Columbus, OH 43218-2074; 614-466-3536, Fax- 614-644-9749; 8AM-4:45PM.

http://statepatrol.ohio.gov/crash.htm

Indexing & Storage: Records available for 5 years to present. Crash records are indexed on computer. New records available for inquiry in 7 to 10 days.

Searching: OSHP will assist to find correct report, but will not accept phone orders. Include in request- full name, date of accident county of occurrence, or crash number if known. This data not released- SSNs.

Access by: mail, in person, online.

Fee & Payment: The fee is $4.00 per record. There is a charge for a no record found. Fee payee- Ohio State Highway Patrol Prepayment required. Personal checks accepted. Credit cards accepted only online.

Mail search: Turnaround time- 3-4 weeks. SASE is not required.

In person: Public access terminals are available in the lobby. Turnaround time is immediate if the record is on file. Assistance is available.

Online search: Crash reports purchased online will be sent to your e-mail account the same day. Crash photographs purchased online will be sent in the mail. Online crash reports are available for crashes that 5 years to present. Search is www.statepatrol.ohio.gov/crash.htm. Reports must be purchased for $4.00 using a credit card.

Vessel Ownership & Registration

DNR-Division of Watercraft, Titles and Registration, 2045 Morse Rd, Bldg A, Columbus, OH 43229-6693; 614-265-6480, Fax- 614-784-5987; 8AM-5PM.

www.dnr.state.oh.us/Watercraft/tabid/2062/Default.aspx

Only Watercraft Agents issue registrations (at the county level). Only Country Clerks of Court write titles. But this agency has access to all records. Registrations are for three years.

Indexing & Storage: Records available from 1960 to the present. Records are indexed on computer for the last 3 years. Any boat operated on public waters must be registered. All boats 14 ft or longer or having a 10+ hp motor must be titled.

Searching: Liens are included on title histories, but you must first request the lien history in writing. Include in request- name or hull ID # or registration # or serial #. This data not released- SSNs.

Access by: mail, phone, fax, in person, online.

Fee & Payment: There is no search fee for registration records. There is a $2.00 fee "per motor" for a title search. Fee payee- Division of Watercraft. Prepayment required. Personal checks accepted, credit cards are not.

Mail search: Turnaround time- 4-5 days. SASE not required.

Phone search: There is a limit of five names per call for registration information. **Fax search:** Same criteria as mail searching.

In person: Simple requests may be processed while you wait.

Online search: A free title inquiry is available at www.dps.state.oh.us/atps/. Note this is through another agency, but people are directed to this site from the DNR site. The title information available from this web page is obtained from Ohio county title offices. Records are from 1993 forward.

Legislation Records

Legislative Service Commission, 77 S High Street, Columbus, OH 43215 (Courier address- Ohio Senate, State House, Columbus, OH 43215); 614-466-3615, 614-466-9745 (Clerk's Office), Fax-614-644-8744; 8:30AM-5PM.

www.legislature.state.oh.us

Records available from 1888 to present on microfiche and are computerized since 1990. Bills for the years 1888-1990 are available on microfilm at many libraries in Ohio. The Internet site offers bill text, status, and enactment back to 1997/98. Access the Ohio Revised Code at www.legislature.state.oh.us/search.cfm.

Voter Registration

Secretary of State, Elections Division, 180 E Broad St, 15th Fl, Columbus, OH 43215; 614-466-2585, Fax- 614-752-4360; 8AM-5PM.

www.sos.state.oh.us

Records are open. Businesses, individual, and political parties may obtain data. Single name search requests are better served at the local level.

Indexing & Storage: Records available for a limited number of years. New records available for inquiry in 3-5 days.

Searching: The agency suggests that all individual requests be done at the county Board of Elections.

Access by: mail, phone, fax, in person.

Fee & Payment: There is no fee for individual searches. Database and list purchases require fees. Fee payee- Secretary of State. Prepayment required. No credit cards accepted.

Mail search: Turnaround time- 1 week to 10 days. SASE not required.

Phone search: Limited name search requests by telephone. **Fax search:** Same criteria as mail requests.

In person: The state is not prepared to handle look-ups, but will assist as necessary.

Other access: Records may obtained on disk in a text format. No customization is possible, only the entire database is released. For more information, contact Robin Fields.

GED Certificates

GED Transcript Office, 25 S Front St, 1st Fl, Columbus, OH 43215-4183; 614-466-1577, Fax-614-752-9445; 8AM-4:30PM.

www.ode.state.oh.us/

Students may review their test scores online and order transcripts with credit card. Online is for students only.

Indexing & Storage: Records available from 1984 to present. Prior records are on microfilm to 1945. New records available for inquiry in 3 to 4 weeks.

Searching: A request form for a transcript copy is found at the webpage. Verification service is only available to prospective employers. Students may obtain proof of GED via online at the web site. Need Ohio DL number to get account. Include in request- name at time of test, SSN, signed release, approx date of test. The DOB and city of test are helpful. Direct questions to ged@ode.state.oh.us. This data not released- personal ID info.

Access by: mail, fax, in person.

Fee & Payment: There is no fee for a verification, a $5.00 fee is charged for a copy of a transcript, $10.00 if expedited. Fee payee- Ohio Testing Services Prepayment required. Personal checks not accepted. Credit cards accepted only online.

Mail search: Turnaround time- 7 to 10 days. SASE not required.

Fax search: Same criteria as mail searching. Will fax back only pass-fail or no record found. No scores given. Cannot search by fax for persons taking GED test prior to 1983.

In person: Simple requests may be processed while you wait.

Expedited service: For one business day processing, the total fee is $10.00. The request can be returned by fax or mail.

Hunting & Fishing License Information

Ohio Department of Natural Resources, Division of Wildlife, 2045 Morse Rd, Bldg G-2, Columbus, OH 43229-6693; 614-265-6300, 800-945-3543; 8AM-5PM.

www.dnr.state.oh.us/wildlife/default.htm

Indexing & Storage: Records available since 1999. Many records are not computerized, but the records that are computerized go back to 1999..

Ohio State Licensing Agencies

For details about the agency responsible for licensing/certifying/registering an item below or in the Agency Quick Finder section, match an item's number with the number of the agency in the *Licensing Agency Information* section.

Ohio Licenses Searchable Online

Accounting Firm #1 .... http://acc.ohio.gov/lookup.htm
Acupuncturist #28........ https://license.ohio.gov/lookup/default.asp
Anesthesiologist Assistant #28........ https://license.ohio.gov/lookup/default.asp
Architect #2 .... https://license.ohio.gov/lookup/
Athlete Agent #32........ www.aco.ohio.gov/pdf/RegAthAg.pdf
Athletic Trainer #29 .... https://license.ohio.gov/lookup/default.asp
Attorney, State #44........ www.sconet.state.oh.us/atty_reg/Public_AttorneyInformation.asp
Audiologist/Audiologist Aide #8 .... https://license.ohio.gov/lookup/default.asp
Backflow Prev. Assembly Insp. #34 .... https://www.comapps.ohio.gov/dic/dico_apps/bdcc/CertifiedBackFlowTesters/
Bank #17 .... http://elicense2-lookup.com.ohio.gov/
Barber #26........ https://license.ohio.gov/lookup/default.asp?division=87
Barber Instructor #26........ https://license.ohio.gov/lookup/default.asp?division=87
Barber School #26........ https://license.ohio.gov/lookup/default.asp?division=87
Barber Shop #26 .... https://license.ohio.gov/lookup/default.asp?division=87
Boiler Contractor #38 .... www.com.state.oh.us/dic/scripts/boilerctrqy.htm
Boiler Inspector #34 .... https://www.comapps.ohio.gov/dic/dico_apps/boil/boiler_contractors/Default.aspx
Boiler Operator #34........ www.com.ohio.gov/OnlineServices.aspx
Boxer/Boxing Professional #32 .... www.aco.ohio.gov/pdf/Boxers.pdf
Cemetery #15........ https://www.com.state.oh.us/real/elicense.aspx
Check Cashing Service #17 .... http://elicense2-lookup.com.ohio.gov/
Check Lending Service #17 .... http://elicense2-lookup.com.ohio.gov/
Child Care Type A or B House #19........ www.odjfs.state.oh.us/cdc/query.asp
Child Day Care Facility #19........ www.odjfs.state.oh.us/cdc/query.asp
Chiropractor #9........ https://license.ohio.gov/lookup/default.asp?division=90
Clinical Nurse Specialist #6........ www.nursing.ohio.gov/verification.stm
Consumer Finance Company #17........ http://elicense2-lookup.com.ohio.gov/
Contractor #14........ www.com.state.oh.us/dic/lics/elicense.aspx
Cosmetic Therapist #28 .... https://license.ohio.gov/lookup/default.asp
Cosmetologist/Managing Cosmetolog't #4... https://license.ohio.gov/lookup/default.asp
Cosmetology Instructor #4 .... https://license.ohio.gov/lookup/default.asp
Day Camp, Children's #19........ www.odjfs.state.oh.us/cdc/query.asp
Dental Assistant Radiologist #33........ https://license.ohio.gov/lookup/default.asp?division=95
Dental Hygienist #33 .... https://license.ohio.gov/lookup/default.asp?division=95
Dentist #33 .... https://license.ohio.gov/lookup/default.asp?division=95
Dialysis Technician #6........ www.nursing.ohio.gov/verification.stm
Dietitian #31 .... https://license.ohio.gov/lookup/default.asp?division=85
Drug Wholesaler/Distributor #7 .... http://pharmacy.ohio.gov/license.htm
Electrical Safety Inspector #3........ www.com.ohio.gov/dico/
Electrician #14........ www.com.state.oh.us/dic/lics/elicense.aspx
Elevator Inspection #3........ https://www.comapps.ohio.gov/dic/dico_apps/elev/elev_lookup/Default.aspx
Emergency Medical Tech. Instr. #22........ https://www.dps.state.oh.us/ems/cert.asp
Emergency Medical Technician #22 .... https://www.dps.state.oh.us/ems/cert.asp
Engineer #23 .... https://license.ohio.gov/lookup/default.asp?division=100
Engineering/Surveying Company #23........ https://license.ohio.gov/lookup/default.asp?division=100
Esthetician/Managing Esthetician #4 .... https://license.ohio.gov/lookup/default.asp
Fire Protection System Designer #3........ www.com.ohio.gov/dico/
Firefighter/Firefighter Instructor #22........ https://www.dps.state.oh.us/ems/cert.asp
Foreign Real Estate Property #15........ https://www.com.state.oh.us/real/elicense.aspx
Heating/Refrigeration (HVAC) #14........ www.com.state.oh.us/dic/lics/elicense.aspx
Hydronic-related Occupation #14........ www.com.state.oh.us/dic/lics/elicense.aspx
Insurance Agent #20 .... www.ohioinsurance.gov/ConsumServ/ocs/agentloc.asp
Landscape Architect #2........ https://license.ohio.gov/lookup/
Legislative Agent/Agent Employer #30 .... www.jlec-olig.state.oh.us/olig2/search_form.aspx
Liquor Distributor #27 .... www.com.ohio.gov/liqr/
Liquor License #27 .... www.com.ohio.gov/liqr/rpts/phone.txt
Liquor License Cancellation #27 .... www.com.ohio.gov/liqr/PermitsActive.aspx
Liquor Permit #27 .... www.com.ohio.gov/liqr/PermitsActive.aspx

Liquor Store #27	www.com.ohio.gov/liqr/rpts/phone.txt
Lobbyist List #30	www.jlec-olig.state.oh.us/AgentandEmployerLists.htm
Lobbyist/Lobbyist Employer #30	www.jlec-olig.state.oh.us/olig2/search_form.aspx
Manicuring/Esthetician Instructor #4	https://license.ohio.gov/lookup/default.asp
Manicurist/Managing Manicurist #4	https://license.ohio.gov/lookup/default.asp
Massage Therapist #28	https://license.ohio.gov/lookup/default.asp
Mechanotherapist #28	https://license.ohio.gov/lookup/default.asp
Medical Doctor #28	https://license.ohio.gov/lookup/default.asp
Midwife Nurse #6	www.nursing.ohio.gov/verification.stm
Milk Processor/Producer/Plant #12	www.ohioagriculture.gov/oda3/_Apps/Admn_License/Default.aspx
Mortgage Broker #17	http://elicense2-lookup.com.ohio.gov/
Naprapath #28	https://license.ohio.gov/lookup/default.asp
Notary Public #10	www.sos.state.oh.us/SOS/Notary/Search.aspx
Nurse Anesthetist #6	www.nursing.ohio.gov/verification.stm
Nurse Practitioner #6	www.nursing.ohio.gov/verification.stm
Nurse-RN/LPN #6	www.nursing.ohio.gov/verification.stm
Occupational Therapist/Assistant #29	https://license.ohio.gov/lookup/default.asp
Ocularist/Ocularist Apprentice #39	https://license.ohio.gov/lookup/default.asp
Optical Dispenser #39	https://license.ohio.gov/lookup/default.asp
Optician/Optician Apprentice #39	https://license.ohio.gov/lookup/default.asp
Optometrist #37	https://license.ohio.gov/lookup/default.asp?division=91
Optometrist, Diagnostic/Therapeutic #37	https://license.ohio.gov/lookup/default.asp?division=91
Osteopathic Physician #28	https://license.ohio.gov/lookup/default.asp
Pawnbroker #17	http://elicense2-lookup.com.ohio.gov/
Pesticide Applicator Business #40	www.ohioagriculture.gov/pubs/divs/plnt/plnt-licensing.stm
Pesticide Applicator/Operator #40	www.ohioagriculture.gov/pubs/divs/plnt/plnt-licensing.stm
Pesticide Dealer #40	www.ohioagriculture.gov/pubs/divs/plnt/plnt-licensing.stm
Pesticide Limited Comm' l Applicator #40	www.ohioagriculture.gov/pubs/divs/plnt/plnt-licensing.stm
Pesticide Private Applicator #40	www.ohioagriculture.gov/pubs/divs/plnt/plnt-licensing.stm
Pesticide Public Operator #40	www.ohioagriculture.gov/pubs/divs/plnt/plnt-licensing.stm
Pharmacist #7	http://pharmacy.ohio.gov/license.htm
Pharmacy/Pharmacy Dispensary #7	http://pharmacy.ohio.gov/license.htm
Physical Therapist/Assistant #29	https://license.ohio.gov/lookup/default.asp
Physician Assistant #28	https://license.ohio.gov/lookup/default.asp
Plumber #14	www.com.state.oh.us/dic/lics/elicense.aspx
Plumbing Inspector #3	https://www.comapps.ohio.gov/dic/dico_apps/bdcc/PlumbingInspectorCertification/
Podiatrist #28	https://license.ohio.gov/lookup/default.asp
Precious Metals Dealer #17	http://elicense2-lookup.com.ohio.gov/
Premium Finance Company #17	http://elicense2-lookup.com.ohio.gov/
Prescriptive Authority #6	www.nursing.ohio.gov/verification.stm
Pressure Piping Inspector #34	www.com.ohio.gov/dico/
Psychologist #36	https://license.ohio.gov/lookup/default.asp?division=83
Public Accountant-CPA #1	http://acc.ohio.gov/lookup.htm
Real Estate Agent/Seller #15	https://www.com.state.oh.us/real/elicense.aspx
Real Estate Appraiser #15	https://www.com.state.oh.us/real/elicense.aspx
Real Estate Broker #15	https://www.com.state.oh.us/real/elicense.aspx
Respiratory Therapist/Student #42	https://license.ohio.gov/lookup/default.asp
Savings & Loan Association #17	http://elicense2-lookup.com.ohio.gov/
Savings Bank #17	http://elicense2-lookup.com.ohio.gov/
School Psychologist #36	https://license.ohio.gov/lookup/default.asp?division=83
Securities Filing #16	https://www.comapps.ohio.gov/secu/secu_apps/offering/
Speech Pathologist/Audiologist #8	https://license.ohio.gov/lookup/default.asp
Sprinkler Equipment Inspector #34	www.com.ohio.gov/dico/
Sprinkler Inspector #3	www.com.ohio.gov/OnlineServices.aspx
Steam Engineer #34	www.com.state.oh.us/dic/scripts/boilerctrqy.htm
Storage Tank Corrective Action #34	https://www.com.state.oh.us/sfm/bustr/CorrectiveActions.htm
Surveyor, Land #23	https://license.ohio.gov/lookup/default.asp?division=100
Underground Storage Tank #34	https://www.com.state.oh.us/sfm/bustr/PublicInquiry.htm
Underground Tank Inspector #34	https://www.com.state.oh.us/sfm/bustr/PDFs/Data/WEBInspectorList
Underground Tank Installer #34	https://www.com.state.oh.us/sfm/bustr/PDFs/Data/WEBInstallerList
Underground Tank Instructor #34	https://www.com.state.oh.us/sfm/bustr/PDFs/TrainerApprovedlist.xls
Veterinarian/Veterinary Tech #45	https://license.ohio.gov/lookup/default.asp?division=88

Ohio Licensing Quick Finder

Accounting Firm #1	614-466-4135
Acupuncturist #28	614-466-3934
Adoption Agency #19	614-466-9274
Adult Care Home #18	614-466-7713
Airline Liquor Permit #27	614-644-2360
Anesthesiologist Assistant #28	614-466-3934
Architect #2	614-466-2316
Athlete Agent #32	330-797-2556
Athletic Trainer #29	614-466-3774
Attorney, Bar Assoc. by Type #13	800-282-6556
Attorney, State #44	614-387-9320
Audiologist/Audiologist Aide #8	614-466-3145
Backflow Prev. Assembly Insp. #34	614-644-2223
Bait Dealer/Whlse/Transporter #21	614-265-6300
Bank #17	614-728-8400
Barber/Barber Instructor/School #26	614-466-5003
Barber Shop #26	614-466-5003
Bedding/Furniture Dealer/Dist/Mfg #38	614-644-2233
Boiler Contr'r/Inspector/Operator #34	614-644-2223
Boxer/Boxing Professional/Event #32	330-797-2556
Building Inspector/Bldg Official #3	614-644-2613
Cemetery #15	216-787-3100
Check Cashing Service #17	614-728-8400
Check Lending Service #17	614-728-8400
Child Care Type A or B House #19	614-466-1043
Child Day Care Facility #19	614-466-1043
Children's Residential Center #19	614-466-1043
Children's Services Agency #19	614-466-1043
Chiropractor #9	614-644-7032
Clinical Nurse Specialist #6	614-466-3947
Coil Cleaner (Liquor/Beverage) #27	614-644-2360
Consumer Finance Company #17	614-728-8400
Contractor #14	614-644-3493
Cosmetic Therapist #28	614-466-3934
Cosmetologist/Mgmt'g Cosmet'g't #4	614-644-3834
Cosmetology Instructor #4	614-644-3834
Counselor #11	614-466-0912
Crematory #5	614-466-4252
Dairy Farm #12	614-466-5550
Day Camp, Children's #19	614-466-1043
Dental Assistant Radiologist #33	614-466-2580
Dental Hygienist #33	614-466-2580
Dentist #33	614-466-2580
Dialysis Technician #6	614-466-3947
Dietitian #31	614-466-3291
Drug Wholesaler/Distributor #7	614-466-4143
Electrical Safety Inspector #3	614-644-2613
Electrical Safety Trainee #3	614-644-2613
Electrician #14	614-644-3493
Elevator Inspection #3	614-644-3524
Elevator Inspector #38	614-644-3524
Embalmer/Embalming Facility #5	614-466-4252
Emergency Medical Technician #22	614-466-9447
Engineer #23	614-466-3650
Engineering/Surveying Company #23	614-466-3650
Esthetician/Managing Esthetician #4	614-644-3834
Explosives #34	614-752-7126
Family Foster Home #19	614-466-9274
Fire Alarm & Detection Inspector #34	614-644-7126
Fire Exting'r (Portable) Inspector #34	614-644-7126
Fire Extinguish'r Equip't Inspector #34	614-644-7126
Fire Protection System Designer #3	614-644-2613
Firefighter/Firefighter Instructor #22	614-466-9447
Fireworks Exhibitor/Assistant #34	614-752-7126
Foreign Real Estate Property #15	614-466-4100
Funeral Director /Home #5	614-466-4252
Group Home Operator #19	614-466-5392
Health Care Facility #18	614-466-7713
Hearing Aid Dealer/Fitter #25	614-466-5215
Heating/Refrigeration (HVAC) #14	614-644-3493
Horse Racing Facility/Owner #41	614-466-2757
Hotel/Motel #34	614-752-7126
Hydronic-related Occupation #14	614-644-3493
Ice Fishing Guide #21	614-265-6300
Independent Living Arranger #19	614-466-9274
Insurance Agent/Solicitor #20	614-644-2665
Insurance Broker, Non-Resident #20	614-644-2665
Investment Advisor/Advisor Rep. #16	614-644-3466
Landscape Architect #2	614-466-2316
Legislative Agent/Agent Employer #30	614-728-5100
Liquor Distributor #27	614-644-2360
Liquor License #27	614-644-2360
Liquor Permit/Store #27	614-644-2360
Lobbyist List #30	614-728-5100
Lobbyist/Lobbyist Employer #30	614-728-5100
Lottery Retailer #35	216-787-3200
Manicuring/Esthetician Instructor #4	614-644-3834
Manicurist/Managing Manicurist #4	614-644-3834
Marriage and Family Therapist #11	614-466-0912
Massage Therapist #28	614-466-3934
Mechanical Inspector #3	614-644-2613
Mechanotherapist #28	614-466-3934
Medical Doctor #28	614-466-3934
Midwife Nurse #6	614-466-3947
Milk Hauler #12	614-466-5550
Milk Processor/Producer/Plant #12	614-466-5550
Milk Tester/Sampler #12	614-466-5550
Mortgage Broker #17	614-728-8400
Naprapath #28	614-466-3934
Notary Public #10	By County
Nurse Anesthetist #6	614-466-3947
Nurse-RN/LPN/Practitioner #6	614-466-3947
Nursing Home /Home Administ'r #18	614-466-5114
Occupational Therapist/Assistant #29	614-466-3774
Ocularist/Ocularist Apprentice #39	614-466-9709
Optical Dispenser #39	614-466-9709
Optician/Optician Apprentice #39	614-466-9709
Optometrist #37	614-466-5115
Optometrist Diagnost'c/Therapeut'c #37	614-466-5115
Osteopathic Physician #28	614-466-3934
Pawnbroker #17	614-728-8400
Pesticide Applicator Business #40	614-728-6987
Pesticide Applicator/Operator #40	614-728-6987
Pesticide Dealer/Ap/Operator #40	614-728-6987
Pesticide Limited Comm' l Applic'r #40	614-728-6987
Pharmacist #7	614-466-4143
Pharmacy/Pharmacy Dispensary #7	614-466-4143
Physical Therapist/Assistant #29	614-466-3774
Physician Assistant #28	614-466-3934
Plan Examiner #3	614-644-2613
Plumber #14	614-644-3493
Plumbing Inspector #3	614-644-2613
Podiatrist #28	614-466-3934
Polygraph Examiner #46	740-845-2614
Precious Metals Dealer #17	614-728-8400
Premium Finance Company #17	614-466-2221
Prescriptive Authority #6	614-466-3947
Pressure Piping Inspector #34	614-644-2223
Psychologist #36	614-466-8808
Public Accountant-CPA #1	614-466-4135
Public Adjuster #20	614-644-2665
Racetrack-related Occupation #41	614-466-2757
Racing Permit #41	614-466-2757
Real Estate Agent/Seller #15	614-466-4100
Real Estate Appraiser #15	216-787-3100
Real Estate Broker #15	614-466-4100
Residential Care Facility #18	614-466-7713
Residential Parenting Org. #19	614-466-9274
Respiratory Therapist/Student #42	614-752-9218
Savings & Loan Association #17	614-728-8400
Savings Bank #17	614-728-8400
School Counselor #43	614-466-3593
School Principal/Administrator #43	614-466-3593
School Psychologist #36	614-466-8808
School Treasurer/Business Mgr. #43	614-466-3593
Scientific Collector #21	614-265-6320
Securities Filing #16	614-644-3466
Securities Salesperson/Dealer #16	614-644-3466
Social Worker #11	614-466-0912
Solid Waste Facility Operator #24	614-644-2621
Speech Pathologist Aide #8	614-466-3145
Speech Pathologist/Audiologist #8	614-466-3145
Sprinkler Equipment Inspector #34	614-644-7126
Sprinkler Inspector #3	614-644-2613
Sprinkler/Fire Alarm/Hazard's Design'r #3	614-644-2613
Steam Engineer #34	614-644-2223
Steam, Stationary #34	614-644-2223
Storage Tank Corrective Action #34	614-752-7921
Surveyor, Land #23	614-466-3650
Teacher/Teacher's Aide #43	614-466-3593
Tough-Person Promoter #32	330-797-2556
Tour Promoter #34	614-644-2223
Travel Agent #34	614-644-2223
Underground Storage Tank #34	614-752-7938
Underground Tank Inspect/Install #34	614-752-7921
Veterinarian/Veterinary Tech #45	614-644-5281
Water Supply Equipment Inspect'r #34	614-644-2223

Ohio Licensing Agency Information

#1 Accountancy Board, 77 S High St, 18th Fl, Columbus, OH 43215-6128; 614-466-4135, Fax- 614-466-2628. Hours- 7:30AM-5PM. http://acc.ohio.gov Search data at- http://acc.ohio.gov/lookup.htm

#2 Architects Board, 77 S High St, 16th Fl, Columbus, OH 43215-6108; 614-466-2316, Fax- 614-644-9048. www.arc.ohio.gov Search data at- https://license.ohio.gov/lookup/

#3 Department of Commerce, Board of Building Standards, 6606 Tussing Rd (PO Box 4009), Reynoldsburg, OH 43068-9009; 614-644-2613, Fax- 614-644-3147. 7:30AM-5PM. www.com.state.oh.us/dic/dicbbs.htm Search data at- www.com.ohio.gov/dico/

#4 Board of Cosmetology, 1929 Gateway Cir, Grove City, OH 43123; 614-466-3834, Fax- 614-466-6880. http://cos.ohio.gov Search data at- https://license.ohio.gov/lookup/default.asp

#5 Board of Embalmers & Funeral Directors of Ohio, 77 S High St, 16th Fl, Columbus, OH 43215-6108; 614-466-4252, Fax- 614-728-6825. http://funeral.ohio.gov Search data at- https://license.ohio.gov/lookup/default.asp

#6 Board of Nursing, 17 S High St, #400, Columbus, OH 43215-7410; 614-466-3947, Fax- 614-466-0388. Hours- 7:30PM-4:30PM. www.nursing.ohio.gov Search data at- www.nursing.ohio.gov/verification.stm Must search by license number or SSN. Prescriptive authority needs name or COA#.

#7 Board of Pharmacy, 77 S High St, Rm 1702, Columbus, OH 43266-0320; 614-466-4143, Fax- 614-752-4836. http://pharmacy.ohio.gov Search at- http://pharmacy.ohio.gov/license.htm

#8 Board of Speech Pathology & Audiology, 77 S High St, 16th Fl, Columbus, OH 43215; 614-466-3145, Fax- 614-995-2286. Hours- 8AM-5PM. www.slpaud.ohio.gov Search data at- https://license.ohio.gov/lookup/default.asp

#9 Chiropractic Board, 77 S High St, 16th Fl, Columbus, OH 43215-6108; 614-644-7032, Fax- 614-752-2539. Hours- 7AM-4PM. http://chirobd.ohio.gov Search data- https://license.ohio.gov/lookup/default.asp?division=90

#10 Commission Clerk, 180 E Broad St, #103, Columbus, OH 43215; By County. www.sos.state.oh.us/SOS/Notary/new.aspx

#11 Counselor & Social Worker Board, 50 W Broad St #1075, Columbus, OH 43215-5919; 614-466-0912, Fax- 614-728-7790. http://cswmft.ohio.gov Search data at- http://cswmft.ohio.gov/ethics.stm

#12 Department of Agriculture, 8995 E Main St, Reynoldsburg, OH 43068-3399; 614-466-5550, Fax- 614-728-2652. www.ohioagriculture.gov/dairy/ Search data at- www.ohioagriculture.gov/oda3/_Apps/Admn_License/Default.aspx

#13 State Bar Association, 1700 Lake Shore Dr (PO Box 16562), Columbus, OH 43204; 800-282-6556, 614-487-2050, Fax- 614-487-1008. www.ohiobar.org/

#14 Department of Commerce, Div of Industrial Compliance, Construction Industry Examination Board, PO Box 4009 (6606 Tussing Rd), Reynoldsburg, OH 43068-9009; 614-644-2223, Fax- 614-644-2618. 7:30AM-5PPM. www.com.ohio.gov/dico/ Search data at- www.com.state.oh.us/dic/lics/elicense.aspx

#15 Department of Commerce, Division of Real Estate & Professional Licensing, 77 S High St, 20th Fl, Columbus, OH 43215-6133; 614-466-4100, Fax- 614-644-0584. www.com.ohio.gov/real/ Search data at- https://www.com.state.oh.us/real/elicense.aspx

#16 Department of Commerce, Division of Securities, 77 S High St, 22nd Fl, Columbus, OH 43215-0548; 614-644-7381, Fax- 614-466-3316. www.com.ohio.gov/secu/

#17 Department of Commerce, Division of Financial Institutions, 77 S High St, 21st Fl, Columbus, OH 43215-6120; 614-728-8400, Fax- 614-466-1631. www.com.ohio.gov/fiin/ Search data at- http://elicense2-lookup.com.ohio.gov

#18 Department of Health, Health Care Facility Program, PO Box 118 (246 N High St 1st Fl), Columbus, OH 43215; 614-466-5114, Fax- 614-466-0271. www.ohiobenha.org

#19 Office For Children & Families, Bureau of Family Svcs, 255 E Main, 3rd Fl, Columbus, OH 43215-5222; 614-466-9274, Fax- 614-728-6726. http://jfs.ohio.gov/ocf/

#20 Department of Insurance, 50 W Town St, #300, Columbus, OH 43215-1067; 614-644-2658, Fax- 614-644-3743. www.ohioinsurance.gov Search at- www.ohioinsurance.gov/ConsumServ/ocs/agentloc.asp

#21 Department of Natural Resources, 2045 Morse Rd, Bldg G, Columbus, OH 43229; 800-945-3543, 614-265-6300, Fax- 614-262-1143. www.dnr.state.oh.us/

#22 Department of Public Safety, Emergency Medical Services Division, PO Box 182073 (1970 W Broad St), Columbus, OH 43218-2073; 614-466-9447, Fax- 614-351-6006. http://ems.ohio.gov Search data at- https://www.dps.state.oh.us/ems/cert.asp

#23 Engineers & Surveyors Board, 50 W Broad St #1820, Columbus, OH 43215-5905; 614-466-3651, Fax- 614-728-3059. www.ohiopeps.org Search data at- https://license.ohio.gov/lookup/default.asp?division=100

#24 Hazardous Waste Facility Board, 50 W Town St #700, Columbus, OH 43215; 614-644-2621, Fax- 614-644-3439. www.epa.state.oh.us/dsiwm/

#25 Hearing Aid Dealers & Fitters Board, 246 N High St, Columbus, OH 43215; 614-466-5215, Fax- 614-466-8692. 7:45AM-4:30PM. www.odh.ohio.gov/odhprograms/dspc/hdlr/hdamain1.aspx

#26 Licensing Boards, Barber Board, 77 S High St, 16th Fl, Columbus, OH 43215-6108; 614-466-5003, Fax- 614-387-1694. http://barber.ohio.gov Search at- https://license.ohio.gov/lookup/default.asp?division=87

#27 Division of Liquor Control, 6606 Tussing Rd, Reynoldsburg, OH 43068-9005; 614-644-2360, Fax- 614-644-2480. Hours- 8AM-5PM. www.com.ohio.gov/liqr/

#28 Medical Board, 30 E Broad St, 3rd Fl, Columbus, OH 43215-6127; 614-466-3934, Fax- 614-728-5946. www.med.ohio.gov Search at- https://license.ohio.gov/lookup/default.asp

#29 OTPTAT - Occupational Therapy - Physical Therapy Board, 77 S High St, 16th Fl, Columbus, OH 43215-6108; 614-466-3774, Fax- 614-995-0816. Hours- 8AM-4:30PM. http://otptat.ohio.gov Search data at- https://license.ohio.gov/lookup/default.asp

#30 Office of Legislative Inspector General, 50 W Broad St, #1308, Columbus, OH 43215-5908; 614-728-5100, Fax- 614-728-5074. www.jlec-olig.state.oh.us Search at- www.jlec-olig.state.oh.us/olig2/search_form.aspx

#31 Board of Dietetics, 77 S High St, 18th Fl, Columbus, OH 43215; 614-466-3291, Fax- 614-728-0723. Hours- 8AM-5PM. www.dietetics.ohio.gov

#32 Athletic Commission, 242 Federal Plaza West, #405, Youngstown, OH 44503; 330-797-2556, Fax- 330-797-2559. Hours- 8AM-4PM. www.aco.ohio.gov/home.htm

#33 Dental Board, 77 S High St, 18th Fl, Riffe Ctr, Columbus, OH 43215-6135; 614-466-2580, Fax- 614-752-8995. Hours- 7:30AM-4:30PM. www.dental.ohio.gov Search data at- https://license.ohio.gov/lookup/default.asp?division=95

#34 Department of Commerce, Div of Industrial Compliance, Testing and Registration, PO Box 4009 (6606 Tussing Rd), Reynoldsburg, OH 43068-9009; 614-644-2223, Fax- 614-644-2618. www.com.ohio.gov/dico/ Search data at- www.com.ohio.gov/dico/

#35 Lottery Commission, 615 W Superior Ave, NW Frank J. Lausche Bldg, Cleveland, OH 44113; 216-787-3200, Fax- 216-787-3718. www.ohiolottery.com

#36 State Board of Psychology, 77 S High St, #1830, Columbus, OH 43215-6108; 614-466-8808, Fax- 614-728-7081. Hours- 8AM-4:30PM. http://psychology.ohio.gov A disc listing all licensed psychologists is $2.00 payable by check or money order to Treasurer, State of Ohio, but mailed to the board address.

#37 Board of Optometry, 77 S High St, 16th Fl, Columbus, OH 43215-6108; 614-466-5115, Fax- 614-644-3937. Hours- 7:45AM-4:30PM. www.optometry.ohio.gov Search data at- https://license.ohio.gov/lookup/default.asp?division=91 Will sell rosters and labels on disk.

#38 Industrial Compliance Division; Operations & Maintenance, Department of Commerce, PO Box 4009 (6606 Tussing Rd), Reynoldsburg, OH 43068-9009; 614-644-3964, Fax- 614-644-8658. https://www.com.state.oh.us/dic/dicbedding.htm Includes the Bedding, Stuffed Toys & Upholstered Furniture Div.

#39 Optical Dispensers Board, 77 S High St, 16th Fl, Columbus, OH 43215-6108; 614-466-9709, Fax- 614-995-5392. Hours- 8AM-5PM. www.optical.ohio.gov Search data at- https://license.ohio.gov/lookup/default.asp

#40 Department of Agriculture, Pesticide Regulations, 8995 E Main St, Reynoldsburg, OH 43068-3399; 614-728-6987, Fax- 614-728-4235. www.ohioagriculture.gov/pesticides/ Search data at- www.ohioagriculture.gov/pubs/divs/plnt/plnt-licensing.stm

#41 Racing Commission, 77 S High St, 18th Fl, Columbus, OH 43215-6108; 614-466-2757, Fax- 614-466-1900. http://racing.ohio.gov

#42 Respiratory Care Board, 77 S High St, 16th Fl, Columbus, OH 43215-6108; 614-752-9218, Fax- 614-728-8691. http://respiratorycare.ohio.gov Search data at- https://license.ohio.gov/lookup/default.asp

#43 Department of Education, Office of Certification/Licensure, 25 S Front St, Columbus, OH 43215-4183; 614-466-3593, Fax- 614-466-1999. www.ode.state.oh.us/gd/gd.aspx

#44 Supreme Court, Attorney Registration Section, 65 S Front St, 5th Fl, Columbus, OH 43215-3431; 614-387-9320, Fax- 614-387-9323. www.sconet.state.oh.us/Atty_Reg/ Search data at- www.sconet.state.oh.us/atty_reg/Public_AttorneyInformation.asp

#45 Veterinary Medical Board, 77 S High St, 16th Fl, Columbus, OH 43215-6108; 614-644-5281, Fax- 614-644-9038. www.ovmlb.ohio.gov Search at- https://license.ohio.gov/lookup/default.asp?division=88

#46 Association of Polygraph Examiners, PO Box 365, London, OH 43140; 740-845-2614, Fax- 614-781-0257. www.ohiopolygraph.org

Ohio Federal Courts

The following list indicates the district and division name for each county in the state. If the bankruptcy court location is different from the district court, then the location of the bankruptcy court appears in parentheses.

Ohio County/Court Cross Reference

County	District	Division
Adams	Southern	Cincinnati
Allen	Northern	Toledo
Ashland	Northern	Cleveland (Canton)
Ashtabula	Northern	Cleveland (Youngstown)
Athens	Southern	Columbus
Auglaize	Northern	Toledo
Belmont	Southern	Columbus
Brown	Southern	Cincinnati
Butler	Southern	Cincinnati (Dayton)
Carroll	Northern	Akron (Canton)
Champaign	Southern	Dayton
Clark	Southern	Dayton
Clermont	Southern	Cincinnati
Clinton	Southern	Cincinnati (Dayton)
Columbiana	Northern	Youngstown
Coshocton	Southern	Columbus
Crawford	Northern	Cleveland (Canton)
Cuyahoga	Northern	Cleveland
Darke	Southern	Dayton
Defiance	Northern	Toledo
Delaware	Southern	Columbus
Erie	Northern	Toledo
Fairfield	Southern	Columbus
Fayette	Southern	Columbus
Franklin	Southern	Columbus
Fulton	Northern	Toledo
Gallia	Southern	Columbus
Geauga	Northern	Cleveland
Greene	Southern	Dayton
Guernsey	Southern	Columbus
Hamilton	Southern	Cincinnati
Hancock	Northern	Toledo
Hardin	Northern	Toledo
Harrison	Southern	Columbus
Henry	Northern	Toledo
Highland	Southern	Cincinnati
Hocking	Southern	Columbus
Holmes	Northern	Akron (Canton)
Huron	Northern	Toledo
Jackson	Southern	Columbus
Jefferson	Southern	Columbus
Knox	Southern	Columbus
Lake	Northern	Cleveland
Lawrence	Southern	Cincinnati
Licking	Southern	Columbus
Logan	Southern	Columbus
Lorain	Northern	Cleveland
Lucas	Northern	Toledo
Madison	Southern	Columbus
Mahoning	Northern	Youngstown
Marion	Northern	Toledo
Medina	Northern	Cleveland (Akron)
Meigs	Southern	Columbus
Mercer	Northern	Toledo
Miami	Southern	Dayton
Monroe	Southern	Columbus
Montgomery	Southern	Dayton
Morgan	Southern	Columbus
Morrow	Southern	Columbus
Muskingum	Southern	Columbus
Noble	Southern	Columbus
Ottawa	Northern	Toledo
Paulding	Northern	Toledo
Perry	Southern	Columbus
Pickaway	Southern	Columbus
Pike	Southern	Columbus
Portage	Northern	Akron
Preble	Southern	Dayton
Putnam	Northern	Toledo
Richland	Northern	Cleveland (Canton)
Ross	Southern	Columbus
Sandusky	Northern	Toledo
Scioto	Southern	Cincinnati
Seneca	Northern	Toledo
Shelby	Southern	Dayton
Stark	Northern	Akron (Canton)
Summit	Northern	Akron
Trumbull	Northern	Youngstown
Tuscarawas	Northern	Akron (Canton)
Union	Southern	Columbus
Van Wert	Northern	Toledo
Vinton	Southern	Columbus
Warren	Southern	Cincinnati (Dayton)
Washington	Southern	Columbus
Wayne	Northern	Akron (Canton)
Williams	Northern	Toledo
Wood	Northern	Toledo
Wyandot	Northern	Toledo

Standards for Federal Courts: Fees are standard unless noted in profile. Search fee is $26.00 per item (one party name or case number). Copy fee is $.50 per page. Certification fee is $9.00 per document, double for exemplification, if available. Most courts require prepayment. Mail requests should enclose a SASE unless otherwise noted. Before releasing records, all courts require prepayment, unless noted.

District courts index by defendant and plaintiff and by case number. Bankruptcy courts usually index by debtor and case number. While most courts now have their indexes on computer, many may still maintain index card files as well. Courts will archive closed case files at different times.

There are numerous public access programs available to online subscribers. Search the U.S. Party/Case Index to find party names and case numbers among all courts. Individual case data is provided on PACER. A search of CM/ECF provides copies of cases filed electronically. For details about PACER, the US Party/Case Index, and CM/ECF see the Appendix or go to http://pacer.psc.uscourts.gov or call 800-676-6856.

US District Court Ohio Northern District

Akron Division Court Clerk, 568 US Courthouse, 2 S Main St, Akron, OH 44308, 330-252-6000. 9-4PM. www.ohnd.uscourts.gov

Counties/Note: Carroll, Holmes, Portage, Stark, Summit, Tuscarawas, Wayne. Northern District is on a central draw system- a case may be assigned Akron or at Cleveland or Youngstown. Cases prior to 1995 for counties in the Youngstown Division may be located at Akron.

Searches/Indexing: Include full name in search request. Results include full name and case number only. Will not fax back documents. New cases are in the index immediately after filing date. Open cases may be located in other district divisions depending on the judge assigned. Case files sent to archives 5 years after closed.

Search Access: Only docket info is available by phone. **Mail:** Search usually completed- 1-2 days. Include SASE for return. **In person:** Public terminals available. Self-serve copies from computer- $.10 each.

Payment: Pay by Visa/MC, money order, cashier's or personal check. Payee: Clerk, US District Court.

E-Services: PACER records go back to 1/1990. Many cases prior to the indicated dates are also online. ECF at https://ecf.ohnd.uscourts.gov. Read Notable Cases at www.ohnd.uscourts.gov/Clerk_s_Office/Notable_Cases/index.html. **Note:** Make copy requests at www.ohnd.uscourts.gov/Clerk_s_Office/Copy_Request/copy_request.html. Access judge's calendars via link at main website.

Cleveland Division Court Clerk, 801 W Superior Ave, Cleveland, OH 44114-1830, 216-357-7000; records- 216-357-7040; Fax- 216-357-7040. 9AM-4PM. www.ohnd.uscourts.gov

Counties/Note: Ashland, Ashtabula, Crawford, Cuyahoga, Geauga, Lake, Lorain, Medina, Richland. Cases prior to 7/1995 for the counties of Ashland, Crawford, Medina and Richland are located in the Akron Division. Cases filed prior to 1995 from the counties in the Youngstown Div. may be located at Cleveland. Northern District is on a central draw system. Rarely a case may be located to Youngstown or Akron Divisions.

Searches/Indexing: Include full name in search request. Results do not include SSN or DOB. Will not fax back documents. New cases are in the index immediately after filing date. Open cases may be located in other district divisions depending on the judge assigned. Case files sent to archives 5 years after closed.

Search Access: Only docket info is available by phone. **Mail:** Search usually completed- 1-2 days. SASE not required. **In person:** 4 public terminals available. Copies printed off computer- $.10 each.

Payment: Pay by Visa/MC/AmEx/Discover, money order, cashier's or personal check. Payee: Clerk, US District Court.

E-Services: PACER records go back to 1/1990. Many cases prior to the indicated dates are also online. New records online after 1 day. ECF at https://ecf.ohnd.uscourts.gov. Read Notable Cases www.ohnd.uscourts.gov/Clerk_s_Office/Notable_Cases/index.html. **Note:** Make copy requests at www.ohnd.uscourts.gov/Clerk_s_Office/Copy_Request/copy_request.html. Access judge's calendars via link at main website.

Toledo Division Court Clerk, 114 US Courthouse, 1716 Spielbusch Ave, Toledo, OH 43624, 419-213-5500. Hours- 9AM-4PM. www.ohnd.uscourts.gov

Counties/Note: Allen, Auglaize, Defiance, Erie, Fulton, Hancock, Hardin, Henry, Huron, Lucas, Marion, Mercer, Ottawa, Paulding, Putnam, Sandusky, Seneca, Van Wert, Williams, Wood, Wyandot. This is known as the Western Division of the Northern District.

Searches/Indexing: Include full name in search request. Results may include last 4 SSN digits, also birth year. Will not fax back documents. New cases are in the index immediately after filing date. Computer index maintained back to 1990. Open cases may be located in other district divisions depending on the judge assigned. Case files sent to archives 5 years after closed.

Search Access: Only docket info is available by phone. **Mail:** Search usually completed- 1-2 days. Include SASE for return. **In person:** Public terminals available. No self-serve copier.

Payment: Pay by Visa/MC, money order, cashier's or personal check. Payee: Clerk, US District Court.

E-Services: PACER records go back to 1/1990. Many cases prior to the indicated dates are also online. New records online after 24 hours. ECF at https://ecf.ohnd.uscourts.gov. Read Notable Cases www.ohnd.uscourts.gov/Clerk_s_Office/Notable_Cases/index.html. **Note:** Make copy requests at www.ohnd.uscourts.gov/Clerk_s_Office/Copy_Request/copy_request.html. Access judge's calendars via link at main website.

Youngstown Division Court Clerk, 337 Federal Bldg, 125 Market St, Youngstown, OH 44503-1780, 330-884-7400. Hours- 9AM-4PM. www.ohnd.uscourts.gov

Counties: Columbiana, Mahoning, Trumbull.

This division was re-activated in the middle of 1995. Older cases will be found in Akron or Cleveland. Northern District is on a central draw system- a case may be assigned to Youngstown or Cleveland or Akron.

Searches/Indexing: Include full name in search request. Results do not include SSN or DOB. Will not fax back documents. New cases are in the index immediately after filing date. Computer index maintained back to 1991. Open cases may be located in other district divisions depending on the judge assigned. Case files sent to archives 5 years after closed.

Search Access: Only docket info is available by phone. **Mail:** Search usually completed- 2-3 days. Include SASE for return. **Fax:** Fax search requests accepted, if prepaid. **In person:** Public terminals available. No self-serve copier.

Payment: Pay by Visa/MC/AmEx/Discover, money order, cashier's or personal check. Payee: Clerk, US District Court.

E-Services: PACER records go back to 1/1990. Many cases prior to the indicated dates are also online. ECF at https://ecf.ohnd.uscourts.gov. Read Notable Cases at www.ohnd.uscourts.gov/Clerk_s_Office/Notable_Cases/index.html. **Online Note:** Make copy requests at www.ohnd.uscourts.gov/Clerk_s_Office/Copy_Request/copy_request.html. Access judge's calendars via link at main website.

US Bankruptcy Court Ohio Northern District

Akron Division Court Clerk, 455 US Courthouse, 2 S Main St, Akron, OH 44308, 330-252-6100; records- 330-252-5145; Fax- 330-252-6115. 9AM-4PM. www.ohnb.uscourts.gov

Counties: Medina, Portage, Summit.

Searches/Indexing: Include SSN in search request. Results include SSN. Will not fax back documents. New cases are in the index 1-2 days after filing date. Both computer and card indexes maintained. Prior to 1995, closed cases sent to Chicago Records Center; case records now sent to Dayton Records Ctr every few years.

Search Access: Voice Case Information Service available, call VCIS at 800-898-6899. **Mail:** Search usually completed- 1-7 days. Include SASE for return. **In person:** 2 public terminals available. Self-serve copies $.25 each.

Payment: Pay by Visa/MC, money order, cashier's, personal, or business check. No debtor checks accepted. Payee: Clerk, US Bankruptcy Ct.

E-Services: PACER records go back to 1/1985. New records online after 1 day. ECF at https://ecf.ohnb.uscourts.gov. **Opinions Online:** www.ohnb.uscourts.gov. These judges' postings include calendars and opinions.

Canton Division Court Clerk, Frank T Bow Federal Bldg, 201 Cleveland Ave SW, Canton, OH 44702, 330-458-2120; Fax- 330-458-2451. Hours-9AM-4PM. www.ohnb.uscourts.gov

Counties: Ashland, Carroll, Crawford, Holmes, Richland, Stark, Tuscarawas, Wayne.

Searches/Indexing: Include SSN in search request. Results include last 4 SSN digits. Will not fax back documents. New cases are in the index 48 hours after filing date. Computer index back to 1990 maintained, Indexed on cards 1982-1989; journalized in books 1984-1990. Pre-1995, closed cases sent to Chicago Records Center; case records now sent to Dayton Records Ctr every few years.

Search Access: Voice Case Information Service available, call VCIS at 800-898-6899. **Mail:** Search usually completed- 1-7 days. Include SASE for return. **Fax:** Fax search requests accepted, prepaid. **In person:** 2 public terminals available. Self-serve copies $.25 each.

Payment: Pay by Visa/MC, money order, cashier's, personal, or business check. No debtor checks accepted. Payee: Clerk, US Bankruptcy Ct.

E-Services: PACER records go back to 6/1990. New records online after 1 day. ECF at https://ecf.ohnb.uscourts.gov. **Opinions Online:** www.ohnb.uscourts.gov. These judges' postings include calendars and opinions.

Cleveland Division Court Clerk, 201 Superior Ave, E, Cleveland, OH 44114-1233, 216-615-4300; Fax- 216-615-4363. Hours-9AM-4PM. www.ohnb.uscourts.gov

Counties: Cuyahoga, Geauga, Lake, Lorain.

Searches/Indexing: Include SSN in search request. Results include SSN. Will not fax back documents. New cases are in the index immediately after filing date. Computer, microfiche and card indexes maintained. Closed cases maintained electronically, available indefinitely, but prior to 1995, closed cases sent to Chicago Records Center; case records now sent to Dayton Records Center.

Search Access: Voice Case Information Service available, call VCIS at 800-898-6899. **Mail:** Search usually completed- 1 week. Include SASE for return. **Fax:** Fax search requests accepted, prepaid. **In person:** 4 public terminals available. No self-serve copier. Outside copy service available.

Payment: Pay by Visa/MC, money order, cashier's, personal or business check. No debtor checks accepted. Payee: Clerk, US Bankruptcy Ct.

E-Services: PACER records go back to 1/1985. New records online immediately. ECF at https://ecf.ohnb.uscourts.gov. **Opinions Online:** www.ohnb.uscourts.gov. These judges' postings include calendars and opinions.

Toledo Division Court Clerk, 411 US Courthouse and Custom House, 1716 Spielbusch Ave, Toledo, OH 43604, 419-213-5600; Fax- 419-213-5647. Hours- 9AM-4PM. www.ohnb.uscourts.gov

Counties: Allen, Auglaize, Defiance, Erie, Fulton, Hancock, Hardin, Henry, Huron, Lucas, Marion, Mercer, Ottawa, Paulding, Putnam, Sandusky, Seneca, Van Wert, Williams, Wood, Wyandot.

Searches/Indexing: Include SSN in search request. Results include SSN. Will not fax back documents. New cases are in the index 1-2 days after filing date. Prior to 1995, closed cases sent to Chicago Records Center; case records now sent to Dayton Records Ctr every few years.

Search Access: Voice Case Information Service available, call VCIS at 800-898-6899. **Mail:** Search usually completed- 2 days. Include SASE for return. **Fax:** Fax search requests accepted, prepaid. **In person:** Public terminals available. No self-serve copier.

Payment: Pay by Visa/MC, money order, cashier's, personal, or business check. No debtor checks accepted. Payee: Clerk, US Bankruptcy Ct.

E-Services: PACER records go back to 1/1985. New records online after 1 day. ECF at https://ecf.ohnb.uscourts.gov. **Opinions Online:** www.ohnb.uscourts.gov. These judges' postings include calendars and opinions.

Youngstown Division Court Clerk, Federal Bldg and US Courthouse, 10 E Commerce St, Youngstown, OH 44503-1621, 330-742-0900; Fax- 330-742-0902. Hours- 9AM - 4PM. www.ohnb.uscourts.gov

Counties: Ashtabula, Columbiana, Mahoning, Trumbull.

Searches/Indexing: Include SSN in search request. Results include last 4 SSN digits. Will not fax back documents. New cases are in the index 24 hours after filing date. A card index is maintained. Prior to 1995, closed cases sent to Chicago Records Center; case records now sent to Dayton Records Ctr every few years.

Search Access: Voice Case Information Service available, call VCIS at 800-898-6899. **Mail:** Search usually completed- 2 days. SASE not required. **In person:** 3 public terminals available. No self-serve copier.

Payment: Pay by Visa/MC, money order, cashier's check, business check. No debtor checks accepted. Payee: Clerk, US Bankruptcy Court.

E-Services: PACER records go back to 1/1985. New records online after 1 day. ECF at https://ecf.ohnb.uscourts.gov. **Opinions Online:** www.ohnb.uscourts.gov. These judges' postings include calendars and opinions.

US District Court Ohio Southern District

Cincinnati Div. Court Clerk, Potter Stewart Courthouse Rm 103, 100 E 5th St, Cincinnati, OH 45202, 513-564-7500; Fax- 513-564-7505. Hours-9AM-4PM. www.ohsd.uscourts.gov

Counties: Adams, Brown, Butler, Clermont, Clinton, Hamilton, Highland, Lawrence, Scioto, Warren .

Searches/Indexing: Include full name in search request. Results do not include SSN or DOB. Will not fax back documents. New cases are in the index 1 day after filing date. Computer index maintained back to 1970. Closed cases sent to archives after 5 years.

Search Access: Only docket info is available by phone. **Mail:** Search usually completed- 3-4 working days. Include SASE for return. **In person:** 4 public terminals available. No self-serve copier.

Payment: Pay by Visa/MC/Discover/AmEx (in person only), money order, cashier's check, business check. No personal checks. Payee: Clerk, US District Court. Give FedEx account number for expedited copy delivery.

E-Services: PACER records go back to 1994. New records online after 1 day. ECF at https://ecf.ohsd.uscourts.gov. **Opinions Online:** www.ohsd.uscourts.gov/opinions.htm.

Columbus Division Court Clerk, Office of the Clerk, Rm 260, 85 Marconi Blvd, Columbus, OH 43215, 614-719-3000; Fax- 614-719-3005. Hours-9AM-4PM. www.ohsd.uscourts.gov

Counties/Note: Athens, Belmont, Coshocton, Delaware, Fairfield, Fayette, Franklin, Gallia, Guernsey, Harrison, Hocking, Jackson, Jefferson, Knox, Licking, Logan, Madison, Meigs, Monroe, Morgan, Morrow, Muskingum, Noble, Perry, Pickaway, Pike, Ross, Union, Vinton, Washington.

Searches/Indexing: Include full name in search request. Results do not include SSN or DOB. Will not fax back documents. New cases are in the index 1-2 days after filing date. Computer, microfiche and card indexes maintained; Microfiche index goes back to 1982. District-wide searches available here. Closed cases sent to archives after 5 years.

Search Access: Only docket info is available by phone. **Mail:** Search usually completed- 1-2 days. Include SASE for return. **In person:** 2 public terminals available. No self-serve copier.

Payment: Pay by Visa/MC/Discover/AmEx (in person only), money order, cashier's check, business check. No personal checks. Payee: Clerk, US District Court.

E-Services: PACER records go back to 1994. New records online after 1 day. ECF at https://ecf.ohsd.uscourts.gov. **Opinions Online:** www.ohsd.uscourts.gov/opinions.htm.

Dayton Division Court Clerk Office, 200 W 2nd, Federal Bldg, Rm 712, Dayton, OH 45402, 937-512-1400. 9-4PM. www.ohsd.uscourts.gov

Counties: Champaign, Clark, Darke, Greene, Miami, Montgomery, Preble, Shelby.

Searches/Indexing: Include full name in search request. Results do not include SSN or DOB. Will not fax back documents. New cases are in the index 1 day after filing date. Computer, microfiche and card indexes maintained. Computer has only open and pending cases back to 1/90. Public can use a view box for cases filed present-day. Closed cases sent to archives after 5 years.

Search Access: By phone, court only reveals whether a case has been filed. Court does not respond to phone requests involving copy work. **Mail:** Search usually completed- 1-2 days. Include SASE for return. **In person:** 2 public terminals available. No self-serve copier.

Payment: Pay by Visa/MC/Discover/AmEx (in person only), money order, cashier's check, business check. No personal checks. Payee: Clerk, US District Court. Provide a wide envelope for return of documents.

E-Services: PACER records go back to 1994. New records online after 1 day. ECF at https://ecf.ohsd.uscourts.gov. **Opinions Online:** www.ohsd.uscourts.gov/opinions.htm.

US Bankruptcy Court Ohio Southern District

Cincinnati Division Court Clerk, 221 E Fourth St, Atrium Two, Rm 800, Cincinnati, OH 45202, 513-684-2572. Hours- 9AM-4PM. www.ohsb.uscourts.gov

Counties/Note: Adams, Brown, Butler, Clermont, Hamilton, Highland, Lawrence, Scioto and part of Butler.

Searches/Indexing: Include debtor name in search request. Results include last 4 SSN digits. Will fax back documents for fee. New cases are in the index 1 day after filing date. Case files sent to archives 6 months after closed.

Search Access: Only docket info is available by phone. Voice Case Information Service available, call VCIS at 800-726-1004. **Mail:** Search usually completed- 1-2 days. Include SASE for return. **In person:** 3 public terminals available. No self-serve copier.

Payment: Pay by Visa/MC (law firms only), money order, cashier's check, business check. No personal or debtor checks. Payee: Clerk, US Bankruptcy Court.

E-Services: PACER records go back to 1990. New records online after 1 day. ECF at https://ecf.ohsb.uscourts.gov. **Opinions Online:** www.ohsb.uscourts.gov/OHSB/OpNet/search.aspx **Online Note:** PDF lists of judges' current schedules free at www.ohsb.uscourts.gov/OHSB/hsnet/hearingschedulejudges.aspx.

Columbus Division Court Clerk, 170 N High St, Columbus, OH 43215, 614-469-6638. Hours-9AM-4PM. www.ohsb.uscourts.gov

Counties/Note: Athens, Belmont, Coshocton, Delaware, Fairfield, Fayette, Franklin, Gallia, Guernsey, Harrison, Hocking, Jackson, Jefferson, Knox, Licking, Logan, Madison, Meigs, Monroe, Morgan, Morrow, Muskingum, Noble, Perry, Pickaway, Pike, Ross, Union, Vinton, Washington. Has satellite hearing offices in Zanesville and in St. Clairesville.

Searches/Indexing: Include debtor name in search request. Results include last 4 SSN digits. Will fax back documents for fee. New cases are in the index 1 day after filing date. Case files sent to archives 6 months after closed.

Search Access: Only docket info is available by phone. Voice Case Information Service available, call VCIS at 800-726-1006 or 937-225-2562. **Mail:** Search usually completed- 1-2 days. SASE not required. **In person:** 2 public terminals available. No self-serve copier. Court also offers on-site copy service to provide copies, fee does not exceed $.50 per page.

Payment: Pay by Visa/MC (law firms only), money order, cashier's check, business check. No personal or debtor checks. Payee: Clerk, US Bankruptcy Court.

E-Services: PACER records go back to 1990. New records online after 1 day. ECF at https://ecf.ohsb.uscourts.gov. **Opinions Online:** www.ohsb.uscourts.gov/OHSB/OpNet/search.aspx **Online Note:** PDF lists of judges' current schedules free at www.ohsb.uscourts.gov/OHSB/hsnet/hearingschedulejudges.aspx.

Dayton Div. Court Clerk, 120 W 3rd St, Dayton, OH 45402, 937-225-2516; Fax- 937-225-7574. Hours-9AM-4PM. www.ohsb.uscourts.gov

Counties/Note: Champaign, Clark, Clinton, Darke, Greene, Miami, Montgomery, Preble, Shelby, Warren; parts of Butler County are handled by Cincinnati Division.

Searches/Indexing: Include debtor name in search request. Results include last 4 SSN digits. Will fax back documents for fee. New cases are in the index 1 day after filing date. Case files sent to archives 6 months after closed.

Search Access: Only docket info is available by phone. Voice Case Information Service available, call VCIS at 800-726-1004 or 937-225-2544. **Mail:** Search usually completed- 1-2 days. Include SASE for return. **In person:** No self-serve copier.

Payment: Pay by Visa/MC (law firms only), money order, cashier's check, in-state business check. No personal or debtor checks. Payee: Clerk, US Bankruptcy Court.

E-Services: PACER records go back to 1990. New records online after 1 day. ECF at https://ecf.ohsb.uscourts.gov. **Opinions Online:** www.ohsb.uscourts.gov/OHSB/OpNet/search.aspx **Online Note:** PDF lists of judges' current schedules free at www.ohsb.uscourts.gov/OHSB/hsnet/hearingschedulejudges.aspx.

Ohio County Courts

Court	Jurisdiction	No. of Courts	How Organized
Court of Common Pleas*	General	88	county
County Courts*	Limited	30	
Municipal Courts*	Limited	134	
Mayors Courts	Municipal	335	
Court of Claims	Special	1	

* Profiled in this Sourcebook.

Court	CIVIL								
	Tort	Contract	Real Estate	Min. Claim	Max. Claim	Small Claims	Estate	Eviction	Domestic Relations
Court of Common Pleas*	X	X	X	$3000/ $10,000	No Max		X		X
County Courts*	X	X	X	$0	$15,000	$3000		X	
Municipal Courts*	X	X	X	$0	$15,000	$3000		X	
Mayors Courts									
Court of Claims					No Max				

Court	CRIMINAL				
	Felony	Misdemeanor	DWI/DUI	Preliminary Hearing	Juvenile
Court of Common Pleas*	X		Juvenile		X
County Courts*		X	X	X	
Municipal Courts*		X	X	X	
Mayors Courts		X	X		
Court of Claims					

Administration

Administrative Director, Supreme Court of Ohio, 65 S Front Street, Columbus, OH 43215-3431; 614-387-9000, Fax: 614-387-9419. www.supremecourtofohio.gov

Court Structure

The Court of Common Pleas is the general jurisdiction court and County/Municipal Courts have limited jurisdiction. Ohio Common Pleas Courts may name their own minimum threshold civil actions. Although most courts elect to use $15,000 as a standard minimum, some use $3,000 and some $10,000. In effect, these Common Pleas courts may take any civil cases. However, civil maximum limits for Ohio's County Courts and Municipal Courts remains the same – $15,000. County and Municipal Courts handle virtually the same subject matter with some minor operational differences.

Probate Courts are divisions of the Court of Common Pleas.

Online Access

There is no statewide computer system for trial court dockets but a number of counties and manymunicipal courts offer online access. Appellate and Supreme Court opinions may be researched from the Supreme Court website.

Searching Tips, Fees, and Other Guidelines

There is no standardization followed for fees. Over 80% of the courts profiled herein offer a public access terminal to view a docket index. All courts are in the Eastern Time Zone (EST).

Adams County

Common Pleas Court 110 W Main, Rm 207, West Union, OH 45693; 937-544-2344; probate phone: 937-544-2921; fax: 937-544-8271; 8:30AM-4PM. ***Felony, Civil Actions over $3,000, Probate.*** Probate fax- 937-544-8911

Civil Records: Access: In person only. Visitors must perform in person searches themselves. Required to search: name, years to search. Civil cases indexed by defendant, plaintiff; index on computer from 4/1993, prior in books, archived from 1910. Civil PAT goes back to 1993.

Criminal Records: Access: Mail, in person. Visitors must perform in person searches themselves. Search fee: $10.00 per name. Required to search: name, years to search, signed release; also helpful: DOB, SSN. Criminal records computerized from 4/93, prior in books, archived from 1910. Mail turnaround time 1 day. Criminal PAT goes back to same as civil.

General Information: Will fax documents to local or toll free line. Court makes copy: $.25 per page. Certification fee: $1.00 per page, includes copy. Payee: Clerk of Court. Personal checks accepted.

County Court 110 W Main, Rm 25, West Union, OH 45693; 937-544-2011; fax: 937-544-8911; 8AM-4PM. ***Misdemeanor, Civil Actions under $15,000, Small Claims.***

Civil Records: Access: Mail, in person. Both court and visitors may perform in person searches. Search fee: $10.00 per name. Required to search: name, years to search. Civil cases indexed by defendant, plaintiff; index on computer from 3/93, index from 1958, prior on dockets and microfilm. Mail turnaround time 1-2 days. Civil PAT goes back to 1993. PAT civil results show middle initial.

Criminal Records: Access: Mail, in person. Both court and visitors may perform in person searches. Search fee: $10.00 per name. Required to search: name, years to search; also helpful: SSN. Criminal records computerized from 3/93, index from 1958, prior on dockets and microfilm. Mail turnaround time 1-2 days. Criminal PAT goes back to same as civil. PAT results show middle initial, DOB. Terminal results may sometimes show SSNs.

General Information: Will fax documents $1.00 per page. Court makes copy: $.25 per page. Self serve: $.25 per page. Certification fee: $1.00. Payee: Adams County Court. Business checks accepted. No credit cards accepted. Mail requests: SASE required.

Allen County

Common Pleas Court PO Box 1243, 301 N Main, Lima, OH 45802; 419-228-3700; fax: 419-222-8427; 8AM-4:30PM. ***Felony, Civil Actions over $15,000, Probate, Domestic Relations.*** www.allencountyohio.com/cle.php

Probate is a separate court at this address.

Civil Records: Access: In person, online. Visitors must perform in person searches themselves. Required to search: name; also helpful: years to search, address. Civil cases indexed by defendant, plaintiff; index on computer back to 1986; in books and archived prior. Civil PAT goes back to 1986. PAT includes domestic cases. Access civil records including judgment liens free at http://65.17.134.12/pa/.

Criminal Records: Access: In person, online. Visitors must perform in person searches themselves. Required to search: name, years to search; also helpful: address, DOB, SSN. Criminal records computerized from 1986; in books and archived prior. Criminal PAT goes back to same as civil. Online access free at http://65.17.134.12/pa/. Records go back to 12/1/1988. Online results show middle initial, DOB.

General Information: No secret indictment records released. Will fax documents $2.00 plus $1.00 per page. Court makes copy: $.25 per page. Certification fee: $3.00. Payee: Clerk of Court. Personal checks accepted; credit cards are not. Mail requests: SASE required for mail return of any copies.

Lima Municipal Court PO Box 1529, 109 N Union St, Lima, OH 45802; 419-221-5275; civil phone: 419-221-5250; criminal fax: 419-998-5526; civil fax: 419-998-5517; 8AM-5PM. ***Misdemeanor, Civil Actions under $15,000, Eviction, Small Claims.*** www.limamunicipalcourt.org

Civil Records: Access: Phone, fax, mail, in person, email, online. Both court and visitors may perform in person searches. No search fee. Required to search: name, years to search; also helpful: address. Civil cases indexed by defendant, plaintiff; index on computer from 4/1990, books and archived prior. Mail turnaround time same day. Civil PAT goes back to 4/1990. PAT results show name only. Search index information at www.limamunicipalcourt.org, click on Case Inquiry. Direct email search requests to limamuni@wcoil.com

Criminal Records: Access: Phone, fax, mail, in person, email, online. Both court and visitors may perform in person searches. No search fee. Required to search: name, years to search; also helpful: address, DOB, SSN. Criminal records computerized from 4/90, index and dockets prior. Mail turnaround time same day. Criminal PAT goes back to same as civil. PAT results show middle initial, DOB. Address included in most search results. Search index information at www.limamunicipalcourt.org, click on Case Inquiry. Direct email search requests to limamuni@wcoil.com Online results show middle initial, DOB.

General Information: Online identifiers in results same as on public terminal. Fee to fax document $.25 per page. Court makes copy: $.25 per page. Certification fee: $2.00. Payee: Clerk of Court. Business checks accepted. Major credit cards accepted. Mail requests: SASE required.

Ashland County

Common Pleas Court 142 W 2nd St, c/o County Clerk of Courts, Ashland, OH 44805; 419-282-4242; probate phone: 419-282-4284; fax: 419-282-4240; 8AM-4PM. ***Felony, Civil Actions over $10,000, Probate.*** www.ashlandcounty.org/clerkofcourts

Probate court is a separate court at the same address. Common Please Ct phone- 419-282-4284.

Civil Records: Access: In person, online. Visitors must perform in person searches themselves. Required to search: name or case number. Civil cases indexed by defendant, plaintiff; index on microfilm from 1800s. Civil PAT goes back to 6/1995. PAT results show middle initial, DOB, SSN. Access records at www.ashlandcountycpcourt.org. Computerized court records go back to 6/7/1995.

Criminal Records: Access: In person, online. Visitors must perform in person searches themselves. Required to search: name or case number. Criminal records on microfilm from 1800s. Criminal PAT goes back to same as civil. PAT results show middle initial, DOB, SSN. Access records at www.ashlandcountycpcourt.org. Computerized court records go back to 6/7/1995.

General Information: Online identifiers in results same as on public terminal. Will fax documents $2.00 transmission fee plus $1.00 per page. Court makes copy: $.10 per page. Certification fee: $1.00 per page includes copy fee. Payee: Ashland County Clerk of Courts. Personal checks accepted; credit cards are not.

Ashland Municipal Court 1209 E Main St, PO Box 385, Ashland, OH 44805; 419-289-8137; civil phone: 419-281-4890; fax: 419-289-8545; 8AM-5PM. ***Misdemeanor, Civil Actions under $15,000, Eviction, Small Claims.*** www.ashland-ohio.com/municipalcourt/index.htm

Civil Records: Access: Phone, mail, fax, in person. Both court and visitors may perform in person searches. No search fee. Required to search: name, years to search. Civil cases indexed by defendant, plaintiff. Civil index in docket books from 1952, computerized since 1995. Mail turnaround time 1-3 days. Civil PAT goes back to 10/1994. PAT results show name only.

Criminal Records: Access: Phone, mail, fax, in person. Both court and visitors may perform in person searches. No search fee. Required to search: name, years to search, SSN. Criminal docket on books from 1952, computerized since 1995. Mail turnaround time 1-3 days. Criminal PAT goes back to 10/1994. PAT results show middle initial, DOB. Terminal also gives DR and plate numbers.

General Information: Fee to fax out file $1.00 per page. Court makes copy: $.10 per page. Certification fee: $1.00. Payee: Municipal Court. Personal checks accepted. Major credit cards accepted for account holders. Mail requests: SASE required.

Ashtabula County

Common Pleas Court 25 W Jefferson St, Jefferson, OH 44047; 440-576-3637; probate phone: 440-576-3451; fax: 440-576-2819; 8AM-4:30PM. ***Felony, Civil Actions over $10,000, Probate.*** http://courts.co.ashtabula.oh.us/pa.htm

Probate is a separate office at the same location. Probate fax is 440-576-3633.

Civil Records: Access: In person, online. Visitors must perform in person searches themselves. Required to search: name, years to search; also helpful: address. Civil cases indexed by defendant, plaintiff; index on computer back to 5/93, in books back to the 1800s. Civil PAT goes back to 5/1993. PAT civil results show middle initial. Access index free http://courts.co.ashtabula.oh.us/pa.htm.

Criminal Records: Access: In person, online. Visitors must perform in person searches themselves. Required to search: name, years to search; also helpful: address, DOB. Criminal records computerized from 5/93, in books back to the 1800s. Criminal PAT goes back to same as civil. PAT results show middle initial, DOB. Access to index is free at http://courts.co.ashtabula.oh.us/pa.htm. Online results show middle initial, DOB.

General Information: Online identifiers in results same as on public terminal. No expungments released. Will not fax documents. Court makes copy: $.25 per page. Certification fee: $1.00 per page. Payee: Clerk of Court. Personal checks accepted; credit cards are not.

County Court Eastern Division 25 W Jefferson St, Jefferson, OH 44047; 440-576-3617; fax: 440-576-3441; 8AM-4:30PM. ***Misdemeanor, Civil Actions under $15,000, Eviction, Small Claims.*** http://courts.co.ashtabula.oh.us/pa.htm

Civil Records: Access: Mail, fax, in person, online. Both court and visitors may perform in person searches. No search fee. Required to search: name, years to search. Civil cases indexed by defendant, plaintiff; index on computer since 1/9/95; in books back to 1960s. Mail turnaround time 1-2 days. Civil PAT goes back to 1995. PAT results show name, DOB. Access to records are free at http://courts.co.ashtabula.oh.us/pa.htm.

Criminal Records: Access: Mail, fax, in person, online. Both court and visitors may perform in person searches. No search fee. Required to search: name, years to search, DOB or SSN. Criminal records on computer since 1/9/95; in books back to 1960s. Mail turnaround time 1-2 days. Criminal PAT goes back to same as civil.PAT results show name, DOB. Access to records are free at http://courts.co.ashtabula.oh.us/pa.htm. Online results show name, DOB.

General Information: Fee to fax document $.50 per page. Court makes copy: $.50 per page. Self serve: same. Certification fee: $1.50. Payee: Eastern County Court. Only cashiers checks and money orders accepted. No credit cards accepted. Mail requests: SASE helpful.

County Court Western Division 117 W Main St, Geneva, OH 44041; 440-466-1184; fax: 440-466-7171; 8AM-4:30PM M; 8AM-N T-F. ***Misdemeanor, Civil Actions under $15,000, Small Claims.*** www.co.ashtabula.oh.us

Civil Records: Access: In person, mail, fax, online. Visitors must perform in person searches themselves. No search fee. Required to search: name, years to search. Civil cases indexed by defendant, plaintiff; index on computer back to 1995; prior records on docket books. Civil PAT goes back to 1995; results show name only. Access records free http://courts.co.ashtabula.oh.us/pa.htm.

Criminal Records: Access: In person, mail, fax, online. Visitors must perform in person searches

themselves. No search fee. Required to search: name, years to search, DOB, SSN, signed release. Criminal records computerized from 1995; prior records on docket books. Mail turnaround time 72 hours. Criminal PAT goes back to 1995. PAT results show name only. Access records free at http://courts.co.ashtabula.oh.us/pa.htm. Online results show name only.
General Information: No confidential records released. Will not fax documents. Court makes copy: $.25 per page. Certification fee: $1.00 per page. Payee: Western County Court. Only cashiers checks and money orders accepted. No credit cards accepted. Mail requests: SASE required.

Ashtabula Municipal Court 110 W 44th St, Ashtabula, OH 44004; criminal phone: 440-992-7112; civil phone: 440-992-7110; fax: 440-998-5786; 8AM-4:30PM. ***Misdemeanor, Civil Actions under $15,000, Eviction, Small Claims.***
www.ashtabulamunicipalcourt.com/
Directory- 440-992-7109. Daily dockets are also available on the website.
Civil Records: Access: In person, online. Visitors must perform in person searches themselves. Required to search: name, years to search. Civil cases indexed by defendant, plaintiff; index on computer from 1992, books back to 1971. Civil PAT goes back to 1988. PAT results show middle initial, DOB. Online access to civil court cases are free at www.ashtabulamunicourt.com/searchcivildocket.asp.
Criminal Records: Access: In person, online. Visitors must perform in person searches themselves. Required to search: name, years to search, DOB, SSN, signed release. Criminal records computerized from 1992, books back to 1971. Criminal PAT goes back to same as civil. PAT results show middle initial, DOB. Online access to court cases, including traffic, are free at www.ashtabulamunicipalcourt.com/searchdocket.asp. Online results show middle initial, DOB.
General Information: No expunged records released. Will fax specific case files for $1.00 per document. Court makes copy: $1.00 per page. Cert fee: $5.00 includes copy fee. Payee: Municipal Court. Personal checks accepted. Visa/MC accepted.

Athens County

Common Pleas Court 1 South Court St, Rm 8, Athens, OH 45701-2824; 740-592-3242; probate phone: 740-592-3251; fax: 740-592-3282; 8AM-4PM. ***Felony, Civil Actions over $10,000, Probate.***
www.athenscountycpcourt.org/
Civil Records: Access: In person, online. Visitors must perform in person searches themselves. Required to search: name, years to search; also helpful: address. Civil cases indexed by defendant, plaintiff; index on computer back to 1/92; prior in books. Civil PAT goes back to 1992. Online access to CP court records are free at http://coc.athenscountygovernment.com/pa/.
Criminal Records: Access: In person, online. Visitors must perform in person searches themselves. Required to search: name, years to search; also helpful: address, DOB, SSN. Criminal records computerized from 1/92; prior in books. Criminal PAT goes back to same as civil. Online access to criminal records is the same as civil.
General Information: Court makes copy: $.05 per page. Self serve: $.05 per page. Certification fee: $1.00. Payee: Clerk of Court. Business checks accepted. No credit cards accepted. Mail requests: SASE required for mail return of any copies.

Athens Municipal Court City Hall, 8 E Washington St, Athens, OH 45701; 740-592-3328; fax: 740-592-3331; 8AM-4PM. ***Misdemeanor, Civil Actions under $15,000, Eviction, Small Claims.***
www.athensmunicipalcourt.com
Civil Records: Access: Mail, in person, online. Visitors must perform in person searches themselves. No search fee. Required to search: name, years to search; also helpful: address. Civil cases indexed by defendant, plaintiff; index on computer back to 1994, prior in books. Civil PAT goes back to 1994. PAT civil results show middle initial. Search by name or case number at http://docket.webxsol.com/athens/index.html. Records available from 1992.
Criminal Records: Access: Mail, in person, online. Visitors must perform in person searches themselves. No search fee. Required to search: name, years to search; also helpful: address, DOB, SSN. Criminal records computerized from 7/1993, prior in books back to 1974. Mail turnaround time 10 days. Criminal PAT goes back to same as civil. PAT results show middle initial, DOB. Search by name or case number at http://docket.webxsol.com/athens/index.html. Records available from 1992. Online results show middle initial, DOB.
General Information: Online identifiers in results same as on public terminal. No expunged or sealed records released. Will not fax documents. Court makes copy: $.05 per page. Certification fee: $1.00 per page. Payee: ACMC. Personal checks and credit cards accepted. Mail requests: SASE required.

Auglaize County

Common Pleas Court PO Box 409, 201 S Willipie St, #211, Wapakoneta, OH 45895; 419-739-6765; probate: 419-739-6778; criminal fax: 419-739-6768; civil fax: 419-738-7953; 8AM-4:30PM. ***Felony, Civil Actions over $10,000, Probate.***
www.auglaizecounty.org/Common_Pleas_Court/index.htm
Probate is a separate index at 201 Willipie St #103. Probate fax- 419-739-7563
Civil Records: Access: In person, online. Visitors must perform in person searches themselves. Required to search: name, years to search; also helpful: address. Civil cases indexed by defendant, plaintiff; index on dockets from 1850, computerized since 2/00. Civil PAT goes back to 2/2000. PAT results show middle initial, DOB. Access civil records back to 2/2000 free at www.auglaizecounty.org/pa/.
Criminal Records: Access: In person, online. Visitors must perform in person searches themselves. Required to search: name, years to search; also helpful: address, DOB, SSN. Criminal docket index from 1850, computerized since 2/00. Criminal PAT goes back to same as civil. PAT results show middle initial, DOB. Access criminal records back to 2/2000 free at www.auglaizecounty.org/pa/.
General Information: Fee to fax specific case file $2.00 per page plus $.25 each copy fee. Court makes copy: $.25 per page. Certification fee: $2.00 per document. Payee: Clerk of Court. Personal checks accepted; credit cards are not.

Auglaize County Municipal Court PO Box 409, Wapakoneta, OH 45895; 419-739-6766; criminal phone: 419-739-6766; civil phone: 419-739-6767; criminal fax: 419-739-6768; civil fax: same; 8AM-4:30PM. ***Misdemeanor, Civil Actions under $15,000, Eviction, Small Claims.***
www.auglaizecounty.org/Municipal_Court/Index.htm
Civil Records: Access: In person, online. Visitors must perform in person searches themselves. Required to search: name, years to search; also helpful: address. Civil cases indexed by defendant, plaintiff; index on computer from 4/1994, docket back to 1976. Civil PAT goes back to 1994. PAT results show middle initial, DOB. Access civil and small claims court records back to 4/1/1994 free at www.auglaizecounty.org/pa/.
Criminal Records: Access: In person, online. Visitors must perform in person searches themselves. Required to search: name, years to search, signed release; also helpful: address, DOB, SSN. Criminal records computerized from 10/1993, docket back to 1976. Criminal PAT goes back to 1993. PAT results show middle initial, DOB. Access criminal and traffic records back to 10/1/1993 free at www.auglaizecounty.org/pa/.
General Information: No records released. Will fax documents $2.00 fax fee plus $.25 per page. Court makes copy: $.25 per page. Certification fee: $2.00. Payee: Clerk of Court. Personal checks accepted. Visa/MC accepted for criminal and traffic only.

Belmont County

Common Pleas Court Belmont County Clerk of Courts, Main St, Courthouse, St Clairsville, OH 43950; 740-695-2121; civil phone: 740-699-2169; probate phone: 740-695-2121 X202; fax: 740-695-5305; 8:30AM-4:30PM. ***Felony, Civil Actions over $3,000, Probate.***
www.belmontcountyohio.org/common_pleas.htm
Civil Records: Access: Mail, in person. Both court and visitors may perform in person searches. Search fee: $3.00 per name. Required to search: name, years to search. Civil cases indexed by defendant, plaintiff. Civil records in books, archived from 1896; computerized from 1995. Mail turnaround time 1 day. Civil PAT goes back to 5/1995. PAT civil results show middle initial.
Criminal Records: Access: Mail, in person. Both court and visitors may perform in person searches. Search fee: $3.00 per name. Required to search: name, years to search. Criminal records in books, archived from 1896; computerized from 1995. Mail turnaround time 1 day. Criminal PAT goes back to 5/1995. PAT criminal results show middle initial.
General Information: No secret criminal records released. Will fax documents to local or toll free line. Court makes copy: $1.00 per page. Certification fee: $5.00. Payee: Clerk of Court. Personal checks accepted; credit cards are not. Mail requests: SASE required.

County Court Eastern Division 400 W 26th St, Bellaire, OH 43906; 740-676-4490; fax: 740-671-6100; 8AM-4PM. ***Misdemeanor, Civil Actions under $15,000, Small Claims.***
Civil Records: Access: Mail, in person. Both court and visitors may perform in person searches. No search fee. Required to search: name, years to search. Civil cases indexed by defendant, plaintiff; index on computer from 9/1994, books back to 1950s. Mail access for attorneys only. Civil PAT goes back to 1994; results show middle initial, DOB.
Criminal Records: Access: Mail, in person. Both court and visitors may perform in person searches. No search fee. Required to search: name, years to search; also helpful: DOB, SSN. Criminal records computerized from 9/1994, books back to 1950s. Mail turnaround time 1 day. Criminal PAT goes back to same as civil; results show middle initial, DOB.
General Information: No sealed or confidential records released. Will fax documents to local or toll-free number. Court makes copy for no fee. Certification fee: $1.00 per page. Payee: Eastern Division. Only cashiers checks and money orders accepted. Visa/MC accepted. Mail requests: SASE required.

County Court Northern Division PO Box 40, Martins Ferry, OH 43935; 740-633-3147; criminal fax: 740-633-6631; civil fax: same; 8AM-4PM. ***Misdemeanor, Civil Actions under $15,000, Small Claims.***
Civil Records: Access: Mail, fax, in person. Both court and visitors may perform in person searches. No search fee. Required to search: name, years to search. Civil cases indexed by defendant, plaintiff; index on computer from 6/1994, books back to 1950s. Mail turnaround time 5-7 days. Civil PAT goes back to 1999; results show middle initial.
Criminal Records: Access: Mail, fax, in person. Both court and visitors may perform in person searches. No search fee. Required to search: name, years to search, DOB; also helpful: SSN, sex, signed release. Criminal records computerized from 6/1994, books back to 1950s. Mail turnaround time 5-7 days. Criminal PAT goes back to same as civil. PAT criminal results show middle initial.
General Information: Will fax documents for no fee. Court makes copy for no fee. Self serve: same. No certification fee. No personal checks or credit cards accepted.

County Court Western Division 147 W Main St, St Clairsville, OH 43950; 740-695-2875; fax: 740-695-7285; 8AM-4PM. ***Misdemeanor, Civil Actions under $15,000, Small Claims.***
Civil Records: Access: Fax, mail, in person. Both court and visitors may perform in person searches. No search fee. Required to search: name, years to

search, address. Civil cases indexed by defendant, plaintiff; index on computer from 1994, books back to 1950s. Mail turnaround time 2 days. Civil PAT goes back to 1994; civil results show middle initial.
Criminal Records: Access: Fax, mail, in person. Both court and visitors may perform in person searches. No search fee. Required to search: name, years to search, address, DOB, SSN. Criminal records computerized from 1994, books back to 1950s. Mail turnaround time 1 week. Criminal PAT goes back to same as civil; crim results show middle initial.
General Information: Pending case information not released. No fee to fax documents. Court makes copy for no fee. No certification fee. Payee: Western Division Court. Only cashiers checks and money orders accepted. No credit cards accepted. Mail requests: SASE required.

Brown County

Common Pleas Court 101 S Main, Georgetown, OH 45121; 937-378-3100; probate phone: 937-378-6549; fax: 937-378-4212; 7:30AM-4:30PM. ***Felony, Civil Actions over $3,000, Probate, Domestic.*** www.browncountyclerkofcourts.org
Probate is a separate court at same address.
Civil Records: Access: Mail, fax, in person, online. Visitors must perform in person searches themselves. No search fee. Required to search: name, years to search; also helpful: address. Civil cases indexed by defendant, plaintiff; index on computer since 1995, in books back to 1860s. Civil PAT goes back to 1995. PAT results show name only. Search court records free at www.browncountyclerkofcourts.org/Search/.
Criminal Records: Access: Mail, fax, in person, online. Visitors must perform in person searches themselves. No search fee. Required to search: name, years to search; also helpful: address, DOB, SSN. Criminal records on computer since 1995, in books back to 1860s. Criminal PAT goes back to same as civil. PAT results show name only. Search court records free at www.browncountyclerkofcourts.org/Search/. Online results show name only.
General Information: No criminal expungment records released. Will fax documents $2.00 per page. Court makes copy: $.10 per page. Self serve: same. Certification fee: $1.00 per certification. Payee: Clerk of Court. Personal checks accepted; credit cards are not. Mail requests: SASE required.

County Municipal Court 770 Mount Orab Pike, Georgetown, OH 45121; 937-378-6358; fax: 937-378-2462; 8AM-4PM. ***Misdemeanor, Civil Actions under $15,000, Eviction, Small Claims.*** www.browncountycourt.org
Civil Records: Access: Mail, in person, online. Both court and visitors may perform in person searches. No search fee. Required to search: name, years to search. Civil cases indexed by defendant, plaintiff. Civil records in books back to 1958, computerized since 1995. Mail turnaround time 3 days. Civil PAT goes back to 1995. PAT results show name only. Access to records are free at www.browncountycourt.org/search.html.
Criminal Records: Access: Mail, in person, online. Both court and visitors may perform in person searches. No search fee. Required to search: name, years to search, DOB; also helpful: SSN. Criminal records in books back to 1958, computerized since 1995. Mail turnaround time 3 days. Criminal PAT goes back to 1995. PAT results show name, DOB, SSN. Access records free at www.browncountycourt.org/search.html. Online results show name, DOB, SSN. Online criminal search results include address and DOB; civil does not.
General Information: Online identifiers in results same as on public terminal. Will not fax documents. Court makes copy: $.10 per page. No certification fee. Payee: Brown County Municipal Court. Only cashiers checks and money orders accepted. Mail requests: SASE required.

Butler County

Common Pleas Court 315 High St, General Division, Gov't Services Ctr, 3rd Fl, Hamilton, OH 45011; 513-887-3278; probate phone: 513-887-3294; fax: 513-887-3089; 8:30AM-4:30PM. ***Felony, Civil Actions over $3,000.*** www.butlercountyclerk.org
Government Service Center phone number is 513-887-3288. Probate Court is a separate entry at the County.
Civil Records: Access: Online, in person. Visitors must perform in person searches themselves. Required to search: name, years to search. Civil cases indexed by defendant, plaintiff; index on computer from 1988, records go back to 1987. Civil PAT goes back to 4/1988. Online access to County Clerk of Courts records are free at www.butlercountyclerk.org/pa/pa.urd/pamw6500-display. Search by name, dates, or case number and type. Online access to Probate Court records is free are http://66.117.197.22/index.cfm?page=courtRecords Search the Estate or Guardianship databases.
Criminal Records: Access: Online, in person. Visitors must perform in person searches themselves. Required to search: name, years to search, DOB; also helpful: SSN. Criminal records computerized from 1988, prior in books. Criminal PAT goes back to same as civil. Online access to criminal records is the same as civil. Online results show name, DOB.
General Information: Online identifiers in results same as on public terminal. Court makes copy: $.25 per page. Certification fee: $2.00. Cert fee includes copy fee, fee is per page. Payee: Butler County Clerk of Court. Personal checks accepted. Major credit cards accepted in person only.

County Court Area #1 118 W High, Oxford, OH 45056; 513-523-4748; fax: 513-523-4737; 8AM-5PM. ***Misdemeanor, Civil Actions under $15,000, Small Claims.***
Civil Records: Access: Phone, mail, in person, online. Both court and visitors may perform in person searches. No search fee. Required to search: name, years to search. Civil cases indexed by defendant, plaintiff; index on index back to 1983. Mail turnaround time 3 days. Civil PAT goes back to 1993. Access to dockets is coming soon and free at www.butlercountyohio.org/areacourts/.
Criminal Records: Access: Mail, in person, phone, online. Both court and visitors may perform in person searches. No search fee. Required to search: name, years to search, DOB. Criminal records on index back to 1983. Mail turnaround time 1-5 days. Criminal PAT goes back to same as civil. Access to dockets is coming soon and free at www.butlercountyohio.org/areacourts/.
General Information: No sealed records released. Will not fax documents. Court makes copy for no fee. No certification fee. Payee: Area 1 Court. No personal checks or credit cards accepted. Mail requests: SASE required.

County Court Area #2 Butler County Courthouse, 101 High St, 1st Fl, Hamilton, OH 45011; 513-887-3459; fax: 513-887-3568; 8AM-5PM. ***Misdemeanor, Civil Actions under $15,000, Small Claims.***
Probate is a separate index; Probate located on Courthouse 2nd Fl.
Civil Records: Access: Phone, in person, online. Visitors must perform in person searches themselves. No search fee. Required to search: name, years to search. Civil cases indexed by defendant, plaintiff; index on computer from 1993, books back to 1983. Civil PAT goes back to 1993. PAT civil results show middle initial. Results include case number. Access to dockets is coming soon and free at www.butlercountyohio.org/areacourts/.
Criminal Records: Access: Phone, mail, in person, online. Visitors must perform in person searches themselves. No search fee. Required to search: name, years to search. Criminal records computerized from 1993, books back to 1983. Mail turnaround time 2 days. Criminal PAT goes back to same as civil. PAT criminal results show middle initial. Results include case number. Access to dockets is coming soon and free at www.butlercountyohio.org/areacourts/.
General Information: No sealed records released. Court makes copy for no fee. Self serve: $.25 per page. No certification fee. Only cashiers checks and money orders accepted. No credit cards accepted. Mail requests: SASE required.

County Court Area #3 9577 Beckett Rd #300, West Chester, OH 45069; 513-867-5070; fax: 513-777-0558; 8AM-5PM. ***Misdemeanor, Civil Actions under $15,000, Small Claims.*** www.butlercountyohio.org/areacourts/
Civil Records: Access: Mail, in person, online. Both court and visitors may perform in person searches. No search fee. Required to search: name, years to search. Civil cases indexed by defendant, plaintiff; index on computer from 1993, books back to 1983. Mail turnaround time 2-3 days. Civil PAT goes back to 7/1993. Access to dockets is coming soon and free at www.butlercountyohio.org/areacourts/.
Criminal Records: Access: Mail, in person, online. Both court and visitors may perform in person searches. No search fee. Required to search: name, years to search. Criminal records computerized from 1993, books back to 1983. Mail turnaround time 1-2 weeks. Criminal PAT goes back to same as civil. Access to dockets is coming soon and free at www.butlercountyohio.org/areacourts/.
General Information: Will not fax documents. Court makes copy: No copy fee for criminal; civil- $.10 per page. Cert fee: $1.00. Payee: Area #3 Court. Personal checks accepted. Mail requests: SASE required.

Fairfield Municipal Court 675 Niles Rd, Fairfield, OH 45014; 513-425-7802; fax: 513-867-6001; 8AM-5PM. ***Misdemeanor, Civil Actions under $15,000, Small Claims.*** www.fairfield-city.org/court/index.cfm
Civil Records: Access: Mail, in person, online. Both court and visitors may perform in person searches. No search fee. Required to search: name, years to search. Civil cases indexed by defendant, plaintiff; index on computer from 1993, books back to 1983. Mail turnaround time 3 days. Civil PAT goes back to 1988. PAT results show middle initial, DOB, SSN. Search records online back to 1988 free at www.fairfield-city.org/MunicipalCourt/index.cfm.
Criminal Records: Access: Mail, in person, online. Both court and visitors may perform in person searches. No search fee. Required to search: name, years to search. Criminal records computerized from 1993, books back to 1983. Mail turnaround time is 3 days. Criminal PAT goes back to 1988. PAT results show middle initial, DOB. Search records online back to 1988 free at www.fairfield-city.org/MunicipalCourt/index.cfm. Online results show middle initial, DOB.
General Information: Online identifiers in results same as on public terminal. No sealed records released. Will fax documents to local or toll free line. Court makes copy: $.05 per page. No certification fee. Payee: City of Fairfield. No personal checks accepted; credit cards are.

Hamilton Municipal Court 345 High St, #2, Hamilton, OH 45011; 513-785-7300; fax: 513-785-7315; 8AM-5PM. ***Misdemeanor, Civil Actions under $15,000, Small Claims.*** www.hamiltonmunicipalcourt.org
Civil Records: Access: Mail, in person, online. Both court and visitors may perform in person searches. No search fee. Required to search: name, years to search. Civil cases indexed by defendant, plaintiff; index on computer from 1993, books back to 1983. Mail turnaround time 3 days. Civil PAT goes back to 1992. PAT results show middle initial, DOB. Search record access free at http://hamiltonmunicipalcourt.org/connect/court/.
Criminal Records: Access: Mail, in person, online. Both court and visitors may perform in person searches. No search fee. Required to search: name, years to search. Criminal records computerized from 1993, books back to 1983. Mail turnaround time is 3 days. Criminal PAT goes back to same as civil. PAT results show middle initial, DOB. Search records free at http://hamiltonmunicipalcourt.org/connect/court/. Online results show middle initial, DOB.
General Information: Online identifiers in results same as on public terminal. No sealed records

released. Will fax documents to local or toll free line. Court makes copy: $.05 per page. No certification fee. Payee: City of Hamilton. Personal checks and credit cards accepted.

Middletown Municipal Court 1 Donham Plaza, Middletown, OH 45042; 513-425-7802; fax: 513-425-7646; 8AM-N, 1-5PM. ***Misdemeanor, Civil Actions under $15,000, Small Claims.***
www.ci.middletown.oh.us/depts/court/
If you mail in a search request, they may just mail back the searchable website so that you can search online.
Civil Records: Access: Mail, In person. Both court and visitors may perform in person searches. No search fee. Required to search: name, years to search. Civil cases indexed by defendant, plaintiff; index on computer from 1993, books back to 1983. Mail turnaround time 2-3 days. Civil PAT goes back to 1993. PAT results show middle initial, DOB.
Criminal Records: Access: In person, online. Both court and visitors may perform in person searches. No search fee. Required to search: name, years to search. Criminal records computerized from 1993, books back to 1983. Criminal PAT goes back to 1993. PAT results show middle initial, DOB. Search criminal and traffic records back to early 1990s and court schedules free at http://court.cityofmiddletown.org/connection/court/index.xsp. Online records go back to 1990.
General Information: No sealed records released. Will fax documents to local or toll free line. Court makes copy: $.05 per page. Certification fee: $3.00 per doc. Payee: City of Middletown. No personal checks or credit cards accepted.

Probate Court 101 High St, Hamilton, OH 45011; 513-887-3294. ***Probate.***
www.butlercountyprobatecourt.org/ Also, search free at http://66.117.197.22/index.cfm?page=home. Click on case type lookups at bottom of webpage.

Carroll County

Common Pleas Court PO Box 367, Carrollton, OH 44615; 330-627-4886; probate phone: 330-627-2323; fax: 330-627-6437; 8AM-4PM. ***Felony, Civil Actions over $15,000, Probate.***
Probate Court address is 119 S Lisbon St, Courthouse.
Civil Records: Access: In person only. Visitors must perform in person searches themselves. Required to search: name, years to search. Civil cases indexed by defendant, plaintiff. Civil records in books back to 1900s. Clerk will assist visitors to find case numbers. Civil PAT goes back to 3/2000. PAT results show name only.
Criminal Records: Access: In person only. Visitors must perform in person searches themselves. Required to search: name, years to search; also helpful: DOB, SSN. Criminal records in books back to 1900s. Clerk will assist visitors to find case numbers. Criminal PAT goes back to same as civil. PAT results show name only.
General Information: Will fax specific case file $2.00 for 1st page plus $1.00 each add'l page. Court makes copy: $.05 per page. Certification fee: $1.00 per document. Payee: Clerk of Court. Personal checks accepted in person with photo ID. No credit cards accepted.

County Municipal Court 119 S Lisbon St, #301, Carrollton, OH 44615; 330-627-5049; fax: 330-627-3662; 8AM-4PM. ***Misdemeanor, Civil Actions under $15,000, Small Claims, Evictions.***
Civil Records: Access: In person only. Visitors must perform in person searches themselves. Required to search: name, years to search. Civil cases indexed by defendant, plaintiff. Civil records in books from 1958; on computer since 11/95. Civil PAT goes back to 1995.
Criminal Records: Access: In person only. Visitors must perform in person searches themselves. Required to search: name, years to search, DOB. Criminal records in books from 1958; on computer since 11/95. Criminal PAT goes back to same as civil. PAT results show middle initial, DOB.
General Information: No confidential records released. Will not fax documents. Court makes copy: $.25 per page. Certification fee: $2.00. Payee: Carroll County Court. Personal checks accepted; credit cards are not.

Champaign County

Common Pleas Court 200 N Main St, Urbana, OH 43078; 937-484-1047; probate phone: 937-484-1028; fax: 937-484-5325; 8AM-4PM. ***Felony, Civil Actions over $10,000, Probate.***
Probate is separate court at same address, 3rd Fl.
Civil Records: Access: Phone, mail, in person. Visitors must perform in person searches themselves. No search fee. Required to search: name, years to search. Civil cases indexed by defendant, plaintiff; index on computer from 6/92, books back to late 1800s. Will only do phone or mail searches with a case number. Even in this situation, requesters are limited to 10 files per month if acting as a retriever. Civil PAT goes back to 1992. PAT results show middle initial, DOB.
Criminal Records: Access: Phone, mail, in person. Visitors must perform in person searches themselves. No search fee. Required to search: name, years to search, DOB, SSN, signed release. Criminal records computerized from 6/92, books back to late 1800s. Court will only do mail or phone searches with a case number. Even in this situation, requesters are limited to 10 files per month if acting as a retriever. Criminal PAT goes back to same as civil. PAT results show middle initial, DOB.
General Information: All records are public. Will fax documents $1.00 per page fee. Court makes copy: $.25 per page. Certification fee: $1.00 per certification. Payee: Clerk of Court. Personal checks over $10.00 not accepted. No credit cards accepted. Mail requests: SASE required.

Champaign County Municipal Court PO Box 85, Urbana, OH 43078; 937-653-7376; fax: 937-652-4333; 8AM-4PM. ***Misdemeanor, Civil Actions under $15,000, Eviction, Small Claims, Traffic.*** www.champaigncountymunicipalcourt.com
Civil Records: Access: Mail, in person, online. Both court and visitors may perform in person searches. No search fee. Required to search: name, years to search. Civil cases indexed by defendant, plaintiff; index on computer from 6/1993, books back to late 1800s. Mail turnaround time 7-10 days. Civil PAT goes back to 1992. Access court records back to 1992 free at www.champaigncountymunicipalcourt.com/Docket.aspx includes civil, criminal and traffic.
Criminal Records: Access: Mail, in person, online. Both court and visitors may perform in person searches. No search fee. Required to search: name, years to search; also helpful: DOB, SSN. Criminal records computerized from 6/1993, books back to late 1800s. Mail turnaround time 7-10 days. Criminal PAT goes back to 1992. PAT results show middle initial, DOB, SSN. Online access to criminal is the same as civil. Online results show middle initial, DOB, SSN. Online results usually show address, civil does not show DOBs.
General Information: No sealed records released. Will not fax documents. Court makes copy: $.25 per page. Certification fee: $2.50 per page includes copies. Payee: Municipal Court. Cashiers checks and money orders accepted. Major credit cards accepted plus $5.00 processing fee. Mail requests: SASE required.

Clark County

Common Pleas Court 101 N Limestone St, Springfield, OH 45502; 937-521-1680; 937-521-1693 (Domestic); probate phone: 937-521-1845; fax: 937-328-2436; 8AM-4:30PM. ***Felony, Civil Actions over $10,000, Probate.***
www.clarkcountyohio.gov/courts/index.htm
Probate Court records at 50 W Columbia St, 5th Fl.
Civil Records: Access: In person, online. Visitors must perform in person searches themselves. Required to search: name, years to search. Civil cases indexed by defendant. Civil records on computer back to 1990, prior in index books. Civil PAT goes back to 1990. PAT results show name, DOB. Online access to clerk's records is free at http://64.56.107.134:80/pa/.
Criminal Records: Access: In person, online. Visitors must perform in person searches themselves. Required to search: name, years to search. Criminal records computerized from 1990, prior in index books. Criminal PAT goes back to same as civil. Online access to clerk's records are free at http://64.56.107.134:80/pa/. The Sheriff's most wanted list is found at www.clarkcountysheriff.com. Online results show name, DOB.
General Information: Online identifiers in results same as on public terminal. Will fax out specific case files for $2.00. Court makes copy: $.25 per page. Certification fee: $1.00. Payee: Clerk of Court. Business checks accepted. No credit cards accepted.

Clark County Municipal Court 50 E Columbia St, Springfield, OH 45502; 937-328-3700; criminal phone: 937-328-3726; civil phone: 937-328-3715; fax: 937-328-3779; 8AM-5PM. ***Misdemeanor, Civil Actions under $15,000, Eviction, Small Claims.***
www.clerkofcourts.municipal.co.clark.oh.us/
Civil Records: Access: Phone, mail, in person, online. Both court and visitors may perform in person searches. No search fee. Required to search: name, years to search. Civil cases indexed by defendant, plaintiff; index on computer since 5/90; prior records go back to 1997. Mail turnaround time 2-3 days. Civil PAT goes back to 5/1990. Online access to case information is free at www.clerkofcourts.municipal.co.clark.oh.us/. Images available back to 4/15/06. Name searching on "New Cases;" other types require a case number. Online records go back to 3/90.
Criminal Records: Access: Mail, in person, online. Both court and visitors may perform in person searches. No search fee. Required to search: name, years to search; also helpful: DOB, SSN. Criminal records on computer since 3/90; prior records go back to 1998. Mail turnaround time 2-3 days. Criminal PAT goes back to 3/1990. Access to criminal records is the same as civil.
General Information: Will fax documents in emergency only. Court makes copy: $.50 per page. Self serve: none. Certification fee: $2.00 includes copy fee. Payee: Clerk of Court. No personal checks. Major credit cards accepted. Mail requests: SASE requested.

Clermont County

Common Pleas Court 270 Main St, Batavia, OH 45103; criminal phone: 513-732-7339; civil phone: 513-732-7560; probate phone: 513-732-7243; fax: 513-732-7050; 8AM-4:30PM. ***Felony, Civil Actions over $10,000, Probate.***
www.clermontclerk.org/Case_Access.htm
Probate court is located at 76 S Riverside Dr, Batavia.
Civil Records: Access: In person, online. Visitors must perform in person searches themselves. Required to search: name, years to search; also helpful: address. Civil cases indexed by defendant, plaintiff; index on computer from 1987, some on microfiche from 1920s, index books from 1959. Civil PAT goes back to 1987. PAT civil results show middle initial. Online access to civil records is the same as criminal, see following.
Criminal Records: Access: In person, online. Visitors must perform in person searches themselves. Required to search: name, years to search, DOB; also helpful: address, SSN. Criminal records computerized from 1987, some on microfiche from 1920s, index books from 1959. Clerk refers criminal record requests to the Sheriff (513-732-7500) who will do searches for $20.00 per name. Criminal PAT goes back to same as civil. PAT results show middle initial, DOB. Online access to court records is free at www.clermontclerk.org/Case_Access.htm. Online records go back to 1/1987. Includes later Municipal Court records. Online results show middle initial.
General Information: Will fax documents $2.00 fee plus $.10 per page. Court makes copy: $.10 per page. Certification fee: $1.00 per page. Payee: Clerk of Court. Business checks accepted. No credit cards accepted.

Clermont County Municipal Court 4430 State Rt 222, Batavia, OH 45103; criminal phone: 513-732-7290; civil phone: 513-732-7292; fax: 513-732-7831; 8AM-5PM. ***Misdemeanor, Civil Actions under $15,000, Eviction, Small Claims.*** www.clermontclerk.org

Civil Records: Access: Mail, in person, online. Visitors must perform in person searches themselves. No search fee. Required to search: name, years to search. Civil cases indexed by defendant, plaintiff. Computerized records from 5/96, civil records in books and microfiche from 1959, docket books back to 1800s. Civil PAT goes back to 1996. PAT results show middle initial, DOB, SSN. Access to court records is the same as criminal, see following.

Criminal Records: Access: Mail, in person, online. Visitors must perform in person searches themselves. No search fee. Required to search: name, years to search, DOB; also helpful: SSN. Computerized records back to 5/96, criminal records in books and microfiche from 1957, docket books back to 1800s. Criminal PAT goes back to 5/1/1996. PAT results show middle initial, DOB, SSN. Access to court records is free at www.clermontclerk.org/Case_Access.htm. Online records go back to 5/1/1996. Online results show middle initial, DOB, SSN.

General Information: Court makes copy: $.25 per page. Certification fee: $4.00 per doc. Payee: Clerk of Court. Only cashiers checks and money orders accepted. No credit cards accepted. Mail requests: SASE required.

Clinton County

Common Pleas Court 46 S South St, Wilmington, OH 45177; 937-382-2316; probate phone: 937-382-2280; fax: 937-383-3455; 8AM-4:30PM. ***Felony, Civil Actions, Probate.***

Probate is a separate office at this same address. Probate fax- 937-383-1158; Probate hours 8AM-4:30PM.

Civil Records: Access: Fax, mail, in person. Both court and visitors may perform in person searches. No search fee. Required to search: name, years to search; also helpful: address. Civil cases indexed by defendant, plaintiff; index on computer since 1995; prior in books back to 1810. Mail turnaround time 1 week. Civil PAT goes back to 1995. PAT results show name only.

Criminal Records: Access: Mail, in person. Both court and visitors may perform in person searches. Search fee: $5.00 per name. Required to search: name, years to search, DOB, SSN; also helpful: address. Criminal records on computer since 1995; prior in books back to 1810. Mail turnaround time 1 week. Criminal PAT goes back to same as civil. PAT results show name only.

General Information: No confidential records released. Will fax out documents $.40 per page. Court makes copy: $.05 per page. Certification fee: $1.00. Payee: Clerk of Court. Personal checks accepted; credit cards are not. Mail requests: SASE required.

Clinton County Municipal Court 69 N South St, PO Box 71, Wilmington, OH 45177; 937-382-8985; fax: 937-383-0130; 8AM-4PM. ***Misdemeanor, Civil Actions under $15,000, Eviction, Small Claims.*** www.clintonmunicourt.org

Civil Records: Access: Fax, mail, in person, online. Both court and visitors may perform in person searches. No search fee. Required to search: name, years to search, SSN. Civil cases indexed by defendant, plaintiff. Civil records in books from 1960; computerized records go back to 1995. Mail turnaround time 1 day. Civil PAT goes back to 1994. Search court records online at www.clintonmunicourt.org/search.html.

Criminal Records: Access: Fax, mail, in person, online. Both court and visitors may perform in person searches. No search fee. Required to search: name, years to search, DOB; also helpful: SSN. Criminal records in books from 1960; computerized records go back to 1995. Mail turnaround time 1 day. Criminal PAT goes back to same as civil. Search court records free online at www.clintonmunicourt.org/search.html.

General Information: Will fax documents to local or toll free line. Court makes copy: $1.00 per page 1st 5; $.25 per page each add'l. No certification fee. Payee: Clerk of Court. Only cashiers checks and money orders accepted. No credit cards accepted. Mail requests: SASE required.

Columbiana County

Common Pleas Court 105 S Market St, Lisbon, OH 44432; 330-424-7777; fax: 330-424-3960; 8AM-4PM. ***Felony, Civil Actions over $15,000.*** www.ccclerk.org

Civil Records: Access: In person, online. Visitors must perform in person searches themselves. Required to search: name, years to search; also helpful: address. Civil cases indexed by defendant, plaintiff; index on computer since 1993; prior in books from 1968, archived back to 1800s. Civil PAT goes back to 3/1993. PAT results show name only. Access all county court index and docket records free at www.ccclerk.org/case_access.htm. Includes probate.

Criminal Records: Access: In person, online. Visitors must perform in person searches themselves. Required to search: name, years to search, DOB; also helpful: address, SSN. Criminal records on computer since 1993; prior in books from 1968, archived back to 1800s. Criminal PAT goes back to same as civil. PAT results show name only. Access all county court index and docket records free at www.ccclerk.org/case_access.htm. Online results show middle initial, DOB.

General Information: Online identifiers in results same as on public terminal. No secret indictment records released. Will not fax documents. Court makes copy: $.05 per page. Self serve: same. Certification fee: $1.00 per page. Payee: Clerk of Court. Personal checks and major credit cards accepted. Mail requests: SASE or postage required for return of any copies.

Municipal Court 38832 Saltwell, Lisbon, OH 44432; 330-424-5326; criminal fax: 330-424-6658; civil fax: same; 8AM-4PM. ***Misdemeanor, Civil Actions under $15,000, Small Claims.*** www.ccclerk.org/the_courts.htm

This court is formerly known as the Southwest Area Court. In Sept. 2005, the Northwest Muni Court in Salem and the Eastern Area Muni Court in East Palestine were merged with this court.

Civil Records: Access: In person, online. Visitors must perform in person searches themselves. Required to search: name, years to search. Civil cases indexed by defendant, plaintiff. Civil records in books from 1950s, archived back to 1800s; on computer back to 1994. Civil PAT goes back to 1994. PAT civil results show middle initial. Access all county court index and docket records free at www.ccclerk.org/case_access.htm.

Criminal Records: Access: In person, online. Visitors must perform in person searches themselves. Required to search: name, years to search; also helpful: DOB, SSN. Criminal records in books from 1950s, archived back to 1800s; on computer back to 1994. Criminal PAT goes back to same as civil. PAT criminal results show middle initial. Access all county court index and docket records free at www.ccclerk.org/case_access.htm. Online results show middle initial, DOB.

General Information: No expungment records released. Will not fax documents. Court makes copy: $.05 per page. Self serve: same. Certification fee: $1.00 per page. Payee: Columbiana County Municipal Court. Personal or cashiers checks, money orders and major credit cards accepted. Mail requests: SASE required for mail return of any copies.

East Liverpool Municipal Court 126 W 6th St, East Liverpool, OH 43920; 330-385-5151; fax: 330-385-1566; 8AM-4PM. ***Misdemeanor, Civil Actions under $15,000, Eviction, Small Claims.*** www.eastliverpool.com/court.html

Civil Records: Access: Phone, fax, mail, in person, online. Both court and visitors may perform in person searches. No search fee. Required to search: name, years to search. Civil cases indexed by defendant, plaintiff. Civil records in books from 1968, archived back to 1800s, computerized since 11/92. Mail turnaround time 1-2 days. Civil PAT goes back to 1992. PAT civil results show middle initial. Access all county court index and docket records free at www.ccclerk.org/case_access.htm.

Criminal Records: Access: Phone, fax, mail, in person, online. Both court and visitors may perform in person searches. No search fee. Required to search: name, years to search, signed release; also helpful: DOB, SSN. Criminal records in books from 1968, archived back to 1800s, computerized since 11/92. Mail turnaround time 1-2 days. Criminal PAT goes back to same as civil. PAT criminal results show middle initial. Access all county court index and docket records free at www.ccclerk.org/case_access.htm. Online results show middle initial, DOB.

General Information: No expungment records released. No fee to fax documents. Court makes copy: $.10 per page. Certification fee: $3.00 each includes copy fee. Copy fee may also apply if more than 4 pages. Payee: East Liverpool Municipal Court. No business or personal checks accepted. Visa/MC accepted. Mail requests: SASE required.

Coshocton County

Common Pleas Court 318 Main St, Coshocton, OH 43812; 740-622-1456; criminal phone: same; probate phone: 740-622-1837; fax: 740-295-0020; 8AM-4PM. ***Felony, Civil Actions over $10,000, Probate.*** www.coshoctoncounty.net

Probate is a separate index at 426 Main St. Probate fax- 740-623-6514

Civil Records: Access: Mail, in person. Both court and visitors may perform in person searches. No search fee. Required to search: name, years to search. Civil cases indexed by defendant, plaintiff. Civil records in books, microfilm back to 1985, archived back to 1800s; on computer back to 1998. Mail turnaround time 2 days. Civil PAT goes back to 1998. Results include name and case number.

Criminal Records: Access: Mail, in person. Both court and visitors may perform in person searches. No search fee. Required to search: name, years to search, DOB; also helpful: SSN. Criminal records in books, microfilm back to 1985, archived back to 1800s; on computer back to 1998. Mail turnaround time 2 days. Criminal PAT goes back to same as civil. Results include name and case number.

General Information: No expunged records released. Will not fax documents. Court makes copy: $.25 per page. Self serve: same. Certification fee: $1.00 per page. Payee: Clerk of Court. Personal checks accepted; credit cards are not.

Coshocton Municipal Court 760 Chestnut St, Coshocton, OH 43812; 740-622-2871; fax: 740-623-5928; 8AM-4:30PM M-W F; 8AM-N TH. ***Misdemeanor, Civil Actions under $15,000, Eviction, Small Claims.*** www.coshoctonmunicipalcourt.com

Civil Records: Access: Phone, fax, mail, in person, online. Both court and visitors may perform in person searches. No search fee. Required to search: name, years to search. Civil cases indexed by defendant, plaintiff; index on computer from 1989, books back to 1952. Mail turnaround time same day. Civil PAT goes back to 1989. Online access to civil records is at the website. Search by name, case number, attorney, date.

Criminal Records: Access: Phone, fax, mail, in person, online. Both court and visitors may perform in person searches. No search fee. Required to search: name, years to search; also helpful: DOB, SSN. Criminal records computerized from 1989, books back to 1952. Mail turnaround time same day. Criminal PAT goes back to same as civil. PAT results show middle initial, DOB. Terminal results also include last known address. Online access to criminal records is the same as civil. Search by name, attorney, citation or case number. Online results show middle initial, DOB.

General Information: Online identifiers in results same as on public terminal. No expunged records released. No fee to fax documents. Court makes copy: $1.00 per page. Certification fee: $5.00. Payee: Clerk of Court. Personal checks accepted. Visa/MC accepted via internet only. Mail requests: SASE requested.

Crawford County

Common Pleas Court 112 E Mansfield St, #204, Bucyrus, OH 44820; 419-562-2766; probate phone: 419-562-8891; fax: 419-562-8011; 8:30AM-4:30PM. ***Felony, Civil Actions over $3,000, Probate.***
www.crawford-co.org/Clerk/default.html
Probate is a separate index, separate office- Probate Court. Probate fax- 419-563-1920
Civil Records: Access: Phone, mail, in person, online. Both court and visitors may perform in person searches. No search fee. Required to search: name, years to search. Civil cases indexed by defendant, plaintiff; index on computer back to 1990, some on microfiche and index books from 1800s. Mail turnaround time usually same day. Civil PAT goes back to 2/1990. PAT civil results show middle initial. Online access to Common Pleas court records is free at www.crawford-co.org/Clerk/default.html and click on "Internet Inquiry."
Criminal Records: Access: Mail, in person, online. Both court and visitors may perform in person searches. No search fee. Required to search: name, years to search. Criminal records computerized from 1990, some on microfiche and index books from 1800s. Mail turnaround time 1-2 days. Criminal PAT goes back to same as civil. PAT results show middle initial, DOB. Online access to criminal cases is the same as civil. Online results show middle initial, DOB.
General Information: No divorce investigations. Will fax documents for no fee. Court makes copy for no fee. Certification fee: $1.00 per page includes copy fee. Payee: Clerk of Court. Personal checks accepted; credit cards are not. Mail requests: SASE required.

Crawford County Municipal Court PO Box 550, 112 E Mansfield, Courthouse, Bucyrus, OH 44820; 419-562-2731; criminal phone: x3; civil phone: x6; fax: 419-562-7064; 8AM-4:30PM. ***Misdemeanor, Civil Actions under $15,000, Eviction, Small Claims.***
Civil Records: Access: Phone, fax, mail, in person. Both court and visitors may perform in person searches. No search fee. Required to search: name, years to search. Civil cases indexed by defendant, plaintiff. Civil records in books back to 1978. Phone search requests must be kept to one name. Mail turnaround time within 1 week. Civil PAT goes back to 1996.
Criminal Records: Access: Mail, fax, in person. Both court and visitors may perform in person searches. No search fee. Required to search: name, years to search, DOB. Criminal records in books back to 1978; on computer back to 1996. Court prefers a fax search request. Mail turnaround time within 1 week. Criminal PAT goes back to 1996. PAT results show middle initial, DOB.
General Information: No counseling report records released. Will fax back documents. Court makes copy: $.10 per page. Certification fee: $2.00 per cert. Payee: Crawford County Municipal Court. No personal checks or credit cards accepted.

Crawford County Municipal Court East Div 301 Harding Way E, Galion, OH 44833; 419-468-6819; fax: 419-468-6828; 8AM-5PM. ***Misdemeanor, Civil Actions under $15,000, Eviction, Small Claims.***
Civil Records: Access: Mail, in person. Both court and visitors may perform in person searches. No search fee. Required to search: name, years to search. Civil cases indexed by defendant, plaintiff. Civil records in books back to 1800s. Mail turnaround time 2-3 days. Civil PAT goes back to 1996.
Criminal Records: Access: Mail, in person. Both court and visitors may perform in person searches. No search fee. Required to search: name, years to search, DOB, SSN, signed release. Criminal records in books back to 1800s. Mail turnaround time 2-3 days. Criminal PAT goes back to same as civil.
General Information: Court makes copy: $.10 per page. Certification fee: $3.00. Payee: Municipal Court. Only cashiers checks and money orders accepted. No credit cards accepted. Mail requests: SASE required.

Cuyahoga County

Common Pleas Court - General Division 1200 Ontario St, Cleveland, OH 44113; 216-443-8560; criminal phone: 216-443-7985; civil phone: 216-443-7960; probate phone: 216-443-8764; fax: 216-443-5424; 8:30AM-4:30PM. ***Felony, Civil Actions over $10,000, Probate.***
http://cp.cuyahogacounty.us/internet/index.aspx
Probate is a separate division with separate records and personnel.
Civil Records: Access: Phone, mail, in person, online. Both court and visitors may perform in person searches. No search fee. Required to search: name, years to search; also helpful: address. Civil cases indexed by defendant, plaintiff; index on index and dockets from 1968, archived from 1800s; computerized since 1975. Phone requests to 216-443-7966. Address mail requests to Gerald Fuerst, 1st Fl, Index Dept. Mail turnaround time 1-2 days. Civil PAT goes back to 1970. PAT results show name, DOB. Online access to Common Please civil courts; click on Civil Case Dockets at http://cpdocket.cp.cuyahogacounty.us/TOS.aspx. Probate at http://probate.cuyahogacounty.us/pa/.
Criminal Records: Access: In person, online. Visitors must perform in person searches themselves. Required to search: name, years to search; also helpful: address, DOB, SSN. Criminal records on index and dockets from 1968, archived from 1800s; computerized since 1975. Criminal Dept on 2nd Floor. Any phone requests must have case number. Criminal PAT goes back to same as civil.PAT results show name, DOB. Online access to criminal records dockets is free at http://cpdocket.cp.cuyahogacounty.us/TOS.aspx. Online results show name, DOB.
General Information: No expungments or sealed records released. Will not fax documents. Court makes copy: $.10 per page.This office is unable to provide change. Certification fee: $1.00 per page includes copy fee. Payee: Clerk of Court. Business checks accepted. No credit cards accepted. Mail requests: SASE required.

Cleveland Municipal Court - Civil Division 1200 Ontario St, Cleveland, OH 44113; 216-664-4870, 216-664-4790; civil phone: small claims- x5; eviction- x4, general- x8; 8AM-4PM. ***Civil Actions under $15,000, Eviction, Small Claims.***
http://clevelandmunicipalcourt.org/home.html
Jurisdiction also includes Village of Bratenahl. Court plans to have online access to case information.
Civil Records: Access: In person only. Both court and visitors may perform in person searches. No search fee. Required to search: name, years to search; also helpful: address. Civil cases indexed by defendant, plaintiff; index on computer from 1988, docket books and index from 1950s, prior archived. Public use terminal has civil records back to 1990. PAT civil results show middle initial.
General Information: Court makes copy: $.25 per page. Certification fee: $1.00 per page. Payee: Municipal Court. Personal checks accepted; credit cards are not.

Cleveland Municipal Court - Criminal Division 1200 Ontario St, Level 3, Cleveland, OH 44113; 216-664-6911, 664-4790; fax: 216-664-4299; 8AM-3:50PM. ***Misdemeanor.***
http://clevelandmunicipalcourt.org/home.html
The court plans to have online access to case information soon.
Criminal Records: Access: In person only. Both court and visitors may perform in person searches. No search fee. Required to search: name, years to search, DOB, SSN, signed release. Criminal records on computer since 1992, on books to 1982, archived prior. Public use terminal has crim records. Public access terminals are available on the 2nd Fl - 8AM-4PM, M-F. Court recommends mail requests for criminal background checks be sent to Cleveland Police Dept, Attn- Criminal Records - Gracie, 1300 Ontario St, Cleveland 44113. For info, phone 216-623-5336. Fee is a nickel per name, do not send cash.
General Information: No adoption or juvenile records released. Will fax documents. Court makes copy: $.25 per page. Certification fee: $5.00. Payee: Cleveland Municipal Clerk of Court. Personal checks accepted. Visa/MC accepted.

Bedford Municipal Court 165 Center Rd, Bedford, OH 44146; 440-232-3420; fax: 440-232-2510; 8:30AM-4:30PM. ***Misdemeanor, Civil Actions under $15,000, Eviction, Small Claims.***
www.bedfordmuni.org/
Civil Records: Access: Fax, mail, in person, online. Both court and visitors may perform in person searches. No search fee. Required to search: name, years to search. Civil cases indexed by defendant, plaintiff; index on computer from 1990 docket books and index from 1970s, prior archived. Mail turnaround time 3 days. Civil PAT goes back to 1990. Access index to court records at www.bedfordmuni.org/ Click on Case Information.
Criminal Records: Access: Fax, mail, in person, online. Both court and visitors may perform in person searches. No search fee. Required to search: name, years to search. Criminal records computerized from 1990, docket books and index from 1970s, prior archived. Mail turnaround time 3 days. Criminal PAT goes back to 1990. PAT results show middle initial, DOB, SSN. Terminal results include perhaps DR number. Access index to court records at www.bedfordmuni.org/ Click on Case Information. Online results show middle initial, DOB, SSN.
General Information: Online identifiers in results same as on public terminal. No fee to fax documents. Court makes copy: $.05 per page. Certification fee: $2.00. Payee: Municipal Court. Personal checks accepted. Visa/MC accepted. Mail requests: SASE required.

Berea Municipal Court 11 Berea Commons, Berea, OH 44017; 440-826-5860; criminal phone: 440-826-5860; civil phone: 440-826-5860; fax: 440-891-3387; 8AM-4:30PM. ***Misdemeanor, Civil Actions under $15,000, Eviction, Small Claims.***
www.bereamunicourt.org/
Traffic fax is same number as criminal fax.
Civil Records: Access: Mail, in person, online. Both court and visitors may perform in person searches. No search fee. Required to search: name, years to search. Civil cases indexed by defendant, plaintiff; index on computer back to 1991, prior in books. Mail turnaround time 7-10 days. Search docket information at www.bereamunicourt.org/info.asp?pageId=5.
Criminal Records: Access: Mail, in person, online. Both court and visitors may perform in person searches. Search fee: $5.00 per name. Required to search: name, years to search; also helpful: address, DOB, SSN. Criminal records computerized from 1991, prior in books. Mail turnaround time 1 week-10 days. Search docket info at www.bereamunicourt.org/info.asp?pageId=5
General Information: No probation records released. No fee to fax documents. Court makes copy: $1.00 per page. Certification fee: $5.00 per doc. Payee: Berea Municipal Court. Personal checks and credit cards accepted. Mail requests: SASE required.

Cleveland Heights Municipal Court 40 Severance Cir, Cleveland Heights, OH 44118; 216-291-4901; fax: 216-291-2459; 8AM-5PM. ***Misdemeanor, Civil Actions under $15,000, Eviction, Small Claims.***
www.clevelandheightscourt.com
Civil Records: Access: In person, online. Visitors must perform in person searches themselves. Required to search: name, years to search; also helpful: address. Civil cases indexed by defendant, plaintiff; index on computer from 1990, prior in books to 1980. Civil PAT goes back to 1990. PAT civil results show middle initial. Search Muni civil (to $15,000) or misdemeanor docket records at http://216.144.36.75/. Search by name or case number.
Criminal Records: Access: In person, online. Visitors must perform in person searches themselves. Required to search: name, years to search; also helpful: address, DOB, SSN. Criminal records computerized from 1990, prior in books to 1980s. Criminal PAT goes back to same as civil. PAT criminal results show middle initial. Online

access to criminal records is the same as civil. Online results show middle initial.
General Information: Online identifiers in results same as on public terminal. No expungments or search warrant records released. Will not fax documents. Court makes copy: $.10 per page. Certification fee: $2.00. Payee: Municipal Court. Personal checks accepted. Credit cards accepted in person only.

East Cleveland Municipal Court 14340 Euclid Ave, East Cleveland, OH 44112; 216-681-2220; fax: 216-681-2217; 8:30AM-4:30PM. ***Misdemeanor, Civil Actions under $15,000, Eviction, Small Claims.***
www.eccourt.com/
Civil Records: Access: In person only. Visitors must perform in person searches themselves. Required to search: name, years to search. Civil cases indexed by defendant, plaintiff. Civil records go back to 1979; on computer from 2000, docket books and index from 1950s, prior archived. Daily dockets available at the website.
Criminal Records: Access: In person only. Visitors must perform in person searches themselves. Required to search: name, years to search, DOB, SSN, signed release; also helpful: address. Criminal records computerized from 1997, docket books and index from 1950s, prior archived. Address mail requests to Police Record Room. Daily dockets available at the website.
General Information: Will fax documents no add'l fee. Court makes copy: $1.00 per page. Certification fee: $10.00. Payee: Municipal Court. Personal checks accepted. Major credit cards accepted; may add $1.00 cc fee.

Euclid Municipal Court 555 E 222 St, Euclid, OH 44123-2099; 216-289-2888; fax: 216-289-8254; 8:30AM-4:30PM. ***Misdemeanor, Civil Actions under $15,000, Eviction, Small Claims.***
www.ci.euclid.oh.us/citydepartments/court.cfm
Civil Records: Access: Mail, in person, online. Both court and visitors may perform in person searches. Search fee: $5.00 per name. Required to search: name, years to search. Civil cases indexed by defendant, plaintiff; index on computer from 2004, docket books and index from 1950s, prior archived. Mail turnaround time 1 week. Civil PAT goes back to 2004. PAT results show middle initial, DOB. Docket index and daily docket lists of civil cases available at www.ci.euclid.oh.us/citydepartments/court.cfm and click on Case Information.
Criminal Records: Access: Mail, in person, online. Both court and visitors may perform in person searches. Search fee: $5.00 per name. Required to search: name, years to search, DOB; also helpful: address, SSN. Criminal records computerized from 1995, docket books and index from 1950s, prior archived. Mail turnaround time 1 week. Criminal PAT goes back to 1995. PAT results show middle initial, DOB. Docket index and daily docket lists of misdemeanor and traffic cases are available at www.ci.euclid.oh.us/citydepartments/court.cfm and click on Case Information.
General Information: Online identifiers in results same as on public terminal. No expunged records released. Will not fax documents. Court makes copy: $.05 per page. Certification fee: $5.00 but normally included in search fee. Payee: Municipal Court. Personal checks accepted. Credit cards accepted except for civil filings. Mail requests: SASE required.

Garfield Heights Municipal Court 5555 Turney Rd, Garfield Heights, OH 44125; 216-475-1900; fax: 216-475-3087; 8:30AM-4:30PM. ***Misdemeanor, Civil Actions under $15,000, Eviction, Small Claims.***
www.ghmc.org
Civil Records: Access: Phone, mail, in person, online. Both court and visitors may perform in person searches. No search fee. Required to search: name, years to search; also helpful: address. Civil cases indexed by defendant, plaintiff; index on computer from 11/91, docket books and index from 1996, prior archived. Phone access depends on age of case. Mail turnaround time 2 weeks. Civil PAT goes back to 1999. Online access is limited to dockets; search by name, date or case number at http://docket.ghmc.org.
Criminal Records: Access: Phone, mail, in person, online. Both court and visitors may perform in person searches. No search fee. Required to search: name, years to search, DOB; also helpful: address, SSN, signed release. Criminal records computerized from 1996, docket books and index from 1995, prior archived. Mail turnaround time 2 weeks. Criminal PAT goes back to same as civil. Online access is limited to dockets; search by name, date or case number at http://docket.ghmc.org.
General Information: No expunged records released. Court makes copy: $.05 per page. Certification fee: $1.00 per page. Cert fee includes copies. Payee: Municipal Court. Personal checks accepted. Visa/MC accepted. Mail requests: SASE required.

Lakewood Municipal Court 12650 Detroit Ave, Lakewood, OH 44107; 216-529-6700; fax: 216-529-7687; 8AM-5PM. ***Misdemeanor, Civil Actions under $15,000, Eviction, Small Claims.***
www.lakewoodcourtoh.com
Civil Records: Access: Phone, fax, mail, in person, online. Both court and visitors may perform in person searches. No search fee. Required to search: name, years to search; also helpful: address. Civil cases indexed by defendant, plaintiff; index on computer from 1987, prior in books. Mail turnaround time 1 week. View weekly dockets only at http://64.227.68.198/casesearch.html.
Criminal Records: Access: Fax, mail, in person, online. Both court and visitors may perform in person searches. No search fee. Required to search: name, years to search, DOB; also helpful: address, SSN. Criminal records on computer since 1983, prior in books. Mail turnaround time 1 week. Search weekly dockets only at http://64.227.68.198/casesearch.html.
General Information: No confidential records released. No fee to fax documents locally only. Court makes copy: $.10 per page. Certification fee: $3.00. Payee: Municipal Court. Personal checks and credit cards accepted. Mail requests: SASE required.

Lyndhurst Municipal Court 5301 Mayfield Rd, Lyndhurst, OH 44124; 440-461-6500; fax: 440-442-1910; 8:30AM-5PM M-TH; till 4PM F. ***Misdemeanor, Civil Actions under $15,000, Eviction, Small Claims.***
www.lyndhurstmunicipalcourt.org
Civil Records: Access: Mail, in person, online. Only the court performs in person searches; visitors may not. No search fee. Required to search: name, years to search; also helpful: address. Civil cases indexed by defendant, plaintiff; index on computer from 1991, prior in books. Mail turnaround time 1 week. Access court records free at www.lyndhurstmunicipalcourt.org/ but may be temporarily down.
Criminal Records: Access: Mail, in person, online. Only the court performs in person searches; visitors may not. No search fee. Required to search: name, years to search, signed release; also helpful: address, DOB, SSN, location. Criminal records computerized from 1991, prior in books. Mail turnaround time 1 week. Access court records free at www.lyndhurstmunicipalcourt.org/ but may be temporarily down.
General Information: Will fax documents to local or toll free line. Court makes copy: $.05 per page. Certification fee: $5.00. Payee: Municipal Court. Personal checks accepted. Visa/MC accepted.

Parma Municipal Court 5555 Powers Blvd, Parma, OH 44125; 440-887-7400; fax: 440-887-7485; 8:30AM-4:30PM. ***Misdemeanor, Civil Actions under $15,000, Eviction, Small Claims.***
www.parmamunicourt.org/
The court blocks the SSN from appearing on search results.
Civil Records: Access: Phone, mail, in person, online. Both court and visitors may perform in person searches. No search fee. Required to search: name, years to search; also helpful: address. Civil cases indexed by defendant, plaintiff; index on computer from 1993, prior in books to 1977. Mail turnaround time up to 1 week. Public use terminal has civil records back to 1993. PAT results show middle initial, DOB, SSN. Access to current and future court dockets only is available free at www.parmamunicourt.org/info.asp?pageId=5.
Criminal Records: Access: Phone, fax, mail, in person, online. Both court and visitors may perform in person searches. No search fee. Required to search: name, years to search, DOB; also helpful: address, SSN. Criminal records computerized from 1993, prior in books to 1992. Mail turnaround time up to 1 week. Access to criminal current and future dockets is the same as civil, see above. Online results show middle initial, DOB, SSN.
General Information: Will not fax documents. Court makes copy: $.05 per page. Certification fee: $1.00. Payee: Parma Municipal Court. Personal checks accepted. Visa/MC/Discover/AmEx accepted in person only. Mail requests: SASE required.

Rocky River Municipal Court 21012 Hilliard Blvd, Rocky River, OH 44116; 440-333-0066; fax: 440-356-5613; 8:30AM-4:30PM. ***Misdemeanor, Civil Actions under $15,000, Eviction, Small Claims.***
www.rrcourt.net
Civil Records: Access: Phone, fax, mail, in person, online. Visitors must perform in person searches themselves. No search fee. Required to search: name, years to search. Civil cases indexed by defendant, plaintiff; index on computer from 1988, prior in books to 1977. Civil PAT goes back to 1/1988. PAT results show name only. Public access to record index at https://rrcourt.net/pa/pa.urd/pamw6500.display.
Criminal Records: Access: Phone, fax, mail, in person, online. Visitors must perform in person searches themselves. No search fee. Required to search: name, years to search, DOB. Criminal records computerized from 1987, prior in books to 1977. Mail turnaround time 2 days. Criminal PAT goes back to 6/1987.PAT results show name, DOB. Access record index free at https://rrcourt.net/pa/pa.urd/pamw6500.display. Online results show middle initial, DOB.
General Information: Online identifiers in results same as on public terminal. Will fax documents to toll free line. Court makes copy: $.05 per page. Certification fee: $10.00. Payee: Municipal Court. Personal checks accepted. Visa/MC accepted. Mail requests: SASE required.

Shaker Heights Municipal Court 3355 Lee Rd, Shaker Heights, OH 44120; 216-491-1300; fax: 216-491-1314; 8:30AM-4:30PM. ***Misdemeanor, Civil Actions under $15,000, Eviction, Small Claims.***
www.shakerheightscourt.org/home/
Criminal Clerk open until 6:30PM on Mondays.
Civil Records: Access: Mail, fax, in person, online. Both court and visitors may perform in person searches. No search fee. Required to search: name, years to search; also helpful: address. Civil cases indexed by defendant, plaintiff; index on computer from 6/86, prior in books for at least 25 years. Mail turnaround time 2 days. Search case records and dockets at www.shakerheightscourt.org/home/.
Criminal Records: Access: Phone, fax, mail, in person, online. Both court and visitors may perform in person searches. No search fee, however complete dockets are $10.00. Required to search: name, years to search, DOB or SSN. Criminal records computerized from 06/86, prior in books. For records prior to 1986 provide month & year to search. Phone access limited to gov't agencies. Mail turnaround time 2 days. Search case records and dockets at www.shakerheightscourt.org/home/.
General Information: No medical or LEADS print-out records released. Fee to fax document $.50 per page. Court makes copy: $.05 per page. Self serve: same. Certification fee: $10.00 per document. Payee: Shaker Heights Municipal Court. Personal checks accepted. Visa, MC, Amex accepted in person only. Mail requests: SASE required.

South Euclid Municipal Court 1349 S Green Rd, South Euclid, OH 44121; 216-381-2880; fax: 216-381-1195; 8AM-4:30PM. ***Misdemeanor, Civil Actions under $15,000, Eviction, Small Claims.***

Civil Records: Access: Phone, fax, mail, in person. Both court and visitors may perform in person searches. No search fee. Required to search: name, years to search; also helpful: address. Civil cases indexed by defendant, plaintiff; index on computer back to 10/97; prior in docket books to 1960s. Mail turnaround time up to 1 week. Civil PAT goes back to 10/1997. PAT civil results show middle initial.
Criminal Records: Access: Mail, in person. Both court and visitors may perform in person searches. No search fee. Required to search: name, years to search, DOB, SSN; also helpful: address. Criminal records computerized from 10/97; prior in docket books to 1960s. Mail turnaround time up to 1 week. Criminal PAT goes back to same as civil. PAT criminal results show middle initial.
General Information: Will fax documents to local or toll free line. Court makes copy: no charge for 1st 10 pages, then $.10 per copy. Certification fee: $1.00 per page. Includes copies but if over 10 pages, add $.10 per page. Payee: Clerk of Court, South Euclid Municipal Court. Personal checks accepted. Major credit cards accepted in person only. Mail requests: SASE required.

Darke County

Common Pleas Court Courthouse, Greenville, OH 45331; 937-547-7335; probate phone: 937-547-7345; fax: 937-547-7305; 8AM-4:30PM. ***Felony, Civil Actions over $15,000, Probate.***
Probate is a separate court located at 300 Garst Ave.
Civil Records: Access: Mail, in person. Both court and visitors may perform in person searches. Search fee: $5.00 per name. Required to search: name, years to search. Civil cases indexed by defendant, plaintiff. Civil records in books to 1832, on microfiche from 1940s, computerized since 1993. Mail turnaround time 1-2 days. Civil PAT goes back to 1993.
Criminal Records: Access: Mail, in person. Both court and visitors may perform in person searches. Search fee: $5.00 per name. Required to search: name, years to search. Criminal records in books to 1832, on microfiche from 1940s, computerized since 1987. Mail turnaround time 1-2 days. Criminal PAT goes back to 1988.
General Information: No secret indictment records released. Will fax out documents. Court makes copy: $.25 per page. Self serve: same. Certification fee: $1.00. Payee: Clerk of Court. Business checks accepted. Mail requests: SASE required.

County Municipal Court Courthouse, Greenville, OH 45331-1990; 937-547-7340; fax: 937-547-7378; 8:30-4:30PM. ***Misdemeanor, Civil Actions under $15,000, Small Claims.***
Civil Records: Access: Mail, in person. Both court and visitors may perform in person searches. No search fee; limit of 5 search requests per month for commercial requesters. Required to search: name, years to search. Civil cases indexed by defendant, plaintiff. Civil records in books since 1959, computerized since 1996. Mail turnaround time 1 week. Civil PAT goes back to 1996.
Criminal Records: Access: Mail, in person. Both court and visitors may perform in person searches. No search fee; limit of 5 search requests per month for commercial requesters. Required to search: name, years to search, DOB; also helpful: SSN. Criminal records in books since 1959. Mail turnaround time 1 week. Criminal PAT goes back to same as civil.
General Information: No sealed or confidential records released. Will fax documents for a fee. Court makes copy: $.25 per page. Certification fee: $5.00 includes copy fee. Payee: County Municipal Court. Cashiers checks and money orders accepted. Visa/MC accepted. Mail requests: SASE required.

Defiance County

Common Pleas Court PO Box 716, Defiance, OH 43512; 419-782-1936; probate phone: 419-782-4181; fax: 419-782-2739; 8:30AM-4:30PM. ***Felony, Civil Actions over $10,000, Probate.***
Common Pleas Court records managed by Clerk of Courts. Probate is a separate office.
Civil Records: Access: Phone, in person. Visitors must perform in person searches themselves. No search fee. Required to search: name, years to search; also helpful: address. Civil cases indexed by defendant, plaintiff; index on computer since 1995. Most recent records are kept here. Civil PAT goes back to 1995. PAT results show name but DOB does not always appear.
Criminal Records: Access: Phone, in person. Visitors must perform in person searches themselves. No search fee. Required to search: name, years to search; also helpful: address, DOB, SSN. Criminal records on computer since 1995; prior records on docket books. Criminal PAT goes back to same as civil. PAT results show name but DOB does not always appear.
General Information: Will fax documents $2.00 1st page, $1.00 each add'l. Court makes copy: $.10 per page. Self serve: same. Certification fee: $1.00 per pleading,. Payee: Clerk of Court. Personal checks accepted; credit cards are not.

Defiance Municipal Court 324 Perry St, Defiance, OH 43512; 419-782-5756; criminal phone: 419-782-5756; civil phone: 419-782-4092; fax: 419-782-2018; 7AM-5PM. ***Misdemeanor, Civil Actions under $15,000, Eviction, Small Claims.***
www.defiancemunicipalcourt.com/
Staff member will perform searches only on Monday, Wednesday, and Fridays.
Civil Records: Access: Fax, mail, in person. Both court and visitors may perform in person searches. Search fee: $9.00 per name; fee only if records in basement storage, otherwise no search fee. Search fee if record on computer- $.10 per computer page. Required to search: name, years to search; also helpful: DOB, SSN, address. Civil cases indexed by defendant, plaintiff; index on computer from 12/89, prior in books to 1958. Mail turnaround time approx. 5 days. Civil PAT goes back to 10/1989. PAT results show name only. Public terminal available M,W,F noon-5PM and Tues, Thur 8AM-5PM.
Criminal Records: Access: Fax, Mail, in person. Both court and visitors may perform in person searches. Search fee: $9.00 per name; fee only if records in basement storage, otherwise no search fee. Required to search: name, years to search; also helpful: address, DOB, SSN. Criminal records computerized from 10/89, prior in books to 1958. Search fee if record on computer- $.05 per computer page. Mail turnaround time approx. 5 days. Criminal PAT goes back to same as civil.PAT results show name, DOB. Public terminal available M,W,F 1-5PM and Tues and Thur 7AM-5PM.
General Information: No confidential records released. Will fax documents. Court makes copy: $.05 per page. Certification fee: $1.00 per page. Payee: Municipal Court. Personal checks and credit cards accepted. Mail requests: SASE required.

Delaware County

Common Pleas Court 91 N Sandusky, Delaware, OH 43015; 740-833-2500; probate phone: 740-833-2680; fax: 740-833-2499; 8:30AM-4:30PM. ***Felony, Civil Actions over $15,000, Probate.***
www.delawarecountyclerk.org
Probate Court is separate and located at 88 N Sandusky St; Probate hours are 8:30AM-4:30PM. Fax number for Probate is not available.
Civil Records: Access: Mail, in person, online. Both court and visitors may perform in person searches. No search fee. Required to search: name, years to search; also helpful: address. Civil cases indexed by defendant, plaintiff; index on computer from 1992, prior books go back to 1800s. Mail turnaround time 1-2 days. Civil PAT goes back to 1992. PAT results show name only. Access to court records is free at www.delawarecountyclerk.org. Probate court index from 1852 to 1920 is free at www.midohio.net/dchsdcgs/probate.html.
Criminal Records: Access: Mail, in person, online. Both court and visitors may perform in person searches. No search fee. Required to search: name, years to search, DOB; also helpful: address, SSN. Criminal records computerized from 1992, prior books go back to 1800s. Mail turnaround time 1-2 days. Criminal PAT goes back to same as civil. PAT results show name only. Access to court records is free at www.delawarecountyclerk.org. Search the sheriff's county database of sex offenders, deadbeat parents, and most wanted list for free at www.delawarecountysheriff.com.
General Information: No grand jury proceedings or expungment records released. Will fax documents $1.00 per page. Court makes copy: $.05 per page. Self serve: same. Certification fee: $1.00. Payee: Clerk of Court. Personal checks accepted; credit cards are not. Mail requests: SASE required.

Delaware Municipal Court 70 N Union St, Delaware, OH 43015; 740-203-1550; criminal phone: 740-203-1570; civil phone: 740-203-1560; fax: 740-203-1549; 8AM-4:30PM. ***Misdemeanor, Civil Actions under $15,000, Eviction, Small Claims.***
www.municipalcourt.org
Civil Records: Access: Phone, mail, in person, online. Both court and visitors may perform in person searches. No search fee. Required to search: name, years to search. Civil cases indexed by defendant, plaintiff; index on computer from 1992, prior in books. Mail turnaround time 1-2 weeks. Civil PAT goes back to 1992. Terminal results also show SSNs. Municipal courts records are at www.municipalcourt.org:81/connection/court/lookup.xsp?in=cv.
Criminal Records: Access: Phone, mail, in person, online. Both court and visitors may perform in person searches. No search fee. Required to search: name, years to search, DOB; also helpful: SSN. Criminal records computerized from 1992, prior in books. Mail turnaround time 1-2 weeks. Criminal PAT goes back to same as civil. PAT criminal results show middle initial. Misdemeanor and traffic case records are free at www.municipalcourt.org:81/connection/court/lookup.xsp?in=ct. Also, search the court's DUI list at www.municipalcourt.org/main_dui.asp.
General Information: Online identifiers in results same as on public terminal. No assessment results or probation records released. Will not fax documents. Court makes copy: $.05 per page. Certification fee: $1.00. Payee: Delaware Municipal Court. Delaware County personal checks accepted. Visa/MC accepted. Mail requests: SASE required.

Erie County

Common Pleas Court 323 Columbus Ave, 1st Fl, Sandusky, OH 44870; 419-627-7705; probate phone: 419-627-7759; fax: 419-627-6684; 8AM-4PM M-TH; 8AM-5PM F. ***Felony, Civil Actions over $10,000, Probate.***
Online access may be available later this year.
Civil Records: Access: In person only. Visitors must perform in person searches themselves. Required to search: name, years to search. Civil cases indexed by defendant, plaintiff; index on books. Civil PAT goes back to 1998. PAT results show name only.
Criminal Records: Access: In person only. Visitors must perform in person searches themselves. Required to search: name, years to search, DOB, SSN, signed release. Criminal docket on books; computerized records since 2001. Criminal PAT goes back to same as civil. PAT results show name only.
General Information: Passports and expungments not released. Will fax documents $2.00 fax fee plus $1.00 per page. Court makes copy: $.25 per page. Certification fee: $1.00 for 1st page, $.25 each add'l. Payee: Clerk of Court. Personal checks accepted. No credit cards accepted; may be accepted later this year.

Erie County Municipal Court 150 W Mason Rd, Milan, OH 44846; 419-499-4689; fax: 419-499-3300; 8AM-4PM. ***Misdemeanor, Civil Actions under $15,000, Small Claims.***
Civil Records: Access: Mail, in person. Only the court performs in person searches; visitors may not. No search fee. Required to search: name, years to search; also helpful: address. Civil cases indexed by defendant, plaintiff; index on computer back to 1990, microfiche back to 1982. Mail turnaround time 3-4 days.
Criminal Records: Access: Mail, in person. Only the court performs in person searches; visitors may not. No search fee. Required to search: name, years to search; also helpful: address, DOB. Criminal records

computerized from 1990, microfiche back to 1982. Mail turnaround time 3-4 days.
General Information: No sealed records released. Will not fax documents. Court makes copy: $.10 per page. No certification fee. Payee: Erie County Municipal Court. No checks accepted. Visa/MC accepted only for court fines and costs. Mail requests: SASE required.

Sandusky Municipal Court 222 Meigs St, Sandusky, OH 44870; 419-627-5921; criminal phone: 419-627-5975; civil phone: 419-627-5924; fax: 419-627-5950; 7AM-4PM. ***Misdemeanor, Civil Actions under $15,000, Eviction, Small Claims.***
www.sanduskymunicipalcourt.org/
Civil Records: Access: Phone, fax, mail, in person, online. Both court and visitors may perform in person searches. No search fee. Required to search: name, years to search; also helpful: case number. Civil cases indexed by defendant, plaintiff; index on computer from 1987, prior in books. Mail turnaround time 3-4 days. Civil PAT goes back to 1991. PAT results show middle initial, DOB. Access Muni court records free at www.sanduskymunicipalcourt.org/search.shtml.
Criminal Records: Access: Phone, fax, mail, in person, online. Both court and visitors may perform in person searches. No search fee. Required to search: name, years to search, DOB; also helpful: SSN, case number. Criminal records computerized from 1987, prior in books. Mail turnaround time 3-4 days. Criminal PAT goes back to same as civil. PAT results show middle initial, DOB. Access Muni court records free at www.sanduskymunicipalcourt.org/search.shtml. Online results show middle initial, DOB.
General Information: No pending, Juvenile crimes of violence records, or expunged records released. Will fax documents $.10 per page. Court makes copy: $.10 per page. Certification fee: $4.00. Payee: Sandusky Municipal Court. No personal checks accepted; credit cards are. Mail requests: SASE requested.

Vermilion Municipal Court 687 Decatur St, Vermilion, OH 44089-1152; 440-204-2430; fax: 440-204-2431; 8AM-4PM. ***Misdemeanor, Civil Actions under $15,000, Eviction, Small Claims.***
www.vermilionmunicipalcourt.org
This court handles cases from both Erie and Lorain counties.
Civil Records: Access: Mail, in person, online. Both court and visitors may perform in person searches. No search fee. Required to search: name, years to search; also helpful: address. Civil cases indexed by defendant, plaintiff; index on computer since late 1991, indexed in books since 1966. Civil PAT goes back to 1991. Results include name of plaintiff and defendant. Online access to Municipal court records at www.vermilionmunicipalcourt.org/search.html.
Criminal Records: Access: Fax, mail, in person, online. Both court and visitors may perform in person searches. No search fee. Required to search: name, years to search; also helpful: SSN. Criminal records on computer since late 1991, indexed in books since 1966. Results include plaintiff's name and defendant's name for civil records, name for criminal records. Criminal PAT goes back to same as civil. PAT results show middle initial, DOB, and may include SSN. Online access to municipal court records is at www.vermilionmunicipalcourt.org/search.html. Online results show name only.
General Information: Online identifiers in results same as on public terminal. no addresses, victim info or confidential report records released without approval from prosecutors office. No fee to fax documents. Court makes copy for no fee. Certification fee: $2.00 includes copies. Payee: Vermilion Municipal Court. Personal checks and credit cards accepted.

Vermilion Municipal Court 687 Decatur St, Vermilion, OH 44089; 440-204-2430; fax: 440-204-2431; 8AM-4PM. ***Misdemeanor, Civil Actions under $15,000, Eviction, Small Claims.***
www.vermilionmunicipalcourt.org
This court handles cases from both Erie and Lorain counties including townships of Vermilion, Florence and Brownhelm and the city of Vermilion.
Civil Records: Access: Fax, mail, in person, online. Both court and visitors may perform in person searches. No search fee. Required to search: name, years to search. Civil cases indexed by defendant, plaintiff; index on computer from 1992, prior in books. Mail turnaround time 1-5 days. Civil PAT goes back to 1992. PAT results show name only. Online access to Municipal court records at the website.
Criminal Records: Access: Fax, mail, in person, online. Both court and visitors may perform in person searches. No search fee. Required to search: name, years to search, DOB; also helpful: SSN. Criminal records computerized from 1992, prior in books. Mail turnaround time 1-5 days. Criminal PAT goes back to 1992. PAT results show name only. Address may also appear on terminal results. Online access to criminal records is the same as civil.
General Information: Will fax documents to local or toll-free number. Court makes copy: No copy fee but $1.00 per page fee for a computer printout. Certification fee: $2.00 includes copies. Payee: Vermilion Municipal Court. Cashiers checks and money orders accepted. Visa/MC accepted. Mail requests: SASE required.

Fairfield County

Common Pleas Court PO Box 370, 224 E Main, Clerk's Office, Lancaster, OH 43130-0370; 740-687-7030; probate phone: 740-687-7090; fax: 740-687-0158; 8AM-4PM. ***Felony, Civil Actions over $10,000, Probate, Domestic.***
www.fairfieldcountyclerk.com
Probate Court is separate from this court but at the same address in Room 303.
Civil Records: Access: In person, online. Visitors must perform in person searches themselves. Required to search: name, years to search; also helpful: address. Civil cases indexed by defendant, plaintiff; index on computer from 10/93, in books to 1970, prior archived to 1800s. Civil PAT goes back to 10/1993. PAT results show middle initial, DOB. Online access to County Clerk's court records database is free at www.fairfieldcountyclerk.com/Search/.
Criminal Records: Access: In person, online. Visitors must perform in person searches themselves. Required to search: name, years to search; also helpful: address, DOB. Criminal records computerized from 10/93, in books to 1970, prior archived to 1800s. Criminal PAT goes back to same as civil. PAT results show middle initial, DOB. Online access to County Clerk's court records database is free at www.fairfieldcountyclerk.com/Search/. Online results show middle initial, DOB.
General Information: No adoption or juvenile records released. Will fax documents $2.00 1st page, $1.00 each add'l. Court makes copy: $.05 per page; first 20 copies are free. Certification fee: $5.00 per doc. Payee: Clerk of Court. Personal checks accepted. Visa/MC accepted in person only. Prepayment of copies is not required.

Fairfield County Municipal Court PO Box 2390, Lancaster, OH 43130; 740-687-6621; fax: 740-681-5014; 8AM-4PM. ***Misdemeanor, Civil Actions under $15,000, Eviction, Small Claims.***
www.fairfieldcountymunicipalcourt.org
Civil Records: Access: Mail, in person, online. Both court and visitors may perform in person searches. No search fee. Required to search: name, years to search. Civil cases indexed by defendant, plaintiff; index on computer from 1990, prior in books. Mail turnaround time 2 days. Civil PAT goes back to 10/1989. PAT results show middle initial, DOB. Search cases online at www.fairfieldcountymunicipalcourt.org/connection/court/.
Criminal Records: Access: Mail, in person, online. Both court and visitors may perform in person searches. No search fee. Required to search: name, years to search. Criminal records computerized from 1989, prior in books. Mail turnaround time 2 days. Criminal PAT goes back to same as civil. PAT results show middle initial, DOB. Search cases online at www.fairfieldcountymunicipalcourt.org/connection/court/.
General Information: Will fax documents to local or toll free line. Court makes copy for no fee. Certification fee: $1.00. Payee: Fairfield County Municipal Court. Personal checks and credit cards accepted. Mail requests: SASE required.

Fayette County

Common Pleas Court 110 E Court St, Washington Court House, OH 43160; 740-335-6371; probate phone: 740-335-0640; fax: 740-333-3522; 9AM-4PM. ***Felony, Civil Actions over $10,000, Probate.***
www.fayette-co-oh.com/Commplea/index.html
Probate is a separate court.
Civil Records: Access: Mail, in person, online. Visitors must perform in person searches themselves. No search fee. Required to search: name, years to search. Civil cases indexed by defendant, plaintiff; index on computer from 1992, prior in books to 1800s. Civil PAT goes back to 1/1992. PAT results show middle initial, DOB. Search docket information free at http://cp.onlinedockets.com/fayettecp/case_dockets/search.aspx.
Criminal Records: Access: Mail, in person, online. Visitors must perform in person searches themselves. No search fee. Required to search: name, years to search, DOB, SSN. Criminal records computerized from 1992, prior in books to 1800s. Mail turnaround time varies. Criminal PAT goes back to same as civil. PAT criminal results show middle initial. Search docket info free at http://cp.onlinedockets.com/fayettecp/case_dockets/search.aspx Online results show middle initial.
General Information: No records released. Fee to fax out file $1.00 per page, plus $2.00 for cover page. Court makes copy: $.25 per page. Self serve: same. Certification fee: $1.00 per cert. Payee: Clerk of Court. Personal checks accepted; credit cards are not. Mail requests: SASE required.

Municipal Court Washington Courthouse, 119 N Main St, Washington Court House, OH 43160; 740-636-2350; criminal fax: 740-636-2359; civil fax: same; 8AM-4PM. ***Misdemeanor, Civil Actions under $15,000, Eviction, Small Claims.***
http://216.29.108.131/
Civil Records: Access: Mail, in person, online. Both court and visitors may perform in person searches. No search fee. Required to search: name, years to search. Civil cases indexed by defendant, plaintiff; index on computer from 1990, prior in books to 1950s. Mail turnaround time 1 week. Civil PAT goes back to 1990. PAT results show name only. Search record index free at http://216.29.108.131/search.shtml.
Criminal Records: Access: Mail, in person, online. Both court and visitors may perform in person searches. No search fee. Required to search: name, years to search, DOB; also helpful: SSN. Criminal records computerized from 1990, prior in books to 1950s. Mail turnaround time 1 week. Criminal PAT goes back to same as civil. PAT results show name only. Search record index free at http://216.29.108.131/search.shtml. Online results show name only.
General Information: Online identifiers in results same as on public terminal. No records protected by the privacy act released. Will not fax documents. Court makes copy for no fee. Certification fee: $5.00 per document includes copies. Payee: Clerk of Court. Cashiers checks and money orders accepted. Credit cards accepted.

Franklin County

Common Pleas Court 373 S High St, 23rd Fl, Clerk of the Court of Common Pleas, Columbus, OH 43215-6311; 614-462-3600; criminal phone: 614-462-3650; civil phone: 614-462-3621; criminal fax: 614-462-5371; civil fax: 614-462-6661; 8AM-5PM. ***Felony, Civil Actions over $15,000.***
www.franklincountyohio.gov/clerk/
Records room address is 369 S High St, 3rd Fl.
Civil Records: Access: Online, in person. Visitors must perform in person searches themselves.

Required to search: name, years to search. Civil cases indexed by defendant, plaintiff. Civil records go back to 1820. Civil PAT goes back to 1978. PAT results show middle initial, DOB. Access records 3AM-11PM at http://fcdcfcjs.co.franklin.oh.us/CaseInformationOnline/ and includes domestic relations cases.
Criminal Records: Access: Online, in person. Both court and visitors may perform in person searches. No search fee. Required to search: name, years to search. Criminal records available since 1935. Criminal PAT goes back to 1980. PAT results show middle initial, DOB. Access records 3AM-11PM at http://fcdcfcjs.co.franklin.oh.us/CaseInformationOnline/. Online results show middle initial, DOB.
General Information: Online identifiers in results same as on public terminal. No sealed or expunged records released. Will fax out documents for fee. Court makes copy: $.10 per page. Self serve: none. Certification fee: $1.00 per page. Payee: Franklin County Clerk of Courts. Only cashiers checks and money orders accepted. No credit cards accepted.

Franklin County Municipal Court - Civil Division 375 S High St, 3rd Fl, Columbus, OH 43215; 614-645-7220; civil phone: 614-645-8161-file room; fax: 614-645-6919; 8AM-5PM. ***Civil Actions under $15,000, Eviction, Small Claims.***
www.fcmcclerk.com
Civil Records: Access: Phone, fax, mail, online, in person. Both court and visitors may perform in person searches. No search fee. Required to search: name, years to search. Civil cases indexed by defendant, plaintiff; index on computer from 1992, prior in books to 1974. Mail turnaround time 2-3 days. Public use terminal has civil records back to 1992. Records from the Clerk of Court Courtview database free online at www.fcmcclerk.com/pa/pa.php. Search by name or case number.
General Information: Online identifiers in results same as on public terminal. No sealed or expunged records released. Will fax documents for free. Court makes copy: $.05 each. Certification fee: $1.00 per page copy fee included. Payee: Franklin County Municipal Court. Personal checks and credit cards accepted. Mail requests: SASE required.

Franklin County Municipal Court - Criminal Division 375 S High St, 2nd Fl, Columbus, OH 43215; criminal phone: 614-645-8186; fax: 614-645-6036; 24 hours a day. ***Misdemeanor, Traffic.***
www.fcmcclerk.com
Criminal Records: Access: Mail, online, in person. Both court and visitors may perform in person searches. No search fee. Required to search: name, years to search; also helpful: DOB, SSN. Criminal records go back to 1987; on computer back to 1992. Mail turnaround time 7 days, usually less. Public use terminal has crim records back to 1992. PAT results show middle initial, DOB. Criminal and traffic records from the Clerk of Court Courtview database free online at www.fcmcclerk.com/pa/pa.php. Search by name, dates, ticket, address or case numbers.
General Information: No sealed or expunged records released. Court makes copy: $.05 per page. Certification fee: $1.00 per page. Payee: Franklin County Municipal Court. Personal checks and credit cards accepted. Mail requests: SASE required.

Probate Court 373 S High St, 22nd Fl, Columbus, OH 43215-6311; 614-462-3894; 8AM-4:30PM. ***Probate.***
www.franklincountyohio.gov/probate/index.cfm
No psych, adoption or estate tax records released. Search probate online at www.co.franklin.oh.us/probate/ProbateSearch.html.

Fulton County

Common Pleas Court 210 S Fulton, Wauseon, OH 43567; 419-337-9230; probate phone: 419-337-9242; 8:30AM-4:30PM. ***Felony, Civil Actions over $3,000, Probate.***
www.fultoncountyoh.com/
Civil Records: Access: In person, online. Visitors must perform in person searches themselves. Required to search: name, years to search. Civil cases indexed by defendant, plaintiff; index on computer from 9/88, prior in books to 1968, archived to 1800s. Civil PAT goes back to 9/1988. Access an index of civil case records at www.fultoncountyoh.com/pa/.
Criminal Records: Access: In person, online. Visitors must perform in person searches themselves. Required to search: name, years to search, DOB; SSN helpful. Criminal records computerized from 9/88, prior in books to 1968, archived to 1800s. Criminal PAT goes back to same as civil. Access the criminal record index at www.fultoncountyoh.com/pa/.
General Information: Will fax documents $2.00 plus $1.00 per page. Court makes copy: $.25 per page first 25 pages, $.13 next 75 pages, $.06 thereafter. Certification fee: $1.00 per page. Payee: Mary Gype Clerk of Court. Personal checks accepted; credit cards are not.

County Court Eastern District 204 S Main St, Swanton, OH 43558; 419-826-5636; fax: 419-825-3324; 8:30AM-4:30PM. ***Misdemeanor, Civil Actions under $15,000, Small Claims.***
www.fultoncountyoh.com/
Civil Records: Access: Mail, fax, in person, online. Both court and visitors may perform in person searches. No search fee. Required to search: name, years to search. Civil cases indexed by defendant, plaintiff; index on computer from 1988, prior in books. Mail turnaround time less than 2 weeks. Access court records back to 1995 free at www.fultoncountyoh.com/pa/.
Criminal Records: Access: Mail, in person, online. Only the court performs in person searches; visitors may not. No search fee. Required to search: name, years to search, DOB; signed release requested. Criminal records computerized from 1988, prior in books. Mail turnaround time under 2 weeks. Access court records back to 1995 free at www.fultoncountyoh.com/pa/.
General Information: No pending case records released. Will fax documents for no fee. Court makes copy: No copy fee but must supply own paper for copies. No certification fee. No personal checks accepted. Visa/MC accepted. Mail requests: SASE required.

County Court Western District 224 S Fulton St, Wauseon, OH 43567; 419-337-9212; fax: 419-337-9286; 8:30AM-4:30PM. ***Misdemeanor, Civil Actions under $15,000, Small Claims.***
www.fultoncountyoh.com
In-person searchers should call first; be aware Tuesdays are busy and hard to get on computer to search. Probate fax is same as main fax number.
Civil Records: Access: Mail, in person, online. Both court and visitors may perform in person searches. No search fee. Required to search: name, years to search. Civil cases indexed by defendant, plaintiff; index on computer from 1989, prior in books. Mail turnaround time 2-3 days. Civil PAT goes back to 1989. PAT civil results show middle initial. Access court records back to 1995 free at www.fultoncountyoh.com/pa/.
Criminal Records: Access: Mail, in person, onlinc. Both court and visitors may perform in person searches. No search fee. Required to search: name, years to search, DOB; also helpful: SSN. Criminal records on computer after 1988, indexed by name and DOB. Mail turnaround time 2-3 days. Criminal PAT goes back to 1988. PAT results show middle initial, DOB. Access court records back to 1995 free at www.fultoncountyoh.com/pa/ Online results show middle initial, DOB.
General Information: Online identifiers in results same as on public terminal. No pending case records released. Will fax documents for no fee. Court makes copy: $.10 per page. Certification fee: $1.00 includes copies. Payee: County Court Western District. No personal checks. Visa/MC accepted. Mail requests: SASE required.

Gallia County

Common Pleas Court - Gallia County Courthouse 18 Locust St, Rm 1290, Gallipolis, OH 45631-1290; 740-446-4612 x223; probate phone: 740-446-4612 x240; fax: 740-441-2932; 8AM-4PM. ***Felony, Civil Actions over $10,000, Probate.***
www.gallianet.net/Gallia/common_pleas.htm
Email questions to commonpleas@gallianet.net. Probate is in room 1293
Civil Records: Access: In person only. Visitors must perform in person searches themselves. Required to search: name, years to search. Civil cases indexed by defendant, plaintiff; index on computer from 7/91, in books to 1968, archived to 1800s. Civil PAT goes back to 7/1991.
Criminal Records: Access: In person only. Visitors must perform in person searches themselves. Required to search: name, years to search. Criminal records computerized from 7/91, in books to 1968, archived to 1800s. Criminal PAT goes back to same as civil.
General Information: No records released. Will fax copies for $1.00 per page if pre-paid. Court makes copy: $.25 per page. Certification fee: $1.00. Payee: Clerk of Court. Personal checks accepted.

Gallipolis Municipal Court 518 2nd Ave, Gallipolis, OH 45631; 740-446-9400; fax: 740-441-6025; 7:30AM-4PM. ***Misdemeanor, Civil Actions under $15,000, Eviction, Small Claims.***
Civil Records: Access: Phone, mail, in person. Both court and visitors may perform in person searches. No search fee. Required to search: name, years to search; also helpful: address. Civil cases indexed by defendant, plaintiff; index on computer from 8/93, prior in books. Mail turnaround time 1 week. Civil PAT goes back to 1993.
Criminal Records: Access: Phone, mail, in person. Both court and visitors may perform in person searches. No search fee. Required to search: name, years to search; also helpful: address, DOB, SSN. Criminal records computerized from 8/93, prior in books. Mail turnaround time 1 week. Criminal PAT goes back to 1993.
General Information: No expunged records released. Will not fax documents. Court makes copy: $.10 per page. Self serve: same. Certification fee: $2.00. Payee: Municipal Court. Personal checks and major credit cards accepted. Mail requests: SASE required.

Geauga County

Common Pleas Court Clerk of Court, 100 Short Court, Ste 300, Chardon, OH 44024; 440-279-1960; fax: 440-286-2127; 8AM-4:30PM. ***Felony, Civil Actions over $10,000, Probate.***
www.co.geauga.oh.us
Civil Records: Access: In person, online. Visitors must perform in person searches themselves. Required to search: name, years to search. Civil cases indexed by defendant, plaintiff; index on computer from 1990, in books from 1968, prior archived. Will not and do not index or search over the phone. Civil PAT goes back to 1990. Online access is free from the Clerk of Courts at www.co.geauga.oh.us/departments/clerk_of_courts/Docket2/Courtintro.asp. Online records go back to 1990. Includes domestic cases.
Criminal Records: Access: In person, online. Visitors must perform in person searches themselves. Required to search: name, years to search. Criminal records computerized from 1990, in books from 1968, prior archived. Will not and do not index or search over the phone. Criminal PAT goes back to same as civil. Online access is same as civil.
General Information: no sealed records released. Will not fax documents. Court makes copy: $.05 per page. Certification fee: $1.00 per page. Cert fee includes copies. Payee: Clerk of Court. Personal checks and major credit cards accepted. Mail requests: SASE required for mail return of any copies.

Chardon Municipal Court 111 Water St, Chardon, OH 44024; 440-286-2670/2684; criminal phone: 440-286-2670; civil phone: 440-286-2684; fax: 440-286-2679; 8AM-4:30PM. ***Misdemeanor, Civil Actions under $15,000, Eviction, Small Claims.***
www.co.geauga.oh.us/departments/muni_court.htm
Civil Records: Access: Mail, in person, online. Both court and visitors may perform in person searches. No search fee. Required to search: name, years to search; also helpful: address. Civil cases indexed by defendant, plaintiff; index on computer from 1990, prior in books. Mail turnaround time 2-4 days. Civil PAT goes back to 1990. PAT results show middle initial, DOB, SSN. Public terminal available 8AM-4:30PM. Search court records free at www.auditor.co.geauga.oh.us/pa/.
Criminal Records: Access: Mail, in person, online. Both court and visitors may perform in person searches. No search fee. Required to search: name, years to search; also helpful: address, DOB, SSN. Criminal records computerized from 1988, prior in books to 1965. Mail turnaround time 2-4 days. Criminal PAT goes back to same as civil. PAT results show middle initial, DOB, SSN. Public terminal available 8AM-4:30PM. Search court records free at www.auditor.co.geauga.oh.us/pa/. Online results show middle initial, DOB.
General Information: No expunged records released. Will fax documents to local or toll free line. Court makes copy: $.05 per page. Certification fee: $1.50 per request. Payee: Chardon Municipal Court. Personal checks accepted. Visa/MC accepted. Mail requests: SASE required.

Greene County

Common Pleas Court 45 N Detroit St, Xenia, OH 45385; 937-562-5290; probate phone: 937-562-5280; fax: 937-562-5309; 8AM-4:30PM. ***Felony, Civil Actions over $15,000, Probate.***
www.co.greene.oh.us/COC/clerk.htm
Probate is separate court at same physical address; closes at 4PM.
Civil Records: Access: In person, online. Visitors must perform in person searches themselves. Required to search: name, years to search. Civil cases indexed by defendant, plaintiff; index on computer from 1982, prior in books and on microfiche. Civil PAT goes back to 1982. PAT results show middle initial, DOB. Online access to clerk of court records is free at www.co.greene.oh.us/pa/pa.htm. Search by name or case number. Also, search probate cases free at www.co.greene.oh.us/Probate/search/case_search.asp.
Criminal Records: Access: In person, online. Visitors must perform in person searches themselves. Required to search: name, years to search; also helpful: DOB, case number. Criminal records computerized from 1982, prior in books and on microfiche. Criminal PAT goes back to same as civil. PAT results show middle initial, DOB. Online access to clerk of court records is free at www.co.greene.oh.us/pa/pa.htm. Search by name or case number. Also, search probate cases free at www.co.greene.oh.us/Probate/search/case_search.asp. Online results show middle initial, DOB.
General Information: No sealed records released. Will fax out specific case files for $2.00 per page, if prepaid. Court makes copy: $.05 per page. Certification fee: $1.00 per page includes copy fee. Payee: Clerk of Court. Personal checks accepted; credit cards are not. Mail requests: SASE required for mail return of any copies.

Fairborn Municipal Court 1148 Kauffman Ave, Fairborn, OH 45324; criminal phone: 937-754-3040; civil phone: 937-754-3044; fax: 937-879-4422; 7:30AM-4PM. ***Misdemeanor, Civil Actions under $20,000, Eviction, Small Claims.***
http://ci.fairborn.oh.us/court.htm
Civil Records: Access: Mail, in person, online. Both court and visitors may perform in person searches. No search fee. Required to search: name, years to search; also helpful: address. Civil cases indexed by defendant, plaintiff; index on computer from 1991, records go back to 1976. Mail turnaround time 1 week. Civil PAT goes back to 1991. PAT civil results show middle initial. The terminal must be set up ahead of time; it is not open to any walk-in person without aid. Website offers free online access to civil, misdemeanor and traffic records, or search at http://70.62.41.228/connection/court/
Criminal Records: Access: Mail, in person, online. Both court and visitors may perform in person searches. No search fee. Required to search: name, years to search, SSN; also helpful: address, DOB. Criminal records computerized from mid 1991, records go back to 1976. Mail turnaround time 1 week. Criminal PAT goes back to same as civil. PAT results show middle initial, DOB. The terminal must be set up ahead of time; it is not open to any walk-in person without aid. Online access same as civil. Online results show middle initial, DOB.
General Information: Online identifiers in results same as on public terminal. Will not fax documents. Court makes copy: $.25 per page. Certification fee: $2.00. Payee: Municipal Court. Personal checks accepted. Visa/MC accepted in person only. Mail requests: SASE required.

Xenia Municipal Court 101 N Detroit, Xenia, OH 45385; 937-376-7294; 376-7297 (Civil Clerk); fax: 937-376-7288; 8AM-4:30PM M,T,W; 8AM-4PM TH,F. ***Misdemeanor, Civil Actions under $15,000, Eviction, Small Claims.***
www.ci.xenia.oh.us/index.php?page=municipal-court
Civil Records: Access: Mail, in person, online. Both court and visitors may perform in person searches. Search fee: $10.00 per name. Required to search: name, years to search; also helpful: address. Civil cases indexed by defendant, plaintiff; index on computer from 1994, prior in books to 1966. Mail turnaround time 2-3 days. Civil PAT goes back to 1/1994. Online access to Municipal Court records free at www.ci.xenia.oh.us/index.php?page=public-access.
Criminal Records: Access: Mail, in person, online. Both court and visitors may perform in person searches. Search fee: $10.00 per name. Required to search: name, years to search; also helpful: address, DOB, SSN. Criminal records computerized from 1994, prior in books to 1966. Mail turnaround time 2-3 days. Criminal PAT goes back to same as civil. Access to criminal records is the same as civil. Online results show name, DOB.
General Information: Online identifiers in results same as on public terminal. No search warrant records released. No fee to fax documents. Court makes copy: $.10 per page. Certification fee: $2.00 includes copies. Payee: Municipal Court. Business checks accepted. Visa/MC accepted. Mail requests: SASE required.

Guernsey County

Common Pleas Court 801 E Wheeling Ave D-300, Cambridge, OH 43725; 740-432-9230; probate phone: 740-432-9262; fax: 740-432-7807; 8:30AM-4PM. ***Felony, Civil Actions over $10,000, Probate.***
http://66.219.161.39/pa/
Probate is a separate division with separate records and personnel.
Civil Records: Access: In person, online. Visitors must perform in person searches themselves. Required to search: name, years to search. Civil cases indexed by defendant, plaintiff; index on computer from 1990, prior in books, archived to 1800s. Civil PAT goes back to 1990. Access case index data free at http://74.218.3.68/pa/.
Criminal Records: Access: In person, online. Visitors must perform in person searches themselves. Required to search: name, years to search, DOB. Criminal records computerized from 1990, prior in books, archived to 1800s. Criminal PAT goes back to 1990. Access case index data free at http://74.218.3.68/pa/.
General Information: Online identifiers in results same as on public terminal. No expunged records released. Will fax documents $1.00 per page. Court makes copy: $.25 per page. Certification fee: $2.00. Payee: Clerk of Court. Personal checks accepted; credit cards are not. Mail requests: SASE required for mail return of any copies.

Cambridge Municipal Court 134 Southgate Pky, Cambridge, OH 43725; 740-439-5585; criminal phone: x226; civil phone: x240; fax: 740-439-5666; 8:30AM-4:30PM. ***Misdemeanor, Civil Actions under $15,000, Eviction, Small Claims.***
www.cambridgeoh.org/court.htm
Civil Records: Access: Mail, fax, in person, online. Both court and visitors may perform in person searches. No search fee. Required to search: name, years to search; also helpful: address. Civil cases indexed by defendant, plaintiff; index on computer from 1988, prior in books. Fax civil court requests to 740-439-9405. Mail turnaround time 3-5 days. Public use terminal available. Access Muni Court records free at http://webconnect03.civicacmi.com/cambridge/court/. An agency login also available; registration required.
Criminal Records: Access: Mail, in person, fax, online. Visitors must perform in person searches themselves. No search fee. Required to search: name, years to search, DOB, SSN; also helpful: address. Criminal records computerized from 1988, prior in books. Mail turnaround time 3-5 days. Public use terminal available. Access criminal and traffic index online- same as civil above.
General Information: No confidential records released. Will fax documents for $5.00 fee. Court makes copy for no fee. Certification fee: $2.00. Payee: Cambridge Municipal Court. Personal checks accepted. Visa/MC accepted. Mail requests: SASE required.

Hamilton County

Common Pleas Court 1000 Main St, Rm 315, Cincinnati, OH 45202; criminal phone: 513-946-5677; civil phone: 513-946-5635; probate phone: 513-946-3580; 8AM-4PM. ***Felony, Civil Actions over $10,000, Probate.***
www.courtclerk.org
Probate is separate court.
Civil Records: Access: Mail, in person, online. Both court and visitors may perform in person searches. No search fee. Required to search: name, years to search. Civil cases indexed by defendant, plaintiff; index on computer since 1960s, prior in books and files. Mail turnaround time 2-3 days. Civil PAT goes back to 1999. Records from the court clerk are free at the website or www.courtclerk.org/queries.aps. Online civil index goes back to 1991. Also, search probate records free at www.probatect.org/case_search/casesearch.asp.
Criminal Records: Access: Mail, online, in person. Both court and visitors may perform in person searches. No search fee. Required to search: name, years to search, signed release; also helpful: DOB, SSN. Criminal records indexed on computer since 1960s, prior in books and files. Mail turnaround time 2-3 days. Criminal PAT goes back to 1989. Online access to criminal records is the same as civil. Online criminal index goes back to 1986.
General Information: Criminal histories not released. Will not fax documents. Court makes copy: $.10 per page. Self serve: same. Certification fee: $1.00. Payee: Clerk of Court. Personal checks and major credit cards accepted. Mail requests: SASE required.

Hamilton County Municipal Court - Civil 1000 Main St, Rm 115, Cincinnati, OH 45202; 513-946-5700; fax: 513-946-5710; 8AM-4PM. ***Civil Actions under $15,000, Eviction, Small Claims.***
www.courtclerk.org
Civil Records: Access: Fax, mail, online, in person. Both court and visitors may perform in person searches. No search fee. Required to search: name; also helpful: years to search. Civil cases indexed by defendant, plaintiff; index on computer from 1989, prior on microfilm. Mail turnaround time 5 days. Public use terminal has civil records back to 1989. PAT civil results show middle initial. Records from the court clerk are free at the website or www.courtclerk.org/queries.aps.
General Information: No expungment records released. No fee to fax documents. Court makes copy: $.10 per page; $5.00 for docket sheet. Certification

fee: $2.00. Payee: Clerk of Courts. Personal checks and credit cards accepted.

Hamilton County Municipal Court - Criminal 1000 Sycamore St #112, Cincinnati, OH 45202; 513-946-6029/6040; 8AM-4PM. ***Misdemeanor.***
www.courtclerk.org
Criminal Records: Access: In person only. Visitors must perform in person searches themselves. Required to search: name, years to search, DOB; also helpful: SSN. Criminal records computerized from 2000, prior on microfiche back to 1973. Court clerk records are no longer online. Public use terminal has crim records back to 1999. PAT results show name only.
General Information: Will fax documents for add'l $.10 per page. Court makes copy: $.10 per page. Certification fee: $2.00. Payee: Clerk of Courts. Personal checks accepted. Visa/MC accepted.

Hancock County

Common Pleas Court 300 S Main St, Findlay, OH 45840; 419-424-7037/7008; probate phone: 419-424-7079; 8:30AM-4:30PM. ***Felony, Civil Actions over $10,000, Probate.***
www.co.hancock.oh.us/commonpleas
Civil Records: Access: Mail, in person, online. Both court and visitors may perform in person searches. Search fee: $15.00 per name. Required to search: name, years to search. Civil cases indexed by defendant, plaintiff; index on computer from 1985, microfiche from 1974, dockets archived to 1800s. Mail turnaround time 10 days. Civil PAT goes back to 1985. PAT results show name, DOB. Search records online back to 1985 at http://pa.co.hancock.oh.us/.
Criminal Records: Access: Mail, in person, online. Both court and visitors may perform in person searches. Search fee: $15.00 per name. Required to search: name, years to search. Criminal records computerized from 1985, microfiche from 1974, dockets archived to 1800s. Mail turnaround time 8-10 days. Criminal PAT goes back to same as civil.PAT results show name, DOB. Search records online back to 1985 at http://pa.co.hancock.oh.us/. Online results show name, DOB.
General Information: Online identifiers in results same as on public terminal. No home investigations, medical records released. Will not fax documents. Court makes copy: $.25 per page. Certification fee: $1.00 per page. Payee: Clerk of Court. Personal checks accepted; credit cards are not. Mail requests: SASE required.

Findlay Municipal Court PO Box 826, Findlay, OH 45839; 419-424-7805; criminal phone: 419-424-7141; civil phone: 419-424-7143; criminal fax: 419-424-7803; civil fax: same; 8AM-5PM; 8AM-7PM T only. ***Misdemeanor, Civil Actions under $15,000, Eviction, Small Claims.***
www.ci.findlay.oh.us/municourt/
Civil Records: Access: Mail, in person, online. Both court and visitors may perform in person searches. Search fee: $2.00 per name/SSN. Required to search: name, years to search. Civil cases indexed by defendant, plaintiff; index on computer from 1984. Mail turnaround time 24 hours. Civil PAT goes back to 1984. Online access from www.ci.findlay.oh.us/municourt/searchcivildocket.asp?pageId=71.
Criminal Records: Access: Mail, in person, online. Both court and visitors may perform in person searches. Search fee: $2.00 per name/SSN. Required to search: name, years to search, DOB, SSN. Criminal records computerized from 1984. Mail turnaround time 24 hours. Criminal PAT goes back to same as civil. Online access same as civil.
General Information: Will not fax documents. Court makes copy: $.10 per page. Self serve: same. Certification fee: $1.00. Payee: Findlay Municipal Court. Hancock County resident's checks accepted. Visa/MC accepted. Mail requests: SASE required.

Hardin County

Common Pleas Court Courthouse, #310, Kenton, OH 43326; 419-674-2278; probate phone: 419-674-2230; fax: 419-674-2273; 8:30AM-4PM. ***Felony, Civil Actions over $15,000.***
http://hardincourts.com/
Civil Records: Access: Mail, in person. Both court and visitors may perform in person searches. Search fee: $5.00 per name. Required to search: full name, years to search, SSN, DOB, reason for request. Civil cases indexed by defendant, plaintiff. Current records on computer as of 1/95. Overall records go back to 1885. Mail turnaround time 2-4 days. Civil PAT goes back to 10/1994.
Criminal Records: Access: Mail, fax, in person. Both court and visitors may perform in person searches. Search fee: $5.00 per name. Required to search: full name, years to search, SSN, DOB, reason for request. Current records on computer as of 1/95. Overall records go back to 1885. Mail turnaround time 2-4 days. Criminal PAT goes back to same as civil. Online access to be available soon.
General Information: Will fax documents $2.00 1st page, $1.00 each add'l. Court makes copy: $.25 per page. Self serve: same. Certification fee: $1.00 per page. Payee: Clerk of Court. Business checks accepted. Major credit cards accepted. Mail requests: SASE required.

Hardin County Municipal Court PO Box 250, 111 W Franklin, Kenton, OH 43326; 419-674-4362; criminal fax: 419-674-4096; civil fax: same; 8:30AM-4PM. ***Misdemeanor, Civil Actions under $15,000, Eviction, Small Claims.***
http://hardincourts.com/
Civil Records: Access: Mail, in person. Both court and visitors may perform in person searches. Search fee: $5.00. Required to search: name, years to search. Civil cases indexed by defendant, plaintiff; index on computer since 1989, prior on books. Mail turnaround time 1-2 days. Civil PAT goes back to 1989.
Criminal Records: Access: Mail, in person. Both court and visitors may perform in person searches. Search fee: $5.00. Required to search: name, years to search; also helpful: SSN. Criminal records on computer since 1989, prior on books. Mail turnaround time 1-2 days. Criminal PAT goes back to same as civil.
General Information: Will fax documents to local or toll-free number. Court makes copy: $.25 per page. Certification fee: $2.00 per page includes copies. Payee: Hardin County Municipal Court. Business checks accepted. Major credit cards accepted; $5.00 usage fee added per transaction. Mail requests: SASE required.

Harrison County

Common Pleas Court 100 W Market, Cadiz, OH 43907; 740-942-8863; probate phone: 740-942-8868; fax: 740-942-4693; 8:30AM-4:30PM. ***Felony, Civil Actions over $15,000, Probate.***
Probate records in separate index at this same address. Probate fax- 740-942-8483.
Civil Records: Access: Phone, fax, mail, in person. Both court and visitors may perform in person searches. No search fee. Required to search: name, years to search; also helpful: address. Civil cases indexed by defendant, plaintiff; index on computer since 1994, in books back to 1800s. Civil PAT goes back to 1994.
Criminal Records: Access: In person only. Visitors must perform in person searches themselves. Required to search: name, years to search; also helpful: address, DOB, SSN. Criminal records on computer since 1994, in books back to 1800s. Criminal PAT goes back to same as civil.
General Information: No secret records released. Will fax documents $.25 per page. Court makes copy: $.25 per page. Certification fee: $1.00. Payee: Clerk of Court. No personal checks or credit cards accepted. Mail requests: SASE required for civil.

Harrison County Court Courthouse, 100 W Market St, Cadiz, OH 43907; 740-942-8865; fax: 740-942-3541; 8AM-4:30PM. ***Misdemeanor, Civil Actions under $15,000, Small Claims.***
Civil Records: Access: In person only. Visitors must perform in person searches themselves. Required to search: name, years to search. Civil cases indexed by defendant, plaintiff. Civil records in books; on computer back to 2/2000. Civil PAT goes back to 2/2000. PAT results show name only.
Criminal Records: Access: In person only. Visitors must perform in person searches themselves. Required to search: name, years to search, DOB; SSN helpful. Criminal records in books; on computer back to 2/2000. Criminal PAT goes back to same as civil. PAT results show name only.
General Information: Will fax specific case file. Court makes copy: $.05 per page. Certification fee: $6.00 per document. Payee: Harrison County Court. Personal or cashier checks and money orders accepted. No credit cards accepted.

Henry County

Common Pleas Court 660 N Perry St #302, Napoleon, OH 43545; 419-592-5926; criminal phone: 419-592-5886; civil phone: 419-592-5886; probate phone: 419-592-7771; criminal fax: 419-592-5888; civil fax: 419-592-5888; 8:30AM-4:30PM. ***Felony, Civil Actions over $15,000, Probate.***
www.henrycountyohio.com
Probate Court is same address, office #203. Probate copies are $1.00 per page. Probate fax- 419-592-7000
Civil Records: Access: Fax, mail, in person. Visitors must perform in person searches themselves. No search fee. Required to search: name, years to search. Civil cases indexed by defendant, plaintiff; index on computer from 10/94, prior in books. Civil PAT goes back to 10/1994. PAT results show name only.
Criminal Records: Access: Fax, mail, in person. Visitors must perform in person searches themselves. No search fee. Required to search: name, years to search. Criminal records computerized from 10/94, prior in books. Mail turnaround time 3 days. Criminal PAT goes back to 10/1994. PAT results show name only.
General Information: No adoption or mental records released. Will fax documents $3.00 1st page, $1.00 each add'l. Court makes copy: $.25 per page first 25 pages; $.12 each up to 75 pages. Certification fee: $1.00 per page. Payee: Henry County Clerk of Courts. No personal checks or credit cards accepted.

Napoleon Municipal Court PO Box 502, Napoleon, OH 43545; 419-592-2851; fax: 419-592-1805; 8AM-5PM. ***Misdemeanor, Civil Actions under $15,000, Eviction, Small Claims.***
Civil Records: Access: Phone, fax, mail, in person. Both court and visitors may perform in person searches. No search fee. Required to search: name, years to search. Civil cases indexed by defendant, plaintiff; index on computer from 1990, prior in books. Mail turnaround time 1-2 days.
Criminal Records: Access: Phone, fax, mail, in person. Both court and visitors may perform in person searches. No search fee. Required to search: name, years to search, DOB; also helpful: SSN. Criminal records computerized from 1990, prior in books. Mail turnaround time 1-2 days.
General Information: No alcohol treatment records released. Will fax documents for no fee. Court makes copy: $.05 per page. Certification fee: $1.00. Payee: Clerk of Court. Personal checks and credit cards accepted. Mail requests: SASE required.

Highland County

Common Pleas Court PO Box 821, Hillsboro, OH 45133; 937-393-9957; probate phone: 937-393-9981; fax: 937-393-9878; 8AM-4:30PM. ***Felony, Civil Actions over $10,000, Probate.***
Probate is a separate court.
Civil Records: Access: Mail, fax, in person. Both court and visitors may perform in person searches. No search fee. Required to search: name, years to search; also helpful: address. Civil cases indexed by defendant, plaintiff. Civil records in books since 1800s; on computer since 1995. Mail turnaround time usually same day. Civil PAT goes back to 1995. PAT civil results show middle initial. Terminal results may also include address.

Criminal Records: Access: Mail, fax, in person. Both court and visitors may perform in person searches. No search fee. Required to search: name, years to search, DOB, signed release; also helpful: SSN. Criminal records in books since 1800s; on computer since 1986. Mail turnaround time same day. Criminal PAT goes back to 1986. PAT results show middle initial, DOB, SSN.
General Information: No sealed records released. Will fax documents to local or toll free line. Court makes copy: $.10 per page. Self serve: same. Certification fee: $1.00 per page. Payee: Clerk of Court. Personal checks accepted; credit cards are not. Mail requests: SASE required.

Hillsboro County Municipal Court 130 Homestead Ave, Hillsboro, OH 45133; 937-393-3022; criminal fax: 937-393-0517; civil fax: same; 7AM-3:30PM M,T,TH,F; 7AM-N W. ***Misdemeanor, Civil Actions under $15,000, Eviction, Small Claims.***
www.hillsboroohio.net
Civil Records: Access: Phone, fax, mail, in person, online. Only the court performs in person searches; visitors may not. No search fee. Required to search: name, years to search. Civil cases indexed by defendant, plaintiff; index on computer from 1991, prior in books. Mail turnaround time 1-2 days. Online access is same as criminal, see below.
Criminal Records: Access: Phone, fax, mail, in person, online. Only the court performs in person searches; visitors may not. No search fee. Required to search: name, years to search, DOB, SSN. Criminal records computerized from 1991, prior in books. Mail turnaround time 1-2 days. Online access is free at http://24.123.13.34/.
General Information: No expunged records released. No fee to fax documents local or toll free only. Court makes copy: $.15 per page. Certification fee: $.50 per page. Payee: Hillsboro Municipal Court. Personal checks accepted; credit cards are not. Mail requests: SASE required.

Hocking County

Common Pleas Court PO Box 108, Logan, OH 43138; 740-385-2616; probate phone: 740-385-3022; fax: 740-385-1822; 8:30AM-4PM. ***Felony, Civil Actions over $10,000.***
www.co.hocking.oh.us/clerk/index.htm
Probate is a separate court at the number given.
Civil Records: Access: Fax, mail, in person, online. Both court and visitors may perform in person searches. No search fee. Required to search: name, years to search; also helpful: address. Civil cases indexed by defendant, plaintiff; index on computer since 1996, in books to late 1800s. Mail turnaround time 1-2 days. Civil PAT goes back to 1996. PAT civil results show middle initial. Access the court case index free at www.court.co.hocking.oh.us/cgi-bin/db2www.pgm/cpq.mbr/main.
Criminal Records: Access: Fax, mail, in person, online. Both court and visitors may perform in person searches. No search fee. Required to search: name, years to search; also helpful: address, DOB, SSN. Criminal records date back to 1980 on docket books. Mail turnaround time 1-2 days. Criminal PAT goes back to same as civil. PAT criminal results show middle initial. Access the court case index free at www.court.co.hocking.oh.us/cgi-bin/db2www.pgm/cpq.mbr/main. Online results show name only.
General Information: No secret records released. Will fax documents $1.00 per page. Court makes copy: $.10 per page, plus $10.00 if extensive/entire case. Self serve: $.10 per page. Certification fee: $1.00 per page. Payee: Clerk of Court. Business checks accepted. No credit cards accepted. Mail requests: SASE required.

Hocking County Municipal Court PO Box 950, 1 E Main St, County Courthouse, 1st Fl, Logan, OH 43138-1278; 740-385-2250; fax: 740-385-3826; 8AM-4PM. ***Misdemeanor, Civil Actions under $15,000, Eviction, Small Claims.***
www.hockingcountymunicipalcourt.com
Civil Records: Access: Mail, in person, fax, online. Both court and visitors may perform in person searches. No search fee. Required to search: name, years to search. Civil cases indexed by defendant, plaintiff; index on computer from 1991, prior in books. Mail turnaround time 1-2 days. Access civil records free at www.hockingcountymunicipalcourt.com/search.shtml. Shows case number, docket entry, charge, case type.
Criminal Records: Access: Mail, in person, fax, online. Both court and visitors may perform in person searches. No search fee. Required to search: name, years to search, DOB, SSN (signed release if for a housing check). Criminal records computerized from 1991 prior in books. Mail turnaround time 1-2 days. Access criminal records free at www.hockingcountymunicipalcourt.com/search.shtml. Shows case number, docket entry, charge, case type. Online results show middle initial.
General Information: Will fax documents to local or toll-free number. Court makes copy: $.10 per page. Certification fee: $1.00 per page. Payee: Hocking County Municipal Court. Personal checks and major credit cards accepted. Mail requests: SASE required.

Holmes County

Common Pleas Court - General Div 1 E Jackson St, #306, Millersburg, OH 44654; 330-674-1876; probate phone: 330-674-5881; fax: 330-674-0289; 8:30AM-4:30PM. ***Felony, Civil Actions over $10,000.***
Juvenile and Probate court at #201 on 2nd Fl; not part of CP General Div.
Civil Records: Access: Fax, mail, in person. Both court and visitors may perform in person searches. Search fee: $5.00 per name. Required to search: name, years to search; also helpful: address. Civil cases indexed by defendant, plaintiff; index on computer from 6/30/94, prior in books to 1850. Mail turnaround time 1-2 days. Civil PAT goes back to 1994. PAT results show name only.
Criminal Records: Access: Fax, mail, in person. Both court and visitors may perform in person searches. Search fee: $5.00 per name. Required to search: name, years to search; also helpful: address, DOB, SSN. Criminal records computerized from 6/30/94, prior in books to 1850. Mail turnaround time 1-2 days. Criminal PAT goes back to same as civil. PAT results show name only.
General Information: No expunged records released. Fee to fax out file $2.00 1st page, $1.00 each add'l. Court makes copy: $.10 per page. Certification fee: $1.00 per document. Payee: Clerk of Court. Personal checks accepted; credit cards are not. Mail requests: SASE required.

Municipal Court 1 E Jackson St, #101, Millersburg, OH 44654; 330-674-4901; fax: 330-674-5514; 8:30AM-4:30PM. ***Misdemeanor, Civil Actions under $15,000, Small Claims.***
The court has separate divisions for Civil and Criminal. Use Room 101 for Civil Div, Room 102 for Criminal Div.
Civil Records: Access: Phone, fax, mail, in person. Both court and visitors may perform in person searches. Search fee: $1.00 per name. Required to search: name, years to search. Civil cases indexed by defendant, plaintiff. Civil records in books going back to 1813; computerized records since 1994. Phone and fax access limited to 1 name. Mail turnaround time 5-10 days. Civil PAT goes back to 1994. PAT civil results show middle initial.
Criminal Records: Access: Phone, fax, mail, in person. Both court and visitors may perform in person searches. Search fee: $1.00 per name. Required to search: name, years to search. Criminal records in books going back to 1813; computerized records since 1994. Phone and fax access limited to 1 name. Mail turnaround time 5-10 days. Criminal PAT goes back to same as civil. PAT criminal results show middle initial.
General Information: No search warrant records released. Will not fax documents. Court makes copy: $.25 each 1-10 pages; $.10 each add'l. Certification fee: $1.00 per page. Payee: Holmes County Court. Personal checks accepted; credit cards are not. Mail requests: SASE required.

Huron County

Common Pleas Court Clerk of Courts, 2 E Main St, Rm 207, Norwalk, OH 44857; 419-668-5113; probate phone: 419-668-4383; fax: 419-663-4048; 8AM-4:30PM. ***Felony, Civil Actions over $10,000, Probate.***
www.huroncountyclerk.com
Probate is separate court at this same address.
Civil Records: Access: In person, online. Both court and visitors may perform in person searches. No search fee. Required to search: name, years to search; also helpful: address. Civil cases indexed by defendant, plaintiff; index on computer from 7/1989, prior in books and on microfiche. Civil PAT goes back to 1989. PAT results show middle initial, DOB. Search court dockets and public records free at the website www.huroncountyclerk.com/html/case_search.html Civil results on internet do not include DOB.
Criminal Records: Access: In person, online. Both court and visitors may perform in person searches. No search fee. Required to search: name, years to search, offense, date of offense; also helpful: address, DOB, SSN. Criminal records on computer since 7/1989, records from 1991 to present in actual files, 1930 to 1991 on microfiche. Criminal PAT goes back to same as civil. PAT results show middle initial, DOB. Search court dockets and public records free at the website www.huroncountyclerk.com/html/case_search.html Online results show middle initial, DOB.
General Information: No secret records released. Will fax out specific case files for $2.00 each plus $1.00 per page. Court makes copy: $.10 per page. Self serve: same. Certification fee: $1.00. Payee: Clerk of Court. Personal checks accepted; credit cards are not.

Bellevue Municipal Court 3000 Seneca Industrial Pky, Bellevue, OH 44811; 419-483-5880; criminal fax: 419-484-8060; civil fax: same; 8:30AM-4:30PM. ***Misdemeanor, Civil Actions under $15,000, Eviction, Small Claims, Traffic.***
Jurisdiction includes City of Bellevue, Sherman, Lyme Township, and York township in Sandusky County. Best time of day to perform searches is afternoons.
Civil Records: Access: Phone, fax, mail, in person. Both court and visitors may perform in person searches. No search fee. Required to search: name, years to search, also case number if known. Civil cases indexed by defendant, plaintiff; index on printed index from 1988, prior in books. Court will only do phone searching if not busy. Mail turnaround time 3-7 days.
Criminal Records: Access: Phone, fax, mail, in person. Both court and visitors may perform in person searches. No search fee. Required to search: name, years to search, DOB; also helpful: SSN. Criminal records computerized from 8/93; paper index goes back further but court will not search for you. Use a retriever or abstractor to come in and search back before 8/1993. Mail turnaround time 3-7 days.
General Information: Will fax documents to local or toll free line. Court makes copy: no fee if less than 5 copies, add'l copy fee varies. Certification fee: $1.00. Payee: Bellevue Municipal Court. Only cashiers checks and money orders accepted. No credit cards accepted. Mail requests: SASE required.

Huron Municipal Court PO Box 468, 417 Main St, Huron, OH 44839; 419-433-5430; fax: 419-433-5120; 8AM-4PM. ***Misdemeanor, Civil Actions under $15,000, Eviction, Small Claims.***
www.cityofhuron.org/muni-court.htm
Civil Records: Access: Fax, mail, in person. Both court and visitors may perform in person searches. Search fee: $1.00 per name. Required to search: name, years to search; also helpful: address. Civil cases indexed by defendant, plaintiff; index on computer back to 1998; prior on docket book to 1976. Mail turnaround time 2-7 days. Civil PAT goes back to 1998.
Criminal Records: Access: Fax, mail, in person. Both court and visitors may perform in person searches. Search fee: $1.00 per name. Required to search: name, years to search, DOB, SSN; also

helpful: address. Criminal records computerized from 1998, prior on docket books to 1976. Mail turnaround time 2-7 days. Criminal PAT goes back to 1998.
General Information: Fee to fax out file $1.00 per page. Court makes copy: $.05 per page. Certification fee: $1.00 per page. Payee: Municipal Court. No personal checks accepted. Major credit cards accepted. Mail requests: SASE required.

Norwalk Municipal Court 45 N Linwood, Norwalk, OH 44857; 419-663-6750; fax: 419-663-6749; 8:30AM-4:30PM. ***Misdemeanor, Civil Actions under $15,000, Eviction, Small Claims.***
www.norwalkmunicourt.com
Access records free at www.norwalkmunicourt.com/search.htm.
Civil Records: Access: Fax, mail, in person, online. Both court and visitors may perform in person searches. Search fee: $1.00 per name. Required to search: name, years to search; also helpful: address. Civil cases indexed by defendant, plaintiff; index on computer from 7/88; prior on docket book to 1976. Mail turnaround time 2-7 days. Civil PAT goes back to 1988. Access records free at www.norwalkmunicourt.com/search.htm.
Criminal Records: Access: Fax, mail, in person, online. Both court and visitors may perform in person searches. Search fee: $1.00 per name. Required to search: name, years to search, DOB, SSN; also helpful: address. Criminal records computerized from 7/88, prior on docket books to 1976. Mail turnaround time 2-7 days. Criminal PAT goes back to same as civil. Access records free at www.norwalkmunicourt.com/search.htm.
General Information: Fee to fax out file $1.00 per page. Court makes copy: $.05 per page. Certification fee: $1.00 per page. Payee: Municipal Court. Personal checks accepted; credit cards are not. Mail requests: SASE required.

Jackson County

Common Pleas Court 226 Main St, Jackson, OH 45640; 740-286-2006; probate phone: 740-286-1401; fax: 740-286-5186; 8AM-4PM. ***Felony, Civil Actions over $10,000, Probate.*** www.jcclerk.com/
Civil Records: Access: In person only. Both court and visitors may perform in person searches. No search fee. Required to search: name, years to search; also helpful: address. Civil cases indexed by defendant, plaintiff. Civil records go back to 1800s, computerized since 6/20/97. Civil PAT goes back to 6/1997. PAT civil results show middle initial.
Criminal Records: Access: In person only. Both court and visitors may perform in person searches. Search fee: Searches only performed in emergency situations. Required to search: name, years to search; also helpful: address, DOB, SSN. Criminal records go back to 1/83; computerized since 06/20/97. Criminal PAT goes back to same as civil. PAT criminal results show middle initial.
General Information: No juvenile or search warrant record released. Will fax documents $3.00 fee. Court makes copy: $.10 per page. Certification fee: $1.00. Payee: Clerk of Court. Personal checks accepted; credit cards are not.

Jackson County Municipal Court 295 Broadway St, #101, Jackson, OH 45640-1764; 740-286-2718; criminal fax: 740-286-0679; civil fax: same; 8AM-4PM. ***Misdemeanor, Civil Actions under $15,000, Eviction, Small Claims.***
www.jacksoncountymunicipalcourt.com/
Civil Records: Access: In person, online. Visitors must perform in person searches themselves. Required to search: name, years to search. Civil cases indexed by defendant, plaintiff. Civil records in books readily available for 8-10 years, prior archived. Civil PAT goes back to 1997. PAT results show middle initial, DOB, SSN. Case information includes personal identifiers. Search record index free at www.jacksoncountymunicipalcourt.com/Search/.
Criminal Records: Access: In person, online. Visitors must perform in person searches themselves. Required to search: name, years to search, DOB, SSN. Criminal records in books readily available for 8-10 years, prior archived. Criminal PAT goes back to same as civil. PAT results show middle initial, DOB, SSN. Case information includes personal identifiers. Search record index www.jacksoncountymunicipalcourt.com/Search/.
General Information: No victim records released. Will fax documents for no fee. Court makes copy: $.10 per page. Certification fee: $5.00. Payee: Clerk of Municipal Court. Cashiers checks and money orders accepted. Visa/MC accepted.

Jefferson County

Common Pleas Court PO Box 1326, 301 Market St, Rm 200, Steubenville, OH 43952; 740-283-8583; probate phone: 740-283-8554; 8:30AM-4:30PM. ***Felony, Civil Actions over $500, Probate.***
www.jeffersoncountyoh.com/cgi-bin/template.pl?countycourts.html
Probate is at PO Box 649.
Civil Records: Access: Mail, in person, online. Both court and visitors may perform in person searches. Search fee: $5.00 per name. Required to search: name, years to search. Civil cases indexed by defendant, plaintiff; index on computer back 10 years or so, prior archived. Computerized domestic records go back to 1972. Mail turnaround time 1-3 days. Civil PAT goes back to 1995. Access court index free at www.jeffersoncountyoh.com/cgi-bin/template.pl?/courts/searchCP.html.
Criminal Records: Access: Mail, in person, online. Both court and visitors may perform in person searches. Search fee: $5.00 per name. Required to search: name, years to search, DOB; also helpful-SSN. Criminal records are computerized to 1988, but can go back many years in archives. Mail turnaround time 1-2 days. Criminal PAT goes back to 1988. Online access to criminal is same as civil, see above.
General Information: Online identifiers in results same as on public terminal. No sealed records released. Will not fax documents. Court makes copy: $.25 per page. Certification fee: $1.00 per page, includes copy fee. Payee: Jefferson County Clerk of Courts. Business checks accepted. No credit cards accepted. Mail requests: SASE required.

County Court #1 1007 Franklin Ave, Toronto, OH 43964; 740-537-2020; fax: 740-537-1866; 8AM-4PM. ***Misdemeanor, Civil Actions under $15,000, Small Claims.***
www.jeffersoncountyoh.com/cgi-bin/template.pl?countycourts.html
Civil Records: Access: Mail, in person, online. Both court and visitors may perform in person searches. Search fee: $5.00 per name. Required to search: name, years to search. Civil cases indexed by defendant, plaintiff. Civil records in books, dating from 1813, computerized records from 6/98. Mail turnaround time 1-2 days. Civil PAT goes back to 6/1998. Search court records free at www.jeffersoncountyoh.com/cgi-bin/template.pl?/courts/search.html.
Criminal Records: Access: Mail, in person, online. Both court and visitors may perform in person searches. Search fee: $5.00 per name. Required to search: name, years to search, DOB, also helpful: SSN, sex, signed release. Criminal records in books, dating from 1813, computerized records from 6/98. Mail turnaround time 1-2 days. Criminal PAT goes back to same as civil. PAT results show middle initial, DOB. Terminal results include SSN. Online access to criminal is same as civil, see above.
General Information: All records are public. Will fax documents to local or toll free line. Court makes copy for no fee. Self serve: $.25 per page. No certification fee. Payee: Jefferson County Court #1. Cashiers checks and money orders accepted. Credit cards accepted. Mail requests: SASE required.

County Court #2 PO Box 2207, 201Talbot Dr, Wintersville, OH 43953; 740-264-7644; fax: 740-264-3909; 8AM-4PM. ***Misdemeanor, Civil Actions under $15,000, Small Claims.***
www.jeffersoncountyoh.com/cgi-bin/template.pl?countycourts.html
Civil Records: Access: Mail, in person, online. Only the court performs in person searches; visitors may not. No search fee. Required to search: name, years to search. Civil cases indexed by defendant, plaintiff; index on computer back to 1998; in books from 1950s, prior archived. Mail turnaround time 1-2 days. Civil PAT goes back to 1998. Search court records free at www.jeffersoncountyoh.com/cgi-bin/template.pl?/courts/search.html.
Criminal Records: Access: Mail, in person, online. Both court and visitors may perform in person searches. Search fee: $5.00 per name. Required to search: name, years to search, DOB or SSN. Criminal records computerized from 1998; in books from 1950s, prior archived. Mail turnaround time 1-2 days. Criminal PAT goes back to same as civil. Online access to criminal is same as civil, see above.
General Information: Online identifiers in results same as on public terminal. Will fax documents to local or toll free line. Court makes copy: $.25 per page. Certification fee: $1.00 per page. Payee: County Court #2. Cashiers checks and money orders accepted. Visa/MC accepted plus $1.00 surcharge. Mail requests: SASE required.

County Court #3 PO Box 495, Dillonvale, OH 43917; 740-769-2903; fax: 740-769-7640; 8AM-4PM. ***Misdemeanor, Civil Actions under $15,000, Small Claims.***
www.jeffersoncountyoh.com/cgi-bin/template.pl?countycourts.html
Civil Records: Access: Mail, fax, in person, online. Both court and visitors may perform in person searches. Search fee: $5.00. Required to search: name, years to search. Civil cases indexed by defendant, plaintiff; index on computer from 1998, prior manual dockets. Mail turnaround time 1-2 days. Civil PAT goes back to 1998. Search court records free at www.jeffersoncountyoh.com/cgi-bin/template.pl?/courts/search.html.
Criminal Records: Access: Mail, in person, online. Both court and visitors may perform in person searches. Search fee: $5.00. Required to search: name, years to search, DOB; also helpful: SSN. Criminal records computerized from 1998, prior manual dockets. Mail turnaround time 1-2 days. Criminal PAT goes back to 1998. Online access to criminal is same as civil, see above.
General Information: Will fax documents $1.00 per page. Court makes copy: $1.00 per page. Certification fee: $1.00. Payee: County Court #3. Cashiers checks and money orders accepted. Credit cards accepted. Mail requests: SASE required.

Steubenville Municipal Court 123 S 3rd St, Steubenville, OH 43952; 740-283-6000 x2200; fax: 740-283-6167; 8:30AM-4PM. ***Misdemeanor, Civil Actions under $15,000, Eviction, Small Claims.***
www.ci.steubenville.oh.us/courts Email questions to municipalcourt@cityofsteubenville.us.
Civil Records: Access: Mail, in person. Both court and visitors may perform in person searches. No search fee. Required to search: name, years to search; also helpful: address. Civil cases indexed by defendant, plaintiff; index on computer from 1991, prior in books. Mail turnaround time 10-14 days. Civil PAT goes back to 1991. PAT results show middle initial, DOB, SSN. Terminal results also include race, sex, hair, eyes.
Criminal Records: Access: Mail, in person. Both court and visitors may perform in person searches. No search fee. Required to search: name, years to search; also helpful: address, DOB, SSN. Criminal records computerized from 1991, prior in books. Mail turnaround time 10-14 days. Criminal PAT goes back to 199. PAT results show middle initial, DOB, SSN. Terminal results also include race, sex, hair, eyes.
General Information: No expunged records released. Will fax documents to local or toll free line. Court makes copy: $1.00 per page. Certification fee: $2.00. Payee: Steubenville Municipal Court. Only cashiers checks and money orders accepted. Visa/MC accepted. Mail requests: SASE required.

Knox County

Common Pleas Court Knox County Clerk of Courts, 117 E High St, #201, Mt Vernon, OH 43050; 740-393-6788; probate phone: 740-393-6798; fax: 740-392-3533; 8AM-4PM. ***Felony, Civil Actions over $15,000.***
www.knoxcountyclerk.org/
Probate is a separate office located at 111 E High St.

Civil Records: Access: Online, in person. Visitors must perform in person searches themselves. Required to search: name, years to search. Civil cases indexed by defendant, plaintiff; index on computer since 9/86, on microfilm from 1960, prior archived. Civil PAT goes back to 1986. PAT results show name only. Search court index, dockets, calendars free online at www.coc.co.knox.oh.us/pa/. Search by name, case, or ticket number.
Criminal Records: Access: Online, in person. Visitors must perform in person searches themselves. Required to search: name, years to search. Criminal records on computer since 9/86, on microfilm from 1960, prior archived. Criminal PAT goes back to same as civil. PAT results show name only. Online access to criminal records is the same as civil.
General Information: If exact case number given, clerk will fax return pages $3.00 1st page, $1.00 each add'l. Court makes copy: $.10 per page. Certification fee: $1.00edPayee: Knox County Clerk of Courts. Personal checks accepted; credit cards are not.

Mount Vernon Municipal Court 5 N Gay St, Mount Vernon, OH 43050; 740-393-9510; fax: 740-393-5349; 8AM-4PM. ***Misdemeanor, Civil Actions under $15,000, Eviction, Small Claims.***
www.mountvernonmunicipalcourt.org
Civil Records: Access: Phone, fax, mail, in person, online. Both court and visitors may perform in person searches. No search fee. Required to search: name, years to search. Civil cases indexed by defendant, plaintiff; index on computer from 6/89, prior in books. Results include name, plaintiff, defendant, case number. Mail turnaround time 1 week. Access the clerk's civil records free at www.mountvernonmunicipalcourt.org/cmiflash/court/home.html.
Criminal Records: Access: Phone, fax, mail, in person, online. Both court and visitors may perform in person searches. No search fee. Required to search: name, years to search. Criminal records computerized from 06/89, prior in books. Results include name, case number, ticket number, drivers license number. Mail turnaround time 1 week. Access the clerk's criminal and traffic records free at www.mountvernonmunicipalcourt.org/cmiflash/court/home.html
General Information: Will fax documents. Court makes copy for no fee. No certification fee. Payee: Mt Vernon Municipal Ct. Personal checks accepted. Credit cards accepted in person. Mail requests: SASE required.

Probate Court 111 E High St, Mt Vernon, OH 43050; 740-393-6796; fax: 740-393-6832; 8AM-4PM. ***Probate.***

Lake County

Common Pleas Court PO Box 490, Painesville, OH 44077; 440-350-2657; probate phone: 440-350-2626; 8AM-4:30PM. ***Felony, Civil Actions over $10,000, Probate.*** www.lakecountyohio.org
Civil Records: Access: In person, online. Visitors must perform in person searches themselves. Required to search: name, years to search; also helpful: address. Civil cases indexed by defendant, plaintiff; index on computer from 1990, microfilm from 1960, prior archived. Civil PAT goes back to 1990. Online access to court records, dockets, and quick index, including probate records, is free at https://phoenix.lakecountyohio.gov/pa/.
Criminal Records: Access: In person, online. Visitors must perform in person searches themselves. Required to search: name, years to search; also helpful: address, DOB, SSN. Criminal records computerized from 1990, microfilm from 1960, prior archived. Criminal PAT goes back to same as civil. Online access to criminal records is the same as civil.
General Information: No adoption or juvenile records released. Will not fax documents. Court makes copy: $.05 per page. Certification fee: $1.00. Payee: Clerk of Court. Business checks accepted. No credit cards accepted.

Mentor Municipal Court 8500 Civic Center Blvd, Mentor, OH 44060-2418; criminal phone: 440-974-5744; civil phone: 440-974-5745; criminal fax: 440-974-5742; civil fax: same; 8AM-4PM; Wed til 6PM. ***Misdemeanor, Civil Actions under $15,000, Eviction, Small Claims.***
www.mentormunicipalcourt.org/
Civil Records: Access: In person, online. Visitors must perform in person searches themselves. Required to search: name. Civil cases indexed by defendant, plaintiff. Civil records go back to 1972; on computer back to 11/1995. Civil PAT goes back to 1995. PAT results show middle initial, DOB. Record searches at www.mentormunicipalcourt.org/search.shtml
Criminal Records: Access: In person, online. Visitors must perform in person searches themselves. Required to search: name, years to search; also helpful: DOB. Criminal records go back to 1972; on computer back to 11/1995. Criminal PAT goes back to same as civil. PAT results show middle initial, DOB. Search records at www.mentormunicipalcourt.org/search.shtml
General Information: Will not fax out case files. Court makes copy: $.25 per page. Certification fee: $1.00. Payee: Mentor Municipal Court. Cashiers checks and money orders accepted; no personal checks. Major credit cards accepted.

Painesville Municipal Court PO Box 601, 7 Richmond St, Painesville, OH 44077; 440-392-5900; criminal fax: 440-352-0028; civil fax: same; 8AM-4:30PM. ***Misdemeanor, Civil Actions under $15,000, Eviction, Small Claims.***
www.pmcourt.com
Probation fax is 440-639-4932.
Civil Records: Access: Fax, mail, in person, online. Visitors must perform in person searches themselves. No search fee. Required to search: name, years to search; also helpful: address. Civil cases indexed by defendant, plaintiff; index on computer from 7/90 (all divisions), prior on books or archived. Civil PAT goes back to 1990. PAT results show name only. Free online access to index at www.pmcourt.com/search.shtml.
Criminal Records: Access: Fax, mail, in person, online. Visitors must perform in person searches themselves. No search fee. Required to search: name, years to search, address; also helpful: DOB, SSN. Criminal records computerized from 7/90 (all divisions), prior on books or archived. Mail turnaround time 1 week. Criminal PAT goes back to 1990. PAT results show middle initial, DOB, SSN. Free online access to index at www.pmcourt.com/search.shtml. Online results show middle initial, DOB.
General Information: Online identifiers in results same as on public terminal. Will fax documents: local $1.00 per page; long distance $3.00 per page. Court makes copy: $1.00 first page. $.20 each add'l. Certification fee: $2.00 plus $1.00 per page after first. Payee: Municipal Court. Personal checks and credit cards accepted. Online payment available for criminal and traffic cases. Mail requests: SASE required.

Willoughby Municipal Court 4000 Erie St, Willoughby, OH 44094; 440-953-4150; criminal phone: 440-953-4150; civil phone: 440-953-4170; fax: 440-953-4149; 7:30AM-4:30 PM, till 7:30PM MH. ***Misdemeanor, Civil Actions under $15,000, Eviction, Small Claims.***
www.willoughbycourt.com
This court serves these communities: Eastlake, Kirtland, Kirtland Hills, Lakeland Community College, Lakeline, Timberlake, Waite Hill, Wickliffe, Willoughby, Willoughby Hills, and Willowick.
Civil Records: Access: Mail, in person, online. Both court and visitors may perform in person searches. No search fee. Required to search: name, years to search. Civil cases indexed by defendant. Civil index on docket books since 1960, computerized back to 1986. Mail turnaround time 1-2 days. Civil PAT goes back to 1993. Access the court's case lookup plus schedules free at www.willoughbycourt.com/connection/court/.
Criminal Records: Access: Mail, in person, online. Both court and visitors may perform in person searches. No search fee. Required to search: name; also helpful: DOB, SSN. Criminal records in docket books since 1960, computerized back to 1988. Mail turnaround time 1-2 days. Criminal PAT goes back to 1989. Access the court's case lookup plus warrants and schedules free at www.willoughbycourt.com/connection/court/.
General Information: Will fax documents $1.00 per page. Court makes copy: $.25 per page. Certification fee: $1.00 per page. Payee: Willoughby Municipal Court. Personal checks and major credit cards accepted.

Lawrence County

Common Pleas Court PO Box 208, Clerk of the Courts, 111 S 4th St, Ironton, OH 45638; 740-533-4355/4356; probate: 740-533-4343; fax: 740-533-4383; 8:30AM-4PM. ***Felony, Civil Actions.***
www.lawrencecountyclkofcrt.org
Probate is a separate court at Veterans Square in Ironton.
Civil Records: Access: In person, online. Visitors must perform in person searches themselves. Required to search: name, years to search; also helpful: address. Civil cases indexed by defendant, plaintiff; index on computer back to 6/88, prior in books going back to 1800s. Civil PAT goes back to 1988. Online access to civil records is free at www.lawrencecountyclkofcrt.org/.
Criminal Records: Access: In person, online. Visitors must perform in person searches themselves. Required to search: name, years to search; also helpful: address, DOB, SSN. Criminal records computerized from 1/88, prior in books going back to 1800s. Criminal PAT goes back to same as civil. Online access to criminal records is free at www.lawrencecountyclkofcrt.org.
General Information: Online identifiers in results same as on public terminal. Will fax out specific case files. Court makes copy: $.25 per page. No certification fee. Payee: Clerk of Court. Personal checks accepted; credit cards are not.

Lawrence County Municipal Court PO Box 126, Chesapeake, OH 45619; 740-867-3128/3127; fax: 740-867-3547; 8:30AM-4PM. ***Misdemeanor, Civil Actions under $15,000, Eviction, Small Claims.***
www.lawcomunicourt.com/
Civil Records: Access: Phone, fax, mail, in person, online. Both court and visitors may perform in person searches. Search fee: $5.00 per name. Required to search: name, years to search. Civil cases indexed by defendant, plaintiff; index on computer from 1991. Mail turnaround time 7-10 days. Click on "Record Search" at the web page for a search of the record index.
Criminal Records: Access: Phone, fax, mail, in person, online. Both court and visitors may perform in person searches. Search fee: $5.00 per name. Required to search: name, years to search, DOB; also helpful: SSN. Criminal records computerized from 1991. Mail turnaround time 7-10 days. Click on "Record Search" at the web page for a search of the record index.
General Information: All records public. Will fax documents if search fee prepaid. Court makes copy: $.25 per page. Self serve: same. Certification fee: $2.00. Payee: Lawrence County Municipal Court. Personal checks accepted. Visa/MC, Discover accepted on the web only. Mail requests: SASE required.

Ironton Municipal Court PO Box 237, 301 S 3rd St, Ironton, OH 45638; 740-532-3062; fax: 740-533-6088; 8:30AM-4PM. ***Misdemeanor, Civil Actions under $15,000, Eviction, Small Claims.***
Searches of index books only allowed Wed and Fri.
Civil Records: Access: Mail, in person. Both court and visitors may perform in person searches. No search fee. Required to search: name, years to search; also helpful: address. Civil cases indexed by defendant, plaintiff; index on computer from 7/89, prior in books. Mail turnaround time 1-2 weeks. Civil PAT goes back to 1989.
Criminal Records: Access: Mail, in person. Both court and visitors may perform in person searches. No search fee. Required to search: name, years to search; also helpful: address, DOB, SSN. Criminal

records computerized from 7/89, prior in books. Searches of the index books only allowed Wed and Fri. Mail turnaround time 1-2 weeks. Criminal PAT goes back to same as civil.
General Information: Will fax documents for fee. Court makes copy: $1.00 per page. Certification fee: $1.00 per page. Payee: Municipal Court. No personal checks or credit cards accepted. Mail requests: SASE required.

Licking County

Common Pleas Court PO Box 4370, Newark, OH 43058-4370; 740-670-5794; probate phone: 740-670-5624; fax: 740-670-5886; 8AM-4:30PM. ***Felony, Civil Actions over $15,000, Probate.***
www.lcounty.com/clerkofcourts/
Probate court has a separate clerk at the same address.
Civil Records: Access: In person, online. Visitors must perform in person searches themselves. Required to search: name, years to search; also helpful: address. Civil cases indexed by defendant, plaintiff; index on computer from 1992, prior in books. Civil PAT goes back to 2/1992. PAT civil results show middle initial. County clerk's office offers free Internet access to current records at www.lcounty.com/pa/pa.urd/pamw6500.display.
Criminal Records: Access: In person, online. Visitors must perform in person searches themselves. Required to search: name, years to search, DOB; also helpful: address, SSN. Criminal records computerized from 1992, prior in books. Criminal PAT goes back to 2/1992. PAT criminal results show middle initial. County clerk's office offers free Internet access to current records at www.lcounty.com/pa/pa.urd/pamw6500.display
General Information: Online identifiers in results same as on public terminal. No sealed records released. Will fax documents $2.00 per transmission and $1.00 per page. Court makes copy: $.05 per page. Certification fee: $1.00. Payee: Clerk of Court. Business checks accepted. Major credit cards accepted in person only.

Licking County Municipal Court 40 W Main St, Newark, OH 43055; criminal phone: 740-670-7800; civil phone: 740-670-7811; fax: 740-345-4250; 8AM-4:30PM. ***Misdemeanor, Civil Actions under $15,000, Eviction, Small Claims.***
www.lcmunicipalcourt.com
Civil Records: Access: Phone, fax, mail, in person, online. Both court and visitors may perform in person searches. No search fee. Required to search: name, years to search. Civil cases indexed by defendant, plaintiff; index on computer from 1990, prior in books. Mail turnaround time 2-3 days. Civil PAT goes back to 1990. PAT civil results show middle initial. Online access to Municipal Court records free at http://67.141.197.6/connection/court/. Results include addresses.
Criminal Records: Access: Phone, fax, mail, in person, online. Both court and visitors may perform in person searches. No search fee. Required to search: name, years to search. Criminal records computerized from 1990, prior in books. Mail turnaround time 2-3 days. Criminal PAT goes back to same as civil. PAT results show middle initial, DOB, SSN. Online access to criminal records is the same as civil. Online results show middle initial, DOB.
General Information: No sealed records released. Will not fax documents. Court makes copy: $.05 per page. Self serve: same. Certification fee: $2.00 per page. Payee: Licking County Municipal Court. Personal checks and credit cards accepted. Mail requests: SASE required.

Logan County

Common Pleas Court 101 S Main St, Rm 18, Bellefontaine, OH 43311-2097; 937-599-7261; criminal phone: 937-599-7256; civil phone: 937-599-7275; criminal fax: 937-599-7281; civil fax: 937-599-7281; 8:30AM-4:30PM. ***Felony, Civil Actions over $10,000, Probate.***
http://co.logan.oh.us/clerkofcourts
Probate is separate index and office.
Civil Records: Access: In person only. Visitors must perform in person searches themselves. Required to search: name, years to search; also helpful: address. Civil cases indexed by defendant, plaintiff; index on computer from 6/88, prior in books to 1943. Civil PAT goes back to 6/1988. PAT civil results show middle initial.
Criminal Records: Access: In person only. Visitors must perform in person searches themselves. Required to search: name, years to search, DOB; also helpful: address, SSN. Criminal records computerized from 6/88, prior in books to 1943. Criminal PAT goes back to same as civil. PAT criminal results show middle initial.
General Information: All records public. Will fax specific case file $2.00 1st page, $1.00 each add'l page. Court makes copy: $.05 per page after first 25 pages. Certification fee: $1.00 per page includes copy fee. Payee: Clerk of Court. Only cashiers checks and money orders accepted. No credit cards accepted.

Bellefontaine Municipal Court 226 W Columbus Ave, Bellefontaine, OH 43311; 937-599-6127; fax: 937-599-2488; 8AM-4:30PM. ***Misdemeanor, Civil Actions under $15,000, Eviction, Small Claims.***
Civil Records: Access: In person, fax, mail. Visitors must perform in person searches themselves. No search fee. Required to search: name, years to search. Civil cases indexed by defendant, plaintiff; index on computer from 1986, prior in books. Civil PAT goes back to 1984.
Criminal Records: Access: In person, fax, mail. Visitors must perform in person searches themselves. No search fee. Required to search: name, years to search, DOB, SSN, signed release; also helpful: address. Criminal records computerized from 1986, prior in books. Mail turnaround time 1-2 days. Criminal PAT goes back to same as civil.
General Information: All records are public. Will fax documents no fee. Court makes copy: $.05 per page. Certification fee: $1.00 per cert. Payee: Bellefontaine Municipal Court. Local checks accepted. Visa/MC accepted for traffic & criminal only. Mail requests: SASE required.

Lorain County

Common Pleas Court 225 Court St., Elyria, OH 44035; 440-329-5536; criminal phone: 440-329-5538; civil phone: 440-329-5536; probate phone: 440-329-5175; criminal fax: 440-329-5404; civil fax: same; 8AM-4:30PM. ***Felony, Civil Actions over $10,000, Probate.***
www.loraincounty.com/clerk
Probate is a separate index in Rm #611. Probate fax-440-328-2157. Court personnel will not do name searches of records.
Civil Records: Access: Online, in person. Visitors must perform in person searches themselves. Required to search: name, years to search. Civil cases indexed by defendant, plaintiff; index on computer from 1988, prior in books archived to 1800s. Some records on microfiche to 1824. Court will not do index searching but they will pull specified records. Civil PAT goes back to 1988. Free access to indices and dockets for common please court cases at http://cp.onlinedockets.com/loraincp/case_dockets/search.aspx. Access probate records at www.loraincounty.com/probate/search.shtml.
Criminal Records: Access: Online, in person. Visitors must perform in person searches themselves. Required to search: name, years to search. Criminal records computerized from 1988, prior in books archived to 1800s. Some records on microfiche to 1960. Court will not do index searching, but they will pull specified records. Criminal PAT goes back to same as civil. Online access to criminal records is the same as civil.
General Information: Online identifiers in results same as on public terminal. No juvenile records released. Will not fax documents. Court makes copy: $.10 per page. Certification fee: $1.00. Payee: Clerk of Court. Personal checks and major credit cards accepted.

Avon Lake Municipal Court 32855 Walker Rd, Avon Lake, OH 44012; 440-930-4103; fax: 440-930-4128; 8:30-4:30PM. ***Misdemeanor, Civil Actions under $15,000, Eviction, Small Claims.***
www.avonlakecourt.com/
Civil Records: Access: Phone, mail, in person, online. Both court and visitors may perform in person searches. No search fee. Required to search: name, years to search. Civil cases indexed by defendant, plaintiff; index on computer from 5/92, records go back to 1976. Mail turnaround time 1-4 days. Civil PAT goes back to 5/1992. PAT results show name only. Search docket index by name at www.avonlakecourt.com/Search/.
Criminal Records: Access: Phone, mail, in person, online. Both court and visitors may perform in person searches. No search fee. Required to search: name, years to search, DOB; also helpful: SSN. Criminal records computerized from 7/92, records go back to 1976. Mail turnaround time 1-2 days. Criminal PAT goes back to same as civil.PAT results show name, DOB. Search docket index by name at www.avonlakecourt.com/Search/. Online results show middle initial, DOB.
General Information: Online identifiers in results same as on public terminal. No non-public records released. Fee to fax out file $3.00 each. Court makes copy: $.10 per page. Certification fee: $1.00. Payee: Avon Lake Municipal Court. Personal checks accepted. Credit cards accepted in person only. Mail requests: SASE required if receipt requested.

Elyria Municipal Court 601 Broad St, Elyria, OH 44035; 440-326-1732; fax: 440-326-1877; 8AM-4:30PM. ***Misdemeanor, Civil Actions under $15,000, Eviction, Small Claims.***
www.elyriamunicourt.org
Civil Records: Access: Fax, mail, online, in person. Both court and visitors may perform in person searches. No search fee. Required to search: name, years to search; also helpful: address. Civil cases indexed by defendant, plaintiff. Civil records in books to 1956, computer from 1996. Mail turnaround time 5 days. Civil PAT goes back to 1996. Search at the Internet site, also you can request information by email to civil@elyriamunicourt.org.
Criminal Records: Access: Fax, mail, in person, online. Both court and visitors may perform in person searches. No search fee. Required to search: name, years to search; also helpful: address, DOB, SSN. Criminal records in books to 1956, computer from 1996. Mail turnaround time 5 days. Criminal PAT goes back to 1992. Search misdemeanor and traffic records back to 1992 at the website, also send email requests to crtr@elyriamunicourt.org. Online results show name, DOB.
General Information: Online identifiers in results same as on public terminal. All records are public. Will fax documents for no fee. Court makes copy: none; may be a charge after 20 pages. Certification fee: $1.00 per page. Personal checks and credit cards accepted. Mail requests: SASE required.

Lorain Municipal Court 200 W Erie Ave, Lorain, OH 44052; 440-204-2140; fax: 440-204-2146; 8:30AM-4:30PM. ***Misdemeanor, Civil Actions under $15,000, Eviction, Small Claims.***
www.lorainmunicourt.org
Civil Records: Access: In person, online. Visitors must perform in person searches themselves. Required to search: name, years to search; also helpful: address. Civil cases indexed by defendant, plaintiff. Civil records in books. Civil PAT goes back to 8/1998. PAT results show name, DOB. Access municipal court records free at www.lorainmunicourt.org/search.shtml. Search by name, date, case number, driver license number or attorney.
Criminal Records: Access: In person, online. Visitors must perform in person searches themselves. Required to search: name, years to search; also helpful: address, DOB, SSN. Criminal records in books. Criminal PAT goes back to same as civil.PAT results show name, DOB. Online access to criminal records is the same as civil. Online results show name, DOB.
General Information: Online identifiers in results same as on public terminal. Will not fax documents. Court makes copy: $.25 per page. No certification fee. Payee: Municipal Court. No personal checks accepted. Major credit cards accepted.

Oberlin Municipal Court 85 S Main St, Oberlin, OH 44074; 440-775-1751; fax: 440-775-0619; 8AM-4PM. ***Misdemeanor, Civil Actions under $15,000, Eviction, Small Claims.***
www.oberlinmunicipalcourt.org
Civil Records: Access: In person, online. Visitors must perform in person searches themselves. Required to search: name, years to search; also helpful: address. Civil cases indexed by defendant, plaintiff; index on computer from 1991, prior in books. Civil PAT goes back to 1991. Access case information free online at www.oberlinmunicipalcourt.org/public.htm.
Criminal Records: Access: In person, online. Visitors must perform in person searches themselves. Required to search: name, years to search; also helpful: address, DOB, SSN. Criminal records computerized from 1991, prior in books. Criminal PAT goes back to same as civil. Access case information free online at www.oberlinmunicipalcourt.org/public.htm.
General Information: Will not fax documents. Court makes copy: $.10 per page. No certification fee. Payee: Oberlin Municipal Court. Cashiers check or money orders accepted. Visa/MC accepted.

Vermilion Municipal Court, OH. ***Misdemeanor, Civil Actions under $15,000, Eviction, Small Claims.***
See Erie County, Vermilion Muni Court. The Erie/Lorain county line is main street. The Court is located on that street.

Lucas County

Common Pleas Court 700 Adams, Courthouse, Toledo, OH 43624; 419-213-4483, 4484; criminal phone: 419-213-4480; civil phone: 419-213-4493; probate phone: 419-213-4775; criminal fax: 419-213-4291; civil fax: 419-213-4487; 8AM-4:50PM. ***Felony, Civil Actions over $10,000, Probate.***
www.co.lucas.oh.us/default.asp?RequestedAlias=clerk
File Rm does searches; crim- 419-213-5540, civ- 419-213-4083. Probate records must be searched separately; probate hours are 8:30-4:30. Probate fax-call for fax number.
Civil Records: Access: Fax, mail, in person, online. Both court and visitors may perform in person searches. No search fee. Required to search: name, years to search. Civil cases indexed by defendant, plaintiff. Civil records computer from 1987, records go back to 1948, prior in books and on film. Mail turnaround time 3 days. Civil PAT goes back to 1986. PAT civil results show middle initial. Online access to clerk of courts dockets is free at http://apps.co.lucas.oh.us/OnlineDockets/. Online records go back to 9/1997. Search probate records at www.lucas-co-probate-ct.org/.
Criminal Records: Access: Fax, mail, in person, online. Both court and visitors may perform in person searches. Search fee: $5.00 per name. Required to search: name, years to search, DOB, SSN; also helpful: sex, signed release. Criminal records computer from 1987, records go back to 1948, prior in books and on film. Mail turnaround time 3 days. Criminal PAT goes back to 1986. PAT criminal results show middle initial. Online access to clerk of courts dockets is free at http://apps.co.lucas.oh.us/OnlineDockets/. Online record go back to 9/1997. Search sex offenders at www.lucascountysheriff.org/sheriff/disclaimer.asp. Online results show middle initial.
General Information: No expunged records released. Will fax documents $3.00 transmittal fee plus copy fees. Court makes copy: $.05 per page. Self serve: same. Certification fee: $1.00 per case. Payee: Clerk of Court. Only cashiers checks and money orders accepted. No credit cards accepted.

Maumee Municipal Court 400 Conant St, Maumee, OH 43537-3397; criminal phone: 419-897-7136; civil phone: 419-897-7145; fax: 419-897-7129; 8AM-4:30PM. ***Misdemeanor, Civil Actions under $15,000, Eviction, Small Claims.***
www.maumee.org/municipal/default.htm
Civil Records: Access: Phone, fax, mail, in person, online. Only the court performs in person searches; visitors may not. No search fee. Required to search: name; also helpful: years to search. Civil cases indexed by defendant, plaintiff. Civil records in docket books since 1964, on computer since 1989. Mail turnaround time 1 week. Online access to web court system database is free at www.maumee.org/municipal/caseinfo.htm. Online includes civil, criminal, traffic.
Criminal Records: Access: Phone, fax, mail, in person, online. Only the court performs in person searches; visitors may not. No search fee. Required to search: name, years to search, DOB; also helpful: SSN. Criminal records in docket books since 1964, on computer since 1987. Mail turnaround time 1 week. Online access to criminal records is the same as civil. Online results show middle initial, DOB. Online results include address if known.
General Information: Will fax documents for no fee. Court makes copy: No copy fee up to 20 pages; $.05 per page over 20. Certification fee: $1.00 per page up to 20 pages includes copy fee. Payee: Maumee Municipal Court. Personal checks accepted. Credit cards not accepted for phone orders. Mail requests: SASE helpful.

Oregon Municipal Court 5330 Seaman Rd, Oregon, OH 43616; criminal phone: 419-698-7173; civil phone: 419-698-7008; fax: 419-698-7013; 8:30AM-4:30PM. ***Misdemeanor, Civil Actions under $15,000, Eviction, Small Claims, Traffic.***
www.ci.oregon.oh.us/ctydpt/court/court.htm
Civil Records: Access: Phone, fax, mail, in person, email, online. Both court and visitors may perform in person searches. No search fee. Required to search: name, years to search. Civil cases indexed by defendant, plaintiff; index on books since 1960, computerized since 1989. Mail turnaround time 1-2 days. Direct email civil search requests to court@ci.oregon.oh.us. Search court cases and schedules free at http://72.240.41.91/.
Criminal Records: Access: Phone, fax, mail, in person, online. Both court and visitors may perform in person searches. No search fee. Required to search: name, years to search; also helpful: DOB, SSN. Criminal docket on books since 1960, computerized since 1989. Mail turnaround time 1-2 days. Search court cases and schedules free at http://72.240.41.91/.
General Information: No fee to fax document; must be local call. Court makes copy: $.25 per page. Certification fee: $2.50 for 1st page, $.10 each add'l. Payee: Oregon Municipal Court. Personal checks accepted. Major credit cards accepted for criminal records only. Mail requests: SASE required.

Sidney Municipal Court 201 W Poplar St, 10 W Court St, Sidney, OH 45365; 937-498-0011; fax: 937-498-8179; 8AM-4:15PM. ***Misdemeanor, Civil Actions under $15,000, Eviction, Small Claims.***
http://sidneyoh.com/court/court.htm
Court located at 110 W Court St.
Civil Records: Access: Fax, mail, in person. Visitors must perform in person searches themselves. No search fee. Required to search: name, years to search. Civil cases indexed by defendant, plaintiff; index on books since 1964, computerized since 1987. Public use terminal available, records go back to 1987.
Criminal Records: Access: Fax, mail, in person. Visitors must perform in person searches themselves. No search fee. Required to search: name, years to search, DOB, SSN. Criminal docket on books since 1964, computerized since 1987. Mail turnaround time 1 week. Public use terminal available, crim records go back to same as civil.
General Information: Will fax documents to local or toll free line. Court makes copy: $.10 per page. Certification fee: $2.00 per page. Payee: Clerk of Court. Business checks accepted. No credit cards accepted.

Sylvania Municipal Court 6700 Monroe St, Sylvania, OH 43560-1995; 419-885-8975; criminal phone: 419-885-8975; civil phone: 419-885-8985; fax: 419-885-8987; 7:30AM-4PM. ***Misdemeanor, Civil Actions under $15,000, Eviction, Small Claims.***
www.sylvaniacourt.com
Civil Records: Access: Fax, mail, in person, online. Visitors must perform in person searches themselves. No search fee. Required to search: name, years to search. Civil cases indexed by defendant, plaintiff; index on books since 1964, computerized since 1987. Civil PAT goes back to 1987. PAT civil results show middle initial. Online access free at http://72.240.45.101/.
Criminal Records: Access: Fax, mail, in person, online. Visitors must perform in person searches themselves. No search fee. Required to search: name, years to search, DOB, SSN. Criminal docket on books since 1964, computerized since 1987. Mail turnaround time 1 week. Criminal PAT goes back to 1987. PAT results show middle initial, DOB. Online access free at http://72.240.45.101/.
General Information: Online identifiers in results same as on public terminal. Will fax documents to local or toll free line. Court makes copy: $.10 per page. Certification fee: $2.00 per page. Payee: Clerk of Court. Business checks accepted. Visa/MC accepted.

Toledo Municipal Court 555 N Erie St, Toledo, OH 43604; 419-936-3650 (Small Claims); criminal phone: 419-936-3650; civil: 419-936-3650; fax: 419-936-3608; 8AM-4:30PM. ***Misdemeanor, Civil Actions under $15,000, Eviction, Small Claims.***
www.tmc-clerk.com
A second website is www.toledomunicipalcourt.org.
Civil Records: Access: Mail, fax, in person, email, online. Both court and visitors may perform in person searches. No search fee. Required to search: name, years to search. Civil cases indexed by defendant. Civil records on computer back to 1986, prior in books since 1960s. Mail turnaround time 3 to 5 days. Public use terminal has civil records back to 1986. PAT results show name, DOB. Daily dockets are online at www.tmc-clerk.com/case/default.asp. Direct email requests to tmc-clerk@noris.org
Criminal Records: Access: Mail, fax, in person, email, online. Both court and visitors may perform in person searches. No search fee. Required to search: name, years to search, DOB, SSN; also helpful: address. Criminal records computerized from 1985, prior in books since 1960s. Have either date of birth or SSN to request a search. Mail turnaround time 3 to 5 days. Daily dockets are online at www.tmc-clerk.com/case/default.asp. Direct email requests to tmc-clerk@noris.org.
General Information: Online identifiers in results same as on public terminal. No sealed records released. Will not fax documents. Court makes copy: $.20 per page. Self serve: No self serve criminal copier; Civil self serve- $.15 each. Certification fee: $6.00. Payee: Toledo Municipal Court. Personal checks accepted for criminal records. Will accept credit cards for criminal records. Mail requests: SASE required.

Madison County

Common Pleas Court PO Box 557, London, OH 43140; 740-852-9776; probate phone: 740-852-0756; fax: 740-845-1778; 8AM-4PM. ***Felony, Civil Actions over $10,000, Probate.***
www.co.madison.oh.us/10206.html
Civil Records: Access: In person, online. Visitors must perform in person searches themselves. Required to search: name, years to search. Civil cases indexed by defendant, plaintiff. Civil records in books since 1981. Civil PAT goes back to 2/2001. PAT results show name only. Search probate records (but no civil records) at http://12.32.69.179/Search/.
Criminal Records: Access: In person only. Visitors must perform in person searches themselves. Required to search: name, years to search; also helpful: address, DOB, SSN. Criminal records in books since 1981. Criminal PAT goes back to same as civil. PAT results show name only.
General Information: No secret indictment records released. Will fax documents for fee; 10 page limit. Court makes copy: $.25 per page. No certification fee. Payee: Clerk of Court. Personal checks accepted; credit cards are not.

Madison County Municipal Court PO Box 646, 1 N Main St, London, OH 43140; 740-852-1669; fax: 740-852-0812; 8-4PM. ***Misdemeanor, Civil Actions under $15,000, Eviction, Small Claims.***
www.co.madison.oh.us/10227.html

Civil Records: Access: Phone, fax, mail, in person, online. Both court and visitors may perform in person searches. No search fee. Required to search: name, years to search. Civil cases indexed by defendant, plaintiff; index on computer from 1989, prior in books indexed from 1958. Mail turnaround time up to 1 week. Civil PAT goes back to 1985. PAT results show name, DOB. Access civil case record free at www.madisonmunict.com/search.shtml. Shows case number, docket entry, charge, case type.
Criminal Records: Access: Phone, fax, mail, in person, online. Both court and visitors may perform in person searches. No search fee. Required to search: name, years to search, DOB, SSN. Criminal records computerized from 1989, prior in books indexed from 1958. Mail turnaround time up to 1 week. Criminal PAT goes back to same as civil.PAT results show name, DOB. Access criminal case record free at www.madisonmunict.com/search.shtml. Shows case number, docket entry, charge, case type. Online results show middle initial, DOB, SSN.
General Information: No probation records released. No fee to fax documents. Court makes copy: $.25 per page. Certification fee: $1.00 per cert. Payee: Madison County Municipal Court. Only cashiers checks and money orders accepted. Mail requests: SASE required.

Mahoning County

Common Pleas Court 120 Market St, Youngstown, OH 44503; 330-740-2103; probate phone: 330-740-2312; fax: 330-740-2105; 8AM-4PM. ***Felony, Civil Actions over $15,000, Probate.***
www.mahoningcountyoh.gov/tabid/810/default.aspx
Civil Records: Access: In person, online. Visitors must perform in person searches themselves. Required to search: name, years to search; also helpful: address. Civil cases indexed by defendant, plaintiff; index on computer from 1989, prior in books indexed from 1946. Civil PAT goes back to 1989. For online access, see criminal section.
Criminal Records: Access: Mail, in person, online. Both court and visitors may perform in person searches. No search fee. Required to search: name, years to search; also helpful: address, DOB, SSN. Criminal records computerized from 1989, prior in books indexed from 1946. Mail turnaround time 2 weeks. Criminal PAT goes back to same as civil. Access integrated justice system cases back to 1995 free at http://courts.mahoningcountyoh.gov/. Attorney searching also available. Online results show middle initial, DOB.
General Information: Online identifiers in results same as on public terminal. No secret indictment records released. Will fax documents $2.00 1st page, $1.00 each add'l. Court makes copy: $.10 per page. Certification fee: $1.00 per cert. Payee: Clerk of Court. Personal checks accepted; credit cards are not. Mail requests: SASE required for criminal.

County Court #2 127 Boardman Canfield Rd, Boardman, OH 44512; 330-726-5546; fax: 330-740-2035; 8:30AM-4:30PM. ***Misdemeanor, Civil Actions under $15,000, Small Claims.***
www.mahoningcountyoh.gov/tabid/810/default.aspx
Civil Records: Access: In person, online. Visitors must perform in person searches themselves. Required to search: name, years to search. Civil cases indexed by defendant, plaintiff. Civil records in books and dockets from 1960; on computer back to 1995. Civil PAT goes back to 1995. For online access, see criminal section.
Criminal Records: Access: In person, online. Only the court performs in person searches; visitors may not. Required to search: name, years to search, DOB, SSN, signed release. Criminal records in books and dockets from 1960; on computer back to 1995. Court will not perform party names searches for in-person requesters. Criminal PAT available. Access integrated justice system cases back to 1995 free at http://courts.mahoningcountyoh.gov/. Attorney searching also available.
General Information: Expunged records are not released. Will not fax documents. Court makes copy: $.10 per page. Certification fee: $1.00 per cert. Payee: County Court #2. Personal checks accepted; credit cards are not. Mail requests: SASE required for mail return of any copies.

County Court #3 605 E Ohio Ave, Sebring, OH 44672; 330-938-9873; fax: 330-938-6518; 8:30AM-4PM. ***Misdemeanor, Civil Actions under $15,000, Small Claims.***
www.mahoningcountyoh.gov/tabid/810/default.aspx
Civil Records: Access: Mail, in person, online. Only the court performs in person searches; visitors may not. Search fee: $5.00. Required to search: name, years to search. Civil cases indexed by defendant, plaintiff. Civil records in books from 1958; on computer back to 8/95. Mail turnaround time 1 week. For online access, see criminal section
Criminal Records: Access: Mail, in person, online. Only the court performs in person searches; visitors may not. Search fee: $5.00. Required to search: name, years to search, DOB; also helpful: SSN. Criminal records in books from 1989; on computer back to 8/95. Mail turnaround time 1 week. Access integrated justice system cases back to 1995 free at http://courts.mahoningcountyoh.gov/. Attorney searching also available.
General Information: No expunged records released. Court makes copy: $.10 per page. Certification fee: $1.00 per page. Payee: Mahoning County Court #3. Personal checks accepted; credit cards are not. Mail requests: SASE required.

County Court #4 6000 Mahoning Ave, Youngstown, OH 44515-2288; 330-740-2001; fax: 330-740-2036; 8:30AM-4PM. ***Misdemeanor, Civil Actions under $15,000, Small Claims.***
www.mahoningcountyoh.gov/tabid/810/default.aspx
Civil Records: Access: Fax, mail, in person, online. Both court and visitors may perform in person searches. No search fee. Required to search: name, years to search. Civil cases indexed by defendant, plaintiff. Civil records in books from the 1940s, on microfiche recent; computerized records since 1996. Phone, fax and mail access limited to out of town requests. Mail turnaround time varies. Civil PAT goes back to 1996. PAT results show middle initial, DOB. For online access, see criminal section.
Criminal Records: Access: Fax, mail, in person, online. Both court and visitors may perform in person searches. No search fee. Required to search: name, years to search, DOB, SSN, signed release. Criminal records in books from the 1940s, on microfiche rec; computerized records since 1996. Mail turnaround time varies. Criminal PAT goes back to same as civil. PAT results show middle initial, DOB. Access integrated justice system cases back to 1995 free at http://courts.mahoningcountyoh.gov/. Attorney searching also available. Online results show middle initial, DOB.
General Information: Online identifiers in results same as on public terminal. No expunged records released. Will fax documents $2.00 1st page, $.50 each add'l. Court makes copy: $.10 per page. Certification fee: $1.00 per page. Payee: County Court #4. Personal checks accepted; credit cards are not. Mail requests: SASE required.

County Court #5 72 N Broad St, Canfield, OH 44406; 330-533-3643; criminal fax: 330-740-2034; civil fax: same; 8:30AM-4PM. ***Misdemeanor, Civil Actions under $15,000, Small Claims.***
www.mahoningcountyoh.gov/tabid/810/default.aspx
Civil Records: Access: In person, online. Visitors must perform in person searches themselves. Required to search: name, years to search; also helpful: address. Civil cases indexed by defendant, plaintiff; index on computer since 1995; overall records go back to 1991. Civil PAT goes back to 1995. For online access, see criminal section.
Criminal Records: Access: Fax, mail, in person, online. Both court and visitors may perform in person searches. Search fee: $5.00 per name. Fee includes certification. Required to search: name, years to search; also helpful: DOB, SSN. Criminal records on computer since 1995; overall records go back to 1991. Mail turnaround time 1-2 days. Criminal PAT goes back to same as civil. Access integrated justice system cases back to 1995 free at http://courts.mahoningcountyoh.gov/. Attorney searching also available.
General Information: No LEADS printout records released. Will fax documents $2.00 1st page, $1.00 each add'l. Court makes copy: $.10 per page. Certification fee: $1.00 per page. Payee: County Court #5. Only cashiers checks and money orders accepted. No credit cards accepted. Mail requests: SASE required for criminal.

Campbell Municipal Court 351 Tenney Ave, Campbell, OH 44405; 330-755-2165; fax: 330-750-3058; 8AM-4PM. ***Misdemeanor, Civil Actions under $15,000, Eviction, Small Claims.***
Civil Records: Access: Fax, mail, in person. Only the court performs in person searches; visitors may not. No search fee. Required to search: name, years to search. Civil cases indexed by defendant, plaintiff. Civil records in books from 1950s; on computer back to 1999. Mail and fax access limited to short searches. Mail turnaround time depends on workload.
Criminal Records: Access: Fax, mail, in person. Only the court performs in person searches; visitors may not. No search fee. Required to search: name, years to search; also helpful: DOB, SSN, signed release. Criminal records in books from 1950s; on computer back to 7/1999. Mail turnaround time depends on workload.
General Information: No sealed records released. Will fax documents to police agencies only. Court makes copy: $.50 per page. Certification fee: $20.00 includes copies. Payee: Campbell Municipal Court. Only cashiers checks and money orders accepted. No credit cards accepted. Mail requests: SASE required.

Struthers Municipal Court 6 Elm St, Struthers, OH 44471; 330-755-1800; criminal phone: x114; civil phone: x113; criminal fax: 330-755-2790; civil fax: same; 8AM-4PM; Public access only-T & TH. ***Misdemeanor, Civil Actions under $15,000, Eviction, Small Claims.***
www.cityofstruthers.com/city_gov/court.htm
Alternative website is www.strutherscourt.com/. This court services several surrounding jurisdictions-Lowellville, Poland Village, Poland Township, New Middletown, and Springfield Township
Civil Records: Access: Mail, in person, online. Both court and visitors may perform in person searches. No search fee. Required to search: name, years to search. Civil cases indexed by defendant, plaintiff. Civil records in books since 1965; on computer since 1996. Mail turnaround time 2-3 days. Civil PAT goes back to 1996. PAT civil results show middle initial. Public terminal up on Tuesdays and Thursdays. Access court records at http://74.219.105.102/searchMC.shtml - records go back to 1996.
Criminal Records: Access: Mail, in person, online. Both court and visitors may perform in person searches. No search fee. Required to search: name, years to search; also helpful: SSN, DOB, signed release. Criminal records in books since 1965; on computer since 1996. Mail turnaround time 2-3 days. Criminal PAT goes back to same as civil. PAT results show middle initial, DOB. Public terminal up on Tuesdays and Thursdays. Terminal results include SSN. Access court records at http://74.219.105.102/searchMC.shtml - records go back to 1996. Onlinc rcsults show middle initial.
General Information: No pending case records released. Will fax documents no fee. Court makes copy: $.25 per page. Self serve: same. Certification fee: $10.00. Payee: Municipal Court. Only cashiers checks and money orders accepted. No credit cards accepted. Mail requests: SASE required.

Youngstown Municipal Court - Civil Records PO Box 6047, Youngstown, OH 44501-6047; 330-742-8863; fax: 330-742-8786; 8AM-4PM. ***Civil Actions under $15,000, Eviction, Small Claims.***
www.youngstownmuniclerk.com/
Civil Records: Access: Phone, fax, mail, in person. Both court and visitors may perform in person searches. No search fee. Required to search: name, years to search; also helpful: address. Civil cases indexed by defendant, plaintiff. Civil records in books since 1970; on computer since 1998. Attorney searching available. Mail turnaround time 1-2

days. Public use terminal has civil records back to 1998. PAT civil results show middle initial. Public terminal has records are small claims and traffic. Online results show middle initial.
General Information: Online identifiers in results same as on public terminal. All records are public. Will fax documents to local or toll-free number. Court makes copy: $.10 per page. Certification fee: $1.00. Cert fee includes copies. Payee: Municipal Court. Personal checks accepted for civil and small claims. Visa cards accepted. Mail requests: SASE required.

Youngstown Municipal Court - Criminal Records 26 S Phelps St, Youngstown, OH 44503; 330-742-8860; fax: 330-742-8786; 8AM-4PM. ***Misdemeanor.***
www.youngstownmuniclerk.com/
Criminal Records: Access: Fax, mail, in person, online. Both court and visitors may perform in person searches. No search fee. Required to search: name, years to search, DOB; also helpful: SSN. Criminal records go back to 1966; kept available since 1994 on docket books, microfiche; also on computer since 1998. Mail turnaround time 1 day. Public use terminal has crim records back to 1998. PAT results show name only. Access integrated justice system cases back to 1995 free at http://courts.mahoningcountyoh.gov/. Attorney searching also available. Online results show middle initial.
General Information: No records released. Will fax documents to local or toll free line. Court makes copy: $1.00 per page. Certification fee: $1.00. Payee: Municipal Court. Cashiers checks and money orders accepted. Visa cards accepted. Mail requests: SASE required.

Marion County

Common Pleas Court 100 N Main St, Marion, OH 43301-1823; 740-223-4270; probate phone: 740-232-4260; fax: 740-223-4279; 8:30AM-4:30PM. ***Felony, Civil Actions over $10,000.***
http://mcoprx.co.marion.oh.us/
Civil Records: Access: Mail, in person, online. Visitors must perform in person searches themselves. No search fee - you supply case number in mail requests. Required to search: name, years to search. Civil cases indexed by defendant, plaintiff; index on computer from 1991, prior in books since 1886. Mail is only used if you have the case number and request a specific document. Mail turnaround time 1-3 days. Civil PAT goes back to 1991. PAT results show middle initial, DOB. Court record access free at http://courtrecords.co.marion.oh.us/pa/.
Criminal Records: Access: Mail, in person, online. Visitors must perform in person searches themselves. No search fee. Required to search: name, years to search; also helpful: DOB, SSN. Criminal records computerized from 1991, prior in books since 1886. Mail requests accepted if you have the case number and request a specific document. Mail turnaround time 1-3 days. Criminal PAT goes back to same as civil. PAT results show middle initial, DOB. Court record access free at http://courtrecords.co.marion.oh.us/pa/.
General Information: No sealed, expunged records released. Fee to fax out file $2.00 per transmission and $1.00 per page. Court makes copy: $.10 per page. Self serve: same. Certification fee: $1.00. Payee: Marion County Clerk of Courts. Personal checks accepted. Major credit cards accepted, in person only. Mail requests: SASE required.

Marion Municipal Court 233 W Center St, Marion, OH 43302-0326; 740-387-0439; criminal phone: 740-382-4031; civil phone: 740-383-5515; fax: 740-382-5274; 8:30AM-4:30PM. ***Misdemeanor, Civil Actions under $15,000, Eviction, Small Claims.***
www.marionmunicipalcourt.org
Civil Records: Access: In person only. Visitors must perform in person searches themselves. Required to search: name, years to search. Civil cases indexed by defendant, plaintiff; index on computer since 1995. Public use terminal available, records go back to 1994. PAT results show name only.
Criminal Records: Access: Mail, in person, online. Both court and visitors may perform in person searches. No search fee. Required to search: name, years to search; also helpful: DOB, SSN. Criminal records computerized from 1986, prior in books. Mail turnaround time 7 days. Public use terminal available, crim records go back to 1994. PAT results show middle initial, DOB. Online case searching to be available at the website.
General Information: Will fax out documents no fee. Court makes copy: $.10 per page. Certification fee: $5.00. Payee: Municipal Court. Cashiers checks and money orders accepted. Credit cards accepted. Mail requests: SASE required for criminal.

Medina County

Common Pleas Court 93 Public Square. Rm 129, Medina, OH 44256; 330-725-9722; criminal phone: 330-725-9721; civil phone: 330-725-9722; probate phone: 330-725-9703; criminal fax: 330-764-8454; civil fax: same; 8AM-4:30PM. ***Felony, Civil Actions over $10,000, Probate.***
www.medinacommonpleas.com
Probate is a separate office at this address. Probate records not managed by the CP clerk.
Civil Records: Access: Mail, in person, online. Both court and visitors may perform in person searches. No search fee. Required to search: name, years to search. Civil cases indexed by defendant, plaintiff; index on computer from 10/92, in books to early 1960s, prior archived. Mail turnaround time 1-2 days. Civil PAT goes back to 1992. Online access is the same as criminal, see below.
Criminal Records: Access: Mail, in person, online. Both court and visitors may perform in person searches. No search fee. Required to search: name, years to search. Criminal records computerized from 10/92, in books to early 1960s, prior archived. Mail turnaround time 1-2 days. Criminal PAT goes back to 1991. Search court documents, motion dockets, sexual predator judgments and court notices at the web page.
General Information: Will not fax documents. Court makes copy: $.25 per page. Certification fee: $1.00 per page plus copy fee; Authentication-Certificate of Record-$5.00. Payee: Clerk of Court. Personal checks accepted. Mail requests: SASE required.

Medina Municipal Court 135 N Elmwood, Medina, OH 44256; 330-723-3287; fax: 330-225-1108; 8AM-4:30PM. ***Misdemeanor, Civil Actions under $15,000, Eviction, Small Claims.***
www.medinamunicipalcourt.org
Civil Records: Access: Mail, in person, online. Both court and visitors may perform in person searches. No search fee. Required to search: name, years to search. Civil cases indexed by defendant, plaintiff; index on computer from 1986, prior in books. Mail turnaround time 7-14 days. Civil PAT goes back to 1987. Access the online Civil Case Lookup free at http://24.144.216.42/connection/court/index.xsp.
Criminal Records: Access: Mail, online, in person. Visitors must perform in person searches themselves. No search fee. Required to search: name, years to search; also helpful: address, DOB, SSN. Criminal records computerized from 1986, prior in books. Mail turnaround time 7-14 days. Criminal PAT goes back to same as civil. Access the online Criminal and Traffic Case Lookup free at http://24.144.216.42/connection/court/index.xsp.
General Information: No expunged records released. Court makes copy: $.10 per page. Certification fee: $1.50. Payee: Medina Municipal Court. Personal checks accepted. Visa/MC accepted for criminal and traffic records only. Mail requests: SASE required.

Wadsworth Municipal Court 120 Maple St, Wadsworth, OH 44281-1825; 330-335-1596; fax: 330-335-2723; 8AM-4PM. ***Misdemeanor, Civil Actions under $15,000, Eviction, Small Claims.***
www.wadsworthmunicipalcourt.com/main.htm
Covers City of Wadsworth and Villages of Gloria Glens, Lodi, Seville, Westfield Center, also Townships of Guilford, Harrisville, Homer, Sharon, Wadsworth, and Westfield.
Civil Records: Access: Fax, mail, in person, online. Both court and visitors may perform in person searches. No search fee. Required to search: name, years to search. Civil cases indexed by defendant, plaintiff; index on computer from 3/90, prior in books. Mail turnaround time 2-4 days. Civil PAT goes back to 1990. Access civil case lookups and case queries free at www.wadsworthmunicipalcourt.com/index.php?folder=1&page=45.
Criminal Records: Access: Fax, mail, in person, online. Both court and visitors may perform in person searches. No search fee. Required to search: name, years to search; also helpful: address, DOB, SSN. Criminal records computerized from 3/90, prior in books. Mail turnaround time up to 1 week. Criminal PAT goes back to same as civil. Online access to criminal case and traffic lookups and case queries is the same as civil, see above.
General Information: No search warrant records released. No fee to fax documents locally only. Court makes copy: $.05 per page after first 25 pages. Certification fee: $1.00. Payee: Wadsworth Municipal Court. Personal checks and credit cards accepted. Mail requests: SASE required.

Meigs County

Common Pleas Court Clerk, PO Box 151, Pomeroy, OH 45769; 740-992-5290; probate phone: 740-992-3096; fax: 740-992-4429; 8:30AM-4:30PM. ***Felony, Civil Actions over $3,000, Probate.***
Probate fax is 740-992-6727.
Civil Records: Access: In person only. Visitors must perform in person searches themselves. Required to search: name, years to search; also helpful: address. Civil cases indexed by defendant, plaintiff; index on computer since 1996, in books to 1800s. Will assist in person searchers. Civil PAT goes back to 1996. PAT civil results show middle initial.
Criminal Records: Access: In person only. Visitors must perform in person searches themselves. Required to search: name, years to search, DOB; also helpful: address, SSN. Criminal records on computer since 1996, in books to 1800s. Court will assist in person searchers. Criminal PAT goes back to same as civil.PAT results show name, DOB. Terminal results include SSN.
General Information: No secret records released. Will fax specific doc to local or toll-free number. Court makes copy: $.25 per page. Certification fee: $1.00. Payee: Clerk of Court. Personal checks accepted; credit cards are not.

Meigs County Municipal Court 100 E 2nd St, Courthouse, Pomeroy, OH 45769; 740-992-2279; fax: 740-992-4570; 8:30-4:30PM. ***Misdemeanor, Civil Actions under $15,000, Small Claims.***
www.meigscountycourt.org
Civil Records: Access: Fax, in person, online. Only the court performs in person searches; visitors may not. Required to search: name, years to search. Civil cases indexed by defendant, plaintiff; index on computer from 8/90, prior in docket books. Phone access limited to records from 1990 to present. Access civil records free at http://docket.webxsol.com/meigs/index.html.
Criminal Records: Access: Fax, in person, online. Only the court performs in person searches; visitors may not. No search fee. Required to search: name, years to search, DOB, SSN, signed release. Criminal records computerized from 8/90, prior in docket books. Phone access limited to records from 1990 to present. Access criminal records free at http://docket.webxsol.c om/meigs/index.html.
General Information: No sealed records released. Will not fax out case files. Court makes copy: $.25 per page. Certification fee: $2.00 includes copy fee. Payee: Meigs County Court. Personal checks accepted; credit cards are not.

Mercer County

Common Pleas Court 101 N Main St, Rm 205, PO Box 28, Celina, OH 45822; 419-586-6461; probate phone: 419-586-2418; fax: 419-586-5826; 8:30AM-4PM. ***Felony, Civil Actions over $10,000, Probate.*** www.mercercountyohio.org/clerk/
Probate records located at 101 N Main ST, Rm 306-307. Probate fax- 419-586-4506
Civil Records: Access: In person, online. Visitors must perform in person searches themselves.

Required to search: name, years to search; also helpful: address. Civil cases indexed by defendant, plaintiff; index on computer back to 1997, microfiche up to and including 1985, prior in books. Online access available http://www2.mercercountyohio.org/pa/. Civil PAT goes back to 1997. PAT results show name only.
Criminal Records: Access: In person, online. Visitors must perform in person searches themselves. Required to search: name, years to search; also helpful: address, DOB, SSN. Criminal records computerized from 1997, microfiche up to and including 1985, prior in books. Online access available http://www2.mercercountyohio.org/pa/. Criminal PAT goes back same as civil; crim results show name only.
General Information: No juvenile or sealed records released. Will fax specific document for $3.00 for 1st page; $1.00 for each add'l page. Court makes copy: $.25 per page. Cert fee: $1.00. Payee: Clerk of Court. Personal checks accepted; credit cards are not.

Celina Municipal Court PO Box 362, Celina, OH 45822; 419-586-6491; criminal fax: 419-586-4735; civil fax: same; 8AM-4:30PM. ***Misdemeanor, Civil Actions under $15,000, Eviction, Small Claims.***
Civil Records: Access: Fax, mail, in person. Both court and visitors may perform in person searches. No search fee. Required to search: name, years to search; also helpful: address. Civil cases indexed by defendant, plaintiff; index on computer from 1990, prior in books. Mail turnaround time 2-3 days. Civil PAT goes back to 1990; results show name only.
Criminal Records: Access: Fax, mail, in person. Both court and visitors may perform in person searches. No search fee. Required to search: name, years to search; also helpful: address, DOB, SSN. Criminal records are on computer since 1989, prior found in books and files. Mail turnaround time 2-3 days. Criminal PAT goes back to 1989. PAT results show middle initial, DOB. Terminal results include SSN.
General Information: No confidential information released. Will fax documents to local or toll free line. Court makes copy: $.05 per page. Self serve: $.25 per page. Cert fee: $1.00 per page. Payee: Municipal Court. In-state personal checks accepted. No credit cards accepted. Mail requests: SASE required.

Miami County

Common Pleas Court & Court of Appeals Safety Bldg, 201 W Main St, 3rd Fl, Troy, OH 45373; 937-440-6010; probate phone: 937-440-6050; fax: 937-440-6011; 8AM-4PM. ***Felony, Civil Actions over $10,000, Probate.***
Probate is a separate division on the 2nd Fl. Probate fax- 937-440-3529
Civil Records: Access: Fax, mail, in person. Both court and visitors may perform in person searches. Search fee: $5.00 per name. Required to search: name, years to search; also helpful: address. Civil cases indexed by defendant, plaintiff. Civil records in books for past 30 years, prior are archived; on computer since 1984. Mail turnaround time 1-2 days. Civil PAT goes back to 1989.
Criminal Records: Access: Fax, mail, in person. Both court and visitors may perform in person searches. Search fee: $5.00 per name. Required to search: name, years to search, DOB, SSN; also helpful: address. Criminal records in books for past 30 years, prior are archived; on computer since 1984. Mail turnaround time 1-2 days. Criminal PAT goes back to same as civil.
General Information: No expunged or sealed records released. Will fax documents $1.00 each. Court makes copy: $.25 per page. Certification fee: $1.00. Payee: Miami County Clerk of Courts. Personal checks accepted; credit cards are not. Mail requests: SASE required.

Miami County Municipal Court 201 W Main St, Courthouse, Troy, OH 45373; 937-440-3918; criminal phone: 937-440-3910; civil phone: 937-440-3919; criminal fax: 937-440-3911; civil fax: 937-440-3537; 8AM-4PM. ***Misdemeanor, Civil Actions under $15,000, Eviction, Small Claims.***
www.co.miami.oh.us/muni/index.htm
If the SSN is not provided by the party doing the search, the court personnel will mask the SSN before providing copies.
Civil Records: Access: Mail, in person, online. Both court and visitors may perform in person searches. Search fee: $5.00 per name. Required to search: name, years to search. Civil cases indexed by defendant, plaintiff. Civil records in books go back 25 years; on computer back to 11/89. Mail turnaround time 2-3 days. Civil PAT goes back to 11/1989. PAT results show middle initial, DOB. Online access to records is free at www.co.miami.oh.us/pa/index.htm.
Criminal Records: Access: Mail, in person, online. Both court and visitors may perform in person searches. Search fee: $5.00 per name. Required to search: name, years to search, SSN. Criminal records computerized from 1985, prior in books. Mail turnaround time 2-3 days. Criminal PAT goes back to 1986. PAT results show middle initial, DOB. Online access to records is free at www.co.miami.oh.us/pa/index.htm. Online results show middle initial, DOB.
General Information: Online identifiers in results same as on public terminal. No search warrant records released. Will fax documents for no fee. Court makes copy: $.25 per page. Self serve: none. Certification fee: $2.00 per page. Payee: Municipal Court. No personal checks accepted. Visa/MC accepted. Mail requests: SASE required.

Monroe County

Common Pleas Court 101 N Main St, Rm 26, Woodsfield, OH 43793; 740-472-0761; probate phone: 740-472-1654; criminal fax: 740-472-2549; civil fax: same; 8:30AM-4:30PM. ***Felony, Civil Actions over $3,000, Probate.***
Probate is a separate index at a separate office.
Civil Records: Access: In person only. Visitors must perform in person searches themselves. Required to search: name, years to search; also helpful: address. Civil cases indexed by defendant, plaintiff. Civil records in books since 1800; computerized records from 11/18/02 to present. Civil PAT goes back to 11/2002. PAT civil results show middle initial.
Criminal Records: Access: Mail, fax, in person. Both court and visitors may perform in person searches. Search fee: $2.00 per name. Clerk of Courts will search more than one name but we do charge $2.00 per name!!!. Required to search: name, years to search; also helpful: address, DOB, SSN. Criminal records in books since 1800; computerized records from 11/18/02 to present. The court will not do party names searches for in-person requesters. Mail turnaround time 3 days. Criminal PAT goes back to same as civil. PAT results show middle initial, DOB. Terminal results include SSN.
General Information: No secret indictment records released. Fee to fax out file $2.00 per page. Court makes copy: $.25 per page. Certification fee: $1.00 per page. Payee: Clerk of Court. Personal checks accepted; credit cards are not. Mail requests: SASE required for criminal.

County Court 101 N Main St, Rm 35, Woodsfield, OH 43793; 740-472-5181; fax: 740-472-2526; 9AM-N, 1-4:30PM. ***Misdemeanor, Civil Actions under $15,000, Small Claims.***
Civil Records: Access: Phone, mail, in person. Both court and visitors may perform in person searches. No search fee. Required to search: name, years to search. Civil cases indexed by defendant, plaintiff. Civil records in books, indexed back to 1950; on computer back to 8/1999. Mail turnaround time 1-2 days. Civil PAT goes back to 1999. PAT results show name only.
Criminal Records: Access: Phone, mail, in person. Both court and visitors may perform in person searches. No search fee. Required to search: name, years to search. Criminal records in books, indexed back to 1979; on computer back to 1999. Mail turnaround time 1-2 days. Criminal PAT goes back to same as civil. PAT results show name only.
General Information: Court makes copy for no fee. Certification fee: $1.00 per page. Payee: Monroe County Court. No personal checks or credit cards accepted. Mail requests: SASE required.

Montgomery County

Common Pleas Court 41 N Perry St, County Clerk of Courts, Dayton, OH 45422; criminal phone: 937-225-4536; civil phone: 937-225-4512; probate phone: 937-225-4640; criminal fax: 937-496-7581; civil fax: 937-496-7220; 8:30AM-4:30PM. ***Felony, Civil Actions over $10,000, Probate.***
www.clerk.co.montgomery.oh.us
Probate located at this address in separate office. Domestic Relations phone- 937-496-7590, same address, Room 9.
Civil Records: Access: Mail, in person, online. Both court and visitors may perform in person searches. No search fee. Required to search: name, years to search; also helpful: address. Civil cases indexed by defendant, plaintiff; index on computer from 1970s, prior in books. Address mail requests to "Montgomery County Clerk of Court Civil Records." Mail Turnaround time 1 week. Civil PAT goes back to 1997. Results may include address if on originating documents. Online access to the Courts countywide PRO system is free at www.clerk.co.montgomery.oh.us/legal/records.cfm. Access probate court-related records free at www.mcohio.org/government/probate/prodcfm/case_search_main.cfm.
Criminal Records: Access: In person, online. Visitors must perform in person searches themselves. Required to search: name, years to search; also helpful: address, DOB, SSN. Criminal records computerized from 1970s, prior in books. Criminal PAT goes back to 1997. PAT criminal results show middle initial. Results may include address if on originating documents. Online access to criminal records is the same as civil. Online results show middle initial.
General Information: Online identifiers in results same as on public terminal. No sealed records released. Will fax documents to local or toll-free number. Court makes copy: $.10 per page. Self serve: same. Certification fee: $1.00 per page. Cert fee includes copies. Payee: Clerk of Court. Personal checks accepted; credit cards are not.

County Court - Area 1 195 S Clayton Rd, New Lebanon, OH 45345-9601; 937-687-9099; fax: 937-687-7119; 8AM-4PM T-TH; 10AM-6PM M; 9AM-4PM F. ***Misdemeanor, Civil Actions under $15,000, Small Claims.*** www.clerk.co.montgomery.oh.us
Civil Records: Access: Mail, in person, online. Both court and visitors may perform in person searches. No search fee. Required to search: name, years to search. Civil cases indexed by defendant, plaintiff; index on computer from 2/92, prior in books, Archives 937-225-6366. Mail turnaround time 2-3 days. PAT results show middle initial, DOB. Results include company name, case number. Search countywide records online at www.clerk.co.montgomery.oh.us/.
Criminal Records: Access: Mail, in person, online. Both court and visitors may perform in person searches. No search fee. Required to search: name, years to search; also helpful: SSN. Criminal records computerized from 2/92, prior in books, Archives 937-225-6366. Mail turnaround time 2-3 days. PAT results show middle initial, DOB. Results include company name, case number. Online access to criminal records is the same as civil.
General Information: No medical, PSI report or LEADS print-out records released. Will fax documents to local or toll-free number. Court makes copy: $.10 per page. Certification fee: $1.00. Payee: Montgomery County Court Area One. Personal checks and credit cards accepted. Mail requests: SASE required.

County Court - Area 2 6111 Taylorsville Rd, Huber Heights, OH 45424; 937-496-7231; civil phone: 937-225-5824; fax: 937-496-7236; 8Am-4PM M-W; N-7PM Th; 9AM-4PM F. ***Misdemeanor, Civil under $15,000, Small Claims under $3,000.***
www.mcohio.org/revize/montgomery/government/clerkofcourts/index.html
Civil Records: Access: Phone, fax, mail, in person, online. Both court and visitors may perform in person searches. No search fee. Required to search: name, years to search; also helpful: address. Civil cases indexed by defendant, plaintiff; index on

computer from 1992, prior in books back to 1974. Mail turnaround time 2-7 days. Search countywide records at www.clerk.co.montgomery.oh.us/.
Criminal Records: Access: Phone, fax, mail, in person, online. Both court and visitors may perform in person searches. No search fee. Required to search: name, years to search; also helpful: address, DOB, SSN. Criminal records computerized from 1992, prior in books back to 1974. Mail turnaround time 2-7 days. Online access to criminal records is the same as civil.
General Information: No confidential, forensic evaluation or medical records released. No fee to fax documents. Court makes copy: $.25 per page. Certification fee: $1.00 per cert. Payee: County Court Area Two. Business checks accepted. Major credit cards accepted. Mail requests: SASE required.

Dayton Municipal Court - Civil Division 301 W 3rd St, PO Box 10700, Dayton, OH 45402-0968; 937-333-4471; fax: 937-333-4468; 8AM-4:30PM. ***Civil Actions under $15,000, Eviction, Small Claims.*** www.daytonmunicipalcourt.org
Civil Records: Access: Phone, fax, mail, in person, online. Both court and visitors may perform in person searches. No search fee. Required to search: name, years to search; also helpful: address. Civil cases indexed by defendant, plaintiff; index on computer back to 1998, prior in books to 1977. Mail turnaround time 2-3 days. Public use terminal has civil records back to 1998. PAT results show name only. Results include case number. Online access to Municipal court records free at www.daytonmunicipalcourt.org/scripts/rgw.dll/Docket; includes traffic and criminal. Online results show name only.
General Information: No expunged case records released. Will fax documents to local or toll-free number. Court makes copy: $.25 per page. No certification fee. Payee: Clerk of Court. Personal checks accepted. Visa/MC accepted. Mail requests: SASE required.

Dayton Municipal Court - Criminal Division 301 W 3rd St, Rm 331, Dayton, OH 45402; 937-333-4315; fax: 937-333-4490; 8AM-4:30PM. ***Misdemeanor.***
www.daytonmunicipalcourt.org
Criminal Records: Access: Phone, in person, online. Visitors must perform in person searches themselves. No search fee. Required to search: name, years to search, DOB; also helpful: address, SSN, signed release. Criminal records computerized from 1992, prior in books. Court is known to allow very limited phone access. Public use terminal has crim records back to 1992. PAT results show middle initial, DOB, SSN. Online access to municipal court records is free at www.daytonmunicipalcourt.org/scripts/rgw.dll/Docket; includes traffic and civil. Online results show name, DOB.
General Information: Online identifiers in results same as on public terminal. All records are public. Will not fax documents. Court makes copy: $.25 per page. No certification fee. Payee: Dayton Municipal Court. Personal checks and credit cards accepted.

Kettering Municipal Court 2325 Wilmington Pike, Kettering, OH 45420; 937-296-2461; fax: 937-534-7017; 8:30AM-4:30PM. ***Misdemeanor, Civil Actions under $15,000, Eviction, Small Claims.***
www.ketteringmunicipalcourt.com
Civil Records: Access: Phone, mail, fax, in person, online. Both court and visitors may perform in person searches. No search fee. Required to search: name, years to search. Civil cases indexed by defendant, plaintiff; index on computer from 1988, prior in books. Mail turnaround time 1-5 days. Civil PAT goes back to 1988. Access case lookups and calendars free at http://caselookup.ketteringmunicipalcourt.com/connection/court/.
Criminal Records: Access: Phone, mail, fax, in person, online. Both court and visitors may perform in person searches. No search fee. Required to search: name, years to search, DOB; also helpful: SSN. Criminal records computerized from 1988, prior in books. Mail turnaround time 1-5 days. Criminal PAT goes back to 1988. Online access same as civil, see above.

General Information: No expungment records released. Will fax documents to local or toll free line. Court makes copy: $.05 per page. Certification fee: $2.50 per page. Payee: Kettering Municipal Court. Personal and business checks accepted. Credit cards accepted. Mail requests: SASE required.

Miamisburg Municipal Court 10 N 1st St, Miamisburg, OH 45342; 937-866-2203; fax: 937-866-0135; 8AM-4PM. ***Misdemeanor, Civil Actions under $15,000, Eviction, Small Claims.***
www.miamisburgcourts.com
Civil Records: Access: Mail, in person, online. Visitors must perform in person searches themselves. No search fee. Required to search: name, years to search; also helpful: address. Civil cases indexed by defendant, plaintiff; index on computer from 1988, prior in books. Call in advance to schedule in person searching. Mail request requires SASE. Access case lookup options and case schedules for free at http://64.56.106.117/connection/court/.
Criminal Records: Access: Mail, in person, online. Only the court performs in person searches; visitors may not. No search fee. Required to search: name, years to search; also helpful: address, DOB, SSN. Criminal records computerized from 1988, prior in books. Call in advance to schedule in person searching. Mail request requires SASE. Mail turnaround time 1-2 weeks. Access case lookup options and case schedules for free at http://64.56.106.117/connection/court/.
General Information: No police reports, search warrants with no returns records released. Will fax documents to local or toll free line. Court makes copy: $.05 per page. No certification fee. Payee: Miamisburg Municipal Court. Personal checks accepted. Visa/MC accepted. Mail requests: SASE required.

Oakwood Municipal Court 30 Park Ave, Dayton, OH 45419; 937-293-3058; fax: 937-297-2939; 8AM-4:30PM. ***Misdemeanor, Civil Actions under $15,000, Eviction, Small Claims.***
Civil Records: Access: Mail, in person. Only the court performs in person searches; visitors may not. No search fee. Required to search: name, years to search; also helpful: address. Civil cases indexed by defendant, plaintiff. Civil records in books since 1976. Mail turnaround time 1-2 weeks. Civil PAT goes back to 1996.
Criminal Records: Access: Mail, in person. Only the court performs in person searches; visitors may not. No search fee. Required to search: name, years to search; also helpful: address, DOB, SSN. Criminal records in books since 1976. Address mail search requests to the Police Records Section. Mail turnaround time 1-2 weeks. Criminal PAT available.
General Information: No sealed, expunged or confidential records released. Will fax documents to local or toll free line. Court makes copy: $.10 per page. No certification fee. Payee: City of Oakwood. Local checks accepted. No credit cards accepted. Mail requests: SASE required.

Vandalia Municipal Court PO Box 429, 245 James Bohanan Dr, Justice Ctr, 2nd Fl, Vandalia, OH 45377; 937-898-3996; fax: 937-898-6648; 8AM-4PM. ***Misdemeanor, Civil Actions under $15,000, Eviction, Small Claims.***
www.vandaliacourt.com
Civil Records: Access: Phone, fax, mail, in person, online. Both court and visitors may perform in person searches. Search fee: $1.00 per page for complete print out. Required to search: name, years to search. Civil cases indexed by defendant, plaintiff; index on computer from 1986. Mail turnaround time 7 days. Civil PAT goes back to 1986. Search records, including traffic, free at http://docket.vandaliacourt.com/.
Criminal Records: Access: Fax, mail, in person, online. Both court and visitors may perform in person searches. No search fee. Required to search: name, years to search, DOB, SSN. Criminal records computerized from 1986. Mail turnaround time 7 days. Criminal PAT available. Search records, including traffic, at http://docket.vandaliacourt.com/.

General Information: No medical, psychological reports or domestic violence report records released. Will fax documents to local or toll-free number. Court makes copy: $1.00 per page. No certification fee. Payee: Clerk of Court. Business checks accepted. Major credit cards accepted. Mail requests: SASE required.

Dayton Municipal Ct - Traffic Division PO Box 10700, 301 W 3rd St, Dayton, OH 45402; 937-333-4313; fax: 937-333-7558; 8AM-4:30PM. ***Misdemeanor, Traffic.***
www.daytonmunicipalcourt.org
It is difficult for the court to provide case information prior to 1995. Search dockets free online at www.daytonmunicipalcourt.org/scripts/rgw.dll/Docket.

Morgan County

Common Pleas Court 19 E Main St, McConnelsville, OH 43756; 740-962-4752; probate phone: 740-962-2861; fax: 740-962-4522; 8AM-4PM M-TH; 8AM-4PM F. ***Felony, Civil Actions over $3,000, Probate.***
Above number is for Clerk. The Common Pleas Court can be reached at 740-962-3371.
Civil Records: Access: Mail, in person. Visitors must perform in person searches themselves. Search fee: $2.00 per name. Required to search: name, years to search; also helpful: address. Civil cases indexed by defendant, plaintiff. Civil records in books, some back to 1850. Mail turnaround time 1-3 days. Civil PAT goes back to 2001.
Criminal Records: Access: Mail, in person. Both court and visitors may perform in person searches. Search fee: $2.00 per name. Required to search: name, years to search; also helpful: address, DOB, SSN. Criminal records in books, some back to 1850. Mail turnaround time 1-3 days. Criminal PAT goes back to same as civil.
General Information: No secret indictment records released. Will not fax documents. Court makes copy for no fee. Certification fee: $1.00 per page. Payee: Clerk of Court. Personal checks accepted; credit cards are not. Mail requests: SASE required.

Morgan County Court 37 E Main St, McConnelsville, OH 43756; 740-962-4031; fax: 740-962-2895; 8AM-4PM. ***Misdemeanor, Civil Actions under $15,000, Small Claims Under $3,000.***
www.morgancounty-oh.gov
Civil Records: Access: Fax, mail, in person. Both court and visitors may perform in person searches. No search fee. Required to search: name, years to search. Civil cases indexed by defendant, plaintiff. Civil records in books from 1950, computerized since 12/02. Mail turnaround time 1-2 days. Civil PAT goes back to 12/2002. PAT results show middle initial, DOB.
Criminal Records: Access: Fax, mail, in person. Both court and visitors may perform in person searches. No search fee. Required to search: name, years to search, DOB; also helpful: SSN. Criminal records in books from 1950, computerized since 12/02. Mail turnaround time 1-2 days. Criminal PAT goes back to same as civil. PAT results show middle initial, DOB.
General Information: No fee to fax documents. Court makes copy: $.10 per page. Self serve: same. Certification fee: $1.00. Payee: Morgan County Court. Personal checks and major credit cards accepted. Mail requests: SASE required.

Morrow County

Common Pleas Court 48 E High St, Mount Gilead, OH 43338; 419-947-2085; probate phone: 419-947-5575; fax: 419-947-5421; 8AM-4PM. ***Felony, Civil Actions over $3,000, Probate.***
Civil Records: Access: Phone, fax, mail, in person. Both court and visitors may perform in person searches. No search fee. Required to search: name, years to search; also helpful: address. Civil cases indexed by defendant, plaintiff. Civil records in books from 1960, computerized since 1/02. Mail turnaround time 1 day. Civil PAT goes back to 2002.
Criminal Records: Access: Phone, fax, mail, in person. Both court and visitors may perform in person searches. No search fee. Required to search: name, years to search; also helpful: address, DOB,

SSN. Criminal records in books from 1960, computerized since 1/02. Mail turnaround time 5-7 days. Criminal PAT goes back to same as civil. PAT results show name only.
General Information: Will fax documents $1.00 per page. Court makes copy: $.05 per page. Self serve: same. Certification fee: $1.00. Payee: Clerk of Court. Personal checks accepted with proper ID. Visa/MC accepted. Mail requests: SASE required.

Municipal Court 48 E High St, Mount Gilead, OH 43338; 419-947-5045; civil phone: x237 or x238; fax: 419-946-4070; 7:30AM-5PM. ***Misdemeanor, Civil under $15,000, Small Claims.***
Civil Records: Access: Phone, fax, mail, in person. Both court and visitors may perform in person searches. No search fee. Required to search: name, years to search; also helpful-DOB or SSN. Civil cases indexed by defendant, plaintiff; index on computer back to 1997, indexed on books from 1970s, archived from 1800s. Mail turnaround time 1-2 days. Court calendars for the week ahead available www.morrowcountymunict.org/. Site may be improved soon to improve case index searching.
Criminal Records: Access: Phone, fax, mail, in person. Both court and visitors may perform in person searches. No search fee. Required to search: name, years to search, DOB, SSN. Criminal records on computer since 1990, indexed on books from 1970s, archived from 1800s. Mail turnaround time 1-2 days. Limited online access, see civil section.
General Information: No confidential records released. Will fax documents for free. Court makes copy: $1.00 per page. Certification fee: $2.00 per cert. Payee: County Municipal Court. No personal checks accepted. Major credit cards accepted. Mail requests: SASE required for mail return of any copies.

Muskingum County

Common Pleas Court 401 Main St, Zanesville, OH 43701; 740-455-7104; probate phone: 740-455-7113; fax: 740-455-7177; 8:30AM-4:30PM. ***Felony, Civil Actions, Probate.***
http://cpc.muskingumcounty.org/
As of 1/1/2001, there is no dollar limit on civil actions; prior, the civil action minimum was $15,000. Probate is separate index at this same address. Ask court's permission before faxing to court.
Civil Records: Access: Mail, in person, online. Both court and visitors may perform in person searches. No search fee. Required to search: name, years to search; also helpful: address. Civil cases indexed by defendant, plaintiff. Civil records in original files back to 1800s. Mail turnaround time 2 weeks. Civil PAT goes back to 10/17/1994. PAT results show name, SSN; DOB and address will appear in results only if available. Online access to court records is at http://clerkofcourts.muskingumc ounty.org/PA/. Records indexed back to 1994.
Criminal Records: Access: Mail, in person, online. Both court and visitors may perform in person searches. No search fee. Required to search: name, years to search, DOB; also helpful: address, SSN. Criminal docket on books to 1960, original files back to 1800s. Mail turnaround time 2 weeks. Criminal PAT goes back to same as civil. PAT results show name, SSN; DOB and address will appear in results if they are available. Online access to criminal index is same as civil, above.
General Information: No grand jury records released. Will not fax documents. Court makes copy: $.05 per page. Self serve: same. Certification fee: $1.00 per page include copy fee. Payee: Clerk of Court. Personal checks and major credit cards accepted. Mail requests: SASE required.

County Court 27 N 5th St, Zanesville, OH 43701; 740-455-7138; fax: 740-455-7157; 8AM-4PM. ***Misdemeanor, Civil under $15,000, Small Claims.***
www.muskingumcountycourt.org
Civil Records: Access: Fax, mail, in person, online. Both court and visitors may perform in person searches. No search fee. Required to search: name, years to search; also helpful: address. Civil cases indexed by defendant, plaintiff. Civil records in books from 1958; on computer back to 1995. Mail turnaround time up to 1 week. Civil PAT goes back to 1995. Access to county court records is free at www.muskingumcountycourt.org/sear.html.
Criminal Records: Access: Fax, mail, in person, online. Both court and visitors may perform in person searches. No search fee. Required to search: name, years to search, DOB; also helpful: address, SSN. Criminal records in books from 1958; on computer back to 1995. Mail turnaround time up to 1 week. Criminal PAT goes back to same as civil. PAT results show middle initial, DOB. Access to county court records is free at www.muskingumcountycourt.org/sear.html. Online results show middle initial, DOB.
General Information: Online identifiers in results same as on public terminal. No expunged records released. No fee to fax documents. Fax available in emergency only. Court makes copy: $.25 per page. Certification fee: $1.00 per page includes copy fee. Payee: Muskingum County Clerk. Personal checks and credit cards accepted. Mail requests: SASE required.

Zanesville Municipal Court PO Box 566, 332 South St, Zanesville, OH 43702; 740-454-3269; criminal fax: 740-455-0739; civil fax: same; 9AM-4:30PM; 9AM-N TH. ***Misdemeanor, Civil Actions under $15,000, Eviction, Small Claims.***
www.coz.org/municipal_court.cfm
Civil Records: Access: Mail, in person, online. Both court and visitors may perform in person searches. No search fee. Required to search: name, years to search; also helpful: address. Civil cases indexed by defendant, plaintiff; index on computer since 1987. In person searches only available for one or two names. Otherwise, searchers are directed to the webpage. Mail turnaround time 1 day. Online access free: http://74.219.84.227/searchMC.shtml
Criminal Records: Access: Mail, in person, fax, online. Both court and visitors may perform in person searches. No search fee. Required to search: name, years to search; also helpful: address, DOB, SSN. Criminal records on computer since 1993. In person searches only available for one or two names. Otherwise, researchers are directed to the webpage. Mail turnaround time 1 day. PAT results show middle initial, DOB. Terminal results include SSN. Online access is free at http://74.219.84.227/searchMC.shtml and includes traffic and civil searching. Online results show middle initial, DOB. Terminal results include SSN.
General Information: Will fax documents no fee. Court makes copy for no fee. Certification fee: $1.00 per page include copies. Payee: Zanesville Municipal Court. Personal checks accepted. Visa/MC accepted for traffic and criminal only. Mail requests: SASE required.

Noble County

Common Pleas Court 350 Courthouse, Caldwell, OH 43724; 740-732-4408; probate phone: 740-732-5047; criminal fax: 740-732-5604; civil fax: same; 8AM-4PM M-W; 8AM-N Th; 8AM-6PM F. ***Felony, Civil Actions over $3,000.*** Probate is a separate office at 270 Courthouse, in Caldwell.
Civil Records: Access: Phone, fax, mail, in person. Both court and visitors may perform in person searches. Search fee: $2.00 per name. Required to search: name, years to search; also helpful: address. Civil cases indexed by defendant, plaintiff. Civil records in books, archived back to mid-1800s. Recent civil records are computerized. Mail turnaround time 1-2 days. Civil PAT goes back to 7/1997.
Criminal Records: Access: Phone, fax, mail, in person. Both court and visitors may perform in person searches. Search fee: $2.00 per name. Required to search: name, years to search; also helpful: address, DOB, SSN. Criminal records in books, archived back to 1800s. Mail turnaround time 1-2 days. Criminal PAT goes back to same as civil.
General Information: No sealed records released. No fee to fax documents. Court makes copy: $.25 per page. Self serve: same. Certification fee: $1.00 per page. Payee: Clerk of Court. Personal checks accepted; credit cards are not. Will bill all court rule copies. Mail requests: SASE required.

Noble County Court 100 Courthouse, Caldwell, OH 43724; 740-732-5795; fax: 740-732-1435; 8:30AM-4PM M-W,F; 8:30AM-N TH. ***Misdemeanor, Civil under $15,000, Small Claims.***
Civil Records: Access: Phone, fax, mail, in person. Both court and visitors may perform in person searches. No search fee. Required to search: name, years to search. Civil cases indexed by defendant, plaintiff. Civil records in books since 1960, on computer back to 2002. Mail turnaround time same day. Civil PAT goes back to 2002. PAT civil results show middle initial.
Criminal Records: Access: Fax, mail, in person. Both court and visitors may perform in person searches. No search fee. Required to search: name, years to search, DOB; also helpful- SSN, signed release. Criminal records in books since 1960; on computer back to 2002. Mail turnaround time same day. Criminal PAT goes back to same as civil. PAT results show middle initial, DOB. Terminal results include SSN.
General Information: Will fax out documents at no charge. Court makes copy: $.25 per page. Self serve: same. Certification fee: $5.00 per document. Payee: County Court. Only cashiers checks and money orders accepted. No credit cards accepted. Mail requests: SASE required.

Ottawa County

Common Pleas Court 315 Madison St, 3rd Fl, Port Clinton, OH 43452; 419-734-6755 (General Division); probate phone: 419-734-6830; fax: 419-734-6875; 8:30AM-4:30PM. ***Felony, Civil Actions over $10,000, Probate Appeals.***
www.ottawacocpcourt.com
Must call first for a "log #" if sending a fax. Probate is a separate court at 315 Madison St., Rm 306.
Civil Records: Access: Mail, online. Visitors must perform in person searches themselves. No search fee. Required to search: name, years to search; also helpful: address. Civil cases indexed by defendant, plaintiff; index on computer from 8/89, prior in books to 1842. Civil PAT goes back to 8/1989. Record search and dockets free at http://96.11.124.244/search.shtml.
Criminal Records: Access: Mail, online. Visitors must perform in person searches themselves. No search fee. Required to search: name, years to search; also helpful: address, DOB, SSN. Criminal records computerized from 8/89, prior in books to 1842. Criminal PAT goes back to same as civil. Record search and dockets free at http://96.11.124.244/search.shtml.
General Information: No sealed records released. Will fax specific case for $3.00. Court makes copy: $.15 per page. Certification fee: $1.00. Payee: Clerk of Courts. Personal checks accepted; credit cards are not. Mail requests: SASE required.

Ottawa County Municipal Court 1860 E Perry St, Port Clinton, OH 43452; 419-734-4143; fax: 419-732-2862; 8:30-4:30PM. ***Misdemeanor, Civil Actions under $15,000, Eviction, Small Claims.***
www.ottawacountymunicipalcourt.com
Civil Records: Access: In person, online. Visitors must perform in person searches themselves. Required to search: name, years to search; also helpful: address. Civil cases indexed by defendant, plaintiff; index on computer from 1989, prior in books. Civil PAT goes back to 1989. PAT results show name, DOB. Search record index is at www.ottawacountymunicipalcourt.com/search.html. Includes small claims.
Criminal Records: Access: In person, online. Visitors must perform in person searches themselves. Required to search: name, years to search, DOB; also helpful: address, SSN. Criminal records computerized from 1989, prior in books. Criminal PAT goes back to same as civil.PAT results show name, DOB. Search records at www.ottawacountymunicipalcourt.com/search.html. Includes traffic. Online results show name, DOB.
General Information: Online identifiers in results same as on public terminal. No sealed records released. Will not fax documents. Court makes copy: $.10 per page. Certification fee: $3.00. Payee: Ottawa County Municipal Court. Only cashiers checks and money orders accepted. No credit cards accepted.

Paulding County

Common Pleas Court 115 N Williams St, Rm 104, Paulding, OH 45879; 419-399-8210; probate phone: 419-399-8256; criminal fax: 419-399-8248; civil fax: same; 8AM-4PM. ***Felony, Civil Actions over $3,000, Probate.***
Probate in separate index at this address. Probate fax-419-399-8261
Civil Records: Access: Fax, mail, in person. Visitors must perform in person searches themselves. Search fee: $5.00 per name. Required to search: name, years to search. Civil cases indexed by defendant, plaintiff. Civil records in books, archived from 1800s. Mail turnaround time same day. Civil PAT goes back to 12/2/2002. PAT civil results show middle initial.
Criminal Records: Access: In person only. Both court and visitors may perform in person searches. No search fee. Required to search: name, years to search; also helpful: address, DOB. Criminal records in books, archived from 1800s. Criminal PAT goes back to same as civil. PAT criminal results show middle initial.
General Information: Will fax documents $2.00 fax fee plus $1.00 per page. Court makes copy: $.05 per page. Certification fee: $1.00. Payee: Clerk of Court. Personal checks accepted; credit cards are not.

County Court 201 E Caroline St, #2, Paulding, OH 45879; 419-399-2792; fax: 419-399-3421; 8AM-4PM. ***Misdemeanor, Civil Actions under $15,000, Small Claims.***
www.pauldingcountycourt.com
Civil Records: Access: Fax, mail, in person, online. Both court and visitors may perform in person searches. Search fee: $5.00 per name. Required to search: name, years to search; also helpful: address. Civil cases indexed by defendant, plaintiff. Civil records in books since 1985; computerized records since 1997. Mail turnaround time 2-4 days. Civil PAT goes back to 1997. Access civil records at www.pauldingcountycourt.com/Search/index.shtml.
Criminal Records: Access: Fax, mail, in person, online. Both court and visitors may perform in person searches. Search fee: $5.00 per name. Required to search: name, years to search; also helpful: address, DOB, SSN. Criminal records in books since 1985; computerized records since 1997. Mail turnaround time 2-4 days. Criminal PAT goes back to same as civil. Access criminal records at www.pauldingcountycourt.com/Search/index.shtml.
General Information: No fee to fax documents. Court makes copy: $.50 per page. Certification fee: $2.00. Payee: Paulding County Court. No personal checks. Mail requests: SASE required.

Perry County

Common Pleas Court PO Box 67, New Lexington, OH 43764; 740-342-1022; probate phone: 740-342-1493; fax: 740-342-5527; 8AM-4PM. ***Felony, Civil Actions over $3,000, Probate.***
Civil Records: Access: In person only. Visitors must perform in person searches themselves. Required to search: name, years to search; also helpful: address. Civil cases indexed by defendant, plaintiff; index on computer since 3/96, in case files prior, indexed from 1940. Civil PAT goes back to 1996. PAT results show name only.
Criminal Records: Access: In person only. Visitors must perform in person searches themselves. Required to search: name, years to search; also helpful: address, DOB, SSN. Criminal records on computer since 3/96, in case files prior, indexed from 1940. Criminal PAT goes back to same as civil. PAT results show name only.
General Information: Will fax documents $2.00 1st page, $1.00 ea add'l page. Court makes copy: $.05 per page. Certification fee: $1.00 per cert. Payee: Clerk of Court. Personal checks accepted; credit cards are not.

Perry County Court PO Box 207, 105 N Main St, New Lexington, OH 43764-0207; 740-342-3156; fax: 740-342-2188; 8:30AM-4:30PM M,W,F; 8AM-4:30PM T,TH. ***Misdemeanor, Civil Actions under $15,000, Small Claims.*** www.perrycountycourt.com
Civil Records: Access: In person, online. Visitors must perform in person searches themselves. Required to search: name, years to search. Civil cases indexed by defendant, plaintiff. Civil records in books 10 to 12 years, computerized since 4/97. Civil PAT goes back to 1997. PAT results show name only. Access court records 24 hours after entry for free at www.perrycountycourt.com/Search/.
Criminal Records: Access: In person, online. Visitors must perform in person searches themselves. Required to search: name, years to search, DOB, SSN, signed release. Criminal records in books 10 to 12 years, computerized since 4/97. Criminal PAT goes back to same as civil. Online access to criminal records is same as civil.
General Information: All records are public. Will not fax documents. Court makes copy: $1.00 per page. Self serve: same. Certification fee: $1.00. Payee: Perry County Court. Personal checks accepted; credit cards are not.

Pickaway County

Common Pleas Court County Courthouse, 207 Court St, PO Box 270, Circleville, OH 43113; 740-474-5231; criminal fax: 740-477-3976; civil fax: same; 8AM-4PM. ***Felony, Civil Actions over $10,000, Probate.*** www.pickawaycountycpcourt.org
Probate is a separate index and separate address.
Civil Records: Access: Mail, in person, online. Both court and visitors may perform in person searches. No search fee. Required to search: name, years to search; also helpful: address. Civil cases indexed by defendant. Civil records on computer back to 1988, indexed to 1940s, archived from 1800s. Mail turnaround time 2-3 days. Civil PAT goes back to 1988. PAT civil results show middle initial. Search docket info at www.pickawaycountycpcourt.org.
Criminal Records: Access: Mail, in person, online. Both court and visitors may perform in person searches. No search fee. Required to search: name, years to search; also helpful: address. Criminal records computerized from 1988, indexed to 1940s, archived from 1800s. Mail turnaround time 2-3 days. Criminal PAT goes back to same as civil. PAT criminal results show middle initial. Search docket info at www.pickawaycountycpcourt.org. Online results show middle initial.
General Information: Will not fax documents. Court makes copy: $.25 per page. Certification fee: $1.00 per doc. Payee: Clerk of Court. No personal checks or credit cards accepted. Mail requests: SASE required.

Circleville Municipal Court PO Box 128, Circleville, OH 43113; 740-474-3171; fax: 740-477-8291; 8AM-4PM. ***Misdemeanor, Civil Actions under $15,000, Eviction, Small Claims.***
www.circlevillecourt.com
Civil Records: Access: Phone, fax, mail, in person, online. Both court and visitors may perform in person searches. No search fee. Required to search: name, years to search. Civil cases indexed by defendant, plaintiff; index on computer from 1989, prior in books. Mail turnaround time 1-2 days. Civil PAT goes back to 1992. Search online at www.circlevillecourt.com/AccessCourtRecords.asp.
Criminal Records: Access: Phone, fax, mail, in person, online. Both court and visitors may perform in person searches. No search fee. Required to search: name, years to search; also helpful: SSN. Criminal records computerized from 1987, prior in books back to 1983. Mail turnaround time 1-2 days. Criminal PAT goes back to 1990. Search at www.circlevillecourt.com/AccessCourtRecords.asp.
General Information: No warrant records released. Will fax documents to local or toll-free number. Court makes copy: $.50 per page. No certification fee. Payee: Circleville Municipal Court. Personal checks and credit cards accepted. Mail requests: SASE required.

Pike County

Common Pleas Court 100 E 2nd St, 2nd Fl, Waverly, OH 45690; 740-947-2715; criminal phone: x103; probate phone: 740-947-2560; fax: 740-947-1729; 8:30AM-4PM. ***Felony, Civil Actions over $15,000, Probate.***
Probate is separate court at 230 Waverly Plaza, #600.
Civil Records: Access: In person only. Visitors must perform in person searches themselves. Search fee: $2.00 per name. Required to search: name, years to search; also helpful: address. Civil cases indexed by defendant, plaintiff. Civil records in books back to 1815; on computer back to 1999. Civil PAT goes back to 11/1999. PAT civil results show middle initial.
Criminal Records: Access: In person only. Visitors must perform in person searches themselves. Search fee: $2.00 per name. Required to search: name, years to search; also helpful: address, DOB, SSN. Criminal records in books back to 1815; on computer back to 1999. Criminal PAT goes back to same as civil. PAT results show middle initial, DOB, SSN.
General Information: No grand jury secret indictment records released. Will fax out documents $2.00 1st page, $1.00 each add'l page. Court makes copy: $.25 per page. Certification fee: $1.00 per cert. Payee: Clerk of Court. Personal checks accepted; credit cards are not.

Pike County Court 230 Waverly Plaza, #900, Waverly, OH 45690; criminal phone: 740-947-4003; fax: 740-947-7644; 8:30AM-4PM. ***Misdemeanor, Civil Actions under $15,000, Small Claims.***
Civil Records: Access: Phone, fax, mail, in person. Both court and visitors may perform in person searches. No search fee. Required to search: name, years to search. Civil cases indexed by defendant, plaintiff. Civil records in books indexed to 1958, computerized since 1996. Mail turnaround time 1 week. Civil PAT goes back to 12/1996. PAT results show middle initial, DOB, SSN.
Criminal Records: Access: Phone, fax, mail, in person. Both court and visitors may perform in person searches. No search fee. Required to search: name, years to search. Criminal records in books indexed to 1958, computerized since 1996. Mail turnaround time 1 week. Criminal PAT goes back to 12/1996; results show middle initial, DOB, SSN
General Information: No sealed or expunged records released. Will fax documents to local or toll free line. Court makes copy for no fee. Self serve: none. No certification fee. Payee: Pike County Court. Personal checks accepted; credit cards are not. Mail requests: SASE required.

Portage County

Common Pleas Court PO Box 1035, Ravenna, OH 44266; 330-297-3644; probate phone: 330-297-3870; criminal fax: 330-297-4554; civil fax: same; 8AM-4PM. ***Felony, Civil Actions over $15,000.***
www.co.portage.oh.us/index.html
Civil Records: Access: In person, online. Visitors must perform in person searches themselves. Required to search: name, years to search; also helpful: address. Civil cases indexed by defendant, plaintiff; index on computer back to 11/1991, prior in books or microfilm back to 1977; Judgments back to 1/1982. Civil PAT goes back to 11/1991 for cases, to 1977 for index. For online records from 1977 forward, go to www.co.portage.oh.us/courtsearch.htm. Case number provided.
Criminal Records: Access: In person, online. Visitors must perform in person searches themselves. Required to search: name, years to search; also helpful: address, DOB. Criminal records index on computer back to 1977, some data on microfilm, case files back to 11/1/1991; prior in books. Criminal PAT goes back to same as civil. Results also includes charge, disposition. For index from 1977 forward or images 06/2005 forward, go to www.co.portage.oh.us/courtsearch.htm. Direct questions about online access to Kathy Postlethwait at 330-297-3648. Online results show middle initial.
General Information: Online identifiers in results same as on public terminal. Will fax out specific case files for $1.00 per page. Court makes copy: $.10 per page. Self serve: same. Certification fee: $1.00 per page includes copy fee. Payee: Clerk of Court. Personal checks accepted. Visa/MC accepted. Monthly accounts available.

Portage County Municipal Ct - Ravenna PO Box 958, Ravenna, OH 44266; criminal phone: 330-297-3639; civil phone: 330-297-3635; criminal fax: 330-297-5867; civil fax: 330-297-3526; 8AM-4PM. ***Misdemeanor, Civil Actions under $15,000, Eviction, Small Claims.*** www.co.portage.oh.us

Civil Records: Access: Mail, in person, online. Visitors must perform in person searches themselves. Search fee: $5.00. Required to search: name, years to search; also helpful: address. Civil cases indexed by defendant, plaintiff; index on computer from 1992. Mail turnaround time 2 days. Civil PAT goes back to 1991. PAT civil results show middle initial. Search records back to 1992 free at http://67.39.103.41/courtsearch.htm.

Criminal Records: Access: Mail, in person, online. Visitors must perform in person searches themselves. Search fee: $5.00. Required to search: name, years to search; also helpful: address, DOB, SSN. Criminal records computerized from 1992. Mail turnaround time 2 days. Criminal PAT goes back to same as civil. Results also include charges, disposition. Search records back to 1992 free at http://67.39.103.41/courtsearch.htm. Direct questions about online access to Cindy W. at 330-297-5654. Online results show middle initial.

General Information: No records released. Will fax documents $3.00 1st page, $1.00 each add'l page. Court makes copy: $.10 per page. Certification fee: $1.00. Payee: Municipal Court. Personal checks & Visa/MC accepted. Mail requests: SASE required.

Portage Municipal Court - Kent Branch 214 S Water, Kent, OH 44240; criminal phone: 330-678-9100; civil phone: 330-678-9170; fax: 330-677-9944; 8AM-4PM. ***Misdemeanor, Civil Actions under $15,000, Eviction, Small Claims.*** www.co.portage.oh.us

Civil Records: Access: In person, online. Both court and visitors may perform in person searches. Search fee: $5.00 per name. Required to search: name, years to search; also helpful: address. Civil cases indexed by defendant, plaintiff; index on computer from 1992, prior in books. Civil PAT goes back to 1992. PAT results show name only. Online records 1992 forward at www.co.portage.oh.us/.

Criminal Records: Access: In person, online. Both court and visitors may perform in person searches. Search fee: $5.00 per name. Required to search: name, years to search; also helpful: address, DOB, SSN. Criminal records computerized from 1992, prior in books. Criminal PAT goes back to same as civil. Records from 1992 forward at www.co.portage.oh.us/. Direct questions about online access to Robyn Godfrey at 330-296-2530.

General Information: No expunged records released. Will fax case file $1.00 per page. Court makes copy: $.10 per page. Self serve: same. Certification fee: $1.00. Payee: Portage County Municipal Court. Personal checks accepted. Credit cards accepted for criminal only, and only if in person.

Probate Court 203 W Main, Ravenna, OH 44266; 330-297-3870; probate: 330-297-3870; 8-4PM. ***Probate.*** www.co.portage.oh.us/index.html

Preble County

Common Pleas Court 101 E Main, 3rd Fl, Eaton, OH 45320; 456-8165; probate phone: 937-456-8138; fax: 937-456-9548; 8AM-4:30PM. ***Felony, Civil, Probate.***

Probate office is separate from this court.

Civil Records: Access: In person, online. Visitors must perform in person searches themselves. Required to search: name, years to search; also helpful: address. Civil cases indexed by defendant, plaintiff; index on computer from 11/89, prior in books indexed to 1840s. Civil PAT goes back to 11/1989. PAT results show name only. Access to court records and calendars free at www.preblecountyohio.net/.

Criminal Records: Access: Mail, in person, online. Both court and visitors may perform in person searches. Search fee: $3.00 per name. Required to search: name, years to search; also helpful: address, DOB, SSN. Criminal records computerized from 11/89, prior in books indexed to 1840s. Mail turnaround time 1 day. Criminal PAT goes back to same as civil. PAT results show name only. Access to court records and calendars free at www.preblecountyohio.net/.

General Information: No secret records released. Will fax documents $.50 per page. Court makes copy: $.50 per page. Certification fee: $1.00 per doc. Payee: Clerk of Court. Personal checks accepted; credit cards are not. Mail requests: SASE required for criminal.

Eaton Municipal Court PO Box 65, 1199 Preble Dr, Eaton, OH 45320; 937-456-4941/6204; fax: 937-456-4685; 8AM-4:30PM. ***Misdemeanor, Civil Actions under $15,000, Eviction, Small Claims.*** www.eatonmunicipalcourt.com

Civil Records: Access: Mail, in person, online. Both court and visitors may perform in person searches. No search fee. Required to search: name, years to search. Civil cases indexed by defendant, plaintiff; index on computer from 1989, prior in books indexed to 1959. Mail turnaround time 1 week. Civil PAT goes back to 1989. PAT results show middle initial, DOB. Search by name or case number free www.eatonmunicipalcourt.com/docket/index.html. Records go back to 1989.

Criminal Records: Access: Mail, in person, online. Both court and visitors may perform in person searches. No search fee. Required to search: name, years to search; also helpful: SSN. Criminal records computerized from 1989, prior in books indexed to 1959. Mail turnaround time 1 week. Criminal PAT goes back to same as civil. PAT results show middle initial, DOB. Search by name or case number free at www.eatonmunicipalcourt.com/docket/index.html. Computerized records begin in 1992 for online civil, criminal and traffic cases. Online results show middle initial, DOB.

General Information: Online identifiers in results same as on public terminal. No driving records released. Court makes copy: $1.00 per page. Self serve: $.35 per page. Certification fee: $1.00. Payee: Eaton Municipal Court. Personal checks and credit cards accepted. Mail requests: SASE required.

Putnam County

Common Pleas Court 245 E Main, Rm 301, Ottawa, OH 45875; 419-523-3110; probate phone: 419-523-3012; criminal fax: 419-523-5284; civil fax: same; 8:30AM-4:30PM. ***Felony, Civil Actions over $10,000, Probate, Domestic.*** www.putnamcountycourtsohio.com/

Probate is a separate court at Rm 204. Probate fax-419-523-9291.

Civil Records: Access: Fax, mail, in person, online. Both court and visitors may perform in person searches. Search fee: $10.00 per name. Required to search: name, years to search. Civil cases indexed by defendant, plaintiff; index on computer from 1992 indexed on docket books back to 1800s. Mail turnaround time 1-4 days. Civil PAT goes back to 1992. PAT results show middle initial, DOB. Online access is free at www.putnamcountycourtsohio.com/.

Criminal Records: Access: Fax, mail, in person, online. Both court and visitors may perform in person searches. Search fee: $10.00 per name. Required to search: name, years to search; also helpful: address, DOB, SSN. Criminal records computerized from 1992 indexed on docket books back to 1800s. Mail turnaround time 1-4 days. Criminal PAT goes back to same as civil. PAT results show middle initial, DOB. Online access is free at www.putnamcountycourtsohio.com/. Online results show middle initial.

General Information: No sealed records released. Will fax documents $3.00 per transmission plus $1.00 per page. Court makes copy: $.25 per page. Certification fee: $1.00 per certification. Payee: Clerk of Court. Putnam County personal checks accepted only. Visa/MC accepted.

Putnam County Court 245 E Main, Rm 303, Ottawa, OH 45875; 419-523-3110; criminal fax: 419-523-5284; civil fax: same; 8:30AM-4:30PM. ***Misdemeanor, Civil Actions under $10,000, Small Claims.***

Civil Records: Access: Mail, fax, in person, online. Both court and visitors may perform in person searches. Search fee: $10.00 per name. Required to search: name, years to search. Civil cases indexed by defendant, plaintiff. Civil records go back to 1800s; computerized records go back to 1992. Court will perform searches when certification is required; you must request this using the courts request form. Mail turnaround time 48 hours. Civil PAT goes back to 1992. PAT results show middle initial, DOB. Online access is free at www.putnamcountycourtsohio.com/.

Criminal Records: Access: Mail, in person, online. Both court and visitors may perform in person searches. Search fee: $10.00 per name. Required to search: name, years to search. Criminal records go back to 1826; computerized records go back to 1992. Court will perform searches when certification is required; you must request this using the courts request form. Mail turnaround time 48 hours. Criminal PAT goes back to same as civil. PAT results show middle initial, DOB. Online access is free at www.putnamcountycourtsohio.com/. Online results show middle initial.

General Information: Will fax documents $3.00 plus $1.00 per page. Court makes copy: $.25 per page. Certification fee: $1.00 per page. Payee: Clerk of Court. Cashiers checks and money orders accepted. Visa/MC accepted. Mail requests: SASE required.

Richland County

Common Pleas Court 50 Park Ave E, Mansfield, OH 44902; 419-774-5543/5690/8969; probate phone: 419-755-5583; fax: 419-774-5547; 8AM-4PM. ***Felony, Civil Actions over $10,000, Probate.*** www.richlandcountyoh.us/coc.htm

Probate is a separate court, separate records. Common Pleas is on the 3rd floor, Probate on the 2nd.

Civil Records: Access: Mail, fax, in person, online. Both court and visitors may perform in person searches. No search fee. Required to search: name, years to search; also helpful: address. Civil cases indexed by defendant, plaintiff; index on computer from 1990, prior in books and on microfiche to 1960. Mail turnaround time 1 week or less. Public use terminal available. Access to civil records is at www.richlandcountyoh.us/courtv.htm.

Criminal Records: Access: Mail, in person, online. Both court and visitors may perform in person searches. No search fee. Required to search: name, years to search, DOB, SSN, signed release; also helpful: address. Criminal records computerized from 1990, prior in books and on microfiche to 1960. Mail turnaround time 1 week or less. Public use terminal available. Access to criminal dockets at www.richlandcountyoh.us/courtv.htm.

General Information: No sealed records released. Will not fax documents. Court makes copy: $.10 per page. Self serve: same. Certification fee: $1.00 per page. Payee: Clerk of Court. Personal checks accepted; credit cards are not.

Mansfield Municipal Court PO Box 1228, Mansfield, OH 44901; 419-755-9633; criminal phone: 419-755-9634; civil phone: 419-755-9637; criminal fax: 419-755-9647; civil fax: 419-755-9641; 8AM-4PM. ***Misdemeanor, Civil Actions under $15,000, Eviction, Small Claims.*** www.ci.mansfield.oh.us/

Civil Records: Access: Phone, fax, mail, in person, online. Both court and visitors may perform in person searches. No search fee. Required to search: name, years to search; also helpful: address. Civil cases indexed by defendant, plaintiff. Criminal records on computer from 1989. Overall records go back to 1940. Phone and fax access limited to short searches. Mail turnaround time 2-3 days. Civil PAT goes back to 1990. PAT civil results show middle initial. Online access at http://docket.webxsol.com/mansfield/index.html for records from 1992 forward.

Criminal Records: Access: Phone, fax, mail, in person, online. Both court and visitors may perform in person searches. No search fee. Required to search: name, years to search; also helpful: address, DOB, SSN. Criminal records computerized from 1989. Overall records go back to 1940. Mail turnaround time 2-3 days. Criminal PAT goes back to 10/1989. PAT results show middle initial, DOB. Online access at http://docket.webxsol.com/mansfield/index.html for records from 1992 forward. Online results show middle initial, DOB.

General Information: Online identifiers in results same as on public terminal. No lead print out records released. No fee to fax documents. Court makes copy: $.25 per page. Certification fee: $1.00 per page. Payee: Clerk of Court or Mansfield Municipal Court. Personal checks accepted except for warrants and forfeitures. Visa/MC accepted. Mail requests: SASE required.

Ross County

Common Pleas Court County Courthouse, 2 N Paint St, #A, Chillicothe, OH 45601; 740-702-3010; probate phone: 740-774-1179; fax: 740-702-3018; 8AM-4PM. ***Felony, Civil Actions over $10,000, Probate.*** www.co.ross.oh.us/ClerkOfCourts/

Civil Records: Access: In person, online. Both court and visitors may perform in person searches. No search fee. Required to search: name, years to search; also helpful: address. Civil cases indexed by defendant, plaintiff; index on computer from 1989, prior in books to 1800s. Civil PAT goes back to 11/1989. Search records back to 11/89 at www.co.ross.oh.us/ClerkOfCourts/.

Criminal Records: Access: In person, online. Both court and visitors may perform in person searches. No search fee. Required to search: name, years to search; also helpful: address, DOB, SSN. Criminal records computerized from 1989, prior in books to 1800s. Criminal PAT goes back to same as civil. Search records back to 11/89 at www.co.ross.oh.us/ClerkOfCourts/.

General Information: No secret indictment records released. Will fax documents to local or toll free line. Court makes copy: $.05 per page. Certification fee: $1.00. Payee: Clerk of Court. Personal checks accepted; credit cards are not.

Chillicothe Municipal Court 26 S Paint St, Chillicothe, OH 45601; 740-773-3515; fax: 740-774-1101; 7:30AM-4:30PM. ***Misdemeanor, Civil Actions under $15,000, Eviction, Small Claims.*** www.chillicothemunicipalcourt.org

Civil Records: Access: Mail, in person, online. Both court and visitors may perform in person searches. No search fee. Required to search: name, years to search; also helpful: address. Civil cases indexed by defendant, plaintiff; index on computer from 6/93, prior in books. Mail turnaround time 10 days. Civil PAT goes back to 6/1993. PAT results show name only. Search docket information at http://216.201.21.130/Search/.

Criminal Records: Access: Mail, in person, online. Both court and visitors may perform in person searches. No search fee. Required to search: name, years to search, DOB, SSN; also helpful: address. Criminal records computerized from 6/93, prior in books. Mail turnaround time 10 days. Criminal PAT goes back to same as civil. PAT results show name only. Search docket info at http://216.201.21.130/Search/. Online results show name only.

General Information: Online identifiers in results same as on public terminal. No confidential records released. Will not fax documents. Court makes copy: $.05 per page. Self serve: same. Certification fee: $1.00 per page includes $.05 copy fee. Payee: Municipal Court. Business checks accepted. Credit cards accepted. Mail requests: SASE required.

Sandusky County

Common Pleas Court 100 N Park Ave, #320, Fremont, OH 43420; 419-334-6161/6163; probate phone: 419-334-6217; criminal fax: 419-334-6164; civil fax: same; 8AM-4:30PM. ***Felony, Civil Actions over $3,000, Probate.***

Probate index is a separate office, Suite 224. Probate fax- 419-334-6210

Civil Records: Access: In person only. Visitors must perform in person searches themselves. Required to search: name, years to search; also helpful: address. Civil cases indexed by defendant, plaintiff; index on computer from 1988, prior in books to 1800s. Civil PAT goes back to 1988.

Criminal Records: Access: In person, online. Visitors must perform in person searches themselves. Required to search: name, years to search; also helpful: address, DOB, SSN. Criminal records computerized from 1988, prior in books to 1800s. Criminal PAT goes back to same as civil. Access misdemeanor traffic and criminal data free at www.sandusky-county.org/Clerk/Clerk_of_Courts/sccoc/search.php.

General Information: No search warrant records released. Will fax documents $2.00 1st page, $1.00 ea add'l page. Court makes copy: $.10 per page. Certification fee: $1.00 per page. Payee: Clerk of Court. Personal checks accepted; credit cards are not.

County Court #1 PO Box 267, 847 E McPherson Hwy, Clyde, OH 43410; 419-547-0915; fax: 419-547-9198; 8AM-4:30PM. ***Misdemeanor, Civil Actions under $15,000, Small Claims.*** www.sandusky-county.org

Civil Records: Access: Phone, fax, mail, in person. Only the court performs in person searches; visitors may not. No search fee. Required to search: name, years to search; also helpful: address. Civil cases indexed by defendant, plaintiff; index on computer from 1998, prior in books for 25 years. Mail turnaround time 2-3 days.

Criminal Records: Access: Phone, fax, mail, in person, online. Only the court performs in person searches; visitors may not. No search fee. Required to search: name, years to search, DOB, SSN; also helpful: address. Criminal records computerized from 1998, prior in books for 25 years. Mail turnaround time 2-3 days. Access misdemeanor traffic and criminal data free at www.sandusky-county.org/Clerk/Clerk_of_Courts/sccoc/search.php.

General Information: No fee to fax documents to toll-free number. Court makes copy: $.10 per page. Self serve: same. Certification fee: $1.00 per document. Cert fee includes copies. Payee: Sandusky County Court. Personal checks and credit cards accepted. Mail requests: SASE required.

County Court #2 215 W Main St, Woodville, OH 43469; 419-849-3961; fax: 419-849-3932; 8AM-4:30PM. ***Misdemeanor, Civil Actions under $15,000, Small Claims.*** www.sandusky-county.org

Civil Records: Access: Phone, fax, mail, in person. Both court and visitors may perform in person searches. No search fee. Required to search: name, years to search; also helpful: address. Civil cases indexed by defendant, plaintiff. Civil records go back to 1983; on computer back to 1998. Mail turnaround time 2-3 days.

Criminal Records: Access: Phone, fax, mail, in person, online. Both court and visitors may perform in person searches. No search fee. Required to search: name, years to search, DOB, SSN. Criminal records go back to 1995; on computer back to 1998. Mail turnaround time 2-3 days. Access misdemeanor traffic and criminal data free at www.sandusky-county.org/Clerk/Clerk_of_Courts/sccoc/search.php.

General Information: No confidential records released. Will fax document $2.00 for 1st page, $1.00 each add'l. Court makes copy: $.10 per page. Certification fee: $1.00 per page. Payee: Sandusky County Court. Personal checks accepted. Visa/MC accepted. Mail requests: SASE required.

Fremont Municipal Court PO Box 886, Fremont, OH 43420-0071; 419-332-1579; fax: 419-332-1570; 8AM-4:30PM. ***Misdemeanor, Civil Actions under $15,000, Eviction, Small Claims.***

Civil Records: Access: Fax, mail, in person. Both court and visitors may perform in person searches. No search fee. Required to search: name, years to search. Civil cases indexed by defendant, plaintiff. Civil records in books from 1960, computerized since 1992. Mail turnaround time 2 days. Civil PAT goes back to 1992.

Criminal Records: Access: Fax, mail, in person, online. Both court and visitors may perform in person searches. No search fee. Required to search: name, years to search; also helpful: DOB, SSN. Criminal records in books from 1960, computerized since 1992. Mail turnaround time 2 days. Criminal PAT goes back to 1992. Access misdemeanor traffic and criminal data at www.sandusky-county.org/Clerk/Clerk_of_Courts/sccoc/search.php.

General Information: No fee to fax documents locally only. Court makes copy: $.10 per page. Certification fee: $1.00 per page. Cert fee includes copy fee. Payee: Fremont Municipal Court. Cashiers checks and money orders accepted. Visa/MC accepted for criminal and traffic only; $2.00 processing fee applies.

Scioto County

Common Pleas Court 602 7th St, Rm 205, Portsmouth, OH 45662; 740-355-8226; probate phone: 740-355-8243; fax: 740-354-2057; 8AM-4:30PM. ***Felony, Civil Actions over $15,000.*** www.sciotocountycpcourt.org

Probate (740-355-8243) is a separate index at the same address in Rm 201.

Civil Records: Access: In person, online. Both court and visitors may perform in person searches. No search fee. Required to search: name, years to search; also helpful: address. Civil cases indexed by defendant, plaintiff; index on computer from 1986, dockets to 1800s. Civil PAT goes back to 1/1986. PAT results show name only. Online access to civil records back to 1/1986 is free at www.sciotocountycpcourt.org/search.htm. Search by court calendar, quick index, general index or docket sheet.

Criminal Records: Access: In person, online. Both court and visitors may perform in person searches. No search fee. Required to search: name, years to search; also helpful: address, DOB. Criminal records computerized from 1986, dockets to 1800s. Criminal PAT goes back to same as civil. PAT results show name only. Online access to criminal records is the same as civil. Online results show name only.

General Information: No sealed or secret records released. Will fax out specific case files for $1.00 per page. Court makes copy: $1.00 per page. Certification fee: $1.00 per page. Payee: Clerk of Court. Local personal checks accepted. No credit cards accepted. Mail requests: SASE required for mail return of any copies.

Portsmouth Municipal Court 728 2nd St, Portsmouth, OH 45662; 740-354-3283; fax: 740-353-6645; 8AM-4PM. ***Misdemeanor, Civil Actions under $15,000, Eviction, Small Claims.*** www.pmcourt.org

Civil Records: Access: Fax, mail, in person, online. Both court and visitors may perform in person searches. Search fee: No fee for computer records search 1989 forward. Required to search: name, years to search. Civil cases indexed by defendant, plaintiff. Criminal records go back to 1985; on computer back to 1995. Mail turnaround time 2-3 days; older records up to 2 weeks. Civil PAT goes back to 11/1989. PAT civil results show middle initial. Access is free at www.pmcourt.org/disc.html.

Criminal Records: Access: Fax, mail, in person, online. Both court and visitors may perform in person searches. Search fee: $20.00 per name if search includes years prior to 1989. No fee for computer records search 1989 forward. Required to search: name, years to search, SSN. Criminal records go back to 1985; on computer back to 1995. Mail turnaround time 2-3 days; older records up to 2 weeks. Criminal PAT goes back to same as civil. PAT criminal results show middle initial. Access criminal records online free at www.pmcourt.org/disc.html. Online results show middle initial.

General Information: Online identifiers in results same as on public terminal. No competency hearing, protection order records released. No fee to fax documents. Court makes copy: $.50 per page. Certification fee: $1.00 per page. Payee: Portsmouth Municipal Court. Personal checks accepted; credit cards are not. Mail requests: SASE required.

Seneca County

Common Pleas Court 117 E Market, Tiffin, OH 44883; 419-447-0671; probate phone: 419-447-3121; criminal fax: 419-443-7919; civil fax: same; 8:30AM-4:30PM. ***Felony, Civil Actions over $10,000.*** www.senecaco.org/clerk/default.html

Probate records with Probate/Juvenile Court, 81 Jefferson St., Tiffin,

Civil Records: Access: In person, online. Both court and visitors may perform in person searches. No search fee. Required to search: name, years to search; also helpful: address. Civil cases indexed by defendant, plaintiff; index on computer from 1/93, prior in books to 1900s, archived to 1800s. Civil PAT goes back to 1/1993. PAT civil results show middle initial. Public terminal located in the Recorder's Office; docket sheets can be printed out for $.10 per page in clerk's office. Search dockets online at www.senecaco.org/clerk/default.html. Click on Internet Inquiry.

Criminal Records: Access: In person, online. Both court and visitors may perform in person searches. No search fee. Required to search: name, years to search, SSN, date of offense. Criminal records computerized from 1/93, prior in books to 1900s, archived to 1800s. Criminal PAT goes back to same as civil. PAT criminal results show middle initial. Public terminal located in the Recorder's Office; docket sheets can be printed out for $.10 per page in clerk's office. Search dockets online at www.senecaco.org/clerk/default.html. Click on Internet Inquiry. Online results show middle initial, DOB.

General Information: Online identifiers in results same as on public terminal. No sealed records released. Will fax out specific case files for $2.00 per transmission. Court makes copy: $.10 per page. Self serve: same. Certification fee: $1.00 per document. Payee: Clerk of Court. Personal checks accepted; credit cards are not. Mail requests: SASE required for mail return of any copies.

Fostoria Municipal Court PO Box 985, Fostoria, OH 44830; 419-435-8139; criminal fax: 419-435-1150; civil fax: same; 8:30AM-5PM. ***Misdemeanor, Civil Actions under $15,000, Eviction, Small Claims.***
www.fostoriamunicipalcourt.com/

Civil Records: Access: Phone, fax, mail, in person. Both court and visitors may perform in person searches. No search fee. Required to search: name, years to search. Civil cases indexed by defendant, plaintiff. Civil records computerized since 1987. Mail turnaround time 1-2 days. Civil PAT goes back to 1987. PAT civil results show middle initial.

Criminal Records: Access: Phone, fax, mail, in person. Both court and visitors may perform in person searches. No search fee. Required to search: name, years to search; also helpful: SSN. Criminal records computerized since 1987. Mail turnaround time 1-2 days. Criminal PAT goes back to 1987. PAT criminal results show middle initial.

General Information: No fee if faxed to local or toll free number. Court makes copy: $.10 per page. Certification fee: $1.00 per page includes copies. Payee: Fostoria Municipal Court. Personal checks accepted; credit cards are not. Mail requests: SASE required.

Tiffin Municipal Court PO Box 694, Tiffin, OH 44883; 419-448-5412; criminal phone: 419-448-5411; civil phone: 419-448-5418; fax: 419-448-5419; 8:30AM-4:30PM. ***Misdemeanor, Civil Actions under $15,000, Eviction, Small Claims.***

Civil Records: Access: Fax, mail, in person, online. Both court and visitors may perform in person searches. No search fee. Required to search: name, years to search; also helpful: address. Civil cases indexed by defendant, plaintiff; index on computer from 8/90, prior in books. Mail turnaround time 3 days. Civil PAT goes back to 8/1990. Access records free at www.tiffinmunicipalcourt.org/search.shtml.

Criminal Records: Access: Fax, mail, in person, online. Both court and visitors may perform in person searches. No search fee. Required to search: name, years to search, DOB, SSN, signed release; also helpful: address. Criminal records computerized from 8/90, prior in books. Mail turnaround time 3 days. Criminal PAT goes back to same as civil. Access records free at www.tiffinmunicipalcourt.org/search.shtml.

General Information: No expunged records released. Fee to fax document $.25 per page. Court makes copy: $.05 per page. Self serve: same. Certification fee: $1.00. Payee: Municipal Court. Personal checks accepted; credit cards are not. Mail requests: SASE required.

Shelby County

Common Pleas Court PO Box 809, Sidney, OH 45365; 937-498-7221; fax: 937-498-4840; 8AM-4PM. ***Felony, Civil over $10,000, Probate.***
http://co.shelby.oh.us/CommonPleasCourt/index.asp

Civil Records: Access: Fax, mail, in person. Both court and visitors may perform in person searches. Search fee: $1.00 per name. Required to search: name, years to search; also helpful: address. Civil cases indexed by defendant, plaintiff; index on computer from 1987, on indexes from 1819. Mail turnaround time 5 days. Civil PAT goes back to 1987. PAT civil results show middle initial.

Criminal Records: Access: Mail, in person. Visitors must perform in person searches themselves. Search fee: $1.00 per name. Required to search: name, years to search DOB, SSN; also helpful: address. Criminal records computerized from 1987, on indexes from 1819. Mail turnaround time 5 days. Criminal PAT goes back to same as civil. PAT results show middle initial, DOB.

General Information: No grand jury tapes released. Fee to fax out file $3.00 plus $3.00 per page. Court makes copy: $.10 per page. Certification fee: $4.00. Payee: Shelby County Clerk of Courts. Personal checks accepted; credit cards are not. Mail requests: SASE required.

Sidney Municipal Court 201 W Poplar, Sidney, OH 45365; 937-498-0011; criminal fax: 937-498-8179; civil fax: same; 8AM-4:15PM. ***Misdemeanor, Civil Actions under $15,000, Eviction, Small Claims.*** www.sidneyoh.com

Send mail requests to the address above; phone and in person searches made at the court at 110 W Court St.

Civil Records: Access: Phone, fax, mail, in person. Both court and visitors may perform in person searches. No search fee. Required to search: name, years to search. Civil cases indexed by defendant, plaintiff; index on computer from 1988; prior on books to 1958. Mail turnaround time 4 days. Civil PAT goes back to 1993. PAT results show middle initial, DOB.

Criminal Records: Access: Phone, fax, mail, in person. Both court and visitors may perform in person searches. No search fee. Required to search: name, years to search; also helpful: address, DOB, SSN. Criminal records computerized from 1988; prior on books to 1958. Mail turnaround time 4 days. Criminal PAT goes back to same as civil. PAT results show middle initial, DOB.

General Information: Confidential and probation records are not released. Will fax documents to toll-free number no charge. Court makes copy: $.10 per page. Certification fee: $1.00 per page. Cert fee includes copies. Payee: Municipal Court. No personal checks or credit cards accepted. Mail requests: SASE required.

Stark County

Common Pleas Court - Civil Division PO Box 21160, Canton, OH 44701; 330-451-7795; fax: 330-451-7066; 8:30AM-4:30PM. ***Civil Actions over $15,000.*** www.starkclerk.org

Civil Records: Access: Phone, fax, mail, in person, online. Both court and visitors may perform in person searches. No search fee. Required to search: name, years to search. Civil cases indexed by defendant, plaintiff; index on computer from 1985, prior in books from 1940s. Mail turnaround time up to 1 week. Public use terminal has civil records back to 1985. PAT civil results show middle initial. Online access to the county case docket database is free at www.starkcourt.org/docket/index.html. Search by name or case number.

General Information: Online identifiers in results same as on public terminal. No sealed records released. Fee to fax out file $2.00 1st page, $1.00 each add'l. Court makes copy: $.10 per page. Certification fee: $1.00 per page. Payee: Clerk of Court. Personal checks accepted; credit cards are not. Mail requests: SASE required.

Common Pleas Court - Criminal Div. PO Box 21160, County Clerk of Courts, Canton, OH 44701-1160; 330-451-7929; fax: 330-451-7066; 8:30AM-4:30PM. ***Felony.***
www.starkclerk.org

Criminal Records: Access: Mail, in person, online. Both court and visitors may perform in person searches. No search fee. Required to search: name, years to search, DOB, SSN. Criminal records computerized from 1985, prior in books to 1940s. Mail turnaround time up to 2 weeks. Public use terminal has crim records back to 1985. PAT criminal results show middle initial. PAT results may also show full middle name. Online access to county case docket database is free at www.starkcourt.org/docket/index.html. Search by name, case number. Online results show middle initial.

General Information: No secret indictments, expungment records released. Will fax documents. Court makes copy: $.10 per page. Certification fee: $1.00 per page includes copy fee. Payee: Clerk of Courts. Personal checks accepted; credit cards are not. Mail requests: SASE required.

Alliance Municipal Court 470 E Market St, Rm 16, Alliance, OH 44601; 330-823-6600; criminal fax: 330-829-2230; civil fax: 330-829-2231; 8:30AM-4:30PM. ***Misdemeanor, Civil Actions under $15,000, Eviction, Small Claims.***
www.alliancecourt.org/

Jurisdiction includes Alliance, Lexington, Marlboro, Washington, Paris, Uniontown, Minerva, Limaville, and Robertsville.

Civil Records: Access: Fax, mail, in person, online. Both court and visitors may perform in person searches. No search fee. Required to search: name. Civil cases indexed by defendant, plaintiff. Civil records go back to 1993. Mail turnaround time 1 day. Civil PAT goes back to 1993. PAT civil results show middle initial. Search the Online Case Docket of the Alliance Court at www.starkcountycjis.org/cjis2/docket/main.html

Criminal Records: Access: Fax, mail, in person, online. Both court and visitors may perform in person searches. No search fee. Required to search: name, years to search; also helpful: DOB, SSN. computerized since 1991. Mail turnaround time 1 day. Criminal PAT goes back to same as civil. PAT results show middle initial, DOB. Search the Online Case Docket of the Alliance Court at www.starkcountycjis.org/cjis2/docket/main.html includes traffic and misdemeanor records. Online results show middle initial, DOB.

General Information: Online identifiers in results same as on public terminal. No fee to fax documents. Court makes copy: $.25 per page. Certification fee: $3.00 per page. Payee: Alliance Municipal Court. Personal checks accepted; credit cards are not. Mail requests: SASE required.

Canton Municipal Court 218 Cleveland Ave SW, PO Box 24218, Canton, OH 44702-4218; 330-489-3203; criminal fax: 330-489-3372; civil fax: 330-489-3075; 8AM-4:30PM. ***Misdemeanor, Civil Actions under $15,000, Eviction, Small Claims.***
www.cantoncourt.org

Jurisdiction includes Canton, North Canton, Louisville, Lake, Plain, Nimishillen, Osnaburg, Pike, Sandy, Hartville, East Canton, Myers Lake, East Sparta, Waynesburg, and Magnolia.

Civil Records: Access: Phone, fax, mail, in person, online. Both court and visitors may perform in person searches. No search fee. Required to search: name, years to search. Civil cases indexed by defendant, plaintiff; index on computer from 1991, prior in books to 1928. Mail turnaround time 1-2 days. Civil PAT goes back to 1990. Search docket information at www.cantoncourt.org/docket.html.

Criminal Records: Access: Phone, fax, mail, in person, online. Both court and visitors may perform in person searches. No search fee. Required to search: name, years to search; also helpful: DOB, SSN. Criminal records computerized from 1986, books to 1928. Mail turnaround time 1-2 days. Criminal PAT goes back to 1996. Search docket info at www.cantoncourt.org/docket.html. Includes traffic.

General Information: No sealed records released. No fee to fax documents. Court makes copy: $.25 per page. Self serve: same. Certification fee: $1.00. Payee: Municipal Court. Personal checks accepted. Mail requests: SASE required.

Massillon Municipal Court PO Box 1040, 2 James Duncan Plaza, Massillon, OH 44646-1040; 330-830-2591; criminal phone: 330-830-1732; civil phone: 330-830-1731; fax: 330-830-3648; 8:30AM-4:30PM. ***Misdemeanor, Civil Actions under $15,000, Eviction, Small Claims.***
www.massilloncourt.org
Jurisdiction includes Massillon, Canal Fulton, Bethlehem, Jackson, Lawrence, Perry, Sugarcreek, Tuscarawas, Beach City, Brewster, Hills and Dales, Navarre, and Wilmot.
Civil Records: Access: Fax, mail, in person, online. Both court and visitors may perform in person searches. No search fee. Required to search: name. Civil cases indexed by defendant, plaintiff. Civil index in docket books from 1986, computerized since 1991. Mail turnaround time 1 week. Civil PAT goes back to 1991. PAT results show name only. Search the Online Case Docket of the Massillon Court at www.massilloncourt.org.
Criminal Records: Access: Fax, mail, in person, online. Both court and visitors may perform in person searches. No search fee. Required to search: name, years to search; also helpful: DOB, SSN. computerized since 1991. Mail turnaround time 1 week. Criminal PAT goes back to same as civil but criminal terminal results may include SSN. Search the Online Case Docket of the Massillon Court at the website, includes traffic and misdemeanor records. Traffic can be reached at 330-830-1732. Online results show name only.
General Information: Online identifiers in results same as on public terminal. No fee to fax documents. Court makes copy: $.05 per page. Certification fee: $2.00 per page. Payee: Massillon Clerk of Court. Personal checks and major credit cards accepted. Mail requests: SASE required.

Summit County

Common Pleas Court 209 S High St, Akron, OH 44308; 330-643-2211, 330-643-2201-Divorce; criminal phone: 330-643-2282; civil phone: 330-643-2217; probate phone: 330-643-2350; fax: 330-643-7772; 9:30AM-4:15PM. ***Felony, Civil Actions over $10,000, Probate.***
www.cpclerk.co.summit.oh.us
For faster service, mail requests to Clerk at 53 University Ave, Akron 44308. Probate is a separate court.
Civil Records: Access: Mail, in person, online. Both court and visitors may perform in person searches. No search fee. Required to search: name, years to search. Civil cases indexed by defendant, plaintiff; index on computer from 1982, prior in books, some microfiche. Mail turnaround time 1 week. Civil PAT goes back to 1982. Access to county clerk of courts records is free at www.cpclerk.co.summit.oh.us. Click on "Case Search." Access to probate records at http://summitohioprobate.com/pa/pa.urd/pamw6500*display.
Criminal Records: Access: Mail, in person, online. Both court and visitors may perform in person searches. Search fee: $2.00 per name. Required to search: name, years to search, DOB; also helpful: SSN. Criminal records computerized from 1982, prior in books, some microfiche. Mail turnaround time 1 week. Criminal PAT goes back to same as civil. Access to county clerk of courts records is free at www.cpclerk.co.summit.oh.us. Click on "Case Search."
General Information: Online identifiers in results same as on public terminal. No secret indictment records released. Will not fax documents. Court makes copy: $.05 per page. Certification fee: $1.00 per page. Payee: Clerk of Court. Only cashiers checks and money orders accepted. No credit cards accepted. Mail requests: SASE required.

Akron Municipal Court 217 S High St, Rm 837, Akron, OH 44308; criminal phone: 330-375-2570; civil phone: 330-375-2920; fax: 330-375-2024; 8AM-4:30PM. ***Misdemeanor, Civil Actions under $15,000, Eviction, Small Claims.***
http://courts.ci.akron.oh.us
Civil Records: Access: Fax, mail, in person, online. Both court and visitors may perform in person searches. No search fee. Required to search: name, years to search. Civil cases indexed by defendant, plaintiff; index on computer from 1988, prior in books to 1975. Mail turnaround time up to 1 week. Civil PAT goes back to 1988. Online access to court records and schedules is free at http://courts.ci.akron.oh.us/disclaimer.htm.
Criminal Records: Access: Fax, mail, in person, online. Both court and visitors may perform in person searches. No search fee. Required to search: name, years to search, DOB, SSN. Criminal records computerized from 1988, prior in books to 1960. Mail turnaround time up to 1 week. Criminal PAT goes back to same as civil. PAT results show middle initial, DOB. Online access to court records and schedules is free at http://courts.ci.akron.oh.us/disclaimer.htm. Online results show name, DOB. Online results include addresses of all parties.
General Information: No sealed records released. Will fax out documents. Court makes copy: first 10 pages free; $.10 each add'l. Certification fee: $1.00 per page. Payee: Akron Municipal Court. No personal checks or credit cards accepted. Mail requests: SASE required.

Barberton Municipal Court Municipal Bldg, 576 W Park Ave, Barberton, OH 44203-2584; 330-753-2261; criminal phone: 330-861-7188; civil phone: 330-861-7192; fax: 330-848-6779; 8AM-4:30PM (civ); Crim/traffic to 8PM. ***Misdemeanor, Civil Actions under $15,000, Eviction, Small Claims.***
www.cityofbarberton.com/clerkofcourts
Civil Records: Access: Phone, fax, mail, in person, online. Both court and visitors may perform in person searches. No search fee. Required to search: name, years to search. Civil cases indexed by defendant, plaintiff. Civil records computerized since 1994. Mail turnaround time 1 week. Civil PAT goes back to 1994. Online records for Barberton, Green, Norton, Franklin, Clinton, Copley and Coventry are free at http://24.123.45.19/.
Criminal Records: Access: Phone, fax, mail, in person, online. Both court and visitors may perform in person searches. No search fee. Required to search: name, years to search; also helpful: DOB, SSN. Criminal records computerized since 1994. Mail turnaround time 1 week. Criminal PAT goes back to same as civil. Online records for Barberton, Green, Norton, Franklin, Clinton, Copley and Coventry are free at http://24.123.45.19/.
General Information: No fee to fax documents. Court makes copy: $.10 per page. Certification fee: $1.00 per page. Payee: Barberton Municipal Court. Personal checks and credit cards accepted.

Cuyahoga Falls Municipal Court 2310 2nd St, Cuyahoga Falls, OH 44221; 330-971-8110; criminal phone: 330-971-8109; civil phone: 330-971-8108; criminal fax: 330-971-8114; civil fax: 330-971-8386; 8AM-8PM (Criminal), 8AM-4:30PM (Civil). ***Misdemeanor, Civil Actions under $15,000, Eviction, Small Claims.***
www.cfmunicourt.com
Civil Records: Access: Phone, mail, in person, online. Both court and visitors may perform in person searches. No search fee. Required to search: name, years to search. Civil cases indexed by defendant, plaintiff, or case number. Civil records indexed back to 1954. Mail turnaround time 1 week. Civil PAT goes back to 1992. PAT results show name, DOBs, case numbers. Court docket information is free at the website.
Criminal Records: Access: Phone, mail, in person, online. Both court and visitors may perform in person searches. No search fee. Required to search: name or case number. Criminal records indexed back to 1954. Results include case number's. Mail turnaround time 1 week. Criminal PAT goes back to same as civil. PAT results show name, DOBs, case numbers. Court docket information is free at the website. Online results show name, DOB.
General Information: Will not fax documents. Court makes copy: $.05 per page. Certification fee: $1.00 per page includes copy. Payee: Cuyahoga Falls Municipal Court. Business checks accepted. Credit cards accepted. Mail requests: SASE required.

Trumbull County

Common Pleas Court 161 High St, Warren, OH 44481; 330-675-2557; criminal phone: 330-675-3058; civil phone: 330-675-2557; probate phone: 330-675-2521; fax: 330-675-2563; 8:30AM-4:30PM. ***Felony, Civil Actions, Probate.***
www.clerk.co.trumbull.oh.us
Probate is located in a separate office at this same address; records in a separate index. Probate fax number- 330-675-3024.
Civil Records: Access: Phone, mail, in person, online. Both court and visitors may perform in person searches. Search fee: $5.00 per name. Required to search: name, years to search. Civil cases indexed by defendant, plaintiff; index in books from 1977, archived from 1800s; on computer back to 5/96. Mail turnaround time 1 week. Civil PAT goes back to 5/1996. Online access to court records is free at www.clerk.co.trumbull.oh.us/search/search.htm. Records go back to May, 1996. Online access to probate court records is free at www.trumbullprobate.org/paccessfront.htm.
Criminal Records: Access: Mail, in person, online. Both court and visitors may perform in person searches. Search fee: $5.00 per name. Required to search: name, years to search, DOB, SSN, signed release. Criminal records indexed in books from 1977, archived from 1800s; on computer back to 5/96. Mail turnaround time 1 week. Criminal PAT goes back to same as civil. Online access to criminal records is the same as civil.
General Information: No secret or sealed records released. Will not fax documents. Court makes copy: $.05 per page. Self serve: same. Certification fee: $1.00 per page. Payee: Clerk of Court. Business checks accepted. No credit cards accepted. Mail requests: SASE required.

Trumbull County Court Central 180 N Mecca St, Cortland, OH 44410; 330-637-5023; 8AM-4PM. ***Misdemeanor, Civil Actions under $15,000, Eviction, Small Claims.***
Civil Records: Access: Phone, fax, mail, in person. Both court and visitors may perform in person searches. No search fee. Required to search: name, years to search. Civil cases indexed by defendant, plaintiff. Records available since 1983. Mail turnaround time 1-2 days. Civil PAT goes back to 1993.
Criminal Records: Access: Phone, fax, mail, in person. Both court and visitors may perform in person searches. No search fee. Required to search: name, years to search; also helpful: DOB, SSN. Same record keeping as civil. Mail turnaround time 1-2 days. Criminal PAT goes back to same as civil.
General Information: No fee to fax documents locally only. Court makes copy: $.25 per page. Self serve: same. Certification fee: $2.00 per page. Payee: Trumbull County Court Central. Personal checks accepted. Credit cards accepted in person only.

Trumbull County Court East 7130 Brookwood Dr, Brookfield, OH 44403; 330-448-1726; fax: 330-448-6310; 8:30AM-4:30PM. ***Misdemeanor, Civil under $15,000, Eviction, Small Claims.***
Civil Records: Access: Phone, fax, mail, in person. Both court and visitors may perform in person searches. No search fee. Required to search: name, years to search. Civil records go back to 1994. Mail turnaround time 1-2 days. Civil PAT goes back to 1994.
Criminal Records: Access: Phone, fax, mail, in person. Both court and visitors may perform in person searches. No search fee. Required to search: name, years to search; also helpful: DOB, SSN. Criminal Records in docket books since 1990, computerized since 1994. Mail turnaround time 1-2 days. Criminal PAT goes back to 1994.PAT results show name, DOB. Results can include SSN and/or address if available.

General Information: No fee to fax documents locally only. Court makes copy: $.25 per page. Self serve: same. Certification fee: $1.00 per page, if "non-copies" are used, then $2.00 per page. Payee: Trumbull County Court East. Personal checks accepted; credit cards are not. Mail requests: SASE required if copies to be returned by mail.

Girard Municipal Court City Hall, 100 N Market St, #A, Girard, OH 44420-2559; criminal phone: 330-545-0069; civil phone: 330-545-3177; fax: 330-545-7045; 8AM-4PM. ***Misdemeanor, Civil Actions under $15,000, Eviction, Small Claims.***
Traffic records: 330-545-3049.
Civil Records: Access: Fax, mail, in person, online. Both court and visitors may perform in person searches. No search fee. Required to search: name, years to search. Civil cases indexed by defendant, plaintiff; index on books since 1990, computerized since 10/96. Mail turnaround time 1 week. Civil PAT goes back to 9/1996. PAT civil results show middle initial. Access available with username and password at www.girardmunicipalcourt.com - contact clerk of court.
Criminal Records: Access: Fax, mail, in person, online. Both court and visitors may perform in person searches. No search fee. Required to search: name, years to search; also helpful: DOB, SSN. Criminal docket on books since 1990, computerized since 10/96. Mail turnaround time 1 week. Criminal PAT goes back to same as civil. PAT results show middle initial, DOB. Access available with username and password at www.girardmunicipalcourt.com -contact clerk of court.
General Information: No fee to fax documents. Court makes copy: 1st 10 pages free; each add'l page $.10. Certification fee: $10.00 per document includes copy fee. Payee: Girard Municipal Court. No personal checks or credit cards accepted. Mail requests: SASE required.

Newton Falls Municipal Court 19 N Canal St, Newton Falls, OH 44444-1302; 330-872-0302; criminal phone: 330-872-0232; civil phone: 330-872-0232; criminal fax: 330-872-3899; civil fax: same; 7:30AM-4PM. ***Misdemeanor, Civil Actions under $15,000, Eviction, Small Claims.*** www.newtonfallscourt.com
Civil Records: Access: Mail, in person, online. Only the court performs in person searches; visitors may not. No search fee. Required to search: name, years to search. Civil cases indexed by defendant, plaintiff. Civil records in books since 1970, computerized since 1992. Mail turnaround time varies, but usually 1 week or less. PAT civil results show middle initial. Search record index free at www.newtonfallscourt.com/Search/.
Criminal Records: Access: Mail, in person, online. Only the court performs in person searches; visitors may not. No search fee. Required to search: name, years to search, DOB or SSN. Criminal records in books since 1970, computerized since 1992. Mail turnaround time varies, usually 1 week or less. PAT criminal results show middle initial. Search record index free at www.newtonfallscourt.com/Search/. Online results show name, DOB, SSN. Online results include violation, hearing info and disposition.
General Information: Will fax documents $2.50 if long distance. Court makes copy: $.10 per page. Certification fee: $1.00 per page. Payee: Newton Falls Municipal Court. Cashiers checks and money orders only accepted. Credit cards accepted, small use fee charged. Mail requests: SASE required.

Niles Municipal Court 15 E State St, Niles, OH 44446-5051; 330-652-5863; fax: 330-544-9025; 8AM-4PM. ***Misdemeanor, Civil Actions under $15,000, Eviction, Small Claims.***
Civil Records: Access: Phone, fax, mail, in person. Both court and visitors may perform in person searches. No search fee. Required to search: name, years to search. Civil cases indexed by defendant, plaintiff; index on computer since 10/96, in books since 1990, in storage from 1930. Mail turnaround times will vary. Civil PAT goes back to 1997. PAT civil results show middle initial.
Criminal Records: Access: Phone, fax, mail, in person. Both court and visitors may perform in person searches. No search fee. Required to search: name, years to search; also helpful: DOB, SSN. Criminal records on computer since 10/96, in books since 1990, in storage from 1930. Mail turnaround time varies. Criminal PAT goes back to same as civil. PAT criminal results show middle initial.
General Information: No fee to fax documents locally only. Court makes copy: $.25 per page. No certification fee. Payee: Niles Municipal Court. Cashiers checks and money orders accepted. Major credit cards accepted.

Warren Municipal Court PO Box 1550, 141 South St SE, Warren, OH 44482; 330-841-2525; criminal phone: 330-841-2525 x105-110; civil phone: 330-841-2525 x112-115; fax: 330-841-2760; 8AM-4:30PM. ***Misdemeanor, Civil Actions under $15,000, Eviction, Small Claims.***
Civil Records: Access: Fax, mail, in person. Both court and visitors may perform in person searches. No search fee. Required to search: name, years to search; also helpful: address. Civil cases indexed by defendant, plaintiff; index on computer since 1995; prior in books to 1978. Mail turnaround time 1-5 days. Civil PAT goes back to 1995. Public cannot print copies from public access terminal.
Criminal Records: Access: Fax, mail, in person. Both court and visitors may perform in person searches. No search fee. Required to search: name, years to search, DOB, SSN, signed release; also helpful: address. Criminal records on computer since 1995; prior in books to 1978. Mail turnaround time 1-5 days. Criminal PAT goes back to same as civil. Public cannot print copies from public access terminal.
General Information: No open case records released. No fee to fax documents. Court makes copy: $.05 per page. Certification fee: $1.00 per document. Payee: Warren Municipal Court. Personal checks and credit cards accepted. Mail requests: SASE required.

Tuscarawas County

Common Pleas Court PO Box 628, 125 E High, New Philadelphia, OH 44663; 330-365-3243; probate phone: 330-365-3266; fax: 330-343-4682; 8AM-4:30PM. ***Felony, Civil Actions over $15,000, Court of Appeals.*** www.co.tuscarawas.oh.us
Probate is a separate court at 101 E High Ave.
Civil Records: Access: In person, online. Visitors must perform in person searches themselves. Required to search: name, years to search; also helpful: address. Civil cases indexed by defendant, plaintiff; index on computer from 1987, prior in books to 1808, archived prior. Civil PAT goes back to 1986. PAT results show middle initial, DOB. Results include redacted images. Search dockets online at www.co.tuscarawas.oh.us/ClerkofCourts/DocketSearch.htm.
Criminal Records: Access: In person, online. Visitors must perform in person searches themselves. Required to search: name, years to search; also helpful: address, DOB, SSN. Criminal records go back to 1868, Criminal records computerized from 1987, prior in books to 1808, archived prior. Criminal PAT goes back to same as civil. PAT results show middle initial, DOB. Results include redacted images. Search dockets online at www.co.tuscarawas.oh.us/ClerkofCourts/DocketSearch.htm Online results show middle initial, DOB.
General Information: Will fax out specific case files for $2.00 transmission fee plus $1.00 per page. Court makes copy: $.10 per page. Certification fee: $1.00 per page. Payee: Clerk of Court. Personal checks and credit cards accepted. Mail requests: SASE required for mail return of any copies.

County Court 336 E 3rd St, Uhrichsville, OH 44683; 740-922-4795; fax: 740-922-7020; 8AM-4:30PM. ***Misdemeanor, Civil Actions under $15,000, Small Claims.*** www.tusccourtsouthern.com/
Probation Office phone: 740-922-3653 & 922-4360 or 866-798-3653.
Civil Records: Access: Fax, mail, in person, online. Both court and visitors may perform in person searches. No search fee. Required to search: name, years to search. Civil cases indexed by defendant, plaintiff. Civil records go back to 1970's, civil records on computer from 2/94, prior in books. Mail turnaround time 1-2 days. Civil PAT goes back to 1992. PAT results show middle initial, DOB. Search records free at http://66.219.135.176/ Warrants are also available on the court website.
Criminal Records: Access: Fax, mail, in person, online. Both court and visitors may perform in person searches. No search fee. Required to search: name, years to search, DOB. Criminal records computerized from 2/94, prior in books. Mail turnaround time 1-2 days. Criminal PAT goes back to same as civil; results show middle initial, DOB. Search records free at http://66.219.135.176/. Warrants are also available on the court website. Online results show middle initial, DOB.
General Information: Online identifiers in results same as on public terminal. No fee to fax documents locally only. Court makes copy: $.10 per page. No certification fee. Payee: Tuscarawas County Court. Only Tuscarawas County personal checks accepted, or money orders or cash. No credit cards accepted. Mail requests: SASE required.

New Philadelphia Municipal Court 166 E High Ave, New Philadelphia, OH 44663; 330-343-6797; criminal phone: 330-343-6797; civil: x231; fax: 330-364-6885; 8AM-4:30PM. ***Misdemeanor, Civil Actions under $15,000, Eviction, Small Claims.*** www.npmunicipalcourt.org
The New Philadelphia Municipal Court has territorial jurisdiction within the municipal corporations of New Philadelphia and Dover, and the villages of Baltic, Bolivar, Midvale, Mineral City, Roswell, Stonecreek, Strasburg, Sugarcreek, and Zoar.
Civil Records: Access: In person only. Visitors must perform in person searches themselves. Required to search: name, years to search. Civil cases indexed by defendant, plaintiff; index on computer back to 4/91, prior in books to 1976. Civil PAT goes back to 4/1991. PAT results show middle initial, DOB.
Criminal Records: Access: In person only. Visitors must perform in person searches themselves. Required to search: name, SSN. Criminal records computerized from 4/91, prior in books to 1976. Criminal PAT goes back to same as civil. PAT results show middle initial, DOB.
General Information: Will not fax documents. Court makes copy: $.25 per page. Certification fee: $1.00 per page. Payee: Municipal Court. Personal checks accepted. Visa/MC accepted in person only.

Union County

Common Pleas Court County Courthouse, Clerk of Courts, 215 W 5th, 2nd Fl, Marysville, OH 43040; criminal phone: 937-645-3140; civil phone: 937-645-3006; probate phone: 937-645-3029; fax: 937-645-3162; 8:30AM-4PM. ***Felony, Civil Actions over $10,000, Probate.*** www.co.union.oh.us/
Forms are available at the website. Probate is located at the same address, separate office. Probate fax is 937-645-3160.
Civil Records: Access: In person, online. Visitors must perform in person searches themselves. Required to search: name, years to search; also helpful: address. Civil cases indexed by defendant, plaintiff; index on computer from 1990, records go back to 1850. Civil PAT goes back to 1990. Online access to the court clerk's public records and index free at http://www3.co.union.oh.us/clerkofcourts/. Records go back to 1/1990, older records added as accessed. Images go back to 1/2002.
Criminal Records: Access: In person, online. Visitors must perform in person searches themselves. Required to search: name, years to search, DOB, also helpful: address. Criminal records computerized from 1990, records go back to 1850. Criminal PAT goes back to same as civil. Online access to court clerk's public record and index is free at http://www3.co.union.oh.us/clerkofcourts/. Records go back to 1/1990, older records added as accessed. Images go back to 1/2002.
General Information: Will fax out specific case files for $1.00 per page. Court makes copy: $.10 per page. Certification fee: $1.00 per page. Payee: Clerk of Court. Only cashiers checks and money orders accepted. No credit cards accepted. Mail requests: SASE required for mail return of any copies.

Marysville Municipal Court City Hall Bldg, 125 E 6th St, Marysville, OH 43040; 937-644-9102; civil phone: x1003; fax: 937-644-1228; 8AM-4PM. ***Misdemeanor, Civil Actions under $15,000, Eviction, Small Claims.***
http://municourt.co.union.oh.us/
If faxing a request for a background check, no more than 2 individuals will be search per request.
Civil Records: Access: Fax, mail, in person. Both court and visitors may perform in person searches. No search fee. Required to search: name, years to search. Civil cases indexed by defendant, plaintiff; index on computer from 1989, prior on microfilm. Mail turnaround time 1-2 days. Civil PAT goes back to 1989.
Criminal Records: Access: Fax, mail, in person. Both court and visitors may perform in person searches. No search fee. Required to search: name, years to search, SSN. Criminal records computerized from 1989, prior on microfilm. Mail turnaround time 1-2 days. Criminal PAT goes back to same as civil.
General Information: No probation records released. No fee to fax documents. Court makes copy: $.20 per page after 1st 5 copies free. No certification fee. Payee: Marysville Municipal Court. Personal checks accepted; credit cards are not. Mail requests: SASE required.

Van Wert County

Common Pleas Court 305 Courthouse, 121 E Main St, Van Wert, OH 45891; 419-238-6935; criminal phone: 419-238-1022; civil phone: 419-238-1022; probate phone: 419-238-0027; fax: 419-238-4760; 8AM-4PM. ***Felony, Civil Actions, Probate.***
www.vwcommonpleas.org
Fax number for Common Pleas Clerk is 419-238-4760. Probate records are at 108 Main St, Van Wert, OH 45891.
Civil Records: Access: In person only. Visitors must perform in person searches themselves. Required to search: name, years to search. Civil cases indexed by defendant, plaintiff. Some early records on microfiche, have docket books and files, indexed on computer since 5/98. Civil PAT goes back to 5/1998. PAT results show name only. Court calendars available online.
Criminal Records: Access: In person only. Visitors must perform in person searches themselves. Required to search: name, years to search; also helpful: address, DOB, SSN. Some early years on microfiche, have docket books and files, indexed on computer since 5/98. Criminal PAT goes back to same as civil. PAT results show name only. Court calendar available online.
General Information: All records public. Will not fax documents. Court makes copy: $.05 per page. Certification fee: $1.00. Payee: Clerk of Court. Personal checks accepted. Major credit cards accepted for copies only.

Van Wert Municipal Court 124 S Market, Van Wert, OH 45891; 419-238-5767; 8AM-4PM. ***Misdemeanor, Civil Actions under $15,000, Eviction, Small Claims.***
http://vanwert.org/gov/court/index.htm
Civil Records: Access: Mail, in person. Both court and visitors may perform in person searches. No search fee. Required to search: name, years to search. Civil cases indexed by defendant, plaintiff; index on computer from 1989. Mail turnaround time 1-2 days. Civil PAT goes back to 1988.
Criminal Records: Access: Mail, in person. Both court and visitors may perform in person searches. No search fee. Required to search: name, years to search; also helpful: SSN. Criminal records computerized from 1989. Mail turnaround time 1-2 days. Criminal PAT goes back to same as civil.
General Information: Fee to fax out file $1.00 per page. Court makes copy: $1.00 per page. Certification fee: $1.00. Payee: Municipal Court. Personal checks accepted. Mail requests: SASE required.

Vinton County

Common Pleas Court County Courthouse, 100 E Main St, McArthur, OH 45651; 740-596-3001; probate phone: 740-596-5480; fax: 740-596-9611; 8:30AM-4PM. ***Felony, Civil Actions over $3,000, Probate.***
Civil Records: Access: In person only. Visitors must perform in person searches themselves. Required to search: name, years to search. Civil cases indexed by defendant, plaintiff. Civil records in books since 1850. Will not mail search requests. Civil PAT goes back to 1/1998.
Criminal Records: Access: In person only. Visitors must perform in person searches themselves. Required to search: name, years to search; also helpful: DOB, SSN. Criminal records in books since 1850. Will not mail search requests. Criminal PAT goes back to same as civil.
General Information: No sealed records released. Will fax documents to local or toll-free number. Court makes copy: $.25 per page. Certification fee: $2.00. Payee: Vinton County Clerk of Court. Personal checks accepted; credit cards are not.

Vinton County Court County Courthouse, McArthur, OH 45651; 740-596-5000; fax: 740-596-9721; 8:30AM-4PM. ***Misdemeanor, Civil Actions under $15,000, Small Claims$3,000.***
Civil Records: Access: In person only. Both court and visitors may perform in person searches. No search fee. Required to search: name, years to search. Civil cases indexed by defendant, plaintiff. Civil records in books from 1980s, archived from 1800s. Civil PAT goes back to 9/1999.
Criminal Records: Access: In person only. Both court and visitors may perform in person searches. No search fee. Required to search: name, years to search, DOB; SSN helpful. Criminal records in books from 1980s, archived from 1800s. Criminal PAT goes back to 9/1999.
General Information: Will not fax out case files. Court makes copy: $.10 per page. Self serve: $.10 per page. No certification fee. Payee: Vinton County Court. No personal checks or credit cards accepted.

Warren County

Common Pleas Court PO Box 238, Lebanon, OH 45036; 513-695-1120; probate phone: 513-695-1180; criminal fax: 513-695-2965; civil fax: same; 8:30AM-4:30PM. ***Felony, Civil Actions over $3,000, Probate.*** www.co.warren.oh.us/clerkofcourt/
Probate located at 570 Justice Dr. Probate fax- 513-695-2945
Civil Records: Access: Phone, mail, in person, online. Both court and visitors may perform in person searches. Search fee: $4.00 per name. Required to search: name, years to search. Civil cases indexed by defendant, plaintiff; index on computer from 1974, archived from 1850. Mail turnaround time 1-4 days. Civil PAT goes back to 1974. PAT civil results show middle initial. Access to court records is free at www.co.warren.oh.us/clerkofcourt/search/index.htm. Index goes back to 1980.
Criminal Records: Access: Mail, in person, online. Both court and visitors may perform in person searches. Search fee: $4.00 per name. Required to search: name, years to search, DOB, signed release; also helpful: SSN. Criminal records computerized from 1974, archived from 1850. Mail turnaround time 1-4 days. Criminal PAT goes back to same as civil. PAT criminal results show middle initial. Access to court records is free at www.co.warren.oh.us/clerkofcourt/search/index.htm. Index goes back to 1980. Online results show middle initial.
General Information: Online identifiers in results same as on public terminal. Will fax documents $2.00 per fax plus $1.00 per page. Court makes copy: $.05 per page. Certification fee: $1.00 per page; exemplification- $5.00 per doc. Payee: Clerk of Court. Personal checks accepted; credit cards are not. Mail requests: SASE required.

County Court 550 Justice Dr, Lebanon, OH 45036; criminal phone: 513-695-1370; civil phone: 513-695-1371; fax: 513-695-2990; 8AM-4:30PM. ***Misdemeanor, Civil Actions under $15,000, Small Claims under $3000.***
www.co.warren.oh.us/countycourt/
Civil Records: Access: Mail, in person, online. Visitors must perform in person searches themselves. No search fee. Required to search: name, years to search; also helpful: address. Civil cases indexed by defendant, plaintiff; index on computer from 1990. No in person searches on Tuesdays thru Thursdays. Civil PAT goes back to 1990. PAT located at 500 Justice Dr. Search court records on the Courtview system free at http://countycourt.co.warren.oh.us/pa/. Online records go back to 1990; no DOBs on civil results.
Criminal Records: Access: Phone, mail, in person, online. Both court and visitors may perform in person searches. No search fee. Required to search: name, years to search, DOB; also helpful: SSN, address. Criminal records computerized from 1990, prior in books. No in person searches on Tuesdays or Thursdays. Mail turnaround time 1-2 weeks. Criminal PAT goes back to 1990. PAT located at 500 Justice Dr. Search court records on the Courtview system free at http://countycourt.co.warren.oh.us/pa/. Online records go back to 1990. Online results show name, DOB.
General Information: Will not fax documents. Court makes copy: $.05 per page. No cert fee. Payee: Warren County Court. Personal checks accepted. Visa/MC accepted. Mail requests: SASE required.

Franklin Municipal Court 1 Benjamin Franklin Way, Franklin, OH 45005; 937-746-2858; criminal fax: 937-743-7751; civil fax: same; 8:30AM-5PM. ***Misdemeanor, Civil Actions under $15,000, Eviction, Small Claims.***
www.franklinohio.org/pages/courtmain.asp
Civil Records: Access: Phone, mail, in person. Both court and visitors may perform in person searches. No search fee. Required to search: name, years to search. Civil cases indexed by defendant, plaintiff; index on computer back to 1990. Mail turnaround time 1-2 days.
Criminal Records: Access: Phone, mail, in person. Both court and visitors may perform in person searches. No search fee. Required to search: name, years to search, signed release; also helpful: DOB, SSN. Criminal records computerized from 1990. Mail turnaround time 1-2 days.
General Information: Will fax documents. Court makes copy: $.50 per page. Certification fee: $.50 per document. Payee: Franklin Municipal Court. Personal checks accepted. Credit cards accepted in person only. Mail requests: SASE required to mail back any docs.

Lebanon Municipal Court City Bldg, 50 S Broadway, Lebanon, OH 45036-1777; 513-932-3060; criminal fax: 513-933-7212; civil fax: same; 8AM-4PM. ***Misdemeanor, Civil Actions, Eviction, Small Claims.*** www.ci.lebanon.oh.us/
Civil Records: Access: Fax, mail, in person. Both court and visitors may perform in person searches. No search fee. Required to search: name, years to search. Civil cases indexed by defendant, plaintiff; index on books since 1956, computerized since 1990. Mail turnaround time 2 days. Civil PAT goes back to 1989.
Criminal Records: Access: Fax, mail, in person. Both court and visitors may perform in person searches. No search fee. Required to search: name, years to search; also helpful: DOB, SSN. Criminal docket on books since 1956, computerized since 1990. Mail turnaround time 2 days. Criminal PAT goes back to same as civil.
General Information: No fee to fax documents locally only. Court makes copy: $.25 per page; first 6 pages free. No certification fee. No personal checks or credit cards accepted.

Mason Municipal Court 5950 S Mason Montgomery Rd, Mason, OH 45040; 513-398-7901; fax: 513-459-8085; 7:30AM-4PM. ***Misdemeanor, Civil Actions under $15,000, Eviction, Small Claims.***
www.masonmunicipalcourt.org
Civil Records: Access: Phone, fax, mail, in person, online. Both court and visitors may perform in

person searches. No search fee. Required to search: name, years to search. Civil cases indexed by defendant, plaintiff. Civil records in docket books since 1985, computerized since 1988. Mail turnaround time 1-2 weeks. Online access to court records is free at http://courtconnect.masonmunicipalcourt.org/connection/court/.
Criminal Records: Access: Phone, fax, mail, in person, online. Both court and visitors may perform in person searches. No search fee. Required to search: name, years to search; also helpful: SSN. Criminal records in docket books since 1985, computerized since 1988. Mail turnaround time 1-2 weeks. Online access to court records is free at http://courtconnect.masonmunicipalcourt.org/connection/court/. Online results show middle initial.
General Information: No fee to fax documents locally only. Court makes copy: n/a. Self serve: $.25 per page. Certification fee: $3.00 per page. Payee: Mason Municipal Court. Cashiers checks and money orders accepted. Credit card okay for in person criminal searching only. Mail requests: SASE required.

Washington County

Common Pleas Court 205 Putnam St, Marietta, OH 45750; 740-373-6623 x366, x 367; probate phone: x253; fax: 740-374-3758; 8AM-4:15PM. ***Felony, Civil Actions over $15,000, Probate.***
www.washingtongov.org
Probate is separate index at this same address, in Annex on 3rd Fl.
Civil Records: Access: In person only. Visitors must perform in person searches themselves. Required to search: name, years to search. Civil cases indexed by defendant, plaintiff; index on computer since 1985, microfilm 1977-1984, index in books from 1795. Civil PAT goes back to 1985. 3 public terminals.
Criminal Records: Access: In person only. Visitors must perform in person searches themselves. Required to search: name, years to search. Criminal records on computer since 1985, microfilm 1977-1984, index in books back to 1795. Criminal PAT goes back to same as civil.
General Information: No sealed, expunged records released. Will not fax out case files. Court makes copy: $.10 per page if 10 pages or over. Certification fee: $1.00 per page. Payee: Clerk of Court. Personal checks & credit cards accepted.

Marietta Municipal Court PO Box 615, 301 Putnam, Marietta, OH 45750; 740-373-4474; fax: 740-373-2547; 8AM-4:30PM. ***Misdemeanor, Civil Actions under $15,000, Eviction, Small Claims.***
www.mariettacourt.com
Civil Records: Access: Mail, in person, online. Both court and visitors may perform in person searches. No search fee. Required to search: name, years to search. Civil cases indexed by defendant, plaintiff; index on computer from 11/91, prior in books. Mail turnaround time 1 week. Civil PAT goes back to 11/1991. PAT civil results show middle initial. Online access to from 1992 of court dockets is free at www.mariettacourt.com.
Criminal Records: Access: Mail, in person, online. Both court and visitors may perform in person searches. No search fee. Required to search: name, years to search. Criminal records computerized from 11/91, prior in books back to 1975. Mail turnaround time 1 week. Criminal PAT goes back to 11/1991. PAT results show middle initial, DOB. Online access to criminal records is the same as civil. Online results show middle initial, DOB.
General Information: Online identifiers in results same as on public terminal. Will not fax documents. Court makes copy: $.05 per page. Certification fee: $1.50. Payee: Municipal Court. Personal checks and major credit cards accepted. Mail requests: SASE required.

Wayne County

Common Pleas Court PO Box 507, 107 W Liberty St, 1st Fl, Wooster, OH 44691; 330-287-5590; probate phone: 330-287-5575; criminal fax: 330-287-5416; civil fax: same; 8AM-4:30PM. ***Felony, Civil Actions over $15,000, Probate.***
www.wayneohio.org/index.html
Probate is a separate court at same address, 2nd Fl
Civil Records: Access: Mail, in person, online. Visitors must perform in person searches themselves. No search fee. Required to search: name, years to search. Civil cases indexed by defendant, plaintiff; index on computer since 1995, in books to 1800s. No name searches are performed by mail. Civil PAT goes back to 1995. Online access same as criminal, see below.
Criminal Records: Access: Mail, in person, online. Visitors must perform in person searches themselves. No search fee. Required to search: name, years to search. Criminal records on computer since 1995, in books to 1800s. Mail turnaround time 1 week. Criminal PAT goes back to same as civil. Online access free at www.wayneohio.org/public_access.php; probate index included.
General Information: No grand jury indictment records released. Will not fax documents. Court makes copy: $.05 per page. Certification fee: $1.00. Payee: Clerk of Court. Personal checks accepted. Visa/MC accepted. Mail requests: SASE required.

Wayne County Municipal Court Clerk 215 N Grant St, Wooster, OH 44691-4817; 330-287-5650; criminal fax: 330-263-4043; civil fax: same; 8AM-4:30PM. ***Misdemeanor, Civil Actions under $15,000, Eviction, Small Claims.***
www.wayneohio.org/clerkofcourts/municipal.html
Civil Records: Access: In person, online. Visitors must perform in person searches themselves. Required to search: name, years to search. Civil cases indexed by defendant, plaintiff; index on computer back to 9/94; in books from 1975. Civil PAT goes back to 9/1994. Online access is same as criminal.
Criminal Records: Access: In person, online. Visitors must perform in person searches themselves. Required to search: name, years to search, offense, date of offense. Criminal records computerized from 9/94; in books from 1975. Criminal PAT goes back to same as civil. Access free at www.wayneohio.org/public_access.php.
General Information: Will fax out specific case files. Court makes copy: $.05 per page. Certification fee: $1.00 per page and includes copy fee. Payee: Wayne County Municipal Court. In state personal checks accepted. Major credit cards accepted.

Williams County

Common Pleas Court 1 Courthouse Sq, Clerk of Court of Common Pleas, Bryan, OH 43506; 419-636-1551; probate phone: 419-636-1548; fax: 419-636-7877; 8:30AM-4:30PM. ***Felony, Civil Actions over $10,000, Probate.*** www.co.williams.oh.us/
Probate Court is at the same address.
Civil Records: Access: Phone, fax, mail, in person. Both court and visitors may perform in person searches. No search fee. Required to search: name, years to search. Civil cases indexed by defendant, plaintiff; index on computer from 1988, records go back to 1840. Mail turnaround time 1-2 days. Civil PAT goes back to 4/1998.
Criminal Records: Access: Mail, in person. Both court and visitors may perform in person searches. No search fee. Required to search: name, years to search. Criminal records computerized from 1988, records go back to 1840. Mail turnaround time 1-2 days. Criminal PAT goes back to same as civil.
General Information: No expunged records released. Will fax documents. Court makes copy: $.10 per page. Self serve: same. Certification fee: $1.00 per page. Payee: Clerk of Court. Personal checks and credit cards accepted. Mail requests: SASE required.

Bryan Municipal Court PO Box 546, 1399 E High St, Bryan, OH 43506; 419-636-6939; fax: 419-636-3417; 8:30AM-4:30PM. ***Misdemeanor, Civil Actions under $15,000, Eviction, Small Claims.***
www.bryanmunicipalcourt.com
Civil Records: Access: Fax, mail, in person, online. Both court and visitors may perform in person searches. No search fee. Required to search: name, years to search. Civil cases indexed by defendant, plaintiff; index on computer from 1988, prior in books to 1966, indexed prior. Mail turnaround time 5 days. Civil PAT goes back to 1988. PAT civil results show middle initial. Muni Ct data available free at www.bryanmunicipalcourt.com/search_courtrecords.asp.
Criminal Records: Access: Fax, mail, in person, online. Both court and visitors may perform in person searches. No search fee. Required to search: name, years to search, DOB; also helpful: SSN. Criminal records computerized from 1988, prior in books to 1966, indexed prior. Mail turnaround time 5 days. Criminal PAT goes back to same as civil. PAT results show middle initial, DOB. Muni Ct data available free at www.bryanmunicipalcourt.com/search_courtrecords.asp.
General Information: Will fax documents $2.00. Court makes copy for no fee. Certification fee: $2.00 per page. Payee: Bryan Municipal Court. Personal checks and credit cards accepted. Mail requests: SASE requested.

Wood County

Common Pleas Court Courthouse Sq, Bowling Green, OH 43402; 419-354-9280; probate phone: 419-354-9235; fax: 419-354-9241; 8:30AM-4:30PM. ***Felony, Civil Actions over $15,000, Probate.*** www.co.wood.oh.us
Probate record searching is separate, with separate fees, separate address. Probate fax- 419-354-9357. Search probate records online at the county website.
Civil Records: Access: In person, online. Both court and visitors may perform in person searches. No search fee. Required to search: name, years to search. Civil cases indexed by defendant, plaintiff; index on computer from 7/90, in books and on microfilm from 1800s, docket books, journals and microfilm back to 1800s. Civil PAT goes back to 7/1990. PAT results show middle initial, DOB. Access court index free at https://pub.clerkofcourt.co.wood.oh.us/pa/.
Criminal Records: Access: In person, online. Both court and visitors may perform in person searches. No search fee. Required to search: name, years to search. Criminal records computerized from 7/90, in books and on microfilm from 1980, docket books, journals and microfilm back to 1800s. Criminal PAT goes back to 1/1960. PAT results show middle initial, DOB. Access court index free at https://pub.clerkofcourt.co.wood.oh.us/pa/.
General Information: No adoption commitment, parental rights, juvenile, mental illness records released. No fee to fax documents. Many documents can be returned via email. Court makes copy: $.25 per page first 25 pages, $.10 each add'l. Certification fee: $1.00. Payee: Wood County Clerk of Courts. Business checks accepted. No credit cards accepted.

Bowling Green Municipal Court 711 S Dunbridge Rd, Bowling Green, OH 43402; 419-352-5263; criminal fax: 419-352-9407; civil fax: same; 8:30AM-4:30PM. ***Misdemeanor, Civil Actions under $15,000, Eviction, Small Claims.***
www.bgcourt.org
Civil Records: Access: Phone, fax, mail, in person, online. Both court and visitors may perform in person searches. No search fee. Required to search: name, years to search. Civil cases indexed by defendant, plaintiff; index on computer from 1988. Mail turnaround time 3 days. Civil PAT goes back to 1988. PAT results show name only. Access is free to civil records at http://bgcourtweb.bgohio.org/connection/court/.
Criminal Records: Access: Phone, fax, mail, in person, online. Both court and visitors may perform in person searches. No search fee. Required to search: name, years to search, DOB; also helpful: SSN. Criminal records computerized from 1988. Mail turnaround time 3 days. Criminal PAT goes back to 1988. PAT results show name only. Terminal results may include DL or vehicle number. Free access to criminal and traffic records from http://bgcourtweb.bgohio.org/connection/court/. Online results show middle initial, DOB.

General Information: No fee to fax documents locally only. Court makes copy: $.05 per page. Certification fee: $1.00 per page. Payee: Bowling Green Municipal Court. Personal checks and credit cards accepted. Mail requests: SASE required.

Perrysburg Municipal Court 300 Walnut St, Perrysburg, OH 43551; criminal phone: 419-872-7900; civil phone: 419-872-7910; criminal fax: 419-872-7905; civil fax: same; 8AM-4:30PM M, W-F; 8AM-6:30PM T. ***Misdemeanor, Civil Actions under $15,000, Eviction, Small Claims.***
www.perrysburgcourt.com
Civil Records: Access: Mail, fax, online, in person. Both court and visitors may perform in person searches. Search fee: $3.00 per name. Fee is $15.00 to look in closed, stored files. Required to search: name, years to search; also helpful: address. Civil cases indexed by defendant, plaintiff; index on computer from 1989, prior in books to 1982, archived from 1972. Mail turnaround time 2 days. Online access to court records is free at www.perrysburgcourt.com/disc.html.
Criminal Records: Access: Mail, fax, online, in person. Both court and visitors may perform in person searches. Search fee: $3.00 per name. Fee is $15.00 to look in closed, stored files. Required to search: name, years to search; also helpful: DOB, SSN. Criminal records computerized from 1989, prior in books to 1982, archived from 1972. Mail turnaround time 2 days. Online access to court records is free at www.perrysburgcourt.com/disc.html.
General Information: No expunged records released. Fee to fax out file $5.00 each. Court makes copy: $.10 per page. Self serve: same. Certification fee: $5.00 per cert. Payee: Municipal Court. Personal checks accepted for criminal and traffic only. Mail requests: SASE required.

Wyandot County

Common Pleas Court 109 S Sandusky Ave, Rm 31, Upper Sandusky, OH 43351; 419-294-1432; probate phone: 419-294-2302; fax: 419-294-6414; 8:30AM-4:30PM. ***Felony, Civil Actions over $10,000, Probate.***
www.co.wyandot.oh.us/clerk/index.html
Civil Records: Access: In person, online. Visitors must perform in person searches themselves. Required to search: name, years to search. Civil cases indexed by defendant, plaintiff; index on computer from 1990, prior in books from late 1800s. Civil PAT goes back to 1/1990. Click on "Common Pleas Inquiry" form web page to view record index.
Criminal Records: Access: Fax, mail, in person, phone, online. Both court and visitors may perform in person searches. No search fee. Required to search: name, years to search; also helpful: SSN. Criminal records computerized from 1990, prior in books from late 1800s. Mail turnaround time 1-2 days. Criminal PAT goes back to same as civil. Click on "Common Pleas Inquiry" at web page to view record index.
General Information: Will fax documents $2.00 1st page, $1.00 ea add'l. Court makes copy: $.10 per page. Self serve: same. Certification fee: $1.00 per page. Payee: Clerk of Court. Personal checks accepted; credit cards are not. Mail requests: SASE required.

Upper Sandusky Municipal Court 119 N 7th St, Upper Sandusky, OH 43351; 419-294-3354; criminal phone: ask for probation dept; civil phone: ask for civil; fax: 419-209-0474; 8AM-4:30PM. ***Misdemeanor, Civil Actions under $15,000, Eviction, Small Claims.***
Civil Records: Access: Mail, in person. Only the court performs in person searches; visitors may not. Search fee: $10.00 per name found if extensive. No charge of SASE or toll free fax provided. Required to search: name, years to search. Civil cases indexed by defendant, plaintiff; index on computer from 5/90, prior in books. Mail turnaround time 1-2 days.
Criminal Records: Access: Mail, in person. Only the court performs in person searches; visitors may not. Search fee: $10.00 per name found if extensive. No charge of SASE or toll free fax provided. Required to search: name, DOB, SSN. Criminal records computerized from 5/90, prior in books. Mail turnaround time 1-2 days.
General Information: No sealed records released. Will fax documents to local or toll-free number. Court makes copy for no fee. Self serve: $.50 per page.The $.50 per page self-serve copy fee includes certification. Certification fee: $1.00 per page includes copy fee. Payee: Upper Sandusky. Personal checks accepted; proper ID required. Credit cards not accepted for phone orders. Mail requests: SASE required.

Ohio Recording Offices

ORGANIZATION: 88 counties, 88 recording offices. The recording officer is the County Recorder. State tax liens are managed by the Clerk of Common Pleas Court. Ohio is entirely in the Eastern Time Zone (EST).

REAL ESTATE RECORDS: Counties will not perform real estate searches. Real estate copy fee is $2.00 per page, self serve copying at most offices. Certification fee is $1.00 per document. Tax records are located at the Auditor's Office.

UCC RECORDS: Ohio was a dual filing state until July 1, 2001. Financing statements were filed both at the state level and with the County Recorder except for consumer goods, farm related and real estate related collateral which were filed only with the County Recorder. As of July 1, 2001, only real estate related collateral is filed at the county level. Where available (most counties), UCC name search fee is usually $20.00 per debtor.

TAX LIEN RECORDS: Federal tax liens are filed in the "Official Records" of each county. All federal tax liens are filed with the County Recorder where the property is located. All state tax liens are filed with the Clerk of Common Pleas Court. Most counties will not perform a separate federal tax lien search.

OTHER LIENS: Mechanics, workers compensation, judgment.

ONLINE ACCESS: A growing number of Ohio counties offer internet access to assessor/real estate data, usually free. Search UCC filings free statewide at www.sos.state.oh.us/SOS/Uniform%20Commercial%20Code.aspx.

Adams County

County Recorder, 110 W Main; Courthouse, West Union, OH 45693. 937-544-2513, R/E recording phone-937-258-3315 or 544-5051; fax-937-544-4616; 8AM-4PM.
Index: All in one. Records indexed on a public use terminal back to 1995. Office personnel or visitors may perform searches. Search fee $20.00 per name. Office will not search real estate records. Copy fee $2.00 per page. Cert fee- $1.00 per cert plus copy fee. Payee- Adams County Recorder. **Other phones:** Treasurer- 937-544-2317; Elections- 937-544-2633; Vital Records- 937-544-5547. **Property tax/Assessing**- 937-544-2364. (Appraiser/Auditor- 937-544-2364) **Online access**- Access the treasurer and auditor property tax data free at http://adamspropertymax.governmaxa.com/propertymax/rover30.asp.

Allen County

County Recorder, PO Box 1243, Lima, OH 45802. 419-223-8517; fax-419-223-8555; 8AM-4:30PM (EST) www.co.allen.oh.us/rec.php
Index: All in one. Records indexed on a public use terminal back to 1989. Only the public may search. Copy fee $2.00 per page. Cert fee- $1.00 per cert plus $.50. Payee- Allen County Recorder. **Online access to Real Estate, Deed, Mortgage, Lien records:** Access recorder index and images free after registration, username and password at http://recorder.allencountyohio.com/ext/logon.asp. Contact the clerk office for sign-up or get user agreement info at www.co.allen.oh.us/rec.php. **Other phones:** Treasurer- 419-223-8515. **Online Records-** Access auditor property data free at http://oh-allen-auditor.governmaxa.com/propertymax/rover30.asp

Ashland County

County Recorder, 142 W 2nd St; Courthouse, Ashland, OH 44805-2193. Recording, R/E & UCC phone-419-282-4238; 8AM-4PM (EST) www.ashlandcounty.org/recorder/index.htm
Index: Separate indices to search include 1846-1995 books, 1995 forward on computer. Records indexed on 3 public use terminals back to 5/1995. Office will perform a UCC search but public must search other records themselves. UCC search per debtor name- $20.00. UCC copy fee $2.00 per page (no self-serve). Self-serve- $.10 per page. Cert fee- $1.00 per cert plus copy fee. Payee- Ashland County Recorder. **Other phones:** Treasurer- 419-282-4229; Elections- 419-282-4224; Vital Records- 419-282-4231. **Property tax/Assessing**- 142 W 2nd St, Courthouse, Ashland, OH 44805-2193; 419-282-4330. (Appraiser 419-282-4330) www.ashlandcounty.org/auditor/index.htm **Online access**- Access property records and sales on the Auditor's database free at www.ashlandcoauditor.org/propertymax/rover30.asp.

Ashtabula County

County Recorder, 25 W Jefferson St, Jefferson, OH 44047. 440-576-3762; fax-440-576-3231; 8AM-4:30PM. www.co.ashtabula.oh.us
Index: All in one. Records indexed on computer from 1984. Office personnel searches UCC, must have UCC search form and $20.00 fee, otherwise visitors perform searches. Office can give specific real estate information - filed date, deed volume/page, etc.- over phone. Copy fee $2.00 per page. Self serve- $.25 each. Cert fee- $1.00 per cert plus copy fee. Payee- Ashtabula County Recorder. Bulk data available for purchase on microfilm, contact Judith A Barta, Recorder. **Online access to Real Estate, Deed records:** Search real estate data back to 1/1984 at www.landaccess.com. **Other phones:** Treasurer- 440-576-3727; Elections- 440-576-6915; Vital Records- 440-576-3627; Auditor- 440-576-3783. **Property tax/Assessing**- 25 W Jefferson St, Jefferson, OH 44047; 440-576-3789. A public access terminal is available. **Online** - Property records on the Auditor's database are free at www.ashtabulacountyauditor.org/propertymax/rover30.asp.

Athens County

County Recorder, 15 S Court St, Rm 236, Athens, OH 45701. 740-592-3228; fax-740-592-3229; 8AM-4PM (EST) www.athenscountygovernment.com
Index: All in one. Records indexed on computer back to 1/1/81. Office will perform a UCC search (with proper search form) but public must search other records themselves. Copy fee $2.00 per page. Cert fee- $1.00 per cert plus copy fee. Payee- Athens County Recorder. Office does sell bulk data, contact ACS Company at 888-363-6720. **Online access to Real Estate, Deed, UCC, Lien, Mortgage records:** Access to county land and UCC records is free at www.landaccess.com. Records go back to 1/1981. **Other phones:** Treasurer- 740-592-3231; Elections- 740-592-3201; Vital Records- 740-592-3251; Auditor- 740-592-3223; Microfilm Dept -740-592-3271. **Property tax/Assessing**- 15 S Court St, 3rd Fl, Athens, 45701; 740-592-3223. (Appraiser - 740-592-3223) **Online** - Search auditor's data by name at www.athenscountyauditor.org/PropertySearch/.

Auglaize County

County Recorder, 209 S Blackhoof St, Rm 103, Wapakoneta, OH 45895-1972. 419-739-6735; fax-419-739-6736; 8AM-4:30PM.
Index: All in one. Records indexed on computer back to 1950. Office will perform a UCC search but public must search other records themselves. UCC search per debtor name- $20.00. Copy fee $2.00 per page, $.25 self serve. Cert fee- $1.00 per cert plus copy fee. Payee- County Recorder. **Online Real Estate, Deed, Lien, UCC records:** Search recorder data free at www.landaccess.com/sites/oh/disclaimer.php?county=auglaize. Records from 1/11950 forward. **Other phones:** Treasurer- 419-739-6745; Elections- 419-739-6720; Auditor- 419-739-6705. **Other Online Records-** Look-up assessor property tax data free at www.auglaizeauditor.ddti.net/.

Belmont County

County Recorder, 101 Main St, St. Clairsville, OH 43950. 740-695-2121; fax-740-699-2140; 8:30AM-4:30PM (EST) www.belmontcountyohio.org
Fax "extension number" is x198. Index: All in one. Records indexed on a public use terminal back to 1992. Office will perform a UCC search but public must search other records themselves. Search fee $20.00 flat fee. Copy fee $2.00 per page, $2.00 for computer printout. Cert fee- $1.00 per cert plus copy fee. Payee- Belmont County Recorder. **Online access to Real Estate, Deed, Mortgage records:** Access to recorder deed data is free at www.landaccess.com/sites/oh/disclaimer.php?county=belmont. **Other phones:** Treasurer- 740-695-2120 x211; Vital Records- 740-695-1202; Auditor- 740-695-2120 x257. **Property tax/Assessing**- 101 Main St, St. Clairsville, OH 43950; 740-699-2130, assessor fax-740-699-2154. A public access terminal is available. www.belmontcountyohio.org/auditor.htm **Online-** property records free at www.belmontcountyohio.org/auditor.htm. Also, search auditor records at http://belmontpropertymax.governmaxa.com/propertymax/rover30.asp.

Brown County

County Recorder, 800 Mt Orab Pike, #151; Admin Bldg, Georgetown, OH 45121. 937-378-6478; fax-937-378-2848; 8AM-4PM.
Index: All in one. Records indexed on a public use terminal back to 1994. Only the public may search. Copy fee $2.00 per page; $.10 each self serve. Cert fee- $1.00 per cert plus $2.00 per page copy fee. Payee- Brown County Recorder. Bulk data available from ACS at 1-888-363-6720. **Online Real Estate, Deed, UCC records:** Access to recordings is free at www.landaccess.com/sites/oh/disclaimer.php?county=brown. Also, access to parcel information for free go to http://brownauditor.ddti.net/ . **Other phones:** Treasurer- 937-378-6705; Elections- 937-378-3008. **Property tax/Assessing**- 800 Mt Orab Pike,

Georgetown, OH 45121; 937-378-6398, assessor fax- 937-378-6038. (Appraiser/Auditor- 937-378-6398) hours- 8AM-4:30PM www.browncountyauditor.org/ **Online**- Visit www.browncountygis.com/PUBLICMAP/PUBLICMAP.HTM for parcel info and maps.

Butler County

County Recorder, 130 High St, Hamilton, OH 45011. 513-887-3192; fax-513-887-3198; 8AM-4:30PM (EST) www.butlercountyohio.org/recorder/
Index: All in one. Records indexed on a public use terminal back to 1987. Office will perform a UCC search but public must search other records themselves. Search fee-$20.00 per name. Copy fee $2.00 per page from books; $.10 per page for computer images (in-house only). Cert fee- $1.00 per cert plus copy fee. Payee- Butler County Recorder. Office does sell bulk data, contact Denise. **Online Real Estate, Deed, UCC, Probate, Voter Registration, Vendor, Veteran records:** Access recorded documents free athttp://66.117.197.57/eSearch/User/Login.aspx; no images available. Login as Guest. Also, county voter records are at www.butlercountyelections.org/index.cfm?page=voterSearch. Also, search county vendors lists free at www.butlercountyauditor.org/index.cfm?page=vl_search. Also, search veteran grave and veteran discharge data free at www.butlercountyohio.org/recorder/index.cfm?page=vetInfo. **Other phones:** Treasurer- 513-887-3181; Elections- 513-887-3700; Vital Records- 513-863-1770; Auditor- 513-887-3295. **Property tax/Assessing**- 130 High St, 3rd & 4th Fl, Hamilton, OH 45011; 513-887-3154, assessor fax- 513-785-5314. (Appraiser 513-887-3147) www.butlercountyauditor.org/ **Online**- Search auditor property records free at http://propertysearch.butlercountyohio.org/butler/Main/Home.aspx. Search tax bills/payments by name free at https://epay.butlercountyohio.org/payment/portal.exe. The sheriff's tax sale list is at www.butlersheriff.org.

Carroll County

County Recorder, PO Box 550, Carrollton, OH 44615-0550. 330-627-4545; fax-330-627-4295; 8AM-4PM www.carrollcountyohio.us/recorder.html
Index: All in one. Records indexed on a public use terminal back to 1990. Only the public may search. Copy fee $2.00 per page. Cert fee- $1.00 per doc plus copy fee. Payee- Carroll County Recorder. **Online access to Real Estate, Deed records:** Free access to recorded documents back to 1/1990 at www.landaccess.com. **Other phones:** Treasurer- 330-627-4221; Elections- 330-627-2610. **Property tax/Assessing**- 119 S Lisbon, Courthouse, Carrollton, OH 44615; 330-327-2250, assessor fax- 330-627-7555. (Appraiser 330-627-2250) **Online**- Access to Auditor's property data is free at http://carrollpropertymax.governmaxa.com/propertymax/rover30.asp.

Champaign County

County Recorder, 1512 S US Hwy 680, #B200, Urbana, OH 43078. 937-484-1630; fax-937-484-1628; 8AM-4PM. www.co.champaign.oh.us/auditor/
Index: Separate indices. Records indexed on a public use terminal back to 1997. Office will perform a UCC search but public must search other records themselves. Search fee- $20.00. Copy fee $2.00 per page if clerk does it, $.25 if you do it yourself. Cert fee- $1.00 per cert plus copy fee. Payee- County Recorder. Bulk data (index only) available for purchase. **Other phones:** Treasurer- 937-484-1640; Auditor- 937-484-1600. **Property tax/Assessing**- 1512 S US Hwy 68, #B300, Urbana, OH 43078; 937-484-1600, assessor fax- 937-484-1626. **Online access**- Online access to property records is free at http://champaignoh.ddti.net/.

Clark County

County Recorder, PO Box 1406, Springfield, OH 45501. 937-521-1705; fax-937-328-4620; 8AM-4:30PM. www.co.clark.oh.us/
Index: All in one. Records indexed on a public use terminal back to 1988. Office will perform a UCC search (with advance payment) but public must search other records themselves. Copy fee $2.00 per page. Cert fee- $1.00 per cert plus copy fee. Payee- Clark County Recorder. **Online access to Real Estate, Deed, UCC records:** Access to county land and UCC records is free at www.landaccess.com. Records go back to 1/1988. **Other phones:** Treasurer- 937-521-1832; Elections- 937-521-2120; Vital Records- 937-390-5600; Auditor- 937-521-1891. **Property tax/Assessing**- PO Box 1325, 31 N Limestone St, Springfield, OH 45501; 937-521-1860. www.clarkcountyohio.gov/auditor/Index.htm **Online access**- Access to property records and GIS/mapping for free go to www.gis.co.clark.oh.us/

Clermont County

County Recorder, 101 E Main St, Batavia, OH 45103-2958. Recording, R/E & UCC phone-513-732-7236; fax-513-732-7891; 8AM-4:30PM (EST) http://recorder.clermontcountyohio.gov/
Index: All in one. Records indexed on a public use terminal back to 1993. Office will perform a UCC search but public must search other records themselves. Search fee $20.00 plus copy fee. Office will not search real estate records. Copy fee $2.00 per page if the clerk does it, $.25 if you do it yourself. Cert fee- $1.00 per doc plus copy fee. Payee- Clermont County Treasurer. Bulk data available for purchase, contact Cindy Hauck. **Online access to Real Estate, Deed, UCC, Property, Sex Offender, Child Support records:** Access to the recorder's property, deed, and UCC records at www.landaccess.com. **Other phones:** Treasurer- 513-732-7254; Elections- 513-732-7275; Auditor- 513-732-7150. **Property tax/Assessing**- Auditor, 101 E Main St, Batavia, OH 45103-2958; 513-732-7150, assessor fax- 513-732-7228. A public access terminal is available for record searches at the office. www.clermontauditorrealestate.org/Main/Home2.aspx **Online access**- Records from the auditor's county property database are free at www.clermontauditorrealestate.org/Main/Home2.aspx.

Clinton County

County Recorder, 46 S South St; Courthouse, Wilmington, OH 45177. Recording, R/E & UCC phone-937-382-2067; fax-937-382-8097; 8AM-4PM (EST) http://co.clinton.oh.us/recorder
Index: All in one. Records indexed on a public use terminal back to 1981. Office will perform a UCC search but public must search other records themselves. UCC search per debtor name- $20.00; $5.00 for limited search of 1 UCC document. Office will not search real estate records. Copy fee $2.00 per page; $.10 self serve. Cert fee- $.10 per page plus copy fee. Payee- Clinton County Recorder. **Online access to Voter Registration records:** Check names to see if registered to vote free at www.voterfind.com/public/ohclinton/pages/vtrlookup.asp. **Other phones:** Treasurer- 937-382-2224; Elections- 937-382-3537; Vital Records- 937-382-3829; Auditor- 937-382-2250. **Property tax/Assessing**- 46 S South St, Wilmington, OH 45177; 937-382-2250. **Online**- Access the Auditor's property database including weekly sales for free at http://clintonoh.ddti.net/PropertySearch/Home.aspx. Access deed references alphabetically by name at www.clintoncountyohgis.org/DeedReferences.htm.

Columbiana County

County Recorder, 105 S Market St, Rm 104; Recorders Office, Lisbon, OH 44432. 330-424-9517 x641, R/E recording phone-330-424-9515, UCC recording phone-330-424-9517; fax-330-424-5067; 8AM-4PM. www.columbianacounty.org
Index: All in one. Records indexed on a public use terminal back to 1983; deeds, mortgages and leases back to 1966. Office personnel or visitors may perform searches. Search fee $20.00. Office will not search real estate records. Copy fee $2.00 per page. Self serve copy $.25; must buy $10.00 copy card. Cert fee- $1.00 per cert plus copy fee. Payee- Columbiana County Recorder. **Online Real Estate, Deed, UCC records:** Access the recorder index of official records back to 1993 and financing statements back to 3/1995 free at www.ccclerk.org/resolution/default.asp. **Other phones:** Treasurer- 330-424-9514. **Other Online Records**- Access property records and tax sale land on the Auditor's database free at www.columbianacntyauditor.org/propertymax/rover30.asp.

Coshocton County

County Recorder, PO Box 817, Coshocton, OH 43812. 740-622-2817; fax-740-295-7352; 8AM-4PM. www.coshoctoncounty.net/
Index: All in one. Records indexed on a public use terminal back to 1980. Office will perform a UCC search but public must search other records themselves. UCC search per debtor name- $20.00. Copy fee $1.00 per page. Computer generated copies- $.25 per page. Fax back fee- $2.00 per page. Cert fee- $1.00 per cert plus $2.00 per page copy fee. Payee- County Recorder. **Online access to Real Estate, Deed, UCC, GIS-mapping records:** Access to county land and UCC records is free at www.landaccess.com. Records go back to 1/1980. Registration required. Also, access to GIS-mapping and deeds for free at www.coshoctoncounty.net/. **Other phones:** Treasurer- 740-622-2713; Elections- 740-622-1117; Auditor- 740-622-1243. **Online**- property tax recs free at www.coshcoauditor.org; click on "Property Search."

Crawford County

County Recorder, 112 E Mansfield St, #206, Bucyrus, OH 44820-0788. Recording, R/E & UCC phone-419-562-6961; fax-419-562-6061; 8:30AM-4:30PM.
Index: All in one. Records indexed on a public use terminal back to 0101/1993. Office will perform a UCC search but public must search other records themselves. UCC search per debtor name- $20.00. Copy fee $2.00 per page. Cert fee- $1.00 per cert plus copy fee. Payee- Crawford County Recorder. **Other phones:** Treasurer- 419-562-7861; Elections- 419-562-8721. **Property tax/Assessing**- 112 E Mansfield St, Bucyrus, OH 44820; 419-562-7941, assessor fax- 419-562-2139. (Appraiser 419-562-7941) **Online**- Access the auditor database free at www.crawford-co.org/auditor/default.html. Access to GIS-mapping for free at http://gis.crawford-co.org/giswebsite/viewer.htm. Owner search is in the lower right.

Cuyahoga County

County Recorder, 1219 Ontario St, Rm 220, Cleveland, OH 44113. 216-443-7300, R/E recording phone-216-443-7300, 216-443-8194, UCC recording phone-216-443-7300; fax-216-443-8193; 8:30AM-4:30PM (EST) http://recorder.cuyahogacounty.us
Records indexed_on a public use terminal. Office personnel or visitors may perform searches. General index search fee $4.00 per 15 minutes. Office will not search real estate records. UCC search per debtor name- $20.00. Will not do federal tax lien search. Copy fee $2.00 per page. Cert fee- $1.00 per cert plus copy fee. Payee- Cuyahoga County Recorder. **Online Real Estate, Deed, Lien, Probate, Marriage, Death records:** Access the Recorders database free at http://recorder.cuyahogacounty.us/Searchs/GeneralSearchs.aspx; includes land documents from 1810-2006. Also, 22 categories of Probate records including marriages at http://probate.cuyahogacounty.us/pa/. **Other phones:** Vitals- 216-664-2317. **Online**- Search the auditor property tax database free at http://auditor.cuyahogacounty.us/repi/default.asp. Access vendors list at https://auditor.cuyahogacounty.us/genservices/vendorList_report.asp. Also, a private company sells county tax claim property, view list free at www.xspand.com/investors/realestate_sale/index.aspx.

Darke County

County Recorder, 504 S Broadway; Courthouse, Greenville, OH 45331. 937-547-7390; 8:30AM-4:30PM (EST) www.co.darke.oh.us
Index: Separate indices to search include abstract indexes, military discharges. Records indexed on a

public use terminal back to 6/96 (scanning 8/00). Office will perform a UCC search but public must search other records themselves. Search fee $20.00 plus $4.00 each name. Copy fee $2.00 per page; self serve- $.25 per page. Cert fee- $1.00 per doc plus copy fee. Payee- Darke County Recorder. **Other phones:** Treasurer- 937-547-7365; Elections- 937-548-1835; Vital Records- 937-547-7361; Auditor- 937-547-7310; Probate Court -937-547-7345. **Property tax/Assessing**- Same address as recording office. 937-547-7310, assessor fax- 937-547-7342. hours- 8AM-4:30PM A public access terminal is available. **Online access**- Property and property tax records on the Darke County database are free at http://darkepropertymax.governmax.com/propertymax/rover30.asp?.

Defiance County

County Recorder, 221 Clinton St; Courthouse, Defiance, OH 43512. Recording, R/E & UCC phone-419-782-4741; fax-419-782-3421; 8:30AM-4:30PM (EST) www.defiance-county.com/recorder/index.html
Index: Separate indices to search up to 1997 had separate indexes; have Official Records beginning 1997. Records indexed on a public use terminal back to 6/94. Office will perform a UCC search for $20.00 per anme but the public must search other records themselves. Copy fee $2.00 per page; self serve $.25. Cert fee- $1.00 per cert plus copy fee. Payee- Defiance County Recorder. **Other phones:** Treasurer- 419-782-8741. **Property tax/Assessing**- 221 Clinton St, Courthouse, Defiance, OH 43512; 419-784-3111. (Appraiser/Auditor- 419-784-3111) A public access terminal is available for record searches. www.defiance-county.com/auditor/index.html **Online access**- Access auditor real estate data free at http://defiance.ddti.net/.

Delaware County

County Recorder, 140 N Sandusky St, Delaware, OH 43015. 740-833-2460; fax-740-833-2459; 8:30AM-4:30PM (EST) www.co.delaware.oh.us
Index: All in one. Records indexed on a public use terminal back to 1990. Office will perform a UCC search but public must search other records themselves. UCC search per debtor name- $20.00 and $2.00 per page for any findings. Copy fee $2.00 per page. Cert fee- $1.00 per cert plus copy fee. Payee- Delaware County Recorder. Bulk data available for purchase, contact Kelley Tenat. **Online access to Real Estate, Deed, UCC records:** Access to the Recorder's data plus UCCs is free at www.landaccess.com. **Other phones:** Treasurer- 740-833-2480. **Property tax/Assessing**- Same address as recording office. 740-833-2900, assessor fax- 740-833-2899. A public access terminal is available. www.delawarecountyauditor.org/ **Online**- Access auditor's property and sales data free at www.delawarecountyauditor.org/propertymax/rover30.asp?.

Erie County

County Recorder, 247 Columbus Ave, Rm 225; Erie County Office Bldg, Sandusky, OH 44870-2635. 419-627-7686, R/E recording phone-419-627-7661, UCC recording phone-419-627-7686; fax-419-627-6639; 8AM-4PM (EST) www.erie-county-ohio.net
Index: Separate indices to search include prior to 1990 are indexed in different categories. Records indexed on computer back to 9/90. Office personnel or visitors may perform searches. Office will search real estate records. Office will not search UCC records. Copy fee $2.00 per page; self serve $.10. Cert fee- $1.00 per doc plus copy fee. Payee- Erie County Recorder. **Online access to Real Estate, Deed records:** Access recorded documents free at www.co-erie-oh-us-recorder.com/recordmax/record40.asp?sid=4D477A86B00549F3BAFE7625E9AE91D1. **Other phones:** Treasurer- 419-627-7201; Auditor- 419-627-7741. **Property tax/Assessing**- 247 Columbus Ave, Rm 210, County Office Bldg, Sandusky, OH 44870; 419-627-7746, assessor fax- 419-627-7740. (Appraiser/Auditor- 419-627-7746) **Online access**- Access the auditor property database including weekly sales for free at www.erie.iviewtaxmaps.com/PropertySearch/Home.aspx

Fairfield County

County Recorder, PO Box 2420, Lancaster, OH 43130-5420. 740-687-7100; fax-740-687-7104; 8AM-4PM (EST) www.co.fairfield.oh.us
Index: Separate indices to search include deed, mortgage, misc, UCC, release, lease, OR. Records indexed on a public use terminal back to 8/96. Only the public may search. Copy fee $2.00 per page. Cert fee- $1.00 per cert plus copy fee. Payee- Fairfield County Recorder. **Online access to Real Estate, Deed, UCC records:** Access to county land and UCC records is free at www.landaccess.com. Records go back to 08/96. Also, access to the sheriff's real estate sale list at www.sheriff.fairfield.oh.us/. **Other phones:** Treasurer- 740-687-7094; Auditor- 740-687-7090. **Property tax/Assessing**- 210 E Main St, Courthouse, Lancaster, OH 43130; 740-687-7028. **Online** - Access to the Auditor's property and sales database is free at http://realestate.co.fairfield.oh.us/. Also, access to the sheriff's real estate sale list at www.sheriff.fairfield.oh.us/.

Fayette County

County Recorder, 133 S Main St, Washington Court House, OH 43160-1393. 740-335-1770; fax-740-333-3521; 8AM-4PM. www.fayette-co-oh.com
Index: Prior to 1997, records are in separate indices- grantor/grantee, deed, mtg release, etc. Records indexed on a public use terminal back to 1978; images go back to 2002. Office will perform a UCC search but public must search other records themselves. Search fee $20.00 per name. Office will not search real estate records. UCC search does not include tax liens. Copy fee $2.00 per page; $.25 self serve. Cert fee- $1.00 per cert plus copy fee. Payee- Recorder. Bulk records may be available from ACS Government Records, a vendor. **Online access to Real Estate, Deed, Lien records:** Access to recorders index database is free at www.landaccess.com. Images go back to 5/20/02. **Other phones:** Treasurer- 740-335-4961; Elections- 740-335-1190; Vital Records- 740-335-5910. **Property tax/Assessing**- 133 S Main St, Washington Court House, OH 43160; 740-335-6461. **Online**- Access the auditor's database for property data at http://fayettepropertymax.governmax.com/propertymax/rover30.asp.

Franklin County

County Recorder, 373 S High St, 18th Fl, Columbus, OH 43215-6307. 614-462-3930, 614-462-3378, R/E recording phone-614-462-3930, UCC recording phone-614-462-3937; fax-614-462-4299; 8:AM-5PM (EST) www.co.franklin.oh.us/recorder/
Index: Separate indices to search include books by year. Plat records indexed on a public use terminal back to 1964, deeds back to 1/2/1914. Office will perform a UCC search but public must search other records themselves. UCC search per debtor name- $20.00. Copy fee $2.00 per page. Cert fee- $1.00 per cert plus copy fee. Payee- Franklin County Recorder. Bulk data is available to purchase on CD-rom, contact Brent Wentzel. **Online access to Real Estate, Deed records:** Access to the recorded data is free at www.co.franklin.oh.us/recorder/search.cfm. **Other phones:** Auditor- 614-462-3894. **Property tax/Assessing**- County Auditor, 373 S High St, 21st Fl, Columbus, Ohio 43215-6310; 614-462-4663. www.franklincountyohio.gov/auditor/ **Online access**- Auditor's property data is at http://franklin.governmaxa.com/propertymax/rover30.asp. Access auditor's GIS-data site with property lookup, history, and more free at http://209.51.193.83/.

Fulton County

County Recorder, 152 S Fulton St, #175, Wauseon, OH 43567. Recording, R/E & UCC phone-419-337-9232; fax-419-337-9282; 8:30AM-4:30PM (EST) www.fultoncountyoh.com
Index: All in one. Records indexed on computer back to 8/95. Office will perform a UCC search but public must search other records themselves. Copy fee $2.00 per page, self serve $.25. Cert fee- $2.00 per cert plus copy fee. Payee- Fulton County Recorder. **Online access to Real Estate, Deed, UCC records:** Access to property, deed, and UCC records is to be free at www.landaccess.com/sites/oh/disclaimer.php?county=ohfulton (indexes only). **Other phones:** Treasurer- 419-337-9252; Elections- 419-335-6841; Vital Records- 419-337-0539; Auditor- 419-337-9200. **Property tax/Assessing**- 152 S Fulton St, #165, Wauseon, OH 43567; 419-337-9200, assessor fax- 419-337-9298. hours- 8:30AM-4PM A public access terminal is available. **Online access**- Search auditor property data and weekly sales free at http://fultonoh-auditor.ddti.net/.

Gallia County

County Recorder, 18 Locust St, Rm 1265, Gallipolis, OH 45631. Recording, R/E-740-446-4612 x246, UCC phone- x315; fax-740-446-4804; 8AM-4PM. www.gallianet.net/Gallia/recorder.htm
Index: Separate indices to search include deeds, mortgages, liens, misc, financing statements. Records indexed on a public use terminal back to 1955 for deeds, 1977 for mortgages, 1995 for leases, 1990 for financial statements, 1986 for Misc. Only the public may search. Copy fee $2.00 per page. Cert fee- $1.00 per cert plus copy fee. Payee- Gallia County Recorder. **Other phones:** Treasurer- 740-446-6004; Auditor- 740-446-4612 x218. **Property tax/Assessing**- 18 Locust St, Rm 1264, Gallipolis, OH 45631; 740-446-4612 x218, assessor fax- 740-446-4804. **Online access**- Property records on the county auditor real estate database are free at http://galliaauditor.ddti.net. Click on "attributes" for property data; click on "sales" to search by real estate attributes. Also, property and GIS-mapping data free at www.gallianet.net/GIS/index.htm.

Geauga County

County Recorder, 231 Main St, #1C; Courthouse Annex, Chardon, OH 44024-1235. Recording, R/E & UCC phone-440-279-2020; 8AM-4:30PM (EST) www.co.geauga.oh.us
Index: All in one. Records indexed on a public use terminal back to 1986. Only the public may search, but will search UCCs if proper form submitted. Search fee-$20.00 for UCC only. Office will not search real estate records. UCC search per debtor name- $20.00. Copy fee $2.00 per page; $.10 self serve. Plat copy- $3.00 per page. Cert fee- $1.00 per cert plus copy fee. Payee- Geauga County Recorder. Bulk data available for purchase, contact Tracy. **Other phones:** Treasurer- 440-279-2000; Elections- 440-279-2030; Vital Records- 440-279-1900. **Property tax/Assessing**- 231 Main St, #1A, Chardon, OH 44024; 440-285-2222 x1640. (Appraiser/Auditor- 440-279-1600) A public access terminal is available for record searches. **Online access**- Search the Auditor's property database at www.co.geauga.oh.us/. Search the sheriff's tax sale lists for free at www.sheriff.geauga.oh.us.

Greene County

County Recorder, PO Box 100, Xenia, OH 45385-0100. Recording, R/E phone-937-562-5270, UCC recording phone-937-562-5278; fax-937-562-5386; 8AM-4:30PM www.co.greene.oh.us/recorder.htm
Index: Separate indices to search include books. Records indexed on a public use terminal back to 1984. Office will perform a UCC search but public must search other records themselves. Search fee $20.00. Copy fee $2.00 per page, self serve $.50. Cert fee- $1.00 per cert plus copy fee. Payee- Greene County Recorder. **Online Real Estate, Grantor/Grantee, Deed, Mortgage, Marriage, Probate records:** Access to the recorders index is free at www.co.greene.oh.us/recorder/documentSearch.asp. Also, search marriages free at www.co.greene.oh.us/Probate/search/marriageLic.asp Search probate cases at www.co.greene.oh.us/Pro

bate/search/case_search.asp. **Other phones:** Treasurer- 937-562-5017; Elections- 937-562-5261; Vital Records- 937-374-5600; Auditor- 937-562-5065. **Property tax/Assessing**- 15 Greene St, Xenia, OH 45385; 937-562-5065, assessor fax- 937-562-5017. (Appraiser/Auditor- 937-562-5064) hours- 7:30AM-4PM **Online access**- Assessor data free at www.co.greene.oh.us/website/gcMaps/. Also, records on Internet Map Server are free at www.co.greene.oh.us/gismapserver.htm - includes owner, address, valuation, taxes, sales data, and parcel ID number.

Guernsey County

County Recorder, 627 Wheeling Ave, #305, Cambridge, OH 43725. 740-432-9275; fax-740-439-6258; 8AM-4PM (EST)
Index: Separate indices to search include 1990 to present full index, prior indexes are separate- deed, mortgage, lien, etc. Records indexed on a public use terminal back to 1990. Office will perform a UCC search but public must search other records themselves. Search fee-$20.00 per name for UCC. Office will not search real estate records. Copy fee $1.00 per page. Cert fee- $1.00 per cert plus copy fee. Payee- Guernsey County Recorder. **Online access to Marriage, Birth, Probate, Will records:** Access to court-related records free at http://74.218.3.68/pa/. **Other phones:** Treasurer- 740-432-9278; Elections- 740-432-2680; Vital Records- 740-432-3577. **Property tax/Assessing**- 627 Wheeling Ave, Rm 301, Cambridge, OH 43725; 740-432-9243, assessor fax- 740-439-6265. (Appraiser/Auditor- 740-432-9243) A public access terminal is available.

Hamilton County

County Recorder, 138 E Court St, Cincinnati, OH 45202. 513-946-4570; fax-513-946-4577; 8AM-4PM (EST) http://recordersoffice.hamilton-co.org
Index: All in one. Records indexed on a public use terminal back to 1988. Office will perform a UCC search but public must search other records themselves. Office will not search real estate records. UCC search does not include tax liens. UCC search per debtor name- $20.00. This agency will not do a state tax lien search. Separate federal tax lien search- $.50 per page. Copy fee $2.00 per page. Cert fee- $1.00 per page plus copy fee. Payee- Hamilton County Recorder. **Online Real Estate, Deed, Lien, Mortgage, UCC, Marriage, Military Discharge, Partnership, Subdivision records:** Access recorder land records free at http://recordersoffice.hamilton-co.org/hcro-pdi/index.jsp. Search the marriage license data at www.probatect.org/case_search/mlsearch.asp. Also, search probate records back to 1/2000 at www.probatect.org/case_search/casesearch.asp. **Other phones:** Treasurer- 513-946-4800. **Other Online Records-** Access the auditor's tax records free at www.hamiltoncountyauditor.org/realestate/.

Hancock County

County Recorder, 300 S Main St; Courthouse, Findlay, OH 45840. Recording, R/E & UCC phone- 419-424-7091; fax-419-423-3017; 8:30AM-4:30PM (EST) http://co.hancock.oh.us/recorder/recorder.htm
Index: Separate indices to search prior to 1986. Records indexed on a public use terminal back to 1986. Office personnel or visitors may perform searches. Office will search real estate records for $20.00 per search plus $2.00 per page for copies. Will search UCC records with proper forms. Copy fee $2.00 per page; self serve $.15. Cert fee- $1.00 per cert plus copy fee. Payee- Hancock County Recorder. Office does not sell bulk data at this time. **Online access to Real Estate, Deed, UCC records:** Access to recorder records is free at www.landaccess.com. Index goes back to 1986; images to 12/19/2000. **Other phones:** Treasurer- 419-424-7213; Elections- 419-422-3245; Vital Records- 419-424-7869; Auditor- 419-424-7083. **Property tax/Assessing**- 300 S Main St, Courthouse, Findlay, OH 45840; 419-424-7015, assessor fax- 419-424-7825. (Appraiser 419-424-7015) **Online access**- Search the auditor's property data free at http://hancock.iviewauditor.com. No name searching.

Hardin County

County Recorder, One Courthouse Sq, #220, Kenton, OH 43326. 419-674-2250; fax-419-675-2802; 8:30AM-4PM; 8:30-4PM Fri. www.co.hardin.oh.us
Index: All in one. Records indexed on a public use terminal back to 1990. Office will perform a UCC search but public must search other records themselves. Office will not search real estate records. UCC search per debtor name- $20.00. Copy fee $.25 per page; fax back- $2.00 per page local, $4.00 if long distance. Cert fee- $2.00 per cert plus copy fee. Payee- Hardin County Recorder. **Other phones:** Treasurer- 419-674-2246; Elections- 419-674-2211. **Property tax/Assessing**- One Courthouse Sq, #229, Kenton, OH 43326; 419-674-2239, assessor fax- 419-674-4023. hours- 8:30AM-4PM **Online access**- Access property records from the auditor's database free at www.co.hardin.oh.us. Click on "Real Estate Internet Inquiry." Also, search property data on the GIS-mapping site at http://hcgis.com. Use QuickSearch.

Harrison County

County Recorder, 100 W Market St; Courthouse, Cadiz, OH 43907. 740-942-8869; fax-740-942-4693; 8:30AM-4:30PM (EST) www.harrisoncountyohio.org
Index: Separate indices to search include grantor/grantee to 12/31/94, abstracts from 1812-current, computer from 1994-current. Records indexed on a public use terminal back to 1994. Images on computer back to 2001. Only the public may search. Copy fee $2.00 per page. Cert fee- $1.00 per cert plus copy fee. Payee- Harrison County Recorder. **Other phones:** Treasurer- 740-942-8864; Elections- 740-942-8866; Vital Records- 740-942-8868; Auditor- 740-942-8861.

Henry County

County Recorder, 660 N Perry St, Rm 202; Courthouse, Napoleon, OH 43545-1747. Recording, R/E & UCC phone-419-592-1766; fax-419-592-1652; 8:30AM-4:30PM (EST) www.henrycountyohio.com
Index: All in one. Records indexed on a public use terminal back to 1990, images back to 2003. Old records purged after 6 years. Only the public may search. Copy fee $2.00 per page; self serve- $.25 per page. Cert fee- $1.00 per cert plus copy fee. Payee- Henry County Recorder. Bulk data available from ACS - Affiliated Computer Services - who manages the recorder data website. **Online Real Estate, Deed, Lien records:** Access recorder data free at www.landaccess.com/sites/oh/disclaimer.php?county=ohhenry. **Other phones:** Treasurer- 419-592-1851. **Property tax/Assessing**- PO Box 546, 660 N. Perry St, 2nd Fl, Courthouse, Napoleon, OH 43545; 419-492-1956, assessor fax- 419-592-4024. www.henrycountyohio.com/auditor.htm **Online-** Access and search property data free at www.co.henry.oh.us/. Click on "Real Estate Internet Inquiry." Also, search sheriff sales list for free at www.henrycountysheriff.com.

Highland County

County Recorder, PO Box 804, Hillsboro, OH 45133. 937-393-9954; fax-937-393-5855; 8:30AM-4PM (EST) www.co.highland.oh.us/
Index: All in one. Records indexed on a public use terminal back to 1989. Office will perform a UCC search but public must search other records themselves. Copy fee $2.00 per item/page. Cert fee- $1.00 per cert plus copy fee. Payee- Highland County Recorder. Bulk data available for purchase, contact Bill Fawley. **Online access to Real Estate, Deed, UCC records:** Access to recorders database is free at www.landaccess.com/sites/oh/disclaimer.php?county=highland. **Other phones:** Treasurer- 937-393-9951; Elections- 937-393-9961; Vital Records- 937-393-1941. **Property tax/Assessing**- PO Box 822, Hillsboro, OH 45133; 937-393-1915, assessor fax- 937-393-3854. (Appraiser/Auditor- 937-393-1915) hours- 7:30AM-4:00PM A public access terminal is available for record searches. www.co.highland.oh.us/ **Online-** Access and search property data free at http://highlandpropertymax.governmaxa.com/propertymax/rover30.asp. Click on "start your search" to begin. Search auditor's tax and sales data for free at www.co.highland.oh.us/. Sheriff's sales lists are free at www.highlandcoso.com/rso.htm.

Hocking County

County Recorder, PO Box 949, Logan, OH 43138. 740-385-2031; fax-740-385-0377; 8:30AM-4PM. www.co.hocking.oh.us
Index: All in one. Records indexed on a public use terminal back to 1992. Office will perform a UCC search but public must search other records themselves. Copy fee $2.00 per page. If self copy-off of computer- fee-$.10 per page. Cert fee- $1.00 per cert plus copy fee. Payee- Recorder. Bulk data available for purchase, contact Auditors office. **Other phones:** Treasurer- 740-385-3517; Elections- 740-380-8683; Vital Records- 740-385-3030; Clerk of Courts- 740-385-2616. **Property tax/Assessing**- 1 E Main St, Courthouse, Logan, OH 43136; 740-385-2127, assessor fax- 740-385-9888. (Appraiser 740-385-2127) hours- 8:30AM-4:30PM A public access terminal is available. www.co.hocking.oh.us/auditor/default.html **Online access**- Access to the auditor's real estate data and dog tag ownership is free at www.co.hocking.oh.us/auditor/default.html.

Holmes County

Recorder, PO Box 213, Millersburg, OH 44654. 330-674-5916; fax-330-674-0782; 8AM-4:30PM (EST)
Index: All in one. Records indexed on a public use terminal back to 1985. Only the public may search. Copy fee $.25 per page. Cert fee- $.25 per cert plus copy fee. Payee- Holmes County Recorder. **Other phones:** Treasurer- 330-674-1896; Auditor- 330-674-1896. **Property tax/Assessing**- 75 E Clilnton St, #107, Millersburg, OH 44654; 330-674-1896, assessor fax- 330-674-9428. hours- 8:30AM-4:30PM www.holmescountyauditor.org **Online access-** Access the auditor's property data and sales free at www.holmescountyauditor.org.

Huron County

County Recorder, 12 E Main St, Norwalk, OH 44857. 419-668-1916; fax-419-663-4052; 8AM-4:30PM. www.huroncountyrecorder.org
Index: All in one. Records indexed on a public use terminal back to 1986. Only the public may search. Copy fee $2.00 per page. Cert fee- $1.00 per cert plus copy fee. Bulk data available for purchase, contact Shannon Thompson. **Online access to Real Estate, Deed, Lien, UCC records:** Search the recorder's land records free at www.huroncountyrecorder.org. **Other phones:** Treasurer- 419-668-2090; Elections- 419-668-8238; Vital Records- 419-668-1652; Auditor- 419-668-4304. **Property tax/Assessing**- 12 E Main St, Norwalk, OH 44857; 419-668-4304. A public access terminal is available. **Online access**- Access to the auditor data and property sales is free at www.huroncountyauditor.org.

Jackson County

County Recorder, 226 E Main St, #1; Courthouse, Jackson, OH 45640. Recording, R/E & UCC phone- 740-286-1919; fax-740-286-8835; 8AM-4PM (EST)
Index: Since 10/2002 the O.R. records in one; prior in individual books. Records indexed on computer, microfiche, abstract books. Office personnel or visitors may perform searches. Search fee $20.00 per name. Office will not search real estate records. Office will not do federal tax lien search. Copy fee $2.00 per page. Self-serve printout from computer is $.10 per page. Cert fee- $1.00 per cert plus copy fee. Payee- Jackson County Recorder. Bulk records may bve available from ACS Government Records, 315-437-1283, a vendor. **Other phones:** Treasurer- 740-286-2402; Elections- 740-286-2905; Auditor- 740-286-4231. **Property tax/Assessing**- 226 E Main St #5, Jackson, OH 45640; 740-286-4231, assessor fax- 740-286-6312. www.jacksoncountyauditor.org/ **Online-**

Access property and sales data free at www.jacksoncountyauditor.org/ -click on Start Search

Jefferson County

County Recorder, 301 Market St; Courthouse, Steubenville, OH 43952. 740-283-8566; fax-740-283-4007; 8:30AM-4:30PM (EST)
Index: All in one. Records indexed on a public use terminal back to 1989. Office will perform a UCC search but public must search other records themselves. Office will search real estate records for $20.00. UCC search per debtor name- $20.00. Copy fee $2.00 per page, $.25 self serve. Cert fee- $2.00 per cert plus copy fee. Payee- Jefferson County Recorder. **Online Voter Registration records:** Search voter names free at www.voterfind.com/public/ohjefferson/pages/vtrlookup.asp. **Other phones:** Treasurer- 740-283-8572; Elections- 740-283-8522. **Property tax/Assessing**- 301 Market St, POB159, Steubenville, 43952; 740-283-8511. www.jeffersoncountyoh.com/cgi-bin/template.pl?auditor/auditor.html **Online access**- Access to the county auditor property data is free at http://public.jeffersoncountyoh.com/realtax/. Download real estate data from auditor's database at http://public.jeffersoncount oh.com/tax/realdown.htm. Access sheriff, treasurer, and auditor foreclosure sales lists free at www.jeffersoncountyoh.com/cgi-bin/template.pl?sheriff/sheriff.html.

Knox County

County Recorder, 117 E High St, Mount Vernon, OH 43050. phone-740-393-6755; 8AM-4PM (EST) www.recorder.co.knox.oh.us
Index: All in one after 1/2003. Records indexed on a public use terminal back to 1981. Office will perform a UCC search but public must search other records themselves. Office will not search real estate records. UCC search per debtor name- $20.00. Copy fee $2.00 per page. Cert fee- $1.00 per cert plus copy fee. Payee- Knox County Recorder. Bulk data available for purchase. **Online Real Estate, Deed, UCC, Plat, Map records:** Access index records free at www.recorder.co.knox.oh.us/Resolution/default.asp. **Other phones:** Treasurer- 740-393-6735; Elections- 740-393-6716; Vital Records- 740-393-2200; Records Center- 740-393-6781. **Property tax/Assessing**- 117 E High St, Mount Vernon, OH 43050; 740-397-6750, fax- 740-393-6806. (Appraiser 740-393-6750) www.knoxcountyauditor.org/ **Online** Online access to property records is available at www.knoxcountyauditor.org/.

Lake County

County Recorder, PO Box 490, Painesville, OH 44077-0490. Recording, R/E phone-440-350-2510, UCC phone-440-350-2511; fax-440-350-5940; 8AM-4PM. www.lakecountyrecorder.org/recorders/
Index: All in one. Records indexed on a public use terminal back to 1986. Office will perform a UCC search (only those currently effective) but public must search other records themselves. Search fee-$20.00 per name. Copy fee $2.00 per page. Cert fee- $1.00 per doc plus copy fee. Payee- Lake County Recorder. Bulk data available for purchase, contact Frank Suponcic. **Online Real Estate, Deed, Lien, UCC records:** Access Recorder's Document Index free at http://www2.lakecountyohio.org/RecordersNewSearch/Search.aspx. Records go back to 1986. UCCs are index only. Images of documents not available. **Other phones:** Treasurer- 440-350-2517; Elections- 440-350-2700; Vital Records- 440-350-2549; Auditor- 440-350-2528. **Property tax/Assessing**- Auditor's Office, 105 Main St, PO Box 490, Painesville, Ohio 44077; 440-350-2534, assessor fax- 440-350-2667. 8AM-4:30PM **Online**- treasurer and auditor's real estate data free at www.lake.iviewauditor.com.

Lawrence County

County Recorder, PO Box 77, Ironton, OH 45638. 740-533-4314; fax-740-533-4411; 8AM-4PM. www.lawrencecountyohiorecorder.org
Index: Separate indices to search include deeds to 1982, liens to 1981, mtgs to 1988. Records (real estate) indexed on computer back to 1988. Office will perform a UCC search but public must search other records themselves. Search fee $20.00. Office will not search real estate or historic UCC records. Copy fee $2.00 per page. Cert fee- $1.00 per cert plus copy fee. Payee- County Recorder. Bulk data available for purchase, contact Chris Kline. **Online access to Real Estate, Deed, Lien, Mortgage records:** Access to the recorders database is free at www.lawrencecountyohiorecorder.org/record_search.htm. Deeds go back to 1982; mortgages to 1988; liens back to 1981. **Other phones:** Treasurer- 740-533-4304; Elections- 740-533-4320; Vital Records- 740-532-2172. **Property tax/Assessing**- 111 S 4th St, Courthouse, Ironton, OH 45638; 740-533-4310, assessor fax- 740-533-4381. A public access terminal is available. **Online access**- Search the auditor's data free at www.lawrencecountyauditor.org.

Licking County

County Recorder, PO Box 520, Newark, OH 43058. 740-670-5300, R/E phone-740-670-5301; fax-740-670-5303; 8AM-4:30PM. www.lcounty.com/rec/
Index: All in one. Records indexed on computer back to 1968. Office will perform a UCC search but public must search other records themselves. Copy fee $2.00 per page. Cert fee- $1.00 per doc plus copy fee. Payee- Licking County Recorder. **Online access to Real Estate, Deed, Lien records:** Access to the recorders database is free at www.lcounty.com/recordings/. Records with images go back to 1984. **Other phones:** Treasurer- 740-670-5010; Elections- 740-670-5080. **Property tax/Assessing**- 20 S 2nd St, Newark, OH 43055; 740-670-5040. (Appraiser/Auditor- 740-670-5040) **Online access**- Access the Assessor's county property database free at www.lcounty.com/itrac/feedback.php

Logan County

County Recorder, 100 S Madriver, #A, Bellefontaine, OH 43311-2075. Recording, R/E & UCC phone-937-599-7201; fax-937-599-7287; 8:30AM-4:30PM (EST) www.co.logan.oh.us/recorder/index.html
Index: All in one after 9/1985. Records indexed on a public use terminal back to 00. Only the public may search, but clerk searches UCC. Search fee-UCC's only $12.00 plus $4.00 per name. Office will not search real estate records. Tax liens not included in UCC search. Copy fee $2.00 per page. If public makes copies without help $.25 per page. Cert fee- $1.00 per cert plus copy fee. Payee- Logan County Recorder. **Online access to Real Estate, Deed, Lien, Delinquent Property records:** recorders data is free http://www3.co.logan.oh.us/recordmax401/record40.asp. Click on "Document Search." Treasurer's delinquent property tax lists free at www.co.logan.oh.us/Treasurer/Delinquent_Real.htm . **Other phones:** Treasurer- 937-599-7223; Elections- 937-599-7255; Vital Records- 937-592-9040; Auditor- 937-599-7213. **Property tax/Assessing**- 100 S Madriver St, Rm 103, Jail Office Complex, Bellefontaine, OH 43311; 937-599-7209. www.co.logan.oh.us/auditor/ **Online access**- Records on the County Auditor's database are free at http://lcaweb.co.logan.oh.us/aweb/. Search sheriff's sales at www.co.logan.oh.us/sheriff/sales.htm.

Lorain County

County Recorder, 226 Middle Ave, 1st Fl, Elyria, OH 44035. 440-329-5148; fax-440-329-5477; 8AM-4:30PM. www.loraincounty.com/recorder/
Index: Separate indices to search. Records indexed on a public use terminal back to 1990. Only the public may search. Copy fee $2.00 per page. Cert fee- $1.00 per page plus copy fee. **Online access to Real Estate, Deed, Lien records:** Access the county Indexed Records database at www.loraincounty.com/recorder/ has been removed from the internet indefinitely. **Other phones:** Treasurer- 440-329-5256. **Property tax/Assessing**- 226 Middle Ave 2nd Fl, Elyria, OH 44035; 440-329-5207. (Appraiser/Auditor- 440-329-5207) www.loraincounty.com/auditor/ **Online access**- Access property records and sales on the County Auditor's database for free at http://oh-lorain-auditor.governmaxa.com/propertymax/rover30.asp. Search sheriff sales lists for free at www.loraincountysheriff.com.

Lucas County

County Recorder, 1 Government Ctr, #700; Jackson St, Toledo, OH 43604. 419-213-4400; fax-419-213-4284; 8AM-5PM (EST) www.co.lucas.oh.us/
Index: All in one. Records indexed on a public use terminal back to 1985. Office will perform a UCC search but public must search other records themselves. Copy fee $2.00 per page, $.05 self serve. Cert fee- $2.00 per cert plus copy fee. Payee- Lucas County Recorder. Office does sell bulk data, contact Julie East. **Online Real Estate, Deed records:** Access to recorder real estate records is free with registration at http://apps.co.lucas.oh.us/rec/logon.asp. **Other phones:** Treasurer- 419-213-4303; Vital Records- 419-213-4100; Auditor- 419-213-4420. **Property tax/Assessing**- 1 Government Ctr, #500, Jackson St, Toledo, OH 43604; see above. **Online access**- Property records go on the County Auditor's Real Estate Information System (AREIS) free at www.co.lucas.oh.us/real_estate/AREISmain/areismain.asp.

Madison County

County Recorder, 1 N Main St, Rm 40; Courthouse, London, OH 43140. 740-852-1854; fax-740-845-1776; 8AM-4PM (EST) www.co.madison.oh.us
Index: All in one. Records indexed on a public use terminal back to 5/1/94. Office will perform a UCC search but public must search other records themselves. Copy fee $2.00 per page. Self-serve- $.10 each. Cert fee- $1.00 per cert plus copy fee. Payee- Madison County Recorder. **Online Real Estate, Deed, UCC records:** Access recorder's office records free at www.co.madison.oh.us/436/41301.html or www.landaccess.com/sites/oh/disclaimer.php?county=madison. Records go back to 5/1994. **Other phones:** Treasurer- 740-852-1936; Elections- 740-852-9425; Vital Records- 740-852-3065; Auditor- 740-852-9717. **Property tax/Assessing**- PO Box 47, London, OH 43140; 740-852-9717, assessor fax- 740-852-5752. **Online access**- Access records on the County Auditor's database free at www.co.madison.oh.us/373/24285.html. Also, access to the sheriff's sale list is at www.madisonsheriff.org.

Mahoning County

County Recorder, PO Box 928, Youngstown, OH 44501. 330-740-2345; fax-330-740-2347; 8AM-4:30PM. www.mahoningcountyoh.gov
Index: Separate indexes to search. Records indexed on a public use terminal back to 1985. Office personnel or visitors may perform searches. Search fee-$20.00. Copy fee $2.00 per page, $.10 per page self serve. Cert fee- $1.00 per cert plus copy fee. Payee- County Recorder. **Online access to Real Estate, Deed, UCC, Lien, Judgment records:** Access to recorder's property, deed, and UCC records is to be free at www.co.madison.oh.us/436/41301.html. Records go back to 1985. **Other phones:** Treasurer- 330-740-2460; Elections- 330-783-2474; Vital Records- 330-743-3333 x231; Auditor- 330-740-2010. **Property tax/Assessing**- 120 Market St, Youngstown, OH 44501; 330-740-2010. (Appraiser 330-740-2010) www.mahoningcountyauditor.org **Online**- Property tax records on the Auditor's database are free at http://ohmahoningpropertymax.governmaxa.com/propertymax/rover30.asp. Also, access property data free on the GIS mapping site at http://gis.mahoningcountyoh.gov/gis/asp.htm.

Marion County

County Recorder, 222 W Center St, Marion, OH 43302-3646. Recording, R/E & UCC phone-740-223-4100; fax-740-223-4109; 8:30AM-4:30PM (EST) http://mcoprx.co.marion.oh.us/recorder/
Index: All in one. Records indexed. In person- only the public may search but staff may help. $20.00 per name. Include SASE with mail requests. Office will search UCC records, but not tax liens or RE. Copy fee

$2.00 per page. Self-serve copies-$.10 per page. Will fax back doc for $4 per page to toll free, $6 per page to non-toll-free. Cert fee- $1.00 per cert plus copy fee. Payee- Marion County Recorder. Office does not sell bulk data at this time. **Online Real Estate, Grantor/ Grantee, Deed, Lien, Plat, UCC, Partnership records:** Access the recorders index after registration at http://recorder.co.marion.oh.us/resolution/. May change URL; check at Recorder website. Official records go back to 1983; UCCs to 1990; plats back to 1820. **Other phones:** Treasurer- 740-223-4030; Elections- 740-223-4090; Auditor- 740-223-4020. **Property tax/Assessing**- 222 W Center St, Marion, OH 43302-3646; 740-223-4020. (Appraiser/Auditor- 740-223-4020) **Online access**- Access to the county auditor real estate database is free at www.co.marion.oh.us/auditor/index1.htm. Click on "Real Estate Internet Inquiry." Also, sheriff sales list at www.co.marion.oh.us/sheriffsales/public_view.asp.

Medina County

County Recorder, 144 N Broadway; County Admin Bldg, Medina, OH 44256-2295. Recording, R/E & UCC phone-330-725-9782; 8AM-4:30PM (EST) www.recorder.co.medina.oh.us

Index: All in one. Records indexed on a public use terminal back to 1970's. Only the public may search. Copy fee $2.00 per page, $.20 per page for maps, $.10 per page if printed from public terminals. Cert fee- $1.00 per cert plus copy fee. Payee- Medina County Recorder. **Online Real Estate, Deed, Mortgage records:** Access to indexes 1983 to present on the recorder database is free at www.recorder.co.medina.oh.us/fcquery.htm. **Property tax/Assessing**- 330-725-9754. **Online**-- Access property records, dog tags, and unclaimed funds on the Medina County Auditor database free at www.medinacountyauditor.org/allsearches.htm. Sheriff's county tax sale list is free at www.medinacountyauditor.org/shersale/.

Meigs County

County Recorder, 100 E 2nd St; Courthouse, Pomeroy, OH 45769. 740-992-3806; fax-740-992-2867; 8:30AM-4:30PM (EST)

Index: Separate indices to search include from 1820 - 1993 index books, 1994 to present on computer. Records indexed on a public use terminal back to 1994. Only the public may search. Copy fee $2.00 per page. Cert fee- $1.00 per cert plus copy fee. Payee- Meigs County Recorder. **Other phones:** Treasurer- 740-992-2004; Auditor- 740-992-5290. **Property tax/Assessing**- 100 E 2nd St, County Courthouse, Pomeroy, Ohio 45769; 740-992-2698, assessor fax- 740-992-6289. (Appraiser/Auditor- 740-992-2004)

Mercer County

County Recorder, 101 N Main St, Rm 203; Courthouse Sq, Celina, OH 45822. 419-586-4232; fax-419-586-3541; 8:30AM-5PM M; 8:30AM-4PM T-F. (EST) www.mercercountyohio.org/recorder/

Index: All in one. Records indexed on a public use terminal back to 1996. Only the public may search. Copy fee $2.00 per page. Cert fee- $1.00 per cert plus copy fee. Payee- Mercer County Recorder. **Online access to Real Estate, Deed, Lien, Mortgage, Judgment, UCC records:** Access recorder data free at http://www2.mercercountyohio.org/oncoreweb42/ . **Other phones:** Treasurer- 419-586-2259; Elections- 419-586-2215. **Property tax/Assessing**- 101 N Main St Rm 105, Celina, OH 45822. (Appraiser/Auditor- 419-586-6402) **Online access**- Access property records on County Auditor Real Estate database free at www.mercercountyohio.org/auditor/ParcelSearch/.

Miami County

County Recorder, PO Box 653, Troy, OH 45373. 937-440-6040, R/E recording phone-937-440-5925, fax-937-440-6041; 7:30AM-4:30PM http://co.miami.oh.us/A55969/mcounty.nsf/All/Recorder

Index: All in one. Records indexed on a public use terminal back to 7/1/97. Only the public may search. Office will help with searches. Search fee $20.00 for UCC. Copy fee $2.00 per page. Cert fee- $1.00 per cert plus copy fee. Payee- Miami County Recorder. Bulk data available for purchase, contact Dona. **Other phones:** Treasurer- 937-440-6045; Elections- 937-440-3900; Auditor- 937-440-5925. **Property tax/Assessing**- 201 W Main St, Troy, OH 45373; 937-440-5925. (Appraiser/Auditor- 937-440-5925) **Online access**- Access auditor data free at www.miamicountyauditor.org.

Monroe County

County Recorder, PO Box 152, Woodsfield, OH 43793-0152. Recording, R/E & UCC phone-740-472-5264; fax-740-472-5264; 8AM-4PM (EST) www.ohiorecorders.com/monroe.html

Index: Separate indices to search include mortgage, deed, lease indexes. Records indexed on computer back to 11/1/93. Office will perform a UCC search (must have request form) but public must search other records themselves. Search fee-$20.00 UCC. Office will not search real estate records. Copy fee $2.00 per page. Cert fee- $1.00 per cert plus copy fee. Payee- Monroe County Recorder. **Other phones:** Treasurer- 740-472-1521; Auditor- 740-472-0873. **Property tax/Assessing**- 101 N Main St, Rm 22, Woodsfield, Ohio 43793-1097; 740-472-0873, fax- 740-472-2523. hours- 8AM-4:30PM http://monroecountyauditor.org/ **Online access**- A commercial subscription program is available from the Auditor's office at http://monroecountyauditor.org. Call first to register, 740-472-0873; $15 fee per month fee applies.

Montgomery County

County Recorder, PO Box 972, Dayton, OH 45422. 937-225-4277, R/E recording phone-937-225-4275; fax-937-225-5980; 8AM-4PM. www.mcrecorder.org

Index: Separate indices to search include document type, address, owners name, legal description. Records indexed on a public use terminal back to 1980. Office will perform a UCC search but public must search other records themselves. Search fee-$20.00 per search. Copy fee $2.00 per page. Cert fee- $1.00 per doc plus copy fee. Payee- Montgomery County Recorder. Office does sell bulk data, contact Ellis Shockley. **Online access to Real Estate, Deed, Lien, Probate, Estate, Marriage, Trade Name, Vendor License, Veterans Gravesites records:** Access to the recorders data is free at www.mcrecorder.org/search_selection.cfm. **Property tax/Assessing**- PO Box 972, 451 W 3rd St, Dayton, OH 45422; 937-225-4326, assessor fax- 937-496-7690. (Appraiser 937-225-4002) hours- 8AM-5PM www.mcohio.org/government/auditor/index.html **Online**- Search auditor's property data and GIS-data free at www.mcrealestate.org/Main/Home.aspx. Property tax records on the county treasurer tax database are free at www.mctreas.org. Also, search auditor's trade name and vendor license free at www.mcauditor.org/VEN_list.cfm?letter=D. Search sheriff sales at www.co.montgomery.oh.us/Sheriff/.

Morgan County

County Recorder, 155 E Main St, Rm 160, McConnelsville, OH 43756. Recording, R/E & UCC phone-740-962-4051; fax-740-962-3364; 8AM-4PM

Index: Separate indices to search before 1/1994. Records indexed on computer back to 1/94. Office will perform a UCC search but public must search other records themselves. Search fee $20.00 for UCC searches only. Copy fee $2.00 per page, self serve $.25 per page. Cert fee- $1.00 per cert plus copy fee. Certified copies must be made by Recorder's office. Payee- Morgan County Recorder. **Other phones:** Treasurer- 740-962-3561; Elections- 740-962-3116; Vital Records- 740-962-4572; Auditor- 740-962-4475. **Property tax/Assessing**- 155 E Main St, Rm 217, McConnelsville, OH 43756; 740-962-4475. **Online access**- Access the auditor property data free at http://morgancountyauditor.org. Use Quick search or Attribute Search. Also, search the Engineer website for tax map property data free at www.morganco engineer.com. Click on Tax Maps.

Morrow County

County Recorder, 48 E High St, Mount Gilead, OH 43338. Recording, R/E & UCC phone-419-947-3060; 8AM-4PM. www.morrowcounty.info/morrowoff.htm

Index: All in one. Records indexed on a public use terminal back to 1994. Only the public may search. Will not search UCC records. Copy fee $2.00 per page. Cert fee- $1.00 per cert plus copy fee. Payee- Morrow County Recorder. **Other phones:** Treasurer- 419-947-6070; Elections- 419-946-4026; Vital Records- 419-947-1545. **Property tax/Assessing**- 48 E High St, Mount Gilead, OH 43338; 419-947-6070, assessor fax- 419-947-6231. (Appraiser/Auditor- 419-946-4060) **Online access**- Access to the county auditor database is free at http://auditor.co.morrow.oh.us/PropertySearch/. Includes property sales data.

Muskingum County

County Recorder, PO Box 2333, Zanesville, OH 43702-2333. 740-455-7107; fax-740-455-7943; 8:30AM-4:30PM (EST) http://recorder.muskingumcounty.org/recorder1024.htm

Index: All in one. Records indexed on a public use terminal back to 1976 for mortgages, 1977 for deeds and 1975 for liens and misc. Office will perform a UCC search but public must search other records themselves. Copy fee $2.00 per page; self serve $.25. Cert fee- $1.00 per cert plus copy fee. Payee- Muskingum County Recorder. **Online access to Real Estate, Deed, Lien, Mortgage, UCC, Plat records:** Access the recorders database free at http://landrecords.muskingumcounty.org/Home.aspx. Click on Indexed Records. Official records go back to 1977. Also, the sheriff's site provides sale lists and sex offender data at www.ohiomuskingumsheriff.org. **Other phones:** Treasurer- 740-455-7118; Elections- 740-455-7120; Auditor- 740-455-7109. **Property tax/Assessing**- 401 Main St, Zanesville, OH 43702; 740-455-7109, assessor fax- 740-455-7182. (Appraiser/Auditor- 740-455-7109) **Online access**- Records on the county auditor database are free at www.muskingumcountyauditor.org/PropertySearch/Home.aspx. Parcel data and GIS-mapping free at www.muskingumcountyauditor.org/PropertySearch/Home.aspx. Also, the sheriff's site provides sale lists at www.ohiomuskingumsheriff.org.

Noble County

County Recorder, 260 Courthouse, Rm 2E, Caldwell, OH 43724. Recording, R/E & UCC phone-740-732-4319; fax-740-732-5702; 8AM-4PM M & W; 8-N Th; 8AM-6PM F. (EST)

Index: Separate indices to search include from 1992 back to 1851; deed, mortgage, lease, federal tax liens, mechanics liens & UCCs. One index from 1992 to present. Records indexed on a public use terminal back to 1992. Office personnel or visitors may perform searches. Search fee-$20.00 per name. Office will search real estate records. Will search UCC records, must have UCCII form. Copy fee $2.00 per page. Cert fee- $1.00 per page plus copy fee. Payee- Noble County Recorder. **Other phones:** Treasurer- 740-732-2457; Elections- 740-732-2057; Vital Records- 740-732-5047.

Ottawa County

County Recorder, 315 Madison St, Rm 204, Port Clinton, OH 43452. Recording, R/E & UCC phone-419-734-6730; fax-419-734-6919; 8:30AM-4:30PM.

Index: All in one. Records indexed on a public use terminal back to 3/94. Only the public may search. Copy fee $2.00 per page if clerk makes copy, $.10 per page if customer makes copy. Cert fee- $1.00 per cert plus copy fee. Payee- Ottawa County Recorder. Treasurer- 419-734-6750; Vital Records- 419-734-6800. **Online Records**- Access to the auditor's property database including sales is free at www.ottawacountyauditor.org/PropertySearch/Home.aspx.

Paulding County

County Recorder, 115 N Williams St, Paulding, OH 45879. Recording, R/E & UCC phone-419-399-8275; fax-419-399-2862; 8AM-4PM.
Index: Separate indices to search include direct, reverse, geographic. Records indexed on a public use terminal back to 0101/1990. Only the public may search. Copy fee $2.00 per page. Cert fee- $1.00 per cert plus copy fee. Payee- County Recorder. **Online access to Real Estate, Deed, Lien, UCC records:** Access recorder data free at www.landaccess.com/sites/oh/disclaimer.php?county=paulding. **Other phones:** Treasurer- 419-399-8280; Elections- 419-399-8230; Vitals- 419-399-3921. **Property tax/Assessing**- 419-399-8205

Perry County

County Recorder, PO Box 147, New Lexington, OH 43764. 740-342-2494, R/E recording phone-740-342-2444, UCC recording phone-740-342-2494; fax-740-342-5539; 8:30AM-4:30PM (EST)
Index: All in one. Records indexed on a public use terminal back to 1983. Office will perform a UCC search (only old ones) but public must search other records themselves. Search fee $20.00. Copy fee $2.00 per page. Cert fee- $1.00 per cert plus copy fee. Payee- Perry County Recorder. **Other phones:** Treasurer- 740-342-1235; Auditor- 740-342-2074.

Pickaway County

County Recorder, 207 S Court St, Circleville, OH 43113. 740-474-5826; fax-740-477-6361; 8AM-4PM.
Index: All in one. Records indexed on a public use terminal back to 1990. Office will perform a UCC search but public must search other records themselves. Search fee $20.00 per name. Copy fee $2.00 per page. Cert fee- $1.00 per doc plus copy fee. Payee- Pickaway County Recorder. Bulk data available for purchase on Film from ACS; contact Barb Dunslow 800-800-0323. **Online Real Estate, Deed, UCC records:** search recorder data free at www.landaccess.com/sites/oh/disclaimer.php?county=pickaway. **Other phones:** Treasurer- 740-474-2370; Elections- 740-474-1100; Vital Records- 740-477-9643; Auditor- 740-474-4765. **Property tax/Assessing**- 207 S Court St, Circleville, OH 43113; 740-474-4765, assessor fax- 740-474-4956. http://pickaway.iviewauditor.com/ **Online access**- Access to the county auditor property data is free at http://pickaway.iviewauditor.com/PropertySearch/.

Pike County

County Recorder, 230 Waverly Plaza, #500; Courthouse, Waverly, OH 45690. 740-947-2622; fax-740-947-7997; hours- 8:30AM-4PM. www.ohiorecorders.com/pike.html
Index: All in one. Records indexed on a public use terminal back to 7/92. Office will perform a UCC search but public must search other records themselves. Search fee $20.00. Copy fee $2.00 per copy. Cert fee- $1.00 per cert plus copy fee. Payee- Pike County Recorder. **Online Real Estate, Deed, Lien, UCC records:** recorder's database is free at www.landaccess.com/sites/oh/disclaimer.php?county=pike. **Other phones:** Treasurer- 740-947-2422; Elections- 740-947-4512; Auditor- 740-947-4125. **Property tax/Assessing**- 230 Waverly Plaza, #300, Waverly, OH 45690; 740-947-4125. **Online access**- Access auditor databases free at www.pike-co.org/ including assessments, parcels, sales, personal property, dog tags, GIS-mapping. Search sheriff sales lists at www.pikecosheriff.com/

Portage County

County Recorder, 449 S Meridian St; 4th Fl, Ravenna, OH 44266. 330-297-3553; fax-330-297-7349; 8AM-4PM. www.co.portage.oh.us/recorder.htm
Index: All in one. Records indexed on computer back to 1995. Office personnel or visitors may perform searches. Office will not search real estate records. Office will not search tax liens. UCC search per debtor name- $20.00. Copy fee $2.00 per page. Cert fee- $1.00 per cert plus copy fee. Payee- Portage County Recorder. Office does sell bulk data, contact Bonnie Howe. **Online access to Deeds, Plats/Tract, Military Service Discharge, Maps, Liens records:** Access to various records for free go to www.co.portage.oh.us/recorder.htm . **Other phones:** Treasurer- 330-297-3586; Elections- 330-297-3511. **Property tax/Assessing**- 449 S Meridian St, Ravenna, OH 44266; see above. (Appraiser/Auditor- 330-297-3570) **Online access**- Access to the auditor's property records and sales is free at http://portagepropertymax.governmaxa.com/propertymax/rover30.asp. Access to the sheriff's property sales list is free at www.co.portage.oh.us.

Preble County

County Recorder, PO Box 371, Eaton, OH 45320-0371. 937-456-8173, R/E recording phone-937-456-8129; fax-none; 8AM-4:30PM (EST)
Index: All in one. Records indexed on computer back to 12/99. Office personnel or visitors may perform searches. Search fee- $20.00 per name. Office will search real estate records. Will search UCC records. Copy fee $2.00 per page. Cert fee- $1.00 per cert plus copy fee. Payee- Preble County Recorder. Data is available fore purchase in mcirofilm format, contact Micro Dept 937-456-8152. **Other phones:** Treasurer- 937-456-8141; Elections- 937-456-8117; Vital Records- 937-472-0087; Microfilm- 937-456-8122. **Property tax/Assessing**- 101 E Main St, Eaton, OH 45320; 937-456-8148, assessor fax- 937-456-8108. **Online**- Property records on the County Auditor's database are free at www.preblecountyauditor.org/.

Putnam County

County Recorder, 245 E Main St, #202; Ottawa, OH 45875-1959. 419-523-6490; fax-419-523-4403; 8:30AM-4:30PM. www.putnamcountyrecorder.com
Index: All in one. Records indexed on a public use terminal back to 1993. Office will perform a UCC search but public must search other records themselves. Office will not search real estate records. UCC search does not include liens. UCC search per debtor name- $20.00. Copy fee $2.00 per copy. Cert fee- $1.00 per cert plus copy fee. Payee- Putnam County Recorder. **Online access to Real Estate, Liens, Property Tax, Grantor/Grantee records:** Access to real estate, property tax back to 1993 go to www.putnamcountyrecorder.com/putnam_county_records_search.htm. Account access may be necessary. **Other phones:** Treasurer- 419-523-6588; Elections- 419-523-3343. **Property tax/Assessing**- 245 E Main St #201, Ottawa, OH 45875; 419-523-6686, assessor fax- 419-523-6390. (Appraiser/Auditor- 419-523-6686) www.co.putnam.oh.us/ **Online access**- Access to real estate for free go to http://co.putnam.oh.us/cgi-bin/db2www.pgm/req.mbr/main?nuser=14:34:19&midf=&midn=

Richland County

County Recorder, 50 Park Ave E, Mansfield, OH 44902. 419-774-5602/5600, R/E recording phone-419-774-5599, UCC recording phone-419-774-5601; fax-419-774-5603; 8AM-4PM (EST) www.richlandcountyauditor.org/Main/Home.aspx
Index: Kept in books before 4/4/1989. Records indexed on computer back to 1989. Office will perform a UCC search (fixture filings only) but public must search other records themselves. Search fee $20.00. Office will not search real estate records. Copy fee $2.00 per page, $.05 per page self serve. Cert fee- $1.00 per cert plus copy fee. Payee- Richland County Recorder. **Online access to Real Estate, Deed records:** Access county land records free at www.landaccess.com. Records go back to 4/1989 (Indices only). **Other phones:** Treasurer- 419-774-5622; Elections- 419-774-5530; Vital Records- 419-774-4500. **Property tax/Assessing**- 50 Park Avenue E, Mansfield, OH 44902; 419-774-5501. (Appraiser/Auditor- 419-774-5503) **Online** - Property records from the County Auditor database are free at www.richlandcountyauditor.org/Main/home.aspx. Also, search the sheriff sales lists for free at www.sheriffrichlandcounty.com.

Ross County

County Recorder, PO Box 6162, Chillicothe, OH 45601. 740-702-3000, R/E phone-740-702-3080; fax-740-702-3006; 8:30AM-4:30PM www.co.ross.oh.us
Index: Before 9/1995, separate indices to search include deed books, mortgages, etc. Records indexed on a public use terminal back to 1/1974. Office will perform a UCC search but public must search other records themselves. Search fee-$20.00 per name for UCC. Copy fee $2.00 per page. Cert fee- $2.00 per cert plus copy fee. Seal is $1.00. Payee- Ross County Recorder. **Online access to Real Estate, Deed, UCC records:** Access to county land, recording and UCC records is free at www.landaccess.com. Index goes back to 1/1974. **Other phones:** Treasurer- 740-702-3080; Elections- 740-775-235-; Vital Records- 740-779-9630. **Property tax/Assessing**- 2 N Panit St #G, Chillicothe, OH 45601; 740-702-3080. http://co.ross.oh.us/auditor/ **Online**- Access the auditor's property and sales data free at www.co.ross.oh.us/Auditor/PropertySearch/Home.aspx.

Sandusky County

County Recorder, 100 N Park Ave; Courthouse, Fremont, OH 43420-2477. 419-334-6226; hours- 8AM-4:30PM (EST) www.sandusky-county.org/Elected%20Officials/Recorder/
Index: All in one. Records indexed on a public use terminal back to 1996. Only the public may search. Copy fee $2.00 per page, $.25 self serve. Cert fee- $1.00 per cert plus copy fee. Payee- Sandusky County Recorder. Treasurer- 419-334-6233. **Property tax/Assessing**- Auditor, 100 N Park Ave #228, Fremont, OH 43420; 419-334-6123, fax- 419-334-6139. www.sandusky-county.org/Elected%20Officials/Auditor/default.asp **Online access**- Access to county auditor and treasurer property data is free at http://ohsanduskypropertymax.governmaxa.com/propertymax/rover30.asp. Click on "Property Search"

Scioto County

County Recorder, 602 7th St, Rm 110, Portsmouth, OH 45662-3950. 740-355-8304; fax-740-355-8355; 8AM-4:30PM (EST) www.sciotocountyohio.com
Index: All in one. Records indexed on a public use terminal back to 6/96. Office will perform a UCC search but public must search other records themselves. UCC search per debtor name- $20.00. General copy fee $2.00 per page; UCC copy fee $2.00 per page. Cert fee- $1.00 per cert plus copy fee. Payee- Recorder. Bulk data available for purchase $1.00 per page, contact Gail Alley. **Other phones:** Treasurer- 740-355-8296; Elections- 740-355-8217; City Birth/Death- 740-353-5153; County Birth/Death -740-354-3241. **Property tax/Assessing**- 602 7th St, Rm 103, Portsmouth, OH 45662; 740-355-8264. (Appraiser/Auditor- 740-355-8264) **Online access**- Access to the auditor's property data is free at www.sciotocountyauditor.org/propertymax/rover30.asp; click on Property Search.

Seneca County

County Recorder, 109 S Washington St, #2104, Tiffin, OH 44883. 419-447-4434; 8:30AM-4:30PM (EST) www.landaccess.com
Index: All in one. Records indexed on a public use terminal back to 9/87. Office will perform a UCC search but public must search other records themselves. Office will not search real estate records. UCC search per debtor name- $20.00. Copy fee $1.00 per page. Cert fee- $1.00 per cert plus copy fee. Payee- Seneca County Recorder. **Online access to Real Estate, Deed records:** Recorder RE data is accessible at www.landaccess.com. **Other phones:** Treasurer- 419-447-1584; Vitals- 419-447-3691. **Property tax/ Assessing**- phone 419-447-1584. (Appraiser/Auditor- 419-447-0692)

Shelby County

County Recorder, 129 E Court St; Shelby County Annex, Sidney, OH 45365. Recording, R/E & UCC phone-937-498-7270; fax-937-498-7272; 8AM-4:30PM. www.co.shelby.oh.us/Recorder/index.asp

Records indexed on computer back to 1989. Office will perform a UCC search but public must search other records themselves. Office will not search real estate records. UCC search per debtor name- $20.00 to start search. Copy fee $2.00 per page. Cert fee- $1.00 per doc plus copy fee. Payee- Shelby County Recorder. **Other phones:** Treasurer- 937-498-7281; Elections- 937-498-7208 or 7209; Vital Records- 937-498-7249 (Birth & Death Certificates); Probate (Wills)- 937-498-7263; Clerk of Courts-Divorce & judgments -937-498-7221. **Property tax/Assessing-** 129 E Court St, Shelby County Annex, Sidney, OH 45365; 937-498-7206, assessor fax- 937-498-2255. (Appraiser/Auditor- 937-498-7202) hours- 8:30AM-4:30PM **Online access-** Access to the sheriff's sale list is free at www.shelbycountysheriff.com

Stark County

County Recorder, 110 Central Plaza S, #170, Canton, OH 44702-1409. 330-451-7443, R/E recording phone-330-451-7443 x4464, UCC recording phone-330-451-7443 x7933; fax-330-451-7394; 8:30AM-4:30PM (recording: 8:30AM-4PM). www.co.stark.oh.us/internet/HOME.DisplayPage?v_page=recorder
Index: All in one. Records indexed on a public use terminal back to 1809. Only the public may search. Copy fee $2.00 per page, $.10 self serve. Cert fee- $1.00 per cert plus copy fee. Payee- Stark County Recorder. Office does sell bulk data, contact Anita. **Online Real Estate, Deed, Mortgage, Lien, UCC records:** Access the recorder's database free after registration at http://app.recorder.co.stark.oh.us/Recorder_Disclaimer.htm. Chose simple, advanced or instrument search. **Other phones:** Treasurer- 330-451-7690. **Property tax/Assessing-** 110 Central Plaza S, #220, Canton, OH 44702; 330-451-7505, assessor fax- 330-451-7630. (Appraiser/Auditor- 330-451-7338) 8:30AM-4:30PM www.auditor.co.stark.oh.us/ **Online access-** Search auditor's property data free at www.auditor.co.stark.oh.us/PropertySearch/. Also, a weekly delinquent taxpayers list is at www.starktaxes.com/list.cgi. Access to sheriff sales lists are at www.sheriff.co.stark.oh.us/RealEstate.htm.

Summit County

Fiscal Officer, Recording Division, 175 S Main St, Akron, OH 44308-1355. Recording, R/E phone-330-643-2720, UCC phone-330-643-8143; 7:30AM-4PM (EST) www.co.summit.oh.us/fiscaloffice/
Index: Pre-1988 indices include deed, mortgage, misc, etc. Records indexed on a public use terminal back to 1988. Office will perform a UCC search but public must search other records themselves. Office will not search real estate records. Will search UCC records. UCC search per debtor name- $20.00. Copy fee $2.00 per page. Cert fee- $1.00 per doc plus copy fee. Payee- Summit County Fiscal Officer. **Other phones:** Treasurer- 330-643-2587; Director of Admin- 330-643-2715. **Other Online Records-** Access tax map data from the county fiscal officer for free at http://scids.summitoh.net/gis/; choose Internactive Online Tax Map Application, then Parcel search. Also property appraisal, images and tax data are on this site. Search property tax bill and appraisal records free at http://megatron.summitoh.net/summit/html/webintg.html. Also, search sheriff tax sale list free at www.co.summit.oh.us/sheriff/.

Trumbull County

County Recorder, 160 High St NW, Warren, OH 44481. Recording, R/E phone-330-675-2401, UCC phone-330-675-2798; fax-330-675-2404; 8:30AM-4:30PM (EST) www.tcrecorder.co.trumbull.oh.us
Index: All in one. Records indexed on a public use terminal back to 1980. Only the public may search. Copy fee $2.00 per page. Cert fee- $1.00 per seal plus copy fee. Payee- Trumbull County Recorder. Monthly listing of Deeds of Conveyance available for purchase at $5.00 each. **Online access to Real Estate, Deed, Mortgage, Lien records:** Access the recorder's database free at http://69.68.42.167:13131/. **Other phones:** Treasurer- 330-675-2736; Elections- 330-675-4050; Auditor- 330-675-2420. **Property tax/Assessing-** County Auditor, 160 High St NW, Warren, OH 44481; 330-675-2420, assessor fax- 330-675-2419. www.co.auditor.trumbull.oh.us/ **Online-** Search auditor property tax data free at http://69.68.42.167:7036/propertysearch/ureca_asp/index.htm. Also, search the Sheriff sales list free at www.tclegalnews.com/subscribe/ssa.php

Tuscarawas County

County Recorder, 125 E High Ave, New Philadelphia, OH 44663. 330-365-3284; 8-4:30PM www.co.tuscarawas.oh.us/Recorder/index.htm
Index: All in one. Records indexed on a public use terminal back to 1991. Only the public may search. Copy fee $2.00 per page. Cert fee- $1.00 per cert plus copy fee. Payee- Tuscarawas County Recorder. Bulk data available for purchase, contact IT Dept. 330-364-8811x3236. **Other phones:** Treasurer- 330-365-3254; Auditor- 330-364-8811 x220. **Property tax/Assessing-** 125 E High Ave, New Philadelphia, OH 44663; 330-365-3325, assessor fax- 330-365-3303. (Appraiser/Auditor- 330-365-3220) A public access terminal is available. **Online access-** County real estate records are free at www.co.tuscarawas.oh.us/tusca208/LandRover.asp. The auditor's delinquent tax list updated in September.

Union County

County Recorder, 233 W 6th St, Marysville, OH 43040. Recording, R/E & UCC phone-937-645-3032; fax-937-642-3397; 8:30AM-4PM (EST) www.co.union.oh.us/Recorder/recorder.html
Index: All in one. Records indexed on a public use terminal back to 1996. Office will perform a UCC search but public must search other records themselves. UCC search per debtor name- $20.00. Copy fee $2.00 per page; self serve $.25. Cert fee- $1.00 per cert plus copy fee. Payee- Union County Recorder. Bulk data available for purchase. **Online Real Estate, Deed, Lien, Mortgage, Judgment, UCC records:** Search recorded documents at www.co.union.oh.us/GD/Templates/Pages/UC/UCCrumbTrail.aspx?page=70. **Other phones:** Treasurer- 937-645-3029; Elections- 937-642-2836; Auditor- 937-645-3003. **Property tax/Assessing-** PO Box 420, 233 W Sixth St, Marysville, OH 43040; 937-645-3003, assessor fax- 937-645-3057. hours- 8AM-4PM A public access terminal is available. **Online access-** Access the Auditors tax assessment/property records database & appraiser property database is free at http://www2.co.union.oh.us/parcelSearch/parcelSearch.aspx/ or www.co.union.oh.us/GD/Templates/Pages/UC/UCDetail.aspx?page=301. Search property via the GIS mapping site at http://www3.co.union.oh.us/website/pub_webgis/viewer.htm. Also, search the treasurers' list of delinquent taxpayers at http://www2.co.union.oh.us/Treasurer/Default.aspx.

Van Wert County

County Recorder, 121 E Main St, Rm 206; Courthouse, Van Wert, OH 45891-1729. Recording, R/E & UCC phone-419-238-2558; fax-419-238-5410; 8:30AM-5PM M; 8:30AM-4PM T-F. (EST) www.vanwertcounty.org/recorder/
Index: Separate indices to search include geographic, daily, grantor/grantee. Records indexed on a public use terminal back to 9/86. Office will perform a UCC search but public must search other records themselves. Office will not search real estate records. UCC search- $20.00 minimum fee. Copy fee $2.00 per page includes lookup; $.05 self serve. Cert fee- $3.00 per page includes copy fee. Payee- Van Wert County Recorder. **Online access to Real Estate, Deed, UCC records:** Access to county land and UCC records is free at www.landaccess.com. Index go back to 1/1994, copies of documents back to 1/94; earlier records being added. **Other phones:** Treasurer- 419-238-5177; Elections- 419-238-4192; Vital Records- 419-238-0808; Auditor- 419-238-0843. **Property tax/Assessing-** 121 E Main St, Van Wert, OH 45891; 419-238-0843, assessor fax- 419-238-1111. www.co.vanwert.oh.us/ **Online access-** Online access to property records free at www.co.vanwert.oh.us/.

Vinton County

County Recorder, 100 E Main St, McArthur, OH 45651. Recording, R/E & UCC phone-740-596-4314; fax-740-596-2265; 8:30AM-4PM (EST)
Index: All in one. Records on a public use terminal. Only the public may search. Copy fee $2.00 per page, $.10 self serve. Cert fee- $2.00 per page plus copy fee. Payee- Vinton County Recorder. **Other phones:** Treasurer- 740-596-4571 x227/228/229; Elections- 740-596-4571; Vital Records- 740-596-5480; Auditor- 740-596-4571 x238/234/232. **Property tax/Assessing-** 100 E Main St, McArthur, OH 45651; 740-596-4571, assessor fax- 740-596-2462. (Appraiser/Auditor- 740-596-4571 x238/234/232);

Warren County

County Recorder, 406 Justice Dr, Lebanon, OH 45036. Recording, R/E phone-513-695-1382, UCC recording phone-513-695-2638; fax-513-695-2949; 8AM-4:30PM (EST) www.co.warren.oh.us/recorder/
Index: All in one. Records indexed on a public use terminal back to 1979. Office will perform a UCC search but public must search other records themselves. Search fee $20.00 per debtor. Copy fee $2.00 per page; self serve $.05 per page. Cert fee- $3.00 per page includes copy fee. Payee- Recorder. Bulk data available for purchase, contact the Data Dept. **Online access to Real Estate, Deed, Lien records:** Access Recorders records free back to 1979 at www.co.warren.oh.us/recorder/. **Other phones:** Treasurer- 513-695-1300; Elections- 513-695-1358; Vital Records- 513-695-1815; Auditor- 513-695-1235. **Property tax/Assessing-** 406 Justice Dr, Lebanon, OH 45036; 513-695-1235, assessor fax-513-695-2960. (Appraiser/Auditor- 513-695-1218) A public access terminal is available. www.co.warren.oh.us/auditor/ **Online access-** Access to the auditor Property Search database is free at www.co.warren.oh.us/auditor/property_search/index.htm. Also, search sheriff sales records free at www.wcsooh.org/sheriff/search/shfentry.htm.

Washington County

County Recorder, 205 Putnam St; Courthouse, Marietta, OH 45750. 740-373-6623 x235 or 236, R/E recording phone-740-373-6623 x235; fax-740-373-9643; 8AM-5PM.
$2.00 per page fee for all incoming faxes and you must have an escrow account. Index: All in one since 1996. Records indexed on a public use terminal back to 12/ 1984. Office personnel or visitors may perform searches. Office will not search real estate records. Office will not search UCC records. Copy fee $2.00 per page; self-serve- $.10 per page. Cert fee- $1.00 per cert plus copy fee. **Online access to Real Estate, Deed, UCC records:** Access to records is free at www.landaccess.com/sites/oh/disclaimer.php?county=washington. **Other phones:** Treasurer- 740-373-6623 x256; Auditor- 740-373-6623 x263. **Other Online-** Access to the county auditor's property search database is free at www.washingtoncountyauditor.org/propertymax/rover30.asp.

Wayne County

County Recorder, 428 W Liberty St, Wooster, OH 44691-5097. Recording, R/E & UCC phone-330-287-5460; fax-330-287-5685; 8AM-4:30PM (EST)
Index: Separate indices to search include official records discharges, plats back to 1996. Records indexed on computer back to May/88. Office will perform a UCC search but public must search other records themselves. UCC search per debtor name- $20.00. Copy fee $2.00 per page. $.10 per computer page. Cert fee- $1.00 per cert plus copy fee. Payee- Wayne County Recorder. **Other phones:** Treasurer- 330-287-5450; Elections- 330-287-5480; Auditor- 330-287-5430. **Property tax/Assessing-** 428 W Liberty St, Wooster, OH 44691; 330-287-5441, fax-330-287-5436. www.waynecountyauditor.org/ **Online** - Access to the auditor's property and sales data is free at www.waynecountyauditor.org. The late taxpayer list appears on the treasurer's website at http://waynecountytreasurer.org/LateTaxpayers.aspx.

Williams County

County Recorder, 1 Courthouse Sq, Bryan, OH 43506. 419-636-3259; fax-419-636-6940; 8:30AM-4:30PM (EST) www.co.williams.oh.us

Index: All in one. Records indexed on a public use terminal back to 1998. Office will perform a UCC search but public must search other records themselves. UCC search per debtor name- $20.00. Copy fee $2.00 per page; self serve $.25. Cert fee- $1.00 per cert plus copy fee. Payee- Williams County Recorder. **Online access to Real Estate, Deed, Lien, UCC records:** Search recorder records free at www.landaccess.com/sites/oh/disclaimer.php?county=williams. **Other phones:** Auditor- 419-636-5639. **Other Online Records-** Access to the auditor's property data and sales is free at http://williamsoh.ddti.net/.

Wood County

County Recorder, 1 Courthouse Sq, Bowling Green, OH 43402-2427. phone-419-354-9140; 8:30AM-4:30PM (EST) www.co.wood.oh.us/recorder/

Index: All in one. Records indexed on a public use terminal back to 1985. Office will perform a UCC search but public must search other records themselves. Office will not search real estate records. Copy fee $2.00 per page. Cert fee- $1.00 per cert plus copy fee. Payee- Wood County Recorder. **Other phones:** Treasurer- 419-354-9130; Elections- 419-354-9120; Vital Records- 419-354-9130. **Property tax/Assessing-** 1 Courthouse Square, 2nd Fl, Bowling Green, OH 43402; 419-354-9150. www.co.wood.oh.us/auditor/ **Online access-** Access to the auditor's property data is free at http://auditor.co.wood.oh.us/. No name searching. Also, search the treasurer's tax data for free at http://woodtaxcollector.governmax.com/collectmax/collect30.asp?

Wyandot County

County Recorder, 109 S Sandusky Ave; Courthouse, Upper Sandusky, OH 43351. Recording, R/E & UCC phone-419-294-1442; fax-419-294-6405; 8:30AM-4:30PM (EST)

Index: Separate indices to search include "official" since 5/1999; prior in grantor/grantee index. Records indexed on a public use terminal back to 0599. Only the public may search. Will not search UCC records. Copy fee $2.00 per page. Cert fee- $1.00 per cert plus copy fee. Payee- Wyandot County. **Other phones:** Treasurer- 419-294-2131; Elections- 419-294-1226; Vital Records- 419-294-2302. **Property tax/Assessing-** 109 S Sandusky Ave, Rm 21, Courthouse, Upper Sandusky, OH 43351; 419-294-1531, assessor fax- 419-209-0408. A public access terminal is available. **Online access-** Access to the Auditor's real estate database is free at www.co.wyandot.oh.us/auditor/default.html. Click on "Real Estate Internet Inquiry." Also may search dog tags.

Ohio County Locator

You will usually be able to find the city name in the City/County Cross Reference below. In that case, it is a simple matter to determine the county from the cross reference. However, only the official US Postal Service city names are included in this index. There are an additional 40,000 place names that people use in their addresses. Therefore, we have also included a ZIP/City Cross Reference immediately following the City/County Cross Reference.

If you know the ZIP Code but the city name does not appear in the City/County Cross Reference index, look up the ZIP Code in the ZIP/City Cross Reference, find the city name, then look up the city name in the City/County Cross Reference. For example, you want to know the county for an address of Menands, NY 12204. There is no "Menands" in the City/County Cross Reference. The ZIP/City Cross Reference shows that ZIP Codes 12201-12288 are for the city of Albany. Looking back in the City/County Cross Reference, Albany is in Albany County.

Ohio City/County Cross Reference

ABERDEEN (45101) Brown(97), Adams(2)
ADA (45810) Hardin(94), Hancock(2), Allen(2)
ADAMSVILLE Muskingum
ADDYSTON Hamilton
ADELPHI Ross
ADENA (43901) Jefferson(77), Harrison(12), Belmont(10)
ADRIAN Seneca
AKRON Summit
ALBANY (45710) Athens(59), Meigs(23), Vinton(16)
ALEXANDRIA Licking
ALGER (45812) Hardin(93), Allen(6)
ALLEDONIA Belmont
ALLIANCE (44601) Stark(90), Mahoning(6), Columbiana(2)
ALPHA Greene
ALVADA (44802) Seneca(61), Hancock(38)
ALVORDTON Williams
AMANDA (43102) Fairfield(90), Hocking(7), Pickaway(1)
AMELIA Clermont
AMESVILLE (45711) Athens(91), Washington(6), Morgan(2)
AMHERST Lorain
AMLIN Franklin
AMSDEN Seneca
AMSTERDAM (43903) Carroll(54), Jefferson(45)
ANDOVER Ashtabula
ANNA Shelby
ANSONIA Darke
ANTWERP (45813) Paulding(98), Defiance(1)
APPLE CREEK Wayne
ARCADIA Hancock
ARCANUM (45304) Darke(98), Preble(1)
ARCHBOLD (43502) Fulton(89), Henry(9)
ARLINGTON Hancock
ASHLAND (44805) Ashland(98), Richland(1)
ASHLEY (43003) Delaware(73), Morrow(26)
ASHTABULA Ashtabula
ASHVILLE Pickaway
ATHENS Athens
ATTICA (44807) Seneca(86), Huron(13)
ATWATER (44201) Portage(96), Stark(3)
AUGUSTA Carroll
AURORA (44202) Portage(89), Summit(8), Geauga(2)
AUSTINBURG Ashtabula
AVA Noble
AVON Lorain
AVON LAKE Lorain
B F GOODRICH CO Summit
BAINBRIDGE (45612) Ross(69), Pike(20), Highland(9)
BAKERSVILLE Coshocton
BALTIC (43804) Holmes(52), Tuscarawas(25), Coshocton(21)
BALTIMORE Fairfield
BANNOCK Belmont
BARBERTON Summit
BARLOW Washington
BARNESVILLE Belmont
BARTLETT Washington
BARTON Belmont
BASCOM Seneca
BATAVIA Clermont
BATH Summit
BAY VILLAGE Cuyahoga
BEACH CITY (44608) Stark(75), Tuscarawas(24)
BEACHWOOD Cuyahoga
BEALLSVILLE (43716) Monroe(73), Belmont(26)
BEAVER (45613) Pike(82), Jackson(17)
BEAVERDAM Allen
BEDFORD Cuyahoga
BELLAIRE Belmont
BELLBROOK Greene
BELLE CENTER (43310) Logan(75), Hardin(24)
BELLE VALLEY Noble
BELLEFONTAINE Logan
BELLEVUE (44811) Huron(41), Sandusky(41), Seneca(11), Erie(6)
BELLVILLE (44813) Richland(85), Knox(7), Morrow(6)
BELMONT Belmont
BELMORE Putnam
BELOIT (44609) Mahoning(60), Columbiana(39)
BELPRE Washington
BENTON RIDGE Hancock
BENTONVILLE Adams
BEREA Cuyahoga
BERGHOLZ (43908) Jefferson(95), Carroll(4)
BERKEY (43504) Lucas(95), Fulton(4)
BERLIN Holmes
BERLIN CENTER Mahoning
BERLIN HEIGHTS Erie
BETHEL (45106) Clermont(86), Brown(13)
BETHESDA Belmont
BETTSVILLE Seneca
BEVERLY (45715) Washington(97), Morgan(2)
BIDWELL Gallia
BIG PRAIRIE (44611) Holmes(94), Wayne(5)
BIRMINGHAM Erie
BLACKLICK Franklin
BLADENSBURG Knox
BLAINE Belmont
BLAKESLEE Williams
BLANCHESTER (45107) Clinton(83), Warren(8), Clermont(4), Brown(3)
BLISSFIELD Coshocton
BLOOMDALE (44817) Wood(91), Hancock(8)
BLOOMINGBURG Fayette
BLOOMINGDALE (43910) Jefferson(96), Harrison(3)
BLOOMVILLE (44818) Seneca(62), Crawford(37)
BLUE CREEK (45616) Adams(82), Scioto(17)
BLUE ROCK (43720) Muskingum(91), Morgan(8)
BLUFFTON (45817) Allen(82), Hancock(15), Putnam(1)
BOLIVAR (44612) Tuscarawas(95), Stark(4)
BOTKINS (45306) Shelby(95), Auglaize(4)
BOURNEVILLE Ross
BOWERSTON (44695) Harrison(56), Carroll(43)
BOWERSVILLE Greene
BOWLING GREEN Wood
BRADFORD (45308) Darke(54), Miami(45)
BRADNER (43406) Wood(92), Sandusky(7)
BRADY LAKE Portage
BRECKSVILLE (44141) Cuyahoga(93), Summit(6)
BREMEN (43107) Fairfield(92), Hocking(5), Perry(2)
BREWSTER Stark
BRICE Franklin
BRIDGEPORT Belmont
BRILLIANT Jefferson
BRINKHAVEN (43006) Coshocton(40), Holmes(40), Knox(19)
BRISTOLVILLE Trumbull
BROADVIEW HEIGHTS Cuyahoga
BROADWAY Union
BROOKFIELD Trumbull
BROOKPARK Cuyahoga
BROOKVILLE Montgomery
BROWNSVILLE Licking
BRUNSWICK Medina
BRYAN (43506) Williams(93), Defiance(6)
BUCHTEL Athens
BUCKEYE LAKE Licking
BUCKLAND Auglaize
BUCYRUS Crawford
BUFFALO Guernsey
BUFORD Highland
BURBANK (44214) Wayne(72), Medina(27)
BURGHILL Trumbull
BURGOON (43407) Sandusky(97), Seneca(2)
BURKETTSVILLE Mercer
BURTON Geauga
BUTLER (44822) Richland(60), Knox(38)
BYESVILLE Guernsey
CABLE Champaign
CADIZ (43907) Harrison(98), Jefferson(1)
CAIRO Allen
CALDWELL (43724) Noble(97), Morgan(1)
CALEDONIA (43314) Marion(87), Morrow(6), Crawford(5)
CAMBRIDGE Guernsey
CAMDEN Preble
CAMERON Monroe
CAMP DENNISON Hamilton
CAMPBELL Mahoning
CANAL FULTON (44614) Stark(97), Summit(1), Wayne(1)
CANAL WINCHESTER (43110) Franklin(73), Fairfield(26)
CANFIELD Mahoning
CANTON (44720) Stark(92), Summit(7)
CANTON (44730) Stark(98), Carroll(1)
CANTON Stark
CARBON HILL Hocking
CARBONDALE Athens
CARDINGTON (43315) Morrow(93), Marion(6)
CAREY (43316) Wyandot(84), Seneca(13), Hancock(1)
CARROLL Fairfield
CASSTOWN (45312) Miami(98), Champaign(1)
CASTALIA (44824) Erie(96), Sandusky(3)
CATAWBA Clark
CECIL (45821) Paulding(89), Defiance(10)
CEDARVILLE (45314) Greene(98), Clark(1)
CELINA Mercer
CENTERBURG (43011) Knox(69), Morrow(11), Delaware(10), Licking(7)
CHAGRIN FALLS (44022) Cuyahoga(77), Geauga(22)
CHAGRIN FALLS Geauga
CHANDLERSVILLE Muskingum
CHARDON (44024) Geauga(97), Lake(2)
CHARM Holmes
CHATFIELD Crawford
CHAUNCEY Athens
CHERRY FORK Adams
CHESAPEAKE Lawrence
CHESHIRE (45620) Gallia(96), Meigs(3)
CHESTER Meigs
CHESTERHILL (43728) Morgan(96), Athens(3)
CHESTERLAND Geauga
CHESTERVILLE Morrow
CHICKASAW Mercer
CHILLICOTHE Ross
CHILO Clermont
CHIPPEWA LAKE Medina
CHRISTIANSBURG Champaign
CINCINNATI (45241) Hamilton(72), Butler(26), Warren(1)
CINCINNATI (45244) Hamilton(57), Clermont(42)
CINCINNATI (45246) Hamilton(92), Butler(7)
CINCINNATI (45249) Hamilton(96), Warren(3)
CINCINNATI (45255) Hamilton(64), Clermont(35)
CINCINNATI Clermont
CINCINNATI Hamilton
CIRCLEVILLE Pickaway
CLARINGTON Monroe
CLARKSBURG (43115) Ross(77), Pickaway(22)
CLARKSVILLE (45113) Clinton(62), Warren(37)
CLAY CENTER Ottawa
CLAYTON Montgomery
CLEVELAND Cuyahoga
CLEVES Hamilton
CLIFTON Greene
CLINTON (44216) Summit(89), Stark(9)

CLOVERDALE (45827) Putnam(84), Paulding(15)
CLYDE (43410) Sandusky(96), Seneca(3)
COAL RUN Washington
COALTON Jackson
COLDWATER Mercer
COLERAIN Belmont
COLLEGE CORNER Butler
COLLINS (44826) Huron(84), Erie(15)
COLLINSVILLE Butler
COLTON Henry
COLUMBIA STATION Lorain
COLUMBIANA (44408) Columbiana(85), Mahoning(14)
COLUMBUS Delaware
COLUMBUS Franklin
COLUMBUS GROVE (45830) Putnam(79), Allen(20)
COMMERCIAL POINT Pickaway
CONESVILLE (43811) Coshocton(98), Muskingum(1)
CONNEAUT Ashtabula
CONOVER (45317) Champaign(47), Miami(40), Shelby(11)
CONTINENTAL (45831) Putnam(96), Defiance(2), Paulding(1)
CONVOY (45832) Van Wert(98), Paulding(1)
COOLVILLE (45723) Athens(87), Meigs(10), Washington(1)
CORNING (43730) Perry(97), Morgan(2)
CORTLAND Trumbull
COSHOCTON Coshocton
COVINGTON Miami
CREOLA (45622) Vinton(97), Hocking(2)
CRESTLINE (44827) Crawford(90), Richland(9)
CRESTON (44217) Wayne(89), Medina(10)
CROOKSVILLE (43731) Perry(85), Morgan(14)
CROTON (43013) Licking(98), Delaware(1)
CROWN CITY (45623) Gallia(83), Lawrence(16)
CUBA Clinton
CUMBERLAND (43732) Guernsey(74), Noble(16), Muskingum(6), Morgan(1)
CURTICE (43412) Lucas(56), Ottawa(43)
CUSTAR (43511) Wood(72), Henry(27)
CUTLER (45724) Washington(98), Athens(1)
CUYAHOGA FALLS Summit
CYGNET Wood
CYNTHIANA Pike
DALTON (44618) Wayne(92), Stark(7)
DAMASCUS Mahoning
DANVILLE Knox
DAYTON (45434) Greene(98), Montgomery(1)
DAYTON (45440) Montgomery(62), Greene(37)
DAYTON (45458) Montgomery(92), Warren(5), Greene(1)
DAYTON (45459) Montgomery(98), Greene(1)
DAYTON Greene
DAYTON Montgomery
DE GRAFF (43318) Logan(79), Champaign(20)
DECATUR Brown
DEERFIELD Portage
DEERSVILLE Harrison
DEFIANCE (43512) Defiance(95), Paulding(3)
DELLROY Carroll
DELPHOS (45833) Allen(56), Van Wert(40), Putnam(3)
DELTA Fulton
DENNISON (44621) Tuscarawas(90), Harrison(8), Carroll(1)
DERBY Pickaway
DERWENT Guernsey
DESHLER (43516) Henry(81), Wood(12), Putnam(4), Hancock(1)
DEXTER CITY Noble
DIAMOND (44412) Portage(80), Mahoning(19)
DILLONVALE (43917) Jefferson(68), Belmont(31)
DOLA Hardin
DONNELSVILLE Clark
DORSET Ashtabula
DOVER Tuscarawas
DOYLESTOWN (44230) Wayne(97), Medina(2)
DRESDEN (43821) Muskingum(86), Coshocton(13)
DUBLIN (43017) Franklin(87), Delaware(11)
DUNBRIDGE Wood
DUNCAN FALLS Muskingum
DUNDEE (44624) Tuscarawas(60), Holmes(27), Wayne(11)
DUNKIRK Hardin
DUPONT Putnam
EAST CLARIDON Geauga
EAST FULTONHAM Muskingum
EAST LIBERTY (43319) Logan(96), Union(3)
EAST LIVERPOOL Columbiana
EAST PALESTINE Columbiana
EAST ROCHESTER (44625) Columbiana(81), Carroll(18)
EAST SPARTA (44626) Stark(94), Tuscarawas(5)
EAST SPRINGFIELD Jefferson
EASTLAKE Lake
EATON Preble
EDGERTON (43517) Williams(78), Defiance(21)
EDISON Morrow
EDON Williams
ELDORADO Preble
ELGIN Van Wert
ELKTON Columbiana
ELLSWORTH Mahoning
ELMORE (43416) Ottawa(93), Sandusky(6)
ELYRIA Lorain
EMPIRE Jefferson
ENGLEWOOD (45322) Montgomery(97), Miami(2)
ENON Clark
ETNA Licking
EUCLID Cuyahoga
EVANSPORT Defiance
FAIRBORN (45324) Greene(96), Clark(3)
FAIRFIELD Butler
FAIRLAWN Summit
FAIRPOINT Belmont
FAIRVIEW Guernsey
FARMDALE Trumbull
FARMER Defiance
FARMERSVILLE (45325) Montgomery(96), Preble(3)
FAYETTE (43521) Fulton(97), Williams(2)
FAYETTEVILLE (45118) Brown(94), Highland(2), Clermont(2)
FEESBURG Brown
FELICITY (45120) Clermont(73), Brown(26)
FINDLAY Hancock
FLAT ROCK Seneca
FLEMING Washington
FLETCHER Miami
FLUSHING (43977) Belmont(80), Harrison(19)
FOREST (45843) Hardin(61), Wyandot(19), Hancock(18)
FORT JENNINGS (45844) Putnam(90), Allen(4), Van Wert(4)
FORT LORAMIE (45845) Shelby(95), Auglaize(3)
FORT RECOVERY (45846) Mercer(84), Darke(15)
FORT SENECA Seneca
FOSTORIA (44830) Seneca(65), Hancock(17), Wood(16)
FOWLER Trumbull
FRANKFORT Ross
FRANKLIN Warren
FRANKLIN FURNACE (45629) Scioto(93), Lawrence(6)
FRAZEYSBURG (43822) Muskingum(61), Licking(19), Coshocton(12), Knox(6)
FREDERICKSBURG (44627) Wayne(68), Holmes(31)
FREDERICKTOWN (43019) Knox(84), Morrow(14)
FREEPORT (43973) Guernsey(52), Harrison(46)
FREMONT Sandusky
FRESNO (43824) Coshocton(91), Tuscarawas(8)
FRIENDSHIP Scioto
FULTON Morrow
FULTONHAM Muskingum
GALENA Delaware
GALION (44833) Crawford(85), Morrow(9), Richland(3), Marion(1)
GALLIPOLIS Gallia
GALLOWAY (43119) Franklin(95), Madison(4)
GAMBIER Knox
GARRETTSVILLE (44231) Portage(88), Geauga(10)
GATES MILLS (44040) Cuyahoga(98), Geauga(1)
GENEVA (44041) Ashtabula(98), Lake(1)
GENOA (43430) Ottawa(94), Wood(3), Sandusky(1)
GEORGETOWN (45121) Brown(98), Clermont(1)
GERMANTOWN (45327) Montgomery(97), Preble(1)
GETTYSBURG Darke
GIBSONBURG (43431) Sandusky(98), Wood(1)
GIRARD Trumbull
GLANDORF Putnam
GLENCOE Belmont
GLENFORD (43739) Perry(64), Licking(35)
GLENMONT (44628) Holmes(61), Knox(38)
GLOUSTER (45732) Athens(92), Perry(5), Hocking(2)
GNADENHUTTEN Tuscarawas
GOMER Allen
GORDON Darke
GOSHEN (45122) Clermont(91), Warren(8)
GRAFTON Lorain
GRAND RAPIDS (43522) Wood(48), Lucas(45), Henry(6)
GRAND RIVER Lake
GRANVILLE Licking
GRATIOT Licking
GRATIS Preble
GRAYSVILLE (45734) Monroe(78), Washington(21)
GRAYTOWN Ottawa
GREEN Summit
GREEN CAMP Marion
GREEN SPRINGS (44836) Seneca(65), Sandusky(34)
GREENFIELD (45123) Highland(55), Ross(25), Fayette(18)
GREENFIELD Highland
GREENFORD Mahoning
GREENTOWN Stark
GREENVILLE Darke
GREENWICH (44837) Huron(75), Richland(12), Ashland(12)
GRELTON Henry
GROVE CITY Franklin
GROVEPORT (43125) Franklin(98), Pickaway(1)
GROVEPORT Franklin
GROVER HILL (45849) Paulding(63), Van Wert(34), Putnam(1)
GUYSVILLE (45735) Athens(94), Meigs(5)
GYPSUM Ottawa
HALLSVILLE Ross
HAMDEN Vinton
HAMERSVILLE (45130) Brown(89), Clermont(10)
HAMILTON Butler
HAMLER Henry
HAMMONDSVILLE (43930) Jefferson(83), Columbiana(16)
HANNIBAL Monroe
HANOVERTON Columbiana
HARBOR VIEW Lucas
HARLEM SPRINGS Carroll
HARPSTER (43323) Wyandot(93), Marion(6)
HARRISBURG Franklin
HARRISON Hamilton
HARRISVILLE Harrison
HARROD (45850) Allen(81), Hardin(12), Auglaize(6)
HARTFORD Trumbull
HARTVILLE (44632) Stark(95), Portage(4)
HARVEYSBURG Warren
HASKINS Wood
HAVERHILL Scioto
HAVILAND Paulding
HAYDENVILLE Hocking
HAYESVILLE Ashland
HEBRON Licking
HELENA Sandusky
HICKSVILLE (43526) Defiance(96), Paulding(3)
HIGGINSPORT Brown
HIGHLAND Highland
HILLIARD Franklin
HILLSBORO (45133) Highland(97), Pike(2)
HINCKLEY Medina
HIRAM (44234) Portage(55), Geauga(44)
HOCKINGPORT Athens
HOLGATE (43527) Henry(89), Defiance(10)
HOLLAND Lucas
HOLLANSBURG Darke
HOLLOWAY Belmont
HOLMESVILLE Holmes
HOMER Licking
HOMERVILLE Medina
HOMEWORTH (44634) Columbiana(80), Stark(19)
HOOVEN Hamilton
HOPEDALE (43976) Harrison(98), Jefferson(1)
HOPEWELL (43746) Muskingum(90), Licking(10)
HOUSTON Shelby
HOWARD Knox
HOYTVILLE Wood
HUBBARD Trumbull
HUDSON (44236) Summit(98), Portage(1)
HUDSON Summit
HUNTSBURG (44046) Geauga(98), Ashtabula(1)
HUNTSVILLE Logan
HURON Erie
IBERIA Morrow
INDEPENDENCE Cuyahoga
IRONDALE (43932) Jefferson(92), Columbiana(7)
IRONTON (45638) Lawrence(94), Scioto(5)
IRWIN (43029) Union(75), Madison(24)
ISLE SAINT GEORGE Ottawa
JACKSON Monroe
JACKSON CENTER (45334) Shelby(88), Auglaize(7), Logan(3)
JACKSONTOWN Licking
JACKSONVILLE Athens
JACOBSBURG Belmont
JAMESTOWN (45335) Greene(95), Clinton(2), Fayette(1)

JASPER Pike
JEFFERSON Ashtabula
JEFFERSONVILLE Fayette
JENERA (45841) Hancock(94), Hardin(5)
JEROMESVILLE (44840) Ashland(98), Wayne(1)
JERRY CITY Wood
JERUSALEM (43747) Monroe(64), Belmont(35)
JEWELL Defiance
JEWETT (43986) Harrison(91), Carroll(8)
JOHNSTOWN (43031) Licking(97), Delaware(2)
JUNCTION CITY Perry
KALIDA Putnam
KANSAS (44841) Seneca(69), Sandusky(30)
KEENE Coshocton
KELLEYS ISLAND Erie
KENSINGTON (44427) Columbiana(57), Carroll(42)
KENT (44240) Portage(98), Summit(1)
KENT Portage
KENTON Hardin
KERR Gallia
KETTLERSVILLE Shelby
KIDRON Wayne
KILBOURNE Delaware
KILLBUCK (44637) Holmes(83), Coshocton(16)
KIMBOLTON (43749) Guernsey(92), Coshocton(4), Tuscarawas(2)
KINGS MILLS Warren
KINGSTON (45644) Ross(64), Pickaway(35)
KINGSVILLE Ashtabula
KINSMAN (44428) Trumbull(96), Ashtabula(3)
KIPLING Guernsey
KIPTON Lorain
KIRBY Wyandot
KIRKERSVILLE Licking
KITTS HILL Lawrence
KUNKLE Williams
LA RUE (43332) Marion(90), Hardin(7), Wyandot(1)
LACARNE Ottawa
LAFAYETTE Allen
LAFFERTY Belmont
LAGRANGE Lorain
LAINGS Monroe
LAKE MILTON (44429) Mahoning(98), Portage(1)
LAKEMORE Summit
LAKESIDE MARBLEHEAD Ottawa
LAKEVIEW (43331) Logan(94), Auglaize(4), Hardin(1)
LAKEVILLE (44638) Holmes(79), Ashland(14), Wayne(7)
LAKEWOOD Cuyahoga
LANCASTER Fairfield
LANGSVILLE Meigs
LANSING Belmont
LATHAM Pike
LATTY Paulding
LAURA (45337) Miami(86), Darke(13)
LAURELVILLE (43135) Hocking(75), Ross(12), Pickaway(11)
LEAVITTSBURG Trumbull
LEBANON Warren
LEES CREEK Clinton
LEESBURG (45135) Highland(77), Fayette(15), Clinton(6)
LEESVILLE Carroll
LEETONIA Columbiana
LEIPSIC (45856) Putnam(97), Henry(2)
LEMOYNE Wood
LEWIS CENTER Delaware
LEWISBURG Preble
LEWISTOWN Logan
LEWISVILLE Monroe
LIBERTY CENTER (43532) Henry(89), Fulton(7), Lucas(3)
LIMA (45806) Allen(94), Auglaize(5)
LIMA Allen
LIMAVILLE Stark
LINDSEY (43442) Sandusky(96), Ottawa(3)
LISBON Columbiana
LITCHFIELD (44253) Medina(82), Lorain(17)
LITHOPOLIS Fairfield
LITTLE HOCKING (45742) Washington(91), Athens(8)
LOCKBOURNE (43137) Franklin(51), Pickaway(48)
LODI Medina
LOGAN (43138) Hocking(98), Perry(1)
LONDON Madison
LONDONDERRY Ross
LONG BOTTOM Meigs
LORAIN Lorain
LORE CITY Guernsey
LOUDONVILLE (44842) Ashland(89), Holmes(9)
LOUISVILLE Stark
LOVELAND (45140) Clermont(40), Hamilton(30), Warren(29)
LOWELL (45744) Morgan(54), Washington(40), Noble(5)
LOWELLVILLE Mahoning
LOWER SALEM (45745) Noble(73), Monroe(14), Washington(12)
LUCAS (44843) Richland(97), Ashland(2)
LUCASVILLE (45648) Scioto(70), Pike(29)
LUCASVILLE Scioto
LUCKEY (43443) Wood(98), Sandusky(1)
LUDLOW FALLS Miami
LYNCHBURG (45142) Highland(90), Clinton(9)
LYNX Adams
LYONS Fulton
MACEDONIA Summit
MACKSBURG (45746) Noble(80), Washington(19)
MADISON Lake
MAGNETIC SPRINGS Union
MAGNOLIA (44643) Stark(42), Tuscarawas(36), Carroll(20)
MAINEVILLE (45039) Warren(98), Hamilton(1)
MALAGA Monroe
MALINTA Henry
MALTA Morgan
MALVERN Carroll
MANCHESTER Adams
MANSFIELD (44904) Richland(89), Morrow(10)
MANSFIELD Richland
MANTUA (44255) Portage(86), Geauga(13)
MAPLE HEIGHTS Cuyahoga
MAPLEWOOD Shelby
MARATHON Clermont
MARENGO (43334) Morrow(94), Delaware(5)
MARIA STEIN (45860) Mercer(98), Darke(1)
MARIETTA Washington
MARK CENTER Defiance
MARSHALLVILLE (44645) Wayne(97), Stark(2)
MARTEL Marion
MARTIN (43445) Ottawa(69), Lucas(30)
MARTINS FERRY Belmont
MARTINSBURG Knox
MARTINSVILLE Clinton
MARYSVILLE Union
MASON Warren
MASSILLON Stark
MASURY Trumbull
MAUMEE Lucas
MAXIMO Stark
MAYNARD Belmont
MC ARTHUR Vinton
MC CLURE (43534) Henry(97), Wood(2)
MC COMB (45858) Hancock(97), Putnam(2)
MC CONNELSVILLE Morgan
MC CUTCHENVILLE (44844) Wyandot(65), Seneca(34)
MC DERMOTT Scioto
MC DONALD (44437) Trumbull(97), Mahoning(2)
MC GUFFEY Hardin
MECHANICSBURG (43044) Champaign(81), Clark(12), Madison(5)
MECHANICSTOWN Carroll
MEDINA Medina
MEDWAY Clark
MELMORE Seneca
MELROSE Paulding
MENDON (45862) Mercer(92), Auglaize(7)
MENTOR Lake
MESOPOTAMIA Trumbull
METAMORA Fulton
MIAMISBURG Montgomery
MIAMITOWN Hamilton
MIAMIVILLE Clermont
MIDDLE BASS Ottawa
MIDDLE POINT Van Wert
MIDDLEBRANCH Stark
MIDDLEBURG Logan
MIDDLEFIELD (44062) Geauga(80), Trumbull(16), Ashtabula(2)
MIDDLEPORT Meigs
MIDDLETOWN Butler
MIDLAND (45148) Clinton(93), Brown(6)
MIDVALE Tuscarawas
MILAN (44846) Erie(92), Huron(7)
MILFORD Clermont
MILFORD CENTER (43045) Union(95), Champaign(4)
MILLBURY (43447) Wood(80), Ottawa(19)
MILLEDGEVILLE Fayette
MILLER CITY Putnam
MILLERSBURG (44654) Holmes(97), Coshocton(2)
MILLERSPORT (43046) Fairfield(91), Licking(8)
MILLFIELD Athens
MILTON CENTER Wood
MINERAL CITY (44656) Tuscarawas(96), Carroll(3)
MINERAL RIDGE (44440) Trumbull(83), Mahoning(16)
MINERVA (44657) Stark(50), Carroll(34), Columbiana(14)
MINFORD Scioto
MINGO Champaign
MINGO JUNCTION Jefferson
MINSTER (45865) Auglaize(78), Shelby(20)
MOGADORE (44260) Portage(70), Summit(24), Stark(5)
MONCLOVA Lucas
MONROE Butler
MONROEVILLE (44847) Huron(70), Erie(29)
MONTEZUMA Mercer
MONTPELIER Williams
MONTVILLE (44064) Geauga(97), Ashtabula(2)
MORRAL (43337) Marion(83), Wyandot(16)
MORRISTOWN Belmont
MORROW Warren
MOSCOW Clermont
MOUNT BLANCHARD (45867) Hancock(94), Wyandot(5)
MOUNT CORY (45868) Hancock(96), Putnam(3)
MOUNT EATON Wayne
MOUNT GILEAD Morrow
MOUNT HOPE Holmes
MOUNT LIBERTY Knox
MOUNT ORAB Brown
MOUNT PERRY (43760) Perry(66), Muskingum(29), Licking(3)
MOUNT PLEASANT Jefferson
MOUNT SAINT JOSEPH Hamilton
MOUNT STERLING (43143) Madison(75), Pickaway(16), Fayette(7)
MOUNT VERNON Knox
MOUNT VICTORY (43340) Hardin(89), Union(10)
MOWRYSTOWN Highland
MOXAHALA Perry
MUNROE FALLS Summit
MURRAY CITY Hocking
NANKIN Ashland
NAPOLEON (43545) Henry(98), Defiance(1)
NASHPORT (43830) Muskingum(88), Licking(11)
NASHVILLE Holmes
NAVARRE (44662) Stark(97), Wayne(2)
NEAPOLIS Lucas
NEFFS Belmont
NEGLEY Columbiana
NELSONVILLE (45764) Athens(88), Hocking(11)
NEVADA (44849) Wyandot(87), Crawford(12)
NEVILLE Clermont
NEW ALBANY Franklin
NEW ATHENS Harrison
NEW BAVARIA (43548) Henry(94), Defiance(2), Putnam(2)
NEW BLOOMINGTON Marion
NEW BREMEN (45869) Auglaize(91), Shelby(4), Mercer(4)
NEW CARLISLE (45344) Clark(82), Miami(14), Montgomery(2)
NEW CONCORD (43762) Muskingum(82), Guernsey(17)
NEW HAMPSHIRE Auglaize
NEW HAVEN Huron
NEW HOLLAND (43145) Pickaway(66), Fayette(33)
NEW KNOXVILLE (45871) Auglaize(77), Shelby(22)
NEW LEBANON Montgomery
NEW LEXINGTON Perry
NEW LONDON (44851) Huron(82), Lorain(12), Ashland(4)
NEW MADISON Darke
NEW MARSHFIELD (45766) Athens(89), Vinton(10)
NEW MATAMORAS (45767) Monroe(66), Washington(33)
NEW MIDDLETOWN Mahoning
NEW PARIS (45347) Preble(93), Darke(6)
NEW PHILADELPHIA Tuscarawas
NEW PLYMOUTH (45654) Vinton(72), Hocking(27)
NEW RICHMOND Clermont
NEW RIEGEL Seneca
NEW RUMLEY Harrison
NEW SPRINGFIELD (44443) Mahoning(95), Columbiana(4)
NEW STRAITSVILLE (43766) Perry(84), Hocking(15)
NEW VIENNA (45159) Clinton(95), Highland(4)
NEW WASHINGTON (44854) Crawford(95), Seneca(4)
NEW WATERFORD Columbiana
NEW WESTON (45348) Darke(98), Mercer(1)
NEWARK Licking
NEWBURY Geauga
NEWCOMERSTOWN (43832) Tuscarawas(84), Coshocton(13), Guernsey(2)
NEWTON FALLS (44444) Trumbull(94), Portage(4), Mahoning(1)
NEWTONSVILLE Clermont
NEY Defiance

NILES Trumbull
NORTH BALTIMORE (45872) Wood(98), Hancock(1)
NORTH BEND Hamilton
NORTH BENTON (44449) Portage(52), Mahoning(47)
NORTH BLOOMFIELD Trumbull
NORTH FAIRFIELD Huron
NORTH GEORGETOWN Columbiana
NORTH HAMPTON Clark
NORTH JACKSON Mahoning
NORTH KINGSVILLE Ashtabula
NORTH LAWRENCE (44666) Stark(80), Wayne(19)
NORTH LEWISBURG (43060) Union(51), Champaign(34), Logan(14)
NORTH LIMA Mahoning
NORTH OLMSTED Cuyahoga
NORTH RIDGEVILLE Lorain
NORTH ROBINSON Crawford
NORTH ROYALTON Cuyahoga
NORTH STAR Darke
NORTHFIELD Summit
NORTHWOOD Wood
NORWALK (44857) Huron(98), Erie(1)
NORWICH Muskingum
NOVA (44859) Ashland(92), Lorain(7)
NOVELTY Geauga
OAK HARBOR (43449) Ottawa(97), Sandusky(2)
OAK HILL (45656) Jackson(87), Gallia(7), Lawrence(4)
OAKWOOD Paulding
OBERLIN Lorain
OCEOLA Crawford
OHIO CITY Van Wert
OKEANA Butler
OKOLONA Henry
OLD FORT Seneca
OLD WASHINGTON Guernsey
OLMSTED FALLS Cuyahoga
ONTARIO Richland
ORANGEVILLE Trumbull
OREGON Lucas
OREGONIA Warren
ORIENT (43146) Pickaway(76), Franklin(21), Madison(1)
ORRVILLE Wayne
ORWELL (44076) Ashtabula(91), Trumbull(8)
OSGOOD Darke
OSTRANDER (43061) Delaware(82), Union(17)
OTTAWA Putnam
OTTOVILLE Putnam
OTWAY (45657) Scioto(80), Adams(17), Pike(2)
OVERPECK Butler
OWENSVILLE Clermont
OXFORD Butler
PAINESVILLE Lake
PALESTINE Darke
PANDORA (45877) Putnam(93), Allen(4), Hancock(1)
PARIS Stark
PARKMAN Geauga
PATASKALA Licking
PATRIOT Gallia
PAULDING Paulding
PAYNE Paulding
PEDRO Lawrence
PEEBLES (45660) Adams(87), Pike(10), Highland(2)
PEMBERTON Shelby
PEMBERVILLE Wood
PENINSULA Summit
PERRY Lake
PERRYSBURG Wood
PERRYSVILLE (44864) Ashland(61), Richland(38)
PETERSBURG (44454) Mahoning(84), Columbiana(15)
PETTISVILLE Fulton
PHILLIPSBURG Montgomery
PHILO Muskingum
PICKERINGTON Fairfield
PIEDMONT (43983) Belmont(57), Guernsey(29), Harrison(14)
PIERPONT Ashtabula
PIKETON Pike
PINEY FORK Jefferson
PIONEER Williams
PIQUA (45356) Miami(96), Shelby(3)
PITSBURG Darke
PLAIN CITY (43064) Madison(52), Union(45), Franklin(1)
PLAINFIELD Coshocton
PLEASANT CITY (43772) Guernsey(58), Noble(41)
PLEASANT HILL Miami
PLEASANT PLAIN (45162) Warren(97), Clermont(2)
PLEASANTVILLE (43148) Fairfield(90), Perry(9)
PLYMOUTH (44865) Richland(49), Huron(45), Crawford(4)
POLK Ashland
POMEROY Meigs
PORT CLINTON Ottawa
PORT JEFFERSON Shelby
PORT WASHINGTON (43837) Tuscarawas(96), Guernsey(3)
PORT WILLIAM Clinton
PORTAGE Wood
PORTLAND Meigs
PORTSMOUTH Scioto
POTSDAM Miami
POWELL (43065) Delaware(85), Franklin(14)
POWHATAN POINT (43942) Belmont(92), Monroe(7)
PROCTORVILLE Lawrence
PROSPECT (43342) Marion(91), Delaware(6), Union(2)
PUT IN BAY Ottawa
QUAKER CITY (43773) Guernsey(54), Noble(39), Belmont(2), Monroe(2)
QUINCY (43343) Logan(89), Champaign(6), Shelby(3)
RACINE Meigs
RADCLIFF Vinton
RADNOR Delaware
RANDOLPH Portage
RARDEN (45671) Scioto(66), Pike(20), Adams(8), Fairfield(4)
RAVENNA Portage
RAWSON Hancock
RAY (45672) Vinton(68), Jackson(26), Ross(4)
RAYLAND (43943) Jefferson(96), Belmont(3)
RAYMOND Union
REEDSVILLE Meigs
REESVILLE Clinton
RENO Washington
REPUBLIC Seneca
REYNOLDSBURG (43068) Franklin(74), Licking(18), Fairfield(7)
REYNOLDSBURG Franklin
RICHFIELD Summit
RICHMOND Jefferson
RICHMOND DALE Ross
RICHWOOD (43344) Union(96), Delaware(2)
RIDGEVILLE CORNERS Henry
RIDGEWAY (43345) Hardin(61), Logan(38)
RIO GRANDE Gallia
RIPLEY Brown
RISINGSUN (43457) Wood(69), Sandusky(26), Seneca(4)
RITTMAN (44270) Wayne(94), Medina(5)
ROBERTSVILLE Stark
ROCK CAMP Lawrence
ROCK CREEK Ashtabula
ROCKBRIDGE Hocking
ROCKFORD (45882) Mercer(94), Van Wert(5)
ROCKY RIDGE Ottawa
ROCKY RIVER Cuyahoga
ROGERS Columbiana
ROME Ashtabula
ROOTSTOWN Portage
ROSEVILLE (43777) Muskingum(55), Perry(44)
ROSEWOOD Champaign
ROSS Butler
ROSSBURG Darke
ROSSFORD Wood
ROUNDHEAD Hardin
RUDOLPH Wood
RUSHSYLVANIA (43347) Logan(89), Hardin(10)
RUSHVILLE (43150) Fairfield(67), Perry(32)
RUSSELLS POINT Logan
RUSSELLVILLE Brown
RUSSIA Shelby
RUTLAND Meigs
SABINA (45169) Clinton(98), Fayette(1)
SAINT CLAIRSVILLE Belmont
SAINT HENRY Mercer
SAINT JOHNS Auglaize
SAINT LOUISVILLE Licking
SAINT MARYS Auglaize
SAINT PARIS Champaign
SALEM (44460) Columbiana(88), Mahoning(11)
SALESVILLE (43778) Guernsey(97), Noble(2)
SALINEVILLE (43945) Columbiana(71), Carroll(19), Jefferson(9)
SANDUSKY Erie
SANDYVILLE Tuscarawas
SARAHSVILLE Noble
SARDINIA Brown
SARDIS Monroe
SAVANNAH Ashland
SCIO (43988) Harrison(71), Carroll(28)
SCIOTO FURNACE Scioto
SCOTT (45886) Van Wert(55), Paulding(45)
SCOTTOWN (45678) Lawrence(80), Gallia(19)
SEAMAN (45679) Adams(92), Highland(7)
SEBRING Mahoning
SEDALIA Madison
SENECAVILLE (43780) Guernsey(69), Noble(30)
SEVEN MILE Butler
SEVILLE Medina
SHADE (45776) Meigs(52), Athens(47)
SHADYSIDE Belmont
SHANDON Butler
SHARON CENTER Medina
SHARPSBURG Athens
SHAUCK Morrow
SHAWNEE Perry
SHEFFIELD LAKE Lorain
SHELBY (44875) Richland(97), Crawford(2)
SHERRODSVILLE (44675) Carroll(70), Tuscarawas(29)
SHERWOOD Defiance
SHILOH (44878) Richland(90), Huron(6), Ashland(3)
SHORT CREEK Harrison
SHREVE (44676) Wayne(82), Holmes(17)
SIDNEY Shelby
SINKING SPRING Highland
SMITHFIELD Jefferson
SMITHVILLE Wayne
SOLON Cuyahoga
SOMERDALE Tuscarawas
SOMERSET Perry
SOMERVILLE Butler
SOUTH BLOOMINGVILLE (43152) Hocking(81), Vinton(18)
SOUTH CHARLESTON (45368) Clark(97), Greene(2)
SOUTH LEBANON Warren
SOUTH POINT Lawrence
SOUTH SALEM Ross
SOUTH SOLON (43153) Madison(76), Fayette(10), Clark(7), Greene(4)
SOUTH VIENNA Clark
SOUTH WEBSTER (45682) Scioto(96), Jackson(2)
SOUTHINGTON (44470) Trumbull(98), Portage(1)
SPARTA Morrow
SPENCER (44275) Medina(93), Lorain(6)
SPENCERVILLE (45887) Allen(75), Auglaize(14), Van Wert(7), Mercer(2)
SPRING HILL NURSERIES Miami
SPRING VALLEY Greene
SPRINGBORO Warren
SPRINGFIELD (45502) Clark(97), Champaign(2)
SPRINGFIELD Clark
STAFFORD Monroe
STERLING Wayne
STEUBENVILLE Jefferson
STEWART Athens
STEWARTSVILLE Belmont
STILLWATER Tuscarawas
STOCKDALE Pike
STOCKPORT (43787) Morgan(92), Washington(7)
STOCKPORT Morgan
STONE CREEK (43840) Coshocton(70), Tuscarawas(29)
STONY RIDGE Wood
STOUT (45684) Scioto(67), Adams(32)
STOUTSVILLE (43154) Fairfield(78), Pickaway(21)
STOW Summit
STRASBURG Tuscarawas
STRATTON Jefferson
STREETSBORO Portage
STRONGSVILLE Cuyahoga
STRUTHERS Mahoning
STRYKER (43557) Williams(81), Henry(12), Fulton(5)
SUGAR GROVE (43155) Fairfield(74), Hocking(25)
SUGARCREEK (44681) Tuscarawas(77), Holmes(22)
SULLIVAN (44880) Ashland(81), Lorain(15), Medina(2)
SULPHUR SPRINGS Crawford
SUMMERFIELD (43788) Noble(76), Monroe(23)
SUMMIT STATION Licking
SUMMITVILLE Columbiana
SUNBURY (43074) Delaware(98), Licking(1)
SWANTON (43558) Fulton(57), Lucas(42)
SYCAMORE (44882) Wyandot(65), Crawford(29), Seneca(5)
SYCAMORE VALLEY Monroe
SYLVANIA Lucas
SYRACUSE Meigs
TALLMADGE (44278) Summit(97), Portage(2)
TARLTON Pickaway
TERRACE PARK Hamilton
THE PLAINS Athens
THOMPSON (44086) Geauga(79), Lake(15), Ashtabula(5)
THORNVILLE (43076) Perry(45), Licking(30), Fairfield(23)
THURMAN (45685) Gallia(72), Jackson(27)
THURSTON Fairfield
TIFFIN Seneca
TILTONSVILLE Jefferson
TIPP CITY (45371) Miami(98), Montgomery(1)

TIPPECANOE (44699) Harrison(72), Tuscarawas(24), Guernsey(2)
TIRO Crawford
TOLEDO (43605) Lucas(97), Wood(2)
TOLEDO Lucas
TOLEDO Wood
TONTOGANY Wood
TORCH Athens
TORONTO Jefferson
TREMONT CITY Clark
TRENTON Butler
TRIMBLE Athens
TRINWAY Muskingum
TROY Miami
TUPPERS PLAINS Meigs
TUSCARAWAS Tuscarawas
TWINSBURG Summit
UHRICHSVILLE (44683) Tuscarawas(91), Harrison(8)
UNION CITY Darke
UNION FURNACE Hocking
UNIONPORT Jefferson
UNIONTOWN (44685) Stark(51), Summit(48)
UNIONVILLE Ashtabula
UNIONVILLE CENTER Union
UNIOPOLIS Auglaize
UPPER SANDUSKY Wyandot
UTICA (43080) Licking(70), Knox(29)
VALLEY CITY (44280) Medina(95), Lorain(4)
VAN BUREN Hancock
VAN WERT Van Wert
VANDALIA Montgomery
VANLUE Hancock
VAUGHNSVILLE Putnam
VENEDOCIA (45894) Van Wert(96), Mercer(2)
VERMILION (44089) Erie(56), Lorain(43)
VERONA Preble
VERSAILLES Darke
VICKERY (43464) Sandusky(76), Erie(23)
VIENNA Trumbull
VINCENT Washington
VINTON Gallia
WADSWORTH Medina
WAKEFIELD Pike
WAKEMAN (44889) Huron(58), Erie(31), Lorain(10)
WALBRIDGE Wood
WALDO (43356) Marion(77), Delaware(14), Morrow(7)
WALHONDING (43843) Coshocton(65), Knox(34)
WALNUT CREEK Holmes
WAPAKONETA (45895) Auglaize(98), Logan(1)
WARNOCK Belmont
WARREN (44481) Trumbull(98), Mahoning(1)
WARREN Trumbull
WARSAW (43844) Coshocton(95), Knox(4)
WASHINGTON COURT HOUSE (43160) Fayette(98), Ross(1)
WASHINGTONVILLE Columbiana
WATERFORD (45786) Washington(93), Morgan(6)
WATERLOO (45688) Lawrence(93), Gallia(6)
WATERTOWN Washington
WATERVILLE Lucas
WAUSEON Fulton
WAVERLY (45690) Pike(92), Ross(7)
WAYLAND Portage
WAYNE Wood
WAYNESBURG (44688) Stark(88), Carroll(11)
WAYNESFIELD (45896) Auglaize(77), Hardin(11), Allen(10)
WAYNESVILLE Warren
WELLINGTON Lorain
WELLSTON Jackson
WELLSVILLE Columbiana
WEST ALEXANDRIA (45381) Preble(93), Montgomery(6)
WEST CHESTER Butler
WEST ELKTON Preble
WEST FARMINGTON (44491) Trumbull(82), Geauga(14), Portage(2)
WEST JEFFERSON Madison
WEST LAFAYETTE Coshocton
WEST LIBERTY (43357) Logan(75), Champaign(24)
WEST MANCHESTER (45382) Preble(77), Darke(22)
WEST MANSFIELD (43358) Logan(57), Union(42)
WEST MILLGROVE Wood
WEST MILTON Miami
WEST POINT Columbiana
WEST PORTSMOUTH Scioto
WEST RUSHVILLE Fairfield
WEST SALEM (44287) Wayne(63), Ashland(29), Medina(6)
WEST UNION Adams
WEST UNITY (43570) Williams(94), Fulton(5)
WESTERVILLE Delaware
WESTERVILLE Franklin
WESTFIELD CENTER Medina
WESTLAKE Cuyahoga
WESTON Wood
WESTVILLE Champaign
WHARTON Wyandot
WHEELERSBURG Scioto
WHIPPLE Washington
WHITE COTTAGE Muskingum
WHITEHOUSE Lucas
WICKLIFFE Lake
WILBERFORCE Greene
WILKESVILLE Vinton
WILLARD Huron
WILLIAMSBURG Clermont
WILLIAMSFIELD Ashtabula
WILLIAMSPORT (43164) Pickaway(95), Ross(4)
WILLIAMSTOWN Hancock
WILLISTON Ottawa
WILLOUGHBY Lake
WILLOW WOOD Lawrence
WILLSHIRE (45898) Van Wert(70), Mercer(29)
WILMINGTON Clinton
WILMOT (44689) Holmes(70), Stark(29)
WINCHESTER (45697) Adams(62), Brown(25), Highland(12)
WINDHAM (44288) Portage(98), Trumbull(1)
WINDSOR (44099) Ashtabula(87), Geauga(12)
WINESBURG Holmes
WINGETT RUN (45789) Washington(96), Monroe(3)
WINONA Columbiana
WINTERSVILLE Jefferson
WOLF RUN Jefferson
WOODSFIELD Monroe
WOODSTOCK (43084) Champaign(91), Union(8)
WOODVILLE (43469) Sandusky(93), Ottawa(5), Wood(1)
WOOSTER Wayne
WREN Van Wert
XENIA Greene
YELLOW SPRINGS (45387) Greene(92), Clark(7)
YORKSHIRE (45388) Darke(95), Mercer(2), Shelby(2)
YORKVILLE (43971) Jefferson(65), Belmont(34)
YOUNGSTOWN (44505) Mahoning(65), Trumbull(34)
YOUNGSTOWN Mahoning
ZALESKI Vinton
ZANESFIELD Logan
ZANESVILLE Muskingum
ZOAR Tuscarawas

Ohio ZIP/City Cross Reference

43001-43001 ALEXANDRIA
43002-43002 AMLIN
43003-43003 ASHLEY
43004-43004 BLACKLICK
43005-43005 BLADENSBURG
43006-43006 BRINKHAVEN
43007-43007 BROADWAY
43008-43008 BUCKEYE LAKE
43009-43009 CABLE
43010-43010 CATAWBA
43011-43011 CENTERBURG
43013-43013 CROTON
43014-43014 DANVILLE
43015-43015 DELAWARE
43016-43017 DUBLIN
43018-43018 ETNA
43019-43019 FREDERICKTOWN
43021-43021 GALENA
43022-43022 GAMBIER
43023-43023 GRANVILLE
43025-43025 HEBRON
43026-43026 HILLIARD
43027-43027 HOMER
43028-43028 HOWARD
43029-43029 IRWIN
43030-43030 JACKSONTOWN
43031-43031 JOHNSTOWN
43032-43032 KILBOURNE
43033-43033 KIRKERSVILLE
43035-43035 LEWIS CENTER
43036-43036 MAGNETIC SPRINGS
43037-43037 MARTINSBURG
43040-43041 MARYSVILLE
43044-43044 MECHANICSBURG
43045-43045 MILFORD CENTER
43046-43046 MILLERSPORT
43047-43047 MINGO
43048-43048 MOUNT LIBERTY
43050-43050 MOUNT VERNON
43054-43054 NEW ALBANY
43055-43058 NEWARK
43060-43060 NORTH LEWISBURG
43061-43061 OSTRANDER
43062-43062 PATASKALA
43064-43064 PLAIN CITY
43065-43065 POWELL
43066-43066 RADNOR
43067-43067 RAYMOND
43068-43069 REYNOLDSBURG
43070-43070 ROSEWOOD
43071-43071 SAINT LOUISVILLE
43072-43072 SAINT PARIS
43073-43073 SUMMIT STATION
43074-43074 SUNBURY
43076-43076 THORNVILLE
43077-43077 UNIONVILLE CENTER
43078-43078 URBANA
43080-43080 UTICA
43081-43082 WESTERVILLE
43083-43083 WESTVILLE
43084-43084 WOODSTOCK
43085-43085 COLUMBUS
43086-43086 WESTERVILLE
43093-43093 NEWARK
43098-43098 HEBRON
43099-43099 BLACKLICK
43101-43101 ADELPHI
43102-43102 AMANDA
43103-43103 ASHVILLE
43105-43105 BALTIMORE
43106-43106 BLOOMINGBURG
43107-43107 BREMEN
43109-43109 BRICE
43110-43110 CANAL WINCHESTER
43111-43111 CARBON HILL
43112-43112 CARROLL
43113-43113 CIRCLEVILLE
43115-43115 CLARKSBURG
43116-43116 COMMERCIAL POINT
43117-43117 DERBY
43119-43119 GALLOWAY
43123-43123 GROVE CITY
43125-43125 GROVEPORT
43126-43126 HARRISBURG
43127-43127 HAYDENVILLE
43128-43128 JEFFERSONVILLE
43130-43132 LANCASTER
43135-43135 LAURELVILLE
43136-43136 LITHOPOLIS
43137-43137 LOCKBOURNE
43138-43138 LOGAN
43140-43140 LONDON
43142-43142 MILLEDGEVILLE
43143-43143 MOUNT STERLING
43144-43144 MURRAY CITY
43145-43145 NEW HOLLAND
43146-43146 ORIENT
43147-43147 PICKERINGTON
43148-43148 PLEASANTVILLE
43149-43149 ROCKBRIDGE
43150-43150 RUSHVILLE
43151-43151 SEDALIA
43152-43152 SOUTH BLOOMINGVILLE
43153-43153 SOUTH SOLON
43154-43154 STOUTSVILLE
43155-43155 SUGAR GROVE
43156-43156 TARLTON
43157-43157 THURSTON
43158-43158 UNION FURNACE
43160-43160 WASHINGTON COURT HOUSE
43162-43162 WEST JEFFERSON
43163-43163 WEST RUSHVILLE
43164-43164 WILLIAMSPORT
43195-43199 GROVEPORT
43200-43299 COLUMBUS
43301-43307 MARION
43310-43310 BELLE CENTER
43311-43311 BELLEFONTAINE
43314-43314 CALEDONIA
43315-43315 CARDINGTON
43316-43316 CAREY
43317-43317 CHESTERVILLE
43318-43318 DE GRAFF
43319-43319 EAST LIBERTY
43320-43320 EDISON
43321-43321 FULTON
43322-43322 GREEN CAMP
43323-43323 HARPSTER
43324-43324 HUNTSVILLE
43325-43325 IBERIA
43326-43326 KENTON
43330-43330 KIRBY
43331-43331 LAKEVIEW
43332-43332 LA RUE
43333-43333 LEWISTOWN
43334-43334 MARENGO
43335-43335 MARTEL
43336-43336 MIDDLEBURG
43337-43337 MORRAL
43338-43338 MOUNT GILEAD
43340-43340 MOUNT VICTORY
43341-43341 NEW BLOOMINGTON
43342-43342 PROSPECT

43343-43343 QUINCY
43344-43344 RICHWOOD
43345-43345 RIDGEWAY
43346-43346 ROUNDHEAD
43347-43347 RUSHSYLVANIA
43348-43348 RUSSELLS POINT
43349-43349 SHAUCK
43350-43350 SPARTA
43351-43351 UPPER SANDUSKY
43356-43356 WALDO
43357-43357 WEST LIBERTY
43358-43358 WEST MANSFIELD
43359-43359 WHARTON
43360-43360 ZANESFIELD
43402-43403 BOWLING GREEN
43406-43406 BRADNER
43407-43407 BURGOON
43408-43408 CLAY CENTER
43410-43410 CLYDE
43412-43412 CURTICE
43413-43413 CYGNET
43414-43414 DUNBRIDGE
43416-43416 ELMORE
43420-43420 FREMONT
43430-43430 GENOA
43431-43431 GIBSONBURG
43432-43432 GRAYTOWN
43433-43433 GYPSUM
43434-43434 HARBOR VIEW
43435-43435 HELENA
43436-43436 ISLE SAINT GEORGE
43437-43437 JERRY CITY
43438-43438 KELLEYS ISLAND
43439-43439 LACARNE
43440-43440 LAKESIDE MARBLEHEAD
43441-43441 LEMOYNE
43442-43442 LINDSEY
43443-43443 LUCKEY
43445-43445 MARTIN
43446-43446 MIDDLE BASS
43447-43447 MILLBURY
43449-43449 OAK HARBOR
43450-43450 PEMBERVILLE
43451-43451 PORTAGE
43452-43452 PORT CLINTON
43456-43456 PUT IN BAY
43457-43457 RISINGSUN
43458-43458 ROCKY RIDGE
43460-43460 ROSSFORD
43462-43462 RUDOLPH
43463-43463 STONY RIDGE
43464-43464 VICKERY
43465-43465 WALBRIDGE
43466-43466 WAYNE
43467-43467 WEST MILLGROVE
43468-43468 WILLISTON
43469-43469 WOODVILLE
43501-43501 ALVORDTON
43502-43502 ARCHBOLD
43504-43504 BERKEY
43505-43505 BLAKESLEE
43506-43506 BRYAN
43510-43510 COLTON
43511-43511 CUSTAR
43512-43512 DEFIANCE
43515-43515 DELTA
43516-43516 DESHLER
43517-43517 EDGERTON
43518-43518 EDON
43519-43519 EVANSPORT
43520-43520 FARMER
43521-43521 FAYETTE
43522-43522 GRAND RAPIDS
43523-43523 GRELTON
43524-43524 HAMLER
43525-43525 HASKINS
43526-43526 HICKSVILLE
43527-43527 HOLGATE
43528-43528 HOLLAND
43529-43529 HOYTVILLE
43530-43530 JEWELL
43531-43531 KUNKLE
43532-43532 LIBERTY CENTER
43533-43533 LYONS
43534-43534 MC CLURE
43535-43535 MALINTA
43536-43536 MARK CENTER
43537-43537 MAUMEE
43540-43540 METAMORA
43541-43541 MILTON CENTER
43542-43542 MONCLOVA
43543-43543 MONTPELIER
43545-43545 NAPOLEON
43547-43547 NEAPOLIS
43548-43548 NEW BAVARIA
43549-43549 NEY
43550-43550 OKOLONA
43551-43552 PERRYSBURG
43553-43553 PETTISVILLE
43554-43554 PIONEER
43555-43555 RIDGEVILLE CORNERS
43556-43556 SHERWOOD
43557-43557 STRYKER
43558-43558 SWANTON
43560-43560 SYLVANIA
43565-43565 TONTOGANY
43566-43566 WATERVILLE
43567-43567 WAUSEON
43569-43569 WESTON
43570-43570 WEST UNITY
43571-43571 WHITEHOUSE
43600-43615 TOLEDO
43616-43616 OREGON
43617-43617 TOLEDO
43618-43618 OREGON
43619-43619 NORTHWOOD
43620-43699 TOLEDO
43701-43702 ZANESVILLE
43711-43711 AVA
43713-43713 BARNESVILLE
43716-43716 BEALLSVILLE
43717-43717 BELLE VALLEY
43718-43718 BELMONT
43719-43719 BETHESDA
43720-43720 BLUE ROCK
43721-43721 BROWNSVILLE
43722-43722 BUFFALO
43723-43723 BYESVILLE
43724-43724 CALDWELL
43725-43725 CAMBRIDGE
43727-43727 CHANDLERSVILLE
43728-43728 CHESTERHILL
43730-43730 CORNING
43731-43731 CROOKSVILLE
43732-43732 CUMBERLAND
43733-43733 DERWENT
43734-43734 DUNCAN FALLS
43735-43735 EAST FULTONHAM
43736-43736 FAIRVIEW
43738-43738 FULTONHAM
43739-43739 GLENFORD
43740-43740 GRATIOT
43746-43746 HOPEWELL
43747-43747 JERUSALEM
43748-43748 JUNCTION CITY
43749-43749 KIMBOLTON
43750-43750 KIPLING
43752-43752 LAINGS
43754-43754 LEWISVILLE
43755-43755 LORE CITY
43756-43756 MC CONNELSVILLE
43757-43757 MALAGA
43758-43758 MALTA
43759-43759 MORRISTOWN
43760-43760 MOUNT PERRY
43761-43761 MOXAHALA
43762-43762 NEW CONCORD
43764-43764 NEW LEXINGTON
43766-43766 NEW STRAITSVILLE
43767-43767 NORWICH
43768-43768 OLD WASHINGTON
43770-43770 STOCKPORT
43771-43771 PHILO
43772-43772 PLEASANT CITY
43773-43773 QUAKER CITY
43777-43777 ROSEVILLE
43778-43778 SALESVILLE
43779-43779 SARAHSVILLE
43780-43780 SENECAVILLE
43782-43782 SHAWNEE
43783-43783 SOMERSET
43786-43786 STAFFORD
43787-43787 STOCKPORT
43788-43788 SUMMERFIELD
43789-43789 SYCAMORE VALLEY
43791-43791 WHITE COTTAGE
43793-43793 WOODSFIELD
43802-43802 ADAMSVILLE
43803-43803 BAKERSVILLE
43804-43804 BALTIC
43805-43805 BLISSFIELD
43811-43811 CONESVILLE
43812-43812 COSHOCTON
43821-43821 DRESDEN
43822-43822 FRAZEYSBURG
43824-43824 FRESNO
43828-43828 KEENE
43830-43830 NASHPORT
43832-43832 NEWCOMERSTOWN
43836-43836 PLAINFIELD
43837-43837 PORT WASHINGTON
43840-43840 STONE CREEK
43842-43842 TRINWAY
43843-43843 WALHONDING
43844-43844 WARSAW
43845-43845 WEST LAFAYETTE
43901-43901 ADENA
43902-43902 ALLEDONIA
43903-43903 AMSTERDAM
43905-43905 BARTON
43906-43906 BELLAIRE
43907-43907 CADIZ
43908-43908 BERGHOLZ
43909-43909 BLAINE
43910-43910 BLOOMINGDALE
43912-43912 BRIDGEPORT
43913-43913 BRILLIANT
43914-43914 CAMERON
43915-43915 CLARINGTON
43916-43916 COLERAIN
43917-43917 DILLONVALE
43920-43920 EAST LIVERPOOL
43925-43925 EAST SPRINGFIELD
43926-43926 EMPIRE
43927-43927 FAIRPOINT
43928-43928 GLENCOE
43930-43930 HAMMONDSVILLE
43931-43931 HANNIBAL
43932-43932 IRONDALE
43933-43933 JACOBSBURG
43934-43934 LANSING
43935-43935 MARTINS FERRY
43937-43937 MAYNARD
43938-43938 MINGO JUNCTION
43939-43939 MOUNT PLEASANT
43940-43940 NEFFS
43941-43941 PINEY FORK
43942-43942 POWHATAN POINT
43943-43943 RAYLAND
43944-43944 RICHMOND
43945-43945 SALINEVILLE
43946-43946 SARDIS
43947-43947 SHADYSIDE
43948-43948 SMITHFIELD
43950-43950 SAINT CLAIRSVILLE
43951-43951 LAFFERTY
43952-43952 STEUBENVILLE
43953-43953 WINTERSVILLE
43960-43960 STEWARTSVILLE
43961-43961 STRATTON
43962-43962 SUMMITVILLE
43963-43963 TILTONSVILLE
43964-43964 TORONTO
43966-43966 UNIONPORT
43967-43967 WARNOCK
43968-43968 WELLSVILLE
43970-43970 WOLF RUN
43971-43971 YORKVILLE
43972-43972 BANNOCK
43973-43973 FREEPORT
43974-43974 HARRISVILLE
43976-43976 HOPEDALE
43977-43977 FLUSHING
43981-43981 NEW ATHENS
43983-43983 PIEDMONT
43984-43984 NEW RUMLEY
43985-43985 HOLLOWAY
43986-43986 JEWETT
43988-43988 SCIO
43989-43989 SHORT CREEK
44001-44001 AMHERST
44003-44003 ANDOVER
44004-44005 ASHTABULA
44010-44010 AUSTINBURG
44011-44011 AVON
44012-44012 AVON LAKE
44017-44017 BEREA
44021-44021 BURTON
44022-44023 CHAGRIN FALLS
44024-44024 CHARDON
44026-44026 CHESTERLAND
44028-44028 COLUMBIA STATION
44030-44030 CONNEAUT
44032-44032 DORSET
44033-44033 EAST CLARIDON
44035-44036 ELYRIA
44039-44039 NORTH RIDGEVILLE
44040-44040 GATES MILLS
44041-44041 GENEVA
44044-44044 GRAFTON
44045-44045 GRAND RIVER
44046-44046 HUNTSBURG
44047-44047 JEFFERSON
44048-44048 KINGSVILLE
44049-44049 KIPTON
44050-44050 LAGRANGE
44052-44053 LORAIN
44054-44054 SHEFFIELD LAKE
44055-44055 LORAIN
44056-44056 MACEDONIA
44057-44057 MADISON
44060-44061 MENTOR
44062-44062 MIDDLEFIELD
44064-44064 MONTVILLE
44065-44065 NEWBURY
44067-44067 NORTHFIELD
44068-44068 NORTH KINGSVILLE
44070-44070 NORTH OLMSTED
44072-44073 NOVELTY
44074-44074 OBERLIN
44076-44076 ORWELL
44077-44077 PAINESVILLE
44080-44080 PARKMAN
44081-44081 PERRY
44082-44082 PIERPONT
44084-44084 ROCK CREEK
44085-44085 ROME
44086-44086 THOMPSON
44087-44087 TWINSBURG
44088-44088 UNIONVILLE
44089-44089 VERMILION
44090-44090 WELLINGTON
44092-44092 WICKLIFFE
44093-44093 WILLIAMSFIELD
44094-44094 WILLOUGHBY
44095-44095 EASTLAKE
44096-44096 WILLOUGHBY
44097-44097 EASTLAKE
44099-44099 WINDSOR
44100-44106 CLEVELAND
44107-44107 LAKEWOOD
44108-44115 CLEVELAND
44116-44116 ROCKY RIVER
44117-44117 EUCLID
44118-44121 CLEVELAND
44122-44122 BEACHWOOD
44123-44123 EUCLID
44124-44130 CLEVELAND

44131-44131 INDEPENDENCE
44132-44132 EUCLID
44133-44133 NORTH ROYALTON
44134-44135 CLEVELAND
44136-44136 STRONGSVILLE
44137-44137 MAPLE HEIGHTS
44138-44138 OLMSTED FALLS
44139-44139 SOLON
44140-44140 BAY VILLAGE
44141-44141 BRECKSVILLE
44142-44142 BROOKPARK
44143-44144 CLEVELAND
44145-44145 WESTLAKE
44146-44146 BEDFORD
44147-44147 BROADVIEW HEIGHTS
44149-44149 STRONGSVILLE
44177-44199 CLEVELAND
44201-44201 ATWATER
44202-44202 AURORA
44203-44203 BARBERTON
44210-44210 BATH
44211-44211 BRADY LAKE
44212-44212 BRUNSWICK
44214-44214 BURBANK
44215-44215 CHIPPEWA LAKE
44216-44216 CLINTON
44217-44217 CRESTON
44221-44223 CUYAHOGA FALLS
44224-44224 STOW
44230-44230 DOYLESTOWN
44231-44231 GARRETTSVILLE
44232-44232 GREEN
44233-44233 HINCKLEY
44234-44234 HIRAM
44235-44235 HOMERVILLE
44236-44238 HUDSON
44240-44240 KENT
44241-44241 STREETSBORO
44242-44243 KENT
44250-44250 LAKEMORE
44251-44251 WESTFIELD CENTER
44253-44253 LITCHFIELD
44254-44254 LODI
44255-44255 MANTUA
44256-44259 MEDINA
44260-44260 MOGADORE
44262-44262 MUNROE FALLS
44264-44264 PENINSULA
44265-44265 RANDOLPH
44266-44266 RAVENNA
44270-44270 RITTMAN
44272-44272 ROOTSTOWN
44273-44273 SEVILLE
44274-44274 SHARON CENTER
44275-44275 SPENCER
44276-44276 STERLING
44278-44278 TALLMADGE
44280-44280 VALLEY CITY
44281-44282 WADSWORTH
44285-44285 WAYLAND
44286-44286 RICHFIELD
44287-44287 WEST SALEM
44288-44288 WINDHAM
44300-44317 AKRON
44318-44318 B F GOODRICH CO
44319-44334 AKRON
44334-44334 FAIRLAWN
44372-44399 AKRON
44401-44401 BERLIN CENTER
44402-44402 BRISTOLVILLE
44403-44403 BROOKFIELD
44404-44404 BURGHILL
44405-44405 CAMPBELL
44406-44406 CANFIELD
44408-44408 COLUMBIANA
44410-44410 CORTLAND
44411-44411 DEERFIELD
44412-44412 DIAMOND
44413-44413 EAST PALESTINE
44415-44415 ELKTON
44416-44416 ELLSWORTH
44417-44417 FARMDALE
44418-44418 FOWLER
44420-44420 GIRARD
44422-44422 GREENFORD
44423-44423 HANOVERTON
44424-44424 HARTFORD
44425-44425 HUBBARD
44427-44427 KENSINGTON
44428-44428 KINSMAN
44429-44429 LAKE MILTON
44430-44430 LEAVITTSBURG
44431-44431 LEETONIA
44432-44432 LISBON
44436-44436 LOWELLVILLE
44437-44437 MC DONALD
44438-44438 MASURY
44439-44439 MESOPOTAMIA
44440-44440 MINERAL RIDGE
44441-44441 NEGLEY
44442-44442 NEW MIDDLETOWN
44443-44443 NEW SPRINGFIELD
44444-44444 NEWTON FALLS
44445-44445 NEW WATERFORD
44446-44446 NILES
44449-44449 NORTH BENTON
44450-44450 NORTH BLOOMFIELD
44451-44451 NORTH JACKSON
44452-44452 NORTH LIMA
44453-44453 ORANGEVILLE
44454-44454 PETERSBURG
44455-44455 ROGERS
44460-44460 SALEM
44470-44470 SOUTHINGTON
44471-44471 STRUTHERS
44473-44473 VIENNA
44481-44488 WARREN
44490-44490 WASHINGTONVILLE
44491-44491 WEST FARMINGTON
44492-44492 WEST POINT
44493-44493 WINONA
44500-44599 YOUNGSTOWN
44601-44601 ALLIANCE
44606-44606 APPLE CREEK
44607-44607 AUGUSTA
44608-44608 BEACH CITY
44609-44609 BELOIT
44610-44610 BERLIN
44611-44611 BIG PRAIRIE
44612-44612 BOLIVAR
44613-44613 BREWSTER
44614-44614 CANAL FULTON
44615-44615 CARROLLTON
44617-44617 CHARM
44618-44618 DALTON
44619-44619 DAMASCUS
44620-44620 DELLROY
44621-44621 DENNISON
44622-44622 DOVER
44624-44624 DUNDEE
44625-44625 EAST ROCHESTER
44626-44626 EAST SPARTA
44627-44627 FREDERICKSBURG
44628-44628 GLENMONT
44629-44629 GNADENHUTTEN
44630-44630 GREENTOWN
44631-44631 HARLEM SPRINGS
44632-44632 HARTVILLE
44633-44633 HOLMESVILLE
44634-44634 HOMEWORTH
44636-44636 KIDRON
44637-44637 KILLBUCK
44638-44638 LAKEVILLE
44639-44639 LEESVILLE
44640-44640 LIMAVILLE
44641-44641 LOUISVILLE
44643-44643 MAGNOLIA
44644-44644 MALVERN
44645-44645 MARSHALLVILLE
44646-44648 MASSILLON
44650-44650 MAXIMO
44651-44651 MECHANICSTOWN
44652-44652 MIDDLEBRANCH
44653-44653 MIDVALE
44654-44654 MILLERSBURG
44656-44656 MINERAL CITY
44657-44657 MINERVA
44659-44659 MOUNT EATON
44660-44660 MOUNT HOPE
44661-44661 NASHVILLE
44662-44662 NAVARRE
44663-44663 NEW PHILADELPHIA
44665-44665 NORTH GEORGETOWN
44666-44666 NORTH LAWRENCE
44667-44667 ORRVILLE
44669-44669 PARIS
44670-44670 ROBERTSVILLE
44671-44671 SANDYVILLE
44672-44672 SEBRING
44675-44675 SHERRODSVILLE
44676-44676 SHREVE
44677-44677 SMITHVILLE
44678-44678 SOMERDALE
44679-44679 STILLWATER
44680-44680 STRASBURG
44681-44681 SUGARCREEK
44682-44682 TUSCARAWAS
44683-44683 UHRICHSVILLE
44685-44685 UNIONTOWN
44687-44687 WALNUT CREEK
44688-44688 WAYNESBURG
44689-44689 WILMOT
44690-44690 WINESBURG
44691-44691 WOOSTER
44693-44693 DEERSVILLE
44695-44695 BOWERSTON
44697-44697 ZOAR
44699-44699 TIPPECANOE
44700-44799 CANTON
44801-44801 ADRIAN
44802-44802 ALVADA
44803-44803 AMSDEN
44804-44804 ARCADIA
44805-44805 ASHLAND
44807-44807 ATTICA
44809-44809 BASCOM
44811-44811 BELLEVUE
44813-44813 BELLVILLE
44814-44814 BERLIN HEIGHTS
44815-44815 BETTSVILLE
44816-44816 BIRMINGHAM
44817-44817 BLOOMDALE
44818-44818 BLOOMVILLE
44820-44820 BUCYRUS
44822-44822 BUTLER
44824-44824 CASTALIA
44825-44825 CHATFIELD
44826-44826 COLLINS
44827-44827 CRESTLINE
44828-44828 FLAT ROCK
44829-44829 FORT SENECA
44830-44830 FOSTORIA
44833-44833 GALION
44836-44836 GREEN SPRINGS
44837-44837 GREENWICH
44838-44838 HAYESVILLE
44839-44839 HURON
44840-44840 JEROMESVILLE
44841-44841 KANSAS
44842-44842 LOUDONVILLE
44843-44843 LUCAS
44844-44844 MC CUTCHENVILLE
44845-44845 MELMORE
44846-44846 MILAN
44847-44847 MONROEVILLE
44848-44848 NANKIN
44849-44849 NEVADA
44850-44850 NEW HAVEN
44851-44851 NEW LONDON
44853-44853 NEW RIEGEL
44854-44854 NEW WASHINGTON
44855-44855 NORTH FAIRFIELD
44856-44856 NORTH ROBINSON
44857-44857 NORWALK
44859-44859 NOVA
44860-44860 OCEOLA
44861-44861 OLD FORT
44862-44862 ONTARIO
44864-44864 PERRYSVILLE
44865-44865 PLYMOUTH
44866-44866 POLK
44867-44867 REPUBLIC
44870-44871 SANDUSKY
44874-44874 SAVANNAH
44875-44875 SHELBY
44878-44878 SHILOH
44880-44880 SULLIVAN
44881-44881 SULPHUR SPRINGS
44882-44882 SYCAMORE
44883-44883 TIFFIN
44887-44887 TIRO
44888-44888 WILLARD
44889-44889 WAKEMAN
44890-44890 WILLARD
44900-44999 MANSFIELD
45001-45001 ADDYSTON
45002-45002 CLEVES
45003-45003 COLLEGE CORNER
45004-45004 COLLINSVILLE
45005-45005 FRANKLIN
45011-45013 HAMILTON
45014-45014 FAIRFIELD
45015-45015 HAMILTON
45018-45018 FAIRFIELD
45020-45026 HAMILTON
45030-45030 HARRISON
45032-45032 HARVEYSBURG
45033-45033 HOOVEN
45034-45034 KINGS MILLS
45036-45036 LEBANON
45039-45039 MAINEVILLE
45040-45040 MASON
45041-45041 MIAMITOWN
45042-45044 MIDDLETOWN
45050-45050 MONROE
45051-45051 MOUNT SAINT JOSEPH
45052-45052 NORTH BEND
45053-45053 OKEANA
45054-45054 OREGONIA
45055-45055 OVERPECK
45056-45056 OXFORD
45061-45061 ROSS
45062-45062 SEVEN MILE
45063-45063 SHANDON
45064-45064 SOMERVILLE
45065-45065 SOUTH LEBANON
45066-45066 SPRINGBORO
45067-45067 TRENTON
45068-45068 WAYNESVILLE
45069-45069 WEST CHESTER
45070-45070 WEST ELKTON
45071-45071 WEST CHESTER
45073-45099 MONROE
45101-45101 ABERDEEN
45102-45102 AMELIA
45103-45103 BATAVIA
45105-45105 BENTONVILLE
45106-45106 BETHEL
45107-45107 BLANCHESTER
45110-45110 BUFORD
45111-45111 CAMP DENNISON
45112-45112 CHILO
45113-45113 CLARKSVILLE
45114-45114 CUBA
45115-45115 DECATUR
45118-45118 FAYETTEVILLE
45119-45119 FEESBURG
45120-45120 FELICITY
45121-45121 GEORGETOWN
45122-45122 GOSHEN
45123-45123 GREENFIELD
45130-45130 HAMERSVILLE
45131-45131 HIGGINSPORT
45132-45132 HIGHLAND
45133-45133 HILLSBORO
45135-45135 LEESBURG
45138-45138 LEES CREEK
45140-45140 LOVELAND

45142-45142 LYNCHBURG
45144-45144 MANCHESTER
45145-45145 MARATHON
45146-45146 MARTINSVILLE
45147-45147 MIAMIVILLE
45148-45148 MIDLAND
45150-45150 MILFORD
45152-45152 MORROW
45153-45153 MOSCOW
45154-45154 MOUNT ORAB
45155-45155 MOWRYSTOWN
45156-45156 NEVILLE
45157-45157 NEW RICHMOND
45158-45158 NEWTONSVILLE
45159-45159 NEW VIENNA
45160-45160 OWENSVILLE
45162-45162 PLEASANT PLAIN
45164-45164 PORT WILLIAM
45165-45165 GREENFIELD
45166-45166 REESVILLE
45167-45167 RIPLEY
45168-45168 RUSSELLVILLE
45169-45169 SABINA
45171-45171 SARDINIA
45172-45172 SINKING SPRING
45174-45174 TERRACE PARK
45176-45176 WILLIAMSBURG
45177-45177 WILMINGTON
45200-45299 CINCINNATI
45301-45301 ALPHA
45302-45302 ANNA
45303-45303 ANSONIA
45304-45304 ARCANUM
45305-45305 BELLBROOK
45306-45306 BOTKINS
45307-45307 BOWERSVILLE
45308-45308 BRADFORD
45309-45309 BROOKVILLE
45310-45310 BURKETTSVILLE
45311-45311 CAMDEN
45312-45312 CASSTOWN
45314-45314 CEDARVILLE
45315-45315 CLAYTON
45316-45316 CLIFTON
45317-45317 CONOVER
45318-45318 COVINGTON
45319-45319 DONNELSVILLE
45320-45320 EATON
45321-45321 ELDORADO
45322-45322 ENGLEWOOD
45323-45323 ENON
45324-45324 FAIRBORN
45325-45325 FARMERSVILLE
45326-45326 FLETCHER
45327-45327 GERMANTOWN
45328-45328 GETTYSBURG
45329-45329 GORDON
45330-45330 GRATIS
45331-45331 GREENVILLE
45332-45332 HOLLANSBURG
45333-45333 HOUSTON
45334-45334 JACKSON CENTER
45335-45335 JAMESTOWN
45336-45336 KETTLERSVILLE
45337-45337 LAURA
45338-45338 LEWISBURG
45339-45339 LUDLOW FALLS
45340-45340 MAPLEWOOD
45341-45341 MEDWAY
45342-45343 MIAMISBURG
45344-45344 NEW CARLISLE
45345-45345 NEW LEBANON
45346-45346 NEW MADISON
45347-45347 NEW PARIS
45348-45348 NEW WESTON
45349-45349 NORTH HAMPTON
45350-45350 NORTH STAR
45351-45351 OSGOOD
45352-45352 PALESTINE
45353-45353 PEMBERTON
45354-45354 PHILLIPSBURG
45356-45356 PIQUA
45358-45358 PITSBURG
45359-45359 PLEASANT HILL
45360-45360 PORT JEFFERSON
45361-45361 POTSDAM
45362-45362 ROSSBURG
45363-45363 RUSSIA
45365-45365 SIDNEY
45366-45366 SPRING HILL NURSERIES
45367-45367 SIDNEY
45368-45368 SOUTH CHARLESTON
45369-45369 SOUTH VIENNA
45370-45370 SPRING VALLEY
45371-45371 TIPP CITY
45372-45372 TREMONT CITY
45373-45374 TROY
45377-45377 VANDALIA
45378-45378 VERONA
45380-45380 VERSAILLES
45381-45381 WEST ALEXANDRIA
45382-45382 WEST MANCHESTER
45383-45383 WEST MILTON
45384-45384 WILBERFORCE
45385-45385 XENIA
45387-45387 YELLOW SPRINGS
45388-45388 YORKSHIRE
45389-45389 CHRISTIANSBURG
45390-45390 UNION CITY
45401-45490 DAYTON
45500-45506 SPRINGFIELD
45601-45601 CHILLICOTHE
45612-45612 BAINBRIDGE
45613-45613 BEAVER
45614-45614 BIDWELL
45616-45616 BLUE CREEK
45617-45617 BOURNEVILLE
45618-45618 CHERRY FORK
45619-45619 CHESAPEAKE
45620-45620 CHESHIRE
45621-45621 COALTON
45622-45622 CREOLA
45623-45623 CROWN CITY
45624-45624 CYNTHIANA
45628-45628 FRANKFORT
45629-45629 FRANKLIN FURNACE
45630-45630 FRIENDSHIP
45631-45631 GALLIPOLIS
45633-45633 HALLSVILLE
45634-45634 HAMDEN
45636-45636 HAVERHILL
45638-45638 IRONTON
45640-45640 JACKSON
45642-45642 JASPER
45643-45643 KERR
45644-45644 KINGSTON
45645-45645 KITTS HILL
45646-45646 LATHAM
45647-45647 LONDONDERRY
45648-45648 LUCASVILLE
45650-45650 LYNX
45651-45651 MC ARTHUR
45652-45652 MC DERMOTT
45653-45653 MINFORD
45654-45654 NEW PLYMOUTH
45656-45656 OAK HILL
45657-45657 OTWAY
45658-45658 PATRIOT
45659-45659 PEDRO
45660-45660 PEEBLES
45661-45661 PIKETON
45662-45662 PORTSMOUTH
45663-45663 WEST PORTSMOUTH
45669-45669 PROCTORVILLE
45670-45670 RADCLIFF
45671-45671 RARDEN
45672-45672 RAY
45673-45673 RICHMOND DALE
45674-45674 RIO GRANDE
45675-45675 ROCK CAMP
45677-45677 SCIOTO FURNACE
45678-45678 SCOTTOWN
45679-45679 SEAMAN
45680-45680 SOUTH POINT
45681-45681 SOUTH SALEM
45682-45682 SOUTH WEBSTER
45683-45683 STOCKDALE
45684-45684 STOUT
45685-45685 THURMAN
45686-45686 VINTON
45687-45687 WAKEFIELD
45688-45688 WATERLOO
45690-45690 WAVERLY
45692-45692 WELLSTON
45693-45693 WEST UNION
45694-45694 WHEELERSBURG
45695-45695 WILKESVILLE
45696-45696 WILLOW WOOD
45697-45697 WINCHESTER
45698-45698 ZALESKI
45699-45699 LUCASVILLE
45701-45701 ATHENS
45710-45710 ALBANY
45711-45711 AMESVILLE
45712-45712 BARLOW
45713-45713 BARTLETT
45714-45714 BELPRE
45715-45715 BEVERLY
45716-45716 BUCHTEL
45717-45717 CARBONDALE
45719-45719 CHAUNCEY
45720-45720 CHESTER
45721-45721 COAL RUN
45723-45723 COOLVILLE
45724-45724 CUTLER
45727-45727 DEXTER CITY
45729-45729 FLEMING
45730-45730 JACKSON
45732-45732 GLOUSTER
45734-45734 GRAYSVILLE
45735-45735 GUYSVILLE
45739-45739 HOCKINGPORT
45740-45740 JACKSONVILLE
45741-45741 LANGSVILLE
45742-45742 LITTLE HOCKING
45743-45743 LONG BOTTOM
45744-45744 LOWELL
45745-45745 LOWER SALEM
45746-45746 MACKSBURG
45750-45750 MARIETTA
45760-45760 MIDDLEPORT
45761-45761 MILLFIELD
45764-45764 NELSONVILLE
45766-45766 NEW MARSHFIELD
45767-45767 NEW MATAMORAS
45768-45768 NEWPORT
45769-45769 POMEROY
45770-45770 PORTLAND
45771-45771 RACINE
45772-45772 REEDSVILLE
45773-45773 RENO
45775-45775 RUTLAND
45776-45776 SHADE
45777-45777 SHARPSBURG
45778-45778 STEWART
45779-45779 SYRACUSE
45780-45780 THE PLAINS
45781-45781 TORCH
45782-45782 TRIMBLE
45783-45783 TUPPERS PLAINS
45784-45784 VINCENT
45786-45786 WATERFORD
45787-45787 WATERTOWN
45788-45788 WHIPPLE
45789-45789 WINGETT RUN
45801-45807 LIMA
45808-45808 BEAVERDAM
45809-45809 GOMER
45810-45810 ADA
45812-45812 ALGER
45813-45813 ANTWERP
45814-45814 ARLINGTON
45815-45815 BELMORE
45816-45816 BENTON RIDGE
45817-45817 BLUFFTON
45819-45819 BUCKLAND
45820-45820 CAIRO
45821-45821 CECIL
45822-45822 CELINA
45826-45826 CHICKASAW
45827-45827 CLOVERDALE
45828-45828 COLDWATER
45830-45830 COLUMBUS GROVE
45831-45831 CONTINENTAL
45832-45832 CONVOY
45833-45833 DELPHOS
45835-45835 DOLA
45836-45836 DUNKIRK
45837-45837 DUPONT
45838-45838 ELGIN
45839-45840 FINDLAY
45841-45841 JENERA
45843-45843 FOREST
45844-45844 FORT JENNINGS
45845-45845 FORT LORAMIE
45846-45846 FORT RECOVERY
45848-45848 GLANDORF
45849-45849 GROVER HILL
45850-45850 HARROD
45851-45851 HAVILAND
45853-45853 KALIDA
45854-45854 LAFAYETTE
45855-45855 LATTY
45856-45856 LEIPSIC
45858-45858 MC COMB
45859-45859 MC GUFFEY
45860-45860 MARIA STEIN
45861-45861 MELROSE
45862-45862 MENDON
45863-45863 MIDDLE POINT
45864-45864 MILLER CITY
45865-45865 MINSTER
45866-45866 MONTEZUMA
45867-45867 MOUNT BLANCHARD
45868-45868 MOUNT CORY
45869-45869 NEW BREMEN
45870-45870 NEW HAMPSHIRE
45871-45871 NEW KNOXVILLE
45872-45872 NORTH BALTIMORE
45873-45873 OAKWOOD
45874-45874 OHIO CITY
45875-45875 OTTAWA
45876-45876 OTTOVILLE
45877-45877 PANDORA
45879-45879 PAULDING
45880-45880 PAYNE
45881-45881 RAWSON
45882-45882 ROCKFORD
45883-45883 SAINT HENRY
45884-45884 SAINT JOHNS
45885-45885 SAINT MARYS
45886-45886 SCOTT
45887-45887 SPENCERVILLE
45888-45888 UNIOPOLIS
45889-45889 VAN BUREN
45890-45890 VANLUE
45891-45891 VAN WERT
45893-45893 VAUGHNSVILLE
45894-45894 VENEDOCIA
45895-45895 WAPAKONETA
45896-45896 WAYNESFIELD
45897-45897 WILLIAMSTOWN
45898-45898 WILLSHIRE
45899-45899 WREN
45944-45999 CINCINNATI

Oklahoma

General Help Numbers:

Governor's Office

State Capitol, Suite 212 — 405-521-2342
Oklahoma City, OK 73105 — Fax 405-521-3353
http://www.governor.state.ok.us — 8AM-5PM

Attorney General's Office

2300 N Lincoln, #112 — 405-521-3921
Oklahoma City, OK 73105 — Fax 405-521-6246
www.oag.state.ok.us/ — 8:30AM-5PM

Legislative Records

Oklahoma Legislature, State Capitol,
Bill Status Info-Rm B-30, Copies-Rm 310 — 405-521-5642
Oklahoma City, OK 73105 — Fax 405-521-5507
www.lsb.state.ok.us — 8:30AM-4:30PM

State Archives

Archives & Records Mgt Divisions — 405-522-3577
200 NE 18th — Fax 405-525-7804
Oklahoma City, OK 73105-3298 — 8AM-5PM
www.odl.state.ok.us

State Specifics:

Capital:	Oklahoma City Oklahoma County
Time Zone:	CST
Number of Counties:	77
Population:	3,642,361
Web Site:	www.ok.gov

State Agencies

Criminal Records

OK State Bureau of Investigation, Criminal History Reporting, 6600 N Harvey, Oklahoma City, OK 73116; 405-848-6724, 405-879-2690, Fax- 405-879-2503; 8:30AM-4:30PM.

www.ok.gov/osbi/

A record request form is available at the website. Questions may be emailed to sylvia@osbi.state.ok.us.

Indexing & Storage: Records available from 1925 on and maintained indefinitely. New records available for inquiry in 5 to 7 days. Per a 2003 DOJ Study, 32% of all arrests in database have final dispositions recorded, 33% for those arrests within last 5 years. However, the agency is working on updating more records and the % numbers are increasing.

Searching: The agency offers billing accounts for entities ordering more than 50 requests per month. Include in request- Full name and DOB or approximate age, also aliases and reason for request. SSN, sex, and race are helpful and provide a better search, but not required. Fingerprints optional. A signed release is not required. 100% of the records are fingerprint-supported. A sex offender search will also be included with search but only if requested. This data not released- juvenile records. FBI checks. Arrest records without dispositions are released if the party was fingerprinted. Computer searches include arrests without dispositions.

Access by: mail, fax, in person.

Fee & Payment: The fee for a computer name search is $15.00. Add $4.00 for a in-state fingerprint search. Fee payee- O.S.B.I. Prepayment or account required. Establish a billing account via Carol at carolk@osbi.state.ok.us or call 405-879-2653, 50 requests per month minimum. Personal checks not accepted. Visa/MC/Discover credit cards are accepted.

Mail search: Turnaround time- 2 weeks. Download a request form from the internet at www.ok.gov/osbi/Criminal_History/index.html. A SASE is requested. Allow 4 weeks turnaround time for requests with fingerprints.

Fax search: Use of credit card and their "Credit Card Fax Form" is required. Call to have them fax you the form or download at www.ok.gov/osbi/Criminal_History/index.html. Results can be returned by fax within 72 hours.

In person: Name requests take 15 minutes; multiple requests same to next day; fingerprint searches take up to four weeks to process.

Expedited service: Requests received via an express service are processed within 1-3 days. For expedited return, include a prepaid return envelope.

Statewide Court Records

Administrative Office of Courts, 1915 N Stiles, #305, Oklahoma City, OK 73105; 405-521-2450, Fax- 405-521-6815; 8AM-5PM.

www.oscn.net

Direct questions to webmaster@oscn.net.

Online search: Free Internet access is available for District Courts in 13 populous counties and all Appellate courts at www.oscn.net. Both civil and criminal docket information is available for the counties involved. Also, the Oklahoma District Court Records free and an advanced pay service for at least 64 courts. More counties are being added as they are readied. The advanced subscription permits searching by DOB, address, and provides email notification and a tracking service. Please note most counties in this system go back at least seven years. Some courts update monthly, but most update daily. Visit www1.odcr.com/search.php. They hope to eventually feature all OK District Courts

Sexual Offender Registry

Oklahoma Department of Corrections, Sex Offender Registry, 3400 Martin Luther King Ave, Oklahoma City, OK 73106; 405-425-2872, Fax- 405-425-7070; 8AM-5PM.

http://docapp8.doc.state.ok.us/servlet/page?_pageid=422&_dad=portal30&_schema=PORTAL30&id=1

Indexing & Storage: Records available from 1989. New records available for inquiry in 7 days.

Searching: Include in request- name and DOB. This data not released- SSN

Access by: mail, phone, fax, online.

Fee & Payment: The copy fee is $.25 per page. Fee payee- OK Dept of Corrections Personal checks not accepted.

Mail search: Turnaround time- 1-3 days. A SASE is not requested. Names searches and geographic lists are available by mail.

Phone search: Telephone requests are accepted.

Fax search: Fax requests are accepted.

Online search: Searching is available from the website. There are a number of search options. A parole status search is available at http://gov.ok.gov/parole/parole_lookup.php.

Other access: Database and bulk purchases can be requested from the IT department. Call for pricing and media.

Incarceration Records

Oklahoma Department of Corrections, Offender Records, PO Box 11400, Oklahoma City, OK 73136 (Courier address- 3400 Martin Luther King Avenue, Oklahoma City, 73136); 405-425-2624, Fax- 405-425-2608; 8AM-5PM.

www.doc.state.ok.us

Indexing & Storage: Records available on current and former offenders.

Searching: Records are maintained indefinitely. Paper records go back 10 years. Include in request- provide first and last name; DOB, SSN and DOC number helpful. Location, DOC number, physical identifiers, conviction and sentencing information, and release dates are provided. This data not released- SSN, offender home address.

Access by: mail, phone, fax, online.

Mail search: Turnaround time- 5 to 10 working days. A SASE is not requested.

Phone search: Limited phone searching available.

Fax search: May request via the fax.

Online search: At the main website, click on Offender Information or visit www.doc.state.ok.us/offenders/offenders.htm. The online system is not available between 3:15 AM to 3:20 AM Monday through Friday, and 3:15 AM to 7:00 AM Saturdays for system maintenance.

Corporation, LLC, LP, LLP, Trade Name, Fictitious Name, Trademark

Secretary of State, Business Records Department, 2300 N Lincoln Blvd, Rm 101, Oklahoma City, OK 73105-4897; 405-521-4211 (Certification), 405-522-4211 (Record Orders), Fax- 405-521-3771; 8AM-5PM.

www.sos.state.ok.us

Officers are available from the Franchise Tax Dept. of the Oklahoma Tax Commission, 405-521-3161.

Indexing & Storage: Records available from late 1800's on. Older records are kept at the State Archives. Most recent records are maintained on a PC-based system. New records available for inquiry immediately.

Searching: The search includes correct name, status, date of registration, service agent and address, state of domicile, authorized shares and par value, amendments, name changes, mergers, and trade names. The records do not include owner names and addresses. Include in request- full name of business. Records include: corporations, limited partnerships, limited liability companies, limited liability partnerships, certificate of partnership fictitious name for general partnerships and trade names.

Access by: mail, phone, fax, in person, online.

Fee & Payment: Copies are $1.00 per page. Certification is $10.00 plus the copy fee. If a certificate is need to state that an entity is NOT registered, the fee is $20.00. See phone fee below. Fee payee- Secretary of State. Prepayment required. Personal checks accepted. Credit cards access for online, fax and phone requests.

Mail search: Turnaround time- 1 to 2 days. A SASE is not requested.

Phone search: The fee is $5.00 per call at the 405-522-4211 line, you are allowed up to 3 record searches per call.

Fax search: Turnaround time 1 to 2 days.

In person: There is no fee to search records on a public access terminal.

Online search: Visit SOONERAccess at https://www.sooneraccess.state.ok.us/home/home-default.asp for free searches on business entities, including registered agents and Trademarks. Customers may also order and receive status certificates as well as certified and plain copies. Fees vary, see the web page for details. There is a list of domestic LLCs. Also, search securities brokers/investment advisors at www.securities.ok.gov/_private/DB_Query/IA_Query/IA_Search_Form.asp. Also securities firms at www.securities.ok.gov/_private/DB_Query/Licensing/IA_Search_FOI.asp.

Uniform Commercial Code

UCC Central Filing Office, Oklahoma County Clerk, 320 R.S. Kerr Ave, County Office Bldg, Rm 105, Oklahoma City, OK 73102; 405-713-1522, Fax- 405-713-2241; 8AM-5PM.

http://countyclerk.oklahomacounty.org/UCC.html

This county agency is the central filing agency for the state.

Indexing & Storage: Records available for since 2/91 on UCC, 10 years on tax liens on computer or one year from lapse. Records are on microfilm from 1977 to present. New records available for inquiry in 2 to 3 days.

Searching: Use search request form UCC-11, the national standard form. Include in request- debtor name. This data not released- SSNs

Access by: mail, in person, online.

Fee & Payment: The search fee is $10.00 per debtor name, the copy fee is $1.00 per page, to certify the document add $1.00 per page. Fee payee- Oklahoma County Clerk. Prepayment required. Personal checks accepted. No credit cards accepted, but may in future.

Mail search: Turnaround time- 2 days. A SASE is not required, but does speed up the process when submitted.

In person: Unless time permits, most record requests must be picked up the next day.

Online search: Records of all UCC financing statements may be viewed free at http://countyclerk.oklahomacounty.org/UCC-SearchSite.html. Search by debtor or secured party. The site gives a strong disclaimer, their may be significant lag time between the date of filing and the date the record is posted on this site. Neither certified searches nor record requests are accepted at the web page.

Other access: The entire database is available on microfilm or computer tapes. The initial history is $500 with $50 per update. Images are available for $.04 per image.

Federal & State Tax Liens

Records not maintained by a state level agency.

All state tax liens and federal tax liens are filed at the local level. Federal tax liens on businesses are filed with the Clerk of Oklahoma County.

Sales Tax Registrations

Taxpayer Assistance, Sales Tax Registration Records, PO Box 26850, Oklahoma City, OK 73126 (Courier address- 2501 N Lincoln Blvd, Oklahoma City 73194); 405-521-3160, 405-521-3200, Fax- 405-521-3826; 7:30AM-4:30PM.

www.tax.ok.gov/bustax.html

Indexing & Storage: Records available for the most recent 10 years on computer, microfilmed back to the 1970's.

Searching: This agency will provide any information found on the face of the permit- business name, address, tax permit number, and SIC code. Payment history is not released. Include in request- permit number or business name. They will also search by owner name, federal tax ID, or by tax permit number.

Access by: mail, phone, in person, online.

Fee & Payment: No search fees, but there is a copy fee of $.25 per page. Fee payee- Oklahoma Tax Commission. Prepayment required. Personal checks accepted.

Mail search: Turnaround time- within 2 weeks. A SASE is requested.

Phone search: Tax permit numbers can be verified by phone, via an automated system. Name searches are not available on an automated basis.

In person: Copies cost $.25 per page.

Online search: A free tax permit look-up is provided at www.oktax.onenet.net/permitlookup/.

Other access: Current sales tax permit holders are permitted to purchase the sales tax database on microfiche or disk. Monthly updates are available. Call for fees.

Birth Certificates

State Department of Health, Vital Records Service, 1000 Northeast 10th, Oklahoma City, OK 73117; 405-271-4040, 877-817-7364 (VitalChek), Fax- 405-232-3311; 8AM-4:30PM.

www.ok.gov/health/

Indexing & Storage: Records available from 1908 on. Records are computerized since 1930. New records available for inquiry immediately.

Searching: Must have a signed release from person of record or immediate family member. Email questions to askvr@health.ok.gov. Include in request- full name, names of parents, mother's maiden name, date of birth, place of birth, reason for information request, and copy of ID of requester and daytime phone number.

Access by: mail, phone, in person.

Fee & Payment: Fee is $10.00, a "Heirloom" record is $35.00. Birth Certificate Substitution (includes one of the following actions: Legitimation, Adoption, Paternity, Sealed Files) is $15.00. Fee payee- Oklahoma State Health Department. Prepayment required. Personal checks accepted. Major cards accepted only for expedited service.

Mail search: Turnaround time- 4 to 6 weeks. A SASE is requested.

Phone search: See expedited service.

In person: Records may also be obtained from the Tulsa Health Department, Central Regional Health Center, 315 S. Utica, Tulsa, Oklahoma 74104-2203. Turnaround time is while you wait.

Expedited service: Expedited service is available for phone requests. Turnaround time- 1-3 days. Add $17.00 for express delivery. Use of credit card required, for an additional $10.95 fee (charged by vendor).

Death Records

State Department of Health, Vital Records Service, 1000 Northeast 10th, Oklahoma City, OK 73117; 405-271-4040, 877-817-7364 (VitalChek), Fax- 405-232-3311; 8AM-4:30PM.

www.ok.gov/health/

Indexing & Storage: Records available from October 1908 on. Records are computerized since 1930. The filing process in many years prior to 1940 are sketchy, esp. pre-1917. New records available for inquiry immediately.

Searching: Records are open to the public. Email questions to askvr@health.ok.gov. Include in request- full name, date of death, place of death, copy of ID of requester. Also, daytime phone number.

Access by: mail, phone, fax, in person.

Fee & Payment: Fee is $10.00 per record. Fee payee- Oklahoma State Health Department. Prepayment required. Personal checks accepted, credit cards are not.

Mail search: Turnaround time- 1 to 2 weeks. A SASE is requested.

Phone search: See expedited service.

Fax search: See expedited service.

In person: Records may also be obtained from the Tulsa Health Department, Central Regional Health Center, 315 S. Utica, Tulsa, Oklahoma 74104-2203. Turnaround time is while you wait, can be one hour.

Expedited service: Expedited service is available for phone requests. Turnaround time- 1-3 days. Add $17.00 for express delivery. Use of credit card required, for an additional $10.95 fee (charged by vendor).

Marriage Certificates, Divorce Records

Records not maintained by a state level agency.

Marriage and divorce records are found at county level. The record should be requested from the county courthouse in the county where the marriage or divorce was filed or granted.

Workers' Compensation Records

Workers Compensation Court, Records, 1915 N Stiles Ave, Oklahoma City, OK 73105-4918; 405-522-8600, 405-522-8640 (Records Dept), 800-269-5353 (Enforcement), 800-522-8210 (General); 8AM-5PM.

www.owcc.state.ok.us

Indexing & Storage: Records available since 1989 on computer. Index to case files are on print-outs and cards since the 1930's. New records available for inquiry in one day.

Searching: Claims information is considered public record. Anyone having a correct case number can access and review files. There are 2 searches involved-1st to get case number, then to do search. Any requests must be on their forms. Include in request- signed release and SSN, use the Prior Claims Request Form found at the web page. Also, to get the claim number, send a written request (Attn: Prior Claims) on their "Request for Information Form," and they will notify you of the case number. With a case number, you can request copies, but you must use their form. This data not released- Form2 content.

Access by: mail, in person.

Fee & Payment: Using their "Request for Information Form" (index card), include a $1.00 search fee to get the case number, unless you are statutorily exempt. The copy fee is $1.00 for the first page and $.50 each add'l page if done by staff; $.25 if by searcher. Fee payee- Workers' Compensation Court. Prepayment required. In-state businesses can set up charge accounts for copies only; payment due within 30 days. Personal checks accepted, credit cards are not.

Mail search: Turnaround time- 5 days. Frequent requesters should set up an account. If payment not included, party will be billed and funds must be received before documents are mailed. A SASE is requested.

In person: One may search on the in-house computer in the basement level and also request and review a file ($1.00 per file). Files are pulled for the public from 8:15AM to 4:45PM.

Other access: PDF versions of most forms are available at the website.

Driver Records

MVR Desk, Records Management Division, PO Box 11415, Oklahoma City, OK 73136-0415 (Courier address- 3600 Martin Luther King Blvd, Rm 206, Oklahoma City, OK 73111); 405-425-2262; 8AM-4:45PM.

www.dps.state.ok.us/dls/default.htm

Copies of tickets may be obtained for $.25 per copy from the address listed above. For certification of copies, add $3.00 per copy.

Indexing & Storage: Records available for 3 years for moving violations, DWIs and suspensions. All violations appear on the driving record. Accidents are recorded if there is a conviction of citation. New records available for inquiry in 30 days.

Searching: Information is available for law enforcement purposes. Anyone else requesting an MVR for another person is required to submit a records request form and consent to release records form signed by both parties. Include in request- full name and date of birth, or driver's license number. Use forms found at www.dps.state.ok.us/recm. Requesters can also visit OK Tag Agencies to obtain record information. This data not released- medical records, SSNs, addresses or personal information (height, weight, sex, eye color, etc.).

Access by: mail, in person, online.

Fee & Payment: The fee is $10.00 per driving record, $13.00 if certified. There is a full fee for a no record found. Online access is $12.50. Fee payee- Department of Public Safety. Prepayment required. No personal checks or credit cards accepted.

Mail search: Turnaround time- 1 week. This agency offers a monthly billing system for high volume requesters. A SASE is not requested.

In person: Records may be requested at an Oklahoma Tag Agency statewide. Up to ten requests may be processed in one day or less.

Many Tag Agency offices across the state will sell records.

Online search: Online access is available for qualified, approved users through www.ok.gov/. Both a batch mode and interactive processes are offered. The $12.50 fee includes a $2.50 service fee. You will not find information about this program on the web since it is not for the general public. For further information, call 800-955-3468.

Vehicle, Vessel Ownership & Registration

Oklahoma Tax Commission, Motor Vehicle Division, Attn: Research, 2501 N Lincoln Blvd, Oklahoma City, OK 73194; 405-521-3770; 7:30AM-4:30PM.

www.tax.ok.gov/motveh.html

Indexing & Storage: Records available for 3 years (registration records); the state keeps title records internally for 20 years. All watercraft must be titled and registered. All motors in excess of 10 HP must be titled. Lien information appears on title records. New records available for inquiry in 2 up to 5 weeks.

Searching: Records are not released to casual requesters. Approved requesters must use the Vehicle Information Request Form 769 completed front and back. (available at web page) Include in request- title number if available, VIN or current plate number and signature of requester. A true signature is required on each form. Name searches are not performed unless related to boating safety or for law enforcement or government.

Access by: mail, in person.

Fee & Payment: Current ownership/lienholder data is $1.00. A computer generated title history is $5.00 (models 1992 & newer), a microfilm title history is $7.50, and a certified microfilm title history is $10.00. Fee payee- Oklahoma Tax Commission, MVD. Prepayment required. Personal checks accepted, credit cards are not.

Mail search: Turnaround time- 7 to 10 days.

In person: Turnaround time is while you wait, depending on the workload.

Other access: Oklahoma does not offer bulk delivery of vehicle and ownership information except for purposes such as vehicle recall.

Accident Reports

Department of Public Safety, Records Management Division, PO Box 11415, Oklahoma City, OK 73136 (Courier address- 3600 Martin Luther King Blvd, Room 206, Oklahoma City, OK 73111); 405-425-2192, Fax- 405-425-2046; 8AM-4:45PM.

www.dps.state.ok.us

This agency refers to these reports as Collision Reports. Reports are held 60 days before release to the public.

Indexing & Storage: Records available for 3 years to present. New records available for inquiry in 20 to 45 days.

Searching: Include in request- date of accident, location of accident, full name of drivers, and county. Qualified requesters include those uses listed under DPPA and members of the media. This data not released- addresses.

Access by: mail, phone, in person.

Fee & Payment: The fee is $7.00 for an uncertified copy and $10.00 for a certified copy. There is no charge for a no record found. Fee payee- Department of Public Safety. Prepayment required. No personal checks or credit cards accepted.

Mail search: Turnaround time- 1 week. A SASE is not required.

Phone search: This agency will reveal whether there is an accident over the phone. No other information will be revealed over the phone.

In person: Normal turnaround time is while you wait.

Legislation Records

Oklahoma Legislature, State Capitol, Bill Status Info-Rm B-30, Copies-Rm 310, Oklahoma City, OK 73105; 405-521-5642 (Bill Status Only), 405-521-5514 (Bill Distribution), 405-528-2546 (Bills in Progress), Fax- 405-521-5507; 8:30AM-4:30PM.

www.lsb.state.ok.us

For session bills prior to 1989, you may call the State Law Library at 405-521-2502, ext. 280.

Indexing & Storage: Records available for current session only. New records available for inquiry in 1 day.

Searching: Include in request- bill number and year.

Access by: mail, phone, in person, online.

Fee & Payment: There is no search fee.

Mail search: Turnaround time- same day. SASE not required.

Phone search: Turnaround time is same day.

In person: Turnaround time is same day.

Online search: The web page provides a variety of legislative information including searching by topic or bill number, and state statutes.

Expedited service: All requests are handled on as soon-as-possible basis.

Voter Registration

State Election Board, Voter Records, PO Box 53156, Oklahoma City, OK 73152 (Courier address- State Capitol-Rm B6, Oklahoma City, OK 73105); 405-521-2391, Fax- 405-521-6457; 8AM-5PM.

www.elections.state.ok.us/

Indexing & Storage: Records available for 4 years. New records available for inquiry in 7 to 10 days.

Searching: Records are open to the public, there are no restriction on use. Records may be accessed at both the state and county levels. Include in request- subject name, address and DOB. This data not released- DL, SSN.

Access by: mail, phone, fax, in person, online.

Fee & Payment: There is no fee for look-ups. Fee payee- OK State Election Board Certified funds or cashier's checks are preferred for database sales. A 2-week hold is placed on order paid for using personal check. No credit cards accepted.

Mail search: Turnaround time- 2 to 5 days. SASE not required.

Phone search: Limited information is given, depending on staff availability.

Fax search: Same criteria as mail search.

In person: Simple requests may be processed while you wait.

Online search: Record requests may be emailed to info@elections.ok.gov

Other access: A statewide database can be purchased on CD for a fee of $150. Large counties are available on CD for $50-75, and smaller counties or precincts or district or school district are available on disk for $10-35.

GED Records

State Dept of Education, Lifelong Learning, 2500 N Lincoln Blvd, Rm 115, Oklahoma City, OK 73105; 405-521-3321, Fax- 405-522-5394; 8AM-4:30PM.

http://sde.state.ok.us

Indexing & Storage: Records available from 1965. New records available for inquiry in up to one week.

Searching: To search, all of the following is required: name, approximate year of test, date of birth, and SSN. This data not released- SSN, DOB, certificate number.

Access by: mail, phone, fax, in person.

Fee & Payment: There is no fee for a verification. There is a $5.00 fee to obtain a transcript, or $10.00 for diploma with transcript attached. Fee payee- State Dept of Education. Prepayment required. Money orders and business checks are accepted. No personal checks or credit cards accepted.

Mail search: Turnaround time- 1 to 2 days. No SASE is required, but helpful.

Phone search: This is for verification only. The agency prefers phone requests over fax requests.

Fax search: The will accept requests for verifications only, not for transcripts.

In person: Turnaround time is typically 30 minutes for verifications.

Hunting & Fishing License Information

Access to Records is Restricted.

Department of Wildlife Conservation, Fish & Game Records, PO Box 53465, Oklahoma City, OK 73152 (Courier address- 1801 N. Lincoln, Oklahoma City, OK 73105); 405-521-3851, 405-521-3852, Fax- 405-521-6535; 8AM-4:30PM.

www.wildlifedepartment.com

They have a central database, but do not release information to the public.

Oklahoma State Licensing Agencies

For details about the agency responsible for licensing/certifying/registering an item below or in the Agency Quick Finder section, match an item's number with the number of the agency in the *Licensing Agency Information* section.

Oklahoma Licenses Searchable Online

Accounting Firm #15 .... www.ok.gov/oab/search.php
Alarm Firm/Employee #37 .... www.ok.gov/health/documents/20080307_OklaLicAlarmAndLocksmithIndustryIndiv_A-Z.pdf
Architect #23 .... https://www.ok.gov/architects/licensee_search.php
Architectural Firm #23 .... https://www.ok.gov/architects/licensee_search.php
Athletic Trainer/Apprentice #8 .... www.okmedicalboard.org/display.php?content=md_search_advanced:md_search_advanced
Attorney #28 .... www.oklahomafindalawyer.com/FindALawyer
Audiologist #6 .... www.obespa.state.ok.us/License%20Data.htm
Bank #35 .... www.state.ok.us/~osbd/
Barber School #37
... ... www.ok.gov/health/documents/OKLAHOMA%20LICENSED%20BARBER%20SCHOOLS_9%2011%2007.pdf
Beauty School #4 .... www.state.ok.us/~cosmo/schools.html
Chiropractor #3 .... www.ok.gov/chiropracticboard/Disciplined_Chiropractors/index.html
Counselor LPC/MLFT/LBP #43 .... www.ok.gov/health/documents/LICENSEE%20SEARCH%20-%20LPC.doc
Credit Services Organization #20 .... www.okdocc.state.ok.us/ROSTERS/rosters.php
Credit Union #35 .... www.state.ok.us/~osbd/
Dental Hygienist #29 .... www.dentist.state.ok.us/lists/index.htm
Dental Laboratory #29 .... www.dentist.state.ok.us/lists/index.htm
Dentist/Dental Assistant #29 .... www.dentist.state.ok.us/lists/index.htm
Dietitian/Provisional Dietitian #8 .... www.okmedicalboard.org/display.php?content=md_search_advanced:md_search_advanced
Electrologist #8 .... www.okmedicalboard.org/display.php?content=md_search_advanced:md_search_advanced
Engineer #13 .... www.pels.state.ok.us/roster/index.html
Health Spa #20 .... www.okdocc.state.ok.us/ROSTERS/rosters.php
Insurance Agent/Representative #32 .... https://www.sircon.com/ComplianceExpress/Inquiry/consumerInquiry.do?nonSscrb=Y
Landscape Architect #23 .... https://www.ok.gov/architects/licensee_search.php
Lobbyist #42 .... www.state.ok.us/~ethics/lobbyist.html
LPG-Liqu'f'd Petrol Dealer/Mfg./Mgr #25 ..... www.oklpgas.org/search/index.php
Medical Doctor #8 .... www.okmedicalboard.org/display.php?content=md_search_advanced:md_search_advanced
Money Order Agent/Order Company #35 ... www.state.ok.us/~osbd/
Mortgage Broker #20 .... www.okdocc.state.ok.us/ROSTERS/rosters.php
Notary Public #26 .... https://www.sooneraccess.state.ok.us/notary/notary_search-menu.asp
Nurse Anesthetist Cert'd, Register'd #30 ..... https://www.ok.gov/nursing/verify/index.php
Nurse Midwife #30 .... https://www.ok.gov/nursing/verify/index.php
Nurse Practitioner, Adv'd Regist'd #30 .... https://www.ok.gov/nursing/verify/index.php
Nurse-RN/LPN/Clinical Specialist #30 .... https://www.ok.gov/nursing/verify/index.php
Occupational Therapist/Assistant #8 .... www.okmedicalboard.org/display.php?content=md_search_advanced:md_search_advanced
Optometrist #7 .... www.arbo.org/index.php?action=findanoptometrist
Orthotist/Prosthetist #8 .... www.okmedicalboard.org/display.php?content=md_search_advanced:md_search_advanced
Osteopathic Physician #10 .... www.docboard.org/ok/df/oksearch.htm
Pawnbroker #20 .... www.okdocc.state.ok.us/ROSTERS/rosters.php
Pedorthist #8 .... www.okmedicalboard.org/display.php?content=md_search_advanced:md_search_advanced
Perfusionist #8 .... www.okmedicalboard.org/display.php?content=md_search_advanced:md_search_advanced
Pesticide Applicator/Dealer #27 .... http://kellysolutions.com/ok/
Pesticide Certification/Registration #27 ...... http://kellysolutions.com/ok/
Pharmacist/Pharm Intern/Techn'c'n #11 .... www.ok.gov/OSBP/License_Verification/index.html
Pharmacy #11 .... www.ok.gov/OSBP/License_Verification/index.html
Physical Therapist/Assistant #8 .... www.okmedicalboard.org/display.php?content=md_search_advanced:md_search_advanced
Physician Assistant #8 .... www.okmedicalboard.org/display.php?content=md_search_advanced:md_search_advanced
Podiatrist #12 .... www.okmedicalboard.org/display.php?content=md_search_advanced:md_search_advanced
Precious Metals & Gem Dealer #20 .... www.okdocc.state.ok.us/ROSTERS/rosters.php
Private Investigator Person/Agency #19 ..... www.opia.com/find_a_pi/default.asp
Prosthetist #8 .... www.okmedicalboard.org/display.php?content=md_search_advanced:md_search_advanced
Psychologist #14 .... https://www.ok.gov/OSBEP/_app/search/index.php
Public Accountant-CPA #15 .... www.ok.gov/oab/search.php
Real Estate Agent/Broker/Sales #38 .... www.ok.gov/OREC/licensee_lookup/lookup.php
Real Estate Corp./Partnership #38 .... www.ok.gov/OREC/licensee_lookup/lookup.php
Registrants Performing Audits/GAS 15 ...... www.ok.gov/oab/search.php

Rent to Own Dealer #20 .... www.okdocc.state.ok.us/ROSTERS/rosters.php
Respiratory Care Practitioner #8 .... www.okmedicalboard.org/display.php?content=md_search_advanced:md_search_advanced
Savings & Loan Association #35 .... www.state.ok.us/~osbd/
Social Worker #24 .... www.osblsw.state.ok.us/licensee_search.php
Speech Pathologist #6 .... www.obespa.state.ok.us/License%20Data.htm
Surveyor, Land #13 .... www.pels.state.ok.us/roster/index.html
Trust Company #35 .... www.state.ok.us/~osbd/

Oklahoma Licensing Quick Finder

Accounting Firm #15 405-521-2397
Alarm Firm/Employee #37 405-271-5779
Alcohol/Drug Influence Tester #17 405-425-2460
Animal Technician #18 405-524-9006
Architect #23 405-949-2383
Architectural Firm #23 405-949-2383
Asbestos Worker #44 .... 405-528-1500 x319
Athletic Trainer/Apprentice #8 .... 405-848-6841 x113
Attorney #28 405-416-7000
Audiologist #6 405-524-4955
Bail Bondsman #32 405-521-6610
Bank #35 405-521-2783
Barber Appren./Instructor/Sch'l #37 405-271-5779
Barber/Barber Shop #37 405-271-5779
Beauty School #4 405-521-2441
Beauty Shop/Salon #4 405-521-2441
Blacksmith #31 405-943-6472
Building Inspector #37 405-271-5779
Burglar Alarm Svc/Instal/Seller #37 405-271-5779
Cemetery #35 405-521-2783
Child/Youth Agency, Priv./Publ. #21 405-521-3561
Chiropractor #3 405-524-6223
Consumer Finance Company #20 405-521-3653
Cosmetician/Dry Hair Stylist #4 405-521-2441
Cosmetology Instructor #4 405-521-2441
Cosmetology Student/Apprentice #4 405-521-2441
Counselor LPC/MLFT/LBP #43 405-271-6030
Credit Services Organization #20 405-521-3653
Credit Union #35 405-521-2783
Dental Hygienist #29 .... 405-524-9037/866-534-9037
Dental Laboratory #29 .... 405-524-9037/866-534-9037
Dentist/Dental Asst #29 405-524-9037/866-534-9037
Dietitian/Provisional Dietitian #8 .... 405-848-6841 x113
Electrical Contrac'r/Inspect'r #37 405-271-5779
Electrician, Journeyman #37 405-271-5779
Electrologist #8 .... 405-848-6841 x113
Embalmer #5 405-522-1790
Engineer #13 405-521-2874
Environmental Specialist #37 405-271-5779
Facial Operator School/Instructor #4 405-521-2441
Facial Operator/Esthetician #4 405-521-2441
Feed/Seed #27 405-522-5894
Fertilizer #27 405-522-5985
Firearm Permit for Ret'd Policeman #19405-425-2484
Forester #16 405-522-6147
Funeral Director/Funeral Home #5 405-522-1790
Ground Water Well Driller #39 405-530-8800
Groundwater Right Permitting #39 405-530-8800
Hairbraider #4 405-521-2441
Health Spa #20 405-521-3653
Hearing Aid Dealer/Fitter #37 405-271-5779
Home Inspector #37 405-271-5779
Horse Racing Professional #31 405-943-6472
Horse Trainer #31 405-943-6472
Insurance Agent/Rep/Adjuster #32 405-521-2828
Insurance Consultant #32 405-521-2828
Investment Adviser/Company #34 405-280-7700
Issuer Agent #34 405-280-7700
Jockey #31 405-943-6472
Jockey Agent #31 405-943-6472
Journeyman #36 405-271-5217
Land Sales Agent #34 405-280-7700
Landscape Architect #23 405-949-2383
Liquor Industry #1 405-521-3484
Lobbyist #42 405-521-3451
Long Term Care Administrator #2 405-522-1616
LPG- Petrol. Dealer/Mfg./Mgr #25 405-879-9828
LPG- Petrol. System Installer #25 405-879-9828
Manicurist #4 405-521-2441
Mechanical Contractor #36 405-271-5217
Mechanical Inspector #36 405-271-5217
Medical Doctor #8 .... 405-848-6841 x113
Mining Operation #22 405-521-3859
Money Order Agent #35 405-521-2783
Money Order Company #35 405-521-2783
Mortgage Broker #20 405-521-3653
Notary Public #26 405-521-2516
Nurse Anesthetist, Cert. Regist'r'd #30 405-962-1800
Nurse Midwife #30 405-962-1800
Nurse Practitioner, Adv'd Registered #30405-962-1800
Nurse Specialist, Clinical #30 405-962-1800
Nurse-RN/LPN #30 405-962-1800
Nursery, Plant #27 405-522-5953
Occupational Therapist/Assist#8 .... 405-848-6841 x113
Optometrist #7 405-733-7836
Orthotist/Prosthetist #8 .... 405-848-6841 x113
Osteopathic Physician #10 405-528-8625
Pawnbroker #20 405-521-3653
Payday Lender #20 405-521-3653
Pedorthist #8 .... 405-848-6841 x113
Perfusionist #8 .... 405-848-6841 x113
Pesticide Applicator #27 405-522-5984
Pesticide Certification/Registration #27405-522-5950
Pesticide Dealer #27 405-522-5984
Pharmacist/Pharmacy Intern #11 405-521-3815
Pharmacy #11 405-521-3815
Pharmacy Facility #11 405-521-3815
Pharmacy Technician #11 405-521-3815
Physical Therapist/Assistant #8 .... 405-848-6841 x113
Physician Assistant #8 .... 405-848-6841 x113
Placement Agency #21 405-521-3561
Plumbing Contractor/Inspector #36 405-271-5217
Podiatrist #12 405-848-6841
Police Officer #19 405-425-2755
Polygraph Examiner/Intern #40 405-425-2778
Precious Metals & Gem Dealer #20 405-521-3653
Private Investigator Person/Agency #19405-425-2775
Prosthetist #8 .... 405-848-6841 x113
Psychologist #14 405-524-9094
Public Accountant-CPA #15 405-521-2397
Pump Installer #39 405-530-8800
Real Estate Agent/Broker/Sales #38 405-521-3387
Real Estate Appraiser #33 405-521-6636
Real Estate Corp./Partnership #38 405-521-3387
Registrants Performing Audits/GAS #15405-521-2397
Rent to Own Dealer #20 405-521-3653
Residential Child Care Facility #21 405-521-3561
Respiratory Care Practitioner #8 .... 405-848-6841 x113
Sanitarian #37 405-271-5779
Savings & Loan Association #35 405-521-2783
School Accreditation #41 405-521-3333
School Transportation #41 405-521-4516
Securities Broker/Dealer #34 405-280-7700
Security Guard/Agency #19 405-425-2775
Self Defense Act Instructor #19 405-425-2760
Shorthand Reporter #9 405-521-2450
Social Worker #24 405-946-7230
Speech Pathologist #6 405-524-4955
Surface Water Right Permit #39 405-530-8800
Surveyor, Land #13 405-521-2874
Teacher #41 405-521-4516
Trust Company #35 405-521-2783
Veterinarian #18 405-524-9006
Veterinary Technician #18 405-524-9006
Waste Water Operator #36 405-702-1000
Weights & Measures, Agricultural #27 405-522-5870
Well Driller/Monitor #39 405-530-8800

Oklahoma Licensing Agency Information

#1 Alcoholic Beverage Laws Enforcement Commission, 4545 N Lincoln Blvd, #270, Oklahoma City, OK 73105; 405-521-3484, Fax- 405-521-6578. www.ok.gov/able/

#2 Board for Nursing Home Administrators, 2401 NW 23rd St #62, Oklahoma City, OK 73107-2431; 405-522-1616, Fax- 405-522-1625. Hours- 8:30AM-5PM. www.ok.gov/osbeltca/

#3 Board of Chiropractic Examiners, 201 NE 38th Terrace, Ste 3, Oklahoma City, OK 73105; 405-524-6223, Fax- 405-524-9542. www.ok.gov/chiropracticboard/index.html

#4 Board of Cosmetology, 2401 NW 23rd St, #84, Shepherd Mall, Oklahoma City, OK 73107-2431; 405-521-2441, Fax- 405-521-2440. 8AM-4PM. www.state.ok.us/~cosmo/

#5 Board of Embalmers & Funeral Directors, 4545 N Lincoln Blvd, #175, Oklahoma City, OK 73105; 405-522-1790, Fax- 405-522-1797. Hours- 8AM-4PM. www.okfuneral.com

#6 Board of Examiners for Speech Pathology/Audiology, PO Box 53592 (3700 N Classen Blvd, #248), Oklahoma City, OK 73152-3592; 405-524-4955, Fax- 405-524-4985. www.obespa.state.ok.us Search data at- www.obespa.state.ok.us/License%20Data.htm

#7 Board of Examiners in Optometry, 2008 S Post Rd, Ste 200, Midwest City, OK 73110-2162; 405-733-7836, Fax- 405-741-3060. 9AM-N, 1-4PM. www.state.ok.us/~optometry/ Search data at- www.arbo.org/index.php?action=findanoptometrist

#8 Board of Medical Licensure & Supervision, PO Box 18256 (5104 N Francis, #C), Oklahoma City, OK 73154-0256; 405-848-6841 x113, Fax- 405-848-8240. www.okmedicalboard.org Search data atwww.okmedicalboard.org/index.php ("Find a Doctor")

#9 Board of Official Shorthand Reporters, 1915 N Stiles, Rm 305, Oklahoma City, OK 73105; 405-521-2450, Fax- 405-521-9688. www.oscn.net/applications/oscn/start.asp

#10 Board of Osteopathic Examiners, 4848 N Lincoln Blvd, Oklahoma City, OK 73105-3335; 405-528-8625, Fax- 405-557-0653. www.docboard.org/ok/ok.htm Search data at- www.docboard.org/ok/df/oksearch.htm

#11 Board of Pharmacy, 4545 N Lincoln Blvd, #112, Oklahoma City, OK 73105-3488; 405-521-3815, Fax- 405-521-3758. 8AM-4:30PM. www.ok.gov/OSBP/ Search data at- www.ok.gov/OSBP/License_Verification/index.html

#12 Board of Podiatry, 5104 N Francis, #C, Oklahoma City, OK 73154-0256; 405-848-6841, Fax- 405-848-8240. 8AM-4:30PM. www.okmedicalboard.org/./display.php?content=md_index:md_index&rmenu=1 Search data- www.okmedicalboard.org/display.php?content=md_search_advanced:md_search_advanced May purchase info on discs or hardcopy.

#13 Board of Professional Engineers & Land Surveyors, 201 NE 27th St, Oklahoma City, OK 73105-2788; 405-521-2874, Fax- 405-523-2135. www.pels.state.ok.us Search data at- www.pels.state.ok.us/roster/index.html

#14 Board of Psychologists Examiners, 201 NE 38th Terrace #3, Oklahoma City, OK 73105; 405-524-9094, Fax- 405-524-9427. 8AM-4:30PM. www.ok.gov/OSBEP/ Agency charges $25 per name.

#15 Accountancy Board, 4545 N Lincoln Blvd, #165, Oklahoma City, OK 73105; 405-521-2397, Fax- 405-521-3118. Hours- 8AM-5PM. www.ok.gov/oab/ Search data at- www.ok.gov/oab/search.php

#16 Board of Registration for Foresters, 2800 N Lincoln Blvd, Agriculture Bldg, Oklahoma City, OK 73105-4298; 405-522-6147, Fax- 405-522-4583. Hours- 8AM-5PM. www.state.ok.us/contact.php?page=62 Will provide list of registered foresters.

#17 Board of Tests for Alcohol & Drug Influence, PO Box 11415 (3600 N Martin Luther King Ave), Oklahoma City, OK 73136-0415; 405-425-2460, Fax- 405-425-2490. www.ok.gov/bot/

#18 Board of Veterinary Medical Examiners, 201 NE 38th Terr, #1, Oklahoma City, OK 73105; 405-524-9006, Fax- 405-524-9012. www.okvetboard.com

#19 Council on Law Enforcement Education & Training, 2401 Egypt Rd, Ada, OK 74820-0669; 580-310-0871, Fax- 580-310-9143. Hours- 8AM-5PM. www.ok.gov/cleet/ Search data at- www.opia.com/find_a_pi/default.asp

#20 Department of Consumer Credit, 4545 N Lincoln Blvd, #104, Oklahoma City, OK 73105-3408; 405-521-3653, Fax- 405-521-6740. www.okdocc.state.ok.us Search data at- www.okdocc.state.ok.us/ROSTERS/rosters.php

#21 Department of Human Services, PO Box 25352, Oklahoma City, OK 73125; 405-521-3646, Fax- 405-522-2564. Hours- 8AM-5PM. www.okdhs.org/divisionsoffices/visd/dcc/

#22 Department of Mines, Mining Commission, 2915 N Classen Blvd., Ste 213, Oklahoma City, OK 73105; 405-521-3859, Fax- 405-427-9646. www.ok.gov/mines/

#23 Board of Governors/Licensed Architects & Landscape Architects, PO Box 53430 (3555 NW 58th St, #640), Oklahoma City, OK 73152; 405-949-2383, Fax- 405-949-1690. www.ok.gov/architects/ Search at- https://www.ok.gov/architects/licensee_search.php

#24 Licensed Social Workers Registration Board, PO Box 18817 (5104 N Francis, Ste E), Oklahoma City, OK 73154; 405-946-7230, Fax- 405-942-1070. www.osblsw.state.ok.us Search data at- www.osblsw.state.ok.us/licensee_search.php

#25 Liquefied Petroleum Gas Board, 6412 N Santa Fe, Ste C, Oklahoma City, OK 73116-9111; 405-879-9828, Fax- 405-879-0304.

#26 Office of Secretary of State, Notary Public Department, 2300 N Lincoln Blvd, #101 (PO Box 53390), Oklahoma City, OK 73105; 405-521-2516, Fax- 405-522-3555. www.sos.state.ok.us/notary/notary_welcome.htm Search data at- https://www.sooneraccess.state.ok.us/notary/notary_search-menu.asp

#27 Department of Agriculture, Food & Forestry, Plant Industry & Consumer Services Division, 2800 N Lincoln Blvd, Oklahoma City, OK 73105-4298; 405-521-3864, Fax- 405-922-0909. www.oda.state.ok.us/

#28 Bar Association, Attorney Certification, PO Box 53036, (1901 Lincoln Blvd), Oklahoma City, OK 73152-3036; 405-416-7000, Fax- 405-416-7001. www.okbar.org Search data at- www.oklahomafindalawyer.com/FindALawyer Will sell labels for $.15 per name.

#29 Board of Dentistry, 201 NE 38th Terr, #2, Oklahoma City, OK 73105; 405-524-9037, Fax- 405-524-2223. Hours- 8:30AM-4:30PM. www.state.ok.us/~dentist/ Search data at- www.dentist.state.ok.us/lists/index.htm

#30 Board of Nursing, 2915 N Classen Blvd, #524, Oklahoma City, OK 73106; 405-962-1800, Fax- 405-962-1821. Hours- 8AM-4:30PM. www.ok.gov/nursing/ Search data at- https://www.ok.gov/nursing/verify/index.php

#31 Horse Racing Commission, 2401 NW 23rd St, #78, Oklahoma City, OK 73107; 405-943-6472, Fax- 405-943-6474. www.ohrc.org

#32 Insurance Department, PO Box 53408 (2401 NW 23 St, #28), Oklahoma City, OK 73152-3408; 405-521-2828, Fax- 405-521-6635. www.ok.gov/oid/ Tulsa office is 3105 E. Skelly Dr #305, Tulsa, 74105, 918-747-7700.

#33 Real Estate Appraiser Board, PO Box 53408, Oklahoma City, OK 73152-3408; 405-521-6636, Fax- 405-522-6909. www.ok.gov/oid/Regulated_Entities/Real_Estate_Appraiser_Board_(REAB)/

#34 State of Oklahoma, Department of Securities, 120 N Robinson, 1st National Ctr #860, Oklahoma City, OK 73102; 405-280-7700, Fax- 405-280-7742. Hours- 8AM-5PM. www.securities.ok.gov

#35 Banking Department, 4545 N Lincoln Blvd, #164, Oklahoma City, OK 73105-3427; 405-521-2782, Fax- 405-522-2993. www.state.ok.us/~osbd/

#36 Department of Environmental Quality, PO Box 1677 (707 N Robinson), Oklahoma City, OK 73101; 405-702-1000, Fax- 405-702-1001. www.deq.state.ok.us

#37 Department of Health, Occupational Licensing, 1000 NE 10th St, Oklahoma City, OK 73117-1299; 405-271-5779, Fax- 405-271-5286. www.health.state.ok.us Search data at- www.health.state.ok.us

#38 Real Estate Commission, 2401 NW 23rd St, #18, Oklahoma City, OK 73107; 405-521-3387, Fax- 405-521-2189. 8AM-4:30PM. www.ok.gov/OREC/ Search data at- www.ok.gov/OREC/licensee_lookup/lookup.php

#39 Water Resources Board, 3800 N Classen Blvd, Oklahoma City, OK 73118; 405-530-8800, Fax- 405-530-8900. Hours- 8AM-5PM. www.owrb.ok.gov/

#40 Polygraph Examiners Board, PO Box 11476, ML King Station, Oklahoma City, OK 73136-0476; 405-425-2778, Fax- 405-425-7314. Hours- 8AM-5PM.

#41 State Department of Education, 2500 N Lincoln Blvd, Rm 1-17, Oklahoma City, OK 73105-4599; 405-521-3301, Fax- 405-521-6205. www.sde.state.ok.us/home/defaultie.html Verifications performed as Open Records Requests; contact info here is for the Records Request Officer.

#42 Ethics Commission, Lobbyist Registration, Sec. of State, 2300 N Lincoln Blvd, RM B5, Oklahoma City, OK 73105-4812; 405-521-3451, Fax- 405-521-4905. www.ok.gov/oec/ Search data at- www.state.ok.us/~ethics/lobbyist.html

#43 Department of Health, Professional Counselor Licensing, 1000 NE 10th St, Oklahoma City, OK 73117-1299; 405-271-6030, Fax- 405-271-1918. Hours- 8AM-5PM. www.ok.gov/health/Protective_Health/Professional_Counselor_Licensing_Division/

#44 Department of Labor, Asbestos Division, 4001 N Lincoln Blvd, Oklahoma City, OK 73105-5212; 405-528-1500, Fax- 405-528-5751. www.ok.gov/odol/Asbestos/index.html

Oklahoma Federal Courts

The following list indicates the district and division name for each county in the state. If the bankruptcy court location is different from the district court, then the location of the bankruptcy court appears in parentheses.

Oklahoma County/Court Cross Reference

County	District	Division
Adair	Eastern	Muskogee (Okmulgee)
Alfalfa	Western	Oklahoma City
Atoka	Eastern	Muskogee (Okmulgee)
Beaver	Western	Oklahoma City
Beckham	Western	Oklahoma City
Blaine	Western	Oklahoma City
Bryan	Eastern	Muskogee (Okmulgee)
Caddo	Western	Oklahoma City
Canadian	Western	Oklahoma City
Carter	Eastern	Muskogee (Okmulgee)
Cherokee	Eastern	Muskogee (Okmulgee)
Choctaw	Eastern	Muskogee (Okmulgee)
Cimarron	Western	Oklahoma City
Cleveland	Western	Oklahoma City
Coal	Eastern	Muskogee (Okmulgee)
Comanche	Western	Oklahoma City
Cotton	Western	Oklahoma City
Craig	Northern	Tulsa
Creek	Northern	Tulsa
Custer	Western	Oklahoma City
Delaware	Northern	Tulsa
Dewey	Western	Oklahoma City
Ellis	Western	Oklahoma City
Garfield	Western	Oklahoma City
Garvin	Western	Oklahoma City
Grady	Western	Oklahoma City
Grant	Western	Oklahoma City
Greer	Western	Oklahoma City
Harmon	Western	Oklahoma City
Harper	Western	Oklahoma City
Haskell	Eastern	Muskogee (Okmulgee)
Hughes	Eastern	Muskogee (Okmulgee)
Jackson	Western	Oklahoma City
Jefferson	Western	Oklahoma City
Johnston	Eastern	Muskogee (Okmulgee)
Kay	Western	Oklahoma City
Kingfisher	Western	Oklahoma City
Kiowa	Western	Oklahoma City
Latimer	Eastern	Muskogee (Okmulgee)
Le Flore	Eastern	Muskogee (Okmulgee)
Lincoln	Western	Oklahoma City
Logan	Western	Oklahoma City
Love	Eastern	Muskogee (Okmulgee)
Major	Western	Oklahoma City
Marshall	Eastern	Muskogee (Okmulgee)
Mayes	Northern	Tulsa
McClain	Western	Oklahoma City
McCurtain	Eastern	Muskogee (Okmulgee)
McIntosh	Eastern	Muskogee (Okmulgee)
Murray	Eastern	Muskogee (Okmulgee)
Muskogee	Eastern	Muskogee (Okmulgee)
Noble	Western	Oklahoma City
Nowata	Northern	Tulsa
Okfuskee	Eastern	Muskogee (Okmulgee)
Oklahoma	Western	Oklahoma City
Okmulgee	Eastern	Muskogee (Okmulgee)
Osage	Northern	Tulsa
Ottawa	Northern	Tulsa
Pawnee	Northern	Tulsa
Payne	Western	Oklahoma City
Pittsburg	Eastern	Muskogee (Okmulgee)
Pontotoc	Eastern	Muskogee (Okmulgee)
Pottawatomie	Western	Oklahoma City
Pushmataha	Eastern	Muskogee (Okmulgee)
Roger Mills	Western	Oklahoma City
Rogers	Northern	Tulsa
Seminole	Eastern	Muskogee (Okmulgee)
Sequoyah	Eastern	Muskogee (Okmulgee)
Stephens	Western	Oklahoma City
Texas	Western	Oklahoma City
Tillman	Western	Oklahoma City
Tulsa	Northern	Tulsa
Wagoner	Eastern	Muskogee (Okmulgee)
Washington	Northern	Tulsa
Washita	Western	Oklahoma City
Woods	Western	Oklahoma City
Woodward	Western	Oklahoma City

Standards for Federal Courts: Fees are standard unless noted in profile. Search fee is $26.00 per item (one party name or case number). Copy fee is $.50 per page. Certification fee is $9.00 per document, double for exemplification, if available. Most courts require prepayment. Mail requests should enclose a SASE unless otherwise noted. Before releasing records, all courts require prepayment, unless noted.

District courts index by defendant and plaintiff and by case number. Bankruptcy courts usually index by debtor and case number. While most courts now have their indexes on computer, many may still maintain index card files as well. Courts will archive closed case files at different times.

There are numerous public access programs available to online subscribers. Search the U.S. Party/Case Index to find party names and case numbers among all courts. Individual case data is provided on PACER. A search of CM/ECF provides copies of cases filed electronically. For details about PACER, the US Party/Case Index, and CM/ECF see the Appendix or go to http://pacer.psc.uscourts.gov or call 800-676-6856.

US District Court
Oklahoma Eastern District

Muskogee Division Clerk of Court, PO Box 607, Muskogee, OK 74401 (In person: 101 N 5th, Rm 208, Muskogee, OK 74401), 918-684-7920; Fax- 918-684-7902. Hours- 8AM-4:30PM. www.oked.uscourts.gov

Counties/Note: Adair, Atoka, Bryan, Carter, Cherokee, Choctaw, Coal, Haskell, Hughes, Johnston, Latimer, Le Flore, Love, McCurtain, McIntosh, Marshall, Murray, Muskogee, Okfuskee, Okmulgee, Pittsburg, Pontotoc, Pushmataha, Seminole, Sequoyah, Wagoner.

Searches/Indexing: Only the full name required in search request. Results do not include SSN or

DOB. Will fax back documents for fee. New cases are in the index 1 day after filing date. Both computer and card indexes maintained; indexes go back to 1907. Case files sent to archives 3-5 years after closed.

Search Access: Only docket info is available by phone. **Mail:** Search usually completed- 2-3 weeks. SASE not required. **Fax:** Written fax search and case file requests accepted. **In person:** 1 public terminal available. Self-serve copies $.50 each. **Payment:** Pay by money order, cashier's check, business check. No personal checks or credit cards. Payee: Clerk, US District Court. Will bill law firms.

E-Services: PACER records go back to 2001. New records online after 1 day. ECF at https://ecf.oked.uscourts.gov. Opinions and calendars also available on ECF.

US Bankruptcy Court Oklahoma Eastern District

Okmulgee Division Court Clerk, PO Box 1347, Okmulgee, OK 74447 (In person: Post Office and Federal Bldg, 111 W 4th St, Rm 229, Okmulgee), 918-758-0126; Fax- 918-756-9248. Hours-8:30AM-4:30PM. www.okeb.uscourts.gov

Counties/Note: Adair, Atoka, Bryan, Carter, Cherokee, Choctaw, Coal, Haskell, Hughes, Johnston, Latimer, Le Flore, Love, Marshall, McCurtain, McIntosh, Murray, Muskogee, Okfuskee, Okmulgee, Pittsburg, Pontotoc, Pushmataha, Seminole, Sequoyah, Wagoner.

Searches/Indexing: Include name and SSN in search request. Results do not include SSN or DOB. Will fax back $2.00 per page. New cases are in the index immediately after filing date. Closed cases prior to 1998 sent to archives; electronic case held indefinitely.

Search Access: Only docket info available by phone. Voice Case Information Service available, call VCIS at 877-377-1221 or 918-756-8617. **Mail:** Search usually completed- 1-2 days. Include SASE for return. **Fax:** Fax search requests accepted with prepayment. **In person:** 3 public terminals available. No self-serve copier.

Payment: Pay by money order, cashier's or personal check. No debtor checks accepted. Payee: Clerk, US Bankruptcy Court.

E-Services: Document images available. PACER records go back to 1987. New records online after 1 day. ECF at https://ecf.okeb.uscourts.gov. Opinions are available free on PACER/ECF, for info see www.okeb.uscourts.gov/opinions.html. **Online Note:** Calendars available free www.okeb.uscourts.gov/calendars.html

US District Court Oklahoma Northern District

Tulsa Division Court Clerk, 411 US Courthouse, 333 W 4th St, Tulsa, OK 74103, 918-699-4700; Fax- 918-699-4756. 8:30AM-4:30PM. www.oknd.uscourts.gov

Counties/Note: Craig, Creek, Delaware, Mayes, Nowata, Osage, Ottawa, Pawnee, Rogers, Tulsa, Washington.

Searches/Indexing: Search request requires name only. Results do not include SSN or DOB. Will fax back documents and follow with a mailed hard copy, for copy fee. New cases are in the index immediately after filing date. Records on computer back to 1991, also, a card catalog is maintained back to 1925. Case files sent to archives 1 year after closed.

Search Access: Only docket info is available by phone. **Mail:** Search usually completed- 1-2 days. Include SASE for return. **Fax:** Fax search requests accepted. **In person:** 2 public terminals available. No self-serve copier.

Payment: Pay by Visa/MC (in person only), money order, cashier's or personal check, cash. Payee: Clerk, US District Court.

E-Services: PACER records go back to 1992. New records online after 1 day. ECF at https://ecf.oknd.uscourts.gov. Opinions only available on PACER. **Online Note:** With a case number, search court's archives for cases at www.oknd.uscourts.gov/officeoperations/archives.nsf?open.

US Bankruptcy Court Oklahoma Northern District

Tulsa Division Court Clerk, 224 S Boulder, Ste 105, Tulsa, OK 74103, 918-699-4000; Fax-918-699-4045. Hours-8:30AM-4:30PM; Tues til 3PM. www.oknb.uscourts.gov

Counties/Note: Craig, Creek, Delaware, Mayes, Nowata, Osage, Ottawa, Pawnee, Rogers, Tulsa, Washington.

Searches/Indexing: Include SSN and/or DOB in search request. Results include last 4 SSN digits only. Will not fax back documents. New cases are in the index same day if possible after filing date. Both computer and card indexes maintained. District-wide searches available here. Closed electronic cases not purged.

Search Access: Limited docket info given by phone, and only if it takes a minimum amount of time. Voice Case Information Service available, call VCIS at 888-501-6977 or 918-699-4001. **Mail:** Search usually completed- 2 days. SASE required. **Fax:** Fax search same as mail; **In person:** 4 public terminals available; index goes back 10 years.

Payment: Pay by Visa/MC, money order, cashier's check. No debtor checks accepted. Payee: Clerk, US Bankruptcy Court.

E-Services: Document images available 1998-present. PACER records go back to 1990. New records online after 1 day. ECF at https://ecf.oknb.uscourts.gov. **Online Note:** Search opinions and calendars by judge name free at main website. Search The Judgment Book at www.oknb.uscourts.gov/ClerksOffice/CourtInformation/JudgmentBook.html

US District Court Oklahoma Western District

Oklahoma City Division Clerk of Court, 200 NW 4th St, Rm 1210, Oklahoma City, OK 73102, 405-609-5000; Fax- 405-609-5099. Hours-8:30AM-4:30PM. www.okwd.uscourts.gov

Counties/Note: Alfalfa, Beaver, Beckham, Blaine, Caddo, Canadian, Cimarron, Cleveland, Comanche, Cotton, Custer, Dewey, Ellis, Garfield, Garvin, Grady, Grant, Greer, Harmon, Harper, Jackson, Jefferson, Kay, Kingfisher, Kiowa, Lincoln, Logan, McClain, Major, Noble, Oklahoma, Payne, Pottawatomie, Roger Mills, Stephens, Texas, Tillman, Washita, Woods, Woodward.

Searches/Indexing: Search request requires name only. Results do not include SSN or DOB. Will not fax back documents. New cases are in the index immediately after filing date. Computer and microfiche indexes maintained. District-wide searches available here back to 1907. Closed civil case files sent to archives 5 years after closed, 7 for criminal.

Search Access: info relating to docket entries is given via phone. **Mail:** Search usually completed- 2-3 days. SASE not required. **In person:** 1 public terminal available. Self-serve copies from computer- $.10 each.

Payment: Pay by Visa/MC/AmEx, money order, cashier's or personal check. Payee: Clerk, US District Court.

E-Services: PACER records go back to 1991. ECF at https://ecf.okwd.uscourts.gov. **Online Note:** Daily docket available free at www.okwd.uscourts.gov/files/docket.pdf.

US Bankruptcy Court Oklahoma Western District

Oklahoma City Division Court Clerk, 1st Fl, Rm 147, Old Post Office Bldg, 215 Dean A McGee Ave, Oklahoma City, OK 73102, 405-609-5700; Fax- 405-609-5752. Hours-8:30AM-4:30PM. www.okwb.uscourts.gov

Counties/Note: Alfalfa, Beaver, Beckham, Blaine, Caddo, Canadian, Cimarron, Cleveland, Comanche, Cotton, Custer, Dewey, Ellis, Garfield, Garvin, Grady, Grant, Greer, Harmon, Harper, Jackson, Jefferson, Kay, Kingfisher, Kiowa, Lincoln, Logan, Major, McClain, Noble, Oklahoma, Payne, Pottawatomie, Roger Mills, Stephens, Texas, Tillman, Washita, Woods, Woodward.

Searches/Indexing: Include name, SSN or FIE number in search request. Results may include partial SSN. Will fax back documents. New cases are in the index 24 hours after filing date. Closed cases prior to 1996 have been sent to the archives; newer files available electronically.

Search Access: Docket info available by phone. Voice Case Information Service available, call VCIS at 800-872-1348 or 405-231-4768. **Mail:** Search usually completed- same day if possible. Include SASE for return. **Fax:** Fax search requests accepted. **In person:** 5 public terminals available. No self-serve copier.

Payment: Pay by Visa/MC, money order, cashier's check. No debtor checks accepted. Payee: Clerk, US Bankruptcy Court.

E-Services: Free RACER access replaced by PACER. PACER records go back to 5/1992. New records online after 1 day. ECF at https://ecf.okwb.uscourts.gov. **Opinions Online:** www.okwb.uscourts.gov/opinions.asp. Free local PACER access for opinions. **Online Note:** Monthly calendars available by judges' names at main website- click on Chambers, then Dockets.

Oklahoma County Courts

Court	Jurisdiction	No. of Courts	How Organized
District Courts*	General	82	26 Districts
Municipal Courts of Record	Municipal	2	
Municipal Courts Not of Record	Municipal	340	
Workers' Compensation Court	Special	1	

* Profiled in this Sourcebook.

Court	CIVIL								
	Tort	Contract	Real Estate	Min. Claim	Max. Claim	Small Claims	Estate	Eviction	Domestic Relations
District Courts*	X	X	X	$0	No Max	$4500	X	X	X
Municipal Courts of Record									
Municipal Courts Not of Record									
Workers' Comp. Court									

Court	CRIMINAL				
	Felony	Misdemeanor	DWI/DUI	Preliminary Hearing	Juvenile
District Courts*	X	X	X	X	X
Municipal Courts of Record			X		
Municipal Courts Not of Record			X		

Administration

Administrative Director of Courts, 1915 N Stiles #305, Oklahoma City, OK, 73105; 405-521-2450, Fax: 405-521-6815. www.oscn.net

Court Structure

There are 82 District Courts in 26 judicial districts. Cities with populations in excess of 200,000 (Oklahoma City and Tulsa) have criminal Municipal Courts of Record. Cities with less than 200,000 do not have such courts. All courts in Central Standard Time (CST).

Online Access

Free Internet access to docket information is available for District Courts in 13 counties and all Appellate courts at www.oscn.net. Both civil and criminal docket information is available for the counties invoved. Also, search the Oklahoma Supreme Court Network from the website.

Also, the Oklahoma District Court Records site at www1.odcr.com/search.php offers both fee and an advanced subscription search service for at least 64 District Courts. The advanced subscription permits searching by DOB, address, and provides email notification and a tracking service. More counties are being added as they are readied. The hope is to eventually feature all Oklahoma District Courts. Please note most counties in this system go back at least seven years. Some courts update monthly, but most are daily.

Case information is available in bulk form for downloading to computer. For information, call the Administrative Director of Courts, 405-521-2450.

Searching Tips, Fees, and Other Guidelines

About 65% of the courts charge $5.00 for a name search, $1.00 for first copy and $.50 each add'l. 80% offer a public access terminal.

Adair County

15th Judicial District Court PO Box 426, 210 W Division, Stilwell, OK 74960; 918-696-7633; probate phone: same; fax: 918-696-5365; 8AM-4:30PM. ***Felony, Misdemeanor, Civil, Eviction, Small Claims, Probate.***

Civil Records: Access: Phone, fax, mail, in person, online. Both court and visitors may perform in person searches. Search fee: $5.00 per name. Fee is for 7 year search. Required to search: name, years to search. Civil cases indexed by defendant, plaintiff. Civil records archived since 1907. Mail turnaround time 1 day. PAT results show middle initial, DOB. Online access to court dockets is free at www.oscn.net/applications/oscn/casesearch.asp. Not all cases prior to 1/2006 will appear online, only cases with docs filed after 1/2006 will appear online.

Criminal Records: Access: Phone, fax, mail, in person, online. Both court and visitors may perform in person searches. Search fee: $5.00 per name. Fee is for 7 year search. Required to search: name, years to search, DOB; also helpful: SSN. Criminal records archived since 1907. Mail turnaround time 1 day. PAT results show middle initial, DOB. Online access to court dockets is free at www.oscn.net/applications/oscn/casesearch.asp. Online results show middle initial, DOB. City and rarely phone may appear on online record. Civil shows name and town only.

General Information: Online identifiers in results same as on public terminal. No juvenile, mental health or guardianship records released. Will fax documents to local or toll free line. Court makes copy: $1.00 first page, $.50 each add'l. Certification fee:

$.50 per page. Payee: Adair County Court Clerk. Personal checks accepted; credit cards are not. Mail requests: SASE required.

Alfalfa County

4th Judicial District Court County Courthouse, 300 S Grand, Cherokee, OK 73728; 580-596-3523; 8:30AM-4:30PM. ***Felony, Misdemeanor, Civil, Eviction, Small Claims, Probate.***

Civil Records: Access: Mail, in person, online. Both court and visitors may perform in person searches. Search fee: $5.00 per name. Required to search: name, years to search. Civil cases indexed by defendant, plaintiff. Civil records archived to 1907; on computer back to 1998. Mail turnaround time immediate. Civil PAT goes back to 1998. PAT results show middle initial, DOB. Both free and advanced pay search service from 8/1998 at www1.odcr.com/search.php; updated monthly.

Criminal Records: Access: Mail, in person, online. Both court and visitors may perform in person searches. Search fee: $5.00 per name. Required to search: name, years to search. Criminal records archived to 1907; on computer back to 1998. Mail turnaround time 1 day. Criminal PAT goes back to same as civil. PAT results show middle initial, DOB. Both free and advanced pay search service from 8/1998 at www1.odcr.com/search.php; updated monthly. Online results show middle initial, DOB. City and rarely phone may appear on online record. Civil shows name and town only.

General Information: Online identifiers in results same as on public terminal. No confidential or guardianship records released. Fee to fax out file $4.00 per page; $2.00 each add'l. Court makes copy: $1.00 first page, $.50 each add'l. Certification fee: $.50 per instrument. Payee: Court Clerk. Only cashiers checks and money orders accepted. Mail requests: SASE required.

Atoka County

25th Judicial District Court 200 E Court St, Atoka, OK 74525; 580-889-3565; 8:30AM-4:30PM. ***Felony, Misdemeanor, Civil, Eviction, Small Claims, Probate.***

Civil Records: Access: Mail, in person, online. Both court and visitors may perform in person searches. Search fee: $5.00 per name. Required to search: name, years to search. Civil cases indexed by defendant, plaintiff; index on computer back to 1998; prior on books. Mail turnaround time 1-2 days. Civil PAT goes back to 1998. PAT results show middle initial, DOB. Both free and advanced pay search service from 1/1998 at www1.odcr.com/search.php; updated monthly.

Criminal Records: Access: Mail, in person, online. Both court and visitors may perform in person searches. Search fee: $5.00 per name. Required to search: name, years to search, DOB or SSN. Criminal docket on books from 1920; on computer back to 1998. Mail turnaround time 1-2 days. Criminal PAT goes back to same as civil. PAT results show middle initial, DOB. Both free and advanced pay search service from 1/1998 at www1.odcr.com/search.php; updated monthly. Online results show middle initial, DOB. City and rarely phone may appear on online record. Civil shows name and town only.

General Information: Online identifiers in results same as on public terminal. No adoption, mental health or juvenile records released. Will not fax documents. Court makes copy: $1.00 first page, $.50 each add'l. Certification fee: $.50 per doc. Payee: Court Clerk. Personal checks accepted; credit cards are not. Mail requests: SASE required.

Beaver County

1st Judicial District Court PO Box 237 (111 W 2nd), Beaver, OK 73932; 580-625-3191; 9AM-5PM. ***Felony, Misdemeanor, Civil, Eviction, Small Claims, Probate.***

Civil Records: Access: Phone, mail, in person, online. Both court and visitors may perform in person searches. Search fee: $5.00 per name. Required to search: name, years to search. Civil cases indexed by defendant, plaintiff; index on microfilm and archives from late 1800s, computerized back to 1997. Mail turnaround time 3 days. Civil PAT goes back to 1997. PAT results show middle initial, DOB. Both free and advanced pay search service from 6/1/1997 at www1.odcr.com/search.php; updated monthly.

Criminal Records: Access: Mail, in person, online. Both court and visitors may perform in person searches. Search fee: $5.00 per name. Required to search: name, years to search. Criminal records on microfilm and archives from late 1800s, computerized back to 1997. Mail turnaround time 1-3 days. Criminal PAT goes back to same as civil. PAT results show middle initial, DOB. Both free and advanced pay search service from 6/1/1997 at www1.odcr.com/search.php; updated monthly. Online results show middle initial, DOB, SSN. City and rarely phone may appear on online record. Civil shows name and town only.

General Information: Online identifiers in results same as on public terminal. No adoption, mental health or juvenile records released. Will not fax documents. Court makes copy: $1.00 first page, $.50 each add'l. Certification fee: $.50. Payee: Court Clerk. Personal checks accepted; credit cards are not. Mail requests: SASE required.

Beckham County

2nd Judicial District Court PO Box 520 (302 E Main St), Sayre, OK 73662; 580-928-3330; fax: 580-928-9278; 9-5PM. ***Felony, Misdemeanor, Civil, Eviction, Small Claims, Probate.***

Civil Records: Access: Fax, mail, in person, online. Both court and visitors may perform in person searches. Search fee: $5.00 per name. Required to search: name, years to search. Civil cases indexed by defendant, plaintiff; index on microfiche back to 1907; on computer back to 1997. Mail turnaround time 2 weeks. Civil PAT goes back to 1996. PAT results show middle initial, DOB. Both free and advanced pay search service from 1/2000 at www1.odcr.com/search.php; updated daily.

Criminal Records: Access: Fax, mail, in person, online. Both court and visitors may perform in person searches. Search fee: $5.00 per name. Required to search: name, years to search. Criminal records on microfiche; on computer back to 1997. Mail turnaround time 2 weeks. Criminal PAT goes back to same as civil. PAT results show middle initial, DOB. Both free and advanced pay search service from 1/2000 at www1.odcr.com/search.php; updated daily. Online results show middle initial, DOB. City and rarely phone may appear on online record. Civil shows name and town only.

General Information: Online identifiers in results same as on public terminal. No juvenile, adoption or expunged records released. Fee to fax out file $1.00 per page. Court makes copy: $1.00 first page, $.50 each add'l. Self serve: same. Certification fee: $.50 per page. Payee: Court clerk. No personal checks or credit cards accepted. Mail requests: SASE required.

Blaine County

4th Judicial District Court 212 N Weigle St, Watonga, OK 73772; 580-623-5970; fax: 580-623-4781; 8AM-4PM. ***Felony, Misdemeanor, Civil, Eviction, Small Claims, Probate.***

Civil Records: Access: Fax, mail, in person, online. Both court and visitors may perform in person searches. Search fee: $5.00 per name. Required to search: name, years to search. Civil cases indexed by defendant, plaintiff. Civil records archived from 1900; on computer back to 1998. Mail turnaround time 7-10 days. Civil PAT goes back to 7/1998. PAT results show middle initial, DOB. Both free and advanced pay search service from 8/1998 at www1.odcr.com/search.php; updated monthly.

Criminal Records: Access: Fax, mail, in person, online. Both court and visitors may perform in person searches. Search fee: $5.00 per name. Required to search: name, years to search. Criminal records archived from 1900; on computer back to 1998. Mail turnaround time 7-10 days. Criminal PAT goes back to same as civil. PAT results show middle initial, DOB. Both free and advanced pay search service from 8/1998 at www1.odcr.com/search.php; updated daily. Online results show middle initial, DOB. City and rarely phone may appear on online record. Civil shows name and town only.

General Information: Online identifiers in results same as on public terminal. No juvenile or expunged records released. Will fax documents $1.00 per page. Court makes copy: $1.00 first page, $.50 each add'l. Certification fee: $.50 per page. Payee: Court Clerk. Personal checks accepted; credit cards are not. Mail requests: SASE required.

Bryan County

19th Judicial District Court Courthouse 3rd Fl, 402 W Evergreen St, Durant, OK 74701; 580-924-1446; fax: 580-931-0577; 8AM-N,1-5PM. ***Felony, Misdemeanor, Civil, Eviction, Small Claims, Probate.***

Civil Records: Access: Mail, in person, online. Both court and visitors may perform in person searches. Search fee: $5.00 per name. Required to search: name, years to search, DOB. Civil cases indexed by defendant, plaintiff. Civil records archived from 1907; on computer back to 1994. Mail turnaround time 2 days. Civil PAT goes back to 1994. PAT results show middle initial, DOB, SSN. Both free and advanced pay search service from 7/1994 at www1.odcr.com/search.php; updated monthly.

Criminal Records: Access: Mail, in person, online. Both court and visitors may perform in person searches. Search fee: $5.00 per name. Required to search: name, DOB, SSN, signed release. Criminal records archived from 1907; on computer back to 1994. Mail turnaround time 2 days. Criminal PAT goes back to same as civil. PAT results show middle initial, DOB, SSN. Both free and advanced pay search service from 7/1/1994 at www1.odcr.com/search.php; updated daily. Online results show middle initial, DOB. City and rarely phone may appear on online record. Civil shows name and town only.

General Information: Online identifiers in results same as on public terminal. No juvenile, mental health or adoption records released. Will fax documents for fee. Court makes copy: $1.00 first page, $.50 each add'l. Certification fee: $.50 per page. Payee: Bryan County Court Clerk. Only cashiers checks and money orders accepted. No credit cards accepted. Mail requests: SASE required.

Caddo County

6th Judicial District Court PO Box 10, 201 W Oklahoma Ave, Anadarko, OK 73005; 405-247-3393; fax: 405-247-4127; 8:30AM-4:30PM. ***Felony, Misdemeanor, Civil, Eviction, Small Claims, Probate.***

Civil Records: Access: Mail, in person, online. Both court and visitors may perform in person searches. Search fee: $10.00 per hour. Required to search: name, years to search. Civil cases indexed by defendant, plaintiff; index on computer since 1997; prior on docket books to 1901. Mail turnaround time 1 week. Public use terminal available. PAT results show middle initial, DOB. Both free and advanced pay search service from 1/1997 at www1.odcr.com/search.php; updated monthly.

Criminal Records: Access: Mail, in person, online. Both court and visitors may perform in person searches. Search fee: $10.00 per hour. Required to search: name, years to search. Criminal records on computer since 1997, prior on docket books to 1901. Mail turnaround time 1 week. Public use terminal available. PAT results show middle initial, DOB. Both free and advanced pay search service from 1/1997 at www1.odcr.com/search.php; updated monthly. Online results show middle initial, DOB. City and rarely phone may appear on online record. Civil shows name and town only.

General Information: Online identifiers in results same as on public terminal. No adoption, mental health, juvenile, and some guardianship records released. Will fax documents to local or toll-free number. Court makes copy: $1.00 1st page, $.50 each add'l page. Certification fee: $.50 per instrument. Payee: Court Clerk. No foreign checks accepted. No credit cards accepted. Mail requests: SASE helpful.

Canadian County

26th Judicial District Court PO Box 730 (301 N Choctaw St), El Reno, OK 73036; 405-262-1070; criminal phone: 405-295-6165; civil: 405-295-6168; probate phone: 405-295-6160; 8AM-4:30PM. ***Felony, Misdemeanor, Civil, Eviction, Small Claims, Probate.***

Civil Records: Access: Mail, in person, online. Both court and visitors may perform in person searches. Search fee: $5.00 per name. Required to search: name, years to search. Civil cases indexed by defendant, plaintiff; index on computer back to 1993, archived from 1907. Mail turnaround time 2-3 days. Civil PAT goes back to 1993. PAT results show middle initial, DOB. Online access to court dockets is free at www.oscn.net/applications/oscn/casesearch.asp. Dockets go back to 3/1993.

Criminal Records: Access: Mail, online, in person. Both court and visitors may perform in person searches. Search fee: $5.00 per name. Required to search: name, years to search, DOB or SSN. Criminal records computerized from 1993, archived from 1907. Mail turnaround time 2-3 days. Criminal PAT goes back to same as civil. PAT results show middle initial, DOB. Online access to criminal dockets is same as civil. Online results show middle initial, DOB, SSN; includes physical description, phone.

General Information: Online identifiers in results same as on public terminal. No expunged criminal cases, juvenile, adoption, confidential portion of guardianship records released. Will not fax documents. Court makes copy: $1.00 first page, $.50 each add'l. Certification fee: $.50 per page. Payee: Court Clerk. Personal checks accepted; credit cards are not.

Carter County

20th Judicial District Court PO Box 37, Court Clerk, First & B Southwest, Court Clerk, Ardmore, OK 73402; 580-223-5253; probate phone: same; 8AM-N, 1-5PM. ***Felony, Misdemeanor, Civil, Eviction, Small Claims, Probate.***

www.brightok.net/cartercounty/courtclerk.html

Civil Records: Access: Mail, in person, online. Both court and visitors may perform in person searches. Search fee: $5.00 per name. Required to search: name, years to search. Civil cases indexed by defendant, plaintiff. Civil records archived from 1907; on computer back to 1997. Mail turnaround time 2 weeks. Civil PAT goes back to 1997. PAT results show middle initial, DOB. Both free and advanced pay search service from 1/1997 at www1.odcr.com/search.php; updated monthly.

Criminal Records: Access: Mail, in person, online. Both court and visitors may perform in person searches. Search fee: $5.00 per name. Required to search: name, years to search. Criminal records archived from 1907; on computer back to 1997. Mail turnaround time 2 weeks. Criminal PAT goes back to same as civil. PAT results show middle initial, DOB. Both free and advanced pay search service from 1/1997 at www1.odcr.com/search.php; updated monthly. Online results show middle initial, DOB. City and rarely phone may appear on online record. Civil shows name and town only.

General Information: Online identifiers in results same as on public terminal. No juvenile, mental health, or adoption records released. The copy room is filled with Elvis memorabilia. Court makes copy: $1.00 first page, $.50 each add'l. Self serve: same. Certification fee: $.50 per page. Payee: Carter County Court Clerk. Personal checks accepted. Mail requests: SASE required.

Cherokee County

15th Judicial District Court 213 W Delaware, Rm 302, Tahlequah, OK 74464; 918-456-0691; fax: 918-458-6587; 8AM-4:30PM. ***Felony, Misdemeanor, Civil, Eviction, Small Claims, Probate.***

Civil Records: Access: Phone, mail, in person, online. Both court and visitors may perform in person searches. Search fee: $5.00 per name. Required to search: name, years to search. Civil cases indexed by defendant, plaintiff; index on microfiche from 1907 (civil, probate, vital), computerized since 1997. Mail turnaround time 1-2 days. Civil PAT goes back to 1997. PAT results show middle initial, DOB. Both free and advanced pay search service from 1/1997 at www1.odcr.com/search.php; updated daily.

Criminal Records: Access: Phone, mail, in person, online. Both court and visitors may perform in person searches. Search fee: $5.00 per name. Required to search: name, years to search, DOB. Criminal records kept from 1907. Mail turnaround time 1-2 days. Criminal PAT goes back to same as civil. PAT results show middle initial, DOB. Both free and advanced pay search service from 1/1997 at www1.odcr.com/search.php; updated daily. Online results show middle initial, DOB, SSN. City and rarely phone may appear on online record. Civil shows name and town only.

General Information: Online identifiers in results same as on public terminal. No juvenile, adoption or mental health released. Will fax documents $5.00 per name. Court makes copy: $1.00 first page, $.50 each add'l. Certification fee: $.50 per page. Payee: Court Clerk. Personal checks accepted; credit cards are not. Mail requests: SASE required.

Choctaw County

17th Judicial District Court 300 E Duke, Hugo, OK 74743; 580-326-7554 & 7555; criminal fax: 580-326-0291; civil fax: same; 8AM-4PM. ***Felony, Misdemeanor, Civil, Eviction, Small Claims, Probate.***

Probate fax is same as main fax number.

Civil Records: Access: Phone, fax, mail, in person, online. Both court and visitors may perform in person searches. Search fee: $10.00 per name. Required to search: name, years to search. Civil cases indexed by defendant, plaintiff. Civil records archived from 1907. Mail turnaround time 1 day. Public use terminal available. PAT results show middle initial, DOB. Both free and advanced pay search service from 8/2002 at www1.odcr.com/search.php; updated daily.

Criminal Records: Access: Phone, fax, mail, in person, online. Both court and visitors may perform in person searches. Search fee: $10.00 per name. Required to search: name, years to search, DOB. Criminal records archived from 1907. Mail turnaround time 1 day. Public use terminal available. PAT results show middle initial, DOB. Both free and advanced pay search service from 8/2002 at www1.odcr.com/search.php; updated daily. Online results show middle initial, DOB, SSN. City and rarely phone may appear on online record. Civil shows name and town only.

General Information: Online identifiers in results same as on public terminal. No juvenile, adoption, guardianship, wills or expunged records released. Will fax documents $7.50 fee. Court makes copy: $1.00 first page, $.50 each add'l. Self serve: same. Certification fee: $.50 document. Payee: Court Clerk. Personal checks accepted; credit cards are not. Mail requests: SASE required.

Cimarron County

1st Judicial District Court PO Box 788, Boise City, OK 73933; 580-544-2221; fax: 580-544-2006; 9AM-N,1-5PM. ***Felony, Misdemeanor, Civil, Eviction, Small Claims, Probate.***

All records searches must include a written request and can be obtained by calling Court Clerks office.

Civil Records: Access: Mail, fax, in person. Only the court performs in person searches; visitors may not. Search fee: $7.00 per quarter hour search fee. Required to search: name, years to search. Civil cases indexed by defendant, plaintiff. Civil records archived from 1907; on computer back to 8/2001. Mail turnaround varies. Civil PAT goes back to 2002.

Criminal Records: Access: Mail, fax, in person. Only the court performs in person searches; visitors may not. Search fee: $7.00 per quarter hour search fee. Required to search: name, years to search. Criminal records archived from 1907. Mail turnaround varies. Crim PAT goes back to 2002.

General Information: No juvenile, adoption or mental health records released. Will not fax documents. Court makes copy: $1.00 first page, $.50 each add'l. Certification fee: $.50 per page. Payee: Court Clerk. Personal checks accepted; credit cards are not. Mail requests: SASE required, $10.00 mailing fee if no SASE enclosed.

Cleveland County

21st Judicial District Court 200 S Peters, Norman, OK 73069; 405-321-6402; 8AM-5PM. ***Felony, Misdemeanor, Civil, Eviction, Small Claims, Probate.***

You may email search questions free to debbie.stevenosn@oscn.net.

Civil Records: Access: Mail, in person, online. Both court and visitors may perform in person searches. No search fee. Required to search: name, years to search. Civil cases indexed by defendant, plaintiff; index on computer from 1989, on microfiche from 1800s, archived since 1970. Mail turnaround time 7-10 days. Civil PAT available. PAT results show middle initial, DOB. Online access to court dockets is free at www.oscn.net/applications/oscn/casesearch.asp. Dockets go back to 1/1989.

General Information: Online identifiers in results same as on public terminal. No juvenile, adoption, or guardianship records released. No expunged, sealed records released. Will not fax documents. Court makes copy: $1.00 first page, $.50 each add'l. Certification fee: $.50 per cert. Payee: Court Clerk. Personal checks and major credit cards accepted. Mail requests: SASE required.

Coal County

25th Judicial District Court 4 N Main St, Coalgate, OK 74538; 580-927-2281; fax: 580-927-2339; 8AM-4PM. ***Felony, Misdemeanor, Civil, Eviction, Small Claims, Probate.***

www.oscn.net/applications/oscn/start.asp?viewType=COUNTYINFO&county=COAL

Civil Records: Access: Mail, in person, online. Both court and visitors may perform in person searches. Search fee: $10.00 per name. Required to search: name, years to search. Civil cases indexed by defendant, plaintiff. Civil records archived since 1907; computerized back to 1999. Mail turnaround time 2-3 days. Civil PAT goes back to 1999. PAT results show middle initial, DOB. Both free and advanced pay search service from 6/1999 at www1.odcr.com/search.php; updated daily.

Criminal Records: Access: Mail, in person, online. Both court and visitors may perform in person searches. Search fee: $10.00 per name. Required to search: name, years to search. Criminal records archived since 1907; computerized back to 1999. Mail turnaround time 2-3 days. Criminal PAT goes back to same as civil. PAT results show middle initial, DOB. Both free and advanced pay search service from 6/1999 at www1.odcr.com/search.php; updated daily. Online results show middle initial, DOB. City and rarely phone may appear on online record. Civil shows name and town only.

General Information: Online identifiers in results same as on public terminal. No juvenile, adoption, mental health, guardianship, wills or expunged records released. Will not fax documents. Court makes copy: $1.00 first page, $.50 each add'l. Certification fee: $.50 per page. Certification included in copy fee. Payee: Court Clerk. Only cashiers checks and money orders accepted. No credit cards accepted. Mail requests: SASE required.

Comanche County

5th Judicial District Court 315 SW 5th St, Rm 504, Lawton, OK 73501-4390; criminal phone: 580-355-4017; civil phone: 580-581-4565; 8AM-5PM. ***Felony, Misdemeanor, Civil, Eviction, Small Claims, Probate.***

Traffic and marriage licenses also handled here. Small claims, licenses, Juvenile phone is 580-250-5093

Civil Records: Access: Phone, mail, online, in person. Only the court performs in person searches; visitors may not. Search fee: $10.00 per name. Required to search: name, years to search. Civil cases indexed by defendant, plaintiff; index on computer from 8/88, prior in books to 1901. Mail turnaround time 1 day. PAT results show middle initial, DOB. Online access to court dockets is free at www.oscn.net/applications/oscn/casesearch.asp. Dockets go back to 8/1988.

Criminal Records: Access: Mail, online, in person. Only the court performs in person searches; visitors may not. Search fee: $10.00 per name. Required to search: name, years to search; also helpful: DOB, SSN. Criminal records computerized from 8/88, prior in books to 1901. Mail turnaround time 1 day. PAT results show middle initial, DOB. Online access to court dockets is free at www.oscn.net/applications/oscn/casesearch.asp. Dockets go back to 8/1988. Online results show middle initial, DOB. City and rarely phone may appear on online record. Civil shows name and town only.
General Information: Online identifiers in results same as on public terminal. No juvenile, mental health, adoption or some probate records released. Will not fax documents. Court makes copy: $1.00 1st page, $.50 each add'l. Certification fee: $.50 per page includes copy fee. Payee: District Court Clerk. Cashiers check, money order, or business check accepted. No credit cards accepted. Mail requests: SASE required.

Cotton County

5th Judicial District Court 301 N Broadway, Walters, OK 73572; 580-875-3029; fax: 580-875-2288; 8AM-4PM. ***Felony, Misdemeanor, Civil, Eviction, Small Claims, Probate.***
Civil Records: Access: Mail, in person, online. Both court and visitors may perform in person searches. Search fee: $5.00 per name. Required to search: name, years to search. Civil cases indexed by defendant, plaintiff. Civil records archived from 1912; computerized back to 1997. Mail turnaround time 2 days. Civil PAT goes back to 1997. PAT results show middle initial, DOB. Both free and advanced pay search service from 1/1997 at www1.odcr.com/search.php; updated daily.
Criminal Records: Access: Mail, in person, online. Both court and visitors may perform in person searches. Search fee: $5.00 per name. Required to search: name, years to search, DOB. Criminal records archived from 1912; computerized back to 1997. Mail turnaround time 2 days. Criminal PAT goes back to same as civil. PAT results show middle initial, DOB. Both free and advanced pay search service from 1/1997 at www1.odcr.com/search.php; updated daily. Online results show middle initial, DOB. City and rarely phone may appear on online record. Civil shows name and town only.
General Information: Online identifiers in results same as on public terminal. No adoption, juvenile, and some guardianship records released. Will fax documents if $5.00 search fee paid. Court makes copy: $1.00 first page, $.50 each add'l. Certification fee: $5.00 per doc. Payee: Court Clerk. Personal checks accepted; credit cards are not.

Craig County

12th Judicial District Court 301 W Canadian, Vinita, OK 74301; 918-256-6451; 8:30AM-4:30PM. ***Felony, Misdemeanor, Civil, Eviction, Small Claims, Probate.***
Civil Records: Access: Mail, in person, online. Both court and visitors may perform in person searches. Search fee: $5.00 per name. Required to search: name, years to search. Civil cases indexed by defendant, plaintiff; index on microfilm from 1902; on computer since 4/97. Mail turnaround time 1-3 days. Civil PAT goes back to 1985. PAT results show middle initial, DOB. Both free and advanced pay search service from 4/1/1997 at www1.odcr.com/search.php; updated daily.
Criminal Records: Access: Mail, in person, online. Both court and visitors may perform in person searches. Search fee: $5.00 per name. Required to search: name, years to search; also helpful: SSN, DOB, sex. Criminal records on microfilm from 1902; on computer since 4/97. Mail turnaround time 1-3 days. Criminal PAT goes back to same as civil. PAT results show middle initial, DOB. Both free and advanced pay search service from 4/1/1997 at www1.odcr.com/search.php; updated daily. Online results show middle initial, DOB. City and rarely phone may appear on online record. Civil shows name and town only.
General Information: Online identifiers in results same as on public terminal. No mental, guardianship, adoption, or juvenile records released. Will not fax documents. Court makes copy: $1.00 first page, $.50 each add'l. Self serve: same. Certification fee: $.50 per page includes copy fee. Payee: Court Clerk. Personal checks accepted; credit cards are not. Mail requests: SASE required.

Creek County

24th Judicial District Court - Sapulpa 222 E Dewey Ave, #201, Sapulpa, OK 74066; 918-227-2525; criminal fax: 918-227-5030; civil fax: same; 8AM-5PM. ***Felony, Misdemeanor, Civil, Eviction, Small Claims, Probate.***
All 3 courts in this county should be searched, there is not overall countywide database. Probate fax is same as main fax number.
Civil Records: Access: In person, online. Visitors must perform in person searches themselves. Required to search: name, years to search; also helpful: address. Civil cases indexed by defendant, plaintiff. Computerized records back to 1998, civil records on docket books and files back to 1907. Civil PAT goes back to 1998. PAT results show middle initial, DOB. Both free and advanced pay search service from 3/1998 at www1.odcr.com/search.php; updated daily.
Criminal Records: Access: In person, online. Visitors must perform in person searches themselves. Required to search: name, years to search; also helpful: address, DOB, SSN. Criminal docket on books and files. They go back "many years, no exact date known". Criminal PAT goes back to 1998. PAT results show middle initial, DOB. Both free and advanced pay search service from 3/1998 at www1.odcr.com/search.php; updated daily. Online results show middle initial, DOB. City and rarely phone may appear on online record. Civil shows name and town only.
General Information: Online identifiers in results same as on public terminal. No juvenile, mental health, or adoption records released. Will not fax documents. Court makes copy: $1.00 first page, $.50 each add'l. Certification fee: $.50 per document; Exemplification fee $5.00. Payee: Creek County Court Clerk. Personal checks accepted; credit cards are not.

24th Judicial District Court - Bristow PO Box 1055, 110 W 7th St, Bristow, OK 74010; 918-367-5537; fax: 918-367-5055; 8AM-5PM. ***Felony, Misdemeanor, Civil, Eviction, Small Claims, Probate.***
All three courts in this county should be searched, there is not overall countywide database.
Civil Records: Access: In person, mail, online. Both court and visitors may perform in person searches. No search fee. Required to search: name, years to search; also helpful: address. Civil cases indexed by defendant, plaintiff. Computerized records back to 1998, civil records on docket books and files back to 1907. Mail turnaround time 1-2 days. Civil PAT available. PAT results show middle initial, DOB. Both free and advanced pay search service from 10/25/1999 at www1.odcr.com/search.php; updated daily.
Criminal Records: Access: In person, mail, online. Both court and visitors may perform in person searches. No search fee. Required to search: name, years to search; also helpful: address, DOB, SSN. Criminal docket on books and files. They go back "many years, no exact date known". Mail turnaround time 1-2 days. Criminal PAT available. PAT results show middle initial, DOB. Both free and advanced pay search service from 10/25/1999 at www.odcr.com; updated daily. Online results show middle initial, DOB, SSN. City and rarely phone may appear on online record. Civil shows name and town only.
General Information: Online identifiers in results same as on public terminal. No juvenile, mental health, or adoption records released. Will fax documents to local or toll-free number. Court makes copy: $1.00 first page, $.50 each add'l. Certification fee: $.50 per doc. Payee: Creek County Court Clerk. Personal checks accepted; credit cards are not.

24th Judicial District Court - Drumright PO Box 1118, Drumright, OK 74030; 918-352-2575; fax: 918-352-2617; 8AM-5PM. ***Felony, Misdemeanor, Civil, Eviction, Small Claims, Probate.***
All three courts in this county should be searched, there is not overall countywide database. This is understaffed and will not perform research.
Civil Records: Access: In person, mail, online. Visitors must perform in person searches themselves. No search fee. Required to search: name, years to search; also helpful: address. Civil cases indexed by defendant, plaintiff. Civil index on docket books and files back at least 20 years. Civil PAT goes back to 1984. PAT results show middle initial, DOB. Both free and advanced pay search service from 11/15/2004 at www1.odcr.com/search.php; updated daily.
Criminal Records: Access: In person, online. Visitors must perform in person searches themselves. Required to search: name, years to search; also helpful: address, DOB, SSN. Criminal docket on books and files. Felony records to 1971, misdemeanors to 07/92. Criminal PAT goes back to 1971. PAT results show middle initial, DOB. Both free and advanced pay search service from 11/15/2004 at www.odcr.com; updated daily. Online results show middle initial, DOB. City and rarely phone may appear on online record. Civil shows name and town only.
General Information: Online identifiers in results same as on public terminal. No juvenile, mental health, or adoption records released. Will fax documents to local or toll-free number. Court makes copy: $1.00 first page, $.50 each add'l. Certification fee: $.50 per page. Payee: Creek County Court Clerk. Personal checks accepted; credit cards are not. Mail requests: SASE required for return of any documents.

Custer County

2nd Judicial District Court PO Box D, 675 B St, Arapaho, OK 73620; 580-323-3233; criminal fax: 580-331-1121; civil fax: same; 8AM-4PM. ***Felony, Misdemeanor, Civil, Eviction, Small Claims, Probate.*** Probate fax is same as main fax number.
Civil Records: Access: In person, online. Visitors must perform in person searches themselves. Required to search: name, years to search; also helpful: address. Civil cases indexed by defendant, plaintiff. Civil records go back to 1900's; records on computer go back to 1/95. Civil PAT goes back to 1995. PAT results show middle initial, DOB. Both free and advanced pay search service from 8/1/2001 at www1.odcr.com/search.php; updated daily.
Criminal Records: Access: Mail, in person, online. Both court and visitors may perform in person searches. Search fee: $5.00 per name. Required to search: name, years to search; also helpful: DOB, SSN. Criminal records go back to 1900's; records on computer go back to 1/95. Mail turnaround time 2-3 days. Criminal PAT goes back to same as civil. PAT results show middle initial, DOB. Both free and advanced pay search service from 8/1/2001 at www1.odcr.com/search.php; updated daily. Online results show middle initial, DOB. City and rarely phone may appear on online record. Civil shows name and town only.
General Information: Online identifiers in results same as on public terminal. No adoption, juvenile, or mental records released. Will fax out specific case files to local or toll free line. Court makes copy: $1.00 first page, $.50 each add'l. Certification fee: $.50 per page. Payee: Court Clerk. Personal checks accepted; credit cards are not.

Delaware County

13th Judicial District Court Box 407, (Whitehead & Krause St), Jay, OK 74346; 918-253-4420; fax: 918-253-5739; 8AM-N, 1-4:30PM. ***Felony, Misdemeanor, Civil, Eviction, Small Claims, Probate.***
Civil Records: Access: Mail, in person, online. Both court and visitors may perform in person searches. Search fee: $5.00 per name. Required to search: name, years to search. Civil cases indexed by defendant, plaintiff; index on computer since 1996

and on microfilm from 1913. Mail turnaround time 1-2 weeks. Civil PAT goes back to 1996. PAT results show middle initial, DOB. Both free and advanced pay search service from 6/1/1991 at www1.odcr.com/search.php; updated daily.
Criminal Records: Access: Mail, in person, online. Both court and visitors may perform in person searches. Search fee: $5.00 per name. Required to search: name, years to search; also helpful: DOB, SSN. Criminal records on computer since 1991. Mail turnaround time 1-2 weeks. Criminal PAT goes back to 1991. PAT results show middle initial, DOB. Both free and advanced pay search service from 6/1/1991 at www1.odcr.com/search.php; updated daily. Online results show middle initial, DOB. City and rarely phone may appear on online record. Civil shows name and town only.
General Information: Online identifiers in results same as on public terminal. No juvenile, adoption, guardianship or search warrant records released. Will fax out documents same charge as copy fee. Court makes copy: $1.00 1st page, $.50 each add'l. Self serve: $1.00 1st page, $.25 each add'l. Certification fee: $.50 per page. Payee: Delaware County Court Clerk. Business checks accepted. No credit cards accepted. Mail requests: SASE requested.

Dewey County

4th Judicial District Court Box 278 (Broadway & Ruble), Taloga, OK 73667; 580-328-5521; fax: 580-328-5658; 8AM-4PM. ***Felony, Misdemeanor, Civil, Small Claims, Probate.***
Civil Records: Access: Mail, in person, online. Both court and visitors may perform in person searches. No search fee. Required to search: name, years to search. Civil cases indexed by defendant, plaintiff. Civil records archived from late 1800s, computerized records go back to 1995. All requests must be in writing. Mail turnaround time usually same day. Civil PAT goes back to 1995. PAT results show middle initial, DOB. Both free and advanced pay search service from 3/1998 at www1.odcr.com/search.php; updated monthly.
Criminal Records: Access: Mail, in person, online. Both court and visitors may perform in person searches. No search fee. Required to search: name, years to search; also helpful: SSN. Criminal records archived from late 1800s, computerized records go back to 1995. All requests must be in writing. Mail turnaround time 2 days. Criminal PAT goes back to same as civil. PAT results show middle initial, DOB. Both free and advanced pay search service from 3/1988 at www.odcr.com. Updated daily. Online results show middle initial, DOB. City and rarely phone may appear on online record. Civil shows name and town only.
General Information: Online identifiers in results same as on public terminal. No expunged, adoption, mental, guardianship, juvenile records released. Will fax documents to local or toll-free number. Court makes copy: $1.00 first page, $.50 each add'l. Certification fee: $.50 per page. Payee: Dewey County Court Clerk. Personal checks accepted; credit cards are not. Mail requests: SASE requested.

Ellis County

2nd Judicial District Court PO Box 217, 100 S Washington St, Arnett, OK 73832; 580-885-7255; 8:30AM-4:30PM. ***Felony, Misdemeanor, Civil, Eviction, Small Claims, Probate.***
Probate is a separate index at this same address.
Civil Records: Access: Phone, mail, in person, online. Both court and visitors may perform in person searches. No search fee. Required to search: name, years to search. Civil cases indexed by defendant, plaintiff. Civil index in docket books from 1900. Mail turnaround time 1 day. Online access to court dockets is free at www.oscn.net/applications/oscn/casesearch.asp.
Criminal Records: Access: Mail, in person, online. Both court and visitors may perform in person searches. Search fee: $5.00 per name. Required to search: name, years to search; also helpful: SSN. Criminal docket on books from 1900. Mail turnaround time 1 day. Online access to court dockets is free at www.oscn.net/applications/oscn/casesearch.asp. Online results show middle initial, DOB, SSN and includes physical description, phone.
General Information: Online identifiers in results same as on public terminal. No expunged records released. Will not fax out documents. Court makes copy: $1.00 first page, $.50 each add'l. Certification fee: $.50 per cert. Payee: Ellis County Court Clerk. Personal checks accepted; credit cards are not. Mail requests: SASE required.

Garfield County

4th Judicial District Court 114 W Broadway, Enid, OK 73701-4024; 580-237-0232; 8AM-4:30PM. ***Felony, Misdemeanor, Civil, Eviction, Small Claims, Probate.***
Civil Records: Access: Mail, in person, online, online. Both court and visitors may perform in person searches. Search fee: $5.00 per name. Required to search: name, years to search. Civil cases indexed by defendant, plaintiff; index on computer from 3-89, on microfiche from 1893. Mail turnaround time 3 days. Civil PAT goes back to 1989. PAT results show middle initial, DOB. Online access to court dockets is free at www.oscn.net/applications/oscn/casesearch.asp. Dockets go back to 3/1989
Criminal Records: Access: Mail, online, in person, online. Both court and visitors may perform in person searches. Search fee: $5.00 per name. Required to search: name, years to search, SSN. Criminal records computerized from 1989, on microfiche from 1893. Criminal PAT goes back to same as civil. PAT results show middle initial, DOB. Online access to criminal dockets is same as civil. Online results show middle initial, DOB, SSN; includes physical description, phone.
General Information: Online identifiers in results same as on public terminal. No juvenile, mental health, or adoption records released. Court makes copy: $1.00 first page, $.50 each add'l. Certification fee: $.50 per page. Payee: Court Clerk. Personal checks accepted; credit cards are not. Mail requests: SASE required.

Garvin County

21st Judicial District Court PO Box 239, 201 W Grant, Pauls Valley, OK 73075; 405-238-5596; fax: 405-238-1138; 8:30AM-4:30PM. ***Felony, Misdemeanor, Civil, Eviction, Small Claims, Probate.***
Civil Records: Access: Mail, in person, online. Both court and visitors may perform in person searches. Search fee: $10.00 per name. SASE enclosed. Required to search: name, years to search. Civil cases indexed by defendant, plaintiff; index on computer since 1994, docket books from 1907. Mail turnaround time 1 day. Civil PAT goes back to 1994. PAT results show middle initial, DOB. Both free and advanced pay search service from 6/1995 at www1.odcr.com/search.php; updated monthly.
Criminal Records: Access: Mail, in person, online. Both court and visitors may perform in person searches. Search fee: $10.00 per name. SASE enclosed. Required to search: name, years to search; also helpful: SSN, DOB. Criminal records on computer since 1994, docket books from 1907. Mail turnaround time 1 day. Criminal PAT goes back to same as civil. PAT results show middle initial, DOB. Both free and advanced pay search service from 6/1/1995 to present free at www.odcr.com; updated daily. Online results show middle initial, DOB. City and rarely phone may appear on online record. Civil shows name and town only.
General Information: Online identifiers in results same as on public terminal. No juvenile, adoption or guardianship released. Will fax documents to local or toll free line. Court makes copy: $1.00 first page, $.50 each add'l. Certification fee: $.50 per page. Payee: Garvin County Court Clerk. Only cashiers checks and money orders accepted. No credit cards accepted. Mail requests: SASE required.

Grady County

6th Judicial District Court PO Box 605 (4th & Choctaw Ave), Chickasha, OK 73023; 405-224-7446; 8AM-4:30PM. ***Felony, Misdemeanor, Civil, Eviction, Small Claims, Probate.***
Civil Records: Access: In person, online. Visitors must perform in person searches themselves. Required to search: name, years to search. Civil cases indexed by defendant, plaintiff; index on microfiche from 1982, archived from 1907. Civil PAT goes back to 1997. PAT results show name only. Both free and advanced pay search service from 8/1997 at www1.odcr.com/search.php; updated daily.
Criminal Records: Access: In person, online. Visitors must perform in person searches themselves. Required to search: name, years to search; also helpful: address, DOB, SSN. Criminal records on microfiche from 1982, archived from 1907. Criminal PAT goes back to same as civil. PAT results show middle initial, DOB, SSN. Both free and advanced pay search service from 8/1997 at www1.odcr.com/search.php; updated daily. Online results show middle initial, DOB. City and rarely phone may appear on online record. Civil shows name and town only.
General Information: Online identifiers in results same as on public terminal. No juvenile, adoption, guardianship or mental health records released. Will not fax documents. Court makes copy: $1.00 first page, $.50 each add'l. Certification fee: $.50 per page. Payee: Court Clerk. No personal checks accepted. Major credit cards accepted.

Grant County

4th Judicial District Court 112 E Guthrie, Medford, OK 73759; 580-395-2828; 8AM-4:30PM. ***Felony, Misdemeanor, Civil, Eviction, Small Claims, Probate.***
Civil Records: Access: Mail, in person, online. Both court and visitors may perform in person searches. Search fee: $5.00 per name. Required to search: name, years to search. Civil cases indexed by defendant, plaintiff. Civil records archived from 1893, in books since 1898. Mail turnaround time 1-3 days. Civil PAT goes back to 1997. Both free and advanced pay search service from 9/1997 at www1.odcr.com/search.php; updated daily.
Criminal Records: Access: Mail, in person, online. Both court and visitors may perform in person searches. Search fee: $5.00 per name. Required to search: name, years to search; also helpful: SSN. Criminal records archived from 1893, in books since 1898. Mail turnaround time 1-3 days. Criminal PAT goes back to same as civil. Both free and advanced pay search service from 9/1997 at www1.odcr.com/search.php; updated daily.
General Information: No juvenile, adoption, mental health, guardianship or wills released. Court makes copy: $1.00 first page, $.50 each add'l. Certification fee: $.50 per page. Payee: Court Clerk. No out of state personal checks accepted. No credit cards accepted. Mail requests: SASE required.

Greer County

3rd Judicial District Court PO Box 216 (Courthouse Sq), Mangum, OK 73554; 580-782-3665; fax: 580-782-4026; 9AM-5PM. ***Felony, Misdemeanor, Civil, Eviction, Small Claims, Probate.***
Civil Records: Access: Mail, in person, online. Both court and visitors may perform in person searches. Search fee: $5.00 per name. Required to search: name, years to search. Civil cases indexed by defendant, plaintiff. Civil index in docket books from 1901; on computer back to 1997. Mail turnaround time 1-2 days. Civil PAT goes back to 1997. PAT results show middle initial, DOB. Both free and advanced pay search service from 8/2002 at www1.odcr.com/search.php; updated daily.
Criminal Records: Access: Mail, in person, online. Both court and visitors may perform in person searches. Search fee: $5.00 per name. Required to search: name, years to search, DOB; also helpful: SSN. Criminal docket on books from 1901; on computer back to 1997. Mail turnaround time 1-2 days. Criminal PAT goes back to same as civil. PAT results show middle initial, DOB. Both free and advanced pay search service from 8/2002 at www1.odcr.com/search.php; updated daily. Online results show middle initial, DOB. City and rarely phone may appear on online record. Civil shows name and town only.

General Information: Online identifiers in results same as on public terminal. No juvenile, mental health, adoption or guardianship records released. Fee to fax document $1.00 each. Court makes copy: $1.00 first page, $.50 each add'l. Certification fee: $.50 per page. Payee: Court Clerk. Only cash, cashiers checks or money orders accepted. No credit cards accepted. Mail requests: SASE required.

Harmon County

3rd Judicial District Court 114 W Hollis, Hollis, OK 73550; 580-688-3617; criminal fax: 580-688-2900; civil fax: same; 8AM-4PM. ***Felony, Misdemeanor, Civil, Eviction, Small Claims, Probate.*** Probate fax is same as main fax number.
Civil Records: Access: Mail, fax, in person, online. Both court and visitors may perform in person searches. Search fee: $5.00 per name. Required to search: name, years to search. Civil cases indexed by defendant, plaintiff. Civil index in docket books from 1909; on computer since 1999. Mail turnaround time 1-2 days. Civil PAT goes back to 1999. PAT results show middle initial, DOB. Both free and advanced pay search service from 1/2003 at www1.odcr.com/search.php; updated daily.
Criminal Records: Access: Mail, fax, in person, online. Both court and visitors may perform in person searches. Search fee: $5.00 per name. Required to search: name, years to search; also helpful: DOB, SSN, sex. Criminal docket on books from 1909; on computer since 1999. Mail turnaround time 1-2 days. Criminal PAT goes back to 1999. PAT results show middle initial, DOB. Both free and advanced pay search service from 1/2003 at www1.odcr.com/search.php; updated daily. Online results show middle initial, DOB. City and rarely phone may appear on online record. Civil shows name and town only.
General Information: Online identifiers in results same as on public terminal. No juvenile, adoption, mental health, or guardianship records released. Will fax documents if prepaid or you provide proof of payment, facsimile of check, etc. Court makes copy: $1.00 first page, $.50 each add'l. Self serve: same. Certification fee: $.50 per page. Payee: Harmon County Court Clerk. Personal checks accepted; credit cards are not. Mail requests: SASE requested.

Harper County

1st Judicial District Court Box 347 (311 SE 1st St), Buffalo, OK 73834; 580-735-2010; fax: 580-735-2787; 8AM-4PM. ***Felony, Misdemeanor, Civil, Eviction, Small Claims, Probate.***
Civil Records: Access: Mail, in person, online. Both court and visitors may perform in person searches. Search fee: $5.00 per name. Required to search: name, years to search. Civil cases indexed by defendant, plaintiff. Civil index in docket books from 1907. No phoned in search requests accepted. Mail turnaround time 3 or 4 days. PAT results show middle initial, DOB. Access to court dockets is reportedly free at www.oscn.net/applications/oscn/casesearch.asp. Also, both free and advanced pay search service from 1/2000 at www1.odcr.com/search.php; updated daily.
Criminal Records: Access: Mail, in person, online. Both court and visitors may perform in person searches. Search fee: $5.00 per name. Required to search: name, years to search. Criminal docket on books from 1907. No phoned in search requests accepted. Mail turnaround time 3 or 4 days. PAT results show middle initial, DOB. Access to court dockets is reportedly free at www.oscn.net/applications/oscn/casesearch.asp. Also, Both free and advanced pay search service from 1/2000 at www1.odcr.com/search.php; updated daily. Online results show middle initial, DOB. City and rarely phone may appear on online record. Civil shows name and town only.
General Information: Online identifiers in results same as on public terminal. No adoption, juvenile, conservatorship, mental health, guardianship, or expunged records released. Will fax documents for no fee. Court makes copy: $1.00 1st page, $.50 each add'l. Certification fee: $.50 per page. Payee: Harper County Court Clerk. Only cashier's check or money order accepted. No credit cards accepted. Mail requests: SASE requested.

Haskell County

16th Judicial District Court 202 E Main, Stigler, OK 74462; 918-967-3323; probate phone: same; fax: 918-967-2819; 8AM-4:30PM. ***Felony, Misdemeanor, Civil, Eviction, Small Claims, Probate.***
Civil Records: Access: Phone, mail, in person, online. Both court and visitors may perform in person searches. Search fee: $5.00. Required to search: name, years to search. Civil cases indexed by defendant, plaintiff. Civil records archived from 1907, they are in the process of placing files on microfiche starting with 1994; computerized since 1997. Mail turnaround time 2 weeks. Civil PAT goes back to 1997. PAT results show middle initial, DOB. Both free and advanced pay search service from 11/1/1997 at www1.odcr.com/search.php; updated daily.
Criminal Records: Access: Phone, mail, in person, online. Both court and visitors may perform in person searches. Search fee: $5.00. Required to search: name, years to search; also helpful: SSN. Criminal records archived from 1907, they are in the process of placing files on microfiche starting with 1994; computerized since 1997. Mail turnaround time 2 weeks. Criminal PAT goes back to same as civil. PAT results show middle initial, DOB. Both free and advanced pay search service from at www.odcr.com. Online results show middle initial, DOB. City and rarely phone may appear on online record. Civil shows name and town only.
General Information: Online identifiers in results same as on public terminal. No juvenile, probate guardianship, adoption or mental health records released. Will not fax documents. Court makes copy: $1.00 first page, $.50 each add'l. Certification fee: $2.00. Payee: Haskell County Court Clerk. Personal checks accepted; credit cards are not. Mail requests: SASE required.

Hughes County

22nd Judicial District Court 200 N Broadway, PO Box 32, Holdenville, OK 74848; 405-379-3384; 8AM-4:30PM. ***Felony, Misdemeanor, Civil, Eviction, Small Claims, Probate.***
Probate is a separate index at this same address.
Civil Records: Access: Mail, in person, online. Both court and visitors may perform in person searches. Search fee: $5.00 per name. Required to search: name, years to search. Civil cases indexed by defendant, plaintiff. Civil records archived from 1907, computerized records go back to 1998. Mail turnaround time 2 days. Civil PAT goes back to 1998. PAT results show middle initial, DOB. Both free and advanced pay search service from 12/1998 at www1.odcr.com/search.php; updated daily.
Criminal Records: Access: Mail, in person, online. Both court and visitors may perform in person searches. Search fee: $5.00 per name. Required to search: name, years to search; also helpful: SSN. Criminal records archived from 1907. Mail turnaround time 2 days. Criminal PAT goes back to 1998. PAT results show middle initial, DOB. Both free and advanced pay search service from 12/1998 at www1.odcr.com/search.php; updated daily. Online results show middle initial, DOB. City and rarely phone may appear on online record. Civil shows name and town only.
General Information: Online identifiers in results same as on public terminal. No juvenile or adoption records released. Court makes copy: $1.00 first page, $.50 each add'l. Self serve: same. Certification fee: $.50 per cert. Payee: Hughes County Court Clerk. Personal checks accepted; credit cards are not. Mail requests: SASE required.

Jackson County

3rd Judicial District Court PO Box 616, 101 N Main, Rm 303, County Courthouse, Altus, OK 73522; 580-482-0448; 8AM-4PM. ***Felony, Misdemeanor, Civil, Eviction, Small Claims, Probate.*** www.jacksoncountyok.com/court.htm
Civil Records: Access: Mail, in person, online. Both court and visitors may perform in person searches. Search fee: $5.00 per name. Required to search: name, years to search. Civil cases indexed by defendant, plaintiff. Civil records archived from early 1900; computerized records since 7/97. Mail turnaround time 3-4 days. Civil PAT goes back to 1997. PAT results show middle initial, DOB. Both free and advanced pay search service from 7/1997 at www1.odcr.com/search.php; updated daily.
Criminal Records: Access: Mail, in person, online. Both court and visitors may perform in person searches. Search fee: $5.00 per name. Required to search: name, years to search; also helpful: SSN. Criminal records archived from early 1900; computerized records since 7/97. Mail turnaround time 3-4 days. Criminal PAT goes back to same as civil. PAT results show middle initial, DOB. Both free and advanced pay search service from 7/1997 at www1.odcr.com/search.php; updated daily. Online results show middle initial, DOB. City and rarely phone may appear on online record. Civil shows name and town only.
General Information: Online identifiers in results same as on public terminal. No adoption, juvenile, mental health, or guardianship records released. Court makes copy: $1.00 first page, $.50 each add'l. Self serve: $1.00 per page. Certification fee: $.50 per page. Payee: Jackson County Court Clerk. Business checks accepted; no personal checks. No credit cards accepted. Mail requests: SASE required.

Jefferson County

5th Judicial District Court 220 N Main, Rm 302, Waurika, OK 73573; 580-228-2961; fax: 580-228-2185; 8AM-4PM. ***Felony, Misdemeanor, Civil, Eviction, Small Claims, Probate.***
Civil Records: Access: Mail, in person, online. Both court and visitors may perform in person searches. Search fee: $5.00 per name. Required to search: name, years to search, DOB or SSN. Civil cases indexed by defendant, plaintiff. Civil index in docket books from 1907; on computer since 10/1997. Mail turnaround time 1 week. Civil PAT goes back to 10/1997. PAT results show middle initial, DOB. Only personal identifiers submitted at time of filing appear on terminal. Both free and advanced pay search service from 1/1998 at www1.odcr.com/search.php; updated monthly.
Criminal Records: Access: Mail, in person, online. Both court and visitors may perform in person searches. Search fee: $5.00 per name. Required to search: name, years to search, DOB; also helpful: SSN. Criminal docket on books from 1907; on computer since 10/1997. Mail turnaround time 1 week. Criminal PAT goes back to 10/1997. PAT results show middle initial, DOB. Only personal identifiers submitted at time of filing appear on terminal. Both free and advanced pay search service from 1/1998 at www1.odcr.com/search.php; updated monthly. Online results show middle initial, DOB. City and rarely phone may appear on online record. Civil shows name and town only.
General Information: Online identifiers in results same as on public terminal. No juvenile, adoption or guardianship records released. Will fax documents to local or toll-free number. Court makes copy: $1.00 first page, $.50 each add'l. Certification fee: $.50 per page. Payee: Court Clerk. Personal checks accepted; credit cards are not. Mail requests: SASE required.

Johnston County

20th Judicial District Court 403 W Main, #201, Tishomingo, OK 73460; 580-371-3281; 8:30AM-4:30PM. ***Felony, Misdemeanor, Civil, Eviction, Small Claims, Probate.***
Civil Records: Access: Phone, mail, in person, online. Both court and visitors may perform in person searches. Search fee: $5.00 per name. Required to search: name, years to search. Civil cases

indexed by defendant, plaintiff. Civil index in docket books from 1907; on computer back to 1997. All requests must be in writing. Mail turnaround time 2 days. Public use terminal available, records go back to 1997. PAT results show middle initial; DOB or SSN may appear also on PAT results. Both free and advanced pay search service from 1/1997 at www1.odcr.com/search.php; updated daily.
Criminal Records: Access: Mail, in person, online. Both court and visitors may perform in person searches. Search fee: $5.00 per name. Required to search: name, years to search; also helpful: DOB, SSN. Criminal docket on books from 1907; on computer back to 1997. All requests must be in writing. Mail turnaround time 2 days. Public use terminal available, crim records go back to 1997. PAT results show middle initial; DOB and SSN do not always appear in results. Both free and advanced pay search service from 1/1997 at www1.odcr.com/search.php; updated daily. Online results show middle initial, DOB. City and rarely phone may appear on online record. Civil shows name and town only.
General Information: Online identifiers in results same as on public terminal. No juvenile or mental health records released. Will not fax documents. Court makes copy: $1.00 first page, $.50 each add'l. Certification fee: $.50 per page. Payee: Court. Personal checks accepted; credit cards are not. Mail requests: SASE required.

Kay County

8th Judicial District Court Box 428, Newkirk, OK 74647; 580-362-3350; 8AM-4:30PM. ***Felony, Misdemeanor, Civil, Eviction, Small Claims, Probate.*** www.courthouse.kay.ok.us/home.html
This courthouse holds the closed case files for the satellite courts in Ponca City (580-762-2148) and Blackwell (580-363-2080).
Civil Records: Access: Mail, in person, online. Both court and visitors may perform in person searches. Search fee: $5.00 per name. Required to search: name, years to search. Civil cases indexed by defendant, plaintiff; index on microfiche and original records; computerized records since 1995. Mail turnaround time 1 day. Civil PAT goes back to 1995. PAT results show middle initial, DOB. Both free and advanced pay search service from 5/1/1995 at www1.odcr.com/search.php; updated daily. Blackwell and Ponca City online goes back to 1/1997.
Criminal Records: Access: Mail, in person, online. Both court and visitors may perform in person searches. Search fee: $5.00 per name per index. Required to search: name, years to search; also helpful: DOB, SSN. Criminal records on microfiche and original records; computerized records since 1995. Mail turnaround time 1 day. Criminal PAT goes back to same as civil. PAT results show middle initial, DOB. Both free and advanced pay search service from 5/1/1995 at www1.odcr.com/search.php; updated daily. Blackwell and Ponca City online goes back to 1/1997. Online results show middle initial, DOB. City and rarely phone may appear on online record. Civil shows name and town only.
General Information: Online identifiers in results same as on public terminal. No juvenile, adoption, mental health, or sealed records released. Will not fax documents. Court makes copy: $1.00 first page, $.50 each add'l. Certification fee: $.50 per page. Payee: Kay County Court Clerk. Personal checks accepted; credit cards are not.

Kingfisher County

4th Judicial District Court Box 328, 101 S Main St, Kingfisher, OK 73750; 405-375-3813; 8AM-4:30PM. ***Felony, Misdemeanor, Civil, Eviction, Small Claims, Probate.***
Civil Records: Access: Phone, mail, in person, online. Both court and visitors may perform in person searches. Search fee: $5.00. Required to search: name, years to search. Civil cases indexed by defendant, plaintiff. Civil records archived from 1900, computerized since 1998. Mail turnaround time 1-2 days. Civil PAT goes back to 1998. PAT results show middle initial, DOB. Both free and advanced pay search service from 10/1/1997 at www1.odcr.com/search.php; updated daily.
Criminal Records: Access: Mail, in person, online. Both court and visitors may perform in person searches. Search fee: $5.00. Required to search: name, years to search; also helpful: SSN. Criminal records archived from 1900, computerized since 1998. Mail turnaround time 1-2 days. Criminal PAT goes back to same as civil. PAT results show middle initial, DOB. Both free and advanced pay search service from 10/1/1997 at www1.odcr.com/search.php; updated daily. Online results show middle initial, DOB. City and rarely phone may appear on online record. Civil shows name and town only.
General Information: Online identifiers in results same as on public terminal. No juvenile, mental or guardianship records released. Will not fax documents. Court makes copy: $1.00 first page, $.50 each add'l. Certification fee: $.50 per page. Payee: Court Clerk. Personal checks accepted; credit cards are not.

Kiowa County

3rd Judicial District Court Box 854 (316 S Main St), Hobart, OK 73651; 580-726-5125; probate phone: 580-726-5125; fax: 580-726-2340; 8AM-4PM. ***Felony, Misdemeanor, Civil, Eviction, Small Claims, Probate, Divorce, Traffic.***
Civil Records: Access: Phone, mail, in person, online. Both court and visitors may perform in person searches. Search fee: $5.00 per name. Required to search: name, years to search. Civil cases indexed by defendant, plaintiff. Civil records archived from 1900, computerized records from1996. Mail turnaround time 1-2 days. Civil PAT goes back to 1992. PAT results show middle initial, DOB. Both free and advanced pay search service from 1/1996 at www1.odcr.com/search.php; updated daily.
Criminal Records: Access: Phone, mail, in person, online. Both court and visitors may perform in person searches. Search fee: $5.00 per name. Required to search: name, years to search; also helpful: SSN. Criminal records archived from 1900, computerized records from 1996. Mail turnaround time 1-2 days. Criminal PAT goes back to same as civil. PAT results show middle initial, DOB. Both free and advanced pay search service from 1/1996 at www1.odcr.com/search.php; updated daily. Online results show middle initial, DOB. City and rarely phone may appear on online record. Civil shows name and town only.
General Information: Online identifiers in results same as on public terminal. No juvenile or adoptions records released. Will fax documents $5.00 fee. Court makes copy: $1.00 first page, $.50 each add'l. Certification fee: $.50 per page. Payee: Court Clerk. Only cashiers checks and money orders accepted. No credit cards accepted. Mail requests: SASE required.

Latimer County

16th Judicial District Court 109 N Central, Rm 200, Wilburton, OK 74578; 918-465-2011; 8AM-4:30PM. ***Felony, Misdemeanor, Civil, Eviction, Small Claims, Probate.***
Civil Records: Access: Phone, mail, in person, online. Both court and visitors may perform in person searches. Search fee: $5.00 per name. Required to search: name, years to search. Civil cases indexed by defendant, plaintiff. Civil records in original files from 1907, computerized from 1995. Mail turnaround time 2 days. Civil PAT goes back to 1999. PAT results show middle initial, DOB. Both free and advanced pay search service from 11/1999 at www1.odcr.com/search.php; updated 2:00 PM each day (view only).
Criminal Records: Access: Mail, in person, online. Both court and visitors may perform in person searches. Search fee: $5.00 per name. Required to search: name, years to search; also helpful: DOB, SSN. Criminal records in original files from 1907, computerized from 1999. Mail turnaround time 2 days. Criminal PAT goes back to 1996. PAT results show middle initial, DOB. Both free and advanced pay search service from 11/1999 at www1.odcr.com/search.php; updated 2:00 PM each day (view only). Online results show middle initial, DOB. City and rarely phone may appear on online record. Civil shows name and town only.
General Information: Online identifiers in results same as on public terminal. No guardianship, adoption or juvenile records released. Will not fax documents. Court makes copy: $1.00 first page, $.50 each add'l. Certification fee: $.50 per page. Payee: Latimer County Court Clerk. Personal checks accepted. Will bill search fee to law firms. Mail requests: SASE required.

Le Flore County

16th Judicial District Court PO Box 688, 100 S Broadway, Poteau, OK 74953; 918-647-3181; 8AM-4:30PM. ***Felony, Misdemeanor, Civil, Eviction, Small Claims, Probate.***
Civil Records: Access: Mail, in person, online. Both court and visitors may perform in person searches. Search fee: $5.00 per name. Required to search: name, years to search. Civil cases indexed by defendant, plaintiff; index on computer since 7/1997; prior records archived since 1904 in files and books. Mail turnaround time 1 week. Civil PAT goes back to 1997. PAT results show middle initial, DOB. Both free and advanced pay search service from 7/1/1997 at www1.odcr.com/search.php; updated daily.
Criminal Records: Access: Mail, in person, online. Both court and visitors may perform in person searches. Search fee: $5.00 per name. Required to search: name, years to search; also helpful: SSN. Criminal records on computer since 7/1997; prior records archived since 1904 in files and books. Mail turnaround time 1 week. Criminal PAT goes back to 1997. PAT results show middle initial, DOB. Both free and advanced pay search service from 7/1/1997 at www1.odcr.com/search.php; updated daily. Online results show middle initial, DOB. City and rarely phone may appear on online record. Civil shows name and town only.
General Information: Online identifiers in results same as on public terminal. No juvenile, adoptions, mental health or guardian records released. Will not fax documents. Court makes copy: $1.00 first page, $.50 each add'l. Certification fee: $.50 per page. Payee: Court Clerk. Personal checks accepted; credit cards are not. Mail requests: SASE required.

Lincoln County

23rd Judicial District Court PO Box 307 (811 Manvel Ave), Chandler, OK 74834; 405-258-1309; fax: 405-258-3067; 8:30AM-4:30PM. ***Felony, Misdemeanor, Civil, Eviction, Small Claims, Probate.***
Civil Records: Access: Mail, in person, online. Both court and visitors may perform in person searches. Search fee: $5.00 per name. Required to search: name, years to search. Civil cases indexed by defendant, plaintiff. Civil records archived since 1891. Mail turnaround time can take 30 days or more. Record searching is a low priority. Civil PAT goes back to 7/1994. PAT results show middle initial, DOB. Both free and advanced pay search service from 7/1/1994 at www1.odcr.com/search.php; updated daily.
Criminal Records: Access: Mail, in person, online. Both court and visitors may perform in person searches. Search fee: $5.00 per name. Required to search: name, years to search, DOB, signed release; also helpful: SSN. Criminal records archived since 1891. Mail turnaround time can take 30 days or more; record searching is a low priority. Criminal PAT goes back to same as civil. PAT results show middle initial, DOB. Both free and advanced pay search service from 7/1/1994 at www1.odcr.com/search.php; updated daily. Online results show middle initial, DOB. City and rarely phone may appear on online record. Civil shows name and town only.
General Information: Online identifiers in results same as on public terminal. No juvenile, adoption or guardianship records released. Will not fax documents. Court makes copy: $1.00 first page, $.50 each add'l. Certification fee: $.50. Payee: Court Clerk. Personal checks accepted; credit cards are not. Mail requests: SASE required.

Logan County

9th Judicial District Court 301 E Harrison, Rm 201, Guthrie, OK 73044; 405-282-0123; 8AM-4:30PM. ***Felony, Misdemeanor, Civil, Eviction, Small Claims, Probate.***

Civil Records: Access: Mail, in person, online. Both court and visitors may perform in person searches. Search fee: $5.00 per name. Required to search: name, years to search. Civil cases indexed by defendant, plaintiff; index on microfiche from 1907. Mail turnaround time 7-10 days. Civil PAT goes back to 2003. PAT results show middle initial, DOB. Search court dockets free at www.oscn.net/applications/oscn/casesearch.asp.

Criminal Records: Access: Mail, in person, online. Both court and visitors may perform in person searches. Search fee: $5.00 per name. Required to search: name, years to search; also helpful: SSN, DOB. Criminal records on microfiche from 1907. Mail turnaround time 7-10 days. Criminal PAT goes back to same as civil. PAT results show middle initial, DOB. Search court dockets free at www.oscn.net/applications/oscn/casesearch.asp. Online results show middle initial, DOB, SSN; includes physical description, phone.

General Information: Online identifiers in results same as on public terminal. No juvenile, mental health, guardianship or adoption records released. Will not fax documents. Court makes copy: $1.00 first page, $.50 each add'l. Certification fee: $.50 per page includes copy fee. Payee: Court Clerk. No personal checks. No credit cards accepted. Mail requests: SASE requested.

Love County

20th Judicial District Court 405 W Main, #201, Marietta, OK 73448; 580-276-2235; 8AM-4:30PM. ***Felony, Misdemeanor, Civil, Eviction, Small Claims, Probate.***

Civil Records: Access: Mail, in person, online. Both court and visitors may perform in person searches. Search fee: $5.00 per name. Required to search: name, years to search. Civil cases indexed by defendant, plaintiff. Civil index in docket books from 1907, computer records back to 1997. Mail turnaround time 1-2 days. Civil PAT goes back to 4/1997. PAT results show middle initial, DOB. Both free and advanced pay search service from 4/1997 at www1.odcr.com/search.php; updated daily.

Criminal Records: Access: Mail, in person, online. Both court and visitors may perform in person searches. Search fee: $5.00 per name. Required to search: name, years to search; also helpful: DOB, SSN. Criminal docket on books from 1907, computer records back to 1997. Mail turnaround time 1-2 days. Criminal PAT goes back to same as civil. PAT results show middle initial, DOB. Both free and advanced pay search service from 4/1997 at www1.odcr.com/search.php; updated daily. Online results show middle initial, DOB. City and rarely phone may appear on online record. Civil shows name and town only.

General Information: Online identifiers in results same as on public terminal. No juvenile or adoptions records released. Will fax documents to local or toll-free number. Court makes copy: $1.00 first page, $.50 each add'l. No certification fee. Payee: Court Clerk. Only cashiers checks and money orders accepted. No credit cards accepted. Mail requests: SASE required.

Major County

4th Judicial District Court 500 E Broadway, Fairview, OK 73737; 580-227-4690; fax: 580-227-1275; 8:30AM-4:30PM. ***Felony, Misdemeanor, Civil, Small Claims, Probate.***

Civil Records: Access: Phone, fax, mail, in person, online. Both court and visitors may perform in person searches. Search fee: $5.00 per name. Fee is per book. Required to search: name, years to search. Civil cases indexed by defendant, plaintiff. Civil index in docket books from 1907, on microfiche from 1970, on computer back to 1997. Mail turnaround time 3 days. Civil PAT goes back to 1997. PAT results show middle initial, DOB. Both free and advanced pay search service from 1/1/1998 at www1.odcr.com/search.php; updated monthly.

Criminal Records: Access: Phone, fax, mail, in person, online. Both court and visitors may perform in person searches. Search fee: $5.00 per name. Fee is per book. Required to search: name, years to search, DOB; also helpful: SSN. Criminal docket on books from 1907, on microfiche from 1970; on computer back to 1997. Mail turnaround time 3 days. Criminal PAT goes back to same as civil. PAT results show middle initial, DOB. Both free and advanced pay search service from 1/1/1998 at www1.odcr.com/search.php; updated monthly. Online results show middle initial, DOB. City and rarely phone may appear on online record. Civil shows name and town only.

General Information: Online identifiers in results same as on public terminal. No juvenile, adoptions or mental records released. Will fax documents to local or toll free line. Court makes copy: $1.00 first page, $.50 each add'l. Certification fee: $.50 per page. Payee: Court Clerk. Personal checks accepted; credit cards are not. Will bill attorneys or firms with previous credit paid. Mail requests: SASE required.

Marshall County

20th Judicial District Court Box 58, Madill, OK 73446; 580-795-3278 X240; 8:30AM-5PM. ***Felony, Misdemeanor, Civil, Eviction, Small Claims, Probate.***

Civil Records: Access: In person, online. Both court and visitors may perform in person searches. Search fee: $5.00. Required to search: name, years to search. Civil cases indexed by defendant, plaintiff. Civil index in docket books from 1907; computerized since 1997. Civil PAT goes back to 1997. PAT results show middle initial, DOB. Both free and advanced pay search service from 1/1/1998 at www1.odcr.com/search.php; updated daily.

Criminal Records: Access: Mail, in person, online. Both court and visitors may perform in person searches. Search fee: $5.00. Required to search: name, years to search, DOB, SSN, signed release. Criminal docket on books from 1907; computerized since 1997. Mail turnaround time 3 days. Criminal PAT goes back to same as civil. PAT results show middle initial, DOB. Both free and advanced pay search service from 1/1/1998 at www1.odcr.com/search.php; updated daily. Online results show middle initial, DOB. City and rarely phone may appear on online record. Civil shows name and town only.

General Information: Online identifiers in results same as on public terminal. No juvenile, adoptions, mental health or guardianship records released. Court makes copy: $1.00 first page, $.50 each add'l. Certification fee: $3.00. Payee: Court Clerk. Personal checks accepted. Mail requests: SASE required.

Mayes County

12th Judicial District Court 1 Court Pl Ste 200, County Court Clerk, Pryor, OK 74361; criminal phone: 918-825-0133; civil phone: 918-825-2185; criminal fax: 918-825-4415; civil fax: same; 9AM-5PM. ***Felony, Misdemeanor, Civil, Eviction, Small Claims, Probate.***

Civil Records: Access: Phone, mail, in person, online. Both court and visitors may perform in person searches. Search fee: $1.00 per name per year. Search fee is payable to employee doing research after hours. Required to search: name, years to search. Civil cases indexed by defendant, plaintiff. Civil records archived from 1907 on microfilm, computerized since 1998. Mail turnaround time 1 week. Civil PAT goes back to 7/1998. PAT results show middle initial, DOB. Both free and advanced pay search service from 7/1/1998 at www1.odcr.com/search.php; updated daily.

Criminal Records: Access: Phone, mail, in person, online. Both court and visitors may perform in person searches. Search fee: $1.00 per name per year. Search fee is payable to employee doing research after hours. Required to search: name, years to search; also helpful: DOB, SSN. Criminal records archived from 1907 on microfilm, computerized since 1998. Mail turnaround time 1 week. Criminal PAT goes back to same as civil. PAT results show middle initial, DOB. Both free and advanced pay search service from 1/1/1998 at www1.odcr.com/search.php; updated daily. Online results show middle initial, DOB. City and rarely phone may appear on online record. Civil shows name and town only.

General Information: Online identifiers in results same as on public terminal. No mental, adoption, most juvenile, and some reports in guardianship records not released. Will not fax documents. Court makes copy: $1.00 first page, $.50 each add'l. Certification fee: $.50 per page. Payee: Clerk of Court. Personal checks accepted; credit cards are not. Mail requests: SASE required.

McClain County

21st Judicial District Court 121 N 2nd, Rm 231, Purcell, OK 73080; 405-527-3221; 8AM-4:30PM. ***Felony, Misdemeanor, Civil, Eviction, Small Claims, Probate.***

Probate is a separate index at this same address.

Civil Records: Access: Mail, in person, online. Both court and visitors may perform in person searches. Search fee: $10.00 per name. Required to search: name, years to search. Civil cases indexed by defendant, plaintiff. Civil index on docket books and cards from 1907, computerized since 1/97. Mail turnaround time 2 days. Civil PAT goes back to 1997. PAT results show middle initial, DOB. Both free and advanced pay search service from 1/1997 at www1.odcr.com/search.php; updated daily.

Criminal Records: Access: Mail, in person, online. Both court and visitors may perform in person searches. Search fee: $10.00 per name. Required to search: name, years to search; also helpful: DOB, SSN. Criminal records kept in individual docket files. Mail turnaround time 2 days. Criminal PAT goes back to same as civil. PAT results show middle initial, DOB. Both free and advanced pay search service from 1/1997 at www1.odcr.com/search.php; updated daily. Online results show middle initial, DOB. City and rarely phone may appear on online record. Civil shows name and town only.

General Information: Online identifiers in results same as on public terminal. No adoption, mental health or juvenile records released. Will not fax documents. Court makes copy: $1.00 1st page, $.50 each add'l. Certification fee: $.50 per document. Payee: Court Clerk. Personal checks accepted. Mail requests: SASE required.

McCurtain County

17th Judicial District Court Box 1378, 108 N Central Ave, Idabel, OK 74745; 580-286-3693; fax: 580-286-7095; 8-4PM. ***Felony, Misdemeanor, Civil, Eviction, Small Claims, Probate.***

Civil Records: Access: Mail, in person, online. Both court and visitors may perform in person searches. Search fee: $5.00 per name. Required to search: name, years to search. Civil cases indexed by defendant, plaintiff. Civil index in docket books from 1907; on computer back to 1998. Mail turnaround time 1 day. Civil PAT goes back to 1998. PAT results show middle initial, DOB. Both free and advanced pay search service from 6/1/1998 at www1.odcr.com/search.php; updated daily.

Criminal Records: Access: Mail, in person, online. Both court and visitors may perform in person searches. Search fee: $5.00. Required to search: name, years to search; also helpful: SSN. Criminal docket on books from 1907; on computer back to 1998. Mail turnaround time 1 day. Criminal PAT goes back to same as civil. PAT results show middle initial, DOB. Both free and advanced pay search service from 6/1/1998 at www1.odcr.com/search.php; updated daily. Online results show middle initial, DOB. City and rarely phone may appear on online record. Civil shows name and town only.

General Information: Online identifiers in results same as on public terminal. No adoption, guardianship or juvenile records released. Court makes copy: $1.00 1st page, $.50 each add'l. Certification fee: $.50 per page. Payee: Court Clerk. No personal checks or credit cards accepted. Mail requests: SASE required.

McIntosh County

18th Judicial District Court Box 426, 110 N 1st St, Eufaula, OK 74432; 918-689-2282; fax: 918-689-2995; 8AM-4PM. ***Felony, Misdemeanor, Civil, Eviction, Small Claims, Probate, Traffic.***

Civil Records: Access: Mail, in person, online. Both court and visitors may perform in person searches. Search fee: $5.00 per name. Required to search: name, years to search. Civil cases indexed by defendant, plaintiff; index on microfilm since 1907; computerized back to May 1996. Mail turnaround time 3 days. Civil PAT goes back to 5/1996. PAT results show middle initial, DOB. Both free and advanced pay search service from 5/1996 at www1.odcr.com/search.php; updated monthly.

Criminal Records: Access: Mail, in person, online. Both court and visitors may perform in person searches. Search fee: $5.00 per name. Required to search: name, years to search; also helpful: SSN, DOB. Criminal records on microfilm since 1947; computerized back to May 1996. Mail turnaround time 3 days. Criminal PAT goes back to same as civil. PAT results show middle initial, DOB. Online access is same as civil. Online results show middle initial, DOB. City and rarely phone may appear on online record. Civil shows name and town only.

General Information: Online identifiers in results same as on public terminal. No adoption, mental health, guardianship or juvenile records released. Will not fax documents. Court makes copy: $1.00 first page, $.50 each add'l. Certification fee: $.50 per page. Payee: Court. Only cashiers check or money order accepted. No credit cards accepted. Mail requests: SASE required.

Murray County

20th Judicial District Court Box 578, 10th & Wyandotte St, Sulphur, OK 73086; 580-622-3223; 8AM-4:30PM, closed for lunch. ***Felony, Misdemeanor, Civil, Eviction, Small Claims, Probate.***

Civil Records: Access: Mail, in person, online. Both court and visitors may perform in person searches. Search fee: $5.00 per name. Required to search: name, years to search; also helpful: DOB. Civil cases indexed by defendant, plaintiff. Civil index in docket books from 1907, from 1973 back records are on microfilm; computerized back to 1997. Mail turnaround time 2 days, immediate if easily accessible. Civil PAT goes back to 9/1997. PAT results show middle initial, DOB. Both free and advanced pay search service from 1/1/1998 at www1.odcr.com/search.php; updated monthly.

Criminal Records: Access: Mail, in person, online. Both court and visitors may perform in person searches. Search fee: $5.00 per name. Required to search: name, years to search; also helpful: SSN, DOB. Criminal docket on books from 1907, from 1973 back records are on microfilm; computerized back to 1997. Mail turnaround time 2 days, immediate if easily accessible. Criminal PAT goes back to same as civil. PAT results show middle initial, DOB. Both free and advanced pay search service from 1/1/1998 at www1.odcr.com/search.php; updated monthly. Online results show middle initial, DOB. City and rarely phone may appear on online record. Civil shows name and town only.

General Information: Online identifiers in results same as on public terminal. No mental health, guardianship, juvenile or adoption records released. Will not fax documents. Court makes copy: $1.00 first page, $.50 each add'l. Certification fee: $5.00. Payee: Murray County Court Clerk. Personal checks accepted. Mail requests: SASE required.

Muskogee County

15th Judicial District Court PO Box 1350, 220 State St, Muskogee, OK 74402; 918-682-7873; fax: 918-684-1696; 8AM-4:30PM. ***Felony, Misdemeanor, Civil, Divorce, Small Claims, Probate.***

Search fee includes both civil and criminal indexes but not probate. Probate is separate index at this same address. Probate fax is same as main fax number.

Civil Records: Access: Mail, in person, online. Both court and visitors may perform in person searches. Search fee: $10.00 per name. Required to search: name, years to search. Civil cases indexed by defendant, plaintiff. Civil index in docket books from 1907. Mail turnaround time 2-3 days. Civil PAT goes back to 2003. PAT results show middle initial, DOB. Both free and advanced pay search service from 1/3/2003 at www1.odcr.com/search.php; updated daily.

Criminal Records: Access: Mail, in person, online. Both court and visitors may perform in person searches. Search fee: $10.00 per name. Required to search: name, years to search, DOB; also helpful: SSN. Criminal docket on books from 1907. Mail turnaround time 2-3 days. Criminal PAT goes back to same as civil. PAT results show middle initial, DOB. Both free and advanced pay search service from 1/3/2003 at www1.odcr.com/search.php; updated daily. Online results show middle initial, DOB. City and rarely phone may appear on online record. Civil shows name and town only.

General Information: Online identifiers in results same as on public terminal. No adoption, mental health, guardianship or juvenile records released. Will fax documents. Court makes copy: $1.00 1st page, $.50 each add'l. Certification fee: $.50 per page. Payee: Court Clerk. Personal checks accepted. Visa/MC accepted but not over the phone. Mail requests: SASE required.

Noble County

8th Judicial District Court 300 Courthouse Dr, x14, Perry, OK 73077; 580-336-5187; 8AM-4:30PM. ***Felony, Misdemeanor, Civil, Eviction, Small Claims, Probate.***

Probate is separate index at this same address.

Civil Records: Access: Mail, in person, online. Both court and visitors may perform in person searches. Search fee: $5.00 per name. Required to search: name, years to search. Civil cases indexed by defendant, plaintiff; index on microfiche from 1893; computerized back to 1997. Mail turnaround time 1 day. Civil PAT goes back to 1997. PAT results show middle initial, DOB. Both free and advanced pay search service from 1/1997 at www1.odcr.com/search.php; updated daily.

Criminal Records: Access: Mail, in person, online. Both court and visitors may perform in person searches. Search fee: $5.00 per name. Required to search: name, years to search, DOB; also helpful: address, SSN. Criminal records on microfiche from 1893; computerized back to 1997. Mail turnaround time 1 day. Criminal PAT goes back to same as civil. PAT results show middle initial, DOB. Both free and advanced pay search service from 1/1997 at www1.odcr.com/search.php; updated daily. Online results show middle initial, DOB. City and rarely phone may appear on online record. Civil shows name and town only.

General Information: Online identifiers in results same as on public terminal. No adoption, mental health, guardianship or juvenile records released. Will not fax documents. Court makes copy: $1.00 1st page, $.50 each add'l. Certification fee: $.50 per instrument. Payee: Noble County Court Clerk. Personal checks accepted; credit cards arc not. Mail requests: SASE appreciated.

Nowata County

11th Judicial District Court 229 N Maple, Nowata, OK 74048; 918-273-0127; fax: 918-273-0322; 8AM-4:30PM. ***Felony, Misdemeanor, Civil, Eviction, Small Claims, Probate.***

Probate is separate index.

Civil Records: Access: Mail, in person, online. Both court and visitors may perform in person searches. Search fee: $5.00 per name. Required to search: name, years to search. Civil cases indexed by defendant, plaintiff. Civil index in docket books from 1907; on computer since 1998. Mail turnaround time 1 day. Civil PAT goes back to 1998. PAT results show middle initial, DOB. Both free and advanced pay search service from 7/1/1998 at www1.odcr.com/search.php; updated monthly.

Criminal Records: Access: Mail, in person, online. Both court and visitors may perform in person searches. Search fee: $5.00 per name. Required to search: name, years to search; also helpful: SSN. Criminal docket on books from 1907; on computer since 1998. Mail turnaround time 1 day. Criminal PAT goes back to same as civil. PAT results show middle initial, DOB. Both free and advanced pay search service from 7/1/1998 at www1.odcr.com/search.php; updated monthly. Online results show middle initial, DOB. City and rarely phone may appear on online record. Civil shows name and town only.

General Information: Online identifiers in results same as on public terminal. No adoption, mental health, guardianship or juvenile records released. Will fax documents to local or toll free line. Court makes copy: $1.00 first page, $.50 each add'l. Certification fee: $.50 per page. Payee: Court Clerk. Personal checks accepted. Mail requests: SASE requested.

Okfuskee County

24th Judicial District Court Box 30 (3rd & Atlanta St), Okemah, OK 74859; 918-623-0525; fax: 918-623-2687; 8:30AM-4:30PM. ***Felony, Misdemeanor, Civil, Eviction, Small Claims, Probate.***

Civil Records: Access: Mail, in person, online. Both court and visitors may perform in person searches. Search fee: $5.00 per name. Required to search: name, years to search. Civil cases indexed by defendant, plaintiff. Civil records in files and docket books from 1907, computerized since 1996. All marriage licenses accessible on the internet site. Mail turnaround time 3 days. Civil PAT goes back to 1996. PAT results show middle initial, DOB. Both free and advanced pay search service from 1/1997 at www1.odcr.com/search.php; updated daily.

Criminal Records: Access: Mail, in person, online. Both court and visitors may perform in person searches. Search fee: $5.00 per name. Required to search: name, years to search; also helpful: SSN. Criminal records in files and docket books from 1907, computerized since 1996. Mail turnaround time 3 days. Criminal PAT goes back to 1990. PAT results show middle initial, DOB. Both free and advanced pay search service from 1/1997 at www1.odcr.com/search.php; updated monthly. Online results show middle initial, DOB. City and rarely phone may appear on online record. Civil shows name and town only.

General Information: Online identifiers in results same as on public terminal. No adoption, mental health, guardianship or juvenile released. Will fax documents to local or toll free line. Court makes copy: $1.00 first page, $.50 each add'l. Certification fee: $.50 per document. Payee: Court Clerk. Personal checks accepted; credit cards are not. Mail requests: SASE required.

Oklahoma County

District Court 320 Robert S Kerr St, Rm 409, Oklahoma City, OK 73102; 405-713-1705; criminal phone: 405-713-1712; civil phone: 405-713-1727; probate phone: 405-713-1727; 8AM-5PM. ***Felony, Misdemeanor, Civil, Eviction, Small Claims, Probate.*** Small claims: 405-713-1738.

Civil Records: Access: Mail, in person, online. Both court and visitors may perform in person searches. Search fee: Lengthy searches are $5.00 per half hour, otherwise no search fee. Required to search: name, years to search. Civil cases indexed by defendant, plaintiff; index on microfiche from 1980, prior archived. Mail turnaround time 5-10 days. Civil PAT goes back to 1984. PAT results show middle initial, DOB. Online access to court dockets is free at www.oscn.net/applications/oscn/casesearch.asp. Civil dockets go back to 12/1984.

Criminal Records: Access: Mail, online, in person. Both court and visitors may perform in person searches. Search fee: Lengthy searches $5.00 per half hour; commercial purpose searches: $25.00. Required to search: name, years to search, DOB; also helpful: SSN. Criminal records on microfiche from 1980, prior archived. Mail turnaround time 5-10 days. Criminal PAT goes back to same as civil. PAT results show middle initial, DOB. Online access to criminal dockets is same as civil. Criminal dockets go back

to 9/1988. The sheriff's current inmates and warrants list is free at www.oklahomacounty.org/cosheriff/. Online results show middle initial, DOB, SSN; includes physical description, phone.
General Information: Online identifiers in results same as on public terminal. No juvenile, sealed, or expunged records released. Will not fax documents. Court makes copy: $1.00 1st page, $.50 each add'l. Certification fee: $.50 per doc. Payee: District Court Clerk. Personal checks accepted; credit cards are not. Mail requests: SASE required.

Okmulgee County

24th Judicial District Court - Henryetta Branch 115 S 4th, Henryetta, OK 74437; 918-652-7142; probate phone: same; fax: 918-650-0287; 8AM-4:30PM. ***Felony, Misdemeanor, Civil, Eviction, Small Claims, Probate.***
You must search at both courts; records are not co-mingled.
Civil Records: Access: Mail, in person, online, limited phone. Both court and visitors may perform in person searches. Search fee: $5.00 per name. Required to search: name, years to search. Civil cases indexed by defendant, plaintiff; index on microfiche from 1970, computerized since 1997. Mail turnaround time 1-2 days. Civil PAT goes back to 1997. PAT results show middle initial, DOB. Both free and advanced pay search service from 1/1998 at www1.odcr.com/search.php; updated monthly.
Criminal Records: Access: Mail, in person, online. Both court and visitors may perform in person searches. Search fee: $5.00 per name. Required to search: name, years to search; also helpful: SSN. Criminal records on microfiche from 1970, books to 6-5-79, computerized since 1997. Mail turnaround time 1-2 days. Criminal PAT goes back to same as civil. PAT results show middle initial, DOB. Both free and advanced pay search service from 1/1998 at www1.odcr.com/search.php; updated monthly. Online results show middle initial, DOB. City and rarely phone may appear on online record. Civil shows name and town only.
General Information: Online identifiers in results same as on public terminal. No expunged or guardianship records released. Will fax documents $1.00 1st page; $.50 each add'l, prepaid. Court makes copy: $1.00 first page, $.50 each add'l. Self serve: same. Certification fee: $.50 per page. Payee: Court Clerk. Business checks accepted. No credit cards accepted. Mail requests: SASE required.

24th Judicial District Court - Okmulgee Branch 314 W 7th, Okmulgee, OK 74447; 918-756-3042; fax: 918-758-1237; 8AM-4:30PM. ***Felony, Misdemeanor, Civil, Eviction, Small Claims, Probate.***
Civil Records: Access: Phone, mail, in person, online. Both court and visitors may perform in person searches. Search fee: $5.00 per name. Required to search: name, years to search. Civil cases indexed by defendant, plaintiff; index on microfiche from 1986, archived from 1907, computerized since 1997. Mail turnaround time 1-2 days. Civil PAT goes back to 1997. PAT results show middle initial, DOB. Both free and advanced pay search service from 1/1998 at www1.odcr.com/search.php; updated monthly.
Criminal Records: Access: Phone, mail, in person, online. Both court and visitors may perform in person searches. Search fee: $5.00 per name. Required to search: name, years to search; also helpful: SSN. Criminal records on microfiche from 1986, archived from 1907, computerized since 1997. Mail turnaround time 1-2 days. Criminal PAT goes back to same as civil. PAT results show middle initial, DOB. Both free and advanced pay search service from 1/1998 at www1.odcr.com/search.php; updated monthly. Online results show middle initial, DOB. City and rarely phone may appear on online record. Civil shows name and town only.
General Information: Online identifiers in results same as on public terminal. No juvenile, mental health, adoption or guardianship records released. Court makes copy: $1.00 first page, $.50 each add'l. Certification fee: $.50 per page. Payee: Court Clerk. Business checks accepted. No credit cards accepted. Mail requests: SASE requested.

Osage County

10th Judicial District Court County Courthouse, 600 Grandview, Pawhuska, OK 74056; 918-287-4104; 8:30-5PM. ***Felony, Misdemeanor, Civil, Eviction, Small Claims, Probate, Divorce.***
Search fee covers a civil and criminal combined.
Civil Records: Access: Mail, in person, online. Both court and visitors may perform in person searches. Search fee: $5.00 per name. Required to search: name, years to search; also helpful: address. Civil cases indexed by defendant, plaintiff. Civil records archived from 1969. Mail turnaround time 1-2 days. Civil PAT goes back to 1996. PAT results show middle initial, DOB. Both free and advanced pay search service from 1/1996 at www1.odcr.com/search.php; updated daily.
Criminal Records: Access: Mail, in person, online. Both court and visitors may perform in person searches. Search fee: $5.00 per name. Required to search: name, years to search; also helpful: address. Criminal records archived from 1969. Mail turnaround time 1-2 days. Criminal PAT goes back to 1995. PAT results show middle initial, DOB. Both free and advanced pay search service from 1/1996 at www1.odcr.com/search.php; updated daily. Online results show middle initial, DOB. City and rarely phone may appear on online record. Civil shows name and town only.
General Information: Online identifiers in results same as on public terminal. No juvenile or adoption records released. Will not fax documents. Court makes copy: $1.00 1st page, $.50 each add'l. Certification fee: $.50 per instrument. Payee: Court Clerk. Only cashiers checks and money orders accepted. No credit cards accepted. Mail requests: SASE required.

Ottawa County

13th Judicial District Court 102 E Central Ave, #300, Miami, OK 74354; 918-542-2801; 9:00AM-5:00PM. ***Felony, Misdemeanor, Civil, Eviction, Small Claims, Probate.***
Civil Records: Access: Phone, mail, in person, online. Both court and visitors may perform in person searches. Search fee: $5.00 per name. Required to search: name, years to search. Civil cases indexed by defendant, plaintiff. Civil index on docket books or cards from 1907, recent records computerized. Mail turnaround time 1-2 days. Civil PAT goes back to 1997. PAT results show middle initial, DOB. Both free and advanced pay search service from 9/1/1997 at www1.odcr.com/search.php; updated daily.
Criminal Records: Access: Mail, in person, online. Both court and visitors may perform in person searches. Search fee: $5.00. Required to search: name, years to search; also helpful: SSN. Criminal docket on books or cards from 1907, recent records computerized. Mail turnaround time 1-2 days. Criminal PAT goes back to same as civil. PAT results show middle initial, DOB. Both free and advanced pay search service from 9/1/1997 at www1.odcr.com/search.php; updated daily. Online results show middle initial, DOB. City and rarely phone may appear on online record. Civil shows name and town only.
General Information: Online identifiers in results same as on public terminal. No juvenile, mental health, adoption or guardianship records released. Will not fax documents. Court makes copy: $1.00 first page, $.50 each add'l. Self serve: same. Certification fee: $.50 per page includes copy fee. Payee: Clerk of Court. Money orders accepted. No credit cards accepted. Mail requests: SASE required.

Pawnee County

14th Judicial District Court Courthouse, 500 Harrison St, Pawnee, OK 74058; 918-762-2547; 8AM-4:30PM. ***Felony, Misdemeanor, Civil, Eviction, Small Claims, Probate.***
Civil Records: Access: Mail, in person, online. Both court and visitors may perform in person searches. Search fee: $5.00. Required to search: name, years to search. Civil cases indexed by defendant, plaintiff; index on docket sheets to 1975, computerized from 1997. Mail turnaround time 1-3 days. Civil PAT goes back to 1997. PAT results show middle initial, DOB. Both free and advanced pay search service from 1/1997 at www1.odcr.com/search.php; updated daily.
Criminal Records: Access: Mail, in person, online. Both court and visitors may perform in person searches. Search fee: $5.00. Required to search: name, years to search; also helpful: SSN. Criminal records on docket sheets to 1975, computerized from 1997. Mail turnaround time 1-3 days. Criminal PAT goes back to same as civil. PAT results show middle initial, DOB. Both free and advanced pay search service from 1/1997 at www1.odcr.com/search.php; updated daily. Online results show middle initial, DOB. City and rarely phone may appear on online record. Civil shows name and town only.
General Information: Online identifiers in results same as on public terminal. No sealed records released. Will not fax documents. Court makes copy: $1.00 first page, $.50 each add'l. Certification fee: $.50 per page. Payee: Court Clerk. Personal checks accepted; credit cards are not. Mail requests: SASE required.

Payne County

9th Judicial District Court 606 S Husband, Rm 206, Stillwater, OK 74074; 405-372-4774; 8AM-5PM. ***Felony, Misdemeanor, Civil, Eviction, Small Claims, Probate.***
Civil Records: Access: Mail, in person, online. Both court and visitors may perform in person searches. Search fee: $5.00 plus $1.00 per name per year. Required to search: name, years to search. Civil cases indexed by defendant, plaintiff. Civil index in docket books from late 1800s, as of 1994 on computer. Mail turnaround time 2 days. Civil PAT goes back to 1994. Online access to court dockets is free at www.oscn.net/applications/oscn/casesearch.asp. Dockets go back to 1/1994.
Criminal Records: Access: Mail, online, in person. Both court and visitors may perform in person searches. Search fee: $5.00 plus $1.00 per name per year. Required to search: name, years to search, DOB, SSN, signed release. Criminal docket on books from late 1800s, as of 1994 on computer. Mail turnaround time 2 days. Criminal PAT goes back to same as civil. PAT results show middle initial, DOB, SSN. Terminal criminal results may also show SSN. Online access to criminal dockets is same as civil. Online results show middle initial, DOB, SSN; includes physical description, phone.
General Information: Online identifiers in results same as on public terminal. No sealed records, juveniles or adoption records released. Will not fax documents. Court makes copy: $1.00 first page, $.50 each add'l. Certification fee: $1.50 per page. Payee: Clerk of Court. Personal checks accepted. Visa/MC accepted. Mail requests: SASE required.

Pittsburg County

18th Judicial District Court Box 460, 122 E Carl Albert Pky, McAlester, OK 74502; 918-423-4859; 8AM-5PM. ***Felony, Misdemeanor, Civil, Eviction, Small Claims, Probate.***
Civil Records: Access: Mail, in person, online. Both court and visitors may perform in person searches. Search fee: $5.00 per name. Required to search: name, years to search. Civil cases indexed by defendant, plaintiff; index on microfiche since 1907; on computer since 1997. Mail turnaround time 1-2 days. Civil PAT goes back to 1997. PAT results show middle initial, DOB. Both free and advanced pay search service from 7/1/1997 at www1.odcr.com/search.php; updated monthly.
Criminal Records: Access: Mail, in person, online. Both court and visitors may perform in person searches. Search fee: $10.00 per name for 10 yr misdemeanor search; add $5.00 to include felonies. Required to search: name, years to search, DOB. Criminal records on microfiche since 1907; on computer since 1997. Mail turnaround time 1-2 days. Criminal PAT goes back to same as civil. PAT results show middle initial, DOB. Both free and advanced pay search service from 7/1/1997 at

www1.odcr.com/search.php; updated monthly. Online results show middle initial, DOB, SSN. City and rarely phone may appear on online record. Civil shows name and town only.
General Information: Online identifiers in results same as on public terminal. No juvenile, adoptions, mental health or guardianship records released. Will not fax documents. Court makes copy: $1.00 first page, $.50 each add'l. Self serve: same. Certification fee: $.50 per page. Payee: Court Clerk. Personal checks accepted; credit cards are not. Mail requests: SASE required.

Pontotoc County

22nd Judicial District Court Box 427 (120 W 13th), Ada, OK 74820; 580-332-5763; fax: 580-332-5766; 8AM-N; 1-5PM. ***Felony, Misdemeanor, Civil, Eviction, Small Claims, Probate.***
Civil Records: Access: Mail, in person, online. Both court and visitors may perform in person searches. Search fee: $5.00 per name. Required to search: name, years to search. Civil cases indexed by defendant, plaintiff; index on card index from 1907; on computer back to 1997. Mail turnaround time 2 days. Civil PAT goes back to 1997. PAT results show middle initial, DOB. Both free and advanced pay search service from 1/1997 at www1.odcr.com/search.php; updated monthly.
Criminal Records: Access: Mail, in person, online. Both court and visitors may perform in person searches. Search fee: $5.00 per name. Required to search: name, years to search; also helpful: DOB, SSN. Criminal records on card index from 1907; on computer back to 1997. Mail turnaround time 2 days. Criminal PAT goes back to 1987. PAT results show middle initial, DOB. Both free and advanced pay search service from 1/1997 at www1.odcr.com/search.php; updated monthly. Online results show middle initial, DOB. City and rarely phone may appear on online record. Civil shows name and town only.
General Information: Online identifiers in results same as on public terminal. No juvenile, adoptions, mental health or guardianship records released. Will fax documents to local or toll-free number if not certified. Court makes copy: $1.00 first page, $.50 each add'l. Certification fee: $.50 per page. Payee: Clerk of Court. Personal checks accepted. Must prepay if out of state. No credit cards accepted. Mail requests: SASE required.

Pottawatomie County

23rd Judicial District Court 325 N Broadway, Shawnee, OK 74801; 405-273-3624; fax: 405-878-5525; 8:30AM-5PM. ***Felony, Misdemeanor, Civil, Eviction, Small Claims, Probate.***
Civil Records: Access: Mail, in person, online. Both court and visitors may perform in person searches. Search fee: $5.00 per name. Required to search: name, years to search. Civil cases indexed by defendant, plaintiff; index on computer from 7/97; prior records on book of names from 1906. Mail turnaround time 2 weeks or less. Civil PAT goes back to 7/1997. PAT results show middle initial, DOB. Both free and advanced pay search service from 7/1/1997 at www1.odcr.com/search.php; updated daily.
Criminal Records: Access: Mail, in person, online. Both court and visitors may perform in person searches. Search fee: $5.00 per name. Required to search: name, years to search; also helpful: SSN. Criminal records computerized from 7/97; prior records on book of names from 1897. Mail turnaround time 2 weeks or less. Criminal PAT goes back to 1997. PAT results show middle initial, DOB. Both free and advanced pay search service from 7/1/1997 at www1.odcr.com/search.php; updated daily. Online results show middle initial, DOB. City and rarely phone may appear on online record. Civil shows name and town only.
General Information: Online identifiers in results same as on public terminal. No juvenile, adoptions, mental health or guardianship records released. Will fax documents $1.00 per page. Court makes copy: $1.00 first page, $.50 each add'l. Certification fee: $.50 per page. Payee: Court Clerk. Personal checks accepted; credit cards are not. Mail requests: SASE requested.

Pushmataha County

17th Judicial District Court Pushmataha County Courthouse, 302 SW B, Antlers, OK 74523; 580-298-2274; fax: 580-298-3696; 8AM-4:30PM. ***Felony, Misdemeanor, Civil, Eviction, Small Claims, Probate.***
Civil Records: Access: Mail, in person, online. Both court and visitors may perform in person searches. Search fee: $5.00 per name. Required to search: name, years to search. Civil cases indexed by defendant, plaintiff; index on docket book from 1907. Mail turnaround time 1 day. PAT results show middle initial, DOB. Online access to court dockets is free at www.oscn.net/applications/oscn/casesearch.asp.
Criminal Records: Access: Mail, in person, online. Both court and visitors may perform in person searches. Search fee: $5.00 per name. Required to search: name, years to search; also helpful: SSN. Criminal records on docket book from 1907. Mail turnaround time 1 day. PAT results show middle initial, DOB. Online access to court dockets is free at www.oscn.net/applications/oscn/casesearch.asp. Online results show middle initial, DOB, SSN; includes physical description, phone.
General Information: Online identifiers in results same as on public terminal. No juvenile or adoption records released. Court makes copy: $1.00 first page, $.50 each add'l. Certification fee: $.50 per page includes copy fee. Payee: Court Clerk. Personal checks accepted; credit cards are not. Mail requests: SASE required.

Roger Mills County

2nd Judicial District Court Box 409 (LL Males Blvd & Broadway), Cheyenne, OK 73628; 580-497-3361; criminal fax: 580-497-2167; civil fax: same; 8AM-4:30PM. ***Felony, Misdemeanor, Civil, Eviction, Small Claims, Probate.***
Probate fax is same as main fax number.
Civil Records: Access: Phone, mail, in person, online. Both court and visitors may perform in person searches. No search fee unless 2 or more, then $5.00. Required to search: name, years to search. Civil cases indexed by defendant, plaintiff; index on computer since 2003, in books since 1893. Mail turnaround time 1 day. Civil PAT goes back to 5 years. PAT results show middle initial, DOB. Online access to court dockets is free at www.oscn.net/applications/oscn/casesearch.asp. No fee to view records.
Criminal Records: Access: Phone, mail, fax, in person, online. Both court and visitors may perform in person searches. No search fee unless 2 or more, then $5.00. Required to search: name, years to search, DOB; also helpful: SSN. Criminal records on computer since 2003, in books since 1893. Mail turnaround time 1 day. Criminal PAT goes back to 4 years. PAT results show middle initial, DOB. Online access is the same as civil. No fee to view records. Online results show middle initial, DOB, SSN; includes physical description, phone.
General Information: Online identifiers in results same as on public terminal. No adoption, juvenile, mental health or guardianship records released. Will fax documents $1.00 per page. Court makes copy: $1.00 first page, $.50 each add'l. Certification fee: $.50 per certification. Payee: Court Clerk. Personal checks accepted; credit cards are not. Mail requests: SASE required.

Rogers County

12th Judicial District Court Box 839 (219 S Missouri), Claremore, OK 74018; 918-341-5711; 8AM-4:30PM. ***Felony, Misdemeanor, Civil, Eviction, Small Claims, Probate.***
Civil Records: Access: Phone, mail, online, in person. Both court and visitors may perform in person searches. No search fee, but phone and mail requests require case number. Required to search: name, years to search. Civil cases indexed by defendant, plaintiff. Civil records in card index since 1907, some computerized. Mail turnaround time 1 day. Civil PAT goes back to 7/1997. PAT results show middle initial, DOB. Online access to court dockets is free at www.oscn.net/applications/oscn/casesearch.asp. Dockets go back to 7/1997.
Criminal Records: Access: Phone, mail, online, in person. Both court and visitors may perform in person searches. No search fee, but phone and mail requests require case number. Required to search: name, years to search, DOB; also helpful: SSN. Criminal records on card index since 1907, some computerized. Mail turnaround time 1 day. Criminal PAT goes back to same as civil. PAT results show middle initial, DOB. Online access to criminal dockets is the same as civil. Online results show middle initial, DOB, SSN; includes physical description, phone.
General Information: Online identifiers in results same as on public terminal. No juvenile or adoption records released. Will not fax documents. Court makes copy: $1.00 first page, $.50 each add'l. Self serve: same. Certification fee: $.50 per page. Payee: Court Clerk. Personal checks accepted; credit cards are not. Mail requests: SASE required.

Seminole County

22nd Judicial District Court - Seminole Branch Box 1320 (401 Main St), Seminole, OK 74868; 405-382-3424; fax: 405-382-9440; 8AM-4PM. ***Civil, Small Claims, Probate.***
Criminal records are now maintained at Seminole County Court Clerk, PO Box 130, Wewoka, OK, 405-257-6236.
Civil Records: Access: Phone, fax, mail, in person. Only the court performs in person searches; visitors may not. Search fee: $5.00 per name. Required to search: name, years to search. Civil cases indexed by defendant, plaintiff. Civil index on cards from 1931, probate from 1969; on computer back to 1996. Mail turnaround time 1 to 2 days. Public use terminal has civil records back to 4,1931 for Superior Ct; 1/1969 for District Ct.
General Information: Court makes copy: $1.00 first page, $.50 each add'l. Certification fee: $1.50 per page. Payee: Court Clerk. Only cashiers checks and money orders accepted. No credit cards accepted. Mail requests: SASE required.

22nd Judicial Dist. Ct - Wewoka Branch PO Box 130, 120 S Wewoka Ave, Wewoka, OK 74884; 405-257-6236; 8AM-4PM. ***Felony, Misdemeanor, Civil, Eviction, Small Claims, Probate.***
Probate records in separate books, but on same computer system.
Civil Records: Access: Mail, in person, online. Both court and visitors may perform in person searches. Search fee: $5.00 per name. Required to search: name, years to search. Civil cases indexed by defendant, plaintiff; index on computer since 1995; prior records on books to 1907. Mail turnaround time 1 day. Civil PAT goes back to 1995. PAT results show middle initial, DOB. Public terminal includes probate. Both free and advanced pay search service from 1/1995 at www1.odcr.com/search.php; updated daily.
Criminal Records: Access: Mail, in person, online. Both court and visitors may perform in person searches. Search fee: $5.00 per name. Required to search: name, years to search; also helpful: SSN. Criminal records indexed on computer since 1995; prior records on books to 1908. Mail turnaround time 1 day. Criminal PAT goes back to same as civil. PAT results show middle initial, DOB. Both free and advanced pay search service from 1/1995 at www1.odcr.com/search.php; updated daily. Online results show middle initial, DOB. City and rarely phone may appear on online record. Civil shows name and town only.
General Information: Online identifiers in results same as on public terminal. No juvenile or adoption records released. Will fax documents to toll-free number. Court makes copy: $1.00 first page, $.50 each add'l. Self serve: same. Cert fee: $.50 per page. Payee: Court Clerk. Personal checks accepted; credit cards are not. Mail requests: SASE required.

Sequoyah County

15th Judicial District Court 120 E Chickasaw, Sallisaw, OK 74955; 918-775-4411; fax: 918-775-1223; 8AM-4PM. ***Felony, Misdemeanor, Civil, Eviction, Small Claims, Probate.***

Probate is a separate office at this same address. Probate fax is same as main fax number.

Civil Records: Access: Mail, in person, online. Both court and visitors may perform in person searches. Search fee: $5.00 per name. Required to search: name, years to search. Civil cases indexed by defendant, plaintiff. Civil records in files and dockets from 1907; on computer back to 1997. Mail turnaround time 1 week. Civil PAT goes back to 1997. PAT results show middle initial, DOB. Both free and advanced pay search service from 7/1/1997 at www1.odcr.com/search.php; updated daily.

Criminal Records: Access: Phone, mail, in person, online. Both court and visitors may perform in person searches. Search fee: $5.00 per name. Required to search: name, years to search; also helpful: SSN. Some Criminal records computerized from 1997, prior in files and dockets. Mail turnaround time 1 week. Criminal PAT goes back to same as civil. PAT results show middle initial, DOB. Both free and advanced pay search service from 7/1/1997 at www1.odcr.com/search.php; updated daily. Online results show middle initial, DOB. City and rarely phone may appear on online record. Civil shows name and town only.

General Information: Online identifiers in results same as on public terminal. No juvenile, adoptions, mental health or guardianship records released. Will fax documents to toll-free or local number. Court makes copy: $1.00 first page, $.50 each add'l. Self serve: same. Cert fee: $5.00 each. Payee: Court Clerk. Personal checks accepted; credit cards are not. Will bill mail requests. Mail requests: SASE required.

Stephens County

5th Judicial District Court 101 S 11th St, Rm 301, Duncan, OK 73533; 580-470-2000; 8:30AM-4:30PM. ***Felony, Misdemeanor, Civil, Eviction, Small Claims, Probate.***

Civil Records: Access: Mail, in person, online. Both court and visitors may perform in person searches. Search fee: $5.00 per name. Required to search: name, years to search. Civil cases indexed by defendant, plaintiff; index on computer from 10/95; prior records on docket books from 1907. Mail turnaround time 1 day. Civil PAT goes back to 1996. PAT results show middle initial, DOB. Both free and advanced pay search service from 1/1996 at www1.odcr.com/search.php; updated daily.

Criminal Records: Access: Mail, in person, online. Both court and visitors may perform in person searches. Search fee: $5.00 per name. Required to search: name, years to search; also helpful: address, DOB, SSN. Criminal records computerized from 10/95; prior records on docket books from 1907. Mail turnaround time 1 day. Criminal PAT goes back to same as civil. PAT results show middle initial, DOB. Both free and advanced pay search service from 1/1996 at www1.odcr.com/search.php; updated daily. Online results show middle initial, DOB. City and rarely phone may appear on online record. Civil shows name and town only.

General Information: Online identifiers in results same as on public terminal. No juvenile, adoptions, mental health or guardianship records released. Will not fax documents. Court makes copy: $1.00 first page, $.50 each add'l. Certification fee: $.50 per page. Payee: Stephens County Court Clerk. No personal checks. No credit cards accepted. Mail requests: SASE required.

Texas County

1st Judicial District Court Box 1081 (319 N Main St), Guymon, OK 73942; 580-338-3003; fax: 580-338-3819; 9-5PM. ***Felony, Misdemeanor, Civil, Eviction, Small Claims, Probate.***

Civil Records: Access: Mail, fax, in person, online. Both court and visitors may perform in person searches. No search fee. Required to search: name, years to search. Fax requests must be on letterhead. Civil cases indexed by defendant, plaintiff; index on microfiche from 1976, archived prior, computerized since 3/95. Mail turnaround time 5 days; 1 day for phone. Civil PAT goes back to 5/1995. PAT results show middle initial, DOB. Both free and advanced pay search service from 1/15/1995 at www1.odcr.com/search.php; updated daily.

Criminal Records: Access: Mail, fax, in person, online. Both court and visitors may perform in person searches. No search fee. Required to search: name, years to search; also helpful: SSN. Fax requests must be on letterhead. Criminal records on microfiche from 1976, archived prior, computerized since 3/95. Mail turnaround time 5 days; 1 day for phone requests. Criminal PAT goes back to same as civil. PAT results show middle initial, DOB. Both free and advanced pay search service from 1/15/1995 at www1.odcr.com/search.php; updated daily. Online results show middle initial, DOB. City and rarely phone may appear on online record. Civil shows name and town only.

General Information: Online identifiers in results same as on public terminal. No juvenile, adoptions, mental health or guardianship records released. Will fax documents. Court makes copy: $1.50 1st page (certified), $.50 ea add'l. Self serve: same. Certification fee: $.50 per pleading or instrument. Payee: Court Clerk. Personal checks accepted; credit cards are not. Mail requests: SASE required.

Tillman County

3rd Judicial District Court Box 116, 201 N Main, Frederick, OK 73542; 580-335-3023; criminal phone: 580-335-5536; civil phone: 580-335-5536; fax: 580-335-5613; 8-4PM. ***Felony, Misdemeanor, Civil, Eviction, Small Claims, Probate.***

Civil Records: Access: Mail, in person, online. Both court and visitors may perform in person searches. Search fee: $5.00 per name. Required to search: name, years to search. Civil cases indexed by defendant, plaintiff. Civil index in docket books from 1907; on computer back to 1998. Mail turnaround time 1 day. Civil PAT goes back to 1998. PAT results show middle initial, DOB. Both free and advanced pay search service from 1/1998 at www1.odcr.com/search.php; updated daily.

Criminal Records: Access: Mail, in person, online. Both court and visitors may perform in person searches. Search fee: $5.00 per name. Required to search: name, years to search, DOB; also helpful: SSN. Criminal docket on books from 1907; on computer back to 1998. Mail turnaround time 1 day. Criminal PAT goes back to same as civil. PAT results show middle initial, DOB. Both free and advanced pay search service from 1/1998 at www1.odcr.com/search.php; updated daily. Online results show middle initial, DOB. City and rarely phone may appear on online record. Civil shows name and town only.

General Information: Online identifiers in results same as on public terminal. No expunged records released. Will fax documents to local or toll-free number. Court makes copy: $1.00 first page, $.50 each add'l. Cert fee: $.50. Payee: District Court. Business checks accepted. No credit cards accepted. Will bill law firms. Mail requests: SASE required.

Tulsa County

14th Judicial District Court 500 S Denver Ave, Tulsa, OK 74103-3832; 918-596-5000; criminal: 918-596-5471; civil: 918-596-5436; probate: 918-596-5440; 8:30AM-5PM. ***Felony, Misdemeanor, Civil, Eviction, Small Claims, Probate.***

Civil Records: Access: Mail, in person, online. Both court and visitors may perform in person searches. Search fee: $5.00 per name. Required to search: name, years to search. Civil cases indexed by defendant, plaintiff; index on computer from 1984, on microfiche from 1907, archived from 1907. Mail turnaround time 1 week. Civil PAT goes back to 1984. PAT results show middle initial, DOB. Online access to court dockets is free at www.oscn.net/applications/oscn/casesearch.asp. Civil dockets go back to 10/1984.

Criminal Records: Access: Online, in person. Both court and visitors may perform in person searches. No search fee. Required to search: name, years to search; also helpful: SSN. Criminal records computerized from 1984, on microfiche from 1907, archived from 1907. For a county criminal search, contact Records Dept at Sheriff's Office, downstairs- 918-596-5670. Fee is $7.50; request should include name, dates, DOB, signed release and also SSN. Criminal PAT goes back to same as civil. PAT results show middle initial, DOB. Online access to criminal dockets is same as civil. Criminal dockets go back to 1/1988. Online results show middle initial, DOB, SSN; includes physical description, phone.

General Information: Online identifiers in results same as on public terminal. No juvenile, adoption or guardianship records released. Court makes copy: $1.00 first page, $.50 each add'l. Cert fee: $.50 per cert. Payee: Court Clerk. Personal checks accepted; credit cards are not. Mail requests: SASE required.

Wagoner County

15th Judicial District Court Box 249, 302 E Cherokee St, Wagoner, OK 74477; 918-485-4508; 8AM-4:30PM. ***Felony, Misdemeanor, Civil, Eviction, Small Claims, Probate.***

Civil Records: Access: Mail, in person, online. Both court and visitors may perform in person searches. Search fee: $5.00 per name. Required to search: name, years to search. Civil cases indexed by defendant, plaintiff. Civil index in docket books from 1980; on computer back to 1997. Mail turnaround time 1-5 days Civil PAT goes back to 1990. PAT results show middle initial, DOB. Both free and advanced pay search service from 1/1990 at www1.odcr.com/search.php; updated monthly.

Criminal Records: Access: Mail, in person, online. Both court and visitors may perform in person searches. Search fee: $5.00 per name if assisted. Required to search: name, years to search; also helpful: SSN. Criminal records are in files and dockets back to 1907; on computer back to 1997. Mail turnaround time 1-5 days. Criminal PAT goes back to same as civil. PAT results show middle initial, DOB. Results may also show DL number. Access to criminal records same as civil. Online results show middle initial, DOB. City and rarely phone may appear on online record. Civil shows name and town only.

General Information: Online identifiers in results same as on public terminal. No juvenile, mental health, adoption or guardianship records released. Will not fax documents. Court makes copy: $1.00 first page, $.50 each add'l. Certification fee: $.50 per page. Payee: Court Clerk. Personal checks accepted; credit cards are not. Mail requests: SASE required.

Washington County

11th Judicial District Court 420 S Johnstone, Rm 101, Bartlesville, OK 74003; 918-337-2870; fax: 918-337-2897; 8-5PM. ***Felony, Misdemeanor, Civil, Eviction, Small Claims, Probate.***

Civil Records: Access: Fax, mail, in person, online. Both court and visitors may perform in person searches. Search fee: $5.00 per name. Required to search: name, years to search. Civil cases indexed by defendant, plaintiff. Civil index in docket books from 1907; computerized records since 1997. Mail turnaround time 2-4 days. Civil PAT goes back to 1998. PAT results show middle initial, DOB. Both free and advanced pay search service from 1/1999 at www1.odcr.com/search.php; updated daily.

Criminal Records: Access: Fax, mail, in person, online. Both court and visitors may perform in person searches. Search fee: $5.00 per name. Required to search: name, years to search, signed release; also helpful: DOB, SSN. Criminal docket on books from 1907; computerized records since 1997. Mail turnaround time 2-4 days. Criminal PAT goes back to 1998. PAT results show middle initial, DOB. Both free and advanced pay search service from 1/1999 at www1.odcr.com/search.php; updated daily. Online results show middle initial, DOB. City and rarely phone may appear on online record. Civil shows name and town only.

General Information: Online identifiers in results same as on public terminal. No juvenile, mental health, adoption or guardianship records released. Will fax documents to local or toll free line. Court makes copy: $1.00 first page, $.50 each add'l.

Certification fee: $.50 per page. Payee: Court Clerk. Personal checks accepted; credit cards are not.

Washita County

2nd Judicial District Court Box 397 (111 E Main St), Cordell, OK 73632; 580-832-3836; fax: 580-832-4123; 8AM-4PM. ***Felony, Misdemeanor, Civil, Small Claims, Probate.***

Civil Records: Access: Mail, in person, online. Both court and visitors may perform in person searches. Search fee: $5.00 per name. Required to search: name, years to search. Civil cases indexed by defendant, plaintiff; index on computer since 1998; prior records on microfiche from 1980s & on docket books from 1892. Mail turnaround time same day. Civil PAT goes back to 1998. PAT results show middle initial, DOB. Both free and advanced pay search service from 10/1/1997 at www1.odcr.com/search.php; updated daily.

Criminal Records: Access: Mail, in person, online. Both court and visitors may perform in person searches. Search fee: $5.00 per name. Required to search: name, years to search; also helpful: DOB, SSN, aliases. Criminal records on computer since 1998; prior records on microfiche from 1980s & on docket books from 1892. Mail turnaround time same day. Criminal PAT goes back to same as civil. PAT results show middle initial, DOB, SSN. Both free and advanced pay search service from 10/1/1997 at www1.odcr.com/search.php; updated daily. Online results also show address. Online results show middle initial, DOB. City and rarely phone may appear on online record. Civil shows name and town only.

General Information: Online identifiers in results same as on public terminal. No juvenile, mental health, adoption or guardianship records released. Will fax documents $1.00 per page. Court makes copy: $1.00 first page, $.50 each add'l. Certification fee: $.50 per doc or $5.00 authenticated certificate. Payee: Court Clerk. Personal checks accepted; credit cards are not. Mail requests: SASE required.

Woods County

4th Judicial District Court Box 924, 407 Government St, Alva, OK 73717; 580-327-3119; fax: 580-327-6237; 8-5PM. ***Felony, Misdemeanor, Civil, Eviction, Small Claims, Probate.***

Civil Records: Access: Mail, in person, online. Both court and visitors may perform in person searches. Search fee: $5.00 per name. Required to search: name, years to search. Civil cases indexed by defendant, plaintiff. Civil index in docket books from 1890. Mail turnaround time 2 days. Civil PAT goes back to 2002. PAT results show middle initial, DOB. Both free and advanced pay search service from 7/2002 at www1.odcr.com/search.php; updated monthly.

Criminal Records: Access: Mail, in person, online. Both court and visitors may perform in person searches. Search fee: $5.00 per name. Required to search: name, years to search. Criminal records on computer since 1987, on dockets and cards from 1890s. Mail turnaround time 2 days. Criminal PAT goes back to same as civil. PAT results show middle initial, DOB. Both free and advanced pay search service from 7/2002 at www1.odcr.com/search.php; updated monthly. Online results show middle initial, DOB. City and rarely phone may appear on online record. Civil shows name and town only.

General Information: Online identifiers in results same as on public terminal. No juvenile, mental health, adoption or guardianship records released. Will not fax documents. Court makes copy: $1.00 first page, $.50 each add'l. Certification fee: $.50 per page. Payee: Clerk of Court. Personal checks accepted; credit cards are not. Mail requests: SASE required.

Woodward County

4th Judicial District Court 1600 Main St, Woodward, OK 73801; 580-256-3413; fax: 580-254-6807; 9AM-5PM. ***Felony, Misdemeanor, Civil, Small Claims, Probate, Divorce.***

Civil Records: Access: Mail, in person, online. Both court and visitors may perform in person searches. Search fee: $5.00 per name. Required to search: name, years to search. Civil cases indexed by defendant, plaintiff. Civil index in docket books from 1890, on microfiche from 1989; on computer from 1997. Mail turnaround time 1-2 days unless older cases found. Civil PAT goes back to 1997. PAT results show middle initial, DOB. Both free and advanced pay search service from 2/1997 at www1.odcr.com/search.php; updated monthly.

Criminal Records: Access: Mail, in person, online. Both court and visitors may perform in person searches. Search fee: $5.00 per name. Required to search: name, years to search; also helpful: DOB, SSN. Criminal docket on books from 1890, on microfiche from 1989; on computer from 1997. Mail turnaround time 1-2 days unless older cases found. Criminal PAT goes back to same as civil. PAT results show middle initial, DOB. Both free and advanced pay search service from 2/1/1997 to present free at www.odcr.com; updated daily. Online results show middle initial, DOB. City and rarely phone may appear on online record. Civil shows name and town only.

General Information: Online identifiers in results same as on public terminal. No mental, juvenile, adoption, guardianship records released. Will not fax documents. Court makes copy: $1.00 first page, $.50 each add'l. Self serve: same. Certification fee: $.50 per page. $5.00 for whole file. Payee: Court Clerk. Personal checks accepted; credit cards are not. Mail requests: SASE required.

Oklahoma Recording Offices

ORGANIZATION: 77 counties, 77 recording offices. The recording officer is the County Clerk. Oklahoma is entirely in the Central Time Zone (CST).

REAL ESTATE RECORDS: Many Oklahoma counties will perform real estate searches by legal description. Real estate record copy fee is $1.00 per page. Certification fee is usually $1.00 per document.

UCC RECORDS: Financing statements are filed centrally with the County Clerk of Oklahoma County. Prior to July, 2001, consumer goods, farm related and real estate related collateral were dual filed with the local County Clerk as well as the County Clerk of Oklahoma County. Now only real estate related collateral is filed at the local level. Most counties will still perform UCC searches. UCC search fees vary from $5.00 to $10.00 per debtor name.

TAX LIEN RECORDS: Federal tax liens on personal property of businesses are filed with the County Clerk of Oklahoma County, which is the central filing office for the state. Other federal and all state tax liens are filed with the County Clerk. Usually state and federal tax liens on personal property are filed in separate indexes, state liens on businesses or individuals usually in the real estate index. Some counties will perform tax lien searches; tax lien search fees vary.

OTHER LIENS: Judgment, mechanics, physicians, hospital.

ONLINE ACCESS: Very little is available online directly from the counties. A private company provides subscription access to assessor indices and property images for all but 1 Oklahoma county; see http://oklahoma.usassessor.com/ or call 800-535-6467 or email tracy@okassessor.com for information. Generally, all records are within 90 days of current. Sub packages: $30 per county or 10 counties $150 or $250 for entire state, except for Osage County which is separate and not on the OKAssessors.com system. Data is also available on CD-rom. Plat Maps also available.

Another second private company offers almost all Oklahoma counties assessment data on CD-rom, also plats and land maps; fees vary by county, see https://secure.vlsmaps.com/ecom_vls/store.php. Also a limited free search is offered for all counties except Texas and Roger Mills at www.pvplus.com/freeaccess/free_login.aspx. Advanced search data is available by subscription.

Good news is www.okcountytreasurers.com/ links to over half of Oklahoma's treasurer offices that offer free online access to parcel and property tax data.

Records of all UCC financing statements may be viewed free at http://countyclerk.oklahomacounty.org/UCC-SearchSite.html.

Adair County

County Clerk, PO Box 169, Stilwell, OK 74960. Recording, R/E phone-918-696-7198; fax-918-696-7198; 8AM-4:30PM.
Index: All in one. Records indexed on computer back to 1978, full records back to 1983-84. Office personnel or visitors may perform searches. General index search fee $5.00 per instrument. Office will search real estate records. UCC search includes tax liens. Copy fee $1.00 per page. Cert fee- $2.00 per page plus copy fee. Payee- Adair County Clerk. **Other phones:** Treasurer- 918-696-7551; Elections- 918-696-7221. **Property tax/Assessing-** PO Box 31, Adair County Courthouse, Stilwell, OK 74960; 918-696-2012, assessor fax- 918-696-6729. A public access terminal is available. **Online** - search assessment data free temporarily at www.pvplus.com/freeaccess/free_login.aspx.

Alfalfa County

County Clerk, 300 S Grand, Cherokee, OK 73728. 580-596-3158; 8:30AM-4:30PM
Index: All in one. Record index not computerized. Office personnel or visitors may perform searches. Search fee-$10.00 per name. Office may search real estate records depending on situation. UCC search includes tax liens. Copy fee $1.00 per page. Cert fee- $1.00 per page plus copy fee. Payee- Alfalfa County Clerk. Bulk data available for purchase, contact Donna. **Other phones:** Treasurer- 580-596-3148; Elections- 580-596-2718. **Property tax/Assessing-** 300 S Grand, Cherokee, OK 73728; 580-596-2145, assessor fax- 580-596-2171.

Atoka County

County Clerk, 200 . Court St, Atoka, OK 74525. 580-889-5157; fax-580-889-5063; 8:30AM-4:30PM
Index: Separate indices to search include liens, UCCs, federal tax liens, judgments, state tax liens. Record index not computerized. Office personnel or visitors may perform searches. Search fee $10.00 per name. Office will not name search real estate records. Copy fee $1.00 per page. Cert fee- $1.00 per cert plus copy fee. Payee- Atoka County Clerk. Bulk data available for purchase, contact Nancy Hill. **Other phones:** Treasurer- 580-889-5283; Elections- 580-889-5297. **Property tax/Assessing-** 200 E Court St, Atoka, OK 74525; 580-889-6036, assessor fax- 580-889-5081. A public access terminal is available. **Online access-** Access to property data is available by subscription at http://oklahoma.usassessor.com.

Beaver County

County Clerk, PO Box 338, Beaver, OK 73932-0338. 580-625-3141, R/E phone-580-625-3418; fax-580-625-3430; 8AM-5PM. http://beaver.okcounties.org/
Index: All in one. Records indexed on computer back to 1998. Office personnel or visitors may perform searches but office will not search UCC or RE. No search fee for general index. Copy fee $1.00 per page. Cert fee- $1.00 per doc plus copy fee. Payee- Beaver County Clerk. **Other phones:** Treasurer- 580-625-3161; Elections- 580-625-4742. **Property tax/Assessing-** PO Box 56, 111 W 2nd St, Beaver, OK 73932-0056; 580-625-3116, assessor fax- 580-625-3493. hours- 8AM-N, 1PM-5PM **Online access-** Access to property data is available by subscription at http://oklahoma.usassessor.com. Also, access treasurer property records free at http://beaver.okcountytreasurers.com/.

Beckham County

County Clerk, PO Box 428, Sayre, OK 73662-0428. 580-928-3383; fax-580-928-5220; 8AM-4PM
Index: Numerous indexes to search. Record index not computerized. Only the public may search. Office will search by written request only. Search fee $10.00 per name. Office will not search real estate records. Copy fee $1.00 per page. Cert fee- $1.00 per page plus copy fee. Payee- Beckham County Clerk. **Online access to Real Estate, Grantor/Grantee, Deed, Lien, Judgment, Fictitious Name records:** Recording records available free online at http://okcountyrecords.com/search.php?County=005. **Other phones:** Treasurer- 580-928-2589; Elections- 580-928-3314. **Property tax/Assessing-** Courthouse, Rm 202, Sayre, OK 73662; 580-928-3329. **Online access-** Access treasurer property data free at http://beckham.okcountytreasurers.com/.

Blaine County

County Clerk, PO Box 138, Watonga, OK 73772. Recording, R/E phone-580-623-5890; fax-580-623-5009; 8AM-4PM. http://blainecountyok.com
Index: Separate indices to search by Section-Township-Range, Town-Lot & Block. Records indexed on a public use terminal back to 2005. Office personnel or visitors may perform searches. Search fee $3.00 per name. Office will search real estate records. Will not search UCC records. Copy fee $1.00 per page. Cert fee- $1.00 per doc plus copy fee. Payee- County Clerk. **Online access to Real Estate, Grantor/Grantee, Deed, Lien, Judgment, Fictitious Name records:** Recording records available free at

http://okcountyrecords.com/search.php. **Other phones:** Treasurer- 580-623-5007; Elections- 580-623-5518; Vital Records- 405-271-4040. **Property tax/Assessing**- PO Box 628, 212 N Weigel, Watonga, OK 73772; 580-623-5123.

Bryan County

County Clerk, PO Box 1789, Durant, OK 74702. Recording, R/E phone-580-924-2202; fax-580-924-2289; 8AM-5PM.
Index: Indices arranged by legal descriptions. Record index not computerized. Office personnel or visitors may perform searches. Search fee $5.00 per name. Office will search real estate records as time permits. Will not search UCC records. Copy fee $1.00 per copy. Cert fee- $1.00 per impression plus copy fee. Payee- County Clerk. **Other phones:** Treasurer- 580-924-0748; Elections- 580-924-3228; Court Records- 580-924-1446. **Property tax/Assessing**- PO Box 931, 402 W Evergreen, Durant, OK 74702; 580-924-2166, assessor fax- 580-924-2166. (Appraiser/Auditor- 580-924-2166) hours- 8AM-4PM Public access terminal available. **Online access**- Access treasurer property data free at http://bryan.okcountytreasurers.com/.

Caddo County

County Clerk, PO Box 68, Anadarko, OK 73005. 405-247-6609; fax-405-247-6510; 8:30AM-4:30PM.
Index: Separate indices to search include computer and index. Records indexed on a public use terminal back to 1993. Office personnel or visitors may perform searches. Will not search UCC records. Copy fee $1.00 per page. Cert fee- $1.00 per doc plus copy fee. Payee- Caddo County Clerk. **Other phones:** Treasurer- 405-247-5151; Elections- 405-247-5001; Vital Records- 405-271-4040; Real Estate- 405-247-6510. **Property tax/Assessing**- PO Box 644, Anadarko, OK 73005; 405-247-2477, assessor fax- 405-247-5718. hours- 8:30AM-4PM A public access terminal is available. **Online** - Access property data free at http://caddo.okcountytreasurers.com/.

Canadian County

County Clerk, PO Box 458, El Reno, OK 73036. 405-262-1070; fax-405-422-2411; 8AM-4:30PM. www.canadiancounty.org/county/Offices/clerk/clerks%20index.htm
Index: All in one. Records indexed on a public use terminal back to 2000 (index to 1987, images to 2000). Only the public may search. Copy fee $1.00 per page. Cert fee- $1.00 per doc plus copy fee. Payee- Canadian County Clerk. **Online access to Real Estate, Grantor/Grantee, Deed, Lien, Judgment records:** Access to recorders database is free http://search.cogov.net/okcana/. **Other phones:** Treasurer- 405-262-1070 x250. **Property tax/Assessing**- 201 N Choctaw, El Reno, OK 73036; 405-262-1070 x269, assessor fax- 405-422-2406. www.canadiancounty.org/county/Offices/Offices%20index.htm **Online access**- Subscriber-based access to Assessor records and free access to property records is at http://canadian.oklahoma.usassessor.com/. Also, access treasurer property data free at www.canadiancountytreasurer.org/.

Carter County

County Clerk, PO Box 1236, Ardmore, OK 73402. 580-223-8162; fax-580-221-5508; 8AM-5PM www.brightok.net/cartercounty/countyclerk.html
Index: All in one. Records indexed on a public use terminal back to 1989. Only the public may search. Copy fee $1.00 per page. Cert fee- $1.00 per doc plus copy fee. Payee- Carter County Clerk. **Online access to All recorded documents records:** Recorded records free at http://okcountyrecords.com/search.php. **Other phones:** Treasurer- 580-223-9467. **Property tax/Assessing**- 20 "B" St SW, Rm 101, Ardmore, OK 73401; 580-223-9594, 800-231-8668 x594 (in county), assessor fax- 580-223-2039. A public access terminal is available. www.cartercountyassessor.org/ **Online** - Search the county assessor database for free at www.cartercountyassessor.org/disclaim.htm. Also, access treasurer property data free at www.cartercountytreasurer.org/cws/c5launch.dll?730634AE/TI.html.

Cherokee County

County Clerk, 213 W Delaware, Rm 200, Tahlequah, OK 74464. Recording, R/E phone-918-456-3171, UCC recording phone-918-458-6512; fax-918-458-6508; 8AM-4:30PM (Recording hours 8AM-4PM).
Index: Separate indices to search include warranty deeds, mortgage, misc. Records indexed on a public use terminal back to 1998. Office personnel or visitors may perform searches. General index search fee $5.00 per name. Office will search real estate records. Copy fee $1.00 per page. Cert fee- $1.50 per cert plus copy fee. Payee- Cherokee County Clerk. **Online access to Real Estate, Grantor/Grantee, Deed, Lien, Judgment, Fictitious Name records:** Recording records available free at http://okcountyrecords.com/search.php. **Other phones:** Treasurer- 918-456-3321; Elections- 918-456-2261. **Property tax/Assessing**- 213 W Delaware, Rm 304, Tahlequah, OK 74464; 918-456-3201, assessor fax- 918-458-6581. hours- 8AM-4:30PM A public access terminal is available.

Choctaw County

County Clerk, 300 E Duke; Courthouse, Hugo, OK 74743. Recording, R/E phone-580-326-3778; fax-580-326-6787; 8AM-4PM.
Index: Separate indices to search. Records indexed on computer back to April, 2001. Office will perform a UCC search but public must search other records themselves. Search fee $10.00 per name. Copy fee $1.00 per page. Cert fee- $1.00 per cert plus copy fee. Payee- County Clerk. **Other phones:** Treasurer- 580-326- 6142; Elections- 580-326-5164; Vital Records- 580-271-4040. **Property tax/Assessing**- 300 E Duke, Courthouse, Hugo, OK 74743; 580-326-2358, assessor fax- 580-326-0633. **Online access**- See notes at beginning of section. With registration you may search assessment data free temporarily at www.pvplus.com/freeaccess/free_login.aspx.

Cimarron County

County Clerk, PO Box 145, Boise City, OK 73933. Recording, R/E phone-580-544-2251; fax-580-544-2250; 8:30AM-N, 1-5PM.
Index: All in one. Record index not computerized. Office personnel or visitors may perform searches. General index search fee $12.00 per hour. Copy fee $1.00 per page. Cert fee- $1.00 per doc plus copy fee. Payee- Cimarron County Clerk. **Other phones:** Treasurer- 580-544-2261; Elections- 580-544-3377; Vital Records- 580-544-2221. **Property tax/Assessing**- PO Box 513, Boise City, OK 73933; 580-544-2701. hours- 9AM-N, 1PM-5PM

Cleveland County

County Clerk, 201 S Jones, #210, Norman, OK 73069. Recording, R/E phone-405-366-0240, UCC recording phone-405-366-0234; fax-405-366-0229; 8AM-5PM. http://search.cogov.net/okclev/
Index: Separate indices to search include real estate, M&M, federal tax, fictitious names, UCCs. Records indexed on a public use terminal back to 1993 for names, 1996 for legals. Office will perform a UCC search but public must search other records themselves. UCC search per debtor name- $10.00. Copy fee $1.00 per page. Cert fee- $1.00 per doc plus copy fee. Payee- County Clerk. **Online access to Real Estate, Deed, Lien, Judgment, UCC, Fictitious Name records:** Access to the Clerk Index is free at http://search.cogov.net/okclev/default.asp. Includes access to various liens, Real Estate, UCCs. **Other phones:** Treasurer- 405-366-0217; Elections- 405-366-0210; Vital Records- 405-271-4040. **Property tax/Assessing**- 201 S Jones, Rm 120, Norman, OK 73069; 405-366-0230, assessor fax- 405-3660695. (Appraiser/Auditor- 405-366-0230) A public access terminal is available. www.clevelandcountyassessor.us/ **Online access**- Access to property records is free at www.clevelandcountyassessor.us/. Also, access treasurer property data free at http://ok-cleveland-treasurer.governmax.com/collectmax/collect30.asp.

Coal County

County Clerk, 4 N Main, #1, Coalgate, OK 74538. Recording, R/E phone-580-927-2103; fax-580-927-4003; 8AM-4PM
Index: Separate indices to search. Records indexed on a public use terminal back to 199. Office personnel or visitors may perform searches. General search fee- $3.00 per name. Office will search real estate records. Will search UCC records. UCC search per debtor name- $10.00. Copy fee $1.00 per page. Cert fee- $1.00 per instrument plus copy fee. Payee- Coal County Clerk. **Other phones:** Treasurer- 580-927-3121; Elections- 580-927-3456; Vital Records- 580-927-2281. **Property tax/Assessing**- 4 N Main, #5, Coalgate, OK 74538; 580-927-3123.

Comanche County

County Clerk, 315 SW 5th, Rm 304, Lawton, OK 73501-4347. Recording, R/E phone-580-355-5214; 8:30AM-5PM
Index: All in one. Records indexed on a public use terminal back to 1989. Office personnel or visitors may perform searches. Copy fee $1.00 per page. Cert fee- $1.00 per doc plus copy fee. Payee- Comanche County Clerk. **Other phones:** Treasurer- 580-355-5763; Elections- 580-353-1880; Vital Records- 405-271-4040. **Property tax/Assessing**- 315 SW 5th, #301, Lawton, OK 73501; 580-355-1052. **Online access**- Access treasurer property data free at http://comanchecountyok.org/cws/c5launch.dll?7266640F/TI.html.

Cotton County

County Clerk, 301 N Broadway, Walters, OK 73572. 580-875-3026; fax-580-875-3756; 8AM-4PM.
Index: Separate indices to search include tract indexes by hand, grantor/grantee indexes on computer. Records indexed on computer back to 1986. Only the public may search. Copy fee $1.00 per page. Cert fee- $1.00 per doc plus copy fee. Payee- Cotton County Clerk. **Other phones:** Treasurer- 580-875-3264; Elections- 580-875-3403; Vital Records- 405-271-4040. **Property tax/Assessing**- Same address as recording office. 580-875-3289.

Craig County

County Clerk, 210 W Delaware Ave, #103, Vinita, OK 74301. 918-256-2507, 918-256-2507 x1702; fax-918-256-3617; 8:30AM-4:30PM.
Index: Separate indices to search include grantor/grantee, land tract. Records indexed on computer back to 05/17/05. Office personnel or visitors may perform searches. Search fee $10.00 per name. Office will search real estate records. Copy fee $1.00 per page. Cert fee- $2.00 1st page; $1.00 each add'l includes copy fee. Payee- Craig County Clerk. **Online access to Real Estate, Grantor/Grantee, Deed, Lien, Judgment, Fictitious Name records:** Recording records available free at http://okcountyrecords.com/search.php. **Other phones:** Treasurer- 918-256-2286; Elections- 918-256-7559. **Property tax/Assessing**- 210 W Delaware Ave, Vinita, OK 74301; 918-256-8766. **Online access**- Access treasurer property data free at http://craig.okcountytreasurers.com/.

Creek County

County Clerk, 317 E Lee, #100, Sapulpa, OK 74066. Recording, R/E phone-918-224-4084, UCC recording phone-918-227-6306; 8AM-5PM
Index: Separate indices to search. Record index not computerized. Only the public may search. Copy fee $1.00 per page. Cert fee- $1.00 per cert plus copy fee. Payee- Creek County Clerk. **Other phones:** Treasurer- 918-227-4501; Mapping- 918-227-6357. **Property tax/Assessing**- 317 E Lee #100, Sapulpa, OK 74066; 918-224-4508. **Online access**- Access to access property records is by subscription from OK Assessors.com, 800-535-6467; weekly and monthly plans available. See note about OKassessors.com at

beginning of section. Also, access treasurer property data free at www.creekcountyok.org/cws/c5launch.dll?351C2089/TI.html.

Custer County

County Clerk, PO Box 300, Arapaho, OK 73620. 580-323-1221; fax-580-331-1117; 8AM-4PM.
Index: All in one. Record index not computerized. Office personnel or visitors may perform searches. Search fee $3.00 per name. Copy fee $1.00 per page. Cert fee- $1.00 per doc plus copy fee. Payee- County Clerk. **Online access to Real Estate, Grantor/Grantee, Deed, Lien, Judgment, Fictitious Name records:** Recording records available free at http://okcountyrecords.com/search.php. **Other phones:** Treasurer- 580-323-2292; Elections- 580-323-2291; Vital Records- 405-171-4040. **Property tax/Assessing**- PO Box 96, Arapaho, OK 73620; 580-323-3271. **Online access**- Access treasurer property data free at www.custercountyok.org.

Delaware County

County Clerk, PO Box 309, Jay, OK 74346. 918-253-4520; fax-918-253-8352; hours- 8AM-4:30PM. www.delawareclerk.org
Index: All in one. Records indexed on a public use terminal back to 1987. Only the public may search. Copy fee $1.00 per page. Cert fee- $1.00 per cert plus copy fee. Payee- Delaware County Clerk. **Online access to Real Estate, Grantor/Grantee, Deed, Lien, Judgment, Fictitious Name records:** Access land records index free at http://okcountyrecords.com/search.php?County=021. Subscription required for images; $10.00 per month. **Other phones:** Treasurer- 918-253-4533; Elections- 918-253-8762; Court Clerk- 918-253-4420. **Property tax/Assessing**- 327 S 5th St, Jay, OK 74346; 918-253-4523, assessor fax- 918-253-8933.

Dewey County

County Clerk, PO Box 368, Taloga, OK 73667. 580-328-5361; fax-580-328-5652; 8AM-4PM
Index: Separate indices to search include judgments. Record index not computerized. Office personnel or visitors may perform searches. Office will not search real estate records. Office will not search tax liens. UCC search per debtor name- $10.00. Copy fee $1.00 per page. Cert fee- $1.00 per cert plus copy fee. Payee- Dewey County Clerk. **Other phones:** Treasurer- 580-328-5501; Elections- 580-328-5668. **Property tax/Assessing**- PO Box 235, Taloga, OK 73667; 580-328-5561, assessor fax- 580-328-5652. **Online**- Access to assessor data may be at www.pvplus.com/freeaccess/free_login.aspx. Registration required. Subscription and fees for full access.

Ellis County

County Clerk, PO Box 197, Arnett, OK 73832. Recording, R/E phone-580-885-7301; fax-580-885-7258; 8:30AM-4:30PM.
Index: All in one. Record index not computerized. Office personnel or visitors may perform searches. Office will search real estate records. No UCC records to search. Copy fee $1.00 per page. Cert fee- $1.00 per instrument; plus copy fee $1.00 per page. Payee- Ellis County Clerk. Treasurer- 580-885-7670; Elections- 580-885-7721; Vital Records- 580-885-7301. **Property tax/Assessing**- PO Box 276, Arnett, 73832; 580-885-7975, assessor fax- 580-885-7258.

Garfield County

County Clerk, PO Box 1664, Enid, OK 73702-1664. Recording, R/E phone-580-237-0226; fax-580-249-5951; 8AM-4:30PM
Index: All in one. Records on a public use terminal. Only the public may search. Copy fee $1.00 per page. Cert fee- $1.00 per page plus copy fee. Payee- Garfield County Clerk. **Other phones:** Treasurer- 580-237-0246; Elections- 580-237-6016; Court Clerk- 580-237-0232. **Property tax/Assessing**- 114 W Broadway, Rm 106, Enid, OK 73703; 580-237-0220, assessor fax- 580-249-5989. (Appraiser/Auditor- 580-237-0220) **Online access**- Access treasurer property data free at www.gctreasurer.org.

Garvin County

County Clerk, PO Box 926, Pauls Valley, OK 73075. 405-238-2772; fax-405-238-6283; 8:30AM-4:30PM.
Index: All in one. Records indexed on a public use terminal back to 1993. Only the public may search. Copy fee $1.00 per page. Cert fee- $1.00 per cert. Payee- Garvin County Clerk. **Online Real Estate, Grantor/Grantee, Deed, Lien, Judgment, Fictitious Name records:** Recording records available free at http://okcountyrecords.com/search.php. **Other phones:** Treasurer- 405-238-7301; Elections- 405-238-3808; Vital Records- 405-271-4040. **Property tax/Assessing**- 201 W Grant, Pauls Valley, OK 73075; 405-238-2409, assessor fax- 405-238-9189. **Online access**- Access treasurer property data free at http://garvin.okcountytreasurers.com/.

Grady County

County Clerk, PO Box 1009, Chickasha, OK 73023. 405-224-7388; fax-405-222-4506; 8AM-4:30PM www.gradycountyok.com/
Index: Separate indices to search include 6 rural, 2 town. Records indexed on a public use terminal back to 1989. Office will perform a UCC search but public must search other records themselves. Search fee $10.00 for UCC per name. Copy fee $1.00 per page. Cert fee- $1.00 per doc plus copy fee. Payee- County Clerk. **Online Real Estate, Grantor/Grantee, Deed, Lien, Judgment, Fictitious Name records:** Recording records available free at http://okcountyrecords.com/search.php. **Other phones:** Treasurer- 405-224-5337; Elections- 405-224-1430; Vital Records- 405-271-4040. **Property tax/Assessing**- 326 Choctaw St, Chickasha, OK 73023; 405-224-4361. **Online access**- Access treasurer property data free at http://grady.okcountytreasurers.com/

Grant County

County Clerk, 112 E Guthrie St, #102, Medford, OK 73759. Recording, R/E phone-580-395-2274; fax-580-395-2086; 8AM-4:30PM
Index: Separate indices to search include individual township & range books, by sections "NW, SW, NE, SE" the numbered books dated instruments. Records indexed on computer back 3 years. Office personnel or visitors may perform searches. Office personell require you to provide the correct legal description. Search fee $5.00 per name. $3.00 for phone search fee if search is complicated. Copy fee $1.00 per page. Cert fee- $1.00 per cert plus copy fee. Payee- Grant County Clerk. **Other phones:** Treasurer- 580-395-2284; Elections- 580-395-2862. **Property tax/Assessing**- 112 E Guthrie, #101, Medford, OK 73759; 580-395-2844, assessor fax- 580-395-2603. **Online access**- Assessor and property data available by subscription at http://grant.oklahoma.usassessor.com/. Access treasurer property data free at http://grant.okcountytreasurers.com/.

Greer County

County Clerk, PO Box 207, Mangum, OK 73554. 580-782-3664; fax-580-782-3803; 8AM-4PM.
Index: Indexes- mtg, deeds, misc, fed & state tax liens, judgments, M&M liens. Record index not computerized. Office personnel or visitors may perform searches. General index search fee $10.00 per name. Office will search real estate records. Will search UCC records. Copy fee $1.00 per page. Cert fee- $1.00 per doc plus copy fee. Payee- Greer County Clerk. **Other phones:** Treasurer- 580-782-5515; Elections- 580-782-2307; Vital Records- 405-271-4040. **Property tax/Assessing**- 106 E Jefferson, #14, County Courthouse, Mangum, OK 73554; 580-782-2740. (Appraiser/Auditor- 580-782-2454) **Online access**- Access treasurer property data free at http://greer.okcountytreasurers.com/.

Harmon County

County Clerk, 114 W Hollis; Courthouse, Hollis, OK 73550. 580-688-3658; fax-580-688-9784; 8AM-4PM
Index: All in one. Record index not computerized. Office personnel or visitors may perform searches. Search fee $5.00 per name. Property transfer searches available. Tax liens not included in UCC search. Copy fee $1.00 per page. Cert fee- $2.00 per doc includes copy fee. Payee- Harmon County Clerk. Treasurer- 580-882-3566; Elections- 580-688-2460. **Property tax/Assessing**- Treasurer's office, 114 W Hollis, Hollis, OK 73550; 580-688-3566, fax- 580- 688-9784. http://harmon.okcountytreasurers.com/ **Online**- Access treasurer property data free at http://harmon.okcountytreasurers.com/.

Harper County

County Clerk, PO Box 369, Buffalo, OK 73834. Recording, R/E phone-580-735-2012; fax-580-735-2612; 8AM-4PM
Index: Separate indices to search. Record index not computerized. Office personnel or visitors may perform searches. General index search fee $10.00. Office will search real estate records. UCC search includes tax liens if requested. UCC search per debtor name- $10.00. Copy fee $1.00 per page. Cert fee- $1.00 per page plus copy fee. Payee- Harper County Clerk. **Other phones:** Treasurer- 580-735-2442; Elections- 580-735-2313; Court Clerk- 580-735-2010. **Property tax/Assessing**- PO Box 352, Buffalo, OK 73834; 580-735-2343.

Haskell County

County Clerk, 202 E Main; Courthouse, Stigler, OK 74462. Recording, R/E phone-918-967-2884; fax-918-967-2885; 8AM-4:30PM.
Index: All in one. Records indexed on computer back to 1994. Office personnel or visitors may perform searches. Search fee $10.00 written; $3.00 phone. Copy fee $1.00 per page. Cert fee- $1.00 per page plus copy fee. Payee- Haskell County Clerk. **Other phones:** Treasurer- 918-967-2441; Elections- 918-967-8792. **Property tax/Assessing**- Same address as recording office. 918-967-2611. **Online access**- Access to property data is available by subscription at http://oklahoma.usassessor.com.

Hughes County

County Clerk, 200 N Broadway St, #5, Holdenville, OK 74848-3400. Recording, R/E phone-405-379-5487; fax-405-379-6890; 8AM-4:30PM
Index: All in one. Record index not computerized. Office will perform a real estate search but public must search other records themselves. Search fee $10.00 per name. Copy fee $1.00 per page. Cert fee- $1.00 per seal plus copy fee. Payee- Hughes County Clerk. **Other phones:** Treasurer- 405-379-5371; Elections- 405-379-2174; Vital Records- 405-379-3384. **Property tax/Assessing**- 200 N Broadway St #4, Holdenville, OK 74848; 405-379-3862, assessor fax- 405-379-0100.

Jackson County

County Clerk, PO Box 515, Altus, OK 73522. Recording, R/E phone-580-482-4070; fax-none; 8AM-4PM
Index: Separate indices to search include taxes, deeds, mortgages. Records indexed on computer back to 2004. Office personnel or visitors may perform searches. General index search fee $10.00 per person. Office will search real estate records. Will search UCC records. Copy fee $1.00 per page. Cert fee- $1.00 per cert plus copy fee. Payee- Jackson County Clerk. **Other phones:** Treasurer- 580-482-4371; Elections- 580-482-2370; Vital Records- 580-482-4070. **Property tax/Assessing**- 101 N Main, Rm 201, Altus, OK 73521; 580-482-0787, assessor fax- 580-482-4462. **Online access**- Access to parcel, treasurer and property tax data free at http://jackson.okcountytreasurers.com/.

Jefferson County

County Clerk, 220 N Main, Rm 103; Courthouse, Waurika, OK 73573. Recording, R/E phone-580-228-2029; fax-580-228-3608; 8AM-4PM www.jeffcoinfo.org/Courts.html
Index: All in one. Record index not computerized. Office will perform a UCC search but public must search other records themselves. Search fee $5.00. Office will not search real estate records. Copy fee $1.00 per page. Cert fee- $1.00 per page plus copy fee. Payee- Jefferson County Clerk. **Other phones:** Treasurer- 580-228-2967; Elections- 580-228-3150; Vital Records- 580-271-4040. **Property tax/Assessing**- 220 N Main, Waurika, OK 73573; 580-228-2397, assessor fax- 580-228-3608. **Online access**- Access assessor property data by subscription at http://jefferson.oklahoma.usassessor.com/. Plats and maps also available. Access treasurer property data free at http://jefferson.okcountytreasurers.com/.

Johnston County

County Clerk, 403 W Main, Rm 101, Tishomingo, OK 73460. Recording, R/E phone-580-371-3184; fax-580-371-3662; 8:30AM-4:30PM
Index: All in one. Records indexed on a public use terminal back to 1992. Office personnel or visitors may perform searches. Search fee $10.00. Limited real estate owner, mortgage, and property transfer searches available. Office will not search UCC records. Tax lien search fee- $3.00 per debtor for uncertified verbal search. Copy fee $1.00 per page. Cert fee- $1.00 per page plus copy fee. Payee- Johnston County Clerk. Copies of bulk recorder records and CD of plats available for purchase. **Online Real Estate, Grantor/Grantee, Deed, Lien, Judgment, Fictitious Name records:** Records free at http://okcountyrecords.com/search.php?County=035. **Other phones:** Treasurer- 580-371-3082; Elections- 580-371-3670; Vital Records- 580-271-4040. **Property tax/Assessing**- 403 W Main, #102, Tishomingo, OK 73460; 580-371-3465. **Online access**- Access treasurer property data free at http://johnston.okcountytreasurers.com/.

Kay County

County Clerk, PO Box 450, Newkirk, OK 74647-0450. Recording, R/E phone-580-362-2537; fax-580-362-3300; 8AM-4:30PM
Index: All in one. Records indexed on a public use terminal back to 1997. Office personnel or visitors may perform searches. No mineral interest searches. Search fee $10.00 per name. Office will search real estate records. Will not search UCC records. Copy fee $1.00 per page. Cert fee- $1.00 per page plus copy fee. Payee- Kay County Clerk. **Online Real Estate, Grantor/Grantee, Deed, Lien, Judgment, Fictitious Name records:** Recording records available free at http://okcountyrecords.com/search.php. **Other phones:** Treasurer- 580-362-2523; Elections- 580-362-2130. **Property tax/Assessing**- County Courthouse, Newkirk, OK 74647; 580-362-2566, assessor fax- 580-362-3668. **Online access**- The assessor office has a subscription service with property data; fee is $10.00 per month with new data being added. A basic index search is to be available. Call 580-362-2565 for details and to request a signup form. Access the treasurer tax lookup page free at www.kaycounty.org/Creek1.htm.

Kingfisher County

County Clerk, 101 S Main St, Rm 3, Kingfisher, OK 73750. 405-375-3887; fax-405-375-6033; 8AM-4:30PM. www.kingfisherco.com/countyclerk.htm
Index: Separate indices to search by type. Record index not computerized. Only the public may search. Copy fee $1.00 per page. Cert fee- $1.00 per doc plus copy fee. Payee- Judy Grellner, County Clerk. **Online access to Real Estate, Grantor/Grantee, Deed, Lien, Judgment, Fictitious Name records:** Recording records available free at http://okcountyrecords.com/search.php. **Other phones:** Treasurer- 405-375-3827; Elections- 405-375-3895. **Property tax/Assessing**- 101 S Main St, Courthouse, Kingfisher, OK 73750; 405-375-3884. (Appraiser- 405-375-3884)

Kiowa County

County Clerk, PO Box 73, Hobart, OK 73651-0073. Recording, R/E phone-580-726-5286; fax-580-726-6033; 8AM-4PM
Index: All in one. Records indexed on a public use terminal back to 12/4/2006. Office personnel or visitors may perform searches. Searches may be requested via telephone. General search fee $3.00 per name. Office will search (within reason) real estate records. Will search UCC records. Copy fee $1.00 per page if a permanent recorded doc; all others are $.25 per copy. Cert fee- $1.00 per doc plus copy fee. Payee- Kiowa County Clerk. **Other phones:** Treasurer- 580-726-2362; Elections- 580-726-2509. **Property tax/Assessing**- PO Box 855, Hobart, OK 73651; 580-726-2150.

Latimer County

County Clerk, 109 N Central, Rm 103, Wilburton, OK 74578. 918-465-3543; fax-918-465-4001; 8AM-4:30PM. www.tax.ok.gov/advalcount/latimer.html
Index: All in one. Records indexed on computer back to 1988. Office personnel or visitors may perform searches. Search fee $10.00 per name. Copy fee $1.00 per page. Cert fee- $1.00 per cert. Payee- Latimer County Clerk. **Other phones:** Treasurer- 918-465-3450. **Property tax/Assessing**- 109 N Central, Rm 104, Wilburton, OK 74578; 918-465-3031. www.tax.ok.gov/advalcount/latimer.html **Online access**- Access treasurer property data free at http://latimer.okcountytreasurers.com/.

Le Flore County

County Clerk, PO Box 218, Poteau, OK 74953-0218. 918-647-5738; fax-918-647-8930; 8AM-4:30PM. http://okcountyrecords.com/search.php?county=040
Index: All in one. Records indexed on a public use terminal back to 1982-1983. Office personnel or visitors may perform searches. Search fee $5.00 per name. Lien search or UCC search- $10.00. Office will not search real estate records; UCCs okay. Copy fee $1.00 per page. Cert fee- $1.00 per cert plus copy fee. Payee- Le Flore County Clerk. **Online access to Real Estate, Grantor/Grantee, Deed, Lien, Judgment, Fictitious Name records:** Access land records index free at http://okcountyrecords.com/search.php. Subscription required for images; $1.00 per copy printed, money has to be credited to account first. **Other phones:** Treasurer- 918-647-3525; Elections- 918-647-3701. **Property tax/Assessing**- PO Box 99, Poteau, OK 74953; 918-647-3652. **Online access**- A subscription is required to access assessment data at http://leflore.oklahoma.usassessor.com/. $30.00 per month. For more info contact Tracy Leniger or Heather Brown at 405-379-5280, or signup online. Also, access treasurer property data free at http://leflore.okcountytreasurers.com/.

Lincoln County

County Clerk, PO Box 126, Chandler, OK 74834-0126. Recording, R/E phone-405-258-1264; fax-405-258-0439; 8:30AM-4:30PM
Index: Separate indices to search include judgments, trust, tax liens, etc. Records indexed on a public use terminal back to 1994. Office personnel or visitors may perform searches. General index search fee $3.00 per legal. Property transfer searches available. Will not search UCC records. Copy fee $1.00 per page. Cert fee- $1.00 per doc plus copy fee. Payee- Lincoln County Clerk. **Other phones:** Treasurer- 405-258-1491; Elections- 405-258-1349. **Property tax/Assessing**- 811 Manvel, #7, Chandler, OK 74834; 405-258-1209. **Online access**- Access treasurer property data free at www.lctreasurer.org/.

Logan County

County Clerk, 301 E Harrison, #102, Guthrie, OK 73044-4999. 405-282-0266; fax-405-282-0267; 8AM-4:30PM www.logancounty-ok.org
Index: All in one. Record index not computerized. Only the public may search. Office offers only a very limited search of real estate records. Copy fee $1.00 per page. Cert fee- $1.00 per cert plus copy fee. Payee- Logan County Clerk. **Online access to Real Estate, Grantor/Grantee, Deed, Lien, Judgment, Fictitious Name, records:** Assess recorded data free at http://okcountyrecords.com/search.php. Images available from 1994 to current. Can not print, call office to request copies. **Other phones:** Treasurer- 405-282-3154; Elections- 405-282-1900; Vital Records- 405-271-4040. **Property tax/Assessing**- 301 E Harrison, #105, Guthrie, OK 73044; 405-282-3509. www.logancounty-ok.org/ **Online access**- Access assessor property records free at http://eland.logancounty-ok.org/display.php. Also, access treasurer property data free at www.loganct.org.

Love County

County Clerk, 405 W Main, Rm 203, Marietta, OK 73448. 580-276-3059; 8AM-N, 12:30-4:30PM
Index: All in one. Records indexed on a public use terminal back to 1992. Only the public may search. Copy fee $1.00 per page. Cert fee- $1.00 per cert. Payee- Love County Clerk. **Online Real Estate, Grantor/Grantee, Deed, Lien, Judgment, Fictitious Name records:** Recording records available free at http://okcountyrecords.com/search.php. **Other phones:** Treasurer- 580-276-2360. **Property tax/Assessing**- 405 W Main, #104, Marietta, 73448; 580-276-2396. **Online**- Access treasurer property data free at http://love.okcountytreasurers.com/.

Major County

County Clerk, PO Box 379, Fairview, OK 73737-0379. 580-227-4732, R/E recording phone-580-227-3918; fax-580-227-2736; 8:30AM-4:30PM
Index: All in one. Records indexed on computer from 2003 forward. Office personnel or visitors may perform searches. Search fee $5.00 per name. Office will search real estate records. Will not search UCC records. Copy fee $1.00 per page. Cert fee- $1.00 plus copy fee. Payee- Major County Clerk. **Online Real Estate, Grantor/Grantee, Deed, Lien, Judgment, Fictitious Name records:** Recording records free at http://okcountyrecords.com/search.php. **Other phones:** Treasurer- 580-227-4782; Elections- 580-227-4520; Vital Records- 580-227-4690. **Property tax/Assessing**- 500 E Broadway, Fairview, 73737; 580-227-4821, assessor fax- 580-227-2736.

Marshall County

County Clerk, PO Box 824, Madill, OK 73446. Recording, R/E phone-580-795-3220; fax-580-795-7596; 8:30AM-N, 12:30-5PM
Index: All in one. Records indexed on a public use terminal back to 2000. Office personnel or visitors may perform searches. Real estate record owner searches available; legal description and name required. UCC search includes tax liens if requested. UCC search per debtor name- $10.00. Copy fee $1.00 per page. Cert fee- $1.00 per cert plus copy fee. Payee- Marshall County Clerk. **Online Real Estate, Grantor/Grantee, Deed, Lien, Judgment, Fictitious Name records:** Recording records available free at http://okcountyrecords.com/search.php. **Other phones:** Treasurer- 580-795-2463; Elections- 580-795-5460; Court Clerk- 580-795-3278; Commissioner -580-795-3165. **Property tax/Assessing**- Marshall County Courthouse, Rm 105, Madill, OK 73446; 580-795-2398, assessor fax- 580-795-7589. (Appraiser/Auditor- 580-795-2398) **Online access**- Access to access property records is by subscription from OK Assessors.com, 800-535-6467; weekly and monthly plans available. See note about OKassessors.com at beginning of section. Access treasurer property data free at http://marshall.okcountytreasurers.com/.

Mayes County

County Clerk, 1 Court Place, #120, Pryor, OK 74361. Recording, R/E phone-918-825-2426; fax-918-825-3803; 9AM-5PM.

Index: All in one. Records indexed on a public use terminal back to 0700. Office personnel or visitors may perform searches. If office personnel searches they are not guaranteed. Search fee $10.00 per debtor; phone searches-$3.00 per search. Will not search UCC records. Copy fee $1.00 per page. Cert fee- $1.00 per doc plus copy fee. Payee- Mayes County Clerk. Bulk data available for purchase, contact Rita Littlefield. **Other phones:** Treasurer- 918-825-0160; Elections- 918-825-1826. **Property tax/Assessing-** PO Box 53, 1 Court Pl, #110, Pryor, OK 74361; 918-825-0625. (Appraiser/Auditor- 918-825-0625) **Online access-** Access treasurer property data free at www.mayescounty.org.

McClain County

County Clerk, PO Box 629, Purcell, OK 73080-0629. Recording, R/E phone-405-527-3360; fax-405-527-5242; 8AM-4:30PM

Index: All in one. Records indexed on computer with name for anything filed after June, 1994. All indexing is hand done on index books. Office personnel or visitors may perform searches. Search fee $3.00. Real estate owner, mortgage, and property transfer searches available. Will not search UCC records. Copy fee $1.00 per page. Cert fee- $1.00 per cert plus copy fee. Payee- McClain County Clerk. **Other phones:** Treasurer- 405-527-3261; Elections- 405-527-3121; Court Clerk- 405-527-3121. **Property tax/Assessing-** 121 N 2nd St, #206, Purcell, OK 73080; 405-527-3520, assessor fax- 405-527-5242. **Online access-** Access to property records is by subscription from OK Assessors.com, 800-535-6467; weekly and monthly plans available. See note about OKassessors.com at beginning of section. Also, search the tax roll inquiry site free at www.mcclaincounty.org/.

McCurtain County

County Clerk, PO Box 1078, Idabel, OK 74745. 580-286-2370, R/E recording phone-580-286-2370x100; fax-580-286-1040; 8AM-4PM

Index: All in one. Records indexed on a public use terminal back to 3/15/01. Office personnel or visitors may perform searches. Search fee $3.00. Office will not search real estate records. Will search UCC records. Copy fee $1.00 per page. Cert fee- $1.00 per cert plus copy fee. Payee- McCurtain County Clerk. **Online Real Estate, Grantor/Grantee, Deed, Lien, Judgment, Fictitious Name records:** Records free at http://okcountyrecords.com/search.php?County=045. **Other phones:** Treasurer- 580-286-5128; Vital Records- 405-271-5600; Voter Registrar- 580-286-7405. **Property tax/Assessing-** 108 N Central, Idabel, OK 74745; 580-286-5272. **Online access-** Access treasurer property data free at http://mccurtain.okcountytreasurers.com/.

McIntosh County

County Clerk, PO Box 110, Eufaula, OK 74432-0110. 918-689-2741; fax-918-689-3385; 8AM-4PM.

Index: indices separated by township and range. Records indexed on computer from 4/15/08 to present. Only the public may search. Copy fee $1.00 per page. Cert fee- $1.00 plus copy fee. Payee- McIntosh County County Clerk. **Other phones:** Treasurer- 918-689-2491. **Property tax/Assessing-** PO Box 107, Eufaula, OK 74432; 918-689-2611, assessor fax- 918-689-3611. **Online access-** Access to property data is by subscription at http://mcintosh.oklahoma.usassessor.com/.

Murray County

County Clerk, PO Box 442, Sulphur, OK 73086. Recording, R/E phone-580-622-3920; fax-580-622-6209; 8AM-4:30PM

Index: All in one. Records indexed on a public use terminal back to 1990. Office personnel or visitors may perform searches. Search fee $5.00. Office will search real estate records. Will search UCC records. Copy fee $1.00 per page. Cert fee- $1.00 per cert plus copy fee. Payee- Murray County Clerk. **Other phones:** Treasurer- 580-622-5622; Elections- 580-622-3800. **Property tax/Assessing-** PO Box 111, 10th & Wyandotte Sts, Sulphur, OK 73086; 580-622-3433, assessor fax- 580-622-6209. **Online access-** With registration, assessment data free temporarily at www.pvplus.com/freeaccess/free_login.aspx.

Muskogee County

County Clerk, PO Box 1008, Muskogee, OK 74402. 918-682-7781; 8AM-4:30PM

Index: All in one. Records indexed on a public use terminal back to 1990. Only the public may search. Copy fee $1.00 per page. Cert fee- $1.00 per cert plus copy fee. Payee- Muskogee County Clerk. **Online access to Real Estate, Grantor/Grantee, Deed, Lien, Judgment, Fictitious Name records:** Recording records available free at http://okcountyrecords.com/search.php. Also, access to public records for free go to http://okcountyrecords.com/search.php?county=051. Data and images from 12/97 -present. **Other phones:** Treasurer- 918-682-0811. **Property tax/Assessing-** 400 W Broadway, Muskogee, OK 74401; 918-682-8781. **Online access-** Access treasurer property data free at www.muskogeetreasurer.org.

Noble County

County Clerk, 300 Courthouse Dr #11; Courthouse, Perry, OK 73077. Recording, R/E phone-580-336-2141; fax-580-336-2481; 8AM-4:30PM.

Index: All in one. Record index not computerized. Office personnel or visitors may perform searches. Search fee $10.00. Office will not search real estate records. Will search UCC records. Copy fee $1.00 per page. Cert fee- $1.00 per page plus copy fee. Payee- Noble County Clerk. **Online access to Real Estate, Grantor/Grantee, Deed, Lien, Judgment, Fictitious Name records:** Recording records available free at http://okcountyrecords.com/search.php. **Other phones:** Treasurer- 580-336-2026; Elections- 580-336-3527. **Property tax/Assessing-** 300 Courthouse Dr, #9, Perry, OK 73077; 580-336-2185. **Online access-** Access treasurer property data free at http://noble.okcountytreasurers.com/.

Nowata County

County Clerk, 229 N Maple, Nowata, OK 74048. Recording, R/E phone-918-273-2480; fax-918-273-2481; 8AM-4:30PM

Index: All records searchable except for DD-214 and personal. Records indexed on a public use terminal back to 1999. Office will perform a UCC search but public must search other records themselves. Search fee $10.00 per name. Copy fee $1.00 per page. Cert fee- $1.00 per instrument plus copy fee. Payee- Nowata County Clerk. **Other phones:** Treasurer- 918-273-3562; Elections- 918-273-0710; Vital Records- 918-273-0127. **Property tax/Assessing-** 229 N Maple, Nowata, 74048; 918-273-0581, fax- 918-273-1448.

Okfuskee County

County Clerk, PO Box 108, Okemah, OK 74859-0108. Recording, R/E phone-918-623-1724; fax-918-623-0739; 8AM-4PM.

Index: All in one. Records on a public use terminal. Office personnel or visitors may perform searches. Search fee-$10.00 per name. Office will search real estate records. Will search UCC records. Copy fee $1.00 per page. Cert fee- $1.00 per seal plus copy fee. Payee- County Clerk. **Other phones:** Treasurer- 918-623-1494; Elections- 918-623-0105; Vital Records- 405-271-4040. **Property tax/Assessing-** PO Box 601, Okemah, 74859; 918-623-1535. 8:30AM-4:30PM

Oklahoma County

County Clerk, 320 Robert S Kerr Ave, Rm 203; Real Estate, Oklahoma City, OK 73102. Recording, R/E phone-405-713-1540, UCC recording phone-405-713-1522; fax-405-713-1810; 8AM-5PM (CT) www.oklahomacounty.org

There is a UCC Section and a real estate/county clerk section. The OK UCC Central Filing Office is operated by the OK County Clerk's Office, Rm 107, 405-713-1522. Index: All in one. UCC records indexed on a public use terminal back to 1961, real estate to 1995. Certain older records are also available. Office will perform a UCC search but public must search other records themselves. UCC search fee $10.00 per debtor name. Copy fee $1.00 per page. Cert fee- $1.00 per page plus copy fee. Payee- Oklahoma County Clerk. Custom orders for bulk data in index format are available. **Online access to Real Estate, Grantor/Grantee, Deed, UCC records:** Real estate, UCC, grantor/grantee records on the county clerk database are free at www.oklahomacounty.org/coclerk/. Images, index and printing available. **Other phones:** Treasurer- 405-713-1300; Elections- 405-713-1515. **Property tax/Assessing-** 320 Robert S Kerr Ave, Oklahoma City, OK 73102; 405-713-1200, assessor fax- 405-713-1220. (Appraiser/Auditor- 405-713-1200) **Online** - Assessor/property data on assessor database is free at www.oklahomacounty.org/assessor/disclaim.htm. Also, search treasurer's property info at www.oklahomacounty.org/treasurer/PublicAccessSearch.htm.

Okmulgee County

County Clerk, PO Box 904, Okmulgee, OK 74447-0904. Recording, R/E phone-918-756-0788; fax-918-758-1261; 8AM-4:30PM.

Index: Separate indices to search include Federal tax lien, M&M liens, liens, judgments. Records indexed on computer back to 1995. Office personnel or visitors may perform searches, depending on type of record. General index search fee $5.00 per legal. If extensive, an hourly rate will be charged. Office will search real estate records. Will not search UCC records. Copy fee $1.00 per page. Cert fee- $1.00 per instrument plus copy fee. **Other phones:** Treasurer- 918-756-3848; Elections- 918-756-2365; Vital Records- 405-271-4040. **Property tax/Assessing-** 314 W 7th, #103, Okmulgee, OK 74447; 918-758-0303. **Online** - Access is free for basic info from a company at www.pvplus.com/freeaccess/register.aspx - free registration is required.

Osage County

County Clerk, PO Box 87, Pawhuska, OK 74056. 918-287-3136; fax-918-287-4979; 8:30AM-5PM

Index: Separate indices to search include Tax Liens, Judgments, Mechanics Liens. Records indexed on a public use terminal back to 1998. Office personnel or visitors may perform searches. Office will not search real estate records. Office will not search tax liens. UCC search per debtor name- $10.00. Copy fee $1.00 per page. Cert fee- $1.00 per cert plus copy fee. Payee- Osage County Clerk. **Online Real Estate, Grantor/Grantee, Deed, Lien, Judgment, Fictitious Name records:** Recording records free at http://okcountyrecords.com/search.php. **Other phones:** Treasurer- 918-287-3101; Elections- 918-287-3036. **Property tax/Assessing-** 600 Grandview, Rm 101, Pawhuska, 74056; 918-287-3448. (Appraiser/Auditor- 918-287-3448)

Ottawa County

County Clerk, 102 E Central, #203, Miami, OK 74354-7043. Recording, R/E phone-918-542-3332; fax-918-542-8260; 9AM-5PM; recording til 4PM

Index: Books, by legal description. Records indexed on a public use terminal back to 1995. Office personnel or visitors may perform searches. Search fee $10.00. Office will search real estate records if time allows. Will not search UCC records. Copy fee $1.00 per page. Cert fee- $1.00 per cert plus copy fee. Payee- Ottawa County Clerk. **Online access to Real Estate, Grantor/Grantee, Deed, Lien, Judgment, Fictitious Name records:** Recording records available free at http://okcountyrecords.com/search.php. **Other phones:** Treasurer- 918-542-8232; Elections- 918-

542-2893; Vital Records- 918-571-2600. **Property tax/Assessing**- 102 E Central, #206, Okmulgee, OK 74447; 918-542-9418. **Online access**- Access to property data is through a subscription with a private company, visit www.pvplus.com. Fee is $10.00 per month per county. Also, access treasurer property data free at http://ottawa.okcountytreasurers.com/.

Pawnee County

County Clerk, 500 Harrison St, Rm 202; Courthouse, Pawnee, OK 74058. 918-762-2732; fax-918-762-6404; 8AM-4:30PM

Index: Separate indices to search by townships. Records indexed on a public use terminal back to 9/94. Only the public may search. Copy fee $1.00 per page. Cert fee- $1.00 per cert plus copy fee. Payee- Pawnee County Clerk. **Other phones:** Treasurer- 918-762-2418; Elections- 918-762-2125. **Property tax/Assessing**- 500 Harrison St, Courthouse, Rm 201, Pawnee, OK 74058; 918-762-2402. **Online access**- Access treasurer property data free at http://pawnee.okcountytreasurers.com/.

Payne County

County Clerk, 315 W 6th Ave, #202, Stillwater, OK 74074. 405-747-8310, R/E recording phone-405-747-8345; fax-405-747-8304; hours - 8AM-5PM http://okcountyrecords.com/search.php?county=060

Index: Separate indices to search include townships, additions. Records indexed on a public use terminal back 15 years; see website for record availability. Office personnel or visitors may perform searches. No mineral searches. Office performs no certified real estate searches. Will not search UCC records. Copy fee $1.00 per page. Cert fee- $1.00 per cert plus copy fee. Payee- Payne County Clerk. **Online Real Estate, Grantor/Grantee, Deed, Lien, Judgment, Fictitious Name records:** Access land records index free at http://okcountyrecords.com/search.php. Index and details only; images available from 1995. **Other phones:** Treasurer- 405-624-9411; Elections- 405-747-8350; Vital Records- 405-271-4040; 405-747-8344. **Property tax/Assessing**- 315 W 6th Ave, #102, Stillwater, OK 74074; 405-747-8300. (Appraiser/Auditor- 405-747-8300) **Online access**- Access treasurer property data free at http://paynecountytreasurer.org.

Pittsburg County

County Clerk, PO Box 3304, McAlester, OK 74502. 918-423-6865; fax-918-423-7304; 8AM-5PM.

Index: Separate indices to search. Records indexed on a public use terminal back to 1993. Office personnel or visitors may perform searches. Search fee $5.00 verbal, $10.00 written per name. Office will search real estate records. Will search UCC records. Copy fee $1.00 per page. Cert fee- $1.00 per page plus copy fee. Payee- Pittsburg County Clerk. **Online Real Estate, Grantor/Grantee, Deed, Lien, Judgment, Fictitious Name records:** Recording records free at http://okcountyrecords.com/search.php. **Other phones:** Treasurer- 918-423-6895; Elections- 918-423-3877. **Property tax/Assessing**- 600 E Choctaw, McAlester, OK 74501; 918-423-4726, assessor fax- 918-423-7321. **Online access**- Access to access property records is by subscription from OK Assessors.com, 800-535-6467; weekly and monthly plans available. See note about OKassessors.com at beginning of section.

Pontotoc County

County Clerk, PO Box 1425, Ada, OK 74821. Recording, R/E phone-580-332-1425; fax-580-332-7269; 8AM-5PM. www.pontotoccountyclerk.org

Index: All in one. Records indexed on a public use terminal back to 1992. Only the public may search. Copy fee $1.00 per page. Cert fee- $1.00 per cert. **Online Real Estate, Deed, UCC, Judgment, Lien, Military records:** Access recorder's index free at http://okcountyrecords.com/search.php?county=062. Access to the clerk's recorded records requires registration and subscription. To register, contact the county clerk. **Other phones:** Treasurer- 580-332-0183; Elections- 580-332-4534; Vital Records- 405-271-5600. **Property tax/Assessing**- PO Box 396, Ada, OK 74821; 580-332-0317. **Online access**- Access treasurer property data free at http://pontotoc.okcountytreasurers.com/.

Pottawatomie County

County Clerk, PO Box 576, Shawnee, OK 74802. 405-273-8222; fax-405-275-6898; 8AM-5PM

Index: All in one. Records indexed on a public use terminal back to 1985. Office personnel or visitors may perform searches. Search fee $5.00. Office will search real estate records if staff is available. Office will not search UCC records. Copy fee $1.00 per page. Cert fee- $1.00 per doc plus copy fee. Payee- County Clerk. CDs of filing available; contact Nancy Bryce County Clerk. **Online access to Real Estate, Deed, Tract, UCC records:** Access property data and UCCs free at www.landaccess.com/sites/ok/pottawatomie/index.php. **Other phones:** Treasurer- 405-273-0213; Elections- 405-273-8367. **Property tax/Assessing**- 325 N Broadway, #204, Shawnee, OK 74801; 405-275-4740. hours- 7:30AM-5PM **Online access**- assessment and property data by subscription at http://pottawatomie.oklahoma.usassessor.com/.

Pushmataha County

County Clerk, 302 SW 'B', Antlers, OK 74523. Recording, R/E phone-580-298-3626; fax-580-298-8452; 8AM-4:30PM

Index: All in one. Record index not computerized. Office will perform a UCC search but public must search other records themselves. Search fee-$5.00 per name. Copy fee $1.00 per page. Cert fee- $2.00 per page includes copy fee. Payee- Pushmataha County Clerk. **Other phones:** Treasurer- 580-298-2580; Elections- 580-298-3292; County Clerk- 580-298-2274. **Property tax/Assessing**- 203 SW 3rd, Antlers, OK 74523; 580-298-3504. (Appraiser/Auditor- 580-298-3504)

Roger Mills County

County Clerk, PO Box 708, Cheyenne, OK 73628. 580-497-3395, R/E recording phone-580-497-3366 or 3395; fax-580-497-3488; 9AM-4:30PM

Index: Separate indices to search include township & range, city. Records indexed on a public use terminal back to 2002. Office will perform a UCC search but public must search other records themselves. Copy fee $1.00 per page. Cert fee- $1.00 per cert plus copies. Payee- Roger Mills County Clerk. **Online access to GIS, Property records:** Access to property records and GIS records for free go to www.oklahomacounty.org/assessor/disclaim.htm . **Other phones:** Treasurer- 580-497-3349; Elections- 580-497-3330. **Property tax/Assessing**- PO Box 424, Cheyenne, OK 73628; 580-497-3350.

Rogers County

County Clerk, PO Box 1210, Claremore, OK 74018. 918-341-2518; fax-918-341-4529; 8AM-4:30PM www.rogerscounty.org

Index: Separate indices to search include land, liens, judgment, legal description. Grantor/grantee records indexed on a public use terminal back to 1986. Only the public may search. Copy fee $1.00 per page. Cert fee- $1.00 per cert plus copy fee. Payee- Rogers County Clerk. Bulk data available for purchase; contact Amie at county clerk office. **Online Real Estate, Grantor/Grantee, Deed, Lien, Judgment, Fictitious Name records:** Recording records free at http://okcountyrecords.com/search.php. Also, access land records at http://etitlesearch.com; for registration and subscription, call 870-856-3055. **Other phones:** Treasurer- 918-341-3159; Elections- 918-314-2965; Vital Records- 405-271-4040. **Property tax/Assessing**- PO Box 5, 219 S Missouri, Rm 1-108, Claremore, OK 74017; 918-341-3290, assessor fax- 918-341-4565. (Appraiser/Auditor- 918-341-0200) **Online access**- Access to the assessor database is free at www.rogerscounty.org/search.html. Also, search the treasurers tax roll database free at www.rogerscounty.org/treasurer/search.html.

Seminole County

County Clerk, PO Box 1180, Wewoka, OK 74884. 405-257-2501; fax-405-257-6422; 8AM-4PM.

Index: All in one. Records indexed on a public use terminal back to 1994. Only the public may search. Copy fee $1.00 per page. Cert fee- $1.00 per instrument. Payee- Seminole County Clerk. **Other phones:** Treasurer- 405-257-6262; Elections- 405-257-2786. **Property tax/Assessing**- PO Box 779, Wewoka, OK 74884; 405-257-3371.

Sequoyah County

County Clerk, 120 E Chickasaw, Sallisaw, OK 74955. 918-775-4516; fax-918-775-1218; 8AM-4PM.

Index: All in one. Records indexed on a public use terminal back to 1982. Only the public may search. Copy fee $1.00 per page. Cert fee- $1.00 per doc plus copy fee. Payee- Sequoyah County Clerk. **Other phones:** Treasurer- 918-775-9321; Elections- 918-775-2614. **Property tax/Assessing**- 120 S Chicasaw, Box 2, Sallisaw, OK 74955; 918-775-2062.

Stephens County

County Clerk, 101 S 11th St, Rm 203, Duncan, OK 73533-4758. 580-255-0977; fax-580-255-0991; 8:30AM-4:30PM.

Index: All in one. Records indexed on a public use terminal back to 1992. Only the public may search. Copy fee $1.00 per page. Cert fee- $1.00 per page plus copy fee. Payee- Stephens County Clerk. Printout of Grantor/Grantee index is available. **Online to Real Estate, Grantor/Grantee, Deed, Lien, Judgment, Fictitious Name records:** Access land records index free at http://okcountyrecords.com/search.php. Subscription required for images; $10.00 per month. **Other phones:** Treasurer- 580-255-0728; Elections- 580-255-8782. **Property tax/Assessing**- 101 S 11th, #208, Duncan, OK 73533; 580-255-1542. **Online access**- Access treasurer property data free at http://stephens.okcountytreasurers.com/.

Texas County

County Clerk, PO Box 197, Guymon, OK 73942-0197. Recording, R/E phone-580-338-3141; fax-580-338-4311; 9AM-5PM

Index: All in one. Records indexed on a public use terminal back to 1986. Office will perform simple searches but it is recommended the public search records themselves. Search fee $3.00 per name. Copy fee $1.00 per page. Cert fee- $1.00 per cert plus copy fee. Payee- Texas County Clerk. **Other phones:** Treasurer- 580-338-7050; Elections- 580-338-7644; Vital Records- 405-271-4040. **Property tax/Assessing**- 319 N Main, Guymon, OK 73942; 580-338-3060, assessor fax- 580-338-1789.

Tillman County

County Clerk, PO Box 992, Frederick, OK 73542. Recording, R/E phone-580-335-3421; fax-580-335-3795; 8AM-4PM www.tillmancounty.org

Index: Separate indices to search include deed, mortgage, misc, platted/unplattted legals, judgment, state/federal tax liens. Record index not computerized. Office personnel or visitors may perform searches. Search fee $10.00 per name. Office will search real estate records. Copy fee $1.00 per page. Cert fee- $1.00 per cert plus copy fee. Payee- County Clerk. Office does sell bulk data in xerox copy form, contact the office. **Other phones:** Treasurer- 580-335-3425; Elections- 580-335-2287; Vital Records- 405-271-4040. **Property tax/Assessing**- 205 N 10th, Frederick, OK 73542; 580-335-3424, assessor fax- 580-335-3795. **Online** - Access treasurer property data free at http://tillman.okcountytreasurers.com/.

Tulsa County

County Clerk, 500 S Denver Ave, Rm 120; County Admin Bldg, Tulsa, OK 74103-3832. Recording, R/E phone-918-596-5801, UCC recording phone-918-596-5864; fax-918-596-5819; 8:30AM-5PM. www.tulsacounty.org

Fax number for UCC dept- 918-596-5867. Index: All in one. Records indexed on a public use terminals back to 1979. Only the public may search. Copy fee $1.00 per page. Cert fee- $1.00 per doc plus copy fee. Payee- County Clerk. **Online Real Estate, Deed, Property records:** Access to Tulsa County's Land Records System requires an approved user agreement, username and password, see https://lrmis.tulsacounty.org/. Monthly access fee is $30.00 and $1.00 per doc printed. Records go back to 1979. For info or signup, contact Dorise at 918-596-5206 **Other phones:** Treasurer- 918-596-5030. **Property tax/Assessing-** 500 S Denver Ave, County Admin Bldg, Tulsa, OK 74103; 918-596-5100. **Online access-** Access to Tulsa County's Land Records System requires an agreement, username and password, and fees, see https://lrmis.tulsacounty.org/.

Wagoner County

County Clerk, PO Box 156, Wagoner, OK 74477. Recording, R/E phone-918-485-2216; fax-918-485-7709; 8AM-4:30PM. www.wagonercountyclerk.com Index: All in one. Records indexed on a public use terminal back to 1995. Only the public may search. Will not search UCC records. Copy fee $1.00 per page. Cert fee- $2.00 per seal. Payee- Wagoner County Clerk. **Online access to Real Estate, Grantor/Grantee, Deed, Lien, Judgment records:** Access recorders official records free at www.edoctecinc.com/. There may be a 2 week to 1 month lag time. Also, access to land records for free go to http://24.173.220.131/wagoner/HomePage.aspx?ID=Wagoner%20County. **Other phones:** Treasurer- 918-485-2149; Elections- 918-485-2142. **Property tax/Assessing-** 307 E Cherokee, Wagoner, OK 74467; 918-485-2367. **Online** - Access treasurer property data free at www.wagonertreasurer.org.

Washington County

County Clerk, 400 S Johnstone, #100, Bartlesville, OK 74003. 918-337-2840, R/E recording phone-918-337-2834; fax-918-337-2894; 8AM-5PM. www.countycourthouse.org Index: Separate indices to search include land descriptions, person names, doc type, date. Records indexed on a public use terminal back to 1995. Only the public may search. General copy fee- $1.00 per page. Cert fee- $1.00 per page plus copy fee. Payee- Washington County Clerk. **Online access to Real Estate, Deed, Mortgage, Lien records:** Access to the recorders database is free at www.countycourthouse.org/countyclerk/disclaimer.htm. **Other phones:** Treasurer- 918-337-2810; Elections- 918-337-2850; Vital Records- 405-271-4040. **Property tax/Assessing-** 400 S Johnstone, #106, Bartlesville, OK 74003; 918-337-2830, assessor fax- 918-337-2893. **Online** - Access treasurer property tax and parcel date free at http://ok-washington-treasurer.governmax.com/collectmax/collect30.asp

Washita County

County Clerk, PO Box 380, Cordell, OK 73632. Recording, R/E phone-580-832-3548; fax-580-832-3526; 8AM-4PM Index: Separate indices to search include land, miscellaneous. Record index not computerized. Office will perform a UCC search but public must search other records themselves. General search fee $5.00. Office will not search real estate records. Tax liens included in UCC search. UCC search per debtor name- $10.00. Copy fee $1.00 per page. Cert fee- $1.00 per page plus copy fee. Payee- Washita County Clerk. **Other phones:** Treasurer- 580-832-2667; Elections- 580-832-3658. **Property tax/Assessing-** 111 E Mains, #6, Coredell, OK 73632; 580-832-2468. **Online access-** Access to property data is by subscription from a private company, registration and login required, see http://washita.oklahoma.usassessor.com/Shared/base/Subscriber/Subscribe.php.

Woods County

County Clerk, PO Box 386, Alva, OK 73717-0386. 580-327-0998, R/E recording phone-580-327-6229, UCC recording phone-580-327-0998; fax-580-327-6222; 9AM-5PM Index: All in one. Record index not computerized. Office will perform a UCC search but public must search other records themselves. Copy fee $1.00 per page. Cert fee- $1.00 per instrument plus copy fee. Payee- Woods County Clerk. **Other phones:** Treasurer- 580-327-0308; Elections- 580-327-1452. **Property tax/Assessing-** 407 Government St, Courthouse, Alva, OK 73717; 580-327-3118, assessor fax- 580-327-6230. hours- 8:30AM-5PM **Online access-** Access treasurer property data free at http://woods.okcountytreasurers.com/.

Woodward County

County Clerk, 1600 Main St, #8, Woodward, OK 73801-3051. 580-256-3625; fax-580-254-6840; 9AM-5PM http://woodwardcounty.org/9322.html Index: All in one. Records indexed on computer back to 11/19/03. Office personnel or visitors may perform searches. Search fee $5.00 per name. Copy fee $1.00 per page. Cert fee- $1.00 per cert plus copy fee. Payee- Woodward County Clerk. **Online access to Real Estate, Grantor/Grantee, Deed, Lien, Judgment, Fictitious Name records:** Recording records free at http://okcountyrecords.com/search.php. **Other phones:** Treasurer- 580-254-7404. **Property tax/Assessing-** 1600 Main St, #11, Woodward; 580-256-5061. http://woodwardcounty.org/9301.html.

Oklahoma County Locator

You will usually be able to find the city name in the City/County Cross Reference below. In that case, it is a simple matter to determine the county from the cross reference. However, only the official US Postal Service city names are included in this index. There are an additional 40,000 place names that people use in their addresses. Therefore, we have also included a ZIP/City Cross Reference immediately following the City/County Cross Reference.

If you know the ZIP Code but the city name does not appear in the City/County Cross Reference index, look up the ZIP Code in the ZIP/City Cross Reference, find the city name, then look up the city name in the City/County Cross Reference. For example, you want to know the county for an address of Menands, NY 12204. There is no "Menands" in the City/County Cross Reference. The ZIP/City Cross Reference shows that ZIP Codes 12201-12288 are for the city of Albany. Looking back in the City/County Cross Reference, Albany is in Albany County.

Oklahoma - City/County Cross Reference

ACHILLE Bryan
ADA Pontotoc
ADAIR (74330) Mayes(97), Craig(2)
ADAMS Texas
ADDINGTON Jefferson
AFTON (74331) Delaware(62), Ottawa(35), Craig(1)
AGRA (74824) Lincoln(88), Payne(11)
ALBANY Bryan
ALBERT Caddo
ALBION Pushmataha
ALDERSON Pittsburg
ALEX (73002) Grady(82), McClain(17)
ALINE (73716) Alfalfa(62), Woods(30), Major(6)
ALLEN (74825) Pontotoc(78), Hughes(21)
ALTUS Jackson
ALTUS AFB Jackson
ALVA Woods
AMBER Grady
AMES (73718) Major(68), Garfield(29), Kingfisher(1)
AMORITA Alfalfa
ANADARKO Caddo
ANTLERS Pushmataha
APACHE (73006) Caddo(52), Comanche(47)
ARAPAHO Custer
ARCADIA (73007) Oklahoma(73), Logan(26)
ARDMORE Carter
ARKOMA Le Flore
ARNETT (73832) Ellis(91), Woodward(8)
ASHER Pottawatomie
ATOKA Atoka
ATWOOD Hughes
AVANT Osage
BACHE Pittsburg
BALKO Beaver
BARNSDALL Osage
BARTLESVILLE (74003) Washington(85), Osage(14)
BARTLESVILLE Washington
BATTIEST McCurtain
BEAVER Beaver
BEGGS Okmulgee
BENNINGTON Bryan
BESSIE Washita
BETHANY Oklahoma
BETHEL McCurtain
BIG CABIN (74332) Craig(87), Mayes(10), Rogers(1)
BILLINGS (74630) Noble(75), Garfield(22), Kay(1)
BINGER Caddo
BISON Garfield
BIXBY Tulsa
BLACKWELL Kay
BLAIR (73526) Jackson(90), Greer(9)
BLANCHARD (73010) McClain(62), Grady(37)
BLANCO Pittsburg
BLOCKER Pittsburg
BLUEJACKET (74333) Ottawa(90), Craig(9)
BOISE CITY Cimarron
BOKCHITO Bryan
BOKOSHE Le Flore
BOLEY Okfuskee
BOSWELL (74727) Choctaw(90), Bryan(9)
BOWLEGS Seminole
BOWRING Osage
BOYNTON (74422) Okmulgee(55), Muskogee(44)
BRADLEY (73011) Grady(98), Garvin(1)
BRAGGS Muskogee
BRAMAN Kay
BRAY Stephens
BRISTOW Creek
BROKEN ARROW Tulsa
BROKEN ARROW Wagoner
BROKEN BOW McCurtain
BROMIDE Johnston
BUFFALO Harper
BUNCH (74931) Cherokee(59), Adair(36), Sequoyah(3)
BURBANK Osage
BURLINGTON Alfalfa
BURNEYVILLE Love
BURNS FLAT Washita
BUTLER Custer
BYARS (74831) McClain(87), Pontotoc(9), Garvin(2)
BYRON Alfalfa
CACHE Comanche
CADDO (74729) Atoka(76), Bryan(23)
CALERA Bryan
CALUMET Canadian
CALVIN Hughes
CAMARGO Dewey
CAMERON Le Flore
CANADIAN Pittsburg
CANEY Atoka
CANTON (73724) Blaine(66), Dewey(33)
CANUTE Washita
CAPRON (73725) Woods(79), Alfalfa(20)
CARDIN Ottawa
CARMEN (73726) Alfalfa(82), Woods(17)
CARNEGIE (73015) Caddo(92), Washita(7)
CARNEY Lincoln
CARRIER Garfield
CARTER Beckham
CARTWRIGHT Bryan
CASHION (73016) Kingfisher(57), Logan(40), Canadian(1)
CASTLE Okfuskee
CATOOSA (74015) Rogers(71), Wagoner(26), Tulsa(1)
CEMENT (73017) Grady(66), Caddo(26), Comanche(6)
CENTRAHOMA Coal
CHANDLER Lincoln
CHATTANOOGA (73528) Comanche(62), Tillman(37)
CHECOTAH McIntosh
CHELSEA (74016) Rogers(93), Mayes(3), Nowata(1), Craig(1)
CHEROKEE Alfalfa
CHESTER (73838) Major(89), Woodward(10)
CHEYENNE Roger Mills
CHICKASHA Grady
CHOCTAW (73020) Oklahoma(97), Cleveland(2)
CHOUTEAU (74337) Mayes(94), Wagoner(5)
CLAREMORE (74019) Rogers(98), Mayes(1)
CLAREMORE Rogers
CLARITA Coal
CLAYTON (74536) Pushmataha(96), Pittsburg(2), Latimer(1)
CLEARVIEW Okfuskee
CLEO SPRINGS (73729) Major(88), Woods(9), Alfalfa(2)
CLEVELAND Pawnee
CLINTON (73601) Custer(97), Washita(2)
COALGATE Coal
COLBERT Bryan
COLCORD Delaware
COLEMAN (73432) Johnston(86), Atoka(13)
COLLINSVILLE (74021) Tulsa(77), Rogers(19), Washington(3)
COLONY (73021) Washita(63), Caddo(36)
COMANCHE Stephens
COMMERCE Ottawa
CONCHO Canadian
CONNERVILLE Johnston
COOKSON Cherokee
COPAN (74022) Washington(96), Osage(3)
CORDELL Washita
CORN Washita
COUNCIL HILL (74428) McIntosh(60), Muskogee(39)
COUNTYLINE Stephens
COVINGTON Garfield
COWETA Wagoner
COYLE (73027) Payne(53), Logan(46)
CRAWFORD Roger Mills
CRESCENT (73028) Logan(93), Kingfisher(6)
CROMWELL Seminole
CROWDER Pittsburg
CUSHING (74023) Payne(96), Lincoln(3)
CUSTER CITY Custer
CYRIL Caddo
DACOMA (73731) Woods(93), Alfalfa(6)
DAISY (74540) Atoka(75), Pushmataha(25)
DAVENPORT Lincoln
DAVIDSON Tillman
DAVIS (73030) Murray(97), Garvin(2)
DEER CREEK Grant
DELAWARE Nowata
DEPEW (74028) Creek(98), Lincoln(1)
DEVOL Cotton
DEWAR Okmulgee
DEWEY Washington
DIBBLE McClain
DILL CITY Washita
DISNEY Mayes
DOUGHERTY Murray
DOUGLAS Garfield
DOVER Kingfisher
DRUMMOND (73735) Garfield(98), Major(1)
DRUMRIGHT (74030) Creek(98), Payne(1)
DUKE (73532) Jackson(94), Greer(4)
DUNCAN Stephens
DURANT Bryan
DURHAM Roger Mills
DUSTIN (74839) Hughes(80), Okfuskee(14), McIntosh(4)
EAGLETOWN McCurtain
EAKLY Caddo
EARLSBORO (74840) Pottawatomie(80), Seminole(19)
EDMOND (73034) Oklahoma(77), Logan(22)
EDMOND Oklahoma
EL RENO Canadian
ELDORADO (73537) Jackson(95), Harmon(4)
ELGIN Comanche
ELK CITY Beckham
ELMER Jackson
ELMORE CITY Garvin
ENID Garfield
ERICK Beckham
EUCHA Delaware
EUFAULA (74432) McIntosh(92), Pittsburg(7)
FAIRFAX Osage
FAIRLAND Ottawa
FAIRMONT Garfield
FAIRVIEW Major
FANSHAWE Le Flore
FARGO (73840) Ellis(66), Woodward(33)
FAXON (73540) Comanche(97), Cotton(2)
FAY (73646) Blaine(44), Dewey(41), Custer(14)
FELT Cimarron
FINLEY Pushmataha
FITTSTOWN Johnston
FITTSTOWN Pontotoc
FITZHUGH Pontotoc
FLETCHER Comanche
FORGAN Beaver
FORT COBB Caddo
FORT GIBSON (74434) Muskogee(97), Wagoner(1)
FORT SILL Comanche
FORT SUPPLY (73841) Woodward(83), Ellis(13), Harper(3)
FORT TOWSON (74735) Choctaw(74), Pushmataha(25)
FOSS (73647) Washita(88), Custer(11)
FOSTER (73434) Stephens(59), Garvin(40)
FOX Carter
FOYIL Rogers
FRANCIS Pontotoc
FREDERICK Tillman
FREEDOM (73842) Woods(66), Woodward(24), Harper(9)
GAGE (73843) Ellis(95), Beaver(4)

GANS Sequoyah
GARBER Garfield
GARVIN McCurtain
GATE (73844) Beaver(51), Harper(48)
GEARY (73040) Blaine(69), Canadian(28), Adair(1)
GENE AUTRY Carter
GERONIMO (73543) Comanche(96), Cotton(3)
GLENCOE (74032) Payne(82), Pawnee(11), Noble(6)
GLENPOOL (74033) Tulsa(93), Creek(6)
GOLDEN McCurtain
GOLTRY (73739) Alfalfa(87), Garfield(12)
GOODWELL Texas
GORE (74435) Sequoyah(88), Muskogee(11)
GOTEBO (73041) Kiowa(79), Washita(20)
GOULD Harmon
GOWEN Latimer
GRACEMONT Caddo
GRAHAM Carter
GRANDFIELD Tillman
GRANITE Greer
GRANT Choctaw
GREENFIELD Blaine
GROVE Delaware
GUTHRIE Logan
GUYMON Texas
HAILEYVILLE Pittsburg
HALLETT Pawnee
HAMMON (73650) Roger Mills(74), Custer(25)
HANNA McIntosh
HARDESTY Texas
HARRAH (73045) Oklahoma(82), Lincoln(12), Pottawatomie(4)
HARTSHORNE (74547) Pittsburg(97), Latimer(2)
HASKELL (74436) Muskogee(59), Okmulgee(30), Wagoner(10)
HASTINGS (73548) Stephens(39), Jefferson(34), Cotton(25)
HAWORTH McCurtain
HAYWOOD Pittsburg
HEADRICK Jackson
HEALDTON Carter
HEAVENER Le Flore
HELENA Alfalfa
HENDRIX Bryan
HENNEPIN (73444) Carter(75), Garvin(12), Murray(12)
HENNESSEY (73742) Kingfisher(96), Garfield(3)
HENRYETTA (74437) Okmulgee(98), McIntosh(1)
HILLSDALE Garfield
HINTON (73047) Caddo(76), Canadian(23)
HITCHCOCK (73744) Blaine(92), Kingfisher(7)
HITCHITA McIntosh
HOBART Kiowa
HODGEN Le Flore
HOLDENVILLE Hughes
HOLLIS Harmon
HOLLISTER Tillman
HOMINY Osage
HONOBIA (74549) Le Flore(94), Pushmataha(5)
HOOKER Texas
HOPETON Woods
HOWE Le Flore
HOYT Haskell
HUGO Choctaw
HULBERT Cherokee
HUNTER (74640) Garfield(93), Grant(6)
HYDRO (73048) Caddo(44), Custer(36), Blaine(18)
IDABEL McCurtain
INDIAHOMA Comanche
INDIANOLA Pittsburg
INOLA (74036) Rogers(96), Mayes(3)
ISABELLA Major
JAY Delaware
JENKS Tulsa
JENNINGS (74038) Pawnee(63), Creek(36)
JET Alfalfa
JONES Oklahoma
KANSAS (74347) Delaware(97), Cherokee(2)
KAW CITY Kay
KELLYVILLE Creek
KEMP Bryan
KEMP CPO Bryan
KENEFIC (74748) Johnston(67), Bryan(18), Atoka(13)
KENTON Cimarron
KEOTA (74941) Haskell(85), Le Flore(14)
KETCHUM Mayes
KEYES Cimarron
KIAMICHI - HONOBIA CPO (74549) Le Flore(94), Pushmataha(5)
KIEFER Creek
KINGFISHER Kingfisher
KINGSTON Marshall
KINTA Haskell
KIOWA (74553) Pittsburg(71), Atoka(28)
KNOWLES Beaver
KONAWA (74849) Seminole(86), Pottawatomie(13)
KREBS Pittsburg
KREMLIN Garfield
LAHOMA (73754) Garfield(90), Major(9)
LAMAR Hughes
LAMONT (74643) Grant(92), Kay(7)
LANE Atoka
LANGLEY Mayes
LANGSTON Logan
LAVERNE (73848) Beaver(50), Harper(47), Ellis(2)
LAWTON Comanche
LEBANON Marshall
LEEDEY (73654) Dewey(62), Roger Mills(28), Custer(9)
LEFLORE Le Flore
LEHIGH (74556) Atoka(60), Coal(40)
LENAPAH Nowata
LEON Love
LEONARD Tulsa
LEQUIRE Haskell
LEXINGTON Cleveland
LINDSAY (73052) Garvin(63), McClain(31), Grady(4)
LOCO Stephens
LOCUST GROVE (74352) Mayes(82), Sequoyah(14), Wagoner(1)
LOGAN Beaver
LONE GROVE Carter
LONE WOLF (73655) Kiowa(97), Greer(2)
LONGDALE (73755) Blaine(62), Major(31), Dewey(6)
LOOKEBA Caddo
LOVELAND Tillman
LOYAL Kingfisher
LUCIEN (73757) Noble(84), Garfield(15)
LUCIEN CPO (73757) Noble(84), Garfield(15)
LUTHER (73054) Oklahoma(77), Lincoln(14), Logan(7)
MACOMB (74852) Pottawatomie(96), Cleveland(3)
MADILL (73446) Marshall(97), Carter(1)
MANCHESTER (73758) Grant(81), Alfalfa(18)
MANGUM (73554) Greer(98), Harmon(1)
MANITOU Tillman
MANNFORD (74044) Creek(69), Pawnee(30)
MANNSVILLE (73447) Johnston(97), Marshall(2)
MARAMEC (74045) Pawnee(98), Payne(1)
MARBLE CITY Sequoyah
MARIETTA Love
MARLAND Noble
MARLOW (73055) Stephens(87), Grady(10), Comanche(2)
MARSHALL (73056) Garfield(65), Logan(29), Kingfisher(4)
MARTHA Jackson
MAUD (74854) Pottawatomie(60), Seminole(39)
MAY (73851) Ellis(51), Harper(48)
MAYFIELD Beckham
MAYSVILLE (73057) Garvin(78), McClain(21)
MAZIE Mayes
MC LOUD (74851) Pottawatomie(74), Cleveland(15), Lincoln(10)
MCALESTER Pittsburg
MCCURTAIN (74944) Haskell(87), Le Flore(12)
MCLOUD (74851) Pottawatomie(74), Cleveland(15), Lincoln(10)
MEAD Bryan
MEDFORD Grant
MEDICINE PARK Comanche
MEEKER (74855) Lincoln(89), Pottawatomie(10)
MEERS Comanche
MENO Major
MERIDIAN Logan
MIAMI Ottawa
MILBURN Johnston
MILFAY Creek
MILL CREEK (74856) Johnston(91), Murray(8)
MILLERTON McCurtain
MINCO (73059) Grady(72), Canadian(14), Caddo(13)
MOFFETT Sequoyah
MONROE Le Flore
MOODYS Cherokee
MOORELAND Woodward
MORRIS Okmulgee
MORRISON Noble
MOUNDS (74047) Okmulgee(51), Creek(28), Tulsa(20)
MOUNTAIN PARK (73559) Kiowa(69), Comanche(30)
MOUNTAIN VIEW Kiowa
MOYERS Pushmataha
MULDROW Sequoyah
MULHALL (73063) Logan(83), Payne(16)
MUSE Le Flore
MUSKOGEE Muskogee
MUSTANG Canadian
MUTUAL Woodward
NARDIN (74646) Kay(89), Grant(10)
NASH (73761) Grant(93), Garfield(6)
NASHOBA Pushmataha
NEWALLA (74857) Cleveland(75), Oklahoma(23), Pottawatomie(1)
NEWCASTLE McClain
NEWKIRK Kay
NICOMA PARK Oklahoma
NINNEKAH Grady
NOBLE Cleveland
NORMAN (73072) Cleveland(95), McClain(4)
NORMAN Cleveland
NORTH MIAMI Ottawa
NOWATA Nowata
OAKHURST Tulsa
OAKS (74359) Delaware(63), Cherokee(36)
OAKWOOD (73658) Dewey(90), Blaine(9)
OCHELATA (74051) Washington(98), Osage(1)
OILTON Creek
OKARCHE (73762) Kingfisher(51), Canadian(48)
OKAY Wagoner
OKEENE (73763) Blaine(89), Major(7), Kingfisher(2)
OKEMAH (74859) Okfuskee(93), Seminole(6)
OKLAHOMA CITY (73128) Oklahoma(87), Canadian(12)
OKLAHOMA CITY (73169) Oklahoma(66), Cleveland(33)
OKLAHOMA CITY (73179) Oklahoma(86), Canadian(13)
OKLAHOMA CITY Cleveland
OKLAHOMA CITY Oklahoma
OKMULGEE Okmulgee
OKTAHA Muskogee
OLUSTEE Jackson
OMEGA (73764) Kingfisher(60), Blaine(39)
OOLOGAH Rogers
ORLANDO (73073) Logan(77), Garfield(19), Noble(2), Payne(1)
OSAGE Osage
OSCAR Jefferson
OVERBROOK (73453) Love(64), Carter(35)
OWASSO (74055) Tulsa(72), Rogers(27)
PADEN Okfuskee
PANAMA Le Flore
PANOLA Latimer
PAOLI (73074) Garvin(86), McClain(13)
PARK HILL Cherokee
PAULS VALLEY Garvin
PAWHUSKA Osage
PAWNEE Pawnee
PEGGS (74452) Cherokee(88), Mayes(11)
PERKINS (74059) Payne(96), Lincoln(3)
PERNELL Garvin
PERRY Noble
PHAROAH Okfuskee
PICHER Ottawa
PICKENS McCurtain
PIEDMONT (73078) Canadian(98), Oklahoma(1)
PITTSBURG Pittsburg
PLATTER Bryan
POCASSET (73079) Grady(91), Caddo(8)
POCOLA Le Flore
PONCA CITY (74604) Kay(70), Osage(29)
PONCA CITY Kay
POND CREEK Grant
PORTER Wagoner
PORUM (74455) Muskogee(80), McIntosh(19)
POTEAU Le Flore
PRAGUE (74864) Lincoln(74), Pottawatomie(25)
PRESTON Okmulgee
PROCTOR Adair
PRUE Osage
PRYOR Mayes
PURCELL McClain
PUTNAM (73659) Dewey(98), Custer(1)
QUAPAW Ottawa
QUINTON (74561) Pittsburg(78), Haskell(21)
RALSTON (74650) Pawnee(65), Osage(34)
RAMONA Washington
RANDLETT Cotton
RATLIFF CITY (73481) Carter(90), Stephens(6), Garvin(2)
RATLIFF CITY Carter
RATTAN Pushmataha
RAVIA Johnston
RED OAK Latimer
RED ROCK (74651) Noble(96), Pawnee(3)
REDBIRD Wagoner
RENTIESVILLE McIntosh
REYDON Roger Mills
RINGLING (73456) Jefferson(65), Carter(25), Love(8)
RINGOLD (74754) McCurtain(67), Pushmataha(30), Choctaw(2)
RINGWOOD Major
RIPLEY Payne
ROCKY (73661) Washita(97), Kiowa(2)

ROFF (74865) Pontotoc(91), Garvin(5), Murray(3)
ROLAND Sequoyah
ROOSEVELT (73564) Kiowa(97), Comanche(2)
ROSE (74364) Delaware(85), Mayes(12), Cherokee(1)
ROSSTON Harper
RUFE McCurtain
RUSH SPRINGS (73082) Grady(96), Comanche(3)
RYAN Jefferson
S COFFEYVILLE (74072) Nowata(97), Craig(2)
SAINT LOUIS Pottawatomie
SALINA (74365) Mayes(81), Delaware(18)
SALLISAW Sequoyah
SAND SPRINGS (74063) Tulsa(74), Osage(20), Creek(5)
SAPULPA (74066) Creek(98), Tulsa(1)
SAPULPA Creek
SASAKWA (74867) Seminole(95), Hughes(4)
SAVANNA Pittsburg
SAWYER Choctaw
SAYRE (73662) Beckham(97), Roger Mills(2)
SCHULTER Okmulgee
SEILING Dewey
SEMINOLE Seminole
SENTINEL Washita
SHADY POINT Le Flore
SHAMROCK Creek
SHARON Woodward
SHATTUCK Ellis
SHAWNEE Pottawatomie
SHIDLER (74652) Osage(96), Kay(3)
SKIATOOK (74070) Osage(60), Tulsa(30), Washington(9)
SLICK Creek
SMITHVILLE (74957) Le Flore(78), McCurtain(21)
SNOW Pushmataha
SNYDER (73566) Kiowa(88), Tillman(11)
SOPER Choctaw
SOUTHARD Blaine
SPARKS Lincoln
SPAVINAW (74366) Mayes(89), Delaware(10)
SPENCER Oklahoma
SPENCERVILLE (74760) Choctaw(65), Pushmataha(34)
SPERRY (74073) Tulsa(65), Osage(34)
SPIRO Le Flore
SPRINGER Carter
STERLING Comanche
STIDHAM McIntosh
STIDHAM COUNTRY CPU McIntosh
STIGLER (74462) Haskell(98), Pittsburg(1)
STILLWATER (74075) Payne(97), Noble(2)
STILLWATER Payne
STILWELL Adair
STONEWALL (74871) Pontotoc(93), Coal(2), Adair(2), Johnston(1)
STRANG Mayes
STRATFORD (74872) Garvin(58), Pontotoc(34), McClain(6)
STRINGTOWN Atoka
STROUD (74079) Lincoln(96), Creek(2)
STUART (74570) Hughes(56), Pittsburg(42), Coal(1)
SULPHUR Murray
SWEETWATER Roger Mills
SWINK Choctaw
TAFT Muskogee
TAHLEQUAH Cherokee
TALALA (74080) Rogers(82), Washington(17)
TALIHINA (74571) Le Flore(60), Latimer(33), Pushmataha(5)
TALOGA Dewey
TATUMS Carter
TECUMSEH Pottawatomie
TEMPLE Cotton
TERLTON (74081) Pawnee(94), Creek(5)
TERRAL Jefferson
TEXHOMA (73949) Cimarron(55), Texas(45)
TEXOLA Beckham
THACKERVILLE Love
THOMAS (73669) Custer(94), Blaine(3), Dewey(2)
TIPTON Tillman
TISHOMINGO Johnston
TONKAWA Kay
TRYON Lincoln
TULLAHASSEE Wagoner
TULSA (74106) Tulsa(94), Osage(5)
TULSA (74108) Tulsa(87), Wagoner(12)
TULSA (74116) Tulsa(62), Rogers(37)
TULSA (74127) Tulsa(60), Osage(39)
TULSA (74132) Tulsa(63), Creek(36)
TULSA Creek
TULSA Tulsa
TUPELO Coal
TURPIN (73950) Beaver(84), Texas(15)
TUSKAHOMA (74574) Pushmataha(51), Latimer(48)
TUSSY Carter
TUTTLE Grady
TWIN OAKS Delaware
TYRONE Texas
UNION CITY Canadian
VALLIANT (74764) McCurtain(90), Choctaw(9)
VELMA Stephens
VERA Washington
VERDEN (73092) Grady(75), Caddo(24)
VERNON McIntosh
VIAN Sequoyah
VICI (73859) Dewey(79), Woodward(17), Ellis(2)
VINITA Craig
VINSON (73571) Harmon(95), Greer(4)
WAGONER Wagoner
WAINWRIGHT Muskogee
WAKITA Grant
WALTERS (73572) Cotton(96), Comanche(3)
WANETTE (74878) Pottawatomie(88), Cleveland(11)
WANN (74083) Nowata(98), Washington(1)
WAPANUCKA (73461) Johnston(92), Atoka(7)
WARDVILLE (74576) Atoka(50), Pittsburg(50)
WARNER Muskogee
WASHINGTON McClain
WASHITA Caddo
WASHITA CPO Caddo
WATONGA Blaine
WATSON McCurtain
WATTS (74964) Adair(84), Delaware(15)
WAUKOMIS Garfield
WAURIKA Jefferson
WAYNE McClain
WAYNOKA (73860) Woods(91), Major(8)
WEATHERFORD (73096) Custer(97), Washita(2)
WEBBERS FALLS Muskogee
WELCH Craig
WELEETKA (74880) Okfuskee(97), Okmulgee(2)
WELLING Cherokee
WELLSTON (74881) Lincoln(90), Logan(9)
WELTY Okfuskee
WESTVILLE Adair
WETUMKA (74883) Hughes(98), Okfuskee(1)
WEWOKA Seminole
WHEATLAND Oklahoma
WHITEFIELD Haskell
WHITESBORO Le Flore
WILBURTON Latimer
WILLOW (73673) Greer(92), Beckham(7)
WILSON (73463) Carter(98), Love(1)
WISTER (74966) Le Flore(96), Latimer(3)
WOODWARD Woodward
WRIGHT CITY McCurtain
WYANDOTTE (74370) Ottawa(91), Delaware(8)
WYNNEWOOD Garvin
WYNONA Osage
YALE Payne
YUKON Canadian

Oklahoma - ZIP/City Cross Reference

73001-73001 ALBERT
73002-73002 ALEX
73003-73003 EDMOND
73004-73004 AMBER
73005-73005 ANADARKO
73006-73006 APACHE
73007-73007 ARCADIA
73008-73008 BETHANY
73009-73009 BINGER
73010-73010 BLANCHARD
73011-73011 BRADLEY
73012-73012 BRAY
73013-73013 EDMOND
73014-73014 CALUMET
73015-73015 CARNEGIE
73016-73016 CASHION
73017-73017 CEMENT
73018-73018 CHICKASHA
73019-73019 NORMAN
73020-73020 CHOCTAW
73021-73021 COLONY
73022-73022 CONCHO
73023-73023 CHICKASHA
73024-73024 CORN
73025-73025 COUNTYLINE
73026-73026 NORMAN
73027-73027 COYLE
73028-73028 CRESCENT
73029-73029 CYRIL
73030-73030 DAVIS
73031-73031 DIBBLE
73032-73032 DOUGHERTY
73033-73033 EAKLY
73034-73034 EDMOND
73035-73035 ELMORE CITY
73036-73036 EL RENO
73037-73037 NORMAN
73038-73038 FORT COBB
73039-73039 FOSTER
73040-73040 GEARY
73041-73041 GOTEBO
73042-73042 GRACEMONT
73043-73043 GREENFIELD
73044-73044 GUTHRIE
73045-73045 HARRAH
73046-73046 HENNEPIN
73047-73047 HINTON
73048-73048 HYDRO
73049-73049 JONES
73050-73050 LANGSTON
73051-73051 LEXINGTON
73052-73052 LINDSAY
73053-73053 LOOKEBA
73054-73054 LUTHER
73055-73055 MARLOW
73056-73056 MARSHALL
73057-73057 MAYSVILLE
73058-73058 MERIDIAN
73059-73059 MINCO
73061-73061 MORRISON
73062-73062 MOUNTAIN VIEW
73063-73063 MULHALL
73064-73064 MUSTANG
73065-73065 NEWCASTLE
73066-73066 NICOMA PARK
73067-73067 NINNEKAH
73068-73068 NOBLE
73069-73072 NORMAN
73073-73073 ORLANDO
73074-73074 PAOLI
73075-73075 PAULS VALLEY
73076-73076 PERNELL
73077-73077 PERRY
73078-73078 PIEDMONT
73079-73079 POCASSET
73080-73080 PURCELL
73081-73081 RATLIFF CITY
73082-73082 RUSH SPRINGS
73083-73083 EDMOND
73084-73084 SPENCER
73085-73085 YUKON
73086-73086 SULPHUR
73087-73087 TATUMS
73088-73088 TUSSY
73089-73089 TUTTLE
73090-73090 UNION CITY
73091-73091 VELMA
73092-73092 VERDEN
73093-73093 WASHINGTON
73094-73094 WASHITA
73094-73094 WASHITA CPO
73095-73095 WAYNE
73096-73096 WEATHERFORD
73097-73097 WHEATLAND
73098-73098 WYNNEWOOD
73099-73099 YUKON
73100-73199 OKLAHOMA CITY
73401-73403 ARDMORE
73425-73425 COUNTYLINE
73430-73430 BURNEYVILLE
73432-73432 COLEMAN
73433-73433 ELMORE CITY
73434-73434 FOSTER
73435-73435 FOX
73436-73436 GENE AUTRY
73437-73437 GRAHAM
73438-73438 HEALDTON
73439-73439 KINGSTON
73440-73440 LEBANON
73441-73441 LEON
73442-73442 LOCO
73443-73443 LONE GROVE
73444-73444 HENNEPIN
73446-73446 MADILL
73447-73447 MANNSVILLE
73448-73448 MARIETTA
73449-73449 MEAD
73450-73450 MILBURN
73453-73453 OVERBROOK
73455-73455 RAVIA
73456-73456 RINGLING
73458-73458 SPRINGER
73459-73459 THACKERVILLE
73460-73460 TISHOMINGO
73461-73461 WAPANUCKA
73463-73463 WILSON
73476-73476 PERNELL
73481-73481 RATLIFF CITY
73487-73487 TATUMS
73488-73488 TUSSY
73491-73491 VELMA
73501-73502 LAWTON

73503-73503	FORT SILL
73505-73507	LAWTON
73520-73520	ADDINGTON
73521-73522	ALTUS
73523-73523	ALTUS AFB
73526-73526	BLAIR
73527-73527	CACHE
73528-73528	CHATTANOOGA
73529-73529	COMANCHE
73530-73530	DAVIDSON
73531-73531	DEVOL
73532-73532	DUKE
73533-73536	DUNCAN
73537-73537	ELDORADO
73538-73538	ELGIN
73539-73539	ELMER
73540-73540	FAXON
73541-73541	FLETCHER
73542-73542	FREDERICK
73543-73543	GERONIMO
73544-73544	GOULD
73546-73546	GRANDFIELD
73547-73547	GRANITE
73548-73548	HASTINGS
73549-73549	HEADRICK
73550-73550	HOLLIS
73551-73551	HOLLISTER
73552-73552	INDIAHOMA
73553-73553	LOVELAND
73554-73554	MANGUM
73555-73555	MANITOU
73556-73556	MARTHA
73557-73557	MEDICINE PARK
73558-73558	MEERS
73559-73559	MOUNTAIN PARK
73560-73560	OLUSTEE
73561-73561	OSCAR
73562-73562	RANDLETT
73564-73564	ROOSEVELT
73565-73565	RYAN
73566-73566	SNYDER
73567-73567	STERLING
73568-73568	TEMPLE
73569-73569	TERRAL
73570-73570	TIPTON
73571-73571	VINSON
73572-73572	WALTERS
73573-73573	WAURIKA
73575-73575	DUNCAN
73601-73601	CLINTON
73620-73620	ARAPAHO
73622-73622	BESSIE
73624-73624	BURNS FLAT
73625-73625	BUTLER
73626-73626	CANUTE
73627-73627	CARTER
73628-73628	CHEYENNE
73632-73632	CORDELL
73638-73638	CRAWFORD
73639-73639	CUSTER CITY
73641-73641	DILL CITY
73642-73642	DURHAM
73644-73644	ELK CITY
73645-73645	ERICK
73646-73646	FAY
73647-73647	FOSS
73648-73648	ELK CITY
73650-73650	HAMMON
73651-73651	HOBART
73654-73654	LEEDEY
73655-73655	LONE WOLF
73656-73656	MAYFIELD
73658-73658	OAKWOOD
73659-73659	PUTNAM
73660-73660	REYDON
73661-73661	ROCKY
73662-73662	SAYRE
73663-73663	SEILING
73664-73664	SENTINEL
73666-73666	SWEETWATER
73667-73667	TALOGA
73668-73668	TEXOLA
73669-73669	THOMAS
73673-73673	WILLOW
73701-73706	ENID
73716-73716	ALINE
73717-73717	ALVA
73718-73718	AMES
73719-73719	AMORITA
73720-73720	BISON
73722-73722	BURLINGTON
73723-73723	BYRON
73724-73724	CANTON
73725-73725	CAPRON
73726-73726	CARMEN
73727-73727	CARRIER
73728-73728	CHEROKEE
73729-73729	CLEO SPRINGS
73730-73730	COVINGTON
73731-73731	DACOMA
73733-73733	DOUGLAS
73734-73734	DOVER
73735-73735	DRUMMOND
73736-73736	FAIRMONT
73737-73737	FAIRVIEW
73738-73738	GARBER
73739-73739	GOLTRY
73741-73741	HELENA
73742-73742	HENNESSEY
73743-73743	HILLSDALE
73744-73744	HITCHCOCK
73746-73746	HOPETON
73747-73747	ISABELLA
73749-73749	JET
73750-73750	KINGFISHER
73753-73753	KREMLIN
73754-73754	LAHOMA
73755-73755	LONGDALE
73756-73756	LOYAL
73757-73757	LUCIEN
73757-73757	LUCIEN CPO
73758-73758	MANCHESTER
73759-73759	MEDFORD
73760-73760	MENO
73761-73761	NASH
73762-73762	OKARCHE
73763-73763	OKEENE
73764-73764	OMEGA
73766-73766	POND CREEK
73768-73768	RINGWOOD
73770-73770	SOUTHARD
73771-73771	WAKITA
73772-73772	WATONGA
73773-73773	WAUKOMIS
73801-73802	WOODWARD
73832-73832	ARNETT
73834-73834	BUFFALO
73835-73835	CAMARGO
73838-73838	CHESTER
73840-73840	FARGO
73841-73841	FORT SUPPLY
73842-73842	FREEDOM
73843-73843	GAGE
73844-73844	GATE
73847-73847	KNOWLES
73848-73848	LAVERNE
73849-73849	LOGAN
73851-73851	MAY
73852-73852	MOORELAND
73853-73853	MUTUAL
73855-73855	ROSSTON
73857-73857	SHARON
73858-73858	SHATTUCK
73859-73859	VICI
73860-73860	WAYNOKA
73901-73901	ADAMS
73931-73931	BALKO
73932-73932	BEAVER
73933-73933	BOISE CITY
73937-73937	FELT
73938-73938	FORGAN
73939-73939	GOODWELL
73942-73942	GUYMON
73944-73944	HARDESTY
73945-73945	HOOKER
73946-73946	KENTON
73947-73947	KEYES
73949-73949	TEXHOMA
73950-73950	TURPIN
73951-73951	TYRONE
74001-74001	AVANT
74002-74002	BARNSDALL
74003-74006	BARTLESVILLE
74008-74008	BIXBY
74009-74009	BOWRING
74010-74010	BRISTOW
74011-74014	BROKEN ARROW
74015-74015	CATOOSA
74016-74016	CHELSEA
74017-74019	CLAREMORE
74020-74020	CLEVELAND
74021-74021	COLLINSVILLE
74022-74022	COPAN
74023-74023	CUSHING
74026-74026	DAVENPORT
74027-74027	DELAWARE
74028-74028	DEPEW
74029-74029	DEWEY
74030-74030	DRUMRIGHT
74031-74031	FOYIL
74032-74032	GLENCOE
74033-74033	GLENPOOL
74034-74034	HALLETT
74035-74035	HOMINY
74036-74036	INOLA
74037-74037	JENKS
74038-74038	JENNINGS
74039-74039	KELLYVILLE
74041-74041	KIEFER
74042-74042	LENAPAH
74043-74043	LEONARD
74044-74044	MANNFORD
74045-74045	MARAMEC
74046-74046	MILFAY
74047-74047	MOUNDS
74048-74048	NOWATA
74050-74050	OAKHURST
74051-74051	OCHELATA
74052-74052	OILTON
74053-74053	OOLOGAH
74054-74054	OSAGE
74055-74055	OWASSO
74056-74056	PAWHUSKA
74058-74058	PAWNEE
74059-74059	PERKINS
74060-74060	PRUE
74061-74061	RAMONA
74062-74062	RIPLEY
74063-74063	SAND SPRINGS
74066-74067	SAPULPA
74068-74068	SHAMROCK
74070-74070	SKIATOOK
74071-74071	SLICK
74072-74072	S COFFEYVILLE
74073-74073	SPERRY
74074-74078	STILLWATER
74079-74079	STROUD
74080-74080	TALALA
74081-74081	TERLTON
74082-74082	VERA
74083-74083	WANN
74084-74084	WYNONA
74085-74085	YALE
74100-74194	TULSA
74301-74301	VINITA
74330-74330	ADAIR
74331-74331	AFTON
74332-74332	BIG CABIN
74333-74333	BLUEJACKET
74335-74335	CARDIN
74337-74337	CHOUTEAU
74338-74338	COLCORD
74339-74339	COMMERCE
74340-74340	DISNEY
74342-74342	EUCHA
74343-74343	FAIRLAND
74344-74345	GROVE
74346-74346	JAY
74347-74347	KANSAS
74349-74349	KETCHUM
74350-74350	LANGLEY
74352-74352	LOCUST GROVE
74353-74353	MAZIE
74354-74355	MIAMI
74358-74358	NORTH MIAMI
74359-74359	OAKS
74360-74360	PICHER
74361-74362	PRYOR
74363-74363	QUAPAW
74364-74364	ROSE
74365-74365	SALINA
74366-74366	SPAVINAW
74367-74367	STRANG
74368-74368	TWIN OAKS
74369-74369	WELCH
74370-74370	WYANDOTTE
74401-74403	MUSKOGEE
74421-74421	BEGGS
74422-74422	BOYNTON
74423-74423	BRAGGS
74425-74425	CANADIAN
74426-74426	CHECOTAH
74427-74427	COOKSON
74428-74428	COUNCIL HILL
74429-74429	COWETA
74430-74430	CROWDER
74431-74431	DEWAR
74432-74432	EUFAULA
74434-74434	FORT GIBSON
74435-74435	GORE
74436-74436	HASKELL
74437-74437	HENRYETTA
74438-74438	HITCHITA
74440-74440	HOYT
74441-74441	HULBERT
74442-74442	INDIANOLA
74444-74444	MOODYS
74445-74445	MORRIS
74446-74446	OKAY
74447-74447	OKMULGEE
74450-74450	OKTAHA
74451-74451	PARK HILL
74452-74452	PEGGS
74454-74454	PORTER
74455-74455	PORUM
74456-74456	PRESTON
74457-74457	PROCTOR
74458-74458	REDBIRD
74459-74459	RENTIESVILLE
74460-74460	SCHULTER
74461-74461	STIDHAM
74461-74461	STIDHAM COUNTRY CPU
74462-74462	STIGLER
74463-74463	TAFT
74464-74465	TAHLEQUAH
74466-74466	TULLAHASSEE
74467-74467	WAGONER
74468-74468	WAINWRIGHT
74469-74469	WARNER
74470-74470	WEBBERS FALLS
74471-74471	WELLING
74472-74472	WHITEFIELD
74477-74477	WAGONER
74501-74502	MCALESTER
74521-74521	ALBION
74522-74522	ALDERSON
74523-74523	ANTLERS
74525-74525	ATOKA
74526-74526	BACHE
74528-74528	BLANCO
74529-74529	BLOCKER
74530-74530	BROMIDE
74531-74531	CALVIN
74533-74533	CANEY
74534-74534	CENTRAHOMA
74535-74535	CLARITA
74536-74536	CLAYTON
74538-74538	COALGATE

74540-74540	DAISY
74542-74542	ATOKA
74543-74543	FINLEY
74545-74545	GOWEN
74546-74546	HAILEYVILLE
74547-74547	HARTSHORNE
74548-74548	HAYWOOD
74549-74549	HONOBIA
74549-74549	KIAMICHI - HONOBIA CPO
74552-74552	KINTA
74553-74553	KIOWA
74554-74554	KREBS
74555-74555	LANE
74556-74556	LEHIGH
74557-74557	MOYERS
74558-74558	NASHOBA
74559-74559	PANOLA
74560-74560	PITTSBURG
74561-74561	QUINTON
74562-74562	RATTAN
74563-74563	RED OAK
74565-74565	SAVANNA
74567-74567	SNOW
74569-74569	STRINGTOWN
74570-74570	STUART
74571-74571	TALIHINA
74572-74572	TUPELO
74574-74574	TUSKAHOMA
74576-74576	WARDVILLE
74577-74577	WHITESBORO
74578-74578	WILBURTON
74601-74604	PONCA CITY
74630-74630	BILLINGS
74631-74631	BLACKWELL
74632-74632	BRAMAN
74633-74633	BURBANK
74636-74636	DEER CREEK
74637-74637	FAIRFAX
74640-74640	HUNTER
74641-74641	KAW CITY
74643-74643	LAMONT
74644-74644	MARLAND
74646-74646	NARDIN
74647-74647	NEWKIRK
74650-74650	RALSTON
74651-74651	RED ROCK
74652-74652	SHIDLER
74653-74653	TONKAWA
74701-74702	DURANT
74720-74720	ACHILLE
74721-74721	ALBANY
74722-74722	BATTIEST
74723-74723	BENNINGTON
74724-74724	BETHEL
74726-74726	BOKCHITO
74727-74727	BOSWELL
74728-74728	BROKEN BOW
74729-74729	CADDO
74730-74730	CALERA
74731-74731	CARTWRIGHT
74733-74733	COLBERT
74734-74734	EAGLETOWN
74735-74735	FORT TOWSON
74736-74736	GARVIN
74737-74737	GOLDEN
74738-74738	GRANT
74740-74740	HAWORTH
74741-74741	HENDRIX
74743-74743	HUGO
74745-74745	IDABEL
74747-74747	KEMP
74747-74747	KEMP CPO
74748-74748	KENEFIC
74750-74750	MILLERTON
74752-74752	PICKENS
74753-74753	PLATTER
74754-74754	RINGOLD
74755-74755	RUFE
74756-74756	SAWYER
74759-74759	SOPER
74760-74760	SPENCERVILLE
74761-74761	SWINK
74764-74764	VALLIANT
74766-74766	WRIGHT CITY
74801-74804	SHAWNEE
74818-74818	SEMINOLE
74820-74821	ADA
74824-74824	AGRA
74825-74825	ALLEN
74826-74826	ASHER
74827-74827	ATWOOD
74829-74829	BOLEY
74830-74830	BOWLEGS
74831-74831	BYARS
74832-74832	CARNEY
74833-74833	CASTLE
74834-74834	CHANDLER
74835-74835	CLEARVIEW
74836-74836	CONNERVILLE
74837-74837	CROMWELL
74838-74838	SHAWNEE
74839-74839	DUSTIN
74840-74840	EARLSBORO
74842-74842	FITTSTOWN
74843-74843	FITZHUGH
74844-74844	FRANCIS
74845-74845	HANNA
74848-74848	HOLDENVILLE
74849-74849	KONAWA
74850-74850	LAMAR
74851-74851	MC LOUD
74851-74851	MCLOUD
74852-74852	MACOMB
74854-74854	MAUD
74855-74855	MEEKER
74856-74856	MILL CREEK
74857-74857	NEWALLA
74859-74859	OKEMAH
74860-74860	PADEN
74862-74862	PHAROAH
74863-74863	FITTSTOWN
74864-74864	PRAGUE
74865-74865	ROFF
74866-74866	SAINT LOUIS
74867-74867	SASAKWA
74868-74868	SEMINOLE
74869-74869	SPARKS
74871-74871	STONEWALL
74872-74872	STRATFORD
74873-74873	TECUMSEH
74875-74875	TRYON
74877-74877	VERNON
74878-74878	WANETTE
74880-74880	WELEETKA
74881-74881	WELLSTON
74882-74882	WELTY
74883-74883	WETUMKA
74884-74884	WEWOKA
74901-74901	ARKOMA
74902-74902	POCOLA
74930-74930	BOKOSHE
74931-74931	BUNCH
74932-74932	CAMERON
74935-74935	FANSHAWE
74936-74936	GANS
74937-74937	HEAVENER
74939-74939	HODGEN
74940-74940	HOWE
74941-74941	KEOTA
74942-74942	LEFLORE
74943-74943	LEQUIRE
74944-74944	MCCURTAIN
74945-74945	MARBLE CITY
74946-74946	MOFFETT
74947-74947	MONROE
74948-74948	MULDROW
74949-74949	MUSE
74951-74951	PANAMA
74953-74953	POTEAU
74954-74954	ROLAND
74955-74955	SALLISAW
74956-74956	SHADY POINT
74957-74957	SMITHVILLE
74959-74959	SPIRO
74960-74960	STILWELL
74962-74962	VIAN
74963-74963	WATSON
74964-74964	WATTS
74965-74965	WESTVILLE
74966-74966	WISTER

General Help Numbers:

Governor's Office

State Capitol Bldg. 503-373-1027
900 Court St NE Fax 503-373-6827
Salem, OR 97301-4047 8AM-5PM
www.governor.state.or.us

Attorney General's Office

Department of Justice 503-378-4400
1162 Court St NE Fax 503-378-4017
Salem, OR 97310 8AM-5PM
www.doj.state.or.us

Legislative Records

Oregon Legislative Assembly, Legislative Publications,
900 Court St, #49 503-986-1180
Salem, OR 97301 Fax 503-373-1527
www.leg.state.or.us 8AM-5PM

State Archives

Archives Division 503-373-0701
800 Summer St NE Fax 503-373-0953
Salem, OR 97301 8AM-4:45PM
http://arcweb.sos.state.or.us

State Specifics:

Capital: Salem
Marion County

Time Zone: PST

Number of Counties: 36

Population: 3,790,060

Web Site: www.oregon.gov

State Agencies

Criminal Records

Oregon State Police, Unit 11, Identification Services Section, PO Box 4395, Portland, OR 97208-4395 (Courier address- 3772 Portland Rd NE, Bldg C, Salem, OR 97301); 503-378-3070, Fax- 503-378-2121; 8AM-5PM M-F.

http://egov.oregon.gov/OSP/ID/

Indexing & Storage: Records available from 1941 on and are computerized. New records available for inquiry in up to 8 days. Approximately 50% of all arrests in database have final dispositions recorded.

Searching: Three types of searches exist: open records search, own record search, and statutorily-required search. The latter can include an FBI fingerprint check for an additional $24.00 fee. Include in request- (for open records) name, date of birth, last known address. Submitting the SSN is helpful, but not required. Fingerprints are required only when subject submits the request. For an open record request, if record exists, person of record will be notified of the request and the record will not be released for 14 additional days. Open record info includes all records with convictions and also all arrests within the past year without disposition. Statutorily-required record searches and own record searches include all records.

Access by: mail, fax, online.

Fee & Payment: Open record search fee is $10.00 per name. A search on oneself is $33.00 and fingerprints are required. Statutorily-required searches are $28.00 ($27 if prints retained by this agency) plus FBI fingerprint fee, if required. $5.00 fee to notarize. Fee payee- Oregon State Police. Prepayment required. Personal checks accepted, credit cards are not.

Mail search: Turnaround time- 2 days.

Fax search: Requesters must be pre-approved, however records are not returned by fax.

Online search: A web based site is available for requesting and receiving criminal records. Website is ONLY for high-volume requesters who must be pre-approved. Results are posted as "No Record" or "In Process" ("In Process" means a record will be mailed in 14 days). Use the "open records" link to get into the proper site. Fee is $10.00 per record. Call 503-373-1808 x230 to receive the application, or visit the website.

Statewide Court Records

Court Administrator, Supreme Court Bldg, 1163 State St, Salem, OR 97301-2563; 503-986-5500, Fax- 503-986-5503; 8AM-5PM.

www.ojd.state.or.us/osca/index.htm

The Appellate Courts office is located at 1163 State St. The profile below indicates how to obtain records online. Otherwise, all requests must be done at the local circuit court.

Access by: online.

Online search: Appellate opinions are found at www.publications.ojd.state.or.us/. Online access through the Oregon Judicial Information Network (OJIN) includes register of cases filed in the Oregon state courts. There is a one-time setup fee of $295.00 plus usage fees of $10-13.00 per hour, plus $10 per month per user. The database contains criminal, civil, small claims, tax, and some probate records. OJIN does not contain any records from municipal or county courts. Searching is done by county, there is no statewide search available. For further information visit www.ojd.state.or.us/ojin/index.htm, or call 800-858-9658 or 503-986-5588.

Other access: Purchase of bulk record for case registers is also available, call 503-986-5588 for details.

Sexual Offender Registry

Oregon State Police, SOR Unit, 255 Capitol St SE, 4th Fl, Salem, OR 97310; 503-378-3725, Fax-503-363-5475; 8AM-5PM.

http://egov.oregon.gov/OSP/SOR/index.shtml

Email questions to Sexoffender.Questions@state.or.us. ORS 181.592 authorizes the Oregon State Police to make information about registered sex offenders available to the public.

Indexing & Storage: New records available for inquiry in up to 10 days.

Searching: As of May 2007 the Unit maintained files on 13,873 individuals who are required to register in Oregon. Include in request- name and DOB. The law allows the release of the names, DOB, photo, physical description, address or city of residence, supervising agency and phone number.

Access by: mail, phone, fax, online.

Fee & Payment: There is no fee for searches, but lists must be purchased. Fee payee- Oregon State Police, SOR Unit Prepayment required. Personal checks accepted.

Mail search: Turnaround time- up to 3 weeks.

Phone search: You can request a list or do a name check by phone. Also, you may leave you name, phone and search info, and the agency will call you back.

Fax search: Requests accepted via fax.

Online search: http://sexoffenders.oregon.gov/ for online searching of sex offenders who have been designated as Predatory. A mapping function is also offered.

Other access: Lists by city or ZIP can usually be requested for no fee, a statewide list be purchased for $85.00.

Incarceration Records

Oregon Department of Corrections, Offender Information & Sentence Computation, PO Box 5670, Wilsonville, OR 97070-5670 (Courier address- 24499 SW Grahams Ferry Rd, Bldg Z, Wilsonville, OR 97070); 503-570-6900, 503-570-6919 (Search Requests), Fax- 503-570-6902; 8AM-4PM.

www.doc.state.or.us

Indexing & Storage: Records available on current and former inmates. New records available for inquiry in up to 4 days.

Searching: Include in request- full name; DOB and SID# helpful. Location, SID number, physical identifiers, conviction and sentencing information, and release dates are provided. This data not released- medical data

Access by: mail, phone, fax, online.

Fee & Payment: Fees are charged for copies as follows: $.50 for paper, $1.25 from microfilm.

Mail search: Turnaround time- 2 to 4 weeks.

Phone search: Name searching permitted by phone.

Fax search: Same criteria as mail.

Online search: A Corrections Most Wanted list in the pull down menu box. Use imate.info@doc.state.or.us to request by email. The agency web page mentions a private company offering free web access at https://www.vinelink.com/vinelink/siteInfoAction.do?siteId=38000; includes state, DOC, and most county jails.

Other access: Bulk sale of information is available. Contact ISSD.

Corporation, LP, LLC, Trademarks/Servicemarks, Fictitious/Assumed Name

Corporation Division, Public Service Building, 255 Capital St NE, #151, Salem, OR 97310-1327; 503-986-2200, 503-986-2317 (Copy Unit), Fax-503-378-4381; 8AM-5PM.

www.filinginoregon.com

Indexing & Storage: Records available on the computer screen for 20 years after inactive. Assumed names are only available for 5 years after inactive. The records prior to 20 years ago are stored in the State Archives back to the 1800's for corporations only. New records available for inquiry immediately.

Searching: All information is public record. Include in request- full name of business. In addition to the articles of organization, business entity records available include: last annual report, Prior (merged) names, Articles of Amendment.

Access by: mail, phone, fax, in person, online.

Fee & Payment: There is no search fee. Copies cost $5.00 per business name or $15.00 if certified, otherwise there is a $1.00 fee per business name for a computer printout. A Good Standing certificate is $10.00. Fee payee- Corporation Division. Prepayment required. Personal checks, Visa, and MasterCard accepted.

Mail search: Turnaround time- 7 to 10 days. A SASE is requested.

Phone search: There is a limit of 3 searches per phone call.

Fax search: Requesters must use a credit card, turnaround time is 3 days or less.

In person: Turnaround time while you wait.

Online search: There is free access at the website for business registry information. Search by name or business registry number. Displays active and inactive records.

Other access: New business lists on email or CDs of the database are available for $50.00 per month or week. Call 503-986-2343 for more information.

Uniform Commercial Code, Federal & State Tax Liens

UCC Division, Attn: Records, 255 Capitol St NE, Suite 151, Salem, OR 97310-1327; 503-986-2200 x6, Fax- 503-373-1166; 8AM-5PM.

www.filinginoregon.com/ucc/index.htm

State tax liens on personal property are filed here; state tax liens on real property are filed at the county level.

Indexing & Storage: Records available on microfiche to 1963. New records available for inquiry in 2 to 4 days.

Searching: Use search request form UCC-11. The search includes tax liens filed here. Include in request- debtor name. This data not released- SSNs.

Access by: mail, fax, in person, online.

Fee & Payment: The search fee is $10.00 per name, with copies is $15.00 per name. A document number request is $5.00. A state seal certificate is $15.00. CD service is $20.00 per CD. Fee payee- Secretary of State. Prepayment required. Personal checks, Visa, and MasterCard accepted.

Mail search: Turnaround time- 1 to 4 days. A SASE is not needed, please do not send.

Fax search: A credit card is required. Results are mailed.

In person: Searches done while you wait.

Online search: Search the web page for information on UCC secured transactions, as well as Farm Product notices, IRS Tax Liens, Agricultural searches Liens, Agricultural Produce Liens, Grain Producer's Liens, Revenue Warrants and Employment Warrants. You can search by debtor name or by lien number. You can also download forms from here.

Other access: UCC database extracts ($200) are offered, this is full extract, not an update service. UCC images are available in bulk for $200 per week. New filings can be purchased weekly or monthly on CD, can give by type of lien for $15.00 per week.

Sales Tax Registrations

State does not impose sales tax.

Birth Certificates

Department of Human Services, Vital Records, PO Box 14050, Portland, OR 97293-0050 (Courier address- 800 NE Oregon St, #205, Portland, OR 97232); 971-673-1190 (Recorded Message), Fax-503-234-8417; 8AM-4:30PM.

http://oregon.gov/DHS/ph/chs/order/index.shtml

Indexing & Storage: Records available for 07/1903 to present. There are some delayed filed, unindexed records with DOBs from 1885 to 1904. Birth indexes prior to 1903 years available at the State Archives. New records available for inquiry in 2 to 4 weeks.

Searching: Investigative searches must have a signed, notarized release from person of record or immediate family member, unless record over 100 years old. Records only available to legal guardians & legal representatives with proof of such. Include in request- full name, names of parents, mother's full maiden name, date of birth, place of birth, relationship to person of record.

Must request "long form" if time of birth, hospital or physician's names is needed. This data not released- original birth record prior to adoption, except to adoptee over age of 21.

Access by: mail, phone, fax, in person, online.

Fee & Payment: The search fee is $20.00. Add $15.00 for each additional copy. Fee payee- DHS Vital Records Prepayment required. Personal checks and major credit cards accepted.

Mail search: Turnaround time- 2 to 3 weeks. Express mail requests are handled immediately. SASE not required.

Phone search: See expedited service.

Fax search: See expedited service.

In person: Turnaround time is under 20 minutes.

Online search: Order records online at www.vitalchek.com, a state designated vendor.

Expedited service: Fax and phone orders are billed to credit cards and processed the same or next day. There is an additional $12.50 service fee plus cost of express delivery. Turnaround time- 2 to 5 days.

Death Records

Department of Human Services, Vital Records, PO Box 14050, Portland, OR 97293-0050 (Courier address- 800 NE Oregon St, #205, Portland, OR 97232); 971-673-1190 (Recorded Message), Fax- 503-234-8417; 8AM-4:30PM.

http://oregon.gov/DHS/ph/chs/order/index.shtml

Indexing & Storage: Records available from 1903 to present. Note that requests for non-certified copies are available from State Archives for reduced fee if record is more than 50 years old (503-373-0701). New records available for inquiry in 2 to 4 weeks.

Searching: Investigative searches must have a signed, notarized release from immediate family member or legal representative or person with a personal or property right. After 50 years, a record becomes public record and there are no restrictions. Include in request- full name, date of death, place of death, relationship to person of record, reason for information request. The name of the spouse is helpful. The date of birth is helpful for common names.

Access by: mail, phone, fax, in person, online.

Fee & Payment: The search fee is $20.00 and additional copies are $15.00 each. Fee payee- DHS Vital Records. Prepayment required. Personal checks and major credit cards accepted.

Mail search: Turnaround time- 2 to 3 weeks. Express mail requests are processed immediately. SASE not required.

Phone search: See expedited service.

Fax search: See expedited service.

In person: Turnaround time is within 20 minutes.

Online search: Records from 1903-1930 are available at www.heritagetrailpress.com/Death_Index/. Order directly on VitalChek's web page at www.VitalChek.com.

Other access: Indexes are available at many state libraries.

Expedited service: Fax and phone orders are billed to credit cards and processed the same or next day. There is an additional $12.50 service fee plus cost of express delivery. Turnaround time- 2 to 5 days.

Marriage Certificates

Department of Human Services, Vital Records, PO Box 14050, Portland, OR 97293-0050 (Courier address- 800 NE Oregon St, #205, Portland, OR 97232); 971-673-1190 (Recorded Message), Fax- 503-234-8417; 8AM-4:30PM.

http://oregon.gov/DHS/ph/chs/order/index.shtml

Indexing & Storage: Records available from 1910 to present. Early records are in an abbreviated form called "Return of Marriage." Records from 1906 to 1910 and 1946- to 1956 are in State Archives. New records available for inquiry in 4 to 8 weeks.

Searching: Records less than 50 years old are only available to family members, legal representatives or those with a personal or property right. Include in request- names of husband and wife, date of marriage, place or county of marriage, and reason for request. Include daytime phone number and as many identifiers as possible. This data not released- SSN, unless record order by registrant.

Access by: mail, phone, fax, in person, online.

Fee & Payment: The search fee is $20.00, additional copies $15.00 per record. Fee payee- DHS Vital Records Prepayment required. Personal checks and major credit cards accepted.

Mail search: Turnaround time- 2 to 3 weeks. If request is expressed, it will be answered ASAP. SASE not required.

Phone search: See expedited service.

Fax search: See expedited service.

In person: Turnaround time is usually within 20 minutes.

Online search: Order online via www.vitalchek.com, a state approved vendor.

Other access: Many state libraries offer record indexes.

Expedited service: Fax and phone orders are billed to credit cards and processed the same or next day. There is an additional $12.50 service fee plus cost of express delivery. Turnaround time- 2 to 5 days.

Divorce Records

Department of Human Services, Vital Records, PO Box 14050, Portland, OR 97293-0050 (Courier address- 800 NE Oregon St, #205, Portland, OR 97232); 971-673-1190 (Recorded Message), Fax- 503-234-8417; 8AM-4:30PM.

http://oregon.gov/DHS/ph/chs/order/index.shtml

Indexing & Storage: Records available from 1925 to present. Records from 1946 to 1956 available from State Archives. New records available for inquiry in 4 to 8 weeks.

Searching: Records less than 50 years old are only available to family members, legal representatives or those with a personal or property right. Include in request- date of divorce. Also include names of husband and wife, and reason for request. This data not released- SSN, unless the record is ordered a person in the divorce.

Access by: mail, phone, fax, in person, online.

Fee & Payment: The search fee is $20.00, additional copies are $15.00 each. Fee payee- DHS Vital Records. Prepayment required. For a mail request, enclose a prepaid, self-addressed envelope for overnight carrier. Personal checks accepted. Major credit cards accepted.

Mail search: Turnaround time- 2 to 3 weeks. Send request by overnight delivery and it will be processed ASAP. SASE not required.

Phone search: See expedited service.

Fax search: See expedited services.

In person: Turnaround time is usually within 20 minutes.

Online search: Order records online at www.vitalchek.com, a state designated vendor.

Other access: Indexes are available in many Oregon libraries.

Expedited service: Fax and phone orders are billed to credit cards and processed the same or next day. There is an additional $12.50 service fee plus cost of express delivery. Turnaround time- 2 to 5 days.

Workers' Compensation Records

Department of Consumer & Business Svcs, Workers Compensation Division, PO Box 14480, Salem, OR 97309-0405 (Courier address- 350 Winter Street NE, Rm 27, Salem, OR 97301-3879); 503-947-7818, 503-947-7810 (Claim Records), 503-947-7624 (History Records), Fax- 503-947-7806; 8AM-5PM M-F.

www.cbs.state.or.us/external/wcd/

Email questions to workcomp.questions@state.or.us. Any person has a right to inspect nonexempt public records. It does not include a right to request blind searches for records not known to exist.

Indexing & Storage: Records available from 1989 to present. New records available for inquiry in 4 days or less.

Searching: Per ORS 192.502(18), claims records are exempt from public disclosure. Access to records is at the discretion of the Director. In general, those with a legitimate business purpose are granted access. Include in request- claimant name, SSN, claim number, name and address of requester. A signed release by subject is honored. Two forms may be downloaded from the web page - Request for Claim File Information and Request for Claims History.

Access by: mail, fax, in person, online.

Fee & Payment: The Department has the authority to charge for staff time and resources for any record request. Records releases only after disclosure requirements are met. Rate is $20.00 per hour and $.02 per page. Fee payee- DCBS. Prepayment required. Personal checks accepted, credit cards are not.

Mail search: Turnaround time- 14 days. SASE not required.

Fax search: Fax requests are accepted if disclosure requirements are met. Completed report may be mailed back.

In person: Completed report may need to be mailed back. Turnaround time: 1 to 14 days.

Online search: Search for employers with coverage or that have coverage ending soon at www.oregonwcd.org/compliance/ecu/empcoverage.html. Claimant names not listed, companies with 10 or fewer employees not listed. Search by claims number or by employer's claim number at http://www4.cbs.state.or.us/ex/imd/reports/rpt/index.cfm?ProgID=CE8039.

Other access: State is allowed to deliver data in other forms to parties that qualify under ORS 192.502(19).

Expedited service: Will expedite if requester agrees to payment.

Driver Records

Driver and Motor Vehicle Services, Record Services, 1905 Lana Ave, NE, Salem, OR 97314; 503-945-5000, 503-945-7950 (Establish Account), Fax- 503-945-5425; 8AM-5PM.

www.oregondmv.com

Oregon differentiates between "employment" and "non-employment" records. Ongoing requesters with a permissible use and qualify to receive personal information per state law may establish a Record Inquiry Account.

Indexing & Storage: Records available for 3 years for accidents, 5 years for minor convictions; 10 years for DUIs and major convictions; and 3 or 5 years after reinstatement for suspensions. If CMV related, 55 years. New records available for inquiry in 2-3 weeks normally.

Searching: Permissible use requesters may open a Record Inquiry Account and are then approved to access via one of the automated systems. Casual requesters who do not present written consent may receive a "sanitized record." Include in request- full name, date of birth, driver's license number. A driver's license report is available which lists the driver's name, address, date of birth, license number, issue and expiration dates, original business date, restrictions, status, and, if applicable, the ID card expiration date. This data not released- medical information, SSNs, photos, mother's maiden name, place of birth.

Access by: mail, phone, fax, online.

Fee & Payment: Fee for a 3 year non-employment driving record is $1.50; $2.00 for a 3 year employment driving record; $3.00 for a "court print" record; $1.50 per record for a driver license information report. There is a charge of $1.50 for no record found. Fee payee- DMV Services. Prepayment required, unless account holder. Personal checks accepted, credit cards are not.

Mail search: Turnaround time- 3 day from receipt. A record request form (Form 7122) and record fee list is available online. SASE not required.

Phone search: Oregon offers "IVR" (DMV's Interactive Voice Response System) to approved accounts. IRV reads information from computer files in a human sounding voice. A variety of records are available on IVR 24 hours a day. Call 503-945-7950 for more information.

Fax search: Records may be requested by fax, but only for approved account holders.

Online search: The Oregon DMV offers a Real-Time Driving Record Service (RADR) that allows qualified customers to access Oregon driving records via a real time connection through AAMVA. Records are $.50 each, including employment, non-employment, and court records. However, a one-time set-up fee of $4,500 is required. Qualified Requestors must meet technical requirements, sign an agreement, and establish a Record Inquiry Account. For more information, contact the Records Policy Unit at 503-945-8905 or 503-945-8906.

Other access: The agency offers an automated "flag program" that informs customers of activity on a name list, for approved account holders only. Call the Automated Reporting Service at 503-945-5427 for more information.

Vehicle Ownership & Registration

Driver and Motor Vehicle Services, Record Services Unit, 1905 Lana Ave, NE, Salem, OR 97314; 503-945-5000, 503-945-7950 (Record Account), 503-945-5300 (IVR), Fax- 503-945-5425; 8AM-5PM.

www.oregondmv.com

Ongoing requesters with a permissible use and qualify for personal information per state law may establish a Record Inquiry Account.

Indexing & Storage: Records available from 1963 to present for titles, 1982 to present for registration. Vehicle title and registration records are archived on microfilm and microfiche (1977 to present). New records available for inquiry in 2-3 weeks from issue.

Searching: Title and registration ownership records are open to the public, for a fee. By law, only certain entities may receive records with personal info. Casual requesters cannot obtain records with personal information without notarized consent of subject. Include in request- name and DOB, or VIN or plate. This data not released- medical information, SSNs, place of birth.

Access by: mail, phone, fax, online.

Fee & Payment: Vehicle record prints are $4.00, information given orally is $2.50 (to account holders). A complete vehicle title history is $22.50, a Previous Owner is $14.00. An insurance information search is $10.00. Generally, $2.50 is charged if no record is found. Fee payee- Driver & Motor Services (DMV). Prepayment required unless account holder. Personal checks accepted, credit cards are not.

Mail search: Turnaround time- 3 days. A SASE is helpful.

Phone search: The automated system called "IVR" is open 24 hours a day. An account is necessary. Call 503-945-7950 for more information.

Fax search: Only available to those entities that have a DMV account.

Online search: Online ordering form option of records is available, but only for approved account holders. The fillable form may be downloaded from the web page. Records are returned by fax or mail, per requester's instructions. Fes range from $4.00 to $22.50 depending on type of record needed.

Other access: Bulk lists available on cartridge to qualified accounts. Call 503-945-8906 for more information.

Accident Reports

Driver & Motor Vehicle Services Division, Accidents Reporting Unit, 1905 Lana Ave, NE, Salem, OR 97314; 503-945-5098, Fax- 503-945-5267; 8AM-5PM.

www.oregondmv.com

Police reports filed with the DMV are available. Copies of individual's reports are not, but information is provided in letter form to those involved or representing someone involved.

Indexing & Storage: Records available for 5 years to present. New records available for inquiry in 2 weeks to 3 months.

Searching: Qualified requesters include legal representatives, involved insurance companies and those involved with property damage or injury. Include in request- full name, dob, date of accident, location of accident (county). Use Request Form 7122. The police report is provided without personal information unless the requester qualifies for personal information under OR law.

Access by: mail, phone, fax, in person.

Fee & Payment: The fee is $8.50 for a police accident report. There is $8.50 charge for a "no record found." The letter described above is no charge to qualified requesters; certification is $13.00 however. Information letters (from personal reports) are $12.50 each. Fee payee- DMV Services. Prepayment required. Personal checks accepted, credit cards are not.

Mail search: Turnaround time- 3 to 5 days. SASE not required.

Phone search: This is only available for pre-approved accounts.

Fax search: This is only available for account holders. Same fees and turnaround time (3-5 days).

In person: Turnaround time will vary, record may not be available same day.

Vessel Ownership & Registration

Oregon State Marine Board, Records, PO Box 14145, Salem, OR 97309 (Courier address- 435 Commercial St NE, #400, Salem, OR 97301); 503-378-8587, Fax- 503-378-4597; 8AM-5PM M-F.

www.boatoregon.com

Lien information is shown on the title records.

Indexing & Storage: Records available from 1997 to present for titles. Records are indexed on computer beginning 1999. Records are on microfiche from the 1978 to 1998. Titles and registrations are issued on all motorized boats and on sailboats 12 ft and over. New records available for inquiry in two days.

Searching: Extremely large pleasure boats which move along the OR-WA-CA border for 60 days or more are sometimes documented with the US Coast Guard. Call 800-799-8362 for more information. Include in request- name, hull ID # or assigned OR certificate of number. Requests can be made via e-mail, from the website.

Access by: mail, phone, fax, in person.

Fee & Payment: There is no fee for one search. Fees for lists are dependent on the time involved. Copies more than 5 pages are $.25 per page. Fee payee- State Marine Board. Prepayment required. Personal checks accepted, credit cards are not.

Mail search: Turnaround time- 7 to 10 days. SASE not required.

Phone search: Limited registration information is released over the phone.

Fax search: Records are available by fax.

In person: If the search is lengthy, the results will be returned by mail.

Other access: An opt out provision is in effect if mailing lists are requested. Records are available on CD. Fee is $165, no credit cards accepted. For more information, call 503-378-2599.

Legislation Records

Oregon Legislative Assembly, Legislative Publications, 900 Court St, #49, Salem, OR 97301; 503-986-1180 (Current Bill Information), 503-373-0701 (Archives), 503-986-1000, Fax- 503-373-1527; 8AM-5PM.

www.leg.state.or.us

Indexing & Storage: Records available for current session only.

Searching: Enrolled bills are available back to 2005. Include in request- bill number, year.

Access by: mail, phone, fax, in person, online.

Fee & Payment: There are no fees for copies of current bills. Copies of enrolled bills and bills from Archives are $.25 per page copy fee and other charges depending on the search requirement. Personal checks accepted.

Mail search: Turnaround time- same day. SASE not required.

Phone search: Records are available by phone.

Fax search: Fax searching available.

In person: Simple requests may be processed while you wait.

Online search: For statutes and codes visit www.leg.state.or.us/ors/home.htm. Find text and histories of measures at the Internet site for no charge. Go to www.leg.state.or.us:8765/. Also, http://arcweb.sos.state.or.us/banners/legis.htm is a great resource.

Voter Registration

Access to Records is Restricted.

Secretary of State, Elections Division, 141 State Capitol, Salem, OR 97310; 503-986-1518, Fax-503-373-7414; 8AM-5PM.

www.sos.state.or.us/elections/

Records cannot be purchased for commercial reasons. Individual records must be researched at the county.

GED Certificates

Dept of Community Colleges/ Workforce Development, Oregon GED Program, 255 Capitol St NE, 3rd Fl, Salem, OR 97310; 503-378-8648 x369, Fax- 503-378-8434; 8AM-5PM M-F.

www.oregon.gov/CCWD/GED/index.shtml

A request form is available at the webpage. Use their search button and type in GED, or email to request a form.

Indexing & Storage: Records available from 1946.

Searching: To verify, the following is a required: name at time of test, date/year of test, DOB, and SSN. If a copy of a transcript is requested, include the above plus a signed release and fee.

Access by: mail, fax, in person, online.

Fee & Payment: There is no fee for verification. Copies of transcripts are $5.00 each. Fee payee- Oregon GED Program Prepayment required. Money orders are accepted. Personal checks accepted, credit cards are not.

Mail search: Turnaround time- 7-10 business days. SASE not required.

Fax search: Fax requests from employers, schools, or agencies accepted with signed release.

In person: Turnaround time is typically 5 minutes.

Online search: For records from 2002 forward, online access is available with the access code provided by the testing center.

Expedited service: Turnaround time- 24 hours. Rush service provided if pre-paid, pre-addressed shipping materials given.

Hunting & Fishing License Information

Fish & Wildlife Department, Licensing Division, 3406 Cherry Ave NE, Salem, OR 97303; 503-947-6101, Fax- 503-947-6117; 8AM-5PM.

www.dfw.state.or.us

Indexing & Storage: Records available from 1996 on computer. New records available for inquiry in 24 hours.

Searching: Include in request- full name, DOB. Fishing licenses and hunting licenses are in the same building in different divisions. This data not released- phone numbers or SSNs.

Access by: mail, fax, in person.

Fee & Payment: The fee for a search is $10.00 for a certified record. If extensive research involved, $28.00 per hour charged, billed in 15 minute increments. Copy fee is $.25 per page first 10, then $.50 per page. Fee payee- O.D.F.W. Prepayment required. Personal checks accepted. Visa/MC/Discover accepted.

Mail search: Turnaround time- 1 to 3 days. SASE not required.

Fax search: Same fees and turnaround time as mail requests. Fax fee is $.30 per page if returned.

In person: Records are usually returned by mail.

Other access: This agency will release bulk data on list or CD for a fee. Fee is $25. plus either cost of the CD or the cost per page. Fax information requests to 503-947-6265 or call the number listed above.

Oregon State Licensing Agencies

For details about the agency responsible for licensing/certifying/registering an item below or in the Agency Quick Finder section, match an item's number with the number of the agency in the *Licensing Agency Information* section.

Oregon Licenses Searchable Online

Acupuncturist #29 .... www.bme.state.or.us/search.html
Animal Euthanasia Tech./Facility #54 .... http://ovmeb.oregonlookups.com
Animal Feed (Livestock) #22 .... http://egov.oregon.gov/ODA/license.shtml
Animal Food Processor #22 .... http://egov.oregon.gov/ODA/license.shtml
Architect #6 .... http://orbae.com/orbae/index.php/search-licensees
Architectural Firm #6 .... http://orbae.com/orbae/index.php/search-licensees
Athletic Trainer #49 .... https://elite.hlo.state.or.us/elitepublic/LPRBrowser.aspx
Attorney #43 .... www.osbar.org/members/start.asp
Audiologist #33 .... http://bspa.oregonlookups.com
Auditor, Municipal #5 .... http://boahost.com/egovlicsearch.lasso
Bakery #23 .... http://egov.oregon.gov/ODA/license.shtml
Barber #7 .... https://elite.hlo.state.or.us/elitepublic/
Body Piercer #7 .... https://elite.hlo.state.or.us/elitepublic/
Brand (Livestock) #22 .... http://egov.oregon.gov/ODA/license.shtml
Brand Inspector #22 .... http://egov.oregon.gov/ODA/license.shtml
Chiropractor/Chiropractic Assistant #8 .... http://obce.alcsoftware.com/liclookup.php
Christmas Tree Grower #25 .... www.oregon.gov/ODA/PLANT/NURSERY/index.shtml
Construction Contractor/Subcontr. #21 .... https://ccbed.ccb.state.or.us/ccb_frames/consumer_info/
Cosmetologist #7 .... https://elite.hlo.state.or.us/elitepublic/
Counselor, Professional #28 .... www.oblpct.state.or.us/OBLPCT/type.shtml
Crematorium #52 .... www.oregon.gov/MortCem/2005_Directory_abbrev_PartA.pdf
Dairy Establishment #23 .... http://egov.oregon.gov/ODA/license.shtml
Dental Hygienist #51 .... http://obd.oregonlookups.com/
Dentist #51 .... http://obd.oregonlookups.com/
Denture Technologist #49 .... https://elite.hlo.state.or.us/elitepublic/LPRBrowser.aspx
Denturist #9 .... https://elite.hlo.state.or.us/elitepublic/LPRBrowser.aspx
Diagnostic Radiologic Technologist #39 .... http://obrt.oregonlookups.com/
Dietitian #11 .... http://bld.oregonlookups.com/
Direct Entry Midwife #49 .... https://elite.hlo.state.or.us/elitepublic/LPRBrowser.aspx
Dog Racing Occupation #42 .... http://licenseinfo.oregon.gov/
Drug Manufacturer/Wholesaler #15 .... http://my.oregon.gov/pharmacy_search/searchResults-submit.do
Drug Outlet, Over-the-Counter #15 .... http://my.oregon.gov/pharmacy_search/searchResults-submit.do
Egg Handler/Breaker #23 .... http://egov.oregon.gov/ODA/license.shtml
Electrologist #7 .... https://elite.hlo.state.or.us/elitepublic/
Electrology Instructor/School #7 .... https://elite.hlo.state.or.us/elitepublic/
Embalmer/Embalmer Apprentice #52 .... www.oregon.gov/MortCem/2005_Directory_abbrev_PartA.pdf
Engineer #10 .... www.osbeels.org
Environmental Health Specialist #49 .... https://elite.hlo.state.or.us/elitepublic/LPRBrowser.aspx
Escrow Agent/Agency #46 .... http://outside.rea.state.or.us/weblookup/
Facial Technician/Technologist #7 .... https://elite.hlo.state.or.us/elitepublic/
Farm Labor Contractor #21 .... http://licenseinfo.oregon.gov/
Fertilizer/Mineral/Lime Registrant #24 .... http://oda.state.or.us/dbs/licenses/search.lasso?&division=pest
Florist #25 .... www.oregon.gov/ODA/PLANT/NURSERY/index.shtml
Food Establishment, Retail #23 .... http://egov.oregon.gov/ODA/license.shtml
Food Exporter/Processing Facility #23 .... http://egov.oregon.gov/ODA/license.shtml
Food Producer/Distributor #23 .... http://egov.oregon.gov/ODA/license.shtml
Food Storage Facility #23 .... http://egov.oregon.gov/ODA/license.shtml
Forest Labor Contractor #21 .... http://licenseinfo.oregon.gov/
Frozen Desert-related Industry #23 .... http://egov.oregon.gov/ODA/license.shtml
Funeral Establishment #52 .... www.oregon.gov/MortCem/2005_Directory_abbrev_PartA.pdf
Funeral Service Practitioner/Apprent' #52 .... www.oregon.gov/MortCem/2005_Directory_abbrev_PartA.pdf
Geologist #12 .... www.oregon.gov/OSBGE/registrants.shtml
Geologist, Engineering #12 .... www.oregon.gov/OSBGE/registrants.shtml
Greenhouse Grower- herbac's plant #25 .... www.oregon.gov/ODA/PLANT/NURSERY/index.shtml
Hair Salon #7 .... https://elite.hlo.state.or.us/elitepublic/
Hair Stylist/Hairdresser #7 .... https://elite.hlo.state.or.us/elitepublic/
Hearing Aid Dealer/Dispenser #2 .... http://elite.hlo.state.or.us/elitepublic/

Hearing Aid Specialist #49 .... https://elite.hlo.state.or.us/elitepublic/LPRBrowser.aspx
Home Inspector #21 .... https://ccbed.ccb.state.or.us/ccb_frames/consumer_info/
Horse Racing Occupation #42 .... http://licenseinfo.oregon.gov/
Insurance Adjuster #27 .... http://www4.cbs.state.or.us/ex/ins/inslic/agent/
Insurance Agency #27 .... www.cbs.state.or.us/external/imd/database/inslic/agency_main.htm
Insurance Agent #27 .... http://www4.cbs.state.or.us/ex/ins/inslic/agent/
Insurance Company #27 .... www.cbs.state.or.us/external/imd/database/inslic/comp_main.htm
Insurance Consultant #27 .... http://www4.cbs.state.or.us/ex/ins/inslic/agent/
Landscape Architect #50 .... www.oregon.gov/LANDARCH/registrants.shtml
Landscaper #25 .... www.oregon.gov/ODA/PLANT/NURSERY/index.shtml
Livestock-Related Business #22 .... http://egov.oregon.gov/ODA/license.shtml
Lobbyist #40 .... www.oregon.gov/OGEC/public_records.shtml
Manicurist/Nail Technician #7 .... https://elite.hlo.state.or.us/elitepublic/
Marriage & Family Therapist #28 .... www.oblpct.state.or.us/OBLPCT/type.shtml
Massage Therapist #38 .... http://obmt.oregonlookups.com/index.asp
Measuring Device #20 .... http://oda.state.or.us/dbs/search.lasso#msd
Medical Doctor/Surgeon #29 .... www.bme.state.or.us/search.html
Milk Hauler/Milk Stabilizer/Handler #23 .... http://egov.oregon.gov/ODA/license.shtml
Motor Fuel Quality #20 .... http://oda.state.or.us/dbs/search.lasso#msd
Nail Technician #7 .... https://elite.hlo.state.or.us/elitepublic/
Naturopathic Physician #34 .... http://obne.oregonlookups.com/
Non-Alcoholic Beverage Plant #23 .... http://egov.oregon.gov/ODA/license.shtml
Notary Public #37 .... www.filinginoregon.com/notary/
Nurse #13 .... www.osbn.state.or.us/search/searchResults-submit.do
Nurse-LPN #13 .... www.osbn.state.or.us/search/searchResults-submit.do
Nursery Dealer #25 .... www.oregon.gov/ODA/PLANT/NURSERY/index.shtml
Nursery Stock/Native Plant Collector #25 .... www.oregon.gov/ODA/PLANT/NURSERY/index.shtml
Nursing Assistant #13 .... www.osbn.state.or.us/search/searchResults-submit.do
Nursing Home Administrator #35 .... http://nhabd.oregonlookups.com
Occupational Therapist #36 .... http://otlb.oregonlookups.com
Occupational Therapy Assistant #36 .... http://otlb.oregonlookups.com
Optometrist #14 .... www.oregonobo.org/doctorinfo.htm
Oral Pathology Endorsement #9 .... https://elite.hlo.state.or.us/elitepublic/LPRBrowser.aspx
Oregon Product #22 .... http://egov.oregon.gov/ODA/license.shtml
Osteopathic Physician/Surgeon #29 .... www.bme.state.or.us/search.html
Permanent Color Technician #7 .... https://elite.hlo.state.or.us/elitepublic/
Pesticide Applicator/Trainee #24 .... http://oda.state.or.us/dbs/licenses/search.lasso?&division=pest
Pesticide Dealer/Consultant #24 .... http://oda.state.or.us/dbs/licenses/search.lasso?&division=pest
Pesticide Product #24 .... http://oda.state.or.us/dbs/licenses/search.lasso?&division=pest
Pharmacy/Pharmacist #15 .... http://my.oregon.gov/pharmacy_search/searchResults-submit.do
Physical Therapist/Assistant #45 .... http://ptlb.oregonlookups.com/
Physician #29 .... www.bme.state.or.us/search.html
Physician Assistant #29 .... www.bme.state.or.us/search.html
Podiatrist #29 .... www.bme.state.or.us/search.html
Political Candidate Statement #40 .... www.oregon.gov/OGEC/public_records.shtml
Polygraph Examiner #18 .... www.oregon.gov/DPSST/SC/Polygraph.shtml
Property Manager #46 .... http://outside.rea.state.or.us/weblookup/
Psychologist #16 .... http://obpe.alcsoftware.com/liclookup.php
Psychologist Associate #16 .... http://obpe.alcsoftware.com/liclookup.php
Public Accountant-CPA #5 .... http://boahost.com/egovlicsearch.lasso
Public Accounting Firm #5 .... http://boahost.com/egovlicsearch.lasso
Pump Installation Contr., Limited #21 .... www.cbs.state.or.us/bcd/licensing.html
Radiologic Technologist Ltd Permit #39 .... http://obrt.oregonlookups.com/
Radiologic Therapy Technologist #39 .... http://obrt.oregonlookups.com/
Real Estate Agent/Seller #46 .... http://outside.rea.state.or.us/weblookup/
Real Estate Appraiser #4 .... http://oregonaclb.org/index.php?option=com_content&task=view&id=20&Itemid=112
Real Estate Branch Office #46 .... http://outside.rea.state.or.us/weblookup/
Real Estate Broker #46 .... http://outside.rea.state.or.us/weblookup/
Refrigerated Plant #23 .... http://egov.oregon.gov/ODA/license.shtml
Respiratory Care Practitioner #32 .... https://elite.hlo.state.or.us/elitepublic/LPRBrowser.aspx
Respiratory Therapist #49 .... https://elite.hlo.state.or.us/elitepublic/LPRBrowser.aspx
Sanitarian #47 .... http://elite.hlo.state.or.us/elitepublic/
Shellfish-related Industry #23 .... http://egov.oregon.gov/ODA/license.shtml
Sign Contractor, Limited #21 .... www.cbs.state.or.us/bcd/licensing.html
Slaughterhouse #23 .... http://egov.oregon.gov/ODA/license.shtml

Social Worker, Clinical #48 .... http://bcsw.oregonlookups.com/
Speech Language Pathologist #33 .... http://bspa.oregonlookups.com
Speech-Language Pathology Ass't #33 .... http://bspa.oregonlookups.com
Surveyor, Land #10 .... www.osbeels.org
Tattoo Artist #49 .... https://elite.hlo.state.or.us/elitepublic/LPRBrowser.aspx
Therapeutic Radiologic Technologist #39 .... http://obrt.oregonlookups.com/
Transaction Verification #20 .... http://oda.state.or.us/dbs/search.lasso#msd
Veterinarian #54 .... http://ovmeb.oregonlookups.com
Veterinary Clinic, Livestock #22 .... http://egov.oregon.gov/ODA/license.shtml
Veterinary Product, Livestock #22 .... http://egov.oregon.gov/ODA/license.shtml
Veterinary Technician #54 .... http://ovmeb.oregonlookups.com
Waste Water System Operator #1 .... www.deq.state.or.us/wq/OpCert/opcert.htm
Water Rights Examiner #10 .... www.osbeels.org
Weighing Device #20 .... http://oda.state.or.us/dbs/search.lasso#msd

Oregon Licensing Quick Finder

Acupuncturist #29 971-673-2700
Aircraft Registration #3 503-378-4880
Airport/Aircraft Landing Area #3 503-378-6275
Amusement Ride Inspector #19 503-378-4133
Animal Euthanasia Tech./Facility #54 971-673-0224
Animal Feed (Livestock) #22 503-986-4691
Animal Food Processor #22 503-986-4680
Architect #6 503-378-4270
Architectural Firm #6 503-378-4270
Athletic Trainer #49 503-378-8667
Attorney #43 503-620-0222
Audiologist #33 971-673-0220
Auditor, Municipal #5 503-378-4181
Bakery #23 503-986-4720
Bank #26 503-378-4140
Bank Registered Agent #26 503-378-4140
Barber #7 503-378-8667
Body Piercer #7 503-378-8667
Boiler Welder #19 503-373-1268
Boilermaker #19 503-373-1268
Boxer #44 503-378-6999
Brand (Livestock) #22 503-986-4681
Brand Inspector #22 503-986-4681
Brewery #41 503-872-5124
Building Official #19 503-373-1248
Building Service Mechanic #19 503-373-1268
Cemetery #52 971-673-1507
Charter School Teacher #53 503-378-3584
Check/Money Order Seller #26 503-378-4140
Chiropractor/Chiropractic Assistant #8 503-378-5816
Christmas Tree Grower #25 503-986-4644
Collection Agency #26 503-378-4140
Construction Contractor/Subcontr. #21 .... 503-378-4621 x4900
Consumer Finance Company #26 503-378-4140
Corrections Officer #18 503-378-2100
Cosmetologist #7 503-378-8667
Counselor, Professional #28 503-378-5499
Court Reporter #31 503-986-5500
Credit Service Organization #26 503-378-4140
Credit Union #26 503-378-4140
Crematorium #52 971-673-1507
Dairy Establishment #23 503-986-4720
Debt Consolidating Agency #26 503-378-4140
Dental Hygienist #51 971-673-3200
Dental Specialist #51 971-673-3200
Dentist #51 971-673-3200
Denture Technologist #49 503-378-8667
Denturist #9 503-378-8667
Diagnostic Radiologic Techn'l'gist #39 971-673-0215
Dietitian #11 971-673-0190
Digital Signature Authority #26 503-378-4140
Direct Entry Midwife #49 503-378-8667
Dog Racing Occupation #42 971-673-0207
Drug Manufacturer/Wholesaler #15 971-673-0001
Drug Outlet, Over-the-Counter #15 971-673-0001
Egg Handler/Breaker #23 503-986-4720
Electrical Installation #19 503-373-1268
Electrician #19 503-373-1268
Electrician, Maintenance #19 503-373-1268
Electrologist #7 503-378-8667
Electrology Instructor/School #7 503-378-8667
Elevator Journeyman, Limited #19 503-373-1268
Embalmer/Embalmer Apprentice #52 971-673-1507
EMD #18 503-378-2100
Endowment Care #26 503-378-4140
Energy Technician, Ltd/Restric'd #19 503-373-1268
Engineer #10 503-362-2666
Environmental Health Specialist #49 503-378-8667
Escrow Agent/Agency #46 503-378-4170
Facial Technician/Technologist #7 503-378-8667
Farm Labor Contractor #21 503-731-4200
Fertilizer/Mineral/Lime Registrant #24 503-986-4600
Firefighter #18 503-378-2100
Florist #25 503-986-4644
Food Establishment, Retail #23 503-986-4720
Food Exporter/Processing Facility #23 503-986-4720
Food Producer/Distributor #23 503-986-4720
Food Storage Facility #23 503-986-4720
Forest Labor Contractor #21 503-731-4200
Frozen Desert-related Industry #23 503-986-4720
Funeral Establishment #52 971-673-1507
Funeral Plan, Prearranged #26 503-378-4140
Funeral Pre-Need Salesperson #52 971-673-1507
Funeral Service Practitioner/Apprentice #52 971-673-1507
Geologist #12 503-566-2837
Geologist, Engineering #12 503-566-2837
Greenhouse Grower- herbaceous plant #25 503-986-4644
Hair Salon #7 503-378-8667
Hair Stylist/Hairdresser #7 503-378-8667
Hearing Aid Dealer/Dispenser #2 503-378-8667
Hearing Aid Specialist #49 503-378-8667
Heliport #3 503-378-6275
Home Inspector #21 .... 503-378-4621 x4900
Horse Racing Occupation #42 971-673-0207
Immediate Disposition Company #52 971-673-1507
Inspector, Building Code #19 503-373-1248
Inspector, Structural/Mechanical #19 503-373-1248
Insurance Adjuster #27 503-947-7981
Insurance Agency #27 503-947-7981
Insurance Agent #27 503-947-7981
Insurance Company #27 503-947-7982
Insurance Consultant #27 503-947-7981
Interpreter, Legal #31 503-986-5695
Investment Advisor #26 503-378-4140
Landscape Architect #50 503-589-0093
Landscape Business #21 503-986-6561
Landscaper #25 503-986-4644
Liquor Control #41 503-872-5000
Liquor Salesman/Agent #41 503-872-5123
Liquor, Wide Shipper #41 503-872-5124
Livestock-Related Business #22 503-986-4680
Lobbyist #40 503-378-5105
Manicurist/Nail Technician #7 503-378-8667
Mfg'd Housing Construction #19 503-373-1248
Marriage & Family Therapist #28 503-378-5499
Massage Therapist #38 503-365-8657
Measuring Device #20 503-986-4670
Medical Doctor/Surgeon #29 971-673-2700
Medical Examiner #51 503-280-6061
Milk Hauler/Milk Stabilizer/Handler #23 503-986-4720
Money Transmitter #26 503-378-4140
Mortgage Banker/Broker/Lender #26 503-378-4140
Motor Fuel Quality #20 503-986-4670
Nail Technician #7 503-378-8667
Naturopathic Physician #34 971-673-0193
Non-Alcoholic Beverage Plant #23 503-986-4720
Notary Public #37 503-986-2593
Nurse #13 971-673-0685
Nurse-LPN #13 971-673-0685
Nursery Dealer #25 503-986-4644
Nursery Stock/Plant Collector #25 503-986-4644
Nursing Assistant #13 971-673-0685
Nursing Home Administrator #35 971-673-0196
Occupational Therapist #36 971-673-0198
Occupational Therapy Assistant #36 971-673-0198
Oil Module #19 503-373-1268
Optometrist #14 503-399-0662
Oral Pathology Endorsement #9 503-378-8667
Oregon Product #22 503-986-4680
Osteopathic Physician/Surgeon #29 971-673-2700
Parole/Probation Officer #18 503-378-2100
Pawnbroker #26 503-378-4140
Permanent Color Technician #7 503-378-8667
Pesticide Applicator/Trainee #24 503-986-4600
Pesticide Dealer/Consultant #24 503-986-4600
Pesticide Product #24 503-986-4600
Pharmacy/Pharmacist #15 971-673-0001
Physical Therapist/Assistant #45 971-673-0200
Physician #29 971-673-2700
Physician Assistant #29 971-673-2700
Pilot #3 503-378-6275
Plans Examiner #19 503-373-1248
Plumber #19 503-373-1268
Podiatrist #29 971-673-2700
Police Chief #18 503-378-2100
Police Officer #18 503-378-2100
Political Candidate Statement #40 503-378-5105
Polygraph Examiner #18 503-378-2100
Pre-Need Salesperson #52 971-673-1507
Pressure Vessel Installer #19 503-373-1268
Private Security Officer #18 503-378-2100
Property Manager #46 503-378-4170
Psychologist #16 503-378-4154
Psychologist Associate #16 503-378-4154
Public Accountant-CPA #5 503-378-4181

Public Accounting Firm #5 503-378-4181
Pump Installation Contr., Limited #21 .. 503-731-4072
Radiologic Technologist Ltd Permit #39 971-673-0215
Radiologic Therapy Technologist #39 .. 971-673-0215
Real Estate Agent/Seller #46 503-378-4170
Real Estate Appraiser #4 503-485-2555
Real Estate Branch Office #46 503-378-4170
Real Estate Broker #46 503-378-4170
Refrigerated Plant #23 503-986-4720
Respiratory Care Practitioner #32 .... 503-378-8667 x4330
Respiratory Therapist #49 503-378-8667
Sanitarian #47 503-378-8667
Savings & Loan Association #26 503-378-4140
School Administrator #53 503-378-3584
School Counselor #53 503-378-3584
School Nurse #53 503-378-3584
School Psychologist #53 503-378-3584
Securities Broker/Dealer/Seller #26 503-378-4140
Shellfish-related Industry #23 503-986-4720
Sign Contractor, Limited #21 503-731-4072
Sign Journeyman, Electrical #19 503-373-1268
Slaughterhouse #23 503-986-4720
Social Worker, Clinical #48 503-378-5735
Special Qualifications Corporation #26 503-378-4140
Speech Language Pathologist #33 971-673-0220
Speech-Language Pathology Ass't #33 971-673-0220
Stage Journeyman, Electrical #19 503-373-1268
Steamfitter #19 503-373-1268
Surveyor, Land #10 503-362-2666
Tattoo Artist #49 503-378-8667
Tax Consultant/Preparer #17 503-378-4034
Teacher #53 503-378-3584
Telecommunicator #18 503-378-2100
Therapeutic Radiologic Techn'gist #39. 971-673-0215
Transaction Verification #20 503-986-4670
Travel Agent #26 503-378-4140
Trust Company #26 503-378-4140
Veterinarian #54 971-673-0224
Veterinary Clinic, Livestock #22 503-986-4680
Veterinary Product, Livestock #22 503-986-4680
Veterinary Technician #54 971-673-0224
Waste Water System Operator #1 503-229-5622
Water Heater Installer, Limited #19 503-373-1268
Water Right #30 503-986-0900
Water Rights Examiner #10 503-362-2666
Water Treatment Installer #19 503-373-1268
Water Well Constructor #30 503-986-0900
Weighing Device #20 503-986-4670
Winery #41 503-872-5124
Wrestler #44 503-378-6999

Oregon Licensing Agency Information

#1 Department of Environmental Quality, Operator Certification Program, Water Quality Division, 811 SW 6th Ave, Portland, OR 97204; 503-229-5696, Fax- 503-229-6124. Hours- 8AM-5PM. www.oregon.gov/DEQ/WQ/index.shtml

#2 Health Licensing Agency, Advisory Council on Hearing Aids, 700 Summer St NE, #320, Salem, OR 97301-1287; 503-378-8667, Fax- 503-585-9114. Hours- 8AM-4:30PM. www.oregon.gov/OHLA Search data at- http://elite.hlo.state.or.us/elitepublic/

#3 Department of Aviation, Aeronautics Section, 3040 25th S SE, Salem, OR 97302-1125; 503-378-4880, Fax- 503-373-1688. Hours- 8AM-5PM. www.aviation.state.or.us/

#4 Appraiser Certification & Licensure Board, 3000 Market St NE, #541, Salem, OR 97301; 503-485-2555, Fax- 503-485-2559. http://oregonaclb.org Search data at- http://oregonaclb.org/index.php?option=com_content&task=view&id=20&Itemid=112

#5 Board of Accountancy, 3218 Pringle Rd SE, #110, Salem, OR 97302-6307; 503-378-4181, Fax- 503-378-3575. Hours- 8AM-5PM. http://egov.oregon.gov/BOA/

#6 Board of Architect Examiners, 205 Liberty St NE, #A, Salem, OR 97301; 503-763-0662, Fax- 503-364-0510. Hours- 8AM-4:30PM. www.orbae.com Search data at- http://orbae.com/orbae/index.php/search-licensees

#7 Health Licensing Agency, Board of Barbers & Hairdressers, 700 Summer St NE, #320, Salem, OR 97301-1287; 503-378-8667, Fax- 503-585-9114. Hours- 8AM-5PM. www.oregon.gov/OHLA Search data at- http://elite.hlo.state.or.us/elitepublic/

#8 Board of Chiropractic Examiners, 3218 Pringle Rd SE, #150, Salem, OR 97302-6311; 503-378-5816, Fax- 503-362-1260. Hours- 8AM-5PM. www.oregon.gov/OBCE/

#9 Board of Denture Technology, 700 Summer St NE, #320, Salem, OR 97301-1287; 503-378-8667, Fax- 503-585-2114. 8AM-4:30PM. www.oregon.gov/HLO/DT/ Search data at- https://elite.hlo.state.or.us/elitepublic/LPRBrowser.aspx

#10 Board of Examiners for Engineer & Land Surveyors, 670 Hawthorne Ave SE, #220, Salem, OR 97301; 503-362-2666, Fax- 503-362-5454. www.osbeels.org

#11 Board of Examiners of Licensed Dietitians, 800 NE Oregon St, #21, Ste 407, Portland, OR 97232; 971-673-0190, Fax- 971-673-0226. Hours- 8AM-5PM. www.bld.state.or.us Search data at- http://bld.oregonlookups.com/ Will sell/provide lists.

#12 Oregon State Board of Geologist Examiners, Sunset Center South, 1193 Royvonne Ave SE, #24, Salem, OR 97302; 503-566-2837, Fax- 503-485-2947. www.oregon.gov/OSBGE/ Search data at- www.oregon.gov/OSBGE/registrants.shtml

#13 Board of Nursing, 17938 SW Upper Boones Ferry Rd, Portland, OR 97224-7012; 971-673-0685, Fax- 971-673-0684. Hours- 8AM-4:30PM. www.oregon.gov/OSBN/ Search data at- www.osbn.state.or.us/search/searchResults-submit.do

#14 Board of Optometry, PO Box 13967, Salem, OR 97309-1967; 503-399-0662, Fax- 503-399-0705. www.oregonobo.org Search data at- www.oregonobo.org/doctorinfo.htm

#15 Board of Pharmacy, 800 NE Oregon St #150, Portland, OR 97232-2162; 971-673-0001, Fax- 971-673-0002. Hours- 8AM-4:30PM. www.pharmacy.state.or.us Search data at- http://my.oregon.gov/pharmacy_search/searchResults-submit.do

#16 Board of Psychologist Examiners, 3218 Pringle Rd SE, #130, Salem, OR 97302-6309; 503-378-4154, Fax- 503-378-3575. Hours- 8AM-5PM. www.obpe.state.or.us Search data at- http://obpe.alcsoftware.com/liclookup.php

#17 Board of Tax Practitioners, 3218 Pringle Rd SE, #120, Salem, OR 97302-6308; 503-378-4034, Fax- 503-378-3575. Hours- 8AM-5PM. www.oregon.gov/OTPB/

#18 Department of Public Safety Standards & Training, 4190 Aumsville Hwy, Salem, OR 97317; 503-378-2100, Fax- 503-378-3306. http://oregon.gov/DPSST/

#19 Department of Consumer & Business Svcs, Building Codes Division, PO Box 14470 (1535 Edgewater NW), Salem, OR 97309-0404; 503-378-4133, Fax- 503-378-2322. www.cbs.state.or.us/bcd/ Search data at- www.cbs.state.or.us/bcd/public_records_request.html

#20 Department of Agriculture, Measurements Standards Division, 635 Capitol St NE, Salem, OR 97301-2532; 503-986-4670, Fax- 503-986-4784. Hours- 8AM-5PM. http://oregon.gov/ODA/MSD/index.shtml Data at- http://oda.state.or.us/dbs/search.lasso#d

#21 Construction & Landscape Contractors Boards, PO Box 14140, 700 Summer St NE #300, Salem, OR 97309-5052; 503-378-4621 x4900, Fax- 503-373-2007. Hours- 8AM-5PM. www.ccb.state.or.us 24-hour Contractor Inquiry Line - 503-378-4610 or 888-366-5635.

#22 Department of Agriculture, Animal Health & Identification Division (State Vet.), 635 Capitol St NE, Salem, OR 97301-2532; 503-986-4680, Fax- 503-986-4734. 8AM-5PM. www.oregon.gov/ODA/AHID/ Search data at- http://egov.oregon.gov/ODA/license.shtml

#23 Department of Agriculture, Food Safety Division, 635 Capitol St NE, Salem, OR 97301-2523; 503-986-4720, Fax- 503-986-4729. http://egov.oregon.gov/ODA/FSD/ Search data at- http://egov.oregon.gov/ODA/license.shtml Updated weekly. Mailing labels available as database formatted ASCII files.

#24 Department of Agriculture, Pesticides Division, 635 Capitol St NE, Salem, OR 97301; 503-986-4635, Fax- 503-986-4735. Hours- 8AM-5PM. http://oregon.gov/ODA/PEST/ Search data at- http://oda.state.or.us/dbs/licenses/search.lasso?&division=pest

#25 Department of Agriculture, Plant Division, 635 Capitol St NE, Salem, OR 97310-0110; 503-986-4640, Fax- 503-986-4786. www.oregon.gov/ODA/PLANT/NURSERY/index.shtml Search data at- www.oregon.gov/ODA/PLANT/NURSERY/index.shtml

#26 Department of Consumer & Business Svcs, Division of Finance and Corporate Securities, 350 Winter St NE, Labor & Industries Bldg, Rm 410, Salem, OR 97301-3881; 503-378-4140, Fax- 503-947-7862. Hours- 8AM-5PM. www.cbs.state.or.us/external/dfcs/ Search data at- www.oregon.gov/DCBS/online.shtml

#27 Department of Consumer and Business Svcs, Insurance Division, PO Box 14480 (350 Winter St NE, Rm 440), Salem, OR 97309-0405; 503-947-7980, Fax- 503-378-4351. Hours- 8AM-5PM. www.insurance.oregon.gov Search data at- http://www4.cbs.state.or.us/ex/ins/inslic/agent/

#28 Licensed Professional Counselors & Therapists, 3218 Pringle Rd SE, #250, Salem, OR 97302-6312; 503-378-5499. Hours- 8AM-5PM. www.oblpct.state.or.us Search data at- www.oblpct.state.or.us/OBLPCT/type.shtml They provide downloadable labels and lists of professionals. They provide a $6.00 disk for labels or a $6.00 annual directory.

#29 Board of Medical Examiners, 1500 SW 1st Ave, #620, Portland, OR 97201; 971-673-2700, Fax- 971-673-2670. Hours- 8AM-5PM. www.oregon.gov/OMB/ Search data at- www.oregon.gov/OMB/online.shtml

#30 Water Resources Department, 725 Summer St NE, #A, Salem, OR 97301-1271; 503-986-0900, Fax- 503-986-0904. Hours- 8AM-5PM. www.wrd.state.or.us

#31 Judicial Department, Office of the State Court Administrator, 1163 State St, Supreme Court Building, Salem, OR 97301-2563; 503-986-5500, Fax- 503-986-5503. www.ojd.state.or.us

#32 Respiratory Therapist Licensing Board, 700 Summer St NE, #320, Salem, OR 97310-1287; 503-378-8667 x4330, F- 503-370-9114. 8AM-4:30PM. www.oregon.gov/HLO/RT/ Search data at- https://elite.hlo.state.or.us/elitepublic/LPRBrowser.aspx

#33 Board of Examiners for Speech-Language Pathology & Audiology, 800 NE Oregon St #407, State Office Bldg, Portland, OR 97232-2162; 971-673-0220, Fax- 971-673-0226. Hours- 8AM-5PM. http://egov.oregon.gov/BSPA/ Search data at- http://bspa.oregonlookups.com

#34 Naturopathic Board of Examiners, 800 NE Oregon, #407, Portland, OR 97232; 971-673-0193, Fax- 971-673-0226. Hours- 8AM-4:30PM. www.oregon.gov/OBNE/index.shtml Search data at- http://obne.oregonlookups.com/

#35 Board of Examiners of Nursing Home Administrators, 800 NE Oregon, #407, Portland, OR 97232; 971-673-0196, Fax- 971-673-0226. Hours- 7AM-4PM. www.oregon.gov/OHLA/NHABD/index.shtml Search data at- http://nhabd.oregonlookups.com

#36 Occupational Therapy Licensing, 800 NE Oregon St, #407, Portland, OR 97232; 971-673-0198, Fax- 971-673-0226. Hours- 8AM-5PM. www.otlb.state.or.us Search data at- http://otlb.oregonlookups.com

#37 Office of Secretary of State, 255 Capitol St NE, #151, Salem, OR 97310-1327; 503 986 2200, Fax- 503-986-2300. Hours- 8AM-5PM. www.filinginoregon.com/notary/

#38 Board of Massage Technicians, 748 Hawthorne Ave NE, Salem, OR 97301-4675; 503-365-8657, Fax- 503-385-4465. Hours- 8AM-4:30PM. www.oregon.gov/OBMT/ Search data at- http://obmt.oregonlookups.com/index.asp

#39 Board of Radiologic Technology, 800 NE Oregon St, #1160A, Portland, OR 97232; 971-673-0215, Fax- 971-673-0218. Hours- 8AM-4PM. www.oregon.gov/RadTech/index.shtml

#40 Government Standards & Practices Commission, Government Ethics Commission, 3218 Pringle Rd SE, #220, Salem, OR 97301-2522; 503-378-5105, Fax- 503-373-1456. Hours- 8AM-5PM. www.gspc.state.or.us Search data at- www.oregon.gov/OGEC/public_records.shtml Search by year.

#41 Liquor Control Commission, 9079 SE McLoughlin Blvd, Milwaukie, OR 97222-7355; 503-872-5000, Fax- 503-872-5266. 8AM-5PM. www.oregon.gov/OLCC/index.shtml

#42 Racing Commission, 800 NE Oregon St, #310, Portland, OR 97232; 971-673-0207, Fax- 971-673-0213. Hours- 8AM-5PM. http://racing.oregon.gov Search data at- http://licenseinfo.oregon.gov/

#43 State Bar Association, PO Box 231935 (16037 SW Upper Boones Ferry Rd), Tigard, OR 97281-1935; 503-620-0222, Fax- 503-684-1366. www.osbar.org Search data at- www.osbar.org/members/start.asp

#44 Boxing & Wrestling Commission, 3400 State St, #G750, Salem, OR 97301; 503-378-6999, Fax- 503-304-9157. Hours- 8AM-5PM. http://oregon.gov/OSP/GAMING/b_w_welcome.shtml

#45 Physical Therapist Licensing Board, 800 NE Oregon St, #407, Portland, OR 97232-2187; 971-673-0200, Fax- 971-673-0226. Hours- 8AM-4:30PM. www.ptboard.state.or.us

#46 Real Estate Agency, 1177 Center St NE, Salem, OR 97301-2505; 503-378-4170, Fax- 503-378-2491. Hours- 8AM-5PM. www.rea.state.or.us Search data at- http://outside.rea.state.or.us/weblookup/

#47 Health Licensing Agency, Sanitarians Registration Board, 700 Summer St NE, #320, Salem, OR 97301-1287; 503-378-8667, Fax- 503-585-9114. www.oregon.gov/OHLA Search data at- http://elite.hlo.state.or.us/elitepublic/

#48 Board of Clinical Social Workers, 3218 Pringle Rd SE, #240, Salem, OR 97302-6310; 503-378-5735, Fax- 503-373-1427. Hours- 8AM-5PM. www.oregon.gov/BCSW/

#49 Health Licensing Agency, Admin Svcs Division Manager, 700 Summer St NE, #320, Salem, OR 97310-1287; 503-378-8667, Fax- 503-585-9114. Hours- 8AM-4:30PM. www.oregon.gov/OHLA/ Search data at- https://elite.hlo.state.or.us/elitepublic/LPRBrowser.aspx

#50 Landscape Architect Board, 1193 Royvonne Ave SE, #24, Salem, OR 97302; 503-589-0093, Fax- 503-485-2947. Hours- 8AM-5PM. www.oregon.gov/LANDARCH/

#51 Board of Dentistry, 1600 SW 4th Ave, #770, Portland, OR 97201; 971-673-3200, Fax- 971-673-3202. Hours- 7:30AM-4:30PM. http://egov.oregon.gov/Dentistry/ Search data at- http://obd.oregonlookups.com/

#52 Mortuary & Cemetery Board, 800 NE Oregon, #430, Portland, OR 97232-2195; 971-673-1500, Fax- 971-673-1501. Hours- 7:30AM-4PM. www.oregon.gov/MortCem/ Search data at- http://licenseinfo.oregon.gov/

#53 Teacher Standards & Practices Commission, 465 Commercial St NE, Salem, OR 97301; 503-378-3586, Fax- 503-378-4448. Hours- 7:30AM-5:30PM. www.tspc.state.or.us Search data at- www.tspc.state.or.us/lookup_query.asp?op=9&id=0

#54 Veterinary Medical Board, 800 NE Oregon, #407, Portland, OR 97232; 971-673-0224, Fax- 971-673-0226. 7:30AM-5PM. www.oregon.gov/OVMEB/ Search data at- http://ovmeb.oregonlookups.com

Oregon Federal Courts

The following list indicates the district and division name for each county in the state. If the bankruptcy court location is different from the district court, then the location of the bankruptcy court appears in parentheses.

Oregon County/Court Cross Reference

County	Court	County	Court
Baker	Portland	Lake	Medford (Eugene)
Benton	Eugene	Lane	Eugene
Clackamas	Portland	Lincoln	Eugene
Clatsop	Portland	Linn	Eugene
Columbia	Portland	Malheur	Portland
Coos	Eugene	Marion	Eugene
Crook	Portland	Morrow	Portland
Curry	Medford (Eugene)	Multnomah	Portland
Deschutes	Eugene (Portland)	Polk	Portland (Eugene)
Douglas	Eugene	Sherman	Portland
Gilliam	Portland	Tillamook	Portland
Grant	Portland	Umatilla	Portland
Harney	Portland	Union	Portland
Hood River	Portland	Wallowa	Portland
Jackson	Medford (Eugene)	Wasco	Portland
Jefferson	Portland	Washington	Portland
Josephine	Medford (Eugene)	Wheeler	Portland
Klamath	Medford (Eugene)	Yamhill	Portland

Standards for Federal Courts: Fees are standard unless noted in profile. Search fee is $26.00 per item (one party name or case number). Copy fee is $.50 per page. Certification fee is $9.00 per document, double for exemplification, if available. Most courts require prepayment. Mail requests should enclose a SASE unless otherwise noted. Before releasing records, all courts require prepayment, unless noted.

District courts index by defendant and plaintiff and by case number. Bankruptcy courts usually index by debtor and case number. While most courts now have their indexes on computer, many may still maintain index card files as well. Courts will archive closed case files at different times.

There are numerous public access programs available to online subscribers. Search the U.S. Party/Case Index to find party names and case numbers among all courts. Individual case data is provided on PACER. A search of CM/ECF provides copies of cases filed electronically. For details about PACER, the US Party/Case Index, and CM/ECF see the Appendix or go to http://pacer.psc.uscourts.gov or call 800-676-6856.

US District Court

Eugene Division Court Clerk, 405 E 8th Ave #2100, Eugene, OR 97401-2712, 541-431-4100; Fax- 541-431-4109. Hours- 8:30AM-4:30PM. www.ord.uscourts.gov

Counties: Benton, Coos, Deschutes, Douglas, Lane, Lincoln, Linn, Marion.

Searches/Indexing: Full name required in search request. Results do not include SSN or DOB. The Documentation index may have DOBs on judgments. Will not fax back documents. New cases are in the index immediately after filing date. Computer index maintained; criminal goes back to 1990, civil to 1988. See microfiche index for criminal records pre-1986. District-wide searches available here. Case files sent to archives 3-5 years after closed.

Search Access: Only docket info is available by phone. **Mail:** Search usually completed- 2-5 days. SASE not required. **In person:** 2 public terminals available. No self-serve copier. **Payment:** Pay by Visa/MC (in person only), money order, cashier's or personal check. Payee: Clerk, US District Court.

E-Services: PACER records go back to 9/1988. New records online immediately. ECF at https://ecf.ord.uscourts.gov. **Opinions Online:** www.ord.uscourts.gov/rulings/rulings.html. A few selected recent rulings only. **Online Note:** Written opinions also available on ECF no extra charge; PACER account required.

Medford Division Court Clerk, 201 James A Redden US Courthouse, 310 W 6th St, Medford, OR 97501, 541-608-8777; Fax- 541-608-8779. Hours-8:30AM-4:30PM. www.ord.uscourts.gov

Counties/Note: Curry, Jackson, Josephine, Klamath, Lake. Court set up in 4/1994; Cases prior to that time were tried in Eugene.

Searches/Indexing: Full name required in search request. Results do not include SSN or DOB. The Documentation index may have DOBs on judgments. Will not fax back documents. New cases are in the index 1 day after filing date. Computer index back to 1980s; microfiche also maintained. District-wide searches available here. Case files sent to archives 3-4 years after closed.

Search Access: Only docket info is available by phone. **Mail:** Search usually completed- 2-5 days. SASE not required. **Fax:** Fax search requests accepted, if prepaid. **In person:** 1 public terminal available. No self-serve copier. **Payment:** Pay by Visa/MC (in person only), money order, cashier's or personal check. Payee: Clerk, USDC.

E-Services: PACER records go back to 9/1988. New records online after 5 days. ECF at https://ecf.ord.uscourts.gov. **Opinions Online:** www.ord.uscourts.gov/rulings/rulings.html. A few selected recent rulings only. **Online Note:** Written opinions also available on ECF no extra charge; PACER account required.

Portland Division Court Clerk, 740 US Courthouse, 1000 SW 3rd Ave, Portland, OR 97204-2902, 503-326-8000; records- 503-326-8020; crim dockets- 503-326-8003; civil dockets- 503-326-8008; Fax- 503-326-8010. Hours-8:30AM-4:30PM. www.ord.uscourts.gov

Counties/Note: Baker, Clackamas, Clatsop, Columbia, Crook, Gilliam, Grant, Harney, Hood River, Jefferson, Malheur, Morrow, Multnomah, Polk, Sherman, Tillamook, Umatilla, Union, Wallowa, Wasco, Washington, Wheeler, Yamhill. There is an unstaffed office in Pendleton, 104 SW Dorian Ave; records at Portland Court.

Searches/Indexing: Full name required in search request. Results do not include SSN or DOB. The Documentation index may have DOBs on judgments. Will not fax back documents. New cases are in the index 24-48 hours after filing date. Computer index back to 1980; microfiche also maintained. All civil cases after 8/88 and all criminal cases after 3/91 maintained here. District-wide searches available here. Case files sent to archives 2-3 years after closed.

Search Access: If case number is provided by phone, docket info is released. **Mail:** Search usually completed- 2-5 days. SASE not required. **Fax:** Will accept fax requests with case number only. **In person:** 2 public terminals available. Self-serve copier available.

Payment: Pay by Visa/MC (in person only), money order, cashier's or personal check. Payee: Clerk, USDC.

E-Services: PACER records go back to 9/1988. New records online after 24-48 hours. ECF at https://ecf.ord.uscourts.gov. **Opinions Online:** www.ord.uscourts.gov/rulings/rulings.html. A few selected recent rulings only. **Online Note:** Written opinions also available on ECF no extra charge; PACER account required.

US Bankruptcy Court

Eugene Division Court Clerk, 405 E 8th Ave, #2600, Eugene, OR 97401, 541-431-4000. Hours-9AM-4:30PM. www.orb.uscourts.gov

Counties/Note: Benton, Coos, Curry, Deschutes, Douglas, Jackson, Josephine, Klamath, Lake, Lane, Lincoln, Linn, Marion.

Searches/Indexing: Search request requires name, also DOB, SSN, other personal identifiers. Results include last 4 SSN digits. Will not fax back documents. New cases are in the index immediately after filing date. Both computer and card indexes maintained. Case files sent to archives irregularly after at least 6 months.

Search Access: Only docket info available by phone. Voice Case Information Service available, call VCIS at 800-726-2227 or 503-326-2249. **Mail:** SASE not required. **In person:** 2 public terminals available. Self-serve copies $.15 each.

Payment: Pay by money order, cashier's check. Payee: Clerk, US Bankruptcy Court.

E-Svcs: PACER- http://pacer.orb.uscourts.gov. PACER records go back to 1989. New records online after one day. ECF at https://ecf.orb.uscourts.gov. **Opinions Online:** www.orb.uscourts.gov/Judges/SearchOpinions.cfm. **Online Note:** Access judges' calendars by judge name and creditor meetings at main website under Calendars.

Portland Division Court Clerk, 1001 SW 5th Ave, #700, Portland, OR 97204, 503-326-1500. Hours-9AM-4:30PM. www.orb.uscourts.gov

Counties/Note: Baker, Clackamas, Clatsop, Columbia, Crook, Gilliam, Grant, Harney, Hood River, Jefferson, Malheur, Morrow, Multnomah, Polk, Sherman, Tillamook, Umatilla, Union, Wallowa, Wasco, Washington, Wheeler, Yamhill.

Searches/Indexing: Search request requires name, also DOB, SSN, other personal identifiers. Results include last 4 SSN digits. Will not fax back documents. New cases are in the index immediately after filing date. Both computer and card indexes maintained. Case files sent to archives irregularly after at least 6 months.

Search Access: Only docket info is available by phone. Voice Case Information Service available, call VCIS at 800-726-2227 or 503-326-2249. **Mail:** Search usually completed- 1-2 days. Include SASE for return. **In person:** 2 public terminals available. Self-serve copies $.15 each.

Payment: Pay by money order, cashier's check. Payee: Clerk, US Bankruptcy Court.

E-Svcs: PACER- http://pacer.orb.uscourts.gov. PACER records go back to 1989. New records online after one day. ECF at https://ecf.orb.uscourts.gov. **Opinions Online:** www.orb.uscourts.gov/Judges/SearchOpinions.cfm. **Online Note:** Access judges' calendars by judge name and creditor meetings at main website under Calendars.

Oregon County Courts

Court	Jurisdiction	No. of Courts	How Organized
Circuit Courts*	General	38	27 Districts
County Courts*	Probate	7	7 Counties
Justice Courts	Municipal	30	
Municipal Courts	Municipal	135	
Tax Court	Special	1	

* Profiled in this Sourcebook.

	CIVIL								
Court	Tort	Contract	Real Estate	Min. Claim	Max. Claim	Small Claims	Estate	Eviction	Domestic Relations
Circuit Courts*	X	X	X	$0	No Max	$5000	X	X	X
County Courts*							X		X
Justice Courts	X	X	X			$5000			
Municipal Courts									
Tax Court									

	CRIMINAL				
Court	Felony	Misdemeanor	DWI/DUI	Preliminary Hearing	Juvenile
Circuit Courts*	X	X	X	X	X
County Courts*					X
Justice Courts		X	X	X	
Municipal Courts		X	X		

Administration

Court Administrator, Supreme Court Building, 1163 State St, Salem, OR, 97301-2563; 503-986-5500, Fax: 503-986-5503. (PST) www.ojd.state.or.us/osca/index.htm

Court Structure

Oregon has two types of state trial courts, the Circuit Courts, which are general jurisdiction courts, and the Oregon Tax Court, whose jurisdiction is limited to cases involving taxes.

Only seven counties, all east of the Cascades, have County Courts: Gilliam, Sherman and Wheeler (both juvenile and probate jurisdiction); Grant, Harney, and Malheur (probate only); and Morrow (juvenile only).

Divorce records are found at the Circuit Court.

The Municipal Courts and Justice Courts oversee minor misdemeanor, traffic, and ordinance cases.

Online Access

Online computer access is available through the Oregon Judicial Information Network (OJIN) which includes cases filed in the Circuit courts. Searching is done by county, there is no statewide search available. There is a one-time setup fee of $295.00 plus usage fees of $10-13.00 per hour, plus $10 per month per user. The database contains criminal, civil, small claims, tax, domestic, usually probate when not at the county court, and some but not all juvenile records. However, it does not contain any records from municipal or county courts. For further information visit www.ojd.state.or.us/ojin, or call 800-858-9658 or 503-986-5588.

Appellate opinions are found at www.publications.ojd.state.or.us.

Searching Tips, Fees, and Other Guidelines

Many Oregon courts indicated that using in person searchers would markedly improve request turnaround time as court offices are understaffed or spread very thin to handle mail requests. Most Circuit Courts with computerized records have public access terminals using the OJIN system. Most records offices close from Noon to 1PM Oregon time for lunch. No staff is available during that period.

The copy fee is generally $.25 per page, the certification fee is $5.00. The courts are permitted to charge $2.00 for the first page and $1.00 for ea add'l page for both incoming and outgoing faxes, but many courts choose not to fax. Prepayment required unless othewise noted.

Baker County

Circuit Court 1995 3rd St, #220, Baker City, OR 97814; 541-523-6305; criminal fax: 541-523-9738; civil fax: same; 8AM-N, 1-5PM. ***Felony, Misdemeanor, Civil, Probate, Divorce, Divorce.*** www.ojd.state.or.us/baker

Probate fax is same as main fax number.

Civil Records: Access: Phone, fax, mail, in person, online. Both court and visitors may perform in person searches. No search fee. Required to search: name, years to search. Civil cases indexed by defendant, plaintiff; index on computer from 1987, archives back to 1865. Mail turnaround time 10 days. Civil PAT goes back to 1987. PAT civil results show middle initial. Index online at the statewide OJIN system, call 800-858-9658 for information.

Criminal Records: Access: Phone, fax, mail, in person, online. Both court and visitors may perform in person searches. No search fee. Required to search: name, years to search. Criminal records computerized from 1987, archives back to 1865. Mail turnaround time 10 days. Criminal PAT goes back to same as civil. PAT results show middle initial, DOB. Online access to criminal records is the same as civil; results show middle initial, DOB.

General Information: Online identifiers in results same as on public terminal. No adoption, mental, juvenile or sealed records released. Fee to fax out file $2.00 1st page; $1.00 each add'l. Court makes copy: $.25 per page. Cert fee: $5.00 per doc. Payee: State of Oregon. Personal checks accepted. Credit cards accepted in person. Mail requests: SASE required.

Benton County

Circuit Court Box 1870, 120 NW 4th St, Corvallis, OR 97339; 541-766-6828; probate phone: 541-766-6825; fax: 541-766-6028; 8AM-N, 1-5PM. ***Felony, Misdemeanor, Civil, Eviction, Small Claims, Probate, Divorce.*** www.ojd.state.or.us/benton

Civil Records: Access: Phone, mail, online, in person. Both court and visitors may perform in person searches. No search fee. Required to search: name, years to search; also helpful: address. Civil cases indexed by defendant, plaintiff, case number. Civil records on computer from 1993, archives and microfiche back to the 1900s. Mail turnaround time up to 1 week. Civil PAT goes back to 1988. Public terminal located outside Rm 106. Results include address if entered. Index online at the statewide OJIN system, call 800-858-9658 for information.

Criminal Records: Access: Phone, mail, online, in person. Both court and visitors may perform in person searches. No search fee. Required to search: name, years to search, DOB, offense; also helpful: address, SSN, case number. Criminal records computerized from 1993, archives and microfiche back to the 1900s. Mail turnaround time up to 1 week. Criminal PAT goes back to same as civil. PAT results show middle initial, DOB. Public terminal located outside Rm 106. Results include address if entered. Online access to criminal records is the same as civil. Criminal index goes back to 1985. Online results show middle initial, DOB.

General Information: No adoption, juvenile, sealed by judge, expunged, mental health records released. Will not fax documents. Court makes copy: $.25 per page. Certification fee: $5.00; Exemplification certificates (3 part cert) $10.00 for cert plus $.25 for each page copied. Payee: State of Oregon. Personal checks accepted. Major credit cards and debit cards accepted. Mail requests: SASE required.

Clackamas County

Circuit Court 807 Main St, Oregon City, OR 97045; 503-655-8447; criminal phone: 503-655-8643; civil phone: 503-655-8447; probate phone: 503-655-8623; 8AM-5PM. ***Felony, Misdemeanor, Civil, Eviction, Small Claims, Probate, Divorce.*** www.ojd.state.or.us/cla/index.htm

Records Management: 503-650-3036.

Civil Records: Access: Mail, in person, online. Only the court performs in person searches; visitors may not. Search fee: $15.00 per hour after first 10 minutes. Required to search: name, years to search, DOB, type of document. Civil cases indexed by defendant, plaintiff; index on computer from 1986, microfilm indexing available 1985 and older, all case types. Mail turnaround time 4-6 weeks. Civil PAT goes back to 1986. PAT civil results show middle initial. Index online at the statewide OJIN system, call 800-858-9658 for information.

Criminal Records: Access: Mail, in person, online. Only the court performs in person searches; visitors may not. Search fee: $15.00 per hour after first 10 minutes. Required to search: name, years to search, DOB. Criminal records computerized from 1986. Mail turnaround time 4-6 weeks. Criminal PAT available. PAT criminal results show middle initial. Index remotely online on the statewide OJIN system, call 800-858-9658 for information.

General Information: No adoption, juvenile, sealed by judge, expunged, mental health records released. Will not fax out nor accept faxes. Court makes copy: $.25 per page. Certification fee: $5.00 per document plus copy fee; exemplification fee $10.00 per document. Payee: State of Oregon. Personal checks accepted. Credit cards only accepted in person. Mail requests: SASE required.

Clatsop County

Circuit Court Box 835, Astoria, OR 97103; 503-325-8583; criminal phone: 503-325-8536; civil phone: 503-325-8555; probate phone: 503-325-8555; criminal fax: 503-325-8677; civil fax: 503-325-9300; 8AM-5PM. ***Felony, Misdemeanor, Civil, Eviction, Small Claims, Probate, Divorce, Traffic.*** www.ojd.state.or.us/clt/index.html

Probate fax- 503-325-9300

Civil Records: Access: Phone, mail, online, in person. Both court and visitors may perform in person searches. No search fee. Required to search: name, years to search. Civil cases indexed by defendant, plaintiff; index on computer from 1987, archives back to 1900. Mail turnaround time 2 weeks. Civil PAT goes back to 1987. Index online at the statewide OJIN system, call 800-858-9658 for information.

Criminal Records: Access: Phone, mail, online, in person. Both court and visitors may perform in person searches. No search fee. Required to search: name, years to search, DOB. Criminal records computerized from 1987, archives back to 1900. Mail turnaround time 2 weeks. Criminal PAT goes back to same as civil. Online access to criminal records is same as civil.

General Information: No adoption, juvenile, sealed by judge, expunged, or mental health records released. Fee to fax out file $5.00 1st page; $1.00 each add'l. Court makes copy: $.25 per page. Certification fee: $5.00 per certification. Payee: Clatsop County Circuit Court. Personal checks and credit cards accepted. Mail requests: SASE required.

Columbia County

Circuit Court Columbia County Courthouse, 230 Strand St, St. Helens, OR 97051; 503-397-2327; probate phone: same; fax: 503-397-3226; 8AM-5PM. ***Felony, Misdemeanor, Civil, Eviction, Small Claims, Probate, Divorce.*** www.ojd.state.or.us/col/

Civil Records: Access: Mail, fax, online, in person. Both court and visitors may perform in person searches. Search fee: Depends upon amount of data needed. Required to search: name, years to search; also helpful: SSN, DOB, address. Civil cases indexed by defendant, plaintiff; index on computer from 9/1987, archives back to 1900. Mail turnaround time 5-7 days. Civil PAT goes back to 1987. Index online at the statewide OJIN system, call 800-858-9658 for information.

Criminal Records: Access: Mail, fax, online, in person. Both court and visitors may perform in person searches. Search fee: Depends upon amount of data needed. Required to search: name, years to search, DOB; also helpful: address, SSN, signed release. Criminal records computerized from 9/1987, archives back to 1900. Mail turnaround time 5-7 days. Criminal PAT goes back to 1987. Online access to criminal records is the same as civil.

General Information: No adoption, juvenile, sealed by Judge, expunged, mental health records released. Will fax documents $2.00 1st page, $1.00 each add'l. Court makes copy: $.25 per page. Certification fee: $5.00 plus copy fee; exemplified copy fee $10.00. Payee: State of Oregon. Personal checks accepted. Visa/MC accepted. Mail requests: SASE required.

Coos County

Circuit Court Courthouse, Coquille, OR 97423; 541-396-3121; criminal phone: X402; civil phone: X401; probate phone: 541-756-2020x556; fax: 541-396-3456; 8AM-N,1-5PM. ***Felony, Misdemeanor, Civil, Eviction, Small Claims, Probate, Divorce.*** http://cooscurrycourts.org

Eviction, Small Claims and Probate records are available at 541-756-2020 ext 556. Probate fax- 541-756-1727. Circuit Court Annex at 1975 McPherson, North Bend, OR 97459.

Civil Records: Access: Phone, mail, online, in person. Both court and visitors may perform in person searches. No search fee. Required to search: name, years to search; also helpful: address. Civil cases indexed by defendant, plaintiff; index on computer from 1987, archives back to 1800. Mail turnaround time 1-2 days. Civil PAT goes back to 1987. Index online at the statewide OJIN system, call 800-858-9658 for information.

Criminal Records: Access: Phone, mail, online, in person. Both court and visitors may perform in person searches. No search fee. Required to search: name, years to search, DOB; also helpful: address, SSN. Criminal records computerized from 1987, archives back to 1800. Mail turnaround time 1-2 days. Criminal PAT goes back to same as civil. Online access to criminal records is same as civil.

General Information: Online identifiers in results same as on public terminal. No adoption, sealed by Judge, expunged, paternity or mental health records released. Will fax documents for a fee. Court makes copy: $.25 per page. Self serve: same. Certification fee: $5.00; exemplified copy- $10.00. Payee: State Courts. Personal checks and credit cards accepted. Mail requests: SASE required.

Crook County

Circuit Court Crook County Courthouse, 300 NE 3rd St, Prineville, OR 97754; 541-447-6541; fax: 541-447-5116; 8AM-Noon; 1PM-5PM. ***Felony, Misdemeanor, Civil, Eviction, Small Claims, Probate, Divorce.*** www.ojd.state.or.us/cro/

Civil Records: Access: Phone, fax, mail, in person, online. Both court and visitors may perform in person searches. No search fee. Required to search: name, years to search; also helpful: address. Civil cases indexed by defendant, plaintiff; index on computer from 1986, microfiche from 1907, archives from 1907. Mail turnaround time 2-4 days. Public use terminal available, records go back to 1987. PAT results show name only. Index online at the statewide OJIN system, call 800-858-9658 for information.

Criminal Records: Access: Phone, fax, mail, in person, online. Both court and visitors may perform in person searches. No search fee. Required to search: name, years to search, DOB; also helpful: address, SSN. Criminal records computerized from 1986, microfiche from 1907, archives from 1907. Mail turnaround time 2-4 days. Public use terminal available, crim records go back to 1987. PAT results show name only. Online access to criminal records is the same as civil.

General Information: Online identifiers in results same as on public terminal. No adoption, juvenile, sealed by Judge, expunged, paternity or mental health records released. Will fax documents $2.00 1st page, $1.00 ea add'l. This also applies to incoming faxes. Court makes copy: $.25 per page. Certification fee: $5.00 per doc. Payee: State of Oregon. Personal checks and credit cards accepted. Mail requests: SASE required.

Curry County

Circuit Court PO Box 810, 29821 Ellensburg Ave., Gold Beach, OR 97444; 541-247-4511; 8AM-N, 1-5PM M,T,W,F; 8AM-N, 1:30-5PM TH. ***Felony, Misdemeanor, Civil, Eviction, Small Claims, Probate, Divorce.*** www.cooscurrycourts.org

Civil Records: Access: Phone, mail, online, in person. Both court and visitors may perform in person searches. No search fee. Required to search:

name, years to search; also helpful: address. Civil cases indexed by defendant, plaintiff; index on computer from 1987, archives back to 1891. Mail turnaround time 1-2 days. Civil PAT goes back to 1987. Index online at the statewide OJIN system, call 800-858-9658 for information.

Criminal Records: Access: Phone, mail, online, in person. Both court and visitors may perform in person searches. No search fee. Required to search: name, years to search, DOB; also helpful: address, SSN. Criminal records computerized from 1987, archives back to 1891. Mail turnaround time 1-2 days. Criminal PAT goes back to same as civil. Online access to criminal records is same as civil.

General Information: No adoption, sealed by Judge, expunged, paternity or mental health records released. Will not fax documents. Court makes copy: $.25 per page. Certification fee: $5.00 per doc plus copy fee for add'l pages. Payee: State Courts. Personal checks and credit cards accepted. Mail requests: SASE required; add postage if SASE not enclosed.

Deschutes County

Circuit Court 1100 NW Bond, Bend, OR 97701; 541-388-5300; criminal phone: x5, 2100, 2040; civil phone: x6, 2090; probate phone: x8, 2080; 8AM-5PM. ***Felony, Misdemeanor, Civil, Eviction, Small Claims, Probate, Divorce.***
www.deschutes-court.ojd.state.or.us

Civil Records: Access: Phone, mail, online, in person. Visitors must perform in person searches themselves. No search fee. Required to search: name, years to search. Civil cases indexed by defendant, plaintiff; index on computer from 9/87, books from 1976, archived from 1916 on microfiche. Civil PAT goes back to 7/1996. Index online at the statewide OJIN system, call 800-858-9658 for information. Also, current calendars are free at www.ojd.state.or.us/des/calendar.nsf/.

Criminal Records: Access: Phone, mail, online, in person. Visitors must perform in person searches themselves. No search fee. Required to search: name, years to search, SSN. Criminal records computerized from 9/87, books from 1976, archived from 1916 on microfiche. Mail turnaround time 3-5 days. Criminal PAT goes back to 7/1996. Criminal Index available remotely online on the statewide OJIN system, call 800-858-9658. Records from 07/86 forward. Also, current calendars are free at www.ojd.state.or.us/des/calendar.nsf/.

General Information: No adoption, juvenile, sealed by Judge, expunged, mental health records released. Will not fax documents. Court makes copy: $.25 per page. Certification fee: $5.00 per doc. Payee: State of Oregon. Personal checks accepted; credit cards are not. Mail requests: SASE required.

Douglas County

Circuit Court 1036 SE Douglas Ave, Rm 201, Roseburg, OR 97470; 541-957-2471; fax: 541-957-2462; 8AM-5PM. ***Felony, Misdemeanor, Civil, Eviction, Small Claims, Probate, Divorce.***
www.ojd.state.or.us/douglas

Civil Records: Access: Phone, mail, online, in person. Both court and visitors may perform in person searches. No search fee. Required to search: name, years to search. Civil cases indexed by defendant, plaintiff; index on computer back to 10/1987, microfiche from 1974 (district) 1962 (circuit), archived from 1910. Mail turnaround time at least 2 weeks. Civil PAT goes back to 10/1987. Index online at the statewide OJIN system, call 800-858-9658 for information.

Criminal Records: Access: Phone, mail, online, in person. Both court and visitors may perform in person searches. No search fee. Required to search: name, years to search, DOB. Criminal records computerized from 10/1987, microfiche from 1974 (district) 1962 (circuit), archived from 1910. Mail turnaround time at least 2 weeks. Criminal PAT goes back to same as civil.PAT results show name, DOB. Terminal results include SSN. Online access to criminal records is the same as civil.

General Information: No adoption, juvenile, sealed by Judge, expunged or mental health records released. Will scan result then send in "PDF" format to an email address at no cost. Court makes copy: $.25 per page. Self serve: same. Certification fee: $5.00. Payee: Oregon Judicial Department. Personal checks accepted. Credit cards accepted in person. Mail requests: SASE required.

Gilliam County

Circuit Court Box 622, Condon, OR 97823; 541-384-3572; fax: 541-384-2170; 1-5PM. ***Felony, Misdemeanor, Civil, Divorce.***
http://seventhdistrict.ojd.state.or.us

Civil Records: Access: Phone, mail, online, in person. Only the court performs in person searches; visitors may not. No search fee. Required to search: name, years to search. Civil cases indexed by defendant, plaintiff; index on computer from 1989, index cards back to 1800s. Mail turnaround time 1-2 days. Index online at the statewide OJIN system, call 800-858-9658 for information.

Criminal Records: Access: Phone, mail, online, in person. Only the court performs in person searches; visitors may not. No search fee. Required to search: name, years to search; also helpful: DOB. Criminal records computerized from 1989, index cards back to 1800s. Mail turnaround time 1-2 days. Online access to criminal records is same as civil.

General Information: No adoption, juvenile, sealed by Judge, expunged, mental health records released. Will fax documents for an add'l fee. Court makes copy: $.25 per page.Add'l postage may be required if copy weight exceeds 1 oz. Certification fee: $5.00 1st page, $1.00 each add'l page. Payee: Gilliam Circuit Court. Personal checks accepted. Visa/MC accepted. Mail requests: SASE required.

County Court PO Box 427, 221 S Oregon, Condon, OR 97823; 541-384-2311; fax: 541-384-2166; 8:30AM-N, 1-5PM. ***Probate, Juvenile.***
www.co.gilliam.or.us/CountyCourt/tabid/5325/Default.aspx Probate index is NOT online on the statewide OJIN system.

Grant County

Circuit Court PO Box 159, 201 S Humbolt St, Canyon City, OR 97820; 541-575-1438; criminal fax: 541-575-2165; civil fax: same; 8AM-N, 1-5PM. ***Felony, Misdemeanor, Civil, Divorce.***
www.ojd.state.or.us/grant

Civil Records: Access: Mail, in person, online. Only the court performs in person searches; visitors may not. No search fee. Required to search: name, years to search. Civil cases indexed by defendant, plaintiff; index on computer from 1987, microfiche from 1950-1965, archives back to 1880. Mail turnaround time 3-5 days. Public use terminal available. Index online at the statewide OJIN system, call 800-858-9658 for information.

Criminal Records: Access: Mail, online, in person. Only the court performs in person searches; visitors may not. No search fee. Required to search: name, years to search. Criminal records computerized from 1987, microfiche from 1950-1965, archives back to 1880. Mail turnaround time 3-5 days. Public use terminal available. Online access to criminal records is the same as civil.

General Information: No adoption, juvenile, sealed by Judge, expunged, mental health records released. Will not fax documents. Court makes copy: $.25 per page. Certification fee: $5.00 per document. Payee: Grant County Circuit Court. Personal checks accepted. Major credit cards accepted in person only. Mail requests: SASE required.

County Court 201 S Humbolt St, #290, Canyon City, OR 97820-6186; 541-575-1675; fax: 541-575-2248; 8AM-5PM. ***Probate.*** Probate index is NOT online on the statewide OJIN system.

Harney County

Circuit Court 450 N Buena Vista, Burns, OR 97720; 541-573-5207; fax: 541-573-5715; 8AM-N; 1PM-5PM. ***Felony, Misdemeanor, Civil, Divorce.***
www.ojd.state.or.us/harney

In this county, misdemeanor records are located at the Justice Court. Call 541-573-2346. The court is located in the same building.

Civil Records: Access: Phone, fax, mail, online, in person. Both court and visitors may perform in person searches. No search fee. Required to search: name, years to search. Civil cases indexed by defendant, plaintiff; index on computer from 1988, microfiche from 1970-1979, archives back to 1880. Mail turnaround time 5 days. Civil PAT goes back to 1988. PAT results show name; terminal results irregularly include DOB, SSN, address. Index online at the statewide OJIN system, call 800-858-9658 for information.

Criminal Records: Access: Phone, fax, mail, online, in person. Both court and visitors may perform in person searches. No search fee. Required to search: name, years to search. Criminal records computerized from 1988, microfiche from 1970-1979, archives back to 1880. Mail turnaround time 1-2 days. Criminal PAT goes back to same as civil. Terminal results irregularly include DOB, SSN, address. Online access to criminal records is the same as civil.

General Information: No adoption, juvenile, sealed by Judge, expunged, paternity or mental health records released. Will fax documents $2.00 1st page, $1.00 each add'l. Court makes copy: $.25 per page. Certification fee: $5.00. Payee: Harney Circuit Court. Personal checks and credit cards accepted. Mail requests: SASE required.

County Court 450 N Buena Vista Ave, Burns, OR 97720-1518; 541-573-6641; fax: 541-573-8370; 8:30AM-N, 1-5PM. ***Probate.***
www.co.harney.or.us/countycourt.htm
Probate index is NOT online on the statewide OJIN system.

Hood River County

Circuit Court 309 State St, Hood River, OR 97031; 541-386-3535; fax: 541-386-3465; 8AM-N, 1-5PM. ***Felony, Misdemeanor, Civil, Eviction, Small Claims, Probate, Divorce.***
http://seventhdistrict.ojd.state.or.us

Civil Records: Access: Phone, fax, mail, online, in person. Both court and visitors may perform in person searches. No search fee. Required to search: name, years to search. Civil cases indexed by defendant, plaintiff; index on computer from 1989, docket books from 1950. Mail turnaround time 7 days. Civil PAT goes back to 1988. Index online at the statewide OJIN system, call 800-858-9658 for information.

Criminal Records: Access: Phone, fax, mail, online, in person. Both court and visitors may perform in person searches. No search fee. Required to search: name, years to search, DOB. Criminal records computerized from 1989, docket books from 1950. Mail turnaround time 7 days. Criminal PAT goes back to same as civil. Online access to criminal records is the same as civil.

General Information: No adoption, juvenile, sealed by Judge, expunged, paternity or mental health records released. Will not fax documents. Court makes copy: $.25 per page. Certification fee: $5.00 per doc. Payee: Hood River Circuit Court. Personal checks and major credit cards accepted. Mail requests: SASE required.

Jackson County

Circuit Court 100 S Oakdale, Medford, OR 97501; 541-776-7171 x0; criminal phone: x583; civil phone: x582; probate phone: x584; criminal fax: 541-776-7057; civil fax: same; 8AM-5PM. ***Felony, Misdemeanor, Civil Actions, Eviction, Small Claims, Probate, Divorce.***
www.ojd.state.or.us/jac/index.htm

For records requests pre-1999, dial x132 for James; for newer records, call Records at x0. Probate fax is same as main fax number.

Civil Records: Access: Mail, fax, online, in person. Visitors must perform in person searches themselves. No search fee. Required to search: name, years to search. Civil cases indexed by defendant, plaintiff; index on computer from 1988, prior records on docket books and microfilm. Civil PAT goes back to late 1980s. PAT results show name only. Public access terminal uses the statewide OJIN system. Index online at the statewide OJIN system, call 800-858-9658 for information.

Criminal Records: Access: Mail, fax, online, in person. Visitors must perform in person searches

themselves. No search fee. Required to search: name, years to search, DOB. Criminal records computerized from 1988, prior records on docket books and microfilm. Mail turnaround time up to 3 weeks depending to volume. Criminal PAT goes back to same as civil.PAT results show name, DOB. Public access terminal uses the statewide OJIN system. Online access to criminal records is the same as civil.
General Information: Online identifiers in results same as on public terminal. No adoption, juvenile, sealed by Judge, expunged, mental health records released. Will fax documents; $2.00 for 1st page, $1.00 each add'l. Court makes copy: $.25 per page. Certification fee: $5.00 per document. Payee: Jackson County Courts. Personal checks and major credit cards accepted. Mail requests: SASE required.

Jefferson County

Circuit Court 75 SE C St, #C, Madras, OR 97741-1750; 541-475-3317; fax: 541-475-3421; 8AM-Noon; 1PM-5PM. ***Felony, Misdemeanor, Civil, Eviction, Small Claims, Probate, Divorce.*** www.ojd.state.or.us/cro/
Civil Records: Access: Mail, fax, online, in person. Both court and visitors may perform in person searches. No search fee. Required to search: name, years to search. Civil cases indexed by defendant, plaintiff; index on computer from 10/1986, archives from 1916-1986. Mail turnaround time 1-2 weeks. Civil PAT goes back to 10/1986. Index online at the statewide OJIN system, call 800-858-9658 for information.
Criminal Records: Access: Mail, fax, online, in person. Both court and visitors may perform in person searches. No search fee. Required to search: name, years to search, DOB. Criminal records computerized from 10/1986, archives from 1916-1986. Mail turnaround time 1-2 weeks. Criminal PAT goes back to same as civil. Online access to criminal records is the same as civil.
General Information: Online identifiers in results same as on public terminal. No adoption, juvenile, sealed by Judge, expunged, mental health records released. Will fax documents $2.00 1st page, $1.00 ea add'l. Court makes copy: $.25 per page. Self serve: same. Certification fee: $5.00 per doc. Payee: State of Oregon. Personal checks and credit cards accepted. Mail requests: SASE required.

Josephine County

Circuit Court Josephine County Courthouse, Dept 17, 500 NW 6th St, Grants Pass, OR 97526; 541-476-2309; fax: 541-471-2079; 8AM-5PM. ***Felony, Misdemeanor, Civil, Eviction, Small Claims, Probate, Divorce.*** www.ojd.state.or.us/jos/
Civil Records: Access: Fax, mail, online, in person. Both court and visitors may perform in person searches. No search fee. Required to search: name, years to search. Civil cases indexed by defendant, plaintiff; index on computer from 1987, microfilm prior to 1980, archives from 1920, index books. Mail turnaround time 8-10 days. Civil PAT goes back to 1987. PAT results show name only. Public terminal located on 2nd Fl Law Library. Index online at the statewide OJIN system, call 800-858-9658 for information.
Criminal Records: Access: Fax, mail, online, in person. Both court and visitors may perform in person searches. No search fee. Required to search: name, years to search, DOB. Criminal records computerized from 1987, microfilm prior to 1980, archives from 1920, index books. Mail turnaround time 5 days. Criminal PAT goes back to same as civil.PAT results show name, DOB. Public terminal located on 2nd Fl Law Library. Online access to criminal records is the same as civil. Online results show name, DOB.
General Information: No adoption, juvenile, sealed by Judge, expunged, mental health records released. No fee to fax out. Court makes copy: $.25 per page. Certification fee: $5.00 per doc. Payee: Josephine County Court. Personal checks and credit cards accepted. Mail requests: SASE required.

Klamath County

Circuit Court 316 Main St, Klamath Falls, OR 97601; 541-883-5503; criminal phone: x232; civil phone: x222; probate phone: x222; fax: 541-882-6109; 8AM-5PM M-TH, 8:30AM-5:30PM Fri. ***Felony, Misdemeanor, Civil, Eviction, Small Claims, Probate, Divorce.***
Civil Records: Access: Mail, fax, in person, online. Both court and visitors may perform in person searches. No search fee. Required to search: name, years to search. Civil cases indexed by defendant, plaintiff; index on computer from 1988, microfiche from 1940-1980. Mail turnaround time 2 weeks. Civil PAT goes back to 1989. PAT civil results show middle initial. Index online at the statewide OJIN system, call 800-858-9658 for information.
Criminal Records: Access: Mail, fax, in person, online. Both court and visitors may perform in person searches. No search fee. Required to search: name, years to search. Criminal records computerized from 1988, felony cases on microfiche from 1940-1980. Mail turnaround time 2 weeks. Criminal PAT goes back to same as civil. PAT results show middle initial, DOB. Online access to criminal records is the same as civil.
General Information: No adoption, juvenile, sealed by Judge, expunged, paternity or mental health records released. Fee to fax out file $2.00 1st page and $1.00 each add'l page. Court makes copy: $.25 per page. Certification fee: $5.00 per doc. Payee: Klamath County Circuit Court. No personal checks accepted. Visa/MC accepted. Mail requests: SASE required.

Lake County

Circuit Court 513 Center St, Lakeview, OR 97630; 541-947-6051; probate phone: 541-947-6051; fax: 541-947-3724; 8AM-N, 1-5PM. ***Felony, Misdemeanor, Civil, Eviction, Small Claims, Probate, Divorce.***
Probate fax is same as main fax number.
Civil Records: Access: Mail, in person, online. Both court and visitors may perform in person searches. No search fee; if pre-1988- $7.50 per name. Required to search: name, years to search. Civil cases indexed by defendant, plaintiff; index on computer from 1988, index cards prior. Mail turnaround time 2 weeks. Civil PAT goes back to 1988. PAT results show middle initial, DOB. Index online at the statewide OJIN system, call 800-858-9658 for information.
Criminal Records: Access: Mail, online, in person. Both court and visitors may perform in person searches. No search fee; if pre-1988- $7.50 per name. Required to search: name, years to search. Criminal records computerized from 1988, index cards prior. Mail turnaround time 2 weeks. Criminal PAT goes back to same as civil. PAT results show middle initial, DOB. Online access to criminal records is the same as civil.
General Information: No adoption, juvenile, sealed by Judge, expunged or mental health records released. Will fax $2.00 1st page, $1.00 each add'l only if local and prepaid. Court makes copy: $.25 per page. Certification fee: $5.00. Payee: Lake County Circuit Court. Personal checks accepted. Visa/MC accepted. Mail requests: SASE required.

Lane County

Circuit Court 125 E 8th Ave, Eugene, OR 97401; 541-682-4020; 8AM-5PM. ***Felony, Misdemeanor, Civil, Eviction, Small Claims, Probate, Divorce.*** www.ojd.state.or.us/lan/
Civil Records: Access: Online, in person. Visitors must perform in person searches themselves. Required to search: name, years to search. Civil cases indexed by defendant, plaintiff; index on computer from 1983, index books prior. Civil PAT goes back to 1983. PAT civil results show middle initial. Index online at the statewide OJIN system, call 800-858-9658 for information.
Criminal Records: Access: Online, in person. Visitors must perform in person searches themselves. Required to search: name, years to search. Criminal records computerized from 1983, index books prior. Criminal PAT goes back to 1982. PAT criminal results show middle initial. Online access to criminal records is the same as civil. Online results show middle initial.
General Information: No adoption, juvenile, sealed by Judge, expunged, mental health records released. Will not fax documents. Court makes copy: $.25 per page. Certification fee: $5.00 per doc. Payee: Lane County Courts. Personal checks accepted. Visa/MC accepted via phone only.

Lincoln County

Circuit Court PO Box 100, 225 W Olive St, Newport, OR 97365; 541-265-4236; fax: 541-265-7561; 8AM-N, 1-5PM. ***Felony, Misdemeanor, Civil, Eviction, Small Claims, Probate, Divorce.*** www.ojd.state.or.us/lincoln
Civil Records: Access: Mail, fax, online, in person. Both court and visitors may perform in person searches. No search fee. Required to search: name. Civil cases indexed by defendant, plaintiff; index on computer from 2/88, archives back to 1893, prior to 1988, years to search must be specified. Mail turnaround time 3 days. Civil PAT goes back to 2/1988. PAT results show name, DOB. Public access terminal found on 3rd Fl. Index online at the statewide OJIN system, call 800-858-9658 for information.
Criminal Records: Access: Mail, fax, online, in person. Both court and visitors may perform in person searches. No search fee. Required to search: name, years to search. Criminal records computerized from 2/88, archives back to 1893, prior to 1988, years to search must be specified. Mail turnaround time 1 week. Criminal PAT goes back to same as civil. Online access to criminal records is the same as civil.
General Information: No adoption, sealed by Judge, expunged, or mental health records released. Will fax documents $2.00 1st page, $1.00 each add'l. Court makes copy: $.25 per page. Certification fee: $5.00. Payee: State of Oregon. Personal checks accepted. Visa/MC accepted; $1.00 minimum payment. Mail requests: SASE required.

Linn County

Circuit Court PO Box 1749, 300 Fourth St SW, #107, Albany, OR 97321; criminal phone: 541-967-3841; civil phone: 541-967-3845; probate phone: 541-967-3845; fax: 541-928-8725; 8AM-5PM. ***Felony, Misdemeanor, Civil, Eviction, Small Claims, Probate, Divorce.*** www.ojd.state.or.us/linn
Public access terminal found in Room 107. Phone for copies/archives- 541-812-877
Civil Records: Access: Mail, in person, online. Both court and visitors may perform in person searches. No search fee. Required to search: name, years to search. Civil cases indexed by defendant, plaintiff; index on computer from 6/1987, archives back to 1863. Mail turnaround time 5-10 days. Civil PAT goes back to 6/1987. PAT results show middle initial, DOB. Index online at the statewide OJIN system, call 800-858-9658 for information.
Criminal Records: Access: Mail, online, in person. Both court and visitors may perform in person searches. No search fee. Required to search: name, years to search, DOB. Criminal records computerized from 6/1987, archives back to 1863. Mail turnaround time 5-10 days. Criminal PAT goes back to same as civil; results show middle initial, DOB. Online access to criminal records is the same as civil.
General Information: No adoption, juvenile, sealed by judge, expunged, paternity or mental health records released. Will fax documents $2.00 1st page, $1.00 ea addl. Court makes copy: $.25 per page. Certification fee: $5.00 per file. Payee: State of Oregon. Personal checks accepted. Visa/MC accepted. Mail requests: SASE required.

Malheur County

Circuit Court PO Box 670, Vale, OR 97918-0670; 541-473-5171; fax: 541-473-2213; 8AM-N, 1-5PM (MST). ***Felony, Misdemeanor, Civil, Eviction, Small Claims.*** www.ojd.state.or.us/malheur
Physical Address: Oregon Judicial Dept., Malheur County Circuit Court, 251 B St W, Vale, OR 97918
Civil Records: Access: Mail, in person, online. Both court and visitors may perform in person searches.

Search fee: No fee, unless access needed to archived records then $15.00 per case. Required to search: name, years to search. Civil cases indexed by defendant, plaintiff; index on computer from 7/1988, archived from 1887. Mail turnaround time 2 weeks minimum. Civil PAT goes back to 1988. PAT results show middle initial, DOB. Index online at the statewide OJIN system, call 800-858-9658 for information.
Criminal Records: Access: Mail, online, in person. Both court and visitors may perform in person searches. Search fee: $15.00 per case, if case number known, then no fee. Required to search: name, years to search, DOB. Criminal records computerized from 7/1988, archived from 1887. Mail turnaround time 2 weeks minimum. Criminal PAT goes back to same as civil. PAT results show middle initial, DOB. Online access to criminal records is the same as civil. Online results show middle initial, DOB.
General Information: No adoption, juvenile, sealed by Judge, expunged, mental health records released. Fee to fax out file $2.00 1st page, $1.00 ea add'l. Incoming fax fee: $2.00 1st page, $1.00 2nd page. Court makes copy: $.25 per page. Self serve: same. Certification fee: $5.00. Payee: State Courts. Personal checks accepted. Visa/MC accepted. Mail requests: SASE requested.

County Court 251 B St West #4, Vale, OR 97918; 541-473-5124; probate phone: 541-473-5151; fax: 541-473-5523; 8:30AM-5PM (MST). ***Probate.*** Probate index NOT online on statewide OJIN system.

Marion County

Circuit Court PO Box 12869, 100 High St NE, Salem, OR 97309; 503-588-5101; fax: 503-373-4360; 7:30AM-5:30PM. ***Felony, Misdemeanor, Civil, Eviction, Small Claims, Probate, Divorce.*** www.ojd.state.or.us/mar/
Civil Records: Access: Mail, in person, online. Both court and visitors may perform in person searches. No search fee. Required to search: name, years to search. Civil cases indexed by defendant, plaintiff; index on computer from 10/1986, prior on microfiche/microfilm. Mail turnaround time minimum 5 days. Civil PAT goes back to 1986. Index online at the statewide OJIN system, call 800-858-9658 for information.
Criminal Records: Access: Mail, online, in person. Both court and visitors may perform in person searches. No search fee. Required to search: name, years to search; also helpful: DOB. Criminal records computerized from 10/1986, prior on microfiche/microfilm. Mail turnaround time minimum 5 days. Criminal PAT goes back to same as civil. Online access to criminal records is the same as civil.
General Information: No adoption, juvenile, sealed by Judge, expunged, paternity or mental health records released. Will fax documents $2.00 1st page; $1.00 each add'l page. Court makes copy: $.25 per page. Certification fee: $5.00. Payee: State of Oregon. Personal checks accepted. Visa/MC accepted. Mail requests: SASE required.

Morrow County

Circuit Court PO Box 609, Heppner, OR 97836; 541-676-5264; fax: 541-676-9902; 8AM-N, 1-5PM. ***Felony, Misdemeanor, Civil, Eviction, Small Claims, Probate, Divorce.*** www.ojd.state.or.us/morrow There is a County Court in Morrow that handles only juvenile cases.
Civil Records: Access: Phone, fax, mail, in person, online. Both court and visitors may perform in person searches. Search fee: $12.65 per hour to locate in 10 minute increments ($2.11). Required to search: name, years to search. Civil cases indexed by defendant, plaintiff; index on computer from 1987, archives back to 1940, index cards, docket books by case #. Mail turnaround time 1-3 days. Index online at the statewide OJIN system, call 800-858-9658 for information.
Criminal Records: Access: Phone, fax, mail, online, in person. Both court and visitors may perform in person searches. Search fee: $12.65 per hour to locate in 10 minute increments ($2.11). Required to search: name, years to search, DOB. Criminal records computerized from 1987, archives back to 1940, index cards, docket books by case #. Mail turnaround time 1-3 days. Online access to criminal records is the same as civil.
General Information: No adoption, juvenile, sealed by Judge, expunged, paternity or mental health records released. No fee to fax documents. Court makes copy: $.25 per page. Certification fee: $5.00. Payee: Circuit Court. Personal checks and major credit cards accepted. Mail requests: SASE required.

Multnomah County

Circuit Court 1021 SW 4th Ave, Rm 131, Portland, OR 97204; 503-988-3003; 8AM-5PM. ***Felony, Misdemeanor, Civil Actions over $10,000, Probate, Divorce.***
Civil Records: Access: Mail, in person, online. Both court and visitors may perform in person searches. No search fee. Required to search: name, years to search. Civil cases indexed by defendant, plaintiff; index on computer from 1988, microfiche, index books, docket books back to 1857. Mail turnaround time 4-5 days. Civil PAT goes back to 1988. Index online at the statewide OJIN system, call 800-858-9658 for information.
Criminal Records: Access: Mail, online, in person. Both court and visitors may perform in person searches. No search fee. Required to search: name, years to search; also helpful: DOB. Criminal records computerized from 1988, microfiche, index books, docket books back to 1857. Mail turnaround time 4-5 days. Criminal PAT goes back to same as civil. Online access to criminal records is the same as civil.
General Information: No adoption, juvenile, sealed by Judge, expunged or mental health records released. Will fax documents to local or toll-free number. Court makes copy: $.25 per page. Certification fee: $5.00. Payee: State of Oregon. Personal checks and major credit cards accepted. Mail requests: SASE required.

Circuit Court - Civil Division 1021 SW 4th Ave, Rm 210, Portland, OR 97204; 503-988-3022 x3; probate phone: 503-988-3022; fax: 503-988-3425; 8:30AM-5PM. ***Civil Actions, Eviction, Small Claims.*** www.ojd.state.or.us/multnomah Records room is #131.
Civil Records: Access: Mail, in person, online. Both court and visitors may perform in person searches. No search fee. Required to search: name, years to search. Civil cases indexed by defendant, plaintiff; index on computer from 1988, microfiche 1984-1988, docket cards by case and year. Some search limitations may apply. Mail turnaround time 5 days. Public use terminal has civil records back to 1988. PAT results show middle initial, DOB. Index online at the statewide OJIN system, call 800-858-9658 for information.
General Information: No adoption, juvenile, sealed by Judge, expunged, paternity or mental health records released. Will not fax documents. Court makes copy: $.25 per page. Certification fee: $5.00 per document; exemplified-$10.00. Payee: State of Oregon. Personal checks accepted. Visa/MC accepted. Mail requests: SASE required.

Polk County

Circuit Court Polk County Courthouse, Rm 301, 850 Main St, Dallas, OR 97338; 503-623-3154; criminal phone: 503-831-1778; civil phone: 503-623-3154; probate phone: 503-623-3154; criminal fax: 503-831-1779; civil fax: 503-623-6614; 8AM-5PM. ***Felony, Misdemeanor, Civil, Eviction, Small Claims, Probate, Divorce, Family.*** www.ojd.state.or.us/plk/index.htm 2nd fax- 503-623-6614. Probate is a separate index at this same address.
Civil Records: Access: Phone, fax, mail, online, in person. Both court and visitors may perform in person searches. No search fee. Required to search: name, years to search. Civil cases indexed by defendant, plaintiff; index on computer from 1985, microfilm, archives from 1969 (District) back to 1800s (Circuit). Mail turnaround time 2 weeks. Civil PAT goes back to 1985. PAT results show middle initial, DOB. Index online at the statewide OJIN system, call 800-858-9658 for information.
Criminal Records: Access: Phone, fax, mail, online, in person. Both court and visitors may perform in person searches. No search fee. Required to search: name, years to search, DOB; also helpful: SSN. Criminal records computerized from 1985, microfilm, archives from 1969 (District) back to 1800s (Circuit). Mail turnaround time 2 weeks. Criminal PAT goes back to same as civil. PAT results show middle initial, DOB. Online access to criminal records is the same as civil. Online results show middle initial, DOB.
General Information: No adoption, juvenile, sealed by Judge, expunged, mental health records released. No fee to fax documents. Court makes copy: $.25 per page. Self serve: same. Certification fee: $5.00. Payee: State of Oregon. Personal checks accepted. Credit cards accepted for in person and phone requests only. Mail requests: SASE required.

Sherman County

Circuit Court PO Box 402, Moro, OR 97039; 541-565-3650; fax: 541-565-3249; 1-5PM. ***Felony, Misdemeanor, Civil, Divorce.***
Civil Records: Access: Phone, mail, online, in person. Both court and visitors may perform in person searches. No search fee. Required to search: name, years to search. Civil cases indexed by defendant, plaintiff; index on computer from 1992, microfiche up to 1987, index books, judgment docket books. Mail turnaround time 2-5 days. Civil PAT goes back to 1992. Index online at the statewide OJIN system, call 800-858-9658 for information.
Criminal Records: Access: Phone, mail, online, in person. Both court and visitors may perform in person searches. No search fee. Required to search: name, years to search, DOB. Criminal records computerized from 1992, microfiche up to 1987, index books, judgment docket books. Mail turnaround time 2-5 days. Criminal PAT goes back to same as civil. Online access to criminal records is the same as civil.
General Information: No adoption, juvenile, sealed by Judge, expunged, paternity or mental health records released. Will fax documents $2.00 1st page, $1.00 each add'l. Court makes copy: $.25 per page. Self serve: same. Certification fee: $5.00 per document. Payee: Sherman County Circuit Court. Personal checks and credit cards accepted. Mail requests: SASE required.

County Court PO Box 365, 500 Court St, Moro, OR 97039; 541-565-3606; fax: 541-565-3312; 8AM-5PM. ***Probate, Juvenile.*** Probate index is NOT online on the statewide OJIN system.

Tillamook County

Circuit Court 201 Laurel Ave, Tillamook, OR 97141; 503-842-2596; criminal fax: 503-842-2597; civil fax: same; 8AM-N; 1PM-5PM. ***Felony, Misdemeanor, Civil, Eviction, Small Claims, Probate, Divorce.*** www.ojd.state.or.us/til Probate fax is same as main fax number.
Civil Records: Access: Mail, fax, online, in person. Both court and visitors may perform in person searches. No search fee, unless massive searching needed. Required to search: name, years to search. Civil cases indexed by defendant, plaintiff; index on computer from 1987, prior on case files. Mail turnaround time- call for estimate. Civil PAT goes back to 1987. Index online at the statewide OJIN system, call 800-858-9658 for information.
Criminal Records: Access: Mail, fax, online, in person. Both court and visitors may perform in person searches. No search fee, unless massive searching needed. Required to search: name, years to search. Criminal records computerized from 1987, prior on case files. Mail turnaround time 2-3 days. Criminal PAT goes back to same as civil; results show name, DOB. Online access to criminal records is the same as civil. Online results show name, DOB.
General Information: No adoption, juvenile, sealed by Judge, expunged, paternity or mental health records released. Will fax documents $2.00 1st page; $1.00 each add'l. Court makes copy: $.25 per page. Certification fee: $5.00. Payee: Tillamook Circuit Court. Personal checks accepted. Visa/MC accepted

with minimum payment of $5.00. Mail requests: SASE required.

Umatilla County

Circuit Court PO Box 1307, 216 SE 4th St, Pendleton, OR 97801; 541-278-0341; criminal phone: x254; civil phone: x236; fax: 541-276-9030; 8AM-N; 1PM-5PM. ***Felony, Misdemeanor, Civil, Eviction, Small Claims, Probate, Divorce.***
www.ojd.state.or.us/uma/index.htm
Civil Records: Access: Mail, in person, online. Both court and visitors may perform in person searches. Search fee: $12.65 per hour. Required to search: name, years to search. Civil cases indexed by defendant, plaintiff; index on computer from 11/86, microfiche, index card, docket books. Mail turnaround time 1-3 weeks. Civil PAT goes back to 1985. PAT results show name, DOB. Public access terminal found in Rm 209. Index online at the statewide OJIN system, call 800-858-9658 for information.
Criminal Records: Access: Mail, online, in person. Both court and visitors may perform in person searches. Search fee: $12.65 per hour. Required to search: name, years to search. Criminal records computerized from 11/86, microfiche, index card, docket books. Mail turnaround time 1-3 weeks. Criminal PAT goes back to same as civil.PAT results show name, DOB. Public access terminal found in Room 209. Online access to criminal records is the same as civil. Online results show name, DOB.
General Information: No adoption, juvenile, sealed by Judge, expunged, paternity or mental health records released. Will not fax documents. Court makes copy: $.25 per page. Self serve: same. Certification fee: $5.00 per document. Payee: Trial Court Administrator. Personal checks accepted. Visa/MC accepted. Mail requests: SASE required.

Union County

Circuit Court 1008 K Ave, La Grande, OR 97850; 541-962-9500; criminal fax: 541-963-0444; civil fax: 541-963-0444; 8AM-N, 1-5PM. ***Felony, Misdemeanor, Civil, Eviction, Small Claims, Probate, Divorce.***
www.ojd.state.or.us/courts/circuit/union.htm
Faxed search requests must be pre-approved. Searches- details other than case number and type are considered a 'detailed search' and may incur copy costs. Limited weekly calendars available at the website. Court at 1007 S 4th St.
Civil Records: Access: Mail, in person, online. Both court and visitors may perform in person searches. No search fee. Required to search: name, years to search. Civil cases indexed by defendant, plaintiff; index on computer from 1986, archives back to 1865, on ledger books/docket books. Mail turnaround time 1-2 weeks. Civil PAT goes back to 1986. PAT results show middle initial, DOB. Index online at the OJIN system, call 800-858-9658 for info.
Criminal Records: Access: Mail, fax, online, in person. Both court and visitors may perform in person searches. No search fee. Required to search: name, years to search, DOB. Criminal records computerized from 1986, archives back to 1800s, on ledger books/docket books. Mail turnaround time 1-2 weeks. Criminal PAT goes back to 1986. PAT results show middle initial, DOB. Online access to criminal records is the same as civil. Online results show middle initial, DOB.
General Information: No adoption, juvenile, sealed by Judge, expunged, paternity or mental health records released. Will fax documents $2.00 1st page, $1.00 ea add'l. Court makes copy: $.25 per page. Certification fee: $5.00 per doc. Payee: Circuit Court. Personal checks and credit cards accepted. Mail requests: SASE required.

Wallowa County

Circuit Court 101 S River St, Rm 204, Enterprise, OR 97828; 541-426-4991; fax: 541-426-4992; 8AM-N; 1-5PM. ***Felony, Misdemeanor, Civil, Eviction, Small Claims, Probate, Divorce.***
www.ojd.state.or.us/courts/circuit/wallowa.htm
Civil Records: Access: Phone, mail, online, in person. Both court and visitors may perform in person searches. No search fee. Required to search: name, years to search. Civil cases indexed by defendant, plaintiff; index on computer from 1987, prior on docket books. Mail turnaround time 1 week. Civil PAT goes back to 1987. Index online at the statewide OJIN system, call 800-858-9658 for information.
Criminal Records: Access: Phone, mail, online, in person. Both court and visitors may perform in person searches. No search fee. Required to search: name, years to search. Criminal records computerized from 1987, prior on docket books. Mail turnaround time 1 week. Criminal PAT goes back to same as civil. Online access to criminal records is the same as civil.
General Information: No adoption, juvenile, sealed by Judge, expunged, paternity or mental health records released. Will not fax documents. Court makes copy: $.25 per page. Certification fee: $5.00. Payee: Circuit Court. Personal checks and credit cards accepted. Copy fees may be billed. Mail requests: SASE required.

Wasco County

Circuit Court PO Box 1400, The Dalles, OR 97058-1400; 541-506-2700; criminal phone: 5506-2716; civil phone: 541-506-2704; probate phone: 541-506-2704; fax: 541-506-2711; 8AM-N,1-5PM. ***Felony, Misdemeanor, Civil, Eviction, Small Claims, Probate, Divorce.***
http://seventhdistrict.ojd.state.or.us/html/wasco.html
Civil Records: Access: Phone, fax, mail, online, in person. Both court and visitors may perform in person searches. No search fee. Required to search: name, years to search. Civil cases indexed by defendant, plaintiff; index on computer from 1989, prior records in docket books by case # and year back to 1900s. Mail turnaround time 2-3 days. Civil PAT goes back to 1989. Index online at the statewide OJIN system, call 800-858-9658 for information.
Criminal Records: Access: Phone, fax, mail, online, in person. Both court and visitors may perform in person searches. No search fee. Required to search: name, years to search, DOB. Criminal records computerized from 1989, prior records in docket books by case # and year back to 1900s. Mail turnaround time 2-3 days. Criminal PAT goes back to same as civil. Online access to criminal records is the same as civil.
General Information: No adoption, juvenile, sealed by Judge, expunged, paternity or mental health records released. Fee to fax out file $2.00 1st page, $1.00 ea add'l. Court makes copy: $.25 per page. Self serve: same. Certification fee: $5.00. Payee: Trial Court Administrator. Personal checks and credit cards accepted. Mail requests: SASE required.

Washington County

Circuit Court 150 N 1st, Hillsboro, OR 97124; 503-846-8888 x8266 (civ) x8252 (crim); probate phone: 503-846-2366; fax: 503-846-6087; 8AM-5PM. ***Felony, Misdemeanor, Civil, Eviction, Small Claims, Probate, Divorce.***
www.ojd.state.or.us/wsh/default.htm
Probate fax- 503-846-8289
Civil Records: Access: Phone, mail, online, in person. Both court and visitors may perform in person searches. No search fee. Required to search: name, years to search. Civil cases indexed by defendant, plaintiff; index on computer from 1982, prior on docket books. Mail turnaround time 2-5 days. Civil PAT goes back to 1983. PAT civil results show middle initial. Index online at the statewide OJIN system, call 800-858-9658 for information.
Criminal Records: Access: Phone, mail, online, in person. Both court and visitors may perform in person searches. No search fee. Required to search: name, years to search, DOB. Criminal records computerized from 1982, prior on docket books. Mail turnaround time 2-5 days. Criminal PAT goes back to same as civil. PAT results show middle initial, DOB. Online access to criminal records is the same as civil. Online results show middle initial, DOB.
General Information: Online identifiers in results same as on public terminal. No adoption, juvenile, sealed by Judge, expunged, paternity or mental health records released. Will fax documents $2.00 1st page, $1.00 ea add'l. Court makes copy: $.25 per page. Certification fee: $5.00. Payee: State of Oregon. Personal checks accepted. Visa/MC accepted.

Wheeler County

Circuit Court PO Box 308, Fossil, OR 97830; 541-763-2541; fax: 541-763-2543; 8:30AM-11:30AM. ***Felony, Misdemeanor, Civil, Divorce.***
http://seventhdistrict.ojd.state.or.us
Civil Records: Access: Phone, mail, online, in person. Both court and visitors may perform in person searches. No search fee. Required to search: name, years to search. Civil cases indexed by defendant. Civil records on computer from 1989, docket books by case # and yr. Mail turnaround time 1 week. Index online at the statewide OJIN system, call 800-858-9658 for information.
Criminal Records: Access: Phone, mail, online, in person. Only the court performs in person searches; visitors may not. No search fee. Required to search: name, years to search, DOB. Criminal records computerized from 1989, docket books by case # and yr. Mail turnaround time 1 week. Online access to criminal records is the same as civil.
General Information: No adoption, juvenile, sealed by Judge, expunged, paternity or mental health records released. Will fax documents to local or toll free line, otherwise extra fee incurred. Court makes copy: $.25 per page. Self serve: same.If postage to return results is over $.39, then add'l postage fees will apply. Certification fee: $5.00 per certification. Payee: Wheeler Circuit Court. Personal checks accepted. Visa/MC accepted. Mail requests: SASE required.

County Court PO Box 327, 701 Adams, Rm 204, Fossil, OR 97830; 541-763-2400; fax: 541-763-2026; 8:30AM-4PM. ***Probate, Juvenile.***
Probate index is NOT online on the statewide OJIN system.

Yamhill County

Circuit Court 535 NE 5th, McMinnville, OR 97128; 503-434-7530; probate phone: 502-434-7493; fax: 503-472-5805; 8AM-N, 1-5PM. ***Felony, Misdemeanor, Civil, Eviction, Small Claims, Probate, Divorce.***
www.ojd.state.or.us/yam/Pages/Home.htm
Civil Records: Access: Mail, in person, online. Both court and visitors may perform in person searches. No search fee, but court may charge fee if search is lengthy. Required to search: name, years to search. Civil cases indexed by defendant, plaintiff; index on computer from 1987, microfiche (10 yrs Dist, unlimited Circuit), archives back to 1900s, docket books by case # and yr. Mail turnaround time 1-7 days. Civil PAT goes back to 1987. PAT civil results show middle initial. Index online at the statewide OJIN system, call 800-858-9658 for information. Current dockets online only at main website.
Criminal Records: Access: Mail, online, in person. Both court and visitors may perform in person searches. No search fee, but court may charge fee if search is lengthy. Required to search: name, years to search, DOB. Criminal records computerized from 1987, microfiche (10 yrs Dist, unlimited Circuit), archives back to 1900s, docket books by case # and yr. Mail turnaround time 1-7 days. Criminal PAT goes back to same as civil. PAT results show middle initial, DOB. Online access to criminal records is the same as civil. Current dockets online only. Also, search sheriff's inmates and most wanted lists free at www.co.yamhill.or.us/sheriff/index.asp. Online results show middle initial, DOB. Note that civil results do not show a DOB.
General Information: Online identifiers in results same as on public terminal. No adoption, juvenile, sealed by Judge, expunged or mental health records released. Will fax documents $2.00 1st page, $1.00 ea add'l. Court makes copy: $.25 per page. Certification fee: $5.00; Exemplification fee- $10.00. Payee: Trial Court. Two party, payroll checks not accepted. Visa/MC accepted. Mail requests: SASE requested.

Oregon Recording Offices

ORGANIZATION: 36 counties, 36 recording offices. The recording officer is the County Clerk. 35 Oregon counties are in the Pacific Time Zone; the exception is Malheur County in the Mountain Time Zone (MST).

REAL ESTATE RECORDS: Some counties will not perform real estate searches and where they do, search fees vary; often a $3.75 Location fee is applied. Copy fee is usually $.25 per page. Certification fee is $3.75 per document. The Assessor keeps tax and ownership records.

UCC RECORDS: Financing statements are filed at the state level except for real estate related collateral. A few county clerks will perform UCC searches; fees vary from $3.50 to $13.50. We suggest to call first.

TAX LIEN RECORDS: All federal and state tax liens on personal property are filed with the Secretary of State. Other federal and state tax liens are filed with the County Clerk. Government agencies file 'warrants' that represent liens for unpaid taxes and other state fees. Certain warrants are filed with the Sec. of State such as those related to income tax and hazardous waste and are included in a UCC search. Other warrants are filed at the county level, such as those relating to employment taxes. A few counties will perform tax lien searches and include them with a UCC search.

OTHER LIENS: County tax, public utility, construction, judgment, hospital.

ONLINE ACCESS: A number of counties offer internet access to assessor records. From a statewide perspective, the ORMAP Tax Viewing System at www.ormap.com/disclaimer.cfm provides maps for free, and searching by county, then by address. Though there is no name searching and maps are pdfs arranged in folders (and you may zoom in to a map location), this is a step toward owner identification.

Search UCCs on the statewide system at www.filinginoregon.com/ucc/index.htm.

Baker County

County Clerk, 1995 3rd St, #150, Baker, OR 97814-3398. Recording, R/E phone-541-523-8207; fax-541-523-8240; 8AM-5PM. www.bakercounty.org

Index: Separate indices to search include deeds, mortgage, liens, county court. Vital records included, except divorce record index must be searched at the circuit court. Records indexed on computer back to 1965. Only the public may search. Location fee $3.75 if recording number not provided. Will not search UCC records. Copy fee $.25 per page. Cert fee- $4.00 1st page, $.25 each add'l page plus copy fee. Payee- Baker County Clerk. **Other phones:** Treasurer- 541-523-8221; Elections- 541-523-8207. **Property tax/Assessing-** 1995 3rd St #130, Baker, OR 97814-3398; 541-523-8203, assessor fax- 541-523-8352. (Appraiser/Auditor- 541-523-8203) hours- 8AM-N 1PM-5PM **Online** - Access assessor property data free at www.bakercounty.org/Assessor/Assessor_Search.html. Access maps via the statewide mapping site free at www.ormap.com/maps/index.cfm.

Benton County

County Clerk, 120 NW 4th St, Rm 4, Corvallis, OR 97330. Recording, R/E phone-541-766-6831; fax-541-766-6675; 8AM-5PM. www.co.benton.or.us/

Index: Separate indices to search include 1987 - present are computer based, all prior records in index books. Vital records included, except divorce record index must be searched at the circuit court. Records indexed on computer back to 1987. Office personnel or visitors may perform searches. Search fee $20.00 per hour in 15 min increments. Office will search real estate records. Will search UCC records. Copy fee $.25 per page. Cert fee- $3.75 per record plus copy fee. Payee- Benton County Recorder. Bulk data available, contact County Info Resource Mgmt Section. **Other phones:** Treasurer- 541-766-6808; Elections- 541-766-6756. **Property tax/Assessing-** 205 NW 5th St, Covallis, OR 97330; 541-766-6855, fax- 541-766-6848. (Appraiser 541-766-6855) **Online access-** Assessor has numerous searches at www.co.benton.or.us/assess/prop_search.php. Also, see note at beginning of section. County is developing a GIS Internet site for viewing property data at www.co.benton.or.us/maps/bentonmaps.php. A fee may apply to purchase of maps, etc.

Clackamas County

County Clerk, 2051 Kaen Rd, Oregon City, OR 97045. 503-650-8551, R/E recording phone-503-655-8551; fax-503-650-5688; 8AM-6PM M; 7AM-6PM T,W,TH; Closed Fri. www.clackamas.us/clerk/

Index: All in one. Vital records included, except divorce record index must be searched at the circuit court. Records indexed on a public use terminal back to 1989. Only the public may search. Copy fee $.25 self serve; copy by clerk is $4.00 1st page, $.25 each add'l. Cert fee- $3.75 per doc plus copy fee. Payee- Clackamas County Clerk. **Other phones:** Treasurer- 503-655-8915; Elections- 503-655-8510; Vital Records- 503-655-8384. **Property tax/Assessing-** Development Services Bldg, 150 Beavercreek Rd, 1st Fl, Oregon City, OR 97045; 503-655-8671, assessor fax- 503-655-8313. hours- 7AM-6PM M-TH; Closed Fri A public access terminal is available for record searches. www.clackamas.us/at/ **Online access-** Parcel records and GIS-Map on the County Metromap database are free at www.metro-region.org/article.cfm?articleid=1055. No name searching. Also, see note at beginning of section.

Clatsop County

County Clerk, 820 Exchange St, #220, Astoria, OR 97103-0178. 503-325-8511; fax-503-325-9307; 8:30AM-5PM. www.co.clatsop.or.us/index.asp

Index: Separate indices to search include computer, microfilm. Vital records included, except divorce record index must be searched at the circuit court. Records indexed on a public use terminal back to 1995. Office personnel or visitors may perform searches. General index search fee $3.75 per document found. Office will search real estate records by name only. Office will not search tax liens. Copy fee $.25 per page. Cert fee- $3.75 per cert. Payee- Clatsop County. **Other phones:** Treasurer- 503-325-8565; Elections- 503-325-8511; Vital Records- 971-673-1190. **Property tax/Assessing-** 820 Exchange St, #200, Astoria, OR 97103; 503-325-8522, assessor fax- 503-338-3638. (Appraiser/Auditor- 503-325-8522) **Online access-** Access property data free at http://maps.co.clatsop.or.us/applications/WebMap/Source/login.asp; click on Agree then click on Search on map page. Other online access available via private companies.

Columbia County

County Clerk, 230 Strand St, Courthouse, St. Helens, OR 97051-2041. Recording, R/E phone-503-397-3796; fax-503-397-7266; Recording hours 9AM-4PM www.co.columbia.or.us

Index: Separate indices to search include deed, mortgage, misc. Vital records included, except divorce record index must be searched at circuit court. Records indexed on a public use terminal back to 1988, prior in books. Office will perform a UCC search but public must search other records themselves. Search fee $3.75 per name, on computer index only. Copy fee $.25 per page. Cert fee- $3.75 per doc plus copy fee. Payee- Columbia County Clerk. **Other phones:** Treasurer- 503-397-7252; Elections- 503-397-7214 & 3796; Vital Records- 503-397-3796. **Property tax/Assessing-** 230 Strand St, Courthouse, St. Helens, OR 97051; 503-397-2240, assessor fax- 503-397-5153. (Appraiser/Auditor- 503-397-2240) hours- 8:30AM-5PM **Online access-** Access maps via the statewide mapping site free at www.ormap.com/maps/index.cfm.

Coos County

County Clerk, 250 N Baxter; Attn: Recording, Coquille, OR 97423-1899. 541-396-3121 x228, 273, 407, 223, R/E recording phone- x223; fax-541-396-6551; 8:30AM-N, 1-4:30PM www.co.coos.or.us

Index: All in one. Vital records included, except divorce record index must be searched at the circuit court. Records indexed on computer from 1990 to present, prior to 1990 in index books. Office personnel or visitors may perform searches. Search fee $12.50 per name. Office will search real estate records. Will search UCC records. Copy fee $4.00 1st page, $.25 each add'l; self serve $.25 per page. Cert fee- $3.75 per cert plus copy fee. Payee- Coos County Clerk. **Other phones:** Treasurer- 541-396-3121 x333; Elections- 541-396-3121 x301. **Property tax/Assessing-** 250 N Baxter, Courthouse, Coquille, OR 97423; 541-396-3121 x274, assessor fax- 541-396-6071. (Appraiser/Auditor- 541-396-3121 x274) hours- 8AM-N 1PM-5PM **Online access-** Access to the assessor property and sales data is free at http://assessor.cooscotax.com. You may name search to lookup account numbers. Also see note at beginning of section.

Crook County

County Clerk, 300 N E 3rd, Prineville, OR 97754. 541-447-6553; fax-541-416-2145; 8AM-5PM. www.co.crook.or.us

Index: Separate indices to search. Vital records included, except divorce record index must be searched at the circuit court. Records indexed on a public use terminal back to 1987. Office personnel or visitors may perform searches. Search fee $3.75 per name location fee; written request only, prepaid. Copy fee $1.00 per page. Cert fee- $3.75 per cert plus copy fee. Payee- Crook County Clerk. **Other phones:** Treasurer- 541-447-6554; Elections- 541-447-6553. **Property tax/Assessing-** 541-447-4133. **Online** - Access property data free on the GIS-mapping site at http://gis.co.crook.or.us/DisclaimerPublic/tabid/74/Default.aspx but no name searching. Also see note at beginning of section.

Curry County

County Clerk, PO Box 746, Gold Beach, OR 97444. Recording, R/E phone-541-247-3295; fax-541-247-9361; 9AM-N 1PM-4PM. www.co.curry.or.us

Index: All in one. Vital records included, except divorce record index must be searched at the circuit court. Records indexed on a public use terminal back to 4/92. Office personnel or visitors may perform searches. General index search fee $3.75 per book or reel pulled by this office. Office will search real estate records. Office will not search UCC records. Copy fee $.25 per page. Cert fee- $7.75 1st page, $.25 each add'l page, plus copy fee. Payee- Curry County Clerk. **Other phones:** Treasurer- 541-247-3299; Elections- 541-247-3297; Vital Records- 971-673-1190. **Property tax/Assessing-** PO Box 746, 29821 Ellensburg Ave, Gold Beach, OR 97444; 541-247-3294. (Appraiser/Auditor- 541-247-3294) A public access terminal available. http://gis.co.curry.or.us/Website/Curry%20PDF/web-content/index.html **Online access-** Access the GIS-mapping site free at www.co.curry.or.us/GIS/WebCoverfix.html but no name searching. You may also choose to search pdf maps. Also, see note at beginning of section.

Deschutes County

County Clerk, 1300 NW Wall St, #202, Bend, OR 97701. Recording, R/E phone-541-388-6549; fax-541-383-4424; 8AM-4PM recording hours. www.deschutes.org/

Index: All in one. Vital records included, except divorce record index must be searched at the circuit court. Records indexed on a public use terminal back to 1985. Office will perform a UCC search but public must search other records themselves. Archives search fee $25.00 per hour. A location fee applies to real estate docs pulled by the office- $3.75 per doc. Copy fee $.25 per page. per page. Cert fee- $3.75 per doc plus copy fee. Payee- Deschutes County Clerk. **Online access to Real Estate, Deed, Mortgage, Lien records:** Search real estate, deeds, mortgages, liens on the clerk's recording system web inquiry for free at http://recordings.co.deschutes.or.us/search.asp. Free registration for username and password required. Index goes back to 1985; images back to 5/1999. **Other phones:** Treasurer- 541-388-6540; Elections- 541-388-6546. **Property tax/Assessing-** 1300 NW Wall St #204, Bend, OR 97701; 541-388-6508, assessor fax- 541-382-1692. hours- 8AM-5PM www.deschutes.org/ **Online access-** View records on the Assessor Inquiry System site at www.co.deschutes.or.us/dial.cfm. There is also business property searching. Access property tax map records on the Lava system free at http://lava.deschutes.org/gisapps/index.cfm but no name searching. Various land/ownership records at www.co.deschutes.or.us/dial.cfm; appraisal details, sales data, transaction-account histories, land use, and lot numbers for no fee. Also a business property search button. Also, see note at beginning of section.

Douglas County

County Clerk, PO Box 10, Roseburg, OR 97470. 541-440-4322, R/E recording phone-541-440-4320; fax-541-440-4408; 8-4PM. www.co.douglas.or.us/clerk/

Index: All in one. Vital records included, except divorce record index must be searched at the circuit court. Records indexed on a public use terminal back to 1996. Office personnel or visitors may perform searches. Search fee $25.00 per hour; $12.50 minumum. Office will not search UCC records. Copy fee $4.00 per doc. Cert fee- $3.75 per doc includes copy fee; $4.25 to return by mail. Payee- Douglas County Clerk. **Other phones:** Treasurer- 541-440-3311; Elections- 541-440-4252. **Property tax/Assessing-** 1036 SE Douglas, Roseburg, OR 97470; 541-440-4222. **Online** - Access assessor property data and sales free at www.co.douglas.or.us/puboaa/cgi/oaasearch.pl. Access to property sales is free at www.co.douglas.or.us/puboaa/ressales.asp. Also see note at beginning of section.

Gilliam County

County Clerk, PO Box 427, Condon, OR 97823. Recording, R/E phone-541-384-2311; fax-541-384-2166; 8:30AM-N, 1-5PM www.co.gilliam.or.us/Clerk/tabid/5192/Default.aspx

Index: Separate indices to search include books, computer. Vital records included, except divorce record index must be searched at the circuit court. Records indexed on a public use terminal, back to 1986. Office personnel or visitors may perform searches. Search fee $3.75 per name location fee; written request only, prepaid. Office will not search real estate records. Copy fee $.25 per page. Cert fee- $3.75 per cert plus copy and location fee. Payee- Gilliam County Clerk. **Other phones:** Treasurer- 541-384-6321; Elections- 541-384-2311; Vital Records- 971-673-1190 (Oregon Vital Records). **Property tax/Assessing-** PO Box 484, 221 S Oregon St, Condon, OR 97823; 541-384-3781, assessor fax- 541-384-2166. hours- 8AM-N, 1PM-5PM www.co.gilliam.or.us/Assessor/tabid/4866/Default.aspx **Online access-** Access maps via the statewide mapping site free at www.ormap.com/maps/index.cfm.

Grant County

County Clerk, 201 S Humbolt, #290, Canyon City, OR 97820. 541-575-1675; fax-541-575-2248; 8AM-5PM. www.gcoregonlive2.com/svc_display.php/526

Index: Vital records included in index, except divorce record index must be searched at the circuit court. Records indexed on computer back to 1990. Office personnel or visitors may perform searches. Search fee $12.50 per name. Copy fee $3.75 per document. Cert fee- $3.75 per copy. Payee- County Clerk. **Other phones:** Treasurer- 541-575-1798; Elections- 541-575-1675. **Property tax/Assessing-** 201 S Humbolt, Canyon City, OR 97820; 541-575-0107. (Appraiser - 541-575-0107) www.gcoregonlive2.com/svc_display.php/524 **Online-** Access maps via statewide mapping site at www.ormap.com/maps/index.cfm.

Harney County

County Clerk, 450 N Buena Vista, Burns, OR 97720. Recording, R/E phone-541-573-6641; fax-541-573-8370; 8:30AM-5PM, closed 1 hr for lunch. www.co.harney.or.us

Index: All in one. Vital records included, except divorce record index must be searched at the circuit court. Records indexed on a public use terminal back to 1984. Office personnel or visitors may perform searches. Search fee $3.75 per name per document. Office will not search real estate records. Will search UCC records. Copy fee- $.50 per page. Cert fee- $3.75 per doc; $.50 per page plus copy fee. Payee- Harney County Clerk. **Other phones:** Treasurer- 541-573-6541; Elections- 541-573-6641. **Property tax/Assessing-** 450 N Buena Vista, Burns, OR 97720; 541-573-8367, assessor fax- 541-573-8193. (Appraiser/Auditor- 541-573-8368) **Online access-** Access maps via the statewide mapping site free at www.ormap.com/maps/index.cfm.

Hood River County

County Clerk, 601 State St, Hood River, OR 97031-1871. 541-386-1442/or/6849, R/E recording phone-541-386-1442; fax-541-387-6864; 8AM-5PM. www.co.hood-river.or.us

Index: All in one. Vital records included, except divorce record index must be searched at the circuit court. Records indexed on a public use terminal back to 1985. Office personnel or visitors may perform searches. Office will not search real estate or UCC records. No fee for search. Copy fee $3.75 1st page; $.25 each add'l. Cert fee- $7.75 per doc plus copy fee. Payee- Hood River County. Contact Kimberly Haack for information on purchasing bulk data. **Other phones:** Treasurer- 541-386-1301; Elections- 541-386-1442. **Property tax/Assessing-** Same address as recording office. 541-386-4522, assessor fax- 541-387-6864. www.co.hood-river.or.us/ **Online access-** Access maps via the statewide mapping site free at www.ormap.com/maps/index.cfm.

Jackson County

County Clerk, 10 S Oakdale, Rm 216A, Medford, OR 97501. 541-774-6152; fax-541-774-6714; 8AM-4PM www.jacksoncounty.org, www.co.jackson.or.us/

Index: All in one. Vital records included, except divorce record index must be searched at the circuit court. Records indexed on a public use terminal back to 1985. Only the public may search. Copy fee $4.00 1st page; $.25 each add'l. Cert fee- $3.75 per cert plus copy fee. Payee- Jackson County Clerk. Bulk data available for purchase, $35.00 per month, contact County Clerk for more information. **Other phones:** Treasurer- 541-774-6541; Elections- 541-774-6148; Vital Records- 503-731-4108. **Property tax/Assessing-** 10 S Oakdale Rm 300 541-774-6059, assessor fax- 541-774-6701. (Appraiser/Auditor- 541-774-6042) www.co.jackson.or.us/ **Online access-** Access property via the Map Book Viewer free at www.smartmap.org/MapBookViewer/Search.asp but no name searching. Also see note at beginning of section.

Jefferson County

County Clerk, 66 SE D St, #C, Madras, OR 97741. Recording, R/E phone-541-475-4451; fax-541-325-5018; 8AM-5PM. www.co.jefferson.or.us/

Index: Vital records included in index, except divorce record index must be searched at the circuit court. Records indexed on a public use terminal back to 1985. Office will accomodate a lien search but public must search other records themselves. General Research fee $35.00 per hour. Copy fee $.50 for microfilm copy; $.25 for scanned image. Cert fee- $3.75 per cert plus copy fee. Payee- Jefferson County. Election data is available in bulk format. **Other phones:** Treasurer- 541-325-5023; Elections- 541-475-4451; Vital Records- 541-475-4456. **Property tax/Assessing-** 66 SE D St, #D, Madras, OR 97741; 541-475-2443, fax- 541-325-5504. (Appraiser - 541-475-2443) www.co.jefferson.or.us/ElectedOfficials/Assessor/tabid/1380/Default.aspx **Online access-** Access assessor property and tax data free at http://159.121.192.44/AandTWebQuery/. Access maps via the statewide mapping site free at www.ormap.com/maps/index.cfm.

Josephine County

County Clerk, PO Box 69, Grants Pass, OR 97528. 541-474-5240; fax-541-474-5246; 9AM-4PM. www.co.josephine.or.us/SectionIndex.asp?SectionID=110

Index: All in one. Vital records included, except divorce record index must be searched at the circuit court. Records indexed on a public use terminal back to 1981. Office will perform a UCC search but public must search other records themselves. Copy fee $4.00 1st page, $.25 each add'l. Cert fee- $3.75 per doc plus copy fee. Payee- Josephine-Co Clerk. **Online access to Real Estate, Deed, Lien, Judgment records:** Access to recording office index and documents is by subscription; fee is $35 per month, minimum 3 months. Contact Art at the recording office for signup, username and password. **Other phones:** Treasurer- 541-474-5235; Elections- 541-474-5243. **Property tax/Assessing**- 500 NW 6th St, Dept 3, Grants Pass, OR 97526; 541-474-5260, assessor fax- 541-474-5261. (Appraiser/Auditor- 541-474-5260) hours- 8AM-5PM **Online access**- Access property via the Map Book Viewer free at www.smartmap.org/MapBookViewer/Search.asp but no name searching. Also, search property data on the LION system free at http://68.185.2.151/website/pumaweb/ but no name searching. Also see note at beginning of section.

Klamath County

County Clerk, 305 Main St, Klamath Falls, OR 97601. 800-377-6094, 541-883-5134, R/E recording phone-541-883-5134; fax-541-885-6757; 8AM-5PM; recording Hours: 8AM-4PM www.co.klamath.or.us

Index: All in one. Vital records included, except divorce record index must be searched at the circuit court. Records indexed on a public use terminal back to 2000. Only the public may search. Copy fee $1.00 per page. This office may choose to add a $3.75 research fee. Cert fee- $7.75 first 2 pages, $1.00 fee for add'l copy pages. Payee- Klamath County Clerk. Treasurer- 541-883-4297; Elections- 541-883-5134. **Property tax/Assessing**- 305 Main St, Klamath Falls, OR 97601; 541-883-5111, fax- 541-885-6757. (Appraiser/Auditor- 541-883-5111) hours- 8AM-5PM www.co.klamath.or.us/Assessor/index.html **Online access**- Assessors property data available by subscription at www.co.klamath.or.us:8008/. Call 541-883-5142 for info and sign-up. Search tax property sales annual list free at www.co.klamath.or.us/PropertySales/index.html. Also see note at beginning of section.

Lake County

County Clerk, 513 Center St, Lakeview, OR 97630-1539. 541-947-6006; fax-541-947-6015; 8:30-5PM

Index: Separate indices to search include tract books, computer. Vital records included, except divorce record index must be searched at the circuit court. Records indexed on a public use terminal back to 1978. Office personnel or visitors may perform searches. Search fee $25.00 per hour plus $3.75 per book; written requests only. UCC search per debtor name- $10.00. General copy fee $4.00 1st page; $.25 each add'l; self serve- $.25 each.Real estate record copy- $.25 per page. Cert fee- $3.75 per doc plus copy fee. Payee- Lake County Clerk. **Property tax/Assessing**- Same address as recording office. 541-947-6000, assessor fax- 541-947-7012. A public access terminal is available. **Online access**- Access maps via the statewide mapping site free at www.ormap.com/maps/index.cfm.

Lane County

County Clerk - Deeds & Records, 125 E 8th Ave, Eugene, OR 97401. 541-682-3654; fax-541-682-3330; 8AM-5PM; recording 9AM-N, 1-4PM

Index: All in one. Vital records included, except divorce record index must be searched at the circuit court. Records indexed on a public use terminal back to 1972. Office personnel or visitors may perform searches. General index search fee $3.75 per document by mail only. Office will do searches by mail request only. Copy fee $.25 per page. Cert fee- $3.75 per cert plus copy fee. Payee- Lane County Clerk. **Online access to Real Estate, Deed records:** Access recorded land data on the Reg. Land Information Database RLID by subscription. Visit www.rlid.org or call Eric at 541-682-4338 for info/signup. Initiation fee is $200; monthly access fee is $80.00. **Other phones:** Treasurer- 541-682-4321; Elections- 541-682-4234; Vital Records- 541-682-4045. **Property tax/Assessing**- 541-687-4321. **Online access**- Access property and sales data on the Reg. Land Information Database RLID by subscription. Visit www.rlid.org or call Eric at 541-682-4338 for info/signup. Initiation fee is $200; monthly access fee is $80.00. Property records on the County Tax Map site are free at www.co.lane.or.us/TaxStatement/Search.aspx. No name searching. Also see note at beginning of section for add'l access.

Lincoln County

County Clerk, 225 W Olive St, Rm 201, Newport, OR 97365-3869. 541-265-4131, R/E recording phone-541-265-4121, UCC recording phone-541-265-4131; fax-541-265-4950; 8:30AM-5PM www.co.lincoln.or.us

Index: All in one. Vital records included, except divorce record index must be searched at the circuit court. Records indexed on a public use terminal back to 1986. Only the public may search. A standard $3.75 locator fee applies to most searches where office participates. Copy fee $.25 per page. Cert fee- $3.75 per cert plus copy fee. Payee- Lincoln County Clerk. Images may be available, please contact Laura, Toni, or Jodi at the county clerk's office. **Other phones:** Treasurer- 541-265-4139; Elections- 541-265-4131; Vital Records- 541-265-4127. **Property tax/Assessing**- 225 W Olive St Rm 207, Newport, OR 97365; 541-265-4102, assessor fax- 541-265-4148. (Appraiser/Auditor- 541-265-4102) **Online**- Access limited property info via the County Map Site free at www.co.lincoln.or.us/assessor/maps.html but no name searching. Download the free viewer and search by Township. Map pdfs also available. Also see note at beginning of section.

Linn County

County Clerk, PO Box 100, Albany, OR 97321. 541-967-3829; fax-541-926-5109; 8:30AM-4:00PM. www.co.linn.or.us

Index: All in one. Vital records included, except divorce record index must be searched at the circuit court. Records indexed on a public use terminal back to 1986. Office will assist the public, but the public performs searches. Separate federal tax lien search- $5.00 per debtor. Copy fee $4.00 1st page, $.25 each add'l. Cert fee- $3.75 per doc. Payee- County Recorder. **Other phones:** Treasurer- 541-967-3859; Elections- 541-967-3831; Vital Records- 503-731-4108; Records- 541-967-3829. **Property tax/Assessing**- Same address as recording office. 541-967-3808, assessor fax- 541-967-7448. **Online access**- Tax assessor rolls and sales may be viewed at www.co.linn.or.us/assessorshomep/assessor.htm. Also, search property via the ELLA Maps site free at www.co.linn.or.us/webmap/. On the map page, click on Search to search by addresses, but no name searching. Also see note at beginning of section.

Malheur County

County Clerk, 251 B St West, #4, Vale, OR 97918. Recording, R/E phone-541-473-5151; fax-541-473-5523; 8:30AM-5PM MST. www.malheurco.org

Index: All in one. Vital records included, except divorce record index must be searched at the circuit court. Records indexed on computer back to 1985. Office personnel or visitors may perform searches. Search fee $3.75 per name and per record. Office will search real estate records. Will not search UCC records. Copy fee $.25 per page. Cert fee- $3.75 per doc plus $.25 per page plus copy fee. Payee- County Clerk. **Other phones:** Treasurer- 541-473-5165; Elections- 541-473-5151; Vital Records- 541-889-7279. **Property tax/Assessing**- 251 B St West, #2, Vale, OR 97918; 541-473-5117, assessor fax- 541-473-5109. **Online access**- Search assessment data free at www.malheurco.org/. Access maps via the statewide mapping site free at www.ormap.com/maps/index.cfm.

Marion County

County Clerk, PO Box 14500, Salem, OR 97309. 503-588-5225; fax-503-373-4408; 8:30AM-5PM. www.co.marion.or.us/co/

Index: Separate indices to search include computer, microfilm. Vital records included, except divorce record index must be searched at the circuit court. Records indexed on a public use terminal back to 1976. Only the public may search. Copy fee $.25 per page. Cert fee- $3.75 per doc plus copy fee and locator fee if applicable. Payee- Marion County Clerk. Treasurer- 503-584-7700; Elections- 503-588-5041; Vitals- 503-588-5406. **Property tax/Assessing**- PO Box 14500, 555 Court St NE #2233 (97301), Salem, OR 97309; 503-588-5144, assessor fax- 503-588-7985. hours- 8AM-5PM www.co.marion.or.us/AO **Online** - Access assessor property data via the GIS-mapping at www.co.marion.or.us/IT/GIS/gisdata.htm. Fee is $82.50; other GIS property-related packages available. Also, property search for free at www.co.marion.or.us/AO. Search free on the Mapper at http://apps.co.marion.or.us/mcim/mcimdis.aspx but no name searching.

Morrow County

County Clerk, PO Box 338, Heppner, OR 97836. 541-676-9061, R/E recording phone-541-676-5604; fax-541-676-9876; hours - 8AM-N, 1PM-5PM. www.morrowcountyoregon.com/clerk/index.html

Index: Separate indices to search include computer to 1984, books to 1885. Vital records included, except divorce record index must be searched at the circuit court. Records indexed on a public use terminal back to 1984. Office personnel or visitors may perform searches. Office will only do a last deed recorded search for $3.75 location fee. Copy fee $.25 per page. Cert fee- $3.75 per doc plus copy fee. **Other phones:** Treasurer- 541-676-5630; Elections- 541-676-5607; Vitals- 541-676-5603. **Property tax/Assessing**- PO Box 247, Room 104, Heppner Courthouse, Heppner, OR 97836; 541-676-5607, assessor fax- 541-676-5610. (Appraiser/Auditor- 541-676-5607) **Online access**- Access maps via the statewide mapping site free at www.ormap.com/maps/index.cfm.

Multnomah County

County Recorder, PO Box 5007, Portland, OR 97208-5007. Recording, R/E phone-503-988-3034; fax-503-988-3330; 8AM-5PM; phone hours: 9AM-4:30PM www.co.multnomah.or.us/dss/at/index.html

Index: Separate indices to search include alpha, numeric by year. Vital records included, except divorce record index must be searched at the circuit court. Record index not computerized. Only the public may search; office will instruct searcher. A standard $3.75 locator fee applies to most searches where office participates. Copy fee $.25 per page; $4.00 per doc if mail return. Cert fee- $3.75 per cert plus copy and locator fee. Payee- Multnomah County Recorder. **Other phones:** Elections- 503-988-3720; Vital Records- 503-731-4095 (State); Tax information line- 503-988-3326. **Property tax/Assessing**- PO Box 2716, Tax Info Office, 501 SE Hawthorne Blvd, 1st Fl, #175, Portland, OR 97208-2716; 503-988-3326, assessor fax- 503-988-3330. (Appraiser - 503-988-3367) 8AM-5PM www.co.multnomah.or.us/ **Online access**- Search assessor maps free at http://gis.co.multnomah.or.us/mcormap/. Records on the County Metromap database are free at http://metromap.metro-region.org/. No name searching. The GIS-mapping site is very similar at http://gis.co.multnomah.or.us/sail/. Also, search property info at http://multcoproptax.com/ or on the Catbird subscription site; fee is $150 setup plus a monthly fee equaling $.25 per page viewed. For info/signup, call 503-988-3345.

Polk County

County Clerk, 850 Main St; Courthouse, Dallas, OR 97338-3179. Recording, R/E phone-503-623-9217; fax-503-623-0717; 8AM-5PM. www.co.polk.or.us

Index: All in one. Vital records included, except divorce record index must be searched at the circuit court. Records indexed on a public use terminal back to 1985 (Do not have birth records, only have death records-if they are recorded). Office personnel or visitors may perform searches (if on computer from 1985 to present). Search fee $3.75. Copy fee $.25 per page. Cert fee- $3.75 plus copy fee. **Other phones:** Treasurer- 503-623-9264 (also Tax); Elections- 503-623-9217; Vital Records- 503-623-8175. **Property tax/Assessing**- 850 Main St, Courthouse, Dallar, OR 97338; 503-623-8391, assessor fax- 503-831-3015.

(Appraiser/Auditor- 503-623-8391) **Online access**- Access property data free at http://apps.co.polk.or.us/webmap/source/login.asp and click on Agree and Accept, then click on Search on left hand side, then choose Tax Lots. Search by name, address, etc. Also, search for assessor maps for free at www.co.polk.or.us/Assessor/MapSearch.htm but no name searching. Also see note at beginning of section.

Sherman County

County Clerk, PO Box 365, Moro, OR 97039. phone-541-565-3606; fax-541-565-3312; 8AM-5PM. www.sherman-county.com/government_contacts.asp Links to assessor and appraiser information at this site. Index: All in one. Vital records included, except divorce record index must be searched at the circuit court. Records indexed on a public use terminal back to 1992. Office personnel or visitors may perform searches. Search fee $13.00 per name. Office will search real estate records. Copy fee $.25 per page. Cert fee- $3.75 per cert plus copy fee. Payee- Sherman County. **Other phones:** Treasurer- 541-565-3553; Elections- 541-565-3606. **Property tax/Assessing**- 541-565-3505. (Appraiser/Auditor-541-565-3505) **Online access**- Access maps via the statewide mapping site free at www.ormap.com/maps/index.cfm.

Tillamook County

County Clerk, 201 Laurel Ave, Tillamook, OR 97141. 503-842-3402; fax-503-842-1599; 8AM-5PM. www.co.tillamook.or.us/gov/clerk/default.htm Index: All in one. Vital records included, except divorce record index must be searched at the circuit court. Records indexed on computer back to 8/1/94. Office personnel or visitors may perform searches. No fee for search. Office will do limited real estate searches. Office will not search UCC records or tax liens. Copy fee $4.00 1st page, $.25 per add'l. Cert fee- $7.75 plus $.25 per add'l page. Payee- Tillamook County Clerk. **Online access to Real Estate, Deed, Lien, Judgment records:** Access to recorded document index free at www.co.tillamook.or.us/gov/clerk/recinq/Login.asp; use username "public" and password "inquiry." Viewing document images is not available online. **Other phones:** Treasurer- 503-842-3425; Elections-503-842-3402; Vital Records- 503-731-4095. **Property tax/Assessing**- 201 Laurel Ave, Tillamook, OR 97141; 503-842-3400. (Appraiser/Auditor- 503-842-3400) **Online access**- Assessment and taxation records on the County Property database are free at www.co.tillamook.or.us/Documents/Search/query.asp Search by property ID number or by name in the general query. Also, search for property info on the GIS-mapping service site at www.co.tillamook.or.us/gov/gis/parcelmaps.htm. Also see note at beginning of section.

Umatilla County

County Clerk, County Records Office, PO Box 1227, Pendleton, OR 97801-1227. 541-278-6236; fax-541-278-6345; 9-5 www.co.umatilla.or.us/records.htm Index: Separate indices to search include computer, older books, microfilm. Vital records included except divorce record index must be searched at the circuit court. Records indexed on a public use terminal back to 1987. Only the public may search but office will do short index name search. No search fee. Copy fee $.25 per page. per page. Cert fee- $3.75 per doc plus copy fee and $3.75 locator fee. Payee- Umatilla County Clerk. **Other phones:** Treasurer- 541-278-6210; Elections- 541-278-6256; Vital Records- 541-278-6236. **Property tax/Assessing**- PO Box 68, 216 SE 4th St, Pendleton, OR 97801; 541-276-7111. **Online access**- Access maps via the statewide mapping site free at www.ormap.com/maps/index.cfm.

Union County

County Clerk, 1001 4th St, #D, La Grande, OR 97850. Recording, R/E phone-541-963-1006; fax-541-963-1013; 8:30AM-5PM M-TH; 9AM-4PM F. www.union-county.org/ Index: All in one. Vital records included, except divorce record index must be searched at the circuit court. Records indexed on computer back to 1990. Only the public may search. Copy fee $.25 per page. Cert fee- $3.75 plus copy fee. Payee- Union County Clerk. Office does sell bulk data, contact Cathy Powell at above phone number. **Other phones:** Treasurer- 541-963-1018; Elections- 541-963-1006; Vital Records- 541-963-1006. **Property tax/Assessing**- 1001 4th St, #A & B, La Grande, OR 97850; 541-963-1002, assessor fax- 541-963-1039. (Appraiser/Auditor- 541-963-1002) hours- 8:30AM-5PM M-TH A public access terminal is available. www.union-county.org/ **Online access**- Access property tax data free at www.union-county.org/assessor_search.html.

Wallowa County

County Clerk, 101 S River, Rm 100, Enterprise, OR 97828. 541-426-4543 x17; fax-541-426-5901; 8:30AM-5PM www.co.wallowa.or.us/cc/ Index: All in one. Recordings start in 1880s. Vital records included; divorce index at circuit court. Records indexed on a public use terminal back to 1990s. Office personnel or visitors may perform searches. General search fee $12.50 per name. Office will not search real estate records. Office will not search UCC records. Copy fee $.25 per page; location fee $3.75. Cert fee- $3.75 per page plus copy fee. Payee- Wallowa County. **Other phones:** Treasurer-541-426-4543 x14; Elections- 541-426-4543 x17; Vital Records- 541-426-4543 x17; State- 503-731-4095. **Property tax/Assessing**- 101 S River, Rm 103, Enterprise, OR 97828; 541-426-4543 x35, assessor fax- 541-426-5901. (Appraiser/Auditor- 541-426-4543 x36) Public access computer in office for index and records searching. **Online access**- Access maps via the statewide mapping site free at www.ormap.com/maps/index.cfm.

Wasco County

County Clerk, 511 Washington St, #201; Courthouse, The Dalles, OR 97058-2237. Recording, R/E phone-541-506-2530; fax-541-506-2531; 9AM-N, 1-4PM www.co.wasco.or.us Index: All in one. Vital records included, except divorce record index must be searched at the circuit court. Records indexed on a public use terminal back to 1985. Only the public may search. Copy fee $3.75 plus $.25 per page. Cert fee- $3.75 per page plus copy fee. Payee- Wasco County Clerk. **Other phones:** Treasurer- 541-506-2772; Elections- 541-506-2530; Vital Records- 503-731-4108. **Property tax/Assessing**- 511 Washington St, #208, The Dalles, OR 97058; 541-506-2510, assessor fax- 541-506-2511. (Appraiser/Auditor- 541-506-2510) Public access computer for records and index searching. www.co.wasco.or.us **Online access**- The GIS-mapping services offers custom designed and also pre-packaged property data products, including the assessor data CD-rom for $300. View product line at www.co.wasco.or.us/gis/GISPrices2002.html. Other online access through private companies.

Washington County

County Clerk, 155 N 1st Ave, Mail Stop 9, Hillsboro, OR 97124. Recording, R/E phone-503-846-8752; fax-503-846-3909; 8:30AM-4:30PM www.co.washington.or.us/deptmts/at/recordng/record.htm Index: All in one 8/1977 to present, direct & indirect separate prior to 12/1988, also fiche index 7/1977-11/1988. Vital records included, except divorce record index must be searched at the circuit court. Records indexed on a public use terminal back to 12/1988. Office personnel or visitors may perform searches, however, the office will only search as time allows. General index search fee $42.50 per hour. Office will search real estate records. Will search UCC records. UCC search- $42.50 per hour, plus material. Copy fee $4.00 1st page, $.25 each add'l page of same doc. Cert fee- $3.75 per cert plus copy fee. Payee- Washington County Clerk. **Other phones:** Elections- 503-846-8670; Vital Records- 503-846-3538; Finance Dept-503-846-8811. **Property tax/Assessing**- 155 N 1st Ave, Mail Stop 8, Hillsboro, OR 97124; 503-846-8741, assessor fax- 503-846-3909. (Appraiser/Auditor- 503-846-8826) hours- 8:30AM-5PM Public access computer in office for index and records searching. **Online access**- Records on County GIS Intermap database are free at www.co.washington.or.us/deptmts/lut/gis/intermap/map_land.htm but no name searching. Also see note at beginning of section.

Wheeler County

County Clerk, PO Box 327, Fossil, OR 97830-0327. 541-763-2400; fax-541-763-2026; 8:30AM-4PM Index: Separate indices to search include deeds and Mtgs. Vital records included, except divorce record index must be searched at the circuit court. Record index not computerized. Office personnel (very limited) or visitors may perform searches. Search fee $3.75 per name location fee; written request only, prepaid. Office will not search real estate records. Will search limited UCC records. Copy fee $.25 per page, $.50 per page for legal-11 x 17. Cert fee- $3.75 per doc plus copy fee. Payee- Wheeler County. **Other phones:** Treasurer- 541-763-2078; Elections- 541-763-2400; Vital Records- 541-763-2400. **Property tax/Assessing**- PO Box 345, Fossil, OR 97830; 541-763-4266, fax- 541-763-2026. (Appraiser/Auditor-541-763-4266) hours- 8AM-N 1PM-5PM

Yamhill County

County Clerk, 414 NE Evans, McMinnville, OR 97128-4607. phone-503-434-7518; fax-503-434-7520; 9AM-5PM www.co.yamhill.or.us/clerk/ Index: All in one. Vital records included, except divorce record index must be searched at the circuit court. Records indexed on a public use terminal back to 1981. Office will perform a real estate search but public must search other records themselves. Search fee- no fee for short name searches; $32.00 per hour for real estate searches, as time allows. Will not search UCC records. Copy fee $.25 per page. Cert fee- $3.50 per cert plus copy fee. Payee- Yamhill County Clerk. **Other phones:** Treasurer- 503-434-7533; Elections-503-434-7518; Vital Records- 503-434-7523. **Property tax/Assessing**- 535 NE 5th St, Rm 42, McMinnville, OR 97128; 503-434-7521, assessor fax-503-434-7352. (Appraiser/Auditor- 503-434-7521) 8:30AM-5PM **Online** - Search assessor property data free www.co.yamhill.or.us/taxinfo/PropSearch.aspx. No name searching. Also, access maps via the statewide mapping site free at www.ormap.com/maps/index.cfm. Limited property data from the county surveyor is free at www.co.yamhill.or.us/surveyor/; no name searching.

Oregon County Locator

You will usually be able to find the city name in the City/County Cross Reference below. In that case, it is a simple matter to determine the county from the cross reference. However, only the official US Postal Service city names are included in this index. There are an additional 40,000 place names that people use in their addresses. Therefore, we have also included a ZIP/City Cross Reference immediately following the City/County Cross Reference.

If you know the ZIP Code but the city name does not appear in the City/County Cross Reference index, look up the ZIP Code in the ZIP/City Cross Reference, find the city name, then look up the city name in the City/County Cross Reference. For example, you want to know the county for an address of Menands, NY 12204. There is no "Menands" in the City/County Cross Reference. The ZIP/City Cross Reference shows that ZIP Codes 12201-12288 are for the city of Albany. Looking back in the City/County Cross Reference, Albany is in Albany County.

Oregon City/County Cross Reference

ADAMS Umatilla
ADEL Lake
ADRIAN Malheur
AGNESS Curry
ALBANY (97321) Linn(75), Benton(24)
ALBANY Linn
ALLEGANY Coos
ALSEA (97324) Benton(90), Lincoln(7), Lane(1)
ALVADORE Lane
AMITY (97101) Yamhill(84), Polk(15)
ANTELOPE Wasco
ARCH CAPE Clatsop
ARLINGTON Gilliam
AROCK Malheur
ASHLAND Jackson
ASHWOOD Jefferson
ASTORIA Clatsop
ATHENA Umatilla
AUMSVILLE Marion
AURORA (97002) Marion(76), Clackamas(23)
AZALEA Douglas
BAKER CITY (97814) Baker(95), Union(4)
BANDON Coos
BANKS Washington
BATES Grant
BAY CITY Tillamook
BEATTY Klamath
BEAVER Tillamook
BEAVERCREEK Clackamas
BEAVERTON Washington
BEND Deschutes
BLACHLY Lane
BLODGETT (97326) Lincoln(63), Benton(36)
BLUE RIVER Lane
BLY Klamath
BOARDMAN Morrow
BONANZA Klamath
BORING Clackamas
BRIDAL VEIL Multnomah
BRIDGEPORT Baker
BRIGHTWOOD Clackamas
BROADBENT Coos
BROGAN Malheur
BROOKINGS Curry
BROTHERS Deschutes
BROWNSVILLE Linn
BURNS Harney
BUTTE FALLS Jackson
BUXTON Washington
CAMAS VALLEY Douglas
CAMP SHERMAN Jefferson
CANBY Clackamas
CANNON BEACH Clatsop
CANYON CITY Grant
CANYONVILLE Douglas
CARLTON Yamhill
CASCADE LOCKS (97014) Multnomah(62), Hood River(37)
CASCADIA Linn
CAVE JUNCTION Josephine
CAYUSE Umatilla
CENTRAL POINT Jackson
CHEMULT (97731) Douglas(76), Klamath(23)
CHESHIRE Lane
CHILOQUIN Klamath
CHRISTMAS VALLEY Lake
CLACKAMAS Clackamas
CLATSKANIE (97016) Columbia(79), Clatsop(20)
CLOVERDALE Tillamook
COLTON Clackamas
COLUMBIA CITY Columbia
CONDON Gilliam
COOS BAY Coos
COQUILLE Coos
CORBETT (97019) Multnomah(95), Clackamas(4)
CORNELIUS Washington
CORVALLIS (97333) Benton(91), Linn(8)
CORVALLIS Benton
COTTAGE GROVE Lane
COVE Union
CRABTREE Linn
CRANE Harney
CRATER LAKE Klamath
CRAWFORDSVILLE Linn
CRESCENT Klamath
CRESCENT LAKE Klamath
CRESWELL Lane
CULP CREEK Lane
CULVER Jefferson
CURTIN Douglas
DAIRY Klamath
DALLAS Polk
DAYS CREEK Douglas
DAYTON Yamhill
DAYVILLE (97825) Grant(98), Wheeler(1)
DEADWOOD Lane
DEER ISLAND Columbia
DEPOE BAY Lincoln
DETROIT Marion
DEXTER Lane
DIAMOND Harney
DILLARD Douglas
DONALD Marion
DORENA Lane
DRAIN Douglas
DREWSEY Harney
DUFUR Wasco
DUNDEE Yamhill
DURKEE Baker
EAGLE CREEK Clackamas
EAGLE POINT Jackson
ECHO Umatilla
EDDYVILLE Lincoln
ELGIN Union
ELKTON Douglas
ELMIRA Lane
ENTERPRISE Wallowa
ESTACADA Clackamas
EUGENE Lane
FAIRVIEW Multnomah
FALL CREEK Lane
FALLS CITY Polk
FIELDS Harney
FLORENCE Lane
FOREST GROVE Washington
FORT KLAMATH Klamath
FORT ROCK Lake
FOSSIL Wheeler
FOSTER Linn
FOX Grant
FRENCHGLEN Harney
GALES CREEK Washington
GARDINER Douglas
GARIBALDI Tillamook
GASTON (97119) Washington(77), Yamhill(22)
GATES (97346) Marion(76), Linn(23)
GERVAIS Marion
GILCHRIST Klamath
GLADSTONE Clackamas
GLENDALE Douglas
GLENEDEN BEACH Lincoln
GLIDE Douglas
GOLD BEACH Curry
GOLD HILL Jackson
GOVERNMENT CAMP Clackamas
GRAND RONDE (97347) Polk(63), Yamhill(35), Tillamook(1)
GRANTS PASS (97527) Josephine(96), Jackson(3)
GRANTS PASS Josephine
GRASS VALLEY Sherman
GREENLEAF Lane
GRESHAM (97080) Multnomah(95), Clackamas(4)
GRESHAM Multnomah
HAINES Baker
HALFWAY Baker
HALSEY Linn
HAMMOND Clatsop
HARPER Malheur
HARRISBURG (97446) Linn(98), Lane(1)
HEBO Tillamook
HELIX Umatilla
HEPPNER Morrow
HEREFORD Baker
HERMISTON Umatilla
HILLSBORO (97123) Washington(96), Yamhill(3)
HILLSBORO Washington
HINES Harney
HOOD RIVER Hood River
HUBBARD (97032) Marion(84), Clackamas(15)
HUNTINGTON (97907) Malheur(66), Baker(33)
IDANHA (97350) Marion(75), Linn(25)
IDLEYLD PARK Douglas
IMBLER Union
IMNAHA Wallowa
INDEPENDENCE Polk
IONE Morrow
IRONSIDE Malheur
IRRIGON Morrow
JACKSONVILLE Jackson
JAMIESON Malheur
JEFFERSON (97352) Marion(97), Linn(2)
JOHN DAY Grant
JORDAN VALLEY Malheur
JOSEPH Wallowa
JUNCTION CITY (97448) Lane(98), Benton(1)
JUNTURA Malheur
KEIZER Marion
KENO Klamath
KENT Sherman
KERBY Josephine
KIMBERLY Grant
KLAMATH FALLS Klamath
LA GRANDE Union
LA PINE (97739) Deschutes(71), Klamath(27)
LAFAYETTE Yamhill
LAKE OSWEGO (97035) Clackamas(92), Multnomah(5), Washington(1)
LAKESIDE Coos
LAKEVIEW Lake
LANGLOIS Curry
LAWEN Harney
LEBANON Linn
LEXINGTON Morrow
LINCOLN CITY Lincoln
LOGSDEN Lincoln
LONG CREEK Grant
LORANE Lane
LOSTINE Wallowa
LOWELL Lane
LYONS (97358) Linn(68), Marion(31)
MADRAS Jefferson
MALIN Klamath
MANNING Washington
MANZANITA Tillamook
MAPLETON Lane
MARCOLA Lane
MARYLHURST Clackamas
MAUPIN Wasco
MCMINNVILLE Yamhill
MEACHAM Umatilla
MEDFORD Jackson
MEHAMA Marion
MERLIN Josephine
MERRILL Klamath
MIDLAND Klamath
MIKKALO Gilliam
MILL CITY (97360) Linn(71), Marion(28)
MILTON FREEWATER Umatilla
MITCHELL Wheeler
MOLALLA Clackamas
MONMOUTH (97361) Polk(97), Benton(2)
MONROE Benton
MONUMENT Grant
MORO Sherman
MOSIER Wasco
MOUNT ANGEL (97362) Marion(96), Clackamas(3)
MOUNT HOOD PARKDALE Hood River
MOUNT VERNON Grant
MULINO Clackamas
MURPHY Josephine
MYRTLE CREEK Douglas

MYRTLE POINT Coos
NEHALEM (97131) Tillamook(98), Clatsop(1)
NEOTSU Lincoln
NESKOWIN Tillamook
NETARTS Tillamook
NEW PINE CREEK (97635) Lake(71), Morrow(28)
NEWBERG (97132) Yamhill(98), Washington(1)
NEWPORT Lincoln
NORTH BEND Coos
NORTH PLAINS (97133) Washington(97), Multnomah(2)
NORTH POWDER (97867) Union(92), Baker(7)
NORWAY Coos
NOTI Lane
NYSSA Malheur
O BRIEN Josephine
OAKLAND Douglas
OAKRIDGE Lane
OCEANSIDE Tillamook
ODELL Hood River
ONTARIO Malheur
OPHIR Curry
OREGON CITY Clackamas
OTIS (97368) Lincoln(94), Tillamook(4), Baker(1)
OTTER ROCK Lincoln
OXBOW Baker
PACIFIC CITY Tillamook
PAULINA Crook
PENDLETON Umatilla
PHILOMATH Benton
PHOENIX Jackson
PILOT ROCK Umatilla
PLEASANT HILL Lane
PLUSH Lake
PORT ORFORD Curry
PORTLAND (97219) Multnomah(97), Clackamas(2)
PORTLAND (97231) Multnomah(90), Washington(6), Columbia(3)
PORTLAND (97266) Multnomah(74), Clackamas(25)
PORTLAND (97229) Washington(84), Multnomah(15)
PORTLAND Clackamas
PORTLAND Multnomah
PORTLAND Washington
POST Crook
POWELL BUTTE Crook
POWERS Coos
PRAIRIE CITY Grant
PRINCETON Harney
PRINEVILLE Crook
PROSPECT Jackson
RAINIER Columbia
REDMOND Deschutes
REEDSPORT Douglas
REMOTE Coos
RHODODENDRON Clackamas
RICHLAND Baker
RICKREALL Polk
RIDDLE Douglas
RILEY Harney
RITTER Grant
RIVERSIDE Malheur
ROCKAWAY BEACH Tillamook
ROGUE RIVER Jackson
ROSE LODGE Lincoln
ROSEBURG Douglas
RUFUS Sherman
SAGINAW Lane
SAINT BENEDICT Marion
SAINT HELENS Columbia
SAINT PAUL Marion
SALEM (97304) Polk(97), Yamhill(2)
SANDY Clackamas
SCAPPOOSE (97056) Columbia(98), Multnomah(1)
SCIO Linn
SCOTTS MILLS (97375) Marion(82), Clackamas(17)
SCOTTSBURG Douglas
SEAL ROCK Lincoln
SEASIDE Clatsop
SELMA Josephine
SENECA Grant
SHADY COVE Jackson
SHANIKO Wasco
SHEDD Linn
SHERIDAN (97378) Yamhill(84), Polk(15)
SHERWOOD (97140) Washington(89), Clackamas(8), Yamhill(1)
SILETZ Lincoln
SILVER LAKE Lake
SILVERTON Marion
SISTERS (97759) Deschutes(96), Jefferson(1), Linn(1)
SIXES Curry
SOUTH BEACH Lincoln
SPRAGUE RIVER Klamath
SPRAY Wheeler
SPRINGFIELD Lane
STANFIELD Umatilla
STAYTON (97383) Marion(96), Linn(3)
SUBLIMITY Marion
SUMMER LAKE Lake
SUMMERVILLE Union
SUMPTER (97877) Grant(82), Baker(18)
SUTHERLIN Douglas
SWEET HOME Linn
SWISSHOME Lane
TALENT Jackson
TANGENT Linn
TENMILE Douglas
TERREBONNE (97760) Jefferson(53), Deschutes(43), Crook(3)
THE DALLES Wasco
THURSTON Lane
TIDEWATER (97390) Lincoln(88), Lane(11)
TILLAMOOK Tillamook
TILLER Douglas
TIMBER Washington
TOLEDO Lincoln
TOLOVANA PARK Clatsop
TRAIL Jackson
TROUTDALE Multnomah
TUALATIN (97062) Washington(84), Clackamas(15)
TURNER Marion
TYGH VALLEY Wasco
UKIAH Umatilla
UMATILLA Umatilla
UMPQUA Douglas
UNITY Baker
VALE Malheur
VENETA Lane
VERNONIA Columbia
VIDA Lane
WALDPORT Lincoln
WALLOWA Wallowa
WALTERVILLE Lane
WALTON Lane
WARM SPRINGS Jefferson
WARREN Columbia
WARRENTON Clatsop
WASCO Sherman
WEDDERBURN Curry
WELCHES Clackamas
WEST LINN Clackamas
WESTFALL Malheur
WESTFIR Lane
WESTLAKE Lane
WESTON Umatilla
WHEELER Tillamook
WHITE CITY Jackson
WILBUR Douglas
WILDERVILLE Josephine
WILLAMINA (97396) Yamhill(53), Polk(46)
WILLIAMS Josephine
WILSONVILLE (97070) Clackamas(83), Washington(15)
WINCHESTER Douglas
WOLF CREEK Josephine
WOODBURN (97071) Marion(97), Clackamas(2)
YACHATS Lincoln
YAMHILL Yamhill
YONCALLA Douglas

Oregon ZIP/City Cross Reference

97001-97001 ANTELOPE
97002-97002 AURORA
97004-97004 BEAVERCREEK
97005-97008 BEAVERTON
97009-97009 BORING
97010-97010 BRIDAL VEIL
97011-97011 BRIGHTWOOD
97013-97013 CANBY
97014-97014 CASCADE LOCKS
97015-97015 CLACKAMAS
97016-97016 CLATSKANIE
97017-97017 COLTON
97018-97018 COLUMBIA CITY
97019-97019 CORBETT
97020-97020 DONALD
97021-97021 DUFUR
97022-97022 EAGLE CREEK
97023-97023 ESTACADA
97024-97024 FAIRVIEW
97026-97026 GERVAIS
97027-97027 GLADSTONE
97028-97028 GOVERNMENT CAMP
97029-97029 GRASS VALLEY
97030-97030 GRESHAM
97031-97031 HOOD RIVER
97032-97032 HUBBARD
97033-97033 KENT
97034-97035 LAKE OSWEGO
97036-97036 MARYLHURST
97037-97037 MAUPIN
97038-97038 MOLALLA
97039-97039 MORO
97040-97040 MOSIER
97041-97041 MOUNT HOOD PARKDALE
97042-97042 MULINO
97044-97044 ODELL
97045-97045 OREGON CITY
97048-97048 RAINIER
97049-97049 RHODODENDRON
97050-97050 RUFUS
97051-97051 SAINT HELENS
97053-97053 WARREN
97054-97054 DEER ISLAND
97055-97055 SANDY
97056-97056 SCAPPOOSE
97057-97057 SHANIKO
97058-97058 THE DALLES
97060-97060 TROUTDALE
97062-97062 TUALATIN
97063-97063 TYGH VALLEY
97064-97064 VERNONIA
97065-97065 WASCO
97067-97067 WELCHES
97068-97068 WEST LINN
97070-97070 WILSONVILLE
97071-97071 WOODBURN
97075-97078 BEAVERTON
97080-97080 GRESHAM
97101-97101 AMITY
97102-97102 ARCH CAPE
97103-97103 ASTORIA
97106-97106 BANKS
97107-97107 BAY CITY
97108-97108 BEAVER
97109-97109 BUXTON
97110-97110 CANNON BEACH
97111-97111 CARLTON
97112-97112 CLOVERDALE
97113-97113 CORNELIUS
97114-97114 DAYTON
97115-97115 DUNDEE
97116-97116 FOREST GROVE
97117-97117 GALES CREEK
97118-97118 GARIBALDI
97119-97119 GASTON
97121-97121 HAMMOND
97122-97122 HEBO
97123-97124 HILLSBORO
97125-97125 MANNING
97127-97127 LAFAYETTE
97128-97128 MCMINNVILLE
97130-97130 MANZANITA
97131-97131 NEHALEM
97132-97132 NEWBERG
97133-97133 NORTH PLAINS
97134-97134 OCEANSIDE
97135-97135 PACIFIC CITY
97136-97136 ROCKAWAY BEACH
97137-97137 SAINT PAUL
97138-97138 SEASIDE
97140-97140 SHERWOOD
97141-97141 TILLAMOOK
97143-97143 NETARTS
97144-97144 TIMBER
97145-97145 TOLOVANA PARK
97146-97146 WARRENTON
97147-97147 WHEELER
97148-97148 YAMHILL
97149-97149 NESKOWIN
97200-97299 PORTLAND
97301-97306 SALEM
97307-97307 KEIZER
97308-97314 SALEM
97321-97322 ALBANY
97324-97324 ALSEA
97325-97325 AUMSVILLE
97326-97326 BLODGETT
97327-97327 BROWNSVILLE
97329-97329 CASCADIA
97330-97333 CORVALLIS
97335-97335 CRABTREE
97336-97336 CRAWFORDSVILLE
97338-97338 DALLAS
97339-97339 CORVALLIS
97341-97341 DEPOE BAY
97342-97342 DETROIT
97343-97343 EDDYVILLE
97344-97344 FALLS CITY
97345-97345 FOSTER
97346-97346 GATES
97347-97347 GRAND RONDE
97348-97348 HALSEY
97350-97350 IDANHA
97351-97351 INDEPENDENCE
97352-97352 JEFFERSON
97355-97355 LEBANON
97357-97357 LOGSDEN
97358-97358 LYONS
97359-97359 MARION
97360-97360 MILL CITY
97361-97361 MONMOUTH
97362-97362 MOUNT ANGEL

97364-97364 NEOTSU
97365-97365 NEWPORT
97366-97366 SOUTH BEACH
97367-97367 LINCOLN CITY
97368-97368 OTIS
97369-97369 OTTER ROCK
97370-97370 PHILOMATH
97371-97371 RICKREALL
97372-97372 ROSE LODGE
97373-97373 SAINT BENEDICT
97374-97374 SCIO
97375-97375 SCOTTS MILLS
97376-97376 SEAL ROCK
97377-97377 SHEDD
97378-97378 SHERIDAN
97380-97380 SILETZ
97381-97381 SILVERTON
97383-97383 STAYTON
97384-97384 MEHAMA
97385-97385 SUBLIMITY
97386-97386 SWEET HOME
97388-97388 GLENEDEN BEACH
97389-97389 TANGENT
97390-97390 TIDEWATER
97391-97391 TOLEDO
97392-97392 TURNER
97394-97394 WALDPORT
97396-97396 WILLAMINA
97401-97405 EUGENE
97406-97406 AGNESS
97407-97407 ALLEGANY
97408-97408 EUGENE
97409-97409 ALVADORE
97410-97410 AZALEA
97411-97411 BANDON
97412-97412 BLACHLY
97413-97413 BLUE RIVER
97414-97414 BROADBENT
97415-97415 BROOKINGS
97416-97416 CAMAS VALLEY
97417-97417 CANYONVILLE
97419-97419 CHESHIRE
97420-97420 COOS BAY
97423-97423 COQUILLE
97424-97424 COTTAGE GROVE
97425-97425 CRESCENT LAKE
97426-97426 CRESWELL
97427-97427 CULP CREEK
97428-97428 CURTIN
97429-97429 DAYS CREEK
97430-97430 DEADWOOD
97431-97431 DEXTER
97432-97432 DILLARD
97434-97434 DORENA
97435-97435 DRAIN
97436-97436 ELKTON
97437-97437 ELMIRA
97438-97438 FALL CREEK
97439-97439 FLORENCE
97440-97440 EUGENE
97441-97441 GARDINER
97442-97442 GLENDALE
97443-97443 GLIDE
97444-97444 GOLD BEACH
97445-97445 GREENLEAF
97446-97446 HARRISBURG
97447-97447 IDLEYLD PARK
97448-97448 JUNCTION CITY
97449-97449 LAKESIDE
97450-97450 LANGLOIS
97451-97451 LORANE
97452-97452 LOWELL
97453-97453 MAPLETON
97454-97454 MARCOLA
97455-97455 PLEASANT HILL
97456-97456 MONROE
97457-97457 MYRTLE CREEK
97458-97458 MYRTLE POINT
97459-97459 NORTH BEND
97460-97460 NORWAY
97461-97461 NOTI
97462-97462 OAKLAND
97463-97463 OAKRIDGE
97464-97464 OPHIR
97465-97465 PORT ORFORD
97466-97466 POWERS
97467-97467 REEDSPORT
97468-97468 REMOTE
97469-97469 RIDDLE
97470-97470 ROSEBURG
97472-97472 SAGINAW
97473-97473 SCOTTSBURG
97476-97476 SIXES
97477-97478 SPRINGFIELD
97479-97479 SUTHERLIN
97480-97480 SWISSHOME
97481-97481 TENMILE
97482-97482 THURSTON
97484-97484 TILLER
97486-97486 UMPQUA
97487-97487 VENETA
97488-97488 VIDA
97489-97489 WALTERVILLE
97490-97490 WALTON
97491-97491 WEDDERBURN
97492-97492 WESTFIR
97493-97493 WESTLAKE
97494-97494 WILBUR
97495-97495 WINCHESTER
97496-97496 WINSTON
97497-97497 WOLF CREEK
97498-97498 YACHATS
97499-97499 YONCALLA
97501-97501 MEDFORD
97502-97502 CENTRAL POINT
97503-97503 WHITE CITY
97504-97504 MEDFORD
97520-97520 ASHLAND
97522-97522 BUTTE FALLS
97523-97523 CAVE JUNCTION
97524-97524 EAGLE POINT
97525-97525 GOLD HILL
97526-97528 GRANTS PASS
97530-97530 JACKSONVILLE
97531-97531 KERBY
97532-97532 MERLIN
97533-97533 MURPHY
97534-97534 O BRIEN
97535-97535 PHOENIX
97536-97536 PROSPECT
97537-97537 ROGUE RIVER
97538-97538 SELMA
97539-97539 SHADY COVE
97540-97540 TALENT
97541-97541 TRAIL
97543-97543 WILDERVILLE
97544-97544 WILLIAMS
97601-97603 KLAMATH FALLS
97604-97604 CRATER LAKE
97620-97620 ADEL
97621-97621 BEATTY
97622-97622 BLY
97623-97623 BONANZA
97624-97624 CHILOQUIN
97625-97625 DAIRY
97626-97626 FORT KLAMATH
97627-97627 KENO
97630-97630 LAKEVIEW
97632-97632 MALIN
97633-97633 MERRILL
97634-97634 MIDLAND
97635-97635 NEW PINE CREEK
97636-97636 PAISLEY
97637-97637 PLUSH
97638-97638 SILVER LAKE
97639-97639 SPRAGUE RIVER
97640-97640 SUMMER LAKE
97641-97641 CHRISTMAS VALLEY
97701-97709 BEND
97710-97710 FIELDS
97711-97711 ASHWOOD
97712-97712 BROTHERS
97720-97720 BURNS
97721-97721 PRINCETON
97722-97722 DIAMOND
97730-97730 CAMP SHERMAN
97731-97731 CHEMULT
97732-97732 CRANE
97733-97733 CRESCENT
97734-97734 CULVER
97735-97735 FORT ROCK
97736-97736 FRENCHGLEN
97737-97737 GILCHRIST
97738-97738 HINES
97739-97739 LA PINE
97740-97740 LAWEN
97741-97741 MADRAS
97750-97750 MITCHELL
97751-97751 PAULINA
97752-97752 POST
97753-97753 POWELL BUTTE
97754-97754 PRINEVILLE
97756-97756 REDMOND
97758-97758 RILEY
97759-97759 SISTERS
97760-97760 TERREBONNE
97761-97761 WARM SPRINGS
97801-97801 PENDLETON
97810-97810 ADAMS
97812-97812 ARLINGTON
97813-97813 ATHENA
97814-97814 BAKER CITY
97817-97817 BATES
97818-97818 BOARDMAN
97819-97819 BRIDGEPORT
97820-97820 CANYON CITY
97821-97821 CAYUSE
97823-97823 CONDON
97824-97824 COVE
97825-97825 DAYVILLE
97826-97826 ECHO
97827-97827 ELGIN
97828-97828 ENTERPRISE
97830-97830 FOSSIL
97831-97831 FOX
97833-97833 HAINES
97834-97834 HALFWAY
97835-97835 HELIX
97836-97836 HEPPNER
97837-97837 HEREFORD
97838-97838 HERMISTON
97839-97839 LEXINGTON
97840-97840 OXBOW
97841-97841 IMBLER
97842-97842 IMNAHA
97843-97843 IONE
97844-97844 IRRIGON
97845-97845 JOHN DAY
97846-97846 JOSEPH
97848-97848 KIMBERLY
97850-97850 LA GRANDE
97856-97856 LONG CREEK
97857-97857 LOSTINE
97859-97859 MEACHAM
97861-97861 MIKKALO
97862-97862 MILTON FREEWATER
97864-97864 MONUMENT
97865-97865 MOUNT VERNON
97867-97867 NORTH POWDER
97868-97868 PILOT ROCK
97869-97869 PRAIRIE CITY
97870-97870 RICHLAND
97872-97872 RITTER
97873-97873 SENECA
97874-97874 SPRAY
97875-97875 STANFIELD
97876-97876 SUMMERVILLE
97877-97877 SUMPTER
97880-97880 UKIAH
97882-97882 UMATILLA
97883-97883 UNION
97884-97884 UNITY
97885-97885 WALLOWA
97886-97886 WESTON
97901-97901 ADRIAN
97902-97902 AROCK
97903-97903 BROGAN
97904-97904 DREWSEY
97905-97905 DURKEE
97906-97906 HARPER
97907-97907 HUNTINGTON
97908-97908 IRONSIDE
97909-97909 JAMIESON
97910-97910 JORDAN VALLEY
97911-97911 JUNTURA
97913-97913 NYSSA
97914-97914 ONTARIO
97917-97917 RIVERSIDE
97918-97918 VALE
97920-97920 WESTFALL

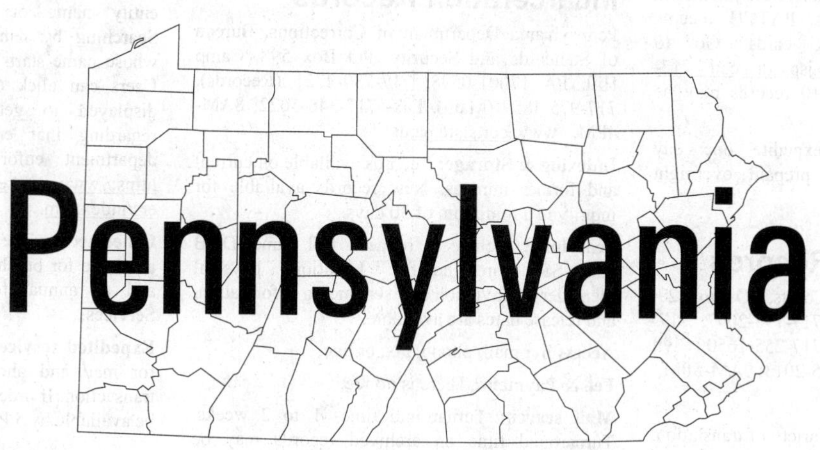

Pennsylvania

General Help Numbers:

Governor's Office

225 Main Capitol Bldg 717-787-2500
Harrisburg, PA 17120 Fax 717-772-8284
www.governor.state.pa.us/ 9AM-4:30PM

Attorney General's Office

Strawberry Square, 16th Floor 717-787-3391
Harrisburg, PA 17120 Fax 717-787-8242
www.attorneygeneral.gov 8AM-5PM

Legislative Records

General Assembly, Legislative Reference Bureau
Main Capitol Bldg, Room 641 717-787-2342
Harrisburg, PA 17120
www.legis.state.pa.us 8:30AM-5PM

State Archives

Bureau of Archives & History 717-783-3281
350 North St Fax 717-787-4822
Harrisburg, PA 17120 9AM-4PM T-F
www.phmc.state.pa.us (click on Archives)

State Specifics:

Capital:	Harrisburg Dauphin County
Time Zone:	EST
Number of Counties:	67
Population:	12,448,279
Web Site:	www.pa.gov/portal/server.pt

State Agencies

Criminal Records

State Police, Central Repository -164, 1800 Elmerton Ave, Harrisburg, PA 17110-9758; 717-783-5494, 717-783-9973, Fax- 717-772-3681; 8:15AM-4:15PM.

www.psp.state.pa.us/psp/site/default.asp

Indexing & Storage: Records available from the 1920s. Records are available for all convictions. New records available for inquiry in 1 day. Per a U.S. Dept of Justice Study, 60% of all arrests in database have final dispositions recorded, 31% for those arrests within last 5 years.

Searching: Must make request on Request Form SP4-164 or the request will be returned. The form can be found on web page (help menu in PATCH section) or call for form. Include in request- full name, date of birth, SSN, sex, race, any aliases, all on proper form. A release is not required. The record database is 100% fingerprint-supported. Statutorily-required fingerprint searches include an FBI fingerprint search. Records include all convictions; all charges that are less then three years from the date of arrest and the Central Repository has not received a disposition; and all charges for which a warrant of arrest has been issued and the Central Repository has been notified of such warrant.

Access by: mail, online.

Fee & Payment: Fee is $10.00 per name search. Add $19.25 for a statutorily-required FBI fingerprint check. Fee payee- Commonwealth of Pennsylvania. Prepayment required. No personal checks accepted. Credit cards accepted online only.

Mail search: Turnaround time- 2-3 weeks. Turnaround can be 6 weeks if a record has a hit. SASE not required.

Online search: Record checks are available for approved agencies through the Internet on the Pennsylvania Access to Criminal History (PATCH). Ongoing requesters may become registered users. This is a commercial system, the $10.00 fee per name applies. PATCH accepts Visa/MC, Discover, AmEx cards. Go to https://epatch.state.pa.us/Home.jsp or call 717-705-1768 to register. Up to 10 records may be requested at one session.

Expedited service: Will expedite one day turnaround if you provide prepaid overnight shipping envelope.

Statewide Court Records

Administrative Office of PA Courts, PO Box 229, Mechanicsburg, PA 17055; 717-795-2097, 717-795-2062 (Communications), 717-255-1650 (Civil Appellate Cases), Fax- 717-795-2013; 9AM-5PM.

www.aopc.org/default.htm

The website offers links to a variety of translation, terminology, and code files that can be viewed or downloaded, along with a brief description.

Access by: mail, online.

Mail search: One may request copies of records from the Appellate level courts - The Superior Court (criminal, family) and Commonwealth Court (civil). A Public Access Request Form is downloadable from the web page.

Online search: The web page offers access to a variety of the Judiciary's Electronic Services (E-Services) such as Web Docket Sheets, DA Link, Superior Court's Web Docketing Statements, etc. Go to http://ujsportal.pacourts.us/. Web Docket provides public access to view and print case docket sheets from the criminal cases of the Courts of Common Pleas and from the Appellate Courts and Criminal Cases. Search by docket number, name or organization. The Infocon County Access System provides a commercial direct dial-up access to court record information for at least 22 counties. There is a $25.00 base set-up fee plus a minimum $25.00 per month based on a $1.10 fee per minute. Visit www.infoconcountyaccess.com.

Sexual Offender Registry

State Police Bureau of Records and Ident., Megan's Law Unit, 1800 Elmerton Ave, Harrisburg, PA 17110-9758; 717-783-4363, 866-771-7130, Fax- 717-705-8839; 7AM-3PM.

www.pameganslaw.state.pa.us

Sexual offenders are required to register for either 10-years or for their lifetime. The length of time a sexual offender is required to register depends on the offense he committed.

Indexing & Storage: Records available from April 21, 1996 forward. As of March 2008, there were over 9,700 active registered sex offenders in the state of Pennsylvania. New records available for inquiry in 24 hours.

Searching: This office provides no searches except via the Internet or email. This data not released- victim information, details of incidents

Access by: online.

Online search: Limited information on all registered sex offenders can be viewed online from the webpage. Complete address information is listed for all active offenders. Upon opening the offender's record, you are provided tabs to click on access details such as alias, address, offense, vehicle, and physical characteristics information.

Incarceration Records

Pennsylvania Department of Corrections, Bureau of Standards and Security, PO Box 598, Camp Hill, PA 17001-0598; 717-730-2721 (Records), 717-975-4859 (Main), Fax- 717-346-5622; 8AM-4PM. www.cor.state.pa.us

Indexing & Storage: Records available on current and former inmates. New records available for inquiry in a minimum of 30 days.

Searching: Include in request- full name. DOB and SSN are helpful. Location, physical identifiers, conviction and sentencing information, and release dates are available.

Access by: mail, phone, fax, online.

Fee & Payment: There is no fee.

Mail search: Turnaround time- 1 to 2 weeks. Turnaround time on archived records may be longer than 2 weeks. A SASE is requested.

Phone search: Includes historical information on released inmates.

Fax search: Can request via fax.

Online search: At the website, click on Inmate Locator for information about each inmate currently under the jurisdiction of the Department of Corrections, or visit www.cor.state.pa.us/inmatelocatorweb/. The site indicates where an inmate is housed, race, date of birth, marital status and other items. The Inmate Locator contains information only on inmates currently residing in a state correctional institution.

Corporation, LP, LLC, LLP, Trademarks/Servicemarks, Fictitious/Assumed Name

Corporation Bureau, Department of State, PO Box 8722, Harrisburg, PA 17105-8722 (Courier - 206 North Office Bldg, Harrisburg, PA 17120); 717-787-1057, Fax- 717-783-2244; 8AM-5PM.

www.dos.state.pa.us/corps/site/default.asp

Indexing & Storage: Records available from 1700's on. Records are indexed on computer since the 1800's. New records available for inquiry in 4 to 7 days.

Searching: Include in request- full name of business. Corporation records include: Articles of Incorporation, Officers, Directors, DBAs, Prior (merged) names, Withdrawn and Reserved (120 days) names. Annual Reports on for-profit corporations are not required by the Department of State.

Access by: mail, phone, fax, in person, online.

Fee & Payment: The search fee is $15.00. Request for copies is $15.00 plus $3.00 per page. Certification is $55.00 plus $3.00 per copy. Printouts from computer or microfilm is $3.00 a page. A Good Standing is $40.00. Fee payee- Department of State. Prepayment required. Ongoing requesters should open a customer deposit account. Personal checks accepted, credit cards are not.

Mail search: Turnaround time- 3 to 5 days. SASE is not required.

Phone search: No fee for telephone request. They will provide basic information only.

Fax search: You must have an account to have materials returned by fax, same fees as above plus a $3.00 per page charge.

In person: There are 2 computer terminals available for public use.

Online search: There is free general searching by entity name or number from the website. Searching by name provides a list of entities whose name starts with the search name entered. Users can click on any one entity in the list displayed to get more detailed information regarding that entity. Also, search securities department enforcement actions database at https://www.secure.psc.state.pa.us/releases/Members/index.cfm.

Other access: The entire database of Image data is available for purchase. There is a $5,000 start fee and an annual fee of $12,000. Contact Web Services.

Expedited service: Expedited service is available for mail and phone searches. Add $70.00 per transaction. If ordered before 1 PM, the record will be available by 5 PM.

Uniform Commercial Code

UCC Division, Department of State, PO Box 8721, Harrisburg, PA 17105-8721 (Courier address- 206 North Office Bldg, Harrisburg, PA 17120); 717-787-1057 x3, Fax- 717-783-2244; 8AM-5PM.

www.dos.state.pa.us/DOS/site/default.asp

Email questions to RA-Corps@state.pa.us.

Indexing & Storage: Records available from 1964 to present on microfiche and computer. New records available for inquiry in 2 to 3 days.

Searching: Use search request form UCC-11. All federal and state tax liens are filed at the Prothonotary of each county. Include in request- debtor name. The agency will not expedite requests.

Access by: mail, fax, in person, online.

Fee & Payment: The search fee is $12.00 per debtor name, copies cost $3.00 per page. Certification is $28.00. Fee payee- Pennsylvania Department of State. Prepayment required. Deposit accounts are accepted. Personal checks accepted. No credit cards accepted for search requests.

Mail search: Turnaround time- 3 to 5 days. SASE not required.

Fax search: There is an additional $3.00 per page fee if returned by fax. A customer deposit account is required.

In person: If the search is conducted by the customer, there is no $12.00 search fee.

Online search: https://www.corporations.state.pa.us/ucc/soskb/SearchStandardRA9.asp allows a search of UCC-1 financing statements filed with the Corporation Bureau by debtor name or financing statement number; a list of financing statements is displayed. The site also allows a search of financing statement records filed with the Corporation Bureau by financing statement number. Note that this database is usually current within three days.

Other access: Daily computer tapes and copies of microfilm are available. Call the number above for details.

Federal & State Tax Liens

Records not maintained by a state level agency.

All federal and state tax liens are filed at the Prothonotary of each county.

Sales Tax Registrations

Revenue Department, Sales Tax Registration Division, Dept 280905, Harrisburg, PA 17128-0905; 717-787-3684, Fax- 717-787-4355; 7:30AM-4:30PM.

www.revenue.state.pa.us

Businesses can register online at www.pa100.state.pa.us/.

Indexing & Storage: Records available from 1971 to present, easily searchable from 1995 to present. New records available for inquiry in 2 to 3 weeks.

Searching: This agency will only confirm that a business is registered. They will provide no other information unless a signed release is presented. Include in request- EIN, state license number, business name. They will only search with a tax permit number.

Access by: mail, fax.

Fee & Payment: There is no search fee.

Mail search: Turnaround time- 2 to 7 days. A SASE is requested.

Fax search: Same criteria as mail searches.

Birth Certificates

PA Department of Health, Division of Vital Records, PO Box 1528, New Castle, PA 16101-1528 (Courier address- 101 S Mercer St, Room 401, New Castle, PA 16101); 724-656-3100 (Message Phone), Fax- 724-652-8951; 8AM-4PM.

www.dsf.health.state.pa.us/health/site/default.asp

Indexing & Storage: Records available from 1906 to present. New records available for inquiry in 1-2 days.

Searching: Records are only released to person of record, legal representative, or immediate family. If subject is deceased, death certificate must be submitted by family. The web pages gives full instructions. Include in request- full name, names of parents, mother's maiden name, date of birth, place of birth, relationship to person of record, reason for information request. Form available on web. Must include daytime phone number and valid government ID of requester. Records may be requested online via a vendor, but are not returned online. The web gives details or see expedited services.

Access by: mail, fax, in person.

Fee & Payment: The fee is $10.00 per record. If the year is not know there is an additional $25.00 fee for each 10 years searched. Fee payee- Vital Records. Prepayment required. Personal checks accepted. Credit cards accepted only by VitalChek.

Mail search: Turnaround time- 3 weeks. Credit cards not accepted for mail requests. A SASE is requested.

Fax search: See expedited services

In person: In person requests are honored in six cities - Erie, Harrisburg, New Castle, Philadelphia, Pittsburgh, and Scranton. Turnaround time is varies depending on workload.

Expedited service: Expedited service is available for request via or fax or online requests. Use of the state form (downloadable from web site) is required. Services is provided by an approved vendor - www.vitalcheck.com. Turnaround time- 2 to 4 days. Add $8.00 for use of credit card, add fees for express delivery, if desired.

Death Records

Department of Health, Division of Vital Records, PO Box 1528, New Castle, PA 16101-1528 (Courier address- 101 S Mercer St, Room 401, New Castle, PA 16101); 724-656-3100 (Message Phone), Fax- 724-652-8951; 8AM-4:30PM.

www.dsf.health.state.pa.us/health/site/default.asp

Indexing & Storage: Records available from 1906 to present. All information is public. New records available for inquiry in up to one month (record always updated on 5th).

Searching: Requester must be at least 18 years of age. An application form may be downloaded from the web. Include in request- full name, date of death, place of death, relationship to person of record, reason for information request. SSN helpful, if known. Include daytime phone number. Records may be requested online via a vendor, but are not returned online. The web gives details or see expedited services.

Access by: mail, fax, in person.

Fee & Payment: The fee is $9.00 per record. If the year is not know there is an additional $25.00 fee for each 10 years searched. Fee payee- Vital Records. Prepayment required. Personal checks accepted. Credit cards accepted only by VitalChek.

Mail search: Turnaround time- 3 to 4 weeks. A SASE is requested.

Fax search: See Expedited Service.

In person: Certified records may obtained from public offices in Erie, Harrisburg, Philadelphia, Pittsburgh, Scranton, and New Castle.

Expedited service: Expedited service is available for request via or fax or online requests. Use of the state form (downloadable from web site) is required. Services is provided by an approved vendor - www.vitalcheck.com. Turnaround time- 2-4 days. Add $8.00 for use of credit card, add fees for express delivery, if desired.

Marriage Certificates, Divorce Records

Records not maintained by a state level agency.

Marriage and divorce records are found at county level at Prothonotary of issue.

Workers' Compensation Records

Bureau of Workers' Compensation, Physical Records Section, 1171 S Cameron St, Rm 324, Harrisburg, PA 17104-2501; 717-772-4447, Fax-717-705-0940; 7:30AM-4PM.

www.dli.state.pa.us/landi/cwp/view.asp?a=138&q=220671

Indexing & Storage: Records available for past 4 years. New records available for inquiry in 1 to 3 days.

Searching: Only the party to the record is allowed full access without a subpoena or a signed release. The Agency will indicate if a record exists for a person, but will not give any other information to the public. Include in request- claimant name, year, date of accident, SSN. If not a party to claim, then include a signed release.

Access by: mail, fax.

Fee & Payment: No fees involved for simple requests.

Mail search: Turnaround time- 14 days. SASE not required.

Fax search: Requests are accepted by fax. Results are mailed.

Driver Records

Department of Transportation, Driver Record Services, PO Box 68695, Harrisburg, PA 17106-8695 (Courier address- 1101 S Front Street, 3rd Fl, Harrisburg, PA 17104); 717-391-6190, 800-932-4600 (In-state only); 7:30AM-4:30PM.

www.dmv.state.pa.us

Indexing & Storage: Records available for minimum of 3 calendar years for moving violations or departmental actions, minimum of 7 yrs for DWIs, and indefinite for suspensions. Accidents are reported on record as involvement only. Driver's address appears on the record. New records available for inquiry in 15 days from conviction receipt.

Searching: The agency must pre-authorize all customers of MVR vendor companies and of pre-employment screening firms. Include in request- driver's license number, full name, date of birth. Non-permissible use requesters submit Form DL-503, which requires the signature of the subject and/or notarized signature of the requester. Large volume requesters must sign an agreement stating the individual authorizations are on file. This data not released- SSN.

Access by: mail, in person, online.

Fee & Payment: The fee is $5.00 for each 3-year record or $10.00 for complete certified record. A 10-year employment record on a commercial driver is available for $5.00. A document pulled from microfilm is also $5.00. Fee payee- Department of Transportation. Prepayment required. Personal checks are accepted. No credit cards accepted.

Mail search: Turnaround time- 7 to 10 days. SASE not required.

In person: The state will process one record request while you wait, additional requests are sent to processing center and mailed to the requester. This is the only location that will provide certified records.

Online search: The online system is available to high volume requesters for three or ten-year records. Fee is $5.00 per record. The driver's license number and first two letters of the last name are required. High volume vendors who represent end-users cannot transmit results via the web unless process and end-user is pre-apporved. The resale of records by vendors to other vendors is generally forbidden. Call 717-705-1051 for more information about establishing an account. Also, PA licensed drivers may order their own record from the web page using a credit card.

Vehicle Ownership & Registration

Department of Transportation, Vehicle Record Services, PO Box 68691, Harrisburg, PA 17106-8691 (Courier address- 1101 South Front St, Harrisburg, PA 17104); 717-391-6190, 800-932-6000 (In-state); 7:30AM-4:30PM.

www.dmv.state.pa.us

This agency also holds records for unattached mobile homes. Encumbrance/lien information is not considered public information and is only released per DPPA guidelines.

Indexing & Storage: New records available for inquiry in 4 to 6 weeks.

Searching: The requester must submit Form DL-135. The state does not authorize the bulk delivery or commercial use of ownership & vehicle information.

Access by: mail, in person.

Fee & Payment: The fee is $5.00 per transaction. Title history may have more than one transaction per vehicle. You can call first to determine the number. There is an additional $5.00 for certification. Fee payee- Department of Transportation. Prepayment required. Personal checks accepted, credit cards are not.

Mail search: Turnaround time- 7 to 10 days. One can order a record in person, but results will be mailed. SASE not required.

In person: Basic info or lien data on one person or vehicle is available over the counter. If microfilm needs to be pulled, results are mailed.

Other access: Bulk information is not sold for commercial purposes. Certain statistical type user requests will be honored.

Accident Reports

State Police Headquarters, Crash Reports Unit, 1800 Elmerton Ave, Harrisburg, PA 17110-9758; 717-783-5516; 8AM-4PM.

www.psp.state.pa.us

Order form is available at the website. Will not do a name search, must have the "Incident Number."

Indexing & Storage: Records available for 10 years to present. New records available for inquiry in 15 days.

Searching: Only those involved, their attorney or insurer may request a copy of the accident report. Include in request- full name, date of accident, State Police incident number. This data not released- medical information or expunged records.

Access by: mail.

Fee & Payment: Reports are $8.00 per record. Fee payee- Commonwealth of Pennsylvania. Prepayment required. Personal checks accepted, credit cards are not.

Mail search: Turnaround time- 3 weeks. Reports may be returned by mail, or email if requested.

Vessel Ownership & Registration

Fish and Boat Commission, Licensing & Registration Section, PO Box 68900, Harrisburg, PA 17106-8900; 717-705-7940, Fax- 717-705-7931; 8AM-4PM.

www.fish.state.pa.us

Any boat powered by a gasoline, diesel or electric motor, including sailboats with auxiliary power must be registered. Boats must be titled if with inboard motor, or outboard motor and 14 ft or longer.

Indexing & Storage: Records available from 1975. New records available for inquiry in 1 month.

Searching: The agency follows the FCRA regarding the release of boat registration and ownership information. Liens are filed here for $5.00 per lien. As of 1998, this agency issues certificates of title. Include in request- signature of requester, reason for request, as much information about the boat or owner as possible. This data not released- address to record holder

Access by: mail.

Fee & Payment: There is a $5.00 fee for either current ownership information or lien information. A title history report is $5.00 for each owner shown on the record chain. Fee payee- Pennsylvania Fish and Boat Commission Personal checks and credit cards accepted.

Mail search: Turnaround time- 1-2 weeks. The Request Boat Title or Security Interest Information form is found at www.fish.state.pa.us/images/pages/forms/pfbc_t9.pdf. SASE not requested.

Legislation Records

Pennsylvania General Assembly, Legislative Reference Bureau, Main Capitol Bldg, Room 641, Harrisburg, PA 17120; 717-787-2342 (Status Room), 717-787-5320 (House Bills), 717-787-6732 (Senate Bills); House- 8:30AM-4:30PM; Senate- 8:30AM-5PM.

www.legis.state.pa.us

The website above is for the PA General Assembly and is not maintained by the Legislative Reference Bureau. Historical data is best obtained from the State Library.

Searching: Include in request- the topic of bill, bill number, or keyword.

Access by: mail, phone, in person, online.

Fee & Payment: There is no search fee or copy fee.

Mail search: Turnaround time- 2 days. SASE not required. Address specific requests to either the Senate or House Bill (document) room.

Phone search: Limited information is released.

In person: Simple requests may be processed while you wait.

Online search: Free access to bill text is available at the Electronic Bill Room found at the web page by selecting "Session Information." Data is available since 1975. The State Code is found at www.pacode.com/.

Voter Registration

Board of Commissions, Elections, & Leg., Voter Registration, 210 N. Office Building, Harrisburg, PA 17120; 717-787-5280, Fax- 717-705-0721; 8AM-5PM.

www.dos.state.pa.us/bcel/site/default.asp

The state has a statewide database. However, single record look-ups should be requested at the county level.

Searching: A request for a list is available from the web. Click on Elections and then click Elections again on the left hand link. Then click on the Request for Voter Lists on the left side. Not for use for commercial purposes. Address and DOB are released on the public lists. This data not released- SSN

Access by: mail, in person.

Mail search: Use the form to request a CD.

In person: Limited verification is available over-the-counter.

Other access: A CD of the entire state or by county can be purchased for $20.00 per disk. Be sure to ask for Voter Registration or go to www.dos.state.pa.us/elections/lib/elections/057request_for_voter_lists/requestvoterlists.pdf for form.

GED Certificates

Commonwealth Diploma Program, GED Office, 333 Market St 12th Fl, Harrisburg, PA 17126-0333; 717-787-6747, 717-787-5532; 8:30AM-4:30PM.

www.paadulted.org/able/site/default.asp

Indexing & Storage: Records available from 1950. New records available for inquiry in minutes.

Searching: This agency will only honor written requests. No verbal or fax verifications are given. Include in request- a signed release, name, approximate year of test, date of birth, SSN, city of test, and a phone number where requester can be reached.

Access by: mail, in person.

Fee & Payment: A verification request is processed as a request of a copy of transcript. The fee is $3.00 per transcript. The fee is non-refundable. Fee payee- Commonwealth of PA. Prepayment required. Cashier's checks and money orders are accepted. No credit cards or personal checks accepted.

Mail search: Turnaround time- up to 8 weeks. SASE not required.

In person: Counter service is available.

Hunting License Information

Access to Records is Restricted.

Game Commission, Hunting License Division, 2001 Elmerton Ave, Harrisburg, PA 17110-9797; 717-787-2084 (Hunting License Division), Fax-717-705-1628; 7:45AM-4PM.

www.theoutdoorshop.state.pa.us/fbg/

Hunting license information is not released to the public.

Fishing License Information

Fish & Boat Commission, Fishing License Division, PO Box 67000, Harrisburg, PA 17106 (Courier address- 1601 Elmerton, Harrisburg, PA 17110); 717-705-7930 (Fishing License Division), Fax- 717-705-7931; 8AM-4PM.

www.fish.state.pa.us/mpag1.htm

Indexing & Storage: Records available for current season only, although records are stored back to 1979. The records are not data based in any media, they are all handwritten.

Searching: Although the records are generally considered open to the public, the agency will not release lists for commercial purposes. Include in request- full name, date of birth, SSN, reason for information request.

Access by: mail, in person.

Fee & Payment: There is no fee.

Mail search: Turnaround time- 1 to 3 days. SASE not required.

In person: Simple requests may be processed while you wait.

Pennsylvania State Licensing Agencies

For details about the agency responsible for licensing/certifying/registering an item below or in the Agency Quick Finder section, match an item's number with the number of the agency in the *Licensing Agency Information* section.

Pennsylvania Licenses Searchable Online

Acupuncturist #20 .... www.licensepa.state.pa.us/
Amphetamine Program #20 .... www.licensepa.state.pa.us/
Anesthesia Permit, Dental #18 .... www.licensepa.state.pa.us/
Animal Health Technician #20 .... www.licensepa.state.pa.us/
Appraiser/Broker #20 .... www.licensepa.state.pa.us/
Architect #20 .... www.licensepa.state.pa.us/
Architectural Firm #20 .... www.licensepa.state.pa.us/
Athletic Agent #15 .... www.licensepa.state.pa.us/
Athletic Trainer #20 .... www.licensepa.state.pa.us/
Attorney #1 .... http://padisciplinaryboard.org/attsearchdc.php
Attorney Discipline Case #1 .... http://padisciplinaryboard.org/attsearchdcd.php
Auction Company/House #20 .... www.licensepa.state.pa.us/
Auctioneer #20 .... www.licensepa.state.pa.us/
Audiologist #20 .... www.licensepa.state.pa.us/
Bank #4 .... www.banking.state.pa.us/Banking/Banking/InstListQuery.asp
Barber #20 .... www.licensepa.state.pa.us/
Barber School/Teacher/Shop Mgr #20 .... www.licensepa.state.pa.us/
Boxer #15 .... www.dos.state.pa.us/sac/cwp/view.asp?a=1090&q=436810&sacNav=|
Builder/Owner, Real Estate #20 .... www.licensepa.state.pa.us/
Campaign Finance Report #21 .... www.campaignfinance.state.pa.us/
Campground Membership Seller #20 .... www.licensepa.state.pa.us/
Cemetery Broker/Seller/Regis. #20 .... www.licensepa.state.pa.us/
Check Casher #4 .... www.banking.state.pa.us/Banking/Banking/InstListQuery.asp
Child Day Care Facility #12 .... https://www.humanservices.state.pa.us/compass/ProviderSearch/PGM/PSADD.aspx
Childcare Complaint/Report #12
.... https://www.pelican.state.pa.us/PPCSPublicFacing/PublicInterface/ComplaintsAndIncidents/PFZIP.aspx
Chiropractor #20 .... www.licensepa.state.pa.us/
Consumer Discount Company #4 .... www.banking.state.pa.us/Banking/Banking/InstListQuery.asp
Continuing Edu. Provider, Financial #4 .... www.banking.state.pa.us/Banking/Banking/InstListQuery.asp
Cosmetologist/Cosmetician #20 .... www.licensepa.state.pa.us/
Cosmetology Shop/Teacher/School #20 .... www.licensepa.state.pa.us/
Counselor, Professional #20 .... www.licensepa.state.pa.us/
Credit Services Loan Broker #4 .... www.banking.state.pa.us/Banking/Banking/InstListQuery.asp
Credit Union #4 .... www.banking.state.pa.us/Banking/Banking/InstListQuery.asp
Debt Collector #4 .... www.banking.state.pa.us/Banking/Banking/InstListQuery.asp
Dental Assist., Expanded Function #18 .... www.licensepa.state.pa.us/
Dentist / Dental Hygienist #18 .... www.licensepa.state.pa.us/
Dietitian/Nutritionist LDN #20 .... www.licensepa.state.pa.us/
Emergency Medical Technician #8 .... https://ems.health.state.pa.us/emsportal/
Engineer #20 .... www.licensepa.state.pa.us/
Evaluator, Appraisal #20 .... www.licensepa.state.pa.us/
Financial Holding Company #4 .... www.banking.state.pa.us/Banking/Banking/InstListQuery.asp
Funeral Director/Supervisor/Establish't #20 .... www.licensepa.state.pa.us/
Geologist #20 .... www.licensepa.state.pa.us/
Hearing Aid Fitter/ Hearing Examiner #20 .... www.licensepa.state.pa.us/
Installment Loan Seller #4 .... www.banking.state.pa.us/Banking/Banking/InstListQuery.asp
Insurance Agent/Company #11 .... http://164.156.71.30/producer/ilist1.asp
Laboratory, Medical #10 .... www.dsf.health.state.pa.us/health/lib/health/labs/clia_certificate.pdf
Landscape Architect #20 .... www.licensepa.state.pa.us/
Loan Correspondent #4 .... www.banking.state.pa.us/Banking/Banking/InstListQuery.asp
Lobbying/Lobbyist/Lobbying Firm #21 .... www.palobbyingservices.state.pa.us/Act134/Public/RegistrationSearch.aspx
Manicurist #20 .... www.licensepa.state.pa.us/
Marriage & Family Therapist #20 .... www.licensepa.state.pa.us/
Medical Doctor #20 .... www.licensepa.state.pa.us/
Midwife #20 .... www.licensepa.state.pa.us/
Money Transmitter #4 .... www.banking.state.pa.us/Banking/Banking/InstListQuery.asp
Mortgage-Related Occupation #4 .... www.banking.state.pa.us/Banking/Banking/InstListQuery.asp

Nuclear Medicine Technologist #20............www.licensepa.state.pa.us/
Nurse #20............www.licensepa.state.pa.us/
Nurses Aide #9............www.asisvcs.com/services/registry/search_fs.asp?CPCat=0639NURSE
Nursing Home #9............http://app2.health.state.pa.us/commonpoc/nhLocatorie.asp
Nursing Home Administrator #20............www.licensepa.state.pa.us/
Occupational Therapist/Assistant #20............www.licensepa.state.pa.us/
Optometrist #20............www.licensepa.state.pa.us/
Osteopathic Acupuncturist #20............www.licensepa.state.pa.us/
Osteopathic Physician/Surgeon/Asst #20 ...www.licensepa.state.pa.us/
Osteopathic Respiratory Care #20............www.licensepa.state.pa.us/
Pawnbroker #4............www.banking.state.pa.us/Banking/Banking/InstListQuery.asp
Pesticide Applicator/Technician #2............https://www.paplants.state.pa.us/PesticideApplicator/ApplicatorExternalSearch.aspx
Pharmacist/Pharmacy #20............www.licensepa.state.pa.us/
Physical Therapist/Assistant #20............www.licensepa.state.pa.us/
Physician Assistant #20............www.licensepa.state.pa.us/
Pilot, Navigational #20............www.licensepa.state.pa.us/
Podiatrist #20............www.licensepa.state.pa.us/
Political Committee/Contributor #21............www.campaignfinance.state.pa.us/
Political Finance Statement #17............www.palobbyingservices.state.pa.us/Act134/Public/RegistrationSearch.aspx
Psychologist #20............www.licensepa.state.pa.us/
Public Accountant-CPA/Corp./Partners #20 .www.licensepa.state.pa.us/
Public Adjuster/ Solicitor #11............http://164.156.71.30/producer/ilist1.asp
Radiation Therapy Technician #20............www.licensepa.state.pa.us/
Radiologic Technologist/Aux/Chiro. #20............www.licensepa.state.pa.us/
Real Estate Agent/Broker/Sales/Sch'l #20 ..www.licensepa.state.pa.us/
Real Estate Appraiser #20............www.licensepa.state.pa.us/
Rental Listing Referral Agent #20............www.licensepa.state.pa.us/
Repossessor #4............www.banking.state.pa.us/Banking/Banking/InstListQuery.asp
Respiratory Care Practitioner #20............www.licensepa.state.pa.us/
Sales Finance Company #4............www.banking.state.pa.us/Banking/Banking/InstListQuery.asp
Savings Association #4............www.banking.state.pa.us/Banking/Banking/InstListQuery.asp
Social Worker #20............www.licensepa.state.pa.us/
Speech-Language Pathologist #20............www.licensepa.state.pa.us/
Surplus Lines Broker #11............http://164.156.71.30/producer/ilist1.asp
Surveyor, Land #20............www.licensepa.state.pa.us/
Table Funder, Wholesale #4............www.banking.state.pa.us/Banking/Banking/InstListQuery.asp
Teacher #6............https://www.tcs.ed.state.pa.us/
Therapist, Drugless #20............www.licensepa.state.pa.us/
Thrift Holding Company #4............www.banking.state.pa.us/Banking/Banking/InstListQuery.asp
Timeshare Salesperson #20............www.licensepa.state.pa.us/
Title Insurance #11............http://164.156.71.30/producer/ilist1.asp
Trust Company #4............www.banking.state.pa.us/Banking/Banking/InstListQuery.asp
Used Vehicle Lot #19............www.licensepa.state.pa.us/
Vehicle Dealer/Mfg/Seller/Dist/Auction #19 .www.licensepa.state.pa.us/
Veterinarian/Veterinary Techn'c'n #20............www.licensepa.state.pa.us/

Pennsylvania Licensing Quick Finder

Acupuncturist #20............717-783-4858
Ambulance Service #8............717-787-8740
Amphetamine Program #20............717-787-2568
Anesthesia Permit, Dental #18............717-783-7162
Animal Health Technician #20............717-783-7134
Appraiser/Broker #20............717-783-4866
Architect #20............717-783-3397
Architectural Firm #20............717-783-3397
Athletic Agent #15............717-787-5720
Athletic Event Professional #15............717-787-5720
Athletic Trainer #20............717-783-4858
Attorney #1............717-731-7073
Attorney Discipline Case #1............717-731-7073
Auction Company/House #20............717-783-3397
Auctioneer #20............717-783-3397
Auctioneer, Real Estate #20............717-783-3658
Audiologist #20............717-783-1389
Bank #4............717-787-3717
Barber #20............717-783-3402
Barber Shop/Mgr/School/Teacher #20.717-783-3402
Boat Registration #13............717-705-7940
Bondsman #11............717-787-3840, 877-336-7479
Boxer #15............717-787-5720
Boxing Judge/Promoter/2nd #15............717-787-5720
Builder/Owner, Real Estate #20............717-783-3658
Campaign Finance Report #21............717-787-5280
Campground Membership Seller #20 ..717-783-3658
Cemetery Broker/Seller/Regis. #20............717-783-3658
Check Casher #4............717-787-3717
Child Day Care Facility #12............717-346-9325
Childcare Complaint/Report #12............717-346-9325
Chiropractor #20............717-783-7155
Consumer Discount Company #4............717-787-3717
Continuing Edu. Provider, Financial #4 717-787-3717
Cosmetologist/Cosmetician #20............717-783-7130
Cosmetology Teacher/School #20............717-783-7130
Cosmetology/Manicurist Shop #20............717-783-7130
Counselor, Professional #20............717-783-1389
Credit Services Loan Broker #4............717-787-3717
Credit Union #4............717-787-3717
Debt Collector #4............717-787-3717
Dental Asst., Expanded Function #18.. 717-783-7162
Entist / Dental Hygienist #18............717-783-7162
Dietitian/Nutritionist LDN #20............717-783-7142
Education Specialist #6............717-787-3356
Emergency Health Professional #8............717-787-8740
Emergency Medical Technician #8............717-787-8740
Engineer #20............717-783-7049
Evaluator, Appraisal #20............717-783-4866
Financial Holding Company #4............717-787-3717
First Responder EMT #8............717-787-8740
Funeral Director/Supervisor #20............717-783-3397
Funeral Establishment #20............717-783-3397
Geologist #20............717-783-7049
Harness Racing #3............717-787-5789
Hearing Aid Dealer #7............717-783-1389
Hearing Aid Fitter/Fitter Apprentice #7. 717-783-1389
Hearing Examiner #20............717-783-1389
Horse Racing #3............717-783-8726
Installment Loan Seller #4............717-787-3717

Insurance Agent/Company #11 .... 717-787-3840, 877-336-7479
Investment Adviser & IA Reps #16 .... 717-783-4216 or 4244
Kickboxer #15 717-787-5720
Laboratory, Medical #10 610-280-3464
Landscape Architect #20 717-772-8528
Liquor Distributor/Retailer/Whlse #14 717-783-8250
Loan Correspondent #4 717-787-3717
Lobbying Principal #21 717-787-5920
Lobbyist/Lobbying Firm #21 717-787-5920
Manicurist #20 717-783-7130
Marriage & Family Therapist #20 717-783-1389
Medical Doctor #20 717-787-2381
Medical School #20 717-783-1400
Midwife #20 717-783-1400
Money Transmitter #4 717-787-3717
Mortgage-Related #4 717-787-3717
Notary Public #5 717-787-5280
Nuclear Medicine Technologist #20 717-787-4858
Nurse #20 717-783-7142
Nurses Aide #9 800-852-0518
Nursing Home #9 .... 610-594-8041, 717-787-1816
Nursing Home Administrator #20 717-783-7155
Occupational Therapist/Assistant #20 717-783-1389
Optometrist #20 717-783-7155
Osteopathic Acupuncturist #20 717-783-4858
Osteopathic Physician Assistant #20 717-783-4858
Osteopathic Physician/Surgeon #20 717-783-4858
Osteopathic Respiratory Care #20 717-783-4858
Paramedic #8 717-787-8740
Pawnbroker #4 717-787-3717
Pesticide Applicator/Technician #2 .... 717-787-5231 x2
Pesticide Dealer/Consultant #2 .... 717-787-5231 x2
Pharmacist/Pharmacy #20 717-783-7156
Physical Therapist/Assistant #20 717-783-7134
Physician Assistant #20 717-787-2381
Pilot, Navigational #20 717-787-6802
Podiatrist #20 717-783-4858
Political Committee/Contributor #21 717-787-5280
Political Finance Statement #17 717-783-1610
Pre-Hospital RN #8 717-787-8740
Private Investigator #15 717-255-2692
Private School Staff #6 717-787-3356
Psychologist #20 717-783-7134
Public Accountant-CPA/Corp. #20 717-783-1404
Public Accounting Partnership #20 717-783-1404
Public Adjuster/ Solicitor #11 .... 717-787-3840, 877-336-7479
Radiation Therapy Technician #20 717-783-7155
Radiologic Auxiliary, Chiropractic #20 717-783-7155
Radiologic Technologist #20 717-783-4858
Real Estate Agent/Broker/Sales #20 717-783-3658
Real Estate Appraiser #20 717-783-4866
Real Estate School #20 717-783-3658
Referee #15 717-787-5720
Rental Listing Referral Agent #20 717-783-3658
Repossessor #4 717-787-3717
Respiratory Care Practitioner #20 717-783-4858
Sales Finance Company #4 717-787-3717
Savings Association #4 717-787-3717
School Administrator/Superintend't #6 717-787-3356
School Intermediate Unit Director #6 717-787-3356
Securities Agent #16 717-783-4212
Securities Broker/Dealer #16 717-783-4211
Social Worker #20 717-783-1389
Speech-Language Pathologist #20 717-783-1389
Surplus Lines Broker #11 .... 717-787-3840, 877-336-7479
Surveyor, Land #20 717-783-7049
Table Funder, Wholesale #4 717-787-3717
Teacher #6 717-787-3356
Therapist, Drugless #20 717-783-4858
Thrift Holding Company #4 717-787-3717
Timeshare Salesperson #20 717-783-3658
Title Insurance #11 .... 717-787-3840, 877-336-7479
Trust Company #4 717-787-3717
Used Vehicle Lot #19 717-783-1697
Vehicle Auction #19 717-783-1697
Vehicle Dealer/Manuf't'r/Dist.Seller #19 717-783-1697
Veterinarian/Veterinary Techn'c'n #20 717-783-7134
Viatical Settlement Broker #11 .... 717-787-3840, 877-336-7479
Wrestling Promoter #15 717-787-5720

Pennsylvania Licensing Agency Information

#1 Disciplinary Board of the Supreme Court, 2 Lemoyne Dr, First Fl, Lemoyne, PA 17055; 717-731-7073, Fax- 717-731-7080. www.padisciplinaryboard.org Data at- www.padisciplinaryboard.org/pa_attorney_search.php

#2 Department of Agriculture, Bureau of Plant Industry, 2301 N Cameron St, Harrisburg, PA 17110-9408; 717-772-5231, Fax- 717-783-3275. Hours- 8AM-4PM. https://www.paplants.state.pa.us/Index.aspx

#3 Department of Agriculture, Racing License Division, 2301 N Cameron St, Agriculture Office Bldg, Rm 304, Harrisburg, PA 17110-9408; 717-787-5196, Fax- 717-787-2271. www.agriculture.state.pa.us/agriculture/cwp/view.asp?a=3&q=129034

#4 Department of Banking, 17 N 2nd St, #1300, Harrisburg, PA 17101-2290; 717-787-2665, Fax- 717-787-8773. www.banking.state.pa.us/banking/site/default.asp Search data at- www.banking.state.pa.us/banking/banking/instlistquery.asp

#5 Department of State, Division of Commissions, Legislation and Notaries, 210 North Office Bldg, Rm 304, Harrisburg, PA 17120; 717-787-5280, Fax- 717-787-2854. www.dos.state.pa.us/bcel/site/default.asp Active and/or commissioned Notaries Public request form at www.dos.state.pa.us/notaries/cwp/ view.asp?a= 1246&q=444958 ¬ariesNav=| and fee is $50.00.

#6 Department of Education, Teacher Certification, 333 Market St, 3rd Fl, Harrisburg, PA 17126-0333; 717-787-3356, Fax- 717-783-6736. www.pde.state.pa.us Search data at- https://www.tcs.ed.state.pa.us/ Use a teacher's SSN to verify certifications.

#7 Bureau of Profession and Occupational Affairs, Board of Examiners in Speech-Language and Hearing, PO Box 2649, Harrisburg, PA 17105; 717-783-1389, Fax- 717-787-7769. www.dos.state.pa.us/bpoa/cwp/view.asp?a=1104&q=433205 Direct list requests to Diane Miller at (717) 772-2244.

#8 Dept. of Health, Emergency Medical Svcs, PO Box 90 (7th & Forster), Harrisburg, PA 17108; 717-787-8740, Fax- 717-772-0910. www.dsf.health.state.pa.us/health/site/

#9 Department of Health, Division of Nursing Care Facilities, Health & Welfare Bldg, 7th & Forster Sts, Rm 526, Harrisburg,, PA 17120; 800-852-0518, Fax- 717-787-1816. www.dsf.health.state.pa.us/health/cwp/browse.asp?a=188&bc=0&c=35675

#10 Department of Health, Bureau of Laboratories, 110 Pickering Way, Lionville, PA 19353; 610-280-3464, Fax- 610-450-1932. www.dsf.health.state.pa.us/health/CWP/view.asp?A=167&QUESTION_ID=202401

#11 Department of Insurance, 1209 Strawberry Sq, Harrisburg, PA 17120; 717-787-2317, Fax- 717-787-8585. www.ins.state.pa.us/ins/default.asp

#12 Department of Public Welfare,OCDEL, Bureau of Certification Services, 333 Market St, 6th Fl, Harrisburg, PA 17126; 717-346-9325, 800-222-2117. www.dpw.state.pa.us/ServicesPrograms/ChildCareEarlyEd/ Search data- https://www.humanservices.state.pa.us/compass/ProviderSearch/PGM/PSADD.aspx There are 4 regional offices - this is the Central Region.

#13 Fish & Boat Commission, PO Box 67000 (1601 Elmerton Ave), Harrisburg, PA 17106-7000; 717-705-7940, Fax- 717-705-7931. www.fish.state.pa.us/registration.htm

#14 Liquor Control Board, PO Box 8940 (Capitol & Forester St), Harrisburg, PA 17105-8940; 717-783-8250, Fax- 717-772-2165. www.lcb.state.pa.us

#15 Department of State, Athletic Commission, 2601 N 3rd St, Harrisburg, PA 17110; 717-787-5720, Fax- 717-783-0824. www.dos.state.pa.us/sac/site/default.asp

#16 Securities Commission, 1010 N 7th St, Eastgate Office Bldg, 2nd Fl, Harrisburg, PA 17102-1410; 717-787-8061, Fax- 717-783-5122. www.psc.state.pa.us

#17 State Ethics Commission, Department of State, PO Box 11470, 309 Finance Bldg, Harrisburg, PA 17108-1470; 717-783-1610, Fax- 717-783-0806. www.ethics.state.pa.us/ethics/site/default.asp

#18 Department of State, Board of Dentistry, PO Box 2649, Harrisburg, PA 17105-2649; 717-783-7162, F- 717-787-7769. www.dos.state.pa.us/bpoa/cwp/view.asp?a=1104&q=432687 Search data at- www.licensepa.state.pa.us/

#19 Dept of State, Professional & Occupational Affairs, Board of Vehicle Manufacturers, Dealers & Salespersons, Box 2649 (2601 Northfield St), Harrisburg, PA 17110; 717-783-1697, Fax- 717-787-0250. www.dos.state.pa.us/bpoa/cwp/view.asp?a=1104&q=433233 Search at- www.licensepa.state.pa.us/ Direct list requests to Diane Miller (717) 772-2244.

#20 Dept of State, Prof & Occupation'l Affairs, P.O. Box 2649 (124 Pine St), Harrisburg, PA 17105; 717-787-8503, Fax- 717-787-7769. www.dos.state.pa.us/bpoa/site/default.asp Search data at- www.licensepa.state.pa.us/

#21 Dept. of State, Bureau of Commissions, Elections, Legislation, 210 North Office Building, Harrisburg, PA 17120; 717-787-5280. www.dos.state.pa.us/bcel/site/default.asp Search at- www.campaignfinance.state.pa.us/

Pennsylvania Federal Courts

The following list indicates the district and division name for each county in the state. If the bankruptcy court location is different from the district court, then the location of the bankruptcy court appears in parentheses.

Pennsylvania County/Court Cross Reference

County	District	Division
Adams	Middle	Harrisburg
Allegheny	Western	Pittsburgh
Armstrong	Western	Pittsburgh
Beaver	Western	Pittsburgh
Bedford	Western	Johnstown (Pittsburgh)
Berks	Eastern	Allentown/Reading (Reading)
Blair	Western	Johnstown (Pittsburgh)
Bradford	Middle	Scranton (Wilkes-Barre)
Bucks	Eastern	Philadelphia
Butler	Western	Pittsburgh
Cambria	Western	Johnstown (Pittsburgh)
Cameron	Middle	Williamsport (Wilkes-Barre)
Carbon	Middle	Scranton (Wilkes-Barre)
Centre	Middle	Williamsport (Harrisburg)
Chester	Eastern	Philadelphia
Clarion	Western	Pittsburgh (Erie)
Clearfield	Western	Johnstown (Pittsburgh)
Clinton	Middle	Williamsport (Wilkes-Barre)
Columbia	Middle	Williamsport (Wilkes-Barre)
Crawford	Western	Erie
Cumberland	Middle	Harrisburg
Dauphin	Middle	Harrisburg
Delaware	Eastern	Philadelphia
Elk	Western	Erie
Erie	Western	Erie
Fayette	Western	Pittsburgh
Forest	Western	Erie
Franklin	Middle	Harrisburg
Fulton	Middle	Harrisburg
Greene	Western	Pittsburgh
Huntingdon	Middle	Harrisburg
Indiana	Western	Pittsburgh
Jefferson	Western	Pittsburgh (Erie)
Juniata	Middle	Harrisburg
Lackawanna	Middle	Scranton (Wilkes-Barre)
Lancaster	Eastern	Allentown/Reading (Reading)
Lawrence	Western	Pittsburgh
Lebanon	Middle	Harrisburg
Lehigh	Eastern	Allentown/Reading (Reading)
Luzerne	Middle	Scranton (Wilkes-Barre)
Lycoming	Middle	Williamsport (Wilkes-Barre)
McKean	Western	Erie
Mercer	Western	Pittsburgh (Erie)
Mifflin	Middle	Harrisburg
Monroe	Middle	Scranton (Wilkes-Barre)
Montgomery	Eastern	Philadelphia
Montour	Middle	Williamsport (Harrisburg)
Northampton	Eastern	Allentown/Reading (Reading)
Northumberland	Middle	Williamsport (Harrisburg)
Perry	Middle	Williamsport (Harrisburg)
Philadelphia	Eastern	Philadelphia
Pike	Middle	Scranton (Wilkes-Barre)
Potter	Middle	Williamsport (Wilkes-Barre)
Schuylkill	Eastern	Allentown/Reading(Wilkes-Barre)
Snyder	Middle	Williamsport (Harrisburg)
Somerset	Western	Johnstown (Pittsburgh)
Sullivan	Middle	Williamsport (Wilkes-Barre)
Susquehanna	Middle	Scranton (Wilkes-Barre)
Tioga	Middle	Williamsport (Wilkes-Barre)
Union	Middle	Williamsport (Harrisburg)
Venango	Western	Erie
Warren	Western	Erie
Washington	Western	Pittsburgh
Wayne	Middle	Scranton (Wilkes-Barre)
Westmoreland	Western	Pittsburgh
Wyoming	Middle	Scranton (Wilkes-Barre)
York	Middle	Harrisburg

Standards for Federal Courts: Fees are standard unless noted in profile. Search fee is $26.00 per item (one party name or case number). Copy fee is $.50 per page. Certification fee is $9.00 per document, double for exemplification, if available. Most courts require prepayment. Mail requests should enclose a SASE unless otherwise noted. Before releasing records, all courts require prepayment, unless noted.

District courts index by defendant and plaintiff and by case number. Bankruptcy courts usually index by debtor and case number. While most courts now have their indexes on computer, many may still maintain index card files as well. Courts will archive closed case files at different times.

There are numerous public access programs available to online subscribers. Search the U.S. Party/Case Index to find party names and case numbers among all courts. Individual case data is provided on PACER. A search of CM/ECF provides copies of cases filed electronically. For details about PACER, the US Party/Case Index, and CM/ECF see the Appendix or go to http://pacer.psc.uscourts.gov or call 800-676-6856.

US District Court
Pennsylvania Eastern District

Allentown - Reading Division c/o Philadelphia Division, US Courthouse, Rm 2609, 601 Market St, Philadelphia, PA 19106-1797, 215-597-7704; records- 267-597-7082; Fax- 267-299-7135. 8:30AM-5PM. www.paed.uscourts.gov

Counties/Note: Berks, Lancaster, Lehigh, Northampton, Schuylkill. The Allentown courthouse is physically located at 504 Hamilton St, Federal Courthouse, Allentown.

Searches/Indexing: Helpful to include DOB in search requests, especially for old records. Results do not include SSN or DOB. Will not fax back documents. New cases are in the index immediately after filing date. Computer index back to 1990 maintained; also microfiche index. Indexes by judgment also available. District-wide searches available here. Closed electronic cases not purged.

Search Access: Docket info available via phone if case number is known. **Mail:** Search usually completed- up to 14 days. Include SASE for return. **Fax:** Written fax search requests accepted, prepaid. **In person:** No self-serve copier.

Payment: Pay by Visa/MC, money order, cashier's, business or personal check. Payee: Clerk, US District Court.

E-Services: PACER records go back to 7/1990. New records online after 1 day. ECF at https://ecf.paed.uscourts.gov. Criminal cases go back to 7/1992. **Opinions Online:** www.paed.uscourts.gov/us03006.asp. Opinions go back to 1997. **Online Note:** Online access is free at www.paed.uscourts.gov/us04000.asp?19. No fee to search; select document type and enter name as search string.

Philadelphia Division Court Clerk, US Courthouse, Rm 2609, 601 Market St, Philadelphia, PA 19106-1797, 215-597-7704; records- 267-299-7082; Fax- 215-597-6390. Hours-8:30AM-5PM. www.paed.uscourts.gov

Counties/Note: Bucks, Chester, Delaware, Montgomery, Philadelphia. This division now hold records for Reading-Allenton court; counties of Berks, Lancaster, Lehigh, Northampton, Schuylkill. There is also a Divisional office in Philadelphia at 900 Market St, also in Easton at 101 Larry Holmes Dr and in Reading at 400 Washington St.

Searches/Indexing: Helpful to include DOB in search requests, especially for old records. Results do not include SSN or DOB; judgment and commitment record may have DOB or SSN. Will fax back docket listings $.10 per page. New cases are in the index immediately after filing date. Computer index back to 1990 maintained; also microfiche index. Indexes by judgment also available. District-wide searches available here. Closed electronic cases not purged.

Search Access: Docket info available via phone if case number is known. **Mail:** Search usually completed- up to 14 days. Include SASE for return. **Fax:** Written fax search requests accepted, prepaid. **In person:** No self-serve copier.

Payment: Pay by Visa/MC, money order, cashier's, business or personal check. Payee: Clerk, US District Court.

E-Services: PACER records go back to 7/1990. New records online after 1 day. ECF at https://ecf.paed.uscourts.gov. Criminal cases go back to 7/1992. **Opinions Online:** www.paed.uscourts.gov/us03006.asp. Opinions go back to 1997. **Online Note:** Online access is free at www.paed.uscourts.gov/. No fee to search; select document type and enter name as search string.

US Bankruptcy Court
Pennsylvania Eastern District

Philadelphia Division Court Clerk, 900 Market St, 4th Fl, Philadelphia, PA 19107, 215-408-2800; records- x2221, x2349. Hours-8:30AM-5PM. www.paeb.uscourts.gov

Counties/Note: Bucks, Chester, Delaware, Lancaster, Montgomery, Philadelphia. As of 7/1/l2006, Lancaster cases will be assigned to Philadelphia, not Reading.

Searches/Indexing: Include debtor name in search request. Results do not include SSN or DOB. Will not fax back documents. New cases are in the index immediately after filing date. Card and microfiche indexes also available. In person searchers may not search the card index. Cases sent to archives as early as 6 months after closed.

Search Access: Voice Case Information Service available, call VCIS at 215-597-2244. **Mail:** Search usually completed- 3 days. Include SASE for return. **In person:** 2 public terminals available. Self-serve copies $.25 each.

Payment: Pay by Visa/MC/Discover, money order, cashier's check, business check. No personal checks. Payee: Clerk, US Bankruptcy Court.

E-Svcs: PACER- http://pacer.paeb.uscourts.gov. PACER records go back to 1988. New records online immediately. ECF at https://ecf.paeb.uscourts.gov. **Opinions Online:** www.paeb.uscourts.gov/pages/pubopins/pub_opinions.htm. **Online Note:** Calendars are listed by judge name; click on Court Information then Judge's Hearings.

Reading Division Court Clerk, The Madison Bldg, 400 Washington St, Reading, PA 19601, 610-320-5255; records- x225. Hours-8AM-4:30PM. www.paeb.uscourts.gov

Counties/Note: Berks, Lehigh, Northampton. As of 7/2006, Lancaster county cases will be assigned to Philadelphia court.

Searches/Indexing: To search, include full name; SSN and DOB may be helpful. Results do not include SSN or DOB. Will not fax back documents. New cases are in the index 1 day after filing date. Both computer and card indexes maintained. Manual case files sent to archives 6 months after closed.

Search Access: Only docket info is available by phone. Voice Case Information Service available, call VCIS at 215-597-2244. **Mail:** Search usually completed- 1-2 days. Include SASE for return. **In person:** 1 public terminal available. No self-serve copier.

Payment: Pay by Visa/MC/Discover, money order, cashier's check, business check. No personal checks. Payee: Clerk, US Bankruptcy Court.

E-Svcs: PACER- http://pacer.paeb.uscourts.gov. PACER records go back to 1988. New records online after one day. ECF at https://ecf.paeb.uscourts.gov. **Opinions Online:** www.paeb.uscourts.gov/pages/pubopins/pub_opinions.htm. **Online Note:** Calendars are listed by judge name; click on Court Information then Judge's Hearings.

US District Court
Pennsylvania Middle District

Harrisburg Division Court Clerk, PO Box 983, Harrisburg, PA 17108-0983 (In person: US Courthouse and Federal Bldg, 228 Walnut St, Harrisburg), 717-221-3920; records-717-221-3924; Fax- 717-221-3959. Hours-8:30AM-5PM. www.pamd.uscourts.gov

Counties/Note: Adams, Cumberland, Dauphin, Franklin, Fulton, Huntingdon, Juniata, Lebanon, Mifflin, York.

Searches/Indexing: To search, include full name only. Results do not include SSN or DOB. Will fax back documents $1.00 per page. New cases are in the index immediately after filing date. Computer index back to 1980 maintained. Both computer and card indexes maintained. Closed electronic cases not purged.

Search Access: Limited search; only accession numbers for a specific case are available by phone. **Mail:** Search usually completed- 2-3 days. Include SASE for return. **Fax:** Fax search requests accepted, if prepaid. **In person:** 1 public terminal available. No self-serve copier.

Payment: Pay by Visa/MC, money order, cashier's or personal check. Payee: Clerk, US District Court.

E-Services: Document images available. PACER records go back to 5/1989. New records online after 1 day. ECF at https://ecf.pamd.uscourts.gov. **Opinions:** www.pamd.uscourts.gov/opinions.htm.

Scranton Division Court Clerk, PO Box 1148, Clerk's Ofc, W J Nealon Federal Bldg and US Courthouse, Scranton, PA 18501-1148 (In person: 235 N Washington Ave, Rm 101, Scranton), 570-207-5680; Fax- 717-207-5689. Hours-8:30AM-5PM. www.pamd.uscourts.gov

Counties/Note: Bradford, Carbon, Lackawanna, Luzerne, Monroe, Pike, Susquehanna, Wayne, Wyoming.

Searches/Indexing: To search, include full name only. Results do not include SSN or DOB. Will fax back documents $1.00 per page. New cases are in the index 1 day after filing date. Computer index back to 1980 maintained; also microfiche index. District-wide searches available here back to 1901. Closed electronic cases not purged.

Search Access: Minimal docket info is released via phone. **Mail:** Search usually completed- 7 days. Include SASE for return. **Fax:** Fax search requests accepted with credit card. **In person:** 2 public terminals available. No self-serve copier.

Payment: Pay by Visa/MC, money order, cashier's or personal check. Payee: Clerk, US District Court.

E-Services: Document images available. PACER records go back to 5/1989. New records online after 1 day. ECF at https://ecf.pamd.uscourts.gov. **Opinions:** www.pamd.uscourts.gov/opinions.htm.

Williamsport Division Court Clerk, Federal Bldg, Rm 218, 240 W 3rd St, Williamsport, PA 17701, 570-323-6380; Fax- 570-323-0636. Hours-8:30AM-5PM. www.pamd.uscourts.gov

Counties/Note: Cameron, Centre, Clinton, Columbia, Lycoming, Montour, Northumberland, Perry, Potter, Snyder, Sullivan, Tioga, Union.

Searches/Indexing: To search, include full name only. Results do not include SSN or DOB. Will fax back documents $1.00 per page. New cases are in the index immediately after filing date. Computer index back to 1980 maintained. Closed electronic cases not purged.

Search Access: Only docket info is available by phone. **Mail:** Search usually completed- 1-2 days. Include SASE for return. **Fax:** Fax requests require the original signature and prepayment. **In person:** 2 public terminals available. No self-serve copier.

Payment: Pay by Visa/MC, money order, cashier's or personal check. Payee: Clerk, US District Court.

E-Services: Document images available. PACER records go back to 5/1989. New records online after 1 day. ECF at https://ecf.pamd.uscourts.gov. **Opinions:** www.pamd.uscourts.gov/opinions.htm.

US Bankruptcy Court
Pennsylvania Middle District

Harrisburg Division Court Clerk, 228 Walnut St, 3rd Fl, Harrisburg, PA 17101, 717-901-2800; Fax- 717-901-2822. 8AM-4PM, phones til 5PM. www.pamb.uscourts.gov

Counties/Note: Adams, Centre, Cumberland, Dauphin, Franklin, Fulton, Huntingdon, Juniata, Lebanon, Mifflin, Montour, Northumberland, Perry, Snyder, Union, York.

Searches/Indexing: Include SSN in search request. Results include last 4 SSN digits. Will not fax back documents. New cases are in the index 1 day after filing date. Case files sent to archives 6 months after closed.

Search Access: Only docket info is available by phone. Voice Case Information Service available, call VCIS at 877-440-2699. **Mail:** Search usually completed- within 1 week. Include SASE for return. **In person:** 2 public terminals available. No self-serve copier available. Court can recommend an outside vendor to make copies.

Payment: Pay by Visa/MC, money order, cashier's check. No debtor checks accepted. Payee: Clerk, US Bankruptcy Court.

E-Svcs: PACER- http://pacer.pamb.uscourts.gov. Document images available. PACER records go back to 8/1986. New records online after 1 day. ECF at https://ecf.pamb.uscourts.gov. Opinions available on the ECF system. **Online Note:** Search judge calendars free by clicking on Court Calendars at www.pamb.uscourts.gov.

Wilkes - Barre Division Clerk's Office, Max Rosen US Courthouse, 197 S Main St, Wilkes-Barre, PA 18701, 570-826-6450; Fax-570-826-6401. Hours-8AM-4PM, phones til 5PM. www.pamb.uscourts.gov

Counties/Note: Bradford, Cameron, Carbon, Clinton, Columbia, Lackawanna, Luzerne, Lycoming, Monroe, Pike, Potter, Schuylkill, Sullivan, Susquehanna, Tioga, Wayne, Wyoming.

Searches/Indexing: Include name and last 4 digits of SSN in search request. Results include last 4 SSN digits. Will not fax back documents. New cases are in the index immediately after filing date. Case files sent to archives 6 months after closed.

Search Access: Court conducts phone searches if name or case number is provided; only docket info is released. Voice Case Information Service available, call VCIS at 877-440-2699. **Mail:** Search usually completed- 1-2 days. Include SASE for return. **Fax:** No fax requests accepted unless approved by a judge. **In person:** 4 public terminals available.

Payment: Pay by Visa/MC, money order, cashier's check. No debtor checks accepted. Payee: Clerk, US Bankruptcy Court.

E-Svcs: PACER- http://pacer.pamb.uscourts.gov. Document images available. PACER records go back to 1987. New records online after 1 day. ECF at https://ecf.pamb.uscourts.gov. Opinions available on the ECF system. **Online Note:** Search judge calendars free by clicking on Court Calendars at www.pamb.uscourts.gov.

US District Court Pennsylvania Western Dist.

Erie Division Court Clerk, PO Box 1820, Erie, PA 16507 (In person: 17 S Park Row, Erie, PA), 814-464-9600. 8:30-4:30. www.pawd.uscourts.gov

Counties: Crawford, Elk, Erie, Forest, McKean, Venango, Warren.

Searches/Indexing: Court prefers that you perform searches at Pittsburgh Division. Include full name only in search request. Results do not include SSN or DOB. Will not fax back documents. New cases are in the index 1 day after filing date. Both computer and card indexes maintained. Closed electronic cases not purged.

Search Access: Only case number, caption and attorneys' names released via phone. **Mail:** Search usually completed- 1-2 days. Include SASE for return. **In person:** 1 public terminal available; index back to 1991. No self-serve copier.

Payment: Pay by Visa/MC, money order, cashier's or personal check. Payee: Clerk, US District Court.

E-Services: PACER records go back to 1989. New records online after 1 day. ECF at https://ecf.pawd.uscourts.gov. **Opinions Online:** www.pawd.uscourts.gov/Pages/opinions.htm. Search opinions by judge name. **Online Note:** Access daily court calendar at www.pawd.uscourts.gov.

Johnstown Div. Court Clerk, Penn Traffic Bldg, Rm 208, 319 Washington St, Johnstown, PA 15901, 814-533-4504; Fax- 814-533-4519. Hours-8:30AM-4:30PM. www.pawd.uscourts.gov

Counties: Bedford, Blair, Cambria, Clearfield, Somerset.

Searches/Indexing: Include full name only in search request. Results do not include SSN or DOB. Will not fax back documents. New cases are in the index 1 day after filing date. Both computer and card indexes maintained; computer back to 6/1992. Card index from 1989 to 1992. Closed electronic cases not purged.

Search Access: Only case number, caption and attorneys' names released via phone. **Mail:** Search usually completed- 1 day. SASE not required. **In person:** 1 public terminal available; index back to 1990-91. No self-serve copier.

Payment: Pay by Visa/MC/Discover, money order, cashier's check. Payee: Clerk, US District Court.

E-Services: PACER records go back to 1989. New records online after 1 day. ECF at https://ecf.pawd.uscourts.gov. **Opinions Online:** www.pawd.uscourts.gov/Pages/opinions.htm. Search opinions by judge name. **Online Note:** Access daily court calendar at www.pawd.uscourts.gov.

Pittsburgh Division Court Clerk, 700 Grant St, US Post Office & Courthouse, Rm 311, Pittsburgh, PA 15219, 412-208-7500, 866-266-2983; records- 412-208-7507; Fax- call for fax number. Hours-8:30AM-4:30PM. www.pawd.uscourts.gov

Counties/Note: Allegheny, Armstrong, Beaver, Butler, Clarion, Fayette, Greene, Indiana, Jefferson, Lawrence, Mercer, Washington, Westmoreland. Erie and Johnstown Divisions send complete paper copies of case records to Pittsburgh; all District case records at Pittsburgh.

Searches/Indexing: Include full name only in search request. Results do not include SSN or DOB. Will not fax back documents. New cases are in the index 2 days after filing date. Both computer and card indexes maintained; computer goes back to 1992. Closed electronic cases not purged.

Search Access: Only docket info is available by phone. **Mail:** Search usually completed- 1 day. Include SASE. **In person:** 3 public terminals available back to 1990. No self-serve copier.

Payment: Pay by Visa/MC/Discover, money order, cashier's or personal check. Payee: Clerk, US District Court.

E-Services: PACER records go back to 1989. New records online after 1 day. ECF at https://ecf.pawd.uscourts.gov. **Opinions Online:** www.pawd.uscourts.gov/Pages/opinions.htm. Search opinions by judge name. **Online Note:** Access daily court calendar at www.pawd.uscourts.gov.

US Bankruptcy Court Pennsylvania Western Dist.

Erie Division Court Clerk, 17 S Park Row, Rm B160, US Courthouse, Erie, PA 16501, 814-464-9740; Fax- 814-464-9747. Hours- 9AM-4:30PM. www.pawb.uscourts.gov

Counties: Clarion, Crawford, Elk, Erie, Forest, Jefferson, McKean, Mercer, Venango, Warren.

Searches/Indexing: Search request requires name only. Results do not include SSN or DOB. Will not fax back documents. New cases are in the index immediately after filing date. Closed cases sent to archives as storage space fills.

Search Access: Docket info available by phone. Voice Case Information Service available, call VCIS at 412-355-3210 or 866-299-8515. **Mail:** Search usually completed- 1-3 days. Include SASE for return. **In person:** 2 public terminals available. No self-serve copier.

Payment: Pay by Visa/MC (in person only), money order, cashier's or personal check. No debtor checks/credit cards accepted. Payee: Clerk, US Bankruptcy Court.

E-Services: PACER records go back to 1991. New records online immediately. ECF at https://ecf.pawb.uscourts.gov. **Opinions Online:** www.pawb.uscourts.gov/cgi-bin/opinions.cgi. **Online Note:** Search calendars by judge name free at www.pawb.uscourts.gov/calendar.htm.

Pittsburgh Division Court Clerk, 600 Grant St #5414, Pittsburgh, PA 15219. 412-644-2700; Fax- 412-644-6512. Hours- 9AM-4:30PM. www.pawb.uscourts.gov

Counties/Note: Allegheny, Armstrong, Beaver, Bedford, Blair, Butler, Cambria, Clearfield, Fayette, Greene, Indiana, Lawrence, Somerset, Washington, Westmoreland. There is also a branch office in Johnstown, PA, 814-533-4246.

Searches/Indexing: Include name and SSN in search request. Results do not include SSN or DOB. Will not fax back documents. New cases are in the index immediately after filing date. Computer and microfiche indexes maintained. District-wide searches available here for cases back to 1986. Closed electronic cases not purged.

Search Access: Limited docket info available by phone. Voice Case Information Service available, call VCIS at 412-355-3210 or 866-299-8515. **Mail:** Search usually completed- 1-2 days. Include SASE for return. **In person:** 6 public terminals available. No self-serve copier available. Court can recommend an outside vendor to make copies.

Payment: Pay by Visa/MC (in person only), money order, personal check. No debtor checks accepted. Payee: Clerk, US Bankruptcy Court.

E-Services: PACER records go back to 1991. New records online immediately. ECF at https://ecf.pawb.uscourts.gov. **Opinions Online:** www.pawb.uscourts.gov/cgi-bin/opinions.cgi. **Online Note:** Search calendars by judge name free at www.pawb.uscourts.gov/calendar.htm.

Pennsylvania County Courts

Court	Jurisdiction	No. of Courts	How Organized
Court of Common Pleas*	General	103	60 Districts
Philadelphia Municipal Court*	Municipal	1	1st District
Philadelphia Traffic Court	Municipal	1	1st District
Pittsburgh Magistrates Court	Municipal	1	Pittsburgh
Register of Wills*	Probate	67	
Magisterial District Courts	Limited	555	60 Districts

* Profiled in this Sourcebook.

Court	CIVIL								
	Tort	Contract	Real Estate	Min. Claim	Max. Claim	Small Claims	Estate	Eviction	Domestic Relations
Court of Common Pleas*	X	X	X	$0	No Max			X	X
Philadelphia Municipal Court*	X	X	X	$0	$10,000	$10000		X	
Philadelphia Traffic Court									
Pittsburgh City Magistrates Court			X	$0	No Max				
Register of Wills*							X		
Magisterial District Courts	X			$0	$8000	$8000			

Court	CRIMINAL				
	Felony	Misdemeanor	DWI/DUI	Preliminary Hearing	Juvenile
Court of Common Pleas*	X	X	X	X	X
Philadelphia Municipal Court*	X	X	X	X	
Philadelphia Traffic Court		X	X		
Pittsburgh City Magistrates Court		X	X	X	
Magisterial District Courts		X	X	X	

Administration

Administrative Office of Pennsylvania Courts, PO Box 229, Mechanicsburg, PA, 17055; 717-795-2097, Fax: 717-795-2013. www.courts.state.pa.us All courts are Eastern Standard Time (EST)

Court Structure

The Courts of Common Pleas are the general trial courts, with jurisdiction over both civil and criminal matters and appellate jurisdiction over matters disposed of by the special courts. Note that the civil records clerk of the Court of Common Pleas is called the Prothonotary. The Prothonotary is elected by the county and is not a state employee. But Allegheny County (Pittsburgh) civil records are an exception - in 2008, a Dept. of Court Records Civil/Family Division was created and civil records were removed from the Prothonotary Office. The Superior Court is a Court of Appeals. Probate is handled by the Register of Wills.

Small claims cases are, usually, handled by the District Justice Courts. These courts, which are designated as "special courts," also handle civil cases up to $8,000. However, all small claims are recorded with the other civil records through the Prothonotary Section of the Court of Common Pleas, which then holds the records. It is not necessary to check with each Magisterial District Court, but rather to check with the Prothonotary for the county.

Online Access

The web page at http://ujsportal.pacourts.us/ offers access to a variety of the Judiciary's Electronic Services (E-Services) such as Web Docket Sheets, DA Link, Superior Court's Web Docketing Statements, etc. Web Docket provides public access to view and print case docket sheets from the criminal cases of the Courts of Common Pleas (with many cross references to Muncipal Court Index Numbers) and from the Appellate Courts. Search by docket number, name or organization.

The Infocon County Access System provides a commercial direct dial-up access to civil (Prothonotary), probate (Register of Wills), and sometimes times criminal record data court record information for at least 28 counties. There is a $25.00 base set-up fee plus a minimum $25.00 per month based on a $1.10 fee per minute. For further information, call Infocon at 814-472-6066 or visit www.infoconcountyaccess.com.

Searching Tips, Fees, and Other Guidelines

Fees vary widely among jurisdictions. Many courts will not conduct searches due to a lack of personnel or, if they do search, turnaround time may be excessively lengthy. Prepayment required at most courts. Many courts offer public access terminals for in-person searches.

Adams County

Court of Common Pleas - Civil 111-117 Baltimore St, Rm 104, Gettysburg, PA 17325; 717-334-6781 x360; fax: 717-334-0532; 8AM-4:30PM. ***Civil, Eviction.***

Civil Records: Access: In person only. Visitors must perform in person searches themselves. Required to search: name, years to search. Civil cases indexed by defendant, plaintiff; index on computer from 1988, some microfiche (dates unsure), on index from 1800s. Public use terminal has civil records back to 1988. PAT results show name but not all terminal results include address.

General Information: No mental health, sealed records released. Will not fax documents. Court makes copy: $.25 per page. Self serve: $.25 per page. Certification fee: $5.00 per doc includes copies. Payee: Prothonotary. Personal checks accepted; credit cards are not.

Court of Common Pleas - Criminal 111-117 Baltimore St, #103, Gettysburg, PA 17325; 717-337-9806; fax: 717-334-9333; 8AM-4:30PM. ***Felony, Misdemeanor.*** www.adamscounty.us/adams/site/default.asp

Criminal Records: Access: Mail, in person, online. Both court and visitors may perform in person searches. Search fee: $9.00 per name. Required to search: name, years to search, DOB. Criminal records on computer since 1986; some not all on microfiche since 1974, some on microfilm to 1800s. Mail turnaround time 1 day. Public use terminal has crim records back to 1986. Search dockets online free at http://ujsportal.pacourts.us/DocketSheets/CP.aspx back to 1986. Also, a most wanted list with photos is available at www.adamscounty.us/adams/. Online results show name, DOB.

General Information: Online identifiers in results same as on public terminal. No juvenile records released. Will fax documents for fee. Court makes copy: $.25 per page. Self serve: same. Certification fee: $9.00 per cert. Payee: Clerk of Courts. Personal checks accepted; no third party checks. No credit cards accepted. Mail requests: SASE required.

Register of Wills 111-117 Baltimore St Rm 102, Gettysburg, PA 17325; 717-337-9826; fax: 717-334-1758; 8AM-4:30PM. ***Probate.*** www.adamscounty.us

Allegheny County

Court of Common Pleas - Civil 414 Grant St, 1st Fl, City County Bldg, Pittsburgh, PA 15219; 412-350-4200; fax: 412-350-5260; 8:30AM-4:30PM. ***Civil.*** www.alleghenycourts.us

The clerk of civil court records was the Prothonotary. However, all civil court records for the county are combined and administered by the Dept. of Court Records - Civil/Family Division.

Civil Records: Access: Mail, in person, online. Both court and visitors may perform in person searches. Search fee: $25.00 per name. Required to search: name, years to search. Civil cases indexed by defendant, plaintiff. Civil records archived from 1700s; on computer since 1/1/95. Mail turnaround time 10 days. Public use terminal has civil records back to 1/1995. Public terminal also offers Family Court records. Search civil cases after registration at http://prothonotary.county.allegheny.pa.us/. Credit card payment or drawn down account; fee is $.15 per search during office hours, $.10 if not. Also, search by case number free at http://dcr.alleghenycounty.us/. Search pre-1995 civil judgment indexes free at http://prothonotary.county.allegheny.pa.us/indices/indices.html. Access opinions free at www.alleghenycourts.us/search/default.asp?source=opinions_civil.

General Information: No juvenile records released. Will not fax documents. Court makes copy: $.50 per page. Self serve: $.25 per page. Certification fee: $8.00 per doc. Payee: Allegheny County. Business checks accepted. No credit cards accepted. Businesses may set up a draw down account. Mail requests: SASE required.

Court of Common Pleas - Criminal 220 Courthouse, 436 Grant St, Pittsburgh, PA 15219; 412-350-5322; fax: 412-350-6154; 8:30AM-4:30PM. ***Felony, Misdemeanor.*** www.alleghenycourts.us

Pittsburgh Magistrate Court phone- 412-350-6715.

Criminal Records: Access: Mail, in person, online. Both court and visitors may perform in person searches. Search fee: $15.00 per name. Required to search: name, years to search, DOB, SSN. Criminal records on files, microfilm back to 1800s; on computer since. Mail turnaround time 2 days. Public use terminal has crim records back to 1988. PAT results show middle initial, DOB. Access to criminal records is free at http://ujsportal.pacourts.us/DocketSheets/CP.aspx back to 1974. Online results show middle initial, DOB, SSN.

General Information: Online identifiers in results same as on public terminal. All records public. Will fax out documents locally only, no add'l fee. Court makes copy: n/a. Self serve: $.50 per page. Cert fee: $10.00 per doc includes copies. Payee: Dept of Court Records. No personal checks. No credit cards accepted. Mail requests: SASE required.

Register of Wills 414 Grant St, City County Bldg, Dept of Court Records. Wills/Orphans Ct, PIttsburgh, PA 15219; 412-350-4183; fax: 412-350-3028; 8:30AM-4PM. ***Probate.*** www.county.allegheny.pa.us/regwills/index.asp

Armstrong County

Court of Common Pleas - Civil 500 E Market St, Kittanning, PA 16201; 724-548-3251; fax: 724-548-3236; 8AM-4:30PM. ***Civil, Eviction.*** www.co.armstrong.pa.us/

Civil Records: Access: Online, in person. Both court and visitors may perform in person searches. No search fee. Required to search: name, years to search. Civil cases indexed by defendant, plaintiff; index on files, microfiche since 1930; on computer since 9/94. Public use terminal has civil records back to 9/1994. PAT results show name only. Online access is by subscription from private company-Infocon at www.infoconcountyaccess.com, 814-472-6066. See note in court summary section for fees. Images are not available; only the index.

General Information: No juvenile, civil commitment records released. Will not fax documents. Court makes copy: $1.00 per page. Certification fee: $3.00 1st page; $1.00 each add'l. Payee: Prothonotary. No out-of-state checks accepted. No credit cards accepted.

Court of Common Pleas - Criminal 500 Market St, Kittanning, PA 16201; 724-548-3252; 8AM-4:30PM. ***Felony, Misdemeanor.*** www.co.armstrong.pa.us/departments/prothonotary-clerk-courts

Criminal Records: Access: Mail, online, in person. Both court and visitors may perform in person searches. Search fee: $10.00 per name. Required to search: name, years to search; also helpful: DOB, SSN. Criminal records in card file from early 1930; on computer since 1994. Mail turnaround time 3 days. Public use terminal has crim records back to 1994. PAT results show name only. Search dockets online free at http://ujsportal.pacourts.us/DocketSheets/CP.aspx back to 1994. Also, see note at beginning of section. Online results show name, DOB.

General Information: No juvenile or mental health records released. Will not fax documents. Court makes copy: $.50 per page, $1.00 if by mail. Self serve: $.50 per page. Cert fee: $5.00 first page. Payee: Clerk of Courts. Personal checks accepted; credit cards are not. Mail requests: SASE required.

Register of Wills 500 Market St, Armstrong County Courthouse, Kittanning, PA 16201; 724-548-3256 X220; fax: 724-548-3236; 8AM-4:30PM. ***Probate.*** www.co.armstrong.pa.us/registerindex.htm

Online access available by subscription from private company-Infocon at www.infoconcountyaccess.com, 814-472-6066. See note at beginning of section. Images are available.

Beaver County

Court of Common Pleas - Civil Beaver County Courthouse, 810 3rd St, Beaver, PA 15009; 724-728-5700; fax: 724-728-3360; 8:30AM-4:30PM. ***Civil, Eviction.*** www.co.beaver.pa.us/prothonotary

Civil Records: Access: In person only. Both court and visitors may perform in person searches. No search fee. Required to search: name, years to search. Civil cases indexed by defendant, plaintiff. Civil records go back to 1800; on computer back to 1995. Public use terminal has civil records back to 1995. PAT civil results show middle initial.

General Information: No sealed records released. Will not fax documents. Court makes copy: $.50 per page. Certification fee: $5.00 per cert includes copies. Payee: Prothonotary. Personal checks accepted; credit cards are not.

Court of Common Pleas - Criminal Beaver County Courthouse, 810 3rd St, Beaver, PA 15009; 724-728-5700 x11323; fax: 724-728-8853; 8:30AM-4:30PM. ***Felony, Misdemeanor.*** www.beavercountypa.gov/Courts/index.htm

Criminal Records: Access: Fax, mail, in person, online. Both court and visitors may perform in person searches. Search fee: $20.00 per name. Required to search: name, years to search; also helpful: DOB, SSN. Criminal records computerized from 1973, on microfiche since 1802. Mail turnaround time 1 week. Public use terminal has crim records. PAT criminal results show middle initial. Terminal results also gives city/town of residence. Search dockets free at http://ujsportal.pacourts.us/DocketSheets/CP.aspx back to 1958. Online results show middle initial, DOB.

General Information: Online identifiers in results same as on public terminal. Records sealed by court order not released. Fee to fax out file $1.75 per page. Court makes copy: $.30 per page. Certification fee: $10.00. Payee: Clerk of Courts Office. Personal checks accepted. Credit cards accepted in person. Mail requests: SASE required.

Register of Wills Beaver County Courthouse, 810 3rd St, Beaver, PA 15009; 724-728-5700 X11265, X11274; fax: 724-728-9810; 8:30AM-4:30PM. ***Probate.*** www.beavercountypa.gov/register/

Online access is by subscription from private company-Infocon at www.infoconcountyaccess.com, 814-472-6066. See note in court summary section for fees. Images are not available; only the index.

Bedford County

Court of Common Pleas - Criminal/Civil

Bedford County Courthouse, Bedford, PA 15522; 814-623-4833; criminal fax: 814-623-4831; civil fax: same; 8:30AM-4:30PM. ***Felony, Misdemeanor, Civil, Eviction.***

Civil Records: Access: Mail, in person, online. Both court and visitors may perform in person searches. Search fee: $20.00 per name. Required to search: name, years to search. Civil cases indexed by defendant, plaintiff; index on file from late 1700s. Mail turnaround time 2 weeks. Civil PAT goes back to 5/1998. Online access is by subscription from company at www.infoconcountyaccess.com, 814-472-6066. See note in court summary section. Images are available.

Criminal Records: Access: Mail, online, in person. Both court and visitors may perform in person searches. Search fee: $20.00 per name. Required to search: name, years to search, DOB. Criminal records on file from late 1700s. Mail turnaround time 2 weeks. Criminal PAT goes back to same as civil. Also, search dockets online free at http://ujsportal.pacourts.us/DocketSheets/CP.aspx back to 1981. Also, access is by subscription from company at www.infoconcountyaccess.com, 814-472-6066. See note at beginning of section. Online results show name, DOB.

General Information: No sex related or juvenile records released. Will fax documents to local or toll free line, if prepaid. Court makes copy: $.50 per page. Self serve: $.25 per page. Certification fee: $4.50 includes copies. Payee: Prothonotary of Bedford County. Personal checks accepted; credit cards are not. Mail requests: SASE required.

Register of Wills

200 S Juliana St, Bedford, PA 15522; 814-623-4836; fax: 814-624-0488; 8:30AM-4:30PM. ***Probate, Ordinance.***

Online access available by subscription from private company-Infocon at www.infoconcountyaccess.com, 814-472-6066. See note at beginning of section. Images are available.

Berks County

Court of Common Pleas - Civil

Prothonotary, 633 Court St, 2nd Fl, Reading, PA 19601; 610-478-6970; fax: 610-478-6969; 8AM-4PM. ***Civil, Eviction.***

www.co.berks.pa.us/courts/site/default.asp

Passports available up to 3:30PM.

Civil Records: Access: Mail, in person, online. Both court and visitors may perform in person searches. No search fee, but you must provide the case number in mail requests. Required to search: name, years to search. Civil cases indexed by defendant, plaintiff. Civil records partially on microfiche, on manual index files from 1750. Mail access limited to docket information only. Mail turnaround time 1-2 days. Public use terminal has civil records back to 1996. PAT results show name only. The Prothonotary has a remote system to access dockets from 2002 forward. Subscription fee is $300 per year. For information, call 610-478-6967.

General Information: No mental, sealed records released. Will fax documents $6.00 1st page, $1.00 each add'l; for emergency only. Court makes copy: $4.00 1st page; $1.00 each add'l. Self serve: $.50 per page printed from computer. Certification fee: $5.95 1st page; $1.50 each add'l. Payee: Prothonotary. Personal checks accepted. Mail requests: SASE required for civil.

Court of Common Pleas - Criminal

4th Fl, 633 Court St, Reading, PA 19601; 610-478-6550; fax: 610-478-6593; 8-5PM. ***Felony, Misdemeanor.***

www.co.berks.pa.us/courts/site/default.asp

Criminal Records: Access: In person, online. Visitors must perform in person searches themselves. Required to search: name, years to search; also helpful: DOB, SSN. Criminal records computerized from 1985 in files from 1992, prior archived. Will not do name lists by mail. Public use terminal has crim records back to 1985. Search dockets online free at http://ujsportal.pacourts.us/DocketSheets/CP.aspx back to 1967. Online results show name, DOB.

General Information: No juvenile records released. Will not fax documents. Court makes copy: $.25 per page first 10, $1.00 each add'l. Certification fee: $8.00. Payee: Berks County Clerk of Courts. Only cashiers checks and money orders accepted. Credit cards accepted for payments on criminal cases only. Mail requests: SASE required.

Register of Wills

633 Court St, 2nd Fl, Reading, PA 19601; 610-478-6600; fax: 610-478-6251; 8AM-5PM. ***Probate.***

www.co.berks.pa.us/rwills/site/default.asp

Blair County

Court of Common Pleas - Criminal/Civil

423 Allegheny St, #144, Hollidaysburg, PA 16648; 814-693-3080; criminal phone: 814-693-3080; fax: 814-371-1600; 8AM-4PM. ***Felony, Misdemeanor, Civil, Eviction.***

Civil Records: Access: In person, online. Visitors must perform in person searches themselves. Required to search: name, years to search. Civil cases indexed by defendant, plaintiff; index on computer from 1989, on index books from 1846 to 1989. Civil PAT goes back to 1989. Online access is by subscription from private company-Infocon at www.infoconcountyaccess.com, 814-472-6066. See note in court summary section. Images are not available.

Criminal Records: Access: Mail, online, in person. Both court and visitors may perform in person searches. Search fee: $10.00 per name. Required to search: name, years to search, DOB; also helpful: SSN. Criminal records computerized from 1989, on index books from 1846 to 1989. Mail turnaround time is 3-5 days. Criminal PAT goes back to same as civil. Search criminal dockets free at http://ujsportal.pacourts.us/DocketSheets/CP.aspx back to 1989. Also, access is by subscription from company at www.infoconcountyaccess.com, 814-472-6066. See note at beginning of section. Online results show name, DOB.

General Information: No adoption records released. Will fax documents for $1.00 per page. Court makes copy: $.50 per page. Self serve: same. Certification fee: $6.00 per cert. Payee: Blair County Prothonotary. Personal checks accepted; credit cards are not. Mail requests: SASE required for criminal.

Register of Wills

423 Allegheny, #145, Hollidaysburg, PA 16648-2022; 814-693-3095; fax: 814-693-3093; 8AM-4PM. ***Probate.***

www.blaircountyrecorder.com/

Online access to the index from 4/29/2005 forward is by subscription from private company-Infocon at www.infoconcountyaccess.com, 814-472-6066. See note in court summary section for fees.

Bradford County

Court of Common Pleas - Criminal/Civil

Courthouse, 301 Main St, Towanda, PA 18848; 570-265-1705; fax: 570-265-1735; 9AM-5PM. ***Felony, Misdemeanor, Civil, Eviction.***

Search fee includes both civil and criminal indexes

Civil Records: Access: Mail, in person. Both court and visitors may perform in person searches. Search fee: $8.00 per name. Required to search: name, years to search. Civil cases indexed by defendant, plaintiff; index on computer from 1986, on microfiche from mid 1800s, archived from mid-1940s. Mail turnaround time 1-2 days. Civil PAT goes back to 1986. DOB and other identifiers may appear on case record, but not in index search results.

Criminal Records: Access: Mail, in person, online. Both court and visitors may perform in person searches. Search fee: $8.00 per name. Required to search: name, years to search, DOB. Criminal records computerized from 1986, on microfiche from mid 1800s, archived from mid-1940s. Mail turnaround time 1-2 days. Criminal PAT goes back to same as civil. DOB and other identifiers may appear on the record, but not in index search results. Search dockets online free at http://ujsportal.pacourts.us/DocketSheets/CP.aspx back to 1984.

General Information: Will not fax documents. Court makes copy: $.25 per page. Self serve: same. Certification fee: $5.00 Civil. $9.00 for criminal records. Payee: Prothonotary. Personal checks accepted; credit cards are not. Mail requests: SASE required.

Register of Wills

301 Main St., Towanda, PA 18848; 570-265-1702; fax: 570-265-1721; 9AM-5PM. ***Probate.***

Access to 'estates' images back to approximately 1997 is by subscription at www.landex.com/remote/. Fee is $.10 per page view, $.50 per fax page.

Bucks County

Court of Common Pleas - Civil

55 E Court St, Doylestown, PA 18901; 215-348-6191; fax: 215-348-6184; 8AM-4:15PM. ***Civil, Eviction.***

www.buckscounty.org/courts

Civil Records: Access: Online, in person. Visitors must perform in person searches themselves. Required to search: name, years to search. Civil cases indexed by defendant, plaintiff; index on computer back to 1980, prior on dockets. This office does not do legal searches with verifications, they only do general searches at no charge. Verified name searches must be done by bonded title searchers. Public use terminal has civil records back to 1980. PAT results show name only. For a limited time, access is free at http://4.43.65.248/autoform.asp?app=cvr. Register of Wills is also included. Domestic and family court dockets are free at http://4.43.65.248/autoform.asp?app=fcr.

General Information: No mental, sealed records released. Court makes copy: $.25 per page. Self serve: $.25 per page. Certification fee: $4.75 plus $1.50 each add'l page, certifications are for documents filed in their office, with the original document in the files. Payee: Prothonotary. Personal checks accepted; credit cards are not.

Court of Common Pleas - Criminal

55 E Court St, Bucks County Courthouse, Doylestown, PA 18901; 215-348-6389; fax: 215-348-6740; 8AM-4:30PM. ***Felony, Misdemeanor.***

www.buckscounty.org/courts

Criminal Records: Access: Mail, online, in person. Both court and visitors may perform in person searches. Search fee: $15.00 per name. Required to search: name, years to search, DOB. Criminal records computerized from 1980, some records on microfiche, on card index from 1932 to 1979. Mail turnaround time 5 days or less. Public use terminal has crim records back to 1980. Access criminal court records free at http://ujsportal.pacourts.us/DocketSheets/CP.aspx back to 1984. Online results show name, DOB.

General Information: No sealed, juvenile or mental records released. Will not fax documents. Court makes copy: $.25 per page. Self serve: same. Certification fee: $8.25. Payee: Clerk of Courts Criminal Division. Personal checks and credit cards accepted. Mail requests: SASE required.

Register of Wills

Bucks County Courthouse, 55 E Court St., Doylestown, PA 18901; 215-348-6265; fax: 215-348-6156; 8AM-4:30PM. ***Probate.***

www.buckscounty.org

Access records online free at http://4.43.65.248/autoform.asp?app=rwr.

Butler County

Court of Common Pleas - Civil

PO Box 1208, 124 W Diamond, Butler County Courthouse, Butler, PA 16001-1208; 724-284-5214; 8:30AM-4:30PM. ***Civil, Eviction.*** www.co.butler.pa.us

Civil Records: Access: Phone, mail, online, in person. Visitors must perform in person searches themselves. No search fee. Required to search: name, years to search. Civil cases indexed by defendant, plaintiff; index on computer from 4/1/93, prior on docket books back to 1800. Public use terminal has civil records back to 4/1/1993. Online access is by subscription from a private company - Infocon at www.infoconcountyaccess.com, 814-472-6066.

See add'l note in court summary section. Images are available.
General Information: No mental records released. Will not fax documents. Court makes copy: $.25 per page criminal; civil- $.50 per page; $1.00 for film copies. Cert fee: $4.50 per doc. Payee: Prothonotary. Personal checks accepted; credit cards are not.

Court of Common Pleas - Criminal PO Box 1208, 124 W Diamond St, County Courthouse, Butler, PA 16003-1208; 724-284-5233; fax: 724-284-5244; 8:30AM-4:30PM. ***Felony, Misdemeanor.*** www.co.butler.pa.us/
Criminal Records: Access: Mail, online, in person. Both court and visitors may perform in person searches. Search fee: $16.00 per name. Required to search: name, DOB; also helpful: years to search. Original records in office for 10 years. Computerized from 1988 to present, prior in Russell Index. Mail turnaround time 1-2 days. Public use terminal has crim records back to 1987. PAT results show middle initial, DOB. Search dockets online free at http://ujsportal.pacourts.us/DocketSheets/CP.aspx back to 1988 for complete index. Also, online access to the index is by subscription from private company at www.infoconcountyaccess.com, 814-472-6066. See note in court summary section for fees. Online results show middle initial, DOB.
General Information: Online identifiers in results same as on public terminal. No mental, sealed, juvenile (16 & under) victim records released. Will fax back to gov't agencies only. Court makes copy: $.50 per page; $1.00 for computer printout. Cert fee: $8.00 per page. Payee: Clerk of Courts. Personal checks accepted. Credit cards accepted in person with ID. Mail requests: SASE required.

Register of Wills PO Box 1208, 124 W Diamond St, Butler County Courthouse, Butler, PA 16003-1208; 724-284-5348; fax: 724-284-5278; 8:30AM-4PM. ***Probate.***
Online access available by subscription from private company-Infocon at www.infoconcountyaccess.com until early to mid 2009. Then search index is free at http://counties.recordfusion.com/index.jsp. Also, see note at beginning of section.

Cambria County

Court of Common Pleas - Civil 200 S Center St, Ebensburg, PA 15931; 814-472-1636; fax: 814-472-5632; 9AM-4PM. ***Civil, Eviction.*** www.co.cambria.pa.us/cambria/site/default.asp
Small claims cases are handled by district judges.
Civil Records: Access: Phone, mail, fax, in person, online. Both court and visitors may perform in person searches. No search fee. Required to search: name, years to search. Civil cases indexed by defendant, plaintiff; index on computer from 1/1/94, prior on dockets from 1800s. Mail turnaround time usually 1 day. Public use terminal has civil records back to 1/1994. PAT civil results show middle initial. Access to civil index is available by subscription at Infocon.com; Signup online or get details at 814-472-6066. Images are not available.
General Information: No divorce or mental records released. Fee to fax out file $1.00 per page. Court makes copy: $.25 per page. Self serve: same. Certification fee: $3.00 includes copies. Payee: Prothonotary. Personal checks accepted; credit cards are not. Mail requests: SASE required for civil.

Court of Common Pleas - Criminal 200 S Center St, County Courthouse, Ebensburg, PA 15931; 814-472-1540; fax: 814-472-0761; 9AM-4PM. ***Felony, Misdemeanor.***
Criminal Records: Access: Mail, fax, in person, online. Only the court performs in person searches; visitors may not. Search fee: $5.00 per name. Required to search: name, years to search, DOB; also helpful: SSN. Criminal conviction records are computerized, indexed from 1800s. Mail turnaround time 5-7 days. Search dockets online free at http://ujsportal.pacourts.us/DocketSheets/CP.aspx back to 1991. Online results include city, state, and ZIP, and year of birth (not full DOB).
General Information: No sealed or child victim records released. Will fax documents to local or toll free number; all fees prepaid. Court makes copy: $.50 per page. Certification fee: $10.10 per doc includes copies. Payee: Clerk of Court. Third party checks not accepted. No credit cards accepted.

Register of Wills 200 S Center St, Ebensburg, PA 15931; 814-472-1440; probate phone: 814-472-1438; fax: 814-472-0762; 9AM-4PM. ***Probate.*** www.co.cambria.pa.us/cambria/CWP/view.asp?A=3&QUESTION_ID=499971
Online access is by subscription from private company-Infocon at www.infoconcountyaccess.com, 814-472-6066. See note in court summary section for fees. Images are available.

Cameron County

Court of Common Pleas - Civil County Courthouse, 20th E 5th St, Emporium, PA 15834; 814-486-3349; 8:30AM-4PM. ***Civil, Eviction.***
Civil Records: Access: Phone, mail, in person. Both court and visitors may perform in person searches. No search fee. Required to search: name, years to search. Civil cases indexed by defendant, plaintiff; index on computer from 1985, archived from 1860 to present. Mail turnaround time same day. Public use terminal has civil records back to 1985. PAT civil results show middle initial.
General Information: No adoption, military discharge records released. Will fax documents to local or toll-free number. Court makes copy: $.50 per page. Certification fee: $10.00 per doc includes copies. Payee: Prothonotary. No personal checks or credit cards accepted. Will bill fees with prior permission from clerk. Mail requests: SASE required.

Court of Common Pleas - Criminal 20 E 5th St, Emporium, PA 15834; criminal phone: 814-486-9330; fax: 814-486-0464; 8:30AM-4PM. ***Felony, Misdemeanor.***
Criminal Records: Access: Phone, fax, mail, in person, online. Both court and visitors may perform in person searches. No search fee. Required to search: name, years to search; also helpful: address, DOB, SSN. Criminal records archived from 1860. Mail turnaround time same day. Public use terminal has crim records back to 4/2004.PAT results show name, DOB. Search dockets online free at http://ujsportal.pacourts.us/DocketSheets/CP.aspx back to 1991. Online results show name, DOB.
General Information: Online identifiers in results same as on public terminal. No juvenile, mental health records released. Will not fax documents. Court makes copy: $.50 per page. Self serve: $.50 per page. Certification fee: $10.00. Cert fee includes copies. Payee: Clerk of Court. Personal checks accepted; credit cards are not. Mail requests: SASE required.

Register of Wills Cameron County Courthouse, 20 E 5th St, Emporium, PA 15834; 814-486-3355; fax: 814-486-0464; 8:30AM-4PM. ***Probate.***

Carbon County

Court of Common Pleas - Civil PO Box 130, Courthouse, Jim Thorpe, PA 18229; 570-325-2481; fax: 570-325-8047; 8:30AM-4:30PM. ***Civil, Small Claims, Eviction.*** www.carboncourts.com
Small Claims and Evictions are found at the local magistrate court and can be reached at 570-325-2751. There are 4 magistrate courts in Carbon County.
Civil Records: Access: In person, online. Visitors must perform in person searches themselves. Required to search: name. Civil cases indexed by defendant, plaintiff; index on computer from 1/84, financing statements from 1/87, on microfiche from 1/84, prior archived. Public use terminal has civil records back to 1984. PAT civil results show middle initial. Online access to the clerk of courts docket records is free at www.carboncourts.com/pubacc.htm. Registration required. Online results show middle initial.
General Information: No abuse, mental health records released. Will fax documents $1.00 per page. Court makes copy: $1.00 per page. Self serve: $.25 per page. Certification fee: $9.20 per cert. Payee: Prothonotary of Carbon County. Personal checks accepted; credit cards are not.

Court of Common Pleas - Criminal County Courthouse, PO Box 107, Jim Thorpe, PA 18229; 570-325-3637; fax: 570-325-5705; 8:30AM-4:30PM. ***Felony, Misdemeanor.*** www.carboncourts.com
Criminal Records: Access: Phone, mail, in person, online. Only the court performs in person searches; visitors may not. No search fee. Required to search: name, years to search, DOB; also helpful: SSN. Criminal records computerized from 1973, on microfiche from 1800. Mail turnaround time 1 day. Online access to clerk of courts docket records is free at www.carboncourts.com/pubacc.htm. Registration required. Also, search dockets online free at http://ujsportal.pacourts.us/DocketSheets/CP.aspx back to 1986. Online results show middle initial, DOB.
General Information: No juvenile, mental health records released. Will not fax documents. Court makes copy for no fee. No certification fee. Payee: Clerk of Courts Carbon County. Personal checks accepted; credit cards are not. Mail requests: SASE required.

Register of Wills PO Box 286, 4 Broadway, Jim Thorpe, PA 18229; 570-325-2261; fax: 570-325-5098; 8:30AM-4:30PM. ***Probate.***
Docket information available free online at www.carboncourts.com/pubacc.htm. Registration required.

Centre County

Court of Common Pleas - Criminal/Civil Centre County Courthouse, Bellefonte, PA 16823; 814-355-6796; 8:30-5PM. ***Felony, Misdemeanor, Civil, Eviction.*** www.co.centre.pa.us/271.asp
Evictions are with the local Magistrate Ct.
Civil Records: Access: In person only. Visitors must perform in person searches themselves. Required to search: name, years to search, DOB. Civil cases indexed by defendant, plaintiff; index on computer from 7-1-94, on docket books from 1986, on microfiche and archived from 1800 to 1992. Civil PAT goes back to 7/1994.
Criminal Records: Access: Mail, in person, online. Both court and visitors may perform in person searches. Search fee: $7.00 per name. Required to search: name, years to search, DOB. Criminal records computerized from 7-1-94, on card files and docket books from 1986, on microfiche and archived from 1800 to 1992. Mail turnaround time 3-5 days. Criminal PAT goes back to same as civil. Search dockets online free at http://ujsportal.pacourts.us/DocketSheets/CP.aspx back to 1979. Online results show name, DOB.
General Information: No sex related, juvenile, mental records released. Will not fax documents. Court makes copy: $.50 per page. Self serve: same. Certification fee: $4.00 1st page, $2.00 ea add'l. Payee: Clerk of Court. Personal checks accepted; credit cards are not. Mail requests: SASE required for criminal.

Register of Wills Willowbank Office Bldg, 414 Holmes Ave, #2, Bellefonte, PA 16823; 814-355-6724, 355-6760; fax: 814-355-8685; 8:30AM-5PM. ***Probate, Orphan's Court.*** www.co.centre.pa.us/224.asp
Some records may be available online; call for current information.

Chester County

Court of Common Pleas - Civil PO Box 2748, 201 W Market St, West Chester, PA 19382; 610-344-6300; criminal phone: 610-344-6135; 8:30AM-4:30PM. ***Civil, Eviction.*** http://dsf.chesco.org
Civil Records: Access: Online, in person. Visitors must perform in person searches themselves. Required to search: name, years to search. Civil cases indexed by defendant, plaintiff; index on dockets from 1985 to present, on microfiche from 1981 to 1984, archived from 1700s. Public use terminal has civil records back to 1990. Internet access to county records including court records requires a sign-up and credit card payment. Application fee: $50. There is a $10.00 per month minimum (no charge for no activity); and $.10 each transaction beyond

100. Sign-up and/or logon at http://epin.chesco.org/. Also, a court case list is free at http://dsf.chesco.org/courts/site/default.asp; click on "Miscellaneous List."
General Information: No sealed records released. Will not fax documents. Court makes copy: $1.00 per page criminal; civil- $1.15 1st page; $.55 each add'l. Certification fee: $5.50. Payee: Prothonotary. Business checks accepted. No credit cards accepted.

Court of Common Pleas - Criminal PO Box 2748, 201 W Market St, #1400, West Chester, PA 19382; 610-344-6135; fax: 610-344-6605; 8:30AM-4:30PM. ***Felony, Misdemeanor.*** http://dsf.chesco.org
Criminal Records: Access: Mail, online, in person. Both court and visitors may perform in person searches. Search fee: $15.00 per name. Required to search: name, years to search; also helpful: DOB. Criminal records on computer and microfiche from mid-70s, archived from the 1700s. Mail turnaround time 1 day, usually. Public use terminal has crim records back to mid-1970's. Search criminal dockets online free at http://ujsportal.pacourts.us/DocketSheets/CP.aspx back to 1978. Online results show name, DOB.
General Information: No juvenile records released. Will not fax documents. Court makes copy: $1.00 per page. Self serve: same. Certification fee: $5.00. Payee: Clerk of Courts. Business checks accepted. No credit cards accepted.

Register of Wills PO Box 2748, 201 W Market St #1400, West Chester, PA 19382; 610-344-6335; fax: 610-344-6218; 8:30AM-4:30PM. ***Probate.***
Internet access to probate records requires a sign-up and payment. Sign-up and/or logon at http://epin.chesco.org.

Clarion County

Court of Common Pleas - Civil 421 Main St, Ste 25, Clarion County Courthouse, Clarion, PA 16214; 814-226-1119; fax: 814-227-2501; 8:30AM-4:30PM. ***Civil, Eviction.*** www.co.clarion.pa.us/
Civil Records: Access: Phone, fax, mail, online, in person. Both court and visitors may perform in person searches. Search fee: $10.00 per name. Required to search: name, years to search. Civil cases indexed by defendant, plaintiff; index on computer from mid-1990s, on dockets from 1800s. Mail turnaround time 2-3 days. Public use terminal has civil records back to 1990. Online access is by subscription from private company-Infocon at www.infoconcountyaccess.com, 814-472-6066. See note in court summary section. Images are not available.
General Information: Online identifiers in results same as on public terminal. No juvenile, mental health records released. Will fax documents $3.00 1st page, $1.00 ea add'l. Court makes copy: $.50 per page. Certification fee: $8.00. Payee: Prothonotary. Personal checks accepted; credit cards are not. Mail requests: SASE required.

Court of Common Pleas - Criminal 421 Main St, Ste 25, Clarion, PA 16214; 814-226-1119; fax: 814-227-2501; 8:30AM-4:30PM. ***Felony, Misdemeanor.***
Criminal Records: Access: Fax, mail, online, in person. Both court and visitors may perform in person searches. Search fee: $10.00 per name. Required to search: name, years to search, DOB. Criminal records computerized from 1990, microfiche 1976-1985, on docket books from 1800s. Mail turnaround time same day. Public use terminal has crim records back to 6/1990. Internet access to court records is by subscription from a private company-Infocon at www.ic-access.com, 814-472-6066. See note at beginning of section. Also, search dockets online free at http://ujsportal.pacourts.us/DocketSheets/CP.aspx back to 1983. Online results show name, DOB. Online search results often show city, state, and zip.
General Information: Online identifiers in results same as on public terminal. No juvenile, mental health records released. Will fax documents $3.00. Court makes copy: $.50 per page. Certification fee: $8.00 per cert. Payee: Clerk of Court. Personal checks accepted; credit cards are not. Mail requests: SASE required.

Register of Wills County Courthouse, 421 Main St, #24, Clarion, PA 16214; 814-226-4000 X3501; fax: 814-226-1117; 8:30AM-4:30PM. ***Probate.***
Online access available by subscription from private company-Infocon at www.infoconcountyaccess.com, 814-472-6066. See note at beginning of section. Images are available.

Clearfield County

Court of Common Pleas - Criminal/Civil PO Box 549, 1 N 2nd St, Clearfield, PA 16830; 814-765-2641; criminal phone: x1336; civil phone: x1330; criminal fax: 814-765-7659; civil fax: same; 8:30AM-4PM. ***Felony, Misdemeanor, Civil, Eviction.*** www.clearfieldco.org
Civil Records: Access: Mail, in person. Both court and visitors may perform in person searches. Search fee: $7.00 per name, 5-years search. Required to search: name, years to search; also helpful: address. Civil cases indexed by defendant, plaintiff; index (Russell System) on dockets from 1820s; on computer back to 11/00. Mail turnaround time same day. Public use terminal has civil records back to 11/2000.
Criminal Records: Access: Mail, in person, online. Both court and visitors may perform in person searches. Search fee: $7.00 per name, 5-year search. Required to search: name, years to search, address, DOB, SSN, signed release. Criminal records indexed (Russell System) on dockets from 1820s; on computer back to 1/95. Mail turnaround time 2 days. PAT results show middle initial, DOB. Search dockets online free at http://ujsportal.pacourts.us/DocketSheets/CP.aspx back to 1990. Online results show middle initial, DOB.
General Information: Online identifiers in results same as on public terminal. No juvenile, sealed or mental health records released. Will not fax documents. Court makes copy: $.25 per page; $1.00 minimum. Self serve: $.25 per page. Certification fee: $1.50. Payee: Prothonotary. Personal checks accepted; credit cards are not. Mail requests: SASE required.

Register of Wills & Clerk of Orphans Court PO Box 361, 1 N 2nd St, Clearfield, PA 16830; 814-765-2641 X1351; fax: 814-765-6089; 8:30AM-4PM. ***Probate.***
Search records 1990 to present by name at www.landex.com; registration and fees required.

Clinton County

Court of Common Pleas - Criminal/Civil 230 E Water St, Lock Haven, PA 17745; 570-893-4007; fax: 570-893-4288; 8AM-5PM M, T,TH,F; 8AM-12:30PM W . ***Felony, Misdemeanor, Civil, Eviction.*** www.clintoncountypa.com/courts.htm
Civil Records: Access: Online, in person. Visitors must perform in person searches themselves. Required to search: name, years to search. Civil cases indexed by defendant, plaintiff; index on computer from 1992, on files from 1839. Civil PAT goes back to 1992. PAT results show name only. Online access is by subscription from private company-Infocon at www.infoconcountyaccess.com, 814-472-6066. See note in court summary section for fees. Images are available.
Criminal Records: Access: Online, in person. Visitors must perform in person searches themselves. Required to search: name, years to search, DOB, SSN, signed release. Criminal records computerized from 1992, on files from 1839. Criminal PAT goes back to same as civil. PAT results show name only. Internet access to court records is by subscription from a private company-Infocon at www.ic-access.com, 814-472-6066. See note at beginning of section. Also, search dockets online free at http://ujsportal.pacourts.us/DocketSheets/CP.aspx back to 1992. Online results show name, DOB.
General Information: No sealed, mental health or minor victim abuse cases records released. Will not fax documents. Court makes copy: $.50 per page. Certification fee: Civil is $4.50 first page, $1.50 ea add'l. Criminal is $5.00 first page. $1.50 ea add'l. Payee: Clerk of Court or Prothonotary. Personal checks accepted; credit cards are not.

Register of Wills PO Box 943, 230 E Water St, Lock Haven, PA 17745; 570-893-4010; fax: 570-893-4273; 8:30AM-5PM M,T,TH,F; 8AM-12:30PM Wed . ***Probate.*** www.clintoncountypa.com
Online access available by subscription from private company-Infocon at www.infoconcountyaccess.com, 814-472-6066. See note at beginning of section. Images are available.

Columbia County

Court of Common Pleas - Criminal/Civil PO Box 380, Bloomsburg, PA 17815; 570-389-5614; fax: 570-389-5620; 8AM-4:30PM. ***Felony, Misdemeanor, Civil, Eviction.*** http://columbiapa.org/courts/index.html
Opinions for civil and criminal cases are listed at the website. Fax to "Attention Barb."
Civil Records: Access: In person only. Both court and visitors may perform in person searches. No search fee. Required to search: name, years to search. Civil cases indexed by defendant, plaintiff; index on computer to 1992, on microfiche from 1814 to present, on dockets from 1814. Civil PAT goes back to 1992. PAT results show name only.
Criminal Records: Access: Mail, fax, in person, online. Both court and visitors may perform in person searches. Search fee: $20.00 per name. Required to search: name, years to search; also helpful: DOB. Criminal records on computer to 1992, on microfiche from 1814 to present, on dockets from 1814. Fax requests must be made on letterhead. Mail turnaround time same or next day. Criminal PAT goes back to same as civil. Search dockets online free at http://ujsportal.pacourts.us/DocketSheets/CP.aspx back to 1991. Online results show name, DOB.
General Information: No juvenile, adoption, mental health petition or OAPSA records released. May fax documents for fee. Court makes copy: $.50 per page. Self serve: same. Certification fee: $4.00. Payee: Prothonotary or Clerk of Court. Personal checks accepted for criminal payment. No credit cards accepted. Mail requests: SASE required for criminal.

Register of Wills 35 W Main St, PO Box 380, Bloomsburg, PA 17815; 570-389-5635/32; fax: 570-389-5636; 8AM-4:30PM. ***Probate.*** www.columbiapa.org/reg_rec/index.html

Crawford County

Court of Common Pleas - Civil Crawford County Courthouse, 903 Diamond Pk, Meadville, PA 16335; 814-333-7324; criminal phone: 814-333-7442; 8:30AM-4:30PM. ***Civil, Eviction.***
Civil Records: Access: Mail, in person. Both court and visitors may perform in person searches. Search fee: $8.00 per name. Required to search: name, years to search. Civil cases indexed by defendant, plaintiff; index on dockets from 1800s. Mail turnaround time 3 days. Public use terminal has civil records back to 10/1999.
General Information: No mental health, sealed records released. Will fax documents $1.60 per page. Court makes copy: $.80 per page; docket copy $1.75 per page. Certification fee: $1.75. Payee: Prothonotary Crawford County. Personal checks accepted with ID. Mail requests: SASE required.

Court of Common Pleas - Criminal Crawford County Courthouse, 903 Diamond Pk, Meadville, PA 16335; 814-333-7442; fax: 814-333-7349; 8:30AM-4:30PM. ***Felony, Misdemeanor.*** http://co.crawford.pa.us/clerk_of_courts/clerk_of_courts_home.htm
Criminal Records: Access: Mail, in person, online. Both court and visitors may perform in person searches. Search fee: $15.00 to search up to 5 names. Required to search: name, years to search, signed release; also helpful: DOB & SSN. Criminal records computerized since 2000, on microfiche from 1974, on dockets from 1914, archived from 1880s. Mail turnaround time 7-14 days. Public use terminal has crim records back to 2000. PAT results show name, DOB, SSN. Clerk will verify identifiers on PAT results. Search dockets online free at

http://ujsportal.pacourts.us/DocketSheets/CP.aspx back to 1981. Online results show name, DOB.
General Information: No juvenile records released. Will not fax documents. Court makes copy: $1.00 per page. Certification fee: $5.00 per cert. Payee: Clerk of Courts. Personal checks accepted; credit cards are not. Mail requests: SASE required.

Register of Wills 903 Diamond Pk, Meadville, PA 16335; 814-373-2537; fax: 814-337-5296; 8:30AM-4:30PM. ***Probate.***

Cumberland County

Court of Common Pleas - Civil Cumberland County Courthouse, Rm 100, One Courthouse Sq, Carlisle, PA 17013-3387; 717-240-6195; fax: 717-240-6573; 8AM-4:30PM. ***Civil, Eviction.***
www.ccpa.net/cumberland/cwp/view.asp?a=1132&Q=452322
Civil Records: Access: In person, online. Visitors must perform in person searches themselves. Required to search: name, years to search; also helpful: address. Civil cases indexed by defendant, plaintiff; index on computer from 1994, on microfiche from 1966-1998, on dockets from 1800s. Selected opinions free at http://records.ccpa.net/weblink_judges/Browse.aspx?dbid=3. Public use terminal has civil records back to 1994. Online access available by subscription from private company at www.infoconcountyaccess.com, 814-472-6066. See note at beginning of section. Images are available. Also, at http://records.ccpa.net/weblink_public/Browse.aspx you may search dockets by year then case number. User name and password must be acquired from Court Clerk Office.
General Information: No mental health records released. Will not fax out case files. Court makes copy: $.50 per page. Self serve: same. Certification fee: $5.00 1st page; $1.00 each add'l. Payee: Office of Prothonotary. No personal checks accepted.

Court of Common Pleas - Criminal Cumberland County Courthouse, East Wing, 1 Courthouse Sq, Carlisle, PA 17013-3387; 717-240-6250; fax: 717-240-6571; 8AM-4:30PM. ***Felony, Misdemeanor.***
www.ccpa.net/index.asp?nid=1129
Criminal Records: Access: Mail, in person, online. Both court and visitors may perform in person searches. Search fee: $19.00 per name. Required to search: name, years to search. Criminal records computerized from 1993, in files from 1976, archived from 1800s. Mail turnaround time same day. Public use terminal has crim records back to 1993. PAT results show middle initial, DOB. Search dockets online free at http://ujsportal.pacourts.us/DocketSheets/CP.aspx back to 1994. Also, you may also search at www.ccpa.net/index.asp?NID=2743 and select Criminal Records and Documents. First acquire username and password from Clerk of Courts Office. Selected opinions free at http://records.ccpa.net/weblink_judges/Browse.aspx?dbid=3. Online results show middle initial, DOB, SSN. Search results include address but only city, state, ZIP.
General Information: Online identifiers in results same as on public terminal. No juvenile records released (Including any case with a juvenile as the victim). Will fax documents as part of search fee. Court makes copy: $.50 per page. No certification fee. Payee: Clerk of Courts. Personal checks accepted; credit cards are not. Mail requests: SASE required.

Register of Wills Cumberland County Courthouse, Rm 102, 1 Courthouse Sq, Carlisle, PA 17013; 717-240-6345; fax: 717-240-7797; 8AM-4:30PM. ***Probate.*** www.ccpa.net/index.asp?nid=125

Dauphin County

Court of Common Pleas - Civil PO Box 945, Harrisburg, PA 17108; criminal phone: 717-780-6530; civil phone: 717-780-6520; 8AM-4:30PM. ***Civil, Eviction.***
www.dauphincounty.org/court-departments/
Civil Records: Access: Phone, mail, in person, online. Both court and visitors may perform in person searches. Search fee: $10.00 per name. Fee is per 5 years searched. Required to search: name, years to search. Civil cases indexed by defendant, plaintiff. Civil judgments on microfilm and dockets from 1970s, archived from 1700s; on computer back to 11/2001. Mail turnaround time 1 day. Public use terminal has civil records back to 1983. Access civil cases back to 11/21, suits (1992-10/31/2001) and judgments back to 1983 free at www.dauphinc.org/onlineservices/public/header.asp.
General Information: No mental health released. Will not fax documents. Court makes copy: $.75 per page. Self serve: $.75 per page. Certification fee: $5.00 1st pg; $1.50 each add'l. Payee: Dauphin County Prothonotary. Business checks accepted; no personal checks. No credit cards accepted. Mail requests: SASE required.

Court of Common Pleas - Criminal Front & Market St, Harrisburg, PA 17101; 717-255-2692; 8AM-4:30PM. ***Felony, Misdemeanor.***
www.dauphincounty.org/court-departments/
Criminal Records: Access: Mail, in person, online. Both court and visitors may perform in person searches. Search fee: $23.00 per name. Required to search: name, years to search; also helpful: DOB, SSN. Criminal records on dockets and computer from 1950, archived from 1700s. Mail turnaround time 1 week. Public use terminal has crim records back to 2002.PAT results show name, DOB. Results include offender city, state, zip. Search dockets free at http://ujsportal.pacourts.us/DocketSheets/CP.aspx back to 1971; results show name, DOB.
General Information: Online identifiers in results same as on public terminal. No juvenile, mental records released. Will not fax documents. Court makes copy: $.50 per page. Certification fee: $10.00 per cert includes 4 copy pages; add copy fee for each add'l page. Payee: Clerk of Court. Business checks accepted. No personal checks. No credit cards accepted.

Register of Wills Front & Market Sts, Rm 103, Harrisburg, PA 17101; 717-780-6500; fax: 717-780-6474; 8AM-4:30PM. ***Probate.***
www.dauphincounty.org/publicly-elected-officials/register-of-wills/

Delaware County

Court of Common Pleas - Criminal/Civil 201 W Front St, Media, PA 19063; 610-891-4370; criminal fax: 610-891-7257; civil fax: 610-891-7257; 8:30AM-4:30PM. ***Felony, Misdemeanor, Civil, Eviction.*** www.co.delaware.pa.us
Civil Records: Access: Online, in person. Visitors must perform in person searches themselves. Required to search: name, years to search. Civil cases indexed by defendant, plaintiff; index on computer from early 1990, on card file from 1920s, archived from 1800s. Public use terminal has civil records back to 1990. Online access to court civil records free (may begin charging in near future) at http://w01.co.delaware.pa.us/pa/publicaccess.asp. Search online by document type, document number, etc.
Criminal Records: Access: Mail, in person, online. Visitors must perform in person searches themselves. No search fee. Required to search: name, years to search; also helpful: DOB, SSN. Criminal records computerized from late 1970s, prior on files. Mail turnaround time 1-3 days. Search dockets online free at http://ujsportal.pacourts.us/DocketSheets/CP.aspx back to 1974. Online results show name, DOB.
General Information: No juvenile, mental health records released. Court makes copy: $1.00 per page. Certification fee: $4.95 civil doc, $7.95 criminal doc,. Payee: Office of Judicial Support. Attorney business checks only accepted. No credit cards accepted. Mail requests: SASE required for criminal.

Register of Wills Delaware County Courthouse, 201 W Front St, Media, PA 19063; 610-891-4400; fax: 610-891-4812; 8:30AM-4:30PM. ***Probate.***

Elk County

Court of Common Pleas - Criminal/Civil PO Box 237, Ridgway, PA 15853; 814-776-5344; fax: 814-776-5303; 8:30AM-4PM. ***Felony, Misdemeanor, Civil, Eviction.***
www.co.elk.pa.us/Courthouse.htm
Civil Records: Access: Phone, fax, mail, in person. Both court and visitors may perform in person searches. Search fee: $8.25 per name. Required to search: name, years to search. Civil cases indexed by defendant, plaintiff; index on dockets from 1843, on computer back to 1998. Mail turnaround time 1 day. Civil PAT goes back to 1998. PAT results show name only.
Criminal Records: Access: Phone, fax, mail, in person, online. Both court and visitors may perform in person searches. Search fee: $10.00 per name. Required to search: name, years to search, DOB. Criminal docket index from 1843, on computer back to 1998. Mail turnaround time 1 day. Criminal PAT goes back to same as civil. PAT results show name only. Search dockets online free at http://ujsportal.pacourts.us/DocketSheets/CP.aspx back to 1998. Online results show name, DOB.
General Information: No mental health or juvenile records released. Will not fax documents. Court makes copy: $.50 per page. Certification fee: $5.00 for civil; $8.50 for criminal. Payee: Elk County Prothonotary. Personal checks accepted; credit cards are not. Mail requests: SASE requested.

Register of Wills PO Box 314, 240 Main St, Ridgway, PA 15853; 814-776-5349; fax: 814-776-5382; 8:30AM-4PM. ***Probate.***

Erie County

Court of Common Pleas - Civil Erie County Courthouse, 140 W 6th St, Erie, PA 16501; 814-451-6080; civil phone: 814-451-6250; probate phone: 814-451-6260; fax: 814-451-7400; 8:30AM-4:30PM. ***Civil, Eviction.*** www.eriecountygov.org/
Civil Records: Access: Mail, in person, online. Both court and visitors may perform in person searches. Search fee: $10.00. Required to search: name, years to search. Civil cases indexed by defendant, plaintiff; index on computer from 1992, on dockets from 1971, on microfilm/microfiche from 1800s. Mail turnaround time same day. Public use terminal has civil records back to 1992. Online access is by subscription from private company at www.infoconcountyaccess.com, 814-472-6066. See note in court summary section. Images are available.
General Information: No sealed records released. Will fax documents to local or toll free line. Court makes copy: $.50 per page. Self serve: same. Certification fee: $5.00. Payee: Prothonotary. Personal checks accepted; credit cards are not. Mail requests: SASE required.

Court of Common Pleas - Criminal Erie County Courthouse, 140 W 6th St, Erie, PA 16501; 814-451-6221; fax: 814-451-6420; 8:30AM-4:30PM. ***Felony, Misdemeanor.***
www.eriecountygov.org/default.aspx?id=courts
Criminal Records: Access: Mail, online, in person. Both court and visitors may perform in person searches. Search fee: $10.00 per name. Required to search: name, years to search, DOB. Criminal records go back to 1950; records computerized back to 1992. Mail turnaround time 1 week. Public use terminal has crim records back to 1992. Search dockets online free at http://ujsportal.pacourts.us/DocketSheets/CP.aspx back to 1992. Online results show name, DOB.
General Information: No juvenile or ARD records released. Will fax documents to local or toll free line. Court makes copy: $.10 per page. No certification fee. Payee: Clerk of Courts. Personal checks accepted; credit cards are not.

Register of Wills Erie County Courthouse, 140 W 6th St, Erie, PA 16501; 814-451-6260; fax: 814-451-7010; 8AM-4:30PM. ***Probate.***
http://eriecountygov.org/default.aspx?id=rw
Online access available by subscription from private company-Infocon at www.infoconcountyaccess.com, 814-472-6066. See note at beginning of section. Images are available.

Fayette County

Court of Common Pleas - Civil 61 E Main St, Uniontown, PA 15401; 724-430-1272; civil phone: 724-430-1272; fax: 724-430-4555; 8AM-4:30PM. ***Civil, Eviction.***

Civil Records: Access: Mail, in person, online. Both court and visitors may perform in person searches. Search fee: $5.00 per name. Required to search: name, years to search. Civil cases indexed by defendant, plaintiff; index on computer from 1999, archived from 1700s. Mail turnaround time 2 weeks. Public use terminal has civil records back to 1999. PAT results show name only. Internet access to court records is by subscription from a private company-Infocon at www.ic-access.com, 814-472-6066. See note at beginning of section. Images are available. Online results show name only.

General Information: No mental records released. Will not fax documents. Court makes copy: $.50 per page. Self serve: same. Certification fee: $11.00 per document includes copy fee. Payee: Prothonotary. Personal checks accepted; credit cards are not. Mail requests: SASE required.

Court of Common Pleas - Criminal 61 E Main St, Uniontown, PA 15401; 724-430-1253; fax: 724-438-8410; 8AM-4:30PM. ***Felony, Misdemeanor.***

www.co.fayette.pa.us/fayette/cwp/view.asp?a=2124&q=516281

Criminal Records: Access: Mail, fax, in person, online. Both court and visitors may perform in person searches. Search fee: $15.00 for 5-year search; $30.00 for 5-yr. plus. Required to search: name, years to search, DOB; also helpful: SSN. Criminal records computerized from 1993, on files from 1800s. Mail turnaround time 3-5 days. Search dockets online free at http://ujsportal.pacourts.us/DocketSheets/CP.aspx back to 1975. Online results show name, DOB.

General Information: No sex related or juvenile records released. Will fax documents $3.00 each. Court makes copy: $.50 per page. Certification fee: $16.50. Payee: Clerk of Courts. No personal checks or credit cards accepted.

Register of Wills 61 E Main St, #1D, Uniontown, PA 15401; 724-430-1206; fax: 724-430-1275; 8AM-N, 1-4:30PM. ***Probate.***

Online access available by subscription from private company-Infocon at www.infoconcountyaccess.com, 814-472-6066. See note at beginning of section. Images are available. Images are not available.

Forest County

Court of Common Pleas 526 Elm St, #2, County Courthouse, Tionesta, PA 16353; 814-755-3526; fax: 814-755-8837; 9AM-4PM. ***Felony, Misdemeanor, Civil, Eviction, Probate.***

Computerized records includes the Register of Wills. Probate records are separate index at same address. Probate fax is same as main fax number.

Civil Records: Access: Mail, fax, in person, online. Both court and visitors may perform in person searches. No search fee. Required to search: name, years to search. Civil cases indexed by defendant, plaintiff. Computerized records from 2002, civil records on dockets since 1995, archived from 1857. Mail turnaround time same day. Civil PAT goes back to 2002. PAT results show name only. Online access available by subscription from private company at www.infoconcountyaccess.com, 814-472-6066. See note at beginning of section. Images are available. Images are not available.

Criminal Records: Access: Mail, fax, in person, online. Both court and visitors may perform in person searches. Search fee: $10.00 per name. Required to search: name, years to search; also helpful: DOB, SSN. Computerized records from 1995, archived from 1857. Mail turnaround time same day. Criminal PAT goes back to 1995.PAT results show name, DOB. Terminal results include SSN. Search dockets online free at http://ujsportal.pacourts.us/DocketSheets/CP.aspx back to 1995. Online results show name, DOB.

General Information: Online identifiers in results same as on public terminal. No adoption records released. Will fax documents $4.00 per document. Court makes copy: $2.00 per docket. Self serve: $.25 per page. Certification fee: $2.00. Payee: Clerk of Courts. Personal checks accepted; credit cards are not. Mail requests: SASE required.

Franklin County

Court of Common Pleas - Civil 157 Lincoln Way E, Chambersburg, PA 17201; 717-261-3858; fax: 717-264-6772; 8:30-4:30PM. ***Civil, Eviction.***

Civil Records: Access: In person, online. Visitors must perform in person searches themselves. Required to search: name, years to search. Civil cases indexed by defendant, plaintiff; index on file from 1985; on computer back to 4/1/1999. Public use terminal has civil records back to 11/1998. PAT results show name only. Public terminal also offers access to liens, division records, custody, protection from abuse and Judgment histories from 1981-1990. Access index by subscription from company at www.infoconcountyaccess.com, 814-472-6066. See note at beginning of section. Images are not available.

General Information: No mental records released. Will fax out specific case files for $1.00 per page. Court makes copy: $.50 per page. Certification fee: $5.00 per document plus copy fee for add'l pages. Payee: Prothonotary. Personal checks accepted; credit cards are not.

Court of Common Pleas - Criminal 157 Lincoln Way E, Chambersburg, PA 17201; 717-261-3805; fax: 717-261-3896; 8:30AM-4:30PM. ***Felony, Misdemeanor.***

Criminal Records: Access: Mail, in person, online. Both court and visitors may perform in person searches. Search fee: $10.00 per name. Required to search: name, years to search, DOB. Computerized back to 1995; criminal records on files for 50 years, archived from 1800s. Mail turnaround time same day. Public use terminal has crim records back to 1995. PAT results show middle initial, DOB. Search dockets online free at http://ujsportal.pacourts.us/DocketSheets/CP.aspx back to 1995. Online results show middle initial, DOB.

General Information: Online identifiers in results same as on public terminal. No juvenile records released. Will fax documents. Court makes copy: $.25 per page. Self serve: same. Certification fee: $5.00 per document. Payee: Clerk of Courts. Personal checks accepted; credit cards are not. Mail requests: SASE requested.

Register of Wills 157 Lincoln Way E, Chambersburg, PA 17201; 717-261-3872; fax: 717-709-7211; 8:30AM-4:30PM. ***Probate.***

Online access available by subscription from private company-Infocon at www.infoconcountyaccess.com, 814-472-6066. See note at beginning of section. Images are not available.

Fulton County

Court of Common Pleas - Criminal/Civil Fulton County Courthouse, 201 N 2nd St, McConnellsburg, PA 17233; 717-485-4212; fax: 717-485-5568; 8:30AM-4:30PM. ***Felony, Misdemeanor, Civil, Eviction.***

Send faxes to Attention-Court of Common Pleas.

Civil Records: Access: In person only. Visitors must perform in person searches themselves. Required to search: name, years to search. Civil cases indexed by defendant, plaintiff; index on docket index from 1850s; on computer back to 1999. Civil PAT goes back to 1999. Online access available by subscription from private company-Infocon at www.infoconcountyaccess.com, 814-472-6066. See note at beginning of section. Images are available. Images are not available.

Criminal Records: Access: Mail, in person, online. Both court and visitors may perform in person searches. Search fee: $5.00 per name. Required to search: name, years to search. Criminal records on docket index from 1850s; on computer back to 1994. Mail turnaround time 3-5 days. Criminal PAT goes back to 1996. Search dockets online free at http://ujsportal.pacourts.us/DocketSheets/CP.aspx back to 1994.

General Information: No juvenile, adoption records released. Will fax documents $5.00 per doc. Court makes copy: $.50 per page. Certification fee: $5.00 per doc includes copy fee. Payee: Prothonotary. Personal checks accepted; credit cards are not. Mail requests: SASE required for criminal.

Register of Wills 201 N 2nd St, McConnellsburg, PA 17233; 717-485-4212; fax: 717-485-5568; 8:30AM-4:30PM. ***Probate.***

Greene County

Court of Common Pleas - Civil Greene County Courthouse, Rm 105, Waynesburg, PA 15370; 724-852-5282; civil phone: 724-852-5289; probate phone: 724-852-5283; fax: 724-852-5353; 8:30AM-4:30PM. ***Civil, Eviction.***

www.co.greene.pa.us/secured/gc/depts/lo/court/coc.htm

Civil Records: Access: Mail, in person. Visitors must perform in person searches themselves. No search fee; if numerous, then $.50 per name. Required to search: name, years to search. Civil cases indexed by defendant, plaintiff. Civil records go back to 1797; on computer back to 1996. Mail turnaround 1 week. Public use terminal has civil records back to 1996.

General Information: No mental health records released. Will not fax documents. Court makes copy: $.50 per page. Self serve: same. Certification fee: $8.00 per record. Payee: Prothonotary. Personal checks accepted; credit cards are not. Mail requests: SASE required.

Court of Common Pleas - Criminal Greene County Courthouse, 10 E High St, Waynesburg, PA 15370; 724-852-5281; fax: 724-852-5316; 8:30AM-4:30PM. ***Felony, Misdemeanor.***

Criminal Records: Access: Mail, in person, online. Both court and visitors may perform in person searches. Search fee: $10.00 per name. Required to search: name, years to search, DOB, signed release; also helpful: SSN. Criminal records indexed in books from 1940s, on computer since 1996. Mail turnaround time same day. Public use terminal has crim records back to 1996. PAT results show middle initial, DOB. Public terminal has limited number of cases only. Search dockets online free at http://ujsportal.pacourts.us/DocketSheets/CP.aspx back to 1974. Online results show middle initial, DOB.

General Information: No juvenile, adoption records released. Fee to fax out file $2.00 1st page; $1.00 each add'l. Court makes copy: $.50 per page. Self serve: $.50 per page. Certification fee: $8.00 per document. Payee: Clerk of Courts. Personal checks accepted; credit cards are not. Mail requests: SASE required.

Register of Wills Greene County Courthouse #100, 10 E High St, Waynesburg, PA 15370; 724-852-5283; fax: 724-627-4716; 8:30AM-4PM. ***Probate.***

www.co.greene.pa.us/secured/gc/depts/lo/rr/index.htm

Huntingdon County

Court of Common Pleas - Criminal/Civil PO Box 39, Courthouse, Huntingdon, PA 16652; 814-643-1610; criminal fax: 814-643-4271; civil fax: same; 8:30AM-4:30PM. ***Felony, Misdemeanor, Civil, Eviction.***

Civil Records: Access: In person, mail, online. Visitors must perform in person searches themselves. No search fee. Required to search: name, years to search; also helpful: address. Civil cases indexed by defendant, plaintiff; index on computer from 8/03/92, on dockets from 1788. Civil PAT goes back to 8/1992. Online access is by subscription from company at www.infoconcountyaccess.com, 814-472-6066. See note in court summary section. Images not shown.

Criminal Records: Access: In person, mail, online. Visitors must perform in person searches themselves. No search fee. Required to search: name, years to search; also helpful: DOB, SSN. Criminal records computerized from 8/03/92, on dockets from 1788. Mail turnaround time 1 day. Criminal PAT goes back to same as civil. Internet access to court records is by subscription from a private company-Infocon at www.ic-access.com, 814-472-6066. See note at beginning of section. Also, search dockets

online free at http://ujsportal.pacourts.us/DocketSheets/CP.aspx back to 1992. Online results show name, DOB.
General Information: No juvenile records released. Will fax documents $1.00 per page. Court makes copy: $.25 per page. Certification fee: $4.50 per cert includes copies. Payee: Prothonotary. Personal checks accepted; credit cards are not.

Register of Wills Courthouse, 223 Penn St, Huntingdon, PA 16652; 814-643-2740; fax: 814-643-8152; 8:30AM-4:30PM. ***Probate.***
When faxing, put "Attn: Recorder's Office."

Indiana County

Court of Common Pleas - Criminal/Civil County Courthouse, 825 Philadelphia St, Indiana, PA 15701; 724-465-3855/3858; fax: 724-465-3968; 8AM-4PM. ***Felony, Misdemeanor, Civil, Eviction.***
Civil Records: Access: Mail, in person, online. Both court and visitors may perform in person searches. Search fee: $7.50 per name. Will not conduct judgment searches. Required to search: name, years to search. Civil cases indexed by defendant, plaintiff; index on computer from 1994, prior on index files to1806. Mail turnaround time same day. Civil PAT goes back to 1994. PAT civil results show middle initial. Online access is by subscription from company at www.infoconcountyaccess.com, 814-472-6066. See note in court summary section. Images not shown.
Criminal Records: Access: Mail, in person, online. Both court and visitors may perform in person searches. Search fee: $10.75 per name. Required to search: name, years to search, DOB, signed release. Criminal records computerized from 1994, prior on index files to 1806. Mail turnaround time same day. Criminal PAT goes back to same as civil. PAT criminal results show middle initial. Search dockets online free at http://ujsportal.pacourts.us/DocketSheets/CP.aspx back to 1975. Online results show name, DOB.
General Information: No juvenile, commitment records released. Will fax documents $.25 per page. Court makes copy: $.25 per page. Certification fee: $3.25 for divorce decrees. Payee: Clerk of Court or Prothonotary. Personal checks accepted; credit cards are not. Mail requests: SASE required.

Register of Wills County Courthouse, 825 Philadelphia St, Indiana, PA 15701; 724-465-3860; fax: 724-465-3863; 8AM-4PM. ***Probate.***

Jefferson County

Court of Common Pleas - Criminal/Civil Courthouse, 200 Main St, Brookville, PA 15825; 814-849-1606 X225; fax: 814-849-1625; 8:30AM-4:30PM. ***Felony, Misdemeanor, Civil, Eviction.***
Civil Records: Access: Mail, in person, online. Both court and visitors may perform in person searches. Search fee: $10.00 per name. Required to search: name, years to search. Civil cases indexed by defendant, plaintiff; index on computer back to 1987; all incoming records microfilmed, records since 1823 on microfilm. Mail turnaround time 2 days. Civil PAT goes back to 1987. PAT results show name only. Online access is by subscription from private company at www.infoconcountyaccess.com, 814-472-6066. See note in court summary section. Images not shown.
Criminal Records: Access: Mail, in person, online. Both court and visitors may perform in person searches. Search fee: $10.00 per name. Required to search: name, years to search, DOB; also helpful: SSN. Criminal records computerized from 1987; all incoming records microfilmed, records since 1947 on microfilm. Mail turnaround time 2 days. Criminal PAT goes back to same as civil. PAT results show name only. Search dockets online free at http://ujsportal.pacourts.us/DocketSheets/CP.aspx back to 1973. Online results show name, DOB.
General Information: No juvenile, mental health, records released, including criminal cases with a minor as a victim. Will fax documents $3.00 1st page; $1.00 ea add'l page. Court makes copy: $.50 per page. Self serve: same. Certification fee: $1.50 per page. Payee: Clerk of Courts. Personal checks accepted; credit cards are not. Mail requests: SASE required.

Register of Wills Jefferson County Courthouse, 200 Main St, Brookville, PA 15825; 814-849-1610; fax: 814-849-1677; 8:30AM-4:30PM. ***Probate.*** $10.00 search fee; $1.00 per page copy fee. Online access is by subscription from private company-Infocon at www.infoconcountyaccess.com, 814-472-6066. See note in court summary section. Images not shown.

Juniata County

Court of Common Pleas - Criminal/Civil Juniata County Courthouse, Mifflintown, PA 17059; 717-436-7715; fax: 717-436-7734; 8AM-4:30PM. ***Felony, Misdemeanor, Civil, Eviction.***
www.co.juniata.pa.us/
This court will not do name searches.
Civil Records: Access: In person only. Visitors must perform in person searches themselves. Required to search: name, years to search. Civil cases indexed by defendant, plaintiff; index on computer go back to 1993, on dockets from 1836. Civil PAT goes back to 1993.
Criminal Records: Access: In person, online. Visitors must perform in person searches themselves. Criminal records on computer go back to 1993, on dockets from 1894. Criminal PAT goes back to same as civil. Search dockets online free at http://ujsportal.pacourts.us/DocketSheets/CP.aspx back to 1975. Online results show name, DOB.
General Information: Online identifiers in results same as on public terminal. No juvenile records released. Will fax documents. Court makes copy: $.50 per page. Certification fee: $2.00 per page. Payee: Prothonotary or Clerk of Courts. Personal checks accepted; credit cards are not.

Register of Wills Juniata County Courthouse, PO Box 68, Mifflintown, PA 17059; 717-436-7709; fax: 717-436-7756; 8AM-4:30PM M-F, 8AM-N Wed (June-Sept) . ***Probate.***
Online access available by subscription from private company-Infocon at www.infoconcountyaccess.com, 814-472-6066. See note at beginning of section. Images not shown.

Lackawanna County

Court of Common Pleas - Civil Clerk of Judicial Records, 436 Spruce St, Brooks Bldg, Scranton, PA 18503-1551; 570-963-6723; fax: 570-963-6387; 9AM-4PM. ***Civil, Eviction.***
www.lackawannacounty.org/viewDepartment.aspx?DeptID=40
Civil Records: Access: In person only. Visitors must perform in person searches themselves. Required to search: name, years to search. Civil cases indexed by defendant, plaintiff. Civil records computerized since 9/95, dockets from 1920s, archived from 1800s. Case number is required. No civil searches performed by court but exceptions made Public use terminal has civil records back to 1995, results show name only
General Information: No juvenile records released. Will not fax documents. Court makes copy: $.50 per page; $1.00 for mail requesters first copy, $.50 each add'l. Self serve: $.50 per page. Certification fee: $4.75. Payee: Clerk of Judicial Records. Business checks accepted. No credit cards accepted.

Court of Common Pleas - Criminal Lackawanna County Courthouse, Scranton, PA 18503; 570-963-6759; fax: 570-963-6459; 9AM-4PM. ***Felony, Misdemeanor.***
Criminal Records: Access: Mail, in person, online. Both court and visitors may perform in person searches. Search fee: $10.00 per name. Required to search: name, years to search, DOB, SSN. Criminal records computerized since 10/95, on dockets from 1983, archived from 1941, indexed by defendant only. Mail turnaround time 1-2 days. Public use terminal has crim records back to 1995. PAT results show middle initial, DOB. Results include LKA. Search dockets online free at http://ujsportal.pacourts.us/DocketSheets/CP.aspx back to 1982. Online results show name, DOB.
General Information: Online identifiers in results same as on public terminal. No juvenile records released. Will fax documents to local or toll free line. Court makes copy: $.50 per page. Certification fee: $8.00 per doc includes copies. Payee: Clerk of Judicial Records. Business checks accepted. Visa/MC in person only accepted. Mail requests: SASE required.

Register of Wills Register of Wills, Scranton Electric Bldg, 507 Linden St, #400, Scranton, PA 18503; 570-963-6702; fax: 570-963-6377; 9AM-4PM. ***Probate.***

Lancaster County

Court of Common Pleas - Civil 50 N Duke St, PO Box 83480, Lancaster, PA 17608-3480; 717-299-8282; fax: 717-293-7210; 8:30AM-5PM. ***Civil, Eviction.***
www.co.lancaster.pa.us/courts/site/default.asp
Civil Records: Access: Online, in person. Visitors must perform in person searches themselves. Required to search: name, years to search; also helpful: address. Civil cases indexed by defendant, plaintiff; index on computer from 7/87, in files from 1987, judgments on dockets from 1800s, others archived from 1800s. Public use terminal has civil records back to 7/1987. PAT results show name only. Access to the Prothonotary's civil court records is free at www.co.lancaster.pa.us/scripts/bannerweb.dll. Also, historical court case schedules are free at www.co.lancaster.pa.us, click on "Court Calendar Archives." Includes Register, Treasurer, and other courthouse record data. Results include addresses. Call Kathy Harris at 717-299-8252 for info. Online results show name only.
General Information: Names and dates naturalization records released. Will fax documents $2.00 1st page, $1.00 each add'l. Fee higher for out of state faxing. Court makes copy: $.50 per page. Certification fee: $5.00 per document. Payee: Prothonotary. Personal checks accepted; credit cards are not. Mail requests: SASE required.

Court of Common Pleas - Criminal Clerk of Courts, 50 N Duke St, Lancaster, PA 17602; 717-299-8275; fax: 717-295-3686; 8:30AM-5PM. ***Felony, Misdemeanor.***
www.co.lancaster.pa.us/courts/site/default.asp
Criminal Records: Access: Mail, in person, online. Both court and visitors may perform in person searches. Search fee: $20.00 per name. Required to search: name, years to search, and SSN, DOB or case docket number. Criminal records computerized from 1988, paper back to 1983, archived from 1901, indexes to 1729. Mail turnaround time 2 days. Public use terminal has crim records back to 1988.PAT results show name, DOB. Search dockets free at http://ujsportal.pacourts.us/DocketSheets/CP.aspx back to 1977. Online results show name, DOB.
General Information: Online identifiers in results same as on public terminal. No juvenile records released. Will not fax documents. Court makes copy: $1.00 per copy or $1.00 for docket page including disposition. Certification fee: $8.00 per doc. Payee: Clerk of Courts. Only cashiers checks and money orders accepted. No credit cards accepted. Mail requests: SASE required.

Register of Wills 50 N Duke St., Lancaster, PA 17602; 717-299-8243; fax: 717-295-5914; 8:30AM-5PM. ***Probate.***
Access probate back to 1933 and marriage records back to 1948 free online at http://paperless.co.lancaster.pa.us/viewerportal/.

Lawrence County

Court of Common Pleas - Criminal/Civil 430 Court St, New Castle, PA 16101-3593; 724-656-2143; criminal phone: 724-656-2188; civil phone: 724-656-1960; fax: 724-656-1988; 8AM-4PM. ***Felony, Misdemeanor, Civil, Eviction.***
www.co.lawrence.pa.us
2nd fax number- 724-656-2479
Civil Records: Access: Fax, mail, online, in person. Both court and visitors may perform in person searches. Search fee: $15.50 per name. Required to search: name, years to search. Civil cases indexed by defendant, plaintiff; index on computer from 1994, on Russell Index from 1885. Mail turnaround time ASAP. Civil PAT goes back to 1987. Online

access is by subscription from private company-Infocon at www.infoconcountyaccess.com, 814-472-6066. See note in court summary section. Images shown.
Criminal Records: Access: Fax, mail, online, in person. Both court and visitors may perform in person searches. Search fee: $17.75 per name. Required to search: name, years to search, signed release; also helpful: DOB, SSN. Criminal records computerized from 1994, on Russell Index from 1885. Mail turnaround time ASAP. Criminal PAT goes back to 1994. Internet access to court records is by subscription from a private company-Infocon at www.ic-access.com, 814-472-6066. See note at beginning of section. Also, search dockets online free at http://ujsportal.pacourts.us/DocketSheets/CP.aspx back to 1968; results show name, DOB.
General Information: No adoption, juvenile, impounded, or juvenile sex crime victim records released. Will fax documents: local $1.00 plus $.50 per pg; long distance $3.00 plus $.50 per pg. Court makes copy: $.90 per page criminal; Civil $.50 per page. Certification fee: $4.50 first certification, $1.50 ea add'l. Payee: Prothonotary. Business checks accepted. No credit cards accepted. Mail requests: SASE requested.

Register of Wills 430 Court St, New Castle, PA 16101-3593; 724-656-2159; fax: 724-656-1966; 8AM-4PM. ***Probate.***
www.co.lawrence.pa.us/rr/index.html
Online access back to 7/7/2006 available by subscription from private company-Infocon at www.infoconcountyaccess.com, 724-656-2128, Record access may also be free or subscription at www.lawrencecountyrecordspa.us/countyweb/login.jsp?countyname=Lawrence.

Lebanon County

Court of Common Pleas - Civil Municipal Bldg, Rm 104, 400 S 8th St, Lebanon, PA 17042; 717-274-2801 x2120; 8:30-4:30PM. ***Civil, Eviction.***
Civil Records: Access: In person only. Visitors must perform in person searches themselves. Required to search: name, years to search; also helpful: address. Civil cases indexed by defendant, plaintiff; index on computer from 1985, on files from 1883. Public use terminal has civil records back to 1985.
General Information: No mental health records released. Will fax documents $.50 per page. Court makes copy: $.50 per page. Certification fee: $10.00 per cert. Payee: Prothonotary. Personal checks accepted; credit cards are not.

Court of Common Pleas - Criminal Municipal Bldg, Rm 102, 400 S 8th St, Lebanon, PA 17042; 717-274-2801 X2118; 8:30AM-4:30PM. ***Felony, Misdemeanor.***
Criminal Records: Access: Mail, in person, online. Both court and visitors may perform in person searches. Search fee: $20.00 per name. Required to search: name, years to search. Criminal records computerized from 1986, indexed from 1800s. Action number required for phone access. Mail turnaround time varies. Public use terminal has crim records back to 1986. Search dockets online free at http://ujsportal.pacourts.us/DocketSheets/CP.aspx back to 1967; results show name, DOB.
General Information: No juvenile records released. Will fax documents to local or toll-free number. Court makes copy: $.50 per page. Cert fee: $10.00 per doc. Payee: Clerk of Court. Personal checks accepted; credit cards are not. Mail requests: SASE required.

Register of Wills Municipal Bldg, Rm 105, 400 S 8th St, Lebanon, PA 17042; 717-274-2801 X2217; probate: x2217/2218; fax: 717-228-4460; 8:30AM-4:30PM. ***Probate.*** Search fee-$5.00 per name.

Lehigh County

Court of Common Pleas - Civil 455 W Hamilton St, Allentown, PA 18101-1614; 610-782-3148; criminal fax: 610-770-3840; civil fax: 610-770-3840; 8:30AM-4:30PM. ***Civil, Eviction.***
www.lccpa.org Probate fax- 610-782-3932
Civil Records: Access: Mail, in person, online. Both court and visitors may perform in person searches. No search fee. Required to search: name, years to search. Civil cases indexed by defendant, plaintiff; index on computer since 1985, on microfilm from 1812, some in books. Mail turnaround time 2 days. Public use terminal has civil records back to 1985. PAT results show name only. Terminal results include litigant names. Access to the county online system requires $300.00 annual usage fee. Search by name or case number. Call Lehigh Cty Fiscal Office at 610-782-3112 for more information.
General Information: Online identifiers in results same as on public terminal. No sealed, confidential, or impounded records released. Will not fax documents. Court makes copy: $.50 per page; docket printout $3.00. Self serve: $.25 per page. Certification fee: $5.00. Payee: Clerk of Courts-Civil. Personal checks and credit cards accepted.

Court of Common Pleas - Criminal Clerk of Judicial Records, 455 W Hamilton St, Allentown, PA 18101-1614; 610-782-3077; fax: 610-770-6797; 8AM-4PM. ***Felony, Misdemeanor.*** www.lccpa.org
Criminal Records: Access: Mail, online, in person. Both court and visitors may perform in person searches. Search fee: $22.50 per name. Fee includes copy of certified docket. Required to search: name, years to search, DOB; SSN helpful. Criminal records computerized from 1990, on alpha index from 1962 to 1990, on microfilm from 1812. Mail turnaround time 1 week. Public use terminal has crim records back to 1962. PAT results show middle initial, DOB. Search dockets online free at http://ujsportal.pacourts.us/DocketSheets/CP.aspx back to 1990. Also, free online access is available for Calendars & Schedules. Online results show name, DOB.
General Information: Online identifiers in results same as on public terminal. No juvenile or impounded records released. Will fax documents if search prepaid. Court makes copy: $.50 per page. Self serve: $.25 per page. Certification fee: $9.30 per doc. Payee: County of Lehigh. Personal checks accepted; credit cards are not. Mail requests: SASE required.

Register of Wills 455 W Hamilton, Allentown, PA 18101-1614; 610-782-3170; fax: 610-782-3932; 8AM-4PM. ***Probate.***
Online access to Wills: call Lehigh Cty Computer Svcs Dept at 610-782-3286 for info.

Luzerne County

Court of Common Pleas - Civil 200 N River St, Office of the Prothonotary, Wilkes Barre, PA 18711-1001; 570-825-1745; fax: 570-825-1757; 9AM-4:30PM. ***Civil, Eviction.***
www.luzernecounty.org/county/row_offices/prothonotary
Civil Records: Access: Phone, mail, in person. Both court and visitors may perform in person searches. Search fee: $19.00 per name for 5 years, $3.00 each add'l year. Required to search: name, years to search, address. Civil cases indexed by defendant, plaintiff. Civil records partially on microfiche and archives, on dockets from 1935. Mail turnaround time 5 days. Public use terminal has civil records back to 3/1995. PAT results show name only.
General Information: No mental, sealed records released. Fee to fax out file $2.25 per page. Court makes copy: $2.25 per page. Self serve: $.25 per page. Certification fee: $7.00 1st page; $3.50 each add'l. Payee: Prothonotary. Personal checks and Visa, MC, AmEx accepted. Mail requests: SASE required.

Court of Common Pleas - Criminal 200 N River St, Wilkes Barre, PA 18711; 570-825-1585; fax: 570-825-1843; 8AM-4:30PM. ***Felony, Misdemeanor.*** www.luzernecountycourts.com/
Criminal Records: Access: Fax, mail, in person, online. Only the court performs in person searches; visitors may not. Search fee: $15.00 per name. Required to search: name, years to search, DOB or SSN. Criminal records on computer, microfiche and archived from 1989, on files from 1972. Records from 1933 to 1959 destroyed in flood. Index starts in 191. Mail turnaround time 1-2 days. Public use terminal has crim records. PAT results show middle initial, DOB. Terminal results include SSN. Search dockets online free at http://ujsportal.pacourts.us/DocketSheets/CP.aspx back to 1989. Online results show middle initial, DOB.
General Information: No "M" number (confidential custody case) records released. No fee to fax documents. Court makes copy: $.35 per page, but copies may be included in search fee. Certification fee: $7.00 per doc. Payee: Clerk of Courts. No personal checks or credit cards accepted.

Register of Wills 20 N Pennsylvania Ave, #231, Penn Place, Wilkes Barre, PA 18701; 570-825-1668, 408-825-8241; fax: 570-826-0869; 9AM-4:30PM. ***Probate.***

Lycoming County

Court of Common Pleas - Criminal/Civil 48 W 3rd St, Williamsport, PA 17701; 570-327-2251; fax: 570-327-2505; 8:30AM-5PM. ***Felony, Misdemeanor, Civil, Eviction. Small Claims.***
www.lyco.org/
Civil Records: Access: In person only. Visitors must perform in person searches themselves. Required to search: name, years to search; also helpful: address. Civil cases indexed by defendant, plaintiff; index on computer from 1983, on dockets from 1795. Civil PAT goes back to 1983. Clerk will verify personal identifiers of PAT results.
Criminal Records: Access: In person, online. Visitors must perform in person searches themselves. Required to search: name, years to search, DOB; also helpful: address. Criminal records computerized from 1910. Criminal PAT goes back to 1910. Clerk will verify personal identifiers of PAT results. Search dockets online free at http://ujsportal.pacourts.us/DocketSheets/CP.aspx back to 1968; results show middle initial, DOB.
General Information: No juvenile, cases involving minors, mental records released. Will not fax documents. Court makes copy: $.50 per page. Self serve: $.50 per page. Certification fee: $7.00 per cert includes copies. Payee: Prothonotary. Personal checks accepted; credit cards are not.

Register of Wills County Courthouse, 48 W 3rd St, Williamsport, PA 17701; 570-327-2263, 327-2258; fax: 570-327-6790; 8:30AM-5PM. ***Probate.***

McKean County

Court of Common Pleas - Criminal/Civil PO Box 273, Smethport, PA 16749; 814-887-3270; fax: 814-887-3219; 8:30AM-4:30PM. ***Felony, Misdemeanor, Civil, Eviction.***
Civil Records: Access: Phone, fax, mail, in person. Both court and visitors may perform in person searches. Search fee: $15.00 per name. Required to search: name, years to search. Civil cases indexed by defendant, plaintiff; index on computer since 1994, on microfiche from 1952 to 1962, on dockets from 1872. Mail turnaround time same day. Civil PAT goes back to 1994.
Criminal Records: Access: Mail, in person, online. Both court and visitors may perform in person searches. Search fee: $15.00 per name. Required to search: name, years to search, DOB. Criminal records on computer since 1994, on dockets from 1872. Mail turnaround time same day. Criminal PAT goes back to same as civil. Search dockets online free at http://ujsportal.pacourts.us/DocketSheets/CP.aspx back to 1994. Online results show name, DOB.
General Information: No sex related, juvenile, mental health records released. Will fax documents $2.00 per page. Court makes copy: $.50 per page. Computer printout $1.00 per page. Self serve: $.50 per page. Cert fee: $10.00. Payee: Prothonotary or Clerk of Courts. Personal checks accepted; credit cards are not. Mail requests: SASE required.

Register of Wills PO Box 202, 500 W Main St, Smethport, PA 16749-0202; 814-887-3260; fax: 814-887-2242; 8:30AM-4:30PM. ***Probate.***

Mercer County

Court of Common Pleas - Civil 105 Mercer County Courthouse, Mercer, PA 16137; 724-662-3800; 8:30AM-4:30PM. ***Civil, Eviction.***
www.mcc.co.mercer.pa.us
Daily court schedule at www.mcc.co.mercer.pa.us/Court_Schedule/Default.htm.
Civil Records: Access: In person, online. Visitors must perform in person searches themselves. Required to search: name, years to search. Civil cases

indexed by defendant, plaintiff; index on computer since 1994; prior records on dockets from 1930s, archived from 1700s. Include SSN and DOB in your search. Public use terminal has civil records back to 1994. PAT civil results show middle initial. Online access is by subscription from private company at www.infoconcountyaccess.com, 814-472-6066. See note in court summary section. Images not shown.

General Information: No mental, sealed records released. Will not fax documents, unless prior arrangement with Prothonotary. Court makes copy: $1.00 per page. Certification fee: $4.50 per cert. Payee: Prothonotary or Clerk of Courts. Personal checks accepted; credit cards are not.

Court of Common Pleas - Criminal 112 Mercer County Courthouse, Mercer, PA 16137; 724-662-3800; criminal phone: X2248; fax: 724-662-1604; 8:30AM-4:30PM. ***Felony, Misdemeanor.***

www.mcc.co.mercer.pa.us

Daily court schedule at www.mcc.co.mercer.pa.us/Court_Schedule/Default.htm.

Criminal Records: Access: Mail, in person, online. Both court and visitors may perform in person searches. Search fee: $10.00 per name. Required to search: name, years to search; also helpful: DOB, SSN. Criminal records on computer since 1993, indexed since 1920, on files from 1980. Mail turnaround time 2-4 days. Public use terminal has crim records back to 1993. Search dockets free at http://ujsportal.pacourts.us/DocketSheets/CP.aspx back to Mercer. Online results show name, DOB.

General Information: Online identifiers in results same as on public terminal. No juvenile records released. Fee to fax document $1.00 1st page, $.25 ea add'l. Court makes copy: $.50 per page. Certification fee: $9.00. Payee: Clerk of Courts. Personal checks and major credit cards accepted. Mail requests: SASE required.

Register of Wills 112 Mercer County Courthouse, Mercer, PA 16137; 724-662-3800 X2253; fax: 724-662-1604; 8:30AM-4:30PM. ***Probate.***

Mifflin County

Court of Common Pleas - Criminal/Civil 20 N Wayne St, Lewistown, PA 17044; 717-248-8146; fax: 717-248-5275; 8AM-4:30PM. ***Felony, Misdemeanor, Civil, Eviction.***

www.co.mifflin.pa.us/mifflin/site/default.asp

This agency will not perform searches.

Civil Records: Access: In person, online. Visitors must perform in person searches themselves. Required to search: name, years to search. Civil cases indexed by defendant, plaintiff; index on computer from 1993, on microfiche from 1971-1990 prior on books. Civil PAT goes back to 1971. PAT civil results show middle initial. Court calendar available at the website. Online access is by subscription from private company-Infocon at www.infoconcountyaccess.com, 814-472-6066. See note in court summary section. Images not shown.

Criminal Records: Access: In person, online. Visitors must perform in person searches themselves. Required to search: name, years to search. Criminal records computerized from 1993, on microfiche from 1971-1990prior on books. Criminal PAT goes back to same as civil. PAT criminal results show middle initial. Court calendar at the website. Internet access to court records is by subscription from a private company-Infocon at www.ic-access.com, 814-472-6066. See note at beginning of section. Also, search dockets free at http://ujsportal.pacourts.us/DocketSheets/CP.aspx back to 1986. Online results show middle initial.

General Information: Online identifiers in results same as on public terminal. No juvenile, mental health records released. Will fax documents $.50 per page. Court makes copy: $.50 per page. Self serve: same. Certification fee: $4.50. Payee: Clerk of Courts. No personal checks or credit cards accepted. Mail requests: SASE required for mail return of any copies.

Register of Wills 20 N Wayne St., Lewistown, PA 17044; 717-242-1449; fax: 717-248-2503; 8AM-4:30PM. ***Probate.***

Online access available by subscription from private company-Infocon at www.infoconcountyaccess.com, 814-472-6066. Images not shown.

Monroe County

Court of Common Pleas - Civil Monroe County Courthouse - Prothonotary, 7th & Monroe St, Stroudsburg, PA 18360; 570-517-3988; 8:30AM-4:30PM. ***Civil, Eviction.***

Passport info 570-517-3370.

Civil Records: Access: In person, online. Visitors must perform in person searches themselves. Required to search: name, years to search; also helpful: DOB, SSN, signed release. Civil cases indexed by defendant, plaintiff; index on computer 1995 to present, prior in dockets, books. Public use terminal has civil records back to 1995. PAT results show name only. Online access is by subscription from private company-Infocon at www.infoconcountyaccess.com, 814-472-6066. See note in court summary section. Images not shown.

General Information: No juvenile records released. Will not fax documents. Court makes copy: $1.00 per page. Self serve: $.25 per page. Certification fee: $3.00. Payee: Monroe County Prothonotary. Only cashiers checks and money orders accepted. No credit cards accepted.

Court of Common Pleas - Criminal Monroe County Courthouse, Rm 312, 7th and Monroe Sts, Stroudsburg, PA 18360-2190; 570-517-3385; criminal phone: 570-517-3339; fax: 570-517-3949; 8:30AM-4:30PM. ***Felony, Misdemeanor.***

Criminal Records: Access: Mail, in person, online. Both court and visitors may perform in person searches. Search fee: $5.00 per name. Required to search: name, years to search; also helpful: address, DOB, SSN. Criminal records on computer since 1995; prior on dockets. Mail turnaround time 1 day. Public use terminal has crim records back to 1995.PAT results show name, DOB. Search dockets online free at http://ujsportal.pacourts.us/DocketSheets/CP.aspx back to 1972. Online results show name, DOB.

General Information: No sex related, juvenile, adoption records released. Will not fax documents. Court makes copy: $1.00 per page. Self serve: $.25 per page. Certification fee: $5.00 per doc. Payee: Clerk of Court. Only cashiers checks and money orders accepted. No credit cards accepted. Mail requests: SASE required.

Register of Wills Monroe County Courthouse, 7th and Monroe, Stroudsburg, PA 18360; 570-517-3359; fax: 570-517-3873; 8:30AM-4PM. ***Probate.***

Access wills records online at www.landex.com/remote/. Fee is $.20 per minute and $.50 per fax page. Wills go back to 11/1836.

Montgomery County

Court of Common Pleas - Civil PO Box 311, Airy & Swede St, Norristown, PA 19404-0311; 610-278-3360; fax: 610-278-5994; 8:30AM-4:15PM. ***Civil, Eviction.***

http://prothy.montcopa.org/prothy/site/default.asp

Civil Records: Access: Mail, in person, online. Visitors must perform in person searches themselves. Search fee: $7.50 per name. Required to search: name, years to search. Civil cases indexed by defendant, plaintiff; index on computer from 4/82, on microfilm from 1800s. Public use terminal has civil records back to 1992. PAT civil results show middle initial. Court and other records are free from prothonotary at http://webapp.montcopa.org/PSI/. This includes active and purged civil cases, also active probate cases, also calendars. Online results show middle initial.

General Information: No mental health, divorce, sealed records released. Will not fax documents. Court makes copy: $1.00 1st 4 pages; $.50 each add'l. Certification fee: $4.50 per cert includes copies. Payee: Prothonotary. Personal checks accepted; credit cards are not. Mail requests: n/a.

Court of Common Pleas - Criminal PO Box 311, Main & Swede St, Norristown, PA 19404-0311; 610-278-3346; fax: 610-278-5188; 8:30AM-4:15PM. ***Felony, Misdemeanor.***

www.courts.montcopa.org/courts/site/default.asp

Criminal Records: Access: Mail, online, in person. Both court and visitors may perform in person searches. Search fee: $18.50 per name. Required to search: name, years to search, DOB, signed release. Criminal records computerized from 10/84, prior archived and on microfiche. Mail turnaround time 2-5 days. Public use terminal has crim records back to 1984. PAT results show middle initial, but terminal gives only DOB year. Search dockets online free at http://ujsportal.pacourts.us/DocketSheets/CP.aspx back to 1979. Online results show middle initial but both online and terminal results give only DOB year.

General Information: No impounded, sealed records released. Will not fax documents. Court makes copy: $1.00 per page, $2.00 per page from microfiche. Certification fee: $8.50 per cert. Payee: Clerk of Courts. Attorney firm checks accepted; no personal checks. Accepts Visa/MC/Discover cards. Mail requests: SASE required.

Register of Wills Airy & Swede St, PO Box 311, Norristown, PA 19404; 610-278-3400; fax: 610-278-3240; 8:30AM-4:15PM. ***Probate, Orphan's Court.***

www.courts.montcopa.org/courts/site/default.asp

Search active cases at www.montcopa.org/registerofwillsorphanscourt/rwocviewer/. Email registerofwillsorphanscourt@mail.montcopa.org. If you provide a name, they will search docket books and computer for a file number.

Montour County

Court of Common Pleas - Criminal/Civil Montour County Courthouse, 29 Mill St, Danville, PA 17821; 570-271-3010; fax: 570-271-3089; 9AM-4PM. ***Felony, Misdemeanor, Civil, Eviction.***

www.montourco.org

Civil Records: Access: Phone, fax, mail, in person, online. Both court and visitors may perform in person searches. Search fee: $20.00 per name. Required to search: name, years to search. Civil cases indexed by defendant, plaintiff; index on books since 1991, on microfiche since 1939, on computer back to 1995. Actual files kept for 20 years. Mail turnaround time 1-2 days. Civil PAT goes back to 1996. Online access is by subscription from private company-Infocon found online at www.infoconcountyaccess.com, or call 814-472-6066. See note in court summary section. Images not shown.

Criminal Records: Access: Phone, fax, mail, in person, online. Both court and visitors may perform in person searches. Search fee: $20.00 per name. Required to search: name, years to search, DOB. Criminal docket on books since 1991, on microfiche since 1939, on computer back to 1995. Mail turnaround time 1-2 days. Criminal PAT goes back to same as civil. Online access is by subscription from private company-Infocon at www.infoconcountyaccess.com, 814-472-6066. See note in court summary section. Images not shown. Search dockets online free at http://ujsportal.pacourts.us/DocketSheets/CP.aspx back to 1992. Online results show middle initial, DOB.

General Information: Online identifiers in results same as on public terminal. No sex related, juvenile or adoption records released. Will fax documents $5.00 fee. Court makes copy: $.50 per page. Certification fee: $5.00. Payee: Prothonotary. Personal checks accepted; credit cards are not. Mail requests: SASE required.

Register of Wills 29 Mill St, Danville, PA 17821; 570-271-3012; fax: 570-271-3071; 9AM-4PM. ***Probate.***

www.montourco.org

Online access available by subscription from private company-Infocon at www.infoconcountyaccess.com, 814-472-6066. See note at beginning of section. Images not shown.

Northampton County

Court of Common Pleas - Civil Gov't Center, 669 Washington St, Lower Level, Easton, PA 18042-7498; 610-559-3060; 8:30AM-4:30PM. ***Civil, Eviction.***
www.nccpa.org
Civil Records: Access: In person only. Visitors must perform in person searches themselves. Required to search: name, years to search; also helpful: address. Civil cases indexed by defendant, plaintiff; index on computer since 1/85 (Civil) and 2/90 (Judgments). Public use terminal has civil records back to 1985. Search calendars and schedules for free at www.nccpa.org/schedule.html. Opinions and judgments may be available.
General Information: No impounded or PFA abuse records released. Will not fax documents. Court makes copy: $1.00 per page. Self serve: $.25 per page. Certification fee: $5.75. Payee: Clerk of Court-Civil or Prothonotary's Office. Business or certified checks accepted; no personal checks. No credit cards accepted.

Court of Common Pleas - Criminal 669 Washington St, Easton, PA 18042-7494; 610-559-3000 X3046; fax: 610-252-4391; 8:30AM-4:30PM. ***Felony, Misdemeanor.***
www.nccpa.org
Criminal Records: Access: Mail, in person, online. Both court and visitors may perform in person searches. Search fee: $10.00 per name. Required to search: name, years to search, DOB; also helpful: SSN. Criminal records computerized from 1984, on files from 1800s. Mail turnaround time 1-2 days. Public use terminal has crim records back to 1984. PAT results show middle initial, DOB. Search calendars and schedules for free online at www.nccpa.org/schedule.html. Opinions to be available soon. Also, search dockets online free at http://ujsportal.pacourts.us/DocketSheets/CP.aspx back to 1995. Online results show middle initial, DOB.
General Information: Online identifiers in results same as on public terminal. No juvenile, expunged records released. Will not fax documents. Court makes copy: $.50 per page. Certification fee: $9.00. Payee: Criminal Division. Business checks accepted, no personal checks. Visa/MC accepted in person only.

Register of Wills Govennment Ctr, 669 Washington St, Easton, PA 18042; 610-559-3094; fax: 610-559-3735; 8:30AM-4:30PM. ***Probate.***

Northumberland County

Court of Common Pleas - Civil County Courthouse, 201 Market St, Rm #7, Sunbury, PA 17801-3468; 570-988-4151; 9AM-5PM M; 9AM-4:30PM T-F . ***Civil, Eviction.***
Civil Records: Access: Phone, mail, in person. Both court and visitors may perform in person searches. Search fee: $7.50 per name. Required to search: name, years to search. Civil cases indexed by defendant, plaintiff; index on file from 1772; on computer back to 1998. Mail turnaround time 1-2 days. Public use terminal has civil records back to 1998.
General Information: No adult abuse, involuntary treatment records released. Court makes copy: $1.10 1st page; $.25 each add'l. Certification fee: $4.00 plus $.25 per page. Payee: Northumberland Prothonotary. Business checks accepted. No credit cards accepted. Mail requests: SASE required.

Court of Common Pleas - Criminal County Courthouse, 201 Market St, Rm 7, Sunbury, PA 17801-3468; 570-988-4148; criminal phone: 570-988-4149; 9AM-5PM M; 9AM-4:30PM T-F . ***Felony, Misdemeanor.***
Criminal Records: Access: Mail, in person, online. Both court and visitors may perform in person searches. Search fee: $10.00 per name. Required to search: name, years to search, DOB; also helpful: SSN. Criminal records indexed in office from 1945, on dockets from 1776, archived from 1776 to 1945, on computer back to 1998. Mail turnaround time 1-2 days. Public use terminal has crim records back to 1998. PAT results show middle initial, but terminal results do not always show DOB or SSN. Search dockets online free at http://ujsportal.pacourts.us/DocketSheets/CP.aspx back to 1983. Online results show name, DOB.
General Information: No juvenile records released. Will not fax documents. Court makes copy: $1.20 for first page, $.25 each add'l. Certification fee: $4.00 1st page, $1.00 each add'l page. Payee: Clerk of Courts Office. Personal checks accepted; credit cards are not. Mail requests: SASE required.

Register of Wills 201 Market St, #6, County Courthouse, Sunbury, PA 17801; 570-988-4143; 570-988-4140; fax: 570-988-4141; 9AM-4:30PM. ***Probate.***

Perry County

Court of Common Pleas - Criminal/Civil PO Box 223 (1 Courthouse Sq), New Bloomfield, PA 17068; 717-582-2131; criminal phone: 717-582-2131 X2241; civil phone: 717-582-2131 X2240; fax: 717-582-5167; 8AM-4PM. ***Felony, Misdemeanor, Civil, Eviction.***
www.perryco.org
Access estate records index back to 1987 via www.landex.com/remote/. Registration and password required.
Civil Records: Access: In person only. Visitors must perform in person searches themselves. Required to search: name, years to search. Civil cases indexed by defendant, plaintiff; index on dockets from 1800s. Civil PAT goes back to 1995.
Criminal Records: Access: Phone, fax, mail, in person, online. Both court and visitors may perform in person searches. Search fee: $10.00 per name. Required to search: name, years to search; also helpful: DOB, SSN. Criminal docket index from 1950. Mail turnaround time 1 week; phone turnaround immediate. Criminal PAT goes back to 1994; 1973-1993 being added. Search dockets online free at http://ujsportal.pacourts.us/DocketSheets/CP.aspx back to 1975. Online results show name, DOB.
General Information: No juvenile records released. Will fax documents $3.00. Court makes copy: $.40 per page. Self serve: same. Certification fee: $7.95 per document includes copy fee. Payee: Prothonotary or Clerk of Courts. Personal checks accepted; credit cards are not. Will bill to attorneys and abstract companies upon approval. Mail requests: SASE required for criminal search reuqests.

Register of Wills PO Box 223, 2 E Main St, New Bloomfield, PA 17068; 717-582-2131; fax: 717-582-5149; 8AM-4PM. ***Probate.***

Philadelphia County

Court of Common Pleas - Civil First Judicial District of PA Prothonotary, Rm 284, City Hall, Philadelphia, PA 19107; 215-686-6653; fax: 215-567-7380 admin; 9AM-5PM. ***Civil Actions Above $10,000.***
http://courts.phila.gov
Has separate search unit (215-686-6656 - 8859), record unit (215-686-6661), and cert unit (215-686-6665). Get case number from web or search unit (Rm 262), then get case files from record unit (Record Rm 264), then certify at Rm 269.
Civil Records: Access: Mail, in person, online. Both court and visitors may perform in person searches. No search fee. Required to search: name, years to search. Civil cases indexed by defendant, plaintiff; index on computer from 1/82 to present, archived on files from 1700s to 1982. Docket number required in any mail request. Current records unit phone- 215-686-6661, Rm 268. Mail turnaround time 1-5 days. Public use terminal has civil records back to 1982. PAT results show name only. Public Terminal in Rm #262. Supply personal info in request to help court match record to name. Access to 1st Judicial District Civil Trial records is free at http://fjdwebserver.phila.gov. Free registration required. Search by name, judgment and docket info. Also search civil free at http://fjd.phila.gov. There is also a civil docket and judgment name search at http://fjdweb2.phila.gov/fjd1/rep l1/zk_fjd_public_qry_00.zp_main_idx.html.
General Information: No mental health, divorce, abuse, adoption records released. Will not fax out documents. Court makes copy: $.50 per page. Self serve: $.50 per page. Certification fee: $37.80 per doc. Payee: Prothonotary. Business checks accepted; no personal checks. Credit cards accepted. Mail requests: SASE required.

Clerk of Quarter Session 1301 Filbert St, #310, Criminal Justice Ctr, Philadelphia, PA 19107; 215-683-7707; fax: 215-683-7713; 9AM-4:30PM. ***Felony, Misdemeanor.***
http://courts.phila.gov
The clerk also holds closed records of misdemeanors for the Municipal Court Misdemeanor Division.
Criminal Records: Access: Mail, fax, in person, online. Both court and visitors may perform in person searches. Search fee: $10.00 per name. Required to search: name, years to search, DOB, signed release; also helpful: address, race, sex. Criminal records on computer and microfiche from 1969, archived from 1800s; has case records back to late 1980s. Mail turnaround time 2-3 weeks. Public use terminal has crim records back to 1969. PAT results show middle initial, DOB. Search dockets online free at http://ujsportal.pacourts.us/DocketSheets/CP.aspx back to 1968. Online results show name, DOB.
General Information: Online identifiers in results same as on public terminal. No sealed, grand jury, mental records released. Will not fax documents. Court makes copy: $.25 per page. Self serve: $.25 per page.Fee is $3.00 per doc for printouts from the computer. Certification fee: $12.50 per doc. Payee: Clerk of Quarter Sessions. Business checks accepted; no personal. No credit cards accepted. Mail requests: SASE required.

Municipal Court - Civil 34 S 11th St, Judgments & Petitions, Philadelphia, PA 19107; 215-686-7950, 7989; 9AM-4PM. ***Civil Actions under $10,000, Eviction, Small Claims.***
http://fjd.phila.gov
Info here is for the Municipal Court who has Active cases only; inactive cases with the Prothonotary ofc.
Civil Records: Access: Phone, mail, in person, online. Only the court performs in person searches; visitors may not. No search fee. Required to search: name, years to search; also helpful- address. Civil cases indexed by defendant, plaintiff; index on computer from 1969. Court will search 1 or 2 names over the phone only - it is best to have a case number. Mail turnaround time 1-2 days. Prothonotary in Rm #262 where you may find a public access terminal. Access Muni court dockets online free at http://fjdclaims.phila.gov/phmuni/publicLogin.jsp or you may register for a username and password. Online results show name only.
General Information: Will not fax documents. Court makes copy: $.50 per page. Self serve: same. Certification fee: $27.00 per. Payee: Municipal Court. Cashiers checks and money orders accepted. Major credit cards accepted in person only. Mail requests: SASE required.

Municipal Court - Misdemeanor 1301 Filbert St, #310, Criminal Justice Ctr, Philadelphia, PA 19107; 215-683-7518; 9AM-4PM. ***Misdemeanor (less than 5 years), Felony Hearings.***
http://courts.phila.gov./municipal/criminal
All closed misdemeanor cases held by Clerk of Quarter Sessions - see separate listing. Info Desk phone- 215-683-7004.
Criminal Records: Access: In person, online. Only the court performs in person searches; visitors may not. Required to search: name, years to search, address, DOB, signed release. Criminal records computerized from 1969. Access disposed cases at Clerk of Quarter Sessions. Public use terminal has crim records back to open cases only. PAT results show middle initial, DOB. Public terminal located at 2nd Fl Information Counter, or in #310. Access docket info free at http://ujsportal.pacourts.us/DocketSheets/MC.aspx. Online results show middle initial, DOB. Results also give city/state/zip.
General Information: Online identifiers in results same as on public terminal. Will not fax documents. Court makes copy: $.25 per page for active cases.Self serve copies available in the attorney review rm. Get

copies of closed Muni misdemeanor records at the Clerk of Quarter Sessions Court. Certification fee: $10.00 per doc. No personal checks accepted. Major credit cards accepted.

Register of Wills City Hall, Rm 180, Broad and Markets Sts, Philadelphia, PA 19107; 215-686-6250; fax: 215-686-6293; 8:30AM-5PM. ***Probate.***
http://secureprod.phila.gov/wills/
Search marriage records free back to 1995 at http://secureprod.phila.gov/wills/marriagesearch.aspx.

Pike County

Court of Common Pleas 412 Broad St, Milford, PA 18337; 570-296-7231; fax: 570-296-1931; 8:30AM-4:30PM. ***Felony, Misdemeanor, Civil, Eviction.***
www.pikepa.org
Civil Records: Access: Phone, mail, online, in person. Both court and visitors may perform in person searches. Search fee: $5.00 per name. Required to search: name, years to search. Civil cases indexed by defendant, plaintiff; index on files for 100 yrs, computerized since 1995. The court will only do searches from 01/95 forward. Mail turnaround time varies. Civil PAT goes back to 1995. Online access is by subscription from private company-Infocon at www.infoconcountyaccess.com, 814-472-6066. See note in court summary section. Images shown.
Criminal Records: Access: Phone, mail, online, in person. Both court and visitors may perform in person searches. Search fee: $5.00 per name. Required to search: name, years to search. Criminal records on files for 100 yrs, computerized since 1995. The court will only do searches from 01/95 forward. Mail turnaround time varies. Criminal PAT goes back to same as civil. Internet access to court records is by subscription from a private company-Infocon at www.ic-access.com, 814-472-6066. See note at beginning of section. Images shown. Also, search dockets online free at http://ujsportal.pacourts.us/DocketSheets/CP.aspx back to 1993. Online results show middle initial, DOB.
General Information: No juvenile, adoption, sealed records released. Will not fax documents. Court makes copy: $.50 per page; $5.00 for docket entries. Self serve: $.50 per page. Certification fee: $5.25 per page. Payee: Prothonotary. Personal checks not exceeding $10.00 accepted. No credit cards accepted. Mail requests: SASE required.

Register of Wills Administration Building, 506 Broad St, Milford, PA 18337; 570-296-3508; fax: 570-296-3514; 8:30AM-4:30PM. ***Probate.***
www.pikepa.org/register.htm
Online access available by subscription from private company-Infocon at www.infoconcountyaccess.com, 814-472-6066. See note at beginning of section. Images not shown.

Potter County

Court of Common Pleas 1 E 2nd St, Rm 23, Coudersport, PA 16915; 814-274-9740; fax: 814-274-3361; 8:30AM-4:30PM. ***Felony, Misdemeanor, Civil, Eviction.***
Civil Records: Access: Phone, fax, mail, in person, online. Both court and visitors may perform in person searches. No search fee. Required to search: name, years to search. Civil cases indexed by defendant, plaintiff; index on dockets from early 1833 to 11/97; on computer since 11/97. Mail turnaround time 2 weeks, phone turnaround immediate unless a lengthy search. Civil PAT goes back to 11/1997. Online access is by subscription from private company at www.infoconcountyaccess.com, 814-472-6066. See note in court summary section. Images shown.
Criminal Records: Access: Phone, fax, mail, in person, online. Both court and visitors may perform in person searches. No search fee. Required to search: name, years to search, DOB. Criminal records on card index from 1983 to 6/27/97; on computer since 6/27/97; archived since 1839. Mail turnaround time 2 weeks; phone turnaround immediate unless a lengthy search. Criminal PAT goes back to 6/27/1997. Search dockets online free at http://ujsportal.pacourts.us/DocketSheets/CP.aspx back to 1992. Online results show name, DOB.
General Information: No juvenile records released. Will fax documents at no charge, but only a limited number of pages. Court makes copy: $.50 per page. Self serve: $.25 per page. Certification fee: $5.00; Exemplification fee-$22.00. Payee: Prothonotary & Clerk of Courts. Personal checks accepted; credit cards are not. Mail requests: SASE required.

Register of Wills 1 N Main St, Coudersport, PA 16915; 814-274-8370; fax: 814-274-3360; 8:30AM-4:30PM. ***Probate.***
Online access available by subscription from private company-Infocon at www.infoconcountyaccess.com, 814-472-6066. See note at beginning of section. Images shown.

Schuylkill County

Court of Common Pleas - Civil 401 N 2nd St, Pottsville, PA 17901-2528; 570-628-1270; fax: 570-628-1261; 8:30AM-4:30PM. ***Civil, Eviction.***
www.co.schuylkill.pa.us
Civil Records: Access: Mail, in person, online. Both court and visitors may perform in person searches. Search fee: $5.00 per name. Required to search: name, years to search. Civil cases indexed by defendant, plaintiff. Civil records (suits) on computer from 1989, judgments on computer from 1999 and on dockets from 1800s. Mail turnaround time 1 day. Public use terminal has civil records back to 1989. PAT civil results show middle initial. Judgments on public terminal go back to 1999. Access civil court records and judgments free at www.co.schuylkill.pa.us/info/Civil/Inquiry/Search.csp. Online results show middle initial.
General Information: Online identifiers in results same as on public terminal. No master reports or sealed records released. Will not fax documents. Court makes copy: $.25 per page. Self serve: same. Certification fee: $6.00 per page. Payee: Prothonotary. Personal checks accepted; credit cards are not. Mail requests: SASE requested.

Court of Common Pleas - Criminal 410 N 2nd St, Pottsville, PA 17901; 570-622-5570 X1141; fax: 570-628-1143; 8:30AM-4:30PM. ***Felony, Misdemeanor.***
www.co.schuylkill.pa.us
Criminal Records: Access: Fax, mail, in person, online. Both court and visitors may perform in person searches. Search fee: $11.50 per name. Required to search: name, years to search, DOB; also helpful: SSN. Criminal records computerized from 4/88, on dockets from 1800s. Mail turnaround time same day. Public use terminal has crim records back to 1988. Search dockets online free at http://ujsportal.pacourts.us/DocketSheets/CP.aspx back to 1974. Online results show name, DOB.
General Information: No juvenile records released. No fee to fax documents. Court makes copy: $.25 per page. Certification fee: $8.75 per doc. Payee: Clerk of Courts. Business checks accepted.

Register of Wills Courthouse 401 N 2nd St, Pottsville, PA 17901-2520; 570-628-1377; fax: 570-628-1384; 8:30AM-4:30PM. ***Probate.***

Snyder County

Court of Common Pleas - Criminal/Civil PO Box 217, 9 W Market St, Snyder County Courthouse, Middleburg, PA 17842; 570-837-4202; fax: 570-837-4275; 8:30AM-4PM. ***Felony, Misdemeanor, Civil, Eviction.***
www.seda-cog.org/snyder/site/default.asp
Civil Records: Access: Mail, in person. Both court and visitors may perform in person searches. Search fee: $17.00 per name. Required to search: name, years to search. Civil cases indexed by defendant, plaintiff; index on dockets from 1855, some on microfilm, computerized since 2001. Mail turnaround time 2 days. Civil PAT goes back to 5/2001.
Criminal Records: Access: Mail, in person, online. Both court and visitors may perform in person searches. Search fee: $17.00 per name per 10 years. Required to search: name, years to search. Criminal docket index from 1855, some on microfilm, computerized since 2001. Mail turnaround time 2 days. Criminal PAT goes back to same as civil. PAT results show middle initial, DOB. Search dockets online free at http://ujsportal.pacourts.us/DocketSheets/CP.aspx back to 1970. Online results show name, DOB.
General Information: No juvenile records released. Will fax back short documents for no fee. Court makes copy: $.35 per page. Self serve: same. Certification fee: $5.00 per cert. Payee: Prothonotary or Clerk of Courts. No out-of-state personal checks. No credit cards accepted. Mail requests: SASE required.

Register of Wills County Courthouse, 9 W Market St, PO Box 217, Middleburg, PA 17842; 570-837-4224; fax: 570-837-4299; 8:30AM-4PM. ***Probate.***
www.seda-cog.org/snyder/ical/calendar.asp

Somerset County

Court of Common Pleas - Civil 111 E Union St, #165, Somerset, PA 15501; 814-445-1428; fax: 814-444-9270; 8:30AM-4PM. ***Civil, Eviction, Divorce.***
www.co.somerset.pa.us
Civil Records: Access: In person only. Both court and visitors may perform in person searches. No search fee. Required to search: name, years to search. Civil cases indexed by defendant, plaintiff; index on computer from 1/92, on microfiche from 1920 to 1972, on dockets (Russell System for all other years prior to 1992). Public use terminal has civil records back to 1992. PAT civil results show middle initial. Court calendars (no names) and daily schedules free at www.co.somerset.pa.us. Also, judgments may appear on the Landex system at www.landex.com/remote/ - registration and password required. Court calendars free at www.co.somerset.pa.us/courtcalendar/ but no name searching.
General Information: No commitment records released. Will fax documents to local or toll-free number. Court makes copy: $.50 per page. Self serve: same. No certification fee. Payee: Prothonotary of Somerset Co. Business checks accepted. No credit cards accepted.

Court of Common Pleas - Criminal 111 E Union St, #110, Somerset, PA 15501; 814-445-1435; fax: 814-444-5851; 8:30AM-4PM. ***Felony, Misdemeanor.***
www.co.somerset.pa.us
When faxing, send to the attention of the Clerk of Courts.
Criminal Records: Access: Phone, mail, in person, online. Both court and visitors may perform in person searches. Search fee: $5.00 per name. Required to search: name, years to search, DOB; also helpful: SSN. Criminal records on microfilm from 1920, archive dates uncertain, computerized since 1996. Mail turnaround time same day; phone turnaround immediate. Public use terminal has crim records back to 1996. Search dockets free at http://ujsportal.pacourts.us/DocketSheets/CP.aspx back to 1990. Court calendars free at www.co.somerset.pa.us/courtcalendar/ but no name searching. Online results show name, DOB.
General Information: No impounded records released. Will fax documents to local or toll-free number. Court makes copy: $.50 per page. Certification fee: $1.00. Payee: Clerk of Courts. Personal checks accepted; credit cards are not. Will bill copy fees.

Register of Wills 111 E Union St, #170, Somerset, PA 15501-1416; 814-445-1548; fax: 814-445-1542; 8:30AM-4PM. ***Probate.***
www.co.somerset.pa.us/RegWills.htm

Sullivan County

Court of Common Pleas - Criminal/Civil Main St, Laporte, PA 18626; 570-946-7351; probate phone: 570-946-7351; fax: 570-946-7105; 8:30AM-4PM. ***Felony, Misdemeanor, Civil, Eviction, Probate.***
www.sullivancounty-pa.us/courthouse.html

Includes the Register of Wills.
Civil Records: Access: In person only. Visitors must perform in person searches themselves. Required to search: name, years to search. Civil cases indexed by defendant, plaintiff; index on dockets from 1847 to present and on computer from 8/2000. Civil PAT goes back to 8/7/2000. PAT results show name, DOB.
Criminal Records: Access: In person, online. Visitors must perform in person searches themselves. Required to search: name, years to search; also helpful: SSN. Criminal docket index from 1847 to present and on computer from 8/2000. Criminal PAT goes back to same as civil.PAT results show name, DOB. search dockets online free at http://ujsportal.pacourts.us/DocketSheets/CP.aspx back to 1999; results show name, DOB.
General Information: No juvenile records released. Will fax documents $3.00 per page. Court makes copy: $2.00 per page. Self serve: $.25 per page. Certification fee: $3.00 per page. Payee: Prothonotary or Clerk of Courts. Personal checks accepted; credit cards are not.

Susquehanna County

Court of Common Pleas - Civil
Susquehanna Courthouse, PO Box 218, Montrose, PA 18801; 570-278-4600 x120; 9AM-4:30PM. ***Civil, Eviction.***
Civil Records: Access: Mail, in person, online. Both court and visitors may perform in person searches. Search fee: $7.50 per name. Required to search: name, years to search. Civil cases indexed by defendant, plaintiff; index on dockets from 1800s. Mail turnaround time usually same day. Public use terminal has civil records back to 8/1996. Online access is by subscription from private company-Infocon at www.infoconcountyaccess.com, 814-472-6066. See note in court summary section. Images not shown.
General Information: No juvenile records released. Will not fax documents. Court makes copy: $.25 per page. Self serve: same. Certification fee: $4.50 per cert. Payee: Prothonotary. Personal checks accepted; credit cards are not. Mail requests: SASE required.

Court of Common Pleas - Criminal
PO Box 218, 11 Maple St, Susquehanna Courthouse, Montrose, PA 18801; 570-278-4600 x321, x320, x323; fax: 570-278-4191; 8:30AM-4:30PM. ***Felony, Misdemeanor.***
Criminal Records: Access: Mail, in person, online. Both court and visitors may perform in person searches. Search fee: $5.00 per name per 5 years. Required to search: name, years to search, DOB, SSN. Criminal docket index from 1800s, archived from 1971, computerized since 8/96. Mail turnaround time 1-2 days. Public use terminal has crim records back to 1996. PAT results show name only. Clerk will verify personal identifiers of public terminal result. Search dockets free at http://ujsportal.pacourts.us/DocketSheets/CP.aspx back to 1996. Online results show middle initial, DOB.
General Information: No juvenile records released. Will not fax out documents. Court makes copy: $.25 per page. Certification fee: $4.50 per cert. Cert and copy fees may be increased early 2009. Payee: Clerk of Courts. Personal checks accepted; credit cards are not. Mail requests: SASE required.

Register of Wills
PO Box 218, 11 Maple St, County Courthouse, Montrose, PA 18801; 570-278-4600 X113; fax: 570-278-2963; 8:30AM-4:30PM. ***Probate.***

Tioga County

Court of Common Pleas - Criminal/Civil
116 Main St, Wellsboro, PA 16901; 570-724-9281; 9AM-4:30PM. ***Felony, Misdemeanor, Civil, Eviction.*** www.tiogacountypa.us
Civil Records: Access: In person only. Visitors must perform in person searches themselves. Required to search: name. Civil cases indexed by defendant, plaintiff; index on dockets from 1827; computerized records since 1997. Civil PAT goes back to 1997.
Criminal Records: Access: Mail, in person, online. Both court and visitors may perform in person searches. Search fee: $5.00 per name and $1.00 for each file found. Required to search: name, years to search, signed release. Criminal docket index from 1827; computerized records since 1965. Mail turnaround time same day when possible. Criminal PAT goes back to 1965. Search dockets online free statewide at http://ujsportal.pacourts.us/DocketSheets/CP.aspx back to 1975. Online results show name, DOB.
General Information: No mental health, juvenile, abuse (14 or younger) records released. Will not fax documents. Court makes copy: $.25 per page. Self serve: same. Cert fee: $5.00. Payee: Tioga County Prothonotary. Personal checks accepted; credit cards are not. Mail requests: SASE required for criminal.

Register of Wills
116 Main St, Wellsboro, PA 16901; 570-724-9260; 9AM-4:30PM. ***Probate.***
Online access to wills is available through a private company at www.landex.com/remote/. Fee is $.20 per minute and $.50 per fax page. Images and wills go back to 2/1999.

Union County

Court of Common Pleas - Criminal/Civil
103 S 2nd St, Lewisburg, PA 17837; 570-524-8751; fax: 570-524-8628; 8:30AM-4:30PM. ***Felony, Misdemeanor, Civil, Eviction.***
www.unionco.org
Civil Records: Access: Phone, mail, in person. Both court and visitors may perform in person searches. No search fee. Required to search: name, years to search. Civil cases indexed by defendant, plaintiff; index on computer from 1988, on microfiche (orphans court 1813 to 1988, marriage 1885 to 2001), on dockets from 1800s to 1988. Mail turnaround time same day schedule permitting. Civil PAT goes back to 1988.
Criminal Records: Access: Phone, mail, in person, online. Both court and visitors may perform in person searches. No search fee. Required to search: name, years to search. Criminal records computerized from 1988, on dockets from 1800s to 1988. Mail turnaround time same day if possible. Criminal PAT goes back to same as civil. Search dockets online free at http://ujsportal.pacourts.us/DocketSheets/CP.aspx back to 1988. Online results show name, DOB.
General Information: Online identifiers in results same as on public terminal. No juvenile records released. Will not fax documents. Court makes copy: $.25 per page. Self serve: same. Certification fee: $5.50. Payee: Prothonotary or Clerk of Courts. Personal checks accepted; credit cards are not. Mail requests: SASE required.

Register of Wills
103 S 2nd St, Lewisburg, PA 17837-1996; 570-524-8761; 8:30AM-4:30PM. ***Probate.***
www.unioncountypa.org/residents/government/courts/wills/default.asp

Venango County

Court of Common Pleas - Criminal/Civil
Venango County Courthouse, 1168 Liberty St, Franklin, PA 16323; 814-432-9577; criminal phone: 814-432-9574; civil phone: 814-432-9577; criminal fax: 814-432-9579; civil fax: same; 8:30AM-4:30PM. ***Felony, Misdemeanor, Civil, Eviction.***
www.co.venango.pa.us
Civil Records: Access: Mail, in person. Both court and visitors may perform in person searches. Search fee: $7.00 per name. Required to search: name, years to search. Civil cases indexed by defendant, plaintiff; index on computer from 1993, on dockets from 1800s. Mail turnaround time same day. Civil PAT goes back to 1993. PAT results show name only.
Criminal Records: Access: Mail, in person, online. Both court and visitors may perform in person searches. Search fee: $7.00 per name. Required to search: name, years to search, DOB; also helpful: SSN. Criminal records computerized from 1993, on dockets from 1800s. Mail turnaround time same day. Criminal PAT goes back to same as civil. PAT results show middle initial, DOB. Search dockets online free at http://ujsportal.pacourts.us/DocketSheets/CP.aspx back to 1975. Online results show name, DOB.
General Information: Online identifiers in results same as on public terminal. No juvenile records released. Fee to fax out file $1.00 per page. Court makes copy: $.50 per page. Self serve: same. Certification fee: $7.50 per case. Payee: Clerk of Courts. Personal checks accepted; credit cards are not. Mail requests: SASE required.

Register of Wills/Recorder of Deeds
PO Box 831, 1168 Liberty St, Franklin, PA 16323; 814-432-9539; probate phone: 814-432-9538; fax: 814-432-9569; 8:30AM-4:30PM. ***Probate, Small Claims.*** Clerk also holds recorded land records.

Warren County

Court of Common Pleas - Criminal/Civil
204 4th Ave, Warren, PA 16365; 814-728-3440; fax: 814-728-3459; 8:30AM-4:30PM. ***Felony, Misdemeanor, Civil, Eviction.***
Search fee includes civil and criminal indexes if you ask for both!
Civil Records: Access: Fax, mail, in person. Both court and visitors may perform in person searches. Search fee: $20.00 per name. Required to search: name, years to search. Civil cases indexed by defendant, plaintiff; index on computer from 2000, on dockets from 1800s. Mail turnaround time 2 days. Civil PAT goes back to 2000. PAT results show middle initial, DOB.
Criminal Records: Access: Fax, mail, in person, online. Both court and visitors may perform in person searches. Search fee: $20.00 per name. Required to search: name, years to search; also helpful: DOB. Criminal records computerized from 2000, on dockets from 1800s. Mail turnaround time 2 days. Criminal PAT goes back to same as civil. PAT results show middle initial, DOB. Search dockets online free at http://ujsportal.pacourts.us/DocketSheets/CP.aspx back to 1999. Online results show name, DOB.
General Information: No juvenile records released. No fee to fax back documents. Court makes copy: $.25 per page. Self serve: same. Certification fee: $4.00 per cert. Payee: Prothonotary or Clerk of Courts. Business checks accepted. No credit cards accepted. Mail requests: SASE required.

Register of Wills
204 4th Ave, Courthouse, Warren, PA 16365; 814-728-3430; fax: 814-728-3476; 8:30AM-4:30PM. ***Probate.***

Washington County

Court of Common Pleas - Civil
1 S Main St, #1001, Washington, PA 15301; 724-228-6770; fax: 724-229-5913; 9AM-4:30PM. ***Civil.***
www.co.washington.pa.us
Civil Records: Access: In person, online. Visitors must perform in person searches themselves. Required to search: name, years to search. Civil cases indexed by defendant, plaintiff; index on computer from 1987, prior on dockets to 1800s. Public use terminal has civil records back to 1987. PAT civil results show middle initial. Access to prothonotary civil records including also orphans court is by subscription; enroll form at www.co.washington.pa.us/downloadpage.aspx?menuDept=28. Also, records available on Common Pleas Ct database at www.co.washington.pa.us/wccourtdocuments/code/login.asp. Registration, username, and password required.
General Information: Will not fax documents. Court makes copy: $1.50 per page. Self serve: $.25 per page. Certification fee: $4.50. Payee: Prothonotary. Only cashiers checks and money orders accepted. Checks from attorneys accepted. No credit cards accepted.

Court of Common Pleas - Criminal
Courthouse, #1005, 1 S Main St, Washington, PA 15301; 724-228-6787; fax: 724-250-4658; 9AM-4:30PM. ***Felony, Misdemeanor, Eviction.***
www.co.washington.pa.us
Criminal Records: Access: Mail, in person, online. Both court and visitors may perform in person searches. Search fee: $10.00 per name. Required to search: name, years to search, DOB; also helpful: address, SSN. Criminal records on computer since 10/87, prior on dockets, archived from 1785. Mail

turnaround time over 1 week. Public use terminal has crim records back to 1987. PAT results show middle initial, DOB. Search dockets online free at http://ujsportal.pacourts.us/DocketSheets/CP.aspx back to 1987. Also, records available on Common Pleas Ct database at www.co.washington.pa.us/wccourtdocuments/code/login.asp. Registration, username, and password required. Online results show middle initial, DOB.

General Information: Online identifiers in results same as on public terminal. No juvenile records released. Will not fax documents. Court makes copy: $.25 per page. Self serve: same. Certification fee: $10.00. Payee: Clerk of Courts. Personal checks and major credit cards accepted. In person only. Mail requests: SASE required.

Register of Wills 1 S Main St, #1002, Courthouse, Washington, PA 15301; 724-228-6775; fax: 724-250-4821; 9AM-4:30PM. ***Probate.*** www.co.washington.pa.us/maindepartment.aspx?menuDept=30

Wills available on Common Pleas Ct database at www.co.washington.pa.us/wccourtdocuments/code/login.asp. Registration, username, and password required.

Wayne County

Court of Common Pleas - Criminal/Civil

925 Court St, Honesdale, PA 18431; 570-253-5970 X1210; criminal fax: 570-253-0687; civil fax: same; 8:30AM-4:30PM. ***Felony, Misdemeanor, Civil, Eviction.***

Civil Records: Access: In person only. Visitors must perform in person searches themselves. Required to search: name, years to search. Civil cases indexed by defendant, plaintiff; index on daily docket entries, computerized since 1996. Civil PAT goes back to 1996. PAT civil results show middle initial.

Criminal Records: Access: In person, online. Visitors must perform in person searches themselves. Required to search: name, years to search. Criminal records on daily docket entries, computerized since 1996. Criminal PAT goes back to same as civil. PAT results show middle initial, DOB. Search dockets online free at http://ujsportal.pacourts.us/DocketSheets/CP.aspx back to 1995. Online results show name, DOB.

General Information: Juvenile records not released. Will not fax documents. Court makes copy: $.50 per page. Self serve: same. No certification fee. Payee: Wayne County Prothonotary. Personal checks accepted; credit cards are not.

Register of Wills 925 Court St, Honesdale, PA 18431; 570-253-5970; probate phone: x4040; 8:30AM-4:30PM. ***Probate.***

Westmoreland County

Court of Common Pleas - Civil

PO Box 1630, 2 N Main St, Rm 501, Courthouse Sq, Greensburg, PA 15601-1168; 724-830-3502; fax: 724-830-3517; 8:30AM-4PM. ***Civil, Eviction.*** www.co.westmoreland.pa.us

Civil Records: Access: Online, in person. Visitors must perform in person searches themselves. Required to search: name, years to search. Civil cases indexed by defendant, plaintiff; index on computer from 9/85, on dockets from 1700s. Public use terminal has civil records back to 1985. Access civil court dockets back to 1985 free at http://westmorelandweb400.us:8088/EGSPublicAccess.htm. Also, search Register of Wills and marriages free back to 1986. Access to full remote online system has $100 setup (no set-up if accessed via Internet) plus $20 monthly minimum. System includes civil, criminal, Prothonotary indexes and recorder data. For info, call 724-830-3874, or click on "e-services" at website.

General Information: Online identifiers in results same as on public terminal. No mental health records released. Will fax documents for $3.00 1st page, $1.00 each add'l. Court makes copy: $.50 per page. Computer printout $1.00 per page. Certification fee: $5.75 per cert. Payee: Prothonotary. Business checks accepted; no personal checks. No credit cards accepted.

Court of Common Pleas - Criminal

Criminal Division, 203 Courthouse Square, Greensburg, PA 15601-1168; 724-830-3734; fax: 724-850-3979; 8:30AM-4PM. ***Felony, Misdemeanor.*** www.co.westmoreland.pa.us

Criminal Records: Access: Fax, mail, online, in person. Both court and visitors may perform in person searches. Search fee: $18.95 per name. Required to search: name, years to search, signed release; also helpful: DOB, SSN. Criminal records computerized from 1941, on microfiche from 1793 to 1950, archived from 1773. Mail turnaround time 7-10 working days. Public use terminal has crim records back to 1941. Search dockets online free at http://ujsportal.pacourts.us/DocketSheets/CP.aspx back to 1971. Online results show name, DOB.

General Information: No juvenile records released. Will fax documents $10.00 per doc. Court makes copy: $1.00 per page. Self serve: same. Certification fee: $9.50 per cert. Payee: Clerk of Courts. Attorney's checks accepted. Major credit cards accepted.

Register of Wills 2 N Main St, #301, Greensburg, PA 15601; 724-830-3177; fax: 724-850-3976; 8:30AM-4PM. ***Probate.*** www.co.westmoreland.pa.us

Search estate indices free back to 1986 at http://westmorelandweb400.us:8088/EGSPublicAccess.htm; marriage index online back to 1885. Fuller data requires registration and fees. Office has births/deaths 1893-1905. Estates start 1773.

Wyoming County

Court of Common Pleas - Criminal/Civil

Wyoming County Courthouse, Tunkhannock, PA 18657; 570-836-3200 X232-234; fax: 570-996-0193; 8:30AM-4PM. ***Felony, Misdemeanor, Civil, Eviction.***

Civil Records: Access: In person only. Visitors must perform in person searches themselves. Required to search: name, years to search. Civil cases indexed by defendant, plaintiff; index on dockets from 1800s. Civil PAT goes back to 1996. PAT civil results show middle initial.

Criminal Records: Access: In person, online. Visitors must perform in person searches themselves. Required to search: name, years to search; also helpful: DOB. Criminal docket index from 1800s. Criminal PAT goes back to same as civil. PAT criminal results show middle initial. Search dockets online free at http://ujsportal.pacourts.us/DocketSheets/CP.aspx back to 1975. Online results show name, DOB.

General Information: No juvenile records released. Will not fax documents. Court makes copy: $.25 per page. Self serve: same. Certification fee: $7.00. Payee: Prothonotary or Clerk of Courts. Personal checks accepted; credit cards are not.

Register of Wills Wyoming County Courthouse, 1 Courthouse Sq, Tunkhannock, PA 18657; 570-836-3200 X2235; fax: 570-996-5053; 8:30AM-4PM. ***Probate.***

York County

Court of Common Pleas - Civil

York County Courthouse, 45 N George St, York, PA 17401; 717-771-9611; 8:30AM-4:30PM. ***Civil.*** www.york-county.org/departments/courts/crtf1.htm

Civil Records: Access: In person only. Visitors must perform in person searches themselves. Required to search: name, years to search. Civil cases indexed by defendant, plaintiff; index on computer from mid-1988, on dockets from 1800s, archived from mid-1700s. Public use terminal has civil records back to mid-1988. PAT civil results show middle initial.

General Information: No mental health records released. Will not fax documents. Court makes copy: $1.00 per page. Self serve: $.50 per page. Certification fee: $6.00 per page. Payee: Prothonotary. Only cashiers checks and money orders accepted. No credit cards accepted.

Court of Common Pleas - Criminal

45 N George St, York County Courthouse, York, PA 17401; 717-771-9612; fax: 717-771-9096; 8:15AM-4:30PM. ***Felony, Misdemeanor.*** www.york-county.org/clerkofcourts.html

Direct search requests to the attention of Beth Ruth.

Criminal Records: Access: Fax, mail, online, in person. Both court and visitors may perform in person searches. Search fee: $11.00 per name. Required to search: name, approximate date to search. Criminal records computerized from 1986, on dockets from 1942, archived from 1700s. Mail turnaround time 1-2 weeks. Public use terminal has crim records back to 1986. PAT criminal results show middle initial. Several public terminals available. Search dockets online free at http://ujsportal.pacourts.us/DocketSheets/CP.aspx back to 1969. Online results show middle initial, DOB.

General Information: Online identifiers in results same as on public terminal. No sex crime, juvenile records released. Will fax back documents - must be prepaid and pre-approved. Court makes copy: $.55 per page. Self serve: $.25 per page.Self serve copier is in law library. Certification fee: $10.00 per doc includes some copies; $.55 each for add'l pages. Payee: Clerk of Courts. Personal checks accepted. MC/Discover cards accepted. Mail requests: SASE required.

Register of Wills York County Judicial Center, 45 N George St, York, PA 17401; 717-771-9263; fax: 717-771-4678; 8AM-4:15PM. ***Probate.***

Pennsylvania Recording Offices

ORGANIZATION: 67 counties, 67 recording offices. Each county has two different recording offices. One is the Prothonotary - Pennsylvania's term for "clerk" - who accepts state, federal and other tax lien filings, also UCC filings until July 1, 2001. The Prothonotary also maintains the Court of Common Pleas Civil Court Cases. The other is the Recorder of Deeds who maintains real estate records. Pennsylvania is entirely in the Eastern Time Zone (EST).

REAL ESTATE RECORDS: County Recorders of Deeds will not perform real estate searches. Real estate copy and certification fees vary widely.

UCC RECORDS: This was a dual filing state. Until July 1, 2001, financing statements were filed both at the state level and with the Prothonotary, except for real estate related collateral which were filed with the Recorder of Deeds. Now, only real estate related collateral is filed locally. Many county offices will not perform UCC searches. If they do, try to use search request form UCC-11. UCC search fee can be up to $59.00 per debtor name. UCC copy fee is usually $.50-$2.00 per page.

TAX LIEN RECORDS: All federal and state tax liens on personal property and on real property are filed with the Prothonotary. Usually, tax liens on personal property are filed in the judgment index of the Prothonotary. Some Prothonotaries will perform tax lien searches, usually $5.00 per name.

OTHER LIENS: Judgment, municipal, mechanics.

ONLINE ACCESS: A number of counties provide web access to assessor data. Also, the Infocon County Access System provides internet and direct dial-up access to recorded record information for over twenty Pennsylvania counties; call Infocon at 814-472-6066 or visit www.infoconcountyaccess.com. https://www.corporations.state.pa.us/ucc/soskb/SearchStandardRA9.asp allows search of UCC-1 financing statements filed with Corporation Bureau by debtor or financing statement number.

Adams County Prothonotary

County Prothonotary, 111-117 Baltimore St, Rm 104, Gettysburg, PA 17325. 717-337-9834, fax-717-334-2091; 8AM-4:30PM

See Recorder for real estate records. Index: All in one. Records indexed on a public use terminal back to 1988. Only the public may search. Copy fee $.25 per page. Cert fee- $5.00 per cert. Payee- Prothonotary.

Adams County Recorder

County Recorder of Deeds, 111-117 Baltimore St, Rm 102; County Courthouse, Gettysburg, PA 17325. 717-337-9826, fax-717-334-1758; 8AM-4:30PM www.adamscounty.us/adams/site/

No tax liens filed here. Index: Misc. Records indexed on a public use terminal back to 1964. All other records back to 1937. Only the public may search. UCC copy fee $2.00 per page.Real estate record copy- $.25 per page. Cert fee- $2.00 per doc plus copy fee. Payee- Adams County Recorder of Deeds. **Other phones:** Treasurer- 717-334-6781 x385; Elections-717-334-6781 x436. **Property tax/Assessing-** 111-117 Baltimore St, Rm 202, Gettysburg, PA 17325; 717-337-9837, assessor fax- 717-334-2091. (Appraiser/Auditor- 717-334-6781 x422) A public access terminal available.

Allegheny County Dept of Real Estate

Dept of Real Estate, 542 Forbes Ave, Recording Div; 101 County Office Bldg, Pittsburgh, PA 15219-2947. 412-350-4226; fax-412-350-6877; 8:30AM-4:30PM www.county.allegheny.pa.us/re/

No tax liens filed here. Starting 1/2008. voters elected to merge these offices into above office- Coroner, Jury Commission, Prothonotary, Clerk of Courts, Register of Wills, and Recorder of Deeds. Index: Books and computer. Records indexed on a public use terminal, (images) deeds and mortgages from 1996 to present; subdivisions back to 1809. Office personnel or visitors may perform searches. Search fee $5.00 per name. Office will search real estate records but only a general search, no details. UCC search per debtor name- $40.00. Copy fee $1.00 per page. Cert fee- $5.00 includes 1st 4 copy pages. Payee- Allegheny County Dept of Real Estate. **Online Real Estate, Deed, Mortgage records:** Access Recorder's Index free at https://www.recorder.county.allegheny.pa.us/palr/pa003/index.jsp. Index goes back to 1986. Fee for doc is $1.00 per page, max fee 10 pages; Commercial draw down account copy fee is $.50 per page. **Other phones:** Treasurer- 412-350-4100. **Property tax/ Assessing-** 436 Grant St, Rm 108, Pittsburgh, PA 15219; 412-350-4100. www.county.allegheny.pa.us/treasure/ **Online-** Access Allegheny County real estate data free at http://www2.county.allegheny.pa.us/realestate/Default.aspx.

Allegheny County Prothonotary

414 Grant St; City County Bldg, Pittsburgh, PA 15219. 412-350-4200, fax-412-350-5260; 8:30AM-4:30PM http://prothonotary.county.allegheny.pa.us

See Recorder for real estate records. Index: All in one. Records indexed on a public use terminal back to 1/1/1995. Office personnel or visitors may perform searches. Search fee $25.00 per name. Copy fee $2.00, if tax lien $1.00 per page. Cert fee- $8.00 per cert plus copy fee. Payee- Allegheny County Prothonotary. **Online access to Civil, Judgment, UCC, Tax Lien records:** Access to Prothonotary pre-1995 indices is free at http://prothonotary.county.allegheny.pa.us/allegheny/welcome.htm. Registration is required for the complete prothonotary system. Credit card purchasing available. UCC records are pre-7-1-2001. Online access to the certified values database is free at the website. Also, there is a free case search.

Armstrong County Prothonotary

Prothonotary, 500 E Market St; County Courthouse, Kittanning, PA 16201. 724-543-2500, fax-724-548-3351; 8AM-4:30PM www.co.armstrong.pa.us

See Recorder for real estate records. Index: Separate indices to search. Records indexed on a public use terminal back to 1994. Office will perform a UCC search but public must search other records themselves. Search fee $5.00 per name. Copy fee $1.00 per page. Cert fee- $3.00 1st page, $1.10 each add'l page. Payee- Armstrong County Prothonotary. **Online access to Judgment, Tax Lien records:** For online access see Register of Deeds.

Armstrong County Recorder

County Recorder of Deeds, 500 Market St; County Courthouse, Kittanning, PA 16201-1495. 724-548-3256; fax-724-548-3236; 8AM-4:30PM

No tax liens filed here. Index: Separate indices to search include computer, books. Records indexed on a public use terminal back to1805, images being added. Only the public may search, but office can do a name lookup (except real estate) on computer. General copy fee $.50 per page; $1.00 per page if mailed.Real estate record copy- $1.00 per page. Cert fee- $1.50 per doc plus copy fee. Payee- Recorder of Deeds. **Online access to Real Estate, Deed, Marriage, Probate, Orphans Court records:** Access is through a private company. For info, call Infocon at 814-472-6066 or www.infoconcountyaccess.com. Includes Orphan Court, Recorder of Deeds, Register of Wills images. **Other phones:** Treasurer- 724-548-3260; Elections-724-548-3222; Vital Records- 724-656-3100. **Property tax/ Assessing-** 450 E Market St, Kittanning, PA 16201; 724-548-3487, assessor fax-724-548-3335. (Appraiser/Auditor- 724-548-3489) A public access terminal available.

Beaver County Prothonotary

Prothonotary, 810 3rd St; County Courthouse, Beaver, PA 15009. 724-728-3934 x11279, fax-724-728-3360; 8:30AM-4:30PM www.co.beaver.pa.us/Prothonotary/

See Recorder for real estate records. Index: All in one. Records indexed on a public use terminal back to 1995. Office personnel or visitors (recommended) may perform searches. Search fee based on time. General copy fee $.50 per page; $1.00 per page is returned by mail. Cert fee- $5.00 per request. Payee-Beaver County Prothonotary.

Beaver County Recorder

County Recorder of Deeds, 810 3rd St; County Courthouse, Beaver, PA 15009. Recording, R/E phone-724-728-5700; fax-724-728-8479; 8:30AM-4:30PM www.co.beaver.pa.us/Recorder/index.htm

No tax liens filed here. Index: All in one. Records indexed on a public use terminal back to 1800's. Only the public may search. Copy fee $1.00 per page. Cert fee- $1.50 per cert plus copy fee. Payee- Beaver County Recorder of Deeds. **Online access to Real Estate, Deed, Mortgage records:** Access to the

Recorder's database is free at www.co.beaver.pa.us/Recorder/disclaimer.htm. Deed index back to 1957, images to 1957. Also, marriages, orphan's ct, Register of Wills indexes by subcription at 814-472-6066 or www.infoconcountyaccess.com.. **Other phones:** Treasurer- 724-728-5700; Elections- 724-728-5700; Switchboard- 724-728-5700. **Property tax/ Assessing**- 810 3rd St, Beaver, PA 15009; 724-728-5700, fax- 724-728-0182. www.beavercountypa.gov/Assessment/index.htm **Online**- Access Assessor office free at www.co.beaver.pa.us/AssessmentPublic/.

Bedford County Prothonotary

County Prothonotary, County Courthouse; Corner of Penn & Julliana, Bedford, PA 15522. 814-623-4833, fax-814-623-4831; 8:30AM-4:30PM
See Recorder for real estate records. Records indexed on computer back to 1930. Office personnel or visitors may perform searches. Search fee $20.00 per name. Copy fee $5.00 per doc; self-serve $.25 per page. Cert fee- $4.50 per cert plus copy fee. Payee- Bedford County Prothonotary. **Online access to Judgment, Tax Lien records:** Access is via a private company; call Infocon at 814-472-6066 or www.infoconcountyaccess.com.

Bedford County Recorder

County Recorder, 200 S Juliana St; County Courthouse, Bedford, PA 15522. Recording, R/E phone-814-623-4836; fax-814-624-0488; 8:30AM-4:30PM www.bedford.net/regrec/home.html
No tax liens filed here. Index: All in one. Records indexed on a public use terminal back to 1771. Only the public may search. Copy fee $.25 per page. Cert fee- $1.00 per doc plus copy fee. Payee- Recorder of Deeds. **Online access to Real Estate, Deed, Probate, Marriage, Tax Claim records:** Access is via a private company; call Infocon at 814-472-6066 or www.infoconcountyaccess.com. Includes Recorder of Deeds and Register of Wills images. **Other phones:** Treasurer- 814-623-4846; Elections- 814-623-4807; Vitals- 814-623-4833. **Property tax/Assessing**- 200 S Juliana St, Bedford, PA 15522; 814-623-4842.

Berks County Prothonotary

County Prothonotary, 633 Court St, Reading, PA 19601. 610-478-6970, fax-610-478-6969; 8AM-4PM www.co.berks.pa.us/
See Recorder for real estate records. Index: All in one. Records indexed on a public use terminal back to 1996. Office will perform a UCC search but public must search other records themselves. Copy fee $.50 per page; if requested by mail- $4.00 1st page, $1.00 each add'l. Cert fee- $5.95 per doc plus copy fee. **Online access to Judgment, Lien, Civil Court records:** Prothonotary offers internet access to info back to 1/1996. Fee is $300. For info, call 610-478-6967.

Berks County Recorder

County Recorder of Deeds, 633 Court St, 3rd Fl, Reading, PA 19601. Recording, R/E phone-610-478-3380; fax-610-478-3359; hours - 8AM-5PM www.co.berks.pa.us/recorder/site/default.asp
No tax liens filed here. Index: Separate indices to search. Records indexed on a public use terminal back to 1980. Office personnel or visitors may perform searches. Search fee $12.00 per name. Office will not search real estate records. Copy fee $1.00 per page; $2.00 per page for UCC. Cert fee- $1.50 per cert plus copy fee. Payee- County Recorder. **Online access to Birth, Death, Marriage records:** Access vital records from Register of Wills searchable indexes free at www.co.berks.pa.us/rwills/s/RegMain.htm and includes county and City of Reading; various dates. **Other phones:** Treasurer- 610-478-6640; Elections- 610-478-6490. **Property tax/Assessing**- 633 Court St, 3rd Fl, Reading, PA 19601; 610-478-6262, assessor fax- 610-478-6261. www.co.berks.pa.us/berks/cwp/view.asp?a=1176&q=455472 **Online**- parcel records free at http://ema.countyofberks.com/Parcel_Search/presentation/chameleon/search.asp.

Blair County Prothonotary

County Prothonotary, 423 Allegheny St, #144, Hollidaysburg, PA 16648. 814-693-3080, R/E recording phone-814-693-3095; 8AM-4PM
See Recorder for real estate records. Index: All in one. Records indexed on a public use terminal back to 1989. Only the public may search. Copy fee $.50 per page. Cert fee- $6.00 per doc includes copy fee. Payee- Blair County Prothonotary. **Online access to Judgment, Tax Lien, Civil Court records:** Access via a private company; call Infocon at 814-472-6066 or www.infoconcountyaccess.com.

Blair Recorder of Deeds

County Recorder of Deeds, 423 Allegheny St, #145; County Courthouse, Hollidaysburg, PA 16648. Recording, R/E phone-814-693-3095; fax-814-693-3093; 8AM-4PM www.blaircountyrecorder.com
No tax liens filed here. Index: All in one. Records indexed on a public use terminal back to 1987. Only the public may search. Copy fee $.25 per page; $.50 for plats, subdivisions, maps. Cert fee- $2.00 per doc plus copy fee. Payee- Blair County Recorder of Deeds. **Online access to Real Estate, Deed, Will, Probate, Marriage records:** Access recorded index back to 1990 and images to 2003 by subscription to www.landex.com, 717-274-5890. Register of Will index goes back to 2000, images to 2005. Landex Remote and Landex Webstore (per piece) both available. Also, access via a private company; call Infocon at 814-472-6066 or www.infoconcountyaccess.com. Includes Recorder of Deeds and Register of Wills indexes, marriage licenses. **Other phones:** Treasurer- 814-693-3120; Elections- 814-693-3287; Prothonotary- 814-693-3080. **Property tax/ Assessing**- 423 Allegheny St, #041, Hollidaysburg, PA 16648; 814-693-3110, assessor fax- 814-396-3115. (Appraiser/Auditor- 814-693-3110) A public access terminal available. **Online**- A private company sells county tax claim property, view list free at www.xspand.com/investors/realestate_sale/index.aspx.

Bradford County Prothonotary

Prothonotary, 301 Main St; Courthouse, Towanda, PA 18848. 570-265-1705, fax-570-265-1735; 9-5PM
See Recorder for real estate records. Index: All in one. Records indexed on a public use terminal back to 1986. Only the public may search. Copy fee $1.00 per page if staff copies, $.25 per page if self serve. Cert fee- $5.00 per doc includes copy fee. Payee- Bradford County Prothonotary. **Online access to Property, GIS/mapping records:** Access to property records and GIS/mapping for free go to www.bradfordappraiser.com/GIS/Search_F.asp .

Bradford County Recorder

County Recorder of Deeds, 301 Main St; Courthouse, Towanda, PA 18848. 570-265-1702; fax-570-265-1721; 9AM-5PM www.bradfordcountypa.org
No tax liens filed here. Index: Separate indices to search include grantor/grantee, mortgagor/mortgagee, lesser/lessee since 1985. (In Prothonotary's office.) Records indexed on a public use terminal back to 1970. Only the public may search. Will not search UCC records. Copy fee $.50 per page. In person copies- $.25 each. Cert fee- $2.00 per cert includes copy fee. Payee- Recorder of Deeds. **Online Real Estate, Deed, Mortgage, Will records:** Access the index free at www.landex.com/webstore/jsp/cart/DocumentSearch.jsp. Full access to Recorder of Deeds and Wills and Orphans Court is by subscription at www.landex.com/remote/. Fee is $.10 per page view, $.50 per fax page. Recorder data goes back to 1971; images to 1970, also 1985-89. Wills and orphan court goes back to 1997. **Other phones:** Treasurer- 570-265-1700; Elections- 570-265-1717. **Property tax/Assessing**- 301 Main St, Towanda, PA 18848; 570-265-1714. (Appraiser/Auditor- 570-265-1714) www.bradfordcountypa.org/CountyDepartments/AssessmentOffice.asp

Bucks County Prothonotary/Civil Division

County Prothonotary/Civil Div, 55 E Court St; Courthouse, Doylestown, PA 18901. 215-348-6191, R/E recording phone-215-348-6209, UCC recording phone-n/a; fax-215-348-6184; 8AM-4:15PM www.buckscounty.org/courts/
See Recorder for real estate records. Index: All in one. Records indexed on a public use terminal back to 1980. Only the public may search. Copy fee $1.50 per page; self serve $.25. Cert fee- $4.75 per doc with a SASE. Payee- Bucks County Prothonotary. **Online access to Property, Tax Lien, Probate, Court, Will, Voter Registration records:** Access prothonotary records free at http://4.43.65.248/menu.asp back to 1980. Includes Register of Wills, sheriff sales, voter registration, civil courts and assessor and records. For info on the fee system, contact Jack Morris 215-348-6579 or view details at website. Search civil cases directly at http://4.43.65.248/autoform.asp?app=cvr. Search family and domestic dockets free at http://4.43.65.248/autoform.asp?app=fcr.

Bucks County Recorder

County Recorder of Deeds, 55 E Court St; Courthouse, Doylestown, PA 18901-4367. 215-348-6209; fax-215-340-8157; 7:30AM-5:15PM; recording 7:30AM-5PM www.buckscounty.org/government/rowOfficers/RecorderofDeeds/index.aspx
No tax liens filed here. Index: All in one. Records indexed on a public use terminal back to 1/1/1980. Only the public may search. Copy fee $1.00 per page. Cert fee- $1.50 per cert plus copy fee. Payee- Bucks County Recorder of Deeds. **Online access to Real Estate, Deed, Mortgage, Lien, Judgment, Voter Registration records:** Access recorder's index and images at www.landex.com/remote/. Fee- $.20 per minute; docs go back to 1980, mortgages back to 1968. Search the index free at www.landex.com/webstore/jsp/cart/DocumentSearch.jsp. Also, access other county records free at http://4.43.65.248/menu.asp back to 1980. Includes Register of Wills, sheriff sales, voter registration, courts, prothonotary as well as property records. For info on the fee system, contact Jack Morris at 215-348-6579 or visit the website. **Other phones:** Treasurer- 215-348-6244; Elections- 215-348-6163; Vital Records- 724-656-3100. **Property tax/ Assessing**- 55 E Court St, Doylestown, PA 18901; 215-348-6219, assessor fax- 215-348-6225. www.buckscounty.org/ **Online**- Access to parcel, sale, and property assessment data is free at http://4.43.65.248/autoform.asp?app=par. Access the index free at www.landex.com/webstore/jsp/cart/DocumentSearch.jsp. Full access to Recorder of Deeds and Wills and Orphans Court is by subscription at www.landex.com/remote/. Fee is $.10 per page view, $.50 per fax page.

Butler County Prothonotary

County Prothonotary, PO Box 1208, Butler, PA 16003-1208. 724-284-5214; 8:30AM-4:30PM www.co.butler.pa.us
See Recorder for real estate records. Index: Separate indices to search include judgment, ejection & miscellaneous, federal lien. Records indexed on computer back to 4/1/93. Only the public may search. Copy fee $.50 per page; $1.00 per microfilm copy. Cert fee- $4.50 per cert plus copy fee. Payee- Butler County Prothonotary. **Online Judgment, Fed Lien, Divorce records:** Private company offers online access to prothonotary records. Call Infocon at 814-472-6066, www.infoconcountyaccess.com.

Butler County Recorder

County Recorder of Deeds, PO Box 1208, Butler, PA 16003-1208. 724-284-5340; fax-724-285-9099; 8:30AM-4:30PM www.co.butler.pa.us
No tax liens filed here. Index: Separate indices to search include mortgages from 1800-1984 (mortgagee/or indexes). Records indexed on a public use terminal back to 1985. Only the public may

search. Copy fee $.50 per page. Cert fee- $1.50 per page plus copy fee. Payee- County Recorder. **Online access to Real Estate, Deed, Marriage, Lien Probate, Orphans Court, Guardianship, Register of Wills records:** Access deeds records free at www.co.butler.pa.us/recorder/. Also, access marriage, probate, and Register of Wills records via a private company; call Infocon at 814-472-6066, www.infoconcountyaccess.com. Images available. Also access probate court estate/guardianship records free at http://66.117.197.22/index.cfm?page=home. At bottom of webpage, click on the type of "lookup" you want. **Other phones:** Treasurer- 724-284-5149; Elections- 724-284-5310. **Property tax/Assessing**- PO Box 1208, 124 W Diamond St, Butler, PA 16003-1208; 724-284-5316, assessor fax- 724-284-5430. A public access terminal available.

Cambria County Prothonotary

County Prothonotary, 200 S Center St, Ebensburg, PA 15931. 814-472-1636, fax-814-472-5632; 9AM-4PM www.co.cambria.pa.us/cambria/site/default.asp
See Recorder for real estate records. Index: Separate indices to search include judgments, misc. Records indexed on a public use terminal back to 1994. Only the public may search. Copy fee $.25 per page. Cert fee- $3.00 per cert plus copy fee. Payee- Cambria County Prothonotary. **Online Judgment, Lien, Civil Court, Divorce records:** Access prothonotary records via a private company. Subscription required. For info, call Infocon at 814-472-6066, www.infoconcountyaccess.com.

Cambria County Recorder

County Recorder of Deeds, County Courthouse; 200 S Center St, Ebensburg, PA 15931. Recording, R/E phone-814-472-1473; fax-814-472-1412; 9AM-4PM www.co.cambria.pa.us/cambria/site/default.asp
No tax liens filed here. Index: Index on computer 1986-present with separate UCC index with recent filings; manual Russell indices 1804-1985; Military discharges unsearchable. Records indexed on a public use terminal back to 100. Only the public may search. Copy fee $.50 per page. Cert fee- $1.50 per doc plus copy fee. Payee- Recorder of Deeds. **Online access to Marriage, Probate, Orphans Court, Will records:** Access county records via a private company. Subscription required; images available. For info, call 814-472-6066, www.infoconcountyaccess.com. **Other phones:** Treasurer- 814-472-1643; Elections- 814-472-1460; Register of Wills- 814-472-1440. **Property tax/Assessing**- 200 S Center St, Ebensburg, PA 15931; 814-472-1451, 814-472-5440 x450, fax-814-472-6573. A public access terminal available.

Cameron County Prothonotary

Prothonotary, 20 E 5th St, Emporium, PA 15834. 814-486-3349, fax-814-486-0464; 8:30AM-4PM
See Recorder for real estate records. Index: All in one. Records indexed on a public use terminal from 1985 to present. Office will perform a UCC search but public must search other records themselves. No fee for search. Copy fee $.50 per page. Cert fee- $10.00 per cert includes copy fee. Payee- Cameron County Prothonotary.

Cameron County Recorder

County Recorder of Deeds, 20 E 5th St, Emporium, PA 15834. Recording, R/E phone-814-486-3349; fax-814-486-0464; 8:30AM-4PM
No tax liens filed here. Index: All in one. Records indexed on a public use terminal from 1990 to present. Only the public may search. Copy fee $.50 per page. Cert fee- $10.00 per copy includes copy fee. Payee- Recorder of Deeds. **Online Real Estate, Deed, Lien, Will records:** Access the index free at www.landex.com/webstore/jsp/cart/DocumentSearch.jsp. Full access to Recorder of Deeds and Wills and Orphans Court is by subscription at www.landex.com/remote/. Index and images go back to 8/2005. **Other phones:** Treasurer- 814-486-3348; Elections- 814-486-2315; Vitals- 814-486-3349. **Property tax/Assessing**- 20 E 5th St, Emporium, PA 15834; 814-486-0723, assessor fax- 814-486-0464.

Carbon County Prothonotary

County Prothonotary, PO Box 130, Jim Thorpe, PA 18229-0130. 570-325-2481, fax-570-325-8047; 8:30AM-4:30PM www.carboncourts.com/prothy.htm
See Recorder for real estate records. Index: All in one. Records indexed on a public use terminal back to 1984. Only the public may search. Copy fee $1.00 per page. Cert fee- $9.20 per cert plus copy fee. Payee- Carbon County Prothonotary. **Online access to Judgment, Lien, UCC, Probate, Will records:** Access to county prothonotary, Register of Wills, and Clerk of Courts remote public access dial-up database is free; 570-325-3288; instructions at www.carboncourts.com/pubacc.htm.

Carbon County Recorder

County Recorder of Deeds, PO Box 89, Jim Thorpe, PA 18229. 570-325-2651, R/E recording phone-570-325-2651, fax-570-325-2726; 8:30AM-4:30PM www.carboncounty.com/deeds.htm
No tax liens filed here. Index: Separate indices to search include computer-1988 to present, Russell index- 1843-1988. Records indexed on a public use terminal back to 1988. Only the public may search. Copy fee $.50 per page. Cert fee- $1.50 per cert plus copy fee. Payee- Carbon Recorder of Deeds. **Online Real Estate, Deed records:** Access the index free at www.landex.com/webstore/jsp/cart/DocumentSearch.jsp. Full access to Recorder of Deeds is by subscription at www.landex.com/remote/. Index goes back to 1988, images to 8/1994. **Other phones:** Treasurer- 570-325-2251; Elections- 570-325-4801. **Property tax/ Assessing**- PO Box 250, Jim Thorpe, PA 18229-0250; 570-325-5254, assessor fax- 570-325-8074. www.carboncounty.com/assessor.htm **Online access**- Access assessor property data free at www.carboncounty.com/records.htm.

Centre County Prothonotary

County Prothonotary, Allegheny & High Sts; County Courthouse, Bellefonte, PA 16823. 814-355-6796; 8:30AM-5PM www.co.centre.pa.us/223.htm
See Recorder for real estate records. Index: Separate indices to search include civil, criminal, UCC. Records indexed on computer back to 7/1/94. Public access terminal available. Only the public may search. Copy fee $.50 per page. Cert fee- $4.00 for 1st page, $2.00 each add'l, plus copy fee. Payee- Centre County Prothonotary. **Online access to Lien, Judgment records:** Access Prothonotary data and more at http://epin.chesco.org; registration and fees required.

Centre County Recorder

Recorder of Deeds, 414 Holmes St, #1, Bellefonte, PA 16823. Recording, R/E phone-814-355-6801; 8:30AM-5PM www.co.centre.pa.us/133.asp
No tax liens filed here. Index: All in one. Records indexed on a public use terminal back to 1900's. Only the public may search. Will not search UCC records. Copy fee $.50 per page. Cert fee- $1.50 per doc plus copy fee. Payee- Recorder of Deeds. **Online access to Real Estate, Deed records:** Access recorded data on the WEB IA subscription system; fee is $10.00 set-up plus $.06 per click or other per click plan. This replaces the old dial-up system. See http://webia.co.centre.pa.us/login.asp. **Other phones:** Treasurer- 814-355-6810; Elections- 814-355-6703; Register of Wills- 814-355-6724. **Property tax/Assessing**- 420 Holmes St, #301, Bellefonte PA 16823-1488; 814-355-6721, assessor fax- 814-355-6747. www.co.centre.pa.us/121.asp **Online access**- Assessment data on the WEB IA subscription system; registration and per page fees apply; see http://webia.co.centre.pa.us/login.asp.

Chester County Prothonotary

County Prothonotary, PO Box 2748, West Chester, PA 19380-0991. 610-344-6301, fax-610-344-5903; 8:30AM-4:30PM http://dsf.chesco.org/
See Recorder for real estate records. Index: All in one. Records indexed on a public use terminal back to 1990. Only the public may search. Copy fee $1.15 1st page; $.55 each add'l. Cert fee- $5.50 1st four pages plus copy fee. Payee- Prothonotary. Bulk data available for purchase, contact 610-344-6884. **Online access to Lien, Court, Judgment records:** Full countywide records including court records requires a sign-up and credit card payment. Application fee is $50. with $10.00 per month minimum; no charge for no activity; $.10 each transaction beyond 100. Sign-up and logon at http://epin.chesco.org.

Chester County Recorder

County Recorder of Deeds, PO Box 2748, West Chester, PA 19380-0991. Recording, R/E phone-610-344-6330, fax-610-344-6408; 8:30AM-4:30PM http://dsf.chesco.org/recorder/site/default.asp
No tax liens filed here. Index: All in one. Records indexed on a public use terminal back to 1920. Only the public may search. Copy fee $5.00 per page; self serve $.50. Cert fee- $1.50. Fee to fax results is $5.00 per page plus copy fee. Payee- Chester County Recorder of Deeds. Purchase county data as reports, labels, magnetic tape, diskettes. **Online access to Real Estate, Deed, Vital Statistic, Archive records:** Search Recorder of Deeds records free at http://rod.chesco.org/icris/splash.jsp. Also, full countywide records including court records requires a sign-up and credit card payment. Application fee is $50. with $10.00 per month minimum - no charge for no activity; $.10 each transaction beyond 100. Sign-up and/or logon at http://epin.chesco.org. Also, genealogical and older vital statistics are free at http://dsf.chesco.org/archives/site/default.asp. **Other phones:** Treasurer- 610-344-6370; Elections- 610-344-6410; Vital Records- 717-783-2548; BLR (Bureau of Land Records-for help with UPI #)- 610-344-5968. **Property tax/Assessing**- 121 N Walnut St,#200, PO Box 2748, West Chester, PA 19380; 610-344-6105, fax- 610-344-5902. (Appraiser- 610-344-6105) http://dsf.chesco.org/chesco/site/default.asp **Online access**- Assessment data available by subscription at http://epin.chesco.org.

Clarion County Prothonotary

County Prothonotary, 421 Main St; Courthouse, Clarion, PA 16214-1092. 814-226-1119, fax-814-227-2501; 8:30AM-4:30PM
Index: includes judgment, general. Records indexed on computer back to 1990. Only the public may search. Copy fee $.50 per page. Cert fee- $8.00 per doc plus copy fee. **Online access to Judgment, Lien records:** Access index through a private company. For info, call Infocon at 814-472-6066 or www.infoconcountyaccess.com.

Clarion County Recorder

Recorder of Deeds, 421 Main St #24; Courthouse, Clarion, PA 16214. 814-226-4000 x2500, R/E recording phone-814-226-4000 x2501; fax-814-226-1117; 8:30AM-4-30PM www.co.clarion.pa.us
No tax liens filed here. Index: All in one. Records indexed on computer back to 1951. Only the public may search. Copy fee $.50 per page; $1.00 per page if mailed back. Cert fee- $4.50 per page includes copy fee for 1st 4 pages. Payee- Gregory K Mortimer, Recorder. **Online access to Real Estate, Deed, OCC/PC, Marriage, Voter Registration, Orphans Court, Probate, Tax Claim records:** Access is through a private company. For info, call Infocon at 814-472-6066 or www.infoconcountyaccess.com. Includes images for Recorder, Register of Wills, and Orphans court. **Other phones:** Treasurer- 814-226-4000 x2861. **Property tax/Assessing**- 421 Main St, Clarion, PA 16214; 814-226-4000 x2301, assessor fax- 814-226-4197. hours- 8:30AM-4:30PM

Clearfield County Prothonotary

County Prothonotary, PO Box 549, Clearfield, PA 16830. 814-765-2641 x1331, R/E recording phone-814-765-2641 x5987; fax-814-765-7659; 8:30AM-4PM www.clearfieldco.org

See Recorder for real estate records. Index: Separate indices to search include docket books and computer. Records indexed on computer from 1100 to present, index books prior to 11/00. Office personnel will make a computer check (5 years) or visitors may perform searches. Search fee $7.00 per name (not certified). Copy fee $.25 per page. Cert fee- $1.50 per doc plus copy fee. Payee- Prothonotary.

Clearfield County Recorder

County Recorder of Deeds, PO Box 361, Clearfield, PA 16830. Recording, R/E phone-814-765-2641 x1350, UCC phone-814-765-2641 x1353; fax-814-765-6089; 8:30AM-4PM www.clearfieldco.org

No tax liens filed here. Index: Multiple indices to search. Records indexed on a public use terminal back to 5/89. Office will perform a UCC search (if it takes a small amount of time), but public must search other records themselves. Copy fee $.50 per page. Maps- $1.00 per page 11x17 inches. Cert fee- $1.00 per doc plus copy fee. Payee- Register & Recording Office. **Online Real Estate, Deed, Mortgage, Probate, Orphans Court records:** Access the index free at www.landex.com/webstore/jsp/cart/DocumentSearch.jsp. Full access to Recorder of Deeds and Wills and Orphans Court is by subscription at www.landex.com/remote/. Fee is $.20 per minute, $1.00 per fax page. Recorder index goes back to 1986; images back to 1989. Wills and orphan court records go back to 1990. **Other phones:** Treasurer- 814-765-2641 x5985; Elections- 814-765-2641 x5996; Vital Records- 724-656-3100. **Property tax/Assessing**- 230 E Market St, #117, Clearfield, PA 16830; 814-765-2641 x5997, assessor fax- 814-765-2640. A public access terminal available. **Online access**- Assessors county tax sale list is updated weekly at www.clearfieldco.org/taxsale.htm.

Clinton County Prothonotary

County Prothonotary, 230 E Water St; Courthouse, Lock Haven, PA 17745. 570-893-4007, fax-570-893-4288; 8AM-5PM M,T,Th,F; 8AM-12:30PM W. www.clintoncountypa.com

See Recorder for real estate records. Index: many indices. Records indexed on a public use terminal back to 1992. Only the public may search. Copy fee $.50 per page. Cert fee- $5.00 per cert plus copy fee. Exemplification $15.00. Payee- Clinton County Prothonotary. **Online access to Judgment, Tax Lien records:** Access images through a private company. For info, call Infocon at 814-472-6066 or www.infoconcountyaccess.com.

Clinton County Recorder

County Recorder of Deeds, PO Box 943, Lock Haven, PA 17745. 570-893-4010; fax-570-893-4273; 8:30AM-5PM M,T,TH,F; 8AM-12:30PM W. www.clintoncountypa.com/register_&_recorder.htm

No tax liens filed here. Index: Separate indices to search include computer, books. Records indexed on a public use terminal back to 1977. Only the public may search. Copy fee $.50 per page. $5.00 fee to fax back document. Cert fee- $1.50 per cert plus copy fee. Payee- Clinton County Recorder of Deeds. **Online Real Estate, Deed, Probate, Orphan Court, Property, Treasurer, Tax Claim records:** Access available via a private company. For info call Infocom at 814-472-6066 or www.infoconcountyaccess.com. Includes images for Recorder, Register of Wills, Orphans Court, Prothonotary. **Other phones:** Treasurer- 570-893-4004; Elections- 570-893-4000; Vitals- 570-893-4010. **Property tax/Assessing**- 230 E Water St, Lock Haven, PA 17745; 570-893-4033, assessor fax- 570-748-4272. (Appraiser- 570-893-4030) www.clintoncountypa.com/assessment.htm **Online access**- Access to gis-mapping property and assessment data is free at www.clintoncountypa.com/giswelcome.htm. Also, access treasure's tax sale lists free at www.clintoncountypa.com/taxsale.htm.

Columbia County Prothonotary

County Prothonotary, PO Box 380, Bloomsburg, PA 17815. 570-389-5614; 8AM-4:30PM

See Recorder for real estate records. Index: All in one. Records indexed on a public use terminal back to 1992. Copy fee $1.00 per page. Cert fee- $4.00 per page includes copy fee. Payee- Columbia County Prothonotary.

Columbia County Recorder

County Recorder of Deeds, PO Box 380, Bloomsburg, PA 17815. Recording, R/E phone-570-389-5632; fax-570-389-5636; 8AM-4:30PM www.columbiapa.org/registerrecorder/index.php

No tax liens filed here. Index: Separate indices to search include all land records from 1974 to 10/99 by book & page, from 10/99 to present-by instrument number. Records indexed on a public use terminal back to 1/1974. Only the public may search. General copy fee $.50 per page. Larger sheets are $1.00 per page. Cert fee- $1.50 per cert plus copy fee. Payee- Columbia County Recorder of Deeds. **Online access to Real Estate, Deed, Mortgage, UCC, Will records:** Access the index free at www.landex.com/webstore/jsp/cart/DocumentSearch.jsp. Full access is via subscription at www.landex.com/remote/. Fee is $.20 per minute. Recorders index goes back to 1974; wills index back to 1995; UCCs to 1992; images go back to 1/1974; wills and UCCs to 10/1999. **Other phones:** Treasurer- 570-389-5626; Elections- 570-389-5640; Vital Records- 570-389-5616 (marriage/divorce). **Property tax/Assessing**- PO Box 380, 35 W Main St, Bloomsburg, PA 17815; 570-389-5645, assessor fax- 570-389-5646. (Appraiser/Auditor- 570-389-5645) www.columbiapa.org **Online access**- Access to gis-mapping property and assessment data is free at www.columbiapa.org/gis/. Click on Search Database.

Crawford County Prothonotary

Prothonotary, 903 Diamond Park; Courthouse, Meadville, PA 16335. 814-333-7324, fax-814-337-5416; 8:30AM-4:30PM www.crawfordcountypa.net/

See Recorder for real estate records. Index: All in one. Records indexed on a public use terminal back to 2000. Office personnel or visitors may perform searches. Copy fee $.80 per page for file copies, $1.60 per page for docket copies. Cert fee- $1.75 per cert. Payee- Crawford County Prothonotary.

Crawford County Recorder

County Recorder of Deeds, 903 Diamond Park; Courthouse, Meadville, PA 16335. Recording, R/E phone-814-373-2537; fax-814-337-5296; 8:30AM-4:30PM www.crawfordcountypa.net/

No tax liens filed here. Index: Index back to 1800. Records indexed on a public use terminal back to 1985. Images back to 1/2/1987. Only the public may search, but will assist genealogical records. Search fee-$5.00 per name. Office will search limited real estate records. Will not search UCC records. Copy fee $1.00 per page. Cert fee- $1.50 per doc plus copy fee. Payee- Crawford County Recorder of Deeds. **Other phones:** Treasurer- 814-333-7332; Elections- 814-333-7307. **Property tax/Assessing**- 903 Diamond Park, Meadville, 16335; 814-333-7302. Public access terminal available. www.crawfordcountypa.net/

Cumberland County Prothonotary

County Prothonotary, 1 Courthouse Sq; County Courthouse, Carlisle, PA 17013-3387. 717-240-6195, fax-717-240-6573; 8AM-4:30PM

See Recorder for real estate records. Index: Separate indices to search include electronically from 1994 to present, 2001 to present are digitally recorded. Records indexed on a public use terminal back to 1994. Only the public may search. Copy fee $.50 per page. Cert fee- No fee for certification. Payee- Cumberland County Prothonotary. **Online access to Judgment, Lien, Civil records:** Civil dockets available free at http://records.ccpa.net/weblink_public/Browse.aspx?dbid=0. Also, access index through a private company. For info, call Infocon at 814-472-6066 or www.infoconcountyaccess.com.

Cumberland County Recorder

County Recorder of Deeds, 1 Courthouse Sq; County Courthouse, Carlisle, PA 17013. Recording, R/E phone-717-240-6370, UCC phone-717-240-5370; fax-717-240-7851; 8AM-4:30PM www.ccpa.net

No tax liens filed here. Index: All in one after 1/1973, before separate index for deeds, mortgages, misc documents. Records indexed on a public use terminal back to 01/73. Only the public may search. Will not search UCC records. Copy fee $.50 per page. Cert fee- $10.00 per cert by mail includes copy fee. Payee- Cumberland Recorder of Deeds. **Online access to Real Estate, Deed, Marriage, Tax Claim, Register of Wills records:** Records index access available via a private company. For info call Infocon at 814-472-6066 or www.infoconcountyaccess.com. Also, access available by sub via www.landex.com/remote/. May include images for Recorder of Deeds records.. **Other phones:** Treasurer- 717-240-6380; Elections- 717-240-6385. **Property tax/Assessing**- 1 Courthouse Sq, Carlisle, PA 17013; 717-240-6350, assessor fax- 717-240-6354. **Online** - Access to the property assessment data is free at www.ccpa.net/index.asp?nid=2677. No name searching. Access property data on the GIS-mapping site free at http://ccgis.ccpa.net/taxmapper/. Search delinquent tax index at http://taxdb.ccpa.net/delin quent/default.asp but no name searching. Tax Sale data at www.ccpa.net/index.asp?nid=2675.

Dauphin County Prothonotary

County Prothonotary, PO Box 945, Harrisburg, PA 17108. 717-780-6520, fax-none; 8AM-4:30PM

See Recorder for real estate records. Index: Separate indices to search include UCC, misc, ejection. Judgments indexed on a public use terminal back to 1992. Office personnel or visitors may perform searches. Search fee $10.00. Copy fee $.75 per page. Cert fee- $5.00 per case includes 1 copy. Payee- Dauphin County Prothonotary. **Online access to UCC records:** At www.dauphinc.org/deeds/ UCCs go back to 10/1/93.

Dauphin County Recorder

County Recorder of Deeds, Front & Market Sts, Rm 102; County Courthouse, Harrisburg, PA 17101. Recording, R/E phone-717-780-6560; fax-717-780-6482; 8AM-4:30PM www.dauphinc.org/deeds/

No tax liens filed here. Index: All in one. Records indexed on a public use terminal back to 1979. Only the public may search. Copy fee $.50 per page. Plan copies $2.00 per page, Microfilm copies $.75 per page. Copy requests via mail $1.00 per page. Cert fee- $2.00 per page plus copy fee. Payee- County Recorder of Deeds. **Online access to Real Estate, Deed, Mortgage, Register of Wills records:** Access the register's land records database free at http://198.185.140.50/oncoreweb/Search.aspx. Access Register of Wills and Orphan Ct docs free at www.landex.com/webstore/jsp/cart/DocumentSearch.jsp. Full access to Register of Wills and Orphans Court is by subscription at www.landex.com/remote/. Images go back 5/2006. **Other phones:** Treasurer- 717-780-6550; Elections- 717-780-6360. **Property tax/Assessing**- 2 S 2nd St, 2nd Fl, Admin Bldg, Harrisburg, PA 17101; 717-780-6101. **Online access**- Access to county assessor property data is free at www.dauphinpropertyinfo.org/propertymax/rover30.asp. To search free, create a limited guest account. Full access fee is $50.00 per month.

Delaware County Prothonotary

County Prothonotary, 201 W Front St, Judicial Support; Delaware County Gov't Ctr Bldg, Media, PA 19063. 610-891-4386, 891-4370, fax-610-891-7257; 8:30AM-4:30PM www.co.delaware.pa.us

See Recorder for real estate records. Index: All in one. Records indexed on public use terminals back to 1970. Only the public may search. Copy fee $1.00 per page. Cert fee- $4.95 per cert plus copy fee. Payee- Office of Judicial Support. Office sells mortage foreclosure and lien reports, contact Dana 610-891-4967. **Online Judgment, Civil records:** Records at http://w01.co.delaware.pa.us/pa/publicaccess.asp.

Delaware County Recorder

County Recorder of Deeds, 201 W Front St, Rm 107; Gov't Ctr Bldg, Media, PA 19063. 610-891-4152; 8:30-4:30 www.co.delaware.pa.us/depts/recorder.html
No tax liens filed here. Index: All in one. Records indexed on a public use terminal back to 1982. Only the public may search. Copy fee $1.00 per page. Cert fee- $7.00 for 1st 4 pages; $1.00 each add'l, includes copy fee. Payee- Delaware County Recorder of Deeds. **Online Real Estate, Deed, Judgment records:** Access to the public access system is free at www.co.delaware.pa.us/depts/recorder.html. **Other phones:** Treasurer- 610-891-4272; Elections- 610-891-4938. **Property tax/Assessing**- 201 W Front St, Media, PA 19063; 610-891-5416, assessor fax- 610-891-4883. **Online access**- Access to Real Estate and Assessment for free at http://w01.co.delaware.pa.us/pa/publicaccess.asp?real.x=71&real.y=50.

Elk County Prothonotary

Prothonotary, PO Box 237, Ridgway, PA 15853-0237. 814-776-5344, fax-814-776-5303; 8:30-4PM
See Recorder for real estate records. Index: All in one. Records indexed on computer back to 1998. Office personnel or visitors may perform searches. Search fee- $8.25 per name. Copy fee $.50 per page. Cert fee- $5.00 per doc plus copy fee; exemplification- $16.50. Payee- Elk County Prothonotary.

Elk County Recorder

County Recorder of Deeds, PO Box 314, Ridgway, PA 15853-0314. 814-776-5349; fax-814-776-5382; 8:30AM-4PM www.co.elk.pa.us/regrecorder/
No tax liens filed here. Index: All in one. Records indexed on a public use terminal back to 1987. Only the public may search. Copy fee $.50 per page. Cert fee- $1.50 per instrument plus copy fee. Payee- Elk County Recorder of Deeds. **Other phones:** Treasurer- 814-776-5322; Elections- 814-776-5337. **Property tax/Assessing**- PO Box 448, 250 Main St, Ridgway, PA 15853; 814-776-5340, assessor fax- 814-776-5305. 8:30AM-4:30PM. Publicterminal available.

Erie County Prothonotary

County Prothonotary, 140 W 6th St, Rm 120, Erie, PA 16501-1080. 814-451-6078, fax-814-451-7400; 8:30AM-4:30PM www.eriecountygov.org
See Recorder for real estate records. Index: All in one. Records indexed on a public use terminal back to 1992. Only the public may search. Copy fee $.50 per page. Cert fee- $5.00 per doc plus copy fee. Payee- Erie County Prothonotary. **Online Judgment, Lien, Civil Court records:** Access is through a private company; call Infocon at 814-472-6066 or www.infoconcountyaccess.com

Erie County Recorder

County Recorder of Deeds, PO Box 1849, Erie, PA 16507-0849. 814-451-6246; fax-814-451-6213; 8AM-4:30PM www.eriecountygov.org
No tax liens filed here. Records indexed on a public use terminal back to 1976. Prior to 1976 in book index. Only the public may search. Will not search UCC records. Copy fee $.50 per page. Cert fee- $1.00 per doc plus copy fee. Payee- Erie County Recorder of Deeds. **Online Real Estate, Deed, Marriage, Probate, Orphan Court records:** Recorder access is through a private company. Includes images, courts, Register of Wills and prothonotary; call Infocon at 814-472-6066 or www.infoconcountyaccess.com. **Other phones:** Treasurer- 814-451-6080. **Property tax/Assessing**- 140 W 6th St, Rm 104, Erie, 16501; 814-451-6225, fax- 814-451-6094. hours- 8:30AM-4:30PM www.eriecountygov.org/default.aspx?id=ao **Online access**- Access property records data free at www.eriecountygov.org/government/assessment/parcelsearch.aspx, no name searching. Also, full data for real estate professionals is available by subscription, click on "sign in" and follow the menu for details. Also, purchase judicial and/or sheriff sale property sale lists for $10.00 each, see www.eriecountygov.org/government/taxclaim/default.aspx.

Fayette County Prothonotary

County Prothonotary, 61 E Main St; Courthouse, Uniontown, PA 15401. 724-430-1272, 8AM-4:30PM
See Recorder for real estate records. Index: All in one. Records indexed on a public use terminal back to 1999. Office will perform a UCC search but public must search other records themselves. Search fee $5.00 per name. Copy fee $.50 per page. Cert fee- $11.00 per doc plus copy fee. Payee- Fayette County Prothonotary. **Online access to Lien, Judgment records:** Access prothonotary index by subscription; call Infocon at 814-472-6066 or www.infoconcountyaccess.com.

Fayette County Recorder

County Recorder of Deeds, 61 E Main St; Courthouse, Uniontown, PA 15401-3389. Recording, R/E phone-724-430-1238, UCC recording phone-724-430-1272; fax-724 430-1458; 8AM-4:30PM www.co.fayette.pa.us/
No tax liens filed here. Index: All in one. Records indexed on a public use terminal back to 1976. Only the public may search. Copy fee $.50 per page. Cert fee- $3.00 per doc plus copy fee. Payee- County Recorder. **Online access to Marriage, Will, Probate, Orphans Court records:** Search marriages, orphan court, and Register of Wills data via a private company; for info call Infocom at 814-472-6066 or www.infoconcountyaccess.com. **Other phones:** Treasurer- 724-430-1256; Elections- 724-430-1289; Vitals- 724-430-1206. **Property tax/Assessing**- 61 E Main St, Uniontown, PA 15401; 724-430-1238, fax-724 430-1458. (Appraiser 724-430-1350) www.co.fayette.pa.us/fayette/cwp/view.asp?a=2092&q=505690 **Online** - Access to property assessments is free at www.fayetteproperty.org/assessor/.

Forest County Recorder
Forest County Prothonotary

526 Elm St, #2, Tionesta, PA 16353. Recording, R/E phone-814-755-3526; fax-814-755-8837; 9AM-4PM www.co.forest.pa.us
Index: All in one. Records indexed on a public use terminal back to 1983. Office will perform a UCC search but public must search other records themselves. Copy fee $.25 per page. Cert fee- $2.00 per doc plus copy fee. Payee- Recorder of Deeds. **Online Real Estate, Deed, Judgment, Lien, Civil Court records:** Access is through a private company; call Infocon at 814-472-6066 or www.infoconcountyaccess.com. **Other phones:** Treasurer- 814-755-3536; Elections- 814-755-3537. **Property tax/Assessing**- 526 Elm St, #1, Tionesta, PA 16353; 814-755-3532, fax- 814-755-8837. 8AM-4PM A public access terminal available.

Franklin County Prothonotary

County Prothonotary, 157 Lincoln Way E; Court house, Chambersburg, PA 17201. 717-261-3860, fax-717-264-6772; 8:30AM-4:30PM www.co.franklin.pa.us/franklin/cwp/view.asp?a=1447&q=464747
See Recorder for real estate records. Index: All in one. Records indexed on a public use terminal from 11/98 to present. Only the public may search. Copy fee $.50 per page. Cert fee- $5.00 1st page, $1.00 each add'l includes copies. Payee- Linda L. Beard, Prothonotary. **Online access to Lien, Judgment records:** Access prothonotary index by subscription; call Infocon at 814-472-6066 or www.infoconcountyaccess.com

Franklin County Recorder

County Recorder of Deeds, 157 Lincoln Way E, Chambersburg, PA 17201. 717-261-3872; fax-717-263-5717; 8:30AM-4:30PM www.co.franklin.pa.us/franklin/cwp/view.asp?a=1447&q=464754
No tax liens filed here. Index: All in one. Records indexed on a public use terminal back to 1986. Only the public may search. Copy fee $.25 per page. Cert fee- $1.50 per page plus copy fee. Payee- County Recorder of Deeds. **Online access to Real Estate, Deed, Probate records:** Access is via a private company; call Infocon at 814-472-6066 or www.infoconcountyaccess.com. **Other phones:** Treasurer- 717-261-3119; Elections- 717-261-3886; UCC/Personal Property- 717-261-3858. **Property tax/Assessing**- 2 N Main St, Old Courthouse, 1st Fl, Chambersburg, PA 17201; 717-261-3801, assessor fax- 717-264-5218. Public terminal is available. www.co.franklin.pa.us/franklin/cwp/view.asp?a=2527&q=567535

Fulton County Prothonotary

County Prothonotary, 201 N 2nd St; County Courthouse, McConnellsburg, PA 17233-1198. 717-485-4212, 8:30AM-4:30PM
See Recorder for real estate records. Index: All in one. Records indexed on a public use terminal back to 1999, prior records in books. Only the public may search. Copy fee $.50 per page. Cert fee- $5.00 per cert plus copy fee. Payee- Fulton County Prothonotary. **Online Judgment, Lien records:** Access is via a private company; call Infocon at 814-472-6066 or www.infoconcountyaccess.com.

Fulton County Recorder

County Recorder of Deeds, 201 N 2nd St; County Courthouse, McConnellsburg, PA 17233-1198. Recording, R/E phone-717-485-4212; fax-717-485-5568; 8:30AM-4:30PM
No tax liens filed here. Index: All in one. Records indexed on a public use terminal back to 1970. Only the public may search. Copy fee $1.00 per page.Real estate record copy- $.50 per page. Cert fee- $5.00 per doc, no page cost, includes copies. Payee- Fulton County Recorder of Deeds. **Online access to Real Estate, Deed, Mortgage records:** Access is via a private company; call Infocon at 814-472-6066 or www.infoconcountyaccess.com. **Other phones:** Treasurer- 717-485-4454; Elections- 717-485-3691. **Property tax/Assessing**- 717-485-3208.

Greene County Prothonotary

Prothonotary, 10 E High St, Rm 105, Waynesburg, PA 15370. 724-852-5289; fax-724-852-5353; 8:30AM-4:30PM www.co.greene.pa.us/secured/gc/depts/lo/court/proth.htm
See Recorder for real estate records. Index: Separate indices to search. Records indexed on a public use terminal back to 1/1/1996. Only the public may search. Copy fee $.50 per page. Cert fee- $6.00 per cert plus copies. Payee- Greene County Prothonotary.

Greene County Recorder

County Recorder of Deeds, 10 E High St, Waynesburg, PA 15370. 724-852-5283; 8:30AM-4:30PM www.co.greene.pa.us/secured/gc/depts/lo/rr/index.htm
No tax liens filed here. Index: All in one. Records indexed on a public use terminal back to 1979. Only the public may search. Office will not search real estate records. Will not search UCC records. Copy fee $.50 per page; UCC copy $1.00. Cert fee- $5.00 per doc plus copy fee. Payee- Greene County Recorder of Deeds. Real estate deed records available on microfilm. Microfilm images are also available. **Online Real Estate, Deed, Mortgage records:** Access real estate deed records may be by subscription at http://216.27.81.170/login.asp. Contact Recorder office for sign-up details. **Other phones:** Treasurer- 724-852-5225; Elections- 724-852-5230; **Property tax/Assessing**- 93 E High St, Rm 202, Waynesburg, PA 15370; 724-852-5211, assessor fax-724-852-5383. **Online**- Access Assessor property records by subscription, see www.co.greene.pa.us/secured/gc/de pts/cc/asses/prop-records.htm or call Pam at 724-852-5210. Fee is $700 per year or $200 per quarter; includes Property Record Card System. A free 30-day trial is offered.

Huntingdon County Prothonotary

Prothonotary, PO Box 39, Huntingdon, PA 16652-814-643-1610; fax-814-643-4271; 8:30AM-4:30PM

See Recorder for real estate records. Index: All in one. Records indexed on a public use terminal back to 8/92. Only the public may search. Copy fee $.25 per page. Cert fee- $4.50 per page includes copy fee. Payee- Prothonotary. **Online access to Judgment, Tax Lien records:** Access is through a private company. Includes courts and prothonotary; call Infocon at 814-472-6066 or www.infoconcountyaccess.com.

Huntingdon County Recorder

County Recorder of Deeds, 223 Penn St; Courthouse, Huntingdon, PA 16652. Recording, R/E phone-814-643-2740, fax-814-643-8152; 8:30AM-4:30PM http://huntingdoncounty.net/hunt_co/site/default.asp
No tax liens filed here. Index: All in one. Records indexed on a public use terminal back to 1987. Only the public may search. Copy fee $.50 or $1.00 per page, depending on format. Cert fee- $1.50 per cert plus copy fee. Payee- Huntingdon County Recorder of Deeds. **Online access to Marriage records:** Access is via a private company; call Infocon at 814-472-6066 or www.infoconcountyaccess.com. **Other phones:** Treasurer- 814-643-3523; Elections- 814-643-3091. **Property tax/Assessing**- 223 Penn St, Huntingdon, PA 16652; 814-643-1000, assessor fax-814-643-8152. A public access terminal available.

Indiana County Prothonotary

Prothonotary & Clerk of Courts, 825 Philadelphia St, 1st Fl; Courthouse, Indiana, PA 15701-3934. 724-465-3855, fax-724-465-3968; 8AM-4PM www.countyofindiana.org
See Recorder for real estate records. Index: All in one. Records indexed on a public use terminal back to 1994. Office personnel or visitors may perform searches. Search fee $7.50 per name. Will not search UCC records. Copy fee $.25 per page. Cert fee- None. Payee- Prothonotary of Indiana County. **Online Lien, Civil, Judgment records:** Access via a private company. Includes courts and prothonotary; Infocon 814-472-6066 or www.infoconcountyaccess.com

Indiana County Recorder

County Recorder of Deeds, 825 Philadelphia St; Courthouse, Indiana, PA 15701. Recording, R/E phone-724-465-3860; fax-724-465-3863; 8AM-4PM www.countyofindiana.org
No tax liens filed here. Index: All in one. Records indexed on a public use terminal back to 1968. Only the public may search. Copy fee $.25 per page. Self address-stamped envelope required for mailings. Cert fee- $3.00 for every 4 pages, includes copy fee. Payee- Recorder of Deeds. **Online Real Estate, Deed records:** Access is available by subscription at http://regrec.countyofindiana.org/countyweb/login.jsp?countyname=Indiana/ but you may login as Guest and search free. **Other phones:** Treasurer- 724-465-3845; Elections- 724-656-3100; Vital Records- 724-656-3100. **Property tax/Assessing**- 825 Philadelphia St, 2nd Fl, Indiana, PA 15701; 724-465-3812, assessor fax- 724-465-3953. hours- 8:30AM-4PM A CD-ROM containing all county tax maps is available for $125. www.countyofindiana.org/assessment

Jefferson County Prothonotary

Prothonotary & Clerk of Courts, 200 Main St, Rm 102; Court House, Brookville, PA 15825. 814-849-1606; fax-814-849-1625; 8:30AM-4:30PM www.jeffersoncountypa.com Index: Separate indices to search. Records indexed on a public use terminal back to 1987. Office will perform a UCC search but public must search other records themselves. Search fee $10.00 per debtor. Copy fee $.50 per page. Cert fee- $1.50 per page includes copy fee. Payee- Jefferson County Prothonotary. Bulk data available for purchase, reports may be run in required fields at $.50 per page. **Online Lien, Judgment records:** Access via a private company, Infocon 814-472-6066 or www.infoconcountyaccess.com

Jefferson County Recorder

County Recorder of Deeds, 200 Main St; Courthouse, Brookville, PA 15825. Recording, R/E phone-814-849-1610; fax-814-849-1677; 8:30AM-4:30PM
No tax liens filed here. Index: All in one. Records indexed on a public use terminal back to 1993. Only the public may search. Copy fee $1.00 per copy. Cert fee- $1.50 per cert plus copy fee. Payee- Recorder of Deeds. **Online access to Real Estate, Deed, Lien, Marriage, Register of Wills records:** Access recording index by subscription; call Infocon at 814-472-6066 or www.infoconcountyaccess.com. **Other phones:** Treasurer- 814-849-1609; Elections- 814-849-1603. **Property tax/Assessing**- 200 Main St, 1st Fl, Courthouse, Brookville, PA 15825; 814-849-1643, fax- 814-849-1638. Public access terminal available.

Juniata County Prothonotary

County Prothonotary, PO Box 68; Courthouse, Mifflintown, PA 17059. 717-436-7715, fax-717-436-7734; 8AM-4:30PM
See Recorder for real estate records. Index: Separate indices to search include computer since 1993, docket books prior to 1993. Records indexed on a public use terminal back to 1993. Office personnel (not recommended) or visitors (recommended) may perform searches. Search fee- none. Copy fee $1.00 per page. Cert fee- $4.50 per doc plus copy fee. Payee- Juniata County Prothonotary.

Juniata County Recorder

County Recorder of Deeds, PO Box 68, Mifflintown, PA 17059. 717-436-7709, fax-717-436-7756; 8AM-4:30PM www.co.juniata.pa.us/recorder.php
No tax liens filed here. Index: Separate indices to search include books up to 1991,computer. Records indexed on a public use terminal back to 1993. Only the public may search. Copy fee $1.00 per page (by mail). In office copy fee is $.35 per page. Cert fee-$5.00 per doc includes copy fee. Payee- Juniata County Recorder of Deeds. **Online Real Estate, Deed, Marriage, Probate, Orphans Court records:** Access is via a private company; call Infocon at 814-472-6066 or www.infoconcountyaccess.com. Includes Recorder of Deeds record images. **Other phones:** Treasurer- 717-436-7742; Elections- 717-436-7706; Vitals- 717-436-7709; **Property tax/Assessing**- PO Box 68, Juniata Courthouse, Bridge & Main Sts, Mifflintown, PA 17059; 717-436-7740, assessor fax- 717-436-7756. hours- 8AM-4:30PM M,T,TH,F; 8AM-N Wed. A public access terminal available in the main courthouse. www.co.juniata.pa.us/assessor.php

Lackawanna County Prothonotary

County Clerk of Judicial Records, Brooks Bldg, 436 Spruce St, Scranton, PA 18503. 570-963-6723, R/E recording phone-570-963-6775; fax-570-963-6387; 9AM-4PM www.lackawannacounty.org/
See Recorder for real estate records. Index: Separate indices to search by type. Records indexed on a public use terminal back to 1970. Only the public may search. General copy fee $.50 per page. Cert fee-$4.50. Payee- Lackawanna County Clerk of Judicial Records.

Lackawanna County Recorder

County Recorder of Deeds, 200 N Washington; Courthouse, Scranton, PA 18503. Recording, R/E phone-570-963-6775; fax-570-963-6390; 9AM-4PM www.lackawannacounty.org
No tax liens filed here. Index: All in one. Records indexed on a public use terminal back to 1980. Only the public may search. Copy fee $.35 per page. Cert fee- $2.00 per doc plus copy fee. Payee- Lackawanna County Recorder of Deeds. **Online access to Real Estate, Deed, Will records:** Access the index free at www.landex.com/webstore/jsp/cart/DocumentSearch.jsp. Full access to Recorder of Deeds and Wills and Orphans Court is by subscription at www.landex.com/remote/. Index and images go back to 8/1994. **Other phones:** Treasurer- 570-963-6731. Elections- 570-963-6737; **Property tax/Assessing**- 507 Linden St, Scranton, PA 18503; 570-963-6728, assessor fax- 570-963-6385. www.lackawannacounty.org/viewDepartment.aspx?DeptID=12 **Online-Access** property data free at http://ao.lackawannacounty.org/agreed.php.

Lancaster County Prothonotary

County Prothonotary, PO Box 83480, Lancaster, PA 17608-3480. 717-299-8282; fax-717-293-7210; 8:30AM-5PM www.co.lancaster.pa.us/
See Recorder of Deeds for real estate records. Index: All in one. Records indexed on a public use terminal back to 1987. Only the public may search. Copy fee $.50 per page. Cert fee- $5.00 per page plus copy fee. Payee- Lancaster County Prothonotary. Bulk data available for purchase. **Online Judgment, Civil records:** Access prothonotary court records free at www.co.lancaster.p a.us/scripts/bannerweb.dll. Civil index goes back to 7/1/1987; judgments back to 8/2/1993.

Lancaster County Recorder

County Recorder of Deeds, PO Box 83480, Lancaster, PA 17608. Recording, R/E phone-717-299-8238; fax-717-299-8393; 8:30AM-4:30PM (recording); 8:30AM-5PM (for public). www.lancasterdeeds.com/lanco_rod/site/default.asp
No tax liens filed here. Index: Separate indices to search include Cris, E-film, infodex. Records indexed on a public use terminal back to 1981. Office personnel or visitors may perform searches. Copy fee $.50 per page. Cert fee- $1.50 per cert plus copy fee. Online certification $5.00 via credit card. Payee- Lancaster County Recorder of Deeds. **Online access to Real Estate, Deed, UCC, Probate, Death, Marriage records:** Access to deeds, UCCs and other recordings is free after registration at http://icris.lancasterdeeds.com/icris/splash.jsp. Also, search probate, death and marriage records free at http://paperless.co.lancaster.pa.us/viewerportal/. **Other phones:** Treasurer- 717-299-8222; Elections-717-299-8293. **Property tax/Assessing**- 717-299-8381. Property data available in bulk from CAMA; basic is $50; full is $500.00. Updated every 6 months. Contact Kathy Harris at 717-299-8252. **Online access**- Access assessor property data free at www.co.lancaster.pa.us/lanco/cwp/view.asp?a=565&q=537155. Property data free on the GIS-mapping site at www.co.lancaster.pa.us/gis/site/default.asp?. Click on GIS-Property Search; choose Query to search by owner name. Sheriff sales list at www.co.lancaster.pa.us/sheriffsoffice/cwp/view.asp?a=3&q=582487.

Lawrence County Prothonotary

County Prothonotary, 430 Court St; Government Ctr, New Castle, PA 16101-3593. 724-656-1943, fax-724-656-1988; 8AM-4PM www.co.lawrence.pa.us
See Recorder for real estate records. Index: All in one. Records indexed on a public use terminal back to 1987. Only the public may search. Copy fee $.50 per page; marriage cert copy- $5.00. Include SASE. Divorce copy $4.90. Cert fee- $1.50 per page plus copy fee. Payee- Lawrence County Prothonotary. **Online access to Judgment, Tax Lien records:** Access is via Infocon, a private company; document images included; call Infocon at 814-472-6066 or www.infoconcountyaccess.com

Lawrence County Recorder

County Recorder of Deeds, 430 Court St; Government Ctr, New Castle, PA 16101. 724-656-2541, R/E recording phone-724-656-2127; fax-724-656-1966; 8AM-4PM www.co.lawrence.pa.us
No tax liens filed here. Index: All in one. Records indexed on a public use terminal back to 1979. Only the public may search in person. Office will honor phone and fax requests, but limit is 2 names. Search fee $5.00 per name. Copy fee $.50 per page. Plats-$1.50 per page. Cert fee- $1.50 per doc plus copy fee. Payee- Recorder of Deeds. **Online Real Estate, Deed, Marriage, Probate, Orphans Court records:** Access back to 12/2005 is via Infocon, a private company; document images included; call Infocon at

814-472-6066 or www.infoconcountyaccess.com. Also, recorder data available by subscription at http://counties.recordfusion.com/countyweb/login.jsp?countyname=Lawrence; registration and fees required, contact Recorder of Deeds office for signup and details. Free trial available. **Other phones:** Treasurer- 724-656-2183; Elections- 724-656-2161; Vitals- 724-656-3100. **Property tax/Assessing-** 430 Court St, New Castle, 16101; 724-656-2191, fax-724-652-9646. www.co.lawrence.pa.us/Assessor/Index.html **Online access-** Access assessment values free at www.co.lawrence.pa.us/Preliminary_Assessment/Preliminary_Assessment.html. Search property records after free registration at. www.lawrencecountyrecordspa.us/assessor/login.jsp?countyname=LawrenceAssessor or by registering at http://counties.recordfusion.com/assessor/login.jsp?countyname=LawrenceAssessor.

Lebanon County Prothonotary

Prothonotary, 400 S 8th St, Rm 104, Lebanon, PA 17042. 717-274-2801 x2120, fax-717-228-4467; 8:30-4:30 www.lebcounty.org/lebanon/site/default.asp

See Recorder for real estate records. Index: All in one. Records indexed on a public use terminal back to 1985. Only the public may search. Copy fee $.50 per page. Cert fee- $10.00 per doc plus copy fee. Payee- Lebanon County Prothonotary.

Lebanon County Recorder

Recorder of Deeds, 400 S 8th St, Rm 107, Lebanon, PA 17042. 717-274-2801 x2223, R/E phone-717-274-2801 x2224, fax-717-228-4456; Recording -8:30AM-4PM http://dsf.pacounties.org/lebanon/site/default.asp

No tax liens filed here. Index: Separate indices to search are in books. Deed and mortgage records indexed on a public use terminal back to 1933; Miscellaneous index back to 1972. Only the public may search. General copy fee $1.00, UCCs $2.00 per page. $.50 per page self serve. Cert fee- $2.00 per cert plus copy fee. Payee- Lebanon County Recorder of Deeds. **Online access to Real Estate, Deed, Mortgage records:** Access the index free at www.landex.com/webstore/jsp/cart/DocumentSearch.jsp. Full access to Recorder of Deeds official records is by subscription at www.landex.com/remote/. For info call OSS at 717-274-5890. Deed and mortgage index goes back to 1933; Misc index back to 1972; Deed images back to 1996; Mortgage images to 2000; Miscellaneous images go back to 2001. Treasurer-717-274-2801 x2229. **Property tax/Assessing-** 400 S 8th St, Rm 118, Municipal Bldg, Lebanon, PA 17042; 717-274-2801 x2250, assessor fax- 717-228-4454. http://dsf.pacounties.org/lebanon/cwp/view.asp?a=3&q=444279 **Online-** Access property data by sub at www.courthouseonline.com/MyProperty.asp. Subcription fee $9.95 3-days, up to $275 per year. A free view available if you have control number and password from tax notice or are registered.

Lehigh County Prothonotary

County Prothonotary, 455 W Hamilton St, Rm 132, Allentown, PA 18101-1614. 610-782-3148, fax-610-770-3840; 8AM-4PM www.lccpa.org

City of Bethlehem is in both Northampton and Lehigh counties. See Recorder for real estate records. Index: Separate indices to search include case file, judgments, ejectments. Records indexed on a public use terminal back to 1985. Office will perform a UCC search ($200.00 minimum?!) but public must search other records themselves. Copy fee $1.00 per page. Cert fee- $5.00 per doc plus copy fee. Payee- Lehigh County Clerk of Courts-Civil Division. **Online access to Judgment, Lien, Court, County Grants records:** County's full-access internet pay system initial cost was $300.00 per year. For signup info, call the Fiscal Office at 610-782-3112. Also, at www.lehighcounty.org, the County Grants database is searched free; free registration required.

Lehigh County Recorder

County Recorder of Deeds, 17 S 7th St, Rm 350, Allentown, PA 18101. 610-782-3162; fax-610-782-3116; 8AM-4PM www.lehighcounty.org

No tax liens filed here. Index: Separate indices to search include computerized index from 1984-present; Russell index book form and computerized from 1812-1983 (grantee/grantor, mortgages). Records indexed on a public use terminal back to 1812. Only the public may search. Copy fee $1.00 per page; $.25 self serve. Cert fee- $1.50 per doc plus copy fee. Payee- Recorder of Deeds. Office does not sell bulk data at this time. **Online access to Real Estate, Grantor/Grantee, Deed, Tax Lien, Game License, Civil, Marriage, Will, Judgment, Naturalization records:** Access to the county's full-access internet pay system 1s $318.00 a year initial cost. Call Lehigh County Computer Svcs Dept at 610-782-3286 for signup or info. Also, subscribe to view naturalization, property tax, assessment, tax records for a fee at www.lehighcounty.org/public/public.cfm. Court records, marriages, and Register of Wills records online by subscription at www.lehighcounty.org/public/public.cfm?doc=ody_home.cfm. Also, access the recorder index via www.landex.com/webstore/jsp/cart/DocumentSearch.jsp. Full access to Recorder of Deeds is by subscription at www.landex.com/remote/. **Other phones:** Treasurer- 610-782-3115; Elections- 610-782-3194; Clerk of Courts- 610-782-3148. **Property tax/Assessing-** 17 S 7th St, Rm 517, Allentown, PA 18101; 610-782-3038, assessor fax- 610-820-3380. **Online access-** Access assessor property data free at www.lehighcounty.org/Assessment/Puba.cfm but no name searching. For deeper access, subscribe at www.lehighcounty.org/public/public.cfm. $300.00 yearly fee applies. Also, view tax sale data free at www.lehighcounty.org/Fiscal/taxsale.cfm. Also, view sheriff's tax sales lists free at www.lehighcounty.org/Fiscal/taxsale.cfm.

Luzerne County Prothonotary

Prothonotary, 200 N River St; County Court House, Wilkes-Barre, PA 18711-1001. 570-825-1745, fax-570-825-1757; 8:30-4:30PM www.luzernecounty.org

See Recorder for real estate records. Index: Separate indices to search. Records indexed on a public use terminal starting 3/1/05. Office personnel or visitors may perform searches. Search fee $19.50 per name per 5 years; $3.50 each add'l year. Copy fee $2.25 per page; self serve copy $.25 per page. Cert fee- $7.00 per doc, add'l $3.00 for each cert of same page or doc plus copy fee. Payee- Prothonotary.

Luzerne County Recorder

County Recorder of Deeds, 200 N River St; Courthouse, Wilkes-Barre, PA 18711. Recording, R/E phone-570-825-1641, UCC recording phone-570-825-1749; fax-570-970-4580; 9AM-4:30PM www.luzernecounty.org

No tax liens filed here. Index: Separate indices to search include records from 2001 forward in one index, prior to 2001, deeds, mortgages, commissions, power of attorney and charters separate. Records indexed on a public use terminal back to 9/1/93. Only the public may search. Will not search UCC records. Copy fee $2.00 per page; $.25 self serve. Cert fee- $1.00 per cert plus copy fee. Payee- Luzerne County Recorder of Deeds. **Online Real Estate, Deed, Mortgage, Register of Wills records:** Access the index free at www.landex.com/webstore/jsp/cart/DocumentSearch.jsp. Full access is through a private company at www.landex.com/remote/. Fee is $.20 per minute. Index goes back to 1/1993; images back to 9/1983. Register of Will data is a separate subscription, also at Landex; Wills index and images go back to 8/2004. **Other phones:** Treasurer- 570-825-1780; Elections- 570-825-1715. **Property tax/Assessing-** 200 N River St, Wilkes-Barre, PA 18711; 570-825-1869, assessor fax- 570-825-1763. www.luzernecounty.org/county/departments_agencies/assessor **Online** - Access data by subscription at www.courthouseonline.com/MyP roperty.asp. $9.95 3-day, up to $275 per year. Get free view with control number & password from tax notice-registration.

Lycoming County Prothonotary

Prothonotary, 48 W 3rd St, Williamsport, PA 17701. 570-327-2251, fax-570-327-2505; 8:30AM-5PM

See Recorder for real estate records. Index: All in one. Records indexed on a public use terminal back to 1983. Only the public may search. Copy fee $.50 per page. Cert fee- $5.00 per doc includes copy fee. Payee- Lycoming County Prothonotary.

Lycoming County Recorder

County Recorder of Deeds, 48 W 3rd St, Williamsport, PA 17701. Recording, R/E phone-570-327-2263; fax-570-327-2511; 8:30AM-5PM

No tax liens filed here. Index: All in one. Records indexed on computer back to 1957. Office will perform a UCC search but public must search other records themselves. Copy fee $.50 per page. Cert fee- $1.50 per cert plus copy fee. Payee- Lycoming County Recorder of Deeds. **Online tax claim records:** Access via a private company, Infocon 814-472-6066 or www.infoconcountyaccess.com. **Other phones:** Treasurer- 570-327-2248; Elections- 570-327-2267. **Property tax/Assessing-** 48 W 3rd St, Williamsport, PA 17701; 570-327-2301, assessor fax-570-327-2309. **Online** - Access property data by sub at www.courthouseonline.com/MyProperty.asp. Sub fee $9.95 3-days, up to $275 per year. A free view available if you have control number and password from tax notice or are registered.

McKean County Prothonotary

Prothonotary, PO Box 273, Smethport, PA 16749. 814-887-3270, fax-814-887-3219; 8:30AM-4:30PM www.mckeancountypa.org/Departments/Prothonotary_Clerk/Index.aspx

There are separate indices to search including Divorces. Records indexed on a public use terminal back to 1994. Office personnel or visitors may perform searches. Search fee $15.00 per name any type search. Copy fee $.50 per page. Cert fee- $10.00 per cert plus $1.00 per page. Payee- Prothonotary.

McKean County Recorder

County Recorder of Deeds, 500 W Main St, Smethport, PA 16749. Recording, R/E phone-814-887-3250; fax-814-887-3255; 8:30AM-4:30PM www.mckeancountypa.org

No tax liens filed here. Index: All in one. Records indexed on a public use terminal back to 1973. Only the public may search. Copy fee $1.00 per page mailed, $.50 per page in person. Cert fee- $1.50 per doc plus copy fee. Payee- Anne Bosworth-Recorder of Deeds. **Online access to Real Estate, Deed, Lien, Mortgage records:** Access the index free at www.landex.com/webstore/jsp/cart/DocumentSearch.jsp. Full access to Recorder of Deeds is by subscription at www.landex.com/remote/. Index goes back to 1973, images to 10/2002. **Other phones:** Treasurer- 814-887-3220; Elections- 814-887-3203; Vital Records- 814-887-3260. **Property tax/Assessing-** 500 W Main St, Courthouse Smethport, PA 16749; 814-887-3215, assessor fax- 814-887-2242.

Mercer County Prothonotary

Prothonotary, 105 Courthouse, Mercer, PA 16137-0066. 724-662-3800 x2261, 8:30AM-4:30PM

See Recorder for real estate records. Records indexed on a public use terminal back to 1994, prior on docket books. Only the public may search. Copy fee $1.00 per page. Cert fee- $4.50 per doc plus copy fee. Payee- Mercer County Prothonotary. **Online access to Judgment, Tax Lien records:** Access via a private company, Infocon 814-472-6066 or www.infoconcountyaccess.com..

Mercer County Recorder

County Recorder of Deeds, 109 Courthouse, Mercer, PA 16137-1293. 724-662-3800, R/E recording phone-

724-662-3800 x2277; fax-724-662-2096; 8:30AM-4:30PM www.mcc.co.mercer.pa.us/
No tax liens filed here. Index: All in one. Records indexed on a public use terminal back to 1972. Images from 2005. Only the public may search. Copy fee $1.00 per page. Plans- $1.50 per page. Cert fee- $2.00 per doc plus copy fee. Payee- Recorder. **Online Real Estate, Grantor/Grantee, Deed, Lien, Occ/PC, Tax Claim records:** general records index back to 1972 at http://recorder.mcc.co.mercer.pa.us/resolution/. Images go back to 7/15/2005. Also, access to index is via a private company; for info, call Infocon at 814-472-6066 or www.infoconcountyaccess.com. **Other phones:** Treasurer- 724-662-3800 x 2514; Elections- 724-662-3803 x2240. **Property tax/Assessing-** 724-662-3800 x2505.

Mifflin County Prothonotary

Prothonotary, 20 N Wayne St, Lewistown, PA 17044. 717-248-8146, fax-717-248-5275; 8AM-4:30PM www.co.mifflin.pa.us/mifflin/cwp/view.asp?a=657&Q=410994
See Recorder for real estate records. Index: All in one. Records indexed on a public use terminal back to 1993. Only the public may search. Copy fee $.50 per page. Cert fee- $4.50 per page plus copy fee. Payee- Mifflin County Prothonotary. **Online Judgment, Tax Lien, GIS-mapping records:** Access via a private company; call Infocon 814-472-6066 or www.infoconcountyaccess.com.

Mifflin County Recorder

Recorder of Deeds, 20 N Wayne St, Lewistown, PA 17044. 717-242-1449; fax-717-248-2503; 8-4:30PM www.co.mifflin.pa.us/mifflin/cwp/view.asp?a=659&Q=411008
No tax liens filed here. Records indexed on computer from 1/93, hard copy-1990-1992, 1981-1989, 1789-1980. Only the public may search. Copy fee $.50 per page. $1.00 for ledgers. Cert fee- $1.50 per cert plus copy fee. Payee- Mifflin County Recorder of Deeds. **Online access to Real Estate, Deed, Probate, Orphans Court, Marriage, Tax Claim records:** Access is via a private company; call Infocon at 814-472-6066 or www.infoconcountyaccess.com; recorder back to 1993, probate, orphans and marriages back to 2000; images soon to be available for Recorder records, indexes for others. **Other phones:** Treasurer-717-248-8439; Elections- 717-248-6571; Vitals- 717-242-1449. **Property tax/Assessing-** 20 N Wayne St, Lewistown, 17044; 717-248-5783, fax-717-242-5465. www.co.mifflin.pa.us/mifflin/cwp/view.asp?a=636&q=408922 **Online access-** Property data is free at http://gis.co.mifflin.pa.us/website/mifflincounty/viewer.htm?. Use the new free Web Mapping Parcel Application to name search for property data.

Monroe County Prothonotary

County Prothonotary, N 7th & Monroe St, Rm 303; Courthouse, Stroudsburg, PA 18360-2190. 570-517-3988; fax-570-517-3865; 8:30AM-4:30PM
See Recorder for real estate records at 570-517-3352. Index: All in one. Records indexed on a public use terminal back to 1995. Only the public may search. Copy fee $1.00 per page. Cert fee- $3.00 per cert plus copy fee. Exemplification fee $10.00. Payee- Monroe County Prothonotary. **Online access to Judgments and Lien records:** Access is via a private company; call Infocon at 814-472-6066 or www.infoconcountyaccess.com. **Other phones:** Tax Claim- 570-517-3172.

Monroe County Recorder

County Recorder of Deeds, 7th & Monroe St; Courthouse, Stroudsburg, PA 18360-2185. 570-517-3352; fax-570-517-3873; 8:30AM-4:30PM www.co.monroe.pa.us/monroe/
No tax liens filed here. Index: All in one. Records indexed on a public use terminal back to 1979. Only the public may search. Copy fee $.25 per page. Cert fee- $3.00 per doc plus copy fee. Payee- Recorder of Deeds. **Online Real Estate, Deed, Will, Mortgage, Marriage, Map records:** Access the index free at www.landex.com/webstore/jsp/cart/DocumentSearch.jsp. Full access is through a private company at www.landex.com/remote/. Fee is $.20 per minute and $.50 per fax page. Land Index goes back to 1/1979; wills index to 11/1836; images of land records back to 1958, Will images to 1990. Map images available. Access Marriages via a private company, Infocon 814-472-6066 www.infoconcountyaccess.com. **Other phones:** Treasurer- 570-517-3180; Elections- 570-517-3165; Clerk of Courts- 570-517-3385. **Property tax/Assessing-** 1 Quaker Plaza, Rm 102, Stroudsburg, PA 18360; 570-517-3133, assessor fax- 570-517-3854. Assessor public access terminal available.

Montgomery County Prothonotary

Prothonotary, PO Box 311, Norristown, PA 19404. 610-278-3360, fax-610-278-5994; 8:30AM-4:15PM http://prothy.montcopa.org/prothy/site/default.asp
See Recorder for real estate records. Index: All in one. Records indexed on a public use terminal back to 1980. Only the public may search. Copy fee- 1st 4 pages $1.00; $.50 each add'l page. Cert fee- $4.50 per page includes copy fee. Exemplification fee-$6.00 (instate), $15.00 (out of state). Payee- Montgomery County Prothonotary. **Online access to Judgment, Lien records:** See Recorder of Deeds. For court-related civil, search at http://webapp.montcopa.org/PSI/Viewer/Search.aspx?c=CaseSearch.

Montgomery County Recorder

County Recorder of Deeds, PO Box 311, Norristown, PA 19404-0311. 610-278-3289, R/E recording phone-610-278-3868; fax-610-278-3869; 8:30AM-4:15PM http://rod.montcopa.org/rod/site/default.asp
No tax liens filed here. Index: Separate indices to search include deeds, mortgages, satisfactions, plans, UCCs, other land related documents. Records indexed on a public use terminal back to 1874. Office will perform a UCC search but public must search other records themselves. Copy fee $.50 per page; $5.00 per doc if by mail. Cert fee- $1.50 per cert plus copy fee; $10.00 if by mail. Payee- Montgomery County Recorder of Deeds. **Online access to Real Estate, Deed, Mortgage, UCC, Lien, Estate, Judgment records:** Recorder of Deeds records are at http://rodviewer.montcopa.org/countyweb/login.jsp?countyname=Montgomery. Login as Guest or subscribe. Records date back to 1990. Lending agency and prothonotary data on system. **Other phones:** Treasurer- 610-278-3066; Elections- 610-278-3075. **Property tax/Assessing-** Board of Assessment Appeals, One Montgomery Plaza, #301, Norristown, PA 19401; 610-278-3761, assessor fax- 610-278-3560. http://boa.montcopa.org/boa/site/default.asp **Online access-** Search property records free at http://propertyrecords.montcopa.org/Main/home.aspx. Also, search parcels and court data at http://webapp.montcopa.org/PSI/Viewer/Search.aspx. Search Tax Claim history lookup free at www.montcopa.org/taxclaim/payment/HistoryLookup.asp. Also, a private company sells county tax claim property, view list free at www.xspand.com/investors/realestate_sale/index.aspx.

Montour County Prothonotary

County Prothonotary, 29 Mill St; Courthouse, Danville, PA 17821. 570-271-3010, fax-570-271-3089; 9AM-4PM www.montourco.org/
Index: Separate indices to search. Records indexed on a public use terminal back to 1995. Office personnel or visitors may perform searches. Search fee-$20.00 per name. Copy fee $.50 per page. UCC copy $1.00 per page. Cert fee- $5.00 per doc plus copy fee. Payee- County Prothonotary. **Online Judgment, Tax Lien records:** Access via a private company, Infocon at 814-472-6066 see www.infoconcountyaccess.com.

Montour County Recorder

County Register & Recorder, 29 Mill St; Courthouse, Danville, PA 17821. 570-271-3012; fax-570-271-3071; 9AM-4PM www.montourco.org
Index: All in one. Records indexed on a public use terminal back to 1/1/1997. Office personnel or visitors may perform searches. Search fee $25.00. Office will search real estate records for present owner only. Copy fee $.50 per page. Cert fee- $.50 per page + $1.50. Payee- Register & Recorder. Bulk data available for purchase in print form or on CD; contact Linda Weaver. **Online access to Real Estate, Deed, Probate, Marriage, Orphans Court, Will records:** Access to Register of Deeds data is by subscription via private company, www.infoconcountyaccess.com. Also includes Prothonotary, Clerk of Courts. Will index 1850 to present is free at www.montour.org, click on Register & Recorder, then Will Index, or see www.montourco.org/montour/cwp/view.asp?a=770&Q=417826&montourNav=|8473|. **Other phones:** Treasurer- 570-271-3016; Elections- 570-271-3000; Vitals- 570-271-3010. **Property tax/Assessing-** 29 Mill St, #5, Danville, PA 17821; 570-271-3006, assessor fax- 570-271-3088. (Appraiser/Auditor- 570-271-3006) A public access terminal is available.

Northampton County Prothonotary

Prothonotary, 669 Washington St, Rm 207; 2nd Fl, Easton, PA 18045. 610-559-3060, 8:30AM-4:30PM www.northamptoncounty.org/northampton/site/default.asp
See Recorder for real estate records. City of Bethlehem is in both Northampton and Lehigh counties. See Recorder for real estate records. Index: All in one. Records indexed on a public use terminal back to 1985. Only the public may search. Copy fee $.25 per page. Cert fee- $5.75 per page plus copy fee. Payee- Northampton County Prothonotary.

Northampton County Recorder

County Recorder of Deeds, 669 Washington St; Government Ctr, Easton, PA 18042. 610-559-3077; fax-610-559-3103; 8:30AM-4:30PM www.northamptoncounty.org/northampton/site/default.asp
No tax liens filed here. City of Bethlehem is in both Northampton and Lehigh counties. Index: Separate indices to search include grantor/grantee, mortgagor/mortgagee, power of attorney, map index. Records indexed on a public use terminal back to 1100. Only the public may search. Copy fee $.25 per page. Map copies $1.00 per page. Cert fee- $2.50 per certification plus copy fee. Payee- Northampton County Recorder of Deeds. **Online Real Estate, Deed, Mortgage, Miscellaneous records:** Access the index free at www.landex.com/webstore/jsp/cart/DocumentSearch.jsp. Full access to recording records is via a private company at www.landex.com/remote/. Fee is $.20 per minute and $.50 per fax page. Deeds data goes back to 11/85; mortgages to 2/86; faxable images go back to 11/85. **Other phones:** Treasurer- 610-559-3102; Elections-610-559-3055; Orphan's Court- 610-559-3095; Register of Wills -610-559-3092. **Property tax/Assessing-** 669 Washington St, Easton, PA 18042-7475, 610-559-3140. **Online access-** Access to assessor's property records data is free at www.ncpub.org/Main/Home.aspx.

Northumberland Prothonotary

County Prothonotary, 201 Market St, Rm 7; Courthouse, Sunbury, PA 17801-3468. 570-988-4151, 9AM-4:30PM (Monday open until 5PM).
See Recorder for real estate records. Index: Separate indices to search include judgments, computer. Records indexed on a public use terminal back to 1998. Office personnel or visitors may perform searches. Search fee $7.00 per name plus $1.00 for each record found. Copy fee $1.00 1st page through the mail, $.25 each add'l. Cert fee- $4.00 per 1st page, $1.00 each add'l page plus copy fee. Payee-Northumberland County Prothonotary.

Northumberland County Recorder

County Recorder of Deeds, 201 Market St; Courthouse, Sunbury, PA 17801. 570-988-4143, R/E recording phone-570-988-4140; fax-570-988-4141; 9AM-4:30PM

No tax liens filed here. Index: All in one. Records indexed on a public use terminal back to 1974. Only the public may search. Copy fee $.50 per page. Cert fee- None. Payee- Northumberland County Recorder of Deeds. **Online Real Estate, Deed, Probate, Will, Orphans Court records:** Access index free at www.landex.com/webstore/jsp/cart/DocumentSearch.jsp. Full access to Recorder of Deeds, Register of Wills and Orphans Court is by subscription at www.landex.com/remote/. Fee is $.22 per minute, $.50 per fax page. Land data and images go back to 1949; images to 1820; Wills back to 1999; Orphans to 1987. **Other phones:** Treasurer- 570-988-4160; Elections- 570-988-4211. **Property tax/Assessing-** 399 S 5th St, Sunbury, PA 17801; 570-988-4112, assessor fax- 570-988-4576. hours- 9AM-5PM M; 9AM-4:30PM T-F. A public terminal available.

Perry County Prothonotary

County Prothonotary, PO Box 325, New Bloomfield, PA 17068-0325. 717-582-2131, fax-717-582-5167; 8AM-4PM. Index: All in one. Records indexed on a public use terminal back to 1976. Only the public may search. Copy fee $.40 per page. Cert fee- $5.00 per cert plus copy fee. Payee- Perry County Prothonotary.

Perry County Recorder

County Recorder of Deeds, PO Box 223, New Bloomfield, PA 17068. 717-582-2131; fax-717-582-5149; 8AM-4PM
No tax liens filed here. Index: All in one. Records indexed on a public use terminal back to 1958. Only the public may search. Copy fee $.40 per page. Cert fee- $2.00 per cert plus copy fee. Payee- Perry County Recorder of Deeds. **Online Real Estate, Deed, Will, Marriage records:** Access to Recorder of Deeds is by subscription at www.landex.com/remote/. Fee is $.22 per minute, $.50 per fax page. Recorder data goes back to 1973; images to 1820. Marriages and wills go back to 1900s. Also, access property data by sub at www.courthouseonline.com/MyProperty.asp. Sub fee $9.95 3-days, up to $275 per year. A free view available if you have control number and password from tax notice or are registered. **Other phones:** Treasurer- 717-582-8984 x4. **Property tax/Assessing-** 717-582-8984 x3. **Online access-** Access property data by subscription at www.courthouseonline.com/MyProperty.asp. Sub fee $9.95 3-days, up to $275 per year. A free view available if you have control number and password from tax notice or are registered.

Philadelphia County Deptartment of Records

County Recorder of Deeds, Broad & Market Sts, Rm 154; City Hall, Philadelphia, PA 19107. 215-686-2260, R/E recording phone-215-686-2291, UCC recording phone-215-686-8864; fax-215-686-2273; 8AM-2PM www.phila.gov/Records/index.html
No tax liens filed here. Index: All in one. Records indexed on a public use terminal back to 1976. Only the public may search. Copy fee $2.00 per page. Cert fee- $2.00 per doc plus copy fee. Payee- Philadelphia County Recorder of Deeds. **Online Real Estate, Deed, UCC records:** Name search recorder data for a fee at http://philadox.phila.gov/picris/splash.jsp; registration required; $15.00 for (1) hour, $40.00 for (1) 24-hour day, $60.00 for (1) 7-day week, $125.00 for (1) full month. Images go back to 1976, index to 1957. **Other phones:** Treasurer- 215-686-2312; Lien Dept- 215-686-8859; Older records -215-686-6669. **Property tax/Assessing-** Property Valuation Ofc/Board of Revision of Taxes, 601 Walnut St 3rd Fl, Philadelphia, PA 19106; 215-686-4334, assessor fax- 215-686-9223. hours- 8AM-5PM **Online access-** Search property assessment data for free at http://brtweb.phila.gov/brt.apps/Search/Disclaimer/disclaimer.aspx?url=search. No name searching. Also, search Board of Revision of Taxes records for free at http://brtweb.phila.gov/index.aspx. No name searches.

Philadelphia County Prothonotary

County Prothonotary, Broad & Market Sts, Rm 262; City Hal, Philadelphia, PA 19107. 215-686-6670. records rm- 215-686-6661, 9AM-3PM
See Recorder for real estate records. Index: Separate indices to search include liens, judgments, older records. Lien records indexed on a public use terminal back to 1980 in Rm 262. Only the public may search. Copy fee $.50 per page. Cert fee- $37.80 per lien doc includes copy fee. Payee- Philadelphia County Prothonotary. Office sells mortgage foreclosure lists, $125 per week, contact Christian Wolzner. **Online access to Judgment, Lien records:** Assess to Prothonotary records is free at http://fjdweb2.phila.gov/fjd1/repl1/zk_fjd_public_qry_00.zp_main_idx.html. Also, includes judgments and liens on behalf of governmental entities.

Pike County Prothonotary

County Prothonotary, 412 Broad St, Milford, PA 18337. 570-296-7231, R/E phone-570-296-3508; fax-570-296-1931; 8:30AM-4:30PM http://pikepa.org
See Recorder for real estate records. Index: All in one. Judgment records indexed on a public use terminal back to 1989. Office will perform a UCC search but public must search other records themselves. UCC search per debtor name- $5.00. Copy fee $.50 per page. Cert fee- $5.25 per doc plus copy fee. Payee- Pike County Prothonotary. **Online access to Judgment, Lien, Civil records:** Access via a private company, Infocon at 814-472-6066 or see www.infoconcountyaccess.com.

Pike County Recorder

County Recorder of Deeds, 506 Broad St, Milford, PA 18337. 570-296-3508; fax-570-296-3514; 8:30AM-4:30PM www.pikepa.org/recorder.htm
No tax liens filed here. Index: Separate indices to search include older deeds, mortgages, also maps, UCCs, SIT. Records indexed on a public use terminal back to 1930. Only the public may search. Copy fee $.50 per page; Up to 10 pages for $5.00-$7.00 if mailed. Cert fee- $7.00 up to 10 pages plus copy fee. Payee- Pike County Recorder of Deeds. **Online Probate, Will, Orphans Court, Marriage records:** Access is via private company; call Infocon at 814-472-6066 or www.infoconcountyaccess.com. **Other phones:** Treasurer- 570-296-3441; Elections- 570-296-3426. **Property tax/Assessing-** 506 Broad St, Milford, PA 18337; 570-296-3417, assessor fax- 570-296-3537. **Online access-** Access parcel data free at www.pikegis.org/pike/viewer.htm.

Potter County Prothonotary

County Prothonotary, 1 E 2nd St, Rm 23; Courthouse, Coudersport, PA 16915. 814-274-9740, fax-814-274-3361; 8:30AM-4:30PM www.pottercountypa.net
See Recorder for real estate records. Index: Separate indices to search include computer, judgment, divorce, ejectment, general plaintiff and defendant, financing statements, equity, mech liens, tax sales. Records indexed on a public use terminal back to 11/1997. Office will perform a UCC search but public must search other records themselves. Search fee $59.00. Copy fee $.25 per page. Cert fee- $5.00 per instrument plus copy fee. Payee- County Prothonotary. **Online Judgment, Tax Lien records:** Access is via a private company; call Infocon at 814-472-6066 or www.infoconcountyaccess.com.

Potter County Recorder

County Recorder of Deeds, Courthouse, Rm 20, Coudersport, PA 16915. Recording, R/E phone-814-274-8370; fax-814-274-3360; 8:30AM-4:30PM
No tax liens filed here. Index: Separate indices to search include books from 1806 to 1996; computer back to 1997. Records indexed on a public use terminal back to 1997. Only the public may search. Copy fee $1.00 per page. Add $3.00 if mailed back. Cert fee- $1.50 per cert plus copy fee. Payee- Potter County Recorder of Deeds. **Online Real Estate, Deed, Probate, Marriage, Orphans Court, Will records:** Access is via private company; call Infocon at 814-472-6066 or www.infoconcountyaccess.com. **Other phones:** Treasurer- 814-274-9775; Elections- 814-274-8467; Vital Records- 814-274-9740. **Property tax/Assessing-** 1 E 2nd St, Coudersport, PA 16915; 814-274-0488, assessor fax- 814-274-3358. A public access terminal available.

Schuylkill County Prothonotary

County Prothonotary, 401 N 2nd St, Pottsville, PA 17901-2520. 570-628-1270, fax-570-628-1261; 8:30AM-4:30PM www.co.schuylkill.pa.us
See Recorder for real estate records. Index: All in one. Records indexed on a public use terminal back to 1999. Only the public may search. Copy fee $.25 per page. Cert fee- $6.00 per page includes copy fee. Payee- Schuylkill County Prothonotary. **Online access to Judgment, Marriage records:** Search marriage dockets free at www.co.schuylkill.pa.us/info/Offices/Archives/MarriageDockets.csp. Also, judgments on civil court files at www.co.schuylkill.pa.us/info/Civil/Inquiry/Search.csp.

Schuylkill County Recorder

County Recorder of Deeds, 401 N 2nd St, Pottsville, PA 17901. Recording, R/E phone-570-628-1480, UCC recording phone-570-628-1270; fax-570-628-1210; 8:30AM-4:30PM www.co.schuylkill.pa.us
No tax liens filed here. Index: All in one. Records indexed on a public use terminal back to 1983. Only the public may search. Copy fee $8.00 per document. Cert fee- $1.50 per cert plus copy fee. Payee- Schuylkill County Recorder of Deeds. **Other phones:** Treasurer- 570-628-1433; Elections- 570-628-3040. **Property tax/Assessing-** 570-628-1025. **Online access-** Access items for the sheriff sale free at www.co.schuylkill.pa.us/Offices/Sheriff/Sale.asp.

Snyder County Prothonotary

Prothonotary, PO Box 217, Middleburg, PA 17842-0217. 570-837-4202, fax-570-837-4275; 8:30-4PM
See Recorder for real estate records. Index: Separate indices to search include books, computer. Records indexed on a public use terminal back to 2001. Only the public may search. Copy fee $.35 per page. Cert fee- $4.50. Payee- Snyder County Prothonotary.

Snyder County Recorder

County Recorder of Deeds, PO Box 217, Middleburg, PA 17842-0217. Recording, R/E phone-570-837-4224, UCC phone-570-837-4225; fax-570-837-4299; 8:30AM-4PM www.snydercounty.org/snyder/
No tax liens filed here. Index: All in one 1973-present, computerized from 1973. Records indexed on computer 1855 to 1972. Only the public may search. General copy fee-$.50-$1.00 for 11 x 17; $.35-$.70 for 8 1/2 x 11 or 14. $1.00 per page to fax local or toll free number. Cert fee- $1.50 per cert plus copy fee. Payee- Snyder County Recorder of Deeds. **Online access to Real Estate, Deed, Lien, Will, Estate, Map records:** Access the index free at www.landex.com/webstore/jsp/cart/DocumentSearch.jsp. Full access to Recorder of Deeds and Wills and Orphans Court is by subscription at www.landex.com/remote/. Index goes back to 2005, and images to 2005, Estates 1855 to 1977. Map images also available. **Other phones:** Treasurer- 570-837-4221; Elections- 570-837-4209. **Property tax/Assessing-** PO Box 217, 9 W Market St, Middleburg, PA 17842-0217; 570-837-4216, assessor fax- 570-837-0392. A public access terminal is available.

Somerset County Prothonotary

County Prothonotary, 111 E Union St, #165, Somerset, PA 15501. 814-445-1428, fax-814-444-9270; 8:30AM-4PM www.co.somerset.pa.us
See Recorder for real estate records. Index: All indices up to 1991 separate; after 1991 all indices on computer. Records indexed on a public use terminal back to 1992. Only the public may search. Copy fee $.50 per page. Cert fee- None. Payee- Somerset County Prothonotary.

Somerset County Recorder

County Recorder of Deeds, 300 N Center Ave, #400, Somerset, PA 15501. 814-445-1547, fax-814-445-1563; 8:30AM-4PM www.co.somerset.pa.us
No tax liens filed here. Index: Records prior to 1985 are indexed by Russell index. Records indexed on computer back to 1985. Office will perform a UCC search but public must search other records themselves. UCC copy fee $2.00 per page.Real estate record copy- $.50 per page. Cert fee- $2.00 per page plus copy fee. Payee- Somerset County Recorder of Deeds. **Online access to Real Estate, Deed, Lien, Mortgage, Map records:** Access property records by monthly subscription; $35.00 start-up fee plus $10.00 per month. For info or signup, call Cindy or John at 814-445-1536. Provide your email, company info and check. System may provide images and comparable sales. Also, access the index free at www.landex.com/webstore/jsp/cart/DocumentSearch.jsp. Full access through that private company by subscription at www.landex.com/remote/. Fee is $.20 per minute and $.50 per fax page. Map images also available. Landex recorders index and images go back to 1/1985. See also separate listing for prothonotary for other online access. **Other phones:** Treasurer- 814-445-1482; Elections- 814-445-1549. **Property tax/Assessing**- 300 N Center Ave, #440, Somerset, PA 15501; 814-445-1536, assessor fax- 814-445-1592. **Online access**- Access property data free at www.co.somerset.pa.us/realpictsearch.asp. Property Sale records also available.

Sullivan County Prothonotary

County Prothonotary, Main St; Courthouse, Laporte, PA 18626. 570-946-7351, fax-570-946-7105; 8:30AM-4PM www.sullivancounty-pa.us
See Recorder for real estate records. Records indexed on computer and books. Only the public may search. Copy fee $.25 per page. Cert fee- $3.00 plus copy fee. Payee- Sullivan County Prothonotary.

Sullivan County Recorder

County Recorder of Deeds, Main St; Courthouse, Laporte, PA 18626. 570-946-7351; fax-570-946-7105; 8:30AM-4PM www.sullivancounty-pa.us
No tax liens filed here. Index: Multiple indexes on computer and old books. Records indexed on computer back to 1/92. Only the public may search. Copy fee $1.00 per financing statement.Real estate record copy- $.25 per page. Cert fee- $3.00 per cert plus copy fee. Payee- Sullivan County Recorder of Deeds. **Online access to Real Estate, Deed, Mortgage, Map records:** Access the index free at www.landex.com/webstore/jsp/cart/DocumentSearch.jsp. Full access through that private company by subscription at www.landex.com/remote/. Fee is $.22 per minute and $.50 per fax page. Index and images go back to 6/2000. Map images also available. **Other phones:** Treasurer- 570-946-7331; Elections- 570-946-5201. **Property tax/Assessing**- 570-946-5061.

Susquehanna County Prothonotary

County Prothonotary, PO Box 218, Montrose, PA 18801-0218. 570-278-4600 x121, fax-570-278-4191; 8:30AM-4:30PM
See Recorder for real estate records. Index: All in one. Records indexed on a public use terminal back to 1996. Only the public may search. Copy fee $.25 per page. Cert fee- $4.50 per name plus copy fee. Payee-Prothonotary. **Online access to Judgment, Tax Lien records:** Access via a private company; call Infocon at 814-472-6066 or www.infoconcountyaccess.com.

Susquehanna County Recorder

County Recorder of Deeds, PO Box 218, Montrose, PA 18801. 570-278-4600 x112/3, R/E recording phone- x112; fax-570-278-2963; 8:30AM-4:30PM www.susqco.com/subsites/gov/pages/govhome.htm
No tax liens filed here. Index: All in one. Records indexed on a public use terminal back to 1974. Only the public may search. General copy fee $.50 per page.Real estate record copy- $2.00 per deed. $5.00 for certified copy of mortgage. Cert fee- $1.50 per doc plus copy fee. Payee- Recorder of Deeds. **Online access to Real Estate, Deed, Lien, Mortgage, Will, Orphans Court records:** Access the index free at www.landex.com/webstore/jsp/cart/DocumentSearch.jsp. Full access to Recorder of Deeds, Register of Wills and Orphans Court is by subscription at www.landex.com/remote/. Fee is $.22 per minute, $.50 per fax page. Index goes back to 1972, images to 2000. Map images also available. **Other phones:** Treasurer- 570-278-4600 x130; Elections- 570-278-4600 x220; Vital Records- 570-278-4600 x112. **Property tax/Assessing**- PO Box 218, Montrose, PA 18801; 570-278-4600 x150, assessor fax- 570-278-9268. www.susqco.com/subsites/gov/pages/assessment/assessment.htm **Online access**- Access property data at www.courthouseonline.com/MyProperty.asp. Sub fee $9.95 3-days, up to $275 per year. A free view available if you have control number and password from tax notice or are registered.

Tioga County Prothonotary

Prothonotary, 116 Main St; Courthouse, Wellsboro, PA 16901. 570-724-9281, fax-570-724-2986; 9AM-4:30PM www.tiogacountypa.us/tioga/site/default.asp
See Recorder for real estate records and other online services. Index: All in one. Records indexed on a public use terminal: Family back to 1980; Civil back to 2001. Only the public may search. Copy fee $.25 per page. Cert fee- $5.00 per cert includes copies-more copy fees if large number of pages. Payee-Tioga County Prothonotary.

Tioga County Recorder

County Recorder of Deeds, 116 Main St; Courthouse, Wellsboro, PA 16901. 570-724-9260; 9AM-4:30PM www.tiogacountypa.us/tioga/site/default.asp
No tax liens filed here. Index: Separate indices to search include grantor/grantee, mortgages. Records indexed on a public use terminal back to 1977. Only the public may search. Copy fee $1.00 per page. Cert fee- $1.50 per cert plus copy fee. Payee- Tioga Recorder of Deeds. **Online Real Estate, Deed, Mortgage, Will records:** Access the index free at www.landex.com/webstore/jsp/cart/DocumentSearch.jsp. Full access to real estate and recorded data by subscription through a private company at www.landex.com/remote/. Fee is $.22 per minute and $.50 per fax page. Recorders data goes back to 1977; images and wills go back to 2/1999. Map images also available. **Other phones:** Treasurer- 570-723-9213; Elections- 570-723-8230. **Property tax/Assessing**- Assessment Office, 118 Main St, Wellsboro, PA 16901; 570-724-9117, fax- 570-723-8118. (Appraiser/Auditor- 570-724-9117) **Online access**- Access property data by subscription at www.courthouseonline.com/MyProperty.asp. Sub fee $9.95 3-days, up to $275 per year. A free view available if you have control number and password from tax notice or are registered. Sheriff sales lists also available free online - web URL too lengthy to show, so see sheriff pages at www.tiogacountypa.us

Union County Prothonotary

County Prothonotary, 103 S 2nd St; Courthouse, Lewisburg, PA 17837. 570-524-8751, fax-570-524-8628; 8:30AM-4:30PM www.unionco.org
See Recorder for real estate records. Index: All in one. Records indexed on a public use terminal back to 1988. Only the public may search. General copy fee $.25 per page.UCC copy fee $2.00. Cert fee- $5.50 per doc plus copy fee. Exemplification fee- $17.50. Payee- Union County Prothonotary.

Union County Recorder

County Recorder of Deeds, 103 S 2nd St; Courthouse, Lewisburg, PA 17837-1996. Recording, R/E phone-570-524-8761; 8:30AM-4:15PM www.unionco.org
No tax liens filed here. Index: All in one, 1813-current. Records indexed on a public use terminal back to 1982. Only the public may search. Copy fee $1.00 per page to mail; $.25 in house. Cert fee- $1.50 per cert and $.25 per page copy fee. Payee- Union County Recorder of Deeds. **Online access to Real Estate, Deed, UCC records:** Access to Register of Deeds land records is free at https://pa.uslandrecords.com/palr_new/PalrApp/index.jsp. Online records go back to 1/1982. **Other phones:** Treasurer- 570-524-8781; Elections- 570-524-8603. **Property tax/Assessing**- 103 S 2nd St, Lewisburg, PA 17837-1996; 570-524-8611, assessor fax- 570-524-8619.

Venango County Prothonotary

County Prothonotary, Courthouse; PO Box 831, Franklin, PA 16323. 814-432-9577, fax-814-432-9579; 8:30AM-4:30PM www.co.venango.pa.us
Index: All in one. Records indexed on a public use terminal back to 1993. Office personnel or visitors may perform searches. Copy fee $1.00 per page. Cert fee- $7.50 per name includes copy fee. Payee-Venango County Prothonotary.

Venango County Recorder

County Recorder of Deeds, PO Box 831, Franklin, PA 16323. 814-432-9539; fax-814-432-9569; 8:30AM-4:30PM www.co.venango.pa.us/Directory/index.htm
No tax liens filed here. Index: All in one. Records indexed on a public use terminal back to 1989. Only the public may search. Copy fee $1.00 per page. Cert fee- $1.50 per page plus copy fee. Payee- Recorder of Deeds. **Other phones:** Treasurer- 814-432-9525; Elections- 814-432-9514; Main Assessment Office-814-432-9520. **Property tax/Assessing**- PO Box 831, 1168 Liberty St, Franklin, PA 16323; 814-432-9515, 814-432-9516, assessor fax- 814-432-9519. **Online**-Access property data by subscription at www.courthouseonline.com/MyProperty.asp. Subscription fee $9.95 3-days, up to $374.95 per year. A free view available if you have control number and password from tax notice.

Warren County Prothonotary

Prothonotary, 204 4th Ave, Warren, PA 16365. 814-728-3440, fax-814-728-3476; 8:30AM-4:30PM
See Recorder for real estate records. Index: All in one. Records indexed on a public use terminal back to 2000. Only the public may search. Copy fee $.25 per page. Cert fee- $4.00 per cert includes copy fee. Payee- Warren County Prothonotary.

Warren County Recorder

County Recorder of Deeds, 204 4th Ave; Courthouse, Warren, PA 16365. Recording, R/E phone-814-728-3430; fax-814-728-3476; 8:30AM-4:30PM
No tax liens filed here. Index: All in one. Records indexed on a public use terminal back to 1985. Only the public may search. Search fee $5.00 per name if the office assists. Copy fee $.25 per page.Real estate record copy- $5.00 per document by mail. Cert fee-$5.00 per cert includes copy fee. Payee- Warren County Recorder of Deeds. Treasurer- 814-723-7550. **Property tax/Assessing**- 814-723-7550.

Washington County Prothonotary

County Prothonotary, 1 S Main St, #1001; Courthouse, Washington, PA 15301. 724-228-6770, fax-724-229-5913; 9AM-4:30PM www.co.washington.pa.us/maindepartment.aspx?menuDept=28
Separate indices to search include judgments, miscellaneous. Records indexed on a public use terminal back to 1988. Office will perform a UCC or naturalization search but public must search other records themselves. Search fee $5.00 per name. Copy fee $1.50 per page. Cert fee- $4.50 per seal includes one copy; add copy fee for add'l pages. Payee-Washington County Prothonotary. **Online Lien, Judgment, Divorce records:** With registration, username/password, access court-related records at www.co.washington.pa.us/wccourtdocuments/code/login.asp.

Washington County Recorder

County Recorder of Deeds, 100 W Beau St, #204; Washington County Courthouse, Washington, PA

15301. 724-228-6806; fax-724-228-6737; 9AM-4:30PM www.co.washington.pa.us
No tax liens filed here. Index: All in one. Records indexed on a public use terminal back to 1952. Only the public may search. Will not search UCC records. Copy fee $.50 per page. By mail-$10.00 per document. Cert fee- $10.00 per cert includes copy fee up to 25 pages. After 25 pages, add $10.00. Payee- Recorder of Deeds. **Online access to Real Estate, Property Tax, Treasurer, Deed, Mortgage, Map records:** Access the recorder index free at www.landex.com/webstore/jsp/cart/DocumentSearch.jsp. Full access to Recorder is by subscription at www.landex.com/remote/. Fee is $.22 per minute, $.50 per fax page. Index goes back to 1952, images to 1995. Map images are also available. Also, public record access available for a fee at Optical Storage Solutions Inc at 800-370-2836, option #4 to set-up account. **Other phones:** Treasurer- 724-228-6780; Elections- 724-228-6750; Vitals- 724-250-6775. **Property tax/Assessing-** 100 W Beau St, #205, Washington, PA 15301; 724-228-6850, assessor fax-724-250-4666. www.co.washington.pa.us/maindepartment.aspx?menuDept=53 **Online access-** Access treasurer real estate tax data free at www.co.washington.pa.us/wcmtp/tri.asp.

Wayne County Prothonotary

County Prothonotary, 925 Court St; Courthouse, Honesdale, PA 18431-1996. 570-253-5970 x1210, fax-570-253-0687; 8:30AM-4:30PM
See Recorder for real estate records. Index: All in one. Records indexed on a public use terminal back to 1996. Office will perform a UCC search but public must search other records themselves. Copy fee $.50 per page. Cert fee- $15.00 per cert. Payee- Wayne County Prothonotary.

Wayne County Recorder

County Recorder of Deeds, 925 Court St, Honesdale, PA 18431-1996. 570-253-5970 x4040; fax-n/a; 8:30AM-4:30PM www.co.wayne.pa.us/?pageid=10
No tax liens filed here. Index: All in one. Records indexed on a public use terminal back to 1941. Only the public may search. Will not search UCC records. Copy fee $.50 per page. Cert fee- $1.50 per doc plus copy fee. Payee- Wayne County Recorder of Deeds. **Other phones:** Treasurer- 570-253-5970 x4210; Elections- 570-253-5970 x1330; Vital Records- 570-253-5970 x4030. **Property tax/Assessing-** 925 Court St, Honesdale, PA 18431-1996; 570-253-5970 x4010, assessor fax- 570-253-5418. www.co.wayne.pa.us/?pageid=19 **Online-** Search assessor property data free after registering at http://taxpub.co.wayne.pa.us/Main.asp.

Westmoreland Prothonotary

County Prothonotary, PO Box 1630, Greensburg, PA 15601. 724-830-3502, fax-724-830-3517; 8:30AM-4PM www.co.westmoreland.pa.us/
See Recorder for real estate records. Index: All in one. (Records indexed on a public use terminal back to 1985. Only the public may search. Copy fee $.50 per page. Cert fee- $5.35 per cert plus copy fee. Payee- Westmoreland County Prothonotary.

Westmoreland County Recorder

County Recorder of Deeds, 2 N Main St, #503; Recorder Office, Greensburg, PA 15601. 724.830.3518, 724-830-3518; fax-724-853-4647; 8:30AM-4:00PM www.co.westmoreland.pa.us
No tax liens filed here. Index: All in one. Records indexed on a public use terminal back to 1943. Only the public may search. Staff will look up 1-2 (limited). Copy fee $.50 per page. Cert fee- $1.50 per page plus copy fee. Payee- Westmoreland County Recorder. **Online access to Real Estate, Deed, Mortgage, UCC records:** Register's old fee-based system has been replaced by a free, searchable site at www.wcdeeds.us/dts/default.asp. Choose simple, advanced, or instrument search. **Other phones:** Treasurer- 724-830-3173; Elections- 724-830-3150. **Property tax/Assessing-** 2 N Main St, #403, Greensburg, PA 15601; 724-830-3490, assessor fax-724-830-3852. www.co.westmoreland.pa.us/westmoreland/site/default.asp **Online access-** Search property and tax parcel data free at http://westmorelandweb400.us:8088/EGSPublicAccess.htm. View data on the GIS site free at www.co.westmoreland.pa.us/gis/Login.aspx?S=1. Search free but $25 monthly minimum fee for full GIS services.

Wyoming County Prothonotary

County Prothonotary, 1 Courthouse Sq; County Courthouse, Tunkhannock, PA 18657-1219. 717-836-3200, 8:30AM-4PM
See Recorder for real estate records. Index: All in one. Records indexed on a public use terminal back to 1996. Only the public may search. Copy fee $.25 per copy. Cert fee- $7.00 per cert includes copy fee. Payee- Wyoming County Prothonotary.

Wyoming County Recorder

County Recorder of Deeds, 1 Courthouse Sq, Tunkhannock, PA 18657. 570-996-2361, R/E recording phone-717-836-3200 x235; fax-570-996-5053; 8:30AM-4PM
No tax liens filed here. Index: All in one. Records indexed on a public use terminal back to 1975. Only the public may search. Copy fee $.25 per page, $.50 per page for index and 11 x 17 sized pages. Cert fee- $5.00 per cert includes up to 8 copies. Payee- Wyoming County Recorder of Deeds. **Other phones:** Treasurer- 717-836-3200 x287; Elections- 717-996-2226; Vital Records- 717-996-2233. **Property tax/Assessing-** 1 Courthouse Sq, Tunkhannock, PA 18657; 570-836-3200 x5, assessor fax- 570-836-5797.

York County Prothonotary

County Prothonotary, 45 N George St, York, PA 17401. 717-771-9611, fax-717-771-4629; 8:30AM-4:30PM www.york-county.org
See Recorder for real estate records. Index: Separate indices to search include new on enact, old on lightspeed. Records indexed on a public use terminal back to 1989. Office will perform a UCC search but public must search other records themselves. Copy fee $1.00 per page. Cert fee- $6.00 per 1st page, $2 each add'l page plus copy fee.

York County Recorder

County Recorder of Deeds, 28 E Market St, York, PA 17401. 717-771-9295, R/E recording phone-717-771-9806, UCC recording phone-717-771-9608; fax-717-771-9582; 8AM-4:30PM www.york-county.org/departments/deeds/deeds.htm
No tax liens filed here. Index: Separate indices to search include grantor/grantee, Mtgor/Mtgee. Records indexed on a public use terminal back to 1981. Office will perform a UCC search but public must search other records themselves. General index search fee $5.00 per search. Copy fee $.50 per page. Cert fee- $1.50 per page plus copy fee. Payee- Recorder of Deeds. **Online Real Estate, Deed, Death, Vital, Registry, Archive records:** Access to recorder land records is by subscription from Landex at www.landex.com/remote/. Base fee is $.20 per minute, $.50 per fax page. Records go back to 1981; images to 1981. Map images also available. Search older vitals, registries, and assorted records from archives free at www.yorkcountyarchives.org/records.asp. **Other phones:** Treasurer- 717-771-9603; Elections- 717-771-9604. **Property tax/Assessing-** 28 E Market St, York, PA 17401; 717-771-9232. (Appraiser/Auditor- 717-771-9232) **Online access-** Online access to the assessor database is free through the GIS data at http://216.174.25.68/york/. Also, search parcel numbers at www.york-county.org/departments/assessment/txasmnt.htm

Pennsylvania County Locator

You will usually be able to find the city name in the City/County Cross Reference below. In that case, it is a simple matter to determine the county from the cross reference. However, only the official US Postal Service city names are included in this index. There are an additional 40,000 place names that people use in their addresses. Therefore, we have also included a ZIP/City Cross Reference immediately following the City/County Cross Reference.

If you know the ZIP Code but the city name does not appear in the City/County Cross Reference index, look up the ZIP Code in the ZIP/City Cross Reference, find the city name, then look up the city name in the City/County Cross Reference. For example, you want to know the county for an address of Menands, NY 12204. There is no "Menands" in the City/County Cross Reference. The ZIP/City Cross Reference shows that ZIP Codes 12201-12288 are for the city of Albany. Looking back in the City/County Cross Reference, Albany is in Albany County.

Pennsylvania City/County Cross Reference

AARONSBURG Centre
ABBOTTSTOWN (17301) Adams(97), York(2)
ABINGTON Montgomery
ACKERMANVILLE Northampton
ACME (15610) Westmoreland(96), Fayette(3)
ACOSTA Somerset
ADAH Fayette
ADAMSBURG Westmoreland
ADAMSTOWN Lancaster
ADAMSVILLE (16110) Crawford(90), Mercer(9)
ADDISON Somerset
ADRIAN Armstrong
AIRVILLE York
AKRON Lancaster
ALBA Bradford
ALBION (16401) Erie(91), Crawford(8)
ALBION Erie
ALBRIGHTSVILLE (18210) Carbon(90), Monroe(9)
ALBURTIS (18011) Berks(61), Lehigh(38)
ALDENVILLE Wayne
ALEPPO Greene
ALEXANDRIA Huntingdon
ALIQUIPPA Beaver
ALLENPORT Washington
ALLENSVILLE (17002) Mifflin(87), Huntingdon(12)
ALLENTOWN (18109) Lehigh(97), Northampton(2)
ALLENTOWN Lehigh
ALLENWOOD (17810) Lycoming(63), Union(36)
ALLISON Fayette
ALLISON PARK Allegheny
ALLPORT Clearfield
ALTOONA Blair
ALUM BANK Bedford
ALVERDA Indiana
ALVERTON Westmoreland
AMBERSON Franklin
AMBLER Montgomery
AMBRIDGE (15003) Beaver(95), Allegheny(4)
AMITY Washington
ANALOMINK Monroe
ANDREAS (18211) Schuylkill(84), Carbon(15)
ANITA Jefferson
ANNVILLE Lebanon
ANTES FORT Lycoming
APOLLO (15613) Westmoreland(50), Armstrong(49)
AQUASHICOLA Carbon
ARCADIA Indiana
ARCHBALD Lackawanna
ARCOLA Montgomery
ARDARA Westmoreland
ARDMORE (19003) Montgomery(62), Delaware(37)
ARENDTSVILLE Adams
ARISTES Columbia
ARMAGH Indiana
ARMBRUST Westmoreland
ARNOT Tioga
ARONA Westmoreland
ARTEMAS Bedford
ASHFIELD Carbon
ASHLAND Schuylkill
ASHVILLE (16613) Cambria(98), Blair(1)
ASPERS Adams
ASTON Delaware
ATGLEN (19310) Chester(98), Lancaster(1)
ATHENS Bradford
ATLANTIC Crawford
ATLASBURG Washington
AUBURN Schuylkill
AUDUBON Montgomery
AULTMAN Indiana
AUSTIN (16720) Potter(58), Cameron(36), McKean(5)
AVELLA Washington
AVIS Clinton
AVONDALE Chester
AVONMORE Westmoreland
BADEN (15005) Beaver(87), Allegheny(12)
BAINBRIDGE Lancaster
BAIRDFORD Allegheny
BAKERS SUMMIT Bedford
BAKERSTOWN Allegheny
BALA CYNWYD Montgomery
BALLY Berks
BANGOR Northampton
BARNESBORO (15714) Cambria(79), Indiana(20)
BARNESVILLE Schuylkill
BART Lancaster
BARTO (19504) Berks(67), Montgomery(32)
BARTONSVILLE Monroe
BATH Northampton
BAUSMAN Lancaster
BEACH HAVEN Luzerne
BEACH LAKE (18405) Wayne(96), Pike(3)
BEALLSVILLE Washington
BEAR CREEK Luzerne
BEAR LAKE Warren
BEAVER FALLS Beaver
BEAVER MEADOWS (18216) Luzerne(69), Carbon(30)
BEAVER SPRINGS Snyder
BEAVERDALE Cambria
BEAVERTOWN Snyder
BECCARIA Clearfield
BECHTELSVILLE (19505) Berks(94), Montgomery(5)
BEDFORD Bedford
BEDMINSTER Bucks
BEECH CREEK (16822) Clinton(91), Centre(8)
BELLE VERNON (15012) Fayette(56), Westmoreland(41), Washington(1)
BELLEFONTE Centre
BELLEVILLE Mifflin
BELLWOOD Blair
BELSANO Cambria
BENDERSVILLE Adams
BENEZETT Elk
BENSALEM Bucks
BENTLEYVILLE Washington
BENTON (17814) Columbia(62), Luzerne(29), Lycoming(4), Sullivan(3)
BERLIN Somerset
BERNVILLE Berks
BERRYSBURG Dauphin
BERWICK (18603) Columbia(79), Luzerne(20)
BERWYN Chester
BESSEMER Lawrence
BETHEL Berks
BETHEL PARK Allegheny
BETHLEHEM (18018) Lehigh(52), Northampton(47)
BETHLEHEM (18017) Northampton(94), Lehigh(5)
BETHLEHEM Lehigh
BETHLEHEM Northampton
BEYER Indiana
BIG COVE TANNERY Fulton
BIG RUN Jefferson
BIGLER Clearfield
BIGLERVILLE (17307) Adams(98), Cumberland(1)
BIRCHRUNVILLE Chester
BIRD IN HAND Lancaster
BIRDSBORO Berks
BLACK LICK Indiana
BLAIN Perry
BLAIRS MILLS Huntingdon
BLAIRSVILLE (15717) Indiana(88), Westmoreland(11)
BLAKESLEE (18610) Monroe(98), Luzerne(1)
BLANCHARD Centre
BLANDBURG Cambria
BLANDON Berks
BLOOMING GLEN Bucks
BLOOMSBURG Columbia
BLOSSBURG Tioga
BLUE BALL Lancaster
BLUE BELL Montgomery
BLUE RIDGE SUMMIT Franklin
BOALSBURG Centre
BOBTOWN Greene
BODINES Lycoming
BOILING SPRINGS Cumberland
BOLIVAR Westmoreland
BOSWELL Somerset
BOVARD Westmoreland
BOWERS Berks
BOWMANSDALE Cumberland
BOWMANSTOWN Carbon
BOWMANSVILLE Lancaster
BOYERS Butler
BOYERTOWN (19512) Berks(95), Montgomery(4)
BOYNTON Somerset
BRACKENRIDGE Allegheny
BRACKNEY Susquehanna
BRADDOCK Allegheny
BRADENVILLE Westmoreland
BRADFORD McKean
BRADFORDWOODS Allegheny
BRANCHDALE Schuylkill
BRANCHTON Butler
BRANDAMORE Chester
BRANDY CAMP Elk
BRAVE Greene
BREEZEWOOD (15533) Bedford(94), Fulton(5)
BREINIGSVILLE Lehigh
BRIDGEPORT Montgomery
BRIDGEVILLE (15017) Allegheny(97), Washington(2)
BRIER HILL Fayette
BRISBIN Clearfield
BRISTOL Bucks
BROAD TOP Huntingdon
BROCKPORT (15823) Elk(81), Jefferson(18)
BROCKTON Schuylkill
BROCKWAY (15824) Jefferson(97), Clearfield(2)
BRODHEADSVILLE Monroe
BROGUE York
BROOKHAVEN Delaware
BROOKLYN Susquehanna
BROOKVILLE Jefferson
BROOMALL Delaware
BROWNFIELD Fayette
BROWNSTOWN Lancaster
BROWNSVILLE (15417) Fayette(62), Washington(37)
BRUIN Butler
BRUSH VALLEY Indiana
BRYN ATHYN Montgomery
BRYN MAWR (19010) Delaware(53), Montgomery(46)
BUCK HILL FALLS Monroe
BUCKINGHAM Bucks
BUENA VISTA Allegheny
BUFFALO MILLS (15534) Bedford(98), Somerset(1)
BULGER Washington
BUNOLA Allegheny
BURGETTSTOWN Washington
BURLINGTON Bradford
BURNHAM Mifflin
BURNSIDE Clearfield
BURNT CABINS (17215) Fulton(82), Huntingdon(17)
BUSHKILL Pike
BUTLER Butler
BYRNEDALE Elk
CABOT Butler
CADOGAN Armstrong
CAIRNBROOK Somerset
CALIFORNIA Washington
CALLENSBURG Clarion

CALLERY Butler
CALUMET Westmoreland
CALVIN Huntingdon
CAMBRA Luzerne
CAMBRIDGE SPRINGS (16403) Crawford(93), Erie(6)
CAMP HILL (17011) Cumberland(98), York(1)
CAMP HILL Cumberland
CAMP HILL Lebanon
CAMPBELLTOWN Lebanon
CAMPTOWN Bradford
CANADENSIS (18325) Monroe(63), Pike(36)
CANONSBURG Washington
CANTON (17724) Bradford(82), Tioga(7), Sullivan(7), Lycoming(3)
CARBONDALE Lackawanna
CARDALE Fayette
CARLISLE Cumberland
CARLTON (16311) Mercer(87), Venango(12)
CARMICHAELS Greene
CARNEGIE Allegheny
CARROLLTOWN Cambria
CARVERSVILLE Bucks
CASHTOWN Adams
CASSANDRA Cambria
CASSVILLE Huntingdon
CASTANEA Clinton
CATASAUQUA (18032) Lehigh(68), Northampton(31)
CATAWISSA (17820) Columbia(96), Montour(3)
CECIL Washington
CEDAR RUN Lycoming
CEDARS Montgomery
CENTER VALLEY Lehigh
CENTERPORT Berks
CENTERVILLE Crawford
CENTRAL CITY Somerset
CENTRALIA Columbia
CENTRE HALL Centre
CHADDS FORD (19317) Delaware(63), Chester(36)
CHALFONT Bucks
CHALK HILL Fayette
CHALKHILL Fayette
CHAMBERSBURG Franklin
CHAMBERSVILLE Indiana
CHAMPION (15622) Westmoreland(84), Fayette(8), Somerset(7)
CHANDLERS VALLEY Warren
CHARLEROI Washington
CHATHAM Chester
CHELTENHAM Montgomery
CHERRY TREE (15724) Indiana(66), Clearfield(26), Cambria(7)
CHERRYVILLE Northampton
CHEST SPRINGS Cambria
CHESTER Delaware
CHESTER HEIGHTS Delaware
CHESTER SPRINGS Chester
CHESTNUT RIDGE Fayette
CHESWICK Allegheny
CHEYNEY (19319) Delaware(97), Chester(2)
CHICORA (16025) Butler(81), Armstrong(18)
CHINCHILLA Lackawanna
CHRISTIANA Lancaster
CLAIRTON Allegheny
CLARENCE Centre
CLARENDON Warren
CLARIDGE Westmoreland
CLARINGTON (15828) Jefferson(92), Forest(5), Elk(2)
CLARION Clarion
CLARK Mercer
CLARKS MILLS Mercer
CLARKS SUMMIT Lackawanna
CLARKSBURG Indiana
CLARKSVILLE (15322) Washington(56), Greene(43)
CLAYSBURG (16625) Bedford(75), Blair(24)
CLAYSVILLE Washington
CLEARFIELD Clearfield
CLEARVILLE Bedford
CLIFFORD Susquehanna
CLIFTON HEIGHTS Delaware
CLIMAX Armstrong
CLINTON (15026) Beaver(78), Allegheny(15), Washington(6)
CLINTONVILLE Venango
CLUNE Indiana
CLYMER Indiana
COAL CENTER Washington
COAL TOWNSHIP Northumberland
COALDALE Schuylkill
COALPORT (16627) Clearfield(93), Cambria(6)
COATESVILLE Chester
COBURN Centre
COCHRANTON (16314) Crawford(90), Mercer(6), Venango(3)
COCHRANVILLE Chester
COCOLAMUS Juniata
CODORUS York
COGAN STATION Lycoming
COKEBURG Washington
COLEBROOK Lebanon
COLLEGEVILLE Montgomery
COLMAR Montgomery
COLUMBIA Lancaster
COLUMBIA CROSS ROADS (16914) Bradford(93), Tioga(6)
COLUMBUS Warren
COLVER Cambria
COMMODORE Indiana
CONCORD Franklin
CONCORDVILLE Delaware
CONESTOGA Lancaster
CONFLUENCE (15424) Somerset(77), Fayette(22)
CONNEAUT LAKE Crawford
CONNEAUTVILLE Crawford
CONNELLSVILLE Fayette
CONNOQUENESSING Butler
CONSHOHOCKEN Montgomery
CONWAY Beaver
CONYNGHAM Luzerne
COOKSBURG (16217) Clarion(91), Forest(8)
COOLSPRING Jefferson
COOPERSBURG (18036) Lehigh(88), Bucks(11)
COOPERSTOWN (16317) Venango(93), Crawford(6)
COPLAY Lehigh
CORAL Indiana
CORAOPOLIS Allegheny
CORNWALL Lebanon
CORRY (16407) Erie(87), Warren(7), Crawford(5)
CORSICA (15829) Jefferson(74), Clarion(25)
COUDERSPORT Potter
COULTERS Allegheny
COUPON Cambria
COURTNEY Washington
COVINGTON Tioga
COWANESQUE Tioga
COWANSVILLE Armstrong
CRABTREE Westmoreland
CRALEY York
CRANBERRY (16319) Venango(60), Clarion(39)
CRANBERRY TWP Butler
CRANESVILLE Erie
CREAMERY Montgomery
CREEKSIDE (15732) Indiana(92), Armstrong(4), Allegheny(2)
CREIGHTON Allegheny
CRESCENT Allegheny
CRESCO (18326) Monroe(98), Pike(1)
CRESSON Cambria
CRESSONA Schuylkill
CROSBY McKean
CROSS FORK (17729) Clinton(59), Potter(40)
CROWN Clarion
CROYDON Bucks
CRUCIBLE Greene
CRUM LYNNE Delaware
CRYSTAL SPRING Fulton
CUDDY Allegheny
CUMBOLA Schuylkill
CURLLSVILLE Clarion
CURRYVILLE Blair
CURTISVILLE Allegheny
CURWENSVILLE Clearfield
CUSTER CITY McKean
CYCLONE McKean
DAGUS MINES Elk
DAISYTOWN Washington
DALLAS (18612) Luzerne(97), Wyoming(2)
DALLAS Luzerne
DALLASTOWN York
DALMATIA (17017) Northumberland(64), Dauphin(35)
DALTON (18414) Lackawanna(78), Wyoming(21)
DAMASCUS Wayne
DANBORO Bucks
DANIELSVILLE Northampton
DANVILLE (17821) Montour(82), Northumberland(16), Columbia(1)
DANVILLE Montour
DARBY Delaware
DARLINGTON Beaver
DARRAGH Westmoreland
DAUBERVILLE Berks
DAUPHIN Dauphin
DAVIDSVILLE Somerset
DAWSON Fayette
DAYTON (16222) Armstrong(66), Jefferson(16), Indiana(16)
DE LANCEY Jefferson
DE YOUNG Elk
DEFIANCE Bedford
DELANO Schuylkill
DELAWARE WATER GAP Monroe
DELMONT Westmoreland
DELTA York
DENBO Washington
DENVER Lancaster
DERRICK CITY McKean
DERRY Westmoreland
DEVAULT Chester
DEVON Chester
DEWART Northumberland
DICKERSON RUN Fayette
DICKINSON Cumberland
DICKSON CITY Lackawanna
DILLINER Greene
DILLSBURG York
DILLTOWN Indiana
DIMOCK Susquehanna
DINGMANS FERRY Pike
DISTANT Armstrong
DIXONVILLE Indiana
DONEGAL Westmoreland
DONORA Washington
DORNSIFE (17823) Northumberland(98), Schuylkill(1)
DOUGLASSVILLE Berks
DOVER York
DOWNINGTOWN Chester
DOYLESBURG Franklin
DOYLESTOWN Bucks
DRAVOSBURG Allegheny
DRESHER Montgomery
DREXEL HILL Delaware
DRIFTING Clearfield
DRIFTON Luzerne
DRIFTWOOD (15832) Cameron(85), Elk(14)
DRUMORE Lancaster
DRUMS Luzerne
DRY RUN Franklin
DU BOIS Clearfield
DUBLIN Bucks
DUDLEY Huntingdon
DUKE CENTER McKean
DUNBAR Fayette
DUNCANNON Perry
DUNCANSVILLE Blair
DUNLEVY Washington
DUNLO Cambria
DUQUESNE Allegheny
DURHAM Bucks
DURYEA Luzerne
DUSHORE (18614) Sullivan(94), Wyoming(3), Bradford(1)
DYSART (16636) Cambria(90), Blair(9)
EAGLES MERE Sullivan
EAGLEVILLE Montgomery
EARLINGTON Montgomery
EARLVILLE Berks
EAST BERLIN (17316) Adams(81), York(18)
EAST BRADY (16028) Clarion(84), Armstrong(15)
EAST BUTLER Butler
EAST EARL Lancaster
EAST FREEDOM Blair
EAST GREENVILLE (18041) Montgomery(70), Lehigh(23), Bucks(3), Berks(2)
EAST HICKORY Forest
EAST MC KEESPORT Allegheny
EAST MILLSBORO Fayette
EAST PETERSBURG Lancaster
EAST PITTSBURGH Allegheny
EAST PROSPECT York
EAST SMETHPORT McKean
EAST SMITHFIELD Bradford
EAST SPRINGFIELD Erie
EAST STROUDSBURG Monroe
EAST TEXAS Lehigh
EAST VANDERGRIFT Westmoreland
EAST WATERFORD (17021) Juniata(87), Huntingdon(6), Franklin(3), Perry(2)
EASTON Northampton
EAU CLAIRE Butler
EBENSBURG Cambria
EBERVALE Luzerne
EDGEMONT Delaware
EDINBORO (16412) Erie(76), Crawford(23)
EDINBORO Erie
EDINBURG Lawrence
EDMON Armstrong
EFFORT Monroe
EIGHTY FOUR Washington
ELCO Washington
ELDERSVILLE Washington
ELDERTON Armstrong
ELDRED McKean
ELGIN Erie
ELIZABETH Allegheny
ELIZABETHTOWN (17022) Lancaster(90), Dauphin(9)
ELIZABETHVILLE Dauphin
ELKINS PARK Montgomery
ELKLAND Tioga
ELLIOTTSBURG Perry
ELLSWORTH Washington
ELLWOOD CITY (16117) Lawrence(67), Beaver(32)
ELM Lancaster
ELMHURST Lackawanna
ELMORA Cambria
ELRAMA Washington
ELTON Cambria
ELVERSON (19520) Chester(69), Berks(30)

ELYSBURG (17824) Northumberland(81), Columbia(17), Montour(1)
EMEIGH Cambria
EMIGSVILLE York
EMLENTON (16373) Venango(49), Clarion(47), Butler(3)
EMMAUS Lehigh
EMPORIUM (15834) Cameron(97), Elk(1)
ENDEAVOR Forest
ENOLA Cumberland
ENON VALLEY (16120) Lawrence(94), Beaver(5)
ENTRIKEN Huntingdon
EPHRATA Lancaster
EQUINUNK Wayne
ERIE Erie
ERNEST Indiana
ERWINNA Bucks
ESSINGTON Delaware
ETTERS York
EVANS CITY Butler
EVERETT Bedford
EVERSON Fayette
EXCELSIOR Northumberland
EXPORT Westmoreland
EXTON Chester
FACTORYVILLE (18419) Wyoming(79), Lackawanna(20)
FAIRBANK Fayette
FAIRCHANCE Fayette
FAIRFIELD Adams
FAIRHOPE Somerset
FAIRLESS HILLS Bucks
FAIRMOUNT CITY Clarion
FAIRVIEW Erie
FAIRVIEW VILLAGE Montgomery
FALLENTIMBER (16639) Cambria(83), Clearfield(16)
FALLS (18615) Wyoming(90), Luzerne(7), Lackawanna(2)
FALLS CREEK (15840) Jefferson(96), Clearfield(3)
FANNETTSBURG Franklin
FARMINGTON Fayette
FARRANDSVILLE Clinton
FARRELL Mercer
FAWN GROVE York
FAYETTE CITY Fayette
FAYETTEVILLE (17222) Franklin(94), Adams(5)
FEASTERVILLE TREVOSE Bucks
FELTON York
FENELTON Butler
FERNDALE Bucks
FINLEYVILLE (15332) Washington(92), Allegheny(7)
FIRST NAT BANK Erie
FISHER Clarion
FISHERTOWN Bedford
FLEETVILLE Lackawanna
FLEETWOOD Berks
FLEMING Centre
FLICKSVILLE Northampton
FLINTON Cambria
FLOURTOWN Montgomery
FOGELSVILLE Lehigh
FOLCROFT Delaware
FOLSOM Delaware
FOMBELL (16123) Beaver(69), Lawrence(30)
FORBES ROAD Westmoreland
FORCE Elk
FORD CITY Armstrong
FORD CLIFF Armstrong
FOREST CITY (18421) Susquehanna(47), Wayne(31), Lackawanna(20)
FOREST GROVE Bucks
FORESTVILLE Butler
FORKSVILLE Sullivan
FORT HILL Somerset
FORT LITTLETON Fulton
FORT LOUDON Franklin
FORT WASHINGTON Bucks
FORT WASHINGTON Montgomery
FOUNTAINVILLE Bucks
FOXBURG Clarion
FRACKVILLE Schuylkill
FRANCONIA Montgomery
FRANKLIN Venango
FRANKLINTOWN York
FREDERICK Montgomery
FREDERICKSBURG (17026) Lebanon(90), Berks(9)
FREDERICKTOWN Washington
FREDONIA Mercer
FREEBURG Snyder
FREEDOM Beaver
FREELAND Luzerne
FREEPORT (16229) Armstrong(64), Butler(23), Westmoreland(10), Allegheny(1)
FRENCHVILLE Clearfield
FRIEDENS Somerset
FRIEDENSBURG Schuylkill
FRIENDSVILLE Susquehanna
FROSTBURG Jefferson
FRYBURG Clarion
FURLONG Bucks
GAINES (16921) Tioga(96), Potter(3)
GALETON Potter
GALLITZIN (16641) Cambria(96), Blair(3)
GANS Fayette
GAP (17527) Lancaster(91), Chester(8)
GARARDS FORT Greene
GARDENVILLE Bucks
GARDNERS (17324) Adams(66), Cumberland(33)
GARLAND Warren
GARRETT Somerset
GASTONVILLE Washington
GEIGERTOWN Berks
GENESEE Potter
GEORGETOWN Beaver
GERMANSVILLE Lehigh
GETTYSBURG Adams
GIBBON GLADE Fayette
GIBSON Susquehanna
GIBSONIA (15044) Allegheny(95), Butler(4)
GIFFORD McKean
GILBERT Monroe
GILBERTON Schuylkill
GILBERTSVILLE Montgomery
GILLETT Bradford
GIPSY Indiana
GIRARD Erie
GIRARDVILLE Schuylkill
GLADWYNE Montgomery
GLASGOW Cambria
GLASSPORT Allegheny
GLEN CAMPBELL (15742) Indiana(91), Clearfield(8)
GLEN HOPE Clearfield
GLEN LYON Luzerne
GLEN MILLS (19342) Delaware(98), Chester(1)
GLEN RICHEY Clearfield
GLEN RIDDLE LIMA Delaware
GLEN ROCK York
GLENMOORE Chester
GLENOLDEN Delaware
GLENSHAW Allegheny
GLENSIDE Montgomery
GLENVILLE York
GLENWILLARD Allegheny
GOODVILLE Lancaster
GORDON Schuylkill
GORDONVILLE Lancaster
GOULDSBORO (18424) Wayne(54), Lackawanna(38), Luzerne(3), Monroe(2)
GOWEN CITY Northumberland
GRADYVILLE Delaware
GRAMPIAN Clearfield
GRAND VALLEY (16420) Warren(81), Crawford(17), Jefferson(1)
GRANTHAM Cumberland
GRANTVILLE (17028) Dauphin(80), Lebanon(19)
GRANVILLE Mifflin
GRANVILLE SUMMIT Bradford
GRAPEVILLE Westmoreland
GRASSFLAT Clearfield
GRATZ Dauphin
GRAY Somerset
GRAYSVILLE Greene
GREAT BEND Susquehanna
GREELEY Pike
GREEN LANE (18054) Montgomery(83), Bucks(16)
GREEN PARK Perry
GREENCASTLE Franklin
GREENOCK Allegheny
GREENSBURG Westmoreland
GREENTOWN Pike
GREENVILLE (16125) Mercer(95), Crawford(4)
GRINDSTONE Fayette
GROVE CITY (16127) Mercer(93), Venango(5)
GROVER Bradford
GUYS MILLS Crawford
GWYNEDD Montgomery
GWYNEDD VALLEY Montgomery
HADLEY Mercer
HALIFAX Dauphin
HALLSTEAD Susquehanna
HAMBURG Berks
HAMILTON Jefferson
HAMLIN Wayne
HANNASTOWN Westmoreland
HANOVER (17331) York(83), Adams(16)
HANOVER York
HARBORCREEK Erie
HARFORD Susquehanna
HARLEIGH Luzerne
HARLEYSVILLE Montgomery
HARMONSBURG Crawford
HARMONY (16037) Butler(82), Lawrence(13), Beaver(3)
HARRISBURG Dauphin
HARRISON CITY Westmoreland
HARRISON VALLEY Potter
HARRISONVILLE Fulton
HARRISVILLE (16038) Venango(53), Butler(46)
HARTLETON Union
HARTSTOWN Crawford
HARVEYS LAKE (18618) Luzerne(86), Wyoming(13)
HARWICK Allegheny
HASTINGS (16646) Cambria(95), Clearfield(4)
HATBORO (19040) Montgomery(96), Bucks(3)
HATFIELD (19440) Montgomery(91), Bucks(8)
HAVERFORD (19041) Montgomery(73), Delaware(26)
HAVERTOWN Delaware
HAWK RUN Clearfield
HAWLEY (18428) Wayne(64), Pike(35)
HAWTHORN Clarion
HAZEL HURST McKean
HAZLETON Luzerne
HEGINS Schuylkill
HEILWOOD Indiana
HELFENSTEIN Schuylkill
HELLERTOWN (18055) Northampton(97), Bucks(2)
HENDERSONVILLE Washington
HENRYVILLE Monroe
HEREFORD Berks
HERMAN Butler
HERMINIE Westmoreland
HERMITAGE Mercer
HERNDON (17830) Northumberland(98), Dauphin(1)
HERRICK CENTER Susquehanna
HERSHEY (17033) Dauphin(96), Lebanon(3)
HESSTON Huntingdon
HIBBS Fayette
HICKORY Washington
HIDDEN VALLEY Somerset
HIGHSPIRE Dauphin
HILLER Fayette
HILLIARDS Butler
HILLSDALE Indiana
HILLSGROVE (18619) Sullivan(81), Lycoming(18)
HILLSVILLE Lawrence
HILLTOWN Bucks
HOLBROOK Greene
HOLICONG Bucks
HOLLIDAYSBURG Blair
HOLLSOPPLE Somerset
HOLMES Delaware
HOLTWOOD Lancaster
HOME Indiana
HOMER CITY Indiana
HOMESTEAD Allegheny
HONESDALE Wayne
HONEY BROOK (19344) Chester(89), Lancaster(10)
HONEY GROVE (17035) Juniata(98), Perry(1)
HOOKSTOWN Beaver
HOOVERSVILLE Somerset
HOP BOTTOM Susquehanna
HOPELAND Lancaster
HOPEWELL Bedford
HOPWOOD Fayette
HORSHAM Montgomery
HOSTETTER Westmoreland
HOUSTON Washington
HOUTZDALE Clearfield
HOWARD Centre
HUGHESVILLE Lycoming
HUMMELS WHARF Snyder
HUMMELSTOWN Dauphin
HUNKER Westmoreland
HUNLOCK CREEK Luzerne
HUNTINGDON Huntingdon
HUNTINGDON VALLEY (19006) Montgomery(91), Bucks(8)
HUNTINGTON MILLS Luzerne
HUSTONTOWN (17229) Fulton(93), Huntingdon(6)
HUTCHINSON Westmoreland
HYDE Clearfield
HYDE PARK Westmoreland
HYDETOWN Crawford
HYNDMAN (15545) Bedford(77), Somerset(22)
HYNER Clinton
ICKESBURG Perry
IDAVILLE Adams
IMLER (16655) Bedford(98), Blair(1)
IMMACULATA Chester
IMPERIAL Allegheny
INDIAN HEAD Fayette
INDIANA Indiana
INDIANOLA Allegheny
INDUSTRY Beaver
INGOMAR Allegheny
INTERCOURSE Lancaster
IRVINE Warren
IRVONA Clearfield
IRWIN Westmoreland
ISABELLA Fayette
JACKSON Susquehanna
JACKSON CENTER Mercer
JACOBS CREEK Westmoreland
JAMES CITY Elk
JAMES CREEK (16657) Huntingdon(98), Bedford(1)
JAMESTOWN (16134) Crawford(90), Mercer(9)
JAMISON Bucks

JEANNETTE Westmoreland
JENKINTOWN Montgomery
JENNERS Somerset
JENNERSTOWN Somerset
JERMYN Lackawanna
JEROME Somerset
JERSEY MILLS Lycoming
JERSEY SHORE (17740) Lycoming(86), Clinton(13)
JERSEY SHORE Lycoming
JESSUP Lackawanna
JIM THORPE Carbon
JOFFRE Washington
JOHNSONBURG Elk
JOHNSTOWN (15905) Cambria(89), Somerset(10)
JOHNSTOWN Cambria
JONES MILLS Westmoreland
JONESTOWN Lebanon
JOSEPHINE Indiana
JULIAN Centre
JUNEAU Indiana
JUNEDALE Carbon
KANE (16735) McKean(71), Elk(28)
KANTNER Somerset
KARNS CITY (16041) Butler(54), Armstrong(45)
KARTHAUS (16845) Clearfield(70), Centre(29)
KEISTERVILLE Fayette
KELAYRES Schuylkill
KELTON Chester
KEMBLESVILLE Chester
KEMPTON (19529) Berks(51), Lehigh(48)
KENNERDELL Venango
KENNETT SQUARE Chester
KENT Indiana
KERSEY Elk
KIMBERTON Chester
KING OF PRUSSIA Chester
KING OF PRUSSIA Montgomery
KINGSLEY Susquehanna
KINGSTON Luzerne
KINTNERSVILLE Bucks
KINZERS Lancaster
KIRKWOOD Lancaster
KITTANNING Armstrong
KLEINFELTERSVILLE Lebanon
KLINGERSTOWN (17941) Schuylkill(84), Northumberland(15)
KNOX Clarion
KNOX DALE Jefferson
KNOXVILLE Tioga
KOPPEL Beaver
KOSSUTH Clarion
KREAMER Snyder
KRESGEVILLE Monroe
KULPMONT Northumberland
KULPSVILLE Montgomery
KUNKLETOWN (18058) Monroe(70), Carbon(29)
KUTZTOWN (19530) Berks(90), Lehigh(9)
KYLERTOWN Clearfield
LA BELLE Fayette
LA JOSE Clearfield
LA PLUME Lackawanna
LACEYVILLE (18623) Wyoming(46), Bradford(38), Susquehanna(15)
LACKAWAXEN Pike
LAFAYETTE HILL Montgomery
LAHASKA Bucks
LAIRDSVILLE Lycoming
LAKE ARIEL (18436) Wayne(67), Lackawanna(32)
LAKE CITY Erie
LAKE COMO Wayne
LAKE HARMONY Carbon
LAKE LYNN Fayette
LAKE WINOLA Wyoming
LAKEVILLE Wayne
LAKEWOOD Wayne
LAMAR Clinton
LAMARTINE Clarion
LAMPETER Lancaster
LANCASTER Lancaster
LANDENBERG Chester
LANDINGVILLE Schuylkill
LANDISBURG Perry
LANDISVILLE Lancaster
LANESBORO Susquehanna
LANGELOTH Washington
LANGHORNE Bucks
LANSDALE Montgomery
LANSDOWNE Delaware
LANSE Clearfield
LANSFORD Carbon
LAPORTE Sullivan
LARIMER Westmoreland
LATROBE Westmoreland
LATTIMER MINES Luzerne
LAUGHLINTOWN Westmoreland
LAURELTON Union
LAURYS STATION Lehigh
LAVELLE Schuylkill
LAWN Lebanon
LAWRENCE Washington
LAWRENCEVILLE Tioga
LAWTON Susquehanna
LE RAYSVILLE (18829) Bradford(95), Susquehanna(4)
LEBANON Lebanon
LECK KILL (17836) Northumberland(78), Schuylkill(21)
LECKRONE Fayette
LECONTES MILLS Clearfield
LEDERACH Montgomery
LEECHBURG (15656) Armstrong(51), Westmoreland(48)
LEEPER Clarion
LEESPORT Berks
LEETSDALE Allegheny
LEHIGH VALLEY Northampton
LEHIGHTON Carbon
LEHMAN Luzerne
LEISENRING Fayette
LEMASTERS Franklin
LEMONT Centre
LEMONT FURNACE Fayette
LEMOYNE Cumberland
LENHARTSVILLE Berks
LENNI Delaware
LENOXVILLE Susquehanna
LEOLA Lancaster
LEROY Bradford
LEVITTOWN Bucks
LEWIS RUN McKean
LEWISBERRY York
LEWISBURG Union
LEWISTOWN Mifflin
LEWISVILLE Chester
LIBERTY (16930) Tioga(73), Lycoming(26)
LIBRARY Allegheny
LICKINGVILLE Clarion
LIGHT STREET Columbia
LIGONIER Westmoreland
LILLY Cambria
LIMEKILN Berks
LIMEPORT Lehigh
LIMESTONE Clarion
LINCOLN UNIVERSITY Chester
LINDEN Lycoming
LINE LEXINGTON (18932) Bucks(93), Montgomery(6)
LINESVILLE Crawford
LIONVILLE Chester
LISTIE Somerset
LITITZ Lancaster
LITTLE MEADOWS (18830) Susquehanna(91), Bradford(8)
LITTLESTOWN Adams
LIVERPOOL (17045) Perry(71), Juniata(23), Snyder(4)
LLEWELLYN Schuylkill
LOCK HAVEN (17745) Clinton(98), Lycoming(1)
LOCUST GAP Northumberland
LOCUSTDALE Schuylkill
LOGANTON Clinton
LOGANVILLE York
LONG POND Monroe
LOPEZ Sullivan
LORETTO Cambria
LOST CREEK Schuylkill
LOWBER Westmoreland
LOYALHANNA Westmoreland
LOYSBURG Bedford
LOYSVILLE Perry
LUCERNEMINES Indiana
LUCINDA Clarion
LUDLOW McKean
LUMBERVILLE Bucks
LURGAN Franklin
LUTHERSBURG Clearfield
LUXOR Westmoreland
LUZERNE Luzerne
LYKENS Dauphin
LYNDELL Chester
LYNDORA Butler
LYON STATION Berks
MACKEYVILLE Clinton
MACUNGIE (18062) Lehigh(89), Berks(10)
MADERA Clearfield
MADISON Westmoreland
MADISONBURG Centre
MAHAFFEY (15757) Clearfield(98), Indiana(1)
MAHANOY CITY Schuylkill
MAHANOY PLANE Schuylkill
MAINESBURG (16932) Tioga(98), Bradford(1)
MAINLAND Montgomery
MALVERN Chester
MAMMOTH Westmoreland
MANCHESTER York
MANHEIM (17545) Lancaster(98), Lebanon(1)
MANNS CHOICE Bedford
MANOR Westmoreland
MANORVILLE Armstrong
MANSFIELD Tioga
MAPLETON DEPOT Huntingdon
MAR LIN Schuylkill
MARBLE Clarion
MARCHAND Indiana
MARCUS HOOK Delaware
MARIANNA Washington
MARIENVILLE (16239) Forest(62), Clarion(37)
MARIETTA Lancaster
MARION Franklin
MARION CENTER Indiana
MARION HEIGHTS Northumberland
MARKLETON Somerset
MARKLEYSBURG Fayette
MARS (16046) Butler(86), Allegheny(13)
MARSHALLS CREEK Monroe
MARSTELLER Cambria
MARTIN Fayette
MARTINDALE Lancaster
MARTINS CREEK Northampton
MARTINSBURG (16662) Blair(69), Bedford(30)
MARY D Schuylkill
MARYSVILLE (17053) Perry(97), Cumberland(2)
MASONTOWN Fayette
MATAMORAS Pike
MATHER Greene
MATTAWANA Mifflin
MAXATAWNY Berks
MAYPORT (16240) Jefferson(55), Clarion(40), Armstrong(3)
MAYTOWN Lancaster
MC ALISTERVILLE Juniata
MC CLELLANDTOWN Fayette
MC CLURE (17841) Mifflin(85), Snyder(14)
MC CONNELLSBURG Fulton
MC CONNELLSTOWN Huntingdon
MC DONALD (15057) Washington(81), Allegheny(18)
MC ELHATTAN Clinton
MC EWENSVILLE Northumberland
MC GRANN Armstrong
MC INTYRE Indiana
MC KEAN Erie
MC KEES ROCKS Allegheny
MC KEESPORT (15131) Allegheny(95), Westmoreland(4)
MC KEESPORT Allegheny
MC KNIGHTSTOWN Adams
MC SHERRYSTOWN Adams
MC VEYTOWN Mifflin
MCADOO (18237) Schuylkill(98), Carbon(1)
MEADOW LANDS Washington
MEADVILLE Crawford
MECHANICSBURG (17055) Cumberland(98), York(1)
MECHANICSBURG Cumberland
MECHANICSVILLE Bucks
MEDIA Delaware
MEHOOPANY Wyoming
MELCROFT Fayette
MENDENHALL Chester
MENGES MILLS York
MENTCLE Indiana
MERCERSBURG (17236) Franklin(92), Fulton(7)
MERION STATION Montgomery
MERRITTSTOWN Fayette
MERTZTOWN (19539) Berks(87), Lehigh(12)
MESHOPPEN (18630) Susquehanna(50), Wyoming(50)
MEXICO Juniata
MEYERSDALE Somerset
MIDDLEBURG Snyder
MIDDLEBURY CENTER Tioga
MIDDLEPORT Schuylkill
MIDDLETOWN Dauphin
MIDLAND Beaver
MIDWAY Washington
MIFFLIN Juniata
MIFFLINBURG Union
MIFFLINTOWN Juniata
MIFFLINVILLE Columbia
MILAN Bradford
MILANVILLE Wayne
MILDRED Sullivan
MILESBURG Centre
MILFORD Pike
MILFORD SQUARE Bucks
MILL CREEK (17060) Huntingdon(88), Mifflin(11)
MILL HALL Clinton
MILL RUN Fayette
MILL VILLAGE Erie
MILLERSBURG Dauphin
MILLERSTOWN (17062) Perry(90), Juniata(9)
MILLERSVILLE Lancaster
MILLERTON (16936) Tioga(87), Bradford(12)
MILLHEIM Centre
MILLMONT Union
MILLRIFT Pike
MILLS Potter
MILLSBORO Washington
MILLVILLE Columbia
MILNESVILLE Luzerne
MILROY Mifflin
MILTON (17847) Northumberland(94), Montour(5)
MINERAL POINT Cambria
MINERAL SPRINGS Clearfield
MINERSVILLE Schuylkill
MINGOVILLE Centre

MINISINK HILLS Monroe
MIQUON Montgomery
MODENA Chester
MOHNTON (19540) Berks(94), Lancaster(5)
MOHRSVILLE Berks
MONACA Beaver
MONESSEN Westmoreland
MONOCACY STATION Berks
MONONGAHELA (15063) Washington(95), Allegheny(3)
MONROETON Bradford
MONROEVILLE Allegheny
MONT ALTO Franklin
MONT CLARE Montgomery
MONTANDON Northumberland
MONTGOMERY Lycoming
MONTGOMERYVILLE Montgomery
MONTOURSVILLE Lycoming
MONTROSE Susquehanna
MOOSIC (18507) Lackawanna(98), Luzerne(1)
MORANN Clearfield
MORGAN Allegheny
MORGANTOWN (19543) Berks(78), Lancaster(17), Chester(3)
MORRIS (16938) Tioga(67), Lycoming(32)
MORRIS RUN Tioga
MORRISDALE Clearfield
MORRISVILLE Bucks
MORTON Delaware
MOSCOW (18444) Lackawanna(93), Wayne(6)
MOSHANNON Centre
MOUNT AETNA Berks
MOUNT BETHEL Northampton
MOUNT BRADDOCK Fayette
MOUNT CARMEL Northumberland
MOUNT GRETNA Lebanon
MOUNT HOLLY SPRINGS Cumberland
MOUNT JEWETT McKean
MOUNT JOY Lancaster
MOUNT MORRIS Greene
MOUNT PLEASANT (15666) Westmoreland(83), Fayette(16)
MOUNT PLEASANT MILLS (17853) Snyder(86), Juniata(13)
MOUNT POCONO Monroe
MOUNT UNION (17066) Huntingdon(70), Mifflin(29)
MOUNT WOLF York
MOUNTAIN TOP Luzerne
MOUNTAINHOME Monroe
MOUNTVILLE Lancaster
MUIR Schuylkill
MUNCY (17756) Lycoming(89), Northumberland(8), Montour(1)
MUNCY VALLEY (17758) Sullivan(65), Lycoming(34)
MUNSON (16860) Clearfield(76), Centre(23)
MURRYSVILLE (15668) Westmoreland(97), Allegheny(2)
MUSE Washington
MYERSTOWN (17067) Lebanon(81), Berks(18)
NANTICOKE Luzerne
NANTY GLO Cambria
NARBERTH Montgomery
NARVON (17555) Lancaster(96), Berks(2), Chester(1)
NATRONA HEIGHTS Allegheny
NAZARETH Northampton
NEEDMORE Fulton
NEELYTON Huntingdon
NEFFS Lehigh
NELSON Tioga
NEMACOLIN Greene
NESCOPECK (18635) Luzerne(74), Columbia(25)
NESQUEHONING (18240) Carbon(85), Schuylkill(14)
NEW ALBANY (18833) Bradford(89), Sullivan(10)
NEW ALEXANDRIA Westmoreland
NEW BALTIMORE Somerset
NEW BEDFORD Lawrence
NEW BERLIN Union
NEW BERLINVILLE Berks
NEW BETHLEHEM (16242) Clarion(92), Armstrong(7)
NEW BLOOMFIELD Perry
NEW BRIGHTON Beaver
NEW BUFFALO Perry
NEW CASTLE Lawrence
NEW COLUMBIA Union
NEW CUMBERLAND (17070) Cumberland(55), York(44)
NEW DERRY Westmoreland
NEW EAGLE Washington
NEW ENTERPRISE Bedford
NEW FLORENCE (15944) Indiana(63), Westmoreland(36)
NEW FREEDOM York
NEW FREEPORT Greene
NEW GALILEE (16141) Lawrence(70), Beaver(29)
NEW GENEVA Fayette
NEW GERMANTOWN Perry
NEW HOLLAND Lancaster
NEW HOPE Bucks
NEW KENSINGTON (15068) Westmoreland(91), Allegheny(8)
NEW KENSINGTON Westmoreland
NEW KINGSTOWN Cumberland
NEW LONDON Chester
NEW MILFORD Susquehanna
NEW MILLPORT Clearfield
NEW OXFORD Adams
NEW PARIS Bedford
NEW PARK York
NEW PHILADELPHIA Schuylkill
NEW PROVIDENCE Lancaster
NEW RINGGOLD Schuylkill
NEW SALEM Fayette
NEW STANTON Westmoreland
NEW TRIPOLI Lehigh
NEW WILMINGTON (16142) Lawrence(69), Mercer(30)
NEW WILMINGTON Lawrence
NEWBURG (17240) Cumberland(68), Franklin(31)
NEWELL Fayette
NEWFOUNDLAND (18445) Wayne(81), Pike(18)
NEWMANSTOWN (17073) Lebanon(93), Lancaster(6)
NEWPORT Perry
NEWRY Blair
NEWTON HAMILTON Mifflin
NEWTOWN Bucks
NEWTOWN SQUARE (19073) Delaware(97), Chester(2)
NEWVILLE Cumberland
NICHOLSON (18446) Wyoming(54), Susquehanna(42), Lackawanna(2)
NICKTOWN Cambria
NINEVEH Greene
NISBET Lycoming
NORMALVILLE Fayette
NORRISTOWN Chester
NORRISTOWN Montgomery
NORTH APOLLO Armstrong
NORTH BEND Clinton
NORTH EAST Erie
NORTH SPRINGFIELD Erie
NORTH VERSAILLES Allegheny
NORTH WALES (19454) Montgomery(81), Bucks(18)
NORTH WALES Montgomery
NORTH WASHINGTON Butler
NORTHAMPTON Northampton
NORTHPOINT Indiana
NORTHUMBERLAND Northumberland
NORVELT Westmoreland
NORWOOD Delaware
NOTTINGHAM (19362) Chester(98), Lancaster(1)
NOXEN (18636) Wyoming(84), Luzerne(15)
NU MINE Armstrong
NUANGOLA Luzerne
NUMIDIA Columbia
NUREMBERG (18241) Luzerne(56), Schuylkill(43)
OAK RIDGE Armstrong
OAKDALE Allegheny
OAKLAND MILLS Juniata
OAKMONT Allegheny
OAKS Montgomery
OHIOPYLE Fayette
OIL CITY Venango
OLANTA Clearfield
OLD FORGE Lackawanna
OLD ZIONSVILLE Lehigh
OLEY Berks
OLIVEBURG Jefferson
OLIVER Fayette
OLYPHANT Lackawanna
ONEIDA Schuylkill
ONO Lebanon
ORANGEVILLE Columbia
ORBISONIA (17243) Huntingdon(98), Juniata(1)
OREFIELD Lehigh
ORELAND Montgomery
ORRSTOWN Franklin
ORRTANNA Adams
ORSON Wayne
ORVISTON Centre
ORWIGSBURG Schuylkill
OSCEOLA Tioga
OSCEOLA MILLS (16666) Clearfield(91), Centre(7), Blair(1)
OSTERBURG Bedford
OTTSVILLE Bucks
OXFORD (19363) Chester(93), Lancaster(6)
PALM (18070) Berks(54), Montgomery(45)
PALMERTON (18071) Carbon(98), Monroe(1)
PALMYRA (17078) Lebanon(94), Dauphin(5)
PAOLI Chester
PARADISE Lancaster
PARDEESVILLE Luzerne
PARKER (16049) Clarion(75), Butler(12), Armstrong(11)
PARKER FORD Chester
PARKESBURG Chester
PARKHILL Cambria
PARRYVILLE Carbon
PATTON Cambria
PAUPACK Pike
PAXINOS Northumberland
PAXTONVILLE Snyder
PEACH BOTTOM Lancaster
PEACH GLEN Adams
PECKVILLE Lackawanna
PEN ARGYL Northampton
PENFIELD Clearfield
PENN Westmoreland
PENN RUN Indiana
PENNS CREEK Snyder
PENNS PARK Bucks
PENNSBURG (18073) Montgomery(91), Bucks(8)
PENNSYLVANIA FURNACE (16865) Centre(88), Huntingdon(11)
PENRYN Lancaster
PEQUEA Lancaster
PERKASIE Bucks
PERKIOMENVILLE Montgomery
PERRYOPOLIS Fayette
PETERSBURG Huntingdon
PETROLIA Butler
PHILADELPHIA Bucks
PHILADELPHIA Delaware
PHILADELPHIA Montgomery
PHILADELPHIA Philadelphia
PHILIPSBURG (16866) Centre(60), Clearfield(39)
PHOENIXVILLE (19460) Chester(98), Montgomery(1)
PICTURE ROCKS Lycoming
PILLOW Dauphin
PINE BANK Greene
PINE FORGE Berks
PINE GROVE Schuylkill
PINE GROVE MILLS Centre
PINEVILLE Bucks
PIPERSVILLE Bucks
PITCAIRN Allegheny
PITMAN (17964) Schuylkill(94), Northumberland(5)
PITTSBURGH (15241) Allegheny(98), Washington(1)
PITTSBURGH Allegheny
PITTSFIELD Warren
PITTSTON (18641) Luzerne(93), Lackawanna(6)
PITTSTON Luzerne
PLAINFIELD Cumberland
PLEASANT HALL Franklin
PLEASANT MOUNT Wayne
PLEASANT UNITY Westmoreland
PLEASANTVILLE (16341) Venango(92), Forest(7)
PLUMSTEADVILLE Bucks
PLUMVILLE Indiana
PLYMOUTH Luzerne
PLYMOUTH MEETING Montgomery
POCONO LAKE Monroe
POCONO LAKE PRESERVE Monroe
POCONO MANOR Monroe
POCONO PINES Monroe
POCONO SUMMIT Monroe
POCOPSON Chester
POINT MARION Fayette
POINT PLEASANT Bucks
POLK (16342) Venango(97), Mercer(2)
POMEROY Chester
PORT ALLEGANY (16743) McKean(95), Potter(4)
PORT CARBON Schuylkill
PORT CLINTON Schuylkill
PORT MATILDA Centre
PORT ROYAL Juniata
PORT TREVORTON Snyder
PORTAGE (15946) Cambria(94), Blair(2), Bedford(2)
PORTERS SIDELING York
PORTERSVILLE (16051) Butler(81), Lawrence(18)
PORTLAND Northampton
POTTERSDALE (16871) Clearfield(87), Clinton(12)
POTTS GROVE Northumberland
POTTSTOWN Chester
POTTSTOWN Montgomery
POTTSVILLE Schuylkill
POYNTELLE Wayne
PRESTO Allegheny
PRESTON PARK Wayne
PRICEDALE Westmoreland
PROMPTON Wayne
PROSPECT Butler
PROSPECT PARK Delaware
PROSPERITY (15329) Washington(88), Greene(11)
PULASKI (16143) Lawrence(89), Mercer(10)
PUNXSUTAWNEY (15767) Jefferson(91), Indiana(7), Clearfield(1)
QUAKAKE Schuylkill
QUAKERTOWN Bucks
QUARRYVILLE Lancaster
QUECREEK Somerset

QUEEN Bedford
QUENTIN Lebanon
QUINCY Franklin
RAILROAD York
RALSTON Lycoming
RAMEY Clearfield
RANSOM Lackawanna
RAVINE Schuylkill
REA Washington
READING Berks
REAMSTOWN Lancaster
REBERSBURG Centre
REBUCK Northumberland
RECTOR Westmoreland
RED HILL Montgomery
RED LION York
REEDERS Monroe
REEDSVILLE Mifflin
REFTON Lancaster
REHRERSBURG Berks
REINHOLDS (17569) Lancaster(80), Berks(19)
RENFREW Butler
RENO Venango
RENOVO Clinton
REPUBLIC Fayette
REVERE Bucks
REVLOC Cambria
REW McKean
REXMONT Lebanon
REYNOLDSVILLE Jefferson
RHEEMS Lancaster
RICES LANDING Greene
RICEVILLE Crawford
RICHBORO Bucks
RICHEYVILLE Washington
RICHFIELD (17086) Juniata(60), Snyder(39)
RICHLAND (17087) Lebanon(54), Berks(45)
RICHLANDTOWN Bucks
RIDDLESBURG Bedford
RIDGWAY (15853) Elk(96), Jefferson(3)
RIDLEY PARK Delaware
RIEGELSVILLE (18077) Bucks(90), Northampton(9)
RILLTON Westmoreland
RIMERSBURG Clarion
RINGGOLD Jefferson
RINGTOWN Schuylkill
RIVERSIDE Northumberland
RIXFORD McKean
ROARING BRANCH (17765) Tioga(57), Lycoming(41)
ROARING SPRING (16673) Blair(68), Bedford(31)
ROBERTSDALE (16674) Huntingdon(98), Fulton(1)
ROBESONIA (19551) Berks(93), Lebanon(4), Lancaster(2)
ROBINSON Indiana
ROCHESTER Beaver
ROCHESTER MILLS Indiana
ROCK GLEN Luzerne
ROCKHILL FURNACE Huntingdon
ROCKTON Clearfield
ROCKWOOD Somerset
ROGERSVILLE Greene
ROME Bradford
RONCO Fayette
RONKS Lancaster
ROSCOE Washington
ROSSITER (15772) Indiana(98), Jefferson(1)
ROSSVILLE York
ROULETTE Potter
ROUSEVILLE Venango
ROUZERVILLE Franklin
ROWLAND Pike
ROXBURY Franklin
ROYERSFORD Montgomery
RUFFS DALE Westmoreland
RURAL RIDGE Allegheny
RURAL VALLEY Armstrong
RUSHLAND Bucks
RUSHVILLE Susquehanna
RUSSELL Warren
RUSSELLTON Allegheny
SABINSVILLE (16943) Potter(56), Tioga(43)
SACRAMENTO Schuylkill
SADSBURYVILLE Chester
SAEGERTOWN Crawford
SAGAMORE Armstrong
SAINT BENEDICT Cambria
SAINT BONIFACE Cambria
SAINT CLAIR Schuylkill
SAINT JOHNS Luzerne
SAINT MARYS Elk
SAINT MICHAEL Cambria
SAINT PETERS Chester
SAINT PETERSBURG Clarion
SAINT THOMAS Franklin
SALFORD Montgomery
SALFORDVILLE Montgomery
SALINA Westmoreland
SALISBURY Somerset
SALIX Cambria
SALONA Clinton
SALTILLO Huntingdon
SALTSBURG (15681) Indiana(70), Westmoreland(29)
SANDY LAKE Mercer
SANDY RIDGE Centre
SARVER (16055) Butler(94), Armstrong(4)
SASSAMANSVILLE Montgomery
SAXONBURG Butler
SAXTON (16678) Bedford(94), Huntingdon(5)
SAYLORSBURG Monroe
SAYRE Bradford
SCENERY HILL Washington
SCHAEFFERSTOWN Lebanon
SCHELLSBURG Bedford
SCHENLEY Armstrong
SCHNECKSVILLE Lehigh
SCHUYLKILL HAVEN Schuylkill
SCHWENKSVILLE Montgomery
SCIOTA Monroe
SCOTLAND Franklin
SCOTRUN Monroe
SCOTTDALE (15683) Westmoreland(88), Fayette(11)
SCRANTON Lackawanna
SEANOR Somerset
SELINSGROVE (17870) Snyder(97), Union(2)
SELLERSVILLE Bucks
SELTZER Schuylkill
SEMINOLE Armstrong
SENECA Venango
SEVEN VALLEYS York
SEWARD (15954) Indiana(72), Westmoreland(27)
SEWICKLEY (15143) Allegheny(94), Beaver(5)
SEWICKLEY Allegheny
SHADE GAP Huntingdon
SHADY GROVE Franklin
SHAMOKIN Northumberland
SHAMOKIN DAM Snyder
SHANKSVILLE Somerset
SHARON Mercer
SHARON HILL Delaware
SHARPSVILLE Mercer
SHARTLESVILLE Berks
SHAVERTOWN Luzerne
SHAWANESE Luzerne
SHAWNEE ON DELAWARE Monroe
SHAWVILLE Clearfield
SHEAKLEYVILLE Mercer
SHEFFIELD (16347) Warren(84), Forest(15)
SHELOCTA (15774) Indiana(51), Armstrong(48)
SHENANDOAH Schuylkill
SHEPPTON Schuylkill
SHERMANS DALE (17090) Perry(98), Cumberland(1)
SHICKSHINNY (18655) Luzerne(92), Columbia(7)
SHINGLEHOUSE (16748) McKean(56), Potter(43)
SHIPPENSBURG (17257) Cumberland(62), Franklin(37)
SHIPPENVILLE Clarion
SHIPPINGPORT Beaver
SHIRLEYSBURG Huntingdon
SHOEMAKERSVILLE Berks
SHOHOLA Pike
SHREWSBURY York
SHUNK Sullivan
SIDMAN Cambria
SIGEL (15860) Jefferson(65), Elk(30), Clarion(3)
SILVER SPRING Lancaster
SILVERDALE Bucks
SINNAMAHONING Cameron
SIPESVILLE Somerset
SIX MILE RUN Bedford
SKIPPACK Montgomery
SKYTOP Monroe
SLATE RUN Lycoming
SLATEDALE Lehigh
SLATINGTON Lehigh
SLICKVILLE Westmoreland
SLIGO Clarion
SLIPPERY ROCK (16057) Butler(78), Lawrence(19), Mercer(2)
SLOVAN Washington
SMETHPORT McKean
SMICKSBURG (16256) Indiana(98), Jefferson(1)
SMITHFIELD Fayette
SMITHMILL Clearfield
SMITHTON Westmoreland
SMOCK Fayette
SMOKERUN Clearfield
SMOKETOWN Lancaster
SNOW SHOE Centre
SNYDERSBURG Clarion
SNYDERTOWN Northumberland
SOLEBURY Bucks
SONESTOWN Sullivan
SOUDERSBURG Lancaster
SOUDERTON (18964) Montgomery(95), Bucks(4)
SOUTH CANAAN Wayne
SOUTH FORK Cambria
SOUTH GIBSON Susquehanna
SOUTH HEIGHTS Beaver
SOUTH MONTROSE Susquehanna
SOUTH MOUNTAIN Franklin
SOUTH PARK Allegheny
SOUTH STERLING Wayne
SOUTHAMPTON Bucks
SOUTHEASTERN Chester
SOUTHVIEW Washington
SOUTHWEST Westmoreland
SPANGLER Cambria
SPARTANSBURG (16434) Crawford(96), Warren(3)
SPINNERSTOWN Bucks
SPRAGGS Greene
SPRANKLE MILLS Jefferson
SPRING CHURCH Armstrong
SPRING CITY Chester
SPRING CREEK Warren
SPRING GLEN (17978) Schuylkill(98), Dauphin(1)
SPRING GROVE York
SPRING HOUSE Montgomery
SPRING MILLS Centre
SPRING MOUNT Montgomery
SPRING RUN Franklin
SPRINGBORO Crawford
SPRINGDALE Allegheny
SPRINGFIELD Delaware
SPRINGS Somerset
SPRINGTOWN Bucks
SPRINGVILLE (18844) Susquehanna(98), Wyoming(1)
SPROUL Blair
SPRUCE CREEK Huntingdon
STAHLSTOWN Westmoreland
STAR JUNCTION Fayette
STARFORD Indiana
STARLIGHT Wayne
STARRUCCA (18462) Wayne(97), Susquehanna(2)
STATE COLLEGE Centre
STATE LINE Franklin
STEELVILLE Chester
STERLING (18463) Pike(63), Wayne(36)
STEVENS Lancaster
STEVENSVILLE Bradford
STEWARTSTOWN York
STILLWATER (17878) Columbia(74), Luzerne(25)
STOCKDALE Washington
STOCKERTOWN Northampton
STONEBORO (16153) Mercer(88), Venango(11)
STONY RUN Berks
STOYSTOWN Somerset
STRABANE Washington
STRASBURG Lancaster
STRATTANVILLE Clarion
STRAUSSTOWN Berks
STRONGSTOWN (15957) Indiana(60), Cambria(40)
STROUDSBURG Monroe
STUMP CREEK Jefferson
STURGEON Allegheny
SUGAR GROVE Warren
SUGAR RUN Bradford
SUGARLOAF Luzerne
SUMMERDALE Cumberland
SUMMERHILL Cambria
SUMMERVILLE (15864) Jefferson(64), Clarion(35)
SUMMIT HILL Carbon
SUMMIT STATION Schuylkill
SUMNEYTOWN Montgomery
SUNBURY Northumberland
SUPLEE Chester
SUSQUEHANNA (18847) Susquehanna(97), Wayne(2)
SUTERSVILLE Westmoreland
SWARTHMORE Delaware
SWEET VALLEY Luzerne
SWENGEL Union
SWIFTWATER Monroe
SYBERTSVILLE Luzerne
SYCAMORE Greene
SYKESVILLE (15865) Jefferson(94), Clearfield(5)
SYLVANIA Bradford
TAFTON Pike
TALMAGE Lancaster
TAMAQUA Schuylkill
TAMIMENT Pike
TANNERSVILLE Monroe
TARENTUM Allegheny
TARRS Westmoreland
TATAMY Northampton
TAYLOR Lackawanna
TAYLORSTOWN Washington
TELFORD (18969) Montgomery(60), Bucks(39)
TEMPLE Berks
TEMPLETON Armstrong
TERRE HILL Lancaster
THOMASVILLE York
THOMPSON (18465) Susquehanna(86), Wayne(13)
THOMPSONTOWN Juniata

THORNDALE Chester
THORNTON Delaware
THREE SPRINGS (17264) Huntingdon(96), Fulton(3)
TIDIOUTE (16351) Warren(95), Forest(4)
TIMBLIN Jefferson
TIOGA Tioga
TIONA Warren
TIONESTA (16353) Clarion(72), Forest(15), Venango(11)
TIPTON Blair
TIRE HILL Somerset
TITUSVILLE (16354) Crawford(64), Venango(34)
TOBYHANNA Monroe
TODD Huntingdon
TOPTON Berks
TORRANCE Westmoreland
TOUGHKENAMON Chester
TOWANDA Bradford
TOWER CITY Schuylkill
TOWNVILLE Crawford
TRAFFORD (15085) Westmoreland(98), Allegheny(1)
TRANSFER Mercer
TREICHLERS Northampton
TREMONT Schuylkill
TRESCKOW Carbon
TREVORTON Northumberland
TREXLERTOWN Lehigh
TROUT RUN Lycoming
TROUTVILLE Clearfield
TROXELVILLE Snyder
TROY (16947) Bradford(92), Tioga(7)
TRUMBAUERSVILLE Bucks
TUNKHANNOCK Wyoming
TURBOTVILLE (17772) Northumberland(55), Montour(44)
TURKEY CITY Clarion
TURTLE CREEK Allegheny
TURTLEPOINT McKean
TUSCARORA Schuylkill
TWIN ROCKS Cambria
TYLER HILL Wayne
TYLERSBURG Clarion
TYLERSPORT Montgomery
TYLERSVILLE Clinton
TYRONE (16686) Blair(73), Huntingdon(20), Centre(6)
ULEDI Fayette
ULSTER Bradford
ULYSSES Potter
UNION CITY (16438) Crawford(55), Erie(44)
UNION DALE (18470) Susquehanna(92), Wayne(7)
UNIONTOWN Fayette
UNIONVILLE Chester
UNITED Westmoreland
UNITY HOUSE Pike
UNITYVILLE (17774) Lycoming(98), Columbia(1)
UNIVERSITY PARK Centre
UPPER BLACK EDDY Bucks
UPPER DARBY Delaware
UPPERSTRASBURG Franklin
URSINA Somerset
UTICA (16362) Venango(86), Mercer(11), Crawford(1)
UWCHLAND Chester
VALENCIA (16059) Butler(92), Allegheny(7)
VALIER Jefferson
VALLEY FORGE Chester
VALLEY FORGE Montgomery
VALLEY VIEW Schuylkill
VAN VOORHIS Washington
VANDERBILT Fayette
VANDERGRIFT (15690) Westmoreland(55), Armstrong(44)
VENANGO Crawford
VENETIA Washington
VENUS (16364) Venango(69), Clarion(30)
VERONA Allegheny
VESTABURG Washington
VICKSBURG Union
VILLA MARIA Lawrence
VILLANOVA (19085) Delaware(56), Montgomery(43)
VINTONDALE (15961) Indiana(90), Cambria(9)
VIRGINVILLE Berks
VOLANT (16156) Lawrence(88), Mercer(11)
VOWINCKEL (16260) Clarion(95), Forest(4)
WAGONTOWN Chester
WALLACETON Clearfield
WALLINGFORD Delaware
WALNUT BOTTOM Cumberland
WALNUTPORT Northampton
WALSTON Jefferson
WALTERSBURG Fayette
WAMPUM (16157) Lawrence(92), Beaver(7)
WAPWALLOPEN Luzerne
WARFORDSBURG Fulton
WARMINSTER Bucks
WARREN Warren
WARREN CENTER Bradford
WARRENDALE Allegheny
WARRINGTON Bucks
WARRIORS MARK (16877) Huntingdon(50), Centre(49)
WASHINGTON BORO Lancaster
WASHINGTON CROSSING Bucks
WASHINGTONVILLE Montour
WATERFALL Fulton
WATERFORD (16441) Erie(95), Crawford(4)
WATERVILLE Lycoming
WATSONTOWN (17777) Northumberland(98), Montour(1)
WATTSBURG Erie
WAVERLY Lackawanna
WAYMART Wayne
WAYNE (19087) Delaware(49), Chester(40), Montgomery(9)
WAYNE Delaware
WAYNESBORO Franklin
WAYNESBURG Greene
WEATHERLY (18255) Carbon(96), Luzerne(3)
WEBSTER Westmoreland
WEEDVILLE Elk
WEIKERT Union
WELLERSBURG Somerset
WELLS TANNERY Fulton
WELLSBORO Tioga
WELLSVILLE York
WENDEL Westmoreland
WERNERSVILLE Berks
WEST ALEXANDER Washington
WEST CHESTER Chester
WEST DECATUR Clearfield
WEST ELIZABETH Allegheny
WEST FINLEY (15377) Washington(90), Greene(9)
WEST GROVE Chester
WEST HICKORY Forest
WEST LEBANON Indiana
WEST LEISENRING Fayette
WEST MIDDLESEX (16159) Mercer(80), Lawrence(19)
WEST MIDDLETOWN Washington
WEST MIFFLIN Allegheny
WEST MILTON Union
WEST NEWTON (15089) Westmoreland(97), Allegheny(2)
WEST PITTSBURG Lawrence
WEST POINT Montgomery
WEST SALISBURY Somerset
WEST SPRINGFIELD Erie
WEST SUNBURY Butler
WEST WILLOW Lancaster
WESTFIELD Tioga
WESTLAND Washington
WESTLINE McKean
WESTMORELAND CITY Westmoreland
WESTON Luzerne
WESTOVER Clearfield
WESTPORT Clinton
WESTTOWN Chester
WEXFORD Allegheny
WHEATLAND Mercer
WHITE Fayette
WHITE DEER Union
WHITE HAVEN (18661) Luzerne(91), Carbon(8)
WHITE MILLS Wayne
WHITEHALL Lehigh
WHITNEY Westmoreland
WICKHAVEN Fayette
WICONISCO Dauphin
WIDNOON Armstrong
WILBURTON Columbia
WILCOX (15870) Elk(94), McKean(5)
WILDWOOD Allegheny
WILKES BARRE Luzerne
WILLIAMSBURG (16693) Blair(93), Huntingdon(6)
WILLIAMSON Franklin
WILLIAMSPORT Lycoming
WILLIAMSTOWN Dauphin
WILLOW GROVE Montgomery
WILLOW HILL Franklin
WILLOW STREET Lancaster
WILMERDING Allegheny
WILMORE Cambria
WINBURNE Clearfield
WIND GAP Northampton
WIND RIDGE Greene
WINDBER (15963) Somerset(85), Cambria(14)
WINDSOR York
WINFIELD (17889) Union(82), Snyder(17)
WITMER Lancaster
WOMELSDORF Berks
WOOD Bedford
WOODBURY Bedford
WOODLAND Clearfield
WOODLYN Delaware
WOODWARD Centre
WOOLRICH Clinton
WORCESTER Montgomery
WORTHINGTON Armstrong
WORTHVILLE Jefferson
WOXALL Montgomery
WRIGHTSVILLE York
WYALUSING Bradford
WYANO Westmoreland
WYCOMBE Bucks
WYNCOTE Montgomery
WYNNEWOOD (19096) Montgomery(95), Delaware(4)
WYOMING Luzerne
WYSOX Bradford
YATESBORO Armstrong
YEAGERTOWN Mifflin
YORK HAVEN York
YORK NEW SALEM York
YORK SPRINGS (17372) Adams(96), York(2)
YOUNGSTOWN Westmoreland
YOUNGSVILLE Warren
YOUNGWOOD Westmoreland
YUKON Westmoreland
ZELIENOPLE (16063) Butler(83), Beaver(16)
ZIEGLERVILLE Montgomery
ZION GROVE (17985) Schuylkill(97), Columbia(2)
ZIONHILL Bucks
ZIONSVILLE (18092) Lehigh(94), Berks(5)
ZULLINGER Franklin

Pennsylvania ZIP/City Cross Reference

15001-15001 ALIQUIPPA
15003-15003 AMBRIDGE
15004-15004 ATLASBURG
15005-15005 BADEN
15006-15006 BAIRDFORD
15007-15007 BAKERSTOWN
15009-15009 BEAVER
15010-15010 BEAVER FALLS
15012-15012 BELLE VERNON
15014-15014 BRACKENRIDGE
15015-15015 BRADFORDWOODS
15017-15017 BRIDGEVILLE
15018-15018 BUENA VISTA
15019-15019 BULGER
15020-15020 BUNOLA
15021-15021 BURGETTSTOWN
15022-15022 CHARLEROI
15024-15024 CHESWICK
15025-15025 CLAIRTON
15026-15026 CLINTON
15027-15027 CONWAY
15028-15028 COULTERS
15029-15029 COURTNEY
15030-15030 CREIGHTON
15031-15031 CUDDY
15032-15032 CURTISVILLE
15033-15033 DONORA
15034-15034 DRAVOSBURG
15035-15035 EAST MC KEESPORT
15036-15036 ELDERSVILLE
15037-15037 ELIZABETH
15038-15038 ELRAMA
15042-15042 FREEDOM
15043-15043 GEORGETOWN
15044-15044 GIBSONIA
15045-15045 GLASSPORT
15046-15046 GLENWILLARD
15046-15046 CRESCENT
15047-15047 GREENOCK
15049-15049 HARWICK
15050-15050 HOOKSTOWN
15051-15051 INDIANOLA
15052-15052 INDUSTRY
15053-15053 JOFFRE
15054-15054 LANGELOTH
15055-15055 LAWRENCE
15056-15056 LEETSDALE
15057-15057 MC DONALD
15059-15059 MIDLAND
15060-15060 MIDWAY
15061-15061 MONACA
15062-15062 MONESSEN
15063-15063 MONONGAHELA
15064-15064 MORGAN
15065-15065 NATRONA HEIGHTS
15066-15066 NEW BRIGHTON
15067-15067 NEW EAGLE
15068-15069 NEW KENSINGTON
15071-15071 OAKDALE
15072-15072 PRICEDALE
15074-15074 ROCHESTER
15075-15075 RURAL RIDGE
15076-15076 RUSSELLTON
15077-15077 SHIPPINGPORT
15078-15078 SLOVAN
15081-15081 SOUTH HEIGHTS
15082-15082 STURGEON
15083-15083 SUTERSVILLE
15084-15084 TARENTUM
15085-15085 TRAFFORD
15086-15086 WARRENDALE
15087-15087 WEBSTER
15088-15088 WEST ELIZABETH
15089-15089 WEST NEWTON
15090-15090 WEXFORD
15091-15091 WILDWOOD
15095-15096 WARRENDALE
15101-15101 ALLISON PARK
15102-15102 BETHEL PARK
15104-15104 BRADDOCK
15106-15106 CARNEGIE
15108-15108 CORAOPOLIS
15110-15110 DUQUESNE
15112-15112 EAST PITTSBURGH
15116-15116 GLENSHAW
15120-15120 HOMESTEAD
15122-15123 WEST MIFFLIN
15126-15126 IMPERIAL
15127-15127 INGOMAR
15129-15129 LIBRARY
15129-15129 SOUTH PARK
15130-15135 MC KEESPORT
15136-15136 MC KEES ROCKS
15137-15137 NORTH VERSAILLES
15139-15139 OAKMONT
15140-15140 PITCAIRN
15142-15142 PRESTO
15143-15143 SEWICKLEY
15144-15144 SPRINGDALE
15145-15145 TURTLE CREEK
15146-15146 MONROEVILLE
15147-15147 VERONA
15148-15148 WILMERDING
15189-15189 SEWICKLEY
15200-15295 PITTSBURGH
15301-15301 WASHINGTON
15310-15310 ALEPPO
15311-15311 AMITY
15312-15312 AVELLA
15313-15313 BEALLSVILLE
15314-15314 BENTLEYVILLE
15315-15315 BOBTOWN
15316-15316 BRAVE
15317-15317 CANONSBURG
15320-15320 CARMICHAELS
15321-15321 CECIL
15322-15322 CLARKSVILLE
15323-15323 CLAYSVILLE
15324-15324 COKEBURG
15325-15325 CRUCIBLE
15327-15327 DILLINER
15329-15329 PROSPERITY
15330-15330 EIGHTY FOUR
15331-15331 ELLSWORTH
15332-15332 FINLEYVILLE
15333-15333 FREDERICKTOWN
15334-15334 GARARDS FORT
15336-15336 GASTONVILLE
15337-15337 GRAYSVILLE
15338-15338 GREENSBORO
15339-15339 HENDERSONVILLE
15340-15340 HICKORY
15341-15341 HOLBROOK
15342-15342 HOUSTON
15344-15344 JEFFERSON
15345-15345 MARIANNA
15346-15346 MATHER
15347-15347 MEADOW LANDS
15348-15348 MILLSBORO
15349-15349 MOUNT MORRIS
15350-15350 MUSE
15351-15351 NEMACOLIN
15352-15352 NEW FREEPORT
15353-15353 NINEVEH
15354-15354 PINE BANK
15356-15356 REA
15357-15357 RICES LANDING
15358-15358 RICHEYVILLE
15359-15359 ROGERSVILLE
15360-15360 SCENERY HILL
15361-15361 SOUTHVIEW
15362-15362 SPRAGGS
15363-15363 STRABANE
15364-15364 SYCAMORE
15365-15365 TAYLORSTOWN
15366-15366 VAN VOORHIS
15367-15367 VENETIA
15368-15368 VESTABURG
15370-15370 WAYNESBURG
15376-15376 WEST ALEXANDER
15377-15377 WEST FINLEY
15378-15378 WESTLAND
15379-15379 WEST MIDDLETOWN
15380-15380 WIND RIDGE
15401-15401 UNIONTOWN
15410-15410 ADAH
15411-15411 ADDISON
15412-15412 ALLENPORT
15413-15413 ALLISON
15415-15415 BRIER HILL
15416-15416 BROWNFIELD
15417-15417 BROWNSVILLE
15419-15419 CALIFORNIA
15420-15420 CARDALE
15421-15421 CHALKHILL
15421-15421 CHALK HILL
15422-15422 CHESTNUT RIDGE
15423-15423 COAL CENTER
15424-15424 CONFLUENCE
15425-15425 CONNELLSVILLE
15427-15427 DAISYTOWN
15428-15428 DAWSON
15429-15429 DENBO
15430-15430 DICKERSON RUN
15431-15431 DUNBAR
15432-15432 DUNLEVY
15433-15433 EAST MILLSBORO
15434-15434 ELCO
15435-15435 FAIRBANK
15436-15436 FAIRCHANCE
15437-15437 FARMINGTON
15438-15438 FAYETTE CITY
15439-15439 GANS
15440-15440 GIBBON GLADE
15442-15442 GRINDSTONE
15443-15443 HIBBS
15444-15444 HILLER
15445-15445 HOPWOOD
15446-15446 INDIAN HEAD
15447-15447 ISABELLA
15448-15448 JACOBS CREEK
15449-15449 KEISTERVILLE
15450-15450 LA BELLE
15451-15451 LAKE LYNN
15454-15454 LECKRONE
15455-15455 LEISENRING
15456-15456 LEMONT FURNACE
15458-15458 MC CLELLANDTOWN
15459-15459 MARKLEYSBURG
15460-15460 MARTIN
15461-15461 MASONTOWN
15462-15462 MELCROFT
15463-15463 MERRITTSTOWN
15464-15464 MILL RUN
15465-15465 MOUNT BRADDOCK
15466-15466 NEWELL
15467-15467 NEW GENEVA
15468-15468 NEW SALEM
15469-15469 NORMALVILLE
15470-15470 OHIOPYLE
15472-15472 OLIVER
15473-15473 PERRYOPOLIS
15474-15474 POINT MARION
15475-15475 REPUBLIC
15476-15476 RONCO
15477-15477 ROSCOE
15478-15478 SMITHFIELD
15479-15479 SMITHTON
15480-15480 SMOCK
15482-15482 STAR JUNCTION
15483-15483 STOCKDALE
15484-15484 ULEDI
15485-15485 URSINA
15486-15486 VANDERBILT
15488-15488 WALTERSBURG
15489-15489 WEST LEISENRING
15490-15490 WHITE
15492-15492 WICKHAVEN
15501-15501 SOMERSET
15502-15502 HIDDEN VALLEY
15510-15510 SOMERSET
15520-15520 ACOSTA
15521-15521 ALUM BANK
15522-15522 BEDFORD
15530-15530 BERLIN
15531-15531 BOSWELL
15532-15532 BOYNTON
15533-15533 BREEZEWOOD
15534-15534 BUFFALO MILLS
15535-15535 CLEARVILLE
15536-15536 CRYSTAL SPRING
15537-15537 EVERETT
15538-15538 FAIRHOPE
15539-15539 FISHERTOWN
15540-15540 FORT HILL
15541-15541 FRIEDENS
15542-15542 GARRETT
15544-15544 GRAY
15545-15545 HYNDMAN
15546-15546 JENNERS
15547-15547 JENNERSTOWN
15548-15548 KANTNER
15549-15549 LISTIE
15550-15550 MANNS CHOICE
15551-15551 MARKLETON
15552-15552 MEYERSDALE
15553-15553 NEW BALTIMORE
15554-15554 NEW PARIS
15555-15555 QUECREEK
15557-15557 ROCKWOOD
15558-15558 SALISBURY
15559-15559 SCHELLSBURG
15560-15560 SHANKSVILLE
15561-15561 SIPESVILLE
15562-15562 SPRINGS
15563-15563 STOYSTOWN
15564-15564 WELLERSBURG
15565-15565 WEST SALISBURY
15601-15606 GREENSBURG
15610-15610 ACME
15611-15611 ADAMSBURG
15612-15612 ALVERTON
15613-15613 APOLLO
15615-15615 ARDARA
15616-15616 ARMBRUST
15617-15617 ARONA
15618-15618 AVONMORE
15619-15619 BOVARD
15620-15620 BRADENVILLE
15621-15621 CALUMET
15622-15622 CHAMPION
15623-15623 CLARIDGE
15624-15624 CRABTREE
15625-15625 DARRAGH
15626-15626 DELMONT
15627-15627 DERRY
15628-15628 DONEGAL
15629-15629 EAST VANDERGRIFT
15630-15630 EDMON
15631-15631 EVERSON
15632-15632 EXPORT
15633-15633 FORBES ROAD
15634-15634 GRAPEVILLE
15635-15635 HANNASTOWN
15636-15636 HARRISON CITY
15637-15637 HERMINIE
15638-15638 HOSTETTER
15639-15639 HUNKER
15640-15640 HUTCHINSON
15641-15641 HYDE PARK
15642-15642 IRWIN
15644-15644 JEANNETTE
15646-15646 JONES MILLS
15647-15647 LARIMER
15650-15650 LATROBE
15655-15655 LAUGHLINTOWN

15656-15656 LEECHBURG
15658-15658 LIGONIER
15660-15660 LOWBER
15661-15661 LOYALHANNA
15662-15662 LUXOR
15663-15663 MADISON
15664-15664 MAMMOTH
15665-15665 MANOR
15666-15666 MOUNT PLEASANT
15668-15668 MURRYSVILLE
15670-15670 NEW ALEXANDRIA
15671-15671 NEW DERRY
15672-15672 NEW STANTON
15673-15673 NORTH APOLLO
15674-15674 NORVELT
15675-15675 PENN
15676-15676 PLEASANT UNITY
15677-15677 RECTOR
15678-15678 RILLTON
15679-15679 RUFFS DALE
15680-15680 SALINA
15681-15681 SALTSBURG
15682-15682 SCHENLEY
15683-15683 SCOTTDALE
15684-15684 SLICKVILLE
15685-15685 SOUTHWEST
15686-15686 SPRING CHURCH
15687-15687 STAHLSTOWN
15688-15688 TARRS
15689-15689 UNITED
15690-15690 VANDERGRIFT
15691-15691 WENDEL
15692-15692 WESTMORELAND CITY
15693-15693 WHITNEY
15695-15695 WYANO
15696-15696 YOUNGSTOWN
15697-15697 YOUNGWOOD
15698-15698 YUKON
15701-15705 INDIANA
15710-15710 ALVERDA
15711-15711 ANITA
15712-15712 ARCADIA
15713-15713 AULTMAN
15714-15714 BARNESBORO
15715-15715 BIG RUN
15716-15716 BLACK LICK
15717-15717 BLAIRSVILLE
15720-15720 BRUSH VALLEY
15721-15721 BURNSIDE
15722-15722 CARROLLTOWN
15723-15723 CHAMBERSVILLE
15724-15724 CHERRY TREE
15725-15725 CLARKSBURG
15727-15727 CLUNE
15728-15728 CLYMER
15729-15729 COMMODORE
15730-15730 COOLSPRING
15731-15731 CORAL
15732-15732 CREEKSIDE
15733-15733 DE LANCEY
15734-15734 DIXONVILLE
15736-15736 ELDERTON
15737-15737 ELMORA
15738-15738 EMEIGH
15739-15739 ERNEST
15740-15740 FROSTBURG
15741-15741 GIPSY
15742-15742 GLEN CAMPBELL
15744-15744 HAMILTON
15745-15745 HEILWOOD
15746-15746 HILLSDALE
15747-15747 HOME
15748-15748 HOMER CITY
15750-15750 JOSEPHINE
15751-15751 JUNEAU
15752-15752 KENT
15753-15753 LA JOSE
15754-15754 LUCERNEMINES
15756-15756 MC INTYRE
15757-15757 MAHAFFEY
15758-15758 MARCHAND
15759-15759 MARION CENTER
15760-15760 MARSTELLER
15761-15761 MENTCLE
15762-15762 NICKTOWN
15763-15763 NORTHPOINT
15764-15764 OLIVEBURG
15765-15765 PENN RUN
15767-15767 PUNXSUTAWNEY
15770-15770 RINGGOLD
15771-15771 ROCHESTER MILLS
15772-15772 ROSSITER
15773-15773 SAINT BENEDICT
15774-15774 SHELOCTA
15775-15775 SPANGLER
15776-15776 SPRANKLE MILLS
15777-15777 STARFORD
15778-15778 TIMBLIN
15779-15779 TORRANCE
15780-15780 VALIER
15781-15781 WALSTON
15783-15783 WEST LEBANON
15784-15784 WORTHVILLE
15801-15801 DU BOIS
15821-15821 BENEZETT
15822-15822 BRANDY CAMP
15823-15823 BROCKPORT
15824-15824 BROCKWAY
15825-15825 BROOKVILLE
15827-15827 BYRNEDALE
15828-15828 CLARINGTON
15829-15829 CORSICA
15831-15831 DAGUS MINES
15832-15832 DRIFTWOOD
15834-15834 EMPORIUM
15840-15840 FALLS CREEK
15841-15841 FORCE
15845-15845 JOHNSONBURG
15846-15846 KERSEY
15847-15847 KNOX DALE
15848-15848 LUTHERSBURG
15849-15849 PENFIELD
15851-15851 REYNOLDSVILLE
15853-15853 RIDGWAY
15856-15856 ROCKTON
15857-15857 SAINT MARYS
15860-15860 SIGEL
15861-15861 SINNAMAHONING
15863-15863 STUMP CREEK
15864-15864 SUMMERVILLE
15865-15865 SYKESVILLE
15866-15866 TROUTVILLE
15868-15868 WEEDVILLE
15870-15870 WILCOX
15901-15915 JOHNSTOWN
15920-15920 ARMAGH
15921-15921 BEAVERDALE
15922-15922 BELSANO
15923-15923 BOLIVAR
15924-15924 CAIRNBROOK
15925-15925 CASSANDRA
15926-15926 CENTRAL CITY
15927-15927 COLVER
15928-15928 DAVIDSVILLE
15929-15929 DILLTOWN
15930-15930 DUNLO
15931-15931 EBENSBURG
15934-15934 ELTON
15935-15935 HOLLSOPPLE
15936-15936 HOOVERSVILLE
15937-15937 JEROME
15938-15938 LILLY
15940-15940 LORETTO
15942-15942 MINERAL POINT
15943-15943 NANTY GLO
15944-15944 NEW FLORENCE
15945-15945 PARKHILL
15946-15946 PORTAGE
15948-15948 REVLOC
15949-15949 ROBINSON
15951-15951 SAINT MICHAEL
15952-15952 SALIX
15953-15953 SEANOR
15954-15954 SEWARD
15955-15955 SIDMAN
15956-15956 SOUTH FORK
15957-15957 STRONGSTOWN
15958-15958 SUMMERHILL
15959-15959 TIRE HILL
15960-15960 TWIN ROCKS
15961-15961 VINTONDALE
15962-15962 WILMORE
15963-15963 WINDBER
16001-16003 BUTLER
16016-16020 BOYERS
16021-16021 BRANCHTON
16022-16022 BRUIN
16023-16023 CABOT
16024-16024 CALLERY
16025-16025 CHICORA
16027-16027 CONNOQUENESSING
16028-16028 EAST BRADY
16029-16029 EAST BUTLER
16030-16030 EAU CLAIRE
16033-16033 EVANS CITY
16034-16034 FENELTON
16035-16035 FORESTVILLE
16036-16036 FOXBURG
16037-16037 HARMONY
16038-16038 HARRISVILLE
16039-16039 HERMAN
16040-16040 HILLIARDS
16041-16041 KARNS CITY
16045-16045 LYNDORA
16046-16046 MARS
16048-16048 NORTH WASHINGTON
16049-16049 PARKER
16050-16050 PETROLIA
16051-16051 PORTERSVILLE
16052-16052 PROSPECT
16053-16053 RENFREW
16054-16054 SAINT PETERSBURG
16055-16055 SARVER
16056-16056 SAXONBURG
16057-16057 SLIPPERY ROCK
16058-16058 TURKEY CITY
16059-16059 VALENCIA
16061-16061 WEST SUNBURY
16063-16063 ZELIENOPLE
16066-16066 CRANBERRY TWP
16101-16108 NEW CASTLE
16110-16110 ADAMSVILLE
16111-16111 ATLANTIC
16112-16112 BESSEMER
16113-16113 CLARK
16114-16114 CLARKS MILLS
16115-16115 DARLINGTON
16116-16116 EDINBURG
16117-16117 ELLWOOD CITY
16120-16120 ENON VALLEY
16121-16121 FARRELL
16123-16123 FOMBELL
16124-16124 FREDONIA
16125-16125 GREENVILLE
16127-16127 GROVE CITY
16130-16130 HADLEY
16131-16131 HARTSTOWN
16132-16132 HILLSVILLE
16133-16133 JACKSON CENTER
16134-16134 JAMESTOWN
16136-16136 KOPPEL
16137-16137 MERCER
16140-16140 NEW BEDFORD
16141-16141 NEW GALILEE
16142-16142 NEW WILMINGTON
16143-16143 PULASKI
16145-16145 SANDY LAKE
16146-16146 SHARON
16148-16148 HERMITAGE
16150-16150 SHARPSVILLE
16151-16151 SHEAKLEYVILLE
16153-16153 STONEBORO
16154-16154 TRANSFER
16155-16155 VILLA MARIA
16156-16156 VOLANT
16157-16157 WAMPUM
16159-16159 WEST MIDDLESEX
16160-16160 WEST PITTSBURG
16161-16161 WHEATLAND
16172-16172 NEW WILMINGTON
16201-16201 KITTANNING
16210-16210 ADRIAN
16211-16211 BEYER
16212-16212 CADOGAN
16213-16213 CALLENSBURG
16214-16214 CLARION
16215-16215 KITTANNING
16216-16216 CLIMAX
16217-16217 COOKSBURG
16218-16218 COWANSVILLE
16220-16220 CROWN
16221-16221 CURLLSVILLE
16222-16222 DAYTON
16223-16223 DISTANT
16224-16224 FAIRMOUNT CITY
16225-16225 FISHER
16226-16226 FORD CITY
16228-16228 FORD CLIFF
16229-16229 FREEPORT
16230-16230 HAWTHORN
16232-16232 KNOX
16233-16233 LEEPER
16234-16234 LIMESTONE
16235-16235 LUCINDA
16236-16236 MC GRANN
16238-16238 MANORVILLE
16239-16239 MARIENVILLE
16240-16240 MAYPORT
16242-16242 NEW BETHLEHEM
16244-16244 NU MINE
16245-16245 OAK RIDGE
16246-16246 PLUMVILLE
16248-16248 RIMERSBURG
16249-16249 RURAL VALLEY
16250-16250 SAGAMORE
16253-16253 SEMINOLE
16254-16254 SHIPPENVILLE
16255-16255 SLIGO
16256-16256 SMICKSBURG
16257-16257 SNYDERSBURG
16258-16258 STRATTANVILLE
16259-16259 TEMPLETON
16260-16260 VOWINCKEL
16261-16261 WIDNOON
16262-16262 WORTHINGTON
16263-16263 YATESBORO
16301-16301 OIL CITY
16311-16311 CARLTON
16312-16312 CHANDLERS VALLEY
16313-16313 CLARENDON
16314-16314 COCHRANTON
16316-16316 CONNEAUT LAKE
16317-16317 COOPERSTOWN
16319-16319 CRANBERRY
16321-16321 EAST HICKORY
16322-16322 ENDEAVOR
16323-16323 FRANKLIN
16326-16326 FRYBURG
16327-16327 GUYS MILLS
16328-16328 HYDETOWN
16329-16329 IRVINE
16331-16331 KOSSUTH
16332-16332 LICKINGVILLE
16333-16333 LUDLOW
16334-16334 MARBLE
16335-16335 MEADVILLE
16340-16340 PITTSFIELD
16341-16341 PLEASANTVILLE
16342-16342 POLK
16343-16343 RENO
16344-16344 ROUSEVILLE
16345-16345 RUSSELL
16346-16346 SENECA
16347-16347 SHEFFIELD
16350-16350 SUGAR GROVE
16351-16351 TIDIOUTE
16352-16352 TIONA
16353-16353 TIONESTA

16354-16354	TITUSVILLE
16360-16360	TOWNVILLE
16361-16361	TYLERSBURG
16362-16362	UTICA
16364-16364	VENUS
16365-16367	WARREN
16368-16368	IRVINE
16368-16368	WARREN
16369-16369	IRVINE
16369-16369	WARREN
16370-16370	WEST HICKORY
16371-16371	YOUNGSVILLE
16372-16372	CLINTONVILLE
16373-16373	EMLENTON
16374-16374	KENNERDELL
16375-16375	LAMARTINE
16388-16388	MEADVILLE
16401-16401	ALBION
16402-16402	BEAR LAKE
16403-16403	CAMBRIDGE SPRINGS
16404-16404	CENTERVILLE
16405-16405	COLUMBUS
16406-16406	CONNEAUTVILLE
16407-16407	CORRY
16410-16410	CRANESVILLE
16411-16411	EAST SPRINGFIELD
16412-16412	EDINBORO
16413-16413	ELGIN
16415-16415	FAIRVIEW
16416-16416	GARLAND
16417-16417	GIRARD
16420-16420	GRAND VALLEY
16421-16421	HARBORCREEK
16422-16422	HARMONSBURG
16423-16423	LAKE CITY
16424-16424	LINESVILLE
16426-16426	MC KEAN
16427-16427	MILL VILLAGE
16428-16428	NORTH EAST
16430-16430	NORTH SPRINGFIELD
16432-16432	RICEVILLE
16433-16433	SAEGERTOWN
16434-16434	SPARTANSBURG
16435-16435	SPRINGBORO
16436-16436	SPRING CREEK
16438-16438	UNION CITY
16440-16440	VENANGO
16441-16441	WATERFORD
16442-16442	WATTSBURG
16443-16443	WEST SPRINGFIELD
16444-16444	EDINBORO
16475-16475	ALBION
16500-16565	ERIE
16566-16566	FIRST NAT BANK
16601-16603	ALTOONA
16611-16611	ALEXANDRIA
16613-16613	ASHVILLE
16614-16614	BAKERS SUMMIT
16616-16616	BECCARIA
16617-16617	BELLWOOD
16619-16619	BLANDBURG
16620-16620	BRISBIN
16621-16621	BROAD TOP
16622-16622	CALVIN
16623-16623	CASSVILLE
16624-16624	CHEST SPRINGS
16625-16625	CLAYSBURG
16627-16627	COALPORT
16629-16629	COUPON
16630-16630	CRESSON
16631-16631	CURRYVILLE
16633-16633	DEFIANCE
16634-16634	DUDLEY
16635-16635	DUNCANSVILLE
16636-16636	DYSART
16637-16637	EAST FREEDOM
16638-16638	ENTRIKEN
16639-16639	FALLENTIMBER
16640-16640	FLINTON
16641-16641	GALLITZIN
16644-16644	GLASGOW
16645-16645	GLEN HOPE
16646-16646	HASTINGS
16647-16647	HESSTON
16648-16648	HOLLIDAYSBURG
16650-16650	HOPEWELL
16651-16651	HOUTZDALE
16652-16654	HUNTINGDON
16655-16655	IMLER
16656-16656	IRVONA
16657-16657	JAMES CREEK
16659-16659	LOYSBURG
16660-16660	MC CONNELLSTOWN
16661-16661	MADERA
16662-16662	MARTINSBURG
16663-16663	MORANN
16664-16664	NEW ENTERPRISE
16665-16665	NEWRY
16666-16666	OSCEOLA MILLS
16667-16667	OSTERBURG
16668-16668	PATTON
16669-16669	PETERSBURG
16670-16670	QUEEN
16671-16671	RAMEY
16672-16672	RIDDLESBURG
16673-16673	ROARING SPRING
16674-16674	ROBERTSDALE
16675-16675	SAINT BONIFACE
16677-16677	SANDY RIDGE
16678-16678	SAXTON
16679-16679	SIX MILE RUN
16680-16680	SMITHMILL
16681-16681	SMOKERUN
16682-16682	SPROUL
16683-16683	SPRUCE CREEK
16684-16684	TIPTON
16685-16685	TODD
16686-16686	TYRONE
16689-16689	WATERFALL
16691-16691	WELLS TANNERY
16692-16692	WESTOVER
16693-16693	WILLIAMSBURG
16694-16694	WOOD
16695-16695	WOODBURY
16698-16698	HOUTZDALE
16699-16699	CRESSON
16701-16701	BRADFORD
16720-16720	AUSTIN
16724-16724	CROSBY
16725-16725	CUSTER CITY
16726-16726	CYCLONE
16727-16727	DERRICK CITY
16728-16728	DE YOUNG
16729-16729	DUKE CENTER
16730-16730	EAST SMETHPORT
16731-16731	ELDRED
16732-16732	GIFFORD
16733-16733	HAZEL HURST
16734-16734	JAMES CITY
16735-16735	KANE
16738-16738	LEWIS RUN
16740-16740	MOUNT JEWETT
16743-16743	PORT ALLEGANY
16744-16744	REW
16745-16745	RIXFORD
16746-16746	ROULETTE
16748-16748	SHINGLEHOUSE
16749-16749	SMETHPORT
16750-16750	TURTLEPOINT
16751-16751	WESTLINE
16801-16801	STATE COLLEGE
16802-16802	UNIVERSITY PARK
16803-16805	STATE COLLEGE
16820-16820	AARONSBURG
16821-16821	ALLPORT
16822-16822	BEECH CREEK
16823-16823	BELLEFONTE
16825-16825	BIGLER
16826-16826	BLANCHARD
16827-16827	BOALSBURG
16828-16828	CENTRE HALL
16829-16829	CLARENCE
16830-16830	CLEARFIELD
16832-16832	COBURN
16833-16833	CURWENSVILLE
16834-16834	DRIFTING
16835-16835	FLEMING
16836-16836	FRENCHVILLE
16837-16837	GLEN RICHEY
16838-16838	GRAMPIAN
16839-16839	GRASSFLAT
16840-16840	HAWK RUN
16841-16841	HOWARD
16843-16843	HYDE
16844-16844	JULIAN
16845-16845	KARTHAUS
16847-16847	KYLERTOWN
16848-16848	LAMAR
16849-16849	LANSE
16850-16850	LECONTES MILLS
16851-16851	LEMONT
16852-16852	MADISONBURG
16853-16853	MILESBURG
16854-16854	MILLHEIM
16855-16855	MINERAL SPRINGS
16856-16856	MINGOVILLE
16858-16858	MORRISDALE
16859-16859	MOSHANNON
16860-16860	MUNSON
16861-16861	NEW MILLPORT
16863-16863	OLANTA
16864-16864	ORVISTON
16865-16865	PENNSYLVANIA FURNACE
16866-16866	PHILIPSBURG
16868-16868	PINE GROVE MILLS
16870-16870	PORT MATILDA
16871-16871	POTTERSDALE
16872-16872	REBERSBURG
16873-16873	SHAWVILLE
16874-16874	SNOW SHOE
16875-16875	SPRING MILLS
16876-16876	WALLACETON
16877-16877	WARRIORS MARK
16878-16878	WEST DECATUR
16879-16879	WINBURNE
16880-16880	BELLEFONTE
16881-16881	WOODLAND
16882-16882	WOODWARD
16901-16901	WELLSBORO
16910-16910	ALBA
16911-16911	ARNOT
16912-16912	BLOSSBURG
16914-16914	COLUMBIA CROSS ROADS
16915-16915	COUDERSPORT
16917-16917	COVINGTON
16918-16918	COWANESQUE
16920-16920	ELKLAND
16921-16921	GAINES
16922-16922	GALETON
16923-16923	GENESEE
16925-16925	GILLETT
16926-16926	GRANVILLE SUMMIT
16927-16927	HARRISON VALLEY
16928-16928	KNOXVILLE
16929-16929	LAWRENCEVILLE
16930-16930	LIBERTY
16932-16932	MAINESBURG
16933-16933	MANSFIELD
16935-16935	MIDDLEBURY CENTER
16936-16936	MILLERTON
16937-16937	MILLS
16938-16938	MORRIS
16939-16939	MORRIS RUN
16940-16940	NELSON
16941-16941	GENESEE
16942-16942	OSCEOLA
16943-16943	SABINSVILLE
16945-16945	SYLVANIA
16946-16946	TIOGA
16947-16947	TROY
16948-16948	ULYSSES
16950-16950	WESTFIELD
17001-17001	CAMP HILL
17002-17002	ALLENSVILLE
17003-17003	ANNVILLE
17004-17004	BELLEVILLE
17005-17005	BERRYSBURG
17006-17006	BLAIN
17007-17007	BOILING SPRINGS
17008-17008	BOWMANSDALE
17009-17009	BURNHAM
17010-17010	CAMPBELLTOWN
17011-17012	CAMP HILL
17013-17013	CARLISLE
17014-17014	COCOLAMUS
17015-17015	COLEBROOK
17016-17016	CORNWALL
17017-17017	DALMATIA
17018-17018	DAUPHIN
17019-17019	DILLSBURG
17020-17020	DUNCANNON
17021-17021	EAST WATERFORD
17022-17022	ELIZABETHTOWN
17023-17023	ELIZABETHVILLE
17024-17024	ELLIOTTSBURG
17025-17025	ENOLA
17026-17026	FREDERICKSBURG
17027-17027	GRANTHAM
17028-17028	GRANTVILLE
17029-17029	GRANVILLE
17030-17030	GRATZ
17031-17031	GREEN PARK
17032-17032	HALIFAX
17033-17033	HERSHEY
17034-17034	HIGHSPIRE
17035-17035	HONEY GROVE
17036-17036	HUMMELSTOWN
17037-17037	ICKESBURG
17038-17038	JONESTOWN
17039-17039	KLEINFELTERSVILLE
17040-17040	LANDISBURG
17041-17041	LAWN
17042-17042	LEBANON
17043-17043	LEMOYNE
17044-17044	LEWISTOWN
17045-17045	LIVERPOOL
17046-17046	LEBANON
17047-17047	LOYSVILLE
17048-17048	LYKENS
17049-17049	MC ALISTERVILLE
17050-17050	MECHANICSBURG
17051-17051	MC VEYTOWN
17052-17052	MAPLETON DEPOT
17053-17053	MARYSVILLE
17054-17054	MATTAWANA
17055-17055	MECHANICSBURG
17056-17056	MEXICO
17057-17057	MIDDLETOWN
17058-17058	MIFFLIN
17059-17059	MIFFLINTOWN
17060-17060	MILL CREEK
17061-17061	MILLERSBURG
17062-17062	MILLERSTOWN
17063-17063	MILROY
17064-17064	MOUNT GRETNA
17065-17065	MOUNT HOLLY SPRINGS
17066-17066	MOUNT UNION
17067-17067	MYERSTOWN
17068-17068	NEW BLOOMFIELD
17069-17069	NEW BUFFALO
17070-17070	NEW CUMBERLAND
17071-17071	NEW GERMANTOWN
17072-17072	NEW KINGSTOWN
17073-17073	NEWMANSTOWN
17074-17074	NEWPORT
17075-17075	NEWTON HAMILTON
17076-17076	OAKLAND MILLS
17077-17077	ONO
17078-17078	PALMYRA
17080-17080	PILLOW
17081-17081	PLAINFIELD
17082-17082	PORT ROYAL
17083-17083	QUENTIN
17084-17084	REEDSVILLE
17085-17085	REXMONT
17086-17086	RICHFIELD
17087-17087	RICHLAND
17088-17088	SCHAEFFERSTOWN

ZIP Range	City
17089-17089	CAMP HILL
17090-17090	SHERMANS DALE
17091-17091	CAMP HILL
17091-17091	LEBANON
17093-17093	SUMMERDALE
17094-17094	THOMPSONTOWN
17097-17097	WICONISCO
17098-17098	WILLIAMSTOWN
17099-17099	YEAGERTOWN
17100-17177	HARRISBURG
17201-17201	CHAMBERSBURG
17210-17210	AMBERSON
17211-17211	ARTEMAS
17212-17212	BIG COVE TANNERY
17213-17213	BLAIRS MILLS
17214-17214	BLUE RIDGE SUMMIT
17215-17215	BURNT CABINS
17217-17217	CONCORD
17218-17218	DICKINSON
17219-17219	DOYLESBURG
17220-17220	DRY RUN
17221-17221	FANNETTSBURG
17222-17222	FAYETTEVILLE
17223-17223	FORT LITTLETON
17224-17224	FORT LOUDON
17225-17225	GREENCASTLE
17228-17228	HARRISONVILLE
17229-17229	HUSTONTOWN
17231-17231	LEMASTERS
17232-17232	LURGAN
17233-17233	MC CONNELLSBURG
17235-17235	MARION
17236-17236	MERCERSBURG
17237-17237	MONT ALTO
17238-17238	NEEDMORE
17239-17239	NEELYTON
17240-17240	NEWBURG
17241-17241	NEWVILLE
17243-17243	ORBISONIA
17244-17244	ORRSTOWN
17246-17246	PLEASANT HALL
17247-17247	QUINCY
17249-17249	ROCKHILL FURNACE
17250-17250	ROUZERVILLE
17251-17251	ROXBURY
17252-17252	SAINT THOMAS
17253-17253	SALTILLO
17254-17254	SCOTLAND
17255-17255	SHADE GAP
17256-17256	SHADY GROVE
17257-17257	SHIPPENSBURG
17260-17260	SHIRLEYSBURG
17261-17261	SOUTH MOUNTAIN
17262-17262	SPRING RUN
17263-17263	STATE LINE
17264-17264	THREE SPRINGS
17265-17265	UPPERSTRASBURG
17266-17266	WALNUT BOTTOM
17267-17267	WARFORDSBURG
17268-17268	WAYNESBORO
17270-17270	WILLIAMSON
17271-17271	WILLOW HILL
17272-17272	ZULLINGER
17294-17294	BLUE RIDGE SUMMIT
17301-17301	ABBOTTSTOWN
17302-17302	AIRVILLE
17303-17303	ARENDTSVILLE
17304-17304	ASPERS
17306-17306	BENDERSVILLE
17307-17307	BIGLERVILLE
17309-17309	BROGUE
17310-17310	CASHTOWN
17311-17311	CODORUS
17312-17312	CRALEY
17313-17313	DALLASTOWN
17314-17314	DELTA
17315-17315	DOVER
17316-17316	EAST BERLIN
17317-17317	EAST PROSPECT
17318-17318	EMIGSVILLE
17319-17319	ETTERS
17320-17320	FAIRFIELD
17321-17321	FAWN GROVE
17322-17322	FELTON
17323-17323	FRANKLINTOWN
17324-17324	GARDNERS
17325-17326	GETTYSBURG
17327-17327	GLEN ROCK
17329-17329	GLENVILLE
17331-17334	HANOVER
17337-17337	IDAVILLE
17339-17339	LEWISBERRY
17340-17340	LITTLESTOWN
17342-17342	LOGANVILLE
17343-17343	MC KNIGHTSTOWN
17344-17344	MC SHERRYSTOWN
17345-17345	MANCHESTER
17346-17346	MENGES MILLS
17347-17347	MOUNT WOLF
17349-17349	NEW FREEDOM
17350-17350	NEW OXFORD
17352-17352	NEW PARK
17353-17353	ORRTANNA
17354-17354	PORTERS SIDELING
17355-17355	RAILROAD
17356-17356	RED LION
17358-17358	ROSSVILLE
17360-17360	SEVEN VALLEYS
17361-17361	SHREWSBURY
17362-17362	SPRING GROVE
17363-17363	STEWARTSTOWN
17364-17364	THOMASVILLE
17365-17365	WELLSVILLE
17366-17366	WINDSOR
17368-17368	WRIGHTSVILLE
17370-17370	YORK HAVEN
17371-17371	YORK NEW SALEM
17372-17372	YORK SPRINGS
17375-17375	PEACH GLEN
17400-17415	YORK
17501-17501	AKRON
17502-17502	BAINBRIDGE
17503-17503	BART
17504-17504	BAUSMAN
17505-17505	BIRD IN HAND
17506-17506	BLUE BALL
17507-17507	BOWMANSVILLE
17508-17508	BROWNSTOWN
17509-17509	CHRISTIANA
17512-17512	COLUMBIA
17516-17516	CONESTOGA
17517-17517	DENVER
17518-17518	DRUMORE
17519-17519	EAST EARL
17520-17520	EAST PETERSBURG
17521-17521	ELM
17522-17522	EPHRATA
17527-17527	GAP
17528-17528	GOODVILLE
17529-17529	GORDONVILLE
17532-17532	HOLTWOOD
17533-17533	HOPELAND
17534-17534	INTERCOURSE
17535-17535	KINZERS
17536-17536	KIRKWOOD
17537-17537	LAMPETER
17538-17538	LANDISVILLE
17540-17540	LEOLA
17543-17543	LITITZ
17545-17545	MANHEIM
17547-17547	MARIETTA
17549-17549	MARTINDALE
17550-17550	MAYTOWN
17551-17551	MILLERSVILLE
17552-17552	MOUNT JOY
17554-17554	MOUNTVILLE
17555-17555	NARVON
17557-17557	NEW HOLLAND
17560-17560	NEW PROVIDENCE
17562-17562	PARADISE
17563-17563	PEACH BOTTOM
17564-17564	PENRYN
17565-17565	PEQUEA
17566-17566	QUARRYVILLE
17567-17567	REAMSTOWN
17568-17568	REFTON
17569-17569	REINHOLDS
17570-17570	RHEEMS
17572-17573	RONKS
17575-17575	SILVER SPRING
17576-17576	SMOKETOWN
17577-17577	SOUDERSBURG
17578-17578	STEVENS
17579-17579	STRASBURG
17580-17580	TALMAGE
17581-17581	TERRE HILL
17582-17582	WASHINGTON BORO
17583-17583	WEST WILLOW
17584-17584	WILLOW STREET
17585-17585	WITMER
17600-17699	LANCASTER
17701-17705	WILLIAMSPORT
17720-17720	ANTES FORT
17721-17721	AVIS
17722-17722	BODINES
17723-17723	JERSEY SHORE
17724-17724	CANTON
17726-17726	CASTANEA
17727-17727	CEDAR RUN
17728-17728	COGAN STATION
17729-17729	CROSS FORK
17730-17730	DEWART
17731-17731	EAGLES MERE
17734-17734	FARRANDSVILLE
17735-17735	GROVER
17737-17737	HUGHESVILLE
17738-17738	HYNER
17739-17739	JERSEY MILLS
17740-17740	JERSEY SHORE
17742-17742	LAIRDSVILLE
17743-17743	LEROY
17744-17744	LINDEN
17745-17745	LOCK HAVEN
17747-17747	LOGANTON
17748-17748	MC ELHATTAN
17749-17749	MC EWENSVILLE
17750-17750	MACKEYVILLE
17751-17751	MILL HALL
17752-17752	MONTGOMERY
17754-17754	MONTOURSVILLE
17756-17756	MUNCY
17758-17758	MUNCY VALLEY
17759-17759	NISBET
17760-17760	NORTH BEND
17762-17762	PICTURE ROCKS
17763-17763	RALSTON
17764-17764	RENOVO
17765-17765	ROARING BRANCH
17767-17767	SALONA
17768-17768	SHUNK
17769-17769	SLATE RUN
17770-17770	SONESTOWN
17771-17771	TROUT RUN
17772-17772	TURBOTVILLE
17773-17773	TYLERSVILLE
17774-17774	UNITYVILLE
17776-17776	WATERVILLE
17777-17777	WATSONTOWN
17778-17778	WESTPORT
17779-17779	WOOLRICH
17801-17801	SUNBURY
17810-17810	ALLENWOOD
17812-17812	BEAVER SPRINGS
17813-17813	BEAVERTOWN
17814-17814	BENTON
17815-17815	BLOOMSBURG
17820-17820	CATAWISSA
17821-17822	DANVILLE
17823-17823	DORNSIFE
17824-17824	ELYSBURG
17825-17825	EXCELSIOR
17827-17827	FREEBURG
17828-17828	GOWEN CITY
17829-17829	HARTLETON
17830-17830	HERNDON
17831-17831	HUMMELS WHARF
17832-17832	MARION HEIGHTS
17833-17833	KREAMER
17834-17834	KULPMONT
17835-17835	LAURELTON
17836-17836	LECK KILL
17837-17837	LEWISBURG
17839-17839	LIGHT STREET
17840-17840	LOCUST GAP
17841-17841	MC CLURE
17842-17842	MIDDLEBURG
17843-17843	BEAVER SPRINGS
17844-17844	MIFFLINBURG
17845-17845	MILLMONT
17846-17846	MILLVILLE
17847-17847	MILTON
17850-17850	MONTANDON
17851-17851	MOUNT CARMEL
17853-17853	MOUNT PLEASANT MILLS
17855-17855	NEW BERLIN
17856-17856	NEW COLUMBIA
17857-17857	NORTHUMBERLAND
17858-17858	NUMIDIA
17859-17859	ORANGEVILLE
17860-17860	PAXINOS
17861-17861	PAXTONVILLE
17862-17862	PENNS CREEK
17864-17864	PORT TREVORTON
17865-17865	POTTS GROVE
17866-17866	COAL TOWNSHIP
17867-17867	REBUCK
17868-17868	RIVERSIDE
17870-17870	SELINSGROVE
17872-17872	SHAMOKIN
17876-17876	SHAMOKIN DAM
17877-17877	SNYDERTOWN
17878-17878	STILLWATER
17880-17880	SWENGEL
17881-17881	TREVORTON
17882-17882	TROXELVILLE
17883-17883	VICKSBURG
17884-17884	WASHINGTONVILLE
17885-17885	WEIKERT
17886-17886	WEST MILTON
17887-17887	WHITE DEER
17888-17888	WILBURTON
17889-17889	WINFIELD
17901-17901	POTTSVILLE
17920-17920	ARISTES
17921-17921	ASHLAND
17922-17922	AUBURN
17923-17923	BRANCHDALE
17925-17925	BROCKTON
17927-17927	CENTRALIA
17929-17929	CRESSONA
17930-17930	CUMBOLA
17931-17932	FRACKVILLE
17933-17933	FRIEDENSBURG
17934-17934	GILBERTON
17935-17935	GIRARDVILLE
17936-17936	GORDON
17938-17938	HEGINS
17939-17939	HELFENSTEIN
17941-17941	KLINGERSTOWN
17942-17942	LANDINGVILLE
17943-17943	LAVELLE
17944-17944	LLEWELLYN
17945-17945	LOCUSTDALE
17946-17946	LOST CREEK
17948-17948	MAHANOY CITY
17949-17949	MAHANOY PLANE
17951-17951	MAR LIN
17952-17952	MARY D
17953-17953	MIDDLEPORT
17954-17954	MINERSVILLE
17957-17957	MUIR
17959-17959	NEW PHILADELPHIA
17960-17960	NEW RINGGOLD
17961-17961	ORWIGSBURG
17963-17963	PINE GROVE
17964-17964	PITMAN
17965-17965	PORT CARBON
17966-17966	RAVINE

17967-17967 RINGTOWN
17968-17968 SACRAMENTO
17970-17970 SAINT CLAIR
17972-17972 SCHUYLKILL HAVEN
17974-17974 SELTZER
17976-17976 SHENANDOAH
17978-17978 SPRING GLEN
17979-17979 SUMMIT STATION
17980-17980 TOWER CITY
17981-17981 TREMONT
17982-17982 TUSCARORA
17983-17983 VALLEY VIEW
17985-17985 ZION GROVE
18001-18003 LEHIGH VALLEY
18010-18010 ACKERMANVILLE
18011-18011 ALBURTIS
18012-18012 AQUASHICOLA
18013-18013 BANGOR
18014-18014 BATH
18015-18025 BETHLEHEM
18030-18030 BOWMANSTOWN
18031-18031 BREINIGSVILLE
18032-18032 CATASAUQUA
18034-18034 CENTER VALLEY
18035-18035 CHERRYVILLE
18036-18036 COOPERSBURG
18037-18037 COPLAY
18038-18038 DANIELSVILLE
18039-18039 DURHAM
18040-18040 EASTON
18041-18041 EAST GREENVILLE
18042-18045 EASTON
18046-18046 EAST TEXAS
18049-18049 EMMAUS
18050-18050 FLICKSVILLE
18051-18051 FOGELSVILLE
18052-18052 WHITEHALL
18053-18053 GERMANSVILLE
18054-18054 GREEN LANE
18055-18055 HELLERTOWN
18056-18056 HEREFORD
18058-18058 KUNKLETOWN
18059-18059 LAURYS STATION
18060-18060 LIMEPORT
18062-18062 MACUNGIE
18063-18063 MARTINS CREEK
18064-18064 NAZARETH
18065-18065 NEFFS
18066-18066 NEW TRIPOLI
18067-18067 NORTHAMPTON
18068-18068 OLD ZIONSVILLE
18069-18069 OREFIELD
18070-18070 PALM
18071-18071 PALMERTON
18072-18072 PEN ARGYL
18073-18073 PENNSBURG
18074-18074 PERKIOMENVILLE
18076-18076 RED HILL
18077-18077 RIEGELSVILLE
18078-18078 SCHNECKSVILLE
18079-18079 SLATEDALE
18080-18080 SLATINGTON
18081-18081 SPRINGTOWN
18083-18083 STOCKERTOWN
18084-18084 SUMNEYTOWN
18085-18085 TATAMY
18086-18086 TREICHLERS
18087-18087 TREXLERTOWN
18088-18088 WALNUTPORT
18091-18091 WIND GAP
18092-18092 ZIONSVILLE
18098-18099 EMMAUS
18100-18195 ALLENTOWN
18201-18202 HAZLETON
18210-18210 ALBRIGHTSVILLE
18211-18211 ANDREAS
18212-18212 ASHFIELD
18214-18214 BARNESVILLE
18216-18216 BEAVER MEADOWS
18218-18218 COALDALE
18219-18219 CONYNGHAM
18220-18220 DELANO
18221-18221 DRIFTON
18222-18222 DRUMS
18223-18223 EBERVALE
18224-18224 FREELAND
18225-18225 HARLEIGH
18229-18229 JIM THORPE
18230-18230 JUNEDALE
18231-18231 KELAYRES
18232-18232 LANSFORD
18234-18234 LATTIMER MINES
18235-18235 LEHIGHTON
18237-18237 MCADOO
18239-18239 MILNESVILLE
18240-18240 NESQUEHONING
18241-18241 NUREMBERG
18242-18242 ONEIDA
18243-18243 PARDEESVILLE
18244-18244 PARRYVILLE
18245-18245 QUAKAKE
18246-18246 ROCK GLEN
18247-18247 SAINT JOHNS
18248-18248 SHEPPTON
18249-18249 SUGARLOAF
18250-18250 SUMMIT HILL
18251-18251 SYBERTSVILLE
18252-18252 TAMAQUA
18254-18254 TRESCKOW
18255-18255 WEATHERLY
18256-18256 WESTON
18301-18301 EAST STROUDSBURG
18320-18320 ANALOMINK
18321-18321 BARTONSVILLE
18322-18322 BRODHEADSVILLE
18323-18323 BUCK HILL FALLS
18324-18324 BUSHKILL
18325-18325 CANADENSIS
18326-18326 CRESCO
18327-18327 DELAWARE WATER GAP
18328-18328 DINGMANS FERRY
18330-18330 EFFORT
18331-18331 GILBERT
18332-18332 HENRYVILLE
18333-18333 KRESGEVILLE
18334-18334 LONG POND
18335-18335 MARSHALLS CREEK
18336-18336 MATAMORAS
18337-18337 MILFORD
18340-18340 MILLRIFT
18341-18341 MINISINK HILLS
18342-18342 MOUNTAINHOME
18343-18343 MOUNT BETHEL
18344-18344 MOUNT POCONO
18346-18346 POCONO SUMMIT
18347-18347 POCONO LAKE
18348-18348 POCONO LAKE PRESERVE
18349-18349 POCONO MANOR
18350-18350 POCONO PINES
18351-18351 PORTLAND
18352-18352 REEDERS
18353-18353 SAYLORSBURG
18354-18354 SCIOTA
18355-18355 SCOTRUN
18356-18356 SHAWNEE ON DELAWARE
18357-18357 SKYTOP
18360-18360 STROUDSBURG
18370-18370 SWIFTWATER
18371-18371 TAMIMENT
18372-18372 TANNERSVILLE
18373-18373 UNITY HOUSE
18401-18401 ALDENVILLE
18403-18403 ARCHBALD
18405-18405 BEACH LAKE
18407-18407 CARBONDALE
18410-18410 CHINCHILLA
18411-18411 CLARKS SUMMIT
18413-18413 CLIFFORD
18414-18414 DALTON
18415-18415 DAMASCUS
18416-18416 ELMHURST
18417-18417 EQUINUNK
18419-18419 FACTORYVILLE
18420-18420 FLEETVILLE
18421-18421 FOREST CITY
18424-18424 GOULDSBORO
18425-18425 GREELEY
18426-18426 GREENTOWN
18427-18427 HAMLIN
18428-18428 HAWLEY
18430-18430 HERRICK CENTER
18431-18431 HONESDALE
18433-18433 JERMYN
18434-18434 JESSUP
18435-18435 LACKAWAXEN
18436-18436 LAKE ARIEL
18437-18437 LAKE COMO
18438-18438 LAKEVILLE
18439-18439 LAKEWOOD
18440-18440 LA PLUME
18441-18441 LENOXVILLE
18443-18443 MILANVILLE
18444-18444 MOSCOW
18445-18445 NEWFOUNDLAND
18446-18446 NICHOLSON
18447-18448 OLYPHANT
18449-18449 ORSON
18451-18451 PAUPACK
18452-18452 PECKVILLE
18453-18453 PLEASANT MOUNT
18454-18454 POYNTELLE
18455-18455 PRESTON PARK
18456-18456 PROMPTON
18457-18457 ROWLAND
18458-18458 SHOHOLA
18459-18459 SOUTH CANAAN
18460-18460 SOUTH STERLING
18461-18461 STARLIGHT
18462-18462 STARRUCCA
18463-18463 STERLING
18464-18464 TAFTON
18465-18465 THOMPSON
18466-18466 TOBYHANNA
18469-18469 TYLER HILL
18470-18470 UNION DALE
18471-18471 WAVERLY
18472-18472 WAYMART
18473-18473 WHITE MILLS
18500-18505 SCRANTON
18507-18507 MOOSIC
18508-18515 SCRANTON
18517-18517 TAYLOR
18518-18518 OLD FORGE
18519-18519 DICKSON CITY
18522-18577 SCRANTON
18601-18601 BEACH HAVEN
18602-18602 BEAR CREEK
18603-18603 BERWICK
18610-18610 BLAKESLEE
18611-18611 CAMBRA
18612-18612 DALLAS
18614-18614 DUSHORE
18615-18615 FALLS
18616-18616 FORKSVILLE
18617-18617 GLEN LYON
18618-18618 HARVEYS LAKE
18619-18619 HILLSGROVE
18621-18621 HUNLOCK CREEK
18622-18622 HUNTINGTON MILLS
18623-18623 LACEYVILLE
18624-18624 LAKE HARMONY
18625-18625 LAKE WINOLA
18626-18626 LAPORTE
18627-18627 LEHMAN
18628-18628 LOPEZ
18629-18629 MEHOOPANY
18630-18630 MESHOPPEN
18631-18631 MIFFLINVILLE
18632-18632 MILDRED
18634-18634 NANTICOKE
18635-18635 NESCOPECK
18636-18636 NOXEN
18637-18637 NUANGOLA
18640-18641 PITTSTON
18642-18642 DURYEA
18643-18643 PITTSTON
18644-18644 WYOMING
18651-18651 PLYMOUTH
18653-18653 RANSOM
18654-18654 SHAWANESE
18655-18655 SHICKSHINNY
18656-18656 SWEET VALLEY
18657-18657 TUNKHANNOCK
18660-18660 WAPWALLOPEN
18661-18661 WHITE HAVEN
18690-18690 DALLAS
18700-18703 WILKES BARRE
18704-18704 KINGSTON
18705-18706 WILKES BARRE
18707-18707 MOUNTAIN TOP
18708-18708 SHAVERTOWN
18709-18709 LUZERNE
18710-18774 WILKES BARRE
18801-18801 MONTROSE
18810-18810 ATHENS
18812-18812 BRACKNEY
18813-18813 BROOKLYN
18814-18814 BURLINGTON
18815-18815 CAMPTOWN
18816-18816 DIMOCK
18817-18817 EAST SMITHFIELD
18818-18818 FRIENDSVILLE
18820-18820 GIBSON
18821-18821 GREAT BEND
18822-18822 HALLSTEAD
18823-18823 HARFORD
18824-18824 HOP BOTTOM
18825-18825 JACKSON
18826-18826 KINGSLEY
18827-18827 LANESBORO
18828-18828 LAWTON
18829-18829 LE RAYSVILLE
18830-18830 LITTLE MEADOWS
18831-18831 MILAN
18832-18832 MONROETON
18833-18833 NEW ALBANY
18834-18834 NEW MILFORD
18837-18837 ROME
18839-18839 RUSHVILLE
18840-18840 SAYRE
18842-18842 SOUTH GIBSON
18843-18843 SOUTH MONTROSE
18844-18844 SPRINGVILLE
18845-18845 STEVENSVILLE
18846-18846 SUGAR RUN
18847-18847 SUSQUEHANNA
18848-18848 TOWANDA
18850-18850 ULSTER
18851-18851 WARREN CENTER
18853-18853 WYALUSING
18854-18854 WYSOX
18901-18901 DOYLESTOWN
18910-18910 BEDMINSTER
18911-18911 BLOOMING GLEN
18912-18912 BUCKINGHAM
18913-18913 CARVERSVILLE
18914-18914 CHALFONT
18915-18915 COLMAR
18916-18916 DANBORO
18917-18917 DUBLIN
18918-18918 EARLINGTON
18920-18920 ERWINNA
18921-18921 FERNDALE
18922-18922 FOREST GROVE
18923-18923 FOUNTAINVILLE
18924-18924 FRANCONIA
18925-18925 FURLONG
18926-18926 GARDENVILLE
18927-18927 HILLTOWN
18928-18928 HOLICONG
18929-18929 JAMISON
18930-18930 KINTNERSVILLE
18931-18931 LAHASKA
18932-18932 LINE LEXINGTON
18933-18933 LUMBERVILLE
18934-18934 MECHANICSVILLE
18935-18935 MILFORD SQUARE
18936-18936 MONTGOMERYVILLE

ZIP Range	City
18938-18938	NEW HOPE
18940-18940	NEWTOWN
18942-18942	OTTSVILLE
18943-18943	PENNS PARK
18944-18944	PERKASIE
18946-18946	PINEVILLE
18947-18947	PIPERSVILLE
18949-18949	PLUMSTEADVILLE
18950-18950	POINT PLEASANT
18951-18951	QUAKERTOWN
18953-18953	REVERE
18954-18954	RICHBORO
18955-18955	RICHLANDTOWN
18956-18956	RUSHLAND
18957-18957	SALFORD
18958-18958	SALFORDVILLE
18960-18960	SELLERSVILLE
18962-18962	SILVERDALE
18963-18963	SOLEBURY
18964-18964	SOUDERTON
18966-18966	SOUTHAMPTON
18968-18968	SPINNERSTOWN
18969-18969	TELFORD
18970-18970	TRUMBAUERSVILLE
18971-18971	TYLERSPORT
18972-18972	UPPER BLACK EDDY
18974-18974	WARMINSTER
18976-18976	WARRINGTON
18977-18977	WASHINGTON CROSSING
18979-18979	WOXALL
18980-18980	WYCOMBE
18981-18981	ZIONHILL
18991-18991	WARMINSTER
19001-19001	ABINGTON
19002-19002	AMBLER
19003-19003	ARDMORE
19004-19004	BALA CYNWYD
19006-19006	HUNTINGDON VALLEY
19007-19007	BRISTOL
19008-19008	BROOMALL
19009-19009	BRYN ATHYN
19010-19010	BRYN MAWR
19012-19012	CHELTENHAM
19013-19013	CHESTER
19014-19014	ASTON
19015-19015	BROOKHAVEN
19016-19016	CHESTER
19017-19017	CHESTER HEIGHTS
19018-19018	CLIFTON HEIGHTS
19019-19019	PHILADELPHIA
19020-19020	BENSALEM
19021-19021	CROYDON
19022-19022	CRUM LYNNE
19023-19023	DARBY
19025-19025	DRESHER
19026-19026	DREXEL HILL
19027-19027	ELKINS PARK
19028-19028	EDGEMONT
19029-19029	ESSINGTON
19030-19030	FAIRLESS HILLS
19031-19031	FLOURTOWN
19032-19032	FOLCROFT
19033-19033	FOLSOM
19034-19034	FORT WASHINGTON
19035-19035	GLADWYNE
19036-19036	GLENOLDEN
19037-19037	GLEN RIDDLE LIMA
19038-19038	GLENSIDE
19039-19039	GRADYVILLE
19040-19040	HATBORO
19041-19041	HAVERFORD
19043-19043	HOLMES
19044-19044	HORSHAM
19046-19046	JENKINTOWN
19047-19048	LANGHORNE
19048-19048	FORT WASHINGTON
19049-19049	LANGHORNE
19049-19049	FORT WASHINGTON
19050-19050	LANSDOWNE
19052-19052	LENNI
19053-19053	FEASTERVILLE TREVOSE
19054-19059	LEVITTOWN
19059-19059	PHILADELPHIA
19061-19061	MARCUS HOOK
19063-19063	MEDIA
19064-19064	SPRINGFIELD
19065-19065	MEDIA
19066-19066	MERION STATION
19067-19067	MORRISVILLE
19070-19070	MORTON
19072-19072	NARBERTH
19073-19073	NEWTOWN SQUARE
19074-19074	NORWOOD
19075-19075	ORELAND
19076-19076	PROSPECT PARK
19078-19078	RIDLEY PARK
19079-19079	SHARON HILL
19080-19080	WAYNE
19081-19081	SWARTHMORE
19082-19082	UPPER DARBY
19083-19083	HAVERTOWN
19085-19085	VILLANOVA
19086-19086	WALLINGFORD
19087-19089	WAYNE
19090-19090	WILLOW GROVE
19091-19091	MEDIA
19092-19093	PHILADELPHIA
19094-19094	WOODLYN
19095-19095	WYNCOTE
19096-19096	WYNNEWOOD
19098-19098	HOLMES
19099-19255	PHILADELPHIA
19301-19301	PAOLI
19310-19310	ATGLEN
19311-19311	AVONDALE
19312-19312	BERWYN
19316-19316	BRANDAMORE
19317-19317	CHADDS FORD
19318-19318	CHATHAM
19319-19319	CHEYNEY
19320-19320	COATESVILLE
19330-19330	COCHRANVILLE
19331-19331	CONCORDVILLE
19333-19333	DEVON
19335-19335	DOWNINGTOWN
19339-19340	CONCORDVILLE
19341-19341	EXTON
19342-19342	GLEN MILLS
19343-19343	GLENMOORE
19344-19344	HONEY BROOK
19345-19345	IMMACULATA
19346-19346	KELTON
19347-19347	KEMBLESVILLE
19348-19348	KENNETT SQUARE
19350-19350	LANDENBERG
19351-19351	LEWISVILLE
19352-19352	LINCOLN UNIVERSITY
19353-19353	LIONVILLE
19354-19354	LYNDELL
19355-19355	MALVERN
19357-19357	MENDENHALL
19358-19358	MODENA
19360-19360	NEW LONDON
19362-19362	NOTTINGHAM
19363-19363	OXFORD
19365-19365	PARKESBURG
19366-19366	POCOPSON
19367-19367	POMEROY
19369-19369	SADSBURYVILLE
19370-19370	STEELVILLE
19371-19371	SUPLEE
19372-19372	THORNDALE
19373-19373	THORNTON
19374-19374	TOUGHKENAMON
19375-19375	UNIONVILLE
19376-19376	WAGONTOWN
19380-19383	WEST CHESTER
19390-19390	WEST GROVE
19395-19395	WESTTOWN
19397-19399	SOUTHEASTERN
19401-19404	NORRISTOWN
19405-19405	BRIDGEPORT
19406-19406	KING OF PRUSSIA
19407-19407	AUDUBON
19408-19408	EAGLEVILLE
19409-19409	FAIRVIEW VILLAGE
19415-19415	EAGLEVILLE
19420-19420	ARCOLA
19421-19421	BIRCHRUNVILLE
19422-19422	BLUE BELL
19423-19423	CEDARS
19424-19424	BLUE BELL
19425-19425	CHESTER SPRINGS
19426-19426	COLLEGEVILLE
19428-19429	CONSHOHOCKEN
19430-19430	CREAMERY
19432-19432	DEVAULT
19435-19435	FREDERICK
19436-19436	GWYNEDD
19437-19437	GWYNEDD VALLEY
19438-19438	HARLEYSVILLE
19440-19440	HATFIELD
19441-19441	HARLEYSVILLE
19442-19442	KIMBERTON
19443-19443	KULPSVILLE
19444-19444	LAFAYETTE HILL
19446-19446	LANSDALE
19450-19450	LEDERACH
19451-19451	MAINLAND
19452-19452	MIQUON
19453-19453	MONT CLARE
19454-19455	NORTH WALES
19456-19456	OAKS
19457-19457	PARKER FORD
19460-19460	PHOENIXVILLE
19462-19462	PLYMOUTH MEETING
19464-19465	POTTSTOWN
19468-19468	ROYERSFORD
19470-19470	SAINT PETERS
19472-19472	SASSAMANSVILLE
19473-19473	SCHWENKSVILLE
19474-19474	SKIPPACK
19475-19475	SPRING CITY
19477-19477	SPRING HOUSE
19478-19478	SPRING MOUNT
19480-19480	UWCHLAND
19481-19485	VALLEY FORGE
19486-19486	WEST POINT
19487-19487	KING OF PRUSSIA
19488-19489	NORRISTOWN
19490-19490	WORCESTER
19492-19492	ZIEGLERVILLE
19493-19496	VALLEY FORGE
19501-19501	ADAMSTOWN
19503-19503	BALLY
19504-19504	BARTO
19505-19505	BECHTELSVILLE
19506-19506	BERNVILLE
19507-19507	BETHEL
19508-19508	BIRDSBORO
19510-19510	BLANDON
19511-19511	BOWERS
19512-19512	BOYERTOWN
19516-19516	CENTERPORT
19517-19517	DAUBERVILLE
19518-19518	DOUGLASSVILLE
19519-19519	EARLVILLE
19520-19520	ELVERSON
19522-19522	FLEETWOOD
19523-19523	GEIGERTOWN
19525-19525	GILBERTSVILLE
19526-19526	HAMBURG
19529-19529	KEMPTON
19530-19530	KUTZTOWN
19533-19533	LEESPORT
19534-19534	LENHARTSVILLE
19535-19535	LIMEKILN
19536-19536	LYON STATION
19538-19538	MAXATAWNY
19539-19539	MERTZTOWN
19540-19540	MOHNTON
19541-19541	MOHRSVILLE
19542-19542	MONOCACY STATION
19543-19543	MORGANTOWN
19544-19544	MOUNT AETNA
19545-19545	NEW BERLINVILLE
19547-19547	OLEY
19548-19548	PINE FORGE
19549-19549	PORT CLINTON
19550-19550	REHRERSBURG
19551-19551	ROBESONIA
19554-19554	SHARTLESVILLE
19555-19555	SHOEMAKERSVILLE
19557-19557	STONY RUN
19559-19559	STRAUSSTOWN
19560-19560	TEMPLE
19562-19562	TOPTON
19564-19564	VIRGINVILLE
19565-19565	WERNERSVILLE
19567-19567	WOMELSDORF
19600-19640	READING

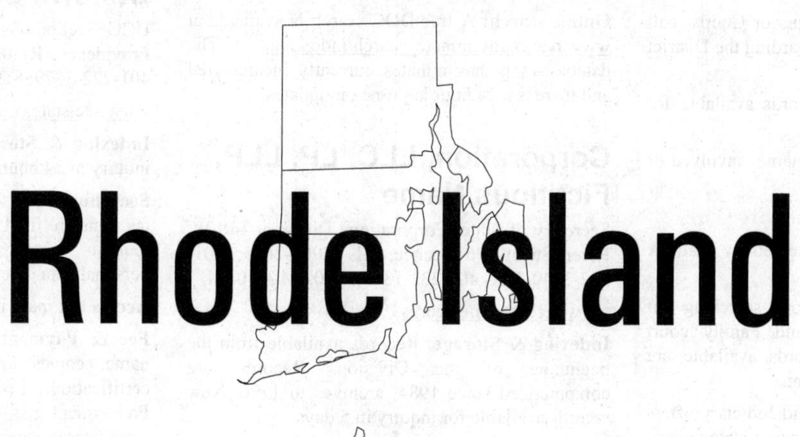

Rhode Island

General Help Numbers:

Governor's Office

State House Rm 115 — 401-222-2080
Providence, RI 02903 — Fax 401-222-8096
www.governor.state.ri.us — 8:30AM-4:30PM

Attorney General's Office

150 S Main St — 401-274-4400
Providence, RI 02903 — Fax 401-222-1331
www.riag.ri.gov/ — 8:30AM-4:30PM

Legislative Records

Secretary of State
Public Information Center — 401-222-3983
State House, Room 38 — Fax 401-222-1404
Providence, RI 02903 — 8:30AM-4:30PM
www.rilin.state.ri.us

State Archives

State Archives & Public Records Admin. — 401-222-2353
337 Westminster St — Fax 401-222-3199
Providence, RI 02903 — 8:30AM-4:30PM M-SA
www.sec.state.ri.us/Archives/

State Specifics:

Capital:	Providence Providence County
Time Zone:	EST
Number of Counties:	5
Population:	1,050,788
Web Site:	www.ri.gov/

State Agencies

Criminal Records

Department of Attorney General, Bureau of Criminal Identification, 150 S Main Street, Providence, RI 02903; 401-274-4400 x2232, Fax-401-222-1331; 8:30AM-4:30PM. www.riag.ri.gov

Indexing & Storage: Records available from 1900's. New records available for inquiry in 1-7 days. 86% of all arrests in database have final dispositions recorded.

Searching: Criminal records are only released to law enforcement agencies, the subject, or to those with a signed notarized authorization from the subject. Include in request- signed notarized release from subject, DOB, picture ID and DOB of the requester. Fingerprints and SSN are optional. They will call the Notary on the authorization for verification. 100% of the records are fingerprint-supported. All arrests and convictions are reported.

Access by: mail, in person.

Fee & Payment: The fee is $5.00 for a name search. If required, the a fingerprint search without an FBI search is $15, with the FBI fingerprint search is $30.00. Fee payee- Department of Attorney General. Prepayment required. Personal checks accepted. No credit cards or cash accepted.

Mail search: Turnaround time- up to 2 weeks. A SASE is required.

In person: Turnaround time is while you wait.

Other access: This agency does not offer online access, but the state court system does offer an information site that should not be substituted as an official search. See that profile for details.

Statewide Court Records

Court Administrator, Supreme Court, 250 Benefit St, Providence, RI 02903; 401-222-3266, Fax-401-222-4224; 8:30AM-4:30PM.

www.courts.state.ri.us

For questions regarding the Superior Courts, call 401-222-2622. For questions regarding the District Courts, call 401-458-5201.

Indexing & Storage: New records available for inquiry in 24 hours.

Searching: Include in request- names involved or case number.

Access by: mail, in person, online.

Mail search: Requests are accepted by mail. A SASE is required.

In person: Limited in-person searching of Supreme, District, Superior, and Family court cases are available. Most records available are from the mid 1980's to the present.

Online search: The Rhode Island Judiciary offers free access to court criminal records statewide at http://courtconnect.courts.state.ri.us. A word of caution, this website is provided as an informational service only and should not be relied upon as an official record of the court. Supreme Court and Appellate opinions are available from the home page.

Other access: Bulk data is available, call for details.

Sexual Offender Registry

Sex Offender Community Notification Unit, Varley Building, 40 Howard Avenue, Cranston, RI 02920; 401-462-0905, Fax- 401-462-0916; 8:30AM-4:30PM. www.paroleboard.ri.gov/

No agency, including any Law Enforcement Agency or any state agency, may direct where the offender does or does not reside, nor can these agencies direct where the offender works or goes to school.

Indexing & Storage: Records available from 07-24-96 (online).

Searching: email questions: parolebd@doc.ri.gov.

Access by: mail, online.

Mail search: the agency will merely respond by sending the web page listing.

Online search: Website information about a sex offender is available to the public only if the Sex Offender Board of Review has classified the offender as a Level 3, or as a Level 2 as of January 1, 2006. Go to www.paroleboard.ri.gov/sexoffender/agree.php. Also, search by town or ZIP.

Incarceration Records

Rhode Island Department of Corrections, Records, PO Box 8249, Cranston, RI 02920 (Courier address- 40 Howard Avenue, Cranston, RI 02920); 401-462-3900, Fax- 401-462-2253; 8AM-4:30PM.

www.doc.ri.gov/index.php

Indexing & Storage: Records available on current and former inmates. New records available for inquiry in 1 to 3 days.

Searching: Include in request- full name; DOB helpful. Location, physical identifiers, conviction and sentencing information, and release dates are provided.

Access by: mail, phone, fax, online.

Fee & Payment: There is no fee.

Mail search: Turnaround time- 30 days. SASE not required.

Phone search: Limited name searching available by phone.

Fax search: Records are available by fax.

Online search: A free DOC search is available at www.doc.ri.gov/inmate_search/index.php. The database only has inmates currently incarcerated and there is a 24 hour lag time on updates.

Corporation, LLC, LP, LLP, Fictitious Name

Secretary of State, Corporations Division, 148 W. River Street, Providence, RI 02904-2615; 401-222-3040, Fax- 401-222-1309; 8:30AM-4:30PM.

www.sec.state.ri.us/corps

Indexing & Storage: Records available from the beginning of the Division. Records are computerized since 1984, archives to 1776. New records available for inquiry in 5 days.

Searching: Include in request- full name of business.

Access by: mail, phone, in person, online.

Fee & Payment: The copy fee is $.15 per page. Certification costs $10.00 per document plus copy fees, $5.00 if a non-profit. A Good Standing is $20.00, $5.00 if for non-profit. There is no search fee. Fee payee- Secretary of State. Personal checks accepted. Credit cards only accepted if online.

Mail search: Turnaround time- 7 to 10 days. A SASE helpful.

Phone search: They will give date of incorporation, registered agent, one officer, status, and whether domestic or foreign. Certified copies and documents can be ordered by phone, but must be picked up in person, takes 48 hours.

In person: Certified copies and certifications may not be available same day.

Online search: At the web, search filings for active and inactive Rhode Island and foreign business corporations, non-profit corporations, limited partnerships, limited liability companies, and limited liability partnerships. Weekly listings of new corporations are also available. There is no fee. A variety of certifications can also be requested, fees involved. Online filing is now available for corporations, LLCs and LPs.

Other access: Various databases may be downloaded or purchased on CD. Call for pricing.

Trademarks/Servicemarks

Secretary of State, Trademark Section, 148 W River St, Providence, RI 02904-2615; 401-222-3040, Fax- 401-222-3879; 8:30AM-4:30PM.

www.sec.state.ri.us/corps/trademark/trademark.html

Indexing & Storage: Records available from the beginning of the Division. A mark is registered for 10 years. New records available for inquiry in less than one week.

Searching: All records are open to the public. Include in request- trademark/servicemark name, registration number and applicant name, if known.

Access by: mail, phone, in person.

Fee & Payment: A search fee may apply depending on how extensive. The copy fee is $.15 per page. Fee payee- Secretary of State Personal checks accepted.

Mail search: Turnaround time- 3 to 5 days. SASE not required.

Phone search: Limited verification information available.

In person: Counter service is available.

Uniform Commercial Code

UCC Section, Secretary of State, 148 River St, Providence, RI 02904-2615; 401-222-3040, Fax- 401-222-3879; 8:30AM-4:30PM.

www.sec.state.ri.us/corps/ucc/ucc.html

Indexing & Storage: New records available for inquiry in 24 hours.

Searching: Use search request form UCC-11. All tax liens are filed at the city/town level. Include in request- debtor name. Office does not index personal data other than name and address.

Access by: mail, in person, online.

Fee & Payment: The search fee is $5.00 per name, copies are $.15 each. Add $5.00 for certification. Fee payee- Secretary of State. Prepayment required. Personal checks accepted. Credit cards accepted only online.

Mail search: Turnaround time- 1 to 2 working days. SASE recommended.

In person: Visitors may use the public access terminal to view records. This is the same system used for online viewing.

Online search: View debtor names in the Pubic Search Index at http://ucc.state.ri.us/psearch/. One may also search by file number or business organization. Rhode Island's UCC Public Search Index allows its users to search using both Standard Search Logic and Non-Standard Logic.

Other access: Bulk data can be purchased by request. Call for details.

Federal & State Tax Liens

Records not maintained by a state level agency.

All records are located at the county level.

Sales Tax Registrations

Taxation Division, Sales & Use Tax Office, One Capitol Hill, Providence, RI 02908-5800; 401-574-8955, Fax- 401-222-6288; 8:30AM-4PM.

www.tax.state.ri.us

Indexing & Storage: Records available from the 1960's. All current permits are on the computer, all inactive records are kept on microfiche. New records available for inquiry immediately.

Searching: This agency will only confirm that a business is registered. They will provide no other information. Include in request- business name or tax permit number.

Access by: mail, phone, fax.

Fee & Payment: There is no search fee nor a copy fee, unless extensive documents are requested.

Mail search: Turnaround time- 7 to 10 days. A SASE is requested.

Phone search: It will take 24 hours for a response.

Fax search: Same criteria as mail searching.

Expedited service: Will try to expedite search, if requested.

Birth Certificates

State Department of Health, Division of Vital Records, 3 Capitol Hill, Room 101, Providence, RI 02908-5097; 401-222-2812, 401-222-2811; 8:30AM-4:30PM. www.health.ri.gov/

If the record is less than 100 years old, it can also be obtained from city/town where birth occurred.

Indexing & Storage: Records available from 100 years to present. Older records are transferred to the RI State Archives, 401-222-2353.

Searching: Birth records are confidential unless over 100 years old. Searches must have a signed release from person of record or immediate family member. Include in request- signed released from person of record or immediate family member, full name, names of parents, mother's maiden name, date of birth, place of birth. Include valid picture ID if family member.

Access by: mail, in person.

Fee & Payment: The fee is $20.00 per record, if uncertain of the date the search covers a 2-year searching period. There is a $2.00 search fee for each additional 2 years searched. Fee payee- General Treasurer, State of Rhode Island. Prepayment required. Personal checks and Mos accepted.

Mail search: Turnaround time- 6 to 8 weeks. For 1 business week service, add an additional $7.00 and mark "rush" on outside of envelope. A SASE is requested. Include photo copy of requester's valid government issued ID.

In person: Turnaround time while you wait.

Expedited service: Turnaround time- 5 days. Add $7.00 for processing.

Death Records

State Department of Health, Division of Vital Records, 3 Capitol Hill, Room 101, Providence, RI 02908-5097; 401-222-2812, 401-222-2811; 8:30AM-4:30PM. www.health.ri.gov/

Records less than 50 years old can also be obtained at the town/city where death took place.

Indexing & Storage: Records available from 50 years to present. Older records are transferred to the RI State Archives, 40-,222-2353.

Searching: Include in request- signed release from immediate family member, full name, date of death, place of death, names of parents, mother's maiden name. Include valid picture ID if family member.

Access by: mail, in person.

Fee & Payment: The fee is $20.00 per record, if uncertain of the date the search covers a 2-year searching period. There is a $2.00 search fee for each additional 2 years searched. Fee payee- General Treasurer, State of Rhode Island. Prepayment required. Personal checks and money orders accepted.

Mail search: Turnaround time- 6 to 8 weeks. For one-week service, add an additional $7.00 and mark "rush" on outside of envelope. A SASE is requested. Include photo copy of requester's valid government issued ID. Include photo copy of requester's ID (DL, passport, etc).

In person: Simple requests may be processed while you wait.

Expedited service: Turnaround time- 5 days. Add $7.00 for processing.

Marriage Certificates

State Department of Health, Division of Vital Records, 3 Capitol Hill, Room 101, Providence, RI 02908-5097; 401-222-2812, 401-222-2811; 8:30AM-4:30PM. www.health.ri.gov/

The record may be also obtained from the town or city where the marriage took place, if the record is less than 100 years old.

Indexing & Storage: Records available from 100 years to present, older records sent to State Archives. New records available for inquiry immediately.

Searching: Requester must be person of record or immediate family members. Include in request- signed release and copy of valid ID of requester, names of husband and wife, date of marriage, place or county of marriage, wife's maiden name.

Access by: mail, in person.

Fee & Payment: The fee is $20.00 per record, if uncertain of the date the search covers a 2-year searching period. There is a $2.00 search fee for each additional 2 years searched. Fee payee- General Treasurer, State of Rhode Island. Prepayment required. Personal checks accepted.

Mail search: Turnaround time- 6 to 8 weeks. For one-week service, add an additional $7.00 and mark "rush" on outside of envelope. A SASE is requested. Include photo copy of requester's valid government issued ID. Include photo copy of requester's ID (DL, passport, etc).

In person: Simple requests may be processed while you wait.

Expedited service: Turnaround time- 5 days. Add $7.00 for processing.

Divorce Records

Records not maintained by a state level agency.

Divorce records are found at one of the 5 county Family Courts.

Workers' Compensation Records

Department of Labor & Training, Division of Workers' Compensation, PO Box 20190, Cranston, RI 02920 (Courier address- 1511 Pontiac Ave, Cranston, RI 02920); 401-462-8100, Fax- 401-462-8105; 8:30AM-4PM. www.dlt.ri.gov

Indexing & Storage: Records available from 1970s. New records available for inquiry immediately.

Searching: Records are not available for employment screening. A first report of injury is not public, by law. Records are released to claimant, attorneys, employer and insurer only if connected to case. Include in request- claimant name, SSN, file number (if known), reason for information request, specific records that you need copies of. Records of insurance carrier coverage only are available for no charge by phone or mail. This data not released- medical records.

Access by: mail, fax, in person.

Fee & Payment: The search fee is $15.00 per hour. Copies are $.15 per page. There is a $.40 per page fee for return by fax. Fee payee- Department of Labor & Training. Prepayment is required for first time requesters. Personal checks accepted, credit cards are not.

Mail search: Turnaround time- 1 to 2 weeks. A SASE is requested.

Fax search: You may request records by fax.

In person: Proof of identity is required.

Other access: Workers' Compensation Court calendars are available free at www.courts.state.ri.us/workers/calendars.htm.

Driver Records

Division of Motor Vehicles, Driving Record Clerk, Operator Control, 30 Howard Ave, Bldg #58, Cranston, RI 02920; 401-462-0800; 8:30AM-3:15PM. www.dmv.ri.gov

The agency follows DPPA. Ongoing requesters should be approved and have an account. Casual requesters must have consent of subject or no record is given.

Indexing & Storage: Records available for 3 years for accidents and moving violations, 5 years for alcohol-related violations or suspensions, 3 years after reinstatement for suspensions. Surrendered licenses are purged 3 years after expiration. New records available for inquiry in 20 days after received from courts.

Searching: Information is not made available for the purpose of commercial solicitation or trade. A description of proposed use must be submitted in advance for departmental approval of high volume requesters. Include in request- driver's license number, full name, date of birth. Use of a state form suggested but not required; find the form at www.dmv.state.ri.us/documents/forms/Reg-DL_App.pdf. Copies of tickets may be obtained without fee by writing to the Traffic Tribunal at 345 Harris Ave, Providence 02908. This data not released- SSNs.

Access by: mail, in person, online.

Fee & Payment: The fee is $17.50 per record request, $19.50 if online. This is the highest fee in the nation for an electronic driving record. Fee payee- Division of Motor Vehicles. Prepayment required. Personal checks accepted, credit cards are not.

Mail search: Turnaround time- 7-10 days. A SASE is requested.

In person: Most requests can be handled immediately.

Online search: Driving records are available in two manners. From the home page above, anyone may request a record online, pay the $19.50 service fee with a credit card and the record will be mailed to the address shown on the DL. This record does not contain the driver's address or SSN. The driver name. DOB and license number must be submitted. Ongoing requesters who qualify to receive records with personal information may obtain a subscription account for interactive service. The same record fee applies. For more information about becoming a subscriber visit www.ri.gov/subscriber/.

Vehicle Ownership & Registration

Division of Motor Vehicles, Vehicle Records, 100 Main Street, Pawtucket, RI 02860; 401-462-4368, 401-462-5774 (Titles), Fax- 401-721-2697; 8:30AM-3:30PM. www.dmv.ri.gov

A Request for Title Information form is downloadable at www.dmv.ri.gov/documents/forms/TitleInfo_Request.pdf, other vehicle record data at www.dmv.ri.gov/documents/forms/Reg-DL_App.pdf.

Indexing & Storage: Records available for 3 years for title information, for 10 years for registration information. New records available for inquiry in 1 week.

Searching: Request must be in writing and the purpose stated. Records will not be released for commercial or solicitation purposes. Casual requesters cannot obtain records unless written consent of subject is given. Include in request- for title: reason for request, VIN, year, make, owner name/address, your signature. For registration: VIN, plate, owner name/address, your name/adr. For DR: DR#, name, address. In all record requests, the agency would like to know the reason for request.

Access by: mail, in person.

Fee & Payment: The fee is $11.50 per record request for registration and license data, and $26.50 for title information. The agency will release lien information. There is a full charge for a no record found request. Fee payee- Registry of Motor Vehicles. Prepayment required. Personal checks accepted, credit cards are not.

Mail search: Turnaround time- 1 week. SASE is requested. Title information turnaround is 4-6 weeks.

In person: Title information can be obtained in person. Registration records are not released in person, but are mailed.

Other access: Bulk retrieval of vehicle and ownership information is limited to statistical purposes.

Accident Reports

Rhode Island State Police, Accident Reports, 311 Danielson Pike, North Scituate, RI 02857-1907; 401-444-1143, Fax- 401-444-1133; 9AM-4PM M,T,F; till 6:30PM on Wed. www.risp.state.ri.us

Indexing & Storage: Records available for the past 2 years plus the current year. Accidents before that are stored in archives. Hard copy files are indexed. New records available for inquiry in 3-5 days.

Searching: Include in request- reason for information request, full name, date of accident, location of accident. An accident report form and example are online at www.dmv.state.ri.us/documents/forms/Accident_Report.pdf.

Access by: mail, phone, in person.

Fee & Payment: The fee is $10.00 per record. Fee payee- Rhode Island State Police Prepayment required. Personal checks accepted, credit cards are not.

Mail search: Turnaround time- 1 week. A SASE is requested.

Phone search: No fee for telephone request. The office will let a requester know if a report is available, but information will not be given over the phone.

In person: Same day processing is available, provided report has been received.

Vessel Ownership & Registration

Dept of Environmental Management, Boat Registration & Licensing, 235 Promenade, Rm 360, Providence, RI 02908; 401-222-6647, Fax- 401-222-1181; 8:30AM-3:30PM M-F.

www.dem.ri.gov/programs/bpoladm/manserv/hfb/boating/boating.htm

Indexing & Storage: Records available from the late 1970s to the present. Records are computer indexed for the last 3 years. This is a title state, lien information shows on the title record. All boats over 14 ft must be titled and registered. New records available for inquiry in 25 days to one year.

Searching: All requests must be in writing on the agency's request form. Call or write for the form. Records cannot be purchased for solicitation or commercial purposes. This agency complies with DPPA. Include in request- name or registration number or RI number. This data not released- street address

Access by: mail, fax, in person.

Fee & Payment: There is no fee, unless extensive searching is involved which is a $15.00 per hour charge.

Mail search: Turnaround time- 1 to 2 weeks or more. SASE not required.

Fax search: Will accept fax requests if on agency Form.

In person: Turnaround time depending on staff availability.

Legislation Records

Secretary of State, Public Information Center, State House, Room 38, Providence, RI 02903; 401-222-3983 (Bill Status Only), 401-222-2473 (State Library), Fax- 401-222-1404; 8:30AM-4:30PM. www.rilin.state.ri.us

All bills are available at the State Law Library.

Indexing & Storage: Records available for current session and previous year only kept on paper, otherwise records are archived. New records available for inquiry in seconds.

Searching: One may search by bill number, subject, word, sponsor, etc.

Access by: mail, phone, fax, in person, online.

Fee & Payment: Copies are made by the Office of Public Information, $.15 per page. There is no search fee. Personal checks accepted.

Mail search: Turnaround time- 2 weeks. SASE not required.

Phone search: Records are available by phone.

Fax search: Fax searching available.

In person: There are public access terminals available.

Online search: The website provides excellent means to search enactments and measures by keywords or bill numbers. The state statutes are found at www.rilin.state.ri.us/Statutes/Statutes.html.

Other access: A CD with legislative information is available for purchase.

Voter Registration

Secretary of State, Elections Division, 148 West River Street, Providence, RI 02904-2615; 401-222-2340, Fax- 401-222-1440; 8:30AM-4:30PM.

www.sec.state.ri.us/elections

The voter registration database is public record. Direct questions to elections@sec.state.ri.us.

Searching: The Local Board of Canvassers keeps records at the town and city level. Although records are open, they may not be purchased for commercial purposes. The record show the voter's DOB. This data not released- SSNs, DLs.

Access by: mail, phone, in person, online.

Mail search: Records are available by mail.

Phone search: Limited record information is available by phone.

In person: Records may be searched in person

Online search: A specific look-up or verification of voter registration is available at www.sec.state.ri.us/vic/. The name, DOB and town is needed. The search shows voter preferences.

Other access: A database of all registered voters, only selected voters by town, is available for $25.00 per CD.

GED Certificates

Department of Education, GED Testing, 255 Westminster, Providence, RI 02908; 401-222-8948, Fax- 401-222-4256; 8AM-3:30PM.

www.ride.ri.gov/

Indexing & Storage: Records available from the 1950's. New records available for inquiry in 1 month.

Searching: Include in request- SSN, date of birth, year of testing name at time of test, and test center name if known. A signed release is also required for a verification or transcript copy.

Access by: mail, phone, in person.

Fee & Payment: The fee for a transcript is $5.00 or duplicate diploma. There is no fee for a verification. Fee payee- General Treasurer, State of Rhode Island. Prepayment required. No personal checks or credit cards accepted.

Mail search: Turnaround time- 7 to 10 days. SASE not required.

Phone search: Limited data is available.

In person: Simple requests may be processed while you wait, but only if emergency; not offered as an ongoing service.

Hunting & Fishing License Information

Boat Registration & Licensing, Licensing, 235 Promenade St, Rm 360, Providence, RI 02908; 401-222-3576, Fax- 401-222-1181; 8:30AM-3:30PM. www.dem.ri.gov/topics/permits.htm

Recreational license information is kept on paper (forwarded to this office by vendors), and is not computerized.

Indexing & Storage: Records available for several years. New records available for inquiry in 25 days to 1 year.

Searching: Although all records are considered open, commercial use of the records is not permitted. Include in request- date of application, date of birth, address. Also, include where purchased. Requests must be in writing. This data not released- street address

Access by: mail, phone, fax, in person.

Fee & Payment: There is no fee for a short search or confirmation. Otherwise, for extensive searches the rate $15.00 per hour. Fee payee- RI DEM. Prepayment required. Personal checks accepted, credit cards are not.

Mail search: Turnaround time- 1 week to 10 days.

Phone search: They will confirm only.

Fax search: Same criteria as mail searches.

In person: They will return by mail.

Rhode Island State Licensing Agencies

For details about the agency responsible for licensing/certifying/registering an item below or in the Agency Quick Finder section, match an item's number with the number of the agency in the *Licensing Agency Information* section.

Rhode Island Licenses Searchable Online

Acupuncturist #13 .... www.health.state.ri.us/hsr/professions/index.php
Ambulatory Care Facility #13 .... www.health.state.ri.us/hsr/professions/index.php
Asbestos Worker #13 .... www.health.state.ri.us/hsr/professions/index.php
Assisted Living Facility #13 .... www.health.state.ri.us/hsr/professions/index.php
Athletic Trainer #13 .... www.health.state.ri.us/hsr/professions/index.php
Auctioneer #11 .... www.dbr.state.ri.us/divisions/commlicensing/auctioneer.php
Audiologist #13 .... www.health.state.ri.us/hsr/professions/index.php
Automobile Body Shop #11 .... www.dbr.state.ri.us/divisions/commlicensing/autobody.php
Automobile Glass Installer #11 .... www.dbr.state.ri.us/divisions/commlicensing/autoglass.php
Automobile Wrecker #11 .... www.dbr.state.ri.us/divisions/commlicensing/autowrecking.php
Barber Shop #13 .... www.health.state.ri.us/hsr/professions/index.php
Barber/Barber Instructor #13 .... www.health.state.ri.us/hsr/professions/index.php
Birth Center #13 .... www.health.state.ri.us/hsr/professions/index.php
Blood Test Screener #13 .... www.health.state.ri.us/hsr/professions/index.php
Business Filing/Annual Report #14 .... www.sec.state.ri.us/corps
Charter School #16 .... www.ride.ri.gov
Chemical Dependency Clinical Spvr #6 .... www.ribccdp.com/LISTS.html
Chemical Dependency Prof./Adv. #6 .... www.ribccdp.com/LISTS.html
Chiropractor #13 .... www.health.state.ri.us/hsr/professions/index.php
Clinical Supervisor, Recognized #6 .... www.ribccdp.com/LISTS.html
Contractor, Resid'l Building #4 .... www.crb.state.ri.us/search.php
Contractor, Watch List #4 .... www.crb.state.ri.us/watchlist.php
Controlled Substance Wholesaler #3 .... https://healthri.mylicense.com/Verification/
Cosmetologist/Cosmetology Instr. #13 .... www.health.state.ri.us/hsr/professions/index.php
Counselor in Training #6 .... www.ribccdp.com/LISTS.html
CPA #1 .... www.dbr.state.ri.us/divisions/accountancy/
Criminal Justice Professional #6 .... www.ribccdp.com/LISTS.html
Day Care, Children #22 .... www.dcyf.state.ri.us/day_care_provider.php
Dental Hygienist #13 .... www.health.state.ri.us/hsr/professions/index.php
Dentist #13 .... www.health.state.ri.us/hsr/professions/index.php
Dietitian/Nutritionist #13 .... www.health.state.ri.us/hsr/professions/index.php
Electrician #8 .... www.dlt.ri.gov/profregs/ElectricianMain.htm
Electrologist #13 .... www.health.state.ri.us/hsr/professions/index.php
Embalmer #13 .... www.health.state.ri.us/hsr/professions/index.php
Emergency Care Facility #13 .... www.health.state.ri.us/hsr/professions/index.php
Emergency Med. Technician/Srvc #13 .... www.health.state.ri.us/hsr/professions/index.php
Esthetician #13 .... www.health.state.ri.us/hsr/professions/index.php
Funeral Director #13 .... www.health.state.ri.us/hsr/professions/index.php
Group Home #13 .... www.health.state.ri.us/hsr/professions/index.php
Hairdresser/Hairdresser Instructor #13 .... www.health.state.ri.us/hsr/professions/index.php
Hazardous Waste Transporter #9 .... www.dem.ri.gov/programs/benviron/waste/transpor/index.htm
Hearing Aid Dispenser #13 .... www.health.state.ri.us/hsr/professions/index.php
Hoisting Engineer #8 .... www.dlt.ri.gov/profregs/HoistMain.htm
Home Care Provider #13 .... www.health.state.ri.us/hsr/professions/index.php
Home Nursing Care #13 .... www.health.state.ri.us/hsr/professions/index.php
Hospice Provider #13 .... www.health.state.ri.us/hsr/professions/index.php
Hospital #13 .... www.health.state.ri.us/hsr/professions/index.php
Hypodermic Dispenser #3 .... https://healthri.mylicense.com/Verification/
Insurance Broker/Producer/Agent #5 .... www.dbr.ri.gov/divisions/insurance/licensed.php
Interpreter for the Deaf #13 .... www.health.state.ri.us/hsr/professions/index.php
Laboratory, Medical #13 .... www.health.state.ri.us/hsr/professions/index.php
Lobbyist Registration #14 .... www.sec.state.ri.us/resources_for/lobbyist.html
Manicurist #13 .... www.health.state.ri.us/hsr/professions/index.php
Manicurist Shop #13 .... www.health.state.ri.us/hsr/professions/index.php
Marriage & Family Therapist #13 .... www.health.state.ri.us/hsr/professions/index.php
Massage Therapist #13 .... www.health.state.ri.us/hsr/professions/index.php

Medical Doctor #13 .... www.health.state.ri.us/hsr/professions/index.php
Medical Waste Transporter #9 .... www.dem.ri.gov/programs/benviron/waste/transpor/index.htm
Mental Health Counselor #13 .... www.health.state.ri.us/hsr/professions/index.php
Midwife #13 .... www.health.state.ri.us/hsr/professions/index.php
Mobile Home Park #11 .... www.dbr.state.ri.us/divisions/commlicensing/mobile.php
Mortgage Broker #5 .... www.dbr.state.ri.us/documents/divisions/banking/program_operations/List_of_Licensees.pdf
Notary Public #15 .... http://ucc.state.ri.us/notaries/notaries.htm#data
Nuclear Medicine Technologist #13 .... www.health.state.ri.us/hsr/professions/index.php
Nurse #13 .... www.health.state.ri.us/hsr/professions/index.php
Nurse-LPN #13 .... www.health.state.ri.us/hsr/professions/index.php
Nursing Assistant #13 .... www.health.state.ri.us/hsr/professions/index.php
Nursing Home Administrator #13 .... www.health.state.ri.us/hsr/professions/index.php
Nursing Service #13 .... www.health.state.ri.us/hsr/professions/index.php
Occupational Therapist #13 .... www.health.state.ri.us/hsr/professions/index.php
Office Operatories (Medical) #13 .... www.health.state.ri.us/hsr/professions/index.php
Open Meeting #14 .... www.sec.state.ri.us/pubinfo/openmeetings
Optician #13 .... www.health.state.ri.us/hsr/professions/index.php
Optometrist #13 .... www.health.state.ri.us/hsr/professions/index.php
Osteopathic Physician #13 .... www.docboard.org/ri/df/search.htm
Outpatient Rehabilitation #13 .... www.health.state.ri.us/hsr/professions/index.php
Pharmacist/Pharmacy Technician #3 .... https://healthri.mylicense.com/Verification/
Pharmacy #3 .... https://healthri.mylicense.com/Verification/
Phlebotomy Station #13 .... www.health.state.ri.us/hsr/professions/index.php
Physical Therapist #13 .... www.health.state.ri.us/hsr/professions/index.php
Physical Therapist Assistant #13 .... www.health.state.ri.us/hsr/professions/index.php
Physician #13 .... www.health.state.ri.us/hsr/professions/index.php
Physician Assistant #13 .... www.health.state.ri.us/hsr/professions/index.php
Physicians Controlled Substance #3 .... https://healthri.mylicense.com/Verification/
Podiatrist #13 .... www.health.state.ri.us/hsr/professions/index.php
Prevention Specialist/Supvr./Adv'c'd #6 .... www.ribccdp.com/LISTS.html
Prosthetist #13 .... www.health.state.ri.us/hsr/professions/index.php
Psychologist #13 .... www.health.state.ri.us/hsr/professions/index.php
Public Accountant-CPA #1 .... www.dbr.state.ri.us/divisions/accountancy/
Public Accounting Firm #1 .... www.dbr.state.ri.us/divisions/accountancy/
Radiation Therapist #13 .... www.health.state.ri.us/hsr/professions/index.php
Radiographer #13 .... www.health.state.ri.us/hsr/professions/index.php
Real Estate Agent/Seller #5 .... www.dbr.state.ri.us/pdf_forms/RE-Real%20Estate%20Salespersons.pdf
Real Estate Appraiser #5 .... www.dbr.state.ri.us/pdf_forms/RE-Real%20Estate%20Appraisers.pdf
Real Estate Broker #5 .... www.dbr.state.ri.us/pdf_forms/RE-Real%20Estate%20Brokers.pdf
Residential Care Facility #13 .... www.health.state.ri.us/hsr/professions/index.php
Respiratory Care Practitioner #13 .... www.health.state.ri.us/hsr/professions/index.php
Roofer, Commercial #4 .... www.crb.state.ri.us/search.php
Salvage Yard #11 .... www.dbr.state.ri.us/divisions/commlicensing/autowrecking.php
Sanitarian #13 .... www.health.state.ri.us/hsr/professions/index.php
School Principal/Superint'nd't/Supvr #16 .... https://www.ricert.ride.ri.gov/RIDE/
Septic Transporter #9 .... www.dem.ri.gov/programs/benviron/waste/transpor/index.htm
Social Worker #13 .... www.health.state.ri.us/hsr/professions/index.php
Speech/Language Pathologist #13 .... www.health.state.ri.us/hsr/professions/index.php
Student Assistance Counselor #6 .... www.ribccdp.com/LISTS.html
Surgery Center, Freestanding #13 .... www.health.state.ri.us/hsr/professions/index.php
Tanning Facility #13 .... www.health.state.ri.us/hsr/professions/index.php
Tattoo Artist #13 .... www.health.state.ri.us/hsr/professions/index.php
Teacher #16 .... https://www.ricert.ride.ri.gov/RIDE/
Travel Agent/Agency #11 .... www.dbr.state.ri.us/divisions/commlicensing/travel.php
Veterinarian #13 .... www.health.state.ri.us/hsr/professions/index.php
X-ray Facility& Portable #13 .... www.health.state.ri.us/hsr/professions/index.php

Rhode Island Licensing Quick Finder

Acupuncturist #13 401-222-2828
Alarm Agent/Company #11 401-222-3857
Ambulatory Care Facility #13 401-222-2566
Arborist #10 401-647-3367
Architect #5 401-222-2565
Asbestos Worker #13 401-222-3601
Assisted Living Facility #13 401-222-5888
Athletic Trainer #13 401-222-5888
Attorney #21 401-222-4233
Auctioneer #11 401-222-3857
Audiologist #13 401-222-2828
Automobile Body Shop #11 401-222-3857
Automobile Glass Installer #11 401-222-3857
Automobile Wrecker #11 401-222-3857
Bail Bondsman #18 401-222-3212
Bank #5 401-222-2405
Bank Holding Company #5 401-222-2405
Barber Shop #13 401-222-2828
Barber/Barber Instructor #13 401-222-2828
Beekeeper #9 .... 401-222-2781 x4519
Birth Center #13 401-222-2827
Blaster #19 401-294-0861
Blood Test Screener #13 401-222-2827
Boxer #5 401-222-6541
Business Filing/Annual Report #14 401-222-2357
Cattle Dealer #9 .... 401-222-2781 x4503
Charter School #16 401-222-4600
Check Casher #5 401-222-2405
Chemical Dependency Clinical Spvr #6 401-233-2215
Chemical Dependency Prof./Adv. #6 ... 401-233-2215
Chiropractor #13 401-222-2828
Clinical Lab Scientist, Cytogenetic #7 .. 401-222-2827
Clinical Lab Scientist/Technician #7 401-222-2827
Clinical Supervisor, Recognized #6 401-233-2215
Contractor, Resid'l Building #4 401-222-1268
Contractor, Watch List #4 401-222-1268
Controlled Substance Wholesaler #3 ... 401-222-2837
Cosmetologist/Cosmetology Instr. #13. 401-222-2828
Counselor in Training #6 401-233-2215
Court Reporter #2 401-222-8663
CPA #1 401-222-3185
Credit Union #5 401-222-2405
Criminal Justice Professional #6 401-233-2215
Cytotechnologist #7 401-222-2827
Day Care, Children #22 401-528-3624
Debt Pooler #5 401-222-2405
Dental Hygienist #13 401-222-2828
Dentist #13 401-222-2828
Dietitian/Nutritionist #13 401-222-5888
Electrician #8 401-462-8571
Electrologist #13 401-222-2828
Electron Microscopy, Lab Scientist #7 . 401-222-2827
Elevator Inspector #8 401-462-8579
Elevator Mechanic #8 401-462-8579
Embalmer #13 401-222-2828
Emergency Care Facility #13 401-222-2401
Emergency Med. Technician/Svc #13 .. 401-222-2401
Esthetician #13 401-222-2828
Family/Group Day Care Home Provider #22
.... 401-528-3624
Financial Institution #5 401-222-2405

Fire Alarm Installer #19 401-294-0861
Fire Extinguisher Installer/Svc #19 401-294-0861
Fireworks Shooter #19 401-294-0861
Fisher, Commercial #9 401-222-6647
Foster Care/Home #22 401-528-3606
Funeral Director #13 401-222-2828
Fur Buyer #9 401-222-6647
Group Home #13 401-222-2566
Hairdresser/Hairdresser Instructor #13 401-222-2828
Hazardous Waste Transp'rt'r #9 401-222-4700 x7517
Health Club #11 401-222-3857
Hearing Aid Dispenser #13 401-222-2828
Histologic Technician, Clinical #7 401-222-2827
Hoisting Engineer #8 401-462-8554
Home Care Provider #13 401-222-2566
Home Nursing Care #13 401-222-2566
Hospice Provider #13 401-222-2566
Hospital #13 401-222-2566
Hypodermic Dispenser #3 401-222-2837
Insurance Adjuster #5 401-222-2223
Insurance Appraiser #5 401-222-2223
Insurance Broker/Producer/Agent #5 ... 401-222-2223
Insurance Solicitor #5 401-222-2223
Interpreter for the Deaf #13 401-222-2828
Investment Advisor #5 401-222-3048
Laboratory, Medical #13 401-222-2827
Landscaper #5 401-222-2565
Lender/Loan Broker #5 401-222-2405
Lifeguard #12 401-222-2632
Liquor Control #5 401-222-2562
Lobbyist Registration #14 401-222-3983
Manicurist #13 401-222-2828
Manicurist Shop #13 401-222-2828
Marriage & Family Therapist #13 401-222-2828
Massage Therapist #13 401-222-2828
Medical Doctor #13 401-222-3855
Medical Waste Transporter #9 .. 401-222-4700 x7517
Mental Health Counselor #13 401-222-2828
Midwife #13 401-222-5700
Mobile Home Park #11 401-222-3857
Mobile/Manufact'd Home Mfg./Dealer #11
.... 401-222-3857
Money Broker #5 401-222-2405
Money Transferer #5 401-222-2405
Mortgage Broker #5 401-222-2405
Notary Public #15 401-222-1487
Nuclear Medicine Technologist #13 401-222-2828
Nurse #13 401-222-5700
Nurse-LPN #13 401-222-5700
Nurseryman #9 .... 401-222-2781 x4516
Nursing Assistant #13 401-222-5888
Nursing Home Administrator #13 401-222-5888
Nursing Service #13 401-222-2827
Occupational Therapist #13 401-222-2827
Office Operatories (Medical) #13 401-222-2827
Open Meeting #14 401-222-2357
Optician #13 401-222-2827
Optometrist #13 401-222-2827
Osteopathic Physician #13 401-222-3855
Outpatient Rehabilitation #13 401-222-2827
Park Ranger #12 401-222-2632

Pesticide Applicator #9 .... 401-222-2781 x4510
Pharmacist/Pharmacy Technician #3 .. 401-222-2837
Pharmacy #3 401-222-2837
Phlebotomy Station #13 401-222-2827
Physical Therapist #13 401-222-2827
Physical Therapist Assistant #13 401-222-2827
Physician #13 401-222-2827
Physician Assistant #13 401-222-2827
Physicians Controlled Substance #3 ... 401-222-3855
Pilot, Ship #20 401-783-5551
Pipefitter #8 401-462-8535
Plumber/Master Plumber/Journey'n #8 401-462-8525
Podiatrist #13 401-222-2827
Prevention Specialist/Supvr./Adv'd #6 . 401-233-2215
Prosthetist #13 401-222-2827
Psychologist #13 401-222-2827
Public Accountant-CPA #1 401-222-3185
Public Accounting Firm #1 401-222-3185
Pyrotechnic Operator #19 401-294-0861
Radiation Therapist #13 401-222-2827
Radiographer #13 401-222-2827
Reading Specialist #16 401-222-4600
Real Estate Agent/Seller #5 401-222-2255
Real Estate Appraiser #5 401-222-2255
Real Estate Broker #5 401-222-2255
Refrigeration Technician #8 401-462-8535
Residential Care Facility #13 401-222-2827
Residential Facility #22 401-528-3623
Respiratory Care Practitioner #13 401-222-2827
Roofer, Commercial #4 401-222-1268
Salvage Yard #11 401-222-3857
Sanitarian #13 401-222-2827
School Coach #16 401-222-4600
School Guidance Counselor #16 401-222-4600
School Principal/Superint'd'nt/Spvr #16 401-222-4600
School Psychol'gist/Social Worker #16 401-222-4600
Securities Broker/Dealer/Seller #5 401-222-3048
Septic Transporter #9 .... 401-222-4700 x7517
Sewage Disposal System Installer #9 .. 401-222-6820
Sheet Metal Technician/Worker #8 401-462-8535
Social Worker #13 401-222-2827
Speech/Language Pathologist #13 401-222-2827
Student Assistance Counselor #6 401-233-2215
Surgery Center, Freestanding #13 401-222-2827
Surveyor, Land #5 401-222-2565
Tanning Facility #13 401-222-2827
Tattoo Artist #13 401-222-2827
Teacher #16 401-222-4600
Telecommunications Technician #8 401-462-8533
Trapper #9 401-222-6647
Travel Agent/Agencies #11 401-222-3857
Upholstery/Bedding Mfg. #11 401-222-3857
Vendor Employee #5 401-222-2405
Veterinarian #13 401-222-2827
Waste Water Treatment Plant Operator #9
.... 401-222-6820
Wildlife Propagator #9 401-222-6647
Wildlife Rehabilitator #17 401-789-0281
Woods Operator #10 401-647-3367
Wrestler #5 401-222-6541
X-ray Facility& Portable #13 401-222-2827

Rhode Island Licensing Agency Information

#1 Department of Business Regulation, Board of Accountancy, 233 Richmond St, Providence, RI 02903-4236;
401-222-3185, Fax- 401-222-6654. www.dbr.state.ri.us/divisions/accountancy/ Search data at- www.dbr.state.ri.us/divisions/accountancy/

#2 Court Administrator Office, Superior Court, 250 Benefit St, #506, Providence, RI 02903; 401-222-8663, Fax- 401-222-2625. Hours- 9AM-5PM. www.courts.ri.gov/

#3 Board of Pharmacy, 3 Capitol Hill, Rm 104, Providence, RI 02908; 401-222-2837, Fax- 401-222-2158. www.health.state.ri.us Search data at- https://healthri.mylicense.com/Verification/

#4 Contractors' Registration Board, 1 Capitol Hill, 2nd Fl, Providence, RI 02908; 401-222-1268, Fax- 401-222-1940. Hours- 8:30AM-4PM. www.crb.state.ri.us Search data at- www.crb.state.ri.us/search.php

#5 Business Regulation Department, Division of Commercial Licensing & Regulation, 233 Richmond St, Providence, RI 02903-4232; 401-222-2246, Fax- 401-222-6098. www.dbr.state.ri.us

#6 Certification of Chemical Dependency Professionals, 31 Smith Ave - 3 Rear, Greenville, RI 02828; 401-349-3822, Fax- 401-349-3833. 9AM-2PM. www.ribccdp.com Search data at- www.ribccdp.com/LISTS.html

#7 Clinical Laboratory Science Board, 3 Capitol Hill, Rm 104, Providence, RI 02908; 401-222-4520, Fax- 401-222-1272. www.health.state.ri.us

#8 Department of Labor & Training, Division of Professional Regulation - Bldg #70, PO Box 20247 (1511 Pontiac Av), Providence, RI 02920-0943; 401-462-8580, Fax- 401-462-8528. Hours- 8AM-4PM. www.dlt.state.ri.us

#9 Department of Environmental Management, Bureau of Natural Resources, 235 Promenade St, #260, Providence, RI 02908-5767; 401-222-4700 x2414, Fax- 401-222-3162. www.dem.ri.gov/programs/bnatres/

#10 Department of Environmental Management, Division of Forest Environment, 1037 Hartford Pike, North Scituate, RI 02857; 401-647-3367, Fax- 401-647-3590. www.dem.ri.gov/programs/bnatres/forest/

#11 Division of Licensing & Consumer Protection, Commercial Licensing, 233 Richmond St, Providence, RI 02903; 401-222-2416, Fax- 401-222-6654. www.dbr.state.ri.us

#12 Division of Parks & Recreation, 2321 Hartford Ave, Johnston, RI 02919; 401-222-2632, Fax- 401-934-0610. 8:30AM-4PM. www.riparks.com

#13 Health Department, Professional Regulation Division, 3 Capitol Hill, Rm 104, Providence, RI 02908-5097; 401-222-2828, Fax- 401-222-3352. Hours- 8:30AM-4:30PM. www.health.state.ri.us/hsr/professions/index.php Search data at- www.health.state.ri.us/hsr/professions/index.php Also, search medical doctors and osteopaths at www.docboard.org/ri/df/search.htm.

#14 Office of Secretary of State, Lobbyist Registration, State House, Smith St, Rm 38, Providence, RI 02903; 401-222-2357, Fax- 401-222-1404. Hours- 8:30AM-4:30PM. www.state.ri.us

#15 Office of Secretary of State, Notary Public Section, 148 W River St, Providence, RI 02903; 401-222-3040, Fax- 401-222-3879. Hours- 8:30AM-4:30PM. http://www3.sec.state.ri.us

#16 Department of Education, Office of Teacher Certification, 255 Westminster St, Providence, RI 02903; 401-222-4600, Fax- 401-222-2048. Hours- 8AM-4PM. www.ride.ri.gov

#17 Department of Environmental Management, Division of Fish & Wildlife, 4808 Tower Hill Road, Wakefield,, RI 02879; 401-789-3094, Fax- 401-783-4460. Hours-8:30AM-4PM. www.dem.ri.gov/programs/bnatres/fishwild/

#18 Superior Court, Bondsman Registration, 250 Benefit St, Rm 533, Providence, RI 02903; 401-222-3212, Fax- 401-272-4645. Hours- 9AM-4:30PM. Direct written requests to Judge Jos. F. Rodgers, Jr. Please make out bonds to "General Chief Clerk". All bonds expire on June 30, 2009, etc.

#19 State Fire Marshall's Office, 118 Parade St, Providence, RI 02909; 401-462-4200, Fax- 401-462-4250. www.fire-marshal.ri.gov/about.php

#20 Pilotage Commission, 301 Great Island Rd, Galilee, RI 02882; 401-783-5551, Fax- 401-783-7285. www.state.ri.us/govtracker/index.php?page=DetailDeptAgency&eid=1554

#21 Supreme Court, Board of Bar Examiners, 250 Benefit St, Providence, RI 02903; 401-222-4233, Fax- 401-222-3599. www.courts.state.ri.us/supreme/bar/barexaminers.htm

#22 Department of Children, Youth & Families, 101 Friendship St #101, Providence, RI 02903; 401-528-3502. www.dcyf.state.ri.us Search data at- www.dcyf.state.ri.us/day_care_provider.php

Rhode Island Federal Courts

The following list indicates the district and division name for each county in the state.

Rhode Island County/Court Cross Reference

Bristol.......... Providence
Kent.......... Providence
Newport.......... Providence
Providence.......... Providence
Washington.......... Providence

US District Court

Rhode Island Division Clerk's Office, One Exchange Terrace, Federal Bldg, Providence, RI 02903, 401-752-7200; Fax- 401-752-7247. Hours-9AM-4:30PM. www.rid.uscourts.gov

Counties: All counties in Rhode Island.

Searches/Indexing: Include names in search request. Results do not include SSN or DOB. Will not fax back documents. New cases are in the index 1-2 days after filing date. Both computer and card indexes maintained; computer goes back to 1992. District-wide searches available here. Case files maintained at court 25 years after closed.

Search Access: Only case number or name released via phone. **Mail:** Search usually completed- 1-2 days. Include SASE for return. **Fax:** Fax search and case file requests accepted. **In person:** 2 public terminals available. Self-serve copies $.50 each.

Payment: Pay by money order, cashier's or personal check. No credit cards accepted. Payee: Clerk, US District Court.

E-Services: PACER records go back to 12/1988. New records online after 1 day. ECF at https://ecf.rid.uscourts.gov. **Opinions Online:** www.rid.uscourts.gov/Judges%20Opinions.asp. **Online Note:** Court calendars at www.rid.uscourts.gov/calendars.asp.

US Bankruptcy Court

Rhode Island Division Court Clerk, 380 Westminster St, 6th Fl, Providence, RI 02903, 401-626-3100; Fax- 401-626-3150. 9AM-4PM. www.rib.uscourts.gov

Counties: All counties in Rhode Island.

Searches/Indexing: Include name and SSN in search request. Results include last 4 SSN digits. Will not fax back documents. New cases are in the index same day after filing date. All closed files on paper have been sent to the archives.

Search Access: Only docket info is available by phone. Voice Case Information Service available, call VCIS at 800-843-2841 or 401-626-3076. **Mail:** Search usually completed- same day. Include SASE for return. **Fax:** Fax search same as mail. **In person:** 2 public terminals available. Self-serve copies from computer- $.10 each.

Payment: Pay by Visa/MC, money order, cashier's or personal check. No debtor checks accepted. Payee: Clerk, US Bankruptcy Court.

E-Services: Document images available. PACER records go back to 1990. New records online immediately. ECF at https://ecf.rib.uscourts.gov. **Opinions Online:** www.rib.uscourts.gov/CourtResources/Opinions/opinions.htm. **Online Note:** Access calendars at www.rib.uscourts.gov/CaseInformation/04/calendar.htm; 341 calendars require ECF registration for access.

Standards for Federal Courts: Fees are standard unless noted in profile. Search fee is $26.00 per item (one party name or case number). Copy fee is $.50 per page. Certification fee is $9.00 per document, double for exemplification, if available. Most courts require prepayment. Mail requests should enclose a SASE unless otherwise noted. Before releasing records, all courts require prepayment, unless noted.

District courts index by defendant and plaintiff and by case number. Bankruptcy courts usually index by debtor and case number. While most courts now have their indexes on computer, many may still maintain index card files as well. Courts will archive closed case files at different times.

There are numerous public access programs available to online subscribers. Search the U.S. Party/Case Index to find party names and case numbers among all courts. Individual case data is provided on PACER. A search of CM/ECF provides copies of cases filed electronically. For details about PACER, the US Party/Case Index, and CM/ECF see the Appendix or go to http://pacer.psc.uscourts.gov or call 800-676-6856.

Rhode Island County Courts

Court	Jurisdiction	No. of Courts	How Organized
Superior Courts*	General	4	4 Divisions
District Courts*	Limited	4	6 Divisions
Municipal Courts	Municipal	16	
Probate Courts*	Probate	39	39 Cities/ Towns
Family Courts	Special	4	4 Divisions
Workers' Compensation Court	Special	1	

* Profiled in this Sourcebook.

Court	CIVIL								
	Tort	Contract	Real Estate	Min. Claim	Max. Claim	Small Claims	Estate	Eviction	Domestic Relations
Superior Courts*	X	X	X	$5000	No Max				
District Courts*	X	X	X	$2500	$10,000	$2500		X	
Municipal Courts									
Probate Courts*							X		
Family Courts									X

Court	CRIMINAL				
	Felony	Misdemeanor	DWI/DUI	Preliminary Hearing	Juvenile
Superior Courts*	X				
District Courts*		X	X	X	
Municipal Courts					
Probate Courts*					
Family Courts					X

Administration

Court Administrator, Supreme Court, 250 Benefit St, Providence, RI, 02903; 401-222-3266, Fax: 401-222-4224. www.courts.state.ri.us

Court Structure

Rhode Island has five counties but only four Superior/District Court Locations— 2nd-Newport, 3rd-Kent, 4th-Washington, and 6th-Providence/Bristol Districts. Bristol and Providence counties are completely merged at the Providence location. Civil claims between $5000 and $10,000 may be filed in either Superior Court or District Court at the discretion of the filer. For questions regarding the Superior Courts, telephone 401-222-2622. For questions regarding the District Courts, telephone 401-458-5201. Probate is handled by the Town Clerk at the 39 cities and towns across the state, not at the courts. The Traffic Tribunal over sees traffic and ordinance violations.

Online Access

The Rhode Island Judiciary offers free access to an index of county criminal cases statewide at http://courtconnect.courts.state.ri.us. The year of birth is shown on results. The site provides a disclaimer that the search is provided only as an informational service and should not be relied upon as an official record of the court. Supreme Court and Appellate opinions are available from the home page.

Searching Tips, Fees, and Other Guidelines

The copy fee has been set at $.15 per page, if the court is willing to make a copy. Limited in-person searching of Supreme, District, Superior, and Family court cases are available. Most records available are from the mid 1980's to the present.

Bristol County

Superior & District Courts, ***Probate.***
Former Bristol civil and criminal cases are handled by the Providence County courts.

Barrington Town Hall 283 County Road, Barrington, RI 02806; 401-247-1900 x4; fax: 401-247-3765; 8:30AM-4:30PM (EST). ***Probate.***

Bristol Town Hall 10 Court St, Bristol, RI 02809; 401-253-7000 x21; fax: 401-253-2647; 8:30AM-4PM (EST). ***Probate.***
www.bristolri.us/

Warren Town Hall 514 Main St, Warren, RI 02885; 401-245-7340; fax: 401-245-7421; 9AM-4PM (EST). ***Probate.***

Kent County

Superior Court 222 Quaker Ln, 4th Fl, Warwick, RI 02886; 401-822-6900; civil phone: 401-822-6906; fax: 401-822-6905; 8:30AM-4:00PM (EST). ***Felony, Civil Actions over $10,000.***
Civil Records: Access: In person only. Visitors must perform in person searches themselves. Required to search: name, years to search. Civil cases indexed by defendant, plaintiff; index on computer from 1987. Civil PAT goes back to 1997. PAT results show middle initial, DOB.
Criminal Records: Access: In person, online. Visitors must perform in person searches themselves. Required to search: name, years to search, signed release; also helpful: DOB. Criminal records computerized from 1987. Criminal PAT goes back to 1987. PAT results show middle initial, DOB. Terminal results show year of birth only. Access criminal records free at http://courtconnect.courts.state.ri.us as an informational service only; should not be relied upon as official court record. Online results show middle initial, year of birth, and include aliases.
General Information: Online identifiers in results same as on public terminal. No adoption, confidential or sealed records released. Will not fax documents. Court makes copy: $.15 per page. Self serve: $.15 per page. Certification fee: $3.00 per page. Exemplified copies: $9.00 each plus cert fee. Payee: Clerk of Superior Court. Personal checks accepted; credit cards are not. Prepayment required.

3rd Division District Court 222 Quaker Ln, 2nd Fl, Warwick, RI 02886-0107; 401-822-6750; criminal phone: x1; civil phone: 401-822-6760; fax: 401-822-6755; 8:30AM-4:30PM, till 4PM in Summer (EST). ***Misdemeanor, Civil Actions under $10,000, Eviction, Small Claims.***
Civil Records: Access: In person only. Visitors must perform in person searches themselves. Required to search: name, years to search. Civil cases indexed by defendant, plaintiff. Civil records 1995-1997 on index cards. Archives stored at RI Judicial Records Ctr, 1 Hill St, Pawtucket, RI 02860, 401-277-3249. Records destroyed after 10 years, but remain in computer.
Criminal Records: Access: In person, online. Visitors must perform in person searches themselves. Required to search: name, years to search, DOB, signed release. Criminal records 1995-1997 on index cards. Archives at RI Judicial Records Ctr. Records destroyed after 10 years, but remain in computer. Public use terminal has crim records. PAT results show middle initial, DOB. Terminal results show year of birth only. Access criminal records free at http://courtconnect.courts.state.ri.us as an informational service only; should not be relied upon as official court record. Online results show middle initial, year of birth, and include aliases.
General Information: Online identifiers in results same as on public terminal. No mental or sealed records released. Will not fax documents. Court makes copy: Court will not make copies. Self serve: $.15 per page. Certification fee: $9.00 per page. Payee: 3rd District Court. No personal checks accepted. Visa/MC accepted. Prepayment required.

Coventry Town Hall 1670 Flat River Rd, Coventry, RI 02816; 401-822-9174; fax: 401-822-9132; 8:30AM-4:30PM (EST). ***Probate.***

East Greenwich Town Hall PO Box 111, 125 Main St, East Greenwich, RI 02818; 401-886-8607; 8604; fax: 401-886-8625; 8:30AM-4:30PM (EST). ***Probate.***

Warwick City Hall 3275 Post Rd, Warwick, RI 02886; 401-738-2000 (x6213); fax: 401-732-7640; 8:30AM-4:30PM (EST). ***Probate.***

West Greenwich Town Hall 280 Victory Hwy, West Greenwich, RI 02817; 401-392-3800; fax: 401-392-3805; 8:30AM-4PM (EST). ***Probate.***

West Warwick Town Hall 1170 Main St, West Warwick, RI 02893-4829; 401-822-9201; fax: 401-822-9266; 8:30AM-4:30PM; 8:30AM-4PM June 1st-Labor Day (EST). ***Probate.***

Newport County

Superior Court Florence K Murray Judicial Complex, 45 Washington Sq, Newport, RI 02840; 401-841-8330; fax: 401-846-1673; 8:30AM-4:30PM (July and August till 4PM) (EST). ***Felony, Civil Actions over $10,000.***
Civil Records: Access: Mail, in person. Both court and visitors may perform in person searches. Search fee: $15.00 per hour for search and review for all searches over 30 minutes. Required to search: name, years to search. Civil cases indexed by defendant, plaintiff; index on computer from 1989. Prior records archived at Rhode Island Records Center. Mail turnaround time 1 day. Civil PAT goes back to mid 1980's.
Criminal Records: Access: Mail, fax, in person, online. Both court and visitors may perform in person searches. Search fee: $15.00 per hour for search and review. Required to search: name, years to search, DOB. Criminal records computerized from 1983, index from 1968. Prior records archived at Records Center. Mail turnaround time 1 day. Criminal PAT goes back to early 1980's. PAT results show middle initial, and terminal results show year of birth. Access criminal records free at http://courtconnect.courts.state.ri.us as an informational service only; should not be relied upon as official court record. Online results show middle initial, year of birth, and include aliases.
General Information: Online identifiers in results same as on public terminal. No child molestation or sexual assault records released. Will not fax documents. Court makes copy: $.15 per page. Certification fee: $3.00 per page. Payee: Clerk Superior Court. Personal checks accepted; credit cards are not. Prepayment required. Mail requests: SASE required.

2nd District Court 45 Washington Square, Newport, RI 02840; 401-841-8350; 8:30AM-4:30PM (4PM-summer hours) (EST). ***Misdemeanor, Civil Actions under $10,000, Eviction, Small Claims.***
Civil Records: Access: In person only. Visitors must perform in person searches themselves. Required to search: name, years to search. Civil cases indexed by defendant, plaintiff. Civil index on cards for past 3 years, prior archived at Pawtucket Judicial Records Center. Civil PAT goes back to 1999.
Criminal Records: Access: In person, online. Visitors must perform in person searches themselves. Required to search: name. Overall records from 1999-2002. Computerized records from 1999-2004. Criminal PAT goes back to 1999. PAT results show middle initial, and terminal results show year of birth. Access criminal records free at http://courtconnect.courts.state.ri.us as an informational service only; should not be relied upon as official court record. Online results show middle initial, year of birth, and include aliases.
General Information: Online identifiers in results same as on public terminal. No juvenile, family court, sealed, expunged or ordered by judge or adoption records released. Will not fax documents. Court makes copy: $.15 per page. Self serve: same. Certification fee: $1.00. Payee: 2nd District Court. No personal checks accepted. Visa/MC accepted. Prepayment required.

Jamestown Town Hall 93 Narragansett Ave, Jamestown, RI 02835; 401-423-7200; fax: 401-423-7230; 8AM-4:30PM (EST). ***Probate.***
Probate Court held on first Wed. of every month at 2PM.

Little Compton Probate Ct 40 Commons, PO Box 226, Little Compton, RI 02837; 401-635-4400; fax: 401-635-2470; 8AM-4PM (EST). ***Probate.***

Middletown Town Hall 350 E Main Rd, Middletown, RI 02842; 401-847-0009; fax: 401-845-0406; 8AM-4PM (EST). ***Probate, Traffic, Ordinance.***

Newport City Hall 43 Broadway, Newport, RI 02840; 401-845-5349, 401-846-9600 x1x3; fax: 401-849-8757; 8:30AM-4:30PM (EST). ***Probate.***
www.cityofnewport.com/departments/city-clerk/probate.cfm

Portsmouth Town Hall 2200 E Main Rd, Portsmouth, RI 02871; 401-683-2101; fax: 401-683-0573; 8:30AM-4:30PM (EST). ***Probate.***

Tiverton Town Hall 343 Highland Rd, Tiverton, RI 02878; 401-625-6700; fax: 401-625-6705; 8:30AM-4PM (EST). ***Probate.***

Providence County

Providence/Bristol Superior Court 250 Benefit St, Providence, RI 02903; 401-222-3250; 8:30AM-4:30PM (EST). ***Felony, Civil Actions over $10,000.***
All civil and criminal cases are handled by the Providence County court & Bristol County court.
Civil Records: Access: Phone, mail, in person. Both court and visitors may perform in person searches. No search fee; only one name may be requested over phone. Required to search: name, years to search. Civil cases indexed by defendant, plaintiff; index on computer since 1983. Mail turnaround time 7-10 days by mail. Civil PAT goes back to 1992. PAT results show name only.
Criminal Records: Access: In person, online. Visitors must perform in person searches themselves. Required to search: name, years to search, DOB. Criminal records on computer since 1983. Criminal PAT goes back to same as civil. PAT results show middle initial, and terminal results show year of birth. Access criminal records free at http://courtconnect.courts.state.ri.us as an informational service only; should not be relied upon as official court record. Online results show middle initial, year of birth, and include aliases.
General Information: Online identifiers in results same as on public terminal. No adoption, confidential or sealed records released. Will not fax documents. Court makes copy: $.15 per page. Self serve: same. Certification fee: $3.00 per page. Payee: Providence Superior Court. Personal checks accepted; credit cards are not. Prepayment required.

6th Division District Court 1 Dorrance Plaza, 2nd Fl, Providence, RI 02903; 401-458-5400; 8:30AM-4PM (EST). ***Misdemeanor, Civil Actions under $10,000, Eviction, Small Claims.***
Phone and fax search requests no longer accepted.
Civil Records: Access: Mail, in person. Both court and visitors may perform in person searches. No search fee. Required to search: name, years to search. Civil cases indexed by defendant, plaintiff; index on card files 2006 to 2007; on computer in 2008. Mail turnaround time varies. Civil PAT goes back to 2008.
Criminal Records: Access: Mail, in person, online. Both court and visitors may perform in person searches. No search fee. Required to search: name, years to search. Criminal records for misdemeanor on computer from 1989; records at court only 2 years. Mail turnaround time varies. Criminal PAT goes back to 1992. PAT results show middle initial, and terminal results show year of birth. Access

criminal records free at http://courtconnect.courts.state.ri.us as an informational service only; should not be relied upon as official court record. Online results show middle initial, year of birth, and include aliases.

General Information: Online identifiers in results same as on public terminal. No adoption, confidential or sealed records released. Will not fax documents. Court makes copy: $.15 per page. Certification fee: $1.50. Payee: 6th Division District Court. Personal checks and credit cards accepted. Prepayment required. Mail requests: SASE required.

Burrillville Town Hall 105 Harrisville Main St, Harrisville, RI 02830; 401-568-4300 x114 or x110; fax: 401-568-0490; 8:30AM-4:30PM M-W; 8:30AM-7:00PM TH; 8:30AM-12:30PM Fri (EST). ***Probate.***
www.burrillville.org/Public_Documents/BurrillvilleRI_Clerk/probate

Central Falls City Hall City Clerk's Office, 580 Broad St, Central Falls, RI 02863; 401-727-7400; fax: 401-727-7406; 8:30AM-4:30PM; summer til 3:30PM (EST). ***Probate.***
www.centralfallsri.us

Cranston City Hall 869 Park Ave, Cranston, RI 02910; 401-461-1000 X3197; probate phone: 401-780-3197; fax: 401-780-3165; 8:30AM-4:30PM (EST). ***Probate.***

Cumberland Town Hall PO Box 7, 45 Broad St, Cumberland, RI 02864; 401-728-2400; civil phone: x154; probate phone: x137; fax: 401-724-1103; 8:30AM-4:30PM; Summer- 9AM-4PM (EST). ***Probate, Traffic, Ordinance.***
www.cumberlandri.org/municipal.htm
Is a Municipal Ct.

East Providence City Hall 145 Taunton Ave, East Providence, RI 02914; 401-435-7595; fax: 401-435-4630; 8AM-4PM (EST). ***Probate.***

Foster Town Hall 181 Howard Hill Rd, Foster, RI 02825; 401-392-9200; fax: 401-702-5010; 9AM-4PM (EST). ***Probate.***

Glocester Town Hall PO Box B, 1145 Putnam Pike, Chepachet, RI 02814; 401-568-6206; fax: 401-568-5850; 8AM-4:30PM (EST). ***Probate.***
www.glocesterri.org

Johnston Town Hall 1395 Atwood Ave, Johnston, RI 02919; 401-351-6618; fax: 401-553-8835; 8:30AM-4:30PM (EST). ***Probate.***

Lincoln Town Hall PO Box 100, 100 Old River Rd, Lincoln, RI 02865; 401-333-8450, 333-8451; fax: 401-333-3648; 9AM-4:30PM (EST). ***Probate.***
Court meets fourth Monday at 9 AM.

North Providence Town Hall 2000 Smith St, North Providence, RI 02911; 401-232-0900; fax: 401-233-1409; 8:30AM-4:30PM (EST). ***Probate.***

North Smithfield 575 Smithfield Rd, Municipal Annex, North Smithfield, RI 02896; 401-767-2200 x326; fax: 401-356-4057; 8AM-4PM M,T,W; 8AM-7PM TH; 8AM-N F (EST). ***Probate.***
Probate Ct sessions held at 83 Greene St.

Pawtucket City Hall 137 Roosevelt Ave, Pawtucket, RI 02860; 401-728-0500 x259 or x223; fax: 401-728-8932; 8:30AM-4:30PM (EST). ***Probate.***

Providence Probate Court 25 Dorrance St, Providence, RI 02903; 401-421-7740; fax: 401-861-6208; 8:30AM-4:00PM (EST). ***Probate.***

Scituate Town Hall 195 Danielson Pike, PO Box 328, North Scituate, RI 02857; 401-647-2822; fax: 401-647-7220; 8:30AM-4PM (EST). ***Probate.***

Smithfield Town Hall 64 Farnum Pike, Smithfield, RI 02917; 401-233-1000 x111; probate phone: 401-233-1000 X114; fax: 401-232-7244; 8:30AM-4:30PM (EST). ***Probate.***
www.smithfieldri.com/

Woonsocket City Hall 169 Main St, Woonsocket, RI 02895; 401-762-6400; probate phone: 401-767-9248; fax: 401-765-0022; 8:30AM-4PM (EST). ***Probate.***

Washington County

Superior Court 4800 Towerhill Rd #173, Wakefield, RI 02879; 401-782-4121; 8:30AM-4:30PM (EST). ***Felony, Civil Actions over $10,000.***

Civil Records: Access: Phone, mail, in person. Both court and visitors may perform in person searches. No search fee. Required to search: name, years to search. Civil cases indexed by defendant, plaintiff; index on computer from 1984, on index prior to 1984. Archived at Record Center, 401-277-3249. Note: Phone requests taken only after 3PM. Mail turnaround time 1 week. Civil PAT goes back to 1984.

Criminal Records: Access: Mail, in person, online. Both court and visitors may perform in person searches. No search fee. Required to search: name, years to search; also helpful: DOB. Criminal records computerized from 1984, on index prior to 1984. Archived at Record Center, 401-277-3249. Mail turnaround time 1 week. Criminal PAT goes back to same as civil. PAT results show middle initial, and terminal results show year of birth. Access criminal records free at http://courtconnect.courts.state.ri.us as an informational service only; should not be relied upon as official court record. Online results show middle initial, year of birth, and include aliases.

General Information: Online identifiers in results same as on public terminal. No confidential or sealed records released. Will fax documents to local or toll free line. Court makes copy: $.15 per page. Self serve: same. Certification fee: $3.00. Payee: Washington Superior Court. Personal checks accepted. Visa/MC accepted. Prepayment required. Mail requests: SASE required.

4th District Court 4800 Towerhill Rd, #123, Wakefield, RI 02879; 401-782-4131; 8:30AM-4:30PM (EST). ***Misdemeanor, Civil Actions under $10,000, Eviction, Small Claims.***

Civil Records: Access: In person only. Visitors must perform in person searches themselves. Required to search: name, years to search. Civil cases indexed by defendant, plaintiff. Civil index on cards, small claims indexed by plaintiff only.

Criminal Records: Access: In person, online. Visitors must perform in person searches themselves. Required to search: name, years to search, DOB. Criminal records available on computer beginning in 1996. Public use terminal has crim records back to 1996. PAT results show middle initial but show year of birth only. Access criminal records free at on the statewide system at http://courtconnect.c ourts.state.ri.us. Records back to 1996. The site is an informational service only and should not be relied upon as official court record. Online results show middle initial, year of birth, and include aliases.

General Information: Online identifiers in results same as on public terminal. No family court records released. Will not fax documents. Court makes copy: $.15 per page. Certification fee: $1.50. Payee: Fourth District Court. Money orders accepted. Personal checks not accepted. Visa/MC accepted. Prepayment required.

North Kingstown Town Hall 80 Boston Neck Rd, North Kingstown, RI 02852-5762; 401-294-3331; probate phone: 401-294-3331 x122; fax: 401-294-2437; 8:30AM-4:30PM (EST). ***Probate.***
www.northkingstown.org

Charlestown Town Hall 4540 S County Tr, Charlestown, RI 02813; 401-364-1200; fax: 401-364-1238; 8:30AM-4:30PM (EST). ***Probate.***
Nothing done on county level. Each city/town has their own Probate Court. Court first Tuesday of the month at 9:30AM.

Exeter Town Hall 675 Ten Rod Rd, Exeter, RI 02822; 401-294-3891 (295-7500); fax: 401-295-1248; 9AM-4PM (EST). ***Probate.***
www.town.exeter.ri.us
Probate Court held 4th Monday monthly at 2:00 PM.

Hopkinton Town Hall 1 Town House Rd, Hopkinton, RI 02833; 401-377-7777; fax: 401-377-7788; 8:30AM-4:30PM or by appointment (EST). ***Probate.***
Civil cases heard in County Courthouse, not Town.

Narragansett Town Hall 25 5th Ave, Narragansett, RI 02882; 401-782-0621; 401-789-1044 X621; fax: 401-783-9637; 8:30AM-4:30PM (EST). ***Probate.***

New Shoreham Town Hall 16 Old Town Rd, PO Drawer 220, Block Island, RI 02807; 401-466-3200; fax: 401-466-3219; 9AM-3PM (EST). ***Probate.***

Richmond Town Hall 5 Richmond Townhouse Rd, Wyoming, RI 02898; 401-539-9000 x9; fax: 401-539-1089; 8:30AM-?? (EST). ***Probate.***

South Kingstown Town 180 High St, Wakefield, RI 02879; 401-789-9331; fax: 401-788-9792; 8:30AM-4:30PM (EST). ***Probate.***

Westerly Municipal and Probate 45 Broad St, Westerly Town Hall, Westerly, RI 02891; 401-348-2535; fax: 401-348-2318; 8:30AM-4:30PM (EST). ***Probate, Misdemeanor, Traffic, Ordinance.***
This court is actually two. Probate held once a month; Judge Linda Urso; Clerk Donna Giordano. Municipal court held every week.

Rhode Island Recording Offices

ORGANIZATION: There are 5 counties in Rhode Island, but there is no county recording of public records in this state. All recording is done at the town/city level at one of 39 locations. The recording officers are the town/city clerks. It is confusing that three locations bear the same name as their respective counties - Bristol, Newport, and Providence. Record searchers must keep in mind that recorded documents within these counties that can relate to property located in cities/towns other than the individual cities of Bristol, Newport, and Providence.

The Town/City Clerk usually also serves as Recorder of Deeds. Rhode Island is in the Eastern Time Zone (EST).

REAL ESTATE RECORDS: Towns will not perform real estate searches. Real estate copy fee is usually $1.50 per page and certification is $3.00 per document.

UCC RECORDS: Financing statements are filed at the state level except for farm related and real estate related collateral which are filed with the Town/City Clerk. Most recording offices will not perform UCC searches; for the few that do, use search request form UCC-11.

TAX LIEN RECORDS: All federal and state tax liens on personal property and on real property are filed with the Recorder of Deeds. Towns will not perform tax lien searches.

OTHER LIENS: Mechanics, municipal, lis pendens.

ONLINE ACCESS: A private vendor has placed assessor records from a number of towns on the internet; visit www.visionappraisal.com/databases/ri/index.htm. View UCC debtor names in the Pubic Search Index at http://ucc.state.ri.us/psearch/ also search by file number or business organization.

Barrington Town

Town Clerk, 283 County Rd; Town Hall, Barrington, RI 02806. 401-247-1900; fax-401-247-3765; 8:30AM-4:30PM (EST) www.barrington.ri.gov

Index: All in one. Records indexed on computer back to 1/84. Only the public may search. Copy fee $1.50 per page. Cert fee- $3.00 per cert plus copy fee. Payee- Town of Barrington. **Other phones:** Treasurer- x2; Elections- x4; Vital Records- x4. **Property tax/Assessing**- 283 County Rd, Barrington, RI 02806; 401-247-1900 x3, assessor fax- 401-247-3765. A public access terminal available. **Online access**- Access property data on a private site at www.appraisalresource.com/Search.aspx?town=Barrington. Also, access assessor property data free at http://data.visionappraisal.com/BarringtonRI/

Bristol Town

Recorder of Deeds, 10 Court St; Town Hall, Bristol, RI 02809. 401-253-7000; fax-401-253-2647; 8:30AM-4PM (EST) www.bristolri.us

Index: All in one. Records indexed on a public use terminal back to 1991. Office will perform a UCC search but public must search other records themselves. Copy fee $1.50 per page. Cert fee- $3.00 per cert plus copy fee. Payee- Town of Bristol. **Other phones:** Treasurer- 401-253-7000; Elections- 401-253-7000; Vital Records- 401-253-7000. **Property tax/Assessing**- 10 Court St, Bristol, RI 02809; 401-253-7000 x138, assessor fax- 401-253-5490. www.bristolri.us/government/finance/tax/ **Online access**- Access property data on a private site at www.clipboardinc.com/bristolsearchpage.html.

Burrillville Town

Town Clerk, 105 Harrisville Main St; Town Hall, Harrisville, RI 02830-1499. 401-568-4300; fax-401-568-0490; 8:30AM-4:30PM M-W; 8:30AM-7PM Th; 8:30AM-12:30PM F. www.burrillville.org

Index: All in one. Records indexed on a public use terminal back to 1990. Only the public may search. Copy fee $1.50 per page. Cert fee- $3.00 per cert plus copy fee. Payee- Burrillville Town Clerk. **Other phones:** Treasurer- 401-568-4300; Elections- 401-568-4300; Vital Records- 401-568-4300. **Property tax/Assessing**- 105 Harrisville Main St, Town Hall, Harrisville, RI 02830-1499; 401-568-4300, assessor fax- 401-568-0490. (Appraiser- 401-568-4300) www.burrillville.org/Public_Documents/BurrillvilleRI_Assessor/assessor **Online**- Access property records free at www.opaldata.net/ritaxbills/search.aspx?municipality=Burrillville&taxyear=2005RP. Also, access property data free at www.crcpropertyinfo.com/crcdb/burrillville.htm.

Central Falls City

City Clerk, 580 Broad St; City Hall, Central Falls, RI 02863. 401-727-7400; fax-401-727-7406; 8:30AM-4:30PM (EST) www.centralfallsri.us

Index: All in one. Records indexed on computer back to 1988. Only the public may search. Copy fee $1.00 per page. Cert fee- $3.00 per page plus copy fee. Payee- City of Central Falls. **Other phones:** Treasurer- 401-727-7470; Elections- 401-727-7450; Vital Records- 401-727-7400. **Property tax/ Assessing**- 580 Broad St, Central Falls, RI 02863; 401-727-7430, assessor fax- 401-727-7472. hours- 8:30AM-4:30PM (Sep-Jun); 8:30AM-3:30PM (Jun-Sep) www.centralfallsri.us/ **Online** - Access to city property data is free at http://data.visionappraisal.com/CentralFallsRI/. Does not require username & password, simply click on link. Also, search property data free at www.appraisalresource.com/Search.aspx?town=Central+Falls.

Charlestown Town

Town Clerk, 4540 South County Trail, Charlestown, RI 02813. 401-364-1200; fax-401-364-1238; 8:30AM-4:30PM. www.charlestownri.org

Index: All in one. Records indexed on a public use terminal back to 1936. Only the public may search. Copy fee $1.50 per page. Cert fee- $3.00 per doc plus copy fee. Payee- Town of Charlestown. **Other phones:** Treasurer- 401-364-1235; Elections- 401-364-1200; Vital Records- 401-364-1200. **Property tax/Assessing**- 4540 S County Tr, Charlestown, RI 02813; 401-364-1233, assessor fax- 401-364-1238. **Online access**- Search town assessor database at http://data.visionappraisal.com/CharlestownRI/.

Coventry Town

Town Clerk, 1670 Flat River Rd; Town Hall, Coventry, RI 02816-8911. 401-822-9174, R/E recording phone-401-822-9170; fax-401-822-9132; 8:30AM-4PM. http://town.coventry.ri.us

Index: All in one. Records indexed on a public use terminal back to 1985. Only the public may search. Copy fee $1.00 per page. Cert fee- $3.00 per doc plus $1.50 per page includes copy fee. Payee- Town of Coventry. **Other phones:** Treasurer- 401-822-9155; Elections- 401-822-9150; Vital Records- 401-822-9170. **Property tax/Assessing**- 1670 Flat River Rd, Coventry, RI 02816-8911; 401-822-9163, assessor fax- 401-822-9132. hours- 8:30AM-4:30PM **Online access**- Property data is listed on a private site at www.appraisalresource.com/Search.aspx?town=Coventry. Also, 2005 Assessment and property data available at www.town.coventry.ri.us/assess.htm.

Cranston City

City Clerk, 869 Park Ave; City Hall, Cranston, RI 02910. 401-461-1000 x3130, R/E recording phone-401-780-3130; fax-401-780-3165; 8:30AM-4:30PM (EST) www.cranstonri.com/

Index: All in one. Records indexed on a public use terminal back to 1986. Only the public may search. Copy fee $1.50 per page. Cert fee- $3.00 per cert plus copy fee. Payee- City of Cranston. **Other phones:** Treasurer- 401-780-3143; Elections- 401-780-3126; Vitals- 401-780-3238. **Property tax/Assessing**- 869 Park Ave, Cranston, RI 02910; 401-461-1000 x3181, assessor fax- 401-780-3361. www.cranstonri.com/generalpage.php?page=36 **Online access**- Records on the city assessor database are online at http://data.visionappraisal.com/CranstonRI/..

Cumberland Town

Town Clerk, PO Box 7, Cumberland, RI 02864-0808. 401-728-2400, R/E recording phone- x135; fax-401-724-1103; 8:30AM-4:30PM (Summer hours) 9AM-4PM (July-Sept). (EST) www.cumberlandri.org

Index: Separate indices to search include grantor/grantee. Records indexed on computer back to 1988. Only the public may search. Will not search UCC records. Copy fee $1.00 per page. Cert fee- $3.00 per cert plus copy fee of $1.50 per page. Payee- Town of Cumberland. **Other phones:** Treasurer- 401-728-2400 x121; Elections- 401-728-2400 x131; Vital Records- 401-728-2400 x137. **Property tax/Assessing**- 45 Broad St, Town Hall, Cumberland, RI 02864; 401-728-2400 x113, assessor fax- 401-475-1851. (Appraiser/Auditor- 401-728-2400 x115) **Online**- Access to property data is free at www.opaldata.net/ritaxbills/search.aspx?municipality=Cumberland&taxyear=2006RP. Also, access the town property data free at www.crcpropertyinfo.com/crcdb/cumberland.htm.

East Greenwich Town

Town Clerk, PO Box 111, East Greenwich, RI 02818. 401-886-8603, R/E phone-401-886-8602; fax-401-886-8625; 8:30-4:30PM. www.eastgreenwichri.com

Index: All in one. Records indexed on computer back to 1969. Only the public may search. Copy fee $1.50 per page. Cert fee- $3.00 per doc plus copy fee. Payee- East Greenwich Town Clerk/Recorder of Deeds. **Online access to Voter Registration records:** Access to voter registration for free go to www.state.ri.us/vic . **Other phones:** Treasurer- 401-886-8608; Elections- 401-886-8603; Vital Records- 401-886-8602. **Property tax/Assessing**- PO Box 111, 125 Main St, East Greenwich, RI 02818; 401-886-8614, assessor fax- 401-886-8613. **Online**- Access property data on a private site at www.appraisalresource.com/Search.aspx?town=East+Greenwich.

East Providence City

City Clerk, 145 Taunton Ave; Recorder of Deeds Office, East Providence, RI 02914. 401-435-7594; fax-401-435-4630; hours- 8AM-3:30PM (EST) www.eastprovidenceri.net/citygov/cityclerk.php

Index: All in one. Records indexed on a public use terminal back to 1981. Only the public may search. Copy fee $1.50 per page. Cert fee- $3.00 per doc plus copy fee. Payee- City of East Providence. **Other phones:** Treasurer- 401-435-7560; Elections- 401-435-7505; Vital Records- 401-435-7596. **Property tax/Assessing**- 145 Taunton Ave, East Providence, RI 02914; 401-435-7574, assessor fax- 401-435-1915. hours- 8AM-4PM www.eastprovidenceri.net **Online access**- Access to Town property data is free at http://data.visionappraisal.com/EastProvidenceRI/.

Exeter Town

Town Clerk, 675 Ten Rod Rd; Town Hall, Exeter, RI 02822. 401-294-3891; fax-401-295-1248; 9AM-4PM. www.town.exeter.ri.us

Index: All in one. Records indexed on a public use terminal back to 1996. Only the public may search. Copy fee $1.50 per page. Generic copy fee- $.15 per page. Cert fee- $3.00 per page plus copy fee. Payee- Town of Exeter. **Other phones:** Treasurer- 401-267-1024; Elections- 401-294-2287; Vital Records- 401-294-3891. **Property tax/Assessing**- 675 Ten Rod Rd, Exeter, RI 02822; 401-294-5734, assessor fax- 401-267-1029. (Appraiser - 401-294-5734) **Online**- Access property data free at www.crcpropertyinfo.com/crcdb/exeter.htm. Access to real estate tax collection data is by subscription from private company www.opaldata.net/OnlineTax/.

Foster Town

Town Clerk, 181 Howard Hill Rd; Town Hall, Foster, RI 02825-1227. 401-392-9200; fax-401-392-9201; 9AM-3:30PM (EST) www.townoffoster.com

Index: Separate indices to search include IHTL. Record index not computerized. Only the public may search. Copy fee $1.50 per page. Cert fee- $3.00 per cert plus copy fee. Payee- Town of Foster. **Other phones:** Treasurer- 401-392-9207; Elections- 401-392-9200; Vital Records- 401-392-9200. **Property tax/Assessing**- 181 Howard Hill Rd, Foster, RI 02825-1227; 401-392-9202, assessor fax- 401-702-5010. hours- 8:30AM-4:30PM www.townoffoster.com/taxassessor.htm **Online**- Access property data free at www.crcpropertyinfo.com/crcdb/foster.htm.

Glocester Town

Town Clerk, PO Drawer B, Glocester/ Chepachet, RI 02814-0702. 401-568-6206 x0, R/E recording phone-401-568-6206x0, UCC recording phone-401-568-6206x1; fax-401-568-5850; 8AM-4:30PM. www.glocesterri.org/townclerk.htm

Index: All in one. Records indexed on a public use terminal back to 1965. Only the public may search. Will not search UCC records. Copy fee $1.00 per page. Minutes pages- $.15 each. If court makes copies $1.50 per page. Cert fee- $3.00 per doc plus $1.50 per page. Payee- Town of Glocester. **Other phones:** Treasurer- 401-568-6206x5; Elections- 401-568-6206x0; Vital Records- 401-568-6206x0; Tax Collector- 401-568-6206x4. **Property tax/Assessing**- 1145 Putnam Pike, PO Drawer B, Glocester/ Chepachet, 02814-0702; 401-568-6206 x3, fax- 401-568-5850. www.glocesterri.org/taxassessor.htm **Online access**- Access tax roll data free at www.opaldata.net/ritaxbills/search.aspx?municipality=Glocester&taxyear=2007RP. Also, access property data free at www.crcpropertyinfo.com/crcdb/glocester.htm.

Hopkinton Town

Town Clerk, 1 Town House Rd; Town Hall, Hopkinton, RI 02833. Recording, R/E & UCC phone-401-377-7777; fax-401-377-7788; 8:30AM-4:30PM (EST) http://hopkintonritownhall.com/

Index: Separate indices to search include plat maps. Records indexed on a public use terminal from to 1/1/90 to present. Only the public may search. Will not search UCC records. Copy fee $1.50 per page. Cert fee- $3.00 per cert plus $1.50 per page. Payee- Town of Hopkinton. **Other phones:** Treasurer- 401-377-7766; Elections- 401-377-7777; Vital Records- 401-377-7777. **Property tax/Assessing**- 1 Town House Rd, Hopkinton, RI 02833; 401-377-7780, fax- 401-377-7775. www.hopkintonri.org/Assessor1.htm **Online access**- Access to town property data is free at www.opaldata.net/ritaxbills/search.aspx?municipality=Hopkinton&taxyear=2007RP. Also, access property data free at www.crcpropertyinfo.com/crcdb/hopkinton.htm.

Jamestown Town

Town Clerk, 93 Narragansett Ave; Town Hall, Jamestown, RI 02835. 401-423-7200; fax-401-423-7230; 8AM-4:30PM, recording 8:30AM-4PM (EST) www.jamestownri.net

Index: All in one. Records indexed on a public use terminal back to 1915. Only the public may search. Copy fee $1.50 per page; self serve $.50. Cert fee- $3.00 per page plus clerk's copy fee. Payee- Town of Jamestown. **Other phones:** Treasurer- 401-423-7200; Elections- 401-423-7200; Vital Records- 401-423-7200. **Property tax/Assessing**- 93 Narragansett Ave, Jamestown, RI 02835; 401-423-7200, assessor fax- 401-423-7230. (Appraiser/Auditor- 401-423-7200) hours- 8:30AM-4:30PM **Online access**- Access property data on a private site at www.appraisalresource.com/Search.aspx?town=Jamestown

Johnston Town

Town Clerk, 1385 Hartford Ave; Town Hall, Johnston, RI 02919. Recording, R/E & UCC phone-401-351-6618; fax-401-553-8835; 8:30AM-4:30PM (EST) www.townofjohnstonri.com

Index: All in one. Records indexed on a public use terminal back to 1984. Office personnel or visitors may perform searches. Search fee varies. Office will not search real estate records. Will not search UCC records. Copy fee $1.00 per page. Cert fee- $3.00 per doc plus copy fee. Payee- Town of Johnston. **Other phones:** Treasurer- 401-351-6618; Elections- 401-351-6618; Vital Records- 401-351-6618. **Property tax/Assessing**- 1385 Hartford Ave, Jonhston, RI 02919; 401-351-6618 x2, assessor fax- 401-553-8861. (Appraiser/Auditor- 401-351-6618) **Online access**- Access to Town property data is free at http://data.visionappraisal.com/JohnstonRI/.

Lincoln Town

Town Clerk, 100 Old River Rd; PO Box 100, Lincoln, RI 02865. 401-333-1100, R/E recording phone-401-333-8452; fax-401-333-3648; 9AM-4:30PM (EST) www.lincolnri.org

Index: Separate indices to search. Record index not computerized. Only the public may search. Copy fee $1.50 per page. Cert fee- $3.00 per instrument. Payee- Town of Lincoln. **Other phones:** Treasurer- 401-333-8441; Elections- 401-333-1140; Vital Records- 401-333-8452. **Property tax/Assessing**- 100 Old River Rd, PO Box 100, Lincoln, RI 02865; 401-333-8449, assessor fax- 401-333-3648. (Appraiser/Auditor- 401-333-1100) hours- 8:30AM-4:30PM www.lincolnri.org/departments/taxassessor.asp **Online access**- Property data free at www.crcpropertyinfo.com/crcdb/lincoln.htm. Values here are the result of a proposed property tax revaluation recently conducted for the Town.

Little Compton Town

Town Clerk, PO Box 226, Little Compton, RI 02837-0226. Recording, R/E & UCC phone-401-635-4400; fax-401-635-2470; 8AM-4PM (EST)

Index: Separate indices to search include liens, attachments. Record index not computerized. Only the public may search. Copy fee $1.50 per page. $1.50 per page for land evidence; $.15 per copy for probate. Cert fee- $3.00 per instrument plus copy fee. Payee- Town of Little Compton. **Other phones:** Treasurer- 401-635-4219; Elections- 401-635-4400; Vital Records- 401-635-4400. **Property tax/Assessing**- PO Box 226, 40 Commons, Town Hall, Little Compton, RI 02837-0226; 401-635-4509, fax- 401-635-2470. hours- 8AM-N 1:30PM-4PM **Online**- Access property data free at http://data.visionappraisal.com/LittleComptonRI/DEFAULT.asp.

Middletown Town

Town Clerk, 350 E Main Rd; Town Hall, Middletown, RI 02842. Recording, R/E & UCC phone-401-847-0009; fax-401-845-0406; hours- 8AM-4PM; 8:30AM-3:30 are the Recording hours. (EST) www.middletownri.com

Index: All in one. Records indexed on a public use terminal back to 7/1/84. Office will perform a UCC search but public must search other records themselves. Copy fee $1.50 per page. Cert fee- $3.00 per doc plus copy fee. Payee- Town of Middletown. **Other phones:** Treasurer- 401-846-4478; Elections- 401-849-5540; Vital Records- 401-847-0009. **Property tax/Assessing**- 350 E Main Rd, Middletown, RI 02842; 401-847-7300, assessor fax- 401-845-0413. hours- 8AM-4PM **Online access**- Records on the town assessor database are online at http://data.visionappraisal.com/MiddletownRI/. Free registration is required for full data.

Narragansett Town

Town Clerk, 25 5th Ave; Town Hall, Narragansett, RI 02882. 401-789-1044, R/E recording phone-401-789-1044 x623, UCC recording phone-401-782-0622; fax-401-783-9637; hours 8:30AM-4:30PM (EST) www.narragansettri.gov

Index: Separate indices to search include books. Records indexed on a public use terminal back to 1985. Office personnel or visitors may perform searches. Office will search real estate records. Will search UCC records. Copy fee $1.00 per page. Cert fee- $3.00 per cert plus $1.50 per page copy fee. Payee- Town of Narragansett. **Other phones:** Treasurer- 401-782-0601; Elections- 401-782-0625; Vitals- 401-782-0624. **Property tax/Assessing**- 25 5th Ave, Narragansett, RI 02882; 401-789-1044 x236, assessor fax- 401-788-2555. **Online access**- Records on the town assessor database are online at http://data.visionappraisal.com/NarragansettRI/. Free registration is required for full data.

New Shoreham Town

Town Clerk, PO Drawer 220, Block Island, RI 02807. Recording, R/E & UCC phone-401-466-3200; fax-401-466-3219; 9AM-3PM (EST)

Index: All in one. Record index not computerized. Only the public may search. Copy fee $1.50 per page. Cert fee- $3.00 plus copy fee. Payee- Town of New Shoreham. **Other phones:** Treasurer- 401-466-3208; Elections- 401-466-3200; Vital Records- 401-466-3200. **Property tax/Assessing**- PO Box 220, 16 Old Town Rd, Block Island, RI 02807; 401-466-3217, assessor fax- 401-466-2752. (Appraiser/Auditor- 401-466-3208) **Online** - Access Town property data free at http://data.visionappraisal.com/NewShorehamRI/.

Newport City

Recorder of Deeds, 43 Broadway; City Hall, Newport, RI 02840-2798. Recording, R/E & UCC phone-401-845-5334; fax-401-849-8757; 8:30AM-

4:30PM (Recording Hours 8:30AM-3:30PM). (EST) www.cityofnewport.com
Index: All in one. Records indexed on a public use terminal back to 1977. Only the public may search. Copy fee $1.50 per page. Cert fee- $3.00 per cert plus copy fee. Payee- City of Newport. **Other phones:** Elections- 401-845-5385 or 5383 or 5384 or 5386; Vital Records- 401-845-5342 or 5340 or 5341 or 5351 or 5349; Timeshare Request:- 401-845-5338. **Property tax/Assessing**- 43 Broadway, Newport City Hall, Newport, RI 02840; 401-845-5365. hours- 8:30AM-4:30PM www.cityofnewport.com/departments/finance/assess/home.cfm **Online access**- Access is via a private company at http://data.visionappraisal.com/NewportRI/.

North Kingstown Town

Town Clerk, 80 Boston Neck Rd; Town Hall, North Kingstown, RI 02852. 401-294-3331, R/E recording phone- x125; fax-401-294-2437; 8:30AM-4:30PM (EST) www.northkingstown.org
Index: Separate indices to search include grantor/grantee. Records indexed on a public use terminal back to 1989 for most records. Only the public may search. Copy fee $1.50 per page. Cert fee- $3.00 per doc plus copy fee. Payee- Town of N Kingstown. **Other phones:** Treasurer- 401-294-3331 x148; Elections- 401-294-3331 x129; Vital Records- 401-294-3331 x122. **Property tax/Assessing**- 80 Boston Neck Rd, North Kingstown, RI 02852; 401-294-3331 x110, assessor fax- 401-294-2435. **Online access**- Access is via a private company at http://data.visionappraisal.com/NorthkingstownRI/. Free registration is required for full data.

North Providence Town

Town Clerk, 2000 Smith St; Town Hall, North Providence, RI 02911. 401-232-0900, R/E recording phone-401-232-0900 x213-214; fax-401-233-1409; 8:30AM-4:30PM (Summer hours 8:30 AM-4PM). (EST) http://NorthProvidenceRI.com
Index: Separate indices. Records indexed on a public use terminal back to 1984. Only the public may search. Will not search UCC records. Copy fee $1.00 per page. Cert fee- $3.00 per cert plus $1.50 per page. Payee- Town of North Providence. **Other phones:** Treasurer- 401-232-0900 x218; Elections- 401-232-0900 x241-235; Vital Records- 401-232-0900 x213-214. **Property tax/Assessing**- 2000 Smith St, Town Hall, North Providence, RI 02911; 401-232-0900 x257. hours- 8:30AM-4:30PM (4PM-Summer) **Online**- Access property data on a private site at www.appraisalresource.com/Search.aspx?town=North+Providence.

North Smithfield Town

Town Clerk, 575 Smithfield Rd; Municipal Annex, North Smithfield, RI 02896. 401-767-2200, R/E recording phone-x504; fax-401-356-4057; 8AM-4PM M-W; 8AM-7PM Th; 8AM-N Fri. (EST) www.northsmithfieldri.com
Index: All in one. Records indexed on a public use terminal back to 3/14/05. Only the public may search. Will not search UCC records. Copy fee $1.50 per page. Cert fee- $3.00 per doc plus copy fee. Payee- Town of North Smithfield. **Other phones:** Treasurer- X304; Elections- x321; Vital Records- 401-767-2200 x321. **Property tax/Assessing**- 575 Smithfield Rd, North Smithfield, RI 02896; 401-767-2200 x325, fax- 401-767-2840. **Online** - Access via private company at http://data.visionappraisal.com/NorthsmithfieldRI/.

Pawtucket City

City Clerk, 137 Roosevelt Ave; City Hall, Pawtucket, RI 02860. 401-728-0500, R/E recording phone-401-728-0500 x262; fax-401-728-8932; 8:30AM-3:30PM (EST) www.pawtucketri.com
Index: All in one. Records indexed on a public use terminal back to 1970. Prior to 1970 indexes are in book form available to the public back to 1765. Only the public may search. Copy fee $1.50 per page. Cert fee- $3.00 per doc plus copy fee. Payee- City of Pawtucket. **Online access to Real Estate, Deed records:** Access real estate data free at http://72.248.180.6/alis/ww400r.pgm. Online indices go back to 1970. **Other phones:** Treasurer- 401-728-0500 x244; Elections- 401-728-0500 x207; Vital Records- 401-728-0500 x224. **Property tax/Assessing**- 137 Roosevelt Ave, Pawtucket, RI 02860; 401-728-0500, assessor fax- 401-727-3041. hours- 8:30AM-4:30PM www.pawtucketri.com **Online access**- Search the assessor database free at http://pawtucket.ias-clt.com/.

Portsmouth Town

Town Clerk, 2200 E Main Rd, Portsmouth, RI 02871. 401-683-2101; Recording hours 9AM-3:45PM (EST) www.portsmouthri.com/frames.htm
Index: Separate indices to search. Records indexed 1950 to 1985 on cards, computerized since. Only the public may search. Will not search UCC records. Copy fee $1.50 per page. Cert fee- $3.00 per cert. Payee- Town of Portsmouth. **Other phones:** Treasurer- 401-683-9118; Elections- 401-683-3157; Vital Records- 401-683-2101. **Property tax/Assessing**- 2200 E Main Rd, Portsmouth, RI 01871; 401-683-1536. (Appraiser/Auditor- 401-683-1536) **Online access**- Search town assessor database at http://data.visionappraisal.com/PortsmouthRI/. Free registration for full data.

Providence City

Recorder of Deeds, 25 Dorrance St; City Hall, Providence, RI 02903. 401-421-7740 x312; fax-401-278-0614; hours - 8:30AM-3:30PM (EST) www.providenceri.com/CityClerk/index.php
Index: Separate indices to search include grantor/grantee, UCC. Records indexed on a public use terminal back to 1984. Only the public may search. This office will give limited information by phone. Copy fee $1.50 per page. Include a SASE if document to be returned by mail. Cert fee- $3.00 per cert plus copy fee. Payee- Providence City Recorder of Deeds. **Property tax/Assessing**- 25 Dorrance St, Rm 208, Providence, RI 02903; 401-421-5900, assessor fax- 401-421-5902. www.providenceri.com/sb/tax_assessor.php **Online access**- Property tax card data available free at http://providence.ias-clt.com/parcel.list.php.

Richmond Town

Town Clerk, 5 Richmond Townhouse Rd; Town Hall, Wyoming, RI 02898. Recording, R/E & UCC phone-401-539-9000 x9; fax-401-539-1089; 9AM-4PM (EST) www.richmondri.com
Index: All in one. Records indexed on a public use terminal back to 1985. Only the public may search. Copy fee $1.50 per page. Cert fee- $3.00 per doc plus copy fee. Payee- Town of Richmond. **Other phones:** Treasurer- 401-539-9000 x8; Elections- 401-539-9000 x9; Vital Records- 401-539-9000 x9. **Property tax/Assessing**- 5 Richmond Townhouse Rd, Wyoming, RI 02898; 401-539-9000 x7, assessor fax- 401-539-1089. hours- 9AM-N 1PM-4PM **Online access**- Search town assessor database at http://data.visionappraisal.com/RichmondRI/.

Scituate Town

Town Clerk, PO Box 328, North Scituate, RI 02857-0328. 401-647-2822; fax-401-647-7220; 8:30AM-4PM (EST) www.scituateri.org/town.htm
Index: All in one. Records indexed on a public use terminal back to 1981. Only the public may search. Copy fee $1.50 per page. Cert fee- $3.00 1st pg, $1.50 each add'l. Payee- Town of Scituate. **Other phones:** Treasurer- 401-647-2547; Elections- 401-647-7466; Vital Records- 401-647-2822. **Property tax/Assessing**- PO Box 328, 195 Danielson Pike, North Scituate, RI 02857-0328; 401-647-2919, fax- 401-647-5960. www.scituateri.org/tax.htm **Online access**- Access to town property data is free at www.crcpropertyinfo.com/crcdb/scituate.htm

Smithfield Town

Town Clerk, 64 Farnum Pike; Town Hall, Esmond, RI 02917. Recording, R/E & UCC phone-401-233-1000; fax-401-232-7244; 8:30AM-4:30PM (EST) www.smithfieldri.com/townclerk.htm
Index: Indices separated by year. Records indexed on a public use terminal back to 1990. Only the public may search. Copy fee $1.50 1st page, $1.00 each add'l. Cert fee- $3.00 per instrument plus copy fee. Payee- Town of Smithfield. **Other phones:** Treasurer- 401-233-1005; Elections- 401-233-1000; Vitals- 401-233-1000. **Property tax/Assessing**- 64 Farnum Pike, Esmond, RI 02917; 401-233-1014, assessor fax- 401-232-7244. (Appraiser/Auditor- 401-233-1014) www.smithfieldri.com/taxassessor.htm **Online access**- Access to town property data is free at http://data.visionappraisal.com/SmithfieldRI/. Tax Rolls and tax bills are also free online at www.opaldata.net/ritaxbills/search.aspx?municipality=Smithfield&taxyear=2007RP.

South Kingstown Town

Town Clerk, PO Box 31, Wakefield, RI 02880. 401-789-9331, R/E recording phone-401-789-9331 x234; fax-401-788-9792; 8:30AM-4:30PM, recording stops-4PM (EST) www.southkingstownri.com
Index: All in one. Records indexed on a public use terminal back to 1980. Only the public may search. Copy fee $1.50 per page. Cert fee- $3.00 per cert plus copy fee. Payee- Town of South Kingstown. **Online access to Real Estate, Deed, Lien, Mortgage, Judgment records:** Access town real estate data free at http://70.168.204.238/ALIS/WW400R.HTM. Land indexes and images go back to 5/2/2005; complete excluding maps. Land indexes only go back to 1980; More to be added. Registration required for full data. **Other phones:** Treasurer- 401-789-9331 x209; Elections- 401-789-9331 x231; Vital Records- 401-789-9331 x230. **Property tax/Assessing**- PO Box 31, 180 High St, Wakefield, RI 02880; 401-789-9331 x220, assessor fax- 401-788-9792. 8:30AM-4:30PM **Online** - Access to the property values data is free at www.southkingstownri.com/code/propvalues_search.cfm. Also, some data available free or by sub at http://70.168.204.238/ALIS/WW400R.HTM under Assessor Document Group. Also, assess to Town property data is free at http://data.visionappraisal.com/SouthKingstownRI/. Does not require a username & password, simply click on link.

Tiverton Town

Town Clerk, 343 Highland Rd; Town Hall, Tiverton, RI 02878. 401-625-6700, R/E recording phone-401-625-6703; fax-401-625-6705; 8:30AM-4PM (EST) www.tiverton.ri.gov/
Index: Separate indices to search. Records indexed on a public use terminal back to 1984. Only the public may search. Copy fee $1.50 per page. Cert fee- $3.00 per cert plus copy fee. Payee- Town of Tiverton. **Other phones:** Treasurer- 401-625-5323; Elections- 401-625-6703; Vital Records- 401-625-6703. **Property tax/Assessing**- 343 Highland Rd, Tiverton, RI 02878; 401-625-6709, assessor fax- 401-625-1966. www.tiverton.ri.gov/government/assessor.html **Online** - Access property data on a private site at www.appraisalresource.com/Search.aspx?town=Tiverton. Also, access tax rolls and tax bills free at www.opaldata.net/ritaxbills/search.aspx?municipality=Tiverton&taxyear=2005RP. Also search free at www.crcpropertyinfo.com/crcdb/tiverton.htm.

Warren Town

Town Clerk, 514 Main St; Town Hall, Warren, RI 02885. 401-245-7340; fax-401-245-7421; 9AM-4PM. www.townofwarren-ri.gov
Index: All in one. Records indexed on a public use terminal back to 1984. Only the public may search. Copy fee $.15 per page, copy of maps $.50 per page.Real estate or tax lien copy- $1.50 per page. Cert fee- $3.00 per doc plus copy fee. Payee- Town of Warren. **Other phones:** Treasurer- 401-245-7341; Elections- 401-245-7340; Vital Records- 401-245-7340; Town Manager- 401-245-7554. **Property tax/**

Assessing- 514 Main St, Warren, RI 02885; 401-245-7342, assessor fax- 401-245-0595. (Appraiser/Auditor- 401-245-7342) **Online-** Access property and assessor data free on private site at www.appraisalresource.com/Search.aspx?town=Warren. Tax bill data is available free at www.opaldata.net/ritaxbills/search.aspx?municipality=Warren&taxyear=2006. Also, plat records are available free at www.townofwarren-ri.gov/services/plats.htm. Requires registration, username and password.

Warwick City

City Clerk, 3275 Post Rd, Warwick, RI 02886. 401-738-2000 x6029, R/E recording phone-401-738-2000 x6218; fax-401-732-7640; hours - 8:30AM-4PM. www.warwickri.gov

Index: All in one. Records indexed on a public use terminal back to 1/1983. Office will perform a UCC search but public must search other records themselves. Search fee $5.00 per request. Copy fee $1.50 per page. Cert fee- $3.00 per cert + $1.50 per page. Payee- City of Warwick. **Other phones:** Treasurer- 401-738-2000 x6228; Elections- 401-738-2000 x6223; Vitals- 401-738-2000 x6215. **Property tax/Assessing-** 3275 Post Rd, Warwick, RI 02886; 401-738-2000 x6016, assessor fax- 401-738-1252. hours- 8:30AM-4:30PM www.warwickri-assessor.org/ **Online access-** Access found at www.warwickri-assessor.org. Click on Property Search.

West Greenwich Town

Town Clerk, 280 Victory Hwy; Town Hall, West Greenwich, RI 02817. 401-392-3800; fax-401-392-3805; 9AM-4PM; 7-9PM Weds. (EST) www.wgtownri.org

Record index not computerized. Only the public may search. Cert fee- $3.00 per doc plus copy fee. Payee- West Greenwich Town Clerk. **Property tax/Assessing-** 401-397-5016 x3. **Online access-** Access property data free at www.crcpropertyinfo.com/crcdb/westgreenwich.htm.

West Warwick Town

Town Clerk, 1170 Main St; Town Hall, West Warwick, RI 02893-4829. Recording, R/E & UCC phone-401-822-9201; fax-401-822-9266; 8:30AM-4:30PM (EST) www.westwarwickri.org

Index: All in one. Records indexed on computer back to 1967. Office will perform a UCC search but public must search other records themselves. Copy fee $1.50 per page. Cert fee- $3.00 per doc plus copy fee. Payee- Town of West Warwick. **Other phones:** Treasurer- 401-822-9216; Elections- 401-822-9201; Vital Records- 401-822-9201. **Property tax/Assessing-** 1170 Main St, West Warwick, RI 02893-4829; 401-822-9208, assessor fax- 401-822-9266. **Online access-** Access property data free at http://westwarwick.univers-clt.com but no name searching. Also, access tax rolls and tax bills free at www.opaldata.net/ritaxbills/. Prior years available.

Westerly Town

Town Clerk, 45 Broad St; Town Hall, Westerly, RI 02891. Recording, R/E & UCC phone-401-348-2500; fax-401-348-2571; 8:30AM-4:30PM (EST) http://westerly.govoffice.com

Index: All in one. Records indexed on a public use terminal back to 1850. Only the public may search. Copy fee $1.50 per page. Cert fee- $3.00 per doc plus copy fee. Payee- Westerly Town Clerk. **Other phones:** Treasurer- 401-348-2618; Elections- 401-348-2503; Vital Records- 401-348-2500. **Property tax/Assessing-** 45 Broad St, Westerly, RI 02891; 401-348-2540, assessor fax- 401-348-2616. (Appraiser/Auditor- 401-348-2540) **Online access-** Access town property assessment data free at http://data.visionappraisal.com/WesterlyRI/. Also, assess 2006 tax rolls and tax bills free at www.opaldata.net/ritaxbills/search.aspx?municipality=Westerly&taxyear=2007RP.

Woonsocket City

Town Clerk, 169 Main St; City Hall, Woonsocket, RI 02895. 401-762-6400, R/E recording phone-401-767-9248; fax-401-765-4569; hours - 8:30AM-4PM. www.ci.woonsocket.ri.us

Index: All in one. Records indexed on computer back to 1991. Only the public may search. Copy fee $1.50 per page. Cert fee- $3.00 per doc plus copy fee. Payee- City Clerks Office. **Other phones:** Treasurer- 401-767-9280; Elections- 401-767-9224; Vital Records- 401-767-8875. **Property tax/Assessing-** 169 Main St, PO Box B, Woonsocket, RI 02895; 401-762-6400 x272, assessor fax- 401-769-4714. A public access terminal is available. **Online access-** Access assessor data free at http://data.visionappraisal.com/woonsocketRI/DEFAULT.asp.

Rhode Island County Locator

You will usually be able to find the city name in the City/County Cross Reference below. In that case, it is a simple matter to determine the county from the cross reference. However, only the official US Postal Service city names are included in this index. There are an additional 40,000 place names that people use in their addresses. Therefore, we have also included a ZIP/City Cross Reference immediately following the City/County Cross Reference.

If you know the ZIP Code but the city name does not appear in the City/County Cross Reference index, look up the ZIP Code in the ZIP/City Cross Reference, find the city name, then look up the city name in the City/County Cross Reference. For example, you want to know the county for an address of Menands, NY 12204. There is no "Menands" in the City/County Cross Reference. The ZIP/City Cross Reference shows that ZIP Codes 12201-12288 are for the city of Albany. Looking back in the City/County Cross Reference, Albany is in Albany County.

Rhode Island City/County Cross Reference

ADAMSVILLE Newport
ALBION Providence
ASHAWAY Washington
BARRINGTON Bristol
BLOCK ISLAND Washington
BRADFORD Washington
BRISTOL Bristol
CAROLINA Washington
CENTRAL FALLS Providence
CHARLESTOWN Washington
CHEPACHET Providence
CLAYVILLE Providence
COVENTRY Kent
CRANSTON Providence
CUMBERLAND Providence
EAST GREENWICH Kent
EAST PROVIDENCE Providence
ESCOHEAG Washington
EXETER Washington
FISKEVILLE Providence
FORESTDALE Providence
FOSTER Providence
GLENDALE Providence
GREENE Kent
GREENVILLE Providence
HARMONY Providence
HARRISVILLE Providence
HOPE Providence
HOPE VALLEY Washington
HOPKINTON Washington
JAMESTOWN Newport
JOHNSTON Providence
KENYON Washington
KINGSTON Washington
LINCOLN Providence
LITTLE COMPTON Newport
MANVILLE Providence
MAPLEVILLE Providence
MIDDLETOWN Newport
NARRAGANSETT Washington
NEWPORT Newport
NORTH KINGSTOWN Washington
NORTH PROVIDENCE Providence
NORTH SCITUATE Providence
NORTH SMITHFIELD Providence
OAKLAND Providence
PASCOAG Providence
PAWTUCKET Providence
PEACE DALE Washington
PORTSMOUTH Newport
PROVIDENCE Providence
PRUDENCE ISLAND Bristol
RIVERSIDE Providence
ROCKVILLE Washington
RUMFORD Providence
SAUNDERSTOWN Washington
SHANNOCK Washington
SLATERSVILLE Providence
SLOCUM Washington
SMITHFIELD Providence
TIVERTON Newport
WAKEFIELD Washington
WARREN Bristol
WARWICK Kent
WEST GREENWICH Kent
WEST KINGSTON Washington
WEST WARWICK Kent
WESTERLY Washington
WOOD RIVER JUNCTION Washington
WOONSOCKET Providence
WYOMING Washington

Rhode Island ZIP/City Cross Reference

02801-02801 ADAMSVILLE
02802-02802 ALBION
02804-02804 ASHAWAY
02806-02806 BARRINGTON
02807-02807 BLOCK ISLAND
02808-02808 BRADFORD
02809-02809 BRISTOL
02812-02812 CAROLINA
02813-02813 CHARLESTOWN
02814-02814 CHEPACHET
02815-02815 CLAYVILLE
02816-02816 COVENTRY
02817-02817 WEST GREENWICH
02818-02818 EAST GREENWICH
02821-02821 ESCOHEAG
02822-02822 EXETER
02823-02823 FISKEVILLE
02824-02824 FORESTDALE
02825-02825 FOSTER
02826-02826 GLENDALE
02827-02827 GREENE
02828-02828 GREENVILLE
02829-02829 HARMONY
02830-02830 HARRISVILLE
02831-02831 HOPE
02832-02832 HOPE VALLEY
02833-02833 HOPKINTON
02835-02835 JAMESTOWN
02836-02836 KENYON
02837-02837 LITTLE COMPTON
02838-02838 MANVILLE
02839-02839 MAPLEVILLE
02840-02841 NEWPORT
02842-02842 MIDDLETOWN
02852-02854 NORTH KINGSTOWN
02857-02857 NORTH SCITUATE
02858-02858 OAKLAND
02859-02859 PASCOAG
02860-02862 PAWTUCKET
02863-02863 CENTRAL FALLS
02864-02864 CUMBERLAND
02865-02865 LINCOLN
02871-02871 PORTSMOUTH
02872-02872 PRUDENCE ISLAND
02873-02873 ROCKVILLE
02874-02874 SAUNDERSTOWN
02875-02875 SHANNOCK
02876-02876 SLATERSVILLE
02877-02877 SLOCUM
02878-02878 TIVERTON
02879-02880 WAKEFIELD
02881-02881 KINGSTON
02882-02882 NARRAGANSETT
02883-02883 PEACE DALE
02885-02885 WARREN
02886-02889 WARWICK
02891-02891 WESTERLY
02892-02892 WEST KINGSTON
02893-02893 WEST WARWICK
02894-02894 WOOD RIVER JUNCTION
02895-02895 WOONSOCKET
02896-02896 NORTH SMITHFIELD
02898-02898 WYOMING
02900-02909 PROVIDENCE
02910-02910 CRANSTON
02911-02911 NORTH PROVIDENCE
02912-02912 PROVIDENCE
02914-02914 EAST PROVIDENCE
02915-02915 RIVERSIDE
02916-02916 RUMFORD
02917-02917 SMITHFIELD
02918-02918 PROVIDENCE
02919-02919 JOHNSTON
02920-02921 CRANSTON
02940-02940 PROVIDENCE

South Carolina

General Help Numbers:

Governor's Office
PO Box 12267
Columbia, SC 29211
www.scgovernor.com/
803-734-2100
Fax 803-734-5167
8AM-6PM

Attorney General's Office
PO Box 11549
Columbia, SC 29211
www.scattorneygeneral.org
803-734-3970
Fax 803-734-4323
8:30AM-5:30PM

Legislative Records
1105 Pendleton St. Blatt Bldg. Rm 223
Columbia, SC 29201
www.scstatehouse.gov
803-2124420
Fax 803-212-4450
9AM-5PM M-F

State Archives
8301 Parklane Rd
Columbia, SC 29223
http://scdah.sc.gov/
803-896-6100
Fax 803-896-6198
8:30AM-5PM M-F

State Specifics:

Capital: Columbia
Richland County

Time Zone: EST

Number of Counties: 46

Population: 4,479,800

Web Site: Www.sc.gov

State Agencies

Criminal Records

South Carolina Law Enforcement Division (SLED), Criminal Records Section, PO Box 21398, Columbia, SC 29221 (Courier address- 4400 Broad River Rd, Columbia, SC 29210); 803-896-7043, Fax- 803-896-7022; 8:30AM-5PM.

www.sled.sc.gov/

Indexing & Storage: Records available from the 1960s. New records available for inquiry in 1 to 12 days. 70% of all arrests in database have final dispositions recorded, 85% for those arrests within last 5 years.

Searching: Criminal records are open without restrictions. Include in request- full name, any aliases, sex, race, and DOB. The SSN is helpful. 100% of the records are fingerprint supported. However, this agency will not do fingerprint searches without state or federal statute. This data not released- juvenile. All records are released, including those without dispositions.

Access by: mail, in person, online.

Fee & Payment: The search fee is $25.00 per individual. The fee is $8.00 for non-profit organizations, pre-approval is required. Fee payee- SLED. Prepayment required. Business checks are accepted. Personal checks not accepted. No credit cards accepted, except online.

Mail search: Turnaround time- 5 to 7 days. They will return by overnight delivery service if prepaid and materials provided. A SASE is requested.

In person: Turnaround time is within minutes for three names or less.

Online search: SLED offers commercial access to criminal record history from 1960 forward on the website. Fees- $25.00 per screening or $8.00 if a charitable organization. Accepts credit card orders. Visit website or call 803-896-7219 for details.

Statewide Court Records

Court Administration, 1015 Sumter St, 2nd Floor, Columbia, SC 29201; 803-734-1800, Fax- 803-734-1355; 8:30AM-5PM M-F.

www.sccourts.org All trial court record access must be done at the local level.

Online search: Appellate and Supreme Court opinions are available from www.sccourts.org/opinions/index.cfm. Calendars available from www.sccourts.org/calendar/index.cfm. Although there is no access to statewide trial court records, a partial system and hot links page to independent online county systems is offered at www.sccourts.org/caseSearch/. At least 25 counties involved; search both criminal and civil indices.

Sexual Offender Registry

Sex Offender Registry, c/o SLED, PO Box 21398, Columbia, SC 29221 (Courier address- 4400 Broad River Rd, Columbia, SC 29210); 803-896-7043, Fax- 803-896-2311; 8:30AM-5PM.

http://services.sled.sc.gov/sor/

Indexing & Storage: Records available from 1994 to present. New records available for inquiry in one hour or less.

Searching: All written requests are screened as to the age of the offender. Therefore, all requests must be on a state form, which can be downloaded from the Internet. This data not released- registrants under 17 unless as required by law.

Fee & Payment: There is no fee unless data is ordered on a CD. Fee payee- SLED

Online search: Access is available from the website. Click on Sexual Offender Registry. Search by name or ZIP Code, county or city. Reports may also be obtained by school name (under the Report Generator).

Incarceration Records

Department of Corrections, Inmate Records Branch, 4444 Broad River Rd, Columbia, SC 29221-1787; 803-896-8531, 877-846-3472 (Inmate Information Line), Fax- 803-896-1217; 8AM-4:30PM. www.doc.sc.gov

The South Carolina Department of Corrections (SCDC) requires individuals requesting information under the FOIA to submit their request in writing to SCDC's FOIA Coordinator at the above address.

Indexing & Storage: Records available on current and former inmates. New records available for inquiry in 1 to 2 days.

Searching: Include in request- provide full name, DOB, SSN. The SCDC number is helpful. Location, SCDC number, physical identifiers, conviction and sentencing information, FBI number, and release dates are provided.

Access by: mail, phone, online.

Fee & Payment: There is no search fee, but there is a copy fee of $.25 per page.

Mail search: Turnaround time- 1-2 weeks. A SASE is requested. Include reason for request and identifying data on the requester. **Phone search:** Name searching available.

Online search: The Inmate Search on the Internet is found at https://sword.doc.state.sc.us/incarceratedInmateSearch/index.jsp, or click on Inmate search at the main website.

Corporation, LP, LLP, LLC, Trademarks/Servicemarks

Corporation Division, Capitol Complex, PO Box 11350, Columbia, SC 29211 (Courier address- Edgar A. Brown Bldg, Room 525, 1205 Pendleton Street, Columbia, SC 29201); 803-734-2158, Fax- 803-734-1614; 8:30PM-5PM. www.scsos.com

This office also handles not-for-profit entity records. Trademarks and service marks are not on the computer, but are in Trademark Division.

Indexing & Storage: Records available from 1800's on. In house computer records are from 1985 on. Older records stored at State Archives. New records available for inquiry immediately.

Searching: This office will not release annual reports, officer names or director names. For that information, call the Dept of Revenue at 803-896-1164. Include in request- full name of business. In addition to the articles of organization, business entity records available include: Prior (merged) names, Inactive, Reserved names. Agency invoices SC lawyers, otherwise prepayment required.

Access by: mail, phone, in person, online.

Fee & Payment: No search fee, copy fee is $1.00 per page for the first page and $.50 per page for each additional. If record is to be certified, the fee is an additional $2.00. A Good Standing is $10.00. Payee- Secretary of State. Prepayment required. Personal checks accepted, credit cards are not.

Mail search: Turnaround time- 1 to 2 days. A SASE is requested. **Phone search:** No fee for telephone request. They will provide basic information only. **In person:** Information requests are available.

Online search: This free web-based program is called the Online Business Filings, the search can be done from the home page. The database provides access to basic filing information about any entity filed with the office. Registered agents' names and addresses, dates of business filings and types of filings are all available. The database is updated every 48 hours.

Fictitious Name, Assumed Name, Trade Names

Records not maintained by a state level agency.

Records are found at the county level.

Annual Reports, Directors and Officers

Department of Revenue, Office Services/Records, Photocopy Section, Columbia, SC 29214; 803-898-5705 x3, 803-896-1171, Fax- 803-898-5888; 8:30AM-5PM. www.sctax.org/default.htm

Indexing & Storage: Records available from 1990 on. Current year records are kept in this office, previous record years are in storage.

Searching: Information on partnerships and on taxes is not public. Include in request- full name of business. A request form is on the web. Download SC4506 and check the third box under Field 11. The annual report gives the director and officer names, and the registered agent information only if it appears on the annual report.

Access by: mail, fax, in person.

Fee & Payment: The fee is $2.50 plus tax (regardless is requester is out of state). Fee payee- South Carolina Department of Revenue. Prepayment required. Personal checks accepted, credit cards are not.

Mail search: Turnaround time- 1 week. A SASE is requested. **Fax search:** Turnaround is usually in 1 day. **In person:** You may request information in person, but will not receive copies the same day.

Uniform Commercial Code

UCC Division, Secretary of State, PO Box 11350, Columbia, SC 29211 (Courier address- Edgar Brown Bldg, 1205 Pendleton St #525, Columbia, SC 29201); 803-734-1116, Fax- 803-734-1610; 8:30AM-5PM.

www.scsos.com/Uniform_Commercial_Code.htm

Effective March 1, 2004, all UCC filings received after October 27, 2003 are not available through Direct Access (online). Records must be requested directly from the UCC Search Division via mail, fax or email.

Indexing & Storage: Records available from 1968. Records are computerized since 1985. New records available for inquiry in 48 hours.

Searching: The agency prefers UCC-11 forms (download form from web), but will still accept UCC-4 for in-state requests. All tax liens filed at the county level. Include in request- debtor name.

Access by: mail, fax, in person, online.

Fee & Payment: The search fee is $5.00. Copies are $2.00 for the first page, plus $1.00 for each page of attachments. Certification is $2.00 per copy. Fee payee- Secretary of State. Prepayment not required. Personal checks accepted, credit cards are not.

Mail search: Turnaround time- 3 to 5 days. A SASE is requested. **Fax search:** There is an additional $5.00 fee for faxing in and $10.00 fee for faxing out, plus $1.00 per page.

In person: Use their PC to look up records, but copies requested are still mailed days later.

Online search: Free access to index of records filed before 10/27/03 at www.scsos.com/Search%20UCC%20Filings. Search by debtor name or number. Information on filings after that date must be obtained by mail or email (SCUCC@INFOAVE.NET).

Federal & State Tax Liens

Records not maintained by a state level agency.

Tax lien data is found at the county level.

Sales Tax Registrations

Revenue Dept, Sales Tax Registration Records, Registration Unit, Columbia, SC 29214 (Courier address- 301 Gervais St, Columbia, SC 29201); 803-896-1350; 8:30AM-4:45PM.

www.sctax.org/default.htm

Direct questions to salesinternet@sctax.org.

Indexing & Storage: Records available for 4 to 5 years, then are archived on hard copy.

Searching: This agency will only confirm that a business is registered. They will provide no other information. Include in request- business name plus one of the following tax permit number, owner name, business name, or federal ID. They can also search by tax permit number, owner name, business name, or federal ID.

Access by: mail, phone.

Mail search: Turnaround time- 7 days. A SASE is requested. No fee for mail request. **Phone search:** No fee for telephone request.

Birth Certificates

South Carolina DHEC, Vital Records, 2600 Bull St, Columbia, SC 29201-1797; 803-898-3630, 877-284-1008 (Expedite Order Line), Fax- 803-898-3761; 8:30AM-4PM.

www.scdhec.gov/administration/vr/

A "short form" wallet size birth certificate can be obtained from any SC county. This form will not show parent names.

Indexing & Storage: Records available from January 1, 1915 to present. New records available for inquiry immediately.

Searching: Records will only be released to the registrant (if 18 or older), parents named on certificate, guardian or legal representative. Include in request- full name, full names of father, mother's full maiden name, date of birth, place of birth. Two types of certificates are issued: wallet-size, and photocopy (actual birth certificate).

Access by: mail, phone, in person, online.

Fee & Payment: The search fee is $12.00 per name, add $3.00 for each additional copy. Fee payee- DHEC. Prepayment required. Personal checks not accepted. Major credit cards accepted for phone requests only.

Mail search: Turnaround time- 4 weeks. SASE not required. **Phone search:** phone requests are accepted, using a credit card. See expedited service from VitalChek. **In person:** Turnaround time is within 1 hour. However, the counter will be closed from 11/3/2008 until 3/2009 for construction.

Online search: Order from state-designated vendor www.vitalchek.com. See expedited svcs.

Expedited service: Expedited service is available for mail requests for an additional $5.00 from this agency. Turnaround is 3-5 days. To have search "expedited" by phone or online from www.vitalchek.com, add $5.00 and fees for express delivery.

Death Records

South Carolina DHEC, Vital Records, 2600 Bull St, Columbia, SC 29201-1797; 803-898-3630, 877-284-1008 (Expedite Order Line), Fax- 803-898-3761; 8:30AM-4PM.

www.scdhec.gov/administration/vr/

Indexing & Storage: Records available from January 1, 1915 to date. New records available for inquiry immediately.

Searching: Copies are available to those who show a direct, tangible interest in a determination of a personal or property right. If less than 5 years, records are at county also. Include in request- full name, date of death, place of death.

Access by: mail, phone, in person, online.

Fee & Payment: The search fee is $12.00 per name, add $3.00 for each additional copy. Fee payee- DHEC. Prepayment required. Personal checks accepted. Major credit cards accepted for phone requests only.

Mail search: Turnaround time- 4 weeks. SASE not required. **Phone search:** phone requests are accepted, using a credit card. See expedited svc from VitalChek. **In person:** Turnaround time is within 1 hour. However, the counter will be closed from 11/3/2008 until 3/2009 for construction.

Online search: Order from state-designated vendor www.vitalchek.com. - see expedited svc.

Expedited service: Expedited service is available for mail requests for an additional $5.00 from this agency. Turnaround is 3-5 days. To have search "expedited" by phone or online from www.vitalchek.com, add $5.00 and fees for express delivery.

Marriage Certificates

South Carolina DHEC, Vital Records, 2600 Bull St, Columbia, SC 29201-1797; 803-898-3630, 877-284-1008 (Expedite Order Line), Fax- 803-898-3761; 8:30AM-4PM.

www.scdhec.gov/administration/vr/

Copies may also be obtained from the Probate Judge in the county where license was issued.

Indexing & Storage: Records available from July 1, 1950 to present. New records available for inquiry in 2 to 3 months.

Searching: Records are released only to the subjects, their adult children, former or present spouses and legal representatives. Others may obtain a statement of marriage date and place. Include in request- names of husband and wife, date of marriage, place or county where marriage license issued.

Access by: mail, phone, in person, online.

Fee & Payment: The search fee is $12.00 per name, add $3.00 for each additional copy. Fee payee- DHEC. Prepayment required. Personal checks accepted. Major credit cards accepted for phone requests only.

Mail search: Turnaround time- 4 weeks. SASE not required.

Phone search: phone requests are accepted, using a credit card. See expedited service from VitalChek.

In person: Turnaround time is within 1 hour. However, the counter will be closed from Nov. 3, 2008 until March 2009 for construction.

Online search: Order from state-designated vendor www.vitalchek.com. See expedited svcs.

Expedited service: Expedited service is available for mail requests for an additional $5.00 from this agency. Turnaround is 3-5 days. To have search "expedited" by phone or online from www.vitalchek.com, add $5.00 and fees for express delivery.

Divorce Records

South Carolina DHEC, Vital Records, 2600 Bull St, Columbia, SC 29201-1797; 803-898-3630, 803-898-3631 (Order Line), Fax- 803-898-3761; 8:30AM-4PM. www.scdhec.gov/administration/vr/

Indexing & Storage: Records available from July 1, 1962 to present. New records available for inquiry immediately.

Searching: Records are available only to the parties, their adult children, a present or former spouse, and their legal representatives. Others may obtain a statement of the date and county of the event. Include in request- names of husband and wife, date of divorce, place of divorce.

Access by: mail, phone, fax, in person, online.

Fee & Payment: The search fee is $12.00 per name, add $3.00 for each additional copy. Fee payee- DHEC. Prepayment required. Personal checks accepted. Major credit cards accepted for phone requests only.

Mail search: Turnaround time- 7 weeks. SASE not required. **Phone search:** phone requests are accepted, using a credit card. See expedited service from VitalChek. **Fax search:** See expedited svc.

In person: Turnaround time is within 1 hour. However, the counter will be closed from Nov. 3, 2008 until March 2009 for construction.

Online search: Order from state-designated vendor www.vitalchek.com. See expedited svcs.

Expedited service: Expedited service is available for mail requests for an additional $5.00 from this agency. Turnaround is 3-5 days. To have search "expedited" by phone, online or fax from www.vitalchek.com, add additional fees for courier delivery.

Workers' Compensation Records

Workers Compensation Commission, Research, PO Box 1715, Columbia, SC 29202 (Courier address- 1612 Marion St, Columbia, SC 29201); 803-737-5700, Fax- 803-737-5768; 8:30AM-5PM.

www.wcc.state.sc.us/

Indexing & Storage: Records available from 1983 on the computer. Some of the older records are at this office and the rest are at the State Archives. Call office first for location of records. New records available for inquiry immediately.

Searching: Include in request- claimant name and signed release, SSN. This data not released- transcripts.

Access by: mail, fax, in person.

Fee & Payment: The search fee is $10.00 per record and includes a computer printout. File copies cost $20.00 for the first up to 20 pages and $.50 for each additional page. Fee payee- SC Workers Compensation Commission. Prepayment required. Personal checks accepted, credit cards are not.

Mail search: Turnaround time- 1 week. A SASE is requested.

Fax search: You can request by fax, but reply is sent by mail, same turnaround time.

In person: Records are still returned by mail.

Driver License Information, Driver Records

Department of Motor Vehicles, Driver Records Section, PO Box 1498, Blythewood, SC 29016-0028; 803-896-5000; 8:30AM-5PM.

www.scdmvonline.com/DMVNew/default.aspx

Copies of tickets are available from this department for a fee of $6.00 per record.

Indexing & Storage: Records available for up to 10 years for moving violations, DWIs and suspensions. Records provided to the public are limited to 3 or 10 years. The state will show moving violations regardless of whether the fine was not paid and license suspended. New records available for inquiry in 1 to 4 weeks.

Searching: Driving records and Identification Card information is confidential by statute. Requests must fall within the guidelines of DPPA. Non-permissible use requesters must submit consent of subject if personal information is to be released. Include in request- Form MV-70 which requires driver's license number or full name and DOB. Consent of driver needed if requester not DPPA approved. This data not released- SSNs or personal info (height, weight, sex, eye color, etc.).

Access by: mail, phone, in person, online.

Fee & Payment: The fee is $6.00 per manual record request, online is higher. Fee payee- Department of Motor Vehicles Prepayment required. Personal checks accepted. Credit cards only accepted for call center and online.

Mail search: Turnaround time- 5 days. Fee and return address must be submitted with each request. SASE not required.

Phone search: Phone searching is only available for account holders.

In person: Most DMV Branch offices in the state will process up to 10 records while you wait.

Online search: Commercial records are available from the portal https://dmvdhr.sc.gov/DriverHistoryRecords/Interactive/CDBLogin.aspx. Authorized businesses must establish an account through a formal approval and acceptance process. The fee is $7.25 per record and a $75.00 annual fee is required. Members have access to additional online services. For more information about setting up an account, call 803-771-0131 or email support@sc-egov.com. For no fee, at www.scdmvonline.com/DMVNew/default.aspx one may view a driver license status. The status includes points history. The DL, SSN and DOB are needed. SC drivers may purchase own record after viewing; a certified copy is mailed for $6.00.

Vehicle Ownership & Registration

Division of Motor Vehicles, Title and Registration Records Section, PO Box 1498, Blythewood, SC 29016; 803-896-5000, Fax- 803-896-6685; 8:30AM-5PM.

www.scdmvonline.com/DMVNew/default.aspx

Indexing & Storage: Records available since 1984. New records available for inquiry in 1 day.

Searching: Information regarding the name, address and telephone number will not be released to the public unless the requester completes form provided by department. Otherwise information is not provided to casual requesters. Requesters must be in compliance with DPPA.

Access by: mail, phone, fax, in person.

Fee & Payment: The standard (over 3 days) search fee is $6.00 per record. Lien ifromation is available. See expedited services. Fee payee- SC Department of Motor Vehicles. Prepayment required. A deposit account is available for ongoing requesters by mail or phone. Personal checks accepted, credit cards are not.

Mail search: Turnaround time- 3 or more days. SASE not required.

Phone search: Telephone searching is available for pre-approved, ongoing requesters. A deposit is required. **Fax search:** See expedited service. This is only available to pre-approved, ongoing requesters. A deposit is required. **In person:** You may search in person.

Other access: South Carolina offers a variety of bulk retrieval programs when permitted by law. There is a minimum charge of $1,000.00. For more information, call customer service department for automated searches.

Expedited service: Expedited service is required to receive the data within 3 days. The fee is $20.00. Request received by 2PM will be counted as next day. Turnaround time- 3 days.

Accident Reports

Accident Reports, Financial Responsibility Office, PO Box 1498, Blythewood, SC 29016-0050; 803-896-5000, Fax- 803-896-8443; 8:30AM-5PM.

www.scdmvonline.com/DMVNew/default.aspx

Indexing & Storage: Records available for 10 years to present. The records are indexed on computer. New records available for inquiry in one week after receipt from enforcement agency.

Searching: Must have full name of all the drivers involved in the accident. Include in request- full name, date of accident, driver's license number or tag number, county.

Access by: mail, phone, in person.

Fee & Payment: The fee is $6.00 for an accident research or insurance research. Fee payee- Department of Motor Vehicles Prepayment usually required. Ongoing requesters may open an account with a $100.00 or more deposit and then will be billed monthly. Personal checks accepted. No credit cards accepted now, but may the near future.

Mail search: Turnaround time- 7 to 10 days. Information requests are available. A SASE is requested. **Phone search:** You may call to find out if record is on file, use number above and option 1.

In person: Records will be processed while you wait, but only at a field office on Shep Road and Blythewood office.

Expedited service: Expedited service is available for an additional $20.00 per report. Turnaround time- 3 days or less.

Vessel Ownership & Registration

Dept of Natural Resources, Registration & Titles, PO Box 167, Columbia, SC 29202 (Courier - 1000 Assembly St, Room 104, Columbia, SC 29201); 803-734-3857, Fax- 803-734-4138; 8:30AM-5PM.

www.dnr.sc.gov/boating/index.html

Boats are registered and titled. Motors are titled. Thus, to search for a boat with a motor, two record checks are required.

Indexing & Storage: Records available from mid 80's to present. Inactive records are put on microfiche seven years after becoming inactive. Records stay on microfiche 75 years. New records available for inquiry in 30 days.

Searching: State law prohibits the release of records for commercial solicitation. The agency does not follow DPPA, they follow Freedom of Information Guidelines. All motorized boats must be titled and registered. All sailboats must be titled, and if used with propulsion then registered. To search, one of the following is required: name and address, hull ID #, title #, or SC (serial) #. This data not released- SSNs.

Access by: mail, in person.

Fee & Payment: The search fee for each type of search is $10.00. Thus to search of boats w/no motor and a search of boats with outboard motor the total fee is $20.00. Fee payee- SC Dept of Natural Resources. Prepayment required. Personal checks accepted, credit cards are not.

Mail search: Turnaround time- 7 to 20 days. SASE not required.

In person: Turnaround time is usually same day.

Legislation Records

Legislative Printing, 1105 Pendleton St, Blatt Bldg Rm 223, Columbia, SC 29201; 803-212-4420, Fax- 803-212-4450; 9AM-5PM.

www.scstatehouse.gov/ Records available for current session only. Session is 2-year. Research older passed bills (prior to 1975) at the Legislative Council on the 4th floor, 803-734-2145.

Voter Registration

State Election Commission, Records, PO Box 5987, Columbia, SC 29250; 803-734-9060, Fax- 803-734-9366; 8:30AM-5PM. www.scvotes.org/

Indexing & Storage: Records available for all active records. New records available for inquiry in one day or less.

Searching: Records are open to the public. Include in request- name with the county, or DOB and/or SSN, plus the requester name, contact information, specifics of the request. This data not released- SSNs.

Access by: mail, phone, fax, in person, online.

Fee & Payment: There is no search fee unless extensive time involved. Copies are $.20 each. Requester must pre-pay if courier service desired. Fee payee- State Election Commission. Prepayment required. Personal checks accepted, credit cards are not.

Mail search: Turnaround time- 1 to 2 days. SASE requested. **Phone search:** Some records are available by phone. **Fax search:** Same criteria as mail searching. $.20 fee per page to return by fax. **In person:** Simple requests may be processed while you wait.

Online search: Intended to check your own registration, free access is offered at www.scvotes.org/check_your_voter_registration. When checking information, must provide the name, street name, county and date of birth exactly as registered.

Other access: Lists, labels, diskettes, and electronic media are available with a variety of sort features. The minimum charge varies from $75 to $160 depending on the media.

GED Certificates

GED Testing Office, 1429 Senate St, #402, Columbia, SC 29201; 803-734-8347 x8, Fax- 803-734-8336; 8:30AM-5PM M-F.

http://ed.sc.gov/agency/Standards-and-Learning/Adult-Education/old/ace/ged/index.html

Indexing & Storage: Records available from 1942. New records available for inquiry in 6 wks.

Searching: To search, all of the following is required: a signed release, name, SSN, and approximate date and city. Specify if for civilian or military use.

Access by: mail, fax, in person.

Fee & Payment: There is no fee for a verification. There is a $5.00 fee for a copy of a transcript by mail, $3.00 if by fax. Fee payee- SC Dept of Education. Prepayment required. Cash and money orders are accepted. No personal checks or credit cards accepted.

Mail search: Turnaround time- up to 4 weeks. No SASE is required, BUT if you express mail or overnight the request, the request will be processed in 24 hours. **Fax search:** After sending fax, call back in 15 minutes for verification. **In person:** Records may be requested in person. Requester must present state-issued ID.

Hunting & Fishing Licenses

Access to Records is Restricted.

SC Department of Natural Resources, Licensing Division, PO Box 167, Columbia, SC 29202; 803-734-3833, Fax- 803-734-9377; 8:30AM-5PM.

www.dnr.sc.gov/ The agency is in the process of creating a centralized database. Most licenses are kept on file within the License Division by the county and agent where the license was sold, however the records are not open to the public.

South Carolina State Licensing Agencies

For details about the agency responsible for licensing/certifying/registering an item below or in the Agency Quick Finder section, match an item's number with the number of the agency in the *Licensing Agency Information* section.

South Carolina Licenses Searchable Online

Accounting Practitioner-AP #2 .... https://verify.llronline.com/LicLookup/
Acupuncturist #39 .... www.llr.state.sc.us/POL/Medical/index.asp?file=licensure.htm
Airport Professional/Contact #35 .... www.scaeronautics.com/directorySearch.asp
Animal Health Technician #43 .... https://verify.llronline.com/LicLookup/
Architect #3 .... https://verify.llronline.com/LicLookup/
Architectural Partnership/Corp #3 .... https://verify.llronline.com/LicLookup/
Attorney #48 .... www.scbar.org/member_resources/member_directory/
Auction Company #50 .... https://verify.llronline.com/LicLookup/
Auctioneer/Auctioneer Apprentice #50 .... https://verify.llronline.com/LicLookup/
Audiologist #22 .... https://verify.llronline.com/LicLookup/
Aviation Facility #35 .... www.scaeronautics.com/AirportSearch.asp
Barber Instructor/School #47 .... https://verify.llronline.com/LicLookup/
Barber/Barber Apprentice #47 .... https://verify.llronline.com/LicLookup/
Bodywork Therapist #47 .... https://verify.llronline.com/LicLookup/
Building Inspector #21 .... https://verify.llronline.com/LicLookup/
Building Official #21 .... https://verify.llronline.com/LicLookup/
Burglar Alarm Contractor #24 .... https://verify.llronline.com/LicLookup/
Certified Public Accountant-CPA #2 .... https://verify.llronline.com/LicLookup/
Chiropractor #4 .... https://verify.llronline.com/LicLookup/
Contact Lens License #14 .... https://verify.llronline.com/LicLookup/
Contractor, General/Mechanical #24 .... https://verify.llronline.com/LicLookup/
Contractor, Specialty Resid'l #45 .... https://verify.llronline.com/LicLookup/
Cosmetologist #5 .... https://verify.llronline.com/LicLookup/
Cosmetology Instructor/School #5 .... https://verify.llronline.com/LicLookup/
Counselor, Professional #8 .... https://verify.llronline.com/LicLookup/
Dental Hygienist #6 .... https://verify.llronline.com/LicLookup/
Dental Specialist/Technician #6 .... https://verify.llronline.com/LicLookup/
Dentist #6 .... https://verify.llronline.com/LicLookup/
Embalmer #11 .... https://verify.llronline.com/LicLookup/
Engineer #7 .... https://verify.llronline.com/LicLookup/
Esthetician #5 .... https://verify.llronline.com/LicLookup/
Forester #38 .... https://verify.llronline.com/LicLookup/LookupMain.aspx
Funeral Director / Funeral Home #11 .... https://verify.llronline.com/LicLookup/
Geologist #20 .... https://verify.llronline.com/LicLookup/
Hair Care Master Specialist #47 .... https://verify.llronline.com/LicLookup/
Home Builder, Residential #45 .... https://verify.llronline.com/LicLookup/
Housing Inspector #21 .... https://verify.llronline.com/LicLookup/
Inspector, Bldg/Housing #21 .... https://verify.llronline.com/LicLookup/
Inspector, Mech./Elec./Plumb./Prov. #21 .... https://verify.llronline.com/LicLookup/
Lobbyist #37 .... www.scstatehouse.gov/reports/ethrpt.htm
Lobbyist Principal #37 .... www.scstatehouse.gov/reports/ethrpt.htm
Manicure Assistant #47 .... https://verify.llronline.com/LicLookup/
Manicurist #5 .... https://verify.llronline.com/LicLookup/
Manufact'd House Sell/Install/Repair #41 .... https://verify.llronline.com/LicLookup/
Manufactured House Mfg/Dealer/Rep #41 .... https://verify.llronline.com/LicLookup/
Marriage & Family Therapist #8 .... https://verify.llronline.com/LicLookup/
Massage Therapist #47 .... https://verify.llronline.com/LicLookup/
Medical Doctor #39 .... www.llr.state.sc.us/POL/Medical/index.asp?file=licensure.htm
Nail Technician #5 .... https://verify.llronline.com/LicLookup/
Nurses, RN / LPN #12 .... https://verify.llronline.com/LicLookup/
Nursing Home Administrator #32 .... https://verify.llronline.com/LicLookup/
Occupational Therapist/Assistant #13 .... https://verify.llronline.com/LicLookup/
Optician #14 .... https://verify.llronline.com/LicLookup/
Optician Apprentice #14 .... https://verify.llronline.com/LicLookup/
Optometrist #9 .... https://verify.llronline.com/LicLookup/
Osteopathic Physician #39 .... www.llr.state.sc.us/POL/Medical/index.asp?file=licensure.htm
Pharmacist/Pharmacy Technician #15 .... https://verify.llronline.com/LicLookup/

Pharmacy/Drug Outlet #15	https://verify.llronline.com/LicLookup/
Physical Therapist/Therapist Asst #16	https://verify.llronline.com/LicLookup/
Physician Assistant #39	www.llr.state.sc.us/POL/Medical/index.asp?file=licensure.htm
Pilot #35	www.scaeronautics.com/AirportSearch.asp
Plans Examiner, Building #21	https://verify.llronline.com/LicLookup/
Podiatrist #17	https://verify.llronline.com/LicLookup/
Produce Whlse Dealer #25	http://agriculture.sc.gov/
Psycho-Educational Specialist #8	https://verify.llronline.com/LicLookup/
Psychologist #18	https://verify.llronline.com/LicLookup/
Public Accountant-PA #2	https://verify.llronline.com/LicLookup/
Real Estate Appraiser #44	http://verify.llronline.com/LicLookup/LookupMain.aspx
Residential Care, Community #32	https://verify.llronline.com/LicLookup/
Respiratory Care Practitioner #39	www.llr.state.sc.us/POL/Medical/index.asp?file=licensure.htm
Shampoo Assistant #47	https://verify.llronline.com/LicLookup/
Social Worker #18	https://verify.llronline.com/LicLookup/
Speech-Language Pathologist #22	https://verify.llronline.com/LicLookup/
Sprinkler Systems Contractor #24	https://verify.llronline.com/LicLookup/
Surveyor, Land #7	https://verify.llronline.com/LicLookup/
Veterinarian #43	https://verify.llronline.com/LicLookup/
Wholesaler/Shipper (Food) #25	http://agriculture.sc.gov/

South Carolina Licensing Quick Finder

Accounting Practitioner-AP #2	803-896-4770
Acupuncturist #39	803-896-4500
Agricultural Dealer/Handler #25	803-734-2182
Airport Professional/Contact #35	803-896-6260
Alcoholic Bev. Sunday Seller #34	803-898-5880
Alcoholic Bev. Vendor/Mfg./Whlse #34	803-898-5864
Amusement Ride #46	803-896-4300
Animal Health Technician #43	803-896-4598
Architect #3	803-896-4408
Architectural Partnership/Corp #3	803-896-4408
Athletic Event/Contest #49	803-896-4571
Athletic Trainer #49	803-896-4571
Attorney #48	803-799-6653
Auction Company #50	803-896-4853
Auctioneer/Auctioneer Apprentice #50	803-896-4853
Audiologist #22	803-896-4650
Aviation Facility #35	803-896-6260
Bank #10	803-734-2001
Barber Instructor/School #47	803-896-4588
Barber Shop #47	803-896-4588
Barber/Barber Apprentice #47	803-896-4588
Bodywork Therapist #47	803-896-4498
Boxer/Boxing Professional #49	803-896-4571
Building Inspector #21	803-896-4688
Building Official #21	803-896-4688
Burglar Alarm Contractor #24	803-896-4686
Butterfat Tester #25	803-737-9700
Certified Public Accountant-CPA #2	803-896-4770
Chiropractor #4	803-896-4587
Constable #29	803-896-7014
Contact Lens License #14	803-896-4681
Contractor, General/Mechanical #24	803-896-4686
Contractor, Specialty Resid'l #45	803-896-4686
Cosmetologist #5	803-896-4494
Cosmetology Instructor/School #5	803-896-4494
Counselor Supervising Profession'l #8	803-896-4658
Counselor, Professional #8	803-896-4658
Counselor, Professional/Intern #8	803-896-4658
Dental Hygienist #6	803-896-4599
Dental Specialist/Technician #6	803-896-4599
Dentist #6	803-896-4599
Electrician #42	803-933-1209
Elevator Service #46	803-896-4300
Embalmer #11	803-896-4497
Emergency Med. Svc./Ambulance #27	803-545-4202
Emergency Medical Technician #27	803-545-4204
Engineer #7	803-896-4422
Esthetician #5	803-896-4494
Ethics Debtors #37	803-253-4192
Feed Manufacturer/Product #25	803-737-9700
Financial Institution #10	803-734-2001
Forester #38	803-896-4675
Funeral Director #11	803-896-4497
Funeral Home #11	803-896-4497
Geologist #20	803-896-4498
Hair Care Master Specialist #47	803-896-4588
Heating & Air/Gas Fitting #42	803-933-1209
Home Builder, Residential #45	803-896-4686
Housing Inspector #21	803-896-4688
Inspector, Bldg/Housing #21	803-896-4688
Inspector, Mech./Elec./Plumb./Prov #21	803-896-4688
Insurance Agency/Company/Filing #31	803-737-6221
Insurance Agent #31	803-737-6095
Investment Advisor #1	803-734-9916
Landscape Architect #40	803-734-9131
Liquor Permit, Special Event #34	803-898-5864
Lobbyist #37	803-253-4192
Lobbyist Principal #37	803-253-4192
Manicure Assistant #47	803-896-4588
Manicurist #5	803-896-4494
Manufact'd House Seller/Install/Repair #41	803-896-4682
Manufactured House Mfg/Dealer/Rep #41	803-896-4682
Marriage & Family Therapist #8	803-896-4658
Massage Therapist #47	803-896-4498
Medical Doctor #39	803-896-4500
Mine Site #30	803-896-4000
Nail Technician #5	803-896-4494
Notary Public #23	803-734-2512
Nurses, RN / LPN #12	803-896-4550
Nursing Home Administrator #32	803-896-4544
Occupational Therapist/Assistant #13	803-896-4683
Optician #14	803-896-4681
Optician Apprentice #14	803-896-4681
Optometrist #9	803-869-4679
Osteopathic Physician #39	803-896-4500
Percolation Test Technician #36	803-896-4430
Pesticide Applicator #33	803-646-2155
Pesticide Dealer #33	803-646-2155
Pharmacist/Pharmacy Technician #15	803-896-4700
Pharmacy/Drug Outlet #15	803-896-4700
Physical Therapist/Therapist Asst #16	803-896-4655
Physician Assistant #39	803-896-4500
Pilot #35	803-896-6260
Pipefitter #42	803-933-1209
Plans Examiner, Building #21	803-896-4688
Plumbing #42	803-933-1209
Podiatrist #17	803-896-4685
Polygraph Examiner #29	803-896-7292
Private Detective #29	803-896-7014
Produce Whlse Dealer #25	803-737-9700
Property Manager #44	803-896-4400
Psycho-Educational Specialist #8	803-896-4658
Psychologist #18	803-896-4664
Public Accountant-PA #2	803-896-4770
Pyrotechnic Technician #19	803-896-9807
Pyrotechnic Whlse./Facility/Jobber #19	803-896-4420
Real Estate Appraiser #44	803-896-4400
Real Estate Broker #44	803-896-4400
Residential Care, Community #32	803-896-4544
Respiratory Care Practitioner #39	803-896-4500
Sanitarian #28	803-896-0655
School Guidance Counselor #26	803-734-8466
School Media Communication Special't #26	803-734-8466
School Principal/Supvr/Super'n'd't #26	803-734-8466
Securities Agent #1	803-734-9916
Securities Broker/Dealer #1	803-734-9916
Security Guard/Security Company #29	803-896-7014
Seed Salesperson #25	803-737-9690
Shampoo Assistant #47	803-896-4588
Sheet Metal #42	803-933-1209
Social Worker #18	803-896-4665
Soil Classifier #40	803-734-9131
Solid Waste Landfill #30	803-896-4148
Solid Waste Landfill Operator #30	803-896-4148
Speech-Language Pathologist #22	803-896-4650
Sprinkler Systems Contractor #24	803-896-4686
Surveyor, Land #7	803-896-4422
Swimming Pool/Spa Operator #36	803-896-4430
Teacher #26	803-734-8466
Timeshare/Land Salesperson #44	803-896-4400
Veterinarian #43	803-896-4598
Waste Water Plant Operator #36	803-896-4430
Water Treatment Registration #36	803-896-4430
Weighman #25	803-737-9700
Weighmaster #25	803-737-9696
Well Driller #36	803-896-4430
Wholesaler/Shipper (Food) #25	803-737-9700
Wrestler/Wrestling Professional #49	803-896-4571

South Carolina Licensing Agency Information

#1 Attorney Generals Office, Securities Division, PO Box 11549 (1000 Assembly St, Rm 519), Columbia, SC 29211-1549; 803-734-9916, Fax- 803-734-0032. www.scattorneygeneral.org/securities/index.html

#2 Department of Labor, Licensing & Regulation, Board of Accountancy, PO Box 11329 (110 Centerview Dr #104), Columbia, SC 29211; 803-896-4770, Fax- 803-896-4554. Hours- 8:30AM-5PM. www.llr.state.sc.us/pol/accountancy/ Search data at- https://verify.llronline.com/LicLookup/

#3 Department of Labor, Licensing & Regulation, Board of Architectural Examiners, PO Box 11419 (110 Centerview Dr, #201), Columbia, SC 29211-1419; 803-896-4408, Fax- 803-734-4410. www.llr.state.sc.us/pol.asp Search data at- https://verify.llronline.com/LicLookup/

#4 Department of Labor, Licensing & Regulation, Division of Chiropractic Examiners, PO Box 11329 (110 Centerview Dr, #306), Columbia, SC 29211-1329; 803-896-4587, Fax- 803-896-4719. Hours- 8:30AM-5PM. www.llr.state.sc.us Search data at- https://verify.llronline.com/LicLookup/

#5 Department of Labor, Licensing & Regulation, Board of Cosmetology, PO Box 11329 (110 Centerview Dr), Columbia, SC 29211-1329; 803-896-4568, Fax- 803-896-4484. Hours- 8:30AM-5PM. www.llr.state.sc.us/pol.asp Search data at- https://verify.llronline.com/LicLookup/ See also Board of Barber examiners for Shampoo Assistant and Master Hair Care Specialist.

#6 Department of Labor, Licensing & Regulation, Board of Dentistry, PO Box 11329 (110 Centerview Dr, #306), Columbia, SC 29211-1329; 803-896-4599, Fax- 803-896-4596. www.llr.state.sc.us/POL/Dentistry/ Search data at- https://verify.llronline.com/LicLookup/

#7 Department of Labor, Licensing & Regulation, Board of Prof. Engineers & Land Surveyors, PO Box 11597 (110 Centerview Dr, #201), Columbia, SC 29211-1597; 803-896-4422, Fax- 803-896-4427. www.llr.state.sc.us/pol.asp Search data at- https://verify.llronline.com/LicLookup/

#8 Department of Labor, Licensing & Regulation, Board of Examiners of Prof. Counselors / Marriage & Family Therapists, PO Box 11329 (110 Centerview, #306), Columbia, SC 29211; 803-896-4658, Fax- 803-896-4719. Hours- 8:30AM-5PM. www.llr.state.sc.us/pol.asp Search data at- https://verify.llronline.com/LicLookup/ List available through email or on diskette for fee of $30.00.

#9 Department of Labor, Licensing & Regulation, Board of Examiners in Optometry, PO Box 11329 (110 Centerview Dr.), Columbia, SC 29211-1329; 803-896-4679, Fax- 803-896-4719. Hours- 8:30AM-5PM. www.llr.state.sc.us/pol.asp Search data at- https://verify.llronline.com/LicLookup/ Online disciplinary records only go back to 1994.

#10 Board of Financial Institutions, 1205 Pendleton St, #305, Columbia, SC 29201; 803-734-2001, Fax- 803-734-2013. http://banking.sc.gov/

#11 Department of Labor, Licensing & Regulation, Board of Funeral Service, PO Box 11329 (110 Centerview Dr, #104), Columbia, SC 29211-1329; 803-896-4497, Fax- 803-896-4484. www.llr.state.sc.us/pol.asp Search data at- https://verify.llronline.com/LicLookup/

#12 Department of Labor, Licensing & Regulation, Board of Nursing, PO Box 12367 (110 Centerview Dr, #202), Columbia, SC 29211-2367; 803-896-4550, Fax- 803-896-4525. Hours- 8:30AM-5PM. www.llr.state.sc.us/pol/nursing/ Search data at- https://verify.llronline.com/LicLookup/

#13 Department of Labor, Licensing & Regulation, Board of Occupational Therapy, PO Box 11329 (110 Centerview Dr, #306), Columbia, SC 29211; 803-896-4683, Fax- 803-896-4719. Hours- 8:30AM-5PM. www.llr.state.sc.us/pol.asp Search data at- https://verify.llronline.com/LicLookup/ Online records only go back to 1994.

#14 Department of Labor, Licensing & Regulation, Board of Examiners in Optometry, PO Box 11329 (110 Centerview Dr #306), Columbia, SC 29211-1329; 803-896-4679, Fax- 803-896-4719. Hours- 8:30AM-5PM. www.llr.state.sc.us/pol.asp Search data at- https://verify.llronline.com/LicLookup/ Online records only go back to 1994.

#15 Department of Labor, Licensing & Regulation, Board of Pharmacy, PO Box 11927, (110 Centerview Dr, Kingstree Bldg, #306), Columbia, SC 29211-1927; 803-896-4700, Fax- 803-896-4596. www.llr.state.sc.us/pol.asp Search data at- https://verify.llronline.com/LicLookup/

#16 Department of Labor, Licensing & Regulation, Board of Physical Therapy Examiners, PO Box 11329 (110 Centerview Dr), Columbia, SC 29211; 803-896-4655, Fax- 803-896-4719. Hours- 8:30AM-5PM. www.llr.state.sc.us/POL/PhysicalTherapy/ Search data at- https://verify.llronline.com/LicLookup/

#17 Department of Labor, Licensing & Regulation, Board of Podiatry Examiners, PO Box 11289 (110 Centerview Dr, #202), Columbia, SC 29211-1289; 803-896-4685, Fax- 803-896-4515. www.llr.state.sc.us/pol/podiatry/ Search data at- https://verify.llronline.com/LicLookup/

#18 Department of Labor, Licensing & Regulation, Board of Examiners in Psychology/Social Work Examiners, PO Box 11329 (110 Centerview Dr), Columbia, SC 29211-1329; 803-896-4665, Fax- 803-896-4687. www.llr.state.sc.us/pol.asp Search at- https://verify.llronline.com/LicLookup/ Online psychologist records only go back to 1994.

#19 Department of Labor, Licensing & Regulation, Board of Pyrotechnic Safety, PO Box 11847 (141 Monticello Tr), Columbia, SC 29211-1329; 803-896-4420, Fax- 803-896-9806. www.llr.state.sc.us/POL/Pyrotechnic/

#20 Department of Labor, Licensing & Regulation, Board of Registration for Geologists, PO Box 11329 (110 Centerview Dr, #104), Columbia, SC 29211-1329; 803-896-4498, Fax- 803-896-4484. www.llr.state.sc.us/pol.asp Search data at- https://verify.llronline.com/LicLookup/

#21 Department of Labor, Licensing & Regulation, Building Codes Council, PO Box 11329 (110 Centerview Dr, #102), Columbia, SC 29211-1329; 803-896-4688, Fax- 803-896-4814. www.llr.state.sc.us/pol.asp Search data at- https://verify.llronline.com/LicLookup/

#22 Department of Labor, Licensing & Regulation, Board of Examiners for Speech-Language Pathology & Audiology, PO Box 11329 (110 Centerview Dr, #306), Columbia, SC 29211-1329; 803-896-4650, Fax- 803-896-4719. Hours- 8:30AM-5PM. www.llr.state.sc.us/POL/Speech/ Search data at- https://verify.llronline.com/LicLookup/

#23 Secretary of State, Notaries & Apostilles Office, PO Box 11350 (1205 Pendleton St, #525), Columbia, SC 29211; 803-734-2512, Fax- 803-734-1661. Hours- 8:30AM-5PM. www.scsos.com/notariesbc.htm State Boards & Agencies- www.sc.gov/portal/orglist.aspx.

#24 Department of Labor, Licensing & Regulation, Contractor's Licensing Board, PO Box 11329 (110 Centerview Dr, #201), Columbia, SC 29211-1329; 803-896-4686, Fax- 803-896-4364. www.llr.state.sc.us/pol.asp Search data at- https://verify.llronline.com/LicLookup/

#25 Department of Agriculture, PO Box 11280 (1200 Senate St), Columbia, SC 29211; 803-734-2210, Fax- 803-734-2192. http://agriculture.sc.gov/content.aspx?MenuID=17

#26 Department of Education, Office of Educator Certification, 3700 Forest Dr, #500, Columbia, SC 29204; 803-734-8466, Fax- 803-734-2873. www.scteachers.org

#27 Department of Health & Environmental Control, EMS Department, 2600 Bull St, Columbia, SC 29201; 803-545-4204, Fax- 803-545-4989. www.scdhec.net/health/ems/

#28 Department of Health & Environmental Control, Bureau of Environmental Health, 2600 Bull St, Columbia, SC 29201; 803-896-0655, Fax- 803-896-0645. www.scdhec.net

#29 Law Enforcement Division, Regulatory Department, PO Box 21398 (4400 Broad River Rd), Columbia, SC 29221; 803-737-9000, Fax- 803-896-7041. www.sled.sc.gov/

#30 Department of Health & Environmental Control, Bureau of Land and Waste Management, 2600 Bull St, Columbia, SC 29201; 803-896-4000, Fax- 803-896-4001. www.scdhec.gov/environment/lwm/html/solidwaste.htm For Landfill Operators, search by county.

#31 Department of Insurance, 1201 Main St, #1000, Columbia, SC 29201; 803-737-6160, Fax- 803-737-6205. www.doi.sc.gov

#32 Department of Labor, Licensing & Regulation, Board of Long Term Care Administrators, PO Box 11329 (110 Centerview Dr), Columbia, SC 29211; 803-896-4544, Fax- 803-896-4555. www.llr.state.sc.us/pol.asp Search data at- https://verify.llronline.com/LicLookup/

#33 Department of Pesticide Regulation, 511 Westinghouse Rd, Pendelton, SC 29670; 864-646-2150, Fax- 864-646-2179. Hours- 8AM-N, 1PM-4:30PM. www.clemson.edu/public/regulatory/pesticide_regulation/

#34 Department of Revenue & Taxation, Alcoholic Beverage Section, PO Box 125, Columbia, SC 29214; 803-898-5864, Fax- 803-898-5899. www.sctax.org/default.htm The state list of Sunday Sales permits for alcoholic beverages is temporarily unavailable.

#35 Division of Aeronautics, PO Box 280068 (2553 Airport Blvd, West Columbia), Columbia, SC 29228-0068; 803-896-6260, 800-922-0574, Fax- 803-896-6277. www.scaeronautics.com

#36 Department of Labor, Licensing & Regulation, Environmental Certification Board, PO Box 11409 (110 Centerview Dr #201), Columbia, SC 29211; 803-896-4430, Fax- 803-896-4424. www.llr.state.sc.us/POL/Environmental/

#37 Ethics Commission, 5000 Thurmond Mall #250, Columbia, SC 29201; 803-253-4192, Fax- 803-253-7539. www.scstatehouse.gov/reports/ethrpt.htm Search data at- www.scstatehouse.gov/reports/ethrpt.htm

#38 Department of Labor, Licensing & Regulation, Board of Registration for Foresters, PO Box 11329 (110 Centerview Dr), Columbia, SC 29211-1329; 803-896-4498, Fax- 803-896-4484. www.llr.state.sc.us/POL/Forestry/ Search at- https://verify.llronline.com/LicLookup/LookupMain.aspx

#39 Department of Labor, Licensing & Regulation, Board of Medical Examiners, PO Box 11289 (110 Centerview Dr, #202), Columbia, SC 29211-1289; 803-896-4500, Fax- 803-896-4515. Hours- 8:30AM-5PM. www.llr.state.sc.us/POL/Medical/ Search data at- www.llr.state.sc.us/POL/Medical/index.asp?file=licensure.htm

#40 Department of Natural Resources, Land, Water & Conservation Div., Licensing Program, 1000 Assembly St. (PO Box 167), Columbia, SC 29202; 803-734-9131, Fax- 803-734-9200. Hours- 8:30AM-5PM. www.dnr.sc.gov

#41 Department of Labor, Licensing & Regulation, Manufactured Housing Board, PO Box 11329 (110 Centerview Dr, #102), Columbia, SC 29211-1329; 803-896-4682, Fax- 803-896-4814. www.llr.state.sc.us/pol.asp Search data at- https://verify.llronline.com/LicLookup/

#42 Municipal Association of South Carolina, Trades Certification Program, PO Box 12109 (1411 Gervais St), Columbia, SC 29211; 803-779-9574, Fax- 803-933-1299. Hours- 9AM-4PM. www.masc.sc/trades/trades.htm Will verify by phone.

#43 Department of Labor, Licensing & Regulation, Board of Veterinary Medical Examiners, PO Box 11329 (110 Centerview Dr #306), Columbia, SC 29211-1329; 803-896-4598, Fax- 803-896-4719. Hours- 8:30AM-5PM. www.llr.state.sc.us/pol.asp Search data at- https://verify.llronline.com/LicLookup/

#44 Real Estate Commission, PO Box 11847 (110 Centerview Dr, #201), Columbia, SC 29211-1847; 803-896-4400, Fax- 803-896-4404. www.llr.state.sc.us/pol.asp Search at- http://verify.llronline.com/LicLookup/LookupMain.aspx

#45 Department of Labor, Licensing & Regulation, Residential Builders Commission, PO Box 11329 (110 Centerview Dr, #201), Columbia, SC 29211-1329; 803-896-4686, Fax- 803-896-4656. www.llr.state.sc.us/pol.asp Search data at- https://verify.llronline.com/LicLookup/

#46 Department of Labor, Licensing & Regulation, Office of Elevators & Amusement Rides, PO Box 11329 (110 Centerview Dr), Columbia, SC 29211-1329; 803-896-7630, Fax- 803-896-7650. www.llr.state.sc.us/Labor/ElevatorAmusement/

#47 Department of Labor, Licensing & Regulation, Board of Barber Examiners, Massage/Bodywork Therapy, PO Box 11329 (110 Centerview Dr, #104), Columbia, SC 29211-1329; 803-896-4491, Fax- 803-896-4484. www.llr.state.sc.us/POL/Barber/ Search data at- https://verify.llronline.com/LicLookup/

#48 Supreme Court, 950 Taylor St, Columbia, SC 29201; 803-799-6653, Fax- 803-799-4118. www.scbar.org Search data at- www.scbar.org/member_resources/member_directory/

#49 Department of Labor, Licensing & Regulation, Athletic Commission, PO Box 11329 (110 Centerview Dr), Columbia, SC 29211; 803-896-4571, Fax- 803-896-4554. www.llr.state.sc.us/pol.asp

#50 Department of Labor, Licensing & Regulation, Auctioneer's Commission, PO Box 11329 (110 Centerview Dr, #104), Columbia, SC 29211-1329; 803-896-4853, Fax- 803-896-4484. www.llr.state.sc.us/POL/Auctioneers/ Search data at- https://verify.llronline.com/LicLookup/

South Carolina Federal Courts

The following list indicates the district and division name for each county in the state. If the bankruptcy court location is different from the district court, then the location of the bankruptcy court appears in parentheses.

All records in the Clerk's Office are filed and retrieved by case number: Rock Hill=0, Aiken=1, Charleston=2, Columbia=3, Florence=4, Orangeburg=5, Greenville=6, Spartanburg=7, Anderson/Greenwood=8, Beaufort=9.

South Carolina County/Court Cross Reference

County	Court	County	Court
Abbeville	Greenwood (Columbia)	Greenwood	Greenwood (Columbia)
Aiken	Aiken (Columbia)	Hampton	Beaufort (Columbia)
Allendale	Aiken (Columbia)	Horry	Florence (Columbia)
Anderson	Anderson (Columbia)	Jasper	Beaufort (Columbia)
Bamberg	Orangeburg (Columbia)	Kershaw	Columbia
Barnwell	Aiken (Columbia)	Lancaster	Rock Hill (Columbia)
Beaufort	Beaufort (Columbia)	Laurens	Greenville (Columbia)
Berkeley	Charleston (Columbia)	Lee	Columbia
Calhoun	Orangeburg (Columbia)	Lexington	Columbia
Charleston	Charleston (Columbia)	Marion	Florence (Columbia)
Cherokee	Spartanburg (Columbia)	Marlboro	Florence (Columbia)
Chester	Rock Hill (Columbia)	McCormick	Greenwood (Columbia)
Chesterfield	Florence (Columbia)	Newberry	Greenwood (Columbia)
Clarendon	Charleston (Columbia)	Oconee	Anderson (Columbia)
Colleton	Charleston (Columbia)	Orangeburg	Orangeburg (Columbia)
Darlington	Florence (Columbia)	Pickens	Anderson (Columbia)
Dillon	Florence (Columbia)	Richland	Columbia
Dorchester	Charleston (Columbia)	Saluda	Greenwood (Columbia)
Edgefield	Greenwood (Columbia)	Spartanburg	Spartanburg (Columbia)
Fairfield	Rock Hill (Columbia)	Sumter	Columbia
Florence	Florence (Columbia)	Union	Spartanburg (Columbia)
Georgetown	Charleston (Columbia)	Williamsburg	Florence (Columbia)
Greenville	Greenville (Columbia)	York	Rock Hill (Columbia)

Standards for Federal Courts: Fees are standard unless noted in profile. Search fee is $26.00 per item (one party name or case number). Copy fee is $.50 per page. Certification fee is $9.00 per document, double for exemplification, if available. Most courts require prepayment. Mail requests should enclose a SASE unless otherwise noted. Before releasing records, all courts require prepayment, unless noted.

District courts index by defendant and plaintiff and by case number. Bankruptcy courts usually index by debtor and case number. While most courts now have their indexes on computer, many may still maintain index card files as well. Courts will archive closed case files at different times.

There are numerous public access programs available to online subscribers. Search the U.S. Party/Case Index to find party names and case numbers among all courts. Individual case data is provided on PACER. A search of CM/ECF provides copies of cases filed electronically. For details about PACER, the US Party/Case Index, and CM/ECF see the Appendix or go to http://pacer.psc.uscourts.gov or call 800-676-6856.

US District Court
District of South Carolina

Aiken Division c/o Columbia Division, 901 Richland St, Columbia, SC 29201, 803-765-5816; Fax- 803-765-5960. Hours- 8:30AM-4:30PM; records rm- 9AM-4:30PM. www.scd.uscourts.gov

Counties/Note: Aiken, Allendale, Barnwell. All records in the Clerk's Office are filed and retrieved by case number: Aiken=1. All counties can be searched electronically at any of the 4 main offices- Columbia, Charleston, Florence, Greenville.

Searches/Indexing: Helpful to include DOB or SSN in criminal search request, but only a full name in civil search. Results do not include SSN or DOB. New cases are in the index 1 month after filing date. Computer index maintained; civil back to 1990, criminal to 1992. Older records indexed on microfiche. District-wide searches available here. Open records not located at Aiken Division. Closed electronic cases not purged.

Search Access: If case number, caption and judge are provided, court gives docket info via phone. Court will not search case numbers or captions via phone. **Mail:** Search usually completed- 2-3 days. SASE not required. **Fax:** Fax search requests accepted with credit card; response returned by mail if prepaid. **In person:** 1 public terminal available; index goes back to 1990. No self-serve copier.

Payment: Pay by Visa/MC, money order, cashier's or personal check. Payee: Clerk, US District Court.

E-Services: Document images available. PACER records go back to 1990. New records online after 1 day. ECF at https://ecf.scd.uscourts.gov. Opinions on subscription WebPacer system.

Anderson Division c/o Greenville Division, PO Box 10768, Greenville, SC 29603 (In person: 300 E Washington St, Greenville, SC), 864-241-2700; Fax- 864-241-2711. 8:30AM-4:30PM. www.scd.uscourts.gov

Counties/Note: Anderson, Oconee, Pickens. All records in the Clerk's Office are filed and retrieved by case number: Anderson=8. All counties can be searched electronically at any of the 4 main offices- Columbia, Charleston, Florence, Greenville.

Searches/Indexing: Include DOB or SSN in search request; only a full name in civil search. Results do not include SSN or DOB. Will not fax back documents. New cases are in the index 1 day after filing date. Open records located at Greenville.

Search Access: Mail: SASE required. **In person:** 1 public terminal available; index back to 1990. No self-serve copier. A copy service can make copies for $.09 per page.

Payment: Pay by Visa/MC, cashier's check, money order. No business or personal checks accepted. Payee: Clerk, US District Court.

E-Services: PACER records go back to 1990. New records online after 1 day. ECF at https://ecf.scd.uscourts.gov. Opinions on subscription WebPacer system.

Beaufort Division c/o Charleston Division, PO Box 835, Charleston, SC 29402 (In person: 85 Broad St, Hollings Judicial Center, Charleston), 843-579-1401; Fax- 803-579-1402. 8:30AM-4:30PM. www.scd.uscourts.gov

Counties/Note: Beaufort, Hampton, Jasper. All records in the Clerk's Office are filed and retrieved by case number: Beaufort=9. All counties can be searched electronically at any of the 4 main offices- Columbia, Charleston, Florence, Greenville.

Searches/Indexing: Helpful to include DOB or SSN in criminal search request, but only a full name in civil search. Results include last 4 SSN digits. Will fax back documents for fee. Computer index goes back to 1991. Open records not available in Beaufort. Civil records sent to Records Ctr 1 year after case closed; criminal records after 5 years.

Search Access: Mail: Include SASE for return. **Fax:** Fax search requests accepted. **In person:** 1 public terminal available; index back to 1990. No self-serve copier.

Payment: Pay by Visa/MC, money order, cashier's check, business check.

E-Services: PACER records go back to 1990. New records online after 1 day. ECF at https://ecf.scd.uscourts.gov. Opinions on subscription WebPacer system.

Charleston Division Court Clerk, PO Box 835, Charleston, SC 29402 (In person: 85 Broad St, Hollings Judicial Center, Charleston), 843-579-1401; civil dockets- 843-579-1401; Fax- 803-579-1402. Hours-8:30AM-4:30PM; records hours- 9AM-4:30PM. www.scd.uscourts.gov

Counties/Note: Berkeley, Charleston, Clarendon, Colleton, Dorchester, Georgetown. All records in the Clerk's Office are filed and retrieved by case number: Charleston=2, Beaufort=9. All counties can be searched electronically at any of the 4 main offices- Columbia, Charleston, Florence, Greenville.

Searches/Indexing: Search request requires name only. Results do not include SSN or DOB. New cases are in the index 1-2 days after filing date. Computer index back to 1991 maintained. Older records indexed on cards and microfiche. District-wide searches available for cases back to 1980. Closed electronic cases not purged.

Search Access: Mail: Search usually completed- 1-2 days. Include SASE for return. **Fax:** Fax search requests accepted. **In person:** 1 public terminal available; index back to 1990. No self-serve copier.

Payment: Pay by Visa/MC, money order, cashier's or personal check. Payee: US District Court.

E-Services: Document images available. PACER records go back to 1990. New records online after 1 day. ECF at https://ecf.scd.uscourts.gov. Opinions on subscription WebPacer system.

Columbia Division Court Clerk, 901 Richland St, Columbia, SC 29201, 803-765-5816; Fax- 803-765-5960. Hours- 8:30AM-4:30PM; records rm- 9AM-4:30PM. www.scd.uscourts.gov

Counties/Note: Kershaw, Lee, Lexington, Richland, Sumter. All records in the Clerk's Office are filed and retrieved by case number: Columbia=3, Rock Hill=0, Aiken=1, Orangeburg=5. All counties can be searched electronically at any of the 4 main offices- Columbia, Charleston, Florence, Greenville.

Searches/Indexing: Helpful to include DOB or SSN in criminal search request, but only a full name in civil search. Results do not include SSN or DOB. New cases are in the index 1 month after filing date. Computer index maintained; civil back to 1990, criminal to 1992. Older records indexed on microfiche. District-wide searches available here. Closed electronic cases not purged.

Search Access: If case number, caption and judge are provided, court gives docket info via phone. Court will not search case numbers or captions via phone. **Mail:** Search usually completed- 2-3 days. SASE not required. **Fax:** Fax search requests accepted with credit card; response returned by mail if prepaid. **In person:** 1 public terminal available; index goes back to 1990. No self-serve copier.

Payment: Pay by Visa/MC, money order, cashier's or personal check. Payee: Clerk, US District Court.

E-Services: Document images available. PACER records go back to 1990. New records online after 1 day. ECF at https://ecf.scd.uscourts.gov. Opinions on subscription WebPacer system.

Florence Division Court Clerk, PO Box 2317, Florence, SC 29503 (In person: 401 W Evans St, McMillan Federal Bldg, Rm 361, Florence), 843-676-3820; Fax- 843-676-3831. Hours-8:30AM-4:30PM; records- 9AM-4:30PM. www.scd.uscourts.gov

Counties/Note: Chesterfield, Darlington, Dillon, Florence, Horry, Marion, Marlboro, Williamsburg. All records in the Clerk's Office are filed and retrieved by case number: Florence=4. All counties can be searched electronically at any of the 4 main offices- Columbia, Charleston, Florence, Greenville.

Searches/Indexing: Helpful to include DOB or SSN in criminal search request, but only a full name in civil search. Results do not include SSN or DOB. New cases are in the index 24-48 hours after filing date. Computer and card indexes maintained; computer back to 1995, Microfiche back to 1982. District-wide searches available here. Closed electronic cases not purged.

Search Access: Mail: Search usually completed- 2-3 days. Include SASE for return. **In person:** 1 public terminal available; index back to 1990. No self-serve copier.

Payment: Pay by Visa/MC, money order, cashier's check. Personal or business check accepted. Payee: Clerk, US District Court. No credit cards.

E-Services: Document images available. PACER records go back to 1995. New records online after 1 day. ECF at https://ecf.scd.uscourts.gov. Opinions on subscription WebPacer system.

Greenville Division Court Clerk, PO Box 10768, Greenville, SC 29603 (In person: 300 E Washington St, Greenville), 864-241-2700; Fax- 864-241-2711. Hours-8:30AM-4:30PM; records hours- 9AM-4:30PM. www.scd.uscourts.gov

Counties/Note: Greenville, Laurens. All records in the Clerk's Office are filed and retrieved by case number: Anderson=8, Greenwood=8, Spartanburg=7, Greenville=6. All counties can be searched electronically at any of the 4 main offices- Columbia, Charleston, Florence, Greenville.

Searches/Indexing: Helpful to include DOB or SSN in criminal search request, but only a full name in civil search. No identifiers on civil records since 2002; none on criminal starting 2005. New cases are in the index 1 day after filing date. Computer index back to 1991 maintained. Older records indexed on microfiche. Closed electronic cases not purged.

Search Access: Only case number, parties and attorneys' names is released via phone. **Mail:** Search usually completed- 1 day. SASE required. **In person:** 1 public terminal available; index back to 1990. No self-serve copier. An authorized contract copy service makes copies for $.09 each.

Payment: Pay by Visa/MC, money order, cashier's or personal check. Payee: Clerk, US District Court.

E-Services: Document images available. PACER records go back to 1990. New records online after 1 day. ECF at https://ecf.scd.uscourts.gov. Opinions on subscription WebPacer system.

Greenwood Division c/o Greenville Division, PO Box 10768, Greenville, SC 29603 (In person: 300 E Washington St, Greenville), 864-241-2700; Fax- 864-241-2711. Hours- 8:30AM-4:30PM. www.scd.uscourts.gov

Counties/Note: Abbeville, Edgefield, Greenwood, McCormick, Newberry, Saluda. All records in the Clerk's Office are filed and retrieved by case number: Greenwood=8. All counties can be searched electronically at any of the 4 main offices- Columbia, Charleston, Florence, Greenville.

Searches/Indexing: Helpful to include DOB or SSN in criminal search request, but only a full name in civil search. Results do not include SSN or DOB. Will fax back documents for fee. New cases are in the index 1 day after filing date. Open records at Greenville Div. Closed electronic cases not purged.

Search Access: Mail: SASE required. **In person:** 1 public terminal available back to 1999. No self-serve copier available. A copy service can make copies for $.09 per page.

Payment: Pay by Visa/MC/AmEx, money order, cashier's check. No business or personal checks accepted. Payee: US District Court.

E-Services: PACER records go back to 1990. New records online after 1 day. ECF at https://ecf.scd.uscourts.gov. Opinions on subscription WebPacer system.

Orangeburg Division c/o Columbia Division, 901 Richland St, Columbia, SC 29201, 803-765-5816; Fax- 803-765-5960. Hours- 8:30AM-4:30PM; records hours- 9AM-4:30PM. www.scd.uscourts.gov

Counties/Note: Bamberg, Calhoun, Orangeburg. All records in the Clerk's Office are filed and retrieved by case number: Orangeburg=5. All counties can be searched electronically at any of the 4 main offices- Columbia, Charleston, Florence, Greenville.

Searches/Indexing: Helpful to include DOB or SSN in criminal search request, but only a full name in civil search. Results do not include SSN or DOB. New cases are in the index 1 month after filing date. Computer index maintained; civil back to 1990, criminal to 1992. Older records indexed on microfiche. District-wide searches available here. Open records not located Orangeburg.. Closed electronic cases not purged.

Search Access: If case number, caption and judge are provided, court gives docket info via phone. Court will not search case numbers or captions via phone. **Mail:** Search usually completed- 2-3 days. SASE not required. **Fax:** Fax search requests accepted with credit card; response returned by mail if prepaid. **In person:** 1 public terminal available; index back to 1990. No self-serve copier.

Payment: Pay by Visa/MC, money order, cashier's or personal check. Payee: Clerk, US District Court.

E-Services: Document images available. PACER records go back to 1990. New records online after 1 day. ECF at https://ecf.scd.uscourts.gov. Opinions on subscription WebPacer system.

Rock Hill Division c/o Columbia Division, 901 Richland St, Columbia, SC 29201, 803-765-5816; Fax- 803-765-5960. Hours- 8:30AM-4:30PM; records hours- 9AM-4:30PM. www.scd.uscourts.gov

Counties/Note: Chester, Fairfield, Lancaster, York All records in the Clerk's Office are filed and retrieved by case number: Rock Hill=0. All counties can be searched electronically at any of the 4 main offices- Columbia, Charleston, Florence, Greenville.

Searches/Indexing: Helpful to include DOB or SSN in criminal search request, but only a full name in civil search. Results do not include SSN or DOB. New cases are in the index 1 month after filing date. Computer index maintained; civil back to 1990, criminal to 1992. Older records indexed on microfiche. District-wide searches available here. Open records not located at Rock Hill. Division. Closed electronic cases not purged.

Search Access: If case number, caption and judge are provided, court gives docket info via phone. Court will not search case numbers or captions via phone. **Mail:** Search usually completed- 2-3 days. SASE not required. **Fax:** Fax search requests accepted with credit card; response returned by mail if prepaid. **In person:** 1 public terminal available; index back to 1990. No self-serve copier.

Payment: Pay by Visa/MC, money order, cashier's or personal check. Payee: Clerk, US District Court.

E-Services: Document images available. PACER records go back to 1990. New records online after 1 day. ECF at https://ecf.scd.uscourts.gov. Opinions on subscription WebPacer system.

Spartanburg Division c/o Greenville Division, PO Box 10768, Greenville, SC 29603 (In person: 300 E Washington St, Greenville), 864-241-2700; Fax- 864-241-2711. Hours- 8:30AM-4:30PM. www.scd.uscourts.gov

Counties/Note: Cherokee, Spartanburg, Union. All records in the Clerk's Office are filed and retrieved by case number: Spartanburg=7. All counties can be searched electronically at any of the 4 main offices- Columbia, Charleston, Florence, Greenville.

Searches/Indexing: Helpful to include DOB or SSN in criminal search request, but only a full name in civil search. Results do not include SSN or DOB. New cases are in the index 1-2 days after filing date.

Search Access: Mail: SASE required. **In person:** 1 public terminal available; index back to 1990. No self-serve copier. A copy service can make copies for $.09 per page.

Payment: Pay by Visa/MC/AmEx. No business or personal checks accepted.

E-Services: PACER records go back to 1990. New records online after 1 day. ECF at https://ecf.scd.uscourts.gov. Opinions on subscription WebPacer system.

US Bankruptcy Court District of South Carolina

Columbia Division Court Clerk, 1100 Laurel St, Columbia, SC 29201, 803-765-5436. Hours- 9AM-4:30PM. www.scb.uscourts.gov

Counties/Note: All counties in South Carolina.

Searches/Indexing: Search request requires name; SSN helpful. Results include last 4 SSN digits. Will not fax back documents. New cases are in the index immediately after filing date. Computer index goes back to 1988. Closed case files sent to archives irregularly.

Search Access: Voice Case Information Service available, call VCIS at 800-669-8767 or 803-765-5211. **Mail:** Search usually completed- 1 week. Include SASE for return. **In person:** 2 public terminals available. No self-serve copier.

Payment: Pay by credit cards (atty only), money order, cashier's or personal check. No debtor checks accepted. Payee: Clerk, US Bankruptcy Ct.

E-Services: Document images and creditor lists available. PACER records go back to 11/1988. New records online immediately. ECF at https://ecf.scb.uscourts.gov. **Opinions Online:** www.scb.uscourts.gov/opinions.html. Calendars at www.scb.uscourts.gov/court_calendars.html

South Carolina County Courts

Court	Jurisdiction	No. of Courts	How Organized
Circuit Courts*	General	46	16 Circuits
Magistrate Courts*	Limited	179	
Municipal Courts	Municipal	204	
Probate Courts*	Probate	46	
Family Courts	Special	46	16 Circuits

* Profiled in this Sourcebook.

Court	CIVIL								
	Tort	Contract	Real Estate	Min. Claim	Max. Claim	Small Claims	Estate	Eviction	Domestic Relations
Circuit Courts*	X	X	X	$5000	No Max	$7500			
Magistrate Courts	X		X	$0	$7500	$7500		X	
Municipal Courts									
Probate Courts*							X		
Family Courts									X

Court	CRIMINAL				
	Felony	Misdemeanor	DWI/DUI	Preliminary Hearing	Juvenile
Circuit Courts*	X	X	X		
Magistrate Courts*		X	X	X	
Municipal Courts		X	X	X	
Family Courts					X

Administration

Court Administration, 1015 Sumter St, 2nd Floor, Columbia, SC, 29201; 803-734-1800, Fax: 803-734-1355. (EST) www.sccourts.org

Court Structure

Circuit Courts are the courts of general jurisdiction and consist of a Court of General Sessions (criminal) and a Court of Common Pleas (civil). The Circuit Court has limited appellate jurisdiction over appeals from the Probate Court, Magistrate's Court, and Municipal Court, A Family Court (juveniale cases) and Probate Court are found in each county. There are over a combined 300 different Magistrate and Municipal Courts (often referred to as "Summary Courts") that handle only handle misdemeanor cases involving a $500 fine and/or thirty days or less jail time.

Online Access

Appellate and Supreme Court opinions are available at www.sccourts.org. Although there is no access to statewide trial court records, a partial system and a page with hot links to 25 independent, searchable online county systems is offered at www.sccourts.org/caseSearch/. Counties are Aiken, Anderson, Beaufort, Charleston, Cherokee, Clarendon, Colleton, Dorchester, Edgefield, Florence, Georgetown, Greenville, Greenwood, Horry, Jasper, Kershaw, Lancaster, Laurens, Lexington, Orangeburg, Pickens, Richland, Spartanburg, Sumter, and York. Plans are to add more counties.

Searching Tips, Fees, and Other Guidelines

If requesting a record in writing, it is recommended that the phrase "Request that General Session, Common Pleas, and Family Court records be searched" be included in the request.

Most South Carolina courts will not conduct searches. However, if a name and case number are provided, many will pull and copy the record. Search fees vary widely as they are set individually by county. Prepayment is required unless otherwise noted.

Abbeville County

Circuit Court PO Box 99, Court Sq, Rm 103, Abbeville, SC 29620; 864-366-5312 x55; fax: 864-366-9188; 8AM-5PM. ***Felony, Misdemeanor, Civil Actions over $7,500.***

www.abbevillecountysc.com/clerkcourt.aspx

Civil Records: Access: In person only. Visitors must perform in person searches themselves. Required to search: name, years to search. Civil cases indexed by defendant, plaintiff; index on card index from 1870. Civil PAT available. Public access terminals available in the records room.

Criminal Records: Access: In person only. Visitors must perform in person searches themselves. Required to search: name, years to search; SSN helpful. Criminal records on card index from 1870. Criminal PAT available. Public access terminals available in the records room.

General Information: No adoption, juvenile, sealed or expunged records released. Will not fax documents. Court makes copy: $.50 per page. Certification fee: $1.00 per page. Payee: Clerk of Court. Personal checks accepted; credit cards are not.

Abbeville Magistrate Court PO Drawer 1156, 21 Old Calhoun Rd, Abbeville, SC 29620; 864-446-6500; fax: 864-446-6555; 9-5PM. ***Misdemeanor, Civil Actions under $7,500, Eviction, Small Claims.***

Probate Court PO Box 70, 102 Court Sq, #102, Abbeville, SC 29620; 864-366-5312 x62; fax: 864-366-4023; 8:30AM-5PM. ***Probate.***

Aiken County

Circuit Court PO Box 583, Aiken, SC 29802; 803-642-1715; 8:30AM-5PM. ***Felony, Misdemeanor, Civil Actions over $7,500.***
www.aikencountysc.gov
Civil Records: Access: In person, online. Both court and visitors may perform in person searches. No search fee. Required to search: name, years to search. Civil cases indexed by defendant, plaintiff; index on computer from 1988; on microfiche, archives and index books from 1800s. Civil PAT goes back to 1988. Access the record index at www.sccourts.org/caseSearch/.
Criminal Records: Access: In person, online. Both court and visitors may perform in person searches. Search fee: Court may charge a search fee. Required to search: name, years to search, DOB; SSN helpful. Criminal records computerized from 1988; on microfiche, archives and index books from 1800s. Criminal PAT goes back to same as civil. Access the record index at www.sccourts.org/caseSearch/.
General Information: No adoption, juvenile, sealed or expunged records released. Will not fax out case files. Court makes copy: $.25 per page. Self serve: same. Certification fee: $1.00. Payee: Clerk of Court. Only cashiers checks and money orders accepted. No credit cards accepted.

Aiken Magistrate Court 1680 Richland Ave W, #70, Aiken, SC 29801; 803-642-1744/1747; fax: 803-642-1749; 9AM-5PM. ***Misdemeanor, Civil Actions under $7,500, Eviction, Small Claims.***

Graniteville Magistrate Court 50 Canal St, #14, Graniteville, SC 29829; 803-663-6634; fax: 803-663-6638; 9AM-5PM. ***Civil Actions under $7,500, Misdemeanor, Eviction, Small Claims.***
Misdemeanor records accessed same as civil.

Langley Magistrate Court PO Box 769, 129 Langley Dam Rd, Langley, SC 29834; 803-593-5171/5172; fax: 803-593-8402; 9AM-5PM. ***Misdemeanor, Civil Actions under $7,500, Eviction, Small Claims.***

Monetta Magistrate Court 5697 Columbia Hwy N, PO Box 190, Monetta, SC 29105; 803-685-7125; fax: 803-685-7988; 8:30AM-12:30PM; 1:30-4:30PM. ***Misdemeanor, Civil Actions under $7,500, Eviction, Small Claims.***

New Ellenton Magistrate Court PO Box 40, 327 Main St, New Ellenton, SC 29809; 803-652-3609; fax: 803-652-2653; 9-5PM. ***Misdemeanor, Civil Actions under $7,500, Eviction, Small Claims.***

North Augusta Magistrate Court PO Box 6493, North Augusta, SC 29861; 803-202-3580/3581; fax: 803-202-3583; 9AM-5PM. ***Misdemeanor, Civil Actions under $7,500, Eviction, Small Claims.***
Physical address: 537 Edgefield Rd, Belvedere, 29841

Probate Court PO Box 1576, 109 Park Ave, Aiken, SC 29802; 803-642-2002; fax: 803-642-2007; 8:30AM-5PM. ***Probate.***

Allendale County

Circuit Court PO Box 126, 292 Barnwell Hwy, Allendale, SC 29810; 803-584-2737; fax: 803-584-7046; 9AM-5PM. ***Felony, Misdemeanor, Civil Actions over $7,500.***
Civil Records: Access: Phone, fax, mail, in person. Both court and visitors may perform in person searches. Search fee: $5.00 per name. Required to search: name, years to search. Civil cases indexed by defendant, plaintiff; index on computer 1988, card index from 1919. Mail turnaround time 2 days. Civil PAT goes back to 1987. PAT results show middle initial, DOB. Terminal results also show SSNs.
Criminal Records: Access: Phone, fax, mail, in person. Both court and visitors may perform in person searches. Search fee: $5.00 per name. Required to search: name, years to search, DOB, signed release; also helpful: SSN. Criminal records kept on computer for 3 years. Mail turnaround time 2 days. Criminal PAT goes back to same as civil. PAT results show middle initial, DOB. Terminal results include SSN.
General Information: No adoption, juvenile, sealed or expunged records released. Will fax documents $1.00 per page fee. Court makes copy: $.50 per page. Certification fee: $2.00. Payee: Clerk of Court. Personal checks accepted; credit cards are not. Mail requests: SASE required.

Allendale Magistrate Court 160 Law Enforcement Court, Fairfax, SC 29827; 803-584-3755; fax: 803-584-7980; 9AM-5PM. ***Misdemeanor, Civil Actions under $7,500, Eviction, Small Claims.***
Now combined with Fairfax Court; address and phone given above.

Fairfax Magistrate Court 160 Law Enforcement Court, PO Box 516, Fairfax, SC 29827; 803-584-3755; fax: 803-584-7980; 9-5PM. ***Misdemeanor, Civil Actions under $7,500, Eviction, Small Claims, Traffic.***

Probate Court PO Box 603, Courthouse Complex, 292 Barnwell Hiway, Allendale, SC 29810; 803-584-3157; fax: 803-584-7082; 9AM-5PM. ***Probate.***

Anderson County

Circuit Court PO Box 8002, 100 S Main St, Courthouse, Anderson, SC 29622; 864-260-4053; fax: 864-260-4715; 8:30AM-5PM. ***Felony, Misdemeanor, Civil Actions over $7,500.***
www.judicial.state.sc.us/index.cfm
Civil Records: Access: In person, online. Visitors must perform in person searches themselves. Required to search: name, years to search. Civil cases indexed by defendant, plaintiff; index on computer back to 1994, prior on cards. Note: Mail searches available to state agencies only. Civil PAT goes back to 1993. PAT results show name only. Access the record index at www.andersoncountysc.org/web/scjdweb/publicindex/.
Criminal Records: Access: In person, online. Visitors must perform in person searches themselves. Required to search: name, years to search, DOB, SSN, signed release. Criminal records computerized from 1994, prior on cards. Criminal PAT goes back to 1992. PAT results show middle initial, DOB, SSN. Terminal results may include SSN. Access to criminal records is the same as civil.
General Information: Online identifiers in results same as on public terminal. No adoption, juvenile, sealed or expunged records released. Will not fax documents. Court makes copy: $.50 per page. No certification fee. Payee: Clerk of Court. No personal checks or credit cards accepted.

Anderson Magistrate Court PO Box 8002, 107 S Main St, Anderson, SC 29622; 864-260-4156/4055; fax: 864-260-4144; 8:30AM-5PM. ***Misdemeanor, Civil Actions under $7,500, Eviction, Small Claims, Traffic.***
www.andersoncountysc.org/web/magistrates_00.asp
Search case details online at www.andersoncountysc.org/web/scjdweb/publicindex/.

Honea Path Magistrate Court PO Box 505, 30 N Main St, Honea Path, SC 29654; 864-369-0015; fax: 864-369-2325; 8:30AM-2PM M,T,TH; 8:30AM-N W. ***Misdemeanor, Civil Actions under $7,500, Eviction, Small Claims.***
www.andersoncountysc.org/web/magistrates_00.asp
Search case details online at www.andersoncountysc.org/web/scjdweb/publicindex/.

Iva Magistrate Court. ***Misdemeanor, Civil Actions under $7,500, Eviction, Small Claims.***
Court closed 2004; records then at Starr Magistrate Court, which closed in 2006; now records assumed to be at Anderson Magistrate Court. Search case details online at www.andersoncountysc.org/web/scjdweb/publicindex/.

Pelzer Magistrate Court PO Box 824, 26 Main St, Pelzer, SC 29669; 864-947-5225; 9AM-4PM M,T, 11AM-3PM W, 9AM-1PM TH, Closed Fri. ***Civil Actions under $7,500, Eviction, Small Claims, Misdemeanor.***
www.andersoncountysc.org/web/magistrates_00.asp
Search case details online at www.andersoncountysc.org/web/scjdweb/publicindex/.

Pendleton Magistrate Court PO Box 76, 100 E Queen, Pendleton, SC 29670; 864-646-6701; 8AM-4PM T W; 8AM-2PM TH. ***Misdemeanor, Civil Actions under $7,500, Eviction, Small Claims.***
www.andersoncountysc.org/web/magistrates_00.asp
Search case details online at www.andersoncountysc.org/web/scjdweb/publicindex/.

Powdersville Magistrate Court PO Box 51312, Piedmont, SC 29673; 864-269-5974; fax: 864-269-5952; 8:30AM-5PM. ***Misdemeanor, Civil Actions under $7,500, Eviction, Small Claims.***
www.andersoncountysc.org/web/magistrates_00.asp
Search case details online at www.andersoncountysc.org/web/scjdweb/publicindex/.

Starr Magistrate Court. ***Misdemeanor, Civil Actions under $7,500, Eviction, Small Claims.***
Starr Magistrate Court closed 2006; records assumed to be at Anderson Magistrate Court. Starr also held records for Iva Magistrate Court which also has been closed. Search case details online at www.andersoncountysc.org/web/scjdweb/publicindex/.

Williamston Magistrate Court 12 W Main St, PO Box 125, Williamston, SC 29697; 864-847-8580; fax: same; 9AM-N; 1PM-5PM T, W, TH. ***Misdemeanor, Civil Actions under $7,500, Eviction, Small Claims.***
www.andersoncountysc.org/web/magistrates_00.asp
Search case details online at www.andersoncountysc.org/web/scjdweb/publicindex/.

Probate Court PO Box 8002, 100 S Main St, Anderson, SC 29622; 864-260-4049; fax: 864-260-4811; 8:30AM-5PM. ***Probate.***
Access to the county probate court, marriage, estate, and guardian records is available free at http://acpass.andersoncountysc.org/Probate_Main.htm

Bamberg County

Circuit Court PO Box 150, 2559 Main Highway, Bamberg, SC 29003; 803-245-3025; fax: 803-245-3088; 9AM-5PM. ***Felony, Misdemeanor, Civil Actions over $7,500.***
Civil Records: Access: Mail, in person fax. Both court and visitors may perform in person searches. Search fee: $5.00 per name. Required to search: name, years to search. Civil cases indexed by defendant, plaintiff. Civil index on docket books, files back to 1890. Mail turnaround time 1-2 days.
Criminal Records: Access: Mail, in person, fax. Both court and visitors may perform in person searches. Search fee: $5.00 per name. Required to search: name, years to search, DOB; also helpful: SSN. Criminal records indexed in books, files back to 1890. Mail turnaround time 1-2 days.
General Information: No adoption, juvenile, sealed or expunged records released. Will not fax documents. Court makes copy: $.25 per page. Self serve: same. Certification fee: $5.00 per cert. Payee: Clerk of Court. No personal checks or credit cards accepted. Mail requests: SASE required.

Bamberg Magistrate Court PO Box 187, 2873 Main Hwy, Bamberg, SC 29003; 803-245-3016; fax: 803-245-3085; 9AM-5PM. ***Misdemeanor, Civil Actions under $7,500, Eviction, Small Claims.***

Probate Court PO Box 180, 2959 Main Hwy, Bamberg, SC 29003; 803-245-3008; fax: 803-245-3008; 9AM-5PM. ***Probate.***

Barnwell County

Circuit Court PO Box 723, 141 Main St, Barnwell, SC 29812; 803-541-1020; fax: 803-541-1025; 9AM-5PM. ***Felony, Misdemeanor, Civil Actions over $7,500.*** Records location is 141 Main St, Barnwell, SC, 29812.

Civil Records: Access: In person only. Visitors must perform in person searches themselves. Required to search: name, years to search. Civil cases indexed by defendant. Civil records on computer from 1988.

Criminal Records: Access: In person only. Visitors must perform in person searches themselves. Required to search: name, years to search, DOB, SSN. Criminal records computerized from 1988.

General Information: No adoption, juvenile, sealed or expunged records released. Will not fax documents. Court makes copy: $.50 per page. Self serve: same. Certification fee: $1.00. Payee: Clerk of Court. Business checks accepted. No credit cards or personal checks accepted.

Barnwell Magistrate Court PO Box 1205, 599 Joey Zorn Blvd, Barnwell, SC 29812; 803-541-1035; fax: 803-541-1055; 9AM-N, 1-5PM. ***Misdemeanor, Civil Actions under $7,500, Eviction, Small Claims.***

Blackville Magistrate Court 5997 Lartigue St, Blackville, SC 29817; 803-284-2765; fax: 803-284-9107; 8AM-5PM M,T,Th,F; 8AM-N W. ***Misdemeanor, Civil Actions under $7,500, Eviction, Small Claims.***

Williston Magistrate Court PO Box 485, 12445 Main St, Williston, SC 29853; 803-266-3700; fax: 803-266-5496; 9AM-5PM. ***Misdemeanor, Civil Actions under $7,500, Eviction, Small Claims.***

Probate Court 57 Wall St, County Courthouse, Rm 108, Barnwell, SC 29812; 803-541-1032; fax: 803-541-1012; 9AM-5PM. ***Probate.***

Beaufort County

Circuit Court PO Drawer 1128, 102 Ribaut Rd, Rm 208, Beaufort, SC 29901; 843-470-5218; fax: 843-470-5248; 8AM-5PM. ***Felony, Misdemeanor, Civil Actions over $7,500.***

Civil Records: Access: Mail, in person, online. Both court and visitors may perform in person searches. Search fee: $10.00 per name. Required to search: name, years to search. Civil cases indexed by defendant, plaintiff; index on computer back to 1985; prior in index books. Mail turnaround time 1 week Civil PAT goes back to 1997. PAT civil results show middle initial. Access public case index and court dockets free at www.beaufortcourt.org.

Criminal Records: Access: Mail, in person, online. Both court and visitors may perform in person searches. Search fee: $10.00 per name. Required to search: name, years to search, DOB; also helpful: SSN. Criminal records computerized from 1985; prior in index books. Mail turnaround time is 1 week. Criminal PAT goes back to 1985. PAT criminal results show middle initial. Access public case index and court dockets free at www.beaufortcourt.org.

General Information: No adoption, juvenile, sealed or expunged records released. Will not fax documents. Court makes copy: $.50 per page. Self serve: same. Certification fee: $1.00. Payee: Clerk of Court. Personal checks accepted. Visa/MC accepted.

Beaufort Magistrate Court PO Box 2207, 100 Ribaut Rd, Beaufort, SC 29901-2207; 843-470-5201; criminal phone: 843-470-5202; civil phone: 843-470-5210; criminal fax: 843-470-5206; civil fax: 843-470-5208; 8AM-4PM M-TH;, 8AM-N F. ***Misdemeanor, Civil Actions under $7,500, Eviction, Small Claims, Traffic.***

This court holds records for the St Helena Island magistrate Court which is now closed. Access court records and dockets free at www.beaufortcourt.org/publicindex/.

Bluffton Magistrate Court PO Box 840, 4819 Bluffton Pky, Bluffton, SC 29910; 843-757-1500; fax: 843-757-1527; 8AM-5PM. ***Misdemeanor, Civil Actions under $7,500, Eviction, Small Claims.***

Access case details free online at www.beaufortcourt.org/publicindex/. Search dockets free at www.beaufortcourt.org/onlinedocket/.

Hilton Head Magistrate Court PO Box 22895, 539 William Hilton Prky, Hilton Head, SC 29925; 843-842-4260, 842-4263; fax: 843-842-4261; 8AM-4PM. ***Misdemeanor, Civil Actions under $7,500, Eviction, Small Claims.***

Access case details free at www.beaufortcourt.org/publicindex/. Search dockets free at www.beaufortcourt.org/onlinedocket/.

Lobeco Magistrate Court PO Box 845, 1860 Trask Pky, Lobeco, SC 29931-0845; 843-846-3902; 5:30PM-7:30P M,W. ***Misdemeanor, Civil Actions under $7,500, Eviction, Small Claims.***

Access case details free online at www.beaufortcourt.org/publicindex/. Search dockets free at www.beaufortcourt.org/onlinedocket/.

St Helena Island Magistrate Court - Closed PO Box 2207, 100 Ribaut Rd, Beaufort, SC 29901-2207; 843-470-5201; fax: 843-470-5206; 8AM-4PM M-TH; 8AM-N F. ***Misdemeanor, Civil Actions under $7,500, Eviction, Small Claims.***

Court is closed; records located at Beaufort Municipal Court, address and telephone given here. Access case details and dockets free at www.beaufortcourt.org.

Probate Court PO Box 1083, 102 Ribaut Rd, Beaufort, SC 29901-1083; 843-470-5319; fax: 843-470-5324; 8AM-5PM. ***Probate.***

www.sccourts.org/probate/index.cfm?countyno=7

Access case details free online at www.beaufortcourt.org/publicindex/. Search dockets free at www.beaufortcourt.org/onlinedocket/.

Berkeley County

Circuit Court PO Box 219, Moncks Corner, SC 29461; 843-719-4400; fax: 843-719-4511; 9AM-5PM. ***Felony, Misdemeanor, Civil Actions over $7,500.*** www.co.berkeley.sc.us/js/coc/

Civil Records: Access: In person only. Visitors must perform in person searches themselves. Required to search: name, years to search. Civil cases indexed by defendant, plaintiff; index on computer from early 1980s, prior on books. Civil PAT goes back to 1984. PAT results show name only.

Criminal Records: Access: In person only. Visitors must perform in person searches themselves. Required to search: name, years to search, DOB, SSN. Criminal records computerized from early 1980s, prior on books. Criminal PAT goes back to 1990. PAT results show name only.

General Information: No adoption, juvenile, sealed or expunged records released. Will not fax documents. Court makes copy: $.35 per page. Certification fee: 1st cert free; $1.00 per doc each add'l. Payee: Berkeley County Clerk of Court. Personal checks accepted; credit cards are not.

Central Summary Court 223 N Live Oak Dr, Moncks Corner, SC 29461; 843-719-4050 or 723-3800 X4050; fax: 843-719-4534; 9AM-5PM. ***Misdemeanor, Civil Actions under $7,500, Eviction, Small Claims, Ordinance.***

www.co.berkeley.sc.us/js/magic/

Formerly Moncks Corner Magistrate Court.

Goose Creek Magistrate Court 303-B Goose Creek Blvd, Goose Creek, SC 29445; 843-553-7080; fax: 843-553-7074; 9AM-5PM. ***Misdemeanor, Civil Actions under $7,500, Eviction, Small Claims.*** www.co.berkeley.sc.us/js/magic/

The former Summerville Magistrate Court merged with this court. Note there is also a Summerville Magistrate Court in Dorchester county. Small Claims phone number- 843-553-6099.

St Stephen Magistrate Court 1158 S Main St, St Stephen, SC 29479; 843-567-7400; fax: 843-567-3102; 9AM-5PM. ***Misdemeanor, Civil Actions under $7,500, Eviction.***

www.co.berkeley.sc.us/js/magic/

Probate Court 300 B California Ave, Moncks Corner, SC 29461; 843-719-4519; fax: 843-719-4527; 9AM-5PM. ***Probate.***

Calhoun County

Circuit Court PO Box 709, 902 S FR Huff Dr, St Matthews, SC 29135-0709; 803-874-3524; criminal fax: 803-874-1942; civil fax: same; 9AM-5PM. ***Felony, Misdemeanor, Civil Actions over $7,500.***

Civil Records: Access: In person only. Visitors must perform in person searches themselves. Required to search: name, years to search. Civil cases indexed by defendant, plaintiff; index on computer from 1984, prior on index books from 1908. Civil PAT goes back to 1962.

Criminal Records: Access: In person only. Both court and visitors may perform in person searches. No search fee. Required to search: name, years to search, DOB. Criminal records computerized from 1984, prior on index books from 1908. Criminal PAT goes back to 1973.

General Information: No adoption, juvenile, sealed or expunged records released. Will not fax out case files. Court makes copy: $.25 per page. Self serve: $.25 per page. No certification fee. Payee: Clerk of Court. Personal checks accepted; credit cards are not.

Cameron Magistrate Court PO Box 663, 204 Boyce Lawton Dr, Cameron, SC 29030; 803-823-2266; fax: 803-823-2288; 1-5PM T,TH. ***Misdemeanor, Civil Actions under $7,500, Eviction, Small Claims, Traffic.***

Cameron Magistrate Court Cameron Town Hall, PO Box 663, Cameron, SC 29030; 803-823-2266; fax: 803-823-2288; 1-5PM T,TH. ***Misdemeanor, Civil Actions under $7,500, Eviction, Small Claims.***

This court is also a Municipal Court.

St Matthews Magistrate Court 1623 Bridge St W, PO Box 191, St Matthews, SC 29135; 803-874-1112; fax: 803-874-1111; 9-4. ***Misdemeanor, Civil Actions under $7,500, Eviction, Small Claims.***

Probate Court 902 Huff Dr., St Matthews, SC 29135; 803-874-3514; fax: 803-874-1942; 9AM-5PM. ***Probate.***

Charleston County

Circuit Court 100 Broad St, #106, Charleston, SC 29401-2210; 843-958-5000; criminal phone: x3; civil phone: same; fax: 843-958-5020; 8:30AM-5PM. ***Felony, Misdemeanor, Civil Actions over $7,500.***

http://www3.charlestoncounty.org

Civil Records: Access: Online, in person. Visitors must perform in person searches themselves. Required to search: name, years to search. Civil cases indexed by defendant, plaintiff; index on computer from 1988, all prior dates indexed in books on microfilm. General Session records available on computer from 4/92, prior in books. Civil PAT goes back to 1975. Access to civil records 1988 forward, also judgments and lis pendens are free at http://www3.charlestoncounty.org/connect. Online document images go back to 1/1/1999. Also accessible via www.sccourts.org/casesearch/.

Criminal Records: Access: Online, in person. Both court and visitors may perform in person searches. No search fee. Required to search: name, years to search, DOB; also helpful: SSN. Criminal records computerized from 4/92, prior on books and microfilm from 1918. Criminal PAT goes back to 1992.PAT results show name, DOB. Access to criminal records from 04/92 forward free at http://www3.charlestoncounty.org/connect. Search by name or case number. Also accessible via www.sccourts.org/casesearch/. Online results show middle initial, DOB, SSN.

General Information: No adoption, juvenile, sealed or expunged records released. No fee to fax documents. Court makes copy: $.25 per page. Self serve: same. Cert fee: $1.00 per cert. Payee: Clerk of Court. Business checks accepted. No credit cards.

Charleston Magistrate Court 4045 Bridgeview Dr, PO Box 60037, Charleston, SC 29419; 843-202-6600; criminal: 843-554-2462; fax: 843-202-6620; 8:30AM-4:30PM. ***Civil under $7,500, Misdemeanor, Eviction, Small Claims.***

http://www3.charlestoncounty.org

17 magistrates under this court. County magistrate requests for background checks forwarded to Sheriff's Office- 843-202-6610.

Civil Records: Access: In person, online. Only the court performs in person searches; visitors may not. Required to search: at court- name, years to search, magistrate who heard the case, case number; also helpful- court date. Access civil records from 1998 forward at http://www3.charlestoncounty.org/connect.

Criminal Records: Access: In person, online. Only the court performs in person searches; visitors may not. Required to search: at court- name, years to search, magistrate who heard the case, ticket or case number; also helpful- court date. Note: Requests for background checks forwarded to Sheriff's Office, except if military personnel. Access criminal and traffic records from 1993 forward free at http://www3.charlestoncounty.org/connect.

General Information: Will not fax documents. Court makes copy: $.25 per page for disposition. Certification fee: $7.00 per doc. Payee: County Treasurer. No credit cards accepted.

Charleston Magistrate Court 995 Morrison Dr, Charleston, SC 29402; 843-724-6720; fax: 843-724-6785; 8:30AM-5PM. ***Small Claims, Evictions.*** http://www3.charlestoncounty.org
Access civil records from 1998 forward free at http://www3.charlestoncounty.org/connect.

East Cooper Magistrate Court 1189 Iron Bridge Rd, #300, PO Box 584, Mt Pleasant, SC 29466; 843-856-1205; fax: 843-856-1188; 8:30-4:30PM. ***Misdemeanor, Civil under $7,500, Eviction.*** http://www3.charlestoncounty.org/docs/CoC/index.html
Access civil records from 1998 forward free at http://www3.charlestoncounty.org/connect.

Edisto Island Magistrate Court 8070 Indigo Hill Rd, PO Box 159, Edisto Island, SC 29438; 843-869-2909; fax: 843-869-4460; 2-6PM M, W. ***Misdemeanor, Civil Actions under $7,500, Eviction, Traffic.*** http://www3.charlestoncounty.org
Access civil records from 1998 forward free at http://www3.charlestoncounty.org/connect. Online misdemeanor and traffic records may be available.

James Island Magistrate Court PO Box 12226, 615 Riverland Dr, James Island, SC 29422; 843-795-1140; fax: 843-406-2753; 8:30AM-12:30PM, 1:30-4:30PM M-TH; 8AM-N F. ***Misdemeanor, Civil Actions under $7,500, Eviction.*** http://www3.charlestoncounty.org
Access civil records from 1998 forward free at http://www3.charlestoncounty.org/connect. Online misdemeanor and traffic records may be available.

Johns Island Magistrate Court 1527 Main Rd, #100, Johns Island, SC 29455; 843-559-1218; fax: 843-559-2378; 8:30AM-12:30PM, 1:30-4:30PM. ***Misdemeanor, Civil Actions under $7,500, Eviction.*** http://www3.charlestoncounty.org
Access civil records from 1998 forward free at http://www3.charlestoncounty.org/connect.

McClellanville Magistrate Court PO Box 7, 10009 Hwy 17 N, McClellanville, SC 29458; 843-887-3334; fax: 843-887-3901; 9AM-N, 1-4PM M & TH. ***Misdemeanor, Civil Actions under $7,500, Eviction, Small Claims.*** http://www3.charlestoncounty.org
Access civil records from 1998 forward free at http://www3.charlestoncounty.org/connect.

North 3 Charleston Magistrate Court 7272 Cross County Rd, North Charleston, SC 29418; 843-767-2743; fax: 843-760-6887; 8:30AM-4:30PM. ***Misdemeanor, Civil Actions under $7,500, Eviction.*** http://www3.charlestoncounty.org
Access civil records from 1998 forward free at http://www3.charlestoncounty.org/connect.

North Area Magistrate Court 4045 Bridge View Dr, #B146, PO Box 70235, North Charleston, SC 29415; 843-202-6650/6610; fax: 843-202-6620; 8:30AM-4:30PM. ***Misdemeanor, Civil Actions under $7,500, Small Claims.*** http://www3.charlestoncounty.org
Fax listed above is for the Magistrate Ct; the Small Claims Ct fax is 843-202-6652. Access civil records from 1998 forward free online at http://www3.charlestoncounty.org/connect.

North Charleston 2 Magistrate Court PO Box 71316, 2145 Melbourne Ave #100, North Charleston, SC 29415; 843-745-2215; fax: 843-745-2334; 8:30AM-1PM, 2-4:30PM. ***Misdemeanor, Civil Actions under $7,500, Eviction, Small Claims.*** http://www3.charlestoncounty.org
Access civil records from 1998 forward free at http://www3.charlestoncounty.org/connect. Online misdemeanor and traffic records may be available.

Ravenel Magistrate Court 5962 Hwy 165, #200, Ravenel, SC 29470; 843-889-8332; fax: 843-889-9202; 8:30AM-4:30PM. ***Misdemeanor, Civil Actions under $7,500, Eviction, Small Claims.*** http://www3.charlestoncounty.org
Access civil records from 1998 forward free at http://www3.charlestoncounty.org/connect.

West Ashley Magistrate Court 1720 Sam Rittenberg Blvd, Unit 11, PO Box 31861, Charleston, SC 29417; 843-766-6531; fax: 843-571-4751; 8:30AM-4:30PM M-TH; 8:30AM-1PM F. ***Civil Actions under $7,500, Eviction.*** http://www3.charlestoncounty.org
Access civil records from 1998 forward free at http://www3.charlestoncounty.org/connect.

Probate Court 84 Broad St, 3rd Fl, Charleston, SC 29401; 843-958-5030, 958-5180; fax: 843-958-5044; 8:30AM-5PM. ***Probate.*** http://www3.charlestoncounty.org
Access to Estate and Wills records is available free at http://www3.charlestoncounty.org/surfer/group2?ref=Conserv.

Cherokee County

Circuit Court PO Drawer 2289, 125 E Floyd-Baker Blvd, Gaffney, SC 29342; 864-487-2571; civil phone: 864-487-2533; probate phone: 864-487-2588; fax: 864-487-2754; 8:30AM-5PM. ***Felony, Misdemeanor, Civil Actions over $7,500.***

Civil Records: Access: In person, online. Visitors must perform in person searches themselves. Required to search: name, years to search. Civil cases indexed by defendant, plaintiff. Civil records go back to 1897; computerized records go back to 1994. Civil PAT goes back to 1991. Access court records at http://publicindex.sccourts.org/cherokee/publicindex/.

Criminal Records: Access: In person, online. Visitors must perform in person searches themselves. Required to search: name, years to search. Criminal records computerized from 1994, prior on books. Criminal PAT goes back to same as civil. Access case details online at http://publicindex.sccourts.org/cherokee/publicindex/.

General Information: No adoption, juvenile, sealed or expunged records released. Will fax documents $5.00 per fax. Court makes copy: $.50 per page. Self serve: same. Certification fee: $1.00. Payee: Clerk of Court. Business checks accepted. No credit cards accepted for copy fees.

Blacksburg Magistrate Court 101 S John St #A, PO Box 427, Blacksburg, SC 29702; 864-839-2492; fax: 864-839-3415; 8:30-5PM. ***Misdemeanor, Civil Actions under $7,500, Eviction, Small Claims.***
Access case details online at http://publicindex.sccourts.org/cherokee/publicindex/.

Cherokee County Magistrate Court PO Box 336, 312 E Frederick St, Gaffney, SC 29342-0336; 864-487-2533/2501; criminal phone: 864-487-2533; civil phone: 864-487-2502; fax: 864-902-8425; 8:30AM-5PM. ***Misdemeanors, Civil Actions under $7,500, Eviction, Small Claims.*** www.cherokeemagistrate.com
Access case details online at http://publicindex.sccourts.org/cherokee/publicindex/.

Probate Court PO Box 22, 1434 N Limestone St, Peachtree Ctr, Gaffney, SC 29342; 864-487-2583; fax: 864-902-8426; 9AM-4:30PM. ***Probate, Marriage.*** www.cherokeecountyprobate.com
Marriage license phone-864-487-2589.

Chester County

Circuit Court PO Drawer 580, 140 9th St, Chester, SC 29706; 803-385-2605; fax: 803-581-7975; 8:30AM-5PM. ***Felony, Misdemeanor, Civil Actions over $7,500.*** www.chestersc.org

Civil Records: Access: In person only. Visitors must perform in person searches themselves. Required to search: name, years to search, address. Civil cases indexed by defendant, plaintiff; index on computer from 1989, microfiche from 1927. Civil PAT goes back to 1992. PAT results show middle initial, DOB. Results may include identifiers entered originally.

Criminal Records: Access: In person only. Visitors must perform in person searches themselves. Required to search: name, years to search, DOB, signed release; also helpful: SSN. Criminal records computerized from 1994, docket books prior. Criminal PAT goes back to only a partial index. PAT results show name only.

General Information: No adoption, juvenile, sealed or expunged records released. Will not fax documents. Court makes copy: $.50 per 11x17 page; $.25 per letter page. Self serve: same. Certification fee: $1.00 per doc. Payee: Clerk of Court. Personal checks accepted; credit cards are not.

Chester Magistrate Court 2740 Dawson Dr, PO Box 727, Chester, SC 29706; 803-581-5136; 581-3040; fax: 803-581-3033; 8:30AM-5PM. ***Misdemeanor, Civil Actions under $7,500, Eviction, Small Claims.***

Probate Court PO Drawer 580, 1476 J A Cochran Bypass, Chester, SC 29706; 803-385-2604; fax: 803-581-5180; 8:30AM-5PM. ***Probate.*** www.chestercounty.org/departments/probate_court.html
Records go back to late 1780s.

Chesterfield County

Circuit Court PO Box 529, Chesterfield, SC 29709; 843-623-2574; probate phone: 843-623-2376; criminal fax: 843-623-6944; civil fax: same; 8:30AM-5PM. ***Felony, Misdemeanor, Civil Actions over $7,500.***

Civil Records: Access: Mail, in person. Both court and visitors may perform in person searches. Search fee: $5.00 per name. Required to search: name, years to search. Civil cases indexed by defendant, plaintiff; index on computer back to 1986, prior on docket books. Mail turnaround time 3 days.

Criminal Records: Access: Mail, in person. Both court and visitors may perform in person searches. Search fee: $5.00 per name. Required to search: name, years to search, DOB, SSN. Criminal records computerized from 1986, prior on docket books. Mail turnaround time 3 days.

General Information: No adoption, juvenile, sealed or expunged records released. Will fax documents $5.00. Court makes copy: $2.00 per document and $.25 per page after 1st 4 pages. Self serve: $.25 per page. No certification fee. Payee: Clerk of Court. Personal checks accepted; credit cards are not. Mail requests: SASE required.

Cheraw Magistrate Court 563 Hwy 52 N, PO Box 364, Cheraw, SC 29520; 843-537-3323; fax: 843-537-3883; 8AM-N. ***Misdemeanor, Civil Actions under $7,500, Eviction, Small Claims.***

Chesterfield I Magistrate Court 1515 E Jackson Rd, Chesterfield, SC 29709; 843-623-7929; 9AM-4PM M-TH. ***Misdemeanor, Civil Actions under $7,500, Eviction, Small Claims.***

Now also hold records for the McBee Court, which is closed.

Chesterfield II Magistrate Court 115 Green St, Chesterfield, SC 29709; 843-623-7829; fax: 843-623-6944; 8:30AM-5PM. ***Misdemeanor, Civil Actions under $7,500, Eviction, Small Claims.***

Magistrate has retired; court records now at Chesterfield, address and phone given above.

McBee Magistrate Court 1515 E Jackson Rd, Chesterfield, SC 29709; 843-623-7929; 9AM-4PM M-TH. ***Misdemeanor, Civil Actions under $7,500, Eviction, Small Claims.***

Court closed, 2008. Records now located at Chesterfield Magistrate Ct, address and phone given here.

Pageland Magistrate Court 310 W McGregor St, PO Box 133, Pageland, SC 29728; 843-672-5685; fax: 843-672-9507; 10AM-3PM. ***Misdemeanor, Civil Actions under $7,500, Eviction, Small Claims.***

Patrick Magistrate Court 10292 Hwy 102, Patrick, SC 29584; 843-498-6398; fax: same; 1-5PM M-TH. ***Misdemeanor, Civil Actions under $7,500, Eviction, Small Claims.***

Fax number is same as voice number. Call first if faxing.

Ruby Magistrate Court PO Box 131, 115 Green St, Ruby, SC 29741; 843-623-9009; 10AM-4PM. ***Misdemeanor, Civil Actions under $7,500, Eviction, Small Claims.***

Physical address is: 1515 E Jackson Rd, Chesterfield, SC 29709.

Probate Court County Courthouse, 200 W Main St, Chesterfield, SC 29709; 843-623-2376; fax: 843-623-9886; 8:30AM-5PM. ***Probate.***

Clarendon County

Circuit Court PO Box 136, Manning, SC 29102; 803-435-4444; criminal phone: 803-435-4210x309; civil phone: 803-435-4443; fax: 803-435-4844; 8:30AM-5PM. ***Felony, Misdemeanor, Civil Actions over $7,500.***

Civil Records: Access: Mail, in person, online. Both court and visitors may perform in person searches. Search fee: $10.00. Includes all copy fees. Required to search: name, years to search. Civil cases indexed by defendant, plaintiff; index on computer from 1988, index books from 1865. Mail turnaround time 5 days. Civil PAT goes back to 1985. PAT civil results show middle initial. Access case details free on state system at http://publicindex.sccourts.org/clarendon/publicindex/.

Criminal Records: Access: Mail, in person, online. Both court and visitors may perform in person searches. Search fee: $10.50. Includes copy fees. Required to search: name, years to search. Criminal records computerized from 1983, index books from 1865. Mail turnaround time 5 days. Criminal PAT goes back to same as civil. PAT results show middle initial, DOB. Terminal results include SSN. Access case details free on state system at http://publicindex.sccourts.org/clarendon/publicindex/. Online results show middle initial, DOB, SSN.

General Information: No adoption, juvenile, sealed or expunged records released. Will fax documents to local or toll-free number. Court makes copy: $.25 per page. Certification fee: $2.00. Payee: Clerk of Court. Personal checks accepted; credit cards are not. Mail requests: SASE required.

Manning Magistrate Court 102 S Mill St, PO Box 371, Manning, SC 29102; 803-435-2670/8925; fax: 803-435-0885; 8:30AM-5PM. ***Misdemeanor, Civil Actions under $7,500, Eviction, Small Claims.*** www.clarendoncounty.sc.gov/magistratepage/

Access case details free on state system at http://publicindex.sccourts.org/clarendon/publicindex/. Results include address.

Summerton Municipal Court 10 W Main St, PO Box 279, Summerton, SC 29148; 803-485-2525 x20; fax: 803-485-2914; 9AM-5PM. ***Misdemeanor, Civil Actions under $7,500, Eviction, Small Claims.***

Access case details free on state system at http://publicindex.sccourts.org/clarendon/publicindex/. Results include address.

Probate Court PO Box 307, 3 W Keitt Street, Manning, SC 29102; 803-435-8774; fax: 803-435-8698; 8:30AM-5PM. ***Probate.***

Colleton County

Circuit Court PO Box 620, Walterboro, SC 29488; 843-549-5791; fax: 843-549-2875; 8AM-5PM. ***Felony, Misdemeanor, Civil Actions over $7,500.*** www.colletoncounty.org/legal/clerk.aspx

Civil Records: Access: Phone, fax, mail, in person, online. Both court and visitors may perform in person searches. Search fee: $10.00 per name. Required to search: name, years to search. Civil cases indexed by defendant, plaintiff; index on computer from 1986, on index books from 1865. Mail turnaround time 2 days. Civil PAT goes back to 1998. Online access to the index is at http://publicindex.sccourts.org/colleton/publicindex/.

Criminal Records: Access: Phone, fax, mail, in person, online. Both court and visitors may perform in person searches. Search fee: $10.00 per name. Required to search: name, years to search; also helpful: SSN, DOB. Criminal records computerized from 1986, on index books from 1865. Mail turnaround time 2 days. Criminal PAT goes back to 1985-6. Online access to the index is at http://publicindex.sccourts.org/colleton/publicindex/.

General Information: No adoption, juvenile, PTI, sealed or expunged records released. Extra $2.00 fee to receive and fax documents. Court makes copy: $.50 per page. Self serve: same. Certification fee: $1.00. Payee: Clerk of Court. Business checks accepted. No credit cards accepted.

Magistrate Court 40 Klein St, PO Box 1732, Walterboro, SC 29488; 843-549-1122; fax: 843-549-9010; 8AM-5PM. ***Misdemeanor, Civil Actions under $7,500, Eviction, Small Claims.***

All magistrate courts were combined, all records are located here.

Probate Court PO Box 1036, 188 N Walter St, Walterboro, SC 29488-0031; 843-549-7216; fax: 843-549-5571; 8AM-5PM. ***Probate.***

Darlington County

Circuit Court PO Box 1177, Darlington, SC 29540; 843-398-4339; fax: 843-393-6871; 8:30AM-5PM. ***Felony, Misdemeanor, Civil Actions over $7,500.*** www.darcosc.com/ClerkofCourt/

Civil Records: Access: In person only. Visitors must perform in person searches themselves. Required to search: name, years to search. Civil cases indexed by defendant, plaintiff; index on computer from 1989, on index books from 1805. Civil PAT goes back to 1989. PAT results show middle initial, DOB, SSN.

Criminal Records: Access: In person only. Visitors must perform in person searches themselves. Required to search: name, years to search; also helpful: DOB, SSN. Criminal records computerized from 1989, on index books from 1805. Note: Court will give disposition & sentence over phone if case number given. Criminal PAT goes back to same as civil. PAT results show middle initial, DOB, SSN.

General Information: No adoption, juvenile, sealed or expunged records released. Will fax documents to local or toll free line; not more that 1 or 2 pages. Court makes copy: $1.00 per page if court make copy. Self serve: $.25 per page. No certification fee. Payee: Clerk of Court. Business checks accepted; no personal checks. No credit cards accepted.

Darlington Magistrate Court 115 Camp Rd, Darlington, SC 29532; 843-398-4340; fax: 843-398-4458; 8:30AM-5PM. ***Misdemeanor, Civil Actions under $7,500, Eviction, Small Claims.***

Hartsville Magistrate Court 404 S 4th St, PO Box 1765, Hartsville, SC 29550; 843-332-9661; fax: 843-332-7212; 8:30AM-5PM. ***Misdemeanor, Civil Actions under $7,500, Eviction, Small Claims.***

Lamar Magistrate Court 103 Warren Ave, PO Box 38, Lamar, SC 29069; 843-326-5441; fax: 843-326-1543; 8AM-6PM T, W, TH. ***Misdemeanor, Traffic.***

Does not handle civil cases.

Probate Court #1 Public Sq, Courthouse, Rm 208, Darlington, SC 29532; 843-398-4310; fax: 843-398-4076; 8:30AM-5PM. ***Probate.***

Dillon County

Circuit Court PO Drawer 1220, 301 W Main St, Dillon, SC 29536; 843-774-1425; fax: 843-841-3706; 8:30AM-5PM. ***Felony, Misdemeanor, Civil Actions over $7,500.***

Civil Records: Access: Mail, in person. Both court and visitors may perform in person searches. Search fee: $10.00 per name. Required to search: name, years to search. Civil cases indexed by defendant, plaintiff; index on computer from 1990, on docket books prior. Note: Public can search index books for free. Mail turnaround time 1 day.

Criminal Records: Access: Mail, in person. Both court and visitors may perform in person searches. Search fee: $10.00 per name. Required to search: name, years to search; also helpful: DOB, SSN. Criminal records computerized from 1990, on docket books prior. Note: Public can search index books for free. Mail turnaround time 1 day.

General Information: No adoption, juvenile, sealed or expunged records released. Will fax documents to local or toll free line. Court makes copy: $.50 per page. Self serve: same. No certification fee. Payee: Clerk of Court. Personal checks accepted; credit cards are not. Mail requests: SASE required.

Dillon Magistrate Court 200 S 5th Ave, PO Box 1016, Dillon, SC 29536; 843-774-1406; fax: 843-774-1453; 8:30AM-5PM. ***Misdemeanor, Civil Actions under $7,500, Eviction, Small Claims.***

Dillon Magistrate Court 200 S 5th Ave, PO Box 1016, Dillon, SC 29536; 843-774-1407; fax: 843-774-1453; 8:30AM-5PM. ***Misdemeanor, Civil Actions under $7,500, Eviction, Small Claims.***

Lake View Municipal Court PO Box 824, 205 N Main St, Lake View, SC 29563; 843-759-2861; fax: 843-759-0177; 9:30AM-Noon M,W,TH,F; 9:30AM-4PM T. ***Misdemeanor, Ordinance.***

Formerly known as a Magistrate Court.

Probate Court PO Box 189, 401 W Main St, Dillon, SC 29536; 843-774-1423; fax: 843-841-3732; 8:30AM-4:30PM. ***Probate.***

Dorchester County

Circuit Court 101 Ridge St, St George, SC 29477; 843-563-0160; criminal phone: 843-563-0121; civil phone: 843-563-0113; criminal fax: 843-563-0178; civil fax: same; 8:30AM-5PM. ***Felony, Misdemeanor, Civil Actions over $7,500, Small Claims.*** www.dorchestercounty.net/

Access case details free online at www.dorchestercounty.net/scjdweb/publicindex/.

Civil Records: Access: In person, online. Visitors must perform in person searches themselves. Required to search: name, years to search. Civil cases indexed by defendant, plaintiff. Civil index on docket books back to 1950s, on computer since 1994. Civil PAT goes back to 1994. Access court records at www.dorchestercounty.net/scjdweb/publicindex/.

Criminal Records: Access: In person, online. Visitors must perform in person searches themselves. Required to search: name, years to search, DOB, signed release; SSN helpful. Criminal records indexed in books back to 1950s, on computer since 1994. Criminal PAT goes back to 1987. Access case details free online at www.dorchestercounty.net/scjdweb/publicindex/. Online results show middle initial, DOB, SSN.

General Information: No adoption, juvenile, sealed or expunged records released. Will not fax out case files. Court makes copy: $.50 per page. Self serve:

same. No certification fee. Payee: Clerk of Court. Personal checks accepted.

St George Magistrate Court 101 Ridge St, St. George, SC 29477; 843-832-0130; fax: 843-563-0123; 8:30AM-5PM. ***Misdemeanor, Civil Actions under $7,500, Eviction, Small Claims.***
www.dorchestercounty.net/
Access case details free online at www.dorchestercounty.net/scjdweb/publicindex/.

Summerville Magistrate Court 212 Deming Way, Box 10, Summerville, SC 29483; 843-832-0370; fax: 843-832-0371; 8:30-5PM. ***Misdemeanor, Civil Actions under $7,500, Eviction, Small Claims.***
www.dorchestercounty.net/
Access case details free online at www.dorchestercounty.net/scjdweb/publicindex/.

Probate Court 101 Ridge St, County Courthouse, St George, SC 29477; 843-563-0105; fax: 843-563-0245; 8:30AM-5PM. ***Probate.***
www.dorchestercounty.net/Probate.htm

Edgefield County

Circuit Court PO Box 34, 129 Courthouse Sq, Edgefield, SC 29824; 803-637-4082; fax: 803-637-4117; 8:30AM-5PM. ***Felony, Misdemeanor, Civil Actions over $7,500.***
www.edgefieldcounty.sc.gov/
Civil Records: Access: Mail, in person, online. Both court and visitors may perform in person searches. Search fee: $5.00 per name. Required to search: name, years to search. Civil cases indexed by defendant, plaintiff. Civil records archived from 1839; on computer back to 1987. Mail turnaround time 1 day. Civil PAT goes back to 1985. PAT results show middle initial, DOB. Access court records at http://publicindex.sccourts.org/edgefield/publicindex/. Also search pending cases free at http://publicindex.sccourts.org/edgefield/courtrosters/PendingCases.aspx.
Criminal Records: Access: Mail, in person, online. Both court and visitors may perform in person searches. Search fee: $5.00 per name. Required to search: name, years to search, DOB; also helpful: SSN. Criminal records archived from 1839; on computer back to 1987. Mail turnaround time 1 day. Criminal PAT goes back to 1985. Access to criminal court records is the same as civil.
General Information: No adoption, juvenile, sealed or expunged records released. Will not fax documents. Court makes copy: $.50 per page. Self serve: same. Certification fee: $10.00 per doc. Payee: Clerk of Court. Business checks accepted. No credit cards accepted. Mail requests: SASE required.

Edgefield Magistrate Court 215 Jeter St, PO Box 664, Edgefield, SC 29824; criminal phone: 803-637-4052/4059; civil phone: 803-637-4090; fax: 803-637-4101; 8:30AM-4:30PM. ***Misdemeanor, Civil Actions under $7,500, Eviction, Small Claims.***
Access case details free online at http://publicindex.sccourts.org/edgefield/publicindex/.

Probate Court 129 Courthouse Square, #212, PO Box 45, Edgefield, SC 29824; 803-637-4076; fax: 803-637-7157; 8:30AM-5PM. ***Probate.***

Fairfield County

Circuit Court PO Drawer 299, Winnsboro, SC 29180; 803-712-6526; fax: 803-712-1506; 9AM-5PM. ***Felony, Misdemeanor, Civil Actions over $7,500.***
Civil Records: Access: In person only. Visitors must perform in person searches themselves. Required to search: name, years to search. Civil cases indexed by defendant, plaintiff. Civil index on docket books. Note: The court provides an index, but will not do record searching for you.
Criminal Records: Access: In person only. Visitors must perform in person searches themselves. Required to search: name, years to search, DOB; SSN helpful. Criminal docket on books.
General Information: No adoption, juvenile, sealed or expunged records released. Will not fax documents. Court makes copy: $.50 per page for ledger size; $.25 per page for letter or legal size. Certification fee: $1.00. Payee: Clerk of Court. No personal checks or credit cards accepted.

Winnsboro Magistrate Court 115-B S Congress St, Winnsboro, SC 29180; 803-635-4525; fax: 803-635-5717; 9AM-5PM. ***Misdemeanor, Civil Actions under $7,500, Eviction, Small Claims.***

Probate Court PO Box 385, Courthouse, Congress St, Winnsboro, SC 29180; 803-712-6519; fax: 803-712-6939; 9AM-5PM. ***Probate.***
www.sccourts.org/trial/probate/probatejudges.cfm?countyno=20

Florence County

Circuit Court Drawer E, City County Complex, 180 N Irby St, Florence, SC 29501; 843-665-3031; fax: 843-665-3097; 8:30AM-5PM. ***Felony, Misdemeanor, Civil Actions over $7,500.***
www.florenceco.org
Civil Records: Access: In person, online. Both court and visitors may perform in person searches. Search fee: $5.00 per name. Required to search: name, years to search. Civil cases indexed by defendant, plaintiff; index on computer from 1984, on microfiche and docket books from 1900s. Civil PAT goes back to 1998. Search judgments back to 1994 at http://web.florenceco.org/cgi-bin/coc/coc.cgi. Also accessible via www.sccourts.org/casesearch/.
Criminal Records: Access: In person, online. Visitors must perform in person searches themselves. Required to search: name, years to search, DOB; also helpful: SSN. Criminal records computerized from 1984, on microfiche and docket books from 1898. Criminal PAT goes back to same as civil. Access criminal record from 1995 forward free at http://web.florenceco.org/cgi-bin/warrants/war.cgi. Also accessible via www.sccourts.org/casesearch/.
General Information: No adoption, juvenile, sealed or expunged records released. Will not fax documents. Court makes copy: $1.00 per page. Self serve: $.25 per page. Certification fee: $1.00. Payee: Clerk of Court. Personal checks accepted; credit cards are not.

Florence Magistrate Court 180 N Irby St, MSC-W, 120 Courthouse Sq, Florence, SC 29501; 843-665-0031; fax: 843-661-7800; 8:30AM-4:30PM. ***Misdemeanor, Civil Actions under $7,500, Eviction, Small Claims.***
www.florenceco.org/Elected/Magistrate/florence.htm

Johnsonville Magistrate Court PO Box 904, 117 W Broadway St, Johnsonville, SC 29555; 843-380-9211; fax: 843-380-9411; 9AM-5PM M,T,W. ***Misdemeanor, Civil Actions under $7,500, Eviction, Small Claims, Traffic.***
www.florenceco.org/Elected/Magistrate/johnsonville.htm

Lake City Magistrate Court PO Box 39, 345 S Ron McNair Blvd, Lake City, SC 29560; 843-394-5461; fax: 843-394-3865; 8:30AM-5PM. ***Misdemeanor, Civil Actions under $7,500, Eviction, Small Claims.***
www.florenceco.org/Elected/Magistrate/lakecity.htm

Olanta Magistrate Court PO Box 362, 220 E Main St, Olanta, SC 29114; 843-396-9056; fax: 843-396-9406; 8:30AM-N, 1-5PM T,W,TH. ***Misdemeanor, Civil Actions under $7,500, Eviction, Small Claims.***
www.florenceco.org/Elected/Magistrate/olanta.htm

Pamplico Magistrate Court PO Box 367, 124 3rd Ave E, Pamplico, SC 29583; 843-493-0072; fax: 843-493-5391; 8:30AM-5PM M-TH. ***Civil Actions under $7,500, Misdemeanor, Eviction, Small Claims, Traffic.***
www.florenceco.org/Elected/Magistrate/pamplico.htm

Timmonsville Magistrate Court PO Box 190, 307 Smith St, Timmonsville, SC 29161; 843-346-7472; fax: 843-346-0660; 8:30AM-5PM. ***Misdemeanor, Civil Actions under $7,500, Eviction, Small Claims.***
www.florenceco.org/Elected/Magistrate/timmonsville.htm

Probate Court 180 N Irby St, Box L, Florence, SC 29501; 843-665-3085; fax: 843-665-3068; 8:30AM-5PM. ***Probate.***

Georgetown County

Circuit Court PO Box 421270, 129 Screven St, Georgetown, SC 29442; criminal phone: 843-545-3053; civil phone: 843-545-3041; fax: 843-545-3003; 8:30AM-5PM. ***Felony, Misdemeanor, Civil Actions over $7,500.***
Civil Records: Access: In person, online. Visitors must perform in person searches themselves. Required to search: name, years to search. Civil cases indexed by defendant, plaintiff; index on index from 1926. Civil PAT goes back to 2000. Access court dockets free at http://secure.georgetowncountysc.org/courtdockets/. Also, Access case details free online at http://secure.georgetowncountysc.org/publicindex/.
Criminal Records: Access: In person, online. Visitors must perform in person searches themselves. Required to search: name, years to search, DOB; SSN helpful. Criminal records indexed from 1926, computerized since 2001. Criminal PAT goes back to same as civil. Access court dockets free at http://secure.georgetowncountysc.org/courtdockets/. Also, access public index search at http://secure.georgetowncountysc.org/publicindex/ Online results show middle initial, DOB, SSN.
General Information: No adoption, juvenile, sealed or expunged records released. Will not fax documents. Court makes copy: $.50 per page. Self serve: $.25 per page. Certification fee: $1.00 per page. Payee: Clerk of Court. In-state business checks accepted. No personal checks accepted. Visa/MC accepted plus $1.45 transaction fee.

Andrews Magistrate Court 110 N Morgan Ave, Andrews, SC 29510; 843-545-3631; 8:30AM-4:30PM. ***Misdemeanor, Civil Actions under $7,500, Eviction, Small Claims.***
Access case details free online at http://secure.georgetowncountysc.org/publicindex/.

Georgetown Magistrate Court 333 Cleland St, Georgetown, SC 29442; 843-545-3381; criminal phone: 843-545-3380; civil phone: 843-545-3391; probate phone: 843-545-3274; fax: 843-545-3394; 8:30AM-5PM. ***Misdemeanor, Civil Actions under $7,500, Eviction, Small Claims.***
www.georgetowncountysc.org/magistrate/default.html
Access case details free online at http://secure.georgetowncountysc.org/publicindex/.

Murrells Inlet Magistrate Court 4450 Murrells Inlet Rd, PO Box 859, Murrells Inlet, SC 29576; 843-545-3635; 8AM-4:30PM. ***Misdemeanor, Civil Actions under $7,500, Eviction, Small Claims.***
Access case details free online at http://secure.georgetowncountysc.org/publicindex/.

Pawleys Island Magistrate Court 291 Parkersville Rd, PO Box 1830, Pawleys Island, SC 29585; 843-545-3633; 8:30AM-4:30PM. ***Misdemeanor, Civil Actions under $7,500, Eviction, Small Claims.***
Access case details free online at http://secure.georgetowncountysc.org/publicindex/.

Pleasant Hill Magistrate Court 9174 Pleasant Hill Dr, Hemingway, SC 29554; 843-558-9711; fax: 843-558-5827; 8:30AM-N, 1PM-5. ***Misdemeanor, Civil Actions under $7,500, Eviction, Small Claims.***
Access case details free online at http://secure.georgetowncountysc.org/publicindex/.

Probate Court PO Box 421270, 129 Screven St, Georgetown, SC 29442; 843-545-3274; fax: 843-545-3572; 8:30AM-5PM. ***Probate.***
www.georgetowncountysc.org/probate/

Greenville County

Circuit Court 305 E North St, Rm 227, Greenville, SC 29601; 864-467-8551; fax: 864-467-8513; 8:30AM-5PM. ***Felony, Misdemeanor, Civil Actions over $7,500.*** www.greenvillecounty.org

Civil Records: Access: In person, online. Visitors must perform in person searches themselves. Required to search: name, years to search. Civil cases indexed by defendant, plaintiff; index on computer from 1985, on docket books from 1900s. Civil PAT goes back to 1982. Family Court and civil index at www.greenvillecounty.org/scjd/publicindex/disclaim23.asp.

Criminal Records: Access: In person, online. Visitors must perform in person searches themselves. Required to search: name, years to search. Criminal records computerized from 1985, on docket books from 1900s. Criminal PAT goes back to same as civil. PAT results show middle initial, DOB. Access case details free at www.greenvillecounty.org/scjd/publicindex/disclaim23.asp. Records go back to 1983. Online results show middle initial, DOB, SSN.

General Information: Online identifiers in results same as on public terminal. No adoption, juvenile, sealed or expunged records released. Will not fax documents. Court makes copy: Court will not make copies. Self serve: $.25 per page. Certification fee: $1.00. Payee: Clerk of Court. Only cashiers checks and money orders accepted. No credit cards accepted.

Bates Magistrate Court 114 N Poinsett Hwy, Travelers Rest, SC 29690; 864-834-6910; fax: 864-834-6911; 9AM-5PM. ***Misdemeanor, Civil Actions under $7,500, Eviction, Small Claims.***
www.greenvillecounty.org/Magistrate_Courts/
Formerly known as Travelers Rest Magistrate Court. Nearby courts are Cleveland, Highlands, and Greer. Access case details free online at www.greenvillecounty.org/scjd/publicindex/disclaim23.asp. Records go back to 1988.

Chick Springs Magistrate Court 1306 W Poinsett St, Greer, SC 29650; 864-244-2922, 864-467-5312; fax: 864-268-1333; 8:30AM-5PM. ***Misdemeanor, Civil Actions under $7,500, Eviction, Small Claims.***
www.greenvillecounty.org/Magistrate_Courts/
Formerly Taylors Magistrate Court. Access case details free online at www.greenvillecounty.org/scjd/publicindex/disclaim23.asp. Records go back to 1988.

Fairview/Austin Magistrate Court 205 N Maple, #4, Simpsonville, SC 29681; 864-963-3457; fax: 864-963-0029; 8:30AM-5PM. ***Misdemeanor, Civil Actions under $7,500, Eviction, Small Claims.***
www.greenvillecounty.org/Magistrate_Courts/
Formerly Simpsonville Magistrate Court. Access case details free at www.greenvillecounty.org/scjd/publicindex/disclaim23.asp. Records go back to 1988.

Gantt Magistrate Court 1103 White Horse Rd, Greenville, SC 29605; criminal phone: 864-277-0856; civil phone: 864-277-4429; fax: 864-277-4376; 8:30AM-5PM. ***Misdemeanor, Civil Actions under $7,500, Eviction, Small Claims.***
www.greenvillecounty.org/Magistrate_Courts/
Access case details free online at www.greenvillecounty.org/scjd/publicindex/disclaim23.asp. Records go back to 1988.

Greenville Magistrate Courts #1 & #2 4 McGhee St, LEC Rm 116A, Greenville, SC 29601; 864-467-5312-City #1, 864-467-5302-City #2; fax: 864-467-5105; 8:30AM-4:30PM. ***Misdemeanor, Civil Actions under $7,500, Eviction, Small Claims.***
www.greenvillecounty.org/Magistrate_Courts/
Access case details free online at www.greenvillecounty.org/scjd/publicindex/disclaim23.asp. Records go back to 1988.

South Greenville Magistrate Court 8150 Augusta Rd, Piedmont, SC 29673; 864-277-9555; fax: 864-277-8345; 8:30AM-5PM. ***Misdemeanor, Civil Actions under $7,500, Eviction, Small Claims.***
www.greenvillecounty.org/Magistrate_Courts/
Formerly known as Piedmont Magistrate Court. Access case details free at www.greenvillecounty.org/scjd/publicindex/disclaim23.asp. Records go back to 1988.

West Greenville Magistrate Court 6247 White Horse Rd, Greenville, SC 29611; 864-294-4810; fax: 864-294-4801; 8:30AM-5PM. ***Misdemeanor, Civil Actions under $7,500, Eviction, Small Claims.***
www.greenvillecounty.org/Magistrate_Courts/
Access case details free online at www.greenvillecounty.org/scjd/publicindex/disclaim23.asp. Records go back to 1988.

Probate Court 301 University Ridge, #1200, Greenville, SC 29601; 864-467-7170; fax: 864-467-7198; 8:30AM-5PM. ***Probate.***
www.greenvillecounty.org/probate/
Search probate records free online at www.greenvillecounty.org/ProbateSearch/default.asp.

Greenwood County

Circuit Court Courthouse, Rm 114, 528 Monument St, Greenwood, SC 29646; 864-943-8089; criminal phone: 864-942-8612; civil phone: 864-942-8089; criminal fax: 864-942-8693; civil fax: same; 8:30AM-5PM. ***Felony, Misdemeanor, Civil Actions over $7,500.***

Civil Records: Access: In person, online. Visitors must perform in person searches themselves. Required to search: name, years to search. Civil cases indexed by defendant, plaintiff. Civil index in docket books from 1897; on computer back to 2000. Civil PAT goes back to 2000. PAT results show name only. Online access to the docket index is at www.sccourts.org/caseSearch/.

Criminal Records: Access: In person, online. Visitors must perform in person searches themselves. Required to search: name, years to search, DOB; also helpful: SSN. Criminal records on alpha index from 1897; on computer back to 2000. Criminal PAT goes back to 1988. PAT results show name only. Online access to the docket index is at www.sccourts.org/caseSearch/.

General Information: No adoption, juvenile, sealed or expunged records released. Will not fax documents. Court makes copy: $.25 per page. Self serve: same. Certification fee: $2.00 per doc. Payee: Clerk of Court. Business and personal checks accepted. No credit cards accepted.

Greenwood Magistrate Court Greenood County Courthouse, 528 Monument, Rm 100, Greenwood, SC 29646; 864-942-8655; fax: 864-942-8663; 8:30AM-5PM. ***Misdemeanor, Civil Actions under $7,500, Eviction, Small Claims.***

Probate Court PO Box 1210, 528 Monument St, Greenwood, SC 29648; 864-942-8625; fax: 864-942-8620; 8:30AM-5PM. ***Probate.***
www.greenwoodsc.gov/probatecourt.aspx
To search online, at the webpage, click on Estate Records Search; site may be temporarily down.

Hampton County

Circuit Court PO Box 7, 1 Elm St, Courthouse Sq, Hampton, SC 29924; 803-943-7510; fax: 803-943-7596; 8AM-5PM. ***Felony, Civil Actions over $7,500.***

Civil Records: Access: Fax, mail, in person. Visitors must perform in person searches themselves. Search fee: $2.00 per name. Required to search: name, years to search. Civil cases indexed by defendant, plaintiff. Civil index on docket books, archived from 1878.

Criminal Records: Access: Fax, mail, in person. Visitors must perform in person searches themselves. Search fee: $2.00 per name. Required to search: name, years to search, DOB; also helpful: SSN. Criminal docket on books, archived from 1878.

General Information: No adoption, juvenile, sealed or expunged records released. Will fax documents $1.00 per page. Court makes copy: $.50 per page. Self serve: $.50 per page. Certification fee: $1.00 per cert. Payee: Clerk of Court. Personal checks accepted; credit cards are not. Mail requests: SASE required.

Estill Magistrate Court PO Box 969, 125 Railroad St. SE, Estill, SC 29918; 803-625-3232; fax: 803-625-2148; 2-5PM. ***Misdemeanor, Civil Actions under $7,500, Eviction, Small Claims.***

Varnville Magistrate Court Law Enforcement Ctr, 411 Cemetery Rd, PO Box 1299, Varnville, SC 29944; 803-943-7511; 8:30-4:30PM. ***Misdemeanor, Civil Actions under $7,500, Eviction, Small Claims.***

Probate Court 1 Elm St, Courthouse Sq, Hampton, SC 29924; 803-914-2172; fax: 803-914-2183; 8AM-5PM. ***Probate.***
Probate office is located in the new building.

Horry County

Circuit Court PO Box 677, 1301 2nd Ave, Conway, SC 29526; 843-915-5080; criminal phone: 843-915-6082; civil phone: 843-915-6081; fax: 843-915-6081; 8AM-5PM. ***Felony, Misdemeanor, Civil Actions over $7,500.***

Civil Records: Access: Phone, mail, in person, online. Both court and visitors may perform in person searches. No search fee. Required to search: name, years to search. Civil cases indexed by defendant, plaintiff; index on computer from 1987, on alpha index from 1920s. Mail turnaround time 2 days. Access case details free online at www.horrycounty.org/publicindex/.

Criminal Records: Access: Phone, mail, in person, online. Both court and visitors may perform in person searches. Search fee: $3.00 per name. Required to search: name, years to search, DOB, SSN, signed release. Criminal records computerized from 1987, on alpha index from 1920s. Mail turnaround time 2 days. Access case details free at www.horrycounty.org/publicindex/. Online results show middle initial, DOB, SSN.

General Information: No adoption, juvenile, sealed or expunged records released. Court makes copy: $.25 per page. Self serve: $.25 per page. Certification fee: $1.00 per page. Payee: Clerk of Court. Business checks accepted. Mail requests: SASE helpful.

Little River Magistrate Court 107 Highway 57 N, Little River, SC 29566; 843-915-5292; fax: 843-399-6792; 8AM-5PM. ***Civil Actions under $7,500, Eviction, Small Claims, Misdemeanors.***
Access case details free online at www.horrycounty.org/publicindex/.

Aynor Magistrate Court 640 9th Ave, Aynor, SC 29511; 843-358-5508; fax: 843-358-0704; 8AM-5PM. ***Misdemeanor, Civil Actions under $7,500, Eviction, Small Claims.***
Access case details free online at www.horrycounty.org/publicindex/.

Conway Magistrate Court 1201 3rd Ave., Conway, SC 29528; 843-915-5290; fax: 843-915-6290; 8AM-5PM. ***Misdemeanor, Civil Actions under $7,500, Eviction, Small Claims.***
Access case details free online at www.horrycounty.org/publicindex/.

Conway Magistrate Court 1201 3rd Ave, 2nd Fl, Conway, SC 29526; 843-915-5290; fax: 843-915-6290; 8AM-5PM. ***Misdemeanor, Civil Actions under $7,500, Eviction, Small Claims.***
Access case details free online at www.horrycounty.org/publicindex/.

Green Sea Magistrate Court 5527 Hwy #9, PO Box 153, Green Sea, SC 29545; 843-392-1219; fax: 843-392-1834; 8AM-5PM. ***Misdemeanor, Civil Actions under $7,500, Eviction, Small Claims.***
Access case details free online at www.horrycounty.org/publicindex/.

Loris Magistrate Court 3817 Walnut St, Loris, SC 29569; 843-756-7918/6674; fax: 843-756-1355; 8AM-5PM. ***Misdemeanor, Civil Actions under $7,500, Eviction, Small Claims.***
Access case details free online at www.horrycounty.org/publicindex/.

Myrtle Beach Magistrate Court 1201 21st Ave N, Myrtle Beach, SC 29577; 843-915-5293; fax: 843-444-6131; 8AM-5PM. ***Misdemeanor, Civil Actions under $7,500, Eviction, Small Claims.***

Access case details free online at www.horrycounty.org/publicindex/.

South Strand Magistrate Court 9630 Scipio Ln, Myrtle Beach, SC 29588-7568; 843-915-5291; fax: 843-915-6291; 8AM-5PM. ***Misdemeanor, Civil Actions under $7,500, Eviction, Small Claims, Ordinance.***
Access case details free online at www.horrycounty.org/publicindex/.

Probate Court PO Box 288, 1301 2nd Ave, Conway, SC 29528; 843-915-5370; fax: 843-915-6370; 8AM-5PM. ***Probate.***
www.horrycounty.org/probatecourt/index.asp

Jasper County

Circuit Court PO Box 248, Ridgeland, SC 29936; 843-726-7710; criminal phone: 843-726-7711; civil: 843-726-7712; fax: 843-726-7782; 8:30AM-5PM. ***Felony, Misdemeanor, Civil Actions over $7,500.***
www.jaspercourt.org/
Civil Records: Access: In person, online. Visitors must perform in person searches themselves. Required to search: name, years to search. Civil cases indexed by defendant, plaintiff; index on computer back to 1999; prior on books to 1912. Civil PAT goes back to 1993. Access court records and dockets free at www.jaspercourt.org/. Access court records at www.jaspercourt.org/publicindex/.
Criminal Records: Access: In person, online. Visitors must perform in person searches themselves. Required to search: name, years to search, DOB; SSN helpful, signed release. Criminal records computerized from 1999; prior on books to 1912. Note: The court refers requests for criminal name searches to the state agency (SLED). Criminal PAT goes back to same as civil. Access court records and dockets free at www.jaspercourt.org/. Access court records at www.jaspercourt.org/publicindex/. Online results show middle initial, DOB, SSN.
General Information: No adoption, juvenile, sealed or expunged records released. Fee to fax specific case file $2.00 per page. Court makes copy: $1.00 per page. Self serve: same. Certification fee: $1.00. Payee: Clerk of Court. No personal checks. No credit cards accepted.

Hardeeville Magistrate Court 21 Martin St, PO Box 1169, Hardeeville, SC 29927; 843-784-2628; 9AM-5PM. ***Misdemeanor, Civil Actions under $7,500, Eviction, Small Claims.***
Access case details free online at www.jaspercourt.org/publicindex/. Online results include address and DOB.

Pineland Magistrate Court 967 Adams St, PO Box 748, Ridgeland, SC 29936; 843-726-7933; fax: 843-726-4191; 9AM-N 1-5PM. ***Misdemeanor, Civil Actions under $7,500, Eviction, Small Claims.***
Pineland Magistrate Court is closed; information here is for the nearby Ridgeland Magistrate Court.

Ridgeland Magistrate Court 800 Jacobsmart Blvd., PO Box 639, Ridgeland, SC 29936; 843-726-7737; fax: 843-726-7745; 9AM-N; 1-5PM. ***Misdemeanor, Civil Actions under $7,500, Eviction, Small Claims.***
Access case details free online at www.jaspercourt.org/publicindex/. Online results include address and DOB.

Probate Court PO Box 1028, 305 Russell St, Ridgeland, SC 29936; 843-726-7719; fax: 843-726-5173; 9AM-5PM. ***Probate.***
Access case details free online at www.jaspercourt.org/publicindex/. Online results include address and DOB.

Kershaw County

Circuit Court County Courthouse, Rm 313, PO Box 1557, Camden, SC 29020; 803-425-1500 x5623; criminal fax: 803-425-1505; civil fax: same; 8:30AM-5PM. ***Felony, Misdemeanor, Civil Actions over $7,500.***
Civil Records: Access: Mail, in person, online. Visitors must perform in person searches themselves. Search fee: $20.00. Required to search: name, years to search. Civil cases indexed by defendant, plaintiff. Civil records archived from 1797, computerized records from 1994. Mail turnaround time 1 day. Civil PAT goes back to 1994. PAT civil results show middle initial. Access to the docket index is at www.sccourts.org/caseSearch/.
Criminal Records: Access: Mail, in person, online. Visitors must perform in person searches themselves. Search fee: $20.00. Required to search: name, years to search, DOB; also helpful: SSN. Criminal records archived from 1890, computerized records from 1994. Mail turnaround time 1 day. Criminal PAT goes back to same as civil. PAT results show middle initial, DOB. Terminal results include SSN. Online access to the docket index is at www.sccourts.org/caseSearch/.
General Information: No adoption, juvenile, sealed or expunged records released. Will not fax documents. Court makes copy: $.50 per page. Self serve: same. Certification fee: $1.00 per document. Payee: Clerk of Court. Personal checks accepted; credit cards are not. Mail requests: SASE required.

Bethune Magistrate Court. ***Misdemeanor, Civil Actions under $7,500, Eviction.***
Court Closed - formerly at 202 N Main St, Bethune.

Camden Magistrate Court PO Box 1528, 1121 Broad St, County Courthouse, #202, Camden, SC 29020; 803-425-1500 x5382; fax: 803-425-6044; 8:30AM-5PM. ***Misdemeanor, Civil Actions under $7,500, Eviction, Small Claims, Traffic.***

Probate Court 1121 Broad St, Camden, SC 29020; 803-425-1500 x5351; fax: 803-425-1526; 8:30AM-5PM. ***Probate.***

Lancaster County

Circuit Court PO Box 1809, Lancaster, SC 29721; 803-285-1581; fax: 803-416-9388; 8:30AM-5PM. ***Felony, Misdemeanor, Civil Actions over $7,500.***
Civil Records: Access: In person, online. Both court and visitors may perform in person searches. No search fee. Required to search: name, years to search. Civil cases indexed by defendant, plaintiff; index on computer from 1987, microfiche from 1937, alpha index from 1764. Civil PAT goes back to 1987. Online access to the docket index is at www.sccourts.org/caseSearch/.
Criminal Records: Access: In person, online. Both court and visitors may perform in person searches. No search fee. Required to search: name, years to search, DOB; SSN helpful. Criminal records computerized from 1987. Criminal PAT goes back to same as civil. Online access to the docket index is at www.sccourts.org/caseSearch/.
General Information: No adoption, juvenile, sealed or expunged records released. Will not fax documents. Court makes copy: $.25 per page. Self serve: same. Certification fee: $2.50. Payee: Clerk of Court. Personal checks accepted.

Lancaster Magistrate Court 761 Lancaster Bypass East, Lancaster, SC 29720; 803-283-3983; fax: 803-416-9407; 8:30AM-5PM. ***Misdemeanor, Civil Actions under $7,500, Eviction, Small Claims.***

Probate Court PO Box 1809, 101 N Main St, Lancaster, SC 29721; 803-283-3379; fax: 803-283-3370; 8:30AM-5PM. ***Probate.***
www.lancastercountysc.net/ProbateCourt

Laurens County

Circuit Court PO Box 287, 100 Hillerst Sq, Laurens, SC 29360; 864-984-3538; fax: 864-984-7023; 9AM-5PM. ***Felony, Misdemeanor, Civil Actions over $7,500.***
Civil Records: Access: In person, online. Both court and visitors may perform in person searches. No search fee. Required to search: name, years to search. Civil cases indexed by defendant, plaintiff. Civil index on docket books back to 1800s; on computer back to 1980. Civil PAT goes back to 1987. Online access to the docket index is at www.sccourts.org/caseSearch/.
Criminal Records: Access: In person, online. Both court and visitors may perform in person searches. No search fee. Required to search: name, years to search, DOB; also helpful: SSN. Criminal records indexed in books back to 1950s; on computer back to 1980. Criminal PAT goes back to 1987. Online access to the docket index is at www.sccourts.org/caseSearch/.
General Information: No adoption, juvenile, sealed or expunged records released. Will not fax documents. Court makes copy: $.50 per page. Self serve: $.50 per page. Certification fee: $1.00 per page. Payee: Clerk of Court. No personal checks or credit cards accepted.

Clinton Magistrate Court 203 W Pitts St, Clinton, SC 29325; 864-833-5879; fax: 864-833-7502; 8AM-5PM M, T; 8AM-N W; 8AM-10AM F. ***Misdemeanor, Civil Actions under $7,500, Eviction, Small Claims.***

Gray Court Magistrate Court 329 Main St, Town Hall, PO Box 438, Gray Court, SC 29645; 864-876-4390; 9AM-5PM,M,T,W; 9AM-2PM Th. ***Misdemeanor, Civil Actions under $7,500, Eviction, Small Claims.***

Laurens Magistrate Court PO Box 925, 154 Templeton Rd, Laurens, SC 29360; 864-683-4485; 9AM-5PM. ***Misdemeanor, Civil Actions under $7,500, Eviction, Small Claims.***

Probate Court PO Box 194, 100 Hillcrest Sq, Ste A, Laurens, SC 29360; 864-984-7315; probate phone: 864-984-7731; fax: 864-984-3779; 9AM-5PM. ***Probate.***
www.sccourts.org/trial/probate/probatejudges.cfm?countyno=30

Lee County

Circuit Court PO Box 387, Bishopville, SC 29010; 803-484-5341; fax: 803-484-1632; 9AM-5PM. ***Felony, Misdemeanor, Civil Actions over $7,500.***
Civil Records: Access: Mail, in person. Both court and visitors may perform in person searches. Search fee: $5.00 per name. Required to search: name, years to search. Civil cases indexed by defendant, plaintiff; index on computer from 1991, on archives from 1900s. Mail turnaround time 2 days. Civil PAT goes back to 1985.
Criminal Records: Access: Mail, in person. Both court and visitors may perform in person searches. Search fee: $2.00 per name. Required to search: name, years to search, DOB; also helpful: SSN. Criminal records computerized from 1991, on archives from 1900s. Mail turnaround time 2 days. Criminal PAT goes back to same as civil.
General Information: No adoption, juvenile, sealed or expunged records released. Will not fax documents. Court makes copy: $.50 per page, $1.00 minimum. Self serve: $.50 per page. Certification fee: $1.00 per page includes copy fee. Payee: Clerk of Court. Business checks accepted. No credit cards accepted. Mail requests: SASE required.

Bishopville Magistrate Court 115 Gregg St, PO Box 2, Bishopsville, SC 29010; 803-484-6463; fax: 803-484-5163; 9AM-5-PM. ***Misdemeanor, Civil Actions under $7,500, Eviction, Small Claims.***

Probate Court PO Box 24, 123 S Main St, Bishopville, SC 29010; 803-484-5341 X338, X339, X361; fax: 803-484-6881; 9AM-5PM. ***Probate.***

Lexington County

Circuit Court Lexington County Judicial Ctr, Rm 107, 205 E Main St, Lexington, SC 29072; 803-785-8212; criminal phone: 803-785-8223; civil phone: 803-785-8252; probate phone: 803-785-8324; fax: 803-785-8314; 8AM-5PM. ***Felony, High Misdemeanor, Civil Actions over $7,500.***
www.lex-co.com/Departments/ClerkOfCourt/Index.html
Civil Records: Access: Mail, in person, online. Both court and visitors may perform in person searches. Search fee: $3.00 per name. Required to search: name, years to search. Civil cases indexed by defendant, plaintiff; index on index from 1936. Mail turnaround time 3 days. Civil PAT goes back to

1984. Search record index free at www.lex-co.com/applications/scjdweb/publicindex/.

Criminal Records: Access: Fax, mail, in person, online. Both court and visitors may perform in person searches. Search fee: $3.00 per name. Required to search: name, years to search, DOB, SSN. Criminal records on computer since 1983. Mail turnaround time 3 days. Criminal PAT goes back to same as civil. Search the record index at www.lex-co.com/applications/scjdweb/publicindex/. Online results show middle initial, DOB, SSN.

General Information: No adoption, juvenile, sealed or expunged records released. Will fax documents $.25 per page. Court makes copy: $.25 per page; included in search fee. Self serve: $.25 per page. Certification fee: $1.25 per cert. Payee: County of Lexington. Personal checks accepted; credit cards are not. Mail requests: SASE required.

Batesburg Leesville Magistrate Court 231 W Church St, Batesburg, SC 29006; 803-359-8330; criminal phone: 803-332-8330; civil phone: 803-332-0204; fax: 803-332-0357; 8AM-5PM. ***Misdemeanor, Civil Actions under $7,500, Eviction, Small Claims.***
Search record index free at www.lex-co.com/applications/scjdweb/publicindex/.

Cayce Magistrate Court 650 Knox Abbott Dr, Cayce, SC 29033; 803-796-7100; fax: 803-796-7635; 8AM-4:30PM. ***Misdemeanor, Civil Actions under $7,500, Eviction, Small Claims.***
Search record index free at www.lex-co.com/applications/scjdweb/publicindex/.

Columbia Magistrate Court 111 Lincreek, Columbia, SC 29212; 803-781-7584/7585; fax: 803-749-4050; 8AM-4:30PM. ***Misdemeanor, Civil Actions under $7,500, Eviction, Small Claims.***
Search record index free at www.lex-co.com/applications/scjdweb/publicindex/.

Lexington Magistrate Court 605 W Main St, #100, Magistrate's Office, Lexington, SC 29072; 803-785-8221; fax: 803-785-8155; 8:30AM-4:30PM. ***Misdemeanor, Civil Actions under $7,500, Eviction, Small Claims.***
Search record index free at www.lex-co.com/applications/scjdweb/publicindex/.

Swansea Magistrate Court 500 Charlie Rast Rd, PO Box 457, Swansea, SC 29160; 803-785-3616; fax: 803-785-4078; 8:30AM-4:30PM. ***Misdemeanor, Civil Actions under $7,500, Eviction, Small Claims.***
www.lex-co.com/Departments/MagistrateCourt/Index.html
Search record index free at www.lex-co.com/applications/scjdweb/publicindex/.

Probate Court 205 E Main St, Suite 134, Lexington, SC 29072; 803-785-8324; 8AM-5PM. ***Probate.***

Marion County

Circuit Court 100 W Court St, Marion, SC 29571; 843-423-8240; fax: 843-423-8242; 8:30AM-5PM. ***Felony, Misdemeanor, Civil Actions over $7,500.***

Civil Records: Access: In person only. Visitors must perform in person searches themselves. Required to search: name, years to search. Civil cases indexed by defendant, plaintiff; index on computer since 1988; prior records on index cards from 1800s. Civil PAT goes back to 1980s.

Criminal Records: Access: In person only. Visitors must perform in person searches themselves. Required to search: name, years to search, DOB; SSN helpful. Criminal records on computer since 1988; prior records on index cards from 1800s. Criminal PAT goes back to 1980s.

General Information: No adoption, juvenile, sealed or expunged records released. Will not fax documents. Court makes copy: $.25 per page. Self serve: $.25 per page. Certification fee: $1.00 per cert. Payee: Circuit Court Clerk. No personal checks or credit cards accepted.

Gresham Magistrate Court 2715 Hwy 76 E., #B, Mullins, SC 25974; fax: 843-423-8394; 8:30AM-5PM. ***Misdemeanor, Civil Actions under $7,500, Eviction, Small Claims.***
For records, call 843-423-8208.

Marion/Mullins Magistrate Court 2715 E Hwy 76, #B, Mullins, SC 29574-6015; 843-423-8208; fax: 843-423-8394; 8:30AM-5PM. ***Misdemeanor, Civil Actions under $7,500, Eviction, Small Claims.***

Probate Court PO Box 583, 201 Court St, Marion, SC 29571; 843-423-8244; fax: 843-431-5026; 8:30AM-5PM. ***Probate.***

Marlboro County

Circuit Court PO Drawer 996, 105 Main St, Bennettsville, SC 29512; 843-479-5613; fax: 843-479-5640; 8:30AM-5PM. ***Felony, Misdemeanor, Civil Actions over $7,500.***

Civil Records: Access: Mail, in person. Visitors must perform in person searches themselves. Search fee: $2.00 per name. Required to search: name, years to search. Civil cases indexed by defendant, plaintiff; index on computer from 1985, on index from 1786. Mail turnaround time 1 day. Public use terminal has civil records back to 1985.

Criminal Records: Access: Mail, in person. Visitors must perform in person searches themselves. Search fee: $2.00 per name. Required to search: name, years to search, DOB; also helpful: SSN. Criminal records computerized from 1985, on index from 1786. Mail turnaround time 1 day.

General Information: No adoption, juvenile, sealed or expunged records released. Will not fax documents. Court makes copy: $2.00 per set. Self serve: $.10 per page. Certification fee: $2.00, complete file $5.00. Payee: Clerk of Court. Personal checks accepted; credit cards are not. Mail requests: SASE required.

Bennettsville Magistrate Court PO Box 418, 211 N Marlboro St, Bennettsville, SC 29512; 843-479-5620; fax: 843-479-5646; 8:30AM-4:30PM M-TH; Civil 4-5PM. ***Misdemeanor, Civil Actions under $7,500, Eviction, Small Claims.***
Court is again active.

Marlboro County Summary Court PO Box 418, 211 N Marlboro St, Bennettsville, SC 29512; 843-479-5620; fax: 843-479-5646; 8:30AM-4:30PM. ***Civil Actions under $7,500, Eviction, Small Claims.***
Same searching and fees as at Circuit Court.

Probate Court PO Box 455, 105 E Main St, Bennettsville, SC 29512; 843-479-5610; fax: 843-479-5668; 8:30AM-5PM. ***Probate.***

McCormick County

Circuit Court 133 S Mine St, Rm 102, McCormick, SC 29835; 864-852-2195; probate phone: 864-852-2630; criminal fax: 864-852-0071; civil fax: same; 9AM-5PM. ***Felony, Misdemeanor, Civil Actions over $7,500.***

Civil Records: Access: In person only. Visitors must perform in person searches themselves. Required to search: name, years to search. Civil cases indexed by defendant, plaintiff. Civil index on docket books from 1916.

Criminal Records: Access: In person only. Visitors must perform in person searches themselves. Required to search: name, years to search, DOB; SSN helpful. Criminal records indexed in books from 1916.

General Information: No adoption, juvenile, sealed or expunged records released. Will not fax out case files. Court makes copy: criminal court $.50 per page. Self serve: $.50 per page. Certification fee: $1.00 per page. Payee: Clerk of Court. Personal checks accepted; credit cards are not.

McCormick Magistrate Court 211 W Augusta Ext., PO Box 1116, McCormick, SC 29835; 864-852-2316; fax: 864-852-2582; 8AM-N, 1-4PM. ***Misdemeanor, Civil Actions under $7,500, Eviction, Small Claims.***

Probate Court 133 S Mine St, #101, McCormick, SC 29835; 864-852-2630; fax: 864-852-0071; 9AM-5PM. ***Probate.***

Newberry County

Circuit Court PO Drawer 10, 1226 College St, Newberry, SC 29108; 803-321-2110; fax: 803-321-2111; 8:30AM-5PM. ***Felony, Misdemeanor, Civil Actions over $7,500.***
www.newberrycounty.net

Civil Records: Access: In person only. Visitors must perform in person searches themselves. Required to search: name, years to search. Civil cases indexed by defendant, plaintiff; index on computer from 1983, docket books from 1776. Civil PAT goes back to 1989. PAT civil results show middle initial.

Criminal Records: Access: In person only. Visitors must perform in person searches themselves. Required to search: name, years to search, DOB; SSN helpful. Criminal records computerized from 1983, docket books from 1776. Criminal PAT goes back to same as civil. PAT criminal results show middle initial.

General Information: No adoption, juvenile, sealed, PTI or expunged records released. Will fax documents $2.00 per page. Court makes copy: $.20 per page. Certification fee: $1.00 per page. Payee: Clerk of Court. Only cashiers checks and money orders accepted. No credit cards accepted.

Little Mountain Magistrate Court PO Box 100, 824 Main St, Little Mountain, SC 29075; 803-345-1040; fax: 803-945-7222; 2PM-5PM T,W. ***Misdemeanor, Civil Actions under $7,500, Eviction, Small Claims.***

Newberry Magistrate Court 3239 Louis Rich Rd, Newberry, SC 29108; criminal phone: 803-321-2144; civil phone: 803-321-2145; probate phone: 803-321-2118; criminal fax: 803-321-2172; civil fax: same; 8:30AM-5PM. ***Misdemeanor, Civil Actions under $7,500, Eviction, Small Claims, Traffic.*** www.newberrycounty.net/
Probate fax is same as main fax number.

Whitmire Magistrate Court 313 Main St, PO Box 61, Whitmire, SC 29178; 803-694-5756; fax: 803-694-5756; 1-5PM T,TH. ***Misdemeanor, Civil Actions under $7,500, Eviction, Small Claims.***

Probate Court PO Box 442, 1309 College St, Newberry, SC 29108; 803-321-2118; fax: 803-321-2119; 8:30AM-5PM. ***Probate.***
www.newberrycounty.net

Oconee County

Circuit Court PO Box 678, 205 W Main St, Walhalla, SC 29691; 864-638-4280; fax: 864-638-4282; 8:30AM-5PM. ***Felony, Misdemeanor, Civil Actions over $7,500.***

Civil Records: Access: In person only. Visitors must perform in person searches themselves. Required to search: name, years to search. Civil cases indexed by defendant, plaintiff. Civil index on cards from 1868; on computer back to 1994. Civil PAT goes back to 1996. PAT results show name only.

Criminal Records: Access: In person only. Visitors must perform in person searches themselves. Required to search: name, years to search; also helpful: DOB, SSN, signed release. Criminal records indexed on cards from 1868; on computer back to 1994. Criminal PAT goes back to same as civil. PAT results show name only.

General Information: No adoption, juvenile, sealed or expunged records released. Will not fax documents. Court makes copy: $1.00 first page, $.50 each add'l. Self serve: $.50 per page. No certification fee. Payee: Clerk of Court. Personal checks accepted; credit cards are not.

Walhalla Magistrate Court 208 Booker Dr, Walhalla, SC 29691; 864-638-4127; criminal phone: 864-638-4125; fax: 864-638-4229; 8:30AM-5PM M,W,F; closed T,TH. ***Misdemeanor, Civil Actions under $7,500, Eviction, Small Claims, Traffic.***
Also known as Oconee County Summary Court. Shares the same clerk as the Westminister Magistrate Court. Fees are charged for record access or copies.

Civil Records: Access: Mail, in person. Only the court performs in person searches; visitors may not. Search fee: fee determined by amount of clerk's time taken. Required to search: name. Indexed by defendant. Small claims and civil in same index. Evictions destroyed annually; complaints after 10 years; claim/delivery records after 3 years. Mail turnaround time 5-7 days.
Criminal Records: Access: Mail, in person. Only the court performs in person searches; visitors may not. Search fee: fee determined by amount of clerk's time taken. Required to search: name.
General Information: Will not fax documents. Court makes copy: Criminal court copy $.50 per page. Payee: Oconee County Summary Court. Personal checks accepted; credit cards are not.

County Summary Court. ***Misdemeanor, Civil Actions under $7,500, Eviction.***
See Walhalla Magistrate Court.

Westminster Magistrate Court 106 E Winston St, Westminster, SC 29693; 864-647-5998; fax: 864-647-4844; 10AM-3:30PM M,W; 8:30AM-4:30PM T,TH, 10AM-3:30 Fri. ***Misdemeanor, Civil Actions under $7,500, Eviction, Small Claims, Traffic.***
Has the same clerk as the Walhalla Magistrate Ct. Same fees and search rules as at Walhalla Ct.

Probate Court PO Box 471, 415 S Pine St, Walhalla, SC 29691; 864-638-4275; fax: 864-638-4278; 8:30AM-5PM. ***Probate.***

Orangeburg County

Circuit Court PO Box 9000, 1540 Ellis Ave NE, Orangeburg, SC 29116; 803-533-6260; criminal phone: 803-533-6262; civil phone: 803-533-6219; fax: 803-534-3848; 8:30AM-5PM. ***Felony, Misdemeanor, Civil Actions over $7,500.***
Civil Records: Access: In person, online. Visitors must perform in person searches themselves. Required to search: name, years to search. Civil cases indexed by defendant, plaintiff. Civil index on cards from 1924. Civil PAT goes back to 1998. Online access to the docket index is at www.sccourts.org/caseSearch/.
Criminal Records: Access: In person, online. Visitors must perform in person searches themselves. Required to search: name, years to search, DOB; SSN helpful. Criminal records indexed on cards from 1924. Criminal PAT goes back to 1998. Online access to the docket index is at www.sccourts.org/caseSearch/.
General Information: No adoption, juvenile, sealed or expunged records released. Will not fax documents. Court makes copy: $.50 per page. Self serve: $.50 per page. Certification fee: $2.00. Payee: Clerk of Court. Personal checks accepted; credit cards are not.

Bowman Magistrate Court ***Misdemeanor, Civil Actions under $7,500, Eviction, Small Claims.***
Direct records search requests to Holly Hill Magistrate Court. Search index online free at www.orangeburgcounty.org/scjdweb/publicindex/.

Branchville Magistrate Court PO Box 85, 7644 Freedom Rd, Branchville, SC 29432; 803-274-8000; fax: 803-274-8760; 8:30AM-5PM. ***Misdemeanor, Civil Actions under $7,500, Eviction, Small Claims.***
Direct records search requests to Orangeburg County Magistrate Court. Search index online free at www.orangeburgcounty.org/scjdweb/publicindex/.

Elloree Magistrate Court. ***Misdemeanor, Civil Actions under $7,500, Eviction, Small Claims.***
Direct record searches to Holly Hill Magistrate Court. Search index online free at www.orangeburgcounty.org/scjdweb/publicindex/.

Eutawville Magistrate Court. ***Misdemeanor, Civil Actions under $7,500, Eviction, Small Claims.***
Direct record searches to Holly Hill Magistrate Court. Search index online free at www.orangeburgcounty.org/scjdweb/publicindex/.

Holly Hill Magistrate Court - Eastern PO Box 154, 7324 Old State Rd, Hwy 176, Holly Hill, SC 29059; 803-496-9533; fax: 803-496-5661; 8:30AM-5PM. ***Misdemeanor, Civil Actions under $7,500, Eviction, Small Claims.***
Also holds records for Magistrate courts in Elloree, Bowman, and Eutawville. Search index online free at www.orangeburgcounty.org/scjdweb/publicindex/.

Neeses Magistrate Court - Western 6357 Savannah Highway, North, SC 29107; 803-247-2011; fax: 803-247-2058; 8:30AM-5PM. ***Misdemeanor, Civil Actions under $7,500, Eviction, Small Claims.***
Also holds records for Magistrate courts in North, Springfield, and Norway. Neeses is a new court location 2007. Search index online free at www.orangeburgcounty.org/scjdweb/publicindex/.

Norway Magistrate Court. ***Misdemeanor, Civil Actions under $7,500, Eviction, Small Claims.***
Direct records search requests to Neeses Magistrate Court. Search index online free at www.orangeburgcounty.org/scjdweb/publicindex/.

Orangeburg Central Region Magistrate Court PO Box 9000, 1540 Ellis Ave NE, Orangeburg, SC 29116; 803-533-5880/5879; fax: 803-516-4011; 8:30AM-5PM. ***Misdemeanor, Civil Actions under $7,500, Eviction, Small Claims.***
Also holds records for Branchville Magistrate Court. Search index online free at www.orangeburgcounty.org/scjdweb/publicindex/.

Orangeburg Magistrate Court PO Box 9000, 1540 Ellis Ave, Orangeburg, SC 29116; 803-533-5843; fax: 803-516-4011; 8:30AM-5PM. ***Misdemeanor, Civil Actions under $7,500, Eviction, Small Claims.***
Search index online free at www.orangeburgcounty.org/scjdweb/publicindex/.

Springfield and North Magistrate Courts. ***Misdemeanor, Civil Actions under $7,500, Eviction, Small Claims.***
Direct records search requests to Neeses Magistrate Court. Search index online free at www.orangeburgcounty.org/scjdweb/publicindex/.

Probate Court PO Drawer 9000, 190 Gibson St, Orangeburg, SC 29116-9000; 803-533-6280; fax: 803-533-6279; 8:30AM-5PM. ***Probate.***
www.sccourts.org/probate/index.cfm?countyno=38

Pickens County

Circuit Court PO Box 215, 214 E Main St, Pickens, SC 29671; 864-898-5857; criminal phone: 864-898-5864; civil phone: 864-898-5862; fax: 864-898-5863; 8:30AM-5PM. ***Felony, Misdemeanor, Civil Actions over $7,500.***
www.co.pickens.sc.us
Civil Records: Access: In person, online. Both court and visitors may perform in person searches. No search fee. Required to search: name, years to search. Civil cases indexed by defendant, plaintiff; index on computer from 1990, on index from 1970. Civil PAT goes back to 1990. PAT results show name, DOB. Terminal results also show SSNs. Access case details free at www.greenvillecounty.org/scjd/publicindex/.
Criminal Records: Access: In person, online. Both court and visitors may perform in person searches. No search fee. Required to search: name, years to search, DOB; also helpful: SSN. Criminal records computerized from 1990, on index from 1970. Criminal PAT goes back to same as civil.PAT results show name, DOB. Terminal results include SSN. Access case details free at www.greenvillecounty.org/scjd/publicindex/. Online results show name, DOB. Terminal results include SSN.
General Information: Online identifiers in results same as on public terminal. No adoption, juvenile, sealed or expunged records released. Will not fax documents. Court makes copy: $.25 per page. Certification fee: $1.00. Payee: Clerk of Court. Personal checks accepted; credit cards are not.

Clemson Magistrate Court 115-B Commons Way, Central, SC 29630; 864-639-8084; fax: 864-639-0701; 8:30AM-4:30PM. ***Misdemeanor, Civil Actions under $7,500, Eviction, Small Claims.***
Access case details free online at www.greenvillecounty.org/scjd/publicindex/.

Easley Magistrate Court 135 Folger Ave, Easley, SC 29640; 864-850-7076; fax: 864-850-7075; 8:30AM-4:30PM. ***Misdemeanor, Civil Actions under $7,500, Eviction, Small Claims.***
Access case details free online at www.greenvillecounty.org/scjd/publicindex/.

Liberty Magistrate Court #147-B Kay Holcombe Rd, Liberty, SC 29657; 864-843-5821 or 5833; criminal phone: 854-843-5833; fax: 864-843-5824; 8:30AM-5PM. ***Misdemeanor, Civil Actions under $7,500, Eviction, Small Claims.***
Access case details free online at www.greenvillecounty.org/scjd/publicindex/.

Pickens Magistrate Court 216-A, Law Enforcement Ctr Rd, Pickens, SC 29671; 864-898-5551/5552; fax: 864-898-5546; 8:30AM-4:30PM. ***Misdemeanor, Civil Actions under $7,500, Eviction, Small Claims.***
Access case details free online at www.greenvillecounty.org/scjd/publicindex/.

Probate Court 222 McDaniel Ave, #B-16, Pickens, SC 29671; 864-898-5903; fax: 864-898-5924; 8AM-5PM. ***Probate.***

Richland County

Circuit Court PO Box 2766, 1701 Main St, Columbia, SC 29202; 803-576-1999; civil phone: 803-576-1939; criminal fax: 803-576-1925; civil fax: 803-748-5039; 8:30AM-5PM. ***Felony, Misdemeanor, Civil Actions over $7,500.***
Civil Records: Access: Mail, in person, online. Both court and visitors may perform in person searches. Search fee: $2.00 per name. Required to search: name, years to search. Civil cases indexed by defendant, plaintiff; index on computer from 1987. Many prior records indexed to 1920's. Civil PAT goes back to 1987. Access case details free at http://www4.rcgov.us/publicindex/default.aspx. Limited court rosters online at www.richlandonline.com/departments/clerkofcourt/courtroster.asp; search by date.
Criminal Records: Access: In person, online. Visitors must perform in person searches themselves. Required to search: name, years to search; also helpful: DOB, SSN. Criminal records on index to 1920's, computerized since 1987. Criminal PAT goes back to same as civil. Access case details free at http://www4.rcgov.us/publicindex/default.aspx. Access limited court rosters at www.richlandonline.com/departments/clerkofcourt/courtroster.asp; search by date. Online results show middle initial, DOB, SSN.
General Information: No adoption, juvenile, sealed or expunged records released. Will fax to gov't agencies only. Court makes copy: $.50 first page, $.15 each add'l. Self serve: $.25 per page. No certification fee. Payee: Richland County Clerk. Personal checks accepted; credit cards are not. Mail requests: SASE required for civil.

Central Magistrate Court 1400 Huger St, PO Box 192, Columbia, SC 29202; 803-576-2300; fax: 803-576-2325; 8:30AM-5PM. ***Misdemeanor, Criminal Domestic Violence, Felony Prelims, Civil Actions under $7,500, Traffic.***
Access case details free online at http://www4.rcgov.us/publicindex/default.aspx.

Columbia Magistrate Court 1515 Richland St, Columbia, SC 29201; 803-576-2510; fax: 803-576-2519; 8:30AM-5PM. ***Misdemeanor, Civil Actions under $7,500, Eviction, Small Claims.***
Access case details free online at http://www4.rcgov.us/publicindex/default.aspx.

Dentsville Magistrate Court 2500 Decker Blvd, #B-1, Box 10, Columbia, SC 29206; 803-576-2560; fax: 803-576-2569; 8:30AM-5PM.

Misdemeanor, Civil Actions under $7,500, Eviction, Small Claims.
Access case details free online at http://www4.rcgov.us/publicindex/default.aspx.

Dutch Fork Magistrate Court 1019 Beatty Rd, Columbia, SC 29210; 803-576-2540; fax: 803-576-2545; 8:30AM-5PM. ***Misdemeanor, Civil Actions under $7,500, Small Claims, Eviction.***
Access case details free online at http://www4.rcgov.us/publicindex/default.aspx.

Hopkins Magistrate Court 6108 Cabin Creek Rd, Hopkins, SC 29061; 803-576-2530; criminal fax: 803-576-2535; civil fax: same; 8:30AM-5PM. ***Misdemeanor, Civil Actions under $7,500, Eviction, Small Claims.***
Access case details free online at http://www4.rcgov.us/publicindex/default.aspx.

Lykesland Magistrate Court 1403 Caroline Rd, Columbia, SC 29209; 803-576-2500; fax: 803-576-2504; 8:30AM-5PM. ***Misdemeanor, Civil Actions under $7,500, Eviction, Small Claims.***
Access case details free online at http://www4.rcgov.us/publicindex/default.aspx.

Olympia Magistrate Court 1601 B Shop Rd, Columbia, SC 29201; 803-576-2550; fax: 803-576-2555; 8:30AM-5PM. ***Misdemeanor, Civil Actions under $7,500, Eviction, Small Claims.***
www.richlandonline.com/departments/magistrate/index.asp
Access case details free online at http://www4.rcgov.us/publicindex/default.aspx.

Pontiac Magistrate Court 10509 Two Notch Rd, #D, Elgin, SC 29045; 803-576-2520; fax: 803-576-2522; 8:30AM-5PM. ***Misdemeanor, Civil Actions under $7,500, Eviction, Small Claims.***
Access case details free online at http://www4.rcgov.us/publicindex/default.aspx.

Upper Township Magistrate Court 4919 Rhett St, Columbia, SC 29203; 803-576-2570; fax: 803-576-2579; 8:30AM-5PM. ***Misdemeanor, Civil Actions under $7,500, Eviction, Small Claims.***
Access case details free online at http://www4.rcgov.us/publicindex/default.aspx.

Waverly Magistrate Court 2712 Middleburg Dr, #106, Columbia, SC 29204; 803-576-2590; fax: 803-576-2599; 8:30AM-5PM. ***Misdemeanor, Civil Actions under $7,500, Eviction, Small Claims.***
Access case details free online at http://www4.rcgov.us/publicindex/default.aspx.

Probate Court PO Box 192 (1701 Main St, #207), Columbia, SC 29202; 803-576-1961; fax: 803-576-1993; 8:30AM-5PM. ***Probate.***
www.richlandonline.com/probate.htm
Access county estate records free at www.richlandonline.com/services/estatesinquiry.asp.

Saluda County

Circuit Court County Courthouse, 100 E Church St, #6, Saluda, SC 29138; 864-445-4500; fax: 864-445-3772; 8:30AM-5PM. ***Felony, Misdemeanor, Civil Actions over $7,500.***
Civil Records: Access: In person. Both court and visitors may perform in person searches. No search fee. Required to search: name, years to search, address. Civil cases indexed by defendant, plaintiff; index on computer from 1995, on index from 1897. Civil PAT goes back to 1995. PAT results show name only.
Criminal Records: Access: In person. Both court and visitors may perform in person searches. No search fee. Required to search: name, years to search, address, DOB, signed release; also helpful: SSN. Criminal records computerized from 1995, on index from 1897. Note: Request must be in writing. Criminal PAT goes back to same as civil. PAT results show name only.
General Information: No adoption, juvenile, sealed or expunged records released. Will not fax documents. Court makes copy: $.25 per page. Self serve: same. Certification fee: $1.00. Payee: Clerk of Court. Personal checks accepted; credit cards are not. Mail requests: SASE required for mail return of any copies.

Saluda Magistrate Court 108 S Rudolph St, Courthouse Annex, Saluda, SC 29138; 864-445-4500; criminal phone: x2236; civil phone: x2239; fax: 864-445-3684; 8AM-5PM. ***Misdemeanor, Civil Actions under $7,500, Eviction, Small Claims.***

Probate Court 100 E Church St, Saluda, SC 29138; 864-445-4500 x2220; fax: 864-445-9726; 8:30AM-5PM. ***Probate.***

Spartanburg County

Circuit Court County Courthouse, 180 Magnolia St, Spartanburg, SC 29306; 864-596-2591; fax: 864-596-2239; 8:30AM-5PM. ***Felony, Misdemeanor, Civil Actions over $7,500.***
www.spartanburgcounty.org/govt/depts/coc/index.htm
Civil Records: Access: In person, online. Visitors must perform in person searches themselves. Required to search: name, years to search. Civil cases indexed by defendant, plaintiff; index on computer from 1975, on microfiche from 1960, on alpha index from 1800s. Public use terminal has civil records back to 1970. Access case details free at http://192.146.148.40/publicindex/.
Criminal Records: Access: In person, online. Visitors must perform in person searches themselves. Required to search: name, years to search, DOB, SSN, signed release. Criminal records computerized from 1975, on microfiche from 1960, on alpha index from 1800s. Note: The public may search the index. Access case details free at http://192.146.148.40/publicindex/.
General Information: No adoption, juvenile, sealed or expunged records released. Will not fax documents. Court makes copy: $1.00 per page. Certification fee: $1.00 per cert. Payee: Clerk of Court. Personal checks accepted.

Chesnee Magistrate Court 201 Cherokee St, Chesnee, SC 29323; 864-461-3402; fax: 864-596-3622; 3:30-9:30PM T, TH. ***Misdemeanor, Civil Actions under $7,500, Eviction, Small Claims.***
Access case details free online at http://192.146.148.40/publicindex/.

Inman Magistrate Court 20 S Main St, Inman, SC 29349; 864-472-4447/6247; fax: 864-596-3622; 9AM-8PM M; 8AM-N T. ***Misdemeanor, Civil Actions under $7,500, Eviction, Small Claims.***
Access case details free online at http://192.146.148.40/publicindex/.

Landrum Magistrate Court 104 E Tucker St, PO Box 744, Landrum, SC 29356; 864-457-7245; fax: 864-457-7245; 8AM-7PM T; 8-11AM TH. ***Misdemeanor, Civil Actions under $7,500, Eviction, Small Claims.***
Access case details free online at http://192.146.148.40/publicindex/.

Pacolet Magistrate Court 980 Sunny Acres Rd, PO Box 416, Pacolet Mills, SC 29373; 864-474-0344/3391; fax: 864-474-4444; 6PM-10PM M & W; 6PM-9PM TH. ***Misdemeanor, Civil Actions under $7,500, Eviction, Small Claims.***
Access case details free online at http://192.146.148.40/publicindex/.

Reidville Magistrate Court 162 Leonard Rd, PO Box 124, Reidville, SC 29375; 864-433-9223; 10AM-5:30PM T; 9AM-2PM TH. ***Misdemeanor, Civil Actions under $7,500, Eviction, Small Claims.***
Access case details free online at http://192.146.148.40/publicindex/.

Spartanburg Magistrate Court County Courthouse, Rm 105, 180 Magnolia St, Spartanburg, SC 29306; 864-596-2564; fax: 864-596-3622; 8:30AM-5PM. ***Misdemeanor, Civil Actions under $7,500, Eviction, Small Claims.***
Access case details free online at http://192.146.148.40/publicindex/.

Probate Court 180 Magnolia St, Rm 302, Spartanburg, SC 29306-2392; 864-596-2556; fax: 864-596-2011; 8:30AM-5PM. ***Probate.***

Sumter County

Circuit Court 141 N Main, Sumter, SC 29150; 803-436-2227; criminal phone: 803-436-2264/65; civil phone: 803-436-2231; fax: 803-436-2223; 8:30AM-5PM. ***Felony, Misdemeanor, Civil Actions over $7,500.***
www.sumtercountysc.org
Civil Records: Access: Mail, in person, online. Both court and visitors may perform in person searches. Search fee: $10.00 per name. Required to search: name, years to search; also helpful: address. Civil cases indexed by defendant, plaintiff; index on computer from 1987, microfiche and books from 1900s. Mail turnaround time 2 days. Civil PAT goes back to 1986. Civil record index is at www.sumtercountysc.org/publicindex/. Family court records online at the website.
Criminal Records: Access: Mail, in person, online. Both court and visitors may perform in person searches. Search fee: $10.00 per name. Required to search: name, years to search, DOB, SSN, signed release; also helpful: address. Criminal records in books. Mail turnaround time 2 days. Criminal PAT goes back to 1986. Access criminal record index is at www.sumtercountysc.org/publicindex/. Online results show middle initial, DOB, SSN.
General Information: No adoption, juvenile, sealed or expunged records released. Will not fax documents. Court makes copy: $.25 per page. Self serve: same. Certification fee: $5.00. Payee: Sumter County Treasurer. Business checks accepted. No credit cards accepted. Mail requests: SASE required.

Mayesville Magistrate Court PO Box 236, Town Hall, Mayesville, SC 29104; 803-436-2280; Thur Eve. ***Misdemeanor, Civil Actions under $7,500, Eviction, Small Claims.***
Access courts records free at www.sumtercountysc.org/publicindex/. The phone number here is for the main magistrate court; ask for Judge Gibson.

Sumter Magistrate Court 115 N Harvin St, PO Box 1428, Sumter, SC 29151; 803-436-2280; fax: 803-436-2789; 8:30AM-5PM. ***Misdemeanor, Civil Actions under $7,500, Eviction, Small Claims.***
Access courts records free at www.sumtercountysc.org/publicindex/.

Probate Court 141 N Main, Rm 111, Sumter, SC 29150; 803-436-2166; fax: 803-436-2407; 8:30AM-5PM. ***Probate.***
www.sumtercountysc.org/probate.htm

Union County

Circuit Court PO Box 703 (210 W Main St), Union, SC 29379; 864-429-1630; fax: 864-429-1715; 8AM-5PM. ***Felony, Misdemeanor, Civil Actions over $7,500.***
www.countyofunion.com/Clerk.html
The court will mail or fax specific case documents, if case number provided. Fees involved.
Civil Records: Access: In person only. Visitors must perform in person searches themselves. Required to search: name, years to search. Civil cases indexed by defendant, plaintiff. All records on computer. Civil PAT goes back to 1981. PAT results show name, DOB. Terminal results also show SSNs.
Criminal Records: Access: In person only. Visitors must perform in person searches themselves. Required to search: name, years to search; SSN helpful, DOB. Criminal records on computer. Criminal PAT goes back to same as civil.PAT results show name, DOB. Terminal results include SSN.
General Information: No adoption, juvenile, sealed or expunged records released. Will fax documents for fee. Fee depends on amount of pages faxed. Court makes copy: $.50 per page. Self serve: same. Certification fee: $1.00 per page. Payee: Clerk of Court. Personal checks accepted; credit cards are not.

Union Magistrate Court 210 W Main St, Union, SC 29379; 864-429-1648; fax: 864-429-1685; 9AM-5PM. ***Misdemeanor, Civil Actions under $7,500, Eviction, Small Claims.***

This is the only Magistrate court bldg in county. There are 3 part-time magistrates who work out of jails or other county offices at night when required.

Probate Court PO Box 447, 210 W Main St, Union, SC 29379; 864-429-1625; fax: 864-427-1198; 9AM-5PM. ***Probate.***

Williamsburg County

Circuit Court 125 W Main St, Kingstree, SC 29556; 843-355-9321 X552; fax: 843-355-7821; 8AM-5PM. ***Felony, Misdemeanor, Civil Actions over $7,500.***

Civil Records: Access: In person. Both court and visitors may perform in person searches. Search fee: $5.00 per name. Required to search: name, years to search. Civil cases indexed by defendant, plaintiff; index on books, archived from 1980-1989, indexed from 1806; computerized records since 1993. Civil PAT goes back to 1994.

Criminal Records: Access: In person. Both court and visitors may perform in person searches. No search fee. Required to search: name, years to search, DOB; also helpful: SSN. Criminal docket on books, archived from 1980-1989, indexed from 1806; computerized records since 1993. Criminal PAT goes back to 1994.

General Information: No adoption, juvenile, sealed or expunged records released. Will not fax documents. Court makes copy: $.25 per page. Certification fee: $3.00 per instrument. Payee: Clerk of Court. Personal checks accepted. Visa/MC accepted.

Hemingway Magistrate Court 206 E Broad St, Hemingway, SC 29554; 843-558-2116; 9AM-Noon, M & T. ***Misdemeanor, Civil Actions under $7,500, Eviction, Small Claims.***

Nesmith Magistrate Court PO Box 673, 209 Short St, Kingstree, SC 29556; 843-355-9565; fax: 843-355-6444; 8AM-5PM. ***Misdemeanor, Civil Actions under $7,500, Eviction, Small Claims.***

Nesmith Court is closed; Nesmith cases now heard in Kingstree (address and phone given here) or Hemingway Magistrate Court.

Williamsburg County Magistrate Court 209 Short St, Kingstree, SC 29556; 843-355-9565; fax: 843-355-6444; 8AM-5PM. ***Civil Actions under $7,500, Eviction, Small Claims, Ordinance.***

www.williamsburgsc.com/magistrate.html

Probate Court PO Box 1005, 125 W Main, Kingstree, SC 29556; 843-355-9321 x558; fax: 843-355-9305; 8AM-5PM. ***Probate.***

York County

Circuit Court PO Box 649, 1675 - 1G York Hwy, York, SC 29745; 803-684-8506; criminal phone: 803-628-3036; civil phone: 803-684-8507; probate phone: 803-684-8513; 8AM-5PM. ***Felony, Misdemeanor, Civil Actions over $7,500.***

www.yorkcountygov.com/

Civil court located at 2 S Congress St.

Civil Records: Access: Mail, in person, online. Both court and visitors may perform in person searches. Search fee: $5.00 per name. Required to search: name, years to search. Civil cases indexed by defendant, plaintiff; index on computer from 1982, in books from 1932. Mail turnaround time 1 day. Civil PAT goes back to 6/1982. Access court records at http://judicial.yorkcountygov.com/scjdpublicindex/.

Criminal Records: Access: Mail, in person, online. Both court and visitors may perform in person searches. Search fee: $5.00 per name. Required to search: name, years to search, DOB; also helpful: SSN. Criminal records computerized from 2005, in books from 1932. Mail turnaround time 1 day. Criminal PAT goes back to 1983. Access case details free online at http://judicial.yorkcountygov.com/scjdpublicindex/ Online results show middle initial, DOB, SSN.

General Information: No adoption, juvenile, sealed or expunged records released. Will not fax documents. Court makes copy: $.40 per page. Self serve: available for civil only. Certification fee: $1.00. Payee: Clerk of Court. No personal checks or credit cards accepted. Mail requests: SASE required.

Clover Magistrate Court 201 S Main St, Clover, SC 29710; 803-222-9404; fax: 803-222-3653; 8AM-5PM. ***Misdemeanor, Civil Actions under $7,500, Eviction, Small Claims.***

Search Summary Court records online free at http://judicial.yorkcountygov.com/scjdpublicindex/.

Fort Mill Magistrate Court 114 Springs St, Fort Mill, SC 29715; 803-547-5572/5573; fax: 803-547-6344; 8AM-5PM. ***Misdemeanor, Civil Actions under $7,500, Eviction, Small Claims.***

Search Summary Court records online free at http://judicial.yorkcountygov.com/scjdpublicindex/.

Hickory Grove Magistrate Court PO Box 37, 5800 Wylie Ave, Hickory Grove, SC 29717; 803-925-2815; 9AM-N, T,3-5PM W, TH, Fri. ***Misdemeanor, Civil Actions under $7,500, Eviction, Small Claims.***

Search Summary Court records online free at http://judicial.yorkcountygov.com/scjdpublicindex/.

Rock Hill Magistrate Court 529 S Cherry Rd, Rock Hill, SC 29730; 803-909-7600; fax: 803-909-7606; 9AM-5:30PM. ***Misdemeanor, Civil Actions under $7,500, Eviction, Small Claims.***

Search Summary Court records online free at http://judicial.yorkcountygov.com/scjdpublicindex/.

York Magistrate Court 1675 York Hwy, York, SC 29745; 803-628-3029; fax: 803-628-3225; 8AM-5PM. ***Misdemeanor, Civil Actions under $7,500, Eviction, Small Claims.***

Search Summary Court records online free at http://judicial.yorkcountygov.com/scjdpublicindex/.

Probate Court PO Box 219, 1 E Liberty St, York, SC 29745; 803-684-8513 X8630; fax: 803-684-8536; 8AM-5PM. ***Probate***

South Carolina Recording Offices

ORGANIZATION: 46 counties, 46 recording offices. The recording officer is either the Register of Mesne Conveyances or Clerk of Court; this varies by county. South Carolina is Eastern Time Zone (EST)

REAL ESTATE RECORDS: Most counties will not perform real estate searches. Copy and certification fees vary. The Assessor keeps tax records.

UCC RECORDS: Financing statements are filed at the state level except for real estate related collateral which are filed with the Register. However, prior to July, 2001, consumer goods and farm collateral were also filed at the Register and these older records can be searched there. At the few recording offices who perform UCC searches, the search fee is usually $5.00 per debtor.

TAX LIEN RECORDS: All federal and state tax liens on personal property and on real property are filed with the Register of Mesne Conveyances or Clerk of Court. A few counties will perform tax lien searches.

ONLINE ACCESS: A number of locations offer free record data via their websites. There is statewide system for lookups on the UCC index.

Abbeville County

Clerk of Court, PO Box 99, Abbeville, SC 29620. 864-366-5312 x200, R/E recording phone-864-366-5312 x203; fax-864-366-9188; 8:30AM-5PM www.abbevillecountysc.com

Index: Separate indices to search. Record index not computerized. Only the public may search. Copy fee $.25 per page. Mailed copies $1.00 per page. Cert fee- $.25 per page. Payee- Abbeville Clerk of Court. Bulk data available for purchase, contact Ann Abaer. **Other phones:** Treasurer- 864-366-5312 x218; Elections- 864-366-5312 x108; Vital Records- 864-366-5312 x102. **Property tax/Assessing**- PO Box 993, 102 Court Sq, Abbeville, SC 29620; 864-366-5312 x102, assessor fax- 864-366-8988. (Appraiser/Auditor- 864-366-5312 x220) A public access terminal is available.

Aiken County

County Register of Mense Conveyances, PO Box 537, Aiken, SC 29802-0537. Recording, R/E phone-803-642-2072, UCC recording phone-803-642-2075; 8:30AM-5PM www.aikencountysc.gov

Index: All in one. Records indexed on a public use terminal back to 1982. Only the public may search. Copy fee $.50 per page; self serve $.25. Cert fee- $1.00 per cert plus copy fee. Payee- Aiken County Register of Mesne Conveyances. **Online access to Real Estate, Deed, Mortgage, Plat, Comparable Sale records:** Access to the county e-services are free at www.aikencountysc.gov/eGovDisclaimer1.cfm but not all modules allow name searching. For full data and name searching, registration and fees are required, $25 per month, $10 if county resident. Registration and password required for Property Cards and Comparable Sales. Also, access to property and deeds indexes and images is via a private company at www.titlesearcher.com. Fee/registration required. Deeds and index goes back to 1/1982; images back to 6/13/2005. **Other phones:** Treasurer- 803-642-2055; Elections- 803-642-2028. **Property tax/Assessing**- PO Box 518, 828 Richland Ave W, Aiken, SC 29802; 803-642-1583, assessor fax- 803-642-1577. (Appraiser/Auditor- 803-642-1583) www.aikencountysc.gov/DspOfc.cfm?qOfcID=ASR **Online access**- Search assessor property data free at http://cxap2.aikencountysc.gov/EGSV2Aiken/RPSearch.do but no name searching.

Allendale County

Clerk of Court, PO Box 126, Allendale, SC 29810. 803-584-2737; fax-803-584-7046; 9AM-5PM

Index: All in one. (Divorce records located here) Records indexed on computer back to 1987. Only office personnel may search. Search fee $5.00 per name. Office will not search real estate records. Copy fee $.50 per page; real estate $.25. Cert fee- $2.00 per page includes copy fee. Payee- Allendale Clerk of Court. **Other phones:** Treasurer- 803-584-3876. **Property tax/Assessing**- 292 Barnwell Hwy, Allendale, SC 29810; 803-584-2572.

Anderson County

Register of Deeds, PO Box 8002, Anderson, SC 29622. 864-260-4054; fax-864-260-4443; 8:30AM-5PM www.andersoncountysc.org

Index: Separate indices to search include land, specials, UCC. Records indexed on a public use terminal back to 1985. Only the public may search. General copy fee $.50 per page. Microfilm/Microfiche- $1.00 per page. Cert fee- $1.00 per doc plus copy fee. Payee- Register. **Online access to Real Estate, Deed records:** Access to the county ACPASS super search site is free at http://acpass.andersoncountysc.org. **Other phones:** Treasurer- 864-260-4033; Elections- 864-260-4035; County Operator -864-260-4444. **Property tax/ Assessing**- 100 S Main St, Courthouse, Anderson, SC 29622; 864-260-4028, assessor fax- 864-260-4099. **Online access**- Search the Property Viewer free at http://gisserve.andersoncountysc.org/propertyviewer/ but no name searching. Access property tax and vehicle tax and other data free at http://acpass.andersoncountysc.org/welcome.shtml.

Bamberg County

Clerk of Court, PO Box 150, Bamberg, SC 29003. Recording, R/E phone-803-245-3025; fax-803-245-3088; 9AM-5PM.

Index: Separate indices to search include deeds, mortgages, Lis Pendens, judgments, fed tax, other liens. Records indexed on computer from 7/1/07 to present. Only the public may search. Separate federal tax lien search- $5.00 per debtor. Copy fee $.25 per page. Cert fee- $5.00 per doc plus copy fee. Payee- Clerk of Court. **Other phones:** Treasurer- 803-245-3003; Elections- 803-245-3028; Auditor- 803-245-3006. **Property tax/Assessing**- PO Box 511, Bamberg, SC 29003; 803-245-3010, assessor fax- 803-245-3010. (Appraiser/Auditor- 803-245-3010).

Barnwell County

Clerk of Court, PO Box 723, Barnwell, SC 29812-0723. 803-541-1020; fax-803-541-1025; 9AM-5PM.

Index: All in one. Records indexed on a public use terminal back to 1980. Only the public may search. Copy fee $.50 per page. Cert fee- $1.00 per page plus copy fee. Payee- Clerk of Court. **Other phones:** Treasurer- 803-541-1050. **Property tax/ Assessing**- PO Box 723, 57 Wall St, Rm 221, Barnwell, 29812; 803-541-1011, fax- 803-541-1046.

Beaufort County

Register of Deeds, PO Box 1197, Beaufort, SC 29901. Recording, R/E phone-843-470-2700, UCC recording phone-843-470-2715; fax-843-470-2709; 8AM-5PM. www.bcgov.net

Index: All in one. Records indexed on a public use terminal back to 1981. Office personnel or visitors may perform searches. Search fee-$5.00 per name. Office will search real estate records for a fee. Will not search UCC records. Copy fee- $.50 per page. Cert fee- $1.00 per doc plus copy fee. Payee- Register of Deeds. **Online access to Real Estate, Deed, Lien records:** Access to the public records search database is free at www.bcgov.net/. **Other phones:** Treasurer- 843-470-2766; Elections- 843-470-3753. **Property tax/Assessing**- PO Box 458, 102 Ribaut Rd, Beaufort, SC 29901; 843-470-2513, assessor fax- 843-470-2512. www.bcgov.net/BC_Assessor/ **Online** - Search assessor data free at www.bcgov.net/RealProperty/New_RealProp/Welcome.php.

Berkeley County

Register of Deeds, PO Box 6122, Moncks Corner, SC 29461. 843-719-4084; fax-843-719-4851; 9AM-5PM. www.co.berkeley.sc.us

Index: Separate indices to search include conveyances, mortgages, tax liens, plats, UCCs. Records indexed on a public use terminal back to 1997. Only the public may search. Copy fee $.35 per page. Print fee determined by machine used. Cert fee- $2.00 per cert plus copy fee. Payee- Berkeley County Register of Deeds. **Online access to Real Estate, Deed, UCC, Lien, Plat, Property Sale records:** Access real estate data at http://server1.co.berkeley.sc.us/esrvmain.html. View comparable sales online. Also, search the clerks document database free at www.sclandrecords.com/sclr/controller. Also, access property records on a private site at www.landaccess.com and click on SC-Berkeley. Records go back to 1/2/1997. **Other phones:** Treasurer- 843-761-3800. **Property tax/Assessing**- PO Box 6122, 1003 Hwy 52, Moncks Corner, SC 29461; 843-761-6900 x4061, assessor fax- 843-719-4271. **Online access**- Search assessor data free at http://server1.co.berkeley.sc.us/EGSBKLY/RPSearch.do. Search personal property and vehicle tax data free at http://server1.co.berkeley.sc.us/esrvmain.html

Calhoun County

Clerk of Court, 902 FR Huff Dr, St. Matthews, SC 29135. 803-874-3524; fax-803-874-1942; 9AM-5PM

Index: All in one. Records indexed on a public use terminal back to 2004. Only the public may search. Copy fee $.25 per page. Cert fee- None. Payee- Calhoun County Treasurer. **Online access to Real Estate, Deed records:** Access to property and deeds indexes and images is via a private company at www.titlesearcher.com. Fee/registration required. Images and indices go back to 8/2004. **Other phones:** Treasurer- 803-874-3519. **Property tax/Assessing**- Court Annex, Rm 107, St. Matthews, SC 29135; 803-874-3613.

Charleston County

Register Mense Conveyances, PO Box 726, Charleston, SC 29402. 843-958-4800; fax-843-958-4803; 8:30AM-5PM. www.charlestoncounty.org Central online search page at www.charlestoncounty.org/publicrecords.htm. Index: Separate indices to search include day book (same day recording), deed, mortgage, misc. Records indexed on a public use terminal back to 1978. Only the public may search. Copy fee $.25 per page. Cert fee- $5.00

per cert plus copy. Payee- Register Mesne Conveyances. **Online access to Real Estate, Deed, Mortgage, Lien, UCC, Plat, Judgment, Marriage, Probate, Will/Estate, Business License records:** Access RMC recording data free at http://www2.charlestoncounty.org - land records go back to 2/1997. Search judgments- http://www3.charlestoncounty.org/connect?ref=MIE. Marriages- http://www3.charlestoncounty.org/connect/LU_GROUP_2?ref=Marriage. Search probate, wills, guardianships free- http://www3.charlestoncounty.org/connect/LU_GROUP_2?ref=Conserv. Business licenses- http://www3.charlestoncounty.org/surfer/group3?s=b. **Other phones:** Treasurer- 843-958-4360; Elections- 843-745-2226; Vital Records- 843-740-0801. **Property tax/Assessing**- PO Box 427, 101 Meeting St, 1st Fl, Charleston, SC 29402; 843-958-4100, assessor fax- 843-958-4182. **Online access**- Access auditor & treasurer's tax system free at http://taxweb.charlestoncounty.org. Access the county's GIS mapping database of property records free at http://gisweb.charlestoncounty.org.

Cherokee County

Clerk of Court, PO Drawer 2289, Gaffney, SC 29342. -864-487-2571; fax-864-487-2754; 8:30AM-5PM http://delisac.web.aplus.net/cherokeecountysouthcarolina/

Index: All in one. Records indexed on a public use terminal back to 1994. Only the public may search. Copy fee $.50 per page. Cert fee- $1.00 per cert plus copy fee. Payee- Cherokee Clerk of Court. **Other phones:** Treasurer- 864-487-2551; Elections- 864-487-2563; Vital Records- 864-487-2571. **Property tax/Assessing**- 312 N Limestone St, Gaffney, SC 29340; 864-487-2552, assessor fax- 864-487-2555. http://delisac.web.aplus.net/cherokeecountysouthcarolina/id26.html

Chester County

Clerk of Court, PO Drawer 580, Chester, SC 29706. 803-385-2605; fax-803-581-7975; 9AM-5PM

Records indexed on a public use terminal back to 1985. Only the public may search. Copy fee $.25 per page. Cert fee- $1.00 per doc plus copy fee. Payee- Clerk of Court. **Other phones:** Treasurer- 803-385-2608. **Property tax/Assessing**- 803-377-4177.

Chesterfield County

Clerk of Court, PO Box 529, Chesterfield, SC 29709. Recording, R/E phone-843-623-2574, UCC phone-843-623-7853; fax-843-623-6944; 8:30AM-5PM.

Index: Separate indices to search include Tax lien, Mental health lien, Common Plea, Mech Lien, Lis Penden, Judgment, General Session. Records indexed on a public use terminal back to 1996. Office will perform a UCC search with required form but public must search other records themselves. Copy fee $2.00 per document if clerk makes, $.25 per page self serve. Cert fee- None. Payee- Clerk of Court. **Other phones:** Treasurer- 843-623-2563; Elections- 843-623-2265; Vital Records- 843-623-2117. **Property tax/Assessing**- 200 W Main St, Chesterfield, SC 29709; 843-623-7362, assessor fax- 843-623-5043. (Appraiser/Auditor- 843-623-7362) A public access terminal available.

Clarendon County

Clerk of Court-Register of Deeds, PO Box 36, Manning, SC 29102. Recording, R/E phone-803-435-4444; fax-803-435-8258; 8:30AM-5PM.

Index: Separate indices to search. Records indexed on a public use terminal back to 1988. Office will perform a UCC search but public must search other records themselves. Copy fee $.25 per page. Cert fee- $2.00 per 4 pages; $.25 each add'l page; all copies must be certified. Payee- Register of Deeds Office. **Other phones:** Treasurer- 803-435-8307; Elections- 803-435-8215. **Property tax/Assessing**- 35 W Boyce St, PO Box 367, Manning, SC 29102; 803-435-4423, assessor fax- 803-435-8905. hours- 8L30AM-5PM

Colleton County

Register of Deeds, PO Box 157, Walterboro, SC 29488-0028. 843-542-2745; fax-843-542-2749; 8AM-5PM. www.colletoncounty.org/secondary.aspx?pageID=116

Index: Separate indices to search include land, UCCs, specials indexes. Records indexed on a public use terminal back to 1986 for lands; 7/1995 for specials; 7/1994 thru 8/1/2001 for UCCs. Only the public may search. Copy fee $1.50 1st page; $.50 each add'l page if to mail, $.25 in person. Cert fee- $1.00 per doc plus copy fee. Payee- Clerk of Court. **Other phones:** Treasurer- 843-549-2233; Elections- 843-549-2842; Vitals- 843-549-1516. **Property tax/Assessing**- PO Box 1166, 31 Klein St/Harrelson Bldg, Rm 307, Walterboro, SC 29488; 843-549-1213, assessor fax-843-549-6185. A public access terminal is available. **Online**- Access property and vehicle tax data free at www.colletoncounty.org/secondary.aspx?pageID=114.

Darlington County

Clerk of Court, PO Box 1177, Darlington, SC 29540. Recording, R/E phone-843-398-4330; fax-843-393-6871; 8:30AM-5PM www.darcosc.com

Index: All in one. Records indexed on a public use terminal back to 1989. Only the public may search. Copy fee $1.00 per page. Self serve $.25 per page. Treasurer- 843-398-4160. **Property tax/Assessing**- #1 Public Sq, Darlington, SC 29540; 843-398-4180. **Online access**- Access property records free at www.darcosc.com/assessor/disclaimer.asp. Lookup tax records at www.darcosc.com/OnlineTaxes/.

Dillon County

Clerk of Court, PO Drawer 1220, Dillon, SC 29536. 843-774-1425; fax-843-841-3706; 8:30AM-5PM

Index: More than one index. Records indexed on computer back to 1982. Office personnel or visitors may perform searches. Search fee $10.00. Office will not search UCC records. Copy fee $.50 per page. Cert fee- None. Payee- Dillon Clerk of Court. **Other phones:** Treasurer- 843-774-1416; Elections- 843-774-1403; Vital Records- 843-774-5611; Auditor-843-774-1418; Probate -8437741423. **Property tax/Assessing**- 843-774-1412. (Appraiser/Auditor-843-774-1412)

Dorchester County

Register of Deeds, PO Box 38, St. George, SC 29477. 843-563-0181, R/E recording phone-843-832-0181, UCC recording phone-843-832-0277; fax-843-563-0182; 8:30AM-5PM. www.dorchestercounty.net

Index: Separate indices to search include grantor/grantee, mortgagor/mortgagee, plat, state tax lien, federal tax lien, UCC, mechanics lien. Records indexed on a public use terminal back to 6/1/94. Only the public may search. Copy fee $.50 per page. Oversized copies of plats $5.00. Cert fee- $5.00 per cert plus copy fee. Payee- Dorchester County Register of Deeds. **Online Real Estate, Deed records:** Access to Register of Deeds real estate records is free at www.dorchestercounty.net/RMC/RMCMain.aspx. A subscription fee may apply in the future. **Other phones:** Treasurer- 843-563-0165; Elections- 843-563-0132; Vital Records- 843-563-0107. **Property tax/Assessing**- 201 Johnson St, St. George, SC 29477; 843-563-0162, assessor fax- 843-563-0174. www.dorchestercounty.net/assessor.htm **Online access**- Search tax and property records free on GIS-site at http://gisweb.dorchestercounty.net/imap/.

Edgefield County

Clerk of Court, PO Box 34, Edgefield, SC 29824. 803-637-4080, R/E phone-803-637-4049; fax-803-637-4117; 8:30-5PM. www.edgefieldcounty.sc.gov

Index: Separate indices to search include grantor/grantee, mortgage/mortgagee, direct/indirect Misc. Records indexed on a public use terminal back to 6/1/95. Office will perform a UCC search but public must search other records themselves. Copy fee $.50 per page. Cert fee- $1.00 per doc plus copy fee. Payee- Registrar of Deeds. **Online access to Real Estate, Grantor/Grantee, Deed, Liens (2006), UCC records:** Access county land record index and images free at www.landaccess.com. **Other phones:** Treasurer- 803-637-4069; Elections- 803-637-4072. **Property tax/Assessing**- 129 Courthouse Sq, #109, Edgefield, SC 29824; 803-637-4066, assessor fax-803-637-4119. (Appraiser/Auditor- 803-637-4057) **Online access**- Access property assessor data free at www.edgefieldcountysc.com/search.aspx.

Fairfield County

Clerk of Court, PO Drawer 299, Winnsboro, SC 29180. 803-712-6526; fax-803-712-1506; 9AM-5PM www.fairfieldsc.com/secondary.aspx?pageID=123

Index: Separate indices to search include deeds, mortgages, liens, lis pendens. Records indexed on a public use terminal back to 1985 for land records and back to 7/2003 for liens and LP. Only the public may search. Copy fee $.25 per page. Cert fee- $1.00 per cert plus copy fee. Payee- Fairfield Clerk of Court. **Other phones:** Treasurer- 803-712 6517. **Property tax/Assessing**- 101 S Congress St, Courthouse, Winnsboro, SC 29180; 803-712-6520. www.fairfieldsc.com/secondary.aspx?pageID=129 **Online access**- Search property/GIS data free at www.emapsplus.com/SCFairfield/maps/.

Florence County

Clerk of Court, MSC-E City/County Complex, Florence, SC 29501. 843-665-3031; fax-843-665-3097; 8:30AM-5PM http://web.florenceco.org

Index: All in one. Records indexed on a public use terminal back to 1984. Only the public may search. Copy fee $1.00 per page. Cert fee- None. Payee- Florence County. **Online Real Estate, Grantor/Grantee, Deed, Lien, Judgment records:** Access recorder data free at http://web.florenceco.org/cgi-bin/coc/coc.cgi. **Other phones:** Treasurer- 843-665-3041; Elections- 843-665-2351. **Property tax/Assessing**- 180 N Irby St, MSC-A, Florence, SC 29501; 843-665-3056, assessor fax- 843-676-1100. **Online access**- Access property tax records free at http://web.florenceco.org/cgi-bin/ta/tax-inq.cgi. Also, access vehicle tax records free at http://web.florenceco.org/cgi-bin/ta/vehinq.cgi.

Georgetown County

Register of Deeds, PO Box 421270, Georgetown, SC 29442. Recording, R/E phone-843-545-3088; 8:30AM-5PM www.georgetowncountysc.org

Index: Separate indices to search include deeds, mortgages, tax liens, plats, misc liens. Records indexed on a public use terminal back to 1977 for deeds, to 700 for mortgages. Only the public may search. Will not search UCC records. Copy fee $.50 per page. UCC record copy fee- $1.00 per page. Cert fee- $1.00 per cert plus copy fee. Payee- Georgetown County Register of Deeds. **Online access to Real Estate, Deed, UCC records:** Access the Register's database free at www.landaccess.com. Click on SC-Georgetown. Index goes back to 1/1977 for deeds, 7/1986 for mortgages, 1/1989 for UCC, 7/1989 for tax liens and 7/2002 for misc liens. **Other phones:** Treasurer- 843-545-3098; Elections- 843-545-3339; Vitals- 843-546-0174. **Property tax/Assessing**- PO Box 421270, Georgetown, SC 29442; 843-545-3014, assessor fax- 843-545-3156. hours- 8AM-6PM www.georgetowncountysc.org/assessor/default.html **Online access**- Access property data on the GIS-mapping site free at http://gismap.georgetowncountysc.org/viewer.htm. Click on the binoculars to get to the name search feature.

Greenville County

Register of Deeds, 301 University Ridge, #1300; County Sq, Greenville, SC 29601-3655. Recording, R/E phone-864-467-7240, UCC recording phone-864-467-7180; fax-864-467-7107; 8:30AM-5PM www.greenvillecounty.org

Index: All in one. Records indexed on a public use terminal back to 1990. Only the public may search. Copy fee $.25 per page. Cert fee- $1.00 per doc plus copy fee. Payee- Register of Deeds. **Online access to**

Real Estate, Deed records: Search the Register of Deeds database free at www.greenvillecounty.org. Click on Register of Deeds Search. Index goes back to 1990, images to 2004. **Other phones:** Treasurer- 864-467-7210. **Property tax/Assessing**- 301 University Ridge #800, Greenville County Sq, Greenville, SC 29601; 864-467-7040. www.greenvillecounty.org/County_Auditor/ **Online access**- Search the property tax and vehicles data at www.greenvillecounty.org/voTaxQry/wcmain.asp. Also, search real estate data at www.greenvillecounty.org/vrealpr24/clrealprop.asp. No name searching.

Greenwood County

Clerk of Court, 528 Monument St, #114; Courthouse, Greenwood, SC 29646. Recording, R/E phone-864-942-8613, UCC phone-864-942-8547; fax-864-942-8693; 8:30AM-5PM www.co.greenwood.sc.us

Index: Separate indices to search include computer and hard copy. Records indexed on a public use terminal back to 1980; judgments back to 2000. Only the public may search. Copy fee $.25 per page. Plat copies are $1-$2 per page. Cert fee- $2.00 per cert plus copy fee. Payee- Greenwood Clerk of Court. **Online Real Estate, Grantor/Grantee, Deed, Mortgage, Lien, Judgment records:** document search for free a www.co.greenwood.sc.us/clerk.aspx or http://gis.greenwoodsc.gov/docsearch/default.aspx. **Other phones:** Treasurer- 864-942-8528; Elections-864-942-8521; Family Court- 864-943-8081; General Phone -864-942-8551. **Property tax/Assessing**- 528 Monument St, Rm 109, Greenwood Sc 29646; 864-942-8536. (Appraiser/Auditor- 864-942-8534) **Online access**- Search Property Tax, Personal Property, Tax Collector data free at www.greenwoodsc.gov/search.aspx.

Hampton County

Clerk of Court, PO Box 7, Hampton, SC 29924. Recording, R/E phone-803-943-7510; fax-803-943-7596; 8AM-5PM

At above address because of courthouse renovation for 1 year. Old address was 1 Elm St, Courthouse Sq #1, Hampton, SC 29924. Index: Separate indices to search include deeds, mortgages, liens, plats, misc. Records indexed on a public use terminal back to 2000. Only the public may search. Copy fee $.25 per page. Cert fee- $1.00 per doc includes copy fee. Payee- Clerk of Court. **Other phones:** Treasurer-803-914-2119; Elections- 803-943-7536; Vital Records- 803-943-3878. **Property tax/Assessing**- PO Box 652, Hampton, SC 29924; 803-943-7507, fax-803-943-7546. (Appraiser/Auditor- 803-914-2115);

Horry County

Register of Deeds, PO Box 470, Conway, SC 29528. 843-915-5000, R/E phone-843-915-5430; fax-843-915-6430; 8-5 www.horrycounty.org/hcgPortal.asp

Index: Separate indices to search include deeds, mortgages, tax liens, condo liens, mechanic liens. Records indexed on computer back to 1984. Only the public may search. Copy fee $8.00 for 1-4 pages, $1.00 each add'l; $1.00 per page self serve. Cert fee- $2.00 per cert plus copy fee. Payee- Register of Deeds. **Online access to Real Estate, Deed, Lien records:** Access the recorders database free at www.horrycounty.org/gateway/disclaimer/idx_rod.html. **Other phones:** Treasurer- 843-915-5470; Elections- 843-915-5440; Vital Records- 843-248-3958; Register of Deeds Main Switchboard- 843-915-5430. **Property tax/Assessing**- 1301 2nd Ave, #1C08, Conway, SC 29526; 843-915-5040, assessor fax- 849-915-6040. (Appraiser/Auditor- 843-915-5050) **Online** - Search real property database free at www.horrycounty.org/gateway/disclaimer/idx_real.html.

Jasper County

Register of Deeds, PO Box 836, Ridgeland, SC 29936. 843-726-4164, R/E recording phone-843-726-7755; fax- 843-726-4207; hours - 9AM-5PM www.jaspercountysc.org

Effective 2006, the Register of Deeds handles land recordings; this had been performed by the Clerk of Court. Index: All in one. Records indexed on a public use terminal back to 1994. Office personnel or visitors may perform searches. Office will only perform a limited real estate name search. Office will only search UCCs back 5 years. Copy fee $1.00 per page. Cert fee- $2.00 per doc plus copy fee. Payee- Jasper County ROD. **Online access to Real Estate, Grantor/Grantee, Deed, Mortgage, Lien, Judgment records:** Access to recorders data is free via a private company website at http://counties.recordfusion.com/countyweb/login.jsp?countyname=Jasper. Liens and judgments go back to 2006. Logon as Guest to search free. **Other phones:** Treasurer- 843-726-7722; Elections- 843-726-7709; Vital Records- 843-726-7790. **Property tax/Assessing**- PO Box 807, 265 Russell St, Ridgeland, SC 29936; 843-726-7732, assessor fax-843-726-7731. (Appraiser/Auditor- 843-726-7725) www.jaspercountysc.org/secondary.aspx?pageID=87

Kershaw County

Register of Deeds, 515 Walnut St, #180, Camden, SC 29020. 803-425-1500, R/E recording phone-803-425-1500 x5365/5367/5434, UCC phone-803-425-1500 x5367/5365/5434; fax-803-425-7673; 8:30AM-5PM www.kershaw.sc.gov/Index.aspx?page=148

Index: Separate indices to search include grantor/grantee, mortgagor/mortgagee, plats-owner, UCCs-debtor/lender, specials-state & federal tax liens-name. Records indexed on a public use terminal back to 12/1990. Only the public may search. Copy fee $.50 per page. Cert fee- $1.00 per doc plus copy fee. Payee- Kershaw Register of Deeds. Assessor's Office sells CD's. **Other phones:** Treasurer- 803-425-1500 x5314; Elections- 803-424-4016/ 424-4017; Vital Records- 803-425-6012. **Property tax/Assessing**- 515 Walnut St, Rm 100, Camden, SC 29020; 803-425-1500 x5332, assessor fax- 803-425-7673. (Appraiser/Auditor- 803-425-1500 x5327) A public access terminal available. **Online access**- Access to property/vehicle tax for free go to www.kershawcountysctax.com/

Lancaster County

Register of Deeds, 101 N Main St, Lancaster, SC 29720. 803-416-9440; fax-803-416-9388; 8:30AM-5:00PM www.lancastercountysc.net

Index: Separate indices to search include Lis Pendens, judgments. Records indexed on computer back to 1980s. Only the public may search. Copy fee $.25 per page. Cert fee- $2.00 per page plus copy fee. Payee- Clerk of Court. **Online access to Real Estate, Deed records:** Access to property and deeds indexes and images is via a private company at www.titlesearcher.com. Fee/registration required. Indices and images go back to 8/27/2002. **Other phones:** Treasurer- 803-285-7939; Elections- 803-285-2969; Vital Records- 803-286-9948. **Property tax/Assessing**- PO Box 1809, 101 N Main St (29720), Lancaster, SC 29721; 803-285-6964, assessor fax- 803-285-3361. **Online** - Access property data free at www.lancastercountysc.net/onlinetaxes/.

Laurens County

Clerk of Court, PO Box 287, Laurens, SC 29360. 864-984-3538; fax-864-984-7023; 9AM-5PM

Index: All in one. Records indexed on computer back to 1986; liens go back to 1993. Only the public may search. Copy fee $1.00 per page.Real estate record copy- $.50 per page. Cert fee- $1.00 per cert plus copy fee. Payee- Laurens Clerk of Court. **Online access to Real Estate, Deed, Treasurer records:** Access to property and deeds indexes and images is via a private company at www.titlesearcher.com. Fee/registration required. Deed records go back to 7/1991; indices back to 6/1/1996; images to 8/26/2006. **Other phones:** Treasurer- 864-984-4742. **Property tax/Assessing**- 864-984-6546. **Online access**- Access property data free at www.laurenscountysctaxes.com.

Lee County

Register of Deeds, PO Box 387, Bishopville, SC 29010. 803-484-5341, R/E recording phone-803-484-5341 x333, UCC recording phone-803-484-5341 x378; fax-803-484-1632; 9AM-5PM.

Index: Separate indices to search. Records indexed on a public use terminal back to 07/94. Only the public may search. Copy fee $.50 per page. Cert fee- $1.00 per doc plus copy fee. Payee- Register of Deeds. **Other phones:** Treasurer- 803-484-5341 x327; Elections- 803-484-5341 x310, 324; GIS/Mapping-Diane G Boykin- 803-484-5341 x355. **Property tax/Assessing**- PO Box 309, 123 Main St, Courthouse, Bishopville, SC 29010-0568; 803-484-5341 x353, assessor fax- 803-484-3518. (Appraiser/Auditor- 803-484-5341 x379, 369) hours-9AM-N, 1PM-5PM

Lexington County

Register of Deeds, 212 S Lake Dr, #301, Lexington, SC 29072. 803-785-8168; fax-803-785-8189; 8AM-5PM www.lex-co.com/Departments/RegisterOfDeeds/Index.html

Index: Separate indices to search include grantor/grantee, UCC, mortgage, plats, original mortgagor. Records indexed on a public use terminal back to 8/1/84. Only the public may search. Copy fee $.50 per page. Cert fee- $1.00 per doc plus copy fee. Payee- County of Lexington. **Online access to Real Estate, Deed, Lien, Mortgage, UCC records:** Access Register of Deeds records free at www.lex-co.com/Departments/RegisterOfDeeds/OnlineServices.html. **Other phones:** Treasurer- 803-785-8217; Customer Service- 803-785-8168; Recording Questions -803-785-8470. **Property tax/Assessing**- 212 S Lake Dr, Lexington, SC 29072; 803-785-8190, fax- 803-785-8249. www.lex-co.com/Departments/Assessor/Index.html **Online access**- Access property and tax data free at www.lex-co.com/GIS/Services.html which includes sales, parcel, property cards, mobile homes, and auto tax.

Marion County

Clerk of Court, PO Box 295, Marion, SC 29571. Recording, R/E phone-843-423-8240; fax-843-423-8306; 8:30AM-5PM

Index: Separate indices to search include real estate and tax liens. Records indexed on a public use terminal back to 1/98. Only the public may search. Copy fee $.25 per page. Cert fee- $1.00 per page plus copy fee. Payee- Marion Clerk of Court. Treasurer-843-423-8230. **Property tax/Assessing**- PO Box 429, 100 W Court St, Marion, SC 29571; 843-423-8227, assessor fax- 843-423-8224. A public access terminal available.

Marlboro County

Clerk of Court, PO Drawer 996, Bennettsville, SC 29512. 843-479-5613; fax-843-479-5640; 8:30AM-5PM www.marlborocounty.sc.gov

Index: All in one. Records indexed on a public use terminal back to 1995. Only the public may search. Copy fee $1.00 per page.Real estate record copy- $.20 per page. Cert fee- $2.00 per cert plus copy fee. Payee- Marlboro Clerk of Court. Treasurer- 843-479-5603; Elections- 843-479-5612. **Property tax/Assessing**- 105 Main St, 2nd Fl, Courthouse, Bennettsville, SC 29512; 843-479-5602, assessor fax-843-479-5660. www.marlborocounty.sc.gov

McCormick County

Clerk of Court, 133 S Mine St, Rm 102; Courthouse, McCormick, SC 29835. 864-852-2195; fax-864-852-0071; 9AM-5PM (EST/EDT)

Index: Separate indices to search include grantor/grantee, Mtgr/Mtge, Judgmnts, Lis Pendens, St &Fed liens, Misc. Record index not computerized. Only the public may search. Will not search UCC records. Copy fee $.50 per page. Cert fee- $1.00 per cert plus copy fee. Payee- Clerk of Court. **Other phones:** Treasurer- 864-852-2332; Elections- 864-852-2089; Vital Records- 864-852-2511; Property Appraiser- 864-852-2931. **Property tax/Assessing-**

PO Box 836, McCormick, SC 29835; 864-852-2931, assessor fax- 864-852-2930. (Appraiser/Auditor- 864-852-2107) A public access terminal available.

Newberry County

Court Clerk, PO Drawer 10, Newberry, SC 29108. Recording, R/E phone-803-321-2110; fax-803-321-2111; 8:30AM-5PM www.newberrycounty.net/
Index: Separate indices to search include land records back to 1983. Records indexed on a public use terminal back to 1990. Office personnel or visitors may perform searches. Search fee- none. Real estate search requests must be in writing; no guarantee on turnaround time. Office will not search UCC records. Copy fee $.20 per page. Cert fee- $1.20. Payee- Newberry County Clerk. **Other phones:** Treasurer- 803-321-2130; Elections- 803-321-2121; Vitals- 803-321-2170. **Property tax/Assessing**- PO Box 362, 1226 College St, Newberry, SC 29108; 803-321-2125, fax- 803-321-2126. www.newberrycounty.net **Online access**- Access to assessor database is free at www.newberrycounty.net/assessor/Index.html.
Access to auditor's property data is free at www.newberrycounty.net/auditor/Index.html. Access to auditor and treasurer property tax data is free at www.newberrycountysctaxes.com/.

Oconee County

Register of Deeds, 415 S Pine St, Walhalla, SC 29691. Recording, R/E phone-864-638-4285; fax-864-638-4287; 8:30AM-5PM www.oconeesc.com
Index: Separate indices to search include deeds, mortgages, tax liens, mechanics liens, assessments. Records indexed on a public use terminal back to 1957 for deeds, 1992 for mortgages. Only the public may search. General copy fee $5.00 for 4 pages; $.50 each add'l.Real estate record copy- $.50 per page. Cert fee- $1.00. Payee- Register of Deeds. **Online access to Land, Deed, Mortgage, Plat records:** Access recorder's index search free at www.oconeesc.com/resolution/default.asp. Deeds go back to 1957; Plats and mortgages to 1992. **Other phones:** Treasurer- 864-638-4162. **Property tax/Assessing**- 415 S Pine St, Walhalla, SC 29691; 864-638-4150, assessor fax- 864-638-4156. www.oconeesc.com/assessor/index.html **Online access**- Access county parcel data complete for free at www.oconeesc.com/gis/indexn.html and click on pdf.

Orangeburg County

Register of Deeds, PO Box 9000, Orangeburg, SC 29116-9000. 803-533-6236, R/E recording phone-803-533-6238, UCC phone-803-533-6236; fax-803-535-2354; 8:30AM-5PM www.orangeburgscrod.org
Index: Separate indices to search include deed, mortgage, plat. Records indexed on computer back to 1989. Only the public may search. Copy fee $.50 per page, self serve $.25 per page. Cert fee- No fee for certification. Payee- Register of Deeds. Bulk data available for purchase, contact Gail Laney at 803-533-6235. **Online access to Property, Deed, Mortgage, UCC, Plat records:** Access free deeds, mortgages and plat records back to 1989 at www.orangeburgscrod.org/Opening.asp. **Other phones:** Treasurer- 803-533-6130; Elections- 803-533-6213; Vital Records- 803-533-6239. **Property tax/Assessing**- PO Box 9000, Admin Bldg on Amelia St, Orangeburg, SC 29116-9000; 803-533-6220, fax-803-533-6223. (Appraiser/Auditor- 803-533-6229) www.orangeburgcounty.org/assessor/DefaultTACT.htm **Online access**- Access to county property tax records is free at www.orangeburgcounty.org/Assessor/main.asp.

Pickens County

Register of Deeds, 222 McDaniel Ave, #B-5, Pickens, SC 29671. 864-898-5868; fax-864-898-5924; 8AM-5PM www.co.pickens.sc.us/regofdeeds/
Index: Separate indices to search include grantor/grantee, mortgagor/mortgagee, plat, liens. Records indexed on a public use terminal back to 1986. Only the public may search. Copy fee per page- $.50 for standard page, $.25 for microfilm, $1.00 for 11x17. Cert fee- $1.00 per doc includes copy fee. Payee- Register of Deeds. **Online access to Real Estate, Deed, Lien, Mortgage, UCC, Plat records:** Access the recorders database back to 12/1986 free at http://67.32.48.38/oncoreweb/. **Other phones:** Treasurer- 864-898-5883; Elections- 864-898-5848; Vitals- 864-898-5965. **Property tax/Assessing**- 222 McDaniel Ave, #B-8, Pickens, SC 29671; 864-898-5872, fax- 864-898-5932. (Appraiser/Auditor- 864-898-5878) www.pickensassessor.org/ **Online access**- Search property tax records at www.co.pickens.sc.us/onlinetaxes/. Also, search assessor property and sales records free at www.pickensassessor.org/

Richland County

Register of Deeds, PO Box 192, Columbia, SC 29202. 803-576-1910, R/E recording phone-803-5761917, UCC phone-803-576-1910; fax-803-576-1922; 8:30AM-5PM. www.richlandonline.com/
Index: Separate indices to search. Records indexed on a public use terminal back to 1985. Only the public may search. Copy fee $.50 per page. Cert fee- $1.00 per doc plus copy fee. Payee- Richland County Treasurer. **Online Real Estate, Deed, Parcel, Marriage records:** Search register of deeds free at www.richlandonline.com/services/rodsearch.asp; no name searching. Also, search marriages free at www.richlandonline.com/services/onlineservices.asp. **Property tax/Assessing**- PO Box 192, 2020 Hampton St, Columbia, SC 29202; 803-576-2640, assessor fax- 803-576-2681. **Online access**- Search assessments at www.richlandonline.com/services/assessorsearch/assessorsearch.asp; no name searching. Access to county property data is free at www.richlandmaps.com. Click on "Property Info" however, there is no name searching.

Saluda County

Clerk of Court, 100 Church St, #6; Courthouse, Saluda, SC 29138. 864-445-4500; fax-864-445-3772; 8:30AM-5PM.
Index: All in one. Records indexed on a public use terminal back to 1000. Only the public may search. Copy fee $.25 per page. Cert fee- $1.00 per cert plus copy fee. Payee- Saluda County Clerk of Court. **Other phones:** Treasurer- 864-445-4500; Elections-864-445-4500. **Property tax/Assessing**- 100 E Church St #1, Saluda, SC 29138; 864-445-4500 x2202, assessor fax- 864-445-4502.

Spartanburg County

County Register of Deeds, 366 N Church St, #100, Spartanburg, SC 29303. 864-596-2514; 8:30AM-5PM www.spartanburgcounty.org
Index: All in one. Records indexed on a public use terminal back to 1970, images from 2003. Only the public may search. Copy fee $.50 per page. Cert fee- $2.00 per cert plus copy fee. Payee- Spartanburg County Register of Mesne Conveyances. **Online access to Real Estate, Deed, Lien, UCC, Plat, Charter records:** Access recording data free at www.spartanburgcounty.org/rmsdmsclient/index.asp. Images being added daily. **Other phones:** Treasurer- 864-596-2603. **Property tax/Assessing**- 366 N Church St, #800, Admin Bldg, Main Level, Spartanburg, SC 29303; 864-596-2544, assessor fax- 864-596-2223. **Online** - Access property tax data free at www.spartanburgcounty.org/asrinfo/index.aspx

Sumter County

Register of Deeds, 141 N Main St, Rm 202; Courthouse, Sumter, SC 29150. Recording, R/E phone-803-436-2177, UCC recording phone-803-436-2179; 8:30AM-5PM www.sumtercountysc.org
Index: Separate indices to search. Records indexed on a public use terminal back to 1980. Only the public may search. Copy fee $.50 per page. Cert fee- $2.00 1st pg, $.50 each add'l. Payee- Sumter County Register of Deeds. **Online access to Real Estate, Deed records:** Search county e-gov data free at www.sumtercountysc.org/disclaim.htm. **Other phones:** Treasurer- 803-436-2213; Elections- 803-436-2310. **Property tax/Assessing**- 13 E Canal St 1st Fl, Sumter, SC 29150; 803-436-2115, assessor fax-803-436-2118. (Appraiser/Auditor- 803-436-2112) www.sumtercountysc.org/asrz.htm **Online access**- Search assessment data and property cards free at www.sumtercountysc.org/EGSV2SMTR/PCSearch.do. Also, search county e-gov data free at www.sumtercountysc.org/disclaim.htm.

Union County

Clerk of Court, PO Box 703, Union, SC 29379. 864-429-1630; fax-864-429-1715; 9AM-5PM www.judicial.state.sc.us/clerks/union/
Index: Separate indices to search. Records indexed on a public use terminal back to 1998. Only the public may search. Copy fee $.50 per page. Cert fee- $1.00 per doc plus copy fee. Payee- Union Clerk of Court. **Other phones:** Treasurer- 864-429-1606; Elections-864-429-1616; Vital Records- 864-429-1690. **Property tax/Assessing**- 203 N Herndon, Union, SC 29379; 864-429-1650, assessor fax- 864-429-2899. (Appraiser - 864-429-1650) A public access terminal is available. www.countyofunion.com/assessor.html

Williamsburg County

Clerk of Court, 125 W Main St, Kingstree, SC 29556. 843-355-9321 x552; fax-843-355-7821; 8AM-5PM.
Index: All in one. Records indexed on a public use terminal back to 1994. Office personnel (Rhonda July) or visitors may perform searches. Search fee $10.00 per name. Copy fee $1.00 per page. Cert fee- $3.00 per page includes copy fee. Payee- Williamsburg County Clerk of Court. CD-rom of plats only available for $650.00. **Other phones:** Treasurer- 843-355-9321 x546; Elections- 843-354-7016. **Property tax/Assessing**- 147 W Main St, Rm 202, Kingtree, SC 29556; 843-355-9321 x516, assessor fax- 843-355-3751. Public use terminal available. www.williamsburgsc.com/assessor.html

York County

Clerk of Court, PO Box 649, York, SC 29745. 803-684-8510; fax-803-684-8560; 8AM-5PM
Index: All in one. Records indexed on a public use terminal back to 1982. Office personnel or visitors may perform searches. Search fee-$5.00 per name. Office will search real estate records. Copy fee $1.00 per page.Real estate or tax lien copy- $.40 per page. Cert fee- $1.00 per doc plus copy fee. Payee- York Clerk of Court. **Other phones:** Treasurer- 803-684-8528; Elections- 803-684-1242; Vital Records- 803-909-7300. **Property tax/ Assessing**- 803-684-8526. **Online access**- Access to the county GIS and property data is free at http://maps.yorkcountygov.com/gisonline/. Click on "GIS Online" and name search at the main map page. Also, search tax records free at http://onlinetaxes.yorkcountygov.com/.

South Carolina County Locator

You will usually be able to find the city name in the City/County Cross Reference below. We have also included a ZIP/City Cross Reference following the City/County Cross Reference.

South Carolina City/County Cross Reference

ABBEVILLE Abbeville
ADAMS RUN (29426) Charleston(78), Dorchester(21)
AIKEN Aiken
ALCOLU (29001) Clarendon(93), Sumter(6)
ALLENDALE Allendale
ANDERSON Anderson
ANDREWS (29510) Georgetown(58), Williamsburg(41)
ARCADIA Spartanburg
AWENDAW Charleston
AYNOR Horry
BALLENTINE Richland
BAMBERG Bamberg
BARNWELL Barnwell
BATESBURG (29006) Lexington(51), Saluda(30), Aiken(17)
BATH Aiken
BEAUFORT Beaufort
BEECH ISLAND Aiken
BELTON (29627) Anderson(93), Greenville(5)
BENNETTSVILLE Marlboro
BETHERA Berkeley
BETHUNE (29009) Kershaw(83), Chesterfield(9), Lee(7)
BISHOPVILLE Lee
BLACKSBURG (29702) Cherokee(96), York(3)
BLACKSTOCK (29014) Chester(58), Fairfield(41)
BLACKVILLE (29817) Barnwell(79), Bamberg(20)
BLAIR Fairfield
BLENHEIM Marlboro
BLUFFTON Beaufort
BLYTHEWOOD (29016) Richland(91), Fairfield(8)
BONNEAU Berkeley
BORDEN Sumter
BOWLING GREEN York
BOWMAN (29018) Orangeburg(93), Dorchester(6)
BRADLEY (29819) Greenwood(80), Abbeville(17), McCormick(1)
BRANCHVILLE (29432) Orangeburg(72), Bamberg(23), Dorchester(4)
BRUNSON Hampton
BUFFALO Union
CADES (29518) Williamsburg(96), Clarendon(3)
CALHOUN FALLS (29628) Abbeville(97), McCormick(2)
CAMDEN (29020) Kershaw(94), Lee(5)
CAMERON (29030) Calhoun(72), Orangeburg(27)
CAMPOBELLO (29322) Spartanburg(98), Greenville(1)
CANADYS Colleton
CARLISLE (29031) Union(47), Chester(34), Fairfield(18)
CASSATT (29032) Kershaw(72), Lee(27)
CATAWBA York
CAYCE Lexington
CENTENARY Marion
CENTRAL (29630) Pickens(93), Anderson(6)
CHAPIN (29036) Lexington(72), Richland(21), Newberry(6)
CHAPPELLS (29037) Newberry(68), Saluda(28), Laurens(3)
CHARLESTON (29406) Charleston(76), Berkeley(23)
CHARLESTON (29418) Charleston(78), Dorchester(21)
CHARLESTON (29420) Dorchester(63), Charleston(36)
CHARLESTON Berkeley
CHARLESTON Charleston
CHARLESTON AFB Charleston
CHERAW Chesterfield
CHEROKEE FALLS Cherokee
CHESNEE (29323) Spartanburg(87), Cherokee(12)
CHESTER Chester
CHESTERFIELD Chesterfield
CLARKS HILL (29821) Edgefield(51), McCormick(48)
CLEARWATER Aiken
CLEMSON Pickens
CLEVELAND (29635) Greenville(73), Pickens(26)
CLIFTON Spartanburg
CLINTON Laurens
CLIO (29525) Marlboro(97), Dillon(2)
CLOVER York
COLUMBIA (29212) Lexington(78), Richland(21)
COLUMBIA (29210) Richland(69), Lexington(30)
COLUMBIA Lexington
COLUMBIA Richland
CONESTEE Greenville
CONVERSE Spartanburg
CONWAY Horry
COOSAWATCHIE Jasper
COPE Orangeburg
CORDESVILLE Berkeley
CORDOVA Orangeburg
COTTAGEVILLE Colleton
COWARD Florence
COWPENS (29330) Spartanburg(64), Cherokee(35)
CROCKETVILLE Hampton
CROSS (29436) Berkeley(94), Orangeburg(5)
CROSS ANCHOR Spartanburg
CROSS HILL (29332) Laurens(90), Newberry(9)
DALE Beaufort
DALZELL (29040) Sumter(81), Lee(18)
DARLINGTON Darlington
DAUFUSKIE ISLAND Beaufort
DAVIS STATION Clarendon
DENMARK Bamberg
DILLON Dillon
DONALDS (29638) Abbeville(86), Greenwood(13)
DORCHESTER Dorchester
DRAYTON Spartanburg
DUE WEST Abbeville
DUNCAN Spartanburg
EARLY BRANCH (29916) Hampton(57), Jasper(42)
EASLEY (29642) Pickens(69), Anderson(30)
EASLEY Pickens
EASTOVER Richland
EDGEFIELD Edgefield
EDGEMOOR Chester
EDISTO ISLAND (29438) Colleton(58), Charleston(41)
EFFINGHAM Florence
EHRHARDT (29081) Bamberg(92), Colleton(7)
ELGIN (29045) Kershaw(56), Richland(39), Fairfield(3)
ELKO Barnwell
ELLIOTT Lee
ELLOREE (29047) Orangeburg(50), Calhoun(49)
ENOREE (29335) Spartanburg(70), Laurens(25), Union(4)
ESTILL Hampton
EUTAWVILLE Orangeburg
FAIR PLAY (29643) Oconee(80), Anderson(19)
FAIRFAX (29827) Allendale(98), Hampton(1)
FAIRFOREST Spartanburg
FINGERVILLE Spartanburg
FLORENCE (29501) Florence(92), Darlington(7)
FLORENCE Florence
FLOYD DALE Dillon
FOLLY BEACH Charleston
FORK Dillon
FORT LAWN Chester
FORT MILL (29715) York(69), Lancaster(30)
FORT MILL York
FOUNTAIN INN (29644) Laurens(60), Greenville(39)
FURMAN Hampton
GABLE (29051) Clarendon(53), Sumter(46)
GADSDEN Richland
GAFFNEY Cherokee
GALIVANTS FERRY Horry
GARNETT (29922) Hampton(69), Jasper(30)
GASTON (29053) Lexington(81), Calhoun(18)
GEORGETOWN Georgetown
GIFFORD Hampton
GILBERT Lexington
GLENDALE Spartanburg
GLOVERVILLE Aiken
GOOSE CREEK Berkeley
GRAMLING Spartanburg
GRANITEVILLE Aiken
GRAY COURT Laurens
GREAT FALLS (29055) Chester(65), Fairfield(34)
GREELEYVILLE (29056) Williamsburg(88), Clarendon(11)
GREEN POND Colleton
GREEN SEA Horry
GREENVILLE (29611) Greenville(93), Anderson(3), Pickens(2)
GREENVILLE Greenville
GREENWOOD Greenwood
GREER (29651) Greenville(54), Spartanburg(45)
GREER Greenville
GRESHAM Marion
GROVER Dorchester
HAMER Dillon
HAMPTON Hampton
HARDEEVILLE Jasper
HARLEYVILLE Dorchester
HARTSVILLE (29550) Darlington(84), Chesterfield(13), Lee(1)
HARTSVILLE Darlington
HEATH SPRINGS (29058) Lancaster(94), Kershaw(5)
HEMINGWAY (29554) Georgetown(52), Williamsburg(44), Florence(2)
HICKORY GROVE York
HILDA Barnwell
HILTON HEAD ISLAND Beaufort
HODGES (29653) Greenwood(93), Abbeville(6)
HODGES Greenwood
HOLLY HILL (29059) Orangeburg(96), Berkeley(3)
HOLLYWOOD Charleston
HONEA PATH (29654) Anderson(59), Abbeville(21), Laurens(11), Greenville(7)
HOPKINS Richland
HORATIO Sumter
HUGER (29450) Berkeley(98), Charleston(1)
INMAN Spartanburg
IRMO (29063) Richland(91), Lexington(8)
ISLANDTON Colleton
ISLE OF PALMS Charleston
IVA (29655) Anderson(58), Abbeville(41)
JACKSON Aiken
JACKSONBORO Colleton
JAMESTOWN Berkeley
JEFFERSON Chesterfield
JENKINSVILLE Fairfield
JOANNA Laurens
JOHNS ISLAND Charleston
JOHNSONVILLE (29555) Florence(93), Williamsburg(6)
JOHNSTON (29832) Edgefield(72), Saluda(27)
JONESVILLE Union
KERSHAW (29067) Lancaster(73), Kershaw(26)
KINARDS (29355) Newberry(54), Laurens(45)
KINGS CREEK Cherokee
KINGSTREE Williamsburg
KLINE Barnwell
LA FRANCE Anderson
LADSON (29456) Dorchester(41), Berkeley(40), Charleston(18)
LADYS ISLAND Beaufort
LAKE CITY (29560) Florence(73), Williamsburg(14), Clarendon(12)
LAKE VIEW Dillon
LAMAR (29069) Darlington(87), Lee(12)
LANDO Chester
LANDRUM (29356) Spartanburg(58), Greenville(41)
LANE Williamsburg
LANGLEY Aiken
LATTA (29565) Dillon(87), Marion(10), Marlboro(2)
LAURENS Laurens
LEESVILLE (29070) Lexington(74), Saluda(25)
LEXINGTON Lexington
LIBERTY (29657) Pickens(86), Anderson(13)
LIBERTY HILL Kershaw
LITTLE MOUNTAIN (29075) Newberry(81), Richland(13), Lexington(5)
LITTLE RIVER Horry
LITTLE ROCK Dillon
LIVINGSTON Orangeburg
LOBECO Beaufort
LOCKHART Union
LODGE (29082) Colleton(92), Bamberg(7)
LONE STAR Calhoun
LONG CREEK Oconee
LONGS Horry
LORIS Horry
LOWNDESVILLE Abbeville
LUGOFF (29078) Kershaw(96), Richland(3)
LURAY (29932) Allendale(56), Hampton(43)

LYDIA Darlington
LYMAN Spartanburg
LYNCHBURG (29080) Lee(50), Sumter(49)
MANNING Clarendon
MARIETTA (29661) Greenville(76), Pickens(23)
MARTIN (29836) Allendale(94), Barnwell(5)
MAULDIN Greenville
MAYESVILLE (29104) Lee(50), Sumter(49)
MAYO Spartanburg
MC BEE (29101) Chesterfield(83), Darlington(16)
MC CLELLANVILLE Charleston
MC COLL Marlboro
MC CONNELLS York
MC CORMICK (29835) McCormick(93), Edgefield(6)
MC CORMICK McCormick
MILEY Hampton
MINTURN Dillon
MODOC (29838) Edgefield(62), McCormick(36), Fairfield(1)
MONCKS CORNER Berkeley
MONETTA (29105) Aiken(66), Saluda(33)
MONTICELLO Fairfield
MONTMORENCI Aiken
MOORE Spartanburg
MOUNT CARMEL McCormick
MOUNT CROGHAN Chesterfield
MOUNT PLEASANT Charleston
MOUNTAIN REST Oconee
MOUNTVILLE Laurens
MULLINS Marion
MURRELLS INLET (29576) Horry(56), Georgetown(43)
MYRTLE BEACH Horry
NEESES Orangeburg
NESMITH Williamsburg
NEW ELLENTON Aiken
NEW ZION (29111) Clarendon(92), Williamsburg(7)
NEWBERRY Newberry
NEWRY Oconee
NICHOLS (29581) Horry(81), Marion(10), Dillon(8)
NINETY SIX (29666) Greenwood(95), Saluda(4)
NORRIS Pickens
NORTH (29112) Orangeburg(91), Calhoun(6), Lexington(2)
NORTH AUGUSTA (29841) Aiken(98), Edgefield(1)
NORTH AUGUSTA (29860) Edgefield(65), Aiken(34)
NORTH AUGUSTA Aiken
NORTH CHARLESTON Berkeley
NORTH CHARLESTON Charleston
NORTH MYRTLE BEACH Horry
NORWAY Orangeburg
OKATIE Beaufort
OLANTA (29114) Florence(59), Sumter(39)
OLAR (29843) Bamberg(90), Barnwell(9)
ORANGEBURG (29118) Orangeburg(94), Calhoun(5)
ORANGEBURG Orangeburg
PACOLET (29372) Spartanburg(69), Union(15), Cherokee(14)
PACOLET MILLS Spartanburg
PAGELAND Chesterfield
PAMPLICO Florence
PARKSVILLE McCormick
PATRICK Chesterfield
PAULINE (29374) Spartanburg(94), Union(6)
PAWLEYS ISLAND Georgetown
PEAK Newberry
PELION Lexington
PELZER (29669) Anderson(65), Greenville(34)
PENDLETON (29670) Anderson(98), Pickens(1)
PERRY Aiken
PICKENS Pickens
PIEDMONT (29673) Anderson(50), Greenville(49)
PINELAND (29934) Jasper(83), Hampton(16)
PINEVILLE Berkeley
PINEWOOD (29125) Clarendon(54), Sumter(45)
PINOPOLIS Berkeley
PLUM BRANCH (29845) McCormick(94), Edgefield(5)
POMARIA Newberry
PORT ROYAL Beaufort
POSTON Horry
PROSPERITY (29127) Newberry(95), Saluda(4)
RAINS Marion
RAVENEL (29470) Charleston(87), Dorchester(12)
REEVESVILLE (29471) Dorchester(96), Orangeburg(3)
REIDVILLE Spartanburg
REMBERT (29128) Sumter(77), Lee(15), Kershaw(7)
RICHBURG Chester
RICHLAND Oconee
RIDGE SPRING (29129) Aiken(47), Saluda(44), Edgefield(8)
RIDGELAND (29936) Jasper(97), Beaufort(2)
RIDGEVILLE (29472) Dorchester(62), Colleton(20), Berkeley(16)
RIDGEWAY (29130) Fairfield(86), Kershaw(11), Richland(1)
RIMINI (29131) Sumter(65), Clarendon(34)
RION Fairfield
ROCK HILL York
ROEBUCK Spartanburg
ROUND O Colleton
ROWESVILLE Orangeburg
RUBY Chesterfield
RUFFIN Colleton
RUSSELLVILLE Berkeley
SAINT GEORGE Dorchester
SAINT HELENA ISLAND Beaufort
SAINT MATTHEWS (29135) Calhoun(97), Orangeburg(2)
SAINT STEPHEN Berkeley
SALEM Oconee
SALLEY (29137) Aiken(85), Orangeburg(14)
SALTERS Williamsburg
SALUDA (29138) Saluda(97), Greenwood(2)
SANDY SPRINGS Anderson
SANTEE Orangeburg
SARDINIA Clarendon
SCOTIA Hampton
SCRANTON Florence
SEABROOK Beaufort
SELLERS (29592) Dillon(70), Marion(29)
SENECA Oconee
SHARON York
SHAW A F B Sumter
SHELDON Beaufort
SILVERSTREET Newberry
SIMPSONVILLE Greenville
SIX MILE Pickens
SLATER Greenville
SMOAKS (29481) Colleton(85), Bamberg(14)
SMYRNA York
SOCIETY HILL (29593) Darlington(53), Chesterfield(46)
SPARTANBURG (29307) Spartanburg(97), Cherokee(2)
SPARTANBURG Spartanburg
SPRINGFIELD (29146) Orangeburg(73), Aiken(26)
STARR Anderson
STARTEX Spartanburg
STATE PARK Richland
SULLIVANS ISLAND Charleston
SUMMERTON Clarendon
SUMMERVILLE (29483) Dorchester(70), Berkeley(29)
SUMMERVILLE (29485) Dorchester(89), Charleston(10)
SUMMERVILLE Dorchester
SUMTER Sumter
SUNSET Pickens
SWANSEA (29160) Lexi'n(52),Calhoun(47)
SYCAMORE Allendale
TAMASSEE Oconee
TATUM Marlboro
TAYLORS Greenville
TIGERVILLE Greenville
TILLMAN Jasper
TIMMONSVILLE (29161) Florence(80), Darlington(19)
TOWNVILLE (29689) Anderson(89), Oconee(10)
TRAVELERS REST Greenville
TRENTON (29847) Edgefield(65), Aiken(34)
TRIO Williamsburg
TROY (29848) Greenwood(85), McCormick(10), Saluda(2), Edgefield(1)
TURBEVILLE (29162) Clarendon(97), Sumter(2)
ULMER Allendale
UNA Spartanburg
VAN WYCK Lancaster
VANCE Orangeburg
VARNVILLE (29944) Hampton(89), Jasper(10)
VAUCLUSE Aiken
WADMALAW ISLAND Charleston
WAGENER Aiken
WALHALLA Oconee
WALLACE Marlboro
WALTERBORO Colleton
WARD Saluda
WARE SHOALS (29692) Laurens(66), Greenwood(24), Abbeville(9)
WARRENVILLE Aiken
WATERLOO Laurens
WEDGEFIELD Sumter
WELLFORD Spartanburg
WEST COLUMBIA Lexington
WEST UNION Oconee
WESTMINSTER Oconee
WESTVILLE Kershaw
WHITE OAK Fairfield
WHITE ROCK Richland
WHITE STONE Spartanburg
WHITMIRE (29178) Newberry(78), Union(16), Laurens(5)
WILLIAMS Colleton
WILLIAMSTON Anderson
WILLISTON (29853) Barnwell(65), Aiken(34)
WINDSOR Aiken
WINNSBORO (29180) Fairfield(97), Richland(2)
WISACKY Lee
WOODRUFF (29388) Spartanburg(93), Laurens(6)
YEMASSEE (29945) Colleton(30), Hampton(29), Jasper(28), Beaufort(11)

South Carolina ZIP/City Cross Reference

ZIP	City
29001-29001	ALCOLU
29002-29002	BALLENTINE
29003-29003	BAMBERG
29006-29006	BATESBURG
29009-29009	BETHUNE
29010-29010	BISHOPVILLE
29014-29014	BLACKSTOCK
29015-29015	BLAIR
29016-29016	BLYTHEWOOD
29017-29017	BORDEN
29018-29018	BOWMAN
29020-29020	CAMDEN
29030-29030	CAMERON
29031-29031	CARLISLE
29032-29032	CASSATT
29033-29033	CAYCE
29036-29036	CHAPIN
29037-29037	CHAPPELLS
29038-29038	COPE
29039-29039	CORDOVA
29040-29040	DALZELL
29041-29041	DAVIS STATION
29042-29042	DENMARK
29044-29044	EASTOVER
29045-29045	ELGIN
29046-29046	ELLIOTT
29047-29047	ELLOREE
29048-29048	EUTAWVILLE
29051-29051	GABLE
29052-29052	GADSDEN
29053-29053	GASTON
29054-29054	GILBERT
29055-29055	GREAT FALLS
29056-29056	GREELEYVILLE
29058-29058	HEATH SPRINGS
29059-29059	HOLLY HILL
29061-29061	HOPKINS
29062-29062	HORATIO
29063-29063	IRMO
29065-29065	JENKINSVILLE
29067-29067	KERSHAW
29069-29069	LAMAR
29070-29070	LEESVILLE
29071-29073	LEXINGTON
29074-29074	LIBERTY HILL
29075-29075	LITTLE MOUNTAIN
29076-29076	LIVINGSTON
29077-29077	LONE STAR
29078-29078	LUGOFF
29079-29079	LYDIA
29080-29080	LYNCHBURG
29081-29081	EHRHARDT
29082-29082	LODGE
29101-29101	MC BEE
29102-29102	MANNING
29104-29104	MAYESVILLE
29105-29105	MONETTA
29106-29106	MONTICELLO
29107-29107	NEESES
29108-29108	NEWBERRY
29111-29111	NEW ZION
29112-29112	NORTH
29113-29113	NORWAY
29114-29114	OLANTA
29115-29118	ORANGEBURG
29122-29122	PEAK
29123-29123	PELION
29124-29124	PERRY
29125-29125	PINEWOOD
29126-29126	POMARIA
29127-29127	PROSPERITY
29128-29128	REMBERT
29129-29129	RIDGE SPRING
29130-29130	RIDGEWAY
29131-29131	RIMINI
29132-29132	RION
29133-29133	ROWESVILLE
29135-29135	SAINT MATTHEWS
29137-29137	SALLEY
29138-29138	SALUDA
29142-29142	SANTEE
29143-29143	SARDINIA
29145-29145	SILVERSTREET
29146-29146	SPRINGFIELD
29147-29147	STATE PARK
29148-29148	SUMMERTON
29150-29151	SUMTER
29152-29152	SHAW A F B

ZIP Code Range	City
29153-29154	SUMTER
29160-29160	SWANSEA
29161-29161	TIMMONSVILLE
29162-29162	TURBEVILLE
29163-29163	VANCE
29164-29164	WAGENER
29166-29166	WARD
29168-29168	WEDGEFIELD
29169-29172	WEST COLUMBIA
29175-29175	WESTVILLE
29176-29176	WHITE OAK
29177-29177	WHITE ROCK
29178-29178	WHITMIRE
29180-29180	WINNSBORO
29183-29183	WISACKY
29200-29292	COLUMBIA
29301-29319	SPARTANBURG
29320-29320	ARCADIA
29321-29321	BUFFALO
29322-29322	CAMPOBELLO
29323-29323	CHESNEE
29324-29324	CLIFTON
29325-29325	CLINTON
29329-29329	CONVERSE
29330-29330	COWPENS
29331-29331	CROSS ANCHOR
29332-29332	CROSS HILL
29333-29333	DRAYTON
29334-29334	DUNCAN
29335-29335	ENOREE
29336-29336	FAIRFOREST
29338-29338	FINGERVILLE
29340-29342	GAFFNEY
29346-29346	GLENDALE
29348-29348	GRAMLING
29349-29349	INMAN
29351-29351	JOANNA
29353-29353	JONESVILLE
29355-29355	KINARDS
29356-29356	LANDRUM
29360-29360	LAURENS
29364-29364	LOCKHART
29365-29365	LYMAN
29368-29368	MAYO
29369-29369	MOORE
29370-29370	MOUNTVILLE
29372-29372	PACOLET
29373-29373	PACOLET MILLS
29374-29374	PAULINE
29375-29375	REIDVILLE
29376-29376	ROEBUCK
29377-29377	STARTEX
29378-29378	UNA
29379-29379	UNION
29384-29384	WATERLOO
29385-29385	WELLFORD
29386-29386	WHITE STONE
29388-29388	WOODRUFF
29390-29391	DUNCAN
29395-29395	JONESVILLE
29401-29403	CHARLESTON
29404-29404	CHARLESTON AFB
29405-29410	CHARLESTON
29410-29410	NORTH CHARLESTON
29411-29415	CHARLESTON
29415-29415	NORTH CHARLESTON
29416-29425	CHARLESTON
29426-29426	ADAMS RUN
29429-29429	AWENDAW
29430-29430	BETHERA
29431-29431	BONNEAU
29432-29432	BRANCHVILLE
29433-29433	CANADYS
29434-29434	CORDESVILLE
29435-29435	COTTAGEVILLE
29436-29436	CROSS
29437-29437	DORCHESTER
29438-29438	EDISTO ISLAND
29439-29439	FOLLY BEACH
29440-29442	GEORGETOWN
29445-29445	GOOSE CREEK
29446-29446	GREEN POND
29447-29447	GROVER
29448-29448	HARLEYVILLE
29449-29449	HOLLYWOOD
29450-29450	HUGER
29451-29451	ISLE OF PALMS
29452-29452	JACKSONBORO
29453-29453	JAMESTOWN
29455-29455	JOHNS ISLAND
29456-29456	LADSON
29457-29457	JOHNS ISLAND
29458-29458	MC CLELLANVILLE
29461-29461	MONCKS CORNER
29464-29466	MOUNT PLEASANT
29468-29468	PINEVILLE
29469-29469	PINOPOLIS
29470-29470	RAVENEL
29471-29471	REEVESVILLE
29472-29472	RIDGEVILLE
29474-29474	ROUND O
29475-29475	RUFFIN
29476-29476	RUSSELLVILLE
29477-29477	SAINT GEORGE
29479-29479	SAINT STEPHEN
29481-29481	SMOAKS
29482-29482	SULLIVANS ISLAND
29483-29485	SUMMERVILLE
29487-29487	WADMALAW ISLAND
29488-29488	WALTERBORO
29492-29492	CHARLESTON
29493-29493	WILLIAMS
29501-29506	FLORENCE
29510-29510	ANDREWS
29511-29511	AYNOR
29512-29512	BENNETTSVILLE
29516-29516	BLENHEIM
29518-29518	CADES
29519-29519	CENTENARY
29520-29520	CHERAW
29525-29525	CLIO
29526-29528	CONWAY
29530-29530	COWARD
29532-29532	DARLINGTON
29536-29536	DILLON
29540-29540	DARLINGTON
29541-29541	EFFINGHAM
29542-29542	FLOYD DALE
29543-29543	FORK
29544-29544	GALIVANTS FERRY
29545-29545	GREEN SEA
29546-29546	GRESHAM
29547-29547	HAMER
29550-29551	HARTSVILLE
29554-29554	HEMINGWAY
29555-29555	JOHNSONVILLE
29556-29556	KINGSTREE
29560-29560	LAKE CITY
29563-29563	LAKE VIEW
29564-29564	LANE
29565-29565	LATTA
29566-29566	LITTLE RIVER
29567-29567	LITTLE ROCK
29568-29568	LONGS
29569-29569	LORIS
29570-29570	MC COLL
29571-29571	MARION
29572-29572	MYRTLE BEACH
29573-29573	MINTURN
29574-29574	MULLINS
29575-29575	MYRTLE BEACH
29576-29576	MURRELLS INLET
29577-29579	MYRTLE BEACH
29580-29580	NESMITH
29581-29581	NICHOLS
29582-29582	NORTH MYRTLE BEACH
29583-29583	PAMPLICO
29584-29584	PATRICK
29585-29585	PAWLEYS ISLAND
29587-29587	MYRTLE BEACH
29588-29588	POSTON
29588-29588	MYRTLE BEACH
29589-29589	RAINS
29590-29590	SALTERS
29591-29591	SCRANTON
29592-29592	SELLERS
29593-29593	SOCIETY HILL
29594-29594	TATUM
29595-29595	TRIO
29596-29596	WALLACE
29597-29598	NORTH MYRTLE BEACH
29601-29617	GREENVILLE
29620-29620	ABBEVILLE
29621-29626	ANDERSON
29627-29627	BELTON
29628-29628	CALHOUN FALLS
29630-29630	CENTRAL
29631-29634	CLEMSON
29635-29635	CLEVELAND
29636-29636	CONESTEE
29638-29638	DONALDS
29639-29639	DUE WEST
29640-29642	EASLEY
29643-29643	FAIR PLAY
29644-29644	FOUNTAIN INN
29645-29645	GRAY COURT
29646-29649	GREENWOOD
29650-29652	GREER
29653-29653	HODGES
29654-29654	HONEA PATH
29655-29655	IVA
29656-29656	LA FRANCE
29657-29657	LIBERTY
29658-29658	LONG CREEK
29659-29659	LOWNDESVILLE
29661-29661	MARIETTA
29662-29662	MAULDIN
29664-29664	MOUNTAIN REST
29665-29665	NEWRY
29666-29666	NINETY SIX
29667-29667	NORRIS
29669-29669	PELZER
29670-29670	PENDLETON
29671-29671	PICKENS
29672-29672	SENECA
29673-29673	PIEDMONT
29675-29675	RICHLAND
29676-29676	SALEM
29677-29677	SANDY SPRINGS
29678-29679	SENECA
29680-29681	SIMPSONVILLE
29682-29682	SIX MILE
29683-29683	SLATER
29684-29684	STARR
29685-29685	SUNSET
29686-29686	TAMASSEE
29687-29687	TAYLORS
29688-29688	TIGERVILLE
29689-29689	TOWNVILLE
29690-29690	TRAVELERS REST
29691-29691	WALHALLA
29692-29692	WARE SHOALS
29693-29693	WESTMINSTER
29695-29695	HODGES
29696-29696	WEST UNION
29697-29697	WILLIAMSTON
29698-29698	GREENVILLE
29702-29702	BLACKSBURG
29703-29703	BOWLING GREEN
29704-29704	CATAWBA
29705-29705	CHEROKEE FALLS
29706-29706	CHESTER
29708-29708	FORT MILL
29709-29709	CHESTERFIELD
29710-29710	CLOVER
29712-29712	EDGEMOOR
29714-29714	FORT LAWN
29715-29716	FORT MILL
29717-29717	HICKORY GROVE
29718-29718	JEFFERSON
29719-29719	KINGS CREEK
29720-29722	LANCASTER
29724-29724	LANDO
29726-29726	MC CONNELLS
29727-29727	MOUNT CROGHAN
29728-29728	PAGELAND
29729-29729	RICHBURG
29730-29734	ROCK HILL
29741-29741	RUBY
29742-29742	SHARON
29743-29743	SMYRNA
29744-29744	VAN WYCK
29745-29745	YORK
29801-29808	AIKEN
29809-29809	NEW ELLENTON
29810-29810	ALLENDALE
29812-29812	BARNWELL
29813-29813	HILDA
29814-29814	KLINE
29816-29816	BATH
29817-29817	BLACKVILLE
29819-29819	BRADLEY
29821-29821	CLARKS HILL
29822-29822	CLEARWATER
29824-29824	EDGEFIELD
29826-29826	ELKO
29827-29827	FAIRFAX
29828-29828	GLOVERVILLE
29829-29829	GRANITEVILLE
29831-29831	JACKSON
29832-29832	JOHNSTON
29834-29834	LANGLEY
29835-29835	MC CORMICK
29836-29836	MARTIN
29838-29838	MODOC
29839-29839	MONTMORENCI
29840-29840	MOUNT CARMEL
29841-29841	NORTH AUGUSTA
29842-29842	BEECH ISLAND
29843-29843	OLAR
29844-29844	PARKSVILLE
29845-29845	PLUM BRANCH
29846-29846	SYCAMORE
29847-29847	TRENTON
29848-29848	TROY
29849-29849	ULMER
29850-29850	VAUCLUSE
29851-29851	WARRENVILLE
29853-29853	WILLISTON
29856-29856	WINDSOR
29860-29861	NORTH AUGUSTA
29899-29899	MC CORMICK
29901-29906	BEAUFORT
29907-29907	LADYS ISLAND
29909-29909	OKATIE
29910-29910	BLUFFTON
29911-29911	BRUNSON
29912-29912	COOSAWATCHIE
29913-29913	CROCKETVILLE
29914-29914	DALE
29915-29915	DAUFUSKIE ISLAND
29916-29916	EARLY BRANCH
29918-29918	ESTILL
29920-29920	SAINT HELENA ISLAND
29921-29921	FURMAN
29922-29922	GARNETT
29923-29923	GIFFORD
29924-29924	HAMPTON
29925-29926	HILTON HEAD ISLAND
29927-29927	HARDEEVILLE
29928-29928	HILTON HEAD ISLAND
29929-29929	ISLANDTON
29931-29931	LOBECO
29932-29932	LURAY
29933-29933	MILEY
29934-29934	PINELAND
29935-29935	PORT ROYAL
29936-29936	RIDGELAND
29938-29938	HILTON HEAD ISLAND
29939-29939	SCOTIA
29940-29940	SEABROOK
29941-29941	SHELDON
29943-29943	TILLMAN
29944-29944	VARNVILLE
29945-29945	YEMASSEE
29948-29948	HILTON HEAD ISLAND

South Dakota

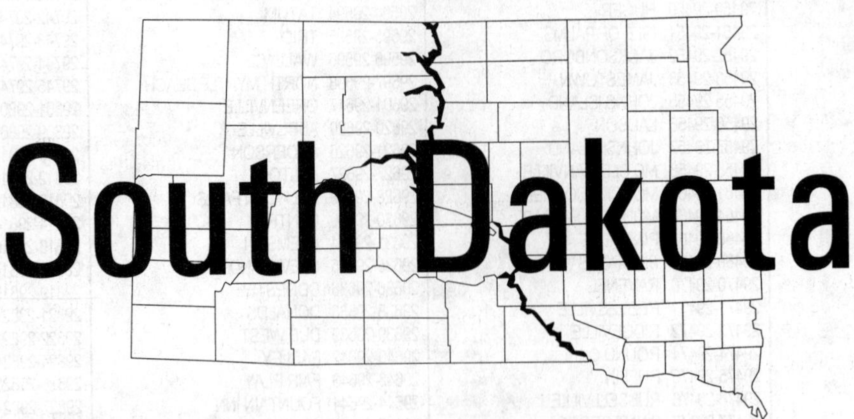

General Help Numbers:

Governor's Office

State Capitol, 500 E Capitol Ave — 605-773-3212
Pierre, SD 57501-5070 — Fax 605-773-4711
www.state.sd.us/governor/ — 8AM-5PM

Attorney General's Office

State Capitol, 500 E Capitol Ave — 605-773-3215
Pierre, SD 57501-5070 — Fax 605-773-4106
www.state.sd.us/attorney/ — 8AM-5PM

Legislative Records

South Dakota Legislature, Capitol Bldg
Legislative Research Council — 605-773-3251
500 E Capitol Ave — Fax 605-773-4576
Pierre, SD 57501 — 8AM-5PM
http://legis.state.sd.us/

State Archives

Cultural Heritage Center/State Archives — 605-773-3804
900 Governors Dr — Fax 605-773-6041
Pierre, SD 57501-2217 — 9AM-4:30PM
www.sdhistory.org/

State Specifics:

Capital: Pierre
Hughes County

Time Zone: CST*

* South Dakota's eighteen western-most counties are MST: They are: Bennett, Butte, Corson, Custer, Dewey, Fall River, Haakon, Harding, Jackson, Lawrence, Meade, Mellette, Pennington, Perkins, Shannon, Stanley, Todd, Ziebach,

Number of Counties: 66

Population: 804,194

Web Site: www.sd.gov/

State Agencies

Criminal Records

Division of Criminal Investigation, Identification Section, 1302 E Highway 14, Ste 5, Pierre, SD 57501-8505; 605-773-3331, Fax- 605-773-2235; 8AM-5PM. http://dci.sd.gov

Indexing & Storage: Records available for 10 years for misdemeanors from sentence date and lifetime for felonies. New records available for inquiry in 1 day. 98% of all arrests in database have final dispositions recorded.

Searching: Include in request- date of birth, full name, set of fingerprints, signed release form. The form requires identifying information: color of hair and eyes, height, weight, date of birth, SSN. This data not released- juvenile records, minor traffic violations or out-of-state or federal charges. All open records without dispositions are released.

Access by: mail.

Fee & Payment: The fee is $20.00 per name. Statutorily-required fingerprint checks will include an FBI fingerprint check for an additional $19.25. Fee payee- Division of Criminal Investigation. Prepayment required. Personal checks accepted, credit cards are not.

Mail search: Turnaround time- 5 to 10 working days. Upon receipt of those requirements, they will conduct a search of their files and supply a copy of any criminal history that is found or a statement that there is no criminal history. A SASE is helpful.

Other access: The State Court Administrator's Office has a statewide database of criminal record information from the state's circuit courts. For more information about setting up a commercial account, contact Jill Gusso at 605-773-3474.

Statewide Court Records

State Court Administrator, State Capitol Bldg, 500 E Capitol Ave, Pierre, SD 57501-5059; 605-773-3474, Fax- 605-773-8437; 8AM-5PM.

www.sdjudicial.com

Indexing & Storage: Records available for criminal records from July 1, 1989 forward. This agency is in the process of developing a statewide civil database also. New records available for inquiry in 6 to 12 months.

Searching: South Dakota has a statewide criminal record search database administrated by this office. Include in request- full name, DOB, and driver license number. Requesters may wish to set up a commercial account by faxing a written request to Jill Gusso, Unified Court System at 605-773-8437 or email jill.gusso@ujs.state.sd.us. Accounts are billed monthly.

Access by: mail, fax, online.

Fee & Payment: The search fee is $15.00 per record. State authorized commercial accounts may order and receive records by fax, there is an add'l $5.00 fee unless a non-toll free line is used.

Mail search: Turnaround time- is usually 1-3 days. Mail requests should be addressed to the Miner County Clerk of Court, PO Box 265, Howard SD 57349 or to Aurora County Clerk of Court, PO Box 366, Plankinton, SD 57368-0366. Providing an SASE is suggested.

Fax search: If authorized, additional minimum fee of $5.00.

Online search: All active judgments and inactive civil money judgments from 04/19/2004 forward are available from a web subscription service offered by this agency. The subscription cost is $250 monthly or $2500 annually. You may also access this system on a pay as you go basis where you deposit from a credit card and the system deducts from your balance. You can get more information on this system at https://apps.sd.gov/applications/judgmentquery/login.aspx. The money judgment system permits bulk downloading of information. However, the agreement with the agency disallows any resell of the data. This subscription system does not include probate or criminal information. For more details contact Ms. Jill Gusso at 605-773-8437. The Supreme Court calendar, opinions, rules and archived oral arguments may be searched from the website.

Other access: Historical civil money judgment data may be purchased, electronic format is provided. Contact Ms. Gusso.

Sexual Offender Registry

Division of Criminal Investigation, Identification Section - SOR Unit, 1302 E Highway 14, #5, Pierre, SD 57501; 605-773-3331, Fax- 605-773-4629; 8AM-5PM.

http://sor.sd.gov/disclaimer.asp?page=search&nav=2

Online access is provided to search from a database of all offenders.

Indexing & Storage: Records available from at least 1994. 1994 was the start-up date, but records are retroactive. New records available for inquiry in 24 hours.

Searching: Mail or phone requests are not often necessary because of the web page. However, under certain circumstances this agency will honor such requests. Email questions- sdsor@state.sd.us.

Online search: Searching available from website.

Incarceration Records

SD Department of Corrections, Central Records Office, PO Box 5911, Pierre, SD 57117; 605-367-5140, Fax- 605-367-5584; 8AM-4PM.

http://doc.sd.gov/

While online searching is not provided for inmates, there is a search for escapees, walkaways, and parole absconders.

Indexing & Storage: Records available on current and former inmates. New records available for inquiry in up to 3 days.

Searching: The computerized records system does not track records back further than those inmates who were discharged in 1985. Include in request- name and DOB or SSN. Location, conviction and sentencing information are available. This data not released- medical, treatment, disciplinary records.

Access by: phone, fax.

Phone search: For phone search, call the number above or for a phone confirmation only the Department's Office of Community Relations at 302-739-5601 x246.

Fax search: Requests accepted by fax.

Other access: A department most wanted list is at www.state.sd.us/corrections/most_wanted.htm.

Corporation, LP, LLC, Trademarks/Servicemarks

Corporation Division, Secretary of State, 500 E Capitol Ave, Suite B-03, Pierre, SD 57501-5070; 605-773-4845, 605-773-3539 (Trademarks), Fax- 605-773-4550; 8AM-5PM.

www.sdsos.gov/corporations/

Trademarks are in a different Division, call 605-773-3539.

Indexing & Storage: Records available from the founding of the state. New records available for inquiry immediately.

Searching: Direct questions to corportations@state.sd.us. Include in request- full name of business. In addition to the articles of organization, business entity records available include: Annual Reports, Officers, Directors, Registered Agent, Prior (merged) names, Inactive and Reserved names.

Access by: mail, phone, fax, in person, online.

Fee & Payment: There is no fee for a general search. A Certificate of Good Standing is available for a fee of $15.00. Copies are $1.00 per page, add $10.00 for certification. Fee payee- Secretary of State. Prepayment required. Personal checks and major credit cards accepted.

Mail search: Turnaround time- 1 to 3 days. A SASE is requested.

Phone search: They will provide basic information only. **Fax search:** Records can be returned by fax for $1.00 per page plus a $5.00 fax fee. **In person:** Turnaround time is immediate.

Online search: Search the Secretary of State Corporations Div. Database free at www.state.sd.us/applications/st02corplook/ASPX/ST32Main.aspx. Trademark searches may be requested via email- marianne.gabriel@state.sd.us.

Other access: The corporate database may be purchased on CD for $1,000 with $500 monthly updates.

Expedited service: Expedited service is available for an additional $20.00 per request.

Fictitious Name, Assumed Name

Records not maintained by a state level agency.

Records are located at the county level.

Uniform Commercial Code, Federal Tax Liens

UCC Division, Secretary of State, 500 East Capitol, Pierre, SD 57501-5077; 605-773-4422, Fax- 605-773-4550; 8AM-5PM.

www.sdsos.gov/ucc

Federal tax liens on business filed here, if on individuals then filed at county level.

Indexing & Storage: Records available for all active records and one year after lapse. New records available for inquiry in less than 1 day.

Searching: Use search request form UCC-11. The search includes federal tax liens on businesses. Include in request- debtor name. This data not released- SSN may be redacted.

Access by: mail, phone, fax, in person, online.

Fee & Payment: The fee is $20.00 per debtor name, ($15.00 if online). Copies are $1.00 per page. There is an additional $10.00 if certification of document desired. Fee payee- Sec. of State. Prepayment required. Personal checks accepted. Major credit cards accepted except Amex.

Mail search: Turnaround time- 1 to 2 days. A SASE is requested.

Phone search: Limited information is given over the phone. Reports can be ordered.

Fax search: Use of a credit card is required or prepay. Fee is additional $5.00 to fax back.

In person: Simple requests may be processed while you wait.

Online search: Dakota Fast File is the filing and searching service available at www.sdsos.gov/busineservices/ucc.shtm. This is a commercial service that requires registration and a $120-$360 fee per year. Certified search also available.

Other access: FTP downloads are available for purchase.

Expedited service: Expedited service is available for mail, phone and fax searches. Turnaround time- 1 day. Add $20.00 per debtor name.

State Tax Liens, Federal Tax Liens

Records not maintained by a state level agency.

All state tax liens and federal tax liens on individuals are filed at the county level.

Sales Tax Registrations

Department of Revenue and Regulation, Business Tax Division, 445 E Capitol, Pierre, SD 57501-3100; 605-773-3311, Fax- 605-773-6729; 8AM-5PM. www.state.sd.us/drr2/revenue.html

Searching: This agency will only confirm if a business is registered and licensed. They will provide no other information. Include in request- business name. Also search by tax permit number or owner name.

Access by: mail, phone, fax, in person.

Mail search: Turnaround time- 2 to 3 weeks. A SASE is requested. No fee for mail request.

Phone search: No fee for telephone request.

Fax search: There is no fee, turnaround time is 2-3 weeks.

In person: No fee for request. Usually requests can be processed while you wait.

Birth Certificates

South Dakota Department of Health, Vital Records, 207 E Missouri, #1A, Pierre, SD 57501; 605-773-4961, Fax- 605-773-2680; 8AM-5PM.

http://doh.sd.gov/VitalRecords/order.aspx

Direct questions to mariah.pokorny@state.sd.us.

Indexing & Storage: Records available from 1905 to present. New records available for inquiry immediately.

Searching: Anyone who submits an application and the applicable fee can obtain an informational copy of a vital record. Only those related or representing the family can request a certified copy, unless permission is given. See web for exact list. Include in request- full name, names of parents, mother's maiden name, date of birth, place of birth, using the state's form. Any county Register of Deeds can provide a computer generated birth certificate for the same fee. This data not released- sealed records.

Access by: mail, phone, fax, in person, online.

Fee & Payment: The search fee is $10.00. Fee payee- South Dakota Department of Health. Prepayment required. Personal checks accepted. Major credit cards accepted only for expedited service.

Mail search: Turnaround time- 4 to 5 days. SASE not required.

Phone search: You must use a credit card, considered expedited service.

Fax search: See expedited service.

In person: Turnaround time 30 minutes.

Online search: Records may be ordered online at the website via a state supported vendor. You can order recent (less than 100 years) birth records at the website, for a fee. You can search free at http://apps.sd.gov/applications/PH14Over100BirthRec/index.asp for birth records over 100 years old.

Expedited service: Expedited service is available for web and phone searches. Turnaround time- overnight delivery. Add $11.50 expedite fee and the delivery fee.

Death Records

South Dakota Department of Health, Vital Records, 207 E Missouri, #1A, Pierre, SD 57501; 605-773-4961, Fax- 605-773-2680; 8AM-5PM.

http://doh.sd.gov/VitalRecords/order.aspx

Direct questions to mariah.pokorny@state.sd.us.

Indexing & Storage: Records available from 1905 to present. New records available for inquiry immediately.

Searching: Anyone who submits an application and the applicable fee can obtain an informational copy of a vital record. Only those related or representing the family can request a certified copy, unless permission is given. See web for exact list. Include in request- full name, date of death, place of death, using the state's form. This data not released- sealed records.

Access by: mail, phone, fax, in person, online.

Fee & Payment: The fee is $10.00 per record. Fee payee- South Dakota Department of Health. Prepayment required. Personal checks accepted. Major credit cards accepted only for expedited service.

Mail search: Turnaround time- 4 to 5 days. SASE not required.

Phone search: You must use a credit card.

Fax search: See expedited service.

In person: Turnaround time is 30 minutes.

Online search: Records may be ordered online at the website via a state supported vendor.

Expedited service: Expedited service is available for Internet and phone searches. Turnaround time- overnight delivery. Add $11.50 expedite fee and the delivery fee.

Marriage Certificates

South Dakota Department of Health, Vital Records, 207 E Missouri, #1A, Pierre, SD 57501; 605-773-4961, Fax- 605-773-2680; 8AM-5PM.

http://doh.sd.gov/VitalRecords/order.aspx

Direct questions to mariah.pokorny@state.sd.us.

Indexing & Storage: Records available from 1905 to present. New records available for inquiry immediately.

Searching: Anyone who submits an application and the applicable fee can obtain an informational copy of a vital record. Only those related or representing the family can request a certified copy, unless permission is given. See web for exact list. Include in request- names of husband and wife, date of marriage, place or county of marriage, using the state's form. Also include wife's maiden name. This data not released- SSN, phone numbers, other information provided by bride or groom not included above.

Access by: mail, phone, fax, in person, online.

Fee & Payment: The fee is $10.00 per record. Fee payee- South Dakota Department of Health. Prepayment required. Personal checks accepted. Major credit cards accepted only for expedited service.

Mail search: Turnaround time- 4 to 5 days. SASE not required.

Phone search: You must use a credit card.

Fax search: See expedited service.

In person: Turnaround time is 30 minutes.

Online search: Records may be ordered online at the website via a state supported vendor.

Expedited service: Expedited service is available for Internet and phone searches. Turnaround time- overnight delivery. Add $11.50 expedite fee and the delivery fee.

Divorce Records

South Dakota Department of Health, Vital Records, 207 E Missouri, #1A, Pierre, SD 57501; 605-773-4961, Fax- 605-773-2680; 8AM-5PM.

http://doh.sd.gov/VitalRecords/order.aspx

Direct questions to mariah.pokorny@state.sd.us.

Indexing & Storage: Records available from 1905 to present. New records available for inquiry immediately.

Searching: Anyone who submits an application and the applicable fee can obtain an informational copy of a vital record. Only those related or representing the family can request a certified copy, unless permission is given. See web for exact list. Include in request- names of husband and wife, date of divorce, place of divorce. This data not released- sealed records.

Access by: mail, phone, fax, in person, online.

Fee & Payment: The fee is $10.00 per record. Fee payee- South Dakota Department of Health. Prepayment required. Personal checks accepted. Major credit cards accepted only for expedited service.

Mail search: Turnaround time- 4 to 5 days. SASE not required.

Phone search: You must use a credit card.

Fax search: See expedited service.

In person: Turnaround time 30 minutes.

Online search: Records may be ordered at the website, the $10.00 fee apples.

Expedited service: Expedited service is available for Internet and phone searches. Turnaround time- overnight delivery. Add $6.50 expedite fee and delivery fee.

Workers' Compensation Records

Labor Department, Workers Compensation Division, 700 Governors Dr, Pierre, SD 57501; 605-773-3681, Fax- 605-773-4211; 8AM-5PM.

http://dol.sd.gov/workerscomp/default.aspx

Indexing & Storage: Records available from 1973. New records available for inquiry immediately.

Searching: Must have a signed release from the claimant. Must also specify which records you are requesting. A computer search will only go back to July 1989. Fraud reports and sealed files are not released. Include in request- claimant name, SSN, date of accident, body part injured.

Access by: mail.

Fee & Payment: Search fee is $20.00 per file or date of injury, copies are included. Fee payee- Division of Labor Management. Prepayment required. Personal checks accepted, credit cards are not.

Mail search: Turnaround time- 2 weeks. SASE not required.

Driver Records

Dept of Public Safety, Office of Driver Licensing, 118 W Capitol, Pierre, SD 57501; 605-773-6883, Fax- 605-773-3018; 8AM-5PM.

www.state.sd.us/dps/dl/

Ticket information is maintained at the local courts, not at the state.

Indexing & Storage: Records available for 3 years for moving violations and DWIs. Speeding violations less than 10 mph over and out-of-state speeding violations (except for commercial drivers), suspensions and revocations are not listed on the record. New records available for inquiry in 1 to 3 weeks.

Searching: Casual requesters can only obtain records with the written permission of the subject. All other requesters must certify for what reason they are obtaining the information and comply with DPPA policies. Request forms can be downloaded from website. Include in request- full name, date of birth. If for a non-permissible (DPPA) use, then notarized signature of driver needed. A secondary search will be done with the license number if no record is found on the name search. Suggest employers and insurance companies use MVR Request Form 2. This data not released- SSNs.

Access by: mail, phone, in person, online.

Fee & Payment: The fee is $4.00 per record. Fee may increase to $5.00 effective July 1, 2009, per legislation introduced. Fee payee- Dept of Public

Safety Prepayment required. Personal checks accepted, credit cards are not.

Mail search: Turnaround time- 48 hours. The DL#, name, and DOB are all needed when requesting records via mail.

Phone search: Pre-approved accounts may order via the telephone. This is a very limited access.

In person: Turnaround time while you wait at this location and at the Sioux Falls Driver Exam Station.

Online search: The system is open for batch requests 24 hours a day. There is a minimum of 250 requests daily. It generally takes 10 minutes to process a batch. The current fee is $4.00 per record (possibly increased to $5.00 in July) and there are some start-up costs. For more information, call 605-773-6883.

Other access: Lists are available to the insurance industry.

Vehicle, Vessel Ownership & Registration

Division of Motor Vehicles, Information Section, 445 E Capitol Ave, Pierre, SD 57501-3185; 605-773-3541, Fax- 605-773-2550; 8AM-5PM.

www.state.sd.us/drr2/motorvehicle/index.htm

The DMV took over the registration and title process for boats in 1992. All boats (except canoes, inflatable's, kayaks, sailboards) over 12 ft in length, and motorized boats must be titled and registered.

Indexing & Storage: Records available on film permanently, original document retained 18 months. New records available for inquiry in 2 weeks.

Searching: The agency requires all requests for vehicle related records be on the Division DPPA Form. Casual requesters (individuals) can only obtain information with written permission of the subject. Include in request- DPPA Form. All requests must be in writing. This data not released- SSN, DL#. Previous owner/address data is extremely limited.

Access by: mail, in person.

Fee & Payment: The fee for VIN, plate, owner, title, or lien searches is $2.00 per record. A complete title history from microfilm is $5.00. Fee payee- Division of Motor Vehicles. Prepayment required. Personal checks accepted, credit cards are not.

Mail search: Turnaround time- 1 day to 1 week. Must provide DPPA request form. A SASE is requested.

In person: You may request records in person, but the request must be in writing on the Division DPPA Form.

Accident Reports

Department of Public Safety, Accident Records, 118 W Capitol Ave, Pierre, SD 57501-2000; 605-773-3868, Fax- 605-773-4156; 8AM-5PM.

Indexing & Storage: Records available for 10 years to present, 5 years on paper. New records available for inquiry in 1 week from receipt from law enforcement agency.

Searching: Include in request- full name, date of accident, location of accident. This data not released- SSN, DL#.

Access by: mail, in person.

Fee & Payment: The fee is $4.00 per record. Fee payee- Accident Records. Prepayment required. Personal checks accepted, credit cards are not.

Mail search: Turnaround time- 5 -15 days. A self addressed envelope is not required.

In person: Normal turnaround time is immediate if the record is on file.

Expedited service: Will return report via fax once record fee is paid.

Legislation Records

South Dakota Legislature, Capitol Bldg - Legislative Research Council, 500 E Capitol Ave, 3rd Fl, Pierre, SD 57501; 605-773-3251, Fax- 605-773-4576; 8AM-5PM.

http://legis.state.sd.us/index.aspx

Signed bills are found at the Secretary of State's office, 605-773-3537. Pending legislation may be obtained here during the session.

Indexing & Storage: Records available from 1951 on. New records available for inquiry immediately.

Searching: Search by bill number, subject, sponsor or by keyword.

Access by: mail, in person, online.

Fee & Payment: Fees are not charged for documents, unless the quantity of copies is large or unless one purchases a subscription to all the bills or journals.

Mail search: Turnaround time- usually same day. SASE is helpful.

In person: Simple requests may be processed while you wait.

Online search: Information is available at their website at no charge. The site is very thorough and has enrolled version of bills and state statutes. The research site at http://legis.state.sd.us/mylrc/index.aspx requires a password (no fees), except for basic searching.

Voter Registration

Secretary of State, Elections Division, 500 E Capitol #204, Pierre, SD 57501; 605-773-3537, Fax- 605-773-6580; 8AM-5PM.

www.sdsos.gov/Elections/

The Secretary of State and County Auditors throughout the state have compiled a statewide voter registration file of the official voter registration files in each county auditor's office. County auditors update the statewide file on a daily basis.

Indexing & Storage: New records available for inquiry in 24 hours.

Searching: Name searching should be done at the county level, this is where the paper records are kept. Include in request- name, dob. Request must in writing with original copy presented. Data files or paper lists of the file or portions of the file may be purchased from the Secretary of State. Information obtained from the statewide file may not be used or sold for any commercial purpose and may not be placed on the internet. This data not released- SSN, DL, date and month of birth.

Access by: mail, in person.

Fee & Payment: Only fees charged are for bulk list purchase or if extensive research needed Fee payee- Secretary of State Prepayment required. personal Checks accepted.

Mail search: Turnaround time- 24 hours. Records are available by mail. A SASE is not requested.

In person: Records may be searched in person.

Other access: The webpage has a list of various files available for purchase on CD or paper. For example, statewide CD is $2,500, statewide printed list is $5,500. Data may be purchased by county or legislative district.

GED Certificates

SD Department of Labor, AEL/GED/Literacy, 700 Governors Drive, Pierre, SD 57501-2291; 605-773-3101, Fax- 605-773-6184; 8AM-5PM.

http://dol.sd.gov/workforce_training/ged_intro.aspx

You may email requests to marcia.hess@state.sd.us.

Indexing & Storage: Records available from 1942 to present. New records available for inquiry in 3-4 weeks.

Searching: Include in request- name at time of test, DOB, SSN and a signed release is required for either a verification or a copy of a transcript.

Access by: mail, fax, in person.

Fee & Payment: The fee for verifications or for a copy of a transcript is $5.00. Fee payee- SD Dept of Labor Prepayment required. Personal checks not accepted.

Mail search: Turnaround time- 1 to 3 days. SASE not required. No fee for mail request.

Fax search: Results will available in 1 day, but will only send transcript after $5.00 fee received.

In person: You can wait for results.

Hunting & Fishing License Information

Game, Fish & Parks Department, License Division, 412 W Missouri Ave, Pierre, SD 57501; 605-773-3393, 605-773-3485, Fax- 605-773-5842; 8AM-5PM. www.sdgfp.info/Index.htm

Indexing & Storage: Records available for current and previous years only.

Searching: Requests must be in writing. They will release address data. The DOB and address are helpful.

Access by: in person.

Fee & Payment: The fee is case dependent per the extent of the names and the search.

In person: There is no fee, if the search request is simple.

Other access: Mailing lists are available for purchase. They have records for big game licensees.

South Dakota State Licensing Agencies

For details about the agency responsible for licensing/certifying/registering an item below or in the Agency Quick Finder section, match an item's number with the number of the agency in the *Licensing Agency Information* section.

South Dakota Licenses Searchable Online

Abstractor, Individual/Company #1 .... www.state.sd.us/drr2/reg/abstracters/New/roster.html
Ambulance Service #20 .... www.state.sd.us/dps/ems/
Animal Remedy (medicine/drug) #19 .... www.state.sd.us/doa/das/hp-af-ar.htm
Architect #23 .... www.state.sd.us/dol/boards/engineer/Roster/roster.htm
Athletic Trainer #10 .... http://doh.sd.gov/boards/medicine/
Attorney #31 .... www.sdbar.net/
Auctioneer #27 .... www.state.sd.us/drr2/reg/realestate/roster_licensees/roster.htm
Audiologist #29 .... http://doh.sd.gov/boards/audiology/roster.aspx
Bail Bond Agent #36 .... www.sd.gov/feedback/
Bank #2 .... www.state.sd.us/drr2/reg/bank/banktrust/banktrust.htm
Barber / Barber Shop #4 .... http://dol.sd.gov/bdcomm/barber/bbrosters.aspx
Beauty Shop/Salon #18 .... http://apps.sd.gov/applications/ld19cosmet/license.asp
Clinical Nurse Specialist #11 .... https://ifmc.sd.gov/lookup.php
Cosmetologist / Salon / Instructor #18 .... http://apps.sd.gov/applications/ld19cosmet/license.asp
Counselor #6 .... http://dhs.sd.gov/brd/Counselor/roster.aspx
Crematory #28 .... http://doh.sd.gov/Boards/FuneralBoard/Roster.aspx
Dentist / Dental Assistant / Hygenist #7 .... www.sdboardofdentistry.com/
Driller, Oil and Gas Supervisor #17 .... www.state.sd.us/denr/DES/Mining/Oil&Gas/NewPermit.htm
Embalmer #28 .... http://doh.sd.gov/Boards/FuneralBoard/Roster.aspx
Engineer #23 .... www.state.sd.us/dol/boards/engineer/Roster/roster.htm
Esthetician #18 .... http://apps.sd.gov/applications/ld19cosmet/license.asp
Fertilizer #19 .... www.state.sd.us/doa/das/hp-fert.htm
Funeral Director/Establishment #28 .... http://doh.sd.gov/Boards/FuneralBoard/Roster.aspx
Gaming Manufacturer #24 .... www.state.sd.us/drr2/reg/gaming/manufac.htm
Health Insurer #36 .... www.sd.gov/feedback/
Hearing Aid Dispenser #29 .... http://doh.sd.gov/boards/audiology/roster.aspx
Home Inspector #27 .... www.state.sd.us/drr2/reg/realestate/roster_licensees/roster.htm
Insurance Company #36 .... www.state.sd.us/drr2/reg/insurance/consumer/index.html
Insurer of Health #36 .... www.sd.gov/feedback/
Landscape Architect #23 .... www.state.sd.us/dol/boards/engineer/Roster/roster.htm
Lobbyist #26 .... www.state.sd.us/applications/ST12ODRS/PublicLobbyistViewlist.asp?cmd=resetall
Manicurist/Nail Technician #18 .... http://apps.sd.gov/applications/ld19cosmet/license.asp
Marriage & Family Therapist #6 .... http://dhs.sd.gov/brd/Counselor/roster.aspx
Midwife Nurse #11 .... https://ifmc.sd.gov/lookup.php
Money Lender #2 .... www.state.sd.us/drr2/reg/bank/licensees/moneylender.htm
Mortgage Broker/Lender #2 .... www.state.sd.us/drr2/reg/bank/licensees/mortgagebrokers.htm
Nail Salon #18 .... http://apps.sd.gov/applications/ld19cosmet/license.asp
Notary #26 .... www.state.sd.us/applications/ST12ODRS/aspx/frmNotaryViewlist.aspx?cmd=resetall
Nurse #11 .... https://ifmc.sd.gov/lookup.php
Nurse Aide Certified #11 .... https://ifmc.sd.gov/lookup.php
Nurse Anesthetist #11 .... https://ifmc.sd.gov/lookup.php
Nurse Practitioner, Certified #11 .... https://ifmc.sd.gov/lookup.php
Nursing Home Administrator #8 .... http://doh.sd.gov/boards/nursingfacility/
Oil & Gas Driller Senior Geologist #17 .... www.state.sd.us/denr/DES/Mining/Oil&Gas/NewPermit.htm
Optometrist #9 .... www.arbo.org/index.php?action=findanoptometrist
Osteopathic Physician #10 .... http://doh.sd.gov/boards/medicine/
Pesticide Applicator/Dealer #19 .... www.state.sd.us/doa/das/
Pet Health Insurer #36 .... www.state.sd.us/drr2/reg/insurance/consumer/pet_companies.pdf
Petrol. Release Assessor/Remediator #23 .... www.state.sd.us/dol/boards/engineer/Roster/roster.htm
Podiatrist #14 .... http://doh.sd.gov/boards/podiatry/
Property Manager #27 .... www.state.sd.us/drr2/reg/realestate/roster_licensees/roster.htm
Psychologist #15 .... http://dhs.sd.gov/brd/Psychologist/roster.aspx
Public Accountant-CPA #3 .... http://dol.sd.gov/bdcomm/
Radiology (Dental) #7 .... www.sdboardofdentistry.com/
Real Estate Agent/Seller/Broker/Firm #27 .... www.state.sd.us/drr2/reg/realestate/roster_licensees/roster.htm
Re-insurer, Accredited/Qualified #36 .... www.sd.gov/feedback/
Residential Rental Agent #27 .... www.state.sd.us/drr2/reg/realestate/roster_licensees/roster.htm

Securities Agent/Broker/Dealer #30 .... http://brokercheck.finra.org/Search/Search.aspx
Social Worker #15 .... http://dhs.sd.gov/brd/SocialWorker/roster.aspx
Storage Tank, Above/Below Ground #35 .... www.state.sd.us/denr/des/ground/tanks/register.htm
Surveyor, Land #23 .... www.state.sd.us/dol/boards/engineer/Roster/roster.htm
Timeshare Project, Registered #27 .... www.state.sd.us/drr2/reg/realestate/roster_licensees/roster.htm
Timeshare Real Estate #27 .... www.state.sd.us/drr2/reg/realestate/roster_licensees/roster.htm
Trust Company #2 .... www.state.sd.us/drr2/reg/bank/banktrust/banktrust.htm
Waste Water System Operator #12 .... www.state.sd.us/denr/des/drinking/PDF/operator.pdf
Water Distributor #12 .... www.state.sd.us/denr/des/drinking/PDF/operator.pdf
Water Treatment Operator #12 .... www.state.sd.us/denr/des/drinking/PDF/operator.pdf
Weapon, Concealed #26 .... www.sdsos.gov/adminservices/concealedpistolpermits.shtm

South Dakota Licensing Quick Finder

9-1-1 Telecommunicator #25 605-773-3331
Abstractor, Individual/Company #1 605-869-2269
Acupuncturist #5 605-668-9017
Alcoholic Beverage Distributor #21 605-773-3311
Ambulance Service #20 605-773-4031
Animal Feed Seller/Producer #19 605-773-4432
Animal Remedy (medicine/drug) #19 605-773-4432
Appliance Contr./Journey'n/Appr'n #33 605-773-3429
Architect #23 605-394-2510
Asbestos Service Company #35 605-773-3153
Asbestos Worker #35 605-773-3153
Athletic Trainer #10 605-367-7781
Attorney #31 605-224-7554
Auctioneer #27 605-773-3600
Audiologist #29 605-642-1600
Bail Bond Agent #36 605-773-3513
Bank #2 605-773-3421
Barber / Barber Shop #4 605-642-1600
Beauty Shop/Salon #18 605-773-6193
Brokerage Firm #30 605-773-4823
Business Opportunities Broker #30 605-773-4823
Canine Team #25 605-773-3331
Chiropractor #5 605-668-9017
Clinical Nurse Specialist #11 605-362-2760
Cosmetologist #18 605-773-6193
Cosmetology Salon/Instructor #18 605-773-6193
Counselor #6 605-331-2927
Court/Shorthand Reporter #37 605-773-3474
Crematory #28 605-642-1600
Dentist/Dental Assistant/Hygienist #7 605-224-1282
Dietitian/Nutritionist #10 605-367-7781
Driller, Oil and Gas Supervisor #17 605-394-2229
Drug Wholesaler #13 605-362-2737
Electrical Inspector #32 605-773-3573
Electrician #32 605-773-3573
Embalmer #28 605-642-1600
Emergency Medical Technician #20 605-773-4031
Engineer #23 605-394-2510
Engineer, Petrol'm Environmen'l #23 605-394-2510
Environmental Site Assessor #35 605-773-3296
Esthetician #18 605-773-6193
Fertilizer #19 605-773-4432
Franchise Sales #30 605-773-4823
Funeral Director/Establishment #28 605-642-1600
Gaming Manufacturer #24 605-773-6050
Gaming, Facility/Personnel #24 605-773-6050
Hazardous Waste #35 605-773-3153
Health Insurer #36 605-773-3563
Hearing Aid Dispenser #29 605-642-1600
Home Inspector #27 605-773-3600
Insurance Agent #36 605-773-3513
Insurance Company #36 605-773-3563
Insurer of Health #36 605-773-3563
Investment Advisor #30 605-773-4823
Landfill #35 605-773-3153
Landscape Architect #23 605-394-2510
Laundromat #21 605-773-3311
Law Enforcement Officer #25 605-773-3331
Livestock Dealer #16 605-773-3321
Loan Production #2 605-773-3421
Lobbyist #26 605-773-3537
Manicurist/Nail Technician #18 605-773-6193
Marriage & Family Therapist #6 605-331-2927
Medical Assistant #10 605-367-7781
Medical Doctor #10 605-367-7781
Midwife Nurse #11 605-362-2760
Milk Grader/Hauler #19 605-773-4294
Milk Tester/Sampler #19 605-773-4294
Mobile Home Contractor #33 605-773-3429
Money Lender #2 605-773-3421
Money Order Business #2 605-773-3421
Mortgage Broker/Lender #2 605-773-3421
Nail Salon #18 605-773-6193
Notary #26 605-773-3537
Nurse #11 605-362-2760
Nurse Aide Certified #11 605-362-2760
Nurse Anesthetist #11 605-362-2760
Nurse Practitioner, Certified #11 605-362-2760
Nurses Aide #34 605-362-2762
Nursing Home Administrator #8 605-331-5040
Occupational Therapist/Assistant #10 605-367-7781
Oil & Gas Driller Senior Geologist #17 605-394-2229
Optometrist #9 605-347-2136
Osteopathic Physician #10 605-367-7781
Paramedic #20 605-773-4031
Pesticide Applicator/Dealer #19 605-773-4432
Pet Health Insurer #36 605-773-3563
Petrol. Release Assessor/Remediator #23 605-394-2510
Pharmacist/Pharmacy #13 605-362-2737
Physical Therapist/Assistant #10 605-367-7781
Physician/Medical Assistant #10 605-367-7781
Plumber #33 605-773-3429
Podiatrist #14 605-642-1600
Polygraph Examiner #25 605-773-3331
Property Manager #27 605-773-3600
Psychologist #15 605-642-1600
Public Accountant-CPA #3 605-367-5770
Racing, Facility/Personnel #24 605-773-6050
Radiologist (Chiropractic) #5 605-668-9017
Radiology (Dental) #7 605-224-1282
Real Estate Agent/Seller #27 605-773-3600
Real Estate Broker/Firm #27 605-773-3600
Recycler #35 605-773-3153
Recycler, Specialty #35 605-773-3153
Re-insurer, Accredited/Qualified #36 605-773-3563
Residential Rental Agent #27 605-773-3600
Respiratory Care Practitioner #10 605-367-7781
School Counselor #22 605-773-3553
School Principal/Superintendent #22 605-773-3553
Scrap Tire Company #35 605-773-3153
Securities Agent/Broker/Dealer #30 605-773-4823
Sewage/Water Installat'n Contractor/Installer #33 605-773-3429
Social Worker #15 605-642-1600
Spill Clean-up Company #35 605-773-3296
Storage Tank, above/below ground #35 605-773-3296
Surveyor, Land #23 605-394-2510
Tank Remover #35 605-773-3296
Teacher #22 605-773-3553
Testing Lab, Environmental #35 605-773-3296
Timeshare Project, Registered #27 605-773-3600
Timeshare Real Estate #27 605-773-3600
Tobacco Wholesaler #21 605-773-3311
Trust Company #2 605-773-3421
Veterinarian/Veterinary Technician #16 605-773-3321
Veterinary Corporation #16 605-773-3321
Waste Water System Operator #12 605-773-3151
Water Conditioning Plumbing Installer #33 605-773-3429
Water Distributor #12 605-773-3151
Water Treatment Operator #12 .... 605-773-3151, 605-773-4208
Weapon, Concealed #26 605-773-3537
Well Driller #35 605-773-3352

South Dakota Licensing Agency Information

#1 Abstractors Board of Examiners, PO Box 4, Kennebec, SD 57544-0187; 605-895-2629, Fax- 605-869-2269. www.state.sd.us/drr2/reg/abstracters/New/index.html Search data at- www.state.sd.us/drr2/reg/abstracters/New/roster.html

#2 Department of Revenue & Regulation, Division of Banking, 217 1/2 W Missouri Ave, Pierre, SD 57501-4590; 605-773-3421, Fax- 866-326-7504. www.state.sd.us/drr2/reg/bank/BANK-HOM.htm

#3 Board of Accountancy, 301 E 14th St, #200, Sioux Falls, SD 57104-5022; 605-367-5770, Fax- 605-367-5773. Hours- 8AM-5PM. http://dol.sd.gov/bdcomm/ Search page may be found at the new accountancy webpage; search, scroll down through the alphabetical listings.

#4 Board of Barber Examiners, c/o Carol Tellinghuisen, Executive Secretary, 135 E Illinois, #214, Spearfish, SD 57783; 605-642-1600, Fax- 605-642-1756. Hours- 8:15AM-4PM M-TH. http://dol.sd.gov/bdcomm/barber/default.aspx Search data at- http://dol.sd.gov/bdcomm/barber/bbrosters.aspx

#5 Board of Chiropractic Examiners, 407 Belmont Ave, Yankton, SD 57078; 605-668-9017, Fax- 605-668-9017. Hours- 8AM-4PM. http://doh.sd.gov/boards/chiropractic/

#6 Board of Counselor Examiners, PO Box 2164, Sioux Falls, SD 57101-1822; 605-331-2927, Fax- 605-331-2043. http://dhs.sd.gov/brd/Counselor/default.aspx Search data at- http://dhs.sd.gov/brd/Counselor/roster.aspx

#7 Board of Dentistry, PO Box 1037, Pierre, SD 57501-1037; 605-224-1282, Fax- 605-224-7426. Hours- 8AM-5PM. Search data at- www.sdboardofdentistry.com/

#8 Board of Examiners for Nursing Home Administrators, PO Box 632, Sioux Falls, SD 57101-0632; 605-331-5040, Fax- 605-331-2043. http://doh.sd.gov/boards/nursingfacility/

#9 Board of Optometry, PO Box 628, 1613 Elk Ct, Sturgis, SD 57785-0628; 605-347-2136, Fax- 605-347-2136. Hours- 8AM-5PM. http://doh.sd.gov/boards/optometry/ Search at- www.arbo.org/index.php?action=findanoptometrist

#10 Board of Medical & Osteopathic Examiners, 123 S Main Ave, #100, Sioux Falls, SD 57104; 605-367-7781, Fax- 605-367-7786. http://doh.sd.gov/boards/medicine/

#11 Board of Nursing, 4305 S Louise Ave, #201, Sioux Falls, SD 57106-3115; 605-362-2760, Fax- 605-362-2768. http://doh.sd.gov/boards/nursing/ Search data at- https://ifmc.sd.gov/lookup.php Online searching/verification system is being updated; check main website.

#12 Department of Environment & Natural Resources, Board of Operator Certification, 523 E Capitol Ave, Foss Bldg, PMB 2020, Pierre, SD 57501; 605-773-3151, Fax- 605-773-6035. Hours- 8AM-5PM. www.state.sd.us/denr/denr.html Search data at- www.state.sd.us/denr/des/drinking/PDF/operator.pdf

#13 Board of Pharmacy, 4305 S Louise Ave, #104, Sioux Falls, SD 57106-3115; 605-362-2737, Fax- 605-362-2738. Hours- 8AM-5PM. http://doh.sd.gov/boards/pharmacy/

#14 Board of Podiatry Examiners, 135 E Illinois, #214, Spearfish, SD 57783; 605-642-1600, Fax- 605-642-1756. Hours- 8:15AM-4PM M-TH. http://doh.sd.gov/boards/podiatry/ Search data at- http://doh.sd.gov/boards/podiatry/

#15 Board of Social Work Examiners/Psychologist Examiners, 135 E Illinois, #214, Spearfish, SD 57783; 605-642-1600, Fax- 605-733 2006. Hours- 8:15AM-4PM M-TH. http://dhs.sd.gov/brd/SocialWorker/default.aspx

#16 Board of Veterinary Medical Examiners, 411 S Fort St, Pierre, SD 57501-4503; 605-773-3321, Fax- 605-773-5459. www.state.sd.us/doa/veterinary/

#17 Department of Environment & Natural Resources, Oil & Gas Section, Minerals & Mining Program, 2050 W Main, #1, Rapid City, SD 57701; 605-394-2229, Fax- 605-394-5317. www.state.sd.us/denr/DES/Mining/Oil&Gas/O&Ghome.htm Search data at- www.state.sd.us/denr/DES/Mining/Oil&Gas/NewPermit.htm Permit records go back five years.

#18 Cosmetology Commission, 500 E Capitol, Pierre, SD 57501-5070; 605-773-6193, Fax- 605-773-7175. http://dol.sd.gov/bdcomm/cosmet/default.aspx Search data at- http://apps.sd.gov/applications/ld19cosmet/license.asp

#19 Department of Agriculture, Division of Ag Services, 523 E Capitol Ave, Foss Bldg, Pierre, SD 57501-3182; 605-773-3724, Fax- 605-773-3481. www.state.sd.us/doa/das/

#20 Department Public Safety, Emergency Medical Services, 118 W Capitol, Pierre, SD 57501; 605-773-4031, Fax- 605-773-6631. www.state.sd.us/dps/ems/

#21 Department of Revenue & Regulation, Property & Special Taxes - Special Tax Division, 445 E Capitol Ave, Pierre, SD 57501-3185; 605-773-3311, Fax- 605-773-5129. www.state.sd.us/drr2/revenue.html

#22 Education & Cultural Affairs Department, Office of Policy & Accountability, 700 Governors Dr, Pierre, SD 57501-2291; 605-773-3134, Fax- 605-773-6139. http://doe.sd.gov/oatq/

#23 Department of Labor, Board of Technical Professions, 2040 W Main St, #304, Rapid City, SD 57702-2447; 605-394-2510, Fax- 605-395-2509. http://dol.sd.gov/lmic/career_licensing_agencies.aspx Search data at- www.state.sd.us/dol/boards/engineer/Roster/roster.htm Roster available for $25.00 by print, disk, or email.

#24 Commission on Gaming, Department of Revenue and Regulation, 221 W Capitol Ave #101 (c/o 1320 E Sioux Ave), Pierre, SD 57501; 605-773-6050, Fax- 605-773-6053. 8AM-5PM. www.state.sd.us/drr2/reg/gaming/ Also has an office in Deadwood at 696 Main St, 605-578-3074.

#25 Division of Criminal Investigation, Criminal Justice Training Center, 1302 E Hwy 14, Suite 5, Pierre, SD 57501; 605-773-3331, Fax- 605-773-4629. http://dci.sd.gov/let/index.htm

#26 Office of Secretary of State, Lobbyist Coordinator, Notaries, 500 E Capitol Ave, State Capitol Bldg, #204, Pierre, SD 57501-5070; 605-773-3537, Fax- 605-773-6580. Hours- 8AM-5PM. http://sdsos.gov

#27 Real Estate Commission, 221 W Capitol, #101, Pierre, SD 57501; 605-773-3600, Fax- 605-773-4356. www.state.sd.us/drr2/reg/realestate/ Search at- www.state.sd.us/drr2/reg/realestate/roster_licensees/roster.htm

#28 Board of Funeral Services, 135 E Illinois, #214, Spearfish, SD 57783-2446; 605-642-1600, Fax- 605-722-1006. Hours-8:15AM-4PM M-TH. http://doh.sd.gov/boards/funeralboard/ Search data at- http://doh.sd.gov/Boards/FuneralBoard/Roster.aspx

#29 Board of Hearing Aid Dispensers and Audiologists, 135 E Illinois, #214, Spearfish, SD 57783-0654; 605-642-1600, Fax- 605-722-1006. Hours- 8:15AM-4PM M-TH. http://doh.sd.gov/boards/audiology/ Search at- http://doh.sd.gov/boards/audiology/roster.aspx

#30 Dept of Revenue & Regulation, Division of Securities, 445 E Capitol Ave, Pierre, SD 57501-3185; 605-773-4823, Fax- 605-773-5953. Hours- 8AM-5PM. www.state.sd.us/drr2/reg/securities/

#31 State Bar, 222 E Capitol Ave, Pierre, SD 57501-2596; 605-224-7554, 800-952-2333, Fax- 605-224-0282. Hours- 8AM-5PM. www.sdbar.net

#32 Electrical Commission, 308 S Pierre St (c/o 1320 E Sioux Ave), Pierre, SD 57501-5070; 605-773-3573, 800-233-7765, Fax- 605-773-6213. http://dol.sd.gov/bdcomm/electric/default.aspx

#33 Plumbing Commission, 308 S. Pierce St (%1320 E Sioux Ave), Pierre, SD 57501; 605-773-3429, Fax- 605-773-5405. http://dol.sd.gov/bdcomm/plumbing/default.aspx

#34 Healthcare Administration, Nurses Aide Testing, 804 N Western Ave, Sioux Falls, SD 57104-2098; 605-362-2762, Fax- 605-339-1354. www.sdhca.org

#35 Department of Environment & Natural Resources, Division of Environmental Svcs, 523 E Capitol Ave, Joe Foss Bldg, PMB 2020, Pierre, SD 57501-3182; 605-773-3153, Fax- 605-773-6035. Hours- 8AM-5PM. www.state.sd.us/denr/denr.html Search data at- www.state.sd.us/denr/DES/WasteMgn/WMPpage1.htm

#36 Department of Commerce & Regulation, Division of Insurance, 445 E Capitol Ave, Pierre, SD 57501; 605-773-3563, Fax- 605-773-5369. www.state.sd.us/drr2/reg/insurance/ Search data at- www.state.sd.us/drr2/reg/insurance/consumer/index.html

#37 Supreme Court, Unified Judicial Court Administrators Office, Capitol Bldg, 500 E Capitol, Pierre, SD 57501; 605-773-3474, Fax- 605-773-5627. www.sdjudicial.com UJS Official Court Reporters names and phone's can be found on the web page above. This info includes only court reporters who are UJS (Unified Judicial System) employees.

South Dakota Federal Courts

The following list indicates the district and division name for each county in the state. If the bankruptcy court location is different from the district court, then the location of the bankruptcy court appears in parentheses.

South Dakota County/Court Cross Reference

County	Court	County	Court
Aurora	Sioux Falls	Hyde	Pierre
Beadle	Sioux Falls	Jackson	Pierre
Bennett	Rapid City (Pierre)	Jerauld	Pierre
Bon Homme	Sioux Falls	Jones	Pierre
Brookings	Sioux Falls	Kingsbury	Sioux Falls
Brown	Aberdeen (Pierre)	Lake	Sioux Falls
Brule	Sioux Falls	Lawrence	Rapid City (Pierre)
Buffalo	Pierre	Lincoln	Sioux Falls
Butte	Aberdeen (Pierre)	Lyman	Pierre
Campbell	Aberdeen (Pierre)	Marshall	Aberdeen (Pierre)
Charles Mix	Sioux Falls	McCook	Sioux Falls
Clark	Aberdeen (Pierre)	McPherson	Aberdeen (Pierre)
Clay	Sioux Falls	Meade	Rapid City (Pierre)
Codington	Aberdeen (Pierre)	Mellette	Pierre
Corson	Aberdeen (Pierre)	Miner	Sioux Falls
Custer	Rapid City (Pierre)	Minnehaha	Sioux Falls
Davison	Sioux Falls	Moody	Sioux Falls
Day	Aberdeen (Pierre)	Pennington	Rapid City (Pierre)
Deuel	Aberdeen (Pierre)	Perkins	Rapid City (Pierre)
Dewey	Pierre	Potter	Pierre
Douglas	Sioux Falls	Roberts	Aberdeen (Pierre)
Edmunds	Aberdeen (Pierre)	Sanborn	Sioux Falls
Fall River	Rapid City (Pierre)	Shannon	Rapid City (Pierre)
Faulk	Pierre	Spink	Aberdeen (Pierre)
Grant	Aberdeen (Pierre)	Stanley	Pierre
Gregory	Pierre	Sully	Pierre
Haakon	Pierre	Todd	Pierre
Hamlin	Aberdeen (Pierre)	Tripp	Pierre
Hand	Pierre	Turner	Sioux Falls
Hanson	Sioux Falls	Union	Sioux Falls
Harding	Rapid City (Pierre)	Walworth	Aberdeen (Pierre)
Hughes	Pierre	Yankton	Sioux Falls
Hutchinson	Sioux Falls	Ziebach	Pierre

Standards for Federal Courts: Fees are standard unless noted in profile. Search fee is $26.00 per item (one party name or case number). Copy fee is $.50 per page. Certification fee is $9.00 per document, double for exemplification, if available. Most courts require prepayment. Mail requests should enclose a SASE unless otherwise noted. Before releasing records, all courts require prepayment, unless noted.

District courts index by defendant and plaintiff and by case number. Bankruptcy courts usually index by debtor and case number. While most courts now have their indexes on computer, many may still maintain index card files as well. Courts will archive closed case files at different times.

There are numerous public access programs available to online subscribers. Search the U.S. Party/Case Index to find party names and case numbers among all courts. Individual case data is provided on PACER. A search of CM/ECF provides copies of cases filed electronically. For details about PACER, the US Party/Case Index, and CM/ECF see the Appendix or go to http://pacer.psc.uscourts.gov or call 800-676-6856.

US District Court

Aberdeen - Northern Division c/o Pierre Division, Federal Bldg & Courthouse, 225 S Pierre St, Rm 405, Pierre, SD 57501, 605-945-4600; Fax- 605-945-4601. Hours- 8AM - 5PM. www.sdd.uscourts.gov

Counties/Note: Brown, Campbell, Clark, Codington, Corson, Day, Deuel, Edmunds, Grant, Hamlin, McPherson, Marshall, Roberts, Spink, Walworth. Judge Battey's closed case records are located at the Rapid City Division. Most records at Pierre Division Clerk Ofc, address and phone given here.

Searches/Indexing: Search request requires name; middle name and alias helpful. Results do not include SSN or DOB. Will fax back documents. New cases are in the index immediately after filing date. Both computer and card indexes maintained; computer goes back to 1985. Case files sent to archives 6 months after closed.

Search Access: Mail: Include SASE for return. **Fax:** Fax search requests accepted with credit card. **In person:** 1 public terminal available; index back to 1990. No self-serve copier.

Payment: Pay by Visa/MC, money order, cashier's check. No business checks accepted. Payee: Clerk, US District Court.

E-Services: PACER records go back to 1991. New records online after 1 day. ECF at https://ecf.sdd.uscourts.gov. Access written opinions free via PACER at www.sdd.uscourts.gov/writop.htm. **Online Note:** Access to very limited court calendar at main website.

Pierre - Central Division Court Clerk, Federal Bldg & Courthouse, Rm 405, 225 S Pierre St, Pierre, SD 57501, 605-945-4600/4460; Fax- 605-945-4601. Hours- 8AM - 5PM. www.sdd.uscourts.gov

Counties: Buffalo, Dewey, Faulk, Gregory, Haakon, Hand, Hughes, Hyde, Jerauld, Jones, Lyman, Mellette, Potter, Stanley, Sully, Todd, Tripp, Ziebach.

Searches/Indexing: Search request requires name; middle name and alias helpful. Results do not include SSN or DOB. New cases are in the index 1 day after filing date. Both computer and card indexes maintained; computer goes back to 1992. Case files sent to archives 6 months after closed.

Search Access: Only docket info is available by phone. **Mail:** Search usually completed- 1-2 days. Include SASE for return. **Fax:** Will accept fax request for fee quote. **In person:** 1 public terminal available; index goes back to 1970. No self-serve copier.

Payment: Pay by Visa/MC, money order, cashier's or personal check. Payee: Clerk, US District Court.

E-Services: PACER records go back to 1991. New records online after 1 day. ECF at https://ecf.sdd.uscourts.gov. Access written opinions free via PACER at www.sdd.uscourts.gov/writop.htm. **Online Note:** Access to very limited court calendar at main website.

Rapid City - Western Division Clerk's Office, PO Box 6080, Rapid City, SD 57709 (In person: 515 9th St, Rm 302, Rapid City), 605-399-6000; Fax- 605-399-6001. 8AM-5PM. www.sdd.uscourts.gov

Counties/Note: Bennett, Butte, Custer, Fall River, Harding, Jackson, Lawrence, Meade, Pennington, Perkins, Shannon. Judge Battey's closed cases are located at Rapid City.

Searches/Indexing: Search request requires name; middle name and alias helpful. Results do not include SSN or DOB. Will fax back documents. New cases are in the index 24 hours after filing date. Both computer and card indexes maintained; computer goes back to 1985. Case files sent to archives 6 months after closed.

Search Access: Only docket info available by phone. **Mail:** Search usually completed- 1-2 days. SASE not required. **Fax:** Fax search requests accepted with credit card. **In person:** 1 public terminal available; index back to 1990. No self-serve copier.

Payment: Pay by Visa/MC, money order, cashier's check. No business checks accepted. Payee: Clerk, US District Court.

E-Services: PACER records go back to 1991. New records online after 1 day. ECF at https://ecf.sdd.uscourts.gov. Access written opinions free via PACER at www.sdd.uscourts.gov/writop.htm. **Online Note:** Access to very limited court calendar at main website.

Sioux Falls - Southern Division Court Clerk, 400 S Phillips Ave, #104, Sioux Falls, SD 57104, 605-330-6600; Fax- 605-330-6601. Hours-8AM-5PM. www.sdd.uscourts.gov

Counties: Aurora, Beadle, Bon Homme, Brookings, Brule, Charles Mix, Clay, Davison, Douglas, Hanson, Hutchinson, Kingsbury, Lake, Lincoln, McCook, Miner, Minnehaha, Moody, Sanborn, Turner, Union, Yankton.

Searches/Indexing: Search request requires name; middle name and alias helpful. Results do not include SSN or DOB. New cases are in the index 1 day after filing date. Computer and card indexes maintained, computer back to 1970. Case files sent to archives 6 months after closed.

Search Access: Only docket info for civil cases is released via phone. **Mail:** Search usually completed- same day if possible. Include SASE for return. **Fax:** Will accept fax request for fee quote. **In person:** 1 public terminal available; index back to 1990. No self-serve copier.

Payment: Pay by Visa/MC, money order, cashier's or personal check. Payee: Clerk, US District Court.

E-Services: PACER records go back to 1991. New records online after 1 day. ECF at https://ecf.sdd.uscourts.gov. Access written opinions free via PACER at www.sdd.uscourts.gov/writop.htm. **Online Note:** Access to very limited court calendar at main website.

US Bankruptcy Court

Pierre Division Clerk of Court, Federal Bldg, 225 S Pierre St, Rm 203, Pierre, SD 57501, 605-945-4460; Fax- 605-945-4461. 8AM-5PM. www.sdb.uscourts.gov

Counties: Bennett, Brown, Buffalo, Butte, Campbell, Clark, Codington, Corson, Custer, Day, Deuel, Dewey, Edmunds, Fall River, Faulk, Grant, Gregory, Haakon, Hamlin, Hand, Harding, Hughes, Hyde, Jackson, Jerauld, Jones, Lawrence, Lyman, Marshall, McPherson, Meade, Mellette, Pennington, Perkins, Potter, Roberts, Shannon, Spink, Stanley, Sully, Todd, Tripp, Walworth, Ziebach.

Searches/Indexing: Helpful to include SSN and also address in search requests. Results include last 4 SSN digits. Will fax back docket listings no extra charge. New cases are in the index immediately after filing date. Computer index goes back to mid-1990s. District-wide searches available here back to 10/1/91. Case files all electronic; never purged.

Search Access: Only docket info available by phone. Voice Case Information Service available, call VCIS at 800-768-6218 or 605-357-2422. **Mail:** Search usually completed- 1 day. Include SASE for return. **Fax:** Fax search requests accepted. **In person:** 2 public terminals available. Self-serve copies $.50 each.

Payment: Pay by Visa/MC, money order, cashier's check, in-state business check. No personal checks accepted. Payee: Clerk, US Bankruptcy Court.

E-Services: Document images available. PACER records go back to 10/1991. New records online immediately. ECF at https://ecf.sdb.uscourts.gov. **Opinions:** www.sdb.uscourts.gov/nDecisions.htm. **Online Note:** Court calendars for the next 2 months are free at https://ecf.sdb.uscourts.gov/cgi-bin/PublicCalendar.pl.

Sioux Falls Division Clerk of Court, 400 S Phillips Ave, #104, Sioux Falls, SD 57102-6851, 605-357-2400; Fax- 605-357-2401. 8AM-5PM. www.sdb.uscourts.gov

Counties/Note: Aurora, Beadle, Bon Homme, Brookings, Brule, Charles Mix, Clay, Davison, Douglas, Hanson, Hutchinson, Kingsbury, Lake, Lincoln, McCook, Miner, Minnehaha, Moody, Sanborn, Turner, Union, Yankton.

Searches/Indexing: Helpful to include SSN and also address in search requests. Results include last 4 SSN digits. Will fax back docket listings no extra charge. New cases are in the index immediately after filing date. Computer index goes back to mid-1990s. District-wide searches available here back to 10/1/91. Case files all electronic; never purged.

Search Access: Only docket info available by phone. Voice Case Information Service available, call VCIS at 800-768-6218 or 605-357-2422. **Mail:** Search usually completed- 1 day. Include SASE for return. **Fax:** Fax search requests accepted. **In person:** 1 public terminal available. Self-serve copies $.50 each.

Payment: Pay by Visa/MC, money order, cashier's check, in-state business check. No personal checks accepted. Payee: Clerk, US Bankruptcy Court.

E-Services: Document images available. PACER records go back to 10/1991. New records online immediately. ECF at https://ecf.sdb.uscourts.gov. **Opinions:** www.sdb.uscourts.gov/nDecisions.htm. **Online Note:** Court calendars for the next 2 months are free at https://ecf.sdb.uscourts.gov/cgi-bin/PublicCalendar.pl

South Dakota County Courts

Court	Jurisdiction	No. of Courts	How Organized
Circuit Courts*	General	64	7 Circuits
Magistrate Courts	Limited	64	

* Profiled in this Sourcebook.

Court	CIVIL								
	Tort	Contract	Real Estate	Min. Claim	Max. Claim	Small Claims	Estate	Eviction	Domestic Relations
Circuit Courts*	X	X	X	$0	No Max	$8000	X	X	X
Magistrate Courts				$0	$10,000	$8000	X	X	X

Court	CRIMINAL				
	Felony	Misdemeanor	DWI/DUI	Preliminary Hearing	Juvenile
Circuit Courts*	X	X	X	X	X
Magistrate Courts		X	X	X	

Administration

State Court Administrator, State Capitol Building, 500 E Capitol Av, Pierre, SD, 57501; 605-773-3474, Fax: 605-773-8437. www.sdjudicial.com

Court Structure

The state re-aligned their circuits from 8 to 7 effective June, 2000. The circuit courts are the general trial courts of the Unified Judicial System. These courts have original jurisdiction in all civil and criminal cases. They are the only court where a criminal felony case can be tried and determined as well as a civil case involving more than $10,000 in damages. Circuit courts also have jurisdiction over appeals from Magistrate Court decisions. Generally, Magistrate Courts assist the circuit courts in processing minor criminal cases and less serious civil actions.

There are 66 counties, but 64 courts. Cases for Buffalo County are handled at the Brule County Circuit Court. Cases for Shannon County are handled by the Fall River County Circuit Court.

Online Access

The Supreme Court calendar, opinions, rules and archived oral arguments may be searched from the website.

All active money judgments and inactive civil money judgments from 04/19/2004 forward are available from a web service offered by SD Court Administrators Office. An unlimited access subscription is $250 monthly or $2500 annually. You may also access this system on a pay as you go basis where you deposit from a credit card and the system deducts from your balance. Charges for searches with a credit/debit card are $4.00 per name or date range search and an additional $1.00 charge to access the judgment docket. Find more information on this system at https://apps.sd.gov/applications/judgmentquery/login.aspx. The money judgment system permits bulk downloading of information. However, the agreement with the agency disallows any resale of the data. This subscription system does not include probate or criminal information. For more details contact Ms. Jill Gusso at 605-773-8437.

Searching Tips, Fees, and Other Guidelines

South Dakota has a statewide criminal record search database administrated by this office. Requesters may wish to set up a commercial account by faxing a written request to Jill Gusso, Unified Court System at 605-773-8437 or email jill.gusso@ujs.state.sd.us. Accounts are billed monthly. The search fee is $15.00 per name search for statewide civil, criminal, or probate searches. The statewide civil search includes money judgments and other civil case data post 2003. For a statewide civil money judgment search, including pre 04/19/04 judgments, there is a fee of $4.00 per name/date range and $1.00 per copy of each judgment docket card. State authorized commercial accounts may order and receive records by fax; there is an additional minimum $5.00 fee unless a non-toll free line is used.

Most South Dakota courts do not allow the public to perform a name search, searches must be performed by the clerk, usually for a fee of $15.00 per name. All clerks offices require written requests. A special Record Search Request Form must be used and can be found at www.sdjudicial.com/downloads/prcdr/rsrf.pdf. An inaccurate date of birth, Social Security Number, driver's license number or other incomplete demographic information may result in inaccurate search results. Clerks are not required to respond to telephone requests, but many courts will return records via fax to ongoing commercial accounts.

Mail Requests - The state asks that all mail requests be directed to one of two processing centers: the Miner County Clerk of Court, PO Box 265, Howard SD 57349, or the Aurora County Clerk of Court, PO Box 366, Plankinton, SD 57368-0366.

Aurora County

Circuit Court PO Box 366, 401 N Main St, Plankinton, SD 57368-0366; 605-942-7165; fax: 605-942-7170; 8AM-N, 1-5PM (CST). ***Felony, Misdemeanor, Civil, Eviction, Small Claims, Probate.***

Civil Records: Access: Fax, mail, in person, online. Both court and visitors may perform in person searches. Search fee: $15.00 per name. Required to search: name, years to search; also helpful: address. Civil cases indexed by defendant, plaintiff; index on manual index since 1879, some computerized since 1988. Mail turnaround time 1 day. Active & inactive judgments from 04/19/2004 forward via web subscription service from Court Administrators Office; see note at the beginning of this section.

Criminal Records: Access: Fax, mail, in person. Only the court performs in person searches; visitors may not. Search fee: $15.00 per name. Required to search: name, years to search, signed release; also helpful: address, DOB, SSN. Criminal records are computerized since 7/89 on a statewide system. Mail turnaround time 1 day.

General Information: No juvenile, sealed, dismissed, adoption or mental health records released. Will fax documents $1.00 per page; $5.00 minimum. Court makes copy: $.20 per page. Certification fee: $2.00 per page. Payee: Aurora County Clerk of Court. Business and personal checks accepted. Visa/MC accepted. Prepayment required. Mail requests: SASE required.

Beadle County

Circuit Court PO Box 1358, 450 3rd St SW, Huron, SD 57350-1358; 605-353-7165; criminal fax: 605-353-0118; civil fax: same; 8AM-5PM (CST). ***Felony, Misdemeanor, Civil, Eviction, Small Claims, Probate.***
www.sdjudicial.com/circuit_courts/index.asp?circuit=3

Searching party must complete form requesting examination of file; clerk will redact any data of a confidential or personal nature. Probate fax is same as main fax number.

Civil Records: Access: Mail, in person, online. Only the court performs in person searches; visitors may not. Search fee: $15.00 per name. Required to search: name, years to search. Civil cases indexed by defendant, plaintiff; index on computer from 1990 (limited), cards from 1900. Not for public use. Mail turnaround time up to 2 weeks. Active & inactive judgments from 04/19/2004 forward via web subscription service from Court Administrators Office; see note at the beginning of this section.

Criminal Records: Access: Mail, in person. Only the court performs in person searches; visitors may not. Search fee: $15.00 per name. Required to search: name, years to search, DOB; also helpful: SSN. Criminal records are computerized since 7/89 on a statewide system. Mail turnaround time up to 2 weeks. For faster service, you may mail search requests to Hand County for processing. See note at beginning of section for locations of the 2 state-recommended processing centers for mail requests.

General Information: No juvenile, sealed, dismissed, adoption, or mental health records released. Will fax documents $5.00 per transmission. Court makes copy: $.20 per page. Certification fee: $2.00 per cert. Payee: Beadle County Clerk of Court. Personal checks accepted. Out of state checks not accepted. Visa/MC accepted. Prepayment required.

Bennett County

Circuit Court PO Box 281, Martin, SD 57551-0281; 605-685-6969; criminal fax: 605-685-1075; civil fax: same; 8AM-4:30PM (MST). ***Felony, Misdemeanor, Civil, Eviction, Small Claims, Probate.***

Probate a separate index at this same address.

Civil Records: Access: Mail, in person, online. Only the court performs in person searches; visitors may not. Search fee: $15.00 per name. Required to search: name, years to search; also helpful: address. Civil cases indexed by defendant, plaintiff; index on index from 1912. Mail turnaround time 48 hours. Active & inactive judgments from 04/19/2004 forward via web subscription service from Court Administrators Office; see note at the beginning of this section.

Criminal Records: Access: Mail, in person. Only the court performs in person searches; visitors may not. Search fee: $15.00 per name. Required to search: name, years to search, DOB; also helpful: address. Request form available. Criminal records are computerized since 7/89 on a statewide system, searchable back to 1912. Mail turnaround time 48 hours. For faster service, you may mail search requests to Potter County for processing. See note at beginning of section for locations of the 2 state-recommended processing centers for mail requests.

General Information: No juvenile, sealed, dismissed, or mental health records released. Will only fax results to ongoing requesters with an account. Court makes copy: $.20 per page. Certification fee: $2.00 includes copy. Payee: Bennett County Clerk of Courts. Business checks accepted. Major credit cards accepted. Prepayment required. Mail requests: SASE required.

Bon Homme County

Circuit Court PO Box 6, Tyndall, SD 57066; 605-589-4215; fax: 605-589-4245; 8AM-4:30PM (CST). ***Felony, Misdemeanor, Civil, Eviction, Small Claims, Probate.***

Civil Records: Access: Fax, mail, in person, online. Both court and visitors may perform in person searches. Search fee: $15.00 per name. Required to search: name, years to search; also helpful: address. Civil cases indexed by defendant, plaintiff; index on alpha index books from 1877. Requests should be in writing. Mail turnaround time 3 days to 1 week. Active & inactive judgments from 04/19/2004 forward via web subscription service from Court Administrators Office; see note at the beginning of this section.

Criminal Records: Access: Mail, in person. Only the court performs in person searches; visitors may not. Search fee: $15.00 per name. Required to search: name, years to search, DOB, signed release; also helpful: address, SSN. Criminal records are computerized since 7/89 on a statewide system. Mail turnaround time 3 days to 1 week. For faster service, you may mail search requests to Douglas County for processing. See note at beginning of section for locations of the 2 state-recommended processing centers for mail requests.

General Information: No juvenile, sealed, dismissed, or mental health records released. Will fax documents $1.00 per page, $5.00 minimum, no fee if local or toll free. Court makes copy: $.20 per page. Self serve: $.10 per page. Certification fee: $2.00 per cert. Cert fee includes copies. Payee: Bon Homme County Clerk of Court. Personal checks accepted; credit cards are not. Prepayment required. Mail requests: SASE required.

Brookings County

Circuit Court 314 6th Ave, Brookings, SD 57006; 605-688-4200; fax: 605-688-4952; 8AM-5PM (CST). ***Felony, Misdemeanor, Civil, Eviction, Small Claims, Probate.***
www.sdjudicial.com/circuit_courts/index.asp?circuit=3

Civil Records: Access: Mail, in person, online. Only the court performs in person searches; visitors may not. Search fee: $15.00 per name. Required to search: name, years to search; also helpful: address. Civil cases indexed by defendant, plaintiff; index on alpha index books from 1900s. Mail turnaround time 3 days. Active & inactive judgments from 04/19/2004 forward via web subscription service from Court Administrators Office; see note at the beginning of this section.

Criminal Records: Access: Mail, in person. Only the court performs in person searches; visitors may not. Search fee: $15.00 per name. Required to search: name, years to search, DOB; also helpful: address, SSN. Criminal records on computer since 7/1989 on a statewide system. Mail turnaround time 3 days. For faster service, you may mail search requests to Hand County for processing. See note at beginning of section for locations of the 2 state-recommended processing centers for mail requests.

General Information: No juvenile, sealed, dismissed, or mental health records released. Fee to fax out file $1.00 per page; $5.00 minimum. Court makes copy: $.20 per page. Self serve: same. Certification fee: $2.00 per document. Payee: Brookings County Clerk of Court. Only cashiers checks and money orders accepted. Visa/MC accepted. Prepayment required. Mail requests: SASE required.

Brown County

Circuit Court 101 1st Ave SE, Aberdeen, SD 57401; 605-626-2451; fax: 605-626-2491; 8AM-5PM (CST). ***Felony, Misdemeanor, Civil, Eviction, Small Claims, Probate.*** http://ujs.sd.gov/5thcircuit/

Civil Records: Access: Mail, in person, online. Both court and visitors may perform in person searches. Search fee: $15.00 per name. Required to search: name, years to search; also helpful: address. Civil cases indexed by defendant, plaintiff; index on registers from 1975 (misdemeanor), registers from 1900s (civil). Mail turnaround time 1-3 days. Active & inactive judgments from 04/19/2004 forward via web subscription service from Court Administrators Office; see note at the beginning of this section.

Criminal Records: Access: Mail, in person. Only the court performs in person searches; visitors may not. Search fee: $15.00 per name. Required to search: name, years to search, DOB; also helpful: address, signed release, SSN. Criminal records on computer since 7/1989 on a statewide system. Mail turnaround time 1-3 days. For faster service, you may mail search requests to Edmunds County for processing. See note at beginning of section for locations of the 2 state-recommended processing centers for mail requests.

General Information: No juvenile, sealed, dismissed, or mental health records released. Will fax documents to local or toll free line. Court makes copy: $.20 per page. Certification fee: $2.00 per cert. Payee: Brown County Clerk of Court. Personal checks and major credit cards accepted. Prepayment required. Mail requests: SASE required.

Brule County

Circuit Court 300 S Courtland, Ste #111, Chamberlain, SD 57325-1599; 605-734-4580; fax: 605-734-4582; 8AM-N, 1-5PM (CST). ***Felony, Misdemeanor, Civil, Eviction, Small Claims, Probate.***

Records from the Buffalo County Circuit Court are housed here.

Civil Records: Access: Mail, in person, online. Only the court performs in person searches; visitors may not. Search fee: $15.00 per name. Required to search: name, years to search; also helpful: address. Civil cases indexed by defendant, plaintiff. Civil index on docket books or docket books from 1875. Mail turnaround time 3-5 days. Active & inactive judgments from 04/19/2004 forward via web subscription service from Court Administrators Office; see note at the beginning of this section.

Criminal Records: Access: Mail, fax, in person. Only the court performs in person searches; visitors may not. Search fee: $15.00 per name. Required to search: name, years to search, DOB; also helpful: address, SSN. Criminal records on computer since 7/1989 on a statewide system. Mail turnaround time 3-5 days. For faster service, you may mail search requests to Miner County for processing. Fax requests accepted for commercial accounts only and are forwarded as well. See note at beginning of section for locations of the 2 state-recommended processing centers for mail requests.

General Information: No juvenile, sealed, dismissed, or mental health records released. Will fax documents $5.00 each. Court makes copy: $.20 per page. Certification fee: $2.00 per doc. Payee: Brule County Clerk of Court. Personal checks and major credit cards accepted. Prepayment required. Mail requests: SASE required.

Buffalo County

Circuit Court 300 S Courtland, Ste #111, Chamberlain, SD 57325; 605-734-4580; fax: 605-293-3240; 9AM-5PM (CST). ***Felony, Misdemeanor, Civil, Eviction, Small Claims, Probate.***
The Brule County Clerk services Buffalo County.

Butte County

Circuit Court PO Box 250, 839 5th Ave, Belle Fourche, SD 57717; 605-892-2516; fax: 605-892-2836; 8AM-N, 1-5PM (MST). ***Felony, Misdemeanor, Civil, Eviction, Small Claims, Probate.***
Civil Records: Access: Mail, in person, online. Only the court performs in person searches; visitors may not. Search fee: $15.00 per name. Required to search: name, years to search; also helpful: DOB, address. Civil cases indexed by defendant, plaintiff. All data on alpha index from 1900s. Mail turnaround time varies. Active & inactive judgments from 04/19/2004 forward via web subscription service from Court Administrators Office; see note at the beginning of this section.
Criminal Records: Access: Mail, in person. Only the court performs in person searches; visitors may not. Search fee: $15.00 per name. Required to search: name, years to search; also helpful: DOB, address. Criminal records on computer since 7/89 on a statewide system. Mail turnaround time varies. See note at beginning of section for locations of the 2 state-recommended processing centers for mail requests.
General Information: No juvenile, sealed, dismissed, or mental health records released. Will fax documents to local or toll free line. Court makes copy: $.20 per page. Certification fee: $2.00 per cert. Payee: Butte County Clerk of Court. Personal checks accepted. Visa/MC accepted. Prepayment required. Mail requests: SASE required.

Campbell County

Circuit Court PO Box 146, 111 2nd St, Mound City, SD 57646; 605-955-3536; fax: 605-955-5303; 8AM-N T-W-F (CST). ***Felony, Misdemeanor, Civil, Small Claims, Probate, Traffic.***
http://ujs.sd.gov/5thcircuit/
Civil Records: Access: Mail, in person, online. Both court and visitors may perform in person searches. Search fee: $15.00 per name. Required to search: name, years to search; also helpful: address. Civil cases indexed by defendant, plaintiff. All data on alpha index from 1800s. Mail turnaround time varies. Active & inactive judgments from 04/19/2004 forward via web subscription service from Court Administrators Office; see note at the beginning of this section.
Criminal Records: Access: Mail, in person. Only the court performs in person searches; visitors may not. Search fee: $15.00 per name. Required to search: name, years to search, DOB; also helpful: address, SSN. Although records are computerized at the state level, this office has records and indices on paper. Mail turnaround time varies. For faster service, you may mail search requests to Edmunds County for processing. To search on computer, you may search at Edmunds Circuit Ct in Ipswich. See note at beginning of section for locations of the 2 state-recommended processing centers for mail requests.
General Information: No juvenile, sealed, dismissed, or mental health records released. Will fax documents to local or toll free line. Court makes copy: $.20 per page. Certification fee: $2.00 per cert. Payee: Campbell County Clerk of Court. Cashiers checks and money orders accepted. Major credit cards accepted. Prepayment required. Mail requests: SASE required.

Charles Mix County

Circuit Court PO Box 640, Main St Courthouse, Lake Andes, SD 57356; 605-487-7511; fax: 605-487-7547; 8-4:30PM (CST). ***Felony, Misdemeanor, Civil, Eviction, Small Claims, Probate.***
Civil Records: Access: Mail, in person, online. Both court and visitors may perform in person searches. Search fee: $15.00 per name. Required to search: name, years to search; also helpful: address. Civil cases indexed by defendant, plaintiff; index on alpha index books from 1917. Mail turnaround time 2-5 days. Active & inactive judgments from 04/19/2004 forward via web subscription service from Court Administrators Office; see note at the beginning of this section.
Criminal Records: Access: Mail, in person. Only the court performs in person searches; visitors may not. Search fee: $15.00 per name. Required to search: name, years to search, DOB; also helpful: address, SSN. Criminal records on computer since 7/89 on a statewide system located in Douglas County. Mail turnaround time 2-5 days. For faster service, fax or mail requests to Douglas County for processing. See note at beginning of section for locations of the 2 state-recommended processing centers for mail requests.
General Information: No juvenile, sealed, dismissed, or mental health records released. Will fax documents $1.00 per page, $5.00 minimum. Court makes copy: $.20 per page. Certification fee: $2.00 per doc. Payee: Charles Mix County Clerk of Court. Personal check accepted with SSN or DL#. Visa/MC accepted. Mail requests: SASE required.

Clark County

Circuit Court PO Box 294, Attn: Clerk of Courts, Clark, SD 57225; 605-532-5851; 8AM-N, 1-5PM (CST). ***Felony, Misdemeanor, Civil, Eviction, Small Claims, Probate.***
www.sdjudicial.com/circuit_courts/index.asp?circuit=3
Civil Records: Access: Mail, in person online. Only the court performs in person searches; visitors may not. Search fee: $15.00 per name. Required to search: name, years to search; also helpful: address, DOB. Civil cases indexed by defendant, plaintiff. All records on alpha index cards from 1969. Mail turnaround time 1-4 days. Active & inactive judgments from 04/19/2004 forward via web subscription service from Court Administrators Office; see note at the beginning of this section.
Criminal Records: Access: Mail, in person. Only the court performs in person searches; visitors may not. Search fee: $15.00 per name. Required to search: name, years to search, DOB; also helpful: address, SSN. Criminal records on computer since 1994 on a statewide system. Mail turnaround time 1-4 days. See note at beginning of section for locations of the 2 state-recommended processing centers for mail requests.
General Information: No juvenile, sealed, dismissed, or mental health records released. Will fax documents $1.00 per page, $5.00 minimum. Court makes copy: $.20 per page. Certification fee: $2.00 per cert. Payee: Clark County Clerk of Court. Personal checks accepted; credit cards are not. Prepayment required.

Clay County

Circuit Court PO Box 377, Vermillion, SD 57069; 605-677-6755/6; fax: 605-677-8885; 8AM-5PM (CST). ***Felony, Misdemeanor, Civil, Eviction, Small Claims, Probate.***
Civil Records: Access: Mail, in person, online. Both court and visitors may perform in person searches. Search fee: $15.00 per name. Required to search: name, years to search; also helpful: address. Civil cases indexed by defendant, plaintiff; index on computer from 1993, in books to 1920, and archived from 1800s. Mail turnaround time 2-4 days. Active & inactive judgments from 04/19/2004 forward via web subscription service from Court Administrators Office; see note at the beginning of this section.
Criminal Records: Access: Mail, in person. Only the court performs in person searches; visitors may not. Search fee: $15.00 per name. Required to search: name, years to search, DOB; also helpful: address, SSN. Criminal records computerized from 1989, in books to 1920, and archived from 1800s. Mail turnaround time 2-4 days. For faster service, you may mail search requests to Aurora or Hanson County for processing. See note at beginning of section for locations of the 2 state-recommended processing centers for mail requests.
General Information: No juvenile, sealed, dismissed, or mental health records released. Will fax documents to local or toll free line. Court makes copy: $.20 per page. Self serve: same. Certification fee: $2.00 per doc. Payee: Clay County Clerk of Court. Personal checks accepted. Visa/MC accepted. Prepayment required. Mail requests: SASE required.

Codington County

Circuit Court Clerk of Court, PO Box 1054, Watertown, SD 57201; 605-882-5095; 8AM-5PM (CST). ***Felony, Misdemeanor, Civil, Eviction, Small Claims, Probate.***
www.sdjudicial.com/circuit_courts/index.asp?circuit=3
Civil Records: Access: Mail, in person, online. Only the court performs in person searches; visitors may not. Search fee: $15.00 per name (includes copies, unless copying entire file). Required to search: name, DOB, years to search. Civil cases indexed by defendant, plaintiff; index on computer from 1991 and alpha index cards back to 1890. Mail turnaround time 2 days. Active & inactive judgments from 04/19/2004 forward via web subscription service from Court Administrators Office; see note at the beginning of this section.
Criminal Records: Access: Mail, in person. Only the court performs in person searches; visitors may not. Search fee: $15.00 per name (includes copies, unless copying entire file). Required to search: name, years to search, DOB. Criminal records on computer since 7/89 on a statewide system. Mail turnaround time 2 days. See note at beginning of section for locations of the 2 state-recommended processing centers for mail requests.
General Information: No juvenile, sealed, dismissed, or mental health records released. Fax fee of $10.00 in and $5.00 out. Court makes copy: $.20 per page. Certification fee: $2.00 per cert. Payee: Codington County Clerk of Court. Business checks accepted. Visa/MC accepted. Prepayment required. Mail requests: SASE required.

Corson County

Circuit Court PO Box 175, 111 2nd Ave E, McIntosh, SD 57641; 605-273-4201; criminal fax: 605-273-4597; civil fax: same; 9:30AM-N, 1-2:30PM (MST). ***Felony, Misdemeanor, Civil, Eviction, Small Claims, Probate.***
Probate fax is same as main fax number.
Civil Records: Access: Mail, in person, online. Only the court performs in person searches; visitors may not. Search fee: $15.00 per name. Required to search: name, years to search; also helpful: address. Civil cases indexed by defendant, plaintiff. All data on alpha index from 1940s. Mail turnaround time 1 day. Civil PAT goes back to 10 years. PAT results show middle initial, DOB. Online results show name only. Active & inactive judgments from 04/19/2004 forward via web subscription service from Court Administrators Office; see note at the beginning of this section.
Criminal Records: Access: Mail, fax, in person. Only the court performs in person searches; visitors may not. Search fee: $15.00 per name. Required to search: name, years to search, DOB; also helpful: address, SSN. Criminal records computerized from 1989. Criminal PAT goes back to 10 years. PAT results show middle initial, DOB. All phone requests are forwarded to Lawrence County for processing. Mail turnaround time 1 day. For faster service you may send search request to Harding County, 603-375-3351. See note at beginning of section for locations of the 2 state-recommended processing centers for mail requests.
General Information: No juvenile, sealed, dismissed, adoption or mental health records released. Will fax documents if you have account with UJS. Set up account with Court Admin Office in Pierre, call 605-773-4873. Court makes copy: $.20 per page. Self serve: same. Certification fee: $2.00 per cert. Payee: Corson County Clerk of Court. No credit cards accepted at the court. Prepayment required.

Custer County

Circuit Court 420 Mt Rushmore Rd, Custer, SD 57730; 605-673-4816; fax: 605-673-3416; 8AM-N, 1-5PM (MST). ***Felony, Misdemeanor, Civil, Eviction, Small Claims, Probate.***
Civil Records: Access: Mail, in person, online. Only the court performs in person searches; visitors may

not. Search fee: $15.00 per name. Required to search: name, years to search, SSN; also helpful: address. Civil cases indexed by defendant, plaintiff. Probate on microfiche from 1915, all other data on docket books and index cards from 1960s. Mail turnaround time 2 days. Active & inactive judgments from 04/19/2004 forward via web subscription service from Court Administrators Office; see note at the beginning of this section.
Criminal Records: Access: Mail, in person. Only the court performs in person searches; visitors may not. Search fee: $15.00 per name. Required to search: name, years to search, DOB, SSN, signed release; also helpful: address. Criminal Mail turnaround time 2 days. records on computer since 7/89 on a statewide system. For faster service you may direct search requests to the Search Center at Harding County Clerk, PO Box 534, Buffalo, SD 57720. See note at beginning of section for locations of the 2 state-recommended processing centers for mail requests.
General Information: No juvenile, sealed, dismissed, or mental health records released. Will not fax out documents. Court makes copy: $.25 per page. Certification fee: $2.00 per doc. Payee: Custer County Clerk of Court. Personal checks accepted. Visa/MC accepted. Mail requests: SASE required.

Davison County

Circuit Court PO Box 927, 200 E Fourth Ave, Mitchell, SD 57301; 605-995-8105; fax: 605-995-8112; 8AM-5PM (CST). ***Felony, Misdemeanor, Civil, Eviction, Small Claims, Probate.***
Civil Records: Access: Mail, in person, online. Both court and visitors may perform in person searches. Search fee: $15.00 per name. Required to search: name, years to search; also helpful: address. Civil cases indexed by defendant. All data on alpha index from 1900s. Mail turnaround time 1 week. Active & inactive judgments from 04/19/2004 forward via web subscription service from Court Administrators Office; see note at the beginning of this section.
Criminal Records: Access: Mail, in person. Only the court performs in person searches; visitors may not. Search fee: $15.00 per name. Required to search: name, years to search, DOB; also helpful: address, SSN. Criminal records are computerized since 7/89 on a statewide system. Mail turnaround time 1 week. For faster service, you may mail search requests to Miner County for processing. See note at beginning of section for locations of the 2 state-recommended processing centers for mail requests.
General Information: No juvenile, sealed, dismissed, or mental health records released. Court makes copy: $.20 per page. Certification fee: $2.00 per doc. Payee: Davison County Clerk of Court. Personal checks accepted. Out of state checks not accepted. Visa/MC accepted. Prepayment required. Mail requests: SASE required.

Day County

Circuit Court 711 W 1st St #201, Webster, SD 57274-1362; 605-345-3771; fax: 605-345-3818; 8AM-5PM (CST). ***Felony, Misdemeanor, Civil, Small Claims, Probate.*** http://ujs.sd.gov/5thcircuit/
Mail requests managed by the Edmonds County Clerk of Courts
Civil Records: Access: In person, online. Only the court performs in person searches; visitors may not. Search fee: $15.00 per name. Required to search: name, years to search; also helpful: address. Civil cases indexed by defendant. Civil index in docket books from 1800s. Active & inactive judgments from 04/19/2004 forward via web subscription service from Court Administrators Office; see note at the beginning of this section.
Criminal Records: Access: In person only. Only the court performs in person searches; visitors may not. Search fee: $15.00 per name. Required to search: name, years to search, DOB; also helpful: address, SSN. Criminal records on computer since 1982 on a statewide system. For faster service, you may mail search requests to Edmunds County for processing. See note at beginning of section for locations of the 2 state-recommended processing centers for mail requests.
General Information: No juvenile, sealed, dismissed, or mental health records released. Court makes copy: $.20 per page. Certification fee: $2.00 per doc. Payee: Day County Clerk of Court. Personal checks accepted; credit cards are not.

Deuel County

Circuit Court 408 Fourth St W, Clear Lake, SD 57226; 605-874-2120; fax: 605-874-3305; 8AM-5PM (CST). ***Felony, Misdemeanor, Civil, Eviction, Small Claims, Probate.***
www.sdjudicial.com/circuit_courts/index.asp?circuit=3
Civil Records: Access: Mail, in person, online. Only the court performs in person searches; visitors may not. Search fee: $15.00 per name. Required to search: name, years to search; also helpful: address. Civil cases indexed by defendant, plaintiff. Civil index on docket books. Mail turnaround time 1-2 days. Active & inactive judgments from 04/19/2004 forward via web subscription service from Court Administrators Office; see note at the beginning of this section.
Criminal Records: Access: Mail, in person. Only the court performs in person searches; visitors may not. Search fee: $15.00 per name. Required to search: name, years to search, DOB; also helpful-signed release. Criminal records on computer since 7/89 on a statewide system. Mail turnaround time 1-2 days. For faster service direct criminal record searches to the Criminal Search Center in Hand County. Also, see note at beginning of section for locations of the 2 state-recommended processing centers for mail requests.
General Information: No juvenile, sealed, dismissed, or mental health records released. Will not fax documents. Court makes copy: $.20 per page. Self serve: same. Certification fee: $2.00 per doc includes copy fee. Payee: Deuel County Clerk of Court. Personal checks accepted; credit cards are not. Prepayment required. Mail requests: SASE required.

Dewey County

Circuit Court PO Box 96, C St, County Courthouse, Timber Lake, SD 57656; 605-865-3566; fax: 605-865-3641; 9:30AM-N, 1-2:30PM (MST). ***Felony, Misdemeanor, Civil, Eviction, Small Claims, Probate.***
Civil Records: Access: Mail, in person, online. Both court and visitors may perform in person searches. Search fee: $15.00 per name. Required to search: name, years to search; also helpful: address. Civil cases indexed by defendant, plaintiff. All data on alpha index and docket books from 1900s; computerized back to 1999. Mail turnaround time 2 days to 1 week. Active & inactive judgments from 04/19/2004 forward via web subscription service from Court Administrators Office; see note at the beginning of this section.
Criminal Records: Access: Mail, in person. Only the court performs in person searches; visitors may not. Search fee: $15.00 per name. Required to search: name, years to search, DOB; also helpful: address, SSN, signed release. Criminal records data on alpha index and docket books from 1900s; computerized back to 1999. Mail turnaround time 2 days to 1 week. For faster service, you may mail search requests to Lawrence County for processing. See note at beginning of section for locations of the 2 state-recommended processing centers for mail requests.
General Information: No juvenile, adoption, sealed, dismissed, or mental health records released. Will fax documents $5.00 each. Court makes copy: $.25 per page. Certification fee: $2.00 per doc. Payee: Dewey County Clerk of Court. Personal checks accepted; credit cards are not. Mail requests: SASE required.

Douglas County

Circuit Court Clerk of Court, PO Box 36, Armour, SD 57313; 605-724-2585; 8AM-3PM M,T,TH (CST). ***Felony, Misdemeanor, Civil, Eviction, Small Claims, Probate.***
Civil Records: Access: Mail, in person, online. Both court and visitors may perform in person searches. Search fee: $15.00 per name. Required to search: name, years to search; also helpful: address. Civil cases indexed by defendant. Civil index in docket books from late 1800s. Mail turnaround time 1 week. Active & inactive judgments from 04/19/2004 forward via web subscription service from Court Administrators Office; see note at the beginning of this section.
Criminal Records: Access: Fax, mail, in person. Only the court performs in person searches; visitors may not. Search fee: $15.00 per name. Required to search: name, years to search, DOB, signed release; also helpful: address, SSN. Criminal records are computerized since 7/89 on a statewide system. Mail turnaround time 1 week. See note at beginning of section for locations of the 2 state-recommended processing centers for mail requests.
General Information: No juvenile, sealed, or mental health records released. Will fax documents to local or toll free line. Court makes copy: $.20 per page. Self serve: same. Certification fee: $2.00 per cert. Payee: Douglas County Clerk of Court. Personal checks accepted; credit cards are not. Prepayment required. Mail requests: SASE required.

Edmunds County

Circuit Court PO Box 384, Ipswich, SD 57451; 605-426-6671; criminal fax: 605-426-6323; civil fax: same; 8AM-N, 1-5PM (CST). ***Felony, Misdemeanor, Civil, Eviction, Small Claims, Probate.*** http://ujs.sd.gov/5thcircuit/
Probate fax is same as main fax number.
Civil Records: Access: Fax, mail, in person, online. Both court and visitors may perform in person searches. Search fee: $15.00 per name. Required to search: name, years to search; also helpful: address. Civil cases indexed by defendant, plaintiff. Civil index in docket books from late 1800s. Mail turnaround time 1 day to 1 week. Active & inactive judgments from 04/19/2004 forward via web subscription service from Court Administrators Office; see note at the beginning of this section.
Criminal Records: Access: Fax, mail, in person. Only the court performs in person searches; visitors may not. Search fee: $15.00 per name. Required to search: name, years to search, DOB; also helpful: DR#, signed release. Criminal records on computer since 7/89; prior records on docket books. Fax requests are for commercial accounts only; results are statewide. Mail turnaround time 24-48 hours. See note at beginning of section for locations of the 2 state-recommended processing centers for mail requests.
General Information: No juvenile, sealed or mental health records released. Will fax documents to local or toll free line. Court makes copy: $.25 per page. Self serve: same. Certification fee: $2.00 per cert. Payee: Edmunds County Clerk of Court. Personal checks and major credit cards accepted. Prepayment required. Mail requests: SASE required.

Fall River County

Circuit Court 906 N River St, Hot Springs, SD 57747; 605-745-5131; 8AM-5PM (MST). ***Felony, Misdemeanor, Civil, Eviction, Small Claims, Probate.***
Also handles cases for Shannon County. Specify which county in any search request, records are not co-mingled.
Civil Records: Access: Mail, in person, online. Only the court performs in person searches; visitors may not. Search fee: $15.00 per name. Required to search: name, years to search; also helpful: DOB. Civil cases indexed by defendant, plaintiff; index on computer from 1992, files from 1889 archived off site. Mail turnaround time 1-2 weeks. Active & inactive money judgments from 4/19/2004 forward are available online at https://apps.sd.gov/applications/judgmentquery/login.aspx. Either unlimited access or individual pay plans are available. See Court Admin's Office profile in the state section or call Jill Gusso-605-773-4874 for more details.
Criminal Records: Access: Mail, in person. Only the court performs in person searches; visitors may not. Search fee: $15.00 per name. Required to search: name, years to search, DOB; also helpful: address, SSN. Criminal records on computer since 7/89 on a statewide system. Mail turnaround time 1-2 weeks. See note at beginning of section for locations of

the 2 state-recommended processing centers for mail requests.
General Information: No juvenile, sealed, adoption, or mental health records released. Will fax documents to local or toll free line. Court makes copy: $.25 per page. Certification fee: $2.00 per doc. Payee: Clerk of Court. Personal checks accepted. Prepayment required. Mail requests: SASE required.

Faulk County

Circuit Court PO Box 357, Faulkton, SD 57438; 605-598-6223; fax: 605-598-6252; 1:00-5:00PM (CST). ***Felony, Misdemeanor, Civil, Eviction, Small Claims, Probate.*** http://ujs.sd.gov/5thcircuit/
Civil Records: Access: Mail, in person, online. Both court and visitors may perform in person searches. Search fee: $15.00 per name. Required to search: name, years to search; also helpful: address. Civil cases indexed by defendant. Civil index in docket books from 1900s. Mail turnaround time 1-2 days. Active & inactive judgments from 04/19/2004 forward via web subscription service from the SD Court Administrators Office, see note at the beginning of this section.
Criminal Records: Access: Mail, in person. Only the court performs in person searches; visitors may not. Search fee: $15.00 per name. Required to search: name, years to search, DOB; also helpful: address, SSN. Criminal records are computerized since 7/89 on a statewide system. Mail turnaround time 1-2 days. See note at beginning of section for locations of the 2 state-recommended processing centers for mail requests.
General Information: No juvenile, sealed, dismissed, adoption, or mental health records released. Will fax documents $1.00 per page, $5.00 minimum. Court makes copy: $.20 per page. Certification fee: $2.00 per cert. Payee: Faulk County Clerk of Court. Personal checks accepted. Prepayment required. Mail requests: SASE required.

Grant County

Circuit Court PO Box 509, 210 E 5th Ave, Milbank, SD 57252; 605-432-5482; 8AM-N, 1-5PM (CST). ***Felony, Misdemeanor, Civil, Eviction, Small Claims, Probate.***
www.sdjudicial.com/circuit_courts/index.asp?circuit=3
Civil Records: Access: Mail, in person, online. Only the court performs in person searches; visitors may not. Search fee: $15.00 per name. Required to search: name, years to search; also helpful: address. Civil cases indexed by defendant, plaintiff; index on computer from 1995, docket books from 1800s. Mail turnaround time 1 week by mail; immediate by phone if on computer. Active & inactive judgments from 04/19/2004 forward via web subscription service from Court Administrators Office; see note at the beginning of this section.
Criminal Records: Access: Mail, in person. Only the court performs in person searches; visitors may not. Search fee: $15.00 per name. Required to search: name, years to search, DOB; also helpful: address, SSN. Criminal records on computer since 7/89 on a statewide system. Mail turnaround time 1 week by mail; immediate by phone if on computer. For faster service, you may mail search requests to and processed by Hand County. See note at beginning of section for locations of the 2 state-recommended processing centers for mail requests.
General Information: No juvenile, sealed, dismissed, adoption or mental health records released. Court makes copy: $.25 per page. Certification fee: $2.00 per doc. Payee: Grant County Clerk of Court. Personal checks accepted. Visa/MC accepted. Prepayment required. Mail requests: SASE required.

Gregory County

Circuit Court PO Box 430, Burke, SD 57523; 605-775-2665; 8AM-N, 1-5PM (CST). ***Felony, Misdemeanor, Civil, Eviction, Small Claims, Probate.***
Probate is a separate index at this same address.
Civil Records: Access: Mail, in person, online. Only the court performs in person searches; visitors may not. Search fee: $15.00 per name. Required to search: name, years to search; also helpful: address. Civil cases indexed by defendant, plaintiff. Civil index in docket books from late 1800s, computerized since 1999. Mail turnaround time 1 week. Active & inactive judgments from 04/19/2004 forward via web subscription service from Court Administrators Office; see note at the beginning of this section.
Criminal Records: Access: Mail, in person. Only the court performs in person searches; visitors may not. Search fee: $15.00 per name. Required to search: name, years to search, DOB, signed release; also helpful: address, SSN. Criminal records computerized from 7/89 on a statewide system. Mail turnaround time 1 week. For faster service, you may mail search requests to Potter County for processing. See note at beginning of section for locations of the 2 state-recommended processing centers for mail requests.
General Information: No juvenile, sealed, dismissed, or mental health records released. Will fax documents for a fee. Court makes copy: $.20 per page. Certification fee: $2.00. Payee: Gregory County Clerk of Court. Cashiers checks and money orders accepted. Mail requests: SASE required.

Haakon County

Circuit Court PO Box 70, Philip, SD 57567; 605-859-2627; criminal fax: 605-859-2257; civil fax: same; 8AM-N (MST). ***Felony, Misdemeanor, Civil, Eviction, Small Claims, Probate.***
Probate fax is same as main fax number.
Civil Records: Access: Mail, in person, online. Only the court performs in person searches; visitors may not. Search fee: $15.00 per name. Required to search: name, years to search; also helpful: address. Civil cases indexed by defendant, plaintiff; index on register from 1915. Mail turnaround time 1 day. Active & inactive judgments from 4/19/2004 forward available on a web subscription service offered by the SD Court Administrators Office, profiled in the state section or call Jill Gusso-605-773-4874 for more details.
Criminal Records: Access: Mail, in person. Only the court performs in person searches; visitors may not. Search fee: $15.00 per name. Required to search: name, years to search, DOB; also helpful: address, SSN. Criminal records are computerized since 7/89 on a statewide system. Mail turnaround time 1 day. For faster service, you may mail search requests to Potter County for processing. See note at beginning of section for locations of the 2 state-recommended processing centers for mail requests.
General Information: No juvenile, sealed, dismissed, or mental health records released. Will not fax out documents. Court makes copy: $.20 per page. Certification fee: $2.00 includes copy fee. Payee: Haakon County Clerk of Court. Local checks accepted only. No credit cards accepted. Prepayment required. Mail requests: SASE required.

Hamlin County

Circuit Court PO Box 256, Hayti, SD 57241; 605-783-3751; criminal fax: 605-783-2157; civil fax: same; 8:30AM-N, 12:30-4:30PM (CST). ***Felony, Misdemeanor, Civil, Eviction, Small Claims, Probate.***
www.sdjudicial.com/circuit_courts/index.asp?circuit=3
Probate fax is same as main fax number.
Civil Records: Access: Mail, in person, online. Only the court performs in person searches; visitors may not. Search fee: $15.00 per name. Required to search: name, years to search; also helpful: address. Civil cases indexed by defendant, plaintiff. Civil index in docket books from 1800s. Mail turnaround time 1 day. Active & inactive judgments from 04/19/2004 forward via web subscription service from the SD Court Administrators Office, see note at the beginning of this section.
Criminal Records: Access: Mail, in person. Only the court performs in person searches; visitors may not. Search fee: $15.00 per name. Required to search: name, years to search, DOB; also helpful: address, SSN. Criminal records on computer since 7/89 on a statewide system. Mail turnaround time 1 day. See note at beginning of section for locations of the 2 state-recommended processing centers for mail requests.
General Information: No juvenile, sealed, dismissed, or mental health records released. Will fax documents $5.00. Court makes copy: $.20 per page. Self serve: same. Certification fee: $2.00 per cert. Payee: Hamlin County Clerk of Court. Personal checks and major credit cards accepted. Prepayment required. Mail requests: SASE required.

Hand County

Circuit Court PO Box 122, Miller, SD 57362; 605-853-3337; criminal fax: 605-853-3779; civil fax: same; 8AM-5PM (CST). ***Felony, Misdemeanor, Civil, Small Claims, Probate.***
www.sdjudicial.com/circuit_courts/index.asp?circuit=3
Probate fax is same as main fax number.
Civil Records: Access: Mail, in person, online. Only the court performs in person searches; visitors may not. Search fee: $15.00 per name. Required to search: name, years to search; also helpful: address. Civil cases indexed by defendant. All data on alpha index and docket books from late 1800s. Mail turnaround time 1 day. Active & inactive judgments from 04/19/2004 forward via web subscription service from Court Administrators Office; see note at the beginning of this section.
Criminal Records: Access: Fax, mail, in person. Only the court performs in person searches; visitors may not. Search fee: $15.00 per name. Required to search: name, years to search, DOB; also helpful: address, SSN. Criminal records on computer since 7/89 on a statewide system. Fax requesting for commercial accounts only. Mail turnaround time 1 day. See note at beginning of section for locations of the 2 state-recommended processing centers for mail requests.
General Information: No juvenile, sealed, dismissed, or mental health records released. Will fax documents; $5.00 fee per doc if non-toll free number; free to toll-free number. Court makes copy: $.20 per page. Certification fee: $2.00. Payee: Hand County Clerk of Court. Business checks accepted. No credit cards accepted. Mail requests: SASE required.

Hanson County

Circuit Court PO Box 127, 720 Fifth St, Alexandria, SD 57311; 605-239-4446; 8AM-4:30PM; Closed- N-12:30PM (CST). ***Felony, Misdemeanor, Civil, Small Claims, Probate.***
Probate fax is same as main fax number.
Civil Records: Access: Mail, in person, online. Only the court performs in person searches; visitors may not. Search fee: $15.00 per name. Required to search: name, years to search; also helpful: address. Civil cases indexed by defendant, plaintiff. Civil index in docket books from 1902; on computer back to 2000. Mail turnaround time varies. Active & inactive judgments from 04/19/2004 forward via web subscription service from Court Administrators Office; see note at the beginning of this section.
Criminal Records: Access: Mail, in person. Only the court performs in person searches; visitors may not. Search fee: $15.00 per name. Required to search: name, years to search, DOB; also helpful: address, SSN. Criminal records computerized since 7/89 on a statewide system. Mail turnaround time varies. See note at beginning of section for locations of the 2 state-recommended processing centers for mail requests.
General Information: No juvenile, sealed, dismissed, adoption or mental health records released. Will fax documents $5.00 each; add $1.00 per page after 5 pages. Court makes copy: $.20 per page. Self serve: same. Certification fee: $2.00 per doc includes copy fee. Payee: Hanson County Clerk of Court. Personal checks accepted. Visa/MC accepted. Prepayment required. Mail requests: SASE required.

Harding County

Circuit Court PO Box 534, Buffalo, SD 57720; 605-375-3351; fax: 605-375-3432; 9AM-N, 1-4PM (MST). ***Felony, Misdemeanor, Civil, Eviction, Small Claims, Probate.***
This court is a designated search center for South Dakota court records. For eviction information the court says to contact Harding County Sheriff, PO Box 293, Buffalo SD 57720.

Civil Records: Access: Mail, in person, online. Only the court performs in person searches; visitors may not. Search fee: $15.00 per name. Required to search: name, years to search, DOB; also helpful: address. Civil cases indexed by defendant. Civil records in archives from 1909 to 1920, index books from 1920. Mail turnaround time 1 week. Active & inactive judgments from 04/19/2004 forward via web subscription service from Court Administrators Office; see note at the beginning of this section.
Criminal Records: Access: Fax, mail, in person. Only the court performs in person searches; visitors may not. Search fee: $15.00 per name. Required to search: name, years to search, DOB; also helpful: address, SSN. Criminal records are computerized since 7/89 on a statewide system. Fax requests for commercial accounts only. Mail turnaround time 1 week. See note at beginning of section for locations of the 2 state-recommended processing centers for mail requests.
General Information: No juvenile, sealed, dismissed, or mental health records released. Will fax documents $1.00 per page, $5.00 minimum, no fee if local or toll free. Court makes copy: $.20 per page. Certification fee: $2.00. Payee: Harding County Clerk of Court. Personal checks accepted. Visa/MC accepted. Mail requests: SASE required.

Hughes County

Circuit Court 104 E Capital, Pierre, SD 57501; 605-773-3713; fax: 605-773-3875; 8AM-5PM (CST). ***Felony, Misdemeanor, Civil, Eviction, Small Claims, Probate.***
Civil Records: Access: Mail, in person, online. Only the court performs in person searches; visitors may not. Search fee: $15.00 per name. Required to search: name, years to search; also helpful: address. Civil cases indexed by defendant, plaintiff; index on microfiche from 1948 to 1973. From 1974 forward have hard copy file, starting 1991 index and docketing on computer. Mail turnaround time approx. 2 days. Active & inactive judgments from 04/19/2004 forward via web subscription service from the SD Court Administrators Office, see note at the beginning of this section.
Criminal Records: Access: Mail, in person. Only the court performs in person searches; visitors may not. Search fee: $15.00 per name. Required to search: name, years to search, DOB; also helpful: address. Criminal records on computer since 1988 on a statewide system. Mail turnaround time approx. 2 days. For faster service, you may mail search requests to Potter County for processing. See note at beginning of section for locations of the 2 state-recommended processing centers for mail requests.
General Information: No juvenile, adoption, any record sealed by the Court or mental health records released. Will not fax out documents. Court makes copy: $.20 per page. Certification fee: $2.00 per cert. Payee: Hughes County Clerk of Court. Personal checks accepted. Visa/MC accepted. Prepayment required. Mail requests: SASE required.

Hutchinson County

Circuit Court 140 Euclid, Rm 36, Olivet, SD 57052-2103; 605-387-4215; fax: 605-387-5035; 8AM-4:30PM (CST). ***Felony, Misdemeanor, Civil, Eviction, Small Claims, Probate.***
Civil Records: Access: Fax, mail, in person, online. Only the court performs in person searches; visitors may not. Search fee: $15.00 per name. Required to search: name, years to search; also helpful: address. Civil cases indexed by defendant, plaintiff. Civil index on docket books and index cards from 1800s, on computer since 1994. Mail turnaround time 1 day. Active & inactive judgments from 04/19/2004 forward via web subscription service from Court Administrators Office; see note at the beginning of this section.
Criminal Records: Access: Fax, mail, in person. Only the court performs in person searches; visitors may not. Search fee: $15.00 per name. Required to search: name, years to search, DOB; also helpful: address, SSN. Older records on docket books and index cards, records since 7/89 are computerized on a statewide system. Mail turnaround time 1 day. For faster service you may fax and mail requests to Douglas County for processing. See note at beginning of section for locations of the 2 state-recommended processing centers for mail requests.
General Information: No juvenile, sealed, dismissed, adoption or mental health records released. Will fax documents $5.00 minimum, $1.00 per page. Court makes copy: $.20 per page. Certification fee: $2.00 per cert. Payee: Hutchinson County Clerk of Court. Business checks accepted. Visa/MC accepted. Prepayment required. Mail requests: SASE required.

Hyde County

Circuit Court PO Box 306, Highmore, SD 57345; 605-852-2512; criminal fax: 605-852-2767; civil fax: same; 8AM-N (CST). ***Felony, Misdemeanor, Civil, Eviction, Small Claims, Probate.***
Probate fax is same as main fax number.
Civil Records: Access: Fax, mail, in person, online. Only the court performs in person searches; visitors may not. Search fee: $15.00 per name. Required to search: name, years to search; also helpful: address. Civil cases indexed by defendant, plaintiff. Civil index in docket books from 1920s, computerized from 2000. Mail turnaround time 1-3 days. Active & inactive judgments from 04/19/2004 forward via web subscription service from Court Administrators Office; see note at the beginning of this section.
Criminal Records: Access: Fax, mail, in person. Only the court performs in person searches; visitors may not. Search fee: $15.00 per name. Required to search: name, years to search, DOB, signed release; also helpful: address, SSN. Criminal records are computerized since 7/89 on a statewide system. Mail turnaround time 1-3 days. For faster service, fax or mail search requests to Potter County for processing. See note at beginning of section for locations of the 2 state-recommended processing centers for mail requests.
General Information: No juvenile, sealed, dismissed, or mental health records released. Will fax documents $5.00 per doc; no fee to local or toll free number. Court makes copy: $.20 per page. Self serve: same. Certification fee: $2.00 per cert includes copies. Payee: Hyde County Clerk of Courts. Personal checks accepted; credit cards are not. Prepayment required. Mail requests: SASE required.

Jackson County

Circuit Court PO Box 128, Kadoka, SD 57543; 605-837-2122; fax: 605-837-2120; 8AM-N, 1-5PM (MST). ***Felony, Misdemeanor, Civil, Eviction, Small Claims, Probate.***
Civil Records: Access: Mail, in person, online. Only the court performs in person searches; visitors may not. Search fee: $15.00 per name. Required to search: name, years to search; also helpful: address. Civil cases indexed by defendant. Civil records on "Register of Action" from 1915; on computer back to 1993. Mail turnaround time 1-2 days. Active & inactive judgments available from a web subscription service offered by the SD Court Administrators Office, profiled in the state section or call Jill Gusso-605-773-4874 for more details.
Criminal Records: Access: Mail, in person. Only the court performs in person searches; visitors may not. Search fee: $15.00 per name. Required to search: name, years to search, DOB; also helpful: address, SSN. Criminal records computerized from 7/89 on a statewide system; other records go back to 1920. Mail turnaround time 1-2 days. For faster service, you may mail search requests to Potter County for processing. See note at beginning of section for locations of the 2 state-recommended processing centers for mail requests.
General Information: No juvenile, sealed, dismissed, or mental health records released. Will fax documents for either $5.00 or $1.00 per page, whichever is greater. Court makes copy: $.20 per page. Self serve: same. Certification fee: $2.00 per cert. Payee: Jackson County Clerk of Court. Personal checks accepted. Mail requests: SASE required.

Jerauld County

Circuit Court PO Box 435, 203 S Wallace St, Wessington Springs, SD 57382; 605-539-1202; fax: 605-539-1203; 8AM-Noon, 1PM-5PM (CST). ***Felony, Misdemeanor, Civil, Eviction, Small Claims, Probate.***
www.sdjudicial.com/circuit_courts/index.asp?circuit=3
Civil Records: Access: Mail, in person, online. Only the court performs in person searches; visitors may not. Search fee: $15.00 per name. Required to search: name, years to search; also helpful: address. Civil cases indexed by defendant. Civil index in docket books from 1900s. Mail turnaround time 2 days. Active & inactive judgments from 04/19/2004 forward via web subscription service from Court Administrators Office; see note at the beginning of this section.
Criminal Records: Access: Mail, in person. Only the court performs in person searches; visitors may not. Search fee: $15.00 per name. Required to search: name, years to search, DOB; also helpful: address, SSN. Criminal records are computerized since 1989 on a statewide system. Fax requesting for commercial accounts only. Mail turnaround time 2 days. See note at beginning of section for locations of the 2 state-recommended processing centers for mail requests.
General Information: No juvenile, sealed, dismissed, or mental health records released. Will fax documents $5.00 per page. Court makes copy: $.25 per page. Certification fee: $2.00 per doc. Payee: Jerauld County Clerk of Court. Personal checks accepted. Visa/MC accepted. Prepayment required. Mail requests: SASE required.

Jones County

Circuit Court PO Box 448, 310 Main St, Murdo, SD 57559; 605-669-2361; fax: 605-669-2641; 8AM-Noon (CST). ***Felony, Misdemeanor, Civil, Eviction, Small Claims, Probate.***
Criminal cases and records at Potter County.
Civil Records: Access: Mail, in person, online. Only the court performs in person searches; visitors may not. Search fee: $15.00 per name. Required to search: name, years to search; also helpful: address. Civil cases indexed by defendant, plaintiff. Civil index in docket books from 1900s. Mail turnaround time 3 days to 1 week. Active & inactive judgments from 04/19/2004 forward via web subscription service from Court Administrators Office; see note at the beginning of this section.
Criminal Records: Access: Mail, in person. Only the court performs in person searches; visitors may not. Search fee: $15.00 per name. Required to search: name, years to search, DOB, SSN; also helpful: address. Criminal records are computerized since 7/89 on a statewide system. Records on books go back to 1917. Mail turnaround time 3 days to 1 week. For faster service you may mail requests to Potter County for processing. See note at beginning of section for locations of the 2 state-recommended processing centers for mail requests.
General Information: No juvenile, sealed, dismissed, or mental health records released. Will fax documents $5.00 each. Court makes copy: $.20 per page. Certification fee: $2.00 per doc. Payee: Jones County Clerk of Court (civil cases); Potter County Clerk of Court (criminal cases). Business checks accepted. No credit cards accepted. Prepayment required. Mail requests: SASE required.

Kingsbury County

Circuit Court PO Box 176, De Smet, SD 57231-0176; 605-854-3811; criminal fax: 605-854-9080; civil fax: same; 8AM-N, 1-5PM (CST). ***Felony, Misdemeanor, Civil, Eviction, Small Claims, Probate.***
www.sdjudicial.com/circuit_courts/index.asp?circuit=3
Probate is a separate index at this same address. Probate fax is same as main fax number.
Civil Records: Access: Mail, in person, online. Both court and visitors may perform in person searches. Search fee: $15.00 per name. Required to search: name, years to search; also helpful: address plus DOB. Civil cases indexed by defendant, plaintiff; index on computer printed index from 1978 and

bound books from 1890. Mail turnaround time same day. Active & inactive judgments from 04/19/2004 forward via web subscription service from the SD Court Administrators Office, see note at the beginning of this section.
Criminal Records: Access: Mail, in person. Only the court performs in person searches; visitors may not. Search fee: $15.00 per name. Required to search: name, years to search, DOB; also helpful: address, SSN. Criminal records on computer since 7/89 on a statewide system. Mail turnaround time same day. You may also mail search requests to Hand County for processing. See note at beginning of section for locations of the 2 state-recommended processing centers for mail requests.
General Information: No juvenile, sealed, dismissed, adoption or mental health records released. Will fax documents $1.00 per page, $5.00 minimum. Court makes copy: $.20 per page. Certification fee: $2.00 per cert includes copy fee. Payee: Kingsbury County Clerk of Court. Personal checks and major credit cards accepted. Prepayment required. Mail requests: SASE required.

Lake County

Circuit Court 200 E Center St, Madison, SD 57042; 605-256-5644; fax: 605-256-5080; 8AM-N, 1-5PM (CST). ***Felony, Misdemeanor, Civil, Eviction, Small Claims, Probate.***
www.sdjudicial.com/circuit_courts/index.asp?circuit=3
Civil Records: Access: Mail, in person, online. Only the court performs in person searches; visitors may not. Search fee: $15.00 per name. Required to search: name, years to search; also helpful: address. Civil cases indexed by defendant. Civil records on computer from 1985, docket books from 1800s. Mail turnaround time 1 day. Active & inactive judgments from 04/19/2004 forward via web subscription service from Court Administrators Office; see note at the beginning of this section.
Criminal Records: Access: Mail, in person. Only the court performs in person searches; visitors may not. Search fee: $15.00 per name. Required to search: name, years to search, DOB, signed release; also helpful: address, SSN. Criminal records on computer since 1989 on a statewide system; prior records on docket books since 1800s. Mail turnaround time 1 day. You may also mail search requests to Miner County for processing. See note at beginning of section for locations of the 2 state-recommended processing centers for mail requests.
General Information: No juvenile, sealed, dismissed, or mental health records released. Court makes copy: $.20 per page. Certification fee: $2.00 per doc. Payee: Lake County Clerk of Court. Personal checks accepted. Visa accepted. Prepayment required. Mail requests: SASE required.

Lawrence County

Circuit Court PO Box 626, 78 Sherman St, Deadwood, SD 57732; 605-578-2040; fax: 605-578-1571; 8AM-N, 1-5PM (MST). ***Felony, Misdemeanor, Civil, Eviction, Small Claims, Probate.***
Civil Records: Access: Mail, in person, online. Only the court performs in person searches; visitors may not. Search fee: $15.00 per name. Required to search: name, years to search; also helpful: address. Civil cases indexed by defendant, plaintiff; index on computer from 1989 and index books from 1800s. Mail turnaround time 2 weeks. Active & inactive judgments from 04/19/2004 forward via web subscription service from Court Administrators Office; see note at the beginning of this section.
Criminal Records: Access: Mail, in person. Only the court performs in person searches; visitors may not. Search fee: $15.00 per name. Required to search: name, years to search, DOB; also helpful: address, SSN. Criminal records on computer since 7/89 on a statewide system. Mail turnaround time 1-3 days. See note at beginning of section for locations of the 2 state-recommended processing centers for mail requests.
General Information: No juvenile, sealed, dismissed, or mental health records released. Will fax documents $5.00 per doc; no fee to local or toll free number. Court makes copy: $.20 per page. Certification fee: $2.00 per doc. Payee: Lawrence County Clerk of Court. Personal checks and major credit cards accepted. Prepayment required. Mail requests: SASE required.

Lincoln County

Circuit Court Clerk of Courts, 104 N Main St, Canton, SD 57013; 605-987-5891; fax: 605-987-9088; 8AM-5PM (CST). ***Felony, Misdemeanor, Civil, Eviction, Small Claims, Probate.***
Civil Records: Access: Mail, in person, online. Both court and visitors may perform in person searches. Search fee: $15.00 per name. Required to search: name, years to search; also helpful: address. Civil cases indexed by defendant, plaintiff. Civil index in docket books from 1900s. Visitor may search written index pre-1993; only the court searches computer records 1994 forward. Mail turnaround time 3 days, longer for probate. Civil PAT goes back to 1996. PAT results show name only. Active & inactive judgments from 04/19/2004 forward via web subscription service from Court Administrators Office; see note at the beginning of this section.
Criminal Records: Access: Mail, in person. Both court and visitors may perform in person searches. Search fee: $15.00 per name. Required to search: name, years to search, DOB; also helpful: address, SSN. Criminal records on computer since 7/89 on a statewide system. Mail turnaround time 3 days, longer for probate. For faster service, you may mail search requests to Douglas County. Criminal PAT goes back to 1989. PAT results show name only. See note at beginning of section for locations of the 2 state-recommended processing centers for mail requests.
General Information: No juvenile, sealed, dismissed, adoption or mental health records released. Court makes copy: $.20 per page. Certification fee: $2.00 per doc. Payee: Lincoln County Clerk of Court. Personal checks accepted. Visa/MC accepted. Prepayment required. Mail requests: SASE required.

Lyman County

Circuit Court PO Box 235, 300 S Main, Courthouse, Kennebec, SD 57544; 605-869-2277; 8AM-5PM (CST). ***Felony, Misdemeanor, Civil, Eviction, Small Claims, Probate.***
A separate search fee for civil and for criminal.
Civil Records: Access: Mail, in person, online. Only the court performs in person searches; visitors may not. Search fee: $15.00 per name. Required to search: name, years to search; also helpful: address. Civil cases indexed by defendant, plaintiff. Civil index in docket books from 1900s; on computer back one year. Mail turnaround time 1 week. Active & inactive judgments from 04/19/2004 forward via web subscription service from Court Administrators Office; see note at the beginning of this section.
Criminal Records: Access: Mail, in person. Only the court performs in person searches; visitors may not. Search fee: $15.00 per name. Required to search: name, years to search, DOB; also helpful: address, SSN. Criminal records on computer since 7/89 on a statewide system. Mail turnaround time 1 week. For faster service, direct search request to Potter county for processing. See note at beginning of section for locations of the 2 state-recommended processing centers for mail requests.
General Information: No juvenile, sealed, dismissed, or mental health records released. Fee to fax out file $5.00 per fax. Court makes copy: $.20 per page. Certification fee: $2.00 per cert. Payee: Lyman County Clerk of Court. Personal checks accepted; credit cards are not. Prepayment required. Mail requests: SASE required.

Marshall County

Circuit Court PO Box 130, Britton, SD 57430; 605-448-5213; 8AM-N, 1-5PM M-TH (CST). ***Felony, Misdemeanor, Civil, Eviction, Small Claims, Probate.*** http://ujs.sd.gov/5thcircuit/
Civil Records: Access: Mail, in person, online. Only the court performs in person searches; visitors may not. Search fee: $15.00 per name. Required to search: name, years to search; also helpful: address. Civil cases indexed by defendant, plaintiff. Civil index in docket books from 1800s. Mail turnaround time 1 week. Active & inactive judgments from 04/19/2004 forward via web subscription service from Court Administrators Office; see note at the beginning of this section.
Criminal Records: Access: Mail, in person. Only the court performs in person searches; visitors may not. Search fee: $15.00 per name. Required to search: name, years to search, DOB; also helpful: address, SSN. Criminal records are computerized since 7/89 on a statewide system. Mail Turnaround time 1 week. For faster service, direct search request to Edmunds County Search Center for processing, 605-426-6671. See note at beginning of section for locations of the 2 state-recommended processing centers for mail requests.
General Information: No juvenile, sealed, dismissed, or mental health records released. Will fax documents to local or toll free line. Court makes copy: $.20 per page. Certification fee: $2.00 per cert. Payee: Marshall County Clerk of Court. Personal checks accepted. Mail requests: SASE required.

McCook County

Circuit Court PO Box 504, Salem, SD 57058; 605-425-2781; fax: 605-425-3144; 8AM-12:30; 1-4:30PM (CST). ***Felony, Misdemeanor, Civil, Eviction, Small Claims, Probate.***
Civil Records: Access: Mail, in person, online. Only the court performs in person searches; visitors may not. Search fee: $15.00 per name. Required to search: name, years to search; also helpful: address, DOB, SSN. Civil cases indexed by defendant, plaintiff. Civil records in index and docket books from late 1800s. Mail turnaround time 1 day. Active & inactive judgments from 04/19/2004 forward via web subscription service from Court Administrators Office; see note at the beginning of this section.
Criminal Records: Access: Mail, in person. Only the court performs in person searches; visitors may not. Search fee: $15.00 per name. Required to search: name, years to search, DOB, signed release; also helpful: address, SSN. Criminal records are computerized since 7/89 on a statewide system. In person requests must be written. Mail turnaround time 1 day. For faster service, you may mail search requests to Miner County for processing. See note at beginning of section for locations of the 2 state-recommended processing centers for mail requests.
General Information: No juvenile, sealed, dismissed, or mental health records released. Will fax documents $5.00 per page. Court makes copy: $.20 per page. Certification fee: $2.00 per cert. Payee: McCook County Clerk of Court. Personal checks accepted. Visa/MC accepted. Prepayment required. Mail requests: SASE required.

McPherson County

Circuit Court PO Box 248, Leola, SD 57456; 605-439-3361; fax: 605-439-3297; 8AM-N (CST). ***Felony, Misdemeanor, Civil, Eviction, Small Claims, Probate.*** http://ujs.sd.gov/5thcircuit/
Civil Records: Access: Mail, in person, online. Both court and visitors may perform in person searches. Search fee: $15.00 per name. Required to search: name, years to search; also helpful: address. Civil cases indexed by defendant, plaintiff; index on register of action from 1910, records are not computerized. When searching in person there is no fee if case number is known. Mail turnaround time 1 day to 1 week. PAT results show name only. Active & inactive judgments from 04/19/2004 forward via web subscription service from Court Administrators Office; see note at the beginning of this section.
Criminal Records: Access: Mail, in person. Only the court performs in person searches; visitors may not. Search fee: $15.00 per name. Required to search: name, years to search, DOB, signed release; also helpful: address, SSN. Criminal records on register of action from 1910, records are not computerized. Mail Turnaround time 1 day to 1 week. For faster service, you may mail search requests to McPherson County for processing. 605-439-3361, See note at beginning of section for locations of the 2 state-recommended processing centers for mail requests.

General Information: No juvenile, sealed, dismissed, adoption or mental health records released. Will fax documents to local or toll free line. Court makes copy: $.25 per page. Self serve: same. Certification fee: $2.00 per cert. Payee: McPherson County Clerk of Court. Personal checks and major credit cards accepted. Prepayment required. Mail requests: SASE required.

Meade County

Circuit Court PO Box 939, 1425 Sherman St, Sturgis, SD 57785; 605-347-4411; fax: 605-347-3526; 8AM-N, 1-5PM (MST). ***Felony, Misdemeanor, Civil, Eviction, Small Claims, Probate.***

Civil Records: Access: Mail, in person, online. Only the court performs in person searches; visitors may not. Search fee: $15.00 per name. Required to search: name, years to search; also helpful: address. Civil cases indexed by defendant, plaintiff. Civil index on cards and docket books from 1800s. Mail turnaround time 1 day to 2 weeks. Active & inactive judgments from 04/19/2004 forward via web subscription service from Court Administrators Office; see note at the beginning of this section.

Criminal Records: Access: Mail, in person. Only the court performs in person searches; visitors may not. Search fee: $15.00 per name. Required to search: name, years to search, DOB, signed release; also helpful: address, SSN. Criminal records on computer since 7/89 on a statewide system. Mail turnaround time 1 day to 2 weeks. For faster service, you may mail search requests to Lawrence County for processing. See note at beginning of section for locations of the 2 state-recommended processing centers for mail requests.

General Information: No juvenile, sealed, dismissed, or mental health records released. Will fax documents $5.00 per fax. Court makes copy: $.20 per page. Certification fee: $2.00 per doc. Payee: Meade County Clerk of Courts. Personal checks (instate only) accepted. Visa/MC accepted. Prepayment required. Mail requests: SASE required.

Mellette County

Circuit Court PO Box 257, White River, SD 57579; 605-259-3230; probate phone: same; 8AM-N (CST). ***Felony, Misdemeanor, Civil, Eviction, Small Claims, Probate.***

Civil Records: Access: Phone, mail, in person, online. Only the court performs in person searches; visitors may not. Search fee: $15.00 per name. Required to search: name, years to search; also helpful: address. Civil cases indexed by defendant. Civil index on cards and docket books from 1900s. Mail turnaround time 3 days; probate up to 1 month. Active & inactive judgments from 04/19/2004 forward via web subscription service from Court Administrators Office; see note at the beginning of this section.

Criminal Records: Access: Mail, in person. Only the court performs in person searches; visitors may not. Search fee: $15.00 per name. Required to search: name, years to search, DOB, signed release; also helpful: address, SSN. Criminal records are computerized since 7/89 on a statewide system. Mail turnaround time 3 days; probate up to 1 month. For faster service, you may mail criminal search requests to Potter County for processing. See note at beginning of section for locations of the 2 state-recommended processing centers for mail requests.

General Information: No juvenile, sealed, dismissed, or mental health records released. Will fax documents $5.00 each. Court makes copy: $.20 per page. Certification fee: $2.00 per cert. Payee: Mellette County Clerk of Court. Personal checks accepted. Prepayment required. Mail requests: SASE required.

Miner County

Circuit Court PO Box 265, Howard, SD 57349; 605-772-4612; criminal fax: 605-772-4412; civil fax: same; 8AM-N; 1-5PM (CST). ***Felony, Misdemeanor, Civil, Eviction, Small Claims, Probate.***

www.sdjudicial.com/circuit_courts/index.asp?circuit=3

Probate fax is same as main fax number.

Civil Records: Access: Mail, in person, online. Both court and visitors may perform in person searches. Search fee: $4.00 per name. Required to search: name, years to search. Civil cases indexed by defendant, plaintiff. Civil index in docket books from 1900's. Mail turnaround time 2 days. Active & inactive judgments from 04/19/2004 forward via web subscription service from Court Administrators Office; see note at the beginning of this section.

Criminal Records: Access: Fax, mail, in person. Only the court performs in person searches; visitors may not. Search fee: $15.00 per name. Required to search: name, years to search, DOB; also helpful: SSN. Criminal records are computerized since 1989. This is a statewide search. Mail turnaround time 2 days.

General Information: No juvenile, sealed, dismissed or mental health records released. Will fax documents $5.00 per doc; no fee to local or toll free number. Court makes copy: $.25 per page criminal; Civil-$1.00 per page. Certification fee: $2.00 per page. Cert fee includes copies. Payee: Miner County Clerk of Court. Personal checks accepted; credit cards are not. Prepayment required. Mail requests: SASE required.

Minnehaha County

Circuit Court 425 N Dakota Ave, Sioux Falls, SD 57104; 605-367-5900; fax: 605-367-5916; 8AM-5PM (CST). ***Felony, Misdemeanor, Civil, Eviction, Small Claims, Probate.***

Please use their request form when requesting search.

Civil Records: Access: Mail, in person, online. Only the court performs in person searches; visitors may not. Search fee: $15.00 per name. Required to search: name, years to search; also helpful: address. Civil cases indexed by defendant, plaintiff; index on computer from 1989, docket books from 1800s. Mail turnaround time 2 weeks. Active & inactive judgments from 04/19/2004 forward via web subscription service from Court Administrators Office; see note at the beginning of this section.

Criminal Records: Access: Mail, in person. Only the court performs in person searches; visitors may not. Search fee: $15.00 per name. Required to search: name, years to search, DOB, signed release; also helpful: address, SSN. Criminal records on computer since 7/89. Mail turnaround time 2 weeks. For faster service, you may mail search requests to either Jerauld (first choice) or Sanborn counties for processing. See note at beginning of section for locations of the 2 state-recommended processing centers for mail requests.

General Information: No juvenile, sealed, dismissed or mental health records released. Will not fax out documents. Court makes copy: $.20 per page. Certification fee: $2.00 per doc. Payee: Minnehaha County Clerk of Court. Personal checks accepted. Visa/MC accepted. Prepayment required. Mail requests: SASE required.

Moody County

Circuit Court 101 E Pipestone, Flandreau, SD 57028; 605-997-3181; criminal fax: 605-997-3861; civil fax: same; 8AM-5PM (CST). ***Felony, Misdemeanor, Civil, Eviction, Small Claims, Probate.***

www.sdjudicial.com/circuit_courts/index.asp?circuit=3&category=counties&nav=913

Probate records are in a separate index at this address. Probate fax is same as main fax number.

Civil Records: Access: Mail, in person, online. Only the court performs in person searches; visitors may not. Search fee: $15.00 per name. Required to search: name, years to search; also helpful: address. Civil cases indexed by defendant, plaintiff; index on computer from 1992 and docket books from 1800s. Mail turnaround time 2-3 days. Active & inactive judgments from 04/19/2004 forward via web subscription service from Court Administrators Office; see note at the beginning of this section.

Criminal Records: Access: Mail, in person. Only the court performs in person searches; visitors may not. Search fee: $15.00 per name. Required to search: name, years to search, DOB; also helpful: address, SSN. Criminal records on computer since 7/89 on a statewide index. Mail turnaround time 2-3 days. For faster service, you may mail search requests to Miner County of processing. See note at beginning of section for locations of the 2 state-recommended processing centers for mail requests.

General Information: No juvenile, sealed, dismissed, adoption or mental health records released. Will fax documents $5.00 each. Court makes copy: $.20 per page. Certification fee: $2.00 per page includes copy fee. Payee: Moody County Clerk of Court. Personal checks accepted; credit cards are not. Prepayment required. Mail requests: SASE required.

Pennington County

Circuit Court PO Box 230, Rapid City, SD 57709; 602-394-2575; criminal phone: 605-394-2570; civil phone: 605-394-2575; probate phone: 605-394-2575; 8AM-5PM (MST). ***Felony, Misdemeanor, Civil, Eviction, Small Claims, Probate.***

Civil Records: Access: Mail, in person, online. Only the court performs in person searches; visitors may not. Search fee: $15.00 per name. Required to search: name, years to search; also helpful: address. Civil cases indexed by defendant, plaintiff; index on computer from 1991, cards and docket books from 1900s. Mail turnaround time 2 weeks. Active & inactive judgments from 04/19/2004 forward via web subscription service from Court Administrators Office; see note at the beginning of this section.

Criminal Records: Access: Mail, in person. Only the court performs in person searches; visitors may not. Search fee: $15.00. Required to search: DOB, years to search. Criminal records computerized to 1989, on other media form 1950. Mail turnaround time 2 weeks. If prior to 1989, you may direct search request here at Pennington County; arrest date and charge is required to conduct search. If 1989 to present, you may direct your mail search request to Ziebach County Clerk. Also, see note at beginning of section for locations of the 2 state-recommended processing centers for mail requests.

General Information: No juvenile, sealed, or mental health records released. Will not fax documents. Court makes copy: $.20 per page. Certification fee: $2.00 per cert. Payee: Clerk of the Court. Personal checks accepted. Visa/MC accepted. Prepayment required. Mail requests: SASE required.

Perkins County

Circuit Court PO Box 426, Bison, SD 57620-0426; 605-244-5626; fax: 605-244-7110; 9AM-N, 1-4PM (MST). ***Felony, Misdemeanor, Civil, Eviction, Small Claims, Probate.***

http://ujs.sd.gov/perkins.htm

Civil Records: Access: Mail, in person, online. Only the court performs in person searches; visitors may not. Search fee: $15.00 per name. Required to search: name, years to search. Civil cases indexed by defendant, plaintiff. Civil index in docket books from 1908; on computer back to 1999. Mail turnaround time varies. Active & inactive judgments from 04/19/2004 forward via web subscription service from Court Administrators Office; see note at the beginning of this section.

Criminal Records: Access: Mail, in person. Only the court performs in person searches; visitors may not. Search fee: $15.00 per name. Required to search: name, years to search, DOB, signed release. Criminal records are computerized back to 7/89 on a statewide system. Mail turnaround time varies. For faster service, fax or mail search requests to Lawrence County for processing. See note at beginning of section for locations of the 2 state-recommended processing centers for mail requests.

General Information: No juvenile, sealed or mental health records released. Will fax documents $5.00 per doc. Court makes copy: $.20 per page. Self serve: same. Certification fee: $2.00 per cert. Payee: Perkins County Clerk of Courts. Only cashiers checks and money orders accepted. No credit cards accepted. Prepayment required. Mail requests: SASE requested.

Potter County

Circuit Court PO Box 67, 201 S Exene St, Gettysburg, SD 57442; 605-765-9472; fax: 605-765-9670; 7:30AM-N, 12:30-5PM M-TH; 7:30AM-N F (CST). ***Felony, Misdemeanor, Civil, Eviction, Small Claims, Probate.***

Civil Records: Access: Mail, in person, online. Only the court performs in person searches; visitors may not. Search fee: $15.00 per name. Required to search: name, years to search; also helpful: address. Civil cases indexed by defendant, plaintiff. Civil index on cards and docket books from 1889. Requests should be in writing. Mail turnaround time 1-2 days. Active & inactive judgments from 04/19/2004 forward via web subscription service from Court Administrators Office; see note at the beginning of this section.

Criminal Records: Access: Mail, in person. Only the court performs in person searches; visitors may not. Search fee: $15.00 per name. Required to search: name, years to search, DOB, signed release; also helpful: address, SSN. Criminal records are indexed on computer since 7/89 on a statewide system. Requests must be in writing. Mail turnaround time 1-2 days. See note at beginning of section for locations of the 2 state-recommended processing centers for mail requests.

General Information: No juvenile, sealed, dismissed, adoption or mental health records released. Will not fax out documents. Court makes copy: $.20 per page. Certification fee: $2.00 per doc. Payee: Potter County Clerk of Court. Personal checks and Visa/MC accepted. Mail requests: SASE required.

Roberts County

Circuit Court 411 2nd Ave E, Sisseton, SD 57262; 605-698-3395; fax: 605-698-7894; 8AM-5PM (CST). ***Felony, Misdemeanor, Civil, Eviction, Small Claims, Probate.*** http://ujs.sd.gov/5thcircuit/

Civil Records: Access: Mail, in person, online. Only the court performs in person searches; visitors may not. Search fee: $15.00 per name. Required to search: name, years to search; also helpful: address. Civil cases indexed by defendant, plaintiff; index on computer from 1992, microfilm from 1920 to 1985 and original files from 1986. Searches performed on a time available basis. Mail turnaround time 2-3 days. Active & inactive judgments from 04/19/2004 forward via web subscription service from Court Administrators Office; see note at the beginning of this section.

Criminal Records: Access: Mail, in person. Only the court performs in person searches; visitors may not. Search fee: $15.00 per name. Required to search: name, years to search, DOB; also helpful: address, SSN. Criminal records on computer since 1988 on a state wide system. Mail turnaround time 2-3 days. For faster service, criminal search requests can be directed to Edmunds County for processing. See note at beginning of section for locations of the 2 state-recommended processing centers for mail requests.

General Information: No juvenile, sealed, dismissed, adoption or mental health records released. Will fax documents to local or toll free line. Court makes copy: $.20 per page. Certification fee: $2.00 includes copy fee. Payee: Roberts County Clerk of Court (or, Edmunds City Clerk, if a criminal search. Personal checks accepted. Visa/MC accepted. Prepayment required. Mail requests: SASE required.

Sanborn County

Circuit Court PO Box 56, 604 W 6th St, Woonsocket, SD 57385; 605-796-4515; fax: 605-796-4502; 9-4:30PM (CST). ***Felony, Misdemeanor, Civil, Eviction, Small Claims, Probate.***
www.sdjudicial.com/circuit_courts/index.asp?circuit=3

Civil Records: Access: Mail, in person, online. Only the court performs in person searches; visitors may not. Search fee: $15.00 per name. Required to search: name, years to search; also helpful: address. Civil cases indexed by defendant, plaintiff. Civil index in docket books from 1890s. Mail turnaround time 1 week. Active & inactive judgments from 04/19/2004 forward via web subscription service from Court Administrators Office; see note at the beginning of this section.

Criminal Records: Access: Mail, in person. Only the court performs in person searches; visitors may not. Search fee: $15.00 per name. Required to search: name, years to search, DOB; also helpful: address, SSN. Criminal records are computerized since 1989 on a statewide system. Mail turnaround time 1 week. See note at beginning of section for locations of the 2 state-recommended processing centers for mail requests.

General Information: No juvenile, sealed, dismissed, or mental health records released. Will fax documents $1.00 per page. Court makes copy: $.20 per page. Certification fee: $2.00 per cert. Payee: Sanborn County Clerk of Courts. Personal checks accepted; no two party checks. Visa/MC and debit cards accepted. Prepayment required. Mail requests: SASE required.

Shannon County

Circuit Court C/O Falls River Circuit Court, 906 N River St, Hot Springs, SD 57747; 605-745-5131; 8AM-5PM (MST). ***Felony, Misdemeanor, Civil, Eviction, Small Claims, Probate.***

Note that cases, proceedings, and records for the Shannon County Circuit Court are handled by the Fall River Circuit Court. Records are not co-mingled. Be specific in your request. Tribal court handles Tribal matters - 605-867-5131.

Civil Records: Access: Mail, in person, online. Only the court performs in person searches; visitors may not. Search fee: $15.00 per name. Required to search: name, years to search; also helpful: address, DOB, SSN. Civil cases indexed by defendant, plaintiff; index on computer from 1992, older files archived off site to 1889. Mail turnaround time 1-2 weeks. Active & inactive judgments from 04/19/2004 forward via web subscription service from Court Administrators Office; see note at the beginning of this section.

Criminal Records: Access: Mail, in person. Only the court performs in person searches; visitors may not. Search fee: $15.00 per name. Required to search: name, years to search, DOB; also helpful: address, SSN. Criminal records on computer since 7/89 on a statewide system. Mail turnaround time 1-2 weeks. See note at beginning of section for locations of the 2 state-recommended processing centers for mail requests.

General Information: No juvenile, sealed, adoption, or mental health records released. Will fax documents to local or toll free line. Court makes copy: $.25 per page. Certification fee: $2.00 per doc. Payee: Shannon County Clerk of Court. Personal checks accepted. No credit cards accepted at this court. Prepayment required. Mail requests: SASE required.

Spink County

Circuit Court 210 E 7th Ave, Redfield, SD 57469; 605-472-4535; criminal fax: 605-472-4352; civil fax: same; 8AM-5PM (CST). ***Felony, Misdemeanor, Civil, Eviction, Small Claims, Probate.***
http://ujs.sd.gov/5thcircuit/

Probate fax is same as main fax number.

Civil Records: Access: Phone, fax, mail, in person, online. Only the court performs in person searches; visitors may not. Search fee: $15.00 per name. Required to search: name, years to search; also helpful: address. Civil cases indexed by defendant, plaintiff. Civil index in docket books from 1882. Mail turnaround time 1 day. Active & inactive judgments from 04/19/2004 forward via web subscription service from Court Administrators Office; see note at the beginning of this section.

Criminal Records: Access: Phone, fax, mail, in person. Only the court performs in person searches; visitors may not. Search fee: $15.00 per name. Required to search: name, years to search, DOB; also helpful: address, SSN. Criminal records on computer since 1988 on a statewide system. Mail turnaround time 1 day. For equally fast service, fax or mail search requests to Edmunds County for processing. See note at beginning of section for locations of the 2 state-recommended processing centers for mail requests.

General Information: No juvenile, sealed, dismissed, or mental health records released. Will fax documents $5.00 per doc; no fee to toll free number; must be a commercial account. Court makes copy: $.20 per page. Cert fee: $2.00 per doc includes copy fee. Payee: Spink County Clerk of Court. Personal checks and major credit cards accepted. Prepayment required. Mail requests: SASE required.

Stanley County

Circuit Court PO Box 758, E. 2nd Ave Courthouse, #8, Fort Pierre, SD 57532; 605-223-7735; fax: 605-223-7738; 8AM-5PM (CST). ***Felony, Misdemeanor, Civil, Eviction, Small Claims, Probate.***

Civil Records: Access: Fax, mail, in person, online. Both court and visitors may perform in person searches. Search fee: $15.00 per name. Required to search: name, years to search; also helpful: address. Civil cases indexed by defendant, plaintiff. Civil index in docket books from 1973. Requests should be in writing. Mail turnaround time 1-2 days. Active & inactive judgments from 04/19/2004 forward via web subscription service from the SD Court Administrators Office. Online results show middle initial, DOB. DOB is on some but not all civil records. See Court Admin's Office profile in the state section or call Jill Gusso-605-773-4874 for more details.

Criminal Records: Access: Fax, mail, in person. Only the court performs in person searches; visitors may not. Search fee: $15.00 per name. Required to search: name, years to search, DOB; also helpful: address, SSN. Criminal records on computer since 1989 on a statewide system. Mail turnaround 1-2 days. For equally fast service, you may direct search requests to Potter County for processing. See note at beginning of section for locations of the 2 state-recommended processing centers for mail requests.

General Information: No juvenile, sealed, dismissed, or mental health records released. Will fax documents $5.00 plus $1.00 per page. Court makes copy: $.20 per page. Certification fee: $2.00 per cert. Payee: Stanley County Clerk of Court. Personal checks accepted. Visa/MC accepted. Prepayment required. Mail requests: SASE required.

Sully County

Circuit Court PO Box 188, Onida, SD 57564; 605-258-2535; fax: 605-258-2270; 8AM-N (CST). ***Felony, Misdemeanor, Civil, Eviction, Small Claims, Probate.***

Civil Records: Access: Mail, in person, online. Both court and visitors may perform in person searches. Search fee: $15.00 per name. Required to search: name, years to search; also helpful: address. Civil cases indexed by defendant, plaintiff. Civil index in docket books from 1900s. Mail turnaround time 1-2 days. Active & inactive judgments from 04/19/2004 forward via web subscription service from Court Administrators Office; see note at the beginning of this section.

Criminal Records: Access: Mail, in person. Both court and visitors may perform in person searches. Search fee: $15.00 per name. Required to search: name, years to search; also helpful: address. Criminal records on computer since 7/89 on statewide system; local computer back to 2000. Mail turnaround time 1-2 days. For equally as fast service, you may mail search requests to Potter County for processing. See note at beginning of section for locations of the 2 state-recommended processing centers.

General Information: No juvenile, sealed, dismissed, or mental health records released. Will fax documents for fee. Court makes copy: $.25 per page plus tax $.02. Self serve: same. Certification fee: $2.00 per cert. Payee: Sully County Clerk of Court. Personal checks accepted; credit cards are not. Prepayment required. Mail requests: SASE required.

Todd County

Circuit Court PO Box 311, 200 E 3rd St, Winner, SD 57580; 605-842-2266; fax: 605-842-2267; 8AM-5PM (MST). ***Felony, Misdemeanor, Civil, Eviction, Small Claims, Probate.***

Court records are maintained by Tripp County.

Tripp County

Circuit Court PO Box 311, 200 E 3rd St, Winner, SD 57580; 605-842-2266; fax: 605-842-2267; 8AM-5PM (CST). ***Felony, Misdemeanor, Civil, Eviction, Small Claims, Probate.***

This court also maintains records for Todd County.

Civil Records: Access: Mail, in person, online. Only the court performs in person searches; visitors may not. Search fee: $15.00 per name. Required to search: name, years to search; also helpful: address. Civil cases indexed by defendant, plaintiff. Civil index in docket books from 1920s. Requests should be in writing. Mail turnaround time 2 days. Active & inactive judgments from 04/19/2004 forward via web subscription service from Court Administrators Office; see note at the beginning of this section.

Criminal Records: Access: Mail, in person. Only the court performs in person searches; visitors may not. Search fee: $15.00 per name. Required to search: name, years to search, DOB, signed release; also helpful: address, SSN. Criminal records on computer since 1989 on statewide system. Mail turnaround time 2 days. For faster service, you may mail search requests to Potter County for processing. See note at beginning of section for locations of the 2 state-recommended processing centers for mail requests.

General Information: No juvenile, sealed, dismissed, or mental health records released. Will fax documents $1.00 per page. Court makes copy: $.25 per page criminal; civil- $.20 per page. Certification fee: $2.00 per doc. Payee: Tripp County Clerk of Court. Personal checks accepted. Visa/MC accepted. Prepayment required. Mail requests: SASE required.

Turner County

Circuit Court PO Box 446, Parker, SD 57053; 605-297-3115; criminal fax: 605-297-2115; civil fax: same; 8:30AM-5PM (CST). ***Felony, Misdemeanor, Civil, Eviction, Small Claims, Probate.***

Civil Records: Access: Mail, in person, online. Only the court performs in person searches; visitors may not. Search fee: $15.00 per name. Required to search: name, years to search; also helpful: address, DOB, and drivers license number. Civil cases indexed by defendant, plaintiff. Civil index on cards and docket books from 1900s. Mail turnaround time 2 days. Active & inactive judgments from 04/19/2004 forward via web subscription service from the SD Court Administrators Office, see note at the beginning of this section.

Criminal Records: Access: Mail, in person. Only the court performs in person searches; visitors may not. Search fee: $15.00 per name. Required to search: name, years to search, DOB, signed release; also helpful: address, drivers license number. Criminal records on computer since 7/89 on a statewide system. Mail turnaround time 2 days. For faster service, you may mail search requests to Hanson County for processing. See note at beginning of section for locations of the 2 state-recommended processing centers for mail requests.

General Information: No juvenile, sealed, dismissed, or mental health records released. Fee to fax out file $1.00 per page; $5.00 minimum. Court makes copy: $.25 per page. Certification fee: $2.00. Payee: Turner County Clerk of Courts. Personal checks and major credit cards accepted. Prepayment required. Mail requests: SASE required.

Union County

Circuit Court 209 E Main St #230, Elk Point, SD 57025; 605-356-2132; fax: 605-356-3687; 8AM-5PM (CST). ***Felony, Misdemeanor, Civil, Eviction, Small Claims, Probate.***

Civil Records: Access: Fax, mail, in person, online. Only the court performs in person searches; visitors may not. Search fee: $15.00 per name. Required to search: name, years to search; also helpful: address. Civil cases indexed by defendant, plaintiff; index on computer from 1990, docket books from 1900s. Mail turnaround time 1-2 days. Active & inactive judgments from 04/19/2004 forward via web subscription service from Court Administrators Office; see note at the beginning of this section.

Criminal Records: Access: Fax, mail, in person. Only the court performs in person searches; visitors may not. Search fee: $15.00 per name. Required to search: name, years to search, DOB; also helpful: address, SSN. Criminal records on computer since 1988 on a statewide system, on docket books from 1900s. Mail turnaround time 1-2 days. For fast service for years 1988 to present direct your criminal search to Douglas County for processing. See note at beginning of section for locations of the 2 state-recommended processing centers for mail requests.

General Information: No juvenile, sealed, dismissed, or mental health records released. Fee to fax out file $5.00 or $1.00 per page, whichever is greater. Court makes copy: $.20 per page. Certification fee: $15.00 per name. Payee: Union County Clerk of Court. Personal checks accepted; credit cards are not. Prepayment required. Mail requests: SASE required.

Walworth County

Circuit Court PO Box 328, Selby, SD 57472; 605-649-7311; fax: 605-649-7624; 8AM-5PM (CST). ***Felony, Misdemeanor, Civil, Eviction, Small Claims, Probate.*** http://ujs.sd.gov/5thcircuit/

Civil Records: Access: Mail, in person, online. Only the court performs in person searches; visitors may not. Search fee: $15.00 per name. Required to search: name, years to search; also helpful: address. Civil cases indexed by defendant, plaintiff. Civil index on cards and docket books from 1900s. Mail turnaround time 1-2 days. Active & inactive judgments from 04/19/2004 forward via web subscription service from Court Administrators Office; see note at the beginning of this section.

Criminal Records: Access: Mail, in person. Only the court performs in person searches; visitors may not. Search fee: $15.00 per name. Required to search: name, years to search, DOB, signed release; also helpful: address, SSN. Criminal records on computer since 7/89 in a statewide system. Mail turnaround time 1-2 days. See note at beginning of section for locations of the 2 state-recommended processing centers for mail requests.

General Information: No juvenile, sealed, dismissed, or mental health records released. Will fax documents $1.00 per page, $10.00 minimum. Court makes copy: $.20 per page. Certification fee: $2.00 per doc. Payee: Walworth County Clerk of Court. Personal checks accepted. Visa/MC accepted. Prepayment required. Mail requests: SASE required.

Yankton County

Circuit Court Clerk of Courts, 410 Walnut St, Yankton, SD 57078; 605-668-3080; criminal fax: 605-668-5411; civil fax: same; 8AM-5PM (CST). ***Felony, Misdemeanor, Civil, Small Claims, Eviction, Probate.***

Probate is a separate index at this same address. Probate fax is same as main fax number.

Civil Records: Access: Mail, in person, online. Both court and visitors may perform in person searches. Search fee: $15.00 per name. Required to search: name, years to search; also helpful: address, DOB, SSN. Civil cases indexed by defendant, plaintiff; index on computer from 1991, docket books from 1900s. Visitors only have access to the book index. Mail turnaround time 1 week. Active & inactive judgments from 04/19/2004 forward via web subscription service from Court Administrators Office; see note at the beginning of this section. Forms online at www.sdjudicial.com/. Online results show name only.

Criminal Records: Access: Mail, in person. Both court and visitors may perform in person searches. Search fee: $15.00 per name. Must be a state authorized account. Required to search: name, years to search, DOB; also helpful: address, SSN. Criminal records on computer since 7/89 on a statewide system, Class II offenses not accessible on computer to public. Visitors only have access to the book index. Mail turnaround time 1 week. For faster service, direct mail requests to Hanson County for processing. See note at beginning of section for locations of the 2 state-recommended processing centers for mail requests.

General Information: No juvenile, sealed, dismissed, or mental health records released. Will fax documents $1.00 per page, $5.00 minimum. Court makes copy: $.20 per page. Certification fee: $2.00 per doc. Payee: Yankton County Clerk of Court. Personal checks accepted. Visa/MC accepted. Prepayment required. Mail requests: SASE required.

Ziebach County

Circuit Court PO Box 306, Dupree, SD 57623; 605-365-5159; 9:30AM-N, 1-2:30PM (MST). ***Felony, Misdemeanor, Civil, Eviction, Small Claims, Probate.***

Probate is a separate index at this same address.

Civil Records: Access: Mail, in person, online. Only the court performs in person searches; visitors may not. Search fee: $15.00 per name. Required to search: name, years to search; also helpful: address. Civil cases indexed by defendant. Civil index on docket books from 1900s. Mail turnaround time 2-3 days. Active & inactive judgments from 04/19/2004 forward via web subscription service from Court Administrators Office; see note at the beginning of this section.

Criminal Records: Access: Mail, in person. Only the court performs in person searches; visitors may not. Search fee: $15.00 per name. Required to search: name, years to search, DOB; also helpful: address, SSN. Criminal records indexed in books from 1900s. Mail turnaround time 2-3 days. For faster service, you may mail search requests to Lawrence County for processing. See note at beginning of section for locations of the 2 state-recommended processing centers for mail requests.

General Information: No juvenile, sealed, dismissed, adoption or mental health records released. Will fax documents to local or toll free line, otherwise $1.00 per page, $5.00 minimum. Court makes copy: $.20 per page. Certification fee: $2.00 per doc includes copies. Payee: Ziebach Clerk of Court. Personal checks accepted. Visa/MC accepted. Prepayment required. Mail requests: SASE required.

South Dakota Recording Offices

ORGANIZATION: 66 counties, 66 recording offices. The recording officer is the Register of Deeds. 48 easternmost South Dakota counties are in the Central Time Zone (CST) and the 18 westernmost are in the Mountain Time Zone (MST).

REAL ESTATE RECORDS: Most counties will not perform real estate searches, though some will assist. Certification fee is now usally $2.00 per seal plus copy fee. The standard copy fee is $1.00 for the first 5 pages, then $.20 each add'l page.

UCC RECORDS: Financing statements are filed at the state level except for real estate related collateral which are filed with the Register of Deeds in the county where the real estate is located. All recording offices should perform UCC searches. All counties have access to a statewide database of UCC filings. Use search request form UCC-11. UCC search fee is usually $10.00 or $20.00 per debtor, $10.00 if online. UCC copy is usually $1.00 per page.

TAX LIEN RECORDS: Federal tax liens on personal property of businesses are filed with the Secretary of State. Other federal and state tax liens are filed with the county Register of Deeds. Tax lien search fees and copy fees vary; rule is $20.00 per name search by mail, $15.00 if verbal.

OTHER LIENS: Mechanics, motor vehicle, materials.

ONLINE ACCESS: Access to UCC records is available through the Secretary of State's Fast File internet access system at www.sdsos.gov/busineservices/ucc.shtm. Registration and annual fee is required. Certified search also available. For the occasional user, a new system named "Expa" is soon to be available.

Aurora County

Register of Deeds, PO Box 397, Plankinton, SD 57368. Recording, R/E & UCC phone-605-942-7161; 8AM-N, 1-5PM.
Index: All in one. Records indexed on computer back to 1995. Office personnel or visitors may perform searches. General search fee- none but $10.00 for marriage or birth records. UCC search per debtor name- $20.00. Copy fee $1.00 per doc; $.20 per page over 5. Cert fee- $2.00 per doc includes copy fee. Payee- Register of Deeds. **Other phones:** Treasurer- 605-942-7162; Vital Records- 605-942-7161. **Property tax/Assessing**- 605-942-7164.

Beadle County

Register of Deeds, PO Box 55, Huron, SD 57350-0055. Recording, R/E & UCC phone-605-353-8412; fax-605-353-8402; 8AM-5PM.
Index: All in one. Records indexed on a public use terminal back to 1993. Office personnel or visitors may perform searches. Search fee-$20.00 for UCC and tax liens with correct form, $5.00 for other searches. Copy fee $1.00 per doc; $.20 per page over 5. Cert fee- $2.00 per doc includes copy fee. Payee- Register of Deeds. **Other phones:** Treasurer- 605-353-8405; Elections- 605-353-8400; Vital Records- 605-353-8412. **Property tax/Assessing**- PO Box 328, Huron, SD 57350; 605-353-8408. (Appraiser/Auditor- 605-353-8408);

Bennett County

Register of Deeds, PO Box 433, Martin, SD 57551-0433. Recording, R/E & UCC phone-605-685-6054; fax-605-685-6311; 8AM-N, 12:30-4:30AM (MST)
Index: All in one. Records indexed on computer back 5 years. Office will perform a UCC search but public must search other records themselves. Office will search real estate records subject to last deed and last mortgage. UCC search per debtor name- $12.00 per person. Copy fee $1.00 per doc; $.20 per page over 5. Cert fee- $2.00 per doc includes copy fee. Payee- Register of Deeds. **Other phones:** Treasurer- 605-685-6092; Vital Records- 605-685-6054. **Property tax/Assessing**- PO Box 426, Martin, SD 57551; 605-685-6991.

Bon Homme County

Register of Deeds, PO Box 3, Tyndall, SD 57066. 605-589-4217, R/E recording phone-605-589-3302; fax-605-589-4202; 8AM-4:30PM (CST)
Office personnel or visitors may perform searches. Search fee $15.00 per name. Office will not search real estate records. Copy fee $1.00 per page. Cert fee- $2.00 per cert plus copy fee. Payee- Bon Homme County Register of Deeds. **Property tax/Assessing**- Director of Equalization/Assessor, Tyndall, SD 57066-0280; 605-589-4210.

Brookings County

Register of Deeds, 314 6th Ave #5, Brookings, SD 57006-2084. 605-696-8240; fax-605-696-8245; 8AM-5PM (CST) www.brookingscountysd.gov
Index: Separate indices to search include deeds and mortgages. Record index not computerized. Office will perform a UCC search (last recorded document) but public must search other records themselves. Search fee $20.00 per name (UCC's). Copy fee $1.00 per doc up to 5 pages. Cert fee- $2.00 per cert plus copy fee. Payee- Brookings County Register of Deeds. **Other phones:** Treasurer- 605-696-8250; Elections- 605-696-8200; Vital Records- 605-696-8240. **Property tax/Assessing**- 601 4th St, #102, 1921 Bldg, Equalization Office 605-696-8220, assessor fax- 605-696-8224. (Appraiser/Auditor- 605-696-8220)

Brown County

Register of Deeds, 25 Market St, #3, Aberdeen, SD 57402-4227. Recording, R/E & UCC phone-605-626-7140; fax-605-626-4010; 8AM-5PM.
Index: All in one. Records indexed on computer back to 1990 (deeds only). Office will perform a UCC search but public must search other records themselves. UCC search per debtor name $20.00. Copy fee $1.00 per page. Cert fee- $2.00 up to 5 pages, $.20 after, includes copy fee. Payee- Register of Deeds. **Other phones:** Treasurer- 605-626-7133; Elections- 605-626-7110; Vital Records- 605-626-7140. **Property tax/Assessing**- 25 Market St, Aberdeen, SD 57402; 605-622-7133. **Online access**- Search assessor property data for a fee on the GIS system at http://beacon.schneidercorp.com/. Registration and username required.

Brule County

Register of Deeds, 300 S Courtland, #110, Chamberlain, SD 57325. 605-234-4454, R/E recording phone-605-234-4434; fax-605-234-4434; 8AM-N,1PM-5PM (CST)
www.brulecounty.org/5.html
Index: Separate indices to search include books, microfilm, computer. Records indexed on a public use terminal back to 1900. Office personnel or visitors may perform searches. Search fee $20.00 per name. Office will not search real estate records. Will search UCC records. Copy fee $1.00 per doc; $.20 per page over 5. Cert fee- $1.00 per doc plus copy fee. Payee- Brule County Register of Deeds. **Other phones:** Treasurer- 605-234-4436; Elections- 605-234-4430; Vital Records- 605-234-4434. **Property tax/Assessing**- 300 S Courtland, Chamberlain, SD 57325; 605-234-4432.

Buffalo County

Register of Deeds, PO Box 174, Gann Valley, SD 57341. Recording, R/E & UCC phone-605-293-3239; fax-605-293-3240; 9AM-5PM.
Index: Separate indices to search include deeds, misc in deed index, mortgages, UCCs in mortgage index. Record index not computerized. Office personnel or visitors may perform searches. Search fee-$10.00 per name. Office will search real estate records. UCC search per debtor name- $12.00. Copy fee $1.00 per page. Cert fee- $1.00 up to 5 pages, $.20 per page thereafter; add'l $1.00 certification fee, $0.25 for non-document copies. Payee- Register of Deeds. **Other phones:** Treasurer- 605-293-3236; Elections- 605-293-3217; Vital Records- 605-293-3239. **Property tax/Assessing**- PO Box 175, Gann Valley, SD 57341; 605-293-3286, assessor fax- 605-293-3240.

Butte County

Register of Deeds, 839 5th Ave, Belle Fourche, SD 57717. Recording, R/E & UCC phone-605-892-2912; fax-605-892-4525; 8AM-5PM (MST)
Index: Separate indices to search include mortgages, deeds. Records indexed on a public use terminal back to 1996. Office personnel or visitors may perform searches. Search fee $20.00. Office will search limited real estate records. Copy fee $1.00 per doc; $.20 per page over 5. Cert fee- $2.00 per doc, plus $.20 per page after 5 pages. Payee- Butte County Register of

Deeds. Contact Belle Butte Title Company for data sale. **Other phones:** Treasurer- 605-892-4456; Elections- 605-892-3950; Vital Records- 605-892-2912. **Property tax/Assessing**- 839 5th Ave, Belle Fourche, SD 57717; 605-892-3950, assessor fax- 605-892-0240. (Appraiser/Auditor- 605-892-4485);

Campbell County

Register of Deeds, PO Box 148, Mound City, SD 57646-0148. Recording, R/E & UCC phone-605-955-3505; fax-605-955-3308; 8AM-N; 12:30-4:30PM.
Index: Separate indices to search include deeds and Mtgs. Record index not computerized. Office personnel or visitors may perform searches. Search fee $20.00. Office will perform last deed on mortgage search only. Copy fee $1.00 per doc; $.20 per page over 5. Cert fee- $2.00 per doc includes copy fee. Payee- Campbell County Register of Deeds. **Other phones:** Treasurer- 605-955-3388; Elections- 605-955-3366; Vital Records- 605-955-3505. **Property tax/Assessing**- 111 2nd St E, PO Box 145, Mound City, SD 57646; 605-955-3577, assessor fax- 605-955-3308. (Appraiser/Auditor- 605-955-3577) hours-8AM-4:30PM

Charles Mix County

Register of Deeds, PO Box 206, Lake Andes, SD 57356-0206. Recording, R/E & UCC phone-605-487-7141; fax-605-487-7221; 8AM-4:30PM.
Index: Separate indices to search include alpha index, legal description. Records indexed on computer back to 1995. Office will perform a UCC search but public must search other records themselves. Search fee $26.00. Copy fee $1.00 per instrument. Cert fee- $2.00 per cert includes copy fee. Payee- Charles Mix County Register of Deeds. **Other phones:** Treasurer- 605-487-7542; Elections- 605-487-7131; Vital Records- 605-487-7141. **Property tax/Assessing**- PO Box 68, Lake Andes, SD 57356; 605-487-7382.

Clark County

Register of Deeds, PO Box 294, Clark, SD 57225-0294. 605-532-5363, R/E recording phone-605-632-5363; fax-605-532-5931; 8AM-5PM.
Index: All in one. Records indexed on computer back to 1995. Office personnel or visitors may perform searches. General index search fee $10.00. Office will search real estate records, just the last index record. Will not search UCC records. Copy fee $1.00 per instrument. Cert fee- $2.00 per cert plus copy fee. Payee- Register of Deeds. **Other phones:** Treasurer- 605-532-5911; Elections- 605-532-5921; Vital Records- 605-532-5363. **Property tax/Assessing**- PO Box 295, 202 N Commercial St, Clark, SD 57225-0295; 605-532-3751, assessor fax- 605-532-5931. hours- 7:30AM-5PM

Clay County

Register of Deeds, 211 W Main St, #202, Vermillion, SD 57069. Recording, R/E & UCC phone-605-677-7130; 8AM-5PM (CST)
Index: Separate indices to search include deeds; land in one index, mortgages have their own. Records indexed on computer back to 1979. Only the public may search. Office will not search real estate records. Will not search UCC records. Copy fee $1.00 per doc; $.20 per page over 5. Cert fee- $1.00 per cert plus copy fee. Payee- Clay County Register of Deeds. **Other phones:** Treasurer- 605-677-7123; Elections-605-677-7120; Vitals- 605-677-7130. **Property tax/Assessing**- 211 W Main St, #1, Vermillion, SD 57069; 605-677-7140, assessor fax- 605-677-7102. www.claycountysd.org/view.php?doc_id=318

Codington County

Register of Deeds, 14 1st Ave SE, Watertown, SD 57201-3695. 605-882-6278; fax-605-882-5230; 8AM-5PM.
Index: Separate indices to search include deeds, Mortgages. Records indexed on a public use terminal back to 2001 for scanned documents. Office personnel or visitors may perform searches. Search fee $20.00. Office will search real estate records only for the last recorded document. Will search UCC records. Copy fee $1.00 per doc; $.20 per page over 5. Cert fee- $2.00 per doc plus copy fee. Payee- Register of Deeds. **Other phones:** Treasurer- 605-886-6285; Elections- 605-882-6297; Vital Records- 605-882-6278. **Property tax/Assessing**- 14 1st Ave SE, Watertown, SD 57201; 605-886-6274, assessor fax-605-882-5387. (Appraiser/Auditor- 605-886-6274);

Corson County

Register of Deeds, PO Box 256, McIntosh, SD 57641-0256. 605-273-4395, R/E recording phone-605-273-4348; fax-605-273-4233; 8AM-N, 1PM-5PM.
Index: Separate indices to search include deeds, mortgages, misc. Record index not computerized. Office personnel or visitors may perform searches. Search fee $10.00 per name. Office will not search real estate records. Copy fee $1.00 per page. Cert fee-$2.00 per cert. Payee- Register of Deeds. **Other phones:** Treasurer- 605-273-4552; Elections- 605-273-4229. **Property tax/Assessing**- Auditor's Office, PO Box 255, McIntosh, SD 57641; 605-273-4229.

Custer County

Register of Deeds, 420 Mount Rushmore Rd, Custer, SD 57730-1934. 605-673-8171; fax-605-673-8148; 8AM-5PM M-Th. (MST)
Index: All in one. Pre-200 records on microfiche cards. Records indexed on a public use terminal back to 2000. Only the public may search. Copy fee $1.00 per doc; $.50 per page over 4. Cert fee- $2.00 per page plus copy fee. Payee- Custer Cuonty Register of Deeds. **Other phones:** Treasurer- 605-673-8172; Elections- 605-673-8173; Vital Records- 605-673-8171. **Property tax/Assessing**- 420 Mount Rushmore Rd, Custer, SD 57730-1934; 605-673-8170, assessor fax- 605-673-8148. (Appraiser/Auditor- 605-673-8170) **Online access**- Search assessor property data for a fee on the GIS system at http://beacon.schneidercorp.com/. Registration and username required.

Davison County

Register of Deeds, 200 E 4th; Courthouse, Mitchell, SD 57301-2692. Recording, R/E & UCC phone-605-995-8616; fax-605-995-8648; 8AM-5PM. www.davisoncounty.org/reg-rodindex.htm
Index: Separate indices to search include index books, grantor/grantee index on computer. Records indexed on a public use terminal back to 4/96. Office personnel or visitors may perform searches. Search fee UCC and federal tax lien $20.00 per name. Office will search only if records have not been destroyed pursuant to destruction schedules. Copy fee $1.00 per doc; $.20 per page over 5. Cert fee- $1.00 per doc plus copy fee up to 5 pages, $.20 per page thereafter. Payee- Davison Cuonty Register of Deeds. **Other phones:** Treasurer- 605-995-8617; Elections- 605-995-8608; Vital Records- 605-995-8616; Court Clerk-605-995-8105; Ausitor/Secretary to the Commission - 605-995-8608. **Property tax/Assessing**- 200 E 4th, Courthouse, Mitchell, SD 57301; 605-995-8613, assessor fax- 605-995-8614. (Appraiser/Auditor- 605-995-8613);

Day County

Register of Deeds, 711 W 1st St, #202, Webster, SD 57274-1363. Recording, R/E & UCC phone-605-345-9506; fax-605-345-9507; 8AM-N, 1-5PM (CST)
Index: All in one. Records indexed on computer back to 1999. Office will perform a UCC and tax lien search but public must search other records themselves. Search fee $12.00 UCCs; tax liens $20.00. Copy fee $1.00 per page. Self serve copy-$.15 per page plus sales tax. Cert fee- $2.00 per page includes copy fee. Payee- Day County Register of Deeds. **Other phones:** Treasurer- 605-345-9510; Elections- 605-345-9500; Vital Records- 605-345-9506. **Property tax/Assessing**- 711 E 1st St, #203, Webster, SD 57274; 605-345-9502. hours- 8AM-5PM

Deuel County

Register of Deeds, PO Box 307, Clear Lake, SD 57226. Recording, R/E & UCC phone-605-874-2268; fax-605-874-1306; 8AM-5PM.
Index: Separate indices to search include deeds, mortgages, state & federal tax liens, UCCs. Record index not computerized. Office personnel or visitors may perform searches. Office will search limited real estate records. UCC search per debtor name- $20.00. Copy fee $1.00 per doc; $.20 per page over 5. Cert fee- $2.00 per doc includes copy fee. Payee- Register of Deeds. **Other phones:** Treasurer- 605-874-2483; Elections- 605-874-2312; Vital Records- 605-874-2268. **Property tax/Assessing**- PO Box 518, Clear Lake, SD 57226; 605-874-2229, assessor fax- 605-874-1306.

Dewey County

Register of Deeds, PO Box 117, Timber Lake, SD 57656-0117. Recording, R/E & UCC phone-605-865-3661; fax-605-865-3691; 8AM-N, 1-5PM.
Public call look up in grantor/grantee book. Record index not computerized. Office personnel or visitors may perform searches. Search fee $10.00 per name for vital records or simple name searches. Will not do RE searches. Office will search real estate records. Search fee $20.00 per name. Copy fee $1.00 per page. Cert fee- $2.00 per cert. Payee- Dewey County Clerk. **Other phones:** Treasurer- 605-865-3501; Elections-605-865-3672; Vitals- 605-865-3661. **Property tax/Assessing**- 605-865-3573. (Appraiser/Auditor-605-865-3730)

Douglas County

Register of Deeds, PO Box 267, Armour, SD 57313-0267. Recording, R/E & UCC phone-605-724-2204; fax-same; 8AM-N, 1-5PM (CST)
Index: Separate indices to search include grantor/grantee, legal description. Record index not computerized. Only office personnel may search. Search fee $20.00 per name. Copy fee $1.00 per page. Cert fee- $2.00 per page includes copy fee. Payee-Register of Deeds. **Other phones:** Treasurer- 605-724-2318; Elections- 605-724-2423; Vital Records-605-724-2204. **Property tax/Assessing**- 605-724-2688. (Appraiser/Auditor- 605-724-2688)

Edmunds County

Register of Deeds, PO Box 386, Ipswich, SD 57451-0386. Recording, R/E & UCC phone-605-426-6431; fax-605-426-6164; 8AM-N,1-5PM (CST)
Index: Separate indices to search include marriage, deaths, burial records. Record index not computerized. Office personnel or visitors may perform searches. Search fee-$20.00. Copy fee $1.00 per doc; $.20 per page over 5. Cert fee- $2.00 per doc includes copy fee. Payee- Edmunds County Register of Deeds. **Other phones:** Treasurer- 605-426-6801; Elections- 605-426-6762; Vital Records- 605-426-6431. **Property tax/Assessing**- 210 2nd Ave, Courthouse, PO Box 247, Ipswich, SD 57451; 605-426-6841. (Appraiser/Auditor- 605-426-6841);

Fall River County

Register of Deeds, 906 N River St, Hot Springs, SD 57747. 605-745-5139; fax-605-745-3708; 8AM-5PM (MST)
Index: All in one. Records indexed on computer. Office will perform a UCC search but public must search other records themselves. Search fee- $7.00 per UCC. Copy fee $1.00 per doc; $.20 per page over 5. Fax back- $3.00 fee. Cert fee- $2.00 per doc includes copy fee. Payee- Fall River County. **Other phones:** Treasurer- 605-745-5145; Elections- 605-745-5130; Vital Records- 605-745-5139. **Property tax/Assessing**- 906 N River St, Hot Springs, SD 57747; 605-745-5136, assessor fax- 605-745-6835. **Online access**- Search assessor property data for a fee at http://beacon.schneidercorp.com/. Registration and username required.

Faulk County

Register of Deeds, PO Box 309, Faulkton, SD 57438. 605-598-6228; fax-605-598-6680; 8AM-N,1-5PM (CST)
Index: Separate indices to search. Record index not computerized. Only the public may search. Copy fee $1.00 per doc; $.20 per page over 5. Vital records- $10.00 per copy. Cert fee- $2.00 per cert includes copy fee. Payee- Faulk County Register of Deeds. Bulk data would have to come from copies made from the books. **Other phones:** Treasurer- 605-598-6232; Elections- 605-598-6224; Vital Records- 605-598-6228. **Property tax/Assessing-** PO Box 309, Faulkton, SD 57438; 605-598-6225, assessor fax- 605-598-6680.

Grant County

Register of Deeds, PO Box 587, Milbank, SD 57252. Recording, R/E & UCC phone-605-432-4752; fax- 605-432-9004; 8AM-5PM (CST)
Index: Separate indices to search include town, rural, and all. Record index not computerized. Office personnel or visitors may perform searches. Search fee $20.00. Office will search real estate records as time permits. Will search UCC records. Copy fee $1.00 per doc; $.20 per page over 5. Cert fee- $2.00 per cert includes copy fee. Payee- Grant County Register of Deeds. **Other phones:** Treasurer- 605-432-5651; Elections- 605-432-6711; Vital Records- 605-432-4752. **Property tax/Assessing-** 210 E 5th Ave, Milbank, SD 57252; 605-432-6532. (Appraiser/Auditor- 605-432-6532);

Gregory County

Register of Deeds, PO Box 437, Burke, SD 57523. 605-775-2624; fax-605-775-9116; 8AM-N,1PM-5PM.
Index: Separate indices to search include deed, mortgage books, computer. Records indexed on a public use terminal back to 2005. Office will perform a UCC search but public must search other records themselves. Search fee-$10.00 per name. Copy fee $.25 per page. Will fax back $2.00 per page. Cert fee- $3.00 per seal includes copy fee. Payee- Gregory County Register of Deeds. **Other phones:** Treasurer- 605-775-2605. **Property tax/Assessing-** 221 E 8th St, Courthouse, PO Box 437, Burke, SD 57523; 605-775-2673.

Haakon County

Register of Deeds, PO Box 100, Philip, SD 57567-0100. 605-859-2785; 8AM-N,1-5PM (MST)
Index: Separate indices to search include deeds, mortgages, misc. Record index not computerized. Office will perform a UCC search but public must search other records themselves. Office will not search real estate records. UCC search per debtor name- $12.00. Copy fee $1.00 per page. Cert fee- $2.00 per cert up to 5 pages, add'l $.25 per page after 5. Payee- Haakon County Register of Deeds. **Other phones:** Treasurer- 605-859-2612. **Property tax/Assessing-** PO Box 668, Philip, SD 57567; 605-859-2824. (Appraiser/Auditor- 605-859-2800);

Hamlin County

Register of Deeds, PO Box 56, Hayti, SD 57241. 605-783-3206; 8AM-N, 1-5PM (CST)
Index: Separate indices to search include deeds, misc, mortgage. Record index not computerized. Only the public may search. Copy fee $1.00 per page. Cert fee- $2.00 per instrument. Fax copies $3.00. Payee- Hamlin County Register of Deeds. **Other phones:** Treasurer- 605-783-3441. **Property tax/Assessing-** 605-783-3331.

Hand County

Register of Deeds, 415 W 1st Ave, Miller, SD 57362-1346. Recording, R/E & UCC phone-605-853-3512; fax-605-853-3512; 8AM-5PM (CST)
Index: Separate indices to search include mortgages and deeds (misc), have separate indexes by land. Records indexed on a public use terminal back to 06/2003. Only the public may search. Copy fee $1.00 per doc up to 4 pages, $.25 each add'l page. Cert fee- $2.00 per copy includes copy fee. Payee- Register of Deeds. Bulk data available for purchase; $2 for fax up to 4 sheets, $.25 per sheet after the fourth. **Other phones:** Treasurer- 605-853-2136; Vital Records- 605-853-3512. **Property tax/Assessing-** 415 W 1st Ave, Miller, SD 57362-1346; 605-853-2115. (Appraiser/Auditor- 605-853-2182);

Hanson County

Register of Deeds, PO Box 500, Alexandria, SD 57311-0500. Recording, R/E & UCC phone-605-239-4512; fax-605-239-4296; 8AM-N; 12:30PM-4:30PM (CST)
Index: Separate indices to search. Records indexed on computer back to 1944. Office personnel or visitors may perform searches. Search fee $20.00 (federal liens). Office will only search real estate for last document recorded. Copy fee $1.00 per doc; $.20 per page over 5. Cert fee- $2.00 per doc; $.20 each page after 5 pages. Payee- Register of Deeds. **Other phones:** Treasurer- 605-239-4723; Elections- 605-239-4714; Vital Records- 605-239-4512. **Property tax/Assessing-** PO Box 500, Alexandria, SD 57311-0500; 605-239-4445, assessor fax- 605-239-4296. (Appraiser/Auditor- 605-239-4445);

Harding County

Register of Deeds, PO Box 101, Buffalo, SD 57720. 605-375-3321; fax-605-375-3310; 8AM-N, 1PM-5PM (MST)
Index: Deeds, oil & gas, misc. Record index not computerized. Office will perform a UCC search but public must search other records themselves. UCC search on UCC-11 form per debtor name- $10.00. Copy fee $1.00 per doc; $.20 per page over 5. Cert fee- $2.00 per doc includes copy fee up to 5 pages. Payee- Harding County Register of Deeds. **Other phones:** Treasurer- 605-375-3542. **Property tax/Assessing-** 410 Ramsland, PO Box 488, Buffalo, SD 57720; 605-375-3234. **Online access-** Search assessor property data on the GIS system at http://beacon.schneidercorp.com/ for free.

Hughes County

Register of Deeds, 104 E Capital, Pierre, SD 57501. Recording, R/E & UCC phone-605-773-7495; fax- 605-773-7479; 8AM-5PM. www.hughescounty.org/index.asp?folderID=5&fileID=9
Index: Separate indices to search include deeds and Mtgs. Records indexed on a public use terminal back to 1920s. Visitors may perform searches. Office personal perform limited searches. Verbal search $15.00; UCC search $10.00 per name; tax lien search $20.00 per name. Office will search real estate records. Copy fee $1.00 per page. Cert fee- $2.00 for 1st 5 pages, $.20 extra thereafter. Payee- Hughes County. **Other phones:** Treasurer- 605-773-7491; Elections- 605-773-7451; Vital Records- 605-773-7495; Auditor- 605-773-7451. **Property tax/ Assessing-** 104 E Capital Ave, Pierre, SC 57501; 605-773-7483, assessor fax- 605-773-7479. (Appraiser/Auditor- 605-773-7483);

Hutchinson County

Register of Deeds, 140 Euclid St, Rm 37, Olivet, SD 57052-2103. Recording, R/E & UCC phone-605-387-4217; fax-605-387-4202; 8AM-4:30PM (CST)
Index: More than one index. Records indexed on computer. Office personnel or visitors may perform searches. Search fee-$20.00 per name. Copy fee $1.00 per doc; $.20 per page over 5. Cert fee- $2.00 per cert includes copy fee. Payee- Hutchinson County Register of Deeds. **Other phones:** Treasurer- 605-387-4213; Elections- 605-387-4212; Vital Records- 605-387-4217. **Property tax/Assessing-** 140 Euclid St Rm 125, Olivet, SD 57052; 605-387-4210, assessor fax- 605-387-4209. (Appraiser/Auditor- 605-387-4210);

Hyde County

Register of Deeds, PO Box 342, Highmore, SD 57345. 605-852-2517; fax-605-852-3178; 8AM-N, 1-5PM (CST)
Record index not computerized. Office will perform a UCC or fed tax lien search but public must search other records themselves. Tax lien or UCC search fee $20.00 per name. Copy fee $1.00 per page; $.20 per page over 5. Cert fee- $2.00 per doc includes copies. Payee- Hyde County Register of Deeds. **Other phones:** Treasurer- 605-852-2510. **Property tax/Assessing-** 412 Commercial SE, Highmore, SD 57345; 605-852-2570.

Jackson County

Register of Deeds, PO Box 248, Kadoka, SD 57453. 605-837-2420; fax-605-837-2447; 8AM-N, 1-5PM (MST)
Index: Separate indices to search include deeds, mortgage index books. Record index not computerized. Office will perform a UCC search but public must search other records themselves. UCC search per debtor name- $10.00. Copy fee $1.00 per doc; $.20 per page over 5. Cert fee- $2.00 per doc includes copy fee. Payee- Jackson County Register of Deeds. **Other phones:** Treasurer- 605-837-2423; Elections- 605-837-2422. **Property tax/Assessing-** 700 Main St, Courthouse, PO Box 407, Kadoka, SD 57453; 605-837-2424, assessor fax- 605-837-2447. hours- 8AM-5PM

Jerauld County

Register of Deeds, PO Box 452, Wessington Springs, SD 57382-0452. 605-539-1221; fax-605-539-9125; 8AM-N, 1-5PM (CST)
Index: Indexes in books. Record index not computerized. Office personnel or visitors may perform searches. Search fee $10.00. Office will search real estate records. Will search UCC records. Copy fee $1.00 per page. Cert fee- $2.00 per cert includes copy fee. Payee- Jerauld County Register of Deeds. **Other phones:** Treasurer- 605-539-1241. **Property tax/Assessing-** PO Box 444, Wessington Springs 57382; 605-539-9701.

Jones County

Register of Deeds, PO Box 446, Murdo, SD 57559. 605-669-7104; fax-605-669-7120; 8AM-N, 1PM-5PM (CST)
Index: Separate indices to search include mortgage, deed books. Record index not computerized. Office personnel or visitors may perform searches. Search fee $20.00 per name. Office will lookup last recorded instrument only. Copy fee $1.00 per doc; $.20 per page over 5. Cert fee- $2.00 per doc includes copy fee. Payee- Jones County Register of Deeds. **Property tax/Assessing-** 310 Main St, Courthouse, PO Box 107, Murdo, SD 57559; 605-669-7103.

Kingsbury County

Register of Deeds, PO Box 146, De Smet, SD 57231-0146. 605-854-3591; fax-605-854-3833; 8AM-N, 1PM-5PM.
Index: Separate indices to search include deed, mortgage books. Record index not computerized. Office personnel or visitors may perform searches. Office will not search real estate records. UCC search per debtor name- $20.00. Copy fee $1.00 per doc; $.20 per page over 5. Cert fee- $2.00 per doc includes copy fee. Payee- Kingsbury County Register of Deeds. **Other phones:** Treasurer- 605-854-3411; Elections- 605-854-3832. **Property tax/Assessing-** 202 2nd St SE, PO Box 158, De Smet, SD 57231; 605-854-3593, assessor fax- 605-854-3833.

Lake County

Register of Deeds, PO Box 266, Madison, SD 57042. Recording, R/E & UCC phone-605-256-7614; fax- 605-256-7622; 8AM-5PM (CST)
Index: All in one. Records indexed on computer back to 1/00. Office personnel or visitors may perform searches. Search fee $10.00 per name. Office will

search real estate records. Will search UCC records. Copy fee $1.00 per page. Cert fee- $2.00 per instrument includes copy fee. Payee- Register of Deeds. Bulk data available for purchase. **Other phones:** Treasurer- 605-256-7618; Vital Records- 605-256-7614. **Property tax/Assessing-** 200 E Center, Madison, SD 57042; 605-256-7605.

Lawrence County

Register of Deeds, PO Box 565, Deadwood, SD 57732. Recording, R/E & UCC phone-605-578-3930; fax-605-722-6212; 8AM-5PM (MST) www.lawrence.sd.us/register.htm
Index: Separate indices to search include numerical, grantor/grantee, Lien, mortgage, deeds, misc, etc. Records indexed on a public use terminal back to 1990. Only the public may search. Office will do limited searches only if proper information is given. Copy fee $1.00 per doc; $.20 per page over 5. UCC copy fee $10.00 certified doc. Cert fee- Certification fees $2.00 per doc plus $.20 per page after 5. Payee- Lawrence County Register of Deeds. **Other phones:** Treasurer- 605-578-1862; Elections- 605-578-1941; Vitals- 605-578-3930. **Property tax** - 605-578-3680.

Lincoln County

Register of Deeds, 104 N Main St #130, Canton, SD 57013-1703. Recording, R/E & UCC phone-605-764-5661; fax-605-764-6623; 8AM-5PM (CST) www.lincolncountysd.org/
Index: Separate indices to search include land records by legal descriptions. Records indexed on a public use terminal back to 1996. Office personnel or visitors may perform searches. Office will search only as time permits. Search fee $20.00 per name. Office will not search real estate records. Office will search UCC records. Copy fee $1.00 per doc; $.20 per page over 5. Cert fee- $1.00 per cert plus copy fee. UCC cert fee- $10.00 per doc. Payee- Lincoln County Register of Deeds. **Other phones:** Treasurer- 605-764-5701; Elections- 605-764-2581; Vital Records- 605-764-5661. **Property tax/Assessing-** 104 N Main St, Canton, 57013; 605-764-2571, fax- 605-764-6078.

Lyman County

Register of Deeds, PO Box 98, Kennebec, SD 57544-0098. phone-605-869-2297; fax-605-869-2203; 8AM-N, 1PM-5PM. http://s92375618.onlinehome.us/content.php?content.5
Index: Separate indices to search include deeds, mortgage books, computer. Records indexed on a public use terminal back to 1985. Office personnel or visitors may perform searches. General search fee- none. UCC search per debtor name- $20.00. Copy fee $1.00 per doc; $.20 per page over 5. Will fax back for $3.00 1st page, $1.00 each add'l. Cert fee- $2.00 per doc includes copy fee. Payee- Lyman Co. Registrar of Deeds. **Other phones:** Treasurer- 605-869-2295; Elections- 605-869-2247; Vital Records- 605-869-2297. **Property tax/Assessing-** 300 S Main St, Courthouse, PO Box 126, Kennebec, SD 57544; 605-869-2206, fax- 605-869-2203. (Appraiser/Auditor- 605-869-2206) hours- 8AM-5PM http://s92375618.onlinehome.us/content.php?content.20

Marshall County

Register of Deeds, PO Box 130, Britton, SD 57430. Recording, R/E & UCC phone-605-448-2352; fax-605-448-2116; 8AM-4:30PM.
Index: Separate indices to search include deeds, satisfactions, mortgages, miscellaneous. Record index not computerized. Office personnel or visitors may perform searches, includes real estate records only if provided with legal description. Search fee $20.00 per debtor name. Will search UCC records. Copy fee $1.00 per doc; $.20 per page over 5. Cert fee- $2.00 per doc plus copy fee. Payee- Marshall County Register of Deeds. **Other phones:** Treasurer- 605-448-2451; Elections- 605-448-2401; Vital Records- 605-448-2352. **Property tax/Assessing-** 911 Vander Horck Ave, Courthouse, Britton, SD 57430; 605-448-5291, assessor fax- 605-448-2116. (Appraiser/Auditor- 605-448-2822);

McCook County

Register of Deeds, PO Box 338, Salem, SD 57058-0338. Recording, R/E & UCC phone-605-425-2701; fax-605-425-2534; 8:30AM-4:30PM (CST)
Index: All in one. Record index not computerized. Only office personnel may search. Search fee $20.00 per name. Copy fee $1.00 per page. Cert fee- $2.00 per cert includes copy fee. Payee- McCook County Register of Deeds. **Other phones:** Treasurer- 605-425-2721; Elections- 605-425-2791; Vital Records- 605-425-2701. **Property tax/Assessing-** PO Box 38, Salem, SD 57058-0038; 605-425-2681. **Online access-** Access assessor property data for a fee on the GIS system at http://beacon.schneidercorp.com/ with registration and password.

McPherson County

Register of Deeds, PO Box 129, Leola, SD 57456. Recording, R/E & UCC phone-605-439-3151; fax-605-439-3394; 8AM-5PM (CST)
Index: Separate indices to search include deeds, mortgages, misc, easements, satisfactions. Record index not computerized. Office will perform a UCC search (will go back one instrument) but public must search other records themselves. Search fee-$20.00 per name. Office will search real estate records. Copy fee $1.00 per page. Cert fee- $2.00 per cert includes copy fee. Payee- Register of Deeds. **Other phones:** Treasurer- 605-439-3544; Elections- 605-439-3314; Vital Records- 605-439-3151. **Property tax/Assessing-** PO Box 50, Leola, SD 57456; 605-439-3663, assessor fax- 605-439-3394. hours- 8AM-N; 1-5PM

Meade County

Register of Deeds, 1425 Sherman St, Sturgis, SD 57785. 605-347-2356; fax-605-720-6619; 8AM-5PM (MST)
www.meadecounty.org/main.asp?SectionID=10
Index: Separate indices to search include satisfactions, mortgage, deed, misc. Record index not computerized. Office will perform a UCC search but public must search other records themselves. Copy fee $1.00 per doc; $.20 per page over 5. Cert fee- $2.00 per page includes copy fee. Payee- Register of Deeds. **Other phones:** Treasurer- 605-347-5871; Elections- 605-347-2360; Vital Records- 605-347-2356. **Property tax/Assessing-** 1425 Sherman St, Sturgis, SD 57785; 605-347-3818, fax- 605-347-6830. www.meadecounty.org/main.asp?SectionID=27
Online access- Search assessor property data for a fee at http://beacon.schneidercorp.com/ with registration and username required.

Mellette County

Register of Deeds, PO Box 183, White River, SD 57579-0183. 605-259-3371; fax-605-259-3194; 8AM-N,1-5PM (MST)
Index: Separate indices to search include deeds, mortgages. Records index not computerized. Office will perform a UCC search but public must search other records themselves. Search fee $20.00 per name. Copy fee $1.00 per doc; $.20 per page over 5. Cert fee- $2.00 per doc plus copy fee. Payee- Mellette County Register of Deeds. **Other phones:** Treasurer- 605-259-3151. **Property tax/Assessing-** PO Box 198, White River, SD 57579; 605-259-3150, assessor fax- 605-259-3194. hours- 8AM-5PM

Miner County

Register of Deeds, PO Box 546, Howard, SD 57349. Recording, R/E & UCC phone-605-772-5621; fax-605-772-4148; 8AM-N, 1PM-5PM (CST)
Index: All in one. Records indexed on computer back to 2005. Only the public may search. Copy fee $1.00 per doc; $.20 per page over 5. Cert fee- $2.00 per page includes copy fee. Payee- Miner County Register of Deeds. **Other phones:** Treasurer- 605-772-4652; Elections- 605-772-4671; Vital Records- 605-772-5621; Auditor- 605-772-4671. **Property tax/Assessing-** PO Box 577, Howard, SD 57349; 605-772-4241, assessor fax- 605-772-4203.

Minnehaha County

Register of Deeds, 415 N Dakota Ave, Sioux Falls, SD 57104-2465. Recording, R/E & UCC phone-605-367-4223; fax-605-367-8314; 8AM-5PM (CST) www.minnehahacounty.org/dept/rd/rd.aspx
Index: Separate indices to search include books, microfilm. Sign in to use the public use terminal; records go back to 1987. Office personnel or visitors may perform searches. Office will not search real estate records. UCC search per debtor name- $20.00. Copy fee $1.00 per doc; $.20 per page over 5. Cert fee- $1.00 per doc plus copy fee. Payee- Minnehaha County Register of Deeds. **Other phones:** Treasurer- 605-367-4212; Elections- 605-367-4220; Vital Records- 605-367-4223. **Property tax/Assessing-** 415 N Dakota Ave, Sioux Falls, SD 57104-2465; 605-367-4228, assessor fax- 605-367-7870. (Appraiser/Auditor- 605-367-4228) www.minnehahacounty.org/dept/eq/eq.aspx **Online access-** Access to the county property tax database is free at www.minnehahacounty.org/property_tax/Index.asp. No name searching at this time.

Moody County

Register of Deeds, PO Box 247, Flandreau, SD 57028-0247. Recording, R/E & UCC phone-605-997-3151; fax-605-997-9996; 8AM-5PM (CST)
Index: All in one. Records indexed on computer back to 2000. Office personnel or visitors may perform searches. Search fee-$20.00 per name. Office will search real estate records for deeds. Copy fee $1.00 per doc; $.20 per page over 5. Cert fee- $2.00 per cert; $.20 per page after 5 pages. Payee- Moody County Register of Deeds. **Other phones:** Treasurer- 605-997-3171; Elections- 605-997-3161; Vital Records- 605-997-3151. **Property tax/Assessing-** 101 E Pipestone Ave, Courthouse, Flandreau, SD 57028; 605-997-3101. (Appraiser/Auditor- 605-997-3161) A public access terminal is available. **Online access-** Search assessor property data for a fee on the GIS system at http://beacon.schneidercorp.com/ with registration and username required.

Pennington County

Register of Deeds, 315 St. Joe St, Rapid City, SD 57701. Recording, R/E & UCC phone-605-394-2177; 8AM-5PM (MST) www.co.pennington.sd.us
Index: Separate indices to search include deeds, mortgages. Records on a public use terminal back to 1990. Office will perform a UCC search but public must search other records themselves. Search fee $20.00. Office will search last deed of record only. Will not search UCC records. Real estate record copy- $1.00 1st 5 pages; $.20 each add'l page. UCC copy fee $1.00 per page. Cert fee- $2.00 per doc plus $.20 per page after 5th page, includes copy fee. Payee- Pennington County Register of Deeds. **Other phones:** Treasurer- 605-394-2161; Elections- 605-394-2153; Vital Records- 605-394-2177. **Property tax/Assessing-** 315 St Joe St, Rapid City, SD 57701; 605-394-2175. **Online access-** Access to the county property tax database is free at www.co.pennington.sd.us/search/search.aspx.

Perkins County

Register of Deeds, PO Box 127, Bison, SD 57620. Recording, R/E & UCC phone-605-244-5620; fax-605-244-7289; 8AM-5PM.
Index: Separate indices to search include grantor/grantee/ mortgages, deed, miscellaneous. Records indexed on computer back to 1996. Office will perform a UCC search (info request form required) but public must search other records themselves. Search fee-$20.00 per name. Office will search real estate records if not too detailed or long legal. Copy fee first 5 pages $1.00 each; $.20 each add'l page. Cert fee- $2.00 each first 5 pages; $.20 each add'l page. Payee- Perkins Co. Registrar of Deeds. **Other phones:** Treasurer- 605-244-5613; Elections- 605-244-5624; Vital Records- 605-773-4961. **Property tax/Assessing-** PO Box 6, Bison, SD 57620; 605-244-5623, assessor fax- 605-244-5623.

Potter County

Register of Deeds, 201 S Exene St, Gettysburg, SD 57442. 605-765-9467; fax-605-765-2836; 7:30AM-N, 12:30-5PM M-TH; 7:30AM-N F.
Index: Separate indices to search include deeds, mortgages. Record index not computerized. Only the public may search. Copy fee $1.00 per doc; $.20 per page over 5. Cert fee- $2.00 per doc includes copy fee. Payee- Potter County Register of Deeds. **Other phones:** Treasurer- 605-765-9403; Elections- 605-765-9408; Vital Records- 605-765-9467. **Property tax/Assessing**- 201 S Exene St, Gettysburg, SD 57442-1596; 605-765-2481.

Roberts County

Register of Deeds, 411 E 2nd Ave, Sisseton, SD 57262. 605-698-7152; fax-605-698-4277; 8AM-5PM (CST)
Index: Separate indices to search include deed, mortgage. Record index not computerized. Office personnel or visitors may perform searches. Search fee-$20.00 per name. Copy fee $1.00 per doc; $.20 per page over 5. Cert fee- $2.00 per doc includes copy fee. Payee- Roberts County Register of Deeds. **Other phones:** Treasurer- 605-698-7245. **Property tax/Assessing**- 411 E 2nd Ave, Sisseton, SD 57262; 605-698-3205.

Sanborn County

Register of Deeds, PO Box 295, Woonsocket, SD 57385. Recording, R/E & UCC phone-605-796-4516; fax-605-796-4509; 8AM-5PM (CST)
Index: Separate indices to search include deeds, mortgages. Most records indexed on computer back to 2004. Office will perform a UCC search but public must search other records themselves. Office will search real estate records, the last deed or mortgage unless customer comes in themselves. UCC search per debtor name- $20.00. Copy fee $1.00 per doc; $.20 per page over 5. Cert fee- $2.00 per doc includes copy fee. Payee- Register of Deeds. **Other phones:** Treasurer- 605-796-4512; Elections- 605-796-4513; Vital Records- 605-796-4516. **Property tax/Assessing**- PO Box 416, Woonsocket, SD 57385; 605-796-4514, assessor fax- 605-796-4509.

Shannon County

Register of Deeds, 906 N River St, Hot Springs, SD 57747. 605-745-5139, R/E recording phone-605-745-5187, UCC recording phone-605-745-5139; fax-605-745-3708; 8AM-5PM (MST)
Index: All in one. Grantor/grantee indexed on computer back to 2000. Office will perform a UCC search but public must search other records themselves. UCC $20.00, Real Estate $7.00 per name. Copy fee $1.00 per doc; $.20 per page over 5. Cert fee- $1.00 per doc plus copy fee. Payee- Shannon County Register of Deeds. **Other phones:** Treasurer- 605-745-5145; Elections- 605-745-5130; Vital Records- 605-745-5139. **Property tax/Assessing**- 906 N River St, Hot Springs, SD 57747; 605-745-5136.

Spink County

Register of Deeds, 210 E 7th Ave, Redfield, SD 57469. Recording, R/E & UCC phone-605-472-4588; fax-605-472-4582; 8AM-5PM.
Index: Separate indices to search include deeds and Mtgs. Record index not computerized. Office personnel or visitors may perform searches. Search fee $13.00 UCCs, $5.00 tax liens. Copy fee $1.00 per document. Copies over 5 pages add'l $.25 per page. Cert fee- $2.00 per page includes copy fee. Payee- Register of Deeds. **Other phones:** Treasurer- 605-472-4583; Elections- 605-472-4580; Vital Records- 605-472-4588. **Property tax/Assessing**- 210 E 7th Ave, Redfield, SD 57469; 605-472-4585, assessor fax- 605-472-4587. A public access terminal is available.

Stanley County

Register of Deeds, PO Box 596, Fort Pierre, SD 57532. Recording, R/E & UCC phone-605-223-7786; fax-605-223-7788; 8AM-N,1PM-5PM (CST)
Index: Separate indices to search include deeds, mortgages. Record index not computerized. Office personnel or visitors may perform searches. No fee for search. Office will search real estate records. Will search UCC records. UCC search per debtor name- $20.00. Separate federal tax lien search- $20.00. Copy fee $1.00 per page. Cert fee- $2.00 1st 5 pg, $.20 each add'l page includes copy fee. Payee- Stanley County Register of Deeds. **Other phones:** Treasurer- 605-223-7783; Elections- 605-223-7780; Vital Records- 605-223-7786. **Property tax/Assessing**- PO Box 623, 8 E 2nd Ave, Courthouse, Fort Pierre SD 57532; 605-223-7789, assessor fax- 605-223-7791.

Sully County

Register of Deeds, PO Box 265, Onida, SD 57564. 605-258-2331; fax-605-258-2590; 8AM-5PM (CST) www.sullycounty.net/content.asp?secId=20&ParentId=14
Index: Separate indices to search include deeds, Mortgages. Record index not computerized. Office will perform a UCC search but public must search other records themselves. UCC search per debtor name- $10.00. Copy fee $1.00 per page.**Other phones:** Treasurer- 605-258-2444; Elections- 605-258-2541; Vital Records- 605-258-2331. **Property tax/Assessing**- Equalization Office, PO Box 265, Onida, SD 57564-0265; 605-258-2522, assessor fax- 605-258-2884. (Appraiser/Auditor- 605-258-2522)

Todd County

Register of Deeds, 200 E 3rd St, Winner, SD 57580-1806. Recording, R/E & UCC phone-605-842-2208; fax-605-842-1116; 8AM-5PM.
Index: Separate indices to search. Records indexed on a public use terminal back to 2003. Public may search but office will look back for the past 2 recorded documents only, no charge. Office will not name search real estate records. Office will search UCC records. UCC search per debtor name- $20.00. Copy fee $1.00 per instrument. Fax back fee- $3.00. Certified copy of UCC is $10.00. Copies over 5 pages add.'l $.20 per page. Cert fee- $2.00 per page includes copy fee. Payee- Todd County Registrar of Deeds. **Other phones:** Treasurer- 605-842-1700; Elections- 605-842-3727; Vital Records- 605-842-2208. **Property tax/Assessing**- PO Box 459, Mission, DS 57555; 605-856-4633.

Tripp County

Register of Deeds, 200 E 3rd St, Courthouse, #202, Winner, SD 57580-1806. Recording, R/E & UCC phone-605-842-2208; fax-605-842-1116; 8AM-5PM (CST)
Index: Separate indices to search include land records, federal and tax lien books. Records indexed on a public use terminal back to 2003. Office will perform a UCC search but public must search other records themselves. Office will not search real estate records but will look back 2 recordings. Copy fee $1.00 per doc; $.20 per page over 5. Fax fee $3.00 per page. Cert fee- $2.00 per cert plus $.20 per page after 1st 5 pages. UCC certified copy- $10.00. Payee- Tripp County Register of Deeds. **Other phones:** Treasurer- 605-842-1700; Elections- 605-842-3727; Vital Records- 605-842-2208. **Property tax/Assessing**- 200 E 3rd St, #201, Winner, SD 57580; 605-842-2300, assessor fax- 605-942-1116.

Turner County

Register of Deeds, PO Box 485, Parker, SD 57053. 605-297-3443; fax-605-297-5556; 8:30AM-5PM.
Index: Separate indices to search include deeds, mortgages. Record index not computerized. Office personnel or visitors may perform searches. General search fee $5.00 per name. Office will not search real estate records. UCC search on UCC-11 form per debtor name- $20.00. Copy fee $1.00 per doc; $.20 per page over 5. Cert fee- $2.00 per doc includes copy fee. Payee- Register of Deeds. **Other phones:** Treasurer- 605-297-4425. **Property tax/Assessing**- PO Box 309, 400 S Main Ave, Parker, SD 57053; 605-297-3424, assessor fax- 605-297-2243.

Union County

Register of Deeds, 209 E Main St, #210, Elk Point, SD 57025. Recording, R/E & UCC phone-605-356-2191; fax-605-356-3047; 8:30AM-5PM.
Index: Separate indices to search include books, computer, microfiche. Records indexed on a public use terminal back to 1993; more being added. Office personnel or visitors may perform searches. Office will search real estate records on computer no fee. UCC or state tax lien search per debtor name- $20.00. Copy fee $1.00 per doc; $.20 per page over 5. Cert fee- $2.00 5 pages, $.20 per add'l page, includes copy fee. Payee- Register of Deeds. **Other phones:** Treasurer- 605-356-2391; Elections- 605-356-2101; Vital Records- 605-356-2191. **Property tax/Assessing**- 209 E Main St, #130, Elk Point, SD 57025; 605-356-2252, assessor fax- 605-356-3047. **Online access**- Search assessor property data for a fee at http://beacon.schneidercorp.com/ with registration and username required.

Walworth County

Register of Deeds, PO Box 159, Selby, SD 57472-0159. 605-649-7057; fax-605-649-7867; 8AM-N,1PM-5PM (CST)
Index: Separate indices to search include books, microfilm, computer. Records indexed on a public use terminal back to 1989 for images. Office will perform a UCC search (must be on the UCC II request form) but public must search other records themselves. Search fee $20.00 per debtor name. Office will not search real estate records. Copy fee $1.00 per doc; $.20 per page over 5. Cert fee- $1.00 per doc plus copy fee. Payee- Walworth County Register of Deeds. **Other phones:** Treasurer- 605-649-7737; Elections- 605-649-7878; Vital Records- 605-649-7057; Clerk of Courts- 605-649-7311. **Property tax/Assessing**- PO Box 292, 4304 4th St, Courthouse, Selby, SD 57472; 605-649-7602, assessor fax- 605-649-7867.

Yankton County

Register of Deeds, PO Box 694, Yankton, SD 57078. 605-260-4400 x5; fax-605-668-9682; 9AM-5PM (CST)
Index: Separate indices to search include grantor/grantee, mortgages. Alpha index on computer back 10 years. Office personnel or visitors may perform searches. Search fee $10.00 per name. Office will not search real estate records. Copy fee $1.00 per page. Cert fee- $2.00 per cert plus copy fee. Payee- Yankton County Register of Deeds. **Other phones:** Treasurer- 605-260-4400 x7. **Property tax/Assessing**- PO Box 1076, Yankton, SD 57078; 605-260-4400 x3.

Ziebach County

Register of Deeds, PO Box 68, Dupree, SD 57623. 605-365-5165; fax-605-365-5204; 8AM-N, 1PM-5PM (MST)
Index: Separate indices to search include deed, mortgage books. Record index not computerized. Only the public may search. Copy fee $1.00 per doc; $.20 per page over 5. Cert fee- $1.00 per cert plus copy fee. Payee- Ziebach County Register of Deeds. **Other phones:** Treasurer- 605-365-5173. **Property tax/Assessing**- 303 Main St, Dupree, SD 57623; 605-365-5129.

South Dakota County Locator

You will usually be able to find the city name in the City/County Cross Reference below. In that case, it is a simple matter to determine the county from the cross reference. However, only the official US Postal Service city names are included in this index. We have also included a ZIP/City Cross Reference immediately following the City/County Cross Reference. If you know the ZIP Code but the city name does not appear in the City/County Cross Reference index, look up the ZIP Code in the ZIP/City Cross Reference, find the city name, then look up the city name in the City/County Cross Reference.

South Dakota City/County Cross Reference

ABERDEEN Brown
AGAR Sully
AKASKA Walworth
ALCESTER (57001) Union(94), Lincoln(5)
ALEXANDRIA (57311) Hanson(97), Hutchinson(1)
ALLEN (57714) Bennett(93), Jackson(6)
ALPENA (57312) Jerauld(58), Beadle(39), Sanborn(1)
AMHERST (57421) Marshall(91), Brown(8)
ANDOVER (57422) Day(95), Brown(4)
ARDMORE Fall River
ARLINGTON (57212) Kingsbury(70), Brookings(22), Hamlin(6)
ARMOUR (57313) Douglas(80), Charles Mix(19)
ARTESIAN Sanborn
ASHTON (57424) Spink(93), Faulk(6)
ASTORIA (57213) Deuel(75), Brookings(24)
AURORA (57002) Brookings(97), Moody(2)
AVON (57315) Bon Homme(98), Charles Mix(1)
BADGER Kingsbury
BALTIC Minnehaha
BANCROFT Kingsbury
BARNARD Brown
BATESLAND (57716) Shannon(86), Bennett(13)
BATH Brown
BEAVER CREEK Tripp
BELLE FOURCHE (57717) Butte(96), Lawrence(2)
BELVIDERE (57521) Jackson(78), Mellette(21)
BERESFORD (57004) Union(62), Lincoln(29), Clay(8)
BETHLEHEM Meade
BIG STONE CITY (57216) Grant(76), Roberts(23)
BISON Perkins
BLACK HAWK (57718) Meade(98), Pennington(1)
BLUNT (57522) Hughes(90), Sully(9)
BONESTEEL Gregory
BOWDLE (57428) Edmunds(79), Walworth(19)
BOX ELDER (57719) Pennington(89), Meade(10)
BRADLEY Clark
BRANDON Minnehaha
BRANDT Deuel
BRENTFORD Spink
BRIDGEWATER (57319) McCook(72), Turner(13), Hutchinson(13)
BRISTOL Day
BRITTON Marshall
BROOKINGS (57006) Brookings(97), Moody(2)
BROOKINGS Brookings
BRUCE Brookings
BRYANT (57221) Hamlin(86), Clark(10), Kingsbury(2)
BUFFALO Harding
BUFFALO GAP (57722) Custer(69), Fall River(22), Shannon(7)
BUFFALO RIDGE Minnehaha
BULLHEAD Corson
BURBANK (57010) Clay(73), Union(26)
BURKE Gregory
CAMP CROOK Harding
CANISTOTA McCook
CANOVA (57321) Hanson(46), Miner(43), McCook(9)
CANTON Lincoln
CAPUTA Pennington
CARPENTER (57322) Beadle(41), Clark(39), Spink(19)
CARTER (57526) Tripp(75), Todd(18), Mellette(5)
CARTHAGE (57323) Miner(90), Kingsbury(8)
CASTLEWOOD (57223) Hamlin(97), Deuel(2)
CAVOUR Beadle
CEDARBUTTE Mellette
CENTERVILLE (57014) Turner(72), Clay(13), Lincoln(13)
CHAMBERLAIN (57325) Brule(98), Buffalo(1)
CHAMBERLAIN Brule
CHANCELLOR (57015) Turner(96), Minnehaha(3)
CHERRY CREEK Ziebach
CHESTER (57016) Lake(89), Minnehaha(10)
CLAIRE CITY Roberts
CLAREMONT (57432) Brown(83), Marshall(16)
CLARK (57225) Clark(90), Deuel(9)
CLEAR LAKE (57226) Deuel(97), Hamlin(2)
COLMAN (57017) Moody(95), Lake(4)
COLOME Tripp
COLTON (57018) Minnehaha(96), Lake(2)
COLUMBIA Brown
CONDE (57434) Spink(67), Brown(16), Day(8), Clark(6)
CORONA (57227) Roberts(97), Grant(2)
CORSICA Douglas
CORSON Minnehaha
CREIGHTON Pennington
CRESBARD (57435) Faulk(90), Edmunds(9)
CROCKER Clark
CROOKS Minnehaha
CUSTER (57730) Custer(97), Pennington(2)
DALLAS (57529) Gregory(69), Tripp(30)
DANTE Charles Mix
DAVIS (57021) Turner(98), Lincoln(1)
DE SMET Kingsbury
DEADWOOD Lawrence
DELL RAPIDS (57022) Minnehaha(88), Moody(11)
DELMONT (57330) Douglas(73), Charles Mix(18), Hutchinson(8)
DIMOCK (57331) Hutchinson(67), Douglas(17), Davison(14)
DOLAND Spink
DRAPER (57531) Jones(98), Lyman(1)
DUPREE (57623) Ziebach(91), Dewey(8)
EAGLE BUTTE Dewey
EDEN (57232) Marshall(97), Day(2)
EDGEMONT (57735) Custer(62), Fall River(37)
EGAN Moody
ELK POINT Union
ELKTON (57026) Brookings(82), Moody(17)
ELLSWORTH AFB Meade
ELM SPRINGS Meade
EMERY (57332) Hutchinson(48), Hanson(38), McCook(12)
ENNING Meade
ERWIN (57233) Kingsbury(96), Hamlin(3)
ESTELLINE (57234) Hamlin(67), Deuel(30), Brookings(2)
ETHAN (57334) Davison(65), Hanson(25), Hutchinson(9)
EUREKA (57437) McPherson(75), Campbell(24)
FAIRBURN Custer
FAIRFAX Gregory
FAIRVIEW Lincoln
FAITH (57626) Meade(52), Perkins(42), Ziebach(5)
FAULKTON Faulk
FEDORA (57337) Miner(94), Sanborn(5)
FERNEY Brown
FIRESTEEL (57628) Corson(50), Dewey(50)
FLANDREAU Moody
FLORENCE (57235) Codington(93), Day(6)
FORT MEADE Meade
FORT PIERRE (57532) Stanley(98), Lyman(1)
FORT THOMPSON Buffalo
FRANKFORT Spink
FREDERICK Brown
FREEMAN (57029) Hutchinson(76), Turner(23)
FRUITDALE Butte
FULTON (57340) Hanson(90), Miner(9)
GANN VALLEY (57341) Buffalo(96), Brule(3)
GARDEN CITY Clark
GARRETSON Minnehaha
GARY Deuel
GAYVILLE (57031) Yankton(81), Clay(18)
GEDDES (57342) Charles Mix(98), Douglas(1)
GETTYSBURG (57442) Potter(96), Dewey(2), Sully(1)
GLAD VALLEY Ziebach
GLENCROSS (57630) Dewey(91), Corson(8)
GLENHAM (57631) Walworth(91), Campbell(9)
GOODWIN (57238) Deuel(72), Codington(23), Hamlin(3), Grant(1)
GREGORY (57533) Gregory(88), Lyman(6), Tripp(5)
GRENVILLE Day
GROTON Brown
HAMILL (57534) Tripp(85), Lyman(14)
HARRISBURG Lincoln
HARRISON Douglas
HARROLD (57536) Hughes(84), Sully(11), Hyde(3)
HARTFORD Minnehaha
HAYES (57537) Stanley(88), Haakon(12)
HAYTI Hamlin
HAZEL (57242) Hamlin(78), Codington(21)
HECLA Brown
HENRY (57243) Codington(95), Clark(4)
HERMOSA (57744) Custer(53), Pennington(45), Shannon(1)
HERREID Campbell
HERRICK Gregory
HETLAND Kingsbury
HIGHMORE (57345) Hyde(90), Faulk(9)
HILL CITY Pennington
HITCHCOCK (57348) Beadle(65), Spink(34)
HOLABIRD Hyde
HOSMER (57448) Edmunds(77), McPherson(22)
HOT SPRINGS (57747) Fall River(97), Custer(2)
HOUGHTON Brown
HOVEN (57450) Potter(61), Walworth(38)
HOWARD Miner
HOWES (57748) Meade(98), Buffalo(1)
HUDSON (57034) Lincoln(93), Union(6)
HUMBOLDT (57035) Minnehaha(97), McCook(2)
HURLEY Turner
HURON Beadle
IDEAL Tripp
INTERIOR (57750) Jackson(96), Pennington(3)
IONA (57542) Lyman(98), Gregory(1)
IPSWICH (57451) Edmunds(95), Brown(4)
IRENE (57037) Yankton(63), Clay(19), Turner(17)
IROQUOIS (57353) Kingsbury(65), Beadle(32), Clark(1)
ISABEL (57633) Dewey(62), Corson(32), Ziebach(5)
JAVA (57452) Walworth(74), Campbell(26)
JEFFERSON Union
KADOKA (57543) Jackson(98), Haakon(1)
KAYLOR Hutchinson
KELDRON Corson
KENNEBEC (57544) Lyman(98), Tripp(1)
KEYSTONE Pennington
KIMBALL (57355) Jerauld(55), Brule(42), Buffalo(2)
KRANZBURG Codington
KYLE (57752) Shannon(80), Jackson(20)
LABOLT Grant
LAKE ANDES Charles Mix
LAKE CITY Marshall
LAKE NORDEN (57248) Hamlin(86), Kingsbury(13)
LAKE PRESTON Kingsbury
LANE Jerauld
LANGFORD (57454) Marshall(79), Day(20)
LANTRY Dewey
LEAD Lawrence
LEBANON Potter
LEMMON (57638) Perkins(96), Corson(3)
LENNOX (57039) Lincoln(94), Turner(5)
LEOLA (57456) McPherson(98), Edmunds(1)
LESTERVILLE (57040) Yankton(95), Bon Homme(4)
LETCHER (57359) Sanborn(76), Aurora(11), Davison(10), Jerauld(1)
LINN (57483) Hand(48), Faulk(35), Spink(16)
LITTLE EAGLE Corson
LODGEPOLE Perkins
LONG VALLEY Jackson
LONGLAKE McPherson
LOWER BRULE Lyman
LUDLOW Harding
LYONS Minnehaha
MAHTO Corson

MANDERSON Shannon
MANSFIELD (57460) Brown(62), Spink(18), Faulk(9), Edmunds(9)
MARCUS Meade
MARION (57043) Turner(94), McCook(3), Hutchinson(1)
MARTIN Bennett
MARTY Charles Mix
MARVIN (57251) Grant(91), Roberts(8)
MC INTOSH Corson
MC LAUGHLIN Corson
MEADOW (57644) Perkins(75), Corson(14), Ziebach(10)
MECKLING Clay
MELLETTE (57461) Spink(98), Brown(1)
MENNO (57045) Hutchinson(86), Yankton(12), Turner(1)
MIDLAND (57552) Haakon(52), Stanley(32), Jackson(9), Mellette(3)
MILBANK (57252) Grant(98), Roberts(1)
MILBANK Grant
MILESVILLE Haakon
MILLER (57362) Hand(98), Buffalo(1)
MINA (57462) Edmunds(86), Brown(13)
MISSION Todd
MISSION HILL Yankton
MISSION RIDGE Stanley
MITCHELL (57301) Davison(98), Hanson(1)
MOBRIDGE Walworth
MONROE (57047) McCook(61), Turner(38)
MONTROSE (57048) McCook(90), Minnehaha(8)
MORRISTOWN Corson
MOUND CITY Campbell
MOUNT VERNON (57363) Davison(91), Aurora(4), Sanborn(3)
MUD BUTTE (57758) Meade(78), Perkins(17), Butte(3)
MURDO (57559) Jones(95), Mellette(4)
NEMO Lawrence
NEW EFFINGTON Roberts
NEW HOLLAND Douglas
NEW UNDERWOOD (57761) Pennington(62), Meade(37)
NEWELL (57760) Butte(80), Meade(17), Harding(1)
NISLAND Butte
NORRIS (57560) Mellette(53), Bennett(28), Jackson(18)
NORTH SIOUX CITY Union
NORTHVILLE (57465) Spink(62), Faulk(38)
NUNDA Lake
OACOMA Lyman
OELRICHS Fall River
OGLALA Shannon
OKATON Jones
OKREEK Todd
OLDHAM (57051) Kingsbury(92), Miner(5), Lake(1)
OLIVET Hutchinson
ONAKA (57466) Faulk(78), Edmunds(19), Potter(1)
ONIDA (57564) Sully(97), Hyde(2)
OPAL Meade
ORAL Fall River
ORIENT (57467) Hand(69), Faulk(30)
ORTLEY (57256) Grant(55), Roberts(33), Day(6), Codington(5)
OWANKA (57767) Pennington(64), Meade(36)
PARADE Dewey
PARKER (57053) Turner(95), McCook(3), Minnehaha(1)
PARKSTON (57366) Hutchinson(94), Douglas(4)
PARMELEE (57566) Todd(82), Mellette(17)
PEEVER Roberts
PHILIP (57567) Haakon(79), Jackson(12), Gregory(7)
PICKSTOWN Charles Mix
PIEDMONT Meade
PIERPONT Day
PIERRE (57501) Hughes(97), Sully(2)
PINE RIDGE Shannon
PLANKINTON Aurora
PLATTE (57369) Charles Mix(95), Aurora(2), Douglas(1)
POLLOCK Campbell
PORCUPINE Shannon
PRAIRIE CITY (57649) Perkins(89), Harding(10)
PRESHO Lyman
PRINGLE Custer
PROVO Fall River
PUKWANA (57370) Brule(83), Buffalo(16)
QUINN (57775) Pennington(56), Haakon(25), Jackson(18)
RALPH Harding
RAMONA (57054) Lake(97), Kingsbury(1), Miner(1)
RAPID CITY (57702) Pennington(98), Meade(1)
RAPID CITY Pennington
RAVINIA Charles Mix
RAYMOND (57258) Clark(87), Spink(12)
RED OWL Meade
REDFIELD (57469) Spink(96), Hand(3)
REDIG Harding
REE HEIGHTS (57371) Hand(96), Hyde(2), Buffalo(1)
RELIANCE Lyman
RENNER Minnehaha
REVA (57651) Harding(66), Perkins(33)
REVILLO (57259) Grant(68), Deuel(31)
RIDGEVIEW Dewey
ROCHFORD Pennington
ROCKHAM (57470) Faulk(54), Hand(45)
ROSCOE Edmunds
ROSEBUD Todd
ROSHOLT Roberts
ROSLYN (57261) Day(98), Marshall(1)
ROWENA Minnehaha
RUTLAND (57057) Lake(97), Moody(2)
SAINT CHARLES Gregory
SAINT FRANCIS Todd
SAINT LAWRENCE Hand
SAINT ONGE (57779) Lawrence(93), Butte(6)
SALEM (57058) McCook(93), Miner(6)
SCENIC (57780) Pennington(94), Shannon(5)
SCOTLAND (57059) Bon Homme(89), Hutchinson(10)
SELBY Walworth
SENECA (57473) Faulk(80), Potter(19)
SHADEHILL Perkins
SHERMAN Minnehaha
SINAI Brookings
SIOUX FALLS (57108) Lincoln(76), Minnehaha(23)
SIOUX FALLS (57106) Minnehaha(92), Lincoln(7)
SIOUX FALLS Minnehaha
SISSETON (57262) Roberts(96), Marshall(3)
SMITHWICK Fall River
SOUTH SHORE (57263) Codington(81), Grant(18)
SPEARFISH Lawrence
SPENCER (57374) Hanson(53), McCook(46)
SPRINGFIELD Bon Homme
STEPHAN Hyde
STICKNEY (57375) Aurora(97), Davison(2)
STOCKHOLM (57264) Grant(98), Codington(1)
STRANDBURG (57265) Grant(70), Deuel(25), Codington(3)
STRATFORD (57474) Brown(94), Spink(5)
STURGIS (57785) Meade(98), Lawrence(1)
SUMMIT (57266) Roberts(55), Grant(44)
TABOR (57063) Bon Homme(84), Yankton(15)
TEA (57064) Lincoln(94), Turner(5)
TIMBER LAKE Dewey
TOLSTOY (57475) Potter(59), Edmunds(38), Walworth(1)
TORONTO (57268) Deuel(76), Brookings(23)
TRAIL CITY (57657) Corson(90), Dewey(9)
TRENT Moody
TRIPP (57376) Hutchinson(86), Bon Homme(12), Charles Mix(1)
TULARE (57476) Spink(86), Hand(13)
TURTON Spink
TUTHILL Bennett
TWIN BROOKS Grant
TYNDALL Bon Homme
UNION CENTER Meade
UTICA Yankton
VALE (57788) Meade(52), Butte(47)
VALLEY SPRINGS Minnehaha
VEBLEN (57270) Marshall(86), Roberts(13)
VERMILLION Clay
VIBORG (57070) Turner(93), Yankton(6)
VIENNA (57271) Clark(76), Hamlin(23)
VIRGIL (57379) Beadle(80), Jerauld(19)
VIVIAN (57576) Lyman(92), Jones(8)
VOLGA (57071) Brookings(95), Lake(3), Moody(1)
VOLIN (57072) Yankton(78), Clay(21)
WAGNER Charles Mix
WAKONDA (57073) Clay(94), Turner(5)
WAKPALA Corson
WALKER Corson
WALL Pennington
WALLACE (57272) Codington(87), Clark(10), Day(2)
WANBLEE (57577) Jackson(98), Bennett(1)
WARD Moody
WARNER Brown
WASTA (57791) Pennington(50), Meade(49)
WATAUGA Corson
WATERTOWN Codington
WAUBAY (57273) Day(88), Roberts(11)
WAVERLY Codington
WEBSTER (57274) Day(98), Clark(1)
WENTWORTH (57075) Lake(98), Moody(1)
WESSINGTON (57381) Beadle(59), Hand(40)
WESSINGTON SPRINGS (57382) Jerauld(94), Aurora(3), Beadle(1)
WESTPORT (57481) Brown(59), McPherson(30), Edmunds(10)
WEWELA Tripp
WHITE Brookings
WHITE LAKE (57383) Aurora(98), Brule(1)
WHITE OWL Meade
WHITE RIVER Mellette
WHITEHORSE Dewey
WHITEWOOD (57793) Lawrence(84), Meade(13), Butte(2)
WILLOW LAKE Clark
WILMOT Roberts
WINFRED (57076) Miner(53), Lake(46)
WINNER (57580) Tripp(98), Todd(1)
WITTEN Tripp
WOLSEY Beadle
WOOD Mellette
WOONSOCKET (57385) Sanborn(83), Jerauld(14), Aurora(1)
WORTHING Lincoln
WOUNDED KNEE Shannon
YALE Beadle
YANKTON Yankton
ZEONA (57795) Perkins(66), Butte(33)

South Dakota ZIP/City Cross Reference

57001-57001 ALCESTER
57002-57002 AURORA
57003-57003 BALTIC
57004-57004 BERESFORD
57005-57005 BRANDON
57006-57007 BROOKINGS
57010-57010 BURBANK
57012-57012 CANISTOTA
57013-57013 CANTON
57014-57014 CENTERVILLE
57015-57015 CHANCELLOR
57016-57016 CHESTER
57017-57017 COLMAN
57018-57018 COLTON
57019-57019 CORSON
57020-57020 CROOKS
57021-57021 DAVIS
57022-57022 DELL RAPIDS
57024-57024 EGAN
57025-57025 ELK POINT
57026-57026 ELKTON
57027-57027 FAIRVIEW
57028-57028 FLANDREAU
57029-57029 FREEMAN
57030-57030 GARRETSON
57031-57031 GAYVILLE
57032-57032 HARRISBURG
57033-57033 HARTFORD
57034-57034 HUDSON
57035-57035 HUMBOLDT
57036-57036 HURLEY
57037-57037 IRENE
57038-57038 JEFFERSON
57039-57039 LENNOX
57040-57040 LESTERVILLE
57041-57041 LYONS
57042-57042 MADISON
57043-57043 MARION
57044-57044 MECKLING
57045-57045 MENNO
57046-57046 MISSION HILL
57047-57047 MONROE
57048-57048 MONTROSE
57049-57049 NORTH SIOUX CITY
57050-57050 NUNDA
57051-57051 OLDHAM
57052-57052 OLIVET
57053-57053 PARKER
57054-57054 RAMONA
57055-57055 RENNER
57056-57056 ROWENA
57057-57057 RUTLAND
57058-57058 SALEM
57059-57059 SCOTLAND
57060-57060 SHERMAN
57061-57061 SINAI
57062-57062 SPRINGFIELD
57063-57063 TABOR
57064-57064 TEA
57065-57065 TRENT
57066-57066 TYNDALL
57067-57067 UTICA
57068-57068 VALLEY SPRINGS
57069-57069 VERMILLION
57070-57070 VIBORG
57071-57071 VOLGA
57072-57072 VOLIN
57073-57073 WAKONDA
57074-57074 WARD
57075-57075 WENTWORTH
57076-57076 WINFRED
57077-57077 WORTHING
57078-57079 YANKTON
57100-57110 SIOUX FALLS
57115-57115 BUFFALO RIDGE
57116-57198 SIOUX FALLS

57201-57201 WATERTOWN
57202-57202 WAVERLY
57212-57212 ARLINGTON
57213-57213 ASTORIA
57214-57214 BADGER
57216-57216 BIG STONE CITY
57217-57217 BRADLEY
57218-57218 BRANDT
57219-57219 BRISTOL
57220-57220 BRUCE
57221-57221 BRYANT
57223-57223 CASTLEWOOD
57224-57224 CLAIRE CITY
57225-57225 CLARK
57226-57226 CLEAR LAKE
57227-57227 CORONA
57229-57229 CROCKER
57231-57231 DE SMET
57232-57232 EDEN
57233-57233 ERWIN
57234-57234 ESTELLINE
57235-57235 FLORENCE
57236-57236 GARDEN CITY
57237-57237 GARY
57238-57238 GOODWIN
57239-57239 GRENVILLE
57241-57241 HAYTI
57242-57242 HAZEL
57243-57243 HENRY
57244-57244 HETLAND
57245-57245 KRANZBURG
57246-57246 LABOLT
57247-57247 LAKE CITY
57248-57248 LAKE NORDEN
57249-57249 LAKE PRESTON
57251-57251 MARVIN
57252-57253 MILBANK
57255-57255 NEW EFFINGTON
57256-57256 ORTLEY
57257-57257 PEEVER
57258-57258 RAYMOND
57259-57259 REVILLO
57260-57260 ROSHOLT
57261-57261 ROSLYN
57262-57262 SISSETON
57263-57263 SOUTH SHORE
57264-57264 STOCKHOLM
57265-57265 STRANDBURG
57266-57266 SUMMIT
57268-57268 TORONTO
57269-57269 TWIN BROOKS
57270-57270 VEBLEN
57271-57271 VIENNA
57272-57272 WALLACE
57273-57273 WAUBAY
57274-57274 WEBSTER
57276-57276 WHITE
57278-57278 WILLOW LAKE
57279-57279 WILMOT
57301-57301 MITCHELL
57311-57311 ALEXANDRIA
57312-57312 ALPENA
57313-57313 ARMOUR
57314-57314 ARTESIAN
57315-57315 AVON
57316-57316 BANCROFT
57317-57317 BONESTEEL
57319-57319 BRIDGEWATER
57321-57321 CANOVA
57322-57322 CARPENTER
57323-57323 CARTHAGE
57324-57324 CAVOUR
57325-57326 CHAMBERLAIN
57328-57328 CORSICA
57329-57329 DANTE
57330-57330 DELMONT
57331-57331 DIMOCK
57332-57332 EMERY
57334-57334 ETHAN
57335-57335 FAIRFAX
57337-57337 FEDORA
57339-57339 FORT THOMPSON
57340-57340 FULTON
57341-57341 GANN VALLEY
57342-57342 GEDDES
57344-57344 HARRISON
57345-57345 HIGHMORE
57346-57346 STEPHAN
57348-57348 HITCHCOCK
57349-57349 HOWARD
57350-57350 HURON
57353-57353 IROQUOIS
57354-57354 KAYLOR
57355-57355 KIMBALL
57356-57356 LAKE ANDES
57357-57357 RAVINIA
57358-57358 LANE
57359-57359 LETCHER
57361-57361 MARTY
57362-57362 MILLER
57363-57363 MOUNT VERNON
57364-57364 NEW HOLLAND
57365-57365 OACOMA
57366-57366 PARKSTON
57367-57367 PICKSTOWN
57368-57368 PLANKINTON
57369-57369 PLATTE
57370-57370 PUKWANA
57371-57371 REE HEIGHTS
57373-57373 SAINT LAWRENCE
57374-57374 SPENCER
57375-57375 STICKNEY
57376-57376 TRIPP
57379-57379 VIRGIL
57380-57380 WAGNER
57381-57381 WESSINGTON
57382-57382 WESSINGTON SPRINGS
57383-57383 WHITE LAKE
57384-57384 WOLSEY
57385-57385 WOONSOCKET
57386-57386 YALE
57399-57399 HURON
57401-57402 ABERDEEN
57420-57420 AKASKA
57421-57421 AMHERST
57422-57422 ANDOVER
57424-57424 ASHTON
57426-57426 BARNARD
57427-57427 BATH
57428-57428 BOWDLE
57429-57429 BRENTFORD
57430-57430 BRITTON
57432-57432 CLAREMONT
57433-57433 COLUMBIA
57434-57434 CONDE
57435-57435 CRESBARD
57436-57436 DOLAND
57437-57437 EUREKA
57438-57438 FAULKTON
57439-57439 FERNEY
57440-57440 FRANKFORT
57441-57441 FREDERICK
57442-57442 GETTYSBURG
57445-57445 GROTON
57446-57446 HECLA
57448-57448 HOSMER
57449-57449 HOUGHTON
57450-57450 HOVEN
57451-57451 IPSWICH
57452-57452 JAVA
57454-57454 LANGFORD
57455-57455 LEBANON
57456-57456 LEOLA
57457-57457 LONGLAKE
57460-57460 MANSFIELD
57461-57461 MELLETTE
57462-57462 MINA
57465-57465 NORTHVILLE
57466-57466 ONAKA
57467-57467 ORIENT
57468-57468 PIERPONT
57469-57469 REDFIELD
57470-57470 ROCKHAM
57471-57471 ROSCOE
57472-57472 SELBY
57473-57473 SENECA
57474-57474 STRATFORD
57475-57475 TOLSTOY
57476-57476 TULARE
57477-57477 TURTON
57479-57479 WARNER
57481-57481 WESTPORT
57483-57483 LINN
57501-57501 PIERRE
57520-57520 AGAR
57521-57521 BELVIDERE
57522-57522 BLUNT
57523-57523 BURKE
57526-57526 CARTER
57527-57527 CEDARBUTTE
57528-57528 COLOME
57529-57529 DALLAS
57531-57531 DRAPER
57532-57532 FORT PIERRE
57533-57533 GREGORY
57534-57534 HAMILL
57536-57536 HARROLD
57537-57537 HAYES
57538-57538 HERRICK
57540-57540 HOLABIRD
57541-57541 IDEAL
57542-57542 IONA
57543-57543 KADOKA
57544-57544 KENNEBEC
57545-57545 BEAVER CREEK
57547-57547 LONG VALLEY
57548-57548 LOWER BRULE
57551-57551 MARTIN
57552-57552 MIDLAND
57553-57553 MILESVILLE
57555-57555 MISSION
57557-57557 MISSION RIDGE
57559-57559 MURDO
57560-57560 NORRIS
57562-57562 OKATON
57563-57563 OKREEK
57564-57564 ONIDA
57566-57566 PARMELEE
57567-57567 PHILIP
57568-57568 PRESHO
57569-57569 RELIANCE
57570-57570 ROSEBUD
57571-57571 SAINT CHARLES
57572-57572 SAINT FRANCIS
57574-57574 TUTHILL
57576-57576 VIVIAN
57577-57577 WANBLEE
57578-57578 WEWELA
57579-57579 WHITE RIVER
57580-57580 WINNER
57584-57584 WITTEN
57585-57585 WOOD
57601-57601 MOBRIDGE
57620-57620 BISON
57621-57621 BULLHEAD
57622-57622 CHERRY CREEK
57623-57623 DUPREE
57625-57625 EAGLE BUTTE
57626-57626 FAITH
57628-57628 FIRESTEEL
57629-57629 GLAD VALLEY
57630-57630 GLENCROSS
57631-57631 GLENHAM
57632-57632 HERREID
57633-57633 ISABEL
57634-57634 KELDRON
57636-57636 LANTRY
57638-57638 LEMMON
57639-57639 LITTLE EAGLE
57640-57640 LODGEPOLE
57641-57641 MC INTOSH
57642-57642 MC LAUGHLIN
57643-57643 MAHTO
57644-57644 MEADOW
57645-57645 MORRISTOWN
57646-57646 MOUND CITY
57647-57647 PARADE
57648-57648 POLLOCK
57649-57649 PRAIRIE CITY
57650-57650 RALPH
57651-57651 REVA
57652-57652 RIDGEVIEW
57653-57653 SHADEHILL
57656-57656 TIMBER LAKE
57657-57657 TRAIL CITY
57658-57658 WAKPALA
57659-57659 WALKER
57660-57660 WATAUGA
57661-57661 WHITEHORSE
57701-57703 RAPID CITY
57706-57706 ELLSWORTH AFB
57708-57708 BETHLEHEM
57709-57709 RAPID CITY
57714-57714 ALLEN
57715-57715 ARDMORE
57716-57716 BATESLAND
57717-57717 BELLE FOURCHE
57718-57718 BLACK HAWK
57719-57719 BOX ELDER
57720-57720 BUFFALO
57722-57722 BUFFALO GAP
57724-57724 CAMP CROOK
57725-57725 CAPUTA
57729-57729 CREIGHTON
57730-57730 CUSTER
57732-57732 DEADWOOD
57735-57735 EDGEMONT
57736-57736 ELM SPRINGS
57737-57737 ENNING
57738-57738 FAIRBURN
57741-57741 FORT MEADE
57742-57742 FRUITDALE
57744-57744 HERMOSA
57745-57745 HILL CITY
57747-57747 HOT SPRINGS
57748-57748 HOWES
57750-57750 INTERIOR
57751-57751 KEYSTONE
57752-57752 KYLE
57754-57754 LEAD
57755-57755 LUDLOW
57756-57756 MANDERSON
57757-57757 MARCUS
57758-57758 MUD BUTTE
57759-57759 NEMO
57760-57760 NEWELL
57761-57761 NEW UNDERWOOD
57762-57762 NISLAND
57763-57763 OELRICHS
57764-57764 OGLALA
57765-57765 OPAL
57766-57766 ORAL
57767-57767 OWANKA
57769-57769 PIEDMONT
57770-57770 PINE RIDGE
57772-57772 PORCUPINE
57773-57773 PRINGLE
57774-57774 PROVO
57775-57775 QUINN
57776-57776 REDIG
57777-57777 RED OWL
57778-57778 ROCHFORD
57779-57779 SAINT ONGE
57780-57780 SCENIC
57782-57782 SMITHWICK
57783-57783 SPEARFISH
57785-57785 STURGIS
57787-57787 UNION CENTER
57788-57788 VALE
57790-57790 WALL
57791-57791 WASTA
57792-57792 WHITE OWL
57793-57793 WHITEWOOD
57794-57794 WOUNDED KNEE
57795-57795 ZEONA
57799-57799 SPEARFISH

Tennessee

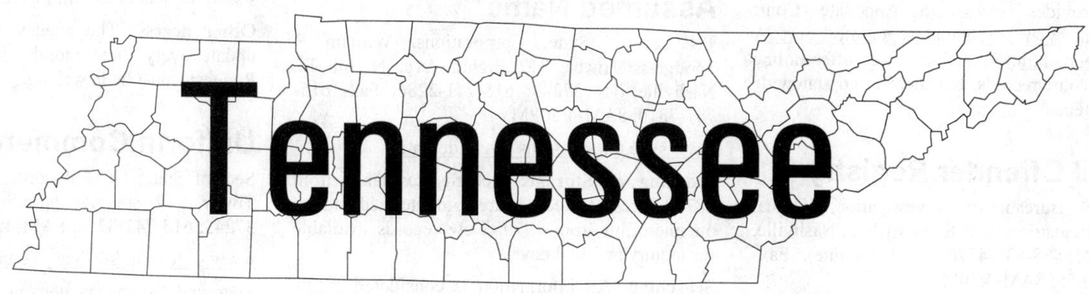

General Help Numbers:

Governor's Office
State Capitol, 1st Floor 615-741-2001
Nashville, TN 37243-0001 Fax 615-532-9711
www.tennesseeanytime.org/governor 8AM-5PM

Attorney General's Office
PO Box 20207 615-741-3491
Nashville, TN 37202-0207 Fax 615-741-2009
www.tn.gov/attorneygeneral/ 8AM-4:30PM

Legislative Records
Office of Legislative Information Services 615-741-3511
Rachel Jackson Bldg, 1st Floor 615-741-0927
Nashville, TN 37243 8AM-4:30PM
www.legislature.state.tn.us

State Archives
State Library & Archives Division 615-741-7996
403 7th Ave N Fax 615-532-2472
Nashville, TN 37243-0312 8AM-6PM M-SA
www.tennessee.gov/tsla/

State Specifics:

Capital: Nashville
Davidson County

Time Zone: CST*
* Tennessee's twenty-nine eastern-most counties are EST: They are: Anderson, Blount, Bradley, Campbell, Carter, Claiborne, Cocke, Grainger, Greene, Hamilton, Hancock, Hawkins, Jefferson, Johnson, Knox, Loudon, McMinn, Meigs, Monroe, Morgan, Polk, Rhea, Roane, Scott, Sevier, Sullivan, Unicoi, Union, Washington.

Number of Counties: 95

Population: 6,214,888

Web Site: www.tennessee.gov

State Agencies

Criminal Records

Tennessee Bureau of Investigation, TN Open Records Information Svcs, 901 R S Gass Blvd, Nashville, TN 37216; 615-744-4057, Fax- 615-744-4289; 24 hours daily. www.tbi.state.tn.us

Per statute, fingerprint-based background checks are to be conducted for paid or volunteer employment or licensing such as such as child care, teachers, security and armed guards, security system contractors, etc.

Indexing & Storage: Records available approx. 80 years on paper. New records available for inquiry in 1 hour. Per a recent U.S. DOJ Study, 23% of all arrests in database have final dispositions recorded, 30% for those arrests within last 5 years.

Searching: The agency maintains a website at www.ticic.state.tn.us for searching of sexual offenders, missing children, and people placed on parole who reside in TN. Include in request- name, DOB, AKA's. Sex, race and current address are helpful. The search system is called TORIS (Tennessee Open Records Information Service). A request form can be downloaded from the webpage. The agency suggests that ongoing requester be registered with an account. This data not released- juvenile records. All records are released to those entitled, including those without dispositions.

Access by: mail, fax, in person, online.

Fee & Payment: The fee is based number of orders per month. 1-300 $29.00; 301-500 $25.00; 501-1000 $22.00; over 1000 $19.00 each. Includes alias name checks. Fee payee- Tennessee Bureau of Investigation Unless a registered account, prepayment required. Business checks accepted, personal checks are not. VISA, MasterCard and Discover accepted.

Mail search: Turnaround time- 2-5 days. SASE not required. **Fax search:** Use of credit card is required unless received from registered customer.

In person: Counter service is available.

Online search: Records may be requested online via email from the website, but this is not an interactive service. Records must still manually searched and will take several days.

Statewide Court Records

Administrative Office of the Courts, Nashville City Center, 511 Union St, Suite 600, Nashville, TN 37219; 615-741-2687, Fax- 615-741-6285; 8AM-4:30PM.

www.tncourts.gov

Except for certain online research capabilities, all court record access must be done at the local level.

Online search: The Administrative Office of Courts provides access to Appellate Court opinions at www.tsc.state.tn.us/geninfo/Courts/AppellateCourts.htm. Several counties offer online access to court records, but there is no statewide access system.

Sexual Offender Registry

Tennessee Bureau of Investigation, Sexual Offender Registry, 901 R S Gass Blvd., Nashville, TN 37216; 888-837-4170 (SOR Hotline), Fax- 615-744-4655; 8AM-4:30PM.

www.ticic.state.tn.us

Indexing & Storage: Records available regardless of date, if offender is tried as an adult. New records available for inquiry in 12 to 84 hours.

Searching: Include in request- name, DOB; SSN is helpful. This data not released- expunged records

Access by: phone, online.

Phone search: Inquiry by name available by name at TBI SOR Hotline.

Online search: Search sexual offenders at www.ticic.state.tn.us/sorinternet/sosearch.aspx by last name, city, county or ZIP Code. One may also search for missing children, and people placed on parole who reside in Tennessee. A map search is found at http://tnmap.state.tn.us/sor/map.aspx.

Incarceration Records

Dept of Corrections-ATTN: PIO/FOIL, Rachel Jackson Building, Ground Fl, 320 6th Avenue, N., Nashville, TN 37243-0465; 615-741-1000, 615-741-1150 (Parole-Probation), Fax- 615-532-1497; 8AM-5PM. www.state.tn.us/correction/

Indexing & Storage: Records available on current and former inmates. New records available for inquiry in 7 days.

Searching: Location, conviction and sentencing information are provided. Include in request- first and last name. The SSN and DOB are helpful. This data not released- medical information, DOB, SSN, and crime or county of crime.

Access by: mail, phone, fax, online.

Fee & Payment: Fees apply when hard copies are needed: $10.00 for search, $.20 per page Fee payee- Tennessee Dept of Corrections Prepayment required.

Mail search: Turnaround time- 10 - 15 working days. Also, historical archived inmate information is available from Operational Support Services; generally, there is a $10.00 archive search fee and $.20 per page copy fee. SASE not required.

Phone search: Limited phone searching is available.

Fax search: Fax requesting available.

Online search: Extensive search capabilities are offered from the website at https://www.tennesseeanytime.org/foil/foil_index.jsp.

Other access: A CD-Rom is available with only public information from current offender database; nominal fee; contact the Planning & Research Division.

Expedited service: Will expedite for law enforcement or subpoena emergency (3 days), but only if shipping is paid in advance.

Corporation, LLC, LP, LLP, Fictitious Name, Assumed Name

TN Sec of State: Corporations, William R Snodgrass Tower, 312 Eighth Ave. N, 6th Fl, Nashville, TN 37243; 615-741-2286, Fax- 615-741-7310; 8AM-4:30PM.

www.state.tn.us/sos/bus_svc/index.htm

Indexing & Storage: Records available from 1875 to present. Records are computerized and are on microfilm from 1979. New records available for inquiry in 2 to 3 days.

Searching: All information is considered public record. Include in request- full name of business. In addition to the articles of organization, business entity records available include: Annual Reports, Officers, Directors, DBAs (assumed names only), Prior (merged) names, Inactive and Reserved names.

Access by: mail, in person, online.

Fee & Payment: Each set of documents per business is $20.00 per entity, which includes certification. Fees are set by statute. Fee payee- Secretary of State. Prepayment required. Personal checks accepted, credit cards are not.

Mail search: Turnaround time- 1 to 3 days. Certificates are usually processed in 1 day. SASE not required.

In person: Turnaround time is immediate unless certified documents are ordered which are ready the next day.

Online search: There is a free online search at www.tennesseeanytime.org/sosname/ for name availability and at www.tennesseeanytime.org/soscorp/ for business records. This gives online access to over 4,000,000 records relating to corporations, limited liability companies, limited partnerships and limited liability partnerships formed or registered in Tennessee. Also, search securities department enforcement actions at www.state.tn.us/commerce/securities/enfaction.html.

Other access: Some data can be purchased in bulk or list format. Call 615-532-9007 for more details.

Expedited service: Send a completed air bill or courier bill and they will overnight the return.

Trademarks/Servicemarks, Trade Names

Secretary of State, Trademarks/Tradenames Division, 312 8th Ave North, 6th Fl, Nashville, TN 37243-0306; 615-741-0531, Fax- 615-741-7310; 8AM-4:30PM.

www.state.tn.us/sos/bus_svc/trademarks.htm

Indexing & Storage: Records available from the 1950s to present on microfilm. New records available for inquiry in 2 to 3 days.

Searching: All records are public information. Include in request- trademark/servicemark name, name of owner, date of application.

Access by: mail, phone, in person, online.

Fee & Payment: There is $20.00 search fee, add $2.00 for certification. Fee payee- Secretary of State. Personal checks accepted, credit cards not.

Mail search: Turnaround time- 1 to 3 days. A SASE is requested.

Phone search: No fee for telephone request.

In person: Turnaround time is while you wait.

Online search: The Internet provides a record search of TN Trademarks, newest records are 3 days old. Search free at http://state.tn.us/sos/bus_svc/iets2/ietm/PgTrademarkSearch.jsp.

Other access: The agency will provide a file update every three months for $1.00 per page. Requests must be in writing.

Uniform Commercial Code

Sec. of State, UCC Records, William Snodgrass Tower, 312 8th Ave N, 6th Fl, Nashville, TN 37243; 615-741-3276; 8AM-4:30PM.

www.state.tn.us/sos/bus_svc/ucc.htm

State and federal tax liens are filed at the county level with the Register of Deeds where the lienee or its property is located.

Indexing & Storage: Records available from 07/01/1964. New records available for inquiry in 2-3 days.

Searching: Use search request form UCC-11. Include in request- debtor name. All information in database is released, if requested properly.

Access by: mail, in person, online.

Fee & Payment: The fee is $15.00 per debtor or debtor address, copies are $1.00 per page. Add $2.00 for certification. See fee schedule at www.state.tn.us/sos/forms/uccfee2001.pdf. Fee payee- Secretary of State. Prepayment required. Personal checks accepted, credit cards are not.

Mail search: Turnaround time- 2-3 days. SASE is not required.

In person: The results are mailed in 2-3 days.

Online search: Free access to general, limited information at http://state.tn.us/sos/bus_svc/iets3/ieuc/PgUCCSearch.jsp. Search by debtor name or file number. Images are not available. Note that this data is current within three days of filing and is not considered an official search. The UCC database is updated between 7:30AM and 11AM (CST). During the update process, secured party information may not be available and/or related UCC document information may not be accurately reflected for a UCC1 filing.

Federal & State Tax Liens

Records not maintained by a state level agency.

State and federal tax liens are filed at the county level with the Register of Deeds where the lienee or its property is located.

Sales Tax Registrations

Access to Records is Restricted.

TN Department of Revenue, Sales Tax Registration, Andrew Jackson Bldg, 500 Deaderick St, Nashville, TN 37242-0100; 615-253-0600, Fax- 615-253-6299; 8AM-4:30PM.

www.state.tn.us/revenue/

The agency will supply information regarding a registered taxpayer with the written permission of the owner of the specific account. This includes confirmation if a submitted tax ID # is either active or inactive. The agency will also release information when presented with a properly issued subpoena.

Birth Certificates

Tennessee Department of Health, Office of Vital Records, 421 5th Ave North, 1st floor, Nashville, TN 37243; 615-741-1763, 615-741-0778 (Credit card order), Fax- 615-741-9860; 8AM-4PM.

http://health.state.tn.us/vr/index.htm

Indexing & Storage: Records available for 100 years to present. For birth records prior, contact the State Library and Archives at 615-741-2764. Short forms are only available since 1949. New records available for inquiry immediately.

Searching: Must have a signed release from person of record or immediate family member for certified copy. Medical and health information is not released. Include in request- full name, names of parents, mother's maiden name, date of birth, place of birth, relationship to person of record. Include copy of government issued ID of requester. Daytime phone helpful.

Access by: mail, phone, fax, in person, online.

Fee & Payment: $12.00 for the long (copy of actual certificate) form; $7.00 for the short computerized form. Add $4.00 per name per copy for additional copies. Fee payee- Tennessee Vital Records. Prepayment required. Personal checks accepted. Major credit cards accepted for expedited srv only.

Mail search: Turnaround time- 2 to 3 weeks. SASE not required.

Phone search: This is expedited service, see below.

Fax search: Same criteria as phone searching. Use 615-726-2559, is considered expedited service.

In person: Requests submitted by 10:30 AM will be available for pickup after 3PM, otherwise records must be picked up the next day.

Online search: Records may be ordered from the website, but are returned by mail. See expedited services.

Expedited service: Expedited service is available for phone, fax or online searches. Turnaround time- 2 to 3 days. Go to https://health.state.tn.us/vrocs/vr.aspx. There is an additional $10.00 fee involved to use this service. Records can be returned overnight for if additional fee for shipping is added.

Death Records

Tennessee Department of Health, Office of Vital Records, 421 5th Ave North, 1st floor, Nashville, TN 37243; 615-741-1763, 615-741-0778 (Credit card order), Fax- 615-741-9860; 8AM-4PM.

http://health.state.tn.us/vr/index.htm

Indexing & Storage: Records available from 01/1914. Previous records are at the State Archives at 615-726-2559. New records available for inquiry in 3 months or less.

Searching: Must have a signed release from immediate family member. Cause of death is restricted to immediate family members or their representatives and must be specifically requested. Include in request- full name, names of parents, mother's maiden name, date of death, place of death, reason for information request, relationship to person of record. Include copy of government issued ID of requester. Daytime phone helpful.

Access by: mail, phone, fax, in person, online.

Fee & Payment: The fee is $7.00 per name. Fee payee- Tennessee Vital Records. Prepayment required. Personal checks accepted. Major credit cards accepted for expedited srv only.

Mail search: Turnaround time- 2 to 3 weeks. SASE not required.

Phone search: is an expedited service, see below.

Fax search: Same criteria as phone searching. Use 615-726-2559, is considered expedited service.

In person: Requests submitted by 10:30 AM will be available for pickup after 3PM, otherwise records must be picked up the next day.

Online search: Records may be ordered from the website, but are returned by mail. See expedited services. The Cleveland (Tennessee) Public Library staff and volunteers have published the 1914-1925 death records of thirty-three counties at www.tennessee.gov/tsla/history/vital/death.htm. Note that the records of children under two years of age have been omitted from this project.

Expedited service: Expedited service is available for phone, fax or online searches. Turnaround time- 2 to 3 days. Go to https://health.state.tn.us/vrocs/vr.aspx. There is an additional $10.00 fee involved to use this service. Records can be returned overnight for if additional fee for shipping is added.

Marriage Certificates

Tennessee Department of Health, Office of Vital Records, 421 5th Ave North, 1st floor, Nashville, TN 37243; 615-741-1763, 615-741-0778 (Credit card order), Fax- 615-741-9860; 8AM-4PM.

http://health.state.tn.us/vr/index.htm

Indexing & Storage: Records available for 50 years. Older records are at the state archives. New records available for inquiry in 1 month.

Searching: Information on race or previous marriages is only released for statistical purposes. Include in request- signed release from persons of record or immediate family member for certified copy, names of husband and wife, date of marriage, place or county of marriage.

Access by: mail, phone, fax, in person, online.

Fee & Payment: The search fee is $12.00. Add $4.00 for each additional copy. Fee payee- Tennessee Vital Records. Prepayment required. Personal checks accepted. Major credit cards accepted for expedited srv only.

Mail search: Turnaround time- 2 to 3 weeks. SASE not required.

Phone search: is an expedited service, see below.

Fax search: Same criteria as phone searching. Use 615-726-2559, is considered expedited service.

In person: Requests submitted by 10:30 AM will be available for pickup after 3PM, otherwise records must be picked up the next day.

Online search: Records may be ordered from the website, but are returned by mail. See expedited services.

Expedited service: Expedited service is available for phone, fax or online searches. Turnaround time- 2 to 3 days. Go to https://health.state.tn.us/vrocs/vr.aspx. There is an additional $10.00 fee involved to use this service. Records can be returned overnight for if additional fee for shipping is added.

Divorce Records

Tennessee Department of Health, Office of Vital Records, 421 5th Ave North, 1st floor, Nashville, TN 37243; 615-741-1763, 615-741-0778 (Credit card order), Fax- 615-741-9860; 8AM-4PM.

http://health.state.tn.us/vr/index.htm

Indexing & Storage: Records available for 50 years. Older records are at the state archives. New records available for inquiry in 2 weeks to 2 months.

Searching: Information on previous marriages and education is released for statistical use only. Include in request- signed release from person of record or immediate family member, names of husband and wife, date of divorce, place of divorce.

Access by: mail, phone, fax, in person, online.

Fee & Payment: The search fee is $12.00. There is an additional $4.00 charge for an extra copy. Fee payee- Tennessee Vital Records. Prepayment required. Personal checks accepted. Major credit cards accepted for expedited srv only.

Mail search: Turnaround time- 2 to 3 weeks. SASE not required.

Phone search: This is expedited service, see below.

Fax search: Same criteria as phone searching. Use 615-726-2559, is considered expedited service.

In person: Requests submitted by 10:30 AM will be available for pickup after 3PM, otherwise records must be picked up the next day.

Online search: Records may be ordered from the website, but are returned by mail. See expedited services.

Expedited service: Expedited service is available for phone, fax or online searches. Turnaround time- 2 to 3 days. Go to https://health.state.tn.us/vrocs/vr.aspx. There is an additional $10.00 fee involved to use this service. Records can be returned overnight for if additional fee for shipping is added.

Workers' Compensation Records

Tennessee Department of Labor, Workers Compensation Division, 710 James Robertson Pkwy, 2nd Floor, Nashville, TN 37243-0661; 615-253-1842, Fax- 615-532-1942; 8AM-4:30PM.

www.state.tn.us/labor-wfd/wcomp.html

Per state law, an employer may ask, in writing, is a job applicant has been truthful about an existing claim or history. However, Per the ADA, a "pre-employment search" is not permitted.

Indexing & Storage: Records available from 09/91 on computer, from 1987 to present on microfiche. Prior records are maintained on index cards. New records available for inquiry in 90 days.

Searching: To receive records, a signed release form the employee is required. An attorney request certain documents such as settlement forms or court papers without a release. Include in request- on letterhead, company name and address, reason for request, and employee SSN. If not a party or representative of a case, a signed release of the employee required.

Access by: mail, fax, in person.

Fee & Payment: The search fee is $10.00 even if no record is found. This agency will invoice. The copy fee is $.25 per page. Fee payee- State of Tennessee Treasurer. Personal checks accepted, credit cards are not.

Mail search: Turnaround time- 1 week. They will invoice you for copies and postage. SASE not required. **Fax search:** This will not effect turnaround time. **In person:** Records are still returned in 2 weeks, but you can pick them up.

Driver Records

Dept. of Safety, Financial Responsibility Section, Attn: Driving Records, PO Box 945, Nashville, TN 37202; 615-741-3954, Fax- 615-253-2093; 8AM-4:30PM. www.tennessee.gov/safety/

Tickets are available from this office for a $5.00 fee per record.

Indexing & Storage: Records available for past 3 years for convictions, if valid; 7 years if the license is suspended, restricted, or revoked. New records available for inquiry in 30 days or more.

Searching: Tennessee passed legislation similar to DPPA. Non permissible use requesters must have written notarized authorization to receive record information with address data. Include in request- license number and last name or DOB.

Access by: mail, in person, online.

Fee & Payment: The fee is $5.00 per record, $7.00 if online. Fee payee- Tennessee Department of Safety. Prepayment required. Certified checks or money orders are preferred. No personal checks accepted.

Mail search: Turnaround time- 2 weeks. SASE not required.

In person: Up to 10 requests will be processed while you wait at this location or at many Driver License Testing Centers throughout the state.

Online search: Driving records are available to subscribers, signup at www.tennesseeanytime.org. There is a $75 registration fee. Records are available 24 hours daily on an interactive basis. Records are $7.00 each. Suggested only for ongoing users. Companies retrieving more than 500 records per month can use a "batch" process in which multiple license numbers can be searched and the results are returned in one file. Call 1-866-886-3468 for more information. Subscribers may obtain a DL status check online for a fee of $1.25.

Other access: Bulk retrieval is available for high volume users. Purchase of the DL file is available for approved requesters. Call Information Systems at 615-251-5322.

Vehicle Ownership & Registration

Motor Vehicle Services, Taxpayer & Vehicle Services, 44 Vantage Way #160, Nashville, TN 37243-8050; 615-741-3101, 888-871-3171, Fax- 615-253-4259; 8AM-4:30PM.

www.tennessee.gov/revenue/

Indexing & Storage: Records available for 12 years to present. New records available for inquiry in 12 weeks.

Searching: The agency follows the DPPA guidelines for permissible requesters.In general, records are not released to casual requesters without consent. The state recommends use of form-RV-F1313801. Include in request- purpose of request, copy of requester's photo ID, and requester's signature.

Access by: mail, in person, online.

Fee & Payment: The fee is $1.00 for general inquiry, $5.00 for photocopy of a current title, an advanced search (complete title history) is $15.00. (advanced record search). Fee payee- Titling and Registration. Prepayment required. Personal checks accepted, credit cards are not.

Mail search: Turnaround time- 4 to 6 weeks. A SASE is requested.

In person: Turnaround time is while you wait, unless photocopy of actual document is required. The office closes at 4PM for walk-in customers. Photo ID required.

Online search: Online access is available for approved subscribers at www.tennesseeanytime.org/ivtr. This is the same subscription system used to pull driving records. The $75.00 annual fee includes 10 users. IVTR allows subscribers to retrieve vehicle, title, and registration information for vehicles registered in Tennessee. Search with license plate or VIN. The fee is $2.00 per search. All subscribers must be approved per DPPA.

Accident Reports

Financial Responsibility Section, Records Unit, 1150 Foster Avenue, Nashville, TN 37210; 615-741-3954, Fax- 615-253-2093; 8AM-4:30PM.

www.tennessee.gov/safety/

Also, one can obtain accident reports from the investigating agency.

Indexing & Storage: Records available from 1992 to present. New records available for inquiry in 30 days.

Searching: Include in request- full name, date of accident, location of accident. Also, include the county of the accident and DL of driver(s). This data not released- SSN

Access by: mail, in person.

Fee & Payment: The fee is $4.00 per record copy. Fee payee- Tennessee Department of Safety. Prepayment required. Agency prefers money orders and certified checks. Personal checks not accepted. Visa and MasterCard accepted for in person only.

Mail search: Turnaround time- 2 weeks. SASE not required. **In person:** Turnaround time is generally while you wait.

Vessel Ownership & Registration

Wildlife Resources Agency, Boating Division, PO Box 40747, Nashville, TN 37204; 615-781-6585, Fax- 615-741-6649; 8AM-4:30PM.

www.state.tn.us/twra/boatmain.html

All liens are filed with the Secretary of State.

Indexing & Storage: Records available for the past 3 years. Records are indexed on computer. The state does not issue titles. All motorized boats and all sailboats must be registered. New records available for inquiry in 30 days.

Searching: Search via email to darren.rider@state.tn.us Include in request- name or SSN or hull ID or TN #.

Access by: mail, phone, fax, in person.

Fee & Payment: There is no fee to do 1 or 2 searches; however, large lists may incur a charge.

Mail search: Turnaround time- 2 days. SASE not required.

Phone search: Whether a phone search will be performed depends on how busy the personnel is at the time of the call. Phone searches are only verbal verifications and require a Tennessee ID # to search.

Fax search: Turnaround time is 2 days. Results will be sent by mail.

In person: Turnaround time is usually immediate, when staff available.

Legislation Records

Tennessee General Assembly, Office of Legislative Information Services, Rachel Jackson Bldg, 1st Floor (320 6th Ave), Nashville, TN 37243; 615-741-3511 (Status), 615-741-0927 (Bill Room); 8AM-4:30PM.

www.legislature.state.tn.us

Records available for the current and past sessions to 1995/6. Earlier records are maintained in the State Library & Archives.

Voter Registration

Access to Records is Restricted.

Secretary of State, Division of Elections, 312 Rosa L Parks Ave, 9th Fl, Snodgrass Twr, Nashville, TN 37243; 615-741-7956, Fax- 615-741-1278; 8AM-4:30PM.

www.state.tn.us/sos/election/index.htm

The statewide database cannot be accessed except for politically-related purposes. A CD is $2500. Local records are open and held by the Administrator of Elections at the county level. Email questions to tennessee.elections@state.tn.us.

GED Certificates

TN Dept of Labor & Workforce Development, Division of Adult Education, 220 French Landing Dr, Nashville, TN 37243; 615-741-7054, Fax- 615-532-4899; 8AM-4:30PM.

www.state.tn.us/labor-wfd/AE/aeged.htm

Indexing & Storage: Records available from 1956. New records available for inquiry in 2 wks.

Searching: Include in request- date of birth, SSN, signed release. Include your daytime telephone number. Year diploma issued also helpful.

Access by: mail, fax, in person.

Fee & Payment: There is no fee for a verification.

Mail search: Turnaround time- 7 to 10 working days. SASE not required. **Fax search:** Turnaround time is generally in 2 days.

In person: Simple requests may be processed while you wait.

Hunting & Fishing License Information

Wildlife Resources Agency, Revenue Division, PO Box 40747, Nashville, TN 37204; 615-781-6500, 800-648-8798, Fax- 615-781-5277; 8AM-4:30PM. www.state.tn.us/twra/

There is a central database of hunting or fishing licenses. Records available since 1999. New records available for inquiry in 24 hours.

Tennessee State Licensing Agencies

For details about the agency responsible for licensing/certifying/registering an item below or in the Agency Quick Finder section, match an item's number with the number of the agency in the *Licensing Agency Information* section.

Tennessee Licenses Searchable Online

Accounting Firm #3 .... http://licsrch.state.tn.us/
Alarm Contractor #3 .... http://licsrch.state.tn.us/
Animal Euthanasia Technician #7 .... http://health.state.tn.us/licensure/index.htm
Architect #3 .... http://licsrch.state.tn.us/
Athletic Trainer #7 .... http://health.state.tn.us/licensure/index.htm
Attorney #12 .... www.tbpr.org/Consumers/AttorneySearch/
Auctioneer/Auction Company #3 .... http://licsrch.state.tn.us/
Audiologist #7 .... http://health.state.tn.us/licensure/index.htm
Barber Shop/Barber School #3 .... http://licsrch.state.tn.us/
Barber/Barber Technician #3 .... http://licsrch.state.tn.us/
Boiler Operator #8 .... http://licsrch.state.tn.us/
Boxing/Racing Personnel #3 .... http://licsrch.state.tn.us/
Chiropractor/Chiropractic Assist. #7 .... http://health.state.tn.us/licensure/index.htm
Clinical Lab Technician/Personnel #6 .... http://health.state.tn.us/licensure/index.htm
Collection Agent/Manager #3 .... http://licsrch.state.tn.us/
Contractor #3 .... http://licsrch.state.tn.us/
Cosmetologist #3 .... http://licsrch.state.tn.us/
Cosmetology Shop/School #3 .... http://licsrch.state.tn.us/
Counselor, Alcohol & Drug Abuse #7 .... http://health.state.tn.us/licensure/index.htm
Counselor, Associate/Professional #7 .... http://health.state.tn.us/licensure/index.htm
Dental Hygienist #7 .... http://health.state.tn.us/licensure/index.htm
Dentist/Dental Assistant #7 .... http://health.state.tn.us/licensure/index.htm
Dietitian/Nutritionist #7 .... http://health.state.tn.us/licensure/index.htm
Electrologist #7 .... http://health.state.tn.us/licensure/index.htm
Electrology Instructor/School #7 .... http://health.state.tn.us/licensure/index.htm
Elevator Inspector #2 .... www.state.tn.us/labor-wfd/elevatorsinsp.html
Embalmer #3 .... http://licsrch.state.tn.us/
Emergency Med. Personnel/Dispatch #7 .... http://health.state.tn.us/licensure/index.htm
Emergency Medical Service #7 .... http://health.state.tn.us/licensure/index.htm
Engineer #3 .... http://licsrch.state.tn.us/
First Responder EMS #7 .... http://health.state.tn.us/licensure/index.htm
Funeral & Burial Director/Apprentice #3 .... http://licsrch.state.tn.us/
Funeral & Burial Est./Cemetery #3 .... http://licsrch.state.tn.us/
Geologist #3 .... http://licsrch.state.tn.us/
Hearing Aid Dispenser #7 .... http://health.state.tn.us/licensure/index.htm
Home Improvement #3 .... http://licsrch.state.tn.us/
Insurance Agent/Firm #3 .... http://licsrch.state.tn.us/
Interior Designer #3 .... http://licsrch.state.tn.us/
Laboratory Personnel, Medical #6 .... http://health.state.tn.us/licensure/index.htm
Landscape Architect/Architect Firm #3 .... http://licsrch.state.tn.us/
Lobbyist #10 .... www.state.tn.us/tref/lobbyists/lobbyists.htm
Manicurist #3 .... http://licsrch.state.tn.us/
Marriage & Family Therapist #7 .... http://health.state.tn.us/licensure/index.htm
Massage Therapist/Establishment #7 .... http://health.state.tn.us/licensure/index.htm
Medical Disciplinary Tracking #6 .... https://health.state.tn.us/AbuseRegistry/default.aspx
Medical Doctor #6 .... http://health.state.tn.us/licensure/index.htm
Midwife #7 .... http://health.state.tn.us/licensure/index.htm
Motor Vehicle Auction #3 .... http://licsrch.state.tn.us/
Motor Vehicle Dealer/Salesperson #3 .... http://licsrch.state.tn.us/
Notary Public #9 .... www.ja.state.tn.us/sos/iets1/ieny/PglenySearch.jsp
Nurse-RN/LPN #6 .... http://health.state.tn.us/licensure/index.htm
Nurses' Aide #6 .... http://health.state.tn.us/licensure/index.htm
Nursing Home Administrator #7 .... http://health.state.tn.us/licensure/index.htm
Occupational Therapist/Assistant #7 .... http://health.state.tn.us/licensure/index.htm
Optician, Dispensing #7 .... http://health.state.tn.us/licensure/index.htm
Optometrist #7 .... http://health.state.tn.us/licensure/index.htm

Orthopedic Physician Assistant #6	http://health.state.tn.us/licensure/index.htm
Osteopathic Physician #6	http://health.state.tn.us/licensure/index.htm
Pastoral Therapist, Clinical #7	http://health.state.tn.us/licensure/index.htm
Personnel Leasing #3	http://licsrch.state.tn.us/
Pharmacist/Pharmacy #3	http://licsrch.state.tn.us/
Pharmacy Researcher #3	http://licsrch.state.tn.us/
Physical Therapist/Assistant #6	http://health.state.tn.us/licensure/index.htm
Physician Assistant #6	http://health.state.tn.us/licensure/index.htm
Plumber/Plumbing Company #8	http://licsrch.state.tn.us/
Podiatrist #7	http://health.state.tn.us/licensure/index.htm
Polygraph Examiner #3	http://licsrch.state.tn.us/
Private Investigative Company #3	http://licsrch.state.tn.us/
Private Investigator #3	http://licsrch.state.tn.us/
Private Security Guard #3	http://licsrch.state.tn.us/
Psychological Examiner #7	http://health.state.tn.us/licensure/index.htm
Psychologist #7	http://health.state.tn.us/licensure/index.htm
Public Accountant-CPA #3	http://licsrch.state.tn.us/
Racetrack #3	http://licsrch.state.tn.us/
Radiologic Assistant #7	http://health.state.tn.us/licensure/index.htm
Real Estate Agent/Broker/Sales #3	http://licsrch.state.tn.us/
Real Estate Appraiser #3	http://licsrch.state.tn.us/
Real Estate Firm #3	http://licsrch.state.tn.us/
Refrigeration Installer/Contractor #8	http://licsrch.state.tn.us/
Respiratory Care Therap't/Tech./Asst. #6	http://health.state.tn.us/licensure/index.htm
School Administrator #5	www.k-12.state.tn.us/tcertinf/Search.asp
School Counselor #5	www.k-12.state.tn.us/tcertinf/Search.asp
School Food Service Supervisor #5	www.k-12.state.tn.us/tcertinf/Search.asp
School Librarian #5	www.k-12.state.tn.us/tcertinf/Search.asp
School Psychologist #5	www.k-12.state.tn.us/tcertinf/Search.asp
School Reading Specialist #5	www.k-12.state.tn.us/tcertinf/Search.asp
School Vocational Endorsement #5	www.k-12.state.tn.us/tcertinf/Search.asp
Security Guard/Company #3	http://licsrch.state.tn.us/
Security Trainer #3	http://licsrch.state.tn.us/
Shampoo Technician #3	http://licsrch.state.tn.us/
Social Worker, Master/Clinical #7	http://health.state.tn.us/licensure/index.htm
Speech Pathologist #7	http://health.state.tn.us/licensure/index.htm
Surveyor, Land #3	http://licsrch.state.tn.us/
Teacher #5	www.k-12.state.tn.us/tcertinf/Search.asp
Timeshare Agent #3	http://licsrch.state.tn.us/
Veterinarian #7	http://health.state.tn.us/licensure/index.htm
X-ray Operator #6	http://health.state.tn.us/licensure/index.htm
X-ray Technologist, Podiatry #6	http://health.state.tn.us/licensure/index.htm

Tennessee Licensing Quick Finder

Accounting Firm #3	615-741-2550
Alarm Contractor #3	615-741-9771
Alcohol Package Store #1	615-741-1602
Alcohol Server #1	615-741-1602
Animal Euthanasia Technician #7	615-532-3202
Animal/Livestock Dealer #11	615-837-5241
Architect #3	615-741-3221
Athletic Trainer #7	615-532-3202
Attorney #12	615-361-7500, 800-486-5714
Auctioneer/Auction Company #3	615-741-3600
Audiologist #7	615-532-3202
Barber Shop/Barber School #3	615-741-2294
Barber/Barber Technician #3	615-741-2294
Bed and Breakfast #4	615-741-7206
Boiler Operator #8	800-544-7693
Boxing/Racing Personnel #3	615-741-6837
Camp/Camping Facility #4	615-741-7206
Chiropractor/Chiropractic Assist. #7	615-532-3202
Clinical Lab Technician/Personnel #6	615-532-5128
Collection Agent/Manager #3	615-741-1741
Contractor #3	615-741-8307
Cosmetologist #3	615-741-2515
Cosmetology Shop/School #3	615-741-2515
Counselor, Alcohol & Drug Abuse #7	615-532-5097
Counselor, Associate/Professional #7	615-532-3202
Court Reporter/Stenographer #2	423-756-0221
Dental Hygienist #7	615-532-3202
Dentist/Dental Assistant #7	615-532-3202
Dietitian/Nutritionist #7	615-532-3202
Electrologist #7	615-532-3202
Electrology Instructor/School #7	615-532-3202
Elevator Inspector #2	615-741-2123
Embalmer #3	615-741-5062
Emerg'cy Med. Personnel/Dispatch #7	615-532-3202
Emergency Medical Service #7	615-532-3202
Engineer #3	615-741-3221
Environmentalist #7	615-532-3202
Fire Protect'n Sprinkler System Cont'r #3	615-741-1322
First Responder EMS #7	615-532-3202
Food Service Establishment #4	615-741-7206
Funeral & Burial Director/Apprent. #3	615-741-5062
Funeral & Burial Est./Cemetery #3	615-741-5062
Geologist #3	615-741-3611
Health Care Facility #6	615-741-7221
Hearing Aid Dispenser #7	615-532-3202
Home Improvement #3	615-741-8307
Hotel #4	615-741-7206
Insurance Agent/Firm #3	615-741-2693
Insurance Education Provider #3	615-741-2693
Interior Designer #3	615-741-3221
Investment Advisor #3	615-741-2947
Laboratory Personnel, Medical #6	615-532-5128
Landscape Architect/Architect Firm #3	615-741-3221
Liquor Sale/Permit #1	615-741-1602
Livestock Brand #11	615-837-5241
Lobbyist #10	615-741-7959
Manicurist #3	615-741-2515
Marriage & Family Therapist #7	615-532-3202
Massage Therapist/Establishment #7	615-532-5083
Medical Disciplinary Tracking #6	615-532-3421
Medical Doctor #6	615-532-4384
Midwife #7	615-532-3202
Milk Tester/Sampler #11	615-837-5151

Motor Vehicle Auction #3 615-741-2711
Motor Vehicle Dealer/Salesperson #3 .. 615-741-2711
Notary Public #9 615-741-3699
Nurse-RN/LPN #6 615-532-5166
Nursery #11 615-837-5512
Nursery Plant Dealer #11 615-837-5512
Nurses' Aide #6 615-741-7670
Nursing Home Administrator #7 615-532-3202
Occupational Therapist/Assistant #7 615-532-3202
Optician, Dispensing #7 615-532-3202
Optometrist #7 615-532-3202
Orthopedic Physician Assistant #6 615-532-4384
Osteopathic Physician #6 615-532-4384
Pastoral Therapist, Clinical #7 615-532-3202
Personnel Leasing #3 615-741-3449
Pest Control Operator #11 615-837-5138
Pharmacist/Pharmacy #3 615-741-2718
Pharmacy Researcher #3 615-741-2718
Physical Therapist/Assistant #6 615-532-5135
Physician Assistant #6 615-532-4384
Plumber/Plumbing Company #8 800-544-7693
Podiatrist #7 615-532-3202
Polygraph Examiner #3 615-741-4827
Private Investigative Company #3 615-741-4827
Private Investigator #3 615-741-4827
Private Security Guard #3 615-741-6382
Psychological Examiner #7 615-532-3202
Psychologist #7 615-532-3202
Public Accountant-CPA #3 615-741-2550
Racetrack #3 615-741-2384
Radiologic Assistant #7 615-532-3202
Radiologic Technician, American #6 ... 615-687-0048
Real Estate Agent/Broker/Sales #3 615-741-2273
Real Estate Appraiser #3 615-741-1831
Real Estate Firm #3 615-741-2273
Refrigeration Installer/Contractor #8 800-544-7693
Respiratory Care Therapist/Tech./Asst. #6 615-532-5096
School Administrator #5 615-532-4885
School Counselor #5 615-532-4885
School Food Service Supervisor #5 615-532-4885
School Librarian #5 615-532-4885
School Psychologist #5 615-532-4885
School Reading Specialist #5 615-532-4885
School Vocational Endorsement #5 615-532-4885
Securities Agent #3 615-741-2947
Securities Broker/Dealer #3 615-741-2947
Security Guard/Company #3 615-741-9771
Security Trainer #3 615-741-9771
Shampoo Technician #3 615-741-2515
Shorthand Reporter #2 423-756-0221
Social Worker, Master/Clinical #7 615-532-3202
Speech Pathologist #7 615-532-3202
Surveyor, Land #3 615-741-3611
Swimming Pool #4 615-741-7206
Tattoo Artist/Apprentice #4 615-741-7206
Teacher #5 615-532-4885
Timeshare Agent #3 615-741-2273
Veterinarian #7 615-532-3202
Water Treatment Plant Operator #13 ... 615-898-8090
Weigh Scales Service Technician #11 . 615-837-5109
Weigher, Public (bulk products) #11 615-837-5109
Weighmaster #11 615-837-5109
Wine Production/Sale/Transport #1 615-741-1602
X-ray Operator #6 615-532-4384
X-ray Technologist, Podiatry #6 615-532-5157

Tennessee Licensing Agency Information

#1 Alcoholic Beverage Commission, 226 Capitol Blvd, Nashville, TN 37219-1804; 615-741-1602, Fax- 615-741-0847. www.state.tn.us/abc/

#2 Department of Labor, Boiler & Elevator Division, Board of Boiler Rules, 220 French Landing Dr, Nashville, TN 37243; 615-741-2123, Fax- 615-532-1469. www.state.tn.us/labor-wfd/boilers.html

#3 Department of Commerce & Insurance, 500 James Robertson Pky, 2nd Fl, Davy Crockett Twr, Nashville, TN 37243; 615-741-2241, Fax- 615-532-2965. www.state.tn.us/commerce/ Search data at- http://licsrch.state.tn.us/ Additional toll-free phone number for insurance-related professional licensing is 888-416-0868 .

#4 Department of Health, Division of General Environmental Health, 425 5th Ave N, Cordell Hull Bldg, 6th Fl, Nashville, TN 37243; 615-741-7206, Fax- 615-741-8510. http://health.state.tn.us/index.shtml

#5 Department of Education, Office of Teacher Licensing, 710 James Robertson Pky, Andrew Johnson Tower, 4th Fl, Nashville, TN 37243-0377; 615-532-4885, Fax- 615-532-1448. www.state.tn.us/education/lic/ Search data at- www.k-12.state.tn.us/tcertinf/Search.asp

#6 Department of Health, Medical Professions, 425 5th Ave N, Cordell Hull Bldg, 1st Fl, Nashville, TN 37243; 615-532-3202, 800-778-4123. Hours- 8AM-4:30PM. http://health.state.tn.us/index.shtml Search data at- http://health.state.tn.us/licensure/index.htm

#7 Department of Health, Allied Health Professions - Licensing, 425 5th Ave N, Cordell Hull Bldg, 1st Fl, Nashville, TN 37247-1010; 615-532-3202, 800-778-4123. 8AM-4:30PM. http://health.state.tn.us/index.shtml Search data at- http://health.state.tn.us/licensure/index.htm

#8 Commerce and Insurance, Tennessee Board of Licensing Contractors, 500 James Robertson Pkwy, Nashville,, TN 37243-1150; 615-741-8307, 800-544-7693, Fax- 615-532-2868. http://tennessee.gov/commerce/boards/contractors/ Search data at- http://licsrch.state.tn.us/

#9 Office of Secretary of State, Notary Commission Services, 312 8th Ave N, 6th Fl, Snodgrass TN Tower, Nashville, TN 37243-0306; 615-741-3699, Fax- 615-741-7310. http://tennessee.gov/sos/bus_svc/notary.htm Search data at- www.ja.state.tn.us/sos/iets1/ieny/PgIenySearch.jsp

#10 Registry of Election Finance, 404 James Robertson Pky, #1614, Nashville, TN 37243; 615-741-7959, Fax- 615-532-8905. http://state.tn.us/tref/ Search data at- www.state.tn.us/tref/lobbyists/lobbyists.htm

#11 Department of Agriculture, PO Box 40627, Melrose Station (440 Hogan Rd, Nashville, TN 37204; 615-837-5120, Fax- 615-837-5335. www.state.tn.us/agriculture/

#12 Supreme Court, Board of Professional Responsibility, 1101 Kermit Dr, #730, Nashville, TN 37217; 615-361-7500, 800-486-5714, Fax- 615-367-2480. 8AM-4:30PM. www.tbpr.org Search data at- www.tbpr.org/Consumers/AttorneySearch/

#13 Dept Of Environment & Conservation, Water & Wastewater Certification Program, 401 Church Street,, Nashville, TN 37243-0435; 615-532-0109. www.tennessee.gov/environment/

Tennessee Federal Courts

The following list indicates the district and division name for each county in the state. If the bankruptcy court location is different from the district court, then the location of the bankruptcy court appears in parentheses.

Tennessee County/Court Cross Reference

County	District	Division
Anderson	Eastern	Knoxville
Bedford	Eastern	Winchester (Chattanooga)
Benton	Western	Jackson
Bledsoe	Eastern	Chattanooga
Blount	Eastern	Knoxville
Bradley	Eastern	Chattanooga
Campbell	Eastern	Knoxville
Cannon	Middle	Nashville
Carroll	Western	Jackson
Carter	Eastern	Greeneville
Cheatham	Middle	Nashville
Chester	Western	Jackson
Claiborne	Eastern	Knoxville
Clay	Middle	Cookeville (Nashville)
Cocke	Eastern	Greeneville
Coffee	Eastern	Winchester (Chattanooga)
Crockett	Western	Jackson
Cumberland	Middle	Cookeville (Nashville)
Davidson	Middle	Nashville
De Kalb	Middle	Cookeville (Nashville)
Decatur	Western	Jackson
Dickson	Middle	Nashville
Dyer	Western	Memphis
Fayette	Western	Memphis
Fentress	Middle	Cookeville (Nashville)
Franklin	Eastern	Winchester (Chattanooga)
Gibson	Western	Jackson
Giles	Middle	Columbia (Nashville)
Grainger	Eastern	Knoxville
Greene	Eastern	Greeneville
Grundy	Eastern	Winchester (Chattanooga)
Hamblen	Eastern	Greeneville
Hamilton	Eastern	Chattanooga
Hancock	Eastern	Greeneville
Hardeman	Western	Jackson
Hardin	Western	Jackson
Hawkins	Eastern	Greeneville
Haywood	Western	Jackson
Henderson	Western	Jackson
Henry	Western	Jackson
Hickman	Middle	Columbia (Nashville)
Houston	Middle	Nashville
Humphreys	Middle	Nashville
Jackson	Middle	Cookeville (Nashville)
Jefferson	Eastern	Knoxville
Johnson	Eastern	Greeneville
Knox	Eastern	Knoxville
Lake	Western	Jackson
Lauderdale	Western	Memphis
Lawrence	Middle	Columbia (Nashville)
Lewis	Middle	Columbia (Nashville)
Lincoln	Eastern	Winchester (Chattanooga)
Loudon	Eastern	Knoxville
Macon	Middle	Cookeville (Nashville)
Madison	Western	Jackson
Marion	Eastern	Chattanooga
Marshall	Middle	Columbia (Nashville)
Maury	Middle	Columbia (Nashville)
McMinn	Eastern	Chattanooga
McNairy	Western	Jackson
Meigs	Eastern	Chattanooga
Monroe	Eastern	Knoxville
Montgomery	Middle	Nashville
Moore	Eastern	Winchester (Chattanooga)
Morgan	Eastern	Knoxville
Obion	Western	Jackson
Overton	Middle	Cookeville (Nashville)
Perry	Western	Jackson
Pickett	Middle	Cookeville (Nashville)
Polk	Eastern	Chattanooga
Putnam	Middle	Cookeville (Nashville)
Rhea	Eastern	Chattanooga
Roane	Eastern	Knoxville
Robertson	Middle	Nashville
Rutherford	Middle	Nashville
Scott	Eastern	Knoxville
Sequatchie	Eastern	Chattanooga
Sevier	Eastern	Knoxville
Shelby	Western	Memphis
Smith	Middle	Cookeville (Nashville)
Stewart	Middle	Nashville
Sullivan	Eastern	Greeneville
Sumner	Middle	Nashville
Tipton	Western	Memphis
Trousdale	Middle	Nashville
Unicoi	Eastern	Greeneville
Union	Eastern	Knoxville
Van Buren	Eastern	Winchester (Chattanooga)
Warren	Eastern	Winchester (Chattanooga)
Washington	Eastern	Greeneville
Wayne	Middle	Columbia (Nashville)
Weakley	Western	Jackson
White	Middle	Cookeville (Nashville)
Williamson	Middle	Nashville
Wilson	Middle	Nashville

Standards for Federal Courts: Fees are standard unless noted in profile. Search fee is $26.00 per item (one party name or case number). Copy fee is $.50 per page. Certification fee is $9.00 per document, double for exemplification, if available. Most courts require prepayment. Mail requests should enclose a SASE unless otherwise noted. Before releasing records, all courts require prepayment, unless noted.

District courts index by defendant and plaintiff and by case number. Bankruptcy courts usually index by debtor and case number. While most courts now have their indexes on computer, many may still maintain index card files as well. Courts will archive closed case files at different times.

There are numerous public access programs available to online subscribers. Search the U.S. Party/Case Index to find party names and case numbers among all courts. Individual case data is provided on PACER. A search of CM/ECF provides copies of cases filed electronically. For details about PACER, the US Party/Case Index, and CM/ECF see the Appendix or go to http://pacer.psc.uscourts.gov or call 800-676-6856.

US District Court Tennessee Eastern District

Chattanooga Division Clerk's Office, 900 Georgia Ave, Rm 309, Chattanooga, TN 37402, 423-752-5200; Fax- 423-752-5205. 8AM-4PM. www.tned.uscourts.gov

Counties/Note: Bledsoe, Bradley, Hamilton, McMinn, Marion, Meigs, Polk, Rhea, Sequatchie.

Searches/Indexing: Include first and last name in search request. Results do not include SSN or DOB. Will not fax back documents. New cases are in the index immediately after filing date. Both computer and card indexes maintained; computer goes back to 1992. Closed electronic cases not purged.

Search Access: Only docket info available by phone. **Mail:** Search usually completed- 1-2 days. SASE required. **Fax:** Written fax search and case file requests accepted. **In person:** 2 public terminals available. Use the computer terminal to search cases back to 10/1992. No self-serve copier. Court can recommend a vendor to make copies.

Payment: Pay by money order, cashier's or personal check. No credit cards accepted. Payee: Clerk, US District Court.

E-Services: Access to the district's Web PACER system requires PACER registration and account. PACER records go back to 1994. New records online immediately. ECF at https://ecf.tned.uscourts.gov. **Opinions Online:** www.tned.uscourts.gov/opinions/search.html. Published opinions only. **Online Note:** Court calendars listed by division free at www.tned.uscourts.gov/calendars.php.

Greeneville Division US District Court Clerk, 220 W Depot St, Ste 200, Greeneville, TN 37743, 423-639-3105; Fax- 423-639-7134. Hours-8AM-4PM. www.tned.uscourts.gov

Counties: Carter, Cocke, Greene, Hamblen, Hancock, Hawkins, Johnson, Sullivan, Unicoi, Washington.

Searches/Indexing: Include first and last name in search request. Results do not include SSN or DOB. Will not fax back documents. New cases are in the index immediately after filing date. Both computer and card indexes maintained; criminal index back to 1994, civil to 1992. Closed electronic cases not purged.

Search Access: Only docket info is available by phone. **Mail:** Search usually completed- 1 day. SASE not required. **Fax:** Written fax search and case file requests accepted. **In person:** 2 public terminals available. No self-serve copier.

Payment: Pay by money order, cashier's or personal check. No credit cards accepted. Payee: Clerk, US District Court.

E-Services: Access to the district's Web PACER system requires PACER registration and account. PACER records go back to 1994. New records online immediately. ECF at https://ecf.tned.uscourts.gov. **Opinions Online:** www.tned.uscourts.gov/opinions/search.html. Published opinions only. **Online Note:** Court calendars listed by division free at www.tned.uscourts.gov/calendars.php.

Knoxville Division Clerk's Office, 800 Market St, Ste 130, Knoxville, TN 37902, 865-545-4228; Fax- 865-545-4247. 8AM-4PM. www.tned.uscourts.gov

Counties/Note: Anderson, Blount, Campbell, Claiborne, Grainger, Jefferson, Knox, Loudon, Monroe, Morgan, Roane, Scott, Sevier, Union.

Searches/Indexing: Include first and last name in search request. Results do not include SSN or DOB. Will not fax back documents. New cases are in the index immediately after filing date. Computer civil index goes back to 6/1992, criminal to 1993; index cards prior. Closed electronic cases not purged.

Search Access: Only docket info is available by phone. **Mail:** Search usually completed- 7 days. SASE not required. **Fax:** Written fax search and case file requests accepted. **In person:** 2 public terminals available. Use the computer terminal to search cases back to 10/1992. No self-serve copier.

Payment: Pay by money order, cashier's or personal check. No credit cards accepted. Payee: Clerk, US District Court.

E-Services: Access to the district's Web PACER system requires PACER registration and account. PACER records go back to 1994. New records online immediately. ECF at https://ecf.tned.uscourts.gov. **Opinions Online:** www.tned.uscourts.gov/opinions/search.html. Published opinions only. **Online Note:** Court calendars listed by division free at www.tned.uscourts.gov/calendars.php.

Winchester Division Court Clerk, 200 S Jefferson St, Rm 201, Winchester, TN 37397, 931-967-1444; Fax- 931-967-9693. Hours- 8AM-12, 1-4PM. www.tned.uscourts.gov

Counties: Bedford, Coffee, Franklin, Grundy, Lincoln, Moore, Van Buren, Warren.

Searches/Indexing: Include first and last name in search request. Results do not include SSN or DOB. Will not fax back documents. New cases are in the index immediately after filing date. Office began maintaining records in 1997. Computer index goes back to 1992. Closed electronic cases not purged.

Search Access: Only docket info available by phone. **Mail:** Search usually completed- 1 day. SASE required. **Fax:** Written fax search and case file requests accepted. **In person:** 2 public terminals available. Use the computer terminal to search cases back to 10/1992. No self-serve copier.

Payment: Pay by money order, cashier's or personal check. No credit cards accepted. Payee: Clerk, US District Court.

E-Services: Access to the district's Web PACER system requires PACER registration and account. PACER records go back to 1994. New records online immediately. ECF at https://ecf.tned.uscourts.gov. **Opinions Online:** www.tned.uscourts.gov/opinions/search.html. Published opinions only. **Online Note:** Court calendars listed by division free at www.tned.uscourts.gov/calendars.php.

US Bankruptcy Court Tennessee Eastern District

Northeastern Division Court Clerk, 220 W Depot St #218, Greenville, TN 37743, 423-787-0113; Fax- 423-787-0714. Hours-8AM-4:30PM. www.tneb.uscourts.gov

Counties: Carter, Cocke, Greene, Hamblen, Hancock, Hawkins, Johnson, Sullivan, Unicoi, Washington.

Searches/Indexing: To obtain positive ID, include SSN or address in search request. Results include last 4 SSN digits only. Will fax back documents for fee. New cases are in the index immediately after filing date. Both computer and card indexes maintained. District-wide searches available here for limited information back to 1/86. Closed records sent to archives 2-3 years after closing.

Search Access: Voice Case Information Service available, call VCIS at 800-767-1512. **Mail:** Search usually completed- 1-2 days. Include SASE for return. **In person:** 1 public terminal available. No self-serve copier.

Payment: Pay by money order, cashier's check. No credit cards except attorneys' cards online. Payee: Clerk, US Bankruptcy Court.

E-Services: PACER records go back to 1/1986. New records online after immediately upon docketing. ECF at https://ecf.tneb.uscourts.gov. **Opinions Online:** www.tneb.uscourts.gov/php/judge-opin-select.php. Search opinions by selecting judge or court location. Opinions after 6/12/06 also on PACER.

Northern Division Court Clerk, 800 Market St, #330, Howard H Baker Jr US Courthouse, Knoxville, TN 37902, 865-545-4279; Hours-8AM-4:30PM. www.tneb.uscourts.gov

Counties/Note: Anderson, Blount, Campbell, Claiborne, Grainger, Jefferson, Knox, Loudon, Monroe, Morgan, Roane, Scott, Sevier, Union.

Searches/Indexing: To obtain positive ID, include SSN or address in search request. Results include last 4 SSN digits only. Will fax back documents for fee. New cases are in the index immediately after filing date. Both computer and card indexes maintained. District-wide searches available here for limited information back to 1/86. Case files sent to archives 2 years after closed. Electronic cases maintained indefinitely since 2004.

Search Access: By phone, court only confirms debtor name, SSN, address, attorney, trustee, chapter filed, date of filing, date of discharge/dismissal, date case closed, in addition to limited data regarding motions, hearings, etc. Voice Case Information Service available, call VCIS at 800-767-1512. **Mail:** Search usually completed- 1-2 days. Include SASE for return. **In person:** 3 public terminals available. Copies from computer terminal $.10 each.

Payment: Pay by money order, cashier's check. No credit cards accepted, except attorneys' cards online. Payee: Clerk, US Bankruptcy Court.

E-Services: PACER records go back to 1/1986. New records online after immediately upon docketing. ECF at https://ecf.tneb.uscourts.gov. **Opinions Online:** www.tneb.uscourts.gov/php/judge-opin-select.php. Search opinions by selecting judge or court location. Opinions after 6/12/06 also on PACER.

Southern Division Court Clerk, 31 E 11th St, Historic US Courthouse, Chattanooga, TN 37402, 423-752-5163. Hours-8AM-4:30PM. www.tneb.uscourts.gov

Counties/Note: Bedford*, Bledsoe, Bradley, Coffee*, Franklin*, Grundy*, Hamilton, Lincoln*, Marion, McMinn, Meigs, Moore*, Polk, Rhea, Sequatchie, Van Buren*, Warren*. This Chattanooga court also holds records for the Winchester Division, 200 South Jefferson St Rm 305, Winchester, 423-752-5163. Winchester Division counties are marked with an asterisk (*).

Searches/Indexing: To obtain positive ID, include SSN or address in search request. Results include last 4 SSN digits only. Will fax back documents for fee. New cases are in the index immediately after filing date. Case files sent to archives 2 years after closed.

Search Access: Court will confirm bankruptcy filings via phone and only honor up to 3 requests per phone call per day. Voice Case Information Service available, call VCIS at 800-767-1512 or 423-752-5272. **Mail:** Search usually completed- 24 hours. SASE not required. **In person:** 2 public terminals available. No self-serve copier.

Payment: Pay by money order, cashier's check, business check. No credit cards except attorneys' cards online. Payee: US Bankruptcy Court.

E-Services: PACER records go back to 1/1986. New records online after immediately upon docketing. ECF at https://ecf.tneb.uscourts.gov. **Opinions Online:** www.tneb.uscourts.gov/php/judge-opin-select.php. Search opinions by selecting judge or court location. Opinions after 6/12/06 also on PACER.

US District Court Tennessee Middle District

Columbia Division c/o Nashville Division, 800 US Courthouse, 801 Broadway, Nashville, TN 37203, 615-736-5498; records- x209; Fax- 615-736-7488. Hours- 8AM - 5PM. www.tnmd.uscourts.gov

Counties: Giles, Hickman, Lawrence, Lewis, Marshall, Maury, Wayne.

Searches/Indexing: Include name and style of case in search request. Results do not include SSN or DOB. Will fax back documents for fee. New cases are in the index immediately after filing date. Computer index goes back to 1991. Case files sent to archives 1 year after closed.

Search Access: **Mail:** Provide a self-addressed, postage-paid envelope or container and account number for express return. SASE not required. **Fax:** Written fax search requests accepted, prepaid. **In person:** 1 public terminal available. No self-serve copier.

Payment: Pay by money order, cashier's or personal check. No credit cards. Payee: Clerk, US District Court.

E-Services: PACER records go back 3 years. New records online after 1 day. ECF at https://ecf.tnmd.uscourts.gov. Opinions and dockets available on ECF; registration required. **Online Note:** Email copy requests to copyrequest@tnmd.uscourts.gov.

Cookeville Division c/o Nashville Division, 800 US Courthouse, 801 Broadway, Nashville, TN 37203, 615-736-5498; Fax- 615-736-7488. Hours-8AM-5PM. www.tnmd.uscourts.gov

Counties: Clay, Cumberland, De Kalb, Fentress, Jackson, Macon, Overton, Pickett, Putnam, Smith, White.

Searches/Indexing: Include name and style of case in search request. Results do not include SSN or DOB. Will fax back documents for fee. New cases are in the index immediately after filing date. Computer index- civil back to 1991, criminal to 1993. Records also indexed on microfiche. Case files sent to archives 1 year after closed.

Search Access: Only docket info is available by phone. **Mail:** Search usually completed- 3 days. Provide a self-addressed, postage-paid envelope or container and account number for express return. Include SASE for return. **Fax:** Written fax search requests accepted, prepaid. **In person:** 1 public terminal available. No self-serve copier.

Payment: Pay by money order, cashier's, business or personal check. No credit cards. Payee: Clerk, US District Court.

E-Services: PACER records go back 3 years. New records online after 1 day. ECF at https://ecf.tnmd.uscourts.gov. Opinions and dockets available on ECF; registration required. **Online Note:** Email copy requests to copyrequest@tnmd.uscourts.gov.

Nashville Division Court Clerk, 800 US Courthouse, 801 Broadway, Nashville, TN 37203, 615-736-5498; records- 615-736-5498; crim dockets- 615-736-7396; civil dockets- 615-736-7178; Fax- 615-736-7488. Hours-8AM-5PM. www.tnmd.uscourts.gov

Counties: Cannon, Cheatham, Davidson, Dickson, Houston, Humphreys, Montgomery, Robertson, Rutherford, Stewart, Sumner, Trousdale, Williamson, Wilson.

Searches/Indexing: Include name and style of case in search request. Results do not include SSN or DOB. Will fax back documents for fee. New cases are in the index immediately after filing date. Computer index back to 1991 maintained; also on microfiche. Closed files sent to archives after 1 year.

Search Access: Only docket info is available by phone. **Mail:** Search usually completed- 2-3 days. Provide a self-addressed, postage-paid envelope or container and account number for express return. SASE not required. **Fax:** Written fax search requests accepted, prepaid. **In person:** 2 public terminals available. No self-serve copier.

Payment: Pay by money order, cashier's or personal check. No credit cards. Payee: Clerk, US District Court.

E-Services: PACER records go back 3 years. New records online after 1 day. ECF at https://ecf.tnmd.uscourts.gov. Opinions and dockets available on ECF; registration required. **Online Note:** Email copy requests to copyrequest@tnmd.uscourts.gov.

US Bankruptcy Court Tennessee Middle District

Nashville Division Court Clerk, PO Box 24890, Nashville, TN 37202-4890 (In person: Customs House, Rm 160, 701 Broadway, Nashville), 615-736-5584; records- 615-695-4980; Hours-8AM-4PM. http://www2.tnmb.uscourts.gov

Counties/Note: Cannon, Cheatham, Clay, Cumberland, Davidson, De Kalb, Dickson, Fentress, Giles, Hickman, Houston, Humphreys, Jackson, Lawrence, Lewis, Macon, Marshall, Maury, Montgomery, Overton, Pickett, Putnam, Robertson, Rutherford, Smith, Stewart, Sumner, Trousdale, Wayne, White, Williamson, Wilson. Nashville holds records for the Columbia and Cookeville Divisions.

Searches/Indexing: Search request requires name only. Results include last 4 SSN digits. Will not fax back documents. New cases are in the index 24 hours after filing date. Both computer and card indexes maintained. Forms are available to request access to files. Closed case files sent to archives at variable intervals.

Search Access: Only docket info is available by phone. Voice Case Information Service available, call VCIS at 615-736-5584 x4. **Mail:** Search usually completed- 24-48 hours. Include SASE for return. **In person:** 2 public terminals available. No self-serve copier.

Payment: Pay by money order, cashier's check, business check. No credit cards or personal checks accepted. Payee: Clerk, US Bankruptcy Court.

E-Services: PACER records go back to 9/1989. New records online immediately. ECF at https://ecf.tnmb.uscourts.gov. **Opinions Online:** http://www2.tnmb.uscourts.gov/modules/opinions/search.php. **Online Note:** A court docket query is free at http://www2.tnmb.uscourts.gov; click on Calendars and then Docket Calendars.

US District Court Tennessee Western District

Jackson Division Court Clerk, US Courthouse 262, 111 S Highland Ave, Jackson, TN 38301, 731-421-9200; Fax- 731-421-9210. Hours-8:30AM-4:30PM. www.tnwd.uscourts.gov

Counties/Note: Benton, Carroll, Chester, Crockett, Decatur, Gibson, Hardeman, Hardin, Haywood, Henderson, Henry, Lake, McNairy, Madison, Obion, Perry, Weakley.

Searches/Indexing: Only full name is required; other identifiers helpful. Results do not include SSN or DOB. Will not fax back documents. New cases are in the index 1-2 days after filing date.

Search Access: Only docket info is available by phone. **Mail:** Search usually completed- 1-2 days. Include SASE for return. **Fax:** Fax search requests accepted. **In person:** 2 public terminals available. No self-serve copier.

Payment: Pay by Visa/MC, money order, cashier's or personal check. Payee: Clerk, US District Court.

E-Services: Document images available. PACER records go back to 1993. New records online after 1 day. ECF at https://ecf.tnwd.uscourts.gov. Opinions on ECF System. **Online Note:** Search Grand Jury criminal filings free at www.tnwd.uscourts.gov/grandjury-returns.php. Monthly court calendars free at www.tnwd.uscourts.gov/calendars/default.htm.

Memphis Division Court Clerk, Federal Bldg, Rm 242, 167 N Main St, Memphis, TN 38103, 901-495-1200; records- 901-495-1221/1222; Fax- 901-495-1206. Hours- 8:30AM-4:30PM. www.tnwd.uscourts.gov

Counties: Dyer, Fayette, Lauderdale, Shelby, Tipton.

Searches/Indexing: Only full name is required; other identifiers helpful. Results do not include SSN or DOB. Will not fax back documents. New cases are in the index 1-2 days after filing date. Computer index back to 1992 maintained.

Search Access: Only docket info is available by phone. **Mail:** Search usually completed- 1-2 days. Include SASE for return. **Fax:** Fax search requests accepted with credit card. **In person:** 3 public terminals available. No self-serve copier.

Payment: Pay by Visa/MC, money order, cashier's or personal check. Payee: Clerk, US District Court.

E-Services: Document images available. PACER records go back to 1993. New records online after 1 day. ECF at https://ecf.tnwd.uscourts.gov. Opinions on ECF System. **Online Note:** Search Grand Jury criminal filings free at www.tnwd.uscourts.gov/grandjury-returns.php. Monthly court calendars free at www.tnwd.uscourts.gov/calendars/default.htm.

US Bankruptcy Court Tennessee Western District

Jackson - Eastern Division Court Clerk, 111 S Highland Ave, Rm 107, Jackson, TN 38301, 731-421-9300; Hours- 8:30AM - 4:30PM. www.tnwb.uscourts.gov

Counties/Note: Benton, Carroll, Chester, Crockett, Decatur, Gibson, Hardeman, Hardin, Haywood, Henderson, Henry, Lake, Madison, McNairy, Obion, Perry, Weakley.

Searches/Indexing: Include debtor name in search request. Results include last 4 SSN digits only. Will not fax back documents. New cases are in the index immediately after filing date. Case files sent to archives 3-6 months after closed.

Search Access: Only docket info is available by phone. Voice Case Information Service available, call VCIS at 888-381-4961. **Mail:** Search usually completed- 1-3 days. SASE not required. **In person:** 2 public terminals available. No self-serve copier.

Payment: Pay by money order, cashier's check, business check. No personal checks or credit cards. Payee: US Bankruptcy Court. A search fee is charged only when certification of the search is issued.

E-Svcs: PACER- http://pacer.tnwb.uscourts.gov. PACER records go back to 1989. New records online after one day. ECF at https://ecf.tnwb.uscourts.gov. **Opinions Online:** www.tnwb.uscourts.gov/Opinions/opinion.asp. **Online Note:** Calendars at www.tnwb.uscourts.gov/vcal/Calendar.asp. Also, case closings located at www.tnwb.uscourts.gov/Web/bankruptcy/CaseInfo/CaseInfo.asp.

Memphis - Western Division Court Clerk, 200 Jefferson Ave, Suite 413, Memphis, TN 38103, 901-328-3500; Fax- 901-328-3500. Hours-8:30AM-4:30PM. www.tnwb.uscourts.gov

Counties: Dyer, Fayette, Lauderdale, Shelby, Tipton.

Searches/Indexing: Include debtor name in search request. Results include last 4 SSN digits only. Will not fax back documents. New cases are in the index immediately after filing date. Case files sent to archives 3-6 months after closed.

Search Access: Only docket info is available by phone. Voice Case Information Service available, call VCIS at 888-381-4961. **Mail:** Search usually completed- 1-3 days. SASE not required. **In person:** 2 public terminals available. No self-serve copier.

Payment: Pay by money order, cashier's check, business check. No personal checks or credit cards. Payee: Clerk, US Bankruptcy Court.

E-Svcs: PACER- http://pacer.tnwb.uscourts.gov. PACER records go back to 1989. New records online after one day. ECF at https://ecf.tnwb.uscourts.gov. **Opinions Online:** www.tnwb.uscourts.gov/Opinions/opinion.asp. **Online Note:** Calendars at www.tnwb.uscourts.gov/vcal/Calendar.asp. Also, case closings located at www.tnwb.uscourts.gov/Web/bankruptcy/CaseInfo/CaseInfo.asp.

Tennessee County Courts

Court	Jurisdiction	No. of Courts	How Organized
Circuit Courts*	General	15	31 Districts
Chancery Courts*	General	87	31 Districts
General Sessions Courts*	Limited	16	By County
Criminal Courts*	General	13	By County
Combined Circuit/ General Sessions*		87	By County
Municipal Courts	Municipal	300	
Probate/County Courts*	Probate	25	By County
Juvenile Courts	Special	17	By County

* Profiled in this Sourcebook.

Court	CIVIL								
	Tort	Contract	Real Estate	Min. Claim	Max. Claim	Small Claims	Estate	Eviction	Domestic Relations
Circuit Courts*	X	X	X	$0	No Max				X
Chancery Court*	X	X	X	$0	No Max		X		X
General Sessions*	X	X	X	$0	$15,000-$25,000	$25,000	X	X	
Municipal Courts									
Probate/County Courts*							X		
Juvenile Courts									X

Court	CRIMINAL				
	Felony	Misdemeanor	DWI/DUI	Preliminary Hearing	Juvenile
Circuit Courts*	X	X	X		
Criminal Courts*	X	X	X		
Chancery Court*					
General Sessions *		X	X	X	X
Municipal Courts		X	X		
Juvenile Courts					X

Administration

Administrative Office of the Courts, 511 Union St (Nashville City Center) #600, Nashville, TN, 37219; 615-741-2687, Fax: 615-741-6285. www.tncourts.gov

Court Structure

Circuit Courts hear civil and criminal cases and appeals of decisions from City, Juvenile, Municipal and General Sessions courts. The jurisdiction of Circuit Courts often overlaps that of the Chancery Courts. Criminal cases are tried in Circuit Court except in districts with separate Criminal Courts established by the General Assembly. Criminal Courts relieve Circuit Courts in areas where they are justified by heavy caseloads. Criminal Courts exist in 13 of the State's 31 judicial districts. The Chancery Courts, in addition to handling probate, also hear certain types of equitable civil cases. Combining of Circuit Court and General Sessions Courts varies by county.

Online Access

Appellate Court opinions are found at www.tsc.state.tn.us/geninfo/Courts/AppellateCourts.htm. Several counties offer online access to court records, but there is no statewide access system.

Searching Tips, Fees, and Other Guidelines

Fees vary widely. Over 2/3's of the general jurisdiction courts offer public access terminals to view docket indices.

Anderson County

7th District Circuit & General Sessions Court 100 N Main St, Rm 301, Clinton, TN 37716; 865-457-5400; criminal phone: 865-463-6822; civil phone: 865-463-6821; fax: 865-259-2345; 8AM-4:30PM (EST). ***Felony, Misdemeanor, Civil, Eviction, Small Claims.***

Civil Records: Access: In person only. Visitors must perform in person searches themselves. Required to search: name, years to search. Civil cases indexed by defendant, plaintiff; index on computer from 1988, archived from 1947. Civil PAT goes back to 1992. PAT civil results show middle initial.

Criminal Records: Access: In person only. Visitors must perform in person searches themselves. Required to search: name, years to search, DOB, SSN. Criminal records computerized from 1988, archived from 1947. Criminal PAT goes back to 1988. PAT results show middle initial, DOB.

General Information: No juvenile records released. Will not fax out case files. Court makes copy: $.50 per page. Self serve: $.25 per page. Certification fee: $5.00 per cert. Payee: Circuit Court Clerk or General Sessions Clerk. Personal checks accepted. Visa, M/C, AMEX accepted by phone to 1-866-347-1902 or online only. Prepayment required.

Chancery Court Anderson County Courthouse, PO Box 501, Clinton, TN 37717; 865-457-5400; probate phone: 865-457-6207; fax: 865-457-6267; 8:30AM-4:30PM (EST). ***Civil, Probate.***

Civil Records: Access: Phone, mail, in person. Visitors must perform in person searches themselves. No search fee. Required to search: name, years to search. Civil cases indexed by defendant, plaintiff; index on computer 1992 to present, prior records on another system.

General Information: No adoption or mental health records released. Will not fax documents. Court makes copy: $.50 per page. Self serve: $.25 per page. Certification fee: $5.00 per cert. Payee: Clerk and Master. Personal checks accepted; credit cards are not. Prepayment required.

Bedford County

17th Dist. Circuit & General Sessions 1 Public Sq, #200, Shelbyville, TN 37160; 931-684-3223; fax: 931-684-4141; 8AM-4PM (CST). ***Felony, Misdemeanor, Civil, Eviction, Small Claims.***

Civil Records: Access: Fax, in person. Both court and visitors may perform in person searches. Search fee: $5.00 per name. Required to search: name, years to search. Civil cases indexed by defendant, plaintiff; index on archives and books from 1934; computerized records since 1994. Civil PAT goes back to 10 years. PAT results show middle initial, DOB, SSN.

Criminal Records: Access: Fax, in person. Both court and visitors may perform in person searches. Search fee: $5.00 per name. Required to search: name, years to search, DOB; SSN helpful. Criminal records on archives and books from 1934; computerized records since 1994. Criminal PAT goes back to 10 years. PAT results show middle initial, DOB, SSN.

General Information: No juvenile, adoptions, mental health, expunged or sealed records released. Court makes copy: $1.00 per page. Self serve: same. Certification fee: $2.00 per cert. Payee: Thomas Smith, Clerk. No personal checks or credit cards accepted. Prepayment required.

Chancery Court Chancery Court, 1 Public Sq, #302, Shelbyville, TN 37160; 931-684-1672; fax: 931-680-0144; 8-4PM (CST). ***Civil, Probate.***

Civil Records: Access: In person only. Visitors must perform in person searches themselves. Required to search: name, years to search. Civil cases indexed by defendant, plaintiff; index on books from 9/82 (probate), prior records back to 1800s filed in county clerk's office.

General Information: No adoption records released. Will not fax documents. Court makes copy: $.50 per page. Certification fee: $5.00 per cert. Payee: Clerk and Master. Personal checks accepted; credit cards are not. Prepayment required.

Benton County

24th District Circuit 1 E Court Sq, Rm 207, Camden, TN 38320; 731-584-6711; fax: 731-584-2081; 8AM-4PM M-TH; 8AM-5PM F (CST). ***Felony, Misdemeanor, Civil, Eviction, Small Claims.*** Sessions court is in room 210. Records room number is 731-584-6165.

Civil Records: Access: In person only. Both court and visitors may perform in person searches. No search fee. Required to search: name, years to search. Civil cases indexed by defendant, plaintiff. Civil records computerized since 1995. Public can only use docket books to search, older records archived to 1800s. Civil PAT goes back to 1996.

Criminal Records: Access: In person only. Both court and visitors may perform in person searches. No search fee. Required to search: name, years to search. Criminal records computerized since 1995. Public can only use docket books to search, older records archived to 1800s. Criminal PAT goes back to 1996.

General Information: No juvenile records released without judge approval. Will not fax documents. Court makes copy: $1.00 per page. Certification fee: $5.00 per cert. Payee: Circuit Court Clerk or General Session. Business checks accepted. No credit cards accepted. Prepayment required.

Chancery Court 1 E Court Sq, Courthouse Rm 206, Camden, TN 38320; 731-584-4435; fax: 731-584-1407; 8AM-4PM M-TH; 8AM-5PM F (CST). ***Civil, Probate.***

Civil Records: Access: In person only. Only the court performs in person searches; visitors may not. Required to search: name, years to search. Civil cases indexed by defendant, plaintiff; index on computer back to 1994; in books since 1880. Public use terminal has civil records back to 1996.

General Information: No adoption or sealed records released. Will fax documents to local or toll-free number. Court makes copy: $.50 per page. Certification fee: $5.00 per cert. Payee: Clerk & Master. Personal checks accepted; credit cards are not.

Bledsoe County

12th Dist. Circuit & General Sessions Court PO Box 455, Pikeville, TN 37367; 423-447-6488; fax: 423-447-2534; 8AM-4PM (CST). ***Felony, Misdemeanor, Civil, Eviction, Small Claims.***

Civil Records: Access: In person only. Visitors must perform in person searches themselves. Required to search: name, years to search. Civil cases indexed by plaintiff. Civil records archived from 1920 in books. Note: Books available for public to search.

Criminal Records: Access: In person only. Visitors must perform in person searches themselves. Required to search: name, years to search, DOB. Criminal records archived from 1920 in books. Note: Books available for public to search.

General Information: No juvenile records released. Will not fax documents. Court makes copy: $.50 per page. Self serve: same. Certification fee: $5.00. Payee: Circuit Court. Checks and money orders accepted. No credit cards. Prepayment required.

Chancery Court PO Box 389, Pikeville, TN 37367; 423-447-2484; 8AM-4PM M,T,W,F; 8AM-N TH (CST). ***Civil, Probate.***

Civil Records: Access: Phone, mail, in person. Both court and visitors may perform in person searches. No search fee. Required to search: name, years to search. Civil cases indexed by defendant, plaintiff; index on books since 1856. Mail turnaround 3 days.

General Information: No juvenile or adoption records released. Will fax documents $2.00 per page. Court makes copy: $.50 per page. Self serve: $.25 per page. Certification fee: $5.00 per cert. Payee: Bledsoe County Clerk and Master. Personal checks accepted; credit cards are not. Prepayment required.

Blount County

5th District General Sessions Court 926 E Lamar Alexander Pky, Maryville, TN 37804-6201; 865-273-5450; crimina/civil phone: 865-273-5400; fax: 865-273-5411; 8AM-4:30PM (EST). ***Misdemeanor, Civil, Eviction, Small Claims.*** www.blountccc.com/generalsessions.aspx

Civil Records: Access: Mail, in person. Both court and visitors may perform in person searches. Search fee: $15.00 per name. Required to search: name, years to search, identifiers. Civil cases indexed by defendant, plaintiff. Civil records in books back to 1991; on computer back to 1997, prior archived not on site. Mail turnaround time 6-10 days. Civil PAT goes back to 1997; results show middle initial.

Criminal Records: Access: Mail, in person. Both court and visitors may perform in person searches. Search fee: $15.00 per name. Required to search: name, years to search, identifiers. Criminal records in books back to 1991; on computer back to 1997, prior archived not on site. Mail turnaround time 6-10 days. Criminal PAT goes back to 1997. PAT criminal results show middle initial.

General Information: No juvenile records released. Will fax documents. Court makes copy: $.50 per page. Self serve: same. Certification fee: $5.00 per document. Payee: Circuit Court Clerk or General Session. Business checks accepted. Credit cards accepted for orders via the internet and at window (no Visa credit cards in person). Prepayment required. Mail requests: SASE required.

Circuit Court 926 E Lamar Alexander Pky, 1st Fl, Maryville, TN 37804; 865-273-5400; probate phone: 865-273-5800; fax: 865-273-5411; 8AM-4:30PM (EST). ***Felony, Misdemeanor, Civil.*** www.blountccc.com/circuitcourt.aspx

Civil Records: Access: Mail, in person. Both court and visitors may perform in person searches. Search fee: $15.00 per name. Required to search: name, years to search, identifiers. Civil cases indexed by defendant. Civil records on books. Civil PAT goes back to 8 years.

Criminal Records: Access: Mail, in person. Visitors must perform in person searches themselves. Search fee: $15.00 per name. Required to search: name, years to search, identifiers. Criminal docket on books. Criminal PAT goes back to 10 years. PAT criminal results show middle initial. Online results show middle initial.

General Information: No juvenile records released. Will fax documents $.50 per page. Court makes copy: $.50 per page. Self serve: same. Certification fee: $5.00 per cert. Payee: Circuit Court Clerk. Only cashiers checks and money orders accepted. Major credit cards accepted. Prepayment required. Mail requests: SASE required.

County Clerk 345 Court St, Old Courthouse, Maryville, TN 37804; 865-273-5800; fax: 865-273-5815; 8AM-4:30PM (EST). ***Probate.***

Bradley County

10th Dist. Circuit & General Sessions Court - Civil Courthouse, Rm 205, 155 N Ocoee St, Cleveland, TN 37311-5068; 423-728-7220; fax: 423-476-0488; 8:30AM-4:30PM M-TH, 8:30AM-5PM Fri (EST). ***Civil, Eviction, Small Claims.***

Civil Records: Access: Mail, in person. Both court and visitors may perform in person searches. Search fee: $25.00 per name. Required to search: name, years to search. Civil cases indexed by defendant, plaintiff. Civil records archived from 1990, on computer from 1990. Mail turnaround time 10 days. Public use terminal has civil records back to 1990. PAT results show middle initial, DOB.

General Information: No juvenile records released. Fee to fax out file $1.00 per page. Court makes copy: $.50 per page. Self serve: $.50 per page. Certification fee: $10.00 per cert. Payee: Circuit Court Clerk or General Session. Personal checks accepted; credit cards are not. Prepayment required. Mail requests: SASE required.

10th District Circuit & General Sessions Court - Criminal 2230 Blythe Ave, County Justice Center, Cleveland, TN; 423-728-7057 circuit; 423-728-7053 Sessions; fax: 423-476-0487; 8:30AM-4:30PM M-TH, 8:30AM-5PM F (EST). ***Felony, Misdemeanor.*** Civil is at old courthouse as of May, 2004, see separate listing.

Criminal Records: Access: Mail, in person. Both court and visitors may perform in person searches. Search fee: $25.00 per name; $5.00 for basic background check for record. Required to search:

name, years to search, signed release. Criminal records archived from 1990, on computer from 1990. Mail turnaround time 10 days. Public use terminal has crim records back to 1998 (10 years). PAT results show middle initial, DOB.
General Information: No juvenile records released. Fee to fax out file $1.00 per page. Court makes copy: $.50 per page. Certification fee: $10.00 per page. Payee: Circuit Court Clerk or General Session. No personal checks accepted. No credit or debit cards accepted. Prepayment required.

Chancery Court 155 N Ocoee St, Rm 203, Cleveland, TN 37311; 423-728-7205; probate phone: 423-728-7208; fax: 423-339-0723; 8:30AM-4:30PM M-TH, 8:30AM-5PM F (EST). ***Civil, Probate.***
Civil Records: Access: Phone, in person. Only the court performs in person searches; visitors may not. No search fee. Required to search: name, years to search. Civil cases indexed by defendant, plaintiff. Civil records filed in books back to 1861, on computer back to 2003.
General Information: No adoption records released. Will fax documents $1.00 per page. Court makes copy: $.50 per page. Certification fee: $5.00 per cert. Payee: Clerk and Master. Personal checks accepted; credit cards are not. Prepayment required.

Campbell County

8th District Circuit & General Sessions Court PO Box 26, 570 Main St, Jacksboro, TN 37757; 423-562-2624; fax: 423-563-0342; 8AM-4:30PM (EST). ***Felony, Misdemeanor, Civil, Eviction, Small Claims.***
Civil Records: Access: Mail, in person. Only the court performs in person searches; visitors may not. No search fee. Required to search: name, years to search. Civil cases indexed by defendant, plaintiff; index on computer since 1991. On microfiche from 1987 and archived since court started located at La Follett Library, La Follett, TN 37766. Mail turnaround time depends on type of search. Civil PAT goes back to 1998.
Criminal Records: Access: Mail, in person. Only the court performs in person searches; visitors may not. No search fee. Required to search: name, years to search, DOB, SSN. Criminal records on computer since 1991. On microfiche from 1987 and archived since court started located at La Follette Library, La Follette, TN 3776. Mail turnaround time depends on type of search. Criminal PAT goes back to 1998.
General Information: No juvenile, adoption and judicial hospitalization records released. Will not fax documents. Court makes copy: $.50 per page. Certification fee: $5.00. Payee: Circuit Court Clerk or General Session. Business checks accepted. Visa/MC accepted. Prepayment required.

Chancery Court PO Box 182 (570 Main St, #110), Jacksboro, TN 37757; 423-562-3496; fax: 423-562-9732; 8-4:30PM (EST). ***Civil, Probate.***
Civil Records: Access: In person, mail. Visitors must perform in person searches themselves. No search fee. Required to search: name, years to search. Civil cases indexed by defendant, plaintiff. Civil records filed in books, microfiche available at LaFollette Library since 1842. Mail turnaround time 1-2 days.
General Information: No adoption records released. Fee to fax document $1.00 1st page, $.50 ea add'l. Court makes copy: $.50 per page. Certification fee: $5.00. Payee: Clerk and Master. Business checks accepted. No credit cards accepted. Prepayment required. Mail requests: SASE preferred.

Cannon County

16th District Circuit & General Sessions Court County Courthouse Public Sq, Woodbury, TN 37190; 615-563-4461; fax: 615-563-6391; 8AM-4PM M,T,TH,F; 8AM-N W (CST). ***Felony, Misdemeanor, Civil, Eviction, Small Claims.***
Civil Records: Access: In person only. Visitors must perform in person searches themselves. Required to search: name, years to search. Civil cases indexed by defendant, plaintiff. Civil records archived on books from 1980s, computerized since 10/2003. Civil PAT goes back to 12/2003. PAT results show name, DOB. Terminal results also show SSNs.
Criminal Records: Access: In person only. Visitors must perform in person searches themselves. Required to search: name, years to search, DOB. Criminal records archived on books from 1980s, computerized since 12/2003. Criminal PAT goes back to same as civil; results show name, DOB.
General Information: No juvenile records released. Court makes copy: $.50 per page. Self serve: same. Certification fee: $5.00. Payee: Circuit Court Clerk or General Session. Personal checks accepted; credit cards are not. Prepayment required.

County Court 1 County Courthouse Public Square, 200 W Main St, Woodbury, TN 37190; 615-563-4278/5936; fax: 615-563-1289; 8AM-4PM M,T,TH,F; 8AM-N Sat (CST). ***Probate.***

Carroll County

24th District Circuit & General Sessions Court 99 Court Sq, #103, Huntingdon, TN 38344; 731-986-1932; criminal phone: 731-986-1927; civil phone: 731-986-1929 (Circuit), 731-986-1926 (Gen Sess); fax: 731-986-1930; 8AM-4PM (CST). ***Felony, Misdemeanor, Civil, Eviction, Small Claims.***
Civil Records: Access: In person only. Only the court performs in person searches; visitors may not. Search fee: $5.00 per name. Required to search: name, years to search. Civil cases indexed by defendant, plaintiff. Civil records archived from 1924; on computer from 1989.
Criminal Records: Access: In person only. Only the court performs in person searches; visitors may not. Search fee: $5.00 per name. Required to search: name, years to search, DOB. Criminal records archived from 1925; on computer from 1989.
General Information: Will not fax out case files. Court makes copy: $.50 per page. No copies by mail. Self serve: same. Certification fee: $5.00 per record. Payee: Circuit Court Clerk or General Session. Only cashiers checks and money orders accepted. No credit cards accepted. Prepayment required.

Chancery Court 99 Court Sq, #105, Huntingdon, TN 38344; 731-986-1920; fax: 731-986-6051; 8AM-4PM (CST). ***Civil, Probate.***
Civil Records: Access: Mail, in person. Both court and visitors may perform in person searches. Search fee: $10.00. Required to search: name, years to search. Civil cases indexed by defendant, plaintiff; index on computer since 6/88, records go back to 1822. Mail turnaround time 5 days.
General Information: No adoption or sealed documents released. Will fax documents $2.00 per page. Court makes copy: $.50 per page. Self serve: same. Certification fee: $5.00 per cert. Payee: Clerk and Master. Checks, money orders and cashiers checks accepted. No credit cards accepted. Mail requests: SASE or $.52 postage required.

Carter County

1st District Circuit & General Sessions Court Carter County Justice Ctr, 900 E Elk Ave, Elizabethton, TN 37643; 423-542-1835; civil phone: 423-542-1825; fax: 423-542-3742; 8AM-4:30PM (EST). ***Felony, Misdemeanor, Civil, Eviction, Small Claims.***
Civil Records: Access: Mail, in person. Visitors must perform in person searches themselves. Search fee: $15.00 per name. Required to search: name, years to search. Civil cases indexed by defendant, plaintiff. Civil records archived from 1800s (partial lost in fire), on computer from 2/92. Civil PAT goes back to 1992.
Criminal Records: Access: Mail, in person. Visitors must perform in person searches themselves. Search fee: $15.00 per name. Required to search: name, years to search. Criminal records archived from 1800s (partial lost in fire), on computer from 4-92. Criminal PAT goes back to 1996. PAT results show middle initial, DOB, SSN. Terminal results include SSN.
General Information: No juvenile, psychiatric or expunged records released. Will not fax documents. Court makes copy: $1.00 per page. Self serve: $1.00 per page. Certification fee: $7.00 per cert. Payee: Circuit Court Clerk or General Session. Personal checks accepted. Visa/MC, Discover accepted.

County Court 801 E Elk Ave., Clerk & Masters Office, Elizabethton, TN 37643; 423-542-1814; fax: 423-547-1502; 8AM-4:30PM (EST). ***Probate.***

Cheatham County

23rd District Circuit Court 100 Public Sq, Rm 225, Ashland City, TN 37015; 615-792-3272; fax: 615-792-3203; 8AM-4PM (CST). ***Felony, Misdemeanor, Civil Actions over $15,000.***
Circuit Court is Rm 225, General Sessions is Rm 223 (615-792-4866); they must be searched separately. Circuit court handles felony, civil actions over $15,000, some misdemeanors; General Sessions handles misdemeanors, small claims, civil under $15,000.
Civil Records: Access: Mail, in person. Both court and visitors may perform in person searches. Search fee: $5.00 per name. Required to search: name, years to search. Civil cases indexed by defendant, plaintiff. Civil records archived on books from 1946 in office, since court started in storage and on computer from 1990. Mail turnaround 2-3 days.
Criminal Records: Access: Mail, in person. Both court and visitors may perform in person searches. Search fee: $5.00 per name. Required to search: name, years to search, and DOB or SSN or Driver's License No. Criminal records archived on books from 1946 in office, since court started in storage and on computer from 1990. Mail turnaround time 2-3 days.
General Information: No juvenile records released. Will not fax documents. Court makes copy: $.50 per page. Certification fee: $5.00. Payee: Circuit Court Clerk. No personal checks or credit cards accepted. Prepayment required. Mail requests: SASE required.

General Sessions 100 Public Sq, Rm 223, Ashland City, TN 37015; 615-792-4866; fax: 615-792-3203; 8AM-4PM (CST). ***Misdemeanor, Civil under $25,000, Eviction, Small Claims.***
Civil Records: Access: Mail, in person. Both court and visitors may perform in person searches. Search fee: $5.00 per name. Required to search: name, years to search. Civil cases indexed by defendant, plaintiff. Civil records archived on books from 1946 in office, since court started in storage and on computer from 1990. Mail turnaround time 2-3 days.
Criminal Records: Access: Mail, in person. Both court and visitors may perform in person searches. Search fee: $5.00 per name. Required to search: name, (DOB, SSN or Drivers License No), and years to search. Criminal records archived on books from 1946 in office, since court started in storage and on computer from 1990. Mail turnaround time 2-3 days.
General Information: No juvenile records released. Will not fax documents. Court makes copy: $.50 per page. Self serve: same. Certification fee: $5.00. Payee: General Sessions Clerk. No personal checks accepted. No credit cards accepted debit cards accepted in-person only. Prepayment required. Mail requests: SASE required.

Chancery Court Clerk & Master, #106, Ashland City, TN 37015; 615-792-4620; fax: 615-792-6059; 8AM-4PM (CST). ***Civil, Probate.***
Civil Records: Access: In person only. Visitors must perform in person searches themselves. Required to search: name, years to search. Civil cases indexed by defendant, plaintiff; index on computer.
General Information: No adoption records released. Will not fax documents. Court makes copy: $.50 per page. Certification fee: $5.00. Payee: Chancery Court. No personal checks accepted. Prepayment required.

Chester County

26th District Circuit & General Sessions Court PO Box 133, Henderson, TN 38340; 731-989-2454; fax: 731-989-9184; 8AM-4PM (CST). ***Felony, Misdemeanor, Civil, Eviction, Small Claims.***
Civil Records: Access: Mail, in person. Both court and visitors may perform in person searches. Search fee: $20.00. Required to search: name, years to search. Civil cases indexed by defendant, plaintiff. Civil records in books and archived from 1892. Mail turnaround time 2 days.
Criminal Records: Access: Mail, in person. Both court and visitors may perform in person searches. Search fee: $20.00 per name. Required to search:

name, years to search, DOB. Criminal records in books and archived from 1892. Mail turnaround time 2 days.
General Information: No juvenile records released. Will not fax documents. Court makes copy: $.50 per page. Certification fee: $5.00. Payee: Circuit Court, or General Sessions Clerk. No personal checks or credit cards accepted. Prepayment required.

Chancery Court Clerk & Master, PO Box 262, Henderson, TN 38340; 731-989-7171; fax: 731-989-7176; 8AM-4PM (CST). ***Civil, Probate.***
Civil Records: Access: Mail, in person. Visitors must perform in person searches themselves. Search fee: $5.00 per name. Required to search: name, years to search. Civil cases indexed by defendant, plaintiff; index on books. Note: Older files are stored off-site. Mail turnaround time 2 days. Public use terminal has civil records back to 10/2003.
General Information: No adoption or sealed records released. Will fax out for fee of $5.00 per certified copy. Court makes copy: $.50 per page. Self serve: $.50 per page. Certification fee: $5.00. Payee: Clerk and Master. Personal checks accepted; credit cards are not. Prepayment required.

Claiborne County

8th District Criminal, Circuit & General Sessions Court 415 Straight Creek Rd, #5, New Tazewell, TN 37825; criminal phone: 423-626-3334; civil phone: 423-626-3334; fax: 423-526-2703; 8:30AM-4:30PM M-TH, 8:30AM-4:30PM F (EST). ***Felony, Misdemeanor, Civil, Eviction, Small Claims.***
Civil Records: Access: Mail, fax, in person. Both court and visitors may perform in person searches. Search fee: $10.00 per name. Required to search: name, years to search. Civil cases indexed by defendant, plaintiff. Civil records archived since 1932; on computer back to 1986. Mail turnaround time 2-3 days. Civil PAT goes back to 1988. PAT civil results show middle initial.
Criminal Records: Access: Mail, fax, in person. Both court and visitors may perform in person searches. Search fee: $10.00 per name. Required to search: name, years to search. Criminal records archived since 1932; on computer back to 1986. Mail turnaround time 2-3 days. Criminal PAT goes back to same as civil.
General Information: No adoption records released. Fee to fax document $.50 per page. Court makes copy: Included in search fee. Self serve: $.50 per page. Certification fee: $5.00. Payee: Circuit Court Clerk or General Sessions. Business checks or in state personal checks accepted. Visa/MC accepted. Prepayment required. Mail requests: SASE required.

Chancery Court PO Box 180, Tazewell, TN 37879; 423-626-3284; fax: 423-626-3604; 8:30AM-N, 1-4PM (EST). ***Civil, Probate.***
Civil Records: Access: Mail, in person. Both court and visitors may perform in person searches. No search fee. Required to search: name, years to search. Civil cases indexed by defendant, plaintiff. Civil records kept on books back to 1932; recent on computer. Mail turnaround time 1-2 days. Public use terminal has civil records back to 1976. PAT results show name only.
General Information: No adoption records released. Will fax documents $.50 per page. Court makes copy: $.50 per page. Certification fee: $5.00 per document; exemplification- $15.00. Payee: Clerk and Master. Personal checks accepted; credit cards are not.

Clay County

13th District Circuit & General Sessions Court PO Box 749, Celina, TN 38551; 931-243-2557; fax: 931-243-2556; 7:30AM-5PM M,T,TH,F; 8AM-N W,Sat (CST). ***Felony, Misdemeanor, Civil, Eviction, Small Claims.***
A local retriever is Jeanie Kirby, 931-858-8786.
Civil Records: Access: In person only. Only the court performs in person searches; visitors may not. Required to search: name, years to search. Civil cases indexed by plaintiff, defendant. Civil records archived from early 1900s, on microfiche from 1986, on computer back to 2000. Note: The court will search the computer back to 2000 for visitors. Civil PAT goes back to 2000. PAT results show name only.
Criminal Records: Access: In person only. Only the court performs in person searches; visitors may not. Required to search: name, years to search. Criminal records archived from early 1900s, on microfiche from 1986, on computer back to 2000. Note: The court will search the computer back to 2000 for visitors. Criminal PAT goes back to 2000. PAT results show name only.
General Information: No juvenile records released. Will fax back $1.00 per page. Court makes copy: $.50 per page. Self serve: same. Certification fee: $5.00. Payee: Circuit Court, or General Sessions Clerk. No personal checks or credit cards accepted. Prepayment required. Mail requests: SASE required for mail return of any copies.

Chancery Court PO Box 332, 100 Courthouse Sq, Celina, TN 38551; 931-243-3145; fax: 931-243-3157; 8AM-4PM M,T,TH,F; 8AM-N Wed (CST). ***Civil, Probate.***
Civil Records: Access: Mail, in person. Both court and visitors may perform in person searches. No search fee. Required to search: name, years to search. Civil cases indexed by defendant, plaintiff; index on books. Mail turnaround time 1 week.
General Information: No juvenile records released. Will not fax documents. Court makes copy: $.50 per page. Certification fee: $5.00 per doc. Payee: Chancery Court Clerk. No credit cards accepted.

Cocke County

4th District Circuit Court 111 Court Ave, Rm 201, Newport, TN 37821; 423-623-6124; fax: 423-625-3889; 8:30AM-5PM (EST). ***Felony, Misdemeanor, Civil Actions over $15,000.***
Civil Records: Access: Mail, in person. Only the court performs in person searches; visitors may not. Search fee: $5.00 per name. Required to search: name, years to search. Civil cases indexed by defendant, plaintiff. Civil records archived from late 1800s. Mail turnaround time ASAP.
Criminal Records: Access: Mail, in person. Only the court performs in person searches; visitors may not. Search fee: $5.00 per name. Required to search: name, years to search, DOB. Criminal records archived from late 1800s. Mail turnaround time ASAP.
General Information: No divorce or sealed records released. Will fax documents to local or toll free line. Court makes copy: $1.00 per page. Certification fee: $5.00. Payee: Circuit Court. Personal checks accepted; credit cards are not. Prepayment required. Mail requests: SASE required.

General Sessions Court 111 Court Ave, Newport, TN 37821; 423-623-8619; fax: 423-623-9808; 8AM-4PM (EST). ***Misdemeanor, Civil Actions under $25,000, Eviction, Small Claims.***
Civil Records: Access: Phone, mail, in person. Both court and visitors may perform in person searches. Search fee: $3.00 per name. Required to search: name, years to search. Civil cases indexed by defendant, plaintiff; index on books at least 10 years. Mail turnaround time varies. Civil PAT goes back to 2000. PAT results show name only.
Criminal Records: Access: Phone, mail, in person. Both court and visitors may perform in person searches. Search fee: $3.00 per name. Required to search: name, years to search. DOB, SSN. Criminal docket on books at least 10 years. Mail turnaround time varies. Criminal PAT goes back to 2001. PAT results show name only.
General Information: Will fax documents, if prepaid. Court makes copy: $.25 per page. Self serve: $3.00 per page. Certification fee: $5.00. Payee: General Sessions Court. Business checks accepted. No credit cards accepted. Prepayment required. Mail requests: SASE required.

Chancery Court Courthouse Annex, 360 E Main St, #103, Newport, TN 37821; 423-623-3321; fax: 423-625-3642; 8AM-4:30PM (EST). ***Civil, Probate.***
Civil Records: Access: Phone, mail, in person. Only the court performs in person searches; visitors may not. No search fee. Required to search: name, years to search. Civil cases indexed by defendant, plaintiff; index on computer since 1984, on books from 1930. Mail turnaround time 1 week.
General Information: No sealed records released. Will fax documents to local or toll free line. Court makes copy: $.50 per page. Self serve: same. Certification fee: $5.00. Payee: Chancery Court, Clerk and Master. Personal checks accepted; credit cards are not. Prepayment required. Mail requests: SASE required.

Coffee County

14th District Circuit & General Sessions Court PO Box 629, 300 Hillsboro Blvd, Manchester, TN 37349; 931-723-5110; fax: 931-723-5116; 8AM-4:30PM (CST). ***Felony, Misdemeanor, Civil, Eviction, Small Claims.***
Civil Records: Access: Mail, in person. Both court and visitors may perform in person searches. Search fee: $5.00 per name per year. Required to search: name, years to search. Civil cases indexed by defendant, plaintiff. Civil records archived from late 1800s, indexed chronologically by court date. Mail turnaround time 1 week. Civil PAT goes back to 1996.
Criminal Records: Access: Mail, in person. Both court and visitors may perform in person searches. Search fee: $5.00 per name per year. Required to search: name, years to search, DOB; also helpful: SSN. Criminal records archived from late 1800s, indexed chronologically by court date. Mail turnaround time 1 week. Criminal PAT goes back to 1995.
General Information: No juvenile record released. Will not fax documents. Court makes copy: $.50 per page. Self serve: none. Certification fee: $3.50 per doc. Payee: General Sessions Clerk. Local personal checks accepted. Major credit cards accepted 4% usage fee charged. Mail requests: SASE required.

Chancery Court 300 Hillsboro Blvd, Manchester, TN 37355; 931-723-5132; fax: 931-723-5116; 8AM-4:30PM (CST). ***Civil, Probate.***
Civil Records: Access: Mail, in person. Both court and visitors may perform in person searches. No search fee. Required to search: name, years to search. Civil cases indexed by defendant, plaintiff; index on books after 1980, before 1980 filed in County Clerk's Office. Mail turnaround time 1-2 days. Public use terminal has civil records back to 1989.
General Information: No juvenile or adoption records released. Will not fax documents. Court makes copy: $.50 per page. Certification fee: $5.00 per doc. Payee: Chancery Court. Personal checks accepted; credit cards are not. Prepayment required. Mail requests: SASE helpful.

Crockett County

Circuit & General Sessions Court 1 S Bell St, #6, Courthouse, Alamo, TN 38001; 731-696-5462; criminal fax: 731-696-2605; civil fax: same; 8AM-4PM (CST). ***Felony, Misdemeanor, Civil, Eviction, Small Claims.***
Civil Records: Access: Mail, fax, in person. Both court and visitors may perform in person searches. Search fee: $10.00 per name. Required to search: name, years to search. Civil cases indexed by defendant, plaintiff. Civil records archived since court started, records prior to 1986 on docket books. Note: All requests must be in writing. Will only accept fax requests if prepaid. Mail turnaround time 1-2 days. Civil PAT goes back to 1992. PAT results show middle initial, DOB, SSN. Terminal results do not always include address.
Criminal Records: Access: Mail, fax, in person. Both court and visitors may perform in person searches. Search fee: $10.00 per name. Required to search: name, years to search, DOB; also helpful: SSN, sex. Criminal docket on books, on computer from 1993. Note: All requests must be in writing. Will only accept fax requests if prepaid. Mail turnaround time 1-2 days. Criminal PAT goes back to 1991. PAT results show middle initial, DOB. Address may be included in terminal results.
General Information: No adoption or mental records released. Will fax documents if fees prepaid. Court makes copy: $1.00 per page. Self serve: same. Certification fee: $6.00 per cert. Payee: Circuit Court, or General Sessions Clerk. Business checks accepted.

No credit cards accepted. Prepayment required. Mail requests: SASE requested.

Chancery Court 1 S Bell St, #5, Alamo, TN 38001; 731-696-5458; fax: 731-696-3028; 8AM-4PM (CST). ***Civil, Probate.***
Civil Records: Access: Mail, in person. Both court and visitors may perform in person searches. No search fee. Required to search: name, years to search. Civil cases indexed by defendant, plaintiff; index on books back to 1872. Mail turnaround time 1-3 days.
General Information: No adoption records released. Will fax documents $10.00. Court makes copy: $.50 per page. Certification fee: $5.00 per cert, plus $.50 per page. Payee: Chancery Court Clerk. Personal checks accepted; credit cards are not. Prepayment required. Mail requests: SASE required.

Cumberland County

13th District Circuit & General Sessions Court 2 N Main St, #302, Crossville, TN 38555; 931-484-6647; fax: 931-456-5013; 8AM-4PM (CST). ***Felony, Misdemeanor, Civil, Eviction, Small Claims.***
Above phone number is for General Sessions; Circuit can be reached at 931-484-5852.
Civil Records: Access: In person only. Visitors must perform in person searches themselves. Required to search: name, years to search. Civil cases indexed by defendant, plaintiff. Civil records archived on books from 1940s approx.; on computer back to 1996. Civil PAT goes back to 1996, results show name only.
Criminal Records: Access: In person only. Visitors must perform in person searches themselves. Required to search: name, years to search, DOB; SSN helpful. Criminal records archived on books from 1940s approx.; on computer back to 1996. Criminal PAT goes back to same as civil. PAT results show name only.
General Information: No sealed records released. Court makes copy for no fee. No certification fee. Payee: Cumberland County Court. No personal checks or credit cards accepted. Prepayment required.

Chancery Court 2 N Main St, #101, Crossville, TN 38555-4583; 931-484-4731; fax: 931-456-4007; 8AM-4PM (CST). ***Civil, Probate.***
Civil Records: Access: Mail, in person. Only the court performs in person searches; visitors may not. No search fee. Required to search: name, years to search. Civil cases indexed by defendant, plaintiff; index on computer since 1991, on books since 1900s. Mail turnaround time 2 days.
General Information: No juvenile, adoption records released. Will not fax documents. Court makes copy: $.50 per page. Certification fee: $5.00 per doc. Payee: Clerk and Master. Business checks accepted. No credit cards accepted. Prepayment required. Mail requests: SASE requested.

Davidson County

20th District Criminal Court 408 2nd Ave N, #2120, Justice A Birch Bldg, Nashville, TN 37201; 615-862-5601; fax: 615-862-5164; 8AM-4:30PM (CST). ***Felony, Misdemeanor.***
http://ccc.nashville.gov
Criminal Records: Access: Mail, online, in person. Both court and visitors may perform in person searches. Search fee: $20.00 per name. Required to search: name, years to search (if over 10 years old), DOB, also helpful: SSN, race. Mail turnaround time 2-3 days. Public use terminal has crim records back to 1996. Terminals are readily available in the afternoon, usually. Access Davidson County Criminal Court database at http://ccc.nashville.gov/portal/page/portal/ccc/home/.
General Information: No records unauthorized by statutes released. Will not fax documents. Court makes copy: $.50 per page. Certification fee: $6.00 per cert. Payee: Criminal Court Clerk. Personal checks accepted but not for record checks. Only Visa credit cards accepted. Prepayment required. Mail requests: SASE required.

Circuit Court PO Box 196303, One Public Sq, Rm 302 Historic Courthouse, Nashville, TN 37201; 615-862-5181; fax: 615-862-5191; 8AM-4:30PM (CST). ***Civil.*** www.nashville.gov/circuit
Civil Records: Access: Mail, fax, in person, phone, online. Both court and visitors may perform in person searches. No search fee. Required to search: name, years to search. Civil cases indexed by defendant, plaintiff. Domestic records go back to 1947. Civil records archived on books from 1800s, on computer from 1975. Mail turnaround time 2-3 days. Public use terminal has civil records back to 1974. PAT results show name, and addresses appear on search results rarely. Three terminals available. Access filed cases online on CaseLink at www.nashville.gov/circuit/caselink/; $35.00 per month fee required plus username, password. Email Caselink@Nashville.Gov for signup or add'l info. I (Fee is $20 thru 10/31, fee increases 11/1/08) Online results show name only.
General Information: Online identifiers in results same as on public terminal. No juvenile or adoption records released. Will not fax documents. Court makes copy: $.50 per page. Certification fee: $5.00 per doc plus $.50 per page, includes copies. Payee: Circuit Court Clerk. No personal checks or credit cards accepted. Prepayment required.

General Sessions Court 408 2nd Ave N, #2110, PO Box 196304, Nashville, TN 37219-6304; 615-862-5195; fax: 615-862-5924; 8AM-4:30PM (CST). ***Civil Actions under $25,000, Eviction, Small Claims.***
www.nashville.gov/circuit/sessions
There is no "Small Claims" court, these type of cases are handled by the General Sessions Civil Division.
Civil Records: Access: Mail, in person, online. Both court and visitors may perform in person searches. No search fee. Required to search: name, years to search. Records indexed on computer since 1990. Public use terminal has civil records back to 1990. PAT results show name only. Access filed cases online on CaseLink at www.nashville.gov/circuit/caselink/; $20.00 per month fee required, plus username and password. Email Caselink@Nashville.Gov for signup or add'l info. Intended to be free searching, soon.
General Information: Online identifiers in results same as on public terminal. No juvenile records released. Will fax documents for fee. Court makes copy: $.50 per page. Certification fee: $5.50 per page. Payee: General Sessions Court Clerk. No personal checks or credit cards accepted. Prepayment required.

Probate Court 1 Public Sq, Rm 303, Nashville, TN 37201; 615-862-5980; fax: 615-862-5987; 8AM-4:30PM (CST). ***Probate.***
Regular address is; 105 Metro Courthouse; temporarily away. See Circuit or General Sessions Court for web access to filed cases.

De Kalb County

13th District Circuit & General Sessions Court 1 Public Sq, Rm 303, Smithville, TN 37166; 615-597-5711; fax: 615-597-9919; 8AM-4:30PM M-TH; 8AM-5PM F (CST). ***Felony, Misdemeanor, Civil, Eviction, Small Claims.***
Civil Records: Access: Mail, fax, In person. Both court and visitors may perform in person searches. No search fee. Required to search: name, years to search. Civil cases indexed by defendant, plaintiff. Civil records archived in office last 10 years. Prior to 1982, records are not very accurate because of fire. Public use terminal available, records go back to 2000. PAT results show middle initial, DOB.
Criminal Records: Access: Mail, fax, in person. Visitors must perform in person searches themselves. No search fee. Required to search: name, years to search, DOB; SSN helpful. Criminal records archived in office last 10 years. Prior to 1982, records are not very accurate because of fire. Public use terminal available, crim records go back to 2000. PAT results show middle initial, DOB.
General Information: No juvenile records released. Will fax specific case file $1.00 per page. Court makes copy: $.50 per page. Certification fee: $5.00 per cert. Payee: Circuit Court, or General Sessions Clerk. Personal checks accepted; credit cards are not. Prepayment required. Mail requests: SASE required.

Chancery Court 1 Public Square, Rm 302, Smithville, TN 37166; 615-597-4360; fax: 615-597-3441; 8AM-4PM (CST). ***Civil, Probate.***
Civil Records: Access: In person only. Visitors must perform in person searches themselves. Required to search: name, years to search. Civil cases indexed by defendant, plaintiff; index on books, computerized as of 6/00. Public use terminal has civil records back to 6/2000. PAT results show middle initial, DOB.
General Information: No adoption, juvenile records released. Will fax documents $5.00 plus $1.00 per page. Court makes copy: $.50 per page. Self serve: same. Certification fee: $5.00 per cert. Payee: Clerk and Master. Personal checks accepted; credit cards are not. Prepayment required.

Decatur County

24th District Circuit & General Sessions Court PO Box 488, 22 Main St, Decaturville, TN 38329; 731-852-3125; fax: 731-852-4172; 8AM-4PM M,T,TH,F; 8AM-N W,Sat (CST). ***Felony, Misdemeanor, Civil, Eviction, Small Claims.***
Civil Records: Access: In person only. Visitors must perform in person searches themselves. Required to search: name, years to search. Civil cases indexed by defendant, plaintiff. Civil records archived on books from 1927; computerized records since 1996. Civil PAT goes back to 8/1996. PAT results show name, DOB.
Criminal Records: Access: In person only. Visitors must perform in person searches themselves. Required to search: name, years to search, DOB, SSN, signed release. Criminal records archived on books from 1927; computerized records since 1996. Criminal PAT goes back to same as civil.PAT results show name, DOB.
General Information: No adoption records released. Will not fax documents. Court makes copy: $.50 per page. Certification fee: $5.00 per doc. Payee: Circuit Court. Business checks accepted. No credit cards accepted. Prepayment required.

Chancery Court Clerk & Master, Decaturville, TN 38329; 731-852-3422; probate phone: same; fax: 731-852-3422; 9M-4PM M,T,TH,F; 9AM-N Wed (CST). ***Civil, Probate.***
www.dcchancery.com/
Civil Records: Access: In person only. Visitors must perform in person searches themselves. Required to search: name, years to search. Civil cases indexed by plaintiff. Probate records in books since 1869 for probate, civil records in books since 1958.
General Information: No adoption records released. Will fax out documents. Court makes copy: $.50 per page. Certification fee: $5.00. Payee: Elizabeth Carpenter, Clerk and Master. Personal checks accepted; credit cards are not. Prepayment required.

Dickson County

23rd District Circuit Court Court Square, PO Box 70, Charlotte, TN 37036; 615-789-7010; fax: 615-789-7018; 8AM-4PM (CST). ***Felony, Misdemeanor, Civil Actions over $25,000.***
Civil Records: Access: Phone, fax, mail, in person. Both court and visitors may perform in person searches. Search fee: $6.00 per name. Required to search: name, years to search. Civil cases indexed by defendant, plaintiff. Civil records archived from 1800s, on computer from 1986, some records back to 1974. Mail turnaround time 1 day.
Criminal Records: Access: Phone, fax, mail, in person. Both court and visitors may perform in person searches. Search fee: $6.00 per name. Required to search: name, years to search; also helpful: DOB. Criminal records archived from 1800s, on computer from 1986, some records back to 1974. Mail turnaround time 1 day.
General Information: No adoption records released. Will fax documents $6.00 plus $.50 per page. Court makes copy: $.50 per page. Self serve: same. Certification fee: $5.00. Payee: Circuit Court Clerk. No personal checks. Major credit cards accepted. Prepayment required. Mail requests: SASE required.

General Sessions PO Box 217, Charlotte, TN 37036; 615-789-5414; fax: 615-789-3456; 8AM-4PM (CST). ***Civil Actions under $25,000, Eviction, Small Claims.***
http://co4.shelbycountytn.gov/court_clerks/gen_sessions_court/civil/sheriff_address.htm
Civil Records: Access: Phone, mail, in person. Both court and visitors may perform in person searches. Search fee: $6.00 per case. Required to search: name, years to search. Civil cases indexed by Defendant, Plaintiff. Civil records archived since court began, on computer from 8/1991. Mail turnaround time 2-3 days. Public use terminal has civil records back to 1991. Public terminal includes Dues.
General Information: No sealed or expunged records released. Will fax documents $4.00 in state or $6.00 out of state fee. Court makes copy: $.50 per page. Self serve: same. Certification fee: $5.00. Payee: General Sessions. No personal checks or credit cards accepted. Prepayment required. Mail requests: SASE required.

County Court Court Square, 4000 Hwy 48 N, #1, Charlotte, TN 37036; 615-789-0250; fax: 615-789-0295; 8AM-4PM (CST). ***Probate.***

Dyer County

29th District Circuit & General Sessions Court
PO Box 1360, 1 Veteran Sq, Courthouse, Dyersburg, TN 38025; 731-286-7809; fax: 731-288-7728; 8:30AM-4:30PM (CST). ***Felony, Misdemeanor, Civil, Eviction, Small Claims.***
Public may search books. Search fee includes both civil and criminal indexes, if asked for.
Civil Records: Access: Mail, fax, in person. Both court and visitors may perform in person searches. Search fee: $25.00 per name. Required to search: name, years to search. Civil cases indexed by defendant, plaintiff. Civil records archived since 1992. Mail turnaround time 2 weeks. Civil PAT goes back to 1992. Terminal results may include DOB, address, and/or SSN.
Criminal Records: Access: Mail, fax, in person. Both court and visitors may perform in person searches. Search fee: $25.00 per name. Required to search: name, years to search, DOB, SSN. Criminal records archived since 1992. Mail turnaround time 2 weeks. Criminal PAT goes back to same as civil. Terminal results may include DOB, address, and/or SSN.
General Information: No juvenile records released. Will fax documents but only if not busy. Court makes copy for no fee. No certification fee. Payee: Circuit Court, or General Sessions Clerk. No personal checks. No credit cards accepted. Prepayment required. Mail requests: SASE required.

Chancery Court PO Box 1360, Dyersburg, TN 38024; 731-286-7818; fax: 731-288-7706; 8:30AM-4:30PM (CST). ***Civil, Probate.***
Civil Records: Access: Mail, in person. Both court and visitors may perform in person searches. No search fee. Required to search: name, years to search. Civil cases indexed by defendant, plaintiff; index on books. Mail turnaround time 1 week. Public use terminal has civil records back to 2001.
General Information: No adoption, juvenile records released. Will fax documents to local or toll-free number. Court makes copy: $.50 per page. Certification fee: $5.50. Payee: Chancery Court Clerk. Personal checks accepted; credit cards are not. Prepayment required. Mail requests: SASE requested.

Fayette County

25th District Circuit & General Sessions Court
PO Box 670, Somerville, TN 38068; 901-465-5205; fax: 901-465-5215; 9AM-5PM (CST). ***Felony, Misdemeanor, Civil, Eviction, Small Claims.***
Civil Records: Access: In person only. Visitors must perform in person searches themselves. Required to search: name, years to search. Civil cases indexed by defendant, plaintiff; index on computer since 1991, prior records archived since court began, some older records destroyed by fire. Civil PAT goes back to 1990. PAT results show middle initial, DOB.
Criminal Records: Access: In person only. Visitors must perform in person searches themselves. Required to search: name, years to search, DOB, SSN. Criminal records on computer since 1991, prior records archived since court began, some older records destroyed by fire. Criminal PAT goes back to same as civil. PAT results show middle initial, DOB.
General Information: No adoption or sealed records released. Court makes copy: $.50 per page. Certification fee: $6.00 per cert. Payee: Circuit Court, or General Sessions Clerk. Personal checks accepted. Major credit cards accepted via phone; only debit cards in person or online. Prepayment required.

Chancery Court PO Drawer 220, Somerville, TN 38068; 901-465-5220; fax: 901-465-5217; 9AM-5PM (CST). ***Civil, Probate.***
Civil Records: Access: In person only. Visitors must perform in person searches themselves. Required to search: name, years to search. Civil cases indexed by defendant, plaintiff; index on computer since 10/92; on books. Public use terminal has civil records back to 1992. PAT civil results show middle initial.
General Information: No adoption records released. Will fax specific case file copies. Court makes copy: $.50 per page. Certification fee: $5.00 per document plus copy fee per page. Payee: Clerk and Master. Personal checks accepted; credit cards are not. Prepayment required.

Fentress County

8th District Circuit & General Sessions Court
PO Box 699, Jamestown, TN 38556; 931-879-7919 Circuit; 931-879-8615 Sessions; fax: 931-879-3014; 8AM-4PM M-F; 8AM-N Sat (CST). ***Felony, Misdemeanor, Civil, Eviction, Small Claims.***
Civil Records: Access: Mail, in person. Both court and visitors may perform in person searches. Search fee: $25.00 per name. Required to search: name, years to search. Civil cases indexed by defendant, plaintiff. Civil records archived from 1800s, readily available for 20 years. Mail turnaround time 5 days.
Criminal Records: Access: Mail, in person, fax. Both court and visitors may perform in person searches. Search fee: $25.00 per name. Required to search: name, years to search, DOB, SSN. Criminal records archived from 1800s, readily available for 20 years. Mail turnaround time 5 days.
General Information: Will not fax documents. Court makes copy: $.50 per page. Certification fee: $20.00 per doc. Payee: Circuit Court Clerk or General Session. Personal checks accepted; credit cards are not. Prepayment required. Mail requests: SASE required.

Chancery Court PO Box 66, Jamestown, TN 38556; 931-879-8615; fax: 931-879-4236; 9AM-5PM M,T,TH,F; 9AM-N Wed (CST). ***Civil, Probate.***
Civil Records: Access: Mail, in person. Both court and visitors may perform in person searches. Search fee: $20.00. Required to search: name, years to search. Civil cases indexed by defendant, plaintiff. Civil records in books. Mail turnaround time 1-5 days.
General Information: No sealed or adoption records released. Will fax documents $1.50 per page. Court makes copy: $.50 per page. Certification fee: $5.00. Payee: Clerk and Master. Personal checks accepted; credit cards are not. Prepayment required.

Franklin County

12th District Circuit Court & General Sessions
101 1st Ave, SW, Winchester, TN 37398; 931-967-2923; criminal fax: 931-962-1479; civil fax: same; 8AM-4:30PM (CST). ***Felony, Misdemeanor, Civil, Eviction, Small Claims.***
The Sessions court clerk now manages Probate records formerly managed by the County Court.
Civil Records: Access: Mail, in person. Both court and visitors may perform in person searches. Search fee: $10.00 per name. Required to search: name, years to search. Civil cases indexed by defendant, plaintiff. Civil records archived on docket books from 1940s, on computer since mid 1991. Mail turnaround time 1 week. Civil PAT goes back to mid-1991.
Criminal Records: Access: Mail, in person. Both court and visitors may perform in person searches. Search fee: $10.00 per name. Required to search: name, years to search, DOB; also helpful: SSN. Criminal records archived on docket books from 1940s, on computer since mid 1991. Mail turnaround time 1 week. Criminal PAT goes back to same as civil. PAT results show middle initial, DOB.
General Information: No juvenile records released. Will fax documents. Court makes copy: $.25 per page. Certification fee: $5.00 per cert includes copy fee. Payee: Circuit Court Clerk or General Session. Business checks accepted. No credit cards accepted. Prepayment required.

County Court 101 1st Ave, SW, Winchester, TN 37398; 931-967-2923. ***Probate.***
Probate Court is now managed by the General Sessions Clerk, address given here.

Gibson County

28th District Circuit & General Sessions Court
295 N College, PO Box 147, Trenton, TN 38382; 731-855-7615; fax: 731-855-7676; 8AM-4:30PM (CST). ***Felony, Misdemeanor, Civil, Eviction, Small Claims.***
Civil Records: Access: Fax, mail, in person. Both court and visitors may perform in person searches. Search fee: $5.00 per name. Required to search: name, years to search; also helpful: address. Civil cases indexed by defendant, plaintiff. Civil records archived in vault mid 1800s, in office since 1982. On computer since 1990. Mail turnaround time 1-3 days. Civil PAT goes back to 1992.
Criminal Records: Access: Fax, mail, in person. Both court and visitors may perform in person searches. Search fee: $5.00 per name. Required to search: name, years to search and either the DOB or the SSN. Criminal records archived in vault mid 1800s, in office since 1982. On computer since 1990. Mail turnaround time 1-3 days. Criminal PAT goes back to 1990. PAT results show middle initial, DOB, SSN.
General Information: No adoption or expunged records released. $5.00 fee to fax back documents. Court makes copy: $.50 per page. Self serve: same. Certification fee: $5.00 per cert. Payee: Circuit Court Clerk. Business checks accepted. In-state checks accepted. No credit cards accepted. Prepayment required. Mail requests: SASE requested.

Chancery Court Clerk & Master, PO Box 290, Trenton, TN 38382; 731-855-7639; fax: 731-855-7655; 8AM-4:30PM (CST). ***Civil, Probate.***
Civil Records: Access: In person only. Both court and visitors may perform in person searches. Search fee: Office will want to know purpose of the search before naming a fee, if any. Required to search: name, years to search. Civil cases indexed by defendant, plaintiff. Probate records in this office since 9/82, prior records filed in County Clerk's office, computerized records go back to 1967. Public use terminal has civil records back to 1958. PAT results show plaintiff and defendant names only.
General Information: No adoption, commitment records released. Will fax documents $10.00 per doc. Court makes copy: $.50 per page. Self serve: $.50 per page. Certification fee: $5.00 per cert. Payee: Clerk & Master. No personal checks or credit cards accepted. Prepayment required.

Giles County

22nd District Circuit & General Sessions Court
PO Box 678, #1 Public Sq, Pulaski, TN 38478; 931-363-5311; fax: 931-424-4790; 8AM-4PM (CST). ***Felony, Misdemeanor, Civil, Eviction, Small Claims.***
Civil Records: Access: mail, fax, in person. Both court and visitors may perform in person searches. No search fee. Required to search: name, years to search. Civil cases indexed by defendant, plaintiff; index on computer from 1/90, remaining records filed in docket books. Mail turnaround time 1 week. Civil PAT goes back to 1990.
Criminal Records: Access: Phone, mail, fax, in person. Both court and visitors may perform in person searches. Required to search: name, years to search, DOB; also helpful: SSN. Criminal records

computerized from 1/90, remaining records filed in docket books. Mail turnaround time 1 week. Criminal PAT goes back to same as civil.
General Information: No juvenile records released without signed release. Will fax documents $5.00 per doc. Court makes copy: $.50 per page from file; $1.00 per page from computer. Self serve: same. Certification fee: $5.50 per doc. Payee: Circuit Court Clerk. No personal checks accepted. Major credit cards accepted. Prepayment required. Mail requests: SASE required.

Chancery Court PO Box 678, 1 Public Sq, Pulaski, TN 38478; 931-363-2620; fax: 931-363-2106; 8AM-4PM (CST). ***Probate.***

Grainger County

4th District Circuit & General Sessions Court PO Box 157, 270 Justice Ctr Dr, Rutledge, TN 37861; 865-828-3605 Circuit; 805-828-4436 Sessions; fax: 865-828-3339; 8:30AM-4:30PM M,T,TH,F (W & Sat 8:30AM-N) (EST). ***Felony, Misdemeanor, Civil, Eviction, Small Claims.***
Civil Records: Access: In person only. Visitors must perform in person searches themselves. Required to search: name, years to search. Civil cases indexed by defendant, plaintiff. Civil records archived from 1977 in office. Civil PAT goes back to 11/2001. PAT results show name, DOB.
Criminal Records: Access: In person only. Visitors must perform in person searches themselves. Required to search: name, years to search, DOB, SSN. Criminal records archived from 1977 in office. Criminal PAT goes back to same as civil.PAT results show name, DOB. Results include driver license number.
General Information: No sealed records released. Will not fax documents. Court makes copy: $.50 per page. Self serve: same. Certification fee: $4.00. Payee: Circuit Court Clerk. Business checks accepted. No credit cards accepted. Prepayment required.

Chancery Court Clerk & Master, PO Box 160, Rutledge, TN 37861; 865-828-4436; fax: 865-828-8714; 8:30AM-4:30PM M,T,TH,F, 8:30AM-N W (EST). ***Civil, Probate.***
Civil Records: Access: Phone, fax, mail, in person. Both court and visitors may perform in person searches. No search fee. Required to search: name, years to search. Civil cases indexed by defendant, plaintiff; index on books. Mail turnaround time varies.
General Information: No adoption records released. Will fax documents to local or toll free line. Court makes copy: $.50 per page. Self serve: same. Certification fee: $4.00. Payee: Clerk & Master. Personal checks accepted; credit cards are not. Prepayment required. Mail requests: SASE requested.

Greene County

3rd District Circuit & General Sessions Court 101 S Main, County Courthouse, Greeneville, TN 37743; 423-798-1760; 8AM-4:30PM (EST). ***Felony, Misdemeanor, Civil, Eviction, Small Claims.***
Civil Records: Access: In person only. Visitors must perform in person searches themselves. Required to search: name, years to search. Civil cases indexed by defendant, plaintiff. Civil records archived since court started, on computer from end of 1990. Civil PAT goes back to 10/1990.
Criminal Records: Access: In person only. Visitors must perform in person searches themselves. Required to search: name, years to search. Criminal records archived since court started, on computer from end of 1990. Criminal PAT goes back to same as civil.
General Information: No adoption records released. Will not fax documents. Court makes copy: $.50 per page. Certification fee: $5.00. Payee: Circuit Court Clerk. Personal checks accepted; credit cards are not. Prepayment required.

County Court 204 N Cutler St, #200, County Courthouse Annex, Greeneville, TN 37745; 423-798-1708, 798-1709; fax: 423-798-1822; 8AM-4:30PM (EST). ***Probate.***

Grundy County

12th District Circuit & General Sessions Court PO Box 161, Altamont, TN 37301; 931-692-3368; fax: 931-692-2414; 8AM-4PM M-TH; 8AM-5PM F (CST). ***Felony, Misdemeanor, Civil, Eviction, Small Claims.***
They have no records from 12/1985 to May 3, 1990.
Civil Records: Access: Mail, fax, in person. Both court and visitors may perform in person searches. Search fee: $5.00 per name. Fee is per court. Required to search: name, years to search. Civil cases indexed by defendant, plaintiff; index on computer since 1993, prior records in books to 1990. Before 1990 on microfiche since 1868. Mail turnaround time 5 days.
Criminal Records: Access: Mail, fax, in person. Both court and visitors may perform in person searches. Search fee: $5.00 per name. Fee is per court. Required to search: name, years to search, DOB; also helpful: SSN. Criminal records on computer since 1993, prior records in books to 1990. Before 1990 on microfiche since 1868. Mail turnaround time 5 days.
General Information: No juvenile records released. Fee to fax out file $4.00 each. Court makes copy: $.50 per page. Certification fee: $5.00. Payee: Circuit Court Clerk. In-state personal checks accepted. No credit cards accepted. Prepayment required. Mail requests: SASE required.

Chancery Court PO Box 174, Altamont, TN 37301; 931-692-3455; fax: 931-692-4125; 8AM-4PM M-TH; 8AM-5PM F (CST). ***Civil, Probate.***
Civil Records: Access: Phone, mail, in person. Only the court performs in person searches; visitors may not. Search fee: $5.00 per name. Required to search: name, years to search. Civil cases indexed by defendant, plaintiff; index on computer since 1993, on books back to 1990. Mail turnaround time 5 days.
General Information: No adoption records released. Will fax documents to local or toll free line. Court makes copy: $.50 per page. Certification fee: $6.00. Payee: Clerk & Master. Personal checks accepted; credit cards are not. Prepayment required. Mail requests: SASE requested.

Hamblen County

3rd District Circuit & General Sessions Court 510 Allison St, Morristown, TN 37814; 423-586-5640; fax: 423-585-2764; 8AM-4PM (CST). ***Felony, Misdemeanor, Civil, Eviction, Small Claims.***
Civil Records: Access: Mail, in person. Both court and visitors may perform in person searches. Search fee: $5.00 per name. Required to search: name, years to search. Civil cases indexed by defendant, plaintiff. Civil records archived from early 1900s, on computer from 1989. Mail turnaround time 1 day. Civil PAT goes back to 1989.
Criminal Records: Access: Mail, in person. Both court and visitors may perform in person searches. Search fee: $5.00 per name. Required to search: name, years to search, DOB; also helpful: SSN. Criminal records archived from early 1900s, on computer from 1989. Mail turnaround time 1 day. Criminal PAT goes back to same as civil.
General Information: No adoption records released. Will fax documents to local or toll-free number. Court makes copy: $.50 per page. Self serve: same. Certification fee: $5.00 per doc. Payee: Circuit Court Clerk or General Sessions. No personal checks or credit cards accepted. Mail requests: SASE required.

Chancery Court 511 W 2nd North St, Morristown, TN 37814; 423-586-9112; fax: 423-318-2510; 8AM-4PM M-TH; 8AM-4:30PM F (EST). ***Civil, Probate.***
Civil Records: Access: Phone, fax, mail, in person. Both court and visitors may perform in person searches. No search fee. Required to search: name, years to search. Civil cases indexed by defendant, plaintiff; index on computer from 1979; prior on books back to 1870's. Mail turnaround time 3-5 days. Public use terminal has civil records back to 1979. PAT civil results show middle initial.
General Information: No adoption records released. Will fax documents $1.00 per page. Court makes copy: $.50 per page. Self serve: same. Certification fee: $5.00 plus per doc. Payee: Clerk & Master. Personal checks accepted; credit cards are not. Prepayment required.

Hamilton County

11th District Civil Court Rm 500, Courthouse, 625 Georgia Ave, Chattanooga, TN 37402; 423-209-6700; fax: 423-209-6701; 8AM-4PM (EST). ***Civil Actions over $15,000.***
www.hamiltontn.gov/courts
Civil Records: Access: Phone, fax, mail, in person, online. Both court and visitors may perform in person searches. No search fee. Required to search: name, years to search. Civil cases indexed by defendant, plaintiff. Civil records archived from 1921, on computer back to 7/89. Court minutes are on microfiche thru 1997, from 1997 forward on digital images. Mail turnaround time 1 week. Public use terminal has civil records back to 1989. Online access to current court dockets are free at www.hamiltontn.gov/courts/Default.aspx.
General Information: No adoption or judicial hospitalization records released. Will fax documents to local numbers only. Court makes copy: $.50 per page. Certification fee: $5.00, Acts of Congress Certification-$10.00. Payee: Circuit Court Clerk. Personal checks accepted; credit cards are not. Prepayment required. Mail requests: SASE required.

11th District General Sessions Court Civil Division, 600 Market St, Rm 111, Chattanooga, TN 37402; 423-209-7630; fax: 423-209-7631; 8AM-4PM (EST). ***Civil Actions under $25,000, Eviction, Small Claims.***
www.hamiltontn.gov/courts/sessions/
Civil Records: Access: Phone, mail, in person, online. Both court and visitors may perform in person searches. No search fee. Required to search: name, years to search. Civil cases indexed by defendant, plaintiff. Civil records archived on docket books, on computer from 6/1985. Mail turnaround time 3-4 days. Public use terminal has civil records back to 1985. PAT civil results show middle initial. Online access to current (7 days) court dockets is free on the web. Search dispositions and calendars free at http://cjusgeneralsessions.hamiltontn.gov/appfolder/GS_Web_Calendar.aspx.
General Information: No mental health records released. Will not fax documents. Court makes copy: $.50 per page. Self serve: same. Certification fee: $4.00. Payee: Sessions Court Clerk. Personal checks accepted; credit cards are not. Prepayment required.

11th District Criminal Court 600 Market St, Rm 102, Chattanooga, TN 37402; 423-209-7500; fax: 423-209-7501; 8AM-4PM (EST). ***Felony, Misdemeanor.*** www.hamiltontn.gov/courts
Criminal Records: Access: Mail, in person, online. Both court and visitors may perform in person searches. Search fee: $10.00 per name. Required to search: name, years to search, DOB, signed release; also helpful: SSN. Criminal records on computer since 1990, prior records in books. Mail turnaround time 1 week. Public use terminal has crim records back to 1990. Search court's disposition records and court dates free at http://cjuscriminal.hamiltontn.gov/AppFolder/CC_Web_Calendar.aspx and records go back to 1989. Also, online access to current court dockets is free at web page.
General Information: No juvenile records released. Will not fax documents. Court makes copy: $.50 per page. No certification fee. Payee: Criminal Court Clerk. Only cashiers checks and money orders accepted. No credit cards accepted. Prepayment required. Mail requests: SASE helpful.

Chancery Court Chancery Court, Clerk & Master, 201 E 7th St, Rm 300, Chattanooga, TN 37402; 423-209-6600; fax: 423-209-6601; 8AM-4PM (EST). ***Civil, Probate.***
www.hamiltontn.gov/courts/Default.aspx
Civil Records: Access: Phone, mail, in person, online. Both court and visitors may perform in person searches. No search fee. Required to search: name, years to search. Civil cases indexed by defendant, plaintiff. Civil index on cards from 1919, on dockets and microfilm; on computer 1995-present. Mail turnaround time 2-3 days. Public use terminal has civil records. PAT civil results show middle initial. Chancery motions/dockets are online at

www.hamiltontn.gov/courts/Default.aspx. Online results show middle initial.
General Information: No mental health, adoption records released. Local fax fee $.50 per page; long distance $1.00 per page. Court makes copy: $.50 per page. Certification fee: $5.00 per cert. Payee: Hamilton County Clerk and Master. Personal checks and major credit cards accepted. Prepayment required. Mail requests: SASE required.

Hancock County

3rd District Circuit & General Sessions Court PO Box 347, Sneedville, TN 37869; 423-733-2954; fax: 423-733-2119; 8AM-4PM M,T,TH,F; 8AM-N Wed,Sat (EST). ***Felony, Misdemeanor, Civil, Eviction, Small Claims.***
Office does not have resources for employment-related searches; suggests using a retriever. Note that some records were destroyed by fire and are not available.
Civil Records: Access: Mail, in person. Both court and visitors may perform in person searches. Search fee: $4.00 per name. Required to search: name, years to search. Civil cases indexed by plaintiff. Civil records archived on books from 1934. Mail turnaround time 5-10 days. Civil PAT goes back to 7 years.
Criminal Records: Access: Mail, in person. Both court and visitors may perform in person searches. Search fee: $4.00 per name. Required to search: name, years to search. Criminal records archived on books from 1934. Mail turnaround time 5-10 days. Criminal PAT goes back to 20 years.
General Information: No juvenile records released. Will fax documents. Court makes copy: $.50 per page. Self serve: same. Certification fee: $4.50 per doc. Payee: Circuit Court Clerk. Personal checks accepted; credit cards are not. Prepayment required. Mail requests: SASE required.

Chancery Court PO Box 347, 1237 Main St, Sneedville, TN 37869; 423-733-4524; fax: 423-733-2762; 8:30AM-N, 1PM-4PM (EST). ***Civil, Probate.***
Civil Records: Access: Mail, in person. Only the court performs in person searches; visitors may not. No search fee. Required to search: name, years to search. Civil cases indexed by defendant, plaintiff; index on books and microfilm back to 1850's. Mail turnaround time 2 days.
General Information: No adoption records released. Will fax documents $1.00 per page. Court makes copy: $.50 per page. Self serve: same. Certification fee: $5.00. Payee: Clerk & Master. Personal checks accepted; credit cards are not. Prepayment required. Mail requests: SASE requested.

Hardeman County

25th District Circuit & General Sessions Court Courthouse, 100 N Main, Bolivar, TN 38008; 731-658-6524; fax: 731-658-4584; 8:30AM-4:30PM M-TH, 8AM-5PM Fri (CST). ***Felony, Misdemeanor, Civil, Eviction, Small Claims.***
Civil Records: Access: In person only. Visitors must perform in person searches themselves. Required to search: name, years to search. Civil cases indexed by defendant, plaintiff; index on computer since 12/92, archived General Sessions from 1960 and Circuit from 1800s. Public use terminal available. PAT results show middle initial, DOB.
Criminal Records: Access: In person only. Visitors must perform in person searches themselves. Required to search: name, years to search, DOB, SSN, signed release. Criminal records on computer since 12/92, archived General Sessions from 1960 and Circuit from 1800s. Public use terminal available. PAT results show middle initial, DOB.
General Information: No juvenile records released. Will not fax out case files. Court makes copy: $.50 per page. Certification fee: $5.00 per cert. Payee: Circuit Court Clerk. Cashiers checks and money orders accepted. Hardeman county personal checks accepted. No credit cards accepted. Prepayment required.

Chancery Court PO Box 45, Bolivar, TN 38008; 731-658-3142; fax: 731-658-4580; 8:30AM-4:30PM M-TH, 8:30AM-5PM F (CST). ***Civil, Probate.***
Civil Records: Access: Phone, mail, fax, in person. Both court and visitors may perform in person searches. No search fee. Required to search: name, years to search. Civil cases indexed by defendant, plaintiff; index on books back to 1825; computerized back to 1975. Mail turnaround time 1 day. Public use terminal has civil records back to 1975.
General Information: No mental health, adoption records released. Fee to fax out file $1.00 per page. Court makes copy: $.50 per page, add'l fee for postage. Certification fee: $5.00 for the seal plus $.50 per page. Payee: Chancery Court Clerk. Business checks accepted. No credit cards accepted. Prepayment required. Mail requests: SASE requested.

Hardin County

24th District Circuit & General Sessions Court 465 Main St, Savannah, TN 38372; 731-925-3583; 8AM-4:30PM M,T,TH,F; 8AM-N W (CST). ***Felony, Misdemeanor, Civil, Eviction, Small Claims.***
Civil Records: Access: In person only. Visitors must perform in person searches themselves. Required to search: name, years to search. Civil cases indexed by defendant, plaintiff. Civil records archived on books and on microfiche from 1800s, on computer from 1996. Civil PAT goes back to 1996.
Criminal Records: Access: In person only. Visitors must perform in person searches themselves. Required to search: name, years to search. Criminal records archived on books and on microfiche from 1800s, on computer from 1996. Criminal PAT goes back to same as civil.
General Information: No juvenile records released. Will not fax documents. Court makes copy: $.50 per page. Certification fee: $5.00. Payee: Circuit Court Clerk. Hardin county personal checks accepted. No credit cards accepted. Prepayment required.

Clerk and Master Office 465 Main St, Savannah, TN 38372; 731-925-8166; fax: 731-925-0255; 8AM-4:30PM M,T,TH,F; 8AM-N W (CST). ***Probate.***
Clerk and Master became managers of probate records in 2004; formerly, records were with County Court clerk.

Hawkins County

3rd District Circuit & General Sessions Court 100 E Main St, Rogersville, TN 37857; 423-272-3397; fax: 423-272-9646; 8AM-4PM (EST). ***Felony, Misdemeanor, Civil, Eviction, Small Claims.***
Records prior to 1950 are kept off-site and are monitored by a genealogical group.
Civil Records: Access: In person only. Visitors must perform in person searches themselves. Required to search: name, years to search. Civil cases indexed by defendant, plaintiff. Civil records archived on books from 1800s. Civil PAT goes back to 1995. PAT results show middle initial, DOB.
Criminal Records: Access: In person only. Visitors must perform in person searches themselves. Required to search: name, years to search. Criminal records archived on books from 1800s. Criminal PAT goes back to same as civil. PAT results show middle initial, DOB.
General Information: No juvenile records released. Will not fax documents. Court makes copy: $.50 per page. Certification fee: $5.00 per cert. Payee: Circuit Court Clerk. No personal checks accepted. Visa/MC accepted.

Chancery Court PO Box 908, 100 E Main St #103, Rogersville, TN 37857; 423-272-8150; fax: 423-272-7347; 8AM-4PM (EST). ***Civil, Probate.***
Civil Records: Access: In person, mail. Visitors must perform in person searches themselves. Search fee: No fee, except for genealogy. Required to search: name, years to search. Civil cases indexed by defendant, plaintiff. Civil index on docket books from 1927 to present. Mail turnaround time 5-10 days
General Information: No adoption records released. Will fax documents $5.00 plus $1.00 per page. Many documents are too large to fax. Court makes copy: $.50 per page. Certification fee: $5.00 per page. Payee: Hawkins County Clerk and Master. Personal checks accepted; credit cards are not. Prepayment required.

Haywood County

28th District Circuit & General Sessions Court 1 N Washington Ave, Brownsville, TN 38012; 731-772-1112; fax: 731-772-8139; 8:30AM-5PM (CST). ***Felony, Misdemeanor, Civil, Eviction, Small Claims.***
This court did not adjust its prices to the new mandated pricing schedule.
Civil Records: Access: Phone, mail, in person. Visitors must perform in person searches themselves. No search fee. Required to search: name, years to search. Civil cases indexed by defendant, plaintiff; index on computer since 8/1991. General Sessions archived since 1960's; Circuit Court archived since 1800s. Civil PAT goes back to 8/1991. PAT results show middle initial, DOB, SSN.
Criminal Records: Access: Phone, mail, in person. Visitors must perform in person searches themselves. No search fee. Required to search: name, years to search, DOB; also helpful: SSN. General Sessions criminal back to 08/1991; Circuit criminal back to 01/1992 on computer. Mail turnaround time depends on search complexity. Criminal PAT goes back to 8/1991. PAT results show middle initial, DOB.
General Information: No juvenile records released. Court makes copy: $.50 per page. Self serve: same. Certification fee: $5.00. Payee: Circuit Court Clerk. Personal checks and major credit cards accepted. Prepayment required. Mail requests: SASE required.

Chancery Court 1 N Washington, PO Box 356, Brownsville, TN 38012; 731-772-0122; fax: 731-772-3197; 8:30AM-5PM (CST). ***Civil, Probate.***
Civil Records: Access: In person only. Visitors must perform in person searches themselves. Required to search: name, years to search. Civil cases indexed by defendant, plaintiff. Probate records on books since 9/82; other records go back to 1800s.
General Information: No adoption or sealed records released. Will fax documents $10.00. Court makes copy: $.50 per page. Self serve: same. Certification fee: $5.00. Payee: Chancery Court. Personal checks accepted; credit cards are not. Prepayment required.

Henderson County

26th District Circuit & General Sessions Court 17 Monroe Ave #9, County Courthouse, Lexington, TN 38351; 731-968-2031; fax: 731-967-9441; 8AM-4:30PM (CST). ***Felony, Misdemeanor, Civil, Eviction, Small Claims.***
Civil Records: Access: In person only. Visitors must perform in person searches themselves. Required to search: name, years to search. Civil cases indexed by defendant, plaintiff; index on cards or books, archived from 1800s; on computer back 5 years. Civil PAT goes back to 1994.
Criminal Records: Access: In person only. Visitors must perform in person searches themselves. Required to search: name, years to search, DOB; also helpful- SSN. Criminal records on cards or books, archived from 1800s; on computer back 5 years. Criminal PAT goes back to same as civil.
General Information: No sealed indictment records released. Will fax documents $10.00 each. Court makes copy: $1.00 per page. Self serve: same. Certification fee: $5.00. Payee: General Sessions Court Clerk. No personal checks or credit cards accepted. Prepayment required.

Chancery Court 17 Monroe, Rm 2, 2nd Fl, Lexington, TN 38351; 731-968-2801; fax: 731-967-5380; 8AM-4:30PM (CST). ***Civil, Probate.***
www.hcchancery.com/
Civil Records: Access: Phone, mail, fax, in person. Only the court performs in person searches; visitors may not. No search fee. Required to search: name, years to search. Civil cases indexed by defendant, plaintiff; index on computer back to 1989; prior in books to 1895. Mail turnaround time depends on search length.
General Information: No confidential adoption records released. Fee to fax out file $2.00 per page. Court makes copy: $.50 per page. Certification fee: $5.00. Payee: Chancery Court. No personal or business checks accepted. No credit cards accepted. Prepayment required. Mail requests: SASE required.

Henry County

24th District Circuit & General Sessions Court PO Box 429, Paris, TN 38242; 731-642-0461; fax: 731-642-1244; 8AM-4:30PM (CST). ***Felony, Misdemeanor, Civil, Eviction, Small Claims.*** The General Sessions Court records date to 1962, when court was created.

Civil Records: Access: Fax, mail, in person. Both court and visitors may perform in person searches. Search fee: $5.00. Required to search: name, years to search. Civil cases indexed by defendant, plaintiff. Civil records archived from 1820s (you search) or 1900s (they search); General Sessions on computer from 1991. Mail turnaround time 1-2 weeks. Civil PAT goes back to 1991 for General Sessions; 2002 for Circuit.

Criminal Records: Access: Fax, mail, in person. Both court and visitors may perform in person searches. Search fee: $5.00. Required to search: name, years to search; also helpful: SSN, DOB. Criminal records archived from 1820s to 1939, (you search) or 1940 present (they search); General Sessions on computer from 1991. Mail turnaround time 1-2 weeks. Criminal PAT goes back to same as civil.

General Information: No juvenile records released. Will fax documents only if account is set up; requests must be prepaid. Court makes copy: $.50 per page. Self serve: same. Certification fee: $5.00 per cert. Payee: Circuit Court Clerk or General Sessions Court Clerk. Personal checks accepted; credit cards are not. Prepayment required. Proof of payment such as account set-up to be paid monthly or fax copy of individual check for payment. Mail requests: SASE required.

County Court PO Box 24, 101 W Washington St, #100, Paris, TN 38242; 731-642-2412; fax: 731-644-0947; 8AM-4:30PM (CST). ***Probate, Juvenile.*** www.henrycountyclerktn.com/

Hickman County

21st District Circuit & General Sessions Court 104 College Ave, #204, Centerville, TN 37033; 931-729-2211; probate phone: 931-729-2522; fax: 931-729-6141; 8AM-4PM (CST). ***Felony, Misdemeanor, Civil, Eviction, Small Claims.***

Civil Records: Access: Mail, fax, in person. Both court and visitors may perform in person searches. Search fee: $10.00 per name. Required to search: name, years to search. Civil cases indexed by defendant, plaintiff; index on computer since 1993, prior records on books to 1849.

Criminal Records: Access: Mail, fax, in person. Both court and visitors may perform in person searches. Search fee: $10.00 per name. Required to search: name, years to search. Criminal records on computer since 1993, prior records on books to 1849.

General Information: No juvenile records released. Will fax documents if copy of check faxed in. Court makes copy: $.50 per page. Certification fee: $5.00. Payee: Circuit Court Clerk. No personal checks or credit cards accepted. Prepayment required.

Chancery Court 104 College Ave, #202, Centerville, TN 37033; 931-729-2522; probate phone: same; fax: 931-729-3726; 8AM-4PM (CST). ***Civil, Probate.***

Civil Records: Access: Mail, in person. Both court and visitors may perform in person searches. No search fee. Required to search: name, years to search. Civil cases indexed by defendant, plaintiff; index on books since 1865; computerized records since 2001. Mail turnaround time 1 week.

General Information: No confidential or adoption records released. Will fax documents $2.00 per page. Court makes copy: $.50 per page. Certification fee: $3.00. Payee: Clerk & Master. Personal checks accepted; credit cards are not. Prepayment required. Mail requests: SASE requested.

Houston County

23rd District Circuit & General Sessions Court PO Box 414, Erin, TN 37061; 931-289-4673; fax: 931-289-5182; 8AM-N, 1-4:30PM (CST). ***Felony, Misdemeanor, Civil, Eviction, Small Claims.***

Civil Records: Access: Mail, in person. Visitors must perform in person searches themselves. Search fee: $10.00 per name. Required to search: name, years to search. Civil cases indexed by defendant, plaintiff. Civil records archived from 1930s in books.

Criminal Records: Access: Mail, in person. Visitors must perform in person searches themselves. Search fee: $10.00 per person. Required to search: name, years to search, DOB; SSN helpful. Criminal records archived from 1930s in books.

General Information: No juvenile records released. Will not fax documents. Court makes copy: $.25 per page. Certification fee: $5.00. Payee: Circuit Court Clerk. Personal checks accepted; credit cards are not. Prepayment required.

Chancery Court PO Box 332, 4725 E Main, Erin, TN 37061; 931-289-3870; fax: 931-289-5679; 8AM-4PM (CST). ***Civil, Probate.***

Civil Records: Access: Mail, in person. Both court and visitors may perform in person searches. No search fee. Required to search: name, years to search. Civil cases indexed by defendant, plaintiff; index on books. Note: All requests must be in writing. Mail turnaround time 2 days.

General Information: No adoption records released. Court makes copy: $.50 per page. Self serve: same. Certification fee: $5.00. Payee: Clerk & Master. Personal checks accepted; credit cards are not. Prepayment required. Mail requests: SASE required.

Humphreys County

23rd District Circuit & General Sessions Court Courthouse, Rm 106, Waverly, TN 37185; 931-296-2461; fax: 931-296-1651; 8AM-4:30PM (CST). ***Felony, Misdemeanor, Civil, Eviction, Small Claims.***

Civil Records: Access: Fax, mail, in person. Only the court performs in person searches; visitors may not. Search fee: $1.00 per name per year minimum 7 years. If more than 15 years, flat $25.00 fee. Required to search: name, years to search. Civil cases indexed by defendant, plaintiff; index on computer back to 1989. Mail turnaround time 10 days.

Criminal Records: Access: Fax, mail, in person. Only the court performs in person searches; visitors may not. Search fee: $1.00 per name per year minimum 7 years. If more than 15 years, flat $25.00 fee. Required to search: name, years to search, DOB, SSN, signed release. Criminal records computerized from 1989. Mail turnaround time 10 days.

General Information: No expunged records released. Will fax documents to local or toll-free number. Court makes copy: $.50 per page. Certification fee: $5.00 seal; plus $1.00 per page. Payee: Circuit Court. Business checks accepted. No credit cards accepted. Prepayment required. Mail requests: SASE required.

County Court Clerk, Rm 2 Courthouse Annex, 102 Thompson St, Waverly, TN 37185; 931-296-7671, 931-296-6503; fax: 931-296-0823; 8AM-4:30PM (CST). ***Probate.***

Jackson County

15th District Circuit & General Sessions Court PO Box 205, Gainesboro, TN 38562; 931-268-9314; fax: 931-268-4555; 8AM-4PM M,T,TH,F; 8AM-2PM W; 8AM-N Sat (CST). ***Felony, Misdemeanor, Civil, Eviction, Small Claims.***

Civil Records: Access: Fax, mail, in person. Both court and visitors may perform in person searches. Search fee: $5.00 per name. Required to search: name, years to search. Civil cases indexed by defendant, plaintiff. Civil records archived from 1900s in books, computerized since 2000. Mail turnaround time 1 week. Civil PAT goes back to 2000.

Criminal Records: Access: Fax, mail, in person. Both court and visitors may perform in person searches. Search fee: $5.00 per name. Required to search: name, years to search, DOB; also helpful: SSN. Criminal records archived from 1900s in books, computerized since 2000. Mail turnaround time 1 week. Criminal PAT goes back to same as civil.

General Information: No juvenile records released. Will not fax documents. Court makes copy: $.50 per page. Certification fee: $5.00 per doc. Payee: Circuit Court Clerk. Business checks accepted. No credit cards accepted. Prepayment required. Mail requests: SASE required.

Chancery Court PO Box 342, 101 E Hull Ave, Gainesboro, TN 38562-0342; 931-268-9516; fax: 931-268-9512; 8AM-4PM M,T,TH,F; 8AM-12PM Wed (CST). ***Probate.***

Jefferson County

4th District Circuit & General Sessions Court PO Box 671, 765 Justice Court Dr, Dandridge, TN 37725; 865-397-2786 Circuit; 865-397-2404 Sessions; fax: 865-397-4894; 8AM-4PM (EST). ***Felony, Misdemeanor, Civil, Eviction, Small Claims.***

Civil Records: Access: In person only. Visitors must perform in person searches themselves. Required to search: name, years to search. Civil cases indexed by defendant, plaintiff. Civil records archived from early 1900s on books. Civil PAT goes back to mid 1990's.

Criminal Records: Access: In person only. Both court and visitors may perform in person searches. No search fee. Required to search: name, years to search, DOB, SSN, signed release. Criminal records archived from early 1900s on books. Note: Searches done by the court are for only 5 years of records. Criminal PAT available. Public record go back to 2005.

General Information: No adoption or juvenile records released. Will not fax documents. Court makes copy: $.50 per page. Certification fee: $3.00. Payee: Circuit Court Clerk. Only cashiers checks and money orders accepted. No credit cards accepted. Prepayment required.

County Court PO Box 710, 214 W Main St, Dandridge, TN 37725; 865-397-2935; fax: 865-397-3839; 8AM-4:30PM M-F, 8AM-11PM Sat (EST). ***Probate.*** www.jeffersoncountytn.gov

Johnson County

1st District Circuit & General Sessions Court PO Box 73, 222 W Main St, Mountain City, TN 37683; 423-727-9012; fax: 423-727-3963; 8:30AM-5PM (EST). ***Felony, Misdemeanor, Civil, Eviction, Small Claims.***

Civil Records: Access: Phone, mail, in person. Both court and visitors may perform in person searches. Search fee: $10.00 per name. Required to search: name, years to search. Civil cases indexed by defendant, plaintiff. Civil records in docket books, sessions 1976, criminal & circuit 1800s. Mail turnaround time 2-3 days. Civil PAT goes back to 2000. PAT results show middle initial, DOB. Terminal results also show SSNs.

Criminal Records: Access: Phone, mail, in person. Both court and visitors may perform in person searches. Search fee: $10.00 per name. Required to search: name, years to search, DOB. Criminal records in docket books, sessions 1976, criminal & circuit 1800s. Mail turnaround time 2-3 days. Criminal PAT goes back to same as civil. PAT results show middle initial, DOB. Terminal results include SSN.

General Information: No adoption, expunged or juvenile records released. Will fax documents $10.00 per name. Court makes copy for no fee. Certification fee: None, but $2.00 if done by the Clerk and Master's Office. Payee: Circuit Court Clerk. Only cashiers checks and money orders accepted. No credit cards accepted. Prepayment required. Mail requests: SASE required.

Chancery Court PO Box 196, Mountain City, TN 37683; 423-727-7853; fax: 423-727-7012; 8:30AM-N; 1-5PM (EST). ***Civil, Probate.***

Civil Records: Access: Mail, in person. Only the court performs in person searches; visitors may not. No search fee. Required to search: name, years to search. Civil cases indexed by defendant, plaintiff; index on books and files. Mail turnaround time same day.

General Information: No adoption records released. Will not fax documents. Court makes copy: $1.00 per page. Certification fee: $2.00 plus $2.00 per page.

Payee: Clerk & Master. Only cashiers checks and money orders accepted. No credit cards accepted. Prepayment required. Mail requests: SASE required.

Knox County

6th District Criminal Court 400 W Main St, Rm 149, Knoxville, TN 37902; 865-215-2492; criminal phone: 865-215-2375 Gen Sessions; fax: 865-215-4291; 8AM-4:30PM (EST). ***Felony, Misdemeanor.***
www.knoxcounty.org
Criminal Records: Access: Fax, mail, in person. Both court and visitors may perform in person searches. Search fee: $10.00 per name. Required to search: name, years to search, DOB; also helpful: address, SSN, signed release. Criminal records computerized from 1980; on books from 1962. Mail turnaround time 48 hours. Criminal PAT goes back to mid-1980s. PAT results show middle initial, DOB.
General Information: No sealed records released. Will not fax documents. Court makes copy: $2.00 per page. Certification fee: $2.00 per page. Payee: Criminal Court Clerk. Personal checks accepted; credit cards are not. Prepayment required.

Circuit Court 400 Main Ave, Rm M-30, PO Box 379, Knoxville, TN 37901; 865-215-2400; fax: 865-215-4251; 8AM-4:30PM (EST). ***Civil Actions over $15,000.***
www.knoxcounty.org
Civil Records: Access: Phone, fax, mail, in person. Both court and visitors may perform in person searches. Search fee: $5.00 per name. Required to search: name, years to search. Civil cases indexed by defendant, plaintiff; index on computer from 1986, prior records archived and on microfilm. Mail turnaround time 2-3 days. Civil PAT goes back to mid-1980s. PAT results show middle initial, DOB.
General Information: No adoption or sealed records released. Court makes copy: $1.00 per page. Self serve: same. Certification fee: $3.50, exemplification fee- $10/50. Payee: Circuit Court Clerk. Personal checks and credit cards accepted. Prepayment required. Mail requests: SASE required.

General Sessions Court 300 Main Ave, Rm 318, PO Box 379, Knoxville, TN 37901; 865-215-2518; fax: 865-215-4296; 8AM-4:30PM (EST). ***Civil Actions under $25,000, Eviction, Small Claims.***
www.knoxcounty.org/gsjudges/index.php
Civil Records: Access: Mail, in person. Both court and visitors may perform in person searches. Search fee: $5.00 per name. Required to search: name, years to search. Civil cases indexed by defendant, plaintiff; index on books and computer. Mail turnaround time 1 week. Public use terminal has civil records back to 2000. PAT civil results show middle initial.
General Information: No juvenile or adoption records released. Will fax out documents. Court makes copy: $1.50 per page. Certification fee: $3.50. Payee: General Sessions Court. Personal checks accepted with DOB, DL#, phone. Visa/MC accepted. Prepayment required.

Chancery Court 400 W Main St, Rm 125, Knoxville, TN 37902; 865-215-2555 (Chancery); probate phone: 865-215-2389; fax: 865-215-2920; 8AM-4:30PM (EST). ***Civil, Probate.***
www.knoxcounty.org
Civil Records: Access: Phone, fax, mail, in person. Visitors must perform in person searches themselves. No search fee. Required to search: name, years to search. Civil cases indexed by defendant, plaintiff; index on computer since 1978, prior records on books. Mail turnaround time 1-2 days. Public use terminal has civil records back to 1904. PAT results show name only.
General Information: No commitment or adoption records released. Will fax documents $1.00 per page. Court makes copy: $1.00 per page. Certification fee: $2.00. Payee: Chancery or Probate Court. Personal checks accepted; credit cards are not. Prepayment required. Mail requests: SASE requested.

Lake County

29th District Circuit & General Sessions Court 229 Church St, PO Box 11, Tiptonville, TN 38079; 731-253-7137; fax: 731-253-8930; 8AM-4PM (CST). ***Felony, Misdemeanor, Civil, Eviction, Small Claims.***
Civil Records: Access: In person only. Visitors must perform in person searches themselves. Required to search: name, years to search. Civil cases indexed by defendant, plaintiff. Civil records archived on books in office up to 30 yrs, vault records before 1960; General Sessions computerized records go back to 1997. Civil PAT goes back to 1996.
Criminal Records: Access: In person only. Visitors must perform in person searches themselves. Required to search: name, years to search, DOB; SSN helpful. Criminal records archived on books in office up to 30 yrs, vault records before 1960. Criminal PAT goes back to 1996.
General Information: No sealed records released. Will not fax out documents to the public. Court makes copy: $.50 per page. Certification fee: $5.00. Payee: Circuit Court Clerk. Only cash and money order accepted. No credit cards accepted. Prepayment required.

Chancery Court 229 Church St, Box 12, Tiptonville, TN 38079; 731-253-8926; fax: 731-253-9815; 9AM-4PM (CST). ***Probate.***

Lauderdale County

25th District Circuit Court PO Box 509, 675 Hwy 51 S, Lauderdale County Justice Ctr, Ripley, TN 38063; 731-635-0101; criminal phone: 731-635-2572; civil phone: 731-635-2572; criminal fax: 731-221-8663; civil fax: same; 8AM-4:30PM (CST). ***Felony, Misdemeanor, Civil Actions over $15,000.***
Civil Records: Access: Phone, mail, in person. Both court and visitors may perform in person searches. Search fee: $10.00 per name. Required to search: name, years to search. Civil cases indexed by defendant, plaintiff. Civil records archived on books from 1800s; on computer back to 1992. Mail turnaround time 2-3 days. Civil PAT goes back to 1992. PAT civil results show middle initial.
Criminal Records: Access: Mail, in person. Both court and visitors may perform in person searches. Search fee: $10.00 per name. Required to search: name, years to search; also helpful: DOB, SSN. Criminal records archived on books from 1800s; on computer back to 1992. Mail turnaround time 2-3 days. Criminal PAT goes back to same as civil. PAT criminal results show middle initial.
General Information: No sealed or adoption records released. Will fax documents $1.00 per page. Court makes copy: $.50 per page. Self serve: same. Certification fee: $5.00 per page. Payee: Circuit Court Clerk. Personal checks accepted in county. No credit cards accepted. Prepayment required. Mail requests: SASE required.

General Sessions Court PO Box 509, Ripley, TN 38063; 731-635-2572; fax: 731-221-8663; 8AM-4:30PM M,T,TH,F; 8AM-N W (CST). ***Civil Actions under $25,000, Eviction, Small Claims.***
Civil Records: Access: Mail, in person. Both court and visitors may perform in person searches. Search fee: $10.00 per name. Required to search: name, years to search. Civil cases indexed by defendant, plaintiff; index on computer since 1992, records prior to 1984 on docket books. Mail turnaround time 2-3 days. Public use terminal has civil records back to 1992. PAT civil results show middle initial.
General Information: No confidential records released. Will fax documents $.50 per page. Court makes copy: $.50 per page. Self serve: same. Certification fee: $5.00 per cert. Payee: General Sessions. Business checks accepted. No credit cards accepted. Prepayment required. Mail requests: SASE required.

County Court Courthouse, 100 Court Sq, Ripley, TN 38063; 731-635-2561; fax: 731-635-4301; 8AM-4:30PM (CST). ***Probate.***

Lawrence County

22nd Dist. Circuit & General Sessions Court NBU #12, 240 W Gaines, Lawrenceburg, TN 38464; 931-762-4398; criminal phone: 931-762-4898; civil: 931-766-4152; fax: 931-766-4471; 8AM-4:30PM (CST). ***Felony, Misdemeanor, Civil, Eviction, Small Claims, Probate.***
Civil Records: Access: In person only. Visitors must perform in person searches themselves. Required to search: name, years to search. Civil cases indexed by defendant, plaintiff. Civil records archived on books since court started in 1940s. Civil PAT goes back to 1994. PAT results show name, DOB.
Criminal Records: Access: In person only. Visitors must perform in person searches themselves. Required to search: name, years to search, DOB, SSN. Criminal records archived on books since court started in 1940s. Criminal PAT goes back to same as civil.PAT results show name, DOB.
General Information: No expunged records released. Will fax specific case file $1.00 per page, maximum 20 pages. Court makes copy: $.50 per page. Certification fee: $5.00 per cert. Payee: Circuit Court Clerk. Only cashiers checks and money orders accepted. No credit cards accepted. Prepayment required.

Lewis County

21st District Circuit & General Sessions Court Courthouse, 110 Park Ave N, Rm 201, Hohenwald, TN 38462; 931-796-3724; fax: 931-796-6021; 8AM-4:30PM (CST). ***Felony, Misdemeanor, Civil, Eviction, Small Claims.***
Civil Records: Access: In person only. Visitors must perform in person searches themselves. Required to search: name, years to search. Civil cases indexed by defendant, plaintiff. Civil records archived 15 years in office, 1800s in vault. Civil PAT goes back to 1995.
Criminal Records: Access: In person only. Visitors must perform in person searches themselves. Required to search: name, years to search; SSN helpful. Criminal records archived 15 years in office, 1800s in vault. Criminal PAT goes back to 1995.
General Information: No juvenile, adoption records released. Will not fax out case files. Court makes copy: $.50 per page. Self serve: same. Certification fee: $5.00 per doc. Payee: Circuit Court Clerk. Personal checks accepted; credit cards are not. Prepayment required.

Chancery Court Lewis County Courthouse, 110 Park Ave N, Rm 208, Hohenwald, TN 38462; 931-796-3734/931-796-6016; fax: 931-796-6017; 8AM-4:30PM (CST). ***Civil, Probate.***
Civil Records: Access: In person only. Visitors must perform in person searches themselves. Required to search: name, years to search. Civil cases indexed by defendant, plaintiff; index on computer since 10/94, prior records indexed on computer by name or case number. Public use terminal has civil records back to 1995.
General Information: No adoption records released. Will fax documents $5.00 fee + $1.00 per page up to $10.00. Court makes copy: $.50 per page. Certification fee: $5.00 plus copy fee for add'l pages. Payee: Clerk & Master. Personal checks accepted; credit cards are not. Prepayment required.

Lincoln County

17th District Circuit & General Sessions Court 112 Main Ave S, Rm 203, Fayetteville, TN 37334; 931-433-2334 Circuit; 931-433-1482 Sessions; fax: 931-438-1577; 8AM-4PM (CST). ***Felony, Misdemeanor, Civil, Eviction, Small Claims.***
Civil Records: Access: Phone, fax, mail, in person. Both court and visitors may perform in person searches. Search fee: $5.00 per name. Fee is for 5 years. Add $1.00 for each add'l year. Required to search: name, years to search. Civil cases indexed by defendant, plaintiff. Civil records archived on books since court started; files go back 10 years; on computer back to 1995. Mail turnaround time 1-2 days. Civil PAT goes back to 1995.
Criminal Records: Access: Phone, fax, mail, in person. Both court and visitors may perform in person searches. Search fee: $5.00 per name. Fee is for 5 years. Add $1.00 for each add'l year. Required to

search: name, years to search, DOB, SSN, signed release. Criminal records archived on books since court started; files go back 10 years; on computer back to 1995. Mail turnaround time 1-2 days. Criminal PAT goes back to 1995.
General Information: No probation records released. Will fax documents $2.00 per page. Court makes copy: $.50 per page. Certification fee: $5.00. Payee: Circuit Court Clerk. No business checks accepted. Visa/MC and debit cards accepted. Prepayment required. Mail requests: SASE required.

Chancery Court 112 Main Ave, Rm B109, Fayetteville, TN 37334; 931-433-1482; fax: 931-433-9313; 8AM-4PM (CST). ***Civil, Probate.***
Civil Records: Access: In person only. Visitors must perform in person searches themselves. Required to search: name, years to search. Civil cases indexed by defendant, plaintiff. Civil records archived on books.
General Information: No adoption, divorce records released. Will fax out 1st 10 pages free; add'l pages $.50 each. Court makes copy: $.50 per page. Certification fee: $5.00 per cert. Payee: Clerk & Master. Personal checks accepted; credit cards are not. Prepayment required.

Loudon County

9th District Criminal & Circuit Court PO Box 280, Loudon, TN 37774; 865-458-2042; fax: 865-458-2043; 8-4:30PM (EST). ***Felony, Civil.***
www.loudoncounty.com/ccc.htm
Civil Records: Access: Phone, fax, mail, in person. Both court and visitors may perform in person searches. Search fee: $5.00 per name. Required to search: name, years to search. Civil cases indexed by defendant, plaintiff. Civil records archived from 1870 on books, on computer from 8/1990. Mail turnaround time 2-4 days.
Criminal Records: Access: Phone, fax, mail, in person. Both court and visitors may perform in person searches. Search fee: $5.00 per name. Required to search: name, years to search. Criminal records archived from 1800s on books, on computer from 8/1990. Mail turnaround time 2-4 days.
General Information: No juvenile, adoption records released. Will fax documents for no fee. Court makes copy: $.50 per page. Certification fee: $5.00 per document. Payee: Circuit Court. Personal checks and major credit cards accepted. Prepayment required. Mail requests: SASE requested.

General Sessions Court 12680 Hwy 11 W, #3, Lenoir City, TN 37771; 865-986-3505; fax: 865-986-7355; 8AM-5PM (EST). ***Misdemeanor, Eviction, Small Claims, Probate.***
www.loudoncounty.com/ccc.htm
Civil Records: Access: Phone, fax, mail, in person. Only the court performs in person searches; visitors may not. Search fee: $5.00 per name. Required to search: name, years to search. Civil cases indexed by defendant, plaintiff. Civil records archived from 1960 on books, on computer from 1995. Mail turnaround time 2-4 days.
Criminal Records: Access: Phone, fax, mail, in person. Only the court performs in person searches; visitors may not. Search fee: $5.00 per name. Required to search: name, years to search. Criminal records archived from 1960 on books, on computer from 1995. Mail turnaround time 2-4 days.
General Information: No juvenile, adoption records released. Will fax documents $5.00 fee. Court makes copy: $.50 per page. Certification fee: $5.00. Payee: General Sessions Court. Cashiers check, money orders or cash accepted. Major credit cards accepted. Prepayment required. Mail requests: SASE requested.

Macon County

15th District Circuit & General Sessions Court Court Clerk, 904 Hwy 52 Bypass, Lafayette, TN 37083; 615-666-2354; probate phone: 615-666-2000; fax: 615-666-3001; 8AM-4PM M-TH; 8AM-4PM F (CST). ***Felony, Misdemeanor, Civil, Eviction, Small Claims, Probate.***
Probate located at 906 Hiway 52 Bypass E; hours are 8AM-4PM. Probate fax- 615-666-8943
Civil Records: Access: In person only. Visitors must perform in person searches themselves. Required to search: name, years to search. Civil cases indexed by defendant, plaintiff. Civil records archived in office from 1975, rest in records room from 1960; on computer since 1997. Civil PAT goes back to 1997. PAT results show middle initial, DOB. Results include case numbers.
Criminal Records: Access: In person only. Visitors must perform in person searches themselves. Required to search: name, years to search, DOB; SSN helpful. Criminal records archived in office from 1975, rest in records room from 1960, on computer since1997. Criminal PAT goes back to same as civil. PAT results show middle initial, DOB. Results include case numbers.
General Information: No juvenile or adoption records released. Will not fax out case files. Court makes copy: $.50 per page. Self serve: same. Certification fee: $5.00 per certification. Payee: Circuit Court Clerk. Personal checks accepted only if from this county. Visa/MC accepted. Prepayment required.

Madison County

26th District Circuit Court 515 S Liberty St, #200, Jackson, TN 38301; 731-423-6035; criminal fax: 731-988-3007; civil fax: same; 8AM-4PM (CST). ***Felony, Misdemeanor, Civil Actions over $25,000.***
www.co.madison.tn.us
Misdemeanor cases here are usually accompanied by felonies. Court has a list of document retrievers who may search for you.
Civil Records: Access: In person only. Visitors must perform in person searches themselves. Required to search: name, years to search. Civil cases indexed by defendant, plaintiff. Civil records archived on books in office from 1963; on computer back to 1995, older records in archives. Civil PAT goes back to 1995. PAT results show name only.
Criminal Records: Access: In person only. Visitors must perform in person searches themselves. Required to search: name, years to search; also helpful: DOB, SSN. Criminal records computerized since 1995, on books from 1965, older records in archives. Criminal PAT goes back to same as civil. PAT results show middle initial, DOB. Terminal results also include gender, race, and sometimes DL or middle initial.
General Information: No sealed records released. Will not fax out case files. Court makes copy: n/a. Self serve: $.50 per page. If searcher supplies paper- $.25 per page. Certification fee: $5.00 per document. Payee: Circuit Court Clerk. Cashiers checks and money orders accepted. Major credit cards accepted online only. Prepayment required.

General Sessions Court 515 S Liberty St, Jackson, TN 38301; criminal phone: 731-423-6128; civil phone: 731-423-6016; fax: 731-265-5398; 8AM-4PM (CST). ***Misdemeanor, Civil Actions under $25,000, Eviction, Small Claims.***
Civil Records: Access: Mail, in person. Visitors must perform in person searches themselves. No search fee. Required to search: name, years to search. Civil cases indexed by defendant, plaintiff. Civil records computerized since 1/98, archived on books in office from 1982, rest stored elsewhere from 1950s. Note: No telephone searches!! Civil PAT goes back to 1994. PAT results show middle initial, DOB.
Criminal Records: Access: In person only. Visitors must perform in person searches themselves. Required to search: name; case number helpful. Records stored since 1950s, computerized since 1/98. Criminal PAT goes back to 1998. PAT results show middle initial, DOB.
General Information: Will fax out docs for $5.00 fee. Court makes copy: $.50 per page. Certification fee: $5.00 per cert. Payee: General Sessions Court. Cashiers checks, money orders accepted. Credit cards accepted at www.paymentchek.com/tn/madisonco. Prepayment required. Mail requests: SASE required.

Probate Division - General Sessions Division II 110 Irby St, #102, Jackson, TN 38301; 731-988-3025; fax: 731-988-3807; 8:30AM-N, 1-4:30PM (CST). ***Probate.***

Marion County

12th District Circuit & General Sessions Court PO Box 789, Courthouse Sq, Jasper, TN 37347; 423-942-2134; fax: 423-942-4160; 8AM-4PM (CST). ***Felony, Misdemeanor, Civil, Eviction, Small Claims.***
Civil Records: Access: Phone, mail, in person. Both court and visitors may perform in person searches. Search fee: $3.00 per name. Required to search: name, years to search. Civil cases indexed by defendant, plaintiff; index on computer from 1988, prior records archived on books and microfiche since 1922. Mail turnaround time 1 week.
Criminal Records: Access: Phone, mail, in person. Both court and visitors may perform in person searches. Search fee: $3.00 per name. Required to search: name, years to search, DOB; also helpful: SSN. Criminal records computerized from 1988, prior records archived on books and microfiche since 1922. Mail turnaround time 1 week.
General Information: No adoption records released. Will fax documents to local or toll free line. Court makes copy: $.50 per page. Self serve: $.50 per page. Certification fee: $3.00. Payee: Circuit Court Clerk. Personal checks accepted; credit cards are not. Prepayment required.

Chancery Court PO Box 789, Jasper, TN 37347; 423-942-2601; fax: 423-942-0291; 8AM-4PM (CST). ***Civil, Probate.***
Civil Records: Access: Mail, in person. Both court and visitors may perform in person searches. No search fee. Required to search: name, years to search. Civil cases indexed by defendant, plaintiff; index on computer since 3/94, prior records on books. Mail turnaround time 1 day. Public use terminal has civil records back to 3/1994. PAT results show name only.
General Information: No adoption records released. Will not fax documents. Court makes copy: $.50 per page. Certification fee: $5.00. Payee: Clerk and Master. Personal checks accepted; credit cards are not. Prepayment required. Mail requests: SASE requested.

Marshall County

17th District Circuit & General Sessions Court 302 Marshall County Courthouse, Lewisburg, TN 37091; 931-359-0536; criminal fax: 931-359-2993; civil fax: same; 8AM-4PM (CST). ***Felony, Misdemeanor, Civil, Eviction, Small Claims.***
Probate fax is same as main fax number.
Civil Records: Access: Mail, in person. Both court and visitors may perform in person searches. Search fee: $10.00 per name. Required to search: name, years to search. Civil cases indexed by plaintiff. Civil records archived on books; also on computer back to 2000. Civil PAT goes back to 2000.
Criminal Records: Access: Mail, in person. Both court and visitors may perform in person searches. Search fee: $10.00 per name. Required to search: name, years to search; also helpful: DOB, SSN. Criminal records go back to 1987; on computer back to 2000. Criminal PAT goes back to same as civil.
General Information: No adoption records released. Will fax specific doc to local or toll-free number. Court makes copy: $.50 per page. Self serve: same. Certification fee: $5.00 per document. Payee: Circuit Court Clerk. No personal checks or credit cards accepted. Prepayment required. Mail requests: SASE required.

Chancery Court 201 Marshall County Courthouse, Lewisburg, TN 37091; 931-359-2181; fax: 931-359-0524; 8AM-4PM (CST). ***Probate.***
Probate is handled by the Clerk & Master.

Maury County

Circuit & General Sessions Court Maury County Courthouse, 41 Public Square, Columbia, TN 38401; 931-381-3690; criminal phone: 931-375-1105/1108; civil phone: 931-375-1109/1112; fax: 931-375-1114; 8AM-4PM (CST). ***Felony, Misdemeanor, Civil, Eviction, Small Claims.***
www.maurycounty-tn.gov/Circuit/circuit.htm
Common court forms available on the website.
Civil Records: Access: Fax, mail, in person. Visitors must perform in person searches themselves. No

search fee. Required to search: name, years to search. Civil cases indexed by defendant, plaintiff; index on books since 1984; on computer back to 1989. Civil PAT goes back to 1989.
Criminal Records: Access: In person only. Visitors must perform in person searches themselves. Required to search: name, years to search; also helpful: DOB, SSN. Criminal records computerized from 1989; others go back to early 1900s. Criminal PAT goes back to same as civil.
General Information: No juvenile records released. Will fax documents $1.00 per page. Court makes copy: $.50 per page. Self serve: same. Certification fee: $6.00 per cert. Payee: Circuit Court Clerk. Only cashiers check or money order accepted. Cedit and Debit cards accpeted over the internet only. Prepayment required.

Probate And Chancery Court Maury County Courthouse, Clerk & Masters Office, 41 Public Square, Columbia, TN 38401; 931-375-1300; fax: 931-375-1319; 8AM-4PM (CST). ***Probate.***
Records on computer go back to 1991.

McMinn County

10th District Circuit & General Sessions Court 6 E Madison Ave, #301, Athens, TN 37303-3666; 423-745-1923; criminal phone: 423-745-1924; civil phone: 423-745-1924; probate phone: 423-745-1281; criminal fax: 423-744-1642; civil fax: same; 8:30AM-4PM (EST). ***Felony, Misdemeanor, Civil, Eviction, Small Claims, Probate.***
Probate records handled by Chancery Court after 07/04; prior in Circuit Court.
Civil Records: Access: Phone, fax, mail, in person. Both court and visitors may perform in person searches. No search fee. Required to search: name, years to search; also helpful: address. Civil cases indexed by defendant, plaintiff. Civil records archived approximately 20 years; computerized back to 1996. Visitor must search using books. Note: Phone searches limited to three names. Mail turnaround time 24-48 hours.
Criminal Records: Access: Phone, fax, mail, in person. Only the court performs in person searches; visitors may not. No search fee. Required to search: name, years to search, DOB, SSN; also helpful: address. Criminal records archived approximately 20 years; computerized back to 1996. Mail turnaround time 24-48 hours.
General Information: No juvenile, adoption records released. Will fax documents. Court makes copy: $.50 per page. Self serve: same. Certification fee: $5.00 per cert plus $2.00 per page. Payee: Circuit Court Clerk. Business checks accepted. No credit cards accepted. Prepayment required.

McNairy County

25th District Circuit & General Sessions Court 300 Industrial Park Dr, Selmer, TN 38375; 731-645-1016/1015; fax: 731-645-1003; 8AM-4:30PM M,T,TH,F; 8AM-N Sat; closed W (CST). ***Felony, Misdemeanor, Civil, Eviction, Small Claims.***
Civil Records: Access: Mail, in person. Both court and visitors may perform in person searches. Search fee: $20.00 per name. Required to search: name, years to search. Civil cases indexed by defendant, plaintiff. Civil records archived on docket books since 1966; computerized records since 2/95. Mail turnaround time 1-2 days. Civil PAT goes back to 1995. PAT results show name only.
Criminal Records: Access: Mail, in person. Both court and visitors may perform in person searches. Search fee: $20.00 per name. Required to search: name, years to search, DOB, SSN. Criminal records archived on docket books since 1966; computerized records since 2/95. Mail turnaround time 1-2 days. Criminal PAT goes back to same as civil.PAT results show name, DOB.
General Information: No juvenile records released. Will not fax documents. Court makes copy: $.25 per page. Self serve: same. Certification fee: $6.00 per cert. Payee: Circuit Court Clerk. Personal checks accepted; credit cards are not. Prepayment required.

Chancery Court Chancery Court, Clerk & Master, Courthouse, Rm 205, Selmer, TN 38375; 731-645-5446; fax: 731-646-1165; 8AM-4PM; closed W (CST). ***Civil, Probate.***
Civil Records: Access: In person only. Visitors must perform in person searches themselves. Required to search: name, years to search. Civil cases indexed by defendant, plaintiff; index on books. Public use terminal has civil records back to 1998.
General Information: No adoption records released. Will fax documents $1.00 per page. Court makes copy: $.50 per page. Self serve: $.50 per page. Certification fee: $5.00. Payee: Clerk & Master. No personal checks accepted. Major credit cards accepted. Prepayment required.

Meigs County

9th District Circuit & General Sessions Court PO Box 205, Decatur, TN 37322; 423-334-5821 Circuit; 423-334-5821 Sessions; fax: 423-334-7201; 8:30AM-5P; till Noon W (EST). ***Felony, Misdemeanor, Civil, Eviction, Small Claims.***
www.meigscountytn.com/
Civil Records: Access: Mail, in person. Both court and visitors may perform in person searches. No search fee; Fee does apply to search of archived records. Required to search: name, years to search. Civil cases indexed by defendant, plaintiff. Civil records archived in office from 1930s, records in storage go further. Note: They refer all name searches to an outside agency. Mail turnaround time 1 week. Civil PAT goes back to 2004. PAT results show name only.
Criminal Records: Access: In person only. Both court and visitors may perform in person searches. No search fee; Fee does apply to search of archived records. Required to search: name, years to search. Criminal records archived in office from 1930s, records in storage go further. Note: They refer name search requests to an outside agency. Criminal PAT goes back to 2004. PAT results show name only.
General Information: No juvenile records released. Will not fax documents. Court makes copy: $.50 per page. Certification fee: $5.00 per cert. Payee: Circuit Court Clerk. Personal checks accepted; credit cards are not. Prepayment required.

Chancery Court PO Box 5, 17214 State Hwy 58 N, Decatur, TN 37322; 423-334-5243; 8AM-5PM M,T,TH,F; 8:30AM-N W (EST). ***Civil, Probate.***
Fax not available.
Civil Records: Access: In person only. Visitors must perform in person searches themselves. Required to search: name, years to search. Civil cases indexed by defendant, plaintiff; index on dockets since 1940.
General Information: No adoption records released. Will fax documents $.25 per page for 3 pages or less. Court makes copy: $.50 per page. Certification fee: $5.00 per cert. Cert fee includes copies. Payee: Meigs County Chancery Court. Personal checks accepted; credit cards are not. Prepayment required.

Monroe County

10th District Circuit I Courts 105 College St #3, Madisonville, TN 37354; 423-442-2396; fax: 423-442-9538; 8AM-4:30PM (EST). ***Felony, Misdemeanor, Civil.*** www.monroegovernment.org
This court does record searches for the General Sessions Court.
Civil Records: Access: Mail, in person. Both court and visitors may perform in person searches. Search fee: $10.00 per name. Required to search: name, years to search. Civil cases indexed by defendant, plaintiff; index on computer since 1991, records on books in office for 10 years, unspecified prior to then. Mail turnaround time 2 days. Civil PAT goes back to 1991. PAT civil results show middle initial. Public terminal also holds records for General Sessions Court.
Criminal Records: Access: Mail, in person. Both court and visitors may perform in person searches. Search fee: $10.00 per name. Required to search: name, years to search. Criminal records on computer since 1991, records on books in office for 10 years, unspecified prior to then. Mail turnaround time 2 days. Criminal PAT goes back to 1992. PAT criminal results show middle initial. Public terminal also holds misdemeanor records for General Sessions Court.
General Information: No juvenile records released. Will fax documents $2.00 per page. Court makes copy: $.50 per page. Certification fee: $5.00. Payee: Circuit Court Clerk. Personal checks accepted; credit cards are not. Prepayment required.

General Sessions Court 310 Tellico St South, #1, Madisonville, TN 37354-1391; 423-442-9537; fax: 423-420-9091; 8AM-4:30PM (EST). ***Civil under $25,000, Eviction, Small Claims.***
Civil Records: Access: Mail, in person. Both court and visitors may perform in person searches. Search fee: $10.00 per name. Required to search: name, years to search. Civil cases indexed by defendant, plaintiff; index on computer since 1991, records on books in this office for 3 years, otherwise in offsite storage. Note: All name searches must be performed at the Circuit Clerk's office. They have a public access terminal there. All mail requests are also forwarded to the Circuit Clerks Office. Mail turnaround time 2 days. Public use terminal has civil records back to 1991. PAT results show name only. Public terminal located at General Sessions Clerk's office.
General Information: No juvenile records released. Will fax documents $2.00 per page. Court makes copy: $.50 per page. Self serve: same. Certification fee: $5.00 per cert. Payee: Circuit Court Clerk. No personal checks or credit cards accepted. Prepayment required.

Chancery Court 105 College St, #2, Madisonville, TN 37354; 423-442-2644; civil phone: 423-442-5940; probate phone: 423-442-4573; fax: 423-420-0048; 8:30AM-4:30PM till 4PM W (EST). ***Civil, Probate.***
www.monroegovernment.org/
Civil Records: Access: Mail, in person. Both court and visitors may perform in person searches. No search fee. Required to search: name, years to search. Civil cases indexed by plaintiff and defendant. Civil records on computer since 05/92, prior records on books. Mail turnaround time 2-3 days.
General Information: No adoption, sealed records released. Will fax documents to local or toll free line. Court makes copy: $.50 per page. Certification fee: $5.00. Payee: Chancery Court. Personal checks accepted; credit cards are not. Prepayment required. Mail requests: SASE requested.

Montgomery County

Montgomery County Circuit & General Sessions Court 2 Millennium Plaza, #115, Clarksville, TN 37040; 931-648-5700; fax: 931-648-5729; 8AM-4:30PM (CST). ***Felony, Misdemeanor, Civil, Evictions, Small Claims.***
Civil Records: Access: Mail, fax, in person. Visitors must perform in person searches themselves. Required to search: name, years to search. Search fee: None. Civil cases indexed by defendant, plaintiff; index on computer back to 11/1999, archived on books in office from 1970s, on microfiche from 1950s. Civil PAT goes back to 11/1999. PAT civil results show middle initial.
Criminal Records: Access: Mail, fax, in person. Both court and visitors may perform in person searches. Search fee: None. Required to search: name, years to search, DOB; also helpful-signed release, SSN. Criminal records computerized from 1985; prior records archived on books from 1970s, on microfiche from 1950s. Mail turnaround time 24 hours. Criminal PAT goes back to 1985. PAT results show middle initial, DOB. Terminal results include SSN.
General Information: No juvenile records released. Will not fax documents. Court makes copy: $.50 per page. Certification fee: $10.00 per doc. Payee: Circuit Court (Criminal or General Sessions Court (civil). Business checks accepted. Major credit cards accepted. Prepayment required. Mail requests: SASE required.

County Court County Courts Center/Clerk & Master, 2 Millennium Plaza, #101, Clarksville, TN 37040; 931-648-5703; probate phone: same; fax: 931-648-5759; 8AM-4:30PM (CST). ***Civil, Probate.***
www.montgomerycountytn.org/county/index.htm
Probate fax is same as main fax number.
Civil Records: Access: Mail, fax, in person. Visitors must perform in person searches themselves. Required to search: name, years to search. Search fee: None. Civil cases indexed by defendant, plaintiff; index on books, microfilm, or computer. Public use terminal has civil records back to 1995. PAT results show name only.
General Information: No adoption or sealed records released. Will not fax documents. Court makes copy: $.50 per page. Certification fee: $5.00 per doc. Payee: County Court. Business checks accepted, also debit cards. No credit cards accepted. Prepayment required.

Moore County

17th District Circuit & General Sessions Court PO Box 206, 196 Main St, Courthouse, Lynchburg, TN 37352; 931-759-7208; 8AM-N, 1-4:30PM M,W,F; 8AM-N Sat (CST). ***Felony, Misdemeanor, Civil, Eviction, Small Claims.***
Civil Records: Access: Mail, in person. Both court and visitors may perform in person searches. Search fee: $5.00 per name. Required to search: name, years to search. Civil cases indexed by defendant, plaintiff. Civil records archived to 1862, on docket books and microfiche from 1862 to 1980s. Mail turnaround time 7-10 days.
Criminal Records: Access: Mail, in person. Both court and visitors may perform in person searches. Search fee: $5.00 per name. Required to search: name, years to search. Criminal records archived to 1862, on docket books and microfiche from 1862 to 1980s. Mail turnaround time 7-10 days.
General Information: No juvenile records released. Will fax documents to local or toll-free number. Court makes copy: $.50 per page. Certification fee: $5.00 per doc. Payee: Circuit Court Clerk. Only cashiers checks and money orders accepted. Prepayment required. Mail requests: SASE required.

Chancery Court PO Box 206, 196 Main St, Courthouse, Lynchburg, TN 37352; 931-759-7028; fax: 931-759-5610; 8AM-N, 1-4:30PM M,W,F; 8AM-N Sat (CST). ***Civil, Probate.***
Civil Records: Access: In person only. Visitors must perform in person searches themselves. Required to search: name, years to search. Civil cases indexed by plaintiff. Civil records on books.
General Information: No adoption or sealed records released. Will not fax documents. Court makes copy: $.50 per page. Self serve: same. Certification fee: $5.00 per document. Payee: Clerk and Master. Only cashiers checks and money orders accepted. Prepayment required.

Morgan County

9th District Circuit & General Sessions Court PO Box 163, 415 N Kingston, Wartburg, TN 37887; 423-346-3503; fax: 423-346-5947; 8AM-4PM (EST). ***Felony, Misdemeanor, Civil, Eviction, Small Claims.***
Civil Records: Access: In person only. Visitors must perform in person searches themselves. Required to search: name, years to search. Civil cases indexed by defendant, plaintiff. Civil records archived on books from 1855.
Criminal Records: Access: In person only. Visitors must perform in person searches themselves. Required to search: name, years to search; also helpful: DOB, SSN. Criminal records archived on books from 1855; computerized since 2/01.
General Information: No sealed records released. Court makes copy: $.50 per page. Certification fee: $5.00 per cert. Payee: Circuit Court Clerk. Only cashiers checks and money orders accepted. No credit cards accepted. Prepayment required.

Chancery Court PO Box 789, Wartburg, TN 37887; 423-346-3881; probate phone: same; fax: 423-346-4217; 8AM-4PM (EST). ***Civil, Probate.***
Probate is separate index at same address. Probate fax is same as main fax number.
Civil Records: Access: Phone, mail, in person. Both court and visitors may perform in person searches. No search fee. Required to search: name, years to search. Civil cases indexed by defendant, plaintiff. Civil records in books since 1883, on microfiche since 1939 at state archives. Mail turnaround 1-8 days.
General Information: No adoption or conservatorship records released. Will fax documents to local or toll free line. Court makes copy: $.50 per page. Certification fee: $5.00 per cert. Payee: Clerk & Master. Personal checks accepted; credit cards are not. Prepayment required. Mail requests: SASE required.

Obion County

27th District Circuit Court 7 Bill Burnett Cir, Union City, TN 38261; 731-885-1372; fax: 731-885-7922; 8:30AM-4:30PM (CST). ***Felony, Misdemeanor, Civil Actions over $25,000.***
Civil Records: Access: Mail, in person. Both court and visitors may perform in person searches. Search fee: $5.00 per name. Required to search: name, years to search. Civil cases indexed by defendant, plaintiff. Civil records archived on books from 1969, civil on books from 1974, rest are located elsewhere. Mail turnaround time 2 days. Civil PAT goes back to 12/1993. PAT civil results show middle initial.
Criminal Records: Access: Mail, in person. Both court and visitors may perform in person searches. Search fee: $5.00. Required to search: name, years to search, DOB, SSN. Criminal records for archived on books from 1969. Mail turnaround time 2 days. Criminal PAT goes back to 12/1993.
General Information: No adoption records released. Will fax documents to local or toll-free number. Court makes copy: $.50 per page. Certification fee: $5.00. Payee: Circuit Court. Business checks accepted. No credit cards accepted. Prepayment required. Mail requests: SASE required.

General Sessions Court 9 Bill Burnett Cir, Union City, TN 38281-0236; 731-885-1811; fax: 731-885-7922; 8:30AM-4:30PM (CST). ***Civil Actions under $25,000, Eviction, Small Claims.***
Civil Records: Access: Mail, in person. Both court and visitors may perform in person searches. Search fee: $5.00 per name, 5 years or less; $10.00 over 5 years. Required to search: name. Civil cases indexed by defendant, plaintiff. Civil records kept in office for last 10 years, computerized since 1994. Mail turnaround time 2 days. Public use terminal has civil records back to 1994. PAT results show name only.
General Information: No juvenile or adoption records released. Will fax documents to local or toll-free number. Court makes copy: $.50 per page. Certification fee: $5.00. Payee: Circuit Court Clerk. Personal checks accepted; credit cards are not. Prepayment required. Mail requests: SASE required.

Chancery Court PO Box 187, Union City, TN 38281; 731-885-2562; fax: 731-885-7922; 8:30AM-4:30PM (CST). ***Civil, Probate.***
Civil Records: Access: Phone, mail, in person. Both court and visitors may perform in person searches. Search fee: $5.00 per name. Required to search: name, years to search. Civil cases indexed by defendant, plaintiff. Civil records (probate) from 9/82 on books in Chancery office, prior records back to 1800s on index books in County Clerk's office. Mail turnaround time 2 days. Public use terminal has civil records.
General Information: No adoption or sealed records released. Will fax documents $5.00 each. Court makes copy: $.50 per page. Certification fee: $5.00. Payee: Clerk and Master. Personal checks accepted; credit cards are not. Prepayment required.

Overton County

13th District Circuit & General Sessions Court Overton County Courthouse, 1000 John Tom Poindexter Dr, Livingston, TN 38570; 931-823-2312; fax: 931-823-9728; 8AM-4:30PM (CST). ***Felony, Misdemeanor, Civil, Eviction, Small Claims.***
Civil Records: Access: Mail, in person. Both court and visitors may perform in person searches. No search fee. Required to search: name, years to search. Civil cases indexed by defendant, plaintiff. Civil records archived on books from late 1800s; computerized records since 1996. Mail turnaround time 3-5 days.
Criminal Records: Access: Mail, in person. Both court and visitors may perform in person searches. No search fee. Required to search: name, years to search, DOB, SSN, signed release. Criminal records archived on books from late 1800s; computerized records since 1996. Mail turnaround time 3-5 days.
General Information: No juvenile records released. Will not fax documents. Court makes copy: $.50 per page. Certification fee: $5.00 per page. Payee: Circuit Court Clerk. Local business checks accepted. No credit cards accepted. Prepayment required. Mail requests: SASE required.

County Court 317 E University St, Livingston, TN 38570; 931-823-2631; fax: 931-823-7631; 8AM-4PM (CST). ***Probate.***

Perry County

21st District Circuit & General Sessions Court PO Box 91, Linden, TN 37096; 931-589-2218; fax: 931-589-2350; 8AM-4PM (CST). ***Felony, Misdemeanor, Civil, Eviction, Small Claims.***
Civil Records: Access: Mail, in person. Both court and visitors may perform in person searches. No search fee. Required to search: name, years to search. Civil cases indexed by defendant, plaintiff. Civil records archived on books from 1941, on microfiche (limited) at library. Mail turnaround time 2-3 days.
Criminal Records: Access: Mail, in person. Both court and visitors may perform in person searches. No search fee. Required to search: name, years to search, DOB, SSN. Criminal records archived on books from 1941, on microfiche (limited) at library. Mail turnaround time 2-3 days.
General Information: No adoption records released. Court makes copy: $.50 per page. Self serve: same. No certification fee. Payee: Circuit Court Clerk. Personal checks accepted only if local. No credit cards accepted. Prepayment required. Mail requests: SASE required.

Chancery Court PO Box 251, Linden, TN 37096; 931-589-2217; fax: 931-589-6369; 8AM-4PM (CST). ***Civil, Probate.***
Civil Records: Access: In person only. Both court and visitors may perform in person searches. No search fee. Required to search: name, years to search. Civil cases indexed by defendant, plaintiff. Civil records (probate) on books from 1982, prior records in County Clerks office. Public use terminal has civil records back to 2002.
General Information: No adoption records released. Will not fax documents. Court makes copy: $.50 per page. Self serve: same. Certification fee: $5.00. Payee: Clerk and Master. Local checks accepted. No credit cards accepted. Prepayment required.

Pickett County

13th District Circuit & General Sessions Court PO Box 188, 1 Courthouse Sq, Byrdstown, TN 38549; 931-864-3958; fax: 931-864-6885; 8AM-4PM, except W 8-11AM (CST). ***Felony, Misdemeanor, Civil, Eviction, Small Claims.***
Civil Records: Access: Mail, in person. Both court and visitors may perform in person searches. Search fee: $10.00 per name. Required to search: name, years to search. Civil cases indexed by defendant. Civil records archived on books but not specific. Mail turnaround time 3-4 days. Civil PAT goes back to 2000.
Criminal Records: Access: Mail, in person. Both court and visitors may perform in person searches. Search fee: $10.00 per name. Required to search: name, years to search; also helpful: SSN. Criminal records not computerized, all on books. Mail turnaround time 3-4 days. Criminal PAT goes back to 2000.
General Information: No adoption or juvenile records released. Will not fax documents. Court makes copy for no fee. No certification fee. Payee: Circuit Court Clerk. Personal checks accepted; credit cards are not. Prepayment required.

County Court 1 Courthouse Sq, Ste 201, Byrdstown, TN 38549; 931-864-3879; fax: 931-864-7087; 8AM-4PM M T,TH,F, 8-11AM W,S (CST). ***Probate.***

Polk County

10th District Circuit & General Sessions Court PO Box 256, Benton, TN 37307; 423-338-4524; fax: 423-338-8611; 8:30AM-4:30PM (EST). ***Felony, Misdemeanor, Civil, Eviction, Small Claims.***

Civil Records: Access: Mail, fax, in person. Both court and visitors may perform in person searches. Search fee: $5.00 per name. Required to search: name, years to search. Civil cases indexed by defendant, plaintiff. Civil records archived from 1936, computerized since 2000. Mail turnaround time 1 day. Civil PAT goes back to 2000.

Criminal Records: Access: Mail, fax, in person. Both court and visitors may perform in person searches. Search fee: $5.00 per name. Required to search: name, years to search, DOB, SSN. Criminal records archived from 1936, computerized since 2000. Mail turnaround time 3 days. Criminal PAT goes back to same as civil. PAT results show middle initial, DOB.

General Information: No juvenile records released. Will fax documents $5.00 per name. Court makes copy: $.50 per page. Self serve: same. Certification fee: $7.50 per cert. Payee: Circuit Court Clerk. Personal checks accepted; credit cards are not. Prepayment required. Mail requests: SASE requested.

Chancery Court PO Box 689, Benton, TN 37307; 423-338-4522; fax: 423-338-4553; 8:30AM-4:30PM (EST). ***Civil, Probate.***

Civil Records: Access: Mail, in person. Both court and visitors may perform in person searches. Search fee: $5.00 per name. Fee varies by document. Required to search: name, years to search. Civil cases indexed by defendant, plaintiff; index on books up to 1800s, computerized since 10/00. Mail turnaround time 2 days.

General Information: No adoption records released. Will fax documents to local or toll free line. Court makes copy: $.50 per page. Certification fee: $5.00 per cert. Payee: Chancery Court. Personal checks accepted; credit cards are not. Prepayment required.

Putnam County

13th District Circuit & General Sessions Court 421 E Spring St, 1C-49A, Cookeville, TN 38501; 931-528-1508; fax: 931-526-2004; 8AM-4PM (CST). ***Felony, Misdemeanor, Civil, Eviction, Small Claims, Probate.***

www.dockets.putnamco.org

Current docket information available at the website. Effective July 1, 2008 this office handles Juvenile and Probate Courts.

Civil Records: Access: In person only. Visitors must perform in person searches themselves. Required to search: name, years to search. Civil cases indexed by defendant, plaintiff. Civil records archived in office from 1980s, unknown before then; computerized records since 1995. Civil PAT goes back to 1995. PAT civil results show middle initial. PAT results may also include a DOB.

Criminal Records: Access: In person. Visitors must perform in person searches themselves. Required to search: name, years to search; also helpful: SSN. Criminal records computerized since 1995. Criminal PAT goes back to 1995. PAT criminal results show middle initial. PAT results may also include a DOB.

General Information: No juvenile or adoption records released. Will fax out documents. Court makes copy: $.50 per page. Self serve: same. Certification fee: $5.00. Payee: Circuit Court Clerk. Business checks accepted, no personal checks. Visa/MC/AmEx/Discover accepted through VitalChek. Prepayment required.

Probate & Juvenile Court 29 N Washington Ave, Cookeville, TN 38501; 931-528-1508; 8AM-4:00PM (CST). ***Probate.***

Prior to July 1, 2008 this court was located at 421 E Spring St, Cookeville, TN.

Rhea County

12th District Circuit & General Sessions Court 1475 Market St, Rm 102, Dayton, TN 37321; 423-775-7805; criminal phone: 423-775-7818; probate phone: 423-775-7806; fax: 423-775-7895; 8AM-4:30PM (EST). ***Felony, Misdemeanor, Civil, Eviction, Small Claims, Probate.***

Probate located at the Rhea County Clerk and Master's Office. Probate fax- 423-775-4046

Civil Records: Access: Phone, mail, in person. Visitors must perform in person searches themselves. No search fee. Required to search: name, years to search. Civil cases indexed by defendant, plaintiff. Civil records in docket books and on computer. Note: Phone and mail search requests are performed on computer back to 7/2002 only.

Criminal Records: Access: Phone, mail, in person. Both court and visitors may perform in person searches. No search fee. Required to search: name, years to search; also helpful: DOB, SSN. Criminal records in docket books and on computer. Note: Phone and mail search requests are performed on computer back to 7/2002 only.

General Information: No adoption records released. Will not fax documents. Court makes copy: $.50 per page. Certification fee: $5.00 per doc. Payee: Circuit Court Clerk. Local personal checks accepted; no out of state checks. No credit cards accepted. Prepayment required. Mail requests: SASE required.

Roane County

9th District Circuit & General Sessions Court PO Box 73, Kingston, TN 37763; 865-376-2390; fax: 865-717-4141; 8:30AM-6PM M; 8:30AM-4:30PM T-F (EST). ***Felony, Misdemeanor, Civil, Eviction, Small Claims.***

General Sessions phone is 865-376-5584, their records are separate from Circuit Court records.

Civil Records: Access: Mail, fax, in person. Both court and visitors may perform in person searches. Search fee: $5.00 per name. Required to search: name, years to search. Civil cases indexed by defendant, plaintiff. Civil records archived since court started, General Sessions and Circuit are on computer since 1991. Mail turnaround time 2-3 days. Civil PAT goes back to 1990; results show name only.

Criminal Records: Access: Mail, fax, in person. Both court and visitors may perform in person searches. Search fee: $5.00 per name. Required to search: name, years to search, DOB; also helpful, SSN, signed release. Criminal records archived since court started, General Sessions and Circuit are on computer since 1991. Mail turnaround time 2-3 days. Criminal PAT goes back to same as civil.PAT results show name, DOB.

General Information: No adoption, expunged records released. Will fax documents. Court makes copy: $.50 per page. Self serve: same. Certification fee: $5.00. Payee: Circuit Court Clerk. Business checks accepted. No credit cards accepted. Prepayment required. Mail requests: SASE required.

Chancery Court PO Box 402, Kingston, TN 37763; 865-376-2487; fax: 865-376-1228; 8:30AM-6PM M, 8:30AM-4:30PM T-F (EST). ***Civil, Probate.***

Civil Records: Access: Phone, mail, in person. Both court and visitors may perform in person searches. Search fee: $5.00. Required to search: name, years to search. Civil cases indexed by defendant, plaintiff; index on books; on computer since 7/95. Tax records on computer since 1982. Note: Searches made by employees are on the computer, searches made by visitor by books. Mail turnaround time same day.

General Information: No adoption records released. Fee to fax out file $1.00 per page. Court makes copy: $.50 per page. Certification fee: $5.00; Exemplification fee- $20.00. Payee: Clerk and Master. Personal checks accepted; credit cards are not. Prepayment required.

Robertson County

County Circuit Court Robertson County Courthouse, Rm 109, Springfield, TN 37172; 615-384-7864; fax: 615-384-0246; 8AM-4:30PM (CST). ***Felony, Misdemeanor.***

Civil Records: Access: Phone, fax, mail, in person. Both court and visitors may perform in person searches. Search fee: $5.00 per name. Required to search: name, years to search. Civil cases indexed by defendant, plaintiff. Civil records archived in office from 2003, archived from 1800s located elsewhere. Mail turnaround time 15 days. Civil PAT goes back to 1994.

Criminal Records: Access: Phone, fax, mail, in person. Both court and visitors may perform in person searches. Search fee: $5.00 per name. Required to search: name, years to search; also helpful: DOB, SSN. Criminal records archived in office from 2003, archived from 1800s located elsewhere. Mail turnaround time 15 days. Criminal PAT goes back to same as civil. PAT results show middle initial, DOB. Terminal results include SSN.

General Information: No sealed records released. Will fax documents to local or toll-free number. Court makes copy: $.50 per page. Self serve: same. Certification fee: $5.00 plus $.50 per page. Payee: Circuit Court Clerk. No personal checks. Credit cards accepted. Prepayment required. Mail requests: SASE required.

General Sessions Court 529 S Brown St., Springfield, TN 37172-2941; 615-382-2324; fax: 615-382-3113; 8AM-4:30PM (CST). ***Misdemeanor, Civil Actions under $25,000, Eviction, Small Claims, Traffic.***

Civil Records: Access: Fax, mail, in person. Both court and visitors may perform in person searches. Search fee: $5.00 per name. Required to search: name, years to search. Civil cases indexed by defendant, plaintiff. Civil records archived in office from 2000, archived from 1800s located elsewhere. Mail turnaround time 7 days. Civil PAT goes back to 1994. PAT civil results show middle initial.

Criminal Records: Access: Fax, mail, in person. Both court and visitors may perform in person searches. Search fee: $5.00 per name. Required to search: name, years to search; also helpful: DOB, SSN. Criminal records archived in office from 2000, archived from 1800s located elsewhere. Mail turnaround time 7 days. Criminal PAT goes back to same as civil. PAT criminal results show middle initial.

General Information: No sealed records released. Will fax documents to local or toll-free number. Court makes copy: $.50 per page. Self serve: same. Certification fee: $5.00 per doc. Payee: General Sessions Court Clerk. No personal checks. Major credit cards accepted. Prepayment required. Mail requests: SASE required.

Chancery Court 501 Main St, Rm 103, County Courthouse, Springfield, TN 37172; 615-384-5650; fax: 615-382-3128; 8AM-4:30PM (CST). ***Civil, Probate.***

Civil Records: Access: Mail, in person. Only the court performs in person searches; visitors may not. Search fee: $5.00. Required to search: name, years to search. Civil cases indexed by defendant, plaintiff. Probate records in books since 1982, computerized from 9/94 to present, all chancery records on books. Mail turnaround time 1-2 days.

General Information: No adoption records released. Will fax documents $2.00 per name. Court makes copy: $.50 per page. Certification fee: $5.00. Payee: Clerk & Master. Personal checks accepted. Prepayment required. Mail requests: SASE required.

Rutherford County

16th District Circuit Court Judicial Bldg, Rm 201, Murfreesboro, TN 37130; criminal phone: 615-898-7812; civil phone: 615-898-7820; criminal fax: 615-217-7120; civil fax: 615-217-7118; 8AM-4:15PM (CST). ***Felony, Misdemeanor, Civil Actions over $15,000.***

Civil Records: Access: In person only. Visitors must perform in person searches themselves. Required to search: name, years to search. Civil cases indexed by defendant, plaintiff. Civil on computer since 1986. Civil PAT goes back to 1986. PAT results show middle initial, DOB, SSN.

Criminal Records: Access: In person only. Visitors must perform in person searches themselves.

Required to search: name, years to search, DOB, signed release; SSN helpful. Criminal on computer since 1990. Criminal PAT goes back to 1990. PAT results show middle initial, DOB, SSN.
General Information: No expunged, sealed criminal records released. Will not fax documents. Court makes copy: $.50 per page. Self serve: $.50 per page. Certification fee: $4.00 plus $.50 per page. Payee: Circuit Court Clerk. Personal checks accepted; credit cards are not. Prepayment required.

General Sessions Court Judicial Bldg, Rm 101, Murfreesboro, TN 37130; 615-898-7831; fax: 615-898-7835; 8AM-4:15PM (CST). ***Civil Actions under $15,000, Eviction, Small Claims.***
Civil Records: Access: In person only. Visitors must perform in person searches themselves. Required to search: name, years to search, DOB, SSN. Civil cases indexed by defendant, plaintiff. Civil records go back to 1948; on computer from 1986. Public use terminal has civil records back to 1986.
General Information: No juvenile records released. Will fax documents. Court makes copy: $.50 per page. Self serve: $.50 per page. Certification fee: $5.00. Payee: General Sessions Court. No personal checks or credit cards accepted. Prepayment required.

County Court 319 N Maple St, Murfreesboro, TN 37130; 615-898-7798; fax: 615-217-6597; 8AM-4PM M-TH; 8AM-5PM F (CST). ***Probate.***

Scott County

Circuit & General Sessions Court PO Box 330, Huntsville, TN 37756; 423-663-2440; fax: 423-663-2595; 8AM-4:30PM ***Felony, Misdemeanor, Civil, Eviction, Small Claims, Probate.***
Probate is a separate index at this same address. Probate fax is same as main fax number.
Civil Records: Access: Phone, mail, in person. Both court and visitors may perform in person searches. Search fee: $10.00 per name per year. Required to search: name, years to search. Civil cases indexed by defendant, plaintiff. Civil records archived in docket books but not specified, on computer from 1991. Mail turnaround time same week.
Criminal Records: Access: Phone, mail, in person. Both court and visitors may perform in person searches. Search fee: $10.00 per name per year. Fee varies according to info requested. Required to search: name, years to search, DOB; also helpful: SSN. Criminal records archived in docket books but not specified, on computer from 1991. Mail turnaround time same week.
General Information: No juvenile records released. Will fax documents to local or toll free line. Court makes copy: $.50 per page. Self serve: same. Certification fee: $5.00 per seal. Payee: Circuit Court Clerk. Personal checks accepted; credit cards are not. Prepayment required. Mail requests: SASE required.

Sequatchie County

12th District Circuit & General Sessions Court 351 Fredonia Rd, Ste B, Dunlap, TN 37327; 423-949-2618; fax: 423-949-2902; 8AM-4PM (CST). ***Felony, Misdemeanor, Civil, Eviction, Small Claims.***
Civil Records: Access: Phone, fax, mail, in person. Both court and visitors may perform in person searches. No search fee. Required to search: name, years to search. Civil cases indexed by defendant, plaintiff. Civil records archived on books but not specified. Mail turnaround time 1 week.
Criminal Records: Access: Phone, fax, mail, in person. Both court and visitors may perform in person searches. No search fee. Required to search: name, years to search, DOB; also helpful: SSN. Criminal records not computerized. Mail turnaround time 1 week.
General Information: No adoption records released. Will fax documents $1.00 per page. Court makes copy: $.50 per page. Certification fee: $4.00. Payee: Circuit Court Clerk. Personal checks accepted; credit cards are not. Prepayment required. Mail requests: SASE required.

Chancery Court PO Box 1651, 22 Cherry St, Dunlap, TN 37327; 423-949-3670; fax: 423-949-2570; 8AM-4PM (CST). ***Civil, Probate.***
Civil Records: Access: In person only. Only the court performs in person searches; visitors may not. Required to search: name, years to search. Civil cases indexed by defendant, plaintiff; index on books.
General Information: No sealed or adoption records released. Will fax documents $1.00 per page. Court makes copy: $.50 per page. Certification fee: $5.00 per cert. Payee: Clerk and Master. Personal checks accepted; credit cards are not. Prepayment required.

Sevier County

4th District Circuit Court 125 Court Ave, #204E, Sevierville, TN 37862; criminal phone: 865-774-3731; civil phone: 865-453-5536; criminal fax: 865-774-3620; civil fax: 865-774-9792; 8AM-4:30PM M-TH, 8AM-6PM F (EST). ***Felony, Misdemeanor, Civil Actions over $15,000.***
Civil Records: Access: Fax, mail, in person. Both court and visitors may perform in person searches. Search fee: $10.00 per name. Required to search: name, years to search. Civil cases indexed by defendant, plaintiff. Civil records computerized back to 1993. Records before 1980s difficult to locate. Mail turnaround time 1 week. Civil PAT goes back to 1993.
Criminal Records: Access: Fax, mail, in person. Both court and visitors may perform in person searches. Search fee: $10.00 per name. Required to search: name, years to search. Criminal records computerized back to 1993. Mail turnaround time 1 week. Criminal PAT goes back to same as civil.
General Information: No expunged records released. Will fax documents $1.00 per page. Court makes copy: $.50 per page. Self serve: same. Certification fee: $4.00 per cert. Payee: Circuit Court or General Sessions Clerk. No personal checks or credit cards accepted. Mail requests: SASE required.

General Sessions Court 125 Court Ave, #107E, Sevierville, TN 37862; 865-453-6116; criminal phone: 865-453-6116; civil phone: 865-429-5671; fax: 865-774-3842; 8AM-4:30PM M-TH, 8AM-6PM F (EST). ***Misdemeanor, Civil Actions under $25,000, Eviction, Small Claims.***
Civil Records: Access: Phone, fax, mail. Only the court performs in person searches; visitors may not. No search fee. Required to search: name, years to search. Civil cases indexed by defendant, plaintiff. Civil records computerized back to 1995. Records before 1980s difficult to locate. Mail turnaround time 1 week. Civil PAT goes back to 6/1995.
Criminal Records: Access: Fax, mail. Only the court performs in person searches; visitors may not. No search fee. Required to search: name, years to search; also helpful: date of arrest. Criminal records computerized back to 1995; index back to 1973. Mail turnaround time 1 week. Criminal PAT goes back to 6/1995. PAT results show middle initial, DOB, SSN.
General Information: No expunged records released. Will fax documents $1.00 per page. Court makes copy: $.50 per page. Self serve: $1.00 per case. Certification fee: $5.00. Payee: General Sessions Clerk. No personal checks. Money order or cash only. No credit cards accepted. Prepayment required.

County Court 125 Court Ave, #202 East, Sevierville, TN 37862; 865-453-5502; fax: 865-453-6830; 8AM-4:30PM (EST). ***Probate.***

Shelby County

Circuit Court 140 Adams Ave, Rm 224, Memphis, TN 38103; 901-545-4006; fax: 901-545-3952; 8AM-4:30PM (CST). ***Civil Actions over $25,000.***
www.circuitcourt.co.shelby.tn.us
The East Office is no longer open.
Civil Records: Access: Fax, mail, in person, online. Both court and visitors may perform in person searches. Search fee: $5.00 per name. Required to search: name; also helpful: years to search. Civil cases indexed by defendant, plaintiff. Civil records archived from early 1900s, on computer from 1991, on microfiche from 1980. Mail turnaround time 5-8 days. Public use terminal has civil records back to 1994. Search clerk's circuit court records for free at the website or at http://gs2.co.shelby.tn.us:7779/pls/crweb/ck_public_qry_main.cp_main_idx.
General Information: Online identifiers in results same as on public terminal. No juvenile or adoption records released. Will fax documents $1.00 per page. Court makes copy: $.50 per page. Self serve: same. Certification fee: $5.00 per cert. Payee: Circuit Court Clerk. Personal checks accepted; credit cards are not. Prepayment required.

30th District Criminal Court Office of the Criminal Court, 201 Poplar, Rm 4-01, Memphis, TN 38103; 901-545-5040; fax: 901-545-3679; 8AM-4:30PM (CST). ***Felony.***
http://co4.shelbycountytn.gov/court_clerks/criminal_court/index.html
Criminal Records: Access: Fax, mail, in person, online. Both court and visitors may perform in person searches. Search fee: $5.00 per name. There is no fee if you do the search yourself. Required to search: name, years to search, DOB, SSN. Criminal records on computer as far back as 1989, prior records archived. Mail turnaround time 3 days. Public use terminal has crim records back to 1989 but may not be complete. PAT results show middle initial, DOB. Search the criminal court records for free at http://jssi.co.shelby.tn.us/. Online results show middle initial, DOB.
General Information: No expunged or sealed records released. Fee to fax out file $4.00 if out of town, $3.00 if in-town. Court makes copy: $.50 per page. Certification fee: $5.00 per cert. Payee: Criminal Court Clerk. Business checks accepted. Visa/MC accepted in person only. Prepayment required.

Chancery Court 140 Adams, Rm 308, Memphis, TN 38103; 901-545-4002; fax: 901-545-2588; 8AM-4:30PM (CST). ***Civil Actions under $25,000, Equity Cases (also, lower Circuit Court Civil issues).***
http://chancerycourt.co.shelby.tn.us
Civil Records: Access: Mail, fax, in person, online. Only the court performs in person searches; visitors may not. Search fee: $5.00 per name. Required to search: name, years to search. Civil cases indexed by defendant, plaintiff. Civil records go back to 1972. Mail turnaround time 1 week. Search court records for free at http://gs2.co.shelby.tn.us:7779/pls/chweb/ck_public_qry_main.cp_main_idx.
General Information: No juvenile or adoption records released. Will not fax documents. Court makes copy: $.50 per page. Certification fee: $5.00 per cert. Payee: Chancery Court Clerk. No personal checks or credit cards accepted. Prepayment required. Mail requests: SASE requested.

General Sessions - Civil 140 Adams, Rm 106, Memphis, TN 38103; 901-545-4031; fax: 901-545-2515; 8AM-4:30PM (CST). ***Civil Actions under $25,000, Eviction, Small Claims.***
http://generalsessionscourt.co.shelby.tn.us
Also an East Division office at 1075 Station Rd, #115 West, ph 901-379-7052, fax 901-379-7053.
Civil Records: Access: In person, online. Visitors must perform in person searches themselves. Required to search: name, years to search. Civil cases indexed by defendant, plaintiff. Civil records archived 10 years in office, some microfiche and on computer from 1982. No paper indexes. Note: Note- Soundex does not always work. Public use terminal has civil records back to 10-20 years, depending on case type. Search court records for free at http://gs2.co.shelby.tn.us:7779/pls/gnweb/ck_public_qry_main.cp_main_idx.
General Information: Online identifiers in results same as on public terminal. No mental commitment records released. Will not fax documents. Court makes copy: $.50 per page. Self serve: same. Certification fee: $5.00 per cert. Payee: General Sessions Court Clerk. Personal checks and major credit cards accepted. Prepayment required.

General Sessions - Criminal 201 Poplar, Rm 81, Memphis, TN 38103; criminal phone: 901-545-5100; fax: 901-545-3655; 8AM-4:30PM (CST). ***Misdemeanor.***
http://generalsessionscourt.co.shelby.tn.us
Criminal Records: Access: Mail, in person, online. Both court and visitors may perform in person searches. Search fee: $10.00 per name. Use of terminal is now free. Required to search: name, years

to search, DOB; also helpful: SSN. Criminal records on computer since 1982, prior records archived since court started. Mail turnaround time 2-5 days. Public use terminal has crim records back to 1982. Search criminal court records free at http://jssi.co.shelby.tn.us/. Online results show middle initial, DOB, SSN.
General Information: No mental records released. Court makes copy: $.50 per page. No certification fee. Payee: General Sessions Court. Personal checks and major credit cards accepted. Prepayment required.

Probate Court 140 Adams Ave, Rm 124, Memphis, TN 38103; 901-545-4040; fax: 901-545-4746; 8AM-4:30PM (CST). ***Probate.***
www.shelbyprobate.com
Probate court records and dockets are free at www.probatedata.co.shelby.tn.us/default2.htm. Search online by name or case number.

Smith County

15th District Circuit & General Sessions Court 211 Main St, Carthage, TN 37030; 615-735-0500 (Gen Sess.); 615-735-8260 (Circuit Ct); fax: 615-735-8261; 8AM-4PM (CST). ***Felony, Misdemeanor, Civil, Eviction, Small Claims.***
Civil Records: Access: Mail, in person. Visitors must perform in person searches themselves. No search fee. Required to search: name, years to search. Civil cases indexed by defendant, plaintiff; index on computer from 3/92, prior records archived on books, questionable to dates. Mail turnaround time 1-2 days.
Criminal Records: Access: Phone, mail, in person. Visitors must perform in person searches themselves. No search fee. Required to search: name, years to search. Criminal records computerized from 3/92, prior records archived on books, questionable to dates. Mail turnaround time 1-2 days.
General Information: No juvenile records released. Will not fax documents. Court makes copy: $.50 per page. Certification fee: $6.00. Payee: Circuit Court Clerk. Only cashiers checks and money orders accepted. Major credit cards accepted. Prepayment required.

Chancery Court 211 N Main St, Carthage, TN 37030; 615-735-2092; fax: 615-735-8431; 8AM-4PM (CST). ***Civil, Probate.***
Civil Records: Access: Fax, mail, in person. Only the court performs in person searches; visitors may not. No search fee. Required to search: name, years to search. Civil cases indexed by defendant, plaintiff; index on books back to 1825. Mail turnaround time 1 day.
General Information: No adoption records released. Fee to fax out file $1.00 per page. Court makes copy: $1.00 per page if mailed, $.50 if in person. Self serve: $.50 per page. Certification fee: $5.00 per doc. Payee: Clerk and Master. Personal checks accepted; credit cards are not. Prepayment required. Mail requests: SASE requested.

Stewart County

23rd District Circuit & General Sessions Court PO Box 193, Dover, TN 37058; 931-232-7042/232-8474; fax: 931-232-3115; 8AM-4:30PM ***Felony, Misdemeanor, Civil, Eviction, Small Claims.***
Civil Records: Access: In person only. Visitors must perform in person searches themselves. Required to search: name, years to search. Civil cases indexed by plaintiff. Civil records archived on books from 1800s, on computer through 8/1993.
Criminal Records: Access: In person only. Visitors must perform in person searches themselves. Required to search: name, years to search. Criminal records archived on books from 1800s, on computer through 8/1993.
General Information: No expunged records released. Will fax documents to local or toll free line. Court makes copy: $.50 per page. Certification fee: $5.00 per doc. No personal checks or credit cards accepted. Prepayment required.

Chancery Court PO Box 102, Dover, TN 37058; 931-232-5665; fax: 931-232-0049; 8AM-4:30PM (CST). ***Civil, Probate.***
Civil Records: Access: Mail, in person. Only the court performs in person searches; visitors may not. No search fee. Required to search: name, years to search. Civil cases indexed by defendant, plaintiff; index on books to 1865; computerized since 1994. Mail turnaround time 1 week.
General Information: No adoption records released. Will fax documents $1.00 per page. Court makes copy: $.50 per page. Certification fee: $5.00. Payee: Clerk and Master. Personal checks accepted; credit cards are not. Mail requests: SASE required.

Sullivan County

Bristol Circuit Court - Civil Division Courthouse, Rm 131, 801 Anderson St, Bristol, TN 37620; 423-989-4354; 8AM-5PM (EST). ***Civil.***
Fax not available.
Civil Records: Access: In person only. Visitors must perform in person searches themselves. Civil cases indexed by defendant, plaintiff. Civil records archived from 1930s (minute books, unsure of docket books), on computer from 1986. Public use terminal has civil records back to 1986.
General Information: No adoption or sealed records released. Will not fax documents. Court makes copy: $.50 per page. Certification fee: $6.00 for seal. Payee: Circuit Court Clerk. Personal checks accepted.

Kingsport Circuit Court - Civil Division 225 W Center St, Kingsport, TN 37660; 423-224-1724; fax: 423-246-1924; 8AM-5PM (EST). ***Civil Actions over $25,000.***
Civil Records: Access: Phone, fax, mail, in person. Both court and visitors may perform in person searches. No search fee. Required to search: name, years to search. Civil cases indexed by defendant, plaintiff. Civil records archived from 1920s, on computer from 1985. Mail turnaround time 2-3 days. Public use terminal has civil records back to 1985.
General Information: No juvenile, adoption records released. Will not fax documents. Court makes copy: $.50 per page. Certification fee: $5.00 per cert. Payee: Circuit Court Clerk. No personal checks or credit cards accepted. Mail requests: SASE requested.

2nd District Circuit Court PO Box 585, 140 Blountville Bypass, Blountville, TN 37617; 423-279-2752; fax: 423-323-3741; 8AM-5PM (EST). ***Felony, Misdemeanor.***
www.sullivancounty.org/circuitcourt.htm
Find civil records in Bristol 423-989-4354, or at Kingsport, 423-224-1724
Criminal Records: Access: In person only. Visitors must perform in person searches themselves. Required to search: name, years to search, DOB; SSN helpful. Criminal records on computer since 12/83; prior records archived since the 1800s. Public use terminal has crim records back to 1984. PAT criminal results show middle initial.
General Information: No juvenile records released. Will not fax documents. Court makes copy: $.50 per page. Certification fee: $5.00 per cert. Payee: Circuit Court Clerk. Personal checks accepted.

Chancery Court PO Box 327, Blountville, TN 37617; 423-323-6483; 8AM-5PM ***Civil, Probate.***
Civil Records: Access: Mail, in person. Both court and visitors may perform in person searches. No search fee. Required to search: name, years to search. Civil cases indexed by defendant, plaintiff; index on books back to 1867; computerized records go back to 1996. Public use terminal civil records back to 1984.
General Information: No adoption records released. Will fax documents $.50 per page. Court makes copy: $.50 per page. Self serve: same. Certification fee: $5.00; Exemplification- $10.00. Payee: Chancery Court. Personal checks accepted; credit cards are not. Prepayment required.

Bristol General Sessions Court Courthouse, 801 Anderson St, Rm 131, Bristol, TN 37620; 423-989-4352; criminal phone: 423-652-1030; fax: 423-968-1138; 8AM-5PM (EST). ***Misdemeanor, Civil Actions under $15,000, Eviction, Small Claims.***
www.bridgeweb.org/docketts.htm
Criminal Records: Access: In person only. Visitors must perform in person searches themselves. Required to search: name, years to search. Criminal records archived since court started (stored in Blountville), on computer from 1986. Criminal PAT goes back to same as civil. PAT results show name only.
General Information: No juvenile records released. Will not fax documents. Court makes copy: $.50 per page. Certification fee: $5.00 per cert. Payee: Circuit Court Clerk. No personal checks accepted. Visa/MC accepted, add 5% usage fee; for use of debit card, add $2.50. Prepayment required.

Kingsport General Sessions 200 Shelby St, Kingsport, TN 37660; 423-224-1711; 8AM-5PM (EST). ***Misdemeanor, Civil Actions under $15,000, Eviction, Small Claims.***
Civil Records: Access: In person only. Visitors must perform in person searches themselves. Required to search: name, years to search. Civil cases indexed by defendant, plaintiff. Civil records archived in office from 1973, on computer from 1981. Civil PAT goes back to 1981.
Criminal Records: Access: In person only. Visitors must perform in person searches themselves. Required to search: name, years to search; SSN helpful. Criminal records archived in office from 1973, on computer from 1981. Criminal PAT goes back to same as civil.
General Information: No juvenile records released. Will fax out documents. Court makes copy: $.50 per page. Certification fee: $5.00 per cert. Payee: General Sessions Clerk. Personal checks accepted; credit cards are not. Prepayment required.

Sumner County

18th District Circuit & General Sessions Court Public Sq, PO Box 549, Gallatin, TN 37066; 615-452-4367; fax: 615-451-6027; 8AM-4:30PM (CST). ***Felony, Misdemeanor, Civil, Eviction, Small Claims.***
General Sessions phone is 615-452-4310.
Civil Records: Access: In person only. Visitors must perform in person searches themselves. Required to search: name, years to search. Civil cases indexed by defendant, plaintiff. Civil records archived on books in office from 1981.
Criminal Records: Access: In person only. Visitors must perform in person searches themselves. Required to search: name, years to search. Criminal records archived on index books in office from 1958; computerized back to 1997. Public use terminal has crim records back to 1997. PAT results show middle initial, DOB.
General Information: No juvenile, adoption records released. Will not fax documents. Court makes copy: $.50 per page. Certification fee: $5.00. Payee: Circuit Court Clerk. Only cashiers checks and money orders accepted. No credit cards accepted.

Chancery Court Rm 400, Sumner County Courthouse, Gallatin, TN 37066; 615-452-4282; fax: 615-451-6031; 8AM-4:30PM (CST). ***Civil, Probate.***
Civil Records: Access: Phone, fax, mail, in person. Both court and visitors may perform in person searches. Search fee: $35.00 charge if search takes 1 hour. Required to search: name, years to search. Civil cases indexed by defendant, plaintiff. Civil records go back to 1983. Mail turnaround time 1-2 days.
General Information: No juvenile or adoption records released. Will fax documents $1.00 per page. Court makes copy: $.50 per page. Certification fee: $5.00 plus $.50 per page. Payee: Clerk and Master. Only money orders, cash, or business checks accepted. No credit cards accepted. Prepayment required.

Tipton County

25th District Circuit & General Sessions Court 1801 S College, Rm 102, Covington, TN 38019; 901-475-3310; fax: 901-475-3318; 8AM-5PM (CST). ***Felony, Misdemeanor, Civil, Eviction, Small Claims.***
Civil Records: Access: Mail, in person. Both court and visitors may perform in person searches. Search fee: $5.00 per name per court. Required to search: name, years to search. Civil cases indexed by defendant, plaintiff. Civil records no computer info prior to 7/1991, prior records on docket books. Civil

PAT goes back to 7/1991. PAT results show middle initial, DOB.
Criminal Records: Access: Mail, in person. Both court and visitors may perform in person searches. Search fee: $5.00 per name per court. Required to search: name, years to search, DOB; also helpful: SSN. Criminal records computerized from 7/1992, prior records on docket books. Criminal PAT goes back to 7/1992, results show middle initial, DOB.
General Information: No juvenile or adoption records released. Will not fax documents. Court makes copy: $.50 per page. Self serve: $.50 per page. Certification fee: $5.00. Payee: Circuit Court Clerk or General Sessions. Business checks, cash or money orders accepted. Debit cards accepted in office. Prepayment required. Mail requests: SASE requested.

Chancery Court Tipton County Justice Ctr, 1801 S College, #110, Covington, TN 38019; 901-476-0209; probate phone: same; fax: 901-476-0246; 8AM-5PM (CST). ***Civil, Probate.***
Civil Records: Access: Phone, fax, mail, in person. Both court and visitors may perform in person searches. Search fee: $5.00. Required to search: name, years to search. Civil cases indexed by defendant, plaintiff; index on books since 1800s, on computer since 1991. Mail turnaround time ASAP. Public use terminal has civil records.
General Information: No adoption records released. Court makes copy: $.50 per page. Self serve: $.25 per page. Certification fee: $4.00 plus $2.00 per page. Payee: Tipton County Chancery Court. Personal checks accepted; credit cards are not. Prepayment required. Mail requests: SASE required.

Trousdale County

15th District Circuit & General Sessions Court 200 E Main St, Rm 5, Hartsville, TN 37074; 615-374-3411; criminal fax: 615-374-1100; civil fax: 615-374-1130; 8AM-4:30PM (CST). ***Felony, Misdemeanor, Civil, Eviction, Small Claims.***
Civil Records: Access: In person only. Visitors must perform in person searches themselves. Required to search: name, years to search. Civil cases indexed by defendant, plaintiff. Civil records archived on books since 1927.
Criminal Records: Access: In person only. Visitors must perform in person searches themselves. Required to search: name, years to search. Criminal records archived on books since 1940.
General Information: No juvenile or adoption records released. Will fax specific case file for fee. Court makes copy: $.50 per page. Certification fee: $.50 per page. Payee: Circuit Court Clerk. Only cashiers checks and money orders accepted. No credit cards accepted. Prepayment required.

Chancery Court Courthouse Rm 1, 200 E Main St, Hartsville, TN 37074; 615-374-2996; fax: 615-374-1100; 8AM-4:30PM (CST). ***Civil, Probate.***
Civil Records: Access: In person only. Visitors must perform in person searches themselves. Required to search: name, years to search. Civil cases indexed by defendant, plaintiff; index on book since 9/80, prior records in County Clerks office.
General Information: No adoption or sealed records released. Will fax documents. Court makes copy: $.50 per page. Certification fee: $5.00 plus $.50 per page. Payee: Clerk and Master. Personal checks accepted; credit cards are not. Prepayment required.

Unicoi County

1st District Circuit & General Sessions Court PO Box 2000, 100 N Main St, Erwin, TN 37650; 423-743-3541; fax: 423-743-1118; 9AM-5PM (EST). ***Felony, Misdemeanor, Civil, Eviction, Small Claims.***
Civil Records: Access: Mail, in person. Only the court performs in person searches; visitors may not. Search fee: $10.00 per name. Required to search: name, years to search. Civil cases indexed by defendant, plaintiff. Civil records archived on books from 1932 (felonies) and 1961 (misdemeanors); only general sessions is on computer back to late 1996. Mail turnaround time 2 days.
Criminal Records: Access: Mail, in person. Only the court performs in person searches; visitors may not. Search fee: $10.00 per name. Required to search: name, years to search, DOB. Criminal records archived on books from 1932 (felonies) and 1961 (misdemeanors); only general sessions is on computer back to late 1996. Mail turnaround time 2 days.
General Information: No adoption records released. Will fax documents to local or toll free line. Court makes copy: $.50 per page. Certification fee: $5.00 per cert. Payee: Circuit Court Clerk. Personal checks accepted; credit cards are not. Prepayment required.

Probate Court PO Box 2000, 100 N Maine Ave, Erwin, TN 37650; 423-743-3541; fax: 423-743-1118; 9AM-5PM M-F, 9AM-N Sat (EST). ***Probate.***

Union County

8th District Circuit & General Sessions Court 901 E Main St, #220, Maynardville, TN 37807; 865-992-5493; criminal fax: 865-992-8099; civil fax: same; 8AM-4PM M-F; 8AM-N Sat (EST). ***Felony, Misdemeanor, Civil, Eviction, Small Claims.***
Civil Records: Access: In person only. Visitors must perform in person searches themselves. Required to search: name, years to search. Civil cases indexed by defendant, plaintiff. Civil records archived on books from 1969. Civil PAT goes back to 1987 civil; Circuit civil back to 2000.
Criminal Records: Access: In person only. Visitors must perform in person searches themselves. Required to search: name, years to search, DOB, SSN. Criminal records archived on books from 1969. Criminal PAT goes back to 1994; General Sessions criminal back to 1994.
General Information: No sealed records released. Will fax documents. Court makes copy: $.50 per page. Self serve: same. Certification fee: $5.00 includes copy fee. Payee: Circuit Court Clerk. No personal checks accepted. Money orders or cash only. No credit cards accepted. Prepayment required.

Chancery Court 901 Main St, #215, Maynardville, TN 37807-3510; 865-992-5942; fax: 865-992-9338; 8AM-4PM (EST). ***Civil, Probate.*** Probate is a separate index at this same address.
Civil Records: Access: Phone, mail, in person. Both court and visitors may perform in person searches. No search fee. Required to search: name, years to search. Civil cases indexed by plaintiff, cross indexed by defendant. Civil records on books back to 1969. Mail turnaround time 1 week.
General Information: No adoption records released. Fee to fax out file $1.00 per page. Court makes copy: $.50 per page. Self serve: same. Certification fee: $5.00 per document plus copies. Payee: Union County Clerk and Master. Personal checks accepted; credit cards are not. Prepayment required.

Van Buren County

31st District Circuit & General Sessions Court PO Box 126, 179 Veteran's Sq, Spencer, TN 38585; 931-946-2153; fax: 931-946-2190; 8AM-5PM (CST). ***Felony, Misdemeanor, Civil, Eviction, Small Claims, Probate.***
Search fee includes both civil and criminal indexes, if asked for. Probate is a function of County Court; records available here.
Civil Records: Access: Mail, in person. Both court and visitors may perform in person searches. Search fee: $10.00 per name. Required to search: name, years to search. Civil cases indexed by defendant. Civil records archived on books, date unspecified. Mail turnaround time 2 weeks.
Criminal Records: Access: Mail, in person. Both court and visitors may perform in person searches. Search fee: $10.00 per name. Required to search: name, years to search, DOB; also helpful: SSN. Criminal records archived on books, date unspecified. Mail turnaround time 2 weeks.
General Information: No juvenile records released. Will fax documents to local or toll free line. Court makes copy: $.50 per page. Certification fee: $3.00 per cerrt. Payee: Circuit Court Clerk. No personal checks or credit cards accepted. Prepayment required. Mail requests: SASE required.

Warren County

31st District Circuit & General Sessions Court 111 Court Sq, PO Box 639, McMinnville, TN 37111; 931-473-2373; probate phone: 931-473-2364; fax: 931-473-3726; 8AM-4:30PM M-TH; 8AM-5PM F (CST). ***Felony, Misdemeanor, Civil, Eviction, Small Claims.***
Civil Records: Access: Mail, in person. Both court and visitors may perform in person searches. Search fee: $5.00 per name. Required to search: name, years to search. Civil cases indexed by defendant, plaintiff; index on computer since 1988 (General Sessions), archived in office from 1939 (Circuit). Mail turnaround time 1-2 days. Civil PAT goes back to 1996.
Criminal Records: Access: Mail, in person. Both court and visitors may perform in person searches. Search fee: $5.00 per name. Required to search: name, years to search, DOB, SSN, offense, date of offense. Criminal records on computer since 1988 (General Sessions), archived in office from 1939 (Circuit). Mail turnaround time 1-2 days. Criminal PAT goes back to same as civil. PAT criminal results show middle initial.
General Information: No adoption or juvenile records released. Will fax documents $5.00 fee. Court makes copy: $1.00 per page. Certification fee: $2.00. Payee: Circuit Court Clerk. Personal checks accepted; credit cards are not. Prepayment required. Mail requests: SASE required.

Chancery Court PO Box 639, McMinnville, TN 37111; 931-473-2364; fax: 931-473-3232; 8AM-4:30PM M-TH, 8AM-5PM F (CST). ***Civil, Probate.***
Civil Records: Access: Mail, in person. Both court and visitors may perform in person searches. No search fee. Required to search: name, years to search. Civil cases indexed by defendant, plaintiff; index on books. Mail turnaround time 1 week.
General Information: No adoption records released. Will fax out documents $.50 per page. Court makes copy: $.50 per page. Certification fee: $5.00 for first page. Payee: Clerk and Master. Personal checks accepted. Major credit cards accepted by phone only. Prepayment required. Mail requests: SASE required.

Washington County

1st District Circuit & General Sessions Court PO Box 356, 100 Main St, Jonesborough, TN 37659; 423-753-1611; fax: 423-926-4862; 8AM-5PM (EST). ***Felony, Misdemeanor, Civil, Eviction, Small Claims.***
Johnson City civil records found in Johnson City. All criminal records for county are found here in Jonesborough.
Civil Records: Access: In person only. Both court and visitors may perform in person searches. No search fee. Required to search: name, years to search. Civil cases indexed by defendant, plaintiff. Civil records archived from 1800s, on computer from 1989. Civil PAT goes back to 1989.
Criminal Records: Access: In person only. Both court and visitors may perform in person searches. No search fee. Required to search: name, years to search, DOB, SSN. Criminal records archived from 1800s, on computer from 1989. Criminal PAT goes back to same as civil.
General Information: No sealed, juvenile, adoption records released. Will not fax documents. Court makes copy: $.50 per page. Certification fee: $5.00. Payee: Circuit Court Clerk. Personal checks accepted; credit cards are not. Prepayment required.

General Sessions 101 E Market St, Johnson City, TN 37604; 423-461-1412; 8AM-5PM (EST). ***Civil Actions under $15,000, Eviction, Small Claims.***
Court will only search for a record if provided a case number. Access criminal records at Jonesborough Ct.
Civil Records: Access: In person only. Visitors must perform in person searches themselves. Required to search: name, years to search. Civil cases indexed by defendant, plaintiff. Civil records archived since court started, computerized since 1990. Public use terminal has civil records back to 1990.
General Information: No sealed records released. Court makes copy: $.50 per page. Self serve: same. Certification fee: $5.00 per cert. Payee: Circuit Court

Clerk. In state checks accepted. No credit cards accepted. Prepayment required.

Johnson City Law Court - Civil 101 E Market St, Johnson City, TN 37604; 423-461-1475; fax: 423-926-4862; 8AM-5PM (EST). ***Civil Actions over $15,000.***

Access criminal records at the Jonesborough Court.

Civil Records: Access: In person only. Visitors must perform in person searches themselves. Required to search: name, years to search. Civil cases indexed by defendant, plaintiff; index on computer from 1988. Public use terminal has civil records back to 1988. PAT results show name only.

General Information: No sealed records released. Will not fax documents. Court makes copy: $.50 per page. Certification fee: $5.00 per doc. Payee: Circuit Court Clerk. No personal or out-of-state checks accepted. Visa/MC accepted. Prepayment required.

Probate Court 100 E Main St, Courthouse, Jonesborough, TN 37659; 423-753-1623 or -0262; fax: 423-753-0190; 8:30AM-5PM (EST). ***Probate.***

Wayne County

22nd District Circuit & General Sessions Court PO Box 869, 100 Court Circle #302, Waynesboro, TN 38485; 931-722-5519; fax: 931-722-9949; 8AM-4PM M,T,TH,F; 8AM-N Wed,Sat (CST). ***Felony, Misdemeanor, Civil, Eviction, Small Claims.***

Civil Records: Access: Phone, mail, in person. Both court and visitors may perform in person searches. No search fee. Required to search: name, years to search. Civil cases indexed by defendant, plaintiff. Civil records archived on books from 1900s. Mail turnaround 7-10 days. Civil PAT goes back to '97.

Criminal Records: Access: Mail, in person. Both court and visitors may perform in person searches. Search fee: $5.00 per name. Required to search: name, years to search, DOB, SSN. Criminal records archived on books from 1900s. Mail turnaround time 7-10 days. Criminal PAT goes back to 1997.

General Information: No juvenile or adoption records released. Will fax documents. Court makes copy: $.50 per page. Certification fee: $5.00. Payee: Circuit Court Clerk. Personal checks accepted; credit cards are not. Prepayment required.

Chancery Court PO Box 101, Waynesboro, TN 38485; 931-722-5517; fax: 931-722-5517; 8AM-4PM (CST). ***Civil, Probate.***

Civil Records: Access: Mail, in person. Both court and visitors may perform in person searches. No search fee. Required to search: name, years to search. Civil cases indexed by defendant, plaintiff; index on books; computerized since 12/92. Mail turnaround time 2 days.

General Information: No adoption records released. Will fax documents to local or toll free line. Court makes copy: $.50 per page. Certification fee: $5.00 minimum or $.50 per page. Payee: Clerk and Master. Personal checks accepted; credit cards are not. Prepayment required. Mail requests: SASE requested.

Weakley County

27th District Circuit & General Sessions Court 116 W Main St - Courthouse, 2nd Fl, Rm 203, Dresden, TN 38225; 731-364-3455; fax: 731-364-6765; 8AM-4:30PM (CST). ***Felony, Misdemeanor, Civil, Eviction, Small Claims.***

www.weakleycountytn.gov/circuitcourtclerk.html

Civil Records: Access: In person only. Visitors must perform in person searches themselves. Required to search: name, years to search. Civil cases indexed by defendant, plaintiff. Civil records archived on since court started, on books; computerized since 1997. Civil PAT goes back to 1997, results show name only.

Criminal Records: Access: In person only. Visitors must perform in person searches themselves. Required to search: name, years to search, DOB; SSN helpful. Criminal records archived on since court started, on books; computerized since 1997. Criminal PAT goes back to 1997, results show name, DOB.

General Information: No adoption or sealed records released. Will not fax documents. Court makes copy: $.50 per page. Self serve: same. Certification fee: $5.00 per cert. Payee: Circuit Court Clerk. No personal checks accepted; credit cards are.

Chancery Court PO Box 197, Dresden, TN 38225; 731-364-3454; fax: 731-364-5247; 8AM-4:30PM (CST). ***Civil, Probate.***

www.weakleycountytn.gov/clerkandmaster.html

Court will not do searches for genealogy.

Civil Records: Access: Mail, in person. Both court and visitors may perform in person searches. No search fee. Required to search: name, years to search. Civil cases indexed by defendant, plaintiff; index on computer since 1982, prior records indexed from 1927; Probate to 1800s. Mail turnaround 1 week.

General Information: No adoption or sealed records released. Will fax documents $1.00 per page, prepaid. Court makes copy: $.50 per page. Self serve: $.50 per page. Certification fee: $5.00. Payee: Clerk and Master. Personal checks accepted; credit cards are not.

White County

13th District Circuit & General Sessions Court 111 Depot St, #1, Sparta, TN 38583; 931-836-3205; fax: 931-836-3526; 8AM-5PM (CST). ***Felony, Misdemeanor, Civil, Eviction, Small Claims.***

www.whiteccc.com/

Civil Records: Access: In person only. Visitors must perform in person searches themselves. Required to search: name, years to search. Civil cases indexed by defendant, plaintiff. Civil records archived since court started, some are offsite, computerized since 1996. Note: Court dockets available free at www.whiteccc.com/ but no historical data. Civil PAT goes back to mid-1996. PAT results show middle initial, DOB, SSN.

Criminal Records: Access: In person only. Visitors must perform in person searches themselves. Required to search: name, years to search. Criminal records archived since court started, some are offsite; computerized records since 1996. Note: Court dockets available free at www.whiteccc.com/ but no historical data. Criminal PAT available. PAT results show middle initial, DOB, SSN.

General Information: No juvenile, adoption records released. Will fax documents $1.00 per page. Court makes copy: $.50 per page. Self serve: $.50 per page. Certification fee: $5.00 per cert. Payee: Circuit Court Clerk. No personal checks or credit cards accepted.

Chancery Court White County Courthouse, Rm 303, Sparta, TN 38583; 931-836-3787; probate phone: same; fax: 931-836-2124; 8AM-4PM (CST). ***Civil, Probate.***

Civil Records: Access: Phone, in person. Visitors must perform in person searches themselves. No search fee. Required to search: name, years to search. Civil cases indexed by defendant, plaintiff. Overall records go back to 1842.

General Information: No adoption records released. Will fax documents if prepaid. Court makes copy: $.50 per page. Self serve: same. Certification fee: $5.00. Payee: Clerk and Master. Personal checks accepted; credit cards are not. Prepayment required. Mail requests: SASE required.

Williamson County

21st District Circuit & General Sessions Court 135 4th Ave, Rm 203, Franklin, TN 37064; 615-790-5454; fax: 615-790-5626; 8AM-4:30PM (CST). ***Felony, Misdemeanor, Civil, Eviction, Small Claims.***

www.williamsoncounty-tn.gov/index.asp?nid=243

Civil Records: Access: In person only. Visitors must perform in person searches themselves. Required to search: name, years to search. Civil cases indexed by defendant, plaintiff. Civil records archived on books from 1810, on computer from 1992. Civil PAT goes back to 1992.

Criminal Records: Access: In person only. Visitors must perform in person searches themselves. Required to search: name, years to search; also helpful: DOB, SSN. Criminal records archived on books from 1810, on computer from 1992. Criminal PAT goes back to same as civil.

General Information: Will not fax documents. Court makes copy: $.50 per page. Self serve: same. Certification fee: $5.00. Payee: Circuit Court Clerk. Personal checks accepted; credit cards are not.

Chancery Court Clerk & Master, PO Box 1666, 135 4th Ave S Rm 236, Franklin, TN 37064; 615-790-5428; fax: 615-790-5626; 8AM-4:30PM (CST). ***Civil, Probate.***

Civil Records: Access: Phone, mail, in person. Both court and visitors may perform in person searches. No search fee. Required to search: name, years to search. Civil cases indexed by defendant, plaintiff; index on computer since 1991, prior records on books since 1800s (no probate on computer). Mail 1-2 weeks. Public use terminal has civil records back to 1991.

General Information: No adoption, sealed records released. Will not fax documents. Court makes copy: $.50 per page. Certification fee: $5.00 per document. Payee: Clerk and Master. Local checks accepted. No credit cards accepted. Prepayment required. Mail requests: SASE requested.

Wilson County

15th District Circuit Court PO Box 518, 134 S College St, Lebanon, TN 37088-0518; 615-444-2042; 8AM-4PM M-TH; 8AM-5PM F (CST). ***Felony, Civil Actions over $15,000.***

Civil Records: Access: In person only. Visitors must perform in person searches themselves. Required to search: name, years to search. Civil cases indexed by defendant, plaintiff. Civil records archived in office from 1982, on computer from 1990, on microfiche from 1940s. Civil PAT goes back to 1990. PAT results show middle initial, DOB.

Criminal Records: Access: In person only. Visitors must perform in person searches themselves. Required to search: name, years to search, DOB. Criminal records archived in office from 1982, on computer from 1990, on microfiche from 1940s. Criminal PAT goes back to same as civil. PAT results show middle initial, DOB.

General Information: No adoption, juvenile records released. Will not fax documents. Court makes copy: $.50 per page. Certification fee: $5.00 per cert. Payee: Circuit Court Clerk. Business checks accepted. No credit cards accepted. Prepayment required.

General Sessions Court 115 E High St, Lebanon, TN 37088; 615-444-2045; fax: 615-443-1186; 8AM-4PM (CST). ***Misdemeanor, Civil Actions under $15,000, Eviction, Small Claims.***

Civil Records: Access: In person only. Visitors must perform in person searches themselves. Required to search: name, years to search. Civil cases indexed by defendant, plaintiff. Civil records archived in office from 1982, on computer from 1990, on microfiche from 1940s. Civil PAT goes back to 1991. PAT results show middle initial, DOB.

Criminal Records: Access: In person only. Visitors must perform in person searches themselves. Required to search: name, years to search, DOB. Criminal records computerized from 1990. Criminal PAT goes back to 1991. PAT results show middle initial, DOB.

General Information: No adoption, juvenile records released. Will not fax documents. Court makes copy: $.50 per page. Certification fee: $5.00 per cert. Payee: Circuit Court Clerk. Personal checks accepted; credit cards are not. Prepayment required.

Probate Court PO Box 1557, 134 S College St, Lebanon, TN 37088; 615-444-2835; fax: 615-443-6191; 8AM-4PM (CST). ***Probate, Civil Actions.***

Probate is now Clerk & Master..

Tennessee Recording Offices

ORGANIZATION: 95 counties, 96 recording offices. The recording officer is the Register of Deeds. Sullivan County has two recording offices. 66 western Tennessee counties including the state capital are in the Central Time Zone (CST) and the remaining 29 eastern counties are in the Eastern Time Zone (EST).

REAL ESTATE RECORDS: Counties will not perform real estate searches. A real estate copy is usually $1.00 per page; copy fees can be lower. Certification fee is generally $1.00 per page. Tax records are kept at the Assessor's Office.

UCC RECORDS: Financing statements are filed at the state level except for real estate related collateral which are filed with the Register of Deeds. However, prior to July, 2001, consumer goods and farm collateral were also filed at the Register of Deeds and these older records can be searched here. Most recording offices will not perform UCC searches.

TAX LIEN RECORDS: All federal tax liens are filed with the county Register of Deeds. State tax liens are filed with the Secretary of State or the Register of Deeds. Counties will not perform tax lien searches.

OTHER LIENS: Judgment, materialman, mechanics, trustee.

ONLINE ACCESS: The State Comptroller of the Treasury Real Estate Assessment Database can be searched free for 88 counties at www.assessment.state.tn.us/. Select a county then search by name for real property information. Counties not on this system are Davidson, Hamilton, Knox, Rutherford, Shelby and Williamson.

Although limited, search the TN UCC index free at http://state.tn.us/sos/bus_svc/iets3/ieuc/PgUCCSearch.jsp.

Online access to a number of county' property and deeds indexes and images is available via a private company at www.titlesearcher.com or email support@TitleSearcher.com. Registration, login, and monthly fee per county required, plus a one-time $20.00 set up fee. A $5 per day plan is also available.

Also, online access to 40 counties' property, deeds, judgment, liens, and UCCs is available via a private company at www.ustitlesearch.net/ or call 615-223-1823. Registration, login, and monthly fee required, plus set up fee. Use DEMO as your username to sample the system.

Also, www.tnrealestate.com offers free and fee services for real estate data from all Tennessee counties.

Anderson County

Register of Deeds, 100 N Main St, Rm 205; Courthouse, Clinton, TN 37716-3688. 865-457-5400; fax-865-457-1638; 8:30AM-4:30PM. www.andersondeeds.com/

Index: All in one. Records indexed on a public use terminal back to 1987 for trust deeds, 1969 for warranty deeds. Office will perform a UCC search as time allows, but public must search other records themselves. No copy fee. Cert fee- $1.00 per page. Payee- Anderson County Register of Deeds. Office can supply bulk data without fee if requester covers costs and supplies; contact Registrar Tim Shelton. **Online access to Real Estate, Deed records:** Access property and deeds indexes/images at http://search.andersondeeds.com/menu.php. Also, see state introduction. **Other phones:** County Clerk- 865-457-6228. **Property tax/Assessing-** 100 N Main St, Clinton, TN 37716; 865-457-5400 x225. **Online access-** Assessment data on state comptroller system is free at www.assessment.state.tn.us/.

Bedford County

Register of Deeds, 108 Northside Sq, Shelbyville, TN 37160. Recording, R/E phone-931-684-5719; fax-931-685-2086; 8AM-4PM (CST)

Index: Separate indices to search include deed, trust deed, lien book, notice of completion, greenbelt, charter. Records indexed on a public use terminal back to 4/96. Only the public may search. Copy fee $.25 per page. Cert fee- $1.00 per page includes copy fee. Payee- Bedford County Register of Deeds. **Online access to Real Estate, Deed records:** Access property and deeds indexes/images at www.titlesearcher.com; fee/registration required. Also, see state introduction. **Other phones:** Treasurer- 931-684-4303; Elections- 931-684-0531; County Clerk- 931-684-1921. **Property tax/Assessing-** 106 Northside Sq, Shelbyville, TN 37160; 931-684-6390, assessor fax- 931-680-1199. Public access terminal available. **Online access-** Assessment data on state comptroller system is free at www.assessment.state.tn.us/.

Benton County

Register of Deeds, 1 E Court Sq, #105, Camden, TN 38320-2070. 731-584-6661; fax-731-584-4651; 8AM-4PM M-Th; 8AM-5PM F. (CST)

Index: Separate indices to search include military discharge, deeds. Records indexed on a public use terminal back to 7/98. Only the public may search. Copy fee $.25 per page. Copy fee is $.50 per page for ledger-size page.Real estate record copy- $.75 per page. Cert fee- $1.00 per cert includes copy fee. Payee- Benton County Register of Deeds. **Other phones:** County Clerk- 731-584-6053. **Property tax/Assessing-** 731-584-7615. **Online access-** Assessment data on state comptroller system is free at www.assessment.state.tn.us/.

Bledsoe County

Register of Deeds, PO Box 385, Pikeville, TN 37367. 423-447-2020; fax-423-447-6856; 8AM-4PM M T W F; 8AM-Noon Sat; Closed on Th.

Index: All in one. Records indexed on a public use terminal back to 02/2002. Only the public may search. Copy fee $.25 per page. Cert fee- $1.00 per page plus copy fee. Payee- Register of Deeds. Bulk data available for purchase, contact Emma Boynton. **Online access to Real Estate, Deed records:** Access property and deeds indexes/images at www.titlesearcher.com; fee/registration required. Also, see state introduction. **Other phones:** Treasurer- 423-447-2369; Elections- 423-447-2776; County Clerk- 423-447-2137; Chancery/Back Taxes - 423-447-2484. **Property tax/Assessing-** 3150 Main St, #200, Pikeville, TN 37367; 423-447-6548. **Online access-** Assessment data on state comptroller system is free at www.assessment.state.tn.us/.

Blount County

Register of Deeds, 349 Court St, Maryville, TN 37804. 865-273-5880; fax-865-273-5890; 8-4:30PM.

Index: Separate indices to search include UCCs, maps. Records indexed on a public use terminal back to 1991. Only the public may search. Copy fee $.50 per page. Cert fee- $1.00 per page includes copy fee. Payee- Blount County Register of Deeds. **Other phones:** Elections- 865-273-5920; Vital Records- 865-983-4582; County Clerk- 865-273-5800. **Property tax/Assessing-** 865-273-5850. **Online access-** Assessment data on state comptroller system is free at www.assessment.state.tn.us/.

Bradley County

Register of Deeds, PO Box 579, Cleveland, TN 37364-0579. 423-728-7240; fax-423-478-8888; 8:30AM-4:30PM.

Index: All in one. Records indexed on computer and public use terminal. Only the public may search. Copy fee $1.00 per page. Cert fee- $1.00 per page plus copy fee. Payee- Register of Deeds. **Online access to Real Estate, Deed records:** Access property and deeds indexes/images at www.titlesearcher.com; fee/registration with software provider is required. Also, see state introduction. **Other phones:** County Clerk- 423-728-7226. **Property tax/Assessing-** PO Box 1412, Cleveland, TN 37364-1412; 423-728-7125, assessor fax- 423-478-8885. www.bradleyco.net/propassesorhome.aspx **Online access-** Assessment data on state comptroller system is free at www.assessment.state.tn.us/.

Campbell County

Register of Deeds, PO Box 85, Jacksboro, TN 37757. 423-562-3864, UCC phone-423-562-8195; fax-423-562-9833; 8AM-4:30PM (EST)

Index: Separate indices to search. Records indexed on computer back to 1965. Only the public may search. Copy fee $1.00 per page. Will fax back $2.00 1st page, $1.00 each add'l.Real estate or tax lien copy- $.25 per copy. Cert fee- $1.00 per page includes copy fee. Payee- Campbell County Register of Deeds. **Online access to Real Estate, Deed records:** Access real estate records at http://www1.ustitlesearch.net/, registration/fee required, images go back to 6/2003. Also, see state introduction. **Other phones:** Treasurer- 423-562-5185; Elections- 423-562-9777; County Clerk- 423-562-4985. **Property tax/Assessing-** PO Box 135, Jacksboro, TN 37757; 423-562-3201. **Online access-** Assessment data on state comptroller system is free at www.assessment.state.tn.us/.

Cannon County

Register of Deeds, Courthouse, Woodbury, TN 37190. 615-563-2041; fax-615-563-1542; 8AM-4PM. Index: All in one. Records indexed on a public use terminal back to 1999. Office will perform a UCC search but public must search other records themselves. Copy fee $.50 per page. Cert fee- $1.00 per page. Payee- Cannon County Register of Deeds. **Online access to Real Estate, Deed, Judgment, Lien, UCC records:** Access RE records at http://www1.ustitlesearch.net/, registration/fee required; also see state introduction. **Other phones:** Elections- 615-563-5650; County Clerk- 615-563-4278. **Property tax/Assessing**- 200 W Main St, Woodbury, TN 37190; 615-563-5437, assessor fax-615-563-3030. hours- 8AM-4PM M,T,Th,F; 8AM-N Sat **Online**- Assessment data on state system is free at www.assessment.state.tn.us/.

Carroll County

Register of Deeds, PO Box 432; Carroll County Office Complex, Huntingdon, TN 38344. 731-986-1952; fax-731-986-1955; 8AM-4PM.
Index: Separate indices to search include warranty deed, trust deed. Records indexed on a public use terminal back to 5/89. Only the public may search. Copy fee $.25 per page. Cert fee- $.50 per cert plus $1.00 per page. Payee- Carroll County Register of Deeds. **Online access to Real Estate, Deed, Judgment, Lien, UCC records:** Access real estate indexes and images at http://www1.ustitlesearch.net/. Registration/monthly fee required. Also, see state introduction. **Other phones:** Elections- 731-986-1968; County Clerk- 731-986-8237. **Property tax/Assessing**- 625 High St #105, Huntingdon, TN 38344; 731-986-1975. **Online access**- Assessment data on state comptroller system is free at www.assessment.state.tn.us/.

Carter County

Register of Deeds, 801 E Elk Ave, Elizabethton, TN 37643. 423-542-1830; 8:00AM-4:30PM (EST) www.carterdeeds.com
Records indexed on computer back to 1997. Only the public may search. Copy fee $.50 per page. Cert fee- $1.00 per page plus copy fee. Payee- Carter County Register of Deeds. **Online access to Real Estate, Deed records:** Access property and deeds indexes/images at www.titlesearcher.com; fees/ registration required. Also, see state introduction. **Other phones:** County Clerk- 423-542-1814. **Property tax/Assessing**- 801 E Elk Ave, Elizabethton, TN 37643; 423-542-1806, assessor fax-423-547-5111. hours- 8AM-4PM **Online access**- Assessment data on state comptroller system is free at www.assessment.state.tn.us/.

Cheatham County

Register of Deeds, PO Box 453, Ashland City, TN 37015. 615-792-4317; fax-615-792-2039; 8AM-4PM. http://cheathamcountytn.gov
Index: Separate indices to search include direct, reverse. Records indexed on a public use terminal back to 98; liens back to 1/95. Only the public may search. Copy fee $.25 per page. Cert fee- $1.00 plus copy fee. Payee- Register of Deeds. **Online Real Estate, Deed, Judgment, Lien, UCC records:** Access real estate indexes/images at http://www1.ustitlesearch.net/; registration/monthly fee required. Also see state introduction. **Other phones:** Treasurer- 615-792-4298; Elections- 615-792-5770; County Clerk- 615-792-4317. **Property tax/Assessing**- 264 S Main St, Ste 101, Ashland City, TN 37015; 615-792-5371, assessor fax- 615-792-2088. http://cheathamcountytn.gov **Online access**- Assessment data on state comptroller system is free at www.assessment.state.tn.us/.

Chester County

Register of Deeds, PO Box 292, Henderson, TN 38340. 731-989-4991; 8AM-4PM (CST)
Index: All in one. Records indexed on a public use terminal back to 6/99. Only the public may search. Will not search UCC records. Copy fee $5.00 per doc if mailed. Cert fee- $1.00 per page includes copy fee up to 4 pages. Payee- Chester County Register of Deeds. **Online access to Real Estate, Deed, Judgment, Lien, UCC records:** Access real estate indexes/images at http://www1.ustitlesearch.net/; registration/monthly fee required. Also see state introduction. **Other phones:** Treasurer- 731-989-3993; County Clerk- 731-989-2233. **Property tax/Assessing**- 159 E Main St, PO Box 332, Henderson, TN 38340; 731-989-4882, assessor fax-731-989-3689. Public access computer available. **Online access**- Assessment data on state comptroller system is free at www.assessment.state.tn.us/.

Claiborne County

Register of Deeds, PO Box 117, Tazewell, TN 37879. 423-626-3325; fax-423-626-5631; 8AM-4:30PM (EST)
Index: All in one. Records indexed on a public use terminal back to 1998. Only the public may search. Copy fee $.25 per page. Cert fee- $4.00 per cert plus copy fee. Payee- Claiborne County Register of Deeds. **Online access to Real Estate, Deed records:** Access property and deeds indexes/images at www.titlesearcher.com; fee/registration required. Also, see state introduction. **Other phones:** Treasurer- 423-626-3275; Elections- 423-626-5128; County Clerk- 423-626-3334. **Property tax/Assessing**- PO Box 57 423-626-3276, assessor fax- 423-626-1661. Public access computer available. **Online access**- Assessment data on state comptroller system is free at www.assessment.state.tn.us/.

Clay County

Register of Deeds, PO Box 430, Celina, TN 38551. Recording, R/E phone-931-243-3298; fax-931-243-6723; 8AM-4PM M,T,TH,F; 8AM-N Sat. (CST)
Index: All in one. Records indexed on computer back to 2001. Only the public may search. Copy fee $.25 per page; fax copy fee $1.00. Cert fee- $1.00 per page includes copy fee. Payee- Clay County Register of Deeds. **Online access to Real Estate, Deed records:** Access property and deeds indexes/images at www.titlesearcher.com; fee/registration required. Also, see state introduction. **Other phones:** Treasurer- 931-243-2310; Elections- 931-243-2536; County Clerk- 931-243-2249. **Property tax/Assessing**- PO Box 350, Celina, TN 38551; 931-243-2599. **Online access**- Assessment data on state comptroller system is free at www.assessment.state.tn.us/.

Cocke County

Register of Deeds, 111 Court Ave, Rm 102; Courthouse, Newport, TN 37821. 423-623-7540; 8AM-4:30PM M,T,Th,F; 8AM-N W,Sat. (EST)
Index: All in one. Records indexed on a public use terminal back to 1998. Only the public may search. Copy fee $.25 per page. Cert fee- None. Payee- Cocke County Register of Deeds. **Online access to Real Estate, Deed records:** Access property and deeds indexes/images at www.titlesearcher.com; fee/registration required. Also, see state introduction. **Other phones:** County Clerk- 423-623-6176; Trustee -423-623-3037. **Property tax/Assessing**- 111 Court Ave, Room 112, Newport, TN 37821-3102; 423-623-7024, assessor fax- 423-623-4655. hours- 8AM-4:30PM M,T,TH,F; 8AM-N W; 8AM-11AM Sat **Online access**- Assessment data on state comptroller system is free at www.assessment.state.tn.us/.

Coffee County

Register of Deeds, PO Box 178, Manchester, TN 37349. Recording, R/E phone-931-723-5130; fax-931-723-8232; 8AM-4:30 PM (CST)
Index: Separate indices to search include deeds, trust deeds and liens. Records indexed on computer back to 1996. Only the public may search. Copy fee $1.00 per page.Real estate or tax lien copy- $.50 per page. Cert fee- $1.00 per page includes copy fee. Payee- Register of Deeds. **Online access to Real Estate, Deed records:** Access property and deeds indexes/images at www.titlesearcher.com; fee/registration required. Also, see state introduction. **Other phones:** County Clerk- 931-723-5106. **Property tax/Assessing**- 931-723-5126. **Online access**- Assessment data on state system is free at www.assessment.state.tn.us/.

Crockett County

Register of Deeds, 1 S Bells St, #2; County Courthouse, Alamo, TN 38001. 731-696-5455; fax-731-696-3028; 8AM-4PM (CST)
Index: Indexes- trust deeds, liens, property deeds. Records indexed on a public use terminal back to 9/02. Only the public may search. Copy fee $.25 per page. Cert fee- $1.00 per page includes copy fee. Payee- Crockett County Register of Deeds. **Online access to Real Estate, Deed, Judgment, Lien, UCC records:** Access real estate indexes/images at http://www1.ustitlesearch.net/; registration/monthly fee required. Also, see state introduction. **Other phones:** Treasurer- 731-696-5454; County Clerk-731-696-5451. **Property tax/Assessing**- 1 S Bells St, #4, County Courthouse, Alamo, TN 38001; 731-696-5456, assessor fax- 731-696-5622. **Online access**- Assessment data on state comptroller system is free at www.assessment.state.tn.us/.

Cumberland County

Register of Deeds, 2 N Main St, #204, Crossville, TN 38555-4583. 931-484-5559; 8AM-4PM (CST)
Index: All in one. Records indexed on a public use terminal back to 1992. Only the public may search. Copy fee $1.00 per page.Real estate or tax lien copy- $5.00 up to 10 pages; $.50 each add'l page. Cert fee- $2.00 1st pg, $1.00 each add'l plus copy fee. Payee- Cumberland County Register of Deeds. **Online Real Estate, Deed records:** Access property and deeds indexes/images at www.titlesearcher.com; fees/ registration required. Also, see state introduction. **Other phones:** Elections- 931-484-4919; County Clerk- 615-484-6442; Trustee -931-484-5730. **Property tax/Assessing**- 2 S Main St, Suite 101, Crossville, TN 38555; 931-484-5745. **Online access**- Assessment data on state comptroller system is at www.assessment.state.tn.us/

Davidson County

Register of Deeds, PO Box 196398, Nashville, TN 37219-6398. 615-862-6790; fax-615-880-2039; 8AM-4:30PM (CST) www.nashville.gov/ROD/
Index: All in one. Records indexed on a public use terminal back to 7/64. Only the public may search. Copy fee $.50 per page. Plats- $3.00 per page. Cert fee- $1.00 per page. Payee- Register of Deeds. A commercial service allows subscribers to download data via FTP. To subscribe fill out application and send $25.00 check. **Online access to Real Estate, Deed, Judgment, Lien records:** Property and mapping records on the Metro Planning Commission Nashville City database are free at http://www3.nashville.org/property/. Click on "text only search." Also, Register of Deeds offers access to recorded docs by subscription; monthly fees vary, a set-up fee is $25.00. For info, call 615-862-6790. Includes books A thru 3784. **Other phones:** County Clerk- 615-862-6050. **Property tax/Assessing**- 615-862-6080. **Online access**- Search county assessments free at http://hobsvtxie01.nashville.org/default.asp.

Decatur County

Register of Deeds, PO Box 488, Decaturville, TN 38329. 731-852-3712; 8AM-4PM M,T,Th,F; 8AM-N Sat. (CST)
Index: All in one. Records indexed on computer back to January, 1998. Only the public may search. Will not search UCC records. Copy fee $1.00 per page. Cert fee- $1.00 per page includes copy fee. Payee- Decatur County Register of Deeds. **Online access to Real Estate, Deed records:** Access property and deeds indexes/images at www.titlesearcher.com; fee/registration required. Also, see state introduction. **Other phones:** Treasurer- 731-852-3723; County Clerk- 731-852-2231. **Property tax/Assessing**- PO Box 488, Decaturville, TN 38329; 731-852-3117,

assessor fax- 731-852-3280. **Online access-** Assessment data on state comptroller system is free at www.assessment.state.tn.us/.

DeKalb County

Register of Deeds, One Public Sq, Rm 201, Smithville, TN 37166. 615-597-4153; fax-615-597-7420; 8AM-4:30PM (CST) www.smithvilletn.com/government/index.htm

Index: All in one. Records indexed on a public use terminal back to 1970. Only the public may search. Copy fee $.25 per page. Cert fee- $1.00. Payee- De Kalb County Register of Deeds. **Other phones:** Treasurer- 615-597-5176; Elections- 615-597-4146; County Clerk- 615-597-5177; Trustee -615-597-5176. **Property tax/Assessing-** 1 Public Sq, Rm 200, Smithville, TN 37166; 615-597-5925, assessor fax- 615-597-7420. **Online-** Assessment data on state system is free at www.assessment.state.tn.us/.

Dickson County

Register of Deeds, PO Box 130, Charlotte, TN 37036. 615-789-5123; fax-615-789-3893; 8AM-4PM.

Index: All in one. Records indexed on a public use terminal back to 10/1996. Only the public may search. Copy fee $1.00 per page. Cert fee- $1.00 includes copy fee. Payee- Dickson County Register of Deeds. **Online access to Real Estate, Deed, Judgment, Lien, UCC records:** Access real estate indexes/images at http://www1.ustitlesearch.net/;, or a 2nd company at www.titlesearcher.com; registration/monthly fee required. Also see state introduction. **Other phones:** Treasurer- 615-789-7006; Elections- 615-789-6021; County Clerk- 615-789-4171. **Property tax/Assessing-** PO Box 270, #4 Court Sq, Charlotte, TN 37036; 615-789-7015, assessor fax- 615-789-3893. **Online access-** Assessment data on state comptroller system is free at www.assessment.state.tn.us/.

Dyer County

Register of Deeds, PO Box 1360, Dyersburg, TN 38025-1360. 731-286-7806; fax-731-288-7724; 8:30AM-4:30PM (CST) www.co.dyer.tn.us

Index: All in one. Records indexed on a public use terminal back to 1996. Only the public may search. Copy fee $.50 per page. Cert fee- $1.00 per instrument plus copy fee. Payee- Dyer County Register. **Online access to Real Estate, Deed, Judgment, Lien, UCC records:** Access real estate indexes/images at http://www1.ustitlesearch.net/; registration/monthly fee required. Also see state introduction. **Other phones:** Treasurer- 731-286-7802; Elections- 731-286-4268; Vital Records- 731-286-7814; County Clerk- 731-286-7814. **Property tax/Assessing-** 101 W Court St, Dyersburg, TN 38025; 731-286-7804. **Online access-** Assessment data on state comptroller system is free at www.assessment.state.tn.us/.

Fayette County

Register of Deeds, PO Box 99, Somerville, TN 38068-0099. 901-465-5251; 9AM-5PM (CST)

Index: All in one. Records indexed on a public use terminal back to 1999. Only the public may search. Copy fee $1.00 per page. Cert fee- $1.00 per cert plus copy fee. Payee- Fayette County Register of Deeds. **Online access to Real Estate, Deed records:** Access property and deeds indexes/images at www.titlesearcher.com; fee/registration required. Also, see state introduction. **Other phones:** Treasurer- 901-465-5224; Elections- 901-465-5223; County Clerk- 901-465-5213. **Property tax/Assessing-** PO Box 446, 17655 Hwy 64, #107, Somerville, TN 38068-0099; 901-465-5226, assessor fax- 901-465-5209. Public access computer available. **Online access-** Assessment data on state comptroller system is free at www.assessment.state.tn.us/.

Fentress County

Register of Deeds, PO Box 341, Jamestown, TN 38556. Recording, R/E phone-931-879-7818; fax-931-879-4502; 8AM-4PM.

Index: All in one. Records indexed on a public use terminal back to 5/00. Only the public may search. Copy fee $1.00 per page.Real estate or tax lien copy- $.25 per page. Cert fee- $1.00 per page plus copy fee. Payee- Register of Deeds. **Online access to Real Estate, Deed records:** Access property and deeds indexes/images at www.titlesearcher.com; fee/registration required. Also, see state introduction. **Other phones:** Treasurer- 931-879-7717; Elections- 931-879-7162; Vital Records- 931-879-8014; County Clerk- 931-879-9936; County Executive -931-879-7713. **Property tax/Assessing-** PO Box 842, Jamestown, TN 38556; 931-879-9194, assessor fax- 931-879-9981. **Online access-** Assessment data on state comptroller system is free at www.assessment.state.tn.us/.

Franklin County

Register of Deeds, 1 S Jefferson St, Rm 6; Franklin County Courthouse, Winchester, TN 37398-0101. 931-967-2840; 8AM-4:30PM; 8AM-N Sat. (CST)

Index: Search separate trust and deed indexes. Records indexed on a public use terminal back to 1999. Only the public may search. Copy fee $1.00 per page. Cert fee- $1.00 per page includes copy fee. Faxed pages $2.00 per page. Payee- Franklin County Register of Deeds. **Online access to Real Estate, Deed records:** Access property and deeds indexes/images at www.titlesearcher.com; fee/registration required. Also, see state introduction. **Other phones:** Treasurer- 931-967-2962; County Clerk- 931-967-2541. **Property tax/Assessing-** 931-967-3869. **Online access-** Assessment data on state system is free at www.assessment.state.tn.us/.

Gibson County

Register of Deeds, 1 Court Sq, Ste 201; Courthouse, Trenton, TN 38382. 731-855-7628; fax-731-855-7650; 8AM-4:30PM M-F; 8AM-N Sat. (CST)

Index: Separate indices up to 10/1999 to search include Deed, Trust Deed, Lien, Greenbelt, UCCs. Records indexed on a public use terminal back to 1099. Only the public may search. Copy fee $.25 per page. Will fax docs for $1.00 per page. Cert fee- $1.00 per page includes copy fee. Payee- Hilda Patterson. **Online access to Real Estate, Deed, Judgment, Lien, UCC records:** Access real estate indexes/images at http://www1.ustitlesearch.net/; registration/monthly fee required. Also see state introduction. **Other phones:** Treasurer- 731-855-7631; Elections- 731-855-7669; County Clerk- 731-855-7642. **Property tax/Assessing-** 1 Court Sq, #202, Trenton, TN 38382; 731-855-7634, assessor fax- 731-855-7650. **Online access-** Assessment data on state system is free at www.assessment.state.tn.us/.

Giles County

Register of Deeds, PO Box 678, Pulaski, TN 38478. 931-363-5137; fax-931-424-4797; 8AM-4PM (CST) www.rackleyhost.com/GilesCounty/CountyOfficials.aspx

Index: Separate indices to search include deeds, deeds of trust, releases, greenbelts, liens, NOC, federal liens. Records indexed on a public use terminal back to 1/1993. Only the public may search. Copy fee $.25 per page. UCC copy fee- $1.00 per page. Cert fee- $1.00 per page includes copy fee. Payee- Giles County Register of Deeds. **Online Real Estate, Deed records:** Access property and deeds indexes/images at www.titlesearcher.com; fee/registration required. **Other phones:** Treasurer- 931-363-1676; Elections- 931-363-2424; County Clerk- 931-363-1509; Trustee -931-363-1676.

Property tax/Assessing- 1 Public Square, PO Box 678, Pulaski, TN 38478; 931-363-2166, fax- 931-424-4795. www.rackleyhost.com/GilesCounty/CountyOfficials.aspx **Online access-** Assessment data on state system is free at www.assessment.state.tn.us/.

Grainger County

Register of Deeds, PO Box 174, Rutledge, TN 37861. 865-828-3523; fax-865-828-4300; 8:30AM-4:30PM M,T,Th,F; 8:30-N W,Sat.

Index: All in one. Records indexed on a public use terminal back to 0600. Office will perform a UCC search but public must search other records themselves. Copy fee $1.00 per page. Cert fee- $5.00 per cert includes copy fee. Payee- Grainger County Register of Deeds. **Online access to Real Estate, Deed records:** Access property and deeds indexes/images at www.titlesearcher.com; fee/registration required. Also, see state introduction. **Other phones:** Treasurer- 865-828-3514; Elections- 865-828-5132; Vital Records- 615-741-1763; County Clerk- 865-828-3511; Trustee -865-828-3514. **Property tax/Assessing-** PO Box 82, Rutledge, TN 37861; 865-828-5858. hours- 8:30AM-4:30PM M,T,TH,F; 8:30AM-Noon W,SAT **Online access-** Assessment data on state comptroller system is free at www.assessment.state.tn.us/.

Greene County

Register of Deeds, 204 N Culter, #215, Greeneville, TN 37743. 423-798-1726, R/E recording phone-423-639-1726; 8AM-4:30PM (EST)

Index: All in one. Records indexed on a public use terminal back to 1999. Only the public may search. Copy fee $1.00 per page. Cert fee- $1.00 per page. Payee- Greene County Register of Deeds. **Online access to Real Estate, Deed records:** Access property and deeds indexes/images at www.titlesearcher.com; fee/registration required. Also, see state introduction. **Other phones:** Treasurer- 423-639-1705; Elections- 423-798-1715; Vital Records- 423-639-1749; County Clerk- 423-639-5321. **Property tax/Assessing-** 204 N Culter, Courthouse, Greeneville, TN 37743; 423-798-1738. **Online access-** Assessment data on state comptroller system is free at www.assessment.state.tn.us/.

Grundy County

Register of Deeds, PO Box 35, Altamont, TN 37301-0035. 931-692-3621; fax-931-692-3627; 8AM-4PM M-Th, 8AM-5PM F. (CST)

Index: All in one. Records indexed on a public use terminal back to 1/1/1990. Only the public may search. Copy fee $.25 per page. Cert fee- $1.00 per page includes copy fee. Payee- Register of Deeds. **Online Real Estate, Deed, Judgment, Lien, UCC records:** Access property and deeds indexes/images at www.titlesearcher.com; fee/registration required. Also, access to property and deeds for a fee go to http://www4.ustitlesearch.net/. **Other phones:** Elections- 931-692-3551; County Clerk- 931-692-3622; Trustee -931-692-3369. **Property tax/Assessing-** PO Box 6, Altamont, TN 37301; 931-692-3596, assessor fax- 931-692-3596. **Online access-** Assessment data on state comptroller system is free at www.assessment.state.tn.us/.

Hamblen County

Register of Deeds, 511 W 2nd North St, Morristown, TN 37814. 423-586-6551; fax-423-318-2505; 8AM-4:30PM N.

Index: All in one. Records indexed on a public use terminal back to 1978. Office personnel or visitors may perform searches. Search fee $1.00 per doc + $.25 per page to mail. Office will not search real estate or UCC records. Copy fee $1.00 per page certified, plus $.25 per page to mail. Cert fee- $1.00 per page includes copy fee. Payee- Register of Deeds. **Online Real Estate, Deed records:** Access property and deeds indexes/images at www.titlesearcher.com; fee/registration required. Also, see state introduction. **Other phones:** Elections- 423-586-7169; County Clerk- 423-586-1993. **Property tax/Assessing-** 511 W 2nd North St, #206, Morristown, TN 37814; 423-586-1852, assessor fax- 423-585-4600. **Online -** Assessment data on state system is free at www.assessment.state.tn.us/.

Hamilton County

Register of Deeds, PO Box 1639, Chattanooga, TN 37401-1639. 423-209-6560; fax-423-209-6561; 7:30AM-5PM (EST) www.hamiltontn.gov/register/
Index: All in one. Records indexed on a public use terminal back to 7/1/69. Only the public may search. Copy fee $.50 per page. Will fax back locally- $1.00 per page; $2.00 long-distance. Cert fee- $1.00 per page includes copy fee. Payee- Hamilton County Register of Deeds. Bulk Data available for purchase; contact Pamela Hurst. **Online access to Real Estate, Deed records:** County Register of Deeds subscription service is $50 per month and $1.00 per fax page. Search by name, address, or book & page. Info, call 423-209-6560 or see www.hamiltontn.gov/Register/. Credit cards accepted. **Other phones:** Treasurer- 423-209-7270; Elections- 423-209-7720; Vital Records- 423-209-8025; County Clerk- 423-209-6500. **Property tax/Assessing**- 625 Georgia Ave, #105, Chattanooga, TN 37402; 423-209-7300. **Online access**- Property assessor records are free at www.hamiltontn.gov/Assessor/. Search property taxes at www.hamiltontn.gov/trustee/default.aspx. Also, search City of Chattanooga property tax database at http://propertytax.chattanooga.gov.

Hancock County

Register of Deeds, PO Box 347, Sneedville, TN 37869. 423-733-4545; 8:30AM-4PM; 8:30AM-N Wed,Sat. (EST)
Index: Deeds in a general index; other documents indexed in the front of each book. Records indexed on computer back to 1/21/03. Only the public may search. Copy fee $.25 per page. Cert fee- $5.00 per doc plus copy fee. Payee- Hancock County Register of Deeds. **Online access to Real Estate, Deed, Judgment, Lien, UCC records:** Access real estate indexes/images at http://www1.ustitlesearch.net/; registration/monthly fee required. Also see state introduction. **Other phones:** Treasurer- 423-733-2939; Elections- 423-733-4549; County Clerk- 423-733-2519; Clerk & Master -423-733-4524. **Property tax/Assessing**- PO Box 347, Main St Courthouse, Sneedville, TN 37869; 423-733-2332, assessor fax- 423-733-2762. hours- 8:30AM-4PM **Online access**- Assessment data on state comptroller system is free at www.assessment.state.tn.us/.

Hardeman County

Register of Deeds, 100 N Main St; Courthouse, Bolivar, TN 38008. 731-658-3476; fax-731-658-3075; 8:30AM-4:30PM; 8:30AM-5PM F. (CST)
Index: Separate indices to search include deeds, Trust deeds, Liens, Military Discharges. Records indexed on a public use terminal back to 1997. Only the public may search. Copy fee $.50 per page. Cert fee- $1.00 per page. Payee- Hardeman County Register of Deeds. **Online access to Real Estate, Deed, Judgment, Lien, UCC records:** Access real estate indexes/images at http://www1.ustitlesearch.net/; registration/monthly fee required. Also see state introduction. **Other phones:** Treasurer- 731-658-5541; Elections- 731-658-4751; County Clerk- 731-658-3541. **Property tax/Assessing**- 731-658-6522. **Online access**- Assessment data on state comptroller system is free at www.assessment.state.tn.us/.

Hardin County

Register of Deeds, Courthouse, Savannah, TN 38372. 731-925-4936; 8AM-4:30PM M,T,Th,F; 8AM-N W. (CST)
Index: Separate indices to search include books and computer. Records indexed on a public use terminal back to 99. Only the public may search. Will not search UCC records. Copy fee $.25 per page. Will fax back for $1.00 per page. Cert fee- $1.00 per cert includes copy fee. Payee- Hardin County Register of Deeds. **Online access to Real Estate, Deed, Judgment, Lien, UCC records:** Access real estate indexes/images at http://www1.ustitlesearch.net/; registration/monthly fee required. Also see state introduction. **Other phones:** Treasurer- 731-925-8180; County Clerk- 731-925-3921. **Property tax/Assessing**- 465 Main St, Courthouse, Savannah, TN 37372; 731-925-9031. **Online access**- Assessment data on state comptroller system is free at www.assessment.state.tn.us/.

Hawkins County

Register of Deeds, PO Box 235, Rogersville, TN 37857. Recording, R/E phone-423-272-8304; fax-423-921-3170; 8AM-4PM; W & Sat 8AM-N. (EST)
Index: All in one. Records indexed on a public use terminal back to 11/1/2002. Only the public may search. Copy fee $1.00 per page. Cert fee- $1.00 per page includes copy. Payee- Register of Deeds. **Online access to Real Estate, Deed records:** Access property and deeds indexes/images at www.titlesearcher.com; fee/registration required. Also, see state introduction. **Other phones:** Treasurer- 423-272-7022 Trustee; Elections- 423-272-8061; County Clerk- 423-272-7002. **Property tax/Assessing**- 110 E Main St, Rm 201, Rogersville, TN 37857; 423-272-8505, assessor fax- 423-272-0159. hours- 8AM-4PM **Online access**- Assessment data on state comptroller system is free at www.assessment.state.tn.us/.

Haywood County

Register of Deeds, 1 N Washington; Courthouse, Brownsville, TN 38012. 731-772-1432; 8:30AM-5PM (CST)
Index: Separate indices to search. Records indexed on a public use terminal back to 1/2005. Only the public may search. Copy fee $1.00 per page; mailed: $5.00 min per doc, must receive request, check & SASE in mail. No fax. Cert fee- $1.00 per doc plus copy fee. Payee- Haywood County Register of Deeds. **Online Real Estate, Deed records:** Access real estate indexes/images at http://www1.ustitlesearch.net/; registration/monthly fee required. Also see state introduction. **Other phones:** Treasurer- 731-772-1722; County Clerk- 731-772-2362. **Property tax/Assessing**- 731-772-0432. **Online access**- Assessment data on state comptroller system is free at www.assessment.state.tn.us/.

Henderson County

Register of Deeds, 17 Monroe Ave, #5, Lexington, TN 38351. 731-968-2941; 8AM-4:30PM (CST)
Index: Separate indices to search include direct, reverse index books, trust book, deed book and misc book. Records indexed on computer back to 2000. Only the public may search. Copy fee $.25 per copy. Cert fee- $1.00 per page plus copy fee. Payee- Henderson County Register of Deeds. **Online access to Real Estate, Deed, Judgment, Lien, UCC records:** Access real estate indexes/images at http://www1.ustitlesearch.net/; registration/monthly fee required. Also see state introduction. **Other phones:** Treasurer- 731-968-2246; County Clerk- 731-968-2856. **Property tax/Assessing**- 731-968-6881. **Online access**- Assessment data on state system is free at www.assessment.state.tn.us/.

Henry County

Register of Deeds, PO Box 44, Paris, TN 38242. 731-642-4081; fax-731-642-2123; 8:30AM-4:30PM.
Index: Pre-7/1999 records in separate indices. Records indexed on a public use terminal back to 99. Only the public may search. Copy fee $.50 per page. Cert fee- $1.00 per page plus $1.00 for certification. Payee- Henry County Register. **Online Real Estate, Deed, Judgment, Lien, UCC records:** Access real estate indexes/images at http://www1.ustitlesearch.net/; registration/monthly fee required. Also see state introduction. **Other phones:** Elections- 731-642-0411; County Clerk- 731-642-2412; Trustee -731-642-6633. **Property tax/Assessing**- 731-642-0162. **Online access**- Assessment data on state comptroller system is free at www.assessment.state.tn.us/.

Hickman County

Register of Deeds, 114 N Central Ave, #104, Centerville, TN 37033-1639. 931-729-4882; fax-931-729-9596; 7:30AM-4PM (CST)
Index: All in one. Records indexed on a public use terminal back to 1996. Office will perform a UCC search but public must search other records themselves. Search fee-$15.00 per name. Office will not search real estate records. Copy fee $.25 per page. Cert fee- $1.00 per page. Payee- Hickman County Register of Deeds. **Online access to Real Estate, Deed records:** Access property and deeds indexes/images at www.titlesearcher.com; fee/registration required. Also, see state introduction. **Other phones:** Treasurer- 931-729-3486; County Clerk- 931-729-3516. **Property tax/Assessing**- 114 N Central Ave, #106, Centerville, TN 37033; 931-729-2169, assessor fax- 931-729-6113. hours- 8AM-4PM **Online access**- Assessment data on state comptroller system is free at www.assessment.state.tn.us/.

Houston County

Register of Deeds, PO Box 412, Erin, TN 37061. 931-289-3510; fax-931-289-3510; 8AM-4:30PM; Sat by appointment. www.houstoncochamber.com/news.php?viewStory=76
Index: Separate indices to search. Records indexed on a public use terminal. Only the public may search. General copy fee $.25 per page. Cert fee- $1.00 per page plus copy fee. Payee- Register of Deeds. **Online access to Real Estate, Deed, Judgment, Lien, UCC records:** Access real estate indexes/images at http://www1.ustitlesearch.net/; registration/monthly fee required. Also see state introduction. **Other phones:** Vital Records- 615-726-2559; County Clerk- 931-289-3141. **Property tax/Assessing**- PO Box 336, 105 Courthouse, Erin, TN 37061; 931-289-3929, assessor fax- 931-289-3929. hours- 8AM-N, 1PM-4PM **Online access**- Assessment data on state system is free at www.assessment.state.tn.us/.

Humphreys County

Register of Deeds, 102 Thompson St, Rm 3; Courthouse Anne, Waverly, TN 37185. Recording, R/E phone-931-296-7681; 8AM-4:30PM (CST)
Index: Separate indices to search include warranty deed, trust deeds, UCC, liens, releases. Records indexed on a public use terminal back to 1994. Office will perform a UCC search but public must search other records themselves. Copy fee $.50 per page; $.25 self serve; $1.00 if mailed. Cert fee- $1.00 per page includes copy fee. Payee- Humphreys County Register of Deeds. **Online access to Real Estate, Deed records:** Access property and deeds indexes/images at www.titlesearcher.com; fee/registration required. Also, see state introduction. **Other phones:** Treasurer- 931-296-2414; County Clerk- 931-296-7681. **Property tax/Assessing**- 931-296-2919. **Online access**- Assessment data on state system is free at www.assessment.state.tn.us/.

Jackson County

Register of Deeds, PO Box 301, Gainesboro, TN 38562. 931-268-9012; fax-931-268-9060; 8AM-4PM M,T,Th,F; 8AM-2PM W; 8AM-N Sat. (CST)
Index: All in one. Records indexed on a public use terminal back to 9/00. Office will perform a UCC search but public must search other records themselves. Copy fee $1.00 per page.Real estate or tax lien copy- $.25 per page. Cert fee- $1.00 per doc includes copy fee. Payee- Jackson County Register of Deeds. **Online access to Real Estate, Deed records:** Access property and deeds indexes/images at www.titlesearcher.com; fee/registration required. Also, see state introduction. **Other phones:** Treasurer- 931-268-9417; Elections- 931-268-9284; County Clerk- 931-268-9212. **Property tax/Assessing**- PO Box 281, Gainesboro, TN 38562; 931-268-0246, assessor fax- 931-268-9512. hours- 8AM-4PM M,T,Th,F; 8AM-Noon W Sat **Online access**- Assessment data on state system is free at www.assessment.state.tn.us/.

Jefferson County

Register of Deeds, PO Box 58, Dandridge, TN 37725. 865-397-2918; hours - 8AM-4PM (EST) www.jeffersoncountytn.gov

Index: All in one. Records indexed on a public use terminal from 9/98 to present. Only the public may search. Copy fee $1.00 per page. Cert fee- $1.00 per page includes copy fee. Payee- Jefferson County Register of Deeds. **Online access to Real Estate, Deed records:** Access property and deeds indexes/images at www.titlesearcher.com; fee/registration required. Also, see state introduction. **Other phones:** Treasurer- 865-397-2101; County Clerk- 865-397-3800. **Property tax/Assessing-** PO Box 975, 202 W Main St, Dandridge, TN 37725; 865-397-3326, assessor fax- 865-397-5645. **Online access-** Assessment data on state comptroller system is free at www.assessment.state.tn.us/.

Johnson County

Register of Deeds, 222 W Main St, Mountain City, TN 37683. 423-727-7841; fax-423-727-9130; 8:30AM-5PM.

Index: All in one. Records indexed on a public use terminal back to 2002. Only the public may search. Copy fee $1.00 per page if mailed or faxed; self-serve- $.25 per page. Cert fee- $1.00 per cert includes copy fee. Payee- Register of Deeds. **Online access to Real Estate, Deed records:** Access property and deeds indexes/images at www.titlesearcher.com; fee/registration required. Also, see state introduction. **Other phones:** Treasurer- 423-727-9062; Elections- 423-727-8592; County Clerk- 423-727-9633. **Property tax/Assessing-** 210 College St, Mountain City, TN 37683; 423-727-7692. **Online access-** Assessment data on state comptroller system is free at www.assessment.state.tn.us/.

Knox County

Register of Deeds, 400 W Main Ave, Rm 225, Knoxville, TN 37902. 865-215-2330; fax-865-215-2332; 8-4:30 (EST) www.knoxcounty.org/register/

Records indexed on a public use terminal back to 1968. Only the public may search. Copy fee $2.00 per page.Real estate or tax lien copy- $.50 per page. Cert fee- $1.00 per page. Payee- Knox County Register of Deeds. **Online access to Real Estate, Deed records:** For online subscription for recorded document records call Ricky Deler at 865-215-3544. **Other phones:** Treasurer- 865-215-2305; County Clerk- 865-215-5100. **Property tax/Assessing-** 400 W Main Ave, Rm 204, Knoxville, TN 37902; 865-215-2360, assessor fax- 865-215-3671. (Appraiser - 865-215-3366) **Online access-** Search property tax rolls free at www.knoxcounty.org/trustee/tax_search/index.php. GIS Dept offers a property map and details report at www.kgis.org/Portal/OnlineData/tabid/38/Default.aspx.

Lake County

Register of Deeds, 229 Church St, Box 5; Courthouse, Tiptonville, TN 38079. 731-253-7462; fax-731-253-9815; 8AM-4PM.

Index: Separate indices to search include deed index and mortgage index. Records indexed on a public use terminal back to 00. Only the public may search. Copy fee $.50 per page. Cert fee- $1.00 per page includes copy fee. Payee- Register of Deeds. **Online access to Real Estate, Deed, Judgment, Lien, UCC records:** Access real estate indexes/images at http://www1.ustitlesearch.net/; registration/monthly fee required. Also see state introduction. **Other phones:** County Clerk- 731-253-7582; Trustee -731-253-7502. **Property tax/Assessing-** 229 Church St, Box 10, Tiptonville, TN 38079; 731-253-7200, assessor fax- 731-253-7200. **Online access-** Assessment data on state comptroller system is free at www.assessment.state.tn.us/.

Lauderdale County

Register of Deeds, Courthouse, Ripley, TN 38063. 731-635-2171; fax-731-635-9682; 8-4:30PM (CST)

Index: All in one. Records indexed on a public use terminal back to 01/1984. Only the public may search. Copy fee $.25 per page; $1.00 to fax back. Cert fee- $1.00 per page plus copy fee. Payee- Lauderdale Cuonty Register of Deeds. **Online access to Real Estate, Deed, Judgment, Lien, UCC records:** Access real estate indexes/images at http://www1.ustitlesearch.net/; registration/monthly fee required. Also see state introduction. **Other phones:** Treasurer- 731-635-0712; Elections- 615-741-7956; County Clerk- 731-635-2561. **Property tax/Assessing-** 100 Court Sq, Ripley, TN 38063; 731-635-9561. **Online access-** Assessment data on state system is free at www.assessment.state.tn.us/.

Lawrence County

Register of Deeds, 240 W Gaines St, NBV #18, Lawrenceburg, TN 38464. 931-766-4100; fax-931-766-5602; 8AM-4:30PM. www.co.lawrence.tn.us

Index: Separate indices to search include trust, warranty, lien. Records indexed on a public use terminal back to 1999. Only the public may search. Copy fee $.25 per page. Cert fee- $1.00 per page includes copy fee. Payee- Teresa Dunkin, Register of Deeds. **Online Real Estate, Deed records:** Access property and deeds indexes/images at www.titlesearcher.com; fees/ registration required.. **Other phones:** Treasurer- 931-766-4110; Elections- 931-766-4130; Vital Records- 615-741-1763; County Clerk- 931-762-7700. **Property tax/Assessing-** 240 W Gaines St, NBU #14, Lawrenceburg, TN 38464; 931-766-4104, assessor fax- 931-766-4103. **Online access-** Assessment data on state system is free at www.assessment.state.tn.us/.

Lewis County

Register of Deeds, 110 N Park Ave, Rm 104; Courthouse, Hohenwald, TN 38462. 931-796-2255; 8AM-4:30PM (CST)

Index: All in one. Records indexed on a public use terminal back to 7/00. Only the public may search. Office will not search real estate records. Will not search UCC records. Copy fee $1.00 per page.Real estate or tax lien copy- $.25 per page. Cert fee- $1.00 per doc plus copy fee. Payee- Lewis County Register of Deeds. **Online access to Real Estate, Deed, Judgment, Lien, UCC records:** Access real estate indexes/images at http://www1.ustitlesearch.net/; registration/monthly fee required. Also see state introduction. **Other phones:** Treasurer- 931-796-2226; Elections- 931-796-3662; County Clerk- 931-796-2200. **Property tax/Assessing-** 110 N Park Ave, Rm B9, Hohenwald, TN 38462; 931-796-5848, assessor fax- 931-796-6013. **Online access-** Assessment data on state comptroller system is free at www.assessment.state.tn.us/.

Lincoln County

Register of Deeds, 112 Main Ave S, Rm 104, Fayetteville, TN 37334. Recording, R/E phone-931-433-5366; fax-931-433-9312; 8AM-4PM (CST)

Index: All in one. Records indexed on a public use terminal back to 99. Only the public may search. Copy fee $.25 per page. Cert fee- $1.00 per page plus copy fee. Payee- Lincoln County Register of Deeds. **Online access to Real Estate, Deed records:** Access property and deeds indexes/images at www.titlesearcher.com; fee/registration required. Also, see state introduction. **Other phones:** Elections- 931-433-6220; County Clerk- 931-433-2454; Trustee -931-433-1371. **Property tax/Assessing-** 112 Main Ave S Rm 105, Fayetteville, TN 37334 931-433-5409. **Online-** Assessment data on state system is free at www.assessment.state.tn.us/. Search property/GIS data free at www.emapsplus.com/TNLincoln/maps/.

Loudon County

Register of Deeds, PO Box 395, Loudon, TN 37774. 865-458-2605; fax-865-458-9028; 8-4:30PM (EST)

Index: All in one. Records indexed on a public use terminal back to 10/1997. Only the public may search. Copy fee $.25 per page in office. Cert fee- $1.00 per page includes copy fee. Payee- Loudon County Register of Deeds. **Online access to Real Estate, Deed records:** Access property and deeds indexes/images at www.titlesearcher.com; fee/registration required. Also, see state introduction. **Other phones:** Treasurer- 865-458-3103; Elections- 865-458-2560; County Clerk- 865-458-3314. **Property tax/Assessing-** 101 Mulberry St, Loudon, TN 37774; 865-458-2050. **Online access-** Assessment data on state comptroller system is free at www.assessment.state.tn.us/.

Macon County

Register of Deeds, Courthouse, Rm 607; Public Sq, Lafayette, TN 37083. 615-666-2353; fax-615-666-2691; 8AM-N; 1-4:30PM M,T,W,F; 8AM-N, 1PM-4PM TH. www.maconcountytn.com/register_of_deeds.htm

Index: Separate indices to search include direct, reverse, mortgage, debtor, charter, lien, POA, release, misc indexes, discharge records, bonds, subdivision, financing statements. Records indexed on a public use terminal back to 1997. Only the public may search. Copy fee $.25 per page. Cert fee- $1.00 per page plus copy fee. Payee- Macon County Register of Deeds. **Online access to Real Estate, Deed records:** Access property and deeds indexes/images at www.titlesearcher.com; fee/registration required. Also, see state introduction. **Other phones:** Elections- 615-666-2199; County Clerk- 615-666-2333; Trustee -615-666-3624. **Property tax/Assessing-** Courthouse, Rm 103, Public Sq, Lafayette, TN 37083; 615-666-3688, assessor fax- 615-666-9115. **Online access-** Assessment data on state comptroller system is free at www.assessment.state.tn.us/.

Madison County

Register of Deeds, 100 Main St, Rm 109; Courthouse, Jackson, TN 38301. Recording, R/E phone-731-423-6028; fax-731-423-6088; 9AM-5PM.

Index: All in one. Records indexed on a public use terminal back to 1985. Only the public may search. Copy fee $1.00 per page if mailed. Cert fee- $1.00 per page. Payee- Register of Deeds. **Online access to Real Estate, Deed records:** Access property and deeds indexes/images at www.titlesearcher.com; fee/registration required. Also, see state introduction. **Other phones:** Treasurer- 731-423-6027; County Clerk- 731-423-6022. **Property tax/Assessing-** 118 E Baltimore, Jackson, TN 38301; 731-423-6100. **Online access-** Assessment data on state comptroller system is free at www.assessment.state.tn.us/.

Marion County

Register of Deeds, PO Box 789, Jasper, TN 37347. 423-942-2573; 8AM-4PM N. (CST)

Index: All in one. Records indexed on a public use terminal back to 1986. Only the public may search. Copy fee $.50 per page. Cert fee- $1.00 per page. Payee- Marion County Register of Deeds. **Online Real Estate, Deed records:** Access property and deeds indexes/images at www.titlesearcher.com; fee/registration required. Also, see state introduction. **Other phones:** County Clerk- 423-942-2515; Trustee -423-942-2681. **Property tax/Assessing-** PO Box 789, Jasper, TN 37347; 423-942-3494, assessor fax-423-942-8009. **Online access-** Assessment data on state system is free at www.assessment.state.tn.us/.

Marshall County

Register of Deeds, 1103 Courthouse Annex, Lewisburg, TN 37091. 931-359-4933; fax-931-270-8262; 8AM-4PM (CST) www.marshallcountytn.com/government/marshall/deeds

Index: All in one. Records indexed on a public use terminal back to 1993. Only the public may search. Copy fee $1.00 per page. Cert fee- $1.00 per page includes copy fee. Payee- Marshall County Register of Deeds. **Online access to Real Estate, Deed, Judgment, Lien, UCC records:** Access real estate indexes/images at http://www1.ustitlesearch.net/ or a 2nd private company at www.titlesearcher.com; registration/monthly fee required. Also see state introduction. **Other phones:** County Clerk- 931-359-1072; Trustee -931-359-4809. **Property tax/Assessing-** 3300 Courthouse Annex, Lewisburg, TN 37091; 931-359-3238, assessor fax- 931-359-0537. **Online access-** Assessment data on state system is free at www.assessment.state.tn.us/.

Maury County

Register of Deeds, PO Box 769, Columbia, TN 38402-0769. 931-375-2101; fax-931-375-2119; 8AM-4PM (CST)

Index: Separate indices to search include liens, notices of completion, greenbelts, charters. Records indexed on a public use terminal back to 8/11/98. Office will perform a UCC search but public must search other records themselves. Copy fee $.50 per page. Cert fee-

$1.00 per page includes copy fee. Payee- Maury County Register of Deeds. Bulk Data available for purchase at: B.I.S., 333 Industrial Park Rd., Piney Flats, TN 37686. **Online access to Real Estate, Deed records:** Access property and deeds indexes/images at www.titlesearcher.com; fee/registration required. Also, see state introduction. **Other phones:** Treasurer- 931-375-2200; Elections- 931-375-6000; County Clerk- 931-381-3690. **Property tax/Assessing-** 6 Public Square, Columbia, TN 38401; 931-375-4000, assessor fax- 931-375-4000. **Online-** Assessment data on state system is free at www.assessment.state.tn.us/. Search property/GIS data free at www.emapsplus.com/TNMaury/maps/.

McMinn County

Register of Deeds, PO Box 1074, Athens, TN 37371-1074. 423-745-1232; 8:30AM-4PM.
Index: All in one. Records indexed on a public use terminal back to 9/99. Only the public may search. Copy fee $.25 per page. Cert fee- $1.00 per page. Payee- Register of Deeds. **Online access to Real Estate, Deed, Judgment, Lien, UCC records:** Access real estate indexes/images back to 9/1999 at http://www1.ustitlesearch.net/; registration/monthly fee required. Also see state introduction. **Other phones:** Treasurer- 423-745-4103; Elections- 423-745-0843; County Clerk- 423-745-4440; Circuit Court Clerk -423-745-1923. **Property tax/Assessing-** 6 E Madison Ave, Athens, TN 37303; 423-745-2743, assessor fax- 423-746-5036. **Online access-** Assessment data on state comptroller system is free at www.assessment.state.tn.us/.

McNairy County

Register of Deeds, PO Box 158, Selmer, TN 38375. 731-645-3656; fax-same; 8AM-4:30PM M T Th F; 8AM-N Sat. (CST)
County Clerk phone- 731-645-3511. Index: All in one. Records indexed on a public use terminal back to 1999. Only the public may search. General copy fee $1.00 per page. Cert fee- $2.00 per doc plus copy fee. Payee- McNairy County Register of Deeds. **Online access to Real Estate, Deed, Judgment, Lien, UCC records:** Access real estate indexes/images at http://www1.ustitlesearch.net/; registration/monthly fee required. Also see state introduction. **Other phones:** Vital Records- 731-645-3511; County Clerk- 731-645-3511. **Property tax/Assessing-** 170 W Court Ave, Selmer, TN 38375; 731-645-5146, assessor fax- 731-645-5146. **Online access-** Assessment data on state system is free at www.assessment.state.tn.us/.

Meigs County

Register of Deeds, PO Box 156, Decatur, TN 37322. 423-334-5228; 8-4:30PM M,T,Th,F; 8-N Sat. (EST)
Courthouse fires for Meigs County happened in 1904 and 1964. Index: All in one. Records indexed on a public use terminal back to 3/03. Only the public may search. General copy fee $1.00 per page. Cert fee- $2.00 per page includes copy fee. Payee- Meigs County Register of Deeds. **Online access to Real Estate, Deed records:** Access real estate indexes/images at http://www1.ustitlesearch.net/; registration/monthly fee required. Also see state introduction. **Other phones:** County Clerk- 423-334-5747; Trustee -423-334-5119. **Property tax/Assessing-** PO Box 215, 17214 State Hwy 58 N, Decatur, TN 37322; 423-334-5231, assessor fax- 423-334-7208. **Online access-** Assessment data on state system is free at www.assessment.state.tn.us/.

Monroe County

Register of Deeds, 103 College St, #4, Madisonville, TN 37354. 423-442-2440; 8:30AM-4:30PM M,T,Th,F; 8:30AM-N W & Sat. (EST)
Index: Prior to 1998 separate indices to search include grantor/grantee. Records indexed on a public use terminal back to 198. Only the public may search. Will not search UCC records. Copy fee $1.00 per page. Cert fee- $1.00 per page. Payee- Monroe County Register of Deeds. **Online access to Real Estate, Deed records:** Access property and deeds indexes/images at www.titlesearcher.com; fee/registration required. Also, see state introduction. **Other phones:** Treasurer- 423-442-2920; Elections- 423-442-2461; County Clerk- 423-442-2220. **Property tax/Assessing-** 103 College St, #27, Madisonville, TN 37354; 423-442-3637, assessor fax- 423-442-6500. **Online access-** Assessment data on state comptroller system is free at www.assessment.state.tn.us/.

Montgomery County

Register of Deeds, PO Box 1124, Clarksville, TN 37041. 931-648-5713; fax-931-553-5157; 7:30AM-4:30PM (CST) www.montgomerycountytn.org/county/register_of_deeds/register_of_deeds.htm
Index: All in one. Records indexed on a public use terminal back to 1986. Only the public may search. Copy fee $.25 per page. Cert fee- $1.00 per page includes copy fee. Payee- Register of Deeds. **Online access to Real Estate, Deed, Judgment, Lien, UCC records:** Access real estate indexes/images at http://www1.ustitlesearch.net/; registration/monthly fee required. Also see state introduction. **Other phones:** Treasurer- 931-648-5710; Elections- 931-648-5707; Vital Records- 931-648-5747; County Clerk- 931-648-5711; Trustee -931-648-5710. **Property tax/Assessing-** 350 Pageant Ln, Clarksville, TN 37040; 931-648-5709. **Online** - Assessment data on state system is free at www.assessment.state.tn.us/.

Moore County

Register of Deeds, PO Box 206, Lynchburg, TN 37352. 931-759-7913; fax-931-759-6394; 8AM-4:30PM; Closed Th; 8AM-N Sat. (CST)
Index: All in one. Records indexed on a public use terminal back to 2002. Only the public may search. Copy fee $1.00 per page.Real estate record copy- $.50 per page. Cert fee- $1.00 per cert plus copy fee. Payee- Moore County Register of Deeds. **Online access to Real Estate, Deed records:** Access property and deeds indexes/images at www.titlesearcher.com; fee/registration required. Also, see state introduction. **Other phones:** County Clerk- 931-759-7346. **Property tax/Assessing-** PO Box 206, Lynchburg, TN 37352; 931-759-7044, assessor fax- 931-759-6394. hours- 8AM-4:30PM M,T,W,F; 8AM-N Sat. **Online** - Assessment data on state system is free at www.assessment.state.tn.us/.

Morgan County

Register of Deeds, PO Box 311, Wartburg, TN 37887. 423-346-3105; 8AM-4PM (EST)
Index: All in one. Records indexed on a public use terminal back to 7/03. Office will perform a UCC search but public must search other records themselves. Copy fee $.50 per page. $.50 per page for fax. Cert fee- $1.00 per page includes copy fee. Payee- Morgan County Register of Deeds. **Online access to Real Estate, Deed, Judgment, Lien, UCC records:** Access real estate indexes/images at http://www1.ustitlesearch.net/; registration/monthly fee required. Also see state introduction. **Other phones:** County Clerk- 423-346-3480; Trustee -423-346-3430. **Property tax/Assessing-** 423-346-3130. **Online access-** Assessment data on state comptroller system is free at www.assessment.state.tn.us/.

Obion County

Register of Deeds, PO Box 514, Union City, TN 38261. 731-885-9351; fax-731-885-7515; 8-4:30PM.
Index: Separate indices to search include warranty deed, trust deed, lien, and misc. Record index not computerized. Only the public may search. Copy fee $.50 per page. Cert fee- $1.00 per page includes copy fee. Payee- Register of Deeds. **Other phones:** Elections- 731-885-1901; County Clerk- 731-885-3831. **Property tax/Assessing-** 731-885-2931. **Online access-** Assessment data on state comptroller system is free at www.assessment.state.tn.us/.

Overton County

Register of Deeds, 317 E University St, Rm 150, Livingston, TN 38570. 931-823-4011; 8AM-4:30PM (CST) _Index: All in one. Records indexed on a public use terminal. Only the public may search. Copy fee $1.00 per page.Real estate or tax lien copy- $.25 per page. Cert fee- $1.00 per page plus copy fee. Payee- Overton County Register of Deeds. **Online access to Real Estate, Deed records:** Access real estate indexes/images at http://www1.ustitlesearch.net/; registration/monthly fee required. Also see state introduction. **Other phones:** Treasurer- 931-832-6220; Elections- 931-823-5985; County Clerk- 931-823-2631. **Property tax/Assessing-** 317 E University St, Rm 34, Livingston, TN 38570; 931-823-1651, assessor fax- 931-823-1130. **Online access-** Assessment data on state comptroller system is free at www.assessment.state.tn.us/.

Perry County

Register of Deeds, PO Box 62, Linden, TN 37096-0062. 931-589-2210; fax-931-589-2215; 8AM-4PM (CST) _Index: All in one. Records indexed on a public use terminal back to 00. Only the public may search. Copy fee $1.00 per page, fax fee $1.25 per page. Cert fee- $5.00 per doc includes copy fee. Payee- Perry County Register of Deeds. **Online Real Estate, Deed records:** Access property and deeds indexes/images at www.titlesearcher.com; fee/registration required. Also, see state introduction. **Other phones:** Treasurer- 931-589-2313; County Clerk- 931-589-2216. **Property tax/Assessing-** PO Box 68, 121 E Main St, Linden, TN 37096; 931-589-2277, assessor fax- 931-589-2765. **Online** - Assessment data on state system is free at www.assessment.state.tn.us/.

Pickett County

Register of Deeds, 1 Courthouse Sq, #204, Byrdstown, TN 38549. 931-864-3316; fax-931-864-7087; 8-11AM, N-4PM. _Index: All in one. Record index not computerized. Only the public may search. Copy fee $.25 per page. Cert fee- $3.00. Payee- Register of Deeds. **Other phones:** Vital Records- 795-296-1400; County Clerk- 931-864-3879. **Property tax/Assessing-** 1 Courthouse Sq, Byrdstown, TN 38549; 931-864-3114. **Online access-** Assessment data on state system is free at www.assessment.state.tn.us/.

Polk County

Register of Deeds, PO Box 293, Benton, TN 37307. 423-338-4537; 8:30AM-4:30PM (EST)
Index: Separate indices to search include grantor/grantee. Records indexed on computer back to 2003. Only the public may search. Copy fee $1.00 per page. Cert fee- $1.00 per page includes copy fee. Payee- Polk County Register of Deeds. **Online access to Real Estate, Deed records:** Access property and deeds indexes/images at www.titlesearcher.com; fee/registration required. Also, see state introduction. **Other phones:** County Clerk- 423-338-4526; Trustee -423-338-4545. **Property tax/Assessing-** 423-338-4505. **Online access-** Assessment data on state system is free at www.assessment.state.tn.us/.

Putnam County

Register of Deeds, PO Box 487, Cookeville, TN 38503-0487. 931-526-7101; fax-931-526-7120; 8AM-4PM (CST)
Index: Separate indices. Record index not computerized. Only the public may search. Copy fee $1.00 per page. Cert fee- $1.00 per page. Payee- Putnam County Register of Deeds. **Online access to Real Estate, Deed, Judgment, Lien, UCC records:** Access real estate indexes/images at http://www1.ustitlesearch.net/; registration/monthly fee required. **Other phones:** Treasurer- 931-526-8845; County Clerk- 931-526-7106. **Property tax/Assessing-** 300 E Spring St, Rm 1, Cookeville, TN 38501; 931-528-8428, assessor fax- 931-520-0468. **Online access-** Assessment data on state system is free at www.assessment.state.tn.us/. Also, search property/GIS data free at www.emapsplus.com/TNputnam/maps/.

Rhea County

Register of Deeds, 375 Church St #106, Dayton, TN 37321. 423-775-7841; 8AM-4:30PM (EST)
Index: All in one. Records indexed on a public use terminal back to 5/03. Only the public may search. Copy fee $.25 per page. Cert fee- $1.00 per page plus copy fee. Payee- Rhea County Register of Deeds. **Online access to Real Estate, Deed records:** Access property and deeds indexes/images at www.titlesearcher.com; fee/registration required. Images go back to 5/28/03. Also, see state introduction. **Other phones:** Treasurer- 423-775-7810; County Clerk- 423-775-7808. **Property tax/Assessing-** 375 Church St, #100, Dayton, TN 37321; 423-775-7840, assessor fax- 423-570-5201.

Online access- Assessment data on state comptroller system is free at www.assessment.state.tn.us/.

Roane County

Register of Deeds, PO Box 181, Kingston, TN 37763. 865-376-4673; 8:30AM-6PM M; 8:30AM-4:30PM T-F. (EST)
Index: Pre-1999 records in 2 indices- warranty deeds and trust deeds/miscellaneous. Records indexed on computer back to 10/99. Only the public may search. Will not search UCC records. Copy fee $1.00 per page. Cert fee- $1.00 per page includes copy fee. Payee- Roane County Register of Deeds. **Online Real Estate, Deed records:** Access property and deeds indexes/images at www.titlesearcher.com; fee/registration required, images go back to 6/5/03. Also, see state introduction. **Other phones:** Elections-865-376-3184; County Clerk- 865-376-5578; Trustee -865-376-4938. **Property tax/Assessing**- 865-376-4362. **Online access**- Assessment data on state system is free at www.assessment.state.tn.us/.

Robertson County

Register of Deeds, 525 S Brown St., Springfield, TN 37172. 615-384-3772; fax-615-384-0256; 8AM-4:30PM (CST)
Index: All in one. Records indexed on a public use terminal back to 1998. Only the public may search. General copy fee $1.00 per page. Cert fee- $1.00 per page plus copy fee. Payee- Robertson County Register of Deeds. **Online access to Real Estate, Deed, Judgment, Lien, UCC records:** Access real estate indexes/images at http://www1.ustitlesearch.net/; registration/monthly fee required. Also see state introduction. **Other phones:** Elections- 615-384-5592; County Clerk-615-384-5895; Trustee -615-384-4238. **Property tax/Assessing**- 521 S Brown St, Springfield, TN 37172; 615-384-4311, assessor fax- 615-384-7297. **Online** - Assessment data on state system is free at www.assessment.state.tn.us/.

Rutherford County

Register of Deeds, PO Box 5050, Murfreesboro, TN 37133. 615-898-7870; fax-615-898-7987; 8AM-4PM.
Index: All in one. Records indexed on a public use terminal back to 1985. Only the public may search. Copy fee $.50 per page. Cert fee- $1.00. Payee-Rutherford County Register of Deeds. **Online access to Real Estate, Deed, Judgment, Lien, UCC records:** Access real estate indexes/images at http://www1.ustitlesearch.net/; registration/monthly fee required. To subscribe call 615-223-1823. Also see state introduction. **Other phones:** County Clerk-615-898-7798. **Property tax/Assessing**- 319 N Maple St, #300, Murfreesboro, TN 37130; 615-898-7750, assessor fax- 615-896-2759. **Online access**-Assessment data on state comptroller system is free at www.assessment.state.tn.us/.

Scott County

Register of Deeds, PO Box 61, Huntsville, TN 37756. 423-663-2417; fax-423-663-8281; 8-4:30PM (EST)
Index: Separate indices to search include direct index book alpha and reverse. Records indexed on computer. Books back to 1850's. Only the public may search. Copy fee $.50 per page; $1.00 per page if UCC. Cert fee- $1.00 per page includes copy fee. Payee- Scott County Register of Deeds. **Other phones:** Treasurer- 423-663-2598; Elections- 423-663-2430; County Clerk- 423-663-2588. **Property tax/Assessing**- 283 Court St, Huntsville, TN 37756; 423-663-2420. **Online access**- Assessment data on state comptroller system is free at www.assessment.state.tn.us/.

Sequatchie County

Register of Deeds, PO Box 174, Dunlap, TN 37327. 423-949-2512; fax-423-949-6554; 8AM-5PM.
Index: All in one. Records indexed on a public use terminal back to 7/01. Only the public may search. Copy fee $.25 per page; fax back $1.00 per page. Cert fee- $1.00 per page includes copy fee. Payee-Sequatchie County Register of Deeds. **Online access to Real Estate, Deed records:** Access property and deeds indexes/images at www.titlesearcher.com; fee/registration required. Also, see state introduction. **Other phones:** County Clerk- 423-949-2522. **Property tax/Assessing**- 423-949-3534. **Online access**- Assessment data on state comptroller system is free at www.assessment.state.tn.us/.

Sevier County

Register of Deeds, 125 Court Ave, #209W; Courthouse, Sevierville, TN 37862. 865-453-2758; 8AM-4:30PM M-Th; 8AM-6PM F. (EST)
Index: All in one. Records indexed on a public use terminal back to 1993. Only the public may search. General copy fee $.20 per page. Cert fee- $1.00 per page includes copy fee. Payee- Sevier County Register of Deeds. For bulk data sales, please contact Business Information Systems at 866-514-5192. **Online access to Real Estate, Deed records:** Access property and deeds indexes/images at www.titlesearcher.com; fee/registration required. Also, see state introduction. **Other phones:** Elections-865-453-6985; County Clerk- 865-453-5502; Trustee -865-453-2767. **Property tax/Assessing**- 865-453-3242. **Online access**- Assessment data on state comptroller system is free at www.assessment.state.tn.us/.

Shelby County

Register of Deeds, 160 N Main St, Rm 519, Memphis, TN 38103. 901-545-4366; fax-901-545-3837; 8AM-4:30PM. http://register.shelby.tn.us
Index: All in one. Records indexed on several public use terminals full from 1201 to present, partial back to 1800s. Only the public may search. Copy fee $.10 per page. Plat copies-$1.50 per page. Cert fee- $1.00 per page includes copy fee. Payee- Shelby County Retister. GIS fly-over data available on DVD, $15 per disc or $210 total, contact Fred in GIS. **Online access to Real Estate, Deed, Lien, Judgment records:** Access the Register of Deeds database free at http://register.shelby.tn.us/index.php. Partial indexes and images go back to 1986; full to 12/2001. Also, access property and deeds indexes/images at www.titlesearcher.com; fee/registration required. Also see state introduction. **Other phones:** County Clerk-901-545-4255. **Property tax/Assessing**- 1075 Mullins Station Rd, Memphis, TN 38134; 901-379-7333, assessor fax- 901-379-7199. Data is available for bulk purchase, call Assessor ofc for details. **Online access**- Access property assessor data free at www.assessor.shelby.tn.us/content.aspx.

Smith County

Register of Deeds, 122 Turner High Circle, #113, Carthage, TN 37030. 615-735-1760; fax-615-735-8263; 8AM-4PM (CST)
Index: Separate indices to search include before 6/28/99 they have different index books. Records indexed on a public use terminal back to 6/99. Office personnel or visitors may perform searches. No fee for search. Office will search real estate records. Will search UCC records. Copy fee $.25 per page. Minimum charge to fax back is $2.50 plus $.50 per page. Will mail back for $.50 per page. Cert fee-$1.00 plus $2.00 processing includes copy fee. Payee-Smith County Register of Deeds. **Online access to Real Estate, Deed records:** Access property and deeds indexes/images at www.titlesearcher.com; fee/registration required. Also, see state introduction. **Other phones:** County Clerk- 615-735-9833. **Property tax/Assessing**- 122 Turner High Circle, #106, Carthage, TN 37030; 615-735-1750, assessor fax- 614-735-8259. **Online access**- Assessment data on state comptroller system is free at www.assessment.state.tn.us/.

Stewart County

Register of Deeds, PO Box 57, Dover, TN 37058. 931-232-5990; fax-931-232-5990; 8-4:30PM (CST)
Index: All in one from 2001 forward. Records indexed on a public use terminal back to 2001. Only the public may search. Copy fee $.25 per page. Cert fee- $1.00 per page plus copy fee. Payee- Stewart County Register of Deeds. **Online access to Real Estate, Deed, Judgment, Lien, UCC records:** Access real estate indexes/images at http://www1.ustitlesearch.net/; registration/monthly fee required. Also see state introduction. **Other phones:** County Clerk- 931-232-7616; Trustee -931-232-7026. **Property tax/Assessing**- 931-232-5252. **Online access**- Assessment data on state comptroller system is free at www.assessment.state.tn.us/.

Sullivan County (Blountville Office)

Register of Deeds, 3411 Hwy 126, #101, Blountville, TN 37617. 423-323-6420; fax-423-279-2771; 8AM-5PM. www.sullivancounty.org/registerdeeds.htm
Index: All in one. Records indexed on a public use terminal back to 1980. Only the public may search. Copy fee $2.00 per page. Cert fee- $1.00. Payee-Sullivan County Register of Deeds. **Other phones:** Elections- 423-323-6444; Vital Records- 423-279-2777; County Clerk- 423-323-6428; Trustee -423-323-6464. **Property tax/Assessing**- 3411 Hwy 126, #103, Blountville, TN 37617; 423-323-6455, assessor fax- 423-279-2808. **Online**- Assessment data on state comptroller system is free at www.assessment.state.tn.us/.

Sullivan County (Bristol Office)

Register of Deeds, 801 Anderson St, Rm 102, Bristol, TN 37620. 423-989-4370; fax-423-989-4371; 8AM-5PM (EST)
Index: All in one. Records indexed on a public use terminal back to 7/1/80. Only the public may search. Copy fee $2.00 for 1-4 pages, add'l pages $.50 per page. Cert fee- $1.00 per page plus copy fee. Payee-Sullivan County Register of Deeds. **Other phones:** Treasurer- 423-323-6464; Elections- 423-323-6444; Vital Records- 423-279-2777; County Clerk- 423-323-6428. **Property tax/Assessing**- 3411 Hwy 126, #103, Blountville, TN 37617; 423-323-6455, assessor fax- 423-279-2808. **Online access**- Assessment data on state comptroller system is free at www.assessment.state.tn.us/.

Sumner County

Register of Deeds, PO Box 299, Gallatin, TN 37066-0299. 615-452-3892; fax-615-442-1105; 8AM-4:30PM (CST) www.deeds.sumnercounty.org
Index: All in one. Records indexed on a public use terminal back to 1989. Books are back to 1977. Only the public may search. Will not search UCC records. Copy fee $1.00 per page. Cert fee- $1.00 per page includes copy fee. Payee- Sumner County Register of Deeds. Bulk data available for purchase on microfilm only. 3 books per roll and $75.00 per roll. **Online access to Real Estate, Deed records:** Access real estate indexes/images back to 10/22/1989 at http://www1.ustitlesearch.net/; registration/monthly fee required. Also see state introduction. **Other phones:** Elections- 615-452-1456; County Clerk-615-452-4063; Trustee -615-452-1260. **Property tax/Assessing**- 355 N. Belvedere Dr, Rm 206, Gallatin, TN 37066; 615-452-2412, assessor fax- 615-442-1108. **Online access**- Assessment data on state comptroller system is free at www.assessment.state.tn.us/. Also, search property data free on the GIS site at http://tn.sumner.geopowered.com. At the map, click on "search for property" then name search.

Tipton County

Register of Deeds, PO Box 626, Covington, TN 38019-0644. Recording, R/E phone-901-476-0204; fax-901-476-0206; 8AM-5PM (CST)
Index: All in one. Records indexed on a public use terminal back to 1000. Only the public may search. Copy fee $1.00 per page. Cert fee- $1.00 per page includes copy fee. Payee- Tipton County Register of Deeds. **Online access to Real Estate, Deed, Judgment, Lien, UCC records:** Access real estate indexes/images back to 10/22/1989 at http://www1.ustitlesearch.net/; registration/monthly fee required. Also see state introduction. **Other phones:** Treasurer- 901-476-0211; Elections- 901-476-0223; County Clerk- 901-476-0207. **Property tax/Assessing**- 901-476-0213. **Online**- Assessments on state system free at www.assessment.state.tn.us/.

Trousdale County

Register of Deeds, 200 E Main St, #8, Hartsville, TN 37074-1706. 615-374-2921; fax-615-374-1100; 8AM-4:30PM (CST)
Index: All in one. Records indexed on a public use terminal back to 3/1/03. Only the public may search. Copy fee $.25 per page. Cert fee- $3.00 per page plus copy fee. Payee- Trousdale County Register of Deeds.

Online access to Real Estate, Deed, Judgment, Lien, UCC records: Access real estate indexes/images back to 10/22/1989 at http://www1.ustitlesearch.net/; registration/monthly fee required. Also see state introduction. **Other phones:** County Clerk- 615-374-2906. **Property tax/Assessing-** 615-374-2553. **Online access-** Assessment data on state comptroller system is free at www.assessment.state.tn.us/.

Unicoi County

Register of Deeds, PO Box 305, Erwin, TN 37650-0305. 423-743-6104; fax-423-743-6278; 9AM-5PM; 9AM-N Sat. (EST) www.unicoicountytn.gov/
Index: All in one. Records indexed on a public use terminal back to 1997. Only the public may search. Will not search UCC records. Copy fee $1.00 per page. Cert fee- $1.00 per page includes copy fee. Payee- Unicoi County Register of Deeds. **Online access to Real Estate, Deed records:** Access property and deeds indexes/images is via a private company at www.titlesearcher.com. Fee/registration required; images go back to 1/1997. Also see state introduction. **Other phones:** Treasurer- 423-743-3011; Elections- 423-743-6521; County Clerk- 423-743-3381; Circuit Court Clerk -423-743-3541. **Property tax/Assessing-** PO Box 257, Erwin, TN 37650; 423-743-3801, assessor fax- 423-743-2001. www.unicoicountytn.gov/ **Online access-** Access to GIS/Mapping for free go to www.unicoicountytn.gov/index.php?option=com_content&task=view&id=33&Itemid=48.

Union County

Register of Deeds, 901 Main S, #108, Maynardville, TN 37807. 865-992-8024; fax-same; 8AM-4PMM,T;W,Th; 8AM-6PM F. (EST)
Index: All in one. Records indexed on a public use terminal back to 12/1400. Only the public may search. Copy fee $.25 per page. Cert fee- $1.00 per page includes copy fee. Payee- Union County Register of Deeds. **Online access to Real Estate, Deed, Judgment records:** Access property and deeds indexes/images at www.titlesearcher.com; fee/registration required. Also, see state introduction. **Other phones:** Treasurer- 865-992-5943; Elections-865-992-3471; Vital Records- 865-992-3867; County Clerk- 865-992-8043; Trustee -865-992-5943. **Property tax/Assessing-** 901 Main St, #115, Maynardville, TN 37807; 865-992-3211. **Online access-** Access assessment data on the state system free at www.assessment.state.tn.us/.

Van Buren County

Register of Deeds, PO Box 9, Spencer, TN 38585. 931-946-7363; fax-931-946-2806; 8AM-4PM M-Th, 8AM-5PM F.
Index: Separate indices to search. Records indexed on a public use terminal back to 2001. Only the public may search. Copy fee $.25 per page. No fee for Military records copied. Cert fee- $3.00 per page plus copy fee. Payee- Linda Simmons, Register of Deeds. **Online access to Real Estate, Deed records:** Access property and deeds indexes/images at www.titlesearcher.com; fee/registration required. Also, see state introduction. **Other phones:** Elections-931-946-2728; County Clerk- 931-946-2121. **Property tax/Assessing-** PO Box 103, Spencer, TN 38585; 931-946-2451, assessor fax- 931-946-2876. **Online access-** Assessment data on state comptroller system is free at www.assessment.state.tn.us/.

Warren County

Register of Deeds, PO Box 128, McMinnville, TN 37111. Recording, R/E phone-931-473-2926, UCC recording phone-931-473-8663; fax-931-474-2114; 8AM-4:30PM M-Th; 8AM-5PM F. (CST)
Index: All in one. Records indexed on a public use terminal back to 1998. Only the public may search. Copy fee $1.00 per page if they pull more that 2 books. Cert fee- $1.00 per page includes copy fee. Payee- Warren County Register of Deeds. Bulk data available for purchase, contact Terry Smith. **Online access to Real Estate, Deed, Judgment, Lien, UCC records:** Access real estate indexes/images at http://www1.ustitlesearch.net/; registration/monthly fee required. Also see state introduction. **Other phones:** County Clerk- 931-473-2623. **Property tax/Assessing-** 201 Locust St, #5, McMinnville, TN 37110; 931-473-3450, assessor fax- 931-474-3455. **Online access-** Assessment data on state comptroller system is free at www.assessment.state.tn.us/.

Washington County

Register of Deeds, PO Box 69, Jonesborough, TN 37659. 423-753-1644, R/E recording phone-423-753-1645, UCC phone-423-753-1648; fax-423-753-1743; 8AM-5PM. www.washingtoncountytn.com
Index: All in one. Records indexed on a public use terminal back to 1972. Office will perform a UCC search but public must search other records themselves. Copy fee $.50 per page. Cert fee- None. Payee- Washington County Register of Deeds. **Online access to Real Estate, Deed, Judgment, Lien, UCC records:** Access property and deeds indexes/images at www.titlesearcher.com; fee/registration required. Also, see state introduction. **Other phones:** Treasurer- 423-753-1610; Elections-423-753-1688; Vital Records- 423-753-1621; County Clerk- 423-753-1621. **Property tax/Assessing-** Jonesborough Courthouse, Jonesborough, TN 37659; 423-753-1670. **Online access-** Assessment data on state comptroller system is free at www.assessment.state.tn.us/.

Wayne County

Register of Deeds, PO Box 465, Waynesboro, TN 38485. 931-722-5518; fax-same; 8AM-4PM M T TH F; 8AM-N W & Sat.
Index: All in one. Records indexed on a public use terminal back to 30 yrs. Only the public may search. Copy fee $.50 per page. Will fax back $1.00 per page includes copies. Cert fee- $1.00 per doc plus $.25 per page. Payee- Wayne County Register. **Online access to Real Estate, Deed records:** Access real estate indexes/images at http://www1.ustitlesearch.net/ or at a 2nd company at www.titlesearcher.com; registration/monthly fee required. Also see state introduction. **Other phones:** Treasurer- 931-722-3269; Elections- 931-722-3517; County Clerk- 931-722-5544. **Property tax/Assessing-** PO Box 466, 100 Court Sq Rm 203, Waynesboro, TN 38485; 931-722-5282, assessor fax- 931-722-5282. hours-8AM04:30PM **Online access-** Assessment data on state system is free at www.assessment.state.tn.us/.

Weakley County

Register of Deeds, PO Box 45, Dresden, TN 38225. 731-364-3646; fax-731-364-5284; 8:30AM-4:30PM
Index: All in one. Records indexed on a public use terminal back to 1995. Only the public may search. Copy fee $.25 per page. Cert fee- $1.00. Payee-Register of Deeds. **Online access to Real Estate, Deed records:** Access property and deeds indexes/images at www.titlesearcher.com; fee/registration required. Also see state introduction. **Other phones:** County Clerk- 731-364-2285; Trustee -731-364-3643. **Property tax/Assessing-** 116 W Main, Rm G01, Dresden, TN 38225; 731-364-3677, assessor fax- 731-364-5389. **Online access-** Assessment data on state comptroller system is free at www.assessment.state.tn.us/.

White County

Register of Deeds, PO Box 86, Sparta, TN 38583-0086. 931-836-2817; fax-931-836-8418; 8AM-5PM. www.spartatn.com
Index: Separate indices to search prior to 1990. Records indexed on a public use terminal back to 1990. Only the public may search. Copy fee $1.00 per page faxed or mailed, $5.00 minimum. Cert fee- $1.00 per page includes copy fee. Payee- Register of Deeds. **Online access to Real Estate, Deed records:** Access property and deeds indexes/images at www.titlesearcher.com; fee/registration required. **Other phones:** Elections- 615-741-7956; County Clerk- 931-836-3712. **Property tax/Assessing-** 1 E Bockman Way, Rm 103, Sparta, TN 38583; 931-836-3480. A public access terminal is available. **Online access-** Assessment data on state comptroller system is free at www.assessment.state.tn.us/.

Williamson County

Register of Deeds, PO Box 808, Franklin, TN 37065-0808. Recording, R/E phone-615-790-5706; fax-615-790-5459; 8AM-4:30PM (CST)
Index: All in one. Records indexed on computer back to 1981. Only the public may search. Copy fee $.50 per page, $1.00 per page if mailed. Cert fee- $1.00 per page plus copy fee. Payee- Williamson County Register of Deeds. **Online access to Real Estate, Deed records:** Access to the Professional Access database by subscription is a $50 per month fee. Info and sign-up at http://williamson-tn.org/co_gov/profacc.htm. Also, access property and deeds indexes/images back to 11/1992 at www.titlesearcher.com; fee/registration required. Also see state introduction. **Other phones:** Treasurer- 615-790-5709; Elections- 615-790-5711; County Clerk-615-790-5412. **Property tax/Assessing-** 1320 W Main St,#300, Franklin, TN 37064; 615-790-5708, fax- 615-790-5760. www.williamsoncounty-tn.gov/index.asp?NID=64 **Online access-** Assessment data on state comptroller system is free at www.assessment.state.tn.us/. Also, access to property search data free go to www.williamson-tn.org/assessor/.

Wilson County

Register of Deeds, PO Box 176, Lebanon, TN 37087-0176. Recording, R/E phone-615-443-2611; fax-615-443-3288; 8AM-4PM. www.wilsondeeds.com
Index: Separate indices to search include 1992 back direct & reverse. Records indexed on a public use terminal back to 1/92. Only the public may search. Copy fee $.25 per page, $2.00 per original size plat. Cert fee- $1.00 per page, $5.00 per certified plat. Payee- Wilson Register. Bulk indices and images available for purchase; contact Jeff Lowe at 866-514-5197. **Online access to Real Estate, Deed, Lien records:** Access to the Register of Deeds database requires a $10 registration fee and $25.00 per month usage fee at www.wilsondeeds.com. Includes indices back to 1925; images back to 1992. Also, online access to property and deeds indexes and images is via a private company at www.titlesearcher.com. A per day only fee/registration required. Also see state introduction. **Other phones:** Treasurer- 615-444-0894; Elections- 615-444-0216; County Clerk- 615-444-0314. **Property tax/Assessing-** 228 E Main St, Lebanon, TN 37087; 615-444-8661. **Online access-** Assessment data on state comptroller system is free at www.assessment.state.tn.us/.

Tennessee County Locator

You will usually be able to find the city name in the City/County Cross Reference below. In that case, it is a simple matter to determine the county from the cross reference. However, only the official US Postal Service city names are included in this index. There are an additional 40,000 place names that people use in their addresses. Therefore, we have also included a ZIP/City Cross Reference immediately following the City/County Cross Reference.

If you know the ZIP Code but the city name does not appear in the City/County Cross Reference index, look up the ZIP Code in the ZIP/City Cross Reference, find the city name, then look up the city name in the City/County Cross Reference. For example, you want to know the county for an address of Menands, NY 12204. There is no "Menands" in the City/County Cross Reference. The ZIP/City Cross Reference shows that ZIP Codes 12201-12288 are for the city of Albany. Looking back in the City/County Cross Reference, Albany is in Albany County.

Tennessee City/County Cross Reference

ADAMS (37010) Robertson(58), Montgomery(41)
ADAMSVILLE (38310) McNairy(56), Hardin(43)
AFTON Greene
ALAMO Crockett
ALCOA Blount
ALEXANDRIA (37012) De Kalb(78), Wilson(11), Smith(10)
ALLARDT Fentress
ALLONS (38541) Overton(66), Clay(33)
ALLRED Overton
ALPINE (38543) Overton(81), Pickett(18)
ALTAMONT Grundy
ANDERSONVILLE (37705) Anderson(68), Union(31)
ANTIOCH Davidson
APISON Hamilton
ARDMORE (38449) Giles(68), Lincoln(31)
ARLINGTON (38002) Shelby(90), Fayette(9)
ARNOLD AFB Coffee
ARRINGTON (37014) Williamson(58), Rutherford(41)
ARTHUR Claiborne
ASHLAND CITY (37015) Cheatham(95), Davidson(3)
ATHENS McMinn
ATOKA (38004) Tipton(94), Shelby(5)
ATWOOD (38220) Carroll(94), Gibson(5)
AUBURNTOWN (37016) Cannon(73), Wilson(26)
BAKEWELL Hamilton
BATH SPRINGS Decatur
BAXTER (38544) Putnam(91), De Kalb(8)
BEAN STATION Grainger
BEECH BLUFF (38313) Madison(51), Henderson(25), Chester(23)
BEECHGROVE (37018) Coffee(97), Bedford(2)
BEERSHEBA SPRINGS Grundy
BELFAST Marshall
BELL BUCKLE (37020) Bedford(79), Rutherford(20)
BELLS (38006) Crockett(78), Haywood(15), Madison(5)
BELVIDERE Franklin
BENTON Polk
BETHEL SPRINGS (38315) McNairy(84), Chester(15)
BETHPAGE (37022) Sumner(73), Trousdale(24), Macon(1)
BIG ROCK Stewart
BIG SANDY Benton
BIRCHWOOD (37308) Hamilton(65), Meigs(34)
BLAINE (37709) Grainger(83), Union(14), Knox(2)
BLOOMINGTON SPRINGS (38545) Jackson(61), Putnam(38)
BLOUNTVILLE Sullivan
BLUFF CITY Sullivan
BOGOTA Dyer
BOLIVAR Hardeman
BON AQUA (37025) Hickman(80), Dickson(17), Williamson(2)
BRADEN Fayette
BRADFORD Gibson
BRADYVILLE (37026) Cannon(90), Coffee(9)
BRENTWOOD (37027) Williamson(82), Davidson(17)
BRENTWOOD Williamson
BRICEVILLE Anderson
BRIGHTON (38011) Tipton(97), Shelby(2)
BRISTOL Sullivan
BROWNSVILLE Haywood
BRUCETON (38317) Carroll(94), Benton(5)
BRUNSWICK Shelby
BRUSH CREEK Smith
BUCHANAN Henry
BUENA VISTA (38318) Carroll(97), Benton(2)
BUFFALO VALLEY (38548) Putnam(76), Smith(23)
BULLS GAP (37711) Greene(60), Hawkins(35), Hamblen(3)
BUMPUS MILLS Stewart
BURLISON Tipton
BURNS Dickson
BUTLER (37640) Johnson(66), Carter(33)
BYBEE Cocke
BYRDSTOWN (38549) Pickett(98), Fentress(1)
CALHOUN (37309) McMinn(87), Polk(12)
CAMDEN Benton
CAMPAIGN Warren
CARTHAGE Smith
CARYVILLE Campbell
CASTALIAN SPRINGS (37031) Sumner(59), Trousdale(40)
CEDAR GROVE Carroll
CEDAR HILL (37032) Robertson(94), Cheatham(4)
CELINA (38551) Clay(98), Jackson(1)
CENTERVILLE Hickman
CHAPEL HILL (37034) Marshall(83), Bedford(16)
CHAPMANSBORO (37035) Cheatham(98), Montgomery(1)
CHARLESTON Bradley
CHARLOTTE (37036) Dickson(93), Cheatham(6)
CHATTANOOGA (37419) Hamilton(87), Marion(12)
CHATTANOOGA Hamilton
CHESTNUT MOUND Smith
CHEWALLA McNairy
CHRISTIANA Rutherford
CHUCKEY (37641) Greene(89), Washington(10)
CHURCH HILL Hawkins
CLAIRFIELD (37715) Claiborne(83), Campbell(16)
CLARKRANGE Fentress
CLARKSBURG Carroll
CLARKSVILLE Montgomery
CLEVELAND Bradley
CLIFTON (38425) Wayne(94), Perry(5)
CLINTON Anderson
COALFIELD Morgan
COALMONT Grundy
COKERCREEK Monroe
COLLEGE GROVE (37046) Williamson(85), Rutherford(12), Marshall(1)
COLLEGEDALE Hamilton
COLLIERVILLE (38017) Shelby(82), Fayette(17)
COLLIERVILLE Shelby
COLLINWOOD Wayne
COLUMBIA Maury
COMO Henry
CONASAUGA Polk
COOKEVILLE (38501) Putnam(92), Jackson(6)
COOKEVILLE (38506) Putnam(82), Overton(12), White(5)
COOKEVILLE Putnam
COPPERHILL Polk
CORDOVA Shelby
CORNERSVILLE (37047) Marshall(79), Giles(19), Lincoln(1)
CORRYTON (37721) Knox(79), Union(20)
COSBY (37722) Cocke(82), Sevier(17)
COTTAGE GROVE (38224) Henry(94), Weakley(5)
COTTONTOWN (37048) Sumner(91), Robertson(8)
COUNCE Hardin
COVINGTON Tipton
COWAN Franklin
CRAB ORCHARD Cumberland
CRAWFORD Overton
CROCKETT MILLS Crockett
CROSS PLAINS Robertson
CROSSVILLE Cumberland
CRUMP Hardin
CULLEOKA (38451) Maury(87), Marshall(12)
CUMBERLAND CITY (37050) Stewart(80), Montgomery(13), Houston(6)
CUMBERLAND FURNACE (37051) Dickson(66), Montgomery(33)
CUMBERLAND GAP Claiborne
CUNNINGHAM (37052) Montgomery(97), Dickson(2)
CYPRESS INN Wayne
DANDRIDGE (37725) Jefferson(98), Sevier(1)
DARDEN (38328) Henderson(76), Decatur(23)
DAYTON (37321) Rhea(98), Bledsoe(1)
DECATUR (37322) Meigs(96), McMinn(3)
DECATURVILLE (38329) Decatur(94), Henderson(5)
DECHERD (37324) Franklin(97), Grundy(2)
DEER LODGE (37726) Morgan(85), Fentress(14)
DEL RIO Cocke
DELANO (37325) Polk(79), McMinn(20)
DELLROSE Lincoln
DENMARK Madison
DENVER Humphreys
DICKSON (37055) Dickson(98), Hickman(1)
DICKSON Dickson
DIXON SPRINGS (37057) Trousdale(48), Macon(29), Smith(21)
DOVER Stewart
DOWELLTOWN De Kalb
DOYLE (38559) White(74), Van Buren(25)
DRESDEN Weakley
DRUMMONDS Tipton
DUCK RIVER Hickman
DUCKTOWN Polk
DUFF Campbell
DUKEDOM Weakley
DUNLAP (37327) Sequatchie(90), Bledsoe(9)
DYER Gibson
DYERSBURG Dyer
EADS (38028) Fayette(56), Shelby(43)
EAGAN Claiborne
EAGLEVILLE (37060) Rutherford(85), Bedford(9), Williamson(4)
EATON Gibson
EIDSON (37731) Hawkins(65), Hancock(34)
ELBRIDGE Obion
ELGIN Scott
ELIZABETHTON Carter
ELKTON Giles
ELLENDALE Shelby
ELMWOOD Smith
ELORA (37328) Lincoln(80), Franklin(19)
ENGLEWOOD (37329) McMinn(93), Monroe(6)
ENVILLE (38332) Chester(89), McNairy(10)
ERIN (37061) Houston(96), Humphreys(3)
ERWIN (37650) Unicoi(95), Washington(4)
ESTILL SPRINGS (37330) Franklin(94), Coffee(5)
ETHRIDGE (38456) Lawrence(77), Giles(22)
ETOWAH McMinn
EVA Benton
EVENSVILLE (37332) Rhea(98), Bledsoe(1)
FAIRVIEW (37062) Williamson(98), Dickson(1)
FALL BRANCH (37656) Greene(49), Washington(43), Sullivan(7)
FARNER Polk
FAYETTEVILLE Lincoln
FINGER (38334) McNairy(80), Chester(19)
FINLEY Dyer
FIVE POINTS Lawrence
FLAG POND Unicoi
FLINTVILLE (37335) Lincoln(96), Franklin(3)
FOSTERVILLE Rutherford
FOWLKES Dyer
FRANKEWING (38459) Giles(56), Lincoln(43)
FRANKLIN Williamson

FRIENDSHIP (38034) Crockett(80), Dyer(19)
FRIENDSVILLE (37737) Blount(92), Loudon(7)
FRUITVALE Crockett
GADSDEN Crockett
GAINESBORO Jackson
GALLATIN Sumner
GALLAWAY Fayette
GATES (38037) Lauderdale(68), Haywood(31)
GATLINBURG Sevier
GEORGETOWN (37336) Meigs(40), Bradley(40), Hamilton(19)
GERMANTOWN Shelby
GIBSON Gibson
GLADEVILLE Wilson
GLEASON (38229) Weakley(98), Henry(1)
GOODLETTSVILLE (37072) Davidson(59), Sumner(32), Robertson(8)
GOODLETTSVILLE Davidson
GOODSPRING Giles
GORDONSVILLE Smith
GRAND JUNCTION (38039) Hardeman(72), Fayette(27)
GRANDVIEW (37337) Cumberland(52), Rhea(47)
GRANVILLE (38564) Jackson(90), Putnam(9)
GRAYSVILLE (37338) Rhea(63), Bledsoe(23), Sequatchie(11), Hamilton(1)
GREENBACK (37742) Loudon(73), Blount(26)
GREENBRIER Robertson
GREENEVILLE Greene
GREENFIELD Weakley
GRIMSLEY Fentress
GRUETLI LAAGER Grundy
GUILD Marion
GUYS McNairy
HALLS (38040) Lauderdale(83), Crockett(11), Dyer(4)
HAMPSHIRE (38461) Maury(93), Lewis(6)
HAMPTON Carter
HARRIMAN (37748) Roane(89), Morgan(10)
HARROGATE Claiborne
HARTFORD Cocke
HARTSVILLE (37074) Trousdale(86), Macon(13)
HEISKELL (37754) Anderson(53), Knox(40), Union(5)
HELENWOOD Scott
HENDERSON (38340) Chester(91), Hardeman(8)
HENDERSONVILLE Sumner
HENNING Lauderdale
HENRY Henry
HERMITAGE (37076) Davidson(95), Wilson(4)
HICKMAN (38567) Smith(95), De Kalb(4)
HICKORY VALLEY (38042) Hardeman(98), Fayette(1)
HICKORY WITHE Fayette
HILHAM (38568) Overton(58), Clay(26), Jackson(14)
HILLSBORO Coffee
HIXSON Hamilton
HOHENWALD Lewis
HOLLADAY (38341) Benton(82), Decatur(13), Henderson(3)
HOLLOW ROCK Carroll
HORNBEAK Obion
HORNSBY (38044) Hardeman(91), McNairy(5), Chester(3)
HUMBOLDT (38343) Gibson(76), Crockett(15), Madison(7)
HUNTINGDON Carroll
HUNTLAND Franklin
HUNTSVILLE Scott
HURON Henderson
HURRICANE MILLS Humphreys
IDLEWILD Gibson
INDIAN MOUND (37079) Stewart(80), Montgomery(19)
IRON CITY (38463) Lawrence(63), Wayne(36)
ISABELLA Polk
JACKS CREEK Chester
JACKSBORO Campbell
JACKSON Madison
JAMESTOWN Fentress
JASPER Marion
JELLICO Campbell
JOELTON (37080) Davidson(51), Cheatham(48)
JOHNSON CITY (37601) Washington(76), Carter(22), Unicoi(1)
JOHNSON CITY Washington
JONESBOROUGH Washington
KELSO Lincoln
KENTON (38233) Gibson(68), Obion(31)
KINGSPORT (37660) Sullivan(95), Hawkins(4)
KINGSPORT (37663) Sullivan(97), Washington(2)
KINGSPORT Sullivan
KINGSTON Roane
KINGSTON SPRINGS Cheatham
KNOXVILLE (37931) Knox(98), Anderson(1)
KODAK (37764) Sevier(89), Knox(9)
KYLES FORD Hancock
LA FOLLETTE Campbell
LA GRANGE Fayette
LA VERGNE (37086) Rutherford(98), Davidson(1)
LA VERGNE Rutherford
LACONIA Fayette
LAFAYETTE Macon
LAKE CITY (37769) Anderson(78), Campbell(21)
LANCASTER (38569) Smith(77), De Kalb(22)
LANCING Morgan
LASCASSAS (37085) Rutherford(79), Wilson(20)
LAUREL BLOOMERY Johnson
LAVINIA Carroll
LAWRENCEBURG (38464) Lawrence(94), Giles(3), Wayne(2)
LEBANON (37087) Wilson(96), Trousdale(2)
LEBANON (37090) Wilson(97), Smith(2)
LEBANON Wilson
LENOIR CITY (37771) Loudon(92), Roane(7)
LENOIR CITY Loudon
LENOX Dyer
LEOMA (38468) Lawrence(90), Giles(9)
LEWISBURG (37091) Marshall(96), Bedford(3)
LEXINGTON Henderson
LIBERTY (37095) De Kalb(76), Cannon(19), Wilson(3)
LIMESTONE (37681) Greene(55), Washington(44)
LINDEN (37096) Perry(88), Wayne(10)
LIVINGSTON Overton
LOBELVILLE (37097) Perry(98), Humphreys(1)
LONE MOUNTAIN Claiborne
LOOKOUT MOUNTAIN Hamilton
LORETTO Lawrence
LOUDON (37774) Loudon(94), Roane(4)
LOUISVILLE Blount
LOWLAND Hamblen
LUPTON CITY Hamilton
LURAY Chester
LUTTRELL (37779) Union(92), Knox(5), Grainger(1)
LUTTS Wayne
LYLES Hickman
LYNCHBURG Moore
LYNNVILLE (38472) Giles(92), Marshall(7)
MACON Fayette
MADISON Davidson
MADISONVILLE (37354) Monroe(98), McMinn(1)
MANCHESTER Coffee
MANSFIELD Henry
MARTIN Weakley
MARYVILLE (37801) Blount(94), Monroe(5)
MARYVILLE Blount
MASCOT (37806) Knox(91), Grainger(8)
MASON (38049) Fayette(78), Tipton(21)
MAURY CITY Crockett
MAYNARDVILLE (37807) Union(98), Knox(1)
MC DONALD (37353) Bradley(88), Hamilton(11)
MC EWEN (37101) Humphreys(89), Houston(5), Hickman(5)
MC KENZIE (38201) Carroll(75), Weakley(14), Henry(10)
MC LEMORESVILLE Carroll
MC MINNVILLE (37110) Warren(97), Grundy(1), Cannon(1)
MC MINNVILLE Warren
MEDINA (38355) Gibson(57), Madison(42)
MEDON (38356) Madison(54), Hardeman(33), Chester(11)
MEMPHIS Shelby
MERCER (38392) Madison(66), Hardeman(33)
MICHIE (38357) McNairy(80), Hardin(19)
MIDDLETON Hardeman
MIDWAY Greene
MILAN Gibson
MILLEDGEVILLE (38359) Chester(77), McNairy(19), Hardin(2)
MILLIGAN COLLEGE Carter
MILLINGTON (38053) Shelby(83), Tipton(16)
MILLINGTON Shelby
MILTON (37118) Rutherford(66), Wilson(24), Cannon(9)
MINOR HILL Giles
MISTON Dyer
MITCHELLVILLE Sumner
MOHAWK Greene
MONROE (38573) Overton(64), Pickett(35)
MONTEAGLE (37356) Marion(83), Grundy(16)
MONTEREY (38574) Putnam(65), Overton(15), Cumberland(14), Fentress(4)
MOORESBURG (37811) Hawkins(95), Grainger(4)
MORLEY Campbell
MORRIS CHAPEL (38361) Hardin(89), McNairy(10)
MORRISON (37357) Warren(58), Coffee(30), Cannon(9), Grundy(1)
MORRISTOWN Hamblen
MOSCOW Fayette
MOSHEIM Greene
MOSS Clay
MOUNT CARMEL Hawkins
MOUNT JULIET (37122) Wilson(96), Rutherford(3)
MOUNT JULIET Wilson
MOUNT PLEASANT (38474) Maury(94), Lewis(3), Giles(1), Lawrence(1)
MOUNT VERNON Monroe
MOUNTAIN CITY Johnson
MOUNTAIN HOME Washington
MULBERRY (37359) Moore(53), Lincoln(46)
MUNFORD Tipton
MURFREESBORO Rutherford
NASHVILLE (37221) Davidson(96), Williamson(3)
NASHVILLE Davidson
NEW JOHNSONVILLE Humphreys
NEW MARKET Jefferson
NEW TAZEWELL (37825) Claiborne(96), Union(3)
NEW TAZEWELL Claiborne
NEWBERN Dyer
NEWCOMB Campbell
NEWPORT Cocke
NIOTA (37826) McMinn(94), Meigs(6)
NOLENSVILLE (37135) Williamson(78), Rutherford(15), Davidson(6)
NORENE Wilson
NORMANDY (37360) Coffee(46), Bedford(38), Moore(14)
NORRIS Anderson
NUNNELLY Hickman
OAK RIDGE (37830) Anderson(93), Roane(5), Knox(1)
OAK RIDGE Anderson
OAKDALE Morgan
OAKFIELD Madison
OAKLAND Fayette
OBION (38240) Obion(93), Dyer(6)
OCOEE Polk
OLD HICKORY (37138) Davidson(68), Wilson(31)
OLDFORT (37362) Bradley(87), Polk(12)
OLIVEHILL (38475) Hardin(86), Wayne(13)
OLIVER SPRINGS (37840) Roane(35), Morgan(32), Anderson(32)
ONEIDA Scott
ONLY Hickman
OOLTEWAH Hamilton
ORLINDA Robertson
OZONE Cumberland
PALL MALL (38577) Fentress(50), Pickett(49)
PALMER (37365) Grundy(90), Sequatchie(7), Marion(1)
PALMERSVILLE Weakley
PALMYRA Montgomery
PARIS (38242) Henry(98), Weakley(1)
PARROTTSVILLE Cocke
PARSONS Decatur
PEGRAM (37143) Cheatham(86), Davidson(13)
PELHAM Grundy
PETERSBURG (37144) Lincoln(56), Marshall(32), Bedford(7), Moore(1)
PETROS Morgan
PHILADELPHIA (37846) Loudon(59), Roane(23), Monroe(15), McMinn(1)
PICKWICK DAM Hardin
PIGEON FORGE Sevier
PIKEVILLE (37367) Bledsoe(84), Cumberland(9), Van Buren(6)
PINEY FLATS Sullivan
PINSON (38366) Chester(52), Madison(47)
PIONEER (37847) Scott(63), Campbell(36)
PLEASANT HILL Cumberland
PLEASANT SHADE (37145) Smith(73), Macon(15), Jackson(11)
PLEASANT VIEW (37146) Cheatham(71), Robertson(28)
PLEASANTVILLE Hickman
POCAHONTAS (38061) Hardeman(63), McNairy(36)
PORTLAND (37148) Sumner(94), Robertson(5)
POWDER SPRINGS (37848) Union(66), Grainger(33)
POWELL (37849) Knox(82), Anderson(17)
PRIMM SPRINGS (38476) Williamson(36), Hickman(35), Maury(27)
PROSPECT Giles
PRUDEN Claiborne
PULASKI Giles
PURYEAR Henry
QUEBECK White
RAMER McNairy
READYVILLE (37149) Rutherford(64), Cannon(35)

REAGAN (38368) Henderson(76), Chester(23)
RED BOILING SPRINGS (37150) Macon(75), Clay(23)
RELIANCE (37369) Polk(81), Monroe(18)
RICEVILLE McMinn
RICKMAN Overton
RIDDLETON Smith
RIDGELY (38080) Lake(62), Dyer(33), Obion(3)
RIDGETOP Robertson
RIPLEY (38063) Lauderdale(94), Haywood(5)
RIVES Obion
ROAN MOUNTAIN Carter
ROBBINS (37852) Scott(90), Morgan(9)
ROCK ISLAND (38581) Warren(77), Van Buren(21)
ROCKFORD (37853) Blount(94), Knox(5)
ROCKVALE (37153) Rutherford(91), Bedford(8)
ROCKWOOD (37854) Roane(76), Cumberland(15), Morgan(7)
ROGERSVILLE Hawkins
ROSSVILLE Fayette
RUGBY Morgan
RUSSELLVILLE Hamblen
RUTHERFORD Gibson
RUTLEDGE Grainger
SAINT ANDREWS Franklin
SAINT BETHLEHEM Montgomery
SAINT JOSEPH Lawrence
SALE CREEK Hamilton
SALTILLO (38370) Hardin(96), Henderson(3)
SAMBURG Obion
SANTA FE Maury
SARDIS (38371) Hardin(59), Henderson(40)
SAULSBURY Hardeman
SAVANNAH Hardin
SCOTTS HILL (38374) Decatur(98), Henderson(1)
SELMER McNairy
SEQUATCHIE Marion
SEVIERVILLE (37876) Sevier(97), Jefferson(2)
SEVIERVILLE Sevier
SEWANEE Franklin
SEYMOUR (37865) Sevier(80), Blount(19)
SHADY VALLEY Johnson
SHARON Weakley
SHARPS CHAPEL Union
SHAWANEE Claiborne
SHELBYVILLE (37160) Bedford(97), Moore(2)
SHELBYVILLE Bedford
SHERWOOD Franklin
SHILOH (38376) Hardin(80), McNairy(19)
SIGNAL MOUNTAIN (37377) Hamilton(88), Sequatchie(11)
SILERTON Hardeman
SILVER POINT (38582) Putnam(71), De Kalb(28)
SLAYDEN Dickson
SMARTT Warren
SMITHVILLE (37166) De Kalb(89), Warren(9), Cannon(1)
SMYRNA Rutherford
SNEEDVILLE (37869) Hancock(65), Hawkins(27), Claiborne(7)
SODDY DAISY (37379) Hamilton(94), Sequatchie(4)
SODDY DAISY Hamilton
SOMERVILLE Fayette
SOUTH FULTON (38257) Obion(94), Weakley(5)
SOUTH PITTSBURG Marion
SOUTHSIDE Montgomery
SPARTA (38583) White(86), De Kalb(6), Cumberland(3), Putnam(2)
SPEEDWELL (37870) Claiborne(76), Campbell(12), Union(10)
SPENCER Van Buren
SPRING CITY (37381) Rhea(95), Bledsoe(4)
SPRING CREEK Madison
SPRING HILL (37174) Maury(56), Williamson(42)
SPRINGFIELD Robertson
SPRINGVILLE Henry
STANTON (38069) Haywood(83), Tipton(8), Fayette(8)
STANTONVILLE McNairy
STEWART (37175) Houston(79), Stewart(20)
STRAWBERRY PLAINS (37871) Knox(44), Jefferson(40), Sevier(15)
SUGAR TREE (38380) Decatur(67), Benton(32)
SUMMERTOWN (38483) Lawrence(76), Lewis(19), Giles(2), Maury(1)
SUMMITVILLE Coffee
SUNBRIGHT (37872) Morgan(95), Scott(4)
SURGOINSVILLE Hawkins
SWEETWATER (37874) Monroe(87), McMinn(6), Loudon(5)
TAFT Lincoln
TALBOTT (37877) Hamblen(61), Jefferson(38)
TALLASSEE Blount
TAZEWELL (37879) Claiborne(95), Hancock(4)
TELFORD Washington
TELLICO PLAINS Monroe
TEN MILE (37880) Roane(58), Meigs(40)
TENNESSEE RIDGE (37178) Houston(86), Stewart(13)
THOMPSONS STATION Williamson
THORN HILL (37881) Grainger(64), Hancock(34)
TIGRETT Dyer
TIPTONVILLE Lake
TOONE Hardeman
TOWNSEND Blount
TRACY CITY (37387) Marion(66), Grundy(33)
TRADE Johnson
TREADWAY Hancock
TRENTON Gibson
TREZEVANT Carroll
TRIMBLE (38259) Dyer(86), Obion(8), Gibson(4)
TROY Obion
TULLAHOMA (37388) Coffee(72), Franklin(18), Moore(8)
TURTLETOWN Polk
UNICOI Unicoi
UNION CITY Obion
UNIONVILLE (37180) Bedford(94), Rutherford(5)
VANLEER (37181) Dickson(98), Houston(1)
VIOLA Warren
VONORE (37885) Monroe(97), Loudon(2)
WALLAND Blount
WALLING White
WARTBURG Morgan
WARTRACE (37183) Bedford(72), Coffee(18), Moore(8)
WASHBURN (37888) Grainger(90), Union(9)
WATAUGA (37694) Carter(76), Sullivan(18), Washington(5)
WATERTOWN (37184) Wilson(96), Smith(3)
WATTS BAR DAM Rhea
WAVERLY Humphreys
WAYNESBORO (38485) Wayne(98), Lewis(1)
WESTMORELAND (37186) Sumner(58), Macon(41)
WESTPOINT (38486) Lawrence(84), Wayne(15)
WESTPORT (38387) Carroll(90), Benton(9)
WHITE BLUFF (37187) Dickson(93), Cheatham(6)
WHITE HOUSE (37188) Robertson(60), Sumner(39)
WHITE PINE (37890) Jefferson(93), Hamblen(6)
WHITES CREEK Davidson
WHITESBURG (37891) Hamblen(68), Hawkins(31)
WHITESIDE Marion
WHITEVILLE (38075) Hardeman(70), Fayette(15), Haywood(14)
WHITLEYVILLE (38588) Jackson(75), Clay(19), Macon(5)
WHITWELL (37397) Marion(95), Sequatchie(4)
WILDER (38589) Overton(54), Fentress(45)
WILDERSVILLE Henderson
WILLIAMSPORT (38487) Maury(94), Hickman(5)
WILLISTON Fayette
WINCHESTER (37398) Franklin(98), Moore(1)
WINFIELD Scott
WINONA Scott
WOODBURY (37190) Cannon(98), Warren(1)
WOODLAND MILLS Obion
WOODLAWN Montgomery
WYNNBURG Lake
YORKVILLE Gibson
YUMA (38390) Carroll(80), Henderson(19)

Tennessee ZIP/City Cross Reference

37010-37010 ADAMS
37011-37011 ANTIOCH
37012-37012 ALEXANDRIA
37013-37013 ANTIOCH
37014-37014 ARRINGTON
37015-37015 ASHLAND CITY
37016-37016 AUBURNTOWN
37018-37018 BEECHGROVE
37019-37019 BELFAST
37020-37020 BELL BUCKLE
37022-37022 BETHPAGE
37023-37023 BIG ROCK
37024-37024 BRENTWOOD
37025-37025 BON AQUA
37026-37026 BRADYVILLE
37027-37027 BRENTWOOD
37028-37028 BUMPUS MILLS
37029-37029 BURNS
37030-37030 CARTHAGE
37031-37031 CASTALIAN SPRINGS
37032-37032 CEDAR HILL
37033-37033 CENTERVILLE
37034-37034 CHAPEL HILL
37035-37035 CHAPMANSBORO
37036-37036 CHARLOTTE
37037-37037 CHRISTIANA
37040-37044 CLARKSVILLE
37046-37046 COLLEGE GROVE
37047-37047 CORNERSVILLE
37048-37048 COTTONTOWN
37049-37049 CROSS PLAINS
37050-37050 CUMBERLAND CITY
37051-37051 CUMBERLAND FURNACE
37052-37052 CUNNINGHAM
37054-37054 DENVER
37055-37056 DICKSON
37057-37057 DIXON SPRINGS
37058-37058 DOVER
37059-37059 DOWELLTOWN
37060-37060 EAGLEVILLE
37061-37061 ERIN
37062-37062 FAIRVIEW
37063-37063 FOSTERVILLE
37064-37065 FRANKLIN
37066-37066 GALLATIN
37067-37069 FRANKLIN
37070-37070 GOODLETTSVILLE
37071-37071 GLADEVILLE
37072-37072 GOODLETTSVILLE
37073-37073 GREENBRIER
37074-37074 HARTSVILLE
37075-37075 HENDERSONVILLE
37076-37076 HERMITAGE
37077-37077 HENDERSONVILLE
37078-37078 HURRICANE MILLS
37079-37079 INDIAN MOUND
37080-37080 JOELTON
37082-37082 KINGSTON SPRINGS
37083-37083 LAFAYETTE
37085-37085 LASCASSAS
37086-37086 LA VERGNE
37087-37088 LEBANON
37089-37089 LA VERGNE
37090-37090 LEBANON
37091-37091 LEWISBURG
37095-37095 LIBERTY
37096-37096 LINDEN
37097-37097 LOBELVILLE
37098-37098 LYLES
37101-37101 MC EWEN
37110-37111 MC MINNVILLE
37115-37116 MADISON
37118-37118 MILTON
37119-37119 MITCHELLVILLE
37121-37122 MOUNT JULIET
37127-37133 MURFREESBORO
37134-37134 NEW JOHNSONVILLE
37135-37135 NOLENSVILLE
37136-37136 NORENE
37137-37137 NUNNELLY
37138-37138 OLD HICKORY
37140-37140 ONLY
37141-37141 ORLINDA
37142-37142 PALMYRA
37143-37143 PEGRAM
37144-37144 PETERSBURG
37145-37145 PLEASANT SHADE
37146-37146 PLEASANT VIEW
37147-37147 PLEASANTVILLE
37148-37148 PORTLAND
37149-37149 READYVILLE
37150-37150 RED BOILING SPRINGS
37151-37151 RIDDLETON
37152-37152 RIDGETOP
37153-37153 ROCKVALE
37155-37155 SAINT BETHLEHEM
37160-37162 SHELBYVILLE
37165-37165 SLAYDEN
37166-37166 SMITHVILLE
37167-37167 SMYRNA
37171-37171 SOUTHSIDE
37172-37172 SPRINGFIELD
37174-37174 SPRING HILL
37175-37175 STEWART
37178-37178 TENNESSEE RIDGE
37179-37179 THOMPSONS STATION
37180-37180 UNIONVILLE
37181-37181 VANLEER
37183-37183 WARTRACE
37184-37184 WATERTOWN
37185-37185 WAVERLY
37186-37186 WESTMORELAND
37187-37187 WHITE BLUFF
37188-37188 WHITE HOUSE
37189-37189 WHITES CREEK
37190-37190 WOODBURY

37191-37191 WOODLAWN
37200-37250 NASHVILLE
37301-37301 ALTAMONT
37302-37302 APISON
37303-37303 ATHENS
37304-37304 BAKEWELL
37305-37305 BEERSHEBA SPRINGS
37306-37306 BELVIDERE
37307-37307 BENTON
37308-37308 BIRCHWOOD
37309-37309 CALHOUN
37310-37310 CHARLESTON
37311-37312 CLEVELAND
37313-37313 COALMONT
37314-37314 COKERCREEK
37315-37315 COLLEGEDALE
37316-37316 CONASAUGA
37317-37317 COPPERHILL
37318-37318 COWAN
37320-37320 CLEVELAND
37321-37321 DAYTON
37322-37322 DECATUR
37323-37323 CLEVELAND
37324-37324 DECHERD
37325-37325 DELANO
37326-37326 DUCKTOWN
37327-37327 DUNLAP
37328-37328 ELORA
37329-37329 ENGLEWOOD
37330-37330 ESTILL SPRINGS
37331-37331 ETOWAH
37332-37332 EVENSVILLE
37333-37333 FARNER
37334-37334 FAYETTEVILLE
37335-37335 FLINTVILLE
37336-37336 GEORGETOWN
37337-37337 GRANDVIEW
37338-37338 GRAYSVILLE
37339-37339 GRUETLI LAAGER
37340-37340 GUILD
37341-37341 HARRISON
37342-37342 HILLSBORO
37343-37343 HIXSON
37345-37345 HUNTLAND
37346-37346 ISABELLA
37347-37347 JASPER
37348-37348 KELSO
37349-37349 MANCHESTER
37350-37350 LOOKOUT MOUNTAIN
37351-37351 LUPTON CITY
37352-37352 LYNCHBURG
37353-37353 MC DONALD
37354-37354 MADISONVILLE
37355-37355 MANCHESTER
37356-37356 MONTEAGLE
37357-37357 MORRISON
37358-37358 MOUNT VERNON
37359-37359 MULBERRY
37360-37360 NORMANDY
37361-37361 OCOEE
37362-37362 OLDFORT
37363-37363 OOLTEWAH
37364-37364 CLEVELAND
37365-37365 PALMER
37366-37366 PELHAM
37367-37367 PIKEVILLE
37369-37369 RELIANCE
37370-37370 RICEVILLE
37371-37371 ATHENS
37372-37372 SAINT ANDREWS
37373-37373 SALE CREEK
37374-37374 SEQUATCHIE
37375-37375 SEWANEE
37376-37376 SHERWOOD
37377-37377 SIGNAL MOUNTAIN
37378-37378 SMARTT
37379-37379 SODDY DAISY
37380-37380 SOUTH PITTSBURG
37381-37381 SPRING CITY
37382-37382 SUMMITVILLE
37383-37383 SEWANEE
37384-37384 SODDY DAISY
37385-37385 TELLICO PLAINS
37387-37387 TRACY CITY
37388-37388 TULLAHOMA
37389-37389 ARNOLD AFB
37391-37391 TURTLETOWN
37394-37394 VIOLA
37395-37395 WATTS BAR DAM
37396-37396 WHITESIDE
37397-37397 WHITWELL
37398-37398 WINCHESTER
37400-37499 CHATTANOOGA
37501-37544 MEMPHIS
37601-37615 JOHNSON CITY
37616-37616 AFTON
37617-37617 BLOUNTVILLE
37618-37618 BLUFF CITY
37620-37625 BRISTOL
37640-37640 BUTLER
37641-37641 CHUCKEY
37642-37642 CHURCH HILL
37643-37644 ELIZABETHTON
37645-37645 MOUNT CARMEL
37650-37650 ERWIN
37656-37656 FALL BRANCH
37657-37657 FLAG POND
37658-37658 HAMPTON
37659-37659 JONESBOROUGH
37660-37669 KINGSPORT
37680-37680 LAUREL BLOOMERY
37681-37681 LIMESTONE
37682-37682 MILLIGAN COLLEGE
37683-37683 MOUNTAIN CITY
37684-37684 MOUNTAIN HOME
37686-37686 PINEY FLATS
37687-37687 ROAN MOUNTAIN
37688-37688 SHADY VALLEY
37690-37690 TELFORD
37691-37691 TRADE
37692-37692 UNICOI
37694-37694 WATAUGA
37699-37699 PINEY FLATS
37701-37701 ALCOA
37705-37705 ANDERSONVILLE
37707-37707 ARTHUR
37708-37708 BEAN STATION
37709-37709 BLAINE
37710-37710 BRICEVILLE
37711-37711 BULLS GAP
37713-37713 BYBEE
37714-37714 CARYVILLE
37715-37715 CLAIRFIELD
37716-37717 CLINTON
37719-37719 COALFIELD
37721-37721 CORRYTON
37722-37722 COSBY
37723-37723 CRAB ORCHARD
37724-37724 CUMBERLAND GAP
37725-37725 DANDRIDGE
37726-37726 DEER LODGE
37727-37727 DEL RIO
37729-37729 DUFF
37730-37730 EAGAN
37731-37731 EIDSON
37732-37732 ELGIN
37733-37733 RUGBY
37737-37737 FRIENDSVILLE
37738-37738 GATLINBURG
37742-37742 GREENBACK
37743-37745 GREENEVILLE
37748-37748 HARRIMAN
37752-37752 HARROGATE
37753-37753 HARTFORD
37754-37754 HEISKELL
37755-37755 HELENWOOD
37756-37756 HUNTSVILLE
37757-37757 JACKSBORO
37760-37760 JEFFERSON CITY
37762-37762 JELLICO
37763-37763 KINGSTON
37764-37764 KODAK
37765-37765 KYLES FORD
37766-37766 LA FOLLETTE
37769-37769 LAKE CITY
37770-37770 LANCING
37771-37772 LENOIR CITY
37773-37773 LONE MOUNTAIN
37774-37774 LOUDON
37777-37777 LOUISVILLE
37778-37778 LOWLAND
37779-37779 LUTTRELL
37801-37804 MARYVILLE
37806-37806 MASCOT
37807-37807 MAYNARDVILLE
37809-37809 MIDWAY
37810-37810 MOHAWK
37811-37811 MOORESBURG
37812-37812 MORLEY
37813-37816 MORRISTOWN
37818-37818 MOSHEIM
37819-37819 NEWCOMB
37820-37820 NEW MARKET
37821-37822 NEWPORT
37824-37825 NEW TAZEWELL
37826-37826 NIOTA
37828-37828 NORRIS
37829-37829 OAKDALE
37830-37831 OAK RIDGE
37840-37840 OLIVER SPRINGS
37841-37841 ONEIDA
37842-37842 OZONE
37843-37843 PARROTTSVILLE
37845-37845 PETROS
37846-37846 PHILADELPHIA
37847-37847 PIONEER
37848-37848 POWDER SPRINGS
37849-37849 POWELL
37851-37851 PRUDEN
37852-37852 ROBBINS
37853-37853 ROCKFORD
37854-37854 ROCKWOOD
37857-37857 ROGERSVILLE
37860-37860 RUSSELLVILLE
37861-37861 RUTLEDGE
37862-37862 SEVIERVILLE
37863-37863 PIGEON FORGE
37864-37864 SEVIERVILLE
37865-37865 SEYMOUR
37866-37866 SHARPS CHAPEL
37867-37867 SHAWANEE
37868-37868 PIGEON FORGE
37869-37869 SNEEDVILLE
37870-37870 SPEEDWELL
37871-37871 STRAWBERRY PLAINS
37872-37872 SUNBRIGHT
37873-37873 SURGOINSVILLE
37874-37874 SWEETWATER
37876-37876 SEVIERVILLE
37877-37877 TALBOTT
37878-37878 TALLASSEE
37879-37879 TAZEWELL
37880-37880 TEN MILE
37881-37881 THORN HILL
37882-37882 TOWNSEND
37883-37883 TREADWAY
37885-37885 VONORE
37886-37886 WALLAND
37887-37887 WARTBURG
37888-37888 WASHBURN
37890-37890 WHITE PINE
37891-37891 WHITESBURG
37892-37892 WINFIELD
37893-37893 WINONA
37900-37999 KNOXVILLE
38001-38001 ALAMO
38002-38002 ARLINGTON
38004-38004 ATOKA
38006-38006 BELLS
38007-38007 BOGOTA
38008-38008 BOLIVAR
38010-38010 BRADEN
38011-38011 BRIGHTON
38012-38012 BROWNSVILLE
38014-38014 BRUNSWICK
38015-38015 BURLISON
38016-38016 CORDOVA
38017-38017 COLLIERVILLE
38018-38018 CORDOVA
38019-38019 COVINGTON
38021-38021 CROCKETT MILLS
38023-38023 DRUMMONDS
38024-38025 DYERSBURG
38027-38027 COLLIERVILLE
38028-38028 EADS
38029-38029 ELLENDALE
38030-38030 FINLEY
38033-38033 FOWLKES
38034-38034 FRIENDSHIP
38036-38036 GALLAWAY
38037-38037 GATES
38039-38039 GRAND JUNCTION
38040-38040 HALLS
38041-38041 HENNING
38042-38042 HICKORY VALLEY
38043-38043 HICKORY WITHE
38044-38044 HORNSBY
38045-38045 LACONIA
38046-38046 LA GRANGE
38047-38047 LENOX
38048-38048 MACON
38049-38049 MASON
38050-38050 MAURY CITY
38052-38052 MIDDLETON
38053-38055 MILLINGTON
38056-38056 MISTON
38057-38057 MOSCOW
38058-38058 MUNFORD
38059-38059 NEWBERN
38060-38060 OAKLAND
38061-38061 POCAHONTAS
38063-38063 RIPLEY
38066-38066 ROSSVILLE
38067-38067 SAULSBURY
38068-38068 SOMERVILLE
38069-38069 STANTON
38070-38070 TIGRETT
38071-38071 TIPTON
38074-38074 BOLIVAR
38075-38075 WHITEVILLE
38076-38076 WILLISTON
38077-38077 WYNNBURG
38079-38079 TIPTONVILLE
38080-38080 RIDGELY
38083-38083 MILLINGTON
38088-38088 CORDOVA
38100-38137 MEMPHIS
38138-38139 GERMANTOWN
38140-38182 MEMPHIS
38183-38183 GERMANTOWN
38184-38197 MEMPHIS
38201-38201 MC KENZIE
38220-38220 ATWOOD
38221-38221 BIG SANDY
38222-38222 BUCHANAN
38223-38223 COMO
38224-38224 COTTAGE GROVE
38225-38225 DRESDEN
38226-38226 DUKEDOM
38227-38227 ELBRIDGE
38229-38229 GLEASON
38230-38230 GREENFIELD
38231-38231 HENRY
38232-38232 HORNBEAK
38233-38233 KENTON
38235-38235 MC LEMORESVILLE
38236-38236 MANSFIELD
38237-38238 MARTIN
38240-38240 OBION
38241-38241 PALMERSVILLE
38242-38242 PARIS
38251-38251 PURYEAR
38253-38253 RIVES
38254-38254 SAMBURG
38255-38255 SHARON
38256-38256 SPRINGVILLE
38257-38257 SOUTH FULTON
38258-38258 TREZEVANT

ZIP Range	City
38259-38259	TRIMBLE
38260-38260	TROY
38261-38261	UNION CITY
38271-38271	WOODLAND MILLS
38281-38281	UNION CITY
38301-38308	JACKSON
38310-38310	ADAMSVILLE
38311-38311	BATH SPRINGS
38313-38313	BEECH BLUFF
38314-38314	JACKSON
38315-38315	BETHEL SPRINGS
38316-38316	BRADFORD
38317-38317	BRUCETON
38318-38318	BUENA VISTA
38320-38320	CAMDEN
38321-38321	CEDAR GROVE
38324-38324	CLARKSBURG
38326-38326	COUNCE
38327-38327	CRUMP
38328-38328	DARDEN
38329-38329	DECATURVILLE
38330-38330	DYER
38331-38331	EATON
38332-38332	ENVILLE
38333-38333	EVA
38334-38334	FINGER
38336-38336	FRUITVALE
38337-38337	GADSDEN
38338-38338	GIBSON
38339-38339	GUYS
38340-38340	HENDERSON
38341-38341	HOLLADAY
38342-38342	HOLLOW ROCK
38343-38343	HUMBOLDT
38344-38344	HUNTINGDON
38345-38345	HURON
38346-38346	IDLEWILD
38347-38347	JACKS CREEK
38348-38348	LAVINIA
38351-38351	LEXINGTON
38352-38352	LURAY
38355-38355	MEDINA
38356-38356	MEDON
38357-38357	MICHIE
38358-38358	MILAN
38359-38359	MILLEDGEVILLE
38361-38361	MORRIS CHAPEL
38362-38362	OAKFIELD
38363-38363	PARSONS
38365-38365	PICKWICK DAM
38366-38366	PINSON
38367-38367	RAMER
38368-38368	REAGAN
38369-38369	RUTHERFORD
38370-38370	SALTILLO
38371-38371	SARDIS
38372-38372	SAVANNAH
38374-38374	SCOTTS HILL
38375-38375	SELMER
38376-38376	SHILOH
38377-38377	SILERTON
38378-38378	SPRING CREEK
38379-38379	STANTONVILLE
38380-38380	SUGAR TREE
38381-38381	TOONE
38382-38382	TRENTON
38387-38387	WESTPORT
38388-38388	WILDERSVILLE
38389-38389	YORKVILLE
38390-38390	YUMA
38391-38391	DENMARK
38392-38392	MERCER
38393-38393	CHEWALLA
38401-38402	COLUMBIA
38425-38425	CLIFTON
38449-38449	ARDMORE
38450-38450	COLLINWOOD
38451-38451	CULLEOKA
38452-38452	CYPRESS INN
38453-38453	DELLROSE
38454-38454	DUCK RIVER
38455-38455	ELKTON
38456-38456	ETHRIDGE
38457-38457	FIVE POINTS
38459-38459	FRANKEWING
38460-38460	GOODSPRING
38461-38461	HAMPSHIRE
38462-38462	HOHENWALD
38463-38463	IRON CITY
38464-38464	LAWRENCEBURG
38468-38468	LEOMA
38469-38469	LORETTO
38471-38471	LUTTS
38472-38472	LYNNVILLE
38473-38473	MINOR HILL
38474-38474	MOUNT PLEASANT
38475-38475	OLIVEHILL
38476-38476	PRIMM SPRINGS
38477-38477	PROSPECT
38478-38478	PULASKI
38481-38481	SAINT JOSEPH
38482-38482	SANTA FE
38483-38483	SUMMERTOWN
38485-38485	WAYNESBORO
38486-38486	WESTPOINT
38487-38487	WILLIAMSPORT
38488-38488	TAFT
38501-38503	COOKEVILLE
38504-38504	ALLARDT
38505-38506	COOKEVILLE
38541-38541	ALLONS
38542-38542	ALLRED
38543-38543	ALPINE
38544-38544	BAXTER
38545-38545	BLOOMINGTON SPRINGS
38547-38547	BRUSH CREEK
38548-38548	BUFFALO VALLEY
38549-38549	BYRDSTOWN
38550-38550	CAMPAIGN
38551-38551	CELINA
38552-38552	CHESTNUT MOUND
38553-38553	CLARKRANGE
38554-38554	CRAWFORD
38555-38555	CROSSVILLE
38556-38556	JAMESTOWN
38557-38558	CROSSVILLE
38559-38559	DOYLE
38560-38560	ELMWOOD
38562-38562	GAINESBORO
38563-38563	GORDONSVILLE
38564-38564	GRANVILLE
38565-38565	GRIMSLEY
38567-38567	HICKMAN
38568-38568	HILHAM
38569-38569	LANCASTER
38570-38570	LIVINGSTON
38571-38572	CROSSVILLE
38573-38573	MONROE
38574-38574	MONTEREY
38575-38575	MOSS
38577-38577	PALL MALL
38578-38578	PLEASANT HILL
38579-38579	QUEBECK
38580-38580	RICKMAN
38581-38581	ROCK ISLAND
38582-38582	SILVER POINT
38583-38583	SPARTA
38585-38585	SPENCER
38587-38587	WALLING
38588-38588	WHITLEYVILLE
38589-38589	WILDER

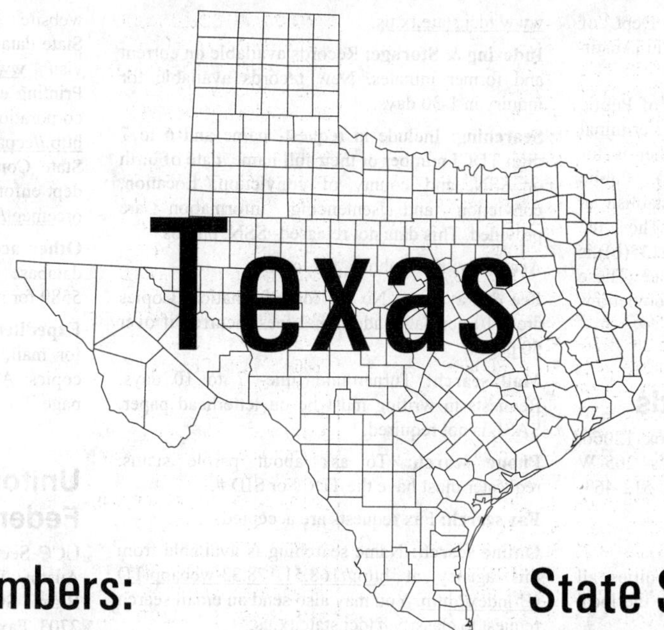

Texas

General Help Numbers:

Governor's Office

PO Box 12428
Austin, TX 78711-2428
www.governor.state.tx.us

512-463-2000
Fax 512-463-1849
7:30AM-5:30PM

Attorney General's Office

PO Box 12548
Austin, TX 78711-2548
www.oag.state.tx.us

512-463-2100
Fax 512-463-2063
7:30AM-5:30PM

Legislative Records

Legislative Reference Library
PO Box 12488
Austin, TX 78711-2488
www.legis.state.tx.us/

512-463-1252
Fax 512-475-4626
8AM-5PM

State Archives

PO Box 12927
Austin, TX 78711-2927
www.tsl.state.tx.us

512-463-5455
Fax 512-463-5430
8AM-5PM
Genealogy 8-5 TU-SA

State Specifics:

Capital: Austin
Travis County

Time Zone: CST*

* Texas' two western-most counties are MST:
They are: El Paso and Hudspeth,

Number of Counties: 254

Population: 24,326,974

Web Site: www.texasonline.com/portal/tol

State Agencies

Criminal Records

DPS - Access & Dissemination Bureau, Crime Records Service, PO Box 15999, Austin, TX 78761-5999; 512-424-2474, Fax- 512-424-5011; 8AM-5PM.

https://records.txdps.state.tx.us/dps_web/Portal/index.aspx

Indexing & Storage: Records available from 1930 to present. New records available for inquiry in 1 day. 66% of all arrests in database have final dispositions recorded. Per a recent study, Travis County sent required updates for only 13 %t of its 2006 charges, while Webb County followed through for just 2 %. Of Texas' 254 counties, only 106 report to DPS electronically.

Searching: To obtain ALL arrest information (conviction and non-conviction), must have a signed release and full set of fingerprints from the person of record. Include in request- fingerprint card (with full name, DOB, sex, race, SSN), reason for request, signed release, full name and address of requester. To obtain conviction and deferred adjudication data only, submit full name, sex, race, and DOB. The SSN is helpful, but not required. No letter of authorization is needed for the conviction only report. This data not released- juvenile records. Fingerprint searches show complete record; name search is conviction only and deferred adjudications. Since 1/1/93 records should include complete info regarding charge, disposition, date of conviction, and county. Data prior to this date may not be complete.

Access by: mail, in person, online.

Fee & Payment: The fee is $15.00 for the full search using fingerprints, and $10.00 for a name-based search. If approved, the FBI fingerprint check is an additional $19.25. Fee payee- Texas Department of Public Safety. Prepayment required. Credit cards are accepted for online searches only. Personal checks, Visa, and MasterCard accepted.

Mail search: Turnaround time- 7 days. SASE not required.

In person: Records requested at the Dept. of Public Safety Crime Records Service in Austin usually takes 1 business day.

Online search: The Texas Department of Public Safety offers two websites for accessing criminal records. One is for the public. The other is for eligible entities (authorized by law). Public requesters may use a credit card and establish an account to pre-purchase credits. The fee established by the Department (Sec. 411.135(b)) is $3.15 per request plus a $.57 handling fee. These checks are instantaneous and provide convictions and deferred adjudications only.

Statewide Court Records

Office of Court Administration, PO Box 12066, Austin, TX 78711-2066 (Courier address- 205 W 14th St, Ste. 600, Austin, TX 78711); 512-463-1625, Fax- 512-463-1648; 8AM-5PM.

www.courts.state.tx.us/oca/

Except for certain online research capabilities, all trial court record access must be done at the local level.

Searching: Trial court records are maintained by each county.

Online search: Case records of the Supreme Court can be searched at www.supreme.courts.state.tx.us. Court of Criminal Appeals opinions at www.cca.courts.state.tx.us. Court case information is searchable free at the website of each Appellate Court, reached online from www.courts.state.tx.us/courts/coa.asp

Sexual Offender Registry

Dept of Public Safety, Sex Offender Registration, PO Box 4143, Austin, TX 78765-4143; 512-424-2800, Fax- 512-424-5666; 8AM-5PM.

https://records.txdps.state.tx.us/DPS_WEB/SorNew/index.aspx

Email any Sex Offender Registration questions to AFIS_CJIS@txdps.state.tx.us.

Indexing & Storage: Records available from 01/1993, in general. New records available for inquiry in 1 day.

Searching: A sex offender's home telephone number, SSN, driver's license number will not be released.

Access by: mail, online.

Fee & Payment: A $10.00 fee is charged for mail searches only. Fee payee- Texas Department of Public Safety. Prepayment required. Personal checks accepted.

Mail search: Turnaround time- 1-2 weeks. There is a $10.00 fee. SASE not required.

Online search: Sex offender data is available at the web page. There is no charge for a sex offender search. Search by name or city/ZIP or by map.

Other access: One may download the offender database from the web page. The data is updated twice a week and is available at no charge to users.

Incarceration Records

Texas Department of Criminal Justice, Bureau of Classification and Records, PO Box 99, Huntsville, TX 77342 (Courier address- 861 IH 45 North, Huntsville, TX 77320); 936-295-6371 (Offender Locator), 936-291-2106 (Parole Status), Fax- 936-437-2125; 8AM-5PM.

www.tdcj.state.tx.us

Indexing & Storage: Records available on current and former inmates. New records available for inquiry in 1-30 days.

Searching: Include in request- name and 6 to 7 digit TDCJ number or their full name, date of birth or SSN, and county of conviction. Location, conviction and sentencing information are provided. This data not released- SSN, photos

Access by: mail, phone, fax, online.

Fee & Payment: No fee for information. Copies are $.10 per page, additional fees incurred if over 50 pages.

Mail search: Turnaround time- 7 to 10 days. Requests in writing must be on letterhead paper. SASE is not required.

Phone search: To ask about parole status, requester must have the TDCJ or SID #.

Fax search: Fax requests are accepted.

Online search: Name searching is available from this agency at http://168.51.178.33/webapp/TDCJ/index2.htm. You may also send an email search request to classify@tdcj.state.tx.us.

Corporation, LLC, LP, Fictitious/Assumed Name, Trademarks/Servicemarks

Secretary of State, Corporation Section, PO Box 13697, Austin, TX 78711-3697 (Courier address- J Earl Rudder Bldg, 1019 Brazos, B-13, Austin, TX 78701); 512-463-5555 (Information), 512-463-5578 (Copies), Fax- 512-463-5709; 8AM-5PM.

www.sos.state.tx.us

Ongoing requesters are encouraged to set-up a Client Account.

Indexing & Storage: Records available from 1871. New records available for inquiry in 1 to 3 days.

Searching: New records are available immediately on the computer, but it takes 3 days before new records are available to be copied. Requests may be ordered via e-mail from the website. Include in request- full name of business, file number. In addition to the certificate of information, records include the following information: public information reports, officers, directors, assumed names, prior names, inactive and reserved names, and histories. This data not released- SSNs, credit card data.

Access by: mail, phone, fax, in person, online.

Fee & Payment: Search fee is $5.00 per name. Certification is $15.00 plus $1.00 per document page. Long form is $25.00. Uncertified copies are $.10 per page, if over 50 copies then $.15 per page. If credit card used, add 2.7%. Fee payee- Secretary of State. Frequent requesters may set up a pre-paid billing account. Personal checks accepted. Visa/MC/Discover accepted.

Mail search: Turnaround time- 3 to 5 days. SASE not required.

Phone search: No fee for telephone request.

Fax search: See below.

In person: Public access terminals are available for walk-in requesters.

Online search: There are several online methods available. Web access is available 24 hours daily. There is a $1.00 fee for each record searched. Filing procedures and forms are available from the website. Also, Corporate and other TX Sec of State data is available via SOSDirect on the Web; visit www.sos.state.tx.us/corp/sosda/index.shtml. Printing and certifying capabilities. Also, general corporation data available at no fee at http://ecpa.cpa.state.tx.us/coa/Index.html from the State Comptroller office. Also, search securities dept enforcement actions- www.ssb.state.tx.us/Enforcement/Recent_Enforcement_Actions.php.

Other access: The agency makes portions of its database available for purchase. Call 512-463-5589 for more information.

Expedited service: Expedited service is available for mail, phone, fax and in person requests for copies. Add $10.00 per document and $2.00 per page if returned by fax.

Uniform Commercial Code, Federal Tax Liens

UCC Section, Secretary of State, PO Box 13193, Austin, TX 78711-3193 (Courier address- 1019 Brazos St, Rm B-13, Austin, TX 78701); 512-475-2703, Fax- 512-463-1423; 8AM-5PM.

www.sos.state.tx.us/ucc/index.shtml

Indexing & Storage: Records available from 1966; imaged and stored in the BEST System. New records available for inquiry in 2 to 3 days.

Searching: Use form UCC-11. The search includes types of filings pursuant to statute. All federal liens on businesses found here. Federal liens on individuals and all state tax liens are filed at the county level. Include in request- debtor's exact full name.

Access by: mail, phone, fax, in person, online.

Fee & Payment: Using the approved form the search fee is $15.00 per name, add $15.00 for a certification stamp. Copies are $1.00 per certified page, non-certified is $.10 per page. Fee payee- Secretary of State. Prepayment required. Personal checks accepted. Major credit cards and LegalEase cards accepted.

Mail search: Turnaround time- 1 to 2 weeks. SASE not required.

Phone search: Debtor and secured party names are released; collateral is listed on imaged documents only.

Fax search: accepted, see expedited svc below.

In person: Counter service available.

Online search: UCC and other Texas Secretary of State data is available via SOSDirect on the Web at www.sos.state.tx.us/corp/sosda/index.shtml. UCC records are $1.00 per search, with printing $1.00 per page and certifying $10.00. General information and forms can also be found at the website.

Other access: This agency offers the database for sale, contact the Information Services Dept at 512-463-5609 for further details.

Expedited service: Expedited service is available for mail, in-person and phone searches. Turnaround time- 24 hours. Add $15.00 per request to expedite. Add $2.00 per page to fax an acknowledgment copy. Expedited mail service is offered. Also, you can include your delivery service account number for fastest return.

State Tax Liens

Records not maintained by a state level agency.

Records are located at the county level.

Sales Tax Registrations

Comptroller of Public Accounts, Sales Tax Permits, PO Box 13528, Capitol Station, Austin, TX 78711-3528 (Courier address- LBJ Office Bldg, 111 E 17th St, Austin, TX 78774); 800-531-5441 x66013, 800-252-1386 (Other Business Searches), Fax- 512-475-1610; 8AM-5PM.

www.window.state.tx.us/taxinfo/sales/

Direct question to open.records@cpa.state.tx.us.

Indexing & Storage: Records available from 1985 to present. New records available for inquiry in 6 weeks.

Searching: This agency will provide the following business information: business name, address, phone number, tax permit number. Audit results are not released. Include in request- business name or permit number.

Access by: mail, phone, fax, in person, online.

Fee & Payment: There is no search fee. Fee payee- Comptroller of Public Accounts. Prepayment required. Personal checks accepted, credit cards are not.

Mail search: Turnaround time- 10 working days. If more than 3 businesses are requested, the agency prefers that you request by mail. No fee for mail request.

Phone search: No fee for telephone request. The agency will provide responses to 3 business names or less over the phone.

Fax search: Fax search requests accepted.

In person: No fee for request. They will verify information or will mail a letter.

Online search: This office makes general corporation information available at http://ecpa.cpa.state.tx.us/vendor/tpsearch1.html. There is no fee. Go to http://cpastar2.cpa.state.tx.us/index.html to search 25,000+ documents by index or collection, including case information. Send email requests, send to open.records@cpa.state.tx.us.

Other access: Sales tax registration lists are available to download as ftp files.

Expedited service: Will expedite at customer expense.

Birth Certificates

Department of State Health Svcs, Bureau of Vital Statistics, PO Box 12040, Austin, TX 78711-2040 (Courier address- 1100 W 49th St, Austin, TX 78756-3191); 512-758-7366, Fax- 512-758-7711; 8AM-5PM. www.dshs.state.tx.us/vs/default.shtm

Indexing & Storage: Records available from 1903 to present. New records available for inquiry in receipt from local registration officials.

Searching: Must have a signed, notarized release from person of record or immediate family member and name and address of requester for records less than 75 years old. Otherwise a Verification of Birth is issued. Include in request- full name, names of parents, mother's maiden name, date of birth, place of birth, relationship to person of record, reason for information request. Must send a copy of requester's photo ID or show a photo ID for in-person searches. This data not released- SSNs.

Access by: mail, fax, in person, online.

Fee & Payment: A certified copy of a birth certificate or a birth verification letter is $22.00 per name. Heirloom certificates are available for $60.00 each. Fee payee- Bureau of Vital Statistics. Prepayment required. Credit cards accepted for fax requests only. Personal checks, Visa, and MasterCard accepted.

Mail search: Turnaround time- 4 to 6 weeks. SASE not required.

Fax search: See expedited service.

In person: Go directly to Local Registrar's office for births that occurred anywhere in Texas. Remote site will issue an abstract of birth facts (a legal birth certificate). Remote Site Access is not available at all county offices. Turnaround time 1-2 hours.

Online search: Records may be ordered online at www.dshs.state.tx.us/vs/default.shtm.

Other access: Birth Indexes from 1926-1995 are available on CD-Rom and microfiche.

Expedited service: Expedited service is available for fax searches at 512-458-7711. Turnaround time- 48 to 96 hours. Add $5.00 expedited service fee, and either $8.00 for UPS ground or $13.65 for US Express mail, if ordered from this agency.

Death Records

Department of State Health Svcs, Bureau of Vital Statistics, PO Box 12040, Austin, TX 78711-2040 (Courier address- 1100 W 49th St, Austin, TX 78756-3191); 512-758-7366, Fax- 512-758-7711; 8AM-5PM.

www.dshs.state.tx.us/vs/default.shtm

Indexing & Storage: Records available from 1903 to present. New records available for inquiry in receipt from local registration officials.

Searching: Must have a signed release from immediate family member and requester's name and current address for records less than 25 years old. Otherwise a Verification of Death is issued. Include in request- full name, date of death, place of death, SSN, relationship to person of record, reason for information request. One must include a copy of requesters' photo ID or show a photo ID for in person requests. Data not released- SSNs.

Access by: mail, fax, in person, online.

Fee & Payment: The search fee is $20.00 per name. Add $3.00 per name per copy for each additional copy. Fee payee- Bureau of Vital Statistics. Prepayment required. Credit cards accepted for fax requests only. Personal checks, Visa, and MasterCard accepted.

Mail search: Turnaround time- 6 to 8 weeks. SASE not required.

Fax search: See expedited service.

In person: Turnaround time 1-2 hours.

Online search: Records may be ordered at www.dshs.state.tx.us/vs/default.shtm. Death records from 1964 thru 1998 may be viewed at http://vitals.rootsweb.ancestry.com/tx/death/search.cgi.

Other access: Death indices from 1964-1998 are available on CD-Rom and microfiche.

Expedited service: Expedited service is available for fax searches at 512-458-7711. Turnaround time- 48 to 96 hours. Add $5.00 expedited service fee, and either $8.00 for UPS ground or $13.65 for US Express mail.

Marriage Certificates

Department of State Health Svcs, Bureau of Vital Statistics, PO Box 12040, Austin, TX 78711-2040 (Courier address- 1100 W 49th St, Austin, TX 78756-3191); 512-758-7366, Fax- 512-758-7711; 8AM-5PM.

www.dshs.state.tx.us/vs/default.shtm

Indexing & Storage: Records available from 1966 to present. New records available for inquiry in delivery from the county clerk.

Searching: This agency will only supply a verification. They only have a copy of the application form and an index to the county record. The actual certificate must be obtained from the county recorder of record. Include in request- names of husband and wife, date of marriage, place or county of marriage. This data not released- SSNs.

Access by: mail, fax, in person, online.

Fee & Payment: The search fee is $20.00 per record. Fee payee- Bureau of Vital Statistics. Prepayment required. Credit cards accepted for fax requests only. Personal checks, Visa, and MasterCard accepted.

Mail search: Turnaround time- 4 to 6 weeks. SASE not required.

Fax search: See expedited service.

In person: Turnaround time while you wait.

Online search: Records may be ordered online at www.dshs.state.tx.us/vs/default.shtm. Department provides marriage data commercially on CD-rom at www.dshs.state.tx.us/vs/marriagedivorce/mindex.shtm, or you may download each year of the marriage index for free, from 1966 to 2005. Also, marriage records for 1966 to 2006 are available through a private company site at www.genlookups.com/texas_marriages/.

Expedited service: Expedited service is available for fax searches. Turnaround time- 48 to 96 hours. Add $5.00 expedited service fee, and either $8.00 for UPS ground or $13.65 for US Express mail.

Divorce Records

Department of State Health Svcs, Bureau of Vital Statistics, PO Box 12040, Austin, TX 78711-2040 (Courier address- 1100 W 49th St, Austin, TX 78756-3191); 512-758-7366, Fax- 512-758-7711; 8AM-5PM. www.dshs.state.tx.us/vs/default.shtm

Indexing & Storage: Records available from 1968 to present. New records available for inquiry in delivery from the county district clerk.

Searching: This agency will only supply a verification. They only have the report of divorce form and an index that directs you to the county district court of record. A copy of the actual record must be obtained at the county level. Include in request- names of husband and wife, date of divorce, year divorce case began, case number (if known).

Access by: mail, fax, in person, online.

Fee & Payment: The search fee is $20.00 per name. Fee payee- Bureau of Vital Statistics. Prepayment required. Credit cards accepted for fax requests only. Personal checks, Visa, and MasterCard accepted.

Mail search: Turnaround time- 4 to 6 weeks. SASE not required.

Fax search: See expedited service.

In person: Turnaround time 1-2 hours.

Online search: Records may be ordered online at www.dshs.state.tx.us/vs/default.shtm. The department provides divorce data commercially on CD-rom at www.dshs.state.tx.us/vs/marriagedivorce/dindex.shtm, or you may download each year of the divorce index for free, from 1968 to 2006. Also, a private company website at www.genlookups.com/texas_divorces/ offers records from 1968 to 2006.

Expedited service: Expedited service is available for fax searches at 512-458-7711. Turnaround time- 48 to 96 hours. Add $5.00 expedited service fee, and either $8.00 for UPS ground or $13.65 for US Express mail.

Workers' Compensation Records

Texas Department of Insurance - Worker's Comp, 7551 Metro Center Dr, #100, MS-92B, Austin, TX 78744; 512-804-4990 x391 (Employment Check), 512-804-4990 x319 (Records), Fax- 512-804-4993; 8AM-5PM.

www.tdi.state.tx.us/wc/indexwc.html

General information about previous work related injuries will only be provided to employers if the applicant has had two or more injuries in the last five years and the employer has made a conditional offer of employment.

Indexing & Storage: Records available back to 1962.

Searching: A signed, notarized release is required to obtain file copies. Use Form TWCC-153 for claim file or medical records or hearing record. Include in request- claimant name, SSN, date of accident. Use of TWCC 153 Form is required. The file number is required to receive copies. If you don't know the file number or date of accident, you must submit Form TWCC-155. Claim file records are confidential; only parties to claim have access.

Access by: mail, fax, online.

Fee & Payment: The fees for TWCC-153 are $1.00 for the first page and $.30 each additional page and $1.00 for certification. The fees for TWCC-155 are $15.00 search fee and $1.00 for certification. Fee payee- Texas Workers' Compensation Commission. Prepayment required. An invoice will be sent when using TWCC 153 Form. Copies are held until payment received. Personal checks accepted, credit cards are not.

Mail search: Turnaround time- 4 to 6 weeks. SASE not required.

Fax search: See expedited service.

Online search: The website gives administrative decisions for cases back to 1991and also permits searching for employers with coverage.

Expedited service: Expedited service is available for mail or fax service, using the TWCC 153 form. Fee for expedited copy service is additional $25.00.

Driver Records

Department of Public Safety, Driver Records Section, PO Box 149246, Austin, TX 78714-9246 (Courier address- 5805 N Lamar Blvd, Austin, TX 78752); 512-424-2032, 512-424-2600, Fax- 512-424-7285; 8AM-5PM.

www.txdps.state.tx.us/administration/driver_licensing_control/dlindex.htm

Tickets are only available from the court system.

Indexing & Storage: Records available for 5 years for moving violations and suspensions, indefinite for DWIs, 11 years for SR judgments. Non-moving violations do not appear on the record. New records available for inquiry in 30 days.

Searching: Requesters must use Form DR-1. This form contains space for written consent if personal information is requested by a casual user. The name and driver's license number or date of birth, are needed when ordering. This data not released- SSNs or medical records, class type listings

Access by: mail, in person, online.

Fee & Payment: Driving record fees of mail or walk-ins are $6.00 for a 3 year driving record, $10.00 if certified. Fees are additional for online access. A license statue including latest address is $4.00 per report. There is a full charge for a "no record found." Fee payee- Texas Department of Public Safety. Prepayment required. Personal checks accepted, credit cards are not.

Mail search: Turnaround time- 7 to 10 days. SASE not required.

In person: Eligible Texas Driver License holders may request their own individual Driver Record online. The printed record is postal mailed by DPS within 5 business days. Normal turnaround time is same day.

Online search: Access is limited to only high volume users who have a permissible use and sign an agreement. The fee is $6.50 for a three-year Type 2 record and $7.50 for a complete Type 3 record. Both batch and interactive modes are available. Call 512-424-5457 to receive a copy of the license agreement. The state also offers access to TX license holders to request their own record, at the web page. Fees vary from $4.50 to $22.00, depending on type of record and if certified.

Other access: Bulk data is available in electronic format for approved requesters. Weekly updates are available. The file does not include driver history data.

Vehicle Ownership & Registration

Department of Transportation, Vehicle Titles and Registration Division,, Austin, TX 78779 (Courier address- 4000 Jackson Ave, Austin, TX 78731); 512-465-7611, Fax- 512-465-7736; 8AM-5PM.

www.txdot.gov/

Submit a "Request for TX Motor Vehicle Information" Form VTR-275. This signed statement certifies that information is requested for a lawful & legitimate purpose, to be used in accordance with 18 USC, Sec 2721-2725 and the TX Trans Code, Ch#730.

Indexing & Storage: Records available as active files until there is no activity for 24 months, upon which records become inactive. After 30 months inactivity, records are archived. Title history information is available on microfilm or digital image for 16 years to present. New records available for inquiry in 48 hours after entry into the system.

Searching: For plate checks and title histories, include a signed/completed Request for Texas Motor Vehicle Information Form VTR-275 certifying your eligibility to receive information. The state does not provide name search capability. Include in request- Form VTR-275. Personal information is not released to casual requesters without attaching written consent of subject or submitting the VTR-275. Data not released- SSNs.

Access by: mail, in person, online.

Fee & Payment: The current fee for VIN and plate checks is $2.30 per record. The fee for a title search/history is $5.75. Add $1.00 for certification. Fee payee- Texas Department of Transportation. Prepayment required. Personal checks accepted, credit cards are not.

Mail search: Turnaround time- 7-10 days for plates. Turnaround time for title histories is 10 working days. Use of the state form is required.

In person: Current record search by license plate number, document number or VIN available at one of the 16 regional offices.

Online search: Online access is available for pre-approved accounts by contract. A $200 deposit is required, there is a $23.00 charge per month and $.12 fee per inquiry. Look-ups are by VIN or plate number. Searching by name or owner is not permitted. For more information, contact Technology Support.

Other access: CD or FTP retrieval is offered for customized searches or the entire database to eligible organizations under signed contract. Weekly updates and batch inquiries are available. Database contains about 29,000,000 records.

Expedited service: The department will overnight the information requested when the customer provides their account number and service provider.

Crash Reports

Texas Department of Public Safety, Crash Records Section, PO Box 149349, Austin, TX 78704 (Courier - 1524 S IH-35, Austin, TX 78704); 512-486-5780, Fax- 512-486-5794; 8AM-5PM.

www.txdot.gov/drivers_vehicles/crash_records/reports.htm

The peace officer's report is CR-3; the driver's report is CR-2. Email questions to crashrecords@dot.state.tx.us.

Indexing & Storage: Records available for 10 years to present. New records available for inquiry in 30 days.

Searching: Crash reports investigated by law enforcement agencies and driver reports are open to the public. Include in request- include two or more of following: full name of any person involved, specific city/county location, and date of incident. A request form can be downloaded from the web page.

Access by: mail.

Fee & Payment: Fee is $6.00 per uncertified report and $8.00 per certified report. There is a $6.00 charge for a no record found search. Fee payee- Texas Department of Transportation Prepayment required. Personal checks accepted, credit cards are not.

Mail search: Turnaround time- 2 weeks. SASE not required.

Vessel Ownership & Registration

Parks & Wildlife Dept, 4200 Smith School Rd, Austin, TX 78744; 512-389-4828, 800-262-8755, Fax- 512-389-4900; 8AM-5PM.

www.tpwd.state.tx.us/fishboat/boat/owner/

Record checks can be processed at any TPWD Boats Law Enforcement Field Office. History requests may be submitted to any field office, but all history requests will be returned by the TPWD Headquarters in Austin.

Indexing & Storage: Records available from 1976 to present for all boats. All motorized boats must be registered and titled. Sailboats 14 ft and over must be registered and titled. Lien data shows on reports. New records available for inquiry in less than 1 day.

Searching: More detailed data is available for most recent 10-year period. Include in request- all known information (TX number, HIN/serial number, make, year, owner of record), a statement of purpose of request, signature, address & phone of requester. The written request must be submitted on completed PWD763 Form (ownership, lien-holder information printout or ownership history request) along with applicable fee.

Access by: mail, in person.

Fee & Payment: There is a $2.00 fee for a record check and a $10.00 fee for a complete history from microfilm. Fee payee- TX Parks & Wildlife Dept. Prepayment required. Personal checks accepted, credit cards are not.

Mail search: Turnaround time- 2 to 3 weeks. Turnaround time is often longer in the summer. SASE not required.

In person: Histories are returned by mail.

Other access: Records are released in bulk format; however, requesters are screened for lawful purpose. The agency requires a copy of any item mailed or distributed as a result of purchase. Media includes tape, labels, and printed lists.

Legislation Records

Legislative Reference Library, PO Box 12488, Austin, TX 78711-2488 (Courier address- State Capitol Building, 2N.3, 1100 N Congress Ave, Austin, TX 78701); 512-463-1252 (Bill Status), 512-463-0252 (Senate Bill Copies), 512-463-1144 (House Bill Copies), Fax- 512-475-4626; 8AM-5PM.

www.legis.state.tx.us/

Call first to determine location of bills. The legislative sessions meets in odd-numbered years from January through May.

Indexing & Storage: Records available from the 63rd session to present of the Legislature in the Library. Records are computerized since 1973.

Searching: Include in request- bill number, year.

Access by: mail, phone, fax, in person, online.

Fee & Payment: There is no search fee. The copy fee is $.25 per page. Will express ship with requester's proper account number of the shipping company. Fee payee- Legislative Reference Library. Business checks or money orders are preferred. No credit cards accepted.

Mail search: Turnaround time- variable. SASE not required.

Phone search: Limited information given by phone.

Fax search: Results may be returned by fax for $.25 per page.

In person: Simple requests may be processed while you wait.

Online search: The web is a thorough searching site of bills and status. State statutes and bill lookups are available from the home page listed above or www.capitol.state.tx.us.

Expedited service: Rush service is $25.00. Turnaround time- same or next day.

Voter Registration

Access to Records is Restricted.

Secretary of State, Elections Division, PO Box 12060, Austin, TX 78711-2060 (Courier address- 208 E 10th St 3rd Fl, Thomas J Rusk Bldg, Austin, TX 78701); 800-252-8683, Fax- 512-475-2811; 8AM-5PM.

www.sos.state.tx.us

To do individual look-ups, go to https://voterinfo.sos.state.tx.us/voterws/viw/faces/SearchSelectionVoter.jsp; The state will sell the entire database, for political purposes, in a variety of media and sort formats.

GED Certificates

Texas Education Agency, GED Unit CC:350, 1701 North Congress Avenue, Austin, TX 78701-1494; 512-463-9292, Fax- 512-305-9493; 8AM-5PM.

http://ritter.tea.state.tx.us/ged/

Direct questions to ged@tea.state.tx.us

Indexing & Storage: Records available from 1942 to present. New records available for inquiry in 2-4 weeks.

Searching: Include in request- name at time test taken, DOB and SSN. Include testing site if known. A signed release is needed for transcript, but not need for only a verification. A request form is found at http://ritter.tea.state.tx.us/ged/verify.html. This data not released- scores, unless signed release specifically mentions.

Access by: mail, phone, fax, in person, online.

Fee & Payment: There is no fee for verification, but $5.00 fee for a record of transcripts. Also, if the subject did not pay the GED fees and the record is prior to 1994, a fee may be charged to the requester. Fee payee- TEA-GED Prepayment required. Personal checks accepted.

Mail search: Turnaround time- 1 to 2 days. SASE not required.

Phone search: Verifications requests accepted.

Fax search: Verifications can be done by fax. To receive copy of grades fax requests require a signed release.

In person: Over-the-counter service available.

Online search: The agency has a excellent verification search at http://ritter.tea.state.tx.us/ged/GEDsearch.html. Search by (SSN) or TEA assigned ID and DOB or by name (maiden) and DOB. Records go back to 1994. One may order a certificate to be sent to an employer.

Hunting & Fishing License Information

TX Parks & Wildlife Department, License Section, 4200 Smith School Rd, Austin, TX 78744; 512-389-4820, Fax- 512-389-4330; 8AM-5PM.

www.tpwd.state.tx.us

Indexing & Storage: Records available from 09/01/92 forward and are computerized. Records between 09/01/96 to 0/31/02 cane provided, but a fee may be required; also, records may be incomplete. New records available for inquiry in seconds.

Searching: All requests must be in writing on their official Form, unless request is for self. They will release address, status, and date of issue. Include in request- driver's DL#, SSN and DOB, or by first and last name with DOB.

Access by: mail, fax, in person.

Fee & Payment: There is no fee, unless for licenses issued between 09/01/96 and 08/31/02 or if extensive time is needed.

Mail search: Turnaround time- 10 days. TPWD abides by Open Records Law. Up to 5 names can be requested by mail.

Fax search: Up to 5 names can be requested by fax. Results are mailed or can be faxed.

In person: Over-the-counter service available only for license holder or signed consent.

Texas State Licensing Agencies

For details about the agency responsible for licensing/certifying/registering an item below or in the Agency Quick Finder section, match an item's number with the number of the agency in the *Licensing Agency Information* section.

Texas Licenses Searchable Online

Acupuncturist #30 .... http://reg.tmb.state.tx.us/OnLineVerif/Phys_NoticeVerif.asp?
Air Condition'g/Refrigeration Contr. #14 .... www.license.state.tx.us/LicenseSearch/
Alarm Installer/Firm/Seller #35 .... www.txdps.state.tx.us/psb/individual/individual_search.aspx
Alarm/Security Instructor #35 .... www.txdps.state.tx.us/psb/individual/individual_search.aspx
Alcoholic Bev. Dist./Mfg./Retail/Permit #46 .... www.tabc.state.tx.us/pubinfo/rosters/default.htm
Architect #61 .... www.tbae.state.tx.us/PublicInfo/FindProfessional_Arch.shtml
Architectural Barrier #14 .... www.license.state.tx.us/LicenseSearch/
Asbesto-related Occupation #12 .... www.dshs.state.tx.us/asbestos/whocan.shtm#lists
Athletic Agent #38 .... www.sos.state.tx.us/statdoc/index.shtml
Athletic Trainer #21 .... www.dshs.state.tx.us/at/at_roster.shtm
Attorney #40 .... www.texasbar.com
Auctioneer #14 .... www.license.state.tx.us/LicenseSearch/
Audiologist/Audiology Assistant #22 .... www.dshs.state.tx.us/plc/default.shtm
Automobile Club #38 .... www.sos.state.tx.us/statdoc/index.shtml
Bank Agency, Foreign #1 .... www.banking.state.tx.us/supreglic_ent.asp
Bank, State Chartered #1 .... www.banking.state.tx.us/supreglic_ent.asp
Barber/Barber Shop/School/Student#2 .... www.license.state.tx.us/LicenseSearch/
Beauty Shop/Salon #8 .... www.license.state.tx.us/LicenseSearch/
Boiler Inspector/Installer #14 .... www.license.state.tx.us/LicenseSearch/
Boxing/Combative Sports Event #14 .... www.license.state.tx.us/LicenseSearch/
Business Opportunity Offering #38 .... www.sos.state.tx.us/statdoc/index.shtml
Career Counselor #14 .... www.license.state.tx.us/LicenseSearch/
Chemical Dependency Counselor #26 .... www.tcada.state.tx.us/licensure/pgSearch.shtml
Child Care Facility #49 .... www.dfps.state.tx.us/Child_Care/Search_Texas_Child_Care/ppFacilitySearchDayCare.asp
Child Care Facility Admin. #49 .... https://www.dfps.state.tx.us/Child_Care/Search_Texas_Child_Care/ppFacilityRegister.asp
Child Care Operation #49
... https://www.dfps.state.tx.us/Child_Care/Search_Texas_Child_Care/CCLNET/Source/CPA/ppSearchTXChildCare2.aspx
Child Support Agency, Private #1 .... www.banking.state.tx.us/supreglic_ent.asp
Chiropractic Facility #25 .... www.tbce.state.tx.us/disc_action_menu.html
Chiropractic Radiologic Technologist #25 .... www.tbce.state.tx.us/verify.html
Chiropractor #25 .... www.tbce.state.tx.us/verify.html
Code Enforcement Officer #26 .... www.dshs.state.tx.us/op/op_roster.shtm
Contact Lens Dispenser #26 .... www.dshs.state.tx.us/contactlens/cl_roster.shtm
Cosmetologist #8 .... www.license.state.tx.us/LicenseSearch/
Counselor, Professional #41 .... www.dshs.state.tx.us/counselor/lpc_rosters.shtm
Courier Company #35 .... www.txdps.state.tx.us/psb/individual/individual_search.aspx
Court Reporter/Court Reporting Firm #9 .... www.crcb.state.tx.us/csr-crf-list.asp
CPA Individual/Firm/Sponsor #43 .... www.tsbpa.state.tx.us/
Credit Service Organization #38 .... www.sos.state.tx.us/statdoc/index.shtml
Currency Exchange #1 .... www.banking.state.tx.us/supreglic_ent.asp
Day Care Center/Residence #49
... https://www.dfps.state.tx.us/Child_Care/Search_Texas_Child_Care/CCLNET/Source/CPA/ppSearchTXChildCare2.aspx
Deaf Service Provider #6 .... www.dars.state.tx.us/dhhs/list.shtml
Dentist / Dental Hygienist / Dental Lab #23 .... www.tsbde.state.tx.us/dbsearch/
Dietitian #22 .... www.dshs.state.tx.us/plc/default.shtm
ECA #27 .... www.dshs.state.tx.us/emstraumasystems/NewCert.shtm
Elevator/Escalator #14 .... www.license.state.tx.us/LicenseSearch/
Emergency Medical Technician #27 .... www.dshs.state.tx.us/emstraumasystems/NewCert.shtm
Engineer/Engineering Firm #5 .... www.tbpe.state.tx.us/downloads.htm
Family Home Day Care #49 .... www.dfps.state.tx.us/Child_Care/Search_Texas_Child_Care/ppFacilitySearchDayCare.asp
Fire Alarm/Extiinguisher Contractor #53 .... www.tdi.state.tx.us/fire/fmli.html
Fire Inspector/Investigator #56 .... https://www.tcfp.state.tx.us/standards/certification/certification_lookup.asp
Fire Protection Sprinkler Contr. #53 .... www.tdi.state.tx.us/fire/fmli.html
Fire Suppression Specialist #56 .... https://www.tcfp.state.tx.us/standards/certification/certification_lookup.asp
Firearm Instructor #35 .... www.txdps.state.tx.us/psb/individual/individual_search.aspx
Firefighter #56 .... https://www.tcfp.state.tx.us/standards/certification/certification_lookup.asp
Fireworks Display #53 .... www.tdi.state.tx.us/fire/fmli.html

Funeral Prepaid Permit Holder #1 .... www.banking.state.tx.us/supreglic_ent.asp
Guard Dog Company #35 .... www.txdps.state.tx.us/psb/individual/individual_search.aspx
Health Spa #38 .... www.sos.state.tx.us/statdoc/index.shtml
Hearing Instrument Dispenser/Fitter #22 .... www.dshs.state.tx.us/plc/default.shtm
Home Equity & 2nd Mortgage Lender #7 .... www.occc.state.tx.us/pages/searches.html
Independent Instructor #28 .... www.dshs.state.tx.us/massage/mt_rosters.shtm
Industrialized Housing #14 .... www.license.state.tx.us/LicenseSearch/
Insurance Adjuster #48 .... www.texasonline.state.tx.us/NASApp/tdi/TdiARManager
Insurance Agency/Agent/Company #48 .... www.texasonline.state.tx.us/NASApp/tdi/TdiARManager
Interior Designer #61 .... www.tbae.state.tx.us/PublicInfo/FindProfessional_IntDes.shtml
Landscape Architect #61 .... www.tbae.state.tx.us/PublicInfo/FindProfessional_LandArch.shtml
Loan Company #7 .... www.occc.state.tx.us/pages/searches.html
Loan Officer #37 .... www.sml.state.tx.us:8080/mblolookup/search.jsp
Lobbyist #50 .... www.ethics.state.tx.us/php/lobsearch.cfm
Manicurist/Manicurist Shop #2 .... www.license.state.tx.us/LicenseSearch/
Marriage & Family Therapist #31 .... www.dshs.state.tx.us/mft/mft_contact.shtm
Massage Therapist/Establishment #28 .... www.dshs.state.tx.us/massage/mt_rosters.shtm
Massage Therapy School/Instructor #28 .... www.dshs.state.tx.us/massage/mt_rosters.shtm
Medical Doctor/Physician #30 .... http://reg.tmb.state.tx.us/OnLineVerif/Phys_NoticeVerif.asp?
Medical Physicist #26 .... www.dshs.state.tx.us/mp/mp_roster.shtm
Medical Specialty (Doctor) #30 .... http://reg.tmb.state.tx.us/OnLineVerif/Phys_NoticeVerif.asp?
Money Service Business #1 .... www.banking.state.tx.us/supreglic_ent.asp
Mortgage Banker/Mortgage Broker #37 .... www.sml.state.tx.us:8080/mblolookup/search.jsp
Motor Vehicle Sales Finance Firm #7 .... www.occc.state.tx.us/pages/searches.html
Notary Public #33 .... https://direct.sos.state.tx.us/notaries/NotarySearch.asp
Nurse - RN/Vocational/Adv'd Practice #63 .... www.bon.state.tx.us/olv/verification.html
Occupational Therapist/Assistant #17 .... www.ecptote.state.tx.us/license/verify_occupational_therapist.php
Occupat'n'l/Physical Therapy Facility #17 .... www.ecptote.state.tx.us/license/verify_physical_therapist.php
Optician #26 .... www.dshs.state.tx.us/optician/opt_roster.shtm
Optometrist #51 .... www.tob.state.tx.us/tob%20verifications.htm
Orthotics & Prosthetics Facility #26 .... www.dshs.state.tx.us/op/op_roster.shtm
Orthotist/Prosthetist #26 .... www.dshs.state.tx.us/op/op_rost.pdf
Paramedic #27 .... www.dshs.state.tx.us/emstraumasystems/NewCert.shtm
Pawn Shop #7 .... www.occc.state.tx.us/pages/searches.html
Perfusionist #26 .... www.dshs.state.tx.us/perfusionist/pf_roster.shtm
Perpetual Care Cemetery #1 .... www.banking.state.tx.us/supreglic_ent.asp
Personal Employment Service #14 .... www.license.state.tx.us/LicenseSearch/
Pesticide Applicator/Dealer #10 .... www.tda.state.tx.us/spcs/PIR/pir.htm
Pharmacist/Pharmacist Intern/Technic'n #24 .... www.tsbp.state.tx.us/dbsearch/Default.htm
Pharmacy #24 .... www.tsbp.state.tx.us/dbsearch/Default.htm
Physical Therapist/Assistant #17 .... www.ecptote.state.tx.us/license/verify_facility.php
Physician Assistant #30 .... http://reg.tmb.state.tx.us/OnLineVerif/Phys_NoticeVerif.asp?
Plumber Master/Journeyman #3 .... www.tsbpe.state.tx.us/license_registration.asp
Podiatrist #20 .... www.foot.state.tx.us/verifications.htm
Political Action Committee List #50 .... www.ethics.state.tx.us/dfs/paclists.htm
Political Contributor #50 .... www.ethics.state.tx.us/php/cesearch.html
Polygraph School #34 .... www.tpeb.state.tx.us/schools.html
Private Business Letter of Authority #35 .... www.txdps.state.tx.us/psb/individual/individual_search.aspx
Private Investigator #35 .... www.txdps.state.tx.us/psb/individual/individual_search.aspx
Property Tax Consultant #14 .... www.license.state.tx.us/LicenseSearch/
Psychological Associate #19 .... www.tsbep.state.tx.us/roster_2008.html
Psychologist #19 .... www.tsbep.state.tx.us/roster_2008.html
Public Accountant-CPA /Firm #43 .... www.tsbpa.state.tx.us/
Public Account't-CPA Educ'r/Sponsor #43 .... www.tsbpa.state.tx.us/
Radiology Technician #16 .... www.dshs.state.tx.us/mrt/mrt_roster.shtm
Real Estate Agent/Broker/Sales #52 .... www.trec.state.tx.us
Real Estate Appraiser #47 .... www.talcb.state.tx.us/appraisers/Appraiser_Search.asp
Real Estate Inspector #52 .... www.trec.state.tx.us
Representative Office-Foreign Bank #1 .... www.banking.state.tx.us/supreglic_ent.asp
Respiratory Care Practitioner #29 .... www.dshs.state.tx.us/respiratory/rc_roster.shtm
Sanitarian #22 .... www.dshs.state.tx.us/plc/default.shtm
Savings & Loan Association #37 .... www.sml.state.tx.us:8080/mblolookup/search.jsp
Savings Bank #37 .... www.sml.state.tx.us:8080/mblolookup/search.jsp
School Psychology Specialist #19 .... www.tsbep.state.tx.us/roster_2008.html
Security Agent/Service/Seller #35 .... www.txdps.state.tx.us/psb/individual/individual_search.aspx

Service Contract Provider #14 .... www.license.state.tx.us/LicenseSearch/
Shorthand Reporter #9 .... www.crcb.state.tx.us/csr-crf-list.asp
Social Worker #26 .... www.dshs.state.tx.us/socialwork/sw_rosters.shtm
Speech-Language Pathologist #22 .... www.dshs.state.tx.us/plc/default.shtm
Staff Leasing #14 .... www.license.state.tx.us/LicenseSearch/
Surveyor, Land #4 .... http://txls.state.tx.us/sect03/rosters.html
Talent Agency #14 .... www.license.state.tx.us/LicenseSearch/
Tax Appraisal Professional #59 .... www.txbtpe.state.tx.us
Teacher #42 .... https://secure.sbec.state.tx.us/SBECONLINE/virtcert.asp
Temporary Common Worker #14 .... www.license.state.tx.us/LicenseSearch/
Transportation Service Provider #54 .... www.license.state.tx.us/LicenseSearch/
Trust Company #1 .... www.banking.state.tx.us/supreglic_ent.asp
Underground Storage Tank Installer #60 .... www.tceq.state.tx.us/comm_exec/cc/cc_db.html
Vehicle Protection Provider #14 .... www.license.state.tx.us/LicenseSearch/
Veterans Organization Solicitation #38 .... www.sos.state.tx.us/statdoc/index.shtml
Veterinarian #18 .... www.tbvme.state.tx.us/verify.asp
Water Well & Pump Installer #14 .... www.license.state.tx.us/LicenseSearch/
Weather Modification Service #14 .... www.license.state.tx.us/LicenseSearch/

Texas Licensing Quick Finder

Acupuncturist #30 512-305-7030
Agricultural Specialty, Perishable #11 .. 512-463-7476
Air Condition'g/Refrigeration Contr. #14 512-463-6599
Alarm Installer/Firm/Seller #35 512-424-7710
Alcoholic Bev. Dist./Mfg./Retailer #46 .. 512-206-3360
Alcoholic Beverage Permit #46 512-206-3360
Architect #61 512-305-9000
Architectural Barrier #14 512-463-6599
Asbestos-related Profession #12 512-834-6600 x2789
Athletic Agent #38 512-475-1769
Athletic Trainer #21 512-834-6615
Attorney #40 512-463-1463
Auctioneer #14 512-463-6599
Audiologist #22 512-834-6627
Audiology Assistant #22 512-834-6627
Automobile Club #38 512-475-1769
Bank/Bank Agency #1 512-475-1300
Barber #2 512-936-6333
Barber School #2 512-936-6333
Barber Shop #2 512-936-6333
Barber Student #2 512-936-6333
Beauty Shop/Salon #8 512-380-7659
Boiler Inspector/Installer #14 800-722-7843
Boxing/Combative Sports Event #14 512-463-5101
Business Opportunity Offering #38 512-475-1769
Career Counselor #14 512-463-6599
Cemetery #15 512-936-2466
Chemical Dependency Counselor #26 .. 800-832-9623
Child Care Facility #49 512-438-3269
Child Care Facility Admin. #49 512-438-3269
Child Care Operation #49 512-438-3269
Child Support Agency, Private #1 512-475-1300
Chiropractic Facility #25 512-305-6700
Chiropractic Radiologic Technol'g't #25 512-305-6700
Chiropractor #25 512-305-6700
Code Enforcement Officer #26 .... 512- 834-4512
Commercial Use of State Seal #38 512-475-1769
Contact Lens Dispenser #26 512-834-4515
Cosmetologist #8 512-380-7659
Counselor, Professional #41 ..... 512-834-6658 x2929
County Librarian #44 512-463-5455
Courier Company #35 512-424-7710
Court Reporter/Reporting Firm #9 512-463-1630
CPA Individual/Firm/Sponsor #43 512-305-7853
Credit Service Organization #38 512-475-0775
Crematory #15 512-936-2466
Currency Exchange #1 512-475-1290
Day Care Center #49 512-438-3269
Day Care, Residential #49 512-438-3269
Deaf Service Provider #6 512-407-3250
Dental Assistant #23 512-463-6400
Dental Hygienist #23 512-463-6400
Dental Laboratory #23 512-463-6400
Dentist #23 512-463-6400
Dietitian #22 512-834-6601
ECA #27 512-834-6700
Egg License #11 512-463-7476
Elevator/Escalator #14 512-463-6599
Embalmer #15 512-936-2474
Emergency Medical Technician #27 512-834-6700
Engineer #5 512-440-7723
Engineering Firm #5 512-440-7723
Family Home Day Care #49 512-438-3269
Farm/Agricultural Service Firm #11 512-463-7476
Fire Alarm System Contractor #53 512-305-7935
Fire Extinguisher Contractor #53 512-305-7934
Fire Inspector/Investigator #56 512-936-3838
Fire Protection Sprinkler Contr. #53 512-305-7933
Fire Suppression Specialist #56 512-936-3838
Firearm Instructor #35 512-424-7710
Firefighter #56 512-936-3838
Fireworks Display #53 512-305-7930
Fish Farmer #11 512-463-7476
Fishing Guide #45 512-389-4818
Funeral Director #15 512-936-2474
Funeral Establishment/Home #15 512-936-2474
Funeral Prepaid Permit Holder #1 512-475-1290
Grain Warehouser #11 512-463-7476
Greyhound Racing #36 512-833-6697
Guard Dog Company #35 512-424-7710
Health Related Registry #22 512-834-6602
Health Spa #38 512-463-6906
Hearing Instrum't Dispenser/Fitter #22 . 512-834-6784
Home Equity & 2nd Mortg. Lender #7 .. 512-936-7600
Home Health Agency #26 512-834-6646
Horse Racing #36 512-833-6697
Independent Instructor #28 512-834-6616
Industrialized Housing #14 512-463-7353
Insurance Adjuster #48 512-322-3503
Insurance Agency/Agent #48 512-322-3503
Insurance Company #48 512-322-3507
Interior Designer #61 512-305-9000
Interpreter for the Deaf #6 512-407-3250
Investment Advisor #39 512-305-8332
Irrigator/Installer #57 512-239-6719
Landscape Architect #61 512-305-9000
Law Enforcement Officer #58 512-936-7700
Lead Abatement-related Profess'n #55 .. 512-834-6600
Loan Company #7 512-936-7600
Loan Officer #37 512-475-1350
Lobbyist #50 512-463-5800
LPG- Petrol. Gas Technician #11 512-462-1441
Mammography System #16 ...... 512-834-6688 x2232
Manicurist/Manicurist Shop #2 512-936-6333
Marriage & Family Therapist #31 512-834-6657
Massage Therapist #28 512-834-6616
Massage Therapy School/Instr. #28 512-834-6616
Medical Doctor/Physician #30 512-305-7030
Medical Laboratory Practitioner #22 512-834-6602
Medical Physicist #26 512-834-6655
Medical Specialty (Doctor) #30 512-305-7030
Medication Aide #13 512-438-3011
Membership Camping Resort #38 512-463-6906
Money Service Business #1 512-475-1290
Mortgage Banker #37 512-475-1350
Mortgage Broker #37 512-475-1350
Motor Vehicle Sales Finance Firm #7 .. 512-936-7600
Notary Public #33 512-463-5705
Nurse-RN/Vocation'l/Adv. Practice #63 512-305-6809
Nursery/Floral #11 512-463-7476
Nurses' Aide #13 .... 800-452-3934, 512-438-3811
Nursing Home Administr'r/Facility #13 .. 512-438-3011
Occupational Therapist/Assistant #17 . 512-305-6900
Occupation'l/Physical Therapy Facility #17 512-305-6900
Optician #26 512-834-6661
Optometrist #51 512-305-8500
Organic Grower #11 512-463-7476
Orthotics & Prosthetics Facility #26 512-834-4520
Orthotist/Prosthetist #26 512-834-4520
Paramedic #27 512-834-6700
Pawn Shop #7 512-936-7600
Perfusionist #26 512-834-6751
Perpetual Care Cemetery #1 512-475-1290
Personal Employment Service #14 512-463-6599
Pesticide Applicator/Dealer #10 512-475-1639
Pharmacist #24 512-305-8012
Pharmacist Intern #24 512-305-8011
Pharmacy #24 512-305-8022
Pharmacy Technician #24 512-305-8031
Physical Therapist/Assistant #17 512-305-6900
Physician Assistant #30 512-305-7030
Plumber Master/Journeyman #3 . 512-458-2145 x227
Plumbing Inspector #3 .... 512-458-2145 x227
Podiatrist #20 512-305-7000
Political Action Committee List #50 512-463-5800
Political Contributor #50 512-463-5800
Polygraph Examiner #34 512-424-2058
Polygraph Examiner of Sex Offenders #26 512-834-6655
Polygraph School #34 512-424-2058
Private Business Letter of Authority #35 512-424-7710
Private Investigator #35 512-424-7710

Property Rights #38 512-475-1769
Property Tax Consultant #14 512-463-6599
Psychologist / Psycholog'l Assoc #19 ... 512-305-7700
Public Accountant-CPA #43 512-305-7853
Public Accountant-CPA Firm #43 512-305-7853
Public Account't-CPA Educ'r/Sponsor #43 512-305-7853
Public Safety Org, Promoter Solicitat'n #38 512-475-0775
Radiology Technician #16 512-834-6617
Real Estate Agent/Broker/Sales #52 512-459-6544
Real Estate Appraiser #47 512-465-3950
Real Estate Inspector #52 512-459-6544
Representative Office-Foreign Bank #1 512-475-1300
Respiratory Care Practitioner #29 512-834-6632
Sanitarian #22 512-834-4517
Sanitation Code Enforcem't Officer #22 512-834-6635
Savings & Loan Association #37 512-475-1350
Savings Bank #37 512-475-1350
School Psychology Specialist #19 512-305-7700
Securities Agent/Seller #39 512-305-8332
Securities Broker/Dealer #39 512-305-8332
Security Agency, Private #35 512-424-7710
Security Agent/Service/Seller #35 512-424-7710
Seed Dealer #11 512-463-7476
Service Contract Provider #14 512-463-6599
Sex Offender Treatment Provider #26 . 512-834-4530
Shorthand Reporter #9 512-463-1630
Social Worker #26 512-719-3521
Speech-Language Pathologist #22 512-834-6627
Staff Leasing #14 512-475-2896
STAP Vendor #6 512-936-7132
Surveyor, Land #4 512-452-9427
Talent Agency #14 512-463-6599
Tax Appraisal Professional #59 512-305-7300
Teacher #42 512-936-8400
Telephone Solicitation #38 512-475-0775
Temporary Common Worker #14 512-463-6599
Third Party Debt Collector Bonds #38 . 512-463-6906
Transportation Service Provider #54 ... 512-416-2860
Trust Company #1 512-475-1300
Undergr'nd Storage Tank Installer #60 512-239-5638
Vehicle Protection Provider #14 512-463-6599
Veterans Organization Solicitation #38 512-475-0775
Veterinarian #18 512-305-7555
Water Well & Pump Installer #14 512-463-7880
Weather Modification Service #14 512-463-6599
Weigher, Public #11 512-463-7607
Weights/Measures Service #11 512-463-7607
Wig Specialist #2 512-936-6333
X-ray Machine #16 ..... 512-834-6688 x2247

Texas Licensing Agency Information

#1 Banking Department, 2601 N Lamar Blvd, Austin, TX 78705-4294; 512-475-1300, Fax-512-475-1313. www.banking.state.tx.us Search at- www.banking.state.tx.us/supreglic_ent.asp Check cashers are not regulated at this time.

#2 Dept of Licensing & Regulation, Board of Barber Examiners, 5717 Balcones Dr, #217, Austin, TX 78731; 512-936-6333, Fax- 512-458-4901. www.license.state.tx.us/barbers/barbers.htm Search data at- www.license.state.tx.us/LicenseSearch/ Online search of individuals requires license number. Cost of bulk record request is estimated based on amount of information requested. Also see cosmetology board for add'l manicurist licenses.

#3 Board of Plumbing Examiners, PO Box 4200 (929 E 41st St), Austin, TX 78765-4200; 512-936-5200, Fax- 512-450-0637. www.tsbpe.state.tx.us/index.html

#4 Board of Professional Land Surveying, 12100 Park 35 Circle Bldg A #156, Austin, TX 78753; 512-239-5263, Fax- 512-239-5253. www.txls.state.tx.us Search data at- http://txls.state.tx.us/sect03/rosters.html

#5 Board of Professional Engineers, 1917 IH-35 S, Austin, TX 78741-3702; 512-440-7723, Fax- 512-442-1414. www.tbpe.state.tx.us Search at- www.tbpe.state.tx.us/downloads.htm Licensing data available as pdf downloads; lists updated twice monthly.

#6 Department of Assistive and Rehabilitative Services, 4800 N Lamar Blvd, Austin, TX 78756; 512-407-3250 Voice; 512-407-3251 TTY, Fax- 512-451-9316. www.dars.state.tx.us/dhhs/

#7 Office of Consumer Credit Commissioner, 2601 N Lamar Blvd, Austin, TX 78705-4207; 512-936-7600, Fax- 512-936-7610. www.occc.state.tx.us

#8 Department of Licensing and Regulation, Cosmetology Commission, 920 Colorado, Austin, TX 78701; 512-463-6599, Fax- 512-475-2871. www.texascosmetologylicenserenewalonline.org/index.html

#9 Court Reporter Certification Board, 205 W 14th, Rm 101, Tom C Clark Bldg, Austin, TX 78701; 512-463-1630, Fax- 512-463-1117. Hours- 8AM-5PM. www.crcb.state.tx.us Interested parties may submit an open records request for a list. Refer to our website link "Making requests from CRCB".

#10 Department of Agriculture, Structural Pest Control Service, PO Box 12847 (1700 Congress Ave), Austin, TX 78711; 512-305-8250, Fax- 888-232-2567. www.agr.state.tx.us/agr/program_render/0,1987,1848_5319_0_0,00.html?channelId=5319 Search at- www.tda.state.tx.us/spcs/PIR/pir.htm

#11 Department of Agriculture, Regulatory Programs, PO Box 12847 (1700 N Congress, Stephen F Austin Bldg), Austin, TX 78711; 512-463-7476, 800-835-5832, Fax- 512-463-1104. www.agr.state.tx.us/agr/sort_render/0,1980,1848_9872_0_0,00.html?channelId=9872

#12 Department of Health, Toxic Substances Control Division, Asbestos Programs Branch, 8407 Wall St, Austin, TX 78754; 512-834-6600 x2479, Fax- 512-834-6614. www.dshs.state.tx.us/asbestos/default.shtm Search data at- www.dshs.state.tx.us/asbestos/whocan.shtm#sts Make in person requests at 8407 Wall St, #N320, Austin, TX.

#13 Aging and Disability Services, Long Term Care Regulatory Credentialing Dept, PO Box 149030, Mail Code Y979 (701 W 51st St), Austin, TX 78714-9030; 512-438-3011, Fax-512-834-6764. www.dads.state.tx.us/services/

#14 Department of Licensing & Regulation, PO Box 12157 (920 Colorado), Austin, TX 78711-2157; 512-463-6599, Fax- 512-475-2871. Hours- 8AM-5PM. www.license.state.tx.us Search data at- www.license.state.tx.us/LicenseSearch/

#15 Funeral Service Commission, PO Box 12217 (333 Guadalupe St, #333), Austin, TX 78704-1718; 512-936-2474, Fax- 512-479-5064. Hours- 8AM-5PM. www.tfsc.state.tx.us

#16 Department of State Health Services, Radiation Safety Licensing, 1100 W 49th St, Austin, TX 78756-3189; 512-834-6688, Fax-512-834-6690. Hours- 8AM-5PM. www.dshs.state.tx.us/radiation/

#17 Council on Physical Therapy & Occupational Therapy Examiners, 333 Guadalupe St, #2-510, Austin, TX 78701; 512-305-6900, Fax- 512-305-6951. Hours- 8AM-5PM. www.ecptote.state.tx.us Search data at- www.ecptote.state.tx.us/license/otverif.php Will sell mailing lists for licensees.

#18 Health Department, State Veterinary Board, 333 Guadalupe, Tower 3, #810, Austin, TX 78701-3998; 512-305-7555, Fax- 512-305-7556. www.tbvme.state.tx.us

#19 Board of Examiners of Psychologists, 333 Guadalupe, #2-450, Austin, TX 78701; 512-305-7700, Fax- 512-305-7701. 8AM-5PM. www.tsbep.state.tx.us/index.html Search data at- www.tsbep.state.tx.us/roster_2008.html

#20 Board of Podiatric Medical Examiners, PO Box 12216 (333 Guadalupe, #2-320), Austin, TX 78711; 512-305-7000, Fax- 512-305-7003. 8AM-5PM. www.foot.state.tx.us/index.htm Data at www.foot.state.tx.us/verifications.htm

#21 Health Department, Advisory Board of Athletic Trainers, 1100 W 49th St, Austin, TX 78756; 512-834-6615, Fax- 512-834-6677. www.dshs.state.tx.us/at/ Search data at- www.dshs.state.tx.us/at/at_roster.shtm

#22 State Health Services, Professional Licensing & Certification - Medical, 1100 W 49th St, Austin, TX 78756-3183; 512-834-6628, Fax- 512-834-6707. www.dshs.state.tx.us/plc/default.shtm

#23 Health Department, Dental Board, 333 Guadalupe, Tower 3, #800, Austin, TX 78701; 512-463-6400, Fax- 512-463-7452. www.tsbde.state.tx.us Search data at- www.tsbde.state.tx.us/dbsearch

#24 Health Department, Board of Pharmacy, 333 Guadalupe, Box 21, Tower 3, #600, Austin, TX 78701-3942; 512-305-8000, Fax- 512-305-8082. www.tsbp.state.tx.us/index.htm Search at- www.tsbp.state.tx.us/dbsearch/Default.htm

#25 Board of Chiropractic Examiners, 333 Guadalupe, Tower 3, #825, Austin, TX 78701; 512-505-6700, Fax- 512-305-6705. www.tbce.state.tx.us

#26 Department of Health, Professional Licensing & Certification Div, 1100 W 49th St,

Austin, TX 78756-3180; 512-834-6628, Fax- 512-834-6677. www.dshs.state.tx.us/plc/default.shtm

#27 Health Department, Office of EMS/Trauma Systems Coordination, 8407 Wall St, #N-410, The Exchange Bldg, Austin, TX 78754; 512-834-6700, Fax- 512-834-6736. Hours- 8AM-5PM. www.dshs.state.tx.us/emstraumasystems/default.shtm Search data at- www.dshs.state.tx.us/emstraumasystems/NewCert.shtm

#28 Health Department, Professional Licensure & Certification, Massage Therapy Registration Program, 1100 W 49th St, MC-1982, Austin, TX 78756; 512-834-6616, Fax- 512-834-6677. www.dshs.state.tx.us/massage/default.shtm Search data at- www.dshs.state.tx.us/massage/mt_rosters.shtm

#29 Health Department, Professional Licensure & Certification, Respiratory Care Division, 1100 W 49th St, Austin, TX 78756; 512-834-6632, Fax- 512-834-6677. www.dshs.state.tx.us/respiratory/ Search data at- www.dshs.state.tx.us/respiratory/rc_roster.shtm

#30 Medical Board, MC 240, PO Box 2018 (333 Guadalupe, #3-610), Austin, TX 78768-2018; 512-305-7010, Fax- 512-463-9416. www.tmb.state.tx.us Search data at- http://reg.tmb.state.tx.us/OnLineVerif/Phys_NoticeVerif.asp? Also search physician on private site at www.docboard.org/tx/df/txsearch.htm.

#31 Health Department, Professional Licensure & Certification, Marriage & Family Therapists, 1100 W 49th St, Austin, TX 78756; 512-834-6657, Fax- 512-834-6677. Hours- 8AM-5PM. www.dshs.state.tx.us/mft/ Search data at- www.dshs.state.tx.us/mft/mft_contact.shtm

#33 Office of Secretary of State, Notary Public Unit, PO Box 13375 (1019 Brazos, Rm 214), Austin, TX 78711; 512-463-5705. Hours- 8AM-5PM. www.sos.state.tx.us/statdoc/ Search data at- https://direct.sos.state.tx.us/notaries/NotarySearch.asp

#34 Polygraph Examines Board, PO Box 4087, MSC-0700 (5805 N Lamar Blvd), Austin, TX 78773-4087; 512-424-2058, 866-448-8610, Fax- 512-424-5739. www.tpeb.state.tx.us

#35 Private Security Bureau, P.O. Box 15999 (5805 N Lamar Blvd), Austin, TX 78761-5999; 512-424-7710, Fax- 512-424-7729. www.txdps.state.tx.us/psb/ Search data at- www.txdps.state.tx.us/psb/individual/individual_search.aspx

#36 Racing Commission, PO Box 12080 (8505 Cross Park Dr, #110), Austin, TX 78711-2080; 512-833-6699, Fax- 512-833-6907. Hours- 8AM-5PM. www.txrc.state.tx.us

#37 Department of Savings and Mortgage Lending, 2601 N Lamar Blvd, #201, Austin, TX 78705; 512-475-1350, Fax- 512-475-1360. www.sml.state.tx.us/ Search data at- www.sml.state.tx.us:8080/mblolookup/search.jsp

#38 Secretary of State, Statutory Documents Section, PO Box 12887 (1019 Brazos), Austin, TX 78711-2887; 512-463-5705, Fax- 512-463-0873. Hours- 8AM-5PM. www.sos.state.tx.us/statdoc/index.shtml Forms found at www.sos.state.tx.us/statdoc/statforms.shtml. List of bad Health Spas on home page.

#39 Securities Board, PO Box 13167 (208 E 10th St, 5th Fl (Rusk Building)), Austin, TX 78711-3167; 512-305-8300, Fax- 512-305-8310. www.ssb.state.tx.us

#40 State Bar of Texas, 1414 Colorado St, Austin, TX 78701-1627; 512-463-1463 x1383, Fax- 512-462-1475. www.texasbar.com

#41 Board of Examiners for Professional Counselors, 1100 W 49th St, MC-1982, Austin, TX 78756; 512-834-6658 x2929, Fax- 512-834-6677. www.dshs.state.tx.us/counselor/ Search data at- www.dshs.state.tx.us/counselor/lpc_rosters.shtm

#42 Board for Educator Certification, 1701 N Congress Ave, WBT 5-100, Austin, TX 78701-1494; 512-936-8400, Fax- 512-936-8277. Hours- 8AM-5PM. www.sbec.state.tx.us/SBECOnline/default.asp Search data at- https://secure.sbec.state.tx.us/SBECONLINE/virtcert.asp

#43 Board of Public Accountancy, 333 Guadalupe St, Tower 3, #900, Austin, TX 78701-3900; 512-305-7800, Fax- 512-505-7875. www.tsbpa.state.tx.us Search data at- www.tsbpa.state.tx.us/

#44 Library & Archives Commission, PO Box 12927, Austin, TX 78711-2927; 512-463-5455, Fax- 512-463-8800. Hours- 8AM-5PM M-F; 9AM-4PM Sat. www.tsl.state.tx.us

#45 State Parks & Wildlife Department, 4200 Smith School Rd, Austin, TX 78744; 512-389-4800, Fax- 512-389-4349. www.tpwd.state.tx.us

#46 Alcoholic Beverage Commission, PO Box 13127 (5806 Mesa Dr), Austin, TX 78711; 512-206-3333, Fax- 512-451-0240. www.tabc.state.tx.us Information regarding licenses/permits to the public in various formats such as 8 1/2" X 11" printouts, PC disks, mailing labels and 3480 tapes for a fee.

#47 Appraisers Licensing & Certification Board, P O Box 12188 (1101 Camino La Costa), Austin, TX 78711-2188; 512-459-2232, Fax- 512-465-3953. Hours- 8AM-5PM. www.talcb.state.tx.us/AgencyInfo/default.asp Search data at- www.talcb.state.tx.us/appraisers/Appraiser_Search.asp

#48 Department of Insurance, PO Box 149104 (333 Guadalupe), Austin, TX 78714; 512-463-6169, Fax- 512-475-2025. www.tdi.state.tx.us Search data at- www.texasonline.state.tx.us/NASApp/tdi/TdiARManager

#49 Department of Protective & Regulatory Services, Child Care Licensing Division, 701 W 51st St, #E-550, Austin, TX 78751; 512-438-4800, Fax- 512-438-3848. www.dfps.state.tx.us/Child_Care/About_Child_Care_Licensing/

#50 Ethics Commission, PO Box 12070, (201 E 14th St 10th Fl), Austin, TX 78711-2070; 512-463-5800, Fax- 512-463-5777. Hours- 8AM-5PM. www.ethics.state.tx.us

#51 Optometry Board, 333 Guadalupe St, #2-420, Austin, TX 78701-3942; 512-305-8500, Fax- 512-305-8501. www.tob.state.tx.us Search at www.tob.state.tx.us/tob%20verifications.htm

#52 Real Estate Commission, PO Box 12188 (1101 Camino La Costa), Austin, TX 78711-2188; 512-459-6544, Fax- 512-465-3913. Hours- 8AM-5PM. www.trec.state.tx.us

#53 State Fire Marshal, PO Box 149104 (333 Guadalupe), Austin, TX 78714; 512- 305-7910, Fax- 512-305-7922. www.tdi.state.tx.us/fire/fmli.html

#54 Department of Transportation, Transportation Service Licensing Dept., 125 E 11th St, Austin, TX 78701; 512-416-2860. www.dot.state.tx.us

#55 Department of State Health Services, Environmental Group - Policy, Standards & Quality Assurance, 1100 W 49th St-MC 2835, Austin, TX 78756-3199; 512-834-6773 x2434, Fax- 512-834-6707. Hours- 8AM-5PM. www.dshs.state.tx.us/elp/default.shtm

#56 Commission on Fire Protection, PO Box 2286, (1701 N Congress #105), Austin, TX 78768-2286; 512-936-3838, Fax- 512-936-3808. www.tcfp.state.tx.us Search data at- https://www.tcfp.state.tx.us/standards/certification/certification_lookup.asp

#57 Commission on Environmental Quality, PO Box 13087, MC-TCEQ (12100 Park 35 Cir), Austin, TX 78711-3087; 512-239-6719, Fax- 512-239-0533. Hours- 8AM-5PM. www.tceq.state.tx.us/compliance/compliance_support/licensing/landscape_lic.html

#58 Commission on Law Enforcement Officer, 6330 US 290 East, #200, Austin, TX 78723; 512-936-7700, Fax- 512-936-7714 or 7766. www.tcleose.state.tx.us

#59 Board of Tax Professional Examiners, 333 Guadalupe St, Tower 2, #520, Austin, TX 78701; 512-305-7300, Fax- 512-305-7304. www.txbtpe.state.tx.us To search online, the board member number is required.

#60 Commission on Environmental Quality, PO Box 13087, MC178, Austin, TX 78711-3087; 512-239-5638, Fax- 512-239-0533. 8AM-5PM. www.tceq.state.tx.us/nav/permits/ Search data at- www.tceq.state.tx.us/comm_exec/cc/cc_db.html

#61 Board of Architectural Examiners, 333 Guadalupe, Ste 2-350, Austin, TX 78701; 512-305-9000, Fax- 512-305-8900. www.tbae.state.tx.us Search data at- www.tbae.state.tx.us/PublicInfo/FindProfessional.shtml

#63 Board of Nurse Examiners, 333 Guadalupe, #3-460, Austin, TX 78701; 512-305-7400, Fax- 512-305-7401. www.bon.state.tx.us/index.html Search data at- www.bon.state.tx.us/olv/verification.htm

Texas Federal Courts

The following list indicates the district and division name for each county in the state. If the bankruptcy court location is different from the district court, then the location of the bankruptcy court appears in parentheses.

Texas County/Court Cross Reference

County	District	Division
Anderson	Eastern	Tyler
Andrews	Western	Midland (Midland/Odessa)
Angelina	Eastern	Texarkana (Beaumont)
Aransas	Southern	Corpus Christi
Archer	Northern	Wichita Falls
Armstrong	Northern	Amarillo
Atascosa	Western	San Antonio
Austin	Southern	Houston
Bailey	Northern	Lubbock
Bandera	Western	San Antonio
Bastrop	Western	Austin
Baylor	Northern	Wichita Falls
Bee	Southern	Corpus Christi
Bell	Western	Waco
Bexar	Western	San Antonio
Blanco	Western	Austin
Borden	Northern	Lubbock
Bosque	Western	Waco
Bowie	Eastern	Texarkana
Brazoria	Southern	Galveston (Houston)
Brazos	Southern	Houston
Brewster	Western	Pecos (Midland/Odessa)
Briscoe	Northern	Amarillo
Brooks	Southern	Corpus Christi
Brown	Northern	San Angelo (Lubbock)
Burleson	Western	Austin
Burnet	Western	Austin
Caldwell	Western	Austin
Calhoun	Southern	Victoria (Corpus Christi)
Callahan	Northern	Abilene (Lubbock)
Cameron	Southern	Brownsville (Corpus Christi)
Camp	Eastern	Marshall
Carson	Northern	Amarillo
Cass	Eastern	Marshall
Castro	Northern	Amarillo
Chambers	Southern	Galveston (Houston)
Cherokee	Eastern	Tyler
Childress	Northern	Amarillo
Clay	Northern	Wichita Falls
Cochran	Northern	Lubbock
Coke	Northern	San Angelo (Lubbock)
Coleman	Northern	San Angelo (Lubbock)
Collin	Eastern	Sherman (Plano)
Collingsworth	Northern	Amarillo
Colorado	Southern	Houston
Comal	Western	San Antonio
Comanche	Northern	Fort Worth
Concho	Northern	San Angelo (Lubbock)
Cooke	Eastern	Sherman (Plano)
Coryell	Western	Waco
Cottle	Northern	Wichita Falls
Crane	Western	Midland (Midland/Odessa)
Crockett	Northern	San Angelo (Lubbock)
Crosby	Northern	Lubbock
Culberson	Western	Pecos (Midland/Odessa)
Dallam	Northern	Amarillo
Dallas	Northern	Dallas
Dawson	Northern	Lubbock
De Witt	Southern	Victoria (Houston)
Deaf Smith	Northern	Amarillo
Delta	Eastern	Sherman (Plano)
Denton	Eastern	Sherman (Plano)
Dickens	Northern	Lubbock
Dimmit	Western	San Antonio
Donley	Northern	Amarillo
Duval	Southern	Corpus Christi
Eastland	Northern	Abilene (Lubbock)
Ector	Western	Midland (Midland/Odessa)
Edwards	Western	Del Rio (San Antonio)
El Paso	Western	El Paso
Ellis	Northern	Dallas
Erath	Northern	Fort Worth
Falls	Western	Waco
Fannin	Eastern	Sherman (Plano)
Fayette	Southern	Houston
Fisher	Northern	Abilene (Lubbock)
Floyd	Northern	Lubbock
Foard	Northern	Wichita Falls
Fort Bend	Southern	Houston
Franklin	Eastern	Texarkana
Freestone	Western	Waco
Frio	Western	San Antonio
Gaines	Northern	Lubbock
Galveston	Southern	Galveston (Houston)
Garza	Northern	Lubbock
Gillespie	Western	Austin
Glasscock	Northern	San Angelo (Lubbock)
Goliad	Southern	Victoria (Corpus Christi)
Gonzales	Western	San Antonio
Gray	Northern	Amarillo
Grayson	Eastern	Sherman (Plano)
Gregg	Eastern	Tyler
Grimes	Southern	Houston
Guadalupe	Western	San Antonio
Hale	Northern	Lubbock
Hall	Northern	Amarillo
Hamilton	Western	Waco
Hansford	Northern	Amarillo
Hardeman	Northern	Wichita Falls
Hardin	Eastern	Beaumont
Harris	Southern	Houston
Harrison	Eastern	Marshall
Hartley	Northern	Amarillo
Haskell	Northern	Abilene (Lubbock)
Hays	Western	Austin
Hemphill	Northern	Amarillo
Henderson	Eastern	Tyler
Hidalgo	Southern	McAllen (Corpus Christi)
Hill	Western	Waco
Hockley	Northern	Lubbock
Hood	Northern	Fort Worth
Hopkins	Eastern	Sherman (Plano)
Houston	Eastern	Texarkana (Beaumont)
Howard	Northern	Abilene (Lubbock)
Hudspeth	Western	El Paso (Midland/Odessa)
Hunt	Northern	Dallas

County	District	Division
Hutchinson	Northern	Amarillo
Irion	Northern	San Angelo (Lubbock)
Jack	Northern	Fort Worth
Jackson	Southern	Victoria (Corpus Christi)
Jasper	Eastern	Beaumont
Jeff Davis	Western	Pecos (Midland/Odessa)
Jefferson	Eastern	Beaumont
Jim Hogg	Southern	Laredo (Houston)
Jim Wells	Southern	Corpus Christi
Johnson	Northern	Dallas
Jones	Northern	Abilene (Lubbock)
Karnes	Western	San Antonio
Kaufman	Northern	Dallas
Kendall	Western	San Antonio
Kenedy	Southern	Corpus Christi
Kent	Northern	Lubbock
Kerr	Western	San Antonio
Kimble	Western	Austin
King	Northern	Wichita Falls
Kinney	Western	Del Rio (San Antonio)
Kleberg	Southern	Corpus Christi
Knox	Northern	Wichita Falls
La Salle	Southern	Laredo (Corpus Christi)
Lamar	Eastern	Sherman (Plano)
Lamb	Northern	Lubbock
Lampasas	Western	Austin
Lavaca	Southern	Victoria (Houston)
Lee	Western	Austin
Leon	Western	Waco
Liberty	Eastern	Beaumont
Limestone	Western	Waco
Lipscomb	Northern	Amarillo
Live Oak	Southern	Corpus Christi
Llano	Western	Austin
Loving	Western	Pecos (Midland/Odessa)
Lubbock	Northern	Lubbock
Lynn	Northern	Lubbock
Madison	Southern	Houston
Marion	Eastern	Marshall
Martin	Western	Midland (Midland/Odessa)
Mason	Western	Austin
Matagorda	Southern	Galveston (Houston)
Maverick	Western	Del Rio (San Antonio)
McCulloch	Western	Austin
McLennan	Western	Waco
McMullen	Southern	Laredo (Houston)
Medina	Western	San Antonio
Menard	Northern	San Angelo (Lubbock)
Midland	Western	Midland (Midland/Odessa)
Milam	Western	Waco
Mills	Northern	San Angelo (Lubbock)
Mitchell	Northern	Abilene (Lubbock)
Montague	Northern	Wichita Falls
Montgomery	Southern	Houston
Moore	Northern	Amarillo
Morris	Eastern	Marshall
Motley	Northern	Lubbock
Nacogdoches	Eastern	Texarkana (Beaumont)
Navarro	Northern	Dallas
Newton	Eastern	Beaumont
Nolan	Northern	Abilene (Lubbock)
Nueces	Southern	Corpus Christi
Ochiltree	Northern	Amarillo
Oldham	Northern	Amarillo
Orange	Eastern	Beaumont
Palo Pinto	Northern	Fort Worth
Panola	Eastern	Tyler
Parker	Northern	Fort Worth
Parmer	Northern	Amarillo
Pecos	Western	Pecos (Midland/Odessa)
Polk	Eastern	Texarkana (Beaumont)
Potter	Northern	Amarillo
Presidio	Western	Pecos (Midland/Odessa)
Rains	Eastern	Tyler
Randall	Northern	Amarillo
Reagan	Northern	San Angelo (Lubbock)
Real	Western	San Antonio
Red River	Eastern	Sherman (Plano)
Reeves	Western	Pecos (Midland/Odessa)
Refugio	Southern	Victoria (Corpus Christi)
Roberts	Northern	Amarillo
Robertson	Western	Waco
Rockwall	Northern	Dallas
Runnels	Northern	San Angelo (Lubbock)
Rusk	Eastern	Tyler
Sabine	Eastern	Texarkana (Beaumont)
San Augustine	Eastern	Texarkana (Beaumont)
San Jacinto	Southern	Houston
San Patricio	Southern	Corpus Christi
San Saba	Western	Austin
Schleicher	Northern	San Angelo (Lubbock)
Scurry	Northern	Lubbock
Shackelford	Northern	Abilene (Lubbock)
Shelby	Eastern	Texarkana (Beaumont)
Sherman	Northern	Amarillo
Smith	Eastern	Tyler
Somervell	Western	Waco
Starr	Southern	McAllen (Corpus Christi)
Stephens	Northern	Abilene (Lubbock)
Sterling	Northern	San Angelo (Lubbock)
Stonewall	Northern	Abilene (Lubbock)
Sutton	Northern	San Angelo (Lubbock)
Swisher	Northern	Amarillo
Tarrant	Northern	Fort Worth
Taylor	Northern	Abilene (Lubbock)
Terrell	Western	Del Rio (San Antonio)
Terry	Northern	Lubbock
Throckmorton	Northern	Abilene (Lubbock)
Titus	Eastern	Texarkana
Tom Green	Northern	San Angelo (Lubbock)
Travis	Western	Austin
Trinity	Eastern	Texarkana (Beaumont)
Tyler	Eastern	Texarkana (Beaumont)
Upshur	Eastern	Marshall
Upton	Western	Midland (Midland/Odessa)
Uvalde	Western	Del Rio (San Antonio)
Val Verde	Western	Del Rio (San Antonio)
Van Zandt	Eastern	Tyler
Victoria	Southern	Victoria (Corpus Christi)
Walker	Southern	Houston
Waller	Southern	Houston
Ward	Western	Pecos (Midland/Odessa)
Washington	Western	Austin
Webb	Southern	Laredo (Houston)
Wharton	Southern	Houston
Wheeler	Northern	Amarillo
Wichita	Northern	Wichita Falls
Wilbarger	Northern	Wichita Falls
Willacy	Southern	Brownsville (Corpus Christi)
Williamson	Western	Austin
Wilson	Western	San Antonio
Winkler	Western	Pecos (Midland/Odessa)
Wise	Northern	Fort Worth
Wood	Eastern	Tyler
Yoakum	Northern	Lubbock
Young	Northern	Wichita Falls
Zapata	Southern	Laredo (Houston)
Zavala	Western	Del Rio (San Antonio)

Standards for Federal Courts: Fees are standard unless noted in profile. Search fee is $26.00 per item (one party name or case number). Copy fee is $.50 per page. Certification fee is $9.00 per document, double for exemplification, if available. Most courts require prepayment. Mail requests should enclose a SASE unless otherwise noted. Before releasing records, all courts require prepayment, unless noted.

District courts index by defendant and plaintiff and by case number. Bankruptcy courts usually index by debtor and case number. While most courts now have their indexes on computer, many may still maintain index card files as well. Courts will archive closed case files at different times.

There are numerous public access programs available to online subscribers. Search the U.S. Party/Case Index to find party names and case numbers among all courts. Individual case data is provided on PACER. A search of CM/ECF provides copies of cases filed electronically. For details about PACER, the US Party/Case Index, and CM/ECF see the Appendix or go to http://pacer.psc.uscourts.gov or call 800-676-6856.

US District Court Texas Eastern District

Beaumont Div. Court Clerk, 300 Willow, Rm 104, Beaumont, TX 77701, 409-654-7000; Fax- 409-654-7080. Hours - 8AM - 5PM. www.txed.uscourts.gov

Counties/Note: Delta*, Fannin*, Hardin, Hopkins*, Jasper, Jefferson, Lamar*, Liberty, Newton, Orange. Counties marked with an asterisk are the old Paris Division, whose case records are maintained at Beaumont. New records are at Sherman Div. Beaumont also maintains records for Paris Division.

Searches/Indexing: Include full name only in search request. Results do not include SSN or DOB. Will not fax back documents. New cases are in the index immediately after filing date. Computer and microfiche indexes maintained. District-wide searches available back to 3/86. View Frequently Requested Cases free on the public access terminal. Case files sent to archives 1 year after closed.

Search Access: Only docket info is available by phone. **Mail:** Search usually completed- 1 week. SASE not required. **In person:** 1 public terminal available. Self-serve copies $.25 each.

Payment: Pay by Visa/MC, money order, cashier's or personal check. Payee: Clerk, US District Court.

E-Services: PACER records go back to 1992. New records online after 1 day. ECF at https://ecf.txed.uscourts.gov. Opinions available on ECF/PACER system.

Lufkin Division Court Clerk, 104 N Third St, Lufkin, TX 75901, 936-632-2739; Fax- 936-632-1210. Hours-8AM-5PM. www.txed.uscourts.gov

Counties: Angelina, Houston, Nacogdoches, Polk, Sabine, San Augustine, Shelby, Trinity, Tyler.

Searches/Indexing: Include full name only in search request. Results do not include SSN or DOB. Will not fax back documents. New cases are in the index immediately after filing date. View Frequently Requested Cases free on the public access terminal.

Search Access: Only docket info is available by phone. **Mail:** Search usually completed- 1 week. Include SASE for return. **In person:** 1 public terminal available. Computer generated copies $.10 each. View Frequently Requested Cases free on the public access terminal. **Payment:** Pay by Visa/MC, money order, cashier's or personal check. Payee: US District Court.

E-Services: PACER records go back to 1992. New records online after 1 day. ECF at https://ecf.txed.uscourts.gov. Opinions available on ECF/PACER system.

Marshall Division Court Clerk, 100 E Houston, Rm 125, Marshall, TX 75670, 903-935-2912; Fax- 903-938-2651. Hours-8AM-5PM. www.txed.uscourts.gov

Camp, Cass, Harrison, Marion, Morris, Upshur.

Searches/Indexing: Include full name only in search request. Results do not include SSN or DOB; you may call and they may verify. Will not fax back documents. New cases are in the index immediately after filing date. View Frequently Requested Cases free on public access terminal.

Search Access: Only docket info is available by phone. **Mail:** Search usually completed- 1 week. Include SASE for return. **In person:** 1 public terminal available. Self-serve copies $.50 each.

Payment: Pay by Visa/MC, money order, cashier's or personal check. Payee: US District Court.

E-Services: PACER records go back to 1992. New records online after 1 day. ECF at https://ecf.txed.uscourts.gov. Opinions available on ECF/PACER system.

Sherman Div. Court Clerk, 101 E Pecan St, Rm 112, Sherman, TX 75090, 903-892-2921; Fax- 903-892-6801. 8-5PM. www.txed.uscourts.gov

Counties/Note: Collin, Cooke, Delta*, Denton, Fannin*, Grayson, Hopkins*, Lamar*. Counties marked with an asterisk were part of the old Paris Division; these old records are at Beaumont. New records are at Sherman. There is also a Plano Divisional Annex Office at 7940 Preston Rd, Rm 210, 214-872-4800.

Searches/Indexing: Include full name only in search request. Results do not include SSN or DOB. Will not fax back documents. New cases are in the index immediately after filing date. District-wide searches available here. View Frequently Requested Cases free on the public access terminal. Case files sent to archives 1 year after closed. **Search Access:** Only docket info is available by phone. **Mail:** Search usually completed- 1 week. Include SASE for return. **In person:** 1 public terminal available. Self-serve copier available. **Payment:** Pay by Visa/MC, money order, cashier's or personal check. Payee: Clerk, US District Court.

E-Services: PACER records go back to 1992. New records online after 1 day. ECF at https://ecf.txed.uscourts.gov. Opinions available on ECF/PACER system.

Texarkana Division Clerk's Office, PO Box 2090, Texarkana, TX 75504 (In person: 500 State Line Ave, Rm 301, Texarkana, TX 75501), 903-794-8561; Fax- 903-794-0600. Hours-8AM-5PM. www.txed.uscourts.gov

Counties: Bowie, Franklin, Red River, Titus.

Searches/Indexing: Include full name only in search request. Results give address but do not include SSN or DOB. Will not fax back documents. New cases are in the index immediately after filing date. Computer, microfiche and card indexes maintained. View Frequently Requested Cases free on the public access terminal. No set time when cases sent to Fort Worth Records Center.

Search Access: Only docket info is available by phone. **Mail:** Search usually completed- 1 week. Include SASE for return. **In person:** 1 public terminal available. Self-serve copies $.50 each.

Payment: Pay by Visa/MC, money order, cashier's or personal check. Payee: Clerk, US District Court.

E-Services: PACER records go back to 1992. New records online after 1 day. ECF at https://ecf.txed.uscourts.gov. Opinions available on ECF/PACER system.

Tyler Div. Clerk of Court, 211 W Ferguson, Rm 106, Tyler, TX 75702, 903-590-1000; Fax- 903-590-1015. 8-5PM. www.txed.uscourts.gov

Anderson, Cherokee, Gregg, Henderson, Panola, Rains, Rusk, Smith, Van Zandt, Wood.

Searches/Indexing: Include first and last name in search request. Results do not include SSN or DOB. Will not fax back documents. New cases are in the index 1-2 days after filing date. View Frequently Requested Cases free on the public access terminal.

Search Access: Only docket info is available by phone. **Mail:** Search usually completed- 1 week. SASE not required. **In person:** 1 public terminal available. Self-serve copier available.

Payment: Pay by Visa/MC, money order, cashier's or personal check. Payee: Clerk, US District Court.

E-Services: PACER records go back to 1992. New records online after 1 day. ECF at https://ecf.txed.uscourts.gov. Opinions available on ECF/PACER system.

US Bankruptcy Court Texas Eastern District

Beaumont Division Court Clerk, 300 Willow St, #100, Beaumont, TX 77701, 409-839-2617. Hours-8AM-4PM. www.txeb.uscourts.gov

Counties/Note: Angelina, Hardin, Houston, Jasper, Jefferson, Liberty, Nacogdoches, Newton, Orange, Polk, Sabine, San Augustine, Shelby, Trinity, Tyler. This Division also has a Courthouse in Luflin at 104 N 3rd St, but no bankruptcy office.

Searches/Indexing: Only the full name required in search request of new court index; SSN helpful in search of older records. Results do not include SSN or DOB. Will not fax back documents. New cases are in the index immediately after filing date. Case files sent to archives 1 year after closed.

Search Access: Only docket info is available by phone. Voice Case Information Service available, call VCIS at 800-466-1694 or 903-590-3251. **Mail:** Search usually completed- 1 week. SASE not required. **In person:** 2 public terminals available. Computer generated copies $.10 each.

Payment: Pay by credit cards, money order, cashier's or personal check. Payee: Clerk, US Bankruptcy Court.

E-Services: Document images available. PACER records go back to 1989. ECF at https://ecf.txeb.uscourts.gov. **Opinions Online:** www.txeb.uscourts.gov/opinions.asp. Also, browse Trustee's Final Reports and Unclaimed Funds at www.txeb.uscourts.gov/reports.asp. Calendars at www.txeb.uscourts.gov/judges.asp.

Marshall Div. c/o Tyler Division, 110 N College Ave, Tyler, TX 75702, 903-590-3200; Fax- 903-590-1226. 8-4. www.txeb.uscourts.gov

Counties/Note: Camp, Cass, Harrison, Marion, Morris, Upshur. All cases at Tyler Div.

Searches/Indexing: Only the full name required in search request of new court index; SSN helpful in search of older records. Results do not include SSN or DOB. Will not fax back documents. New cases are in the index immediately after filing date. Case files sent to archives 1 year after closed.

Search Access: Only docket info is available by phone. Voice Case Information Service available, call VCIS at 800-466-1694 or 903-590-3251. **Mail:** Search usually completed- 2-3 days. SASE not required. **In person:** 3 public terminals available. Self-serve copies from computer- $.10.

Payment: Pay by credit cards, money order, cashier's check only. Payee: Clerk, Bankruptcy Ct.

E-Services: Document images available. PACER records go back to 1989. New records online after 1 day. ECF at https://ecf.txeb.uscourts.gov. **Opinions:** www.txeb.uscourts.gov/opinions.asp. Also, browse Trustee's Reports and Unclaimed Funds at www.txeb.uscourts.gov/reports.asp. Calendars at www.txeb.uscourts.gov/judges.asp.

Plano Division Court Clerk, 660 N Central Expressway, Ste 300B, Plano, TX 75074, 972-509-1240; Fax- 972-509-1245. Hours-8AM-4PM. www.txeb.uscourts.gov

Counties/Note: Collin, Cooke, Delta, Denton, Fannin, Grayson, Hopkins, Lamar, Red River.

Searches/Indexing: Only the full name required in search request of new court index; SSN helpful in search of older records. Results do not include SSN or DOB. Will not fax back documents. New cases are in the index immediately after filing date. Case files sent to archives 1 year after closed.

Search Access: Only docket info is available by phone. Voice Case Information Service available, call VCIS at 800-466-1694 or 903-590-5251. **Mail:** Search usually completed- same day if possible. SASE not required. **In person:** 3 public terminals available. Computer generated copies $.10 each. **Payment:** Pay by credit cards, money order, cashier's or personal check. Payee: Clerk, US Bankruptcy Court.

E-Services: Document images available. PACER records go back to 1989. ECF at https://ecf.txeb.uscourts.gov. **Opinions Online:** www.txeb.uscourts.gov/opinions.asp. Also, browse Trustee's Final Reports and Unclaimed Funds at www.txeb.uscourts.gov/reports.asp. Calendars at www.txeb.uscourts.gov/judges.asp.

Texarkana Division c/o Plano Division, 660 N Central Expressway, Suite 300B, Plano, TX 75074, 972-509-1240; Fax- 972-509-1245. Hours-8AM-4PM. www.txeb.uscourts.gov

Counties/Note: Bowie, Franklin, Titus. Courthouse is located 500 N. Stateline in Texarkana but there is no bankruptcy office.

Searches/Indexing: Only the full name required in search request of new court index; SSN helpful in search of older records. Results do not include SSN or DOB. Will not fax back documents. New cases are in the index immediately after filing date. Case files sent to archives 1 year after closed.

Search Access: Only docket info is available by phone. Voice Case Information Service available, call VCIS at 800-466-1694 or 903-590-3251. **Mail:** Search usually completed same day. SASE not required. **In person:** 3 public terminals available. No self-serve copier. **Payment:** Pay by credit cards, money order, cashier's or personal check. Payee: Clerk, US Bankruptcy Court.

E-Services: Document images available. PACER records go back to 1989. ECF at https://ecf.txeb.uscourts.gov. **Opinions Online:** www.txeb.uscourts.gov/opinions.asp. Also, browse Trustee's Final Reports and Unclaimed Funds at www.txeb.uscourts.gov/reports.asp. Calendars at www.txeb.uscourts.gov/judges.asp.

Tyler Division Court Clerk, 110 N College Ave, 9th Fl, Tyler, TX 75702, 903-590-3200; Fax- 903-590-1226. Hours- 8AM - 4PM. www.txeb.uscourts.gov **Counties:** Anderson, Cherokee, Gregg, Henderson, Panola, Rains, Rusk, Smith, Van Zandt, Wood.

Searches/Indexing: Only the full name required in search request of new court index; SSN helpful in search of older records. Results do not include SSN or DOB. Will not fax back documents. New cases are in the index immediately after filing date. Computer, microfiche and card indexes maintained. Card index for cases prior to 10/1987 only. This Court maintains automated case records and finance records for entire Eastern district. District-wide searches available back to 10/87. Case files sent to archives 1 year after closed.

Search Access: Via phone, this court will answer questions pertaining to info not found on VCIS. Voice Case Information Service available, call VCIS at 800-466-1694 or 903-590-3251. **Mail:** Search usually completed- 2-3 days. SASE not required. **In person:** 3 public terminals available. Computer generated copies $.10 each. **Payment:** Pay by credit cards, money order, cashier's or personal check. Payee: Clerk, US Bankruptcy Ct.

E-Services: Document images available. PACER records go back to 1989. New records online after 1 day. ECF at https://ecf.txeb.uscourts.gov. **Opinions:** www.txeb.uscourts.gov/opinions.asp. Also, browse Trustee's Reports and Unclaimed Funds at www.txeb.uscourts.gov/reports.asp. Calendars at www.txeb.uscourts.gov/judges.asp.

US District Court
Texas Northern District

Abilene Division Court Clerk, 341 Pine St, Rm 2008, Abilene, TX 79601, 325-677-6311. 8:30AM-N, 1-4:30PM. www.txnd.uscourts.gov

Counties: Callahan, Eastland, Fisher, Haskell, Howard, Jones, Mitchell, Nolan, Shackelford, Stephens, Stonewall, Taylor, Throckmorton.

Searches/Indexing: Search request requires name only. Results do not include SSN or DOB. Will not fax back documents. New cases are in the index immediately after filing date. Computer index goes back to 1990, entire district included. 1981-1991 records on microfiche, entire district. Each division has its own 1957 through 1981 case files on microfiche at its court. Open records- civil go back 2 years and criminal back 3 years. Closed case files sent to archives yearly.

Search Access: Only a name or case number is released via phone. **Mail:** Search usually completed- 1-2 days. SASE not required. **In person:** 1 public terminal available. No self-serve copier. **Payment:** Pay by money order, cashier's or personal check. Payee: Clerk, US District Court. **E-Services:** Document images available. PACER records go back to 6/1991. New records online after 1 day. ECF at https://ecf.txnd.uscourts.gov. **Opinions Online:** www.txnd.uscourts.gov/judges/.

Amarillo Division Court Clerk, 205 E 5th St, Rm 133, Amarillo, TX 79101, 806-468-3800; Fax- 806-468-3862. Hours- 8:30AM-N, 1-4:30PM. www.txnd.uscourts.gov

Counties/Note: Armstrong, Briscoe, Carson, Castro, Childress, Collingsworth, Dallam, Deaf Smith, Donley, Gray, Hall, Hansford, Hartley, Hemphill, Hutchinson, Lipscomb, Moore, Ochiltree, Oldham, Parmer, Potter, Randall, Roberts, Sherman, Swisher, Wheeler.

Searches/Indexing: Search request requires name only. Results do not include SSN or DOB. Will not fax back documents. New cases are in the index immediately after filing date. Computer index goes back to 1996; entire district included. 1981-1996 records on microfiche, entire district. Each division has its own 1957 through 1981 case files on microfiche at its court. Open records- civil go back 2 years and criminal back 3 years. Closed case files sent to archives yearly.

Search Access: No party info is released via phone. Only pleadings are released via phone. **Mail:** Search usually completed- 1-2 days. SASE not required. **In person:** 1 public terminal available. No self-serve copier.

Payment: Pay by Visa/MC, money order, cashier's or personal check. Payee: Clerk, US District Court.

E-Services: Document images available. PACER records go back to 6/1991. New records online after 1 day. ECF at https://ecf.txnd.uscourts.gov. **Opinions:** www.txnd.uscourts.gov/judges/.

Dallas Division Court Clerk, 1100 Commerce St, Rm 1452, Dallas, TX 75242, 214-753-2200; records- 214-753-2196. 8:30AM-N, 1-4:30PM. www.txnd.uscourts.gov **Counties:** Dallas, Ellis, Hunt, Johnson, Kaufman, Navarro, Rockwall.

Searches/Indexing: Search request requires name only. Results do not include SSN or DOB. Will not fax back documents. New cases are in the index immediately after filing date. Computer index goes back to 1990, entire district included. 1981-1991 records on microfiche, entire district. Each division has its own 1957 through 1981 case files on microfiche at its court. Open records- civil go back 2 years and criminal back 3 years. Closed case files sent to archives yearly.

Search Access: Only computerized docket info is released via phone. **Mail:** Search usually completed- 1-2 days. Include SASE for return. **In person:** 1 public terminal available. No self-serve copier. **Payment:** Pay by Visa/MC, money order, cashier's or personal check. Payee: Clerk, US District Court.

E-Services: Document images available. PACER records go back to 6/1991. New records online after 1 day. ECF at https://ecf.txnd.uscourts.gov. **Opinions:** www.txnd.uscourts.gov/judges/.

Fort Worth Division Clerk's Office, 501 W Tenth St, Rm 310, Fort Worth, TX 76102, 817-850-6600; Fax- 817-850-6633. Hours-8:30AM-N, 1-4:30PM. www.txnd.uscourts.gov

Counties/Note: Comanche, Erath, Hood, Jack, Palo Pinto, Parker, Tarrant, Wise.

Searches/Indexing: Search request requires name only. Results do not include SSN or DOB. Will not fax back documents. New cases are in the index immediately after filing date. Computer index goes back to 1990, entire district included.

1981-1991 records on microfiche, entire district. Each division has its own 1957 through 1981 case files on microfiche at its court. Open records- civil go back 2 years and criminal back 3 years. Closed case files sent to archives yearly. **Search Access:** If provided a case number via phone, this court will only release minimal case information. Court will not search for case numbers via phone. **Mail:** Search usually completed 1-2 days. No SASE required. **In person:** 1 public terminal available. No self-serve copier.

Payment: Pay by Visa/MC, money order, cashier's or personal check. Payee: Clerk, US District Court.

E-Services: Document images available. PACER records go back to 6/1991. New records online after 1 day. ECF at https://ecf.txnd.uscourts.gov. **Opinions:** www.txnd.uscourts.gov/judges/.

Lubbock Div. Clerk of Court, 1205 Texas Ave, Rm 209, Lubbock, TX 79401, 806-472-1900, 806-472-7624; Fax- 806-472-7639. Hours-8:30AM-N, 1-4:30PM. www.txnd.uscourts.gov

Counties/Note: Bailey, Borden, Cochran, Crosby, Dawson, Dickens, Floyd, Gaines, Garza, Hale, Hockley, Kent, Lamb, Lubbock, Lynn, Motley, Scurry, Terry, Yoakum.

Searches/Indexing: Search request requires name only. Results do not include SSN or DOB. Will not fax back documents. New cases are in the index immediately after filing date. Computer index goes back to 1990, entire district included. 1981-1991 records on microfiche, entire district. Each division has its own 1957 through 1981 case files on microfiche at its court. Open records- civil go back 2 years and criminal back 3 years. Closed case files sent to archives yearly.

Search Access: Only docket info available by phone. **Mail:** Search usually completed- 1-2 days. Include SASE for return. **In person:** 1 public terminal available. No self-serve copier. **Payment:** Pay by Visa/MC, money order, cashier's or personal check. Payee: Clerk, US District Court.

E-Services: Document images available. PACER records go back to 6/1991. New records online after 1 day. ECF at https://ecf.txnd.uscourts.gov. **Opinions:** www.txnd.uscourts.gov/judges/.

San Angelo Div. Clerk's Office, 33 E Twohig St, Rm 202, San Angelo, TX 76903, 325-655-4506; Fax- 325-658-6826. Hours-8:30AM-N, 1-4:30PM. www.txnd.uscourts.gov

Counties/Note: Brown, Coke, Coleman, Concho, Crockett, Glasscock, Irion, Menard, Mills, Reagan, Runnels, Schleicher, Sterling, Sutton, Tom Green.

Searches/Indexing: Search request requires name only. Results do not include SSN or DOB. Will not fax back documents. New cases are in the index immediately after filing date. Computer index goes back to 1990, entire district included. 1981-1991 records on microfiche, entire district. Each division has its own 1957 through 1981 case files on microfiche at its court. Open records- civil go back 2 years and criminal back 3. Civil records retained 3 years; criminal records 7 to 8 years.

Search Access: Only docket info available by phone. **Mail:** Search usually completed- 1-2 days. Include SASE for return. **In person:** 1 public terminal available. No self-serve copier.

Payment: Pay by money order, cashier's or personal check. Payee: Clerk, US District Court.

E-Services: Document images available. PACER records go back to 6/1991. New records online after 1 day. ECF at https://ecf.txnd.uscourts.gov. **Opinions:** www.txnd.uscourts.gov/judges/.

Wichita Falls Division Court Clerk, 1000 Lamar, Rm 203, Wichita Falls, TX 76301, 940-767-1902; Fax- 940-767-2526. Hours-8:30AM-N, 1-4:30PM. www.txnd.uscourts.gov

Counties: Archer, Baylor, Clay, Cottle, Foard, Hardeman, King, Knox, Montague, Wichita, Wilbarger, Young.

Searches/Indexing: Search request requires name only. Results do not include SSN or DOB. Will not fax back documents. New cases are in the index immediately after filing date. Computer index goes back to 1990, entire district included. 1981-1991 records on microfiche, entire district. Each division has its own 1957 through 1981 case files on microfiche at its court. Open records- civil go back 2 years and criminal back 3 years. Closed case files sent to archives yearly.

Search Access: Only docket info is available by phone. **Mail:** Search usually completed- 1-2 days. Include SASE for return. **In person:** 1 public terminal. No self-serve copier. **Payment:** Pay by money order, cashier's or personal check. No credit cards. Payee: Clerk, US District Court.

E-Services: Document images available. PACER records go back to 6/1991. New records online after 1 day. ECF at https://ecf.txnd.uscourts.gov. **Opinions:** www.txnd.uscourts.gov/judges/.

US Bankruptcy Court Texas Northern District

Amarillo Division Court Clerk, 624 S Polk St #100, Amarillo, TX 79101-2320, 806-324-2302. Hours-8AM-4PM. www.txnb.uscourts.gov

Counties/Note: Armstrong, Briscoe, Carson, Castro, Childress, Collingsworth, Dallam, Deaf Smith, Donley, Gray, Hall, Hansford, Hartley, Hemphill, Hutchinson, Lipscomb, Moore, Ochiltree, Oldham, Parmer, Potter, Randall, Roberts, Sherman, Swisher, Wheeler.

Searches/Indexing: Include full name and SSN in search request. Results include last 4 SSN digits, address and name. New cases are in the index immediately after filing date. Both computer and card indexes maintained. Card index available prior to 6/1988. Search fee required should the court have to pull a file and count pages. Open records not physically at this court, only electronically. Case files sent to archives 6 months after closed. **Search Access:** Only docket info is available by phone. Voice Case Information Service available, call VCIS at 800-886-9008 or 214-753-2128. **Mail:** Search usually completed- 1-2 days. Include SASE for return. **In person:** 1 public terminal available back to 1990. Self-serve copies available. **Payment:** Pay by money order, cashier's check, business check. No personal checks or credit cards. Payee: Clerk, US Bankruptcy Court.

E-Services: Document images available back to 2/03. PACER records go back to 1994. New records online after 1 day. ECF at https://ecf.txnb.uscourts.gov. **Opinions Online:** www.txnb.uscourts.gov/opinions/. **Online Note:** Calendars free at www.txnb.uscourts.gov/judges.

Dallas Division Court Clerk, 1100 Commerce St, Suite 1254, Dallas, TX 75242-1496, 214-753-2000; Fax- 214-753-2038. 8:30AM-4:30PM. www.txnb.uscourts.gov

Counties/Note: Dallas, Ellis, Hunt, Johnson, Kaufman, Navarro, Rockwall. This court maintains records for the Wichita Falls Division.

Searches/Indexing: Include full name and SSN in search request. Results include last 4 SSN digits, address and name. New cases are in the index 1-2 days after filing date. Both computer and card indexes maintained. District-wide searches available back to 8/92. No search fee for searching docket sheets or claims registers in person. Case files sent to archives 6 months after closed.

Search Access: Only docket info is available by phone. Voice Case Information Service available, call VCIS at 800-886-9008 or 214-753-2128. **Mail:** Search usually completed- 2-3 days. Include SASE for return. **In person:** No self-serve copier.

Payment: No business or personal checks accepted. Payee: Clerk, US Bankruptcy Court.

E-Services: Document images available back to 2/03. PACER records go back to 1994. New records online after 1 day. ECF at https://ecf.txnb.uscourts.gov. **Opinions Online:** www.txnb.uscourts.gov/opinions/. **Online Note:** Calendars free at www.txnb.uscourts.gov/judges.

Fort Worth Division Court Clerk, 501 W 10th, Suite 147, Fort Worth, TX 76102, 817-333-6000; Fax- 817-333-6001. 8:30AM-4:30PM. www.txnb.uscourts.gov

Counties/Note: Comanche, Erath, Hood, Jack, Palo Pinto, Parker, Tarrant, Wise.

Searches/Indexing: Include full name and SSN in search request. Results include last 4 SSN digits, address and name. New cases are in the index 1-2 days after filing date. Both computer and card indexes maintained. 1987 to 8/1992 records indexed manually; records up to 1986 on index cards. Computer records go back to 8/1992. Open records not physically at this court, only electronically. Closed cases held in-house as space permits; sent year end to Fort Worth Records Ctr.

Search Access: Only docket info is available by phone; court will search by debtor's name for records back to 1987. Voice Case Information Service available, call VCIS at 800-886-9008 or 214-753-2128. **Mail:** Search usually completed- 1-2 days. Include SASE for return. **In person:** Self-serve copies $.25 each. **Payment:** Pay by money order, cashier's or personal check. No debtor checks accepted. Payee: Clerk, US Bankruptcy Ct.

E-Services: Document images available back to 2/03. PACER records go back to 1994. New records online after 1 day. ECF at https://ecf.txnb.uscourts.gov. **Opinions Online:** www.txnb.uscourts.gov/opinions/. **Online Note:** Calendars free at www.txnb.uscourts.gov/judges.

Lubbock Division Court Clerk, 1205 Texas Ave, 306 Federal Bldg, Lubbock, TX 79401-4002, 806-472-5000. 8-4PM. www.txnb.uscourts.gov

Counties/Note: Bailey, Borden, Brown, Callahan, Cochran, Cooke, Coleman, Concho, Crockett, Crosby, Dawson, Dickens, Eastland, Fisher, Floyd, Gaines, Garza, Glasscock, Hale, Haskell, Hockley, Howard, Irion, Jones, Kent, Lamb, Lubbock, Lynn, Menard, Mills, Mitchell, Motley, Nolan, Reagan, Runnels, Schleicher, Scurry, Shackelford, Stephens, Sterling, Stonewall, Sutton, Taylor, Terry, Throckmorton, Tom Green, Yoakum. The Lubbock Division also holds records for the San Angelo Div. and the Abilene Div.

Searches/Indexing: Include full name and SSN in search request. Results include last 4 SSN digits, address and name. New cases are in the index immediately after filing date. Records back to 2/2003 maintained on computer. Case files sent to archives 6 months after closed.

Search Access: Only basic case info from 1987 to present available by phone. Voice Case Information Service available, call VCIS at 800-886-9008 or 214-753-2128. **Mail:** Search usually completed- 3 days. Include SASE for return. **In person:** No self-serve copier.

Payment: Pay by Visa/MC (but not from debtor), money order, cashier's check, business check. No personal checks. Payee: Clerk, US Bankruptcy Ct.

E-Services: Document images available back to 2/03. PACER records go back to 1994. New records online immediately. ECF at https://ecf.txnb.uscourts.gov. **Opinions Online:** www.txnb.uscourts.gov/opinions/. **Online Note:** Calendars free at www.txnb.uscourts.gov/judges.

Wichita Falls Division c/o Dallas Division, 1100 Commerce St, Rm 1254, Dallas, TX 75242-1496, 214-753-2000; records- 214-767-0814. Hours-8:30AM-4:30PM. www.txnb.uscourts.gov

Counties/Note: Archer, Baylor, Clay, Cottle, Foard, Hardeman, King, Knox, Montague, Wichita, Wilbarger, Young.

Searches/Indexing: Include full name and SSN in search request. Results include last 4 SSN digits, address and name. New cases are in the index 1-2 days after filing date. Both computer and card indexes maintained. Case files sent to archives 6 months after closed. **Search Access:** Voice Case Information Service available, call VCIS at 800-886-9008 or 214-753-2128. **Mail:** Include SASE for return. **In person:** No self-serve copier.

Payment: Pay by money order, cashier's check. No business/personal checks or credit cards accepted. Payee: Clerk, US Bankruptcy Court.

E-Services: Document images available back to 2/03. PACER records go back to 1994. New records online after 1 day. ECF at https://ecf.txnb.uscourts.gov. **Opinions Online:** www.txnb.uscourts.gov/opinions/. **Online Note:** Calendars free at www.txnb.uscourts.gov/judges.

US District Court Texas Southern District

Brownsville Division Court Clerk, 600 E Harrison St, Rm 101, Brownsville, TX 78520-7114, 956-548-2500; crim dockets- 956-548-2528; Fax- 956-548-2598. Hours - 8AM - 5PM. www.txs.uscourts.gov **Counties/Note:** Cameron, Willacy. Also holds bankruptcy court records. You may search entire Southern District electronically at any of the seven courthouse locations.

Searches/Indexing: May be helpful to include DOB with full name or case number. Results do not include SSN or DOB. Will not fax back documents. New cases are in the index immediately after filing date. Computer index goes back to 1995. District-wide searches available here back to 1979. Files sent to archives after 6 months.

Search Access: Only docket info available by phone. **Mail:** Search usually completed- 1 week. Include SASE for return. **Fax:** Written fax search requests accepted, prepaid. **In person:** 1 public terminal available. No self-serve copier.

Payment: Pay by money order, cashier's or business checks. No personal checks or credit cards. Payee: Clerk, US District Court.

E-Services: PACER records go back to 6/1990. New records online after 1 day. ECF at https://ecf.txsd.uscourts.gov. **Opinions Online:** www.txsd.uscourts.gov/district/opinions/. Selected opinions only. **Online Note:** Search notable cases free at www.txs.uscourts.gov/cgi-bin/notablecases/notablecases.pl. 2 week court calendars of some, judges at www.txsd.uscourts.gov/district/judges/.

Corpus Christi Div. Clerk's Office, 1133 N Shoreline Blvd, #208, Corpus Christi, TX 78401, 361-888-3142. 8:30-4:30. www.txs.uscourts.gov

Counties/Note: Aransas, Bee, Brooks, Duval, Jim Wells, Kenedy, Kleberg, Live Oak, Nueces, San Patricio. Search entire Southern District electronically at any of the seven courthouse locations. Bankruptcy Court co-located in Corpus.

Searches/Indexing: May be helpful to include DOB with full name or case number. Results do not include SSN or DOB. Will not fax back documents. New cases are in the index immediately after filing date. Computer and microfiche indexes maintained. District-wide searches available here back to 1979. Case files sent to archives 6 months after closed.

Search Access: Only docket info available by phone. **Mail:** Search usually completed- 1-2 days. Include SASE for return. **Fax:** Written fax search requests accepted, prepaid. **In person:** 2 public terminals available. No self-serve copier. Request for copies filled as personnel are available.

Payment: Pay by money order, cashier's or business checks. No personal checks or credit cards. Payee: Clerk, US District Court.

E-Services: Document images available. PACER records go back to 6/1990. New records online after 1 day. ECF at https://ecf.txsd.uscourts.gov. **Opinions:** www.txsd.uscourts.gov/district/opinions/. Selected opinions only. **Online Note:** Search notable cases at www.txs.uscourts.gov/cgi-bin/notablecases/notablecases.pl. 2 week court calendars of some, not all judges at www.txsd.uscourts.gov/district/judges/.

Galveston Division Clerk's Office, **Temporarily closed** - See Houston Division, Galveston, TX 77553 (In person: 601 Rosenberg, Rm 411, Temporarily closed - See Houston, Galveston, TX 77550), 713-250-5500 for info; Galveston- 409-766-3530. Hours-8:30AM-5PM. www.txs.uscourts.gov **Counties/Note:** Brazoria, Chambers, Galveston, Matagorda. Also holds bankruptcy court records. You may search entire Southern District electronically at any of 7 courthouse locations.

Searches/Indexing: May be helpful to include DOB with full name or case number. Results do not include SSN or DOB. Will not fax back documents. New cases in the index immediately after filing date. Computer index goes back to 1990. District-wide searches available here back to 1979. Case files sent to archives after 6 months.

Search Access: Only docket info available by phone. **Mail:** Search usually completed- 1-2 days. Include SASE for return. **Fax:** Written fax search requests accepted, prepaid. **In person:** Self-serve copies $.50 each. **Payment:** Pay by money order, cashier's or business checks. No personal checks or credit cards. Payee: Clerk, US District Court.

E-Services: Document images available. PACER records go back to 6/1990. New records online after 1 day. ECF at https://ecf.txsd.uscourts.gov. **Opinions:** www.txsd.uscourts.gov/district/opinions/. Selected opinions only. **Online Note:** Search notable cases free at www.txs.uscourts.gov/cgi-bin/notablecases/notablecases.pl. 2 week court calendars of some, not all judges at www.txsd.uscourts.gov/district/judges/.

Houston Division Court Clerk, PO Box 61010, Houston, TX 77208 (In person: 515 Rusk, Rm 1217, United States Courthouse, Houston, TX 77002), 713-250-5500; records- 713-250-5500; crim dockets- 713-250-5786; civil dockets- 713-250-5786. 8:30AM-5PM. www.txs.uscourts.gov

Counties/Note: Austin, Brazos, Colorado, Fayette, Fort Bend, Grimes, Harris, Madison, Montgomery, San Jacinto, Walker, Waller, Wharton. Criminal docketing for the district is performed in Houston. You may search entire Southern District electronically at any of seven courthouse locations. Bankruptcy Court also co-located in Houston.

Searches/Indexing: May be helpful to include DOB with full name or case number. Results include last 4 SSN digits. Will not fax back documents. New cases are in the index immediately after filing date. Computer, microfiche and card indexes maintained. District-wide searches available here back to 1979. Court personnel will assist searchers. Case files sent to archives 6 months after closed.

Search Access: Only docket info available by phone. **Mail:** Search usually completed- 1-2 days. Court Clerk can recommend an outside vendor to search for you. SASE not required. **Fax:** Written fax search requests accepted, prepaid. **In person:** No self-serve copier available. Court can recommend an outside vendor to make copies.

Payment: Pay by money order, cashier's or business checks. No personal checks or credit cards. Payee: Clerk, US District Court.

E-Services: Document images available. PACER records go back to 6/1990. New records online after 1 day. ECF at https://ecf.txsd.uscourts.gov. **Opinions:** www.txsd.uscourts.gov/district/opinions/. Selected opinions only. **Online Note:** Search notable cases at www.txs.uscourts.gov/cgi-bin/notablecases/notablecases.pl. 2 week court calendars of some, not all judges at www.txsd.uscourts.gov/district/judges/.

Laredo Division Court Clerk, 1300 Victoria St #1131, Laredo, TX 78040, 956-723-3542. Hours-9AM-4PM. www.txs.uscourts.gov

Counties/Note: Jim Hogg, La Salle, McMullen, Webb, Zapata. Also holds bankruptcy court records at Laredo. You may search entire Southern District electronically at any of the seven courthouse locations.

Searches/Indexing: May be helpful to include DOB with full name or case number. Results do not include SSN or DOB. Will not fax back documents. New cases are in the index immediately after filing date. District-wide searches available here back to 1979. Case files sent to archives 6 months after closed.

Search Access: Only docket info available by phone. **Mail:** Search usually completed- 1-2 days. SASE not required. **Fax:** Written fax search requests accepted, prepaid. **In person:** 3 public terminals available. No self-serve copier.

Payment: Pay by money order, cashier's or business checks. No personal checks or credit cards. Payee: Clerk, US District Court.

E-Services: PACER records go back to 6/1990. New records online after 1 day. ECF at https://ecf.txsd.uscourts.gov. **Opinions online:** www.txsd.uscourts.gov/district/opinions/. Selected opinions only. **Online Note:** Search notable cases free at www.txs.uscourts.gov/notablecases/. 2 week court calendars of some, not all judges at www.txsd.uscourts.gov/district/judges/.

McAllen Division Court Clerk, PO Box 5059, McAllen, TX 78501 (In person: Bentsen Tower, Suite 1011, 1701 W Business Hwy 83, McAllen), 956-618-8065. 8AM-5PM. www.txs.uscourts.gov

Counties/Note: Hidalgo, Starr. Also holds bankruptcy court records. You may search entire Southern District electronically at any of the seven courthouse locations. Court in operation 12 years.

Searches/Indexing: May be helpful to include DOB with full name or case number. Results do not include SSN or DOB. Will not fax back documents. New cases are in the index immediately after filing date. Both computer and card indexes maintained; computer goes back to 1988. District-wide searches available here back to 1979. Case files sent to archives after 6 months.

Search Access: Only docket info available by phone. **Mail:** Search usually completed- 1 week. Include SASE for return. **Fax:** Written fax search requests accepted, prepaid. **In person:** No self-serve copier.

Payment: Pay by money order, cashier's or business checks. No personal checks or credit cards. Payee: Clerk, US District Court.

E-Services: Document images available. PACER records go back to 6/1990. New records online after 1 day. ECF at https://ecf.txsd.uscourts.gov. **Opinions:** www.txsd.uscourts.gov/district/opinions/. Selected opinions only. **Online Note:** Search notable cases free at www.txs.uscourts.gov/cgi-bin/notablecases/notablecases.pl. 2 week court calendars of some, not all judges at www.txsd.uscourts.gov/district/judges/.

Victoria Division Court Clerk, PO Box 1638, Victoria, TX 77902 (In person: 312 S Main, Rm 406, Martin Luther King, Jr. Federal Building, Victoria), 361-788-5000. Hours-8:30AM-4:30PM. www.txs.uscourts.gov

Counties/Note: Calhoun, De Witt, Goliad, Jackson, Lavaca, Refugio, Victoria. Also holds bankruptcy court records at Victoria. You may search entire Southern District electronically at any of the seven courthouse locations.

Searches/Indexing: May be helpful to include DOB with full name or case number. Results do not include SSN or DOB. Will not fax back documents. New cases are in the index immediately after filing date. Both computer and card indexes maintained; computer goes back to 1996. District-wide searches available here back to 1979. Case files sent to archives after 6 months.

Search Access: Only docket info available by phone. **Mail:** Search usually completed- 2-3 days. Include SASE for return. **Fax:** Written fax search requests accepted, prepaid. **In person:** Self-serve copies $.50 each.

Payment: Pay by money order, cashier's or business checks. No personal checks or credit cards. Payee: Clerk, US District Court.

E-Services: Document images available. PACER records go back to 6/1990. New records online after 1 day. ECF at https://ecf.txsd.uscourts.gov. **Opinions:** www.txsd.uscourts.gov/district/opinions/. Selected opinions only. **Online Note:** Search notable cases free at www.txs.uscourts.gov/cgi-bin/notablecases/notablecases.pl. 2 week court calendars of some, not all judges at www.txsd.uscourts.gov/district/judges/.

US Bankruptcy Court Texas Southern District

Corpus Christi Division Court Clerk, 1133 N Shoreline Blvd, 2nd Fl, Corpus Christi, TX 78401, 361-888-3484. Hours-8:30AM-4:30PM. www.txsd.uscourts.gov

Counties/Note: Aransas, Bee, Brooks, Cameron*, Duval, Hidalgo**, Jim Wells, Kenedy, Kleberg, Live Oak, Nueces, San Patricio, Starr**, Willacy*. Files from Brownsville, Corpus Christi, and McAllen maintained at Corpus Christi. Houston office also holds old Victoria Div. records. Open case records for counties with a single asterisk (*) at Galveston Div. (see US Dist Court). Open case records for counties with a double asterisk (**) at McAllen Div. (see US Dist Court). Search entire Southern Dist. electronically at any of the 7 courthouse locations.

Searches/Indexing: Search request requires name only. Results include last 4 SSN digits only. Will not fax back documents. New cases are in the index 1-2 days after filing date. Computer and microfiche indexes maintained. Case files sent to archives 6 months after closed.

Search Access: Voice Case Information Service available, call VCIS at 800-745-4459 or 713-250-5049. **Mail:** Search usually completed- 1-2 days. Include SASE for return. **In person:** 3 public terminals available back to 1990. Self-serve copies $.25 each; off computer- $.10 each.

Payment: Pay by Visa/MC, money order, cashier's or personal check. Payee: Clerk, Bankruptcy Ct.

E-Services: Document images available. PACER records go back to 6/1991. New records online after 1 day. ECF at https://ecf.txsb.uscourts.gov. **Opinions:** www.txsd.uscourts.gov/bankruptcy/opinions/. Search opinions by year back to 2001 free. **Online Note:** 2 weeks of judge hearing calendars free at www.txsd.uscourts.gov/bankruptcy/judges/.

Houston Division Court Clerk, PO Box 61010, Houston, TX 77008 (In person: 515 Rusk Ave, Rm 1217, Houston), 713-250-5500. Hours-8AM-5PM. www.txs.uscourts.gov

Counties/Note: Austin, Brazoria**, Brazos, Calhoun***, Chambers**, Colorado, De Witt***, Fayette, Fort Bend, Galveston**, Goliad***, Grimes, Harris, Jackson***, Jim Hogg*, La Salle*, Lavaca***, Madison, Matagorda**, McMullen*, Montgomery, Refugio*** San Jacinto, Victoria***,Walker, Waller, Wharton, Webb* Zapata*. Open case records for counties with single asterisk (*) at Laredo Div (see US Dist Court). Open case records for counties with double asterisk (**) at Galveston Div. (see US Dist Court). Open case records for counties with 3 asterisks (***) at Victoria Div (see US Dist Court). Search all Southern Dist. electronically at any of 7 courthouses.

Searches/Indexing: Search request requires name only. Results include last 4 SSN digits only. Will not fax back documents. New cases are in the index same day after filing date. Earliest case files from 1987. Files sent to archives after 6 months.

Search Access: Only docket info available by phone. Voice Case Information Service available, call VCIS at 800-745-4459 or 713-250-5049. **Mail:** Search usually completed- 2-3 weeks. Include SASE for return. **Fax:** Fax search and case file requests accepted. **In person:** 3 public terminals available back to 1990. No self-serve copier available; on-site copy service.

Payment: Pay by Visa/MC, money order, cashier's or personal check. Payee: Clerk, US District Court.

E-Services: Document images available. PACER records go back to 6/1991. New records online after 1 day. ECF at https://ecf.txsb.uscourts.gov. **Opinions:** www.txsd.uscourts.gov/bankruptcy/opinions/. 2 weeks of judge hearing calendars free at www.txsd.uscourts.gov/bankruptcy/judges/.

US District Court Texas Western District

Austin Div. Court Clerk, 200 W 8th St, Rm 130, Austin, TX 78701, 512-916-5896; Fax- 512-916-5894. 8AM-5PM. www.txwd.uscourts.gov

Counties/Note: Bastrop, Blanco, Burleson, Burnet, Caldwell, Gillespie, Hays, Kimble, Lampasas, Lee, Llano, McCulloch, Mason, San Saba, Travis, Washington, Williamson.

Searches/Indexing: Include SSN and DOB in search request. Results do not include SSN or DOB. Will fax back documents $.50 per page. New cases are in the index 1-2 days after filing date. Computer and microfiche indexes maintained. Case files kept a minimum 2 years before sending to archives.

Search Access: Only docket info is available by phone. **Mail:** Search usually completed- 7-10 days. Include SASE for return. **Fax:** Written fax requests accepted, prepaid. **In person:** 1 public terminal available. Self-serve copies $.25 each.

Payment: Pay by money order, cashier's or personal check. No credit cards accepted. Payee: Clerk, US District Court.

E-Services: PACER and ECF online at www.txwd.uscourts.gov/ecf/. PACER records go back to 1994. New records online after 1 day. ECF at https://ecf.txwd.uscourts.gov. **Opinions Online:** www.nysd.uscourts.gov/courtweb/PubMain.htm. Also, view notable cases free at www.txwd.uscourts.gov/opinions/notable.asp. **Online Note:** Access judges' calendars free at www.txwd.uscourts.gov/calendar/default.asp.

Del Rio Div. Court Clerk, 111 E Broadway, Rm L100, Del Rio, TX 78840, 830-703-2054; Fax- 830-703-2071. Hours - 8AM-N, 1-5PM. www.txwd.uscourts.gov

Counties/Note: Edwards, Kinney, Maverick, Terrell, Uvalde, Val Verde, Zavala.

Searches/Indexing: Include full name in search request. Results do not include SSN or DOB. Will not fax back documents. New cases are in the index 1-2 days after filing date. Case files sent to archives 2 years after closed.

Search Access: Only docket info is available by phone. **Mail:** Search usually completed- 4-5 days. Include SASE for return. **Fax:** Written fax requests accepted, prepaid. **In person:** 1 public terminal available. No self-serve copier.

Payment: Pay by money order, cashier's or personal check. No credit cards accepted. Payee: Clerk, US District Court.

E-Services: PACER and ECF online at www.txwd.uscourts.gov/ecf/. PACER records go back to 1994. New records online after 1 day. ECF at https://ecf.txwd.uscourts.gov. **Opinions Online:** www.nysd.uscourts.gov/courtweb/PubMain.htm. Also, view notable cases free at www.txwd.uscourts.gov/opinions/notable.asp. **Online Note:** Access judges' calendars free at www.txwd.uscourts.gov/calendar/default.asp.

El Paso Division US District Clerk Office, 511 E San Antonio, Rm 219, El Paso, TX 79901, 915-534-6725; records- 915-534-6722. Hours-8AM-5PM MST. www.txwd.uscourts.gov

Counties/Note: El Paso, Hudspeth.

Searches/Indexing: Include full name in search request; also helpful- DOB. Results do not include SSN or DOB. Will not fax back documents. New cases are in the index 1-2 days after filing date. Computer, microfiche and card indexes maintained. Closed cases archived after 3 years.

Search Access: Only docket info is available by phone. **Mail:** Search usually completed- 7-10 days. Include SASE for return. **Fax:** Written fax requests accepted, prepaid. **In person:** 1 public terminal available. Self-serve copies $.25 each.

Payment: Pay by money order, cashier's or personal check. No credit cards accepted. Payee: Clerk, US District Court.

E-Services: PACER and ECF online at www.txwd.uscourts.gov/ecf/. PACER records go back to 1994. New records online after 1 day. ECF at https://ecf.txwd.uscourts.gov. **Opinions Online:** www.nysd.uscourts.gov/courtweb/PubMain.htm. Also, view notable cases free at www.txwd.uscourts.gov/opinions/notable.asp. **Online Note:** Access judges' calendars free at www.txwd.uscourts.gov/calendar/default.asp.

Midland-Odessa Div. Clerk, US District Court, 200 E Wall St, Rm 107, Midland, TX 79701, 432-686-4001. Hours-8AM-5PM. www.txwd.uscourts.gov **Counties:** Andrews, Crane, Ector, Martin, Midland, Upton.

Searches/Indexing: Include SSN and DOB in search request. Results do not include SSN or DOB. Will not fax back documents. New cases are in the index immediately after filing date. Computer index goes back to 1985. Case files sent to archives 5 years after closed. **Search Access:** Most info is released via phone. **Mail:** Search usually completed- 1-2 days. Include SASE for return. **Fax:** Written fax requests accepted, prepaid. **In person:** 1 public terminal available. Self-serve copies $.25; bring your own change.

Payment: Pay by money order, cashier's or personal check. No credit cards accepted. Payee: Clerk, US District Court.

E-Services: PACER and ECF online at www.txwd.uscourts.gov/ecf/. PACER records go back to 1994. New records online after 1 day. ECF at https://ecf.txwd.uscourts.gov. **Opinions Online:** www.nysd.uscourts.gov/courtweb/PubMain.htm. Also, view notable cases free at www.txwd.uscourts.gov/opinions/notable.asp. **Online Note:** Access judges' calendars free at www.txwd.uscourts.gov/calendar/default.asp.

Pecos Division Court Clerk, 410 S Cedar St, US Courthouse, Pecos, TX 79772, 432-445-4228; Fax- 432-445-9859. Hours- 8AM-N, 1-5PM. www.txwd.uscourts.gov

Counties/Note: Brewster, Culberson, Jeff Davis, Loving, Pecos, Presidio, Reeves, Ward, Winkler. Pecos Division also has a court in Alpine, 2450 State Hwy. 118, 432-837-7323.

Searches/Indexing: Include SSN and DOB in search request. Results do not include SSN or DOB. Will not fax back documents. New cases are in the index immediately after filing date. Computer and card indexes maintained; computer index back to 1991. Case files kept a minimum 2 years before sending to archives.

Search Access: Only docket info is available by phone. **Mail:** Search usually completed- 2-3 days. Include SASE for return. **Fax:** Written fax requests accepted, prepaid. **In person:** 1 public terminal available. Self-serve copies $.25 each.

Payment: Pay by money order, cashier's or personal check. No credit cards accepted. No debtor checks accepted. Payee: Clerk, District Ct.

E-Services: PACER and ECF online at www.txwd.uscourts.gov/ecf/. PACER records go back to 1994. New records online after 1 day. ECF at https://ecf.txwd.uscourts.gov. **Opinions Online:** www.nysd.uscourts.gov/courtweb/PubMain.htm. Also, view notable cases free at www.txwd.uscourts.gov/opinions/notable.asp. **Online Note:** Access judges' calendars free at www.txwd.uscourts.gov/calendar/default.asp.

San Antonio Division Clerk, US District Court, 655 E Durango Blvd, Suite G-65, San Antonio, TX 78206, 210-472-6550. 8AM-5PM. www.txwd.uscourts.gov

Counties/Note: Atascosa, Bandera, Bexar, Comal, Dimmit, Frio, Gonzales, Guadalupe, Karnes, Kendall, Kerr, Medina, Real, Wilson.

Searches/Indexing: Include SSN and DOB in search request. Results do not include SSN or DOB. Will not fax back documents. New cases are in the index 1-2 days after filing date. Computer and microfiche indexes maintained. Case files kept a minimum 2 years before sending to archives.

Search Access: Only docket info is available by phone. **Mail:** Search usually completed- soon as work load permits. Include SASE for return. **Fax:** Written fax requests accepted, prepaid. **In person:** 1 public terminal available. Self-serve copies $.25 each. **Payment:** Pay by money order, cashier's or personal check. No credit cards accepted. Payee: Clerk, US District Court.

E-Services: PACER and ECF online at www.txwd.uscourts.gov/ecf/. PACER records go back to 1994. New records online after 1 day. ECF at https://ecf.txwd.uscourts.gov. **Opinions Online:** www.nysd.uscourts.gov/courtweb/PubMain.htm. Also, view notable cases free at www.txwd.uscourts.gov/opinions/notable.asp. **Online Note:** Access judges' calendars free at www.txwd.uscourts.gov/calendar/default.asp.

Waco Division Clerk of Court, 800 Franklin, Rm 380, Waco, TX 76701, 254-750-1501. Hours-8AM-5PM. www.txwd.uscourts.gov

Counties/Note: Bell, Bosque, Coryell, Falls, Freestone, Hamilton, Hill, Leon, Limestone, McLennan, Milam, Robertson, Somervell. Waco Div also has offices in Ft Hood 254-287-3487, and in Temple 254-778-7204.

Searches/Indexing: Include SSN and DOB in search request. Results do not include SSN or DOB. Will not fax back documents. New cases are in the index 1-2 days after filing date. A card index is maintained. Case files kept a minimum 2 years before sending to archives. **Search Access:** Only docket info is available by phone. **Mail:** Search usually completed- 1-2 days. Include SASE for return. **Fax:** Written fax requests accepted, prepaid. **In person:** 1 public terminal available. Self-serve copies $.25 each. **Payment:** Pay by money order, cashier's or personal check. No credit cards accepted. Payee: Clerk, US District Ct.

E-Services: PACER and ECF online at www.txwd.uscourts.gov/ecf/. PACER records go back to 1994. New records online after 1 day. ECF at https://ecf.txwd.uscourts.gov. **Opinions Online:** www.nysd.uscourts.gov/courtweb/PubMain.htm. Also, view notable cases free at www.txwd.uscourts.gov/opinions/notable.asp. **Online Note:** Access judges' calendars free at www.txwd.uscourts.gov/calendar/default.asp.

US Bankruptcy Court Texas Western District

Austin Division Court Clerk, Homer Thornberry Judicial Bldg, 903 San Jacinto, # 322, Austin, TX 78701, 512-916-5237; records- 888-436-7477; Fax- 512-916-5278. Hours-8AM-4PM. www.txwb.uscourts.gov

Counties/Note: Bastrop, Blanco, Burleson, Burnet, Caldwell, Gillespie, Hays, Kimble, Lampasas, Lee, Llano, Mason, McCulloch, San Saba, Travis, Washington, Williamson.

Searches/Indexing: Include tax ID number, SSN, and full name and aliases for court to identify results. Results do not include SSN or DOB; clerk will verify if your SSN is correct. Will not fax back documents. New cases are in the index 24 hours after filing date. Computer and microfiche indexes maintained. Case files sent to archives 6-8 months after closed.

Search Access: Only docket info is available by phone. Voice Case Information Service available, call VCIS at 888-436-7477 or 210-472-4023. **Mail:** Search usually completed- 3 days. Include SASE. **In person:** 2 public terminals available.

Payment: Pay by Visa/MC, debit cards, money order, cashier's check. No debtor checks/credit cards accepted. Payee: US Bankruptcy Court.

E-Services: PACER records go back to 5/1987. New records online after 1 day. ECF at https://ecf.txwb.uscourts.gov. **Opinions Online:** www.txwb.uscourts.gov/opinions/judges.php. **Note:** Calendars free at www.txwb.uscourts.gov/information/calendars/calendar_index.htm.

El Paso Division Court Clerk, PO Box 971040, El Paso, TX 79925 (In person: US Bankruptcy Courthouse, 8515 Lockheed, El Paso), 915-779-7362; Fax- 915-779-5693. Hours-8AM-4PM MST. www.txwb.uscourts.gov

Counties: El Paso.

Searches/Indexing: Include SSN and full name and aliases for court to identify results. Results do not include SSN or DOB; clerk will verify if your SSN is correct. Will not fax back documents. New cases are in the index 24 hours after filing date. Computer index back to 1987 maintained; index to 1987 and microfiche up to 1980. Case files sent to archives 6-8 months after closed.

Search Access: Only docket info is available by phone. Voice Case Information Service available, call VCIS at 888-436-7477 or 210-472-4023. **Mail:** Search usually completed- 10 days. Include SASE for return. **In person:** 2 public terminals available. Self-serve copies $.25 each.

Payment: Pay by Visa/MC, debit cards, money order, cashier's check. No debtor checks/credit cards accepted. Payee: Clerk, US Bankruptcy Ct.

E-Services: PACER records go back to 5/1987. New records online after 1 day. ECF at https://ecf.txwb.uscourts.gov. **Opinions Online:** www.txwb.uscourts.gov/opinions/judges.php. Calendars free at www.txwb.uscourts.gov/information/calendars/calendar_index.htm.

Midland/Odessa Div. Court Clerk, US Post Office Annex, Rm P-163, 100 E Wall St, Midland, TX 79701, 432-683-1650; Fax- 432-683-1643. Hours-8AM-N, 1-4PM. www.txwb.uscourts.gov

Counties/Note: Andrews, Brewster, Crane, Culberson, Ector, Hudspeth, Jeff Davis, Loving, Martin, Midland, Pecos, Presidio, Reeves, Upton, Ward, Winkler. Records from the Pecos Division, which closed, were transferred to Midland/Odessa.

Searches/Indexing: Include SSN and full name and aliases for court to identify results. Results do not include SSN or DOB; clerk will verify if your SSN is correct. Will not fax back documents. New cases are in the index immediately after filing date. Computer and card indexes maintained. Court can return documents via email if requested. Case files sent to archives 6-8 months after closed.

Search Access: Only docket info is available by phone. Voice Case Information Service available, call VCIS at 888-436-7477 or 210-472-4023. **Mail:** Search usually completed- same day if possible. Include SASE for return. **In person:** 2 public terminals available. Self-serve copies $.25 each; bring your own change or else.

Payment: Pay by Visa/MC, debit cards, money order, cashier's check. No debtor checks/credit cards accepted. Payee: Clerk, US Bankruptcy Ct.

E-Services: PACER records go back to 5/1987. New records online after 1 day. ECF at https://ecf.txwb.uscourts.gov. **Opinions Online:** www.txwb.uscourts.gov/opinions/judges.php. Calendars free at www.txwb.uscourts.gov/information/calendars/calendar_index.htm.

San Antonio Division Court Clerk, PO Box 1439, San Antonio, TX 78295 (In person: 615 E Houston St, Rm 137, San Antonio, TX 78205), 210-472-6720; Fax- 210-472-5916. 8AM-4PM. www.txwb.uscourts.gov

Counties/Note: Atascosa, Bandera, Bexar, Comal, Dimmit, Edwards, Frio, Gonzales, Guadalupe, Karnes, Kendall, Kerr, Kinney, Maverick, Medina, Real, Terrell, Uvalde, Val Verde, Wilson, Zavala.

Searches/Indexing: Include SSN and full name and aliases for court to identify results. Results do not include SSN or DOB; clerk will verify if your SSN is correct. Will not fax back documents. New cases are in the index 24 hours after filing date. District-wide searches available here back 10 years. Case files sent to archives after 6-8 months.

Search Access: Only docket info is available by phone. Voice Case Information Service available, call VCIS at 888-436-7477 or 210-472-4023. **Mail:** Search usually completed- 1 week. Include SASE for return. **In person:** 2 public terminals available. Self-serve copies $.35 each. A copy service is on site.

Payment: Pay by Visa/MC, debit cards, money order, cashier's check. No debtor checks/credit cards accepted. Payee: Clerk, US Bankruptcy Ct.

E-Services: PACER records go back to 5/1987. New records online after 1 day. ECF at https://ecf.txwb.uscourts.gov. **Opinions Online:** www.nysd.uscourts.gov/courtweb/PubMain.htm. **Online Note:** Access judges' calendars free at www.txwd.uscourts.gov/calendar/default.asp.

Waco Div. Court Clerk, 800 Franklin Ave #140, Waco, TX 76701, 254-750-1513; Fax- 254-750-1529. Hours-8AM-4PM. www.txwb.uscourts.gov

Counties/Note: Bell, Bosque, Coryell, Falls, Freestone, Hamilton, Hill, Leon, Limestone, McLennan, Milam, Robertson, Somervell.

Searches/Indexing: Include SSN and full name and aliases for court to identify results. Results do not include SSN or DOB; clerk will verify if your SSN is correct. Will not fax back documents. New cases are in the index same day after filing date. Case files sent to archives 6-8 months after closed.

Search Access: Only docket info is available by phone. Voice Case Information Service available, call VCIS at 888-436-7477 or 210-472-4023. **Mail:** Search usually completed- 3 days. Include SASE for return. **In person:** 2 public terminals available. Computer generated copies $.10 each.

Payment: Pay by Visa/MC, debit cards, money order, cashier's check. No debtor checks/credit cards accepted. Payee: Clerk, US Bankruptcy Ct.

E-Services: PACER records go back to 5/1987. New records online after 1 day. ECF at https://ecf.txwb.uscourts.gov. **Opinions Online:** www.txwb.uscourts.gov/opinions/judges.php. Calendars free at www.txwb.uscourts.gov/information/calendars/calendar_index.htm.

US District Court Texas Western District

Austin Division Court Clerk, Rm 130, 200 W 8th St, Austin, TX 78701, 512-916-5896; Fax-512-916-5894. 8-5PM. www.txwd.uscourts.gov

Counties: Bastrop, Blanco, Burleson, Burnet, Caldwell, Gillespie, Hays, Kimble, Lampasas, Lee, Llano, McCulloch, Mason, San Saba, Travis, Washington, Williamson.

Searches & Indexing: Include SSN and DOB in search request. Results do not include SSN or DOB. 1 public terminal available. Will not fax back documents. Computer and microfiche indexes maintained. Case files kept a minimum 2 years before sending to archives. **Search Access:** Only docket information is available by phone. **Mail:** Search usually completed- 7-10 days. Include SASE for return. **In Person:** Fee charged if court performs your in person search. Self-serve copies $.25 each.

Payment: Pay by money order, cashier's or personal check. No credit cards accepted. Payee: Clerk, US District Court. Prepayment required.

E-Services: PACER and ECF online at www.txwd.uscourts.gov/ecf/. PACER records go back to 1994. **Opinions Online:** www.nysd.uscourts.gov/courtweb/public.htm. **Online Note:** Access judges' calendars free at www.txwd.uscourts.gov/calendar/default.asp.

Del Rio Div. Court Clerk, 111 E Broadway, Rm 100, Del Rio, TX 78840, 830-703-2054; Fax-830-703-2071. 8-5PM. www.txwd.uscourts.gov **Counties:** Edwards, Kinney, Maverick, Terrell, Uvalde, Val Verde, Zavala.

Searches & Indexing: Include full name and/or case number in search request. Results do not include SSN or DOB. 1 public terminal available. Will fax back documents no add'l fee; hardcopies also mailed. Case files sent to archives 2 years after case closed. **Search Access:** Only docket information is available by phone. **Mail:** Search usually completed- 4-5 days. Include SASE for return. **Fax:** search requests accepted with prepayment. **In Person:** Fee charged if court performs your in person search. No self-serve copier. **Payment:** Pay by money order, cashier's or personal check. No credit cards accepted. Payee: Clerk, US District Court. Prepayment required.

E-Services: PACER and ECF online at www.txwd.uscourts.gov/ecf/. PACER records go back to 1994. **Opinions Online:** www.nysd.uscourts.gov/courtweb/public.htm. **Online Note:** Access judges' calendars free at www.txwd.uscourts.gov/calendar/default.asp.

El Paso Div. US District Clerk Office, 511 E San Antonio, Rm 219, El Paso, TX 79901, 915-534-6725; records- 915-534-6722; records room fax- x243, x244; fax record requests to-x243, or x244. Hours- 8AM-5PM. www.txwd.uscourts.gov

Counties: El Paso.

Searches & Indexing: Include full name in search request; also helpful- DOB. Results do not include SSN or DOB. 1 public terminal available. Will not fax back documents. Computer, microfiche and card indexes maintained. Closed cases are archived after 3 years. **Search Access:** Only docket information is available by phone. **Mail:** Search usually completed- 7-10 days. Include SASE for return. **Fax:** Fax search and document requests accepted. **In Person:** Fee charged if court performs your in person search. Self-serve $.25.

Payment: Pay by money order, cashier's or personal check. No credit cards accepted. Payee: Clerk, US District Court. Prepayment required.

E-Services: PACER and ECF online at www.txwd.uscourts.gov/ecf/. PACER records go back to 1994. **Opinions Online:** www.nysd.uscourts.gov/courtweb/public.htm. **Online Note:** Access judges' calendars free at www.txwd.uscourts.gov/calendar/default.asp.

Midland Div. Clerk, US District Court, 200 E Wall St, Rm 107, Midland, TX 79701, 432-686-4001. 8AM-5PM. www.txwd.uscourts.gov

Counties: Andrews, Crane, Ector, Martin, Midland, Upton.

Searches & Indexing: Include SSN and DOB in search request. Results do not include SSN or DOB. 1 public terminal available. Will not fax back documents. Computer index goes back to 1985. Case files sent to archives after 5 years.

Search Access: Most information is released via phone. **Mail:** Search usually completed- 1-2 days. Include SASE for return. **In Person:** Fee charged if court performs your in person search. Self-serve copies $.25 each; bring your own change or else.

Payment: Pay by money order, cashier's or personal check. No credit cards accepted. Payee: Clerk, US District Court. Prepayment required.

E-Services: PACER and ECF online at www.txwd.uscourts.gov/ecf/. PACER records go back to 1994. **Opinions Online:** www.nysd.uscourts.gov/courtweb/public.htm. **Online Note:** Access judges' calendars free at www.txwd.uscourts.gov/calendar/default.asp.

Pecos Div. Court Clerk, 410 S Cedar St, US Courthouse, Pecos, TX 79772, 432-445-4228; Fax- 432-445-9859. Hours - 8AM - 5PM. www.txwd.uscourts.gov **Counties:** Brewster, Culberson, Hudspeth, Jeff Davis, Loving, Pecos, Presidio, Reeves, Ward, Winkler.

Searches & Indexing: Include SSN and DOB in search request. Results do not include SSN or DOB. 1 public terminal available. Will not fax back documents. Computer and card indexes maintained; computer index back to 1991. Files kept minimum 2 years before sending to archives.

Search Access: Only docket information is available by phone. **Mail:** Search usually completed- 2-3 days. Include SASE. **Fax:** search requests accepted with prepayment. **In Person:** Fee charged if court performs your in person search. Self-serve copies $.25 each.

Payment: Pay by money order, cashier's or personal check. No credit cards accepted. No debtor's checks accepted. Payee: Clerk, US District Court. Prepayment required.

E-Services: PACER and ECF online at www.txwd.uscourts.gov/ecf/. PACER records go back to 1994. **Opinions Online:** www.nysd.uscourts.gov/courtweb/public.htm. **Online Note:** Access judges' calendars free at www.txwd.uscourts.gov/calendar/default.asp.

San Antonio Div. Clerk, US District Court, 655 E Durango Blvd, Suite G-65, San Antonio, TX 78206, 210-472-6550; Fax- 210-472-6573. Hours- 8AM-5PM. www.txwd.uscourts.gov

Counties: Atascosa, Bandera, Bexar, Comal, Dimmit, Frio, Gonzales, Guadalupe, Karnes, Kendall, Kerr, Medina, Real, Wilson.

Searches & Indexing: Include SSN and DOB in search request. Results do not include SSN or DOB. 1 public terminal available. Will not fax back documents. Computer and microfiche indexes maintained. Case files kept a minimum 2 years before sending to archives. **Search Access:** Only docket information is available by phone. **Mail:** Search usually completed as soon as work load permits. Include SASE. **In Person:** Self-serve copies $.25 each. **Payment:** Pay by money order, cashier's or personal check. No credit cards accepted. Payee: Clerk, US District Court.

E-Services: PACER and ECF online at www.txwd.uscourts.gov/ecf/. PACER records go back to 1994. **Opinions Online:** www.nysd.uscourts.gov/courtweb/public.htm. **Online Note:** Access judges' calendars free at www.txwd.uscourts.gov/calendar/default.asp.

Waco Division Clerk of Court, 800 Franklin, Rm 380, Waco, TX 76701, 254-750-1501. Hours- 8AM-5PM. www.txwd.uscourts.gov

Counties: Bell, Bosque, Coryell, Falls, Freestone, Hamilton, Hill, Leon, Limestone, McLennan, Milam, Robertson, Somervell.

Searches & Indexing: Include SSN and DOB in search request. Results do not include SSN or DOB. 1 public terminal available. Will not fax back documents. A card index is maintained. Files kept minimum 2 years before sending to archives.

Search Access: Only docket information is available by phone. **Mail:** Search usually completed- 1-2 days. Include SASE for return. **In Person:** Fee charged if court performs your in person search. Self-serve copies $.25 each.

Payment: Pay by money order, cashier's or personal check. No credit cards accepted. Payee: Clerk, US District Court. Prepayment required.

E-Services: PACER and ECF online at www.txwd.uscourts.gov/ecf/. PACER records go back to 1994. **Opinions Online:** www.nysd.uscourts.gov/courtweb/public.htm. **Online Note:** Access judges' calendars free at www.txwd.uscourts.gov/calendar/default.asp.

US Bankruptcy Court Texas Western District

Austin Division Court Clerk, Homer Thornberry Judicial Bldg, 903 San Jacinto, # 322, Austin, TX 78701, 512-916-5237; records- 888-436-7477; Fax- 512-916-5278. Hours- 8AM-4PM. www.txwb.uscourts.gov

Counties: Bastrop, Blanco, Burleson, Burnet, Caldwell, Gillespie, Hays, Kimble, Lampasas, Lee, Llano, Mason, McCulloch, San Saba, Travis, Washington, Williamson.

Searches & Indexing: Include tax ID number, SSN, and full name and aliases for court to identify results. Results do not include SSN or DOB; clerk will verify if your SSN is correct. 2 public terminals available. Will not fax back documents. Computer and microfiche indexes maintained. Case files sent to archives 6-8 months after closed. **Search Access:** Only docket information is available by phone. Voice Case Information Service available, call VCIS at 888-436-7477 or 210-472-4023. **Mail:** Search usually completed- 3 days. Include SASE for return.

Payment: Pay by Visa/MC (in person only), money order, cashier's or personal check. No debtor's checks accepted. Payee: US Bankruptcy Court. Prepayment required.

E-Services: PACER records go back to 5/1987. ECF at https://ecf.txwb.uscourts.gov. **Opinions:** www.txwb.uscourts.gov/opinions/judges.php. **Note:** Calendars free at www.txwb.uscourts.gov/information/calendars/calendar_index.htm.

El Paso Division Court Clerk, PO Box 971040, El Paso, TX 79925 (In person: 8515 Lockheed, El Paso), 915-779-7362; Fax- 915-779-5693. Hours- 8AM-4PM. www.txwb.uscourts.gov

Counties: El Paso.

Searches & Indexing: Include SSN and full name and aliases for court to identify results. Results do not include SSN or DOB; clerk will verify if your SSN is correct. 2 public terminals available. Computer index back to 1987 maintained; index to 1987 and microfiche up to 1980. Case files sent to archives 6-8 months after closed.

Search Access: Only docket information is available by phone. Voice Case Information Service available, call VCIS at 888-436-7477 or 210-472-4023. **Mail:** Search usually completed- 10 days. Include SASE for return. **In Person:** Fee charged if court performs your in person search. Self-serve copies $.25 each.

Payment: Pay by credit cards, money order, cashier check only. No debtor's checks accepted. Payee: Clerk, US Bankruptcy Court.

E-Services: PACER records go back to 5/1987. ECF at https://ecf.txwb.uscourts.gov. **Opinions:** www.txwb.uscourts.gov/opinions/judges.php. Calendars free at www.txwb.uscourts.gov/information/calendars/calendar_index.htm.

Midland/Odessa Division Court Clerk, 100 E Wall St, US Post Office Annex, Rm P-163, Midland, TX 79701, 432-683-1650. Hours- 8AM-N, 1-4PM. www.txwb.uscourts.gov

Counties: Andrews, Brewster, Crane, Culberson, Ector, Hudspeth, Jeff Davis, Loving, Martin, Midland, Pecos, Presidio, Reeves, Upton, Ward, Winkler. Records from the Pecos Division, which closed, were transferred here.

Searches & Indexing: Include SSN and full name and aliases for court to identify results. Results do not include DOB but may include last 4 digits of SSN; clerk will verify if your SSN is correct. 2 public terminals. Will fax back documents. Computer and card indexes maintained. Court can return documents via email if requested. Case files sent to archives 6-8 months after closed. **Search Access:** Only docket information is available by phone. Voice Case Information Service available, call VCIS at 888-436-7477 or 210-472-4023. **Mail:** Search usually completed-same day if possible. Include SASE for return. **In Person:** Fee charged if court performs your in person search. Self-serve copies $.25 each; bring your own change or else. **Payment:** Pay by credit cards, money order, cashier's or personal check. No debtor's checks accepted. Payee: Clerk, US Bankruptcy Court. Prepayment required.

E-Services: PACER records go back to 5/1987. ECF at https://ecf.txwb.uscourts.gov. **Opinions:** www.txwb.uscourts.gov/opinions/judges.php. **Note:** Calendars free at www.txwb.uscourts.gov/information/calendars/calendar_index.htm.

San Antonio Division Court Clerk, PO Box 1439, San Antonio, TX 78295 (In person: 615 E Houston St, Rm 147, San Antonio, TX 78205), 210-472-6720; Fax- 210-472-5916. Hours- 8AM-4PM. www.txwb.uscourts.gov

Counties: Atascosa, Bandera, Bexar, Comal, Dimmit, Edwards, Frio, Gonzales, Guadalupe, Karnes, Kendall, Kerr, Kinney, Maverick, Medina, Real, Terrell, Uvalde, Val Verde, Wilson, Zavala.

Searches & Indexing: Include SSN and full name and aliases for court to identify results. Results do not include SSN or DOB; clerk will verify if your SSN is correct. 2 public terminals. District-wide searches available here back 10 years. Case files sent to archives 6-8 months after closed. **Search Access:** Only docket information is available by phone. Voice Case Information Service available, call VCIS at 888-436-7477 or 210-472-4023. **Mail:** Search usually completed- 1 week. Include SASE for return. **In Person:** Fee charged if court performs your search. Self-serve copies $.35 each. A copy service is on site. **Payment:** Pay by Visa/MC/AmEx, money order, cashier's check. No debtor's checks accepted. Payee: Clerk, US Bankruptcy Court.

E-Services: PACER records go back to 5/1987. ECF at https://ecf.txwb.uscourts.gov. **Opinions:** www.nysd.uscourts.gov/courtweb/public.htm. **Online Note:** Access judges' calendars free at www.txwd.uscourts.gov/calendar/default.asp.

Waco Division Court Clerk, 800 Franklin Ave #140, Waco, TX 76701, 254-750-1513; Fax- 254-750-1529. 8AM-4PM. www.txwb.uscourts.gov

Counties: Bell, Bosque, Coryell, Falls, Freestone, Hamilton, Hill, Leon, Limestone, McLennan, Milam, Robertson, Somervell.

Searches & Indexing: Include SSN and full name and aliases for court to identify results. Results do not include SSN or DOB; clerk will verify if your SSN is correct. 2 public terminals available. Case files sent to archives 6-8 months after closed. **Search Access:** Only docket information is available by phone. Voice Case Information Service available, call VCIS at 888-436-7477 or 210-472-4023. **Mail:** Search usually completed- 3 days. Include SASE for return. **In Person:** Fee charged if court performs your in person search. Computer generated copies $.10 each. **Payment:** Pay by credit cards, money order, cashier's or personal check. No debtor's checks accepted. Payee: Clerk, US Bankruptcy Court..

E-Services: PACER records go back to 5/1987. ECF at https://ecf.txwb.uscourts.gov. **Opinions:** www.txwb.uscourts.gov/opinions/judges.php. **Note:** Calendars free at www.txwb.uscourts.gov/information/calendars/calendar_index.htm

Texas County Courts

Court	Jurisdiction	No. of Courts	How Organized
District Courts*	General	449	449 Districts
County Constitutional Courts*	Limited	254	254 Counties
County Courts at Law Courts*	Limited	227	84 Counties
Justice of the Peace Courts	By Precinct	821	
Municipal Courts	Municipal	916	
Probate Courts*	Probate	18	10 Counties

* Profiled in this Sourcebook.

Court	CIVIL Tort	Contract	Real Estate	Min. Claim	Max. Claim	Small Claims	Estate	Eviction	Domestic Relations
District Courts*	X	X	X	$200	No Max				X
County Constitu-tional*	X	X	X	$200	$10,000		X		X
County At Law*	X	X	X	$200	$100,000		X		X
Justice Courts	X	X		$0	$10,000	$5000		X	
Municipal Courts									
Probate Courts*							X		

Court	CRIMINAL Felony	Misdemeanor	DWI/DUI	Preliminary Hearing	Juvenile
District Courts*	X				X
County Courts*		X	X		X
Justice of the Peace Courts		X		X	
Municipal Courts		X			

Administration

Office of Court Administration, PO Box 12066, Austin, TX, 78711; 512-463-1625, Fax: 512-463-1648. All but two Texas Counties are in Central Time Zone. The exceptions are El Paso and Hudspeth Counties, in Mountain Time Zone. www.courts.state.tx.us

Court Structure

The legal court structure for Texas is explained extensively in the "Texas Judicial Annual Report." Generally, Texas District Courts have general civil jurisdiction and exclusive felony jurisdiction, along with typical variations such as contested probate and divorce. There can be multiple districts and multiple Disctrict Courts in one courthouse, with one searchable database.

The County Court structure consists of two forms of courts - "Constitutional" and "At Law." The Constitional upper civil claim limit is $10,000 while the At Law upper limit is $100,000 and some jurisdictions are higher. For civil matters up to $10,000, we recommend searchers start at the Constitutional County Court as they, generally, offer a shorter waiting time for cases in urban areas. District Courts handle felonies. County Courts have orginal jurisdcition for misdemeanors with fines greater than $500 or jail sentences. They also handle general civil cases. Justice courts handle misdemeanors where the fine is less than $500 and no jail sentences. In some counties the District Court or County Court handles evictions. In 69 counties, District Court and County Court are combined.

Probate is handled in Probate Court in the ten largest counties and in District Courts or County Courts At Law elsewhere. The County Clerk is responsible for the records in every county.

Online Access

A number of local county courts offer online access to their records but there is no statewide system of local level court records. 45+ counties use www.idocket.com. Case records of the Supreme Court can be searched at www.supreme.courts.state.tx.us. Appellate Court case information is searchable free at the website of each Appellate Court, reached online from www.courts.state.tx.us/courts/coa.asp. Court of Criminal Appeals opinions are found at www.cca.courts.state.tx.us.

Searching Tips, Fees, and Other Guidelines

Often, a record search is automatically combined for two courts, for example a District Court with a County Court, or both County Courts. Most District Courts charge $5.00 to do a name search and $1.00 for a copy. Less than half the courts have public access terminals to view docket indices. Prepayment is almost always required.

Anderson County

Court PO Box 1159, Palestine, TX 75802-1159; 903-723-7412; fax: 903-723-7491; 8AM-N, 1-5PM (CST). ***Felony, Civil, Family.*** www.co.anderson.tx.us
The court also holds family Cases.
Civil Records: Access: Phone, mail, in person. Both court and visitors may perform in person searches. Search fee: $5.00 per name. Required to search: name, years to search. Civil cases indexed by defendant, plaintiff; index on computer from 1984; prior on card index back to 1946. Mail turnaround time 2-4 days. Civil PAT goes back to 1984. PAT civil results show middle initial.
Criminal Records: Access: Mail, in person. Both court and visitors may perform in person searches. Search fee: $5.00 per name. Required to search: name, years to search, DOB, SSN. Criminal records computerized from 1984; prior on index. Mail turnaround time 2-4 days. Criminal PAT goes back to same as civil. PAT criminal results show middle initial.
General Information: No juvenile or adoption records released. Will not fax documents. Court makes copy: $1.00 per page. Cert fee: $1.00 per page. Payee: Anderson County District Clerk. Personal checks accepted; credit cards are not. Mail requests: SASE required.

County Court 500 N Church, Palestine, TX 75801; 903-723-7432; probate phone: 903-723-7437; fax: 903-723-4625; 8AM-5PM (CST). ***Misdemeanor, Civil, Probate.***
Probate fax is same as main fax number.
Civil Records: Access: Mail, in person. Both court and visitors may perform in person searches. Search fee: $5.00 per name. Required to search: name, years to search. Civil cases indexed by defendant, plaintiff; index on computer from 1982, land cases from 1983. Mail turnaround time 1 week. Civil PAT goes back to 1982. PAT civil results show middle initial.
Criminal Records: Access: Mail, in person. Both court and visitors may perform in person searches. Search fee: $5.00 per name. Required to search: name, years to search, DOB. Criminal records computerized from 1969. Mail turnaround time 1 week. Criminal PAT goes back to 1969. PAT results show middle initial, DOB. Terminal results include SSN.
General Information: Will not fax documents. Court makes copy: $1.00 per page. Self serve: same. Cert fee: $5.00. Payee: County Clerk. Personal checks accepted; credit cards are not. Mail requests: SASE required.

Andrews County

District Court PO Box 328, Andrews, TX 79714; 432-524-1417; 8AM-5PM (CST). ***Felony, Civil.***
Civil Records: Access: Mail, in person. Only the court performs in person searches; visitors may not. Search fee: $5.00 per name. Required to search: name, years to search. Civil cases indexed by defendant, plaintiff. Civil records computerized since 1975. Mail turnaround time 1 day.
Criminal Records: Access: Mail, in person. Only the court performs in person searches; visitors may not. Search fee: $5.00 per name. Required to search: name, years to search, DOB; also helpful: SSN. Criminal records computerized back to 1910. Mail turnaround time 1 day.
General Information: No juvenile, mental, sealed, terminations or adoption records released. Will not fax documents. Court makes copy: $1.00 first page, $.50 each add'l. Cert fee: $2.00. Payee: District Clerk. Personal checks accepted; credit cards are not. Mail requests: SASE required.

County Court PO Box 727, Andrews, TX 79714; 432-524-1426; fax: 432-524-1464; 8AM-5PM (CST). ***Misdemeanor, Civil, Probate.***
Probate in a separate index at this same address
Civil Records: Access: Phone, mail, in person. Both court and visitors may perform in person searches. Search fee: $10.00 per name. Required to search: name, years to search. Civil cases indexed by defendant, plaintiff; index on computer since 1980; prior records in manual index. Mail turnaround 1 day.
Criminal Records: Access: Phone, mail, in person. Both court and visitors may perform in person searches. Search fee: $10.00 per name. Required to search: name, years to search, DOB or SSN; also helpful: sex. Criminal records on computer since 1985; prior records in manual index. Mail turnaround time 1 day.
General Information: No juvenile, mental, sealed, or adoption records released. Will not fax documents. Court makes copy: $1.00 per page. Cert fee: $5.00 per document. Payee: F. Wm. Hoermann County Clerk. Personal checks accepted if in state. No credit cards accepted.

Angelina County

District Court PO Box 908, Lufkin, TX 75902; 936-634-4312; fax: 936-634-5915; 8AM-5PM (CST). ***Felony, Civil.*** www.angelinacounty.net
Civil Records: Access: Mail, in person. Both court and visitors may perform in person searches. Search fee: $5.00 per name. Required to search: name, years to search. Civil cases indexed by defendant, plaintiff; index on computer from 1996, on index books from 1800s. Note: Must state whether search is on plaintiff or defendant. Mail turnaround time 2-3 days. Civil PAT goes back to 1986. PAT results show middle initial, DOB. Terminal results also show SSNs.
Criminal Records: Access: Mail, in person. Both court and visitors may perform in person searches. Search fee: $5.00 per name. Required to search: name, years to search, DOB; also helpful: SSN. Criminal records computerized from 1984, on index books from 1800s. Mail turnaround time 2-3 days. Criminal PAT goes back to 1986. Terminal results include SSN.
General Information: No juvenile, mental, sealed, or adoption records released. Will fax documents $5.00 fee. Court makes copy: $1.00 per page. Cert fee: $2.00 per document. Payee: District Clerk. No personal checks. No credit cards accepted. Mail requests: SASE required.

County Court PO Box 908, 215 E Lufkin Ave, Lufkin, TX 75902; 936-634-8339; fax: 936-634-8460; 8AM-5PM ***Misdemeanor, Civil, Probate.*** www.angelinacounty.net
Civil Records: Access: Mail, in person, online. Both court and visitors may perform in person searches. Search fee: $5.00 per name plus 10-year period. Required to search: name, years to search. Civil cases indexed by defendant, plaintiff. Civil records go back to 1893; computerized records go back to 8/1995. Mail turnaround time 1-2 days. Online access to dockets is through www.idocket.com; registration and password required. Civil cases from 11/30/96; probate from 1/31/95. One free name search permitted per day, otherwise subscription required.
Criminal Records: Access: Mail, in person, online. Both court and visitors may perform in person searches. Search fee: $5.00 per name plus 10-year period. Will search back to 1984. Required to search: name, years to search; also helpful: DOB. Criminal records go back to 1893; computerized records go back to 1983. Mail turnaround time 1-2 days. Online access to misdemeanor dockets is through www.idocket.com; registration and password required. Misdemeanor cases from 12/31/83. One free name search permitted per day, otherwise subscription required.
General Information: No mental or sealed records released. These records are not filed in our office. Will not fax documents. Court makes copy: $1.00 per page. Cert fee: $5.00. Payee: County Clerk. Business checks accepted. No credit cards accepted. Mail requests: SASE required.

Aransas County

District Court 301 N Live Oak, Rockport, TX 78382; 361-790-0128; fax: 361-790-5211; 8AM-5PM (CST). ***Felony, Civil.***
Civil Records: Access: Mail, in person. Both court and visitors may perform in person searches. Search fee: $5.00 per name. Required to search: name, years to search. Civil cases indexed by defendant, plaintiff. Civil records in index books from 1800s, computerized since 1999. Mail turnaround time 1-2 days. Civil PAT goes back to 2000. PAT results show middle initial, DOB.
Criminal Records: Access: Mail, in person. Both court and visitors may perform in person searches. Search fee: $5.00 per name. Required to search: name, years to search. Criminal docket on books from 1800s, computerized since 1999. Mail turnaround time 1-2 days. Criminal PAT goes back to 1965. PAT results show name only.
General Information: Online identifiers in results same as on public terminal. No juvenile, mental, sealed, or adoption records released. Will not fax documents. Court makes copy: $1.00 per page. Self serve: same. Cert fee: $1.00 per document. Payee: District Clerk. Personal checks accepted. Discover CC accepted. Mail requests: SASE required.

County Court 301 N Live Oak, Rockport, TX 78382; 361-790-0122; fax: 361-790-0119; 8AM-4:30PM (CST). ***Misdemeanor, Civil, Probate.***
Civil Records: Access: Mail, in person. Both court and visitors may perform in person searches. Search fee: $10.00 per name. Required to search: name, years to search. Civil cases indexed by defendant, plaintiff. Civil records in index books from 1947, computerized records go back to 1998. Mail turnaround time 2 days. Civil PAT goes back to 1995. PAT results show name only.
Criminal Records: Access: Mail, in person. Both court and visitors may perform in person searches. Search fee: $10.00 per name. Required to search: name, years to search, DOB. Criminal docket on books from 1947; computerized records go back to 1995. Mail turnaround time 2 days. Criminal PAT goes back to 1992. PAT criminal results show middle initial.
General Information: No mental or sealed records released; we do not have juvenile or adoption records in our office. Will fax documents to local or toll free line. Court makes copy: $1.00 per page. Cert fee: $5.00 per doc. Payee: County Clerk. Personal checks accepted; credit cards are not. Mail requests: SASE required.

Archer County

District Court PO Box 815, Archer City, TX 76351; 940-574-4615; fax: 940-574-2432; civil fax: same; 8:30AM-5PM (CST). ***Felony, Civil.***
Civil Records: Access: Mail, in person. Both court and visitors may perform in person searches. Search fee: $5.00 per name. Fee is per index searched. Required to search: name, years to search. Civil cases indexed by defendant, plaintiff. Civil records in index books from 1900s. Mail turnaround time 2-3 days.
Criminal Records: Access: Mail, in person. Both court and visitors may perform in person searches. Search fee: $5.00 per name. Fee is per index searched. Required to search: name, years to search. Criminal docket on books from 1900s. Mail turnaround time 2-3 days.
General Information: No juvenile, mental, sealed, or adoption records released. Will fax documents after search fee is paid. Court makes copy: $1.00 per page. Self serve: same. Cert fee: $1.00 per doc. Payee: District Clerk. Personal checks accepted; credit cards are not. Mail requests: SASE helpful.

County Court PO Box 427, Archer City, TX 76351; 940-574-4302; criminal fax: 940-574-2876; civil fax: same; 8:30AM-5PM (CST). ***Misdemeanor, Civil, Probate.*** Probate is a separate index at this same address. Probate fax same as main fax number.

Civil Records: Access: Phone, mail, in person. Both court and visitors may perform in person searches. Search fee: $5.00 per name. Fee is per index searched. Required to search: name, years to search. Civil cases indexed by defendant, plaintiff. Civil records in index books from 1900s. Mail turnaround time 1 day.

Criminal Records: Access: Phone, mail, in person. Both court and visitors may perform in person searches. Search fee: $5.00 per name. Fee is per index searched. Required to search: name, years to search. Criminal docket on books from 1900s. Mail turnaround time 1 day.

General Information: No juvenile, mental, sealed, or adoption records released. Will fax documents $2.00 per page. Court makes copy: $1.00 per page. Self serve: same. Cert fee: $5.00 per doc. Payee: County Clerk. Personal checks accepted; credit cards are not. Mail requests: SASE required.

Armstrong County

District & County Court PO Box 309, 100 Trice St., Claude, TX 79019; 806-226-2081; fax: 806-226-5301; 8AM-N, 1-5PM (CST). ***Felony, Misdemeanor, Civil, Probate.***

Probate is a separate index at this same address. Probate fax is same as main fax number.

Civil Records: Access: Mail, in person. Both court and visitors may perform in person searches. Search fee: $5.00 per name. Required to search: name, years to search. Civil cases indexed by defendant, plaintiff. Civil records in index books from 1800s. Mail turnaround time 1-2 days.

Criminal Records: Access: Mail, in person. Both court and visitors may perform in person searches. Search fee: $5.00 per name. Required to search: name, years to search. Criminal docket on books from 1800s; computerized back to 1992. Mail turnaround time 1-2 days. Public use terminal has crim records back to 1912.

General Information: No juvenile, mental, sealed, or adoption records released. Will fax documents $1.00 per fax. Court makes copy: $1.00 per page. Self serve: same. Cert fee: $5.00 per cert. Payee: County Clerk. Personal checks accepted; credit cards are not. Mail requests: SASE required.

Atascosa County

District Court Courthouse Circle, #4-B, Jourdanton, TX 78026; 830-769-3011; fax: 830-769-1332; 8AM-N, 4PM (CST). ***Felony, Civil.***

Civil Records: Access: Mail, in person. Both court and visitors may perform in person searches. Search fee: $5.00 per name. Required to search: name, years to search; also helpful: address. Civil cases indexed by defendant, plaintiff. Civil records in index books from 1857.

Criminal Records: Access: Mail, in person. Both court and visitors may perform in person searches. Search fee: $5.00 per name. Required to search: name, years to search; also helpful: DOB, SSN. Criminal docket on books from 1857.

General Information: No juvenile, mental, sealed, or adoption records released. Fee to fax out file $2.00 per page. Court makes copy: $1.00 per page. Self serve: same. Cert fee: $1.00. Payee: District Clerk. Personal checks accepted; credit cards are not. Mail requests: SASE required.

County Court #1 Courthouse Circle, #102, Jourdanton, TX 78026; 830-767-2511; fax: 830-769-2349; 8-4:30PM ***Misdemeanor, Civil, Probate.***

Civil Records: Access: Mail, in person. Both court and visitors may perform in person searches. No search fee. Required to search: name, years to search. Civil cases indexed by defendant, plaintiff. Civil records in index books from 1900s; on computer back to 2000. Mail turnaround time 1 week Civil PAT goes back to 2000.

Criminal Records: Access: In person only. Visitors must perform in person searches themselves. Required to search: name, years to search. Criminal docket on books from 1900s; on computer back to 2000. Criminal PAT goes back to 2000.

General Information: No juvenile, mental, sealed, or adoption records released. Will fax documents $1.50 per page. Court makes copy: $1.00 per page. Cert fee: $5.00. Payee: County Clerk. Personal checks accepted; credit cards are not. Mail requests: SASE required for civil.

Austin County

District Court 1 E Main, Bellville, TX 77418-1598; 979-865-5911 x257; fax: 979-865-8350; 8AM-N, 1-5PM (CST). ***Felony, Civil.***
www.austincounty.com/dclerk.html

155 District website is www.cvtv.net/~tx155district/. Daily dockets available.

Civil Records: Access: Mail, in person. Both court and visitors may perform in person searches. Search fee: $5.00 per name. Required to search: name, years to search. Civil cases indexed by defendant, plaintiff. Civil records in index books from 1843; on computer back to 1995. Mail turnaround time 1 day. Civil PAT goes back to 1995. Terminal results also show SSNs.

Criminal Records: Access: Mail, in person. Both court and visitors may perform in person searches. Search fee: $5.00 per name. Required to search: name, years to search; also helpful: DOB, SSN. Criminal docket on books from 1843; on computer back to 1996. Mail turnaround 1 day. Criminal PAT goes back to 1996. Terminal results include SSN.

General Information: No juvenile, mental, sealed, or adoption records released. Fee to fax out file $2.00 each. Court makes copy: $1.00 per page. Self serve: same. Cert fee: Included in copy fee; will certify only if document is complete. Payee: District Clerk. Personal checks accepted; credit cards are not. Mail requests: SASE required.

County Court at Law 1 E Main, Bellville, TX 77418; 979-865-5911; criminal phone: x233; civil phone: x234; probate phone: x233; fax: 979-865-0336; 8AM-5PM (CST). ***Misdemeanor, Civil, Probate.*** Probate fax is same as main fax number.

Civil Records: Access: Mail, in person. Both court and visitors may perform in person searches. Search fee: $5.00 per name. Required to search: name, years to search. Civil cases indexed by defendant, plaintiff; index on computer from 1983, index books from 1843. Mail turnaround time 2-3 days. Civil PAT goes back to 1983. PAT results show name only.

Criminal Records: Access: Mail, in person. Both court and visitors may perform in person searches. Search fee: $5.00 per name. Required to search: name, years to search, DOB; also helpful: SSN. Criminal records computerized from 1/85; index books from 1876. Mail turnaround time 2-3 days. Criminal PAT goes back to 1985. PAT results show middle initial, DOB. PAT results may include SSN and DL number.

General Information: No juvenile, mental, sealed, or adoption records released. Will fax documents $2.00 per page. Court makes copy: $1.00 per page. Self serve: same. Cert fee: $5.00 per document. Payee: Carrie Gregor, County Clerk. Personal checks accepted; credit cards are not.

Bailey County

District Court 300 S 1st St, Muleshoe, TX 79347; 806-272-3165; criminal fax: 806-272-3124; civil fax: same; 8AM-5PM (CST). ***Felony, Civil.***

Civil Records: Access: Phone, mail, fax, in person, online. Both court and visitors may perform in person searches. Search fee: $5.00 per name. Required to search: name, years to search. Civil cases indexed by defendant, plaintiff. Civil records in index books, archived from 1925, computerized back to 1995. Mail turnaround time 1 day. Online access is through www.idocket.com; registration and password required. Records go back to 12/31/1995. One free name search permitted per day, otherwise subscription required.

Criminal Records: Access: Phone, mail, in person, online. Both court and visitors may perform in person searches. Search fee: $5.00 per name. Required to search: name, years to search. Criminal index in books, archived from 1925, computerized back to 1995. Mail turnaround time 1 day. Online access is through www.idocket.com; registration and password required. Records go back to 12/31/1995. One free name search permitted per day, otherwise subscription required.

General Information: No juvenile, mental, sealed, or adoption records released. Will fax documents $1.00 per page. Court makes copy: $1.00 per page. Self serve: same. Cert fee: $1.00 per page. Payee: District Clerk. Personal checks accepted; credit cards are not. Mail requests: SASE required.

County Court 300 S 1st St, Muleshoe, TX 79347; 806-272-3044; criminal fax: 806-272-3538; civil fax: same; 8:30AM-N, 1-5PM (CST). ***Misdemeanor, Civil, Probate*** Probate has a separate index. Probate fax is same as main fax number.

Civil Records: Access: Mail, in person, online. Both court and visitors may perform in person searches. Search fee: $10.00 per name. Required to search: name, years to search. Civil cases indexed by defendant, plaintiff. Civil records in index books, archived from 1925. Mail turnaround time 10 days. Online access is through www.idocket.com; registration and password required. Civil records go back to 12/31/1995 and 13/31/96 for probate. One free name search permitted per day, otherwise subscription required.

Criminal Records: Access: Mail, in person, online. Both court and visitors may perform in person searches. Search fee: $10.00 per name. Required to search: name, years to search. Criminal index in books, archived from 1925. Mail turnaround time 10 days. Online access is through www.idocket.com; registration and password required. Records go back to 12/31/1996. One free name search permitted per day, otherwise subscription required.

General Information: No juvenile, mental, sealed, or adoption records released. Will fax documents. Court makes copy: $1.00 per page. Self serve: same. Cert fee: $5.00 per document. Payee: County Clerk. Personal checks accepted; credit cards are not. Mail requests: SASE required.

Bandera County

District Court PO Box 2688, 500 Main St, Bandera, TX 78003; 830-796-4606; fax: 830-796-8499; 7:30-4:30PM (CST). ***Felony, Civil, Probate.***
www.banderacounty.org/departments/district_clerk.htm

Civil Records: Access: Phone, fax, mail, in person, online. Both court and visitors may perform in person searches. Search fee: $5.00 per name. Required to search: name, years to search; also helpful: address. Civil cases indexed by defendant, plaintiff; index on computer back to 1988, index books from 1857. Mail turnaround time 2 days. Civil PAT goes back to 1990. PAT civil results show middle initial. Civil case information is free at www.idocket.com. Registration and password required. Records go back to 12/31/1990. One free name search permitted per day, otherwise subscription required.

Criminal Records: Access: Fax, mail, in person, online. Both court and visitors may perform in person searches. Search fee: $5.00 per name. Required to search: name, years to search, signed release; also helpful: address, DOB, SSN. Criminal records computerized from 1988, index books from 1857. Mail turnaround time 2 days. Criminal PAT goes back to same as civil. PAT criminal results show middle initial. Felony record index access is through www.idocket.com; registration and password required; records go back to 12/31/1990. One free name search permitted per day, otherwise subscription required. Online results show middle initial, DOB.

General Information: Online identifiers in results same as on public terminal. No juvenile, mental or sealed records released. Fee to fax out file $2.00 1st page, $1.00 each add'l. Court makes copy: $1.00 per page certified; non-certified is $1.00 1st pg, $.25 each add'l pg per doc. Cert fee: $5.00. Payee: Bandera District Clerk. Personal checks and major credit cards accepted. Mail requests: SASE required.

County Court PO Box 823, 500 Main St, Bandera, TX 78003; 830-796-3332; fax: 830-796-8323; 8AM-N, 1-4:30PM (CST). ***Misdemeanor, Civil, Eviction, Probate.***
www.banderacounty.org/departments/county_clerk.htm

Civil Records: Access: Fax, mail, in person, online. Both court and visitors may perform in person searches. Search fee: $5.00 per name. Required to search: name, years to search; also helpful: address. Civil cases indexed by defendant, plaintiff; index on computer back to 1994, index books back to 1857. Mail turnaround time 2 days. Public use terminal available, records go back to 1994. Online access to dockets is through www.idocket.com; registration and password required. Civil cases from 1/1994; probate from 1/1991. One free name search permitted per day, otherwise subscription required.

Criminal Records: Access: Fax, mail, in person, online. Both court and visitors may perform in person searches. Search fee: $5.00 per name. Required to search: name, years to search, signed release; also helpful: address, DOB, SSN. Criminal records computerized from 1990, index books back to 1857. Mail turnaround time 2 days. Public use terminal available, crim records go back to 1990. Online access to dockets is through www.idocket.com; registration and password required. Misdemeanor cases from 1/1992. One free name search permitted per day, otherwise subscription required. Online results show name, DOB.

General Information: No juvenile, mental or sealed records released. Fee to fax out file $2.00 1st page, $1.00 each add'l. Court makes copy: $1.00 per page. Cert fee: $5.00 per document. Payee: Bandera County Clerk. Personal checks, major credit cards accepted. Mail requests: SASE required.

Bastrop County

District Court PO Box 770, Bastrop, TX 78602; 512-332-7244; fax: 512-332-7249; 8AM-5PM (CST). ***Felony, Civil.*** www.co.bastrop.tx.us/ips/cms/districtcourt/districtClerk.html

Civil Records: Access: Mail, in person, fax. Both court and visitors may perform in person searches. Search fee: $5.00 per name. Required to search: name, years to search. Civil cases indexed by defendant, plaintiff; index on microfilm from 1986, archived from early 1800s. Mail turnaround time 1 day. Civil PAT goes back to 1995.

Criminal Records: Access: Mail, in person, fax. Both court and visitors may perform in person searches. Search fee: $5.00 per name. Required to search: name, years to search, signed release. Criminal records on computer since 1989; prior on microfilm from 1986, archived from early 1800s. Mail turnaround 1 day. Criminal PAT goes back to 1989.

General Information: No juvenile, mental, sealed, or adoption records released. Court makes copy: $.50 per page. Self serve: same. Cert fee: $1.00 per page. Payee: District Clerk. Personal checks and major credit cards accepted. Mail requests: SASE required.

County Court PO Box 577, Bastrop, TX 78602; 512-332-7234; fax: 512-332-7241; 8AM-5:PM (CST). ***Misdemeanor, Probate.***

Criminal Records: Access: Mail, in person. Both court and visitors may perform in person searches. Search fee: $5.00 per name. Required to search: name, years to search, DOB, SSN. Criminal records on computer since 1986, prior on index books. Mail turnaround time 1-2 days. Public use terminal has crim records back to 1986. .PAT results show name, DOB.

General Information: No juvenile, mental, sealed, or adoption records released. Fee to fax out file $5.00. Court makes copy: $1.00 per page. Cert fee: $5.00. Payee: Bastrop County Clerk. Personal checks accepted, include DL number and DOB on back. Credit cards accepted; $3.00 convenience fee will be added. Mail requests: SASE required.

Baylor County

District & County Court 101 S Washington St, #C, Seymour, TX 76380-2566; 940-889-3322; fax: 940-889-4300; 8:30AM-5PM (CST). ***Felony, Misdemeanor, Civil, Probate.***

Civil Records: Access: Phone, mail, in person. Both court and visitors may perform in person searches. Search fee: $10.00 per name. Required to search: name, years to search. Civil cases indexed by defendant, plaintiff. Civil records in books from 1900s. Mail turnaround time 1-2 days.

Criminal Records: Access: Phone, mail, in person. Both court and visitors may perform in person searches. Search fee: $10.00 per name. Required to search: name, years to search. Criminal records in books from 1900s. Mail turnaround time 1-2 days.

General Information: No juvenile, mental, sealed, or adoption records released. Will not fax documents. Court makes copy: $1.00 per page. Cert fee: $3.00 felony, $6.00 misdemeanor County Court certification. Payee: Baylor County Clerk. Personal checks accepted; credit cards are not. Mail requests: SASE required.

Bee County

District Court PO Box 666, 105 Corpus Christi, Beeville, TX 78104-0666; 361-362-3242; fax: 361-362-3282; 8AM-5PM (CST). ***Felony, Civil.*** www.co.bee.tx.us/ips/cms/districtcourt/

Civil Records: Access: Mail, in person, online. Both court and visitors may perform in person searches. Search fee: $5.00 per name. Required to search: name, years to search. Civil cases indexed by defendant, plaintiff. Civil index on docket books from 1856, computerized since 2000. Mail turnaround time 1-3 days. Civil PAT goes back to 2000. Online access is at www.idocket.com; registration and password required. A fee service; only one free name search per day. Records may go back to 12/31/1987.

Criminal Records: Access: Mail, in person, online. Both court and visitors may perform in person searches. Search fee: $5.00 per name. Required to search: name, years to search, signed release. Criminal records indexed in books from 1856, computerized since 2000. Mail turnaround time 1-3 days. Criminal PAT goes back to same as civil. Felony case record access at www.idocket.com; registration and password required. A fee service; only one free name search a day. Records may go back to 12/31/1994.

General Information: No juvenile, mental, sealed, or adoption records released. Will fax documents. Court makes copy: $1.00 per page. Cert fee: $5.00. Payee: District Clerk. Personal checks & Visa/MC accepted. Mail requests: SASE required.

County Court 105 W Corpus Christi St, Rm 108, Beeville, TX 78102; 361-362-3245; fax: 361-362-3247; 8AM-N, 1-5PM (CST). ***Misdemeanor, Civil, Probate.*** Probate fax is same as main fax number.

Civil Records: Access: Mail, in person. Both court and visitors may perform in person searches. Search fee: $5.00 per name. Required to search: name, years to search. Civil cases indexed by defendant, plaintiff. Civil index on docket books from 1900. Mail turnaround time 10 days.

Criminal Records: Access: Mail, in person. Both court and visitors may perform in person searches. Search fee: $6.00 per name. Required to search: name, years to search, DOB; also helpful: SSN. Criminal records indexed in books from 1900. Mail turnaround time 10 days.

General Information: Fee to fax out file $2.00 per page. Court makes copy: $1.00 per page. Cert fee: $2.00 per page includes copy fee. Add $5.00 for cert. Payee: County Clerk. Personal checks accepted; credit cards are not. Mail requests: SASE required.

Bell County

District Court PO Box 909, 1201 Huey Rd, Belton, TX 76513; 254-933-5197; criminal phone: 254-933-5957; civil phone: 254-933-5195; fax: 254-933-5199; 8AM-5PM (CST). ***Felony, Civil.*** www.bellcountytx.com/districtclerk/index.htm

Civil Records: Access: Mail, in person. Both court and visitors may perform in person searches. Search fee: $5.00 per name. Required to search: name, years to search. Civil cases indexed by defendant, plaintiff; index on computer back to 1987, alpha index from 1982, chrono from 1800. Mail turnaround time 1-2 days. Civil PAT goes back to 1987. PAT results show middle initial, DOB.

Criminal Records: Access: Mail, in person. Both court and visitors may perform in person searches. Search fee: $5.00 per name. Required to search: name, years to search, DOB; also helpful, SSN, signed release, cause number. Criminal records computerized from 1987, alpha index from 1982, chrono from 1800. Mail turnaround time 1-2 days. Criminal PAT goes back to same as civil. PAT results show middle initial, DOB.

General Information: No juvenile, mental, sealed, or adoption records released. Will fax documents. Court makes copy: $.50 per page. Self serve: same. Cert fee: $1.00 per page. Payee: District Clerk, Bell County. No personal checks accepted. Major credit cards accepted. Mail requests: SASE required.

County Court Bell County Clerk's Office, PO Box 480, Belton, TX 76513; 254-933-5160; criminal phone: 254-933-5170; civil phone: 254-933-5174; probate phone: 254-993-5167; fax: 254-933-5176; 8AM-5PM (CST). ***Misdemeanor, Civil, Probate.*** www.co.bell.tx.us/countyclerk/index.htm

Civil Records: Access: Mail, in person. Both court and visitors may perform in person searches. Search fee: $5.00 per name. Required to search: name, years to search. Civil cases indexed by defendant, plaintiff; index on computer back to 9/1989. Mail turnaround time 5 days. Civil PAT goes back to 1989.

Criminal Records: Access: Mail, in person. Both court and visitors may perform in person searches. Search fee: $5.00 per name. Required to search: name, years to search, DOB, SSN. Criminal records computerized from 1984. Note: In person searching closed for lunch hour. Mail turnaround time 5 days. Criminal PAT goes back to 1986. PAT results show middle initial, DOB, SSN.

General Information: No juvenile, mental, sealed, or adoption records released. Will not fax documents. Court makes copy: $1.00 per page. Self serve: same. Cert fee: $1.00. Payee: County Clerk. Local checks accepted only. No credit cards accepted.

Bexar County

District Court - Central Records 100 Dolorosa, County Courthouse, Chief Court Clerk/Records, San Antonio, TX 78205; 210-335-2113; criminal phone: 210-335-2591; civil phone: 210-335-2661; criminal fax: 210-335-3424; civil fax: 210-335-0536; 8AM-5PM (CST). ***Felony, Civil.*** www.bexar.org/dclerk/

Civil Records: Access: Mail, fax, online, in person. Both court and visitors may perform in person searches. Search fee: $5.00 per name. Required to search: name, years to search. Civil cases indexed by defendant, plaintiff; index on computer from 1982-present, chrono index from 1909. Note: For fax requests, call court clerk to request form, or find form on website, then submit form with payment with Discover Card. Mail turnaround time up to 10 days. Civil PAT goes back to 1982. Access to the remote online system back to 1980 requires $100 setup fee, plus a $25 monthly fee, plus inquiry fees. Call BCIS for info at 210-335-0212. Also, search civil litigants free at www.co.bexar.tx.us/webapps/html/dklitinq01.asp.

Criminal Records: Access: Mail, fax, online, in person. Both court and visitors may perform in person searches. Search fee: $5.00 per name. Required to search: name, years to search, signed release, DOB; also helpful- SSN, DR number. Criminal records computerized from 1974, chrono index from 1909. Note: For fax requests, call criminal department clerk to request form or find it online, then submit form with payment with Discover Card. Mail turnaround time up to 10 days. Criminal PAT goes back to 1974. Access to the remote online system back to 1980 requires $100 setup fee, plus a $25 monthly fee, plus inquiry fees. Call BCIS for info at 210-335-0212.

General Information: No juvenile, mental, sealed, or adoption records released. Will not fax documents. Court makes copy: $.75 per page. Self serve: same. Cert fee: $1.00 per page. Cert fee includes copy fee. Payee: District Clerk. Only cashiers checks, money orders accepted. Discover cards accepted. Mail requests: SASE required.

County Court - Civil Central Filing Department 100 Dolorosa, San Antonio, TX 78205-3083; 210-335-2231; fax: 210-335-2097; 8AM-5PM (CST). ***Civil.***

There are twelve hearing locations in this county where open cases are held. All closed cases are forwarded here.

Civil Records: Access: Mail, in person. Both court and visitors may perform in person searches. Search fee: $5.00 per name. Fee is for 10 year search. Required to search: name, years to search. Civil cases indexed by defendant, plaintiff; index on computer go back 10 years, index books prior. Open and closed records maintained. Mail turnaround time 5-7 days. Public use terminal has civil records back to 1980. PAT civil results show middle initial.

General Information: No mental, sealed records released. Will not fax documents. Court makes copy: $1.00 per page. Cert fee: $5.00. Payee: County Clerk. Personal checks accepted; credit cards are not. Mail requests: SASE required.

County Court - Criminal 100 Dolorosa, Rm 104, San Antonio, TX 78205-3083; 210-335-2238; fax: 210-335-3938; 8-5PM (CST). ***Misdemeanor.*** www.bexar.org/judges/html/countycourts.asp

Criminal Records: Access: Mail, online, in person. Both court and visitors may perform in person searches. Search fee: $5.00 per name. Fee is per 10 year period. $1.00 for each add'l year. Required to search: name, years to search, DOB, signed release; also helpful: SSN. Criminal records on computer since 1983, alpha index since 1983, on card index from 1909, records go back to 1899. Note: This court requires an $11.00 search and cert fee for a background check with a certified letter. Mail turnaround time 2-3 days. Public use terminal has crim records back to 1983. Access to the criminal online system requires $100 setup fee, plus a $25 monthly fee, plus inquiry fees. Call Roxanne Arellano at 210-335-0212 for more information.

General Information: No sealed records released. Will fax documents $1.00 per page. Court makes copy: $1.00 per page. Cert fee: $5.00 per document. Payee: County Clerk. Personal checks accepted; credit cards are not.

Probate Courts #1 and #2 100 Dolorosa St, Rm 204, San Antonio, TX 78205; 210-335-2546; probate phone: 210-335-2241- Admin; fax: 210-335-2029; 8AM-5PM (CST). ***Probate.*** www.co.bexar.tx.us/pcourt/probatecourts.htm

Blanco County

County Court PO Box 65, Johnson City, TX 78636; 830-868-7357; fax: 830-868-4158; 8AM-4:30PM (CST). ***Misdemeanor, Civil, Probate.*** Probate is separate index at this same address.

Civil Records: Access: Mail, in person. Both court and visitors may perform in person searches. Search fee: $5.00 per name. Required to search: name, years to search. Civil cases indexed by defendant, plaintiff; index on computer from 1994, index books back to 1876. Mail turnaround time 2 days. Civil PAT goes back to 1994. PAT results show name only.

Criminal Records: Access: Mail, in person. Both court and visitors may perform in person searches. Search fee: $5.00 per name. Required to search: name, years to search, DOB, SSN. Criminal records computerized from 1994, index books back to 1876. Mail turnaround time 1 day. Criminal PAT goes back to same as civil.PAT results show name, DOB. Terminal results include SSN.

General Information: No juvenile, mental, sealed, or adoption records released. Will fax back search documents. Court makes copy: $1.00 per page. Self serve: same. Cert fee: $5.00 per doc. Payee: County Clerk. Personal checks accepted; credit cards are not. Mail requests: SASE required.

District Court PO Box 382, Johnson City, TX 78636; 830-868-0973; fax: 830-868-2084; 8AM-4:30PM (CST). ***Felony, Civil, Probate.*** http://dcourt.org
Probate fax is same as main fax number.

Civil Records: Access: Mail, in person. Both court and visitors may perform in person searches. Search fee: $5.00 per name. Required to search: name, years to search. Civil cases indexed by defendant, plaintiff; index on computer from 1994, index books back to 1876. Mail turnaround time 1 day. Civil PAT goes back to 1992. PAT civil results show middle initial.

Criminal Records: Access: Mail, in person. Both court and visitors may perform in person searches. Search fee: $5.00 per name. Required to search: name, years to search, DOB, SSN. Criminal records computerized from 1994, index books back to 1876. Mail turnaround time 1 day. Criminal PAT goes back to 1992. PAT results show middle initial, DOB. Also gives DR number, arrest and disposition dates, offense.

General Information: No juvenile, mental, sealed, or adoption records released. Will not fax documents. Court makes copy: $1.00 first page; $.25 per page add'l. Cert fee: $1.00 per page includes copy fee. Payee: District Clerk. Personal checks accepted; credit cards are not. Mail requests: SASE required.

Borden County

District & County Court PO Box 124, Gail, TX 79738; 806-756-4312; fax: 806-756-4405; 8AM-5PM (CST). ***Felony, Misdemeanor, Civil, Probate.*** Probate fax is same as main fax number.

Civil Records: Access: Mail, in person. Both court and visitors may perform in person searches. Search fee: $5.00 per name. Required to search: name, years to search. Civil cases indexed by defendant, plaintiff. Civil records in index books, archived from 1900. Mail turnaround time 1 week.

Criminal Records: Access: Mail, in person. Both court and visitors may perform in person searches. Search fee: $5.00 per name. Required to search: name, years to search. Criminal index in books, archived from 1900. Mail turnaround time 1 week.

General Information: No juvenile, mental, sealed, or adoption records released. Fee to fax out file $1.00 per page. Court makes copy: $1.00 per page. Cert fee: $5.00 per cert. Payee: District Clerk. Personal checks accepted; credit cards are not. Mail requests: SASE required.

Bosque County

District Court PO Box 674 (Main & Morgan St), Meridian, TX 76665; 254-435-2334; 8AM-5PM (CST). ***Felony, Civil.*** In person searches are conducted by viewing index books.

Civil Records: Access: Mail, in person. Both court and visitors may perform in person searches. Search fee: $5.00 per name. Required to search: name, years to search. Civil cases indexed by defendant, plaintiff. Some civil records on computer from 1994, files/books from 1870s. Mail turnaround time 1 day.

Criminal Records: Access: Mail, in person. Both court and visitors may perform in person searches. Search fee: $5.00 per name. Required to search: name, years to search, DOB or SSN. Some computerized records from 1994, criminal records on books/files from 1856. Mail turnaround time 1 day.

General Information: No juvenile, mental, sealed, or adoption records released. Will not fax documents. Court makes copy: $1.00 per page. Self serve: same. Cert fee: $1.00. Payee: District Clerk. Personal checks accepted; credit cards are not. Mail requests: SASE required.

County Court PO Box 617, Meridian, TX 76665; 254-435-2201; fax: 254-435-2152; 8AM-5PM (CST). ***Misdemeanor, Civil, Probate.***

Civil Records: Access: Mail, in person. Both court and visitors may perform in person searches. Search fee: $5.00 per name. Required to search: name, years to search. Civil cases indexed by defendant, plaintiff. Civil records in index books from 1854; on computer back to 1997. Mail turnaround time 1-2 days.

Criminal Records: Access: Mail, in person. Only the court performs in person searches; visitors may not. Search fee: $5.00 per name. Required to search: name, years to search, DOB, SSN. Criminal docket on books from 1854; on computer back to 1997. Mail turnaround time 1-2 days.

General Information: No juvenile, mental, sealed, or adoption records released. Will not fax documents. Court makes copy: $1.00 per page. Self serve: $1.00 per page. Cert fee: $5.00. Payee: County Clerk. In state personal checks accepted for civil records. Major credit cards acceptance planned. Mail requests: SASE required.

Bowie County

District & County Court at Law 710 James Bowie Dr, PO Box 248, New Boston, TX 75570; 903-628-6750; criminal phone: 903-628-6766; civil phone: 903-628-6751; probate phone: 903-628-6743; fax: 903-628-6761; 8AM-5PM (CST). ***Felony, Misdemeanor, Civil, Probate.*** www.co.bowie.tx.us
Probate records are at this address in the County Clerk's office.

Civil Records: Access: Mail, in person. Both court and visitors may perform in person searches. Search fee: $5.00 per name. Required to search: name, years to search. Civil cases indexed by defendant, plaintiff; index on computer from 1978, on microfiche from 1900s, chrono index from 1800s. Mail turnaround time 1 day. Civil PAT available.

Criminal Records: Access: Mail, in person. Both court and visitors may perform in person searches. Search fee: $5.00 per name. Required to search: name, years to search, DOB. Criminal records computerized from 1978, on microfiche from 1900s, chrono index from 1800s. Mail turnaround time 1 day. Criminal PAT available.

General Information: No juvenile, mental, sealed, or adoption records released. Will fax documents $5.00 each. Court makes copy: $1.00 per page. Cert fee: $1.00. Payee: District Clerk. Personal checks accepted. Visa/MC accepted. Mail requests: SASE required.

Brazoria County

District Court Clerk's Office, 111 E Locust, #500, Angleton, TX 77515-4678; 979-864-1316; 8AM-5PM (CST). ***Felony, Civil.*** www.brazoria-county.com/dclerk

Civil Records: Access: Phone, mail, in person, online. Both court and visitors may perform in person searches. Search fee: $5.00 per name. Fee is per 10 year period. Required to search: name, years to search. Civil cases indexed by defendant, plaintiff; index on computer from 1987, index chrono from 1900, prior alpha. Mail turnaround time 1-2 days. Civil PAT goes back to 1987. PAT results show name only. Access civil record docket free at http://records.brazoria-county.com/.

Criminal Records: Access: Phone, mail, in person, online. Both court and visitors may perform in person searches. Search fee: $5.00 per name. Fee is per 10 year period. Required to search: name, years to search, DOB, signed release; also helpful: SSN. Criminal records computerized from 1986, index chrono from 1900, prior alpha. Mail turnaround time 1-2 days. Criminal PAT goes back to same as civil. PAT results show middle initial, DOB. Drivers' License number may show up on the public terminal and online results. Access criminal record docket free at http://records.brazoria-county.com; Sheriff bond and jail records also available. Online results show middle initial, DOB.

General Information: Online identifiers in results same as on public terminal. No juvenile, mental, sealed, or adoption records released. Will fax documents $10.00 each. Court makes copy: $1.00 per page. Self serve: same. Cert fee: $1.00. Payee: District Clerk. No personal checks accepted; credit cards are. Mail requests: SASE required.

County Court 111 E Locust, #200, Angleton, TX 77515; criminal phone: 979-864-1380; civil phone: 979-864-1385; fax: 979-864-1020; 8AM-4:30PM (CST). ***Misdemeanor, Civil.*** www.brazoria-county.com

Civil Records: Access: Fax, mail, in person, online. Both court and visitors may perform in person searches. Search fee: $5.00 per name. Required to search: name, years to search. Civil cases indexed by defendant, plaintiff; index on computer from 1984; prior on books or microfiche back to 1800s. Note: Fee must be prepaid before faxing in a search request. Mail turnaround time 2 days. Civil PAT goes back to 1/1986. Results include name and case number. Access civil record docket free at http://records.brazoria-county.com/. Also, access index and docs back to 1/1/1986 at www.idocket.com; registration and password required. This is a fee service; only one free name search per day.

Criminal Records: Access: Fax, mail, in person, online. Both court and visitors may perform in person searches. Search fee: $5.00 per name. Required to search: name, years to search, DOB. Criminal records computerized from 1986; prior on books or microfiche back to 1800s. Note: Results include name and case number. Mail turnaround time 2 days. Criminal PAT goes back to same as civil. Results include name and case number. Access criminal court and county inmate and bond records free at http://records.brazoria-county.com. Also, access index and docs back to 1/1/1986 at www.idocket.com; registration and password

required. This is a fee service, unless only one name searched a day.
General Information: Online identifiers in results same as on public terminal. No juvenile, mental, sealed records released. Will not fax documents. Court makes copy: $1.00 per page. Cert fee: $5.00 per document. Payee: Joyce Hudman, County Clerk. Personal checks accepted; credit cards are not. Mail requests: SASE required.

Probate Court 111 E Locust, #200, Angleton, TX 77515; 979-864-1367; fax: 979-864-1031; 8AM-5PM (CST). ***Probate.*** Access probate records free at http://records.brazoria-county.com/.

Brazos County

District Court 300 E 26th St, #216, Bryan, TX 77803; 979-361-4240; fax: 979-361-0197; 8AM-5PM (CST). ***Felony, Civil.***
www.co.brazos.tx.us/courts
Civil Records: Access: Mail, in person, online. Both court and visitors may perform in person searches. Search fee: $5.00 per name. Required to search: name, years to search. Civil cases indexed by defendant, plaintiff; index on computer, index chromo from 1800s. Mail turnaround time 10 days. Civil PAT available. Civil case index and hearing index at http://justiceweb.co.brazos.tx.us/judicialsearch/.
Criminal Records: Access: Mail, in person, online. Both court and visitors may perform in person searches. Search fee: $5.00 per name. Required to search: name, years to search; also helpful: DOB, SSN, cause number. Criminal records on computer, index chrono from 1800s. Mail turnaround time 10 days. Criminal PAT available. Criminal case index and hearing index available at http://justiceweb.co.brazos.tx.us/judicialsearch/. Online results show middle initial, DOB.
General Information: No juvenile, mental, sealed, or adoption records released. Will fax documents to toll free number. Court makes copy: $.50 per page. Cert fee: $1.00 per page. Payee: District Clerk. Personal checks accepted; credit cards are not. Mail requests: SASE required.

County Court 300 E 26th St, #120, Bryan, TX 77803; 979-361-4128; criminal phone: 979-361-4132; fax: 979-361-4125; 8AM-5PM (CST). ***Misdemeanor, Civil under $500, Probate.***
www.co.brazos.tx.us/courts/countyCourts.php
County Clerk holds misdemeanor records prior to 1986 only. Newer cases are filed at the District Clerks Office. The current docket may be viewed at the web page, sorted by Judge.
Civil Records: Access: Mail, in person, online. Both court and visitors may perform in person searches. Search fee: $5.00 per name. Required to search: name, years to search. Civil cases indexed by defendant, plaintiff; index on computer from 1986, index chrono from 1958. Mail turnaround 2-3 days. Civil PAT goes back to 1986. PAT civil results show middle initial. Current dockets at web page.
Criminal Records: Access: Mail, in person, online. Both court and visitors may perform in person searches. Search fee: $5.00 per name. Required to search: name, years to search, DOB. Criminal records computerized from 1986, index chrono from 1958. Mail turnaround time 2-3 days. Criminal PAT goes back to same as civil. PAT results show middle initial, DOB. Current dockets at web page.
General Information: No juvenile, mental, sealed, or adoption records released. Will fax documents $1.00 per page. Court makes copy: $1.00 per page. Cert fee: $5.00. Payee: County Clerk or District Clerk. Only cashiers checks and money orders accepted. No credit cards accepted. Mail requests: SASE required.

Brewster County

District Court PO Box 1024, Alpine, TX 79831; 432-837-6216; fax: 432-837-6217; 9AM-12, 1-5PM (CST). ***Felony, Civil.***
Civil Records: Access: Phone, fax, mail, in person. Both court and visitors may perform in person searches. Search fee: $8.00. Required to search: name; also helpful: years to search. Civil cases indexed by defendant, plaintiff. Civil records are computerized since 1994, indexed from 1899. Mail turnaround time 2-3 days.
Criminal Records: Access: Phone, fax, mail, in person. Both court and visitors may perform in person searches. Search fee: $8.00. Required to search: name, DOB; also helpful: years to search. Criminal records are computerized since 1994, indexed from 1899. Mail turnaround time 2-3 days.
General Information: No fee to fax documents to local number. Court makes copy: $1.00 per page. Cert fee: $1.00 per page. Payee: District Clerk. Personal checks accepted. Major credit cards may be accepted in 2009.

County Court PO Box 119 (201 W Ave. E), Alpine, TX 79831; 432-837-3366; fax: 432-837-6217; 8:30AM-5PM (CST). ***Misdemeanor, Civil, Probate.***
Civil Records: Access: Mail, fax, in person. Both court and visitors may perform in person searches. Search fee: $10.00 per name. Required to search: name, years to search. Civil cases indexed by defendant, plaintiff. Civil records in index books from 1950s; computerized since 1995. Mail turnaround time 1 week. Civil PAT goes back to 1994. PAT results show name only.
Criminal Records: Access: Mail, fax, in person. Both court and visitors may perform in person searches. Search fee: $10.00 per name. Required to search: name, years to search, DOB, signed release; also helpful: SSN. Criminal docket on books from 1920s, computerized since 1994. Mail turnaround time 1 week. Criminal PAT goes back to same as civil. PAT results show middle initial, DOB.
General Information: No juvenile, mental, sealed, or adoption records released. Fee to fax out file $2.00 per page. Court makes copy for no fee. Self serve: $1.00 per page. Cert fee: $5.00. Payee: County Clerk. Personal checks accepted; credit cards are not.

Briscoe County

District & County Court PO Box 555, Silverton, TX 79257; 806-823-2134; fax: 806-823-2359; 8AM-5PM (CST). ***Felony, Misdemeanor, Civil, Probate.***
Civil Records: Access: Fax, mail, in person. Both court and visitors may perform in person searches. Search fee: $5.00 per name. Required to search: name, years to search. Civil cases indexed by defendant, plaintiff. Civil records in index books from 1892. Mail turnaround time 1 day.
Criminal Records: Access: Fax, mail, in person. Both court and visitors may perform in person searches. Search fee: $5.00 per name. Required to search: name, years to search, DOB. Criminal docket on books from 1892. Mail turnaround time 1 day.
General Information: No juvenile, mental, sealed, or adoption records released. Will fax documents $5.00 per name if prepaid or copy of check faxed in. Court makes copy: $1.00 per page. Cert fee: $5.00. Payee: District or County Clerk. Personal checks accepted. Visa/MC/Discover/AMEx accepted. Mail requests: SASE required.

Brooks County

District Court PO Box 534, Falfurrias, TX 78355; 361-325-5604; criminal phone: x239; civil phone: x237; fax: 361-325-5679; 8AM-5PM (CST). ***Felony, Civil.***
Civil Records: Access: Phone, fax, mail, online, in person. Both court and visitors may perform in person searches. Search fee: $5.00 per name. Required to search: name, years to search; also helpful: address. Civil cases indexed by defendant, plaintiff; index on computer back to 1992, index books since 1920. Mail turnaround time 1 week. Civil PAT goes back to 1993. PAT results show name only. Civil case index and doc online at www.idocket.com. Records go back to 12/31/1993. One free name search permitted per day, otherwise subscription required.
Criminal Records: Access: Phone, fax, mail, online, in person. Both court and visitors may perform in person searches. Search fee: $5.00 per name. Required to search: name, years to search, DOB, SSN; also helpful: address. Criminal records computerized from 1992, index books since 1920, microfiche since 1939. Mail turnaround time 1 week. Criminal PAT available. PAT results show name only. Criminal case index and docs online through www.idocket.com; registration and password required. Records go back to 12/31/1993. One free name search permitted per day, otherwise subscription required. Online results show middle initial.
General Information: No juvenile, mental, sealed, or adoption records released. Fee to fax out file $1.00 per page. Court makes copy: $1.00 per page. Self serve: $.25 per page. Cert fee: $2.00 per document. Payee: District Clerk. Business checks accepted. Major credit cards accepted. Mail requests: SASE required.

County Court PO Box 427, 408 W Travis, Falfurrias, TX 78355; 361-325-5604 x6; criminal phone: x245; civil phone: x247; fax: 361-325-4944; 8AM-N, 1-5PM (CST). ***Misdemeanor, Civil Actions Less Than $5000, Probate.***
This court recommends that civil be cases be filed in District Court, thus there are very few civil records here. The search fee includes both the civil and criminal indexes if you ask for both.
Civil Records: Access: Phone, fax, mail, in person. Both court and visitors may perform in person searches. Search fee: $10.00 per name. Required to search: name, years to search. Civil cases indexed by plaintiff. Civil records in index books since 1911. Mail turnaround time 1-2 days.
Criminal Records: Access: Phone, fax, mail, in person, online. Both court and visitors may perform in person searches. Search fee: $10.00 per name. Required to search: name, years to search, DOB. Criminal docket on books from 1911. Mail turnaround time 1-2 days. Access misdemeanor case info back to 12/31/94 at www.idocket.com; registration and password required. This is a fee service; only one free name search per day.
General Information: No juvenile, mental, sealed, or adoption records released. Will fax documents $5.00 1st page, $2.00 each add'l. Court makes copy: $1.00 per page. Self serve: same. Cert fee: $5.00 per cert plus copy fees. Payee: County Clerk. Personal checks accepted; credit cards are not. Mail requests: SASE required.

Brown County

District Court 200 S Broadway, Brownwood, TX 76801; 325-646-5514; 8AM-5PM (CST). ***Felony, Civil.***
Civil Records: Access: Mail, in person. Both court and visitors may perform in person searches. Search fee: $5.00 per name. Required to search: name, years to search. Civil cases indexed by defendant, plaintiff; index on computer since 1995; prior records on books to 1930s. Mail turnaround time 2-3 days. Civil PAT goes back to 1995.
Criminal Records: Access: In person. Both court and visitors may perform in person searches. Search fee: $5.00 per name. Required to search: name, years to search. Criminal records on computer since 1995; prior records on books to 1930s. Criminal PAT goes back to same as civil.PAT results show name, DOB. Terminal results include SSN.
General Information: No juvenile, mental, sealed, or adoption records released. Will not fax documents. Court makes copy: $1.00 per page. Self serve: $.50 per page. Cert fee: $1.00 per page. Payee: District Clerk. Business checks accepted. No credit cards accepted. Mail requests: SASE required.

County Court 200 S Broadway, Brownwood, TX 76801; 325-643-2594; 8:30AM-5PM (CST). ***Misdemeanor, Civil, Probate.***
Civil Records: Access: Mail, in person. Both court and visitors may perform in person searches. Search fee: $5.00 per name. Required to search: name, years to search. Civil cases indexed by defendant, plaintiff; index on computer from 1988 on microfiche from 1900s. Mail turnaround time 1-2 days. Civil PAT goes back to 1987.
Criminal Records: Access: Mail, in person. Both court and visitors may perform in person searches. Search fee: $5.00 per name. Required to search: name, years to search; also helpful: DOB, SSN. Criminal records computerized from 1987, on microfiche from 1900s. Mail turnaround time 1-2 days. Criminal PAT goes back to same as civil. PAT results show middle initial, DOB.
General Information: No juvenile, mental, sealed records released. Will not fax documents. Court makes copy: $1.00 per page. Self serve: $.25 per

page. Cert fee: $5.00. Payee: Brown County Clerk. Personal checks accepted; credit cards are not.

Burleson County

District Court 100 W Buck, #303, Caldwell, TX 77836; 979-567-2336; 8AM-N, 1-5PM (CST). ***Felony, Civil.***

Civil Records: Access: Mail, in person. Both court and visitors may perform in person searches. Search fee: $10.00 per name. Required to search: name, years to search. Civil cases indexed by defendant, plaintiff; index on microfilm from 1980, index books prior. Mail turnaround time 1-2 days.

Criminal Records: Access: Mail, in person. Both court and visitors may perform in person searches. Search fee: $10.00 per name. Required to search: name, years to search. Criminal records on microfilm from 1980, index books prior. Mail turnaround time 1-2 days.

General Information: No juvenile, mental, sealed, or adoption records released. Will fax to toll-free number. Court makes copy: $1.00 per page. Self serve: same. Cert fee: $1.00. Payee: District Clerk. Personal checks accepted; credit cards are not. Mail requests: SASE or toll-free phone number required.

County Court 100 W Buck, #203, Caldwell, TX 77836; 979-567-2329; probate phone: same; fax: 979-567-2376; 8AM-5PM (CST). ***Misdemeanor, Civil, Probate.***

Civil Records: Access: Phone, mail, fax, in person. Both court and visitors may perform in person searches. Search fee: $10.00 per name, per case. Required to search: name, years to search. Civil cases indexed by defendant, plaintiff; index to 1900, records archived to 1900s. Mail turnaround time 2-4 days.

Criminal Records: Access: Mail, fax, in person. Visitors must perform in person searches themselves. Search fee: $10.00 per name, per case. Required to search: name, years to search, DOB, SSN. Criminal records indexed to 1990, records archived to 1900s. Mail turnaround time 2-4 days.

General Information: No juvenile, mental, or sealed records released. Fee to fax out file $1.00 per page. Court makes copy: $1.00 per page. Cert fee: $5.00. Payee: County Clerk. Personal checks accepted; cashiers check or money order is faster return. No credit cards accepted. Mail requests: SASE required.

Burnet County

District Court 1701 E Polk St, #90, Burnet, TX 78611; 512-756-5450; fax: 512-756-5023; 8AM-4PM (CST). ***Felony, Civil, Family.*** http://dcourt.org

Civil Records: Access: Mail, in person. Both court and visitors may perform in person searches. Search fee: $5.00 per name. Required to search: name, years to search. Civil cases indexed by defendant, plaintiff; index on computer from 1991, index books to 1856. Signup for email notifications of civil dockets at www.dcourt.org/_attys/dockets.htm. Mail turnaround time 3 days. Civil PAT goes back to 1990. PAT results show name, DOB. Terminal results also show SSNs.

Criminal Records: Access: Mail, in person. Both court and visitors may perform in person searches. Search fee: $5.00 per name. Required to search: name, years to search; also helpful: DOB, SSN. Criminal records computerized from 1990, index book from 1856. Mail turnaround time 3 days. Criminal PAT goes back to same as civil.PAT results show name, DOB. Terminal results include SSN. Signup for email notifications of criminal dockets at www.dcourt.org/_attys/dockets.htm.

General Information: No juvenile, mental, sealed, or adoption records released. Will fax documents $2.00 per page. Court makes copy: $1.00 per page. Cert fee: $2.00 per doc. Certification included in copy fee. Personal checks not accepted. Major credit cards accepted. Mail requests: SASE required.

County Court 220 S Pierce, Burnet, TX 78611; 512-756-5403; criminal phone: 512-756-5407; civil:: 512-756-5481; probate: 512-756-5408; fax: 512-756-5410; 9-5PM (CST). ***Misdemeanor, Civil, Probate.*** Probate fax is same as main fax number.

Civil Records: Access: Fax, mail, in person. Both court and visitors may perform in person searches. Search fee: $10.00 per name. Required to search: name, years to search. Civil cases indexed by defendant, plaintiff; index on computer from 1989, on microfiche from 1852. Mail turnaround time 2 days. Civil PAT goes back to 1989. Results include name and case number.

Criminal Records: Access: Fax, mail, in person. Both court and visitors may perform in person searches. Search fee: $10.00 per name. Required to search: name, years to search, offense, date of offense. Criminal records computerized from 1989, on microfiche from 1852. Mail turnaround time 2 days. Criminal PAT goes back to same as civil. Results include name and case number.

General Information: No juvenile, mental, sealed, or adoption records released. Will fax documents $3.00 per page. Court makes copy: $1.00 per page. Self serve: same. Cert fee: $5.00 per doc. Payee: County Clerk. Personal checks, major credit cards accepted. Mail requests: SASE required.

Caldwell County

District Court 201 E San Antonio St, Lockhart, TX 78644; 512-398-1806; fax: 512-398-1805; 8:30AM-N, 1-5PM (CST). ***Felony, Civil.*** www.co.caldwell.tx.us/ips/cms

Civil Records: Access: Phone, fax, mail, in person. Both court and visitors may perform in person searches. Search fee: $5.00 per name. Required to search: name, years to search. Civil cases indexed by defendant, plaintiff; index on computer since 1988, index books from 1846. Mail turnaround time 1-3 days. Civil PAT goes back to 1988.

Criminal Records: Access: Phone, fax, mail, in person. Both court and visitors may perform in person searches. Search fee: $5.00 per name. Required to search: name, years to search; also helpful: DOB, SSN. Criminal records on computer since 1988, index books from 1846. Mail turnaround 1-3 days. Criminal PAT goes back to same as civil.

General Information: No juvenile, mental, sealed, or adoption records released. Will fax documents to local or toll free line. Court makes copy: $1.00 per page. Cert fee: $1.00. Payee: District Clerk. Personal checks and credit cards accepted. Mail requests: SASE required.

County Court PO Box 906, Lockhart, TX 78644; 512-398-1804; criminal: 512-398-1824; 8:30AM-N, 1-5PM (CST). ***Misdemeanor, Civil, Probate.*** Probate is a separate index at this same address.

Civil Records: Access: Mail, in person. Both court and visitors may perform in person searches. Search fee: $5.00 per name. Required to search: name, years to search. Civil cases indexed by defendant, plaintiff. Civil records in index books since 1967. Mail turnaround time 2-4 days.

Criminal Records: Access: Mail, in person. Both court and visitors may perform in person searches. Search fee: $5.00 per name. Required to search: name, years to search, DOB, offense, date of offense. Criminal docket on books from 1967. Mail turnaround time 2-4 days.

General Information: No juvenile, mental, sealed, or adoption records released. Will not fax documents. Court makes copy: $1.00 per page. Cert fee: $5.00 per document. Payee: Caldwell County Clerk. Personal checks accepted; credit cards are not..

Calhoun County

District Court District Clerk, 211 S Ann Courthouse, Port Lavaca, TX 77979; 361-553-4630; fax: 361-553-4637; 8AM-N, 1-5PM (CST). ***Felony, Civil.***

Civil Records: Access: Fax, mail, in person. Both court and visitors may perform in person searches. Search fee: $5.00 per name. Required to search: name, years to search. Civil cases indexed by defendant, plaintiff. Civil records in index books from 1852. Mail turnaround time 3-5 days.

Criminal Records: Access: Fax, mail, in person. Both court and visitors may perform in person searches. Search fee: $5.00 per name. Required to search: name, years to search, signed release; also helpful: DOB. Criminal docket on books from 1852. Mail turnaround time 3-5 days.

General Information: No mental, sealed, or adoption records released. Will not fax documents. Court makes copy: $1.00 per page. Self serve: same. Cert fee: $1.00 per page. Payee: District Clerk. Personal checks accepted; credit cards are not. Mail requests: SASE required.

County Court At Law 211 S Ann, Port Lavaca, TX 77979; 361-553-4411; criminal phone: 361-553-4414; civil phone: 361-553-4415; probate phone: 361-553-4413; fax: 361-553-4420; 8AM-5PM (CST). ***Misdemeanor, Civil, Probate.*** Established 11/1986.

Civil Records: Access: Phone, mail, in person. Both court and visitors may perform in person searches. Search fee: $5.00 per name. Required to search: name, years to search. Civil cases indexed by defendant, plaintiff. Civil records in index books from 11/1986; indexed on computer back to 2000. Mail turnaround 1-2 days. Civil PAT back to 6/2005. Expected to be online with iDocket.com in 2009.

Criminal Records: Access: Phone, mail, in person. Both court and visitors may perform in person searches. Search fee: $5.00 per name. Required to search: name, years to search. Criminal docket on books from 11/1986; indexed on computer back to 1993. Mail turnaround time 1-2 days. Criminal PAT goes back to 6/2005. Expected to be online with iDocket.com in 2009.

General Information: No juvenile, mental, sealed, or adoption records released. Will not fax documents. Court makes copy: $1.00 per page. Cert fee: $5.00. Payee: County Clerk. Personal checks accepted; credit cards are not. Mail requests: SASE required.

Callahan County

District Court 100 W 4th St, #300, Baird, TX 79504-5396; 325-854-5825; fax: 325-854-5826; 8AM-5PM (CST). ***Felony, Civil.*** www.callahancounty.org/

Civil Records: Access: Mail, in person. Both court and visitors may perform in person searches. Search fee: $5.00 per name. Required to search: name, years to search. Civil cases indexed by defendant, plaintiff. Civil records in index books since 1879. Mail turnaround time 1-2 days.

Criminal Records: Access: Mail, in person. Both court and visitors may perform in person searches. Search fee: $5.00 per name. Required to search: name, years to search. Criminal docket on books from 1879. Mail turnaround time 1-2 days.

General Information: No juvenile, mental, sealed, or adoption records released. Will fax documents to local or toll-free number. Court makes copy: $1.00 per page. Cert fee: $1.00. Payee: District Clerk. Personal checks accepted; credit cards are not. Mail requests: SASE required.

County Court 100 W 4th St, #104, Baird, TX 79504-5300; 325-854-5815; fax: 325-854-5816; 8AM-N, 1-5PM ***Misdemeanor, Civil, Probate.*** www.callahancounty.org/

Civil Records: Access: Mail, in person. Both court and visitors may perform in person searches. Search fee: $6.00 per name. Required to search: name, years to search. Civil cases indexed by defendant, plaintiff. Civil records go back to 1877; computerized records go back to 1992. Mail turnaround time 1-2 days.

Criminal Records: Access: Phone, fax, mail, in person. Both court and visitors may perform in person searches. Search fee: $6.00 per name. Required to search: name, years to search. Criminal records go back to 1877; computerized records go to 1992. Mail turnaround time 1-2 days.

General Information: No juvenile, mental, sealed, or adoption records released. Fee to fax out file $1.50 per page. Court makes copy: $1.00 per page. Self serve: same. Cert fee: $5.00 per document. Payee: County Clerk. Personal checks accepted; credit cards are not. Mail requests: SASE required.

Cameron County

District Court 974 E Harrison St, Brownsville, TX 78520; 956-544-0839; criminal phone: 956-544-0839; civil phone: 956-544-0838; fax: 956-548-9591; 8Am-5PM (CST). ***Felony, Civil.***

Civil Records: Access: Mail, in person, online. Both court and visitors may perform in person searches. Search fee: $5.00 per name. Required to search: name, years to search. Civil cases indexed by defendant, plaintiff; index on computer from 1989. Mail turnaround time 1 week. On cases prior to

1990 turnaround can be more than 1 week. Civil PAT goes back to 1989. Results include name and case number. Online access to cases is at www.idocket.com; registration and password required. A fee service; only one free name search per day.
Criminal Records: Access: Mail, in person, online. Only the court performs in person searches; visitors may not. Search fee: $5.00 per name. Required to search: name, years to search, DOB, SSN, signed release, offense. Criminal records on computer since 1989. Note: All mail requests are forwarded to Edmunds County for processing. Mail turnaround time 1 week; cases prior to 1990 turnaround can be more than 1 week. Criminal PAT goes back to 1990. PAT results show name, DOB, SSN. Felony records access is at www.idocket.com; registration and password required. This is a fee service, unless only one name search a day. Records may go back to 12/31/1988.
General Information: No juvenile, mental, sealed, or adoption records released. Will fax documents to local or toll-free number. Court makes copy: $1.00 per page. No certification fee. Payee: Cameron County District Clerk. Personal checks accepted. MC credit cards accepted. Mail requests: SASE required.

County Court No. 1, 2 & 3 PO Box 2178, 974 E Harrison, Brownsville, TX 78522-2178; criminal phone: 956-544-0848; civil phone: 956-544-0867; probate phone: 956-544-0867; criminal fax: 956-544-0894; civil fax: 956-550-7215; 8AM-5PM (CST). ***Misdemeanor, Civil, Probate.*** www.co.cameron.tx.us
Probate fax is same as main fax number.
Civil Records: Access: Mail, in person, online. Both court and visitors may perform in person searches. Search fee: $5.00 per name. Required to search: name, years to search. Civil cases indexed by defendant, plaintiff; index on optical imaging since 1994, on computer from 1987, index books from 1912. Mail turnaround time 1-2 days. Civil PAT goes back to 1993. Access case records back to 12/01/93 including probate at www.idocket.com; registration and password required. A fee service; only one free name search per day.
Criminal Records: Access: Mail, in person, online. Both court and visitors may perform in person searches. Search fee: $5.00 per name. Required to search: name, years to search, DOB. Criminal records on optical imaging since 1994, on computer from 1987, index books from 1912. Mail turnaround time 1-2 days. Criminal PAT goes back to 1987. Criminal online access same as civil, see above.
General Information: No juvenile, mental, sealed, or adoption records released. Will not fax out documents. Court makes copy: $1.00 per page. Self serve: same. Cert fee: $5.00 per document. Payee: Joe G Rivera, County Clerk. No personal checks. No credit cards accepted. Mail requests: SASE required.

Camp County

District Court 126 Church St, Rm 204, Pittsburg, TX 75686; 903-856-3221; fax: 903-856-0560; 8AM-5PM (CST). ***Felony, Civil.***
Civil Records: Access: Mail, fax, in person. Both court and visitors may perform in person searches. Search fee: $5.00 per name. Required to search: name, years to search. Civil cases indexed by defendant, plaintiff. Civil records in index books from 1874; computerized since 1995. Mail turnaround time 1 week.
Criminal Records: Access: Mail, in person. Both court and visitors may perform in person searches. Search fee: $5.00 per name. Required to search: name, years to search, signed release. Criminal docket on books from 1874; computerized since 1993. Mail turnaround time 1 week.
General Information: No juvenile, mental, sealed, or adoption records released. Fee to fax document $.25 per page. Court makes copy: $1.00 per page. Self serve: same. Cert fee: $2.00 first page; $1.00 each add'l. Payee: District Clerk. Personal checks accepted; credit cards are not. Mail requests: SASE required.

County Court 126 Church St, Rm 102, Pittsburg, TX 75686; 903-856-2731; probate phone: 903-856-2731; fax: 903-856-6112; 8AM-N, 1-5PM (CST). ***Misdemeanor, Civil, Probate.***
Civil Records: Access: Fax, mail, in person. Both court and visitors may perform in person searches. Search fee: $10.00 per name. Required to search: name, years to search. Civil cases indexed by defendant, plaintiff. Civil records in index books from 1960; computerized since 1999. Note: Fax access is only allowed if fees prepaid. Mail turnaround time 1 day.
Criminal Records: Access: Fax, mail, in person. Both court and visitors may perform in person searches. Search fee: $10.00 per name. Required to search: name, years to search, signed release, offense. Criminal docket on books from 1960; computerized since 1999. Mail turnaround time 1 day.
General Information: No juvenile, mental, sealed, or adoption records released. Will fax documents $1.00 per page. Court makes copy: $1.00 per page. Self serve: same. Cert fee: $5.00. Payee: Camp County Clerk. Personal checks accepted; credit cards are not. Mail requests: SASE required.

Carson County

District & County Court PO Box 487, Panhandle, TX 79068; 806-537-3873; fax: 806-537-3623; 8AM-N, 1-5PM (CST). ***Felony, Misdemeanor, Civil, Probate.***
This court will not perform criminal record searches but welcomes researchers. Probate is a separate index at this address. Probate fax same as main fax number.
Civil Records: Access: Mail, fax, in person. Both court and visitors may perform in person searches. Search fee: $5.00 per name. Required to search: name, years to search. Civil indexed by defendant, plaintiff; index on computer from 1981, index books from 1800s. Mail turnaround 1 day or less.
Criminal Records: Access: In person only. Visitors must perform in person searches themselves. Required to search: name, years to search. Criminal records are not computerized.
General Information: No juvenile, mental, sealed, or adoption records released. Will fax documents if fees prepaid. Court makes copy: $1.00 per page. Cert fee: $5.00 per document. Payee: Carson County Clerk. Personal checks and major credit cards accepted. Mail requests: SASE required for civil.

Cass County

District Court PO Box 510, Linden, TX 75563; 903-756-7514; fax: 903-756-5253; 8AM-5PM (CST). ***Felony, Civil.*** www.co.cass.tx.us/ips/cms
Civil Records: Access: Mail, in person. Both court and visitors may perform in person searches. Search fee: $5.00 per name. Required to search: name, years to search. Civil cases indexed by defendant, plaintiff; index on computer from 1953, index books from 1900s. Mail turnaround time 1 day. Civil PAT goes back to 1953. PAT civil results show middle initial.
Criminal Records: Access: Mail, in person. Both court and visitors may perform in person searches. Search fee: $5.00 per name. Required to search: name, years to search. Criminal records computerized from 1985, index books from 1900s. Mail turnaround time 1 day. Criminal PAT goes back to 1985. PAT results show middle initial, DOB.
General Information: No juvenile, mental, sealed, or adoption records released. Fee to fax document $.25 per minute; minimum $3.00. Court makes copy: $1.00 per page. Cert fee: n/a. Payee: District Clerk. Personal checks accepted; credit cards are not. Mail requests: SASE required.

County Court PO Box 449, 101 E Rush St, Linden, TX 75563; 903-756-5071; fax: 903-756-8051; 8AM-5PM (CST). ***Misdemeanor, Probate.***
Probate is a separate index at same address. Probate fax is same as main fax number.
Criminal Records: Access: Mail, in person. Both court and visitors may perform in person searches. Search fee: $10.00 per name. Required to search: name, years to search. Criminal docket on books from 1983, computerized since 1999. Mail turnaround time 1 day.
General Information: No juvenile, mental, sealed, or adoption records released. Will not fax documents. Court makes copy: $1.00 per page. Cert fee: $5.00 per doc. Payee: County Clerk. Personal checks accepted; credit cards are not. Mail requests: SASE required.

Castro County

District & County Court 100 E Bedford, Rm 101, Dimmitt, TX 79027; 806-647-3338; fax: 806-647-5438; 8AM-5PM (CST). ***Felony, Misdemeanor, Civil, Probate.*** www.242ndcourt.com
Civil Records: Access: Mail, in person. Both court and visitors may perform in person searches. Search fee: $5.00 per name. Required to search: name, years to search. Civil cases indexed by defendant, plaintiff. Civil index in books. Mail turnaround time 1 day.
Criminal Records: Access: Mail, in person. Both court and visitors may perform in person searches. Search fee: $5.00 per name. Required to search: name, years to search; also helpful: DOB, SSN. Criminal index in books; computerized records since 2000. Mail turnaround time 1 day.
General Information: No juvenile, mental, sealed, or adoption records released. Will fax documents $3.00 plus $1.00 per page. Court makes copy: $1.00 per page. Self serve: same. Cert fee: $5.00 per doc in county court, $1.00 in district per page. Payee: County or District Court Clerk. Personal checks accepted; credit cards are not. Mail requests: SASE required.

Chambers County

District Clerk Drawer NN, Anahuac, TX 77514; 409-267-8276; fax: 409-267-8209; 8AM-N, 1-5PM (CST). ***Felony, Civil.***
www.co.chambers.tx.us/offices/distclrk.html
Civil Records: Access: Mail, in person, online. Both court and visitors may perform in person searches. Search fee: $5.00 per name. Required to search: name, years to search. Civil cases indexed by defendant, plaintiff; index on computer back to 1800s. Mail turnaround time 1 day. Search online after registering free for login and password at www.chambersonline.net/districtclerk/
Criminal Records: Access: Mail, in person, online. Both court and visitors may perform in person searches. Search fee: $5.00 per name. Required to search: name, years to search, DOB, SSN. Criminal records computerized from 1940s. Mail turnaround time 1 day. Online access same as civil, see above.
General Information: No juvenile, mental, sealed, or adoption records released. Will not fax documents. Court makes copy: $1.00 per page. Self serve: same. Cert fee: $5.00. Payee: R B Scherer Jr, District Clerk. Personal checks accepted; credit cards are not. Mail requests: SASE required.

County Court PO Box 728, Anahuac, TX 77514; 409-267-8309; criminal phone: 409-267-8313; civil phone: 409-267-8313; probate phone: 409-267-8313; criminal fax: 409-267-8405; civil fax: 409-267-8315; 8AM-5PM (CST). ***Misdemeanor, Civil, Probate.*** www.co.chambers.tx.us
Probate fax is same as the civil fax number.
Civil Records: Access: Mail, in person. Both court and visitors may perform in person searches. Search fee: $5.00 per name. Required to search: name, years to search; also helpful: address. Civil cases indexed by defendant, plaintiff; index on computer from 2000, index books in office from 1905. Mail turnaround time 2-3 days.
Criminal Records: Access: Mail, in person. Both court and visitors may perform in person searches. Search fee: $5.00 per name. Required to search: name, years to search, DOB, offense; also helpful: address. Criminal records computerized from 2000, index books in office from 1905. Mail turnaround time 2-3 days.
General Information: No juvenile or mental records released. Will fax documents $1.00 per page if local; long-distance fee $1.50 per page. Court makes copy: $1.00 per page. Cert fee: $5.00 per document. Payee: Chambers County Clerk. Personal checks accepted. Visa/MC accepted.

Cherokee County

District Court Drawer C, Rusk, TX 75785; 903-683-4533; criminal phone: 903-683-6908; civil phone: 903-683-5945/5883; fax: 903-683-2971; 8AM-N, 1-5PM (CST). ***Felony, Civil.***

Civil Records: Access: Mail, fax, in person. Both court and visitors may perform in person searches. Search fee: $5.00 per name. Required to search: name, years to search. Civil cases indexed by defendant, plaintiff; index on computer from 1992, index books from 1848. Mail turnaround time 1-2 days. Civil PAT goes back to 1992. PAT results show name only.
Criminal Records: Access: Mail, fax, in person. Both court and visitors may perform in person searches. Search fee: $5.00 per name. Required to search: name, years to search. Criminal records computerized from 1992, index books from 1848. Mail turnaround 1-2 days. Criminal PAT goes back to 1992. PAT results show middle initial, DOB.
General Information: No juvenile, mental, sealed, or adoption records released. Will not fax documents. Court makes copy: $1.00 per page. Cert fee: $1.00 per page. Payee: District Clerk. Personal checks accepted; credit cards are not. Mail requests: SASE required.

County Court Cherokee County Clerk, PO Box 420, 502 N Main, Rusk, TX 75785; 903-683-2350; fax: 903-683-5931; 8-5PM ***Misdemeanor, Civil, Probate.*** Probate fax is same as main fax number.
Civil Records: Access: Mail, in person, online. Both court and visitors may perform in person searches. Search fee: $5.00 per name. Required to search: name, years to search. Civil cases indexed by defendant, plaintiff; index on computer back to 1987, index books from 1846. Mail turnaround 2-4 days. Access cases back to 1988 at www.idocket.com; registration and password required. A fee service; only one free name search per day.
Criminal Records: Access: Mail, in person, online. Both court and visitors may perform in person searches. Search fee: $10.00 per name. Required to search: name, years to search. Criminal records computerized from 1984, index books from 1920s. Mail turnaround time 2-4 days. Access cases back to 1988 at www.idocket.com; registration and password required. A fee service; only one free name search per day.
General Information: No juvenile, mental, sealed, or adoption records released. Will not fax documents. Court makes copy: $1.00 per page. Cert fee: $5.00 per document. Payee: County Clerk. Personal checks accepted; credit cards are not. Mail requests: SASE required.

Childress County

District & County Court Courthouse, Box 4, Childress, TX 79201; 940-937-6143; fax: 940-937-3708; 8:30AM-N, 1-5PM (CST). ***Felony, Misdemeanor, Civil, Probate.***
Probate fax is same as main fax number.
Civil Records: Access: Mail, in person. Both court and visitors may perform in person searches. Search fee: $5.00 per name. Required to search: name, years to search. Civil cases indexed by defendant, plaintiff; index on computer from 1995, index books from 1920. Mail turnaround time 1 day.
Criminal Records: Access: Mail, in person. Both court and visitors may perform in person searches. Search fee: $5.00 per name. Required to search: name, years to search, DOB. Criminal records computerized from 1995, index books from 1920. Mail turnaround time 1 day.
General Information: No juvenile, mental, sealed, or adoption records released. Will fax documents. Court makes copy: $1.00 per page. Self serve: same. Cert fee: $1.00 per cert. County Court cert fee is $5.00 per document. Payee: District or County Clerk. Personal checks accepted; credit cards are not.

Clay County

District Clerk PO Box 568, Henrietta, TX 76365; 940-538-4561; fax: 940-538-4431; 8AM-N, 1-5PM (CST). ***Felony, Civil.***
Civil Records: Access: Mail, in person. Both court and visitors may perform in person searches. Search fee: $5.00 per name. Required to search: name, years to search. Civil cases indexed by defendant, plaintiff. Civil records in index books from 1873. Mail turnaround time 1-2 days.
Criminal Records: Access: Mail, in person. Both court and visitors may perform in person searches. Search fee: $5.00 per name. Required to search: name, years to search. Criminal docket on books from 1873. Mail turnaround time 1-2 days.
General Information: No juvenile, mental, sealed, or adoption records released. Will fax documents to local or toll-free number. Court makes copy: $1.00 per page. Self serve: $.25 per page. Cert fee: $1.00 per page includes copy fee. Payee: District Clerk. Personal checks accepted; credit cards are not.

County Court PO Box 548, Henrietta, TX 76365; 940-538-4631; fax: 940-538-5597; 8AM-N, 1-5PM (CST). ***Misdemeanor, Civil, Probate.***
Probate is a separate index at this same address.
Civil Records: Access: Mail, in person. Both court and visitors may perform in person searches. Search fee: $5.00 per name. Required to search: name, years to search. Civil cases indexed by defendant, plaintiff. Civil records in index books from 1873, records go back to 1910; no computerized records. Mail turnaround time 2-4 days.
Criminal Records: Access: Mail, in person. Both court and visitors may perform in person searches. Search fee: $5.00 per name. Required to search: name, years to search. Criminal docket on books from 1873, records go back to 1910; no computerized records. Mail turnaround time 2-4 days.
General Information: No juvenile, mental, sealed, or adoption records released. Will not fax documents. Court makes copy: $1.00 per page. Self serve: same. Cert fee: $5.00 per document. Payee: County Clerk. Personal checks accepted; credit cards are not. Mail requests: SASE required.

Cochran County

District & County Court County Courthouse, Rm 102, Morton, TX 79346; 806-266-5450; fax: 806-266-9027; 8AM-5PM (CST). ***Felony, Misdemeanor, Civil, Probate.***
Probate fax is same as main fax number.
Civil Records: Access: Phone, fax, mail, in person, online. Only the court performs in person searches; visitors may not. Search fee: $5.00 per name. Required to search: name, years to search. Civil cases indexed by defendant, plaintiff. Civil records in index books go back to 1925. Mail turnaround time 1 day. Email address for requests is cclerk@door.net.
Criminal Records: Access: Fax, mail, in person, online. Only the court performs in person searches; visitors may not. Search fee: $5.00 per name. Required to search: name, years to search, DOB; also helpful: sex. Criminal docket on booksgo back to 1925. Mail turnaround time 1 day. Email address for search requests is cclerk@door.net.
General Information: No juvenile, mental, sealed, or adoption records released. Will fax documents to 800 number free; otherwise fax fee $5.00. Court makes copy: $1.00 per page. Self serve: same. Cert fee: $5.00 per document. Payee: District or County Clerk. Personal checks accepted; credit cards are not. Mail requests: SASE required.

Coke County

District & County Court PO Box 150, Robert Lee, TX 76945; 325-453-2631; fax: 325-453-2650; 8AM-5PM (CST). ***Felony, Misdemeanor, Civil, Probate.*** Probate fax is same as main fax number.
Civil Records: Access: Mail, in person. Both court and visitors may perform in person searches. Search fee: $10.00 per name. Required to search: name, years to search. Civil records in index books since 1889, computerized since 1993. Mail turnaround time 2 days.
Criminal Records: Access: Mail, in person. Both court and visitors may perform in person searches. Search fee: $10.00 per name. Required to search: name, years to search. Criminal docket on books from 1889. Mail turnaround time 2 days.
General Information: No juvenile, mental, sealed, or adoption records released. Will fax documents $2.00 per page. Court makes copy: $1.00 per page. Self serve: same. Cert fee: $5.00. Payee: Coke County Clerk. Personal checks accepted; credit cards are not.

Coleman County

District Court PO Box 512, Coleman, TX 76834; 325-625-2568; 8AM-4:30PM (CST). ***Felony, Civil.***
Civil Records: Access: Mail, in person. Both court and visitors may perform in person searches. Search fee: $5.00 per name. Required to search: name, years to search. Civil cases indexed by defendant, plaintiff. Civil records in index books since 1934; earlier records not indexed. Mail turnaround time up to 5 days.
Criminal Records: Access: Mail, in person. Both court and visitors may perform in person searches. Search fee: $5.00 per name. Required to search: name, years to search; also helpful are DOB. Criminal docket on books from 1931; earlier records not indexed. Mail turnaround time up to 5 days.
General Information: No juvenile, mental, sealed, or adoption records released. Will not fax documents. Court makes copy: $1.00 per page. Cert fee: $1.00. Payee: District Clerk. Personal checks accepted. Mail requests: SASE required.

County Court 100 W Liveoak, #105, Coleman, TX 76834; 325-625-2889; fax: 325-625-2889; 8AM-5PM (CST). ***Misdemeanor, Civil, Probate.***
Civil Records: Access: Mail, in person. Both court and visitors may perform in person searches. Search fee: $5.00 per name. Required to search: name, years to search. Civil cases indexed by defendant, plaintiff. Civil records in index books from 1971. Mail turnaround time 1-2 days.
Criminal Records: Access: Mail, in person. Both court and visitors may perform in person searches. Search fee: $5.00 per name. Required to search: name, years to search. Criminal docket on books from 1977, archived to 1900s. Mail turnaround time 1-2 days.
General Information: No juvenile, mental, sealed, or adoption records released. Will not fax documents. Court makes copy: $1.00 per page. Cert fee: $5.00. Payee: County Clerk. Personal checks accepted; credit cards are not. Mail requests: SASE required.

Collin County

District Clerk PO Box 578, McKinney, TX 75070; criminal phone: 972-548-4430; civil phone: 972-548-4320; criminal fax: 972-548-4764; civil fax: 972-548-4697; 8AM-4:30PM (CST). ***Felony, Civil.*** www.co.collin.tx.us/district_courts/index.jsp
Civil Records: Access: Mail, fax, online, in person. Both court and visitors may perform in person searches. Search fee: $5.00 per name. Required to search: name, years to search. Civil cases indexed by defendant, plaintiff; index on computer and microfiche from 1986 (some records are on computer through the 1970s), index books from 1846. Note: Fax service only to ongoing subscriber. Mail turnaround time 2-3 days. Civil PAT goes back to 1986. PAT civil results show middle initial. Name and case look up is at www.co.collin.tx.us/rsp-bin/pbkr125.pgm. Search case schedules for free at www.co.collin.tx.us/ShowScheduleSearchServlet. There is also a commercial system- see county courts. Call 972-548-4503 for subscription info.
Criminal Records: Access: Mail, fax, online, in person. Both court and visitors may perform in person searches. Search fee: $5.00 per name. Required to search: name, years to search, DOB. Criminal records on computer and microfiche from 1986 (some records are on computer through the 1970s), index books from 1846. Note: Fax service only to ongoing subscriber. Mail turnaround time 2-3 days. Criminal PAT goes back to same as civil. PAT results show middle initial, DOB. Online access to criminal records is the same as civil. Online results show middle initial, DOB.
General Information: Online identifiers in results same as on public terminal. No juvenile, mental, sealed, or adoption records released. Will return items by fax, if subscriber. Court makes copy: $1.00 per page. No certification fee. Payee: District Clerk. Personal checks accepted; credit cards are not. Mail requests: SASE required.

County Court At Law 1800 N Graves, #110, McKinney, TX 75069; criminal phone: 972-548-6420; civil phone: 972-548-6423; probate phone: 972-548-6465; fax: 972-548-6433; 8AM-4:30PM (CST). ***Misdemeanor, Civil, Probate.***
www.collincountytexas.gov
Probate is in #115; Probate fax is 972-548-6468.
Civil Records: Access: Mail, in person, online. Both court and visitors may perform in person searches. Search fee: $5.00 per name. Required to search: name, years to search. Civil cases indexed by

defendant, plaintiff; index on computer and microfiche from 1975. Mail turnaround time 2-4 days. Civil PAT goes back to 1970s. Online access is free at www.co.collin.tx.us/ShowCaseLookupServlet?district_or_county_court=county.
Criminal Records: Access: Mail, online, in person. Both court and visitors may perform in person searches. Search fee: $5.00 per name. Required to search: name, DOB. Criminal records computerized since 1975. Mail turnaround time 2-4 days. Criminal PAT goes back to same as civil. Online access to misdemeanor records is the same as civil.
General Information: No juvenile, mental, sealed, or adoption records released. Will not fax documents. Court makes copy: $1.00 per page. Cert fee: $5.00. Payee: County Clerk. Personal checks and major credit cards accepted. Mail requests: SASE required.

Collingsworth County

District & County Court County Courthouse, Rm 3, 800 W Ave, Box 10, Wellington, TX 79095; 806-447-2408; fax: 806-447-2409; 9AM-5PM (CST). ***Felony, Misdemeanor, Civil, Probate.***
Civil Records: Access: Phone, fax, mail, in person. Both court and visitors may perform in person searches. Search fee: $10.00 per name. Required to search: name, years to search. Civil cases indexed by defendant, plaintiff. Civil index on docket books from 1800s. Mail turnaround time 2 days.
Criminal Records: Access: Mail, in person. Both court and visitors may perform in person searches. Search fee: $10.00 per name. Required to search: name, years to search, DOB. Criminal records indexed in books to 1800s. Mail turnaround 2 days.
General Information: No juvenile, mental health, sealed, or adoption records released. Will fax documents $1.50 per page. Court makes copy: $1.00 per page. Self serve: same. Cert fee: $5.00. Payee: Collingsworth County Clerk. Personal checks accepted. Mail requests: SASE required.

Colorado County

District Court County Courthouse, Rm 210E, 400 Spring St, Columbus, TX 78934; 979-732-2536; fax: 979-732-2591; 8AM-N, 1-5PM (CST). ***Felony, Civil.*** Civil and criminal indexes are usually considered separate searches.
Civil Records: Access: Mail, in person. Both court and visitors may perform in person searches. Search fee: $5.00 per name. Required to search: name, years to search. Civil cases indexed by defendant, plaintiff. Civil records in index books from 1837. Mail turnaround time 1-3 days.
Criminal Records: Access: Mail, in person. Both court and visitors may perform in person searches. Search fee: $5.00 per name. Required to search: name, years to search. Criminal docket on books from 1837. Mail turnaround time 1-3 days.
General Information: No juvenile, mental, sealed, or adoption records released. Will not fax documents. Court makes copy: $1.00 per page. Cert fee: No fee to certify. Payee: District Clerk. Personal checks accepted; credit cards are not. Mail requests: SASE required.

County Court 400 Spring St #103, County Courthouse, Columbus, TX 78934; 979-732-2155; fax: 979-732-8852; 8AM-5PM (CST). ***Misdemeanor, Civil, Probate.***
Civil Records: Access: Mail, in person. Both court and visitors may perform in person searches. Search fee: $10.00 per name. Required to search: name, years to search. Civil cases indexed by defendant, plaintiff. Civil records in index books from 1850, computerized since 1996. Mail turnaround time 1-2 days.
Criminal Records: Access: Mail, in person. Both court and visitors may perform in person searches. Search fee: $10.00 per name. Required to search: name, years to search. Criminal docket on books from 1850, computerized since 1996. Mail turnaround time 1-2 days.
General Information: No juvenile, mental, sealed, or adoption records released. Will fax documents $5.00 plus $1.00 per page. Court makes copy: $1.00 per page. Cert fee: $5.00. Payee: County Clerk. Personal checks and major credit cards accepted. Mail requests: SASE requested.

Comal County

District Court Clerk's Office, 150 N Seguin, #304, New Braunfels, TX 78130-5161; 830-620-5574; fax: 830-608-2006; 8AM-4:30PM (CST). ***Felony, Civil.*** www.co.comal.tx.us
Civil Records: Access: Fax, mail, in person, online. Both court and visitors may perform in person searches. Search fee: $5.00 per name. Required to search: name, years to search. Civil cases indexed by defendant, plaintiff; index on computer from 1984, index books from 1846. Mail turnaround time 10 days. Civil PAT goes back to 1985. Online access county judicial records free at www.co.comal.tx.us/recordsearch.htm. Search by either party name.
Criminal Records: Access: Fax, mail, in person, online. Both court and visitors may perform in person searches. Search fee: $5.00 per name. Required to search: name, years to search, DOB; also helpful: SSN, sex. Criminal records computerized from 1984, index books from 1846. Mail turnaround time 10 days. Criminal PAT goes back to same as civil. Access county criminal judicial records free at www.co.comal.tx.us/recordsearch.htm.
General Information: No juvenile, sealed, or adoption records released. Will fax documents $5.00 per page. Fee is for incoming or outgoing faxes. Court makes copy: $1.00 first page, $.25 each add'l. Cert fee: $1.00 per page. Cert fee includes copies. Payee: District Clerk. Personal checks accepted. Credit cards accepted in person. Mail requests: SASE required.

County Court at Law 100 Main Plaza, #303, New Braunfels, TX 78130; 830-608-8615; criminal phone: 830-620-5582; civil phone: 830-620-5586; probate phone: 830-620-5539; fax: 830-608-2021; 8AM-4:30PM (CST). ***Misdemeanor, Civil, Probate.*** www.comalcounty.net
Civil Records: Access: Phone, fax, mail, in person, online. Both court and visitors may perform in person searches. Search fee: $5.00 per name. Required to search: name, years to search. Civil cases indexed by defendant, plaintiff. Civil records go back to 1977. Mail turnaround time 1 week. Civil PAT goes back to 1989. Access county judicial records free at www.co.comal.tx.us/recordsearch.htm. Search by either party name.
Criminal Records: Access: Phone, fax, mail, in person, online. Both court and visitors may perform in person searches. Search fee: $5.00 per name. Required to search: name, years to search; also helpful: address, DOB. Criminal records go back to 1977. Mail turnaround time 1 week. Criminal PAT goes back to 1977. Access county criminal records free at www.co.comal.tx.us/recordsearch.htm.
General Information: No juvenile, mental, sealed or adoption records released. Will fax documents $1.00 per page. Court makes copy: $1.00 per page. Self serve: same. Cert fee: $5.00. Payee: County Court at Law. Cashiers checks and money orders accepted. Credit cards accepted.

Comanche County

District Court County Courthouse, Box 206, Comanche, TX 76442; 325-356-2342; fax: 325-356-2150; 8:30AM-N, 1-5PM (CST). ***Felony, Civil.***
Civil Records: Access: Mail, in person. Only the court performs in person searches; visitors may not. Search fee: $5.00 per name. Required to search: name, years to search. Civil cases indexed by defendant, plaintiff; index on computer back 1 year, index books from 1876. Mail turnaround time 1 day.
Criminal Records: Access: Mail, in person. Only the court performs in person searches; visitors may not. Search fee: $5.00 per name. Required to search: name, years to search. Criminal records computerized from 1990, index books from 1876. Mail turnaround time 1 day.
General Information: No juvenile, mental, sealed, or adoption records released. Will not fax documents. Court makes copy: $1.00 per page. Cert fee: $2.00. Payee: District Clerk. Personal checks accepted; credit cards are not. Mail requests: SASE required.

County Court County Courthouse, Comanche, TX 76442; 325-356-2655; fax: 325-356-5764; 8:30AM-5PM (CST). ***Misdemeanor, Civil, Probate.***
Civil Records: Access: Mail, in person. Both court and visitors may perform in person searches. Search fee: $5.00 per name. Required to search: name, years to search. Civil cases indexed by defendant, plaintiff. Civil records in index books from 1856. Mail turnaround time 1 day.
Criminal Records: Access: Mail, in person. Both court and visitors may perform in person searches. Search fee: $5.00 per name. Required to search: name, years to search. Criminal docket on books from 1856. Mail turnaround time 1 day.
General Information: No juvenile, mental, sealed, or adoption records released. Will fax documents $1.50 per fax. Court makes copy: $1.00 per page. Cert fee: $5.00. Payee: County Clerk. Personal checks accepted; credit cards are not. Mail requests: SASE required.

Concho County

District & County Court PO Box 98, Paint Rock, TX 76866; 325-732-4322; fax: 325-732-2040; 8:30AM-5PM (CST). ***Felony, Misdemeanor, Civil, Probate.*** www.co.concho.tx.us/ips/cms/districtcourt/
Probate is in a separate index at this address. Probate fax is same as main fax number.
Civil Records: Access: Mail, in person. Both court and visitors may perform in person searches. Search fee: $5.00 per name. Required to search: name, years to search. Civil cases indexed by defendant, plaintiff. Civil records in index books from 1879; computerized back to 1994. Mail turnaround time 1 day.
Criminal Records: Access: Mail, in person. Only the court performs in person searches; visitors may not. Search fee: $5.00 per name. Required to search: name, years to search, DOB; also helpful: SSN. Criminal docket on books from 1879; computerized back to 1994. Mail turnaround time 1 day.
General Information: No juvenile, mental, sealed, or adoption records released. Will not fax documents. Court makes copy: $1.00 per page. Cert fee: $5.00 for County Court; $1.00 for District. Payee: District or County Clerk. Personal checks and major credit cards accepted. Mail requests: SASE required.

Cooke County

District Court 100 S Dixon, County Courthouse, Gainesville, TX 76240; 940-668-5450; fax: 940-668-5476; 8AM-N, 1-5PM (CST). ***Felony, Civil.***
Civil Records: Access: Mail, in person. Both court and visitors may perform in person searches. Search fee: $5.00 per name. Required to search: name, years to search. Civil cases indexed by defendant, plaintiff; index on microfiche from late 1900s, index books from 1800s. Note: Must request specifically if you wish to search back more than 10 years. Mail turnaround time varies.
Criminal Records: Access: Mail, in person. Both court and visitors may perform in person searches. Search fee: $5.00 per name. Required to search: name, years to search. Criminal records on microfiche from late 1900,s, index books from 1800s. Mail turnaround time varies.
General Information: No juvenile, mental, sealed, or adoption records released. Will fax documents. Court makes copy: $1.00 per page. Self serve: same. Cert fee: $5.00 per page includes copy fee. Payee: District Clerk. Only cashiers checks and money orders accepted. Visa/MC accepted. Mail requests: SASE required.

County Court County Courthouse, Gainesville, TX 76240; 940-668-5422/5437; fax: 940-668-5486; 8AM-5PM ***Misdemeanor, Civil, Probate.***
Civil Records: Access: Mail, in person. Both court and visitors may perform in person searches. Search fee: $5.00 per name. Required to search: name, years to search. Civil cases indexed by defendant, plaintiff. Civil records in index books and original papers from late 1850s. Mail turnaround time 1 day. Civil PAT goes back to 2006.
Criminal Records: Access: Mail, in person. Both court and visitors may perform in person searches. Search fee: $5.00 per name. Required to search: name, years to search, DOB. Criminal records go back to 1969. Mail turnaround time 1 day. Criminal PAT goes back to 2006.
General Information: No juvenile, mental, sealed, or adoption records released. Will fax out files to toll free lines or when prepaid. Court makes copy: $1.00 per

page. Self serve: same. Cert fee: $5.00 per instrument. Payee: Cooke Clerk. Personal checks accepted; credit cards are not.

Coryell County

District Court PO Box 4, Gatesville, TX 76528; 254-865-5911; fax: 254-865-5064; 8AM-5PM (CST). ***Felony, Civil.***
www.coryellcounty.org/district_clerk.htm
Civil Records: Access: Fax, mail, in person. Both court and visitors may perform in person searches. Search fee: $5.00 per name. Required to search: name, years to search. Civil cases indexed by defendant, plaintiff. Civil records in index books from 1854; computerized back to 2000. Mail turnaround time 1 day. Civil PAT goes back to 1999. PAT results show name only.
Criminal Records: Access: Fax, mail, in person. Both court and visitors may perform in person searches. Search fee: $5.00 per name. Required to search: name, years to search, DOB, SSN. Criminal docket on books from 1854; computerized back to 2000. Mail turnaround time 1 day. Criminal PAT goes back same as civil; results show name only.
General Information: No juvenile, sealed, or adoption records released. Fee to fax out file $1.50 per page. Court makes copy: $1.00 per page. No certification fee. Payee: District Clerk. Personal checks accepted from Coryell County residents only. Money order, cashiers check accepted for others. Credit cards accepted. Mail requests: SASE required.

County Court PO Box 237, Gatesville, TX 76528; 254-865-5911 x235; fax: 254-865-8631; 8AM-N, 1-5PM (CST). ***Misdemeanor, Civil, Probate.*** Court intends to be online in 2009.
Civil Records: Access: Mail, in person. Visitors must perform in person searches themselves. Search fee: $10.00 per name per 10 years. Required to search: name, years to search. Civil cases indexed by defendant, plaintiff; index on computer back to 1993, index books from 1846. Mail turnaround time 1-5 days. Civil PAT back to 1993 shows name only.
Criminal Records: Access: Mail, in person. Visitors must perform in person searches themselves. Search fee: $10.00 per name per 10 years. Required to search: name, years to search, DOB, SSN. Criminal records computerized from 1993; index books from 1846. Mail turnaround 1-5 days. Criminal PAT goes back to same as civil; results show name only.
General Information: No juvenile, mental, sealed, or adoption records released. Will fax documents $1.00 per page. Out of county fax is $5.00 plus $1.00 per page. Court makes copy: $1.00 per page. Self serve: same. Cert fee: $5.00 per doc. Payee: County Clerk. Business checks accepted. Personal checks must be in county. Visa/MC accepted. Will mail only when a $10.00 search fee is paid in advance of search (10 year). Mail requests: SASE required.

Cottle County

District & County Court PO Box 717, Paducah, TX 79248; 806-492-3823; fax: 806-492-2625; 9-N, 1-5PM ***Felony, Misdemeanor, Civil, Probate.***
Civil Records: Access: Mail, in person. Both court and visitors may perform in person searches. Search fee: $5.00 per name. Required to search: name, years to search. Civil cases indexed by defendant, plaintiff. Civil records in index books from 1892. Mail turnaround time 2-3 days.
Criminal Records: Access: Mail, in person. Both court and visitors may perform in person searches. Search fee: $5.00 per name. Required to search: name, years to search. Criminal docket on books from 1892. Mail turnaround time 2-3 days.
General Information: No juvenile, mental, sealed, or adoption records released. Will not fax documents. Court makes copy: $1.00 per page. Cert fee: $1.00 in District Court; $5.00 for County Court. Payee: Cottle County Clerk. Personal checks accepted; credit cards are not. Mail requests: SASE required.

Crane County

District & County Court PO Box 578, Crane, TX 79731; 432-558-3581; fax: 432-558-1148; 8AM-N, 1-5PM (CST). ***Felony, Misdemeanor, Civil, Probate.*** www.co.crane.tx.us/ips/cms/districtcourt/
Probate is a separate index at this same address.
Civil Records: Access: Mail, in person, online. Visitors must perform in person searches themselves. Search fee: $5.00 per name per 10 years searched. Required to search: name, years to search. Civil cases indexed by defendant, plaintiff. Limited civil records on computer from 1990; index books from 1927. Mail turnaround time 2-5 days. Civil PAT goes back to 1990. Access to dockets is free at www.edoctecinc.com but may be 2 weeks to a month lag time.
Criminal Records: Access: Mail, in person, online. Both court and visitors may perform in person searches. Search fee: $5.00 per name per 10 years searched. Required to search: name, years to search, offense. Limited Criminal records computerized from 1990; index books from 1927. Mail turnaround time 2-5 days. Criminal PAT goes back to same as civil. Online access is same as civil, above.
General Information: No juvenile, mental, sealed or adoption records released. Court makes copy: $1.00 per page. Cert fee: $5.00 per doc County Court; $1.00 per doc in Dist Court. Payee: District or County Clerk. Only cashiers checks and money orders accepted. No credit cards accepted. Mail requests: SASE requested.

Crockett County

District & County Court PO Drawer C, Ozona, TX 76943; 325-392-2022; 8AM-5PM (CST). ***Felony, Misdemeanor, Civil, Probate.***
www.co.crockett.tx.us/ips/cms
Civil Records: Access: Mail, in person. Both court and visitors may perform in person searches. Search fee: $10.00 per name. Required to search: name, years to search. Civil cases indexed by defendant, plaintiff; index on computer from 1982, index books from 1800s. Mail turnaround 1 week.
Criminal Records: Access: Mail, in person. Both court and visitors may perform in person searches. Search fee: $10.00 per name. Required to search: name, years to search, DOB, SSN, signed release. Criminal records computerized from 1982, index books from 1800s. Mail turnaround time 1 week.
General Information: No juvenile, mental, sealed, or adoption records released. Fee to fax out file $2.00 per page. Court makes copy: $1.00 per page. Self serve: same. Cert fee: $5.00 per document. Payee: District or County Clerk. Personal checks accepted; credit cards are not.

Crosby County

District Court 201 W Aspen St, #207, Crosbyton, TX 79322-2500; 806-675-2071; fax: 806-675-2433; 8AM-N, 1-5PM (CST). ***Felony, Civil.***
Civil Records: Access: Phone, fax, mail, in person. Both court and visitors may perform in person searches. Search fee: $5.00 per name. Required to search: name, years to search. Civil cases indexed by defendant, plaintiff. Civil records in index books from 1896. Mail turnaround time 1 day.
Criminal Records: Access: Phone, fax, mail, in person. Both court and visitors may perform in person searches. Search fee: $5.00 per name. Required to search: name, years to search. Criminal docket on books from 1896. Mail turnaround 1 day.
General Information: No juvenile, mental, sealed, or adoption records released. Will fax documents to local or toll free numbers only. Court makes copy: $1.00 per page. Cert fee: $1.00. Payee: District Clerk. Personal checks accepted; credit cards are not. Mail requests: SASE required.

County Court 201 W Aspen St, #102, Crosbyton, TX 79322-2500; 806-675-2334; 8AM-N, 1-5PM (CST). ***Misdemeanor, Civil, Probate.*** Search fees are per index. Probate is separate index at this address.
Civil Records: Access: Mail, in person. Both court and visitors may perform in person searches. Search fee: $5.00 per name. Required to search: name, years to search. Civil cases indexed by defendant, plaintiff; index on microfiche from 1990, index books from 1886. Mail turnaround time 1 day.
Criminal Records: Access: Mail, in person. Both court and visitors may perform in person searches. Search fee: $5.00 per name. Required to search: name, years to search. Criminal records on microfiche from 1990, index books from 1886. Mail turnaround time 1 day. **General Information:** No juvenile, mental, sealed, or adoption records released. Will fax documents $1.00 per page. Court makes copy: $1.00 per page. Cert fee: $5.00 per doc. Payee: County Clerk. Personal checks accepted; credit cards are not.

Culberson County

District & County Court PO Box 158, 300 La Caverna, Van Horn, TX 79855; 432-283-2058; 8AM-N; 1PM-5PM (CST). ***Felony, Misdemeanor, Civil, Probate.*** All search requests must be in writing.
Civil Records: Access: Mail, in person. Both court and visitors may perform in person searches. Search fee: $5.00 per name. Required to search: name, years to search. Civil cases indexed by defendant, plaintiff. Civil records in index books since 1911. Mail turnaround time 2 days.
Criminal Records: Access: Phone, mail, in person. Both court and visitors may perform in person searches. Search fee: $5.00 per name. Required to search: name, years to search, signed release. Criminal docket on books from 1911. Mail turnaround 2 days.
General Information: No juvenile, mental, sealed, or adoption records released. Fee to fax out file $1.00 per page. Court makes copy: $1.00 per page. Cert fee: $5.00. Payee: District or County Clerk. Personal checks accepted. Mail requests: SASE required.

Dallam County

District & County Court PO Box 1352, Dalhart, TX 79022; 806-244-4751; fax: 806-244-3751; 9AM-5PM (CST). ***Felony, Misdemeanor, Civil, Probate.***
Civil Records: Access: Fax, mail, in person. Both court and visitors may perform in person searches. Search fee: $5.00 per name. Required to search: name, years to search. Civil cases indexed by defendant, plaintiff. Civil records in index books from 1800s; computerized since 1991. Mail turnaround time 1 day. **Criminal Records:** Access: Fax, mail, in person. Both court and visitors may perform in person searches. Search fee: $5.00 per name. Required to search: name, years to search. Criminal docket on books from 1800s; computerized since 1991. Mail turnaround time 1 day.
General Information: No juvenile, mental, sealed, or adoption records released. Fee to fax out file $5.00 1st page, $1.00 each add'l. Court makes copy: $1.00 per page. Cert fee: $5.00. Payee: Dallam County Clerk. Personal checks and major credit cards accepted. Mail requests: SASE required.

Dallas County

District Court - Civil 600 Commerce St, Dallas, TX 75202-4606; 214-653-7421; fax: 214-653-6634; 8AM-6:00PM (CST). ***Civil.***
www.dallascounty.org
Civil Records: Access: Mail, in person, online. Both court and visitors may perform in person searches. Search fee: $5.00 per name. Required to search: name, case number. Civil cases indexed by defendant, plaintiff; index on computer since 1967; on dockets back to 1940; records prior to 1940 are maintained by Texas Historical Div. of the Dallas Public Lib. Public use terminal has civil records. Search civil judgment index at www.dallascounty.org/pars2/. No fee unless a record is viewed. Also, search district civil and family case index free at http://courts.dallascounty.org/. Cases go back to early 1960s.
General Information: Online identifiers in results same as on public terminal. No sealed records released. Will not fax documents. Court makes copy: $1.00 per page. Cert fee: $1.00 per page. Payee: District Clerk. Cashiers checks, money orders and major credit cards accepted.

District Court - Criminal 133 N Industrial Blvd, LB12, Attn: District Clerk, Dallas, TX 75207-4313; 214-653-5950, 214-653-5069 records dept; fax: 214-653-5986; 8AM-4:30PM (CST). ***Felony.***
www.dallascounty.org
Criminal Records: Access: Mail, online, in person. Both court and visitors may perform in person searches. Search fee: $5.00 per name. Required to search: name, years to search, DOB. Criminal records computerized from 1972, on microfiche from 1979. Mail turnaround time 1-2 days. Public use terminal has crim records back to 1972. PAT results show middle initial, DOB. PAT terminal in law library but may also be at court. Name search free at

www.dallascounty.org/pars2/# and free results exhaustive, but there is a small fee to view a document using a credit card for payment. Online results show middle initial; not all records show DOB but most show race and gender.
General Information: Online identifiers in results same as on public terminal. No juvenile, mental, sealed, or adoption records released. Will not fax documents. Court makes copy: $1.00 per page. Cert fee: $1.00 per page. Payee: District Clerk. Only cashiers checks and money orders accepted. Major credit cards accepted. Mail requests: SASE required.

County Court - Misdemeanor 133 N Industrial Blvd, #LB43, Dallas, TX 75207-4313; 214-653-5740; fax: 214-653-5778; 8AM-4PM (CST). ***Misdemeanor.*** www.dallascounty.org
Criminal Records: Access: Mail, online, in person. Both court and visitors may perform in person searches. Search fee: $5.00 per name. Required to search: name, DOB. Criminal records computerized from 1975. Physical records go back to only 1993. For older searches call 214-653-5763, same fees apply. Mail turnaround time 10-11 days. Public use terminal has crim records back to 1975. PAT results show middle initial, DOB. PAT terminal in law library but may also be at court. Name search free at www.dallascounty.org/pars2/#. Criminal index includes DOB. There is no fee unless a record is viewed but most records info is viewed for free. Online results show middle initial, not all records have DOBs but most show race and gender.
General Information: No juvenile, mental, sealed, or adoption records released. Court makes copy: $1.00 per page. Cert fee: $6.00 per jacket. Payee: County Clerk. Only cashiers checks and money orders accepted or cash if in person. No credit cards accepted. Mail requests: SASE required.

Criminal District Courts 1-5 133 N Industrial Blvd, LB12, Attn: District Clerk, Records Department, Dallas, TX 75207; 214-653-5950; fax: 214-653-5986; 8AM-4:30PM (CST). ***Felony.***
www.dallascounty.org
This is the same criminal court as the main Dallas Criminal Court. Name search free at www.dallascounty.org/pars2/# but there is a small fee to view a document using a credit card for payment. Records are also on PATs as far back as 1975.

County Court - Civil 600 Commerce St, #101, Dallas, TX 75202; 214-653-7131; civil phone: 214-653-7442, 653-7096; fax: 214-653-7779; 8AM-4:30PM (CST). ***Civil.*** www.dallascounty.org
No civil claims limit as of 05/23/97.
Civil Records: Access: Phone, mail, in person, online. Both court and visitors may perform in person searches. Search fee: $5.00 per name per 10 years. Required to search: name, years to search. Civil cases indexed by defendant, plaintiff; index on computer from 1964, index books from 1800s. Mail turnaround time 1 day. Public use terminal has civil records back to 1964. Search civil judgment index at www.dallascounty.org/pars2/. No fee unless a record is viewed.
General Information: No juvenile, mental, sealed, or adoption records released. Will not fax documents. Court makes copy: $1.00 per page.Copy of a page from the archives- $2.00. Cert fee: $5.00 per doc; same to exemplify. Payee: County Clerk. Personal checks accepted; credit cards are not. Mail requests: SASE required.

Probate Court #3 509 Main St, #209, Records Bldg, 2nd Fl, Dallas, TX 75202; 214-653-6166; 8AM-4:30PM (CST). ***Probate.***
Search the probate civil judgment index at http://courts.dallascounty.org/. There is no fee unless a record is viewed.

Dawson County

District Court Drawer 1268, Lamesa, TX 79331; 806-872-7373; fax: 806-872-9513; 8:30AM-5PM (CST). ***Felony, Civil.***
Civil Records: Access: Mail, in person. Both court and visitors may perform in person searches. Search fee: $5.00 per name. Required to search: name, years to search. Civil cases indexed by defendant, plaintiff. Civil records in index books/files from 1905; computerized records since 1995. Mail turnaround time 1 day.
Criminal Records: Access: Mail, in person. Both court and visitors may perform in person searches. Search fee: $5.00 per name. Required to search: name, years to search, signed release. Criminal index in books/files from 1900s; computerized records since 1995. Mail turnaround time 1 day.
General Information: No juvenile, mental, sealed, or adoption records released. Will fax documents $1.00 per page. Court makes copy: $1.00 per page. Cert fee: $1.00 per page. Payee: Dawson County District Clerk. Personal checks accepted; credit cards are not.

County Court Drawer 1268, Lamesa, TX 79331; 806-872-3778; probate phone: same; criminal fax: 806-872-2473; civil fax: same; 8:30AM-N;1-5PM (CST). ***Misdemeanor, Civil, Probate.***
Probate fax is same as main fax number.
Civil Records: Access: Fax, mail, in person. Both court and visitors may perform in person searches. Search fee: $5.00 per name. Required to search: name, years to search. Civil cases indexed by defendant, plaintiff. Civil records in index files since 1906, on computer back to 1992. Note: Fees must be prepaid before fax access is allowed. Mail turnaround 1 day. Civil PAT goes back to 1992.
Criminal Records: Access: Mail, fax, in person. Both court and visitors may perform in person searches. Search fee: $5.00 per name. Required to search: name, years to search, DOB; also helpful-signed release, offense, date of offense. Criminal records in index files since 1906; on computer back to 1986. Note: Fees must be prepaid before fax access is allowed. Mail turnaround time 1 day. Criminal PAT goes back to 1982. PAT criminal results show middle initial.
General Information: No juvenile, mental or sealed records released. Fee to fax out file $5.00 each plus $1.00 per page. Court makes copy: $1.00 per page. Self serve: same. Cert fee: $5.00 per document. Payee: County Clerk. Personal checks and major credit cards accepted.

De Witt County

District Court PO Box 845, Cuero, TX 77954; 361-275-2221; fax: 361-275-5910; 8AM-5PM (CST). ***Felony, Civil.***
Civil Records: Access: Mail, in person. Both court and visitors may perform in person searches. Search fee: $5.00 per name. Required to search: name, years to search. Civil cases indexed by defendant, plaintiff. Mail turnaround time 1 week.
Criminal Records: Access: Mail, in person. Both court and visitors may perform in person searches. Search fee: $5.00 per name. Required to search: name, years to search, DOB, SSN, signed release. Criminal records maintained on books. Mail turnaround time 1 week.
General Information: No juvenile, mental, sealed, or adoption records released. Will not fax documents. Court makes copy: $1.00 per page. Cert fee: $1.00. Payee: DeWitt County District Clerk. Personal checks accepted; credit cards are not. Mail requests: SASE required.

County Court 307 N Gonzales, Cuero, TX 77954; 361-275-3724; probate phone: same; fax: 361-275-8994; 8AM-5PM (CST). ***Misdemeanor, Probate.***
Probate is in a separate index at this same address. Probate fax is same as main fax number.
Criminal Records: Access: Mail, in person. Both court and visitors may perform in person searches. Search fee: $5.00 per name. Required to search: name, years to search; also helpful: DOB, SSN. Criminal records go back to 1960s; on computer back to 1998.
General Information: No juvenile, mental, sealed, or adoption records released. Fee to fax out file $1.00 per page. Court makes copy: $1.00 per page. Cert fee: $5.00 per document. Payee: DeWitt County Clerk. Personal checks accepted; credit cards are not.

Deaf Smith County

District Court 235 E 3rd St, Rm 304, Hereford, TX 79045; 806-364-3901; fax: 806-363-7007; 8AM-5PM (CST). ***Felony, Civil.***
Civil Records: Access: Fax, mail, in person. Both court and visitors may perform in person searches. Search fee: $5.00 per name. Required to search: name, years to search, DOB, SSN. Civil cases indexed by defendant, plaintiff; index on computer from 2/1993; prior on microfiche from 5/15/1981. Mail turnaround time 3 days. Civil PAT goes back to 2/1993. PAT results show name only.
Criminal Records: Access: Fax, mail, in person. Both court and visitors may perform in person searches. Search fee: $5.00 per name. Required to search: name, years to search; also helpful: DOB, SSN, case number. Criminal records computerized from 2/1993; prior on microfiche from 5/15/1981. Mail turnaround time 3 days. Criminal PAT goes back to same as civil. PAT results show name only. Aliases may also be included in PAT search results.
General Information: No juvenile, mental, sealed, or adoption records released. Fee to fax out file $2.00 per page. Court makes copy: $1.00 per page. Cert fee: $1.00. Payee: District Clerk. Personal checks accepted; credit cards are not. Mail requests: SASE required.

County Court Deaf Smith Courthouse, 235 E 3rd, Rm 203, Hereford, TX 79045; 806-363-7077; fax: 806-363-7023; 8AM-5PM (CST). ***Misdemeanor, Civil, Probate.***
Civil Records: Access: Mail, in person. Both court and visitors may perform in person searches. Search fee: $5.00 per name. Required to search: name, years to search, DOB. Civil cases indexed by defendant, plaintiff; index on computer from 1989, microfiche from 1981, index books from early 1900s. Mail turnaround time 1 day. Civil PAT goes back to 1989. PAT results show name only.
Criminal Records: Access: Mail, in person. Both court and visitors may perform in person searches. Search fee: $5.00 per name. Required to search: name, years to search; DOB and SSN helpful. Criminal records computerized from 1993, microfiche from 1981, index books from early 1900s. Note: Records also available on CD-rom special order, usually $22.00 minimum. Mail turnaround time 1 day, usually. Criminal PAT goes back to 1993. PAT results show middle initial, DOB. Terminal results include SSN.
General Information: No juvenile, mental, sealed, or adoption records released. Will fax documents $2.00 plus $1.00 copy fee for each page faxed. Court makes copy: $1.00 per page. Self serve: same.Volume discounts for copies, usually $.10 per page if over 10 pages. Copies for ongoing criminal investigations/prosecutions are no charge. Cert fee: $5.00 per document. Payee: County Clerk. Personal checks accepted. Major credit cards accepted; 5% usage fee added.

Delta County

District & County Court 200 W Dallas Ave, Cooper, TX 75432; 903-395-4400 x223; criminal phone: 903-395-4400; civil phone: 903-395-4400; probate phone: 903-395-4400; fax: 903-395-4260; 8-5PM (CST). ***Felony, Misdemeanor, Civil, Probate.***
Probate is a separate index at this same address. Probate fax is same as main fax number.
Civil Records: Access: Phone, mail, in person. Both court and visitors may perform in person searches. Search fee: $5.00 per name per court. Required to search: name, years to search. Civil cases indexed by defendant, plaintiff. Civil records in index books from late 1800s. Note: Phone searches must be pre-paid. Mail turnaround time 1 day. Public use terminal has civil records but record index not complete.
Criminal Records: Access: Phone, mail, in person. Both court and visitors may perform in person searches. Search fee: $5.00 per name per court. Required to search: name, years to search, DOB. Criminal docket on books from late 1800s. Note: Phone searches must be prepaid. Mail turnaround time 1 day.
General Information: No juvenile, mental, sealed, or adoption records released. Fee to fax out file $2.00 1st page, $1.00 each add'l. Court makes copy: $1.00 per page. Self serve: same. Cert fee: $5.00 per doc. Payee: County or District Clerk. Personal checks and major credit cards accepted. Mail requests: SASE required.

Denton County

District Court PO Box 2146, Denton, TX 76202; criminal phone: 940-349-2210; civil phone: 940-349-2201; criminal fax: 940-349-2211; civil fax: 940-349-2201; 8AM-4:30PM (CST). ***Felony, Civil.***
http://dentoncounty.com/dept/main.asp?Dept=26
Civil Records: Access: Phone, mail, fax, online, in person. Only the court performs in person searches; visitors may not. Search fee: $5.00 per name. Required to search: name, years to search. Civil cases indexed by defendant, plaintiff; index on computer from 1990, archived from 1936. Mail turnaround time 1-2 weeks. Search civil records free at http://justice.dentoncounty.com. Search by name or cause number.
Criminal Records: Access: Mail, fax, online, in person. Only the court performs in person searches; visitors may not. Search fee: $5.00 per name. Required to search: name, years to search, DOB. Criminal records computerized from 1990, archived from 1936. Mail turnaround 1-2 weeks. Criminal searches free at http://justice.dentoncounty.com. Records go back to 1994 forward. Access also includes sheriff bond and jail records.
General Information: No juvenile, mental, sealed, expunctions or adoption records released. Fee to fax out file $1.00 per page. Court makes copy: $1.00 1st page, $.25 each add'l, same document. Cert fee: $1.00 per document. No personal checks accepted. Use of credit card requires a 5% surcharge. Mail requests: SASE required.

County Court PO Box 2187, Attn: County Clerk, 1450 McKinney, Denton, TX 76202-2187; 940-349-2012; criminal phone: 940-349-2014; civil phone: 940-349-2016; probate phone: 940-349-2036; criminal fax: 940-349-2015; civil fax: 940-349-2141; 8AM-5PM, W til 4:30PM (CST). ***Misdemeanor, Civil, Probate.***
http://dentoncounty.com/deptall.asp
Civil Records: Access: Mail, in person, online. Both court and visitors may perform in person searches. Search fee: $5.00 per name. Add $1.00 per year prior to 1989. Required to search: name, years to search. Civil cases indexed by defendant, plaintiff; index on computer back to 1990. Mail turnaround time 1-2 weeks. Civil PAT goes back to 1990. Public terminal in Law Library. Online access civil court records free at http://justice.dentoncounty.com/CivilSearch/civfrmd.htm.
Criminal Records: Access: Mail, in person, online. Both court and visitors may perform in person searches. Search fee: $5.00 per name. Add $1.00 per year over first 5. Required to search: name, years to search, DOB. Criminal records computerized from 1990. Mail turnaround time 1-2 weeks. Criminal PAT goes back to 1990. Public terminal in Law Library. Access county criminal records free at http://justice.dentoncounty.com/CrimSearch/crimfrmd.htm. Jail, bond, and parole records are also available at http://justice.dentoncounty.com. Search registered sex offenders by ZIP Code at http://sheriff.dentoncounty.com/sex_offenders/default.htm.
General Information: No juvenile, mental, sealed, or adoption records released. Will not fax documents. Court makes copy: $.25 per page. Cert fee: $5.00 per doc. Payee: Denton County Clerk. Cashiers checks and money orders accepted. Visa/MC accepted. Mail requests: SASE required.

Dickens County

District & County Court PO Box 120, Dickens, TX 79229; 806-623-5531; fax: 806-623-5319; 8AM-5PM ***Felony, Misdemeanor, Civil, Probate.***
Civil Records: Access: Mail, fax, phone, in person. Both court and visitors may perform in person searches. Search fee: $5.00 per name. Required to search: name, years to search, DOB, SSN and signed release. Civil cases indexed by defendant, plaintiff. Civil records in index books since late 1891. Mail turnaround time 1-2 days.
Criminal Records: Access: Mail, fax, phone, in person. Both court and visitors may perform in person searches. Search fee: $5.00 per name. Required to search: name, years to search; also helpful: DOB, SSN and signed release. Criminal docket on books from late 1891. Mail turnaround time 1-2 days.
General Information: No juvenile, mental, sealed or adoption records released. Will fax documents $1.00 per page. Court makes copy: $1.00 per page. Self serve: same. Cert fee: $5.00. Payee: District Court. Personal checks accepted; credit cards are not. Mail requests: SASE required.

Dimmit County

District Court 103 N 5th St, Carrizo Springs, TX 78834; 830-876-4243 x111, x112; criminal phone: 830-876-4280; fax: 830-876-4200; 8AM-N; 1PM-5PM (CST). ***Felony, Civil.***
Probate is in the county clerk office.
Civil Records: Access: Mail, in person. Both court and visitors may perform in person searches. Search fee: $10.00 per name. Required to search: name, years to search; also helpful: address. Civil cases indexed by defendant, plaintiff. Civil records in index books, archived from 1922. Mail turnaround time 2-3 days.
Criminal Records: Access: Mail, in person. Both court and visitors may perform in person searches. Search fee: $10.00 per name. Required to search: name, years to search; also helpful: DOB, SSN. Criminal index in books, archived from 1936. Mail turnaround time 2-3 days.
General Information: No juvenile, mental, sealed, or adoption records released. Will not fax documents. Court makes copy: $1.00 per page. Self serve: same. Cert fee: $5.00 per doc. Payee: District Clerk. Personal checks accepted; credit cards are not. Mail requests: SASE required.

County Court 103 N 5th, Carrizo Springs, TX 78834; 830-876-4238/9; fax: 830-876-4205; 8AM-5PM (CST). ***Misdemeanor, Civil, Probate.***
Probate is a separate index. Probate fax is same as main fax number.
Civil Records: Access: Fax, mail, in person. Both court and visitors may perform in person searches. Search fee: $10.00 per name. Required to search: name, years to search. Civil cases indexed by defendant, plaintiff; index on microfiche from 1992, index books prior. Mail turnaround time 1 day.
Criminal Records: Access: Fax, mail, in person. Both court and visitors may perform in person searches. Search fee: $10.00 per name. Required to search: name, years to search, signed release, DOB; also helpful: sex, SSN. Mail turnaround time 1 day.
General Information: No juvenile, mental, sealed, or adoption records released. Fee to fax out file $1.50 1st page; $1.00 each add'l. Court makes copy: $1.00 per page. Self serve: same. Cert fee: $5.00 per certification. Payee: County Clerk. Personal checks accepted; credit cards are not. Mail requests: SASE required.

Donley County

District & County Court PO Drawer U, Clarendon, TX 79226; 806-874-3436; fax: 806-874-3351; 8AM-N, 1-5PM (CST). ***Felony, Misdemeanor, Civil, Probate.***
Civil Records: Access: Mail, in person. Both court and visitors may perform in person searches. Search fee: $5.00 per name. Required to search: name, years to search. Civil cases indexed by defendant, plaintiff; index on computer from 1991, index books from 1890s. Mail turnaround time 1 day. Civil PAT goes back to 1994.
Criminal Records: Access: Mail, in person. Both court and visitors may perform in person searches. Search fee: $5.00 per name. Required to search: name, years to search, DOB, signed release, aliases; also helpful: SSN. Criminal records computerized from 1991, index books from 1890s. Mail turnaround 1 day. Criminal PAT goes back to same as civil.
General Information: No juvenile, mental, sealed, or adoption records released. Will not fax documents. Court makes copy: $1.00 per page. Self serve: same. Cert fee: $5.00. Payee: County Clerk. Personal checks accepted; credit cards are not. Mail requests: SASE required.

Duval County

District Court PO Drawer 428, 400 E Gravis, San Diego, TX 78384; 361-279-3322 x239; criminal phone: 361-279-6209; civil phone: 361-279-6284; 8AM-5PM (CST). ***Felony, Civil.***
Civil Records: Access: Mail, in person. Both court and visitors may perform in person searches. Search fee: $15.00 per name. Fee is for large cases. Required to search: name, years to search. Civil cases indexed by defendant, plaintiff. Civil index on docket books from 1900s. Mail turnaround time 1-2 days.
Criminal Records: Access: Phone, mail, in person. Both court and visitors may perform in person searches. Search fee: $15.00 per name. Fee is for large cases. Required to search: name, years to search. Criminal records not computerized, indexed in books since 1900's. Mail turnaround time 1-2 days.
General Information: No sealed, or adoption records released. Will not fax documents. Court makes copy: $1.00 per page. Cert fee: $5.00. Payee: District Clerk. Personal checks accepted; credit cards are not. Mail requests: SASE required.

County Court PO Box 248, San Diego, TX 78384; 361-279-6249/6272; fax: 361-279-3159; 8AM-N, 1-5PM ***Misdemeanor, Civil, Probate.***
Civil Records: Access: Mail, in person. Both court and visitors may perform in person searches. Search fee: $10.00 per name. Required to search: name, years to search. Civil cases indexed by defendant, plaintiff. Civil records in index books from 1800s, records go back to the early 1900's. Mail turnaround time 2 days.
Criminal Records: Access: Mail, in person. Both court and visitors may perform in person searches. Search fee: $10.00 per name. Required to search: name, years to search, offense, date of offense. Criminal docket on books from 1800s. Mail turnaround time 2 days.
General Information: No juvenile, mental, sealed, or adoption records released. Will not fax documents. Court makes copy: $1.00 per page. Cert fee: $5.00. Payee: County Clerk. Personal checks accepted; credit cards are not. Mail requests: SASE required.

Eastland County

District Court 100 W Main St, #206, Eastland, TX 76448; 254-629-2664; fax: 254-629-6070; 8AM-5PM (CST). ***Felony, Civil.***
Civil Records: Access: Mail, in person. Both court and visitors may perform in person searches. Search fee: $5.00. Required to search: name, years to search. Civil cases indexed by defendant, plaintiff; index on computer from 1930. Mail turnaround time 1 day.
Criminal Records: Access: Mail, in person. Both court and visitors may perform in person searches. Search fee: $5.00. Required to search: name, years to search. Criminal records computerized from 1976, archived from 1875. Mail turnaround time 1 day.
General Information: No juvenile, mental, sealed, or adoption records released. Will fax documents to toll free line. Court makes copy: $1.00 per page. Cert fee: $5.00 per document. Payee: District Clerk. Personal checks and credit cards accepted. Mail requests: SASE required.

County Court PO Box 110, Eastland, TX 76448; 254-629-1583; fax: 254-629-8125; 8AM-5PM (CST). ***Misdemeanor, Probate.***
No civil records after 1977; criminal and probate records only thereafter. Probate is in a separate index at this same address.
Criminal Records: Access: Mail, in person. Both court and visitors may perform in person searches. Search fee: $5.00 per name. Required to search: name, years to search, DOB; also helpful: SSN. Signed release required if subject is a minor. Criminal docket on books and on computer from 1987; name searches only. Mail turnaround time 1-2 days. Public use terminal has crim records back to 1987.
General Information: No juvenile, mental, sealed, or adoption records released. Will fax documents $5.00 fee. Court makes copy: $1.00 per page. Cert fee: $5.00 per cert. Payee: Eastland County Clerk. Personal checks accepted; checks must include phone number & DL number. No credit cards accepted.

Ector County

District Court County Courthouse, 300 N Grant, Rm 301, Odessa, TX 79761; 432-498-4290; fax: 432-498-4292; 8AM-5PM (CST). ***Felony, Civil.***

Civil Records: Access: Phone, fax, mail, in person. Both court and visitors may perform in person searches. Search fee: $5.00 per name. Required to search: name, years to search. Civil cases indexed by defendant, plaintiff; index on computer from 1989, index books from 1880. Mail turnaround time 2 weeks. Civil PAT goes back to 1989.
Criminal Records: Access: Phone, mail, in person. Both court and visitors may perform in person searches. Search fee: $5.00 per name. Required to search: name, years to search. Criminal records computerized from 1989, index books from 1880. Mail turnaround time 2 weeks. Criminal PAT goes back to same as civil.
General Information: No juvenile, mental, sealed, or adoption records released. Will fax documents $2.00 per page. Court makes copy: $.25 per page. Cert fee: $1.00 per page includes copy fee. Payee: Ector County District Clerk. Business checks accepted. No credit cards accepted. Mail requests: SASE required.

County Court PO Box 707, Odessa, TX 79760; 432-498-4130; fax: 432-498-4177; 8AM-4:30PM (CST). ***Misdemeanor, Civil, Probate.***
Civil Records: Access: Mail, in person. Both court and visitors may perform in person searches. Search fee: $10.00 per name per ten years. Required to search: name, years to search. Civil cases indexed by defendant, plaintiff; index on computer from 1992, index books from 1900s. Mail turnaround time 5 days. Civil PAT goes back to 1992. PAT results show middle initial, DOB. Results on public terminal may show DR.
Criminal Records: Access: Mail, in person. Both court and visitors may perform in person searches. Search fee: $10.00 per name per ten years. Required to search: name, years to search; also helpful: DOB, SSN. Criminal records computerized from 1989, index books from 1900s. Mail turnaround time 5 days. Criminal PAT goes back to 1989. PAT results show middle initial, DOB. Results on public terminal may show DR.
General Information: No juvenile, mental, sealed, or adoption records released. Fee to fax out file $2.00 each. Court makes copy: $1.00 per page. Cert fee: $5.00 per doc. Payee: County Clerk. Personal checks and credit cards accepted. Mail requests: SASE required.

Edwards County

District & County Court PO Box 184, Rocksprings, TX 78880; 830-683-2235; fax: 830-683-5376; 8AM-N, 1-5PM (CST). ***Felony, Misdemeanor, Civil, Probate.***
Civil Records: Access: Phone, fax, mail, in person. Both court and visitors may perform in person searches. Search fee: $10.00 per name. Required to search: name, years to search. Civil cases indexed by defendant, plaintiff. Real Property on computer from 2003, index books from 1885. Mail turnaround time 1 day or less.
Criminal Records: Access: Phone, fax, mail, in person. Both court and visitors may perform in person searches. Search fee: $10.00 per name. Required to search: name, years to search. Index books from 1960. Mail turnaround time 1 day.
General Information: No juvenile, mental, sealed, or adoption records released. Fee to fax out file $3.00. Court makes copy: $1.00 per page. Cert fee: $5.00. Payee: Edwards County Clerk. Personal checks accepted; credit cards are not. Mail requests: SASE required.

El Paso County

District Court 500 E San Antonio, Rm 103, El Paso, TX 79901; 915-546-2021; criminal phone: 915-834-8255; civil phone: 915-834-8256; fax: 915-546-8139; 8AM-5PM (MST). ***Felony, Civil.*** www.co.el-paso.tx.us/districtclerk
No fee to request a name search of indexes, however a $10 charge per individual if a certified document stating the presence or absence of felony charges against that individual is requested. Each 10 year period prior to 1986 carries an add'l $5 charge.
Civil Records: Access: Mail, in person, online, fax, phone. Both court and visitors may perform in person searches. Search fee: See above statement regarding fees. Required to search: name, years to search. Civil cases indexed by defendant, plaintiff; index on computer from 1986, microfiche from 1971, index books from 1800s. Mail turnaround time 1-3 days. Civil PAT goes back to 1986. All records disposed or active on public access terminal. Access civil court records free at www.co.el-paso.tx.us/JIMSSearch/CivilRecordsearch.asp. Also, access index and images at www.idocket.com; registration and password required; online civil records go back to 12/31/1986.
Criminal Records: Access: Mail, in person, online, fax, phone. Both court and visitors may perform in person searches. Search fee: See above statement regarding fees. Required to search: name, years to search, DOB, signed release; also helpful: sex. Criminal records computerized from 1986, microfiche from 1971, index books from 1800s. Mail turnaround time 1-3 days. Criminal PAT goes back to same as civil. All records disposed or active on public access terminal. Online access to criminal court active records is free at www.co.el-paso.tx.us/JIMSSearch/CriminalRecordsearch.asp Also, online access index and images at www.idocket.com; registration and password required; online records go back to 12/31/1986.
General Information: No juvenile, mental, sealed, or adoption records released. Will fax documents $10.00 plus $.25 per page. Court makes copy: $.25 per page. Self serve: same. Cert fee: $1.00. Payee: District Clerk. Business checks accepted. Major credit cards accepted for mail or phone searches. Mail requests: SASE required.

County Court 500 E San Antonio St, Rm 105, El Paso, TX 79901; 915-546-2072; fax: 915-546-2012; 8AM-4:45PM (MST). ***Misdemeanor, Civil.*** www.co.el-paso.tx.us
Civil Records: Access: Mail, fax, in person, online. Both court and visitors may perform in person searches. Search fee: $5.00 per name. Required to search: name, years to search. Civil cases indexed by defendant, plaintiff; index on computer from 1989, on microfiche and archived from 1952. Mail turnaround time up to 1 week. Civil PAT goes back to 1989. PAT results show name only. Access civil court records free online at www.co.el-paso.tx.us/JIMSSearch/CivilRecordsearch.asp. Also, search vital records and recordings. Also, access index and images at www.idocket.com; registration and password required. Civil records go back to 12/31/1986, probate to 12/31/1989.
Criminal Records: Access: Phone, mail, fax, in person, online. Both court and visitors may perform in person searches. Search fee: $5.00 per name. Required to search: name, years to search, DOB, SSN. Criminal records computerized since 1989. Mail turnaround time up to 1 week. Criminal PAT goes back to same as civil. PAT results show name only. Online access to misdemeanor criminal records is the same as civil at www.co.el-paso.tx.us/JIMSSearch/CriminalRecordsearch.asp and also at www.idocket.com with signup, see civil above.
General Information: Online identifiers in results same as on public terminal. No juvenile, mental, sealed, or adoption records released. Will not fax documents. Court makes copy: $.25 per page. Cert fee: $5.00 per document. Payee: County Clerk. No personal checks or credit cards accepted. Mail requests: SASE required.

Probate Court #1 El Paso County Courthouse, 500 E San Antonio, Rm 703, El Paso, TX 79901; 915-546-2161; fax: 915-875-8527; 8AM-Noon,1-5PM (MST). ***Probate.*** Access probate records through www.idocket.com; registration and password required. Records go back to 12/31/1986.

Ellis County

District Court 1201 N Highway 77, #103, Waxahachie, TX 75165; 972-825-5091; fax: 972-825-5010; 8AM-5PM (CST). ***Felony, Civil.***
Civil Records: Access: Mail, in person. Both court and visitors may perform in person searches. Search fee: $5.00 per name. Required to search: name, years to search. Civil cases indexed by defendant, plaintiff; index on computer from 1992, index books from 1800s. Mail turnaround time 1 week. Civil PAT goes back to 1992. PAT results show name, DOB, and SSNs.
Criminal Records: Access: Mail, in person. Both court and visitors may perform in person searches. Search fee: $5.00 per name. Required to search: name, years to search, DOB, offense. Criminal records computerized from 1992, index books from 1800s. Mail turnaround time 1 week. Criminal PAT goes back to same as civil.PAT results show name, DOB. Terminal results include SSN.
General Information: No juvenile, mental, sealed, or adoption records released. Will not fax documents. Court makes copy: $.50 per page. Cert fee: $1.00 per page. Payee: District Clerk's Office. Cashiers checks money orders, Visa/MC accepted. Mail requests: SASE required.

County Court PO Box 250, Waxahachie, TX 75168; 972-923-5070; criminal phone: 972-923-5078; civil phone: 972-923-5083; probate phone: 972-923-5082; fax: 972-923-5075; 8AM-4:30PM (CST). ***Misdemeanor, Civil, Probate.*** www.co.ellis.tx.us
Probate fax is same as main fax number.
Civil Records: Access: Mail, in person. Both court and visitors may perform in person searches. Search fee: $5.00 per name. Fee is per 5 year period. Required to search: name, years to search. Civil cases indexed by defendant, plaintiff; index on computer go back to 1995. Prior to computer records go back to 1969. Mail turnaround time 1-5 days. Civil PAT goes back to 1992.
Criminal Records: Access: Mail, in person. Both court and visitors may perform in person searches. Search fee: $5.00 per name. Fee is per 5 year period. Required to search: name, years to search, DOB, SSN. Criminal records on computer since 1992, index books from 1959. Mail turnaround time 1-5 days. Criminal PAT goes back to same as civil.
General Information: No juvenile, mental, sealed, or adoption records released. Will not fax documents. Court makes copy: $1.00 per page. Self serve: same. Cert fee: $5.00 per doc. Payee: Ellis Clerk. Personal checks with ID accepted. Credit cards accepted. Mail requests: SASE required.

Erath County

District Court 112 W College, Courthouse Annex, Stephenville, TX 76401; 254-965-1486; fax: 254-965-7156; 8AM-5PM (CST). ***Felony, Civil.*** www.co.erath.tx.us/ips/cms
Civil Records: Access: Mail, in person, online. Both court and visitors may perform in person searches. Search fee: $5.00 per name. Fee is per name per search. Required to search: name, years to search. Civil cases indexed by defendant, plaintiff. Limited civil records on computer last 10 years, in person must be done using docket books. Mail turnaround time 1-2 days. Civil PAT goes back to 5 years. PAT results show name, DOB. Access to District Clerk records requires registration, login and password; signup online at www.erathcountyonline.net/districtclerk/
Criminal Records: Access: Mail, in person, online. Both court and visitors may perform in person searches. Search fee: $5.00 per name. Required to search: name, years to search, DOB; also helpful: SSN. Limited criminal records on computer last 10 years, in person must be done using docket books. Mail turnaround time 1-2 days. Criminal PAT goes back to same as civil.PAT results show name, DOB. Access to District Clerk records requires registration, login and password; signup online at www.erathcountyonline.net/districtclerk/
General Information: No juvenile, mental, sealed, or adoption records released. Fee to fax out file $1.00 per page. Court makes copy: $1.00 per page. Cert fee: $5.00 per doc. Payee: District Clerk. Personal checks and major credit cards accepted. Mail requests: SASE required.

County Court Erath County Courthouse, 100 W Washington, Stephenville, TX 76401; 254-965-1482; criminal phone: 254-965-1407; civil phone: 254-965-1428; probate phone: 254-965-1428; fax: 254-965-5732; 8AM-4PM (CST). ***Misdemeanor, Civil, Probate.***
Probate is a separate index at this same address. Probate fax is same as main fax number.
Civil Records: Access: Mail, in person, online. Both court and visitors may perform in person searches. Search fee: $5.00 per name. Required to search:

name, years to search. Civil cases indexed by defendant, plaintiff; index on computer back to 1993, index books since 1970. Mail turnaround time 1 week. Civil PAT goes back to 1993. PAT civil results show middle initial. Access to County Court records requires registration, login and password; signup online at www.erathcountyonline.net/countyclerk/.
Criminal Records: Access: Mail, in person, online. Both court and visitors may perform in person searches. Search fee: $10.00 per name. Required to search: name, years to search, DOB. Criminal records computerized from 1993, index books from 1960. Mail turnaround time 1 week. Criminal PAT goes back to same as civil. Results include name and case number. Access to County Court records requires registration, login and password; signup online at www.erathcountyonline.net/countyclerk/.
General Information: No juvenile, mental, sealed, or adoption records released. Will fax documents $1.75 fee for the 1st page and $.75 for each additional page. Court makes copy: $1.00 per page. Self serve: same. Cert fee: $5.00 per document. Payee: County Clerk. Personal checks accepted; credit cards are not. Mail requests: SASE required.

Falls County

District Court PO Box 229, 125 Bridge St, Rm 301, Marlin, TX 76661; 254-883-1419; 8AM-N, 1-4:30PM (CST). ***Felony, Civil.*** Mail requests to PO Box 229 in care of the District Clerk.
Civil Records: Access: Mail, in person. Both court and visitors may perform in person searches. Search fee: $5.00 per name. Required to search: name, years to search. Civil cases indexed by defendant, plaintiff. Overall records go back to 1850's. Computerized records go back to 1998. Mail turnaround time 1-5 days. Public terminal has civil records back to 1998; results show name, DOB.
Criminal Records: Access: Mail, in person. Both court and visitors may perform in person searches. Search fee: $5.00 per name. Required to search: name, years to search; also helpful: DOB. Criminal index in books. Mail turnaround time 1-5 days.
General Information: No juvenile, mental, sealed, child support or adoption records released. Court makes copy: $1.00 per page. No certification fee. Payee: District Clerk. Personal checks accepted; credit cards are not. Mail requests: SASE required.

County Court PO Box 458, Marlin, TX 76661; 254-883-1408; fax: 254-883-1406; 8AM-5PM (CST). ***Misdemeanor, Civil, Probate.***
Civil Records: Access: Phone, mail, in person. Both court and visitors may perform in person searches. Search fee: $5.00 per name. Required to search: name, years to search. Civil cases indexed by defendant, plaintiff. Civil records in index books from 1985. Note: Court allows phone search only if fee prepaid. Mail turnaround time 1 day.
Criminal Records: Access: Phone, mail, in person. Both court and visitors may perform in person searches. Search fee: $5.00 per name. Required to search: name, years to search, DOB, SSN. Criminal docket on books from 1985. Note: Phone search only if fee is prepaid. Mail turnaround time 1 day.
General Information: No juvenile, mental, sealed, or adoption records released. Will not fax documents. Court makes copy: $1.00 per page. Cert fee: $5.00 per instrument. Payee: County Clerk. Local personal and business checks accepted. No credit cards accepted. Mail requests: SASE required.

Fannin County

District Court 101 E Sam Rayburn Dr, #201, Bonham, TX 75418; 903-583-7459; fax: 903-640-1826; 8AM-5PM (CST). ***Felony, Civil.*** www.co.fannin.tx.us/ips/cms
Civil Records: Access: Fax, mail, in person. Both court and visitors may perform in person searches. Search fee: $5.00 per name. Required to search: name, years to search. Civil cases indexed by defendant, plaintiff. Civil records in index books, archived from 1865. Mail turnaround time 10 days.
Criminal Records: Access: Fax, mail, in person. Both court and visitors may perform in person searches. Search fee: $5.00 per name. Fee is for felonies only. Required to search: name, years to search, address, DOB, SSN. Criminal records computerized from 1985, books from 1975, archived from 1865. Mail turnaround time 5 days.
General Information: No juvenile, mental, sealed, or adoption records released. Will not fax documents. Court makes copy: $1.00 per page. Self serve: same. Cert fee: $2.00. Payee: District Clerk, Fannin County. Personal checks accepted; credit cards are not. Mail requests: SASE required.

County Court County Courthouse, 101 E Sam Rayburn, Bonham, TX 75418; 903-583-7486; criminal phone: 903-583-8502; civil: 903-640-2008; probate phone: 903-640-2008; fax: 903-583-9598; 8AM-5PM (CST). ***Misdemeanor, Civil, Probate.*** Address requests to Ste 103 for criminal and Ste 106 for civil or probate.
Civil Records: Access: Mail, in person. Only the court performs in person searches; visitors may not. Search fee: $10.00 per name. Required to search: name, years to search. Civil cases indexed by defendant, plaintiff. Civil index in books. Mail turnaround time 1 day.
Criminal Records: Access: Mail, in person. Only the court performs in person searches; visitors may not. Search fee: $10.00 per name. Required to search: name, years to search, DOB; also helpful-SSN. Criminal records computerized from 1979; prior on index books. Mail turnaround time 1 day.
General: No juvenile, mental, sealed, or adoption records released. Will not fax documents. Court makes copy: $1.00 per page. Cert fee: $5.00. Payee: County Clerk. Personal checks accepted if local. No credit cards accepted. Mail requests: SASE required.

Fayette County

District Court Fayette County Courthouse, 151 N Washington, La Grange, TX 78945; 979-968-3548; fax: 979-968-2618; 8AM-5PM (CST). ***Felony, Civil over $5,000.*** www.cvtv.net/~tx155district
Civil Records: Access: Mail, in person. Both court and visitors may perform in person searches. Search fee: $5.00 per name. Required to search: name, years to search. Civil cases indexed by defendant, plaintiff. Civil records in index books, on computer since 1990. Mail turnaround time 2-3 days. Civil PAT goes back to 1990. PAT results show middle initial, DOB. **Criminal Records:** Access: Mail, in person. Both court and visitors may perform in person searches. Search fee: $5.00 per name. Required to search: name, years to search. Criminal index in books, on computer since 1990. Mail turnaround 2-3 days. Criminal PAT goes back to 1987. PAT results show middle initial, DOB.
General Information: No juvenile, mental, sealed, or adoption records released. Will fax documents $5.00 per page. Court makes copy: $1.00 per page. Cert fee: $2.00. Payee: Fayette County District Clerk. Personal checks accepted; credit cards are not. Mail requests: SASE required.

County Court PO Box 59, 246 W Colorado, La Grange, TX 78945; 979-968-3251; fax: 979-968-8531; 8AM-5PM (CST). ***Misdemeanor, Civil under $5,000, Probate.*** www.co.fayette.tx.us
Civil Records: Access: Mail, in person. Both court and visitors may perform in person searches. Search fee: $5.00 per name. Required to search: name, years to search. Civil cases indexed by defendant, plaintiff. Civil records in index books, archived from 1970. Mail turnaround time 1 day. Public terminal has civil back to 4/15/2008.
Criminal Records: Access: Mail, in person. Both court and visitors may perform in person searches. Search fee: $5.00 per name. Required to search: name, years to search. Criminal records computerized from 1980, index books prior. Mail turnaround 1 day.
General Information: No juvenile, mental, sealed, or adoption records released. Will fax documents for double the copy fee, prepaid. Court makes copy: $1.00 per page. Cert fee: $5.00. Payee: County Clerk. Personal checks and major credit cards accepted.

Fisher County

District Court PO Box 88, Roby, TX 79543; 325-776-2279; fax: 325-776-3253; 8AM-5PM (CST). ***Felony, Civil.*** **Civil Records:** Access: Mail, in person. Both court and visitors may perform in person searches. Search fee: $5.00 per name. Required to search: name, years to search; also helpful: address. Civil cases indexed by defendant, plaintiff. Civil records in index books from 1886. Mail turnaround 1-2 days.
Criminal Records: Access: Mail, in person. Both court and visitors may perform in person searches. Search fee: $5.00 per name. Required to search: name, years to search, signed release; also helpful: address, DOB. Criminal docket on books from 1886. Mail turnaround time 1-2 days.
General Information: No juvenile, mental, sealed, or adoption records released. Fee to fax out file $1.00 per page. Court makes copy: $.50 per page. Self serve: same. Cert fee: $1.00 per page. Payee: District Clerk. Business checks accepted. No credit cards accepted. Mail requests: SASE required.

County Court Box 368, Roby, TX 79543-0368; 325-776-2401; fax: 325-776-3274; 8AM-N, 1-5PM (CST). ***Misdemeanor, Civil, Probate.***
Civil Records: Access: Mail, in person. Both court and visitors may perform in person searches. Search fee: $5.00 per name. Required to search: name, years to search. Civil cases indexed by defendant, plaintiff; index on computer from 1994 index books from 1880. Mail turnaround time 1 day. Civil PAT available. **Criminal Records:** Access: Mail, in person. Both court and visitors may perform in person searches. Search fee: $5.00 per name. Required to search: name, years to search, signed release, offense. Criminal records computerized from 1994, index books from 1886. Mail turnaround 1 day. Criminal PAT available.
General Information: No juvenile, mental, sealed, or adoption records released. Will not fax documents. Court makes copy: n/a. Self serve: $1.00 per page. Cert fee: $5.00 per document. Payee: Fisher County Clerk. Personal checks accepted; credit cards are not. Mail requests: SASE required.

Floyd County

District Court PO Box 67, Floydada, TX 79235; 806-983-4923; 8:30AM-N, 1-4:45PM (CST). ***Felony, Civil.***
Civil Records: Access: Mail, in person. Both court and visitors may perform in person searches. Search fee: $5.00 per name. Required to search: name, years to search. Civil cases indexed by defendant, plaintiff. Civil records in index books from early 1891. Mail turnaround time 1 day.
Criminal Records: Access: Mail, in person. Both court and visitors may perform in person searches. Search fee: $5.00 per name. Required to search: name, years to search. Criminal docket on books from early 1891. Mail turnaround time 1 day.
General Information: No juvenile, mental, sealed, or adoption records released. Will fax out documents for $1.50 per page. Court makes copy: $1.00 per page. Cert fee: $1.00. Payee: District Clerk. Personal checks accepted; credit cards are not. Mail requests: SASE required.

County Court Courthouse, Rm 101, Main St, Floydada, TX 79235; 806-983-4900; fax: 806-983-4926; 8:30AM-N, 1-5PM (CST). ***Misdemeanor, Civil, Probate.***
Civil Records: Access: Phone, mail, in person. Both court and visitors may perform in person searches. Search fee: $5.00 per name. Required to search: name, years to search. Civil cases indexed by defendant, plaintiff. Civil records in index books from 1890. Mail turnaround time 2-4 days.
Criminal Records: Access: Phone, mail, in person. Both court and visitors may perform in person searches. Search fee: $5.00 per name. Required to search: name, years to search, DOB. Criminal docket on books from 1890. Mail turnaround time 1-5 days.
General Information: No juvenile, mental, sealed, or adoption records released. Will fax documents $1.00 fee plus $1.00 per page. Court makes copy: $1.00 per page. Self serve: same. Cert fee: $5.00. Payee: County Clerk. Personal checks accepted; credit cards are not.

Foard County

District & County Court PO Box 539, Crowell, TX 79227; 940-684-1365; fax: 940-684-1918; 9AM-4:30PM (CST). ***Felony, Misdemeanor, Civil, Probate.***

Civil Records: Access: Mail, in person. Both court and visitors may perform in person searches. Search fee: $10.00 per name. Required to search: name, years to search. Civil cases indexed by defendant, plaintiff. Civil records go back to 1908, civil records in index books from 1910; on computer from 1989. Mail turnaround time varies.
Criminal Records: Access: Mail, in person. Both court and visitors may perform in person searches. Search fee: $10.00 per name. Required to search: name, years to search, DOB. Criminal records go back to 1908, Criminal index in books from 1910; on computer from 1989. Mail turnaround time varies.
General Information: No juvenile, mental, sealed, or adoption records released. Fee to fax out file $2.50 1st page, $.25 per page each add'l. Court makes copy: $1.00 per page. Self serve: same. Cert fee: $5.00. Payee: Foard County Clerk. Personal checks accepted; credit cards are not. Mail requests: SASE required.

Fort Bend County

District Court 301 Jackson, Richmond, TX 77469; 281-341-4515; fax: 281-341-4519; 8AM-5PM (CST). ***Felony, Civil.*** www.co.fort-bend.tx.us
Physical court location is 401 Jackson.
Civil Records: Access: Phone, mail, online, in person. Both court and visitors may perform in person searches. Search fee: $5.00 per name. In person search no fee. Required to search: name, years to search. Civil cases indexed by defendant, plaintiff; index on computer from 1991, index books from early 1900s. Mail turnaround time approx. 5 days. Civil PAT goes back to 1991. PAT civil results show middle initial. Public terminal located at 401 Jackson, Rm 100, Richmond. Search court and jail data free at http://tylerpaw.co.fort-bend.tx.us/default.aspx. Records go back to 9/2000; no DOBs. Also, search court records free at http://ccweb.co.fort-bend.tx.us/localization/menu.asp.
Criminal Records: Access: Mail, online, in person. Both court and visitors may perform in person searches. Search fee: $5.00 per name. In person search no fee. Required to search: name, years to search, DOB, SSN. Criminal records computerized from 1981, index books from early 1900s. Mail turnaround time approx. 5 days. Criminal PAT goes back to 1982. PAT results show middle initial, DOB. Public terminal located at 401 Jackson, Rm 100, Richmond. Search criminal records free at www.co.fort-bend.tx.us/getSitePage.asp?sitePage=5608. Online results show middle initial, DOB.
General Information: Online identifiers in results same as on public terminal. No juvenile, mental, sealed, termination or adoption records released. Court makes copy: $1.00 per page. Cert fee: Included in copy fee. Exemplification fee- $2.00 per doc. Payee: District Clerk. No out of state personal checks accepted. Credit cards accepted, but a convenience fee is added. Mail requests: SASE required.

County Court Attn: Clerk, 301 Jackson St, #101, Richmond, TX 77469; 281-341-8685; criminal fax: 281-341-8681; civil fax: 281-341-4520; 8AM-4PM (CST). ***Misdemeanor, Civil, Probate.*** www.co.fort-bend.tx.us Probate fax- 281-341-4520
Civil Records: Access: Mail, in person, online. Both court and visitors may perform in person searches. Search fee: $10.00 per name. Search fee is for each type record to be searched. Required to search: name, years to search. Civil cases indexed by defendant, plaintiff; index on computer from 1984, also 1984-present optical imaged. Mail turnaround time 1-2 days. Civil PAT goes back to 1984. PAT civil results show middle initial. Online access to the civil records index free at www.co.fort-bend.tx.us/getSitePage.asp?sitePage=11895. The site includes probate records index online. Also search free at http://ccweb.co.fort-bend.tx.us/localization/menu.asp.
Criminal Records: Access: Mail, online, in person. Both court and visitors may perform in person searches. Search fee: $10.00 per name. A search fee for each type record to be searched required. Required to search: name, years to search, DOB. Criminal records computerized from 1983, also 1983 to present optical imaged. Mail turnaround time 1-2 days. Criminal PAT available. PAT results show middle initial, DOB. Online access to misdemeanor index is the same as civil. Online results show middle initial, DOB.
General Information: Online identifiers in results same as on public terminal. No juvenile, mental, sealed, or adoption records released. Fee to fax out file $1.00 per page. Court makes copy: $1.00 per page. Cert fee: $5.00 per document. Payee: Ft Bend County Clerk. Personal checks and credit cards accepted.

Franklin County

District Court PO Box 750, Mount Vernon, TX 75457; 903-537-4786; 8AM-5PM ***Felony, Civil.***
Civil Records: Access: Mail, in person. Both court and visitors may perform in person searches. Search fee: $5.00 per name. Required to search: name, years to search. Civil cases indexed by defendant, plaintiff; index on computer from 1987, index books from 1800s. Mail turnaround time 1 day.
Criminal Records: Access: Mail, in person. Both court and visitors may perform in person searches. Search fee: $5.00 per name. Required to search: name, years to search; also helpful: DOB, SSN. Criminal records computerized from 1987, index books from 1800s. Mail turnaround time 1 day.
General Information: No juvenile, mental, sealed, or adoption records released. Will fax documents $1.00 per page. Court makes copy: $1.00 per page. Self serve: same. Payee: District Clerk. Personal checks accepted; credit cards are not. Mail requests: SASE required.

County Court 200 N Caufman St, Mount Vernon, TX 75457; 903-537-4252 x2; fax: 903-537-2962; 8AM-5PM (CST). ***Misdemeanor, Civil, Probate.***
Probate fax is same as main fax number.
Civil Records: Access: Mail, fax, in person. Both court and visitors may perform in person searches. Search fee: $5.00 per name. Required to search: name, years to search. Civil cases indexed by defendant, plaintiff; index on computer from 1993, index books from 1847. Mail turnaround time 1 week. Civil PAT goes back to 1993. PAT results show middle initial, DOB.
Criminal Records: Access: Mail, fax, in person. Both court and visitors may perform in person searches. Search fee: $5.00 per name. Required to search: name, years to search, DOB and SSN. Criminal records computerized from 1993, index books from 1847. Mail turnaround time 1 week. Criminal PAT goes back to same as civil. PAT results show middle initial, DOB.
General Information: No juvenile, mental, sealed, or adoption records released. Fee to fax out file $1.00 per page. Court makes copy: $1.00 per page. Self serve: same. Cert fee: $5.00 per document. Payee: County Clerk. personal and business checks not accepted. No credit cards accepted. Mail requests: SASE required.

Freestone County

District Court PO Box 722, 118 Commerce St, Fairfield, TX 75840; 903-389-2534; 8AM-5PM (CST). ***Felony, Civil.***
Civil Records: Access: Mail, in person. Both court and visitors may perform in person searches. Search fee: $5.00 per name. Required to search: name, years to search. Civil cases indexed by defendant, plaintiff. Civil records in index books from 1830s. Mail turnaround time 1 day.
Criminal Records: Access: Mail, in person. Both court and visitors may perform in person searches. Search fee: $5.00 per name. Required to search: name, years to search. Criminal docket on books from 1830s. Mail turnaround time 1 day.
General Information: No juvenile, mental, sealed, or adoption records released. Will not fax documents. Court makes copy: $1.00 per page. Cert fee: $1.00 per page. Payee: District Clerk. Personal checks accepted; credit cards are not.

County Court PO Box 1010, Fairfield, TX 75840; 903-389-2635; fax: 903-389-6956; 8AM-5PM M-TH; 8AM-4:30PM Fri (CST). ***Misdemeanor, Civil, Probate.***
Civil Records: Access: In person only. Visitors must perform in person searches themselves. Required to search: name, years to search. Civil cases indexed by defendant, plaintiff. Civil records in index books from 1967. Civil PAT goes back to 2000.
Criminal Records: Access: Mail, in person. Visitors must perform in person searches themselves. Search fee: $5.00 per name, 10-year search. Required to search: name, years to search. Criminal docket on books from 1967. Mail turnaround time 2 days. Criminal PAT goes back to same as civil.
General Information: No juvenile, mental, sealed, or adoption records released. Will not fax documents. Court makes copy: $1.00 per page. Cert fee: $5.00 per document. Payee: Freestone County Clerk. Personal checks accepted; credit cards are not.

Frio County

District Court 500 E San Antonio, Box 8, Pearsall, TX 78061; 830-334-8073; fax: 830-334-0047; 8AM-5PM (CST). ***Felony, Civil.***
Civil Records: Access: Mail, in person. Both court and visitors may perform in person searches. Search fee: $10.00 per name. Required to search: name, years to search; also helpful: address. Civil cases indexed by defendant, plaintiff. Civil records in index books from 1948. Mail turnaround 2-3 days.
Criminal Records: Access: Mail, in person. Both court and visitors may perform in person searches. Search fee: $10.00 per name. Required to search: name, years to search, DOB; also helpful: address. Criminal docket on books from 1950. Mail turnaround time 2-3 days.
General Information: No juvenile, mental, sealed, or adoption records released. Fee to fax out file $2.00 per page. Court makes copy: $1.00 per page. Self serve: same. Cert fee: $1.00 per page includes copy fee. Payee: District Clerk. Business checks accepted. No credit cards accepted. Mail requests: SASE required.

County Court 500 E San Antonio St, #6, Pearsall, TX 78061; 830-334-2214; fax: 830-334-0021; 8AM-N, 1-5PM (CST). ***Misdemeanor, Civil, Probate.***
Probate fax is same as main fax number.
Civil Records: Access: Fax, mail, in person. Both court and visitors may perform in person searches. Search fee: $10.00 per name. Required to search: name, years to search. Civil cases indexed by defendant, plaintiff. Civil records go back to 1800s, civil records in index books from 1876, on computer back to 2005. Mail turnaround time 2-4 days. Civil PAT goes back to 2005.
Criminal Records: Access: Fax, mail, in person. Both court and visitors may perform in person searches. Search fee: $10.00 per name. Required to search: name, years to search. Criminal records go back to 1800s, Criminal index in books from 1876; no computerized records. Mail turnaround time 2-4 days. Criminal PAT goes back to 2005.
General Information: No juvenile, mental, sealed, or adoption records released. Will fax documents $2.00 per page; $1.00 if faxing to a toll-free number. Court makes copy: $1.00 per page. Self serve: same. Cert fee: $5.00 per certificate. Payee: County Clerk. Personal checks accepted; credit cards are not. Mail requests: SASE required.

Gaines County

District Court 101 S Main, Rm 213, Seminole, TX 79360; 432-758-4013; fax: 432-758-4036; 8AM-N, 1-5PM (CST). ***Felony, Civil.***
Civil Records: Access: Phone, mail, in person. Only the court performs in person searches; visitors may not. Search fee: $5.00 per name. Required to search: name, years to search. Civil cases indexed by defendant, plaintiff; index on computer from 1980, index books from 1900s. Mail turnaround time 1 day.
Criminal Records: Access: Phone, mail, in person. Only the court performs in person searches; visitors may not. Search fee: $5.00 per name. Required to search: name, years to search. Criminal records computerized from 1980, index books from 1900s. Mail turnaround time 1 day.
General Information: No juvenile, mental, sealed, or adoption records released. Will fax documents to local or toll free line. Court makes copy: $1.00 per page. Self serve: same. Cert fee: $5.00 per certification. Payee: District Clerk. Personal checks accepted; credit cards are not. Mail requests: SASE required.

County Court 101 S Main, Rm 107, Seminole, TX 79360; 432-758-4003; fax: 432-758-1442; 8AM-5PM (CST). ***Misdemeanor, Civil, Probate.***

Civil Records: Access: Mail, in person. Both court and visitors may perform in person searches. Search fee: $5.00 per name. Required to search: name, years to search. Civil cases indexed by defendant, plaintiff. Civil records available from 1900s, computerized since 1991. Note: Probate records may be accessed with same criteria as civil records. Mail turnaround time 1 day. Civil PAT goes back to 1991. PAT results show name only.
Criminal Records: Access: Mail, in person. Both court and visitors may perform in person searches. Search fee: $5.00 per name. Required to search: name, years to search. Criminal records available from 1900s, computerized since 1991. Mail turnaround time 1 day. Criminal PAT goes back to same as civil. PAT results show name only.
General Information: No juvenile, mental, sealed, or adoption records released. Will fax documents $1.00 per page plus $2.00 per call. Court makes copy: $1.00 per page. Self serve: same. Cert fee: $5.00. Payee: County Clerk. Personal checks and major credit cards accepted. Mail requests: SASE required.

Galveston County

District Court 600 59th St #4001, Galveston, TX 77551; 409-766-2424; criminal phone: 409-770-5233; civil phone: 409-766-2441; fax: 409-766-2292; 8AM-5PM (CST). ***Felony, Civil.*** www.co.galveston.tx.us/District_Courts/default.htm
Civil Records: Access: Fax, mail, in person, online. Both court and visitors may perform in person searches. Search fee: $5.00 per name. Required to search: name, years to search. Civil cases indexed by defendant, plaintiff; index on computer from 1984, on microfiche from 1982, archived from 1849. Note: Fax access is only allowed with prepaid accounts. Mail turnaround time 2-5 days. Civil PAT goes back to 1984. Online access to judge's daily calendars is free at the website. Civil cases under $100,000 are found at http://207.80.116.33/.
Criminal Records: Access: Fax, mail, in person. Both court and visitors may perform in person searches. Search fee: $5.00 per name. Required to search: name, years to search, DOB. Criminal records computerized from 1984, on microfiche from 1982, archived from 1849. Note: There is a $1.50 per page for incoming faxes. Mail turnaround time 2-5 days. Criminal PAT available. Online access to Judge's daily calendars is free at the website.
General Information: No juvenile, mental, sealed, or adoption records released. Will fax documents long distance for $5.00 fax fee plus $1.50 per page. Local fax- $1.50 per page. Court makes copy: $1.00 per page; over 15 pages is $.25 each add'l. Cert fee: $2.00 for an affidavit. Payee: District Clerk. Personal checks accepted if under $50.00. Credit cards accepted. Mail requests: SASE required.

County Court PO Box 17253, Galveston, TX 77552-7253; 409-766-2200; criminal phone: 409-766-2389; civil phone: 409-766-2203; probate phone: 409-766-2202; fax: 409-765-3160; 8AM-5PM (CST). ***Misdemeanor, Civil, Probate.*** http://www2.co.galveston.tx.us/County_Clerk/
Civil Records: Access: Mail, in person, online. Both court and visitors may perform in person searches. Search fee: $5.00 per name. Required to search: name, years to search; DOB or SSN helpful. Civil cases indexed by defendant, plaintiff; index on computer from 1984, index books from 1947. Mail turnaround time 1-2 days. Civil PAT goes back to 1984. PAT civil results show middle initial. Online access, including probate, is at http://207.80.116.33/. Records go back to 1995 generally. Access to the GCNET remote online service has been suspended.
Criminal Records: Access: Mail, in person, online. Both court and visitors may perform in person searches. Search fee: $5.00 per name. Required to search: name, years to search, DOB; also helpful: SSN. Criminal records computerized from 1984, index books from 1947. Mail turnaround time 1-2 days. Criminal PAT goes back to 1984. PAT results show middle initial, DOB. Online access is at http://207.80.116.33/. Index search if free; records go back to 1995 generally. Online results show middle initial.
General Information: No juvenile, mental, sealed, or adoption records released. Will not fax documents. Court makes copy: $1.00 per page. Cert fee: $5.00 per document. Payee: County Clerk. Personal checks accepted; credit cards are not. Mail requests: SASE required.

Garza County

District & County Court PO Box 366, Post, TX 79356; 806-495-4430; fax: 806-495-4431; 8AM-N,1-5PM (CST). ***Felony, Misdemeanor, Civil, Probate.*** www.garzacounty.net/id26.html
Civil Records: Access: Mail, in person. Both court and visitors may perform in person searches. Search fee: $5.00 per name. Required to search: name, years to search. Civil cases indexed by defendant, plaintiff. Civil index on docket books. Mail turnaround time 2-3 days.
Criminal Records: Access: Mail, in person. Both court and visitors may perform in person searches. Search fee: $5.00 per name. Required to search: name, years to search, DOB. Criminal records indexed in books. Mail turnaround time 2-3 days.
General Information: Fee to fax out file $3.00 1st page $1.00 ea add'l. Court makes copy: $1.00 per page. Cert fee: $5.00. Payee: District or County Clerk. Personal checks accepted; credit cards are not.

Gillespie County

District Court 101 W Main, Rm 204, Fredericksburg, TX 78624; 830-997-6517; 8AM-4:30PM (CST). ***Felony, Civil.***
Civil Records: Access: Mail, in person. Both court and visitors may perform in person searches. Search fee: $5.00 per name. Required to search: name, years to search. Civil cases indexed by defendant, plaintiff. Civil records in index books from 1800s. Index #1 from 1800s-1927, Index #2 from 1927-1988, Index #3 from 1989-present. Mail turnaround time 1-2 days.
Criminal Records: Access: Mail, in person. Both court and visitors may perform in person searches. Search fee: $5.00 per name. Required to search: name, years to search; also helpful: DOB, SSN. Criminal docket on books from 1800s. Index #1 from 1800s-1927, Index #2 from 1927-1988, Index #3 from 1989-present. Mail turnaround time 1-2 days.
General Information: No juvenile, mental, sealed, or adoption records released. Will fax documents if only a page or 2. Court makes copy: $1.00 for 1st page, $.25 each add'l. Cert fee: $1.00 per page includes copy fee. Payee: Gillespie County District Clerk. Personal checks accepted; credit cards are not. Mail requests: SASE required.

County Court 101 W Main, #13, Fredericksburg, TX 78624; 830-997-6515; fax: 830-997-9958; 8AM-4PM (CST). ***Misdemeanor, Civil, Probate.*** Probate fax is same as main fax number.
Civil Records: Access: Mail, in person. Both court and visitors may perform in person searches. Search fee: $5.00 per name. Required to search: name, years to search; also helpful: address. Civil cases indexed by defendant, plaintiff; index on computer from 1988, on microfiche from 1990, index books from 1900s. Mail turnaround time 1-2 days.
Criminal Records: Access: Mail, in person. Both court and visitors may perform in person searches. Search fee: $5.00 per name. Required to search: name, years to search, aliases; also helpful: DOB, SSN. Criminal records (not at public viewing) on computer from 1988, on microfiche from 1990, index books from 1900s. Mail turnaround time 1-2 days.
General Information: No juvenile, mental, sealed, or adoption record released. Will fax documents for no add'l fee. Court makes copy: $1.00 per page. Cert fee: $10.00 per document. Payee: County Clerk. No out-of-town personal checks accepted. No credit cards accepted. Mail requests: SASE required.

Glasscock County

District & County Court PO Box 190, 117 E Currie, Garden City, TX 79739; 432-354-2371; fax: 432-354-2616; 8:30AM-4PM (CST). ***Felony, Misdemeanor, Civil, Probate.***
Civil Records: Access: Mail, in person. Both court and visitors may perform in person searches. Search fee: $10.00 per name. Required to search: name, years to search. Cases indexed by defendant, plaintiff. Civil records in index books from 1893.
Criminal Records: Access: Mail, in person. Both court and visitors may perform in person searches. Search fee: $10.00 per name. Required to search: name, years to search, DOB. Criminal docket on books from 1893.
General Information: No juvenile, mental, or adoption records released. Will fax documents $2.00 per page. Court makes copy: $1.00 per page. Cert fee: $5.00 per document. Payee: District or County Clerk. Personal checks accepted. Mail requests: SASE required.

Goliad County

District & County Court PO Box 50 (127 N Courthouse Sq), Goliad, TX 77963; 361-645-3294; fax: 361-645-3858; 8AM-5PM, closed 1 hour at noon (CST). ***Felony, Misdemeanor, Civil, Probate.*** Probate fax is same as main fax number.
Civil Records: Access: Mail, in person. Both court and visitors may perform in person searches. Search fee: $10.00 per name. Fee is per court. Required to search: name, years to search; also helpful: address. Civil cases indexed by defendant, plaintiff; index on computer since 1983 (real property only), on microfiche and index books from 1870. Mail turnaround time 1-2 days.
Criminal Records: Access: Mail, in person. Both court and visitors may perform in person searches. Search fee: $10.00 per name. Fee is per court. Required to search: name, years to search; also helpful: address, DOB, SSN, offense. Criminal docket on books and folders from 1870. Mail turnaround time 1-2 days.
General Information: No juvenile, mental, sealed, or adoption records released. Fee to fax out file $2.00 per page includes copy fee. Court makes copy: $1.00 per page. Cert fee: $5.00 for County Court; $1.00 per page in District Court. Payee: Goliad County/District Clerk. Personal checks accepted. No credit cards accepted at this time.

Gonzales County

District Court 414 St Joseph #300, Gonzales, TX 78629; 830-672-2326; fax: 830-672-9313; 8AM-N 1PM-5PM (CST). ***Felony, Civil.***
Civil Records: Access: Phone, fax, mail, in person. Both court and visitors may perform in person searches. Search fee: $5.00 per name. Required to search: name, years to search; also helpful: address. Civil cases indexed by defendant, plaintiff; index on computer from 1991, index books from 1800s. Mail turnaround time 1-2 days.
Criminal Records: Access: Phone, fax, mail, in person. Both court and visitors may perform in person searches. Search fee: $5.00 per name. Required to search: name, years to search; also helpful: address, DOB, SSN. Criminal records computerized from 1991, index books from 1800s. Mail turnaround time 1-2 days.
General Information: No juvenile, mental, sealed, or adoption records released. Fee to fax out file $1.00 per page. Court makes copy: $1.00 per page. Self serve: same. No certification fee. Payee: District Clerk. Personal checks accepted; credit cards are not.

County Court PO Box 77, Gonzales, TX 78629; 830-672-2801; criminal fax: 830-672-2636; civil fax: same; 8AM-5PM (CST). ***Misdemeanor, Civil, Probate.*** Probate fax is same as main fax number.
Civil Records: Access: Fax, mail, in person. Both court and visitors may perform in person searches. Search fee: $5.00 per name. Required to search: name, years to search, DOB. Civil cases indexed by defendant, plaintiff; index on computer since 1993, original jackets since 1975, index books from 1900s. Mail turnaround time 1-2 days.
Criminal Records: Access: Mail, in person. Both court and visitors may perform in person searches. Search fee: $5.00 per name. Required to search: name, years to search, DOB, offense, date of offense. Criminal records on computer since 1993, original jackets, index books from 1900s. Mail turnaround time 1-2 days.
General Information: No mental or drug dependant commitment records released. Fee to fax out file $5.00. Court makes copy: $1.00 per page. Self serve: same. Cert fee: $5.00 per instrument. Payee: County Clerk. Personal checks accepted; credit cards are not. Mail requests: SASE required.

Gray County

District Court PO Box 1139, Pampa, TX 79066-1139; 806-669-8010; fax: 806-669-8053; 8:30AM-5PM (CST). ***Felony, Civil.***

Civil Records: Access: Fax, mail, in person. Both court and visitors may perform in person searches. Search fee: $5.00 per name. Required to search: name, years to search, DOB. Civil cases indexed by defendant, plaintiff; index on computer from 1940, index books from 1910. Note: All requests must be in writing. Mail turnaround time 1-2 days. Civil PAT goes back to 1930.

Criminal Records: Access: Fax, mail, in person. Both court and visitors may perform in person searches. Search fee: $5.00 per name. Required to search: name, years to search; also helpful: DOB. Criminal records go back to 1930; Criminal records computerized from 1965. Note: All requests must be in writing. Mail turnaround time 1-2 days. Criminal PAT goes back to 1930.

General Information: No juvenile, mental, sealed, or adoption records released. Will fax documents $1.00 per page. Court makes copy: $.50 per page.$1.00 per page to mail copies. Cert fee: $1.00 per page. Payee: District Clerk. Personal checks accepted; credit cards are not. Mail requests: SASE required.

County & Probate Court PO Box 1902, Pampa, TX 79066-1902; 806-669-8004; fax: 806-669-8054; 8:30-5PM ***Misdemeanor, Civil, Probate.***

Civil Records: Access: Phone, fax, mail, in person. Both court and visitors may perform in person searches. Search fee: $10.00 per name. Fee is per index. Required to search: name, years to search. Civil cases indexed by defendant, plaintiff; index on type written indices from 1900s. Mail turnaround time 1-2 days. Civil PAT goes back to 4/19/02.

Criminal Records: Access: Phone, fax, mail, in person. Both court and visitors may perform in person searches. Search fee: $10.00 per name. Fee is per index. Required to search: name, years to search, DOB. Criminal records on type written indices from 1900s. Mail turnaround time 1-2 days. Criminal PAT goes back to 1983.

General Information: No juvenile, mental, sealed, or adoption records released. They will not release any records with the SSN on it. Will fax documents $2.50 1st page, $1.00 each add'l. Court makes copy: $1.00 per page. Self serve: same. Cert fee: $5.00. Payee: Susan Winborne, County Clerk. Personal checks accepted. Mail requests: SASE required.

Grayson County

District Court 200 S Crockett, Rm 120-A, Sherman, TX 75090; 903-813-4352; fax: 903-870-0609; 8AM-5PM (CST). ***Felony, Civil, Family.*** www.co.grayson.tx.us

Civil Records: Access: Mail, in person, online. Both court and visitors may perform in person searches. Search fee: $5.00 per name. Required to search: name, years to search. Civil cases indexed by defendant, plaintiff; index on computer from 1988, microfilm since 1939, index books since 1900s. Mail turnaround time 1-2 days. Civil PAT goes back to 1989. PAT results show middle initial, DOB. Terminal results also show SSNs. Access judicial records free http://24.117.89.66:3004/judsrch.asp.

Criminal Records: Access: Mail, in person, online. Both court and visitors may perform in person searches. Search fee: $5.00 per name. Required to search: name, years to search, DOB; also helpful: SSN. Criminal records on computer since 1988, microfilm since 1939, index books since 1900s. Mail turnaround time 1-2 days. Criminal PAT goes back to 1983. PAT results show middle initial, DOB. Terminal results include SSN. Access judicial records free http://24.117.89.66:3004/judsrch.asp.

General Information: No juvenile, mental, sealed, expunction or adoption records released. Will not fax documents. Court makes copy: $1.00 per page. Cert fee: $1.00. Payee: District Clerk. Personal checks accepted; credit cards are not. SASE required.

County Court 200 S Crockett, Sherman, TX 75090; 903-813-4336; civil phone: 903-813-4335; probate phone: 903-813-4241; fax: 903-892-8300; 8AM-5PM (CST). ***Misdemeanor, Civil, Probate.*** www.co.grayson.tx.us/courtsmain.htm
Criminal Clerk #2 is at 903-813-4334

Civil Records: Access: Mail, in person, online. Both court and visitors may perform in person searches. Search fee: $10.00 per name per 10 years. Required to search: name, years to search. Civil cases indexed by defendant, plaintiff; index on computer since 1992, index books since 1952. Mail turnaround time 1-2 days. Civil PAT goes back to 1982. PAT results show middle initial, DOB. Online access to civil and probate records is free at http://24.117.89.66:3004/judsrch.asp. Includes sheriffs' bail, and sheriff's jail searching.

Criminal Records: Access: In person, online. Both court and visitors may perform in person searches. Search fee: $10.00 per name per 10 years. Required to search: name, years to search, also helpful: DOB, SSN. Criminal records computerized from 1982. Criminal PAT goes back to same as civil. PAT results show middle initial, DOB. Online access to criminal records is the same as civil. Online results show middle initial, DOB.

General Information: Online identifiers in results same as on public terminal. No juvenile, mental, sealed, or adoption records released. Court makes copy: $1.00 per page. Cert fee: $5.00. Payee: Grayson County Clerk. Personal checks accepted; credit cards are not. Mail requests: SASE required.

Gregg County

District Court PO Box 711, Longview, TX 75606; criminal phone: 903-236-8459; civil phone: 903-237-2663; fax: 903-236-8474; 8AM-5PM (CST). ***Felony, Civil.*** www.co.gregg.tx.us/government/courts.asp

Civil Records: Access: Phone, fax, mail, in person, online. Both court and visitors may perform in person searches. Search fee: $5.00 per name. Required to search: name, years to search. Civil cases indexed by defendant, plaintiff; index on computer back to 1981, index books from 1873. Mail turnaround time 1-2 days. Public use terminal available, records go back to 1981. Online access to county judicial records is free at www.co.gregg.tx.us/judsrch.htm. Search by name, cause number, status.

Criminal Records: Access: Phone, fax, mail, in person, online. Both court and visitors may perform in person searches. Search fee: $5.00 per name. Required to search: name, years to search. Criminal records computerized from 1977, index books from 1873. Mail turnaround time 1-2 days. Public use terminal available, crim records go back to 1977. Online access to criminal records is the same as civil, also includes jail and bond search. Online results show name, DOB.

General Information: No juvenile, mental, sealed, or adoption records released. Will fax documents $1.00 per page. Court makes copy: $1.00 per page. Cert fee: $1.00 per page. Payee: District Clerk. Only cashiers checks and money orders accepted. No credit cards accepted. Mail requests: SASE required.

County Court 101 E Methvin, #200, Longview, TX 75606; 903-236-8430; fax: 903-237-2574; 8AM-5PM (CST). ***Misdemeanor, Civil, Probate.*** www.co.gregg.tx.us/government/county_courts/countyclerk.asp

Civil Records: Access: Mail, in person, online. Both court and visitors may perform in person searches. Search fee: $5.00 per name. Required to search: name, years to search. Civil cases indexed by defendant, plaintiff; index on computer from 1983, index books after 1962. Mail turnaround time 1 week. Civil PAT goes back to 1876. PAT civil results show middle initial. Public terminal probate index goes back to 1908. Online access to judicial records is free at www.co.gregg.tx.us/judsrch.htm. Search by name, cause number, or status.

Criminal Records: Access: Mail, in person, online. Both court and visitors may perform in person searches. Search fee: $5.00 per name. Required to search: name, years to search, DOB or SSN. Criminal records computerized from 1983, index books after 1932. Mail turnaround time 1 week. Criminal PAT goes back to 1983. PAT results show middle initial, DOB. Online access to criminal records is the same as civil. Jail and bond search available.

General Information: No juvenile, mental, sealed, or adoption records released. Fee to fax out file $1.00 per page. Court makes copy: $1.00 per page. Self serve: same. Cert fee: $5.00 per cert. Payee: Gregg County Clerk. Only in-state personal checks accepted. No credit cards accepted. Mail requests: SASE required.

Grimes County

District Court PO Box 234, Anderson, TX 77830; 936-873-2111 x240; fax: 936-873-2514; 8AM-5PM, closed 1 hour at noon (CST). ***Felony, Civil.***

Civil Records: Access: Phone, fax, mail, in person. Both court and visitors may perform in person searches. Search fee: $5.00 per name. Required to search: name, years to search. Civil cases indexed by defendant, plaintiff; index on computer from 1990, index books from 1800s. Mail turnaround time 1-2 days. Civil PAT goes back to 10 years.

Criminal Records: Access: Phone, fax, mail, in person. Both court and visitors may perform in person searches. Search fee: $5.00 per name. Required to search: name, years to search, DOB, SSN. Criminal records computerized from 1990, index books from 1800s. Mail turnaround time 1-2 days. Criminal PAT goes back to 10 years.

General Information: No juvenile, mental, sealed, or adoption records released. Will fax documents $1.00 per page. Court makes copy: $1.00 per page. Cert fee: $1.00. Payee: District Clerk. Personal checks OK. Visa/MC/AmEx on Official Payments System.

County Court PO Box 209, Anderson, TX 77830; 936-873-2606 X251; fax: 936-873-3308; 8AM-4:45PM (CST). ***Misdemeanor, Civil, Probate.***

Civil Records: Access: Mail, in person. Only the court performs in person searches; visitors may not. Search fee: $5.00 per name. Required to search: name, years to search. Civil cases indexed by defendant, plaintiff. Civil records in index books from 1850. Mail turnaround time 1-2 days.

Criminal Records: Access: Mail, in person. Only the court performs in person searches; visitors may not. Search fee: $5.00 per name. Required to search: name, years to search, offense, date of offense. Criminal docket on books from 1850. Mail turnaround time 1-2 days.

General Information: No juvenile, mental, sealed, or adoption records released. Will not fax documents. Court makes copy: $1.00 per page. Cert fee: $5.00. Payee: County Clerk. Personal checks accepted; credit cards are not. Mail requests: SASE required.

Guadalupe County

District Court 101 E Court St, #308, Seguin, TX 78155; 830-303-4188; criminal phone: x276; civil phone: x262; criminal fax: 830-379-1943; civil fax: same; 8AM-4:30PM (CST). ***Felony, Civil.*** www.co.guadalupe.tx.us/dist_Clerk.htm
Will look up case record if case number is known.

Civil Records: Access: In person, online. Visitors must perform in person searches themselves. Required to search: name, years to search. Civil cases indexed by defendant, plaintiff; index on computer from 1987, index books from 1846. Access to court records and hearings is free at www.co.guadalupe.tx.us/judicialsearch/judsrch.asp.

Criminal Records: Access: In person, online. Both court and visitors may perform in person searches. Search fee: $5.00 per name. Required to search: name, years to search, DOB; also helpful: SSN. Criminal records computerized from 1985, index books from 1846. Note: Also search sheriff's jail and bond records. Access to court records and hearings is available free at www.co.guadalupe.tx.us/judicialsearch/judsrch.asp. Search sheriff's jail and bond records also. Dockets go back to 12/31/1991. Online results show middle initial, DOB.

General Information: No juvenile, mental, sealed, or adoption records released. Will fax out specific case files for $5.00 fee plus $1.00 per page after 1st page. Court makes copy: $1.00 per page. Cert fee: $1.00 per page and includes copy fee. Payee: District Clerk. Checks accepted for civil only. Criminal payments-cash, money orders, cashiers check. Credit cards OK.

County Court 101 E Court St #302, Seguin, TX 78155; 830-303-4188 x2; 830-303-8869; fax: 830-303-5325; 8AM-4:30PM (CST). ***Misdemeanor, Civil, Probate.*** www.co.guadalupe.tx.us/ccl_1.htm

Civil Records: Access: Mail, in person, online. Both court and visitors may perform in person searches.

Search fee: $10.00 per year. Required to search: name, years to search. Civil cases indexed by defendant, plaintiff; index on computer from 1988, index books from 1968. Mail turnaround time 5 days. Civil PAT goes back to 1988. Access to court records and hearings is free at www.co.guadalupe.tx.us/judicialsearch/judsrch.asp.

Criminal Records: Access: Mail, in person, online. Both court and visitors may perform in person searches. Search fee: $10.00 per year. Required to search: name, years to search, DOB; also helpful: SSN. Criminal records computerized from 1988, index books from 1968. Mail turnaround time 5 days. Criminal PAT goes back to same as civil. Access to court records and hearings is available free at www.co.guadalupe.tx.us/judicialsearch/judsrch.asp. Also search sheriff's jail and bond records.

General Information: Online identifiers in results same as on public terminal. No juvenile, mental, sealed, or adoption records released. Will not fax documents. Court makes copy: $1.00 per page. Cert fee: $5.00 per doc. Payee: County Clerk. Personal checks not accepted for records. No credit cards accepted. Mail requests: SASE required.

Hale County

District Court 225 Broadway, #4, Plainview, TX 79072-8050; 806-291-5226; fax: 806-291-5206; 8AM-N; 1-5PM (CST). ***Felony, Civil.***
www.242ndcourt.com

Civil Records: Access: Phone, fax, mail, in person, online. Both court and visitors may perform in person searches. Search fee: $5.00 per name. Required to search: name, years to search. Civil cases indexed by defendant, plaintiff; index on computer back to 1990; index cards from 1975; prior back to 1897. Mail turnaround time 1-2 days. Civil PAT goes back to 1990. PAT results show name only. Access docket data from 01/1990 online at www.idocket.com; registration and password required. A fee service; only one free name search per day.

Criminal Records: Access: Phone, fax, mail, in person, online. Both court and visitors may perform in person searches. Search fee: $5.00 per name. Required to search: name, years to search, SSN; also helpful: DOB. Criminal records computerized from 1990, index cards from 1975; prior back to 1897. Mail turnaround time 1-2 days. Criminal PAT goes back to same as civil. PAT results show name only. Access docket data from 01/1990 online at www.idocket.com; registration and password required. A fee service; only one free name search per day.

General Information: No juvenile, mental, sealed, or adoption records released. Will fax documents $2.00 each. Court makes copy: $1.00 per page. Self serve: same. Cert fee: $1.00 each. Payee: District Clerk. Personal checks and credit cards accepted. Mail requests: SASE required.

County Court 500 Broadway, #140, Plainview, TX 79072-8030; 806-291-5261; criminal phone: 806-291-5218; civil phone: 806-291-5261; probate phone: 806-291-5261; fax: 806-291-9810; 8AM-N, 1-5PM (CST). ***Misdemeanor, Civil, Probate.***
Probate records are in a separate index. Probate fax is same as main fax number.

Civil Records: Access: Mail, fax, in person, online. Both court and visitors may perform in person searches. Search fee: $5.00 per name. Required to search: name, years to search, address. Civil cases indexed by defendant, plaintiff. Civil records in index books from 1928; on computer back to 1995. Mail turnaround time same day if before 3PM. Civil PAT goes back to 1995. PAT results show name, DOB. Clerk guarantees accuracy of computer records from 1995 forward on access terminal, which includes SSNs. Online access is through www.idocket.com; registration and password required. Civil and probate data back to 01/1991. One free name search permitted per day, otherwise subscription required.

Criminal Records: Access: Mail, fax, in person, online. Both court and visitors may perform in person searches. Search fee: $5.00 per name. Required to search: name, years to search, DOB. Criminal docket on books from 1928; on computer back to 1995, limited records back to 1990. Mail turnaround time 1-2 days. Criminal PAT goes back to same as civil.PAT results show name, DOB. Clerk guarantees accuracy of computer records from 1995 forward on access terminal. SSNs appear in results. Online access to misdemeanor docket from 01/91 forward is through www.idocket.com; registration and password required. One free name search permitted per day, otherwise subscription required.

General Information: No juvenile, mental, sealed, or adoption records released. Will fax documents for copy fee plus $1.00 for long distance call. Court makes copy: $1.00 per page. Self serve: same. Cert fee: $5.00 per document. Payee: County Clerk. Personal checks accepted. Visa/MC accepted. Mail requests: SASE required.

Hall County

District & County Court County Courthouse, 512 Main St, #8, Memphis, TX 79245; 806-259-2627; fax: 806-259-5078; 8:30AM-N; 1-5PM (CST). ***Felony, Misdemeanor, Civil, Probate.***

Civil Records: Access: Mail, in person. Both court and visitors may perform in person searches. Search fee: $5.00 per name. Required to search: name, years to search. Civil cases indexed by defendant, plaintiff; index on computer from 1992, index books from 1890. Mail turnaround 1-2 days.

Criminal Records: Access: Mail, in person. Both court and visitors may perform in person searches. Search fee: $5.00 per name. Required to search: name, years to search, offense. Criminal records computerized from 1992, index books from 1890. Mail turnaround time 1-2 days.

General Information: No juvenile, mental, sealed, or adoption records released. Will fax documents to local or toll free line. Court makes copy: $1.00 per page. Self serve: $.25 per page. Cert fee: $5.00. Payee: Hall County Clerk. Personal checks accepted; credit cards are not. Mail requests: SASE required.

Hamilton County

District Court County Courthouse, Hamilton, TX 76531; 254-386-3417; fax: 254-386-8610; 8AM-5PM M-TH; 8AM-4:30PM Fri (CST). ***Felony, Civil.***

Civil Records: Access: Fax, mail, in person. Both court and visitors may perform in person searches. Search fee: $5.00 per name. Required to search: name, years to search. Civil cases indexed by defendant, plaintiff. Civil records since 1985 in index books, computerized since 1999. Mail turnaround time 2-4 days.

Criminal Records: Access: Fax, mail, in person. Both court and visitors may perform in person searches. Search fee: $5.00 per name. Required to search: name, years to search. Criminal docket on books from 1985, computerized since 1999. Mail turnaround time 2-4 days.

General Information: No juvenile, mental, sealed, or adoption records released. No fee to fax documents. Court makes copy: $1.00 per page. Self serve: same. Cert fee: $2.00 per document. Payee: District Clerk. Personal checks accepted. Mail requests: SASE required.

County Court 101 E Main St, County Courthouse, Hamilton, TX 76531; 254-386-3518; fax: 254-386-8727; 8AM-5PM (CST). ***Misdemeanor, Civil, Probate.***
Probate fax is same as main fax number.

Civil Records: Access: Mail, fax, in person. Both court and visitors may perform in person searches. Search fee: $5.00 per name. Required to search: name, years to search. Civil cases indexed by defendant, plaintiff. Civil records in index books; on computer since. Mail turnaround time 1-2 days.

Criminal Records: Access: Mail, fax, in person. Both court and visitors may perform in person searches. Search fee: $5.00 per name. Required to search: name, years to search, DOB or SSN. Criminal index in books; on computer since. Mail turnaround time 1-2 days.

General Information: No juvenile, mental, sealed, or adoption records released. Will fax documents for fee. Court makes copy: $1.00 per page. Self serve: same. Cert fee: $1.00 per page. Payee: County Clerk. Personal checks accepted; credit cards are not. Mail requests: SASE required.

Hansford County

District & County Court 15 NW Court, Spearman, TX 79081; 806-659-4110; criminal fax: 806-659-4168; civil fax: same; 8AM-5PM (CST). ***Felony, Misdemeanor, Civil, Probate.***

Civil Records: Access: Phone, fax, mail, in person. Both court and visitors may perform in person searches. Search fee: $10.00 per name. Required to search: name, years to search. Civil cases indexed by defendant, plaintiff; index on computer from 1/92, index books from 1900s. Mail turnaround time ASAP. Civil PAT goes back to 1992.

Criminal Records: Access: Phone, fax, mail, in person. Both court and visitors may perform in person searches. Search fee: $10.00 per name. Required to search: name, years to search; also helpful: DOB, SSN. Criminal records on computer since 6/92, archived from 1900s. Mail turnaround 1-2 days. Criminal PAT goes back to same as civil.

General Information: No juvenile, mental, sealed, or adoption records released. Will fax documents $3.00 fee. Court makes copy: $1.00 per page. Cert fee: $2.00 in District Court; $5.00 in County Court. Payee: District/County Clerk. Personal checks accepted; credit cards are not. Mail requests: SASE required.

Hardeman County

District & County Court PO Box 30, Quanah, TX 79252; 940-663-2901; fax: 940-663-5161; 8:30AM-5PM ***Felony, Misdemeanor, Civil, Probate.***
Probate is separate index at this same address. Probate fax- 940-663-5161

Civil Records: Access: Mail, in person. Both court and visitors may perform in person searches. Search fee: $10.00 per name. Required to search: name, years to search. Civil cases indexed by defendant, plaintiff. Civil records in index books from 1900s. Mail turnaround time 1-2 days. Civil PAT goes back to 2006.

Criminal Records: Access: Mail, in person. Both court and visitors may perform in person searches. Search fee: $10.00 per name. Required to search: name, years to search. Criminal docket on books from 1920. Mail turnaround time 1-2 days. Criminal PAT goes back to 2006.

General Information: No juvenile, mental, sealed, or adoption records released. Will not fax documents. Court makes copy: $1.00 per page. Self serve: same. Cert fee: $5.00 per cert. Payee: District Clerk. Personal checks accepted; credit cards are not. Mail requests: SASE required.

Hardin County

District Court PO Box 2997, 300 Monroe, Kountze, TX 77625; 409-246-5150; 8AM-4PM (CST). ***Felony, Civil.***

Civil Records: Access: Mail, in person. Both court and visitors may perform in person searches. Search fee: $5.00 per name. Required to search: name, years to search. Civil cases indexed by defendant, plaintiff. Civil records in index books since 1920, computerized since 1997. Mail turnaround time 1-2 days.

Criminal Records: Access: Mail, in person. Both court and visitors may perform in person searches. Search fee: $5.00 per name. Required to search: name, years to search, DOB; also helpful: SSN, sex. Criminal docket on books from 1920, computerized since 1997. Mail turnaround time 1-2 days.

General Information: No juvenile, mental, sealed, or adoption records released. Fee to fax out file $1.00 per page. Court makes copy: $1.00 per page. Self serve: $.50 per page. Cert fee: $2.00 per doc. Payee: District Clerk. Business checks accepted. No credit cards accepted. Mail requests: SASE required.

County Court PO Box 38, Kountze, TX 77625; 409-246-5185; 8AM-5PM (CST). ***Misdemeanor, Civil, Probate.***

Civil Records: Access: Mail, in person, phone. Both court and visitors may perform in person searches. Search fee: $5.00 per name. Required to search: name, years to search. Civil cases indexed by defendant, plaintiff. Civil records in index books since 1850; on computer back to 1999. Mail turnaround time 1-2 days.

Criminal Records: Access: Mail, in person, phone. Both court and visitors may perform in person

searches. Search fee: $5.00 per name. Required to search: name, years to search. Criminal records on computer since 1992, index books from 1850. Mail turnaround time 1-2 days.
General Information: No juvenile, mental, sealed, or adoption records released. Will not fax documents. Court makes copy: $1.00 per page. Self serve: same. Cert fee: $5.00 per doc plus $1.00 per copy. Payee: Hardin County Clerk. Personal checks accepted; credit cards are not.

Harris County

District Court District Clerk, PO Box 4651, Houston, TX 77210-4651; 713-755-5734, 888-545-5577; criminal phone: 713-755-7801; civil phone: 713-755-5711 x2; criminal fax: 713-755-5480; civil fax: 713-755-5751; 7:30M-5PM (CST). ***Felony, Misdemeanor, Civil over $100,000.*** www.hcdistrictclerk.com/Home/Home.aspx
Civil Records: Access: Fax, online, in person. Both court and visitors may perform in person searches. Search fee: $5.00 per search, with up to 3 names per search. Required to search: name, years to search. Civil cases indexed by defendant, plaintiff; index on computer from 1969. Civil PAT goes back to 1968. PAT results show middle initial, DOB. First, an online case lookup service is free at http://legacy.hcdistrictclerk.com/Edocs/Public/search.aspx. Online records go back to 10/1989. Second, register for free-to-view e-docs service at https://e-docs.hcdistrictclerk.com/eDocs.Web/Login.aspx and pay $1 per page (credit cards accepted) for civil documents. Qualified JIMs subscribers may access at www.jims.hctx.net.
Criminal Records: Access: Mail, online, in person. Both court and visitors may perform in person searches. Search fee: $5.00 per name. Required to search: name, years to search, DOB. Criminal records on computer since 1976. Criminal PAT goes back to 1985. Online criminal index case lookup is the same as civil. The e-docs service does not offer access to criminal records.
General Information: No juvenile or sealed records released. Will fax out docs for fee; requires credit card prepayment. Court makes copy: $1.00 per page. Cert fee: $1.00, called Exemplification Fee. Payee: Harris County District Clerk. Business check accepted from attorney with TX Bar Card, corporate or company check with Harris Co. address. Major credit cards accepted. Mail requests: SASE required.

County Court PO Box 1525, 201 Caroline, 3rd Fl, Houston, TX 77251-1525; 713-755-6421; fax: 713-755-4710; 8AM-4:30PM (CST). ***Civil under $100,000.*** www.cclerk.hctx.net
The Information Department (for record information) telephone is 713-755-6405, located at County Civil Courthouse, 210 Caroline, 3rd Fl. Small claims and evictions are handled by county Justice of Peace Courts; usually there are two per precinct.
Civil Records: Access: Phone, mail, online, in person. Both court and visitors may perform in person searches. Search fee: $5.00 for mail requests. Required to search: name, years to search. Civil cases indexed by defendant, plaintiff; index on computer and microfiche from 1963. Mail turnaround time 24-48 hours. Public use terminal has civil records back to 1977. Public terminal also includes Probate records. Online access is free at www.cclerk.hctx.net. System includes civil data search and county civil settings inquiry and other county clerk functions. For further information, visit the website or call 713-755-6421. Also, civil case online access back to 12/31/1997 at www.idocket.com; registration and password required. A fee service; only one free name search a day.
General Information: Will fax documents $1.00 per page. Court makes copy: $1.00 per page. Cert fee: $5.00. Payee: Harris County Clerk. Business checks and personal checks accepted in person with ID. Credit cards accepted. Mail requests: SASE required.

Probate Court 201 Caroline ST, #800, Houston, TX 77002; 713-755-6425; fax: 713-755-5468; 8AM-4:30PM (CST). ***Probate.***
Probate dockets are available through the Harris County online system. Call 713-755-7815 for information. Dockets free at www.cclerk.hctx.net/coolice/default.asp?Category=ProbateCourt&Service=pc_inquiry. Records go back to 1837.

Harrison County

District Court PO Box 1119, 200 W Houston St #234, Marshall, TX 75671-1119; 903-935-8409; fax: 903-927-1918; 8AM-5PM (CST). ***Felony, Civil.*** www.co.harrison.tx.us
Civil Records: Access: Mail, in person. Both court and visitors may perform in person searches. Search fee: $5.00 per name. Required to search: name, years to search; also helpful: address. Civil cases indexed by defendant, plaintiff; index on computer from 1988, index books from 1845. Mail turnaround time 1-2 days. Civil PAT goes back to 1987. PAT results show middle initial, DOB. Terminal results also show SSNs.
Criminal Records: Access: Mail, in person. Both court and visitors may perform in person searches. Search fee: $5.00 per name. Required to search: name, years to search, DOB; also helpful: address, SSN. Criminal records computerized from 1988, index books from 1845. Mail turnaround time 1-2 days. Criminal PAT goes back to same as civil. PAT results show middle initial, DOB. Terminal results include SSN.
General Information: No juvenile, mental, sealed, or adoption records released. Will not fax documents. Court makes copy: $1.00 per page. Self serve: $.50 per page. No certification fee. Payee: Harrison County District Clerk. Personal checks accepted. Visa/MC accepted. Mail requests: SASE required.

County Court PO Box 1365, Marshall, TX 75671; 903-935-8403; fax: 903-935-4877; 8AM-5PM (CST). ***Misdemeanor, Civil, Probate.***
Probate is a separate index at this same address.
Civil Records: Access: Mail, in person. Both court and visitors may perform in person searches. Search fee: $5.00 per name. Required to search: name, years to search. Civil cases indexed by defendant, plaintiff. Civil records in docket books from 1800; on computer back to 2001. Mail turnaround time 10 days. Civil PAT goes back to 2002. PAT results show middle initial, DOB, SSN.
Criminal Records: Access: Mail, in person. Both court and visitors may perform in person searches. Search fee: $5.00 per name. Required to search: name, years to search, DOB. Criminal records in docket books from 1800; on computer back to 2001. Mail turnaround 10 days. Criminal PAT goes back to 2002. PAT results show middle initial, DOB.
General: No juvenile, mental, sealed, birth, death or adoption records released. Fee to fax out file $4.00. Court makes copy: $1.00 per page. Self serve: same. Cert fee: $5.00 per document. Payee: County Clerk. No personal checks accepted; credit cards are.

Hartley County

District & County Court PO Box Q, Channing, TX 79018; 806-235-3582; fax: 806-235-2316; 8:30AM-N, 1-5PM (CST). ***Felony, Misdemeanor, Civil, Probate.*** www.co.hartley.tx.us/ips/cms
Probate is a separate index at this same address
Civil Records: Access: Mail, in person. Both court and visitors may perform in person searches. Search fee: $5.00 per name. Charge is for each book searched. Required to search: name, years to search. Civil cases indexed by defendant, plaintiff; index on computer from 1994, index books from 1890. Mail turnaround time 1-2 days. Civil PAT goes back to 1994. Results include case style.
Criminal Records: Access: Mail, in person. Both court and visitors may perform in person searches. Search fee: $5.00 per name, per book searched (misdemeanor or felony). Required to search: name, years to search, DOB. Criminal records computerized from 1994, index books from 1890. Mail turnaround time 1-2 days. Criminal PAT goes back to same as civil. Results include style of case.
General Information: No juvenile, mental, sealed, or adoption records released. Will fax documents if prepaid. Court makes copy: $1.00 per page County Ct; $1.00 for District Ct. Cert fee: $5.00 per cert plus copy fee for county; $1.00 per page plus copy fee for district. Payee: Hartley County Clerk. Personal checks accepted. Credit card payments must be made via OfficialPaymentCorporation.com. Mail requests: SASE required.

Haskell County

District Court PO Box 27, 1 Ave D, 2nd Fl, Haskell, TX 79521; 940-864-2030; fax: 940-864-6164; 8:30AM-N, 1-5PM M-TH; 8:30AM-4:30PM F (CST). ***Felony, Civil.***
Civil Records: Access: Mail, in person. Both court and visitors may perform in person searches. Search fee: $5.00 per name. Required to search: name, years to search. Civil cases indexed by defendant, plaintiff; index on computer from 1992, index books from 1896. Mail turnaround 1-2 days.
Criminal Records: Access: Mail, in person. Both court and visitors may perform in person searches. Search fee: $5.00 per name. Required to search: name, years to search, signed release. Criminal records computerized from 1992, index books from 1896. Mail turnaround time 1-2 days.
General Information: No juvenile, mental, sealed, or adoption records released. Will fax documents $1.00 per page. Court makes copy: $1.00 per page. Cert fee: $1.00. Payee: District Clerk. Business checks accepted. In-state checks accepted. No credit cards accepted. Mail requests: SASE required.

County Court PO Box 725, Haskell, TX 79521; 940-864-2451; probate phone: same; fax: 940-864-6164; 8AM-N, 1-5PM ***Misdemeanor, Civil, Probate.***
Civil Records: Access: Phone, fax, mail, in person. Both court and visitors may perform in person searches. Search fee: $5.00 per name. Required to search: name, years to search. Civil cases indexed by defendant, plaintiff. Civil records in index books from 1903; computerized records since 1994. Mail turnaround time 1-2 days.
Criminal Records: Access: Fax, mail, in person. Both court and visitors may perform in person searches. Search fee: $5.00 per name. Required to search: name, years to search. Criminal docket on books from 19; computerized records since 1994. Mail turnaround time 1-2 days.
General Information: No juvenile, mental, sealed, or adoption records released. Will fax documents $2.00 per page. Court makes copy: $1.00 per page. Self serve: same. Cert fee: $5.00. Payee: County Clerk. Personal checks accepted; credit cards are not. Mail requests: SASE helpful.

Hays County

District Court 110 E Martin Luther King, #123, San Marcos, TX 78666; 512-393-7660; fax: 512-393-7674; 8AM-5PM (CST). ***Felony, Civil.*** www.co.hays.tx.us
Civil Records: Access: Phone, mail, in person, online. Both court and visitors may perform in person searches. Search fee: $5.00 per name. Required to search: name, years to search. Civil cases indexed by defendant, plaintiff; index on computer from 1987, index books from 1890s. Mail turnaround time 1-5 days. Civil PAT goes back to 1989. Online access is through www.idocket.com; registration and password required. Case records go back to 12/31/1986. One free name search permitted per day, otherwise subscription required.
Criminal Records: Access: Phone, mail, in person, online. Both court and visitors may perform in person searches. Search fee: $5.00 per name. Required to search: name, years to search; also helpful: DOB, SSN. Criminal records computerized from 1987, index books from 1890s. Mail turnaround time 1-5 days. Criminal PAT goes back to same as civil. Online criminal access is through www.idocket.com; registration and password required. Case records go back to 12/31/1986. One free name search permitted per day, otherwise subscription required.
General: No sealed or adoption records released. Court makes copy: $.50 per page. Cert fee: $1.00 per page. Payee: District Clerk. Personal checks and credit cards accepted. Mail requests: SASE required.

County Court Justice Center, 110 E Martin L King Dr, San Marcos, TX 78666; 512-393-7738; criminal phone: 512-393-2198; civil phone: 512-393-7739; probate phone: 512-393-7734; fax: 512-393-7735; 8AM-5PM. ***Misdemeanor, Civil, Probate.*** www.co.hays.tx.us
Probate fax is same as main fax number.
Civil Records: Access: Mail, in person, online. Both court and visitors may perform in person searches.

Search fee: $10.00 per name. Required to search: name, years to search. Civil cases indexed by defendant, plaintiff; index on computer from 1988, index books from 1848. Mail turnaround time 1-2 weeks. Civil PAT goes back to 1987. PAT results show middle initial, DOB. Online access is through www.idocket.com; registration and password required. Includes probate. Case records from 01/88. One free name search permitted per day, otherwise subscription required.
Criminal Records: Access: Mail, in person, online. Both court and visitors may perform in person searches. Search fee: $10.00 per name. Required to search: name, years to search, DOB. Criminal records computerized from 1987, index books from 1848. Mail turnaround time 1-2 weeks. Criminal PAT goes back to same as civil. PAT results show middle initial, DOB. Misdemeanor records online access is through www.idocket.com; registration and password required. Case records go back to 12/31/1987. One free name search permitted per day, otherwise subscription required. Online results show middle initial, DOB.
General Information: No juvenile, mental, sealed, or adoption records released. Will fax documents if all fees paid. Court makes copy: $1.00 per page. Self serve: same. Cert fee: $5.00 per document. Payee: Hays County Clerk. Personal checks accepted; credit cards are not.

Hemphill County

District & County Court PO Box 867, 400 Main St, Canadian, TX 79014; 806-323-6212; 8AM-N. 1-5PM ***Felony, Misdemeanor, Civil, Probate.***
Probate is a separate index at this same address.
Civil Records: Access: Phone, mail, in person. Both court and visitors may perform in person searches. Search fee: $10.00 per name per index. Required to search: name, years to search. Civil cases indexed by defendant, plaintiff; index from 1890s, in storage. Mail turnaround time 1-2 weeks.
Criminal Records: Access: Phone, mail, in person. Both court and visitors may perform in person searches. Search fee: $10.00 per name per index. Required to search: name, years to search, DOB. Criminal records indexed from 1890s, in storage. Mail turnaround time 1-2 weeks.
General Information: No juvenile, mental, sealed, or adoption records released. Will not fax documents. Court makes copy: $1.00 per page. Self serve: $.50 per page. Cert fee: $5.00 per page. Payee: Hemphill County Clerk. Personal checks accepted; credit cards are not. Mail requests: SASE required.

Henderson County

District Court District Clerk Henderson County, 100 E Tyler, Rm 203, Athens, TX 75751; criminal phone: 903-675-6116; civil phone: 903-675-6115; fax: 903-677-7274; 7:30AM-N, 1PM-4:30PM (CST). ***Felony, Civil.*** www.co.henderson.tx.us/ips/cms/districtcourt/districtClerk.html
This office accepts no fax over 5 pages.
Civil Records: Access: Mail, in person. Both court and visitors may perform in person searches. Search fee: $5.00 per name. Required to search: name, years to search. Civil cases indexed by defendant, plaintiff; index on computer from 1987, index books from 1849. Mail turnaround time 1-2 days. Civil PAT goes back to 1987. PAT results show middle initial, DOB, SSN.
Criminal Records: Access: Mail, in person. Both court and visitors may perform in person searches. Search fee: $5.00 per name. Required to search: name, years to search, DOB; also helpful: SSN. Criminal records computerized from 1984, index books from 1849. Mail turnaround time 1-2 days. Criminal PAT goes back to 1984. PAT results show middle initial, DOB, SSN.
General Information: No juvenile, mental, sealed, or adoption records released. Will fax documents to local or toll-free number, 4 pages maximum. Court makes copy: $1.00 per page. No certification fee. Payee: District Clerk. Personal checks and major credit cards accepted. Mail requests: SASE required.

County Court PO Box 632, 100 E Tyler, Athens, TX 75751; 903-675-6140; criminal phone: 903-677-4022; civil phone: 903-675-6144; probate phone: 903-677-7206; fax: 903-675-6105; 8AM-5PM (CST). ***Misdemeanor, Civil, Probate.*** www.co.henderson.tx.us/ips/cms/countyoffices/countyClerk.html
Civil Records: Access: Phone, mail, fax, in person. Both court and visitors may perform in person searches. Search fee: $5.00 per name. Required to search: name, years to search. Civil cases indexed by defendant, plaintiff; index on computer back to 1984, index books from 1960s. Note: Docket calendars available on the website. Mail turnaround time 1-2 weeks. Civil PAT goes back to 1984. PAT results show name only.
Criminal Records: Access: Mail, fax, in person. Both court and visitors may perform in person searches. Search fee: $5.00 per name. Required to search: name, years to search, DOB, SSN. Criminal records computerized from 1984, index books from 1960s. Note: Docket calendars available on the website. Mail turnaround time 1-2 weeks. Criminal PAT goes back to same as civil. PAT results show name only.
General Information: No juvenile, mental, sealed, or adoption records released. Fee to fax out file $2.00 per page. Court makes copy: $1.00 per page. Self serve: same. Cert fee: $1.00 per document. Payee: County Clerk. Personal checks accepted; credit cards are not. Mail requests: SASE required.

Hidalgo County

District Court PO Box 87, 100 N Closner, Edinburg, TX 78540; 956-318-2200; fax: 956-318-2251; 7:30AM-5:30PM (CST). ***Felony, Civil.*** www.co.hidalgo.tx.us/dc/
Extension numbers for the various clerks are: 92nd- x6204 93rd- x6206, 139th- x6208, 206th- 6210, 275th- 6212, 332nd- x6215, 370th- x6217, 389th- x6219; 398th- x6221. Dial 0 for main clerk switchboard.
Civil Records: Access: Mail, in person, online. Only the court performs in person searches; visitors may not. Search fee: $5.00 per name. Required to search: name, years to search. Civil cases indexed by defendant, plaintiff; index on computer from 1987. Mail turnaround time 1-2 days. Online case access is through www.idocket.com; registration and password required. Records go back to 12/31/1986. One free name search permitted per day, otherwise subscription required.
Criminal Records: Access: Mail, in person, online. Only the court performs in person searches; visitors may not. Search fee: $5.00 per name. Required to search: name, years to search, DOB. Criminal records computerized from 1987. Mail turnaround time 1-2 days. Online case access is through www.idocket.com; registration and password required. Records go back to 12/31/1986. One free name search permitted per day, otherwise subscription required.
General Information: No juvenile, mental, sealed, or adoption records released. Will fax documents $4.25 1st page, $2.25 ea add'l. Court makes copy: $1.00 per page. Cert fee: $1.00 per page. Payee: District Clerk. Business checks accepted. Visa/MC, Discover accepted. Mail requests: SASE required.

County Court PO Box 58, Hidalgo County County Clerk, Edinburg, TX 78540; 956-318-2100; fax: 956-318-2105; 7:30AM-5:30PM (CST). ***Misdemeanor, Civil, Probate.*** www.hidalgo.tx.us.landata.com/
Civil Records: Access: Mail, in person, online. Both court and visitors may perform in person searches. Search fee: $5.00 per name. Required to search: name, years to search. Civil cases indexed by defendant, plaintiff; index on computer from 1986, index books before 1986. Mail turnaround time 1-2 days. Civil PAT goes back to 1986. PAT results show name only. Online case access is through www.idocket.com; registration and password required. Civil and probate records go back to 12/31/1986. One free name search permitted per day, otherwise subscription required.
Criminal Records: Access: Mail, in person, online. Both court and visitors may perform in person searches. Search fee: $5.00 per name. Required to search: name, years to search. Criminal records computerized from 1986, index books before 1986. Mail turnaround time 1-2 days. Criminal PAT goes back to same as civil.PAT results show name, DOB. Misdemeanor case records access is through www.idocket.com; registration and password required. Records go back to 12/31/1991. One free name search permitted per day, otherwise subscription required.
General Information: No juvenile, mental, sealed, or adoption records released. Will not fax documents. Court makes copy: $1.00 per page. Self serve: same. Cert fee: $5.00 per doc. Payee: County Clerk. Business checks accepted. Credit cards accepted. Mail requests: SASE required.

Hill County

District Court PO Box 634, Hillsboro, TX 76645; 254-582-4042; fax: 254-582-4035; 8AM-5PM (CST). ***Felony, Misdemeanor, Civil.***
Civil Records: Access: Mail, in person, online. Both court and visitors may perform in person searches. Search fee: $5.00 per name. Required to search: name, years to search. Civil cases indexed by defendant, plaintiff; index on optical imaging from 9/1993, on computer from 1991, microfilm from 1930s to 1950s, index books from 1900s. Mail turnaround time 1-2 days. Civil PAT goes back to 1990. PAT civil results show middle initial. Online case access is through www.idocket.com. One search a day is free; subscription required for more. Records go back to 12/31/1990.
Criminal Records: Access: Mail, in person, online. Both court and visitors may perform in person searches. Search fee: $5.00 per name. Required to search: name, years to search; also helpful: DOB, SSN. Criminal records on optical imaging from 9/1993, on computer from 1989, microfilm from 1930s to 1950s, index books from 1900s. Mail turnaround time 1-2 days. Criminal PAT goes back to same as civil. PAT criminal results show middle initial. Criminal case access is through www.idocket.com; registration and password required. Records go back to 12/31/1990. One free name search permitted per day, otherwise subscription required. Results show name only.
General Information: Online identifiers in results same as on public terminal. No juvenile, mental, sealed, or adoption records released. Will fax documents $1.50 per page. Court makes copy: $1.00 per page. Cert fee: $1.00. Payee: District Clerk. Personal checks accepted in person. Visa/MC accepted in person only; DL number required. Mail requests: SASE required.

County Court PO Box 398, 1 Courthouse Sq, Hillsboro, TX 76645; 254-582-4030; probate phone: 254-582-4030; fax: 254-582-4003; 8AM-5PM (CST). ***Probate.*** Online access to Probate court records is through www.idocket.com.

Hockley County

District Court 802 Houston St, #316, Levelland, TX 79336; 806-894-8527; fax: 806-894-3891; 9AM-5PM (CST). ***Felony, Civil.***
Civil Records: Access: Phone, mail, in person. Both court and visitors may perform in person searches. Search fee: $5.00 per name. Required to search: name, years to search. Civil cases indexed by defendant, plaintiff; index on computer from 1990, archived from 1922. Mail turnaround time 1-2 days. Civil PAT goes back to 1990. PAT results show name, DOB.
Criminal Records: Access: Phone, mail, in person. Both court and visitors may perform in person searches. Search fee: $5.00 per name. Required to search: name, years to search. Criminal records computerized from 1990, archived from 1922. Mail turnaround time 1-2 days. Criminal PAT goes back to same as civil.PAT results show name, DOB.
General Information: No juvenile, mental, sealed, or adoption records released. Will fax documents $1.00 per page. Court makes copy: $1.00 per page. Cert fee: $2.00. Payee: District Clerk. Only cashiers checks and money orders accepted. No credit cards accepted. Mail requests: SASE required.

County Court County Courthouse, 802 Houston St, #213, Levelland, TX 79336; 806-894-3185; 9AM-5PM (CST). ***Misdemeanor, Civil, Probate.***

Civil Records: Access: Mail, in person. Both court and visitors may perform in person searches. No search fee. Required to search: name, years to search. Civil cases indexed by defendant, plaintiff; index on computer from 1990, index books from 1960. Mail turnaround 1-2 days. Civil PAT goes back to 1990.
Criminal Records: Access: Mail, in person. Both court and visitors may perform in person searches. Search fee: $5.00 per name. Required to search: name, years to search; also helpful: DOB. Criminal records computerized from 1990, index books from 1960. Mail turnaround time 1-2 days. Criminal PAT goes back to 1986.
General Information: No juvenile, mental, sealed, or adoption records released. Will not fax documents. Court makes copy: $1.00 per page. Self serve: $1.00 per page. Cert fee: $5.00 per document. Payee: Hockley County Clerk. Only cashiers checks and money orders accepted. No credit cards accepted. Mail requests: SASE required.

Hood County

District Court County Justice Center, 1200 W Pearl St, Granbury, TX 76048; 817-579-3236; fax: 817-579-3239; 8AM-5PM (CST). ***Felony, Civil.*** www.co.hood.tx.us/text_only/districtclerk.htm
Civil Records: Access: Mail, in person. Both court and visitors may perform in person searches. Search fee: $5.00 per name. Required to search: name, years to search. Civil cases indexed by defendant, plaintiff; index on computer and microfiche from 1983, index books before 1983. Mail turnaround time 1-2 days.
Criminal Records: Access: Mail, in person. Both court and visitors may perform in person searches. Search fee: $5.00 per name. Required to search: name, years to search, DOB, SSN, signed release. Criminal records on computer and microfiche from 1983, index books before 1983. Mail turnaround time 1-2 days.
General Information: No juvenile, mental, sealed, or adoption records released. Will not fax documents. Court makes copy: $1.00 1st page; $.25 each add'l. Cert fee: $1.00 per page includes copy fee. Payee: District Clerk. Personal checks accepted; credit cards are not. Mail requests: SASE required.

County Court PO Box 339, Granbury, TX 76048; 817-579-3222; fax: 817-579-3227; 8AM-5PM (CST). ***Misdemeanor, Civil, Probate.***
Civil Records: Access: Mail, in person. Both court and visitors may perform in person searches. Search fee: $5.00 per name. Required to search: name, years to search. Civil cases indexed by defendant, plaintiff. Civil index in books. Mail turnaround time 1 day.
Criminal Records: Access: Mail, in person. Both court and visitors may perform in person searches. Search fee: $5.00 per name. Required to search: name, years to search; also helpful: DOB. Criminal records on computer and microfiche from 1982, index books before 1982. Mail turnaround time 1 day.
General Information: No juvenile, mental, sealed, or adoption records released. Will fax documents if prepaid. Court makes copy: $1.00 per page. Self serve: same. Cert fee: $5.00. Payee: Hood County Clerk. Personal checks accepted. Visa/MC accepted in person only. Mail requests: SASE required.

Hopkins County

District Court 118 Church St, Sulphur Springs, TX 75483; 903-438-4081; criminal phone: 903-438-4083; civil phone: 903-438-4084; 8AM-5PM (CST). ***Felony, Civil.***
Civil Records: Access: Mail, in person. Both court and visitors may perform in person searches. Search fee: $5.00 per name. Required to search: name, years to search. Civil cases indexed by defendant, plaintiff; index on computer from 1987, index books from 1840. Mail turnaround time 2 days. Civil PAT goes back to 1980.
Criminal Records: Access: Mail, in person. Both court and visitors may perform in person searches. Search fee: $5.00 per name. Required to search: name, years to search. Criminal records computerized from 1987, index books from 1840. Mail turnaround time 2 days. Criminal PAT goes back to 1998.
General Information: No juvenile, mental, sealed, or adoption records released. Will not fax documents. Court makes copy: $1.00 per page. Cert fee: $2.00 per doc. Payee: District Clerk. Personal checks accepted; credit cards are not. Mail requests: SASE required.

County Court PO Box 288, 306 N Davis, Sulphur Springs, TX 75483; 903-438-4074; probate phone: 903-438-4074; criminal fax: 903-438-4110; civil fax: same; 8AM-5PM (CST). ***Misdemeanor, Civil, Probate.*** www.hopkinscountytx.org/
Probate index is here; Probate Court at 118 Church St at the County Courthouse. Probate records fax is same as main fax number.
Civil Records: Access: Mail, in person, online. Both court and visitors may perform in person searches. Search fee: $5.00 per name. Required to search: name, years to search. Civil cases indexed by defendant, plaintiff; index on computer since 1992, index books from 1846. Mail turnaround time 1-2 days. Civil PAT goes back to 1992. PAT results show name only. Search county court index free after registering for login and password at www.hopkinscountyonline.net/countyclerk/.
Criminal Records: Access: Mail, in person, online. Both court and visitors may perform in person searches. Search fee: $5.00 per name. Required to search: name, years to search; also helpful-DOB, SSN, signed release. Criminal records computerized from 1985, index books from 1846. Mail turnaround time 1-2 days. Criminal PAT goes back to 1985.PAT results show name, DOB. Terminal results may include DL number. Online access is the same as civil, see above.
General Information: No juvenile, mental, or sealed records released. Will fax documents $2.00 per page. Court makes copy: $1.00 per page. Self serve: same. Cert fee: $5.00 per document. Payee: County Clerk. In-state personal checks accepted. No out-of-state checks. Major credit cards accepted. Mail requests: SASE required.

Houston County

District Court Houston County Courthouse, 401 E Houston, PO Box 1186, Crockett, TX 75835; 936-544-3255 x228; criminal phone: 936-544-3255 x229; civil phone: 936-544-3255 x235; fax: 936-544-9523; 8AM-4:30PM (CST). ***Felony, Civil, Family.***
Civil Records: Access: Fax, mail, in person. Both court and visitors may perform in person searches. Search fee: $5.00 per name. Required to search: name, years to search. Civil cases indexed by plaintiff. Civil records on computer from 1/97, index books since 1800s. Mail turnaround time 2-5 days. Civil PAT goes back to 1800s. PAT civil results show middle initial.
Criminal Records: Access: Fax, mail, in person. Both court and visitors may perform in person searches. Search fee: $5.00 per name. Required to search: name, years to search, signed release; also helpful: DOB, SSN. Criminal records on computer since 01/98, index books since 1800s. Mail turnaround time 2-5 days. Criminal PAT goes back to same as civil. PAT criminal results show middle initial.
General Information: No juvenile, mental, sealed, or adoption records released. Will fax documents $3.50 1st page, $.50 each add'l. Court makes copy: $1.00 per page. No certification fee. Payee: District Clerk. Personal checks accepted; credit cards are not.

County Court PO Box 370, Crockett, TX 75835; 936-544-3255; criminal phone: x241; civil phone: x239; probate phone: x239 or x241; fax: 936-544-1954; 8AM-4:30PM (CST). ***Misdemeanor, Civil, Probate.*** Probate fax is same as main fax number.
Civil Records: Access: Mail, in person. Both court and visitors may perform in person searches. Search fee: $5.00 per name. Required to search: name, years to search. Civil cases indexed by defendant, plaintiff; index on computer since 2000, microfiche since 1983, index books since 1881 (probate). Mail turnaround 1-2 days. Civil PAT goes back to 1999; results show middle initial.
Criminal Records: Access: Mail, in person. Both court and visitors may perform in person searches. Search fee: $5.00 per name. Required to search: name, years to search. Criminal records on computer since 2000, index books since 1881. Mail turnaround time 1-2 days. Criminal PAT goes back to same as civil. PAT criminal results show middle initial.
General Information: No juvenile, mental, sealed, or adoption records released. Will fax documents to local or toll-free number $1.00 per document. Court makes copy: $1.00 per page. Self serve: same. Cert fee: $5.00 per document. Payee: Houston County Clerk. Personal checks accepted; credit cards are not.

Howard County

District Court PO Box 2138, Big Spring, TX 79721; 432-264-2223; fax: 432-264-2256; 8AM-5PM (CST). ***Felony, Civil.***
Civil Records: Access: Mail, in person. Both court and visitors may perform in person searches. Search fee: $5.00 per name. Required to search: name, years to search. Civil cases indexed by defendant, plaintiff; index on computer from 1990, index books from 1881. Mail turnaround 1-2 days.
Criminal Records: Access: Mail, in person. Both court and visitors may perform in person searches. Search fee: $5.00 per name. Required to search: name, years to search. Criminal records computerized from 1990, index books from 1881. Mail turnaround time 1-2 days.
General Information: No juvenile, mental, sealed or adoption records released. Fee to fax out file $1.00 per page. Court makes copy: $1.00 per page. Cert fee: $1.00 per page. Payee: District Clerk. Personal checks accepted; credit cards are not. Mail requests: SASE required.

County Court PO Box 1468, Big Spring, TX 79721; 432-264-2213; fax: 432-264-2215; 8AM-5PM (CST). ***Misdemeanor, Civil, Probate.***
Civil Records: Access: Phone, mail, in person. Both court and visitors may perform in person searches. Search fee: $5.00 per name. Required to search: name, years to search. Civil cases indexed by defendant, plaintiff. Civil records in index books since 1881. Mail turnaround time 1-2 days.
Criminal Records: Access: Phone, mail, in person. Both court and visitors may perform in person searches. Search fee: $5.00 per name. Required to search: name, years to search. Criminal docket on books from 1881. Mail turnaround time 1-2 days.
General Information: No juvenile, mental, sealed, or adoption records released. Will fax documents $5.00 per doc. Court makes copy: $1.00 per page. Cert fee: $5.00. Payee: County Clerk. Business checks accepted. Credit card payments can only be made through officialpayments.com.

Hudspeth County

District & County Court PO Drawer 58, 109 W Millican St, Sierra Blanca, TX 79851; 915-369-2301; fax: 915-369-0055; 8AM-5PM (MST). ***Felony, Misdemeanor, Civil, Probate.***
Search fee covers both courts, both civil and criminal.
Civil Records: Access: Phone, mail, in person. Both court and visitors may perform in person searches. Search fee: $5.00 per name. Required to search: name, years to search. Civil cases indexed by defendant, plaintiff. Civil records in index books from 1900s; on computer since 1988. Mail turnaround time 1-2 days. Civil PAT goes back to 10 years. PAT results show name only.
Criminal Records: Access: Phone, mail, in person. Both court and visitors may perform in person searches. Search fee: $5.00 per name. Required to search: name, years to search, DOB. Criminal docket on books from 1900s; on computer since 1998. Mail turnaround time 1-2 days. Criminal PAT goes back to same as civil. PAT results show name only.
General Information: No juvenile, mental, sealed, or adoption records released. Will fax documents $1.00 per page. Court makes copy: $1.00 per page. Self serve: same. Cert fee: $5.00 per doc. Payee: District/County Clerk. Personal checks accepted; credit cards are not. Mail requests: SASE required.

Hunt County

District Court Court Clerk, PO Box 1437, Greenville, TX 75403; 903-408-4172; 8AM-5PM (CST). ***Felony, Civil.*** www.huntcounty.net/
Civil Records: Access: Mail, in person. Both court and visitors may perform in person searches. Search fee: $5.00 per name. Required to search: name, years to search. Civil cases indexed by defendant, plaintiff; index on computer from 1992,

microfiche from 1973, index books from 1900s. Mail turnaround 1-2 days. Civil PAT goes back to 1992.
Criminal Records: Access: Mail, in person. Both court and visitors may perform in person searches. Search fee: $5.00 per name. Required to search: name, years to search, DOB. Criminal records computerized from 1992, microfilm from 1973, index books from 1900s. Mail turnaround time 1-2 days. Criminal PAT goes back to 1992.
General: No juvenile, sealed, or adoption records released. Will not fax documents. Court makes copy: $1.00 per page. Self serve: same. Cert fee: $1.00. Payee: District Clerk. Personal checks accepted; credit cards are not. Mail requests: SASE required.

County Court PO Box 1316, Greenville, TX 75403-1316; 903-408-4130; criminal phone: 903-408-4129; civil phone: 903-408-4260; probate phone: 903-408-4136; fax: 903-408-4287; 8AM-4:30PM (CST). ***Misdemeanor, Civil, Probate.***
Civil Records: Access: Mail, in person. Both court and visitors may perform in person searches. Search fee: $5.00 per name. Required to search: name, years to search. Civil cases indexed by defendant, plaintiff; index on computer since 1986, index books from 1940; on microfilm prior to 1986. Mail turnaround 1-2 days. Civil PAT goes back to 1986. PAT civil results show middle initial.
Criminal Records: Access: Mail, in person. Both court and visitors may perform in person searches. Search fee: $5.00 per name. Required to search: name, years to search, DOB. Criminal records on computer since 1986, index books from 1940; on microfilm prior to 1986. Mail turnaround time 1-2 days. Criminal PAT goes back to 1987. PAT results show middle initial, DOB. Terminal results may show DL number.
General Information: No juvenile, mental, sealed, or adoption records released. Will not fax documents. Court makes copy: $1.00 per page. Self serve: same. Cert fee: $5.00. Payee: County Clerk. Personal checks accepted; credit cards are not. Mail requests: SASE required.

Hutchinson County

District Court PO Box 580, Stinnett, TX 79083; 806-878-4017; fax: 806-878-4042; 9AM-5PM (CST). ***Felony, Civil.***
Civil Records: Access: Mail, in person, online. Both court and visitors may perform in person searches. Search fee: $5.00 per name. Required to search: name, years to search. Civil cases indexed by defendant, plaintiff; index on computer from 1990, docket books from 1920. Mail turnaround time 3 to 5 days. Civil PAT goes back to 3/1990. PAT results show name, DOB. Online case access is available by subscription at www.idocket.com including civil (no probate) back to 1/1/1990. One free name search permitted per day, otherwise subscription required.
Criminal Records: Access: Mail, in person, online. Both court and visitors may perform in person searches. Search fee: $5.00 per name. Required to search: name, years to search, signed release; also helpful: DOB, SSN. Criminal records computerized from 1989, docket books from 1920. Mail turnaround time 2 days. Criminal PAT goes back to 3/1990. PAT results show middle initial, DOB. Includes DR number. Online case access is available by subscription at www.idocket.com including criminal back to 1/1/1989. One free name search permitted per day, otherwise subscription required. Online results show middle initial.
General Information: No juvenile, mental, sealed, or adoption records released. Fee to fax out file $1.00 per page. Court makes copy: $1.00 1st page, $.25 each add'l. Cert fee: $1.00 per page. Payee: District Clerk. Personal checks and major credit cards accepted. Mail requests: SASE required.

County Court PO Box 1186, County Clerk, Stinnett, TX 79083; 806-878-4002; fax: 806-878-3497; 9AM-5PM ***Misdemeanor, Civil, Probate.***
When the court performs the search, the computer is used; when a visitor searches, index books are used.
Civil Records: Access: Mail, in person. Both court and visitors may perform in person searches. Search fee: $5.00 per name. Required to search: name, years to search. Civil cases indexed by defendant, plaintiff. Civil records in index books from 1900s. Mail turnaround time 2 days.
Criminal Records: Access: Mail, in person. Both court and visitors may perform in person searches. Search fee: $5.00 per name. Required to search: name, years to search. Criminal records on computer since 1990, index books from 1900s. Mail turnaround time 2 days.
General Information: No juvenile, mental, sealed, or adoption records released. Will not fax documents. Court makes copy: $1.00 per page. Cert fee: $5.00. Payee: Hutchinson County Clerk. Business checks accepted. No credit cards accepted.

Irion County

District & County Court PO Box 736, 209 N Parkview, Mertzon, TX 76941-0736; 325-835-2421; fax: 325-835-7941; 8AM-N, 1-5PM (CST). ***Felony, Misdemeanor, Civil, Probate.***
Civil Records: Access: Mail, in person. Both court and visitors may perform in person searches. Search fee: $5.00 per name. Fee is per court. Required to search: name, years to search. Civil cases indexed by defendant, plaintiff. Civil records in index books from 1889. Mail turnaround time 1-2 days.
Criminal Records: Access: Mail, in person. Both court and visitors may perform in person searches. Search fee: $5.00 per name. Fee is per court. Required to search: name, years to search; also helpful: DOB, DL. Criminal records indexed in books from 1886. Mail turnaround time 1-2 days.
General Information: No juvenile, mental, or sealed records released. Will fax documents $1.00 per page if long distance, $.50 per page if local. Court makes copy: $1.00 per page. Cert fee: $5.00 per doc. Payee: District/County Clerk. Personal checks and major credit cards accepted. Mail requests: SASE requested.

Jack County

District Court 100 Main, County Courthouse, Jacksboro, TX 76458; 940-567-2141; fax: 940-567-2696; 8AM-5PM (CST). ***Felony, Civil.***
Civil Records: Access: Mail, in person. Both court and visitors may perform in person searches. Search fee: $10.00 per name. Required to search: name, years to search. Civil cases indexed by defendant, plaintiff. Civil records in index books from 1857. Mail turnaround time 2 days.
Criminal Records: Access: Mail, in person. Both court and visitors may perform in person searches. Search fee: $10.00 per name. Required to search: name, years to search. Criminal docket on books from 1857. Mail turnaround time 2 days.
General Information: No juvenile, mental, sealed, or adoption records released. Court makes copy: $1.00 per page. Self serve: same. Cert fee: $10.00. Payee: Jack County District Clerk. Personal checks accepted; credit cards are not. Mail requests: SASE required.

County Court 100 Main, Jacksboro, TX 76458; 940-567-2111; fax: 940-567-6441; 8AM-5PM (CST). ***Misdemeanor, Civil, Probate.***
Civil Records: Access: Mail, in person, online. Both court and visitors may perform in person searches. Search fee: $5.00 per name. Required to search: name, years to search. Civil cases indexed by defendant, plaintiff. Civil records in index books from 1856, computerized since 2005. Mail turnaround time 1-2 days. Online case access is available by subscription at www.idocket.com including civil and probate back to 1/2000. One free name search permitted per day, otherwise subscription required.
Criminal Records: Access: Phone, mail, in person, online. Both court and visitors may perform in person searches. Search fee: $5.00 per name. Required to search: name, years to search. Criminal docket on books from 1856, computerized since 2002. Mail turnaround time 1-2 days. Public use terminal has crim records. Online misdemeanor case access is available by subscription at www.idocket.com including criminal back to 1/1999. One free name search permitted per day, otherwise subscription required.
General Information: No juvenile, mental, sealed, or adoption records released. Will fax documents $1.00 per page. Court makes copy: $1.00 per page. Self serve: same. Cert fee: $5.00. Payee: Jack County Clerk. Personal checks and credit cards accepted. Mail requests: SASE required.

Jackson County

District Court 115 W Main, Rm 203, Edna, TX 77957; 361-782-3812; fax: 361-782-3056; 8AM-5PM (CST). ***Felony, Civil.*** www.co.jackson.tx.us/ips/cms/districtcourt/districtClerk.html
Civil Records: Access: Phone, mail, in person. Both court and visitors may perform in person searches. Search fee: $5.00 per name. Required to search: name, years to search. Civil cases indexed by defendant, plaintiff. Civil records in index books from 1850. Mail turnaround time 1 day.
Criminal Records: Access: Mail, in person. Both court and visitors may perform in person searches. Search fee: $5.00 per name. Required to search: name, years to search. Criminal records on microfiche from 1981, index books from 1850. Mail turnaround time 1-2 days.
General Information: No sealed, or adoption records released. Will fax documents. Court makes copy: $1.00 per page. Self serve: same. Cert fee: $1.00. Payee: District Clerk. Personal checks accepted; credit cards are not. Mail requests: SASE required.

County Court 115 W Main, Rm 101, Edna, TX 77957; 361-782-3563; fax: 361-782-3132; 8AM-N, 1-4PM (CST). ***Misdemeanor, Civil, Probate.***
Probate is separate index at this same address.
Civil Records: Access: Mail, in person. Both court and visitors may perform in person searches. Search fee: $5.00 per name. Required to search: name, years to search. Civil cases indexed by defendant, plaintiff. Civil records in index books from 1900s; computerized back to 1993.
Criminal Records: Access: Mail, in person. Both court and visitors may perform in person searches. Search fee: $5.00 per name. Required to search: name, years to search, DOB, offense, date of offense. Criminal docket on books from 1900s. Mail turnaround time 1-2 days.
General Information: No juvenile, mental, sealed, or adoption records released. Fee to fax out file $4.25 for the 1st page, $2.25 per page thereafter. Court makes copy: $1.00 per page. Cert fee: $5.00 per document. Payee: County Clerk. Personal checks and credit cards accepted.

Jasper County

District Court County Courthouse, #202, PO Box 2088, Jasper, TX 75951; 409-384-2721; fax: 409-383-7501; 8AM-4:30PM (CST). ***Felony, Civil.***
Civil Records: Access: Mail, in person. Both court and visitors may perform in person searches. Search fee: $5.00 per name. Required to search: name, years to search. Civil cases indexed by defendant, plaintiff; index on computer since 1991, index books and microfilm since 1850s. Mail turnaround time 1-2 days. Civil PAT goes back to 1990. PAT results show name only.
Criminal Records: Access: Mail, in person. Only the court performs in person searches; visitors may not. Search fee: $5.00 per name. Required to search: name, years to search. Criminal records on computer since 12/96; index books and microfilm since 1850s. Mail turnaround time 1-2 days. Criminal PAT available. PAT results show name only.
General Information: No juvenile, mental, sealed, or adoption records released. Will fax documents $5.00 up to 10 pages; fee $10.00 if more than 10 pages. Court makes copy: $1.00 per page. Self serve: same. Cert fee: $5.00. Payee: District Clerk/Court. Personal checks accepted. Mail requests: SASE required.

County Court Rm 103, Courthouse, Main at Lamar, PO Box 2070, Jasper, TX 75951; 409-384-2632; criminal phone: 409-384-5078; civil phone: 409-384-2632; probate phone: 409-384-2632; criminal fax: 409-384-7198; civil fax: same; 8AM-4:30PM (CST). ***Misdemeanor, Civil, Probate.***
Probate fax is same as main fax number.
Civil Records: Access: Mail, fax, in person. Both court and visitors may perform in person searches. Search fee: $10.00 per name. There is no fee if you do the search yourself. Required to search: name, years to search. Civil cases indexed by defendant, plaintiff. Civil records in index books; on computer back to 1987. Mail turnaround time 1 day. Civil PAT goes back to 1991. PAT results show middle initial, DOB. Terminal results also show SSNs.

Criminal Records: Access: Mail, fax, in person. Both court and visitors may perform in person searches. Search fee: $10.00 per name. There is no fee if you do the search yourself. Required to search: name, years to search, DOB; also helpful: SSN. Criminal index in books; on computer back to 1987. Mail turnaround time 1 day. Criminal PAT goes back to 1990. PAT results show middle initial, DOB. Terminal results include SSN.
General Information: No juvenile, mental, sealed, or adoption records released. Fee to fax out file $3.00 per page. Court makes copy: $1.00 per page. Cert fee: $5.00 per document. Payee: Debbie Newman County Clerk. Personal checks require drivers license. Major credit cards accepted at www.officialpayments.com.

Jeff Davis County

District & County Court PO Box 398, Fort Davis, TX 79734; 432-426-3251; criminal fax: 432-426-3760; civil fax: same; 9AM-N, 1-5PM (CST). ***Felony, Misdemeanor, Civil, Probate.***
Probate fax is same as main fax number.
Civil Records: Access: Mail, in person. Both court and visitors may perform in person searches. Search fee: $5.00 per name. Required to search: name, years to search. Civil cases indexed by defendant, plaintiff. Civil index in books. Mail turnaround time 2 days.
Criminal Records: Access: Mail, in person, fax. Both court and visitors may perform in person searches. Search fee: $5.00 per name. Required to search: name, years to search. Criminal index in books. Mail turnaround time 2 days.
General Information: No juvenile, mental, sealed, or adoption records released. Will fax documents to local or toll free line. Court makes copy: $1.00 per page. Cert fee: $5.00 per certification. Payee: County Clerk. No personal checks or credit cards accepted. Mail requests: SASE helpful.

Jefferson County

District Court 1001 Pearl St, Pearl St Courthouse, Beaumont, TX 77701; 409-835-8580; criminal phone: 409-835-8583; civil phone: 409-835-8580; fax: 409-835-8527; 8AM-5PM (CST). ***Felony, Civil.***
www.co.jefferson.tx.us/dclerk/dc_home.htm
Civil Records: Access: Mail, in person, online. Both court and visitors may perform in person searches. Search fee: $10.00 per name. Required to search: name, years to search. Civil cases indexed by defendant, plaintiff; index on computer and index books since 1940s. Mail turnaround time 2-4 days. Civil PAT goes back to 1945. PAT civil results show middle initial. Public terminal has civil, family, and E-file on selected cases. Online access to the civil records index at www.co.jefferson.tx.us/dclerk/civil_index/main.htm. Search by year by defendant or plaintiff by year 1985 to present. Index goes back to 1995; images back to 12/1998. There is also a Doemestic Index.
Criminal Records: Access: Mail, online, in person. Both court and visitors may perform in person searches. Search fee: $10.00 per name. Required to search: name, years to search; also helpful: DOB, SSN. Criminal records on computer and index books since 1940s. Mail turnaround time 2-4 days. Criminal PAT goes back to 1936. PAT criminal results show middle initial. Online access to criminal records index is at www.co.jefferson.tx.us/dclerk/criminal_index/main.htm. Search by name by year 1981 to present. Online results show middle initial.
General Information: No juvenile, mental, sealed, or adoption records released. Will fax documents local for $3.00 1st page, $1.00 each add'l. Long distance 1st page is $5.00. A similar fee applies to fax send to them. Court makes copy: $1.00 per page. Self serve: same. Cert fee: $5.00 per instrument; search results are not certified unless done by the court itself. Payee: District Clerk. Only cashiers checks and money orders accepted. No credit cards accepted. Mail requests: SASE required.

County Court PO Box 1151, Beaumont, TX 77704; 409-835-8479; probate phone: 409-835-8483; criminal fax: 409-839-2394; civil fax: same; 8AM-5PM (CST). ***Misdemeanor, Civil, Probate.***
www.co.jefferson.tx.us/cclerk/clerk.htm
Search probate records back to 1988 free at http://jeffersontxclerk.manatron.com/. Images go back to 1998. Probate records in a separate index. Probate fax is same as main fax number.
Civil Records: Access: Mail, in person, online. Both court and visitors may perform in person searches. Search fee: $10.00 per name. Required to search: name, years to search. Civil cases indexed by defendant, plaintiff; index on computer since 11/1/95, index books to 1836. Mail turnaround time 1 day. Civil PAT goes back to 11/1/1995 for index; 12/14/1998 for images. PAT results show name only. Public terminal probate index goes back to 10/1988. Search county clerk's civil index free at http://jeffersontxclerk.manatron.com. Index goes back to 1995; images back to 12/1998. $2.00 per page to obtain online docs.
Criminal Records: Access: Mail, in person, online. Both court and visitors may perform in person searches. Search fee: $10.00 per name. Required to search: name, years to search, DOB. Criminal records on computer since 1-1-82, index books to 1836. Mail turnaround time 1 day. Criminal PAT goes back to 1/1983 for index; 12/14/1998 for images.PAT results show name, DOB. Access to Class A&B and C Misdemeanor that are appealed indexes back to 1982 are free at http://jeffersontxclerk.manatron.com/. $1.00 per page to obtain online docs, $2.50 minimum. Add'l criminal records being added. Online results show name only.
General Information: No juvenile, mental, sealed, or adoption records released. Will fax documents $2.50 1st page, $.25 each add'l. Court makes copy: $1.00 per page. Cert fee: $5.00 per cause number. Payee: County Clerk. Personal checks accepted. Major credit cards accepted plus $2.50 transaction fee.

Jim Hogg County

District & County Court PO Box 878, Hebbronville, TX 78361; 361-527-4031; fax: 361-527-5843; 9AM-5PM (CST). ***Felony, Misdemeanor, Civil, Probate.***
Probate records are in a separate index. Probate fax is same as main fax number.
Civil Records: Access: Mail, fax, in person. Both court and visitors may perform in person searches. Search fee: $15.00 per name. Required to search: name, years to search. Civil cases indexed by defendant, plaintiff. Civil index in books.
Criminal Records: Access: In person only. Only the court performs in person searches; visitors may not. Search fee: $15.00 per name. Required to search: name, years to search. Criminal index in books.
General Information: No juvenile, mental, sealed, or adoption records released. Fee to fax out file $3.00 per page. Court makes copy: $1.00 per page. Self serve: same. Cert fee: $5.00 per document. Payee: District Clerk. Personal checks accepted; credit cards are not. Mail requests: SASE required for civil.

Jim Wells County

District Court PO Drawer 2219, Alice, TX 78333; 361-668-5717; fax: 361-668-5732; 8AM-N, 1-5PM (CST). ***Felony, Civil.***
Fax filings are not accepted.
Civil Records: Access: Mail, in person. Both court and visitors may perform in person searches. Search fee: $5.00 per name. Required to search: name, years to search. Civil cases indexed by defendant, plaintiff; index on computer since 1992, index books since 1912. Mail turnaround 2 days.
Criminal Records: Access: Mail, in person. Both court and visitors may perform in person searches. Search fee: $5.00 per name. Required to search: name, years to search; also helpful: SSN, DOB. Criminal records on computer since 1992, index books since 1912. Mail turnaround time 2 days.
General Information: No juvenile, mental, sealed, or adoption records released. Will fax documents $2.00 1st page, $1.00 ea add'l. Court makes copy: $1.00 per page. Cert fee: $2.00. Payee: District Clerk. Personal checks cashier's checks or money orders only accepted. Mail requests: SASE required.

County Court PO Box 1459, 200 N Almond St, Alice, TX 78333; 361-668-5702; 8AM-N, 1-5PM (CST). ***Misdemeanor, Civil, Probate.***
Civil Records: Access: Mail, in person. Both court and visitors may perform in person searches. Search fee: $10.00 per name. Required to search: name, years to search. Civil cases indexed by defendant, plaintiff. Civil records in index books from 1911. Mail turnaround time 1 day.
Criminal Records: Access: Phone, mail, in person. Both court and visitors may perform in person searches. Search fee: $10.00 per name. Required to search: name, years to search, address, DOB. Criminal records on computer since 1992, index books from 1911. Mail turnaround time 1 day.
General Information: No juvenile, mental, sealed, or adoption records released. Will not fax documents. Court makes copy: $1.00 per page. Cert fee: $5.00 per doc. Payee: County Clerk. Personal checks accepted; credit cards are not.

Johnson County

District Court PO Box 495, Cleburne, TX 76033-0495; 817-556-6839; fax: 817-556-6120; 8AM-5PM (CST). ***Felony, Civil.***
www.johnsoncountytx.org
Civil Records: Access: Fax, mail, in person, online. Both court and visitors may perform in person searches. Search fee: $5.00 per name. Required to search: name; also helpful: years to search. Civil cases indexed by defendant, plaintiff; index on computer from mid-1989, index books back to 1800s. Mail turnaround time 2-4 days. Civil PAT goes back to mid-1989. Access index and images online at www.idocket.com; registration and password required. A fee service; only one free name search per day. Records go back to 11/10/1989. Images available.
Criminal Records: Access: Fax, mail, in person, online. Both court and visitors may perform in person searches. Search fee: $5.00 per name. Required to search: name; also helpful: years to search, aliases. Criminal records computerized from mid-1989, index books back to 1800s. Mail turnaround time 2-4 days. Criminal PAT goes back to same as civil. Access index and images online at www.idocket.com; registration and password required. A fee service; only one free name search per day. Records go back to 11/10/1989. Images available.
General Information: No juvenile, mental, sealed, or adoption records released without a court order on file. Fee to fax out file $2.00 per page. Court makes copy: $.50 per page criminal; Civil- $1.00 per page. Self serve: same. Cert fee: $1.00 per page include copy fee. Payee: District Clerk. Business checks accepted. No credit cards accepted. Mail requests: SASE required.

County Court Guinn Justice Center, 204 S Buffalo Ave #407, Cleburne, TX 76033-0662; 817-556-6323; criminal phone: ext 1326; civil phone: ext 1311; probate phone: ext 1308; fax: 817-556-6170; 8AM-N, 1-4:30PM (CST). ***Misdemeanor, Civil, Probate.*** www.johnsoncountytx.org
Civil Records: Access: Mail, in person, online. Both court and visitors may perform in person searches. Search fee: $5.00 per name. Required to search: name, years to search. Civil cases indexed by defendant, plaintiff; index on computer since 1988, index books from 1985. Note: Only searches made by court will be certified. Mail turnaround time 2-3 days. Civil PAT goes back to 1985. PAT results show name, DOB. Results include name and case number. Access index and images online at http://idocket.com/homepage2.htm. Registration required. Civil records back to 12/31/85, probate to 12/31/88. One free name search permitted per day, otherwise subscription required.
Criminal Records: Access: Mail, in person, online. Both court and visitors may perform in person searches. Search fee: $5.00 per name. Required to search: name, years to search, and DOB or SSN. Criminal records on computer since 1988, index books from 1985. Note: Only searches made by court will be certified. Mail turnaround time 1-2 days. Criminal PAT goes back to 1988. Results include name and case number. Access misdemeanor index and images online at http://idocket.com/homepage2.htm. Registration required. Records back to 12/31/88. One free name

search permitted per day, otherwise subscription required.
General Information: No juvenile, mental, sealed, or adoption records released. Will not fax documents. Court makes copy: $1.00 per page. Cert fee: $5.00. Payee: County Clerk. Business checks accepted. No personal checks accepted; credit cards are. Mail requests: SASE required.

Jones County

District & County Court PO Box 308, 12th and Commercial Sts, Anson, TX 79501; 325-823-3731; fax: 325-823-4200; 8AM-5PM (CST). ***Felony, Misdemeanor, Civil.***
Civil Records: Access: Mail, in person. Both court and visitors may perform in person searches. Search fee: $5.00 per name. Required to search: name, years to search. Civil cases indexed by defendant, plaintiff; index on computer since 1990, index books since 1881. Mail turnaround same day.
Criminal Records: Access: Mail, in person. Both court and visitors may perform in person searches. Search fee: $5.00 per name. Required to search: name, years to search, DOB. Criminal records on computer since 1986, index books since 1881. Mail turnaround time same day.
General Information: No juvenile, mental, sealed, or adoption records released. Will fax documents to local or toll free line. Court makes copy: $1.00 per page. Self serve: same. Cert fee: $1.00. Payee: Nona Carter, District Clerk. Personal checks accepted; deposit accounts can be setup. No credit cards accepted. Mail requests: SASE required.

Karnes County

District Court County Courthouse, 101 N Panna Maria Ave, Karnes City, TX 78118-2930; 830-780-2562; criminal fax: 830-780-3227; civil fax: same; 8AM-N, 1-5PM (CST). ***Felony, Civil.***
Civil Records: Access: Mail, in person. Both court and visitors may perform in person searches. Search fee: $5.00 per name. Required to search: name, years to search. Civil cases indexed by defendant, plaintiff. Civil records in index books from 1858. Mail turnaround time 1-2 days.
Criminal Records: Access: Mail, in person. Both court and visitors may perform in person searches. Search fee: $5.00 per name. Required to search: name, years to search, DOB, SSN or other identifiers. Criminal docket on books from 1906. Mail turnaround time 1-2 days.
General Information: No juvenile, mental, sealed, or adoption records released. Will fax documents $.25 per page. Court makes copy: $1.00 per page. Cert fee: $5.00. Payee: District Clerk. Personal checks accepted; credit cards are not. Mail requests: SASE required.

County Court 101 N Panna Maria Ave, #9 Courthouse, Karnes City, TX 78118-2929; 830-780-3938; criminal fax: 830-780-4576; civil fax: same; 8AM-5PM (CST). ***Misdemeanor, Civil, Probate.***
Probate fax is same as main fax number.
Civil Records: Access: Mail, in person. Both court and visitors may perform in person searches. Search fee: $10.00 per name. Required to search: name, years to search. Civil cases indexed by defendant, plaintiff. Civil records in index books from 1920, no computerization. Mail turnaround time 2 days. Civil PAT goes back to 2005.
Criminal Records: Access: Mail, in person. Both court and visitors may perform in person searches. Search fee: $10.00 per name. Required to search: name, years to search. Criminal docket on books from 1900, computerized since 1991. Mail turnaround time 2 days. Criminal PAT goes back to 1992.
General Information: No juvenile, mental, sealed, or adoption records released. Fee to fax out file $2.00 per page. Court makes copy: $1.00 per page. Self serve: same. Cert fee: $5.00 per doc. Payee: Alva Jonas, County Clerk. Personal checks and credit cards accepted. Mail requests: SASE required.

Kaufman County

District Court County Courthouse, 100 W Mulberry St, Kaufman, TX 75142; 972-932-0274; 8AM-5PM (CST). ***Felony, Civil, Family.***
Civil Records: Access: Mail, in person, online. Both court and visitors may perform in person searches. Search fee: $5.00 per name. Required to search: name, years to search. Civil cases indexed by defendant, plaintiff; index on computer or books from 1849. Mail turnaround up to 1 week. Civil PAT goes back to 1849. Access court records free at http://12.14.175.23/Login.aspx?ReturnUrl=/default.aspx and login as 'public' and password 'public.'
Criminal Records: Access: Mail, in person, online. Both court and visitors may perform in person searches. Search fee: $5.00 per name. Required to search: name, years to search. Criminal records on computer or books from 1849. Mail turnaround time up to 1 week. Criminal PAT goes back to same as civil. Access to criminal records online is same as civil.
General Information: No sealed, or adoption records released. Will not fax documents. Court makes copy: $1.00 per page. Self serve: same. Cert fee: $1.00. Payee: Kaufman District Clerk. Personal checks accepted; credit cards are not. Mail requests: SASE required.

County Court County Courthouse, Kaufman, TX 75142; 972-932-4331 x1101; criminal fax: 972-932-4086; civil fax: 972-932-0659; 8AM-4:30PM (CST). ***Misdemeanor, Civil, Probate.***
www.kaufmancountyclerk.com/
Probate fax- 972-932-0659
Civil Records: Access: Mail, in person, online. Both court and visitors may perform in person searches. Search fee: $5.00 per name; probate is $10.00 per name. Required to search: name, years to search. Civil cases indexed by defendant, plaintiff; index on computer from 1985, index books to 1959. Mail turnaround time 10 days. Civil PAT goes back to 1985. PAT civil results show middle initial. Access court records free at http://12.14.175.23/Login.aspx?ReturnUrl=/default.aspx and login as 'public' and password 'public.'
Criminal Records: Access: Mail, in person, online. Both court and visitors may perform in person searches. Search fee: $5.00 per name. Required to search: name, years to search. Criminal records computerized from 1985, index books to 1870. Mail turnaround time 10 days. Criminal PAT goes back to same as civil. PAT criminal results show middle initial. Access to criminal records online is same as civil. Online results show middle initial.
General Information: Online identifiers in results same as on public terminal. No juvenile, mental, sealed, or adoption records released. Will fax documents $3.00 each. Court makes copy: $1.00 per page. Self serve: same. Cert fee: $5.00 first page; $1.00 each add'l page,. Payee: County Clerk. Personal checks and major credit cards accepted. Mail requests: SASE required.

Kendall County

District Court - 216th Judicial District 201 E. San Antonio, #201, Boerne, TX 78006; 830-249-9343; fax: 830-249-1763; 8AM-N, 1-5PM (CST). ***Felony, Civil.***
Civil Records: Access: Mail, in person. Both court and visitors may perform in person searches. Search fee: $5.00 per name. Required to search: name, years to search. Civil cases indexed by defendant, plaintiff. Civil index in docket books from early 1900s. Mail turnaround time 1-2 days.
Criminal Records: Access: Mail, in person. Both court and visitors may perform in person searches. Search fee: $5.00 per name. Required to search: name, DOB, years to search, signed release; also helpful: SSN. Criminal docket on books back to early 1900s. Mail turnaround time 2-4 days.
General Information: No juvenile, mental, sealed, or adoption records released. Will not fax documents. Court makes copy: $.50 per page. Cert fee: $1.00 per page. Payee: District Clerk. Personal checks accepted; credit cards are not. Mail requests: SASE required.

County Court 201 E San Antonio, #127, Boerne, TX 78006; 830-249-9343; probate phone: same; fax: 830-249-3472; 8AM-5PM (CST). ***Misdemeanor, Probate.***
Criminal Records: Access: Mail, in person. Both court and visitors may perform in person searches. Search fee: $5.00 per name. Required to search: name, years to search. Criminal docket on books from 1860s. Mail turnaround time 2-4 days.
General Information: No juvenile, mental, sealed, or adoption records released. No fee to fax documents. Court makes copy: $1.00 per page. Self serve: same. Cert fee: $5.00. Payee: County Clerk. Personal checks accepted; credit cards are not. Mail requests: SASE required.

Kenedy County

District & County Court PO Box 227, Sarita, TX 78385; 361-294-5220; fax: 361-294-5218; 8:30AM-N, 1:30PM-4:30PM (CST). ***Felony, Misdemeanor, Civil, Probate.***
Civil Records: Access: Phone, fax, mail, in person. Both court and visitors may perform in person searches. Search fee: $5.00 per name. Required to search: name, years to search. Civil cases indexed by defendant, plaintiff; index on microfilm since 1991, minute books since 1921. Mail turnaround time 5 days.
Criminal Records: Access: Phone, fax, mail, in person. Both court and visitors may perform in person searches. Search fee: $5.00 per name. Required to search: name, years to search. Criminal records on microfilm since 1991, minute books since 1921. Mail turnaround time 5 days.
General Information: No juvenile, mental, sealed, or adoption records released. Will fax documents $5.00 1st page, $2.00 ea add'l. Court makes copy: $1.00 per page. Cert fee: $5.00 per doc. Payee: District/County Clerk. Personal checks accepted; credit cards are not.

Kent County

District & County Court PO Box 9, Jayton, TX 79528; 806-237-3881; fax: 806-237-2632; 8:30AM-N, 1-5PM (CST). ***Felony, Misdemeanor, Civil, Probate.***
Probate fax is same as main fax number.
Civil Records: Access: Mail, in person. Visitors must perform in person searches themselves. Search fee: $5.00 per name. Required to search: name, years to search. Civil cases indexed by defendant, plaintiff. Civil index in books. Mail turnaround time ASAP.
Criminal Records: Access: Mail, in person. Visitors must perform in person searches themselves. Search fee: $5.00 per name. Required to search: name, years to search. Criminal index in books. Mail turnaround time ASAP.
General Information: No juvenile, mental, sealed, or adoption records released. Will not fax documents. Court makes copy: $1.00 per page. Self serve: same. Cert fee: $5.00 per document. Payee: County Clerk. Cashiers checks, money orders and major credit cards accepted. Mail requests: SASE required.

Kerr County

District Court 700 Main, County Courthouse, Kerrville, TX 78028; 830-792-2281; fax: 830-792-2289; 8AM-5PM (CST). ***Felony, Civil.***
www.co.kerr.tx.us/dclerk/districtclerk.html
Civil Records: Access: Mail, in person, online. Both court and visitors may perform in person searches. Search fee: $5.00 per name. Required to search: name, years to search. Civil cases indexed by defendant, plaintiff; index on computer from late 1991, index books prior to 1991. Mail turnaround time 2-4 days. Civil PAT goes back to early 1990s. PAT results show name only. Search all court indexes also jail and bond indexes free at http://public.co.kerr.tx.us/CaseManagement/PublicAccess/default.aspx.
Criminal Records: Access: Mail, in person, Online. Both court and visitors may perform in person searches. Search fee: $5.00 per name. Required to search: name, years to search. Criminal records computerized from late 1990, index books prior. Mail turnaround time 2-4 days. Criminal PAT goes back to same as civil. PAT results show name only. Online access is the same as civil.
General Information: No juvenile, mental, sealed, or adoption records released. Fee to fax out file $1.00 per page. Court makes copy: $1.00 1st page; $.25 each add'l. Self serve: same. Cert fee: $1.00 per page. Payee: District Clerk. Personal checks and credit cards accepted. Mail requests: SASE required.

County Court & County Court at Law 700 Main St, #122, Kerrville, TX 78028-5389; 830-792-2262; probate phone: 830-792-2261; fax: 830-792-2274; 8:30AM-5PM (CST). ***Misdemeanor, Probate.*** www.co.kerr.tx.us/

Probate fax is same as main fax number. All other civil cases in District Court, upstairs.

Civil Records: Access: Mail, fax, in person, online. Both court and visitors may perform in person searches. Search fee: $5.00 per name. Required to search: name, years to search. Civil cases indexed by defendant, plaintiff; index on computer since 1988, microfiche since 1985, index books prior to 1985. Mail turnaround time 3 days. Civil PAT goes back to 1986. PAT civil results show middle initial. For online access, see criminal section, below.

Criminal Records: Access: Mail, fax, in person, online. Both court and visitors may perform in person searches. Search fee: $5.00 per name. Required to search: name, years to search, DOB; also helpful: SSN. Criminal records on computer since 1985, index books prior to 1918. Mail turnaround time 3 days. Criminal PAT goes back to same as civil. PAT results show middle initial, DOB. Terminal results include SSN. Search all court records also jail and bond records free at http://public.co.kerr.tx.us/CaseManagement/PublicAccess/default.aspx.

General Information: No juvenile, mental, sealed, or adoption records released without judge's approval. Fee to fax out file $1.00 per page. Court makes copy: $1.00 per page. Self serve: $.10 per page. Cert fee: $5.00 per document. Payee: Kerr County Clerk. Only cashiers checks and money orders accepted. Major credit cards accepted.

Kimble County

District & County Court 501 Main St, Junction, TX 76849; 325-446-3353; fax: 325-446-2986; 8AM-N, 1-5PM (CST). ***Felony, Misdemeanor, Civil, Probate.*** www.co.kimble.tx.us/ips/cms

Probate records are in a separate index. Probate fax is same as main fax number.

Civil Records: Access: In person only. Visitors must perform in person searches themselves. Required to search: name, years to search. Civil cases indexed by defendant, plaintiff. Civil records in index books (records are micro-filmed for security only).

Criminal Records: Access: Mail, in person. Both court and visitors may perform in person searches. Search fee: $5.00 per name. Required to search: name, years to search, DOB. Criminal docket on books(records are micro-filmed for security only). Note: The clerk will search back 7 years. Request for criminal search must be in writing and can be faxed if you have prearranged for payment. Mail turnaround time 3-4 days.

General Information: No juvenile, mental, sealed, or adoption records released. Will fax documents to local or toll free line, fee is $5.00. Court makes copy: $1.00 per page. Cert fee: $5.00. Payee: Kimble County/District Clerk. Personal checks accepted; credit cards are not. Mail requests: SASE required for criminal.

King County

District & County Court PO Box 135, Guthrie, TX 79236; 806-596-4412; criminal phone: 806-596-4412; civil phone: 806-596-4412; probate phone: 806-596-4412; fax: 806-596-4664; 9AM-N, 1-5PM (CST). ***Felony, Misdemeanor, Civil, Probate.***

Civil Records: Access: Mail, in person. Both court and visitors may perform in person searches. Search fee: $5.00 per name. Required to search: name, years to search. Civil cases indexed by defendant, plaintiff. Civil index in books. Mail turnaround time 2-4 days.

Criminal Records: Access: Mail, in person. Both court and visitors may perform in person searches. Search fee: $5.00 per name. Required to search: name, years to search, DOB. Criminal index in books. Mail turnaround time 2-4 days.

General Information: No juvenile, mental, sealed, or adoption records released. Will fax documents $1.00 per page. Court makes copy: $1.00 per page. Self serve: same. Cert fee: $5.00. Payee: District Clerk. Personal checks accepted; credit cards are not. Mail requests: SASE required.

Kinney County

District & County Court PO Drawer 9, 501 S "N" St, Brackettville, TX 78832; 830-563-2521; fax: 830-563-2644; 8AM-5PM (CST). ***Felony, Misdemeanor, Civil, Probate.***

Civil Records: Access: Phone, fax, mail, in person. Both court and visitors may perform in person searches. Search fee: $10.00 per name. Required to search: name, years to search. Civil cases indexed by defendant, plaintiff. Civil records in index books from late 1800s; computerized back to 1996. Mail turnaround time 1 week.

Criminal Records: Access: Phone, fax, mail, in person. Both court and visitors may perform in person searches. Search fee: $10.00 per name. Required to search: name, years to search, DOB. Criminal docket on books from late 1800s; computerized records back to 1996. Mail turnaround time 1 week.

General Information: No juvenile, mental, sealed, or adoption records released. Will fax documents $3.00 1st page; $2.00 ea add'l. Court makes copy: $1.00 per page. Self serve: same. Cert fee: $5.00 in County court; $1.00 in District. Payee: County & District Clerk. Personal checks accepted; credit cards are not. Mail requests: SASE required.

Kleberg County

District & County Court at Law PO Box 312, Kingsville, TX 78364-0312; 361-595-8561; fax: 361-595-8525; 8AM-N, 1-5 PM (CST). ***Felony, Civil.***

Civil Records: Access: Phone, fax, mail, in person, online. Both court and visitors may perform in person searches. Search fee: $5.00 per name. Required to search: name, years to search. Civil cases indexed by defendant, plaintiff. Civil records in index books since 1916. Computerized records go back to 1992. Mail turnaround time 1-2 days. Civil PAT goes back to 1992. PAT civil results show middle initial. Online access is at www.idocket.com; registration and password required. A fee service, only one free name search per day. Records go back to 1/1992.

Criminal Records: Access: Phone, fax, mail, in person, online. Both court and visitors may perform in person searches. Search fee: $5.00 per name. Required to search: name, years to search; also helpful: DOB. Criminal docket on books from 1916. Computerized records go to 1992. Mail turnaround time 1-2 days. Criminal PAT goes back to same as civil. PAT results show middle initial, DOB. Online case access is at www.idocket.com; registration and password required. A fee service; only one free name search per day. Records go back to 12/31/1995. Online results show middle initial.

General Information: Online identifiers in results same as on public terminal. No sealed or adoption records released. Will fax documents $5.00 per doc; incoming fax fee $1.00 per page. Court makes copy: $1.00 1st page, $.25 each add'l. Cert fee: $1.00 per page. Payee: District Clerk. Local personal checks accepted only. No credit cards accepted. Mail requests: SASE required.

County Court - Criminal PO Box 1327, Kingsville, TX 78364; 361-595-8548; fax: 361-593-1355; 8AM-5PM (CST). ***Misdemeanor, Probate.*** www.co.kleberg.tx.us/courtatlaw.html

Court also handles civil cases dealing with occupational licenses and bond forfeitures.

Criminal Records: Access: Phone, mail, in person, online. Both court and visitors may perform in person searches. Search fee: $10.00 per name per 10 years. Required to search: name, years to search, DOB. Criminal records on computer since 1989, index books since 1913. Mail turnaround time 3 to 5 days. Public use terminal has crim records back to 1983. PAT results show middle initial, DOB. Online case access at www.idocket.com; registration and password required. A fee service; only one free name search per day. Records go back to 1/1/1983. Online results show middle initial, DOB.

General Information: Online identifiers in results same as on public terminal. No juvenile or mental records released. Will not fax documents. Court makes copy: $1.00 per page. Cert fee: $5.00. Payee: Kleberg County Clerk. Business checks and major credit cards accepted. Mail requests: SASE requested.

Knox County

District & County Court PO Box 196, Benjamin, TX 79505; 940-459-2441; criminal fax: 940-459-2005; civil fax: same; 8AM-5PM (CST). ***Felony, Misdemeanor, Civil, Probate.***

Probate is separate index at this same address. Probate fax is same as main fax number.

Civil Records: Access: Mail, in person. Both court and visitors may perform in person searches. Search fee: $5.00 per name. Required to search: name, years to search. Civil cases indexed by defendant, plaintiff. Civil index in books. Mail turnaround time same day.

Criminal Records: Access: Mail, in person. Both court and visitors may perform in person searches. Search fee: $5.00 for a misdemeanor search; $5.00 for a felony search. Required to search: name, years to search, DOB, SSN, signed release. Criminal docket on books back to 1885. Mail turnaround time 1 day.

General Information: No juvenile, mental, sealed, or adoption records released. Fee to fax out file $1.00 per page. Court makes copy: $1.00 per page. Self serve: same. Cert fee: $5.00 per document. Payee: District/County Clerk. Personal checks accepted; credit cards are not. Mail requests: SASE required.

La Salle County

District & County Courts Courthouse Square, #107, Cotulla, TX 78014; 830-879-4432; criminal fax: 830-879-2933; civil fax: same; 8AM-5PM (CST). ***Misdemeanor, Civil, Probate.***

Probate fax is same as main fax number.

Civil Records: Access: Phone, mail, in person. Both court and visitors may perform in person searches. Search fee: $5.00 per name. Required to search: name, years to search. Civil cases indexed by defendant, plaintiff; index on computer since 1994, prior on index books. Mail turnaround time 1-2 days.

Criminal Records: Access: Mail, in person. Both court and visitors may perform in person searches. Search fee: $5.00 per name. Required to search: name, years to search. Criminal records on computer since 1994, prior on index books. Mail turnaround time 1-2 days.

General Information: No juvenile, mental, sealed, or adoption records released. Will fax documents $1.00 per page. Court makes copy: $1.00 per page. Self serve: same. Cert fee: $5.00 per document. Payee: District & County Clerk. Personal checks accepted; credit cards are not.

Lamar County

District Court 119 N Main, Rm 405, Paris, TX 75460; 903-737-2427; 8AM-5PM ***Felony, Civil.*** www.co.lamar.tx.us

Civil Records: Access: Mail, in person, online. Both court and visitors may perform in person searches. Search fee: $5.00 per name. Required to search: name, years to search. Civil cases indexed by defendant, plaintiff; index on computer since 1/1994, index books prior to 1994. Mail turnaround time 1-2 days. Civil PAT goes back to 1994. Access to county judicial records is free at www.co.lamar.tx.us/. Search by either party name.

Criminal Records: Access: Mail, in person, online. Both court and visitors may perform in person searches. Search fee: $5.00 per name. Required to search: name, years to search. Criminal records on computer since 1/1994, index books prior to 1994. Mail turnaround time 1-2 days. Criminal PAT goes back to 1987. Access to county judicial records is free online at www.co.lamar.tx.us. Search by defendant name.

General Information: No juvenile, mental, sealed, or adoption records released. Court makes copy: $1.00 per page. Self serve: same. No certification fee. Payee: District Clerk. Personal checks accepted. Mail requests: SASE required.

County Court 119 N Main, Paris, TX 75460; 903-737-2420; fax: 903-782-1111; 8AM-5PM (CST). ***Misdemeanor, Civil, Probate.***

Civil Records: Access: Phone, fax, mail, in person, online. Both court and visitors may perform in

person searches. Search fee: $10.00 per name. Required to search: name, years to search. Civil cases indexed by defendant, plaintiff. Civil records in index books since 1913; on computer back to 1998. Mail turnaround time 2-3 days. Access to county judicial records is free at http://68.89.102.225/. Search by either party name.
Criminal Records: Access: Phone, fax, mail, in person, online. Both court and visitors may perform in person searches. Search fee: $5.00 per name. Required to search: name, years to search, DOB; SSN or drivers license number also required. Criminal records computerized from 1988, index books since 1913. Mail turnaround time 2-3 days. Access to county judicial records is free online at www.co.lamar.tx.us. Search by defendant name.
General Information: No juvenile, mental, sealed, or adoption records released. Will not fax documents. Court makes copy: $1.00 per page. Cert fee: $5.00 per document. Payee: County Clerk. Business checks accepted; will accept local personal checks. No credit cards accepted.

Lamb County

District Court 100 6th Dr, Rm 212, Courthouse, Littlefield, TX 79339; 806-385-4222; criminal phone: x1; civil phone: x1; fax: 806-385-3554; 8:30AM-5PM (CST). ***Felony, Civil.***
Search fee includes both civil and criminal indexes if you ask for both.
Civil Records: Access: Mail, in person. Both court and visitors may perform in person searches. Search fee: $5.00 per name. Required to search: name, years to search. Civil cases indexed by defendant, plaintiff; index on computer since 1987; on index books back to 1940. Mail turnaround 2-3 days.
Criminal Records: Access: Mail, in person. Both court and visitors may perform in person searches. Search fee: $5.00 per name. Required to search: name, years to search; also helpful: DOB, SSN. Criminal docket on booksto 1940s; on computer since 1987. Mail turnaround time 2-3 days.
General Information: No juvenile, mental, sealed, or adoption records released. Will fax documents to local or toll free line. Court makes copy: $1.00 per page. Self serve: same. No certification fee To certify, indicate that "it needs to be certified.". Payee: District Court. Personal checks accepted; credit cards are not. Mail requests: SASE required.

County Court County Courthouse, Rm 103, Littlefield, TX 79339-3366; 806-385-4222 X214; fax: 806-385-6485; 8:30AM-N, 1-5PM (CST). ***Misdemeanor, Civil, Probate.*** www.co.lamb.tx.us
Civil Records: Access: Mail, in person. Both court and visitors may perform in person searches. Search fee: $5.00 per name. Required to search: name, years to search. Civil cases indexed by defendant, plaintiff. Civil index in books. Mail turnaround time 1-7 working days.
Criminal Records: Access: Mail, in person. Both court and visitors may perform in person searches. Search fee: $5.00 per name. Required to search: name, years to search; also helpful: DOB, SSN. Criminal index in books. Mail turnaround time 1-7 working days.
General Information: No juvenile, mental, sealed, or adoption records released. Court makes copy: $1.00 per page. Cert fee: $5.00 per document. Payee: Lamb County Clerk. Personal checks accepted. Major credit cards accepted online only; $5.95 usage charge added.

Lampasas County

District Court PO Box 327, Lampasas, TX 76550; 512-556-8271 X240; fax: 512-556-9463; 8AM-5PM (CST). ***Felony, Civil.***
Civil Records: Access: Mail, in person. Both court and visitors may perform in person searches. Search fee: $5.00 per name. Required to search: name, years to search. Civil cases indexed by defendant, plaintiff. Civil records in index books, computerized since 1997. Mail turnaround 2-4 days.
Criminal Records: Access: Mail, in person. Both court and visitors may perform in person searches. Search fee: $5.00 per name. Required to search: name, years to search. Criminal index in books; on computer for 5 years. Mail turnaround time 2-4 days.
General Information: No juvenile, mental, sealed, or adoption records released. Fee to fax out file $1.00 per page. Court makes copy: $1.00 per page. Self serve: same. Cert fee: $2.00 per document. Payee: District Clerk. Business checks accepted. No credit cards accepted. Mail requests: SASE required.

County Court PO Box 347, 409 S Pecan, Lampasas, TX 76550; 512-556-8271 x202; 8AM-5PM (CST). ***Misdemeanor, Civil, Probate.***
Probate is separate index at this same address.
Civil Records: Access: Mail, in person. Both court and visitors may perform in person searches. Search fee: $5.00 per name. Required to search: name, years to search. Civil cases indexed by defendant, plaintiff. Civil index in books. Mail turnaround time 1-2 days.
Criminal Records: Access: Mail, in person. Both court and visitors may perform in person searches. Search fee: $5.00 per name. Required to search: name, years to search; also helpful: DOB, SSN. Criminal index in books. Mail turnaround 1-2 days.
General Information: No juvenile, mental, sealed, or adoption records released. Will not fax documents. Court makes copy: $1.00 per page. Self serve: same. Cert fee: $5.00 per document. Payee: County Clerk. Personal checks must be in state. No credit cards accepted. Mail requests: SASE requested.

Lavaca County

District Court PO Box 306, Hallettsville, TX 77964; 361-798-2351; fax: 361-798-5674; 8AM-N, 1-5PM (CST). ***Felony, Civil.***
Civil Records: Access: Phone, mail, in person. Both court and visitors may perform in person searches. Search fee: $5.00 per name. Required to search: name, years to search. Civil cases indexed by defendant, plaintiff. Civil records in index books from 1847. Note: Information released to attorneys only. Mail turnaround time same day.
Criminal Records: Access: Mail, in person. Both court and visitors may perform in person searches. Search fee: $5.00 per name. Required to search: name, years to search. Criminal docket on books from 1847. Note: Information released to law enforcement only. Mail turnaround time same day.
General Information: No juvenile, Department of Human Services, adoptions and expunction records released. Will fax documents to local or toll free line. Court makes copy: $1.00 per page. Self serve: same. Cert fee: $2.00. Payee: Lavaca County District Clerk. Personal checks accepted; credit cards are not. Mail requests: SASE required.

County Court PO Box 326, Hallettsville, TX 77964; 361-798-3612; fax: 361-798-1610; 8AM-5PM (CST). ***Misdemeanor, Civil, Probate.***
Civil Records: Access: Mail, in person. Both court and visitors may perform in person searches. Search fee: $5.00 per name per 10 years. Required to search: name, years to search, DOB; also helpful: address, SSN, DL#. Civil cases indexed by defendant, plaintiff; index on computer go back to late 1993; earlier in index books. Mail turnaround time same day as received. Civil PAT goes back to 12/1993. PAT results show middle initial, DOB.
Criminal Records: Access: Mail, in person. Both court and visitors may perform in person searches. Search fee: $5.00 per name per 5 years. Required to search: name, years to search; also helpful: address, DOB, DL#, SSN. Records on computer go back to late 1993; earlier in index books. Mail turnaround time same day as received. Criminal PAT goes back to same as civil. PAT results show middle initial, DOB.
General Information: No mental health or sealed records released. Will fax out documents $2.00 per page fee. Court makes copy: $1.00 per page. Self serve: same. Cert fee: $5.00 per document. Payee: County Clerk. Personal checks accepted. Visa/MC accepted at www.certifiedpayments.net.

Lee County

District Court PO Box 176, Giddings, TX 78942; 979-542-2947; criminal fax: 979-542-2444; civil fax: same; 8AM-N, 1-5PM (CST). ***Felony, Civil.***
Civil Records: Access: Mail, in person. Both court and visitors may perform in person searches. Search fee: $5.00 per name. Required to search: name, years to search. Civil cases indexed by defendant, plaintiff. Civil index on docket books from 1800s. Mail turnaround time 1-2 days.
Criminal Records: Access: Mail, in person. Both court and visitors may perform in person searches. Search fee: $5.00 per name. Required to search: name, years to search; also helpful: DOB, SSN. Criminal records on computer since 1989. Mail turnaround time 1-2 days.
General Information: No juvenile or adoption records released. Will fax documents to local or toll free line. Court makes copy: $1.00 per page. Self serve: same. Cert fee: $2.00 per cert. Payee: District Clerk, Lee County. Personal checks accepted; credit cards are not. Mail requests: SASE required.

County Court PO Box 419, Giddings, TX 78942; 979-542-3684; criminal fax: 979-542-2623; civil fax: same; 8AM-5PM (CST). ***Misdemeanor, Civil, Probate.*** Probate fax is same as main fax number.
Civil Records: Access: Mail, in person. Both court and visitors may perform in person searches. Search fee: $5.00 per name. Required to search: name, years to search. Civil cases indexed by defendant, plaintiff. Civil records in index books since 1874 (beginning 1995 on computer). Mail turnaround time 1-3 days.
Criminal Records: Access: Mail, in person. Both court and visitors may perform in person searches. Search fee: $5.00 per name. Required to search: name, years to search. Criminal records on computer since 1992, index books since 1874. Mail turnaround time 1-3 days.
General: No juvenile, mental, sealed or adoption records released. Will fax documents to local or toll free line. Court makes copy: $1.00 per page. Cert fee: $5.00. Payee: County Clerk. Personal checks and credit cards accepted. Mail requests: SASE required.

Leon County

District Court PO Box 39, 139 E Main St, Centerville, TX 75833; 903-536-2227; 8AM-5PM (CST). ***Felony, Civil.*** www.co.leon.tx.us
Fax available by permission only; call ahead.
Civil Records: Access: Mail, in person. Both court and visitors may perform in person searches. Search fee: $5.00 per name. Required to search: name, years to search. Civil cases indexed by defendant, plaintiff. Civil records in index books. Mail turnaround time 2-10 days.
Criminal Records: Access: Mail, in person. Both court and visitors may perform in person searches. Search fee: $5.00 per name. Required to search: name, years to search. Criminal index in books. Mail turnaround time 2-10 days.
General Information: No juvenile, mental, sealed, or adoption records released. Will not fax documents. Court makes copy: $1.00 per page. Cert fee: $1.00. Payee: Leon County District Clerk. Personal checks accepted; credit cards are not. Mail requests: SASE required.

County Court PO Box 98, 204 E St Mary St, Centerville, TX 75833; 903-536-2352; 8AM-5PM (CST). ***Misdemeanor, Civil, Probate.***
Civil Records: Access: Mail, in person. Both court and visitors may perform in person searches. Search fee: $5.00 per name. Required to search: name, years to search. Civil cases indexed by defendant, plaintiff. Civil index in books. Mail turnaround time 1-3 days.
Criminal Records: Access: Mail, in person. Both court and visitors may perform in person searches. Search fee: $5.00 per name. Required to search: name, years to search, signed release. Criminal records only 1950 to present. Mail turnaround time 1-3 days.
General Information: No juvenile, mental, sealed records released. Will not fax documents. Court makes copy: $1.00 per page. Cert fee: $5.00 per doc. Payee: Leon County Clerk. Business checks accepted. Personal checks accepted in person only. No credit cards accepted. Mail requests: SASE required.

Liberty County

District Court 1923 Sam Houston, #115, Liberty, TX 77575; 936-336-4600 x4; criminal phone: 936-336-4682; civil phone: 936-336-4683; 8AM-N, 1-5PM (CST). ***Felony, Civil.***

Civil Records: Access: Mail, in person. Both court and visitors may perform in person searches. Search fee: $5.00 per name. Required to search: name, years to search. Civil cases indexed by defendant, plaintiff; index on computer since 1993, index books prior. Mail turnaround time 2-4 days. Civil PAT goes back to 1875. PAT results show name only.
Criminal Records: Access: Mail, in person. Both court and visitors may perform in person searches. Search fee: $5.00 per name. Required to search: name, years to search. Criminal records on computer since 1993, index books prior. Mail turnaround time 2-4 days. Criminal PAT goes back to 1894. PAT results show name only.
General Information: No juvenile, mental, sealed, or adoption records released. Will not fax documents. Court makes copy: $1.00 per page. Payee: District Clerk. Personal checks and major credit cards accepted. Mail requests: SASE required.

County Court PO Box 369, 1923 Sam Houston #208, Liberty, TX 77575; 936-336-4670; 8AM-5PM (CST). ***Misdemeanor, Civil, Probate.***
Civil Records: Access: Mail, in person. Both court and visitors may perform in person searches. Search fee: $5.00 per name. Required to search: name, years to search. Civil cases indexed by defendant, plaintiff. Civil records in index books; later on computer. Mail turnaround time 2-4 days. Civil PAT goes back to 1995.
Criminal Records: Access: Mail, in person. Both court and visitors may perform in person searches. Search fee: $5.00 per name. Required to search: name, years to search, DOB, SSN, signed release. Criminal index in books; later on computer. Mail turnaround time 2-4 days. Criminal PAT goes back to same as civil.
General Information: No juvenile, mental, sealed, or adoption records released. Will not fax documents. Court makes copy: $1.00 per page. Cert fee: $5.00 per doc. Payee: County Clerk. Business checks accepted. Personal checks accepted in person only. Major credit cards accepted. Mail requests: SASE required.

Limestone County

District Court PO Box 230, Groesbeck, TX 76642; 254-729-3206; fax: 254-729-2960; 8AM-5PM (CST). ***Felony, Civil.***
Civil Records: Access: Mail, in person. Both court and visitors may perform in person searches. Search fee: $5.00 per name. Required to search: name, years to search. Civil cases indexed by defendant, plaintiff; index on computer since 9/1990, index books since 1883. Mail turnaround time 1 week. Civil PAT goes back to 1991.
Criminal Records: Access: Mail, in person. Both court and visitors may perform in person searches. Search fee: $5.00 per name. Required to search: name, years to search, DOB; also helpful: SSN. Criminal records on computer since 9/1990, index books since 1911. Mail turnaround time 1 week. Criminal PAT goes back to same as civil. PAT results show middle initial, DOB.
General Information: No juvenile, mental, sealed, or adoption records released. Will fax documents $1.00 1st page, $.25 each add'l. Court makes copy: $1.00 per page. Self serve: $.50 per page. Cert fee: $2.00 per cert. Payee: District Clerk. Personal checks accepted; credit cards are not.

County Court PO Box 350, Groesbeck, TX 76642; 254-729-5504; fax: 254-729-2951; 8AM-5PM (CST). ***Misdemeanor, Civil, Probate.***
Civil Records: Access: Mail, in person. Both court and visitors may perform in person searches. Search fee: $5.00 per name. Required to search: name, years to search. Civil cases indexed by defendant, plaintiff. Civil records in index books to early 1900s, computerized since 1985. Mail turnaround time 2 days. Public use terminal available. PAT civil results show middle initial.
Criminal Records: Access: Mail, in person. Both court and visitors may perform in person searches. Search fee: $5.00 per name. Required to search: name, years to search; also helpful: DOB, SSN, signed release. Criminal docket on booksto 1900s, computerized since 1985. Mail turnaround time 2 days. Public use terminal available. PAT criminal results show middle initial.
General Information: No juvenile, mental, sealed, or adoption records released. Fee to fax out file $2.00 per page. Court makes copy: $1.00 per page. Cert fee: $5.00. Payee: Limestone County Clerk. Personal checks and major credit cards accepted.

Lipscomb County

District & County Court PO Box 70, Lipscomb, TX 79056; 806-862-3091; fax: 806-862-3004; 8:30AM-N, 1-5PM (CST). ***Felony, Misdemeanor, Civil, Probate.***
Civil Records: Access: Fax, mail, in person. Both court and visitors may perform in person searches. Search fee: $10.00 per name. Required to search: name. Civil cases indexed by defendant, plaintiff. Civil records in index books since 1887; on computer back to 1999. Mail turnaround time 2 days.
Criminal Records: Access: Fax, mail, in person. Both court and visitors may perform in person searches. Search fee: $5.00 per name. Required to search: name; also helpful: DOB. Criminal docket on books from 1887; on computer back to 1999. Mail turnaround time 2 days.
General Information: No juvenile, mental, sealed, or adoption records released. Will fax documents $1.00 1st page, $.50 each add'l. Court makes copy: $1.00 per page. Self serve: same. Cert fee: $5.00 in County Court; $1.00 in District. Payee: County Clerk. Personal checks accepted; credit cards are not. Can pay on 'Official Payments.'. Mail requests: SASE required.

Live Oak County

District Court PO Drawer 440, George West, TX 78022; 361-449-2733 X105; fax: 361-449-2992; 8AM-5PM (CST). ***Felony, Civil.***
Civil Records: Access: Phone, fax, mail, in person. Both court and visitors may perform in person searches. Search fee: $10.00 per name. Required to search: name, years to search. Civil cases indexed by defendant, plaintiff. Civil records in index books and microfiche since 1850s. Mail turnaround 1-2 days.
Criminal Records: Access: Phone, fax, mail, in person. Both court and visitors may perform in person searches. Search fee: $10.00 per name. Required to search: name, years to search, DOB; also helpful: SSN. Criminal docket on books and microfiche since 1850s. Mail turnaround 1-2 days.
General Information: No juvenile, mental, sealed, or adoption records released. Will fax documents $1.00 per page. Court makes copy: $1.00 per page. Self serve: same. Cert fee: $1.00. Payee: District Clerk. Personal checks accepted; credit cards are not. Mail requests: SASE required.

County Court PO Box 280, George West, TX 78022; 361-449-2733; criminal phone: x129; civil phone: x103; probate phone: x103; 9AM-4PM (CST). ***Misdemeanor, Civil, Probate.***
Civil Records: Access: Mail, in person. Both court and visitors may perform in person searches. Search fee: $10.00 per name. Required to search: name, years to search. Civil cases indexed by defendant, plaintiff. Civil index in books. Mail turnaround time 1-2 days.
Criminal Records: Access: Mail, in person. Both court and visitors may perform in person searches. Search fee: $10.00 per name. Required to search: name, years to search. Criminal index in books. Mail turnaround time 1-2 days.
General Information: No juvenile, mental, sealed, or adoption records released. No fax machine. Court makes copy: $1.00 per page. Cert fee: $5.00. Payee: County Clerk. Personal checks and major credit cards accepted.

Llano County

District Clerk 832 Ford St, Llano, TX 78643-0877; 325-247-5036; fax: 325-248-0492; 8AM-4:30PM (CST). ***Felony, Civil.*** http://dcourt.org
Signup for email notifications of civil and criminal dockets at www.dcourt.org/_attys/dockets.htm.
Civil Records: Access: Mail, in person, online. Both court and visitors may perform in person searches. Search fee: $5.00 per name. Fee is per 5 year period. Required to search: name, years to search. Civil cases indexed by defendant, plaintiff. Civil index in docket books from 1900, computerized back to 1995. Mail turnaround time 1-3 days. Civil PAT goes back to 1995. PAT results show name only. Signup for email notifications of civil and criminal dockets at www.dcourt.org/_attys/dockets.htm.
Criminal Records: Access: Mail, in person, online. Both court and visitors may perform in person searches. Search fee: $5.00 per name. Fee is per 5 year period. Required to search: name, years to search. Criminal docket on books back to 1900, computerized back to 1995. Mail turnaround time 1-3 days. Criminal PAT goes back to same as civil. PAT results show name only. Signup for email notifications of civil and criminal dockets at www.dcourt.org/_attys/dockets.htm.
General Information: No juvenile, mental, sealed, or adoption records released. Will fax documents to local or toll free line. Court makes copy: $1.00 per page. Self serve: same. Cert fee: $1.00 per page. Payee: Llano County District Clerk. Personal checks accepted; credit cards are not. Mail requests: SASE required.

County Court PO Box 40, Llano, TX 78643-0040; 325-247-4455; fax: 325-247-2406; 8AM-4:30PM (CST). ***Misdemeanor, Civil, Probate.***
Civil Records: Access: Phone, mail, in person. Both court and visitors may perform in person searches. Search fee: $5.00 per name. Required to search: name, years to search. Civil cases indexed by defendant, plaintiff; index on computer since 1985, index books prior. Mail turnaround time 2-4 days. Civil PAT goes back to 1985. PAT civil results show middle initial.
Criminal Records: Access: Phone, mail, in person. Both court and visitors may perform in person searches. Search fee: $5.00 per name. Required to search: name, years to search; also helpful: DOB. Criminal records on computer since 1985, index books prior. Mail turnaround time 2-4 days. Criminal PAT goes back to same as civil. PAT criminal results show middle initial.
General Information: No juvenile, mental, sealed, or adoption records released. Will fax documents to local or toll free line. Court makes copy: $1.00 per page. Self serve: same. Cert fee: $5.00. Payee: County Clerk. Personal checks accepted; credit cards are not.

Loving County

District & County Court PO Box 194, Mentone, TX 79754; 432-377-2441; fax: 432-377-2701; 9AM-N, 1-5PM (CST). ***Felony, Misdemeanor, Civil, Probate.***
Civil Records: Access: Mail, in person. Both court and visitors may perform in person searches. Search fee: $5.00 per name. Required to search: name, years to search. Civil cases indexed by defendant, plaintiff. Civil records in index books from 1935. Mail turnaround time 2 days.
Criminal Records: Access: Mail, in person. Visitors must perform in person searches themselves. Search fee: $5.00 per name. Required to search: name, years to search. Criminal docket on books from 1935; computerized back to 1987. Mail turnaround time 2 days.
General Information: No juvenile, mental, sealed, or adoption records released. Fee to fax out file $1.50 per page. Court makes copy: $1.00 per page. Cert fee: $5.00 per doc. Payee: Loving County Clerk. Personal checks accepted; credit cards are not.

Lubbock County

District Court PO Box 10536 (904 Broadway #105), Lubbock, TX 79408-3536; 806-775-1623; criminal fax: 806-775-1382; civil fax: same; 8AM-5PM (CST). ***Felony, Civil.***
www.co.lubbock.tx.us/DClerk/d_clerk.htm
Civil Records: Access: Fax, mail, in person. Both court and visitors may perform in person searches. Search fee: $5.00 per name. Required to search: name, years to search. Civil cases indexed by defendant, plaintiff; index on computer back to 1979, in index books to 1908. Mail turnaround time 2 business days. Civil PAT goes back to 1979. PAT civil results show middle initial.
Criminal Records: Access: Fax, mail, in person. Both court and visitors may perform in person searches. Search fee: $5.00 per name. Required to

search: name, years to search, DOB; also helpful: SSN, signed release. Criminal records computerized from 1979, in index books to 1908. Mail turnaround 2 business days. Criminal PAT goes back to same as civil. PAT criminal results show middle initial.
General Information: No juvenile, sealed, or adoption records released. Will fax documents $5.00 plus $1.00 per page copy fee. Court makes copy: $1.00 per page. Cert fee: $1.00. Payee: District Clerk. Money order or cashiers checks accepted. Visa/MC accepted. Mail requests: SASE required.

County Courts Courthouse, Rm 207, PO Box 10536, Lubbock, TX 79408; criminal phone: 806-775-1044; civil: 806-775-1047; probate: 806-775-1053; 8:30AM-5PM ***Misdemeanor, Civil, Probate.*** www.co.lubbock.tx.us/CCourt/c_courts.htm
Civil Records: Access: In person only. Both court and visitors may perform in person searches. Search fee: $10.00 per name. Fee is for each 10 year period. Required to search: name, years to search. Civil cases indexed by defendant, plaintiff; index on computer back to 1986, index books prior. Civil PAT goes back to 1986. PAT results show name only.
Criminal Records: Access: Mail, in person, online. Both court and visitors may perform in person searches. Search fee: $10.00 per name. Required to search: name, years to search; DOB helpful. Criminal records computerized from 1988, index books prior. Mail turnaround time 3-5 days. Criminal PAT goes back to 1988. Access criminal court data by subscription; for information call David Slayton, 806-775-1020. Online results show name, DOB.
General Information: No juvenile, mental, sealed, or adoption records released. Court makes copy: $1.00 per page. Cert fee: $5.00 per doc. Payee: County Clerk. Personal checks accepted; include your DR# and your phone. No credit cards accepted. Mail requests: SASE required.

Lynn County

District Court PO Box 939, Tahoka, TX 79373; 806-561-4274; fax: 806-561-4151; 8:30AM-5PM (CST). ***Felony, Civil.***
Civil Records: Access: Fax, mail, in person. Both court and visitors may perform in person searches. Search fee: $5.00 per name. Required to search: name, years to search. Civil cases indexed by defendant, plaintiff; index on computer from 1997, index books from 1916. Mail turnaround time 2 days.
Criminal Records: Access: Fax, mail, in person. Both court and visitors may perform in person searches. Search fee: $5.00 per name. Required to search: name, years to search. Criminal records computerized from 1997, index books from 1916. Mail turnaround time 2 days.
General: No juvenile, mental, sealed, or adoption records released. Will fax documents $2.00 per page. Court makes copy: $1.00 per page. Cert fee: $1.00 per page. Payee: District Clerk. Personal checks accepted; credit cards are not. Mail requests: SASE required.

County Court PO Box 937, Tahoka, TX 79373; 806-561-4750; fax: 806-561-4988; 8:30AM-5PM (CST). ***Misdemeanor, Civil, Probate.***
Civil Records: Access: Mail, in person. Both court and visitors may perform in person searches. Search fee: $5.00. Required to search: name, years to search. Civil cases indexed by defendant, plaintiff. Civil records in index books from 1903; on computer back to 1997. Mail turnaround time same day. Civil PAT goes back to 1997.
Criminal Records: Access: Mail, in person. Both court and visitors may perform in person searches. Search fee: $5.00. Required to search: name, years to search. Criminal docket on books from 1903; on computer back to 1997. Mail turnaround time same day. Criminal PAT goes back to same as civil.
General: No juvenile, mental, sealed, or adoption records released. Fee to fax out file $2.00 per page. Court makes copy: $1.00 per page. Cert fee: $5.00. Payee: Lynn County Clerk. Personal checks and major credit cards accepted. Mail requests: SASE required.

Madison County

District Court 101 W Main, Rm 226, Madisonville, TX 77864; 936-348-9203; 8AM-N, 1-5PM (CST). ***Felony, Civil.***
Civil Records: Access: Mail, in person. Both court and visitors may perform in person searches. Search fee: $5.00 per name. Required to search: name, years to search. Civil cases indexed by defendant, plaintiff. Civil records in index books to 1935, in archives to 1873. Mail turnaround 1 day.
Criminal Records: Access: Mail, in person. Both court and visitors may perform in person searches. Search fee: $5.00 per name. Required to search: name, years to search. Criminal docket on booksto 1835. Mail turnaround time 1 day.
General Information: No juvenile, mental, sealed, or adoption records released. Will not fax documents. Court makes copy: $1.00 per page. Self serve: same. No certification fee. Payee: District Clerk. Personal checks accepted; credit cards are not. Mail requests: SASE required.

County Court 101 W Main, Rm 102, Madisonville, TX 77864; 936-348-2638; 8AM-4:30PM ***A & B Misdemeanors, Civil, Probate.*** www.co.madison.tx.us/ips/cms/countyoffices/countyClerk.html Probate fax is same as main fax number.
Civil Records: Access: Mail, in person. Both court and visitors may perform in person searches. Search fee: $10.00 per name. Required to search: name, years to search. Civil cases indexed by defendant, plaintiff; index on computer from 1/00; index books back to 1970. Mail turnaround time as soon as fees are paid. Public use terminal records go back to 2000 and show middle initial, DOB.
Criminal Records: Access: Mail, in person. Both court and visitors may perform in person searches. Search fee: $10.00 per name. Required to search: name, years to search, DOB. Criminal records computerized from 1982; records go back to early 1900's (not indexed). Mail turnaround time 1 day. Public use terminal available, crim records go back to 1985. PAT results show middle initial, DOB.
General Information: No juvenile, mental, sealed, or adoption records released. Fee to fax out file $1.00 per page. Court makes copy: $1.00 per page. Cert fee: $5.00 per document. Payee: Madison County Clerk. Personal checks accepted. Visa/MC/Discover/AmEx cards accepted. Mail requests: SASE required.

Marion County

District Court PO Box 628, Jefferson, TX 75657; 903-665-2441/2013; fax: 903-665-2102; 8AM-5PM (CST). ***Felony, Civil.*** www.co.marion.tx.us/ips/cms/districtcourt/
Civil Records: Access: Mail, in person. Both court and visitors may perform in person searches. Search fee: $5.00 per name. Required to search: name, years to search. Civil cases indexed by defendant, plaintiff; index on computer from 1997, index books up to 1996. Mail turnaround time 1 week. Civil PAT goes back to 1997.
Criminal Records: Access: Mail, in person. Both court and visitors may perform in person searches. Search fee: $5.00 per name. Required to search: name, years to search. Criminal records computerized from 1997, index books up to 1996. Mail turnaround time 1 week. Criminal PAT goes back to 1997.
General Information: No juvenile, mental, sealed, or adoption records released. Will not fax documents. Court makes copy: $1.00 per page. Self serve: same. Cert fee: $1.00. Payee: District Clerk. Personal checks accepted; credit cards are not. Mail requests: SASE required.

County Court 102 W Austin St, #206, Jefferson, TX 75657; 903-665-3971; fax: 903-665-8732; 8AM-N, 1-5PM (CST). ***Misdemeanor, Probate.***
Criminal Records: Access: Phone, mail, in person. Both court and visitors may perform in person searches. No search fee. Required to search: name, years to search. Criminal docket on books from 1966; computerized back to '97. Mail turnaround 2-4 days.
General Information: No juvenile, mental, sealed, or adoption records released. Will not fax documents. Court makes copy: $1.00 per page. Self serve: same. Cert fee: $5.00. Payee: County Clerk. Personal checks accepted; credit cards are not. Mail requests: SASE required.

Martin County

District & County Court PO Box 906, Stanton, TX 79782; 432-756-3412; fax: 432-607-2212; 8AM-N, 1-5PM (CST). ***Felony, Misdemeanor, Civil, Probate.***
Civil Records: Access: Mail, in person. Both court and visitors may perform in person searches. Search fee: $5.00 per name. Required to search: name, years to search. Civil cases indexed by defendant, plaintiff. Civil records in index books to 1900. Mail turnaround time 2-4 days.
Criminal Records: Access: Mail, in person. Both court and visitors may perform in person searches. Search fee: $5.00 per name. Required to search: name, years to search. Criminal docket on booksto 1900, computerized since 1980. Mail turnaround time 2-4 days.
General: No juvenile, mental, sealed, or adoption records released. Fee to fax out file $2.00. Court makes copy: $1.00 per page. Cert fee: $5.00. Payee: County/District Clerk. Personal checks accepted; credit cards are not. Mail requests: SASE required.

Mason County

District & County Court PO Box 702, Mason, TX 76856; 325-347-5253; criminal fax: 325-347-6868; civil fax: same; 8AM-N, 1-4PM (CST). ***Felony, Misdemeanor, Civil, Probate.***
Search fee includes a search in both county and district courts. Probate fax same as main fax number.
Civil Records: Access: Mail, in person. Both court and visitors may perform in person searches. Search fee: $10.00 per name. Required to search: name, years to search. Civil cases indexed by defendant, plaintiff. Civil records in index books to 1858; on computer back to 1993. Mail turnaround time 2 days. Civil PAT goes back to 1993.
Criminal Records: Access: Mail, in person. Both court and visitors may perform in person searches. Search fee: $10.00 per name. Required to search: name, years to search; also helpful: DOB, SSN. Criminal records go back to 1877; on computer back to 1993. Mail turnaround time 2 days. Criminal PAT goes back to same as civil.
General Information: No juvenile, mental, sealed, or adoption records released. Will fax documents for no add'l fee. Court makes copy: $1.00 per page. Self serve: same. Cert fee: $5.00 per doc County Ct; $1.00 per cert for District Ct. Payee: County/District Clerk. Personal checks accepted; credit cards are not. Mail requests: SASE required.

Matagorda County

District Court 1700 7th St, Rm 307, Bay City, TX 77414-5092; 979-244-7621; 8AM-N, 1-5PM (CST). ***Felony, Civil.*** www.co.matagorda.tx.us
Civil Records: Access: Mail, in person. Both court and visitors may perform in person searches. Search fee: $5.00 per name. Required to search: name, years to search. Civil cases indexed by defendant, plaintiff. Civil index in docket books from 1910; computerized back to 1994. Mail turnaround time 1-2 days. Civil PAT goes back to 1994.
Criminal Records: Access: Mail, in person. Both court and visitors may perform in person searches. Search fee: $5.00 per name. Required to search: name, years to search, DOB. Criminal docket on books back to 1910; computerized back to 1994. Mail turnaround time 1-2 days. Criminal PAT goes back to same as civil.
General Information: No juvenile, sealed, or adoption records released. Will not fax documents. Court makes copy: $1.00 per page. Cert fee: $2.00. Payee: District Clerk. Personal checks accepted; credit cards are not. Mail requests: SASE required.

County Court 1700 7th St, Rm 202, Bay City, TX 77414-5094; 979-244-7680; criminal phone: 979-244-7682; civil phone: 979-244-7683; probate phone: 979-244-7685; criminal fax: 979-244-7688; civil fax: same; 8AM-5PM (CST). ***Misdemeanor, Civil, Probate.***
Probate is a separate index at this address. Probate fax is same as main fax number.
Civil Records: Access: Mail, in person. Both court and visitors may perform in person searches. Search fee: $10.00 per name. Required to search: name, years to search. Civil cases indexed by defendant, plaintiff; index on computer from 1994, index books prior. Mail turnaround time 1-10 days. Civil PAT goes back to 1987. PAT civil results show middle initial.

Criminal Records: Access: Mail, in person. Both court and visitors may perform in person searches. Search fee: $10.00 per name. Required to search: name, years to search, DOB; also helpful: SSN, DL number. Criminal records computerized from 1994, index books prior. Mail turnaround time 1-10 days. Criminal PAT goes back to same as civil. PAT criminal results show middle initial.
General Information: No juvenile, mental, sealed, or adoption records released. Fee to fax out file $2.00 per page. Court makes copy: $1.00 per page. Self serve: same. Cert fee: $5.00 per document. Payee: County Clerk. Provide ID then personal checks accepted. Visa/MC accepted. Mail requests: SASE required.

Maverick County

District Court 500 Quarry St, #5, Eagle Pass, TX 78853; 830-773-2629; fax: 830-773-4439; 8AM-5PM (CST). ***Felony, Civil.***
Civil Records: Access: Mail, in person, online. Both court and visitors may perform in person searches. Search fee: $5.00 per name. Required to search: name, years to search. Civil cases indexed by defendant, plaintiff. Civil records in index books; recent records computerized. Mail turnaround time 1 week. Civil PAT goes back to 1986. Access cases online back to 11/1994 at www.idocket.com; registration and password required. A fee service; only one free name search per day.
Criminal Records: Access: Mail, in person, online. Both court and visitors may perform in person searches. Search fee: $5.00 per name. Required to search: name, years to search. Criminal index in books; recent records computerized. Mail turnaround time 2-4 days. Criminal PAT goes back to 1986. Access felony cases back to 8/1/1995 at www.idocket.com; registration and password required. A fee service; only one free name search per day.
General Information: No juvenile, mental, sealed, or adoption records released. Fee to fax back $1.00 per page. Court makes copy: $1.00 per page. Self serve: same. Cert fee: $5.00. Payee: District Clerk. No personal checks. No credit cards accepted. Mail requests: SASE required.

County Court 500 Quarry St, #2, Eagle Pass, TX 78853; 830-773-2829 x228; criminal fax: 830-752-4479; civil fax: same; 8AM-5PM (CST). ***Misdemeanor, Civil, Probate.***
www.co.maverick.tx.us/ips/cms
Civil Records: Access: Mail, in person, online. Both court and visitors may perform in person searches. Search fee: $10.00 per name. Required to search: name, years to search. Civil cases indexed by defendant, plaintiff; index on index books. Mail turnaround time 1-2 days. Access cases online back to 1/2006 at www.idocket.com; registration and password required. A fee service; only one free name search per day.
Criminal Records: Access: Mail, in person, online. Both court and visitors may perform in person searches. Search fee: $10.00 per name. Required to search: name, years to search, DOB, SSN. Criminal records indexed in books. Mail turnaround time 1-2 days. Access misdemeanor cases back to 1/1999 at www.idocket.com; registration and password required. A fee service; only one free name search per day.
General Information: No juvenile, mental, sealed, or adoption records released. Fee to fax out file $1.00 per page. Court makes copy: $1.00 per page. Cert fee: $5.00 per cert. Payee: County Clerk. Personal checks accepted. Major credit cards accepted but there is a usage fee charged. Mail requests: SASE required.

McCulloch County

District Court County Courthouse, Rm 205, Brady, TX 76825; 325-597-0733; criminal fax: 325-597-0606; civil fax: same; 8:30AM-5PM (CST). ***Felony, Civil.***
Civil Records: Access: Mail, fax, in person, online. Both court and visitors may perform in person searches. Search fee: $5.00 per name. Required to search: name, years to search. Civil cases indexed by defendant, plaintiff. Civil index in docket books from 1900s. Mail turnaround time 2-4 days. Civil PAT goes back to 1995. PAT results show name only. Access civil cases at www.idocket.com. Records go back to 12/31/1995. One free name search permitted per day, otherwise subscription required.
Criminal Records: Access: Mail, fax, in person, online. Both court and visitors may perform in person searches. Search fee: $5.00 per name. Required to search: name, years to search; also helpful: DOB, SSN. Criminal docket on books back to 1990; on computer back to 1995. Mail turnaround time 2-4 days. Criminal PAT goes back to same as civil. PAT results show middle initial, DOB. Access felony cases online through www.idocket.com; registration and password required. Records go back to 12/31/1995. One free name search permitted per day, otherwise subscription required. Online results show middle initial, DOB.
General Information: No juvenile, mental, sealed, or adoption records released. Will fax documents $2.00 per page. Court makes copy: $1.00 per page. Cert fee: $2.00. Payee: District Clerk. Personal checks accepted; credit cards are not. Mail requests: SASE required.

County Court County Courthouse, Brady, TX 76825; 325-597-0733; fax: 325-597-1731; 8AM-Noon; 1-5PM (CST). ***Misdemeanor, Civil, Probate.***
Civil Records: Access: Mail, in person, online. Both court and visitors may perform in person searches. Search fee: $5.00 per name. Required to search: name, years to search. Civil cases indexed by defendant, plaintiff. Civil records in index books since early 1900's, computerized since 10/95. Mail turnaround time 7-10 days. Online case access is through www.idocket.com; registration and password required. Records go back to 12/31/1996; includes probate. One free name search permitted per day, otherwise subscription required.
Criminal Records: Access: Mail, in person, online. Both court and visitors may perform in person searches. Search fee: $5.00 per name. Required to search: name, years to search. Criminal docket on books from 1900's, computerized since 10/95. Mail turnaround time 7-10 days. Online misdemeanor case access is through www.idocket.com; registration and password required. Records go back to 12/31/1996. One free name search permitted per day, otherwise subscription required.
General Information: No juvenile, mental, sealed, or adoption records released. Court makes copy: $1.00 per page. Cert fee: $1.00 per page plus $5.00 for the certification. Payee: County Clerk. Personal checks accepted. Mail requests: SASE required.

McLennan County

District Court PO Box 2451, 501 Washington Ave, 300 Courthouse Annex, Waco, TX 76703; criminal phone: 254-757-5054; civil: 254-757-5057; fax: 254-757-5060; 8AM-5PM (CST). ***Felony, Civil.***
www.co.mclennan.tx.us/distclerk/index.html
Civil Records: Access: Fax, mail, in person, online. Both court and visitors may perform in person searches. Search fee: $5.00 per name. Required to search: name, years to search. Civil cases indexed by defendant, plaintiff; index on computer since 1959, index books from 1850. Mail turnaround time 3 days. Civil PAT goes back to 1959. PAT results show name only. Online index and image access is through http://idocket.com/homepage2.htm; registration, password and fees required. Records go back to 1/1955; no probate. One free name search permitted per day, otherwise subscription required.
Criminal Records: Access: Mail, fax, in person, online. Both court and visitors may perform in person searches. Search fee: $5.00 per name. Required to search: name, years to search. Criminal records on computer since 1959, index books from 1850. Mail turnaround time 3 days. Criminal PAT goes back to same as civil. PAT results show name only. Online index and image access is through www.idocket.com; registration and password required. Felony records go back to 1/1981. One free name search permitted per day, otherwise subscription required.
General Information: No juvenile, mental, sealed, or adoption records released. Will fax documents to local or toll-free number for $3.00 1st page, $1.00 ea add'l. If long distance then $5.00 1st page $2.00 ea add'l. The court will charge $1.00 per page when receiving a fax. Court makes copy: $1.00 per page. Cert fee: $3.00 per doc. Payee: Karen C Matkin, District Clerk. Personal checks accepted. Visa/MC accepted. Mail requests: SASE required.

County Clerk's Office PO Box 1727, Waco, TX 76703; criminal phone: 254-757-5140/5185; civil phone: 254-757-5189; probate phone: 254-757-5186; fax: 254-757-5146; 8AM-5PM (CST). ***Misdemeanor, Civil, Probate.***
Civil Records: Access: Mail, in person. Both court and visitors may perform in person searches. Search fee: $5.00 per name. Required to search: name, years to search. Civil cases indexed by defendant, plaintiff. Civil index in docket books from 1876 computerized since 2000. Probate to 1850, computerized since 1967. Mail turnaround time 1-3 days. Civil PAT goes back to 2000.
Criminal Records: Access: Mail, in person. Both court and visitors may perform in person searches. Search fee: $5.00 per name. Required to search: name, years to search; also helpful: DOB, SSN. Criminal records on computer since 1993; in index books to 1935. Mail turnaround time 2-4 days. Criminal PAT goes back to 1993.
General Information: No mental or sealed records released. Court makes copy: $1.00 per page. Cert fee: $5.00. Payee: County Clerk. Business checks accepted. No credit cards accepted. Mail requests: SASE required.

McMullen County

District & County Court PO Box 235, Tilden, TX 78072; 361-274-3215; fax: 361-274-3858; 8AM-4PM (CST). ***Felony, Misdemeanor, Civil, Probate.***
Civil Records: Access: Mail, in person. Both court and visitors may perform in person searches. Search fee: $5.00 per name. Required to search: name, years to search. Civil cases indexed by defendant, plaintiff. Civil records in index books from 1918. Mail turnaround time 2-4 days.
Criminal Records: Access: Mail, in person. Both court and visitors may perform in person searches. Search fee: $10.00 per name. Required to search: name, years to search. Criminal docket on books from 1918. Mail turnaround time 2-4 days.
General Information: No juvenile, mental, sealed, or adoption records released. Will fax documents $3.00 1st page, $1.00 each add'l. Court makes copy: $1.00 per page. Cert fee: $5.00. Payee: County Clerk. Personal checks accepted. Mail requests: SASE required.

Medina County

District Court County Courthouse, Rm 209, 1100 16th St, Hondo, TX 78861; criminal phone: 830-741-6070; civil phone: 830-741-6070; 8AM-5PM (CST). ***Felony, Civil, Family.***
Civil Records: Access: Phone, mail, in person. Both court and visitors may perform in person searches. Search fee: $5.00 per name. Required to search: name, years to search. Civil cases indexed by defendant, plaintiff; index on computer since 1990, index books since 1849. Mail turnaround time 2-3 days. Civil PAT goes back to 1990.
Criminal Records: Access: Mail, in person. Both court and visitors may perform in person searches. Search fee: $5.00 per name. Required to search: name, years to search, DOB, SSN. Criminal records on computer since 1990, index books since 1849. Mail turnaround time 2-3 days. Criminal PAT goes back to same as civil.
General Information: No juvenile, mental, sealed, or adoption records released. Will not fax documents. Court makes copy: $1.00 first page; $.50 each add'l. Cert fee: $1.00 per page. Payee: Medina County District Clerk. No personal or out-of-state checks accepted. No credit cards accepted. Mail requests: SASE required.

County Court at Law 1100 16th St, Rm 109, Hondo, TX 78861; 830-741-6040; fax: 830-741-6015; 8AM-N, 1-5PM ***Misdemeanor, Civil, Probate.***
Civil Records: Access: Phone, mail, in person. Both court and visitors may perform in person searches. Search fee: $5.00 per name. Required to search: name, years to search. Civil cases indexed by

defendant, plaintiff; index on computer since late 1993, index books prior to 1881. Mail turnaround time 1-2 days.
Criminal Records: Access: Phone, mail, in person. Both court and visitors may perform in person searches. No search fee. Required to search: name, years to search; also helpful: address, DOB, SSN. Criminal records on computer since late 1985, index books prior to 1953. Mail turnaround time 1-2 days.
General Information: No juvenile, mental, or sealed records released. Will fax documents $3.00 plus $1.00 per page. Court makes copy: $1.00 per page. Self serve: same. Cert fee: $5.00 plus $1.00 per page per document. Payee: County Clerk. Personal checks accepted. Major credit cards accepted only for criminal fees. Mail requests: SASE helpful.

Menard County

District & County Court PO Box 1038, 206 E San Saba Ave, Menard, TX 76859; 325-396-4682; fax: 325-396-2047; 8AM-N, 1-5PM M-TH; 8AM-N, 104PM F (CST). ***Felony, Misdemeanor, Civil, Probate.***
Civil Records: Access: Fax, mail, in person. Both court and visitors may perform in person searches. Search fee: $10.00 per name. Required to search: name, years to search. Civil cases indexed by defendant, plaintiff. Civil index in docket books from 1900s. Mail turnaround time 2-4 days.
Criminal Records: Access: Mail, in person. Both court and visitors may perform in person searches. Search fee: $10.00 per name. Required to search: name, years to search. Criminal docket on books back to 1900s. Mail turnaround time 2-4 days.
General Information: No juvenile, mental, sealed, or adoption records released. Will fax documents $1.00 per page. Court makes copy: $1.00 per page. Cert fee: $5.00 per doc. Payee: District/County Clerk. Personal checks accepted; credit cards are not. Mail requests: SASE required.

Midland County

District Court 200 W Wall, #301, Midland, TX 79701; 432-688-4500; criminal phone: x4; civil phone: x3; fax: 432-688-4934; 8AM-5PM (CST). ***Felony, Civil.***
www.co.midland.tx.us/DC/default.asp
Civil Records: Access: Mail, in person, online. Both court and visitors may perform in person searches. Search fee: $5.00 per name. Required to search: name, years to search. Civil cases indexed by defendant, plaintiff; index on computer back to 1965, index books prior. Mail turnaround time 2 days. Civil PAT goes back to 1965. PAT results show name only. Online access to district clerk database at www.co.midland.tx.us/DC/Database/search.asp. Registration and password required; Fee is $120 per year plus $.10 per image. Contact the clerk for access restrictions.
Criminal Records: Access: Mail, in person, online. Both court and visitors may perform in person searches. Search fee: $5.00 per name. Required to search: name, years to search. Criminal records computerized from 1940, index books prior. Mail turnaround time 2 days. Criminal PAT goes back to 1940. PAT results show middle initial, DOB. Online access to criminal records is same as civil.
General Information: No juvenile, mental, sealed, or adoption records released. Fee to fax out file $1.00 per page, but it must be prepaid. Court makes copy: $1.00 per page. No certification fee. Payee: District Clerk. Business checks accepted; no personal checks. No credit cards accepted. Mail requests: SASE required.

County Court PO Box 211, Midland, TX 79702; 432-688-4402; civil phone: 432-688-4405; probate phone: 432-688-4480; criminal fax: 432-688-4926; civil fax: same; 8AM-5PM (CST). ***Misdemeanor, Civil, Probate.***
www.co.midland.tx.us/CC/default.asp
Probate fax is same as main fax number.
Civil Records: Access: Mail, in person, online. Both court and visitors may perform in person searches. Search fee: $5.00 per name. Required to search: name; also helpful: years to search, address. Civil cases indexed by defendant, plaintiff; index on computer since 1987, index books since 1885. Probate records on computer since 1887. Mail turnaround time 1-2 days. Civil PAT goes back to 1985. PAT results show middle initial, DOB, SSN. Online access to the County Clerk database is free at www.co.midland.tx.us/CC/Database/default.asp.
Criminal Records: Access: Mail, in person, online. Both court and visitors may perform in person searches. Search fee: $5.00 per name. Required to search: name; also helpful: years to search, address, DOB, SSN. Criminal records on computer since 1978, index books since 1885. Mail turnaround time 1-2 days. Criminal PAT goes back to 1978. PAT results show middle initial, DOB, SSN. Online access to criminal records is the same as civil. Online results show middle initial, DOB.
General Information: Online identifiers in results same as on public terminal. No juvenile, mental, sealed, or adoption records released. Will fax documents $2.00. Court makes copy: $1.00 per page. Cert fee: $5.00 per cert. Payee: County Clerk. Cashiers checks and money orders accepted; no personal checks. Credit cards accepted at www.officialpayments.com.

Milam County

District Court 102 S Fannin Ave #5, Cameron, TX 76520; 254-697-7052; 8AM-5PM (CST). ***Felony, Civil.***
Civil Records: Access: Mail, in person. Both court and visitors may perform in person searches. Search fee: $5.00 per name. Required to search: name, years to search. Civil cases indexed by defendant, plaintiff; index on microfilm and index books. Mail turnaround time same day.
Criminal Records: Access: Mail, in person. Both court and visitors may perform in person searches. Search fee: $5.00 per name. Required to search: name, years to search. Criminal records on microfilm and index books. Mail turnaround time same day.
General Information: No juvenile, mental, sealed, or adoption records released. Will not fax documents. Court makes copy: $1.00 per page. Cert fee: $1.00 per doc. Payee: District Clerk. Only cashiers checks, money orders and personal checks accepted. No credit cards accepted. Mail requests: SASE required.

County Court 107 W Main St, Cameron, TX 76520; 254-697-7049; criminal fax: 254-697-7055; civil fax: same; 8AM-5PM (CST). ***Misdemeanor, Civil, Probate.***
Probate fax is same as main fax number.
Civil Records: Access: Mail, in person. Both court and visitors may perform in person searches. Search fee: $5.00 per name. Required to search: name, years to search. Civil cases indexed by defendant, plaintiff. Civil records in books go back to 1874, computerized since 1992. Mail turnaround time 1-2 days. Civil PAT goes back to 1992.
Criminal Records: Access: Mail, in person. Both court and visitors may perform in person searches. Search fee: $5.00 per name. Required to search: name, years to search, signed release, SSN. Criminal records in books go back to 1874, computerized since 1992. Mail turnaround time 1-2 days. Criminal PAT goes back to same as civil.
General Information: No juvenile, mental, sealed, or adoption records released. Fee to fax out file $2.00 plus $1.00 per page. Court makes copy: $1.00 per page. Self serve: same. Cert fee: $5.00 per document. Payee: Milam County Clerk. Personal checks accepted; credit cards are not.

Mills County

District & County Court PO Box 646, Goldthwaite, TX 76844; 325-648-2711; criminal fax: 325-648-3251; civil fax: same; 8AM-N, 1-5PM (CST). ***Felony, Misdemeanor, Civil, Probate.***
Probate fax is same as main fax number.
Civil Records: Access: Fax, mail, in person. Both court and visitors may perform in person searches. Search fee: $5.00 per search for felony or misdemeanor. Required to search: name, years to search; also helpful: cause number. Civil cases indexed by defendant, plaintiff. Civil records in index books since 1887; no computerized records. Mail turnaround time 1-2 days.
Criminal Records: Access: Mail, fax, in person. Both court and visitors may perform in person searches. Search fee: $5.00 per search for felony or misdemeanor. Required to search: name, years to search, DOB, signed release; also helpful: cause number. Criminal docket on books from 1887; no computerized records. Mail turnaround 1-2 days.
General Information: No juvenile, mental, sealed, or adoption records released. Will not fax documents. Court makes copy: $1.00 per page. Self serve: same. Cert fee: $5.00 per cert. Payee: County-District Clerk. Personal checks accepted; credit cards are not. Mail requests: SASE requested.

Mitchell County

District Court County Courthouse, 349 Oak St, Rm 302, Colorado City, TX 79512; 325-728-5918; 9AM-4PM (CST). ***Felony, Civil.***
Civil Records: Access: Mail, in person, online. Both court and visitors may perform in person searches. Search fee: $5.00 per name. Required to search: name, years to search. Civil cases indexed by defendant, plaintiff. Civil index in books. Mail turnaround time 1 day. Access to dockets is free at www.edoctecinc.com but may be a 2 weeks to a month lag time. Site may be down.
Criminal Records: Access: Mail, in person, online. Only the court performs in person searches; visitors may not. Search fee: $5.00 per name. Required to search: name, years to search. Criminal index in books. Mail turnaround 1 day. Online access to criminal dockets is same as civil.
General Information: No juvenile, mental, sealed, or adoption records released. Will not fax documents. Court makes copy: $.35 per page. Cert fee: $1.00 per document. Payee: District Clerk. No personal checks or credit cards accepted. Mail requests: SASE required.

County Court 349 Oak St, Rm 103, Colorado City, TX 79512; 325-728-3481; criminal fax: 325-728-5322; civil fax: same; 8AM-N, 1-5PM (CST). ***Misdemeanor, Civil, Probate.***
Probate fax is same as main fax number.
Civil Records: Access: Fax, mail, in person, online. Both court and visitors may perform in person searches. Search fee: $5.00 per name. Required to search: name, years to search. Civil cases indexed by defendant, plaintiff. Civil index in docket books from 1882; on computer from 4/1984 to present. Mail turnaround time 2-4 days. Civil PAT goes back to 4/1984. Access to dockets is free at www.edoctecinc.com but may be a 2 wk to a month lag time. Site may be down.
Criminal Records: Access: Mail, in person, online. Both court and visitors may perform in person searches. Search fee: $5.00 per name. Required to search: name, years to search; also helpful: DOB. Criminal docket on books back to 1948; on computer from 5/1973 to present. Mail turnaround time 2-4 days. Criminal PAT goes back to 5/1973. Results include DL#. Online access to criminal dockets is same as civil. Online results show middle initial.
General Information: No juvenile, mental, sealed, or adoption, commitment records released. Will fax documents long distance for $3.00 for 1st page, $1.00 per add'l page. Fax to local or toll-free number for $2.00 for 1st page and $1.00 per add'l page. Court makes copy: $1.00 per page. Self serve: same. Cert fee: $5.00 per cert. Payee: Mitchell County Clerk. No out of state personal checks. Money orders accepted. Credit Cards accepted with 4% fee added.

Montague County

District Clerk PO Box 155, Montague, TX 76251; 940-894-2571; 8AM-5PM (CST). ***Felony, Civil.***
Civil Records: Access: Mail, in person. Both court and visitors may perform in person searches. Search fee: $5.00 per name. Required to search: name, years to search. Civil cases indexed by defendant, plaintiff; index on computer and index books. Mail turnaround time 2-4 days.
Criminal Records: Access: Mail, in person. Both court and visitors may perform in person searches. Search fee: $5.00 per name. Required to search: name, years to search. Criminal records on computer and index books. Mail turnaround time 2-4 days.
General Information: No juvenile, mental, sealed, or adoption records released. Will not fax documents. Court makes copy: $1.00 per page. No certification fee. Payee: District Clerk. No personal checks. No credit cards accepted. Mail requests: SASE required.

County Court PO Box 77, Montague, TX 76251; 940-894-2461; fax: 940-894-6601; 8AM-4:45PM (CST). ***Misdemeanor, Civil, Probate.***
Civil Records: Access: Mail, in person. Both court and visitors may perform in person searches. Search fee: $10.00 per 10 years per name. Required to search: name, years to search. Civil cases indexed by defendant, plaintiff; index on computer since 1993, index books prior. Mail turnaround time 1-2 days. Public use terminal available. PAT civil results show middle initial.
Criminal Records: Access: Mail, in person. Both court and visitors may perform in person searches. Search fee: $5.00 per 10 years per name. Required to search: name, years to search, DOB. Criminal records on computer since 1993, index books prior. Mail turnaround time 1-2 days. Public use terminal available, crim records go back to 1993. PAT criminal results show middle initial.
General Information: No juvenile, mental, sealed, or adoption records released. Will fax documents $2.75 1st page, $.75 each add'l page. Court makes copy: $1.00 per page. Self serve: same. Cert fee: $5.00. Payee: County Clerk. Personal checks and major credit cards accepted. Mail requests: SASE required.

Montgomery County

District Court PO Box 2985, 301 N Main, Conroe, TX 77305; 936-539-7855; criminal fax: 936-539-7829; civil fax: 936-538-8138; 8AM-5PM; 8AM-4PM 1st Wed of month (CST). ***Felony, Civil.***
www.co.montgomery.tx.us/dcourts/index.shtml
Probate is a separate index at this same courthouse.
Civil Records: Access: Mail, in person. Both court and visitors may perform in person searches. Search fee: $5.00 per name. Required to search: name, years to search. Civil cases indexed by defendant, plaintiff. Civil records in index books since 1900, on computer since 1990. Mail turnaround time 3-6 days. Civil PAT goes back to 1990. PAT results show middle initial, DOB. Terminal results also show SSNs.
Criminal Records: Access: Mail, in person. Both court and visitors may perform in person searches. Search fee: $5.00 per name. Required to search: name, years to search. Criminal docket on books from 1900, on computer since 1990. Mail turnaround time 3-6 days. Criminal PAT goes back to same as civil. PAT results show middle initial, DOB.
General Information: No juvenile, mental, sealed, or adoption records released. Will not fax documents. Court makes copy: $1.00 per page. No certification fee. Payee: Barbara Adamick, District Clerk. No personal checks. Visa/MC accepted. Mail requests: SASE required.

County Court PO Box 959, Conroe, TX 77305; 936-539-7885; probate phone: 936-539-7892; fax: 936-760-6990; 8AM-5PM (CST). ***Misdemeanor, Civil, Probate.***
www.co.montgomery.tx.us/cclerk/index.shtml
There is also a South County Annex (Mon,Wed,Fri) and an East County Annex (Tues,Thur).
Civil Records: Access: Mail, in person. Visitors must perform in person searches themselves. Search fee: $5.00 per name. Required to search: name, years to search. Civil cases indexed by defendant, plaintiff; index on computer since 1971, and index books. Mail turnaround time 2-5 days. Civil PAT goes back to 1971. PAT results show name only.
Criminal Records: Access: Mail, in person, online. Visitors must perform in person searches themselves. Search fee: $5.00 per name. Required to search: name, years to search, DOB and SSN. Criminal records on computer since 1985, and index books. Mail turnaround time 2-5 days. Criminal PAT goes back to 1985.PAT results show name, DOB. Search county clerk's misdemeanor records free at www.co.montgomery.tx.us/cclerk/kiosk/criminalinquiry.asp. Access misdemeanor cases online at www.idocket.com; registration and password required. A fee service; only one free name search per day. Records go back to 12/31/1989. Online results show name, DOB, SSN. Online search results give physical features.
General Information: No mental or sealed records released. Fee to fax out file $2.00 per page. Court makes copy: $1.00 per page. Cert fee: $5.00 plus $1.00 per page. Payee: County Clerk. Personal checks accepted; credit cards are not. Mail requests: SASE required.

Moore County

District Court 715 Dumas Ave, #109, Dumas, TX 79029; 806-935-4218; fax: 806-935-6325; 8:30AM-5PM (CST). ***Felony, Civil.***
Civil Records: Access: Mail, in person. Both court and visitors may perform in person searches. Search fee: $5.00 per name. Required to search: name, years to search. Civil cases indexed by defendant, plaintiff; index on computer back to 1990; docket books and original files thru 2006. Mail turnaround time 1 day. Civil PAT goes back to 2006. PAT civil results show middle initial.
Criminal Records: Access: Mail, in person. Both court and visitors may perform in person searches. Search fee: $5.00 per name. Required to search: name, years to search, DOB; also helpful: SSN. Criminal records computerized from 1990; docket books and original file thru 2006. Mail turnaround time 1 day. Criminal PAT goes back to same as civil. PAT criminal results show middle initial.
General Information: No juvenile, mental, sealed, or adoption records released. Will fax documents to toll free number. Court makes copy: $1.00 per page. Cert fee: $1.00 per page. Payee: District Clerk. Personal checks accepted. Visa/MC accepted. Mail requests: SASE required.

County Court 715 Dumas Ave, Rm 107, Dumas, TX 79029; 806-935-6164/2009; probate phone: same; fax: 806-935-9004; 8:30AM-5PM (CST). ***Misdemeanor, Civil, Probate.***
Civil Records: Access: Mail, in person. Both court and visitors may perform in person searches. Search fee: $5.00 per name. Required to search: name, years to search. Civil cases indexed by defendant, plaintiff; index on computer back to 1996, in index books prior. Mail turnaround time 24 hours. Civil PAT goes back to 1986. PAT results show middle initial, DOB, SSN.
Criminal Records: Access: Mail, fax, in person. Both court and visitors may perform in person searches. Search fee: $5.00 per name. Required to search: name, years to search, signed release, DOB or SSN. Criminal records computerized from 1987, in index books prior. Mail turnaround time 24 hours. Criminal PAT goes back to 1986. PAT results show middle initial, DOB, SSN.
General Information: No juvenile, mental, sealed, or adoption records released. Fee to fax out file $5.00 plus $1.00 per page. Court makes copy: $1.00 per page. Self serve: same. Cert fee: $5.00. Payee: Moore County Clerk. Business checks accepted. No credit cards accepted. Mail requests: SASE required.

Morris County

District Court 500 Broadnax, Daingerfield, TX 75638; 903-645-2321; fax: 903-645-3433; 8AM-5PM (CST). ***Felony, Civil.***
Civil Records: Access: Mail, in person. Both court and visitors may perform in person searches. Search fee: $5.00 per name. Required to search: name, years to search. Civil cases indexed by defendant, plaintiff. Civil records in index books and file folders from 1930s, computerized since 2000. Mail turnaround time 1 day.
Criminal Records: Access: Mail, in person. Both court and visitors may perform in person searches. Search fee: $5.00 per name. Required to search: name, years to search, DOB. Criminal docket on books and file folders from 1930s, computerized since 2000. Mail turnaround time 1 day.
General Information: No juvenile, mental, sealed, or adoption records released. Will not fax documents. Court makes copy: $1.00 per page. Cert fee: $1.00. Payee: Morris County District Clerk. Personal checks accepted; credit cards are not. Mail requests: SASE required.

County Court 500 Broadnax, Daingerfield, TX 75638; 903-645-3911; probate phone: 903-645-3911; fax: 903-645-4026; 8AM-N, 1-5PM (CST). ***Misdemeanor, Probate.***
Probate fax is same as main fax number.
Criminal Records: Access: Mail, in person. Both court and visitors may perform in person searches. Search fee: $5.00 per name. Required to search: name, DOB, years to search. Criminal record on index books, computerized since 1999. Mail turnaround time 1 day.
General Information: No juvenile, mental, sealed, or adoption records released. Will fax documents $3.00 fee. Court makes copy: $1.00 per page. Cert fee: $5.00. Payee: County Clerk. Personal checks and credit cards accepted. Mail requests: SASE requested.

Motley County

District & County Court PO Box 660, Matador, TX 79244; 806-347-2621; criminal fax: 806-347-2220; civil fax: same; 9AM-N, 1-5PM (CST). ***Felony, Misdemeanor, Civil, Probate.***
Civil Records: Access: Mail, fax, in person. Both court and visitors may perform in person searches. Search fee: $10.00 per name. Required to search: name, years to search, address. Civil cases indexed by defendant, plaintiff. Civil records in docket books, archived from 1891. Mail turnaround time 1-2 days.
Criminal Records: Access: Mail, fax, in person. Only the court performs in person searches; visitors may not. Search fee: $10.00 per name. Required to search: name, years to search, DOB. Criminal records in docket books, archived from 1891. Mail turnaround time 1-2 days.
General Information: No juvenile, mental, sealed or adoption records released. Will fax documents to local or toll free number. Court makes copy: $1.00 per page. Cert fee: $5.00 per instrument. Payee: Motley County Clerk. Personal checks accepted; credit cards are not. Mail requests: SASE required.

Nacogdoches County

District Court 101 W Main, Rm #120, Nacogdoches, TX 75961; 936-560-7730; criminal phone: 936-560-7740; civil phone: 936-560-7729; criminal fax: 936-560-7839; civil fax: same; 8AM-5PM (CST). ***Felony, Civil.***
Civil Records: Access: In person, online. Both court and visitors may perform in person searches. No search fee. Required to search: name, years to search. Civil cases indexed by defendant, plaintiff; index on computer from 1987, index books prior. Civil PAT goes back to 1987. PAT results show name only. Online case access is available by subscription at www.idocket.com including civil and family back to 12/31/1986. One free name search permitted per day, otherwise subscription required.
Criminal Records: Access: Mail, in person, online. Both court and visitors may perform in person searches. Search fee: $5.00 per name. Required to search: name, years to search, signed release. Criminal records computerized from 1987, index books prior. Mail turnaround time 5-6 days. Criminal PAT goes back to same as civil. PAT results show name only. Online case access is available by subscription at www.idocket.com; online records go back to 12/31/1986. One free name search permitted per day, otherwise subscription required. Online results show name only.
General Information: No juvenile, mental, sealed, or adoption records released. Will fax documents to local or toll free line. Court makes copy: $1.00 per page. No certification fee. Payee: District Clerk. Business checks accepted. No credit cards accepted. Mail requests: SASE required.

County Court County Clerk, 101 W Main, Rm 205, Nacogdoches, TX 75961; 936-560-7733; fax: 936-559-5926; 8AM-5PM (CST). ***Misdemeanor, Civil, Probate.***
www.co.nacogdoches.tx.us
The County Clerk is the Clerk for County Court at Law, except for Juvenile, Family Law, including Divorce & Adoption (for these, see District Clerk).
Civil Records: Access: Mail, in person, online. Both court and visitors may perform in person searches. Search fee: $5.00 per name. Required to search: name, years to search. Civil cases indexed by defendant, plaintiff; index on computer since 6/1986, index books prior. Mail turnaround time 2-4 days. Civil PAT goes back to 1986. Online case access is available by subscription at www.idocket.com including civil and probate back to 12/31/1986. One free name search permitted per day, otherwise subscription required.

Criminal Records: Access: Mail, in person, online. Both court and visitors may perform in person searches. Search fee: $5.00 per name. Required to search: name, years to search. Criminal records on computer since 1986, index books prior. Mail turnaround time 2-4 days. Criminal PAT goes back to same as civil. Online case access is available by subscription at www.idocket.com; online records go back to 12/31/1986. One free name search permitted per day, otherwise subscription required.
General Information: Online identifiers in results same as on public terminal. No sealed released. Will fax documents to local or toll free line. Court makes copy: $1.00 per page. Self serve: same. Cert fee: $5.00. Exemplification- add $2.00. Payee: County Clerk. Personal checks accepted; credit cards are not. Mail requests: SASE required.

Navarro County

District Court PO Box 1439, Corsicana, TX 75151; 903-654-3040; fax: 903-654-3088; 8AM-5PM (CST). ***Felony, Civil.***
www.co.navarro.tx.us/ips/cms/districtcourt/
Civil Records: Access: Phone, fax, mail, online, in person. Both court and visitors may perform in person searches. Search fee: $5.00 per name. Required to search: name, years to search. Civil cases indexed by defendant, plaintiff; index on computer since 1990, index books and microfiche since 1900s. Mail turnaround time 1-2 days. Civil PAT goes back to 1990. Online civil case access is through www.idocket.com. Records go back to 12/31/1990. One free name search permitted per day, otherwise subscription required.
Criminal Records: Access: Phone, fax, mail, in person, online. Both court and visitors may perform in person searches. Search fee: $5.00 per name. Required to search: name, years to search. Criminal records on computer since 1990, index books and microfiche since 1900s. Mail turnaround time 1-2 days. Criminal PAT goes back to same as civil. Online criminal case access is through www.idocket.com; registration and password required. Records go back to 12/31/1990. One free name search permitted per day, otherwise subscription required.
General Information: No juvenile, sealed, or adoption records released. Will fax documents $5.00 1st page, $1.00 each add'l. Court makes copy: $1.00 first page, $.25 each add'l. Cert fee: $1.00 per page. Payee: District Clerk. Personal checks and credit cards accepted. Mail requests: SASE required.

County Court PO Box 423, 300 W 3rd Ave Ste 101, Corsicana, TX 75151; 903-654-3035; probate phone: same; fax: 903-872-7329; 8AM-5PM (til 4PM for instruments) (CST). ***Misdemeanor, Civil, Probate.*** www.co.navarro.tx.us/ips/cms
Civil Records: Access: Mail, in person. Both court and visitors may perform in person searches. Search fee: $5.00 per name. Fee is for 10 year period. Required to search: name, years to search. Civil cases indexed by defendant, plaintiff. Civil records in index books to 1960's; on computer back to 1995. Mail turnaround time 2-4 days. Civil PAT goes back to 1995.
Criminal Records: Access: Mail, in person. Both court and visitors may perform in person searches. Search fee: $5.00 per name. Fee is for 10 year period. Required to search: name, years to search, DOB or SSN. Criminal docket on booksto 1930's; on computer back to 1999. Mail turnaround time 2-4 days. Criminal PAT goes back to 1999. PAT results show middle initial, DOB, SSN.
General Information: No mental, sealed records released. Will not fax documents. Court makes copy: $1.00 per page. Self serve: same. Cert fee: $5.00. Payee: County Clerk. Personal checks and credit cards accepted. Mail requests: SASE requested.

Newton County

District Court PO Box 535, Newton, TX 75966; 409-379-3951; fax: 409-379-9087; 8AM-4:30PM (CST). ***Felony, Civil.***
Civil Records: Access: Mail, in person. Both court and visitors may perform in person searches. Search fee: $5.00 per name. Required to search: name, years to search. Civil cases indexed by defendant, plaintiff. Civil index in books. Mail turnaround time same day.
Criminal Records: Access: Mail, in person. Both court and visitors may perform in person searches. Search fee: $5.00 per name. Required to search: name, years to search. Criminal index in books. Mail turnaround time same day.
General Information: No juvenile, mental, sealed, or adoption records released. Will fax documents $2.00 per page. Court makes copy: $1.00 per page. Cert fee: $2.00. Payee: District Clerk. Personal checks accepted; credit cards are not. Mail requests: SASE required.

County Court PO Box 484, Newton, TX 75966; 409-379-5341; fax: 409-379-9049; 8AM-4:30PM (CST). ***Misdemeanor, Civil, Probate.***
Civil Records: Access: Mail, in person. Both court and visitors may perform in person searches. Search fee: $5.00 per name. Required to search: name, years to search. Civil cases indexed by defendant, plaintiff. Civil index on docket books from 1953. Mail turnaround time 1-2 days. Public use terminal available. PAT civil results show middle initial.
Criminal Records: Access: Mail, in person. Both court and visitors may perform in person searches. Search fee: $5.00 per name. Required to search: name, years to search. Criminal records indexed in books from 1953. Mail turnaround time 1-2 days. Public use terminal available. PAT criminal results show middle initial.
General Information: No juvenile, mental, sealed, or adoption records released. Fee to fax document $.50 per page. Court makes copy: $1.00 per page. Cert fee: $5.00. Payee: County Clerk. Personal checks accepted; credit cards are not.

Nolan County

District Court 100 E 3rd, #200A, Sweetwater, TX 79556; 325-235-2111; 8:30AM-N, 1-5PM (CST). ***Felony, Civil.***
Civil Records: Access: Mail, in person. Both court and visitors may perform in person searches. Search fee: $5.00 per name. Required to search: name, years to search. Civil cases indexed by defendant, plaintiff. Civil index in docket books from 1800s; records are computerized a few years back. Mail turnaround time same day. Civil PAT available.
Criminal Records: Access: Mail, in person. Only the court performs in person searches; visitors may not. Search fee: $5.00 per name. Required to search: name, years to search. Criminal docket on books back to 1900, records are computerized 7 years or more. Note: Include which years to search. If requester provides a toll-free number, the court will call with results if asked. Mail turnaround time same day. Criminal PAT available.
General Information: No juvenile, mental, sealed, or adoption records released. Will not fax documents. Court makes copy: $1.00 first page, $.50 each add'l. Self serve: $.25 per page. Cert fee: $1.00 per page. Payee: District Clerk. Personal checks accepted; credit cards are not. Mail requests: SASE required.

County Court 100 E 3rd St, #108, Sweetwater, TX 79556-4546; 325-235-2462; probate phone: same; fax: 325-236-9416; 8:30AM-5PM (CST). ***Misdemeanor, Civil, Probate.***
Direct faxes to "Attn County Clerk;" no fax search requests accepted without payment.
Civil Records: Access: Mail, in person. Both court and visitors may perform in person searches. Search fee: $5.00 per name. Required to search: name, years to search. Civil cases indexed by defendant, plaintiff. Civil records in index books, computerized since 1999. Mail turnaround time same day. Civil PAT goes back to 1999. PAT results show middle initial, DOB. Terminal results also show SSNs.
Criminal Records: Access: Mail, in person. Both court and visitors may perform in person searches. Search fee: $5.00 per name. Required to search: name, years to search. Criminal index in books, computerized since 1999. Mail turnaround time same day. Criminal PAT goes back to same as civil. PAT results show name only.

General Information: No juvenile, mental, sealed, or adoption records released. Will fax out documents $2.00 per doc. Court makes copy: $1.00 per page. Cert fee: $5.00 per doc. Payee: County Clerk. Personal checks accepted; credit cards are not. Mail requests: SASE required.

Nueces County

District & County Court PO Box 2987, Corpus Christi, TX 78403-2987; 361-888-0450; criminal phone: 361-888-0495; fax: 361-888-0571; 8AM-5PM (CST). ***Felony, Misdemeanor, Civil, Probate.***
www.co.nueces.tx.us/districtclerk
Records are combined at this location.
Civil Records: Access: Mail, in person, online. Both court and visitors may perform in person searches. Search fee: $5.00 per name. Required to search: name, years to search. Civil cases indexed by defendant, plaintiff; index on computer since 1980, index books prior. Mail turnaround time 2-4 days. Civil PAT goes back to 1980. PAT civil results show middle initial. Online access to civil District & County Court records are free at www.co.nueces.tx.us/districtclerk/. Click on Civil/Criminal Case Search, register, then search by name, company, or cause number.
Criminal Records: Access: Mail, in person, online. Both court and visitors may perform in person searches. Search fee: $5.00 per name. Required to search: name, years to search. Criminal records on computer since 1980, index books prior. Mail turnaround time 2-4 days. Criminal PAT goes back to same as civil. PAT results show middle initial, DOB. Terminal results include SSN. Online access to criminal District & County Court records are free at www.co.nueces.tx.us/districtclerk/. Click on Civil/Criminal Case Search, register, then search by name, SID number, or cause number. Online results show middle initial, DOB. Terminal results include SSN.
General Information: No juvenile, mental, sealed, or adoption records released. Will fax documents to local or toll-free number, fee is $5.00 1st page then $2.50 ea add'l. Court makes copy: $1.00 per page. Self serve: same. Cert fee: $1.00. Payee: District Clerk. Personal checks accepted; credit cards are not. Mail requests: SASE required.

Ochiltree County

District Court 511 S Main, Perryton, TX 79070; 806-435-8054; criminal fax: 806-435-8058; civil fax: same; 8:30AM-5PM (CST). ***Felony, Civil.***
Civil Records: Access: Fax, mail, in person. Both court and visitors may perform in person searches. Search fee: $5.00 per name. Required to search: name, years to search. Civil cases indexed by defendant, plaintiff. Civil records in index books; on computer back to 1995. Mail turnaround time 7 days.
Criminal Records: Access: Fax, mail, in person. Only the court performs in person searches; visitors may not. Search fee: $5.00 per name. Required to search: name, years to search. Criminal index in books; on computer back to 1995. Mail turnaround time 7 days.
General Information: No juvenile, mental, sealed, or adoption records released. Will fax documents $1.00 per page. Court makes copy: $1.00 per page. Cert fee: $1.00. Payee: District Clerk. Personal checks accepted; credit cards are not. Mail requests: SASE required.

County Court 511 S Main St, Perryton, TX 79070; 806-435-8039; criminal fax: 806-435-2081; civil fax: same; 8:30AM-N, 1-5PM (CST). ***Misdemeanor, Civil, Probate.***
Probate fax is same as main fax number.
Civil Records: Access: Fax, mail, in person. Visitors must perform in person searches themselves. Search fee: $5.00 per name. Required to search: name, years to search. Civil cases indexed by defendant, plaintiff. Civil index in books. Mail turnaround time same day.
Criminal Records: Access: Fax, mail, in person. Visitors must perform in person searches themselves. Search fee: $5.00 per name. Required to search: name, years to search. Criminal index in books. Mail turnaround time usually mailed same day as received.

General Information: No juvenile, mental, sealed, or adoption records released. Will fax documents $2.00 per page. Court makes copy: $1.00 per page. Cert fee: $5.00 per cert. Payee: Ochiltree County Clerk. Personal checks accepted; credit cards are not. Mail requests: SASE requested.

Oldham County

District & County Court PO Box 360, Vega, TX 79092; 806-267-2667; 8:30AM-N, 1-5PM (CST). ***Felony, Misdemeanor, Civil, Probate.***
Civil Records: Access: Mail, in person, online. Both court and visitors may perform in person searches. Search fee: $5.00 per name. Required to search: name, years to search. Civil cases indexed by defendant, plaintiff. Civil index in books. Mail turnaround time 2-4 days. Online case access is through www.idocket.com; registration and password required. Records go back to 3/1998, probate to 2/1996. Civil County cases to 3/1/1998, civil District cases to 03/01/1994. One free name search permitted per day, otherwise subscription required.
Criminal Records: Access: Mail, in person, online. Both court and visitors may perform in person searches. Search fee: $5.00 per name. Required to search: name, years to search. Criminal index in books. Mail turnaround time 2-4 days. Online case access is through www.idocket.com; registration and password required. Misdemeanor records go back to 1/1993, felony to 1/1992. One free name search permitted per day, otherwise subscription required.
General Information: No juvenile, mental, sealed, or adoption records released. Will not fax documents. Court makes copy: $1.00 per page. Cert fee: $5.00 in county court, $1.00 in district. Payee: Oldham County/District Clerk. Personal checks accepted; credit cards are not. Mail requests: SASE required.

Orange County

District Court 801 W Division Ave, Orange, TX 77630; 409-883-7740; fax: 409-882-7083; 8AM-5PM (CST). ***Felony, Civil.***
Civil Records: Access: Mail, in person. Both court and visitors may perform in person searches. Search fee: $5.00 per name. Required to search: name, years to search. Civil cases indexed by defendant, plaintiff; index on computer since 1986, index books prior. Mail turnaround time 2-4 days. Civil PAT goes back to 1986.
Criminal Records: Access: Mail, in person, fax. Both court and visitors may perform in person searches. Search fee: $5.00 per name. Required to search: name, years to search. Criminal records computerized since 1986. Mail turnaround time 2-4 days. Criminal PAT goes back to same as civil.
General Information: No juvenile, mental, sealed, or adoption records released. Court makes copy: $1.00 per page. Self serve: $.50 per page. Cert fee: $1.00. Payee: District Clerk. Only cashiers checks and money orders accepted. No credit cards accepted. Mail requests: SASE required.

County Court 123 S 6th St, Orange, TX 77630; 409-882-7055; fax: 409-882-7012; 8AM-5PM (CST). ***Misdemeanor, Civil, Probate.***
www.co.orange.tx.us
Civil Records: Access: Mail, in person. Both court and visitors may perform in person searches. Search fee: $5.00. Required to search: name, years to search. Civil cases indexed by defendant, plaintiff. Civil records back to 1852; on computer back to 1982. Mail turnaround time 7-10 days. Civil PAT goes back to 1982; results show middle initial.
Criminal Records: Access: Mail, in person. Both court and visitors may perform in person searches. Search fee: $5.00. Required to search: name, years to search. Criminal records back to 1897, on computer back to 1897. Mail turnaround time 7-10 days. Criminal PAT goes back to 1897. PAT results show middle initial, DOB. Search misdemeanor warrants free at www.co.orange.tx.us/Misdomeanor%20Warrants.htm.
General Information: No juvenile, mental, sealed. Fee to fax out file $1.00 per page. Court makes copy: $1.00 per page. Self serve: $.50 per page. Cert fee: $5.00. Payee: Karen Jo Vance, County Clerk. Personal checks accepted; credit cards are not.

Palo Pinto County

District Court PO Box 189, Palo Pinto, TX 76484-0189; 940-659-1279; 8AM-4:30PM (CST). ***Felony, Civil.***
Civil Records: Access: Mail, in person. Both court and visitors may perform in person searches. Search fee: $5.00 per name. Required to search: name, years to search. Civil cases indexed by defendant, plaintiff; index on computer since 1993, index books prior. Mail turnaround time 1-2 days. Civil PAT goes back to 1890.
Criminal Records: Access: Mail, in person. Both court and visitors may perform in person searches. Search fee: $5.00 per name. Required to search: name, years to search. Criminal records on computer since 1993, index books prior. Mail turnaround time 1-2 days. Criminal PAT goes back to same as civil.
General Information: No juvenile, mental, sealed, or adoption records released. Will not fax documents. Court makes copy: $1.00 per page. Cert fee: $1.00. Payee: District Clerk. Personal checks accepted; credit cards are not. Mail requests: SASE required.

County Court PO Box 219, Palo Pinto, TX 76484; 940-659-1277; criminal phone: 940-659-1218; civil phone: 940-659-1220; probate phone: 940-659-1220; criminal fax: 940-659-2289; civil fax: same; 8:30AM-4:30PM (CST). ***Misdemeanor, Civil, Probate.***
Probate in separate index at this same address. Probate fax is same as main fax number.
Civil Records: Access: Mail, in person, phone. Both court and visitors may perform in person searches. Search fee: $5.00 per name. Required to search: name, years to search. Civil cases indexed by defendant, plaintiff; index on computer back to 1998 index books from 1857. Mail turnaround next day.
Criminal Records: Access: Mail, in person. Both court and visitors may perform in person searches. Search fee: $5.00 per name. Required to search: name, years to search, DOB; also helpful: SSN. Criminal records computerized from 1986; index books from 1857. Mail turnaround time next day.
General Information: No juvenile, mental, sealed records released. Will not fax documents. Court makes copy: $1.00 per page. Self serve: same. Cert fee: $5.00 per instrument. Payee: County Clerk. Personal checks accepted; credit cards are not.

Panola County

District Court 110 S Sycamore St, #227, Carthage, TX 75633; 903-693-0306; criminal fax: 903-693-6914; civil fax: same; 8AM-5PM (CST). ***Felony, Civil.***
Civil Records: Access: Mail, in person, online. Both court and visitors may perform in person searches. Search fee: $5.00 per name. Required to search: name, years to search. Civil cases indexed by defendant, plaintiff. Civil records in index books from 1865; computerized back to 1994. Mail turnaround time 3 days. Civil PAT goes back to 1994. PAT civil results show middle initial. Access to civil records is free at www.panolacountyjudicial.com/.
Criminal Records: Access: Mail, in person, online. Both court and visitors may perform in person searches. Search fee: $5.00 per name. Required to search: name, years to search, DOB. Criminal docket on books from 1900's; computerized back to 1994. Mail turnaround time 3 days. Criminal PAT goes back to same as civil. PAT criminal results show middle initial. Access to criminal records is free at www.panolacountyjudicial.com/.
General Information: No sealed, or adoption records released. Fee to fax out file $1.00 per page. Court makes copy: $1.00 per page. Self serve: same. Cert fee: $1.00 per page includes copy fee. Exemplified copy- $5.00. Payee: District Clerk. Personal checks accepted; credit cards are not. Mail requests: SASE required.

County Court County Courthouse, Rm 201, 110 S Sycamore, Carthage, TX 75633; 903-693-0302; fax: 903-693-0328; 8AM-5PM (CST). ***Misdemeanor, Civil, Probate.***
Probate is a separate index at this same address.
Civil Records: Access: Mail, in person. Both court and visitors may perform in person searches. Search fee: $5.00 per name. Required to search: name, years to search. Civil cases indexed by defendant, plaintiff. Civil records in index books; computerized since 1996. Mail turnaround time 2-4 days. Civil PAT available. PAT results show name only. Clerk will verify personal identifiers you provide.
Criminal Records: Access: Mail, in person, fax. Both court and visitors may perform in person searches. Search fee: $5.00 per name. Required to search: name, years to search, DOB. Criminal index in books; computerized since 1996. Mail turnaround time 2-4 days. Criminal PAT available. PAT results show name only. Clerk will verify personal identifiers you provide.
General Information: No juvenile, mental, sealed, or adoption records released. Will fax documents $1.00 per 10 pages. Court makes copy: $1.00 per page. Self serve: same. Cert fee: $5.00 per document. Payee: County Clerk. Personal checks require ID. No credit cards accepted.

Parker County

District Court PO Box 2050, 117 Ft. Worth Ave, Weatherford, TX 76086; 817-598-6194; criminal phone: 817-598-6054; civil phone: 817-598-6114; criminal fax: 817-598-6131; civil fax: same; 8AM-5PM (CST). ***Felony, Civil.*** www.parkercountytx.com
All civil cases filed with District Clerk.
Civil Records: Access: Mail, in person, online. Both court and visitors may perform in person searches. Search fee: $5.00 per name. Required to search: name, years to search, and/or cause number. Civil cases indexed by defendant, plaintiff. Civil index in books. Mail turnaround time same day. Civil PAT available. PAT results show name only. Results also include both party names, case style, atty. Access to court records is free at www.parkercountytx.com. Online civil records go back to 1/2003. Civil results include party names, case type, atty.
Criminal Records: Access: Mail, in person, online. Both court and visitors may perform in person searches. Search fee: $5.00 per name. Required to search: name, years to search, DOB, and/or cause number; also helpful: SSN. Criminal index in books; on computer back to 7/1988. Mail turnaround time same day. Criminal PAT available. PAT results show name only. Results also include atty, offense, disposition. Access to criminal records and sheriff inmates and bonds search is free at www.parkercountytx.com. Online criminal records go back to 7/88. Online results include atty, offense, disposition.
General Information: Online identifiers in results same as on public terminal. No juvenile, mental, sealed, or adoption records released. Will not fax documents. Court makes copy: $1.00 per page. Cert fee: Cert fee included in copy fee. Payee: District Clerk. Personal checks accepted with valid DR number. Mail requests: SASE required.

County Court Parker County Clerk - Court Division, PO Box 819, Weatherford, TX 76086-0819; 817-594-1632; 8AM-N, 1-5PM (CST). ***Misdemeanor.***
www.parkercountytx.com
There are two District Courts (43rd & 415th) and two County Courts-at-Law at this location. The County Court records are co-mingled, but not with District Court records.
Civil Records: Access: Phone, mail, in person, online. Both court and visitors may perform in person searches. Search fee: $5.00 per name. Required to search: name, years to search. Civil cases indexed by defendant, plaintiff. Civil records in index books; on computer since 8/1985. Mail turnaround time 1-2 days. Civil PAT goes back to 2003. Online access to civil is same as criminal, see below.
Criminal Records: Access: Phone, mail, in person, online. Both court and visitors may perform in person searches. Search fee: $5.00 per name. Required to search: name, years to search, DOB; signed release. Criminal records on computer since 8/1985, index books and archived since 1900s. Mail turnaround time 1-2 days. Criminal PAT goes back to 1985. Online access is free at www.parkercountytx.com. Search the sheriff bond and jail lists here also.

General Information: No juvenile, mental, sealed, or adoption records released. Will not fax documents. Court makes copy: $1.00 per page. Cert fee: $5.00 per cert. Payee: County Clerk. Personal checks accepted; credit cards are not. Mail requests: SASE required.

Probate Court 1112 Santa Fe Dr, Weatherford, TX 76086; 817-594-7461; fax: 817-598-6147; 8AM-4PM (CST). ***Probate.***

Parmer County

District Court PO Box 195, Farwell, TX 79325-0195; 806-481-3419; fax: 806-481-9416; 8:30AM-N, 1-5PM (CST). ***Felony, Civil.***

Civil Records: Access: Fax, mail, in person, online. Both court and visitors may perform in person searches. Search fee: $5.00 per name. Required to search: name, years to search. Civil cases indexed by defendant, plaintiff. Civil records in index books since 1917. Mail turnaround time 1 day. Online case access is through www.idocket.com; registration and password required. Records go back to 12/31/1995. One free name search permitted per day, otherwise subscription required.

Criminal Records: Access: Fax, mail, in person, online. Both court and visitors may perform in person searches. Search fee: $5.00 per name. Required to search: name, years to search. Criminal docket on books from 1917. Mail turnaround time 1 day. Online case access is through www.idocket.com; registration and password required. Records go back to 12/31/1995. One free name search permitted per day, otherwise subscription required. Online results show name only.

General Information: No juvenile, mental, sealed, or adoption records released. Will fax documents $1.00 per page. Court makes copy: $1.00 per page. No certification fee. Payee: District Clerk. Personal checks accepted; credit cards are not. Mail requests: SASE required.

County Court PO Box 356, Farwell, TX 79325; 806-481-3691; probate phone: same; fax: 806-481-9154; 8:30AM-N; 1-5PM (CST). ***Misdemeanor, Civil, Probate.***

Probate fax is same as main fax number.

Civil Records: Access: Mail, in person. Both court and visitors may perform in person searches. Search fee: $5.00 per name. Required to search: name, years to search. Civil cases indexed by defendant, plaintiff. Civil records in index books to 1924, computerized since 1996. Mail turnaround time 2-4 days. Civil PAT goes back to 1996.

Criminal Records: Access: Mail, in person. Both court and visitors may perform in person searches. Search fee: $5.00 per name. Required to search: name, years to search. Criminal docket on booksto 1920, computerized since 1996. Mail turnaround time 2-4 days. Criminal PAT goes back to same as civil.

General Information: No juvenile, mental, sealed, or adoption records released. Will fax documents $1.50 per page. Court makes copy: $1.00 per page. Cert fee: $5.00. Payee: County Clerk. Personal checks accepted; credit cards are not. Mail requests: SASE required.

Pecos County

District Court 400 S Nelson, Fort Stockton, TX 79735; 432-336-3503; fax: 432-336-6437; 8AM-5PM (CST). ***Felony, Civil.***

Civil Records: Access: Mail, in person. Both court and visitors may perform in person searches. Search fee: $5.00 per name. Required to search: name, years to search, SSN. Civil cases indexed by defendant, plaintiff; index on computer since 1996, index books prior to the 1920's. Note: A seven year search is performed. Mail turnaround 2-4 days.

Criminal Records: Access: Mail, in person. Both court and visitors may perform in person searches. Search fee: $5.00 per name. Required to search: name, years to search, DOB, signed release; also helpful-address, SSN. Criminal records on computer since 1996, index books prior to 1924. Mail turnaround time 2-4 days.

General Information: No juvenile, mental, sealed, or adoption records released. Fee to fax out file $2.00 per page. Court makes copy: $1.00 per page. Self serve: same. Cert fee: $1.00. Payee: District Clerk. Personal checks accepted; credit cards are not. Mail requests: SASE required.

County Court 103 W Callaghan, Fort Stockton, TX 79735; 432-336-7555; fax: 432-336-7557; 8AM-5PM (CST). ***Misdemeanor, Civil, Probate.***

Civil Records: Access: Mail, in person. Both court and visitors may perform in person searches. Search fee: $5.00 per name. Required to search: name, years to search. Civil cases indexed by defendant, plaintiff. Civil records index books to 1955. Mail turnaround time same day.

Criminal Records: Access: Mail, in person. Both court and visitors may perform in person searches. Search fee: $5.00 per name. Required to search: name, years to search. Criminal records computerized from 1989 and index books to 1955. Mail turnaround time same day.

General Information: No juvenile, mental, or sealed records released. Will fax documents $5.00 plus $1.00 per page. Court makes copy: $1.00 per page. Cert fee: $5.00. Payee: County Clerk. Personal checks accepted; credit cards are not. Mail requests: SASE required.

Polk County

District Court 101 W Church, #205, Livingston, TX 77351; 936-327-6814; fax: 936-327-6851; 8AM-5PM (CST). ***Felony, Civil.***

Search fee for civil with criminal indexes is $15.00 per name.

Civil Records: Access: Fax, mail, in person. Both court and visitors may perform in person searches. Search fee: $10.00 per name per 10 year period. Required to search: name, years to search. Civil cases indexed by defendant, plaintiff. Civil records in index books, computerized since 1996. Mail turnaround time 2-4 days. Civil PAT goes back to mid-1996. PAT civil results show middle initial.

Criminal Records: Access: Fax, mail, in person. Both court and visitors may perform in person searches. Search fee: $5.00 per name per 10 year period. Required to search: name, years to search; also helpful: DOB. Criminal index in books, computerized since 1996. Mail turnaround time 2-4 days. Criminal PAT goes back to mid-1996. PAT results show name only.

General Information: No juvenile, mental, sealed, or adoption records released. Will not fax documents. Court makes copy: $1.00 per page. Cert fee: $2.00 per doc. Payee: District Clerk. No personal checks or credit cards accepted. Mail requests: SASE required.

County Court PO Drawer 2119, Livingston, TX 77351; 936-327-6804; criminal phone: 936-327-6805; civil phone: 936-327-6804; probate phone: 936-327-6804; criminal fax: 936-327-6874; civil fax: same; 8AM-5PM (CST). ***Misdemeanor, Civil, Probate.***

Probate is a separate index at this same address. Probate fax is same as main fax number.

Civil Records: Access: Mail, in person, online. Both court and visitors may perform in person searches. Search fee: $5.00 per name. Required to search: name, years to search. Civil cases indexed by defendant, plaintiff. Civil records in index books, on computer since 1988, available since 1846. Mail turnaround time 2-4 days. Civil PAT goes back to 1846. Civil case information is free at www.idocket.com. Registration and password required. One free name search permitted per day, otherwise subscription required.

Criminal Records: Access: Mail, in person, online. Both court and visitors may perform in person searches. Search fee: $5.00 per name. Required to search: name, years to search; also helpful: DOB, SSN. Criminal index in books; on computer back to 1982. Mail turnaround time 2-4 days. Criminal PAT goes back to 1987. PAT results show middle initial, DOB. Terminal results include SSN. Criminal case information is free at www.idocket.com. Registration and password required. One free name search permitted per day, otherwise subscription required.

General Information: No mental records released. Fee to fax out file $2.00 each plus $1.00 per page. Court makes copy: $1.00 per page. Self serve: same. Cert fee: $5.00 per document. Payee: County Clerk. Personal checks accepted for civil only. Major credit cards accepted. Mail requests: SASE required.

Potter County

District Court PO Box 9570, Amarillo, TX 79105-9570; 806-379-2300; criminal phone: 806-379-2311; civil phone: 806-379-2307; criminal fax: 806-372-5061; civil fax: same; 7:30AM-5:30PM (CST). ***Felony, Civil.***
www.co.potter.tx.us/districtclerk

Civil Records: Access: Fax, mail, online, in person. Both court and visitors may perform in person searches. Search fee: $5.00 per name. Required to search: name, years to search. Civil cases indexed by defendant, plaintiff; index on computer since 9/87, index books prior. Mail turnaround time less than 10 days. Civil PAT goes back to 1988. PAT results show name only. Civil index and images back to 1988 online at www.idocket.com. One free name search permitted per day, otherwise subscription required.

Criminal Records: Access: Fax, mail, online, in person. Both court and visitors may perform in person searches. Search fee: $5.00 per name. Required to search: name, years to search. Criminal records on computer since 9/87, index books prior. Mail turnaround time 2-4 days. Criminal PAT goes back to same as civil. PAT results show name only. Felony cases online at www.idocket.com. Felonies go back to 1/1989. One free name search permitted per day, otherwise subscription required.

General Information: Online identifiers in results same as on public terminal. No juvenile, mental, sealed, or adoption records released. Will fax documents $1.00 per page. Court makes copy: $.50 per page. Self serve: same. Cert fee: $1.00 per page. Payee: District Clerk. Business checks accepted; no personal checks. Visa/MC accepted; Add 5% of transaction total for credit card use fee. Mail requests: SASE required.

County Court & County Courts at Law 1 & 2 PO Box 9638, 500 S Fillmore St, Amarillo, TX 79105; 806-379-2285; criminal phone: 806-379-2283; probate phone: 806-379-2280; fax: 806-379-2296; 8AM-5PM (CST). ***Misdemeanor, Probate (Civil under $5,000 Lmt'd).***
www.co.potter.tx.us/countyclerk/index.html

Limited civil records filed here, most are with the District Clerk. Any civil after 1987 are with the District Clerk. Probate records on a separate index at this address.

Civil Records: Access: Mail, in person, online. Both court and visitors may perform in person searches. No search fee, but must pay the certificate of fact fee. Required to search: exact name, years to search. Civil cases indexed by defendant, plaintiff; index on in books and microfiche to 1987, probate from early 1800s. Mail turnaround time 1-2 days. Civil PAT goes back to - civil records end as of 1987. PAT civil results show middle initial. Online case access is through www.idocket.com; registration and password required. Records go back to 9/1/1987, probate back to 1/1886. One free name search permitted per day, otherwise subscription required.

Criminal Records: Access: Mail, in person, online. Both court and visitors may perform in person searches. No search fee, but must pay the certificate of fact fee. Required to search: exact name, years to search, DOB, offense. Criminal records on computer since 1889. Mail turnaround time 1-2 days. Criminal PAT goes back to ealy 1990s. PAT criminal results show middle initial. Misdemeanor cases online at www.idocket.com. Misdemeanors go back to 1/1991. One free name search permitted per day, otherwise subscription required. Online results show name only.

General Information: No juvenile, mental or sealed records released. Will fax documents for fee. Court makes copy: $1.00 per page. Self serve: same. Cert fee: $5.00 per doc; Exemplification- $7.00; Certification of Fact- $5.00. Payee: Potter County Clerk. Personal checks accepted. Credit cards accepted; add 5% surchage. Mail requests: SASE required.

Presidio County

District & County Court PO Box 789, 320 N Highland, Marfa, TX 79843; 432-729-4812; Dist.-729-3857; fax: 432-729-4313; 8AM-N, 1-4PM (CST). ***Felony, Misdemeanor, Civil, Probate.***
Probate is a separate index as this same address. Probate fax is same as main fax number.

Civil Records: Access: Mail, in person. Both court and visitors may perform in person searches. Search fee: $6.00 per name. Required to search: name, years to search. Civil cases indexed by defendant, plaintiff. Civil index in docket books from 1800s. Note: Requests must be in writing. Mail turnaround time 2-4 days.

Criminal Records: Access: Mail, in person. Both court and visitors may perform in person searches. Search fee: $6.00 per name. Required to search: name, years to search. Criminal docket on books back to 1800s. Note: Search requests must be in writing. Mail turnaround time 2-4 days.

General Information: No juvenile, mental, sealed, or adoption records released. Will fax documents $3.00 each. Court makes copy: $1.00 per page. Self serve: same. Cert fee: $5.00 per document. Payee: District Clerk. Personal checks accepted; credit cards are not. Mail requests: SASE required.

Rains County

District Court PO Box 187, Emory, TX 75440; 903-473-5000 x101; fax: 903-473-0163; 8AM-5PM (CST). ***Felony, Civil.***

Civil Records: Access: Mail, fax, in person. Both court and visitors may perform in person searches. Search fee: $5.00 per name. Required to search: name. Civil cases indexed by defendant, plaintiff; index on computer back to 1990, index books back to 1903. Mail turnaround time same day. Civil PAT available. Terminal to be available Summer '08.

Criminal Records: Access: Mail, fax, in person. Both court and visitors may perform in person searches. Search fee: $5.00 per name. Required to search: name; also helpful: DOB. Criminal records computerized from 1990, index books back to 1880. Mail turnaround time same day. Criminal PAT available. Terminal to be available Summer '08.

General Information: No juvenile, mental, sealed, or adoption records released. Will fax documents to local or toll-free number. Court makes copy: $1.00 per page. Self serve: same. No certification fee. Payee: Rains County District Clerk. Personal checks accepted if proper ID provided; DL, DOB. No credit cards accepted. Mail requests: SASE required.

County Court PO Box 187, Emory, TX 75440; 903-473-5000 x103; probate phone: 903-473-5000 x105; fax: 903-474-9390; 8AM-5PM (CST). ***Misdemeanor, Civil, Probate.***
Probate fax- 903-474-9390.

Civil Records: Access: Mail, In person. Visitors must perform in person searches themselves. Search fee: $5.00 per name. Required to search: name. Civil cases indexed by defendant, plaintiff; index on paper indices in 10 year increments back to 1989, index books prior to 1903. Mail turnaround time 2-3 days.

Criminal Records: Access: Mail, in person. Visitors must perform in person searches themselves. Search fee: $5.00 per name. Required to search: name; also helpful: DOB. Criminal records on paper indices in 10 year increments back to 1989, index books prior to 1880. Mail turnaround time 2-3 days.

General Information: No juvenile, mental, sealed, or adoption records released. Will fax documents to local or toll-free number. Court makes copy: $1.00 per page. Self serve: same. Cert fee: $5.00 per cert. Payee: Rains County Clerk. Personal checks accepted; credit cards are not. Mail requests: SASE required.

Randall County

District Courts 2309 Russell Long Blvd, Canyon, TX 79015; 806-468-5600; fax: 806-468-5604; 8AM-5PM (CST). ***Felony, Civil.***
www.randallcounty.org

Civil Records: Access: Fax, mail, online, in person. Both court and visitors may perform in person searches. Search fee: $5.00 per name. Required to search: name, years to search. Civil cases indexed by defendant, plaintiff; index on computer since 1984. Mail turnaround time 1-2 days. Civil PAT goes back to 1983. PAT results show name only. Civil case information at www.idocket.com. Records from 12/31/84. Subscription required.

Criminal Records: Access: Fax, mail, online, in person. Both court and visitors may perform in person searches. Search fee: $5.00 per name. Required to search: name, years to search. Criminal records on computer since 1985; prior in docket books. Mail turnaround time 1-2 days. Criminal PAT goes back to 1985. PAT results show name only. Felony cases online at idocket at http://idocket.com/counties.htm. This is a fee service. Felony records go back to 1/1992. Subscription required.

General Information: No juvenile, mental, sealed, or adoption records released. Fee to fax out file $5.00 1st pg; $1.00 each add'l. Court makes copy: $1.00 per page. Self serve: $.50 per page. Cert fee: $1.00 per page includes copy fee. Payee: District Clerk. Personal checks accepted. Credit cards accepted; surcharge of.025 added.

County Court PO Box 660, Canyon, TX 79015; 806-468-5505; criminal phone: x4001; civil phone: 806-468-5548; fax: 806-468-5509; 8AM-5PM (CST). ***Misdemeanor, Civil, Probate.***
www.randallcounty.org/cclerk/default.htm
Probate is separate index at this same address.

Civil Records: Access: Mail, fax, in person, email, online. Both court and visitors may perform in person searches. Search fee: $10.00 per name. Required to search: name, years to search, SASE. Civil cases indexed by defendant, plaintiff. Civil records in index books 1900 to present. Mail turnaround time 2-4 days. Civil PAT goes back to 1999. PAT results show name only. Most records have name only, but a few have some personal identifiers. Civil case information at www.idocket.com. Records go back to 1/2000; probate back to 9/11/1969. One free name search permitted per day, otherwise subscription required. Direct email records requests to countyclerk@randallcounty.org.

Criminal Records: Access: Mail, fax, in person, online, email. Both court and visitors may perform in person searches. Search fee: $10.00 per name. Required to search: name, years to search; also helpful: DOB. Criminal records on computer since 1984; prior records in index books. Mail turnaround time 2-4 days. Criminal PAT goes back to 1991. PAT results show name only. Misdemeanor cases online at idocket at http://idocket.com/counties.htm. Is a fee service. Misd. records go back to 1/1985. One free name search permitted per day, otherwise subscription required. Direct email records requests to countyclerk@randallcounty.org.

General Information: No juvenile, mental, sealed, or adoption records released. Fee to fax out file $1.00 per page, $5.00 fee add'l if call is long distance. Court makes copy: $1.00 per page. Self serve: same. Cert fee: $5.00 per document. Payee: Randall County Clerk. Personal checks accepted. Major credit cards accepted but not over the phone. Court charges a 2.5% credit card fee. Mail requests: SASE required.

Reagan County

District & County Court PO Box 100, 3rd St at Plaza, Big Lake, TX 76932; 325-884-2442; fax: 325-884-1503; 8:30AM-5PM M-TH, 8:30AM-4PM F (CST). ***Felony, Misdemeanor, Civil, Probate.***

Civil Records: Access: Mail, in person. Both court and visitors may perform in person searches. Search fee: $5.00 per name. Required to search: name, years to search. Civil cases indexed by defendant, plaintiff. Civil records in index books to 1903. Mail turnaround time same day. Civil PAT available.

Criminal Records: Access: Mail, in person. Both court and visitors may perform in person searches. Search fee: $5.00 per name. Required to search: name, years to search. Criminal docket on booksto 1903. Mail turnaround time same day. Criminal PAT available.

General Information: No juvenile, mental, sealed, or adoption records released. Will fax documents $2.00; no fee to a toll-free number. Court makes copy: $1.00 per page. Cert fee: $5.00 per doc. Payee: County/District Clerk. Personal checks not accepted if out-of-state. No credit cards accepted. Mail requests: SASE required.

Real County

District & County Court PO Box 750, Leakey, TX 78873; 830-232-5202; criminal fax: 830-232-6888; civil fax: same; 8AM-5PM (CST). ***Felony, Misdemeanor, Civil, Probate.***

Civil Records: Access: Mail, in person. Both court and visitors may perform in person searches. Search fee: $5.00 per name. Required to search: name, years to search. Civil cases indexed by defendant, plaintiff. Civil index in books.

Criminal Records: Access: Mail, in person only. Both court and visitors may perform in person searches. Search fee: $5.00 per name. Required to search: name, years to search, DOB. Criminal index in books.

General Information: No juvenile, mental, sealed, or adoption records released. Will fax documents for fee. Fee varies. Court makes copy: $1.00 per page. Cert fee: $5.00 per document. Payee: District/County Court. Personal checks accepted; credit cards are not. Mail requests: SASE required.

Red River County

District Court 400 N Walnut, Clarksville, TX 75426; 903-427-3761; fax: 903-427-1201; 8:30AM-N, 1-5PM (CST). ***Felony, Civil.***

Civil Records: Access: Mail, in person. Both court and visitors may perform in person searches. Search fee: $5.00 per name. Required to search: name, years to search. Civil cases indexed by defendant, plaintiff. Civil records in index books and on microfilm to 1800s. Mail turnaround time same day. Civil PAT goes back to 2002. PAT results show name only.

Criminal Records: Access: Mail, in person. Both court and visitors may perform in person searches. Search fee: $5.00 per name. Required to search: name, years to search. Criminal docket on books and on microfilm to 1800s. Mail turnaround time same day. Criminal PAT goes back to same as civil.PAT results show name, DOB. Terminal results include SSN.

General Information: No juvenile, mental, sealed, or adoption records released. Will fax documents to local or toll free line. Court makes copy: $1.00 per page. Cert fee: $1.00 per page includes copies. Payee: District Clerk. Personal checks accepted; credit cards are not. Mail requests: SASE required.

County Court 200 N Walnut, Clarksville, TX 75426; 903-427-2401; fax: 903-427-3589; 8:30AM-5PM (CST). ***Misdemeanor, Probate.***

Criminal Records: Access: Mail, in person. Both court and visitors may perform in person searches. Search fee: $5.00 per name. Required to search: name, years to search, SSN. Criminal records on computer (name only) since 1980, in index books since 1960s. Mail turnaround time 1-2 days. Public use terminal has crim records back to 1980. PAT results show middle initial, DOB. Results may also show DL number.

General Information: No mental, sealed, or adoption records released. Will fax documents $2.00 per page. Court makes copy: $1.00 per page. Self serve: same. Cert fee: $5.00 per instrument. Payee: County Clerk. Personal checks accepted; credit cards are not.

Reeves County

District Court PO Box 848, Pecos, TX 79772; 432-445-2714; fax: 432-445-7455; 8AM-N, 1-5PM (CST). ***Felony, Civil.***
Probate records handled by County Clerk.

Civil Records: Access: Phone, mail, in person. Both court and visitors may perform in person searches. Search fee: $5.00 per name. Required to search: name, years to search. Civil cases indexed by defendant, plaintiff; index on computer since 1/91, index books prior. Mail turnaround time 2 days.

Criminal Records: Access: Mail, in person. Both court and visitors may perform in person searches. Search fee: $5.00 per name. Required to search: name, years to search. Criminal records computerized from 1/90, index books prior. Mail turnaround time 2-4 days.

General Information: No juvenile, mental, sealed, or adoption records released. Will not fax documents. Court makes copy: $.50 per page. Self serve: same. Cert fee: $1.00 per page. Payee: District Clerk Reeves County. Personal checks accepted; credit cards are not. Mail requests: SASE required.

County Court PO Box 867, Pecos, TX 79772; 432-445-5467; criminal fax: 432-445-3997; civil fax: same; 8AM-5PM (CST). ***Misdemeanor, Civil, Probate.***

Probate is a separate index at this same address. Probate fax is same as main fax number.

Civil Records: Access: Mail, in person. Both court and visitors may perform in person searches. Search fee: $10.00 per name. Required to search: name, years to search; also helpful: address. Civil cases indexed by defendant, plaintiff; index on computer go back 10 years, index books prior. Mail turnaround 1-3 days. Civil PAT goes back to 1993.

Criminal Records: Access: Mail, in person. Both court and visitors may perform in person searches. Search fee: $10.00 per name. Required to search: name, years to search, DOB; also helpful: address. Criminal records on computer go back 10 years; index books prior. Mail turnaround time 5 days. Criminal PAT goes back to 1993.

General Information: No juvenile, mental, sealed, or adoption records released. Will fax documents $.50 per page. Court makes copy: $1.00 per page. Cert fee: $5.00 per cert includes copy fee. Payee: Reeves County Clerk. Personal checks accepted; credit cards are not. Mail requests: SASE required.

Refugio County

District Court PO Box 736, Refugio, TX 78377; 361-526-2721; 8AM-N, 1-5PM ***Felony, Civil.***

Civil Records: Access: Mail, in person, online. Both court and visitors may perform in person searches. Search fee: $5.00 per name. Required to search: name, years to search. Civil cases indexed by defendant, plaintiff; index on computer back to 1992, index books back to 1879. Mail turnaround time 2-4 days. Access cases back to 1/1994 at www.idocket.com; registration and password required. A fee service; only one free name search per day.

Criminal Records: Access: Mail, in person. Both court and visitors may perform in person searches. Search fee: $5.00 per name. Required to search: name, years to search, date of birth; also helpful-SSN, signed release. Criminal records computerized from 1992, index books back to 1879. Mail turnaround time 2-4 days.

General Information: No juvenile, mental, sealed, or adoption records released. Will not fax documents. Court makes copy: $1.00 per page. Cert fee: $1.00 per seal. Payee: District Clerk. Personal checks accepted; credit cards are not. Mail requests: SASE required.

County Court PO Box 704, Refugio, TX 78377; 361-526-2233 x306; fax: 361-526-1325; 8AM-5PM (CST). ***Misdemeanor, Civil, Probate.***

Civil Records: Access: Mail, in person, online. Both court and visitors may perform in person searches. Search fee: $10.00 per name. Required to search: name, years to search. Civil cases indexed by defendant, plaintiff. Civil records in index books, began computerization in 2003. Mail turnaround time 5-10 days. Access cases back to 1/1994 at www.idocket.com; registration and password required. A fee service; only one free name search per day.

Criminal Records: Access: Mail, in person, online. Both court and visitors may perform in person searches. Search fee: $10.00 per name. Required to search: name, years to search. Criminal records on computer since 1992, index books prior. Mail turnaround time 5-10 days. Access misdemeanor cases back to 1/1991 at www.idocket.com; registration and password required. A fee service; only one free name search per day.

General Information: No juvenile, mental, sealed, or adoption records released. Will not fax documents. Court makes copy: $1.00 per page. Cert fee: $5.00 per document. Payee: Ruby Garcia, County Clerk. Personal checks accepted; credit cards are not.

Roberts County

District & County Court PO Box 477, Miami, TX 79059; 806-868-2341; fax: 806-868-3381; 8AM-N, 1-5PM (CST). ***Felony, Misdemeanor, Civil, Probate.***

Civil Records: Access: Mail, in person. Both court and visitors may perform in person searches. Search fee: $5.00 per name. Required to search: name, years to search. Civil cases indexed by defendant, plaintiff. Civil index in books. Note: Written search requests only. Mail turnaround time 2-4 days.

Criminal Records: Access: Mail, in person. Both court and visitors may perform in person searches. Search fee: $5.00 per name. Required to search: name, years to search, DOB, SSN. Criminal index in books. Note: Written search requests only. Mail turnaround time 2-4 days.

General Information: No juvenile, mental, sealed, or adoption records released. Will fax documents $3.00 1st page; $1.00 each add'l. Court makes copy: $1.00 per page. Include postage with copy fee. Cert fee: $5.00 per doc in County Court; $1.00 per page in District Court. Payee: Roberts County. Personal checks accepted; credit cards are not. Mail requests: SASE required.

Robertson County

District Court PO Box 250, Franklin, TX 77856; 979-828-3636; 8AM-5PM (CST). ***Felony, Civil.***
www.co.robertson.tx.us

Civil Records: Access: Mail, in person. Both court and visitors may perform in person searches. Search fee: $5.00 per name. Required to search: name, years to search, SSN. Civil cases indexed by defendant, plaintiff; index on computer since 1987 and index books. Mail turnaround time 1-2 days. Civil PAT available.

Criminal Records: Access: Mail, in person. Both court and visitors may perform in person searches. Search fee: $5.00 per name. Required to search: name, years to search, DOB; also helpful: SSN. Criminal records on computer since 1987 and index books. Mail turnaround time 1-2 days. Criminal PAT available.

General Information: No juvenile, sealed, or adoption records released. Will not fax documents. Court makes copy: $1.00 per page. Self serve: same. Cert fee: $1.00 per page. Payee: Robertson County District Clerk. No personal checks accepted. Cash or money orders only. No credit cards accepted. Mail requests: SASE required.

County Court PO Box 1029, Franklin, TX 77856; 979-828-4130; probate phone: same; fax: 979-828-1260; 8AM-5PM (CST). ***Misdemeanor, Civil, Probate.***

Civil Records: Access: Mail, fax, in person. Both court and visitors may perform in person searches. Search fee: $5.00 per name. Required to search: name, years to search. Civil cases indexed by defendant, plaintiff; index on computer back from 1990 to present, index books from 1985 to present. Mail turnaround time same day.

Criminal Records: Access: Mail, fax, in person. Both court and visitors may perform in person searches. Search fee: $5.00 per name. Required to search: name, years to search, DOB. Criminal records computerized from 1986 to present, index books from 1918. Mail turnaround time same day.

General Information: No juvenile, mental, sealed, or adoption records released. Will not fax documents. Court makes copy: $1.00 per page. Self serve: same. Cert fee: $5.00. Payee: Robertson County Clerk. Personal checks accepted; credit cards are not.

Rockwall County

District Court 1101 Ridge Rd, #209, Rockwall, TX 75087; 972-204-6610; fax: 972-204-6619; 8AM-5PM (CST). ***Felony, Civil.***
www.rockwallcountytexas.com

Civil Records: Access: Mail, in person, online. Both court and visitors may perform in person searches. Search fee: $5.00 per name. Fee is per 5 year period. Required to search: name, years to search. Civil cases indexed by defendant, plaintiff; index on computer back to 1994, index books prior. Mail turnaround time 2-4 days. Civil PAT goes back to 1994. PAT civil results show middle initial. Online access is same as criminal, see below.

Criminal Records: Access: Mail, in person, online. Both court and visitors may perform in person searches. Search fee: $5.00 per name. Required to search: name, years to search, DOB. Criminal records computerized from 1980, index books prior. Mail turnaround time 2-4 days. Criminal PAT goes back to 1981. PAT results show middle initial, DOB. Online access is free at http://65.70.178.219/judicialsearch/. Search sheriff bond and jail lists too.

General Information: No juvenile, mental, sealed, or adoption records released. Will not fax documents. Court makes copy: $1.00 per page. Cert fee: $1.00 per page. Payee: District Clerk. Personal checks accepted; credit cards are not. Mail requests: SASE required.

County Court at Law 1101 Ridge Rd, #101, Attn- County Clerk, Rockwall, TX 75087; 972-204-6410; probate phone: same; fax: 972-204-6419; 8AM-5PM (CST). ***Misdemeanor, Civil, Probate.***
www.rockwallcountytexas.com/index.asp?nid=77

Civil Records: Access: Phone, mail, in person, online. Both court and visitors may perform in person searches. Search fee: $5.00 per name. Required to search: name, years to search. Civil cases indexed by defendant, plaintiff; index on computer back to 1985 and in index books from 1800s. Mail turnaround time 2-4 days. Civil PAT goes back to 2000. PAT results show name, DOB. Online access is same as criminal, see below.

Criminal Records: Access: Phone, mail, in person, online. Both court and visitors may perform in person searches. Search fee: $5.00 per name. Required to search: name, years to search. Criminal records computerized from 1987 and in index books from 1800s. Mail turnaround time 2-4 days. Criminal PAT goes back to same as civil.PAT results show name, DOB. Online access is free at http://65.70.178.219/judicialsearch/. Search sheriff bond and jail lists too. Online results show name, DOB.

General Information: Online identifiers in results same as on public terminal. No juvenile, mental, sealed, or adoption records released. Fee to fax out file $5.00 each. Court makes copy: $1.00 per page. Self serve: same. Cert fee: $5.00. Payee: County Clerk. Personal checks and major credit cards accepted. Mail requests: SASE required.

Runnels County

District Court PO Box 166, Ballinger, TX 76821; 325-365-2638; criminal fax: 325-365-9229; civil fax: same; 8:30AM-5PM (CST). ***Felony, Civil.***

Civil Records: Access: Phone, fax, mail, in person. Both court and visitors may perform in person searches. Search fee: $5.00 per name. Required to search: name; also helpful: years to search. Civil cases indexed by defendant, plaintiff. Civil records in index books since 1882. Mail turnaround time 1-2 days. Public use terminal available. PAT results show name only.

Criminal Records: Access: Phone, fax, mail, in person. Both court and visitors may perform in person searches. Search fee: $5.00 per name. Required to search: name; also helpful: years to search, DOB, SSN. Criminal docket on books from 1882. Mail turnaround time 1-2 days. Public use terminal available. PAT results show middle initial, DOB.

General Information: No juvenile, mental, sealed or adoption records released. Will fax documents $1.00 per page. Court makes copy: $1.00 per page. Self serve: same. Cert fee: $1.00 per cert. Payee: District Clerk. Personal checks accepted; credit cards are not.

County Court PO Box 189, Ballinger, TX 76821; 325-365-2720; criminal fax: 325-365-3408; civil fax: same; 8:30AM-N, 1-5PM (CST). ***Misdemeanor, Civil, Probate.***

Probate fax is same as main fax number.

Civil Records: Access: Phone, mail, in person. Both court and visitors may perform in person searches. Search fee: $5.00. Required to search: name, years to search. Civil cases indexed by defendant, plaintiff. Civil records in docket books with alphabetical index and file jacket by number; computerized since 1992. Mail turnaround 1-2 days. Civil PAT available.

Criminal Records: Access: Phone, mail, in person. Both court and visitors may perform in person searches. Search fee: $5.00. Required to search: name, years to search; also helpful: DOB. Criminal records in docket books with alphabetical index and file jacket by number; computerized since 1992. Mail turnaround time 1-2 days. Criminal PAT available.
General Information: No juvenile or mental records released. Will fax documents to toll-free number. Court makes copy: $1.00 per page. Self serve: $.50 per page. Cert fee: $5.00. Payee: County Clerk, Runnels County. Personal checks accepted; credit cards are not.

Rusk County

District Court PO Box 1687, 115 N Main St #301, Henderson, TX 75653; 903-657-0353; fax: 903-657-1914; 8AM-5PM (CST). ***Felony, Civil.***
Civil Records: Access: Mail, in person. Both court and visitors may perform in person searches. Search fee: $5.00 per name. Required to search: name, years to search. Civil cases indexed by defendant, plaintiff. Civil records in index books; on computer back to 1973. Mail turnaround time 2-4 days. Civil PAT goes back to 1985. PAT results show name only.
Criminal Records: Access: Mail, in person. Both court and visitors may perform in person searches. Search fee: $5.00 per name. Required to search: name, years to search, DOB, SSN, signed release. Criminal index in books; on computer back to 1973. Mail turnaround time 2-4 days. Criminal PAT goes back to same as civil. PAT results show name only.
General Information: No juvenile, mental, sealed, or adoption records released. Will not fax documents. Court makes copy: $1.00 per page. Cert fee: $1.00 per page includes copy fee. Payee: District Clerk. No personal checks or credit cards accepted. Mail requests: SASE required.

County Court at Law PO Box 758, 115 N Main St #206, Henderson, TX 75653-; 903-657-0330; fax: 903-657-0062; 8AM-5PM (CST). ***Misdemeanor, Civil, Probate.***
Misdemeanor & probate records are at County Clerk.
Civil Records: Access: Mail, in person. Both court and visitors may perform in person searches. Search fee: $5.00 per name. Required to search: name, years to search. Civil cases indexed by defendant, plaintiff. Civil index in books. Mail turnaround time 2-4 days. Civil PAT goes back to 1997. PAT results show name only.
Criminal Records: Access: Mail, in person. Both court and visitors may perform in person searches. Search fee: $5.00 per name. Required to search: name, years to search, DOB, SSN. Criminal records computerized. Mail turnaround time 2-4 days. Criminal PAT goes back to 1997.
General Information: No juvenile, mental, sealed, or adoption records released. Will not fax documents. Court makes copy: $1.00 per page. Cert fee: $5.00 per doc. Payee: County Clerk. Business checks accepted. No credit cards accepted. Mail requests: SASE required.

Sabine County

District Court PO Box 850, Hemphill, TX 75948; 409-787-2912; fax: 409-787-2623; 8AM-4:00PM (CST). ***Felony, Civil.***
Civil Records: Access: Mail, in person. Both court and visitors may perform in person searches. Search fee: $10.00 per name. Required to search: name, years to search. Civil cases indexed by defendant, plaintiff; index on computer since 1992. Overall records go back to 1900. Mail turnaround time 1-2 days.
Criminal Records: Access: Mail, in person. Both court and visitors may perform in person searches. Search fee: $10.00 per name. Required to search: name, years to search. Criminal records on computer since 1992. Overall records go back to 1900. Mail turnaround time 1-2 days.
General Information: No juvenile, mental, sealed, or adoption records released. Will not fax documents. Court makes copy: $1.00 per page. Self serve: same. No certification fee. Payee: District Clerk. Personal checks accepted; credit cards are not. Mail requests: SASE required.

County Court PO Drawer 580, Hemphill, TX 75948-0580; 409-787-2889; fax: 409-787-3795; 8AM-4PM (CST). ***Misdemeanor, Probate.***
Criminal Records: Access: Mail, in person. Both court and visitors may perform in person searches. Search fee: $10.00 per name. Required to search: name, years to search. Criminal records on computer since 1992, index books prior. Note: Court will search 10 years, no further. Mail turnaround time 2 days.
General Information: No juvenile, mental, sealed, or adoption records released. Will not fax documents. Court makes copy: $1.00 per page. Self serve: same. Cert fee: $5.00. Payee: Sabine County Clerk. Business checks accepted. No credit cards accepted. Mail requests: SASE required.

San Augustine County

District Court County Courthouse, Rm 202, San Augustine, TX 75972; 936-275-2231; fax: 936-275-2389; 8AM-4PM (CST). ***Felony, Civil.***
Civil Records: Access: Phone, mail, in person. Both court and visitors may perform in person searches. Search fee: $5.00 per name. Required to search: name, years to search. Civil cases indexed by plaintiff. Civil index in books. Mail turnaround time 2-4 days.
Criminal Records: Access: Phone, mail, in person. Only the court performs in person searches; visitors may not. Search fee: $5.00 per name. Required to search: name, years to search. Criminal index in books. Mail turnaround time 2-4 days.
General Information: No juvenile, mental, sealed, or adoption records released. Will fax documents to local or toll free line. Court makes copy: $1.00 per page. Self serve: same. Cert fee: $1.00. Payee: District Clerk. Personal checks accepted; credit cards are not. Mail requests: SASE required.

County Court 100 W Columbia, Rm 106, San Augustine, TX 75972; 936-275-2452; fax: 936-275-9579; 8AM-4PM (CST). ***Misdemeanor, Probate.***
Criminal Records: Access: Phone, mail, in person. Both court and visitors may perform in person searches. Search fee: $10.00 per name. Required to search: name, years to search; also helpful: address, DOB, SSN. Criminal records go back to 1984; on computer since 1990. Mail turnaround time 2-3 days.
General Information: No juvenile, mental, sealed, or adoption records released. Will fax documents $4.00 plus $1.00 per page. Court makes copy: $1.00 per page. Self serve: same.Copies must be paid for in advance. Cert fee: $5.00. Payee: County Clerk. Personal checks accepted; credit cards are not. Mail requests: SASE required.

San Jacinto County

District Court 1 State Hwy 150, Rm 4, Coldspring, TX 77331; 936-653-2909; fax: 936-653-4659; 8AM-N, 1-5PM (CST). ***Felony, Civil.***
Civil Records: Access: Mail, in person. Both court and visitors may perform in person searches. Search fee: $5.00 per name. Required to search: name, years to search. Civil cases indexed by plaintiff. Civil records in index books. Mail turnaround time 2-4 days. Civil PAT goes back to 1999. PAT results show middle initial, DOB. Not all records show personal identifiers; SSNs sometimes appear.
Criminal Records: Access: Mail, in person. Both court and visitors may perform in person searches. Search fee: $5.00 per name. Required to search: name, years to search. Criminal records on computer since 1999. Mail turnaround time 2-4 days. Criminal PAT goes back to same as civil. PAT results show middle initial, DOB. Not all records show personal identifiers, some show SSNs.
General Information: No juvenile, mental, sealed, or adoption records released. Will fax documents $1.00 per page. Court makes copy: $1.00 per page. Cert fee: $5.00. Payee: District Clerk. Personal checks accepted; credit cards are not. Mail requests: SASE required.

County Court 1 State Hwy 150, Rm 2, Coldspring, TX 77331; 936-653-2324; fax: 936-653-8312; 8AM-4:30PM (CST). ***Misdemeanor, Civil, Probate.*** www.co.san-jacinto.tx.us/ips/cms/countyoffices/countyClerk.html
Civil Records: Access: Mail, in person. Both court and visitors may perform in person searches. Search fee: $11.00 per name. Required to search: name, years to search. Civil cases indexed by defendant, plaintiff. Civil records in index books and on computer. Mail turnaround time 1 week. Civil PAT goes back to 1995. PAT results show name only.
Criminal Records: Access: Mail, in person. Both court and visitors may perform in person searches. Search fee: $11.00 per name. Required to search: name, years to search; also helpful: address, DOB, SSN. Criminal index in books. Mail turnaround time 1 week. Criminal PAT goes back to 1997. PAT results show name only.
General Information: No juvenile, mental, sealed, or adoption records released. Will fax documents $3.00 fee. Court makes copy: $1.00 per page. Cert fee: $5.00. Payee: County Clerk. Personal checks accepted. Only cashiers checks and money orders accepted for criminal searches. No credit cards accepted. Mail requests: SASE required.

San Patricio County

District Court PO Box 1084, Sinton, TX 78387; 361-364-6225; fax: 361-364-6137; 8AM-5PM (CST). ***Felony, Civil.*** www.co.san-patricio.tx.us/ips/cms/districtcourt/districtClerk.html
Civil Records: Access: Mail, fax, in person, online. Both court and visitors may perform in person searches. Search fee: $5.00 per name. Required to search: name, years to search. Civil cases indexed by defendant, plaintiff. Civil records in index books from 1800s; computerized from 1993 forward. Mail turnaround time 2-4 days. Civil PAT goes back to 1993. Access civil cases online back to 11/1992 at www.idocket.com; registration and password required. One free name search permitted per day, otherwise subscription required.
Criminal Records: Access: Mail, fax, in person, online. Both court and visitors may perform in person searches. Search fee: $5.00 per name. Required to search: name, years to search. Criminal docket on books from 1800s; computerized from 1993 forward. Mail turnaround time 2-4 days. Criminal PAT goes back to same as civil. Online access to felony cases back to 1/1994 at www.idocket.com; registration and password required. One free name search permitted per day, otherwise subscription required.
General Information: No juvenile, mental, sealed, or adoption records released. Will not fax documents. Court makes copy: $1.00 per page. Self serve: same. Cert fee: $1.00. Payee: District Clerk. Business checks accepted. Credit cards accepted. Mail requests: SASE required.

County Court PO Box 578, Sinton, TX 78387; 361-364-9350; fax: 361-364-9450; 8AM-5PM (CST). ***Misdemeanor, Civil, Probate.*** www.co.san-patricio.tx.us
Civil Records: Access: Mail, in person, online. Both court and visitors may perform in person searches. Search fee: $5.00 per name. Required to search: name, years to search; also helpful: address. Civil cases indexed by defendant, plaintiff. Civil records in index books and microfilm, some as far back as 1824; computerized back to 1997. Mail turnaround time 2-3 days. Public use terminal has civil records back to 1998. PAT results show middle initial, DOB. Access civil cases including probate online back to 1/1997 at www.idocket.com; registration and password required. One free name search permitted per day, otherwise subscription required.
Criminal Records: Access: Mail, in person, online. Both court and visitors may perform in person searches. Search fee: $5.00 per name. Required to search: name, years to search; also helpful: address, DOB, SSN, anything. Criminal docket on books and microfilm; computerized back to 1997. Mail turnaround time 2-3 days. Online access to Misd. cases back to 1/1994 at www.idocket.com; registration and password required. One free name search permitted per day, otherwise subscription required.
General Information: No juvenile, mental, or sealed records released. Will not fax documents. Court makes copy: $1.00 per page. Cert fee: $5.00. Payee: County Clerk. Personal checks accepted for civil only. Major credit cards accepted. Mail requests: SASE required.

San Saba County

District & County Court County Courthouse, 500 E Wallace, #202, San Saba, TX 76877; 325-372-3375; 8AM-N, 1-4:30PM (CST). ***Felony, Misdemeanor, Civil, Probate.*** http://dcourt.org

Civil Records: Access: Phone, mail, in person. Both court and visitors may perform in person searches. Search fee: $10.00 per name. Required to search: name, years to search. Civil cases indexed by defendant, plaintiff. Civil index in books. Mail turnaround time 2-3 days.

Criminal Records: Access: Mail, in person. Both court and visitors may perform in person searches. Search fee: $5.00 per name. Required to search: name, years to search; also helpful: DOB. Criminal index in books. Mail turnaround time 2-3 days.

General Information: No juvenile, mental, sealed, or adoption records released. Will not fax documents. Court makes copy: $1.00 per page. Cert fee: $5.00. Payee: District/County Clerk. Personal checks accepted; credit cards are not. Mail requests: SASE required.

Schleicher County

District & County Court PO Drawer 580, Courthouse Sq, Eldorado, TX 76936; 325-853-2833; fax: 325-853-2768; 9AM-N, 1-5PM (CST). ***Felony, Misdemeanor, Civil, Probate.***

Civil Records: Access: Mail, in person. Both court and visitors may perform in person searches. Search fee: $10.00 per name. Required to search: name, years to search. Civil cases indexed by defendant, plaintiff. Civil index in books. Mail turnaround time 1 day in order received.

Criminal Records: Access: Mail, in person. Both court and visitors may perform in person searches. Search fee: $10.00 per name. Required to search: name, years to search. Criminal index in books. Mail turnaround time 1 day in order received.

General Information: No juvenile, mental, sealed, or adoption records released. Will fax documents $2.00 per page, must be paid before search. Court makes copy: $1.00 per page. Self serve: same. Cert fee: $5.00 per doc. Payee: District/County Clerk. Personal checks accepted; credit cards are not. Mail requests: SASE required.

Scurry County

District Court 1806 25th St, #402, County District Clerk Office, Snyder, TX 79549; 325-573-5641; fax: 325-573-1081; 8:15AM-N, 1-5PM (CST). ***Felony, Civil.***

Civil Records: Access: Mail, in person. Both court and visitors may perform in person searches. Search fee: $5.00 per name. Required to search: name, years to search. Civil cases indexed by defendant, plaintiff. Civil records go back to 1890; computerized records since 1994. Note: All requests must be in writing. Mail turnaround time 2-3 days.

Criminal Records: Access: Mail, in person. Both court and visitors may perform in person searches. Search fee: $5.00 per name. Required to search: name, years to search, address, DOB, SSN, sex. Criminal records go back to 1890; computerized records since 1994. Note: All requests must be in writing. Mail turnaround time 2-3 days.

General Information: No juvenile, mental, sealed, or adoption records released. Fee to fax out file $1.00 per page. Court makes copy: $1.00 first page, $.25 each add'l per doc. Cert fee: $1.00 per page. Cert fee includes copies. Payee: District Clerk. Personal checks accepted; credit cards are not. Mail requests: SASE required.

County Court County Courthouse, 1806 25th St, #300, Snyder, TX 79549; 325-573-5332; fax: 325-573-7396; 8:30AM-5PM (CST). ***Misdemeanor, Civil, Probate.***

Civil Records: Access: Mail, in person. Both court and visitors may perform in person searches. Search fee: $10.00 per name. Required to search: name, years to search. Civil cases indexed by defendant, plaintiff. Civil records in index books since 1900s; on computer back to 1996. Mail turnaround time 1-2 days. Civil PAT goes back to 1996. PAT results show middle initial, DOB.

Criminal Records: Access: Mail, in person. Both court and visitors may perform in person searches. Search fee: $5.00 per name. Fee includes copies. Required to search: name, years to search; also helpful: address, DOB, SSN. Criminal docket on books from 1900s; on computer back to 1996. Note: Written request always required. Mail turnaround time 1-2 days. Criminal PAT goes back to same as civil. PAT results show middle initial, DOB.

General Information: No mental or sealed records released. Fee to fax out file $1.00 per page. Court makes copy: $1.00 per page. Cert fee: $5.00. Payee: County Clerk Scurry County. Personal checks and major credit cards accepted.

Shackelford County

District & County Court PO Box 247, Albany, TX 76430; 325-762-2232 x100; criminal fax: 325-762-2830; civil fax: same; 8:30AM-N, 1-5PM (CST). ***Felony, Misdemeanor, Civil, Probate.***

Civil Records: Access: Mail, in person. Both court and visitors may perform in person searches. Search fee: $5.00 per name. Fee is per court. Required to search: name, years to search. Civil cases indexed by defendant, plaintiff; index on computer since 1987, index books since 1867. Mail turnaround time 7 days after receipt. Civil PAT goes back to 1987. PAT civil results show middle initial.

Criminal Records: Access: Mail, in person. Both court and visitors may perform in person searches. Search fee: $5.00 per name. Fee is per court. Required to search: name, years to search. Criminal records on computer since 1987, index books since 1867. Mail turnaround time 7 days after received. Criminal PAT goes back to same as civil. PAT criminal results show middle initial.

General Information: No juvenile, mental, sealed, or adoption records released. Will not fax documents. Court makes copy: $1.00 per page. Cert fee: $5.00 per document District Ct; $1.00 if County Ct. Payee: Clerk, Shackelford County. Personal checks accepted; credit cards are not. Mail requests: SASE required.

Shelby County

District Court PO Drawer 1953, Clerk's Office, 200 S Augustine St, Ste. B, Center, TX 75935; 936-598-4164; 8AM-4:30PM (CST). ***Felony, Civil.***

Civil Records: Access: Mail, in person, online. Both court and visitors may perform in person searches. Search fee: $5.00 per name. Required to search: name, years to search. Civil cases indexed by defendant, plaintiff. Civil records in index books; on computer back to 2000. Mail turnaround time 2-3 days. Access court records free at http://cc.co.shelby.tx.us/.

Criminal Records: Access: Mail, in person, online. Both court and visitors may perform in person searches. Search fee: $5.00 per name. Required to search: name, years to search, signed release. Criminal index in books; on computer back to 2000. Mail turnaround time 2-3 days. Access court records free at http://cc.co.shelby.tx.us/.

General Information: No juvenile, mental, sealed, or adoption records released. Will not fax documents. Court makes copy: $1.00 per page. Cert fee: $1.00 per doc. Payee: District Clerk. Personal checks accepted; credit cards are not. Mail requests: SASE required.

County Court PO Box 1987, Center, TX 75935; 936-598-6361; criminal fax: 936-598-3701; civil fax: same; 8AM-4:30PM (CST). ***Misdemeanor, Civil, Probate.***

Probate records in a separate index at this same address. Probate fax is same as main fax number.

Civil Records: Access: Mail, in person, online. Both court and visitors may perform in person searches. Search fee: $10.00 per name. Required to search: name, years to search. Civil cases indexed by defendant, plaintiff. Civil & probate records in index books back to 1882; on computer back to 1990. Mail turnaround time 1-2 days. Civil PAT goes back to 1993. Access court records free at http://cc.co.shelby.tx.us/.

Criminal Records: Access: Mail, in person, online. Both court and visitors may perform in person searches. Search fee: $10.00 per name. Required to search: name, years to search, SSN, DOB; also helpful: signed release. Criminal docket on books back to 1920; on computer back to 1990. Note: All requests must be in writing. Mail turnaround time 1-2 days. Criminal PAT goes back to 1993. Access court records free at http://cc.co.shelby.tx.us/.

General Information: No juvenile, mental, sealed, or adoption records released. Will fax documents for fee. Court makes copy: $1.00 per page. Cert fee: $5.00 per certification. Payee: Shelby County Clerk. Personal checks and major credit cards accepted. Mail requests: SASE required.

Sherman County

District & County Court PO Box 270, 701 N 3rd St, Stratford, TX 79084; 806-366-2371; criminal fax: 806-366-5670; civil fax: same; 8AM-N, 1-5PM (CST). ***Felony, Misdemeanor, Civil, Probate.***

Probate fax is same as main fax number.

Civil Records: Access: Mail, fax, in person. Both court and visitors may perform in person searches. Search fee: $5.00 per name, per 5 years, per record, per court. Required to search: name, years to search. Civil cases indexed by plaintiff. Civil records to 1930. Note: Fax search requests must be prepaid. Mail turnaround time 3-5 days.

Criminal Records: Access: Mail, fax, in person. Only the court performs in person searches; visitors may not. Search fee: $5.00 per name, per 5 years, per record, per court. Required to search: name, years to search. Criminal records to 1947. Note: Fax search requests must be prepaid. Mail turnaround time 2-3 days.

General Information: No juvenile, mental, sealed, or adoption records released. Will fax documents $5.00 1st page, $1.00 each add'l. Court makes copy: $1.00 per page. Cert fee: $5.00 per document,. Payee: Sherman County Clerk. Personal checks accepted; credit cards are not. Mail requests: SASE required.

Smith County

District Court PO Box 1077, Attn: District Clerk, Tyler, TX 75710; 903-590-590-1660/1672; fax: 903-590-1661; 8AM-5PM (CST). ***Felony, Civil.*** www.smith-county.com/

Civil Records: Access: Mail, in person, online. Both court and visitors may perform in person searches. Search fee: $5.00 per name. Required to search: name, years to search. Civil cases indexed by defendant, plaintiff. Civil index in books. Mail turnaround time 2-3 days. Civil PAT goes back to 1999. PAT results show name only. Name or cause number needed. Access court indexes and sheriff's jail and bond data free at http://judicial.smith-county.com/judsrch.asp.

Criminal Records: Access: Mail, in person, online. Both court and visitors may perform in person searches. Search fee: $5.00 per name. Required to search: name, years to search. Criminal docket on books to 1846, computerized since 1/99. Mail turnaround time 2-3 days. Criminal PAT goes back to 1999. PAT results show name only. Name and cause number needed. Online access to criminal is same as civil above.

General Information: No juvenile, mental, sealed, or adoption records released. Will not fax documents. Court makes copy: $1.00 per page. Cert fee: $1.00 per doc. Payee: District Clerk. Cashiers checks and money orders accepted. Major credit cards accepted. Mail requests: SASE required.

County Court at Law 1, 2, 3 PO Box 1018, 200 E Ferguson, #300, Tyler, TX 75710; 903-590-4670; criminal phone: 903-590-4681; civil phone: 903-590-4673; probate phone: 903-590-4673; fax: 903-590-4689; 8AM-5PM ***Misdemeanor, Civil, Probate.*** www.smith-county.com/

There are three Courts at Law at this location.

Civil Records: Access: Mail, in person, online. Both court and visitors may perform in person searches. Search fee: $5.00 per name. Required to search: name, years to search. Civil cases indexed by defendant, plaintiff. Civil index in books. Mail turnaround time 2-4 days. Civil PAT goes back to 1997. PAT civil results show middle initial. Probates records on public access terminal back to 1992. Access court and probate indexes and sheriff's jail and bond data free at http://judicial.smith-county.com/judsrch.asp.

Criminal Records: Access: Mail, in person, online. Both court and visitors may perform in person searches. Search fee: $5.00 per name. Required to search: name, years to search; also helpful: DOB,

SSN. Criminal index in books. Mail turnaround time 2-4 days. Criminal PAT goes back to 1995. PAT results show middle initial, DOB. Online access to criminal is same as civil above.
General Information: No juvenile, mental, sealed, or adoption records released. Will fax documents $1.00 per page. Court makes copy: $1.00 per page. Cert fee: $5.00 per certificate. Payee: Smith County Clerk. No personal checks accepted. All major credit cards accepted. Mail requests: SASE required.

Somervell County

District & County Court PO Box 1098, Glen Rose, TX 76043; 254-897-4427; fax: 254-897-3233; 8AM-5PM (CST). ***Felony, Misdemeanor, Civil, Probate.***
Evictions are handled by Justice of the Peace, POB 237, Glen Rose, TX 76043, 254-897-2120.
Civil Records: Access: Mail, in person. Visitors must perform in person searches themselves. Search fee: $5.00 per name. Required to search: name, years to search; also helpful: address. Civil cases indexed by defendant, plaintiff; index on microfilm since 1980, index books since 1875. Mail turnaround time same day.
Criminal Records: Access: Mail, in person. Visitors must perform in person searches themselves. Search fee: $5.00 per name. Required to search: name, years to search, DOB, SSN, signed release; also helpful: address. Criminal records on microfilm since 1980, index books since 1875. Mail turnaround time same day.
General Information: No juvenile, mental, sealed, or adoption records released. Fee to fax out file $1.00 per page. Court makes copy: $1.00 per page. Self serve: same. Cert fee: $5.00. Payee: County/District Clerk. Personal checks accepted; credit cards are not. Mail requests: SASE preferred.

Starr County

District & County Court Starr County Courthouse, Rm 304, 401 N Britton, Rio Grande City, TX 78582; 956-487-8482 (Dist) 487-8485 (County); criminal phone: 956-487-8485; civil phone: 956-487-8482; probate phone: 956-487-8032; criminal fax: 956-487-8493; civil fax: same; 8AM-5PM (CST). ***Felony, Misdemeanor, Civil, Probate.***
The civil court also here handles civil county court cases. Probate fax is same as main fax number.
Civil Records: Access: Phone, fax, mail, in person, online. Both court and visitors may perform in person searches. Search fee: $7.00 per name. Required to search: name, years to search. Civil cases indexed by defendant, plaintiff. Civil index on docket books from 1920s, computerized since 9/07. Mail turnaround time 2 days. Access index and images online at www.idocket.com; registration and password required. A fee service; only one free name search per day. Records go back to 1/1999.
Criminal Records: Access: Phone, fax, mail, in person, online. Only the court performs in person searches; visitors may not. Search fee: $7.00 per name. Required to search: name, years to search, SSN; also helpful: DOB. Criminal records on computer since 9/07; in docket books to 1800s. Mail turnaround time 2 days. Public use terminal has crim records back to 2006. Access felony index and images online at www.idocket.com; registration and password required. A fee service; only one free name search per day. Felony records go back to 1/2003.
General Information: No adoption records released. Will fax documents $5.00 1st page; $1.00 each add'l. Court makes copy: $1.00 per page. Cert fee: $5.00 per document. Payee: District Clerk. Personal checks accepted; credit cards are not. Mail requests: SASE required.

County Court Starr County Courthouse, Rm 201, 401 N Britton Ave, Rio Grande City, TX 78582; 956-487-8032; fax: 956-487-8674; 8AM-5PM (CST). ***Misdemeanor, Probate.***
See District & County Court for civil county court cases. Probate is here, but is not available online.
Criminal Records: Access: Mail, in person, online. Both court and visitors may perform in person searches. Search fee: $10.00 per name. Required to search: name, years to search; also helpful: SSN, DOB. Criminal records on computer since 1997, in index books since 1984, archived prior. Mail turnaround time 2-4 days. Online access is at www.idocket.com; registration and password required. A fee service; only one free name search per day. Records go back to 12/31/96.
General Information: No juvenile, mental, sealed, or adoption records released. Fee to fax out file $1.00 per page. Court makes copy: $1.00 per page. Cert fee: $5.00 per doc. Payee: County Clerk. Personal checks accepted; credit cards are not. Mail requests: SASE requested.

Stephens County

District Court 200 W Walker, Breckenridge, TX 76424; 254-559-3151; fax: 254-559-8127; 8:30AM-5PM (CST). ***Felony, Civil, Misdemeanor.***
Civil Records: Access: Fax, mail, in person. Both court and visitors may perform in person searches. Search fee: $5.00 per name. Required to search: name, years to search. Civil cases indexed by defendant, plaintiff. Civil records in index books, archived from 1900; on computer back to 1995. Mail turnaround time same day.
Criminal Records: Access: Fax, mail, in person. Both court and visitors may perform in person searches. Search fee: $5.00 per name. Required to search: name, years to search, DOB. Criminal index in books, archived from 1900; on computer back to 1995. Mail turnaround time same day.
General Information: No juvenile, mental, sealed, or adoption records released. Will fax documents $1.00 per page; available to local and 800 numbers only. Court makes copy: $1.00 per page. Cert fee: $1.00. Payee: District Clerk. Personal checks accepted; credit cards are not. Mail requests: SASE required.

County Clerk 200 W Walker, Stephens County Courthouse, Breckenridge, TX 76424; 254-559-3700; fax: 254-559-5892; 8:30AM-N, 1-5PM (CST). ***Probate.***

Sterling County

District & County Court PO Box 55, Sterling City, TX 76951; 325-378-5191; fax: 325-378-3111; 8AM-4PM M-TH; 8AM-1:30PM F (CST). ***Felony, Misdemeanor, Civil, Probate.***
Probate is a separate index at this same address.
Civil Records: Access: Mail, in person. Both court and visitors may perform in person searches. No search fee. Required to search: name, years to search; also helpful: address. Civil cases indexed by defendant, plaintiff. Civil records in index books from 1900s. Mail turnaround time 1-2 days.
Criminal Records: Access: Mail, in person. Both court and visitors may perform in person searches. Search fee: $5.00 per name. Required to search: name, years to search; also helpful: DOB, SSN. Criminal docket on books from 1900s. Mail turnaround time 1-2 days.
General Information: No juvenile, mental, sealed, or adoption records released. Fee to fax out file $1.00 per page. Court makes copy: $1.00 per page. Cert fee: $5.00 per document. Payee: Sterling County/District Clerk. In-state personal checks accepted only. No credit cards accepted. Mail requests: SASE helpful.

Stonewall County

District & County Court PO Drawer P, Aspermont, TX 79502; 940-989-2272; fax: 940-989-2715; 8AM-N, 1-4:30PM (CST). ***Felony, Misdemeanor, Civil, Probate.***
Civil Records: Access: Phone, mail, in person. Both court and visitors may perform in person searches. Search fee: $5.00 per name. Required to search: name, years to search. Civil cases indexed by defendant, plaintiff. Civil records in index books to 1900's. Mail turnaround time 2 days.
Criminal Records: Access: Phone, mail, in person. Both court and visitors may perform in person searches. Search fee: $5.00 per name. Required to search: name, years to search. Criminal docket on booksto 1900's. Mail turnaround time 2 days.
General Information: No juvenile, mental, sealed, or adoption records released. Will fax documents $2.00 per page. Court makes copy: $1.00 per page. Self serve: same. Cert fee: $5.00. Payee: County Clerk. Personal checks accepted; credit cards are not. Mail requests: SASE required.

Sutton County

District & County Court 300 E Oak, #3, Sonora, TX 76950; 325-387-3815; fax: 325-387-6028; 8:30AM-4:30PM (CST). ***Felony, Misdemeanor, Civil, Probate.***
Civil Records: Access: Phone, mail, in person. Both court and visitors may perform in person searches. Search fee: $10.00 per name. Required to search: name, years to search. Civil cases indexed by defendant, plaintiff; index on computer back to 1992, index books prior. Mail turnaround time 2-4 days.
Criminal Records: Access: Mail, in person. Both court and visitors may perform in person searches. Search fee: $10.00 per name. Required to search: name, years to search. Criminal records computerized from 1995, index books prior to 1890. Mail turnaround time 2-4 days.
General Information: No juvenile, mental, sealed, or adoption records released. Will fax documents to local or toll free line. Court makes copy: $1.00 per page. Self serve: same. Cert fee: $5.00. Payee: County Clerk. Personal checks accepted; credit cards are not. Mail requests: SASE required.

Swisher County

District & County Court County Courthouse, 119 S Maxwell, Tulia, TX 79088; 806-995-4396; criminal fax: 806-995-4121; civil fax: same; 8AM-5PM (CST). ***Felony, Misdemeanor, Civil, Probate.***
www.242ndcourt.com
Probate is a separate index at this same address. Probate fax is same as main fax number.
Civil Records: Access: Mail, fax, in person, email. Both court and visitors may perform in person searches. Search fee: $5.00 per name. Required to search: name, years to search. Civil cases indexed by defendant, plaintiff; index on computer since 1992, index books prior. Note: Direct email search requests to brenda.hudson@swisher-tx.net. Mail turnaround time 1 day. Only daily docket and monthly calendar for 242nd Court are online.
Criminal Records: Access: Mail, fax, in person, email. Both court and visitors may perform in person searches. Search fee: $5.00 per name. Required to search: name, years to search, DOB and SSN. Criminal records on computer since 1992, index books prior to early 1900's. Note: Direct email search requests to brenda.hudson@swisher-tx.net. Mail turnaround time 1-2 days. Only daily docket and monthly calendar for 242nd Court are online.
General Information: No juvenile, mental, sealed, or adoption records released. Fee to fax out file $3.00 per page plus $1.00 ea add'l. Court makes copy: $1.00 per page. Self serve: $.50 per page. Cert fee: $1.00 per page. Payee: County/District Clerk. Personal checks accepted. Will accept credit cards for email or fax requests and at the counter. Mail requests: SASE requested.

Tarrant County

District Court 401 W Belknap, County District Clerk's Office, Fort Worth, TX 76196-0402; 817-884-1574 (884-1265 Family Division); criminal phone: 817-884-1342; civil phone: 817-884-1240; 8AM-5PM (CST). ***Felony, Civil, Family.***
www.tarrantcounty.com/ecourts/site/default.asp
Civil Records: Access: Mail, in person, online. Both court and visitors may perform in person searches. Search fee: $5.00 per name if the office does the search. Required to search: full name and DOB. Civil cases indexed by defendant, plaintiff; index on computer since 1989, file jackets prior to 1989; records go back to 1800s. Mail turnaround time 1-3 days. Civil PAT goes back to 1975. PAT results show middle initial, DOB, SSN. Access to the remote online system requires $50 setup fee and $35.00 monthly with add'l month prepaid; for 1 to 5 users; fees increase with more users. Call 817-884-1345 for info and signup. Index records are available for free at http://cc.co.tarrant.tx.us/CivilCourts/ccl/default.asp.
Criminal Records: Access: Mail, online, in person. Both court and visitors may perform in person searches. Search fee: $5.00 per name if the office does the search. Required to search: full name, years to search, DOB; also helpful: SSN. Criminal records computerized from 1975, microfilm since 1970, index

books and case files since 1800s. Mail turnaround time 1-3 days. Criminal PAT goes back to same as civil. PAT results show middle initial, DOB, SSN. Online access same as civil. Online results show middle initial, DOB, SSN.
General Information: No juvenile, mental, sealed, or adoption records released. Will not fax documents. Court makes copy: $.35 per page. Cert fee: $1.00 per page. Payee: District Clerk. Business checks accepted. Major credit cards accepted.

County Court - Criminal 401 W Belknap, County Clerk's Office, Fort Worth, TX 76196-0402; 817-884-1195; criminal phone: 817-884-1066; fax: 817-884-3409; 7:30AM-4:30PM (CST). ***Misdemeanor.***
www.tarrantcounty.com/ecourts/site/default.asp
Small Claims, Evictions, and low-level civil cases are handled by JP/Municipal Courts.
Criminal Records: Access: Mail, online, in person. Both court and visitors may perform in person searches. Search fee: $5.00 per name. Required to search: name, years to search, DOB. Criminal records on computer back 25 years. Mail turnaround time 1-3 days. Public use terminal has crim records back to 25 years. PAT results show middle initial, DOB, SSN. Access to the remote online system requires $50 setup fee and $35.00 monthly with add'l month prepaid; this is for 1 to 5 users. Fees increase with more users. The District Court records are on this system also. Call 817-884-1345 for more information. Online results show middle initial, DOB, SSN.
General Information: No juvenile, mental, sealed, or adoption records released. Will not fax documents. Court makes copy: $1.00 per page. Cert fee: $5.00 per case. Payee: County Clerk. Business and personal checks accepted. No credit cards accepted. Mail requests: SASE required.

Probate Court County Courthouse, 100 W Weatherford St, Probate Court #1 Rm 260A, Fort Worth, TX 76196; 817-884-1200; probate phone: 817-884-1254; fax: 817-884-3178; 8AM-4:30PM (CST). ***Probate.***
www.tarrantcounty.com/ecourts/site/default.asp
Search probate records by name or case number at http://cc.co.tarrant.tx.us/CivilCourts/Probate/default.asp or http://cc.co.tarrant.tx.us/CivilCourts/Probate/default.asp?eprobatecourtsNav=|

Taylor County

District Court 300 Oak St, Abilene, TX 79602; 325-674-1316; 8AM-N, 1-5PM (CST). ***Felony, Civil.*** www.taylorcountytexas.org/
Civil Records: Access: Mail, in person. Both court and visitors may perform in person searches. Search fee: $5.00 per name. Required to search: name, years to search. Civil cases indexed by defendant, plaintiff; index on computer since 1984; prior records in index books to 1885. Mail turnaround time 5 days. Civil PAT goes back to 1984.
Criminal Records: Access: Mail, in person. Both court and visitors may perform in person searches. Search fee: $5.00 per name. Required to search: name, years to search, DOB; also helpful: SSN. Criminal records on computer since 1982; prior records in index books to 1885. Mail turnaround time 5 days. Criminal PAT goes back to 1982.
General Information: No juvenile, mental, sealed, or adoption records released. Will not fax documents. Court makes copy: $1.00 per page. Cert fee: $1.00. Payee: Taylor County District Clerk. Business checks accepted. No credit cards accepted. Mail requests: SASE required.

County Court 300 Oak St, Abilene, TX 79602; 325-674-1202; probate phone: same; fax: 325-674-1279; 8AM-5PM (CST). ***Misdemeanor, Civil, Probate.*** www.taylorcountytexas.org
Civil Records: Access: Mail, in person. Both court and visitors may perform in person searches. Search fee: $5.00 per name per 10 years searched. Probate searches are $5.00, years not applicable. Required to search: name, years to search. Civil cases indexed by defendant, plaintiff; index on computer less than ten years, index books prior. Mail turnaround time 2-4 days. Civil PAT goes back to 1981. Public access terminal has probate back to 1888. Results include name and case number.
Criminal Records: Access: Mail, in person. Both court and visitors may perform in person searches. Search fee: $5.00 per name per 10 years searched. Required to search: name, years to search, DOB; also helpful: address, SSN. Criminal records computerized from 1980; overall records go back to 1949. Mail turnaround time 2-4 days. Criminal PAT goes back to same as civil. PAT results show middle initial, DOB.
General Information: No juvenile, mental, sealed, or adoption records released. Fee to fax out file $1.00 per page, $2.00 per doc. Court makes copy: $1.00 per page. Self serve: same. Cert fee: $5.00. Payee: County Clerk. No personal checks accepted. Major credit cards accepted. Mail requests: SASE required.

Terrell County

District & County Court PO Drawer 410, Sanderson, TX 79848; 432-345-2391; fax: 432-345-2740; 9AM-N, 1-5PM (CST). ***Felony, Misdemeanor, Civil, Probate.***
Civil Records: Access: Mail, in person. Both court and visitors may perform in person searches. Search fee: $10.00 per name. Required to search: name, years to search. Civil cases indexed by defendant, plaintiff. Civil index in books. Note: All requests must be in writing. Mail turnaround time 2-4 days. Civil PAT goes back to 1994.
Criminal Records: Access: Mail, in person. Both court and visitors may perform in person searches. Search fee: $10.00 per name. Required to search: name, years to search. Criminal index in books. Note: All requests must be in writing. Mail turnaround time 2-4 days. Criminal PAT goes back to same as civil.
General Information: No juvenile, mental, sealed, or adoption records released. Will not fax documents. Court makes copy: $1.00 per page. No certification fee. Payee: County Clerk. Personal checks accepted; credit cards are not.

Terry County

District Court 500 W Main, Rm 209E, Brownfield, TX 79316; 806-637-4202; fax: 806-637-1333; 8:30AM-5PM (CST). ***Felony, Civil.***
Civil Records: Access: Mail, in person. Both court and visitors may perform in person searches. Search fee: $5.00 per name. Required to search: name, years to search. Civil cases indexed by defendant, plaintiff. Civil records in index books and on computer. Mail turnaround time same day.
Criminal Records: Access: Mail, in person. Only the court performs in person searches; visitors may not. Search fee: $5.00 per name. Required to search: name, years to search, DOB; also helpful: SSN. Criminal docket on books and on computer. Mail turnaround time same day.
General Information: No juvenile, mental, sealed, or adoption records released. Will fax documents to local or toll free line. Court makes copy: $1.00 per page. Cert fee: $1.00 per document. Payee: District Clerk. Personal checks accepted; credit cards are not. Mail requests: SASE required.

County Court 500 W Main, Rm 105, Brownfield, TX 79316-4398; 806-637-8551; 8:30AM-5PM (CST). ***Misdemeanor, Civil, Probate.***
Civil Records: Access: Mail, in person. Both court and visitors may perform in person searches. Search fee: $10.00 per name. Required to search: name, years to search. Civil cases indexed by defendant, plaintiff. Civil records in index books to 1904, computerized since 1981. Mail turnaround time 2-3 days.
Criminal Records: Access: Mail, in person. Both court and visitors may perform in person searches. Search fee: $10.00 per name. Required to search: name, years to search; also helpful: address, DOB, SSN. Criminal docket on books back to 1904, computerized since 1981. Mail turnaround 1-2 days.
General Information: No juvenile, mental, sealed, or adoption records released. Fee to fax out file $1.00 per page. Court makes copy: $1.00 per page. Cert fee: $5.00. Payee: County Clerk. Personal checks accepted; credit cards are not. Mail requests: SASE required.

Throckmorton County

District & County Court PO Box 309, Throckmorton, TX 76483; 940-849-2501; probate phone: same; fax: 940-849-3032; 8AM-N, 1-4:30PM M,TH; 8AM-N F (CST). ***Felony, Misdemeanor, Civil, Probate.***
Civil Records: Access: Mail, in person. Both court and visitors may perform in person searches. Search fee: $10.00 per name. Required to search: name, years to search. Civil cases indexed by defendant, plaintiff. Civil records in index books; computerized records go back to 1990. Mail turnaround 1 week. Civil PAT goes back to 1990.
Criminal Records: Access: Mail, in person. Both court and visitors may perform in person searches. Search fee: $10.00 per name. Required to search: name, years to search. Criminal index in books; computerized records go back to 1990. Mail turnaround time 2-4 days. Criminal PAT goes back to 1990.
General Information: No juvenile, mental, sealed, or adoption records released. Will fax documents $2.00 per page. Court makes copy: $1.00 per page. Self serve: same. Cert fee: $5.00. Payee: County/District Clerk. Personal checks accepted; $35.00 is charged if it is returned to court. No credit cards accepted. Mail requests: SASE required.

Titus County

District Court 105 W 1st St, PO Box 492, Mount Pleasant, TX 75455; criminal phone: 903-577-6723; civil phone: 903-577-6721; fax: 903-577-6719; 8AM-5PM (CST). ***Felony, Civil.***
www.co.titus.tx.us/district_clerk/index.htm
Civil Records: Access: Phone, mail, in person. Both court and visitors may perform in person searches. Search fee: $5.00 per name. Required to search: name, years to search. Civil cases indexed by defendant, plaintiff. Civil records in index books from 1895; computerized back to 1992. Mail turnaround time 2-3 days. Civil PAT goes back to 10 years. Results include name and case number.
Criminal Records: Access: Phone, mail, in person. Both court and visitors may perform in person searches. Search fee: $5.00 per name. Required to search: name, years to search. Criminal docket on books from 1895; computerized back to 1992. Mail turnaround time 2-3 days. Criminal PAT goes back to same as civil. PAT criminal results show middle initial.
General Information: No juvenile, mental, sealed, or adoption records released. Will not fax documents. Court makes copy: $1.00 per page. Self serve: same. Cert fee: $5.00. Payee: District Clerk. Personal checks accepted; credit cards are not. Mail requests: SASE required.

County Court 100 W 1st St, #204, Mount Pleasant, TX 75455; 903-577-6796; fax: 903-572-5078; 8AM-4:45PM ***Misdemeanor, Civil, Probate.***
Civil Records: Access: Mail, in person, online. Both court and visitors may perform in person searches. Search fee: $10.00 per name. Required to search: name, years to search; also helpful: address. Civil cases indexed by defendant, plaintiff; index on computer since 1/1994, index books since 1895. Mail turnaround time 7-10 days. Civil PAT available. Access to court records is to be online at www.tituscountyonline.net/countyclerk/. Registration required.
Criminal Records: Access: Mail, in person, online. Both court and visitors may perform in person searches. Search fee: $10.00 per name. Required to search: name, years to search; also helpful: address, DOB, SSN. Criminal records on computer since 1/1994, index books since 1930. Mail turnaround time 1 week to 10 days. Criminal PAT available. Access to criminal court records is to be online, probably at www.tituscountyonline.net/countyclerk/. Registration required.
General Information: No juvenile, mental, sealed, or adoption records released. Will not fax documents. Court makes copy: $1.00 per page. Self serve: same. Cert fee: $5.00. Payee: County Clerk. Business checks accepted. Major credit cards accepted. Mail requests: SASE required.

Tom Green County

District Court County Courthouse, 112 W Beauregard, San Angelo, TX 76903; 325-659-6579; fax: 325-659-3241; 8AM-5PM (CST). ***Felony, Civil.*** www.co.tom-green.tx.us/distclrk/

Civil Records: Access: Mail, in person, online. Both court and visitors may perform in person searches. Search fee: $5.00 per name per 5 years searched. Required to search: name, years to search; also helpful. Civil cases indexed by defendant, plaintiff. Civil records in index books from 1900s; on computer back to 1993. Mail turnaround time 1 week. Civil PAT goes back to 1994. Online access to civil case records back to 1994 is online at http://justice.co.tom-green.tx.us. Search by name, case number. Also, online case access back to 4/4/1992 at www.idocket.com; registration and password required.

Criminal Records: Access: Mail, in person, online. Both court and visitors may perform in person searches. Search fee: $5.00 per name per 5 years searched. Required to search: name, years to search, DOB. Criminal docket on books from 1900s; on computer back to 1993. Mail turnaround time 1 week. Criminal PAT goes back to same as civil. Online access to criminal case records back to 1994 at http://justice.co.tom-green.tx.us. Search by name, case number. Also, online felony case access back to 10/1/1991 at www.idocket.com; registration and password required.

General Information: No juvenile, mental, sealed, or adoption records released. Fee to fax out file $1.50 per page. Court makes copy: $1.00 per page. Self serve: $.25 per page. No certification fee. Payee: District Clerk. Business checks accepted. Visa/MC accepted. Mail requests: SASE required.

County Court 124 W Beauregard, San Angelo, TX 76903; 325-659-6551; criminal phone: 325-659-6555; civil phone: 325-659-6554; fax: 325-659-3251; 8AM-4:30PM (CST). ***Misdemeanor, Civil, Probate.*** http://justice.co.tom-green.tx.us

Civil Records: Access: Mail, in person, online. Both court and visitors may perform in person searches. Search fee: $5.00 per name. Required to search: name, years to search; also helpful: address. Civil cases indexed by defendant, plaintiff; index on computer since 1994, index books prior. Mail turnaround time same day. Civil PAT goes back to 1994. Online access to civil records back to 1994 is free at http://justice.co.tom-green.tx.us.

Criminal Records: Access: Mail, in person, online. Both court and visitors may perform in person searches. Search fee: $5.00 per name. Required to search: name, years to search, DOB; also helpful: address, SSN. Criminal records on computer since 1994, index books prior. Mail turnaround time same day. Criminal PAT goes back to same as civil. Online access to criminal records is the same as civil. Website includes sheriff's jail-bond records.

General Information: No juvenile, mental, sealed, or adoption records released. Will fax documents to local or toll free line. Court makes copy: $1.00 per page. Self serve: same. Cert fee: $5.00. Payee: County Clerk. Personal checks and major credit cards accepted. Certified payments may be made online. Mail requests: SASE required.

Travis County

District Court PO Box 679003, 1001 Guadalupe St #103, Austin, TX 78767; 512-854-9420; criminal phone: 512-854-9457; civil phone: 512-854-9457; criminal fax: 512-854-9549; civil fax: same; 8AM-5PM (CST). ***Felony, Civil.***

Civil Records: Access: Mail, in person. Both court and visitors may perform in person searches. Search fee: $5.00 per name. Add $2.00 per year prior to 1988. Required to search: name, years to search. Civil cases indexed by defendant, plaintiff; index on computer since 1986, microfiche and index books. Mail turnaround time 2-3 days. Civil PAT goes back to 1986. PAT results show name, DOB, SSN.

Criminal Records: Access: Fax, mail, in person. Both court and visitors may perform in person searches. Search fee: $5.00 per name. Add $2.00 per year prior to 1988. Required to search: name, years to search, DOB. Criminal records on computer since 1988, index books prior to 1988. Mail turnaround time 2-3 days, usually. Criminal PAT goes back to 1988. PAT results show name only.

General Information: No juvenile, mental, sealed, or adoption records released (all felony cases are public record). Will not fax documents. Court makes copy: $.50 per page. Self serve: $.25 per page. Cert fee: $1.00 per cert. Payee: District Clerk. Personal checks and credit cards accepted. Mail requests: SASE required.

County Court PO Box 149325, Misdemeanor Div; Civil/Probate Div., 1000 Guadalupe St., #222, Austin, TX 78714-9325; 512-854-9188; criminal fax: 512-854-4220; civil fax: 512-854-3129; 8AM-5PM (CST). ***Misdemeanor, Civil, Probate.*** www.co.travis.tx.us/county_clerk

Records include appeals from the Travis County JP Courts. All phone inquiries routed through the Call Center 512-854-9188. Probate fax- 512-854-3129

Civil Records: Access: Phone, mail, in person, online. Both court and visitors may perform in person searches. Search fee: $10.00 per name per 10 years. Fee applies to cases opened prior to June 1986. Required to search: name, years to search. Civil cases indexed by defendant, plaintiff; index on computer since 6/86, microfilm 1845 to 1986, probate from 1/1992 forward. Mail turnaround time 2-5 days. Civil PAT goes back to 6/1986. Online results show name only. Access to probate court records only is free at http://deed.co.travis.tx.us/search.aspx?cabinet=probate.

Criminal Records: Access: Mail, in person. Both court and visitors may perform in person searches. Search fee: $5.00 per name. $10.00 per name for microfilm. Required to search: name, years to search; also helpful: address, DOB, SSN. Criminal misdemeanor records on computer since 1981; prior records on microfilm to 1845. Mail turnaround time 2-10 days. Criminal PAT goes back to 1981. PAT results show middle initial, DOB.

General Information: No juvenile, mental, sealed, or adoption records released. Will fax documents $1.00 per page. Court makes copy: $1.00 per page. Self serve: $.25 per page. Cert fee: $5.00 per doc. Payee: Travis County Clerk. Personal checks and major credit cards accepted.

Trinity County

District Court PO Box 549, Groveton, TX 75845; 936-642-1118; 8AM-5PM (CST). ***Felony, Civil.***

Civil Records: Access: Mail, in person. Both court and visitors may perform in person searches. Search fee: $5.00 per name. Required to search: name, years to search. Civil cases indexed by defendant, plaintiff; index on computer since 1980, index books prior. Mail turnaround time 1 day.

Criminal Records: Access: Mail, in person. Both court and visitors may perform in person searches. Search fee: $5.00 per name. Required to search: name, years to search. Criminal records on computer since 1980, index books prior. Mail turnaround 1 day.

General Information: No juvenile, mental, sealed, or adoption records released. Will not fax documents. Court makes copy: $1.00 per page. Self serve: same. Cert fee: $1.00 per page. Payee: District Clerk. Personal checks accepted.

County Court PO Box 456, 162 W 1st St, Groveton, TX 75845; 936-642-1208; criminal fax: 936-642-3004; civil fax: same; 8AM-5PM (CST). ***Misdemeanor, Civil, Probate.***

Probate fax is same as main fax number.

Civil Records: Access: Mail, in person, online. Both court and visitors may perform in person searches. Search fee: $5.00 per name. Required to search: name, years to search; also helpful: address. Civil cases indexed by defendant, plaintiff. Civil index in docket books from 1982. Date of birth helpful for searching. Mail turnaround time 1 day. Online case access is through www.idocket.com; registration and password required. One free name search permitted per day, otherwise subscription required.

Criminal Records: Access: Mail, in person, online. Both court and visitors may perform in person searches. Search fee: $5.00 per name. Required to search: name, years to search, SSN; also helpful: address, DOB, sex. Criminal docket on books back to 1982. Mail turnaround time 1 day. Online case access is through www.idocket.com; registration and password required. One free name search permitted per day, otherwise subscription required.

General Information: No juvenile, mental, sealed, or adoption records released. Fee to fax out file $2.00 per page. Court makes copy: $1.00 per page. Self serve: same. Cert fee: $5.00 1st page, $1.00 each add'l. Payee: County Clerk. Personal checks accepted; credit cards are not. Mail requests: SASE required.

Tyler County

District Court 203 Courthouse, 100 W Bluff, Woodville, TX 75979; 409-283-2162; 8AM-N, 1-4:30PM (CST). ***Felony, Civil.***

Civil Records: Access: Mail, in person. Both court and visitors may perform in person searches. Search fee: $5.00 per name. Required to search: name, years to search. Civil cases indexed by defendant, plaintiff. Civil index in books. Mail turnaround time same day.

Criminal Records: Access: Mail, in person. Both court and visitors may perform in person searches. Search fee: $5.00. Required to search: name, years to search. Criminal index in books. Mail turnaround time same day.

General Information: No juvenile, mental, sealed, or adoption records released. Will not fax documents. Court makes copy: $1.00 per page. Self serve: same. No certification fee. Payee: District Clerk. Business checks accepted. No credit cards accepted. Mail requests: SASE required.

County Court County Courthouse, Rm 110, 100 W Bluff, Woodville, TX 75979; 409-283-2281; fax: 409-283-6305; 8AM-4:30PM (CST). ***Misdemeanor, Civil, Probate.***

Civil Records: Access: Phone, mail, in person. Both court and visitors may perform in person searches. Search fee: $5.00 per name. Required to search: name, years to search. Civil cases indexed by defendant, plaintiff; index on computer back to 1989, microfilm since 1973, index books from 1800s. Mail turnaround time 3-5 days. Civil PAT goes back to 1989. PAT results show name only.

Criminal Records: Access: Mail, in person. Both court and visitors may perform in person searches. Search fee: $5.00 per name. Required to search: name, years to search; also helpful: address, DOB, SSN. Criminal records computerized from 1989, microfilm since 1973, index books from 1800s. Mail turnaround time 3-5 days. Criminal PAT goes back to same as civil. PAT results show name only.

General Information: No juvenile, mental, sealed or adoption records released. Will fax documents $3.00 per page. Court makes copy: $1.00 per page. Self serve: same. Cert fee: $5.00. Payee: County Clerk. Personal checks accepted; credit cards are not.

Upshur County

District Court PO Box 950, 405 N Titus, Gilmer, TX 75644; 903-843-5031; criminal fax: 903-843-3540; civil fax: same; 8AM-5PM M-TH; 8AM-4:30PM Fri (CST). ***Felony, Misdemeanor, Civil, Probate.*** www.countyofupshur.com

Civil Records: Access: Mail, in person, online. Both court and visitors may perform in person searches. Search fee: $5.00 per name. Required to search: name, years to search. Civil cases indexed by defendant, plaintiff. Civil records in index books to 1800s. Mail turnaround time same day. Civil PAT goes back to 1975. Results include name and case number. Access court records and hearings free at www.countyofupshur.com/judicialsearch/.

Criminal Records: Access: Mail, in person, online. Both court and visitors may perform in person searches. Search fee: $5.00 per name. Required to search: name, years to search. Criminal docket on booksto 1800s. Note: Results include name and case number. Mail turnaround time same day. Criminal PAT goes back to 1992.PAT results show name, DOB. Results include name and case number. Access court records and hearings free at www.countyofupshur.com/judicialsearch/.

General Information: No juvenile, mental, sealed or adoption records released. Will not fax documents. Court makes copy: $1.00 per page. Cert fee: $1.00 per document. Payee: District Clerk. No personal checks or credit cards accepted. Mail requests: SASE required.

County Court PO Box 730, Courthouse Sq, Hwy 154 West, Gilmer, TX 75644; 903-843-4015; fax: 903-843-5492; 8AM-4:30PM (CST). ***Misdemeanor, Civil, Probate.*** www.countyofupshur.com/

Civil Records: Access: Mail, in person, online. Both court and visitors may perform in person searches. Search fee: $5.00 per name per 10 year period. Required to search: name, years to search. Civil cases indexed by defendant, plaintiff. Civil records in index books to 1936; on computer back to 1993. Mail turnaround time same day. Civil PAT goes back to 1993. PAT civil results show middle initial. Access court records and hearings free at www.countyofupshur.com/judicialsearch/.

Criminal Records: Access: Mail, in person, online. Both court and visitors may perform in person searches. Search fee: $5.00 per name per 10 year period. Required to search: name, years to search, DOB, offense, signed release. Criminal docket on booksto 1936; on computer back to 1993. Mail turnaround time same day. Criminal PAT goes back to same as civil. PAT criminal results show middle initial. Access court records and hearings free at www.countyofupshur.com/judicialsearch/. Online results show middle initial.

General Information: Online identifiers in results same as on public terminal. No juvenile, mental, sealed or adoption records released. Will fax documents $1.00 per page, prepaid. Court makes copy: $1.00 per page. Self serve: $1.00 per page. Cert fee: $5.00 per doc. Payee: County Clerk. Personal checks accepted; credit cards are not. Mail requests: SASE required.

Upton County

District & County Court PO Box 465, Rankin, TX 79778; 432-693-2861; criminal fax: 432-693-2129; civil fax: same; 8AM-5PM (CST). ***Felony, Misdemeanor, Civil, Probate.*** www.co.upton.tx.us

Probate fax is same as main fax number.

Civil Records: Access: Fax, mail, in person. Both court and visitors may perform in person searches. Search fee: $5.00 per name. Required to search: name, years to search. Civil cases indexed by defendant, plaintiff; index on computer back to 1987; in index books to 1910. Mail turnaround time 1-2 days.

Criminal Records: Access: Fax, mail, in person. Both court and visitors may perform in person searches. Search fee: $5.00 per name. Required to search: name, years to search, signed release; also helpful: address, DOB. Criminal records computerized from 1987; in index books to 1910. Mail turnaround time 1-2 days.

General Information: No juvenile, mental, sealed, or adoption records released. Fee to fax out file $2.00 per page. Court makes copy: $1.00 per page. Cert fee: $5.00 per document. Payee: District/County Clerk. Personal checks accepted; credit cards are not. Mail requests: SASE required.

Uvalde County

District Court County Courthouse, #15, Uvalde, TX 78801; 830-278-3918; 8AM-5PM (CST). ***Felony, Civil.***

Civil Records: Access: Phone, mail, in person. Both court and visitors may perform in person searches. Search fee: $5.00 per name. Required to search: name, years to search. Civil cases indexed by defendant, plaintiff. Civil index in books. Mail turnaround time 2-3 days.

Criminal Records: Access: Mail, in person. Both court and visitors may perform in person searches. Search fee: $5.00 per name. Required to search: name, years to search, DOB, SSN. Criminal index in books. Mail turnaround time 2-3 days.

General Information: No juvenile, mental, sealed, or adoption records released. Will not fax documents. Court makes copy: $.75 per page. Cert fee: $1.00 per page. Payee: District Clerk. No personal checks or credit cards accepted. Mail requests: SASE required.

County Clerk PO Box 284, 100 Getty St, Uvalde, TX 78802; 830-278-6614; fax: 830-278-8692; 8AM-5PM (CST). ***Misdemeanor, Civil, Probate.***

Civil Records: Access: Mail, in person. Both court and visitors may perform in person searches. Search fee: $10.00 per name; 10 year search. Required to search: name, years to search. Civil cases indexed by defendant, plaintiff. Civil records in index books from 1856, computerized records from 1997. Mail turnaround time 1-2 days. Civil PAT goes back to 1997. PAT results show name only.

Criminal Records: Access: In person. Visitors must perform in person searches themselves. Required to search: name, years to search, DOB, SSN. Criminal docket on books from 1856, computerized records from 1997. Criminal PAT goes back to 6/1997. PAT results show name only.

General Information: No juvenile, mental, sealed, or adoption records released. Will fax documents to local or toll-free number. Court makes copy: $1.00 per page. Cert fee: $5.00 per page. Payee: Lucille C Hutcherson, Uvalde County Clerk. Personal checks accepted; credit cards are not.

Val Verde County

District Court PO Box 1544, 100 E Broadway, 1st Fl, Del Rio, TX 78841; 830-774-7538; criminal phone: 830-774-7539; fax: 830-774-7643; 8AM-4:30PM (CST). ***Felony, Civil.***

Civil Records: Access: Mail, in person, online. Both court and visitors may perform in person searches. Search fee: $5.00 per name. Required to search: name, years to search. Civil cases indexed by defendant, plaintiff; index on computer since 1990, index books prior. Mail turnaround time 2-5 days. Civil PAT goes back to 1989. Public terminal results may contain DOB, SSN, address if included at time of filing. Access civil cases except probate at www.idocket.com; registration and password required. A fee service; only one free name search per day. Records go back to 12/31/89.

Criminal Records: Access: Mail, in person, online. Both court and visitors may perform in person searches. Search fee: $5.00 per name. Required to search: name, years to search. Criminal records on computer since 1990, index books prior. Mail turnaround time 2-5 days. Criminal PAT goes back to 1993. Public terminal criminal results may contain DOB, address and more. Access felonies at www.idocket.com; registration and password required. A fee service; only one free name search per day. Felonies go back to 12/31/93.

General Information: No juvenile, mental, sealed, or adoption records released. Will not fax documents. Court makes copy: $.50 per page. Cert fee: $1.00 per page includes copy fee. Payee: District Clerk. Business and local checks accepted. No credit cards accepted. Mail requests: SASE required.

County Court PO Box 1267, 400 Pecan St, Del Rio, TX 78841-1267; 830-774-7564; fax: 830-774-7608; 8AM-N, 1-4:30PM (CST). ***Misdemeanor, Civil, Probate.***

Civil Records: Access: Mail, in person. Both court and visitors may perform in person searches. Search fee: $10.00 per name. Required to search: name, years to search. Civil cases indexed by defendant, plaintiff. Civil index in docket books from 1885, computerized since 1999. Mail turnaround time 1-2 days.

Criminal Records: Access: Mail, in person. Both court and visitors may perform in person searches. Search fee: $10.00 per name. Required to search: name, years to search; also helpful: address, DOB, SSN. Criminal index in books, computerized since 1999. Mail turnaround time 1-2 days.

General Information: No juvenile, mental, sealed, or adoption records released. Will not fax documents. Court makes copy: $1.00 per page. Cert fee: $5.00 per doc. Payee: County Clerk. Personal checks accepted; credit cards are not. Mail requests: SASE required.

Van Zandt County

District Court 121 E Dallas St, Rm 302, Canton, TX 75103; 903-567-6576; fax: 903-567-1283; 8AM-5PM (CST). ***Felony, Civil.***

Civil Records: Access: Phone, fax, mail, in person. Both court and visitors may perform in person searches. Search fee: $5.00 per name. Required to search: name, years to search. Civil cases indexed by defendant, plaintiff. Civil index in docket books from 1800s; on computer back to 1980. Mail turnaround time 2-4 days. Civil PAT goes back to 1990. PAT civil results show middle initial.

Criminal Records: Access: Mail, fax, in person. Both court and visitors may perform in person searches. Search fee: $5.00 per name. Required to search: name, years to search, DOB. Criminal docket on books back to 1800s; on computer back to 1980. Mail turnaround time 2-4 days. Criminal PAT goes back to same as civil. PAT results show middle initial, DOB.

General Information: No juvenile, mental, sealed, or adoption records released. Will fax documents $1.00 per page. Court makes copy: $1.00 per page. Cert fee: $1.00. Payee: District Clerk. Personal checks accepted; credit cards are not. Mail requests: SASE required.

County Court 121 E Dallas St, #202, Canton, TX 75103; 903-567-6503; criminal fax: 903-567-6722; civil fax: same; 8AM-4:30PM (CST). ***Misdemeanor, Civil, Probate.*** www.vanzandtcounty.org/ips/cms

Probate fax is same as main fax number. Searching on the public access terminals to be available again, soon.

Civil Records: Access: Mail, in person. Only the court performs in person searches; visitors may not. Search fee: $5.00 per name. Required to search: name, years to search. Civil cases indexed by defendant, plaintiff; index on computer back to 1993. Mail turnaround time 2-4 days.

Criminal Records: Access: Mail, in person. Only the court performs in person searches; visitors may not. Search fee: $5.00 per name. Required to search: name, years to search; also helpful: address, DOB, SSN. Criminal records computerized from 1987. Mail turnaround time 2-4 days.

General Information: No juvenile, mental, sealed, or adoption records released. Fee to fax out file $3.00 each plus $1 per page. Court makes copy: $1.00 per page. Self serve: $.50 per page. Cert fee: $5.00 1st page; $1.00 each add'l. Payee: County Clerk. Personal checks accepted; credit cards are not.

Victoria County

District Court PO Box 2238, 115 N. Bridge St, 3rd Fl, Victoria, TX 77902; 361-575-0581; fax: 361-572-5682; 8AM-5PM (CST). ***Felony, Civil.*** www.vctx.org/departments/dclerk/dclerk.htm

Civil Records: Access: Mail, in person, online. Both court and visitors may perform in person searches. Search fee: $5.00 per name. Required to search: name, years to search. Civil cases indexed by defendant, plaintiff; index on computer since 1990, index books since 1838. Mail turnaround time 1-2 days. Civil PAT goes back to 1990. PAT civil results show middle initial. Online index and images at www.idocket.com; registration and password required. Records go back to 12/31/1993. One free name search permitted per day, otherwise subscription required. Images available.

Criminal Records: Access: Mail, in person, online. Both court and visitors may perform in person searches. Search fee: $5.00 per name. Required to search: name, years to search, DOB. Criminal records on computer since 1990, index books since 1838s. Note: Civil online results include middle initial, criminal online results include DOB, SSN, middle initial. Mail turnaround time 1-2 days. Criminal PAT goes back to same as civil. PAT results show middle initial, DOB. Terminal results include SSN. Access felony index and images at www.idocket.com; registration and password required. Records go back to 12/31/1993. One free name search permitted per day, otherwise subscription required.

General Information: Online identifiers in results same as on public terminal. No juvenile, mental, sealed, or adoption records released. No fee for local fax; Long distance fax fee $5.00 plus $1.00 per pg. Court makes copy: $1.00 per page. Cert fee: $1.00 per document. Payee: District Clerk. Personal checks accepted; credit cards are not. Mail requests: SASE required.

County Court 115 N Bridge, Rm 103, Victoria, TX 77901; 361-575-1478; fax: 361-575-6276; 8AM-5PM (CST). ***Misdemeanor, Civil, Probate.*** www.vctx.org

Probate fax is same as main fax number.

Civil Records: Access: Phone, mail, in person, online. Both court and visitors may perform in

person searches. Search fee: $10.00 per name. Required to search: name, years to search. Civil cases indexed by defendant, plaintiff; index on Cox index back to 1838; on computer back to 1991. Mail turnaround time 1 day. Civil PAT goes back to 1991. PAT results show name only. Results include case type. Online case access at www.idocket.com; registration and password required. Civil records go back to 12/31/1991; probate to 6/31//1991. One free name search permitted per day, otherwise subscription required.
Criminal Records: Access: Phone, fax, mail, in person, online. Both court and visitors may perform in person searches. Search fee: $10.00 per name. Required to search: name, years to search; also helpful: address, DOB, SSN. Criminal records on Cox index back to 1838; on computer back to 1989. Mail turnaround time 1 day. Criminal PAT goes back to 1989. PAT results show name only. Results include case type. Access Misd. cases online at www.idocket.com; registration and password required. Records go back to 12/31/1989. One free name search permitted per day, otherwise subscription required. Online results show name.
General Information: No juvenile, mental, sealed, birth, death or adoption records released. Will fax documents $3.50 each or $3.50 plus $1.50 per page to non-toll-free number. Court makes copy: $1.00 per page. Self serve: same. Cert fee: $5.00 per document. Payee: Victoria County Clerk. Personal checks &. Visa/MC accepted. Mail requests: SASE required.

Walker County

District Court 1100 University Ave, Rm 209, Huntsville, TX 77340; 936-436-4972; fax: 936-436-4973; 8AM-N, 1-5PM (CST). ***Felony, Civil.***
Civil Records: Access: Mail, in person. Both court and visitors may perform in person searches. Search fee: $5.00 per name. Required to search: name, years to search. Civil cases indexed by defendant, plaintiff. Civil index on docket books. Mail turnaround time 1-2 days.
Criminal Records: Access: Mail, in person. Both court and visitors may perform in person searches. Search fee: $5.00 per name. Required to search: name, years to search. Criminal records indexed in books. Mail turnaround time 1-2 days.
General Information: No juvenile, mental, sealed, abortion or adoption records released. Will fax documents to local or toll free line. Court makes copy: $1.00 per page. No certification fee. Payee: District Clerk. Business checks accepted. No credit cards accepted. Mail requests: SASE required.

County Court PO Box 210, Huntsville, TX 77342-0210; 936-436-4922; criminal fax: 936-436-4928; civil fax: 936-436-4928; 8AM-4:45PM (CST). ***Misdemeanor, Civil, Probate.***
www.co.walker.tx.us/courts.htm
Civil and Probate fax- 936-436-4928
Civil Records: Access: Mail, in person. Both court and visitors may perform in person searches. Search fee: $5.00 per name. Required to search: name, years to search. Civil cases indexed by defendant, plaintiff. Civil index in books. Note: This office will not search probate records. Mail turnaround time 3-5 days.
Criminal Records: Access: Mail, in person. Both court and visitors may perform in person searches. Search fee: $5.00 per name. Required to search: name, years to search; also helpful: address, DOB, SSN. Criminal docket on booksto 1977, computerized since 1998. Mail turnaround time 3-5 days. Public use terminal has crim records back to 1991; records back to 9/1977 being added. PAT results show middle initial, DOB.
General Information: No juvenile, mental, sealed, or adoption records released. Will not fax documents. Court makes copy: $1.00 per page. Cert fee: $5.00 per doc. Payee: County Clerk. Personal checks and major credit cards accepted. Mail requests: SASE required.

Waller County

District Court 836 Austin St, Rm 318, Hempstead, TX 77445; 979-826-7735; fax: 979-826-7738; 8AM-N, 1-5PM (CST). ***Felony, Civil.***
www.wallercotx.com
Civil Records: Access: Mail, in person. Both court and visitors may perform in person searches. Search fee: $5.00 per name. Required to search: name, years to search, DOB, SSN. Civil cases indexed by defendant, plaintiff; index on index books to 1866, computerized in 2000. Mail turnaround time 2 days. Civil PAT goes back to 5/2000.
Criminal Records: Access: Mail, in person. Both court and visitors may perform in person searches. Search fee: $5.00 per name. Required to search: name, years to search, DOB, SSN. Criminal records on computer since 9/99, archived to early 1900s. Mail turnaround time 2 days. Criminal PAT goes back to 1/1998.
General Information: No juvenile, mental, sealed, or adoption records released. Will not fax documents. Court makes copy: $1.00 per page. Cert fee: $1.00. Payee: District Clerk. Personal checks accepted; credit cards are not. Mail requests: SASE required.

County Court 836 Austin St, Rm 217, Hempstead, TX 77445; 979-826-7711; 8AM-N, 1-5PM (CST). ***Misdemeanor, Civil, Probate.***
Civil Records: Access: Mail, in person. Both court and visitors may perform in person searches. Search fee: $5.00 per name. Required to search: name, years to search. Civil cases indexed by defendant, plaintiff. Civil records in index books; on computer back to 1994. Mail turnaround time same day if possible. Civil PAT goes back to 1994.
Criminal Records: Access: Mail, in person. Both court and visitors may perform in person searches. Search fee: $5.00 per name. Required to search: name, years to search, signed release; also helpful: DOB, SSN. Criminal index in books; on computer back to 1994. Mail turnaround time 2-3 days. Criminal PAT goes back to same as civil.
General Information: No juvenile, mental, sealed, or adoption records released. Court makes copy: $1.00 per page. Cert fee: $5.00. Payee: Waller County Clerk. No personal checks accepted for copies. No credit cards accepted. Mail requests: SASE required.

Ward County

District Court PO Box 440, Monahans, TX 79756; 432-943-2751; fax: 432-943-3810; 8AM-N-1-5PM (CST). ***Felony, Civil.***
Civil Records: Access: Mail, in person. Both court and visitors may perform in person searches. Search fee: $5.00 per name. Required to search: name, years to search. Civil cases indexed by defendant, plaintiff; index on computer since 1980, index books prior. Mail turnaround time 1-2 days.
Criminal Records: Access: Mail, in person. Both court and visitors may perform in person searches. Search fee: $5.00 per name. Required to search: name, years to search. Criminal docket on books, computerized since 1980. Mail turnaround 1-2 days.
General Information: No juvenile, mental, sealed, or adoption records released. Will fax documents $2.00 per page, if prepaid. Court makes copy: $.50 per page. Cert fee: $1.00 per page; Exemplification fee- $5.00. Payee: District Clerk. Business checks accepted. No credit cards accepted. Mail requests: SASE required.

County Court 400 S Allen, #101, c/o Ward County Clerk, Monahans, TX 79756; 432-943-3294; fax: 432-943-6054; 8AM-5PM (CST). ***Misdemeanor, Civil, Probate.***
Civil Records: Access: Mail, in person. Both court and visitors may perform in person searches. Search fee: $5.00 per name. Required to search: name, years to search. Civil cases indexed by defendant, plaintiff. Civil records in index books; computerized records go back 10 years. Note: In person requests must be accompanied by written request. Mail turnaround time 1-2 days.
Criminal Records: Access: Mail, in person. Both court and visitors may perform in person searches. Search fee: $5.00 per name. Required to search: name, years to search, DOB, signed release; also helpful: address, SSN. Criminal index in books; computerized records go back 10 years. Note: In person requests must be accompanied by a written request. Mail turnaround time 1-2 days.
General Information: No juvenile, mental, sealed, or adoption records released. Fee to fax out file $3.00 per page, prepaid. Court makes copy: $1.00 per page. Cert fee: $5.00. Payee: County Clerk. No personal checks or credit cards accepted. Mail requests: SASE required.

Washington County

District Court 100 E Main, #304, Brenham, TX 77833-3753; 979-277-6200; 8AM-5PM (CST). ***Felony, Civil.***
Civil Records: Access: Mail, in person, online. Both court and visitors may perform in person searches. Search fee: $5.00 per name. Required to search: name, years to search. Civil cases indexed by defendant, plaintiff. Civil records in index books since 1800s; on computer back to 1988. Mail turnaround time 3-5 days. Civil PAT goes back to 1988. Online case access at www.idocket.com. Dockets from 12/30/1988. One search a day is free; subscription required for more.
Criminal Records: Access: Mail, in person, online. Both court and visitors may perform in person searches. Search fee: $5.00 per name. Required to search: name, years to search; also helpful: DOB. Criminal docket on books from 1800s; on computer back to 1988. Mail turnaround time 3-5 days. Criminal PAT goes back to same as civil. Access felony cases at www.idocket.com. Dockets from 12/30/1988. One search a day is free; subscription required for more.
General Information: No juvenile, sealed, or adoption records released. Court makes copy: $.50 per page. Self serve: same. Cert fee: $1.00 per page. Payee: District Clerk. Personal checks accepted; credit cards are not.

County Court 100 E Main, #102, Brenham, TX 77833; 979-277-6200; fax: 979-277-6278; 8AM-5PM (CST). ***Misdemeanor, Civil, Probate.***
Civil Records: Access: Mail, in person, online. Both court and visitors may perform in person searches. Search fee: $5.00 per name. Required to search: name, years to search. Civil cases indexed by defendant, plaintiff. Civil records in index books from 1868; computerized back to 1985. Note: In person request must be accompanied by a written request. Mail turnaround time 1-2 days. Civil PAT goes back to 1985. PAT civil results show middle initial. Online case access at www.idocket.com; registration and password required. Civil records go back to 12/31/85; probate to 12/31/68. One free name search permitted per day, otherwise subscription required.
Criminal Records: Access: Mail, in person, online. Both court and visitors may perform in person searches. Search fee: $5.00 per name. Required to search: name, years to search; also helpful: address, DOB. Criminal docket on books from 1870; computerized back to 1992. Note: In person request must be accompanied by a written request. Mail turnaround time 1-2 days. Criminal PAT goes back to 1990. PAT results show middle initial, DOB. Access Misd. cases at www.idocket.com; registration and password required. Misdemeanor records back to 12/31/1985. One free name search permitted per day, otherwise subscription required. Online results show middle initial, DOB.
General: no juvenile, mental, sealed records released. Fee to fax out file $1.00 per page prepaid. Court makes copy: $1.00 per page. Cert fee: $5.00 per seal. Payee: County Clerk. Personal checks and . Visa/MC/AmEx accepted. Mail requests: SASE required.

Webb County

District Court PO Box 667, 1110 Victoria #203, Laredo, TX 78042-0667; 956-523-4268; fax: 956-523-5063; 8AM-5PM (CST). ***Felony, Civil.***
www.webbcountytx.gov
Add'l fax number- 956-523-5121.
Civil Records: Access: Phone, mail, fax, in person, online. Both court and visitors may perform in person searches. Search fee: $5.00 per name. Required to search: name, years to search, address; also helpful: DOB, SSN. Civil cases indexed by defendant, plaintiff; index on computer back to 11/1988, index books prior. Mail turnaround time 1 week. Civil PAT goes back to 1988. Online case access at www.idocket.com; registration and password required. Civil records (no probate) go back to 12/31/1988. One free name search permitted per day, otherwise subscription required.
Criminal Records: Access: Mail, fax, in person, online. Both court and visitors may perform in person searches. Search fee: $5.00 per name.

Required to search: name, years to search, DOB or SSN, signed release. Criminal records computerized from 11/1988, index books prior. Mail turnaround time 1 week. Criminal PAT goes back to same as civil. Online felony cases at www.idocket.com; registration and password required. Felonies go back to 12/31/1988. One free name search permitted per day, otherwise subscription required.
General Information: No juvenile, mental, sealed, or adoption records released. Will fax documents $5.00 plus add'l $1.00 per page. Court makes copy: $1.00 per page. Cert fee: $1.00 per page includes copy fee. Payee: District Clerk. Personal checks accepted; credit cards are not. Mail requests: SASE required.

County Court 1110 Victoria, #201, Laredo, TX 78040; 956-523-4266; criminal phone: 956-523-4261; civil phone: 956-523-4259; probate phone: 956-523-4257; fax: 956-523-5035; 8AM-5PM (CST). ***Misdemeanor, Civil under $5,000, Probate.*** www.webbcountytx.gov/
Court does not have public access terminal but staff will assist you with searches on their computers. Any records before 1975 can be found at the District Clerk's Office.
Civil Records: Access: Mail, in person. Both court and visitors may perform in person searches. Search fee: $5.00 per name. Required to search: name, years to search. Civil cases indexed by defendant, plaintiff; index on computer since 1988, index books prior. Mail turnaround time 2-3 days. Civil PAT goes back to 1989. PAT results show middle initial, DOB, SSN.
Criminal Records: Access: Mail, in person. Both court and visitors may perform in person searches. Search fee: $5.00 per name. Required to search: name, years to search, DOB; also helpful: address, SSN. Criminal records on computer since 1988, index books prior to 10/75. Mail turnaround time 2-3 days. Criminal PAT goes back to 1989. PAT results show middle initial, DOB.
General Information: No juvenile, mental, sealed, or adoption records released. Will fax documents $4.00 1st page; $.50 each add'l page; half that fee per page for incoming faxes. Court makes copy: $1.00 per page. Self serve: same. Cert fee: $5.00. Payee: County Clerk. Personal checks accepted; credit cards are not. Mail requests: SASE required.

Wharton County

District Court PO Drawer 391, Wharton, TX 77488; 979-532-5542; fax: 979-532-1299; 8AM-N, 1-4:30PM (CST). ***Felony, Civil.***
Civil Records: Access: Mail, fax, in person. Both court and visitors may perform in person searches. Search fee: $5.00 per name. Required to search: name, years to search. Civil cases indexed by defendant, plaintiff; index on computer since 1989, index books prior to 1848. Mail turnaround time same day. Civil PAT goes back to 1989.
Criminal Records: Access: Mail, fax, in person. Both court and visitors may perform in person searches. Search fee: $5.00 per name. Required to search: name, years to search. Criminal records on computer since 1989, index books prior to 1932. Mail turnaround time same day. Criminal PAT goes back to 1989. PAT results show middle initial, DOB. DR may also appear on terminal.
General Information: No juvenile, mental, or adoption records released. Will fax documents $5.00 plus add'l $1.00 per page. Court makes copy: $1.00 per page. Self serve: $1.00 per page. Cert fee: $2.00 per document. Payee: District Clerk of Wharton. Personal checks accepted; credit cards are not. Mail requests: SASE required.

County Court PO Box 69, Wharton, TX 77488; 979-532-2381; fax: 979-532-8426; 8AM-5PM (CST). ***Misdemeanor, Civil, Probate.***
Civil Records: Access: Mail, in person. Both court and visitors may perform in person searches. Search fee: $5.00 per name per 10 years searched. Required to search: name, years to search. Civil cases indexed by defendant, plaintiff; index on computer since 1991, index books since 1978, prior indexes in storage to 1893. Mail turnaround time 1-2 days. Civil PAT goes back to 1991. PAT results show name only.
Criminal Records: Access: Mail, in person. Both court and visitors may perform in person searches. Search fee: $5.00 per name per 10 years searched. Required to search: name, years to search, DOB, signed release; also helpful: address, SSN, copy of ID. Criminal records on computer since 1991, index books since 1978, prior indexes in storage to 1893. Mail turnaround time 1-2 days. Criminal PAT goes back to 1991.PAT results show name, DOB. Cases older than 2005 do not include the DOB, only 2005 and later.
General Information: No juvenile, mental, sealed, or adoption records released. Fee to fax out file $2.00 plus $1.00 per page. Court makes copy: $1.00 per page. Self serve: same. Cert fee: $5.00. Payee: County Clerk. Business checks accepted; personal checks accepted only if local resident. No credit cards accepted. Mail requests: SASE required.

Wheeler County

District Court PO Box 528, Wheeler, TX 79096; 806-826-5931; fax: 806-826-5503; 8AM-5PM (CST). ***Felony, Civil.***
Civil Records: Access: Phone, mail, in person. Both court and visitors may perform in person searches. Search fee: $5.00 per name. Required to search: name, years to search. Civil cases indexed by defendant, plaintiff. Civil index in books. Mail turnaround time 2-3 days.
Criminal Records: Access: Phone, mail, in person. Both court and visitors may perform in person searches. Search fee: $5.00 per name. Required to search: name, years to search. Criminal index in books. Mail turnaround time 2-3 days.
General Information: No juvenile, mental, sealed, or adoption records released. Will fax documents $2.00 per page. Court makes copy: $1.00 per page. Self serve: same. Cert fee: $1.00. Payee: District Clerk. Personal checks accepted. All major credit cards accepted.

County Court PO Box 465, 401 Main St, Wheeler, TX 79096; 806-826-5544; fax: 806-826-3282; 8AM-5PM ***Misdemeanor, Civil, Probate.***
Civil Records: Access: Mail, in person. Both court and visitors may perform in person searches. Search fee: $10.00 per name. Required to search: name, years to search. Civil cases indexed by defendant, plaintiff. Civil index in docket books from 1800s. Mail turnaround time 1 day.
Criminal Records: Access: Mail, in person. Both court and visitors may perform in person searches. Search fee: $10.00 per name. Required to search: name, years to search; also helpful: DOB, SSN. Criminal index in books. Mail turnaround time 1 day.
General Information: No juvenile, mental, sealed, or adoption records released. Will fax documents $1.00 per page. Court makes copy: $1.00 per page. Cert fee: $5.00 per doc. Payee: Wheeler County Clerk. Business checks accepted. No credit cards accepted. Mail requests: SASE required.

Wichita County

District Court 900 7th St, #303, Wichita Falls, TX 76301; criminal phone: 940-766-8187; civil phone: 940-766-8190; 8AM-5PM (CST). ***Felony, Civil.*** www.co.wichita.tx.us/district_clerk.htm
Civil Records: Access: Phone, mail, in person. Both court and visitors may perform in person searches. Search fee: $5.00 per name. Required to search: name, years to search. Civil cases indexed by defendant, plaintiff; index on computer since 1984, index books prior. Note: Phone searches must be prepaid. Mail turnaround time 2-3 days. Civil PAT goes back to 1800s.
Criminal Records: Access: Phone, mail, in person. Both court and visitors may perform in person searches. Search fee: $5.00 per name. Required to search: name, years to search. Criminal records on computer since 1984, index books before, some older record dockets are computerized. Note: Phone searches must be prepaid. Mail turnaround time 2-3 days. Criminal PAT goes back to same as civil.
General Information: No juvenile, mental, sealed, or adoption records released. Will not fax documents. Court makes copy: $1.00 per page. Self serve: same. Cert fee: $1.00. Payee: District Clerk. Personal checks accepted; credit cards are not. Mail requests: SASE required.

County Court PO Box 1679, Wichita Falls, TX 76307; criminal phone: 940-766-8173; probate phone: 940-766-8172; fax: 940-716-8554; 8AM-5PM (CST). ***Misdemeanor, Probate.***
Criminal Records: Access: Phone, mail, in person. Both court and visitors may perform in person searches. Search fee: $10.00 per name searched. Required to search: name, years to search; also helpful: DOB, SSN. Criminal records on computer or printed index from 1980 to present. Mail turnaround time 1 week or less. Public use terminal has crim records back to 1980. PAT results show middle initial, DOB. Terminal results include SSN.
General Information: No juvenile, mental, sealed, or adoption records released. Mental can be released with an order from the judge. Will fax to toll-free numbers only. Court makes copy: $1.00 per page. Self serve: same. Cert fee: $5.00 per document. Payee: Wichita County Clerk. No personal checks or credit cards accepted. Mail requests: SASE required.

Wilbarger County

District Court 1700 Wilbarger, Rm 33, Vernon, TX 76384; 940-553-3411; criminal fax: 940-553-2316; civil fax: same; 8AM-5PM (CST). ***Felony, Civil.***
Civil Records: Access: Mail, in person. Both court and visitors may perform in person searches. Search fee: $5.00 per name. Required to search: name, years to search. Civil cases indexed by defendant, plaintiff. Civil records go back to 1800s; computerized records go back 4 years. Mail turnaround time 2-3 days.
Criminal Records: Access: Mail, in person. Both court and visitors may perform in person searches. Search fee: $5.00 per name. Required to search: name, years to search, DOB. Criminal records go back to 1800s; computerized records go back 4 years. Mail turnaround time 2-3 days.
General Information: No juvenile, mental, sealed, or adoption records released. Will return results by fax or phone if an 800 number is provided. Will fax documents to toll-free number. Court makes copy: $1.00 per page. Self serve: same. Cert fee: $5.00 per document. Payee: District Clerk. Business checks accepted. No credit cards accepted. Mail requests: SASE required.

County Court 1700 Wilbarger, Rm 15, Vernon, TX 76384; 940-552-5486; fax: 940-553-1202; 8AM-5PM (CST). ***Misdemeanor, Civil, Probate.*** Probate is a separate index at this same address.
Civil Records: Access: Mail, in person. Both court and visitors may perform in person searches. Search fee: $5.00 per 7 year search. Required to search: name, years to search. Civil cases indexed by Plaintiff. Civil records go back to 1887; no computerized records. Mail turnaround time same day.
Criminal Records: Access: Mail, in person. Both court and visitors may perform in person searches. Search fee: $5.00 per 7 year search. Required to search: name, years to search; also helpful: address, DOB, SSN. Criminal records go back to 1887; computerized records go back to 1999. Mail turnaround time same day.
General Information: No juvenile, mental, sealed, or adoption records released. Fee to fax out file $1.00 per page. Court makes copy: $1.00 per page. Self serve: same. Cert fee: $5.00 per document. Payee: County Clerk. Personal checks accepted; credit cards are not.

Willacy County

District Court County Courthouse, Raymondville, TX 78580; 956-689-2532; fax: 956-689-5713; 8AM-5PM (CST). ***Felony, Civil.***
Civil Records: Access: Mail, in person, phone. Both court and visitors may perform in person searches. Search fee: $5.00 per name. Required to search: name, years to search. Civil cases indexed by defendant, plaintiff. Civil index in books. Mail turnaround time 2-3 days.
Criminal Records: Access: Mail, in person. Both court and visitors may perform in person searches. Search fee: $5.00 per name. Required to search: name, years to search. Criminal index in books. Mail turnaround time 2-3 days.
General Information: No juvenile, mental, sealed, or adoption records released. Will fax documents $2.00

per page. Court makes copy: $1.00 per page. Self serve: same. No certification fee. Payee: District Clerk. Personal checks accepted; credit cards are not. Mail requests: SASE required.

County Court 540 W Main, Raymondville, TX 78580; 956-689-2710; fax: 956-689-9849; 8AM-N, 1-5PM (CST). ***Misdemeanor, Civil, Probate.***

Civil Records: Access: Mail, in person. Both court and visitors may perform in person searches. Search fee: $10.00 per name, ten year search only. Required to search: name, years to search; also helpful: address. Civil cases indexed by defendant, plaintiff. Civil records go back to 1920's. Mail turnaround time 2-3 days.

Criminal Records: Access: Mail, in person. Both court and visitors may perform in person searches. Search fee: $10.00 per name. Required to search: name, years to search; also helpful: address, DOB, SSN. Criminal records go back to 1921, computerized since 1990. Mail turnaround time 2-3 days.

General Information: No juvenile, mental, sealed, or adoption records released. Will not fax documents. Court makes copy: $1.00 per page. Self serve: same. Cert fee: $5.00. Payee: County Clerk. No personal checks or credit cards accepted. Mail requests: SASE required.

Williamson County

District Court PO Box 24, 405 Martin Luther King, Georgetown, TX 78627; 512-943-1212; fax: 512-943-1222; 8AM-5PM (CST). ***Felony, Civil.*** www.williamson-county.org

Civil Records: Access: Mail, in person. Both court and visitors may perform in person searches. Search fee: $5.00 per name. Required to search: name, years to search. Civil cases indexed by defendant, plaintiff; index on computer since 1989, index books prior. Mail turnaround time 2-3 days. Civil PAT goes back to 1989.

Criminal Records: Access: Mail, in person. Both court and visitors may perform in person searches. Search fee: $5.00 per name. Required to search: name, years to search, DOB, signed release; also helpful: SSN. Criminal records on computer since 1989, index books prior. Mail turnaround time 2-3 days. Criminal PAT goes back to same as civil. Sheriff bond and inmate data is at http://judicialsearch.wilco.org.

General Information: No juvenile, mental, sealed, or adoption records released. Will not fax documents. Court makes copy: $1.00 1st page; $.25 each add'l. Cert fee: Cert fee included in copy fee. Payee: District Clerk. Personal checks accepted; credit cards are not. Mail requests: SASE required.

County Court 405 MLK St, Box 14, Georgetown, TX 78626; criminal phone: 512-943-1150; civil phone: 512-943-1140; probate phone: 512-943-1140; criminal fax: 512-943-1445; civil fax: 512-943-1154; 8AM-5PM (CST). ***Misdemeanor, Civil, Probate.*** www.wilcogov.org/

Separate search fees for civil and criminal.

Civil Records: Access: Mail, in person, online. Both court and visitors may perform in person searches. Search fee: $10.00 per name. Required to search: name, years to search. Civil cases indexed by defendant, plaintiff; index on computer since 1985, index books since 1848.GA. Mail turnaround time 2 days. Civil PAT goes back to 1985. PAT civil results show middle initial. Access to limited civil records is free at http://judicialsearch.wilco.org. Also various court records available for free at https://deed.wilco.org/. JP Court #1 records are free at www.edoctecinc.com but there may be a 2 week to 1 month lag time.

Criminal Records: Access: Mail, in person, online. Both court and visitors may perform in person searches. Search fee: $10.00 per name. Required to search: name, years to search; also helpful: DOB, SSN. Criminal records on computer since 1983. Overall records go back to 1800. Mail turnaround time 2 days. Criminal PAT goes back to 1983. PAT criminal results show middle initial. Access to a criminal case records from 1983 is free at http://judicialsearch.wilco.org. Sheriff bond and inmate data is also available. Also various court records available for free at https://deed.wilco.org/. Results include DOB. Online results show middle initial.

General Information: No juvenile, mental, sealed, or adoption records released. Fee to fax out file $1.00 per page to local numbers only. Court makes copy: $1.00 per page. Cert fee: $5.00 per case. Payee: County Clerk. Personal checks and credit cards accepted. Mail requests: SASE required.

Wilson County

District Court PO Box 812, 1420 3rd St 2nd Fl, Floresville, TX 78114; 830-393-7322; fax: 830-393-7319; 8AM-N, 1-5PM (CST). ***Felony, Civil.***

Request must be in writing if court personnel are to do search.

Civil Records: Access: Fax, mail, in person. Both court and visitors may perform in person searches. Search fee: $5.00 per name. Required to search: name, years to search. Civil cases indexed by Defendant, Plaintiff. Civil records go back to 1960. Mail turnaround time 2-3 days.

Criminal Records: Access: Fax, mail, in person. Both court and visitors may perform in person searches. Search fee: $5.00 per name. Required to search: name, years to search; also helpful: DOB. Criminal records go back to 1975. Mail turnaround time 2 days.

General Information: No juvenile, mental, sealed, or adoption records released. Will fax documents to local or toll free line. Court makes copy: $.50 per page. Self serve: same. Cert fee: $1.00. Payee: District Clerk. Personal checks accepted w/ proper ID. No credit cards accepted. Mail requests: SASE required.

County Court PO Box 27, Floresville, TX 78114; 830-393-7308; fax: 830-393-7334; 8AM-5PM (CST). ***Misdemeanor, Civil, Probate.***

Civil Records: Access: Phone, mail, fax, in person. Both court and visitors may perform in person searches. No search fee. Required to search: name, years to search. Civil cases indexed by defendant, plaintiff. Civil records available from 1862. Mail turnaround time same day.

Criminal Records: Access: Phone, mail, fax, in person. Both court and visitors may perform in person searches. No search fee. Required to search: name, years to search, DOB. Criminal records stored since 1917, computerized since 11/2002. Mail turnaround time same day.

General Information: Will not fax documents. Court makes copy: $1.00 per page. Self serve: same. Cert fee: $5.00. Payee: Eva S Martinez, County Clerk. Personal checks accepted; credit cards are not.

Winkler County

District Court PO Box 1065, Kermit, TX 79745; 432-586-3359; 8AM-5PM (CST). ***Felony, Civil.***

Civil Records: Access: Phone, mail, in person. Both court and visitors may perform in person searches. Search fee: $5.00 per name. Required to search: name, years to search. Civil cases indexed by defendant, plaintiff; index on computer since 1991 (child-support only), index books prior. Mail turnaround time 3-4 days.

Criminal Records: Access: Mail, in person. Both court and visitors may perform in person searches. Search fee: $5.00 per name. Required to search: name, years to search, DOB, SSN. Criminal records on computer since 1991, index books prior. Mail turnaround time 3-4 days.

General Information: No juvenile, mental, sealed, or adoption records released. Will not fax documents. Court makes copy: $1.00 per page. No certification fee. Payee: District Clerk. Personal checks accepted; credit cards are not. Mail requests: SASE required.

County Court PO Box 1007, 100 E Winkler St, Kermit, TX 79745; 432-586-3401; 8AM-5PM (CST). ***Misdemeanor, Civil, Probate.***

Civil Records: Access: Mail, in person. Visitors must perform in person searches themselves. Search fee: $5.00 per name. Required to search: name, years to search. Civil cases indexed by defendant, plaintiff. All civil records in index books. Mail turnaround time 2-3 days.

Criminal Records: Access: Mail, in person. Visitors must perform in person searches themselves. Search fee: $5.00 per name. Required to search: name, years to search; also helpful: address, DOB, SSN. Criminal records computerized from 1991; prior in index books. Mail turnaround time 2-3 days.

General Information: No juvenile, mental, sealed, or adoption records released. Will not fax documents. Court makes copy: $1.00 per page. Cert fee: $5.00. Payee: County Clerk. Business checks accepted. No credit cards accepted. Mail requests: SASE required.

Wise County

District Court PO Box 308, Decatur, TX 76234; 940-627-5535; fax: 940-627-0705; 8AM-5PM (CST). ***Felony, Civil.***

Civil Records: Access: Mail, in person. Both court and visitors may perform in person searches. Search fee: $5.00 per name. Required to search: name, years to search. Civil cases indexed by defendant, plaintiff. Civil records in index books since 1895, computerized since 1999. Mail turnaround time same day. Civil PAT goes back to 1999. PAT civil results show middle initial.

Criminal Records: Access: Mail, in person. Both court and visitors may perform in person searches. Search fee: $5.00 per name. Required to search: name, years to search; also helpful-DOB, SSN. Criminal records in docket books to 1896, computerized since 1999. Mail turnaround time same day. Criminal PAT goes back to 1999. PAT criminal results show middle initial.

General Information: No juvenile, mental, sealed, or adoption records released. Will fax documents. Court makes copy: $1.00 per page. Cert fee: exemplification- $2.00. Payee: Wise County District Clerk. Personal checks accepted; credit cards are not. Mail requests: SASE required.

County Court at Law PO Box 359, Decatur, TX 76234; 940-627-3351; fax: 940-627-3790; 8AM-5PM (CST). ***Misdemeanor, Civil, Probate.***

Civil Records: Access: Mail, in person. Both court and visitors may perform in person searches. Search fee: $10.00 per name. Required to search: name, years to search. Civil cases indexed by defendant, plaintiff. Civil records in index books since sovereignty; on computer back to 1998. Mail turnaround time 1 day. Civil PAT goes back to 1998. PAT results show name only.

Criminal Records: Access: Mail, in person. Both court and visitors may perform in person searches. Search fee: $10.00 per name. Required to search: name, years to search; also helpful: DOB, SSN. Criminal docket on books from sovereignty; on computer back to 1997. Mail turnaround time 1 day. Criminal PAT goes back to 1997. PAT results show name only.

General Information: No mental health or sealed records released. Will fax documents for fee. Court makes copy: $1.00 per page. Cert fee: $5.00. Payee: Wise County Clerk. Personal checks accepted; credit cards are not. Mail requests: SASE required.

Wood County

District Court PO Box 1707, Quitman, TX 75783; 903-763-2361; fax: 903-763-1511; 8AM-5PM ***Felony, Civil.*** http://judicial.co.wood.tx.us

Civil Records: Access: Mail, fax, in person, online. Both court and visitors may perform in person searches. Search fee: $5.00 per name. Required to search: name, years to search. Civil cases indexed by defendant, plaintiff; index on computer since 1990, microfilm since 1981, index books since 1890. Mail turnaround time 2-3 days. Civil PAT goes back to 1980. PAT results show name only. Search civil case index at http://judicial.co.wood.tx.us/CivilSearch/civfrmd.asp.

Criminal Records: Access: Mail, fax, in person, online. Both court and visitors may perform in person searches. Search fee: $5.00 per name. Required to search: name, years to search; also helpful: DOB, SSN. Criminal records on computer since 1990, microfilm since 1981, index books since 1890. Mail turnaround time 2-3 days. Criminal PAT goes back to same as civil. Results include name, charge, DOB, SSN. Search criminal case index at http://judicial.co.wood.tx.us/CrimSearch/crimfrmd.asp. Online results show middle initial, DOB. Terminal results include SSN.

General Information: No juvenile, mental, sealed, or adoption records released. Will not fax documents. Court makes copy: $1.00 per page. Cert fee: $1.00 per document. Payee: District Clerk. Personal checks accepted; credit cards are not. Mail requests: SASE required.

County Court PO Box 1796, Quitman, TX 75783; 903-763-2711; fax: 903-763-5641; 8AM-5PM (CST). ***Misdemeanor, Civil, Probate.***
www.co.wood.tx.us/ips/cms
Probate is a separate index at this same address.
Civil Records: Access: Mail, in person, online. Both court and visitors may perform in person searches. Search fee: $5.00 per name. Required to search: name, years to search. Civil cases indexed by defendant, plaintiff; index on computer since 1980; index books since early 1900s. Mail turnaround time same day. Civil PAT goes back to 1980. PAT results show name only. Search all courts free at http://judicial.co.wood.tx.us/.
Criminal Records: Access: Mail, in person, online. Both court and visitors may perform in person searches. Search fee: $5.00 per name. Required to search: name, years to search; also helpful DOB, SSN, signed release, DL#. Criminal records computerized from 1986; index books from 1965, archived to 1900. Mail turnaround time same day. Criminal PAT goes back to same as civil.PAT results show name, DOB. Search all courts and Sheriff bond and inmate lists free at http://judicial.co.wood.tx.us/. Online results show name, DOB.
General Information: No mental or sealed records released. Will fax documents $2.00 per page. Court makes copy: $1.00 per page. Cert fee: $5.00 per document. Payee: Wood County Clerk. Personal checks accepted, if proper ID. No credit cards accepted. Mail requests: SASE required.

Yoakum County

District Court PO Box 899, Plains, TX 79355; 806-456-7491 x297; criminal fax: 806-456-8767; civil fax: same; 8AM-5PM (CST). ***Felony, Civil.***
www.co.yoakum.tx.us/ips/cms/districtcourt/
Civil Records: Access: Fax, mail, in person. Both court and visitors may perform in person searches. Search fee: $5.00 per name. Required to search: name, years to search. Civil cases indexed by defendant, plaintiff; index on computer since 1980, index books since 1907. Mail turnaround time same day. Civil PAT goes back to 1980. PAT results show name only. Results include case type.
Criminal Records: Access: Fax, mail, in person. Both court and visitors may perform in person searches. Search fee: $5.00 per name. Required to search: name, years to search, DOB; also helpful: SSN. Criminal records on computer since 1980, index books since 1910. Mail turnaround time same day. Criminal PAT goes back to same as civil. PAT results show name only. Results include offense.
General Information: No juvenile, mental, sealed, or adoption records released. Will not fax documents. Court makes copy: $1.00 1st page, $.25 each add'l. Cert fee: $1.00 per page. Payee: District Clerk. Personal checks and credit cards accepted. Mail requests: SASE required.

County Court PO Box 309, Cowboy Way and Avenue G, Plains, TX 79355; 806-456-7491; fax: 806-456-2258; 8AM-5PM (CST). ***Misdemeanor, Civil, Probate.***
Civil Records: Access: Phone, mail, in person. Both court and visitors may perform in person searches. Search fee: $5.00 per name. Required to search: name, years to search; also helpful: address. Civil cases indexed by defendant, plaintiff. Civil records in minutes books and microfilm since 9/1986; on computer back to 1/1986. Mail turnaround time same day. Civil PAT goes back to 9/1986. PAT results show name only.
Criminal Records: Access: Mail, in person. Both court and visitors may perform in person searches. Search fee: $5.00 per name. Required to search: name, years to search, DOB; also helpful: address, SSN. Criminal minutes books and microfilm since 9/1986; on computer back to 1/1986. Mail turnaround time same day. Criminal PAT goes back to same as civil. PAT results show name only.
General Information: No juvenile or mental records released. Will fax documents $2.00 per fax plus $1.00 per page, prepaid. Court makes copy: $1.00 per page. Cert fee: $5.00 per document. Payee: County Clerk, Yoakum County. Personal checks and major credit cards accepted.

Young County

District Court 516 4th St, Rm 201, Courthouse, Graham, TX 76450; 940-549-0029; fax: 940-549-4874; 8:30AM-N, 1-5PM (CST). ***Felony, Civil.***
www.co.young.tx.us/ips/cms/index.html
Civil Records: Access: Mail, in person, online. Both court and visitors may perform in person searches. Search fee: $5.00 per name. Required to search: name, years to search. Civil cases indexed by defendant, plaintiff; index on computer since 1989, index books prior. Note: Search fee must be prepaid before fax access is allowed. Mail turnaround time 1-2 days. Civil PAT goes back to 1989. Access civil cases except probate at www.idocket.com; registration and password required. A fee service; only one free name search per day. Civil cases go back to 3/1/1998.
Criminal Records: Access: Mail, in person, online. Both court and visitors may perform in person searches. Search fee: $5.00 per name. Required to search: name, years to search; also helpful: DOB, SSN. Criminal records on computer since 1989, index books prior. Mail turnaround time 1-2 days. Criminal PAT goes back to 1989. Access felony cases at www.idocket.com; registration and password required. A fee service; only one free name search per day. Records go back to 3/1/1998.
General Information: No juvenile, mental, sealed, or adoption records released. No fee to fax documents. Court makes copy: $1.00 first page, $.50 each add'l. Cert fee: $1.00 per page. Payee: District Clerk. Personal checks and major credit cards accepted. Mail requests: SASE required.

County Court 516 4th St, Rm 104, Graham, TX 76450; 940-549-8432; fax: 940-521-0305; 8:30AM-N, 1-5PM ***Misdemeanor, Civil, Probate.***
Civil Records: Access: Mail, in person. Both court and visitors may perform in person searches. Search fee: $5.00 per name. Required to search: name, years to search. Civil cases indexed by defendant, plaintiff; index on computer since 1991, index books prior to 1800s. Mail turnaround time same day. Civil PAT goes back to 1991. PAT results show name only.
Criminal Records: Access: Mail, in person. Both court and visitors may perform in person searches. Search fee: $5.00 per name. Required to search: name, years to search. Criminal records on computer since 1991, index books prior to 1800s. Mail turnaround time same day. Criminal PAT goes back to same as civil; results show name only.
General Information: No juvenile, mental, sealed, or adoption records released. Fee to fax out file $1.00 per page. Court makes copy: $1.00 per page. Self serve: same. Cert fee: $5.00. Payee: County Clerk. Personal checks accepted; credit cards are not.

Zapata County

District Court PO Box 788, Clerk's Office, Zapata, TX 78076; 956-765-9930; fax: 956-765-9931; 8AM-N, 1-5PM (CST). ***Felony, Civil.***
Civil Records: Access: Mail, in person. Both court and visitors may perform in person searches. Search fee: $5.00 per name. Required to search: name, years to search. Civil cases indexed by plaintiff. Civil index in books. Mail turnaround time 1-3 days. Civil PAT goes back to 15 years.
Criminal Records: Access: Mail, in person. Both court and visitors may perform in person searches. Search fee: $5.00 per name. Required to search: name, years to search. Criminal index in books. Mail turnaround time 1-3 days. Criminal PAT goes back to 15 years.
General Information: No juvenile, mental, sealed, or adoption records released. Will not fax documents. Court makes copy: $1.00 per page. Self serve: same. Cert fee: $5.00 per document. Payee: District Clerk/County Clerk. Personal checks accepted; credit cards are not. Mail requests: SASE required.

County Court PO Box 789, Zapata, TX 78076; 956-765-9915; fax: 956-765-9933; 8AM-N, 1-5PM (CST). ***Misdemeanor, Civil, Probate.***
Probate fax is same as main fax number.
Civil Records: Access: Mail, in person. Both court and visitors may perform in person searches. Search fee: $5.00 per name. Required to search: name, years to search. Civil cases indexed by plaintiff only. Civil records in index books since 1800s, computerized records back to 1990. Mail turnaround time 1-2 days.
Criminal Records: Access: Mail, in person. Both court and visitors may perform in person searches. Search fee: $5.00 per name. Required to search: name, years to search, DOB, SSN. Criminal docket on books from 1800s, computerized records back to 1930. Mail turnaround time 1-2 days.
General Information: No juvenile, mental, sealed, or adoption records released. Will fax documents $5.00 for 1st page, $1.00 each add'l. Court makes copy: $1.00 per page. Self serve: same. Cert fee: $5.00 per doc. Payee: County Clerk. Personal checks accepted; credit cards are not.

Zavala County

District Court PO Box 704, Crystal City, TX 78839; 830-374-3456; fax: 830-374-2632; 8AM-N, 1-5PM (CST). ***Felony, Civil.***
Civil Records: Access: Phone, mail, in person. Both court and visitors may perform in person searches. Search fee: $10.00 per name. Required to search: name, years to search. Civil cases indexed by defendant, plaintiff. Civil records in index books from 1900s. Mail turnaround time 1-2 days.
Criminal Records: Access: Phone, mail, in person. Both court and visitors may perform in person searches. Search fee: $10.00 per name. Required to search: name, years to search. Criminal docket on books from 1900s. Mail turnaround time 1-2 days.
General Information: No juvenile, mental, sealed, or adoption records released. Will fax back documents for no fee. Court makes copy: $1.00 per page. Self serve: same. No certification fee. Payee: Zavala District Clerk. Personal checks accepted; credit cards are not. Mail requests: SASE required.

County Court Zavala County Courthouse, 200 E Uvalde, Crystal City, TX 78839; 830-374-2331; probate phone: same; fax: 830-374-5955; 8AM-5PM (CST). ***Misdemeanor, Civil, Probate.***
Probate fax is same as main fax number.
Civil Records: Access: Mail, in person. Both court and visitors may perform in person searches. Search fee: $10.00 per name. Required to search: name, years to search. Civil cases indexed by defendant, plaintiff. Civil records in index books from 1880s. Mail turnaround time 1-2 days. Civil PAT goes back to 1988. PAT results show name only.
Criminal Records: Access: Mail, in person. Both court and visitors may perform in person searches. Search fee: $10.00 per name. Required to search: name, years to search, DOB. Criminal docket on books from 1880s. Mail turnaround time 1-2 days. Criminal PAT goes back to 1988.PAT results show name, DOB.
General Information: No juvenile, mental, sealed, or adoption records released. Will fax documents $8.00 1st page, $2.00 ea add'l. Court makes copy: $1.00 per page. Self serve: same. Cert fee: $1.00 per doc. Payee: Zavala County Clerk. Personal checks accepted; credit cards are not. Mail requests: SASE required.

Texas Recording Offices

ORGANIZATION: 254 counties, 254 recording offices. The recording officer is the County Clerk. 252 Texas counties are in the Central Time Zone (CST) Two - El Paso and Hudspeth - are in the Mountain Time Zone (MST).

REAL ESTATE RECORDS: About one-half of Texas' counties will perform real estate searches. Real estate copy fee is usually $1.00 per page. Certification fee is usually $5.00 per document or per seal. Each county has an "Appraisal District" which is responsible for collecting taxes.

UCC RECORDS: Financing statements are filed at the state level except for real estate related collateral which are filed with the County Clerk. Most Texas recording offices will perform UCC searches. UCC search fee is usually $10.00 to $15.00 per debtor name using the approved UCC-11 request form, but can be $31.00 for using a non-Texas form. UCC copy fee is usually $1.00-$2.00 per page.

TAX LIEN RECORDS: Federal tax liens on personal property of businesses are filed with the Secretary of State. Other federal and all state tax liens are filed with the County Clerk. Most counties will perform tax lien searches. Tax lien search fees and copy fees can vary; tax lien records are usually provided as part of a UCC search.

OTHER LIENS: Mechanics, judgment, hospital, labor, lis pendens.

ONLINE ACCESS: A search at the State Archives' TRAIL website at www.tsl.state.tx.us/trail/ lets you locate information from over 180 Texas state agency web servers. A good place to link to county appraisal districts is http://appraisaldistrict.net/ where you can click through to many county appraisers, many with free searching.

Texas has a statewide UCC system that is accessible with subscription and registration.

Numerous counties offer online access to assessor and recorded document data via vendors summarized below.

www.txcountydata.com - Assessor and property information records for many Texas counties on this TX site are available for no fee. At this site click on "County Search" then use the pull down menu in the county field to select the county to search. Generally, you can search any county account, owner name, address, or property ID number. A search allows you to access owner address, property address, legal description, taxing entities, exemptions, deed, account number, abstract/subdivision, neighborhood, valuation info, and more.

www.taxnetusa.com - TaxNetUSA offers appraisal district and property information records for a large number of Texas counties. They offer a free search as well as online subscriptions services using a sliding fee scale, or you may purchase bulk data as downloads. Visit the website or call 877-652-2707 for info. To search free at the TaxNetUSA site, click on the "Coverage Area" and select a county.

www.titlex.com - This site offers recording office records in county grantor/grantee indices - including real estate, deeds, liens, judgments records and more - free for many Texas counties.

www.texaslandrecords.com - The site offers free land index searching at a group of 26 or more Texas counties, plus a deeper real estate subscription service for those counties which require fees, registration, and password.

Anderson County

County Clerk, 500 N Church St, Rm 10, Palestine, TX 75801. 903-723-7432, R/E recording phone-903-723-7431, UCC recording phone-903-723-7484; fax-903-723-4625; 8AM-5PM (CST)

Index: All in one. Records indexed on a public use terminal back to 1982. Office personnel or visitors may perform searches. General index search fee $5.00 per name. Office will search real estate records for years of 1985 to present. Office will search UCC records prior to 7/2001 and current fixture (land) files. Will search tax liens. UCC search per debtor name- $10.00. Copy fee $1.00 per page. Cert fee- $5.00 per doc plus copy fee. Payee- Anderson County Clerk. Bulk data available for purchase, contact Casey Brown. **Online access to Real Estate, Grantor/Grantee, Deed, Judgment, Lien records:** Access recorded records free at www.titlex.com; select Anderson county. Records range is 6/1972 to 12/2003. **Other phones:** Treasurer- 903-723-7408; Elections- 903-723-7438; Vital Records- 903-723-7432. **Property tax/Assessing**- PO Box 1990, 703 N Malard, Ste 104, Palestine, TX 75801; 903-723-7438, assessor fax- 903-723-7801. (Appraiser/Auditor- 903-723-2949) hours- 8AM-4:45PM **Online**- make poperty tax inquiries at www.taxnetusa.com/texas/ and www.txcountydata.com/county.asp?County=001.

Andrews County

County Clerk, PO Box 727, Andrews, TX 79714. Recording, R/E phone-432-524-1426; fax-432-524-1464; 8AM-5PM. www.co.andrews.tx.us

Index: All in one. Only the public may search. Copy fee $1.00 per page. Cert fee- $5.00 per doc plus copy fee. Payee- Andrews County Clerk. **Other phones:** Treasurer- 432-524-1410; Elections- 432-524-1426; Vital Records- 432-524-1426. **Property tax/Assessing**- PO Box 18, 201 N Main, Rm 101, Andrews, TX 79714; 432-524-1409, assessor fax-432-524-1450. (Appraiser/Auditor- 432-523-9111);

Angelina County

County Clerk, PO Box 908, Lufkin, TX 75902-0908. 936-634-8339; fax-936-634-8460; 8AM-4:30PM (CST) www.angelinacounty.net

Index: All in one. Records indexed on a public use terminal back to 1962. Office will perform a UCC search but public must search other records themselves. General index search fee $5.00 per name. Copy fee $1.00 per page. Cert fee- $5.00 per cert plus copy fee. Payee- Angelina County Clerk. Bulk data available for purchase, contact Mr. Shanklin. **Online access to Real Estate, Grantor/Grantee, Deed, Lien, Vital Statistic, Judgment records:** Search grantor/grantee index free at www.texaslandrecords.com. Registration and fees required for full data. Search probate records and judgment records back to 1996 at http://idocket.com/countycourt.htm. Also see note at beginning of section for add'l property data. **Other phones:** Treasurer- 936-634-7312; Elections- 936-634-8376; Vital Records- 936-634-8339. **Property tax/Assessing**- 606 E Lufkin Ave, PO Box 1344, Lufkin, TX 75902; 936-634-8376, assessor fax- 936-634-2690. (Appraiser/Auditor- 936-634-8456) A public access terminal is available. www.angelinacounty.net/tax/ **Online access**- Access appraisal district data free at www.angelinacad.org/Appraisal/PublicAccess/. Also, access assessment records at www.txcountydata.com.

Aransas County

County Clerk, 301 N Live Oak, Rockport, TX 78382. 361-790-0122; fax-361-790-0119; 8AM-4:30PM (CST) www.aransascounty.org

Index: Pre-10/1984 has separate indices to search. Records indexed on a public use terminal back to 1993. Office will perform a UCC search but public must search other records themselves. Search fee- $10.00 per name per search. Copy fee $1.00 per page. Cert fee- $5.00 per cert plus copy fee. Payee- Aransas County Clerk. Bulk data of official records available for purchase on CD; contact County Clerk. **Other phones:** Treasurer- 361-790-0132; Elections- 361-729-7431; Vital Records- 361-790-0122. **Property tax/Assessing**- 319 N Church St, Rockport, TX 78382; 361-790-0160, assessor fax- 361-729-4373. (Appraiser/Auditor- 361-729-9733) **Online access**- Access dated appraiser and property tax data at www.aransascad.org/Appraisal/PublicAccess/. Also, property tax inquiries can be made via www.txcountydata.com/selectCounty.asp. Other online access through private companies.

Archer County

County Clerk, PO Box 427, Archer City, TX 76351. 940-574-4302; fax-940-574-2876; 8:30AM-4:30PM (CST) www.co.archer.tx.us/ips/cms

Index: All in one. Record index not computerized. Only the public may search. Copy fee $1.00 per page. Cert fee- $5.00 per cert plus copy fee. Payee- Archer County Clerk. Hard copies of bulk data are available for purchase, contact the County Clerk. **Other phones:** Treasurer- 940-574-4822; Elections- 940-574-4302; Vital Records- 940-574-4302. **Property tax/Assessing**- PO Box 700, Archer City, TX 76351;

940-574-4531, assessor fax- 940-574-4625. (Appraiser/Auditor- 940-574-2172) hours- 8:30AM-5PM **Online access**- Access property records free at www.taxnetusa.com/texas/. For full info registration and password required; fee is $99 per year.

Armstrong County

County Clerk, PO Box 309, Claude, TX 79019-0309. Recording, R/E phone-806-226-2081; fax-806-226-5301; 8AM-N, 1-5PM (CST)
Index: Separate indices to search include Probate, Civil, and Criminal. Records indexed on a public use terminal back to 1993. Office will perform a UCC search but public must search other records themselves. Copy fee $1.00 per page. Cert fee- $5.00 per cert includes copy fee. Payee- Armstrong County Clerk. **Other phones:** Treasurer- 806-226-3651; Elections- 806-226-2081; Vital Records- 806-226-2081. **Property tax/Assessing**- PO Box 835, Claude, TX 79019; 806-226-4481, assessor fax- 806-226-2654. (Appraiser/Auditor- 806-226-4481);

Atascosa County

County Clerk, #1 Courthouse Circle, #102, Jourdanton, TX 78026. Recording, R/E phone-830-767-2511; fax-830-769-1021; 8AM-4:30PM (CST)
Index: Various indexes for early pre-1995 records. Records indexed on a public use terminal back to 1995. Only the public may search (court will only search Fed and State Tax Liens for $5.00). Tax lien search fee-. Copy fee $1.00 per page. Cert fee- $5.00 per cert plus copy fee. Payee- Atascosa County Clerk. **Online access to Real Estate, Grantor/Grantee, Judgment, Deed, Lien records:** Access recording records free at www.titlex.com; select Atascosa County. Also, see note at beginning of section. **Other phones:** Treasurer- 830-769-3024; Elections- 830-769-1472; Vital Records- 830-767-2511. **Property tax/Assessing**- 1001 Oak St, Jourdanton, TX 78026; 830-769-3142, assessor fax- 830-769-2115. (Appraiser/Auditor- 830-742-3591) hours- 9AM-5PM **Online access**- Access appraisal data free at www.txcountydata.com/county.asp?County=007.

Austin County

County Clerk, 1 E Main, Bellville, TX 77418-1551. Recording, R/E phone-979-865-5911; fax-979-865-0336; 8AM-5PM (CST)
Index: All in one. Records indexed on a public use terminal back to 1995. Office personnel or visitors may perform searches. Search fee $10.00 per name. Office will not search real estate records. Copy fee $1.00 per page. Cert fee- $5.00 per cert plus copy fee. Payee- Austin County Clerk. **Online access to Real Estate, Grantor/Grantee, Deed, Judgment, Lien records:** Access recording records free at www.titlex.com; select Austin county. Records range is 8/1997 to 9/2005. Also, see note at beginning of section for add'l property data. **Other phones:** Elections- 979-865-8633; Vital Records- 979-865-5911. **Property tax/Assessing**- 20 S Holland, Bellville, TX 77418; 979-865-8633. **Online**- Search property tax records for free at www.austincad.org. Also, property tax inquiries can be made via www.txcountydata.com/selectCounty.asp.

Bailey County

County Clerk, 300 S 1st, #200, Muleshoe, TX 79347. Recording, R/E phone-806-272-3044; fax-806-272-3538; 8:30AM-N 1-5PM.
Index: Separate indices to search. Records indexed on computer back to 1995. Office personnel or visitors may perform searches. Search fee-$10.00 per name. Office will search real estate records. Will search UCC records. Copy fee $1.00 per page. Cert fee- $5.00 per cert and $1.00 per page. Payee- Bailey County Clerk. **Online access to Probate, Judgment records:** Search probate records and judgment records free at http://idocket.com/countycourt.htm. **Other phones:** Treasurer- 806-272-3239; Elections- 806-272-3044; Vitals- 806-272-3044. **Property tax/Assessing**- 300 S 1st #200, Muleshoe, TX 79347; 806-272-3022. (Appraiser/Auditor- 806-272-5501)

Bandera County

County Clerk, PO Box 823, Bandera, TX 78003. 830-796-3332; fax-830-796-8323; 8AM-4:30PM (CST) www.banderacounty.org
Index: All in one. Records indexed on a public use terminal back to 1983. Office personnel or visitors may perform searches. Search fee $5.00 per name. Office will search real estate records. Office will not search UCC records or liens. Copy fee $1.00 per page. Cert fee- $5.00 per cert plus copy fee. Payee- Bandera County Clerk. Bulk data available for purchase, contact Anne Ruthven at anner@indian-creek.net or 830-796-3332. **Online access to Real Estate, Deed, Probate, Judgment records:** Access to public record search is free at www.taxnetusa.com/publicrecords/. Also, See note at beginning of section. Also, to search probate records and judgment records go to http://idocket.com/countycourt.htm. **Other phones:** Treasurer- 830-796-4573; Elections- 830-796-3731; Vital Records- 830-796-3332; State Vital Records- 512-458-7111. **Property tax/Assessing**- PO Box 368, Bandera, TX 78003; 830-796-3731, assessor fax- 830-796-8140. (Appraiser/Auditor- 830-796-3030) hours- 7:30AM - 5PM M-F; 8:00 - 12:00 1st Sat of month **Online**-Access appraisal district records free at http://propaccess.banderaproptax.org/clientdb/?cid=1. Search Tax Collector data a www.banderacounty.org/departments/tax.htm. Also, ccess property search is free at www.taxnetusa.com/publicrecords/.

Bastrop County

County Clerk, PO Box 577, Bastrop, TX 78602. Recording, R/E phone-512-332-7234; fax-512-332-7241; 8AM-5PM (CST) www.cc.co.bastrop.tx.us
Index: Separate indices to search include computer and paper-1837-1920,1920-1973, 1973-1993, 1994-1995. Records indexed on computer back to 1996. Office will perform a UCC search but public must search other records themselves. Copy fee $1.00 per page. Cert fee- $5.00 per cert plus copy fee. Exemplification fee- $7.00. Payee- Bastrop County Clerk. CDs of bulk information available; contact Rose Pietsch, County Clerk. **Online access to Real Estate, Grantor/Grantee, Deed, Judgment, Lien, UCC, Marriage records:** Access county clerk public access page for recorded documents free at www.cc.co.bastrop.tx.us. Also, access recording records free at www.titlex.com; select Bastrop county. Record range is 3/2001 to 8/31/2001. **Other phones:** Treasurer- 512-332-7204; Elections- 512-332-7260; Vital Records- 512-332-7234; Voter Registrar- 512-332-7260; Tax Collector -512-332-7261. **Property tax/Assessing**- PO Box 579, Bastrop, TX 78602; 512-581-7160. (Appraiser/Auditor- 512-303-3536) **Online access**- Access to tax office records is free at www.bastroptac.com/Appraisal/PublicAccess/. Also, property tax inquiries can be made via www.txcountydata.com/selectCounty.asp. Also, see note at beginning of section.

Baylor County

County Clerk, 101 S Washington, Seymour, TX 76380. Recording, R/E phone-940-889-3322; fax-940-889-4300; 8:30AM-5PM (CST)
Index: All in one. Record index not computerized. Office personnel or visitors may perform searches. Search fee $5.00 per name. Real estate owner, mortgage, and property transfer searches available. Office will search UCC records prior to 7/2001 and current fixture (land) files. UCC search includes tax liens if requested. Copy fee $1.00 per page. Cert fee- $6.00 per cert plus copy fee. Payee- Baylor County Clerk. **Other phones:** Treasurer- 940-889-1846; Elections- 940-889-3322; Vitals - 940-889-3322. **Property tax/Assessing**- 211 N Washington, Seymour, TX 76380; 940-889-3169. (Appraiser/Auditor- 940-888-5636)

Bee County

County Clerk, 105 W Corpus Christi St, Rm 108, Beeville, TX 78102. Recording, R/E phone-361-362-3245; fax-361-362-3247; 8AM-N, 1-5PM (CST)
Index: Separate indices to search include Official Public Records as of June, 1995, prior to June, 1995 each has own index. Records indexed on a public use terminal back to 6/1/95. Office personnel or visitors may perform searches. General search fee $5.00 per book per name, also applied to UCC search. Office will search real estate records; written request required. Copy fee $1.00 per page. Cert fee- $5.00 per cert plus copy fee. Payee- Bee County Clerk. **Online Real Estate, Grantor/Grantee, Deed records:** Access Grantor/Grantee index by subscription at https://www.texaslandrecords.com/txlr/TxlrApp/index.jsp. Day or monthly pay plans. **Other phones:** Elections- 361-362-3245; Vital Records- 361-362-3245; Auditor- 361-362-3200. **Property tax/Assessing**- PO Box 1900, 411 E Houston, Beeville, TX 78102; 361-362-3250, assessor fax- 361-358-5417. (Appraiser/Auditor- 361-358-0193) hours- 8:15AM-5PM **Online access**- Access property records free at www.beecad.org/. Also, access delinquent sales list free at www.co.bee.tx.us/ips/cms/countyoffices/taxAssessorCollector.html.

Bell County

County Clerk, PO Box 480, Belton, TX 76513-0480. 254-933-5160, R/E recording phone-254-933-5772; fax-254-933-5176; 8AM-5PM (CST) www.bellcountytx.com/countyclerk/index.htm
Index: All in one. Records indexed on a public use terminal back to 1988. Only the public may search. Copy fee $1.00 per page. Cert fee- $1.00 per cert plus copy fee. Payee- Bell County Clerk. **Other phones:** Treasurer- 254-933-5252; Elections- 254-933-5780; Vital Records- 254-933-5165; Appraiser- 254-939-3909. **Property tax/Assessing**- 411 E Central, Belton, TX 76513; 254-939-5841, assessor fax- 254-939-3909. (Appraiser/Auditor- 254-939-5841) hours- 8AM-4:45PM A public access terminal is available. www.bellcad.org/ **Online access**- Search property and parcel data free at http://propaccess.bellcad.org/clientdb/?cid=1.

Bexar County

County Clerk, 100 Dolorosa, Rm 104; Bexar County Courthouse, San Antonio, TX 78205-3083. 210-335-2581, 335-2273, 335-3041, R/E recording phone-210-335-2581; fax-210-335-2813; 8AM-5PM (CST) www.countyclerk.bexar.landata.com
Index: All in one. Records indexed on a public use terminal back to 1964. Office personnel or visitors may perform searches. General search fee $1.00 per year. Real estate owner, mortgage, and property transfer searches available. Office will search UCC records prior to 7/2001 and current fixture (land) files. Tax liens not included in UCC search. Copy fee $1.00 per page. Cert fee- $5.00 per cert plus copy fee. Payee- Bexar County Clerk. **Online access to Real Estate, Grantor/Grantee, Deed, Mortgage, Foreclosure, Marriage, UCC, Assumed Name, Probate records:** Access to the County Clerk database is free after free registration at www.countyclerk.bexar.landata.com. Includes land records, deeds, UCCs, assumed names and foreclosure notices, and more. Probate is recently added. Images are to be added on a new subscription service. **Other phones:** Elections- 210-335-8683; Vital Records- 210-335-2585; Appraisal- 210-224-8511. **Property tax/Assessing**- PO Box 839950, 233 N Pecos-LaTrinidad, San Antonio, TX 78283; 210-335-6585. (Appraiser/Auditor- 210-224-8511) hours- 8AM-4:45PM; 6:45PM W A public access terminal is available. www.bexar.org **Online access**- Access the county Central Appraisal District database free at www.bcad.org/clientdb/?cid=1.

Blanco County

County Clerk, PO Box 65, Johnson City, TX 78636. 830-868-7357; fax-830-868-4158; 8AM-4:30PM (CST) www.co.blanco.tx.us
Index: All in one. Records indexed on a public use terminal back to 10/1991. Office personnel or visitors may perform searches. Search fee $5.00 per name. Office will not search real estate records. Office will

not search UCC or real estate records, but will search tax liens. Tax lien search fee- $5.00 per debtor. Copy fee $1.00 per page. Cert fee- $5.00 per cert plus copy fee. Payee- Blanco County Clerk. **Other phones:** Treasurer- 830-868-4566; Vital Records- 830-868-7357. **Property tax/Assessing**- PO Box 465, 200 N Ave G, Johnson City, TX 78636; 830-868-7178, fax-830-868-2228. (Appraiser 830-868-4013) hours 8AM-5PM **Online** - Access property data at www.txcountydata.com/county.asp?County=016. Other online access through private companies.

Borden County

County Clerk, PO Box 124, Gail, TX 79738-0124. Recording, R/E phone-806-756-4312; fax-806-756-4405; 8AM-N, 1PM-5PM (CST)
Index: All in one. Record index not computerized. Office personnel or visitors may perform searches. General search fee $5.00 per name. Office will not search real estate records. Will search UCC records. UCC search per debtor name- $10.00. Copy fee $2.00, if tax lien or real estate $1.00 per page. Cert fee- $5.00 per cert plus copy fee. Payee- Borden County Clerk. Bulk data available in paper form. **Other phones:** Treasurer- 806-756-4386; Elections- 806-756-4312; Vital Records- 806-756-4312. **Property tax/Assessing**- PO Box 115, 116 E Wilbourn, Gail, TX 79738-0115; 806-756-4415, assessor fax- 806-756-4431. (Appraiser/Auditor- 806-756-4484);

Bosque County

County Clerk, PO Box 617, Meridian, TX 76665. 254-435-2201; fax-254-435-2152; 8AM-5PM (CST)
Index: Pre-1997 records in paper index. Records indexed on computer back to 1990. Office personnel or visitors may perform searches. Search fee $5.00 per name. Real estate owner, mortgage, and property transfer searches available only. Office will not search UCC records. Copy fee $1.00 per page. Cert fee- $5.00 per cert plus copy fee. Payee- Bosque County Clerk. Bulk data available for purchase in CD's, available back to 1990 (index) and 1997 (images), contact the Clerk. **Other phones:** Treasurer- 254-435-2931; Elections- 254-435-2201; Vital Records- 254-435-2201; Appraisal District- 254-435-2304. **Property tax/Assessing**- PO Box 393, 102 W Morgan, Meridian, TX 76665; 254-435-2301, assessor fax- 254-435-2822. (Appraiser/Auditor- 254-435-2304) **Online access**- Access property records at www.txcountydata.com/county.asp?County=018. Other online access through private companies.

Bowie County

County Clerk, PO Box 248, New Boston, TX 75570. 903-628-6740; fax-903-628-6729; 8AM-5PM. www.co.bowie.tx.us
Index: All in one. Record index not computerized. Only office personnel may search. Search fee $10.00 per name with written verification. Office will not search real estate records. Office will search UCC records prior to 7/2001 and current fixture (land) files. Copy fee $1.00 per page. Cert fee- $5.00 per doc plus copy fee. Payee- County Clerk. **Other phones:** Treasurer- 903-628-6722; Elections- 903-628-6810; Vital Records- 903-628-6744; Courthouse Operator- 903-628-6700. **Property tax/Assessing**- PO Box 248, 710 James Bowie Dr, New Boston, TX 75570-0248; 903-628-6730, assessor fax- 903-628-6780. (Appraiser/Auditor- 903-628-6724) www.co.bowie.tx.us/ips/cms/countyoffices/taxAssessorCollector.html **Online access**- Access to Appraisal District's Appraisal Roll data is free at www.bowiecad.org/Search.htm.

Brazoria County

County Clerk, 111 E Locust, #200, Angleton, TX 77515-4654. 979-849-5711, R/E recording phone-979-864-1355 x5, UCC recording phone-979-864-1355 x9; fax-979-864-1358; 8AM-4:30PM. www.brazoria.tx.us.landata.com
Index: All in one. Records indexed on a public use terminal back to 1826. Office personnel or visitors may perform searches. General search fee $5.00 per name. Office will not search real estate records. UCC search per debtor name- $10.00. Copy fee $1.00 per page. Cert fee- $5.00 per cert plus copy fee. Payee- County Clerk. **Online access to Real Estate, Grantor/Grantee, Deed, Lien, Judgment records:** Access recording records free at www.titlex.com; select Brazoria county. Records range from 3/2001 to 4/2007. Also, see note at beginning of section for add'l property data. **Other phones:** Treasurer- 979-849-5711; Elections- 979-864-1355 x8; Vital Records- 979-864-1355 x6. **Property tax/Assessing**- 451 N Velasco, #150, Angleton, TX 77515; 979-849-1320, assessor fax- 979-864-1346. (Appraiser/Auditor- 979-849-7792) hours- 8AM-5PM A public access terminal is available. **Online access**- Access to the county Central Appraisal District database is free at www.brazoriacad.org. Click on "appraisal roll." Also, property tax inquiries can be made at www.txcountydata.com/selectCounty.asp.

Brazos County

County Clerk, 300 E 26th St, #120, Bryan, TX 77803. 979-361-4132; fax-979-361-4125; 8AM-5PM (CST) http://co.brazos.tx.us
Index: All in one. Records indexed on a public use terminal back to 1967. Office personnel or visitors may perform searches. General index search fee $5.00 per name. Office will not search real estate records. Will not search UCC records. Copy fee $1.00 per page. Cert fee- $5.00 per cert plus copy fee. Payee- Brazos County Clerk. Bulk data available for purchase, documents and indexes from 2000 to present, contact Karen McQueen, County Clerk. **Online access to Real Estate, Grantor/Grantee, Deed, Lien, Vital Statistic, Fictitious Name records:** Search grantor/grantee index free at www.texaslandrecords.com. Registration and fees required for full data. **Other phones:** Treasurer- 979-361-4340; Elections- 979-361-4124; Vital Records- 979-361-4528. **Property tax/Assessing**- 300 E Wm J Bryan Pky, Bryan, TX 77803; 97-361-4470, assessor fax- 979-361-4487. (Appraiser/Auditor- 979-774-4100) **Online access**- Access Appraisal District data free at http://propaccess.trueautomation.com/clientdb/?cid=65. Also, property tax inquiries can be made via www.txcountydata.com/selectCounty.asp. Also, see notes at beginning of section.

Brewster County

County Clerk, PO Box 119, Alpine, TX 79831. Recording, R/E phone-432-837-3366; fax-432-837-6217; 8:30AM-5PM.
Index: All in one. Records indexed on computer from 9/98 to present. Office personnel or visitors may perform searches. Search fee $10.00 per name. Office will search real estate records. Office will not search UCC records. Copy fee $1.00 per page. Cert fee- $5.00 per cert plus copy fee. Payee- County Clerk Office. **Other phones:** Treasurer- 432-837-6200; Elections- 432-837-6230; Vital Records- 432-837-3366. **Property tax/Assessing**- 107 W Ave E, #1, Alpine, TX 79830; 432-837-2214, assessor fax- 432-837-3871. (Appraiser/Auditor- 432-837-2558) hours- 8:30AM-N, 1-5PM

Briscoe County

County Clerk, PO Box 555, Silverton, TX 79257. Recording, R/E phone-806-823-2134; fax-806-823-2359; 8AM-5PM.
Index: All in one. Record index not computerized. Office personnel or visitors may perform searches. General index search fee $5.00 per name. Office will search UCC records prior to 7/2001 only. Tax liens not included in UCC search. UCC search per debtor name- $11.00. Copy fee $1.00 per page. Cert fee- $5.00 per doc plus copy fee. Payee- County Clerk. **Other phones:** Treasurer- 806-823-2133; Elections- 806-823-2134; Vital Records- 806-823-2134. **Property tax/ Assessing**- 806-823-2136. (Appraiser/Auditor- 806-823-2161)

Brooks County

County Clerk, PO Box 427, Falfurrias, TX 78355. 361-325-5604, R/E recording phone-361-325-5604 x1; fax-361-325-4944; 8AM-N, 1-5PM. www.co.brooks.tx.us/ips/cms/countyoffices/countyClerk.html
Index: All in one. Records indexed on computer back to 1993. Only office personnel may search. Search fee $10.00. Office will search real estate records. Office will search UCC records. Copy fee $1.00 per page. Cert fee- $5.00 per doc plus copy fee. Payee- Brooks County Clerk. **Online access to Real Estate, Deed, Probate, Judgment records:** Access recording office land data at www.etitlesearch.com; registration required, fee based on usage. Also, to search probate records and judgment records go to http://idocket.com/countycourt.htm . **Other phones:** Treasurer- 361-325-5604 x229; Elections- 361-325-5604 x234; Vital Records- 361-325-5604 x247. **Property tax/Assessing**- PO Box 558, 408 W Travis, Falfurrias, TX 78355; 361-325-5604 x4, assessor fax-361-325-2529. (Appraiser/Auditor- 361-325-5681) www.co.brooks.tx.us/ips/cms/countyoffices/taxAssessorCollector.html **Online** - Access to property tax searches for free go to www.co.brooks.tx.us/ips/cms/countyoffices/taxAssessorCollector.html

Brown County

County Clerk, 200 S Broadway; Courthouse, Brownwood, TX 76801. 325-643-2594; fax-n/a; 8:30AM-5PM (CST)
Index: All in one. Records indexed on a public use terminal back to 1992. Office personnel or visitors may perform searches. Search fee $10.00 for federal and state lien; $5.00 for abstract of judgment, hospital lien, criminal, probate and civil. Office will not search real estate records. Will not search UCC records. Copy fee $1.00 per page. Cert fee- $5.00 per doc plus copy fee. Payee- Brown County Clerk. **Other phones:** Treasurer- 325-646-6033; Elections- 325-643-6433; Vitals- 325-643-2594. **Property tax/ Assessing**- 403 Fisk, Brownwood, TX; 325-643-5676, assessor fax- 325-643-1647. (Appraiser/Auditor- 325-643-5676) hours- 8AM-4:30PM **Online**- Access Appraisal District records free at http://clientdb.trueautomation.com/clientdb/main.asp?id=30. Other online access through private companies.

Burleson County

County Clerk, 100 W Buck St, #203, Caldwell, TX 77836. Recording, R/E phone-979-567-2329; fax-979-567-2376; 8AM-5PM (CST)
Index: Separate indices to search include several years per each index. Records indexed on a public use terminal back to 1975. Only the public may search. Will not search UCC records. Copy fee $1.00 per page. Cert fee- $5.00 per cert plus copy fee. Payee- Burleson County Clerk. **Other phones:** Treasurer- 979-567-2305; Elections- 979 567 2000; Vital Records- 979-567-2329. **Property tax/Assessing**- 100 W Buck, #202, Caldwell, TX 77836; 979-567-2326, assessor fax- 979-567-2369. (Appraiser/Auditor- 979-567-2318) A public access terminal is available.

Burnet County

County Clerk, 220 S Pierce St, Burnet, TX 78611. Recording, R/E phone-512-756-5406; fax-512-756-5410; 9AM-5PM (CST) www.burnetcountytexas.org/default.aspx?name=cclerk.home
Index: All in one. Records indexed on a public use terminal back to 1989. Office personnel or visitors may perform searches. Search fee $10.00 per debtor. Office will not search real estate records. Office will search UCC records prior to 7/2001 and current fixture (land) files. Tax liens not included in UCC search. Copy fee $1.00 per page. Cert fee- $5.00 per cert plus copy fee. Payee- Burnet County Clerk. CDs ranged in date format are available for purchase. **Online access to Real Estate, Grantor/Grantee, Deed, Lien, Judgment records:** Access recording records free at www.titlex.com; select Burnett county. Records range from 1/1998 to 11/2001. Also, see note

at beginning of section. **Other phones:** Treasurer- 512-756-5498; Elections- 512-756-5406; Vital Records- 512-756-5406. **Property tax/Assessing-** 1701 E Polk, #96, Burnet, TX 78611; 512-756-5494, assessor fax- 512-756-7873. (Appraiser/Auditor- 512-756-8291) hours- 8AM-5PM A public access terminal is available. www.burnet-cad.org/ **Online access-** Property tax inquiries made at http://clientdb.trueautomation.com/clientdb/main.asp?id=19.

Caldwell County

County Clerk, PO Box 906, Lockhart, TX 78644-0906. 512-398-1804; 8:30AM-5PM (CST)
Index: All in one. Records indexed on a public use terminal back to 5/92. Office personnel or visitors may perform searches. Search fee $5.00. Real estate owner, mortgage, and property transfer searches available. Office will search UCC records prior to 7/2001 only. Copy fee $1.00 per page. Cert fee- $5.00 per cert plus copy fee. Payee- Caldwell County Clerk. **Other phones:** Treasurer- 512-398-1800; Elections- 512-398-1830; Vital Records- 512-398-1804. **Property tax/Assessing-** 610 San Jacinto 512-398-5550. (Appraiser/Auditor- 512-398-5550) hours- 8AM-5PM **Online access-** Access the county Appraisal District database now free at www.txcountydata.com. Also, see online notes in state summary at beginning of section.

Calhoun County

County Clerk, 211 S Ann, Port Lavaca, TX 77979. Recording, R/E phone-361-553-4411; fax-361-553-4420; 8AM-5PM.
Index: Separate indices to search include deed records, official records. Records indexed on a public use terminal back to 1992. Only the public may search. Copy fee $1.00 per page. Cert fee- $5.00 per cert plus copy fee. Payee- County Clerk. Hard copies can be made, fees paid before copies made. **Online access to Real Estate, Grantor/Grantee, Deed, Judgment, Lien records:** Access recording records free at www.titlex.com; select Calhoun county; login and password required. Records range up to 9/2003. **Other phones:** Treasurer- 361-553-4620; Elections- 361-553-4440; Vital Records- 361-553-4411. **Property tax/Assessing-** PO Box 49, 426 W Main, Port Lavaca, TX 77979; 361-552-4560, assessor fax- 361-552-4787. (Appraiser/Auditor- 361-552-8808) A public access terminal is available. **Online access-** Access Appraisal District records free at http://clientdb.trueautomation.com/clientdb/main.asp?id=24.

Callahan County

County Clerk, 100 W 4th, #104; Courthouse, Baird, TX 79504. Recording, R/E phone-325-854-5815; fax-325-854-5816; 8AM-N 1PM-5PM (CST) www.callahancounty.org
Index: All in one. Records indexed on a public use terminal back to 1984. Office personnel or visitors may perform searches. Search fee $11.00 per name. Copy fee $1.00 per page. Cert fee- $5.00 per cert plus copy fee. Payee- Callahan County Clerk. **Other phones:** Treasurer- 325-854-5840; Elections- 325-854-5815; Vital Records- 325-854-5815. **Property tax/Assessing-** 100 W 4th, Courthouse, Baird, TX 79504; 325-854-5820, assessor fax- 325-854-5821. (Appraiser/Auditor- 325-854-5865) hours- 8AM-N, 1PM-4:30PM **Online access-** Find appraisal district data free at http://208.75.248.98/.

Cameron County

County Clerk, PO Box 2178, Brownsville, TX 78522. Recording, R/E phone-956-544-0815, UCC recording phone-956-550-1329; fax-956-547-7080; 8AM-5PM. www.co.cameron.tx.us/countyclerks/countyclerk.html
Index: All in one. Records indexed on a public use terminal back to 1926. Office personnel or visitors may perform searches. General search fee $5.00 per name. Office will search real estate records. Will search UCC records. UCC search per debtor name- $10.00. Copy fee $1.00 per page. Cert fee- $5.00 per doc plus copy fee. Payee- Cameron County Clerk. **Online access to Real Estate, Grantor/Grantee, Deed, Lien records:** Search grantor/grantee index free at www.texaslandrecords.com. Registration and fees required for full data. Also, access probate and judgment records free at http://idocket.com/countycourt.htm. Records go back to 1993. Also, see note at beginning of section for add'l property data. **Other phones:** Treasurer- 956-544-0819; Elections- 956-544-0809; Vital Records- 956-544-0817. **Property tax/Assessing-** 964 E Harrison, Brownsville, TX 78520; 956-544-0800, assessor fax- 956-544-0808. (Appraiser/Auditor- 956-399-9322 or 541-3365) hours- 8AM-4:30PM A public access terminal is available. **Online access-** Access appraisal district property records free at www.cameroncad.org/ClientDB/PropertySearch.aspx?cid=1.

Camp County

County Clerk, 126 Church St, Rm 102, Pittsburg, TX 75686. Recording, R/E phone-903-856-2731; fax-903-856-2309; 8AM-5PM.
Index: All in one. Records indexed on computer back to 1997. Office personnel or visitors may perform searches. Office will not search old UCC records. Search fee $10.00 per name. Copy fee $1.00 per page. Cert fee- $5.00 per page includes copy fee. Payee- Camp County Clerk. Paper copies of bulk information available for purchase. **Other phones:** Treasurer- 903-855-1756; Elections- 903-856-2731; Vital Records- 903-856-2731. **Property tax/Assessing-** 115 North Ave, Pittsburg, TX 75686; 903-856-3391, assessor fax- 903-856-0811. (Appraiser/Auditor- 903-856-6538) hours- 8AM-4:30PM **Online access-** Access property tax records free at www.campcad.org.

Carson County

County Clerk, PO Box 487, Panhandle, TX 79068. Recording, R/E phone-806-537-3873; fax-806-537-3623; 8AM-N, 1-5PM (CST)
Index: All in one. Records indexed on a public use terminal back to 5/81. Only the public may search. Copy fee $1.00 per page. Cert fee- $5.00 per cert plus copy fee. Payee- Carson County Clerk. **Other phones:** Treasurer- 806-537-3753; Elections- 806-537-3873; Vital Records- 806-537-3873. **Property tax/Assessing-** Same address as recording office. 806-537-3412. (Appraiser/Auditor- 806-537-3488)

Cass County

County Clerk, PO Box 449, Linden, TX 75563. Recording, R/E phone-903-756-5071; fax-903-756-8057; 8AM-4:30PM.
Index: All in one. Records indexed on a public use terminal back to 1846. Office will perform a UCC search but public must search other records themselves. Search fee $10.00. Copy fee $1.00 per page. Cert fee- $5.00 per page plus copy fee. Payee- Cass County Clerk. **Other phones:** Treasurer- 903-756-7626; Elections- 903-756-5071; Vital Records- 903-756-5071. **Property tax/Assessing-** PO Box 870, Linden, TX 75563; 903-756-5313, assessor fax- 903-756-7431. (Appraiser/Auditor- 903-756-7545) **Online access-** Access to property records is free at www.casscad.org. Click on Search Our Data.

Castro County

County Clerk, 100 E Bedford, Rm 101, Dimmitt, TX 79027-2643. Recording, R/E phone-806-647-3338; fax-806-647-5438; 8AM-5PM (CST)
Index: All in one. Records indexed on a public use terminal from 1999 to 2004. Office will perform a UCC search but public must search other records themselves. Search fee $16.00 per name. Copy fee $1.00 per page. Cert fee- $5.00 per cert plus copy fee. Payee- Castro County Clerk. Bulk data available for purchase on CD's from 2004 to present. **Other phones:** Treasurer- 806-647-5534; Elections- 806-647-3338; Vital Records- 806-647-3338. **Property tax/Assessing-** 100 E Bedford, Bimmitt, TX 79027; 806-647-5336. (Appraiser/Auditor- 806-647-5131);

Chambers County

County Clerk, PO Box 728, Anahuac, TX 77514. 409-267-8309; fax-409-267-8315; 8AM-N 1PM-5PM (CST) www.co.chambers.tx.us
Has a sub-office in Mont Belvieu, 10616 Eagle Dr, 281-576-6982. Index: Separate indices to search include official public records indexes; miscellaneous indexes contain marriage license, assumed name certificates, plats. Records indexed on computer back to 1990. Office personnel or visitors may perform searches. Search fee $5.00 each 10 year search. Must provide specific information. Office will search real estate records. Office will not search UCC records. Copy fee $1.00 per page. Cert fee- $5.00 per cert plus copy fee. Payee- Chambers County Clerk. **Online access to Real Estate, Deed, Mortgage records:** Access county clerk's real property records free after registering for a login name and password at www.chambersonline.net/realproperty/. **Other phones:** Treasurer- 409-267-8286; Elections- 409-267-8309. **Property tax/Assessing-** PO Box 519, Anahuac, TX 77514; 409-267-8301. (Appraiser/Auditor- 409-267-3795) **Online access-** Search the appraiser property tax database for free at www.chamberscad.org. Also, see note at beginning of section.

Cherokee County

County Clerk, PO Box 420, Rusk, TX 75785. Recording, R/E phone-903-683-2350; fax-903-683-5931; 8AM-5PM.
Index: All in one. Records indexed on a public use terminal back to 1976. Office personnel or visitors may perform searches. Search fee $10.00. Office will not search real estate records. Copy fee $1.00 per page. Cert fee- $5.00 per page plus copy fee. Payee- Cherokee County Clerk. **Online access to Real Estate, Grantor/Grantee, Deed, Judgment, Lien, Birth, Death, Marriage, Probate records:** Access recording records free at www.titlex.com; select Cherokee county. Records range from 5/1973 to 2/2004. Also, see note at beginning of section. Also, search grantor/grantee index free at www.texaslandrecords.com. Registration and fees apply for full data. Also, search probate and judgment records at http://idocket.com/countycourt.htm . **Other phones:** Treasurer- 903-683-4935; Elections- 903-683-2350; Vital Records- 903-683-2350. **Property tax/Assessing-** 135 S Main, Rusk, TX 75785; 903-683-5478, assessor fax- 903-683-2362. (Appraiser/Auditor- 903-683-2296) hours- 8AM-5:45PM M-Th; 8AM-N Fri Public access terminal available. **Online access-** Search the Cherokee CAD database for free at http://clientdb.trueautomation.com/clientdb/main.asp?id=2.

Childress County

County Clerk, Courthouse Box 4, Childress, TX 79201. Recording, R/E phone-940-937-6143; fax-940-937-3708; 8:30AM-5PM (CST)
Index: All in one. Record index not computerized. Office personnel or visitors may perform searches. Search fee $5.00 per name. Office will search real estate records. Office will not search UCC records. Copy fee $1.00 per page. Cert fee- $5.00 per instrument plus copy fee. Payee- County Clerk, Zona Prince. **Other phones:** Treasurer- 940-937-6271; Elections- 940-937-6143; Vital Records- 940-937-6143; Appraisal- 940-937-6062. **Property tax/Assessing-** 100 Ave E NW, Courthouse Box 4, Childress, TX 79201; 940-937-2232. (Appraiser/Auditor- 940-937-6062) hours- 8:30AM-4:30PM www.co.childress.tx.us/ips/cms/countyoffices/taxAssessorCollector.html

Clay County

County Clerk, PO Box 548, Henrietta, TX 76365. 940-538-4631; fax-none; 8AM-Noon, 1PM-5PM (CST) www.co.clay.tx.us/ips/cms
Index: Separate indices to search include deed, deed of trust, tax lien, abstracts, judgments, mechanic liens. Record index not computerized. Only the public may search. Will not search UCC records. Copy fee $1.00

per page. Cert fee- $5.00 per cert plus copy fee. Payee- Clay County Clerk. **Other phones:** Treasurer- 940-538-5911; Elections- 940-538-4631; Vital Records- 940-538-4631. **Property tax/Assessing-** 100 N Bridge St, Henrietta, TX 76365; 940-538-4356. (Appraiser/Auditor- 940-538-4311) **Online access-** Access property tax records free at www.claycad.org/. Also, see note at beginning of section.

Cochran County

County Clerk, 100 N Main; Courthouse, Morton, TX 79346-2598. -806-266-5450; fax-806-266-9027; 8AM-5PM (CST) http://co.cochran.tx.us/ips/cms
Index: All in one. Record index not computerized. Office personnel or visitors may perform searches. Search fee $5.00 per name. Office will search limited real estate records. Will search UCC records. Copy fee $1.00 per page. Cert fee- $5.00 per cert includes copy fee. Payee- Cochran County Clerk. Office does sell bulk data in paper form only. **Other phones:** Treasurer- 806-266-5161; Elections- 806-266-5450; Vital Records- 806-266-5450. **Property tax/Assessing-** Courthouse, Rm 101, Morton, TX 79346; 806-266-5171, assessor fax- 806-266-5629. (Appraiser/Auditor- 806-266-5584);

Coke County

County Clerk, 13 E 7th St; Courthouse, Robert Lee, TX 76945. Recording, R/E phone-325-453-2631; fax-325-453-2650; 8AM-5PM M-Th, 8AM-1PM Fri.. (CST)
Index: All in one. Records indexed on a public use terminal back to 1970. Office will perform a UCC search but public must search other records themselves. General search fee $10.00 per name. Office will not search real estate records. Copy fee $1.00 per page. $2.00 per page for UCC. Cert fee- $5.00 per cert plus copy fee. Payee- Coke County Clerk. **Other phones:** Treasurer- 325-453-2713; Elections- 325-453-2631; Vital Records- 325-453-2631. **Property tax/Assessing-** 13 E 7th St, Robert Lee, TX 76945; 325-453-2614, assessor fax- 325-453-2328. (Appraiser/Auditor- 325-453-4528) No public access terminal.

Coleman County

County Clerk, PO Box 591, Coleman, TX 76834. 325-625-2889; 8AM-5PM (CST)
Index: Separate indices to search include deed, deed of trust, mechanics lien, state tax lien, federal tax lien, abstract judgment. Record index not computerized. Office will perform a UCC search and some limited real estate, but public is advised to search records themselves. UCC search per debtor name $10.00. Office will not search real estate records. Copy fee $1.00 per page. Cert fee- $5.00 per cert plus copy fee. Payee- Coleman County Clerk. **Other phones:** Treasurer- 325-625-4221. **Property tax/Assessing-** 100 W Liveoat, #104, Coleman, TX 76834; 325-625-2153, assessor fax- 325-625-2154. (Appraiser/Auditor- 325-625-4155) hours- 8AM-4:30PM No public access terminal. **Online access-** Property tax inquiries can be made at www.txcountydata.com/county.asp?County=042`. Other access may be available through private companies.

Collin County

County Clerk, 200 S McDonald, #120; Annex "A", McKinney, TX 75069. Recording, R/E phone-972-548-4185; fax-972-547-5731; 8AM-5PM (8AM-4PM land recording). (CST) www.co.collin.tx.us
Index: All in one. Records indexed on a public use terminal back to 1974. Office personnel or visitors may perform searches. No phone searches. Search fee $10.00. Office will search real estate records. Will search UCC records. Copy fee $1.00 per page. Plats- $5.00 per copy. Cert fee- $5.00 per cert plus copy fee. Payee- Collin County Clerk. Images, indexes, land records and assumed names available for purchase, please contact Brenda Cavender, Land Admin. **Online access to Real Estate, Deed, Lien, Judgment, Vital Statistic, Mortgage records:** Access to the county clerk Deeds database is free at http://countyclerkrecords.co.collin.tx.us/webinquiry/. Also, see note at beginning of section for more property data. **Other phones:** Elections- 972-547-1900; Vital Records- 972-548-4185. **Property tax/Assessing-** 1800 N Graves, McKinney TX 75070; 972-547-5020, assessor fax- 972-548-5040. (Appraiser/Auditor- 469-742-9200) **Online access-** Search the Appraiser's property tax and business property database free at www.collincad.org/search.php. Also, search the tax assessor and collector look up free at www.co.collin.tx.us/tax_assessor/taxstmt_search.jsp.

Collingsworth County

County Clerk, 800 West Ave, Box 10, Wellington, TX 79095. Recording, R/E phone-806-447-2408; fax-806-447-2409; 9AM-5PM (CST)
Index: All in one. Record index not computerized. Office personnel or visitors may perform searches. General index search fee $10.00 per search. Office will search real estate records. Tax liens not included in UCC search. UCC search per debtor name- $16.00. UCC search request using non-standard form (per name)- $31.00. Copy fee $1.00 per page. Cert fee- $5.00 per cert plus copy fee. Payee- Collingsworth County Clerk. **Other phones:** Treasurer- 806-447-2616; Elections- 806-447-2408; Vital Records- 806-447-2408. **Property tax/Assessing-** 800 West Ave, Box 2, Wellington, TX 79095; 806-447-5606, assessor fax- 806-447-2251. (Appraiser/Auditor- 806-447-5172) hours- 9AM-N, 1PM-5PM No public access terminal.

Colorado County

County Clerk, 400 Spring St, Rm 103; Courthouse, Columbus, TX 78934. 979-732-2155, R/E recording phone-979-732-6561 or 2155; fax-979-732-8852; 8AM-5PM (CST) www.co.colorado.tx.us/ips/cms
Index: All in one. Records indexed on computer back to 1971. Only the public may search. Copy fee $1.00 per page. Cert fee- $5.00 per cert plus copy fee. Payee- Colorado County Clerk. Bulk data available by paper. **Online access to Real Estate, Grantor/Grantee, Deed, Judgment, Lien records:** Access recording records free at www.titlex.com; select Colorado county. Records range is 5/1997 to 9/2001. For more land data, see note at beginning of section. **Other phones:** Treasurer- 979-732-2865; Vital Records- 979-732-6561 or 2155. **Property tax/Assessing-** PO Box 10, 106 Cardinal Ln, Columbus, TX 78934; 979-732-2710, assessor fax-979-732-6485. (Appraiser/Auditor- 979-732-8222) Public access terminal available. **Online access-** For property search go to www.coloradocad.org/ and click on property search. Also, see note at beginning of section.

Comal County

County Clerk, 150 N Seguin, #101, New Braunfels, TX 78130. 830-221-1230; fax-830-620-3410; 8AM-4:30PM (CST) www.co.comal.tx.us
Index: All in one. Records indexed on a public use terminal back to 1974. Office personnel or visitors may perform searches. General search fee $10.00 per name. Office will search real estate records. Will not search UCC records. Copy fee $1.00 per page; plats/maps- $5.00 per copy. Cert fee- $5.00 per doc plus copy fee. Payee- Comal County Clerk. Bulk data available for purchase, contact Denise Rainey in writing or by email at cckdmr@co.comal.tx.us. **Other phones:** Treasurer- 830-221-1220; Elections- 830-221-1233; Vital Records- 830-221-1230. **Property tax/Assessing-** PO Box 311445, 205 N Seguin St, New Braunfels, TX 78131-1445; 830-620-5521, assessor fax- 830-620-5525. (Appraiser/Auditor- 830-625-8597) hours- 8AM-5PM Public access terminal available. **Online access-** Access property free at www.comalcad.org/. Search property tax data free at http://taxweb.co.comal.tx.us/clientdb/?cid=1.

Comanche County

County Clerk, 101 W Central Ave; Courthouse, Comanche, TX 76442. Recording, R/E phone-325-356-2655; fax-325-356-5764; 8:30AM-5PM (CST)
Index: Separate indices to search include deeds of trust, judgments, tax liens, lis pendens. Records indexed on computer back to 2003. Office personnel or visitors may perform searches. General search fee $5.00. Office will not search real estate records. Office will search UCC records prior to 7/2001 and current fixture (land) files. UCC search includes tax liens if requested. UCC search per debtor name- $10.00. UCC search request using non-standard form (per name)- $25.00. Copy fee $1.00 per page. Vital records have varying fees. Cert fee- $5.00 per cert plus copy fee. Payee- Comanche County Clerk. **Other phones:** Treasurer- 325-356-2838; Elections- 325-356-2655; Vital Records- 325-356-2655. **Property tax/Assessing-** 8 Huett Circle, PO Box 6, Comanche, TX 76442; 325-356-5253. (Appraiser/Auditor- 325-356-5253) **Online access-** Access Appraisal District records free at http://propaccess.trueautomation.com/clientdb/?cid=24.

Concho County

County Clerk, PO Box 98, Paint Rock, TX 76866-0098. Recording, R/E phone-325-732-4322; fax-325-732-2040; 8:30AM-5PM (CST)
Index: Separate indices to search include misc, liens, land. Records indexed on computer back to 1991. Office will perform a UCC search but public must search other records themselves. Search fee $5.00 per name per search. Real estate record owner and mortgage searches available. Copy fee $1.00 per page. Cert fee- $5.00 per cert plus copy fee. Payee- Concho County Clerk. **Other phones:** Treasurer- 325-732-4279; Elections- 325-732-2031; Vital Records- 325-732-4322. **Property tax/Assessing-** PO Box 68, 121 S Roberts, Paint Rock, TX 76866-0067; 325-732-4389, assessor fax- 325-732-4234. (Appraiser/Auditor- 325-732-4389) hours- 8AM-4:30PM No public access terminal.

Cooke County

County Clerk, Courthouse, Gainesville, TX 76240. Recording, R/E phone-940-668-5420, UCC recording phone-940-668-5474; fax-940-668-5486; 8AM-5PM. www.co.cooke.tx.us
Index: By years. Records indexed on computer from 1994-2008 in their office. Office will perform a UCC and Tax lien search but public must search other records themselves. Search fee $10.00. Copy fee $1.00 per page. Cert fee- $5.00 per cert plus copy fee. Payee- County Clerk. Office does not sell bulk data at this time. **Other phones:** Treasurer- 940-668-5423; Elections- 940-668-5420; Vital Records- 940-668-5421. **Property tax/Assessing-** 100 S Dixon, Gainesville, TX 76240; 940-668-5425, assessor fax-940-668-5497. (Appraiser/Auditor- 940-665-7651) No public access terminal.

Coryell County

County Clerk, PO Box 237, Gatesville, TX 76528. 254-865-5911, R/E recording phone-254-865-5911 x235; fax-254-865-8631; 8AM-N, 1PM-5PM. www.co.coryell.tx.us
Index: Separate indices to search include computer, older books. Records indexed on a public use terminal back to 1993. Office personnel or visitors may perform searches. Search fee $10.00 per name per year. Office will not search real estate records. Will not search UCC records. Copy fee $1.00 per page. Cert fee- $5.00 plus $1.00 per page. Payee- Coryell County Clerk. **Other phones:** Treasurer- x225; Elections- x296. **Property tax/Assessing-** PO Box 6, 201 S 7th St, County Annex/Gatesville, Gatesville, Texas 76528; 254-865-5911 x265, assessor fax- 254-865-2519. (Appraiser/Auditor- 254-865-6593) 8AM-4:30PM
www.coryellcounty.org/tax_assessor_collector.html

Cottle County

County Clerk, PO Box 717, Paducah, TX 79248. 806-492-3823; fax-806-492-2625; 9AM-N; 1-5PM (CST)
Index: All in one. Records indexed on computer back to 10/1/03. Office personnel or visitors may perform searches. Search fee $10.00. Office will search real estate records. Will search UCC records, request must be in writing. Copy fee $1.00 per page if court copies, $.25 per page if you copy. Cert fee- $5.00 per cert plus copy fee. Payee- Cottle County Clerk. **Other phones:** Treasurer- 806-492-3738; Elections- 806-492-3823; Vital Records- 806-492-3823. **Property tax/Assessing**- PO Box 908, 9th and Backus, Paducah, TX 79248; 806-492-3345, assessor fax-806-492-3107. (Appraiser/Auditor- 806-492-3345) No public access terminal.

Crane County

County Clerk, PO Box 578, Crane, TX 79731. 432-558-3581; fax-432-558-1148; 8AM-N, 1-5PM (CST) www.co.crane.tx.us
Index: All in one. Records indexed on computer back to 1990. Only the public may search. Copy fee $1.00 per page. Cert fee- $5.00 per cert plus copy fee. Payee- Crane County Clerk. **Online access to Real Estate, Grantor/Grantee, Deed, Lien, Birth, Death, Marriage, Probate, Court records:** Search official records after choosing county at www.edoctecinc.com/. If records are Unofficial, you search or copy them freely; if not Unofficial, a $1.00 per page fee applies. For details and signup, contact clerk or Jerry Anderson at 800-578-7746. **Other phones:** Treasurer- 432-558-3372; Elections- 432-558-3581; Vital Records- 432-558-3581. **Property tax/Assessing**- PO Box 878, 201 W 6th St #111, Crane, TX 79731; 432-558-2622, assessor fax- 432-558-1198. (Appraiser/Auditor- 432-558-1021) hours- 8AM-5PM No public access terminal.

Crockett County

County Clerk, PO Drawer C, Ozona, TX 76943. Recording, R/E phone-325-392-2022; 8AM-5PM, M-Th, 8AM-4PM Fri.
Index: Books. Records indexed on a public use terminal back to 1980. Office personnel or visitors may perform searches. Search fee $10.00 per hour. Office will not search UCC records. Copy fee $1.00 per page. Cert fee- $5.00 per cert plus copy fee. Payee- Crockett County Clerk. **Other phones:** Treasurer- 325-392-3376; Elections- 325-392-2022; Vital Records- 325-392-2022. **Property tax/Assessing**- PO Drawer H, 909 Ave D, Ozona, TX 76943; 325-392-2674, assessor fax- 325-392-2906. (Appraiser/Auditor- 325-392-2674) hours- 8:30AM-N 1-5PM M-Th; 8:30AM-N 1-4PM Fri. No public access terminal.

Crosby County

County Clerk, 201 W Aspen St, Rm 102, Crosbyton, TX 79322. 806-675-2334; 8AM-N, 1-5PM (CST)
Index: All in one. Record index not computerized. Only the public may search. Copy fee $1.00 per page. UCC copy $2.00 per page. Cert fee- $5.00 per cert plus copy fee. Payee- Crosby County Clerk. **Property tax/Assessing**- 806-675-2311. (Appraiser/Auditor-806-675-2356)

Culberson County

County Clerk, PO Box 158, Van Horn, TX 79855. 432-283-2058; fax-432-283-9234; 8AM-N, 1-5PM.
Index: All in one. Record index not computerized. Office personnel or visitors may perform searches. General index search fee $10.00 per name. Office will search real estate records, must have written request only. Copy fee $1.00 per page. Cert fee- $5.00 per cert plus copy fee. Payee- County Clerk. **Other phones:** Treasurer- 432-283-1419; Elections- 432-283-2058; Vital Records- 432-283-2058. **Property tax/Assessing**- PO Box 668, 300 La Caverna Dr, Van Horn, TX 79855; 432-283-2130, assessor fax- 432-283-1939. (Appraiser/Auditor- 432-283-2977) No public access terminal.

Dallam County

County Clerk, PO Box 1352, Dalhart, TX 79022. Recording, R/E phone-806-244-4751; fax-806-244-3751; 8AM-5PM (CST) www.dallam.org
Index: All in one. Records indexed on computer back to 1995. Only the public may search. Copy fee $1.00 per page. Cert fee- $5.00 per doc plus copy fee. Payee- Dallam County District Clerk. **Other phones:** Treasurer- 806-244-2530; Elections- 806-244-4751; Vital Records- 806-244-4751. **Property tax/Assessing**- PO Box 1299, Dalhart, TX 79022; 806-244-2801. (Appraiser/Auditor- 806-249-6767) www.dallam.org/county/tax.shtml

Dallas County

County Clerk, 509 Main St; Records Bldg, 2nd Fl, Dallas, TX 75202-3502. Recording, R/E phone-214-653-7275, UCC 214-653-7135; 8AM-4:30PM (CST) www.dallascounty.org/department/countyclerk/cclerk_index.html
Index: Separate indices to search include real property, personal property, assumed name filed with real property indexes. Records indexed on a public use terminal back to 1964. Office will perform a UCC and Tax lien search but public must search other records themselves. Copy fee $1.00. Internet watermarked copies free. Certified copies In Office or by mail. Cert fee- $5.00 per cert plus copy fee. Payee- Dallas County Clerk. **Online Real Estate, Deed, Lien, UCC, Voter Registration, Marriage, Assumed Name, Probate records:** Search most records at www.dallascounty.org/pars2/. Name search indices of deeds, marriages, assumed names, UCCs, probate, court records and real estate back to 1964 at www.realestate.countyclerk.dallascounty.org. Indices include DOB. Fee to view and print documents; credit cards accepted. Purchase per item, or subscribe for annual fee. Also, access County Voter Registration Records free at www.dalcoelections.org/voters.asp. Shows if registered and precinct. **Other phones:** Treasurer- 214-653-7321; Elections- 214-819-6300; Vital Records- 314-653-7478. **Property tax/Assessing**- 500 Elm St, Dallas, TX 75202-3304; 214-653-7811, assessor fax- 214-653-7887. (Appraiser/Auditor- 214-631-0520) hours- 7AM-5PM Public access terminal available. **Online access**- Access Central Appraisal District data free at www.dallascad.org/SearchOwner.aspx. Also search De Soto City and Glenn Heights tax office records free at www.texaspayments.com/057906/, and City of Garland taxes at www.texaspayments.com/057120/

Dawson County

County Clerk, PO Drawer 1268, Lamesa, TX 79331. Recording, R/E phone-806-872-3778; fax-806-872-2473; 8:30AM-5PM (CST)
Index: Separate indices to search. Records indexed on a public use terminal back to 1992. Office will perform a UCC search but public must search other records themselves. Search fee $5.00 per name. Copy fee $1.00 per page. Cert fee- $5.00 per cert plus copy fee. Payee- Dawson County Clerk. **Other phones:** Treasurer- 806-872-7474; Elections- 806-872-3778; Vital Records- 806-872-3778. **Property tax/Assessing**- 1806 Lubbock Hwy, Lamosa, TX 79331; 806-872-7060. (Appraiser/Auditor- 806-872-7060) hours- 8AM-5PM www.dawsoncad.org.

De Witt County

County Clerk, 307 N Gonzales; Courthouse, Cuero, TX 77954. 361-275-3724; fax-361-275-8994; 8AM-N, 1-5PM (CST) www.co.dewitt.tx.us/ips/cms
Index: All in one. Records indexed on official public records since January, 1996. Office will perform a UCC search but public must search other records themselves. General search fee $10.00 per debtor. Office may search real estate records for $5.00. Tax lien search fee-$10.00 per name. Copy fee $1.00 per page. Cert fee- $5.00 per doc plus copy fee. Payee- De Witt County Clerk. **Other phones:** Treasurer- 361-275-3478; Elections- 361-275-3724; Vital Records-361-275-3724; District Clerk Tabeth Gardner- 361-275-2221. **Property tax/Assessing**- PO Box 489, 115 N Gonzales, Cuero, TX 77954; 361-275-0879, assessor fax- 361-275-0883. (Appraiser/Auditor- 361-275-5312) 8AM-5PM No public access terminal. www.co.dewitt.tx.us/ips/cms/countyoffices/taxAssessorCollector.html **Online access**- Access appraisal district property data free at www.dewittcad.org/ and click on Search our data. Also, access assessor tax payment data free at www.dewittcountyonline.net/tax/taxonline.jsp.

Deaf Smith County

County Clerk, 235 E 3rd, Rm 203, Hereford, TX 79045-5542. Recording, R/E phone-806-363-7077; fax-806-363-7023; 8AM-5PM (CST)
Index: All in one. Records indexed on a public use terminal back to 1972. Office personnel or visitors may perform searches. Office only performs federal tax lien searches. Search fee $5.00 per federal tax lien debtor. General copy fee- $1.00 per page. Cert fee- $5.00 per cert plus copy fee. Payee- Deaf Smith County Clerk. Images on CD-rom available for $25.00 each; contact County Clerk David Ruland. **Other phones:** Treasurer- 806-363-7088; Elections-806-363-7077; Vital Records- 806-363-7077. **Property tax/Assessing**- PO Box 2298, 140 E 3rd St, Hereford, TX 79045; 806-364-0625, assessor fax-806-364-6895. (Appraiser/Auditor- 806-364-0625) hours- 8AM-N, 1-5PM Assessor and Appraiser in one office; public access terminal available. **Online access**- Access property and appraiser data free at http://clientdb.trueautomation.com/clientdb/main.asp.

Delta County

County Clerk, 200 W Dallas Ave, Cooper, TX 75432. 903-395-4400, R/E recording phone-903-395-4400 x222; fax-903-395-2178; 8AM-5PM (CST)
Index: All in one. Records indexed on a public use terminal back to 1/100. Office personnel or visitors may perform searches. Search fee $10.00; $5.00 per name per court. Office will search real estate records. Separate state/federal tax lien search fee- $5.00 per debtor. Copy fee $1.00 per page; $2.00 each if faxed back. Cert fee- $5.00 per cert plus copy fee. Payee- Delta County Clerk. **Other phones:** Treasurer- 903-395-4400 x225; Elections- 903-395-4400 x222; Vital Records- 903-395-4400 x222. **Property tax/Assessing**- 200 W Dallas Ave, Cooper, TX 75432; 903-395-4400 x228, assessor fax- 903-395-4638. (Appraiser/Auditor- 903-395-4118) Public access terminal available. **Online access**- Access Appraisal District records free at http://clientdb.trueautomation.com/clientdb/main.asp?id=39.

Denton County

County Clerk, PO Box 2187, Denton, TX 76202-2187. Recording, R/E phone-940-349-2010; fax-940-349-2019; 8AM-5PM; 8AM-4:30 Wed. (CST) www.dentoncounty.com/dept/ccl.htm
Index: Separate indices to search include deed of trust, release, mechanics lien, abstract of judgment, misc. Records indexed on a public use terminal from 1974 to present. Office personnel (mail only) or visitors may perform searches. General index search fee $5.00 per 5 years, per name. Office will search real estate records through the mail w/fee. Office will search UCC records prior to 7/2001 and current fixture (land) files. Tax liens not included in UCC search. UCC search per debtor name- $10.00. UCC search request using non-standard form (per name)- $25.00. Copy fee $1.00 per page. Cert fee- $5.00 per cert plus copy fee. Payee- Denton County Clerk, Cynthia Mitchell. Contact Cynthia Mitchell with individual bulk data request. **Online access to Real Estate, Grantor/Grantee, Deed, Lien, Voter Registration records:** Access county property database indices free for name/instrument searches; no fee for access, but to view and print images is $1.00 per page; see https://www.texaslandrecords.com/txlr/TxlrApp/index.jsp. With a full subscription search full indices and download images. Also, search voter registration rolls free at https://elections.dentoncounty.com/goVR.asp?Dept=82&Link=292. **Other phones:**

Treasurer- 940-349-3150; Elections- 940-349-3200; Vital Records- 940-349-2018; Admin- 940-349-2012. **Property tax/Assessing-** PO Box 90223, 1505 E McKinney, Denton, TX 76202; 940-349-3500, assessor fax- 940-349-3501. (Appraiser/Auditor- 940-349-3800) hours- 8AM-4:30PM No public access terminal available. **Online access-** Property tax inquiries can be made at www.dentoncad.com. Tax records are also at http://taxweb.dentoncounty.com/tax/ but no name searching.

Dickens County

County Clerk, PO Box 120, Dickens, TX 79229. 806-623-5531; fax-806-623-5319; 8AM-N, 1PM-5PM (CST)
Index: All in one. Record index not computerized. Office personnel or visitors may perform searches. General index search fee $5.00. Office will search real estate records. Office will not search UCC records. Copy fee $1.00 per page. Cert fee- $5.00 per cert includes copy fee. Payee- Dickens County Clerk. Bulk data available for purchase in paper format; contact county clerk. **Other phones:** Treasurer- 806-623-5542; Elections- 806-623-5531. **Property tax/Assessing-** PO Box 119, 512 Montgomery St, Dickens, TX 79229; 806-623-5216, assessor fax- 806-623-5361. (Appraiser/Auditor- 806-623-5216) No public access terminal.

Dimmit County

County Clerk, 103 N 5th St, Carrizo Springs, TX 78834. 830-876-4238/4239, R/E recording phone-830-876-4238; fax-830-876-4205; 8AM-5PM.
Index: All in one as of 7/2003. Record index not computerized. Office personnel or visitors may perform searches. General index search fee $10.00 per 10 years. Office will search real estate records. Office will not search UCC records. Copy fee $1.00 per page. Cert fee- $5.00 per doc plus copy fee. Payee- Dimmit County Clerk. **Other phones:** Treasurer- 830-876-4246 x3; Elections- 830-876-4238; Vital Records- 830-876-4238. **Property tax/Assessing-** 407 W Houston, Carrizo Springs, TX 78834; 830-876-4246 x1, assessor fax- 830-876-4203. (Appraiser/Auditor- 830-876-3420) hours- 8AM-N, 1-5PM Public access terminal available.

Donley County

County Clerk, PO Drawer U, Clarendon, TX 79226. Recording, R/E phone-806-874-3436; fax-806-874-3351; 8AM-N, 1-5PM.
Index: All in one. Records indexed on a public use terminal back to 9/94. Office personnel or visitors may perform searches. Search fee $5.00. UCC search $10.00. Office will search real estate records. Will search UCC records. Copy fee $1.00 per page. Cert fee- $5.00 per page plus copy fee. Payee- Donley County District Clerk. **Other phones:** Treasurer- 806-874-2328; Elections- 806-874-3436; Vital Records- 806-874-3436. **Property tax/Assessing-** PO Box 638, Clarendon, TX 79226; 806-874-2193, assessor fax- 806-874-3165. (Appraiser/Auditor- 806-874-2744);

Duval County

County Clerk, PO Box 248, San Diego, TX 78384. 361-279-6272 or 6274, R/E recording phone-361-279-6272; fax-361-279-3159; 8AM-N, 1-5PM (CST)
Index: All in one. Records indexed on a public use terminal back to 1986. Office personnel or visitors may perform searches. General index search fee $10.00 per search. Office will search real estate records. Office will search UCC records prior to 7/2001 and current fixture (land) files. Tax liens not included in UCC search. UCC search per debtor name- $10.00. Tax lien search fee- $10.00 per debtor. Copy fee $1.00 per page. Cert fee- $5.00 per cert plus copy fee. Payee- Duval County Clerk. **Other phones:** Treasurer- 361-279-6327; Elections- 361-279-6278; Vital Records- 361-279-6272. **Property tax/Assessing-** PO Box 337, 100 S Bexar, San Diego, TX 78384; 361-279-6340 or 6338, assessor fax- 361-279-2193. (Appraiser/Auditor- 361-279-3305) hours- 8AM-5PM No public access terminal.

Eastland County

County Clerk, PO Box 110, Eastland, TX 76448-0110. 254-629-1583; fax-254-629-8125; 8AM-5PM (CST)
Index: All in one. Records indexed on a public use terminal back to 1983. Office personnel or visitors may perform searches. Search fee $5.00 per name. Office will not search real estate records. Office will not search UCC records. Copy fee $1.00 per page. Cert fee- $5.00 per cert plus copy fee. Payee- Eastland County Clerk. **Other phones:** Treasurer- 254-629-2672; Elections- 254-629-1583; Vital Records- 254-629-1583. **Property tax/Assessing-** 100 W Main, #101 & 103, 1st FL, Eastland County Courthouse, Eastland, TX 76448; 254-629-1564 or 2211. (Appraiser/Auditor- 254-629-8597) hours- 8AM-11:30AM, 12:30PM-4:30PM www.eastlandcountytexas.com/County%20Tax%20Assessor-Collector.htm

Ector County

County Clerk, PO Box 707, Odessa, TX 79760. 432-498-4130; fax-432-498-4177; 8AM-4:30PM. www.co.ector.tx.us
Index: All in one. Records indexed on computer back to 1994. Office will perform a UCC or tax lien search but public must search other records themselves. Search fee $10.00 per debtor. Office will search real estate records only if volume and page number is provided. Copy fee $1.00 per page. Cert fee- $5.00 per cert plus copy fee. Payee- Linda Haney, County Clerk. **Online access to Real Estate, Grantor/Grantee, Deed, Lien, Judgment records:** Search the grantor/grantee index free at www.texaslandrecords.com. Also has a subscription service with search/payment options for full document viewing. Also, public record searches for a fee at https://www.countygovernmentrecords.com/texas/web/ **Other phones:** Treasurer- 432-498-4060; Elections- 432-498-4030. **Property tax/Assessing-** 1301 E 8th, Odessa, TX 79761; 432-498-4050. (Appraiser/Auditor- 432-332-6834) hours- 8AM-5PM Public access terminal available. **Online access-** Search appraisal district property data and personal property free at www.ectorcad.org.

Edwards County

County Clerk, PO Box 184, Rocksprings, TX 78880-0184. 830-683-2235; fax-830-683-5376; 8AM-5PM (CST)
Index: All in one. Records indexed on computer back to 2003. Office personnel or visitors may perform searches. Search fee $10.00 per name. Separate federal, state, or combined tax lien search- $10.00 per debtor. Copy fee $1.00 per page. Cert fee- $5.00 per cert plus copy fee. Payee- Edwards County Clerk. **Other phones:** Treasurer- 830-683-5116. **Property tax/Assessing-** PO Box 378, 204 N Sweden St, Rocksprings, TX 78880; 830-683-2337, assessor fax- 830-683-4195. (Appraiser/Auditor- 830-683-4189) 8AM-N, 1-4:30PM. Public access terminal available.

El Paso County

County Clerk, 500 E San Antonio, Rm 105, El Paso, TX 79901-2496. 915-546-2071, R/E recording phone-915-546-2074, UCC recording phone-915-546-2071; fax-915-546-2012; 8AM-5:30PM (MST) www.epcounty.com/clerk/
Index: All in one. Records indexed on a public use terminal back to 1981. Only the public may search. Copy fee $1.00 per page. Cert fee- $5.00 per cert plus copy fee. Payee- El Paso County Clerk. **Online access to Real Estate, Deed, Lien, Mortgage, Assumed Name, Vital Records, Judgment records:** Search official records including recordings, vital statistics and property free at www.epcounty.com/clerk/deedsearch.asp, also marriages at www.epcounty.com/clerk/marriagesearch.asp. Also, to search probate judgment records go to http://idocket.com/countycourt.htm. Search assumed names free at www.epcounty.com/clerk/assumed_search.asp. For county births, search www.epcounty.com/clerk/birthsearch.asp; deaths- www.epcounty.com/clerk/deaths.asp. Also, see note at beginning of section. **Other phones:** Elections- 915-546-2154; Vital Records- 915-546-2071. **Property tax/Assessing-** Appraisal District, 5801 Trowbridge, El Paso, TX 79925; 915-780-2000, assessor fax- 915-780-2130. (Appraiser/Auditor- 915-780-2000) hours- 8AM-5PM No public access terminal. www.elpasocad.org/ **Online access-** Search property tax data free at www.elpasocad.org. Also, see note at beginning of section. Search foreclosure notices free at www.epcounty.com/foreclosures/.

Ellis County

County Clerk, PO Box 250, Waxahachie, TX 75168. Recording, R/E phone-972-923-5070; fax-972-923-5075; 8AM-4:30PM (CST)
Index: All in one 1992 forward. Office personnel or visitors may perform searches. General search fee $5.00 per 5 years per name; UCCs $10.00 per 5 years. Real estate owner, mortgage, and property transfer searches available. Office will search UCC records prior to 7/2001 and current fixture (land) files. UCC search includes tax liens if requested. Copy fee $1.00 per page. Cert fee- $5.00 per cert plus copy fee. Payee- Ellis County Clerk. **Other phones:** Treasurer- 972-825-5125; Elections- 972-923-5195; Vital Records- 972-923-5070. **Property tax/Assessing-** 114 S Rogers, Waxahachie, TX 75165; 972-923-5150. (Appraiser/Auditor- 972-937-3552) **Online access-** Search the property appraiser database for free at www.elliscad.org. Access to property tax information is at www.elliscountytax.com. Other online access through private companies.

Erath County

County Clerk, 100 W Washington St; Courthouse, Stephenville, TX 76401. Recording, R/E phone-254-965-1482; fax-254-965-5732; 8AM-4PM (CST)
Index: All in one. Records indexed on a public use terminal back to 1988. Only the public may search. Copy fee $1.00 per page. Cert fee- $5.00 per cert plus copy fee. Payee- Erath County Clerk. **Other phones:** Treasurer- 254-965-1483; Elections- 254-965-1482; Vitals- 254-965-1410. **Property tax/Assessing-** 320 W College St, Stephenville, TX 76401; 254-965-8630, assessor fax- 254-965-4025. (Appraiser/Auditor- 254-965-7301) Public access terminal available. **Online access-** Find appraisal district data free at http://208.75.248.98/. Also, search tax office records free at www.texaspayments.com/072000/. Also, see note at beginning of section.

Falls County

County Clerk, PO Box 458, Marlin, TX 76661. Recording, R/E phone-254-883-1408, UCCs-254-883-1521; fax-254-883-1406; 8AM-N, 1-5PM (CST)
Index: All in one. Record index not computerized. Office personnel or visitors may perform searches. General search fee $5.00. UCC search fee- $10.00. Office will not search real estate records. Will search UCC records. Copy fee $1.00 per page. Cert fee- $5.00 per cert plus copy fee. Payee- Falls County Clerk. **Other phones:** Treasurer- 254-883-1433; Elections- 254-883-1521; Vital Records- 254-883-1408. **Property tax/Assessing-** PO Box 59, 125 Bridge St, #207, Marlin, TX 76661; 254-883-1436, assessor fax- 254-883-1438. (Appraiser/Auditor- 254-883-2543) hours- 8AM-4:30PM No public access terminal. **Online access-** Access property data free at www.fallscad.org. Click on Search Our Data. Maps may also be available.

Fannin County

County Clerk, 101 E Sam Rayburn Dr, #102; Courthouse, Bonham, TX 75418-4346. 903-583-7486; fax-903-583-7811; 8AM-5PM (CST) www.co.fannin.tx.us/ips/cms
Index: Indices now combined all-in-one. Records indexed on a public use terminal back to 1968. Office will perform a UCC search but public must search other records themselves. Copy fee $1.00 per page. Cert fee- $5.00 per cert plus copy fee. Payee- Fannin County Clerk. **Other phones:** Elections- 903-583-7488; Auditor- 903-583-7451. **Property**

tax/Assessing- 210 S Main St, Bonham, TX 75418; 903-583-7493, assessor fax- 903-583-1244. (Appraiser/Auditor- 903-583-8701) www.co.fannin.tx.us/ips/cms/departments/taxAssessorCollector.html

Fayette County

County Clerk, PO Box 59, La Grange, TX 78945. 979-968-3251, R/E recording phone-409-968-3251; fax-979-968-8531; 8AM-N, 1-5PM (CST) www.co.fayette.tx.us

Index: Separate indices to search. Records indexed on computer back to 1993. Only the public may search. Copy fee $1.00 per page. Cert fee- $5.00 per cert plus copy fee. Payee- Fayette County Clerk. **Online access to Real Estate, Grantor/Grantee, Deed, Lien, Judgment records:** Access recording records free at www.titlex.com; select Fayette County. **Other phones:** Elections- 979-968-6563; Vital Records- 979-968-3251. **Property tax/Assessing**- 151 N Washington St, Rm 107, Courthouse, LaGrange, TX 78945; 979-968-3164, assessor fax- 979-968-5840. (Appraiser/Auditor- 979-968-8383) hours- 8AM-5PM No public access terminal. **Online access**- Access assessor property records free at http://clientdb.trueautomation.com/clientdb/main.asp.

Fisher County

County Clerk, PO Box 368, Roby, TX 79543-0368. 325-776-2401; fax-325-776-3274; 8AM-5PM (CST)

Index: All in one. Records indexed on a public use terminal back to 1986. Office will perform a UCC search but public must search other records themselves. General index search fee $5.00 per name. Office will not search real estate records. UCC search per debtor name- $10.00. Copy fee $1.00 per page. Cert fee- $5.00 per page plus copy fee. Payee- Fisher County Clerk. **Other phones:** Treasurer- 325-776-3257; Elections- 325-776-2401; Vital Records- 325-776-2401. **Property tax/Assessing**- 109 N Angelo, Courthouse, Roby, TX 79543; 325-776-2733. (Appraiser/Auditor- 325-776-2733)

Floyd County

County Clerk, 105 Main St, Rm 101; Courthouse, Floydada, TX 79235. Recording, R/E phone-806-983-4900; fax-806-983-4909; 8:30AM-N, 1-5PM (CST)

Index: All in one. Record index not computerized. Office personnel or visitors may perform searches. Search fee $10.00 per debtor. Office will search real estate records. Office will not search UCC records. Copy fee $1.00 per page. Cert fee- $5.00 per cert plus copy fee. Payee- Floyd County Clerk. **Other phones:** Treasurer- 806-983-4910; Elections- 806-983-4900; Vital Records- 806-983-4900. **Property tax/Assessing**- 100 Main St, Courthouse, Rm 116, Floydada, TX 79235; 806-983-4908, assessor fax-806-983-4909. (Appraiser/Auditor- 806-983-5256) No public access terminal. **Online access**- Find appraisal district data free at http://208.75.248.98/.

Foard County

County Clerk, PO Box 539, Crowell, TX 79227. Recording, R/E phone-940-684-1365; fax-940-684-1918; 9AM-4:30PM (CST)

Index: All in one. Records indexed on computer back to 1989. Office personnel or visitors may perform searches. General index search fee $10.00 per name. Office will search real estate records. Office will search UCC records prior to 7/2001 and current fixture (land) files. Tax liens not included in UCC search. UCC search request using non-standard form (per name)- $25.00. Separate state tax lien search- $10.00 per debtor. Copy fee $1.00 per page. Cert fee- $5.00 plus copy fees. Payee- Foard County Clerk. **Other phones:** Treasurer- 940-684-1818; Elections- 940-684-1365; Vital Records- 940-684-1365. **Property tax/Assessing**- PO Box 309, 110 S First, Crowell, TX 79227; 940-684-1501, assessor fax- 940-684-1947. (Appraiser/Auditor- 940-684-1225) hours- 9AM-N, 1-4:30PM. Public access terminal available.

Fort Bend County

County Clerk, 301 Jackson, #101, Richmond, TX 77469. Recording, R/E phone-281-341-8685; fax-281-341-8669; 8AM-4PM (CST) www.co.fort-bend.tx.us

All UCC records purged 7/1/08 from this office. Index: All in one. Records indexed on a public use terminal back to 1836. Office will perform a fed tax lien search but public must search other records themselves. Search fee $10.00. Will not search UCC records. Copy fee $1.00 per page, Plats- $5.00 per page, CD Rom- $20.00. Cert fee- $5.00 per cert plus copy fee. Payee- Fort Bend County Clerk. Credit cards accepted (M/C or Visa). Bulk data available for purchase; contact Diane Shepard at 281-341-8664. **Online access to Real Estate, Grantor/Grantee, Deed, Lien, Judgment, Marriage, Death, Birth, Probate records:** Recorded records can be searched for free at http://ccweb.co.fort-bend.tx.us/. Also, see note at beginning of section. **Other phones:** Treasurer- 281-341-3750; Elections- 281-341-8670; Vitals- 281-341-8685. **Property tax/Assessing**- 500 Liberty St, Richmond, TX 77469; 281-341-3710, assessor fax- 281-341-3774. (Appraiser/Auditor- 281-344-8623) **Online access**- Access appraisal records free at www.fbcad.org/Appraisal/PublicAccess/. Also, property tax inquiries can be made free at www.txcountydata.com/selectCounty.asp.

Franklin County

County Clerk, 200 N Kaufman St, Mount Vernon, TX 75457-0068. Recording, R/E phone-903-537-4252 x2, UCC recording phone- ext 6; fax-903-537-2962; 8AM-N 1PM-5PM (CST) www.co.franklin.tx.us

Office will do basic searches, no extensive searches for public. Search for records is not guaranteed. Index: All in one. Deed records indexed on a public use terminal back to 1843. Office personnel or visitors may perform searches. General index search fee $5.00 per name. Office will search (limited) real estate records. Will not search UCC records. Copy fee $1.00 per page. Cert fee- $5.00 per cert plus copy fee. $23.00 for cert Birth, $21.00 for cert Death ($4.00 each for add'l copy purchased at same time). Payee- Franklin County Clerk. **Other phones:** Treasurer- 903-537-8334; Elections- 903-537-2358; Vital Records- 903-537-4252 x2. **Property tax/Assessing**- PO Box 70, 208 Highway 37S, Mount Vernon, TX 75457; 903-537-2358, assessor fax- 903-537-3483. (Appraiser/Auditor- 903-537-2286) hours- 8AM-4:45PM Public access terminal available. **Online access**- Access to property data is free at www.franklincad.com. Click on Search Our Data. Also, see note at beginning of section.

Freestone County

County Clerk, PO Box 1010, Fairfield, TX 75840. 903-389-2635; 8AM-5PM M-Th; 8AM-4:30PM F. (CST)

Index: All in one. Records indexed on a public use terminal back to 1981. Only the public may search. Copy fee $1.00 per page. Cert fee- $5.00 per cert plus copy fee. Payee- Freestone County Clerk. **Other phones:** Treasurer- 903-389-2180; Elections- 903-389-2635; Vital Records- 903-389-2635. **Property tax/Assessing**- PO Box 257, 112 E Main, Fairfield, TX 75840; 903-389-2336, assessor fax- 903-389-6533. (Appraiser/Auditor- 903-389-5510) Public access terminal available. **Online access**- Access to Appraiser's property data is free at www.freestonecad.org. Click on Search Our Data.

Frio County

County Clerk, 500 E San Antonio St, #6, Pearsall, TX 78061. Recording, R/E phone-830-334-2214; fax-830-334-0021; 8AM-N; 1PM-5PM.

Index: Separate indices to search. Records indexed on a public use terminal back 2 years. Only the public may search. Copy fee $1.00 per page. Cert fee- $5.00 per cert plus copy fee. Payee- Frio County Clerk. **Other phones:** Treasurer- 830-334-0040; Elections-830-334-2214; Vital Records- 830-334-2214. **Property tax/Assessing**- 500 E San Antonio St, #6, Pearsall, TX 78061; 830-334-2152. (Appraiser/Auditor- 830-334-4163);

Gaines County

County Clerk, 101 S Main, Rm 107, Seminole, TX 79360. Recording, R/E phone-432-758-4003, UCC recording phone-432-758-4033; fax-432-758-1442; 8AM-5PM (CST) www.co.gaines.tx.us

Index: All in one. Records indexed on a public use terminal back to 1964. Office personnel or visitors may perform searches. Search fee $5.00 per name. Office will not search real estate records. Tax liens not included in UCC search. Copy fee $1.00 per page. Cert fee- $5.00 per cert plus copy fee. Payee- Gaines County Clerk. **Other phones:** Treasurer- 432-758-4009; Elections- 432-758-4033 or 758-4003; Vital Records- 432-758-4033. **Property tax/Assessing**- 302 SE Ave B, Seminole, TX 79360; 432-758-4008, assessor fax- 432-758-3674. (Appraiser/Auditor- 432-758-3263) hours- 8:30AM-5PM A public access terminal is available. **Online access**- Access county parcel data free at www.taxnetusa.com/texas/. Tax Assessor located at 101 S Main, #108,

Galveston County

County Clerk, PO Box 17253, Galveston, TX 77552. 409-766-2200, R/E recording phone-409-766-2208; fax-409-765-3160; 8AM-5PM (CST) www.co.galveston.tx.us/County_Clerk/

Index: All in one. Records indexed on a public use terminal back to 1965. Only the public may search. Office will search real estate records. General copy fee $1.00 per page. Cert fee- $5.00 per cert plus copy fee. Payee- Galveston County Clerk. Bulk data available for purchase; call Dick Dickinson at 409-770-5115. **Online access to Real Estate, Grantor/Grantee, Deed, Lien, Judgment, UCC, Vital Statistic records:** Several sources exist. Access the county online official records index free at http://207.80.116.33/. Also, a Grantor/Grantee index is at www.titlex.com; select Galveston County; records go back to 1/1965. Also, see note at beginning of section. **Other phones:** Treasurer- 409-770-5395; Elections- 409-766-1005; Vital Records- 409-766-2207. **Property tax/Assessing**- PO Box 1169, 722 Moody Ave, Galveston, TX 77553-1169; 409-766-2280, assessor fax- 409-766-2280. (Appraiser/Auditor- 409-935-1980) A public access terminal is available. **Online access**- Search Central Appraisal Dist. database free at www.galvestoncad.org/Appraisal/PublicAccess/. For info, call 409-766-5115.

Garza County

County Clerk, PO Box 366, Post, TX 79356-0366. Recording, R/E phone-806-495-4430; fax-806-495-4431; 8AM-N, 1-5PM (CST) www.garzacounty.net

Index: All in one. Records indexed on computer back to 1987. Office personnel or visitors may perform searches. Search fee $5.00 per name. Copy fee $1.00 per page. Cert fee- $5.00 per cert plus copy fee. Payee- Garza County Clerk. **Other phones:** Treasurer- 806-495-4423; Elections- 806-495-4430; Vitals- 806-495-4430. **Property tax/Assessing**- PO Box 26, Post, TX 79356; 806-495-4448, assessor fax-806-495-4483. (Appraiser/Auditor- 806-495-3518) No public access terminal.

Gillespie County

County Clerk, 101 W Main, Rm 109, Unit #13, Fredericksburg, TX 78624. 830-997-6515; fax-830-997-9958; 8AM-4PM (CST)

Index: All in one. Records indexed on a public use terminal back to 9/89. Office personnel or visitors may perform searches. Search fee $5.00 per name; must be written request. Office will not search real estate records. Will not search UCC records. Copy fee $1.00; tax lien or real estate $1.00 per page. Cert fee- $10.00 per cert plus copy fee. Payee- Gillespie County Clerk. **Other phones:** Treasurer- 830-997-6521; Elections- 830-997-6515; Vital Records- 830-997-6515. **Property tax/Assessing**- 101 W Main, Unit #2, Fredericksburg, TX 78624; 830-997-6519, assessor fax- 830-990-2756. (Appraiser/Auditor- 830-997-9807) hours- 8AM-4:30PM No public access terminal. **Online**- Access Appraiser property data free http://propaccess.trueautomation.com/clientDB/?cid=52. Also, make Property tax inquiries at www.txcountydata.com/selectCounty.asp. Other online access through private companies.

Glasscock County

County Clerk, PO Box 190, Garden City, TX 79739. Recording, R/E phone-432-354-2371; fax-432-354-2616; 7:30AM-4PM (CST)
Index: All in one. Record index not computerized. Only the public may search. Office will not search real estate records. Will not search UCC records. Copy fee $1.00 per page. Cert fee- $5.00 per cert plus copy fee. Payee- Glasscock County Clerk. **Other phones:** Treasurer- 432-354-2415; Elections- 432-354-2371; Vital Records- 432-354-2371. **Property tax/Assessing**- PO Box 89, 124 S Myrl, Garden City, TX 79739; 432-354-2361, assessor fax- 432-354-2661. (Appraiser/Auditor- 432-354-2580) hours-8:30AM-N, 1-4PM No public access terminal.

Goliad County

County Clerk, PO Box 50, Goliad, TX 77963. 361-645-3294; fax-361-645-3858; 8AM-N, 1PM-5PM (CST) www.co.goliad.tx.us/ips/cms
Index: All in one. (Divorce records located here) Real property records indexed by last name and year on a public use terminal back to 1/1/1983. Office will perform UCC and RE search but public must search other records themselves. Search fee $10.00 per name. Copy fee $1.00 per page. Cert fee- $5.00 per cert plus copy fee. Payee- County Clerk. **Online access to Real Estate, Grantor/Grantee, Deed, Lien, Judgment records:** Access recording records free at www.titlex.com; select Goliad county. Records range is 1/1950 to 12/2003. Also, see note at beginning of section. **Other phones:** Treasurer- 361-645-3551; Elections- 361-645-3294; Vital Records- 361-645-3294. **Property tax/Assessing**- PO Box 800, 329 W Franklin, Goliad, TX 77963; 361-645-3354 or 2541, assessor fax- 361-645-8544. (Appraiser/Auditor- 361-645-2492) hours- 8AM-5PM. No public access terminal.

Gonzales County

County Clerk, PO Box 77, Gonzales, TX 78629. Recording, R/E phone-830-672-2801; fax-830-672-2636; 8AM-5PM (CST)
Index: Separate indices to search include prior to 1980, deed, deed of trust, oil & gas, cont sale, judgment, state & federal tax liens. Records indexed on a public use terminal back to 1981. Office personnel or visitors may perform searches. Search fee $5.00 per name. Copy fee $1.00 per page. Cert fee- $5.00 per instrument plus copy fee. Payee- County Clerk. **Other phones:** Treasurer- 830-672-2621; Vital Records- 830-672-2801. **Property tax/Assessing**- PO Box 677, 522 St Matthews St, Gonzales, TX 78629; 830-672-2841, assessor fax-830-672-3476. (Appraiser/Auditor- 830-672-2879) hours- 8AM-4:45PM No public access terminal.

Gray County

County Clerk, PO Box 1902, Pampa, TX 79066-1902. Recording, R/E phone-806-669-8004; fax-806-669-8054; 8:30AM-5PM (CST)
Index: All in one. Records indexed on a public use terminal back to 1990. Office personnel or visitors may perform searches. Search fee $10.00 per name. Office will not search real estate records. Copy fee $1.00 per page. Cert fee- $5.00 per cert plus copy fee. Payee- Gray County Clerk. **Other phones:** Treasurer-806-669-8009; Elections- 806-669-4003; Vital Records- 806-669-8004. **Property tax/Assessing**- PO Box 382, 205 N Russell, Courthouse, Pampa, TX 79065; 806-669-8018, assessor fax- 806-669-8051. (Appraiser/Auditor- 806-665-0791) No public access terminal.

Grayson County

County Clerk, 100 W Houston, #17, Sherman, TX 75090. 903-813-4242, R/E recording phone-903-813-4238, UCC phone-903-813-4239; fax-903-813-4382; 8AM-5PM (CST) www.co.grayson.tx.us/main.htm
Index: All in one. Records indexed on a public use terminal back to 1968. Only the public may search. Office will not search real estate records. Copy fee $1.00, if tax lien or real estate $1.00 per page. Cert fee- $5.00 per cert plus copy fee. Payee- Grayson County Clerk. **Online access to Real Estate, Grantor/Grantee, Deed, Mortgage, Lien, Death, Marriage, Judgment records:** Search grantor/grantee index free at www.texaslandrecords.com. Registration and fees required for full data. Access recording records free at www.titlex.com; select Grayson county. **Other phones:** Treasurer- 903-813-4251; Elections- 903-813-4260; Vital Records- 903-813-4243. **Property tax/Assessing**- 100 W Houston, Sherman, TX 75090; 903-893-8683. (Appraiser/Auditor- 903-893-9673) **Online access**- Search appraiser property data free at www.graysoncad.org/. Search the Grayson CAD system for mortgage, and property data at http://clientdb.trueautomation.com/clientdb/main.asp?id=15.

Gregg County

County Clerk, PO Box 3049, Longview, TX 75606. 903-236-8430, R/E recording phone-903-236-8430 x846, UCC recording phone-903-236-8430 x746 or 846; fax-903-237-2574; 8AM-5PM (CST) www.co.gregg.tx.us
Index: All in one. Records indexed on a public use terminal back to 1981. Office will perform a UCC search but public must search other records themselves. Search fee $10.00 per debtor for UCC's. Copy fee $1.00 per page. Cert fee- $5.00 per cert plus copy fee. Payee- Gregg County Clerk. **Online access to Real Estate, Grantor/Grantee, Deed, Mortgage, Lien, Judgment, Vital Statistic, UCC records:** Access to the County Clerk's Official Public Records database is free to view at www.co.gregg.tx.us/A2WebUI/. Fee to copy documents. Also, access recording records free at www.titlex.com; select Gregg county. Records range is 4/1977 to 5/2005. Also, see note at beginning of section. **Other phones:** Treasurer- 903-236-8430 x853; Elections- 903-236-8458; Vital Records- 903-236-8430 x637. **Property tax/Assessing**- 101 E Methvin, #215, Longview, TX 75606; 903-237-2552, assessor fax- 903-237-2607. (Appraiser/Auditor- 903-238-8823) hours- 8AM-4:30PM. Public access terminal available. **Online access**- Search property tax records for free at www.co.gregg.tx.us/appraisal/publicaccess/. Also, property tax inquiries made at http://propaccess.trueautomation.com/clientdb/?cid=38.

Grimes County

County Clerk, PO Box 209, Anderson, TX 77830. 936-873-2111, R/E recording phone-936-873-2111 x252, UCC recording phone-936-873-2606 x252; fax-936-873-3308; 8AM-N, 1-4:45PM (CST)
Index: All in one. Records indexed on a public use terminal back to 1967. Office will perform a UCC search by form only, but public must search other records themselves. Search fee $5.00 per name. Copy fee $1.00 per page. Cert fee- $5.00 per cert plus copy fee. Payee- Grimes County Clerk. **Other phones:** Treasurer- 936-873-2606 x233; Elections- 936-873-2606 x246; Vital Records- 936-873-2606 x250. **Property tax/Assessing**- PO Box 455, 114 W Buffington, Anderson, TX 77830; 936-873-2606 x231, assessor fax- 936-873-2623. (Appraiser/Auditor- 936-873-2163) hours- 8AM-4:30PM No public access terminal. **Online access**- Access property appraisal data free at http://67.76.234.90/Appraisal/PublicAccess/. Other online access through private companies.

Guadalupe County

County Clerk, 101 E Court St, Rm 209, Seguin, TX 78155. 830-303-4188 x236; fax-830-401-0300; 8AM-4:30PM (CST) www.co.guadalupe.tx.us
Index: Separate indices to search include indexes back to the 1800's. Records indexed on a public use terminal back to 1974. Office will perform a UCC search but public must search other records themselves. Office will not perform real estate title searches but will retrieve files. Copy fee $1.00 per page. Cert fee- $5.00 per cert plus copy fee. Payee- Guadalupe County Clerk. **Other phones:** Treasurer-830-303-4188 x338; Elections- 830-303-6363; Vital Records- 830-303-4188 x233. **Property tax/Assessing**- 307 W Court St, Seguin, TX 78155; 830-303-3421 x511, assessor fax- 830-372-9940. (Appraiser/Auditor- 830-372-2871 or 830-303-3313) No public access terminal. **Online access**- Search appraisal roll, parcel tax data free at www.co.guadalupe.tx.us/Appraisal/PublicAccess/.

Hale County

County Clerk, 500 Broadway, #140, Plainview, TX 79072-8030. 806-291-5261; fax-806-291-9810; 8AM-N,1-5PM (CST)
Index: All in one. Records indexed on computer from 1995 to present; 1994 and back in books. Office personnel or visitors may perform searches. Search fee $5.00 per name. Office will search real estate records. Will not search UCC records or liens. Copy fee $1.00 per page. Cert fee- $5.00 per cert plus copy fee. Payee- Hale County Clerk. CDs of bulk data available for purchase. **Other phones:** Treasurer-806-291-5213; Elections- 806-291-5261; Vitals- 806-291-5219. **Property tax/Assessing**- 302 W 8th, Plainview, TX 79072; 806-293-4226, assessor fax-806-293-1834. (Appraiser/Auditor- 806-293-4226) hours- 8AM-5PM Public access terminal available.

Hall County

County Clerk, 512 Main St S, #8; Courthouse, Memphis, TX 79245. 806-259-2627; fax-806-259-5078; 8:30AM-N, 1-5PM (CST)
Index: Books, computer. Records indexed on a public use terminal back to 1992. Office personnel or visitors may perform searches. Search fee $10.00. Office will search real estate records. Copy fee $1.00 per page. Cert fee- $5.00 per cert plus copy fee. Payee- Hall County Clerk. **Other phones:** Treasurer- 806-259-2421. **Property tax/Assessing**- 516 6th St #5, Memphis, TX 79245; 806-259-2125, assessor fax-806-259-3322. (Appraiser/Auditor- 806-259-2393) 8:30AM-N, 1-4:30PM. Public access terminal available.

Hamilton County

County Clerk, 101 E Main St; Courthouse, Hamilton, TX 76531. Recording, R/E phone-254-386-3518; fax-254-386-8727; 8AM-5PM.
Index: All in one. Record index not computerized. Office personnel or visitors may perform searches. Search fee $10.00 per name (FTL, STL, AJ). Office will search limited real estate records. Will search UCC records. General copy fee $1.00 per page. Cert fee- $1.00 per doc plus copy fee. Payee- Hamilton County Clerk. **Other phones:** Treasurer- 254-386-5315; Elections- 254-386-3518; Vital Records- 254-386-3518. **Property tax/Assessing**- 119 E Henry, Hamilton, TX 76531; 254-386-8945, assessor fax-254-386-3841. (Appraiser/Auditor- 254-386-8945) No public access terminal. **Online access**- Access property appraisal data free at www.txcountydata.com/county.asp?County=097.

Hansford County

County Clerk, 15 NW Court, Spearman, TX 79081. Recording, R/E phone-806-659-4110; fax-806-659-4168; 8AM-5PM.
Index: All in one. Records indexed on computer from 1980, prior in index books. Only office personnel may search. Search fee $10.00. Copy fee $1.00 per page. Cert fee- $5.00 per cert plus copy fee. Payee- County Clerk. **Other phones:** Treasurer- 806-659-4125;

Elections- 806-659-4110; Vital Records- 806-659-4110. **Property tax/Assessing**- 14 NW Court, Spearman, TX 79081; 806-659-4120, assessor fax-806-659-4124. (Appraiser/Auditor- 806-659-5575) hours- 8AM-4:45PM No public access terminal.

Hardeman County

County Clerk, PO Box 30, Quanah, TX 79252-0030. Recording, R/E phone-940-663-2901; fax-940-663-5161; 8:30AM-5PM (CST)
Index: All in one. Record index not computerized. Only the public may search. Copy fee $1.00 per page. Cert fee- $5.00 per cert plus copy fee. Payee-Hardeman County Clerk. **Other phones:** Treasurer-940-663-5401; Elections- 940-663-2901; Vital Records- 940-663-2901. **Property tax/Assessing**- PO Box 30, 300 Main St, Quanah, TX 79252; 940-663-5221, assessor fax- 940-663-2770. (Appraiser/Auditor- 940-663-2532) hours- 8:30AM-N, 1-5PM No public access terminal.

Hardin County

County Clerk, PO Box 38, Kountze, TX 77625. Recording, R/E phone-409-246-5185; fax-409-246-3208; 8AM-5PM (CST)
Index: All in one. Records indexed on a public use terminal back to 1992. Office personnel or visitors may perform searches. Search fee $5.00. Include the approximate date in any real estate search request. Will not search UCC records. Copy fee $1.00 per page. Cert fee- $5.00 per cert plus copy fee. Payee-Hardin County Clerk. Bulk data available for purchase, contact 409-246-5185. **Other phones:** Treasurer- 409-246-5121; Elections- 409-246-5185; Vital Records- 409-246-5185. **Property tax/Assessing**- PO Box 2260, 300 Monroe #B101, Kountze, TX 77625; 409-246-5180, assessor fax-409-246-4718. (Appraiser/Auditor- 409-246-2507) Public access terminal available.

Harris County

County Clerk, PO Box 1525, Houston, TX 77251-1525. Recording, R/E phone-713-755-6405, UCC recording phone-713-755-6439; fax-713-755-4977; 8AM-4:30PM (CST) www.cclerk.hctx.net
Personal checks are not accepted for mail requests.
Index: Separate indices to search include real property, marriage license, assumed name, county civil courts at law, probate. Records indexed on computer back to 1961. Office will perform a UCC search but public must search other records themselves. General copy fee $5.00 for 1-3 pages; $1.50 each add'l.Real estate record copy- $1.00 per page. Cert fee- $5.00 per doc plus copy fee. Payee-Harris County Clerk. **Online access to Real Estate, Grantor/Grantee, Lien, Judgment, Appraiser, Voter, UCC, Assumed Name, Vital Statistic, Probate records:** Access to Assumed Name records, UCC filings, vital statistic, and Real Property are at www.cclerk.hctx.net/coolice/default.asp?Category=RealProperty&Service=mastermenu. County Court Civil, marriage and informal marriage records also available. Also, access recording records free at www.titlex.com; select Harris county. Search voter registrations free at www.tax.co.harris.tx.us/voter/voter.asp. Also, search probate records and judgment records at http://idocket.com/countycourt.htm. **Other phones:** Treasurer- 713-755-5120; Elections- 713-755-5792; Vital Records- 713-755-6438. **Property tax/Assessing**- 1001 Preston, Houston, TX 77002; 713-368-2200, assessor fax- 713-368-2409. (Appraiser/Auditor- 713-957-5291) hours- 7:45AM-4:45PM Public access terminals available. **Online access**- Appraiser records are at www.hcad.org/Records/. Search tax assessor data free at www.tax.co.harris.tx.us/dbsearch/dbsearch.asp. Also, search tax statements free at www.hctax.net/propertytax/current/currentsearch.asp

Harrison County

County Clerk, PO Box 1365, Marshall, TX 75671. Recording, R/E phone-903-935-8403; fax-903-935-4877; 8AM-5PM (CST)
Index: All in one. Records indexed on a public use terminal back to 8/13/76. Office personnel or visitors may perform searches; office personnel will not search for real estate titles. Search fee $5.00 per name per 10 years. Office will not search real estate records. Office will search UCC records prior to 7/2001 and current fixture (land) files. UCC search includes tax liens if requested. Copy fee $1.00 per page. Cert fee- $5.00 per cert plus copy fee. Payee- Harrison County Clerk. Bulk data available for purchase on CD's, contact Patsy Cox. **Other phones:** Treasurer- 903-935-8404; Elections- 903-935-4822; Vital Records-903-935-8403. **Property tax/Assessing**- PO Box 967, 200 W Houston, Marshall, TX 75671; 903-935-8411, assessor fax- 903-935-5564. (Appraiser/Auditor- 903-935-1991) Public access terminals are available. **Online access**- Find appraisal district data free at http://208.75.248.98/.

Hartley County

County Clerk, PO Box Q, Channing, TX 79018. 806-235-3582; fax-806-235-2316; 8:30AM-N 1PM-4:30PM. www.co.hartley.tx.us/ips/cms/countyoffices/countyClerk.html
Index: All in one. Records indexed on a public use terminal back to 1990. Only the public may search. Will not search UCC records. Copy fee $1.00 per page. Cert fee- $5.00 per doc plus copy fee. Payee-Hartley County Clerk. **Other phones:** Treasurer-806-235-3572; Elections- 806-235-3582; Vital Records- 806-235-3582; Judge- 806-235-3442. **Property tax/Assessing**- PO Box I, Channing, TX 79018; 806-235-3142, fax- 806-235-2003. (Appraiser/Auditor- 806-365-4515) www.co.hartley.tx.us/ips/cms/countyoffices/taxAssesorCollector.html **Online access**- Find appraisal district data free at http://208.75.248.98/.

Haskell County

County Clerk, PO Box 725, Haskell, TX 79521-0725. Recording, R/E phone-940-864-2451; fax-940-864-6164; 8AM-5PM.
Index: All in one. Records indexed on computer back to 1994. Office personnel or visitors may perform searches. General index search fee $5.00 per name. Office will not search real estate records. UCC search per debtor name- $10.00. Separate tax lien search-$10.00 per debtor. Copy fee $1.00 per page. Cert fee-$5.00 per doc plus copy fee. Payee- Haskell County Clerk. **Other phones:** Treasurer- 940-864-3448; Elections- 940-864-2451; Vital Records- 940-864-2451. **Property tax/Assessing**- 1 Ave D, Courthouse, Haskell, TX 79521; 940-864-3805, assessor fax- 940-864-6164. (Appraiser/Auditor- 940-864-3805) hours-8:30AM-5PM M-Th, 8:30AM-4:30PM Fri **Online access**- Property tax inquiries can be made at www.txcountydata.com/county.asp?County=104. Other online access through private companies.

Hays County

County Clerk, 137 N Guadalupe; Hays County Records Bldg, San Marcos, TX 78666. 512-393-7329; fax-512-393-7337; 8AM-4:30PM (CST) www.co.hays.tx.us
Index: All in one. Records indexed on a public use terminal back to 1/1/1990. Office personnel or visitors may perform searches. General index search fee $10.00 per name per 10 years. Office will search real estate records. Will not search UCC records. Copy fee $1.00 per page. Cert fee- $5.00 per cert plus copy fee. Payee- Hays County Clerk. **Online Real Estate, Grantor/Grantee, Deed, Line, Vital Statistic, Judgment, Probate records:** Search Grantor/Grantee index free at www.texaslandrecords.com. Registration and fees apply for full data. Access probate and judgment records back to 1997 free at http://idocket.com/countycourt.htm . **Other phones:** Treasurer- 512-393-2236; Elections- 512-393-7310; Vital Records- 512-393-7326. **Property tax/Assessing**- 102 N LBJ, San Marcos, TX 78666; 512-393-5545, assessor fax- 512-393-5545. (Appraiser/Auditor- 512-268-2522) Public access terminals available. **Online** - Access property appraiser data free at www.hayscad.com/Appraisal/PublicAccess/default.aspx. Access tax collector property data free at http://66.90.254.60/appraisal/publicaccess/. Also, see notes at beginning of section for add'l property data.

Hemphill County

County Clerk, PO Box 867, Canadian, TX 79014. 806-323-6212; 8AM-5PM (CST)
Index: All in one. Record index not computerized. Only the public may search real estate. General index search fee $5.00 per name. Copy fee $1.00 per page. Cert fee- $5.00 per cert plus copy fee. Payee-Hemphill County Clerk. **Other phones:** Treasurer-806-323-6671; Elections- 806-323-6212; Vital Records- 806-323-6212. **Property tax/Assessing**-400 Main St, Canadian, TX 79014; 806-323-6661, assessor fax- 806-323-9745. (Appraiser/Auditor- 806-323-8022) hours- 8AM-N, 1-5PM No public access terminal. **Online access**- Access to county property data is free at www.hemphillcad.org. Site may be under construction.

Henderson County

County Clerk, PO Box 632, Athens, TX 75751-0632. Recording, R/E phone-903-675-6140; fax-903-675-6105; 8AM-5PM (CST) http://co.henderson.tx.us
Index: All in one. Records indexed on a public use terminal back to 1967. Office personnel or visitors may perform searches. Search fee $5.00. Office will search real estate records. Will search UCC records. Copy fee $1.00 per page; marriage cert copy- $5.00. Cert fee- $1.00 per cert plus copy fee. Payee-Henderson County Clerk. CDs of bulk data available for purchase; contact Evelyn Anderson or Barbara Cox. **Other phones:** Treasurer- 903-675-6119; Elections- 903-675-6140; Vital Records- 903-675-6140. **Property tax/Assessing**- 101 E Tyler, Athens, TX 75751; 903-675-6134, assessor fax- 903-677-3858. (Appraiser/Auditor- 903-675-9296) hours-8AM-4:45PM No public access terminal. **Online access**- Find appraisal district data free at http://208.75.248.98/. Add'l online access through private companies.

Hidalgo County

County Clerk, PO Box 58, Edinburg, TX 78540. 956-318-2100; fax-956-318-2105; 7:30AM-5:30PM (CST) www.hidalgocountyclerk.us
Index: Books, computer. Records indexed on a public use terminal back to 1980. Office personnel or visitors may perform searches. Search fee $5.00 per name. Office will search real estate records. Office will not search UCC records. Copy fee $1.00 per page. Cert fee- $5.00 per cert plus copy fee. Payee- Hidalgo County Clerk. **Online access to Real Estate, Grantor/Grantee, Deed, Judgment, Vital Statistic, Probate records:** Search grantor/grantee index free at www.texaslandrecords.com. Registration and fees apply for full data. Access probate and judgment records back to 1986 free at http://idocket.com/countycourt.htm. **Other phones:** Treasurer- 956-318-2504; Elections- 956-318-2570. **Property tax/Assessing**- 2812 S Bus Hwy 281, Edinburg, TX 78540; 956-318-2157, assessor fax-956-318-2733. (Appraiser/Auditor- 956-381-8466) hours- 8AM-5PM **Online access**- Search appraiser property records for free at www.hidalgoad.org/appraisal/publicaccess/. Also, see note at beginning of section for add'l property data.

Hill County

County Clerk, PO Box 398, Hillsboro, TX 76645. 254-582-4030; fax-254-582-4003; 8AM-5PM (CST)
Index: All in one. Records indexed on a public use terminal back to 1993. Office personnel or visitors may perform searches. Search fee $10.00. Office will not search real estate records. Will search UCC records. Copy fee $1.00 per page. Cert fee- $5.00 per cert plus copy fee. Payee- Hill County Clerk. Bulk data available for purchase on CD, contact Martha. **Online access to Probate, Judgment records:** Search probate court records and judgment records at

http://idocket.com/countycourt.htm Also, see note at beginning of section. **Other phones:** Treasurer- 254-582-4050; Elections- 254-582-4072; Vital Records-254-582-4030. **Property tax/Assessing**- PO Box 412, #40 Waco St, Hillsboro, TX 76645; 254-582-4000, assessor fax- 254-582-4001. (Appraiser/Auditor- 254-582-2508) Public access terminal available. **Online access**- Access appraisal district property records free at www.hillcad.org/in/reportshome.php.

Hockley County

County Clerk, 800 Houston St, #213, Levelland, TX 79336. 806-894-3185; fax-none; 9AM-5PM (CST) www.co.hockley.tx.us/coclerk.html
Index: Indices arranged by years. Records indexed on a public use terminal back to 1960. Only the public may search. Copy fee $1.00 per page. Cert fee- $5.00 per cert plus copy fee. Payee- Hockley County Clerk. **Other phones:** Treasurer- 806-894-3718; Elections-806-894-3185; Vital Records- 806-894-3185. **Property tax/Assessing**- 802 Houston St, #106, Levelland, TX 79336; 806-894-4938, assessor fax-806-894-6917. (Appraiser/Auditor- 806-894-6070) Public access terminal available. **Online access**-Access property records free at http://clientdb.trueautomation.com/clientdb/main.asp?id=50.

Hood County

County Clerk, PO Box 339, Granbury, TX 76048-0339. 817-579-3222; fax-817-579-3227; 8AM-4:30PM (CST) www.co.hood.tx.us
Index: Separate indices to search include before 1996 recorded in deed records, after 1996 real records, deeds, leases, deed trust, assignments, etc. Records indexed on a public use terminal back to 1982. Office personnel or visitors may perform searches. General index search fee $5.00 per name. Office will not search real estate or UCC records. Copy fee $1.00 per page. Cert fee- $5.00 per cert plus copy fee. Payee-Hood County Clerk. Weekly filings available on CD for $25.00 each. Also, recorded images from 1998 to present available in bulk, contact Mary Burnett. **Other phones:** Treasurer- 817-579-3208; Elections-817-408-2525; Vital Records- 817-579-3222. **Property tax/Assessing**- 1902 W Pearl, Granbury, TX 76048; 817-579-3295, assessor fax- 817-573-6451. (Appraiser/Auditor- 817-573-2471) Public access terminal available. **Online access**- Find appraisal district data free at http://208.75.248.98/. Add'l online access through private companies.

Hopkins County

County Clerk, PO Box 288, Sulphur Springs, TX 75483. 903-438-4074, R/E recording phone-903-885-4074, UCC phone-903-438-4074; fax-903-438-4110; 8AM-5PM (CST) www.hopkinscountytx.org
Index: All in one. Records indexed on a public use terminal back to 1967. Office will perform a UCC search but public must search other records themselves. UCC search per debtor name- $10.00 per name. Copy fee $1.00 per page. Cert fee- $5.00 per cert plus copy fee. Payee- Hopkins County Clerk. Images and indexes are available from June 2001 to present, contact Kay Penn. **Online access to Real Estate, Deed records:** Access real property records free after registering for login and password at www.hopkinscountyonline.net/countyclerk/. **Other phones:** Treasurer- 903-438-4003; Elections- 903-438-4074; Vital Records- 903-438-4074; Voter Registrar- 903-438-4063. **Property tax/Assessing**-118 Main St, Sulpur Springs, TX 75482; 903-438-4063, assessor fax- 903-438-4015. (Appraiser/Auditor- 903-885-2173) Public access terminal available. **Online access**- Find appraisal district data free at http://208.75.248.98/.

Houston County

County Clerk, PO Box 370, Crockett, TX 75835-0370. 936-544-3255, R/E recording phone-936-544-3255 x241; fax-936-544-1954; 8AM-4:30PM (CST) www.co.houston.tx.us
Index: All in one. Records indexed on a public use terminal back to 199. Only the public may do name searches; this office will retrieve specific documents for a fee. Search fee $10.00 per name. Office will search limited real estate records. Office will search UCC records. Copy fee $1.00 per page. Cert fee-$5.00 per doc plus copy fee. Payee- Houston County Clerk. land data is available in bulk format, contact Bridget Lamb, 936-544-3255 x240. **Online access to Real Estate, Deed, Official records:** Search official records after choosing county at www.edoctecinc.com/. If records are Unofficial, you search or copy them freely; if not Unofficial, a $1.00 per page fee applies. For details and signup, contact clerk or Jerry Anderson at 800-578-7746. **Other phones:** Treasurer- 936-544-3255 x236; Elections-936-544-3255 x241; Vital Records- 936-544-3255 x241. **Property tax/Assessing**- PO Box 112, Crockett, TX 75835; 936-544-9655, assessor fax-936-544-8213. (Appraiser/Auditor- 936-544-9655) A public access terminal is available. **Online**- Access to property tax records is free at www.houstoncad.org/.

Howard County

County Clerk, PO Box 1468, Big Spring, TX 79721-1468. Recording, R/E phone-432-264-2213, UCC recording phone-432-264-2214; fax-432-264-2215; 8AM-5PM (CST) www.howard-county.net
Index: All in one. Records indexed on a public use terminal back to 1983. Only the public may search. Copy fee $1.00 per page. Cert fee- $5.00 per cert plus copy fee. Payee- Howard County Clerk. **Other phones:** Treasurer- 432-264-2218; Elections- 432-264-2273; Vital Records- 432-264-2214. **Property tax/Assessing**- PO Box 1111, 315 Main St, Big Springs,TX 79721-1111; 432-264-2232, assessor fax-432-264-2282. (Appraiser/Auditor- 432-263-8301) A public access terminal is available. www.co.howard.tx.us/ips/cms/countyoffices/taxAssessorCollector.html

Hudspeth County

County Clerk, PO Drawer 58, Sierra Blanca, TX 79851. Recording, R/E phone-915-369-2301; fax-915-369-0055; 8AM-N, 1PM-5PM (MST)
Index: All in one. Records indexed on a public use terminal back to mid-1986. Office personnel or visitors may perform searches. General search fee $5.00 per name. Office will search real estate records. Office will search UCC records prior to 7/2001 and current fixture (land) files. UCC search per debtor name- $10.00. Copy fee $1.00 per page. Cert fee-$5.00 per doc plus copy fee. Payee- County Clerk. **Other phones:** Treasurer- 915-369-3511; Elections-915-369-2301; Vital Records- 915-369-2301; Auditor- 915-369-4147. **Property tax/Assessing**- PO Box 158, 109 Brown St, Sierra Blanca, TX 79851; 915-369-2331, assessor fax- 915-369-3005. (Appraiser/Auditor- 915-369-4118) hours- 8AM-5PM Public access terminal available.

Hunt County

County Clerk, PO Box 1316, Greenville, TX 75403-1316. Recording, R/E phone-903-408-4130; fax-none; 8AM-4:30PM (CST) www.huntcounty.net
Index: All in one. Records indexed on a public use terminal back to 1966. Office personnel or visitors may perform searches. Search fee $10.00 per name/debtor. Office will not search real estate records. Office will not search UCC records. Copy fee $1.00 per page. Cert fee- $5.00 per cert plus copy fee. Payee- Hunt County Clerk. Bulk data available for purchase (index & images of real property). Ask for Linda Brooks-Co Clerk. **Other phones:** Treasurer-903-408-4171; Elections- 903-454-5467; Vital Records- 903-408-4130. **Property tax/Assessing**-2500 Stonewall St, Greenville, TX 75401; 903-408-4000, assessor fax- 903-408-3202. (Appraiser/Auditor- 903-454-3510) hours- 8AM-5PM No pubic access terminal. **Online access**- Access property tax data and sheriff sales data free at www.hctax.info. Also, search property information free at http://propaccess.trueautomation.com/clientdb/?cid=37. Also see notes at beginning of section for add'l property data.

Hutchinson County

County Clerk, PO Box 1186, Stinnett, TX 79083. Recording, R/E phone-806-878-4002; fax-806-878-3497; 9AM-5PM (CST)
Index: Separate indices to search include property, probate, civil, criminal and others. Records indexed on computer back to 0601/92. Office suggests internet search. Search fee $5.00 per name. Copy fee $1.00 per page. Cert fee- $5.00 per cert plus copy fee. Payee- Hutchinson County Clerk. **Other phones:** Treasurer- 806-878-4010; Elections- 806-878-4002; Vital Records- 806-878-4002. **Property tax/Assessing**- PO Box 989, 5th & Main Sts, Stinnett, TX 79083; 806-878-4005, assessor fax- 806-878-4008. (Appraiser/Auditor- 806-274-2294) hours-9AM-4PM No public access terminal. **Online access**-Access to property tax data is free at www.hutchinsoncad.org/.

Irion County

County Clerk, PO Box 736, Mertzon, TX 76941-0736. Recording, R/E phone-325-835-2421; fax-325-835-7941; 8AM-N; 1PM-5PM.
Index: All in one. Record index not computerized. Office personnel (office will search names only) or visitors may perform searches. Search requests must be in writing. Search fee $5.00 per name. General copy fee- $1.00 per page. Cert fee- $5.00 per doc plus copy fee. Payee- Irion County Clerk. Bulk data sold in paper form, $1.00 per page. **Other phones:** Treasurer- 325-835-4111; Elections- 325-835-2421; Vital Records- 325-835-2421. **Property tax/Assessing**- PO Box 859, 209 N Parkview, Mertzon, TX 76941; 325-835-7771, assessor fax-325-835-2195. (Appraiser/Auditor- 325-835-3551) hours- 8AM-5PM. Public access terminal available.

Jack County

County Clerk, 100 Main St, Jacksboro, TX 76458. Recording, R/E phone-940-567-2111; fax-940-567-6441; 8AM-5PM (CST)
Index: All in one. Records indexed on a public use terminal back to 4/02. Office personnel or visitors may perform searches. Search fee $5.00 per name. Office will not search real estate records. Will search UCC records. Copy fee $1.00 per page; UCC copy $1.00 per page. Cert fee- $5.00 per cert plus copy fee. Payee- Jack County Clerk. **Other phones:** Treasurer-940-567-2251; Elections- 940-567-2111; Vital Records- 940-567-2111. **Property tax/Assessing**-100 Main St, #209, Jacksboro, TX 76458; 940-567-2352, assessor fax- 940-567-5322. (Appraiser/Auditor- 940-567-6301)

Jackson County

County Clerk, 115 W Main, Rm 101, Edna, TX 77957. 361-782-3563; fax-361-782-3132; 8AM-4PM (CST) www.co.jackson.tx.us
Index: Separate indices to search include grantor/grantee back to 1/1993, also various year indexes back to 1918. Records indexed on computer back to 1993. Office personnel or visitors may perform searches. Search fee $5.00. Office will search name index but not titles on RE records. Copy fee $1.00 per page. Cert fee- $5.00 per cert plus copy fee. Payee- Jackson County Clerk. **Online access to Real Estate, Grantor/Grantee, Deed, Lien, Judgment records:** Access recording records free at www.titlex.com; select Jackson county. Records range is 1/1993 to 9/2004. Also, see note at beginning of section. Also, property tax inquiries can be made at www.txcountydata.com/selectCounty.asp. **Other phones:** Treasurer- 361-782-3402; Elections- 361-782-3563; Vital Records- 361-782-3563. **Property tax/Assessing**- 115 W Main, Rm 102, Edna, TX 77957; 361-782-3473, assessor fax- 361-782-3645. (Appraiser/Auditor- 361-782-7115) hours- 8AM-5PM No public access terminal. **Online access**- Access appraiser property records free at www.jacksoncad.org/Appraisal/PublicAccess/. Also, property tax inquiries can be made at www.txcountydata.com/selectCounty.asp.

Jasper County

County Clerk, PO Box 2070, Jasper, TX 75951. Recording, R/E phone-409-384-2632; fax-409-384-7198; 8AM-4:30PM (CST) www.co.jasper.tx.us/ips/cms/countyoffices/countyClerk.html
Index: All in one. Records indexed on a public use terminal back to 1987. Office personnel or visitors may perform searches. Search fee $10.00 per name. Office will not search real estate records. Will search UCC records. Copy fee $1.00 per page. Cert fee- $5.00 per doc plus copy fee. Payee- County Clerk. **Other phones:** Treasurer- 409-384-2461; Elections- 409-384-3399; Vital Records- 409-384-2632. **Property tax/Assessing**- PO Box 1970, Jasper, TX 75951; 409-384-4684, assessor fax- 409-384-8226. (Appraiser/Auditor- 409-384-2544) www.co.jasper.tx.us/ips/cms/countyoffices/taxAssessorCollector.html

Jeff Davis County

County Clerk, PO Box 398, Fort Davis, TX 79734. 432-426-3251; fax-432-426-3760; 9AM-N, 1PM-5PM.
Index: All in one. Record index not computerized. Office personnel or visitors may perform searches. Search fee-$10.00 per name. Office will search real estate records. Will search UCC records. Copy fee $1.00 per page. Cert fee- $5.00 per doc plus copy fee. Payee- County Clerk. **Other phones:** Treasurer- 432-426-3242. **Property tax/Assessing**- PO Box 1061, 105 Court Ave, Ft. Davis, TX 79734; 432-426-3213, assessor fax- 432-426-3937. (Appraiser/Auditor- 432-857-3333 or 426-3210) No public access terminal.

Jefferson County

County Clerk, PO Box 1151, Beaumont, TX 77704-1151. 409-835-8475, R/E recording phone-409-835-8435, UCC recording phone-409-835-8475; fax-409-839-2394; 8AM-4:30PM (phones till 5PM). (CST) www.co.jefferson.tx.us
Index: Separate indices to search include Official Public Records, assumed names, marriages, criminal, misdemeanors, probate, civil, UCCs. Records indexed on a public use terminal. Office personnel or visitors may perform searches. Search fee $10.00 per name. Office will assist public with RE searches. Office will not search UCC records. Copy fee $1.00 per page. Cert fee- $5.00 per cert plus copy fee. Payee- Jefferson County Clerk. Bulk data available for purchase. **Online access to Probate, Civil, Criminal, Real Estate, Deed, Lien, Judgment, Marriage, UCC, Assumed Name records:** Access the recorder database free at http://jeffersontxclerk.manatron.com/. Recording index goes back to 1983; images to 1983. Marriages go back to 1995; UCCs to 7/2001. Also, see note at beginning of section. **Other phones:** Treasurer- 409-835-8509; Elections- 409-835-8760; Vital Records- 409-835-8475. **Property tax/Assessing**- PO Box 2112, 1149 Pearl St, Beaumont, TX 77701; 409-835-8516, assessor fax- 409-784-5848. (Appraiser/Auditor- 409-835-4611) hours- 8AM-4:30PM A public access terminal is available. **Online access**- Access property tax records free at www.jcad.org/search/.

Jim Hogg County

County Clerk, PO Box 878, Hebbronville, TX 78361. Recording, R/E phone-361-527-4031; fax-361-527-5843; 9AM-5PM.
Index: All in one. Record index not computerized. Office personnel or visitors may perform searches. General index search fee $15.00 per search. Office will not search real estate records. Office will search UCC records prior to 7/2001 and current fixture (land) files. Copy fee $1.00 per page. Cert fee- $5.00 per doc plus copy fee. Payee- Jim Hogg- County Clerk. **Online access to Real Estate, Deed records:** Access recording office land data at www.etitlesearch.com; registration required, fee based on usage. **Other phones:** Treasurer- 361-527-3164; Elections- 361-527-4031; Vital Records- 361-527-4031. **Property tax/Assessing**- PO Box 160, Hebbronville, TX 78361; 361-527-5841, assessor fax- 361-527-4034. (Appraiser/Auditor- 361-527-4033) hours- 8AM-5PM No public access terminal.

Jim Wells County

County Clerk, PO Box 1459, Alice, TX 78333. 361-668-5702; 8AM-N, 1-5PM (CST)
Index: All in one. Records indexed on computer back to 1995. Office personnel or visitors may perform searches. Search fee $10.00 per name. Office will not search real estate records. Office will search UCC records prior to 7/2001 and current fixture (land) files. Will search tax liens. Copy fee $1.00 per page. Cert fee- $5.00 per cert plus copy fee. Payee- Jim Wells County Clerk. Bulk data (indexes and images) available for purchase, contact Bea Sharp. **Online access to Real Estate, Deed records:** Access recording office land data at www.etitlesearch.com; registration required, fee based on usage. **Other phones:** Treasurer- 361-668-5713; Elections- 361-668-5711; Vital Records- 361-668-5702. **Property tax/Assessing**- 200 N Almond St, Alice, TX 78332; 361-668-5711, assessor fax- 361-6685754. (Appraiser/Auditor- 361-668-9656) hours- 8:15AM-N, 1:30-4PM Public access terminal available.

Johnson County

County Clerk, PO Box 1986, Cleburne, TX 76033-0662. 817-556-6323, R/E recording phone-817-556-6313; fax-817-556-6327; 8AM-N, 1PM-4:30PM (CST) www.johnsoncountytx.org/departments/countyclerk/
Index: All in one. Records indexed on a public use terminal back to 1988. Office personnel or visitors may perform searches. General search fee $5.00. Office will search UCC records prior to 7/2001 and current fixture (land) files. UCC search includes tax liens if requested. UCC search per debtor name- $10.00. Copy fee $1.00 per page. Cert fee- $5.00 per doc plus copy fee. Payee- Johnson County Clerk. **Online access to Judgment, Probate records:** Search probate records and judgment records at http://idocket.com/countycourt.htm. Records go back to 1980s. Also, see note at beginning of section for add'l property data. **Other phones:** Treasurer- 817-566-6340; Elections- 817-556-6382; Vital Records- 817-556-6191. **Property tax/Assessing**- 2 N Mill St, Rm #B, Bank of America Bldg, Cleburne, TX 76033; 817-558-0122, assessor fax- 817-556-0826. (Appraiser/Auditor- 817-558-8100) www.johnsoncountytx.org/departments/profile.php/Tax-Assessor-Collector-54/ **Online access**- Records from the County Appraiser are free at www.johnsoncountytaxoffice.org/accountSearch.asp or at Taxnet site at www.johnsoncad.com/search_appr.php.

Jones County

County Clerk, PO Box 552, Anson, TX 79501-0552. Recording, R/E phone-325-823-3762; fax-325-823-4223; 8AM-5PM (CST) www.co.jones.tx.us
Index: Separate indices to search. Records indexed on a public use terminal back to 1991. Office personnel or visitors may perform searches. Search fee $5.00 per name. Office will not search real estate records. Will search UCC records, must have written request and fee is $5.00 per name. Copy fee $1.00 per page. Cert fee- $5.00 per doc. Payee- Jones County Clerk. Bulk data available for purchase for $1.00 per page (paper copies). Contact County Clerk. **Other phones:** Treasurer- 325-823-3742; Elections- 325-823-3762; Vital Records- 325-823-3762. **Property tax/Assessing**- PO Box 511, Anson, TX 79501-0552; 325-823-2437. (Appraiser/Auditor- 325-823-2422) **Online access**- Access property tax records free at www.jonescad.org/Appraisal/PublicAccess/.

Karnes County

County Clerk, 101 N Panna Maria Ave, #9; Courthouse, Karnes City, TX 78118-2929. Recording, R/E phone-830-780-3938; fax-830-780-4576; 8AM-5PM. www.co.karnes.tx.us/ips/cms
Index: Separate indices to search. Records indexed on a public use terminal back to 06/2003. Office will perform a UCC or tax lien search but public must search other records themselves. Search fee $10.00 per name. Office will not search real estate records. Copy fee $1.00 per page. Cert fee- $5.00 per doc plus copy fee. Payee- Karnes County Clerk. **Other phones:** Treasurer- 830-780-2312; Elections- 830-780-3938; Vital Records- 830-780-3938. **Property tax/Assessing**- 200 E Culvert, Karnes City, TX 78118; 830-780-2431, assessor fax- 830-780-4530. (Appraiser/Auditor- 830-780-2433) hours- 8AM-4:30PM No public access terminal.

Kaufman County

County Clerk, 100 W Mulberry St; Courthouse, Kaufman, TX 75142. Recording, R/E phone-972-932-4331; fax-972-962-8018; 8AM-4:30PM (CST) www.kaufmancountyclerk.com
Index: Separate indices to search include computer, grantor, grantee, book. Records indexed on a public use terminal back to 1968. Office personnel or visitors may perform searches. Office will not search liens. General index search fee $10.00 per name. Office will search real estate records. Will not search UCC records. Copy fee $1.00 per page. Cert fee- $6.00 1st page, $1.00 each add'l page, includes copy fee. Payee- Kaufman County Clerk. Recoding data on CD-rom available for purchase by written request. **Online access to Real Estate, Grantor/Grantee, Deed, Lien, Judgment records:** Access recording records free at www.titlex.com; select Kaufman county. Records go back to 3/1/1969. Also, search grantor/grantee recording index free at https://www.texaslandrecords.com/txlr/TxlrApp/index.jsp; click on free search. Registration and fees or 1-day pass is required for full data. Also, see note at beginning of section. **Other phones:** Treasurer- 972-932-4331; Elections- 972-932-0288; Vital Records- 972-932-4331. **Property tax/Assessing**- PO Box 339, 100 N Washington, Kaufman, TX 75142; 972-932-4331 x5, x3. (Appraiser/Auditor- 972-932-6081) **Online access**- Search appraisal roll data free at http://clientdb.trueautomation.com/clientdb/main.asp?id=66.

Kendall County

County Clerk, 201 E San Antonio, #127, Boerne, TX 78006. Recording, R/E phone-830-249-9343; fax-830-249-3472; 8AM-5PM (CST)
Index: All in one. Records indexed on a public use terminal back to 1983. Office personnel or visitors may perform searches. Search fee $5.00. Office will not search real estate records. Will search UCC records. Copy fee $1.00 per page. Cert fee- $5.00 per cert plus copy fee. Payee- Kendall County Clerk. Office sells data on Jaz Tape. Availabe is index from 1983-1996 and image and index 1997 to present. $19.00 per tape; tape has to be 1 GB. **Online access to Real Estate, Grantor/Grantee, Deed, Lien, Judgment records:** Access recording records free at www.titlex.com; select Kendall county. Also see note at beginning of section. **Other phones:** Treasurer- 830-249-9343; Elections- 830-249-9343; Vital Records- 830-249-9343. **Property tax/Assessing**- 121 S Main, Boerne, TX 78006; 830-249-9343, assessor fax- 830-249-3975. (Appraiser/Auditor- 830-249-8012) Public access terminal available. www.kendallad.org/ **Online** - Access property data free at http://clientdb.trueautomation.com/clientdb/main.asp?id=69.

Kenedy County

County Clerk, PO Box 227, Sarita, TX 78385-0227. Recording, R/E phone-361-294-5220; fax-361-294-5218; 8:30AM-N, 1-4:30PM (CST)
Index: Separate indices to search include official records, liens, probate, courts. Record index not computerized. Office personnel or visitors may perform searches. Search fee $5.00 per name. Copy fee $1.00 per page. Cert fee- $5.00 per cert plus copy fee. Payee- Kenedy County Clerk. **Other phones:** Treasurer- 361-294-5304; Elections- 361-294-5255; Vital Records- 361-294-5220. **Property tax/Assessing**- PO Box 129, 101 Malorie, Sarita, TX 78385-0129; 361-294-5202, assessor fax- 361-294-

5710. (Appraiser/Auditor- 361-321-1695) hours- 8:30AM-4:30PM No public access terminal.

Kent County

County Clerk, PO Box 9, Jayton, TX 79528-0009. Recording, R/E phone-806-237-3881; fax-806-237-2300; 8:30AM-N, 1PM-5PM (CST) www.co.kent.tx.us

Index: All in one. Records indexed on computer back to 1987. Office personnel or visitors may perform searches. General index search fee $5.00 per name per instrument. Office will search real estate records. Will search UCC records. Copy fee $1.00 per page. Cert fee- $5.00 per cert plus copy fee. Payee- Kent County Clerk. **Other phones:** Treasurer- 806-237-3075; Elections- 806-237-3881; Vital Records- 806-237-3881. **Property tax/Assessing-** 101N Main St, Jayton, TX 79528; 806-237-3746, assessor fax- 806-237-3306. (Appraiser/Auditor- 806-237-3066) hours- 8AM-N, 1PM-5PM

Kerr County

County Clerk, 700 Main St, Rm 122; Courthouse, Kerrville, TX 78028-5389. Recording, R/E phone-830-792-2255; fax-830-792-2274; 8AM-5PM (CST) www.co.kerr.tx.us/

Index: All in one. Records indexed on a public use terminal back to 1986. Imaged records from 1/1/98. Only the public may search. Copy fee $1.00 per page. Cert fee- $5.00 per doc plus copy fee. Payee- Kerr County Clerk. Bulk data available for purchase, contact Jannett Pieper at 830-792-2255. **Online access to Real Estate, Deed, Lien, Assumed Name, Marriage records:** Access to recorder land data by subscription at www.kerr.tx.us.landata.com. Registration and login required; $50.00 monthly fee. Also, search the old records system for deeds, assumed names, and marriage records free at www.edoctecinc.com/. **Other phones:** Treasurer- 830-792-2275; Elections- 830-792-2242; Vital Records- 830-792-2255. **Property tax/Assessing-** 700 Main St, Courthouse, Kerrville, TX 78028; 830-792-2242, assessor fax- 830-792-2253. (Appraiser/Auditor- 830-895-5223) hours- 8:30AM-4:30PM Public access terminal available. **Online access-** Access appraiser's property records free at http://public.co.kerr.tx.us:8088/Appraisal/PublicAccess/. Also, see note at beginning of section. Also, access to property records free at http://propaccess.trueautomation.com/clientdb/?cid=35.

Kimble County

County Clerk, 501 Main St, Junction, TX 76849. Recording, R/E phone-325-446-3353; fax-325-446-2986; 8AM-N, 1PM-5PM (CST) www.co.kimble.tx.us/ips/cms

Index: Property-related records 2006 forward all in OPR index. Separate indices to search include deed, DT, abstract, liens, Lis Penden, District Min., County Min, etc. Record index not computerized. Only the public may search. Copy fee $1.00 per page. Cert fee- $5.00 per cert plus copy fee. Payee- Kimble County Clerk. **Other phones:** Treasurer- 325-446-2847; Elections- 325-446-3353; Vital Records- 325-446-3353. **Property tax/Assessing-** PO Box 307, 501 Main St, Junction, TX 76849-0307; 325-446-3717, assessor fax- 325-446-4361. (Appraiser/Auditor- 325-446-3717) hours- 8AM-N, 1PM-4:55PM. A public access terminal is available. **Online** - Access appraiser's property data at www.txcountydata.com/county.asp?County=134.

King County

County Clerk, PO Box 135, Guthrie, TX 79236. Recording, R/E phone-806-596-4412; fax-806-596-4664; 9AM-N, 1-5PM (CST)

Index: All in one. Record index not computerized. Office personnel or visitors may perform searches. General index search fee $5.00 per book. Office will search real estate records. Office will search UCC records prior to 7/2001 and current fixture (land) files. Tax liens not included in UCC search. Copy fee $1.00 per page. Cert fee- $5.00 per cert plus copy fee. Payee- King County Clerk. **Other phones:** Treasurer- 806-596-4319; Elections- 806-596-4412; Vital Records- 806-596-4412. **Property tax/Assessing-** PO Box 105, 800 S Baker, Guthrie, TX 79236; 806-596-4318, assessor fax- 806-596-4030. (Appraiser/Auditor- 806-596-4588) No public access terminal.

Kinney County

County Clerk, PO Drawer 9, Brackettville, TX 78832. Recording, R/E phone-830-563-2521; fax-830-563-2644; 8AM-N; 1PM-5PM.

Index: All in one. Records indexed on computer back to 1986. Office personnel or visitors may perform searches. Search fee $5.00 per name. Office will search real estate records. Will search UCC records. Copy fee $1.00 per page. Cert fee- $5.00 per page plus copy fee. Payee- County Clerk. **Other phones:** Treasurer- 830-563-2777; Elections- 830-563-2521; Vital Records- 830-563-2521. **Property tax/Assessing-** PO Box 1220, 501 S Ann, Brackettville, TX 78832; 830-563-2688, assessor fax- 830-563-9563. (Appraiser/Auditor- 830-563-2323) No public access terminal.

Kleberg County

County Clerk, PO Box 1327, Kingsville, TX 78364-1327. 361-595-8548; fax-361-593-1355; 8AM-5PM (CST) www.co.kleberg.tx.us/ips/cms

Index: All in one. Records indexed on a public use terminal back to 03/171994. Office personnel or visitors may perform searches. Search fee $5.00 per name per 5 years. Office will search real estate records. Will search UCC records if applicable. Copy fee $1.00 per page. Cert fee- $5.00 per cert plus copy fee. Payee- Kleberg County Clerk. We now have data available on CD's. You may ask for any of the three names listed at the clerk's office for additional informaion and pricing. **Online access to Judgment, Property records:** Search judgment records back to 1991 at http://idocket.com/countycourt.htm. County Clerk does not offer a searchable website at this time. **Other phones:** Treasurer- 361-595-8535; Elections- 361-595-8548; Vital Records- 361-595-8548. **Property tax/Assessing-** PO Box 1457, 700 E Kleberg, Kingsville, TX 78363; 361-595-8542, assessor fax- 361-595-8546. (Appraiser/Auditor- 361-595-5775) 8AM-4:30PM No public access terminal. www.co.kleberg.tx.us/ips/cms/countyoffices/taxAssessorCollector.html **Online access-** Access to county appraisal rolls and property data is free at www.klebergcad.org/search_appr.php.

Knox County

County Clerk, PO Box 196, Benjamin, TX 79505. Recording, R/E phone-940-459-2441; fax-940-459-2005; 8AM-N, 1-5PM (CST)

Index: All in one. Record index not computerized. Office personnel or visitors may perform searches. Search fee $5.00 per name. Copy fee $1.00 per page. Cert fee- $5.00 per doc plus copy fee. Payee- Knox County Clerk. **Online access to Real Estate, Grantor/Grantee, Deed, Lien, Judgment records:** Access recording records at www.titlex.com; select Knox county; login and password required. **Other phones:** Treasurer- 817-459-2251; Elections- 940-459-2441; Vital Records- 940-459-2441. **Property tax/Assessing-** PO Box 47, 1 Main Place, Benjamin, TX 79505; 940-459-2411, assessor fax- 940-459-2004. (Appraiser/Auditor- 940-459-3891) hours- 8AM-5PM No public access terminal.

La Salle County

County Clerk, 201 NE Lane, Cotulla, TX 78014. Recording, R/E phone-830-879-4432; fax-830-879-2933; 8AM-N; 1-5PM (CST) www.co.la-salle.tx.us/

Index: All in one. Record index not computerized. Only office personnel may search. General search fee $5.00. Office will not search real estate records. Office will search UCC records prior to 7/2001 and current fixture (land) files. Copy fee $1.00 per page. Cert fee- $5.00 per cert plus copy fee. Payee- LaSalle Co Clerk. **Online access to Property, Appraiser, Real Estate, Deed records:** Access recording office land data at www.etitlesearch.com; registration required, fee based on usage. **Other phones:** Treasurer- 830-879-4440; Elections- 830-879-4432; Vitals- 830-879-4432. **Property tax/Assessing-** PO Box 737, 101 Courthouse Sq, #120, Cotulla, TX 78014; 830-879-4437, assessor fax- 830-879-4438. (Appraiser/Auditor- 830-879-2415/4331) No public access terminal. Appraisal Dist Ofc- 101 N Baylor. www.lasallecountytx.org/Tax_Collector/tax_collector.html **Online access-** Access property tax data free at http://propaccess.trueautomation.com/clientdb/?cid=23. Search tax sales lists free at http://tax.acttax.com/pls/sales/property_taxsales_pkg.search_page?PI_STATE=TX and chose Struck Off as sales type.

Lamar County

County Clerk, 119 N Main, #109; Courthouse, Paris, TX 75460. Recording, R/E phone-903-737-2420; fax-903-782-1111; 8AM-N, 1-5PM (CST)

Index: Separate indices to search include deeds, liens up to 1988, then official records; RE, marriage, births & death, oil/gas, FTL indices are separate. Records indexed on a public use terminal back to 1971. Office personnel or visitors may perform searches. Search fee $10.00 per name. Office will not search real estate records. Tax liens not included in UCC search. Copy fee $1.00 per page. Cert fee- $5.00 per cert plus copy fee. Payee- Lamar County Clerk. **Other phones:** Treasurer- 903-737-2418; Elections- 903-737-2420; Vital Records- 903-737-2420. **Property tax/Assessing-** 521 Bonham St, Paris, TX 75460; 903-785-7822, assessor fax- 903-785-8322. (Appraiser/Auditor- 903-785-7822) hours- 8AM-5PM Public access terminal available.

Lamb County

County Clerk, 100 6th Dr; Rm 103, Littlefield, TX 79339-3366. 806-385-4222 x210, R/E recording phone-806-385-4222; fax-806-385-6485; 8:30AM-5PM (CST) www.co.lamb.tx.us

Index: All in one. Records indexed on computer back to 1989. Office personnel or visitors may perform searches. Office will search real estate records. Will search UCC records. Copy fee $1.00 per page. Cert fee- $5.00 per cert plus copy fee. Payee- Lamb County Clerk. **Other phones:** Treasurer- 806-385-4222 x204; Elections- 806-385-4222; Vital Records- 806-385-4222. **Property tax/Assessing-** 100 6th Dr, #105, Littlefield, TX 79339; 806-385-4222 x230, assessor fax- 806-385-6485. (Appraiser/Auditor- 806-385-6474) hours- 8:30AM-N, 1PM-5PM www.co.lamb.tx.us/ips/cms/countyoffices/taxAssessorCollector.html **Online access-** Online access through private companies.

Lampasas County

County Clerk, PO Box 347, Lampasas, TX 76550. 512-556-8271; 8AM-5PM (CST) www.co.lampasas.tx.us/ips/cms

Index: Separate indices to search include tax liens, judgments, probate, criminal, deed of trust. Record index not computerized. Office will perform a UCC but public must search other records themselves. Search fee $5.00. Copy fee $1.00 per page. Cert fee- $5.00 per cert plus copy fee. Payee- Lampasas County Clerk. **Other phones:** Treasurer- 512-556-8271; Elections- 512-556-8271 x206; Vital Records- 512-556-8271. **Property tax/Assessing-** 109 E 5th St, Lampasas, TX 76550; 512-556-8058. (Appraiser/Auditor- 512-556-8058)

Lavaca County

County Clerk, PO Box 326, Hallettsville, TX 77964-0326. Recording, R/E phone-361-798-3612; fax-361-798-1610; 8AM-5PM (CST)

Index: Separate indices to search. Records indexed on computer back to 12/93. The public performs searches. If the office searches, which they rarely do, the search fee is $5.00. Copy fee $1.00 per page. Cert fee- $5.00 per cert plus copy fee. Payee- Lavaca County Clerk. Printed versions of bulk data are available to purchase, contact Joyce or Barbara.

Other phones: Treasurer- 361-798-2181; Elections- 361-798-3612; Vital Records- 361-798-3612. **Property tax/Assessing**- PO Box 293, 204 E Fourth St, Hallettsville, TX 77964; 361-798-3601, assessor fax- 361-798-5229. (Appraiser/Auditor- 361-798-4396) No public access terminal. **Online access**- Access appraiser's property data free at www.txcountydata.com/county.asp?County=143.

Lee County

County Clerk, PO Box 419, Giddings, TX 78942. 979-542-3684; fax-979-542-2623; 8AM-5PM (CST) www.co.lee.tx.us/ips/cms/countyoffices/countyClerk.html

Index: All in one. Records indexed on a public use terminal back to 1874. Only the public may search. Copy fee $1.00 per page. Cert fee- $5.00 per cert plus copy fee. Payee- Lee County Clerk. Bulk data available for purchase, contact Kristy Gholson. **Other phones:** Treasurer- 979-542-2161; Elections- 979-542-3684; Vital Records- 979-542-3684. **Property tax/Assessing**- 898 E Richmond, Giddings, TX 78942; 979-542-2640, assessor fax- 979-542-3787. (Appraiser/Auditor- 979-542-9618) hours- 8AM-4PM No public access terminal. **Online**- Access Appraisal District records free at http://clientdb.trueautomation.com/clientdb/main.asp?id=9.

Leon County

County Clerk, PO Box 98, Centerville, TX 75833. Recording, R/E phone-903-536-2352; 8AM-5PM.

Index: All in one. Records indexed on a public use terminal back to 1949. Only the public may search. Copy fee $1.00 per page. Cert fee- $5.00. Payee- Leon County Clerk. **Other phones:** Treasurer- 903-536-2915; Elections- 903-536-2352; Vital Records- 903-536-2352. **Property tax/Assessing**- PO Box 37, 204 E St Mary's, Centerville, TX 75833; 903-536-2543, assessor fax- 903-536-2431. (Appraiser/Auditor- 903-536-2252) hours- 8AM-N, 1-4PM No public access terminal.

Liberty County

County Clerk, PO Box 369, Liberty, TX 77575. 936-336-4670, R/E recording phone-936-336-4674, UCC recording phone-936-336-4673; 8AM-5PM (CST)

Index: Separate indices to search include all records from 1983 to present on computer, records prior to 1983 indexed alphabetically by year. Records indexed on a public use terminal back to 1983. Office personnel or visitors may perform searches. Search fee $10.00 per name. Office will not search real estate records. Will search UCC records. Copy fee $1.00 per page. Cert fee- $5.00 per cert plus copy fee. Payee- Liberty County Clerk. **Other phones:** Elections- 936-336-4676; Vital Records- 936-336-4673. **Property tax/Assessing**- 1923 Sam Houston, Liberty, TX 77575; 936-336-4629. (Appraiser/Auditor- 409-336-5722) **Online**- Access Appraisal District records at http://clientdb.trueautomation.com/clientdb/main.asp?id=41. Online access through private companies.

Limestone County

County Clerk, PO Box 350, Groesbeck, TX 76642. 254-729-5504; fax-254-729-2951; 8AM-5PM (CST)

Index: All in one. Records indexed on a public use terminal back to 1985. Office personnel or visitors may perform searches. Search fee $10.00. Office will not search real estate records. Copy fee $1.00 per page. Cert fee- $5.00 per cert plus copy fee. Payee- Limestone County Clerk. Bulk data available for purchase, from 2003 forward. Contact Peggy Beck at 254-729-5504. **Other phones:** Treasurer- 254-729-3314; Elections- 254-729-5504; Vital Records- 254-729-5504; District Clerk- 254-729-3206. **Property tax/Assessing**- PO Box 539, Groesbeck, TX 76642; 254-729-3405, assessor fax- 254-729-3533. (Appraiser/Auditor- 254-729-3009) Public access terminal available. **Online**- Access appraiser's property data free at http://limestonecad.txcountydata.com/Appraisal/PublicAccess/. Also, see notes at beginning of section.

Lipscomb County

County Clerk, PO Box 70, Lipscomb, TX 79056. 806-862-3091; fax-806-862-3004; 8:30AM-N. 1PM-5PM. www.co.lipscomb.tx.us/ips/cms

Index: Separate indices to search include general, grantor/grantee. Records indexed on computer back to 1999. Visitors may perform searches; office personnel may perform searches if time permits. General index search fee $10.00 per name. If time permits office will search real estate records. Office will not search UCC records. Copy fee $1.00 per page. Cert fee- $5.00 per page plus copy fee. Payee- Lipscomb County Clerk. **Other phones:** Treasurer- 806-862-3821. **Property tax/Assessing**- PO Box 129, 101 S Main St, Lipscomb, TX 79056; 806-862-2911, assessor fax-806-862-3004. (Appraiser/Auditor- 806-624-2881) No public access terminal. **Online access**- Find appraisal district data free at http://208.75.248.98/.

Live Oak County

County Clerk, PO Box 280, George West, TX 78022. 361-449-2733 x103, R/E recording phone-361-449-2733; 8AM-N, 1-5PM (CST) www.co.live-oak.tx.us

Divorce/Dissolution searches at the district clerk's office. Index: All in one. Records indexed on computer back to 3/00. Office personnel or visitors may perform searches. Search fee $10.00 per name per book. Office will not search real estate or UCC records. Office will not search UCC records. Copy fee $1.00 per page. Cert fee- $5.00 per cert plus copy fee. Payee- Live Oak County Clerk. **Other phones:** Treasurer- 361-449-2641 x109; Elections- 361-449-2733 x129 or 110; Vital Records- 361-449-2733 x129 or 103. **Property tax/Assessing**- 205 Bowie St, George West, TX 78022; 361-449-2733 x111, fax-361-449-2774. (Appraiser/Auditor- 361-449-2641) hours- 8AM-5PM. No public access terminal.

Llano County

County Clerk, PO Box 40, Llano, TX 78643-0040. 325-247-4455; fax-325-247-2406; 8-4:30PM (CST)

Index: All in one. Records indexed on a public use terminal back to 1986. Office will perform a UCC search but public must search other records themselves. Copy fee $1.00 per page. Cert fee- $5.00 per cert plus copy fee. Payee- Llano County Clerk. CD of official public images in TIF format available; contact Marai. **Other phones:** Treasurer- 325-247-7743; Elections- 325-247-4455; Vital Records- 325-247-4455 (Llano County Only). **Property tax/Assessing**- 100 W Sandstone, Llano, TX 78643; 325-247-4165, assessor fax- 325-247-5205. (Appraiser/Auditor- 325-247-7739) Public access terminal available. **Online access**- Search tax office data free by selecting county at http://208.75.248.98/. Other online access through private companies.

Loving County

County Clerk, PO Box 194, Mentone, TX 79754. Recording, R/E phone-432-377-2441; fax-432-377-2701; 9AM-N, 1-5PM (CST)

Index: All in one. Records indexed on computer back to 1987. Office personnel or visitors may perform searches. UCC search per debtor name $15.00. Separate tax lien search fee-$2.00 per debtor. Office will search real estate records. Will search UCC records. Copy fee $1.00 per page. Cert fee- $5.00 per doc plus copy fee. Payee- County Clerk. Bulk data available for purchase from books for $1.00 per page. **Other phones:** Treasurer- 432-377-2311; Elections-432-377-2441; Vital Records- 432-377-2441. **Property tax/Assessing**- PO Box 104, 121 N Pecos St, Mentone, TX 79754; 432-377-2411, assessor fax-432-377-2025. (Appraiser/Auditor- 432-377-2201) hours- 6:30AM-2:30PM No public access terminal.

Lubbock County

County Clerk, PO Box 10536, Lubbock, TX 79408-0536. 806-775-1630, R/E recording phone-806-775-1060; fax-806-775-1660; 8:30AM-5PM. www.co.lubbock.tx.us

Index: Separate indices to search. Records indexed on a public use terminal back to 1974. Book indexes back to 1881. Only the public may search. Search fee $10.00 per name for AJ, FTL and STL only. Office will not search real estate or UCC records. Copy fee $1.00 per page, $1.50 for plats. Cert fee- $5.00 each per doc plus copy fee. Payee- Lubbock County Clerk. **Other phones:** Treasurer- 806-775-1018; Elections-806-775-1339; Vital Records- 806-775-2926 (birth/death), 806-775-1054(marriage). **Property tax/Assessing**- 1715 26th St, Lubbock, TX 79401; 806-755-1344, assessor fax- 806-762-2451. (Appraiser/Auditor- 806-762-5000) Public access terminal available. **Online access**- Search the property appraiser database for free at www.lubbockcad.org/Appraisal/PublicAccess/. Also, see note at beginning of section.

Lynn County

County Clerk, PO Box 937, Tahoka, TX 79373. 806-561-4750; fax-806-561-4988; 8:30AM-5PM (CST) www.co.lynn.tx.us/ips/cms

Index: All in one. Records indexed on computer back to 1997. Office suggests internet search. Search fee $10.00. Office will not search real estate records. Will not search UCC records. Copy fee $1.00 per page. Cert fee- $5.00 per cert plus copy fee. Payee- Lynn County Clerk. Office not sell bulk data in paper form. **Other phones:** Treasurer- 806-561-4055; Elections-806-561-4750; Vital Records- 806-561-4750. **Property tax/Assessing**- PO Box 789, 615 Main St, Tahoka, TX 79373; 806-561-5477. (Appraiser - 806-561-5477) No public access terminal. www.co.lynn.tx.us/ips/cms/countyoffices/taxAssessorCollector.html

Madison County

County Clerk, 101 W Main, Rm 102, Madisonville, TX 77864. 936-348-2638; fax-936-348-5858; 8AM-4:30PM (CST) www.co.madison.tx.us/ips/cms

Index: All in one. Records indexed on a public use terminal back to 1974. Only the public may search. Copy fee $1.00 per page. Cert fee- $5.00 per cert plus copy fee. Payee- Madison County Clerk. Bulk data of current recordings available for purchase on CD's; contact Anna Eubank: 936-348-2638. All other bulk records - ACS Gov't records, Dallas TX. **Online access to Real Estate, Grantor/Grantee, Deed, Lien, Judgment records:** Search land records index free at www.texaslandrecords.com. Subscription and fees required for full records. Indexes back to 1974; images back to mid 1974. **Other phones:** Treasurer-936-348-5141; Elections- 936-348-2638; Vital Records- 936-348-2638. **Property tax/Assessing**- PO Box 417, 101 W Main St, Madisonville, TX 77864; 936-348-2654, assessor fax- 936-348-2655. (Appraiser/Auditor- 936-348-2783) A public access terminal is available. www.madisontax.org/ **Online access**- Access Appraisal District tax records free at www.txcountydata.com/county.asp?County=157.

Marion County

County Clerk, PO Box 763, Jefferson, TX 75657. Recording, R/E phone-903-665-3971; fax-903-665-8732; 8AM-N, 1PM-5PM (CST)

Index: All in one. Records indexed on a public use terminal back to 1976. Office personnel or visitors may perform searches. General search fee $5.00 per name. Real estate owner, mortgage, and property transfer searches available if not busy. Will search UCC records. UCC search per debtor name- $16.00. Copy fee $1.00 per page. UCC copy $2.00 per page. Cert fee- $5.00 per cert plus copy fee. Payee- Marion County Clerk. **Online access to Real Estate, Grantor/Grantee, Deed, Lien, Judgment records:** Access recording records free at www.titlex.com; select Marion county. **Other phones:** Treasurer- 903-665-2472; Elections- 903-665-3971; Vital Records-903-665-3971. **Property tax/Assessing**- 114 W Austin, #100, Jefferson, TX 75657; 903-665-3281, assessor fax- 903-665-3132. (Appraiser/Auditor- 903-665-2519) hours- 8AM-N, 1PM-4:30PM No public access terminal. **Online access**- Access property tax records free at www.marioncad.org.

Martin County

County Clerk, PO Box 906, Stanton, TX 79782. Recording, R/E phone-432-756-3412; fax-432-607-2212; 8AM-5PM (CST)
Index: Separate indices to search. Record index not computerized. Office personnel or visitors may perform searches. Search fee $10.00 per name. Office will not search OPR or UCC records. Copy fee $1.00 per page. Cert fee- $5.00 per cert plus copy fee. Payee- Martin County Clerk. **Other phones:** Treasurer- 432-756-3631; Elections- 432-756-3412; Vital - 432-756-3412. **Property tax/Assessing**- 301 N St. Peter St, Stanton, TX 79782; 432-756-3397. (Appraiser/Auditor- 432-756-2823) hours- 8AM-N 1PM-5PM **Online access**- Access to property data is free at www.martincad.org/.

Mason County

County Clerk, PO Box 702, Mason, TX 76856-0702. Recording, R/E phone-325-347-5253; fax-325-347-6868; 8AM-N, 1-4PM (CST)
Records indexed on a public use terminal back to 1900. Office personnel or visitors may perform searches. Search fee $10.00 per name. Office will not search real estate records. Office will not search UCC records. Copy fee $1.00 per page. Cert fee- $5.00 per cert plus copy fee. Payee- Mason County Clerk. **Other phones:** Treasurer- 325-347-5251; Elections- 325-347-5253; Vital Records- 325-347-5253. **Property tax/Assessing**- PO Box 391, Mason, TX 76856; 325-347-6937. (Appraiser - 325-347-5989) www.co.mason.tx.us/ips/cms/countyoffices/taxAssessorCollector.html

Matagorda County

County Clerk, 1700 7th St, Rm 203, Bay City, TX 77414. Recording, R/E phone-979-244-7680; fax-979-244-7688; 8AM-5PM. www.co.matagorda.tx.us
Index: All in one. Records indexed on a public use terminal back to 1987. Office personnel or visitors may perform searches, but office will not search UCCs or RE. Search fee $5.00 per name. Copy fee $1.00 per page. Cert fee- $5.00 per doc plus copy fee. Payee- County Clerk. **Other phones:** Treasurer- 979-244-7609; Elections- 979-244-7680; Vital Records- 979-244-7680. **Property tax/Assessing**- Same address as recording office. 979-244-7670, assessor fax- 979-244-7678. (Appraiser/Auditor- 979-244-2031) Public access terminal available. **Online access**- Access to Appraisal District records is free at http://clientdb.trueautomation.com/clientdb/main.asp?id=25.

Maverick County

County Clerk, 500 Quarry St, #2, Eagle Pass, TX 78852. 830-773-2829 or 772-4480, R/E recording phone-830-773-2829; fax-830-752-4479; 8AM-5PM (CST) www.co.maverick.tx.us/ips/cms/countyoffices/countyClerk.html
Index: All in one. Records indexed on a public use terminal back to 1992. Office personnel or visitors may perform searches. Search fee $10.00 per name. Office will not search real estate records. Copy fee $2.00, if tax lien or real estate $1.00 per page. Cert fee- $5.00 per cert plus copy fee. Payee- Maverick County Clerk. **Other phones:** Treasurer- 830-773-2413; Elections- 830-757-4175; Vital Records- 830-773-2829. **Property tax/Assessing**- 370 N Monroe #3, Eagle Pass, TX 78852; 830-773-9273, assessor fax- 830-773-6378. (Appraiser - 830-773-0255) www.co.maverick.tx.us/ips/cms/countyoffices/taxAssessorCollector.html **Online access**- Visit www.maverickcad.org/searchaccounts.htm for the appraisal roll. Other online access through private companies.

McCulloch County

County Clerk, Courthouse, Brady, TX 76825. 325-597-0733, R/E recording phone-325-597-0733 x103; fax-325-597-1731; 8AM-N; 1PM-5PM. www.co.mcculloch.tx.us/ips/cms
Index: Separate indices to search include state/federal tax liens, abstract of judgment. Records indexed on computer back to 10/95. Office personnel or visitors may perform searches. Search fee $5.00 per name. Office will search real estate records only if name of grantee & grantor provided with year of purchase. Copy fee $1.00 per page. Cert fee- $5.00 per instrument plus $1.00 per page. Payee- McCulloch County Clerk. **Online access to Judgment, Court records:** Search judgment records at http://idocket.com/countycourt.htm. **Other phones:** Treasurer- 325-597-0773 x116; Elections- 325-597-8733 x103; Vital Records- 325-597-0733; Voter Registrar- 325-597-7607. **Property tax/Assessing**- 302 W Commerce, Brady, Texas 76825; 325-597-7607, fax- 325-597-2408. (Appraiser/Auditor- 325-597-1627) 8AM-5PM **Online access**- Search assessor property records free at www.taxnetusa.com/texas/. Subscription service also available.

McLennan County

McLennan County Clerk, PO Box 1727, Waco, TX 76703-1727. Recording, R/E phone- 254-757-5078; fax-254-757-5146; 8AM-5PM (CST) www.co.mclennan.tx.us/cclerk/index.aspx
Index: Pre-1996 indices include deed, D/T, M/L, judgment, lien, etc. Records indexed on computer back to 1996. Office personnel or visitors may perform searches. Search fee $10.00 per name. Office will not search real estate records. Copy fee $1.00 per page. UCC copy fee- $1.50 per page, $5.00 minimum. Cert fee- $5.00 per cert plus copy fee. Payee- McLennan County Clerk. Bulk data available for purchase. **Online access to Real Estate, Grantor/Grantee, Deed, Lien, Judgment, Property Tax records:** Access recording records free at www.titlex.com; select McLennan county. Records range from 1/1996 to 12/2002. Also, see note at beginning of section. Also, access land records at http://etitlesearch.com. You can do a name search; choose from $50.00 monthly subscription or per-click account. Also, see note at beginning of section. **Other phones:** Treasurer- 254-757-5020; Elections- 254-757-5043; Vital Records- 254-757-5188; County Auditor- 254-757-5156. **Property tax/Assessing**- 215 N 5th St, 1st Fl, Waco, TX 76701; 254-757-5151, assessor fax- 254-757-2666. (Appraiser/Auditor- 254-752-9864) hours- 7:30AM-4:30PM **Online access**- Search real estate appraisal records at www.mclennancad.org or at http://propaccess.trueautomation.com/clientDB/?cid=20. Property Tax balance information free at https://actweb.acttax.com/act_webdev/mclennan/index.jsp.

McMullen County

County Clerk, PO Box 235, Tilden, TX 78072-0235. Recording, R/E phone-361-274-3215; fax-361-274-3858; 8AM-4PM (CST)
Index: All in one. Record index not computerized. Office personnel or visitors may perform searches. Search fee $5.00 per name. Office will search real estate records. Copy fee $1.00 per page. Cert fee- $5.00 per cert plus copy fee. Payee- McMullen County Clerk. **Other phones:** Treasurer- 361-274-3685; Elections- 361-274-3215; Vitals- 361-274-3215. **Property tax/Assessing**- PO Box 38, 503 River, Tilden, TX 78072; 361-274-3233, assessor fax- 361-274-3618. (Appraiser/Auditor- 361-274-3233) No public access terminal.

Medina County

County Clerk, 1100 16th St, Rm 109; Courthouse, Hondo, TX 78861. 830-741-6041; fax-830-741-6015; 8AM-5PM. www.medina.tx.us.landata.com
Index: All in one. Records indexed on a public use terminal back to 1991. Office personnel or visitors may perform searches. Search fee $5.00 per name. Office will search real estate records, but not lien searches. Office will not search UCC records. Copy fee $1.00 per page. Cert fee- $5.00 per page plus copy fee. Payee- Medina County Clerk. Bulk data available for purchase in CD form on real estate records, contact Sandy Young at 830-741-6043. **Online Real Estate, Deed, Lien records:** Access to recorder's index free at www.medina.tx.us.landata.com but there is a $4.00 fee per document image, or you may subscribe for $50.00 per month and pay $2.00 per document image. There is a $150.00 per doc processing fee. Visa/MC credit cards accepted online. **Other phones:** Treasurer- 830-741-6110; Elections- 830-741-6104; Vital Records- 830-741-6041. **Property tax/Assessing**- 1102 15th St, Hondo, TX 78861; 830-741-6100, assessor fax- 830-741-6105. (Appraiser/Auditor- 830-741-3035) Public access terminal available.

Menard County

County Clerk, PO Box 1038, Menard, TX 76859. Recording, R/E phone-325-396-4682; fax-325-396-2047; 8AM-N; 1PM-5PM M-TH; 8AM-N 1-4PM F.
Index: All in one. Records indexed on computer back to 1990. Office personnel or visitors may perform searches. Search fee $10.00 per name. Office will search real estate records. Will search UCC records. Copy fee $1.00 per page. Cert fee- $5.00 per cert plus copy fee. Payee- Menard County Clerk. **Other phones:** Treasurer- 325-396-2748; Elections- 325-396-4682; Vital Records- 325-396-4682. **Property tax/Assessing**- 210 E San Saba, Menard, TX 76859; 325-396-4523, assessor fax- 915-396-2047. (Appraiser/Auditor- 325-396-4784)

Midland County

County Clerk, PO Box 211, Midland, TX 79702. Recording, R/E phone-432-688-4401; fax-432-688-4925; 8AM-5PM (CST) www.co.midland.tx.us
Index: All in one. Records indexed on a public use terminal back to 1981. Office personnel or visitors may perform searches. Search fee $10.00. Office will not search real estate or UCC records. Copy fee $1.00 per page. Cert fee- $5.00 per cert plus copy fee. Payee- Midland County Clerk. **Online access to Real Estate, Grantor/Grantee, Deed, Lien, Judgment, Divorce, Voter Registration records:** Access recording records free at www.titlex.com; select Midland county. Also, search Grantor/Grantee and divorce index free at www.texaslandrecords.com or www.uslandrecords.com. Registration and fees required for full data. Also, access voter registration data free at www.co.midland.tx.us/Elections/VoterDatabase/input.asp. **Other phones:** Treasurer- 432-688-4880; Elections- 432-688-4890; Vitals- 432-688-4401. **Property tax/Assessing**- 2110 N "A" St, Midland, TX 79701; 432-688-4810, assessor fax- 432-688-4918. (Appraiser/Auditor- 432-699-4991) hours- 8AM-5PM M,T,W,F; 8AM-6PM Th Public access terminal available. **Online access**- Access property tax data and delinquent taxes free at www.co.midland.tx.us/tax/Property/default.asp. Also, find appraisal district data free at http://208.75.248.98/. Also, search property data on the mapping page at www.midcad.org/Search/index.htm.

Milam County

County Clerk, 107 W Main, Cameron, TX 76520. 254-697-7049/800-216-0490, R/E recording phone-254-697-7049; fax-254-697-7055; 8AM-5PM (CST)
Phone number for Cindy Fechner, District Clerk is 254-697-7052. Index: Separate indices to search include deed, deed of trust, federal, state and release, abstract of judgment, assumed name, execution, etc prior to 1983. As of 1983 all records in Official Records. Records indexed on computer back to 1983. Office personnel or visitors may perform searches. Search fee $10.00 per name. Office will not search real estate records. Will not search UCC records. Copy fee $1.00 per page. Cert fee- $5.00 per cert plus copy fee. Payee- Milam County Clerk. **Online access to Real Estate, Grantor/Grantee, Deed, Lien, Judgment records:** Access recording records free at www.titlex.com; select Milam county. Records range is 5/2000 to 8/2001. Also, see note at beginning of section. **Other phones:** Treasurer- 254-697-7032; Elections- 254-697-7049; Vital Records- 254-697-7049. **Property tax/Assessing**- PO Box 551, 101 S Fannin, Cameron, TX 76520; 254-697-7017, assessor fax- 254-697-7020. (Appraiser/Auditor- 254-697-

6638) Public access terminal available. **Online access-** Search appraisal district data free at www.txcountydata.com/county.asp?County=166. Also see note at beginning of section.

Mills County

County Clerk, PO Box 646, Goldthwaite, TX 76844-0646. Recording, R/E phone-325-648-2711; fax-325-648-3251; 8AM-N, 1PM-5PM (CST)

Index: Separate indices to search include deeds, civil, Probate. Record index not computerized. Office personnel or visitors may perform searches. Office personnel searches are very limited. Search fee $5.00 per name. Office will not search real estate records. Office will not search UCC records. Copy fee $1.00 per page. Cert fee- $5.00 per cert plus copy fee. Payee- Mills County Clerk. **Other phones:** Treasurer- 325-648-2636; Elections- 325-648-2711; Vital Records- 325-648-2711. **Property tax/Assessing-** PO Box 565, 901 6th St, Goldthwaite, TX 76844; 325-648-2253, assessor fax- 325-648-3458. (Appraiser/Auditor- 325-648-2253) Public access terminal available. **Online access-** Find appraisal district data free at http://208.75.248.98/.

Mitchell County

County Clerk, 349 Oak St, #103, Colorado City, TX 79512-6213. Recording, R/E phone-325-728-3481; fax-325-728-5322; 8AM-N, 1-5PM (CST)

Index: Separate indices to search include document type, name or volume & page. Records indexed on a public use terminal back to 00. Office personnel or visitors may perform searches. Search fee $5.00 for docket searches. Office will not search real estate records. Office will not search UCC records. Copy fee $1.00 per page. Cert fee- $5.00 per cert plus copy fee. Exemplification fee $10.00 plus copy fee. Payee- Mitchell County Clerk. Bulk data available on CD or DVD images for $11.00, full - $8.00 for partial. **Online access to Land, Deed, Lien, Marriage, Death, Probate records:** Search official records after choosing county at www.edoctecinc.com/. If records are stamped Unofficial, you can copy them freely; Official, a $1.00 per page fee applies. For details and signup, contact Edoc Tec at 800-578-7746. **Other phones:** Treasurer- 325-728-8356; Vital Records- 325-728-3481; Property Auditor- 325-728 2196; Votor Registration -325-728-2606. **Property tax/Assessing-** 438 E 2nd, Colorado City, TX 79512; 325-728-2606, assessor fax- 325-728-3963. (Appraiser/Auditor- 325-728-5028) hours- 8AM-N, 1-4:45PM No public access terminal. **Online access-** Access to real property searches for free found at www.mitchellcad.org/

Montague County

County Clerk, PO Box 77, Montague, TX 76251-0077. 940-894-2461; fax-940-894-6601; 8AM-4:45PM.

Index: All in one. Records indexed on a public use terminal back to 1993. Office personnel or visitors may perform searches. Search fee $10.00 per name per 10 year interval. Copy fee $1.00 per page. Cert fee- $5.00 per doc plus copy fee. Payee- Montague Co. Clerk. **Other phones:** Treasurer- 940-894-2161. **Property tax/Assessing-** 101 E Franklin, Courthouse, Montague, TX 76251; 940-894-3881. (Appraiser/Auditor- 940-894-2081) **Online access-** Find appraisal district data free at http://208.75.248.98/.

Montgomery County

County Clerk, PO Box 959, Conroe, TX 77305. 936-539-7885; fax-936-760-6990; 8:30AM-4:30PM (CST) www.co.montgomery.tx.us

Index: Separate indices prior to 1980- deeds of trusts, judgments, tax liens. Records indexed on a public use terminal back to 1970. Office will perform a UCC search but public must search other records themselves. Search fee $10.00 per name. OPR copy fee $1.00 per page; UCC copy fee $1.50 per page, $5.00 minimum. Cert fee- $5.00 per cert plus copy fee. Payee- Montgomery County Clerk. OPR images on hard drive back to 1993 availalbe for bulk purchase. **Online access to Real Estate, Grantor/Grantee, Deed, Lien, Judgment, Probate records:** Access recording records free at www.titlex.com; select Montgomery county. Records go back to 1/1966. Similar index search may also be performed free at www.courthousedirect.com/IndexSearches.aspx. Registration and password required for full data. Also, to search probate records and judgment records go to http://idocket.com/countycourt.htm . **Other phones:** Treasurer- 936-759-7844; Elections- 936-539-7843; Vital Records- 936-538-8114. **Property tax/Assessing-** 400 N San Jacinto, Conroe, TX 77301; 936-539-7844. (Appraiser/Auditor- 936-756-3354) www.mcad-tx.org/ **Online access-** Access property appraiser data free at www.mcad-tx.org/html/records.html.

Moore County

County Clerk, 715 Dumas Ave, Rm 107, Dumas, TX 79029. 806-935-2009; fax-806-935-9004; 8:30AM-5PM (CST)

Index: All in one. Records indexed on a public use terminal back to 1990. Office personnel or visitors may perform searches. General search fee $5.00. $15.00 for UCC's. Office will not search real estate records. Separate federal tax lien search- $10.00 per debtor. Will search UCC records. Copy fee $1.00 per page; UCC copy $2.00 per page. Cert fee- $5.00 per cert plus copy fee. Payee- Moore County Clerk. **Other phones:** Treasurer- 806-935-2019; Elections- 806-935-2009; Vital Records- 806-935-2009. **Property tax/Assessing-** 700 S Bliss, Dumas, TX 79029; 806-935-2008, assessor fax- 806-935-2344. (Appraiser/Auditor- 806-935-4193) www.co.moore.tx.us/ips/cms/countyoffices/taxAssessorCollector.html **Online access-** Access to property data is free at www.moorecad.org.

Morris County

County Clerk, 500 Broadnax St, Daingerfield, TX 75638. Recording, R/E phone-903-645-3911; fax-903-645-4026; 8AM-N, 1-5PM (CST)

Index: All in one. Records indexed on a public use terminal back to 1965. Office personnel or visitors may perform searches. Search fee $10.00 per name. Copy fee $1.00 per page. Cert fee- $5.00 per cert plus copy fee. Payee- Morris County Clerk. **Other phones:** Treasurer- 903-645-2916; Elections- 903-645-3911; Vital Records- 903-645-3911. **Property tax/Assessing-** 501 Crockett St, Daingerfield, TX 75638; 903-645-5601. (Appraiser/Auditor- 903-645-5061) hours- 8AM-N 12:30PM-4:30PM **Online access-** Find appraisal district data free at http://208.75.248.98/.

Motley County

County Clerk, PO Box 660, Matador, TX 79244. Recording, R/E phone-806-347-2621; fax-806-347-2220; 8:30AM-5PM.

Index: Separate indices to search. Record index not computerized. Office personnel or visitors may perform searches. Search fee $10.00 per name. Office will search real estate records. Will search UCC records. Copy fee $1.00 per page. Cert fee- $5.00 per cert plus copy fee. Payee- Motley County Clerk. **Other phones:** Treasurer- 806-347-2800; Elections- 806-347-2621; Vital Records- 806-347-2621. **Property tax/Assessing-** PO Box 727, 701 Dundee St, Matador, TX 79244; 806-347-2252, assessor fax- 806-347-2220. (Appraiser/Auditor- 806-347-2273) hours- 9AM-N, 1PM-5PM. No public access terminal.

Nacogdoches County

County Clerk, 101 W Main, Rm 205, Nacogdoches, TX 75961. 936-560-7733; fax-936-559-5926; 8AM-5PM (CST) www.co.nacogdoches.tx.us

Index: All in one. Records indexed on a public use terminal back to 1965. Only the public may search real estate. Search fee $10.00 per name. Will not search UCC records. Copy fee $1.00 per page. Cert fee- $5.00 per cert plus copy fee. Payee- Nacogdoches County Clerk. **Online access to Real Estate, Grantor/Grantee, Lien, Judgment, Deed, Death, Marriage, Court records:** Access, view and search the Real Property grantor/grantee index free at https://www.texaslandrecords.com/txlr/TxlrApp/index.jsp. Monthly subscription is recommended; there is a pay as you go plan for $1 per document. Also, access court records at www.idocket.com. Fees involved. **Other phones:** Treasurer- 936-560-7703; Elections- 936-560-7825; Vital Records- 936-560-7733. **Property tax/Assessing-** 101 W Main, Rm 100, Nacogdoches, TX 75961; 936-560-7769, assessor fax- 936-564-2217. (Appraiser/Auditor- 409-560-3447) hours- 8AM-4:30PM Public access terminal available. Appraisal Dist. Ofc located at 216 W Hospital St. **Online access-** Access property tax data free at www.nacocad.org. Click on Search Our Data. Also, access to county Appraisal Roll from TaxNetUSA MAY be at www.taxnetusa.com/texas/.

Navarro County

County Clerk, PO Box 423, Corsicana, TX 75151. 903-654-3035; fax-903-872-7329; 8AM-5PM (CST) www.co.navarro.tx.us/ips/cms

Index: All in one. Records indexed on computer from 1995 to present; before 1995 manual indexes, UCCs and tax liens in different indexes. Office will perform a UCC search but public must search other records themselves. General search fee $5.00 per 10 years. Copy fee $1.00 per page. Cert fee- $5.00 per cert plus copy fee. Payee- Navarro County Clerk. **Online Judgment, Civil records:** Access civil and judgment records free at http://idocket.com/countycourt.htm. Also, see note at beginning of section for "Advanced" fee service. **Other phones:** Treasurer- 903-654-3090; Elections- 903-654-3330; Vital Records- 903-654-3035. **Property tax/Assessing-** 300 W 3rd Ave, Corsicana, TX 75110; 903-654-3080. (Appraiser - 903-872-2476) **Online access-** Find appraisal district data free at http://208.75.248.98/.

Newton County

County Clerk, PO Box 484, Newton, TX 75966-0484. Recording, R/E phone-409-379-5341; fax-409-379-9049; 8AM-4:30PM (CST)

Index: All in one. Records indexed on a public use terminal back to 1987; add'l computer indexes go back to 1985 and 1949. Office will perform a UCC search but public must search other records themselves. Separate federal tax or state tax lien search- $10.00 per debtor. Copy fee $1.00 per page. Cert fee- $5.00 per cert plus copy fee. Payee- Newton County Clerk. **Other phones:** Treasurer- 409-379-8127; Vital Records- 409-379-5341. **Property tax/Assessing-** PO Box 456, 113 Court St, Newton, TX 75966; 409-379-4241, assessor fax- 409-379-5944. (Appraiser/Auditor- 409-379-3710) Public access terminal available. **Online access-** Access Appraiser/property tax records free at www.newtoncad.org/Appraisal/PublicAccess/. Also, see note at beginning of section.

Nolan County

County Clerk, 100 E 3rd St, #108, Sweetwater, TX 79556-0098. Recording, R/E phone-325-235-2462; fax-325-236-9416; 8:30AM-5PM (CST)

Index: Separate indices to search include grantor/grantee. Records indexed on a public use terminal back to 1982. Only the public may search. Copy fee $1.00 per page. Cert fee- $5.00 per cert plus copy fee. Payee- Nolan County Clerk. **Other phones:** Treasurer- 325-236-6932; Elections- 325-235-2462; Vital Records- 325-235-2462. **Property tax/Assessing-** PO Box 1256, 208 Elm St, Sweetwater, TX 79556; 325-235-3331, assessor fax- 325-235-8165. (Appraiser/Auditor- 325-235-8421) hours- 8AM-4PM No public access terminal.

Nueces County

County Clerk, PO Box 2627, Corpus Christi, TX 78403. 361-888-0111, R/E recording phone-361-888-

0611, UCC recording phone-361-888-0580; fax-361-888-0329; 8AM-5PM (CST) www.co.nueces.tx.us
Index: All in one. Records indexed on a public use terminal back to 1981. Office personnel or visitors may perform searches. General search fee $5.00 per name. Office will not search real estate records. UCC search per debtor name- $14.00. UCC search request using non-standard form (per name)- $29.00. Copy fee $1.00 per page. Cert fee- $5.00 per cert plus copy fee. Payee- Nueces County Clerk. **Online access to Real Estate, Grantor/Grantee, Deed, Judgment, Lien records:** Access to county clerk recording records is free after registration at www.co.nueces.tx.us/countyclerk/records/; access is also free at www.titlex.com; select Nueces county. Also, see notes at beginning of section. **Other phones:** Treasurer- 361-888-0515; Elections- 361-888-0483; Vital Records- 361-888-0580. **Property tax/Assessing**- 361-888-0475. (Appraiser/Auditor-361-881-8022) **Online access**- Access County Appraiser records free at www.ncadistrict.com/ and click on Property to choose search mode. Also, see notes at beginning of section.

Ochiltree County

County Clerk, 511 S Main, Perryton, TX 79070. Recording, R/E phone-806-435-8039; fax-806-435-2081; 8:30AM-N, 1-5PM (CST)
Index: Separate indices to search include grantor/grantee, and numerical. Record index not computerized. Only the public may search. Copy fee $1.00 per page. Cert fee- $5.00 per cert plus copy fee. Payee- Ochiltree County Clerk. **Other phones:** Treasurer- 806-435-8046; Elections- 806-435-8039; Vital Records- 806-435-8039. **Property tax/Assessing**- 511 S Main, Perryton, TX 79070; 806-435-8025, assessor fax- 806-435-2899. (Appraiser/Auditor- 806-435-9623) hours- 8AM-N, 1-5PM except Th 8AM-5PM. No public access terminal.

Oldham County

County Clerk, PO Box 360, Vega, TX 79092. 806-267-2667; 8:30AM-5PM (CST)
Index: All in one. Record index not computerized. Only the public may search; office will perform limited searches. Search fee $5.00. Copy fee $1.00 per page. Cert fee- $5.00 per cert plus copy fee. Payee- Oldham County Clerk. **Other phones:** Treasurer-806-267-2329; Elections- 806-267-2667; Vital Records- 806-267-2667. **Property tax/Assessing**-806-267-2280. (Appraiser/Auditor- 806-267-2442)

Orange County

County Clerk, 123 S 6th St, Orange, TX 77630. Recording, R/E phone-409-882-7055; fax-409-882-7012; 8AM-5PM. www.co.orange.tx.us
Index: Separate indices to search include year and doc type. Records indexed on a public use terminal back to 00. Office personnel or visitors may perform searches. Search fee $5.00 unless otherwise indicated. Copy fee $1.00 per page; self-serve $.50 per page. Cert fee- $5.00 per doc plus copy fee. Payee- County Clerk. Data available (deeds & official public records images from 1852 to present) for bulk purchase; contact Michael Gilbert, Chief Deputy at 409-882-7055. **Other phones:** Treasurer- 409-882-7991; Elections- 409-882-7973; Vital Records- 409-882-7055. **Property tax/Assessing**- 123 S 6th St, Orange, TX 77630; 409-882-7971, assessor fax- 409-882-7912. (Appraiser/Auditor- 409-745-4777) hours-8AM-5PM except Wed 8:30AM-5PM Public access terminal available. **Online access**- Access to the county appraisal district records is free at www.orangecad.org/ or at the county site directly at www.orangecad.net/Appraisal/PublicAccess/.

Palo Pinto County

County Clerk, PO Box 219, Palo Pinto, TX 76484. Recording, R/E phone-940-659-1277; fax-940-659-2289; 8:30AM-4:30PM (CST)
Index: Separate indices to search. Records indexed on a public use terminal back to 1986. Only the public may search. Copy fee $1.00 per page. Cert fee- $5.00 per cert plus copy fee. Payee- Palo Pinto County Clerk. **Other phones:** Treasurer- 940-659-1260; Elections- 940-659-1277; Vital Records- 940-659-1277. **Property tax/Assessing**- PO Box 160, 520 Oak St, Palo Pinto, TX 76484; 940-659-1271, assessor fax- 940-659-3628. (Appraiser/Auditor- 940-659-1281) No public access terminal. **Online access**- Access to property data is free at www.palopintocad.org. Click on Search Our Data.

Panola County

County Clerk, Sabine & Sycamore, Rm 201; Courthouse Bldg, Carthage, TX 75633. Recording, R/E phone-903-693-0302; fax-903-693-0328; 8AM-5PM (CST)
Index: All in one. Records indexed on a public use terminal back to 5/1/79. Only the public may search. Copy fee $1.00 per page. Cert fee- $5.00 per cert plus copy fee. Payee- Panola County Clerk. **Online access to Real Estate, Grantor/Grantee, Deed, Lien, Judgment, Death, Marriage records:** Access recording records free at www.titlex.com; select Panola county. Also, search grantor/grantee index free at www.texaslandrecords.com. Registration and fees required for full access. **Other phones:** Treasurer-903-693-0325; Elections- 903-693-0370; Vital Records- 903-693-0302. **Property tax/Assessing**-Panola County Courthouse, 110 S Sycamore, #211, Carthage, TX 75633; 903-693-0340, assessor fax-903-694-2909. (Appraiser/Auditor- 903-693-2891) hours- 8AM-4:30PM Public access terminal available.

Parker County

County Clerk, PO Box 819, Weatherford, TX 76086. 817-594-7461; fax-817-594-9540; 8AM-4PM (CST) www.co.parker.tx.us/ips/cms
Index: Onsite indices are by year in books. Records indexed on computer back to 1981. Only the public may search. Office will not search real estate records. Will not search UCC records. Copy fee $1.00 per page. Cert fee- $5.00 per cert plus copy fee. Payee-Parker County Clerk. **Online access to Real Estate, Deed, Lien, Marriage, Birth, Death records:** Access county clerk's index free after registration at www.parker.tx.us.landata.com/. Fees required for full data, $2.00 per doc. **Other phones:** Treasurer- 817-598-6150; Elections- 817-598-6185; Vital Records-817-594-7461. **Property tax/Assessing**- 1108 Santa Fe Dr, Weatherford, TX 76086; 817-599-7671, assessor fax- 817-613-8092. (Appraiser/Auditor- 817-596-0077) hours- 8AM-5PM Public access terminal available. **Online access**- Find appraisal district data free at http://208.75.248.98/. Add'l online access through private companies.

Parmer County

County Clerk, PO Box 356, Farwell, TX 79325. Recording, R/E phone-806-481-3691; fax-806-481-9154; 8:30AM-5PM (CST)
Index: All in one. Records indexed on a public use terminal back to 1996. Office personnel or visitors may perform searches. Search fee $10.00. Office will not search real estate records. Will search UCC records. Copy fee $1.00 per page. Cert fee- $5.00 per cert plus copy fee. Payee- Parmer County Clerk. Bulk data available for purchase from ACS. **Other phones:** Treasurer- 806-481-9152; Elections- 806-481-3691; Vital Records- 806-481-3691. **Property tax/ Assessing**- PO Drawer G, Farwell, TX 79325; 806-481-3691, assessor fax- 806-481-9548. (Appraiser/Auditor- 806-481-1405) hours- 8:30AM-N, 1PM-4:45PM No public access terminal.

Pecos County

County Clerk, 200 S Nelson, Fort Stockton, TX 79735. 432-336-7555; fax-432-336-7557; 8AM-N, 1-5PM. www.co.pecos.tx.us/
Index: All in one. Records indexed on computer back to April, 1983. Only the public may search. Copy fee $1.00 per page. Cert fee- $5.00 per doc plus copy fee. Payee- Pecos County Clerk. **Other phones:** Treasurer- 432-336-3461; Elections- 432-336-7555; Vital Records- 432-336-7555. **Property tax/Assessing**- 200 S Nelson, Fort Stockton, TX 79735; 432-336-3386, assessor fax- 432-336-3382. (Appraiser/Auditor- 432-336-7587) hours- 8AM-5PM Public access terminal available. www.pecoscad.org/ **Online access**- Access to property data is free at www.pecoscad.org/. Click on Search Our Data.

Polk County

County Clerk, PO Drawer 2119, Livingston, TX 77351. Recording, R/E phone-936-327-6804; fax-936-327-6874; 8AM-5PM (CST) www.co.polk.tx.us
Index: All in one. Records indexed on a public use terminal back to 1846. Office personnel or visitors may perform searches. General index search fee $5.00 per name. Office will search real estate records. Will search UCC records. Copy fee $1.00 per page. Cert fee- $5.00 per cert plus copy fee. Payee- Polk County Clerk. **Online access to Real Estate, Deed, Lien records:** Access to County Clerk's data is by subscription at www.co.polk.tx.us/ips/cms/countyoffices/countyClerk.html. Username and password required. **Other phones:** Treasurer- 936-327-6816; Elections- 936-327-6804; Vital Records- 936-327-6804; Court Clerk- 936-327-6805. **Property tax/Assessing**- 416 N Washington St, Livingston, TX 77351; 936-327-6801, assessor fax- 936-327-6885. (Appraiser/Auditor- 936-327-6811) hours- 8AM-4:30PM No public access terminal.

Potter County

County Clerk, PO Box 9638, Amarillo, TX 79105. 806-379-2275, R/E recording phone-806-379-2292, UCC recording phone-806-379-2276; fax-806-379-2296; 8AM-5PM (CST)
Index: All in one. Records indexed on a public use terminal back to 1/1980. Office personnel or visitors may perform searches. Search fee $10.00 per name. Office will search real estate records. Will search UCC records. UCC search per debtor name- $15.00. Copies requested at the same time are $.10 each. Copy fee $1.00 per page. Cert fee- $5.00 per cert plus copy fee. Payee- Potter County Clerk. Bulk data available for purchase. **Online access to Real Estate, Grantor/Grantee, Deed, Lien, Marriage, Divorce, Judgment, Probate records:** Access recording records free at www.titlex.com; select Potter county. Also, search grantor/grantee index free at www.texaslandrecords.com. Registration and fees required for full data. Search probate and judgment records go to http://idocket.com/countycourt.htm. Also, see note at beginning of section. **Other phones:** Treasurer- 806-349-4832; Elections- 806-379-2299; Vital Records- 806-379-2290. **Property tax/Assessing**- PO Box 2289, 900 South Polk, Amarillo, TX 79105; 806-342-2600 x2. (Appraiser/Auditor- 806-358-1601) **Online access**-Records on the Potter-Randall Appraisal District database are free at www.prad.org. Records periodically updated; for current tax info call Potter-806-342-2600 or Randall- 806-665-6287.

Presidio County

County Clerk, PO Box 789, Marfa, TX 79843. 432-729-4812; fax-432-729-4313; 8AM-N; 1PM-4PM (CST) www.co.presidio.tx.us
Index: All in one. Records indexed on a public use terminal back to 6/13/02. Only the public may search. Copy fee $1.00 per page. Cert fee- $5.00 per cert plus copy fee. Payee- Presidio County Clerk. **Other phones:** Treasurer- 432-729-4076; Elections- 432-729-4812; Vital Records- 432-729-4812. **Property tax/Assessing**- PO Box 848, 301 N Highland Ave, Marfa, TX 79843; 432-729-4081, assessor fax- 432-729-4920. (Appraiser/Auditor- 432-729-3431);

Rains County

County Clerk, PO Box 1150, Emory, TX 75440. Recording, R/E phone-903-473-5000, UCC phone-903-373-5000; fax-903-474-9390; 8AM-4:30PM.
Index: Separate indices to search. Records indexed on computer back to 1992. Only the public may search; office computer not for public use. Copy fee $1.00 per

page. Cert fee- $5.00 per cert plus copy fee. Payee- Rains County Clerk. **Other phones:** Treasurer- 903-474-9999; Elections- 903-473-5000; Vital Records- 903-474-5000. **Property tax/Assessing**- 903-474-2391. (Appraiser/Auditor- 903-473-2391)

Randall County

County Clerk, PO Box 660, Canyon, TX 79015. Recording, R/E phone-806-468-5505; fax-806-468-5509; 8AM-5PM (CST) www.randallcounty.org

Index: Separate indices to search include books, computer. Records indexed on a public use terminal back to 2000. Office personnel or visitors may perform searches. Search fee $10.00 per name. Office will not search real estate records. UCC search per debtor name- $15.00. Copy fee $1.00 per page. Cert fee- $5.00 per cert plus copy fee. Payee- Randall County Clerk. OPR records available for bulk pruchase; contact Renee Calhoun or Dawn Wauer. **Online access to Real Estate, Deed, Lien, Deed, Marriage, Probate, Judgment records:** Access Real Estate records from 2000 forward free at http://ccopr.randallcounty.org/, click on Official Public Records and then OPR search, or marriages, or Comm. Court for Commissioner's Court data. Also, criminal, probate and civil records found at www.idocket.com. Also, see notes at beginning of section for add'l property records. **Other phones:** Treasurer- 806-468-5535; Elections- 806-468-5510; Vital Records- 806-468-5505. **Property tax/Assessing**- 400 16th St, Canyon, TX 79015; 806-468-5540, assessor fax- 806-468-5541. (Appraiser/Auditor- 806-358-1601) **Online access**- Randall County appraisal and personal property records are combined online with Potter County; see Potter County for access info or visit www.prad.org. Randall County sheriff sales records are combined online with Potter County; see Potter County for access info or visit www.prad.org.

Reagan County

County Clerk, PO Box 100, Big Lake, TX 76932. Recording, R/E phone-325-884-2442; fax-325-884-1503; 8:30AM-5PM; 4PM F. (CST)

Index: All in one. Records indexed on a public use terminal back to 2001. Office personnel or visitors may perform searches. Search fee $10.00 per name. Office will not search real estate records. Office will search UCC records. Copy fee $1.00 per page. Cert fee- $5.00 per cert plus copy fee. Payee- Reagan County Clerk. **Online access to Real Estate, Grantor/Grantee, Divorce records:** Access to public record search is free at www.taxnetusa.com/publicrecords/. Also, See note at beginning of section. **Other phones:** Treasurer- 325-884-2090; Elections- 325-884-2442; Vital Records- 325-884-2442. **Property tax/Assessing**- 300 Plaza, Courthouse, Big Lake, TX 76932; 325-884-2131, assessor fax- 325-884-4104. (Appraiser/Auditor- 325-884-3275)

Real County

County Clerk, PO Box 750, Leakey, TX 78873-0750. Recording, R/E phone-830-232-5202; fax-830-232-6888; 8AM-5PM (CST) www.co.real.tx.us/ips/cms

Index: All in one. Records indexed on computer back to 12/92. Only the public may search real estate. Search fee $5.00 per name. Copy fee $1.00 per page. Cert fee- $5.00 per doc plus copy fee. Payee- Bella A. Rubio, County Clerk. **Other phones:** Treasurer- 830-232-6627; Elections- 830-232-5202; Vital Records- 830-232-5202. **Property tax/Assessing**- PO Box 898, 101 S Market St, Leakey, TX 78873; 830-232-6210, assessor fax- 830-232-6888. (Appraiser/Auditor- 830-232-6248);

Red River County

County Clerk, 200 N Walnut; Courthouse Annex, Clarksville, TX 75426-3075. 903-427-2401; fax-903-427-3589; 8:30AM-5PM (CST) www.co.red-river.tx.us/ips/cms/countyoffices/countyClerk.html

Index: All in one. Records indexed on a public use terminal back to 1968 for deeds, other records back to 1984. Only the public may search. Copy fee $1.00 per page. Cert fee- $5.00 per cert plus copy fee. Payee- Red River County Clerk. **Other phones:** Treasurer- 903-427-3748; Elections- 903-427-2401; Vital Records- 903-427-2401. **Property tax/Assessing**- 200 N Walnut, Courthouse Annex, Clarksville, TX 75426; 903-427-3009. (Appraiser - 903-427-4181) www.co.red-river.tx.us/ips/cms/countyoffices/taxAssessorCollector.html **Online access**- Access to county appraisal district records is free at www.redrivercad.org.

Reeves County

County Clerk, PO Box 867, Pecos, TX 79772. Recording, R/E phone-432-445-5467; fax-432-445-3997; 8AM-5PM.

Index: All in one. Records indexed on computer back to 1984. Office personnel or visitors may perform searches. Search fee $10.00 per name. Office will not search real estate records. Office will not search UCC records. Copy fee $1.00 per page. Cert fee- $5.00 per cert plus copy fee. Payee- Reeves County Clerk. **Other phones:** Treasurer- 432-445-2631; Elections- 432-445-5467; Vital Records- 432-445-5467. **Property tax/Assessing**- PO Box 700, 100 E 4th St, Rm 104, Pecos, TX 79772; 432-445-5473, assessor fax- 432-445-5096. (Appraiser - 432-445-5122);

Refugio County

County Clerk, PO Box 704, Refugio, TX 78377. 361-526-2233; fax-361-526-1325; 8AM-4PM (CST) www.co.refugio.tx.us

Index: All in one. Records indexed. Only office personnel may search. Search fee $10.00. Real estate record owner and property searches available. Office will search UCC records. Copy fee $1.00 per page. Cert fee- $5.00 per cert plus copy fee. Payee- Refugio County Clerk. Bulk data available for purchase, contact Ida Turner. **Other phones:** Treasurer- 361-526-4223; Elections- 361-526-2151; Vital Records- 361-526-2233. **Property tax/Assessing**- PO Box 1001, 808 Commerce Rm109, Refugio, TX 78377; 361-526-2023, assessor fax- 361-526-2279. (Appraiser/Auditor- 361-526-5994) hours- 8AM-4:15PM www.co.refugio.tx.us **Online access**- Access property data free at www.refugiocad.org. Click on Search Our Data.

Roberts County

County Clerk, PO Box 477, Miami, TX 79059-0477. 806-868-2341; fax-806-868-3381; 8AM-N; 1-5PM.

Index: Separate indices to search include deed, lease, probate, judgment, liens, etc. Records indexed on computer back to 1996. Only the public may search. Copy fee $1.00 per page. Cert fee- $5.00 per doc plus copy fee. Payee- Pay fees to Robert Co Clerk. **Other phones:** Treasurer- 806-868-2411; Elections- 806-868-2341; Vital Records- 806-868-2341; Voter Registrar- 806-868-3611. **Property tax/Assessing**- Courthouse, Miami, TX 79059; 806-868-3611. (Appraiser/Auditor- 806-868-5281)

Robertson County

County Clerk, PO Box 1029, Franklin, TX 77856. Recording, R/E phone-979-828-4130; fax-979-828-1260; 8AM-5PM (CST)

Index: Separate indices to search include grantor/grantee by years. Records indexed on a public use terminal back to 1/1/1983. Only the public may search. Copy fee $1.00 per page. Cert fee- $5.00 per cert plus copy fee. Payee- Robertson County Clerk. Bulk data available for purchase, contact Carolyn Bancroft or Kathryn Brimhall. **Online access to Real Estate, Grantor/Grantee, Deed, Lien, Judgment records:** Access recording records free at www.titlex.com; select Robertson county. Also, access grantor/grantee index free at www.texaslandrecords.com but registration and fees required for full data. **Other phones:** Treasurer- 979-828-3201; Elections- 979-828-5726; Vital Records- 979-828-4130; County Judge- 979-828-3542. **Property tax/Assessing**- PO Box 220, 315 N Center St, Franklin, TX 77856; 979-828-3337, assessor fax- 979-828-4011. (Appraiser/Auditor- 979-828-5800) hours- 8AM-4:30PM

Rockwall County

County Clerk, 1101 Ridge Rd, #101, Rockwall, TX 75087. 972-204-6300, R/E recording phone-972-882-0220, UCC recording phone-972-882-0226; fax-972-204-6309; hours - -8AM-5PM (CST) www.rockwallcountytexas.com/index.asp?nid=108

Index: All in one. Records indexed on a public use terminal back to 1978. Office personnel or visitors may perform searches. Office will not search real estate records. Office will search UCC records prior to 7/2001 and current fixture (land) files. UCC search includes tax liens if requested. UCC search per debtor name- $10.00. Copy fee $1.00 per page. Cert fee- $5.00 per cert plus copy fee. Payee- Rockwall County Clerk. **Online access to Real Estate, Grantor/Grantee, Deed, lien, Judgment, Vital Statistic records:** Access grantor/grantee index free at www.texaslandrecords.com. Registration and fees required for full data. **Other phones:** Treasurer- 972-882-0290; Elections- 972-882-0240; Vital Records- 972-882-0220. **Property tax/Assessing**- Auditor's Office, 101 E Rusk St, #101, Rockwall, TX 75087; 972-204-6050, fax- 972-204-6059. (Appraiser- 972-771-2034) www.rockwallcountytexas.com/index.asp?NID=219 **Online access**- Access appraisal district property records free at www.rockwallcad.com.

Runnels County

County Clerk, PO Box 189, Ballinger, TX 76821-0189. Recording, R/E phone-325-365-2720; fax-325-365-3408; 8:30AM-N, 1-5PM (CST)

Index: Indexes separated by date. Records indexed on a public use terminal back to 1996. Office personnel or visitors may perform searches. Office will only do limited searching. Search fee $10.00 per name per document. Office will not search real estate records. Office will search UCC records prior to 7/2001 and current fixture (land) files. Tax liens not included in UCC search. Copy fee $1.00 per page. Cert fee- $5.00 per cert plus copy fee. Payee- County Clerk, Runnels County. **Other phones:** Treasurer- 325-365-2428; Elections- 325-365-2720; Vital Records- 325-365-2720. **Property tax/Assessing**- PO Box 517, Ballinger, TX 76821-0517; 325-365-2339. (Appraiser/Auditor- 325-365-3583) **Online access**- Find appraisal district data free at http://208.75.248.98/.

Rusk County

County Clerk, PO Box 758, Henderson, TX 75653-0758. Recording, R/E phone-903-657-0330; fax-903-657-0062; 8AM-5PM (CST) www.co.rusk.tx.us

Index: All in one. Records indexed on a public use terminal back to 1976. Office personnel or visitors may perform searches. Search fee $5.00 per name. Office will not search real estate records. Will not search UCC records. Copy fee $1.00 per page. Cert fee- $5.00 per cert plus copy fee. Payee- Rusk County Clerk. **Online access to Real Estate, Grantor/Grantee, Deed, Judgment, Lien records:** Access to grantor/grantee index free at www.texaslandrecords.com. Registration and fees required for full access. Also, see note at beginning of section. **Other phones:** Treasurer- 903-657-0352; Elections- 903-657-0321; Vital Records- 903-657-0301; 903-657-0327. **Property tax/Assessing**- 202 N Main St, Henderson, TX 75652; 903-657-0321. (Appraiser/Auditor- 903-657-3578) **Online access**- Access property data free at www.ruskcad.org. Click on Search Our Data. Also see www.taxnetusa.com for property tax records.

Sabine County

County Clerk, PO Drawer 580, Hemphill, TX 75948-0580. Recording, R/E phone-409-787-3786; fax-409-787-4973; 8AM-4PM (CST)

Index: All in one. Records indexed on computer back to 1991. Only the public may search. Copy fee $1.00 per page. Cert fee- $5.00 per cert plus copy fee. Payee- Sabine County Clerk. **Other phones:**

Treasurer- 409-787-2210; Elections- 409-787-3786; Vital Records- 409-787-3786; Registrar of Deeds- 409-787-3786. **Property tax/Assessing-** PO Box 310, Hemphill, TX 75948; 409-787-2257. (Appraiser - 409-787-2777)

San Augustine County

County Clerk, 100 W Columbia, #106; Courthouse, San Augustine, TX 75972-1335. 936-275-2452; fax-936-275-9579; 8AM-4PM (CST)
Index: All in one. Record index not computerized. Office will not perform UCC or tax lien searches. Search fee $10.00 per name. Time permitting, office may perform an unguaranteed real estate search. Copy fee $1.00 per page but not less than $5.00 per debtor. Cert fee- $5.00 per cert plus copy fee. Payee- San Augustine County Clerk. **Other phones:** Treasurer- 936-275-9472; Elections- 936-275-0989; Vital Records- 936-275-2452. **Property tax/Assessing-** 936-275-2300. (Appraiser/Auditor- 936-275-3496)

San Jacinto County

County Clerk, 1 State Hwy 150, Rm 2, Coldspring, TX 77331. Recording, R/E phone-936-653-2324; fax-936-653-8312; 8AM-4:30PM (CST)
Index: All in one. Records indexed on a public use terminal back to 1996. Office personnel or visitors may perform searches. Search fee $11.00 per name for civil, criminal and probate. Office will not search UCC or real estate records. Will not search UCC records. Copy fee $1.00 per page. Cert fee- $5.00 per cert plus copy fee. Payee- San Jacinto County Clerk. Bulk data available for purchase on CD-rom; contact Angelia Steele. **Other phones:** Treasurer- 936-653-2353; Elections- 936-653-5804; Vital Records- 936-653-5804. **Property tax/Assessing-** 111 State Hwy, Rm C5, Coldspring, TX 77331; 936-653-3292, assessor fax- 936-653-2533. (Appraiser/Auditor- 936-653-1450) hours- 8AM-N, 1PM-4PM **Online access-** Online access available through private companies.

San Patricio County

County Clerk, PO Box 578, Sinton, TX 78387. 361-364-6290, R/E recording phone-361-364-9350; fax-361-364-6112; 8AM-5PM (CST) www.co.san-patricio.tx.us/ips/cms
Index: All in one. Records indexed on a public use terminal back to 10/1/2001. Office personnel or visitors may perform searches. Search fee $10 per name. Office will not search real estate records. Tax liens not included in UCC search. State and federal tax lien search fee- $10.00 per debtor per 10 years. Copy fee $1.00 per page. Cert fee- $5.00 per cert plus copy fee. Payee- San Patricio County Clerk. CD available, $8.00 per week, contact Dalia Sanchez. **Other phones:** Treasurer- 361-364-9335; Elections- 361-364-9365; Vital Records- 361-364-9350. **Property tax/Assessing-** PO Box 280, 400 W Sinton St, Rm 144, Sinton, TX 78387; 361-364-9373, assessor fax- 361-364-9473. (Appraiser/Auditor- 361-364-5402) A public access terminal is available. www.co.san-patricio.tx.us **Online access-** Search the Appraiser database for free at www.taxnetusa.com/texas/ OR search via the county site, http://12.105.136.220/appraisal/publicaccess/.

San Saba County

County Clerk, 500 E Wallace, San Saba, TX 76877. 325-372-3614; 8-4:30PM. www.sansabacounty.org
Index: All in one. Records indexed on computer back to 5/01. Office will perform a UCC and Tax lien search but public must search other records themselves. Search fee $15.00. Copy fee $1.00 per page. Cert fee- $5.00 per doc plus copy fee. Payee- Clerk. **Other phones:** Treasurer- 325-372-3337; Elections- 325-372-3614; Vital Records- 325-372-3614. **Property tax/Assessing-** 423 E Wallace St, San Saba, TX 76877; 325-372-5031. (Appraiser/Auditor- 325-372-5031) 8:30AM-4:30PM

Schleicher County

County Clerk, PO Drawer 580, Eldorado, TX 76936. 325-853-2833 ext 72, R/E recording phone-325-853-2833; fax-325-853-2768; 9AM-N, 1-5PM.
Index: All in one. Record index not computerized. Office personnel or visitors may perform searches. Search fee $10.00 per name. Office will search real estate records. Will search UCC records. Copy fee $1.00 per page. Cert fee- $5.00 per cert plus copy fee. Payee- Schleicher County Clerk. **Other phones:** Treasurer- 325-853-2594; Elections- 325-853-2302; Vital Records- 325-853-2833. **Property tax/Assessing-** 164 E US Hwy 190, Eldorado, TX 76936; 325-853-3066, assessor fax- 325-853-2603. (Appraiser/Auditor- 325-853-2617) hours- 9AM-5PM

Scurry County

County Clerk, 1806 25th St, #300, Snyder, TX 79549-2530. 325-573-5332; fax-325-573-7396; 8:30AM-5PM (CST)
Index: All in one. Records indexed on a public use terminal back to 1997 and some of 1996. Office will perform a UCC search but public must search other records themselves. Search fee $10.00. Copy fee $1.00 per page. Cert fee- $5.00 per doc plus copy fee. Payee- County Clerk. **Online access to Real Estate, Grantor/Grantee, Deed, Lien, Judgment records:** Search index free at www.texaslandrecords.com. Fees and registration required for full data. **Other phones:** Treasurer- 325-573-5382; Elections- 325-573-5332; Vital Records- 325-573-5332. **Property tax/Assessing-** 1806 25th St, #300, Snyder, TX 79549; 325-573-9316, assessor fax- 325-574-1687. (Appraiser/Auditor- 325-573-8549);

Shackelford County

County Clerk, PO Box 247, Albany, TX 76430. 325-762-2232, R/E recording phone-325-762-2232 x102, UCC phone-x100; fax-325-762-2830; 8:30AM-N, 1PM-5PM (CST) www.co.shackelford.tx.us/ips/cms
Index: All in one. Records indexed on a public use terminal back to 1987. Office will perform an in-person search or public may search themselves. General index search fee $5.00 per name. UCC search fee $10.00. No major RE or UCC searches. Copy fee $1.00 per page. Include SASE for mail return. Cert fee- $5.00 per cert plus copy fee. Payee- Shackelford County Clerk. **Other phones:** Treasurer- x121; Elections- x101; Vital Records- x102. **Property tax/Assessing-** PO Box 565, Albany, TX 76430; 325-762-2207. (Appraiser/Auditor- 325-762-2207) hours- 8AM-5PM

Shelby County

County Clerk, PO Box 1987, Center, TX 75935. 936-598-6361; fax-936-598-3701; 8AM-4:30PM (CST) http://cc.co.shelby.tx.us/
Index: Separate indices to search include (pre-1990)-deed, DT, MML. AJ, FTL, STL. Records indexed on computer back to 1986. Only the public may search. Copy fee $1.00 per page. Cert fee- $5.00 per cert plus copy fee. Payee- Shelby County Clerk. **Online access to Real Estate, Deed, Lien, Judgment, UCC, Marriage, Court, Probate records:** Access the recorder's databases of records free at http://cc.co.shelby.tx.us/. **Other phones:** Treasurer- 936-598-3581; Elections- 936-598-6361; Vital Records- 936-598-6361. **Property tax/Assessing-** PO Box 1987, 200 San Augustine St #A, Center, TX 75935; 936-598-4441, fax- 936-598-8942. (Appraiser - 936-598-6171) www.shelbycad.com **Online access-** Search appraisal district records free at www.txcountydata.com/county.asp?county=210.

Sherman County

County Clerk, PO Box 270, Stratford, TX 79084. 806-366-2371; fax-806-366-5670; 8AM-N, 1-5PM.
Index: Separate indices to search include grantor/grantee, Daily Register. Record index not computerized. Only the public may search. Will not search UCC records. Do not have any old UCC's. Copy fee $1.00 per page. Cert fee- $5.00 per page plus copy fee. Payee- Sherman County Clerk. **Other phones:** Treasurer- 806-396-5842; Elections- 806-366-2371; Vitals- 806-366-2371; Property Tax Appraiser- 806-396-5566. **Property tax/Assessing-** 806-396-2150.

Smith County

County Clerk, PO Box 1018, Tyler, TX 75710. 903-590-3102, R/E recording phone-903-590-4751; fax-903-590-4689; 8AM-5PM. www.smith-county.com
Index: All in one. Records indexed on a public use terminal back to 9/1/81. Office personnel or visitors may perform searches. Search fee $10.00 UCCs, $5.00 tax lien. Office will search real estate records. Will search UCC records. Copy fee $1.00 per page. Cert fee- $5.00 per cert plus copy fee. Payee- Smith County Clerk. **Online access to Real Estate, Grantor/Grantee, Deed, Lien, Judgment records:** Search grantor/grantee index free at www.texaslandrecords.com. Registration and fees required for full data access. Also, see note at beginning of section. **Other phones:** Treasurer- 903-590-4730; Elections- 903-590-4777; Vital Records- 903-590-4697. **Property tax/Assessing-** 1517 W Front St, Tyler, TX 75702; 903-590-2920. (Appraiser - 903-510-8600) www.smithcad.org **Online access-** Access to county appraisal district records is free at www.smithcountymapsite.org/. Also, access property data on the GIS-mapping site free at www.smithcad.org/scadarc/viewer_temp.htm. Also, see note at beginning of section.

Somervell County

County/District Clerk, PO Box 1098, Glen Rose, TX 76043. Recording, R/E phone-254-897-4427; fax-254-897-3233; 8AM-5PM (CST)
Index: All in one. Records indexed on computer back to 1989. Only the public may search. Copy fee $1.00 per page. Cert fee- $5.00 per cert plus copy fee. Payee- Somervell County Clerk. CDs of bulk data available for purchase; contact Virginia Fuentes. **Other phones:** Treasurer- 254-897-4814; Elections-254-897-4427; Vital Records- 254-897-4427. **Property tax/Assessing-** PO Box 305, Glen Rose, TX 76043; 254-897-2419, assessor fax- 254-897-3018. (Appraiser/Auditor- 254-897-4094) **Online access-** Access Appraisal District records free at http://clientdb.trueautomation.com/clientdb/main.asp?id=29 or via http://somervellcad.org. Other online access through private companies.

Starr County

County Clerk, Courthouse, Rio Grande City, TX 78582. 956-487-8032; 8AM-5PM (CST)
Index: All in one. Records indexed on computer back to 1984. Office personnel or visitors may perform searches. General index search fee $10.00 per name. Office will search real estate records. Copy fee $1.00 per page. Cert fee- $5.00 per cert plus copy fee. Payee- Starr County Clerk. **Online access to Probate, Judgment records:** Access probate and judgment records free at http://idocket.com/countycourt.htm . **Other phones:** Treasurer- 956-487-8106; Elections-956-488-2648; Vital Records- 956-487-8032. **Property tax/ Assessing-** 956-487-8136. (Appraiser/Auditor- 956-487-5613)

Stephens County

County Clerk, Courthouse, Breckenridge, TX 76424. Recording, R/E phone-254-559-3700; fax-254-559-5892; 8:30AM-5PM (CST)
Index: Separate indices to search include books, computer. Records indexed on a public use terminal back to 1977. Office personnel or visitors may perform searches. General search fee $5.00 per name. Office will not search real estate records. UCC search includes tax liens if requested. UCC search per debtor name- $10.00. Copy fee $1.00 per page. Cert fee- $5.00 per cert plus copy fee. Payee- Stephens County Clerk. **Other phones:** Treasurer- 254-559-3181; Elections- 254-559-3700; Vital Records- 254-559-3700. **Property tax/Assessing-** 200 W Walker, Breckenridge, TX 76424; 254-559-2732, assessor fax- 254-559-2960. (Appraiser/Auditor- 254-559-

8233) A public access terminal is available. **Online access-** Find appraisal district data free at http://208.75.248.98/.

Sterling County

County Clerk, PO Box 55, Sterling City, TX 76951-0055. Recording, R/E phone-325-378-5191; fax-325-378-3111; 8AM-4PM M-Th; 8AM-1:30PM Fri. (CST) www.co.sterling.tx.us

Index: Separate indices to search include official public records (1/1/1999 - present), grantor/grantee. Before 1999, separate indexes for deed, deed of trust, bill of sale, abstract of judgments, tax liens, mechanic liens, assumed name cert, patents, etc. Record index not computerized. Office personnel or visitors may perform searches. Search fee $15.00 per name. Office will search real estate records. Will search UCC records. Copy fee $1.00 per page. Cert fee- $5.00 per cert plus copy fee. Payee- Sterling County Clerk. **Other phones:** Treasurer- 325-378-8511; Elections-325-378-5191; Vital Records- 325-378-5191. **Property tax/Assessing-** PO Box 888, Sterling City, TX 76951; 325-378-7711, assessor fax- 325-378-2266. (Appraiser/Auditor- 325-378-7711);

Stonewall County

County Clerk, PO Drawer P, Aspermont, TX 79502. Recording, R/E phone-940-989-2272; fax-940-989-2715; 8AM-4:30PM (CST)

Alternate fax number- 940-989-2032. Index: All in one. Records indexed on computer back to 2002. Only the public may search. Copy fee $1.00 per page. Cert fee- $5.00 per cert plus copy fee. Payee-Stonewall County Clerk. **Other phones:** Treasurer-940-989-3520; Elections- 940-989-2272; Vital Records- 940-989-2272. **Property tax/Assessing-** Drawer N, Apermont, TX 79502; 940-989-2633, assessor fax- 940-989-2715. (Appraiser/Auditor- 940-989-3363)

Sutton County

County Clerk, 300 E Oak, #3; Sutton County Annex, Sonora, TX 76950. 325-387-3815; fax-325-387-6028; 8:30AM-4:30PM (CST)

Index: All in one. Records indexed on computer 1992. Office will perform a UCC search but public must search other records themselves. Copy fee $1.00 per page. Cert fee- $5.00 per instrument or document. Payee- Sutton County Clerk. **Other phones:** Treasurer- 325-387-2886; Appraiser- 325-387-2809; Auditor -325-387-5380. **Property tax/Assessing-** PO Box 858, Sonora, TX 76938; 325-387-2342.

Swisher County

County Clerk, 119 S Maxwell; Courthouse, Tulia, TX 79088. 806-995-3294; fax-806-995-4121; 8AM-5PM (CST) www.co.swisher.tx.us/ips/cms

Index: All in one. Records indexed on computer back to 1992. Office personnel can only search tax lien & judgment lien records, but public must search other records themselves. Copy fee $1.00 per page. Self serve- $.50 per page. Cert fee- $5.00 per cert plus copy fee. Payee- Swisher County Clerk. **Other phones:** Treasurer- 806-995-2204; Elections- 806-995-3294; Vital Records- 806-995-3294. **Property tax/Assessing-** 119 S Maxwell, Tulia, TX 79088; 806-995-3513, assessor fax- 806-995-4572. (Appraiser/Auditor- 806-995-4118);

Tarrant County

County Clerk, 100 W Weatherford, Rm B-30; Courthouse, Ft. Worth, TX 76196. 817-884-1069, R/E recording phone-817-884-1060; fax-817-884-3295; 8AM-4:30PM (CST) www.tarrantcounty.com/eCountyClerk/site/default.asp

Index: All in one. Records indexed on a public use terminal back to 1970. Office will perform a UCC search but public must search other records themselves. UCC search per debtor name $16.00. Copy fee $1.00 per page. Cert fee- $5.00 per cert plus copy fee. Payee- Tarrant County Clerk. **Online access to Real Estate, Grantor/Grantee, Lien, Judgment, Deed, Assumed Name, Marriage, UCC records:** Search grantor/grantee index at http://ccanthem.co.tarrant.tx.us/search.aspx?cabinet=opr. Also, access a real estate and grantor/grantee index free at www.titlex.com where records range from 4/1997 to 11/2001 only; select Tarrant County. Also, search assumed names, marriages, courts, UCCs, Traffic at www.tarrantcounty.com/ecountyclerk/cwp/view.asp?A=735&Q=427570. Also see note at beginning of section. **Other phones:** Elections- 817-884-1115. **Property tax/Assessing-** 100 E Weatherford St, Ft Worth, TX 76196; 817-884-1100. (Appraiser/Auditor- 817-284-0024) Public access terminal at Appraiser Ofc, 2500 Handly-Ederville Rd, Ft Worth 76118, 817-284-4063. www.tarrantcounty.com/eTax/site/default.asp **Online access-** Access Appraisal District Property data free at www.tad.org/Datasearch/datasearch.htm. Access assessor's accounts search for tax data free at http://taxoffice.tarrantcounty.com/AccountSearch.asp. Access City of Grapevine and Coffeyville tax office free at www.texaspayments.com/validate.asp.

Taylor County

County Clerk, 300 Oak St, Abilene, TX 79602-1581. 325-674-1202; fax-325-674-1279; 8AM-5PM (CST)

Index: All in one. Records indexed on a public use terminal back to 1981. Only the public may search. Copy fee $1.00 per page. Cert fee- $5.00 per cert plus copy fee. Payee- Taylor County Clerk. **Online access to Real Estate, Grantor/Grantee, Deed, Vital Statistic records:** Access land records index free at www.texaslandrecords.com. Registration and fees required for full data. Also, see note at beginning of section for add'l property data. **Other phones:** Treasurer- 325-674-1231; Elections- 325-674-1216; Vital Records- 325-674-1202. **Property tax/Assessing-** 400 Oak St, Abilene, TX 79602; 325-674-1224. (Appraiser/Auditor- 325-676-9381) **Online access-** Access to the county Central Appraisal District database is free at www.taxnetusa.com/texas/. Also, access Appraisal District records free at http://propaccess.trueautomation.com/clientdb/?cid=32. Search the treasurer's list of unclaimed property at www.taylorcountytexas.org/unclaime.html.

Terrell County

County Clerk, PO Drawer 410, Sanderson, TX 79848. Recording, R/E phone-432-345-2391; fax-432-345-2740; 9AM-5PM (CST) www.sandersontx.info

Index: All in one. Records indexed on computer back to 6/1/94. Office personnel or visitors may perform searches. Search fee $5.00 per name. Office will search real estate records. Will search UCC records. Copy fee $1.00 per page. Cert fee- $5.00 per cert plus copy fee. Payee- Terrell County Clerk. **Other phones:** Treasurer- 432-345-2992. **Property tax/Assessing-** PO Box 320, Sanderson, TX 79848; 432-345-2499, assessor fax- 432-345-3056. (Appraiser/Auditor- 432-345-2251) hours- 8AM-5PM

Terry County

County Clerk, 500 W Main, Rm 105, Brownfield, TX 79316-4398. Recording, R/E phone-806-637-8551; fax-806-637-4874; 8:30AM-5PM (CST) www.co.terry.tx.us/ips/cms/countyoffices/countyClerk.html

Index: All in one. Records indexed on computer back to 1981. Only office personnel may search. Search fee $10.00. Copy fee $1.00 per page. Cert fee- $5.00 per doc includes copy fee. Payee- Terry County Clerk. Bulk data available for purchase contact Ronnie Burran. **Other phones:** Treasurer- 806-637-3616; Elections- 806-637-8551; Vital Records- 806-637-8551. **Property tax/Assessing-** 421 W Powell, Brownfield, TX 79316; 806-637-6966, assessor fax-806-637-4675. (Appraiser/Auditor- 806-637-6966) **Online access-** Tax roll information is available at www.terrycad.org/.

Throckmorton County

County Clerk, PO Box 309, Throckmorton, TX 76483. Recording, R/E phone-940-849-2501; fax-940-849-3032; 8AM-N 1PM-5PM M-TH; 8AM-N 1PM-4PM F.

Index: All in one. Records indexed on a public use terminal back to 1990. Office personnel or visitors may perform searches. Search fee $10.00 per name. Office will search real estate records, very limited. Copy fee $1.00 per page. Cert fee- $1.00 per page includes copy fee. Payee- County/Disrtict Clerk. **Other phones:** Treasurer- 940-849-2921; Elections-940-849-2501; Vital Records- 940-849-2501. **Property tax/Assessing-** PO Box 578, Throckmorton, TX 76483; 940-849-5691. hours-8AM-4PM

Titus County

County Clerk, 100 W 1st St, 2nd Fl, #204, Mount Pleasant, TX 75455. Recording, R/E phone-903-577-6796; fax-903-572-5078; 8AM-5PM (CST)

Index: Separate indices to search include grantor/grantee. Records indexed on computer from 1973 forward. Office personnel or visitors may perform searches. Search fee $10.00 per name. Copy fee $1.00 per page. Cert fee- $5.00 per cert plus copy fee. Payee- Titus County Clerk. Bulk real property data availalbe for purchase on CD's. **Other phones:** Treasurer- 903-572-8723; Elections- 903-575-0902; Vital Records- 903-577-6796. **Property tax/Assessing-** 105 W 1st St #101, Mt Pleasant, TX 75455; 903-572-6712. (Appraiser - 903-577-7939) **Online** - Access property and other tax data free at http://clientdb.trueautomation.com/clientdb/main.asp?id=71. Also, search the tax payments database free at www.co.titus.tx.us/.

Tom Green County

County Clerk, 124 W Beauregard, San Angelo, TX 76903-5835. Recording, R/E phone-325-659-6552, UCC phone-325-659-3262; fax-325-659-3251; 8AM-4:30 (CST) http://countyclerk.tomgreencountytx.gov

Index: Separate indices include grantor and grantee. Records indexed on a public use terminal back to 1982. Office personnel or visitors may perform searches. General index search fee $5.00 per name; financing statements such as UCCs, tax liens- $10.00 per name. Copy fee $1.00 per page. UCC copy or Fed tax lien copy- $1.50 per page. Cert fee- $5.00 per cert plus copy fee. Payee- Tom Green County Clerk. Bulk RE scanned miages available for purchase, contact Sue Baulos 325-659-6552. **Online access to Real Estate, Grantor/Grantee, Deed, Lien, Judgment, Marriage, Birth, Death, Fictitious Name records:** Access official public records including vital stats and fictitious names free at http://countyclerk.tomgreencountytx.gov/. Also, access recording records free at www.titlex.com; select Tom Green County. **Other phones:** Elections-325-659-6541; Vital Records- 325-659-6556. **Property tax/Assessing-** 113 W Beauregard, San Angelo, TX 76903; 325-658-5575, assessor fax- 325-655-3450. (Appraiser/Auditor- 325-658-5575) **Online access-** Access appraisal district property data free at www.tomgreencad.com/.

Travis County

County Clerk, 5501 Airport Blvd, Austin, TX 78701. 512-854-9188, R/E recording phone-512-854-4526, fax-512-854-4526; hours - 8AM-5PM (CST) www.co.travis.tx.us/county_clerk/default.asp

Judgments and other court records found at 100 Guadalupe, #222, Austin, TX 78751. Index: All in one. Records indexed on a public use terminal back to 1987/. Office personnel or visitors may perform searches. Search fee $10.00 per debtor for 10 years. Copy fee $1.00 per page. Self serve- $.25 each. Cert fee- $5.00 per cert plus copy fee. Payee- Travis County Clerk. All recording data avialble for purchase on CD, monthly; contact Bill Vaught. **Online access to Real Estate, Grantor/Grantee, Deed, UCC, Marriage, Probate, Voter Registration records:** Access to recorders official records is free at http://deed.co.travis.tx.us/. Images available back to 1/1/88. Also, See note at beginning of section for add'l property records. **Other phones:** Treasurer- 512-854-9000; Elections- 512-854-9075; Vital Records- 512-458-7111. **Property tax/Assessing-** 5501 Airport

Blvd, Austin, TX 78701; 512-854-9473. (Appraiser/Auditor- 512-854-9317) **Online access**- Access the Central Appraisal District database free at www.traviscad.org/search.htm. Also search business personal property. Also, you may search on the county tax payment system at www.texasonline.state.tx.us/NASApp/rap/BaseRap.

Trinity County

County Clerk, PO Box 456, Groveton, TX 75845. Recording, R/E phone-936-642-1208; fax-936-642-3004; 8AM-5PM (CST)

Index: All in one. Records indexed on computer back to 1999. Office personnel or visitors may perform searches. Search fee $10.00. Office will search real estate records. Tax liens not included in UCC search. Copy fee $1.00 per page. Cert fee- $5.00 per cert includes copy fee. Payee- Trinity County Clerk. **Other phones:** Treasurer- 936-642-1443; Elections- 936-642-1208; Vital Records- 936-642-1208. **Property tax/Assessing**- PO Box 369, 162 W 1st, Groveton, TX 75845; 936-642-1637, assessor fax- 936-642-2609. (Appraiser/Auditor- 936-642-1502) hours- 8AM-N, 1PM-5PM. A public access terminal is available. **Online access** - Access property appraisal district data free at www.txcountydata.com/county.asp?County=228.

Tyler County

County Clerk, 110 W Bluff, Rm 110, Woodville, TX 75979. 409-283-2281, R/E recording phone-409-283-2281 x10, UCC recording phone-409-283-2281 x13; 8AM-4:30PM (CST)

Searches not guaranteed, they are only a computerized index print out. Index: All in one. Records indexed on computer back to 1978. Office personnel or visitors may perform searches. General search fee $5.00 per name. Real estate owner, mortgage, and property transfer searches available. Office will search UCC records prior to 7/2001 and current fixture (land) files. Tax liens not included in UCC search. UCC search per debtor name- $10.00. UCC search request using non-standard form (per name)- $25.00. Separate fed and/or state tax lien search fee- $10.00 per debtor. Copy fee $1.00 per page. Cert fee- $5.00 per cert plus copy fee. Payee- Tyler County Clerk. **Other phones:** Treasurer- 409-283-3054; Elections- 409-283-2281 x10; Vital Records- 409-283-2281 x15. **Property tax/Assessing**- 1001 West Bluff, Woodville, TX 75979; 409-283-2734, assessor fax- 409-283-5967. (Appraiser/Auditor- 409-283-3736) No public access terminal. **Online** - Access to the county appraisal district records is free at www.tylercad.org and also at www.txcountydata.com/county.asp?County=229

Upshur County

County Clerk, PO Box 730, Gilmer, TX 75644. 903-843-4015, R/E recording phone-903-680-8123, 8124, 8125, UCC phone-903-843-4015; fax-903-843-5492; 8AM-4:30PM (CST) www.countyofupshur.com

Index: All in one. Records indexed on a public use terminal back to 8/79. Only the public may search. Copy fee $1.00 per page. Cert fee- $5.00 per cert plus copy fee. Payee- Upshur County Clerk. **Online access to Real Estate, Grantor/Grantee, Deed, Lien, Judgment, Marriage, Birth, Death, Probate records:** Access County Clerks' OPR and other recorder records including civil and probate free at http://countyofupshur.com:8000/. Also, access recording records free at www.titlex.com; select Upshur county. Also, see note at beginning of section. **Other phones:** Treasurer- 903-680-8135, 8136, 8138; Elections- 903-680-8123; Vital Records- 903-680-8123; Civil, Criminal & Probate- 903-680-8123. **Property tax/Assessing**- 215 N Titus, Gilmer TX 75644; 903-843-3085, assessor fax- 903-843-3083. (Appraiser/Auditor- 903-843-3041) hours- 7:30AM-5PM **Online access**- To view property information for free go to www.trueautomation.com.

Upton County

County Clerk, PO Box 465, Rankin, TX 79778. 432-693-2861; fax-432-693-2129; 8AM-5PM. www.co.upton.tx.us

Index: All in one. Records indexed on a public use terminal back to 1992. Office personnel or visitors may perform searches. General index search fee $5.00 per name per document. Office will not search RE or UCC records. Copy fee $1.00 per page. Exemplification fee, $10.00 per doc plus copy fee. Cert fee- $5.00 per doc plus copy fee. Payee- Upton County Clerk. **Online access to Real Estate, Grantor/Grantee, Deed, Lien records:** Search grantor/grantee index free at www.texaslandrecords.com. Registration and fees required for fuller data, but images not available. **Other phones:** Treasurer- 432-693-2401; Elections- 432-693-2861; Vital Records- 432-693-2861. **Property tax/Assessing**- PO Box 14, Rankin, TX 79778; 432-693-2572, assessor fax- 432-693-2243. (Appraiser/Auditor- 432-652-3221) hours- 9AM-N, 1-5PM

Uvalde County

County Clerk, PO Box 284, Uvalde, TX 78802-0284. Recording, R/E phone-830-278-6614; fax-830-278-8692; 8AM-5PM (CST) www.uvaldecounty.com

Index: All in one. Records indexed on a public use terminal back to 1997. Only the public may search. Will not search UCC records. Copy fee $1.00 per page. Cert fee- $5.00 per cert plus copy fee. Payee- Uvalde County Clerk. Bulk data available on CD's of OPR, Probate, Image, Index for $30.00 per CD; contact Mary Flores (830) 278-6614. **Other phones:** Treasurer- 830-278-5821; Elections- 830-278-3225; Vital Records- 830-278-6614. **Property tax/Assessing**- 209 N High St, Uvalde, TX 78801; 830-278-1106, assessor fax- 830-278-8150. (Appraiser/Auditor- 830-278-1106) hours- 8AM-N, 1-5PM **Online access**- Access to county appraisal district tax data may be available through www.uvaldecounty.com; search page may be temporarily down.

Val Verde County

County Clerk, PO Box 1267, Del Rio, TX 78841-1267. 830-774-7564; fax-830-774-7608; 8AM-4:30PM (CST)

Index: Separate indices to search include records from 1885-1992, official public records, 1992-present. Records indexed on computer. Office will perform a UCC search but public must search other records themselves. Search fee $5.00 plus $1.00 per page. Copy fee $1.00 per page. Cert fee- $5.00 per cert plus copy fee. Payee- Val Verde County Clerk. **Online access to Probate, Judgment records:** Search probate records and judgment records at http://idocket.com/countycourt.htm . **Other phones:** Treasurer- 210-774-4602. **Property tax/Assessing**- 830-774-7535. (Appraiser/Auditor- 830-774-4602) **Online** - Access Appraisal District records free at http://clientdb.trueautomation.com/clientdb/main.asp?id=42.

Van Zandt County

County Clerk, 121 E Dallas St, Rm 202; Courthouse, Canton, TX 75103. Recording, R/E phone-903-567-6503; fax-903-567-6722; 8AM-4:30PM (CST) www.vanzandtcounty.org

Index: All in one. Records indexed on computer back to 1971. Office will perform a tax lien search or see if a filing was made but generally the public must search records themselves. Search fee $10.00 per name. Copy fee $1.00 per page. Cert fee- $6.00 1st page, $2.00 each add'l page, includes copy fee. Payee- Van Zandt County Clerk. **Online access to Real Estate, Grantor/Grantee, Deed, Judgment, Lien records:** Access recorded document index 1971 to present free after registration at https://www.countygovernmentrecords.com/texas/web/ but there may be a fee to view images. Also, access recording records 1/1971 to current free at www.titlex.com; select Van Zandt county. Registration required; pay by tokens. Also, see note at beginning of section. **Other phones:** Treasurer- 903-567-2551; Elections- 903-567-6503; Vital Records- 903-567-6503. **Property tax/Assessing**- 27867 Hwy 64, Canton, TX 75103; 903-567-6551. (Appraiser/Auditor- 903-567-6171) **Online access**- Search the county appraisal rolls for free at www.vanzandtcad.org/; includes plat maps online. Also, find property data at www.myswdata.com/. Also, find appraisal district data free at http://208.75.248.98/.

Victoria County

County Clerk, PO Box 1968, Victoria, TX 77902. Recording, R/E phone-361-575-1478; fax-361-575-6276; 8AM-5PM (CST)

Index: All in one. Records indexed on computer. Only the public may search, but office can assist. Search fee $10.00. Office will not name search real estate records. Office will search UCC records prior to 7/2001 and current fixture (land) files. Tax liens not included in UCC search. Copy fee $1.00 per page. Cert fee- $5.00 per cert plus copy fee. Payee- Victoria County Clerk. Bulk data available for purchase; contact Chief Deputy Betty Tovar. **Online access to Real Estate, Grantor/Grantee, Deed, Judgment, Lien, Probate records:** Access recording records free at www.titlex.com; select Victoria county. Records range is 1/1964 to 5/26/2005 only. Also, to search probate records and judgment records go to http://idocket.com/countycourt.htm. Also, see note at beginning of section . **Other phones:** Treasurer- 361-575-8588; Elections- 361-576-0124; Vital Records- 361-575-1478 (county); Vital Records (city) -361-485-3040. **Property tax/Assessing**- 205 N Bridge, Rm 101, Victoria, TX 77901; 361-576-3671, assessor fax- 361-576-0477. (Appraiser/Auditor- 361-576-3621) **Online access**- Access to appraisal district records is free at www.victoriacad.org.

Walker County

County Clerk, PO Box 210, Huntsville, TX 77342-0210. 936-436-4922; fax-936-436-4928; 8AM-4:45PM (CST) www.co.walker.tx.us

Index: Separate indices to search include numerous indexes from 1846 to present. Records indexed on computer from 1960 to present. Office will perform a UCC search but public must search other records themselves. Copy fee $1.00 per page. Cert fee- $5.00 per cert plus copy fee. Payee- James D. Patton, County Clerk. **Online access to Real Estate, Grantor/Grantee, Deed, Lien, Death, Divorce, Marriage records:** Search land records index free at www.texaslandrecords.com. Indexes from 1960-forward; images of the records back to 1/1/2003. Subscription required for full data. **Other phones:** Treasurer- 936-436-4933; Elections- 936-436-4950; Vital Records- 936-436-4922; Voter Registration-936-436-4959. **Property tax/Assessing**- 1301 Sam Houston Ave, Huntsville, TX 77340; 936-436-4950, assessor fax- 936-436-4961. (Appraiser/Auditor- 936-295-0402) hours- 8:15AM-4:45PM **Online access**- Access to county appraisal district records is free at http://clientdb.trueautomation.com/clientdb/main.asp?id=4.

Waller County

County Clerk, 836 Austin St, Rm 217, Hempstead, TX 77445. Recording, R/E phone-979-826-7711; fax-979-826-8317; hours - 8AM-N, 1-5PM (CST) www.co.waller.tx.us/ips/cms/countyoffices/countyClerk.html

Index: All in one. Records indexed on a public use terminal back to 1994. Office will perform a UCC search but public must search other records themselves. UCC search per debtor name $10.00. Office will not search real estate records. Copy fee $1.00 per page. Cert fee- $5.00 per cert plus copy fee. Payee- Waller County Clerk. **Other phones:** Treasurer- 979-826-7707; Elections- 979-826-7643; Vital Records- 979-826-7711. **Property tax/Assessing**- 730 9th St, Hempstead, TX 77445; 979-826-7620. (Appraiser/Auditor- 281-396-6100) hours- 8AM-5PM **Online access**- Access appraiser property data free at www.txcountydata.com/county.asp?County=237.

Ward County

County Clerk, Corner of 4th & Allen, Monahans, TX 79756. 432-943-3294; fax-432-943-6054; 8AM-5PM.
Index: All in one. Record index not computerized. Only the public may search. Copy fee $1.00 per page. Cert fee- $5.00 per doc plus copy fee. Payee- Ward County Clerk. **Other phones:** Treasurer- 432-943-2841; Elections- 432-943-3294; Vital Records- 432-943-3294. **Property tax/Assessing**- 400 S Allen #102, Monahans, TX 79756; 432-943-2546/2547, fax- 432-943-2745. (Appraiser/ - 432-943-3224) www.co.ward.tx.us/ips/cms/countyoffices/taxAssessorCollector.html

Washington County

County Clerk, 100 E Main, #102, Brenham, TX 77833. 979-277-6200; fax-979-277-6278; 8AM-5PM. www.co.washington.tx.us
Index: All in one. Records indexed on a public use terminal back to 1951. Only the public may search. Office will not search real estate records. Office will not search UCC records. Copy fee $1.00 per page. Cert fee- $5.00 per doc plus copy fee. Payee- Washington County Clerk. **Online access to Real Estate, Grantor/Grantee, Deed, Judgment, Lien, Probate, Marriage, Birth, Death, Military Discharge records:** Access recording records free at www.titlex.com; select Washington county. Records go back to 1/1965. Also, search probate and judgment records at http://idocket.com/countycourt.htm. Also, see note at beginning of section. Also, search official records after choosing county at www.edoctecinc.com/. If records are Unofficial, you search or copy them free; if not Unofficial, a $1.00 per page fee applies. For details and signup, contact clerk or Jerry Anderson at 800-578-7746. **Other phones:** Treasurer- 979-277-6200; Elections- 979-277-6200; Vitals- 979-277-6200. **Property tax/Assessing**- 100 E Main #100, Brenham, TX 77833; 979-277-6218, fax- 979-277-6282. (Appraiser - 979-277-3740) www.co.washington.tx.us/ips/cms/countyoffices/TAX/ **Online** - Access appraisal district property records free at www.washingtoncad.org:8008/Appraisal/PublicAccess/

Webb County

County Clerk, PO Box 29, Laredo, TX 78042. 956-523-4622, R/E recording phone-956-523-4266; fax-956-523-5035; hours - 8AM-5PM (CST) www.webbcounty.com
Index: All in one. Records indexed on a public use terminal back to 1982. Office personnel or visitors may perform searches. Search fee $10.00. Copy fee $1.00 per page. Cert fee- $5.00 per cert plus copy fee. Payee- Webb County Clerk. **Online access to Real Estate, Deed, Probate, Judgment records:** Access recording office land data at www.etitlesearch.com; registration required, fee based on usage. Also, to search probate records and judgment records go to http://idocket.com/countycourt.htm. Also, see note at beginning of section for add'l property data. **Other phones:** Treasurer- 956-523-4150; Elections- 956-523-4050; Vital Records- 956-523-4266 (outside city limits); Vital Records (inside city limits) -956-795-4929. **Property tax/Assessing**- Same address as recording office. 956-523-4200. (Appraiser/Auditor- 956-718-4091) **Online access**- Search the county Central Appraisal District database at www.webbcad.org/Propertysearch/propertysearch.html.

Wharton County

County Clerk, PO Box 69, Wharton, TX 77488. Recording, R/E phone-979-532-2381; fax-979-532-8426; 8AM-5PM (CST)
Index: All in one. Real property records indexed on computer from 1978 to present, criminal, civil and probate-1991 to present, 1978 and prior-separate, deed of trust, judgment, mechanic liens and tax liens. Only the public may search. Copy fee $1.00 per page. Cert fee- $5.00 per cert plus copy fee. Payee- Wharton County Clerk. **Online access to Real Estate, Grantor/Grantee, Deed, Lien, Judgment records:** Access recording records free at www.titlex.com; select Wharton county. Records go up to 11/2003. **Other phones:** Treasurer- 979-532-2971; Elections- 979-532-0193; Vital Records- 979-532-2381. **Property tax/Assessing**- PO Box 189, Wharton, TX 77488; 979-532-3312. (Appraiser/Auditor- 979-532-8931) **Online**- Access appraisal district property data at www.txcountydata.com/county.asp?County=241.

Wheeler County

County Clerk, PO Box 465, Wheeler, TX 79096. 806-826-5544; fax-806-826-3282; 8AM-5PM (CST)
Index: Separate indices to search. Record index not computerized. Office personnel or visitors may perform searches. Search fee $10.00 per name. Office will not search real estate or UCC records. Copy fee $1.00 per page. Cert fee- $5.00 per cert plus copy fee. Payee- Wheeler County Clerk. **Other phones:** Treasurer- 806-826-3122. **Property tax/Assessing**- County Courthouse, Wheeler, TX 79096; 806-826-3131. (Appraiser/Auditor- 806-826-5900) **Online access**- Find tax office data free at http://208.75.248.98/.

Wichita County

County Clerk, PO Box 1679, Wichita Falls, TX 76307-1679. 940-766-8144, R/E recording phone-940-766-8160; fax-940-716-8554; 8AM-5PM (CST)
Index: All in one. Records indexed on a public use terminal back to 1986; images back to 1986. Office personnel or visitors may perform searches. Search fee $10.00 per name. Office will search real estate records. Will search UCC records. Copy fee $1.00 per page. Marriage license cert copy- $10.00. Plats- $5.00 each. Cert fee- $5.00 per cert plus copy fee. Payee- Wichita County Clerk. **Online access to Real Estate, Grantor/Grantee, Deed, Lien, Judgment, Marriage records:** Search grantor/grantee index free at www.texaslandrecords.com. Registration and fees required for full data. Some, not all, UCCs are available. Also, see note at beginning of section. **Other phones:** Treasurer- 940-766-8245; Elections-940-766-8174; Vital Records- 940-766-8127; Auditor- 940-766-8138. **Property tax/Assessing**- 600 Scott St, Wichita Falls, TX 76301; 940-766-8203, assessor fax- 940-766-8189. (Appraiser/Auditor- 940-322-2435) **Online** - Access appraisal district records free at http://propaccess.wadtx.com/clientdb/?cid=1. Also, see online notes in state summary at beginning of section.

Wilbarger County

County Clerk, 1700 Willbarger, #15; Courthouse, Vernon, TX 76384. Recording, R/E phone-940-552-5486; fax-940-553-1202; 8AM-5PM (CST)
Index: Indices are in books arranged by year, some 20 yr, some 5, some single year. Record index not computerized. Only the public may search, except UCC and tax liens. Search fee $5.00 per 10 year period. Office will not search real estate records. Office will search UCC records prior to 7/2001 and current fixture (land) files. Tax liens not included in UCC search. UCC search per debtor name- $13.00. Separate state or federal tax lien search- $5.00 per search per 10 year period. Copy fee $1.00 per page. Cert fee- $5.00 per cert plus copy fee. Payee- Wilbarger County Clerk. **Other phones:** Treasurer-940-553-2302; Elections- 940-552-5486; Vital Records- 940-552-5486. **Property tax/Assessing**- 1700 Willbarger, #17, Vernon, TX 76384; 940-552-9341, assessor fax- 940-553-2324. (Appraiser/Auditor- 940-553-1857) **Online access**- Access to property data is free at www.wilbargerappraisal.org/. Also, search the appraisal rolls for free at www.taxnetusa.com. Also see note at beginning of section.

Willacy County

County Clerk, 576 W Main St, Raymondville, TX 78580. Recording, R/E phone-956-689-2710; fax-956-689-9849; 8AM-N, 1-5PM (CST)
Index: Separate indices to search include grantor/grantee, by yrs. Record index not computerized. Office personnel or visitors may perform searches. Search fee $10.00 per name for every 10 yrs. Office will search one real estate record if your provided. UCC search per debtor name- $16 on standard form, $31 non-standard. Copy fee $1.00 per page. Cert fee- $5.00 per cert plus copy fee. Payee- Willacy County Clerk. **Online access to Real Estate, Grantor/Grantee, Deed, Judgment, Lien records:** Access recording records free at www.titlex.com; select Willacy county. Record range is 8/1998 to 1/2004. Also, access land records back 20 years at www.landtitleusa.com. **Other phones:** Treasurer- 956-689-2772; Elections- 956-689-2387; Vital Records- 956-689-2710. **Property tax/Assessing**- 190 N 3rd, Raymondville, TX 78580; 956-689-3621, assessor fax- 956-689-4817. (Appraiser/Auditor- 956-689-5979) **Online access**- See note at beginning of section.

Williamson County

County Clerk, PO Box 18, Georgetown, TX 78627-0018. Recording, R/E phone-512-943-1515, UCC recording phone-512-943-1514; fax-512-943-1616; 8AM-5PM (CST) www.wilcogov.org/
Index: All in one. Record index not computerized. Visitors must perform searches except office will search Abstract of Judgment, state/and/fed tax liens, and assumed names. Search fee $10.00 per name. Office will not name search real estate or UCC records. Copy fee $1.00 per page. Fed tax lien copy fee- $1.50 per page. Cert fee- $5.00 per cert plus copy fee. Payee- Williamson County Clerk. **Online access to Real Estate, Grantor/Grantee, Deed, Lien, Judgment records:** Access recording records free at www.titlex.com; select Williamson county. Records go back to 5/1999. **Other phones:** Treasurer- 512-943-1587; Elections- 512-943-1630; Vital Records-512-943-1526. **Property tax/Assessing**- 904 S Main, Georgetown, TX 78626; 512-943-1603. (Appraiser - 512-930-3787) www.wilcogov.org **Online access**- Access the appraiser database free at www.wcad.org. Also, access the monthly delinquent tax sale list at http://wcportals.wilco.org/tax%5Fassessor/. Also, see note at beginning of section.

Wilson County

County Clerk, PO Box 27, Floresville, TX 78114. 830-393-7308; fax-830-393-7334; 8AM-5PM (CST) www.co.wilson.tx.us/ips/cms/countyoffices/countyClerk.html
Index: All in one. Records indexed on a public use terminal back to 1/1992. Only the public may search. Copy fee $1.00 per page. Cert fee- $5.00 per cert plus copy fee. Payee- Wilson County Clerk. **Other phones:** Treasurer- 830-393-7310; Elections- 830-393-7368; Vital Records- 830-393-7308. **Property tax/Assessing**- 2 Library Ln, Floresville, TX 78114; 830-393-7313, assessor fax- 830-393-7359. (Appraiser/Auditor- 830-393-3065) hours- 7:30AM-6PM **Online access**- See note at beginning of section.

Winkler County

County Clerk, PO Box 1007, Kermit, TX 79745. 432-586-3401; 8AM-5PM (CST)
Index: All in one. Record index not computerized. Only the public may search. Copy fee $1.00 per page; UCC copy- $1.50 per page. Cert fee- $5.00 per cert plus copy fee. Payee- Winkler County Clerk. **Other phones:** Treasurer- 432-586-6604. **Property tax/Assessing**- PO Drawer T, Kermit, TX 79745; 432-586-3465. (Appraiser/Auditor- 432-586-2832)

Wise County

County Clerk, PO Box 359, Decatur, TX 76234. 940-627-3351; fax-940-627-2138; 8AM-4:30PM (CST)
Index: All in one. Records indexed on a public use terminal back to 1982. Office personnel or visitors

may perform searches. Search fee $10.00; will not search UCCs. Office will search real estate records. Copy fee $1.00 per page; 11 x 17 copies $2.00. Cert fee- $5.00 per cert plus copy fee. Payee- Wise County Clerk. **Online access to Real Estate, Grantor/Grantee, Deed, Lien, Mortgage, Divorce, Marriage records:** Search land records and vital records at www.texaslandrecords.com. Index search is free; subscription required for full data. **Other phones:** Treasurer- 940-627-3540; Elections- 940-626-4453; Vital Records- 940-627-3351. **Property tax/Assessing**- 404 W Walnut, Decatur, TX 76234; 940-627-3523. (Appraiser/Auditor- 940-627-3081) **Online access**- Find appraisal district data free at http://208.75.248.98/. Also, search county property tax data free at www.taxnetusa.com/texas/.

Wood County

County Clerk, PO Box 1796, Quitman, TX 75783. 903-763-2711; fax-903-763-5641; 8AM-5PM (CST) www.co.wood.tx.us

Index: Indices by year. Records indexed on a public use terminal back to 1960; images go back to 1990. Office personnel or visitors may perform searches. Search fee $5.00 per name. Office will not search real estate records. Copy fee $1.00 per page; faxed back- $2.00 per page. Cert fee- $5.00 per cert plus copy fee. Payee- Wood County Clerk. **Online access to Real Estate, Grantor/Grantee, Deed, Lien, Judgment records:** Access recording records at www.titlex.com; select Wood county. Registration and login required; purchase tokens in order to search. **Other phones:** Treasurer- 903-763-4186; Elections- 903-763-2400; Vital Records- 903-763-2711. **Property tax/Assessing**- PO Box 1919, Quitman, TX 75783; 903-763-2261, assessor fax- 903-763-5753. (Appraiser/Auditor- 903-763-4946) **Online access**- Search property tax records free at http://taxinfo.co.wood.tx.us/Appraisal/PublicAccess/.

Yoakum County

County Clerk, PO Box 309, Plains, TX 79335. 806-456-2721, R/E recording phone-806-456-7491; fax-806-456-2258; 8AM-5PM (CST)

Index: All in one. Records indexed on a public use terminal back to 1986. Office personnel or visitors may perform searches. Office personnel will only perform small searches. Search fee $5.00 per name plus $2.00 if faxed back. Office will not search real estate records. Will not search UCC records. Copy fee $1.00 per page. Cert fee- $5.00 per cert plus copy fee. Payee- Yoakum County Clerk. Paper copies available for purchase in bulk. **Other phones:** Treasurer- 806-456-7491; Elections- 806-456-7491; Vital Records- 806-456-7491. **Property tax/Assessing**- PO Box 250, Courthouse, Plains, TX 79355; 806-456-7491 x295, fax- 806-456-7118. (Appraiser - 806-456-7491) www.co.yoakum.tx.us/ips/cms/countyoffices/taxAssessorCollector.html

Young County

County Clerk, 516 4th St #104, Graham, TX 76450-3063. Recording, R/E phone-940-549-8432; fax-940-521-0305; 8:30AM-N, 1-5PM (CST)

Index: All in one. Records indexed on a public use terminal back to 1991. Office will perform a UCC search but public must search other records themselves. Copy fee $1.00, tax lien or real estate $1.00 per page. Cert fee- $5.00 per cert plus copy fee. Payee- Young County Clerk. **Other phones:** Treasurer- 940-549-2633; Elections- 940-521-9483; Vital Records- 940-539-8432; 940-539-8433. **Property tax/Assessing**- 724 Oak St, Graham, TX 76450 940-549-1393. (Appraiser/Auditor- 940-549-2392) hours- 8AM-N, 1-5PM **Online access**- Access to property data is free at www.youngcad.org. Click on Search Our Data.

Zapata County

County Clerk, PO Box 789, Zapata, TX 78076. 956-765-9915; fax-956-765-9933; 8AM-5PM (CST)

Index: All in one. Records indexed on a public use terminal back to 1994. Office personnel or visitors may perform searches. General index search fee $5.00 per name. UCCs $10.00. Office will search real estate records. Copy fee $1.00 per page. Cert fee- $5.00 per doc plus copy fee. Payee- Zapata County Clerk. **Online access to Real Estate, Deed records:** Access recording office land data at www.etitlesearch.com; registration required, fee based on usage. **Other phones:** Treasurer- 956-765-9925; Elections- 956-765-9915; Vital Records- 956-765-9945. **Property tax/Assessing**- 956-765-9971. (Appraiser/Auditor- 956-765-9117) **Online** - Access to appraisal district records is free at http://clientdb.trueautomation.com/clientdb/main.asp?id=28.

Zavala County

County Clerk, Zavala Courthouse, Crystal City, TX 78839. 830-374-2331; fax-830-374-5955; 8AM-5PM (CST) www.co.zavala.tx.us

Index: All in one. Record index from 7/06 to present not computerized. Office personnel or visitors may perform searches. Search fee $10.00 per name. Office will search real estate records. Will search UCC records. Copy fee $1.00 per page. Cert fee- $5.00 per cert plus copy fee. Payee- Zavala County Clerk. **Other phones:** Treasurer- 830-374-2442; Elections- 830-374-2331; Vital Records- 830-374-2331. **Property tax/Assessing**- 323 W Zavala, Crystal City, TX 78839; 830-347-3475, assessor fax- 830-374-2331. (Appraiser/Auditor- 830-374-3476) hours- 8AM-4:30PM (closed for lunch)

Texas County Locator

You will usually be able to find the city name in the City/County Cross Reference below. In that case, it is a simple matter to determine the county from the cross reference. However, only the official US Postal Service city names are included in this index. We have also included a ZIP/City Cross Reference immediately following the City/County Cross Reference. If you know the ZIP Code but the city name does not appear in the City/County Cross Reference index, look up the ZIP Code in the ZIP/City Cross Reference, find the city name, then look up the city name in the City/County Cross Reference.

Texas City/County Cross Reference

ABBOTT (76621) Hill(94), McLennan(5)
ABERNATHY (79311) Hale(68), Lubbock(31)
ABILENE (79601) Taylor(77), Jones(16), Callahan(3), Shackelford(2)
ABILENE (79602) Taylor(94), Callahan(5)
ABILENE Taylor
ACE Polk
ACKERLY (79713) Martin(38), Dawson(29), Howard(25), Borden(7)
ADDISON Dallas
ADKINS (78101) Bexar(82), Wilson(17)
ADRIAN (79001) Oldham(70), Deaf Smith(30)
AFTON Dickens
AGUA DULCE Nueces
AIKEN Floyd
ALAMO Hidalgo
ALANREED Gray
ALBA (75410) Wood(72), Rains(27)
ALBANY Shackelford
ALEDO (76008) Parker(84), Tarrant(15)
ALICE (78332) Jim Wells(98), Duval(1)
ALICE Jim Wells
ALIEF Harris
ALLEN Collin
ALLEYTON Colorado
ALLISON Wheeler
ALPINE Brewster
ALTAIR Colorado
ALTO Cherokee
ALVARADO Johnson
ALVIN (77511) Brazoria(93), Galveston(6)
ALVIN Brazoria
ALVORD Wise
AMARILLO (79124) Potter(93), Randall(6)
AMARILLO (79121) Randall(76), Potter(23)
AMARILLO Potter
AMARILLO Randall
AMHERST Lamb
ANAHUAC Chambers
ANDERSON Grimes
ANDREWS Andrews
ANGLETON Brazoria
ANNA Collin
ANNONA Red River
ANSON Jones
ANTHONY El Paso
ANTON (79313) Hockley(74), Lamb(17), Lubbock(5), Hale(1)
APPLE SPRINGS Trinity
AQUILLA (76622) Hill(92), McLennan(7)
ARANSAS PASS (78336) San Patricio(88), Aransas(11)
ARANSAS PASS San Patricio
ARCHER CITY Archer
ARGYLE Denton
ARLINGTON Tarrant
ARMSTRONG Kenedy
ARP Smith
ART Mason
ARTESIA WELLS La Salle
ARTHUR CITY Lamar
ASHERTON Dimmit
ASPERMONT Stonewall
ATASCOSA Bexar
ATHENS (75751) Henderson(98), Anderson(1)
ATHENS (75752) Henderson(93), Van Zandt(6)
ATLANTA Cass
AUBREY Denton
AUSTIN (78737) Hays(57), Travis(42)
AUSTIN (78728) Travis(94), Williamson(5)
AUSTIN (78736) Travis(97), Hays(2)
AUSTIN (78750) Travis(51), Williamson(48)
AUSTIN (78729) Williamson(92), Travis(7)
AUSTIN Travis
AUSTIN Williamson
AUSTWELL Refugio
AVALON Ellis
AVERY (75554) Red River(95), Bowie(4)
AVINGER (75630) Marion(55), Cass(44)
AXTELL (76624) McLennan(95), Limestone(4)
AZLE (76020) Tarrant(51), Parker(45), Wise(3)
AZLE Parker
BACLIFF Galveston
BAGWELL Red River
BAILEY Fannin
BAIRD Callahan
BALLINGER Runnels
BALMORHEA Reeves
BANDERA Bandera
BANGS (76823) Brown(88), Coleman(11)
BANQUETE Nueces
BARDWELL Ellis
BARKER Harris
BARKSDALE (78828) Edwards(68), Real(31)
BARNHART (76930) Irion(58), Crockett(41)
BARRY Navarro
BARSTOW Ward
BARTLETT (76511) Bell(53), Williamson(28), Milam(18)
BASTROP Bastrop
BATESVILLE Zavala
BATSON Hardin
BAY CITY Matagorda
BAYSIDE Refugio
BAYTOWN (77521) Harris(96), Chambers(3)
BAYTOWN Harris
BEASLEY Fort Bend
BEAUMONT Jefferson
BEBE Gonzales
BECKVILLE Panola
BEDFORD Tarrant
BEDIAS Grimes
BEEVILLE Bee
BELLAIRE Harris
BELLEVUE (76228) Clay(88), Montague(11)
BELLS Grayson
BELLVILLE Austin
BELMONT Gonzales
BELTON Bell
BEN ARNOLD Milam
BEN BOLT Jim Wells
BEN FRANKLIN Delta
BEN WHEELER Van Zandt
BENAVIDES Duval
BEND San Saba
BENJAMIN Knox
BERCLAIR Goliad
BERGHEIM Kendall
BERTRAM Burnet
BIG BEND NATIONAL PARK Brewster
BIG LAKE Reagan
BIG SANDY (75755) Upshur(52), Wood(47)
BIG SANDY Upshur
BIG SPRING (79720) Howard(98), Glasscock(1)
BIG SPRING Howard
BIG WELLS Dimmit
BIGFOOT Frio
BIROME Hill
BISHOP Nueces
BIVINS Cass
BLACKWELL (79506) Nolan(55), Coke(44)
BLANCO (78606) Blanco(90), Comal(7), Kendall(1)
BLANKET (76432) Brown(94), Comanche(5)
BLEDSOE Cochran
BLEIBLERVILLE Austin
BLESSING Matagorda
BLOOMBURG Cass
BLOOMING GROVE Navarro
BLOOMINGTON Victoria
BLOSSOM Lamar
BLUE RIDGE (75424) Collin(92), Fannin(7)
BLUEGROVE Clay
BLUFF DALE (76433) Erath(72), Hood(17), Somervell(9)
BLUFFTON Llano
BLUM Hill
BOERNE (78015) Bexar(64), Kendall(32), Comal(3)
BOERNE (78006) Kendall(82), Bexar(16), Comal(1)
BOGATA Red River
BOLING (77420) Wharton(92), Matagorda(6), Fort Bend(1)
BON WIER Newton
BONHAM Fannin
BOOKER (79005) Lipscomb(63), Ochiltree(36)
BORGER Hutchinson
BOVINA Parmer
BOWIE (76230) Montague(87), Jack(8), Clay(4)
BOYD (76023) Wise(96), Parker(3)
BOYS RANCH (79010) Oldham(83), Potter(16)
BRACKETTVILLE Kinney
BRADY (76825) McCulloch(98), Mason(1)
BRANDON Hill
BRASHEAR (75420) Hopkins(96), Rains(3)
BRAZORIA Brazoria
BRECKENRIDGE Stephens
BREMOND (76629) Robertson(95), Falls(4)
BRENHAM Washington
BRIDGE CITY Orange
BRIDGEPORT (76426) Wise(95), Jack(4)
BRIGGS Burnet
BRISCOE (79011) Hemphill(59), Wheeler(40)
BROADDUS San Augustine
BRONSON (75930) Sabine(72), San Augustine(27)
BRONTE (76933) Coke(61), Runnels(38)
BROOKELAND (75931) Sabine(82), Jasper(16)
BROOKESMITH (76827) Brown(98), Coleman(1)
BROOKSHIRE (77423) Waller(94), Fort Bend(5)
BROOKSTON Lamar
BROWNFIELD Terry
BROWNSBORO (75756) Henderson(94), Van Zandt(5)
BROWNSVILLE Cameron
BROWNWOOD Brown
BRUCEVILLE (76630) McLennan(97), Falls(2)
BRUNI (78344) Webb(91), Duval(8)
BRYAN (77808) Brazos(91), Robertson(8)
BRYAN Brazos
BRYSON Jack
BUCHANAN DAM Llano
BUCKHOLTS Milam
BUDA (78610) Hays(75), Travis(22), Caldwell(2)
BUFFALO (75831) Leon(96), Freestone(3)
BUFFALO GAP Taylor
BULA (79320) Bailey(81), Lamb(18)
BULLARD (75757) Smith(70), Cherokee(29)
BULVERDE Comal
BUNA Jasper
BURKBURNETT Wichita
BURKETT Coleman
BURKEVILLE Newton
BURLESON (76028) Johnson(77), Tarrant(22)
BURLESON Johnson
BURLINGTON (76519) Milam(50), Bell(37), Falls(11)
BURNET (78611) Burnet(96), Llano(3)
BURTON Washington
BUSHLAND Potter
BYERS Clay
BYNUM Hill
CACTUS Moore
CADDO Stephens
CADDO MILLS Hunt
CALDWELL Burleson
CALL (75933) Newton(71), Jasper(28)
CALLIHAM McMullen
CALVERT Robertson
CAMDEN Polk
CAMERON Milam
CAMP WOOD (78833) Real(84), Edwards(15)
CAMPBELL Hunt
CAMPBELLTON (78008) Atascosa(97), Live Oak(2)
CANADIAN (79014) Hemphill(93), Lipscomb(6)
CANTON Van Zandt
CANUTILLO El Paso
CANYON Randall
CANYON LAKE Comal
CARBON Eastland
CAREY Childress
CARLSBAD Tom Green
CARLTON (76436) Hamilton(61), Comanche(35), Erath(2)
CARMINE (78932) Fayette(95), Washington(4)
CARRIZO SPRINGS Dimmit

CARROLLTON (75007) Denton(90), Dallas(9)
CARROLLTON Dallas
CARROLLTON Denton
CARTHAGE Panola
CASON Morris
CASTELL (76831) Llano(65), Mason(35)
CASTROVILLE Medina
CAT SPRING (78933) Colorado(64), Austin(35)
CATARINA Dimmit
CAYUGA Anderson
CEDAR CREEK (78612) Bastrop(93), Travis(6)
CEDAR HILL Dallas
CEDAR LANE Matagorda
CEDAR PARK (78613) Williamson(85), Travis(14)
CEDAR PARK Williamson
CEE VEE Cottle
CELESTE (75423) Hunt(95), Fannin(4)
CELINA (75009) Collin(95), Denton(4)
CENTER (75935) Shelby(98), San Augustine(1)
CENTER POINT Kerr
CENTERVILLE Leon
CENTRALIA Trinity
CHALK Cottle
CHANDLER (75758) Henderson(88), Van Zandt(11)
CHANNELVIEW Harris
CHANNING (79018) Hartley(58), Moore(41)
CHAPMAN RANCH Nueces
CHAPPELL HILL (77426) Washington(90), Austin(9)
CHARLOTTE Atascosa
CHATFIELD Navarro
CHEROKEE San Saba
CHESTER (75936) Tyler(72), Polk(27)
CHICO (76431) Wise(96), Jack(3)
CHICOTA Lamar
CHILDRESS (79201) Childress(95), Cottle(2), Hall(2)
CHILLICOTHE (79225) Hardeman(93), Wilbarger(6)
CHILTON Falls
CHINA Jefferson
CHINA SPRING (76633) McLennan(91), Bosque(8)
CHIRENO Nacogdoches
CHRIESMAN Burleson
CHRISTINE Atascosa
CHRISTOVAL (76935) Tom Green(78), Schleicher(21)
CIBOLO (78108) Guadalupe(80), Bexar(17), Comal(1)
CISCO (76437) Eastland(92), Callahan(4), Stephens(3)
CLARENDON (79226) Donley(88), Armstrong(7), Hall(1), Briscoe(1)
CLARKSVILLE Red River
CLAUDE (79019) Armstrong(93), Randall(6)
CLAY Burleson
CLAYTON Panola
CLEBURNE (76033) Johnson(97), Somervell(1)
CLEBURNE Johnson
CLEVELAND (77328) Montgomery(40), San Jacinto(38), Liberty(20)
CLEVELAND Liberty
CLIFTON Bosque
CLINT El Paso
CLUTE Brazoria
CLYDE Callahan
COAHOMA (79511) Howard(76), Borden(23)
COLDSPRING San Jacinto
COLEMAN Coleman
COLLEGE STATION Brazos
COLLEGEPORT Matagorda
COLLEYVILLE Tarrant
COLLINSVILLE (76233) Grayson(75), Cooke(24)
COLMESNEIL Tyler
COLORADO CITY Mitchell
COLUMBUS Colorado
COMANCHE Comanche
COMBES Cameron
COMFORT (78013) Kendall(87), Kerr(12)
COMMERCE Hunt
COMO (75431) Hopkins(78), Wood(21)
COMSTOCK Val Verde
CONCAN Uvalde
CONCEPCION Duval
CONCORD Leon
CONE Crosby
CONROE Montgomery
CONVERSE Bexar
COOKVILLE Titus
COOLIDGE Limestone
COOPER Delta
COPEVILLE Collin
COPPELL Dallas
COPPERAS COVE (76522) Coryell(94), Lampasas(5)
CORPUS CHRISTI Nueces
CORRIGAN Polk
CORSICANA Navarro
COST Gonzales
COTTON CENTER Hale
COTULLA La Salle
COUPLAND (78615) Williamson(68), Travis(31)
COVINGTON Hill
COYANOSA Pecos
CRANDALL Kaufman
CRANE Crane
CRANFILLS GAP (76637) Bosque(98), Hamilton(1)
CRAWFORD McLennan
CRESSON (76035) Hood(56), Parker(33), Johnson(9)
CROCKETT Houston
CROSBY Harris
CROSBYTON Crosby
CROSS PLAINS (76443) Callahan(90), Brown(7), Coleman(2)
CROWELL (79227) Knox(59), Foard(40)
CROWLEY (76036) Tarrant(81), Johnson(18)
CRYSTAL CITY (78839) Zavala(98), Dimmit(1)
CUERO De Witt
CUMBY (75433) Hopkins(96), Hunt(3)
CUNEY Cherokee
CUNNINGHAM Lamar
CUSHING (75760) Nacogdoches(87), Rusk(12)
CYPRESS Harris
D HANIS Medina
DAINGERFIELD Morris
DAISETTA Liberty
DALE (78616) Caldwell(90), Bastrop(9)
DALHART (79022) Dallam(68), Hartley(30)
DALLARDSVILLE Polk
DALLAS (75252) Collin(97), Dallas(2)
DALLAS (75287) Collin(49), Denton(48), Dallas(2)
DALLAS Dallas
DAMON (77430) Fort Bend(53), Brazoria(46)
DANBURY Brazoria
DANCIGER Brazoria
DANEVANG Wharton
DARROUZETT Lipscomb
DAVILLA Milam
DAWN Deaf Smith
DAWSON Navarro
DAYTON (77535) Liberty(94), Chambers(5)
DE BERRY Panola
DE KALB Bowie
DE LEON Comanche
DEANVILLE Burleson
DECATUR (76234) Wise(98), Denton(1)
DEER PARK Harris
DEL RIO Edwards
DEL RIO Val Verde
DEL VALLE (78617) Travis(86), Bastrop(13)
DELL CITY Hudspeth
DELMITA (78536) Starr(86), Hidalgo(13)
DENISON Grayson
DENNIS Parker
DENTON Denton
DENVER CITY (79323) Yoakum(94), Gaines(5)
DEPORT (75435) Lamar(86), Red River(13)
DESDEMONA (76445) Eastland(82), Comanche(15), Erath(1)
DESOTO Dallas
DETROIT (75436) Red River(89), Lamar(10)
DEVERS Liberty
DEVINE Medina
DEWEYVILLE Newton
DIANA (75640) Upshur(67), Harrison(31), Marion(1)
DIBOLL Angelina
DICKENS Dickens
DICKINSON Galveston
DIKE Hopkins
DILLEY Frio
DIME BOX Lee
DIMMITT (79027) Castro(97), Lamb(1)
DINERO Live Oak
DOBBIN Montgomery
DODD CITY Fannin
DODGE Walker
DODSON (79230) Collingsworth(83), Childress(16)
DONIE (75838) Freestone(79), Limestone(20)
DONNA Hidalgo
DOOLE McCulloch
DOSS Gillespie
DOUCETTE Tyler
DOUGHERTY Floyd
DOUGLASS Nacogdoches
DOUGLASSVILLE Cass
DRIFTWOOD Hays
DRIPPING SPRINGS (78620) Hays(90), Travis(9)
DRISCOLL Nueces
DRYDEN Terrell
DUBLIN (76446) Erath(85), Comanche(14)
DUMAS Moore
DUMONT King
DUNCANVILLE Dallas
DUNN Scurry
DYESS AFB Taylor
EAGLE LAKE (77434) Colorado(98), Wharton(1)
EAGLE PASS Maverick
EARLY Brown
EARTH (79031) Lamb(77), Castro(18), Bailey(3)
EAST BERNARD (77435) Wharton(78), Fort Bend(20), Colorado(1)
EASTLAND Eastland
EASTON Gregg
ECLETO Karnes
ECTOR Fannin
EDCOUCH Hidalgo
EDDY (76524) McLennan(77), Falls(22)
EDEN Concho
EDGEWOOD Van Zandt
EDINBURG Hidalgo
EDMONSON Hale
EDNA Jackson
EDROY San Patricio
EGYPT Wharton
EL CAMPO Wharton
EL INDIO Maverick
EL PASO (79938) El Paso(97), Hudspeth(2)
EL PASO El Paso
ELBERT Throckmorton
ELDORADO Schleicher
ELECTRA (76360) Wichita(88), Wilbarger(11)
ELGIN (78621) Bastrop(77), Travis(13), Lee(5), Williamson(3)
ELIASVILLE Young
ELKHART Anderson
ELLINGER Fayette
ELM MOTT McLennan
ELMATON Matagorda
ELMENDORF (78112) Bexar(98), Wilson(1)
ELMO Kaufman
ELSA Hidalgo
ELYSIAN FIELDS Harrison
EMORY Rains
ENCINAL La Salle
ENCINO Brooks
ENERGY Comanche
ENLOE Delta
ENNIS (75119) Ellis(98), Navarro(1)
ENNIS Ellis
ENOCHS (79324) Bailey(93), Lamb(6)
EOLA (76937) Tom Green(69), Concho(30)
ERA Cooke
ESTELLINE Hall
ETOILE Nacogdoches
EULESS Tarrant
EUSTACE (75124) Henderson(77), Van Zandt(22)
EVADALE Jasper
EVANT (76525) Coryell(65), Hamilton(25), Lampasas(8)
FABENS El Paso
FAIRFIELD Freestone
FALCON HEIGHTS Starr
FALFURRIAS (78355) Brooks(95), Jim Wells(4)
FALLS CITY (78113) Wilson(41), Karnes(36), Atascosa(21)
FANNIN Goliad
FARMERSVILLE (75442) Collin(87), Hunt(12)
FARNSWORTH Ochiltree
FARWELL (79325) Parmer(92), Bailey(7)
FATE Rockwall
FAYETTEVILLE (78940) Fayette(86), Austin(12)
FENTRESS Caldwell
FERRIS (75125) Ellis(83), Dallas(16)
FIELDTON Lamb
FISCHER Comal
FLAT Coryell
FLATONIA (78941) Fayette(87), Bastrop(6), Gonzales(5)
FLINT Smith
FLOMOT (79234) Motley(85), Floyd(14)
FLORENCE (76527) Williamson(97), Bell(1), Burnet(1)
FLORESVILLE Wilson
FLOWER MOUND Denton
FLOYDADA (79235) Floyd(96), Crosby(3)
FLUVANNA (79517) Scurry(71), Borden(28)
FLYNN Leon
FOLLETT Lipscomb
FORESTBURG (76239) Montague(73), Cooke(26)
FORNEY (75126) Kaufman(97), Rockwall(2)
FORRESTON Ellis
FORSAN Howard
FORT DAVIS Jeff Davis
FORT HANCOCK Hudspeth
FORT MC KAVETT (76841) Menard(87), Kimble(8), Schleicher(3)
FORT STOCKTON Pecos

FORT WORTH (76126) Tarrant(87), Parker(12)
FORT WORTH (76178) Tarrant(96), Denton(3)
FORT WORTH Tarrant
FOWLERTON (78021) La Salle(80), Atascosa(10), McMullen(10)
FRANCITAS Jackson
FRANKLIN Robertson
FRANKSTON (75763) Anderson(52), Henderson(47)
FRED Tyler
FREDERICKSBURG (78624) Gillespie(86), Kendall(13)
FREDONIA (76842) Mason(54), San Saba(40), McCulloch(5)
FREEPORT Brazoria
FREER Duval
FRESNO Fort Bend
FRIENDSWOOD (77546) Galveston(68), Harris(31)
FRIENDSWOOD Galveston
FRIONA (79035) Parmer(94), Deaf Smith(4), Castro(1)
FRISCO (75034) Collin(55), Denton(44)
FRISCO Collin
FRITCH (79036) Hutchinson(94), Carson(5)
FROST Navarro
FRUITVALE Van Zandt
FULSHEAR Fort Bend
FULTON Aransas
GAIL Borden
GAINESVILLE Cooke
GALENA PARK Harris
GALLATIN Cherokee
GALVESTON Galveston
GANADO Jackson
GARCIASVILLE Starr
GARDEN CITY (79739) Glasscock(84), Reagan(15)
GARDENDALE Ector
GARLAND (75048) Dallas(80), Collin(19)
GARLAND Dallas
GARRISON (75946) Nacogdoches(53), Rusk(46)
GARWOOD Colorado
GARY (75643) Panola(94), Shelby(5)
GATESVILLE (76528) Coryell(97), Bell(2)
GATESVILLE Coryell
GAUSE Milam
GENEVA Sabine
GEORGE WEST Live Oak
GEORGETOWN Williamson
GERONIMO Guadalupe
GIDDINGS Lee
GILCHRIST Galveston
GILLETT Karnes
GILMER (75645) Upshur(98), Gregg(1)
GILMER Upshur
GIRARD Kent
GIRVIN Pecos
GLADEWATER (75647) Gregg(52), Upshur(37), Smith(9)
GLEN FLORA Wharton
GLEN ROSE Somervell
GLIDDEN Colorado
GOBER Fannin
GODLEY Johnson
GOLDEN Wood
GOLDSBORO (79519) Taylor(38), Coleman(33), Runnels(27)
GOLDSMITH Ector
GOLDTHWAITE Mills
GOLIAD Goliad
GONZALES Gonzales
GOODFELLOW AFB Tom Green
GOODRICH Polk
GORDON (76453) Palo Pinto(86), Erath(13)
GORDONVILLE Grayson
GOREE (76363) Knox(96), Haskell(2), Throckmorton(1)
GORMAN (76454) Eastland(73), Comanche(26)
GOULDBUSK Coleman
GRAFORD Palo Pinto
GRAHAM (76450) Young(93), Stephens(3), Palo Pinto(3)
GRANBURY (76048) Hood(98), Somervell(1)
GRANBURY (76049) Hood(96), Parker(2)
GRAND PRAIRIE (75052) Dallas(62), Tarrant(36)
GRAND PRAIRIE (75054) Tarrant(71), Dallas(28)
GRAND PRAIRIE Dallas
GRAND SALINE (75140) Van Zandt(98), Smith(1)
GRANDFALLS Ward
GRANDVIEW (76050) Johnson(90), Ellis(5), Hill(4)
GRANGER Williamson
GRAPELAND (75844) Houston(73), Anderson(26)
GRAPEVINE (76051) Tarrant(98), Dallas(1)
GRAPEVINE Tarrant
GREENVILLE Hunt
GREENWOOD Wise
GREGORY San Patricio
GROESBECK Limestone
GROOM (79039) Carson(64), Gray(33), Donley(1)
GROVES Jefferson
GROVETON Trinity
GRULLA Starr
GRUVER (79040) Hansford(60), Sherman(39)
GUERRA (78360) Jim Hogg(80), Starr(20)
GUNTER Grayson
GUSTINE Comanche
GUTHRIE King
GUY (77444) Fort Bend(75), Brazoria(24)
HALE CENTER (79041) Hale(97), Lamb(2)
HALLETTSVILLE Lavaca
HALLSVILLE Harrison
HALTOM CITY Tarrant
HAMILTON Hamilton
HAMLIN (79520) Jones(95), Fisher(4)
HAMSHIRE (77622) Jefferson(91), Chambers(8)
HANKAMER Chambers
HAPPY (79042) Randall(60), Swisher(19), Castro(12), Armstrong(7)
HARDIN Liberty
HARGILL Hidalgo
HARKER HEIGHTS Bell
HARLETON (75651) Harrison(95), Marion(4)
HARLINGEN Cameron
HARPER (78631) Gillespie(64), Kimble(26), Kerr(10)
HARROLD Wilbarger
HART (79043) Castro(76), Lamb(20), Hale(3)
HARTLEY Hartley
HARWOOD (78632) Gonzales(52), Caldwell(47)
HASKELL Haskell
HASLET (76052) Tarrant(88), Wise(6), Denton(5)
HASSE Comanche
HAWKINS Wood
HAWLEY Jones
HEARNE Robertson
HEBBRONVILLE Jim Hogg
HEDLEY Donley
HEIDENHEIMER Bell
HELOTES (78023) Bexar(91), Medina(8)
HEMPHILL Sabine
HEMPSTEAD Waller
HENDERSON Rusk
HENRIETTA (76365) Clay(98), Jack(1)
HEREFORD (79045) Deaf Smith(91), Castro(8)
HERMLEIGH (79526) Scurry(95), Fisher(3)
HEWITT McLennan
HEXT (76848) Menard(94), Mason(5)
HICO (76457) Hamilton(63), Erath(30), Bosque(5)
HIDALGO Hidalgo
HIGGINS (79046) Lipscomb(87), Hemphill(12)
HIGH ISLAND Galveston
HIGHLANDS Harris
HILLISTER Tyler
HILLSBORO Hill
HITCHCOCK Galveston
HOBSON Karnes
HOCHHEIM De Witt
HOCKLEY (77447) Harris(47), Waller(36), Montgomery(15)
HOLLAND Bell
HOLLIDAY Archer
HONDO Medina
HONEY GROVE (75446) Fannin(91), Lamar(8)
HOOKS Bowie
HOUSTON (77053) Fort Bend(56), Harris(43)
HOUSTON (77099) Harris(96), Fort Bend(3)
HOUSTON Harris
HOWE Grayson
HUBBARD (76648) Hill(91), Navarro(5), Limestone(2)
HUFFMAN Harris
HUFSMITH Harris
HUGHES SPRINGS (75656) Cass(89), Morris(10)
HULL Liberty
HUMBLE (77339) Harris(81), Montgomery(18)
HUMBLE Harris
HUNGERFORD Wharton
HUNT (78024) Kerr(96), Real(3)
HUNTINGTON Angelina
HUNTSVILLE (77320) Walker(91), San Jacinto(8)
HUNTSVILLE Walker
HURST Tarrant
HUTCHINS Dallas
HUTTO (78634) Williamson(98), Travis(1)
HYE Blanco
IDALOU Lubbock
IMPERIAL Pecos
INDUSTRY Austin
INEZ Victoria
INGLESIDE San Patricio
INGRAM Kerr
IOLA Grimes
IOWA PARK Wichita
IRA (79527) Scurry(81), Borden(18)
IRAAN Pecos
IREDELL (76649) Bosque(86), Erath(13)
IRENE Hill
IRVING Dallas
ITALY Ellis
ITASCA Hill
IVANHOE Fannin
JACKSBORO (76458) Jack(98), Wise(1)
JACKSONVILLE Cherokee
JARRELL Williamson
JASPER Jasper
JAYTON (79528) Kent(83), Stonewall(16)
JEFFERSON (75657) Marion(87), Cass(9), Harrison(2)
JERMYN (76459) Jack(95), Young(5)
JEWETT (75846) Leon(90), Limestone(9)
JOAQUIN (75954) Shelby(91), Panola(8)
JOHNSON CITY Blanco
JOINERVILLE Rusk
JONESBORO (76538) Hamilton(52), Coryell(47)
JONESVILLE (75659) Harrison(80), Rusk(20)
JOSEPHINE Collin
JOSHUA Johnson
JOURDANTON Atascosa
JUDSON Gregg
JUNCTION Kimble
JUSTICEBURG Garza
JUSTIN (76247) Denton(98), Wise(1)
KAMAY Wichita
KARNACK Harrison
KARNES CITY Karnes
KATY (77494) Fort Bend(90), Harris(8), Waller(1)
KATY (77450) Harris(69), Fort Bend(30)
KATY (77493) Harris(82), Waller(15), Fort Bend(1)
KATY Harris
KAUFMAN Kaufman
KEENE Johnson
KELLER Tarrant
KEMAH Galveston
KEMP (75143) Henderson(63), Kaufman(36)
KEMPNER (76539) Lampasas(82), Bell(8), Coryell(4), Burnet(3)
KENDALIA Kendall
KENDLETON Fort Bend
KENEDY Karnes
KENNARD (75847) Trinity(52), Houston(47)
KENNEDALE Tarrant
KENNEY Austin
KERENS Navarro
KERMIT Winkler
KERRICK Dallam
KERRVILLE (78028) Kerr(95), Gillespie(4)
KERRVILLE Kerr
KILDARE Cass
KILGORE (75662) Gregg(74), Rusk(24), Smith(1)
KILGORE Gregg
KILLEEN (76544) Bell(65), Coryell(34)
KILLEEN (76549) Bell(98), Burnet(1)
KILLEEN Bell
KINGSBURY Guadalupe
KINGSLAND (78639) Llano(87), Burnet(12)
KINGSVILLE Kleberg
KIRBYVILLE (75956) Jasper(98), Newton(1)
KIRKLAND Childress
KIRVIN Freestone
KLONDIKE Delta
KNICKERBOCKER Tom Green
KNIPPA Uvalde
KNOTT (79748) Howard(75), Martin(25)
KNOX CITY (79529) Knox(96), Haskell(3)
KOPPERL Bosque
KOSSE (76653) Limestone(87), Falls(10), Robertson(1)
KOUNTZE Hardin
KRESS (79052) Swisher(91), Hale(7), Castro(1)
KRUM Denton
KURTEN Brazos
KYLE (78640) Hays(98), Caldwell(1)
LA BLANCA Hidalgo
LA COSTE (78039) Medina(78), Bexar(21)
LA FERIA Cameron
LA JOYA Hidalgo
LA MARQUE Galveston
LA PORTE Harris
LA PRYOR Zavala
LA SALLE Jackson
LA VERNIA (78121) Wilson(76), Guadalupe(23)
LA VILLA Hidalgo
LA WARD Jackson
LADONIA (75449) Fannin(91), Hunt(8)
LAIRD HILL Rusk
LAKE CREEK Delta
LAKE DALLAS Denton

LAKE JACKSON Brazoria
LAKEVIEW Hall
LAMESA (79331) Dawson(97), Martin(1)
LAMPASAS Lampasas
LANCASTER Dallas
LANE CITY Wharton
LANEVILLE Rusk
LANGTRY Val Verde
LAREDO Webb
LARUE Henderson
LASARA Willacy
LATEXO Houston
LAUGHLIN A F B Val Verde
LAVON Collin
LAWN (79530) Taylor(93), Runnels(6)
LAZBUDDIE Parmer
LEAGUE CITY Galveston
LEAKEY Real
LEANDER (78641) Williamson(59), Travis(40)
LEANDER Travis
LEANDER Williamson
LEDBETTER (78946) Fayette(78), Washington(14), Lee(6)
LEESBURG (75451) Camp(89), Wood(6), Upshur(4)
LEESVILLE Gonzales
LEFORS Gray
LEGGETT Polk
LELIA LAKE Donley
LEMING Atascosa
LENORAH Martin
LEON JUNCTION Coryell
LEONA Leon
LEONARD (75452) Fannin(86), Hunt(7), Collin(6)
LEROY McLennan
LEVELLAND Hockley
LEWISVILLE Denton
LEXINGTON (78947) Lee(98), Milam(1)
LIBERTY Liberty
LIBERTY HILL (78642) Williamson(98), Burnet(1)
LILLIAN Johnson
LINCOLN Lee
LINDALE Smith
LINDEN Cass
LINDSAY Cooke
LINGLEVILLE Erath
LINN (78563) Hidalgo(94), Starr(5)
LIPAN (76462) Hood(45), Palo Pinto(20), Parker(16), Erath(12)
LIPSCOMB Lipscomb
LISSIE Wharton
LITTLE ELM Denton
LITTLE RIVER Bell
LITTLE RIVER ACADEMY Bell
LITTLEFIELD (79339) Lamb(92), Hockley(7)
LIVERPOOL Brazoria
LIVINGSTON Polk
LLANO Llano
LOCKHART Caldwell
LOCKNEY (79241) Floyd(97), Swisher(1)
LODI Marion
LOHN (76852) McCulloch(98), Concho(1)
LOLITA Jackson
LOMETA (76853) Lampasas(95), Mills(3)
LONDON (76854) Kimble(77), Menard(21)
LONE OAK (75453) Hunt(73), Rains(19), Hopkins(7)
LONE STAR (75668) Morris(86), Marion(11), Henderson(1)
LONG BRANCH (75669) Panola(98), Rusk(1)
LONG MOTT Calhoun
LONGVIEW (75602) Gregg(65), Harrison(34)
LONGVIEW (75603) Gregg(81), Rusk(18)
LONGVIEW (75604) Gregg(97), Upshur(2)
LONGVIEW (75605) Gregg(81), Harrison(17), Upshur(1)
LONGVIEW Gregg
LOOP Gaines
LOPENO Zapata
LORAINE (79532) Mitchell(94), Scurry(3), Nolan(2)
LORENA McLennan
LORENZO (79343) Crosby(71), Lubbock(28)
LOS EBANOS Hidalgo
LOS FRESNOS Cameron
LOS INDIOS Cameron
LOTT Falls
LOUISE (77455) Wharton(91), Jackson(8)
LOVELADY (75851) Houston(67), Trinity(32)
LOVING Young
LOWAKE Concho
LOZANO Cameron
LUBBOCK (79407) Lubbock(91), Hockley(8)
LUBBOCK Lubbock
LUEDERS (79533) Jones(58), Shackelford(37), Haskell(4)
LUFKIN Angelina
LULING (78648) Caldwell(91), Guadalupe(7), Gonzales(1)
LUMBERTON Hardin
LYFORD Willacy
LYONS Burleson
LYTLE (78052) Atascosa(79), Medina(13), Bexar(7)
MABANK (75156) Henderson(95), Kaufman(2), Van Zandt(1)
MABANK (75147) Kaufman(47), Van Zandt(46), Henderson(5)
MACDONA Bexar
MADISONVILLE Madison
MAGNOLIA (77355) Montgomery(98), Waller(1)
MAGNOLIA Montgomery
MAGNOLIA SPRINGS Bowie
MAGNOLIA SPRINGS Jasper
MALAKOFF Henderson
MALONE Hill
MANCHACA (78652) Travis(74), Hays(25)
MANOR Travis
MANSFIELD (76063) Tarrant(92), Johnson(7)
MANVEL Brazoria
MAPLE Bailey
MARATHON Brewster
MARBLE FALLS (78654) Burnet(95), Travis(4)
MARBLE FALLS (78657) Burnet(50), Llano(47), Blanco(1)
MARFA Presidio
MARIETTA Cass
MARION (78124) Guadalupe(93), Bexar(6)
MARKHAM Matagorda
MARLIN Falls
MARQUEZ Leon
MARSHALL Harrison
MART (76664) McLennan(83), Limestone(13), Falls(2)
MARTINDALE (78655) Caldwell(78), Guadalupe(21)
MARTINSVILLE Nacogdoches
MARYNEAL Nolan
MASON (76856) Mason(98), Menard(1)
MASTERSON (79058) Moore(58), Potter(41)
MATADOR Motley
MATAGORDA Matagorda
MATHIS (78368) San Patricio(94), Live Oak(5)
MAUD Bowie
MAURICEVILLE Orange
MAXWELL (78656) Caldwell(95), Hays(4)
MAY Brown
MAYDELLE Cherokee
MAYPEARL Ellis
MAYSFIELD Milam
MC CAMEY Upton
MC CAULLEY Fisher
MC COY Atascosa
MC DADE Bastrop
MC GREGOR (76657) McLennan(98), Coryell(1)
MC KINNEY Collin
MC LEOD Cass
MC NEIL Travis
MC QUEENEY Guadalupe
MCADOO (79243) Crosby(52), Dickens(47)
MCALLEN Hidalgo
MCFADDIN Victoria
MCLEAN (79057) Gray(70), Wheeler(20), Donley(9)
MEADOW (79345) Terry(86), Lynn(11), Taylor(1)
MEDINA Bandera
MEGARGEL Archer
MELISSA Collin
MELVIN (76858) McCulloch(60), Concho(39)
MEMPHIS (79245) Hall(97), Collingsworth(2)
MENARD (76859) Menard(78), Kimble(21)
MENTONE Loving
MERCEDES Hidalgo
MERETA Tom Green
MERIDIAN Bosque
MERIT Hunt
MERKEL (79536) Taylor(75), Jones(24)
MERTENS (76666) Hill(96), Navarro(3)
MERTZON Irion
MESQUITE Dallas
MEXIA (76667) Limestone(95), Freestone(4)
MEYERSVILLE (77974) De Witt(51), Victoria(48)
MIAMI (79059) Roberts(78), Gray(21)
MICO Medina
MIDFIELD Matagorda
MIDKIFF (79755) Upton(82), Midland(14), Reagan(2)
MIDLOTHIAN Ellis
MIDWAY (75852) Madison(97), Walker(1)
MILAM Sabine
MILANO (76556) Milam(98), Burleson(2)
MILES (76861) Tom Green(61), Runnels(36), Concho(1)
MILFORD (76670) Ellis(91), Navarro(7), Hill(1)
MILLERSVIEW Concho
MILLICAN Brazos
MILLSAP (76066) Parker(94), Palo Pinto(5)
MINDEN Rusk
MINEOLA (75773) Wood(91), Smith(7)
MINERAL Bee
MINERAL WELLS (76067) Palo Pinto(96), Parker(3)
MINERAL WELLS Palo Pinto
MINGUS (76463) Erath(75), Palo Pinto(23)
MIRANDO CITY Webb
MISSION Hidalgo
MISSOURI CITY (77489) Fort Bend(95), Harris(4)
MISSOURI CITY Fort Bend
MOBEETIE (79061) Wheeler(89), Gray(7), Hemphill(2)
MONAHANS Ward
MONT BELVIEU Chambers
MONTAGUE Montague
MONTALBA (75853) Anderson(98), Henderson(1)
MONTGOMERY (77356) Montgomery(98), Grimes(1)
MOODY (76557) McLennan(55), Bell(33), Coryell(10)
MOORE (78057) Medina(92), Frio(7)
MORAN (76464) Shackelford(81), Stephens(11), Callahan(6)
MORGAN Bosque
MORGAN MILL Erath
MORSE (79062) Hutchinson(87), Hansford(12)
MORTON (79346) Cochran(95), Bailey(4)
MOSCOW (75960) Polk(91), Tyler(8)
MOULTON Lavaca
MOUND Coryell
MOUNT CALM (76673) Hill(87), Limestone(9), McLennan(3)
MOUNT ENTERPRISE Rusk
MOUNT PLEASANT (75455) Titus(98), Franklin(1)
MOUNT PLEASANT Titus
MOUNT VERNON Franklin
MOUNTAIN HOME Kerr
MUENSTER Cooke
MULDOON Fayette
MULESHOE (79347) Bailey(83), Parmer(10), Lamb(4), Castro(1)
MULLIN Mills
MUMFORD Robertson
MUNDAY Knox
MURCHISON (75778) Henderson(65), Van Zandt(34)
MYRA Cooke
NACOGDOCHES Nacogdoches
NADA Colorado
NAPLES (75568) Morris(90), Cass(9)
NASH Bowie
NATALIA Medina
NAVAL AIR STATION/ JRB Tarrant
NAVASOTA Brazos
NAVASOTA Grimes
NAZARETH Castro
NECHES Anderson
NEDERLAND Jefferson
NEEDVILLE Fort Bend
NEMO (76070) Somervell(86), Johnson(13)
NEVADA Collin
NEW BADEN Robertson
NEW BOSTON Bowie
NEW BRAUNFELS (78130) Comal(83), Guadalupe(16)
NEW BRAUNFELS Comal
NEW CANEY Montgomery
NEW DEAL Lubbock
NEW HOME Lynn
NEW LONDON Rusk
NEW SUMMERFIELD Cherokee
NEW ULM (78950) Austin(64), Colorado(34)
NEW WAVERLY (77358) Walker(48), San Jacinto(39), Montgomery(12)
NEWARK (76071) Wise(96), Tarrant(3)
NEWCASTLE (76372) Young(78), Throckmorton(21)
NEWGULF Wharton
NEWPORT Clay
NEWTON (75966) Newton(95), Jasper(4)
NIXON (78140) Gonzales(88), Wilson(8), Guadalupe(3)
NOCONA Montague
NOLAN Nolan
NOLANVILLE Bell
NOME Jefferson
NORDHEIM (78141) De Witt(93), Karnes(6)
NORMANGEE (77871) Leon(59), Madison(40)
NORMANNA Bee
NORTH HOUSTON Harris
NORTH RICHLAND HILLS Tarrant
NORTH ZULCH Madison
NORTON Runnels
NOTREES Ector
NOVICE (79538) Coleman(51), Runnels(48)
NURSERY Victoria
O BRIEN Haskell
OAKHURST San Jacinto
OAKLAND Colorado
OAKVILLE Live Oak

OAKWOOD (75855) Leon(77), Freestone(22)
ODELL Hardeman
ODEM San Patricio
ODESSA (79766) Ector(89), Crane(6), Midland(3)
ODESSA (79765) Midland(52), Ector(47)
ODESSA Ector
ODONNELL (79351) Borden(40), Lynn(39), Dawson(19)
OGLESBY (76561) Coryell(90), McLennan(9)
OILTON Webb
OKLAUNION Wilbarger
OLD GLORY (79540) Stonewall(98), Haskell(1)
OLD OCEAN Brazoria
OLDEN Eastland
OLMITO Cameron
OLNEY (76374) Young(97), Archer(1), Throckmorton(1)
OLTON (79064) Lamb(79), Hale(20)
OMAHA Morris
ONALASKA Polk
ORANGE GROVE Jim Wells
ORANGEFIELD Orange
ORCHARD Fort Bend
ORE CITY (75683) Upshur(73), Marion(26)
ORLA Reeves
OTTINE Gonzales
OTTO Falls
OVALO (79541) Taylor(90), Callahan(9)
OVERTON (75684) Rusk(87), Smith(12)
OZONA (76943) Crockett(87), Val Verde(12)
PADUCAH (79248) Cottle(90), King(5), Foard(4)
PAIGE (78659) Bastrop(78), Lee(21)
PAINT ROCK Concho
PALACIOS (77465) Matagorda(73), Jackson(25)
PALESTINE (75803) Anderson(98), Henderson(1)
PALESTINE Anderson
PALMER Ellis
PALO PINTO Palo Pinto
PALUXY Hood
PAMPA (79065) Gray(97), Roberts(2)
PAMPA Gray
PANDORA Wilson
PANHANDLE (79068) Carson(97), Potter(1)
PANNA MARIA Karnes
PANOLA Panola
PARADISE Wise
PARIS Lamar
PASADENA Harris
PATTISON Waller
PATTONVILLE Lamar
PAWNEE Bee
PEACOCK Stonewall
PEAR VALLEY McCulloch
PEARLAND (77581) Brazoria(96), Harris(3)
PEARLAND Brazoria
PEARSALL Frio
PEASTER Parker
PECAN GAP (75469) Delta(91), Hunt(8)
PECOS Reeves
PEGGY Atascosa
PENDLETON Bell
PENELOPE Hill
PENITAS Hidalgo
PENNINGTON (75856) Trinity(68), Houston(31)
PENWELL Ector
PEP (79353) Hockley(96), Cochran(3)
PERRIN (76486) Jack(47), Palo Pinto(26), Parker(26)
PERRY Falls
PERRYTON Ochiltree
PETERSBURG (79250) Hale(48), Lubbock(22), Floyd(17), Crosby(11)
PETROLIA Clay
PETTUS Bee
PETTY Lamar
PFLUGERVILLE Travis
PHARR Hidalgo
PICKTON (75471) Hopkins(61), Wood(38)
PIERCE Wharton
PILOT POINT (76258) Denton(90), Grayson(9)
PINEHURST Montgomery
PINELAND Sabine
PIPE CREEK Bandera
PITTSBURG (75686) Camp(85), Upshur(7), Titus(5), Morris(1)
PLACEDO Victoria
PLAINS Yoakum
PLAINVIEW Hale
PLANO (75093) Collin(95), Denton(4)
PLANO Collin
PLANTERSVILLE (77363) Grimes(98), Waller(1)
PLEASANTON Atascosa
PLEDGER Matagorda
PLUM Fayette
POINT (75472) Rains(98), Hopkins(1)
POINT COMFORT Calhoun
POINTBLANK San Jacinto
POLLOK Angelina
PONDER Denton
PONTOTOC (76869) Llano(58), Mason(31), San Saba(9)
POOLVILLE (76487) Parker(68), Wise(22), Jack(8)
PORT ARANSAS Nueces
PORT ARTHUR Jefferson
PORT BOLIVAR Galveston
PORT ISABEL Cameron
PORT LAVACA Calhoun
PORT MANSFIELD Willacy
PORT NECHES Jefferson
PORT O CONNOR Calhoun
PORTER (77365) Montgomery(98), Harris(1)
PORTLAND San Patricio
POST (79356) Garza(91), Lynn(5), Crosby(2)
POTEET Atascosa
POTH Wilson
POTTSBORO Grayson
POTTSVILLE Hamilton
POWDERLY Lamar
POWELL Navarro
POYNOR Henderson
PRAIRIE HILL Limestone
PRAIRIE LEA Caldwell
PRAIRIE VIEW Waller
PREMONT Jim Wells
PRESIDIO Presidio
PRICE Rusk
PRIDDY Mills
PRINCETON Collin
PROCTOR Comanche
PROGRESO Hidalgo
PROSPER (75078) Collin(94), Denton(5)
PURDON Navarro
PURMELA (76566) Coryell(76), Hamilton(24)
PUTNAM Callahan
PYOTE Ward
QUAIL Collingsworth
QUANAH Hardeman
QUEEN CITY Cass
QUEMADO (78877) Maverick(98), Kinney(1)
QUINLAN (75474) Hunt(96), Kaufman(3)
QUITAQUE (79255) Briscoe(64), Motley(21), Floyd(13), Hall(1)
QUITMAN Wood
RAINBOW Somervell
RALLS Crosby
RANDOLPH Fannin
RANGER (76470) Eastland(85), Stephens(14)
RANKIN Upton
RANSOM CANYON Lubbock
RATCLIFF Houston
RAVENNA Fannin
RAYMONDVILLE Willacy
RAYWOOD Liberty
REAGAN Falls
REALITOS Duval
RED OAK (75154) Ellis(78), Dallas(21)
RED ROCK (78662) Bastrop(96), Caldwell(3)
REDFORD Presidio
REDWATER Bowie
REESE AIR FORCE BASE Lubbock
REFUGIO Refugio
REKLAW (75784) Cherokee(88), Rusk(11)
RHOME (76078) Wise(95), Denton(4)
RICE (75155) Navarro(94), Ellis(5)
RICHARDS (77873) Montgomery(54), Grimes(35), Walker(10)
RICHARDSON (75082) Collin(74), Dallas(25)
RICHARDSON (75080) Dallas(84), Collin(15)
RICHARDSON Dallas
RICHLAND Navarro
RICHLAND SPRINGS (76871) San Saba(95), Lampasas(3)
RICHMOND Fort Bend
RIESEL (76682) McLennan(96), Falls(3)
RINGGOLD (76261) Montague(92), Clay(8)
RIO FRIO Real
RIO GRANDE CITY Starr
RIO HONDO Cameron
RIO MEDINA Medina
RIO VISTA (76093) Johnson(92), Hill(7)
RISING STAR (76471) Eastland(79), Brown(16), Comanche(4)
RIVERSIDE Walker
RIVIERA Kleberg
ROANOKE (76262) Denton(63), Tarrant(36)
ROANOKE Denton
ROANS PRAIRIE Grimes
ROARING SPRINGS (79256) Motley(52), Dickens(47)
ROBERT LEE (76945) Coke(94), Tom Green(5)
ROBSTOWN Nueces
ROBY Fisher
ROCHELLE (76872) McCulloch(80), San Saba(19)
ROCHESTER Haskell
ROCK ISLAND Colorado
ROCKDALE (76567) Milam(94), Burleson(5)
ROCKLAND Tyler
ROCKPORT Aransas
ROCKSPRINGS Edwards
ROCKWALL (75087) Rockwall(97), Collin(2)
ROCKWALL Rockwall
ROCKWOOD Coleman
ROGERS (76569) Bell(86), Milam(13)
ROMA Starr
ROMAYOR Liberty
ROOSEVELT (76874) Sutton(66), Kimble(33)
ROPESVILLE (79358) Hockley(78), Lubbock(19), Terry(1)
ROSANKY (78953) Bastrop(53), Caldwell(46)
ROSCOE (79545) Nolan(93), Scurry(3), Fisher(3)
ROSEBUD (76570) Falls(85), Milam(13)
ROSENBERG Fort Bend
ROSHARON (77583) Brazoria(78), Fort Bend(21)
ROSS McLennan
ROSSER Kaufman
ROSSTON Cooke
ROTAN (79546) Fisher(95), Stonewall(3)
ROUND MOUNTAIN (78663) Blanco(88), Travis(8), Hays(3)
ROUND ROCK (78664) Williamson(95), Travis(4)
ROUND ROCK Williamson
ROUND TOP (78954) Fayette(97), Austin(2)
ROUND TOP Fayette
ROWENA (76875) Runnels(85), Concho(14)
ROWLETT (75089) Dallas(94), Rockwall(5)
ROWLETT Dallas
ROXTON Lamar
ROYALTY Ward
ROYSE CITY (75189) Rockwall(56), Hunt(26), Collin(16)
RULE (79547) Haskell(97), Stonewall(2)
RULE Haskell
RUNGE (78151) Karnes(94), De Witt(3), Goliad(1)
RUSK Cherokee
RYE Liberty
SABINAL Uvalde
SABINE PASS Jefferson
SACUL Nacogdoches
SADLER Grayson
SAINT HEDWIG Bexar
SAINT JO (76265) Montague(81), Cooke(18)
SALADO Bell
SALINENO Starr
SALT FLAT (79847) Hudspeth(74), Culberson(25)
SALTILLO (75478) Hopkins(87), Franklin(12)
SAMNORWOOD Collingsworth
SAN ANGELO Tom Green
SAN ANTONIO (78223) Bexar(98), Wilson(1)
SAN ANTONIO (78253) Bexar(89), Medina(10)
SAN ANTONIO (78264) Bexar(93), Atascosa(6)
SAN ANTONIO (78266) Comal(95), Bexar(4)
SAN ANTONIO Bexar
SAN AUGUSTINE San Augustine
SAN BENITO Cameron
SAN DIEGO (78384) Duval(94), Jim Wells(5)
SAN ELIZARIO El Paso
SAN FELIPE Austin
SAN ISIDRO Starr
SAN JUAN Hidalgo
SAN MARCOS (78666) Hays(92), Guadalupe(6), Caldwell(1)
SAN MARCOS Hays
SAN PERLITA Willacy
SAN SABA San Saba
SAN YGNACIO Zapata
SANDERSON Terrell
SANDIA (78383) Jim Wells(60), Nueces(35), Live Oak(4)
SANDY Blanco
SANFORD Hutchinson
SANGER Denton
SANTA ANNA Coleman
SANTA ELENA Starr
SANTA FE Galveston
SANTA MARIA Cameron
SANTA ROSA Cameron
SANTO Palo Pinto
SARAGOSA Reeves
SARATOGA Hardin
SARITA Kenedy
SATIN Falls
SAVOY Fannin
SCHERTZ (78154) Guadalupe(73), Bexar(23), Comal(2)

SCHULENBURG (78956) Fayette(89), Lavaca(10)
SCHWERTNER Williamson
SCOTLAND Archer
SCOTTSVILLE Harrison
SCROGGINS (75480) Franklin(95), Wood(4)
SCURRY Kaufman
SEABROOK Harris
SEADRIFT Calhoun
SEAGOVILLE (75159) Dallas(86), Kaufman(13)
SEAGRAVES (79359) Gaines(74), Terry(13), Yoakum(12)
SEALY Austin
SEBASTIAN Willacy
SEGUIN Guadalupe
SELMAN CITY Rusk
SEMINOLE Gaines
SEYMOUR (76380) Baylor(96), Knox(3)
SHAFTER Presidio
SHALLOWATER (79363) Lubbock(97), Hockley(1)
SHAMROCK (79079) Wheeler(90), Collingsworth(9)
SHAMROCK Wheeler
SHEFFIELD Pecos
SHEPHERD San Jacinto
SHEPPARD AFB Wichita
SHERIDAN Colorado
SHERMAN Grayson
SHINER (77984) Lavaca(91), Gonzales(8)
SHIRO Grimes
SIDNEY (76474) Comanche(98), Brown(1)
SIERRA BLANCA Hudspeth
SILSBEE Hardin
SILVER Coke
SILVERTON Briscoe
SIMMS Bowie
SIMONTON Fort Bend
SINTON (78387) San Patricio(92), Bee(7)
SKELLYTOWN (79080) Hutchinson(80), Carson(20)
SKIDMORE Bee
SLATON (79364) Lubbock(96), Lynn(3)
SLIDELL Wise
SMILEY Gonzales
SMITHVILLE (78957) Bastrop(98), Fayette(1)
SMYER Hockley
SNOOK Burleson
SNYDER Scurry
SOMERSET (78069) Atascosa(64), Bexar(35)
SOMERVILLE Burleson
SONORA Sutton
SOUR LAKE Hardin
SOUTH BEND Young
SOUTH HOUSTON Harris
SOUTH PADRE ISLAND Cameron
SOUTH PLAINS Floyd
SOUTHLAKE Tarrant
SOUTHLAND Garza
SOUTHMAYD Grayson
SPADE Lamb
SPEAKS Lavaca
SPEARMAN (79081) Hansford(92), Hutchinson(4), Ochiltree(3)
SPICEWOOD (78669) Travis(71), Burnet(26), Blanco(2)
SPLENDORA (77372) Montgomery(88), Liberty(11)
SPRING Harris
SPRING Montgomery
SPRING BRANCH Comal
SPRINGLAKE (79082) Lamb(84), Castro(15)
SPRINGTOWN (76082) Parker(78), Wise(21)
SPUR (79370) Dickens(89), Crosby(6), Kent(3)
SPURGER Tyler

STAFFORD (77477) Fort Bend(91), Harris(8)
STAFFORD Fort Bend
STAMFORD (79553) Jones(91), Haskell(8)
STANTON (79782) Martin(70), Glasscock(25), Midland(3)
STAPLES Guadalupe
STAR Mills
STEPHENVILLE Erath
STERLING CITY (76951) Sterling(98), Glasscock(1)
STINNETT (79083) Hutchinson(66), Moore(30), Hansford(2)
STOCKDALE Wilson
STONEWALL (78671) Gillespie(97), Blanco(2)
STOWELL Chambers
STRATFORD (79084) Sherman(95), Dallam(4)
STRAWN (76475) Eastland(76), Palo Pinto(23)
STREETMAN (75859) Freestone(65), Navarro(34)
SUBLIME Lavaca
SUDAN (79371) Lamb(62), Bailey(37)
SUGAR LAND Fort Bend
SULLIVAN CITY Hidalgo
SULPHUR BLUFF Hopkins
SULPHUR SPRINGS Hopkins
SUMMERFIELD (79085) Castro(85), Parmer(14)
SUMNER Lamar
SUNDOWN Hockley
SUNNYVALE Dallas
SUNRAY (79086) Moore(50), Sherman(48), Hansford(1)
SUNSET (76270) Montague(57), Wise(42)
SUTHERLAND SPRINGS Wilson
SWEENY (77480) Brazoria(95), Matagorda(4)
SWEET HOME Lavaca
SWEETWATER (79556) Nolan(95), Fisher(4)
SYLVESTER (79560) Fisher(89), Jones(10)
TAFT San Patricio
TAHOKA Lynn
TALCO (75487) Franklin(74), Titus(25)
TALPA (76882) Coleman(63), Runnels(36)
TARPLEY Bandera
TARZAN Martin
TATUM Rusk
TAYLOR Williamson
TEAGUE Freestone
TEHUACANA Limestone
TELEGRAPH (76883) Edwards(69), Kimble(30)
TELEPHONE Fannin
TELFERNER (77988) Lavaca(77), Victoria(22)
TELL (79259) Childress(56), Hall(43)
TEMPLE Bell
TENAHA (75974) Shelby(63), Panola(36)
TENNESSEE COLONY Anderson
TENNYSON Coke
TERLINGUA Brewster
TERRELL (75160) Kaufman(91), Hunt(8)
TERRELL Kaufman
TEXARKANA Bowie
TEXAS CITY Galveston
TEXLINE Dallam
THE COLONY Denton
THICKET Hardin
THOMASTON De Witt
THOMPSONS Fort Bend
THORNDALE (76577) Milam(95), Williamson(4)
THORNTON (76687) Limestone(73), Robertson(25)
THRALL (76578) Williamson(94), Milam(4), Lee(1)
THREE RIVERS Live Oak

THROCKMORTON Throckmorton
TILDEN McMullen
TIMPSON (75975) Shelby(97), Panola(1), Rusk(1)
TIOGA (76271) Grayson(88), Cooke(11)
TIVOLI (77990) Refugio(67), Calhoun(32)
TOKIO (79376) Yoakum(72), Terry(27)
TOLAR Hood
TOM BEAN Grayson
TOMBALL Harris
TORNILLO El Paso
TOW Llano
TOYAH Reeves
TOYAHVALE Reeves
TRENT (79561) Taylor(43), Nolan(36), Fisher(11), Jones(8)
TRENTON (75490) Fannin(97), Grayson(2)
TRINIDAD Henderson
TRINITY (75862) Trinity(95), Walker(4)
TROUP (75789) Smith(82), Cherokee(16), Rusk(1)
TROY (76579) Bell(95), Falls(4)
TRUSCOTT Knox
TULETA Bee
TULIA (79088) Swisher(96), Castro(1), Briscoe(1)
TURKEY (79261) Hall(92), Briscoe(7)
TUSCOLA Taylor
TYE Taylor
TYLER Smith
TYNAN Bee
UMBARGER Randall
UNIVERSAL CITY Bexar
UTOPIA Uvalde
UVALDE Uvalde
VALENTINE (79854) Presidio(57), Jeff Davis(42)
VALERA Coleman
VALLEY MILLS (76689) Bosque(59), McLennan(27), Coryell(13)
VALLEY SPRING Llano
VALLEY VIEW (76272) Cooke(98), Denton(1)
VAN (75790) Van Zandt(97), Smith(2)
VAN ALSTYNE (75495) Grayson(55), Collin(44)
VAN HORN Culberson
VAN VLECK Matagorda
VANCOURT (76955) Tom Green(51), Concho(48)
VANDERBILT Jackson
VANDERPOOL Bandera
VEGA (79092) Oldham(56), Deaf Smith(43)
VENUS (76084) Johnson(72), Ellis(27)
VERA (76383) Knox(91), Baylor(8)
VERIBEST Tom Green
VERNON Wilbarger
VICTORIA (77905) Victoria(91), Goliad(8)
VICTORIA Victoria
VIDOR Orange
VILLAGE MILLS Hardin
VOCA McCulloch
VON ORMY (78073) Bexar(89), Atascosa(10)
VOSS Coleman
VOTAW Hardin
VOTH Jefferson
WACO McLennan
WADSWORTH Matagorda
WAELDER (78959) Gonzales(70), Fayette(19), Bastrop(7), Caldwell(3)
WAKA Ochiltree
WALBURG Williamson
WALL Tom Green
WALLER (77484) Waller(73), Harris(21), Grimes(5)
WALLIS (77485) Austin(66), Fort Bend(32)
WALLISVILLE Chambers
WALNUT SPRINGS (76690) Bosque(75), Somervell(23), Erath(1)
WARDA Fayette
WARING Kendall

WARREN Tyler
WASKOM Harrison
WATER VALLEY Tom Green
WAXAHACHIE Ellis
WAYSIDE (79094) Armstrong(92), Swisher(7)
WEATHERFORD (76087) Parker(96), Hood(3)
WEATHERFORD Parker
WEBSTER Harris
WEESATCHE Goliad
WEIMAR (78962) Colorado(98), Fayette(1)
WEINERT Haskell
WEIR Williamson
WELCH (79377) Dawson(63), Terry(27), Gaines(9)
WELLBORN Brazos
WELLINGTON (79095) Collingsworth(94), Childress(5)
WELLMAN Terry
WELLS Cherokee
WESLACO Hidalgo
WEST McLennan
WEST COLUMBIA Brazoria
WEST POINT Fayette
WESTBROOK Mitchell
WESTHOFF De Witt
WESTMINSTER Collin
WESTON Collin
WHARTON Wharton
WHEELER Wheeler
WHEELOCK Robertson
WHITE DEER (79097) Carson(96), Gray(3)
WHITE OAK Gregg
WHITEFACE Cochran
WHITEHOUSE Smith
WHITESBORO (76273) Grayson(71), Cooke(28)
WHITEWRIGHT (75491) Grayson(73), Fannin(26)
WHITHARRAL Hockley
WHITNEY Hill
WHITSETT Live Oak
WHITT (76490) Parker(58), Palo Pinto(41)
WHON Coleman
WICHITA FALLS (76305) Wichita(62), Clay(37)
WICHITA FALLS (76310) Wichita(64), Archer(18), Clay(16)
WICHITA FALLS Wichita
WICKETT Ward
WIERGATE Newton
WILDORADO (79098) Deaf Smith(44), Randall(23), Oldham(22), Potter(9)
WILLIS (77378) Montgomery(81), San Jacinto(18)
WILLIS Montgomery
WILLOW CITY Gillespie
WILLS POINT (75169) Van Zandt(83), Hunt(9), Kaufman(6)
WILMER Dallas
WILSON Lynn
WIMBERLEY Hays
WINCHESTER Fayette
WINDOM Fannin
WINDTHORST (76389) Archer(61), Clay(29), Jack(8)
WINFIELD Titus
WINGATE (79566) Taylor(58), Runnels(34), Nolan(6)
WINK Winkler
WINNIE (77665) Chambers(98), Jefferson(1)
WINNSBORO (75494) Wood(72), Franklin(20), Hopkins(6)
WINONA Smith
WINTERS (79567) Runnels(97), Taylor(2)
WODEN Nacogdoches
WOLFE CITY (75496) Hunt(79), Fannin(20)
WOLFFORTH Lubbock
WOODLAKE Trinity
WOODLAWN Harrison

WOODSBORO Refugio
WOODSON (76491) Throckmorton(96), Stephens(3)
WOODVILLE Tyler
WOODWAY McLennan
WORTHAM (76693) Freestone(88), Navarro(7), Limestone(3)
WRIGHTSBORO Gonzales
WYLIE (75098) Collin(88), Dallas(9), Rockwall(1)
YANCEY Medina
YANTIS (75497) Wood(87), Hopkins(10), Rains(1)
YOAKUM (77995) Lavaca(51), De Witt(32), Victoria(16)
YORKTOWN De Witt
ZAPATA Zapata
ZAVALLA Angelina
ZEPHYR (76890) Brown(95), Mills(2), Comanche(1)

Texas ZIP/City Cross Reference

73301-73344 AUSTIN
75001-75001 ADDISON
75002-75002 ALLEN
75006-75008 CARROLLTON
75009-75009 CELINA
75010-75011 CARROLLTON
75013-75013 ALLEN
75014-75017 IRVING
75019-75019 COPPELL
75020-75021 DENISON
75022-75022 FLOWER MOUND
75023-75026 PLANO
75027-75028 FLOWER MOUND
75029-75029 LEWISVILLE
75030-75030 ROWLETT
75032-75032 ROCKWALL
75034-75035 FRISCO
75037-75039 IRVING
75040-75049 GARLAND
75050-75054 GRAND PRAIRIE
75056-75056 THE COLONY
75057-75057 LEWISVILLE
75058-75058 GUNTER
75060-75063 IRVING
75065-75065 LAKE DALLAS
75067-75067 LEWISVILLE
75068-75068 LITTLE ELM
75069-75071 MC KINNEY
75074-75075 PLANO
75076-75076 POTTSBORO
75077-75077 LEWISVILLE
75078-75078 PROSPER
75080-75083 RICHARDSON
75084-75084 IRVING
75085-75085 RICHARDSON
75086-75086 PLANO
75087-75087 ROCKWALL
75088-75089 ROWLETT
75090-75092 SHERMAN
75093-75094 PLANO
75097-75097 WESTON
75098-75098 WYLIE
75099-75099 COPPELL
75101-75101 BARDWELL
75102-75102 BARRY
75103-75103 CANTON
75104-75104 CEDAR HILL
75105-75105 CHATFIELD
75106-75106 CEDAR HILL
75109-75110 CORSICANA
75114-75114 CRANDALL
75115-75115 DE SOTO
75116-75116 DUNCANVILLE
75117-75117 EDGEWOOD
75118-75118 ELMO
75119-75120 ENNIS
75121-75121 COPEVILLE
75123-75123 DE SOTO
75123-75123 DESOTO
75124-75124 EUSTACE
75125-75125 FERRIS
75126-75126 FORNEY
75127-75127 FRUITVALE
75132-75132 FATE
75134-75134 LANCASTER
75135-75135 CADDO MILLS
75137-75138 DUNCANVILLE
75140-75140 GRAND SALINE
75141-75141 HUTCHINS
75142-75142 KAUFMAN
75143-75143 KEMP
75144-75144 KERENS
75146-75146 LANCASTER
75147-75147 MABANK
75148-75148 MALAKOFF
75149-75150 MESQUITE
75151-75151 CORSICANA
75152-75152 PALMER
75153-75153 POWELL
75154-75154 RED OAK
75155-75155 RICE
75156-75156 MABANK
75157-75157 ROSSER
75158-75158 SCURRY
75159-75159 SEAGOVILLE
75160-75161 TERRELL
75163-75163 TRINIDAD
75164-75164 JOSEPHINE
75165-75165 WAXAHACHIE
75166-75166 LAVON
75167-75168 WAXAHACHIE
75169-75169 WILLS POINT
75172-75172 WILMER
75173-75173 NEVADA
75180-75181 MESQUITE
75182-75182 SUNNYVALE
75185-75187 MESQUITE
75189-75189 ROYSE CITY
75200-75398 DALLAS
75401-75404 GREENVILLE
75407-75407 PRINCETON
75409-75409 ANNA
75410-75410 ALBA
75411-75411 ARTHUR CITY
75412-75412 BAGWELL
75413-75413 BAILEY
75414-75414 BELLS
75415-75415 BEN FRANKLIN
75416-75416 BLOSSOM
75417-75417 BOGATA
75418-75418 BONHAM
75420-75420 BRASHEAR
75421-75421 BROOKSTON
75422-75422 CAMPBELL
75423-75423 CELESTE
75424-75424 BLUE RIDGE
75425-75425 CHICOTA
75426-75426 CLARKSVILLE
75428-75429 COMMERCE
75431-75431 COMO
75432-75432 COOPER
75433-75433 CUMBY
75434-75434 CUNNINGHAM
75435-75435 DEPORT
75436-75436 DETROIT
75437-75437 DIKE
75438-75438 DODD CITY
75439-75439 ECTOR
75440-75440 EMORY
75441-75441 ENLOE
75442-75442 FARMERSVILLE
75443-75443 GOBER
75444-75444 GOLDEN
75446-75446 HONEY GROVE
75447-75447 IVANHOE
75448-75448 KLONDIKE
75449-75449 LADONIA
75450-75450 LAKE CREEK
75451-75451 LEESBURG
75452-75452 LEONARD
75453-75453 LONE OAK
75454-75454 MELISSA
75455-75456 MOUNT PLEASANT
75457-75457 MOUNT VERNON
75458-75458 MERIT
75459-75459 HOWE
75460-75462 PARIS
75468-75468 PATTONVILLE
75469-75469 PECAN GAP
75470-75470 PETTY
75471-75471 PICKTON
75472-75472 POINT
75473-75473 POWDERLY
75474-75474 QUINLAN
75475-75475 RANDOLPH
75476-75476 RAVENNA
75477-75477 ROXTON
75478-75478 SALTILLO
75479-75479 SAVOY
75480-75480 SCROGGINS
75481-75481 SULPHUR BLUFF
75482-75483 SULPHUR SPRINGS
75485-75485 WESTMINSTER
75486-75486 SUMNER
75487-75487 TALCO
75488-75488 TELEPHONE
75489-75489 TOM BEAN
75490-75490 TRENTON
75491-75491 WHITEWRIGHT
75492-75492 WINDOM
75493-75493 WINFIELD
75494-75494 WINNSBORO
75495-75495 VAN ALSTYNE
75496-75496 WOLFE CITY
75497-75497 YANTIS
75501-75507 TEXARKANA
75550-75550 ANNONA
75551-75551 ATLANTA
75554-75554 AVERY
75555-75555 BIVINS
75556-75556 BLOOMBURG
75557-75557 MAGNOLIA SPRINGS
75558-75558 COOKVILLE
75559-75559 DE KALB
75560-75560 DOUGLASSVILLE
75561-75561 HOOKS
75562-75562 KILDARE
75563-75563 LINDEN
75564-75564 LODI
75565-75565 MC LEOD
75566-75566 MARIETTA
75567-75567 MAUD
75568-75568 NAPLES
75569-75569 NASH
75570-75570 NEW BOSTON
75571-75571 OMAHA
75572-75572 QUEEN CITY
75573-75573 REDWATER
75574-75574 SIMMS
75599-75599 TEXARKANA
75601-75615 LONGVIEW
75630-75630 AVINGER
75631-75631 BECKVILLE
75633-75633 CARTHAGE
75636-75636 CASON
75637-75637 CLAYTON
75638-75638 DAINGERFIELD
75639-75639 DE BERRY
75640-75640 DIANA
75641-75641 EASTON
75642-75642 ELYSIAN FIELDS
75643-75643 GARY
75644-75645 GILMER
75647-75647 GLADEWATER
75650-75650 HALLSVILLE
75651-75651 HARLETON
75652-75654 HENDERSON
75656-75656 HUGHES SPRINGS
75657-75657 JEFFERSON
75658-75658 JOINERVILLE
75659-75659 JONESVILLE
75660-75660 JUDSON
75661-75661 KARNACK
75662-75663 KILGORE
75666-75666 LAIRD HILL
75667-75667 LANEVILLE
75668-75668 LONE STAR
75669-75669 LONG BRANCH
75670-75672 MARSHALL
75680-75680 MINDEN
75681-75681 MOUNT ENTERPRISE
75682-75682 NEW LONDON
75683-75683 ORE CITY
75684-75684 OVERTON
75685-75685 PANOLA
75686-75686 PITTSBURG
75687-75687 PRICE
75688-75688 SCOTTSVILLE
75689-75689 SELMAN CITY
75691-75691 TATUM
75692-75692 WASKOM
75693-75693 WHITE OAK
75694-75694 WOODLAWN
75701-75713 TYLER
75750-75750 ARP
75751-75752 ATHENS
75754-75754 BEN WHEELER
75755-75755 BIG SANDY
75756-75756 BROWNSBORO
75757-75757 BULLARD
75758-75758 CHANDLER
75759-75759 CUNEY
75760-75760 CUSHING
75762-75762 FLINT
75763-75763 FRANKSTON
75764-75764 GALLATIN
75765-75765 HAWKINS
75766-75766 JACKSONVILLE
75770-75770 LARUE
75771-75771 LINDALE
75772-75772 MAYDELLE
75773-75773 MINEOLA
75778-75778 MURCHISON
75779-75779 NECHES
75780-75780 NEW SUMMERFIELD
75782-75782 POYNOR
75783-75783 QUITMAN
75784-75784 REKLAW
75785-75785 RUSK
75788-75788 SACUL
75789-75789 TROUP
75790-75790 VAN
75791-75791 WHITEHOUSE
75792-75792 WINONA
75797-75797 BIG SANDY
75798-75799 TYLER
75801-75803 PALESTINE
75831-75831 BUFFALO
75832-75832 CAYUGA
75833-75833 CENTERVILLE
75834-75834 CENTRALIA
75835-75835 CROCKETT
75838-75838 DONIE
75839-75839 ELKHART
75840-75840 FAIRFIELD
75844-75844 GRAPELAND
75845-75845 GROVETON
75846-75846 JEWETT
75847-75847 KENNARD
75848-75848 KIRVIN
75849-75849 LATEXO
75850-75850 LEONA
75851-75851 LOVELADY
75852-75852 MIDWAY
75853-75853 MONTALBA
75855-75855 OAKWOOD

75856-75856 PENNINGTON
75858-75858 RATCLIFF
75859-75859 STREETMAN
75860-75860 TEAGUE
75861-75861 TENNESSEE COLONY
75862-75862 TRINITY
75865-75865 WOODLAKE
75880-75880 TENNESSEE COLONY
75882-75882 PALESTINE
75884-75886 TENNESSEE COLONY
75901-75915 LUFKIN
75925-75925 ALTO
75926-75926 APPLE SPRINGS
75928-75928 BON WIER
75929-75929 BROADDUS
75930-75930 BRONSON
75931-75931 BROOKELAND
75932-75932 BURKEVILLE
75933-75933 CALL
75934-75934 CAMDEN
75935-75935 CENTER
75936-75936 CHESTER
75937-75937 CHIRENO
75938-75938 COLMESNEIL
75939-75939 CORRIGAN
75941-75941 DIBOLL
75942-75942 DOUCETTE
75943-75943 DOUGLASS
75944-75944 ETOILE
75946-75946 GARRISON
75947-75947 GENEVA
75948-75948 HEMPHILL
75949-75949 HUNTINGTON
75951-75951 JASPER
75954-75954 JOAQUIN
75956-75956 KIRBYVILLE
75957-75957 MAGNOLIA SPRINGS
75958-75958 MARTINSVILLE
75959-75959 MILAM
75960-75960 MOSCOW
75961-75965 NACOGDOCHES
75966-75966 NEWTON
75968-75968 PINELAND
75969-75969 POLLOK
75970-75970 ROCKLAND
75972-75972 SAN AUGUSTINE
75973-75973 SHELBYVILLE
75974-75974 TENAHA
75975-75975 TIMPSON
75976-75976 WELLS
75977-75977 WIERGATE
75978-75978 WODEN
75979-75979 WOODVILLE
75980-75980 ZAVALLA
75990-75990 WOODVILLE
76000-76007 ARLINGTON
76008-76008 ALEDO
76009-76009 ALVARADO
76010-76019 ARLINGTON
76020-76020 AZLE
76021-76022 BEDFORD
76023-76023 BOYD
76028-76028 BURLESON
76031-76033 CLEBURNE
76034-76034 COLLEYVILLE
76035-76035 CRESSON
76036-76036 CROWLEY
76039-76040 EULESS
76041-76041 FORRESTON
76043-76043 GLEN ROSE
76044-76044 GODLEY
76048-76049 GRANBURY
76050-76050 GRANDVIEW
76051-76051 GRAPEVINE
76052-76052 HASLET
76053-76054 HURST
76055-76055 ITASCA
76058-76058 JOSHUA
76059-76059 KEENE
76060-76060 KENNEDALE
76061-76061 LILLIAN
76063-76063 MANSFIELD
76064-76064 MAYPEARL
76065-76065 MIDLOTHIAN
76066-76066 MILLSAP
76067-76068 MINERAL WELLS
76070-76070 NEMO
76071-76071 NEWARK
76073-76073 PARADISE
76077-76077 RAINBOW
76078-76078 RHOME
76082-76082 SPRINGTOWN
76084-76084 VENUS
76085-76088 WEATHERFORD
76092-76092 SOUTHLAKE
76093-76093 RIO VISTA
76094-76094 ARLINGTON
76095-76095 BEDFORD
76096-76096 ARLINGTON
76097-76097 BURLESON
76098-76098 AZLE
76099-76099 GRAPEVINE
76100-76116 FORT WORTH
76117-76117 HALTOM CITY
76118-76126 FORT WORTH
76127-76127 NAVAL AIR STATION/ JRB
76129-76179 FORT WORTH
76180-76180 NORTH RICHLAND HILLS
76181-76181 FORT WORTH
76182-76182 NORTH RICHLAND HILLS
76185-76199 FORT WORTH
76201-76210 DENTON
76225-76225 ALVORD
76226-76226 ARGYLE
76227-76227 AUBREY
76228-76228 BELLEVUE
76230-76230 BOWIE
76233-76233 COLLINSVILLE
76234-76234 DECATUR
76238-76238 ERA
76239-76239 FORESTBURG
76240-76241 GAINESVILLE
76244-76244 KELLER
76245-76245 GORDONVILLE
76246-76246 GREENWOOD
76247-76247 JUSTIN
76248-76248 KELLER
76249-76249 KRUM
76250-76250 LINDSAY
76251-76251 MONTAGUE
76252-76252 MUENSTER
76253-76253 MYRA
76254-76254 NEWPORT
76255-76255 NOCONA
76258-76258 PILOT POINT
76259-76259 PONDER
76261-76261 RINGGOLD
76262-76262 ROANOKE
76263-76263 ROSSTON
76264-76264 SADLER
76265-76265 SAINT JO
76266-76266 SANGER
76267-76267 SLIDELL
76268-76268 SOUTHMAYD
76270-76270 SUNSET
76271-76271 TIOGA
76272-76272 VALLEY VIEW
76273-76273 WHITESBORO
76299-76299 ROANOKE
76301-76310 WICHITA FALLS
76311-76311 SHEPPARD AFB
76351-76351 ARCHER CITY
76352-76352 BLUEGROVE
76354-76354 BURKBURNETT
76357-76357 BYERS
76359-76359 ELBERT
76360-76360 ELECTRA
76363-76363 GOREE
76364-76364 HARROLD
76365-76365 HENRIETTA
76366-76366 HOLLIDAY
76367-76367 IOWA PARK
76369-76369 KAMAY
76370-76370 MEGARGEL
76371-76371 MUNDAY
76372-76372 NEWCASTLE
76373-76373 OKLAUNION
76374-76374 OLNEY
76377-76377 PETROLIA
76379-76379 SCOTLAND
76380-76380 SEYMOUR
76383-76383 VERA
76384-76385 VERNON
76388-76388 WEINERT
76389-76389 WINDTHORST
76401-76402 STEPHENVILLE
76424-76424 BRECKENRIDGE
76426-76426 BRIDGEPORT
76427-76427 BRYSON
76429-76429 CADDO
76430-76430 ALBANY
76431-76431 CHICO
76432-76432 BLANKET
76433-76433 BLUFF DALE
76435-76435 CARBON
76436-76436 CARLTON
76437-76437 CISCO
76438-76438 ELIASVILLE
76439-76439 DENNIS
76442-76442 COMANCHE
76443-76443 CROSS PLAINS
76444-76444 DE LEON
76445-76445 DESDEMONA
76446-76446 DUBLIN
76448-76448 EASTLAND
76449-76449 GRAFORD
76450-76450 GRAHAM
76452-76452 ENERGY
76453-76453 GORDON
76454-76454 GORMAN
76455-76455 GUSTINE
76456-76456 HASSE
76457-76457 HICO
76458-76458 JACKSBORO
76459-76459 JERMYN
76460-76460 LOVING
76461-76461 LINGLEVILLE
76462-76462 LIPAN
76463-76463 MINGUS
76464-76464 MORAN
76465-76465 MORGAN MILL
76466-76466 OLDEN
76467-76467 PALUXY
76468-76468 PROCTOR
76469-76469 PUTNAM
76470-76470 RANGER
76471-76471 RISING STAR
76472-76472 SANTO
76474-76474 SIDNEY
76475-76475 STRAWN
76476-76476 TOLAR
76481-76481 SOUTH BEND
76483-76483 THROCKMORTON
76484-76484 PALO PINTO
76485-76485 PEASTER
76486-76486 PERRIN
76487-76487 POOLVILLE
76490-76490 WHITT
76491-76491 WOODSON
76501-76508 TEMPLE
76511-76511 BARTLETT
76513-76513 BELTON
76517-76517 BEN ARNOLD
76518-76518 BUCKHOLTS
76519-76519 BURLINGTON
76520-76520 CAMERON
76522-76522 COPPERAS COVE
76523-76523 DAVILLA
76524-76524 EDDY
76525-76525 EVANT
76526-76526 FLAT
76527-76527 FLORENCE
76528-76528 GATESVILLE
76530-76530 GRANGER
76531-76531 HAMILTON
76533-76533 HEIDENHEIMER
76534-76534 HOLLAND
76537-76537 JARRELL
76538-76538 JONESBORO
76539-76539 KEMPNER
76540-76547 KILLEEN
76548-76548 HARKER HEIGHTS
76549-76549 KILLEEN
76550-76550 LAMPASAS
76552-76552 LEON JUNCTION
76554-76554 LITTLE RIVER
76554-76554 LITTLE RIVER ACADEMY
76555-76555 MAYSFIELD
76556-76556 MILANO
76557-76557 MOODY
76558-76558 MOUND
76559-76559 NOLANVILLE
76561-76561 OGLESBY
76564-76564 PENDLETON
76565-76565 POTTSVILLE
76566-76566 PURMELA
76567-76567 ROCKDALE
76569-76569 ROGERS
76570-76570 ROSEBUD
76571-76571 SALADO
76573-76573 SCHWERTNER
76574-76574 TAYLOR
76576-76576 GATESVILLE
76577-76577 THORNDALE
76578-76578 THRALL
76579-76579 TROY
76596-76599 GATESVILLE
76621-76621 ABBOTT
76622-76622 AQUILLA
76623-76623 AVALON
76624-76624 AXTELL
76625-76625 BIROME
76626-76626 BLOOMING GROVE
76627-76627 BLUM
76628-76628 BRANDON
76629-76629 BREMOND
76630-76630 BRUCEVILLE
76631-76631 BYNUM
76632-76632 CHILTON
76633-76633 CHINA SPRING
76634-76634 CLIFTON
76635-76635 COOLIDGE
76636-76636 COVINGTON
76637-76637 CRANFILLS GAP
76638-76638 CRAWFORD
76639-76639 DAWSON
76640-76640 ELM MOTT
76641-76641 FROST
76642-76642 GROESBECK
76643-76643 HEWITT
76644-76644 CLIFTON
76645-76645 HILLSBORO
76648-76648 HUBBARD
76649-76649 IREDELL
76650-76650 IRENE
76651-76651 ITALY
76652-76652 KOPPERL
76653-76653 KOSSE
76654-76654 LEROY
76655-76655 LORENA
76656-76656 LOTT
76657-76657 MC GREGOR
76660-76660 MALONE
76661-76661 MARLIN
76664-76664 MART
76665-76665 MERIDIAN
76666-76666 MERTENS
76667-76667 MEXIA
76670-76670 MILFORD
76671-76671 MORGAN
76673-76673 MOUNT CALM
76675-76675 OTTO
76676-76676 PENELOPE
76677-76677 PERRY
76678-76678 PRAIRIE HILL
76679-76679 PURDON
76680-76680 REAGAN
76681-76681 RICHLAND

76682-76682 RIESEL
76684-76684 ROSS
76685-76685 SATIN
76686-76686 TEHUACANA
76687-76687 THORNTON
76689-76689 VALLEY MILLS
76690-76690 WALNUT SPRINGS
76691-76691 WEST
76692-76692 WHITNEY
76693-76693 WORTHAM
76700-76711 WACO
76712-76712 WOODWAY
76714-76799 WACO
76801-76801 BROWNWOOD
76802-76802 EARLY
76803-76804 BROWNWOOD
76820-76820 ART
76821-76821 BALLINGER
76823-76823 BANGS
76824-76824 BEND
76825-76825 BRADY
76827-76827 BROOKESMITH
76828-76828 BURKETT
76831-76831 CASTELL
76832-76832 CHEROKEE
76834-76834 COLEMAN
76836-76836 DOOLE
76837-76837 EDEN
76841-76841 FORT MC KAVETT
76842-76842 FREDONIA
76844-76844 GOLDTHWAITE
76845-76845 GOULDBUSK
76848-76848 HEXT
76849-76849 JUNCTION
76852-76852 LOHN
76853-76853 LOMETA
76854-76854 LONDON
76855-76855 LOWAKE
76856-76856 MASON
76857-76857 MAY
76858-76858 MELVIN
76859-76859 MENARD
76861-76861 MILES
76862-76862 MILLERSVIEW
76864-76864 MULLIN
76865-76865 NORTON
76866-76866 PAINT ROCK
76867-76867 PEAR VALLEY
76869-76869 PONTOTOC
76870-76870 PRIDDY
76871-76871 RICHLAND SPRINGS
76872-76872 ROCHELLE
76873-76873 ROCKWOOD
76874-76874 ROOSEVELT
76875-76875 ROWENA
76877-76877 SAN SABA
76878-76878 SANTA ANNA
76880-76880 STAR
76882-76882 TALPA
76883-76883 TELEGRAPH
76884-76884 VALERA
76885-76885 VALLEY SPRING
76886-76886 VERIBEST
76887-76887 VOCA
76888-76888 VOSS
76889-76889 WHON
76890-76890 ZEPHYR
76901-76906 SAN ANGELO
76908-76908 GOODFELLOW AFB
76909-76909 SAN ANGELO
76930-76930 BARNHART
76932-76932 BIG LAKE
76933-76933 BRONTE
76934-76934 CARLSBAD
76935-76935 CHRISTOVAL
76936-76936 ELDORADO
76937-76937 EOLA
76939-76939 KNICKERBOCKER
76940-76940 MERETA
76941-76941 MERTZON
76943-76943 OZONA
76945-76945 ROBERT LEE
76949-76949 SILVER
76950-76950 SONORA
76951-76951 STERLING CITY
76953-76953 TENNYSON
76955-76955 VANCOURT
76957-76957 WALL
76958-76958 WATER VALLEY
77000-77299 HOUSTON
77301-77306 CONROE
77315-77315 NORTH HOUSTON
77316-77316 MONTGOMERY
77318-77318 WILLIS
77320-77320 HUNTSVILLE
77325-77325 HUMBLE
77326-77326 ACE
77327-77328 CLEVELAND
77331-77331 COLDSPRING
77332-77332 DALLARDSVILLE
77333-77333 DOBBIN
77334-77334 DODGE
77335-77335 GOODRICH
77336-77336 HUFFMAN
77337-77337 HUFSMITH
77338-77339 HUMBLE
77340-77344 HUNTSVILLE
77345-77347 HUMBLE
77348-77349 HUNTSVILLE
77350-77350 LEGGETT
77351-77351 LIVINGSTON
77353-77355 MAGNOLIA
77356-77356 MONTGOMERY
77357-77357 NEW CANEY
77358-77358 NEW WAVERLY
77359-77359 OAKHURST
77360-77360 ONALASKA
77362-77362 PINEHURST
77363-77363 PLANTERSVILLE
77364-77364 POINTBLANK
77365-77365 PORTER
77367-77367 RIVERSIDE
77368-77368 ROMAYOR
77369-77369 RYE
77371-77371 SHEPHERD
77372-77372 SPLENDORA
77373-77373 SPRING
77374-77374 THICKET
77375-77375 TOMBALL
77376-77376 VOTAW
77377-77377 TOMBALL
77378-77378 WILLIS
77379-77383 SPRING
77384-77385 CONROE
77386-77393 SPRING
77396-77396 HUMBLE
77399-77399 LIVINGSTON
77401-77402 BELLAIRE
77404-77404 BAY CITY
77406-77406 RICHMOND
77410-77410 CYPRESS
77411-77411 ALIEF
77412-77412 ALTAIR
77413-77413 BARKER
77414-77414 BAY CITY
77415-77415 CEDAR LANE
77417-77417 BEASLEY
77418-77418 BELLVILLE
77419-77419 BLESSING
77420-77420 BOLING
77422-77422 BRAZORIA
77423-77423 BROOKSHIRE
77426-77426 CHAPPELL HILL
77428-77428 COLLEGEPORT
77429-77429 CYPRESS
77430-77430 DAMON
77431-77431 DANCIGER
77432-77432 DANEVANG
77433-77433 CYPRESS
77434-77434 EAGLE LAKE
77435-77435 EAST BERNARD
77436-77436 EGYPT
77437-77437 EL CAMPO
77440-77440 ELMATON
77441-77441 FULSHEAR
77442-77442 GARWOOD
77443-77443 GLEN FLORA
77444-77444 GUY
77445-77445 HEMPSTEAD
77446-77446 PRAIRIE VIEW
77447-77447 HOCKLEY
77448-77448 HUNGERFORD
77449-77450 KATY
77451-77451 KENDLETON
77452-77452 KENNEY
77453-77453 LANE CITY
77454-77454 LISSIE
77455-77455 LOUISE
77456-77456 MARKHAM
77457-77457 MATAGORDA
77458-77458 MIDFIELD
77459-77459 MISSOURI CITY
77460-77460 NADA
77461-77461 NEEDVILLE
77462-77462 NEWGULF
77463-77463 OLD OCEAN
77464-77464 ORCHARD
77465-77465 PALACIOS
77466-77466 PATTISON
77467-77467 PIERCE
77468-77468 PLEDGER
77469-77469 RICHMOND
77470-77470 ROCK ISLAND
77471-77471 ROSENBERG
77473-77473 SAN FELIPE
77474-77474 SEALY
77475-77475 SHERIDAN
77476-77476 SIMONTON
77477-77477 STAFFORD
77478-77479 SUGAR LAND
77480-77480 SWEENY
77481-77481 THOMPSONS
77482-77482 VAN VLECK
77483-77483 WADSWORTH
77484-77484 WALLER
77485-77485 WALLIS
77486-77486 WEST COLUMBIA
77487-77487 SUGAR LAND
77488-77488 WHARTON
77489-77489 MISSOURI CITY
77491-77494 KATY
77496-77496 SUGAR LAND
77497-77497 STAFFORD
77501-77508 PASADENA
77510-77510 SANTA FE
77511-77512 ALVIN
77514-77514 ANAHUAC
77515-77516 ANGLETON
77517-77517 SANTA FE
77518-77518 BACLIFF
77519-77519 BATSON
77520-77522 BAYTOWN
77530-77530 CHANNELVIEW
77531-77531 CLUTE
77532-77532 CROSBY
77533-77533 DAISETTA
77534-77534 DANBURY
77535-77535 DAYTON
77536-77536 DEER PARK
77538-77538 DEVERS
77539-77539 DICKINSON
77541-77542 FREEPORT
77545-77545 FRESNO
77546-77546 FRIENDSWOOD
77547-77547 GALENA PARK
77549-77549 FRIENDSWOOD
77550-77555 GALVESTON
77560-77560 HANKAMER
77561-77561 HARDIN
77562-77562 HIGHLANDS
77563-77563 HITCHCOCK
77564-77564 HULL
77565-77565 KEMAH
77566-77566 LAKE JACKSON
77568-77568 LA MARQUE
77571-77572 LA PORTE
77573-77574 LEAGUE CITY
77575-77575 LIBERTY
77577-77577 LIVERPOOL
77578-77578 MANVEL
77580-77580 MONT BELVIEU
77581-77581 PEARLAND
77582-77582 RAYWOOD
77583-77583 ROSHARON
77584-77584 PEARLAND
77585-77585 SARATOGA
77586-77586 SEABROOK
77587-77587 SOUTH HOUSTON
77588-77588 PEARLAND
77590-77592 TEXAS CITY
77597-77597 WALLISVILLE
77598-77598 WEBSTER
77611-77611 BRIDGE CITY
77612-77612 BUNA
77613-77613 CHINA
77614-77614 DEWEYVILLE
77615-77615 EVADALE
77616-77616 FRED
77617-77617 GILCHRIST
77619-77619 GROVES
77622-77622 HAMSHIRE
77623-77623 HIGH ISLAND
77624-77624 HILLISTER
77625-77625 KOUNTZE
77626-77626 MAURICEVILLE
77627-77627 NEDERLAND
77629-77629 NOME
77630-77632 ORANGE
77639-77639 ORANGEFIELD
77640-77643 PORT ARTHUR
77650-77650 PORT BOLIVAR
77651-77651 PORT NECHES
77655-77655 SABINE PASS
77656-77656 SILSBEE
77657-77657 LUMBERTON
77659-77659 SOUR LAKE
77660-77660 SPURGER
77661-77661 STOWELL
77662-77662 VIDOR
77663-77663 VILLAGE MILLS
77664-77664 WARREN
77665-77665 WINNIE
77670-77670 VIDOR
77700-77708 BEAUMONT
77709-77709 VOTH
77710-77710 BEAUMONT
77711-77711 LUMBERTON
77713-77726 BEAUMONT
77801-77808 BRYAN
77830-77830 ANDERSON
77831-77831 BEDIAS
77833-77834 BRENHAM
77835-77835 BURTON
77836-77836 CALDWELL
77837-77837 CALVERT
77838-77838 CHRIESMAN
77839-77839 CLAY
77840-77845 COLLEGE STATION
77850-77850 CONCORD
77852-77852 DEANVILLE
77853-77853 DIME BOX
77855-77855 FLYNN
77856-77856 FRANKLIN
77857-77857 GAUSE
77859-77859 HEARNE
77861-77861 IOLA
77862-77862 KURTEN
77863-77863 LYONS
77864-77864 MADISONVILLE
77865-77865 MARQUEZ
77866-77866 MILLICAN
77867-77867 MUMFORD
77868-77869 NAVASOTA
77870-77870 NEW BADEN
77871-77871 NORMANGEE
77872-77872 NORTH ZULCH
77873-77873 RICHARDS
77875-77875 ROANS PRAIRIE

77876-77876 SHIRO
77878-77878 SNOOK
77879-77879 SOMERVILLE
77880-77880 WASHINGTON
77881-77881 WELLBORN
77882-77882 WHEELOCK
77901-77905 VICTORIA
77950-77950 AUSTWELL
77951-77951 BLOOMINGTON
77954-77954 CUERO
77957-77957 EDNA
77960-77960 FANNIN
77961-77961 FRANCITAS
77962-77962 GANADO
77963-77963 GOLIAD
77964-77964 HALLETTSVILLE
77967-77967 HOCHHEIM
77968-77968 INEZ
77969-77969 LA SALLE
77970-77970 LA WARD
77971-77971 LOLITA
77972-77972 LONG MOTT
77973-77973 MCFADDIN
77974-77974 MEYERSVILLE
77975-77975 MOULTON
77976-77976 NURSERY
77977-77977 PLACEDO
77978-77978 POINT COMFORT
77979-77979 PORT LAVACA
77982-77982 PORT O CONNOR
77983-77983 SEADRIFT
77984-77984 SHINER
77985-77985 SPEAKS
77986-77986 SUBLIME
77987-77987 SWEET HOME
77988-77988 TELFERNER
77989-77989 THOMASTON
77990-77990 TIVOLI
77991-77991 VANDERBILT
77993-77993 WEESATCHE
77994-77994 WESTHOFF
77995-77995 YOAKUM
78001-78001 ARTESIA WELLS
78002-78002 ATASCOSA
78003-78003 BANDERA
78004-78004 BERGHEIM
78005-78005 BIGFOOT
78006-78006 BOERNE
78007-78007 CALLIHAM
78008-78008 CAMPBELLTON
78009-78009 CASTROVILLE
78010-78010 CENTER POINT
78011-78011 CHARLOTTE
78012-78012 CHRISTINE
78013-78013 COMFORT
78014-78014 COTULLA
78015-78015 BOERNE
78016-78016 DEVINE
78017-78017 DILLEY
78019-78019 ENCINAL
78021-78021 FOWLERTON
78022-78022 GEORGE WEST
78023-78023 HELOTES
78024-78024 HUNT
78025-78025 INGRAM
78026-78026 JOURDANTON
78027-78027 KENDALIA
78028-78029 KERRVILLE
78039-78039 LA COSTE
78040-78049 LAREDO
78050-78050 LEMING
78052-78052 LYTLE
78053-78053 MC COY
78054-78054 MACDONA
78055-78055 MEDINA
78056-78056 MICO
78057-78057 MOORE
78058-78058 MOUNTAIN HOME
78059-78059 NATALIA
78060-78060 OAKVILLE
78061-78061 PEARSALL
78062-78062 PEGGY
78063-78063 PIPE CREEK
78064-78064 PLEASANTON
78065-78065 POTEET
78066-78066 RIO MEDINA
78067-78067 SAN YGNACIO
78069-78069 SOMERSET
78070-78070 SPRING BRANCH
78071-78071 THREE RIVERS
78072-78072 TILDEN
78073-78073 VON ORMY
78074-78074 WARING
78075-78075 WHITSETT
78076-78076 ZAPATA
78101-78101 ADKINS
78102-78104 BEEVILLE
78107-78107 BERCLAIR
78108-78108 CIBOLO
78109-78109 CONVERSE
78111-78111 ECLETO
78112-78112 ELMENDORF
78113-78113 FALLS CITY
78114-78114 FLORESVILLE
78115-78115 GERONIMO
78116-78116 GILLETT
78117-78117 HOBSON
78118-78118 KARNES CITY
78119-78119 KENEDY
78121-78121 LA VERNIA
78122-78122 LEESVILLE
78123-78123 MC QUEENEY
78124-78124 MARION
78125-78125 MINERAL
78130-78132 NEW BRAUNFELS
78133-78133 CANYON LAKE
78135-78135 NEW BRAUNFELS
78140-78140 NIXON
78141-78141 NORDHEIM
78142-78142 NORMANNA
78143-78143 PANDORA
78144-78144 PANNA MARIA
78145-78145 PAWNEE
78146-78146 PETTUS
78147-78147 POTH
78148-78150 UNIVERSAL CITY
78151-78151 RUNGE
78152-78152 SAINT HEDWIG
78154-78154 SCHERTZ
78155-78156 SEGUIN
78159-78159 SMILEY
78160-78160 STOCKDALE
78161-78161 SUTHERLAND SPRINGS
78162-78162 TULETA
78163-78163 BULVERDE
78164-78164 YORKTOWN
78200-78299 SAN ANTONIO
78330-78330 AGUA DULCE
78332-78333 ALICE
78335-78336 ARANSAS PASS
78338-78338 ARMSTRONG
78339-78339 BANQUETE
78340-78340 BAYSIDE
78341-78341 BENAVIDES
78342-78342 BEN BOLT
78343-78343 BISHOP
78344-78344 BRUNI
78347-78347 CHAPMAN RANCH
78349-78349 CONCEPCION
78350-78350 DINERO
78351-78351 DRISCOLL
78352-78352 EDROY
78353-78353 ENCINO
78355-78355 FALFURRIAS
78357-78357 FREER
78358-78358 FULTON
78359-78359 GREGORY
78360-78360 GUERRA
78361-78361 HEBBRONVILLE
78362-78362 INGLESIDE
78363-78364 KINGSVILLE
78368-78368 MATHIS
78369-78369 MIRANDO CITY
78370-78370 ODEM
78371-78371 OILTON
78372-78372 ORANGE GROVE
78373-78373 PORT ARANSAS
78374-78374 PORTLAND
78375-78375 PREMONT
78376-78376 REALITOS
78377-78377 REFUGIO
78379-78379 RIVIERA
78380-78380 ROBSTOWN
78381-78382 ROCKPORT
78383-78383 SANDIA
78384-78384 SAN DIEGO
78385-78385 SARITA
78387-78387 SINTON
78389-78389 SKIDMORE
78390-78390 TAFT
78391-78391 TYNAN
78393-78393 WOODSBORO
78400-78480 CORPUS CHRISTI
78501-78505 MCALLEN
78516-78516 ALAMO
78520-78526 BROWNSVILLE
78535-78535 COMBES
78536-78536 DELMITA
78537-78537 DONNA
78538-78538 EDCOUCH
78539-78541 EDINBURG
78543-78543 ELSA
78545-78545 FALCON HEIGHTS
78547-78547 GARCIASVILLE
78548-78548 GRULLA
78549-78549 HARGILL
78550-78553 HARLINGEN
78557-78557 HIDALGO
78558-78558 LA BLANCA
78559-78559 LA FERIA
78560-78560 LA JOYA
78561-78561 LASARA
78562-78562 LA VILLA
78563-78563 LINN
78564-78564 LOPENO
78565-78565 LOS EBANOS
78566-78566 LOS FRESNOS
78567-78567 LOS INDIOS
78568-78568 LOZANO
78569-78569 LYFORD
78570-78570 MERCEDES
78572-78574 MISSION
78575-78575 OLMITO
78576-78576 PENITAS
78577-78577 PHARR
78578-78578 PORT ISABEL
78579-78579 PROGRESO
78580-78580 RAYMONDVILLE
78582-78582 RIO GRANDE CITY
78583-78583 RIO HONDO
78584-78584 ROMA
78585-78585 SALINENO
78586-78586 SAN BENITO
78588-78588 SAN ISIDRO
78589-78589 SAN JUAN
78590-78590 SAN PERLITA
78591-78591 SANTA ELENA
78592-78592 SANTA MARIA
78593-78593 SANTA ROSA
78594-78594 SEBASTIAN
78595-78595 SULLIVAN CITY
78596-78596 WESLACO
78597-78597 SOUTH PADRE ISLAND
78598-78598 PORT MANSFIELD
78599-78599 WESLACO
78602-78602 BASTROP
78603-78603 BEBE
78604-78604 BELMONT
78605-78605 BERTRAM
78606-78606 BLANCO
78607-78607 BLUFFTON
78608-78608 BRIGGS
78609-78609 BUCHANAN DAM
78610-78610 BUDA
78611-78611 BURNET
78612-78612 CEDAR CREEK
78613-78613 CEDAR PARK
78614-78614 COST
78615-78615 COUPLAND
78616-78616 DALE
78617-78617 DEL VALLE
78618-78618 DOSS
78619-78619 DRIFTWOOD
78620-78620 DRIPPING SPRINGS
78621-78621 ELGIN
78622-78622 FENTRESS
78623-78623 FISCHER
78624-78624 FREDERICKSBURG
78626-78628 GEORGETOWN
78629-78629 GONZALES
78630-78630 CEDAR PARK
78631-78631 HARPER
78632-78632 HARWOOD
78634-78634 HUTTO
78635-78635 HYE
78636-78636 JOHNSON CITY
78638-78638 KINGSBURY
78639-78639 KINGSLAND
78640-78640 KYLE
78641-78641 LEANDER
78642-78642 LIBERTY HILL
78643-78643 LLANO
78644-78644 LOCKHART
78645-78646 LEANDER
78648-78648 LULING
78650-78650 MC DADE
78651-78651 MC NEIL
78652-78652 MANCHACA
78653-78653 MANOR
78654-78654 MARBLE FALLS
78655-78655 MARTINDALE
78656-78656 MAXWELL
78657-78657 MARBLE FALLS
78658-78658 OTTINE
78659-78659 PAIGE
78660-78660 PFLUGERVILLE
78661-78661 PRAIRIE LEA
78662-78662 RED ROCK
78663-78663 ROUND MOUNTAIN
78664-78664 ROUND ROCK
78665-78665 SANDY
78666-78667 SAN MARCOS
78669-78669 SPICEWOOD
78670-78670 STAPLES
78671-78671 STONEWALL
78672-78672 TOW
78673-78673 WALBURG
78674-78674 WEIR
78675-78675 WILLOW CITY
78676-78676 WIMBERLEY
78677-78677 WRIGHTSBORO
78680-78683 ROUND ROCK
78691-78691 PFLUGERVILLE
78700-78799 AUSTIN
78801-78802 UVALDE
78827-78827 ASHERTON
78828-78828 BARKSDALE
78829-78829 BATESVILLE
78830-78830 BIG WELLS
78832-78832 BRACKETTVILLE
78833-78833 CAMP WOOD
78834-78834 CARRIZO SPRINGS
78835-78835 DEL RIO
78836-78836 CATARINA
78837-78837 COMSTOCK
78838-78838 CONCAN
78839-78839 CRYSTAL CITY
78840-78842 DEL RIO
78843-78843 LAUGHLIN A F B
78847-78847 DEL RIO
78850-78850 D HANIS
78851-78851 DRYDEN
78852-78853 EAGLE PASS
78860-78860 EL INDIO
78861-78861 HONDO
78870-78870 KNIPPA
78871-78871 LANGTRY
78872-78872 LA PRYOR

78873-78873 LEAKEY
78877-78877 QUEMADO
78879-78879 RIO FRIO
78880-78880 ROCKSPRINGS
78881-78881 SABINAL
78883-78883 TARPLEY
78884-78884 UTOPIA
78885-78885 VANDERPOOL
78886-78886 YANCEY
78931-78931 BLEIBLERVILLE
78932-78932 CARMINE
78933-78933 CAT SPRING
78934-78934 COLUMBUS
78935-78935 ALLEYTON
78938-78938 ELLINGER
78940-78940 FAYETTEVILLE
78941-78941 FLATONIA
78942-78942 GIDDINGS
78943-78943 GLIDDEN
78944-78944 INDUSTRY
78945-78945 LA GRANGE
78946-78946 LEDBETTER
78947-78947 LEXINGTON
78948-78948 LINCOLN
78949-78949 MULDOON
78950-78950 NEW ULM
78951-78951 OAKLAND
78952-78952 PLUM
78953-78953 ROSANKY
78954-78954 ROUND TOP
78956-78956 SCHULENBURG
78957-78957 SMITHVILLE
78959-78959 WAELDER
78960-78960 WARDA
78961-78961 ROUND TOP
78962-78962 WEIMAR
78963-78963 WEST POINT
78964-78964 WINCHESTER
79001-79001 ADRIAN
79002-79002 ALANREED
79003-79003 ALLISON
79005-79005 BOOKER
79007-79008 BORGER
79009-79009 BOVINA
79010-79010 BOYS RANCH
79011-79011 BRISCOE
79012-79012 BUSHLAND
79013-79013 CACTUS
79014-79014 CANADIAN
79015-79016 CANYON
79018-79018 CHANNING
79019-79019 CLAUDE
79021-79021 COTTON CENTER
79022-79022 DALHART
79024-79024 DARROUZETT
79025-79025 DAWN
79027-79027 DIMMITT
79029-79029 DUMAS
79031-79031 EARTH
79032-79032 EDMONSON
79033-79033 FARNSWORTH
79034-79034 FOLLETT
79035-79035 FRIONA
79036-79036 FRITCH
79039-79039 GROOM
79040-79040 GRUVER
79041-79041 HALE CENTER
79042-79042 HAPPY
79043-79043 HART
79044-79044 HARTLEY
79045-79045 HEREFORD
79046-79046 HIGGINS
79051-79051 KERRICK
79052-79052 KRESS
79053-79053 LAZBUDDIE
79054-79054 LEFORS
79056-79056 LIPSCOMB
79057-79057 MCLEAN
79058-79058 MASTERSON
79059-79059 MIAMI
79061-79061 MOBEETIE
79062-79062 MORSE
79063-79063 NAZARETH
79064-79064 OLTON
79065-79066 PAMPA
79068-79068 PANHANDLE
79070-79070 PERRYTON
79072-79073 PLAINVIEW
79077-79077 SAMNORWOOD
79078-79078 SANFORD
79079-79079 SHAMROCK
79080-79080 SKELLYTOWN
79081-79081 SPEARMAN
79082-79082 SPRINGLAKE
79083-79083 STINNETT
79084-79084 STRATFORD
79085-79085 SUMMERFIELD
79086-79086 SUNRAY
79087-79087 TEXLINE
79088-79088 TULIA
79090-79090 SHAMROCK
79091-79091 UMBARGER
79092-79092 VEGA
79093-79093 WAKA
79094-79094 WAYSIDE
79095-79095 WELLINGTON
79096-79096 WHEELER
79097-79097 WHITE DEER
79098-79098 WILDORADO
79100-79189 AMARILLO
79201-79201 CHILDRESS
79220-79220 AFTON
79221-79221 AIKEN
79222-79222 CAREY
79223-79223 CEE VEE
79224-79224 CHALK
79225-79225 CHILLICOTHE
79226-79226 CLARENDON
79227-79227 CROWELL
79229-79229 DICKENS
79230-79230 DODSON
79231-79231 DOUGHERTY
79232-79232 DUMONT
79233-79233 ESTELLINE
79234-79234 FLOMOT
79235-79235 FLOYDADA
79236-79236 GUTHRIE
79237-79237 HEDLEY
79238-79238 KIRKLAND
79239-79239 LAKEVIEW
79240-79240 LELIA LAKE
79241-79241 LOCKNEY
79243-79243 MCADOO
79244-79244 MATADOR
79245-79245 MEMPHIS
79247-79247 ODELL
79248-79248 PADUCAH
79250-79250 PETERSBURG
79251-79251 QUAIL
79252-79252 QUANAH
79255-79255 QUITAQUE
79256-79256 ROARING SPRINGS
79257-79257 SILVERTON
79258-79258 SOUTH PLAINS
79259-79259 TELL
79260-79260 TRUSCOTT
79261-79261 TURKEY
79311-79311 ABERNATHY
79312-79312 AMHERST
79313-79313 ANTON
79314-79314 BLEDSOE
79316-79316 BROWNFIELD
79320-79320 BULA
79321-79321 CONE
79322-79322 CROSBYTON
79323-79323 DENVER CITY
79324-79324 ENOCHS
79325-79325 FARWELL
79326-79326 FIELDTON
79329-79329 IDALOU
79330-79330 JUSTICEBURG
79331-79331 LAMESA
79336-79338 LEVELLAND
79339-79339 LITTLEFIELD
79342-79342 LOOP
79343-79343 LORENZO
79344-79344 MAPLE
79345-79345 MEADOW
79346-79346 MORTON
79347-79347 MULESHOE
79350-79350 NEW DEAL
79351-79351 ODONNELL
79353-79353 PEP
79355-79355 PLAINS
79356-79356 POST
79357-79357 RALLS
79358-79358 ROPESVILLE
79359-79359 SEAGRAVES
79360-79360 SEMINOLE
79363-79363 SHALLOWATER
79364-79364 SLATON
79366-79366 RANSOM CANYON
79367-79367 SMYER
79368-79368 SOUTHLAND
79369-79369 SPADE
79370-79370 SPUR
79371-79371 SUDAN
79372-79372 SUNDOWN
79373-79373 TAHOKA
79376-79376 TOKIO
79377-79377 WELCH
79378-79378 WELLMAN
79379-79379 WHITEFACE
79380-79380 WHITHARRAL
79381-79381 WILSON
79382-79382 WOLFFORTH
79383-79383 NEW HOME
79400-79464 LUBBOCK
79489-79489 REESE AIR FORCE BASE
79490-79499 LUBBOCK
79501-79501 ANSON
79502-79502 ASPERMONT
79503-79503 STAMFORD
79504-79504 BAIRD
79505-79505 BENJAMIN
79506-79506 BLACKWELL
79508-79508 BUFFALO GAP
79510-79510 CLYDE
79511-79511 COAHOMA
79512-79512 COLORADO CITY
79516-79516 DUNN
79517-79517 FLUVANNA
79518-79518 GIRARD
79519-79519 GOLDSBORO
79520-79520 HAMLIN
79521-79521 HASKELL
79525-79525 HAWLEY
79526-79526 HERMLEIGH
79527-79527 IRA
79528-79528 JAYTON
79529-79529 KNOX CITY
79530-79530 LAWN
79532-79532 LORAINE
79533-79533 LUEDERS
79534-79534 MC CAULLEY
79535-79535 MARYNEAL
79536-79536 MERKEL
79537-79537 NOLAN
79538-79538 NOVICE
79539-79539 O BRIEN
79540-79540 OLD GLORY
79541-79541 OVALO
79542-79542 PEACOCK
79543-79543 ROBY
79544-79544 ROCHESTER
79545-79545 ROSCOE
79546-79546 ROTAN
79547-79548 RULE
79549-79550 SNYDER
79553-79553 STAMFORD
79556-79556 SWEETWATER
79560-79560 SYLVESTER
79561-79561 TRENT
79562-79562 TUSCOLA
79563-79563 TYE
79565-79565 WESTBROOK
79566-79566 WINGATE
79567-79567 WINTERS
79600-79606 ABILENE
79607-79607 DYESS AFB
79608-79699 ABILENE
79701-79712 MIDLAND
79713-79713 ACKERLY
79714-79714 ANDREWS
79718-79718 BALMORHEA
79719-79719 BARSTOW
79720-79721 BIG SPRING
79730-79730 COYANOSA
79731-79731 CRANE
79733-79733 FORSAN
79734-79734 FORT DAVIS
79735-79735 FORT STOCKTON
79738-79738 GAIL
79739-79739 GARDEN CITY
79740-79740 GIRVIN
79741-79741 GOLDSMITH
79742-79742 GRANDFALLS
79743-79743 IMPERIAL
79744-79744 IRAAN
79745-79745 KERMIT
79748-79748 KNOTT
79749-79749 LENORAH
79752-79752 MC CAMEY
79754-79754 MENTONE
79755-79755 MIDKIFF
79756-79756 MONAHANS
79758-79758 GARDENDALE
79759-79759 NOTREES
79760-79769 ODESSA
79770-79770 ORLA
79772-79772 PECOS
79776-79776 PENWELL
79777-79777 PYOTE
79778-79778 RANKIN
79779-79779 ROYALTY
79780-79780 SARAGOSA
79781-79781 SHEFFIELD
79782-79782 STANTON
79783-79783 TARZAN
79785-79785 TOYAH
79786-79786 TOYAHVALE
79788-79788 WICKETT
79789-79789 WINK
79821-79821 ANTHONY
79830-79832 ALPINE
79834-79834 BIG BEND NATIONAL PARK
79835-79835 CANUTILLO
79836-79836 CLINT
79837-79837 DELL CITY
79838-79838 FABENS
79839-79839 FORT HANCOCK
79842-79842 MARATHON
79843-79843 MARFA
79845-79845 PRESIDIO
79846-79846 REDFORD
79847-79847 SALT FLAT
79848-79848 SANDERSON
79849-79849 SAN ELIZARIO
79850-79850 SHAFTER
79851-79851 SIERRA BLANCA
79852-79852 TERLINGUA
79853-79853 TORNILLO
79854-79854 VALENTINE
79855-79855 VAN HORN
79900-79999 EL PASO
88510-88595 EL PASO

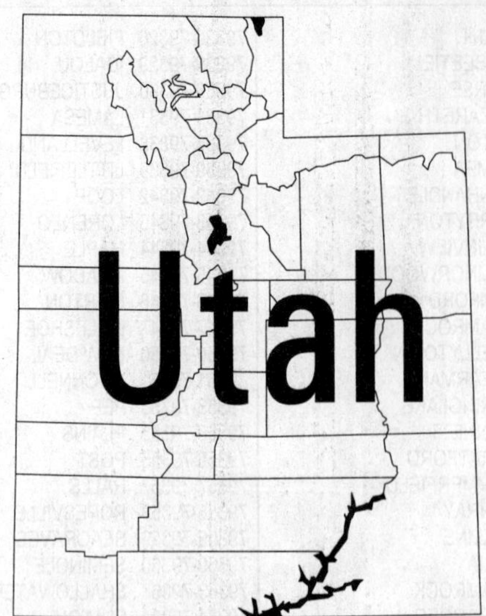

General Help Numbers:

Governor's Office

East Office Bldg. Suite220 — 801-538-1000
Salt Lake City, UT 84114 — Fax 801-538-1528
www.utah.gov/governor/index.html — 8AM-5PM

Attorney General's Office

East Office Bldg. Suite 320 — 801-538-9600
Salt Lake City, UT 84114 — Fax 801-538-1121
http://attorneygeneral.utah.gov — 8AM-5:30PM

State Court Administrator

Office of Legislative Research and General Counsel
W 210 State Capitol Complex — 801-538-1588
Salt Lake City, UT 84114 — Fax 801-538-1712
http://le.utah.gov — 8AM-5PM

State Archives

346 S Rio Grande — 801-538-3848
Salt Lake City, UT 84101 — Fax 801-538-3854
http://archives.utah.gov/index.html — 8AM-5PM

State Specifics:

Capital:	Salt Lake City Salt Lake County
Time Zone:	MST
Number of Counties:	29
Population:	2,736,424
Web Site:	www.utah.gov/

State Agencies

Criminal Records

Access to Records is Restricted.

Bureau of Criminal Identification, Records Supervisor, Box 148280, Salt Lake City, UT 84114-8280 (Courier address- 3888 West 5400 South, Salt Lake City, UT 84118); 801-965-4555, Fax- 801-965-4749; 7AM-6PM M,T,W,TH only.

http://publicsafety.utah.gov/bci/

Employers not identified by state statute cannot request records, even with notarized release from prospective employee. Records are not open to the public nor to employers not identified by statute signature This agency recommends the subject state in request for the report to be sent directly to the employer or third party. Include name, DOB, SSN, driver's license number, notarized signature of subject, fingerprints.

Statewide Court Records

Court Administrator, PO Box 140241, Salt Lake City, UT 84114-0241 (Courier address- 450 S State, Salt Lake City, UT 84114); 801-578-3800, Fax- 801-578-3859; 8AM-5PM.

www.utcourts.gov

Indexing & Storage: Records available for many district court locations since late 1980's, smaller courts from mid 1990's. Complete, consistent data is available for all district court locations since 1998. New records available for inquiry in seconds.

Searching: Include in request- full name, DOB, specific counties or geographic area to search. The SSN is optional.

Online search: Case information from all Utah District Court locations and 43 Justice Courts is available through Xchange, the other 91 Justice Courts do not participate. Note that Justice courts oversee B and C misdemeanors, infractions and small claims cases. Fees include $25.00 registration and $30.00 per month which includes 200 searches. Each additional search is billed at $.10 per search. Information about XChange and the subscription agreement is found at www.utcourts.gov/records/. One can search for supreme or appellate opinions at the website.

Sexual Offender Registry

Sex Offenders Registration Program, 14717 S Minuteman Dr, Draper, UT 84020; 801-495-7700; 8AM-5PM.

http://corrections.utah.gov/asp-bin/sonar.asp

Utah Code § 77-27-21.5 requires the Utah Dept. of Corrections to operate, and maintain a registry of persons who have been convicted of certain sex offenses. The offenses are listed within the subsections.

Indexing & Storage: New records available for inquiry in 60 days after sentencing.

Searching: Email questions to registry@utah.gov. Include in request- name, DOB or SSN, requester name address and phone number.

Access by: mail, phone, in person, online.

Mail search: Turnaround time- 20 days. Records are searchable by petitioner submitting name and phone number, then search by ZIP Code, or by name and an identifier (such as DOB, SSN, etc.)

Phone search: Searches may be requested by phone, but results are mailed.

In person: They will respond by mail only.

Online search: The Registry may be searched from the web page. Records are searchable by name, ZIP Code, or name and ZIP Code. The information released includes photos, descriptions, addresses, vehicles, offenses, and targets.

Incarceration Records

Utah Department of Corrections, Records Bureau, 14717 Minuteman Dr, Draper, UT 84020; 801-545-5500, 877-884-8463 (Phone Service- vendor), Fax- 801-545-5702; 8AM-4PM.

www.cr.ex.state.ut.us

The Utah Most Wanted List is found at www.cr.ex.state.ut.us/community/mostwanted/index.html.

Indexing & Storage: Records available on current and former inmates. New records available for inquiry in 1 to 20 days.

Searching: Direct questions to corrections@utah.gov. Include in request- full name and DOB. The SSN and inmate number are helpful. Location, conviction and sentencing information, and release dates are provided. This data not released- SSN, DOB and specific prison housing location.

Access by: mail, phone, fax, online.

Fee & Payment: There is a $.25 fee per copy. Fee payee- Utah State Prison Personal checks accepted if amount in excess of $50.

Mail search: Turnaround time- 7 to 10 days. A SASE is requested.

Phone search: The agency outsources to a private company; see toll free line listed above. This service provides custody status and release dates and offers notification if an inmate is released or moved.

Fax search: Searching by fax is permitted.

Online search: Access free at www.cr.ex.state.ut.us/contentservices/offendersearch.asp. The site includes information on only current inmates; historical data is not available.

Other access: Records are released in bulk on tape or CD. Call 801-545-5625 for details.

Corporation, LLC, LP, Fictitious/Assumed Name, Trademarks/Servicemarks

Commerce Department, Corporate Division, PO Box 146705, Salt Lake City, UT 84114-6705 (Courier address- 160 E 300 S, 2nd fl, Salt Lake City, UT 84111); 801-530-4849 (Call Center), Fax- 801-530-6438; 8AM-5PM.

www.corporations.utah.gov/

Indexing & Storage: Records available for active entities only. New records available for inquiry in 5-10 days.

Searching: Include in request- full name of business. In addition to the articles of organization, business entity records available include: Annual Reports, Officers, Directors, DBAs, Prior (merged) names and Reserved names.

Access by: mail, phone, fax, in person, online.

Fee & Payment: Search fee is $12.00. Certification is $12.00. Copies are $.30 per page, no charge if under 10 copies. Fax transmittals are $5.00 for the first page and $1.00 each page after. Fee payee- State of Utah. Prepayment required. Personal checks and major credit cards accepted.

Mail search: Turnaround time- 5-10 days. A SASE is requested.

Phone search: Copies cost $.30 per page. They will answer questions on name availability, status, agent and officer information.

Fax search: Turnaround time is 5-10 days. There is an additional fee of $5.00 for the first page and $1.00 for each add'l.

In person: However, usually turnaround time is 5-10 days unless expedited fee paid.

Online search: A business entity/principle search service is available at www.utah.gov/services/business.html?type=citizen. Also search available names. Basic information (name, address, agent) is free. Detailed data is available for minimal fees, but registration is required. The website also offers an Unclaimed Property search page. Also, search securities professions database free at www.securities.utah.gov/search.html.

Other access: State allows e-mail access for orders of Certification of Existence at orders@br.state.ut.us.

Expedited service: Expedited service is available. Turnaround time- 24-48 hours. Add $75.00 per business name.

Uniform Commercial Code

Department of Commerce, UCC Division, Box 146705, Salt Lake City, UT 84114-6705 (Courier address- 160 E 300 South, Heber M Wells Bldg, 2nd Fl, Salt Lake City, UT 84111); 801-530-4849 x4, 877-526-3994 (In State), Fax- 801-530-6438; 8AM-5PM.

http://corporations.utah.gov/

The phone number above is the "only way in" and caller can experience 5-30 minute waits. Suggest faxing or email questions to corpucc@utah.gov

Indexing & Storage: Records available from 1965. Records are computerized since 1995. New records available for inquiry in 24 hours or less.

Searching: Use search request form UCC-11 (can be downloaded from web). All tax liens are filed at the county level. Include in request- file number(s) and/or debtor name(s), name and address of requesting party, and daytime phone number. Check out the search instructions page at http://corporations.utah.gov/pdf/ra9_search_instructions.pdf.

Access by: mail, fax, in person, online.

Fee & Payment: For a certified search, the fee is $12.00 per file number or name certified plus copies are $.30 per page. For uncertified searches, the fee is only $.30 per page. There is no fee if under 10 specified copies. Fee payee- State of Utah. Prepayment required. Personal checks accepted. Major credit cards accepted for online system.

Mail search: Turnaround time- 10 working days. A SASE is requested.

Fax search: Same fees and turnaround time as mail search apply. They will invoice.

In person: Counter service is available.

Online search: UCC uncertified records are available free online at https://secure.utah.gov/uccsearch/uccs. Search by debtor individual name or organization, or by filing number. Certified searches may also be ordered for $12.00 per search. To receive certified searches, you may be a registered user or use a credit card. The website gives details. Note for subscribers there is a $70 annual registration fee which includes 10 user logins. Email requests are accepted at orders@br.state.ut.us.

Other access: Records are available on CD-ROM. Suggest writing or faxing.

Expedited service: Expedited service is available for mail and phone searches. Add $75.00 per name. Turnaround time is 24 hours.

Federal & State Tax Liens

Records not maintained by a state level agency.

Records are found at the local level.

Sales Tax Registrations

Taxpayer Services, Technical Research, 210 N 1950 W, Salt Lake City, UT 84134; 801-297-2200, Fax- 801-297-7697; 8AM-5PM.

http://tax.utah.gov/

Records are not accessible by the public; access is limited to the owner(s) of the account(s) or by power of attorney. General forms and tax law information can be downloaded from the website.

Indexing & Storage: Records available for 15 years for business records, for 10 years for individual records. New records available for inquiry in 30 days.

Searching: Requester must have written consent. This agency will only confirm that a business is registered and active if a tax permit number is provided. They will provide no other information. Include in request- use of Form TC880 if a specific record is requested.

Access by: mail, in person.

Fee & Payment: Copies are $6.50 per record. Fee payee- Utah Tax Commission. Prepayment required. Personal checks accepted, credit cards are not.

Mail search: Turnaround time- 1 to 2 weeks. SASE not required. Must use the required form.

In person: Must use the required form. Turnaround time is 24 hours.

Birth Certificates

Department of Health, Office of Vital Records & Statistics, Box 141012, Salt Lake City, UT 84114-1012 (Courier address- 288 N 1460 W, Salt Lake City, UT 84114); 801-538-6105 (This Agency), 801-538-6380 (VitalChek), Fax- 801-538-9467; 9AM-5PM M-TH (walk-in counter closes at 4:30 PM).

http://health.utah.gov/vitalrecords/

Must have a signed release from person of record or immediate family member.

Indexing & Storage: Records available from 1905 on. Index computer files go back to 1978. Indexes are not available to the public. New records available for inquiry in 1-2 weeks.

Searching: At the website you can download an application or order online from the state. The expedited service described below is for faster service via a vendor; www.vitalchek.com. Include in request- full name, names of parents, mother's maiden name, date of birth, place of birth, relationship to person of record, reason for information request, and photo ID of requester. Be sure to sign the request and include a daytime phone number. You may phone, fax or email to request an application form. This data not released- medical records.

Access by: mail, fax, in person, online.

Fee & Payment: Search fee is $15.00. Add $8.00 per name for second copies. Fee payee- Vital Records. Prepayment required. Personal checks and major credit cards accepted.

Mail search: Turnaround time- 2 to 3 weeks. SASE not required.

Fax search: See expedited service.

In person: Turnaround time 30-40 minutes.

Online search: Orders can be placed via a state designated vendor. Go to www.vitalchek.com. Extra fees are involved. See expedited service.

Expedited service: Expedited service is available for mail, phone and fax searches, via www.vitalchek.com. Turnaround time- overnight delivery. Check the vendor web page for fees. Extra fees are incurred for use of credit card, expedited service and priority shipping if requested.

Death Records

Department of Health, Office of Vital Records & Statistics, Box 141012, Salt Lake City, UT 84114-1012 (Courier address- 288 N 1460 W, Salt Lake City, UT 84114); 801-538-6105 (This Agency), 801-538-6380 (VitalChek), Fax- 801-538-9467; 9AM-5PM M-TH (walk-in counter closes at 4:30 PM).

http://health.utah.gov/vitalrecords/

Certificates can be obtained by an immediate family member or with written permission from the immediate family.

Indexing & Storage: Records available from 1905 on. Index computer files go back since 1978. Indexes are not available to the public. New records available for inquiry in 1-2 weeks.

Searching: At the website you can download an application or order online from the state. The Expedited Service described below is for faster service via a vendor; www.vitalchek.com. Include in request- full name, date of death, place of death, relationship to person of record, reason for information request. If you do not know the date of death, include last known date alive. You may phone, fax or email to request an application form.

Access by: mail, fax, in person, online.

Fee & Payment: Search fee is $13.00, add $8.00 for each additional copy. Fee payee- Vital Records. Prepayment required. Personal checks and major credit cards accepted.

Mail search: Turnaround time- 2 weeks. SASE not required.

Fax search: See expedited service.

In person: Turnaround time 30-40 minutes.

Online search: Utah's Death Certificate index search is found at http://archives.utah.gov/research/indexes/20842.htm. Orders can be placed via a state designated vendor. Go to www.vitalchek.com. Extra fees are involved. See expedited service.

Other access: Search the state's Cemetery and Burials database for free at http://history.utah.gov/apps/burials/execute/searchburials.

Expedited service: Expedited service is available for mail, phone and fax searches, via www.vitalchek.com. Turnaround time- overnight delivery. Check the vendor web page for fees. Extra fees are incurred for use of credit card, expedited service and priority shipping if requested.

Marriage Certificates

Department of Health, Office of Vital Records & Statistics, Box 141012, Salt Lake City, UT 84114-1012 (Courier address- 288 N 1460 W, Salt Lake City, UT 84114); 801-535-6105 (This Agency), 801-538-6380 (VitalChek), Fax- 801-538-9467; 9AM-5PM M-TH (walk-in counter closes at 4:30 PM).

http://health.utah.gov/vitalrecords/

Certification of marriage occurring in Utah from 1978 through 2001 are issued in this office. Requests for certified copies of marriage prior to 1978 are issued by the county where the marriage license was obtained.

Indexing & Storage: New records available for inquiry in up to 1 year.

Searching: Records are certification summaries and not copies of the original records. Download an application at the Forms link on the website navigation bar. Mail or bring the application to the Service Window in-person, or you may write a letter. Include in request- date & place of occurrence, groom's name, bride's maiden name. One may phone, fax or email to request an application form.

Access by: mail, in person, online.

Fee & Payment: $9.00 is for the abstract certificate. Fee payee- Vital Records. Prepayment required Personal checks accepted Major credit cards accepted.

Mail search: Turnaround time- 2-3 weeks.

In person: Turn in your order form for a certificate before 4:30 p.m., and wait while it is processed. Requests received at the counter after 4:30 p.m. are processed the following day.

Online search: Orders can be placed via a state designated vendor. Go to www.vitalchek.com. Extra fees are involved.

Expedited service: Expedited service is available for mail, phone and fax searches, via www.vitalchek.com. Turnaround time- same day service. Check the vendor web page for fees. Extra fees are incurred for use of credit card, expedited service and priority shipping if requested.

Divorce Records

Department of Health, Office of Vital Records & Statistics, Box 141012, Salt Lake City, UT 84114-1012 (Courier address- 288 N 1460 W, Salt Lake City, UT 84114); 801-538-6101 (This Agency), 801-538-6380 (VitalChek), Fax- 801-538-9467; 9AM-5PM M-TH (walk-in counter closes at 4:30 PM).

http://health.utah.gov/vitalrecords/

The offices releases certificates of abstract; actual records at county. Copies can only be obtained from the state by an immediate family member or with written permission from the immediate family.

Indexing & Storage: Records available from 1978 forward. Requests for certified copies of divorce prior to 1978 are issued by the county where the divorce occurred. New records available for inquiry in up to 1 year.

Searching: Records are certification summaries and not copies of the original records. Download an application at the Forms link on the website navigation bar. Mail or bring the application to the Service Window in-person, or you may write a letter. Include in request- date and place of occurrence, date and place of marriage, husband's name, wife's name. One may phone or fax to request an application form.

Access by: mail, in person, online.

Fee & Payment: $13.00 for an abstract only. Fee payee- Vital Records. Prepayment required Personal checks accepted Credit cards accepted: Visa/MC/Discover/AmEx.

Mail search: Turnaround time- 2-3 weeks.

In person: Turn in your order form for a certificate before 4:30 p.m., and wait while it is processed the same day.

Online search: Orders can be placed via a state designated vendor. Go to www.vitalchek.com. Extra fees are involved.

Expedited service: Expedited service is available for mail, phone and fax searches, via www.vitalchek.com. Turnaround time- 1-2 days. Check the vendor web page for fees. Extra fees are incurred for use of credit card, expedited service and priority shipping if requested.

Workers' Compensation Records

Labor Commission, Division of Industrial Accidents, PO Box 146610, Salt Lake City, UT 84114-6610 (Courier address- 160 E 300 S, 3rd Floor, Salt Lake City, UT 84114); 801-530-6800, Fax- 801-530-6804; 7AM-6PM M-TH.

www.laborcommission.utah.gov

Indexing & Storage: Records available from 1970 to 1988 on microfiche, from 1989 to present on computer. New records available for inquiry in one week.

Searching: Must have a notarized release from claimant (not over 90 days old). If a conditional job has been offered, then include a statement of such with employer's name and signature. Include in request- SSN, date of birth, as well as release form. Phone or fax to request form.

Access by: mail, fax, in person.

Fee & Payment: The search fee is $15.00 per name, copies are $.50 per page. Fee payee- Division of Industrial Accidents. Prepayment required. Personal checks accepted, credit cards are not.

Mail search: Turnaround time- 2 to 3 days. Include requester's telephone number so they can call with the total charge, which must be paid before records are released. SASE not required.

Fax search: Prepayment is required.

In person: Same criteria as mail requests.

Driver Records

Department of Public Safety, Driver License Division, Customer Service Section, PO Box 144501, Salt Lake City, UT 84114-4501 (Courier address- 4501 South 2700 West, 3rd Floor South, Salt Lake City, UT 84119); 801-965-4437, Fax- 801-965-4496; 8AM-5PM.

http://publicsafety.utah.gov/dld/

Copies of tickets can be purchased for $5.00 per record.

Indexing & Storage: Records available for 3 years for moving violations, 10 years for DWIs and 3 years for suspensions (alcohol related suspensions are 10 years). Records on commercial drivers are kept for 10 years. New records available for inquiry in 2 weeks to 6 months.

Searching: Interstate speeding convictions less than 10 mph over are not shown. Accidents are reported only if driver had citation. Addresses removed from report to comply with DPPA. Requests must comply with DPPA permissible uses. Include in request- driver's full name and DOB and/or license number. This data not released- medical records.

Access by: mail, fax, in person, online.

Fee & Payment: The fee is $6.00 per record, $10.75 if certified and $9.00 if online. Fee payee- Department of Public Safety. Prepayment required. Personal checks and major credit cards accepted.

Mail search: Turnaround time- approx. 1 week. Will FedEx if requester has account or submits pre-paid envelope. A SASE is requested.

Fax search: Requests may be faxed, but results are returned by mail.

In person: Up to 10 requests can be processed immediately; any additional requests are available the next day. Driving records can be obtained at any one of 17 branch offices throughout the state.

Online search: Driving records are available to eligible organizations through the eUtah. The system is available 24 hours daily. The fee per driving record is $9.00. There is an annual $75.00 subscription fee which includes access for 10 users. For more information, visit the website at www.utah.gov/registration/.

Vehicle, Vessel Ownership & Registration

State Tax Commission, Motor Vehicle Records Section, 210 North 1950 West, Salt Lake City, UT 84134; 801-297-3507, Fax- 801-297-3570; 7AM-6PM M-Th. http://dmv.utah.gov

Note offices are closed on Fridays.

Indexing & Storage: Records available for 15 years. All boats 1985 or newer must be titled. All motors over 25 HP must be titled. All boats, except canoes, must be registered. New records available for inquiry in 2 weeks.

Searching: Access is not open to casual requesters without notarized consent of subject. Requesters should use Form TC-890. Include in request- vehicle ID or registration number or hull ID and other information as required by TC-890 form. The agency will not do a name check for the public. This data not released- medical records or SSNs.

Access by: mail, phone, fax, in person, online.

Fee & Payment: The current fee is $3.00 per record, $4.00 if by fax, and $6.50 for each microfilm record requested. State has established accounts for dealerships and financial institutions requesting lien-holder information. Fee payee- State Tax Commission. Prepayment required. Personal checks accepted, credit cards are not.

Mail search: Turnaround time- 5 - 7 days. Boat records can take as long as 1 week to process.

Phone search: Searching is available for pre-approved, established accounts.

Fax search: Results may be returned by fax at $4.00 per record, for pre-approved accounts only.

In person: Turnaround time while you wait for small amounts.

Online search: The "Title, Lien and Motor Vehicle Information Service (TLRIS) is offered to qualified requesters. There is a $75 annual fee PLUS one must be a subscriber to the online system at www.utah.gov/registration/. That fee is also $75 per year. The record fee is $2.00 per record accessed.

Other access: Bulk requests are available for approved entities. Submit all requests in writing.

Accident Reports

Driver's License Division, Accident Reports Section, PO Box 144501, Salt Lake City, UT 84130-0560 (Courier address- 4501 South 2700 West, 3rd Floor South, Salt Lake City, UT 84119); 801-965-4428, Fax- 801-964-4536; 8AM-5PM.

http://publicsafety.utah.gov/dld/

Indexing & Storage: Records available from ten years; 1995 to 2002 on microfilm and 2002 to present on optical imaging system and the UT Highway patrol system. New records available for inquiry in 2 weeks or more.

Searching: Records are restricted only to those involved or with an interest. Members of the news media received limited information. Include in request- full name, date of accident, location of accident, name of requestor and reason for request. Use of their form is strongly suggested. Request must be in writing. Call to have the request form faxed or mailed to you.

Access by: mail, fax, in person.

Fee & Payment: The fee is $5.00 per record. Fee payee- Department of Public Safety. Prepayment required. The state will allow ongoing requesters to pre-pay with an account. Personal checks accepted. Credit cards accepted if in person.

Mail search: Turnaround time- 2 weeks or more.

Fax search: Requests may be sent by fax, but results are returned by mail.

In person: Records will be mailed, or can be picked up if pre-paid.

Legislation Records

Utah Legislature, Office of Legislative Research and General Counsel, W210 State Capitol Complex, Salt Lake City, UT 84114; 801-538-1588 (Bill Room), 801-326-1600 (Library), Fax- 801-538-1712; 8AM-5PM. http://le.utah.gov

General Session convenes annually, 3rd Tuesday in January. Records available from 1990 forward online. Records archived back to 1896.

Voter Registration

Access to Records is Restricted.

Elections - Office of Lt Governor, PO Box 142325, State Capital, Ste 220, Salt Lake City, UT 84114-2325; 801-538-1041, 800-995-8683, Fax- 801-538-1133; 8AM-5PM.

http://elections.utah.gov

Individual record requests are referred to the county clerk offices. Records that have not been secured by the registrant are open to the public; however, the counties will not release the SSN or DL. The entire state voter registration database (current records only) can be purchased from this office for $1,050. The website contains financial disclosures for political parties, action committees, lobbyists, corporations and political issue committees.

GED Certificates

Utah State Office of Education, GED Testing Records, PO Box 144200, Salt Lake City, UT 84114-4200; 801-538-7921, Fax- 801-538-7868; 8AM-4PM.

www.usoe.k12.ut.us/adulted/ged/index.html

Records prior to 1990 may be at the testing sites in hard copy. Storage depends on the site. Testing sites may have fees to verify or release records.

Indexing & Storage: Records available from 1970 to present. New records available for inquiry in 7 to 10 days.

Searching: The agency would rather fax than mail responses. Include in request- SSN, signed release, DOB, name at time of testing, current name if different, name and phone number of the requester. The date/year of test and city of test. The year is especially helpful for records prior to 1991.

Access by: mail, fax.

Fee & Payment: There is no fee for verification.

Mail search: Turnaround time- 7 to 10 days. SASE not required.

Fax search: Same criteria as mail searching.

Hunting & Fishing License Information

Utah Division of Wildlife Resources, PO Box 146301, Salt Lake City, UT 84114-6301 (Courier address- 1594 West North Temple, #2110, Salt Lake City, UT 84116); 801-538-4700, 877-592-5169, Fax- 801-538-4709; 7AM-6PM M-TH.

http://wildlife.utah.gov/index.php

Records available for the current year plus the 3 previous years are kept on computer.

Utah State Licensing Agencies

For details about the agency responsible for licensing/certifying/registering an item below or in the Agency Quick Finder section, match an item's number with the number of the agency in the *Licensing Agency Information* section.

Utah Licenses Searchable Online

Acupuncturist #5 ... https://secure.utah.gov/llv/llv
ADRP/Arbitrator/Negotiator #5 ... https://secure.utah.gov/llv/llv
Architect #5 ... https://secure.utah.gov/llv/llv
Athletic Agent #5 ... https://secure.utah.gov/llv/llv
Attorney #9 ... www.utahbar.org/forms/members_directory_search.html
Bank #10 ... www.dfi.utah.gov/Banks.htm
Building Inspector, Combo or Ltd #5 ... https://secure.utah.gov/llv/llv
Burglar Alarm Firm/Agent/Temp #5 ... https://secure.utah.gov/llv/llv
Check Cashier/Payday Lender #10 ... www.dfi.utah.gov/ckcash.htm
Chiropractic Physician/or/Temp. #5 ... https://secure.utah.gov/llv/llv
Consumer Lender #10 ... www.dfi.utah.gov/consumer.htm
Contractor-All #5 ... https://secure.utah.gov/llv/llv
Control'd Subst. Precurs'r Dist/Prch #5 ... https://secure.utah.gov/llv/llv
Cosmetologist/Barber #5 ... https://secure.utah.gov/llv/llv
Cosmetology/Barber School/Instruct #5 ... https://secure.utah.gov/llv/llv
Counselor, Professional #5 ... https://secure.utah.gov/llv/llv
Counselor, Tranie/Intern #5 ... https://secure.utah.gov/llv/llv
Court Reporter, Shorthand/Voice #5 ... https://secure.utah.gov/llv/llv
CPA/Firm #5 ... https://secure.utah.gov/llv/llv
Credit Union #10 ... www.dfi.utah.gov/CreditUn.htm
Deception Detection Examiner/Intern #5 ... https://secure.utah.gov/llv/llv
Dental Hygienist/Local Anesthesia #5 ... https://secure.utah.gov/llv/llv
Dentist w/ Anesthesia Class I-IV #5 ... https://secure.utah.gov/llv/llv
Dentist/or/Dental Hygienist #5 ... https://secure.utah.gov/llv/llv
Dietitian, Certified or Temporary #5 ... https://secure.utah.gov/llv/llv
Electrician, Appren./Journey'n/Master #5 ... https://secure.utah.gov/llv/llv
Electrician, Resid'l/Journeym'n/Master #5 ... https://secure.utah.gov/llv/llv
Electrologist Instructor/School #5 ... https://secure.utah.gov/llv/llv
Engineer, Structural Professional #5 ... https://secure.utah.gov/llv/llv
Engineer/Land Surveyor #5 ... https://secure.utah.gov/llv/llv
Enviro'l Health Scientist/or/in-training #5 ... https://secure.utah.gov/llv/llv
Escrow Agent #10 ... www.dfi.utah.gov/escrow.htm
Esthetician Master/Instructor/School #5 ... https://secure.utah.gov/llv/llv
Factory Built Housing Dealer #5 ... https://secure.utah.gov/llv/llv
Funeral Service Director/Apprentice #5 ... https://secure.utah.gov/llv/llv
Funeral Service Establishment #5 ... https://secure.utah.gov/llv/llv
Genetic Counselor/Temp Counselor #5 ... https://secure.utah.gov/llv/llv
Geologist #5 ... https://secure.utah.gov/llv/llv
Health Facility Administrator/Temp #5 ... https://secure.utah.gov/llv/llv
Hearing Instrument Specialist/Intern #5 ... https://secure.utah.gov/llv/llv
Holding Company #10 ... www.dfi.utah.gov/HCSList.htm
Industrial Banks #10 ... www.dfi.utah.gov/industbk.htm
Insurance Agent #8 ... https://secure.utah.gov/cas/search?page=index
Insurance Establishment #8 ... https://secure.utah.gov/cas/search?page=index
Landscape Architect #5 ... https://secure.utah.gov/llv/llv
Liquor License #1 ... http://javaweb.abc.state.ut.us/NASApp/orderweb/LLoginJsp.jsp
Liquor Store (Retail Liquor License) #1 ... www.abc.utah.gov/license_permit/licensee_list.pdf
Lobbyist/Lobbyist Report #12 ... https://secure.utah.gov/lobbyist/lobbysearch
Marriage/Family Therapist/Temporary #5 ... https://secure.utah.gov/llv/llv
Massage Therapist/Apprentice #5 ... https://secure.utah.gov/llv/llv
Mortgage Broker, Residential #2 ... http://realestate.utah.gov/database/index.html
Mortgage Loan Service #10 ... www.dfi.utah.gov/mortgage.htm
Nail Technician/Instructor/School #5 ... https://secure.utah.gov/llv/llv
Naturopath #5 ... https://secure.utah.gov/llv/llv
Naturopathic Physician #5 ... https://secure.utah.gov/llv/llv
Nurse Midwife, Certified #5 ... https://secure.utah.gov/llv/llv
Nurse, Controlled Substance #5 ... https://secure.utah.gov/llv/llv

Nurse, LPN/RN/Practical #5	https://secure.utah.gov/llv/llv
Nurse/APRN/Cont'd Substance/Intern #5	https://secure.utah.gov/llv/llv
Nurse-LPN #5	https://secure.utah.gov/llv/llv
Occupational Therapist/Assist. Temp #5	https://secure.utah.gov/llv/llv
Optometrist/Cont'd Subst./Diagnostic #5	https://secure.utah.gov/llv/llv
Osteo. Phys'n/Surg'n/Cont'd Subst. #5	https://secure.utah.gov/llv/llv
Pesticide Dealer/Applicator #3	www.kellysolutions.com/UT/pesticideindex.htm
Pharm. E -Control'd substance license #5	https://secure.utah.gov/llv/llv
Pharmac't/Intern/Tech./Contr'd Subst. #5	https://secure.utah.gov/llv/llv
Pharmacy Class A/Retail #5	https://secure.utah.gov/llv/llv
Pharmacy Class B Facility/Clinic #5	https://secure.utah.gov/llv/llv
Pharmacy Class C/Mfgtr/Whlse/Distr. #5	https://secure.utah.gov/llv/llv
Pharmacy Class D/Mail Order #5	https://secure.utah.gov/llv/llv
Pharmacy Class E - Lab/Med'l Gases #5	https://secure.utah.gov/llv/llv
Physical Therapist #5	https://secure.utah.gov/llv/llv
Physician Assistant #5	https://secure.utah.gov/llv/llv
Physician/Surgeon, Cont'd Substance #5	https://secure.utah.gov/llv/llv
Plumber Apprentice/Journeyman #5	https://secure.utah.gov/llv/llv
Podiatric Physic'n/Control'd Substance #5	https://secure.utah.gov/llv/llv
Political Candidate #12	http://elections.utah.gov/candidates.html
Pre-Need Provider/Sales Agent #5	https://secure.utah.gov/llv/llv
Probation Provider, Private #5	https://secure.utah.gov/llv/llv
Psychologist/Resident/Temporary #5	https://secure.utah.gov/llv/llv
Radiology Practical Technician #5	https://secure.utah.gov/llv/llv
Radiology Technologist/or/Temp #5	https://secure.utah.gov/llv/llv
Real Estate Agent/Broker/Company #2	http://realestate.utah.gov/database/index.html
Real Estate Appraiser #2	http://realestate.utah.gov/database/index.html
Recreational Therapist/master/Spec'l'st #5	https://secure.utah.gov/llv/llv
Respiratory Care Practitioner #5	https://secure.utah.gov/llv/llv
Savings & Loan #10	www.dfi.utah.gov/sls.htm
Security Company/Officer, Private #5	https://secure.utah.gov/llv/llv
Social Worker-Clinical/Certified #5	https://secure.utah.gov/llv/llv
Speech Pathologist/Audiologist #5	https://secure.utah.gov/llv/llv
Substance Abuse Counselor/Temp #5	https://secure.utah.gov/llv/llv
Third Party Payment Issuer #10	www.dfi.utah.gov/montrans.htm
Title Lender #10	www.dfi.utah.gov/titlelen.htm
Trust Company #10	www.dfi.utah.gov/trslist.htm
Veterinarian/Vet Intern/cont'l subst. #5	https://secure.utah.gov/llv/llv
Wine Store #1	www.alcbev.state.ut.us/Stores/wine_stores.html

Utah Licensing Quick Finder

Acupuncturist #5	801-530-6628
ADRP/Arbitrator/Negotiator #5	801-530-6628
Architect #5	801-530-6628
Athletic Agent #5	801-530-6628
Attorney #9	801-531-9077
Bank #10	801-538-8835
Bedding/Upholst'y Mfg/Whls/Dealer #3	801-538-7151
Beekeeper #3	801-538-7184
Brand Inspector #3	801-538-7137
Building Inspector, Combo or Ltd #5	801-530-6628
Burglar Alarm Firm/Agent/Temp #5	801-530-6964
Check Cashier/Payday Lender #10	801-538-8842
Chiropractic Physician/or/Temp. #5	801-530-6628
Consumer Lender #10	801-538-8830
Contractor-All #5	801-530-6628
Control'd Substance Precurs'r Dist/Purch'r #5	801-530-6964
Cosmetologist/Barber #5	801-530-6628
Cosmetology/Barber School/Instruct #5	801-530-6628
Counselor, Professional #5	801-530-6628
Counselor, Tranie/Intern #5	801-530-6628
Court Reporter, Shorthand/Voice #5	801-530-6628
CPA/Firm #5	801-530-6628
Credit Union #10	801-538-8840
Deception Detection Examiner/Intern #5	801-530-6628
Dental Hygienist/Local Anesthesia #5	801-530-6628
Dentist w/ Anesthesia Class I-IV #5	801-530-6628
Dentist/or/Dental Hygienist #5	801-530-6628
Dietitian, Certified or Temporary #5	801-530-6628
Egg & Poultry Inspector #3	801-538-7124
Electrician, Appren./Journey'n/Master #5	801-530-6628
Electrician, Resid'l/Journeym'n/Master #5	801-530-6628
Electrologist Instructor/School #5	801-530-6628
Engineer, Structural Professional #5	801-530-6628
Engineer/Land Surveyor #5	801-530-6628
Enviro'l Health Scientist/or/in-training #5	801-530-6628
Escrow Agent #10	801-538-8842
Esthetician Master/Instructor/School #5	801-530-6628
Factory Built Housing Dealer #5	801-530-6628
Feed #3	801-538-7183
Food & Dairy Inspector #3	801-538-7145
Funeral Service Director/Apprentice #5	801-530-6628
Funeral Service Establishment #5	801-530-6628
Genetic Counselor/Temp Counselor #5	801-530-6628
Geologist #5	801-530-6628
Grain & Seed #3	801-538-7183
Health Facility Administrator/Temp #5	801-530-6628
Hearing Instrument Specialist/Intern #5	801-530-6628
Holding Company #10	801-538-8842
Industrial Banks #10	801-538-8841
Insurance Agent #8	801-538-3805
Insurance Establishment #8	801-538-3805
Interpreter for the Deaf #7	801-263-4860
Landscape Architect #5	801-530-6628
Liquor License #1	801-977-6800
Liquor Store (Retail Liquor License) #1	801-977-6800
Lobbyist/Lobbyist Report #12	801-538-1041
Marriage/Family Therapist/or/Temp. #5	801-530-6628
Massage Therapist/Apprentice #5	801-530-6628
Meat Inspector #3	801-538-7161
Mortgage Broker, Residential #2	801-530-6747
Mortgage Loan Service #10	801-538-8830
Nail Technician/Instructor/School #5	801-530-6628
Naturopath #5	801-530-6628
Naturopathic Physician #5	801-530-6628

Notary Public #4 ....801-538-1180 x4
Nurse Midwife, Certified #5 801-530-6628
Nurse, Controlled Substance #5 801-530-6628
Nurse, LPN/RN/Practical #5..................801-530-6628
Nurse/APRN/Cont'd Substance/Intern #5801-530-6628
Nurse-LPN #5..801-530-6628
Occupational Therapist/Asst. Temp #5 .801-530-6628
Optometrist/Cont'd Subst./Diagn'st'c#5. 801-530-6628
Osteo. Phys'n/Surg'n/Cont'd Substance #5 801-530-6628
Pesticide Dealer/Applicator #3 801-538-7188
Pharm. E -Control'd substance license #5 801-530-6628
Pharmac't/Intern/Tech./Contr'd Substance #5 801-530-6628
Pharmacy Class A/Retail #5.................801-530-6628
Pharmacy Class B Facility/Clinic #5......801-530-6628
Pharmacy Class C/Mfgtr/Whls/Distr. #5 801-530-6628
Physical Therapist #5...........................801-530-6628
Physician Assistant #5 801-530-6628
Physician/Surgeon, Con'd Subst'nce #5801-530-6628
Plumber Apprentice/Journeyman #5.... 801-530-6628
Podiatric Physic'n/Control'd Substance #5 801-530-6628
Political Candidate #12.........................801-538-1041
Polygraph Examiner #11 801-965-4484
Pre-Need Provider/Sales Agent #5......801-530-6628
Probation Provider, Private #5 801-530-6628
Psychologist/Resident/Temporary #5 .. 801-530-6628
Radiology Practical Technician #5.......801-530-6628
Radiology Technologist/or/Temp #5 801-530-6628
Real Estate Agent/Broker/Firm #2 801-530-6747
Real Estate Appraiser #2 801-530-6747
Recreational Therapist/master/Spec'l'st #5 801-530-6628
Respiratory Care Practitioner #5..........801-530-6628
Savings & Loan #10 801-538-8842
School Administrator #6.......................801-538-7740
School Librarian #6 801-538-7740
Security Company/Officer, Private #5.. 801-530-6628
Social Worker-Clinical/Certified #5 801-530-6628
Speech Pathologist/Audiologist #5 801-530-6628
Substance Abuse Counselor/Temp #5 801-530-6628
Teacher #6 801-538-7740
Third Party Payment Issuer #10 801-538-8842
Title Lender #10 801-538-8842
Trust Company #10...............................801-538-8842
Upholst'r/Upholstery Mfg/Whlse/Dealer #3 801-538-7151
Veterinarian/Vet Intern/cont'l substance #5 801-530-6628
Weights & Measures #3........................801-538-7158
Wine Store #1..801-977-6800

Utah Licensing Agency Information

#1 Alcoholic Beverage Control Department, 1625 S 900 W, Salt Lake City, UT 84130; 801-977-6800, Fax- 801-977-6888. www.alcbev.state.ut.us

#2 Commerce Department, Real Estate Division, PO Box 146711 (160 E 300 S, 2nd Fl), Salt Lake City, UT 84114-6711; 801-530-6747, Fax- 801-526-4387. Hours- 8AM-5PM. http://realestate.utah.gov Search data at- http://realestate.utah.gov/database/index.html

#3 Department of Agriculture and Food, Regulatory Services, PO Box 146500 (350 North Redwood Rd), Salt Lake City, UT 84114-6500; 801-538-7100, Fax- 801-538-7126. Hours- 8AM-5PM. http://ag.utah.gov/about.html

#4 Notary Public and Authentication Office, Office of the Lieutenant Governor, PO Box 142325, Notary Office, Ste 220, Salt Lake City, UT 84114; 801-538-1041, Fax- 801-538-1133. Hours- 9AM-4PM. http://notary.utah.gov

#5 Department of Commerce, Division of Occupational & Professional Licensing, PO Box 146741 (160 E 300 S, Heber M Wells Bldg), Salt Lake City, UT 84114-6741; 801-530-6628, Fax- 801-530-6511. Hours- 8AM-5PM. www.dopl.utah.gov Search data at- https://secure.utah.gov/llv/llv

#6 Educator Quality Services, Office of Education, PO Box 144200 (250 E 500 S), Salt Lake City, UT 84114-4200; 801-538-7740, Fax- 801-538-7973. www.usoe.k12.ut.us/cert/ Formerly Educator Licensing.

#7 Division of Services for the Deaf & Hard of Hearing, Interpreter Program, 5709 S 1500 W, Salt Lake City, UT 84123-5217; 801-263-4861, Fax- 801-263-4865. Hours- 8AM-5PM. www.deafservices.utah.gov/

#8 Insurance Department, PO Box 146901 (3110 State Office Bldg #3110), Salt Lake City, UT 84114-6901; 801-538-3800, Fax- 801-538-3829. www.insurance.utah.gov/index.html Search data at- https://secure.utah.gov/cas/search?page=index

#9 State Bar Association, 645 S 200 E, Salt Lake City, UT 84111; 801-531-9077, Fax- 801-531-0660. www.utahbar.org Search data at- www.utahbar.org/forms/members_directory_search.html

#10 Department of Financial Institutions, PO Box 146800, (324 S State St, #201), Salt Lake City, UT 84114-6800; 801-538-8830, Fax- 801-538-8894. Hours- 8AM-5PM. www.dfi.utah.gov

#11 Bureau of Regulatory Licensing, Department of Public Safety, 4501 S 2700 W, Salt Lake City, UT 84119; 801-965-4484.

#12 State Elections Office, Lieutenant Governor Office, PO Box 142325, (Utah State Capitol, Ste 220), Salt Lake City, UT 84114; 801-538-1041, Fax- 801-538-1133. 8AM-5PM. http://elections.utah.gov/stateelectionsoffice.html Search data at- https://secure.utah.gov/lobbyist/lobb.

Utah Federal Courts

County/Court Cross Reference

All counties report to Salt Lake City.

Standards for Federal Courts: Fees are standard unless noted in profile. Search fee is $26.00 per item (one party name or case number). Copy fee is $.50 per page. Certification fee is $9.00 per document, double for exemplification, if available. Most courts require prepayment. Mail requests should enclose a SASE unless otherwise noted. Before releasing records, all courts require prepayment, unless noted.

District courts index by defendant and plaintiff and by case number. Bankruptcy courts usually index by debtor and case number. While most courts now have their indexes on computer, many may still maintain index card files as well. Courts will archive closed case files at different times.

There are numerous public access programs available to online subscribers. Search the U.S. Party/Case Index to find party names and case numbers among all courts. Individual case data is provided on PACER. A search of CM/ECF provides copies of cases filed electronically. For details about PACER, the US Party/Case Index, and CM/ECF see the Appendix or go to http://pacer.psc.uscourts.gov or call 800-676-6856.

US District Court District of Utah

Utah Division Clerk's Office, Rm 150, 350 S Main St, Salt Lake City, UT 84101-2180, 801-524-6100; Fax- 801-526-1175. Hours-8:30AM-4:30PM. www.utd.uscourts.gov

Counties/Note: All counties in Utah. Though all cases are heard at Salt Lake, the district is divided into Northern and Central Divisions. Northern Division includes the counties of Box Elder, Cache, Rich, Davis, Morgan and Weber; Central Division includes all other counties.

Searches/Indexing: Include full name only in search request. Results do not include SSN or DOB. Will fax back documents for $.50 per page fee prepaid. New cases are in the index 1 day after filing date. Older records on microfiche. Case files sent to archives 3-4 years after closed.

Search Access: Limited info released via telephone. **Mail:** Search usually completed- 2-3 days. SASE not required. **Fax:** Fax search requests accepted. **In person:** 3 public terminals available. Self-serve copies $.15 each.

Payment: Pay by Visa/MC/AmEx/Discover, money order, cashier's or personal check. Payee: Clerk, US District Court.

E-Services: Document images available. PACER records go back to 7/1989. New records online immediately. ECF at https://ecf.utd.uscourts.gov. **Opinions Online:** https://ecf.utd.uscourts.gov/cgi-bin/opinions.pl. These are opinions over the past six months. For more opinions, search in PACER; registration and login required. **Online Note:** Calendars at www.utd.uscourts.gov/reports/cal.php.

US Bankruptcy Court District of Utah

Utah Division Clerk of Court, Frank E Moss Courthouse, 350 S Main St, Rm 301, Salt Lake City, UT 84101, 801-524-6687; Fax- 801-524-4409. Hours-8AM-4:30PM. www.utb.uscourts.gov

Counties/Note: All counties in Utah. Although all cases are handled at Salt Lake City, the court divides itself into 2 divisions. Northern Division includes counties of Box Elder, Cache, Rich, Davis, Morgan and Weber, and the Central Division includes the remaining counties. Court is held once a month in St. George for southern division. Court is no longer held in Ogden.

Searches/Indexing: Search request requires name only. Results include last 4 SSN digits only. Will not fax back documents. New cases are in the index as soon as workload permits after filing date.

Search Access: Only docket info is available by phone. Voice Case Information Service available, call VCIS at 800-733-6740 or 801-524-3107. **Mail:** Search usually completed- 1 week. Include SASE for return. **In person:** No self-serve copier. Imaged copies available.

Payment: Pay by credit cards, money order or cashier's check. No debtor checks or personal checks accepted. Payee: Clerk, US Bankruptcy Court.

E-Services: Document images available. PACER records go back to 1/1985. ECF at https://ecf.utb.uscourts.gov. **Opinions Online:** www.utb.uscourts.gov/slopinions.htm. **Online Note:** Calendars free at www.utb.uscourts.gov/. Also search recent filings.

Utah County Courts

Court	Jurisdiction	No. of Courts	How Organized
District Courts*	General	38	8 Districts
Justice Courts	Limited	134	Cities/ Counties
Juvenile Courts	Special		8 Districts

* Profiled in this Sourcebook.

Court	CIVIL Tort	Contract	Real Estate	Min. Claim	Max. Claim	Small Claims	Estate	Eviction	Domestic Relations
District Courts*	X	X	X	$0	No Max	$7500	X	X	X
Justice Courts	X	X		$0	$7500	$7500			
Juvenile Courts									

Court	CRIMINAL Felony	Misdemeanor	DWI/DUI	Preliminary Hearing	Juvenile
District Courts*	X	X	X	X	
Justice Courts		X	X		
Juvenile Courts					X

Administration

Court Administrator, 450 S State St, Salt Lake City, UT, 84114; 801-578-3800, Fax: 801-578-3859. (MST) www.utcourts.gov

Court Structure

41 District Courts are arranged in eight judicial districts. Branch courts in larger counties, such as Salt Lake, which were formerly Circuit Courts and now elevated to District Courts have full jurisdiction over felony as well as misdemeanor cases. Justice Courts are established by counties and municipalities and have the authority to deal with class B and C misdemeanors, violations of ordinances, small claims, and infractions committed within their territorial jurisdiction. The Justice Court shares jurisdiction with the Juvenile Court over minors 16 or 17 years old who are charged with certain traffic offenses– automobile homicide, alcohol or drug related traffic offenses, reckless driving, fleeing an officer, and driving on a suspended license are excepted. Those charges are handled through Juvenile Court.

Online Access

Case information from all Utah District Court locations and 43 Justice Courts is available online through Xchange. Since misdemeanor B's, C's, Infractions and Small Claims cases are often filed in Justice Courts, this information is not available statewide on this system. Fees include $25.00 registration and $30.00 per month which includes 200 searches. Each additional search is billed at $.10 per search. The search provides a summary of the docket index; case files and copies are not available. Information about Xchange, the subscription agreement, and a list of the participating 43 Justice Courts can be found at http://www.utcourts.gov/records or call 801-578-3850.

One may search for Supreme Court or Appellate Courts opinions at the main website.

Searching Tips, Fees, and Other Guidelines

Most District Courts charge $15.00 per hour to do a name search, some give the first 15-20 minutes free. Most courts charge $.25 for a copy and $4.00 for certification. The Salt Lake District Court has an automated information phone line that provides court appearance look-ups, outstanding fine balance look-ups, and judgment/divorce decree lookups. Call 801-238-7830.

Beaver County

5th Judicial District Court PO Box 1683, 2270 South 525 West, Beaver, UT 84713; 435-438-5309; fax: 435-438-5395; 8AM-5PM (MST). ***Felony, Misdemeanor, Civil, Eviction, Probate.***

Civil Records: Access: Fax, mail, in person, online. Both court and visitors may perform in person searches. Search fee: No fee for name search unless extensive, then $15.00 per hour fee. Required to search: name, years to search. Civil cases indexed by defendant, plaintiff; index on computer back to 1997. Mail turnaround time 2-7 days. Civil PAT goes back to 1997. Online access through Xchange, see www.utcourts.gov/records/. Also, see state introduction.

Criminal Records: Access: Fax, mail, in person, online. Both court and visitors may perform in person searches. Search fee: No fee for name search unless extensive, then $15.00 per hour fee. Required to search: name, years to search, DOB. Criminal records computerized from 1997. Mail turnaround time 2-7 days. Criminal PAT goes back to 1997. Online access through Xchange, see www.utcourts.gov/records/. Also, see state introduction.

General Information: No adoption, juvenile, sealed records released. Fee to fax out file $5.00 minimum, $.50 each page over 10. Court makes copy: $.25 per page. Certification fee: $4.00 plus $.50 per page includes copies. Payee: 5th District Court. Personal checks accepted. Visa/MC accepted. Prepayment required. Mail requests: SASE required or postage.

Box Elder County

1st District Court PO Box 873, 43 N Main St, Brigham City, UT 84302; 435-734-4600; fax: 435-734-4610; 8AM-5PM (MST). ***Felony, Misdemeanor, Civil, Eviction, Small Claims, Probate.***

Civil Records: Access: Phone, fax, mail, online, in person. Both court and visitors may perform in person searches. No search fee, but after 30 minutes a minimum $22 per hour fee applies. Required to search: name, years to search; helpful- case number. Civil cases indexed by defendant, plaintiff; index on computer from 3/87, books, microfiche, archived from 1856. Mail turnaround time 3-4 days Civil PAT goes back to 3/1987. PAT results show middle initial, DOB. Identifiers, particularly SSNs, do not appear on all records. Online access

through Xchange, see www.utcourts.gov/records/. Also, see state introduction.
Criminal Records: Access: Phone, fax, mail, online, in person. Both court and visitors may perform in person searches. No search fee, but after 30 minutes a minimum $22 per hour fee applies. Required to search: name, years to search; also helpful: DOB, SSN. Criminal records computerized from 3/87, books, microfiche, archived from 1856. Mail turnaround time 3-4 days. Criminal PAT goes back to same as civil. PAT results show middle initial, DOB. Identifiers do not show on all records. Online access through Xchange, see www.utcourts.gov/records/. Also, see state introduction.
General Information: No adoption, sealed records released. Fee to fax out file $5.00 up to 10 pages, then $.50 per add'l page. Court makes copy: $.25 per page. Certification fee: $4.00 plus $.50 per page; Exemplification fee- $6.00 plus $.50 per page. Payee: 1st District Court. Personal checks accepted. Visa/MC accepted. Prepayment required. Mail requests: SASE required.

Cache County

1st District Court 135 N 100 W, Logan, UT 84321; 435-750-1300; probate phone: same; fax: 435-750-1355; 8AM-5PM (MST). ***Felony, Misdemeanor, Civil, Eviction, Small Claims, Probate.***
Civil Records: Access: Phone, mail, online, in person. Both court and visitors may perform in person searches. Search fee: $15.00 per hour. Required to search: name, years to search. Civil cases indexed by defendant, plaintiff; index on computer from 11-87, archived from 1983, microfiche in Salt Lake City. Mail turnaround time 10 days. Civil PAT goes back to 1987. PAT results show middle initial, DOB. Online access through Xchange, see www.utcourts.gov/records/. Also see state introduction.
Criminal Records: Access: Phone, mail, online, in person. Both court and visitors may perform in person searches. Search fee: $15.00 per hour. Required to search: name, years to search; also helpful: DOB, SSN. Criminal records computerized from 11-87, archived from 1983, microfiche in Salt Lake City. Mail turnaround time 2 weeks. Criminal PAT goes back to same as civil. PAT results show middle initial, DOB. Online access through Xchange, see www.utcourts.gov/records/. Also see state introduction. Online results show middle initial, DOB.
General Information: No sealed records released. Fee to fax out file $5.00 for up to 10 pages. Court makes copy: $.25 per page. Certification fee: $4.00 plus $.50 per page. Payee: 1st Judicial District. Personal checks and credit cards accepted. Prepayment required. Mail requests: SASE required.

Carbon County

7th District Court 149 E 100 S, Price, UT 84501; 435-636-3400; fax: 435-637-7349; 8AM-5PM (MST). ***Felony, Misdemeanor, Civil, Eviction, Probate.***
http://utcourts.gov/directory/courthouse.cgi?county=4
Misdemeanor records are Class A.
Civil Records: Access: Phone, mail, online, in person. Both court and visitors may perform in person searches. Search fee: $15.00 per hour. Required to search: name, years to search. Civil cases indexed by defendant, plaintiff; index on computer from 1988, on microfiche from 1985, archived prior to 1988. Mail turnaround time 48 hours. Civil PAT goes back to 1987. Online access through Xchange, see www.utcourts.gov/records/. Also see state introduction.
Criminal Records: Access: Phone, mail, online, in person. Both court and visitors may perform in person searches. Search fee: $15.00 per hour. Required to search: name, years to search, DOB; also helpful: SSN. Criminal records computerized from 1988, on microfiche from 1985, archived prior to 1988. Mail turnaround time 48 hours. Criminal PAT goes back to same as civil. Online access through Xchange, see www.utcourts.gov/records/. Also see state introduction.
General Information: No sealed records released. Fee to fax out file $5.00 1st 10 pages, $.50 each add'l page. Court makes copy: $.25 per page. Certification fee: $4.00 plus $.50 per page includes copies. Payee: 7th District Court. Personal checks accepted. Visa/MC accepted. Prepayment required. Mail requests: SASE required.

Daggett County

8th District Court PO Box 219, 95 N 1st W, Manila, UT 84046; 435-784-3154; fax: 435-784-3335; 8AM-N, 1-5PM (MST). ***Felony, Misdemeanor, Civil, Eviction, Probate.***
Faxed in search requests require prior approval. Any phone search requests will only be on clerk's computer.
Civil Records: Access: Phone, fax, mail, in person, online. Both court and visitors may perform in person searches. Search fee: $15.00 per hour, 1st 15 minutes no charge. Required to search: name, years to search. Civil cases indexed by defendant, plaintiff. Civil records archived from 1918; on computer at least 5 years. Mail turnaround time 10 days. Online access through Xchange, see www.utcourts.gov/records/. Also see state introduction.
Criminal Records: Access: Fax, mail, in person, online. Both court and visitors may perform in person searches. Search fee: $15.00 per hour, 1st 15 minutes no charge. Required to search: name, years to search, DOB; signature and record request form required. Criminal records archived from 1918; on computer at least 5 years. Mail turnaround time 10 days. Online access through Xchange, see www.utcourts.gov/records/. Also see state introduction. Online results show name, DOB. Terminal results include SSN.
General Information: No sealed records released. Will fax back file $5.00 each up to 10 pages, $.50 per add'l page. Court makes copy: $.25 per page. Self serve: same. Certification fee: $4.00 per doc. Payee: Daggett County. Personal checks accepted; credit cards are not. Prepayment required. Mail requests: SASE required.

Davis County

2nd District Court PO Box 769, Farmington, UT 84025; 801-447-3800; fax: 801-447-3881; 8AM-5PM (MST). ***Felony, Civil, Probate.***
www.daviscountyutah.gov/justice_court/default.cfm
Probate fax is same as main fax number.
Civil Records: Access: Phone, mail, online, in person. Both court and visitors may perform in person searches. Search fee: $15.00 per hour. First 15 minutes no charge. Required to search: name, years to search. Civil cases indexed by defendant, plaintiff; index on computer back to 1982, prior on microfiche and archived to 1896. Mail turnaround time 2-3 days. Civil PAT goes back to 1982. PAT civil results show middle initial. Online access through Xchange, see www.utcourts.gov/records/. Also see state introduction.
Criminal Records: Access: Phone, mail, online, in person. Both court and visitors may perform in person searches. Search fee: $15.00 per hour. First 15 minutes no charge. Required to search: name, years to search, DOB; also helpful: SSN. Criminal records computerized from 1989, prior on microfiche and archived to 1896. Mail turnaround time 2-3 days. Criminal PAT goes back to 1990. PAT results show middle initial, DOB. Online access through Xchange, see www.utcourts.gov/records/. Also see state introduction. Online results show middle initial, DOB.
General Information: No adoption, criminal pre-sentence investigation records released. Will fax documents $5.00. Court makes copy: $.25 per page. Self serve: same. Certification fee: $4.00 per document plus $.50 per page. Payee: 2nd District Court. Personal checks accepted. Visa/MC accepted. Prepayment required. Mail requests: SASE required.

2nd District Court - Bountiful Dept. 805 S Main, Bountiful, UT 84010; 801-397-7008; criminal phone: 801-397-7007; civil phone: 801-397-7004; fax: 801-397-7010; 8AM-5PM (MST). ***Felony, Misdemeanor, Civil, Eviction, Small Claims, Probate.***
Small Claims x2; Traffic at x1.
Civil Records: Access: Phone, online, in person. Both court and visitors may perform in person searches. No search fee. Required to search: name, years to search; also helpful: address. Civil cases indexed by defendant, plaintiff; index on computer since 10/86. Civil PAT available. PAT results show name only. Online access through Xchange, see www.utcourts.gov/records/. Also see state introduction.
Criminal Records: Access: Phone, mail, online, in person. Both court and visitors may perform in person searches. No search fee. Required to search: name, years to search; helpful- DOB. Criminal records on computer since 10/86. Mail turnaround time 1 week. Criminal PAT available. PAT results show name only. Online access through Xchange, see www.utcourts.gov/records/. Also see state introduction.
General Information: Will fax documents $5.00 1st 10 pages, then $.25 each add'l page. Court makes copy: $.25 per page. Certification fee: $4.00 plus $.50 per page. Payee: Second District Court. Personal checks accepted. Visa/MC accepted. Prepayment required. Mail requests: SASE required.

2nd District Court - Layton Department 425 Wasatch Dr, Layton, UT 84041; 801-444-4300; fax: 801-546-8224; 8AM-5PM (MST). ***Misdemeanor, Civil, Eviction, Small Claims, Probate, Traffic.***
Civil Records: Access: Mail, in person, online. Visitors must perform in person searches themselves. No search fee, for first 20 minutes. Required to search: name, years to search. Civil cases indexed by defendant, plaintiff; index on computer from 1988, archived from start of court. Computer index alpha and case number, archives by alpha from 1982, prior to 1982 n. Civil PAT goes back to 1988. Online access through Xchange, see www.utcourts.gov/records/. Also see state introduction.
Criminal Records: Access: Mail, online, in person. Both court and visitors may perform in person searches. No search fee, for first 20 minutes. Required to search: name, years to search; also helpful: DOB, SSN. Criminal records computerized from 1988, archived from start of court. Computer index alpha and case number, archives by alpha from 1982, prior to 198. Mail turnaround time 1 day. Criminal PAT goes back to same as civil. Online access via Xchange, www.utcourts.gov/records/. Also see state introduction.
General Information: No confidential records, probation reports, sealed records released. Will fax documents $5.00 per page. Court makes copy: $.25 per page. Certification fee: $4.00 plus $.50 per add'l page includes copy fee. Payee: 2nd District Court. Personal checks accepted. Visa/MC accepted. Prepayment required. Mail requests: SASE requested.

Duchesne County

8th District Court PO Box 990, Duchesne, UT 84021; 435-738-2753; fax: 435-738-2754; 8AM-5PM (MST). ***Felony, Misdemeanor, Civil, Eviction, Small Claims, Probate.***
Probate fax is same as main fax number.
Civil Records: Access: Phone, mail, fax, online, in person. Both court and visitors may perform in person searches. Search fee: $15.00 per hour. First 15 minutes no charge. Required to search: name, years to search. Civil cases indexed by defendant, plaintiff; index on computer back to 6/1993, civil on microfiche back to 1912. Mail turnaround time 1-5 days. Civil PAT goes back to 6/1993. Online access through Xchange, see www.utcourts.gov/records/.
Criminal Records: Access: Phone, mail, fax, online, in person. Both court and visitors may perform in person searches. Search fee: $15.00 per hour. First 15 minutes no charge. Required to search: name, years to search. Criminal records computerized from 1993; index books back to 1912. Mail turnaround time 1-5 days. Criminal PAT goes back to same as civil. Criminal records access through Xchange. For information contact Jolene Cox 578-3831. Also, see state introduction.
General Information: No confidential records released. Fee to fax out file $5.00 for 10 pages or less;

$.50 each add'l over 10 pages. Court makes copy: $.25 per page. Certification fee: $4.00 per doc plus $.50 per page. Payee: 8th District Court. Personal checks and money orders accepted. Visa/MC accepted. Prepayment required. Mail requests: SASE required.

8th District Court - Roosevelt Dept. PO Box 1286, 255 S State St, Roosevelt, UT 84066; 435-722-0235; fax: 435-722-0236; 8AM-5PM (MST). ***Felony, Misdemeanor, Civil, Eviction, Probate.***

Civil Records: Access: Mail, fax, online, in person. Both court and visitors may perform in person searches. Search fee: $15.00 per hour, first 15 minutes no charge. Required to search: name, years to search. Civil cases indexed by defendant, plaintiff; index on computer since 1993. Mail turnaround time 2-5 days. Civil PAT goes back to 1991. Online access through Xchange, see www.utcourts.gov/records/. Also see state introduction.

Criminal Records: Access: Mail, fax, online, in person. Both court and visitors may perform in person searches. Search fee: $15.00 per hour, first 15 minutes no charge. Required to search: name, years to search; also helpful: DOB. Criminal records on computer since 1994. Mail turnaround time 2-5 days. Criminal PAT goes back to same as civil. Online access through Xchange, see www.utcourts.gov/records/. Also see state introduction.

General Information: No confidential, sealed, expunged or juvenile records released. Will fax documents $5.00 plus $.50 each add'l page. Court makes copy: $.25 per page. Certification fee: $4.00 plus $.50 per page includes copies. Payee: 8th District. Personal checks accepted. Visa/MC accepted. Prepayment required. Mail requests: SASE required.

Emery County

7th District Court PO Box 635, 1850 N 560 W, Castle Dale, UT 84513; 435-381-2619; fax: 435-381-5625; 8AM-5PM (MST). ***Felony, Misdemeanor, Civil, Eviction, Probate.***

Phone for hearing impaired is 800-992-0172.

Civil Records: Access: Phone, fax, mail, in person, online. Both court and visitors may perform in person searches. Search fee: $15.00 per hour; first 20 minutes no charge. Required to search: name, years to search. Civil cases indexed by defendant, plaintiff; index on computer from 1997, older on microfilm and archived. Mail turnaround time 1 week. Civil PAT goes back to 1997. Online access through Xchange, see www.utcourts.gov/records/. Also see state introduction.

Criminal Records: Access: Phone, fax, mail, in person, online. Both court and visitors may perform in person searches. Search fee: $15.00 per hour; first 20 minutes no charge. Required to search: name, years to search, DOB. Criminal records computerized from 1997, older on microfilm and archived. Mail turnaround time 1 week. Criminal PAT goes back to same as civil. Online access through Xchange, see www.utcourts.gov/records/. Also see state introduction.

General Information: No adoption, sealed records released. Will fax documents $5.00 1st page, $.50 each add'l. Court makes copy: $.25 per page. Certification fee: $4.00 plus $.50 per page includes copy fee; Exemplification fee $6.00 plus $.50 per page. Payee: 7th District Court. Personal checks accepted. Visa/MC accepted. Prepayment required. Mail requests: SASE required.

Garfield County

6th District Court PO Box 77, Panguitch, UT 84759; 435-676-8826 X104; fax: 435-676-8629; 9AM-5PM (MST). ***Felony, Misdemeanor, Civil, Eviction, Small Claims, Probate.***

Civil Records: Access: Phone, fax, mail, in person, online. Only the court performs in person searches; visitors may not. Search fee: $15.00 per hour. Required to search: name, years to search. Civil cases indexed by defendant, plaintiff. Civil records archived for 100 years; on computer back to 2000. Mail turnaround time 1 day. Online access through Xchange, see www.utcourts.gov/records/. Also see state introduction.

Criminal Records: Access: Fax, mail, in person, online. Only the court performs in person searches; visitors may not. Search fee: $15.00 per hour. Required to search: name, years to search. Criminal records archived for 100 years; on computer back to 2000. Mail turnaround time 1 day. Online access through Xchange, see www.utcourts.gov/records/. Also see state introduction.

General Information: No adoption records released. Fee to fax out file $1.00 for 1st page, $.50 each add'l. Court makes copy: $.25 per page. Self serve: $.10 per page. Certification fee: $4.00 plus $.50 per page. Payee: 6th District Court. Personal checks accepted; credit cards are not. Prepayment required.

Grand County

7th District Court 125 E Center St, Moab, UT 84532; 435-259-1349; probate phone: same; fax: 435-259-4081; 8AM-5PM (MST). ***Felony, Misdemeanor, Civil, Eviction, Probate.***

Phone search requests are limited one or two index names, less if clerk doesn't emphasize.

Civil Records: Access: Phone, mail, online, in person. Both court and visitors may perform in person searches. No search fee for 1st 20 minutes; $15.00 per hour thereafter. Required to search: name, years to search. Civil cases indexed by defendant, plaintiff. District records on computer from Spring 1990, Circuit from spring 1989, archived since court started. Mail turnaround time 5 days. Civil PAT goes back to 1990. PAT results show middle initial, DOB. Online access through Xchange, see www.utcourts.gov/records/. Also see state introduction.

Criminal Records: Access: Phone, mail, online, in person. Both court and visitors may perform in person searches. No search fee for 1st 20 minutes; $15.00 per hour thereafter. Required to search: name, years to search; also helpful: DOB, SSN. District records on computer from spring 1990, Circuit from spring 1989, archived since court started. Mail turnaround time 1-5 days. Criminal PAT goes back to same as civil. PAT results show middle initial, DOB. Online access through Xchange, see www.utcourts.gov/records/. Also see state introduction. Online results show middle initial, DOB.

General Information: No adoption, expunged records released. Will fax documents $5.00 flat rate for 1-10 pages, then $.50 each after 10. Court makes copy: $.25 per page. Certification fee: $4.00 plus $.50 per page. Payee: 7th District Court. Personal checks accepted. Visa/MC accepted. Prepayment required. Mail requests: SASE required.

Iron County

Fifth District Court 40 N 100 E, Cedar City, UT 84720; 435-867-3250; criminal fax: 435-867-3212; civil fax: same; 8AM-5PM (MST). ***Felony, Misdemeanor, Civil, Eviction, Probate, Domestic.***

Hearing location also in Parowan, but records held here. Probate fax is same as main fax number.

Civil Records: Access: Mail, phone, in person, online. Both court and visitors may perform in person searches. Search fee: varies. Required to search: name. Civil cases indexed by defendant, plaintiff. District records on computer from 4/89, former Circuit Court records on computer from 1987, archived from 1900. Mail turnaround time 2-3 days. Civil PAT goes back to 1987. PAT results show name only. Online access through Xchange, see www.utcourts.gov/records/. Also see state introduction.

Criminal Records: Access: Mail, phone, online, in person. Both court and visitors may perform in person searches. Search fee: varies. Required to search: name, years to search, DOB, SSN. District records on computer from 4/89, former Circuit Court records on computer from 1987, archived from 1900. Mail turnaround time 2-3 days. Criminal PAT goes back to 1987. PAT results show name only. Online access through Xchange, see www.utcourts.gov/records/. Also see state introduction.

General Information: No sealed records released. Will fax documents $5.00 up to 10 pages. Court makes copy: $.25 per page. Certification fee: $4.00 per doc plys $.50 per page; exemplification- $6.00 plus $.50 per page. Payee: 5th District Court. Personal checks and major credit cards accepted. Prepayment required. Mail requests: SASE required.

Juab County

4th District Court 160 N. Main, PO Box 249, Nephi, UT 84648; 435-623-0901; fax: 435-623-0922; 8AM-5PM (MST). ***Felony, Misdemeanor, Civil, Eviction, Probate.***

Probate fax is same as main fax number.

Civil Records: Access: Phone, mail, online, in person. Both court and visitors may perform in person searches. Search fee: $15.00 per hour. First 15 minutes are no charge. Required to search: name, years to search. Civil cases indexed by defendant, plaintiff; index on computer from 11/94, archived since court started. Mail turnaround time 1 week. Civil PAT goes back to 11/1994. PAT results show name only. Online access through Xchange, see www.utcourts.gov/records/. Also see state introduction.

Criminal Records: Access: Phone, mail, online, in person. Both court and visitors may perform in person searches. Search fee: $15.00 per hour. First 15 minutes are no charge. Required to search: name, years to search. Criminal records computerized from 11/94, archived since court started. Mail turnaround time 1 week. Criminal PAT goes back to same as civil. PAT results show name only. Online access through Xchange, see www.utcourts.gov/records/. Also see state introduction. Online results show name only.

General Information: Online identifiers in results same as on public terminal. All records must be viewed in this office. Will not fax documents. Court makes copy: $.25 per page. Certification fee: $4.00 plus $.50 per page includes copies. Payee: 4th District Court. Personal checks accepted. Visa/MC accepted. Prepayment required. Mail requests: SASE required.

Kane County

6th District Court 76 N Main, Kanab, UT 84741; 435-644-2458; fax: 435-644-4939; 8AM-5PM (MST). ***Felony, Misdemeanor, Civil, Eviction, Small Claims, Probate.***

http://kane.utah.gov/deptinfo.cfm?deptID=11

Civil Records: Access: Phone, fax, mail, in person, online. Only the court performs in person searches; visitors may not. Search fee: First 15 minutes of search is free, thereafter $25.00 per hour. Required to search: name, years to search. Civil cases indexed by defendant, plaintiff; index on computer from 1985, archived since court started. Mail turnaround time 2-3 days. PAT results show name only. Online access through Xchange, see www.utcourts.gov/records/. Also see state introduction.

Criminal Records: Access: Phone, fax, mail, in person, online. Only the court performs in person searches; visitors may not. Search fee: First 15 minutes of search is free, thereafter $25.00 per hour. Required to search: name, years to search. Criminal records computerized from 1985, archived since court started. Mail turnaround time 2-3 days. PAT results show name only. Online access through Xchange, see www.utcourts.gov/records/. Also see state introduction.

General Information: No sealed, expunged records released. Fee to fax document $.50 per page. Court makes copy: $.25 per page. Self serve: same. Certification fee: $4.00 per doc plus $.50 per page. Payee: Sixth District Court. Personal checks accepted; credit cards are not. Prepayment required. Mail requests: SASE required.

Millard County

4th District Court 765 S Hwy 99, #6, Fillmore, UT 84631; 435-743-6223; fax: 435-743-6923; 8AM-5PM (MST). ***Felony, Misdemeanor, Civil, Eviction, Small Claims, Probate.***

Civil Records: Access: Phone, mail, online, in person. Both court and visitors may perform in person searches. Search fee: $10.00 per hour. Required to search: name, years to search. Civil cases indexed by defendant, plaintiff; index on computer from 1988, archived from 1896. Mail turnaround time 1 day. Civil PAT goes back to 1988. PAT civil

results show middle initial. Online access through Xchange, see www.utcourts.gov/records/. Also see state introduction.
Criminal Records: Access: Phone, mail, online, in person. Both court and visitors may perform in person searches. Search fee: $10.00 per hour. Required to search: name, years to search. Criminal records computerized from 1988, archived from 1896. Mail turnaround time 1 day. Criminal PAT goes back to same as civil. PAT results show middle initial, DOB. Online access through Xchange, see www.utcourts.gov/records/. Also see state introduction. Online results show middle initial, DOB.
General Information: No pre-sentence, expunged or sealed records released. Will not fax documents. Court makes copy: $.25 per page. Certification fee: $4.00 plus $.50 per page. Payee: 4th District Court. Business checks accepted. No credit cards accepted. Prepayment required. Mail requests: SASE required.

Morgan County

2nd District Court PO Box 886, Morgan, UT 84050; 801-845-4020; fax: 801-829-6176; 8AM-5PM (MST). ***Felony, Misdemeanor, Civil, Eviction, Small Claims, Probate.***
Civil Records: Access: Phone, fax, mail, online, in person. Both court and visitors may perform in person searches. Search fee: $25.00 per name, if extensive. Required to search: name, years to search. Civil cases indexed by defendant, plaintiff; index on computer since 1992; on microfiche, books, archived from 1862. Mail turnaround time several days. Civil PAT goes back to 1992. Online access through Xchange, see www.utcourts.gov/records/. Also see state introduction. Extensive (special) search requests must be in writing.
Criminal Records: Access: Phone, fax, mail, online, in person. Both court and visitors may perform in person searches. Search fee: $25.00 per name, if extensive. Required to search: name, years to search, DOB; also helpful: SSN. Criminal records on computer since 1992, prior in books. Mail turnaround time several days. Criminal PAT goes back to same as civil. Online access through Xchange, see www.utcourts.gov/records/. Also see state introduction. Extensive (special) search requests must be in writing.
General Information: No sealed records released. Will fax documents $5.00 fee. Court makes copy: $.25 per page. Certification fee: $4.00 plus $.50 per page. Payee: Morgan District. Personal checks accepted. Visa/MC accepted. Prepayment required. Mail requests: SASE requested.

Piute County

6th District Court PO Box 99, 550 N Main St, Junction, UT 84740; 435-577-2840; fax: 435-577-2433; 9AM-N, 1-5PM (MST). ***Felony, Misdemeanor, Civil, Eviction, Small Claims, Probate.***
Civil Records: Access: Mail, in person, online. Both court and visitors may perform in person searches. No search fee. Required to search: name, years to search. Civil cases indexed by defendant, plaintiff. Civil records archived from 1889. Mail turnaround time 2-3 days. Online access through Xchange, see www.utcourts.gov/records/. Also see state introduction.
Criminal Records: Access: Mail, in person, online. Both court and visitors may perform in person searches. No search fee. Required to search: name, years to search. Criminal records archived from 1889. Mail turnaround time 2-3 days. Online access through Xchange, see www.utcourts.gov/records/. Also see state introduction.
General Information: No sealed records released. Will fax out documents in emergency for $.50 per page. Court makes copy: $.25 per page. Certification fee: $4.00 plus $.50 per page. Payee: Piute County District Court. Personal checks accepted. Search fees may be billed if prior arrangement made. Mail requests: SASE required.

Rich County

1st District Court PO Box 218, Randolph, UT 84064; 435-793-2415; criminal fax: 435-793-2410; civil fax: same; 9AM-5PM (MST). ***Felony, Misdemeanor, Civil, Eviction, Probate.***
Probate fax is same as main fax number.
Civil Records: Access: Phone, fax, mail, in person, online. Both court and visitors may perform in person searches. Search fee: $10.00 per hour. Required to search: name, years to search; also helpful: address. Civil cases indexed by defendant, plaintiff. Civil records ago back to 1896; computerized records since 2000. Mail turnaround time 2-3 days. Online access through Xchange, see www.utcourts.gov/records/. Also see state introduction.
Criminal Records: Access: Phone, fax, mail, in person, online. Both court and visitors may perform in person searches. Search fee: $10.00 per hour. Required to search: name, years to search; also helpful: address, DOB, SSN. Criminal records go back to 1896; computerized records since 2000. Mail turnaround time 2-3 days. Online access through Xchange, see www.utcourts.gov/records/. Also see state introduction.
General Information: No sealed records released. Will fax documents to local or toll free line. Court makes copy: $.25 per page. Self serve: same. Certification fee: $4.00 per page. Payee: Rich County. Personal checks accepted; credit cards are not. Prepayment required. Mail requests: SASE required.

Salt Lake County

3rd District Court - Salt Lake Dept. PO Box 1860, 450 S State St, Salt Lake City, UT 84111; 801-238-7300; probate phone: 801-238-7162; fax: 801-238-7396; 8AM-5PM (MST). ***Felony, Misdemeanor, Civil, Eviction, Small Claims, Probate.*** Probate fax- 801-238-7396.
Civil Records: Access: Mail, in person, online. Both court and visitors may perform in person searches. Search fee: First 20 minutes no charge, then $15.00 per hour. Required to search: name, years to search. Civil cases indexed by defendant, plaintiff; index on computer from 1985, archived after 1969. Mail turnaround time 2-3 days. Civil PAT goes back to 1985. PAT results show middle initial, DOB. Terminal results also show SSNs. Online access through Xchange, see www.utcourts.gov/records/. Also see state introduction. An automated court information line allows phone access to court dates, fine balances, and judgment/divorce decrees (case or citation number required) at 801-238-7830.
Criminal Records: Access: Mail, online, in person. Both court and visitors may perform in person searches. Search fee: First 20 minutes no charge, then $15.00 per hour. Required to search: name, years to search, DOB; also helpful: SSN. Criminal records computerized from 1986, archived after satisfaction or dismissal, destroyed prior to 1985. Mail turnaround time 2-3 days. Criminal PAT goes back to 1986. PAT results show middle initial, DOB. Terminal results include SSN. Online access through Xchange, see www.utcourts.gov/records/. Also see state introduction. Online results show middle initial, DOB. Terminal results include SSN.
General Information: No confidential records released. Will fax documents $5.00 up to 10 pages; $.50 per each add'l page. Court makes copy: $.25 per page. Certification fee: $4.00 per doc and $.50 per page; exemplification- $6.00 per doc and $.50 per page. Payee: 3rd District Court. Business checks accepted. Visa/MC accepted. Prepayment required.

3rd District Court - Sandy Department, West Jordan, UT 84088. ***Felony, Misdemeanor, Civil, Eviction, Small Claims.***
Now combined with the old West Valley Dept. to form the new West Jordan Dept.

3rd District Court - West Jordan Department 8080 S Redwood Rd, Ste 1701, West Jordan, UT 84084; 801-233-9700; criminal fax: 801-233-9727; civil fax: 801-233-9761; 8AM-5PM (MST). ***Felony, Misdemeanor, Civil, Eviction, Domestic, Probate.***
Now combined with old Sandy Division; formerly known as the West Valley Dept.
Civil Records: Access: Mail, in person, online. Both court and visitors may perform in person searches. Search fee: $15.00 per hour. Required to search: name, years to search. Civil cases indexed by defendant, plaintiff; index on computer since 1986, archived from 1983. Mail turnaround time 1 week. Civil PAT goes back to 1986. Online access through Xchange for a fee, see www.utcourts.gov/records/. Also see state introduction.
Criminal Records: Access: Mail, online, in person. Both court and visitors may perform in person searches. Search fee: $15.00 per hour. Required to search: name, years to search. Criminal records on computer since 1986, archived from 1983. Mail turnaround time 1 week. Criminal PAT goes back to same as civil. Online access through Xchange for a fee, see www.utcourts.gov/records/. Also see state introduction.
General Information: No sealed records released. Will fax documents $5.00 1st 10 pages; $.50 ea add'l page. Court makes copy: $.25 per page. Certification fee: $4.00 plus $.50 per page. Payee: 3rd District Court. Personal checks and credit cards accepted. Prepayment required. Mail requests: SASE required.

San Juan County

7th District Court PO Box 68, Monticello, UT 84535; 435-587-2122; fax: 435-587-2372; 8AM-5PM (MST). ***Felony, Misdemeanor, Civil, Eviction, Probate.***
Civil Records: Access: Phone, mail, fax, online, in person. Both court and visitors may perform in person searches. Search fee: $15.00 per hour. Required to search: name, years to search. Civil cases indexed by defendant, plaintiff; index on computer since 1991; on index books from 1919 to 1991. Mail turnaround time 1 week. Civil PAT goes back to 1991. PAT results show middle initial, DOB. Results include last 4 digits on SSN. Online access through Xchange, see www.utcourts.gov/records/. Also see state introduction.
Criminal Records: Access: Mail, fax, online, in person. Both court and visitors may perform in person searches. Search fee: $15.00 per hour. Required to search: name, years to search. Criminal records on computer since 1991; on index books from 1919 to 1991. Note: Results include last 4 digits on SSN. Mail turnaround time 1 week. Criminal PAT goes back to same as civil. PAT results show middle initial, DOB. Results include last 4 digits on SSN. Online access through Xchange, see www.utcourts.gov/records/. Also see state introduction. Online results show middle initial, DOB.
General Information: No juvenile records released. Fee to fax out file $5.00 up to 10 pages; $.50 per each add'l page. Court makes copy: $.25 per page. Certification fee: $4.00 plus $.50 per page. Payee: 7th District Court. Personal checks accepted. Visa/MC accepted in person and by phone. Prepayment required. Mail requests: SASE required or postage.

Sanpete County

6th District Court 160 N Main, Manti, UT 84642; 435-835-2121; fax: 435-835-2135; 8AM-5PM (MST). ***Felony, Misdemeanor, Civil, Eviction, Small Claims, Probate.***
Civil Records: Access: Phone, fax, mail, in person, online. Both court and visitors may perform in person searches. Search fee: $15.00 per hour after first 15 minutes free. Required to search: name, years to search. Civil cases indexed by defendant, plaintiff; index on computer from 1998. Mail turnaround time 10 days. Civil PAT goes back to 9/1998. PAT civil results show middle initial. Online access through Xchange, see www.utcourts.gov/records/. Also see state introduction.
Criminal Records: Access: Phone, fax, mail, in person, online. Both court and visitors may perform in person searches. Search fee: $15.00 per hour. Required to search: name, years to search; also helpful: DOB. Criminal records computerized from 1998. Mail turnaround time 10 days. Criminal PAT goes back to 9/1998. PAT criminal results show

middle initial. Online access through Xchange, see www.utcourts.gov/records/. Also see state introduction.
General Information: No criminal, expunged, or sealed records released. Will fax documents $5.00 fee; add $1.00 per page over 10. Court makes copy: $.25 per page. Certification fee: $4.00 plus $.50 per page. Payee: 6th District Court. Personal checks accepted; credit cards are not. Prepayment required. Mail requests: SASE requested.

Sevier County

6th District Court 895 E 300 N, Richfield, UT 84701-2345; 435-896-2700; fax: 435-896-8047; 8AM-5PM (MST). ***Felony, Misdemeanor, Civil, Eviction, Probate.***
Civil Records: Access: Phone, fax, mail, online, in person. Both court and visitors may perform in person searches. Search fee: $15.00 per hour. For search requiring 15 minutes or less, no charge. Required to search: name, years to search. Civil cases indexed by defendant, plaintiff. Circuit records on computer from 1989, District on computer from 1991. Mail turnaround time 2-3 days. Civil PAT goes back to 1992. PAT results show middle initial, DOB, SSN. Online access through Xchange, see www.utcourts.gov/records/. Also see state introduction.
Criminal Records: Access: Fax, mail, online, in person. Both court and visitors may perform in person searches. Search fee: $15.00 per hour. For search requiring 15 minutes or less, no charge. Required to search: name, years to search, DOB, SSN. Circuit records on computer from 1989, District on computer from 1991. Mail turnaround time 2-3 days. Criminal PAT goes back to same as civil. PAT results show middle initial, DOB, SSN. Online access through Xchange, see www.utcourts.gov/records/. Also see state introduction. Online results show middle initial, DOB.
General Information: No sealed records released. Will fax documents $5.00 1st page, $.50 each add'l. Court makes copy: $.25 per page. Self serve: computer access terminal copies $.05 each. Certification fee: $4.00 plus $.50 per page includes copies; Exemplications fee- $6.00. Payee: 6th District Court. Personal checks accepted. Visa/MC accepted. Prepayment required. Mail requests: SASE required.

Summit County

3rd District Court 6300 N Silver Creek, Park City, UT 84098; 435-615-4300; fax: 435-658-1067; 8AM-5PM. ***Felony, Misdemeanor, Civil, Small Claims, Evictions, Probate.***
Civil Records: Access: Mail, in person, online. Both court and visitors may perform in person searches. Search fee: $15.00 per hour, first 15 minutes free. Required to search: name, years to search; also helpful: DOB. By plaintiff and defendant. All indexes on computer back to 1993, records archived back to 1900's. Mail turnaround time 2 days. Civil PAT goes back to 9/1993. Online access through Xchange, see www.utcourts.gov/records/. Also see state introduction.
Criminal Records: Access: Mail, online, in person. Both court and visitors may perform in person searches. Search fee: $15.00 per hour. First 15 minutes no charge. Required to search: name, years to search; also helpful: DOB. Criminal records on computer since 1993. Mail turnaround time 2 days. Criminal PAT goes back to same as civil. Online access through Xchange, see www.utcourts.gov/records/. Also see state introduction.
General Information: Will fax documents $5.00 1st 1-10 pages, then $.50 per page. Court makes copy: $.25 per page. Certification fee: $4.00 plus $.50 per page. Payee: 3rd District Court. Personal checks and major credit cards accepted. Prepayment required. Mail requests: SASE required.

3rd District Court, Park City, UT 84098; 435-615-4300 main ofc. ***Probate.***
This courts closed as of 2008. Online access through Xchange, see www.utcourts.gov/records/. Also see state introduction.

Tooele County

3rd District Court 74 South 100 East, #14, Tooele, UT 84074; 435-833-8000; fax: 435-833-8058; 8AM-5PM (MST). ***Felony, Misdemeanor, Civil, Eviction, Small Claims, Probate.***
Civil Records: Access: Fax, mail, online, in person. Both court and visitors may perform in person searches. Search fee: $15.00 per hour. First 20 minutes no charge. Required to search: name, years to search. Civil cases indexed by defendant, plaintiff; index on computer from 1982, archived since court started. Mail turnaround time 2-3 days. Civil PAT goes back to 1982. Online access through Xchange, see www.utcourts.gov/records/. Also see state introduction.
Criminal Records: Access: Fax, mail, online, in person. Both court and visitors may perform in person searches. Search fee: $15.00 per hour. First 20 minutes no charge. Required to search: name, years to search; also helpful: SSN. Criminal records computerized from 1989, archived since court started. Mail turnaround time 2-3 days. Criminal PAT goes back to 1989. Online access through Xchange, see www.utcourts.gov/records/. Also see state introduction.
General Information: No adoption records released. Will fax documents $5.00 for 10 pages; $.50 each add'l. Court makes copy: $.25 per page. Self serve: same. Certification fee: $4.00 plus $.50 per page; exemplifications $6.00 plus $.50 per page. Payee: 3rd District Court. Personal checks and credit cards accepted. Prepayment required. Mail requests: SASE required.

Uintah County

8th District Court 920 E Hwy 40, Vernal, UT 84078; 435-781-9300; fax: 435-789-0564; 8AM-5PM (MST). ***Felony, Misdemeanor, Civil, Eviction, Probate.***
Civil Records: Access: Mail, in person, online. Both court and visitors may perform in person searches. Search fee: $15.00 per hour. First 20 minutes no charge. Required to search: name, years to search. Civil cases indexed by defendant, plaintiff. Circuit records on computer from 1987, everything else from 1989, archived since court started. Mail turnaround time 2-3 days. Civil PAT goes back to 1987. PAT results show middle initial, DOB. Online access through Xchange, see www.utcourts.gov/records/. Also see state introduction.
Criminal Records: Access: Mail, online, in person. Both court and visitors may perform in person searches. Search fee: $15.00 per hour. First 20 minutes no charge. Required to search: name, years to search. Circuit records on computer from 1987, everything else from 1989, archived since court started. Mail turnaround time 2-3 days. Criminal PAT goes back to same as civil. PAT results show middle initial, DOB. Online access through Xchange, see www.utcourts.gov/records/. Also see state introduction. Online results show middle initial, DOB.
General Information: Online identifiers in results same as on public terminal. No sealed records released. Will fax documents to local or toll free line. Court makes copy: $.25 per page. Certification fee: $4.00 plus $.50 per page. Payee: 8th District Court. Personal checks and credit cards accepted. Prepayment required. Mail requests: SASE required.

Utah County

4th District Court 125 N 100 W, Provo, UT 84601; 801-429-1000; criminal phone: 801-429-1171; civil phone: 801-429-1172; probate phone: 1-801-429-1172; fax: 801-429-1033; 8AM-5PM (MST). ***Felony, Misdemeanor, Civil, Eviction, Small Claims, Probate.***
Civil Records: Access: Phone, mail, fax, in person, online. Both court and visitors may perform in person searches. Search fee: $15.00 per hour. Required to search: name, years to search. Civil cases indexed by defendant, plaintiff. Civil and probate on computer from 1986, judgments, tax liens, and divorce decrees on microfiche from 1900 to 1975, archived from 1900s. Mail turnaround time 7-10 days. Civil PAT goes back to 1986. PAT results show name only. Online access through Xchange, see www.utcourts.gov/records/. Also see state introduction.
Criminal Records: Access: Phone, mail, fax, in person, online. Both court and visitors may perform in person searches. Search fee: $15.00 per hour. Required to search: name, years to search; also helpful: DOB. Felony on computer from 1989; archived from 1900s. Mail turnaround time 7-10 days. Criminal PAT goes back to 1989. PAT results show middle initial, DOB. Online access through Xchange, see www.utcourts.gov/records/. Also see state introduction. Online results show middle initial, DOB.
General Information: Online identifiers in results same as on public terminal. No sealed records released. Will fax documents $5.00 up to 10 pages, then $.50 per page. Court makes copy: $.25 per page. Certification fee: $4.00 plus $.50 per page. Payee: 4th District Court. Personal checks accepted. Visa/MC accepted. Prepayment required. Mail requests: SASE required.

4th District Court - Orem Department 97 E Center, Orem, UT 84057; 801-764-5860; criminal phone: 801-764-5865; civil phone: 801-764-5864; fax: 801-226-5244; 8AM-5PM (MST). ***Misdemeanor, Civil, Eviction, Small Claims.***
Civil Records: Access: Mail, in person, online. Both court and visitors may perform in person searches. Search fee: $15.00 per hour. First 20 minutes no charge. Required to search: name, years to search. Civil cases indexed by defendant, plaintiff; index on computer since 1988. Mail turnaround time 5-7 days. Civil PAT goes back to 1988. PAT results show name only. Online access through Xchange, see www.utcourts.gov/records/. Also see state introduction.
Criminal Records: Access: Mail, online, in person. Both court and visitors may perform in person searches. Search fee: $15.00 per hour. First 20 minutes no charge. Required to search: name, years to search; also helpful: DOB. Criminal records on computer since 1988. Mail turnaround time 5-7 days. Criminal PAT goes back to same as civil. PAT results show name only. Online access through Xchange, see www.utcourts.gov/records/. Also see state introduction.
General Information: No sealed, expunged or confidential records released. Will fax documents to local or toll-free number. Court makes copy: $.25 per page. Certification fee: $4.00 plus $.50 per page. Payee: 4th District Court. Personal checks and credit cards accepted. Prepayment required.

4th District Court - Spanish Forks Dept. 775 W Center, Spanish Forks, UT 84660; 801-798-8674; fax: 801-798-1377; 8AM-5PM (MST). ***Misdemeanor, Civil, Eviction, Small Claims.***
Civil Records: Access: Phone, fax, mail, online, in person. Both court and visitors may perform in person searches. Search fee: $15.00 per hour. First 15 minutes no charge. Required to search: name, years to search. Civil cases indexed by defendant, plaintiff. Civil records stored from 1978, on computer since 1987. Mail turnaround time 5-7 days. Civil PAT goes back to 1987. Online access through Xchange, see www.utcourts.gov/records/. Also see state introduction.
Criminal Records: Access: Phone, fax, mail, online, in person. Both court and visitors may perform in person searches. Search fee: $15.00 per hour. First 15 minutes no charge. Required to search: name, years to search; also helpful: DOB. Criminal records stored from 1978, on computer since 1987. Mail turnaround time 5-7 days. Criminal PAT goes back to same as civil. Online access through Xchange, see www.utcourts.gov/records/. Also see state introduction.
General Information: No sealed, expunged or confidential records released. No fee to fax documents. Fax requires prior arrangement. Court makes copy: $.25 per page. Self serve: same. Certification fee: $4.00 plus $.50 per page. Payee: 4th District Court. Personal checks and credit cards accepted. Prepayment required.

4th District Court - American Fork Dept. 75 E 80 N, #202, American Fork, UT 84003-; 801-756-9654; fax: 801-763-0153; 8AM-5PM (MST). ***Misdemeanor, Civil, Eviction, Small Claims.***

Civil Records: Access: Mail, in person, online. Both court and visitors may perform in person searches. Search fee: $15.00 per hour. First 15 minutes no charge. Required to search: name, years to search. Civil cases indexed by defendant, plaintiff; index on computer since 1988. Mail turnaround time 5-7 days. Civil PAT goes back to 5/1988. PAT civil results show middle initial. Terminal results also show SSNs. Online access through Xchange, see www.utcourts.gov/records/. Also see state introduction.

Criminal Records: Access: Mail, online, in person. Both court and visitors may perform in person searches. Search fee: $15.00 per hour. First 15 minutes no charge. Required to search: name, years to search; also helpful: DOB. Criminal records stored since 1988. Mail turnaround time 5-7 days. Criminal PAT goes back to same as civil. PAT results show middle initial, DOB. Terminal results include SSN. Online access through Xchange, see www.utcourts.gov/records/. Also see state introduction. Online results show middle initial, DOB. Terminal results include SSN.

General Information: Online identifiers in results same as on public terminal. No sealed, expunged or confidential records released. Will fax documents $5.00 per fax. Court makes copy: $.25 per page. Certification fee: $4.00 plus $.50 per page. Payee: 4th District Court. Personal checks accepted. Visa/MC accepted. Prepayment required. Mail requests: SASE required.

Wasatch County

4th District Court 1361 S Hwy 40, PO Box 730, Heber City, UT 84032; 435-654-4676; criminal fax: 435-654-5281; civil fax: same; 8AM-5PM (MST). ***Felony, Misdemeanor, Civil, Eviction, Probate, Domestic.***

Small claims are handled at one of two Justice Courts. Heber City Justice Court- 435-654-1662, Wasatch County Justice Court- 435-654-2679. Probate fax is same as main fax number.

Civil Records: Access: Phone, fax, mail, online, in person. Both court and visitors may perform in person searches. No search fee. Required to search: name, years to search. Civil cases indexed by defendant, plaintiff; index on computer since 1/95; records archived since court started. Mail turnaround time 1-2 days. Civil PAT goes back to 1/1995. PAT results show name only. Online access through Xchange, see www.utcourts.gov/records/. Also see state introduction.

Criminal Records: Access: Phone, fax, mail, online, in person. Both court and visitors may perform in person searches. No search fee. Required to search: name, years to search; also helpful: DOB, signed release. Criminal records on computer since 1/95; records archived since court started. Mail turnaround time 1-2 days. Criminal PAT goes back to same as civil. PAT results show name only. Online access through Xchange, see www.utcourts.gov/records/. Also see state introduction.

General Information: Online identifiers in results same as on public terminal. No adoption records released. Will not fax documents. Court makes copy: $.25 per page. Certification fee: $4.00 plus $.50 per page. Payee: 4th District Court. Personal checks and credit cards accepted. Prepayment required. Mail requests: SASE required.

Washington County

5th District Court 220 N 200 E, St. George, UT 84770; criminal phone: 435-986-5700; civil phone: 435-986-5701; fax: 435-986-5723; 8AM-5PM (MST). ***Felony, Misdemeanor, Civil, Eviction, Small Claims, Probate.***

Civil Records: Access: Mail, fax, online, in person. Both court and visitors may perform in person searches. No search fee; fee will apply if search exceeds 15 minutes. Required to search: name. Civil cases indexed by defendant, plaintiff. District Court records on computer from 4/1990; Circuit Court on computer from 1987. Mail turnaround time 2-3 days. Public use terminal available. PAT results show name only. Online access through Xchange, see www.utcourts.gov/records/. Also see state introduction.

Criminal Records: Access: Mail, online, in person, fax. Both court and visitors may perform in person searches. No search fee; fee will apply if search exceeds 15 minutes. Required to search: name, years to search. District Court records on computer from 4/1990; Circuit Court on computer from 1987. Mail turnaround time 2-3 days. Public use terminal available. PAT results show middle initial, DOB. Online access through Xchange, see www.utcourts.gov/records/. Also see state introduction. Online results show middle initial, DOB.

General Information: Online identifiers in results same as on public terminal. No mental health, sealed, private, or adoption records released. Fee to fax out file extra $.25 per page; minimum $5.00 charge. Court makes copy: $.25 per page. Certification fee: $4.00 plus $.50 per page; exemplification fee- $6.00 per doc plus $.50 per page. Payee: 5th District Court. Personal checks and credit cards accepted. Prepayment required. Mail requests: SASE required.

Wayne County

6th District Court PO Box 189, Loa, UT 84747; 435-836-1301; fax: 435-836-2479; 9AM-5PM (MST). ***Felony, Misdemeanor, Civil, Eviction, Small Claims, Probate.***

Civil Records: Access: Phone, mail, fax, in person, online. Both court and visitors may perform in person searches. Search fee: $15.00 per hour. Required to search: name, years to search. Civil cases indexed by defendant, plaintiff. Civil records archived since court started; computerized from 10/2000. Mail turnaround time 2-3 days. Online access through Xchange, see www.utcourts.gov/records/. Also see state introduction.

Criminal Records: Access: Phone, mail, fax, in person, online. Both court and visitors may perform in person searches. Search fee: $15.00 per hour. Required to search: name, years to search; also helpful: SSN. Criminal records archived since court started; computerized from 10/2000. Mail turnaround time 2-3 days. Online access through Xchange, see www.utcourts.gov/records/. Also see state introduction.

General Information: No sealed records released. Fee to fax out file $1.00 per page. Court makes copy: $.25 per page. Certification fee: $4.00 plus $.50 per page. Payee: 6th District Court. Personal checks accepted; credit cards are not. Prepayment required. Mail requests: SASE required.

Weber County

2nd District Court 2525 Grant Ave, Ogden, UT 84401; 801-395-1079; criminal phone: 801-395-1071; civil phone: 801-395-1091; probate phone: 801-395-1173; fax: 801-395-1182; 8AM-5PM (MST). ***Felony, Misdemeanor, Civil, Eviction, Small Claims, Probate.***

Until 12/02, there was a District Court also in Roy. However, this court is now a Justice Court; its records are held in Ogden.

Civil Records: Access: Phone, mail, online, in person. Both court and visitors may perform in person searches. Search fee: $15.00 per hour. First 15 minutes no charge. Visitors may search on office computer only, not in paper files. Required to search: name, years to search. Civil cases indexed by defendant, plaintiff; index on computer the past 20 years, books prior to that. Mail turnaround time 2-9 days. Civil PAT goes back to 1987. PAT results show middle initial, DOB. Online access through Xchange, see www.utcourts.gov/records/. Also see state introduction. An automated court information line allows phone access to court dates, fine balances, and judgment/divorce decrees (case or citation number required) at 888-824-2678.

Criminal Records: Access: Phone, mail, online, in person. Both court and visitors may perform in person searches. Search fee: $15.00 per hour. First 15 minutes no charge. Required to search: name, years to search, DOB, SSN. Criminal records on computer the past 20 years, books prior to that. Mail turnaround time 2-9 days. Criminal PAT goes back to same as civil. PAT results show middle initial, DOB. Online access through Xchange, see www.utcourts.gov/records/. Also see state introduction. Online results show middle initial, DOB.

General Information: Online identifiers in results same as on public terminal. No adoption, voluntary commitments, expunged criminal records released. Will fax documents $5.00 includes up to 10 pages; add $.50 per page over 10. Court makes copy: $.25 per page. Certification fee: $4.00 plus $.50 per page. Payee: Ogden District Court. Personal checks accepted. Visa/MC accepted. Prepayment required. Mail requests: SASE required.

Utah Recording Offices

ORGANIZATION: 29 counties, 29 recording offices. The recording officers are the County Recorder for real estate and the Clerk of District Court for state tax liens. Utah is entirely in the Mountain Time Zone (MST)

REAL ESTATE RECORDS: County Recorders will not perform real estate searches. Real estate record copy fees vary from $.25 to $1.00 per page. Certification fee is usually $5.00 per seal.

UCC RECORDS: Financing statements are filed at the state level except for real estate related collateral which are filed with the Register of Deeds (and at the state level in certain cases). Many filing offices will not perform UCC searches. UCC copy fees vary but is usually $1.00 per page.

TAX LIEN RECORDS: All federal tax liens are filed with the County Recorder. They do not perform searches. All state tax liens are filed with Clerk of District Court, many of which have online access and most all will perform searches.

ONLINE ACCESS: A number of counties offer online access; some are fee-based. Search the statewide UCC database free at https://secure.utah.gov/uccsearch/uccs.

Beaver County

County Recorder, PO Box 431, Beaver, UT 84713. 435-438-6480; fax-435-438-6481; 9AM-5PM www.beaver.state.ut.us

Index: All in one. Records indexed on a public use terminal back to 1999. Only the public may search. Copy fee $1.00 per page. Cert fee- $5.00 per cert plus copy fee. Payee- Beaver County Recorder. **Other phones:** Treasurer- 435-438-6410; County Clerk- 435-438-6465. **Property tax/Assessing-** PO Box 352, Beaver, UT 84713; 435-438-6400, assessor fax- 435-438-6481. (Appraiser/Auditor- 435-438-6460);

Box Elder County

County Recorder, 1 S Main St; Courthouse, Brigham City, UT 84302-2599. 435-734-3351, R/E recording phone-435-734-3391; fax-435-723-7562; 8AM-5PM www.boxeldercounty.org/

Index: All in one. Records indexed on computer back to 1986. Only the public may search. Copy fee $1.00 1st page; $.25 each add'l. Cert fee- $5.00 1st page plus copy fee. Payee- Box Elder County Recorder. Office does sell customized portions from existing database, call 435-734-3330. **Online access to Real Estate, Deed, Lien, Tax Roll, Plat records:** Access to county recordings data is available by subscription at www.boxeldercounty.org/opis.html. Monthly subscriptions and per doc payment plans available, contact Chad at 435-734-3301 . **Other phones:** Treasurer- 435-734-3333; Elections- 435-734-3391; County Clerk- 435-734-3391. **Property tax/ Assessing-** 1 S Main St, Courthouse, Brigham City, UT 84302-2599; 435-734-3333, assessor fax- 435-734-3380. (Appraiser/Auditor- 435-734-3317) www.boxeldercounty.org/ **Online access-** Access to GIS/mapping for free go to www.boxeldercounty.org/

Cache County

County Recorder, 179 N Main St, #101, Logan, UT 84321. 435-755-1530; 7AM-6PM M-Th, closed Fri. www.cachecounty.org/recorder/

Index: All in one. Records indexed on a public use terminal back to 1980. Only the public may search. Copy fee $1.00 per page. Cert fee- $5.00 per doc plus copy fee. Payee- Cache County Recorder. **Online access to Real Estate, Grantor/Grantee, Deed, Lien records:** Access to recording records is via subscription at www.landlight.com. Choose from 3 subscription plans; short free trial is offered. Grantor/Grantee Index goes back to 10/1980; Abstracts to 7/1984; images to 12/1992. Call 435-787-9003 for more info on online access. **Other phones:** Treasurer- 435-755-1500; County Clerk- 435-755-1460. **Property tax/Assessing-** 179 N. Main St, #205, Logan, UT 84321; 435-755-1590, assessor fax- 435-755-2173. (Appraiser/Auditor- 435-716-7123) **Online access-** A subscription service is available at www.landlight.com/ for assessor records.

Carbon County

County Recorder, 120 E Main; Courthouse Bldg, Price, UT 84501. Recording, R/E phone-435-636-3244; fax-435-636-3730; 8AM-5PM. www.carbon.utah.gov/recorder/index.html

Index: Separate indices to search include older abstract books; newer records on computer. Records indexed on computer back to 1983; brief legals go back to 2/94 only. Only the public may search. Copy fee $.25 per page, $2.00 for 18 x 18 plats; $5.00 for mylar or large plats. Cert fee- $5.00 1st page; $1.00 each add'l page includes copy. Payee- Carbon County Recorder. **Other phones:** Treasurer- 435-636-3258; Elections- 435-636-3220; County Clerk- 435-636-3220. **Property tax/Assessing-** 120 E Main, Price, UT 84501; 435-636-3249, assessor fax- 435-636-3232. (Appraiser/Auditor- 435-636-3227) www.carbon.utah.gov/assessor/index.htm

Daggett County

County Recorder, PO Box 219, Manila, UT 84046-0219. 435-784-3210; fax-435-784-3335; 9AM-N; 1-5PM.

Index: Books and computer, by name and legal description. Records indexed on computer back 4 years. Only the public may search. Copy fee $.25 per page. Cert fee- $2.00 per page plus copy fee. Exemplification fee $6.00 per page. Payee- Dagget Co. Recorder. **Other phones:** Treasurer- 435-784-3154; Elections- 435-784-3154; Vital Records- 435-784-3154; County Clerk- 435-784-3154. **Property tax/Assessing-** PO Box 387, Manila, UT 84046; 435-784-3222x410, assessor fax- 435-784-3335. (Appraiser/Auditor- 435-784-3210) hours- 9AM-5PM

Davis County

County Recorder, PO Box 618, Farmington, UT 84025. Recording, R/E phone-801-451-3225; fax-801-451-3141; 8:30AM-5PM www.co.davis.ut.us

Index: All in one. Records indexed on a public use terminal back to 1981. Only the public may search. Copy fee $1.00 per page. Cert fee- $5.00 per doc plus copy fee. Payee- Davis County Recorder. **Online access to Real Estate, Deed, Lien records:** Access to the recorder's land records database requires written registration and $15.00 per month fee plus $.10 per transaction. Records go back to 1981. For info and sign-up, contact Janet at 801-451-3347. **Other phones:** Treasurer- 801-451-3243; Elections- 801-451-3213; Vital Records- 801-451-3337; County Clerk- 801-451-3324. **Property tax/Assessing-** 801-451-3252. (Appraiser/Auditor- 801-451-3214) **Online access-** Search property and tax data free at www.co.davis.ut.us/recorder/property_search/property_search.cfm.

Duchesne County

County Recorder, PO Box 916, Duchesne, UT 84021. Recording, R/E phone-435-738-1160; fax-435-738-1220; 8:30AM-5PM

Index: Separate indices to search include surface and misc and mineral. Records indexed on a public use terminal back to 1986. Only the public may search. Will not search UCC records. Copy fee $1.00 per copy. Cert fee- $5.00 per cert plus copy fee. Payee- County Recorder. **Other phones:** Treasurer- 435-738-1193; Elections- 435-738-1101; County Clerk- 435-738-1100 or 1103. **Property tax/Assessing-** 734 N Center, Rm 30, Duchesne, UT 84021; 435-738-1110. (Appraiser/Auditor- 435-738-1123) www.duchesnegov.net/assessor/assesor.html

Emery County

County Recorder, PO Box 698, Castle Dale, UT 84513-0698. 435-381-2414; fax-435-381-2614; 8:30AM-5PM. www.emerycounty.com

Index: All in one. Records indexed on computer back to 1986. Only the public may search. Copy fee $.25 per page. Cert fee- $5.00 per cert plus $.50 per page includes copy fee. Payee- Emery County Recorder. Bulk data available for purchase of parcel data with different attributes. Must sign users agreement, contact IT Dept at 435-381-5281. **Online access to Plat, Real Estate records:** Access plat map data by parcel ID number or location on county map free at www.emerycounty.com/recorder/needa_plat.htm . **Other phones:** Treasurer- 435-381-2510; Elections- 435-381-5106; County Clerk- 435-381-5106; IT Department -435-381-5281. **Property tax/Assessing-** PO Box 727, Castle Dale, UT 84513; 435-381-2474, assessor fax- 435-381-5529. (Appraiser/Auditor- 435-381-2474).

Garfield County

County Recorder, PO Box 77, Panguitch, UT 84759. 435-676-1112; fax-435-676-8239; 9AM-N, 1-5PM

Index: All in one. Records indexed on a public use terminal back to 1/1/2002. Only the public may search. Copy fee $1.00 1st page, $.50 each add'l page. Cert fee- $5.00 per doc includes copy fee. Payee- Garfield County Recorder. **Other phones:** Treasurer- 435-676-1109; County Clerk- 435-676-1000. **Property tax/Assessing-** 55 S Main, Panguitch, UT 84759; 435-676-1107. (Appraiser/Auditor- 435-676-8826 x100)

Grand County

County Recorder, 125 N Center St, Moab, UT 84532. 435-259-1331; fax-435-259-1320; 8AM-5PM. www.grandcountyutah.net/recorder.htm

Index: Separate indices to search. Records indexed on computer back to 1997. Only the public may search. Copy fee $1.00 per page. Cert fee- $5.00 1st page; $1.00 each add'l page includes copy. fee. Payee-

Grand County Recorder. **Other phones:** Treasurer- 435-259-1337; County Clerk- 435-259-1323. **Property tax/Assessing-** 125 E Center, Moab, UT 84532; 435-295-1329, assessor fax- 435-295-1382. (Appraiser/ - 435-259-1322) hours- 7AM-6:00PM M-TH www.grandcountyutah.net/assessor.htm

Iron County

County Recorder, PO Box 506, Parowan, UT 84761. 435-477-8350; fax-435-477-8359; 8:30AM-5PM http://archives.utah.gov/research/agencyhistories/537.html

Index: All in one. Records indexed on a public use terminal back to 1984. Only the public may search. Copy fee $1.00 per page. Cert fee- $5.00 per cert plus copy fee. Payee- Iron County Recorder. **Other phones:** Treasurer- 435-477-8360; County Clerk- 435-477-8340. **Property tax/Assessing-** 68 S 100 E, Parowan, UT 84761; 435-477-8311. (Appraiser/Auditor- 435-477-8331)

Juab County

County Recorder, 160 N Main, Nephi, UT 84648. 435-623-3430; 8:30AM-5PM www.co.juab.ut.us

Index: Separate indices to search include hand written and computer. Records indexed on a public use terminal back to 1993. Only the public may search. $1.00 for a computer printout. Office will not search real estate records. Will not search UCC records. Copy fee $1.00 per page. Cert fee- $5.00 per cert plus copy fee. Payee- Juab County Recorder. **Other phones:** Treasurer- 435-623-3420; County Clerk- 435-623-3410 or 3411. **Property tax/Assessing-** 160 N Main, Nephi, UT 84648; 435-623-3425. (Appraiser/Auditor- 435-623-3425)

Kane County

County Recorder, 76 N Main St, Kanab, UT 84741-3209. 435-644-2360; 8AM-5PM http://kane.utah.gov

Index: Separate indices to search include grantor/grantee, mortgage, misc., Fed tax, judgment. Records indexed on a public use terminal back to 08/26/06. Only the public may search. Will not search UCC records. Copy fee $.50 per page. Cert fee- $5.00 per cert plus copy fee. Payee- Kane County Recorder. **Online access to Real Estate, Property, Lien records:** Access county property records free at http://eagleweb.kane.utah.gov/eaglesoftware/web/login.jsp. **Other phones:** Treasurer- 435-644-5659; Elections- 435-644-2458; County Clerk- 435-644-2458. **Property tax/Assessing-** 76 N Main st, Kanab, UT 84741; 435-644-2647, assessor fax- 435-644-2052. www.kane.utah.gov **Online** - Access property data free at http://eagleweb.kane.utah.gov/eaglesoftware/web/login.jsp but no name searches.

Millard County

County Recorder, 50 S Main, Fillmore, UT 84631. Recording, R/E phone-435-743-6210; fax-435-743-4221; 8AM-5PM

Index: Separate indices to search include alphabetical, abstract retrieval, parcel ownership retrieval. Records indexed on a public use terminal back to 1985. Only the public may search. Copy fee $1.00 per page. Cert fee- $5.00 per doc plus copy fee. Payee- Millard County Recorder. **Other phones:** Treasurer- 435-743-5322; County Clerk- 435-743-6223. **Property tax/Assessing-** 50 S Main, Fillmore, UT 84631; 435-743-5719, assessor fax- 435-743-4221. (Appraiser/Auditor- 435-743-5227)

Morgan County

County Recorder, PO Box 886, Morgan, UT 84050. Recording, R/E phone-801-829-3277; fax-801-845-4066; 9AM-6PM M,T. www.morgan-county.net

Index: Separate indices to search include grantor/grantee, parcel abstract, UCC, Fed liens, judgments. Records indexed on a public use terminal; grantor/grantee-brief legal, back to 1985, grantor/grantee brief & full legal back to 1993 (June). Only the public may search. Copy fee $1.50 per page. Cert fee- $5.00 per doc plus copy fee. Payee- Morgan Co. Recorder. Office does not sell bulk data yet. **Other phones:** Treasurer- 801-845-4030; Elections- 801-845-4012; County Clerk- 801-845-4011. **Property tax/Assessing-** PO Box 680, 48 W Young St, Rm 2, Morgan, UT 84050; 801-845-4000, assessor fax- 801-845-4091. (Appraiser/Auditor- 801-845-4011) www.morgan-county.net

Piute County

County Recorder, PO Box 116, Junction, UT 84740. 435-577-2505; fax-435-577-2433; 9AM-5PM

Index: Separate indices to search include deeds, mortgages. Records indexed on a public use terminal back to 1999. Only the public may search. Office will not search real estate records as a practice. Copy fee $.50 per page. Cert fee- $4.00 plus copy fee. Payee- Piute County Recorder. **Other phones:** Treasurer- 435-577-2505; County Clerk- 435-577-2840. **Property tax/Assessing-** 550 N Main, Courthouse, Junction, UT 84740; 435-577-2988. (Appraiser/Auditor- 435-577-2840)

Rich County

County Recorder, PO Box 322, Randolph, UT 84064. 435-793-2005; fax-435-793-2007; 9AM-N,1-5PM

Index: Separate indices to search. Records indexed on a public use terminal back to 1990. Only the public may search. Copy fee $1.00 per page. Cert fee- $5.00 per cert plus copy fee. Payee- Rich County Recorder. Recorder can sell prior year ownership plans on CD ($250.00) and tax rolls in MS Access. **Other phones:** Treasurer- 435-793-5155; County Clerk- 435-793-2415. **Property tax/Assessing-** PO Box 343, Randolph, UT 84064; 435-793-5215, assessor fax-435-793-2410. (Appraiser/Auditor- 435-793-2415) **Online access-** Access current tax sale data at http://richcountyut.org/documents/delinquent_taxes.htm. Check main website for other record types to be added.

Salt Lake County

County Recorder, 2001 S State St, Rm N-1600; Government Center, Salt Lake City, UT 84190-1150. 801-468-3391; fax-801-468-3335; 8AM-5PM http://slcorecorder.siredocs.com/rechome/main.aspx

Index: Separate indices to search include books by property description, computer back to 1981. Records indexed on a public use terminal back to 1981. Only the public may search. Copy fee $2.00 per page. Cert fee- $5.00 per cert plus copy fee. Payee- Salt Lake County Recorder. Bulk recording office data available to purchase, call office for details. **Online access to Real Estate, Deed, Lien, UCC, Judgment, Voter Registration records:** Access to recording office records is by subscription; minimum $150 sign-up, $25.00 monthly, plus $.01 per screen view or image. Tax maps $1.00. Add'l info at http://slcorecorder.siredocs.com/RecHome/SiteOverview.aspx or phone 801-468-3013 x2 for signup. Check an address on voter registration rolls free at https://secure.slco.org/cl/elections/index.cfm. **Other phones:** Treasurer- 801-468-3140; Elections- 801-468-3427; Vital Records- 801-534-4657 (death, birth); County Clerk- 801-468-3425. **Property tax/Assessing-** 2001 S State St, Rm N-2300, Salt Lake City, UT 84190; 801-468-3050, assessor fax-801-468-3329. (Appraiser/Auditor- 801-468-3389) www.assessor.slco.org/ **Online access-** Name search assessor records free at www.assessor.slco.org/cfml/Query/query2.cfm and also on the Truth-In-Tax Information website are free at www.slpropertyinfo.org but no name searching. Also, search parcel data at http://maps.slco.org/website/assessor/public_parcelviewer/viewer.htm but no name searching. Also, search property data free on the GIS-map site at www.assessor.slco.org/cfml/GIS.cfm but no name searching.

San Juan County

County Recorder, PO Box 789, Monticello, UT 84535. 435-587-3228; fax-435-587-2425; 8AM-5PM www.sanjuancounty.org/recorder.htm

Index: All in one. Records indexed on a public use terminal back to 0701/1991. Only the public may search. Copy fee $1.00 per page; $.50 if computer print.Real estate or tax lien copy- $.75 per page. Cert fee- $5.00 per doc plus copy fee. Payee- San Juan County Recorder. **Other phones:** Treasurer- 435-547-3237; Elections- 435-587-3223; Vital Records- 435-587-2021; County Clerk- 435-587-3443. **Property tax/Assessing-** PO Box 787, Monticello, UT 84535; 435-587-3221, assessor fax- 435-587-3233. (Appraiser/Auditor- 435-587-3223);

Sanpete County

County Recorder, PO Box 129, Manti, UT 84642. 435-835-2181; fax-435-835-2182; 8:00AM-5PM

Index: Separate indices to search include grantor/grantee, fee entry, brief legal, ownership name. Records indexed on a public use terminal back to 1988. Only the public may search. Copy fee $1.00 per page. Cert fee- $5.00 per cert plus copy fee. Payee- Sanpete County Recorder. **Other phones:** Treasurer- 435-835-2101; Elections- 435-835-2131; County Clerk- 435-835-2131. **Property tax/Assessing-** PO Box 158, Manti, UT 84642; 435-835-2111, assessor fax- 435-835-2110. (Appraiser/Auditor- 435-835-2142) Assessor records on a public access terminal in the Recorders office.

Sevier County

County Recorder, 250 N Main, Richfield, UT 84701. 435-893-0411, R/E recording phone-435-893-0410; fax-435-893-0456; 8AM-5PM. www.sevierutah.net

Index: All in one. Records indexed on a public use terminal back to 1984. Only the public may search. Will not search UCC records. Copy fee $.25 per page. Fax fee $2.00 per doc. Cert fee- $5.00 per doc plus copy fee. Payee- Sevier County Recorder. Bulk data available on CD and microfilm; contact Dick Jensen 435-893-0450 or Carolyn Bagley 435-843-0410. **Online Real Estate, Grantor/Grantee, Deed, Lien, Judgment, UCC records:** Access to recorder's database index of data is available with free login at http://qdocs.sevierutah.net/recorder/web/login.jsp. No images available. **Other phones:** Treasurer- 435-893-0440; Elections- 435-893-0404; County Clerk- 435-893-0401. **Property tax/Assessing-** 250 N Main, Richfield, UT 84701; 435-893-0400x2, assessor fax-435-896-8888. (Appraiser/Auditor- 435-893-0434) www.sevierutah.net/assessor/assessor.html **Online access-** Assessor data and sales included in recorder document search lookup with free login at http://qdocs.sevierutah.net/recorder/web/login.jsp.

Summit County

County Recorder, PO Box 128, Coalville, UT 84017. Recording, R/E phone-435-336-3238; fax-435-336-3055; 8AM-5PM www.co.summitcounty.org

Index: Separate indices to search include parcels, FLT, UCC, POA, Judgment, Mining, Water. Records indexed on a public use terminal back to 1983 alphabetical; 1992 for abstracts. Only the public may search. Copy fee $.50 per page, $.25 self serve. Copy fee if mail return- $5.00 minimum. Fax return- $4.00 1st page; $1.00 each add'l. Cert fee- $5.00 per page plus copy fee. Payee- Summit County Recorder. Bulk data available for purchase on CD's; $50.00 per CD. **Online Real Estate, Deed, Mortgage, Lien, Judgment, UCC records:** Access the county Document search page free at http://property.summitcounty.org:8080/eaglesoftware/web/login.jsp?submit=Enter. For free search use username public and password public. **Other phones:** Treasurer- 435-336-3266; County Clerk- 435-336-3203. **Property tax/Assessing-** 60 N Main, Coalville, UT 84017; 435-336-3248, assessor fax- 435-336-3049. (Appraiser/Auditor- 435-336-3254) **Online access-** Access property data free at http://property.summitcounty.org:8080/eaglesoftware/web/login.jsp?submit=Enter. For free search use username public and password public.

Tooele County

County Recorder, 47 S Main St, Rm 213, Tooele, UT 84074-2194. 435-843-3180; fax-435-882-7317; 7AM-6PM. www.co.tooele.ut.us/recorder.htm

Index: All in one. Records indexed on a public use terminal back to 1990. Only the public may search. Copy fee $1.00 per page. Cert fee- $7.00 1st page, $2.00 each add'l page. Payee- County Recorder. **Other phones:** Treasurer- 435-843-3191; Elections- 435-843-3140; Vital Records- 435-843-2300; County Clerk- 435-843-3140. **Property tax/Assessing**- 47 S Main St, Rm 221, Tooele, UT 84074; 435-843-3101, assessor fax- 435-843-3139. (Appraiser/Auditor- 435-843-3130) **Online access**- Access the property information database free at www.co.tooele.ut.us/taxinfo.html.

Uintah County

County Recorder, 147 E Main St; County Bldg, Vernal, UT 84078. 435-781-5461, R/E recording phone-435-781-5398; fax-435-781-5319; 8AM-5PM www.co.uintah.ut.us

Index: All in one. Records indexed on a public use terminal back to 1995. Only the public may search. Copy fee $.50 per page. Cert fee- $5.00 per cert includes copy fee. Payee- Uintah County Recorder. **Online access to Real Estate, Lien, Judgment, UCC, Plat records:** For a small subscription fee you can access public records at www.co.uintah.ut.us. **Other phones:** Treasurer- 435-781-5362; County Clerk- 435-781-5361. **Property tax/Assessing**- 435-781-5349. (Appraiser/Auditor- 435-781-5360) **Online access**- Access assessor property data free at www.co.uintah.ut.us/recorder/ownerqueryform.php.

Utah County

County Recorder, PO Box 122, Provo, UT 84603. Recording, R/E phone-801-851-8179; fax-801-851-8181; 8:30AM-5PM www.utahcountyonline.org

Index: Separate indices to search include 22 categories. Records indexed on a public use terminal back to 1978. Only the public may search. Copy fee $1.00 per page. Cert fee- $5.00 per cert plus copy fee. Payee- Utah County Recorder. **Online access to Real Estate, Deed, Lien, Building records:** Access the land records database and also map searching free at www.utahcountyonline.org/Dept/Record/LandRecordsandMaps/WebAccess.asp. Indexes go back to 1978; parcel indexes back to 1981. Document images go back to 1924. Building and GIS data is also online. **Other phones:** Treasurer- 801-851-8259; Elections- 801-951-8123; Vital Records- 801-851-4526; County Clerk- 801-851-8179 #5. **Property tax/Assessing**- 100 E Center #1100, Provo, UT 84606; 801-851-8286, assessor fax- 801-851-8282. (Appraiser/Auditor- 801-851-8291) **Online access**- Property and assessment data can be searched free at www.utahcountyonline.org/Dept/Record/LandRecordsandMaps/index.asp. Also, name search property data free at http://pbw.co.utah.ut.us/scripts/pbcgi70.exe/uc/u_functions/uof_namesearch. Delinquent tax list- http://pbw.co.utah.ut.us/scripts/pbcgi70.exe/ucl/u_functions/delinq_list.

Wasatch County

County Recorder, 25 N Main, Heber, UT 84032. 435-657-3210; 8AM-5PM www.co.wasatch.ut.us/d/recorder.html

Index: All in one. Records indexed on a public use terminal back to 1997. Only the public may search. Will not search UCC records. Copy fee $1.00 per page, $2.00 for 18 x 18; $4.00 for 24 x 36; $6.00 and up for larger. Cert fee- $5.00 per cert plus copy fee. Payee- Wasatch County Recorder. **Online access to Real Estate, Grantor/Grantee, Deed, Marriage, Parcel Map records:** Access to a limited grantor/grantee index (entry#, book & page/date/KOI). Also, surveys & subdivisions www.co.wasatch.ut.us/SIRE/portal.aspx?sun=wasatch. Documents from 09/20/1993 to present are accessible. Grantor/Grantee data back to 5/20/2002. **Other phones:** Treasurer- 435-657-3217; Elections- 434-657-3190; Vital Records- 435-654-2700; County Clerk- 435-657-3190; IT Dept -435i-657-3334. **Property tax/Assessing**- 25 N Main, Heber, UT 84032; 435-657-3221, assessor fax- 435-654-9924. (Appraiser/Auditor- 435-657-3221) **Online access**- The county GIS Dept. plans to have "metadata" property information free at its GIS mapping site at in the future. All parcel maps by number are free at www.co.wasatch.ut.us/plan/index.html.

Washington County

County Recorder, 87 N 200 E, #101, St. George, UT 84770. Recording, R/E phone-435-634-5709; fax-435-652-5895; 8AM-5PM. www.washco.utah.gov/

Index: All in one. Records indexed on a public use terminal back to 1983. Only the public may search. Copy fee $1.00 per page. Plats- $2.00; subdivision plat C- $4.00. Cert fee- $5.00 per cert includes copy fee. Payee- Washington County Recorder. **Online access to Real Estate, Deed, Mortgage, Lien records:** Access recorder data free at http://eweb.washco.utah.gov/recorder/web/login.jsp. **Other phones:** Treasurer- 435-652-5711; Elections- 435-634-5712; County Clerk- 435-634-5712. **Property tax/Assessing**- 87 N 200 E, #201, St. George, UT 84770; 435-634-5703, assessor fax- 435-652-5887. (Appraiser/Auditor- 435-634-5703) **Online access**- Search GIS property data free at http://maps.washco.utah.gov/imf/imf.jsp?site=washco_main and click on Locate but no name searching. Delinquent tax parcels at www.washco.utah.gov/treasurer/delinquents.php. Access the treasurer's property tax data free at www.washco.utah.gov/treasurer/AccountQuery.php but no name searching.

Wayne County

County Recorder, PO Box 187, Loa, UT 84747-0187. 435-836-2765 x2; fax-435-836-2479; 9AM-5PM www.waynecnty.com

Index: All in one. Records indexed on computer back to 1998. Only the public may search. Copy fee $.50 per page. Cert fee- $4.00 per cert, $1.00 per page of doc. Payee- Wayne County Recorder. **Other phones:** Treasurer- 435-836-2765 x2; County Clerk- 435-836-2765. **Property tax/Assessing**- 18 S Main, Loa, UT 84747; 435-836-2765 x3, assessor fax- 435-836-2479. (Appraiser/Auditor- 435-836-2765 x1);

Weber County

County Recorder, 2380 Washington Blvd, #370, Ogden, UT 84401. 801-399-8441; 8AM-5PM http://www1.co.weber.ut.us/rs/recorder/index.php

Index: Separate indices to search include pre-1980 abstract books, computer. Records indexed on a public use terminal back to 1980. Only the public may search. Copy fee $1.00 per page. Cert fee- $5.00 per cert plus copy fee. Payee- Weber County Recorder. Office does sell bulk data online, contact Debbie Conley at 399-8020-Fee is $100.00 per quarter. **Online access to Plats records:** Access recorder's dedicated plats data free at www.co.weber.ut.us/ded_plats.php. **Other phones:** Treasurer- 801-399-8454; Elections- 801-399-8400; Vital Records- 801-399-7130; County Clerk- 801-399-8400. **Property tax/Assessing**- PO Box 9700, 2380 Washington Blvd, #380, Ogden, UT 84409; 801-399-8572, fax- 801-399-8308. (Appraiser - 801-399-8400) http://www1.co.weber.ut.us/ **Online access**- Property records on the County Parcel Search site are free at www.co.weber.ut.us/psearch/. Also, access Abstract Title Registrations for a monthly fee at www.co.weber.ut.us/abstract.php is being redeveloped. Multiple GIS-mapping aps avaialbe free at www.co.weber.ut.us/gis/?content=interactive.

Utah County Locator

You will usually be able to find the city name in the City/County Cross Reference below. In that case, it is a simple matter to determine the county from the cross reference. However, only the official US Postal Service city names are included in this index. There are an additional 40,000 place names that people use in their addresses. Therefore, we have also included a ZIP/City Cross Reference immediately following the City/County Cross Reference.

If you know the ZIP Code but the city name does not appear in the City/County Cross Reference index, look up the ZIP Code in the ZIP/City Cross Reference, find the city name, then look up the city name in the City/County Cross Reference. For example, you want to know the county for an address of Menands, NY 12204. There is no "Menands" in the City/County Cross Reference. The ZIP/City Cross Reference shows that ZIP Codes 12201-12288 are for the city of Albany. Looking back in the City/County Cross Reference, Albany is in Albany County.

Utah City/County Cross Reference

ALPINE Utah
ALTAMONT Duchesne
ALTON Kane
ALTONAH Duchesne
AMERICAN FORK Utah
ANETH San Juan
ANNABELLA Sevier
ANTIMONY Garfield
AURORA Sevier
AXTELL Sanpete
BEAR RIVER CITY Box Elder
BERYL Iron
BICKNELL Wayne
BINGHAM CANYON Salt Lake
BLANDING San Juan
BLUEBELL Duchesne
BLUFF San Juan
BONANZA Uintah
BOULDER Garfield
BOUNTIFUL Davis
BRIAN HEAD Iron
BRIDGELAND Duchesne
BRIGHAM CITY Box Elder
BRYCE Garfield
BRYCE CANYON Garfield
CACHE JUNCTION Cache
CANNONVILLE Garfield
CASTLE DALE Emery
CEDAR CITY Iron
CEDAR VALLEY Utah
CENTERFIELD Sanpete
CENTERVILLE Davis
CENTRAL Washington
CHESTER Sanpete
CIRCLEVILLE Piute
CISCO Grand
CLARKSTON Cache
CLAWSON Emery
CLEARFIELD Davis
CLEVELAND Emery
COALVILLE Summit
COLLINSTON Box Elder
CORINNE Box Elder
CORNISH Cache
CROYDON Morgan
DAMMERON VALLEY Washington
DELTA Millard
DEWEYVILLE Box Elder
DRAPER Salt Lake
DUCHESNE Duchesne
DUCK CREEK VILLAGE Kane
DUGWAY Tooele
DUTCH JOHN Daggett
EAST CARBON Carbon
ECHO Summit
EDEN Weber
ELBERTA Utah
ELMO Emery
ELSINORE Sevier
EMERY Emery
ENTERPRISE Washington
EPHRAIM Sanpete
ESCALANTE Garfield
EUREKA Juab
FAIRVIEW Sanpete
FARMINGTON Davis
FAYETTE Sanpete
FERRON Emery
FIELDING Box Elder
FILLMORE Millard
FORT DUCHESNE Uintah
FOUNTAIN GREEN Sanpete
FRUITLAND Duchesne
GARDEN CITY Rich
GARLAND Box Elder
GARRISON Millard
GLENDALE Kane
GLENWOOD Sevier
GOSHEN Utah
GRANTSVILLE Tooele
GREEN RIVER Emery
GREENVILLE Beaver
GREENWICH Piute
GROUSE CREEK Box Elder
GUNLOCK Washington
GUNNISON Sanpete
GUSHER Uintah
HANKSVILLE Wayne
HANNA Duchesne
HATCH Garfield
HEBER CITY Wasatch
HELPER Carbon
HENEFER Summit
HENRIEVILLE Garfield
HIAWATHA Carbon
HILDALE Washington
HILL AFB Davis
HINCKLEY Millard
HOLDEN Millard
HONEYVILLE Box Elder
HOOPER (84315) Weber(92), Davis(7)
HOWELL Box Elder
HUNTINGTON Emery
HUNTSVILLE Weber
HURRICANE Washington
HYDE PARK Cache
HYRUM Cache
IBAPAH Tooele
IVINS Washington
JENSEN Uintah
JOSEPH Sevier
JUNCTION Piute
KAMAS (84036) Summit(86), Wasatch(13)
KANAB Kane
KANARRAVILLE Iron
KANOSH Millard
KAYSVILLE Davis
KENILWORTH Carbon
KINGSTON Piute
KOOSHAREM Sevier
LA SAL San Juan
LA VERKIN Washington
LAKE POWELL San Juan
LAKETOWN Rich
LAPOINT Uintah
LAYTON Davis
LEAMINGTON Millard
LEEDS Washington
LEHI Utah
LEVAN Juab
LEWISTON Cache
LINDON Utah
LOA Wayne
LOGAN Cache
LYMAN Wayne
LYNNDYL Millard
MAGNA Salt Lake
MANILA Daggett
MANTI Sanpete
MANTUA Box Elder
MAPLETON Utah
MARYSVALE Piute
MAYFIELD Sanpete
MEADOW Millard
MENDON Cache
MEXICAN HAT San Juan
MIDVALE Salt Lake
MIDWAY Wasatch
MILFORD Beaver
MILLVILLE Cache
MINERSVILLE Beaver
MOAB Grand
MODENA Iron
MONA Juab
MONROE Sevier
MONTEZUMA CREEK San Juan
MONTICELLO San Juan
MONUMENT VALLEY San Juan
MORGAN Morgan
MORONI Sanpete
MOUNT CARMEL Kane
MOUNT PLEASANT Sanpete
MOUNTAIN HOME Duchesne
MYTON (84052) Duchesne(75), Uintah(24)
NEOLA Duchesne
NEPHI Juab
NEW HARMONY Washington
NEWCASTLE Iron
NEWTON Cache
NORTH SALT LAKE Davis
OAK CITY Millard
OAKLEY Summit
OASIS Millard
OGDEN (84405) Weber(87), Davis(12)
OGDEN Weber
ORANGEVILLE Emery
ORDERVILLE Kane
OREM Utah
PANGUITCH Garfield
PARADISE Cache
PARAGONAH Iron
PARK CITY (84060) Summit(96), Wasatch(3)
PARK CITY Summit
PARK VALLEY Box Elder
PAROWAN Iron
PAYSON Utah
PEOA Summit
PINE VALLEY Washington
PLEASANT GROVE Utah
PLYMOUTH Box Elder
PORTAGE Box Elder
PRICE Carbon
PROVIDENCE Cache
PROVO Utah
RANDLETT Uintah
RANDOLPH Rich
REDMOND Sevier
RICHFIELD Sevier
RICHMOND Cache
RIVERSIDE Box Elder
RIVERTON Salt Lake
ROOSEVELT (84066) Duchesne(94), Uintah(5)
ROY Weber
RUSH VALLEY Tooele
SAINT GEORGE Washington
SALEM Utah
SALINA Sevier
SALT LAKE CITY Salt Lake
SANDY Salt Lake
SANTA CLARA Washington
SANTAQUIN Utah
SCIPIO Millard
SEVIER Sevier
SIGURD Sevier
SMITHFIELD Cache
SNOWVILLE Box Elder
SOUTH JORDAN Salt Lake
SPANISH FORK Utah
SPRING CITY Sanpete
SPRINGVILLE Utah
STERLING Sanpete
STOCKTON Tooele
SUMMIT Iron
SUNNYSIDE Carbon
SYRACUSE Davis
TABIONA Duchesne
TALMAGE Duchesne
TEASDALE Wayne
THOMPSON Grand
TOOELE Tooele
TOQUERVILLE Washington
TORREY Wayne
TREMONTON Box Elder
TRENTON Cache
TRIDELL Uintah
TROPIC Garfield
VERNAL Uintah
VERNON Tooele
VEYO Washington
VIRGIN Washington
WALES Sanpete
WALLSBURG Wasatch
WELLINGTON Carbon
WELLSVILLE Cache
WENDOVER Tooele
WEST JORDAN Salt Lake
WHITEROCKS Uintah
WILLARD Box Elder
WOODRUFF Rich
WOODS CROSS Davis

Utah ZIP/City Cross Reference

84001-84001 ALTAMONT
84002-84002 ALTONAH
84003-84003 AMERICAN FORK
84004-84004 ALPINE
84006-84006 BINGHAM CANYON
84007-84007 BLUEBELL
84008-84008 BONANZA
84010-84011 BOUNTIFUL
84012-84012 BRIDGELAND
84013-84013 CEDAR VALLEY
84014-84014 CENTERVILLE
84015-84016 CLEARFIELD
84017-84017 COALVILLE
84018-84018 CROYDON
84020-84020 DRAPER
84021-84021 DUCHESNE
84022-84022 DUGWAY
84023-84023 DUTCH JOHN
84024-84024 ECHO
84025-84025 FARMINGTON
84026-84026 FORT DUCHESNE
84027-84027 FRUITLAND
84028-84028 GARDEN CITY
84029-84029 GRANTSVILLE
84030-84030 GUSHER
84031-84031 HANNA
84032-84032 HEBER CITY
84033-84033 HENEFER
84034-84034 IBAPAH
84035-84035 JENSEN
84036-84036 KAMAS
84037-84037 KAYSVILLE
84038-84038 LAKETOWN
84039-84039 LAPOINT
84040-84041 LAYTON
84042-84042 LINDON
84043-84043 LEHI
84044-84044 MAGNA
84046-84046 MANILA
84047-84047 MIDVALE
84049-84049 MIDWAY
84050-84050 MORGAN
84051-84051 MOUNTAIN HOME
84052-84052 MYTON
84053-84053 NEOLA
84054-84054 NORTH SALT LAKE
84055-84055 OAKLEY
84056-84056 HILL AFB
84057-84059 OREM
84060-84060 PARK CITY
84061-84061 PEOA
84062-84062 PLEASANT GROVE
84063-84063 RANDLETT
84064-84064 RANDOLPH
84065-84065 RIVERTON
84066-84066 ROOSEVELT
84067-84067 ROY
84068-84068 PARK CITY
84069-84069 RUSH VALLEY
84070-84070 SANDY
84071-84071 STOCKTON
84072-84072 TABIONA
84073-84073 TALMAGE
84074-84074 TOOELE
84075-84075 SYRACUSE
84076-84076 TRIDELL
84078-84079 VERNAL
84080-84080 VERNON
84082-84082 WALLSBURG
84083-84083 WENDOVER
84084-84084 WEST JORDAN
84085-84085 WHITEROCKS
84086-84086 WOODRUFF
84087-84087 WOODS CROSS
84088-84088 WEST JORDAN
84089-84089 CLEARFIELD
84090-84094 SANDY
84095-84095 SOUTH JORDAN
84097-84097 OREM
84098-84098 PARK CITY
84100-84199 SALT LAKE CITY
84201-84244 OGDEN
84301-84301 BEAR RIVER CITY
84302-84302 BRIGHAM CITY
84304-84304 CACHE JUNCTION
84305-84305 CLARKSTON
84306-84306 COLLINSTON
84307-84307 CORINNE
84308-84308 CORNISH
84309-84309 DEWEYVILLE
84310-84310 EDEN
84311-84311 FIELDING
84312-84312 GARLAND
84313-84313 GROUSE CREEK
84314-84314 HONEYVILLE
84315-84315 HOOPER
84316-84316 HOWELL
84317-84317 HUNTSVILLE
84318-84318 HYDE PARK
84319-84319 HYRUM
84320-84320 LEWISTON
84321-84323 LOGAN
84324-84324 MANTUA
84325-84325 MENDON
84326-84326 MILLVILLE
84327-84327 NEWTON
84328-84328 PARADISE
84329-84329 PARK VALLEY
84330-84330 PLYMOUTH
84331-84331 PORTAGE
84332-84332 PROVIDENCE
84333-84333 RICHMOND
84334-84334 RIVERSIDE
84335-84335 SMITHFIELD
84336-84336 SNOWVILLE
84337-84337 TREMONTON
84338-84338 TRENTON
84339-84339 WELLSVILLE
84340-84340 WILLARD
84341-84341 LOGAN
84400-84415 OGDEN
84501-84501 PRICE
84510-84510 ANETH
84511-84511 BLANDING
84512-84512 BLUFF
84513-84513 CASTLE DALE
84515-84515 CISCO
84516-84516 CLAWSON
84518-84518 CLEVELAND
84520-84520 EAST CARBON
84521-84521 ELMO
84522-84522 EMERY
84523-84523 FERRON
84525-84525 GREEN RIVER
84526-84526 HELPER
84527-84527 HIAWATHA
84528-84528 HUNTINGTON
84529-84529 KENILWORTH
84530-84530 LA SAL
84531-84531 MEXICAN HAT
84532-84532 MOAB
84533-84533 LAKE POWELL
84534-84534 MONTEZUMA CREEK
84535-84535 MONTICELLO
84536-84536 MONUMENT VALLEY
84537-84537 ORANGEVILLE
84539-84539 SUNNYSIDE
84540-84540 THOMPSON
84542-84542 WELLINGTON
84601-84606 PROVO
84620-84620 AURORA
84621-84621 AXTELL
84622-84622 CENTERFIELD
84623-84623 CHESTER
84624-84624 DELTA
84626-84626 ELBERTA
84627-84627 EPHRAIM
84628-84628 EUREKA
84629-84629 FAIRVIEW
84630-84630 FAYETTE
84631-84631 FILLMORE
84632-84632 FOUNTAIN GREEN
84633-84633 GOSHEN
84634-84634 GUNNISON
84635-84635 HINCKLEY
84636-84636 HOLDEN
84637-84637 KANOSH
84638-84638 LEAMINGTON
84639-84639 LEVAN
84640-84640 LYNNDYL
84642-84642 MANTI
84643-84643 MAYFIELD
84644-84644 MEADOW
84645-84645 MONA
84646-84646 MORONI
84647-84647 MOUNT PLEASANT
84648-84648 NEPHI
84649-84649 OAK CITY
84650-84650 OASIS
84651-84651 PAYSON
84652-84652 REDMOND
84653-84653 SALEM
84654-84654 SALINA
84655-84655 SANTAQUIN
84656-84656 SCIPIO
84657-84657 SIGURD
84660-84660 SPANISH FORK
84662-84662 SPRING CITY
84663-84663 SPRINGVILLE
84664-84664 MAPLETON
84665-84665 STERLING
84667-84667 WALES
84701-84701 RICHFIELD
84710-84710 ALTON
84711-84711 ANNABELLA
84712-84712 ANTIMONY
84713-84713 BEAVER
84714-84714 BERYL
84715-84715 BICKNELL
84716-84716 BOULDER
84717-84717 BRYCE CANYON
84718-84718 CANNONVILLE
84719-84719 BRIAN HEAD
84720-84721 CEDAR CITY
84722-84722 CENTRAL
84723-84723 CIRCLEVILLE
84724-84724 ELSINORE
84725-84725 ENTERPRISE
84726-84726 ESCALANTE
84728-84728 GARRISON
84729-84729 GLENDALE
84730-84730 GLENWOOD
84731-84731 GREENVILLE
84732-84732 GREENWICH
84733-84733 GUNLOCK
84734-84734 HANKSVILLE
84735-84735 HATCH
84736-84736 HENRIEVILLE
84737-84737 HURRICANE
84738-84738 IVINS
84739-84739 JOSEPH
84740-84740 JUNCTION
84741-84741 KANAB
84742-84742 KANARRAVILLE
84743-84743 KINGSTON
84744-84744 KOOSHAREM
84745-84745 LA VERKIN
84746-84746 LEEDS
84747-84747 LOA
84749-84749 LYMAN
84750-84750 MARYSVALE
84751-84751 MILFORD
84752-84752 MINERSVILLE
84753-84753 MODENA
84754-84754 MONROE
84755-84755 MOUNT CARMEL
84756-84756 NEWCASTLE
84757-84757 NEW HARMONY
84758-84758 ORDERVILLE
84759-84759 PANGUITCH
84760-84760 PARAGONAH
84761-84761 PAROWAN
84762-84762 DUCK CREEK VILLAGE
84763-84763 ROCKVILLE
84764-84764 BRYCE
84765-84765 SANTA CLARA
84766-84766 SEVIER
84767-84767 SPRINGDALE
84770-84771 SAINT GEORGE
84772-84772 SUMMIT
84773-84773 TEASDALE
84774-84774 TOQUERVILLE
84775-84775 TORREY
84776-84776 TROPIC
84779-84779 VIRGIN
84780-84780 WASHINGTON
84781-84781 PINE VALLEY
84782-84782 VEYO
84783-84783 DAMMERON VALLEY
84784-84784 HILDALE
84790-84791 SAINT GEORGE

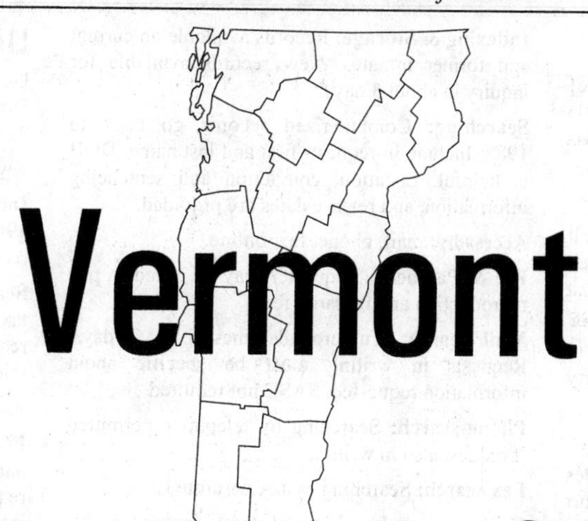

Vermont

General Help Numbers:

Governor's Office
Pavillion Office Bldg
109 State St
Montpelier, VT 05609-0101
http://governor.vermont.gov/
802-828-3333
Fax 802-828-3339
7:45AM-4:30PM

Attorney General's Office
109 State St
Montpelier, VT 05609-1001
www.atg.state.vt.us/
802-828-3171
Fax 802-828-2154
7:45AM-4:30PM

Legislative Records
State House-Legislative Council
115 State Street, Drawer 33
Montpelier, VT 05633
www.leg.state.vt.us
802-828-2231
Fax 802-828-2424
8AM-4:30PM

State Archives
State Archives Division
26 Terrace-Redstone Bldg
Montpelier, VT 05609-1103
http://vermont-archives.org
802-828-2308
Fax 802-828-1135
7:45AM-4:30PM

State Specifics:

Capital: Montpelier
Washington County

Time Zone: EST

Number of Counties: 14

Population: 621,270

Web Site: http://vermont.gov/

State Agencies

Criminal Records

Criminal Record Check Section, Vermont Criminal Information Center, 103 S. Main St., Waterbury, VT 05671-2101; 802-244-8727, 802-241-5237, Fax- 802-241-5552; 8AM-4:30PM.

www.dps.state.vt.us

Indexing & Storage: New records available for inquiry in 10 to 20 days. 96% of records in the state database have dispositions.

Searching: 35% of records are fingerprint supported. Include in request- subject's notarized signature, DOB, SSN, telephone number. The requester must have a User Agreement in place. Copies of the User Agreement and the Request Form may both be downloaded from the web page. A copy of the record must be given by the employer to the hiree within 10 days. The employer may be represented by an agency or third party. This data not released- location of court, docket number, juvenile records unless the juvenile was prosecuted in District Court as an adult. Only conviction data is released, unless requester is law enforcement. Charges arraigned in Family Court, the Traffic Ticket Bureau or the Municipal Ordinance Bureau are not reported.

Access by: mail, online.

Fee & Payment: The fee is $20.00 per record. The fee will increase to $25 in July 2009. Fee payee- Vermont Criminal Information Center Prepayment required. Personal checks accepted.

Mail search: Turnaround time- 5 to 7 days. SASE required,

Online search: Access to District Court criminal records is at https://secure.vermont.gov/DPS/criminalrecords/. Search by name and DOB. One may use a credit or billing is available to subscribers to Vermont.gov. The fee is $20.00 per record. Results are immediate and can be printed. A validation service is also offered. Search results report the date of conviction, charge, sentence and venue. It won't show the original charge filed, or give information about the victim or the circumstances of the crime. Disclosure of the contents of the conviction report to anyone other than the subject of the record or properly designated employees of any agency with a documented need to know the contents of the record is prohibited.

Statewide Court Records

Court Administrator, Administrative Office of Courts, 109 State St, Montpelier, VT 05609-0701; 802-828-3278, Fax- 802-828-3457; 7:45AM-4:30PM.

www.vermontjudiciary.org/default.aspx

Except for certain online research capabilities, all court record access must be done at the local level. A list of statewide court fees is found at www.vermontjudiciary.org/Resources/courtfees.aspx.

Searching: Include in request- docket # or party name with DOB, if by mail.

Access by: online.

Online search: Vermont Courts Online provides access to civil and small claim cases and court calendar information from 12 of the county Superior Courts. Not available for Chittenden and Franklin. Not available for criminal, domestic and juvenile cases. Go to https://secure.vermont.gov/vtcdas/user. Records are in real-time mode. There is a $12.50 activation fee plus a fee of $.50 per case for look-up after the 1st 5 cases. Supreme Court opinions are available from the main web site and are also maintained by Vermont Dept. of Libraries at http://libraries.vermont.gov/law/supct.

Sexual Offender Registry

State Repository, Vermont Criminal Information Center, 103 S. Main St., Waterbury, VT 05671-2101; 802-244-8727, 802-241-5400, Fax- 802-241-5552; 8AM-4:30PM.

www.dps.state.vt.us/cjs/s_registry.htm

13 V.S.A. section 5401 et seq., requires the DPS to establish and maintain a registry of persons who are required to register as sex offenders and to post electronically information on sex offenders. The website contains only high-risk offenders.

Indexing & Storage: Records available from 1996. New records available for inquiry in 24 hours.

Searching: The complete record database is not publicly available and is accessible only by those authorized by law (employers with employees working with children, elderly, or disabled) or by the subject. Otherwise, requesters must search at local level. The Registry is prohibited from releasing lists of offenders in response to general questions regarding the whereabouts of sex offenders in a particular community. This data not released- victim information and exact address of offender.

Access by: phone, online.

Phone search: Telephone requests are accepted if search is not extensive.

Online search: The webpage gives access to the high-risk offenders only. The requestor must also acknowledge a statement which specifies the conditions under which the registry information is being released.

Incarceration Records

Vermont Department of Corrections, Inmate Information Request, 103 S. Main Street, Waterbury, VT 05671-1001; 802-241-2276, Fax-802-241-2565; 8AM-4:30PM.

www.doc.state.vt.us

Indexing & Storage: Records available on current and former inmates. New records available for inquiry in about 3 days.

Searching: Computerized records go back to 1988. Include in request- first and last name. DOB is helpful. Location, conviction and sentencing information, and release dates are provided.

Access by: mail, phone, fax, online.

Fee & Payment: Requester may be asked to pay reproduction and research fees.

Mail search: Turnaround time- 5 to 7 days. Requests in writing must be specific about information requested. SASE not required.

Phone search: Searching by telephone permitted if request also in writing.

Fax search: Searching by fax permitted.

Online search: The website provides an Incarcerated Offender Locator to ascertain where an inmate is located. Click at the top of main page, or go directly to http://doc.vermont.gov/offender-locator/ Search results give name, DOB, location and case worker. This is not designed to provide complete inmate records nor is it a database of all inmates past and present in the system.

Corporation, LLC, LLP, LP, L3C, Trade Name, Trademarks/Servicemarks

Secretary of State, Corporation Division, 81 River St, Montpelier, VT 05609-1104; 802-828-2386, Fax- 802-828-2853; 7:45AM-4:30PM.

www.sec.state.vt.us/corps/index.htm

Indexing & Storage: Records available from beginning of record keeping. Records are on computer if active. Inactive records are indexed by a card file. New records available for inquiry in 24-48 hours.

Searching: Include in request- full name of business. One search tip provided by agency is not to use the "corp" ending as part of the name search.

Access by: mail, phone, fax, in person, online.

Fee & Payment: There is no search fee. The fee for certification is $20.00 plus $1.00 per page for copies. Fee payee- Secretary of State. Prepayment required. Personal checks accepted, credit cards are not.

Mail search: Turnaround time- 3 to 5 days. SASE requested.

Phone search: They will only confirm if business is active.

Fax search: Same criteria as mail searching. They will return a page or two by fax, if local number, otherwise results are mailed.

In person: Simple requests may be processed while you wait.

Online search: Information on Corporate and trademark records can be accessed from the Internet for no fee. For the corporation name search, go to www.sec.state.vt.us/seek/database.htm#2. Many records, included corporation, UCC, trademark, trade name, and name look-ups are available. Search securities investment professionals at www.bishca.info/php/BDIA/bdia01.htm.

Other access: There is an option on the web to download the entire corporation (and trade name) database.

Uniform Commercial Code

UCC Division, Secretary of State, 81 River St, Drawer 4, Montpelier, VT 05609-1101; 802-828-2386, Fax- 802-828-2853; 7:45AM-4:30PM.

www.sec.state.vt.us/tutor/dobiz/ucc/ucchome.htm

Indexing & Storage: Records available from 1967. All active records are computerized. New records available for inquiry in 3 to 5 days.

Searching: Use search request form UCC-11. All tax liens are filed at the town/city level. Include in request- debtor name, business name. This data not released- SSNs

Access by: mail, fax, in person, online.

Fee & Payment: Certified searches are $20.00 per name. Fee payee- Secretary of State. Prepayment required. Personal checks accepted, credit cards are not.

Mail search: Turnaround time- 4 days. A SASE is requested for listings. Individual copies can be obtained via the web.

Fax search: Same criteria as mail searching, if account established.

In person: Turnaround time depends on workload, may not be immediate.

Online search: UCC searches available free at www.sec.state.vt.us/seek/ucc_seek.htm. Search by debtor or business name.

Other access: The database may be downloaded from the web. The data file is in a self extracting, IBM compatible, generic dbf format. Also the last 30 days of images may be downloaded in a ZIP format.

Expedited service: Expedited service is available for account holders.

Federal & State Tax Liens

Records not maintained by a state level agency.

Records are found at the local town level.

Sales Tax Registrations

Administrative Agency/Tax Department, Taxpayers Services Division, PO Box 547, Montpelier, VT 05602-0457; 802-828-2551, Fax-802-828-5787; 7:45AM-4:30PM.

www.state.vt.us/tax/

Indexing & Storage: Records available for 4 years on computer database, then records are archived. New records available for inquiry in 30 days.

Searching: This agency will only confirm that a business is registered. Taxpayer records are considered confidential, as provided by law. Include in request- business name or tax permit number or owner name or federal tax ID.

Access by: mail, phone, fax.

Fee & Payment: There is no fee to confirm whether a business is registered to collect sales tax.

Mail search: Turnaround time- 7 to 10 days. A SASE is requested.

Phone search: No fee for telephone request.

Fax search: Requests may be faxed.

Birth Certificates

Reference & Research, Vital Records Section, US Rte 2, Drawer 33, Montpelier, VT 05633-7601; 802-828-3286, Fax- 802-828-3710; 8AM-4PM.

www.bgs.state.vt.us/gsc/pubrec/referen/

Only certified records are sold.

Indexing & Storage: Records available from 1760 to 2003. For records for the past 5 years only, contact the Department of Health at 802-863-7300.

Searching: The records are open to the public, but use of the state form is required. The form may be downloaded from the web page. Include in request- full name, names of parents, mother's maiden name, date of birth, place of birth.

Access by: mail, in person, online.

Fee & Payment: The search fee is $10.00 per name. Fee payee- BGS State of VT Prepayment required. Personal checks and major credit cards accepted.

Mail search: Turnaround time- 5 to 7 days. A SASE is requested.

In person: You may view the records for no charge.

Online search: The online Vital Records Request Service allows users to request certified copies of vital records including: birth, death, marriage, civil union, divorce, or dissolution. The fee is $10.00. Visit https://secure.vermont.gov/BGS/vitalrecords/. Use of a credit card is required. Records are returned by mail in 5 to 7 days.

Death Records

Reference & Research, Vital Records, US Rte 2, Drawer 33, Montpelier, VT 05633-7601; 802-828-3286, Fax- 802-828-3710; 8AM-4PM.

www.bgs.state.vt.us/gsc/pubrec/referen/

Only certified records are sold.

Indexing & Storage: Records available from 1760 to 2003. For records for the past 5 years only, contact the Department of Health at 802-863-7300.

Searching: Records are open to the public. Include in request- full name, date of death, place of death, names of parents.

Access by: mail, in person, online.

Fee & Payment: The search fee is $10.00 per name. Fee payee- BGS State of VT Prepayment required. Credit cards accepted. Personal checks accepted.

Mail search: Turnaround time- 5 to 7 days. A SASE is requested.

In person: You may view records at no charge.

Online search: The online Vital Records Request Service allows users to request certified copies of vital records including: birth, death, marriage, civil union, divorce, or dissolution. Fee is $10.00. Visit https://secure.vermont.gov/BGS/vitalrecords/. Use of a credit card is required. Records are returned by mail in 5 to 7 days.

Marriage Certificates

Reference & Research, Vital Records Section, US Rte 2, Drawer 33, Montpelier, VT 05633-7601; 802-828-3286, Fax- 802-828-3710; 8AM-4PM.

www.bgs.state.vt.us/gsc/pubrec/referen/

Only certified records are sold.

Indexing & Storage: Records available from 1760 to 2003. For records for the past 5 years only, contact the Department of Health at 802-863-7300.

Searching: Records are open. Include in request- names of husband and wife, date of marriage, place or county of marriage, names of parents.

Access by: mail, in person, online.

Fee & Payment: The search fee is $10.00 per name. Fee payee- BGS State of VT Prepayment required. Personal checks and credit cards accepted.

Mail search: Turnaround time- 5 to 7 days. A SASE is requested.

In person: Records may be viewed in person at no charge.

Online search: The online Vital Records Request Service allows users to request certified copies of vital records including: birth, death, marriage, civil union, divorce, dissolution. Fee is $10.00. Visit https://secure.vermont.gov/BGS/vitalrecords/. Use of a credit card is required. Records are returned by mail in 5 to 7 days.

Divorce Records

Research & Reference, Vital Records Section, US Rte 2, Drawer 33, Montpelier, VT 05633-7601; 802-828-3286, Fax- 802-828-3710; 8AM-4PM.

www.bgs.state.vt.us/gsc/pubrec/referen/

Only certified records are sold.

Indexing & Storage: Records available from 1760 to 2003. For records for the past 5 years only, contact the Department of Health at 802-863-7300.

Searching: Records are open. Include in request- names of husband and wife, date of divorce, place of divorce.

Access by: mail, in person, online.

Fee & Payment: The search fee is $10.00 per name. Fee payee- BGS/State of VT Prepayment required. Personal checks and credit cards accepted.

Mail search: Turnaround time- 5 to 7 days. A SASE is requested.

In person: There is no fee to view records.

Online search: The online Vital Records Request Service allows users to request certified copies of vital records including: birth, death, marriage, civil union, divorce, dissolution. Fee is $10.00. Visit https://secure.vermont.gov/BGS/vitalrecords/. Use of a credit card is required. Records are returned by mail in 5 to 7 days.

Workers' Compensation Records

Department of Labor, Workers Compensation Division, PO Box 488, Montpelier, VT 056201-0488 (Courier address- 5 Green Mountain Drive, Montpelier, VT 05602); 802-828-2286, Fax- 802-828-2195; 7:45AM-4:30PM.

www.labor.vermont.gov/

Indexing & Storage: Records available on site. New records available for inquiry immediately.

Searching: Must be a party to the claim or have a signed release from the claimant. You also will get only the employer's first report of injury. Include in request- claimant name, SSN, place of employment at time of accident. This data not released- medical records.

Access by: mail, fax, in person.

Fee & Payment: No search fee, copy fee is $.05 per page. Fee payee- State of Vermont. Personal checks accepted, credit cards are not.

Mail search: Turnaround time- 2 weeks. A SASE is requested.

Fax search: Turnaround time is 2 weeks.

In person: Turnaround time is while you wait if staff is available.

Driver Records, Driver License Information

Department of Motor Vehicles, DI - Records Unit, 120 State St, Montpelier, VT 05603-0001; 802-828-2050, Fax- 802-828-2098; 7:45AM-4:30PM.

http://dmv.vermont.gov/

Ticket information is available from the Vermont Judicial Bureau, PO Box 607, White River Junction, VT 05001, 802-295-8869. There is no charge, but no information is given over the phone.

Indexing & Storage: Records available for convictions and accidents. Records are sold as 3-year records or as complete (8+ years) records. New records available for inquiry in 5-7 days normally.

Searching: Ongoing permissible users must use Form TA-VG-118. Otherwise, use TA-VG-116 for written authorization from the subject to release personal information to the requester. Include in request- name, DOB, signed release, if necessary. Mail or walk-in requesters need the driver's full name and DOB; the license number is optional. Online requesters need only the license number, but the last name and DOB are helpful. This data not released- addresses, SSNs, medical information or personal information (height, weight, sex, eye color, etc.).

Access by: mail, in person, online.

Fee & Payment: The charge for mail or in-person records is $10.00 for 3-year record and $16.00 for the "complete" certified record. The three-year record can be accessed online for $13.00 per record. There is a full charge for a "no record found." Fee payee- Vermont Department of Motor Vehicles. Prepayment required. Personal checks accepted, credit cards are not.

Mail search: Turnaround time- 5 to 7 days. A SASE is requested.

In person: Normal turnaround time is while you wait.

Online search: Record access is available to approved requesters as a premium service from Vermont.gov. The fee is $13.00 per record; a $75.00 annual subscription fee is also required. Single inquiry and batch mode are both available. The system is open 24 hours a day, 7 days a week (except for file maintenance periods). Only the license number is needed when ordering, the system does not ask for the name and DOB. For more information about setting up an account, call Driver Improvement at 802-828-2061. To reach Vermont.gov visit www.vermont.gov or email vt_mvr@nicusa.gov.

Other access: This agency will sell its license file to approved requesters for non-commercial use, but customization is not available.

Vehicle, Vessel Ownership & Registration

Department of Motor Vehicles, Registration & License Information/Records, 120 State St, Montpelier, VT 05603; 802-828-2000, Fax- 802-828-2872; 7:45AM-4:30PM.

http://dmv.vermont.gov/

Ongoing permissible users must be authorized first. Occasional requesters must use form TA-VG 116(d). If record use is not "permissible" per DPPA, written authorization is needed from subject. Otherwise, records with no personal data are released.

Indexing & Storage: Records available for 15 years to present. All motorized boats must be registered. New records available for inquiry in 1 to 3 weeks.

Searching: Potential lien-holders are provided a "yes or no" answer when asked about liens on a record. One must have name and DOB or plate # or VIN. To receive personal information, you must include signed release by individual, unless ongoing account. Use of Vermont DMV Record Request Form is advised. This data not released- SSNs, residence addresses, bulk information or lists for commercial purposes or medical information.

Access by: mail, in person.

Fee & Payment: $6.00 for each group (1-4) of registration records and $20.00 for an ownership (lien) search. Vessel fees are different: registration check is $6.00, title search is $13.00. Extensive research is $35.00 per hour. Fee payee- Vermont Department of Motor Vehicles. Prepayment required. Personal checks accepted, credit cards are not.

Mail search: Turnaround time- 7 to 10 days. A SASE is requested.

In person: The turnaround time is generally 30 minutes for vehicle records. Vessel records are returned by mail.

Other access: High volume requesters can obtain records electronically. Bulk release of the database is not available except for statistical purposes. Apply to the Commissioner's Office.

Accident Reports

Department of Motor Vehicles, Accident Report Section, 120 State St, Montpelier, VT 05603; 802-828-2050; 7:45AM-4PM.

http://dmv.vermont.gov/

Indexing & Storage: Records available for 4 years to present, 3 years on paper. Only records involving damage in excess of $1,000 or if injuries involved are reportable. New records available for inquiry in 45 days after the incident.

Searching: Include in request- full name, date of accident, location of accident, address of person involved. If accident involves a criminal action or fatality it may take up to 3 months after accident date to get the report. This data not released- SSNs.

Access by: mail, in person.

Fee & Payment: The fee for certified copies are $15.00 for the police report, $10.00 for a copy of the individual's report, and $6.00 for insurance information of the accident. Fee payee- Vermont Department of Motor Vehicles. Prepayment required. Personal checks accepted, credit cards are not.

Mail search: Turnaround time- 15 days. A SASE is requested.

In person: Simple requests may be processed while you wait.

Legislation Records

Vermont General Assembly, State House- Legislative Council, 115 State Street, Drawer 33, Montpelier, VT 05633; 802-828-2231, 802-828-2247 (House Clerk), Fax- 802-828-2424; 8AM-4:30PM.

www.leg.state.vt.us

Indexing & Storage: Records available from 1940 at Legislative Council.

Searching: Include in request- bill number.

Access by: mail, phone, fax, in person, online.

Fee & Payment: There is no fee.

Mail search: Turnaround time- same day. SASE not required.

Phone search: Records are available by phone.

Fax search: Fax searching available.

In person: No fee for request. A public access terminal is available in the public lobby of the legislature.

Online search: The website offers access to extensive information about bills and statutes.

Other access: A subscription service is available for bill text.

Voter Registration

Access to Records is Restricted.

Secretary of State, Election Division, 26 Terrace St, Montpelier, VT 05609-1101; 802-828-2464, 802-828-0175, Fax- 802-828-5171; 7:45AM-4:30PM.

http://vermont-elections.org/soshome.htm

Individual name searches must be done at the municipal level. This agency will sell an electronic file of voter records but only if the list is used for political purposes.

GED Certificates

Department of Education, GED Testing, 120 State Street, Montpelier, VT 05620; 802-828-5161, Fax- 802-828-3146; 8AM-4:30PM.

http://education.vermont.gov/

Indexing & Storage: Records available from 1943. New records available for inquiry in 2 weeks.

Searching: Include in request- name, date of birth, SSN, signed release.

Access by: mail, phone, fax, in person.

Fee & Payment: The fee is $3.00 for a transcript copy. There is no fee for a simple verification. Fee payee- Treasurer, State of Vermont. Prepayment required. Personal checks accepted, credit cards are not.

Mail search: Turnaround time- 1 week. SASE not required.

Phone search: The agency will give a verification over the phone.

Fax search: You may use the fax to verify a GED, but not for a transcript purchase unless money previously sent.

In person: If staff available, requests will be processed while you wait.

Expedited service: Rush service is available for emergency situations.

Hunting & Fishing License Information

Access to Records is Restricted.

Fish & Wildlife Department, Licensing Division, 103 South Main Street - Bldg 10 South, Waterbury, VT 05671-0501; 802-241-3700, Fax- 802-241-3295; 7:45AM-4:30PM.

www.vtfishandwildlife.com

Although they maintain a central database on computer, the records are not open to the public.

Vermont State Licensing Agencies

For details about the agency responsible for licensing/certifying/registering an item below or in the Agency Quick Finder section, match an item's number with the number of the agency in the *Licensing Agency Information* section.

Vermont Licenses Searchable Online

Accounting Firm #15 .... www.sec.state.vt.us/seek/lrspseek.htm
Acupuncturist #15 .... www.sec.state.vt.us/seek/lrspseek.htm
Anesthesiologist Assistant #14 .... http://healthvermont.gov/hc/med_board/docfinder.aspx
Architect #15 .... www.sec.state.vt.us/seek/lrspseek.htm
Asbestos Contractor/Worker #13 .... http://healthvermont.gov/enviro/asbestos/documents/asbestos_list.pdf
Athletic Trainer #15 .... www.sec.state.vt.us/seek/lrspseek.htm
Attorney #2 .... www.vermontjudiciary.org/bbe/bbelibrary/publicattorneyinformation.htm
Auctioneer #15 .... www.sec.state.vt.us/seek/lrspseek.htm
Bank #5 .... www.bishca.state.vt.us/BankingDiv/banking_index.htm
Barber #15 .... www.sec.state.vt.us/seek/lrspseek.htm
Body Piercer #15 .... www.sec.state.vt.us/seek/lrspseek.htm
Boxing Manager/Promoter #15 .... www.sec.state.vt.us/seek/lrspseek.htm
Boxing Professional #15 .... www.sec.state.vt.us/seek/lrspseek.htm
Chemical Suppression TQP Cert #8 .... www.dps.state.vt.us/fire/index.html
Chimney Sweep TQP Cert #8 .... www.dps.state.vt.us/fire/index.html
Chiropractor #15 .... www.sec.state.vt.us/seek/lrspseek.htm
Cosmetologist #15 .... www.sec.state.vt.us/seek/lrspseek.htm
Courier, Armed #15 .... www.sec.state.vt.us/seek/lrspseek.htm
Credit Union #5 .... www.bishca.state.vt.us/BankingDiv/banking_index.htm
Crematory #15 .... www.sec.state.vt.us/seek/lrspseek.htm
Dental Assistant #15 .... www.sec.state.vt.us/seek/lrspseek.htm
Dental Hygienist #15 .... www.sec.state.vt.us/seek/lrspseek.htm
Dentist #15 .... www.sec.state.vt.us/seek/lrspseek.htm
Dietitian #15 .... www.sec.state.vt.us/seek/lrspseek.htm
Electrician #8 .... www.dps.state.vt.us/fire/index.html
Electrologist #15 .... www.sec.state.vt.us/seek/lrspseek.htm
Elevator Inspector #8 .... www.dps.state.vt.us/fire/index.html
Elevator Mechanic #8 .... www.dps.state.vt.us/fire/index.html
Embalmer #15 .... www.sec.state.vt.us/seek/lrspseek.htm
Engineer #15 .... www.sec.state.vt.us/seek/lrspseek.htm
Esthetician #15 .... www.sec.state.vt.us/seek/lrspseek.htm
Fire Alarm System Instal'r/Dealer #8 .... www.dps.state.vt.us/fire/index.html
Fire Sprinkler System Design/Installer #8 .... www.dps.state.vt.us/fire/index.html
Funeral Director #15 .... www.sec.state.vt.us/seek/lrspseek.htm
Hearing Aid Dispenser #15 .... www.sec.state.vt.us/seek/lrspseek.htm
Lead Abatement Contractor/Worker #13 .... http://healthvermont.gov/enviro/asbestos/documents/lead_list.pdf
Lift Mechanic #8 .... www.dps.state.vt.us/fire/index.html
Liquor, Retail/Wholesale #10 .... www.state.vt.us/dlc/downloads.html#licensing
Lobbyist #19 .... http://vermont-elections.org/elections1/lobbyist.html
Lobbyist Employer/Firm #19 .... http://vermont-elections.org/elections1/lobbyist.html
Lobbyist Gift #19 .... http://vermont-elections.org/elections1/lobbyist.html
LPG/Propane Installer #8 .... www.dps.state.vt.us/fire/index.html
Manicurist #15 .... www.sec.state.vt.us/seek/lrspseek.htm
Marriage & Family Therapist #15 .... www.sec.state.vt.us/seek/lrspseek.htm
Medical Doctor/Surgeon #14 .... http://healthvermont.gov/hc/med_board/docfinder.aspx
Mental Health Counselor, Clinical #15 .... www.sec.state.vt.us/seek/lrspseek.htm
Midwife, Licensed #15 .... www.sec.state.vt.us/seek/lrspseek.htm
Natural Gas System Installer #8 .... www.dps.state.vt.us/fire/index.html
Naturopathic Physician #15 .... www.sec.state.vt.us/seek/lrspseek.htm
Notary Public #15 .... http://vermont-archives.org/notary/notary.asp
Nurse/Nurse Practitioner/LNA #15 .... www.sec.state.vt.us/seek/lrspseek.htm
Nursing Home Administrator #15 .... www.sec.state.vt.us/seek/lrspseek.htm
Occupational Therapist #15 .... www.sec.state.vt.us/seek/lrspseek.htm
Oil Burning Equipment Installer #8 .... www.dps.state.vt.us/fire/index.html
Optician #15 .... www.sec.state.vt.us/seek/lrspseek.htm
Optometrist #15 .... www.sec.state.vt.us/seek/lrspseek.htm
Osteopathic Physician #15 .... www.sec.state.vt.us/seek/lrspseek.htm

Pesticide Applicator #4................................ www.vermontagriculture.com/pest.htm
Pharmacist/Pharmacy #15................................ www.sec.state.vt.us/seek/lrspseek.htm
Physical Therapist/Assistant #15................................ www.sec.state.vt.us/seek/lrspseek.htm
Physician, Assistant #14................................ http://healthvermont.gov/hc/med_board/docfinder.aspx
Plumber #8................................ www.dps.state.vt.us/fire/licensing/plicenses.htm
Podiatrist #14................................ http://healthvermont.gov/hc/med_board/docfinder.aspx
Private Investigator #15................................ www.sec.state.vt.us/seek/lrspseek.htm
Psychoanalyst #15................................ www.sec.state.vt.us/seek/lrspseek.htm
Psychologist/Psychotherapist #15................................ www.sec.state.vt.us/seek/lrspseek.htm
Radiation Tech #15................................ www.sec.state.vt.us/seek/lrspseek.htm
Real Estate Agent/Broker/Seller #12................................ www.sec.state.vt.us/seek/lrspseek.htm
Real Estate Appraiser #12................................ www.sec.state.vt.us/seek/lrspseek.htm
Respiratory Therapy #15................................ www.sec.state.vt.us/seek/lrspseek.htm
Security Guard #15................................ www.sec.state.vt.us/seek/lrspseek.htm
Social Worker #15................................ www.sec.state.vt.us/seek/lrspseek.htm
Tattooist #15................................ www.sec.state.vt.us/seek/lrspseek.htm
Teacher #6................................ http://education.vermont.gov/new/html/licensing/disciplinary.html
Veterinarian #15................................ www.sec.state.vt.us/seek/lrspseek.htm
Waste Water Treatm't Plant Operator #1................................ www.anr.state.vt.us/dec/ww/opcert/WW_Operator_List.pdf

Vermont Licensing Quick Finder

Accounting Firm #15................................ 802-828-2363
Acupuncturist #15................................ 802-828-2363
Alcohol/Drug Abuse Counselor #18................................ 802-878-7776
Anesthesiologist Assistant #14................................ 802-657-4220
Architect #15................................ 802-828-2363
Asbestos Contractor/Worker #13................................ 802-863-7231
Athletic Trainer #15................................ 802-828-2363
Attorney #2................................ 802-828-3281
Auctioneer #15................................ 802-828-2363
Audiologist #6................................ 802-828-2445
Bank #5................................ 802-828-3307
Barber #15................................ 802-828-2363
Body Piercer #15................................ 802-828-2363
Boiler & Pressure Vessel Inspec #9................................ 802-879-2304
Boxing Manager/Promoter #15................................ 802-828-2363
Boxing Professional #15................................ 802-828-2363
Chemical Suppression TQP Cert #8................................ 802-479-7563
Chimney Sweep TQP Cert #8................................ 802-479-7563
Chiropractor #15................................ 802-828-2363
Cosmetologist #15................................ 802-828-2363
Counselor, Alcohol & Drug Abuse #18................................ 802-878-7776
Courier, Armed #15................................ 802-828-2363
Credit Union #5................................ 802-828-3307
Crematory #15................................ 802-828-2363
Dealer/Repair Weigh/Measure Devices #4................................ 802-828-2436
Dental Assistant #15................................ 802-828-2363
Dental Hygienist #15................................ 802-828-2363
Dentist #15................................ 802-828-2363
Dietitian #15................................ 802-828-2363
Driver Training Instructor #11................................ 802-828-2114
Driving Instructor/School, Commerc'l #11................................ 802-828-2114
Electrician #8................................ 802-479-7564
Electrologist #15................................ 802-828-2363
Elevator Inspector #8................................ 802-479-7563
Elevator Mechanic #8................................ 802-479-7563
Embalmer #15................................ 802-828-2363
Emergency Care Attendant #7................................ 802-863-7310
Emergency Medical Technician #7................................ 802-863-7310
Engineer #15................................ 802-828-2363
Esthetician #15................................ 802-828-2363
Fire Alarm System Instal'r/Dealer #8................................ 802-479-7563
Fire Sprinkler System Design/Installer #8................................ 802-479-7563
Funeral Director #15................................ 802-828-2363
Hearing Aid Dispenser #15................................ 802-828-2363
Horse Racing Trainer/Owner/Profes'n'l #17................................ 802-786-5050
Insurance Adjuster #5................................ 802-828-3303
Insurance Agent/Consultant #5................................ 802-828-3303
Insurance Appraiser #5................................ 802-828-3303
Insurance Broker #5................................ 802-828-3303
Investment Advisor #5................................ 802-828-3420
Issuer Agent #5................................ 802-828-3420
Lead Abatement Contr'r/Worker #13................................ 802-863-7231
Lift Mechanic #8................................ 802-479-7563
Liquor, Retail/Wholesale #10................................ 802-828-2339
Livestock Dealer #4................................ 802-828-2421
Lobbyist #19................................ 802-828-0771
Lobbyist Employer/Firm #19................................ 802-828-0771
Lobbyist Gift #19................................ 802-828-0771
Lottery Retailer #16................................ 802-479-5686
LPG/Propane Installer #8................................ 802-479-7563
Manicurist #15................................ 802-828-2363
Marriage & Family Therapist #15................................ 802-828-2363
Meat Inspection Laboratory #4................................ 802-244-4510
Medical Doctor/Surgeon #14................................ 802-657-4220
Mental Health Counselor, Clinical #15................................ 802-828-2363
Midwife, Licensed #15................................ 802-828-2363
Milk & Cream Tester #4................................ 802-244-4510
Natural Gas System Installer #8................................ 802-479-7563
Naturopathic Physician #15................................ 802-828-2363
Notary Public #15................................ 802-828-2363
Nurse/Nurse Practitioner/LNA #15................................ 802-828-2363
Nursing Home Administrator #15................................ 802-828-2363
Occupational Therapist #15................................ 802-828-2363
Oil Burning Equipment Installer #8................................ 802-479-7563
Optician #15................................ 802-828-2363
Optometrist #15................................ 802-828-2363
Osteopathic Physician #15................................ 802-828-2363
Pari-Mutuel Seller #17................................ 802-786-5050
Pesticide Applicator #4................................ 802-828-3475
Pharmacist/Pharmacy #15................................ 802-828-2363
Physical Therapist/Assistant #15................................ 802-828-2363
Physician, Assistant #14................................ 802-657-4220
Plumber #8................................ 802-828-2107
Podiatrist #14................................ 802-657-4220
Polygraph Examiner #3................................ 802-872-4003
Private Investigator #15................................ 802-828-2363
Psychoanalyst #15................................ 802-828-2363
Psychologist/Psychotherapist #15................................ 802-828-2363
Public Adjuster #5................................ 802-828-3303
Radiation Tech #15................................ 802-828-2363
Real Estate Agent/Broker/Seller #12................................ 802-828-3228
Real Estate Appraiser #12................................ 802-828-3228
Respiratory Therapy #15................................ 802-828-2363
School Guidance Counselor #6................................ 802-828-2445
School Librarian/Media Specialist #6................................ 802-828-2445
School Nurse #6................................ 802-828-2445
School Principal/Superintendent #6................................ 802-828-2445
Securities Broker/Dealer #5................................ 802-828-3420
Securities Sales Rep. #5................................ 802-828-3420
Security Guard #15................................ 802-828-2363
Social Worker #15................................ 802-828-2363
Speech Language Pathologist #6................................ 802-828-2445
Tattooist #15................................ 802-828-2363
Teacher #6................................ 802-828-2445
Vehicle Dealer #11................................ 802-828-2038
Veterinarian #15................................ 802-828-2363
Vocational Education Teacher #6................................ 802-828-2445
Waste Water Plant Operator #1................................ 802-241-3822

Vermont Licensing Agency Information

#1 Agency of Natural Resources, Department of Environmental Conservation, 103 S Main St, Sewing Bldg, Waterbury, VT 05671-0405; 802-241-3822, Fax- 802-241-2596. www.anr.state.vt.us/dec/ww/wwmd.cfm

#2 Board of Bar Examiners, 2418 Airport Rd, #2, Barre, VT 05641; 802-828-3281, Fax- 802-828-1695. Hours- 7:45AM-4:30PM. www.vermontjudiciary.org/BBE/bbelibrary/attylic.aspx Will not sell mailing lists.

#3 Department of Public Safety, Polygraph Unit, 103 S Main St, Waterbury State Complex, Waterbury, VT 05671-2101; 802-244-8781, Fax- 802-241-5420. www.dps.state.vt.us/vtsp/polygraph.html

#4 Department of Agriculture, Consumer Assurance, 103 S Main St, Waterbury, VT 05671; 802-828-2436, Fax- 802-241-3008. www.vermontagriculture.com/ARMES/

#5 Department of Banking, Securities, Insurance & Health Care Admin., 89 Main St, City Ctr, Drawer 20, Montpelier, VT 05620-3101; 802-828-3301, Fax- 802-828-3306. www.bishca.state.vt.us.

#6 Department of Education, Licensing Professional Standards, 120 State St, Montpelier, VT 05620-2501; 802-828-2445, Fax- 802-828-5107. Hours- 7:45AM-4:30AM. http://education.vermont.gov/new/html/maincert.html

#7 Department of Health, Emergency Medical Services Division, PO Box 70 (108 Cherry St), Burlington, VT 05402-0070; 802-863-7310, Fax- 802-863-7577. http://healthvermont.gov/hc/ems/ems_index.aspx

#8 Department of Public Safety, Division of Fire Safety, 1311 US Rte 302 - Berlin #600, Barre, VT 05641-2351; 802-479-7561, Fax- 802-479-7562. Hours- 7:45AM-4:30PM. www.dps.state.vt.us/fire/ Search data at- www.dps.state.vt.us/fire/index.html

#9 Department of Public Safety, Fire Safety-Boiler Inspector, 372 Hurricane Ln #102, Williston, VT 05495-2080; 802-879-2304, Fax- 802-879-2312. www.dps.state.vt.us/fire/index.html

#10 Department of Liquor Control, PO Drawer 20 (13 Green Mountain Dr), Montpelier, VT 05620-4501; 802-828-2339, Fax- 802-828-2803. www.state.vt.us/dlc/ Search data at- www.state.vt.us/dlc/downloads.html#censing

#11 Department of Motor Vehicles, 120 State St, Montpelier, VT 05603; 802-828-2114, Fax- 802-828-2092. www.dmv.state.vt.us

#12 Real Estate Commission, National Life Bldg, North 2nd Fl, Montpelier, VT 05620-3402; 802-828-3228, Fax- 802-828-2368. www.sec.state.vt.us Search data at- www.sec.state.vt.us/seek/lrspseek.htm

#13 Department of Health, Environmental Health, PO Box 70 (108 Cherry St), Burlington, VT 05402; 802-863-7220, Fax- 802-865-7754. http://healthvermont.gov/index.aspx Search at- http://healthvermont.gov/enviro/asbestos/asbestos.aspx

#14 Board of Medical Practice, Department of Health, PO Box 70 (108 Cherry St), Burlington, VT 05402-0070; 802-657-4220 (800-745-7371 within Vermont), Fax- 802-657-4227. http://healthvermont.gov/hc/med_board/bmp.aspx Search data at- http://healthvermont.gov/hc/med_board/docfinder.aspx Written verifications available for $20 each; suggested to search files (dbf, delimited, or excel) at the website. Searching also available at private firm at www.docboard.org/vt/df/vtsearch.htm.

#15 Secretary of State, Office of Professional Regulation, National Life Bldg, North 2nd Fl, Montpelier, VT 05620-3402; 802-828-2363, Fax- 802-828-2496. www.sec.state.vt.us Search data at- www.sec.state.vt.us/seek/lrspseek.htm

#16 Lottery Commission, 1311 US Rte 302 - Berlin, Barre, VT 05641; 802-479-5686, Fax- 802-479-4294. Hours- 7:45AM-4:30PM. www.vtlottery.com

#17 Racing Commission, , Montpelier, VT ; 802-786-5050, Fax- 802-786-5051. Currently no horse racing active in Vermont.

#18 Alcohol & Drug Abuse Certification Board, PO Box 8566, Essex, VT 05451; 802-878-7776, Fax- 802-879-6211. www.vtcertificationboard.org/main/

#19 Secretary of State, Elections Division, 26 Terrace St, Montpelier, VT 05609-1101; 800-439-8683, Fax- 802-828-5171. http://vermont-elections.org/elections1/lobbyist.html Search data at- http://vermont-elections.org/elections1/lobbyist.html Lobbyist lists also available in pdf format.

Vermont Federal Courts

The following list indicates the district and division name for each county in the state. If the bankruptcy court location is different from the district court, then the location of the bankruptcy court appears in parentheses.

Vermont County/Court Cross Reference

County	Court	County	Court
Addison	Rutland	Lamoille	Burlington (Rutland)
Bennington	Rutland	Orange	Rutland
Caledonia	Burlington (Rutland)	Orleans	Burlington (Rutland)
Chittenden	Burlington (Rutland)	Rutland	Rutland
Essex	Burlington (Rutland)	Washington	Burlington (Rutland)
Franklin	Burlington (Rutland)	Windham	Rutland
Grand Isle	Burlington (Rutland)	Windsor	Rutland

Standards for Federal Courts: Fees are standard unless noted in profile. Search fee is $26.00 per item (one party name or case number). Copy fee is $.50 per page. Certification fee is $9.00 per document, double for exemplification, if available. Most courts require prepayment. Mail requests should enclose a SASE unless otherwise noted. Before releasing records, all courts require prepayment, unless noted.

District courts index by defendant and plaintiff and by case number. Bankruptcy courts usually index by debtor and case number. While most courts now have their indexes on computer, many may still maintain index card files as well. Courts will archive closed case files at different times.

There are numerous public access programs available to online subscribers. Search the U.S. Party/Case Index to find party names and case numbers among all courts. Individual case data is provided on PACER. A search of CM/ECF provides copies of cases filed electronically. For details about PACER, the US Party/Case Index, and CM/ECF see the Appendix or go to http://pacer.psc.uscourts.gov or call 800-676-6856.

US District Court

Burlington Division Clerk's Office, PO Box 945, Burlington, VT 05402-0945 (In person: 11 Elmwood Ave, Rm 506, Burlington), 802-951-6301. Hours-8:30AM-5PM. www.vtd.uscourts.gov

Counties/Note: Caledonia, Chittenden, Essex, Franklin, Grand Isle, Lamoille, Orleans, Washington. However, cases from all Vermont counties are randomly assigned to either Burlington or Rutland. Brattleboro is a hearing location only, 204 Main St; 802-254-0250; no records searching.

Searches/Indexing: Search request requires name only. Results do not include SSN or DOB. Will fax back docs, but only a few pages free. New cases are in the index 1 working day after filing date. Computer index maintained; criminal back 6 years, civil back 10. Pre-1991 cases indexed on microfilm. New cases filed back to 1/1991 on computer. Court scans all documents; fully computerized 1/1/06. District-wide computer searches available from both Division locations. Closed electronic cases not purged.

Search Access: Only general info accessed by computer is released via phone. **Mail:** Search usually completed- 1 day. Include SASE for return. **In person:** 1 public terminal available. Self-serve copies $.50 each; from computer- $.10.

Payment: Pay by Visa/MC, money order, cashier's check, personal or business check. Payee: Clerk, US District Court.

E-Services: Login to RACER at https://pacer.login.uscourts.gov/cgi-bin/login.pl?court_id=r_vtdc. PACER records go back to 1/1991. New records online after 1 day. ECF at https://ecf.vtd.uscourts.gov. **Opinions Online:** http://nysd.uscourts.gov/cwrulings.fwx?mode=rptform&cascode=D02VTXC. Filings of interest free at www.vtd.uscourts.gov/Decisions.html. **Online Note:** Search monthly court calendar at www.vtd.uscourts.gov/Calendars.htm.

Rutland Division Court Clerk, PO Box 607, Rutland, VT 05702-0607 (In person: 151 West St, Rutland), 802-773-0245. Hours-8:30AM-5:30PM. www.vtd.uscourts.gov

Counties/Note: Addison, Bennington, Orange, Rutland, Windsor, Windham. However, cases from all Vermont counties are randomly assigned to either Burlington or Rutland. Brattleboro is a hearing location only, 204 Main St; 802-254-0250; no records searching.

Searches/Indexing: Search request requires name only. Results do not include SSN or DOB. Will fax back docs, but only a few pages free. New cases are in the index 1 day after filing date. Computer index maintained; criminal back 6 years, civil back 10. Pre-1991 cases indexed on microfilm. New cases filed back to 1/1991 on computer. Court scans all documents; fully computerized 1/1/06. District-wide computer searches available from both Division locations. Closed electronic cases not purged.

Search Access: Only docket info available by phone. **Mail:** Search usually completed- 1-2 weeks. Include SASE for return. **In person:** 1 public terminal available. Self-serve copies $.50 each; from computer- $.10 each.

Payment: Pay by Visa/MC, money order, cashier's check, personal or business check. Payee: Clerk, US District Court.

E-Services: Login to PACER at https://pacer.login.uscourts.gov/cgi-bin/login.pl?court_id=r_vtdc. PACER records go back to 1/1991. New records online after 1 day. ECF at https://ecf.vtd.uscourts.gov. **Opinions:** http://nysd.uscourts.gov/cwrulings.fwx?mode=rptform&cascode=D02VTXC. Filings of interest free at www.vtd.uscourts.gov/Decisions.html. **Online Note:** Search monthly court calendar at www.vtd.uscourts.gov/Calendars.htm.

US Bankruptcy Court

Rutland Division Court Clerk, PO Box 6648, Rutland, VT 05702-6648 (In person: 67 Merchants Row, Rutland), 802-776-2000; Fax- 802-776-2020. Hours-8AM-5PM. www.vtb.uscourts.gov

Counties/Note: All counties in Vermont. Court is held in Rutland or Burlington, but records at Rutland.

Searches/Indexing: Helpful to include SSN in search request. Results include last 4 SSN digits and possibly address. Will fax back documents no add'l fee. New cases are in the index immediately after filing date. All records now maintained on computer back to 2002; some cases on computer back to 1999. Closed electronic cases not purged.

Search Access: Basic docket data is available by phone. Voice Case Information Service available, call VCIS at 800-260-9956. **Mail:** Search usually completed- 1-2 days. SASE not required. **Fax:** Fax search requests accepted with credit card. **In person:** 1 public terminal available. No self-serve copier.

Payment: Pay by Visa/MC/Discover, money order, cashier's check, cash. No personal checks accepted. Payee: US Bankruptcy Court

E-Services: Document images available. PACER records go back to 1992; limited information prior. New records online after 1 day. ECF at https://ecf.vtb.uscourts.gov. **Opinions Online:** www.vtb.uscourts.gov/opinions.php. **Online Note:** Calendars on main website.Court.

Vermont County Courts

Court	Jurisdiction	No. of Courts	How Organized
Superior Courts*	General	11	14 Counties
District Courts*	Limited	11	3 Circuits
Combined Courts*		3	
Probate Courts*	Probate	18	Judges
Family Courts	Special	14	14 Counties
Environmental Court	Special	1	

* Profiled in this Sourcebook.

	CIVIL								
Court	Tort	Contract	Real Estate	Min. Claim	Max. Claim	Small Claims	Estate	Eviction	Domestic Relations
Superior Courts*	X	X	X	$0	No Max	$5000		X	
District Courts*									
Probate Courts*							X		
Family Courts									X

	CRIMINAL				
Court	Felony	Misdemeanor	DWI/DUI	Preliminary Hearing	Juvenile
Superior Courts*					
District Courts*	X	X	X	X	
Family Courts					X

Administration

Administrative Office of Courts (AOC), Court Administrator, 109 State St, Montpelier, VT, 05609-0701; 802-828-3278, Fax: 802-828-3457. (EST) www.vermontjudiciary.org

Court Structure

The Superior Court hears predominantly civil, tort, real estate, and small claims cases. On rare occasion it hears criminal cases, but the District Court hears predominantly criminal cases. Specialty courts include Probate Courts and Family Courts. In Vermont, the Judicial Bureau has jurisdiction over traffic, municipal ordinances, and Fish and Game violations, minors in possession, and hazing.

Online Access

Vermont Courts Online provides access to civil and small claim cases and court calendar information from 12 of the county Superior Courts. Access is not offered for Chittenden and Franklin. Go to https://secure.vermont.gov/vtcdas/user. Records are in real-time mode. There is a $12.50 activation fee plus a fee of $.50 per case for look-up after the 1st 5 cases.

In a cooperative program with the AOC, the Vermont Criminal Information Center sells online criminal record checks from submitted conviction data from the District Courts. The fee is $20.00 per record. Visit https://secure.vermont.gov/DPS/criminalrecords/.

Supreme Court opinions are available from the main web site and are also maintained by the Vermont Department of Libraries at http://dol.state.vt.us.

Probate court contacts and locations are listed at www.vermontjudiciary.org/courts/probate/probateinfo/index.htm.

Searching Tips, Fees, and Other Guidelines

The statewide search, certification, and copy fees set by the legislature are as follows: search fee- $30.00 per name; certification fee- $5.00 per document plus copy fee; copy fee- $.25 per page with a $1.00 minimum. Be aware that some courts vary slightly from this schedule and a number of courts do not charge for a search of civil records.

Addison County

Superior Court 7 Mahady Ct, Middlebury, VT 05753; 802-388-7741; fax: 802-388-4621; 8AM-4:30PM. ***Civil, Eviction, Small Claims.***

Civil Records: Access: Fax, mail, in person, online. Only the court performs in person searches; visitors may not. No search fee. Required to search: name, years to search. Civil cases indexed by defendant, plaintiff. Civil index on cards and recording books, computerized since 1995. Mail turnaround time 2-3 days. Access civil and small claims case records by web subscription, $12.50 activation plus $.50 per page; registration info at https://secure.vermont.gov/vtcdas/user. Also, click on Calendars by Date and County to view calendars free. Online results show name, DOB.

General Information: No sealed or unserved records released. Will not fax documents. Court makes copy: $.25 per page, $1.00 minimum. Certification fee: $5.00 per doc. Payee: Addison Superior Court. Personal checks accepted; credit cards are not. Prepayment required.

District Court 7 Mahady Ct, Middlebury, VT 05753; 802-388-4237; 8-4:30 ***Felony, Misdemeanor.***

Criminal Records: Access: Mail, in person. Only the court performs in person searches; visitors may not. Search fee: $30.00 per name. Required to search: name, years to search, DOB. Criminal records on computer since mid 1991; prior on dockets and index cards. Mail turnaround time up to 1 week. Click on Calendars by Date and County at https://secure.vermont.gov/vtcdas/user.

General Information: No adoption, juvenile, sealed, or expunged records released. Will not fax documents. Court makes copy: $.25 per page, $1.00 minimum. Certification fee: $5.00 per doc. Payee: Addison District Court. Personal checks accepted; credit cards are not. Prepayment required.

Probate Court 7 Mahady Ct, Middlebury, VT 05753; 802-388-2612; fax: 802-388-4621; 8AM-4:30PM. ***Probate.***

Bennington County

Superior Court 207 South St, PO Box 4157, Bennington, VT 05201; 802-447-2700; fax: 802-447-2703; 8-4:30PM. ***Civil, Eviction, Small Claims.***

Civil Records: Access: Fax, phone, mail, in person, online. Both court and visitors may perform in person searches. No search fee. Required to search: name, years to search. Civil cases indexed by defendant, plaintiff; index on computer from 1989, index from 1968. Mail turnaround time 2-3 days. Access civil and small claims case records by web subscription, $12.50 activation plus $.50 per page; registration info at https://secure.vermont.gov/vtcdas/user. Also, click on Calendars by Date and County to view calendars free. Online results show name, DOB.

General Information: No deposition, adoption, juvenile, sealed or expunged records released. Will not fax documents. Court makes copy: $.25 per page, $1.00 minimum. Self serve: $.10 per page. Certification fee: $5.00 per doc. Payee: Bennington County. Personal checks accepted; credit cards are not. Prepayment required.

District Court 150 Veterans Memorial Dr, Bennington, VT 05201; 802-447-2727; fax: 802-447-2750; 7:45AM-4:30PM. ***Felony, Misdemeanor.***

Criminal Records: Access: Mail, in person. Only the court performs in person searches; visitors may not. Search fee: $30.00 per name includes copy of docket sheet. Required to search: name, years to search, DOB. Criminal records indexed on cards, docket books, and computer. Mail turnaround time varies. Public use terminal has crim records back to 1990. PAT results show middle initial, DOB. Click on Calendars by Date and County at https://secure.vermont.gov/vtcdas/user.

General Information: No sealed, diversion case records released. Will fax documents to toll free line. Court makes copy: $.25 per page. $1.00 minimum. Certification fee: $5.00 per doc. Payee: Vermont District Court. Personal checks accepted; credit cards are not. Prepayment required. Mail requests: SASE requested.

Probate Court - Bennington District 207 South St, PO Box 65, Bennington, VT 05201; 802-447-2705; fax: 802-447-2703; 8AM-N, 1-4pm. ***Probate.*** Fax to "Attention Probate Court."

Probate Court - Manchester District PO Box 446, 3588 Main St, Manchester, VT 05254; 802-362-1410; 8AM-N, 1-4:20PM. ***Probate.***

Caledonia County

Superior Court 1126 Main St, #1, St Johnsbury, VT 05819; 802-748-6600; fax: 802-748-6603; 8AM-4:30PM. ***Civil, Eviction, Small Claims.***

Civil Records: Access: Phone, mail, in person, online. Only the court performs in person searches; visitors may not. No search fee. Required to search: name, years to search. Civil cases indexed by defendant, plaintiff; index on computer from 1992, in archives before 1985, index from 1985, all other records on index cards. Mail turnaround time 1 week. Access civil and small claims case records by web subscription, $12.50 activation plus $.50 per page; registration info at https://secure.vermont.gov/vtcdas/user. Also, click on Calendars by Date and County to view calendars free.

General Information: No adoption, juvenile, sealed or expunged records released. Will fax documents $2.00 per page. Court makes copy: $.25 per page, $1.00 minimum. Certification fee: $5.00 per doc. Payee: Caledonia Superior Court. Personal checks accepted; credit cards are not. Prepayment required. Mail requests: SASE requested.

District Court 1126 Main St, #1, St Johnsbury, VT 05819; 802-748-6600; fax: 802-748-6603; 8AM-4:30PM. ***Felony, Misdemeanor.***

Criminal Records: Access: Fax, mail, in person. Both court and visitors may perform in person searches. Search fee: $30.00 per name. Required to search: name, years to search, DOB. Criminal records on computer since 1991, prior on index cards to 1950. Mail turnaround time less than 1 week. Click on Calendars by Date and County at https://secure.vermont.gov/vtcdas/user.

General Information: No adoption, juvenile, sealed or expunged records released. Will fax documents $2.00 per page. Court makes copy: $.25 per page; $1.00 minimum. Certification fee: $5.00 per doc. Payee: Caledonia District Court. Personal checks accepted; credit cards are not. Prepayment required. Mail requests: SASE required.

Probate Court 1126 Main St, PO Box 406, St Johnsbury, VT 05819; 802-748-6605; fax: 802-748-6603; 8AM-4:30PM. ***Probate.***

Chittenden County

Superior Court PO Box 187, 175 Main St, Burlington, VT 05402; 802-863-3467; 8AM-4:30PM. ***Civil, Eviction, Small Claims.*** www.chittendensuperiorcourt.com/index.htm

Civil Records: Access: Phone, mail, in person. Only the court performs in person searches; visitors may not. No search fee. Required to search: name, years to search. Civil cases indexed by defendant, plaintiff; index on computer back to 1983, small claims since 1996, prior records on books from 1800s. Mail turnaround 1 week. Access case information free at www.chittendensuperiorcourt.com/index.htm and click on Cases. Calendars also online.

General Information: No adoption, juvenile, sealed or expunged records released. Will not fax documents. Court makes copy: $.25 per page, $1.00 minimum. Certification fee: $5.00 per doc. Payee: Chittenden County Superior Court. Personal checks accepted; credit cards are not. Prepayment required.

District Court 32 Cherry St, #300, Burlington, VT 05401; 802-651-1950; fax: 802-651-1759; 8AM-4:30PM. ***Felony, Misdemeanor.***

Criminal Records: Access: Mail, in person. Both court and visitors may perform in person searches. Search fee: $30.00 per name. Required to search: name, years to search; also helpful: DOB. Criminal records on new computer from 6/90, on old computer from 6/85 to 6/90, books by alpha name from 12/69 to 1980, on index cards from 1970. Mail turnaround time 1-2 days. Public use terminal has crim records back to 6/1990.PAT results show name, DOB. Click on Calendars by Date and County at https://secure.vermont.gov/vtcdas/user.

General Information: No adoption, juvenile, sealed or expunged records released. Will not fax out documents. Court makes copy: $.25 per page, $1.00 minimum. Certification fee: $5.00 per doc. Payee: Vermont District Court. Personal checks accepted; credit cards are not. Prepayment required. Mail requests: SASE required.

Probate Court PO Box 511, 175 Main St, Burlington, VT 05402; 802-651-1518; 8AM-4:30PM; till 4PM F. ***Probate.***

Essex County

District & Superior Court Box 75, Guildhall, VT 05905; 802-676-3910; fax: 802-676-3463; 8AM-4:30PM. ***Felony, Misdemeanor, Civil, Eviction, Small Claims.***

Civil Records: Access: Phone, fax, mail, in person, online. Only the court performs in person searches; visitors may not. No search fee. Required to search: name, years to search. Civil cases indexed by defendant, plaintiff; index from 1974; on computer from 5/94. Note: Will not accept phone requests for more than 2 names. Mail turnaround time 1 week. Access case records by internet subscription, $12.50 activation plus $.50 per page; registration info at https://secure.vermont.gov/vtcdas/user. Also, click on Calendars by Date and County to view calendars free.

Criminal Records: Access: Mail, in person. Only the court performs in person searches; visitors may not. Search fee: $30.00 per name. Required to search: name, years to search, DOB. Criminal records indexed from 1974; on computer from 5/94. Mail turnaround 1 week. Click on Calendars by Date and County at https://secure.vermont.gov/vtcdas/user.

General Information: No adoption, juvenile, sealed or expunged records released. Will fax documents $1.00 per page. Court makes copy: $.25 per page, $1.00 minimum. Certification fee: $5.00 per doc. Payee: Depends on court (Superior or District). Only cashiers checks and money orders accepted. No credit cards accepted. Prepayment required. Mail requests: SASE required.

Probate Court PO Box 426, 49 Mill St Ext., Island Pond, VT 05846; 802-723-4770; fax: 802-723-4770; 8:30AM-N, 1-3:30PM. ***Probate.***

Franklin County

Superior Court PO Box 808, 17 Church St, St Albans, VT 05478; 802-524-3863; fax: 802-524-7996; 8AM-12:15PM, 1PM-4:30PM. ***Civil, Eviction, Small Claims.***

Civil Records: Access: Mail, in person. Only the court performs in person searches; visitors may not. No search fee. Required to search: name, years to search; or by docket number. Civil cases indexed by defendant, plaintiff; index on computer since 1996; prior on index cards from 1840. Mail turnaround time 1 week.

General Information: No adoption, juvenile, sealed or expunged records released. Will not fax documents. Court makes copy: $.25 per page, $1.00 minimum. Certification fee: $5.00 per doc. Payee: Franklin Superior Court. Personal checks accepted; credit cards are not. Prepayment required. Mail requests: SASE requested.

District Court 36 Lake St, St Albans, VT 05478; 802-524-7997; fax: 802-524-7946; 8AM-4:30PM. ***Felony, Misdemeanor.***

Criminal Records: Access: Mail, in person. Both court and visitors may perform in person searches. Search fee: $30.00 per name. Required to search: name, years to search; also helpful: DOB, SSN. Criminal records on computer since 1987. Note: Court will perform in person searches only if time permits. Mail turnaround time 7-10 days. Public use terminal has crim records back to 1990.PAT results show name, DOB. Click on Calendars by Date and County at https://secure.vermont.gov/vtcdas/user.

General Information: No adoption, juvenile, sealed or expunged records released. Fee to fax document

$1.00 each plus $.25 per page. Court makes copy: $.25 per page, $1.00 minimum. Certification fee: $5.00 per doc. Payee: Vermont District Court. Personal checks accepted; credit cards are not. Prepayment required. Mail requests: SASE required.

Franklin Probate Court 17 Church St, St Albans, VT 05478; 802-524-4112; 8AM-N, 1-4:30PM. ***Probate, Marriage.***

Grand Isle County

District & Superior Court PO Box 7, North Hero, VT 05474; 802-372-8350; fax: 802-372-3221; 8AM-4:30PM. ***Felony, Misdemeanor, Civil, Eviction, Small Claims.***

Civil Records: Access: Phone, fax, mail, in person, online. Both court and visitors may perform in person searches. No search fee. Required to search: name, years to search. Civil cases indexed by defendant, plaintiff; index on computer from 1990, on index 1940, in-house from 1970. Mail turnaround time 1-2 days. Access case records by internet subscription, $12.50 activation plus $.50 per page; registration info at https://secure.vermont.gov/vtcdas/user. Also, click on Calendars by Date and County to view calendars free.

Criminal Records: Access: Fax, mail, in person. Both court and visitors may perform in person searches. Search fee: $30.00 per name. Required to search: name, years to search; also helpful: DOB, SSN. Criminal records computerized from 1990, on index from 1940, in-house from 1979. Note: Fax requests not processed until payment received; court suggest just to mail in your request. Mail turnaround time 1-2 days. Click on Calendars by Date and County at https://secure.vermont.gov/vtcdas/user.

General Information: No adoption, juvenile, sealed or expunged records released. Will not fax documents. Court makes copy: $.25 per page, $1.00 minimum. Self serve: $.25 per page. Certification fee: $5.00 per doc. Payee: Grand Isle Superior or District Court. Personal checks accepted; credit cards are not. Prepayment required.

Probate Court PO Box 7, 3677 US Route 2, North Hero, VT 05474; 802-372-8350; fax: 802-372-3221; 8AM-12:30, 1:30-4:30PM. ***Probate.***

Lamoille County

Superior Court Box 490, 154 Main St, Hyde Park, VT 05655; 802-888-2207; 8AM-Noon; 12:30-4:30PM except Wed 12:30-4:30PM. ***Civil, Eviction, Small Claims.***

Civil Records: Access: Mail, in person, online. Only the court performs in person searches; visitors may not. No search fee. Required to search: name, years to search. Civil cases indexed by defendant, plaintiff; index on computer from 1989, index from 1970s. Mail turnaround time 1 week. Public use terminal has civil records back to 1994. PAT results show name only. Access civil and small claims case records by web subscription, $12.50 activation plus $.50 per page; registration info at https://secure.vermont.gov/vtcdas/user. Also, click on Calendars by Date and County to view calendars free.

General Information: No adoption, juvenile, sealed or expunged records released. Will not fax documents. Court makes copy: $.25 per page, $1.00 minimum. Certification fee: $5.00 per doc. Payee: Lamoille Superior Court. Personal checks accepted; credit cards are not. Prepayment required. Mail requests: SASE required.

District Court PO Box 489, Hyde Park, VT 05655-0489; 802-888-3887; fax: 802-888-2591; 8AM-4:30PM. ***Felony, Misdemeanor.***

Criminal Records: Access: Mail, in person. Only the court performs in person searches; visitors may not. Search fee: $30.00 per name. Required to search: name, DOB; also helpful: years to search. Criminal records on computer since 6/88; prior on index cards. Mail turnaround time 3 days if record on-site; 1 week if off-site. Click on Calendars by Date and County at https://secure.vermont.gov/vtcdas/user.

General Information: No adoption, juvenile, sealed or expunged records released. Will fax documents to toll free or local line only. Court makes copy: $.25 per page; $1.00 minimum. Certification fee: $5.00 per doc. Payee: Vermont District Court. Personal checks accepted. Planning to accept credit cards. Prepayment required. Mail requests: SASE required.

Probate Court PO Box 102, 154 Main St, Hyde Park, VT 05655-0102; 802-888-3306; fax: 802-888-0669; 8AM-Noon, 12:30-4:30PM. ***Probate.***

Orange County

District & Superior Court 5 Court St, Chelsea, VT 05038-9746; 802-685-4610; fax: 802-685-3173; 8AM-4:30PM. ***Felony, Misdemeanor, Civil, Eviction, Small Claims.***

Civil Records: Access: Fax, mail, in person, online. Only the court performs in person searches; visitors may not. No search fee. Required to search: name, years to search; also helpful: address. Civil cases indexed by defendant, plaintiff; index on computer from 7/94, on index from 1967. Mail turnaround time 1 week. Access case records by internet subscription, $12.50 activation plus $.50 per page; registration info at https://secure.vermont.gov/vtcdas/user. Also, click on Calendars by Date and County to view calendars free.

Criminal Records: Access: Phone, fax, mail, in person. Only the court performs in person searches; visitors may not. Search fee: $30.00 per name. Required to search: name, years to search, DOB; also helpful: address. Criminal records computerized from 1990, on index from 1967. Mail turnaround time 1 week. Click on Calendars by Date and County at https://secure.vermont.gov/vtcdas/user.

General Information: No adoption, juvenile, sealed or expunged records released. Fee to fax out file $1.00 per page. Court makes copy: $.25 per page, $1.00 minimum. Certification fee: $5.00 per doc. Payee: depends on court- District Court or Superior Court. Personal checks accepted. No credit cards accepted at Superior Court. Prepayment required.

Probate Court 5 Court St, County Courthouse, Chelsea, VT 05038-9746; 802-685-4610; fax: 802-685-3173; 8AM-4:30PM. ***Probate.***

The Bradford and Randolph Districts were consolidated into this one probate court 6/1/1994.

Orleans County

Superior Court 247 Main St, #1, Newport, VT 05855-1203; 802-334-3344; fax: 802-334-4429; 8AM-4:30PM M,W,TH,F; 12:30-4:30PM T. ***Civil, Eviction, Small Claims.***

Civil Records: Access: Phone, fax, mail, in person, online. Only the court performs in person searches; visitors may not. No search fee. Required to search: name; also helpful: years to search. Civil cases indexed by defendant, plaintiff; index on computer since 1994; prior records on index from 1800s. Mail turnaround time 1 week or so. Results include county. Access civil and small claims case records by web subscription, $12.50 activation plus $.50 per page; registration info at https://secure.vermont.gov/vtcdas/user. Also, click on Calendars by Date and County to view calendars free.

General Information: No juvenile records released. Will not fax documents. Court makes copy: $.25 per page, $1.00 minimum. Certification fee: $5.00 per doc. Payee: Orleans Superior Court. Personal checks accepted; credit cards are not. Prepayment required. Mail requests: SASE required.

District Court 217 Main St, #4, Newport, VT 05855; 802-334-3325; 8AM-4:30PM. ***Felony, Misdemeanor.***

Criminal Records: Access: Mail. Only the court performs in person searches; visitors may not. Search fee: $30.00 per name. Required to search: name, years to search, DOB. Criminal records on computer since 1/91; prior on index cards back to 1971. Mail turnaround time 1 week. Click on Calendars by Date and County at https://secure.vermont.gov/vtcdas/user.

General Information: No adoption, juvenile, sealed or expunged records released. Will fax documents to toll-free number only. Court makes copy: $.25 per page, $1.00 minimum; add $5.00 if copies retrieved from public records. Self serve: $.25 per page. Certification fee: $5.00 per doc. Payee: District Court of Vermont. Personal checks accepted; credit cards are not. Prepayment required. Mail requests: SASE required.

Probate Court 247 Main St, Newport, VT 05855; 802-334-3366; fax: 802-334-3385; 8AM-N, 1-4PM. ***Probate.***

Rutland County

Superior Court 83 Center St, Rutland, VT 05701; 802-775-4394; fax: 802-775-2291; 8AM-4:30PM. ***Civil, Eviction, Small Claims.***

Civil Records: Access: Mail, in person, online. Only the court performs in person searches; visitors may not. No search fee; a fee may apply for more sophisticated searches. Required to search: name, years to search. Civil cases indexed by defendant, plaintiff; index on computer from 1987, on index from late 1700s. Mail turnaround time 1 week. Access civil and small claims case records by web subscription, $12.50 activation plus $.50 per page; registration info at https://secure.vermont.gov/vtcdas/user. Also, click on Calendars by Date and County to view calendars free.

General Information: No adoption, juvenile, sealed or expunged records released. Will fax documents to local or toll free line. Court makes copy: $.25 per page; $1.00 minimum. Certification fee: $5.00 per cert. Payee: Rutland Superior Court. Personal checks accepted; credit cards are not. Prepayment required. Mail requests: SASE required.

District Court 9 Merchants Row, Rutland, VT 05701-2886; 802-786-5880; 8AM-4:30PM. ***Felony, Misdemeanor.***

Criminal Records: Access: Phone, mail, in person. Both court and visitors may perform in person searches. Search fee: $30.00 per name. Required to search: name, years to search, DOB. Criminal records computerized from mid 1991. Mail turnaround time 1 week. Public use terminal has crim records back to 1991. Click on Calendars by Date and County at https://secure.vermont.gov/vtcdas/user.

General Information: No sealed, expunged records released. Court makes copy: $.25 per page. $1.00 minimum. Certification fee: $5.00 per doc. Payee: District Court of Vermont. Personal checks accepted. No credit cards accepted for searches or copy fees. Prepayment required. Mail requests: SASE required.

Probate Court - Fair Haven District 3 N Park Pl, Fair Haven, VT 05743; 802-265-3380; fax: 802-265-3380; 8AM-4PM. ***Probate.***

Probate Court - Rutland District 83 Center St, Rutland, VT 05701; 802-775-0114; fax: 802-775-1671; 8AM-4:30PM. ***Probate.***

Washington County

Superior Court 65 State St, Montpelier, VT 05602-3594; 802-828-2091; 8AM-4:30PM. ***Civil, Eviction, Small Claims #828-5551.***

Civil Records: Access: Phone, mail, in person, online. Only the court performs in person searches; visitors may not. No search fee. Required to search: name, years to search; also helpful: address. Civil cases indexed by defendant, plaintiff; index on computer from 1987, archives from 1900s. Mail turnaround time 1-2 days. Access civil and small claims case records by web subscription, $12.50 activation plus $.50 per page; registration info at https://secure.vermont.gov/vtcdas/user. Also, click on Calendars by Date and County to view calendars free. Online results show name, DOB.

General Information: No adoption, juvenile or expunged records released. Will fax documents $1.00 per page. Court makes copy: $.25 per page, $1.00 minimum. Certification fee: $5.00 per doc. Payee: Washington County Superior Court. Personal checks accepted; credit cards are not. Prepayment required. Mail requests: SASE requested.

District Court 255 N Main, Barre, VT 05641; 802-479-4252; 8-4:30PM. ***Felony, Misdemeanor.***

Criminal Records: Access: Mail, in person. Only the court performs in person searches; visitors may not. Search fee: $30.00 per name. Required to search:

name, years to search; also helpful: DOB. Criminal records on computer since 1989; prior records in index from 1970s. Mail turnaround time 3-5 days. PAT results show name, DOB. Click on Calendars by Date and County at https://secure.vermont.gov/vtcdas/user.
General Information: No adoption, juvenile, sealed or expunged records released. Court makes copy: $.25 per page. $1.00 minimum. Certification fee: $5.00 per doc. Payee: Washington District Court. Personal checks accepted; credit cards are not. Prepayment required. Mail requests: SASE requested.

Probate Court 10 Elm St, #2, Montpelier, VT 05602; 802-828-3405; 8AM-N, 1-4PM. ***Probate.***

Windham County

Superior Court Box 207, 7 Court St, Newfane, VT 05345; 802-365-7979; fax: 802-365-4360; 9AM-4PM. ***Civil, Eviction, Small Claims.***
Civil Records: Access: Phone, fax, mail, in person, online. Both court and visitors may perform in person searches. No search fee. Required to search: name, years to search. Civil cases indexed by defendant, plaintiff; index on computer from 1994, on index from 1919. Note: Fax access available only in emergency. Mail turnaround time 1-2 days. Access civil and small claims case records by web subscription, $12.50 activation plus $.50 per page; registration info at https://secure.vermont.gov/vtcdas/user. Also, click on Calendars by Date and County to view calendars free.
General Information: No adoption, juvenile, sealed or expunged records released. No fee to fax documents. Court makes copy: $.25 per page, $1.00 minimum. Certification fee: $5.00 per doc. Payee: Windham Superior Court. Personal checks accepted; credit cards are not. Prepayment required. Mail requests: SASE required.

District Court 30 Putney Rd, #2, Brattleboro, VT 05301; 802-257-2800; 8AM-4:30PM. ***Felony, Misdemeanor, Civil Suspension.***
Criminal Records: Access: Mail, in person. Both court and visitors may perform in person searches. Search fee: $30.00 per name. Required to search: name, years to search; also helpful: address, DOB, SSN. Criminal record go back to 1969s; computer since 1990; prior on index cards and docket books. Mail turnaround time 5-7 days. Public use terminal has crim records back to 1991.PAT results show name, DOB. Click on Calendars by Date and County at https://secure.vermont.gov/vtcdas/user.
General Information: No adoption, juvenile, sealed or expunged records released. Fee to fax document $.25 per page. Court makes copy: $.25 per page, $1.00 minimum. Certification fee: $5.00 per doc. Payee: Vermont District Court. Personal checks accepted; credit cards are not. Prepayment required. Mail requests: SASE requested.

Probate Court - Marlboro District 80 Flat St, #104, Brattleboro, VT 05301; 802-257-2898; fax: 802-251-2139; 8AM-N, 1-4:30PM. ***Probate.***

Probate Court - Westminster District PO Box 47, 39 Square, Bellows Falls, VT 05101-0047; 802-463-3019; fax: 802-463-0144; 8AM-N,1-4:30PM. ***Probate.***

Windsor County

Superior Court Box 458, Woodstock, VT 05091; 802-457-2121; 8AM-4:30PM. ***Civil, Eviction, Small Claims.***
Civil Records: Access: Phone, mail, in person, online. Only the court performs in person searches; visitors may not. Search fee: Up to $10.00. Required to search: name, years to search. Civil cases indexed by defendant, plaintiff. Civil records available since on computer 1990. Mail turnaround time 48 hours. Access civil and small claims case records by web subscription, $12.50 activation plus $.50 per page; registration info at https://secure.vermont.gov/vtcdas/user. Also, click on Calendars by Date and County to view calendars free.
General Information: No sealed or expunged records released. Court makes copy: $.25 per page, $1.00 minimum. Certification fee: $5.00 per doc. Payee: Windsor County Clerk or Windsor Superior Court. Personal checks accepted; credit cards are not. Prepayment required. Mail requests: SASE required.

District Court Windsor Circuit Unit 1, 82 Railroad Row, White River Junction, VT 05001-1962; 802-295-8865; fax: 802-295-8897; 8AM-4:30PM. ***Felony, Misdemeanor.***
Criminal Records: Access: Mail, in person. Only the court performs in person searches; visitors may not. Search fee: $30.00 per name. Required to search: name, years to search; also helpful: DOB, SSN. Criminal records computerized from 1990, index from 1968. Note: Record request forms available, please use. Mail turnaround time 7 days. Click on Calendars by Date and County at https://secure.vermont.gov/vtcdas/user.
General Information: No adoption, juvenile, sealed or expunged records released. Will fax documents to local or toll-free number. Court makes copy: $.25 per page, $1.00 minimum. Certification fee: $5.00 per doc. Payee: Vermont District Court. Personal checks accepted; credit cards are not. Prepayment required. Mail requests: SASE requested.

Probate Court - Hartford District 62 Pleasant St, Woodstock, VT 05091; 802-457-1503; fax: 802-457-5203; 8AM-N, 1-4:30PM. ***Probate.***

Probate Court - Windsor District PO Box 402, Rte 106, Cota Fuel Bldg, North Springfield, VT 05150; 802-886-2284; fax: 802-886-2285; 8AM-N, 1-4:30PM. ***Probate.***

Vermont Recording Offices

ORGANIZATION: Vermont has 14 counties and 246 towns/cities which have 246 recording offices. There is **no county recording** in this state. All recording is done at the city/town level. Many towns are so small that their mailing addresses are in different towns. 4 towns had the same names as cities - Barre, Newport, Rutland, and St. Albans. 11 cities or towns bear the same name as a Vermont county - Addison, Bennington, Chittenden, Essex, Franklin, Grand Isle, Orange, Rutland, Washington, Windham, and Windsor. Vermont is in the Eastern Time Zone (EST)

Many towns charge a $2.00 per hour vault time fee for in person searches.

REAL ESTATE RECORDS: Most towns/cities will not perform real estate searches. Real estate record copy fees and certification fees vary. Copy fee is usually $1.00 per page. Certified copy fee varies; many counties still charge $7.00 per page, most charge $8.00, some $10.00.

UCC RECORDS: Vermont was a dual filing state until December 31, 1994. From January 1, 1995, only consumer goods and real estate related collateral were filed with Town/City Clerks. Since July 1, 2001, only real estate collateral is filed at the local level. Some but not all recording offices will perform UCC searches. Use search request form UCC-11. The UCC search fee is usually $10.00 per name.

TAX LIEN RECORDS: All federal and state tax liens on personal property and on real property are filed with the Town/City Clerk in the lien/attachment book and indexed in real estate records. Most towns/cities will not perform tax lien searches.

OTHER LIENS: Mechanics, local tax, judgment, foreclosure.

ONLINE ACCESS: There is limited online access to county recorded documents, and a growing number of towns have contracted out online services, usually offering property assessment records or property cards. State recorded UCC data is available online from the Vermont Secretary of State; search free at www.sec.state.vt.us/seek/ucc_seek.htm

Addison Town

Town Clerk, 7099 Vermont Rte 22A, Addison, VT 05491. 802-759-2020; fax-802-759-2233; 8:30AM-N, 1-4:30PM.

Index: All in one. Record index not computerized. Only the public may search. Copy fee $1.00 per page. Cert fee- $8.00 per page plus copy fee. Payee- Addison Town Clerk. **Property tax/Assessing-** 65 Rte 17 W, Addison,VT 05491; 802-759-2020.

Albany Town

Town Clerk, PO Box 284, Albany, VT 05820-0284. 802-755-6100; 9AM-4PM T,Th; 9AM-7PM W.

Index: All in one. Record index not computerized. Office personnel or visitors may perform searches. General search fee $5.00 per hour. Office will not search real estate records. Office will search UCC records, but not tax liens. UCC search per debtor name- $10.00. Copy fee $1.00 per page. Cert fee- $8.00 per page includes copy fee. Payee- Albany Town Clerk. **Property tax/Assessing-** PO Box 284, Albany, VT 05820-0284; 802-755-6100.

Alburg Town

Town Clerk, 1 N Main St, Alburg, VT 05440-4404. 802-796-3468; fax-802-796-3939; 9AM-N; 1-5PM.

Index: Separate indices to search include liens and attachments, UCCs. Record index not computerized. Office will perform a UCC search but public must search other records themselves. Copy fee $1.00 per page. Cert fee- $2.00 per page plus copy fee. Payee- Town of Alburg. Treasurer- 802-796-3468; Elections- 802-796-3468. **Property tax/ Assessing-** 1 N Main St, Alburgh, VT 05440; 802-796-4061.

Andover Town

Town Clerk, 953 Weston-Andover Rd, Andover, VT 05143. 802-875-2765; fax-802-875-6647; 9AM-1PM M,T,TH,F; Wed 11AM-3PM.

Index: Separate indices to search include general index through 3/93, card index 3/93 to present. Record index not computerized. Office personnel or visitors may perform searches. Office will search on a case by case basis. Will not search UCC records. Copy fee $1.00 per page. Cert fee- $10.00 per doc includes copy fee. Payee- Town of Andover. **Property tax/Assessing-** 953 Weston-Andover Rd, Andover, VT 05143; 802-875-2765.

Arlington Town

Town Clerk, PO Box 304, Arlington, VT 05250. 802-375-2332; fax-802-375-2332; 9AM-2PM.

Index: All in one. Records indexed on a public use terminal back to 1978 for deeds, all the way back for liens, surveys and R.O.W. Only the public may search. Search fee $2.00 per hour vault time. Copy fee $1.00 per page. Cert fee- $8.00 per page includes copies. Payee- Arlington Town Clerk. Buld data available for purchase on CD for $5.00. Contact listers office 802-375-9022. **Other phones:** Treasurer- 802-375-1260. **Property tax/Assessing-** PO Box 268, Arlington, VT 05250; 802-375-9022.

Athens Town

Town Clerk, 56 Brookline Rd, Athens, VT 05143. 802-869-3370; fax-same; 9AM-1PM or by appointment.

Index: All in one. Record index not computerized. Office personnel or visitors may perform searches. Search fee $15.00. General copy fee $7.00 per doc.Real estate record copy- $2.00 per page. Cert fee- $5.00 per page includes copy fee. Payee- Athens Town Clerk. **Property tax/Assessing-** PO Box 651, Saxton River, VT 05143; 802-869-3995.

Bakersfield Town

Town Clerk, PO Box 203, Bakersfield, VT 05441. 802-827-4495; fax-802-827-3106; 9AM-N N.

Index: Separate indices to search include pre 1983 general index book, after 1983- card file. Indexes include RE, Liens, Vitals, Old UCC. Record index not computerized. Office personnel or visitors may perform searches. Search fee $10.00 per hour; plus $2.00 per hour vault time. Copy fee $1.00 per page; $2.00 minimum. Cert fee- $7.00 per page includes copy fee. Payee- Kathy-Town Clerk. **Other phones:** Treasurer- 802-827-4495; Elections- 802-827-4495; Vital Records- 802-827-4495. **Property tax/Assessing-** Same address as recording office. 802-827-4495, assessor fax- 802-827-3106. (Appraiser/Auditor- 802-827-4495)

Baltimore Town

Town Clerk, 1902 Baltimore Rd, Baltimore, VT 05143. 802-263-5274; fax-same; 4-6PM W; 9-11AM TH. www.virtualvermont.com/towns/baltimore.html

Before faxing, call ahead. Index: Separate indices to search. Record index not computerized. Office personnel or visitors may perform searches. General index search fee $2.00 per hour. Copy fee $1.00 per page. Cert fee- $10.00 per doc includes copy fee. Payee- Town of Baltimore.

Barnard Town

Town Clerk, PO Box 274, Barnard, VT 05031-0274. Recording, R/E phone-802-234-9211; 8AM-3:30PM M-W.

Index: All in one. Records indexed. Only the public may search. Copy fee $1.00 per page. Cert fee- $7.00 per page plus copy fee. Payee- Town of Barnard. Treasurer- 802-234-9211; Elections- 802-234-9211; Vitals- 802-234-9211. **Property tax/Assessing-** 802-243-9576. (Appraiser/Auditor- 802-234-9576)

Barnet Town

Town Clerk, PO Box 15, Barnet, VT 05821-0015. 802-633-2256; fax-802-633-4315; 9AM-N, 1PM-4:30PM. www.barnetvt.org/townclerk.htm

Index: All in one. Records indexed on computer back to 2000. Office personnel or visitors may perform searches. Search fee $10.00. Office will perform a limited search of real estate records. Will search UCC records. Copy fee $1.00 per page. Cert fee- $8.00 per page plus copy fee. Payee- Town of Barnet. **Property tax/Assessing-** Treasurers Office, PO Box 15, Barnet, VT 05821-0015; 802-633-2256, assessor fax- 802-633-4315. www.barnetvt.org/taxcollector.htm

Barre City

City Clerk, PO Box 418, Barre, VT 05641. Recording, R/E phone-802-476-0242; fax-802-476-0264; 7:30AM-4:30PM www.barrecity.org

Index: All in one. Records indexed on computer back to 2000. Only the public may search. Copy fee $1.00 per page. Cert fee- $10.00 per page includes copy fee. Payee- Barre City. **Other phones:** Treasurer- 802-476-0242; Elections- 802-476-0242; Vital Records-

802-476-0242. **Property tax/Assessing**- 6 N Main St, Barre, VT 05641; 802-476-0244. (Appraiser/Auditor- 802-476-0244) hours- 7:30AM-N 1PM-4:30PM www.barrecity.org/index.asp

Barre Town

Town Clerk, PO Box 124, Websterville, VT 05678-0124. Recording, R/E phone-802-479-9391; fax-802-479-9332; 8AM-4:30. www.barretown.org
Index: Books and computer. Record index not computerized. Only the public may search. Search fee $2.00 per hour vault time. Copy fee $1.00 per page, fax fee $1.00 per page. Cert fee- $10.00 per page plus copy fee. Payee- Town of Barre. **Other phones:** Treasurer- 802-479-9391; Elections- 802-479-9391; Vital Records- 802-479-9391; Town Manager- 802-479-9331. **Property tax/Assessing**- PO Box 116, Websterville, VT 05678; 802-479-2595, assessor fax- 802-479-9332. (Appraiser/Auditor- 802-479-2595) hours- 8AM-4PM

Barton Town

Town Clerk, 34 Main St, Barton, VT 05822-1386. Recording, R/E phone-802-525-6222; fax-802-525-8856; 7:30AM-4PM.
Index: Separate indices to search include grantor/grantee, card files. Record index not computerized. Office will perform a UCC search but public must search other records themselves. UCC search per debtor name- $20.00. Copy fee $1.00 per page; UCC $2.00 per dock. Cert fee- $8.00 per page includes copies. Payee- Barton Town Clerk. **Other phones:** Treasurer- 802-525-6222; Elections- 802-525-6222; Vital Records- 802-525-6222. **Property tax/Assessing**- 34 Main St, Barton, VT 05822; 802-525-6222, assessor fax- 802-525-8836. (Appraiser/Auditor- 802-525-6222)

Belvidere Town

Town Clerk, 3996 Vermont Rte 109, Belvidere Center, VT 05492. 802-644-6621; fax-802-644-6621; 8:30AM-3:30PM T W Th.
Index: Separate indices to search include map surveys, UCCs. Record index not computerized. Office personnel or visitors may perform searches. Search fee $2.00 per hour for public; $5.00 per hour by clerk. Copy fee $.40 per page. Cert fee- $8.00 per doc includes copy fee. Payee- Town of Belvidere. **Other phones:** Tax Collector- 802-644-5427.

Bennington Town

Town Clerk, 205 South St, Bennington, VT 05201. Recording, R/E phone-802-442-1043; fax-802-442-1068; 8AM-5PM. www.bennington.com/local.html
Index: All in one. Record index not computerized. Only the public may search. Copy fee $1.00 per page. Cert fee- $8.00 per page includes copy fee. Payee- Bennington Town Clerk. **Other phones:** Treasurer- 802-442-1046; Elections- 802-442-1043; Vital Records- 802-442-1043. **Property tax/Assessing**- 205 South St, Bennington, VT 05201; 802-442-1042, assessor fax- 802-442-1068. (Appraiser/Auditor- 802-442-1042) **Online access**- Access to the Grand List search program is free at www.bennington.com/government/grandlist/index.html. No name searching at this time; site may be under construction and data incomplete.

Benson Town

Town Clerk, PO Box 163, Benson, VT 05731-0163. 802-537-2611; fax-802-537-2612; 9AM-N, 1PM-4:30PM M-Th. www.benson-vt.com/
Index: Separate indices to search include recording, liens. Record index not computerized. Office will perform a UCC search but public must search other records themselves. Search fee $2.00 per hour vault time. Copy fee $1.00 per page; lister's cards- $.25 each. Cert fee- $10.00 per cert includes copy fee. Payee- Benson Town Clerk.

Berkshire Town

Town Clerk, 4454 Watchtower Rd, Enosburg Falls, VT 05450. 802-933-2335; fax-802-933-5913; 9AM-N, 1-4PM M,T,Th,F; 9AM-N W.
Index: All in one. Record index not computerized. Only the public may search. Copy fee $1.00 per name. Cert fee- $6.00 per page includes copy fee. Payee- Berkshire Town Clerk. **Property tax/Assessing**- Same address as recording office. see above. hours- 9AM-N, 1-4PM

Berlin Town

Town Clerk, 108 Shed Rd, Berlin, VT 05602. Recording, R/E phone-802-229-9298; fax-802-229-9530; 8:30AM-3:30 PM M-Th. www.berlinvt.org/
Index: All in one. Record index not computerized. Office will perform a UCC search but public must search other records themselves. Office will not search real estate records. UCC search per debtor name- $10.00. Copy fee $.25 per page. Cert fee- $7.00 per doc includes copy fee. Payee- Berlin Town Clerk. Office does sell bulk data on paper. **Other phones:** Treasurer- 802-229-9380; Elections- 802-229-9298; Vital Records- 802-229-9298; Zoning Admin.- 802-229-2529. **Property tax/Assessing**- 108 Shed Rd, Berlin, VT 05602; 802-229-4880.

Bethel Town

Town Clerk, PO Box 404, Bethel, VT 05032. Recording, R/E phone-802-234-9722; fax-802-234-6840; 8AM-12:30PM-1PM-4PM, M, TH; 8AM-Noon T, F.
Index: All in one. Record index not computerized. Only the public may search. Office will not search real estate records. Will not search UCC records. Copy fee $1.00 per page. Copies of filed documents $.10 a copy. Cert fee- $8.00 per page. Payee- Bethel Town Clerk. **Other phones:** Treasurer- 802-234-9722; Elections- 802-234-9722; Vital Records- 802-234-9722; Tax Collector- 802-234-9340. **Property tax/Assessing**- 134 S Main St, Town Office, Bethel, VT 05032; 802-234-9722, fax- 802-234-6840.

Bloomfield Town

Town Clerk, PO Box 336, No. Stratford, VT 03590. 802-962-5191; fax-802-962-5191; 9AM-3PM Tues & Thurs. ndex: All in one. Record index not computerized. Only the public may search. Copy fee $1.00 per page. Cert fee- $10.00 per page. Payee- Town Clerk.

Bolton Town

Town Clerk, 3045 Theodore Roosevelt Hwy, Waterbury, VT 05676. Recording, R/E phone-802-434-3064; fax-802-434-6404; 8AM-N, 12:30-4PM M-TH.
Index: All in one card index. Record index not computerized. Only the public may search. Copy fee $1.00 per page. Cert fee- $10.00 per page plus copy fee. Payee- Town of Bolton. **Other phones:** Treasurer- 802-434-5075; Elections- 802-434-5075; Vital Records- 802-434-5075. **Property tax/Assessing**- 3045 Theodore Roosevelt Hwy, Waterbury, VT 05676; 802-434-3064, assessor fax- 802-434-6404. (Appraiser/Auditor- 802-434-3064) hours- 8AM-4PM

Bradford Town

Town Clerk, PO Box 339, Bradford, VT 05033-0339. 802-222-4727, R/E recording phone-x300; fax-802-222-3520; 8:30AM-4:30 M-TH; 9AM-Noon F.
Index: All in one. Record index not computerized. Only the public may search. Copy fee $1.00 per page. Cert fee- $10.00 per page includes copy fee. Payee- Town of Bradford. Call clerk with individual requests for bulk data. **Other phones:** Treasurer- x303; Elections- x300; Vital Records- x300; Water/Sewer- 802-222-4727 x307; Town Admin & Zoning -802 222 4727 x304. **Property tax/Assessing**- 172 N Main St, Bradford, VT 05033; 802-222-4727 x306, assessor fax- 802-222-3520. (Appraiser/Auditor- 802-222-4727 x306) hours- 9AM-N T & TH

Braintree Town

Town Clerk, 932 Vermont Rte 12A, Braintree, VT 05060. 802-728-9787; fax-802-728-9787; 8AM-N, 1-5PM T,W,Th. www.braintreevt.com/townclerk.htm
Index: All in one. Record index not computerized. Office personnel or visitors may perform searches. Search fee $2.00 per hour; $5.00 if clerk helps. Office will not search real estate records. Office will not search UCC records. General copy fee $2.00 per page.Real estate or tax lien copy- $1.00 per page. Cert fee- $10.00 per doc plus copy fee. Payee- Braintree Town Clerk. **Other phones:** Treasurer- 802-728-9787; Elections- 802-728-9787; Vital Records- 802-728-9787. **Property tax/Assessing**- 937 Vermont Rte 12A, Braintree, VT 05060; 802-728-9787, assessor fax- 802-728-9787. hours- 8AM-N T

Brandon Town

Town Clerk, 49 Center St, Brandon, VT 05733. Recording, R/E phone-802-247-5721; fax-802-247-5481; 8AM-4PM. www.town.brandon.vt.us
Index: Separate indices to search include grantor and grantee by time periods. Records indexed on computer back to 1995. Only the public may search. Copy fee $1.00 per page. Copy of UCC filing- $20.00 per doc. Cert fee- $7.00 per page includes copy fee. Payee- Town of Brandon. **Other phones:** Treasurer- 802-247-5721; Elections- 802-247-5721; Vital Records- 802-247-5721. **Property tax/Assessing**- 49 Center St, Brandon, VT 05733; 802-247-0226, assessor fax- 802-247-5481. (Appraiser/Auditor- 802-247-0226) hours- 8:30AM-4PM T; 8:30AM-N TH

Brattleboro Town

Town Clerk, 230 Main St, #108, Brattleboro, VT 05301-2885. 802-251-8157, R/E recording phone-802-802-251-8157, UCC recording phone-802-251-8157; fax-802-257-2312; 8:30AM-5PM. www.brattleboro.org
Index: All in one. Records indexed on a public use terminal back to 1987. Only the public may search. Copy fee $1.00 per page; $2.00 minimum. Cert fee- $8.00 per page. Payee- Brattleboro Town Clerk. **Other phones:** Treasurer- 802-251-8123; Elections- 802-251-8129; Vital Records- 802-251-8157. **Property tax/Assessing**- 230 Main St, #115, Brattleboro, VT 05301; 802-251-8119, fax- same as phone.

Bridgewater Town

Town Clerk, 7335 US Rte 4; Clerk's Office, Bridgewater, VT 05034. Recording, R/E phone-802-672-3334; fax-802-672-5395; 8AM-4PM M-Th.
Index: All in one. Record index not computerized. Only the public may search. Will not search UCC records. Copy fee $1.00 per page. Cert fee- $8.00 per page plus copy fee. Payee- Town of Bridgewater. **Other phones:** Treasurer- 802-672-3334; Elections- 802-672-3334; Vital Records- 802-672-3334; Tax Collector- 802-672-3334. **Property tax/Assessing**- 7335 US Rte 4, Bridgewater, VT 05034; 802-672-3334, assessor fax- 802-672-5395. (Appraiser/Auditor- 802-672-3334) **Online access**- Access assessor property data free at www.visionappraisal.com/databases/.

Bridport Town

Town Clerk, PO Box 27, Bridport, VT 05734-0027. Recording, R/E phone-802-758-2483; fax-n/a; 9AM-4PM M,T,F; 9AM-N 1-4PM Wed; 9AM-N Th.
Index: All in one. Record index not computerized. Only the public may search, but town clerk may perform searches as a private contractor. Search fee $5.00 per hour. Office will not search real estate records. Office will search UCC records. Copy fee $.10 per page. Cert fee- $8.00 per doc includes copy fee. Payee- Bridport Town Clerk. **Other phones:** Treasurer- 802-758-2483. **Property tax/Assessing**- 82 Crown Pt Rd, Bridport, VT 05734; 802-758-2483.

Brighton Town

Town Clerk, PO Box 377, Island Pond, VT 05846. Recording, R/E phone-802-723-4405; fax-802-723-4405; 8AM-3:30PM.
Index: Separate indices to search include general, alpha. Record index not computerized. Office will perform a UCC search but public must search other records themselves. Copy fee $.25; real estate $1.00 per page. Cert fee- $10.00 per doc plus copy fee. Payee- Brighton Town Clerk. **Other phones:** Treasurer- 802-723-4405; Elections- 802-732-4405; Vital Records- 802-732-4405. **Property tax/Assessing**- 49 Mill St Extension, Island Pond, VT 05846; 802-723-4405, assessor fax- 802-723-4405. (Appraiser/Auditor- 802-723-6672);

Bristol Town

Town Clerk, PO Box 249, Bristol, VT 05443. 802-453-2486; fax-802-453-5188; 8AM-4:30PM.
Index: All in one back to 1986, general index before that. Record index not computerized. Only the public may search. Search fee $2.00 per hour vault time. Copy fee $1.00 per page; tax maps and permits are $.05 each. Cert fee- $8.00 per page plus copy fee. Payee- Town of Bristol. **Other phones:** Treasurer-802-453-2486; Elections- 802-453-2486; Vital Records- 802-453-2486. **Property tax/Assessing**-Same address as recording office. 802-453-2486, assessor fax- 802-453-5188.

Brookfield Town

Town Clerk, PO Box 463, Brookfield, VT 05036-0463. 802-276-3352; fax-802-276-3926; 8:30AM-N, 1-4:30PM T,W,Th.
Index: Separate indices to search include land records, permit files, lister cards, vital statistics, UCCs. Record index not computerized. Office will perform a UCC search but public must search other records themselves. Copy fee $1.00 each for land records, $.25 per page for others. Cert fee- $8.00 per page includes copy fee. Payee- Town of Brookfield.

Brookline Town

Town Clerk, PO Box 403, Brookline, VT 05345. 802-365-4648; fax-same; 9AM-2PM Wed.
Index: All in one. Record index not computerized. Only the public may search. Copy fee $1.00 per page. Cert fee- none. Payee- Brookline Town Clerk.

Brownington Town

Town Clerk, 509 Dutton Brook Ln, Orleans, VT 05860. 802-754-8401; fax-802-754-8401; 9AM-4PM
Index: All in one. Record index not computerized. Office personnel or visitors may perform searches. Search fee-$2.00 per hour vault time. Office will search real estate records. Copy fee $1.00 per page. Cert fee- $7.00 per page includes copies. Payee-Brownington Town Clerk. Bulk data available for purchase, contact Cheryl Perry. **Other phones:** Treasurer- 802-754-6559. **Property tax/Assessing**- . (Appraiser/Auditor- 802-754-8401)

Brunswick Town

Town Clerk, 994 Vermont Rte 102, Brunswick, VT 05905. Recording, R/E phone-802-962-5514; fax-802-962-5522; 4PM-6PM Th or by app't.
Index: Books. Record index not computerized. Office will perform a UCC search but public must search other records themselves. Search fee $10.00. Office will not search real estate records. Copy fee $1.00 per page. Cert fee- $2.00 per page. Payee- Brunswick Town Clerk. **Other phones:** Treasurer- 802-962-5514; Elections- 802-962-5514; Vital Records- 802-962-5514. **Property tax/Assessing**- 994 Vermont Rte 102, Brunswick, VT 05905; 802-962-5514, assessor fax- 802-962-5522.

Burke Town

Town Clerk, 212 School St, West Burke, VT 05871. Recording, R/E phone-802-467-3717; fax-802-467-8623; 8AM-4PM. www.burkevt.org Index: All in one. Record index not computerized. Only the public may search. Office will charge fee for vault time. Copy fee $.25 per page. Deeds are $1.00 per copy; maps $.50 per copy. Cert fee- $10.00 per page plus copy fee. Payee- Town of Burke. **Other phones:** Treasurer- 802-467-3717; Elections- 802-467-3717; Vital Records- 802-467-3717. **Property tax/Assessing**- 212 School St, Town Office, West Burke, VT 05871; 802-467-3717.

Burlington City

Town Clerk, 149 Church St, Rm 20; City Hall, Burlington, VT 05401. 802-865-7135, R/E recording phone-802-865-7133, UCC recording phone-802-865-7135; fax-802-865-7014; 8AM-4:30PM. www.ci.burlington.vt.us ndex: All in one. Records indexed on computer back to 1986. Only the public may search. Copy fee $1.00 per page. Cert fee-$20.00 per page plus copy fee,UCC. Payee-Burlington City Clerk. **Other phones:** Treasurer-802-865-7000; Elections- 802-865-7137; Vital Records- 802-865-7000. **Property tax/Assessing**-802-865-7114.

Online access- Access to city property tax data is free at http://ci.burlingtontelecom.com/assessor/search/.

Cabot Town

Town Clerk, PO Box 36, Cabot, VT 05647-0036. Recording, R/E phone-802-563-2279; fax-802-563-2423; 9AM-5PM M-Th; 9AM-1PM F.
Index: All in one. Record index not computerized. Only the public may search. Will not search UCC records. Copy fee $2.00 per page. Cert fee- $7.00 per cert plus copy fee. Payee- Town of Cabot. **Other phones:** Treasurer- 802-563-2279; Elections- 802-563-2279; Vital Records- 802-563-2279. **Property tax/Assessing**- 3084 Main St, Town Hall, Cabot, VT 05647; 802-563-2279, assessor fax- 802-563-2423. (Appraiser/Auditor- 802-563-2279)

Calais Town

Town Clerk, 3120 Pekin Brook Rd, East Calais, VT 05650. 802-456-8720; 8AM-5PM M,T,Th; 8AM-N Sat. www.calaisvermont.gov/
Index: Separate indices to search. Card file back to 1942, books prior. Office personnel or visitors may perform searches. Office will not search real estate or UCC records. Will search UCC records. Copy fee $1.00 per page. Cert fee- $7.00 per doc plus copy fee. Payee- Calais Town Clerk. **Other phones:** All offices- 802-456-8720. **Property tax/Assessing**-3120 Pekin Brook Rd, East Calais, VT 05650; 802-456-8720.

Cambridge Town

Town Clerk, PO Box 127, Jeffersonville, VT 05464. Recording, R/E phone-802-644-2251; fax-802-644-8348; 8AM-4PM. _Index: All in one. Record index not computerized. Only the public may search. Search fee $2.00 per hour vault time. Copy fee $.25 per page. Cert fee- $10.00 per cert plus copy fee. **Other phones:** Elections- 802-644-8348; Vital Records-802-644-2251. **Property tax/Assessing**- 802-644-2251. (Appraiser/Auditor- 802-644-2200)

Canaan Town

Town Clerk, PO Box 159, Canaan, VT 05903-0159. Recording, R/E phone-802-266-3370; fax-802-266-8253; 9AM-3PM
Index: All in one. Record index not computerized. Office will perform a UCC search (only current records) but public must search other records themselves. Search fee $2.00 per hour vault time. Copy fee $1.00 per page. Cert fee- $7.00 per page. Payee- Town of Canaan. **Other phones:** Treasurer-802-266-3370; Elections- 802-266-3370; Vital Records- 802-266-3370. **Property tax/Assessing**-Town Hall, Canaan, VT 05903; 802-266-3370, assessor fax- 802-266-8253. (Appraiser/Auditor- 802-266-3370);

Castleton Town

Town Clerk, PO Box 727, Castleton, VT 05735. Recording, R/E phone-802-468-2212 x214, UCC recording phone-802-468-2212 x 214; fax-802-468-5482; 8:30AM-N; 1PM-4:30PM www.bsi-vt.com/castleton/towninfo.htm
Index: Separate indices to search include grantor/grantee indexes. Record index not computerized. Only the public may search. Search fee $2.00 per hour vault time. General copy fee $1.00 per page; tax maps $.25 per page. Cert fee- $8.00 per page (land records), $10.00 per page (vital records). Payee-Town of Castleton. **Other phones:** Treasurer- 802-468-5319; Elections- 802-468-2212 x214; Vital Records- 802-468-2212 x214. **Property tax/Assessing**- 556 Main St, Castleton, VT 05735; 802-468-5319 x217 or 224, assessor fax- 802-468-5482. (Appraiser/Auditor- 802-468-2751) 9AM-N M,W,F www.bsi-vt.com/castleton/towninfo.htm

Cavendish Town

Town Clerk, PO Box 126, Cavendish, VT 05142-0126. Recording, R/E phone-802-226-7292; fax-802-226-7290; 9AM-N, 1PM-4:30PM.
Index: Index is grantor/grantee back to 1952. Record index not computerized. Only the public may search. Copy fee $1.00 per page. Cert fee- $5.00 per page. Payee- Cavendish Town Clerk. **Other phones:** Treasurer- 802-226-7292; Elections- 802-226-7292; Vital Records- 802-226-7292. **Property tax/Assessing**- PO Box 126, High St, Town Hall, Cavendish, VT 05142; 802-226-7289, assessor fax-802-226-7290. (Appraiser/Auditor- 802-226-7292);

Charleston Town

Town Clerk, 5063 VT Rte 105, West Charleston, VT 05872-7902. 802-895-2814; fax-802-895-2814; 8AM-3PM M,T,TH (Closed Wed) 8AM-12:30PM F. www.charlestonvt.org
Index: All in one. Records indexed on computer back to 1930. Only the public may search. Copy fee $1.00 per page. Deed copies $2.00 minimum. Cert fee-$7.00 per page plus copy fee. Payee- Town of Charleston. **Other phones:** Treasurer- 802-895-2814; Vital Records- 802-895-2814. **Property tax/Assessing**- 5063 VT Rte 105, West Charleston, VT 05872 802-895-2814, fax- 802-895-2814.

Charlotte Town

Town Clerk, PO Box 119, Charlotte, VT 05445-0119. Recording, R/E phone-802-425-3071; fax-802-425-4241; 8AM-4PM www.charlottevt.org
Index: All in one. Record index not computerized. Office will perform a UCC search but public must search other records themselves. Office will not search real estate records. Copy fee $1.00 per page. Cert fee- $8.00 per page includes copy fee. Payee-Town of Charlotte. **Other phones:** Treasurer- 802-425-3071; Elections- 802-425-3071; Vital Records-802-425-3071; Planning & Zoning- 802-425-3533. **Property tax/Assessing**- 159 Ferry Rd, Charlotte, VT 05445; 802-425-3855, assessor fax- 802-425-4241. (Appraiser/Auditor- 802-425-3855)

Chelsea Town

Town Clerk, PO Box 266, Chelsea, VT 05038. 802-685-4460; fax-Same; 8AM-N, 1-4PM M-Th.
Index: Separate indices to search. Record index not computerized. Only the public may search. Copy fee $1.00 per page. Cert fee- $10.00 per doc plus copy fee. Payee- Chelsea Town Clerk. **Property tax/Assessing**- 802-685-4460.

Chester Town

Town Clerk, PO Box 370, Chester, VT 05143. 802-875-2173; fax-802-875-2237; hours - 8AM-5PM. www.chester.govoffice.com
Index: All in one. Record index not computerized. Only the public may search. Copy fee $.50 per page. Cert fee- $8.00 per page plus copy fee. Payee- Town of Chester. **Property tax/Assessing**- Same address as recording office. 802-875-2173.

Clarendon Town

Town Clerk, PO Box 30, North Clarendon, VT 05759-0030. Recording, R/E phone-802-775-4274;

fax-802-775-4274; 10AM-4PM M-TH. www.clarendonvt.org/government.htm
Index: Separate indices to search include lien, mobile home transfers, land records, UCCs. Records indexed on computer back to 1/1/03. Only the public may search. Search fee $2.00 per hour vault time. Copy fee $2.00 per UCC.Real estate or tax lien copy- $1.00 per page. Cert fee- $10.00 per page plus copy fee. Payee- Town of Clarendon. Treasurer- 802-775-1536; Elections- 802-775-4274; Vital Records- 802-775-4274. **Property tax/Assessing**- 279 Middle Rd, North Clarendon, VT 05759; 802-775-1536, assessor fax- 802-775-2474. (Appraiser/Auditor- 802-775-1536)

Colchester Town

Town Clerk, PO Box 55, Colchester, VT 05446. Recording, R/E phone-802-264-5520, UCC recording phone-802-264-5522; fax-802-264-5503; 8AM-4PM. www.town.colchester.vt.us
Index: All in one. Records indexed on a public use terminal back to 05/96. Office will perform a UCC (with search request form) search but public must search other records themselves. Search fee $2.00 per hour vault time. Copy fee $1.00 per page. UCC copy fee is $20.00 plus $2.00 per copy. Cert fee- $8.00 per page plus copy fee. Payee- Town of Colchester. **Other phones:** Treasurer- 802-264-5525; Elections- 203-264-5520; Vital Records- 203-264-5520. **Property tax/Assessing**- 835 Blakely Rd, Colchester, VT 05446; 802-264-5671, assessor fax- 802-654-0757. (Appraiser/Auditor- 802-264-5671);

Concord Town

Town Clerk, PO Box 317, Concord, VT 05824-0317. 802-695-2220; fax-802-695-2220; 7:30AM-3:30PM M-Th; 9AM-2PM F.
Index: Separate indices to search include books, general index. Land records indexed on a public use terminal back to 1999. Only the public may search. Copy fee $1.00 per page. Cert fee- $7.00 per page plus copy fee. Payee- Town of Concord. **Other phones:** Treasurer- 802-695-2220; Elections- 802-695-2220; Vital Records- 802-695-2220. **Property tax/Assessing**- 274 Main St, Concord, VT 05824; 802-695-2220. (Appraiser/Auditor- 802-695-2220)

Corinth Town

Town Clerk, PO Box 461, Corinth, VT 05039. Recording, R/E phone-802-439-5850; fax-802-439-5850; 8AM-4PM M,T; 10AM-6PM TH; 8:30AM-3PM F. www.corinthvt.org
Index: Separate indices to search include books, computer. Records indexed on computer back to 2004. Only the public may search. Copy fee $1.00 per page. Cert fee- $10.00 per page includes copy fee. Payee- Town of Corinth. **Other phones:** Treasurer- 802-439-5850; Elections- 802-439-5850; Vital Records- 802-439-5850. **Property tax/Assessing**- 134 Cookeville Rd, Town Hall, Corinth, VT 05039; 802-439-5098.

Cornwall Town

Town Clerk, 2629 Rte 30, Cornwall, VT 05753-9299. 802-462-2775; fax-802-462-2606; 9AM-5PM T-F.
Index: Separate indices. Record index not computerized. Only the public may search. Copy fee $1.00 per page. Cert fee- $7.00 per doc plus copy fee. Payee- Town Clerk. **Property tax/Assessing**- 2629 Rte 30, Cornwall, VT 05753; 802-462-2855.

Coventry Town

Town Clerk, PO Box 104, Coventry, VT 05825. 802-754-2288; fax-802-754-6274; 8AM-N M,T,Th, Fri; 4-7PM Wed.
Index: All in one. Record index not computerized. Only the public may search. Search fee $2.00 per hour vault time. Copy fee $1.00 per page. Cert fee- $10.00 per page includes copy fee. Payee- Coventry Town Clerk. **Property tax/Assessing**- 168 Coventry Community Center, E Fremont, Coventry, VT 05825; 802-754-2288, assessor fax- 802-754-6274.

Craftsbury Town

Town Clerk, PO Box 55, Craftsbury, VT 05826. 802-586-2323; fax-same; 8:30AM-4PM T,W,Th, F. www.townofcraftsbury.com/
Index: All in one. Records indexed on a public use terminal back to 1900s. Office personnel or visitors may perform searches. Search fee $5.00 per hr; flat $10.00 for UCC search. Copy fee $1.00 per page. Cert fee- $9.50 per doc includes copy fee. Payee- Town of Craftsbury. **Property tax/Assessing**- 85 Craftbury Rd, Town Hall, Craftsbury, 05826; 802-586-2835.

Danby Town

Town Clerk, PO Box 231, Danby, VT 05739-0231. Recording, R/E phone-802-293-5136; fax-802-293-5311; 9AM-N, 1-4PM M-Th.
Index: All in one. Record index not computerized. Only the public may search. Copy fee $1.00 per page. Cert fee- $7.00 per page. Payee- Town of Darby. Bulk data available for purchase, contact the listers. **Other phones:** Treasurer- 802-293-5136; Elections- 802-293-5136; Vital Records- 802-293-5136. **Property tax/Assessing**- 130 Brook Rd, Danby, VT 05739; 802-293-5136, assessor fax- 802-293-5311. (Appraiser/Auditor- 802-293-5136) hours- 9AM-2PM

Danville Town

Town Clerk, PO Box 183, Danville, VT 05828. 802-684-3352; fax-802-684-9606; 8AM-4PM.
Index: All in one. Record index not computerized. Only the public may search. Copy fee $1.00 per page. Lister cards copy fee $.50, non-recorded copies $.20. Cert fee- $8.00 per page includes copy fee. Payee- Town of Danville. Bulk data is available for purchase in print form. Contact recording office. **Property tax/Assessing**- 36 Rte 2 W, Town Hall, Danville, VT 05828; 802-684-3352.

Derby Town

Town Clerk, PO Box 25, Derby, VT 05829. 802-766-4906; fax-802-766-2027; 8AM-4PM; 7AM-4:30PM M-Th; Closed Fri (Summer). www.derbyvt.org
Index: Separate indices to search include general index. Records indexed on computer back 40 years. Only the public may search. Copy fee $1.00 per page. Cert fee- $10.00 per cert plus copy fee. Payee- Derby Town Clerk. **Other phones:** Treasurer- 802-766-4906; Elections- 802-766-4906; Vital Records- 802-766-4906; Zoning- 802-766-2017. **Property tax/Assessing**- 802-766-4906. (Appraiser/Auditor- 802-766-2012) Public access terminal available.

Dorset Town

Town Clerk, PO Box 24, East Dorset, VT 05253. 802-362-1178; fax-802-362-5156; 8:30AM-3:30PM M-TH; 8AM-N Fri.
Index: All in one. Records indexed on a public use terminal back to 1999 (currently going backwards to a 40 year search). Office personnel or visitors may perform searches. Search fee $5.00 hour, not to exceed $25.00. Office will not search real estate records. Will search UCC records. Copy fee $1.00 per page. Cert fee- $8.00 per page plus copy fee. Payee- Dorset Town Clerk. **Property tax/Assessing**- 112 Mad Tom Rd, Town Hall, East Dorset, VT 05253; 802-362-0162, assessor fax- 802-362-5156. hours- 9AM-3:30PM T & TH

Dover Town

Town Clerk, PO Box 527, Dover, VT 05356-0527. Recording, R/E phone-802-464-5100; fax-802-464-8721; 9AM-5PM. www.doververmont.com/
Index: Book 1793-1967, cards 1967-present, computer. Records indexed on a public use terminal back to 2002. Only the public may search. Copy fee $1.00 per page. Lister cards and zoning records $.10. Cert fee- $7.00 per page includes copy fee. Payee- Dover Town Clerk. **Other phones:** Treasurer- 802-464-8723; Elections- 802-464-5100; Vital Records- 802-464-5100. **Property tax/Assessing**- PO Box 428, Dover, VT 05356; 802-464-8724, assessor fax- 802-464-8721. (Appraiser - 802-464-8724) 10AM-4PM

Dummerston Town

Town Clerk, 1523 Middle Rd, East Dummerston, VT 05346. 802-257-1496; fax-802-257-4671; hours- 9AM-3PM M T TH F; 11AM-5PM Wed. http://townclerk.dummerston.org/
Index: All in one. Record index not computerized. Only the public may search. Copy fee $1.00 per page. Cert fee- $10.00 per page. Payee- Town of Dummerston. **Other phones:** Treasurer- 802-257-1496; Elections- 802-257-1496; Vital Records- 802-257-1496. **Property tax/Assessing**- 1523 Middle Rd, E Dummerston, VT 05346; 802-257-1496, assessor fax- 802-257-4671. hours- 9AM-N T,TH

Duxbury Town

Town Clerk, 5421 Vermont Rte 100, Duxbury, VT 05676. 802-244-6660; fax-802-244-5442; 8AM-4PM M; 10AM-6PM W; 7:30AM-3:30 PM T, Th, F. www.duxburyvermont.org
Index: All in one. Records indexed on computer back to 1990, on card file back to 1790's. Only the public may search. General copy fee $1.00 per page. Cert fee- $10.00 per page total. Payee- Town of Duxbury. **Property tax/Assessing**- 5421 VT Rte 100, Duxbury, VT 05676; 802-244-6660, fax- 802-244-5442.

East Haven Town

Town Clerk, PO Box 10, East Haven, VT 05837-0010. 802-467-3772; 1-6PM T; 8AM-1PM Th; and by appt.
Index: Pre-1984 indices in books. Record index not computerized. Office will perform a UCC search but public must search other records themselves. Search fee $2.00 per hour. Copy fee $1.00 per page for deeds; $.15 per page for other papers. Cert fee- $7.00 per doc plus copy fee. Payee- Town of East Haven. Treasurer- 802-467-3772; Elections- 802-467-3772; Vital Records- 802-467-3772. **Property tax/Assessing**- 17 Maple St, East Haven, VT 05837; 802-467-3772. (Appraiser - 802-467-3772);

East Montpelier Town

Town Clerk, PO Box 157, East Montpelier, VT 05651-0157. Recording, R/E phone-802-223-3313; fax-802-223-4467; 9AM-5PM M-Th; 9AM-N Fri.
Index: Separate indices to search include land record index books 1-2-3 before 7/1988, after on card record index file; beginning 11/30/2000- index on computer. Records indexed on a public use terminal back to 11/3000. Only the public may search; office will perform minor searches. No search fee for minor searches. $1.00 per half hour for extended searches. Copy fee $1.00 per page; $.10 per page for tax map or lister card; UCC copy- $2.00 per doc. Cert fee- $7.00 per page plus copy fee. Payee- East Montpelier Town Clerk. **Other phones:** Treasurer- 802-223-3313; Elections- 802-223-3313; Vital Records- 802-223-3313. **Property tax/Assessing**- 40 Kelton Rd, Municipal Bldg, East Montpelier, VT 05651; 802-223-3313, assessor fax- 802-223-4467. (Appraiser/Auditor- 802-223-3313);

Eden Town

Town Clerk, 71 Old Schoolhouse Rd, Eden Mills, VT 05653. 802-635-2528; fax-802-635-1724; 8AM-12:30-1:30-4PM M-Th.
Index: All in one. Record index not computerized. Only the public may search. Will not search UCC records. Copy fee $1.00 per page. Cert fee- $10.00 per page includes copy fee. Payee- Eden Town Clerk. **Other phones:** Vital Records- 802-635-2528. **Property tax/Assessing**- 71 Old Schoolhouse Rd, Eden Mills, VT 05653; 802-635-2554, assessor fax- 802-635-1724.

Elmore Town

Town Clerk, PO Box 123, Lake Elmore, VT 05657. 802-888-2637; fax-802-888-2637; 9AM-3PM T,W,Th. Index: Separate indices to search include grantor/grantee. Record index not computerized. Office personnel (limited searches) or visitors may perform searches. Office will search real estate records. Fee is $5.00 per hour. UCC search fee is $5.00 per hour. Copy fee $1.00 per page. Cert fee- $10.00 per page plus copy fee. Payee- Elmore Town Clerk. **Property tax/Assessing**- 1175 Vermont Rte 12, Town Hall, Lake Elmore, VT 05657; 802-888-2637.

Enosburgh Town

Town Clerk, PO Box 465, Enosburg Falls, VT 05450. Recording, R/E phone-802-933-4421; fax-802-933-4832; 8AM-4PM www.enosburghvt.org
Index: All in one. Record index not computerized. Only the public may search. Copy fee $1.00 per page. Cert fee- $8.00 per doc plus copy fee. UCC's-$20.00. Payee- Town of Enosburgh. **Other phones:** Treasurer- 802-933-4421; Elections- 802-933-4421; Vital Records- 802-933-4421. **Property tax/Assessing**- 239 Main St, Enosburg Falls, VT 05450; 802-933-4421, assessor fax- 802-933-4832. (Appraiser/Auditor- 802-933-4421);

Essex Town

Town Clerk, 81 Main St, Essex Junction, VT 05452. Recording, R/E phone-802-879-0413; fax-802-878-1353; 7:30AM-4:30PM (CST) www.essex.org
Index: All in one. Record index not computerized. Only the public may search. Copy fee $1.00 per page. Cert fee- $8.00 per page plus copy fee. Payee- Town of Essex. **Other phones:** Treasurer- 802-879-0413; Elections- 802-879-0413; Vital Records- 802-879-0413. **Property tax/Assessing**- 81 Main St, Essex Junction, VT 05452; 802-878-1345, assessor fax-802-878-1353. (Appraiser/Auditor- 802-878-1345);

Fair Haven Town

Town Clerk, 3 N Park Pl, Fair Haven, VT 05743. Recording, R/E phone-802-265-3610; fax-802-265-2158; 8AM-4PM.
Index: Separate indices to search include computer and books. Records indexed on a public use terminal back to 1948. Only the public may search. Search fee $2.00 per hour vault time. Copy fee $1.00 per page. Cert fee- $8.00 per cert plus copy fee. Payee- Town of Fair Haven. **Other phones:** Treasurer- 802-265-3010; Elections- 802-265-3610; Vital Records- 802-265-3610. **Property tax/Assessing**- Same address as recording office. 802-265-3610, assessor fax- 802-265-3176. (Appraiser/Auditor- 802-265-3610)

Fairfax Town

Town Clerk, PO Box 27, Fairfax, VT 05454. Recording, R/E phone-802-849-6111; fax-802-849-6276; 9AM-4PM
Index: Separate indices to search. Records indexed on computer back to 1954. Office will perform a UCC search but public must search other records themselves. Copy fee $1.00 per page. Cert fee- $7.00 per page plus copy fee. Payee- Fairfax Town Office. Treasurer- 802-849-6111; Vital Records- 802-849-6111. **Property tax/Assessing**- 67 Hunt St, Town Office, Fairfax, VT 05454; 802-849-6111, assessor fax- 802-849-6276. hours- 9AM-4PM M-F; 6PM-8PM M

Fairfield Town

Town Clerk, PO Box 5, Fairfield, VT 05455. 802-827-3261; fax-802-827-3653; 9AM-3PM; N-7PM W. http://fairfieldvermont.us/html/contact_us.html
Index: All in one. Record index not computerized. Only the public may search. Search fee $2.00 per hour vault time. Copy fee $1.00 per page, $2.00 minimum. Cert fee- $1.00 per page. Payee- Fairfield Town. **Property tax/Assessing**- Town Hall, Fairfield, VT 05455; 802-827-3261. hours- Varies

Fairlee Town

Town Clerk, PO Box 95, Fairlee, VT 05045-0095. 802-333-4363; fax-802-333-9214; 8:30AM-3:30PM M-TH. www.fairleevt.org/townclerk.htm Index: Separate indices to search include general index, card file. Records indexed on computer back to Book 61 in 2004. Only the public may search. Search fee $2.00 per hour vault time. Copy fee $1.00 per page, $2.00 minimum. Cert fee- $6.00 per page includes copy fee. Payee- Fairlee Town Clerk. **Other phones:** Treasurer- 802-333-4363; Elections- 802-333-4363; Vital Records- 802-333-4363; Zoning Admin- 802-333-4158. **Property tax/Assessing**- 75 Town Common Rd, Fairlee, VT 05045; 802-333-9829, assessor fax- 802-333-9214. (Appraiser/Auditor- 802-333-9829) hours- Mornings M-TH

Fayston Town

Town Clerk, 866 N Fayston Rd, No. Fayston, VT 05660. 802-496-2454 x21 or 23; fax-802-496-9850; 9AM-N, 12:30-3:30PM M-Th, Fri 9AM-3PM www.faystonvt.com/
Index: Separate indices to search include books by volume number. Record index not computerized. Only the public may search. Will not search UCC records. Copy fee $1.00 per page. Cert fee- $8.00 per page includes copy fee. Payee- Town of Fayston. **Other phones:** Treasurer- 802-496-2454 x23; Elections- 802-496-2454 x23; Town Clerk/Tax Collector- 802-496-2454 x21. **Property tax/Assessing**- 866 N Fayston Rd, No. Fayston, VT 05660; 802-496-2454 x24.

Ferrisburgh Town

Town Clerk, PO Box 6, Ferrisburgh, VT 05456-0006. 802-877-3429; fax-802-877-6757; 8AM-4PM. www.twp.ferrisburgh.vt.us
Index: All in one. Records indexed on computer from 2003 to present, card index from 1970 to 3/00, general index from 1970-back. Office will perform a UCC search but public must search other records themselves. Copy fee $1.00 per page. Cert fee- $8.00 per doc includes copy fee. Payee- Town of Ferrisburg.

Fletcher Town

Town Clerk, 215 Cambridge Rd, Cambridge, VT 05444. Recording, R/E phone-802-849-6616; fax-802-849-2500; 8AM-3:30PM M-Th;6:30PM-8:30PM M; closed Fri. _Index: All in one. Record index not computerized. Only the public may search. Copy fee $1.00 per page. Cert fee- $7.00 per page includes copy fee. Payee- Town of Fletcher. **Other phones:** Treasurer- 802-849-6616; Elections- 802-849-6616; Vital Records- 802-849-6616. **Property tax/Assessing**- 215 Cambridge Rd, Town Office, Cambridge, VT 05444; 802-849-6616, fax- 802-849-2500. (Appraiser - 802-849-6616);

Franklin Town

Town Clerk, PO Box 82, Franklin, VT 05457-0082. Recording, R/E phone-802-285-2101; fax-802-285-2181; 8:30AM-3:30PM M,T,F; 8:30AM-6PM Th; 8:30AM-N Wed. www.franklinvermont.com
Index: All in one except old UCCs separate. Records indexed on computer. No public access terminal available. Only the public may search. Search fee $2.00 per hour vault time. Will not search UCC records. Copy fee $2.00 per doc; UCC copy $1.00 per page. Cert fee- $8.00 per doc includes copy fee. Payee- Town of Franklin. **Other phones:** Treasurer- 802-285-2101; Elections- 802-285-2101; Vital Records- 802-285-2101. **Property tax/Assessing**- PO Box 82, Franklin, VT 05457; 802-285-2101, assessor fax- 802-285-2181. (Appraiser/Auditor- 802-285-2101);

Georgia Town

Town Clerk, 47 Town Common Rd N, St. Albans, VT 05478. Recording, R/E phone-802-524-3524; fax-802-524-3543; 8AM-4PM. www.townofgeorgia.com
Office will charge in person searches for vault time-$2.00 per hour. Index: Separate indices to search include general indexes to 1970, cards-1970-4/1/2001, computer 2001 to present. Records indexed on a public use terminal back to 1995. Only the public may search. Search fee $2.00 per hour; $1.00 per half hour. Copy fee $1.00 per page. Cert fee- $8.00 per page plus copy fee. Payee- Town of Georgia. **Other phones:** Treasurer- 802-524-3524; Elections- 802-524-3524; Vital Records- 802-524-3524; Town Administrator- 802-524-9794. **Property tax/Assessing**- 47 Town Common Rd N, Town Hall, St. Albans, VT 05478; 802-524-3524, assessor fax-802-524-3543. (Appraiser/Auditor- 802-524-3524)

Glover Town

Town Clerk, 51 Bean Hill, Glover, VT 05839. Recording, R/E phone-802-525-6227; fax-802-525-4115; 8AM-4PM,.
Index: All in one. Record index not computerized. Only the public may search. Copy fee $1.00 per page. Cert fee- $8.00 per page includes copy fee. Payee-Town of Glover. **Other phones:** Treasurer- 802-525-6227; Elections- 802-525-6227; Vital Records- 802-525-6227. **Property tax/Assessing**- 51 Bean Hill, Glover, VT 05839; 802-525-6227. (Appraiser/Auditor- 802-525-6227);

Goshen Town

Town Clerk, 50 Carlisle Hill Rd, Goshen, VT 05733. 802-247-6455; fax-802-247-6740; 9AM-1PM Tues.
Index: Separate indices; in process of combining last 15 years into 1 index. Record index not computerized. Only the public may search. Search fee- after 1/2 hour fee is $5.00. Will not search UCC records. Copy fee $1.00 per page; UCC copies- $2.00 minimum. Cert fee- $7.00 per doc includes copy fee. Payee- Town Clerk. **Property tax/Assessing**- 50 Carlisle Hill Rd, Goshen, VT 05733; 802-247-6455. hours- by appointment only

Grafton Town

Town Clerk, PO Box 180, Grafton, VT 05146. 802-843-2419; 9AM-N, 1-4PM M,T,Th,F.
Index: All in one. Record index not computerized. Office personnel will only search if time; suggests visitors to perform searches. Search fee $5.00. Office will not search real estate records. Office will not search UCC records or tax liens. Copy fee $1.00 per page. Cert fee- $10.00 per page. Payee- Grafton Town Clerk. Bulk data available for purchase, contact Lyle Morrison.

Granby Town

Town Clerk, PO Box 56, Granby, VT 05840. 802-328-3611; fax-802-328-2200; Tues or Thurs by appointment.
Index: Separate indices to search include individual and general books. Record index not computerized. Office will perform a UCC search but public must search other records themselves. Copy fee $1.00 per page. Cert fee- $2.00 per page plus copy fee. Payee-Town of Grandby. **Property tax/Assessing**- 9005 Granby Rd, Granby, VT 05840; 802-328-2191, assessor fax- 802-328-2200.

Grand Isle Town Clerk

Town Clerk, PO Box 49, Grand Isle, VT 05458. Recording, R/E phone-802-372-8830; fax-802-372-8815; 8:30AM-3:30PM M-F; 5PM-7PM T; 10AM-N Sat. www.grandislevt.org
Index: Separate indices to search include books by name. Record index not computerized. Only the public may search. Copy fee $1.00 per page. Cert fee- $10.00 per page plus copy fee. Payee- Town of Grand Isle. **Other phones:** Treasurer- 802-372-8830; Elections- 802-372-8830; Vital Records- 802-372-8830. **Property tax/Assessing**- 9 Hyde Rd, Grand Isle, VT 05458; 802-372-5233. (Appraiser/Auditor- 802-372-5233)

Granville Town

Town Clerk, PO Box 66, Granville, VT 05747-0066. 802-767-4403; 9AM-2PM M-Th; closed Fri.
Index: All in one. Record index not computerized. Only the public may search. Search fee $1.00 per hour public fee. Copy fee $1.00 per page; $7.00 for mortgages, quit claims, etc. Cert fee- $7.00 per page total. Payee- Granville Town Clerk. **Other phones:** Treasurer- 802-767-4403. **Property tax/Assessing**- Same address as recording office. 802-767-4403.

Greensboro Town

Town Clerk, PO Box 119, Greensboro, VT 05841. 802-533-2911; fax-802-533-2191; 9AM-N, 1PM-4:30PM T-F. www.greensborovt.com/

Index: Separate indices to search include liens & attachments separate, zoning separate, deeds & mortgages. Record index not computerized. Only the public may search. Copy fee $1.00 per page. Cert fee- $8.00 per page includes copy fee. Payee- Greensboro Town Clerk.

Groton Town

Town Clerk, 1476 Scott Hwy, Groton, VT 05046. Recording, R/E phone-802-584-3276; fax-802-584-3276; 8:30AM-12:30, 1PM-5PM M T Th; 8:30AM-N W F. www.grotonvt.com

Index: Separate indices to search include card files. Record index not computerized. Only the public may search. Search fee $2.00 per hour vault time. Copy fee $1.00 per page. Cert fee- $8.00 per doc includes copy fee. Payee- Town of Groton. **Other phones:** Treasurer- 802-584-3131; Elections- 802-584-3276; Vital Records- 802-584-3276. **Property tax/Assessing**- 1476 Scott Hwy, Groton, VT 05046; 802-584-3276/ 584-3155, assessor fax- 802-584-3276. (Appraiser/Auditor- 802-584-3155) hours- 8:30AM-12:30PM, 1PM-5PM

Guildhall Town

Town Clerk, PO Box 10, Guildhall, VT 05905. 802-676-3797; fax-802-676-3518; 9AM-2PM T, 9AM-6PM Th.

Index: All in one. Record index not computerized. Only the public may search. Copy fee $1.00 per page from any records book, others $.50 per page. Cert fee- $9.50 per page includes copy fee. Payee- Town of Guildhall. **Property tax/Assessing**- Rte 102, Guildhall, VT 05905; see above.

Guilford Town

Town Clerk, 236 School Rd, Guilford, VT 05301-8319. 802-254-6857; fax-802-257-5764; 9AM-6PM M; 9AM-4PM T,TH; 9AM-N W; Closed Fri. www.guilfordschool.org/town_office/index.php

Index: All in one. Record index not computerized. Office will perform a UCC search but public must search other records themselves. Search fee $10.00 per name. Copy fee $1.00 per page. Vital records- $10.00 each. Cert fee- $8.00 per page includes copy fee. Payee- Town of Guilford. **Other phones:** Treasurer- 802-254-6857; Elections- 802-254-6857; Vital Records- 802-254-6857. **Property tax/Assessing**- 236 School Rd, Guilford, VT 05301; 802-254-6857, assessor fax- 802-257-5764. (Appraiser/Auditor- 802-254-6857);

Halifax Town

Town Clerk, PO Box 127, West Halifax, VT 05358. Recording, R/E phone-802-368-7390; fax-802-368-7390; 9AM-4PM M,T,F; 9AM-N Sat. www.halifaxvermont.com

Index: Card index and books. Record index not computerized. Only the public may search. Copy fee $1.00; real estate or tax lien $1.00 per copy. Cert fee- $8.00 per page includes copy fee. Payee- Halifax Town Clerk. **Other phones:** Treasurer- 802-368-7160; Elections- 802-368-7390; Vitals- 802-368-7390. **Property tax/Assessing**- 246 Branch Rd, West Halifax, VT 05358; 802-368-7390, assessor fax- 802-368-7390. (Appraiser/Auditor- 802-368-7390);

Hancock Town

Town Clerk, PO Box 100, Hancock, VT 05748. 802-767-3660; fax-802-767-3660; 9AM-3PM M-Th.

Index: Separate indices to search. Record index not computerized. Only the public may search. Will not search UCC records. Copy fee $1.00 per page, $2.00 minimum. Cert fee- $10.00 per page includes copy fee. Payee- Town of Hancock. **Other phones:** Treasurer- 802-767-3660; Elections- 802-767-3660; Vital Records- 802-767-3660. **Property tax/Assessing**- 48 Rte 125, Hancock, VT 05748; 802-767-3301, assessor fax- 413-738-5310. (Appraiser/Auditor- 802-767-3660)

Hardwick Town

Town Clerk, PO Box 523, Hardwick, VT 05843. Recording, R/E phone-802-472-5971; fax-802-472-3793; 9AM-4PM.

Index: All in one. Record index not computerized. Only the public may search. Search fee $2.00 per hour vault time. Copy fee $1.00 per page; maps- $.50 per page. Cert fee- $9.50 per page includes copy fee. Payee- Town of Hardwick. **Other phones:** Treasurer- 802-472-5971; Elections- 802-472-5971; Vital Records- 802-472-5971. **Property tax/Assessing**- PO Box 523, Hardwick, VT 05843; 802-472-5971, assessor fax- 802-472-3793. (Appraiser/Auditor- 802-472-5971)

Hartford Town

Town Clerk, 171 Bridge St, White River Junction, VT 05001-1920. Recording, R/E phone-802-295-2785; fax-802-295-6382; 8AM-N, 1-5PM www.hartford-vt.org

Index: Separate indices to search include UCC. Records indexed on computer back to 2005. Only the public may search. Office will not search real estate records. Office will not search UCC record or tax liens. Copy fee $2.00 per page. Must provide self addressed-stamped envelope. Cert fee- $8.00 per page includes copy fee. Payee- Town of Hartford. **Other phones:** Treasurer- 802-295-3002; Elections- 802-295-2785; Vital Records- 802-295-2785. **Property tax/Assessing**- 171 Bridge St, White River Junction, VT 05001; 802-295-3077, assessor fax- 802-295-6382. (Appraiser - 802-295-3077) hours- 8:30AM-4:30PM **Online** - Access assessor property data free at http://data.visionappraisal.com/hartfordvt/DEFAULT.asp.

Hartland Town

Town Clerk, PO Box 349, Hartland, VT 05048-0349. Recording, R/E phone-802-436-2444; fax-802-436-2464; 7AM-5PM. www.hartland.govoffice.com/

Index: Separate indices to search include card files. Record index not computerized. Office will perform a UCC search but public must search other records themselves. No fee for search, generally. Copy fee $1.00 per page. Cert fee- $10.00 per page includes copy fee. Payee- Town of Hartland. Bulk data may be available for purchase; contact Town Clerk. **Other phones:** Treasurer- 802-436-2464; Elections- 802-436-2444; Vital Records- 802-436-2444. **Property tax/Assessing**- 1 Queechee Rd, Hartland, VT 05048; 802-436-2464, assessor fax- 802-436-2464. hours- 9AM-N T & TH

Highgate Town

Town Clerk, PO Box 189, Highgate Center, VT 05459. 802-868-4697; fax-802-868-3064; 8:30AM-N, 1PM-4:30PM

Index: Separate indices to search include general, books by name, property cards. Record index not computerized. Only the public may search. Copy fee- $1.00 per page. Cert fee- $10.00 per page includes copy fee. Payee- Town of Highgate. **Property tax/Assessing**- Municipal Bldg, Rte 78, Highgate Center, VT 05459; 802-868-2741.

Hinesburg Town

Town Clerk, PO Box 133, Hinesburg, VT 05461. 802-482-2281; fax-802-482-5404; 8AM-4PM M T TH F; 11AM-7PM W. www.hinesburg.org

Index: All in one. Records indexed on computer back to 2000. Carded to mid 1960's. Only the public may search. Will not search UCC records. Copy fee $1.00 per page. Tax map- $.25 per copy. Cert fee- $8.00 per page includes copies. Payee- Town of Hinesburg. **Other phones:** Treasurer- 802-482-2281; Elections- 802-482-2281; Vital Records- 802-482-2281. **Property tax/Assessing**- 10632 Rte 116, Town Hall, Hinesburg, VT 05461; 802-482-3619, assessor fax- 802-482-5404. hours- 8AM-4PM

Holland Town

Town Clerk, 120 School Rd, Holland/Derby Line, VT 05830. Recording, R/E phone-802-895-4440; fax-802-895-4440; 8AM-4:30PM M,T,TH.

Index: Separate indices to search include liens, UCCs. Records indexed on a public use terminal. Only the public may search. Copy fee $1.00 per page. Cert fee- $8.00 per page plus copy fee. Payee- Town of Holland. Treasurer- 802-895-4440; Elections- 802-895-4440; Vital Records- 802-895-4440. **Property tax/Assessing**- 120 School Rd, Holland, VT 05830; 802-895-4440. hours- By Appointment

Hubbardton Town

Town Clerk, 1831 Monument Hill Rd, Castleton, VT 05735. 802-273-2951; fax-802-273-3729; 9AM-2PM M,W,F.

Index: All in one. Record index not computerized. Office personnel or visitors may perform searches. Search fee $5.00 per hour. Real estate owner, mortgage, and property transfer searches available as time permits. Will search UCC records. Copy fee $1.00 per page. Cert fee- $10.00 per doc includes copy fee. For certified land records- $8.00 per page, Vital statistics- $10.00 per page. Payee- Hubbardton Town Clerk. **Property tax/Assessing**- 1831 Monument Hill Rd, Castleton, 05735; 802-273-2951.

Huntington Town

Town Clerk, 4930 Main Rd, Huntington, VT 05462. Recording, R/E phone-802-434-2032; fax-802-434-4731; 7AM-7PM M; 8AM-3PM T-W; 7AM-5PM TH. www.huntingtonvt.org

Index: All in one. Record index not computerized. Only the public may search. Copy fee $1.00 per page. Cert fee- $8.00 per page plus copy fee and/or fax fee. Payee- Town of Huntington. **Other phones:** Treasurer- 802-434-2032; Elections- 802-434-2032; Vital Records- 802-434-2032; Administrator- 802-434-4779. **Property tax/Assessing**- 4930 Main Rd, Huntington, VT 05462; 802-434-5783. (Appraiser/Auditor- 802-434-5783);

Hyde Park Town

Town Clerk, PO Box 98, Hyde Park, VT 05655-0098. Recording, R/E phone-802-888-2300; fax-802-888-6878; 8AM-4PM. www.hydeparkvt.com

Index: Separate indices to search include 1970 to present-cards, before 1970 general index. Record index not computerized. Only the public may search. Will not search UCC records. Copy fee $1.00 per page. Cert fee- $8.00 per record plus copy fee. Payee- Hyde Park Town. Bulk data available for purchase, contact Gary Anderson. **Other phones:** Treasurer- 802-888-2300; Elections- 802-888-2300; Vital Records- 802-888-2300; Zoning/Health Officer- 802-888-7784. **Property tax/Assessing**- 344 Vermont Rte 15W, Hyde Park, VT 05655; 802-888-7786, assessor fax- 802-888-6878. (Appraiser - 802-888-7786)

Ira Town

Town Clerk, PO Box 870, West Rutland, VT 05777. Recording, R/E phone-802-235-2745; 9AM-2:30PM M; 2:15-7:15PM T.

Index: All in one. Record index not computerized. Office personnel or visitors may perform searches. Search fee $2.00 per hour for public; $5.00 per hour if clerk searches. Office will not search real estate records. Office will not search UCC records. Copy fee $1.00 per page. Cert fee- $8.00 per page plus copy fee. Payee- Ira Town Clerk. **Other phones:** Treasurer- 802-235-2745; Elections- 802-235-2745; Vital Records- 802-235-2745. **Property tax/Assessing**- PO Box 870, West Rutland, VT 05777; 802-235-2745. (Appraiser - 802-235-2745)

Irasburg Town

Town Clerk, PO Box 51, Irasburg, VT 05845. Recording, R/E phone-802-754-2242; fax-802-754-2242; 9AM-3PM M,W,Th. Index: All in one. Record index not computerized. Office personnel or visitors may perform searches. General search fee $2.00 per hour. Office will search real estate records. Office will search UCC records and tax liens. UCC search per debtor name- $10.00. Copy fee $1.00 per page. Cert fee- $2.00 per page includes copy fee. Payee- Irasburg Town Clerk. **Other phones:** Treasurer- 802-754-2242; Elections- 802-754-2242; Vital Records- 802-754-2242. **Property tax/Assessing**- Same address as recording office. 802-754-2242. (Appraiser/Auditor- 802-754-2242)

Isle La Motte Town

Town Clerk, PO Box 250, Isle La Motte, VT 05463. Recording, R/E phone-802-928-3434; fax-802-928-3002; 7:30AM-3PM T,Th; 2-6PM W; 8AM-N S.
Index: All in one. Records indexed on computer. Office will perform a UCC search but public must search other records themselves. Copy fee $1.00 per page. Cert fee- $7.00 per doc includes copy fee. Payee- Town of Isle LaMotte. Treasurer- 802-928-3434; Elections- 802-928-3434; Vital Records- 802-928-3434. **Property tax/Assessing**- 204 Lakehurst Rd, Isle Lamotte, VT 05463; 802-928-3266. (Appraiser/Auditor- 802-928-3266)

Jamaica Town

Town Clerk, PO Box 173, Jamaica, VT 05343. 802-874-4681; 9AM-N, 1-4PM T,W,Th,F. www.jamaicavermont.org
Index: All in one. Record index not computerized. Only the public may search. Copy fee $1.00 per page, $2.00 minimum. Cert fee- $10.00 per page includes copy fee. Payee- Town of Jamaica. **Property tax/Assessing**- 802-874-4908.

Jay Town

Town Clerk, 1036 Vermont Rte 242, Jay, VT 05859-9820. 802-988-2996; fax-802-988-2996; 7AM-4PM M-TH. www.jayvt.com/
Index: Separate indices to search include zoning permits, UCCs, vital records. Record index not computerized. Only the public may search. Copy fee $1.00 per page, $2.00 minimum. Cert fee- $8.00 per page includes copy fee. Payee- Town of Jay. **Other phones:** Treasurer- 802-988-2996; Elections- 802-988-2996; Vital Records- 802-988-2996. **Property tax/Assessing**- 1036 Vermont Rte 242, Jay, VT 05859; 802-988-2996.

Jericho Town

Town Clerk, PO Box 67, Jericho, VT 05465. Recording, R/E phone-802-899-4936 x1; fax-802-899-5549; 8AM-5PM M-TH, 8AM-3PM F. www.jerichovt.gov/index.asp
Index: Separate indices to search include UCCs, cards back to 1960s, books, general back to late 1700s. Records indexed on computer back to 1999. Only the public may search. Search fee $2.00 per hour vault time. Copy fee $1.00 per page. Cert fee- $8.00 per page includes copy fee. Payee- Town of Jericho. **Other phones:** Treasurer- 802-899-4786 x5; Elections- 802-899-4936; Vital Records- 802-899-4936 x1. **Property tax/Assessing**- PO Box 39, 67 Vermont Rte 15, Jericho, VT 05465; 802-899-2640 x4. (Appraiser/Auditor- 802-899-2640 x4) hours- 9AM-N www.jerichovt.gov/index.asp **Online**- Property appraisal lists in pdf format available at the website - click on Town Government then Listers/Assessors.

Johnson Town

Town Clerk, PO Box 383, Johnson, VT 05656. Recording, R/E phone-802-635-2611; fax-802-635-2393; 7:30AM-4PM. www.townofjohnson.com
Index: All in one. No computer access terminal for the public. Only the public may search. Search fee $2.00 per hour vault time. Copy fee $2.00 1st page, $1.00 each add'l page. Cert fee- $10.00 per doc includes copy fee. Payee- Town of Johnson. **Other phones:** Treasurer- 802-635-2611; Elections- 802-635-2611; Vital Records- 802-635-2611. **Property tax/Assessing**- 293 Main St, Johnson, VT 05656; 802-635-2611, assessor fax- 802-635-2393. (Appraiser/Auditor- 802-635-2611);

Killington Town

Town Clerk, PO Box 429, Killington, VT 05751-0429. Recording, R/E phone-802-422-3243; fax-802-422-3030; 9AM-3PM. www.killingtontown.com
Formerly known as Town of Sherburne. Index: Separate indices to search include land records, UCC; card index 1960-1980. Records indexed on computer back to 1960. Only the public may search. Search fee $2.00 per hour vault time. Copy fee $1.00 per page. Cert fee- $8.00 per page includes copy fee. Payee- Killington Town Clerk. **Other phones:** Treasurer- 802-422-3241; Elections- 802-422-3243; Vital Records- 802-422-3243. **Property tax/Assessing**- PO Box 429, Killington, VT 05751; 802-422-3241, assessor fax- 802-422-3030. 10AM-2PM T-TH

Kirby Town

Town Clerk, 346 Town Hall Rd; Town of Kirby, Lyndonville, VT 05851-9802. Recording, R/E phone-802-626-9386; fax-802-626-9386; 8AM-3PM; T,TH.
Index: All in one. Record index not computerized. Office will perform a UCC search but public must search other records themselves. Search fee $10.00 per debtor. Office will not search real estate records. Copy fee $1.00 per page. Cert fee- $2.00 per page plus copy fee. Payee- Town of Kirby. Bulk data is available for purchase; contact Wanda Grant 802-626-9386. **Other phones:** Treasurer- 802-626-9386; Elections- 802-626-9386; Vital Records- 802-626-9386. **Property tax/Assessing**- 346 Town Hall Rd, Lyndonville, VT 05851; 802-626-9386, assessor fax- 802-626-9386. (Appraiser/Auditor- 802-626-9386);

Landgrove Town

Town Clerk, PO Box 508, Londonderry, VT 05148. Recording, R/E phone-802-824-3716; fax-Same; 9AM-1PM.
Index: Separate indices to search include land records, UCCs, Liens. Record index not computerized. Office will perform a UCC and Tax lien search but public must search other records themselves. Search fee $10.00. Copy fee $1.00 per page. Cert fee- $7.00 per page. Payee- Landgrove Town Clerk. **Other phones:** Treasurer- 802-824-3716; Elections- 802-824-3716; Vital Records- 802-824-3716. **Property tax/Assessing**- 15 Cody Rd, Londonderry, VT 05148; 802-824-3716, assessor fax- 802-824-4677. (Appraiser/Auditor- 802-824-3716)

Leicester Town

Town Clerk, 44 Schoolhouse Rd, Leicester, VT 05733. Recording, R/E phone-802-247-5961; fax-n/a; 8AM-Noon M-W; 8AM-1PM Th. www.leicestervt.org
Index: All in one. Record index not computerized. Only the public may search. Search fee $2.00 per hour vault time. Will not search UCC records. Copy fee $1.00 per page. Cert fee- $8.00 per doc includes copy fee. Payee- Leicester Town Clerk. **Other phones:** Treasurer- 802-247-5961; Elections- 802-247-5961; Vitals- 802-247-5961. **Property tax/Assessing**- 44 Schoolhouse Rd, Leicester, VT 05733; 802-247-5961. (Appraiser/Auditor- 802-247-5961)

Lemington Town

Town Clerk, 2549 River Rd, VT Rte 102, Lemington, VT 05903. 802-277-4814; fax-802-277-4091; 9AM-Noon Th.
Index: All in one. Records indexed on computer. No public access terminal available. Only the public may search. Copy fee $.50 per page; $1.50 per page UCC. Cert fee- $6.00 per page includes copy fee. Payee- Town of Lemington. **Property tax/Assessing**- 2549 River Rd, VT Rte 102, Lemington, VT 05903-9610; 802-277-4814, assessor fax- 802-277-4091.

Lincoln Town

Town Clerk, 62 Quaker St, Lincoln, VT 05443. 802-453-2980; fax-802-453-2975; 8AM-2PM M-Th, Weds 4-7PM; also by appointment.
Index: All in one. Record index not computerized. Only the public may search. Public search fee $2.00 per hour. Copy fee $1.00 per page. Cert fee- $8.00 per doc includes copy fee. Payee- Town of Lincoln. **Property tax/Assessing**- 62 Quaker St, Lincoln, VT 05443; 802-453-2980, assessor fax- 802-453-2975. hours- irregular **Online access**- The Torn Grand List is available from the Listers at the Assessor office.

Londonderry Town

Town Clerk, PO Box 118, South Londonderry, VT 05155-0118. 802-824-3356; fax-802-824-4259; hours - 9AM-3PM T-F; 9AM-12 Sat. www.londonderryvt.org/directory.html
Index: Separate indices to search include card file drawers, old records in books. Records on computer back to 1965. Only the public may search. Copy fee $1.00 per page. Cert fee- $8.00 per page includes copy fee. Payee- Londonderry Town Clerk. Office does sell bulk data on CD's and paper copy.

Lowell Town

Town Clerk, 2170 Vermont Rte 100, Lowell, VT 05847-0007. Recording, R/E phone-802-744-6559; fax-802-744-2357; 9AM-2:30PM Mon & Th.
Index: Separate indices to search include volume index, general, map, permits, transfers. Record index not computerized. Only the public may search. Search fee $2.00 per hour vault time. Copy fee $1.00 per page. Cert fee- $8.00 per doc includes copy fee. Payee- Lowell Town. **Other phones:** Treasurer- 802-744-6559; Elections- 802-744-6559; Vital Records- 802-744-6559. **Property tax/Assessing**- 2170 Vermont Rte 100, Lowell, VT 05847; 802-744-6559, assessor fax- 802-744-2357. (Appraiser/Auditor- 802-744-6559) hours- Appointments

Ludlow Town

Town Clerk, PO Box 307, Ludlow, VT 05149. Recording, R/E phone-802-228-3232; fax-802-228-8399; 8:30AM-4:30PM www.ludlow.vt.us
Index: All in one. Record index not computerized. Only the public may search. Copy fee $1.00 per page. Cert fee- $8.00 per page includes copy fee. Payee- Town of Ludlow. **Other phones:** Treasurer- 802-228-3232; Elections- 802-228-3232; Vital Records- 802-228-3232. **Property tax/Assessing**- PO Box 161, 37 Depot St, Ludlow, VT 05149; 802-228-7206. (Appraiser/Auditor- 802-228-7206);

Lunenburg Town

Town Clerk, PO Box 54, Lunenburg, VT 05906. Recording, R/E phone-802-892-5959; fax-802-892-5100; 8:30AM-N, 1PM-3PM
Index: All in one. Record index not computerized. Office will perform a UCC search but public must search other records themselves. Copy fee $1.00 per page. UCC or deed copy- $2.00 per page. Cert fee- $8.00 per doc plus copy fee. Payee- Lunenburg Town Clerk. **Other phones:** Treasurer- 802-892-5959; Elections- 802-892-5959; Vital Records- 802-892-5959. **Property tax/Assessing**- Main St, Lunenburg, VT 05906; 802-892-1162, assessor fax- 802-892-5100. (Appraiser/Auditor- 802-892-1162)

Lyndon Town

Town Clerk, PO Box 167, Lyndonville, VT 05851. Recording, R/E phone-802-626-5785; fax-802-626-1265; 7:30AM-4:30PM.
Index: Separate indices to search include computer (2000 to present) and card files (1940 to present). Records indexed on computer back to 2000. Office will perform a UCC search but public must search other records themselves. Search fee $2.00 per hour. Office will not search real estate records. Copy fee $1.00 per page. Cert fee- $8.00 per cert plus copy fee. Payee- Lyndon Town Clerk. **Other phones:** Treasurer- 802-626-5785; Elections- 802-626-5785; Vital Records- 802-626-5785; Zoning Admin- 802-626-1269. **Property tax/Assessing**- 119 Park Ave, Lyndonville, VT 05851; 802-626-1270. (Appraiser/Auditor- 802-626-1270)

Maidstone Town

Town Clerk, PO Box 118, Guildhall, VT 05905-0118. Recording, R/E phone-802-676-3210; fax-802-676-3210; 9AM-N M-TH.
Index: Separate indices to search include books and cards. Records index not computerized. Office personnel or visitors may perform searches. General search fee $5.00 per hour. Office will search real estate records. Office will search UCC records, tax liens not included. UCC search per debtor name- $10.00. Copy fee $1.00 per page; $2.00 minimum. Cert fee- $8.00 per doc plus copy fee. Payee- Maidstone Town Clerk. **Other phones:** Treasurer- 802-676-3210; Elections- 802-676-3210; Vital Records- 802-676-3210. **Property tax/Assessing**- 508 State Rte 102, Guildhall, VT 05905; 802-676-3210, assessor fax- 802-676-3210.

Manchester Town

Town Clerk, PO Box 830, Manchester Center, VT 05255. 802-362-1315; fax-802-362-1315; 8AM-4:30PM. www.town.manchester.vt.us
Index: All in one. Records indexed on a public use terminal back to 11/0300. Office will perform a UCC search but public must search other records themselves. General index search fee $5.00 per hour. Copy fee $1.00 per page. UCC copy fee $2.00 per page. Cert fee- $8.00 per doc includes copy fee. Payee- Manchester Town Clerk. **Other phones:** Treasurer- 802-362-1197; Elections- 802-362-1315; Vital Records- 802-362-1315; Town Manager- 802-362-1313. **Property tax/Assessing**- 6039 Main St, Manchester Center, VT 05255; 802-362-1373. (Appraiser/Auditor- 802-362-1373);

Marlboro Town

Town Clerk, PO Box E, Marlboro, VT 05344-0305. Recording, R/E phone-802-254-2181; fax-802-257-2447; 9AM-4PM M,W,Th.
Index: All in one. General indexes on computer 1700's to 1900; Card Index 1900 - 4/1/2006; 4/1/2006 - present computerized. Office personnel (at their discretion; not required) or visitors may perform searches. Search fee $2.00 per hour; $5.00 per hour if done by clerk. Office will not search real estate records. Office will not search UCC records. General copy fee $1.00 per page, minimum $2.00. Cert fee- $8.00 per page includes copy fee. Payee- Town of Marlboro. Treasurer- 802-254-2181; Elections- 802-254-2181; Vital Records- 802-254-2181. **Property tax/Assessing**- 510 South Rd, Town Office, Marlboro, VT 05344; 802-254-2181, assessor fax- 802-257-2447. (Appraiser/Auditor- 802-254-2181)

Marshfield Town

Town Clerk, 122 School St, Rm 1, Marshfield, VT 05658. 802-426-3305; fax-802-426-3045; 8AM-N, 12:30-4PM. www.town.marshfield.vt.us
Index: Separate indices to search include surveys and UCCs. Record index not computerized. Only the public may search. Search fee $2.00 per hour vault time. Copy fee $1.00 per page, $2.00 minimum. Cert fee- $8.00 per page includes copy fee. Payee- Town of Marshfield. Treasurer- 802-426-3305; Elections- 802-426-3305; Vital Records- 802-426-3305; Delinquent Tax Collector- 802-426-3305. **Property tax/Assessing**- 122 School St, Marshfield, VT 05658; 802-426-3305. (Appraiser/Auditor- 802-426-3305)

Mendon Town

Town Clerk, 34 US Rte 4, Mendon, VT 05701. 802-775-1662; fax-802-773-9682; 8AM-5PM M-Th; closed Fri. www.mendonvt.org
Index: Land records and attachments on one index. Records indexed on computer back to 02/02. Only the public may search. Copy fee $1.00 per page. Cert fee- $8.00 per cert plus copy fee. Payee- Mendon Town Clerk. Office does sell bulk data, CD's and paper copy. **Other phones:** Treasurer- 802-775-1662; Elections- 802-775-1662; Vital Records- 802-775-1662. **Property tax/Assessing**- 34 US Rte 4, Mendon, VT 05701; 802-496-9689, assessor fax- 802-773-9682.

Middlebury Town

Town Clerk, 94 Main St, Middlebury, VT 05753-1334. Recording, R/E phone-802-388-8100 x211, 212, UCC recording phone-802-388-8102 x237; fax-802-388-4261; 7:30AM-5:30PM M-TH. www.middlebury.govoffice.com
Index: Separate indices to search include UCCs, maps. Records indexed on computer back to 1955. Only the public may search. Copy fee $8.00 per record. Cert fee- $8.00 per page includes copy fee. Vital records- $10.00. Payee- Town of Middlebury. **Other phones:** Treasurer- 802-388-8100 x203; Elections- 802-388-8100 x211, 212; Vital Records- 802-388-8100 x211, 212. **Property tax/Assessing**- 94 Main St, Municipal Bldg, Middlebury, VT 05753; 802-388-8100 x207, assessor fax- 802-388-4261. (Appraiser/Auditor- 802-388-4100) hours- 8:30AM-N 1PM-4:30PM www.middlebury.govoffice.com/

Middlesex Town

Town Clerk, 5 Church St, Middlesex, VT 05602. Recording, R/E phone-802-223-5915; fax-802-223-1298; 8:30AM-N, 1-4:30PM M-Th. www.middlesex-vt.org
Index: All in one. Record index not computerized. Only the public may search. Search fee $2.00 per hour vault time. Copy fee $1.00 per page. Cert fee- $10.00 per cert includes copy fee. Payee- Town Clerk. **Other phones:** Treasurer- 802-223-5915; Elections- 802-223-5915; Vital Records- 802-223-5915. **Property tax/Assessing**- Town Hall, Middlesex, CT 05602; 802-223-5915. (Appraiser/Auditor- 802-223-5915)

Middletown Springs Town

Town Clerk, PO Box 1232, Middletown Springs, VT 05757-1197. 802-235-2220; fax-802-235-2066; 9AM-N, 1-4PM M, T; 1-4PM F; 9AM-N Sat.
Record index not computerized. Office will not search UCC records. Copy fee $1.00 per page. Cert fee- $10.00 per page. Payee- Middletown Springs Town Clerk.

Milton Town

Town Clerk, PO Box 18, Milton, VT 05468. Recording, R/E phone-802-893-4111; fax-802-893-1005; 8AM-5PM. www.milton.govoffice2.com
Index: All in one. Record index not computerized. Only the public may search. Copy fee $1.00 per page. Cert fee- $8.00 per page includes copy fee. Payee- Town of Milton. **Other phones:** Treasurer- 802-893-4111; Elections- 802-893-4111; Vital Records- 802-893-4111. **Property tax/Assessing**- 43 Bombardier Rd, Milton, VT 05468; 802-893-4325, assessor fax- 802-893-1005. (Appraiser/Auditor- 802-893-4325)

Monkton Town

Town Clerk, PO Box 12, North Ferrisburg, VT 05469. Recording, R/E phone-802-453-3800; fax-802-453-5612; 8AM-1PM M,T,Th; 8:30AM-N Sat. www.monktonvt.com
Record index not computerized. Only the public may search. Search fee $2.00 per hour vault time. Will not search UCC records. Copy fee $.50 per page. UCC and deeds-copy fee is $1.00 per page. Cert fee- $10.00 includes copy fee. Payee- Monkton Town Clerk. **Other phones:** Treasurer- 802-453-3800; Elections- 802-453-3800; Vital Records- 802-453-3800. **Property tax/Assessing**- 280 Monkton Ridge, North Ferrisburg, VT 05469; 802-453-4515, assessor fax- 802-453-4515. (Appraiser/Auditor- 802-453-4515) hours- 8AM-11AM M,W,Sat

Montgomery Town

Town Clerk, PO Box 356, Montgomery Center, VT 05471-0356. Recording, R/E phone-802-326-4719; fax-802-326-4939; 8-Noon, 1-6PM M; 8-Noon 1-4PM T,TH,F; Closed Wed. www.montgomeryvt.us/clerk.htm
Index: Separate indices to search include index cards 1994 to present, and general index back to 2002. Records indexed on computer back to 1/2/03. Only the public may search. Search fee $2.00 per hour vault time. Copy fee $1.00 per page; $2.00 minimum. Cert fee- $6.00 per page includes copy fee. Payee- Town of Montgomery. Treasurer- 802-326-4719; Elections- 802-326-4719; Vital Records- 802-326-4719. **Property tax/Assessing**- PO Box 356, Montgomery Center, VT 05471-0356; 802-326-4719, assessor fax- 802-326-4939. (Appraiser/Auditor- 802-326-4719)

Montpelier City

City Clerk, 39 Main St; City Hall, Montpelier, VT 05602. 802-223-9500; fax-802-223-9523; 8AM-4:30PM.
Index: Separate indices to search include date logs, books, computer. Records indexed on a public use terminal back to 1993; can be up to 4 months from current. Only the public may search. Copy fee $1.00 per page. Cert fee- $10.00 per doc includes copy fee. Payee- City of Montpelier. **Property tax/Assessing**- 39 Main St, City Hall, Montpelier, VT 05602; 802-223-9504. **Online access**- Access city property assessor data free at http://data.visionappraisal.com/ coming soon.

Moretown Town

Town Clerk, PO Box 666, Moretown, VT 05660. 802-496-3645; fax-802-496-2385; 7AM-3PM M-TH; Closed Fri.
Index: All in one. Records indexed on computer. Office personnel or visitors may perform searches. Search fee $2.00 per hour vault time. Copy fee $1.00 per page. Cert fee- $7.00 per page plus copy fee. Payee- Moretown Town Clerk. **Other phones:** Treasurer- 802-496-3645. **Property tax/Assessing**- Rte 100B, Moretown, VT 05660; 802-496-3645.

Morgan Town

Town Clerk, PO Box 45, Morgan, VT 05853-0045. 802-895-2927; fax-802-895-4204; 8AM-2PM M, 7AM-2PM T-TH, 7AM-N Fri.
Index: All in on as of 2001. Record index not computerized. Only the public may search. Search fee $2.00 per hour vault time. Copy fee $1.00 per page. Cert fee- $7.00 per page includes copy fee. Payee- Morgan Town Clerk, Town of Morgan. **Other phones:** Treasurer- 802-895-2927; Elections- 802-895-2927; Vital Records- 802-895-2927. **Property tax/Assessing**- 41 Meade Hill Rd, Morgan, VT 05853; 802-895-2858. (Appraiser - 802-875-2858)

Morristown Town

Town Clerk, PO Box 748, Morrisville, VT 05661-0748. 802-888-6370; fax-802-888-6375; 8:30AM-4:30PM, M,T,TH,F; 8:30AM-12:30PM Wed. www.morristownvt.org
Index: All in one. Records indexed on computer back to 00. Office will perform a UCC search but public must search other records themselves. UCC search per debtor name- $5.00 per hour. UCC search request using non-standard form (per name)- $20.00. Copy fee $2.00 per page.Real estate or tax lien copy- $1.00 per page. Cert fee- $8.00 per page includes copy fee. Payee- Town of Morristown. Grand list on CD-rom available from Lister's Office; call 802-888-6371. **Property tax/Assessing**- 43 Portland St, Morrisville, VT 05661; 802-888-6371, assessor fax- 802-888-6377. hours- 8:30AM-12:30PM

Mount Holly Town

Town Clerk, PO Box 248, Mount Holly, VT 05758. Recording, R/E phone-802-259-2391; fax-802-259-2391; 8:30AM-4PM M-Th.
Index: Liens in a separate book. Record index not computerized. Only the public may search. Copy fee $1.00 per page. Cert fee- $8.00 per page includes copy fee. Payee- Town Clerk. **Other phones:** Treasurer- 802-259-2391; Elections- 802-259-2391; Vitals- 802-259-2391. **Property tax/Assessing**- 802-259-2391, assessor fax- 802-259-2391. (Appraiser/Auditor- 802-259-2391)

Mount Tabor Town

Town Clerk, PO Box 245, Mt Tabor, VT 05739. Recording, R/E phone-802-293-5282; fax-802-293-5287; 9AM-Noon Tu-W.
Index: All in one. Records indexed on computer. No public access terminal available. Only the public may search. Copy fee $1.00 per page. Cert fee- $7.00 per copy includes copy fee. Payee- Mt. Tabor Town Clerk. Treasurer- 802-293-5282; Elections- 802-293-5282; Vital Records- 802-293-5282. **Property tax/Assessing-** 522 Brooklyn Rd, Town Office, Mt Tabor, VT 05739; 802-293-5282, assessor fax- 802-293-5287. (Appraiser/Auditor- 802-293-5282);

New Haven Town

Town Clerk, 78 North St, New Haven, VT 05472. 802-453-3516; fax-802-453-3516; 9AM-3PM www.newhavenvt.com
Index: Separate indices to search include general index cards up to 1987, booklets past 1987, current year booklet. Records indexed on a public use terminal back to 1987. Only the public may search. Copy fee if tax lien or real estate $1.00 per page. UCC copy- $2.00 per page. Cert fee- $8.00 per doc. Payee-Town of New Haven. **Property tax/Assessing-** 78 North St, New Haven, VT 05472; 802-453-3516.

Newark Town

Town Clerk, 1336 Newark St, Newark, VT 05871. 802-467-3336; 9AM-4PM M,W,Th.
Index: All in one. Record index not computerized. Only the public may search. Will not search UCC records. Copy fee $1.00 per page. Cert fee- $10.00 per page total. Payee- Newark Town Clerk. **Property tax/Assessing-** 1336 Newark St, Newark, VT 05871; 802-467-3687.

Newbury Town

Town Clerk, PO Box 126, Newbury, VT 05051. Recording, R/E phone-802-866-5521; fax-802-866-5301; 8:30AM-2:30PM; 2:30PM-6PM T.
Index: Separate indices to search. Record index not computerized. Only the public may search. Copy fee $1.00 per page. Cert fee- $10.00 per page includes copy fee. Payee- Newbury Town Clerk. **Other phones:** Treasurer- 802-866-5521; Elections- 802-866-5521; Vital Records- 802-866-5521. **Property tax/Assessing-** 12 Main St S, Newbury, VT 05051; 802-866-5521, assessor fax- 802-866-5301. (Appraiser/Auditor- 802-866-5521);

Newfane Town

Town Clerk, PO Box 36, Newfane, VT 05345-0036. 802-365-7772; fax-802-365-7692; 9AM-3PM. www.newfanevt.com
Index: Records are in 3 general indexes. Record index not computerized. Only the public may search. Copy fee $1.00 per page. Cert fee- $8.00 per page includes copy fee. Payee- Town of Newfane. **Other phones:** Treasurer- 802-365-7772 x12; Elections- 802-365-7772 x10. **Property tax/Assessing-** 555 Vermont Rte 30, Newfane, VT 05345; 802-365-7772 x11, assessor fax- 802-365-7692.

Newport City

Town Clerk, 222 Main St, Newport, VT 05855. Recording, R/E phone-802-334-2112; fax-802-334-5632; 8:30AM-4:30PM
Index: All in one. Record index not computerized. Office personnel or visitors may perform searches. Search fee $25.00 per name. Copy fee $1.00 per page. Cert fee- $7.00 per page includes copy fee. Payee-City of Newport. **Other phones:** Treasurer- 802-334-2112; Elections- 802-334-2112; Vital Records- 802-334-2112. **Property tax/Assessing-** 222 Main St, Newport, VT 05855; 802-334-6992, assessor fax-802-334-5632. (Appraiser/Auditor- 802-334-6992) hours- 8AM-4:30PM TH **Online access-** Access to Newport City assessor data is free at http://data.visionappraisal.com/newportvt/.

Newport Town

Town Clerk, PO Box 85, Newport Center, VT 05857. 802-334-6442; fax-802-334-6442; 7AM-4:30PM,M-Th, Closed Fri.
Index: Separate indices to search include books by doc type. Record index not computerized. Only the public may search. Copy fee $1.00 per page. Cert fee-$10.00 per page includes copy fee. Payee- Newport Town Clerk. **Property tax/Assessing-** 102 Vance Hill Rd, Newport Center, VT 05857; 802-334-6442, assessor fax- 802-334-6442. **Online-** Search assessor records at http://data.visionappraisal.com/newportvt/.

North Hero Town

Town Clerk, PO Box 38, North Hero, VT 05474-0038. Recording, R/E phone-802-372-6926; fax-802-372-3806; 8AM-4:40 M,T,TH; 8AM-N W,F; 8:30AM-N Sat. www.northherovt.com/
Index: All in one. Records indexed on a public use terminal back to 12/1500. Only the public may search. Copy fee $1.00 per page. Cert fee- $7.00 per page plus copy fee. Payee- Town of North Hero+. **Other phones:** Treasurer- 802-372-6926; Elections- 802-372-6926; Vital Records- 802-372-6926. **Property tax/Assessing-** 2681 US Rte 2, North Hero, VT 05474; 802-372-6926, assessor fax- 802-372-3806. (Appraiser/Auditor- 802-372-6926) 9AM-N M,T,W

Northfield Town

Town Clerk, 51 S Main St, Northfield, VT 05663. Recording, R/E phone-802-485-5421; fax-802-485-8426; 8AM-4:30PM www.northfield.vt.us
Index: Separate indices to search include land records, vital statistics. Records (land records) indexed on computer back to 1999. Only the public may search. Copy fee $1.00 per page. Cert fee- $8.00 per page includes copy fee. Payee- Town of Northfield. **Other phones:** Treasurer- 802-485-5421; Elections- 802-485-5421; Vital Records- 802-485-5421. **Property tax/Assessing-** 51 S Main St, Northfield, VT 05663; 802-485-6004, assessor fax- 802-485-8426. (Appraiser/Auditor- 802-485-6004)

Norton Town

Town Clerk, 12 VT Rte 114E, Norton, VT 05907. Recording, R/E phone-802-822-9935; fax-802-822-9965; 2-4PM M, 10AM-4PM T; 10AM-N last Sat of month. Index: All in one. Record index not computerized. Office personnel or visitors may perform searches. Search fee $5.00 per hour. Copy fee $1.00 per page. Cert fee- $10.00 per doc includes copy fee. Payee- Town of Norton. **Other phones:** Treasurer- 802-822-9935; Elections- 802-822-9935; Vitals- 802-822-9935. **Property tax/Assessing-** 12 VT Rte 114E, Norton, VT 05907; see above.

Norwich Town

Town Clerk, PO Box 376, Norwich, VT 05055. 802-649-1419, R/E recording phone-802-649-1419 x103; fax-802-649-0123; 8:30AM-4:30PM; 8:30-6PM Th. www.norwich.vt.us
Email for Assessor's Office is lister@norwich.vt.us.
Index: All in one. Record index not computerized. Office will perform a UCC search for a fee but public must search other records themselves. Search fee $5.00 per hour. Copy fee $1.00 per page. Cert fee-$8.00 per cert includes copy fee. Payee- Norwich Town Clerk. **Other phones:** Treasurer- 802-649-1419 x105; Elections- 802-649-1419 x103; Vital Records- 802-649-1419 x103. **Property tax/Assessing-** PO Box 376, Norwich, VT 06055; 802-649-1419 x110, assessor fax- 802-649-0123. hours- 8:30AM-11AM M-TH

Orange Town

Town Clerk, PO Box 233, East Barre, VT 05649. 802-479-2673; fax-802-479-2673; 8AM-N, 1-4PM.
Records filed by town not county. Index: All in one. Record index not computerized. Only the public may search. Will not search UCC records. Copy fee $1.00 per page. Cert fee- $7.00 per page includes copy fee. Payee- Town Clerk. Treasurer- 802-479-2673; Deliquent Tax- 802-439-5828. **Property tax/Assessing-** US Rte 302, East Barre, VT 05649; 802-479-2673.

Orwell Town

Town Clerk, PO Box 32, Orwell, VT 05760-0032. 802-948-2032; fax-n/a; 9:30AM-N 1PM-3:30PM M T TH; 9:30AM-N, 1PM-6PM F Closed W.
Index: Separate indices to search include general index books to 1997; cards 1997 to present. Record index not computerized. Only the public may search. Office will not search real estate records. Will not search UCC records. General copy fee $1.00 per page; $5.00 if oversize. UCC copy fee $20.00. Cert fee- $8.00 per page includes copy fee. Payee- Town of Orwell. **Other phones:** Treasurer- 802-948-2811. **Property tax/Assessing-** 436 Main St, Orwell, VT 05760; 802-948-2665.

Panton Town

Town Clerk, PO Box 174, Vergennes, VT 05491-0174. 802-475-2333; fax-802-475-2785; 8:30AM-5:30PM M,Th; 8:30AM-2:30PM T, F; 4-7PM W. www.pantonvt.us/clerk.html
Index: All in one. Records indexed not computerized. Only the public may search. Copy fee $1.00; tax liens $.25 per page. Cert fee- $10.00 per page plus copy fee. Payee- Panton Town Clerk. **Property tax/Assessing-** 802-496-9689.

Pawlet Town

Town Clerk, PO Box 128, Pawlet, VT 05761-0128. Recording, R/E phone-802-325-3309; fax-802-325-6109; 11AM-6PM T; 9AM-4PM W; 8:30AM-3:30PM TH; 8AM-Noon F.
Index: All in one. Record index not computerized. Office will perform a UCC search but public must search other records themselves. Search fee $2.00 per hour vault time. Copy fee $1.00 per deed. Maps-$1.00, Card-$.50 per side. Cert fee- $10.00 per page includes copy fee. Payee- Town of Pawlet. **Other phones:** Treasurer- 802-325-3302; Elections- 802-325-3309; Vital Records- 802-325-3309. **Property tax/Assessing-** 122 School St, Town Hall, Pawlet, VT 05761; 802-325-3302, assessor fax- 802-325-6109.

Peacham Town

Town Clerk, PO Box 244, Peacham, VT 05862. 802-592-3218; fax-802-592-3218; 8:30AM-12:30 M-F; 3-7PM Wed. www.peacham.net
Index: All in one. Record index not computerized. Only the public may search. Copy fee $1.00 per page. Cert fee- $10.00 per page includes copy fee. Payee-Town of Peacham. **Property tax/Assessing-** 79 Church St, PO Box 244, Peacham, VT 05862; 802-592-3011. (Appraiser/Auditor- 802-592-3011) hours-8:30AM-N M & TH or by appointment

Peru Town

Town Clerk, PO Box 127, Peru, VT 05152. 802-824-3065; fax-802-824-3065; 8:30AM-4PM T, Th.
Index: Separate indices to search include 3 index books; separate lien & attachments. Record index not computerized. Only the public may search. Will not search UCCs. Copy fee $1.00 per page. Cert fee-$10.00 per page plus copy fee. Payee- Town of Peru.

Pittsfield Town

Town Clerk, PO Box 556, Pittsfield, VT 05762-0556. 802-746-8170; fax-802-746-8170; N-6PM T; 9AM-3PM W,Th. www.pittsfieldvt.org/townclerk.htm
Only the public may search. Copy fee $1.00 per page. Cert fee- $8.00 per page. Payee- Town of Pittsfield. **Other phones:** Treasurer- 802-746-8050. **Property tax/Assessing-** 802-746-8113.

Pittsford Town

Town Clerk, PO Box 10, Pittsford, VT 5763. 802-483-2931, R/E recording phone-802-483-6500 x12; fax-802-483-6612; 8AM-4:30PM M-W; 8AM-6PM Th; 8AM-3PM F. www.town.pittsford.vt.us
Index: All in one. Record index not computerized. Office personnel or visitors may perform searches.

Search fee $10.00 per name. Office will not search real estate records. Copy fee $1.00 per UCC. Cert fee- $8.00 per page includes copy fee. Payee- Town of Pittsford. **Other phones:** Treasurer- 802-483-6500 x12; Elections- 802-483-6500 x12; Vital Records- 802-483-6500 x12. **Property tax/Assessing**- Same address as recording office. 802-483-6500 x15, assessor fax- 802-483-6612. (Appraiser/Auditor- 802-483-6500 x12) **Online access**- Access property assessor data free at http://data.visionappraisal.com/ coming soon.

Plainfield Town

Town Clerk, PO Box 217, Plainfield, VT 5667. Recording, R/E phone-802-454-8461; fax-802-454-8467; 7:30AM-N, 12:30PM-4PM M,W,F.
Index: All in one. Record index not computerized. Only the public may search. At last report, records available for in person searching M/W/F 7:30AM-N 12:30PM-4PM. Search fee $2.00 per hour for use of records. Copy fee $1.00 per page. Cert fee- $8.00 per doc includes copy fee. Payee- Town of Plainfield. **Other phones:** Treasurer- 802-454-8461; Elections- 802-454-8461. **Property tax/Assessing**- Town of Plainfield, PO Box 217, Plainfield, VT 05667; 802-454-8461, assessor fax- 802-454-8467. (Appraiser/Auditor- 802-454-8461);

Plymouth Town

Town Clerk, 68 Town Office Rd, Plymouth, VT 05056. 802-672-3655; fax-802-672-5466; 8AM-4PM. www.plymouthvt.org/
Index: All in one. Record index not computerized. Only the public may search. Search fee $2.00 per hour vault time. Copy fee $1.00 per page. Cert fee- $8.00. Payee- Plymouth Town Clerk. Bulk data available for purchase, contact Keeley Crosssman. **Property tax/Assessing**- Clerk and Treasurer' Office, 68 Town Office Rd, Plymouth, VT 05056; 802-672-5000, assessor fax- 802-672-5466.

Pomfret Town

Town Clerk, PO Box 64, South Pomfret, VT 05067. Recording, R/E phone-802-457-3861; fax-none; 8:30AM-2:30PM M,W,F.
Index: Surveys in a card file index; all others in general index. Record index not computerized. Only the public may search. Will not search UCC records. Copy fee $8.00 per page. Cert fee- $10.00 per doc includes copy fee. Payee- Pomfret Town Clerk. **Other phones:** Treasurer- 802-457-3861; Elections- 802-457-3861; Vital Records- 802-457-3861. **Property tax/Assessing**- 802-457-3861.

Poultney Town

Town Clerk, 9 Main St, #2, Poultney, VT 05764. 802-287-5761; fax-802-287-5110; 8:30AM-12:30, 1:30-4PM www.poultneyvt.com/
Index: All in one. Record index not computerized. Office will perform a UCC search but public must search other records themselves. Office will not search real estate records. Husband and wife considered as one debtor. UCC search per debtor name- $10.00. Copy fee $1.00 per page. UCC copy fee $2.00 per page. Cert fee- $10.00 per doc includes copy fee. Payee- Poultney Town Clerk. **Property tax/Assessing**- 802-287-5761.

Pownal Town

Town Clerk, PO Box 411, Pownal, VT 05261. Recording, R/E phone-802-823-7757; fax-802-823-0116; 9AM-2PM M W F; 9AM-4PM T and by appointment.
Index: Separate indices to search. Record index not computerized. Office personnel or visitors may perform searches. Search fee $10.00 per name. Office will not search real estate records. Office will not search UCC records. General copy fee $3.00 per page. Cert fee- $8.00 (land records), $10.00 (Vital records) per cert plus copy fee. Payee- Pownal Town Clerk. **Property tax/Assessing**- 467 Center St, Pownal, VT 05261; 802-823-5644.

Proctor Town

Town Clerk, 45 Main St, Proctor, VT 05765. 802-459-3333; fax-802-459-2356; 8AM-4PM.
Index: Separate indices to search include index cards, books. Record index not computerized. Only the public may search. Copy fee- $1.00 per page. Cert fee- $10.00 per doc includes copy fee. Payee- Twon of proctor. **Property tax/Assessing**- 45 Main St, Proctor, VT 05765; 802-459-2504.

Putney Town

Town Clerk, PO Box 233, Putney, VT 05346. 802-387-5862 x14; fax-802-387-4708; 9AM-2PM M, Th, F; 9AM-2PM, 7-9PM W; 9AM-N Sat.
Recording is by town not county. Index: Indices in 5 separate books. Record index not computerized. Only the public may search. Search fee $2.00 per hour vault time. Will not search UCC records. Copy fee $1.00 per page. Cert fee- $7.00 per page includes copy fee. Payee- Putney Town Clerk. **Property tax/Assessing**- 127 Main St, Town Hall, Putney, VT 05346; 802-387-5862 x15, fax- 802-387-4708. hours- Noon-4PM

Randolph Town

Town Clerk, Drawer B, Randolph, VT 05060. Recording, R/E phone-802-728-5682; fax-802-728-5818; 8AM-4:30PM. www.randolphvt.com
Index: Separate indices to search include card, general. Record index not computerized. Only the public may search. Copy fee $2.00, if tax lien or real estate $1.00 per page. Cert fee- $8.00 per page plus copy fee. Payee- Town of Randolph. **Other phones:** Treasurer- 802-728-5682; Elections- 802-728-5682; Vitals- 802-728-5682. **Property tax/Assessing**- Same address as recording office. 802-728-5682.

Reading Town

Town Clerk, PO Box 72, Reading, VT 05062. Recording, R/E phone-802-484-7250; fax-same; 8AM-4PM M-Th. www.readingvt.govoffice.com
Index: All in one. Record index not computerized. Only the public may search. Copy fee $1.00 per page. Cert fee- $8.00 per page includes copy fee. Payee- Town of Reading. **Other phones:** Treasurer- 802-484-7250; Elections- 802-484-7250; Vital Records- 802-484-7250. **Property tax/Assessing**- 799 Rte 106, Reading, VT 05062; 802-484-7258. (Appraiser/Auditor- 802-484-7258)

Readsboro Town

Town Clerk, PO Box 187, Readsboro, VT 05350. Recording, R/E phone-802-423-5405; fax-802-423-5423; 9AM-3PM.
Index: Separate indices to search include A-Z, Frank Ross; A-Z Readsboro, Volume 3; Computer print outs begin with Volume 4. Records indexed on computer back to part of 1989. Only the public may search. Copy fee $1.00 per page. Cert fee- $8.00 per page includes copy fee. Payee- Town of Readsboro. **Other phones:** Treasurer- 802-423-5405; Elections- 802-423-5405; Vital Records- 802-423-5405. **Property tax/Assessing**- PO Box 354, Readsboro, VT 05350; 802-423-7023, assessor fax- 802-423-5423. hours- 9AM-N W

Richford Town

Town Clerk, PO Box 236, Richford, VT 05476-0236. Recording, R/E phone-802-848-7751; fax-802-848-7752; 8:30AM-4PM www.richfordvt.com
Index: All in one. Record index not computerized. Only the public may search. Search fee $2.00 per hour vault time. Copy fee $1.00 per page, $2.00 minimum. Cert fee- $7.00 per page includes copy fee. Payee- Town of Richford. **Other phones:** Treasurer- 802-848-7751; Elections- 802-848-7751; Vital Records- 802-848-7751. **Property tax/Assessing**- 94 Main St, Town Hall, Richford, VT 05476; 802-848-7751, assessor fax- 802-848-7751. (Appraiser/Auditor- 802-848-7751) hours- 8:30AM-N Monday only

Richmond Town

Town Clerk, PO Box 285, Richmond, VT 05477. 802-434-2221; fax-802-434-5570; 8AM-5PM M; 8AM-4PM T-Th, 8AM-N F. www.richmondvt.com
Index: All in one. Record index not computerized. Only the public may search. Office charges $2.00 per hour vault time. Copy fee $1.00 per page. Cert fee- $8.00 per doc plus copy fee. Payee- Town of Richmond. **Other phones:** Elections- 802-434-2221. **Property tax/Assessing**- PO Box 285, Richmond, VT 05477; see above.

Ripton Town

Town Clerk, PO Box 10, Ripton, VT 05766-0010. 802-388-2266; fax-802-388-0012; 2-6PM M; 9AM-1PM T,W,Th; closed Fridays.
Index: Separate indices to search include cards, books. Record index not computerized. Only the public may search. Office will search simple information on real estate records, but is not responsible for a title search. Copy fee $.25 per page. Uncertified copies (photocopies) of recorded & filed doc-$1.00. Cert fee- $10.00 per page plus copy fee. Payee- Town of Ripton. **Property tax/Assessing**- 1311 Rte 125, Ripton, VT 05766; 802-388-2266, assessor fax- 802-388-0012.

Rochester Town

Town Clerk, PO Box 238, Rochester, VT 05767-0238. Recording, R/E phone-802-767-3631; fax-802-767-6028; 8AM-4PM Tu-F.
Index: Separate indices to search include vital records. Record index not computerized. Only the public may search. Search fee $2.00 per hour vault time. Copy fee $1.00 per page for deeds; $.25 for regular copies. Cert fee- $9.50 per page plus copy fee. Payee- Town of Rochester. **Other phones:** Treasurer- 802-767-3631; Elections- 802-767-3631; Vital Records- 802-767-3631. **Property tax/Assessing**- 67 School St, Rochester, VT 05767; 802-767-3631, assessor fax- 802-767-6028.

Rockingham Town

Town Clerk, PO Box 339, Bellows Falls, VT 05101-0339. Recording, R/E phone-802-463-4336; fax-802-463-1228; 8:30AM-4:30PM www.rockbf.org
Index: Separate indices to search include UCCs, everything else in 1. Records indexed on computer from 2000 forward. Office will search UCC file but public must search other records themselves. UCC search per debtor name $10.00 per search, tax liens not included. UCC records- office will not locate if filed in land records. Copy fee $1.00 per page, $2.00 minimum. Vital records copy- $10.00. Cert fee- $8.00 per page.Payee- Town of Rockingham. **Other phones:** Treasurer- 802-463-3964; Elections- 802-463-4336; Vital Records- 802-463-4336; Health & Zoning -802-463-3964. **Property tax/Assessing**- PO Box 370, Bellows Falls, VT 05101-0370; 802-463-1229, assessor fax- 802-463-1228. hours- Usually mornings

Roxbury Town

Town Clerk, PO Box 53, Roxbury, VT 05669. Recording, R/E phone-802-485-7840; fax-802-485-9160; 9AM-N; 1PM-4PM T-F.
Index: All in one. Record index not computerized. Only the public may search. Copy fee $1.00 per page. Cert fee- $10.00 per page plus copy fee. Payee- Town of Roxbury. **Other phones:** Treasurer- 802-485-7860; Elections- 802-485-7840; Vital Records- 802-485-7840. **Property tax/Assessing**- 1664 Roxbury Rd, Roxbury, VT 05669; 802-485-7860, assessor fax- 802-485-9160. (Appraiser/Auditor- 802-485-7840 or 485-7860);

Royalton Town

Town Clerk, PO Box 680, South Royalton, VT 05068-0680. Recording, R/E phone-802-763-7207; fax-same; 8AM-3PM M-Th. www.royaltonvt.com
Index: All in one. Record index not computerized. Only the public may search. Search fee $2.00 per hour

vault time. Copy fee $1.00 per page. Cert fee- $2.00 per page plus copy fee. Payee- Town of Royalton. Grand list available for purchase; contact listers. **Other phones:** Treasurer- 802-763-7207; Elections- 802-763-7207; Vital Records- 802-763-7207; Second Phone- 802-763-7967. **Property tax/Assessing-** 23 Alexander Pl, Royalton Memorial Library, South Royalton, VT 05068; 802-763-2202, assessor fax- 802-763-7967.

Rupert Town

Town Clerk, PO Box 140, West Rupert, VT 05776. 802-394-7728; fax-802-394-2524; 11-7PM M; 12-5PM T,W; 8:30AM-3:30PM Th.
Index: All in one. Records indexed on index cards back to 1950. Prior in general index books. Office personnel or visitors may perform searches. General search fee $5.00 per hour. UCC search per debtor name- $10.00. UCC and tax lien copy fee $7.00; real estate is $1.00. per page. Cert fee- $8.00 per doc plus copy fee. Payee- Rupert Town Clerk. Bulk data available for purchase, zoning bylaws, town plan, septic regs., subdivision regs., tax maps on CD. Contact the town clerk. **Other phones:** Treasurer- 802-394-7728; Elections- 802-394-7728; Vital Records- 802-394-7728. **Property tax/Assessing-** PO Box 140, 187 E St, West Rupert, VT 05776; 802-394-7728, assessor fax- 802-394-2524.

Rutland City

City Clerk, PO Box 969, Rutland, VT 05702. Recording, R/E phone-802-773-1801; fax-802-773-1846; 8:30AM-5PM www.rutlandcity.com
Index: Separate indices to search. Currently in process of computerizing the records; a public use terminal available. Only the public may search. Search fee $2.00 per hour vault time. Office will not search UCC records or tax liens. Copy fee $1.00 per page. Cert fee- $8.00 per page total includes copy fee. Payee- City of Rutland. **Other phones:** Treasurer- 802-773-1800; Elections- 802-773-1801; Vital Records- 802-773-1801. **Property tax/Assessing-** 52 Washington St, 2nd Fl, Rutland, VT 05701; 802-773-1800, assessor fax- 802-773-2112. (Appraiser/Auditor- 802-773-1800) www.rutlandcity.com/

Rutland Town

Town Clerk, PO Box 225, Center Rutland, VT 05736. Recording, R/E phone-802-773-2528; fax-802-773-7295; 8AM-4:30PM.
Index: All in one. Record index not computerized. Only the public may search. Copy fee $1.00; $10.00 for vital records. per page. Cert fee- $7.00 per page plus copy fee. Payee- Rutland Town Clerk. **Other phones:** Treasurer- 802-773-2528. **Property tax/Assessing-** 181 Business Rte 4, Center Rutland, VT 05736; 802-773-2528. Public access terminal available.

Ryegate Town

Town Clerk, PO Box 332, Ryegate, VT 05042. Recording, R/E phone-802-584-3880; fax-802-584-3880; 1-5PM M,T,W; 9AM-1PM F.
Index: Card file index. Record index not computerized. Only the public may search. Copy fee $1.00 per page. Tax maps $.08 per page. Cert fee- $10.00 per doc plus copy fee. Payee- Town of Ryegate. **Other phones:** Treasurer- 802-584-4247; Elections- 802-584-3880; Vital Records- 802-584-3880. **Property tax/Assessing-** 18 S Bayley-Hazen Rd, Town Hwy #1, Ryegate, VT 05042; 802-584-4247. (Appraiser/Auditor- 802-584-4247)

Salisbury Town

Town Clerk, PO Box 66, Salisbury, VT 05769-0066. 802-352-4228; fax-802-352-9832; 11AM-5:30PM Mon; 10AM-2PM Tues, TH; Closed Wed, Fri. http://townclerk.salisburyvt.com/
Index: All in one. Record index not computerized. Only the public may search. Copy fee $1.00 per page. Cert fee- $8.00 per page. Payee- Town of Salisbury. **Other phones:** Treasurer- 802-352-4228; Elections- 802-352-4228; Vital Records- 802-352-4228; Listers- 802-352-9390. **Property tax/Assessing-** 25 Schoolhouse Rd, Salisbury, VT 05769; see above, assessor fax- 802-352-9832. hours- 11AM-1PM Monday only

Sandgate Town

Town Clerk, 3266 Sandgate Rd, Sandgate, VT 05250. 802-375-9075; fax-802-375-8350; 9AM-3PM T, W.
Index: Some card files, also original handwritten index book, computer. Records indexed on computer back to 1962. Only the public may search. Will not search UCC records. Copy fee $1.00 per page. Cert fee- $7.00 per doc plus copy fee if more than 1 page. Payee- Sandgate Town Clerk. **Other phones:** Treasurer- 802-375-9075; Elections- 802-375-9075; Vital Records- 802-375-9075; Liters- 802-375-9270. **Property tax/Assessing-** 3266 Sandgate Rd, Sandgate, VT 05250; 802-375-9075, assessor fax- 802-375-8350. (Appraiser/Auditor- 802-375-9075)

Searsburg Town

Town Clerk, PO Box 157, Wilmington, VT 05363. Recording, R/E phone-802-464-8081; fax-802-464-7610; 8AM-4PM M; 8AM-Noon T F.
Index: All in one. Record index not computerized. Office personnel or visitors may perform searches. Search fee $2.00 per hour vault time. Office will not search real estate records. Copy fee $1.00 per page. Cert fee- $8.00 per page. Payee- Searsburg Town Clerk. **Other phones:** Treasurer- 802-464-8081; Elections- 802-464-8081; Vital Records- 802-464-8081. **Property tax/Assessing-** PO Box 157, Wilmington, VT 05363; 802-464-8081, assessor fax- 802-464-7610. hours- call for app'm't

Shaftsbury Town

Town Clerk, PO Box 409, Shaftsbury, VT 05262. 802-442-4038; fax-802-442-0955; 9AM-5PM Mon; 9AM-3PM T-F. www.shaftsbury.net
Index: All in one. Record index not computerized. Only the public may search. Copy fee $1.00 per page. Cert fee- $8.00 per cert plus copy fee. Payee- Shaftsbury Town Clerk. **Other phones:** Treasurer- 802-442-6242; Elections- 802-442-4038; Vital Records- 802-442-4038. **Property tax/Assessing-** 61 Buck Hill Rd, Shaftsbury, VT 05262; 802-442-5740.

Sharon Town

Town Clerk, PO Box 250, Sharon, VT 05065. 802-763-8268; fax-802-763-7392; 7AM-5PM
Index: Separate indices to search include general, card. Record index not computerized. Only the public may search. Copy fee $1.00 per page. Cert fee- $7.00 per cert includes copy fee. Payee- Sharon Town Clerk. **Property tax/Assessing-** PO Box 250, Sharon, VT 05065; 802) 763-8268, assessor fax- 802-763-7392.

Sheffield Town

Town Clerk, PO Box 165, Sheffield, VT 05866-0165. 802-626-8862; fax-802-626-8862; 8AM-2PM M W F; 5PM-8PM W.
Index: All in one. Record index not computerized. Only the public may search. Copy fee $1.00 per page. Cert fee- $8.00 per page includes copy fee. Payee- Sheffield Town Clerk. **Other phones:** Treasurer- 802-626-8862; Elections- 802-626-8862. **Property tax/Assessing-** Town Hwy Yard, 37 Dane Rd, Sheffield, VT 05866; 802-626-9273.

Shelburne Town

Town Clerk, PO Box 88, Shelburne, VT 05482. Recording, R/E phone-802-985-5116; fax-802-985-9550; 8:30AM-4:30PM. www.shelburneVT.org
Index: All in one. Records indexed on a public use terminal back to 1992. Office will perform a UCC search but public must search other records themselves. Copy fee $1.00 per page. Cert fee- $8.00 per doc plus copy fee. Payee- Town of Shelburne. **Other phones:** Treasurer- 802-985-5116; Elections- 802-985-5116; Vital Records- 802-985-5116; 802-985-5117. **Property tax/Assessing-** 5420 Shelburne Rd, Shelburne, VT 05482; 802-985-5115. (Appraiser/Auditor- 802-985-5115)

Sheldon Town

Town Clerk, PO Box 66, Sheldon, VT 05483. 802-933-2524; fax-802-933-4951; 8AM-3PM
Index: All in one. Records indexed on a public use terminal. Only the public may search. Copy fee $2.00 per page for deeds; $1.00 for lister card. Cert fee- $5.00 per cert includes copy fee. Payee- Sheldon Town Clerk. **Other phones:** Treasurer- 802-933-2524. **Property tax/Assessing-** 1640 Main St, Sheldon, VT 05483; 802-933-2524, assessor fax- 802-933-4951.

Shoreham Town

Town Clerk, 297 Main St, Shoreham, VT 05770-9759. Recording, R/E phone-802-897-5841; fax-802-897-2545; 9AM-N 1PM-4PM; closed Thurs. www.shorehamvt.org/town/
Index: Separate indices to search include land, UCC, maps, vital records. Record index not computerized. Only the public may search. Will not search UCC records. Copy fee $1.00 per page. Cert fee- $10.00 per page includes one copy. Payee- Town of Shoreham. **Other phones:** Treasurer- 802-897-5841; Elections- 802-897-5841; Vital Records- 802-897-5841; Tax Collector- 802-897-7811. **Property tax/Assessing-** 297 Main St, Shoreham, VT 05770; 802-897-5841, assessor fax- 802-897-2545.

Shrewsbury Town

Town Clerk, 9823 Cold River Rd, Shrewsbury, VT 05738. 802-492-3511; fax-802-492-3511; 9AM-3PM M-TH. www.shrewsburyvt.org/townclerk.htm
Index: Records in separate books and indexes pre-1996. Records indexed on computer back to 1994. Office will perform a UCC search but public must search other records themselves. Search fee $2.00 per hour vault time, $5.00 per hour for assistance by clerk. Copy fee $1.00 per page. Cert fee- $8.00 per page includes copy fee. Payee- Anne Haley, Town Clerk. **Other phones:** Treasurer- 802-492-3558. **Property tax/Assessing-** 9823 Cold River Rd, Shrewsbury, VT 05738; 802-492-3511, assessor fax- 802-492-3511.

South Burlington City

Town Clerk, 575 Dorset St, South Burlington, VT 05403. 802-846-4105; 8AM-4:30PM, M W TH F; 8AM-5:30PM T. www.sburl.com
Index: All in one. Record index not computerized. Only the public may search. Search fee $2.00 per hour vault time. Will not search UCC records. Copy fee $1.00 per page. Cert fee- $8.00 per doc includes copy fee. Payee- City of South Burlington. **Other phones:** Treasurer- 802-846-4119; Elections- 802-846-4105; Vital Records- 802-846-4105; Taxes- 802-846-4109. **Property tax/Assessing-** 575 Dorset St, South Burlington, VT 05403; 802-846-4103. (Appraiser/Auditor- 802-846-4103) 8AM-4:30PM

South Hero Town

Town Clerk, PO Box 175, South Hero, VT 05486. Recording, R/E phone-802-372-5552; 8:30AM-N, 1-4:30PM M-W; 8:30AM-N,1-5PM Th.
Index: All in one. Record index not computerized. Only the public may search. Office will not search real estate records. Will not search UCC records. Copy fee $1.00 per page. Cert fee- $8.00 per page plus copy fee. Payee- Town of South Hero. **Other phones:** Treasurer- 802-372-5552; Elections- 802-372-5552; Vital Records- 802-372-5552. **Property tax/Assessing-** 333 Rte 2, PO Box 175, South Hero, VT 05486; 802-372-5552. (Appraiser/Auditor- 802-372-5552)

Springfield Town

Town Clerk, 96 Main St, Springfield, VT 05156. Recording, R/E phone-802-885-2104; fax-802-885-1617; 8AM-4:30PM
Index: All in one. Records indexed on computer back to 1994. Only the public may search. Search fee $10.00 per hour for assistance. Copy fee $1.00 per

page, $2.00 minimum. Cert fee- $8.00 per page includes copy fee. Payee- Town of Springfield. **Other phones:** Treasurer- 802-885-2104; Elections- 802-885-2104; Vital Records- 802-885-2104. **Property tax/Assessing-** 96 Main St, Springfield, VT 05156; 802-885-2104. (Appraiser/Auditor- 802-885-2104)

St. Albans City

City Clerk, PO Box 867, St. Albans, VT 05478-0867. Recording, R/E phone-802-524-1501; 7:30AM-4PM

Index: UCCs indexed separately. Record index not computerized. Only the public may search. Will not search UCC records. Copy fee $2.00 per page. Cert fee- $6.00 per page includes copy fee. Payee- St. Albans City. **Other phones:** Treasurer- 802-524-1501; Elections- 802-524-1501; Vital Records- 802-524-1501; Accounting- 802-524-1506. **Property tax/Assessing-** 100 N Main, St. Albans, VT 05478; 802-524-1502. (Appraiser/Auditor- 802-524-1502)

St. Albans Town

Town Clerk, PO Box 37, St. Albans Bay, VT 05481. Recording, R/E phone-802-524-2415; fax-802-524-9609; 8AM-4PM; closed to public Wed. www.stalbanstown.com

Index: Separate indices to search include UCCs, trailers. Records indexed on a public use terminal back to 0599. Office personnel or visitors may perform searches. Search fee $2.00 per hour vault time. Office will not search real estate records. Office will not search UCC records. Copy fee $1.00 per page. Cert fee- $8.00 per page plus copy fee. Payee- Town of St. Albans. **Other phones:** Treasurer- 802-524-2415; Elections- 802-524-2415; Vital Records- 802-524-2415. **Property tax/Assessing-** 579 Lake Rd, St. Albans Bay, VT 05481; 802-524-7589, assessor fax- 802-524-9609. (Appraiser/Auditor- 802-524-7589)

St. George Town

Town Clerk, 1 Barber Rd, St. George, VT 05495. 802-482-5272; fax-802-482-5548; 8AM-N. http://stgeorgevt.com

Index: All in one. Record index not computerized. Only the public may search. Copy fee $1.00 per copy. Cert fee- $1.00 per page plus copy fee. Payee- Town of St. George. **Other phones:** Treasurer- 802-482-5272; Elections- 802-482-5272; Vital Records- 802-482-5272. **Property tax/Assessing-** PO Box 616, Wartsfield,Vt 05673; 802-496-9689.

St. Johnsbury Town

Town Clerk, 1187 Main St, #2, St. Johnsbury, VT 05819-2288. Recording, R/E phone-802-748-4331; fax-802-748-1267; 8AM-5PM; summer 7AM-4PM. www.town.st-johnsbury.vt.us

Index: All in one. Record index not computerized. Only the public may search. Copy fee $1.00 per page. Cert fee- $8.00 per page includes copy fee. Payee- Town of Johnsbury. **Other phones:** Treasurer- 802-748-1260; Elections- 802-748-4331; Vital Records- 802-748-4331. **Property tax/Assessing-** 1189 Main St, St. Johnsbury, VT 05819; 802-748-4272, assessor fax- 802-748-1267. (Appraiser - 802-748-4272)

Stamford Town

Town Clerk, 986 Main Rd, Stamford, VT 05352-9601. Recording, R/E phone-802-694-1361; fax-n/a; 11AM-4PM T & W; Noon-4PM, 7-9PM Th; Noon-4PM F.

Index: All in one. Record index not computerized. Only the public may search. Office will not search real estate records. Will not search UCC records. Copy fee $1.00 per page. Cert fee- $8.00 per page includes copy fee. Payee- Town of Stamford. **Other phones:** Treasurer- 802-694-1361; Elections- 802-694-1361; Vital Records- 802-694-1361. **Property tax/Assessing-** 986 Main Rd, Stamford, VT 05352-9601; 802-694-1361. (Appraiser - 802-694-1361)

Stannard Town

Town Clerk, PO Box 94, Greensboro Bend, VT 05842-0094. 802-533-2577; 8AM-N Wed.

Call before faxing; fax same as phone. Index: All in one. Record index not computerized. Office personnel or visitors may perform searches. Search fee $2.00 per hour vault time. Office will not search real estate records or tax liens. UCC search per debtor name- $10.00. UCC search request using non-standard form (per name)- $15.00. Copy fee $1.00 per page. Real estate record copy- $2.00 per page. Cert fee- $7.00 per page. Payee- Stannard Town Clerk.

Starksboro Town

Town Clerk, PO Box 91, Starksboro, VT 05487-0091. 802-453-2639; fax-802-453-7293; 8:30AM-4:30PM M-Th. www.starksboro.org

Index: All in one. Record index not computerized. Only the public may search. Search fee $5.00 per hour for search assistance. Will not search UCC records. Copy fee $1.00 per page for land record docs, all other records $.25 per page. Cert fee- $1.00 per page plus copy fee. Payee- Town of Starksboro. **Other phones:** Treasurer- 802-453-2639; Elections- 802-453-2639; Vitals- 802-453-2639. **Property tax/Assessing-** 2849 Vermont Rte 116, Starksboro, VT 05487; 802-453-4949, assessor fax- 802-453-7293.

Stockbridge Town

Town Clerk, PO Box 39, Stockbridge, VT 05772-0039. 802-746-8400; fax-802-746-8400; 8AM-4:30PM T W TH; 8AM-N Fri. Index: All in one. Record index not computerized. Only the public may search. Copy fee $1.00 per page. Cert fee- $7.00 per page. Payee- Town of Stockbridge. **Property tax/Assessing-** PO Box 39, 1722 Vt Rte 100, Stockbridge, VT 05772-0039; 802-746-8400.

Stowe Town

Town Clerk, PO Box 248, Stowe, VT 05672. Recording, R/E phone-802-253-6133; fax-802-253-6143; 7:30AM-4:30PM.

Index: All in one. Records indexed on a public use terminal back to 10/100. Only the public may search. Search fee $2.00 per hour vault time. Copy fee $1.00 per page. Cert fee- $7.00 per page includes copy fee. Payee- Stowe Town Clerk. Bulk data available for purchase, contact Tom Vickey. **Other phones:** Treasurer- 802-253-6133; Elections- 802-253-6133; Vitals- 802-253-6133. **Property tax/Assessing-** 802-253-6144. (Appraiser/Auditor- 802-253-6144)

Strafford Town

Town Clerk, PO Box 27, Strafford, VT 05072. 802-765-4411; fax-802-765-9621; 7:30AM-4:30PM M-Th, closed Fri. Index: Separate indices to search include prior to book 44 - index books, 44 to current card file. Records indexed on computer from 2002. Office will perform a UCC search but public must search other records themselves. Search fee $5.00 an hour. Copy fee $1.00 per page. Cert fee- $9.50 per page includes copy fee. Payee- Town of Strafford. **Property tax/Assessing-** 227 Justin Morrill Hwy, Strafford, VT 05072; 802-765-4411.

Stratton Town

Town Clerk, PO Box 166, West Wardsboro, VT 05360. Recording, R/E phone-802-896-6184; fax-802-896-6630; 9AM-3PM M-TH.

Index: Separate indices to search. Records indexed on cards back to 1987, index prior. Office will perform a UCC search but public must search other records themselves. Copy fee $1.00 per page. Cert fee- $8.00 per page includes copy fee. Payee- Town of Stratton. **Other phones:** Treasurer- 802-896-6184; Elections- 802-896-6184; Vital Records- 802-896-6184. **Property tax/Assessing-** 9 W Jamaica Rd, West Wardsboro, VT 05360; 802-896-6184, assessor fax- 802-896-6630. (Appraiser/Auditor- 802-896-6184) **Online access-** Access assessor property data free at www.visionappraisal.com/databases/.

Sudbury Town

Town Clerk, 36 Blacksmith Ln, Sudbury, VT 05733. Recording, R/E phone-802-623-7296; fax-802-623-7296; 9AM-4PM M; 7PM-9PM W; 9AM-3PM Fri.

Index: All in one. Record index not computerized. Office personnel or visitors may perform searches. Search fee $5.00 per name. Office will not search title or mortgage records. Will not search UCC records. Copy fee $1.00 per page. Cert fee- $10.00 per page. Payee- Sudbury Town Clerk. **Other phones:** Treasurer- 802-623-7296; Elections- 802-623-7296; Vital Records- 802-623-7296. **Property tax/Assessing-** 36 Blacksmith Ln, Sudbury, VT 05733; 802-623-7296, assessor fax- 802-623-7296. (Appraiser/Auditor- 802-623-7296);

Sunderland Town

Town Clerk, PO Box 295, East Arlington, VT 05252. 802-375-6106; fax-same; 8AM-2PM M,T,Th; 8AM-N, 6-8PM W.

Index: Separate indices to search include books by year, alpha index. Record index not computerized. Only the public may search. Copy fee $1.00 per page. Cert fee- $7.00 per page includes copies. Payee- Sunderland Town Clerk. **Property tax/Assessing-** 802-375-9390.

Sutton Town

Town Clerk, Box 106, Sutton, VT 05867. 802-467-3377; fax-802-467-1052; 9AM-5PM,M,T,Th, F; 9AM-N Wed. Index: All in one. Record index not computerized. Office will perform a UCC search but public must search other records themselves. Office will not search real estate records. Copy fee $1.00 per page. Cert fee- $8.00 plus copy fee. Payee- Sutton Town Clerk. **Property tax/Assessing-** 167 Underpass Rd, Sutton,VT 05867; 802-467-3964, assessor fax- 802-467-1052.

Swanton Town

Town Clerk, PO Box 711, Swanton, VT 05488. Recording, R/E phone-802-868-4421; fax-802-868-4957; 8AM-4PM www.swantonvermont.org

Index: Separate indices to search include land records, attachments by index and card file; UCC in separate card file. Record index not computerized. Office personnel or visitors may perform searches. Search fee $5.00 per hour. Copy fee $1.00 per page, with a $2.00 minimum. Cert fee- $10.00 per page included copy fee. UCC's- $20.00. Payee- Town of Swanton. **Other phones:** Treasurer- 802-868-4421; Elections- 802-868-4421; Vital Records- 802-868-4421. **Property tax/Assessing-** 1 Academy St, Swanton, VT 05488; 802-868-2232, assessor fax- 802-868-4957. (Appraiser/Auditor- 802-868-4421) hours- 9AM-11AM

Thetford Town

Town Clerk, PO Box 126, Thetford Center, VT 05075-0126. Recording, R/E phone-802-785-2922; fax-802-785-2031; 8:30AM-3:30PM T-F (summer: T,W,Th only). www.thetfordvermont.us

Index: Separate indices to search include card file from 1967-2004; general index pre-1967 and 3/1/2004 forward. Records indexed on computer back to 2002. Public access terminal will be available in 2009. Office personnel or visitors may perform searches. Search fee $2.00 per hour; $5.00 per hour if clerk searches. Office will not search real estate or UCC records. Copy fee $1.00 per page. Cert fee- $8.00 per page includes copy fee. Payee- Town of Thetford. **Other phones:** Treasurer- 802-785-2922 x19; Elections- 802-785-2922; Vital Records- 802-785-2922. **Property tax/Assessing-** 3910 Rte 113, Thetford Center, VT 05075; 802-785-2922 x15, assessor fax- 802-785-2031. (Appraiser/Auditor- 802-785-2922 x15);

Tinmouth Town

Town Clerk, 515 N End Rd, Tinmouth, VT 05773. Recording, R/E phone-802-446-2498; fax-802-446-2498; 8AM-N, 1-5PM M & Th & 8AM-N Sat Jan-May only.

Index: Separate indices to search by date. Record index not computerized. Office will perform a UCC search but public must search other records themselves. Copy fee $1.00 per page. Cert fee- $8.00

per page plus copy fee. Payee- Timmouth Town Clerk. **Other phones:** Treasurer- 802-446-2498; Elections- 802-446-2498; Vital Records- 802-446-2498. **Property tax/Assessing-** 515 N End Rd, Tinmouth, VT 05773; 802-446-2498, assessor fax-802-446-2498. (Appraiser/Auditor- 802-446-2498)

Topsham Town

Town Clerk, PO Box 69, Topsham, VT 05076. Recording, R/E phone-802-439-5505; fax-802-439-5505; 1PM-6PM M; 9AM-4PM T-F; Closed W.
Index: Separate indices to search include cards 1967-present, prior in general index. Record index not computerized. Only the public may search. Search fee $2.00 per hour vault time. Copy fee $1.00 per page. For non-recorded documents $.15. Cert fee- $10.00 per page includes copy fee. Payee- Topsham Town. **Other phones:** Treasurer- 802-439-5505; Elections-802-439-5505; Vital Records- 802-439-5505; Delinquent Tax Collector- 802-439-5550. **Property tax/Assessing-** 6 Harts Rd, Topsham, VT 05076; 802-439-5505. (Appraiser/Auditor- 802-439-5505)

Town of Chittenden

Town Clerk, PO Box 89, Chittenden, VT 05737. 802-483-6647; fax-802-483-2504; 1:30-5PM; till 7PM W. Chittenden is in Rutland County, not Chittenden County. Uninformed secured parties continue to attempt filings at the county level here even though there is no county filing in Vermont. Index: Separate indices to search include liens and other recorded documents. Record index not computerized. Only the public may search. Copy fee $1.00 per page. Cert fee-$8.00 per doc includes copy fee. Payee- Chittenden Town Clerk.

Townshend Town

Town Clerk, PO Box 223, Townshend, VT 05353-0223. 802-365-7300 x2; fax-802-365-7309; 9AM-4PM M,T,W,F.
Index: All in one. Record index not computerized. In books back to 1935. Only the public may search. Copy fee $1.00 per page. Cert fee- $8.00 per doc plus copy fee. Payee- Town of Townshend. **Other phones:** Treasurer- 802-365-7300 x3. **Property tax/Assessing-** 2006 VT Rte 30, Town Hall, Townshend, VT 05353; 802-365-7300 x4.

Troy Town

Town Clerk, PO Box 80, North Troy, VT 05859. 802-988-2663; fax-802-988-4692; 8AM-N, 1-4PM
Index: All in one. Record index not computerized. Office personnel or visitors may perform searches. Office will not search real estate records. UCC search includes tax liens if requested. UCC search per debtor name- $5.00. Copy fee $1.00 per page; $2.00 minimum. Cert fee- $8.00 per cert plus copy fee. Payee- Troy Town Clerk. **Property tax/Assessing-** 142 Main St, North Troy, VT 05859; 802-988-4692. hours- Varies

Tunbridge Town

Town Clerk, PO Box 6, Tunbridge, VT 05077. Recording, R/E phone-802-889-5521; fax-802-889-3744; 8AM-N, 1PM-4PM M-Th.
Index: Separate indices to search include card index 1974-current grantor/grantee cards. General index from beginning of time to 1974. Record index not computerized. Only the public may search. Copy fee $1.00 per page. Cert fee- $10.00 per page includes copy fee. Payee- Town of Tunbridge. For grand list information please call 802-889-3571. **Other phones:** Treasurer- 802-889-5521; Elections- 802-889-5521; Vitals- 802-889-5521. **Property tax/Assessing-** Main St, Tunbridge, VT 05077; 802-889-5521, assessor fax- 802-889-3744. (Appraiser - 802-889-3571);

Underhill Town

Town Clerk, PO Box 32, Underhill, VT 05490. Recording, R/E phone-802-899-4434; fax-802-899-2137; 8AM-4PM M-F. www.underhillvt.gov
Index: All in one. Record index not computerized. Office will perform a limited UCC search but public must search other records themselves. Search fee $2.00 per hour vault time. Copy fee $1.00 per page. Cert fee- $8.00 per page plus copy fee. Payee-Underhill Town Clerk. **Other phones:** Treasurer-802-899-4434; Elections- 802-899-4434; Vital Records- 802-899-4434. **Property tax/Assessing-** 12 Pleasant Valley Rd, Underhill, VT 05490; 802-899-4434, assessor fax- 802-899-2137. (Appraiser/Auditor- 802-899-4434)

Vergennes City

Town Clerk, PO Box 35, Vergennes, VT 05491-0035. Recording, R/E phone-802-877-2841; fax-802-877-1160; 8AM-3:30PM M,W,F; 8AM-4PM T,Th. www.vergennes.org
Index: Separate indices to search include liens, maps, mobile homes, birth, deaths, marriage, land records, UCCs. Record index not computerized. Only the public may search. Search fee $2.00 per hour vault time. Copy fee $1.00 per page. Cert fee- $7.00 per page includes copy fee. Payee- City Clerk. **Other phones:** Treasurer- 802-877-2841; Elections- 802-877-2841; Vital Records- 802-877-2841. **Property tax/Assessing-** 120 Main St, Vergennes, VT 05491; 802-877-1163, assessor fax- 802-877-1160. (Appraiser/Auditor- 802-877-2841)

Vernon Town

Town Clerk, 567 Governor Hunt Rd, Vernon, VT 05354. 802-257-0292; fax-802-254-3561; 8AM-4PM. www.sover.net/~vernontc/
Index: All in one. Records indexed on a public use terminal back to Book 17. Office will perform a UCC search but public must search other records themselves. Copy fee $1.00 per page; $2.00 minimum. Cert fee- $8.00 per page plus copy fee. Payee- Town Clerk. Treasurer- 802-257-3077; Elections- 802-257-0292; Vitals- 802-257-0292. **Property tax/Assessing-** 567 Governor Hunt Rd, Vernon, VT 05354; 802-257-3077, assessor fax- 802-254-3561. (Appraiser - 802-257-0292) 8AM-4:30PM

Vershire Town

Town Clerk, 6894 Vermont Rte 113, Vershire, VT 05079. Recording, R/E phone-802-685-2227; fax-same; 8:30AM-3PM T-Th.
Index: Separate indices to search include UCC, attachments, vital. Record index not computerized. Only the public may search. Copy fee $1.00 per page. Cert fee- $10.00 per page includes copy fee. Payee-Vershire Town Clerk. **Other phones:** Treasurer- 802-685-2227; Elections- 802-685-2227; Vital Records-802-685-2227. **Property tax/Assessing-** 6894 Vermont Rte 113, Vershire, 05079; 802-685-2227.

Victory Town

Town Clerk, PO Box 609, North Concord, VT 05858. 802-328-2400; fax-same; 10PM-6PM Tu; 10AM-3 Th by appt.
Index: Separate indices in vault books. Record index not computerized. Office personnel or visitors may perform searches. Search fee $2.00 per hour. Office will not search real estate records. Office will not search UCC records. General copy fee $2.00 per page. Cert fee- $7.00 per page includes copy fee. Payee-Victory Town Clerk. **Other phones:** Treasurer- 802-328-2400. **Property tax/Assessing-** 102 Radar Rd, North Concord, VT 05858; 802-328-2400.

Waitsfield Town

Town Clerk, 9 Bridge St, Waitsfield, VT 05673-0390. Recording, R/E phone-802-496-2218; fax-802-496-9284; 9AM-4PM
Index: All in one. Record index not computerized. Only the public may search. General copy fee- $1.00 per page. Cert fee- $10.00 per page includes copy fee. Payee- Town of Waitsfield. **Other phones:** Treasurer- 802-496-2218; Elections- 802-496-2218; Vital Records- 802-496-2218. **Property tax/Assessing-** 9 Bridge St, Waitsfield, VT 05673; 802-496-9689.

Walden Town

Town Clerk, 12 Vermont Rte 215, West Danville, VT 05873. 802-563-2220; fax-802-563-3008; 9AM-4PM www.danvillevt.com/town_clerks_office.htm
Index: All in one. Record index not computerized. Only the public may search. Copy fee $1.00 per page. Cert fee- $7.00 per doc includes copy fee. Payee-Walden Town Clerk. **Property tax/Assessing-** 12 VT Rte 215, West Danville, VT 05873-9859; 802-563-2220, assessor fax- 802-563-3008.

Wallingford Town

Town Clerk, PO Box 327, Wallingford, VT 05773. 802-446-2336; fax-802-446-3174; 8AM-4:30PM M-Th; 8AM-N F. www.wallingfordvt.com
Index: Separate indices to search include card, books by number. Record index not computerized. Only the public may search. Copy fee $.25 per page. Cert fee-$10.00 per page includes copy fee. Payee-Wallingford Town Clerk. **Other phones:** Treasurer-802-446-2336; Elections- 802-446-2336; Vital Records- 802-446-2336. **Property tax/Assessing-** 75 School St, Wallingford, VT 05773; 802-446-2974, assessor fax- 802-446-3174.

Waltham Town

Town Clerk, PO Box 175, Vergennes, VT 05491. 802-877-3641; fax-802-877-3641; 9AM-3PM T; 9AM-3PM F.
Index: All in one. Record index not computerized. Office will perform a UCC search but public must search other records themselves. Search fee $2.00 per hour vault time. Copy fee $1.00 per page. Cert fee-$1.00 per page plus copy fee. Payee- Waltham Town Clerk. **Other phones:**Zoning Admin- 802-877-6734. **Property tax/Assessing-** PO Box 175, Vergennes, VT 05491.

Wardsboro Town

Town Clerk, PO Box 48, Wardsboro, VT 05355-0048. 802-896-6055; fax-802-896-1000; 9AM-N, 1-4:30PM, M-Th.
Index: All in one. Record index not computerized. Only the public may search. Copy fee $1.00 per page. Cert fee- $8.00 per cert plus copy fee. Payee-Wardsboro Town Clerk. **Property tax/Assessing-** 71 Main St, Wardsboro, VT 05355; 802-896-6055.

Warren Town

Town Clerk, PO Box 337, Warren, VT 05674. Recording, R/E phone-802-496-2709 x21; fax-802-496-2418; 9AM-4:30PM www.warrenvt.org
Index: Separate indices to search include card files to 1976, general index. Record index not computerized. Office personnel or visitors may perform searches. No fee for search. Copy fee $1.00 per page. Cert fee-$9.50 per page includes copies. Payee- Warren Town Clerk. **Other phones:** Treasurer- 802-496-2709 x22; Elections- 802-496-2709 x21; Vital Records- 802-496-2709 x21. **Property tax/Assessing-** 42 Cemetery Rd, Warren, VT 05674; 802-496-2709 x26. (Appraiser/Auditor- 802-496-2709 x26)

Washington Town

Town Clerk, 2895 Rte 110; Clerk's Office, Washington, VT 05675. Recording, R/E phone-802-883-2218; fax-802-883-2218; 8:30AM-2PM M,T.
Do not confuse this Washington Town with Washington County. Index: All in one. Record index not computerized. Office personnel or visitors may perform searches. Real estate record owner searches available. UCC search includes tax liens if requested. UCC search per debtor name- $10.00. UCC search request using non-standard form (per name)- $15.00. Copy fee $1.00 per page. Cert fee- $1.00 per page includes copy fee. Payee- Washington Town Clerk. **Other phones:** Treasurer- 802-883-2218; Elections-802-883-2218; Vital Records- 802-883-2218. **Property tax/Assessing-** 802-883-2218.

Waterbury Town

Town Clerk, 51 S Main St, Waterbury, VT 05676. Recording, R/E phone-802-244-8447; fax-802-244-1014; 8AM-4:30PM. www.waterburyvt.com

Index: Separate indices to search include index card file. Records indexed on a public use terminal back 3 years. Only the public may search. Will not search UCC records. Copy fee $1.00 per page. Cert fee- $8.00 per page plus copy fee. Payee- Town Clerk. **Other phones:** Treasurer- 802-244-8447; Elections- 802-244-8447; Vital Records- 802-244-8447. **Property tax/Assessing**- 51 S Main St, Waterbury, VT 05676; 802-244-1013, assessor fax- 802-244-1014. (Appraiser/Auditor- 802-244-8447);

Waterford Town

Town Clerk, PO Box 56, Lower Waterford, VT 05848. Recording, R/E phone-802-748-2122; fax-802-748-8196; 8:30AM-3:30PM, M, TH, F; Noon-6PM, T.

Index: Separate indices to search include card file from book 44 to present, general index book for previous books. Record index not computerized. Office will perform a UCC search but public must search other records themselves. Copy fee $1.00 per page. Cert fee- 8.00 per page includes copy fee. Payee- Town of Waterford. Bulk data available for purchase, contact Joanne Jarenthuff. **Other phones:** Treasurer- 802-748-2122; Elections- 802-748-2122; Vital Records- 802-748-2122. **Property tax/Assessing**- 532 Maple St, Lower Waterford, VT 05848; 802-748-2122, assessor fax- 802-748-8196. (Appraiser/Auditor- 802-748-2122)

Waterville Town

Town Clerk, PO Box 31, Waterville, VT 05492. Recording, R/E phone-802-644-8865; fax-802-644-8865; 9AM-1:30PM M,T,TH; closed W,F.

Index: All in one. Record index not computerized. Office personnel or visitors may perform searches. Search fee $5.00 per hour. Office will not search real estate records. Office will not search UCC records. Copy fee $1.00 per page. Cert fee- $8.00 per doc includes copy fee. Payee- Waterville Town Clerk. **Other phones:** Treasurer- 802-644-8865; Elections- 802-644-8865; Vital Records- 802-644-8865. **Property tax/Assessing**- 850 Vermont Rte 109, Waterville, VT 05492; 802-644-8865, assessor fax- 802-644-8865. (Appraiser/Auditor- 802-644-8865);

Weathersfield Town

Town Clerk, PO Box 550, Ascutney, VT 05030-0550. Recording, R/E phone-802-674-9500; fax-802-674-2117; 9AM-4PM M-W; 9AM-5PM TH. www.weathersfield.org/pages/townclerk.htm

Index: Separate indices to search include UCC, surveys, older lien, zoning permit. Record index not computerized. Only the public may search. Copy fee $1.00 per page. Cert fee- $8.00 per doc includes copy fee. Payee- Weathersfield Town Clerk. **Other phones:** Elections- 802-674-9500; Vital Records- 802-674-9500. **Property tax/Assessing**- 5259 Rte 5, Martin Memorial Hall, Weathersfield, VT 05030; 802-674-2626, assessor fax- 802-674-2117. hours- 8AM-4PM M-W; 8AM-5PM TH; 8AM-3PM F

Wells Town

Town Clerk/Tax Collector, PO Box 585, Wells, VT 05774. 802-645-0486; fax-802-645-0464; 8:30AM-4PM M-Th.

Index: All in one. Records indexed on a public use terminal back to 1987. Only the public may search. Copy fee $1.00 per page. Cert fee- $10.00 per doc plus copy fee. Payee- Wells Town Clerk. **Other phones:** Treasurer- 802-645-0486; Lister- 802-645-0188. **Property tax/Assessing**- 108 Vermont Rte 30, Wells, VT 05774; see above. hours- by appointment Public access terminal available.

West Fairlee Town

Town Clerk, Box 615, West Fairlee, VT 05083. 802-333-9696; fax-802-333-9611; 8:30AM-2:30PM M,T,Th. www.westfairleevt.com

Index: Indices in front of books. Records indexed on computer back to 1927. No public terminal available. Only the public may search. Copy fee $1.00 per page. Cert fee- $2.00 per page includes copy fee. Payee- Town of West Fairlee. Treasurer- 802-333-9696; Elections- 802-333-9696; Vital Records- 802-333-9696. **Property tax/Assessing**- 908 VT Rte 113, West Fairlee, VT 05083; 802-333-9696, assessor fax- 802-333-9611. hours- 8:30AM-10:30AM M

West Haven Town

Town Clerk, 2919 Main Rd, West Haven, VT 05743-9610. 802-265-4880; fax-same; 1-3:30PM

Index: All in one. Record index not computerized. Office personnel or visitors may perform searches. Office will not search real estate records. UCC search includes tax liens. UCC search per hour- $2.00. Separate state tax lien search- $3.00 per hour. Separate federal tax lien search- $5.00 per hour. Copy fee $1.00 per page. Cert fee- $7.00 per doc includes copy fee. Payee- Town of West Haven. **Other phones:** Treasurer- 802-265-3675; Elections- 802-265-4880; Vital Records- 802-265-4880. **Property tax/Assessing**- 2813 Main Rd, West Haven, VT 05743; 802-265-7996. (Appraiser - 802-265-7996)

West Rutland Town

Town Clerk, 35 Marble St, West Rutland, VT 05777. Recording, R/E phone-802-438-2204; fax-802-438-5133; 9AM-4PM M-Th; Fri by appointment. www.wrutland.org/

Index: Separate indices to search include written book, card index, computer. Records indexed on computer back to 2000. Office will perform a UCC search but public must search other records themselves. UCC search per debtor name- $20.00. Copy fee $2.00 1st page, $1.00 per add'l page. Cert fee- $8.00 per page includes copy fee. Payee- Town of West Rutland. **Other phones:** Treasurer- 802-438-2263; Elections- 802-438-2204; Vital Records- 802-438-2204. **Property tax/Assessing**- 35 Marble St, West Rutland, VT 05777; 802-438-2263, assessor fax- 802-438-5133. (Appraiser - 802-438-2263)

West Windsor Town

Town Clerk, PO Box 6, Brownsville, VT 05037. Recording, R/E phone-802-484-7212; fax-802-484-3518; 9AM-N, 1:30PM-4:30PM.

Index: Separate indices to search include grantor/grantee index, books. Record index not computerized. Only the public may search. Copy fee $1.00 per page. Cert fee- $10.00 per page plus copy fee. Payee- Town of West Windsor. **Other phones:** Treasurer- 802-484-7212. **Property tax/Assessing**- 22 Brownsville-Hartland Rd, PO Box 6 (05037), West Windsor, VT 05089; 802-484-3113, assessor fax- 802-484-3518. (Appraiser - 802-484-7212)

Westfield Town

Town Clerk, 1257 Vermont Rte 100, Westfield, VT 05874. Recording, R/E phone-802-744-2484; fax-802-744-6224; 8AM-4PM M,T,W,TH.

Index: All in one. Record index not computerized. Office will perform a UCC search but public must search other records themselves. Copy fee $1.00 per page. Cert fee- $10.00 per page includes copy fee. Payee- Westfield Town Clerk. **Other phones:** Treasurer- 802-744-2484; Vital Records- 802-744-2484. **Property tax/Assessing**- 38 School St, Westfield, VT 05874; 802-744-2484, assessor fax- 802-744-6224.

Westford Town

Town Clerk, 1713 Vermont Rte 128, Westford, VT 05494. Recording, R/E phone-802-878-4587; fax-802-879-6503; 8:30AM-4:30PM.

Index: Separate indices to search include Land records (general index and card index), liens, UCC, surveys carded separately. Record index not computerized. Only the public may search. Copy fee $1.00 per page. Cert fee- $10.00 per page includes copy fee. Payee- Town of Westford. **Other phones:** Treasurer- 802-878-4587; Elections- 802-878-4587; Vital Records- 802-878-4587. **Property tax/Assessing**- 1713 Vermont Rte 128, Westford, VT 05494; 802-878-4587, fax- 802-879-6503. (Appraiser - 802-878-4587)

Westminster Town

Town Clerk, PO Box 147, Westminster, VT 05158-0147. 802-722-4091; fax-802-722-9816; 8:30AM-4PM http://westminster.govoffice.com

Index: All in one. Records indexed on computer back to 2001. Only the public may search. Search fee $2.00 per hour vault time. Will not search UCC records. General copy fee $1.00 per page; zoning files & tax maps $.25 per page. Cert fee- $8.00 per page plus copy fee. Payee- Town of Westminster. Grand list is available for purchase, $2.00 CD-rom. **Other phones:** Treasurer- 802-722-4091; Elections- 802-722-4091; Vital Records- 802-722-4091; Taxes, Current & Delinquent- 802-722-4091. **Property tax/Assessing**- 3651 US Rte 5, Town Hall, Westminster, VT 05158; 802-722-9516, assessor fax- 802-722-9816. (Appraiser/Auditor- 802-722-9516) hours- By Appointment

Westmore Town

Town Clerk, 54 Hinton Hill Rd, Orleans, VT 05860. 802-525-3007; fax-802-525-1131; 8:30AM-4PM M-Th. www.westmoreonline.org/main/?page_id=6

Index: Books. Record index not computerized. Only the public may search. Copy fee $1.00 per page. For Maps $.50 per page. Cert fee- $10.00 per page plus copy fee. Payee- Town of Westmore. Grand List is available for purchase, $6.00 on CD, $35.00 paperback. **Property tax/Assessing**- 54 Hinton Hill Rd, Orleans, VT 05860; 802-525-3235, assessor fax- 802-525-1131. hours- 9AM-4PM T,TH

Weston Town

Town Clerk, PO Box 98, Weston, VT 05161. 802-824-6645; fax-802-824-4121; 8AM-1PM www.westonvt.org

Index: Separate indices to search include liens. Record index not computerized. Only the public may search. Copy fee $1.00 per page for land records, tax bills, lister cards; general copy fee $.25 per side. Cert fee- $10.00 per page plus copy fee. Payee- Town Clerk. **Other phones:** Treasurer- 802-824-6645; Elections- 802-824-6645; Vital Records- 802-824-6645. **Property tax/Assessing**- 12 Lawrence Hill Rd, Weston, VT 05161; 802-824-6645, assessor fax- 802-824-4449. hours- by appointment

Weybridge Town

Town Clerk, 1727 Quaker Village Rd, Weybridge, VT 05753. Recording, R/E phone-802-545-2450; fax-802-545-2624; 9AM-2PM M,T,TH,F.

Index: All in one. Record index not computerized. Only the public may search. Copy fee $1.00 per page. Cert fee- $.50 per page. Payee- Weybridge Town. **Other phones:** Treasurer- 802-545-2450; Elections- 802-545-2450; Vitals- 802-545-2450. **Property tax/Assessing**- 802-545-2450. (Appraiser/Auditor- 802-545-2450)

Wheelock Town

Town Clerk, PO Box 1328, Lyndonville, VT 05851-1328. Recording, R/E phone-802-626-9094; fax-802-626-9094; 8AM-4PM M-Th.

Index: All in one. Record index not computerized. Only the public may search. Real estate record owner searches available. Copy fee $1.00 per page. Cert fee- $8.00 per page includes copy fee. Payee- Wheelock Town Clerk. **Other phones:** Treasurer- 802-626-9094; Elections- 802-626-9094; Vital Records- 802-626-9094. **Property tax/Assessing**- 1192 Rte 122, Wheelock, VT 05851; 802-626-9094.

Whiting Town

Town Clerk, 29 S Main St, Whiting, VT 05778. Recording, R/E phone-802-623-7813; 9AM-N M,W,F and by App't.
Index: Separate indices to search include grantee/grantor. Record index not computerized. Office personnel or visitors may perform searches. Search fee $10.00 per name. Office will not search real estate records. Office will not search UCC records. Copy fee $1.00 per page; UCC copy $.25 per page. Cert fee- $8.00 per page plus copy fee. Payee- Whiting Town Clerk. **Other phones:** Treasurer- 802-623-7813. **Property tax/Assessing**- 29 S Main St 802-623-7813.

Whitingham Town

Town Clerk, PO Box 529, Jacksonville, VT 05342. 802-368-7887; fax-802-368-7519; 9AM-2PM (5-7PM W); 1st Sat of month 9AM-N.
Index: All in one. Public use terminal has records as far back as 1991. Records indexed on a public use terminal. Office personnel or visitors may perform searches. Office will not search real estate records. UCC search includes tax liens if requested. UCC search per debtor name- $2.00 per hour. Copy fee $1.00 per page. Cert fee- $7.00 per cert plus copy fee. Payee- Whitingham Town Clerk. **Other phones:** Treasurer- 802-368-7543; Elections- 802-368-7887; Vital Records- 802-368-7887. **Property tax/Assessing**- PO Box 350, Jacksonville, VT 05342; 802-368-7887, assessor fax- 802-368-7519. (Appraiser/Auditor- 802-368-2838)

Williamstown Town

Town Clerk, PO Box 646, Williamstown, VT 05679. Recording, R/E phone-802-433-5455; fax-802-433-2160; 8AM-4:30PM www.williamstownvt.org
Index: Separate indices to search. Records indexed with card file and paper index after 1001. Office will perform a UCC search but public must search other records themselves. Copy fee $1.00 per page. Cert fee- 8.00 per cert includes copy fee. Payee- Williamstown Town Clerk. **Other phones:** Treasurer- 802-433-5455; Elections- 802-433-5455; Vital Records- 802-433-5455. **Property tax/Assessing**- 2470 Vermont Rte 14, Williamstown, VT 05679; 802-433-5455, assessor fax- 802-433-2160. (Appraiser/Auditor- 802-433-5455);

Williston Town

Town Clerk, 7900 Williston Rd, Williston, VT 05495. 802-878-5121; fax-802-764-1140; 8AM-4:30PM www.town.williston.vt.us/website/
St. George is a separate town with a Williston mailing address. Index: Separate indices to search include books, card index back to 1944. Record index not computerized. Office will perform a UCC search but public must search other records themselves. UCC search per debtor name $20.00. Copy fee $1.00 per page. Cert fee- $7.00 per page includes copy fee. Payee- Town of Williston. **Other phones:** Treasurer- 802-878-5121; Elections- 802-878-5121; Vital Records- 802-878-5121. **Property tax/Assessing**- 7900 Williston Rd, Williston, VT 05495; 802-878-1091, assessor fax- 802-764-1140. (Appraiser/Auditor- 802-878-1091) hours- 9AM-1PM

Wilmington Town

Town Clerk, PO Box 217; Town Hall, Wilmington, VT 05363-0217. Recording, R/E phone-802-464-5836; fax-802-464-1238; 8:30AM-N, 1-4PM M-Th; Fri 8:30AM-6:30PM. www.wilmingtonvermont.us
Index: Books; 1797-1965 (vol 1&2), 1966-2000 (card file), and computer, 1989-present. Records indexed on computer back to 1989. Office will perform a UCC search but public must search other records themselves. Copy fee $1.00 per page. Cert fee- $8.00 per page includes copy fee. Payee- Town of Wilmington. **Other phones:** Treasurer- 802-464-8591; Elections- 802-464-5836; Vital Records- 802-464-5836. **Property tax/Assessing**- 2 E Main St, Wilmington, VT 05363; 802-464-8591, assessor fax-802-464-8477. (Appraiser/Auditor- 802-464-8591) hours- 8AM-1PM M,W,F **Online access**- The Grand List is available as a pdf in the Documents section of the main website www.wilmingtonvermont.us/.

Windham Town

Town Clerk, 5976 Windham Hill Rd, Windham, VT 05039. 802-874-4211; fax-802-874-4144; 10AM-3PM T,Th,F.
Office's jurisdiction includes ONLY Windham Town; DO NOT CONFUSE WINDHAM TOWN WITH WINDHAM COUNTY. Index: Separate indices to search include card system. Record index not computerized. Only the public may search. General copy fee $1.00 per page, $2.00 minimum on deeds. Cert fee- $8.00 per page plus copy fee. Payee- Windham Town Clerk. **Property tax/Assessing**- 5976 Windham Hill Rd, Windham, VT 05039; 802-874-4211, assessor fax- 802-874-4144.

Windsor Town

Town Clerk, PO Box 47, Windsor, VT 05089. Recording, R/E phone-802-674-5610; fax-802-674-1017; 8AM-5PM M-Th. www.vermont-towns.org/windsor/
Index: UCCs indexed separately at Sec of State. Record index not computerized. Only the public may search. Copy fee $1.00 per page. Cert fee- $8.00 per page. Payee- Town Clerk. **Other phones:** Treasurer- 802-674-6788; Elections- 802-674-5610; Vital Records- 802-674-5610. **Property tax/Assessing**- PO Box 47, Windsor, VT 05089; 802-674-5414, assessor fax- 802-674-1017. (Appraiser - 802-674-5414)

Winhall Town

Town Clerk, PO Box 389, Bondville, VT 05340. Recording, R/E phone-802-297-2122; fax-802-297-2582; 9AM-N; Closed Th.
Index: Separate indices to search. Records indexed on cards, 3 indices prior to 1985; 1 index after 00. Only the public may search. Search fee $2.00 per hour vault time. Copy fee $1.00 per page. Cert fee- $8.00 per doc includes copy fee. Payee- Winhall Town Clerk. **Other phones:** Treasurer- 802-297-1994; Elections- 802-297-2122; Vital Records- 802-297-2122. **Property tax/Assessing**- #3 River Rd, Bondville, VT 05340; 802-297-2151. (Appraiser - 802-297-2151);

Winooski City

Town Clerk, 27 W Allen St, Winooski, VT 05404. 802-655-6419; fax-802-655-6414; 8AM-4PM T-TH; N-6PM M; N-4PM F. www.onioncity.com/
Index: All in one. Record index not computerized. Office will perform a UCC search but public must search other records themselves. Copy fee $1.00 per page. Cert fee- $8.00 per cert plus copy fee. Payee- Winooski City. **Property tax/Assessing**- 27 W Allen St, Winooski, VT 05404; 802-655-6410, assessor fax-802-655-6414. hours- 8AM-8PM M; 8AM-4PM T,W,TH; 8AM-N F

Wolcott Town

Town Clerk, PO Box 100, Wolcott, VT 05680-0100. Recording, R/E phone-802-888-2746; fax-same; 8AM-6PM T; 8AM-4PM W-F.
Index: Separate indices to search. Records indexed on computer back to 1999. Office personnel or visitors may perform searches. Search fee $5.00 per hour. Office will search real estate records for name only. No title searches. Copy fee $1.00 per page. Cert fee- $8.00 per page includes copy fee. Payee- Town of Wolcott. **Other phones:** Treasurer- 802-888-2746; Elections- 802-888-2746; Vital Records- 802-888-2746; Listers- 802-888-6858. **Property tax/Assessing**- 4186 Vermont Rte 15, Wolcott, VT 05680; 802-888-2746, assessor fax- 802-888-2746. (Appraiser/Auditor- 802-888-6858)

Woodbury Town

Town Clerk, PO Box 10, Woodbury, VT 05681. 802-456-7051; fax-802-456-8834; 8:30AM-1PM T-W-Th; 6-8PM Th evening.
Index: Separate indices to search include card file. Records indexed on computer. Office prefers public do their own research. Office will search real estate records. Office will search UCC records, but not tax liens. UCC search per debtor name- $10.00. UCC search request using non-standard form (per name)- $15.00. Copy fee $1.00 per page, $2.00 minimum. Cert fee- $7.00 per page includes copy fee. Payee- Woodbury Town Clerk. **Property tax/Assessing**- 1672 Rte 14, Woodbury, VT 05681; 802-456-8836, assessor fax- 802-456-8834.

Woodford Town

Town Clerk, 1391 Vermont Rte 9, Bennington, VT 05201. Recording, R/E phone-802-442-4895; fax-802-442-4816; 8:30AM-4PM.
Above hours for Town Clerk office. Town office hours- 8:30AM-4PM. Index: Separate indices to search include prior to 1967 records indexed in books, 1967 to present index cards used. Record index not computerized. Only the public may search. Copy fee $1.00 per page. Fax fee $1.00 plus $1.00 per page. Cert fee- $10.00 per page includes copy fee. Payee- Town Clerk. **Other phones:** Treasurer- 802-442-4895; Elections- 802-442-4895; Vital Records- 802-442-4895. **Property tax/Assessing**- 1391 Vermont Rte 9, Woodford, VT 05201; 802-442-4895, assessor fax- 802-442-4816. (Appraiser - 802-442-4895);

Woodstock Town

Town Clerk, 31 The Green, Woodstock, VT 05091. 802-457-3611 x5, R/E recording phone-802-457-3611; fax-802-457-2329; 8AM-N, 1-4:30PM www.townofwoodstock.org
Index: Separate indices to search include land, UCC, survey maps. Record index not computerized. Only the public may search. Search fee $2.00 per hour vault time. Copy fee $1.00 per page. Cert fee- $7.00 per page plus copy fee. Payee- Town of Woodstock. **Other phones:** Treasurer- 802-457-3456. **Property tax/Assessing**- PO Box 488, 31 The Green, Woodstock, VT 05091; 802-457-2607. **Online access**- Access to the Lister's Grand Lists and Sales List is available free at www.townofwoodstock.org/listers/index.html.

Worcester Town

Town Clerk, Drawer 161, Worcester, VT 05682-0161. 802-223-6942; fax-802-229-5216; 8:30AM-N 1PM-4:30PM M,W,TH.
Index: Pre-2004 liens and attachments in separate books; Pre-1988 not indexed. Record index not computerized. Only the public may search. Search fee $2.00 per hour vault time. Copy fee $1.00 per page. Cert fee- $8.00 per page plus copy fee. Payee- Town of Worcester.

Vermont County Locator

You will usually be able to find the city name in the City/County Cross Reference below. In that case, it is a simple matter to determine the county from the cross reference. However, only the official US Postal Service city names are included in this index. We have also included a ZIP/City Cross Reference immediately following the City/County Cross Reference. If you know the ZIP Code but the city name does not appear in the City/County Cross Reference index, look up the ZIP Code in the ZIP/City Cross Reference, find the city name, then look up the city name in the City/County Cross Reference.

Vermont City/County Cross Reference

ADAMANT Washington
ALBANY Orleans
ALBURG Grand Isle
ARLINGTON Bennington
ASCUTNEY Windsor
AVERILL Essex
BAKERSFIELD Franklin
BARNARD Windsor
BARNET Caledonia
BARRE Washington
BARTON Orleans
BEEBE PLAIN Orleans
BEECHER FALLS Essex
BELLOWS FALLS Windham
BELMONT Rutland
BELVIDERE CENTER Lamoille
BENNINGTON Bennington
BENSON Rutland
BETHEL Windsor
BOMOSEEN Rutland
BONDVILLE Bennington
BRADFORD Orange
BRANDON (05733) Rutland(94), Addison(5)
BRATTLEBORO Windham
BRIDGEWATER Windsor
BRIDGEWATER CORNERS Windsor
BRIDPORT Addison
BRISTOL Addison
BROOKFIELD Orange
BROWNSVILLE Windsor
BURLINGTON Chittenden
CABOT (05647) Washington(98), Caledonia(1)
CAMBRIDGE (05444) Chittenden(94), Franklin(3), Lamoille(2)
CAMBRIDGEPORT Windham
CANAAN Essex
CASTLETON Rutland
CAVENDISH Windsor
CENTER RUTLAND Rutland
CHARLOTTE Chittenden
CHELSEA Orange
CHESTER Windsor
CHESTER DEPOT Windsor
CHITTENDEN Rutland
COLCHESTER Chittenden
CONCORD Essex
CORINTH Orange
COVENTRY Orleans
CRAFTSBURY Orleans
CRAFTSBURY COMMON Orleans
CUTTINGSVILLE Rutland
DANBY Rutland
DANVILLE Caledonia
DERBY Orleans
DERBY LINE Orleans
DORSET Bennington
EAST ARLINGTON Bennington
EAST BARRE (05649) Washington(93), Orange(6)
EAST BERKSHIRE Franklin
EAST BURKE Caledonia
EAST CALAIS Washington
EAST CHARLESTON Orleans
EAST CORINTH Orange
EAST DORSET (05253) Bennington(98), Rutland(1)
EAST DOVER Windham
EAST FAIRFIELD Franklin
EAST HARDWICK Caledonia
EAST HAVEN Essex
EAST MIDDLEBURY Addison
EAST MONTPELIER Washington
EAST POULTNEY Rutland
EAST RANDOLPH Orange
EAST RYEGATE Caledonia
EAST SAINT JOHNSBURY Caledonia
EAST THETFORD Orange
EAST WALLINGFORD Rutland
EDEN Lamoille
EDEN MILLS Lamoille
ELY Orange
ENOSBURG FALLS Franklin
ESSEX Chittenden
ESSEX JUNCTION Chittenden
FAIR HAVEN Rutland
FAIRFAX (05454) Chittenden(93), Franklin(6)
FAIRFIELD Franklin
FAIRLEE Orange
FERRISBURG Addison
FLORENCE Rutland
FOREST DALE Rutland
GAYSVILLE Windsor
GILMAN Essex
GLOVER Orleans
GRAFTON Windham
GRANBY Essex
GRAND ISLE Grand Isle
GRANITEVILLE (05654) Washington(88), Orange(11)
GRANVILLE Addison
GREENSBORO Orleans
GREENSBORO BEND Orleans
GROTON Caledonia
GUILDHALL Essex
HANCOCK Addison
HARDWICK Caledonia
HARTFORD Windsor
HARTLAND Windsor
HARTLAND FOUR CORNERS Windsor
HIGHGATE CENTER Franklin
HIGHGATE SPRINGS Franklin
HINESBURG Chittenden
HUNTINGTON Chittenden
HYDE PARK Lamoille
HYDEVILLE Rutland
IRASBURG Orleans
ISLAND POND Essex
ISLE LA MOTTE Grand Isle
JACKSONVILLE Windham
JAMAICA Windham
JEFFERSONVILLE Lamoille
JERICHO Chittenden
JOHNSON Lamoille
JONESVILLE Chittenden
KILLINGTON Rutland
LAKE ELMORE Lamoille
LONDONDERRY Windham
LOWELL Orleans
LOWER WATERFORD Caledonia
LUDLOW Windsor
LUNENBURG Essex
LYNDON Caledonia
LYNDON CENTER Caledonia
LYNDONVILLE Caledonia
MANCHESTER Bennington
MANCHESTER CENTER Bennington
MARLBORO Windham
MARSHFIELD Washington
MC INDOE FALLS Caledonia
MIDDLEBURY Addison
MIDDLETOWN SPRINGS Rutland
MILTON (05468) Chittenden(96), Franklin(3)
MONKTON Addison
MONTGOMERY Franklin
MONTGOMERY CENTER (05471) Franklin(97), Orleans(2)
MONTPELIER Washington
MORETOWN Washington
MORGAN Orleans
MORRISVILLE Lamoille
MOSCOW Lamoille
MOUNT HOLLY Rutland
NEW HAVEN Addison
NEWBURY Orange
NEWFANE Windham
NEWPORT Orleans
NEWPORT CENTER Orleans
NORTH BENNINGTON Bennington
NORTH CLARENDON Rutland
NORTH CONCORD Essex
NORTH FERRISBURG Addison
NORTH HARTLAND Windsor
NORTH HERO Grand Isle
NORTH HYDE PARK Lamoille
NORTH MONTPELIER Washington
NORTH POMFRET Windsor
NORTH POWNAL Bennington
NORTH SPRINGFIELD Windsor
NORTH THETFORD Orange
NORTH TROY Orleans
NORTHFIELD Washington
NORTHFIELD FALLS Washington
NORTON Essex
NORWICH Windsor
ORLEANS Orleans
ORWELL (05760) Addison(97), Rutland(2)
PASSUMPSIC Caledonia
PAWLET (05761) Rutland(98), Bennington(1)
PEACHAM Caledonia
PERKINSVILLE Windsor
PERU Bennington
PITTSFIELD (05762) Rutland(96), Windsor(3)
PITTSFORD Rutland
PLAINFIELD Washington
PLYMOUTH Windsor
POST MILLS Orange
POULTNEY Rutland
POWNAL Bennington
PROCTOR Rutland
PROCTORSVILLE Windsor
PUTNEY Windham
QUECHEE Windsor
RANDOLPH Orange
RANDOLPH CENTER Orange
READING Windsor
READSBORO Bennington
RICHFORD Franklin
RICHMOND Chittenden
RIPTON Addison
ROCHESTER (05767) Windsor(97), Addison(1)
ROXBURY (05669) Addison(91), Washington(7), Orange(1)
RUPERT Bennington
RUTLAND Rutland
SAINT ALBANS BAY Franklin
SAINT JOHNSBURY Caledonia
SAINT JOHNSBURY CENTER Caledonia
SALISBURY Addison
SAXTONS RIVER Windham
SHAFTSBURY Bennington
SHARON Windsor
SHEFFIELD Caledonia
SHELBURNE Chittenden
SHELDON Franklin
SHELDON SPRINGS Franklin
SHOREHAM Addison
SOUTH BARRE Washington
SOUTH BURLINGTON Chittenden
SOUTH HERO Grand Isle
SOUTH LONDONDERRY Windham
SOUTH NEWFANE Windham
SOUTH POMFRET Windsor
SOUTH ROYALTON Windsor
SOUTH RYEGATE Caledonia
SOUTH STRAFFORD Orange
SOUTH WOODSTOCK Windsor
SPRINGFIELD Windsor
STARKSBORO Addison
STOCKBRIDGE Windsor
STOWE Lamoille
STRAFFORD Orange
SUTTON Caledonia
SWANTON Franklin
TAFTSVILLE Windsor
THETFORD Orange
THETFORD CENTER Orange
TOWNSHEND Windham
TROY Orleans
TUNBRIDGE Orange
UNDERHILL Chittenden
UNDERHILL CENTER Chittenden
VERGENNES Addison
VERNON Windham
VERSHIRE Orange
WAITSFIELD Washington
WALLINGFORD Rutland
WARDSBORO Windham
WARREN Washington
WASHINGTON Orange
WATERBURY (05676) Washington(86), Chittenden(13)
WATERBURY Washington
WATERBURY CENTER Washington
WATERVILLE Lamoille
WEBSTERVILLE Washington
WELLS Rutland
WELLS RIVER Orange
WEST BURKE Caledonia
WEST CHARLESTON Orleans
WEST DANVILLE Caledonia
WEST DOVER Windham
WEST DUMMERSTON Windham
WEST FAIRLEE Orange
WEST GLOVER Orleans
WEST HALIFAX Windham
WEST HARTFORD Windsor
WEST NEWBURY Orange
WEST PAWLET (05775) Rutland(98), Bennington(2)
WEST RUPERT Bennington
WEST RUTLAND Rutland
WEST TOPSHAM Orange
WEST TOWNSHEND Windham

WEST WARDSBORO Windham
WESTFIELD Orleans
WESTFORD Chittenden
WESTMINSTER Windham
WESTMINSTER STATION Windham
WESTON Windsor
WHITE RIVER JUNCTION Windsor
WHITING (05778) Addison(96), Rutland(3)
WHITINGHAM Windham
WILDER Windsor
WILLIAMSTOWN Orange
WILLIAMSVILLE Windham
WILLISTON Chittenden
WILMINGTON Windham
WINDSOR Windsor
WINOOSKI Chittenden
WOLCOTT Lamoille
WOODBURY Washington
WOODSTOCK Windsor
WORCESTER Washington

Vermont ZIP/City Cross Reference

05001-05009 WHITE RIVER JUNCTION
05030-05030 ASCUTNEY
05031-05031 BARNARD
05032-05032 BETHEL
05033-05033 BRADFORD
05034-05034 BRIDGEWATER
05035-05035 BRIDGEWATER CORNERS
05036-05036 BROOKFIELD
05037-05037 BROWNSVILLE
05038-05038 CHELSEA
05039-05039 CORINTH
05040-05040 EAST CORINTH
05041-05041 EAST RANDOLPH
05042-05042 EAST RYEGATE
05043-05043 EAST THETFORD
05044-05044 ELY
05045-05045 FAIRLEE
05046-05046 GROTON
05047-05047 HARTFORD
05048-05048 HARTLAND
05049-05049 HARTLAND 4 CORNERS
05050-05050 MC INDOE FALLS
05051-05051 NEWBURY
05052-05052 NORTH HARTLAND
05053-05053 NORTH POMFRET
05054-05054 NORTH THETFORD
05055-05055 NORWICH
05056-05056 PLYMOUTH
05058-05058 POST MILLS
05059-05059 QUECHEE
05060-05060 RANDOLPH
05061-05061 RANDOLPH CENTER
05062-05062 READING
05065-05065 SHARON
05067-05067 SOUTH POMFRET
05068-05068 SOUTH ROYALTON
05069-05069 SOUTH RYEGATE
05070-05070 SOUTH STRAFFORD
05071-05071 SOUTH WOODSTOCK
05072-05072 STRAFFORD
05073-05073 TAFTSVILLE
05074-05074 THETFORD
05075-05075 THETFORD CENTER
05076-05076 EAST CORINTH
05077-05077 TUNBRIDGE
05079-05079 VERSHIRE
05081-05081 WELLS RIVER
05083-05083 WEST FAIRLEE
05084-05084 WEST HARTFORD
05085-05085 WEST NEWBURY
05086-05086 WEST TOPSHAM
05088-05088 WILDER
05089-05089 WINDSOR
05091-05091 WOODSTOCK
05101-05101 BELLOWS FALLS
05141-05141 CAMBRIDGEPORT
05142-05142 CAVENDISH
05143-05143 CHESTER
05144-05144 CHESTER DEPOT
05146-05146 GRAFTON
05148-05148 LONDONDERRY
05149-05149 LUDLOW
05150-05150 NORTH SPRINGFIELD
05151-05151 PERKINSVILLE
05152-05152 PERU
05153-05153 PROCTORSVILLE
05154-05154 SAXTONS RIVER
05155-05155 SOUTH LONDONDERRY
05156-05156 SPRINGFIELD
05158-05158 WESTMINSTER
05159-05159 WESTMINSTER STATION
05161-05161 WESTON
05201-05201 BENNINGTON
05250-05250 ARLINGTON
05251-05251 DORSET
05252-05252 EAST ARLINGTON
05253-05253 EAST DORSET
05254-05254 MANCHESTER
05255-05255 MANCHESTER CENTER
05257-05257 NORTH BENNINGTON
05260-05260 NORTH POWNAL
05261-05261 POWNAL
05262-05262 SHAFTSBURY
05301-05304 BRATTLEBORO
05340-05340 BONDVILLE
05341-05341 EAST DOVER
05342-05342 JACKSONVILLE
05343-05343 JAMAICA
05344-05344 MARLBORO
05345-05345 NEWFANE
05346-05346 PUTNEY
05350-05350 READSBORO
05351-05351 SOUTH NEWFANE
05352-05352 READSBORO
05353-05353 TOWNSHEND
05354-05354 VERNON
05355-05355 WARDSBORO
05356-05356 WEST DOVER
05357-05357 WEST DUMMERSTON
05358-05358 WEST HALIFAX
05359-05359 WEST TOWNSHEND
05360-05360 WEST WARDSBORO
05361-05361 WHITINGHAM
05362-05362 WILLIAMSVILLE
05363-05363 WILMINGTON
05401-05402 BURLINGTON
05403-05403 SOUTH BURLINGTON
05404-05404 WINOOSKI
05405-05406 BURLINGTON
05407-05407 SOUTH BURLINGTON
05439-05439 COLCHESTER
05440-05440 ALBURG
05441-05441 BAKERSFIELD
05442-05442 BELVIDERE CENTER
05443-05443 BRISTOL
05444-05444 CAMBRIDGE
05445-05445 CHARLOTTE
05446-05446 COLCHESTER
05447-05447 EAST BERKSHIRE
05448-05448 EAST FAIRFIELD
05449-05449 COLCHESTER
05450-05450 ENOSBURG FALLS
05451-05451 ESSEX
05452-05453 ESSEX JUNCTION
05454-05454 FAIRFAX
05455-05455 FAIRFIELD
05456-05456 FERRISBURG
05457-05457 FRANKLIN
05458-05458 GRAND ISLE
05459-05459 HIGHGATE CENTER
05460-05460 HIGHGATE SPRINGS
05461-05461 HINESBURG
05462-05462 HUNTINGTON
05463-05463 ISLE LA MOTTE
05464-05464 JEFFERSONVILLE
05465-05465 JERICHO
05466-05466 JONESVILLE
05468-05468 MILTON
05469-05469 MONKTON
05470-05470 MONTGOMERY
05471-05471 MONTGOMERY CENTER
05472-05472 NEW HAVEN
05473-05473 NORTH FERRISBURG
05474-05474 NORTH HERO
05476-05476 RICHFORD
05477-05477 RICHMOND
05478-05479 SAINT ALBANS
05481-05481 SAINT ALBANS BAY
05482-05482 SHELBURNE
05483-05483 SHELDON
05485-05485 SHELDON SPRINGS
05486-05486 SOUTH HERO
05487-05487 STARKSBORO
05488-05488 SWANTON
05489-05489 UNDERHILL
05490-05490 UNDERHILL CENTER
05491-05491 VERGENNES
05492-05492 WATERVILLE
05494-05494 WESTFORD
05495-05495 WILLISTON
05601-05633 MONTPELIER
05640-05640 ADAMANT
05641-05641 BARRE
05647-05647 CABOT
05648-05648 CALAIS
05649-05649 EAST BARRE
05650-05650 EAST CALAIS
05651-05651 EAST MONTPELIER
05652-05652 EDEN
05653-05653 EDEN MILLS
05654-05654 GRANITEVILLE
05655-05655 HYDE PARK
05656-05656 JOHNSON
05657-05657 LAKE ELMORE
05658-05658 MARSHFIELD
05660-05660 MORETOWN
05661-05661 MORRISVILLE
05662-05662 MOSCOW
05663-05663 NORTHFIELD
05664-05664 NORTHFIELD FALLS
05665-05665 NORTH HYDE PARK
05666-05666 NORTH MONTPELIER
05667-05667 PLAINFIELD
05669-05669 ROXBURY
05670-05670 SOUTH BARRE
05671-05671 WATERBURY
05672-05672 STOWE
05673-05673 WAITSFIELD
05674-05674 WARREN
05675-05675 WASHINGTON
05676-05676 WATERBURY
05677-05677 WATERBURY CENTER
05678-05678 WEBSTERVILLE
05679-05679 WILLIAMSTOWN
05680-05680 WOLCOTT
05681-05681 WOODBURY
05682-05682 WORCESTER
05701-05702 RUTLAND
05730-05730 BELMONT
05731-05731 BENSON
05732-05732 BOMOSEEN
05733-05733 BRANDON
05734-05734 BRIDPORT
05735-05735 CASTLETON
05736-05736 CENTER RUTLAND
05737-05737 CHITTENDEN
05738-05738 CUTTINGSVILLE
05739-05739 DANBY
05740-05740 EAST MIDDLEBURY
05741-05741 EAST POULTNEY
05742-05742 EAST WALLINGFORD
05743-05743 FAIR HAVEN
05744-05744 FLORENCE
05745-05745 FOREST DALE
05746-05746 GAYSVILLE
05747-05747 GRANVILLE
05748-05748 HANCOCK
05750-05750 HYDEVILLE
05751-05751 KILLINGTON
05753-05753 MIDDLEBURY
05757-05757 MIDDLETOWN SPRINGS
05758-05758 MOUNT HOLLY
05759-05759 NORTH CLARENDON
05760-05760 ORWELL
05761-05761 PAWLET
05762-05762 PITTSFIELD
05763-05763 PITTSFORD
05764-05764 POULTNEY
05765-05765 PROCTOR
05766-05766 MIDDLEBURY
05766-05766 RIPTON
05767-05767 ROCHESTER
05768-05768 RUPERT
05769-05769 SALISBURY
05770-05770 SHOREHAM
05772-05772 STOCKBRIDGE
05773-05773 WALLINGFORD
05774-05774 WELLS
05775-05775 WEST PAWLET
05776-05776 WEST RUPERT
05777-05777 WEST RUTLAND
05778-05778 WHITING
05819-05819 SAINT JOHNSBURY
05820-05820 ALBANY
05821-05821 BARNET
05822-05822 BARTON
05823-05823 BEEBE PLAIN
05824-05824 CONCORD
05825-05825 COVENTRY
05826-05826 CRAFTSBURY
05827-05827 CRAFTSBURY COMMON
05828-05828 DANVILLE
05829-05829 DERBY
05830-05830 DERBY LINE
05832-05832 EAST BURKE
05833-05833 EAST CHARLESTON
05836-05836 EAST HARDWICK
05837-05837 EAST HAVEN
05838-05838 EAST SAINT JOHNSBURY
05839-05839 GLOVER
05840-05840 GRANBY
05841-05841 GREENSBORO
05842-05842 GREENSBORO BEND
05843-05843 HARDWICK
05845-05845 IRASBURG
05846-05846 ISLAND POND
05847-05847 LOWELL
05848-05848 LOWER WATERFORD
05849-05849 LYNDON
05850-05850 LYNDON CENTER
05851-05851 LYNDONVILLE
05853-05853 MORGAN
05855-05855 NEWPORT
05857-05857 NEWPORT CENTER
05858-05858 NORTH CONCORD
05859-05859 NORTH TROY
05860-05860 ORLEANS
05861-05861 PASSUMPSIC
05862-05862 PEACHAM
05863-05863 SAINT JOHNSBURY CENTER
05866-05866 SHEFFIELD
05867-05867 SUTTON
05868-05868 TROY
05871-05871 WEST BURKE
05872-05872 WEST CHARLESTON
05873-05873 WEST DANVILLE
05874-05874 WESTFIELD
05875-05875 WEST GLOVER
05901-05901 AVERILL
05902-05902 BEECHER FALLS
05903-05903 CANAAN
05904-05904 GILMAN
05905-05905 GUILDHALL
05906-05906 LUNENBURG
05907-05907 NORTON

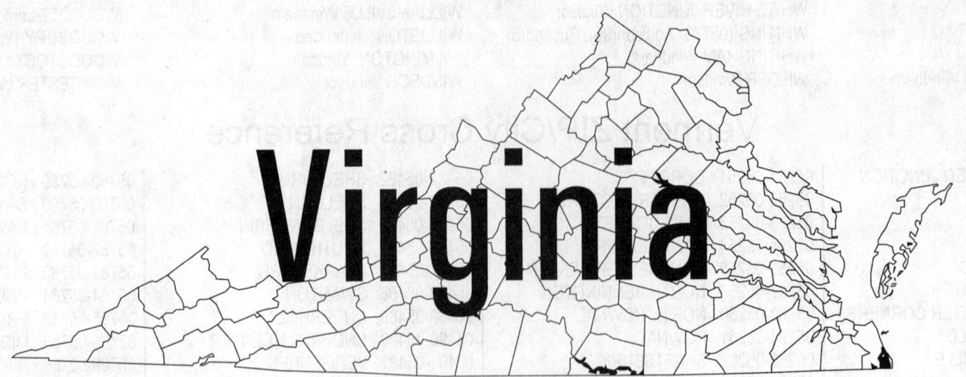

General Help Numbers:

Governor's Office

Capitol Bldg, 3rd Floor
Richmond, VA 23219
www.governor.virginia.gov

804-786-2211
Fax 804-371-6351
8:30AM-5:30PM

Attorney General's Office

900 E Main St
Richmond, VA 23219
www.oag.state.va.us

804-786-2071
Fax 804-786-1991
8:30AM-5PM

Legislative Records

Information & Public Relations
PO Box 406
Richmond, VA 23218
http://leg1.state.va.us/

804-698-1500
Fax 804-786-3215
8AM-5PM

State Archives

800 E. Broad St
Richmond, VA 23219-8000
www.lva.lib.va.us

804-692-3500
Fax 804-692-3556
9AM-5PM T-SA

State Specifics:

Capital:	Richmond Richmond City County
Time Zone:	EST
Number of Counties:	95
Population:	7,769,089
Web Site:	www.virginia.gov

State Agencies

Criminal Records

Virginia State Police, CCRE, PO Box 85076, Richmond, VA 23261-5076 (Courier - 7700 Midlothian Turnpike, Richmond, VA 23235); 804-674-6750, Fax- 804-674-8529; 8AM-5PM.

www.vsp.state.va.us Email questions to: Thomas.Turner@vsp.virginia.gov.

Indexing & Storage: Records available from 1966. New records available for inquiry in 1 to 3 days. 84% of all arrests in database have final dispositions recorded.

Searching: Section 19.2-389 Code of Virginia outlines that non-criminal entities can receive conviction only records. Certain agencies may receive complete records. The website gives complete details. Include in request- full name, date of birth, sex, race. The SSN is optional. The general public and employers not covered by statute must have a signed release from person of record, including notarized signatures for both subject and requester. These requesters must use form "SP-167" which is downloadable from website. This data not released- dismissals, nolled pressed, whenever the disposition is missing, or if not guilty Certain agencies receive complete records; non-criminal justice entities receive conviction only records.

Access by: mail, online.

Fee & Payment: The fee is $15.00 per name; $20 if sex offender registry search included. When required, statutorily-required fingerprint check is $13; $37 if an FBI fingerprint check is also required. Not for profit fee is $8.00. Fee payee- Virginia State Police. Prepayment required. Pay by certified check or money order. Personal checks not accepted. Visa and MasterCard accepted.

Mail search: Turnaround time- 1 to 2 weeks. General users must use the state form SP-167 which can be downloaded from www.vsp.state.va.us/FormsPublications.shtm. There is also a form SP-230 which you can use depending on your exempt status.

Online search: Certain entities, including screening companies, are can apply for online access via the NCJI System. The system is ONLY available to IN-STATE accounts and allows you to submit requests faster. Fees are same as manual submission-$15.00 per record or $20.00 SOR record search. Username and password required. There is a minimum usage requirement of 10 requests per month. Turnaround time 24-72 hours.

Statewide Court Records

Executive Secretary, Administrative Office of Courts, 100 N 9th St, 3rd Floor, Richmond, VA 23219; 804-786-6455, Fax- 804-786-4542; 8AM-5PM.

www.courts.state.va.us

Online search: There are several searchable systems for trial courts. None are statewide inclusive. In addition, each county must be searched separately and the records from General

District Courts are separated from Circuit Courts. For records from all but 3 General District Courts and over 90% of the Circuit Courts go to www.courts.state.va.us/ and click on type of court. Searching is by name only. Results show address of subject and the day and month of birth, but not year. A older dial-up access system known as LOPAS (Law Office & Public Access System) is available for all District and most Circuit Cts. Results include full name & address. This system may not be fully supported in the future. Call Marguerite Steele, 804-786-6455 for LOPAS details. Also, the home page offers access to Supreme Court and Appellate opinions.

Sexual Offender Registry

Virginia State Police - Criminal records, Sex Offender and Crimes Against Minors Registry, PO Box 85076, Richmond, VA 23261-5076; 804-674-6750, Fax- 804-674-8529; 8AM-5PM.

http://sex-offender.vsp.virginia.gov/sor/

Email questions to Lt.CJIS@vsp.virginia.gov.

Indexing & Storage: Records available from 1994 when the Registry was implemented. New records available for inquiry in 1 to 3 days.

Searching: There are two searches. Form SP-266 is a sex offender search. Form SP-167 is a combined sex offender and criminal record search. Include in request- name, race, sex, DOB; also helpful-SSN, residence address, notarized signature of requester. This data not released-DOB, SSN

Access by: mail, online.

Fee & Payment: $15.00 for the sex offender search (SP-266), but $8.00 if for a not-for profit. The combined search is $20.00, and $16.00 if for a not for profit. No fee for the Internet search. Prepayment required. No Personal checks, Visa, and MasterCard accepted.

Mail search: Turnaround time- 1 to 2 weeks. It is suggested to use one of the two forms described above.

Online search: Search by name, city, county or ZIP Code, or from a map at a link at the home page.

Incarceration Records

Virginia Department of Corrections, Records Unit, PO Box 26963, Richmond, VA 23261-6963 (Courier address- 6900 Atmore Drive, Richmond, VA 23225); 804-674-3131, 804-674-3000, Fax-804-674-3598; 8AM-5PM.

www.vadoc.state.va.us

Requesters can email requests to docmail@vadoc.virginia.gov.

Indexing & Storage: Records available on current and former inmates (only current if request is online). New records available for inquiry in up to 10 days.

Searching: Computer records go back to 1986 Include in request- full name; DOB and race are helpful. Location, conviction and sentencing information, and release dates are provided.

Access by: mail, phone, online.

Fee & Payment: There is no fee.

Mail search: Turnaround time- 1 to 2 days. SASE not required.

Phone search: A phone search provides inmate location, address, and approximate release date.

Online search: Visit http://www2.vipnet.org/cgi-bin/vadoc/doc.cgi for an Inmate Status/Locator to ascertain where an inmate is located. Searcher must have either the inmates' Department of Corrections' six digit identification number or exact first and last name, middle initial plus the inmate's race and sex. A DOC wanted/fugitives list is found at www.vadoc.virginia.gov/offenders/wanted/fugitive.shtm.

Corporation, LLC, LP, Fictitious Name, Business Trust Records

State Corporation Commission, Clerks Office, PO Box 1197, Richmond, VA 23218-1197 (Courier address- Tyler Bldg, 1st Floor, 1300 E Main St, Richmond, VA 23219); 804-371-9733 (Call Center), Fax- 804-371-9133; 8:15AM-5PM.

www.scc.virginia.gov/clk/bussrch.aspx

Indexing & Storage: Records available for all active entities on computer. Older inactive records must be researched from the State Library.

Searching: Records are public and are open for inspection. Original documents are microfilmed/imaged. Images are maintained permanently at the VA State Library. Include in request- full name of business. In addition to the articles of organization, business entity records available include: Annual Reports, Officers, Directors, DBAs, Prior (merged) names, Inactive (back to 1976 on computer) and Reserved names, and Registered Agents.

Access by: mail, phone, fax, in person, online.

Fee & Payment: Plain copies cost $.50 per page. Certification is $3.00 in addition to copy fee. A Good Standing (corporations only) or Certificate of Fact is $6.00. Fee payee- Treasurer of Virginia. Prepayment required. Requesters with billing accounts are encouraged to fax orders. Personal checks accepted, credit cards are not.

Mail search: Turnaround time- 3- 5 business days. Be sure to include your phone number and contact person with all written requests. SASE not required.

Phone search: No fee for telephone request. Agency will provide limited information (screen data only) and name availability over the phone.

Fax search: Turnaround time is 3-5 business days.

In person: Information is available via public access terminals and microfilm. Certificates of Fact and Good Standing are generally available in 3 to 5 business days.

Online search: An business entity search is at www.scc.virginia.gov/clk/bussrch.aspx. There is a limited amount of searchers who can be on at once, expect error messages during peak hours. The Docket Search is available for the status of any case, public filings (by date or by company), the Commission's case calendar, and selected public documents associated with cases before the Commission. Visit http://docket.scc.virginia.gov:8080/vaprod/main.asp. Images of business entity documents are not currently available for electronic or online viewing, except for Corporate Annual Reports. Also, search securities companies, agents, and franchises registered with the state at www.scc.virginia.gov/srf/index.aspx.

Other access: The database is available for bulk purchase. Call for details.

Trademarks, Service Marks

State Corporation Commission, Virginia Securities Division, PO Box 1197 (1300 Main St, 9th Fl), Richmond, VA 23218 (Courier address- 1300 Main St, 9th Fl, Richmond, VA 23219); 804-371-9187, Fax- 804-371-9911; 8:15AM-5PM.

www.scc.virginia.gov/srf/bus/tmsm.aspx

Indexing & Storage: Records available from the 1970s on a computerized basis. New records available for inquiry in less than 1 day.

Searching: Include in request- name of mark or owner.

Access by: mail, phone, fax, in person, online.

Fee & Payment: There is no search fee. The copy fee is $.50 per page. Fee payee- Treasurer of Virginia. Prepayment required. Personal checks accepted, credit cards are not.

Mail search: Turnaround time- 1 to 5 days. SASE not required.

Phone search: Limited to 1 or 2 searches per call.

Fax search: Fax searching available.

In person: in person requests available as time permits.

Online search: Search Trademarks and Service Marks at www.scc.virginia.gov/srf/bus/tmsm.aspx.

Uniform Commercial Code, Federal Tax Liens

UCC Division, State Corporation Commission, PO Box 1197, Richmond, VA 23218-1197 (Courier address- 1300 E Main St, 1st Floor, Richmond, VA 23219); 804-371-9733, Fax- 804-371-9133; 8:15AM-5PM.

www.scc.virginia.gov/clk/uccsrch.aspx

Indexing & Storage: Records available from the 1960s on microfiche and from mid 1992 on computer. New records available for inquiry in 5 days.

Searching: Use search request form UCC-11. The search includes federal tax liens on businesses if specifically requested. Federal tax liens on individuals and all state tax liens are filed at the local level, which may be a county or independent city. Include in request- debtor name. Turnaround time for copies of UCC searches is generally 5 days.

Access by: mail, phone, in person, online.

Fee & Payment: Search request is $7.00, copies are $.50 each, certification is an additional $3.00. Fee payee- State Corporation Commission. Prepayment required. Personal checks accepted, credit cards are not.

Mail search: Turnaround time- 5 days. A SASE is requested.

Phone search: No fee for telephone request. They will do limited verification on a yes or no basis.

In person: Counter service provides free access to microfilm records.

Online search: Their system is called Clerk's Information System (CIS) and is available free at www.scc.virginia.gov/clk/uccsrch.aspx. Images of UCC filings and tax liens are not available for electronic or online viewing. Collateral information is not available in CIS but can be obtained if a search is ordered and the associated fee paid.

State Tax Liens

Records not maintained by a state level agency.

All information is found at the local city or county level.

Sales Tax Registrations

Taxation Department, Sales Tax Licenses, PO Box 1115, Richmond, VA 23218-1115 (Courier address- 2220 W Broad St, Richmond, VA 23220); 804-367-8037, Fax- 804-254-6111; 8:30AM-4:30PM.

www.tax.virginia.gov

Registration information of businesses is available from the Corporation Commission.

Indexing & Storage: Records available for three years on computer, then put on microfilm for ten years, then purged.

Searching: This agency will provide no information without a written, signed, notarized authorization from the business itself; they will then provide the business name, address, phone, and tax permit number. Include in request- business name, tax permit number. iFile is an Internet filing application offered by the Virginia Department of Taxation and the Virginia Employment Commission that allows businesses to file and pay taxes online via the Internet.

Access by: mail.

Mail search: Turnaround time- 1 week to 10 days. SASE not required. No fee for mail request.

Birth Certificates

State Health Department, Office of Vital Records, PO Box 1000, Richmond, VA 23218-1000 (Courier address- 1601 Willow Lawn Drive, #275, Richmond, VA 23220); 804-662-6200; 8AM-4:45PM, 8AM-12 Sat.

www.vdh.virginia.gov/vital_Records/index.htm

An application for certification may be downloaded from the website.

Indexing & Storage: Records available from 1912 on. Records from 1853 to 1896 are located at the State Archives. New records available for inquiry immediately.

Searching: Recent vital records are available to immediate family members only. Birth records are public information 100 years after the date of the event. Include in request- name at birth, date of birth, place of birth, mother's maiden name, father's name, relationship to the person on the certificate, photocopy ID of requester. Include your area code and daytime phone number, your return address, and be sure to sign your request and provide copy of ID.

Access by: mail, phone, fax, in person.

Fee & Payment: The fee is $12.00 per certificate. If certificate needs to be authorized, fee is additional an $12.00 per authentication. Fee payee- The State Health Department. Prepayment required. Personal checks and major credit cards accepted.

Mail search: Turnaround time- 2-4 weeks. SASE not required.

Phone search: You must use a credit card. See Expedited Service.

Fax search: You must use a credit card. See Expedited Service.

In person: Turnaround time 15 minutes.

Expedited service: Expedited service available from VitalChek Express Service. Phone 877-572-6333, select option #2. Website: www.vitalchek.com; email: vitals.reply@vitalchek.com. Turnaround time- 2 - 5 days. Total fee including delivery is $49.25.

Death Records

State Health Department, Office of Vital Records, PO Box 1000, Richmond, VA 23218-1000 (Courier address- 1601 Willow Lawn Drive, #275, Richmond, VA 23220); 804-662-6200; 8AM-4:45PM, 8AM-12 Sat.

www.vdh.virginia.gov/vital_Records/index.htm

An application for certification may be downloaded from website. Also, recent death records are available at the local health department where the death certificate was filed

Indexing & Storage: Records available from 1912 on. Records from 1853 to 1896 are located at the State Archives. New records available for inquiry immediately.

Searching: Recent vital records are available to immediate family members only. Death records are public information 50 years after the date of the event. Include in request- name of deceased, date of death, place of death, relationship to the deceased, reason for the certificate. Include your area code and daytime phone number, your return address, and be sure to sign your request and provide copy of ID.

Access by: mail, phone, fax, in person.

Fee & Payment: The fee is $12.00 per certificate. If certificate needs to be authorized, fee is additional an $12.00 per authentication. Fee payee- The State Health Department. Prepayment required. Personal checks and major credit cards accepted.

Mail search: Turnaround time- 2 to 4 weeks. SASE not required.

Phone search: You must use a credit card. See Expedited Service.

Fax search: You must use a credit card. See Expedited Service.

In person: Turnaround time 15 minutes.

Expedited service: Expedited service available from VitalChek Express Service. Phone 877-572-6333, select option #2. Check their website at www.vitalchek.com; email address is vitals.reply@vitalchek.com. Turnaround time- 2 - 5 days. Total fee including delivery is $49.25.

Marriage Certificates

State Health Department, Office of Vital Records, PO Box 1000, Richmond, VA 23218-1000 (Courier address- 1601 Willow Lawn Drive, #275, Richmond, VA 23220); 804-662-6200; 8AM-4:45PM, 8AM-12 Sat.

www.vdh.virginia.gov/vital_Records/index.htm

An application for certification may be downloaded from website. Marriage and divorce records are available at the Circuit Court in which the event took place.

Indexing & Storage: Records available from 1853 to present. New records available for inquiry immediately.

Searching: Recent vital records are available to immediate family members only. Marriage records are public information 50 years after the date of the event. Include in request- name, date of marriage, place of marriage, relationship to the person on the certificate, reason for the certificate. Include your area code and daytime phone number, your return address, and be sure to sign your request.

Access by: mail, phone, fax, in person.

Fee & Payment: The fee is $12.00 per certificate. If certificate needs to be authorized, fee is additional an $12.00 per authentication. Fee payee- The State Health Department. Prepayment required. Personal checks and major credit cards accepted.

Mail search: Turnaround time- 2 to 4 weeks. SASE not required.

Phone search: You must use a credit card. See Expedited Service.

Fax search: You must use a credit card. See Expedited Service.

In person: Turnaround time 15 minutes.

Expedited service: Expedited service available from VitalChek Express Service. Phone 877-572-6333, select option #2. See their website at www.vitalchek.com or e-mail to vitals.reply@vitalchek.com for fee information. Turnaround time- 2 - 5 days. Total fee including delivery is $49.25.

Divorce Records

State Health Department, Office of Vital Records, PO Box 1000, Richmond, VA 23218-1000 (Courier address- 1601 Willow Lawn Drive, #275, Richmond, VA 23220); 804-662-6200; 8AM-4:45PM, 8AM-12 Sat.

www.vdh.virginia.gov/vital_Records/index.htm

An application for certification may be downloaded from website. Marriage and divorce records are available at the Circuit Court in which the event took place.

Indexing & Storage: Records available from 1918 to present. New records available for inquiry immediately.

Searching: Recent vital records are available to immediate family members only. Divorce records are public information 50 years after the date of the event. Include in request- name, date of divorce, place of divorce, relationship to the person on the certificate, reason for the certificate. Include your area code and daytime phone number, your return address, and be sure to sign your request and provide copy of ID.

Access by: mail, phone, fax, in person.

Fee & Payment: The fee is $12.00 per certificate. If certificate needs to be authorized, fee is additional an $12.00 per authentication. Fee payee- The State Health Department. Prepayment required. Personal checks and major credit cards accepted.

Mail search: Turnaround time- 2 to 4 weeks. SASE not required.

Phone search: You must use a credit card. See Expedited Service.

Fax search: You must use a credit card. See Expedited Service.

In person: Turnaround time 15 minutes.

Expedited service: Expedited service available from VitalChek Express Service. Phone 877-572-6333, select option #2. See their website at www.vitalchek.com or e-mail to vitals.reply@vitalchek.com for fee information. Turnaround time- 2 - 5 days. Total fee including delivery is $49.25.

Workers' Compensation Records

Workers' Compensation Commission, 1000 DMV Dr, Richmond, VA 23220; 804-367-8633, 877-664-2566, Fax- 804-367-9740; 8:15AM-5PM.

www.vwc.state.va.us

Commission opinions are available at the website.

Indexing & Storage: Records available from 1977 on. New records available for inquiry immediately.

Searching: To receive file copies, you must have a notarized release from the claimant unless requester is a party in a case. Awards issued are public information. Include in request- claimant name, SSN, claim number. All requests must be in writing. This data not released- sealed records.

Access by: mail, in person.

Fee & Payment: The search fee is $10.00 (prepaid). Copy fee for non-parties is $.50 per page for first 50 pages then $.25 ea add'l. $1.00 per page for imaged documents. Fee payee- Treasurer - State of Virginia. Prepayment required. Personal checks accepted, credit cards are not.

Mail search: Turnaround time- 1 to 4 days. An SASE is not required if records readily available.

In person: Request must be in writing.

Driver Records

Department of Motor Vehicles, Customer Records Work Center, PO Box 27412, Richmond, VA 23269; 804-367-0538, Fax- 804-367-0390; 8:30AM-5:30PM M-F; 8AM-12 noon S.

www.dmvnow.com/

Copies of tickets from non-computerized courts are available at this address for $8.00 per record only to driver or driver's authorized representative. Ticket information from computerized courts must be obtained from each court.

Indexing & Storage: Records available for 3 years for moving violations & misc convictions, 5 years for speeding & unauthorized use of a motor vehicle, 11 years for 3 reckless driving offenses and DWI, and 24 months from the complied date for suspensions. New records available for inquiry in 12 days from receipt.

Searching: Access to records follows DPPA guidelines. Casual requesters can only obtain records with consent using from CRD93 which can be downloaded form the web. Include in request- full name, date of birth, sex. Insurance records display 5 years, employment records the last 7 years. Surrendered licenses are purged after 5 years.

Access by: mail, phone, fax, in person, online.

Fee & Payment: The current fee is $8.00 for mail or walk-in requests and $7.00 for online requests. Add $5.00 for certification. Fee payee- Department of Motor Vehicles. Prepayment required. Personal checks and major credit cards accepted.

Mail search: Turnaround time- 5 days. The driver's name, DOB, and sex must "match" to get a record. Request must be on a DMV form or on letterhead. A SASE is requested.

Phone search: Requests accepted by phone.

Fax search: Requests accepted by fax.

In person: Normal turnaround time is while you wait. There are 62 field offices where records can be requested.

Online search: Online service is provided by the Virginia Interactive. Online reports are provided via the Internet on an interactive basis 24 hours daily. There is a $95 annual administrative fee and records are $7.00 each. Go to www.virginiainteractive.org/cmsportal2/ for more information (search "online services") or call 804-786-4718.

Other access: The agency offers several monitoring programs for employers. Call 804-497-7155 for details.

Vehicle Ownership & Registration

Department of Motor Vehicles, Vehicle Records Work Center, PO Box 27412, Richmond, VA 23269; 804-367-0538, Fax- 804-367-9705; 8:30AM-5:30PM M-F; 8AM-12PM S.

www.dmvnow.com/

Lien information is only released to lending institutions, collection agencies, and businesses.

Indexing & Storage: Records available for 10 years. New records available for inquiry in 12 days from receipt.

Searching: Casual requesters cannot obtain records without consent. High volume requesters must sign an agreement or contract and will be assigned a user number. Records cannot be purchased and resold for marketing purposes. Include in request- Form CRD93. Private investigators who are registered as compliance agents by the Department of Justice Services may obtain address information by submitting a license plate number.

Access by: mail, fax, in person, online.

Fee & Payment: The fee is $8.00 for vehicle ownership and registration information or $8.00 per vehicle on a name search. Add $5.00 for certification. Lien information is $8.00 to approved requesters. A verification search for vehicle buyers is $12.00. Fee payee- Department of Motor Vehicles. Prepayment required. Personal checks accepted, credit cards are not.

Mail search: Turnaround time- 7-10 days. A SASE is requested.

Fax search: Fax requests accepted.

In person: Turnaround time while you wait, usually limited to five at one time.

Online search: The online system, managed by the Virginia Interactive, open 24 hours daily. There is an annual $95.00 administration fee and records are $7.00 each. All accounts must be approved by both the DMV and Virginia Interactive. Call 804-786-4718 to request an information use agreement application. The URL is www.virginiainteractive.org/cmsportal2/.

Also, a $12.00 vehicle verification search is for prospective vehicle buyers available at https://www.dmv.virginia.gov/dmvnet/ppi/intro.asp.

Other access: Bulk release of vehicle or ownership information is not available except for statistical and vehicle recall purposes.

Accident Reports

Department of Motor Vehicles, Customer Records Work Center, Rm 514, PO Box 27412, Richmond, VA 23269-0001; 804-367-0538, 866-368-5463, Fax- 804-367-0390; 8:30AM-5PM M-F; 8:30AM-12:30PM Sat.

www.dmvnow.com

Indexing & Storage: Records available for 40 months to present. Records are scanned into computer. New records available for inquiry in 25-30 days.

Searching: All requests must be in writing. Records are only released to those involved or with a tangible interest. Include in request- full name of driver, date of accident, location of accident.

Access by: mail, fax, in person.

Fee & Payment: The fee is $8.00 per report. Prepayment is required, except for attorneys and insurance companies. Fee payee- Department of Motor Vehicles. Prepayment required. Personal checks and major credit cards accepted.

Mail search: Turnaround time- 5 days. SASE is not required.

Fax search: Must pay with a credit card or bill to Fed tax ID#.

In person: Turnaround time is while you wait, if personnel available.

Vessel Ownership & Registration

Game & Inland Fisheries Dept, Boat Registration Dept, 4010 W Broad St, Richmond, VA 23230; 804-367-6135, Fax- 804-367-1064; 8:15AM-5PM.

www.dgif.virginia.gov

The records are open to the public to the extent that information is released with either a registration or hull #. FOIA requests are directed to 804-267-8341

Indexing & Storage: Records available from 1960 to the present. Records are indexed on computer from 1989 to the present. All motorized boats must be registered and titled. Non-motorized sailboats if over 18 ft are titled. Lien information will show on record.

Searching: Include in request- either registration or hull #. This data not released- SSN, credit card numbers.

Access by: mail, phone, fax, in person, online.

Fee & Payment: If history or extensive research is required, there is a fee of $50.00 per boat. There is no fee for a simple registration search. Fee payee- Game & Inland Fisheries Dept. Prepayment required. Personal checks and credit cards accepted.

Mail search: Turnaround time- 3 to 4 working days. SASE not required.

Phone search: They will report the owner if a boat number is given, or if a lien exists, on a single request basis.

Fax search: Call first, depends on need.

In person: Turnaround time is usually immediate.

Online search: The VA boat registration database may be searched on the web at www.virginiainteractive.org/cmsportal2/. There are two options, one for commercial use, and for non-commercial use. Both require a subscription, which is $95.00 a year and record fees are incurred. Additional services are provided.

Other access: CDs with data can be sold to approved requesters.

Legislation Records

Legislative Reference Center, General Assembly Building, 2nd Floor, 910 Capitol Street, Richmond, VA 23219; 804-786-3591 (Reference Center), 804-698-1500 (House Information), 804-698-7410 (Senate Information), Fax- 804-371-0169; 8AM-5PM.

http://dls.state.va.us/lrc.htm?OpenDocument within Capitol Square, on the corner of 9th and Broad Streets

Indexing & Storage: Records available from 1994 on computer.

Searching: A request in writing to the Clerk of the House of Delegates is necessary to obtain a member's voting record and statements of economic interests. Include in request- bill number, topic of bill, year. The name of the bill sponsor (patron) and topic of bill are helpful.

Access by: mail, phone, in person, online.

Fee & Payment: There is no search fee or copy fee. Fee payee- Treasurer of Virginia. Personal checks accepted, credit cards are not.

Mail search: Turnaround time- 1 to 2 days. SASE not required.

Phone search: Records are available by phone.

In person: Simple requests may be processed while you wait.

Online search: Bill status information can be found on the website. There is no fee. Visit http://leg1.state.va.us/000/src.htm for the Code of Virginia.

Other access: Lists of General Assembly members, information on General Assembly, documents summarizing bills introduced and enacted are all available through this office.

Voter Registration

State Board of Elections, 200 N 9th Street, #101, Richmond, VA 23219-3485; 804-786-6551, 804-864-8901, Fax- 804-371-0194; 8:30AM-5PM.

www.sbe.virginia.gov/cms/

Individual searches must be done at the county or city level with the General Registrars.

Searching: The state will sell all or portions of its statewide database (95 counties, 39 cities) to authorized entities meaning candidates, political parties, etc.

Access by: mail, online.

Mail search: Limited record data is released.

Online search: Verify registration status at www.sbe.virginia.gov/cms/Voter_Information/Index.html.

GED Certificates

Virginia Dept of Education, GED Services, PO Box 2120, Richmond, VA 23218-2120; 804-786-4642, 804-371-2334, Fax- 804-225-3352; 8:15AM-5PM.

www.doe.virginia.gov/

The records are not considered open to the public; a signed release is required. Questions can be directed to gedinfo@doe.virginia.gov.

Indexing & Storage: Records available from 1942. New records available for inquiry in 1 week.

Searching: Include in request- signed release, name at time of test, DOB, SSN, location and year of test.

Access by: mail, in person.

Fee & Payment: There is a $5.00 fee for a verification or for a transcript, the fee is $10.00 for a certified certificate. Fee payee- Treasurer of Virginia Prepayment required. Personal checks are accepted. No credit cards accepted.

Mail search: Turnaround time- 1 week. A SASE is not requested.

In person: Turnaround time is typically immediate.

Hunting & Fishing License Information

Records not maintained by a state level agency.

The Game & Inland Fisheries Dept does not have a central database because there are hundreds of vendors throughout the state that sell licenses.

Virginia State Licensing Agencies

For details about the agency responsible for licensing/certifying/registering an item below or in the Agency Quick Finder section, match an item's number with the number of the agency in the *Licensing Agency Information* section.

Virginia Licenses Searchable Online

Acupuncturist #6 ..... http://www2.vipnet.org/dhp/cgi-bin/search_publicdb.cgi
Alcoholic Beverage Distributor #1 ..... www.abc.virginia.gov/licenseeSearch/jsp/controller.jsp
Architect #10 ..... www.dpor.virginia.gov/regulantlookup/selection_input.cfm
Asbestos-related Occupation #10 ..... www.dpor.virginia.gov/regulantlookup/selection_input.cfm
Athletic Trainer #6 ..... http://www2.vipnet.org/dhp/cgi-bin/search_publicdb.cgi
Attorney/Attorney Assoc #14 ..... www.vsb.org/attorney/attSearch.asp?S=D
Auctioneer/Auction Firm #10 ..... www.dpor.virginia.gov/regulantlookup/selection_input.cfm
Audiologist #6 ..... http://www2.vipnet.org/dhp/cgi-bin/search_publicdb.cgi
Bank #7 ..... www.scc.virginia.gov/bfi/index.aspx
Barber/Barber School/Business #10 ..... www.dpor.virginia.gov/regulantlookup/selection_input.cfm
Boxer #10 ..... www.dpor.virginia.gov/regulantlookup/selection_input.cfm
Boxing/Wresting Occupation #10 ..... www.dpor.virginia.gov/regulantlookup/selection_input.cfm
Carpenter #10 ..... www.dpor.virginia.gov/regulantlookup/selection_input.cfm
Cemetery Company/Seller #10 ..... www.dpor.virginia.gov/regulantlookup/selection_input.cfm
Check Casher #7 ..... www.scc.virginia.gov/bfi/index.aspx
Chiropractor #6 ..... http://www2.vipnet.org/dhp/cgi-bin/search_publicdb.cgi
Clinical Nurse Specialist #6 ..... http://www2.vipnet.org/dhp/cgi-bin/search_publicdb.cgi
Contractor #10 ..... www.dpor.virginia.gov/regulantlookup/selection_input.cfm
Cosmetic Procedure Certification #6 ..... http://www2.vipnet.org/dhp/cgi-bin/search_publicdb.cgi
Cosmetologist/Cosmo School/Firm #10 ..... www.dpor.virginia.gov/regulantlookup/selection_input.cfm
Counselor, Professional #6 ..... http://www2.vipnet.org/dhp/cgi-bin/search_publicdb.cgi
Crematory #6 ..... http://www2.vipnet.org/dhp/cgi-bin/search_publicdb.cgi
Dental Hygienist #6 ..... http://www2.vipnet.org/dhp/cgi-bin/search_publicdb.cgi
Dentist #6 ..... http://www2.vipnet.org/dhp/cgi-bin/search_publicdb.cgi
Embalmer #6 ..... http://www2.vipnet.org/dhp/cgi-bin/search_publicdb.cgi
Engineer #10 ..... www.dpor.virginia.gov/regulantlookup/selection_input.cfm
Fair Housing #10 ..... www.dpor.virginia.gov/regulantlookup/selection_input.cfm
Funeral Director/Establ./Trainee #6 ..... http://www2.vipnet.org/dhp/cgi-bin/search_publicdb.cgi
Funeral Service Provider #6 ..... http://www2.vipnet.org/dhp/cgi-bin/search_publicdb.cgi
Gas Fitter #10 ..... www.dpor.virginia.gov/regulantlookup/selection_input.cfm
Geologist #10 ..... www.dpor.virginia.gov/regulantlookup/selection_input.cfm
Hair Braider #10 ..... www.dpor.virginia.gov/regulantlookup/selection_input.cfm
Hearing Aid Specialist #10 ..... www.dpor.virginia.gov/regulantlookup/selection_input.cfm
Home Inspector #10 ..... www.dpor.virginia.gov/regulantlookup/selection_input.cfm
Humane Society #6 ..... http://www2.vipnet.org/dhp/cgi-bin/search_publicdb.cgi
Interior Designer #10 ..... www.dpor.virginia.gov/regulantlookup/selection_input.cfm
Investment Advisor/Advisor Agency #12 ..... www.scc.virginia.gov/srf/index.aspx
Landscape Architect #10 ..... www.dpor.virginia.gov/regulantlookup/selection_input.cfm
Lead-Related Occupation #10 ..... www.dpor.virginia.gov/regulantlookup/selection_input.cfm
Lobbyist #11 ..... http://secure01.virginiainteractive.org/lobbyist/cgi-bin/search_lobbyist.cgi
Marriage & Family Therapist #6 ..... http://www2.vipnet.org/dhp/cgi-bin/search_publicdb.cgi
Massage Therapist #6 ..... http://www2.vipnet.org/dhp/cgi-bin/search_publicdb.cgi
Medical Doctor #6 ..... http://www2.vipnet.org/dhp/cgi-bin/search_publicdb.cgi
Medical Equipment Supplier #6 ..... http://www2.vipnet.org/dhp/cgi-bin/search_publicdb.cgi
Medical Wholesaler/Mfg #6 ..... http://www2.vipnet.org/dhp/cgi-bin/search_publicdb.cgi
Money Transmitter #7 ..... www.scc.virginia.gov/bfi/index.aspx
Mortgage Lender/Broker #7 ..... www.scc.virginia.gov/bfi/index.aspx
Nail Technician #10 ..... www.dpor.virginia.gov/regulantlookup/selection_input.cfm
Nurse/Nurse's Aide #6 ..... http://www2.vipnet.org/dhp/cgi-bin/search_publicdb.cgi
Nurse-LPN #6 ..... http://www2.vipnet.org/dhp/cgi-bin/search_publicdb.cgi
Nurse-RN #6 ..... http://www2.vipnet.org/dhp/cgi-bin/search_publicdb.cgi
Nursing Home Administ'tor/Preceptor #6 ..... http://www2.vipnet.org/dhp/cgi-bin/search_publicdb.cgi
Occupational Therapist #6 ..... http://www2.vipnet.org/dhp/cgi-bin/search_publicdb.cgi
Optician #10 ..... www.dpor.virginia.gov/regulantlookup/selection_input.cfm
Optometrist #6 ..... http://www2.vipnet.org/dhp/cgi-bin/search_publicdb.cgi
Oral/Maxillofacial Surgeon #6 ..... http://www2.vipnet.org/dhp/cgi-bin/search_publicdb.cgi

Osteopathic Physician #6	http://www2.vipnet.org/dhp/cgi-bin/search_publicdb.cgi
Payday Lender #7	www.scc.virginia.gov/bfi/index.aspx
Pharmacist/Pharmacy #6	http://www2.vipnet.org/dhp/cgi-bin/search_publicdb.cgi
Physical Therapist #6	http://www2.vipnet.org/dhp/cgi-bin/search_publicdb.cgi
Physician #6	http://www2.vipnet.org/dhp/cgi-bin/search_publicdb.cgi
Physician Assistant #6	http://www2.vipnet.org/dhp/cgi-bin/search_publicdb.cgi
Pilot, Branch #10	www.dpor.virginia.gov/regulantlookup/selection_input.cfm
Podiatrist #6	http://www2.vipnet.org/dhp/cgi-bin/search_publicdb.cgi
Polygraph Examiner #10	www.dpor.virginia.gov/regulantlookup/selection_input.cfm
Prescriptive Authorization #6	http://www2.vipnet.org/dhp/cgi-bin/search_publicdb.cgi
Property Association #10	www.dpor.virginia.gov/regulantlookup/selection_input.cfm
Psychologist at School #6	http://www2.vipnet.org/dhp/cgi-bin/search_publicdb.cgi
Psychologist, Clinical/Applied #6	http://www2.vipnet.org/dhp/cgi-bin/search_publicdb.cgi
Psychology School #6	http://www2.vipnet.org/dhp/cgi-bin/search_publicdb.cgi
Radiologic Technologist-limited #6	http://www2.vipnet.org/dhp/cgi-bin/search_publicdb.cgi
Real Estate Agent/Business/School #10	www.dpor.virginia.gov/regulantlookup/selection_input.cfm
Real Estate Appraiser/Appraiser Firm #10	www.dpor.virginia.gov/regulantlookup/selection_input.cfm
Rehabilitation Provider #6	http://www2.vipnet.org/dhp/cgi-bin/search_publicdb.cgi
Respiratory Care Practitioner #6	http://www2.vipnet.org/dhp/cgi-bin/search_publicdb.cgi
Savings Institution #7	www.scc.virginia.gov/bfi/index.aspx
School Guidance Counselor #8	https://p1pe.doe.virginia.gov/tinfo/
School Library Media Specialist #8	https://p1pe.doe.virginia.gov/tinfo/
School Principal/Superintendent #8	https://p1pe.doe.virginia.gov/tinfo/
Securities Broker/Dealer/Agent #12	www.scc.virginia.gov/srf/index.aspx
Securities Brokerage #12	www.scc.virginia.gov/srf/index.aspx
Social Worker, Clinical/Registered #6	http://www2.vipnet.org/dhp/cgi-bin/search_publicdb.cgi
Soil Scientist #10	www.dpor.virginia.gov/regulantlookup/selection_input.cfm
Speech Pathologist at School #6	http://www2.vipnet.org/dhp/cgi-bin/search_publicdb.cgi
Speech Pathologist/Audiologist #6	http://www2.vipnet.org/dhp/cgi-bin/search_publicdb.cgi
Substance Abuse Counselor #6	http://www2.vipnet.org/dhp/cgi-bin/search_publicdb.cgi
Substance Abuse Treatm't Practitioner #6	http://www2.vipnet.org/dhp/cgi-bin/search_publicdb.cgi
Surveyor, Land #10	www.dpor.virginia.gov/regulantlookup/selection_input.cfm
Tattoo Artist/Body Piercing #10	www.dpor.virginia.gov/regulantlookup/selection_input.cfm
Teacher #8	https://p1pe.doe.virginia.gov/tinfo/
Tradesman #10	www.dpor.virginia.gov/regulantlookup/selection_input.cfm
University Limited Medical License #6	http://www2.vipnet.org/dhp/cgi-bin/search_publicdb.cgi
Veterinarian/Veterinary Technician #6	http://www2.vipnet.org/dhp/cgi-bin/search_publicdb.cgi
Warehouser, Medical #6	http://www2.vipnet.org/dhp/cgi-bin/search_publicdb.cgi
Waste Management Facility Operator #10	www.dpor.virginia.gov/regulantlookup/selection_input.cfm
Waste Water Plant Operator #10	www.dpor.virginia.gov/regulantlookup/selection_input.cfm
Wax Technician #10	www.dpor.virginia.gov/regulantlookup/selection_input.cfm
Wetlands Delineator #10	www.dpor.virginia.gov/regulantlookup/selection_input.cfm
Wrestler #10	www.dpor.virginia.gov/regulantlookup/selection_input.cfm

Virginia Licensing Quick Finder

Acupuncturist #6	804-662-9908
Alarm Respondent #5	804-786-0460
Alcoholic Beverage Distributor #1	804-213-4400
Architect #10	804-367-8506
Armored Car Personnel #5	804-786-0460
Asbestos-related Occupation #10	804-367-8595
Athletic Trainer #6	804-662-9924
Attorney/Attorney Assoc #14	804-775-0500
Auctioneer/Auction Firm #10	804-367-8506
Audiologist #6	804-662-9907
Bank #7	804-371-9704
Barber/Barber School/Business #10	804-367-8509
Boxer #10	804-367-0186
Boxing/Wresting Occupation #10	804-367-0186
Carpenter #10	804-367-8511
Cemetery Company/Seller #10	804-367-0115
Central Station Dispatcher #5	804-786-0460
Check Casher #7	804/371-9701
Chiropractor #6	804-662-9908
Clinical Nurse Specialist #6	804-662-9909
Contractor #10	804-367-8511
Cosmetic Procedure Certification #6	804-662-9906
Cosmetologist/Cosmo Sch'l/Firm #10	804-367-8509
Counselor, Professional #6	804-662-9907
Credit Union #7	804-371-9267
Crematory #6	804-662-9900
Dental Hygienist #6	804-662-9906
Dentist #6	804-662-9906
Electr'c Security Sales Rep/Tech/Asst #5	804-786-0460
Embalmer #6	804-662-9907
Emergency Medical Technician #15	804-864-7628
EMT Enhanced/Intermediate #15	804-864-7628
Engineer #10	804-367-8506
Fair Housing #10	804-367-8530
Funeral Director/Establ./Trainee #6	804-662-9907
Funeral Service Provider #6	804-662-9907
Gas Fitter #10	804-367-8511
Geologist #10	804-367-0524
Hair Braider #10	804-367-8509
Hearing Aid Specialist #10	804-367-8509
Home Inspector #10	804-367-8595
Horse Racing Professional #13	804-966-7400
Humane Society #6	804-662-9911
Insurance Agent/Agency #2	804-371-9631
Interior Designer #10	804-367-8506
Investment Advisor/Advisor Agncy #12	804-371-9686
Landscape Architect #10	804-367-8506
Lead-Related Occupation #10	804-367-8595
Lobbyist #11	804-786-2441
Marriage & Family Therapist #6	804-662-9912
Massage Therapist #6	804-662-9912
Medical Doctor #6	804-662-9908
Medical Equipment Supplier #6	804-662-9911
Medical Wholesaler/Mfg #6	804-662-9911
Money Transmitter #7	804/371-9701
Mortgage Lender/Broker #7	804/371-9701
Nail Technician #10	804-367-8509
Notary Public #9	804-786-2441
Nurse/Nurse's Aide #6	804-662-9909
Nurse-LPN #6	804-662-9909
Nurse-RN #6	804-662-9909
Nursing Home Admin'r/Preceptor #6	804-662-9906
Occupational Therapist #6	804-662-9908
Optician #10	804-367-8509
Optometrist #6	804-662-9910

Oral/Maxillofacial Surgeon #6 804-662-9906
Osteopathic Physician #6.....................804-662-9908
Paramedic #15......................................804-864-7628
Payday Lender #7...................................804/371-9701
Personal Protection Specialist #5.........804-786-0460
Pesticide Applicator (Private) #4.........804-786-3798
Pesticide Applicat'r/Firm #4.................804-786-3798
Pharmacist/Pharmacy #6.....................804-662-9911
Physical Therapist #6..........................804-662-9911
Physician #6..804-662-9908
Physician Assistant #6.........................804-662-9908
Pilot, Branch #10..................................804-367-8514
Podiatrist #6..804-662-9908
Polygraph Examiner #10.......................804-367-6166
Prescriptive Authorization #6...............804-662-9908
Private Investigator #5..........................804-786-0460
Property Association #10......................804-367-8510
Psychologist at School #6.....................804-662-9913
Psychologist, Clinical/Applied #6..........804-662-9913
Psychology School #6............................804-662-9913
Radiologic Technologist-limited #6......804-662-9908
Real Estate Agent/Business/Sch'l #10..804-367-8526
Real Estate Apprais'r/Apprais.Firm #10 804-367-2039
Rehabilitation Provider #6...................804-662-9912
Respiratory Care Practitioner #6..........804-662-9908
Savings Institution #7..........................804-371-9704
School Guidance Counselor #8.............804-371-2522
School Library Media Specialist #8......804-371-2522
School Principal/Superintendent #8.....804-371-2522
Securities Broker/Dealer/Dealer Agent #12
....804-371-9686
Securities Brokerage #12.....................804-371-9187
Security Canine Handler #5.................804-786-0460
Security Officer, Unarmed/Armed #5...804-786-0460
Security Technic'n (elect. security) #5.804-786-0460
Social Worker, Clinical/Registered #6..804-662-9914
Soil Scientist #10..................................804-367-8506
Special Conservator of the Peace #5...804-786-0460
Speech Pathologist at School #6.........804-662-9900
Speech Pathologist/Audiologist #6.......804-662-9111
Substance Abuse Counselor #6..........804-662-9912
Substance Abuse Treatment Practitioner #6
....804-662-9912
Surveyor, Land #10...............................804-367-8506
Tattoo Artist/Body Piercing #10..........804-367-8509
Teacher #8..804-371-2522
Tradesman #10......................................804-367-8511
Unarmed Security Officer/Courier #5...804-786-0460
University Limited Medical License #6. 804-662-9900
Veterinarian/Veterinary Technician #6. 804-662-9915
Veterinary Facility #6..........................804-662-9915
Warehouser, Medical #6.......................804-662-9900
Waste Management Facility Operator #10
....804-367-0219
Waste Water Plant Operator #10.........804-367-2176
Wax Technician #10..............................804-367-8509
Wetlands Delineator #10......................804-367-8506
Wrestler #10..804-367-0186

Virginia Licensing Agency Information

#1 Alcoholic Beverage Control Board, PO Box 27491 (2901 Hermitage Rd), Richmond, VA 23261-7491; 804-213-4577, Fax- 804-213-4586. Hours- 8:15AM-5PM. www.abc.virginia.gov

#2 Bureau of Insurance, Agent Regulation, PO Box 1157 (Tyler Bldg, 1300 E Main St), Richmond, VA 23218; 804-371-9631, Fax- 804-371-9349. www.scc.virginia.gov/division/boi/

#4 Department of Agriculture & Consumer Services, Office of Pesticide Services, 102 Governor St, 1st Fl, Richmond, VA 23219; 804-786-3798, 371-6558, Fax- 804.786.9149. www.vdacs.virginia.gov/pesticides/index.shtml 786-9149 is the fax number for license applications.

#5 Department of Criminal Justice, Private Security, PO Box 1300 (202 N 9th St, 5th Fl), Richmond, VA 23218; 804-786-4700, Fax- 804-786-6344. Hours- 8:30AM-4:30PM. www.dcjs.virginia.gov/pss/ Private Security Services may apply or renew at www.dcjs.virginia.gov/pss/howto/index.cfm?menuLevel=9&mID=30.

#6 Department of Health Professions, 9960 Mayland Dr, Ste 300, Perimeter Ctr, Richmond, VA 23233-1463; 804-367-4400, Fax- 804-527-4475. 8:15AM-5PM. www.dhp.virginia.gov Search data at- http://www2.vipnet.org/dhp/cgi-bin/search_publicdb.cgi Automated License Verification: 804-270-6836. License/case decision alert service tracks licensing status and disciplinary actions for healthcare people at www.vipnet.org/dhp/demo/dhpserviceinfo.html to join. Licensee lists also available.

#7 Corporation Commission, Bureau of Financial Institutions, PO Box 640 (1300 E Main St, 8th Fl, Tyler Bldg), Richmond, VA 23218-0640; 804-371-9657, Fax- 804-371-9416. Hours- 8:15AM-5PM. www.scc.virginia.gov/bfi/index.aspx Search data at- www.scc.virginia.gov/bfi/index.aspx

#8 Department of Education, Division of Teacher Education & Licensure, PO Box 2120 (101 N 14th St, James Monroe Bldg), Richmond, VA 23218-2120; 804-371-2522, Fax- 804-786-6759. www.doe.virginia.gov/ Search data at- https://p1pe.doe.virginia.gov/tinfo/

#9 Secretary of the Commonwealth, Notary Public Division, PO Box 1795, Richmond, VA 23218; 804-786-2441, Fax- 804-371-0017. www.soc.state.va.us/OfficialDocuments/Notary/notary.cfm

#10 Department of Professional & Occupation Regulation, 9960 Mayland Dr, Ste 400, Richmond, VA 23233; 804-367-8500, Fax- 804-367-9537. Hours- 8:15AM-5PM. www.dpor.virginia.gov Search data at- www.dpor.virginia.gov/regulantlookup/selection_input.cfm

#11 Secretary of the Commonwealth, PO Box 2454 (1111 E Broad St, 4th Fl), Richmond, VA 23218; 804-781-2441, Fax- 804-371-0017. www.soc.state.va.us Search data at- http://secure01.virginiainteractive.org/lobbyist/cgi-bin/search_lobbyist.cgi

#12 Corporation Commission, Securities Division, PO Box 1197 (1300 E Main, 9th Fl), Richmond, VA 23218; 804-371-9187, Fax- 804-371-9911. www.scc.virginia.gov/srf/index.aspx Search data at- www.scc.virginia.gov/srf/index.aspx

#13 Racing Commission, 10700 Horsemens Rd, New Kent, VA 23124; 804-966-7400, Fax- 804-966-7418. Hours- 8:30AM-4:30PM. www.vrc.virginia.gov

#14 State Bar Association, 707 E Main St, #1500, Richmond, VA 23219-2800; 804-775-0500, Fax- 804-775-0501. Hours- 8:15AM-4:45PM. www.vsb.org Search data at- www.vsb.org/attorney/attSearch.asp?S=D

#15 Department of Health, Emergency Medical Services, 109 Governor St, Ste UB-55, Richmond, VA 23219; 804-864-7600, Fax- 804-864-7580. Hours- 8:30AM-5PM. www.vdh.virginia.gov/OEMS/

Virginia Federal Courts

The following list indicates the district and division name for each county in the state. If the bankruptcy court location is different from the district court, then the location of the bankruptcy court appears in parentheses.

Virginia County/Court Cross Reference

County	District	Division
Accomack	Eastern	Norfolk
Albemarle	Western	Charlottesville (Lynchburg)
Alexandria City	Eastern	Alexandria
Alleghany	Western	Roanoke (Harrisonburg)
Amelia	Eastern	Richmond
Amherst	Western	Lynchburg
Appomattox	Western	Lynchburg
Arlington	Eastern	Alexandria
Augusta	Western	Harrisonburg
Bath	Western	Harrisonburg
Bedford	Western	Lynchburg
Bedford City	Western	Lynchburg
Bland	Western	Roanoke
Botetourt	Western	Roanoke
Bristol City	Western	Abingdon (Roanoke)
Brunswick	Eastern	Richmond
Buchanan	Western	Abingdon (Roanoke)
Buckingham	Western	Lynchburg
Buena Vista City	Western	Lynchburg (Harrisonburg)
Campbell	Western	Lynchburg
Caroline	Eastern	Richmond
Carroll	Western	Roanoke
Charles City	Eastern	Richmond
Charlotte	Western	Danville (Lynchburg)
Charlottesville City	Western	Charlottesville (Lynchburg)
Chesapeake City	Eastern	Norfolk
Chesterfield	Eastern	Richmond
Clarke	Western	Harrisonburg
Clifton Forge City	Western	Roanoke (Harrisonburg)
Colonial Heights City	Eastern	Richmond
Covington City	Western	Roanoke (Harrisonburg)
Craig	Western	Roanoke
Culpeper	Western	Charlottesville (Lynchburg)
Cumberland	Western	Lynchburg
Danville City	Western	Danville (Lynchburg)
Dickenson	Western	Big Stone Gap (Roanoke)
Dinwiddie	Eastern	Richmond
Emporia City	Eastern	Richmond
Essex	Eastern	Richmond
Fairfax	Eastern	Alexandria
Fairfax City	Eastern	Alexandria
Falls Church City	Eastern	Alexandria
Fauquier	Eastern	Alexandria
Floyd	Western	Roanoke
Fluvanna	Western	Charlottesville (Lynchburg)
Franklin	Western	Roanoke
Franklin City	Eastern	Norfolk
Frederick	Western	Harrisonburg
Fredericksburg City	Eastern	Richmond
Galax City	Western	Roanoke
Giles	Western	Roanoke
Gloucester	Eastern	Newport News
Goochland	Eastern	Richmond
Grayson	Western	Roanoke
Greene	Western	Charlottesville (Lynchburg)
Greensville	Eastern	Richmond
Halifax	Western	Danville (Lynchburg)
Hampton City	Eastern	Newport News
Hanover	Eastern	Richmond
Harrisonburg City	Western	Harrisonburg
Henrico	Eastern	Richmond
Henry	Western	Danville (Lynchburg)
Highland	Western	Harrisonburg
Hopewell City	Eastern	Richmond
Isle of Wight	Eastern	Norfolk
James City	Eastern	Newport News
King George	Eastern	Richmond
King William	Eastern	Richmond
King and Queen	Eastern	Richmond
Lancaster	Eastern	Richmond
Lee	Western	Big Stone Gap (Roanoke)
Lexington City	Western	Lynchburg (Harrisonburg)
Loudoun	Eastern	Alexandria
Louisa	Western	Charlottesville (Lynchburg)
Lunenburg	Eastern	Richmond
Lynchburg City	Western	Lynchburg
Madison	Western	Charlottesville (Lynchburg)
Manassas City	Eastern	Alexandria
Manassas Park City	Eastern	Alexandria
Martinsville City	Western	Lynchburg
Mathews	Eastern	Newport News
Mecklenburg	Eastern	Richmond
Middlesex	Eastern	Richmond
Montgomery	Western	Roanoke
Nelson	Western	Charlottesville (Lynchburg)
New Kent	Eastern	Richmond
Newport News City	Eastern	Newport News
Norfolk City	Eastern	Norfolk
Northampton	Eastern	Norfolk
Northumberland	Eastern	Richmond
Norton City	Western	Big Stone Gap (Roanoke)
Nottoway	Eastern	Richmond
Orange	Western	Charlottesville (Lynchburg)
Page	Western	Harrisonburg
Patrick	Western	Danville (Lynchburg)
Petersburg City	Eastern	Richmond
Pittsylvania	Western	Danville (Lynchburg)
Poquoson City	Eastern	Newport News
Portsmouth City	Eastern	Norfolk
Powhatan	Eastern	Richmond
Prince Edward	Eastern	Richmond
Prince George	Eastern	Richmond
Prince William	Eastern	Alexandria
Pulaski	Western	Roanoke
Radford City	Western	Roanoke
Rappahannock	Western	Charlottesville (Harrisonburg)
Richmond	Eastern	Richmond
Richmond City	Eastern	Richmond
Roanoke	Western	Roanoke
Roanoke City	Western	Roanoke
Rockbridge	Western	Lynchburg (Harrisonburg)
Rockingham	Western	Harrisonburg
Russell	Western	Abingdon (Roanoke)
Salem City	Western	Roanoke
Scott	Western	Big Stone Gap (Roanoke)
Shenandoah	Western	Harrisonburg
Smyth	Western	Abingdon (Roanoke)
South Boston City	Western	Danville (Lynchburg)
Southampton	Eastern	Norfolk
Spotsylvania	Eastern	Richmond
Stafford	Eastern	Alexandria
Staunton City	Western	Harrisonburg
Suffolk City	Eastern	Norfolk
Surry	Eastern	Richmond
Sussex	Eastern	Richmond
Tazewell	Western	Abingdon (Roanoke)
Virginia Beach City	Eastern	Norfolk
Warren	Western	Harrisonburg
Washington	Western	Abingdon (Roanoke)
Waynesboro City	Western	Harrisonburg
Westmoreland	Eastern	Richmond
Williamsburg City	Eastern	Newport News
Winchester City	Western	Harrisonburg
Wise	Western	Big Stone Gap (Roanoke)
Wythe	Western	Roanoke
York	Eastern	Newport News

Standards for Federal Courts: Fees are standard unless noted in profile. Search fee is $26.00 per item (one party name or case number). Copy fee is $.50 per page. Certification fee is $9.00 per document, double for exemplification, if available. Most courts require prepayment. Mail requests should enclose a SASE unless otherwise noted. Before releasing records, all courts require prepayment, unless noted.

District courts index by defendant and plaintiff and by case number. Bankruptcy courts usually index by debtor and case number. While most courts now have their indexes on computer, many may still maintain index card files as well. Courts will archive closed case files at different times.

There are numerous public access programs available to online subscribers. Search the U.S. Party/Case Index to find party names and case numbers among all courts. Individual case data is provided on PACER. A search of CM/ECF provides copies of cases filed electronically. For details about PACER, the US Party/Case Index, and CM/ECF see the Appendix or go to http://pacer.psc.uscourts.gov or call 800-676-6856.

US District Court Virginia Eastern District

Alexandria Division Court Clerk, 401 Courthouse Square, Alexandria, VA 22314, 703-299-2100; records- 703-299-2128; crim dockets- 703-299-2102; civil dockets- 703-299-2101. Hours-8:30AM-5PM. www.vaed.uscourts.gov

Counties/Note: Arlington, Fairfax, Fauquier, Loudoun, Prince William, Stafford, City of Alexandria, City of Fairfax, City of Falls Church, City of Manassas, City of Manassas Park.

Searches/Indexing: Only full name required in search request. Results do not include SSN or DOB. Will not fax back documents. New cases are in the index 1 day after filing date. Computer index maintained; civil back to 1995, criminal to 2000. Records indexed and stored in numerical case order. Closed electronic cases not purged.

Search Access: Only docket info available by phone. **Mail:** Search usually completed- 1 week. SASE not required. **In person:** No self-serve copier. A copy service is available.

Payment: Pay by Visa/MC, money order, cashier's or personal check. Payee: Clerk, US District Court.

E-Services: PACER records go back to 6/1990. ECF at https://ecf.vaed.uscourts.gov. **Opinions:** www.vaed.uscourts.gov/opinions/index.htm. This opinions webpage gives instructions for viewing opinions on PACER for free with registration. Also, view notable cases free at www.vaed.uscourts.gov/notablecases/index.html.

Newport News Division Clerk's Office, 2400 West Ave, Newport News, VA 23607, 757-247-0784; Fax- 757-928-0137. Hours-8:30AM-5PM. www.vaed.uscourts.gov

Counties/Note: Gloucester, James City, Mathews, York, City of Hampton, City of Newport News, City of Poquoson, City of Williamsburg. This division houses misdemeanor records only. Direct civil and felony record requests to Norfolk Div.

Searches/Indexing: Only full name required in search request. Results do not include SSN or DOB. Will not fax back documents. New cases are in the index 1 day after filing date. Open records located at Norfolk Division. Records indexed and stored in numerical case order.

Search Access: Only docket info released by phone. **Mail:** Search usually completed- 1 week. Mail requests for civil and felony records are forwarded to Norfolk. SASE not required. **In person:** 1 public terminal available. No self-serve copier.

Payment: Pay by Visa/MC, money order or cashier's or personal checks. Payee: Clerk, US District Court.

E-Services: PACER records go back to 6/1990. New records online after 1 day. ECF at https://ecf.vaed.uscourts.gov. **Opinions Online:** www.vaed.uscourts.gov/opinions/index.htm. This opinions webpage gives instructions for viewing opinions on PACER for free with registration. Also, view notable cases free at www.vaed.uscourts.gov/notablecases/index.html.

Norfolk Division Court Clerk, US Courthouse, Rm 193, 600 Granby St, Norfolk, VA 23510, 757-222-7204; crim dockets- 757-222-7202; civil dockets- 757-222-7201; Fax- 757-222-7236. Hours-8:30AM-5PM. www.vaed.uscourts.gov

Counties/Note: Accomack, City of Chesapeake, City of Franklin, Isle of Wight, City of Norfolk, Northampton, City of Portsmouth, City of Suffolk, Southampton, City of Virginia Beach.

Searches/Indexing: Only full name required in search request. Results do not include SSN or DOB. Will not fax back documents. New cases are in the index 1 day after filing date. Computer, microfiche and card indexes maintained; Index on microfiche 1/1981 to 6/1991; prior to 1981 in card index. Records indexed and stored in numerical case order.

Search Access: Only docket info released by phone. **Mail:** Search usually completed- 1 week. SASE not required. **In person:** 1 public terminal available. Court will only do searches if the public terminal is down. No self-serve copier.

Payment: Pay by Visa/MC, business or personal checks. Payee: Clerk, US District Court. A private copy service available onsite, 757-624-9990.

E-Services: PACER records go back to 6/1990. New records online after 1 day. ECF at https://ecf.vaed.uscourts.gov. **Opinions Online:** www.vaed.uscourts.gov/opinions/index.htm. This opinions webpage gives instructions for viewing opinions on PACER for free with registration. Also, view notable cases free at www.vaed.uscourts.gov/notablecases/index.html.

Richmond Division Clerk, Federal Courthouse, 701 E Broad St, Richmond, VA 23219, 804-916-2200; crim dockets- 804-916-2230; civil dockets- 804-916-2220. Hours-8:30AM-5PM. www.vaed.uscourts.gov

Counties/Note: Amelia, Brunswick, Caroline, Charles City, Chesterfield, Dinwiddie, Essex, Goochland, Greensville, Hanover, Henrico, King and Queen, King George, King William, Lancaster, Lunenburg, Mecklenburg, Middlesex, New Kent, Northumberland, Nottoway, City of Petersburg, Powhatan, Prince Edward, Prince George, Richmond, City of Richmond, Spotsylvania, Surry, Sussex, Westmoreland, City of Colonial Heights, City of Emporia, City of Fredericksburg, City of Hopewell.

Searches/Indexing: Only full name required in search request. Results do not include SSN or DOB. Will not fax back documents. New cases are in the index 1 day after filing date. Records indexed and stored in numerical case order.

Search Access: Only docket info available by phone. This court will not honor requests for lists of names via phone. **Mail:** Search usually completed 1 week. SASE not required. **In person:** No self-serve copier. A copy service is available.

Payment: Pay by Visa/MC, money order, cashier's or personal check. Payee: Clerk, US District Court.

E-Services: PACER records go back to 6/1990. ECF at https://ecf.vaed.uscourts.gov. **Opinions:** www.vaed.uscourts.gov/opinions/index.htm. This opinions webpage gives instructions for viewing opinions on PACER for free with registration. Also, view notable cases free at www.vaed.uscourts.gov/notablecases/index.html. **Online Note:** Richmond court schedules at www.vaed.uscourts.gov/schedule/main.html.

US Bankruptcy Court Virginia Eastern District

Alexandria Division Court Clerk, 200 S Washington St #100, Alexandria, VA 22314, 703-258-1200. 9AM-4PM. www.vaeb.uscourts.gov

Counties/Note: City of Alexandria, Arlington, Fairfax, City of Fairfax, City of Falls Church, Fauquier, Loudoun, City of Manassas, City of Manassas Park, Prince William, Stafford.

Searches/Indexing: Search request requires name only. Results include last 4 SSN digits. Will not fax back documents. New cases are in the index immediately after filing date. Both computer and card indexes maintained. Cases prior to 12/1989 on index cards. Closed electronic cases not purged. A creditor register is also kept for each case. Copy requests are managed by an outside vendor, 757-624-9990 or creativeassistant@verizon.net.

Search Access: Only docket info released via phone. Voice Case Information Service available, call VCIS at 800-326-5879. **Mail:** Search usually completed- 3 days. Include SASE for return. **In person:** No self-serve copier. Court can recommend an outside vendor to make copies.

Payment: Pay by money order, cashier's check. No debtor checks/credit cards accepted. Attorney checks/credit cards accepted. Payee: Clerk, US Bankruptcy Court.

E-Services: PACER records go back to mid 1989. New records online immediately. ECF at https://ecf.vaeb.uscourts.gov. **Opinions Online:** www.vaeb.uscourts.gov/dtsearch.html. **Calendars** at www.vaeb.uscourts.gov/cal/calroot/judges.htm.

Newport News Div. Bankruptcy Court Clerk, c/o Norfolk US Bankruptcy Ct, 600 Granby St, 4th Fl, Norfolk, VA 23510-1915 (In person: 2400 W Ave, #110, Newport News), 757-222-7500. Hours-9AM-4PM. www.vaeb.uscourts.gov

Counties/Note: Newport News City. Records are at the Norfolk Bankruptcy Court.

Searches/Indexing: Search request requires name only. Results include last 4 SSN digits. Will not fax back documents. New cases are in the index immediately after filing date. Computer index maintained back to 1990. Copy requests are managed by an outside vendor, 757-624-9990 or creativeassistant@verizon.net.

Search Access: Only docket info released via phone. Voice Case Information Service available, call VCIS at 800-326-5879. **Mail:** Search usually completed- within 2 days. Include SASE for return. **In person:** No self-serve copier. Court can recommend an outside vendor to search and make copies; they may perform searches for $10.

Payment: Pay by money order, cashier's check. No debtor checks/credit cards accepted. Attorney checks/credit cards accepted. Payee: Clerk, US Bankruptcy Court.

E-Services: New records online immediately. ECF at https://ecf.vaeb.uscourts.gov. **Opinions Online:** www.vaeb.uscourts.gov/dtsearch.html. Calendars at www.vaeb.uscourts.gov/cal/calroot/judges.htm.

Norfolk Division Court Clerk, Walter E Hoffman US Courthouse, Rm 400, 600 Granby St, 4th Fl, Norfolk, VA 23510-1915, 757-222-7500. Hours-9AM-4PM. www.vaeb.uscourts.gov

Counties/Note: Accomack, City of Cape Charles, City of Chesapeake, City of Franklin, Gloucester, City of Hampton, Isle of Wight, James City, Matthews, City of Norfolk, Northampton, City of Poquoson, City of Portsmouth, Southampton, City of Suffolk, City of Virginia Beach, City of Williamsburg, York.

Searches/Indexing: Search request requires name only. Results include last 4 SSN digits. Will not fax back documents. New cases are in the index immediately after filing date. Computer index maintained back to 1989. Copy requests are managed by an outside vendor, 757-624-9990 or creativeassistant@verizon.net. Closed electronic cases not purged.

Search Access: Only docket info released via phone. Voice Case Information Service available, call VCIS at 800-326-5879. **Mail:** Search usually completed- within 2 days. Include SASE for return. **In person:** No self-serve copier. Court can recommend an outside vendor to make copies; they will perform searches for $10.

Payment: Pay by money order, cashier's check. No debtor checks/credit cards accepted. Attorney checks/credit cards accepted. Payee: Clerk, US Bankruptcy Court.

E-Services: New records online immediately. ECF at https://ecf.vaeb.uscourts.gov. **Opinions Online:** www.vaeb.uscourts.gov/dtsearch.html. **Online Note:** Court calendars at www.vaeb.uscourts.gov/cal/calroot/judges.htm.

Richmond Division Office of the Clerk, 701 E Broad St, 23219-1888, 804-916-2400; Hours-8:30AM-5PM. www.vaeb.uscourts.gov

Counties/Note: Amelia, Brunswick, Caroline, Charles City, Chesterfield, City of Colonial Heights, Dinwiddie, City of Emporia, Essex, City of Fredericksburg, Goochland, Greensville, Hanover, Henrico, City of Hopewell, King and Queen, King George, King William, Lancaster, Lunenburg, Mecklenburg, Middlesex, New Kent, Northumberland, Nottoway, City of Petersburg, Powhatan, Prince Edward, Prince George, Richmond, City of Richmond, Spotsylvania, Surry, Sussex, Westmoreland.

Searches/Indexing: Search request requires name only. Results include last 4 SSN digits. Will not fax back documents. New cases are in the index immediately after filing date. Computer index maintained back to 1990. Copy requests are managed by an outside vendor, 757-624-9990 or creativeassistant@verizon.net.

Search Access: Only docket info released via phone. Voice Case Information Service available, call VCIS at 800-326-5879. **Mail:** Search usually completed- 2 days. Include SASE for return. **In person:** 3 public terminals available. No self-serve copier. Court can recommend an outside vendor to make copies; they will perform searches for $10.

Payment: Pay by money order, cashier's check. No debtor checks/credit cards accepted. Attorney checks/credit cards accepted. Payee: Clerk, US Bankruptcy Court.

E-Services: New records online immediately. ECF at https://ecf.vaeb.uscourts.gov. **Opinions Online:** www.vaeb.uscourts.gov/dtsearch.html. Calendars at www.vaeb.uscourts.gov/cal/calroot/judges.htm.

US District Court Virginia Western District

Abingdon Division Clerk's Office, 180 W. Main St, #104, Abingdon, VA 24212, 276-628-5116; Fax- 276-628-1028. Hours-8:30AM-4:30PM. www.vawd.uscourts.gov

Counties/Note: Buchanan, City of Bristol, Russell, Smyth, Tazewell, Washington.

Searches/Indexing: In addition to full name, search requests may include last 4 digits of SSN, DOB year, gender and/or City and State of address. Results may include last 4 SSN digits. Will not fax back documents. New cases are in the index immediately after filing date. Computer and card indexes maintained. Automated in-house records system goes back to 1992. District-wide searches available for all records. Case files sent to archives 1 year after closed.

Search Access: Docket info available via phone. **Mail:** Search usually completed- 2-3 days. SASE not required. **Fax:** Written, prepaid fax search requests accepted. **In person:** 1 public terminal available. Computer generated copies $.10 each.

Payment: Pay by Visa/MC, money order, cashier's or personal check. Payee: Clerk, US District Court. Court will bill for searches and copies.

E-Services: PACER records go back to mid 1990. New records online immediately. ECF at https://ecf.vawd.uscourts.gov. **Opinions Online:** www.vawd.uscourts.gov/opinion.asp. **Online Note:** Judges' calendars free at www.vawd.uscourts.gov/judgescal/default.asp. Opinions and calendars also on PACER.

Big Stone Gap Division Court Clerk, PO Box 490, Big Stone Gap, VA 24219 (In person: 322 E Wood Ave, Rm 204, Big Stone Gap, VA 24219), 276-523-3557; records- 276-523-3557; Fax- 276-523-6214. Hours-8:30AM-4:30PM. www.vawd.uscourts.gov

Counties/Note: Dickenson, Lee, Scott, Wise, City of Norton.

Searches/Indexing: In addition to full name, search requests may include last 4 digits of SSN, DOB year, gender and/or City and State of address. Results may include last 4 SSN digits. Will fax back docket listings only. New cases are in the index immediately after filing date. Computer index maintained; older cases on microfilm index. Automated in-house records system goes back to 1992. Case files sent to archives 1 year after closed.

Search Access: Only docket info is available by phone. **Mail:** Search usually completed- 2 days. Include SASE for return. **In person:** 1 public terminal available. No self-serve copier.

Payment: Pay by Visa/MC/AmEx, money order, cashier's or personal checks. Payee: Clerk, US District Court.

E-Services: PACER records go back to mid 1990. New records online immediately. ECF at https://ecf.vawd.uscourts.gov. **Opinions Online:** www.vawd.uscourts.gov/opinion.asp. **Online Note:** Judges' calendars free at www.vawd.uscourts.gov/judgescal/default.asp. Opinions and calendars also on PACER.

Charlottesville Division Court Clerk, 255 W Main St, Rm 304, Charlottesville, VA 22902, 434-296-9284; Fax- 434-295-8909. Hours-8:30AM-4:30PM. www.vawd.uscourts.gov

Counties/Note: Albemarle, Culpeper, Fluvanna, Greene, Louisa, Madison, Nelson, Orange, Rappahannock, City of Charlottesville.

Searches/Indexing: In addition to full name, search requests may include last 4 digits of SSN, DOB year, gender and/or City and State of address. Results do not include SSN or DOB. Will not fax back documents. New cases are in the index immediately after filing date. Computer index maintained; older cases on microfilm index. Automated in-house records system goes back to 1992. Automated in-house records system goes back to 1992. District-wide searches available here. Case files sent to archives 1 year after closed.

Search Access: Mail: Search usually completed- 2-3 days. Include SASE for return. **Fax:** Written, prepaid fax search requests accepted. **In person:** 1 public terminal available. Self-serve copies $.50.

Payment: Pay by Visa/MC, money order, cashier's or personal check. Payee: Clerk, US District Court.

E-Services: PACER records go back to mid 1990. New records online immediately. ECF at https://ecf.vawd.uscourts.gov. **Opinions Online:** www.vawd.uscourts.gov/opinion.asp. **Online Note:** Judges' calendars free at www.vawd.uscourts.gov/judgescal/default.asp. Opinions and calendars also on PACER.

Danville Division Court Clerk, PO Box 1400, Danville, VA 24543-0053 (In person: Post Office Bldg, 700 Main St, Rm 202, Danville, VA 24541), 434-793-7147; Fax- 434-793-0284. Hours-8:30AM-4:30PM. www.vawd.uscourts.gov

Counties/Note: Charlotte, Halifax, Henry, Patrick, Pittsylvania, City of Danville, City of Martinsville, City of South Boston.

Searches/Indexing: Search requests may include last 4 digits of SSN, DOB year, gender and/or City and State of address. Results may include last 4 SSN digits. Will fax back documents for same fee as hard copies. New cases are in the index immediately after filing date. Computer, microfiche and card indexes maintained. Automated in-house records system goes back to 1992. District-wide searches available for all records. Closed cases sent to records center after 1 year. **Search Access:** For expedited requests where fees are prepaid, this court will call to give info then follow with a written response. **Mail:** Search usually completed- 2-3 days. SASE not required. **Fax:** Fax requests for searches and case files accepted. **In person:** 1 public terminal available. No self-serve copier.

Payment: Pay by Visa/MC, money order, cashier's or personal check. Payee: Clerk, US District Court.

E-Services: PACER records go back to mid 1990. New records online immediately. ECF at https://ecf.vawd.uscourts.gov. **Opinions Online:** www.vawd.uscourts.gov/opinion.asp. **Online Note:** Judges' calendars free at www.vawd.uscourts.gov/judgescal/default.asp. Opinions and calendars also on PACER.

Harrisonburg Division Clerk of Court, 116 N Main St, Rm 314, Harrisonburg, VA 22802, 540-434-3181; Fax- 540-434-3319. Hours-8:30AM-4:30PM. www.vawd.uscourts.gov

Counties/Note: Augusta, Bath, Clarke, Frederick, Highland, Page, Rockingham, Shenandoah, Warren, City of Harrisonburg, City of Staunton, City of Waynesboro, City of Winchester.

Searches/Indexing: In addition to full name, search requests may include last 4 digits of SSN, DOB year, gender and/or City and State of address. Results may include last 4 SSN digits. Will not fax back documents. New cases are in the index 1-2 days after filing date. Computer, microfiche and card indexes maintained. Automated in-house system goes back to 1992. District-wide searches available here, but court prefers searches be conducted where case is filed. Case files sent to archives 1 year after closed.

Search Access: Limited info available by phone. **Mail:** Search usually completed- 1-2 days. SASE not required. **Fax:** Fax search requests accepted. **In person:** 1 public terminal available. No self-serve copier. **Payment:** Pay by Visa/MC, money order, cashier's or personal checks. Payee: Clerk, US District Court.

E-Services: PACER records go back to mid 1990. New records online immediately. ECF at https://ecf.vawd.uscourts.gov. **Opinions Online:** www.vawd.uscourts.gov/opinion.asp. **Online Note:** Judges' calendars free at www.vawd.uscourts.gov/judgescal/default.asp. Opinions and calendars also on PACER.

Lynchburg Division Clerk of Court, 1101 Court St #A66, Lynchburg, VA 24504, 434-847-5722; Fax- 434-847-2002. Hours-8:30AM-4:30PM. www.vawd.uscourts.gov

Counties/Note: Amherst, Appomattox, Bedford, Buckingham, Campbell, Cumberland, Rockbridge, City of Bedford, City of Buena Vista, City of Lexington, City of Lynchburg.

Searches/Indexing: In addition to full name, search requests may include last 4 digits of SSN, DOB year, gender and/or City and State of address. Results may include last 4 SSN digits. Will not fax back documents. New cases are in the index 1-2 days after filing date. Computer, microfiche, and card indexes maintained. Automated in-house records system goes back to 1992. District-wide searches available for all records. Case files sent to archives after 1 year.

Search Access: Only docket info is available by phone. **Mail:** Search usually completed- 2 days. SASE not required. **Fax:** Fax search requests accepted. **In person:** 1 public terminal available. No self-serve copier.

Payment: Pay by Visa/MC, money order, cashier's or personal checks. Payee: Clerk, US District Ct.

E-Services: PACER records go back to mid 1990. New records online immediately. ECF at https://ecf.vawd.uscourts.gov. **Opinions Online:** www.vawd.uscourts.gov/opinion.asp. **Online Note:** Judges' calendars free at www.vawd.uscourts.gov/judgescal/default.asp. Opinions and calendars also on PACER.

Roanoke Division Clerk of Court, PO Box 1234, Roanoke, VA 24006 (In person: 210 Franklin Rd, Rm 308, Roanoke, VA 24011), 540-857-5100; crim dockets- 540-857-5102; civil dockets- 540-857-5101; Fax- 540-857-5110. Hours-8:30AM-4:30PM. www.vawd.uscourts.gov

Counties/Note: Alleghany, Bland, Botetourt, Carroll, Craig, Floyd, Franklin, Giles, Grayson, Montgomery, Pulaski, Roanoke, Wythe, City of Covington, City of Clifton Forge, City of Galax, City of Radford, City of Roanoke, City of Salem.

Searches/Indexing: In addition to full name, search requests may include last 4 digits of SSN, DOB year, gender and/or City and State of address. Results may include last 4 SSN digits. Will not fax back documents. New cases are in the index immediately after filing date. Computer, microfiche and card indexes maintained. Automated in-house records system goes back to 1992. District-wide searches available for all records. Case files sent to archives 1 year after closed.

Search Access: For expedited requests where fees are prepaid, this court will call to give info then follow with a written response. **Mail:** Search usually completed- 1 week. SASE not required. **Fax:** Fax search requests accepted. **In person:** 1 public terminal available. No self-serve copier.

Payment: Pay by credit cards (in person or by phone), money order, cashier's or personal checks. Payee: Clerk, US District Court.

E-Services: PACER records go back to mid 1990. New records online immediately. ECF at https://ecf.vawd.uscourts.gov. **Opinions Online:** www.vawd.uscourts.gov/opinion.asp. **Online Note:** Judges' calendars free at www.vawd.uscourts.gov/judgescal/default.asp. Opinions and calendars also on PACER.

US Bankruptcy Court Virginia Western District

Harrisonburg Division Court Clerk, 116 N Main St, Rm 223, Harrisonburg, VA 22802, 540-434-8327; records- x2; Fax- 540-434-9715. Hours-8AM-4:30PM. www.vawb.uscourts.gov

Counties: Alleghany, Augusta, Bath, City of Buena Vista, Clarke, City of Clifton Forge, City of Covington, Frederick, City of Harrisonburg, Highland, City of Lexington, Page, Rappahannock, Rockbridge, Rockingham, Shenandoah, City of Staunton, Warren, City of Waynesboro, City of Winchester.

Searches/Indexing: Include SSN in search request. Results include last 4 SSN digits. Will not fax back documents. New cases are in the index immediately after filing date. Both computer and card indexes maintained; computer goes back to 1986. Paper case files sent to archives 2 years after closed. Electronic cases maintained indefinitely.

Search Access: Only docket info is available by phone and only if it is on computer. **Mail:** Search usually completed- 7-10 days. Include SASE for return. **In person:** 1 public terminal available. No self-serve copier.

Payment: Pay by money order, cashier's check, business check. No credit cards or personal checks accepted. Payee: Clerk, US Bankruptcy Court.

E-Services: PACER records go back to 3/1986. New records online after same day. ECF at https://ecf.vawb.uscourts.gov. **Opinions Online:** http://pacer.vawb.uscourts.gov/courtweb/enter1.html. **Online Note:** Calendars back to 1999 at http://pacer.vawb.uscourts.gov/Calendars/2005calendar.html.

Lynchburg Division Court Clerk, 1101 Court St, Rm 166, Lynchburg, VA 24504, 434-845-0317; Fax- 434-845-1801. Hours-8AM-4:30PM. www.vawb.uscourts.gov

Counties: Albemarle, Amherst, Appomattox, Bedford, City of Bedford, Buckingham, Campbell, Charlotte, City of Charlottesville, Culpeper, Cumberland, City of Danville, Fluvanna, Greene, Halifax, Henry, Louisa, Lynchburg City, Madison, Martinsville City, Nelson, Orange, Patrick, Pittsylvania, City of South Boston.

Searches/Indexing: Include SSN in search request. Results include last 4 SSN digits. Will not fax back documents. New cases are in the index same day if possible after filing date. Computer index back to 1986 maintained. Paper case files sent to archives 2 years after closed. Electronic cases maintained indefinitely.

Search Access: Only name, date filed and chapter is released via phone. **Mail:** Search usually completed- 5 days. Include SASE for return. **In person:** 1 public terminal available. No self-serve copier.

Payment: Pay by money order, cashier's check, business check. No credit cards or personal checks accepted. Payee: Clerk, US Bankruptcy Court.

E-Services: PACER records go back to 3/1986. New records online after 1 day. ECF at https://ecf.vawb.uscourts.gov. **Opinions Online:** http://pacer.vawb.uscourts.gov/courtweb/enter1.html. **Online Note:** Calendars back to 1999 at http://pacer.vawb.uscourts.gov/Calendars/2005calendar.html.

Roanoke Division Court Clerk, 210 Church Ave SW, #200, Roanoke, VA 24011-1525, 540-857-2391; Fax- 540-857-2873. Hours-8AM-4:30PM. www.vawb.uscourts.gov

Counties: Bland, Botetourt, City of Bristol, Buchanan, Carroll, Craig, Dickenson, Floyd, Franklin, City of Galax, Giles, Grayson, Lee, Montgomery, City of Norton, Pulaski, City of Radford, Roanoke, City of Roanoke, Russell, City of Salem, Scott, Smyth, Tazewell, Washington, Wise, Wythe.

Searches/Indexing: Include SSN in search request. Results include last 4 SSN digits. Will not fax back documents. New cases are in the index same day if possible after filing date. Records indexed numerically; for example- 7-92-00123 = office number, year and 5 digit case number. Paper case files sent to archives 2 years after closed. Electronic cases maintained indefinitely.

Search Access: Limited search; only the number of pages of the requested items is given via phone. **Mail:** Search usually completed- 2 days. Include SASE for return. **Fax:** Fax search requests accepted. **In person:** 2 public terminals available. No self-serve copier.

Payment: Pay by money order, cashier's check, law firm check. No business or personal checks accepted. Debtor credit and debit cards not accepted. Payee: Clerk, US Bankruptcy Court.

E-Services: PACER records go back to 3/1986. New records online after 1 day. ECF at https://ecf.vawb.uscourts.gov. **Opinions Online:** http://pacer.vawb.uscourts.gov/courtweb/enter1.html. **Online Note:** Calendars back to 1999 at http://pacer.vawb.uscourts.gov/Calendars/2005calendar.html.

Virginia County Courts

Court	Jurisdiction	No. of Courts	How Organized
Circuit Courts*	General	117	31 Circuits
District Courts*	Limited	132	32 Circuits
Combined Courts*		11	

* Profiled in this Sourcebook.

Court	CIVIL: Tort	Contract	Real Estate	Min. Claim	Max. Claim	Small Claims	Estate	Eviction	Domestic Relations
Circuit Courts*	X	X	X	$4,500	No Max		X		X
District Courts*	X	X	X	$0	$15,000	$5,000		X	X

Court	CRIMINAL: Felony	Misdemeanor	DWI/DUI	Preliminary Hearing	Juvenile
Circuit Courts*	X				
District Courts*		X	X	X	X

Administration

Executive Secretary, Administrative Office of Courts, 100 N 9th Street, 3rd Fl, Supreme Court Building, Richmond, Virginia, 23219; 804-786-6455, Fax: 804-786-4542. All courts are Eastern Standard Time www.courts.state.va.us

Court Structure

The Circuit Courts in 31 districts are the courts of general jurisdiction. Please note that a district can comprise a county or a city. The General District Court decides all criminal offenses involving ordinances laws, and by-laws of the county or city where it is located and all misdemeanors under state law. A misdemeanor is any charge that carries a penalty of no more than one year in jail or a fine of up to $2,500, or both.

Records of civil action from $4,500 to $15,000 can be at either the Circuit Court or District Court as either can have jurisdiction. It is necessary to check both record locations as there is no concurrent database nor index.

Online Access

There are 3 systems. Each county or county equivelent must be searched separately. The case docket index may be searched for over 90% of the Circuit Courts and all but three of the General District Courts (Charlottesville City, Clifton Forge City, and Radford City). Visit the home page at www.courts.state.va.us/ to find the participating courts and do searches. These 2 online systems usually include partial DOBs in criminal results, and civil results sometimes include addresses. Also, a dial-up access system known as LOPAS (Law Office & Public Access System) provides free searching for all Circuit and most District Courts. Results include full name and address. Call Marguerite Steele, 804-786-6455 for LOPAS details. Also, the home page provides access to Supreme Court and Appellate opinions.

Searching Tips, Fees, and Other Guidelines

In most Circuit Courts the certification fee is $2.00 per document plus copy fee which is usually $.50 per page. The General District Court fees are more varied by location.

Fifteen independent cities share the Clerk of Circuit Court with the county - Bedford, Covington (Alleghany County), Emporia (Greenville County), Fairfax, Falls Church (Arlington or Fairfax County), Franklin (Southhampton County), Galax (Carroll County), Harrisonburg (Rockingham County), Lexington (Rockbridge County), Manassas and Manassas Park (Prince William County), Norton (Wise County), Poquoson (York County), South Boston (Halifax County), and Williamsburg (James City County).

Charles City and James City are counties, not cities. The City of Franklin is not in Franklin County, but is its own separate jurisdiction. The City of Richmond is not in Richmond County, but is its own separate jurisdiction. The City of Roanoke is not in Roanoke County, but is its own separate jurisdiction.

Accomack County

2nd Circuit Court PO Box 126, Accomac, VA 23301; 757-787-5776; probate phone: 757-787-5778; fax: 757-787-1849; 9AM-5PM. ***Felony, Civil Actions over $15,000, Probate.***
www.courts.state.va.us/courts/circuit.html

Civil Records: Access: Fax, mail, online, in person. Both court and visitors may perform in person searches. No search fee. Required to search: name, years to search. Civil cases indexed by defendant, plaintiff; index on microfiche and archived from 1663; on computer back to 1998. Mail turnaround time 1-2 days. Search free at www.courts.state.va.us/. Results show address of subject and day and month of birth, but not year.

Criminal Records: Access: Fax, mail, online, in person. Both court and visitors may perform in person searches. No search fee. Required to search: name, years to search, DOB; also helpful: SSN. Criminal records on microfiche and archived from 1663; on computer back to 1994. Note: Results include full name Mail Turnaround time 1-2 days. Search free at www.courts.state.va.us/. Searching is by name only. Results show address of subject and day & month of birth, but not year.

General Information: No juvenile, sealed, probate, tax return or adoption records released. Fee to fax out file $2.00 1st page, $.50 each add'l. Court makes copy: $.50 per page. Self serve: same. Certification fee: $2.00. Payee: Samuel H Cooper Jr, Clerk of Court. Personal checks accepted. Visa/MC accepted. Prepayment required. Mail requests: SASE required.

2A General District Court PO Box 276, Accomac, VA 23301; 757-787-0923; criminal phone: x117; civil phone: x123; 8:30AM-4:30PM. ***Misdemeanor, Civil Actions under $15,000, Eviction, Small Claims.***

Civil Records: Access: Phone, mail, online, in person. Both court and visitors may perform in person searches. No search fee. Required to search: name, years to search. Civil cases indexed by defendant. Civil records retained ten years. Mail turnaround time 1-3 days. Civil PAT goes back to 1996. Search free at www.courts.state.va.us/.

Results show address of subject and day & month of birth, but not year.
Criminal Records: Access: Phone, mail, online, in person. Both court and visitors may perform in person searches. No search fee. Required to search: name, years to search, DOB; also helpful: SSN. Criminal records retained ten years. Mail turnaround time 1-3 days. Criminal PAT goes back to same as civil. Search free at www.courts.state.va.us/. Results show address of subject and day & month of birth, but not year.
General Information: No juvenile, sealed, adoption records released. Will not fax documents. Court makes copy: no fee if less than 10 pages. No certification fee. Payee: Accomack District Court. Personal checks and credit cards accepted. Prepayment required. Mail requests: SASE required.

Albemarle County

16th Circuit & District Court 501 E Jefferson St, Charlottesville, VA 22902; criminal phone: 424-972-4086; civil phone: 434-972-4085; fax: 434-972-4071; 8:30AM-4:30PM. ***Felony, Misdemeanor, Civil, Eviction, Probate.***
www.courts.state.va.us/courts/circuit.html
Civil Records: Access: Mail, in person, online. Both court and visitors may perform in person searches. Search fee: $5.00 per name. Required to search: name, years to search. Civil records on microfiche from 1980 to present and archived from 1700s to 1990. Mail turnaround time 7-10 days. Public use terminal has civil records back to 2001. Search free at www.courts.state.va.us/. Results show address of subject and day & month of birth, but not year. Also search LOPAS; call 804-786-5511 to apply.
Criminal Records: Access: Mail, online, in person. Both court and visitors may perform in person searches. Search fee: $5.00 per name. Required to search: name, years to search. Criminal records on microfiche from 1980 to present and archived from 1700s to 1990. Mail turnaround time 7-10 days. Search free at www.courts.state.va.us/. Results show address of subject and day & month of birth, but not year. Remote online access to court case indexes via LOPAS; call 804-786-5511 to apply. Online results show middle initial, DOB.
General Information: No juvenile, sealed records released. Will not fax documents. Court makes copy: $.50 per page. Certification fee: $2.00. Payee: Albemarle Clerk of Court. Personal checks accepted; credit cards are not. Prepayment required.

Alexandria City

18th Circuit Court 520 King St, #307, Alexandria, VA 22314; criminal phone: 703-838-4047; civil phone: 703-838-4044; probate phone: 703-838-4055; 9AM-5PM. ***Felony, Civil over $15,000, Probate.*** http://alexandriava.gov/clerkofcourt/
Civil Records: Access: In person, online. Visitors must perform in person searches themselves. Required to search: name, years to search. Civil cases indexed by defendant, plaintiff; index on computer from 1983 to present, microfiche from 1970s to present. Civil PAT goes back to 1983. Images are available. There is limited free online access to civil docket information from 01/01/1983, and a subscription service ($500 per year or $50 per month) to full data including images. Visit https://cheyenne.alexandriava.gov/ajis/index.php.
Criminal Records: Access: In person, online. Visitors must perform in person searches themselves. Required to search: name, years to search; also helpful: DOB. Criminal records on computer since 7/87. Criminal PAT goes back to 1987. PAT results show middle initial, DOB. Images are available. Online access to criminal records is same as civil, available from 7/01/1987. Online results show middle initial, DOB.
General Information: No juvenile, sealed, adoption or expunged records released. Will not fax documents. Court makes copy: $.50 per page. Self serve: same. Certification fee: $2.00. Payee: Clerk of Court. Only cashiers checks and money orders accepted. No credit cards accepted. Prepayment required.

18th General District Court PO Box 320489, 520 King St, #201, Alexandria, VA 22320; 703-838-4041; criminal phone: 703-838-4030; civil phone: 703-838-4021; 8AM-4PM. ***Misdemeanor, Civil Actions under $15,000, Eviction, Small Claims.***
Civil Records: Access: Online, in person. Both court and visitors may perform in person searches. No search fee. Required to search: name, years to search. Civil cases indexed by defendant. Civil records on computer from 1993 to present. Public use terminal available. PAT results show name; SSNs may appear on some records. Search free at www.courts.state.va.us/. Results show address of subject and day & month of birth, but not year.
Criminal Records: Access: Online, in person. Visitors must perform in person searches themselves. Required to search: name. Criminal records computerized from 1993 to present. Public use terminal available. PAT results show middle initial, DOB. SSNs may also appear as an identifier on some records. Search free at www.courts.state.va.us/. Results show address of subject and day & month of birth, but not year.
General Information: Will not fax documents. Court makes copy: $1.00 each first 2 pages, $.50 each add'l. No certification fee. Payee: 18th District Court. Visa/MC accepted.

Alleghany County

25th Circuit Court PO Box 670, 266 W Main St, Covington, VA 24426; 540-965-1730; fax: 540-965-1732; 8:30AM-5PM. ***Felony, Civil Actions over $15.000, Probate.***
Civil Records: Access: In person, online. Visitors must perform in person searches themselves. Required to search: name. Civil cases indexed by plaintiff. Civil records available from 1822, all on microfilm. Search free at www.courts.state.va.us/. Results show address of subject and day & month of birth, but not year.
Criminal Records: Access: In person, online. Required to search: name. Criminal records available from 1822, all on microfilm. Search free at www.courts.state.va.us/. Searching is by name only. Results show address of subject and day & month of birth, but not year. Only month and day of DOB appears, plus sex, race.
General Information: No juvenile, adoption or sealed records released. Will not fax documents. Court makes copy: $.50 per page. Self serve: same. Certification fee: $2.00 per doc. Payee: Clerk of Court. Personal checks discouraged. No credit cards accepted. Prepayment required.

25th General District Court PO Box 139, 266 W Main St, Covington, VA 24426; 540-965-1720; fax: 540-965-1722; 9AM-5PM. ***Misdemeanor, Civil Actions under $15,000, Eviction, Small Claims.***
Civil Records: Access: Online, in person. Visitors must perform in person searches themselves. Required to search: name, years to search. Civil cases indexed by defendant, plaintiff; index on computer from 1/90, prior on index cards. Civil PAT goes back to 10 years. Search free at www.courts.state.va.us/. Results show address of subject and day & month of birth, but not year. Also search LOPAS; call 804-786-5511 to apply.
Criminal Records: Access: Online, in person. Visitors must perform in person searches themselves. Required to search: name, years to search; also helpful: DOB, SSN. Criminal records computerized from 1/90, prior on index cards. Criminal PAT goes back to 10 years. Search free at www.courts.state.va.us/. Results show address of subject and day & month of birth, but not year.
General Information: No juvenile, sealed records released. Will fax back documents. Court makes copy: $.50 per page. No certification fee. Payee: Court. Personal checks accepted. Visa/MC accepted.

Amelia County

11th Circuit Court PO Box 237 (1 E Main St, B-5), Amelia, VA 23068; 804-561-2128; fax: 804-561-6364; 8:30AM-4:30PM. ***Felony, Civil Actions over $15,000, Probate.***
Court will search on phone request if not busy.
Civil Records: Access: Mail, in person, online. Both court and visitors may perform in person searches. No search fee. Required to search: name, years to search. Civil cases indexed by defendant, plaintiff; index on microfiche 1735 to present, indexed on books. Mail turnaround time 3-5 days. Civil PAT goes back to 6/7/2002. PAT civil results show middle initial. Search free at www.courts.state.va.us/. Results show subject address and day & month of birth, but not year. Also search LOPAS; call 804-786-5511 to apply.
Criminal Records: Access: Mail, online, in person. Both court and visitors may perform in person searches. No search fee. Required to search: name, years to search, DOB; also helpful: SSN. Criminal records on microfiche 1735 to present, indexed on books. Mail turnaround time 3-5 days. Criminal PAT goes back to same as civil. PAT results show name only. Online access to criminal records is the same as civil. Online results show only month and day of DOB plus sex, race.
General Information: No juvenile, sealed records released. Will not fax documents. Court makes copy: $.50 per page. Self serve: same. Certification fee: $2.00. Payee: Amelia County Circuit Court. Personal checks accepted; credit cards are not. Prepayment required. Mail requests: SASE required.

11th General District Court PO Box 24, Amelia, VA 23002; 804-561-2456; fax: 804-561-6956; 8:30AM-4:30PM. ***Misdemeanor, Civil Actions under $15,000, Eviction, Small Claims.***
Civil Records: Access: Online, in person. Visitors must perform in person searches themselves. Required to search: name, years to search. Civil cases indexed by defendant, plaintiff; index on computer since 12/20/92. Civil PAT available. PAT civil results show middle initial. Search free at www.courts.state.va.us/. Results show address of subject and day & month of birth, but not year. Also search LOPAS; call 804-786-5511 to apply.
Criminal Records: Access: Online, in person. Visitors must perform in person searches themselves. Required to search: name, years to search, DOB; also helpful: SSN. Criminal records on computer since 12/20/92. Criminal PAT available. PAT results show middle initial, DOB. Search free at www.courts.state.va.us/. Results show address of subject and day & month of birth, but not year.
General Information: Online identifiers in results same as on public terminal. No juvenile, sealed records released. Will not fax documents. Court makes copy: $1.00 1st 2 pages, $.50 each add'l. No certification fee. Payee: Amelia District Court. Personal checks and Visa/MC accepted. Prepayment required. Mail requests: SASE required for mail return of any copies.

Amherst County

24th Circuit Court PO Box 462, Amherst, VA 24521; 434-946-9321; probate phone: same; fax: 434-946-9323; 8AM-5PM. ***Felony, Civil Actions over $15,000, Probate.***
www.courts.state.va.us/courts/circuit.html
Civil Records: Access: In person, online. Visitors must perform in person searches themselves. Required to search: name, years to search. Civil cases indexed by defendant, plaintiff. Civil index on docket books from 1761; on computer back to 1997. Civil PAT goes back to 1998. Search free at www.courts.state.va.us/. Results show address of subject and day & month of birth, but not year. Also, remote online access to court case indexes may also be at LOPAS; 804-786-5511 to apply.
Criminal Records: Access: In person, online. Visitors must perform in person searches themselves. Required to search: name, years to search, date of offense. Criminal records indexed in books back to 1761; on computer back to 1997. Criminal PAT goes back to same as civil. Access to criminal court records is same as civil, see above. Online results show only month and day of DOB, sex, race.
General Information: No juvenile, sealed or adoption records released. Will not fax documents. Court makes copy: $.50 per page. Self serve: same. Certification fee: $2.00. Payee: Clerk of Circuit Court. Personal checks accepted. Prepayment required.

24th General District Court PO Box 513, Amherst, VA 24521; 434-946-9351; criminal fax: 434-946-9359; civil fax: same; 8AM-4PM. ***Misdemeanor, Civil Actions under $15,000, Eviction, Small Claims.***
Has handled misdemeanor cases since 1985.
Civil Records: Access: Mail, fax, online, in person. Both court and visitors may perform in person searches. Search fee: $10.00. Required to search: name, years to search. Civil cases indexed by defendant, plaintiff; index on computer 10 years prior. Mail turnaround time 48 hours. Civil PAT goes back to 10 years. Search free at www.courts.state.va.us/. Results show address of subject and day & month of birth, but not year. Also search via LOPAS; 804-786-5511 to apply.
Criminal Records: Access: Mail, online, in person. Both court and visitors may perform in person searches. Search fee: $10.00. Required to search: name, years to search, DOB, SSN. Criminal records on computer 10 years prior. Mail turnaround time 48 hours. Criminal PAT goes back to same as civil. Search free at www.courts.state.va.us/. Results show address of subject and day & month of birth, but not year.
General Information: No sealed records released. Will fax documents. Court makes copy: $1.00 per page. No certification fee. Payee: Clerk of Court. Personal checks and credit cards accepted. Prepayment required. Mail requests: SASE required for mail return of any copies.

Appomattox County

10th Circuit Court PO Box 672, 297 Court St, Ste B, Appomattox, VA 24522; 434-352-5275; fax: 434-352-2781; 8:30AM-4:30PM. ***Felony, Civil Actions over $15,000, Probate.***
www.courts.state.va.us/courts/circuit.html
Civil Records: Access: In person, online. Visitors must perform in person searches themselves. Required to search: name, years to search. Civil cases indexed by defendant, plaintiff; index on books from 1892 to present; on computer since 1997. Civil PAT goes back to 7/1997. Search free at www.courts.state.va.us/. Results show address of subject and day & month of birth, but not year. Also search LOPAS; call 804-786-5511 to apply.
Criminal Records: Access: In person, online. Visitors must perform in person searches themselves. Required to search: name, years to search. Criminal docket on books from 1892 to present; on computer since 1997. Criminal PAT goes back to same as civil.PAT results show name, DOB. Online access to criminal records is the same as civil. Online results show only month and day of DOB plus sex, race.
General Information: No juvenile, sealed records released. Will not fax documents. Court makes copy: $.50 per page. No certification fee. Payee: Clerk of Circuit Court. Personal checks accepted; credit cards are not. Prepayment required.

10th General District Court PO Box 187, 297 Court St, Appomattox, VA 24522; 434-352-5540; fax: 434-352-0717; 8:30AM-4:30PM. ***Misdemeanor, Civil Actions under $15,000, Eviction, Small Claims.***
Civil Records: Access: Fax, mail, online, in person. Both court and visitors may perform in person searches. No search fee. Required to search: name, years to search. Civil cases indexed by defendant, plaintiff; index on computer back to 1997. Mail turnaround time 1-5 days. Civil PAT goes back to 1997. Results include name and case number. Search free at www.courts.state.va.us/. Results show address of subject and day & month of birth, but not year. Also search via LOPAS; call 804-786-5511 to apply.
Criminal Records: Access: Fax, mail, online, in person. Both court and visitors may perform in person searches. No search fee. Required to search: name, years to search; also helpful: SSN. Criminal records computerized from 1997. Note: Results include address and case number. Mail turnaround time 1-5 days. Criminal PAT goes back to 1997. PAT results show middle initial, DOB, SSN. Search free at www.courts.state.va.us/. Results show address of subject and day & month of birth, but not year.
General Information: Online identifiers in results same as on public terminal. No juvenile, sealed records released. No fee to fax documents. Court makes copy: $1.00 1st page; $.50 each add'l. No certification fee. Payee: General District Court. Personal checks and credit cards accepted. Prepayment required. Mail requests: SASE required.

Arlington County

17th Circuit Court 1425 N Courthouse Rd, Arlington, VA 22201; 703-228-7010; criminal phone: 703-228-4399; civil phone: 703-228-7010; probate phone: 703-228-4376; 8AM-4PM. ***Felony, Civil Actions over $15,000, Probate.***
www.courts.state.va.us/courts/circuit.html
Court info line- 703-228-4370,
Civil Records: Access: In person, online. Visitors must perform in person searches themselves. Required to search: name, years to search. Civil cases indexed by defendant, plaintiff; index on computer from 1987; prior on books from mid-1930 to present. Civil PAT goes back to 1987. Search free at www.courts.state.va.us/. Results show address of subject and day & month of birth, but not year.
Criminal Records: Access: In person, online. Visitors must perform in person searches themselves. Required to search: name, years to search. Criminal records computerized from 1987; prior on books from mid-1930 to present. Criminal PAT goes back to same as civil. Online access to criminal records is the same as civil. Online results show only month and day of DOB plus sex, race.
General Information: No juvenile, adoption or sealed records released. Will not fax documents. Court makes copy: $.50 per page. Certification fee: $2.00. Payee: Clerk of Court. Personal checks accepted. Prepayment required.

17th General District Court 1425 N Courthouse Rd, Rm 2500, Arlington, VA 22201; 703-228-7900; civil phone: 703-228-4485; fax: 703-228-4593; 8AM-4PM. ***Misdemeanor, Civil Actions under $15,000, Eviction, Small Claims.***
Phone access limited to 4 requests.
Civil Records: Access: Phone, mail, online, in person. Both court and visitors may perform in person searches. No search fee. Required to search: name, years to search, case number. Civil cases indexed by defendant. Civil records on computer back 10 years, books from early 1970s. Mail turnaround time 5 days. Civil PAT goes back to 10 years. PAT results show name, DOB. Search free at www.courts.state.va.us/. Results show address of subject and day & month of birth, but not year. Also search via LOPAS; 804-786-5511 to apply.
Criminal Records: Access: Phone, mail, online, in person. Both court and visitors may perform in person searches. No search fee. Required to search: name, years to search, DOB; also helpful-SSN. Criminal records on computer back 10 years. Mail turnaround time 5 days. Criminal PAT goes back to same as civil.PAT results show name, DOB. Search free at www.courts.state.va.us/. Results show address of subject and day & month of birth, but not year.
General Information: No juvenile, sealed records released. Will not fax documents. Court makes copy: $1.00 each first 2 pages, $.25 each add'l. Certification fee: $2.00. Payee: Clerk of Court. Personal checks accepted. Visa/MC accepted. Prepayment required.

Augusta County

25th Circuit Court PO Box 689, Staunton, VA 24402-0689; 540-245-5321; probate phone: same; fax: 540-245-5318; 8AM-5PM. ***Felony, Civil Actions over $15,000, Probate.***
www.courts.state.va.us/courts/circuit.html
Court prefers that searches be done in person. Mail access is limited; they will only search back to 1987. Phone available for very short search only.
Civil Records: Access: Mail, in person, online. Both court and visitors may perform in person searches. No search fee. Required to search: name, years to search. Civil cases indexed by defendant, plaintiff; index on computer from 1987 to present, books from 1745 to 1986. Mail turnaround time 1-2 days. Civil PAT goes back to 1987. Search free at www.courts.state.va.us/. Results show address of subject and day & month of birth, but not year.
Criminal Records: Access: Mail, in person, online. Both court and visitors may perform in person searches. No search fee. Required to search: name, years to search; also helpful: DOB, SSN. Criminal records go back to 1987 felonies only. Mail turnaround time 1-2 days. Criminal PAT available. Online access to criminal records is the same as civil. Online results show only month and day of DOB, sex, race.
General Information: No juvenile, adoption or sealed records released. Will not fax documents. Court makes copy: $.50 per page. Self serve: same. Certification fee: $2.00. Payee: Clerk, Augusta County Circuit Court. Personal checks accepted; credit cards are not. Prepayment required. Mail requests: SASE required.

25th General District Court 6 E Johnson St, 2nd Fl, Staunton, VA 24401; 540-245-5300; criminal fax: 540-245-5365; civil fax: same; 8:30AM-4:30PM. ***Misdemeanor, Civil Actions under $15,000, Eviction, Small Claims.***
www.courts.state.va.us/courts/gd/Augusta/home.html
This court also handles traffic infractions.
Civil Records: Access: Mail, in person, online. Both court and visitors may perform in person searches. No search fee. Required to search: name, years to search. Civil cases indexed by defendant, plaintiff. Civil records kept for 10 years on computer. Mail turnaround time 5-7 days. Civil PAT goes back to 10 years. PAT civil results show middle initial. Search online free at http://epwsgdp1.courts.state.va.us/gdcourts/caseSearch.do?index=index. Results show name and sometimes address.
Criminal Records: Access: Mail, online, in person. Both court and visitors may perform in person searches. No search fee. Required to search: name, years to search. Criminal records kept for 10 years on computer, then destroyed. Mail turnaround time 5-7 days. Criminal PAT goes back to same as civil. PAT criminal results show middle initial. Search free at www.courts.state.va.us/. Results show address of subject and day & month of birth, but not year.
General Information: Online identifiers in results same as on public terminal. Will not fax documents. Court makes copy: $.50 per page. No certification fee. Payee: Augusta General District Court. Personal checks accepted. Visa/MC accepted. Prepayment required. Mail requests: SASE requested.

Bath County

25th Circuit Court PO Box 180, Warm Springs, VA 24484; 540-839-7226; probate phone: 540-839-7226; fax: 540-839-7248; 8:30AM-4:30PM. ***Felony, Civil Actions over $15,000, Probate.***
www.courts.state.va.us/courts/circuit.html
Probate fax- 540-839-7248
Civil Records: Access: Mail, in person, online. Both court and visitors may perform in person searches. No search fee. Required to search: name, years to search. Civil cases indexed by defendant, plaintiff; index on books from 1791 to present. Mail turnaround time 3-4 days Remote online access to court case indexes is via LOPAS; call 804-786-5511 to apply. Search free by name only or case number at www.courts.state.va.us/. Results show address of subject and day & month of birth, but not year.
Criminal Records: Access: In person, online. Visitors must perform in person searches themselves. Required to search: name, years to search; also helpful: DOB. Criminal docket on books from 1791 to present. Online access to criminal records is the same as civil. Online results show only month and day of DOB plus sex, race.
General Information: No juvenile, sealed or adoption records released. Will not fax documents. Court makes copy: $.50 per page. Self serve: same. Certification fee: $2.00. Payee: Bath County Circuit Court. Personal checks accepted; credit cards are not. Prepayment required.

25th General District Court PO Box 96, Warm Springs, VA 24484; 540-839-7241; fax: 540-

839-7242; 8:30AM-4:30PM. ***Misdemeanor, Civil Actions under $15,000, Eviction, Small Claims.***
Civil Records: Access: Phone, fax, mail, online, in person. Both court and visitors may perform in person searches. No search fee. Required to search: name, years to search. Civil cases indexed by defendant, plaintiff; index on files from 1985 to present, Prior records in Circuit Court. Mail turnaround time 2 days; will give immediate response on phone if not an extensive search. Search free at www.courts.state.va.us/. Results show address of subject and day & month of birth, but not year. Also search LOPAS; call 804-786-5511 to apply.
Criminal Records: Access: Phone, fax, mail, online, in person. Both court and visitors may perform in person searches. No search fee. Required to search: name, years to search, DOB; also helpful: SSN. Criminal records on files back 10 years, Prior records in Circuit Court. Mail turnaround time 2 days; immediate response by phone if not extensive search. Search free at www.courts.state.va.us/. Results show address of subject and day & month of birth, but not year.
General Information: No juvenile, sealed records released. Will fax documents $.50 per page. Court makes copy: $.50 per page. No certification fee. Payee: Bath County Combined Court. Personal checks and credit cards accepted. Prepayment required. Mail requests: SASE requested.

Bedford County

County Circuit Court 123 E Main St, #201, Bedford, VA 24523; 540-586-7632; fax: 540-586-6197; 8:30AM-5PM. ***Felony, Civil Actions over $15,000, Probate.***
www.courts.state.va.us/courts/circuit.html
Civil Records: Access: In person, online. Visitors must perform in person searches themselves. Required to search: name, years to search. Civil cases indexed by defendant, plaintiff; index on computer from 1998, index books. Civil PAT goes back to 1998. PAT results show name only. Search free at www.courts.state.va.us/. Results show address of subject and day & month of birth, but not year.
Criminal Records: Access: In person, online. Visitors must perform in person searches themselves. Required to search: name, years to search, DOB. Criminal records computerized from 1988, index books. Criminal PAT goes back to 1999. PAT results show name only. Remote online access to court case indexes via LOPAS; call 804-786-5511 to apply. Remote online access to court case indexes via LOPAS; call 804-786-5511 to apply. Online results show middle initial.
General Information: Online identifiers in results same as on public terminal. No juvenile, sealed records released. Will not fax documents. Court makes copy: $.50 per page. Self serve: $.50 per page. Certification fee: $2.00. Payee: Bedford Clerk of Court. Personal checks accepted; credit cards are not. Prepayment required.

24th General District Court 123 E Main St, #202, Bedford, VA 24523; 540-586-7637; fax: 540-586-7684; 8AM-4PM. ***Misdemeanor, Civil Actions under $15,000, Eviction, Small Claims, Traffic.***
The court will not perform name searches.
Civil Records: Access: Mail, in person, online. Visitors must perform in person searches themselves. No search fee. Required to search: name. Civil cases indexed by defendant. Civil records on computer for ten years. Civil PAT goes back to 10 years. Search free at www.courts.state.va.us/. Results show address of subject and day & month of birth, but not year. Also search LOPAS; call 804-786-5511 to apply.
Criminal Records: Access: Mail, online, in person. Visitors must perform in person searches themselves. No search fee. Required to search: name. Criminal records on computer for ten years. Criminal PAT goes back to same as civil. PAT results show middle initial, DOB. Search free at www.courts.state.va.us/. Results show address of subject and day & month of birth, but not year.
General Information: Online identifiers in results same as on public terminal. No sealed records released. Will not fax documents. Court makes copy: $1.00 1st 2 pages, $.50 each add'l. No certification fee. Payee: Bedford General District Court. Personal checks and credit cards accepted. Prepayment required. Mail requests: SASE required.

Bedford City

Circuit & District Courts
See Bedford County.

Bland County

27th Circuit Court PO Box 295, Bland, VA 24315; 276-688-4562; fax: 276-688-2438; 8AM-6PM. ***Felony, Civil Actions over $15,000, Probate.***
www.courts.state.va.us/courts/circuit.html
Civil Records: Access: Phone, fax, mail, in person, online. Both court and visitors may perform in person searches. Search fee: $10.00 per name. Required to search: name, years to search. Civil cases indexed by defendant, plaintiff; index on books from 1861 to present. Mail turnaround time 2 days. Civil PAT available. Search free at www.courts.state.va.us/. Results show address of subject and day & month of birth, but not year. Also search LOPAS; call 804-786-5511 to apply.
Criminal Records: Access: Phone, fax, mail, in person, online. Both court and visitors may perform in person searches. Search fee: $10.00 per name. Required to search: name, years to search, signed release; also helpful: SSN. Criminal docket on books from 1861 to present. Mail turnaround time 2 days. Criminal PAT available. Online access to criminal records is the same as civil. Online results show only month and day of DOB plus sex, race.
General Information: No juvenile, sealed or adoption records released. Will fax documents $1.00 per page. Court makes copy: $.50 per page. Self serve: same. Certification fee: $2.00. Payee: Clerk of Court. Personal checks accepted; credit cards are not. Prepayment required. Mail requests: SASE required.

27th General District Court PO Box 157, Bland, VA 24315; 276-688-4433; fax: 276-688-4789; 8AM-4:30PM. ***Misdemeanor, Civil Actions under $15,000, Eviction, Small Claims.***
www.bland.org/government/generaldistrictcourt.html
Civil Records: Access: Phone, fax, mail, online, in person. Both court and visitors may perform in person searches. No search fee. Required to search: name, years to search. Civil cases indexed by defendant. Civil records on computer from 4/23/95. Mail turnaround time 1-2 days. Civil PAT goes back to 1995. PAT civil results show middle initial. Search free at www.courts.state.va.us/. Results show address of subject and day & month of birth, but not year. Also search LOPAS; call 804-786-5511 to apply.
Criminal Records: Access: Phone, fax, mail, online, in person. Both court and visitors may perform in person searches. No search fee. Required to search: name, years to search; also helpful: DOB, SSN. Criminal records computerized from 4/23/92. Note: Phone access limited to specific cases only. Mail turnaround time 1-2 days. Criminal PAT goes back to 1996. PAT criminal results show middle initial. Search free at www.courts.state.va.us/. Results show address of subject and day & month of birth, but not year.
General Information: No juvenile, sealed or adoption records released. Will fax documents to local or toll-free number. Court makes copy: $1.00 1st 2 pages, $.50 each add'l. No certification fee. Payee: General District Court. Personal checks and credit cards accepted. Mail requests: SASE required.

Botetourt County

25th Circuit Court PO Box 219, 1 W Main St, Courthouse, Fincastle, VA 24090; 540-473-8274; fax: 540-473-8209; 8:30AM-4:30PM. ***Felony, Civil Actions over $15,000, Probate.***
www.courts.state.va.us/courts/circuit/Botetourt/home.html
Civil Records: Access: Mail, in person, online. Both court and visitors may perform in person searches. No search fee. Required to search: name, years to search. Civil cases indexed by defendant, plaintiff; index on computer 7/1/91 to present, books back to 1770. Mail turnaround time same day. Civil PAT goes back to 1991. Search free at www.courts.state.va.us/. Results show address of subject and day & month of birth, but not year. Also search LOPAS; call 804-786-5511 to apply.
Criminal Records: Access: Mail, online, in person. Only the court performs in person searches; visitors may not. No search fee. Required to search: name, years to search, DOB, SSN. Criminal records on computer 7/1/91 to present, books back to 1770. Mail turnaround time same day. Criminal PAT goes back to 1991. Online access to criminal records is the same as civil. Online results show only month and day of DOB plus sex, race.
General Information: No juvenile, sealed or adoption records released. Will not fax documents. Court makes copy: $.50 per page. Certification fee: $2.00. Payee: Clerk of Court. Personal checks accepted; credit cards are not. Prepayment required. Mail requests: SASE required.

25th General District Court PO Box 858, Fincastle, VA 24090-0858; 540-473-8244; fax: 540-473-8344; 8AM-4PM. ***Misdemeanor, Civil Actions under $15,000, Eviction, Small Claims.***
Civil Records: Access: Mail, in person, online. Both court and visitors may perform in person searches. No search fee. Required to search: name, years to search. Civil cases indexed by defendant, plaintiff; index on computer back to 1998. Civil records on files back to 1997. Mail turnaround time 3-4 days. Civil PAT goes back to 1998. Search free at www.courts.state.va.us/. Results show address of subject and day & month of birth, but not year. Also search LOPAS; call 804-786-5511 to apply.
Criminal Records: Access: Mail, online, in person. Both court and visitors may perform in person searches. No search fee. Required to search: name, years to search. Criminal records computerized from 1998. Mail turnaround time 3-4 days. Criminal PAT goes back to same as civil. Search free at www.courts.state.va.us/. Results show address of subject and day & month of birth, but not year.
General Information: No juvenile, sealed records released. Will not fax documents. Court makes copy: $.50 per page. Self serve: $.10 per page. No certification fee. Payee: General District Court. Personal checks accepted; checks requiring verification calls not accepted. Credit cards accepted. Prepayment required. Mail requests: SASE required.

Bristol City

28th Circuit Court 497 Cumberland St, Bristol, VA 24201; 276-645-7321; fax: 276-821-6097; 9AM-5PM. ***Felony, Civil over $15,000, Probate.***
www.courts.state.va.us/courts/circuit.html
Civil Records: Access: Mail, in person, online. Visitors must perform in person searches themselves. Search fee: $5.00 per name. Required to search: name, years to search. Civil cases indexed by defendant, plaintiff; index from 1890 to present; on computer back to 1994. Civil PAT goes back to 1994. PAT results show name only. Search free at www.courts.state.va.us/. Results show address of subject and day & month of birth, but not year. Also search LOPAS; call 804-786-5511 to apply.
Criminal Records: Access: Mail, in person, online. Visitors must perform in person searches themselves. Search fee: $5.00 per name. Required to search: name, years to search. Criminal records indexed from 1890 to present; on computer back to 1994. Criminal PAT goes back to same as civil. PAT results show name only. Online access to criminal records index is the same as civil. Online results show only month and day of DOB plus sex, race.
General Information: Online identifiers in results same as on public terminal. No juvenile, sealed or adoption records released. Will not fax documents. Court makes copy: $.50 per page. Self serve: $.50 per page. Certification fee: $2.00 per doc plus copy fee; Exemplification fee- $2.50. Payee: Clerk of Circuit Court. Personal checks accepted; credit cards are not. Prepayment required. Mail requests: SASE required.

28th General District Court 497 Cumberland St, Bristol, VA 24201; 276-645-7341; fax: 276-645-7342; 8:30AM-4:30PM. ***Misdemeanor, Civil Actions under $15,000, Eviction, Small Claims.***
www.courts.state.va.us/courts/circuit/Bristol/home.html
Civil Records: Access: Online, in person. Both court and visitors may perform in person searches. No search fee. Required to search: name, years to search. Civil cases indexed by defendant, plaintiff; index on computer from 1997, card file 1983 to 1988. Search free at www.courts.state.va.us/. Results show address of subject and day & month of birth, but not year. Also search LOPAS; 804-786-5511.
Criminal Records: Access: Online, in person. Visitors must perform in person searches themselves. Required to search: name, years to search, DOB, SSN. Criminal records computerized from 1997, card file 1983 to 1988. Note: Results include name and case number. Search free at www.courts.state.va.us/. Results show address of subject and day & month of birth, but not year.
General Information: No juvenile, sealed records released. Will not fax documents. Court makes copy for no fee. No certification fee. Payee: General District Court. Personal checks accepted. Visa/MC accepted. Prepayment required.

Brunswick County

6th Circuit Court 216 N Main St, Lawrenceville, VA 23868; 434-848-2215; fax: 434-848-4307; 8:30AM-5PM. ***Felony, Civil, Probate.***
www.courts.state.va.us/courts/circuit.html
Civil Records: Access: In person, online. Visitors must perform in person searches themselves. Required to search: name, years to search. Civil cases indexed by defendant, plaintiff. Civil records in books back to 1732; on computer since 1992 (office use only). Access record images via http://208.210.219.102/cgi-bin/p/rms.cgi; registration and password required. Search free by name only or case number at www.courts.state.va.us/. Results show address of subject and day & month of birth, but not year. Also search LOPAS; call 804-786-5511 to apply.
Criminal Records: Access: In person, online. Visitors must perform in person searches themselves. Required to search: name, years to search. Criminal records in books back to 1732; on computer back to 1992 (office use only). Online access to criminal records is the same as civil. Online results show only month and day of DOB plus sex, race.
General Information: No juvenile, sealed or adoption records released. Will not fax documents. Court makes copy: $.50 per page. Certification fee: $2.00. Payee: Clerk of Court. Personal checks accepted; credit cards are not. Prepayment required.

6th General District Court 202 Main St, Albertis S. Harrison Jr. Courthouse, Lawrenceville, VA 23868-0066; 434-848-2315; fax: 434-848-2550; 8AM-4PM. ***Misdemeanor, Civil under $15,000, Eviction, Small Claims.*** www.courts.state.va.us/courts/combined/Brunswick/home.html
Civil Records: Access: Mail, in person, online. Both court and visitors may perform in person searches. No search fee. Required to search: name, years to search. Civil cases indexed by defendant, plaintiff. Civil records computerized since 1988, records go back to 1988. Note: Court will search time permitting. Mail turnaround time 1-2 days. Civil PAT goes back to 10 years. Search free at www.courts.state.va.us/. Results show address of subject and day & month of birth, but not year. Also search LOPAS; call 804-786-5511 to apply.
Criminal Records: Access: Mail, in person, online. Both court and visitors may perform in person searches. No search fee. Required to search: name, years to search, DOB; also helpful: SSN, signed release. Criminal records computerized since 1991; records go back ten years. Note: Court will perform in person searches only if time permits. Mail turnaround time 1-2 days. Criminal PAT goes back to same as civil. Search free at www.courts.state.va.us/. Results show address of subject and day & month of birth, but not year.
General Information: Online identifiers in results same as on public terminal. No juvenile, sealed records released. Will not fax documents. Court makes copy: $1.00 per page. No certification fee. Payee: Brunswick G D Court. Personal checks accepted. Visa/MC accepted. Prepayment required. Mail requests: SASE required.

Buchanan County

29th Circuit Court PO Box 929, Grundy, VA 24614; 276-935-6567; criminal phone: 276-935-6575; civil phone: 276-935-6575; fax: 276-935-7086; 8:30AM-5PM. ***Felony, Misdemeanor, Civil Actions over $15,000, Probate.***
www.courts.state.va.us/courts/circuit.html
This court has records of Misdemeanors under appeal. See the 29th Judicial District Court for originating Misdemeanor records.
Civil Records: Access: Phone, mail, online, in person. Both court and visitors may perform in person searches. No search fee. Required to search: name, years to search; also helpful: address. Civil cases indexed by defendant, plaintiff; index on computer back to 1991, in books back to 1923. Mail turnaround time 1 week. Civil PAT goes back to 1991. PAT results show middle initial, DOB. Search free at www.courts.state.va.us/. Also search LOPAS; call 804-786-5511 to apply.
Criminal Records: Access: Online, in person. Visitors must perform in person searches themselves. Required to search: name, years to search, DOB; also helpful: address, SSN. Criminal records computerized from 1991; in books back to 1928. Criminal PAT goes back to 1991. PAT criminal results show middle initial. Search free at www.courts.state.va.us. Also, remote online access to court case indexes is via LOPAS; call 804-786-5511 to apply. Online results show only month and day of DOB plus sex, race.
General Information: Online identifiers in results same as on public terminal. No juvenile, sealed records released. Will not fax documents. Court makes copy: $.50 per page. Self serve: same. Certification fee: $2.00. Payee: Clerk of Circuit Court. Personal checks accepted if in state. Visa/MC accepted.

29th General District Court PO Box 654, Grundy, VA 24614; 276-935-6526; fax: 276-935-5479; 8AM-4PM. ***Misdemeanor, Civil Actions under $15,000, Eviction, Small Claims, Traffic.***
Also search the Circuit Court for appealed Misdemeanor records.
Civil Records: Access: Fax, mail, in person, phone, online. Both court and visitors may perform in person searches. No search fee. Required to search: name; also helpful: years to search. Civil cases indexed by defendant, plaintiff. Civil records are indexed for 10 years, computerized back to 1993. Mail turnaround time 1 week. Civil PAT available. PAT civil results show middle initial. Search free at www.courts.state.va.us/. Results show address of subject and day & month of birth, but not year. Also search LOPAS; call 804-786-5511 to apply.
Criminal Records: Access: Fax, mail, in person, online. Both court and visitors may perform in person searches. No search fee. Required to search: name; also helpful: years to search. Criminal Records computerized back to 1993. Criminal PAT available. PAT criminal results show middle initial. Search free at http://epwsgdp1.courts.state.va.us/gdcourts/caseSearch.do?index=index. Results show DOB month and day, sex, race. Also search LOPAS; call 804-786-5511 to apply. Online results show middle initial, DOB.
General Information: Online identifiers in results same as on public terminal. Will fax to toll-free or local numbers only. Court makes copy for no fee. No certification fee. Payee: General District Court. Personal checks accepted. Visa/MC accepted. Prepayment required. Mail requests: SASE required.

Buckingham County

10th Circuit Court PO Box 107, Rte 60, Buckingham, VA 23921; 434-969-4734; fax: 434-969-2043; 8:30AM-4:30PM. ***Felony, Civil Actions over $15,000, Probate.***
www.courts.state.va.us/courts/circuit.html
Civil Records: Access: Mail, in person, online. Both court and visitors may perform in person searches. No search fee. Required to search: name, years to search. Civil cases indexed by defendant, plaintiff; index on books from 1869 to present, computerized since 2001. Public use terminal has civil records back to 2001. Search free at www.courts.state.va.us/. Results show address of subject and day & month of birth, but not year. Also search LOPAS; call 804-786-5511 to apply.
Criminal Records: Access: In person, online. Only the court performs in person searches; visitors may not. Required to search: name, years to search; also helpful: DOB. Criminal docket on books from 1869 to present. Search free by name only or case number at www.courts.state.va.us/. Results show address of subject and day & month of birth, but not year. Also search LOPAS; call 804-786-5511 to apply. Online results show middle initial, DOB.
General Information: No juvenile, sealed or adoption records released. Will fax documents $2.00 per page. Court makes copy: $.50 per page. Self serve: same. Certification fee: $2.00. Payee: Clerk of Court. Personal checks accepted; credit cards are not. Mail requests: SASE required.

Buckingham General District Court PO Box 127, Buckingham, VA 23921; 434-969-4755; fax: 434-969-1762; 8:30-4:30PM. ***Misdemeanor, Civil Actions under $15,000, Eviction, Small Claims.***
Civil Records: Access: Mail, in person, online, fax. Only the court performs in person searches; visitors may not. No search fee. Required to search: name, years to search. Civil cases indexed by defendant. Civil records on computer or hard copy from 1993, prior records on index cards. Mail turnaround time 2 weeks. Search free at www.courts.state.va.us/. Results show address of subject and day & month of birth, but not year. Also search LOPAS; call 804-786-5511 to apply.
Criminal Records: Access: Mail, online, in person, fax. Only the court performs in person searches; visitors may not. No search fee. Required to search: name, years to search, DOB, SSN, signed release. Criminal records on computer or hard copy from 1993, prior records on index cards. Mail turnaround 2 weeks. Search free at www.courts.state.va.us/. Results show address of subject and day & month of birth, but not year.
General Information: No juvenile, sealed records released. Will not fax documents. Court makes copy for no fee. No certification fee. Payee: Buckingham. Personal checks accepted. Visa/MC accepted. Prepayment required.

Buena Vista City

25th Circuit & District Court 2039 Sycamore Ave, Buena Vista, VA 24416; 540-261-8627; fax: 540-261-8625; 8:30AM-5PM. ***Felony, Misdemeanor, Civil, Eviction, Probate.***
www.courts.state.va.us/courts/circuit.html
Probate fax is same as main fax number.
Civil Records: Access: Mail, in person, online. Both court and visitors may perform in person searches. No search fee. Required to search: name, years to search. Civil cases indexed by defendant, plaintiff; index on manual records 1892 to present, computerized since 1996. Mail turnaround time 1 day. Public use terminal has civil records back to 1/1993. Search free at www.courts.state.va.us/. Results show address of subject and day & month of birth, but not year. Also search LOPAS; call 804-786-5511 to apply.
Criminal Records: Access: Mail, online, in person. Both court and visitors may perform in person searches. No search fee. Required to search: name, years to search. Criminal records on manual records 1892 to present, computerized since 1996. Mail turnaround time 1 day. Search free by name only or case number at www.courts.state.va.us/. Results show address of subject and day & month of birth, but not year.
General Information: Online identifiers in results same as on public terminal. No juvenile, sealed records released. Will not fax documents. Court makes copy: $.50 per page. Self serve: same. Cert fee: $2.00 per cert. Payee: Buena Vista Circuit Court.

Personal checks accepted; credit cards are not. Prepayment required. Mail requests: SASE required.

Campbell County

24th Circuit Court 732 Village Hwy, PO Box 7, Rustburg, VA 24588; 434-592-9517; criminal phone: 434-592-9614; civil phone: 434-592-9610; probate phone: 434-592-9517; fax: 434-332-9598; 8:30AM-4:30PM. ***Felony, Civil over $15,000, Probate.***
www.courts.state.va.us/courts/circuit.html

Civil Records: Access: Mail, in person, online. Both court and visitors may perform in person searches. No search fee. Required to search: name, years to search. Civil cases indexed by defendant, plaintiff. Civil index on docket books. Mail turnaround time 5 days. Civil PAT goes back to 1994-95. Search free at www.courts.state.va.us/. Results show address of subject and day & month of birth, but not year. Also search LOPAS; call 804-786-5511 to apply.

Criminal Records: Access: Mail, online, in person. Both court and visitors may perform in person searches. No search fee. Required to search: name, years to search; also helpful: DOB. Criminal records indexed in books. Mail turnaround time 5 days. Criminal PAT goes back to same as civil. Search free by name only or case number at www.courts.state.va.us/. Results show address of subject and day & month of birth, but not year. Also search LOPAS; call 804-786-5511 to apply. Online results show middle initial, DOB.

General Information: No juvenile, sealed or adoption records released. Will not fax documents. Court makes copy: $.50 per page. Self serve: same. Certification fee: $2.00 per cert. Payee: Clerk of Court. Personal checks accepted; credit cards are not. Prepayment required. Mail requests: SASE required.

24th General District Court PO Box 97, 732 Village Hwy, Rustburg, VA 24588; 434-332-9546; fax: 434-332-9694; 8AM-4PM. ***Misdemeanor, Civil Actions under $15,000, Eviction, Small Claims.***
www.courts.state.va.us/courts/gd/Campbell/home.html

Civil Records: Access: Online, in person. Visitors must perform in person searches themselves. Required to search: name, years to search. Civil cases indexed by defendant, plaintiff; index on computer for 10 years. Public use terminal available, records go back to 1998 (back 10 years). PAT civil results show middle initial. Search free at www.courts.state.va.us/. Results show address of subject and day & month of birth, but not year. Also search LOPAS; call 804-786-5511 to apply.

Criminal Records: Access: Online, in person. Visitors must perform in person searches themselves. Required to search: name, years to search. Criminal records on computer for 10 years. Public use terminal available, crim records go back to 1998 (back 10 years). PAT criminal results show middle initial. Search free at www.courts.state.va.us/. Results show address of subject and day & month of birth, but not year.

General Information: Online identifiers in results same as on public terminal. Will fax documents if copy fee is prepaid. Court makes copy: $1.00 1st 2 pages, $.50 each add'l. No certification fee. Payee: Clerk of Court. Personal checks accepted. Credit cards accepted in person. Prepayment required.

Caroline County

15th Circuit Court 112 Courthouse Ln, #A, PO Box 309, Bowling Green, VA 22427-0309; 804-633-5800; criminal phone: 804-633-1093; civil phone: 804-633-1094; probate phone: 804-633-1093; fax: 804-633-0519; 8:30AM-4PM. ***Felony, Civil Actions over $15,000, Probate.***
www.courts.state.va.us/courts/circuit.html

Civil Records: Access: In person, online. Visitors must perform in person searches themselves. Required to search: name, years to search. Civil cases indexed by defendant, plaintiff; index on books from early 1900s to present. Civil PAT goes back to 1991. Search free at www.courts.state.va.us/. Results show address of subject and day & month of birth, but not year. Also search LOPAS; call 804-786-5511 to apply.

Criminal Records: Access: In person, online. Visitors must perform in person searches themselves. Required to search: name, years to search; also helpful: DOB. Criminal docket on books from early 1900s to present, computerized since 1896. Criminal PAT goes back to same as civil. Search free by name only or case number at www.courts.state.va.us/. Results show address of subject and day & month of birth, but not year. Also search LOPAS; call 804-786-5511 to apply. Online results show middle initial, DOB.

General Information: No juvenile, sealed, adoption records released. Will not fax documents. Court makes copy: $.50 per page. Self serve: same. Certification fee: $2.50. Payee: Clerk of Court. Personal checks accepted. Credit cards accepted for payment of fines and costs only. Not accepted over the phone. Prepayment required. Mail requests: SASE required for mail return of any copies.

15th General District Court PO Box 511, 111 Ennis St, Bowling Green, VA 22427; 804-633-5720; fax: 804-633-3033; 8AM-4PM. ***Misdemeanor, Civil Actions under $15,000, Eviction, Small Claims.***

Civil Records: Access: Online, in person. Both court and visitors may perform in person searches. No search fee. Required to search: name, years to search. Civil cases indexed by defendant, plaintiff; index on computer from 1/92. Note: At the court's discretion, usually for high volume, you may have to fill out a research request form before they'll search. Civil PAT goes back to 10 years. PAT results show middle initial, DOB. Search free at www.courts.state.va.us/. Results show address of subject and day & month of birth, but not year. Also search LOPAS; call 804-786-5511 to apply.

Criminal Records: Access: Online, in person. Both court and visitors may perform in person searches. No search fee. Required to search: name, years to search, SSN. Criminal records on computer back 10 years. Records older than 10 years are destroyed/expunged/purged. Note: At the court's discretion, usually for high volume, you may have to fill out a research request form before they'll search. Criminal PAT goes back to 10 years. Search free at www.courts.state.va.us/. Results show address of subject and day & month of birth, but not year.

General Information: Will not fax documents. Court makes copy for no fee. No certification fee. No credit cards accepted.

Carroll County

27th Circuit Court PO Box 218, Hillsville, VA 24343; 276-730-3070; fax: 276-730-3071; 8AM-5PM. ***Felony, Civil Actions over $15,000, Probate.***
www.courts.state.va.us/courts/circuit.html

Civil Records: Access: Mail, in person, online. Both court and visitors may perform in person searches. Search fee: $5.00 per name. Required to search: name, years to search, also helpful: SSN. Civil cases indexed by defendant, plaintiff; index on books from 1842 to present, on computer back to 1991. Mail turnaround time 3 days. Search free at www.courts.state.va.us/. Results show address of subject and day & month of birth, but not year. Also search LOPAS; call 804-786-5511 to apply.

Criminal Records: Access: Mail, in person, online. Both court and visitors may perform in person searches. Search fee: $5.00 per name. Required to search: name, years to search; also helpful: SSN. Criminal docket on books from 1842 to present; on computer back to 1991. Mail turnaround time 3 days. Online access to criminal records is the same as civil. Online results show only month and day of DOB, sex, race.

General Information: No juvenile, sealed, adoption records released. Will fax documents $2.50 per page. Court makes copy: $.50 per page. Self serve: same. Certification fee: $2.00. Payee: Clerk of Court. Personal checks accepted. Visa/MC accepted. Prepayment required. Mail requests: SASE required.

Carroll Combined District Court PO Box 698, 605 Pine St, Hillsville, VA 24343; 276-730-3050; fax: 276-730-3054; 8AM-4:30PM. ***Misdemeanor, Civil Actions under $15,000, Eviction, Small Claims.***

Civil Records: Access: In person, online. Visitors must perform in person searches themselves. Required to search: name, years to search. Civil cases indexed by defendant, plaintiff; index on books from 1800s, on computer from 1988; no plaintiff index prior to computerization. Civil PAT goes back to 1996. PAT civil results show middle initial. Search free at www.courts.state.va.us/. Results show address of subject and day & month of birth, but not year. Also search LOPAS; call 804-786-5511 to apply.

Criminal Records: Access: In person, online. Visitors must perform in person searches themselves. Required to search: name, years to search, DOB. Criminal docket on books from 1800s, on computer 10 years. Criminal PAT goes back to same as civil. PAT results show middle initial, DOB. Search free at www.courts.state.va.us/. Results show address of subject and day & month of birth, but not year.

General Information: No juvenile, sealed records released. Will not fax documents. Court makes copy for no fee. No certification fee. Payee: Carroll County. Personal checks accepted. Visa/MC accepted. Prepayment required.

Charles City

9th Circuit Court PO Box 86, 10780 Courthouse Rd, Charles City, VA 23030-0086; 804-652-2105; fax: 804-829-5647; 8:30AM-4:30PM. ***Felony, Civil Actions over $15,000, Probate.***
www.courts.state.va.us/courts/circuit/Charles_City/home.html

Civil Records: Access: In person only, online. Visitors must perform in person searches themselves. No search fee. Required to search: name, years to search. Civil cases indexed by defendant, plaintiff; index on computer from 2000, on books from 1789-2000. Civil PAT goes back to 2000. Search free at www.courts.state.va.us/. Results show address of subject and day & month of birth, but not year. Also search LOPAS; call 804-786-5511 to apply.

Criminal Records: Access: In person, online. Visitors must perform in person searches themselves. Required to search: name, years to search, DOB. Criminal records computerized from 2000, on books from 1789-2000. Criminal PAT goes back to same as civil. Online access to criminal records is the same as civil. Online results show only month and day of DOB plus sex, race.

General Information: No juvenile, sealed records released. Fee to fax document $.50 per page. Court makes copy: $.50 per page. Self serve: same. Certification fee: $2.00. Payee: Clerk of Circuit Court. Personal checks accepted; credit cards are not. Prepayment required.

9th General District Court PO Box 57, Charles City Courthouse, 10780 Courthouse Rd, Charles City, VA 23030; 804-652-2188; fax: 804-829-6390; 8:30AM-4PM. ***Misdemeanor, Civil Actions under $15,000, Eviction, Small Claims.***
www.courts.state.va.us/courts/combined/Charles_City/home.html

Civil Records: Access: Mail, in person, online. Both court and visitors may perform in person searches. No search fee. Required to search: name, years to search. Civil cases indexed by defendant, plaintiff; index on computer back to 1997. Mail turnaround time 3 days. Civil PAT goes back to 1997. Search free at www.courts.state.va.us/. Results show address of subject and day & month of birth, but not year. Also search LOPAS; call 804-786-5511 to apply.

Criminal Records: Access: Mail, online, in person. Both court and visitors may perform in person searches. No search fee. Required to search: name, years to search, DOB, SSN. Criminal records computerized from 1997. Mail turnaround time 3 days. Criminal PAT goes back to 1997. Search free at www.courts.state.va.us/. Results show address of subject and day & month of birth, but not year.

General Information: No juvenile, sealed records released. Will not fax documents. Court makes copy for no fee. No cert fee. Personal checks accepted. Prepayment required. Mail requests: SASE required.

Charlotte County

10th Circuit Court PO Box 38, 125 David Bruce Ave, Charlotte Courthouse, VA 23923; 434-542-5147; fax: 434-542-4336; 8:30AM-4:30PM. ***Felony, Civil Actions over $15,000, Probate.***
www.courts.state.va.us/courts/circuit/Charlotte/home.html
Civil Records: Access: In person, online. Visitors must perform in person searches themselves. Required to search: name, years to search. Civil cases indexed by defendant, plaintiff; index on books from 1765, in folders by case number. Search free at www.courts.state.va.us/. Results show address of subject and day & month of birth, but not year. Also search LOPAS; call 804-786-5511 to apply.
Criminal Records: Access: In person, online. Visitors must perform in person searches themselves. Required to search: name, years to search, DOB. Criminal docket on books from 1765, in folders by case number. Search free by name only or case number at www.courts.state.va.us/. Results show address of subject and day & month of birth, but not year. Also search LOPAS; call 804-786-5511 to apply. Online results show middle initial, DOB.
General Information: No juvenile, sealed records released. Will not fax documents. Court makes copy: $.50 per page. Certification fee: $3.00. Payee: Clerk of Circuit Court. Personal checks accepted; credit cards are not. Prepayment required.

Charlotte General District Court PO Box 127, 111 Lagrand Ave, Charlotte Courthouse, VA 23923; 434-542-5600; fax: 434-542-5902; 8:30AM-4:30PM. ***Misdemeanor, Civil Actions under $15,000, Eviction, Small Claims.***
www.courts.state.va.us/courts/gd/Charlotte/home.html
Civil Records: Access: Online, in person. Visitors must perform in person searches themselves. Required to search: name, years to search. Civil cases indexed by defendant, plaintiff; index on computer back to 5/97. Civil PAT goes back to 10 years. Search free at www.courts.state.va.us/. Results show address of subject and day & month of birth, but not year. Also search LOPAS; call 804-786-5511 to apply.
Criminal Records: Access: Online, in person. Visitors must perform in person searches themselves. Required to search: name, years to search, DOB; also helpful-SSN, signed release. Criminal records computerized from 5/97. Criminal PAT goes back to 10 years. Search free at www.courts.state.va.us/. Results show address of subject and day & month of birth, but not year.
General Information: No juvenile, sealed records released. Will not fax documents. Court makes copy: $.50 per page. Self serve: same. No cert fee. Payee: Clerk of General District Court. Personal checks accepted. Visa/MC accepted. Prepayment required.

Charlottesville City

16th Circuit Court 315 E High St, Charlottesville, VA 22902; 434-970-3766; 8:30AM-4:30PM. ***Felony, Civil over $15,000, Probate.***
www.courts.state.va.us/courts/circuit/Charlottesville/home.html
Civil Records: Access: In person. Visitors must perform in person searches themselves. Required to search: name, years to search. Civil cases indexed by defendant, plaintiff; index on books from 1888 to present.
General Information: No juvenile, sealed or adoption records released. Will not fax documents. Court makes copy: $.50 per page. Certification fee: $2.00. Payee: Charlottesville Circuit Court Clerk's Office. No out of state checks accepted. No credit cards accepted. Prepayment required.

Charlottesville General District Court PO Box 2677, 606 E Market St, Charlottesville, VA 22902-2677; 434-970-3388; criminal phone: 434-970-3366; civil phone: 434-970-3392; fax: 434-970-3387; 8:30AM-4:30PM. ***Misdemeanor, Civil Actions under $15,000, Eviction, Small Claims.***
www.courts.state.va.us/courts/gd/Charlottesville/home.html Traffic phone- 434-970-3386.
Civil Records: Access: Mail, in person, online. Both court and visitors may perform in person searches. No search fee. Required to search: name, years to search. Civil cases indexed by defendant, plaintiff. Civil records kept for 10 years. Mail turnaround time 3 days. Civil PAT goes back to 10 years. PAT civil results show middle initial. Search via LOPAS; call 804-786-5511 to apply.
Criminal Records: Access: Mail, online, in person. Both court and visitors may perform in person searches. No search fee. Required to search: name, years to search; also helpful: DOB, SSN. Criminal records kept for 10 years. Mail turnaround time 3 days. Criminal PAT goes back to same as civil. PAT criminal results show middle initial. Search via LOPAS; call 804-786-5511 to apply. Online results show middle initial, DOB.
General Information: Online identifiers in results same as on public terminal. No juvenile, sealed, confidential records released. Will fax documents to local or toll-free number. Court makes copy: $1.00 first page, $.50 each add'l. Self serve: $.50 per page. Certification fee: Included in copy fee. Payee: General District Court. Personal checks accepted. Visa/MC accepted. Prepayment required. Mail requests: SASE required.

Chesapeake County

1st Circuit Court 307 Albemarle Dr, #300A, Chesapeake, VA 23322-5579; 757-382-3000; fax: 757-382-3034; 8AM-4PM. ***Felony, Civil Actions over $15,000, Probate.***
www.courts.state.va.us/courts/circuit.html
Civil Records: Access: Mail, fax, online, in person. Visitors must perform in person searches themselves. No search fee. Required to search: name, years to search. Civil cases indexed by defendant, plaintiff; index on books from 1637, on computer from 1989. Mail turnaround time 1 week. Civil PAT goes back to 1989. Search free at www.courts.state.va.us/. Results show address of subject and day & month of birth, but not year. Also search LOPAS; call 804-786-5511 to apply.
Criminal Records: Access: Mail, fax, online, in person. Visitors must perform in person searches themselves. No search fee. Required to search: name, years to search, DOB; also helpful: SSN, sex, signed release. Criminal docket on books from 1800s; on computer from 1989. Mail turnaround time 1 week. Criminal PAT goes back to same as civil. Online access to criminal records is the same as civil. Online results show only month and day of DOB plus sex, race.
General Information: No juvenile, sealed records released. Fee to fax document $.50 per page. Court makes copy: $.50 per page. Certification fee: $2.00. Payee: Clerk of Circuit Court. Personal checks accepted. Visa/MC accepted. Mail requests: SASE required.

1st General District Court 307 Albemarle Dr, #100, Chesapeake, VA 23322; 757-382-3100; criminal phone: 757-382-3134; civil: 757-382-3143; fax: 757-382-3171; 8AM-4PM. ***Misdemeanor, Civil Actions under $15,000, Eviction, Small Claims, Traffic.***
Indicate division (civil, criminal or traffic) in address. Alternative fax- 757-382-3113. Traffic phone- 757-382-3119.
Civil Records: Access: Mail, in person, online. Both court and visitors may perform in person searches. No search fee. Required to search: name, years to search. Civil cases indexed by defendant, plaintiff; index on computer back to 1990; prior on books. Mail turnaround time up to 4 weeks. Civil PAT goes back to 1990. Search free at www.courts.state.va.us/. Results show address of subject and day & month of birth, but not year.
Criminal Records: Access: Mail, online, in person. Both court and visitors may perform in person searches. Required to search: name, years to search, DOB; also helpful: SSN. Criminal records computerized from 1990; prior on books. Mail turnaround time 2-14 days. Criminal PAT goes back to same as civil. Search free at www.courts.state.va.us/. Results show address of subject and day & month of birth, but not year.
General Information: Online identifiers in results same as on public terminal. No juvenile, sealed records released. Will not fax documents. Court makes copy: $1.00 per page. Certification fee: $2.00. Payee: General District Court. Personal checks accepted. Visa/MC accepted. Prepayment required.

Chesterfield County

12th Circuit Court 9500 Courthouse Rd, PO Box 125, Chesterfield, VA 23832; 804-748-1241; fax: 804-796-5625; 8AM-4:30PM. ***Felony, Civil Actions over $15,000, Probate.***
www.co.chesterfield.va.us/JusticeAdministration/CircuitCourtClerk/clerhome.asp
The probate clerk will not search probate court records for you.
Civil Records: Access: Mail, in person, online. Both court and visitors may perform in person searches. No search fee. Required to search: name, years to search. Civil cases indexed by defendant, plaintiff; index on computer go back to 1989; prior on index books. Mail turnaround time 1-2 days. Public use terminal has civil records back to 1989. PAT results show middle initial, DOB. Remote online access to court case indexes is via LOPAS; call 804-786-5511 to apply.
Criminal Records: Access: Mail, in person, online. Only the court performs in person searches; visitors may not. No search fee. Required to search: name, years to search; also helpful: DOB, SSN, charge. Criminal records on computer go back to 1989, prior on index books. Mail turnaround time 1 week. Remote online access to court case indexes is via LOPAS; call 804-786-5511 to apply.
General Information: No juvenile, adoption, sealed records released. Will not fax documents. Court makes copy: $.50 per page. Certification fee: $2.00. Payee: Chesterfield Circuit Court. Personal checks accepted; credit cards are not. Prepayment required. Mail requests: SASE required.

12th General District Court PO Box 144, 9500 Courthouse Rd, Chesterfield, VA 23832; 804-748-1231; fax: 804-748-1757; 8-4. ***Misdemeanor, Civil under $15,000, Eviction, Small Claims.***
www.courts.state.va.us/courts/gd/Chesterfield/home.html
Civil Records: Access: Mail, in person, online. Both court and visitors may perform in person searches. No search fee. Required to search: name, years to search. Civil cases indexed by defendant, plaintiff; index on computer from 1986 to present, index books from 1975 to 1986. Mail turnaround time 2 days. Search free at www.courts.state.va.us/. Results show address of subject and day & month of birth, but not year. Also search LOPAS; call 804-786-5511 to apply.
Criminal Records: Access: Mail, online, in person. Both court and visitors may perform in person searches. No search fee. Required to search: name, years to search, DOB, SSN. Criminal records computerized from 1986 to present, index books from 1975 to 1986. Note: Results include name and address. Mail turnaround time 2 days. Search free at www.courts.state.va.us/. Results show address of subject and day & month of birth, but not year.
General Information: No sealed records released. Will not fax documents. Court makes copy: $.50 per page. Certification fee: $2.00. Payee: Court. Personal checks accepted. Visa/MC accepted. Prepayment required.

Clarke County

26th Circuit Court PO Box 189, Berryville, VA 22611; 540-955-5116; fax: 540-955-0284; 9AM-5PM. ***Felony, Civil Actions over $15,000, Probate.***
www.courts.state.va.us/courts/circuit.html
Civil Records: Access: In person, online. Visitors must perform in person searches themselves. Required to search: name, years to search. Civil cases indexed by defendant, plaintiff; index on books from 1920s. Search free at www.courts.state.va.us/. Results show address of subject and day & month of birth, but not year. Also search LOPAS; call 804-786-5511 to apply.
Criminal Records: Access: In person, online. Visitors must perform in person searches

themselves. Required to search: name, years to search, signed release. Criminal docket on books from 1920s. Search free by name only or case number at www.courts.state.va.us/. Results show address of subject and day & month of birth, but not year. Also search LOPAS; call 804-786-5511 to apply. Online results show middle initial, DOB.
General Information: No juvenile, sealed or adoption records released. No criminal records by mail. Fee to fax document $.50 per page. Court makes copy: $.50 per page. Self serve: same. No certification fee. Payee: Clerk of Court. Personal checks accepted. Prepayment required.

General District Court PO Box 612, 104 N Church St, Berryville, VA 22611; 540-955-5128; fax: 540-955-1195; 8:30-4:30PM. ***Misdemeanor, Civil Actions under $15,000, Eviction, Small Claims.***
www.co.clarke.va.us
Civil Records: Access: Online, in person. Visitors must perform in person searches themselves. Required to search: name, years to search. Civil cases indexed by defendant, plaintiff; index on computer back 10 years, on index cards prior. Civil PAT goes back to 10 years. Search free at www.courts.state.va.us/. Results show address of subject and day & month of birth, but not year. Also search LOPAS; call 804-786-5511 to apply.
Criminal Records: Access: Online, in person. Visitors must perform in person searches themselves. Required to search: name, years to search, DOB, date of conviction, charge; also helpful: docket number, defendant's name. Criminal records on computer back 10 years. Criminal PAT goes back to 10 years. Search free at www.courts.state.va.us/. Results show address of subject and day & month of birth, but not year.
General Information: Online identifiers in results same as on public terminal. Will not fax documents. Court makes copy: $.50 per page. Self serve: same. No certification fee. Payee: Clarke County General District Court. Personal checks require name and address. Major credit cards accepted. Mail requests: SASE required for mail return of any copies.

Clifton Forge City

25th Circuit Court ***Felony, Civil Actions over $15,000, Probate.***
This court closed 7/1/01 and was combined with the Alleghany County Circuit Court.

25th General District Court PO Box 139, 266 W Main St, Covington, VA 24426; 540-965-1720; fax: 540-965-1722; 9AM-5PM. ***Misdemeanor, Civil Actions under $15,000, Eviction, Small Claims.***
As of 7/1/2001, the Clifton Forge Court combined with the Alleghany County District Court to form the 25th Combined District Court.

Colonial Heights City

12th Circuit Court 401 Temple Ave, PO Box 3401, Colonial Heights, VA 23834; 804-520-9364; fax: 804-524-8726; 8:30AM-5PM. ***Felony, Civil Actions over $15,000, Probate.***
www.courts.state.va.us/courts/circuit.html
Civil Records: Access: Mail, in person, online. Both court and visitors may perform in person searches. Search fee: $5.00 per name. Required to search: name, years to search. Civil cases indexed by defendant, plaintiff; index on books from 1961, on computer from 1990. Mail turnaround time 2 days. Search via LOPAS; call 804-786-5511 to apply.
Criminal Records: Access: Mail, in person, online. Both court and visitors may perform in person searches. Search fee: $5.00 per name. Required to search: name, years to search; also helpful: DOB, SSN. Criminal docket on books from 1961, on computer from 1990. Mail turnaround time 2 days. Online access to criminal records is the same as civil.
General Information: No juvenile, sealed or adoption records released. Court makes copy: $.50 per page. Self serve: same. Certification fee: $2.00 per document. Payee: Clerk of Circuit Court. Personal checks accepted; credit cards are not. Prepayment required. Mail requests: SASE required.

12th General District Court PO Box 279, 401 Temple Ave, Colonial Heights, VA 23834; 804-520-9346 (dial 0); fax: 804-520-9370; 8AM-4PM. ***Misdemeanor, Civil Actions under $15,000, Eviction, Small Claims.***
Civil Records: Access: Mail, fax, online, in person. Both court and visitors may perform in person searches. No search fee. Required to search: name, years to search. Civil cases indexed by defendant, plaintiff; index on computer from 1989 to present, index cards from 1985. Mail turnaround time 1 week. Civil PAT goes back to 10 years. PAT civil results show middle initial. Results include name and case number, but only a partial SSN. Search free at www.courts.state.va.us/. Results show address of subject and day & month of birth, but not year. Also search LOPAS; call 804-786-5511 to apply.
Criminal Records: Access: Mail, fax, online, in person. Both court and visitors may perform in person searches. No search fee. Required to search: name, years to search, DOB, SSN. Criminal records computerized from 1989 to present, index cards from 1985. Mail turnaround time 1 week. Criminal PAT goes back to 10 years. PAT results show middle initial, DOB. Results include name and case number. Search free at www.courts.state.va.us/. Results show address of subject and day & month of birth, but not year.
General Information: No juvenile, sealed records released. Will not fax documents. Court makes copy: $.50 per page. No certification fee. Payee: Colonial Heights Combined Court. Personal checks accepted. Visa/MC accepted. Prepayment required. Mail requests: SASE requested.

Covington City

Circuit & District Courts
See Alleghany County.

Craig County

25th Circuit Court 182 Main St, #4, New Castle, VA 24127-0185; 540-864-6141; fax: 540-864-7471; 9AM-5PM. ***Felony, Civil Actions over $15,000, Probate.***
www.courts.state.va.us/courts/circuit.html
Civil Records: Access: Online, in person. Visitors must perform in person searches themselves. Required to search: name, years to search. Civil cases indexed by defendant. Civil records on books from mid 1800s. Civil PAT goes back to 1984. Remote online access to court case indexes is via LOPAS; call 804-786-5511 to apply.
Criminal Records: Access: Online, in person. Visitors must perform in person searches themselves. Required to search: name, years to search; also helpful: SSN. Criminal docket on books from mid 1800s. Criminal PAT goes back to 1984.PAT results show name, DOB. Online access to criminal records is the same as civil. Online results show only month and day of DOB plus sex, race.
General Information: No juvenile, sealed or adoption records released. Will not fax documents. Court makes copy: $.50 per page. Self serve: same. Certification fee: $2.00. Payee: Clerk of Court. Personal checks accepted; credit cards are not. Prepayment required.

25th General District Court Craig County General District Court, PO Box 232, New Castle, VA 24127; 540-864-5989; fax: 540-864-7385; 8:15AM-4:45PM. ***Misdemeanor, Civil Actions under $15,000, Eviction, Small Claims.***
Civil Records: Access: Mail, in person, online. Visitors must perform in person searches themselves. No search fee. Required to search: name, years to search. Civil cases indexed by defendant, plaintiff. Civil records in files 10 years back. Mail turnaround time 2-3 days. Civil PAT goes back to 10 years. PAT results show name only. Search free at www.courts.state.va.us/. Results show address of subject and day & month of birth, but not year. Also search LOPAS; call 804-786-5511 to apply.
Criminal Records: Access: Mail, online, in person. Visitors must perform in person searches themselves. No search fee. Required to search: name, years to search; also helpful: SSN. Criminal records in files 10 years back. Note: Lengthy searches must be performed in person. Mail turnaround time is 2-3 days. Criminal PAT goes back to same as civil. PAT results show name only. Search free at www.courts.state.va.us/. Results show address of subject and day & month of birth, but not year.
General Information: No juvenile, sealed records released. Will not fax documents. Court makes copy: $.50 per page. No certification fee. Payee: Craig County District Court. Personal checks and credit cards accepted. Prepayment required. Mail requests: SASE required.

Culpeper County

16th Circuit Court 135 W Cameron St, Culpeper, VA 22701-3097; 540-727-3438; 8:30AM-4:30PM. ***Felony, Civil over $15,000, Probate.***
www.courts.state.va.us/courts/circuit/Culpeper/home.html
Civil Records: Access: In person, online. Visitors must perform in person searches themselves. Required to search: name, years to search. Civil cases indexed by defendant, plaintiff; index on computer from 1991, docket books from 1800s. Civil PAT goes back to 1991. Search free at www.courts.state.va.us/. Results show address of subject and day & month of birth, but not year. Also search LOPAS; call 804-786-5511 to apply.
Criminal Records: Access: In person, online. Visitors must perform in person searches themselves. Required to search: name, years to search, signed release. Criminal records computerized from 1991, docket books from 1800s. Criminal PAT goes back to same as civil. Online access to criminal records is same as civil. Online results show only month and day of DOB plus sex, race.
General Information: No juvenile, sealed records released. Will not fax documents. Court makes copy: $.50 per page. Self serve: $.50 per page. Certification fee: $2.00. Payee: Clerk of Court. No personal checks. No credit cards accepted. Prepayment required.

16th General District Court 135 W Cameron St, Culpeper, VA 22701; 540-727-3417; fax: 540-727-3474; 8:30AM-4:30PM. ***Misdemeanor, Civil Actions under $15,000, Eviction, Small Claims.***
Civil Records: Access: Mail, in person, online. Both court and visitors may perform in person searches. No search fee. Required to search: name, years to search. Civil cases indexed by defendant, plaintiff; index on computer from 1987 to present, prior on index cards. Mail turnaround time 1-5 days. Civil PAT goes back to back 10 years. Search free at www.courts.state.va.us/. Results show address of subject and day & month of birth, but not year. Also search LOPAS; call 804-786-5511 to apply.
Criminal Records: Access: Mail, online, in person. Both court and visitors may perform in person searches. No search fee. Required to search: name, years to search. Criminal records computerized from 1987 to present, prior on index cards. Mail turnaround time 1-5 days. Criminal PAT goes back to same as civil. Search free at www.courts.state.va.us/. Results show address of subject and day & month of birth, but not year.
General Information: No juvenile, sealed records released. Will not fax documents. Court makes copy: $1.00 1st 2 pages, $.50 each add'l. Certification fee: $1.00 per page. Payee: General District Court. Personal checks accepted. Visa/MC accepted. Prepayment required. Mail requests: SASE required.

Cumberland County

10th Circuit Court PO Box 8, Cumberland, VA 23040; 804-492-4442; fax: 804-492-4876; 8:30AM-4:30PM. ***Felony, Civil Actions over $15,000, Probate.***
www.courts.state.va.us/courts/circuit.html
Civil Records: Access: Online, in person. Visitors must perform in person searches themselves. Civil cases indexed by defendant, plaintiff. Civil records computerized from 1/2001. Note: Phone access only for simple requests. Public use terminal available. Search free at www.courts.state.va.us/. Results show address of subject and day & month of birth, but not year. Also search LOPAS; call 804-786-5511 to apply.

Criminal Records: Access: Online, in person. Visitors must perform in person searches themselves. Criminal records computerized from 1/2001. Public use terminal available. Online access to criminal records is same as civil. Online results show only month and day of DOB plus sex, race.
General Information: No juvenile, sealed records released. Will fax documents $1.00 per page. Court makes copy: $.50 per page. Self serve: same. Certification fee: $.50 per page. Payee: Clerk of Circuit Court. Personal checks accepted. Prepayment required.

10th General District Court PO Box 24, Cumberland, VA 23040; 804-492-4848; fax: 804-492-9455; 8:30AM-4:30PM. ***Misdemeanor, Civil Actions under $15,000, Eviction, Small Claims.***
Civil Records: Access: Phone, fax, mail, online, in person. Only the court performs in person searches; visitors may not. No search fee. Required to search: name, years to search. Civil cases indexed by defendant, plaintiff; index on computer from 1993. Mail turnaround time 2 days. Search free at http://epwsgdp1.courts.state.va.us/gdcourts/caseSearch.do?index=index. Results show name and sometimes address
Criminal Records: Access: Phone, fax, mail, online, in person. Only the court performs in person searches; visitors may not. No search fee. Required to search: name, years to search; also helpful: DOB, SSN, sex. Criminal records computerized from 1993. Mail turnaround time 2 days. Online access to criminal records is the same as civil. Results show DOB month and day only. Online results show middle initial, DOB.
General Information: No juvenile, sealed records released. Will not fax documents. Court makes copy: $1.00 per page. No certification fee. Payee: Clerk of District Court. Personal checks and credit cards accepted. Prepayment required. Mail requests: SASE required.

Danville City

22nd Circuit Court PO Box 3300 (401 Patton St), Danville, VA 24543; 434-799-5168; fax: 434-799-6502; 9AM-4:30PM. ***Felony, Civil Actions over $15,000, Probate.*** www.danville-va.gov/home.asp
Civil Records: Access: In person, online. Visitors must perform in person searches themselves. Required to search: name, years to search. Civil cases indexed by defendant, plaintiff. Civil records in index books from 1841, judgments on computer since 1990. Civil PAT goes back to 1988. Search free at www.courts.state.va.us/. Results show address of subject and day & month of birth, but not year. Also, search daily docket from the web page.
Criminal Records: Access: In person, online. Visitors must perform in person searches themselves. Required to search: name, years to search. Criminal docket on books from 1841. Criminal records computerized from 1988. Criminal PAT goes back to same as civil. Online access to criminal records is the same as civil. Online results show only month and day of DOB plus sex, race.
General Information: No juvenile, sealed or adoption records released. Will not fax documents. Court makes copy: $.50 per page. Self serve: same. Certification fee: $2.00. Payee: Gerald A Gibson, Clerk. Personal checks accepted; credit cards are not. Prepayment required.

22nd General District Court PO Box 3300, Danville, VA 24543; 434-799-5179; fax: 434-797-8814; 8:30AM-4:30PM. ***Misdemeanor, Civil Actions under $15,000, Eviction, Small Claims, Traffic.***
Civil Records: Access: Mail, in person, online. Both court and visitors may perform in person searches. No search fee. Required to search: name, years to search. Civil cases indexed by defendant, plaintiff. Civil records go back 10 years on computer. Mail turnaround time 2 days. Civil PAT goes back to 10 years. PAT results show name only. Select and search District Courts at http://epwsgdp1.courts.state.va.us/gdcourts/caseSearch.do?index=index. Results show name and sometimes address. For information about the statewide online systems, see the state introduction.

Criminal Records: Access: Mail, online, in person. Both court and visitors may perform in person searches. No search fee. Required to search: name, years to search. Criminal records go back 10 years; on computer back to 1994. Mail turnaround time 2 days. Criminal PAT goes back to same as civil. PAT results show name only. Search free at www.courts.state.va.us/. Results show address of subject and day & month of birth, but not year.
General Information: Online identifiers in results same as on public terminal. No juvenile, sealed records released. Court makes copy: $1.00 1st 2 pages, $.50 each add'l. No certification fee. Payee: General District Court. Personal checks and credit cards accepted. Prepayment required. Mail requests: SASE required.

Dickenson County

29th Circuit Court PO Box 190, 293 Clintwood Main St, Clintwood, VA 24228; 276-926-1616; fax: 276-926-6465; 8AM-4:30PM. ***Felony, Civil Actions over $15,000, Probate.***
www.courts.state.va.us/courts/circuit.html
Civil Records: Access: Mail, in person, online. Both court and visitors may perform in person searches. No search fee. Required to search: name, years to search. Civil cases indexed by defendant, plaintiff; index on computer from 1989, index book from 1880. Mail turnaround time 1 week. Civil PAT goes back to 1989. Search free at www.courts.state.va.us/. Results show address of subject and day & month of birth, but not year.
Criminal Records: Access: Mail, online, in person. Both court and visitors may perform in person searches. No search fee. Required to search: name, years to search, DOB; also helpful: SSN. Criminal records computerized from 1989, index book from 1880. Note: Results include name, address and case number. Mail turnaround time 1 week. Criminal PAT goes back to same as civil. Online access to criminal records is the same as civil. Online results show only month and day of DOB plus sex, race.
General Information: Online identifiers in results same as on public terminal. No juvenile, sealed, adoption, confidential records released. Will not fax documents. Court makes copy: $.50 per page. Self serve: same. Certification fee: $2.50. Payee: Joe Tate, Clerk of Circuit Court. No personal checks. No credit cards accepted. Prepayment required. Mail requests: SASE requested.

29th General District Court PO Box 128, Clintwood, VA 24228; 276-926-1630; fax: 276-926-4815; 8:30AM-4:30PM. ***Misdemeanor, Civil Actions under $15,000, Eviction, Small Claims.***
Civil Records: Access: Phone, mail, in person, online. Both court and visitors may perform in person searches. No search fee. Required to search: name, years to search. Civil cases indexed by defendant. Civil records on computer back 10 years. Mail turnaround time 1 week. Civil PAT goes back to 10 years. PAT civil results show middle initial. Search free at www.courts.state.va.us/. Results show address of subject and day & month of birth, but not year. Also search LOPAS; call 804-786-5511 to apply.
Criminal Records: Access: Phone, mail, in person, online. Both court and visitors may perform in person searches. No search fee. Required to search: name, years to search. Criminal records on computer back 10 years. Mail turnaround time 1 week. Criminal PAT goes back to 10 years. PAT criminal results show middle initial. Search free at www.courts.state.va.us/. Results show address of subject and day & month of birth, but not year.
General Information: Online identifiers in results same as on public terminal. No juvenile, sealed records released. Will fax documents. Court makes copy: $.10 per page. No certification fee. Payee: Dickenson Combined Court or General District Court. Personal checks and credit cards accepted. Prepayment required. Mail requests: SASE requested.

Dinwiddie County

11th Circuit Court PO Box 63, Dinwiddie, VA 23841; 804-469-4540; fax: 804-469-5386; 8:30AM-4:30PM. ***Felony, Civil Actions over $15,000, Probate.***
www.courts.state.va.us/courts/circuit.html
Probate is separate index at this same address.
Civil Records: Access: Mail, in person, online. Both court and visitors may perform in person searches. No search fee. Required to search: name, years to search; also helpful: address. Civil cases indexed by defendant, plaintiff. Civil index on cards from 1833; deeds on computer since 1989. Mail turnaround time 3 days. Search free at www.courts.state.va.us/. Results show address of subject and day & month of birth, but not year.
Criminal Records: Access: Mail, online, in person. Both court and visitors may perform in person searches. No search fee. Required to search: name, years to search; also helpful: DOB, SSN. Criminal records indexed on cards from 1833; deeds on computer since 1989. Mail turnaround time 3 days. Online access to criminal records is the same as civil. Online results show only month and day of DOB, sex, race.
General Information: No juvenile, sealed or expunged records released. Will not fax documents. Court makes copy: $.50 per page. Self serve: same. Certification fee: $2.00. Payee: Clerk of Court. Personal checks accepted. Visa/MC accepted for criminal payments only accepted. Prepayment required. Mail requests: SASE requested.

11th General District Court PO Box 280, Dinwiddie, VA 23841; 804-469-4533; fax: 804-469-5383; 8:30AM-4:30PM. ***Misdemeanor, Civil Actions under $15,000, Eviction, Small Claims.***
Civil Records: Access: Mail, in person, online. Only the court performs in person searches; visitors may not. No search fee. Required to search: name, years to search. Civil cases indexed by Defendant, Plaintiff. Civil records go back 10 years. Mail turnaround time 3 days. Civil PAT goes back to 10 years. Search free at www.courts.state.va.us/. Results show address of subject and day & month of birth, but not year. Also search LOPAS; call 804-786-5511 to apply.
Criminal Records: Access: Mail, online, in person. Only the court performs in person searches; visitors may not. No search fee. Required to search: name, years to search. Criminal records computerized from 1989. Mail turnaround time 3 days. Criminal PAT goes back to 10 years. Search free at www.courts.state.va.us/. Results show address of subject and day & month of birth, but not year.
General Information: No juvenile, sealed records released. Will not fax documents. Court makes copy: $.50 per page. Payee: District Court. Personal checks and credit cards accepted. Prepayment required. Mail requests: SASE required.

Emporia City

Circuit Court
See Greensville County

6th General District Court 315 S Main, Emporia, VA 23847; 434-634-5400; fax: 434-634-0049; 8:30AM-4PM. ***Misdemeanor, Civil Actions under $15,000, Eviction, Small Claims.***
Civil Records: Access: Online, in person. Visitors must perform in person searches themselves. Required to search: name, years to search. Civil cases indexed by defendant, plaintiff; index on computer back to 1991. Civil PAT goes back to 10 years. Search free at www.courts.state.va.us/. Results show address of subject and day & month of birth, but not year. Also search LOPAS; call 804-786-5511 to apply.
Criminal Records: Access: Online, in person. Visitors must perform in person searches themselves. Required to search: name, years to search. Criminal records computerized from 1991. Criminal PAT goes back to 10 years. Search free at www.courts.state.va.us/. Results show address of subject and day & month of birth, but not year.
General Information: No juvenile records released. Will not fax documents. Court makes copy: $1.00 per

page; $.25 each add'l. No certification fee. Payee: The Court. Visa/MC accepted. Prepayment required.

Essex County

15th Circuit Court PO Box 445, 305 Prince St, Tappahannock, VA 22560; 804-443-3541; fax: 804-445-1216; 8:30AM-5PM. ***Felony, Civil Actions over $15,000, Probate.*** www.courts.state.va.us/courts/circuit.html

Civil Records: Access: In person, online. Visitors must perform in person searches themselves. Required to search: name, years to search. Civil cases indexed by defendant, plaintiff; index on books from 1656; deed index on computer back to 2006. Search free at www.courts.state.va.us/. Results show address of subject and day & month of birth, but not year. Also search LOPAS; call 804-786-5511 to apply.

Criminal Records: Access: In person, online. Visitors must perform in person searches themselves. Required to search: name, years to search. Criminal docket on books from 1656. Public use terminal has crim records. Online access to criminal records is the same as civil. Online results show only month and day of DOB plus sex, race.

General Information: No juvenile, sealed records released. Will fax documents $.50 per page. Court makes copy: $.50 per page. Self serve: same. Certification fee: $2.00. Payee: Clerk of Court. Personal checks accepted. Prepayment required.

15th General District Court PO Box 66, 300 Prince St, Tappahannock, VA 22560; 804-443-3744; fax: 804-443-4122; 8AM-4PM. ***Misdemeanor, Civil Actions under $15,000, Eviction, Small Claims.***

Civil Records: Access: Online, in person. Both court and visitors may perform in person searches. No search fee. Required to search: name, years to search. Civil cases indexed by defendant, plaintiff; index on computer from 5/92. Civil PAT goes back to 10 years. Search free at www.courts.state.va.us/. Results show address of subject and day & month of birth, but not year. Also search LOPAS; call 804-786-5511 to apply.

Criminal Records: Access: Online, in person. Visitors must perform in person searches themselves. Required to search: name, years to search, DOB, SSN. Criminal records computerized from 5/92. Criminal PAT goes back to same as civil. Search free at www.courts.state.va.us/. Results show address of subject and day & month of birth, but not year.

General Information: No juvenile, sealed records released. Will not fax documents. Court makes copy: $1.00 per page. No certification fee. Payee: Court. Personal checks accepted. Visa/MC accepted. Prepayment required.

Fairfax County

19th Circuit Court 4110 Chain Bridge Rd, Fairfax, VA 22030; criminal phone: 703-246-2228; civil phone: 703-691-7320 x3-1-1; fax: 703-273-6564; 8AM-4PM. ***Felony, Civil Actions over $15,000, Probate.*** www.fairfaxcounty.gov/courts/circuit

Civil Records: Access: In person, online. Visitors must perform in person searches themselves. Required to search: name, years to search. Civil cases indexed by defendant, plaintiff. Civil records computerized from 1979; index books for prior years; scanned back to 1700s. Civil PAT goes back to 1979. PAT results show middle initial, DOB. Access to current court case indexes is via CPAN subscription; call 703-246-2366 or see www.fairfaxcounty.gov/courts/circuit/cpan.htm to apply. Fee is $25.00 per month per user. Also, Friday's Motion dockets are available free at www.fairfaxcounty.gov/courts/circuit/dockets/.

Criminal Records: Access: In person, online. Visitors must perform in person searches themselves. Required to search: name, years to search, DOB; also helpful: SSN. Criminal records computerized from 1979. Criminal PAT goes back to same as civil. PAT results show middle initial, DOB. Online access to criminal same as civil, see above. Online results show only month and day of DOB plus sex, race.

General Information: Online identifiers in results same as on public terminal. No juvenile, sealed records released. Will not fax documents. Court makes copy: $.50 per page.Separate fees for electronically generated docs. Certification fee: $2.00 per doc, paper or electronic. Payee: Fairfax Circuit Court. No personal checks. Credit cards accepted. Prepayment required.

19th General District Court 4110 Chain Bridge Rd, Fairfax, VA 22030; criminal phone: 703-246-3305; civil phone: 703-246-3012; fax: 703-591-2349; 8AM-4PM. ***Misdemeanor, Civil Actions under $15,000, Eviction, Small Claims.*** www.fairfaxcounty.gov/courts/gendist Traffic Division- 703-246-3764.

Civil Records: Access: In person, online. Visitors must perform in person searches themselves. Required to search: name, years to search. Civil cases indexed by defendant, plaintiff. Civil indexes for 10 years; onsite records held only 3 years before archiving; on computer back 10 years. Civil PAT goes back to 10 years. PAT results show name only. Search free at www.courts.state.va.us/. Results show address of subject and day & month of birth, but not year.

Criminal Records: Access: In person, online. Both court and visitors may perform in person searches. No search fee. Required to search: name, years to search; also helpful: DOB, SSN, offense. Criminal & traffic records on computer for 10 years; onsite records held only 3 years before archiving. Criminal PAT goes back to 10 years. PAT results show name only. Search free at www.courts.state.va.us/. Results show address of subject and day & month of birth, but not year.

General Information: No juvenile, sealed records released. Will not fax documents as a general rule. Court makes copy: $.50 per page. Self serve: same. No certification fee. Payee: Fairfax General District Court. Personal checks accepted. Visa/MC accepted. Prepayment required.

Fairfax City

Circuit Court
See Fairfax County.

19th General District Court 10455 Armstrong St, #101, Fairfax, VA 22030; 703-385-7866; fax: 703-352-3195; 8:30AM-4:30PM. ***Misdemeanor, Traffic.*** www.courts.state.va.us/courts/gd/Fairfax_City/home.html
Find Circuit Court cases and General District civil cases for this city in Fairfax County.

Criminal Records: Access: Mail, in person, online. Only the court performs in person searches; visitors may not. No search fee. Required to search: name, years to search; also helpful: SSN. Criminal records on computer and index from 1996. Mail turnaround time same day. Public use terminal has crim records back to 1998. Search free at www.courts.state.va.us/. Results show address of subject and day & month of birth, but not year.

General Information: No juvenile or sealed records released. Will not fax documents. Court makes copy: $1.00 for first 2 pages, $.50 each add'l. No certification fee. Payee: General District Court. Personal checks accepted. Visa/MC accepted. Prepayment required. Mail requests: SASE requested.

Falls Church City

Circuit Court
See Arlington County.

17th General District Courts Combined
Falls Church District, 300 Park Ave, Falls Church, VA 22046-3305; 703-248-5096 (GDC); civil phone: 703-248-5098; fax: 703-241-1407; 8AM-4PM. ***Misdemeanor, Civil Actions under $15,000, Eviction, Small Claims.*** www.fallschurchva.gov
Small claims phone is 703-248-5157; juvenile and domestic relations is 703-248-5099.

Civil Records: Access: Fax, online. Only the court performs in person searches; visitors may not. No search fee. Required to search: name, years to search. Civil cases indexed by defendant, plaintiff; index on computer back to 1997. Search free at www.courts.state.va.us/. Results show address of subject and day & month of birth, but not year. Also search LOPAS; call 804-786-5511 to apply.

Criminal Records: Access: Fax, online, in person. Only the court performs in person searches; visitors may not. No search fee. Required to search: name, years to search; also helpful: DOB, SSN. Criminal records computerized from 1997. Search free at www.courts.state.va.us/. Results show address of subject and day & month of birth, but not year.

General Information: No juvenile or sealed records released. No fee to fax documents. Court makes copy: $1.00 1st page; $.50 each add'l. No certification fee. Payee: Falls Church District Court. Personal checks accepted. Visa/MC accepted. Prepayment required.

Fauquier County

Circuit Court 29 Ashby St, Circuit Clerk Office, Warrenton, VA 20186-3298; 540-347-8610; criminal phone: 540-347-8609; civil phone: 540-347-8607; probate phone: 540-347-8606; 8AM-4:30PM. ***Felony, Civil Actions over $15,000, Probate.*** www.fauquiercounty.gov/government/departments/circuitcourt

Civil Records: Access: Mail, in person, online. Visitors must perform in person searches themselves. Search fee: $5.00 per name. Required to search: name, years to search. Civil cases indexed by defendant, plaintiff; index on computer back to 1988. Mail turnaround time 1-5 days. Civil PAT goes back to 1988. PAT results show name only. Search free at www.courts.state.va.us/. Results show address of subject and day & month of birth, but not year.

Criminal Records: Access: Mail, in person, online. Visitors must perform in person searches themselves. Search fee: $5.00 per name. Required to search: name, years to search. Criminal records computerized from 1988. Note: Court recommends you contact the VA State Police. Mail turnaround time 1-5 days. Criminal PAT goes back to same as civil. PAT results show name only. Online access to criminal records is the same as civil. Online results show only month and day of DOB plus sex, race.

General Information: No juvenile, sealed, adoption records released. Will not fax documents. Court makes copy: $.50 per page. Self serve: same.Self serve copier requires $10.00 purchase of encoder device. Certification fee: $2.00 per doc. Payee: Clerk of Fauquier Circuit Court. No personal checks. No credit cards accepted. Prepayment required.

20th General District Court 6 Court St, Warrenton, VA 20186; 540-347-8627; fax: 540-347-5756; 8:30AM-4:30PM. ***Misdemeanor, Civil Actions under $15,000, Eviction, Small Claims.***

Civil Records: Access: Online, in person. Visitors must perform in person searches themselves. Required to search: name, years to search. Civil cases indexed by defendant, plaintiff; index on computerized back 10 years. Civil PAT goes back to 10 years. PAT civil results show middle initial. Search free at www.courts.state.va.us/. Results show address of subject and day & month of birth, but not year. Also search LOPAS; call 804-786-5511 to apply.

Criminal Records: Access: Online, in person. Visitors must perform in person searches themselves. Required to search: name, years to search. Criminal records computerized back 10 years, criminal records only go back 10 years. Note: In the rare instances when the court performs a search, there is no fee. Criminal PAT goes back to same as civil. PAT criminal results show middle initial. Search free at www.courts.state.va.us/. Results show address of subject and day & month of birth, but not year.

General Information: Online identifiers in results same as on public terminal. No juvenile, sealed records released. Will not fax documents. Court makes copy: $1.00 1st 2 pages, $.50 each add'l. No certification fee. Payee: General District Court. Personal checks and credit cards accepted. Prepayment required. Mail requests: SASE required for mail return of any copies.

Floyd County

27th Circuit Court 100 E Main St, #200, Floyd, VA 24091; 540-745-9330; fax: 540-745-9303; 8:30AM-4:30PM, 8:30AM-N Sat. ***Felony, Civil Actions over $15,000, Probate.***
www.floydcova.org/departments/circuit_court.shtml
Closed on Saturdays if it is a holiday.
Civil Records: Access: In person, online. Visitors must perform in person searches themselves. Required to search: name, years to search. Civil cases indexed by defendant, plaintiff; index on files from 1831. Civil PAT goes back to 1996. PAT results show name only. Search free at www.courts.state.va.us/. Results show address of subject and day & month of birth, but not year. Also search LOPAS; call 804-786-5511 to apply.
Criminal Records: Access: In person, online. Visitors must perform in person searches themselves. Required to search: name, years to search; also helpful: DOB, SSN. Criminal records on files from 1831. Criminal PAT goes back to 1996. PAT results show name only. Online access to criminal records is the same as civil. Online results show only month and day of DOB plus sex, race.
General Information: Online identifiers in results same as on public terminal. No juvenile, sealed records released. Will not fax documents. Court makes copy: $.50 per page. Certification fee: $2.00 per cert. Payee: Clerk of Circuit Court. Personal checks accepted; credit cards are not. Prepayment required.

27th General Combined District Court 100 E Main St, #208, Floyd, VA 24091-2101; 540-745-9327; fax: 540-745-9329; 8AM-4:30PM. ***Misdemeanor, Civil Actions under $15,000, Eviction, Small Claims.***
Civil Records: Access: In person, online. Visitors must perform in person searches themselves. Required to search: name, years to search. Civil cases indexed by defendant, plaintiff. Civil records computerized since 1993. Note: Phone search results may be of limited content. Civil PAT goes back to 1996. PAT civil results show middle initial. Search free at www.courts.state.va.us/. Results show address of subject and day & month of birth, but not year. Also, remote online access to court case indexes is via LOPAS; call 804-786-5511 to apply.
Criminal Records: Access: In person, online. Visitors must perform in person searches themselves. Required to search: name, years to search, DOB. Criminal records computerized since 1993. Note: Phone search results may be of limited content. Criminal PAT goes back to 1996. PAT criminal results show middle initial. Search free at www.courts.state.va.us/. Results show address of subject and day & month of birth, but not year.
General Information: No juvenile, sealed records released. Will not fax documents. Court makes copy: $.50 per page. Certification fee: None reported. Payee: Clerk of District Court. Personal checks accepted; credit cards are not. Prepayment required.

Fluvanna County

16th Circuit Court PO Box 550, Palmyra, VA 22963; 434-591-1970; fax: 434-591-1971; 8AM-4:30PM. ***Felony, Civil over $15,000, Probate.***
www.courts.state.va.us/courts/circuit.html
Civil Records: Access: Mail, in person, online. Both court and visitors may perform in person searches. Search fee: $5.00 per name. Required to search: name, years to search. Civil cases indexed by defendant, plaintiff. Civil index on docket books from 1777; computerized back to 1985. Mail turnaround time same 1-2 days. Search free at www.courts.state.va.us/. Results show address of subject and day & month of birth, but not year. Also search LOPAS; call 804-786-5511 to apply.
Criminal Records: Access: Mail, in person, online. Both court and visitors may perform in person searches. Search fee: $5.00 per name. Required to search: name, years to search, DOB; also helpful: SSN. Criminal records indexed in books from 1777; computerized back to 1985. Mail turnaround time 1-2 days. Online access to criminal records is the same as civil. Online results show only month and day of DOB, sex, race.
General Information: No juvenile or sealed records released. Fee to fax out file $2.00 each. Court makes copy: $.50 per page. Self serve: $.25 per page. Certification fee: $2.00. Payee: Clerk of Circuit Court. Personal checks accepted; credit cards are not. Prepayment required. Mail requests: SASE required.

16th General District Court PO Box 417, 72 Main St #B, County Courthouse, Palmyra, VA 22963; 434-591-1980; 8:30AM-4PM. ***Misdemeanor, Civil Actions under $15,000, Eviction, Small Claims.***
www.courts.state.va.us/courts/combined/Fluvanna/home.html For fax, dial, wait for answer, then press 4.
Civil Records: Access: Online, in person. Visitors must perform in person searches themselves. Required to search: name, years to search. Civil cases indexed by defendant, plaintiff; index on computer since 12/91, on books since 1984. Civil PAT goes back to 10 years. PAT civil results show middle initial. Search free at www.courts.state.va.us/. Results show address of subject and day & month of birth, but not year. Also search LOPAS; call 804-786-5511 to apply.
Criminal Records: Access: Online, in person. Visitors must perform in person searches themselves. Required to search: name, years to search; also helpful: DOB, SSN. Criminal records on computer since 12/91, on books since 1984. Criminal PAT goes back to same as civil. PAT criminal results show middle initial. Search free at www.courts.state.va.us/. Results show address of subject and day & month of birth, but not year.
General Information: Online identifiers in results same as on public terminal. No juvenile records released. Will not fax documents. Court makes copy: $.50 per page. No certification fee. Payee: Fluvanna District Court. Personal checks accepted; credit cards are not. Prepayment required.

Franklin County

22nd Judicial Circuit Court PO Box 567, 275 S Main St, #212, Rocky Mount, VA 24151; 540-483-3065; fax: 540-483-3042; 8:30AM-5PM. ***Felony, Civil Actions over $15,000, Probate.***
www.courts.state.va.us/courts/circuit/Franklin/home.html
Note that Franklin City is not the same as Franklin County. Only Franklin County information is given here. Contact the Sheriff's office at 540-483-3000 for record searches.
Civil Records: Access: In person, online. Visitors must perform in person searches themselves. Required to search: name. Civil cases indexed by defendant, plaintiff. Criminal records file on computer. Civil PAT goes back to 1986. Search free at www.courts.state.va.us/. Results show address of subject and day & month of birth, but not year.
Criminal Records: Access: In person, online. Visitors must perform in person searches themselves. Required to search: name, years to search. Criminal records file on computer. Criminal PAT goes back to same as civil. Online access to criminal records is the same as civil. Online results show only month and day of DOB plus sex, race.
General Information: Online identifiers in results same as on public terminal. No juvenile records released. Will fax documents $.50 per page. Court makes copy: $.50 per page. Self serve: $.50 per page. Certification fee: $2.00 per page. Payee: Court. Personal checks accepted; credit cards are not. Prepayment required. Mail requests: SASE required for mail return of any copies.

22nd General District Court PO Box 569, 275 S Main St, #111, Rocky Mount, VA 24151; 540-483-3060; fax: 540-483-3036; 8:30AM-4:30PM. ***Misdemeanor, Civil Actions under $15,000, Eviction, Small Claims.***
www.courts.state.va.us/courts/gd/Franklin_County/home.html
Contact the Sheriff's office at 540-483-3000 for criminal record searches.
Civil Records: Access: Online, in person. Visitors must perform in person searches themselves. Required to search: name, years to search. Civil cases indexed by defendant, plaintiff. Civil records file on computer from 1996. Civil PAT goes back to 10 years. PAT civil results show middle initial. Search free at www.courts.state.va.us/. Results show address of subject and day & month of birth, but not year. Also search LOPAS; call 804-786-5511 to apply.
Criminal Records: Access: Online, in person. Visitors must perform in person searches themselves. Required to search: name, years to search. Criminal records file on computer from 1996. Criminal PAT goes back to 10 years. PAT criminal results show middle initial. Search free at www.courts.state.va.us/. Results show address of subject and day & month of birth, but not year.
General Information: Online identifiers in results same as on public terminal. Will not fax documents. Court makes copy: $.25 per page. No certification fee. Personal checks accepted. Visa/MC accepted. Prepayment required.

Franklin City

Circuit Court
See Southampton County Circuit Court.

5th Judicial General District Combined 1020 Pretlow St, Franklin, VA 23851; 757-562-8550; 8AM-4PM. ***Misdemeanor, Civil Actions under $15,000, Eviction, Traffic.***
www.courts.state.va.us/courts/combined/Franklin_City/home.html
Southampton County serves as the Circuit Court for City of Franklin.
Civil Records: Access: Mail, in person, online. Both court and visitors may perform in person searches. No search fee. Required to search: name, years to search. Civil cases indexed by plaintiff. Civil records on computer since 1990. Mail turnaround time 5 days. Civil PAT goes back to 1990. Search free at www.courts.state.va.us/. Results show address of subject and day & month of birth, but not year. For info on the statewide online systems, see the state introduction.
Criminal Records: Access: Mail, online, in person. Both court and visitors may perform in person searches. No search fee. Required to search: name, years to search; also helpful: SSN. Criminal records on computer since 1990. Mail turnaround time 5 days. Criminal PAT goes back to same as civil. Search free at www.courts.state.va.us/. Results show address of subject and day & month of birth, but not year.
General Information: No juvenile records released. Will not fax documents. Court makes copy: $1.00 1st page; $.50 each add'l. No certification fee. Payee: Clerk of the District Court. Personal checks accepted. Visa/MC accepted. Prepayment required.

Frederick County

Circuit Court 5 N Kent St, Winchester, VA 22601; 540-667-5770; probate phone: 540-665-5659; fax: 540-545-8711; 9AM-5PM. ***Felony, Misdemeanor, Civil, Probate.***
www.winfredclerk.com
Civil Records: Access: Mail, in person, online. Both court and visitors may perform in person searches. No search fee. Required to search: name, years to search. Civil cases indexed by defendant, plaintiff; index on books from 1970s. Note: Mail access limited to simple requests. Mail turnaround time 1-2 days. Civil PAT goes back to 1985. Search free at www.courts.state.va.us/. Results show address of subject and day & month of birth, but not year. Also search LOPAS; call 804-786-5511 to apply.
Criminal Records: Access: In person, online. Visitors must perform in person searches themselves. Required to search: name, years to search. Criminal docket on books from 1970s. Criminal PAT goes back to same as civil. Online access to criminal records is the same as civil. Online results show only month and day of DOB plus sex, race.
General Information: No juvenile, sealed or adoption records released. Will not fax documents. Court makes copy: $.50 per page. Certification fee: $3.00. Payee: Clerk of Circuit Court. Personal checks accepted; credit cards are not. Prepayment required. Mail requests: SASE required.

26th General District Court 5 N Kent St, Judicial Ctr, Winchester, VA 22601; 540-722-7208; fax: 540-722-1063; 8AM-4PM. ***Misdemeanor, Civil Actions up to $15,000.***
www.courts.state.va.us/courts/gd/Frederick~Winchester/home.html
Civil Records: Access: In person, online. Visitors must perform in person searches themselves. Required to search: name, years to search. Civil records go back to 1987. Civil PAT goes back to 10 years. Search free at www.courts.state.va.us/. Results show address of subject and day & month of birth, but not year. Also search LOPAS; call 804-786-5511 to apply.
Criminal Records: Access: In person, online. Visitors must perform in person searches themselves. Required to search: name, years to search. Criminal records go back to 1987. Criminal PAT goes back to same as civil. Search free at www.courts.state.va.us/. Results show address of subject and day & month of birth, but not year.
General Information: Will not fax documents. Court makes copy: $.50 per page. Payee: Frederick District Court. Personal checks accepted. Visa/MC accepted. Prepayment required.

Fredericksburg City

15th Circuit Court PO Box 359 (601 Caroline St. 2nd Fl), Fredericksburg, VA 22404-0359; 540-372-1066; 8:30AM-4PM. ***Felony, Civil Actions over $15,000, Probate.***
www.courts.state.va.us/courts/circuit.html
Civil Records: Access: In person, online. Visitors must perform in person searches themselves. Required to search: name, years to search. Civil cases indexed by defendant, plaintiff. Civil index on docket books from 1765; computerized records since 1987. Civil PAT goes back to 1987. Search free at www.courts.state.va.us/. Results show address of subject and day & month of birth, but not year.
Criminal Records: Access: In person, online. Visitors must perform in person searches themselves. Required to search: name, years to search, DOB. Criminal records indexed in books from 1765; computerized records since 1987. Criminal PAT goes back to same as civil. Online access to criminal records is the same as civil. Online results show only month and day of DOB plus sex, race.
General Information: No juvenile, probate tax returns, sealed or adoption records released. Will not fax documents. Court makes copy: $.50 per page. Certification fee: $2.00 per doc. Payee: Clerk of Circuit Court. Personal checks accepted. Prepayment required.

15th General District Court PO Box 180, 615 Princess Ann St, Fredericksburg, VA 22404; criminal phone: 540-372-1043; civil phone: 540-372-1044; criminal fax: 540-372-1228; civil fax: 540-370-1729; 8AM-4PM. ***Misdemeanor, Civil Actions under $15,000, Eviction, Small Claims.***
Civil Records: Access: Mail, fax, online, in person. Both court and visitors may perform in person searches. No search fee. Required to search: name, years to search. Civil cases indexed by defendant, plaintiff; index on computer the past 10 years, prior on index books. Mail turnaround time 5-7 days. Civil PAT goes back to 10 years. Search free at www.courts.state.va.us/. Results show address of subject and day & month of birth, but not year. Also search LOPAS; call 804-786-5511 to apply.
Criminal Records: Access: Mail, fax, online, in person. Both court and visitors may perform in person searches. No search fee. Required to search: name, years to search, DOB, SSN. Criminal records on computer the past 10 years, prior on index books. Mail turnaround time 5-7 days. Criminal PAT goes back to 10 years. Search free at www.courts.state.va.us/. Results show address of subject and day & month of birth, but not year.
General Information: Online identifiers in results same as on public terminal. No sealed records released. Will fax out documents. Court makes copy: $1.00 1st page, $.50 each add'l. Self serve: same. Certification fee: $2.00 per doc. Payee: Fredricksburg District Court. Personal checks accepted. Major credit cards accepted for criminal only. Prepayment required. Mail requests: SASE required.

Galax City

Circuit Court
For Galax City area Circuit Court records, see Carroll County for Hillsville area and Grayson County for Independence area.

27th General District Court 353 N Main St, PO Box 214, Galax, VA 24333-0214; 276-236-8731; fax: 276-236-2754; 8AM-4:30PM. ***Misdemeanor, Civil Actions under $15,000, Eviction, Small Claims.*** Circuit Court jurisdiction for this city can be in Carroll County or Grayson County depending on side of the city the offense occurred.
Civil Records: Access: Mail, fax, online, in person. Both court and visitors may perform in person searches. No search fee. Required to search: name, years to search. Civil cases indexed by defendant, plaintiff; index on computer since 1990, prior on index books. Mail turnaround time 1-5 days. Public use terminal available, records go back to 10 years. Search free at www.courts.state.va.us/. Results show address of subject and day & month of birth, but not year. Also search LOPAS; call 804-786-5511 to apply.
Criminal Records: Access: Mail, fax, online, in person. Both court and visitors may perform in person searches. No search fee. Required to search: name, years to search. Criminal records on computer since 1990, prior on index books. Mail turnaround time 1-5 days. Public use terminal available, crim records go back to 10 years. Search free at www.courts.state.va.us/. Results show address of subject and day & month of birth, but not year.
General Information: No juvenile, sealed records released. Will not fax documents. Court makes copy: $.25 per page. No certification fee. Payee: Clerk of District Court Galax District. Personal checks and credit cards accepted. Prepayment required.

Giles County

27th Circuit Court 501 Wenonah Ave, PO Box 502, Pearisburg, VA 24134; 540-921-1722; fax: 540-921-3825; 8:30AM-5PM. ***Felony, Civil Actions over $15,000, Probate.***
www.courts.state.va.us/courts/circuit.html
Civil Records: Access: Mail, in person, online. Visitors must perform in person searches themselves. No search fee. Required to search: name, years to search. Civil cases indexed by defendant, plaintiff. Civil records go back to 1994. Mail turnaround time 1-2 days. Search free at www.courts.state.va.us/. Results show address of subject and day & month of birth, but not year.
Criminal Records: Access: In person, online. Visitors must perform in person searches themselves. Required to search: name, years to search, DOB; SSN helpful. Criminal records go back to 1994. Online access to criminal records is the same as civil. Online results show middle initial, DOB.
General Information: No juvenile, sealed records released. Will not fax documents. Court makes copy: $.25 per page. Self serve: $.25 per page. Certification fee: $3.00. Payee: Clerk of Circuit Court. Personal checks accepted; credit cards are not. Prepayment required. Mail requests: SASE required if copies to be mailed back.

27th General District Court 120 N Main St, #1, Pearisburg, VA 24134; 540-921-3533; fax: 540-921-3752; 8:30AM-4:30PM. ***Misdemeanor, Civil Actions under $15,000, Eviction, Small Claims.***
www.courts.state.va.us/courts/combined/Giles/home.html
Civil Records: Access: Fax, mail, online, in person. Both court and visitors may perform in person searches. No search fee. Required to search: name, years to search. Civil cases indexed by defendant, plaintiff; index on computer since 1990. Mail turnaround time 3-7 days. Civil PAT goes back to 1990. Terminal results also show SSNs. Search free at www.courts.state.va.us/. Results show address of subject and day & month of birth, but not year. Also search LOPAS; call 804-786-5511 to apply.
Criminal Records: Access: Fax, mail, online, in person. Both court and visitors may perform in person searches. No search fee. Required to search: name, years to search; also helpful: SSN. Criminal records on computer since 1990. Mail turnaround time 3-7 days. Criminal PAT goes back to same as civil. PAT criminal results show middle initial. Search free at www.courts.state.va.us/. Results show address of subject and day & month of birth, but not year.
General Information: Online identifiers in results same as on public terminal. No juvenile, sealed records released. Fee to fax out file $1.00 per page. Court makes copy: $1.00 first page, $.50 each add'l. No certification fee. Payee: General District Court. Personal checks accepted. Visa/MC accepted.

Gloucester County

9th Circuit Court 7400 Justice Dr #327, Gloucester, VA 23061-0570; 804-693-2502; fax: 804-693-2186; 8AM-4:30PM. ***Felony, Civil Actions over $15,000, Probate.***
www.gloucesterva.info
Civil Records: Access: Online, in person. Both court and visitors may perform in person searches. No search fee. Required to search: name, years to search. Civil cases indexed by defendant, plaintiff. Civil index on docket books from 1862; on computer since 1990. Civil PAT goes back to 1994. Search free at www.courts.state.va.us/. Results show address of subject and day & month of birth, but not year.
Criminal Records: Access: Online, in person. Visitors must perform in person searches themselves. Required to search: name, years to search, DOB. Criminal records indexed in books from 1862; on computer since 1990. Criminal PAT goes back to same as civil. Online access free at www.courts.state.va.us/caseinfo/circuit.html. Online results show only month and day of DOB plus sex, race.
General Information: No juvenile, sealed or adoption records released. Will not fax documents. Court makes copy: $.50 per page. Self serve: same. Certification fee: $2.00; $2.50 if judge's signature required. Payee: Clerk of Circuit Court. Personal checks and major credit cards accepted. Prepayment required.

9th General District Court PO Box 873, Gloucester, VA 23061; 804-693-4860; fax: 804-693-6669; 8:30AM-4:30PM. ***Misdemeanor, Civil Actions under $15,000, Eviction, Small Claims.***
Civil Records: Access: Fax, mail, online, in person. Both court and visitors may perform in person searches. No search fee. Required to search: name, years to search. Civil cases indexed by defendant, plaintiff. Civil index on docket books from 1985; computerized back to 1992. Mail turnaround time 1 week. Civil PAT goes back to 10 years. Search free at www.courts.state.va.us/. Results show address of subject and day & month of birth, but not year. Also search LOPAS; call 804-786-5511 to apply.
Criminal Records: Access: Fax, mail, online, in person. Both court and visitors may perform in person searches. No search fee. Required to search: name, years to search; also helpful: DOB, SSN. Criminal records indexed in books for 10 years; computerized back to 1992. Mail turnaround time 1 week. Criminal PAT goes back to same as civil. Search free at www.courts.state.va.us/. Results show address of subject and day & month of birth, but not year.
General Information: No juvenile, sealed records released. No fee to fax documents. Court makes copy: $.50 per page. No certification fee. Payee: Gloucester District Court. Personal checks and credit cards accepted. Prepayment required. Mail requests: SASE requested.

Goochland County

16th Circuit Court PO Box 196, 2938 River Rd W, Bldg B, Goochland, VA 23063; 804-556-5353; fax: 804-556-4962; 8:30AM-5PM. ***Felony, Civil Actions over $15,000, Probate.***
www.courts.state.va.us/courts/circuit.html
Civil Records: Access: Online, in person. Visitors must perform in person searches themselves. Required to search: name, years to search. Civil cases indexed by defendant, plaintiff. Civil index on docket

books from 1850. Public use terminal has civil records back to 2001. Results include name and case number. Search free at www.courts.state.va.us/. Results show address of subject and day & month of birth, but not year. Also search LOPAS; call 804-786-5511 to apply.
Criminal Records: Access: Online, in person. Visitors must perform in person searches themselves. Required to search: name, years to search. Criminal records indexed in books from 1850. Note: Results include name and case number. Search free by name only or case number at www.courts.state.va.us/. Results show address of subject and day & month of birth, but not year. Also search LOPAS; call 804-786-5511 to apply. Online results show middle initial, DOB.
General Information: Online identifiers in results same as on public terminal. No juvenile, sealed or adoption records released. Will not fax documents. Court makes copy: $.50 per page. Certification fee: $1.00. Payee: Clerk of Circuit Court. Personal checks accepted. Visa/MC accepted for criminal cases only. Prepayment required.

General District Court PO Box 47, Goochland, VA 23063; 804-556-5309; fax: 804-556-4494; 8:30AM-4:30PM. ***Misdemeanor, Civil Actions under $15,000, Eviction, Small Claims.***
Civil Records: Access: Online, in person. Visitors must perform in person searches themselves. Required to search: name, years to search. Civil cases indexed by defendant, plaintiff. Civil index on docket books and computer back to 1995. Civil PAT goes back to 1995. Search free at www.courts.state.va.us/. Results show address of subject and day & month of birth, but not year. Also search LOPAS; call 804-786-5511 to apply.
Criminal Records: Access: Online, in person. Visitors must perform in person searches themselves. Required to search: name, years to search, DOB. Criminal records indexed in books and computer back to 1995. Criminal PAT goes back to same as civil. Search free at www.courts.state.va.us/. Results show address of subject and day & month of birth, but not year.
General Information: No juvenile records released. Court makes copy for no fee. No certification fee. Personal checks and credit cards accepted. Prepayment required.

Grayson County

27th Circuit Court PO Box 130, Independence, VA 24348; 276-773-2231; fax: 276-773-3338. 8AM-5PM. ***Felony, Civil over $15,000, Probate.***
www.courts.state.va.us/courts/circuit.html
Probate is a separate index at this address. Probate fax is same as main fax number.
Civil Records: Access: Mail, in person, online. Both court and visitors may perform in person searches. No search fee. Required to search: name, years to search. Civil cases indexed by defendant, plaintiff. Civil index on docket books since 1793. Mail turnaround time 2-3 days. Civil PAT goes back to 2001. Search free at www.courts.state.va.us/. Results show address of subject and day & month of birth, but not year.
Criminal Records: Access: Mail, online, in person. Visitors must perform in person searches themselves. No search fee. Required to search: name, years to search, DOB. Criminal records indexed in books since 1793. Mail turnaround time 2-3 days. Criminal PAT goes back to same as civil. Online access to criminal records is the same as civil. Online results show only month and day of DOB plus sex, race.
General Information: No juvenile, sealed or adoption records released. Will fax documents $.50 per page. Court makes copy: $.50 per page. Self serve: same. Certification fee: $2.00 per instrument. Payee: Clerk of Circuit Court. Personal checks accepted; credit cards are not. Prepayment required. Mail requests: SASE requested.

27th General District Court PO Box 280, 129 Davis St, Independence, VA 24348; 276-773-2011; fax: 276-773-3174; 8AM-4:30PM. ***Misdemeanor, Civil Actions under $15,000, Eviction, Small Claims.***
Civil Records: Access: Mail, in person, online. Both court and visitors may perform in person searches. No search fee. Required to search: name, years to search. Civil cases indexed by defendant. Civil records on computer from 1989. Mail turnaround time 1 week. Civil PAT goes back to 1989. Search free at www.courts.state.va.us/. Results show address of subject and day & month of birth, but not year. Also search LOPAS; call 804-786-5511 to apply.
Criminal Records: Access: Mail, online, in person. Both court and visitors may perform in person searches. No search fee. Required to search: name, years to search; also helpful: DOB, SSN. Criminal records computerized from 1997. Note: Results include name and address. Mail turnaround time 1 week. Criminal PAT goes back to same as civil. Search free at www.courts.state.va.us/. Results show address of subject and day & month of birth, but not year.
General Information: Online identifiers in results same as on public terminal. No juvenile, sealed records released. Will fax documents to local or toll free line. Court makes copy for no fee. No certification fee. Payee: Grayson District Court. Personal checks accepted. Visa/MC accepted.

Greene County

16th Circuit Court PO Box 386, Stanardsville, VA 22973; 434-985-5208; fax: 434-985-6723 8:15AM-4:30PM. ***Felony, Civil Actions over $15,000, Probate.***
www.courts.state.va.us/courts/circuit.html
Probate is a separate index at this same address. Probate fax is same as main fax number.
Civil Records: Access: Mail, in person, online. Both court and visitors may perform in person searches. No search fee. Required to search: name, years to search. Civil cases indexed by defendant, plaintiff. Civil index on docket books from 1838. Mail turnaround time 7-10 days. Remote online access to court case indexes is via LOPAS; call 804-786-5511 to apply.
Criminal Records: Access: Mail, in person. Both court and visitors may perform in person searches. No search fee. Required to search: name, years to search. Criminal records indexed in books from 1838. Mail turnaround time 7-10 days.
General Information: No juvenile, sealed or adoption records released. Will not fax documents. Court makes copy: $.50 per page. Self serve: same. Certification fee: $2.00 per instrument. Payee: Clerk of Circuit Court or Greene County Circuit. Personal checks accepted; credit cards are not. Prepayment required. Mail requests: SASE required.

16th General District Court PO Box 245, 22 Court St, County Courthouse, Stanardsville, VA 22973; 434-985-5224; fax: 434-985-1448; 8:30AM-4PM. ***Misdemeanor, Civil Actions under $15,000, Eviction, Small Claims.***
Civil Records: Access: Fax, mail, online, in person. Both court and visitors may perform in person searches. No search fee. Required to search: name, years to search. Civil cases indexed by defendant, plaintiff. Civil index on docket books from 1838, on computer back to 10/93. Civil PAT goes back to 1995. Search free at www.courts.state.va.us/. Results show address of subject and day & month of birth, but not year. Also search LOPAS; call 804-786-5511 to apply.
Criminal Records: Access: In person, online. Visitors must perform in person searches themselves. Required to search: name, years to search, DOB; also helpful: SSN. Criminal records computerized from 1/92, prior on cards, books. Note: Results include name and address. Criminal PAT goes back to same as civil. Search free at www.courts.state.va.us/. Results show address of subject and day & month of birth, but not year.
General Information: No juvenile, sealed records released. No fee to fax documents. Court makes copy: $.50 per page. No certification fee. Payee: Clerk of General District Court or Greene County Combined Court. Personal checks and credit cards accepted. Prepayment required. Mail requests: SASE required.

Greensville County

6th Circuit Court PO Box 631, 337 S Main St, Emporia, VA 23847; 434-348-4215; fax: 434-348-4020; 9AM-5PM. ***Felony, Civil Actions over $15,000, Probate.***
www.courts.state.va.us/courts/circuit.html
Civil Records: Access: In person, online. Visitors must perform in person searches themselves. Required to search: name, years to search. Civil cases indexed by defendant, plaintiff. Civil index on docket books from 1781; on computer since 1989. Civil PAT goes back to 1989. PAT results show name only. Search free at www.courts.state.va.us/. Results show address of subject and day & month of birth, but not year. Also search LOPAS; call 804-786-5511 to apply.
Criminal Records: Access: In person, online. Visitors must perform in person searches themselves. Required to search: name, years to search. Criminal records indexed in books from 1781; on computer since 1989. Note: Court does not conduct criminal searches. Criminal PAT goes back to same as civil. PAT results show name only. Online access to criminal records is the same as civil. Online results show only month and day of DOB, sex, race.
General Information: No juvenile, sealed records released. Will not fax documents. Court makes copy: $.50 per page. Certification fee: $2.00. Payee: Clerk of Circuit Court. Business checks accepted. No credit cards accepted. Prepayment required.

Greenville/Emporia Combined Court 333 S Main St, Emporia, VA 23847; 434-348-4215; fax: 434-634-0049; 8:30AM-4PM. ***Misdemeanor, Civil Actions under $15,000, Eviction, Small Claims.***
Civil Records: Access: Online, in person. Visitors must perform in person searches themselves. Required to search: name, years to search. Civil cases indexed by defendant, plaintiff. Civil index on docket books from 1800s; on computer back 10 years. Civil PAT goes back to 10 years. Select and search District Courts at http://epwsgdp1.courts.state.va.us/gdcourts/caseSearch.do?index=index. Results show name only.
Criminal Records: Access: Online, in person. Visitors must perform in person searches themselves. Required to search: name, years to search, DOB; also helpful: SSN. Criminal records indexed in books from 1800s; on computer back 10 years. Criminal PAT goes back to same as civil. Search free at http://epwsgdp1.courts.state.va.us/gdcourts/caseSearch.do?index=index. Results show DOB month and day, sex, race.
General Information: No juvenile, sealed records released. Will not fax documents. Court makes copy: $.50 per page. No certification fee. Payee: Clerk of General District Court. Personal checks accepted. Visa/MC accepted.

Halifax County

10th Circuit Court PO Box 729, Halifax, VA 24558; 434-476-6211; fax: 434-476-2890; 8:30AM-4:30PM. ***Felony, Civil Actions over $15,000, Probate.***
www.courts.state.va.us/courts/circuit.html
Civil Records: Access: Online, in person. Visitors must perform in person searches themselves. Required to search: name, years to search. Civil cases indexed by defendant, plaintiff; index on computer from 1988, on index books from 1752. Civil PAT goes back to 1989. Search free at www.courts.state.va.us/. Results show address of subject and day & month of birth, but not year.
Criminal Records: Access: Mail, online, in person. Only the court performs in person searches; visitors may not. Search fee: No search fee, copy and certifictaion fees can be charged. Required to search: name, years to search. Criminal records computerized from 1988, on index books from 1752. Mail turnaround time 1-5 days. Criminal PAT available. Online access to criminal records same as civil, above. Online results show only month and day of DOB, sex, race.
General Information: No juvenile, sealed records released. Will fax documents $.50 per page plus search fee per telephone call. Court makes copy: $.50

per page. Self serve: same. Certification fee: $2.00 per document. Payee: Circuit Court. Personal checks accepted; credit cards are not. Prepayment required. Mail requests: SASE required for criminal.

10th General District Court PO Box 458, 8 S Main St, Courthouse Sq, Halifax, VA 24558; 434-476-3385; fax: 434-476-3387; 8:30AM-4:30PM. ***Misdemeanor, Civil Actions under $15,000, Eviction, Small Claims.***

Civil Records: Access: Fax, mail, online, in person. Both court and visitors may perform in person searches. No search fee. Required to search: name, years to search, address. Civil cases indexed by defendant, plaintiff; index on computer from 1993. Mail turnaround time within 7 days. Civil PAT goes back to 10 years. PAT civil results show middle initial. Search free at www.courts.state.va.us/. Results show address of subject and day & month of birth, but not year. Also search LOPAS; call 804-786-5511 to apply.

Criminal Records: Access: Fax, mail, online, in person. Both court and visitors may perform in person searches. No search fee. Required to search: name. Criminal records computerized from 1993. Mail turnaround time within 7 days. Criminal PAT goes back to same as civil. PAT criminal results show middle initial. Search free at http://epwsgdp1.courts.state.va.us/gdcourts/caseSearch.do?index=index. Results show DOB month and day, sex, race. Also, search on LOPAS; LOPAS shows the DOB. Online results show middle initial, DOB.

General Information: No juvenile, sealed records released. Fax back fee only charged for large number of pages. Court makes copy: $.50 per page. Self serve: same. No certification fee. Payee: General District Court. Personal checks accepted. Prepayment required.

Hampton City

8th Circuit Court PO Box 40, 101 King's Way, Hampton, VA 23669-0040; 757-727-6105; fax: 757-728-3505; 8:30AM-4PM. ***Felony, Civil Actions over $15,000, Probate.***

www.courts.state.va.us/courts/circuit.html

Civil Records: Access: Phone, mail, fax, in person, online. Both court and visitors may perform in person searches. Search fee: $10.00 per name. Required to search: name, years to search. Civil cases indexed by defendant, plaintiff. Computerized records back to 1991, civil records on index books since 1834. Mail turnaround time 5-10 days. Civil PAT goes back to 1995. Search free at www.courts.state.va.us/. Results show address of subject and day & month of birth, but not year.

Criminal Records: Access: Mail, online, in person. Both court and visitors may perform in person searches. Search fee: $10.00 per name. Required to search: name, years to search. Computerized records back to 1991, criminal records on index books since1949. Mail turnaround time 3 days. Criminal PAT goes back to same as civil. Online access to criminal records is the same as civil. Online results show only month and day of DOB, sex, race.

General Information: No pre-sentence, criminal correspondence, chancery, judges notes or medical records released. Will fax documents. Court makes copy: $.50 per page. Self serve: same. Certification fee: $2.00. Payee: Clerk of Court. No out of state checks accepted. No credit cards accepted. Prepayment required. Mail requests: SASE required.

8th General District Court PO Box 70, 236 King St, Courthouse, Hampton, VA 23669-0070; criminal phone: 757-727-6260; civil phone: 757-727-6480; fax: 757-727-6035; 8AM-4PM. ***Misdemeanor, Civil Actions under $15,000, Eviction, Small Claims.***

Civil Records: Access: Online, in person. Visitors must perform in person searches themselves. Required to search: name, years to search. Civil cases indexed by defendant, plaintiff. Civil index on docket books and computer for 10 years. Note: Mail access limited to specific case and two names. Civil PAT goes back to 10 years. Search free at www.courts.state.va.us/. Results show address of subject and day & month of birth, but not year. Also search LOPAS; call 804-786-5511 to apply.

Criminal Records: Access: Online, in person. Visitors must perform in person searches themselves. Required to search: name, years to search. Criminal records indexed in books and computer for 10 years. Criminal PAT goes back to same as civil. Search free at www.courts.state.va.us/. Results show address of subject and day & month of birth, but not year.

General Information: No sealed records released. Will not fax documents. Court makes copy: $1.00 for 1st and 2nd copy, $.50 each add'l copy. Certification fee: $7.00. Payee: Hampton District Court. Personal checks accepted. Credit Cards accepted for fines only. Prepayment required.

Hanover County

15th Circuit Court 7507 Library Dr, PO Box 39, Hanover, VA 23069; 804-365-6151; criminal phone: 804-365-6843; civil phone: 804-365-6148; probate phone: 804-365-6478; fax: 804-365-6278; 8:30AM-4:30PM. ***Felony, Civil over $15,000, Probate.***

www.co.hanover.va.us/circuitct/default.htm

Civil Records: Access: Online, in person. Visitors must perform in person searches themselves. Required to search: name, years to search; helpful-case number. Civil cases indexed by defendant, plaintiff. Civil records index in books, older records date from 1865. Civil PAT goes back to 1990. PAT civil results show middle initial. Search free at www.courts.state.va.us/. Results show address of subject and day & month of birth, but not year. Also search LOPAS; call 804-786-5511 to apply.

Criminal Records: Access: Online, in person. Visitors must perform in person searches themselves. Required to search: name, years to search; helpful- case number. Criminal records index in books, older records date from 1865. Criminal PAT goes back to 1990. PAT results show middle initial, DOB, SSN. Online access to criminal records is the same as civil. Online results show middle initial, DOB, SSN; only month and day of DOB appears, plus sex, race and partial address.

General Information: No juvenile, sealed records released. Will not fax documents. Court makes copy: $.50 per page. Certification fee: $2.00 per cert. Payee: Clerk of Circuit Court. Personal checks accepted; credit cards are not. Prepayment required.

15th General District Court PO Box 176, County Courthouse, Hanover, VA 23069; 804-365-6191; civil phone: 804-365-6457; criminal fax: 804-365-6290; civil fax: 804-365-6436; 8AM-4PM. ***Misdemeanor, Civil Actions under $15,000, Eviction, Small Claims.***

Civil Records: Access: Online, in person. Visitors must perform in person searches themselves. Required to search: name, years to search. Civil cases indexed by defendant, plaintiff; index on computer back 10 years. Civil PAT goes back to 10 years. Search free at www.courts.state.va.us/. Results show address of subject and day & month of birth, but not year. Also search LOPAS; call 804-786-5511 to apply.

Criminal Records: Access: Online, in person. Visitors must perform in person searches themselves. Required to search: name, years to search, DOB; also helpful: SSN. Criminal records on computer back 10 years. Criminal PAT goes back to same as civil. PAT results show middle initial, SSN but DOB results show month and day only. Address also usually on results. Search free at www.courts.state.va.us/. Results show address of subject and day & month of birth, but not year.

General Information: Will not fax documents. Court makes copy: $1.00 per page 1st 2 pages, $.50 each add'l up to 10 pages. No certification fee. Payee: Hanover General District Court. Only cash accepted for the copy fee. Visa/MC accepted.

Harrisonburg City

Circuit & District Courts

See Rockingham County.

Henrico County

14th Circuit Court PO Box 27032, Richmond, VA 23273-7032; 804-501-4202; criminal phone: 804-501-5448; civil phone: 804-501-5422; probate phone: 804-501-4316; fax: 804-501-5214; 8AM-4:30PM. ***Felony, Civil over $15,000, Probate.***

www.co.henrico.va.us/clerk/

Civil Records: Access: In person, online. Visitors must perform in person searches themselves. Required to search: name, years to search. Civil cases indexed by defendant, plaintiff; index on computer from 11/88, on index cards from 1850. Civil PAT goes back to 11/1988. PAT civil results show middle initial. Remote online access to court case indexes is via LOPAS; call 804-786-5511 to apply.

Criminal Records: Access: In person, online. Visitors must perform in person searches themselves. Required to search: name, years to search. Criminal records computerized from 11/88, on index cards from 1850. Criminal PAT goes back to 1989. PAT criminal results show middle initial. Results include partial data of birth. Remote online access to court case indexes via LOPAS; call 804-786-5511 to apply. Online results show middle initial. Online results include partial date of birth.

General Information: No juvenile, judges notes, adoption sealed records released. Will not fax documents. Court makes copy: $.50 per page. Self serve: same. Certification fee: $2.00 per document. Payee: Clerk of Circuit Court. Personal checks accepted; credit cards are not. Prepayment required. Mail requests: SASE required for mail return of any copies.

14th General District Court PO Box 27032, Richmond, VA 23273; criminal phone: 804-501-4723; civil phone: 804-501-4727; criminal fax: 804-501-7388; civil fax: 804-501-4141; 8AM-4PM. ***Misdemeanor, Civil Actions under $15,000, Eviction, Small Claims.***

Civil Records: Access: Online, in person. Visitors must perform in person searches themselves. Required to search: name, years to search. Civil cases indexed by defendant. Civil records on computer back to 1998. Civil PAT goes back to 1998. Search free at www.courts.state.va.us/. Results show address of subject and day & month of birth, but not year. Also search LOPAS; call 804-786-5511 to apply.

Criminal Records: Access: Online, in person. Visitors must perform in person searches themselves. Required to search: name, years to search, DOB. Criminal records computerized from 1998. Criminal PAT goes back to same as civil. Search free at www.courts.state.va.us/. Results show address of subject and day & month of birth, but not year.

General Information: No juvenile, sealed records released. Will not fax documents. Court makes copy: $1.00 minimum for 1st 2 pages, $.50 ea add'l; Civil- $1.00 per page. No certification fee. Payee: Clerk of General District Court. Personal checks accepted. Visa/MC accepted but not over the phone. Prepayment required.

Henry County

Circuit Court 3160 Kings Mountain Rd, #B, Martinsville, VA 24112; 276-634-4880; criminal phone: 276-634-4889 or 276-634-4885; civil phone: 276-634-4884; probate phone: 276-634-4883; 9AM-5PM. ***Felony, Civil Actions over $15,000, Probate.***

www.courts.state.va.us/courts/circuit/Henry/home.html

Civil Records: Access: Online, in person. Visitors must perform in person searches themselves. Required to search: name, years to search. Civil cases indexed by defendant, plaintiff; index on computer since 4/92, index back to 1777. Civil PAT goes back to 1992. Search free at www.courts.state.va.us/. Results show address of subject and day & month of birth, but not year.

Criminal Records: Access: Online, in person. Visitors must perform in person searches themselves. Required to search: name, years to search, DOB; also helpful: SSN. Criminal records computerized since 7/92, index back to 1777. Criminal PAT goes back to same as civil. Online access to criminal records is same as civil. Online

results show only month and day of DOB plus sex, race.
General Information: Online identifiers in results same as on public terminal. No juvenile, expungments, sealed or adoption records released. Will not fax documents. Court makes copy: $.50 per page. Self serve: same. Certification fee: $2.00. Payee: Clerk of Circuit Court. Personal checks accepted; credit cards are not. Prepayment required.

21st General District Court 3160 King's Mountain Rd #A, Martinsville, VA 24112; 276-634-4815; fax: 276-634-4825; 9AM-5PM. ***Misdemeanor, Civil Actions under $15,000, Eviction, Small Claims.***
www.courts.state.va.us/courts/gd/Henry/home.html
Civil Records: Access: Online, in person. Visitors must perform in person searches themselves. Required to search: name, years to search; also helpful: address. Civil cases indexed by defendant, plaintiff; index on computer from 1998 (maintained for 10 years). Civil PAT goes back to 1998. PAT results show name only. Search free at www.courts.state.va.us/. Results show address of subject and day & month of birth, but not year. Also search LOPAS; call 804-786-5511 to apply.
Criminal Records: Access: Online, in person. Visitors must perform in person searches themselves. Required to search: name, years to search, DOB; also helpful: address, SSN. Criminal records computerized from 1998 (maintained for 10 years). Criminal PAT goes back to same as civil. PAT results show name only. Search free at www.courts.state.va.us/. Results show address of subject and day & month of birth, but not year.
General Information: No sealed records released. Will not fax documents. Court makes copy: $.50 per page. No certification fee. Payee: Henry County General District Court. Personal checks accepted; credit cards are not. Prepayment required.

Highland County

25th Circuit Court PO Box 190, Monterey, VA 24465; 540-468-2447; probate phone: same; fax: 540-468-3447; 8:30AM-4:30PM. ***Felony, Civil Actions over $15,000, Probate.***
www.courts.state.va.us/courts/circuit.html
Civil Records: Access: Mail, in person, online. Both court and visitors may perform in person searches. No search fee. Required to search: name, years to search. Civil cases indexed by defendant, plaintiff. Civil index on docket books from 1868. Mail turnaround time up to 1 week. Search free at www.courts.state.va.us/. Results show address of subject and day & month of birth, but not year. Also search LOPAS; call 804-786-5511 to apply.
Criminal Records: Access: Mail, online, in person. Both court and visitors may perform in person searches. No search fee. Required to search: name, years to search. Criminal records indexed in books from 1868. Mail turnaround time up to 1 week. Online access to criminal records is same as civil. Online results show only month and day of DOB plus sex, race.
General Information: No juvenile, sealed records released. Will fax documents $2.00 plus $.50 per page. Court makes copy: $.50 per page. Self serve: same. Certification fee: $2.00. Payee: Clerk of Circuit Court. Personal checks accepted; credit cards are not. Prepayment required.

25th General District Court PO Box 88, Highland County Courthouse, 165 W Main St, Monterey, VA 24465; 540-468-2445; fax: 540-468-3449; 8:30AM-5PM. ***Misdemeanor, Civil Actions under $15,000, Eviction, Small Claims.***
Civil Records: Access: Fax, mail, online, in person. Both court and visitors may perform in person searches. No search fee. Required to search: name, years to search. Civil cases indexed by defendant, plaintiff. Civil index on docket books from 1997; computerized to present. Mail turnaround time 2-3 days. Civil PAT goes back to 1997. PAT civil results show middle initial. Search free at www.courts.state.va.us/. Results show address of subject and day & month of birth, but not year. Also search LOPAS; call 804-786-5511 to apply.
Criminal Records: Access: Fax, mail, online, in person. Both court and visitors may perform in person searches. No search fee. Required to search: name, years to search; also helpful: DOB, SSN, signed release. Criminal records indexed in books from 1997; computerized to present. Mail turnaround time 2-3 days. Criminal PAT goes back to same as civil. PAT criminal results show middle initial. Search free at www.courts.state.va.us/. Results show address of subject and day & month of birth, but not year.
General Information: No juvenile, sealed records released. Will fax back documents. Court makes copy: $1.00 first 2 pages; $.50 each add'l. No certification fee. Payee: General District Court. Personal checks accepted. Visa/MC accepted. Prepayment required. Mail requests: SASE requested.

Hopewell City

6th Circuit Court 100 E Broadway, PO Box 310, 2nd Fl, Rm 251, Hopewell, VA 23860; 804-541-2239; fax: 804-541-2438; 8:30AM-4PM. ***Felony, Civil Actions over $15,000, Probate.***
www.courts.state.va.us/courts/circuit.html
Civil Records: Access: In person, online. Visitors must perform in person searches themselves. Required to search: name, years to search. Civil cases indexed by defendant, plaintiff. Civil index on docket books since 1916. Civil PAT goes back to 1990. PAT results show name, DOB. Search free at www.courts.state.va.us/. Results show address of subject and day & month of birth, but not year. Also search LOPAS; call 804-786-5511 to apply.
Criminal Records: Access: Online, in person. Visitors must perform in person searches themselves. Required to search: name, years to search, DOB. Criminal records indexed in books since 1916. Criminal PAT goes back to same as civil.PAT results show name, DOB. Online access to criminal records is the same as civil. Online results show only month and day of DOB plus sex, race.
General Information: Online identifiers in results same as on public terminal. No juvenile, sealed records released. Will not fax documents. Court makes copy: $.50 per page. Self serve: same. Certification fee: $2.00. Payee: Clerk of Circuit Court. Personal checks accepted; credit cards are not. Prepayment required. Mail requests: SASE required for mail return of any copies.

Hopewell General District Court 100 E Broadway, Hopewell, VA 23860; 804-541-2257; fax: 804-541-2364; 8:30-4:30PM. ***Misdemeanor, Civil Actions under $15,000, Eviction, Small Claims.***
www.courts.state.va.us/courts/combined/Hopewell/home.html
Civil Records: Access: Mail, in person, online. Both court and visitors may perform in person searches. No search fee. Required to search: name, years to search. Civil cases indexed by defendant, plaintiff; index on computer from 1988, older case records archived. Mail turnaround time 3-5 days. Civil PAT goes back to 1988. Search free at www.courts.state.va.us/. Results show address of subject and day & month of birth, but not year. Also search LOPAS; call 804-786-5511 to apply.
Criminal Records: Access: Mail, online, in person. Both court and visitors may perform in person searches. No search fee. Required to search: name, years to search, DOB; also helpful: SSN. Criminal records computerized from 1988, older case records are archived. Mail turnaround time 3-5 days. Criminal PAT goes back to same as civil. Search free at www.courts.state.va.us/. Results show address of subject and day & month of birth, but not year.
General Information: No juvenile, sealed or domestic relations records released. Will not fax documents. Court makes copy: $1.00 per page 1st 2 pages, then $.50 each. No certification fee. Payee: Clerk of General District Court. Personal checks and credit cards accepted. Prepayment required. Mail requests: SASE requested.

Isle of Wight County

5th Circuit Court 17122 Monument Circle, PO Box 110, Isle of Wight, VA 23397; 757-365-6233; fax: 757-357-0884; 9AM-5PM. ***Felony, Civil Actions over $15,000, Probate.***
www.courts.state.va.us/courts/circuit.html
Civil Records: Access: Online, in person. Visitors must perform in person searches themselves. Required to search: name, years to search. Civil cases indexed by defendant, plaintiff. Civil index on docket books from 1800s; on computer back to 1988. Note: Court will only search the computer indices for you to determine is a name exists. Civil PAT goes back to 1988. PAT civil results show middle initial. Search free at www.courts.state.va.us/. Results show address of subject and day & month of birth, but not year. Also search LOPAS; call 804-786-5511 to apply.
Criminal Records: Access: Online, in person. Visitors must perform in person searches themselves. Required to search: name, years to search, DOB. Criminal records indexed in books from 1800s; on computer back to 1988. Note: Court will only search the computer indices for you to determine is a name exists. Criminal PAT goes back to same as civil. PAT criminal results show middle initial. Online access to criminal records is same as civil. Online results show only month and day of DOB plus sex, race.
General Information: Online identifiers in results same as on public terminal. No juvenile, sealed records released. Will not fax documents. Court makes copy: $.50 per page. Certification fee: $2.00. Payee: Clerk of Circuit Court. Personal checks accepted; credit cards are not. Prepayment required. Mail requests: SASE required for mail return of any copies.

5th General District Court PO Box 122, Isle of Wight Courthouse, 17110 Monument Circle, Isle of Wight, VA 23397; 757-365-6243; fax: 757-365-6246; 8AM-4PM. ***Misdemeanor, Civil Actions under $15,000, Eviction, Small Claims.***
The Clerk can be reached at 757-365-6244.
Civil Records: Access: Online, in person. Visitors must perform in person searches themselves. Required to search: name, years to search. Civil cases indexed by defendant, plaintiff. Civil index on docket books back to 1800s; on computer back 10 years. Civil PAT goes back to 10 years. Search free at www.courts.state.va.us/. Results show address of subject and day & month of birth, but not year. Also search LOPAS; call 804-786-5511 to apply.
Criminal Records: Access: Online, in person. Visitors must perform in person searches themselves. Required to search: name, years to search. Criminal records indexed in books back to 1800s; on computer back 10 years. Note: This court suggests that background checks be directed to the Sheriff's Office. Criminal PAT goes back to same as civil. Records purged after 10 years. Search free at www.courts.state.va.us/. Results show address of subject and day & month of birth, but not year.
General Information: Juvenile and sealed records not released. Court makes copy for no fee. Certification fee: $1.00. Payee: Clerk of GDC. Personal checks accepted. Visa/MC accepted. Prepayment required.

James City County

Williamsburg-James City Circuit Court 5201 Monticello Ave #6, Williamsburg, VA 23188-8218; 757-564-2242; fax: 757-564-2329; 8:30AM-4:30PM. ***Felony, Civil over $15,000, Probate.***
www.courts.state.va.us/courts/circuit.html
Court will assist - and tell if a name exists - but not perform searches.
Civil Records: Access: Phone, in person, online. Visitors must perform in person searches themselves. No search fee. Required to search: name, years to search. Civil cases indexed by defendant, plaintiff; index on computer since 1987, archived from 1970, prior on index books. Note: Phone access very limited. Civil PAT goes back to 1987. PAT civil results show middle initial. Search free at www.courts.state.va.us/. Results show address of subject and day & month of birth, but not year.

Criminal Records: Access: Phone, in person, online. Visitors must perform in person searches themselves. Search fee: $10.00 per name. Required to search: name, years to search, DOB; also helpful: SSN. Criminal records on computer since 1987, archived from 1970, prior on index books. Note: Phone access very limited. Criminal PAT goes back to same as civil. PAT results show middle initial, DOB. Online access to criminal records is the same as civil. Online results show only month and day of DOB plus sex, race.
General Information: No juvenile, sealed, adoption records released. Fee to fax out file $1.00 per page. Court makes copy: $.50 per page. Self serve: same. Certification fee: $2.00. Payee: Clerk of Circuit Court. No personal checks. No credit cards accepted. Prepayment required.

King and Queen County

9th Circuit Court PO Box 67, 234 Allen's Circle, King & Queen Court House, VA 23085; 804-785-5984; fax: 804-785-5698; 9AM-5PM. ***Felony, Civil Actions over $15,000, Probate.***
www.courts.state.va.us/courts/circuit.html
Civil Records: Access: In person, online. Visitors must perform in person searches themselves. Required to search: name, years to search. Civil cases indexed by plaintiff. Civil records archived from 1864, computerized since 1995 for index, images back to 2005. Civil PAT goes back to 1995. Search via LOPAS; call 804-786-5511 to apply.
Criminal Records: Access: Online, in person. Visitors must perform in person searches themselves. Required to search: name, years to search. Criminal records archived from 1864, computerized since 1995 for index, images back to 2005. Criminal PAT goes back to same as civil. Search via LOPAS; call 804-786-5511 to apply. Online results show middle initial, DOB.
General Information: No juvenile, sealed or adoption records released. Will fax documents $1.00 per page. Court makes copy: $.50 per page. Certification fee: $2.00. Payee: Clerk of Circuit Court. Personal checks accepted; credit cards are not. Prepayment required.

King & Queen General District Court PO Box 86, 242 Allen's Circle, Ste F, King & Queen Courthouse, VA 23085-0086; 804-785-5982; fax: 804-785-5694; 8:30-4:30PM. ***Misdemeanor, Civil Actions under $15,000, Eviction.***
www.kingandqueenco.net/html/Govt/gendist.html
The General District Court also holds preliminary hearings in felony cases.
Civil Records: Access: Fax, mail, online, in person. Both court and visitors may perform in person searches. No search fee. Required to search: name, years to search. Civil cases indexed by defendant, plaintiff; index on computer back to 1995. Mail turnaround time 1-5 days. Civil PAT goes back to 1991. Search free at www.courts.state.va.us/. Results show address of subject and day & month of birth, but not year. Also search LOPAS; call 804-786-5511 to apply.
Criminal Records: Access: Fax, mail, online, in person. Both court and visitors may perform in person searches. No search fee. Required to search: name, years to search, DOB; also helpful: SSN, signed release. Criminal records computerized from 1995. Mail turnaround time 1-5 days. Criminal PAT goes back to same as civil. Search free at www.courts.state.va.us/. Results show address of subject and day & month of birth, but not year.
General Information: Online identifiers in results same as on public terminal. No fee to fax documents. Court makes copy: $1.00 first page, $.50 each add'l. No certification fee. Payee: General District Court. Personal checks accepted. Visa/MC accepted. Prepayment required. Mail requests: SASE required.

King George County

15th Circuit Court 9483 Kings Highway, #3, King George, VA 22485; 540-775-3322; fax: 540-775-5466; 8:30AM-4:30PM. ***Felony, Civil Actions over $15,000, Probate.***
www.courts.state.va.us/courts/circuit/King_George/home.html
Civil Records: Access: Mail, in person, online. Both court and visitors may perform in person searches. Search fee: $10.00 per name. Required to search: name, years to search. Civil cases indexed by defendant, plaintiff. Civil index on docket books from 1800s; computerized records since 1990. Mail turnaround time 30 days. Civil PAT goes back to 1990. PAT civil results show middle initial. Search free at www.courts.state.va.us/. Results show address of subject and day & month of birth, but not year.
Criminal Records: Access: Mail, in person, online. Both court and visitors may perform in person searches. Search fee: $10.00 per name. Required to search: name, years to search. Criminal records indexed in books from 1800s; computerized records since 1990. Mail turnaround time 30 days. Criminal PAT goes back to same as civil. PAT results show middle initial, DOB. Online access to criminal records is same as civil. Only month and day of birth shown in results. Online results show only month and day of DOB plus sex, race.
General Information: No sealed records released. Will not fax documents. Court makes copy: $.50 per page. Self serve: same. Certification fee: $2.00. Payee: Clerk of Circuit court. Personal checks accepted; credit cards are not. Prepayment required. Mail requests: SASE required.

15th General District Combined Court 9483 Kings Hwy, County Courthouse, King George, VA 22485; 540-775-3573; 8AM-4:00PM. ***Misdemeanor, Civil Actions under $15,000, Eviction, Small Claims.***
Civil Records: Access: Mail, in person, online. Both court and visitors may perform in person searches. No search fee. Required to search: name, years to search. Civil cases indexed by defendant, plaintiff. Civil index on docket books from early 1900s; computerized records since 1992. Mail turnaround time 1-5 days. Civil PAT goes back to 1992. Online access is at http://epwsgdp1.courts.state.va.us/gdcourts/caseSearch.do?index=index. Results show name and sometimes address.
Criminal Records: Access: Mail, in person, online. Both court and visitors may perform in person searches. No search fee. Required to search: name, years to search, DOB; also helpful: SSN. Criminal records indexed in books from early 1900s; computerized records since 1992. Mail turnaround time 1-5 days. Criminal PAT goes back to same as civil. Search free at www.courts.state.va.us/. Results show address of subject and day & month of birth, but not year.
General Information: No juvenile, sealed records released. Will not fax documents. Court makes copy: $1.00 per page 1st 2 pages, $.50 each add'l. No certification fee. Payee: Clerk of General District Court. Personal checks accepted. Visa/MC accepted. Prepayment required. Mail requests: SASE required.

King William County

9th Circuit Court 351 Courthouse Ln, PO Box 216, King William, VA 23086; 804-769-4936; criminal phone: 804-769-4938; civil phone: 804-769-4936; probate phone: 804-769-4936; fax: 804-769-4991; 8:30AM-4:30PM. ***Felony, Civil Actions over $15,000, Probate.***
www.courts.state.va.us/courts/circuit.html
Probate fax is same as main fax number.
Civil Records: Access: Mail, in person, online. Both court and visitors may perform in person searches. No search fee. Required to search: name, years to search. Civil cases indexed by defendant, plaintiff. Civil index on docket books from 1885. Mail turnaround time 1 week. Civil PAT goes back to 1999. PAT civil results show middle initial. Search free at www.courts.state.va.us/. Results show address of subject and day & month of birth, but not year. Also search LOPAS; call 804-786-5511 to apply.
Criminal Records: Access: Mail, in person, online. Both court and visitors may perform in person searches. No search fee. Required to search: name, years to search, DOB; also helpful: SSN. Criminal records indexed in books from 1885, computerized records from 1999. Mail turnaround time 1 week. Criminal PAT goes back to same as civil. PAT results show middle initial, DOB. Online access to criminal records is the same as civil. Online results show only month and day of DOB plus sex, race.
General Information: Online identifiers in results same as on public terminal. No juvenile, sealed records released. Will fax documents to local or toll free line. Court makes copy: $.50 per page. Self serve: same. Certification fee: $2.00 per instrument. Payee: Clerk of Circuit Court. Personal checks accepted; credit cards are not. Prepayment required. Mail requests: SASE required.

King William General District Court POB 5, 351 Courthouse Lane, King William, VA 23086; 804-769-4948; fax: 804-769-4971; 8:30AM-4:30PM. ***Misdemeanor, Civil Actions under $15,000, Eviction, Small Claims.***
Civil Records: Access: Fax, mail, online, in person. Both court and visitors may perform in person searches. No search fee. Required to search: name, years to search. Civil cases indexed by defendant, plaintiff; index on computer since 1998. Mail turnaround time 1-3 days. Civil PAT goes back to 1998. PAT civil results show middle initial. Search free at www.courts.state.va.us/. Results show address of subject and day & month of birth, but not year. Also search LOPAS; call 804-786-5511 to apply.
Criminal Records: Access: Fax, mail, online, in person. Both court and visitors may perform in person searches. No search fee. Required to search: name, years to search, DOB; also helpful: signed release, SSN. Criminal records computerized from 1998. Mail turnaround time 1-3 days. Criminal PAT goes back to 1998. PAT results show middle initial, DOB. Search free at www.courts.state.va.us/. Results show address of subject and day & month of birth, but not year.
General Information: Online identifiers in results same as on public terminal. No juvenile, sealed records released. No fee to fax documents. Court makes copy: $1.00 first page, $.50 each add'l. Self serve: same. No certification fee. Payee: General District Court. Personal checks and credit cards accepted. Prepayment required. Mail requests: SASE requested.

Lancaster County

15th Circuit Court PO Box 99, Courthouse Bldg, 8311 Mary Ball Rd, Lancaster, VA 22503; 804-462-5611; fax: 804-462-9978; 8:30AM-4:30PM. ***Felony, Civil Actions over $15,000, Probate.***
www.courts.state.va.us/courts/circuit.html
Civil Records: Access: Mail, in person, online. Only the court performs in person searches; visitors may not. No search fee. Required to search: name, years to search. Civil cases indexed by defendant, plaintiff. Civil index on docket books from 1845. Mail turnaround time same day. Search free at www.courts.state.va.us/. Results show address of subject and day & month of birth, but not year. Also search LOPAS; call 804-786-5511 to apply.
Criminal Records: Access: Mail, online, in person. Both court and visitors may perform in person searches. No search fee. Required to search: name, years to search. Criminal records indexed in books from 1845. Mail turnaround time same day. Online access to criminal records is the same as civil. Online results show only month and day of DOB plus sex, race.
General Information: No juvenile, sealed records released. Will not fax documents. Court makes copy: $.50 per page. Certification fee: $2.00. Payee: Clerk of Circuit Court. Personal checks accepted. Out of state checks not accepted. No credit cards accepted. Prepayment required. Mail requests: SASE required.

15th General District Court PO Box 129, 8311 Mary Ball Rd #205, Lancaster, VA 22503; 804-

462-0012; fax: 804-462-0371; 8AM-N; 1-4:30PM. ***Misdemeanor, Civil Actions under $15,000, Eviction, Small Claims.***

Civil Records: Access: Mail, in person, online. Both court and visitors may perform in person searches. No search fee. Required to search: name, years to search. Civil cases indexed by defendant. Civil records kept for 10 years. Mail turnaround time 1-2 days. Civil PAT goes back to 12/1996. PAT civil results show middle initial. Search free at www.courts.state.va.us/. Results show address of subject and day & month of birth, but not year. Also search LOPAS; call 804-786-5511 to apply.

Criminal Records: Access: Mail, online, in person. Both court and visitors may perform in person searches. No search fee. Required to search: name, years to search, DOB; also helpful: SSN. Criminal records computerized from 11/93. Hard copies kept 10 years. Mail turnaround time 1-2 days. Criminal PAT goes back to same as civil. PAT criminal results show middle initial. Search free at www.courts.state.va.us/. Results show address of subject and day & month of birth, but not year.

General Information: No sealed records released. Will not fax documents. Court makes copy: $1.00 1st page; $1.00 2nd page, $.50 each add'l. No certification fee. Payee: Clerk of General District Court. Personal checks accepted. Visa/MC accepted but no debit cards. Prepayment required. Mail requests: SASE helpful.

Lee County

30th Circuit Court PO Box 326, Jonesville, VA 24263; 276-346-7763; fax: 276-346-3440; 8:30AM-5PM. ***Felony, Civil over $15,000, Probate.***
www.courts.state.va.us/courts/circuit/Lee/home.html

Civil Records: Access: Phone, fax, mail, online, in person. Both court and visitors may perform in person searches. No search fee. Required to search: name, years to search. Civil cases indexed by defendant, plaintiff. Civil index on docket books from 1800s. Note: Phone & fax access limited to short searches. Mail turnaround time 1-3 days. Civil PAT goes back to 1988. Search free at www.courts.state.va.us/. Results show address of subject and day & month of birth, but not year.

Criminal Records: Access: Phone, fax, mail, online, in person. Both court and visitors may perform in person searches. No search fee. Required to search: name, years to search, DOB; also helpful: SSN. Criminal records indexed in books from 1800s. Mail turnaround time 1-3 days. Criminal PAT goes back to same as civil. Online access to criminal records is the same as civil. Online results show only month and day of DOB plus sex, race.

General Information: No juvenile, sealed records released. Will fax documents to local or toll free line. Court makes copy: $.50 per page. Self serve: same. Certification fee: $2.00. Payee: Clerk of Circuit Court. Personal checks accepted; credit cards are not. Prepayment required. Mail requests: SASE required.

30th General District Court PO Box 306, County Courthouse, #108, Jonesville, VA 24263; 276-346-7729; fax: 276-346-7701; 8AM-4:30PM. ***Misdemeanor, Civil Actions under $15,000, Eviction, Small Claims.***

Civil Records: Access: Mail, in person, online. Both court and visitors may perform in person searches. No search fee. Required to search: name, years to search. Civil cases indexed by defendant, plaintiff. Civil index on docket books from 1800s, on computer from 11/7/90. Mail turnaround time 1-2 days. Civil PAT goes back to 1990. PAT results show name, DOB. Search free at www.courts.state.va.us/. Results show address of subject and day & month of birth, but not year. Also search LOPAS; call 804-786-5511 to apply.

Criminal Records: Access: Mail, online, in person, fax. Both court and visitors may perform in person searches. No search fee. Required to search: name, years to search. Criminal records indexed in books from 1800s, on computer from 11/7/90. Mail turnaround time 1-2 days. Criminal PAT goes back to same as civil.PAT results show name, DOB. Search free at www.courts.state.va.us/. Results show address of subject and day & month of birth, but not year.

General Information: No juvenile, sealed records released. Will fax back documents. Court makes copy: $1.00 first page, $.50 each add'l. No certification fee. Payee: Clerk of General District Court. Personal checks accepted. Visa/MC accepted. Prepayment required. Mail requests: SASE helpful.

Lexington City

Circuit & District Courts
See Rockbridge County

Loudoun County

20th Circuit Court PO Box 55, 18 E Market St, MS33, Leesburg, VA 20178; 703-777-0270; probate phone: 703-777-0272; fax: 703-777-0376; 8:30AM-4:30PM. ***Felony, Civil over $15,000, Probate.***
www.loudoun.gov/clerk
Probate fax- 703-737-8096.

Civil Records: Access: Phone, online, in person. Both court and visitors may perform in person searches. No search fee. Required to search: name, years to search. Civil cases indexed by defendant, plaintiff; index on computer since 1995; prior on index books from 1700s. Note: Phone access limited to simple requests. Civil PAT goes back to 1987. PAT civil results show middle initial. Search free at www.courts.state.va.us/. Results show address of subject and day & month of birth, but not year. Also search LOPAS; call 804-786-5511 to apply. Also, docket lists are free at www.loudoun.gov/Default.aspx?tabid=318&fmpath=/Dockets.

Criminal Records: Access: Online, in person. Both court and visitors may perform in person searches. No search fee. Required to search: name, years to search, DOB; also helpful: SSN. Criminal records on computer since 1995; prior on index books from 1700s. Criminal PAT goes back to same as civil. PAT criminal results show middle initial. Search free by name only or case number at www.courts.state.va.us/. Results show address of subject and day & month of birth, but not year. Also search LOPAS; call 804-786-5511 to apply. Also, docket lists are online free at www.loudoun.gov/Default.aspx?tabid=318&fmpath=/Dockets. Online results show only month and day of DOB plus sex, race.

General Information: Online identifiers in results same as on public terminal. No juvenile, sealed or adoption records released. Will not fax documents. Court makes copy: $.50 per page. Certification fee: $2.00 per doc. Payee: Clerk of Circuit Court. Business checks accepted. Personal checks accepted if in state. No credit cards accepted. Prepayment required.

20th General District Court 18 E Market St, Leesburg, VA 20176; 703-777-0310; fax: 703-771-5284; 8AM-4PM. ***Misdemeanor, Civil Actions under $15,000, Eviction.***
www.courts.state.va.us/courts/gd/Loudoun/home.html

Civil Records: Access: Mail, fax, online, in person. Both court and visitors may perform in person searches. No search fee. Required to search: name, years to search. Civil cases indexed by defendant, plaintiff; index on computer back 10 years. Mail turnaround time 5 days. Civil PAT goes back to 10 years. Search free at www.courts.state.va.us/. Results show address of subject and day & month of birth, but not year. Also search LOPAS; call 804-786-5511 to apply.

Criminal Records: Access: Mail, fax, online, in person. Both court and visitors may perform in person searches. No search fee. Required to search: name, years to search. Criminal records on computer back 10 years. Mail turnaround time 5 days. Criminal PAT goes back to same as civil. Search free at www.courts.state.va.us/. Results show address of subject and day & month of birth, but not year.

General Information: Will not fax documents. Court makes copy: $.50 per page. Certification fee: $.50. Payee: General District Court. Personal checks and credit cards accepted. Prepayment required. Mail requests: SASE required.

Louisa County

16th Circuit Court PO Box 37, 100 W Main St, Louisa, VA 23093; 540-967-5312; fax: 540-967-2705; 8:30AM-5PM. ***Felony, Civil Actions over $15,000, Probate.***
www.courts.state.va.us/courts/circuit/Louisa/home.html

Civil Records: Access: Online, in person. Visitors must perform in person searches themselves. Required to search: name, years to search. Civil cases indexed by defendant, plaintiff. Civil records archived from 1742; on computer back to 1989. Civil PAT available. Search free at www.courts.state.va.us/. Results show address of subject and day & month of birth, but not year. Also search LOPAS; call 804-786-5511 to apply.

Criminal Records: Access: Online, in person. Both court and visitors may perform in person searches. No search fee. Required to search: name, years to search, DOB or SSN. Criminal records archived from 1742; on computer back to 1989. Criminal PAT available. Online access to criminal records is the same as civil. Online results show only month and day of DOB plus sex, race.

General Information: No juvenile, sealed records released. Will not fax documents. Court makes copy: $.50 per page. Self serve: same. Certification fee: $2.00. Payee: Clerk of Circuit Court. Personal checks accepted. Prepayment required.

16th General District Court PO Box 452, Louisa, VA 23093; 540-967-5330; fax: 540-967-2369; 8:30AM-4:30PM. ***Misdemeanor, Civil Actions under $15,000, Eviction, Small Claims.***

Civil Records: Access: Online, in person. Visitors must perform in person searches themselves. Required to search: name, years to search. Civil cases indexed by defendant, plaintiff; index on computer from 1997. Civil PAT goes back to 1997. PAT results show name only. Search free at www.courts.state.va.us/. Results show address of subject and day & month of birth, but not year. Also search LOPAS; call 804-786-5511 to apply.

Criminal Records: Access: Online, in person. Visitors must perform in person searches themselves. Required to search: name, years to search. Criminal records computerized from 1997. Criminal PAT goes back to same as civil.PAT results show name, DOB. Search free at www.courts.state.va.us/. Results show address of subject and day & month of birth, but not year.

General Information: No juvenile, sealed records released. Will not fax documents. Court makes copy: $1.00 first page, $.50 each add'l. Payee: Louisa District Court. Personal checks and major credit cards accepted. Prepayment required.

Lunenburg County

10th Circuit Court 11435 Courthouse Rd, Lunenburg, VA 23952; 434-696-2230; fax: 434-696-3931; 8:30AM-4:30PM. ***Felony, Civil Actions over $15,000, Probate.***
www.courts.state.va.us/courts/circuit.html

Civil Records: Access: Online, in person. Visitors must perform in person searches themselves. Required to search: name, years to search. Civil cases indexed by defendant, plaintiff. Civil index on docket books from 1700s; computerized records since 2002. Civil PAT goes back to 2000. Search free at www.courts.state.va.us/. Results show address of subject and day & month of birth, but not year. Also search LOPAS; call 804-786-5511 to apply.

Criminal Records: Access: In person, mail, online. Visitors must perform in person searches themselves. Search fee: Varies by numbers of yrs searched. Required to search: name, years to search. Criminal records indexed in books from 1700s; computerized records since 2002. Mail turnaround time 1-2 days. Criminal PAT goes back to 2001. Online access to criminal records is the same as civil. Online results show only month and day of DOB plus sex, race.

General Information: No juvenile, sealed records released. No fee to fax documents. Court makes copy: $.50 per page. Certification fee: $2.00 per page. Payee: Clerk of Circuit Court. Personal checks accepted; credit cards are not. Prepayment required.

10th General District Court 160 Courthouse Sq, #201, Lunenburg, VA 23952; 434-696-5508; fax: 434-696-3665; 8:30-4:30PM. ***Misdemeanor, Civil Actions under $15,000, Eviction, Small Claims.***
Civil Records: Access: Mail, in person, online. Both court and visitors may perform in person searches. No search fee. Required to search: name, years to search. Civil cases indexed by defendant, plaintiff. Civil records computerized since 1995, on index books and cards from 1991, prior to 1985 at Circuit Court. Mail turnaround time 3 days. Civil PAT goes back to 1995. Search free at www.courts.state.va.us/. Results show address of subject and day & month of birth, but not year. Also search LOPAS; call 804-786-5511 to apply.
Criminal Records: Access: Mail, online, in person. Both court and visitors may perform in person searches. No search fee. Required to search: name, years to search, DOB, SSN. Criminal records computerized since 1995, on index books and cards from 1991, prior to 1985 at Circuit Court. Mail turnaround time 3 days. Criminal PAT goes back to same as civil. Search free at www.courts.state.va.us/. Results show address of subject and day & month of birth, but not year.
General Information: Online identifiers in results same as on public terminal. No juvenile records released. Will not fax documents. Court makes copy: $.50 per page. No certification fee. Payee: Lunenburg District Court. Personal checks and major credit cards accepted. Mail requests: SASE required.

Lynchburg City

24th Circuit Court 900 Court St, PO Box 4, Lynchburg, VA 24505-0004; 434-455-2620; fax: 434-847-1864; 8:15AM-4:45PM. ***Felony, Civil Actions over $15,000, Probate.***
www.courts.state.va.us/courts/circuit.html
Civil Records: Access: In person, online. Both court and visitors may perform in person searches. No search fee. Required to search: name, years to search. Civil cases indexed by defendant, plaintiff. Civil index on docket books from 1800s, on computer since 1993. Civil PAT goes back to 2000. Search free at www.courts.state.va.us/. Results show address of subject and day & month of birth, but not year. Also search LOPAS; call 804-786-5511 to apply.
Criminal Records: Access: In person, online. Both court and visitors may perform in person searches. No search fee. Required to search: name, years to search; also helpful: DOB, SSN. Criminal records indexed in books from 1800s, on computer since 1993. Criminal PAT goes back to same as civil. Online access to criminal records is the same as civil. Online results show only month and day of DOB plus sex, race.
General Information: No juvenile, sealed records released. Court makes copy: $.50 per page. Self serve: same. Certification fee: $2.00. Payee: Clerk of Circuit Court. Personal checks accepted; credit cards are not. Prepayment required.

24th General District Ct - Civil Division 905 Court St, Public Safety Bldg, Lynchburg, VA 24504; civil phone: 434-455-2640; fax: 434-847-1779; 8AM-4PM. ***Civil Actions under $15,000, Eviction, Small Claims.***
Civil Records: Access: Online, in person. Both court and visitors may perform in person searches. No search fee. Required to search: name, years to search. Civil cases indexed by defendant, plaintiff. On computer since 1987. Public use terminal has civil records back to 10 years. Public terminal also has traffic cases. Search free at www.courts.state.va.us/. Results show address of subject and day & month of birth, but not year. Also search LOPAS; call 804-786-5511 to apply.
General Information: No juvenile, sealed records released. Will not fax documents. Court makes copy: $1.00 first 2 pages, $.50 each add'l. No certification fee. Payee: Lynchburg General District Court. Personal checks accepted; credit cards are not. Prepayment required.

24th General District Court - Criminal Division 905 Court St, Public Safety Bldg, Lynchburg, VA 24504; 434-455-2630; fax: 434-847-1779; 8AM-4PM. ***Misdemeanor.***
Criminal Records: Access: Online, in person. Visitors must perform in person searches themselves. Required to search: name, years to search. Criminal records indexed in books and computer go back 10 years. Note: Mail access limited to specific cases only; no name searches. Public use terminal has crim records back to 10 years. PAT results show name only. Search free at www.courts.state.va.us/. Results show address of subject and day & month of birth, but not year.
General Information: No juvenile, sealed records released. Will not fax documents. Court makes copy: $1.00 for first 2 pages, $.50 each add'l. No certification fee. Payee: Lynchburg General District Court. Personal checks accepted; credit cards are not. Prepayment required.

Madison County

16th Circuit Court PO Box 220, 1 Main St, Madison, VA 22727; 540-948-6888; fax: 540-948-3759; 8:30AM-4:30PM. ***Felony, Civil Actions over $15,000, Probate.***
www.courts.state.va.us/courts/circuit.html
Civil Records: Access: Mail, in person, online. Visitors must perform in person searches themselves. No search fee. Required to search: name, years to search. Civil cases indexed by defendant, plaintiff. Civil index on docket books from 1792, on computer since 1989. Mail turnaround time 1 week. Search free at www.courts.state.va.us/. Results show address of subject and day & month of birth, but not year.
Criminal Records: Access: Mail, online, in person. Visitors must perform in person searches themselves. No search fee. Required to search: name, years to search, DOB; also helpful: SSN. Criminal records indexed in books from 1792, on computer since 1989. Mail turnaround time 1 week. Online access to criminal records is the same as civil. Online results show only month and day of DOB plus sex, race.
General Information: No juvenile, sealed records released. Will not fax documents. Court makes copy: $.50 per page. Self serve: $.50 per page. Certification fee: $2.00. Payee: Clerk of Circuit Court. Personal checks accepted; credit cards are not. Prepayment required. Mail requests: SASE required.

16th General District Court 2 Main St, PO Box 470, Madison, VA 22727; 540-948-4657; fax: 540-948-5649; 8:30-4:30PM. ***Misdemeanor, Civil Actions under $15,000, Eviction, Small Claims.***
Civil Records: Access: Phone, fax, mail, online, in person. Only the court performs in person searches; visitors may not. No search fee. Required to search: name, years to search. Civil cases indexed by defendant, plaintiff. Civil index on docket books and computer back to 1996. Mail turnaround time 3-4 days. Search free at www.courts.state.va.us/. Results show address of subject and day & month of birth, but not year. Also search LOPAS; call 804-786-5511 to apply.
Criminal Records: Access: Phone, fax, mail, online, in person. Only the court performs in person searches; visitors may not. No search fee. Required to search: name, years to search, DOB; also helpful: address, SSN. Criminal records indexed in books and computer back to 1997. Mail turnaround time 3-4 days. Search free at www.courts.state.va.us/. Results show address of subject and day & month of birth, but not year.
General Information: No juvenile, sealed or pre-trial records released. No fee to fax documents. Court makes copy for no fee. No certification fee. Payee: Madison Combined Court. Personal checks accepted. Visa/MC accepted. Mail requests: SASE required.

Manassas City

Circuit & District Courts
See Prince William County.

Manassas Park City

Circuit & District Courts
See Prince William County.

Martinsville City

21st Circuit Court PO Box 1206, Martinsville, VA 24114-1206; 276-403-5106; fax: 276-403-5232; 9AM-5PM. ***Felony, Civil Actions over $15,000, Probate.***
www.ci.martinsville.va.us/circuitclerk
Civil Records: Access: Online, in person. Visitors must perform in person searches themselves. Required to search: name, years to search. Civil cases indexed by defendant, plaintiff; index on computer since 1988, on index books from 1942. Civil PAT goes back to 2002. PAT civil results show middle initial. Search free at www.courts.state.va.us/. Results show address of subject and day & month of birth, but not year. Also, with subscription and password, access judgments at https://www.ci.martinsville.va.us/crms/.
Criminal Records: Access: Online, in person. Visitors must perform in person searches themselves. Required to search: name, years to search; also helpful: DOB, SSN. Criminal records on computer since 1988, on index books from 1942. Criminal PAT goes back to same as civil. PAT criminal results show middle initial. Online access to criminal records is the same as civil. Online results show only month and day of DOB plus sex, race.
General Information: Online identifiers in results same as on public terminal. No juvenile, sealed records released. Will not fax documents. Court makes copy: $.50 per page. Self serve: same. Certification fee: $2.00. Payee: Clerk of Circuit Court. Personal checks accepted. Visa/MC accepted. Prepayment required.

21st General District Court PO Box 1402, 55 W Church St, Martinsville, VA 24112; 276-403-5125; fax: 276-403-5114; hours - 8AM-5PM. ***Misdemeanor, Civil Actions under $15,000, Eviction, Small Claims.***
www.courts.state.va.us/courts/gd/Martinsville/home.html
Civil Records: Access: Online, in person. Visitors must perform in person searches themselves. Required to search: name, years to search. Civil cases indexed by defendant, plaintiff; index on computer back to 1997. Civil PAT goes back to 1997. PAT results show name only. Public terminals available in County General District Court, 3160 Kings Mountain Rd, Martinsville, VA. Search free at www.courts.state.va.us/. Results show address of subject and day & month of birth, but not year. Also search LOPAS; call 804-786-5511 to apply.
Criminal Records: Access: Online, in person. Visitors must perform in person searches themselves. Required to search: name, years to search. Criminal records computerized from 1996. Criminal PAT goes back to 1997. PAT results show name only. Public terminals available in County General District Court, 3160 Kings Mountain Rd, Martinsville, VA. Search free at www.courts.state.va.us/. Results show address of subject and day & month of birth, but not year. Electronic results show name as appears on case papers.
General Information: Online identifiers in results same as on public terminal. No sealed or expunged records released. Will not fax documents. Court makes copy: $.50 per page. No certification fee. Payee: Martinsville General Dist Ct. Personal checks accepted. Visa/MC accepted. Prepayment required.

Mathews County

9th Circuit Court PO Box 463, Mathews, VA 23109; 804-725-2550; 8AM-4PM. ***Felony, Civil Actions over $15,000, Probate.***
www.courts.state.va.us/courts/circuit/Mathews/home.html
Civil Records: Access: In person, online. Visitors must perform in person searches themselves. Required to search: name, years to search. Civil cases indexed by defendant, plaintiff. Civil index on docket books from 1800s. Public use terminal has civil records back to 7/1/2006. Search free at www.courts.state.va.us/. Results show address of subject and day & month of birth, but not year.

Criminal Records: Access: In person, online. Visitors must perform in person searches themselves. Required to search: name, years to search; also helpful: DOB, SSN. Criminal records indexed in books from 1800s. Online access same as civil. Online results show middle initial, DOB.
General Information: No juvenile, sealed records released. Will not fax documents. Court makes copy: $.50 per page. Certification fee: $2.00. Payee: Clerk of Circuit Court. Personal checks accepted; credit cards are not. Prepayment required.

9th General District Court PO Box 169, Saluda, VA 23149; 804-758-4312; fax: 804-758-4343; 8:30AM-4:30PM. ***Misdemeanor, Civil Actions under $15,000, Eviction, Small Claims.***
Civil Records: Access: Mail, in person, online. Both court and visitors may perform in person searches. No search fee. Required to search: name, years to search. Civil cases indexed by defendant. Civil records on computer 10 years back. Mail turnaround time 7-10 days. Civil PAT goes back to 10 years. Search free at www.courts.state.va.us/. Results show address of subject and day & month of birth, but not year. Also search LOPAS; call 804-786-5511 to apply.
Criminal Records: Access: Mail, online, in person. Both court and visitors may perform in person searches. No search fee. Required to search: name, years to search, DOB, date of offense; also helpful: SSN. Criminal records on computer 10 years back. Mail turnaround time 7-10 days. Criminal PAT goes back to same as civil. Search free at www.courts.state.va.us/. Results show address of subject and day & month of birth, but not year.
General Information: Online identifiers in results same as on public terminal. No juvenile, sealed records released. Will not fax documents. Court makes copy: $.50 per page. No certification fee. Payee: Clerk of General District Court. Personal checks accepted; credit cards are not. Prepayment required. Mail requests: SASE required.

Mecklenburg County

10th Circuit Court PO Box 530, 1294 Jefferson St, Courthouse, Boydton, VA 23917; 434-738-6191 x4220; criminal phone: x4210; civil phone: x4210; fax: 434-738-6861; 8:30AM-5PM. ***Felony, Civil Actions over $15,000, Probate.***
www.courts.state.va.us/courts/circuit/Mecklenburg/home.html
Civil Records: Access: Online, in person. Visitors must perform in person searches themselves. Civil cases indexed by Defendant, Plaintiff. Civil index on docket books from 1800s, on computer from 1988. Civil PAT goes back to 1988. PAT civil results show middle initial. Search free at www.courts.state.va.us/. Results show address of subject and day & month of birth, but not year. Also search LOPAS; call 804-786-5511 to apply.
Criminal Records: Access: Online, in person. Visitors must perform in person searches themselves. Required to search: name, years to search. Criminal records indexed in books from 1800s, on computer from 1987. Criminal PAT goes back to same as civil. PAT criminal results show middle initial. Online access same as civil. Online results show middle initial, DOB.
General Information: No juvenile, adoption, and sealed or direct indictments (drug offenses) records released. Will fax specific case file data $1.00 per page to local or toll-free numbers. Court makes copy: n/a. Self serve: $.50 per page. Certification fee: $2.00. Payee: Clerk of Circuit Court. Personal checks accepted; credit cards are not. Prepayment required.

10th General District Court PO Box 306, 911 Madison St, Boydton, VA 23917; 434-738-6260; fax: 434-738-0761; 8:30AM-4:30PM. ***Misdemeanor, Civil Actions under $15,000, Eviction, Small Claims.***
www.courts.state.va.us/courts/gd/Mecklenburg/home.html
Civil Records: Access: Fax, mail, online, in person. Both court and visitors may perform in person searches. Search fee: $5.00. Required to search: name, years to search. Civil cases indexed by defendant, plaintiff; index on computer back to 1998. Mail turnaround time 2 days. Civil PAT goes back to 1998. PAT civil results show middle initial. Search free at www.courts.state.va.us/. Results show address of subject and day & month of birth, but not year. Also search LOPAS; call 804-786-5511 to apply.
Criminal Records: Access: Fax, mail, online, in person. Both court and visitors may perform in person searches. Search fee: $5.00. Required to search: name, years to search; also helpful: DOB, SSN. Criminal records on computer since 1998. Mail turnaround time 2 days. Criminal PAT goes back to 1998. PAT criminal results show middle initial. Search free at www.courts.state.va.us/. Results show address of subject and day & month of birth, but not year.
General Information: Online identifiers in results same as on public terminal. Sealed, and adoption records not released. Will fax documents $1.00 per page. Court makes copy: $.50 per page. No certification fee. Payee: Clerk of General District Court. Personal checks and credit cards accepted. Prepayment required. Mail requests: SASE required.

Middlesex County

9th Circuit Court PO Box 158, 73 Bowden St, Saluda, VA 23149; 804-758-5317; fax: 804-758-8637; 8:30AM-4:30PM. ***Felony, Civil Actions over $15,000, Probate.***
www.courts.state.va.us/courts/circuit.html
Civil Records: Access: In person, online. Visitors must perform in person searches themselves. Required to search: name, years to search. Civil cases indexed by defendant, plaintiff. Civil index on docket books from 1672; on computer back to 1992. Search free at www.courts.state.va.us/. Results show address of subject and day & month of birth, but not year. Also search LOPAS; call 804-786-5511 to apply.
Criminal Records: Access: In person, online. Visitors must perform in person searches themselves. Required to search: name, years to search, DOB, SSN. Criminal records indexed in books from 1674; on computer back to 1992. Public use terminal has crim records back to 2006. Online access same as civil. Online results show middle initial, DOB.
General Information: No juvenile, sealed records released. Will fax documents to local number only. Court makes copy: $.50 per page. Self serve: same. Certification fee: $2.00 per doc. Payee: Clerk of Circuit Court. Personal checks accepted; credit cards are not. Prepayment required.

9th General District Court PO Box 169, 73 Bowden St, Saluda, VA 23149; 804-758-4312; fax: 804-758-4343; 8:30-4:30PM. ***Misdemeanor, Civil Actions under $15,000, Eviction, Small Claims.***
Civil Records: Access: Mail, in person, online. Both court and visitors may perform in person searches. No search fee. Required to search: name, years to search. Civil cases indexed by defendant. Civil records held 10 years, computerized since 1997. Mail turnaround time 2-3 days. Civil PAT goes back to 1997. PAT results show name only. Search free at http://epwsgdp1.courts.state.va.us/gdcourts/caseSearch.do?index=index. Results include name and sometimes address. Also search LOPAS; call 804-786-5511 to apply.
Criminal Records: Access: Mail, online, in person. Both court and visitors may perform in person searches. No search fee. Required to search: name, years to search. Criminal records held 10 years, computerized since 1997. Mail turnaround time 2-3 days. Criminal PAT goes back to same as civil. PAT results show middle initial, DOB month and day, sex, race. Search free at www.courts.state.va.us/. Results show address of subject and day & month of birth, but not year.
General Information: Online identifiers in results same as on public terminal. No juvenile, sealed records released. Will not fax documents. Court makes copy: $.50 per page. No certification fee. Payee: Clerk of General District Court. Personal checks accepted. Visa/MC accepted. Prepayment required. Mail requests: SASE required.

Montgomery County

27th Circuit Court PO Box 6309, Christiansburg, VA 24068; 540-382-5760; probate phone: 540-382-3384; fax: 540-382-6937; 8:30AM-4:30PM. ***Felony, Civil Actions over $15,000, Probate.***
www.courts.state.va.us/courts/circuit.html
Search requests must be in writing and prepaid, and include SASE for return; call first to learn the copy fee.
Civil Records: Access: Phone, mail, online, in person. Both court and visitors may perform in person searches. No search fee. Required to search: name, years to search. Civil cases indexed by defendant, plaintiff. Civil index on docket books from 1800s, on computer from 1/94. Note: Phone and mail access limited to cases filed 7/1993-to-present. Civil PAT goes back to 1994. PAT results show name, DOB. Search free at www.courts.state.va.us/. Results show address of subject and day & month of birth, but not year.
Criminal Records: Access: Online, in person. Visitors must perform in person searches themselves. Required to search: name, years to search; also helpful: DOB, SSN. Criminal records on computer since 9/93, prior in books. Criminal PAT goes back to 6/1993.PAT results show name, DOB. Online access to criminal records is the same as civil. Online results show only month and day of DOB plus sex, race.
General Information: No juvenile, sealed records released. Will not fax documents. Court makes copy: $.50 per page. Self serve: same. Certification fee: $2.00 per doc. Payee: Clerk of Circuit Court. Personal checks accepted. Visa/MC accepted. Prepayment required. Mail requests: SASE required.

27th General District Court Montgomery County Courthouse, 1 E Main St, #201, Christiansburg, VA 24073; 540-382-5735; criminal phone: 540-394-2086; civil: 540-394-2085; fax: 540-382-6988; 8:30AM-4:30PM. ***Misdemeanor, Civil Actions under $15,000, Eviction, Small Claims.***
Civil Records: Access: Online, in person. Only the court performs in person searches; visitors may not. Required to search: name, years to search. Civil cases indexed by defendant, plaintiff; index on computerized records go back ten years. Search free at www.courts.state.va.us/. Results show address of subject and day & month of birth, but not year. Also search LOPAS; call 804-786-5511 to apply. Separate searches required for Blacksburg or Christiansburg.
Criminal Records: Access: In person, online. Only the court performs in person searches; visitors may not. Required to search: name, years to search. Computerized records go back ten years. Search free at www.courts.state.va.us/. Results show address of subject and day & month of birth, but not year. Separate searches required for Blacksburg or Christiansburg. Online results show middle initial, DOB.
General Information: No juvenile records released. Will fax documents to local or toll-free number. Court makes copy: $.50 per page. No certification fee. Payee: Clerk General District Court. Personal checks and major credit cards accepted. Prepayment required. Mail requests: SASE required for mail return of any copies.

Nelson County

24th Circuit Court PO Box 10, Lovingston, VA 22949; 434-263-7020; fax: 434-263-7027; 8AM-5PM. ***Felony, Civil Actions over $15,000, Probate.***
www.courts.state.va.us/courts/circuit.html
Civil Records: Access: Online, in person. Visitors must perform in person searches themselves. Required to search: name, years to search. Civil cases indexed by defendant, plaintiff. Civil index on docket books from 1800s, deeds on computer from 7/93. Search free at www.courts.state.va.us/. Results show address of subject and day & month of birth, but not year.
Criminal Records: Access: Online, in person. Visitors must perform in person searches themselves. Required to search: name, years to search; also helpful- DOB, SSN. Criminal records indexed in books from 1800s, deeds on computer

from 7/93. Online access to criminal records is the same as civil. Online results show only month and day of DOB plus sex, race.
General Information: No juvenile, sealed records released. Will fax documents $1.00 1st page, $.50 ea add'l. Court makes copy: $.50 per page. Certification fee: $2.50. Payee: Clerk of Circuit Court. Personal checks accepted; credit cards are not. Prepayment required. Mail requests: SASE required for mail return of any copies.

24th General District Court PO Box 514, 84 Courthouse Sq, County Courthouse, Lovingston, VA 22949; 434-263-7040; fax: 434-263-7033; 8AM-4PM. ***Misdemeanor, Civil Actions under $15,000, Eviction, Small Claims.***
Civil Records: Access: Fax, mail, online, in person. Both court and visitors may perform in person searches. No search fee. Required to search: name, years to search. Civil cases indexed by defendant, plaintiff; index on computer for 10 years. Mail turnaround time 3-4 days. Search free at www.courts.state.va.us/. Results show address of subject and day & month of birth, but not year. Also search LOPAS; call 804-786-5511 to apply.
Criminal Records: Access: Fax, mail, online, in person. Both court and visitors may perform in person searches. No search fee. Required to search: name, years to search. Criminal records on computer for 10 years. Mail turnaround time 3-4 days. Search free at www.courts.state.va.us/. Results show address of subject and day & month of birth, but not year.
General Information: No sealed records released. No fee to fax documents. Court makes copy: $.50 per page. No certification fee. Payee: Clerk of General District Court. Personal checks accepted; credit cards are not. Prepayment required. Mail requests: SASE required.

New Kent County

9th Circuit Court PO Box 98, 12001 Court House Circle, New Kent, VA 23124; 804-966-9520; fax: 804-966-9528; 8:30AM-4:30PM. ***Felony, Civil Actions over $15,000, Probate.***
www.courts.state.va.us/courts/circuit.html
Civil Records: Access: Online, in person. Visitors must perform in person searches themselves. Required to search: name, years to search. Civil cases indexed by defendant, plaintiff. Civil index on docket books from 1865, some on cards; computerized back to 1990. Civil PAT goes back to 1990. Search free at www.courts.state.va.us/. Results show address of subject and day & month of birth, but not year.
Criminal Records: Access: Online, in person. Visitors must perform in person searches themselves. Required to search: name, years to search, DOB, SSN. Criminal records indexed in books from 1923, some on cards; computerized back to 1990. Criminal PAT goes back to same as civil. Online access to criminal records is same as civil. Online results show only month and day of DOB plus sex, race.
General Information: No juvenile, sealed, adoption records released. Court makes copy: $.50 per page. Self serve: $.50 per page. Certification fee: $2.00. Payee: Circuit Court. Personal checks accepted; credit cards are not. Prepayment required.

9th General District Court PO Box 127, 12001 Courthouse Circle, New Kent, VA 23124; 804-966-9531; fax: 804-966-9535; 8:30AM-4:30PM. ***Misdemeanor, Civil Actions under $15,000, Eviction, Small Claims, Traffic.***
In person requests are not processed on demand; SASE must be included for mail return within 10 days.
Civil Records: Access: Mail, in person, online. Both court and visitors may perform in person searches. No search fee. Required to search: name, years to search. Civil cases indexed by defendant, plaintiff. Civil records go back to 1998 and on computer back 10 years. Mail turnaround time 10 days. Search free at www.courts.state.va.us/. Results show address of subject and day & month of birth, but not year. Also search LOPAS; call 804-786-5511 to apply.
Criminal Records: Access: In person, online. Both court and visitors may perform in person searches. No search fee. Required to search: name, years to search; also helpful: DOB and signed release. Criminal records go back to 1998 and on computer back 10 years. Note: Provide case number and SASE and written mail request and clerk will process. The sheriff department or Commonwealth attorney are both alternative sources for criminal records. Search free at www.courts.state.va.us/. Results show address of subject and day & month of birth, but not year.
General Information: No juvenile, sealed records released. Court makes copy: $1.00 per page. No certification fee. Payee: General District Court. Personal checks and credit cards accepted. Prepayment required. Mail requests: SASE required.

Newport News City

7th Circuit Court 2500 Washington Ave, Newport News, VA 23607; 757-926-8561; fax: 757-926-8531; 8AM-4:45PM. ***Felony, Civil Actions over $15,000, Probate.***
www.courts.state.va.us/courts/circuit/Newport_News/home.html
Civil Records: Access: Mail, in person, online. Both court and visitors may perform in person searches. No search fee. Required to search: name, years to search. Civil cases indexed by defendant, plaintiff; index on computer from 1987, prior on index books. Note: Mail access only available for old records. Mail turnaround time 1-2 days. Civil PAT goes back to 1983. Search free at www.courts.state.va.us/. Results show address of subject and day & month of birth, but not year.
Criminal Records: Access: In person, online. Visitors must perform in person searches themselves. Required to search: name, years to search. Criminal records computerized from 1987, on index books from 1985 to 1987, prior on judgment books. Criminal PAT goes back to same as civil. Online access to criminal records is the same as civil. Online results show only month and day of DOB plus sex, race. No IDs on civil results.
General Information: No adoption, juvenile, sealed records released. Will not fax documents. Court makes copy: $.50 per page. Self serve: same. Certification fee: $2.00. Payee: Clerk of Circuit Court. In state personal checks accepted. Visa/MC accepted. Prepayment required. Mail requests: SASE required for civil.

7th General District Court 2500 Washington Ave, Newport News, VA 23607; criminal phone: 757-926-8811; civil phone: 757-926-3520; fax: 757-926-8496; 7:30AM-4PM. ***Misdemeanor, Civil Actions under $15,000, Eviction, Small Claims.***
Civil Records: Access: Phone, fax, mail, in person, online. Visitors must perform in person searches themselves. No search fee. Required to search: name, years to search. Civil records go back to 10 years. Civil PAT goes back to 10 years. PAT civil results show middle initial. Search free at www.courts.state.va.us/. Results show address of subject and day & month of birth, but not year. Also search LOPAS; call 804-786-5511 to apply.
Criminal Records: Access: Phone, fax, mail, online, in person. Both court and visitors may perform in person searches. No search fee. Required to search: name, years to search. Criminal records on computer back 10 years. Mail turnaround time varies. Criminal PAT goes back to same as civil. PAT results show middle initial, DOB. Search free at www.courts.state.va.us/. Results show address of subject and day & month of birth, but not year. Traffic is a separate search. Online results show middle initial, DOB. Partial, not full, DOB may appear.
General Information: Online identifiers in results same as on public terminal. No juvenile, sealed records released. Court makes copy: $.50 per page. No certification fee. Payee: General District Court. Personal checks accepted. Visa/MC accepted for criminal records only. Prepayment required.

Norfolk City

4th Circuit Court 100 St Paul's Blvd, Norfolk, VA 23510; 757-664-4380; criminal phone: 757-664-4384; civil phone: 757-664-4387; probate phone: 757-664-4385; fax: 757-664-4581; 8:45AM-4:45PM. ***Felony, Civil Actions over $15,000, Probate.***
www.courts.state.va.us/courts/circuit.html
Civil Records: Access: In person, online. Both court and visitors may perform in person searches. Search fee: $10.00 if years to search prior to 1996, none if later. Required to search: name, years to search. Civil cases indexed by defendant, plaintiff; index on computer back to 1996, docket books back to 1800s. Search free at www.courts.state.va.us/. Results show address and the day/month of birth, but not year. Also access record images via http://208.210.219.102/cgi-bin/p/rms.cgi; registration and password required. Also, the Clerk of Circuit court subscription online system contains judgment records, wills, marriages, recorded documents etc at www.norfolk.gov/Circuit_Court/remoteaccess.asp. Fee is $50 per month. Judgments, Wills, Marriages, etc back to 1993.
Criminal Records: Access: In person, online. Both court and visitors may perform in person searches. Search fee: $10.00 if years to search prior to 1996, none if later. Required to search: name, years to search, DOB, SSN, signed release. Criminal records go back to 1972; on computer back to 1996, docket books back to 1800s. Online same as civil. Online results show only month and day of DOB plus sex, race.
General Information: No juvenile, sealed records released. Will not fax documents. Court makes copy: $.50 per page. Certification fee: $2.00. Payee: Clerk of Circuit Court. Personal checks accepted. Visa/MC accepted. Prepayment required.

4th General District Court 811 E City Hall Ave, Norfolk, VA 23510; 757-664-4910; criminal phone: 757-664-4915/6; civil phone: 757-664-4913/4; 8AM-4PM. ***Misdemeanor, Civil Actions under $15,000, Eviction, Small Claims.***
Civil Records: Access: Mail, in person, online. Visitors must perform in person searches themselves. Search fee: $10.00 per name. Required to search: name, years to search. Civil cases indexed by defendant, plaintiff. Civil records in files, on computer back 10 years. Mail turnaround time 1-2 weeks. Civil PAT goes back to 1998. PAT results show name only. Search free at www.courts.state.va.us/. Results show address of subject and day & month of birth, but not year. Also search LOPAS; call 804-786-5511 to apply.
Criminal Records: Access: Mail, online, in person. Visitors must perform in person searches themselves. Search fee: $10.00. Required to search: name, years to search. Criminal records in files, on computer back 10 years. Mail turnaround time 1-2 weeks. Criminal PAT goes back to 1998.PAT results show name, DOB. Search free at www.courts.state.va.us/. Results show address of subject and day & month of birth, but not year.
General Information: No juvenile, sealed, or adoption records released. Court makes copy: $1.00 per page. Certification fee: $1.00. Payee: Norfolk General District Court. Personal checks accepted. Visa/MC accepted. Prepayment required.

Northampton County

2nd Circuit Court PO Box 36, 5229 The Hornes, Eastville, VA 23347-0036; 757-678-0465; fax: 757-678-5410; 9AM-4:30PM. ***Felony, Civil Actions over $15,000, Probate.***
www.courts.state.va.us/courts/circuit.html
Oldest continuous records in the USA. Probate fax is same as main fax number.
Civil Records: Access: Phone, fax, mail, online, in person. Both court and visitors may perform in person searches. No search fee. Required to search: name, years to search. Civil cases indexed by defendant, plaintiff. Civil index on docket books from 1632; on computer back to 1993. Mail turnaround time 1 week. Civil PAT goes back to 7/1997. Search free at www.courts.state.va.us/. Results show address of subject and day & month of birth,

but not year. Also search LOPAS; call 804-786-5511 to apply.

Criminal Records: Access: Phone, mail, online, in person. Both court and visitors may perform in person searches. No search fee. Required to search: name, years to search, DOB. Criminal records indexed in books from 1632; on computer back to 1993, some previous. Mail turnaround time 1 week. Criminal PAT goes back to same as civil. Online access to criminal index is same as civil. Online results show only month and day of DOB plus sex, race.

General Information: No juvenile, sealed records released. Will fax documents $1.00 per page. Court makes copy: $.50 per page. Self serve: same. Certification fee: $2.00 per instrument. Payee: Clerk of Circuit Court. Personal checks accepted. Visa/MC accepted. Prepayment required. Mail requests: SASE required.

Northampton General District Court PO Box 1289, Eastville, VA 23347; 757-678-0466; 8:30AM-4:30PM. ***Misdemeanor, Civil Actions under $15,000, Eviction, Small Claims.***

Civil Records: Access: Mail, in person, online. Only the court performs in person searches; visitors may not. No search fee. Required to search: name, years to search. Civil cases indexed by defendant, plaintiff; index on computer since 1990. Mail turnaround time 1-2 days. Civil PAT goes back to 1999. Search free at www.courts.state.va.us/. Results show address of subject and day & month of birth, but not year. Also search LOPAS; call 804-786-5511 to apply.

Criminal Records: Access: Mail, online, in person. Only the court performs in person searches; visitors may not. No search fee. Required to search: name, years to search, DOB or SSN. Criminal records on computer since 1990. Mail turnaround time 1-2 days. Criminal PAT goes back to 1999. Search free at www.courts.state.va.us/. Results show address of subject and day & month of birth, but not year.

General Information: Will not fax documents. Court makes copy: $.50 per page. No certification fee. Payee: General District Court. Personal checks accepted; credit cards are not. Prepayment required. Mail requests: SASE required.

Northumberland County

15th Circuit Court PO Box 217, Heathsville, VA 22473; 804-580-3700; fax: 804-580-2261; 8:30AM-4:45PM. ***Felony, Civil Actions over $15,000, Probate.***

www.courts.state.va.us/courts/circuit.html

Civil Records: Access: Mail, in person, online. Both court and visitors may perform in person searches. No search fee. Required to search: name, years to search. Civil cases indexed by defendant, plaintiff. Civil index on docket books from 1650. Mail turnaround time 1-2 days. Search free at www.courts.state.va.us/. Results show address of subject and day & month of birth, but not year.

Criminal Records: Access: Mail, online, in person. Both court and visitors may perform in person searches. No search fee. Required to search: name, years to search, DOB. Criminal records indexed in books from 1650. Mail turnaround time 1-2 days. Online access to criminal records is the same as civil. Online results show only month and day of DOB plus sex, race.

General Information: No juvenile, sealed records released. Court makes copy: $.50 per page. Self serve: same. No certification fee. Payee: Clerk of Circuit Court. Personal checks accepted; credit cards are not. Mail requests: SASE required.

15th General District Court PO Box 114, 39 Judicial Pl, Northumberland Courthouse, Heathsville, VA 22473; 804-580-4323; fax: 804-580-6702; 8AM-4:30PM. ***Misdemeanor, Civil Actions under $15,000, Eviction, Small Claims.***

Civil Records: Access: Online, in person. Visitors must perform in person searches themselves. Required to search: name, years to search. Civil cases indexed by defendant, plaintiff; index on computer back 10 years. Civil PAT goes back to 10 years. Search free at www.courts.state.va.us/. Results show address of subject and day & month of birth, but not year. Also search LOPAS; call 804-786-5511 to apply.

Criminal Records: Access: Online, in person. Visitors must perform in person searches themselves. Required to search: name, years to search, DOB; also helpful: SSN. Criminal records on computer back 10 years. Criminal PAT goes back to same as civil. Search free at www.courts.state.va.us/. Results show address of subject and day & month of birth, but not year.

General Information: No juvenile, sealed records released. Will fax documents to local or toll-free number. Court makes copy: $.50 per page. No certification fee. Payee: Northumberland General District Court. Personal checks accepted. Visa/MC accepted. Prepayment required. Mail requests: SASE required for mail return of any copies.

Norton City

Circuit & District Courts

See Wise County.

Nottoway County

11th Circuit Court 328 W Courthouse Rd, Nottoway, VA 23955; 434-645-9043; fax: 434-645-2201; 8:30AM-4:30PM. ***Felony, Civil Actions over $15,000, Probate.***

Civil Records: Access: Mail, in person, online. Both court and visitors may perform in person searches. Search fee: $10.00 per hour. Required to search: name, years to search. Civil cases indexed by defendant, plaintiff. Civil index on docket books from late 1700s; on computer back to 2000. Civil PAT goes back to 2000. Search free at www.courts.state.va.us/. Results show address of subject and day & month of birth, but not year. Also search LOPAS; call 804-786-5511 to apply.

Criminal Records: Access: In person, online. Visitors must perform in person searches themselves. Required to search: name, years to search; also helpful: DOB, SSN. Criminal records indexed in books from late 1700s; on computer back to 2000. Criminal PAT goes back to same as civil. Online access to criminal records is the same as civil. Online results show only month and day of DOB plus sex, race.

General Information: No juvenile, sealed records released. Will not fax documents. Court makes copy: $.50 per page. Self serve: same. Certification fee: $2.00. Payee: Clerk's Office. Personal checks accepted; credit cards are not. Prepayment required. Mail requests: SASE required for civil.

11th General District Court PO Box 25, 328 W Courthouse Rd, Nottoway, VA 23955; 434-645-9312; fax: 434-645-8584; 8AM-4:15PM. ***Misdemeanor, Civil Actions under $15,000, Eviction, Small Claims.***

Civil Records: Access: Mail, in person, online. Both court and visitors may perform in person searches. No search fee. Required to search: name, years to search. Civil cases indexed by defendant, plaintiff. Civil index on cards from 1986, on computer the past 10 years. Only court can search prior to 1989. Mail turnaround time 2-3 days. Search free at www.courts.state.va.us/. Results show address of subject and day & month of birth, but not year. Also search LOPAS; call 804-786-5511 to apply.

Criminal Records: Access: Mail, online, in person. Both court and visitors may perform in person searches. No search fee. Required to search: name, years to search; also helpful: DOB, SSN. Criminal records indexed on cards from 1986, on computer the past 10 years Only court can search prior to 1989. Mail turnaround time 2-3 days. Search free at www.courts.state.va.us/. Results show address of subject and day & month of birth, but not year.

General Information: No juvenile records released. Will not fax documents. Court makes copy: $1.00 first page, $.50 each add'l. No certification fee. Payee: Nottoway District Court. Personal checks accepted. Visa/MC accepted. Prepayment required. Mail requests: SASE required.

Orange County

16th Circuit Court PO Box 230, Orange, VA 22960; 540-672-4030; fax: 540-672-2939; 8:30AM-4:30PM. ***Felony, Civil Actions over $15,000, Probate.***

www.courts.state.va.us/courts/circuit.html

Probate fax is same as main fax number.

Civil Records: Access: Online, in person. Both court and visitors may perform in person searches. No search fee. Required to search: name, years to search. Civil cases indexed by defendant, plaintiff; index on computer since 1989, in index books from 1734 for deeds, from 1853 for births, from 1912 for marriages. Civil PAT goes back to 2000. PAT results show name only. Search free at www.courts.state.va.us/. Results show address of subject and day & month of birth, but not year. Also search LOPAS; call 804-786-5511 to apply.

Criminal Records: Access: Phone, fax, mail, online, in person. Both court and visitors may perform in person searches. No search fee. Required to search: name, years to search, DOB; also helpful: SSN. Criminal records on computer since 1989, in index books from 1734. Mail turnaround time 1 week-10 days. Criminal PAT goes back to same as civil. PAT results show name only. Online access to criminal records is the same as civil. Online results show only month and day of DOB plus sex, race.

General Information: No juvenile, sealed records released. No fee to fax documents. Court makes copy: $.50 per page. Self serve: same. No certification fee. Payee: Clerk of Circuit Court. Personal checks accepted; credit cards are not. Prepayment required.

16th General District Court Orange County Courthouse, PO Box 821, Orange, VA 22960; 540-672-3150; 8:30AM-4:30PM. ***Misdemeanor, Civil Actions under $15,000, Eviction, Small Claims.***

Civil Records: Access: Mail, in person, online. Only the court performs in person searches; visitors may not. No search fee. Required to search: name, years to search. Civil cases indexed by defendant, plaintiff. Civil index on docket books from 1800s, on computer from 1990. Mail turnaround time 1-2 days. Civil PAT goes back to 1998. Search free at www.courts.state.va.us/. Results show address of subject and day & month of birth, but not year. Also search LOPAS; call 804-786-5511 to apply.

Criminal Records: Access: Mail, online, in person. Only the court performs in person searches; visitors may not. No search fee. Required to search: name, years to search, DOB; also helpful: SSN. Criminal records indexed in books from 1800s, on computer from 1990. Mail turnaround time 1-2 days. Criminal PAT available. Search free at www.courts.state.va.us/. Results show address of subject and day & month of birth, but not year.

General Information: No juvenile, sealed records released. Will not fax documents. Court makes copy: $1.00 first page, $.50 each add'l. Certification fee: $1.00 for 1st page, $.50 each add'l. Payee: Clerk of District Court. In state checks accepted. Visa/MC accepted. Prepayment required.

Page County

26th Circuit Court 116 S Court St, #A, Luray, VA 22835; 540-743-4064; fax: 540-743-2338; 9AM-5PM. ***Felony, Civil over $15,000, Probate.***

www.courts.state.va.us/courts/circuit.html

Civil Records: Access: Online, in person. Visitors must perform in person searches themselves. Required to search: name, years to search. Civil cases indexed by defendant, plaintiff. Civil index on docket books from 1831. Computerized records go back to 1995. Civil PAT goes back to 1995. PAT results show middle initial, DOB. Terminal results also show SSNs. Search free at www.courts.state.va.us/. Results show address of subject and day & month of birth, but not year.

Criminal Records: Access: Online, in person. Visitors must perform in person searches themselves. Required to search: name, years to search, DOB; also helpful: SSN. Criminal records indexed in books from 1831. Computerized records go back to 1995. Criminal PAT goes back to same as civil. PAT results show middle initial, DOB. Terminal results include SSN. Online access to

criminal records is the same as civil. Online results show only month and day of DOB plus sex, race.
General Information: Online identifiers in results same as on public terminal. No juvenile, sealed records released. Will fax documents after payment. Court makes copy: $.50 per page. Self serve: same. Certification fee: $2.00. Payee: Ron Wilson, Clerk. No 2-party checks accepted. No credit cards accepted. Prepayment required.

26th General District Court 116 S Court St, Luray, VA 22835; 540-743-5705; fax: 540-743-5334; 8AM-4:30PM. ***Misdemeanor, Civil Actions under $15,000, Eviction, Small Claims.***
www.co.page.va.us/
Civil Records: Access: Mail, in person, online. Both court and visitors may perform in person searches. No search fee. Required to search: name, years to search. Civil cases indexed by defendant, plaintiff; index on computer go back 10 years. Mail turnaround time 7-10 days. Civil PAT goes back to 10 years. PAT results show middle initial, DOB. Search free at www.courts.state.va.us/. Results show address of subject and day & month of birth, but not year. Also search LOPAS; call 804-786-5511 to apply.
Criminal Records: Access: Mail, online, in person. Both court and visitors may perform in person searches. No search fee. Required to search: name, years to search; also helpful: DOB. Criminal records on computer go back 10 years. Mail turnaround time 7-10 days. Criminal PAT goes back to same as civil. PAT results show middle initial, DOB. Search free at www.courts.state.va.us/. Results show address of subject and day & month of birth, but not year.
General Information: Online identifiers in results same as on public terminal. No sealed records released. Will fax documents to local or toll-free number. Court makes copy: $.50 per page. Self serve: same. Certification fee: $2.00 per page. Payee: District Court. Personal checks accepted. Visa/MC accepted. Prepayment required. Mail requests: SASE requested.

Patrick County

21st Circuit Court PO Box 148, Main St Courthouse, Stuart, VA 24171; 276-694-7213; fax: 276-694-6943; 9AM-5PM. ***Felony, Civil Actions over $15,000, Probate.***
www.courts.state.va.us/courts/circuit.html
Records available in office from 4/7/02 to present for both civil and criminal.
Civil Records: Access: In person, online. Visitors must perform in person searches themselves. Required to search: name, years to search. Civil cases indexed by plaintiff. Civil index on docket books from 1791. Search free at www.courts.state.va.us/. Results show address of subject and day & month of birth, but not year.
Criminal Records: Access: Online, in person. Visitors must perform in person searches themselves. Required to search: name, years to search; also helpful: DOB, SSN. Criminal records indexed in books from 1791. Online access to criminal records is the same as civil. Online results show only month and day of DOB plus sex, race.
General Information: No juvenile, sealed records released. Will not fax documents. Court makes copy: $.50 per page. Self serve: same. Certification fee: $2.00. Payee: Clerk of Circuit Court. Personal checks accepted; credit cards are not. Prepayment required.

21st General District Court PO Box 149, 106 Rucker St, #319, Stuart, VA 24171; 276-694-7258; fax: 276-694-5614; 8:30AM-5PM. ***Misdemeanor, Civil Actions under $15,000, Eviction, Small Claims.***
www.courts.state.va.us/courts/gd/Patrick/home.html
Civil Records: Access: Mail, fax, online, in person. Both court and visitors may perform in person searches. No search fee. Required to search: name, years to search. Civil cases indexed by defendant, plaintiff. Civil records go back to 1992; on computer from 10/94. Mail turnaround time 1 week. Civil PAT goes back to 10/1998. Search free at www.courts.state.va.us/. Results show address of subject and day & month of birth, but not year. Also search LOPAS; call 804-786-5511 to apply.
Criminal Records: Access: Mail, online, in person. Both court and visitors may perform in person searches. No search fee. Required to search: name, years to search, DOB; also helpful: SSN. Criminal records go back to 1992; on computer from 10/94. Mail turnaround time 1 week. Criminal PAT goes back to same as civil. Search free at www.courts.state.va.us/. Results show address of subject and day & month of birth, but not year.
General Information: Online identifiers in results same as on public terminal. No juvenile, sealed records released. Will not fax documents. Court makes copy: $.50 per page. No certification fee. Payee: Court. Personal checks accepted. Visa/MC accepted. Mail requests: SASE requested.

Petersburg City

11th Circuit Court 7 Courthouse Ave, Petersburg, VA 23803; 804-733-2367; fax: 804-732-5548; 8AM-4PM. ***Felony, Civil Actions over $15,000, Probate.***
www.courts.state.va.us/courts/circuit.html
Civil Records: Access: In person, online. Visitors must perform in person searches themselves. Required to search: name, years to search. Civil cases indexed by defendant, plaintiff. Civil index on docket books back to 1784; on computer back to 1988. Public use terminal has civil records. Search free at www.courts.state.va.us/. Results show address of subject and day & month of birth, but not year.
Criminal Records: Access: In person, online. Visitors must perform in person searches themselves. Required to search: name, years to search; also helpful: DOB, SSN. Criminal records go back to 1970; on computer back to 1996. Online access to criminal records is the same as civil. Online results show only month and day of DOB plus sex, race.
General Information: No juvenile, sealed or adoption records released. Will not fax documents. Court makes copy: $.50 per page. Self serve: same. Certification fee: $2.00. Payee: Petersburg Circuit Court Clerk. Personal checks accepted. Out of state checks not accepted. No credit cards accepted. Prepayment required. Mail requests: SASE required for mail return of any copies.

11th General District Court 35 E Tabb St, Petersburg, VA 23803; 804-733-2374; criminal phone: X4152; civil phone: X4153; fax: 804-733-2375; 8AM-4PM. ***Misdemeanor, Civil Actions under $15,000, Eviction, Small Claims.***
www.courts.state.va.us/courts/gd/Petersburg/home.html
When faxing, put to attention of civil or criminal.
Civil Records: Access: Mail, in person, online. Both court and visitors may perform in person searches. No search fee. Required to search: name, years to search. Civil cases indexed by defendant, plaintiff. Civil index on docket books back to 1997, computerized back 10 years. Mail turnaround time 1 week. Civil PAT goes back to 10 years. Public terminal available M,W,TH,F after 1PM. Results show partial address. Search free at http://epwsgdp1.courts.state.va.us/gdcourts/caseSearch.do?index=index. Results show partial address. Also search LOPAS; call 804-786-5511 to apply.
Criminal Records: Access: Mail, online, in person. Both court and visitors may perform in person searches. No search fee. Required to search: name, years to search, DOB; also helpful: SSN. Criminal records indexed on books for 10 years; on computer back ten years. Mail turnaround time 1 week. Criminal PAT goes back to 10 years. PAT results show middle initial, DOB. Public terminal available M,W,TH,F after 1PM. Results show partial address. Search free at www.courts.state.va.us/. Results show address of subject and day & month of birth, but not year.
General Information: No sealed records released. Will fax out documents. Court makes copy: $1.00 first 2 pages. $.50 each add'l. No certification fee. Payee: General District Court. In state personal checks accepted. Visa/MC accepted. Prepayment required. Mail requests: SASE required.

Pittsylvania County

22nd Circuit Court PO Drawer 31, 3 N Main St, Chatham, VA 24531; 434-432-7887; probate phone: 434-432-7892; fax: 434-432-7913; 8:30AM-5PM. ***Felony, Civil Actions over $15,000, Probate.***
www.courts.state.va.us/courts/circuit.html
Civil Records: Access: In person, online. Visitors must perform in person searches themselves. Required to search: name, years to search. Civil cases indexed by defendant, plaintiff. Civil index on docket books back to 1767; computerized records since 1995. Search free at www.courts.state.va.us/. Results show address of subject and day & month of birth, but not year. If documents mailed, add $.50 per page if SASE not included.
Criminal Records: Access: In person, online. Visitors must perform in person searches themselves. Required to search: name, years to search, DOB, SSN. Criminal records indexed in books back to 1767; computerized records since 1995. Search free by name only or case number at www.courts.state.va.us/. Results show address of subject and day & month of birth, but not year. Only month and day of DOB appears, plus sex, race.
General Information: No juvenile, sealed records released. Will not fax documents. Court makes copy: $.50 per page.If documents mailed, add $.50 per page if SASE not included. Certification fee: $2.00. Payee: Clerk of Circuit Court. Personal checks accepted; credit cards are not. Prepayment required.

22nd General District Court PO Box 695, Courthouse Annex, 11Bank St, 201, Chatham, VA 24531; 434-432-7880; fax: 434-432-7915; 8:30AM-4:30PM. ***Misdemeanor, Civil Actions under $15,000, Eviction, Small Claims, Traffic.***
www.courts.state.va.us/courts/gd/Pittsylvania/home.html
Civil Records: Access: Online, in person. Visitors must perform in person searches themselves. Required to search: name, years to search. Civil cases indexed by defendant, plaintiff; index on computer since 1995. Civil PAT goes back to 10 years. PAT results show name only. Search free at www.courts.state.va.us/. Results show address of subject and day & month of birth, but not year. Also search LOPAS; call 804-786-5511 to apply.
Criminal Records: Access: Online, in person. Visitors must perform in person searches themselves. Required to search: name, years to search. Criminal records on computer since 1995. Criminal PAT goes back to 10 years. PAT results show name only. Search free at www.courts.state.va.us/. Results show address of subject and day & month of birth, but not year.
General Information: No juvenile records released. Will not fax documents. Court makes copy: $.50 per page. No certification fee. Payee: General District Court. Personal checks and major credit cards accepted. Prepayment required.

Poquoson City

Circuit & District Courts
See York County.

Portsmouth City

Circuit Court PO Drawer 1217, 601 Crawford St, Portsmouth, VA 23705; 757-393-8671; criminal phone: x5143; civil phone: x5129; probate phone: x5127; fax: 757-399-4826; 8:30AM-5PM. ***Felony, Civil Actions over $15,000, Probate.***
www.courts.state.va.us/courts/circuit.html
Civil Records: Access: Mail, in person, online. Visitors must perform in person searches themselves. Search fee: $10.00 per name. Required to search: name, years to search. Civil cases indexed by defendant, plaintiff; index on computer back to 6/1987, prior on index books back to 1858. Note: Phone access limited to simple requests. Mail turnaround time 5 days or less. Civil PAT goes back to 1993. PAT results show name only. Search free at www.courts.state.va.us/. Results show address of subject and day & month of birth, but not year.
Criminal Records: Access: Mail, online, in person. Both court and visitors may perform in person

searches. Search fee: $10.00 per name. Required to search: name, years to search, DOB; also helpful: SSN. Criminal records computerized from 6/1987, prior indexed on books back to 1858. Mail turnaround time 48 hours for records before 2000. Criminal PAT goes back to same as civil. PAT results show name only. Online access to criminal records is same as civil. Online results show only month and day of DOB plus sex, race.
General Information: No juvenile, sealed records released. Will not fax documents. Court makes copy: $.50 per page. Self serve: same. Certification fee: $2.00. Payee: Cynthia P Morrison, Clerk. Business checks accepted. No credit cards accepted. Prepayment required.

General District Court PO Box 129, Portsmouth, VA 23705; criminal phone: 757-393-8681; civil phone: 757-393-8624; fax: 757-393-8634; 8:30AM-4:30PM. ***Misdemeanor, Civil Actions under $15,000, Eviction, Small Claims.***
Traffic Division: 757-393-8506.
Civil Records: Access: Online, in person. Visitors must perform in person searches themselves. Required to search: name, years to search. Civil cases indexed by defendant, plaintiff; index on computer from 4/87, from 1983 to 4/87 paper files only. Civil PAT goes back to 1996. Search free at www.courts.state.va.us/. Results show address of subject and day & month of birth, but not year. Also search LOPAS; call 804-786-5511 to apply.
Criminal Records: Access: Mail, fax, online, in person. Visitors must perform in person searches themselves. Search fee: $7.00 per name. Required to search: name, years to search; also helpful: DOB, SSN. Criminal records on computer and case (paper files) maintained for 10 years. Mail turnaround time within 14 days. Criminal PAT goes back to same as civil. Search free at www.courts.state.va.us/. Results show address of subject and day & month of birth, but not year.
General Information: Juvenile, sealed records not released. Will not fax documents. Court makes copy: $.50 1st 3 copies, $1.00 each add'l 3 copies. No certification fee. Payee: General District Court. Personal checks and credit cards accepted. Prepayment required. Mail requests: SASE required for criminal.

Powhatan County

11th Circuit Court PO Box 37, Powhatan, VA 23139-0037; 804-598-5660; criminal fax: 804-598-5608; civil fax: same; 8:30AM-5PM. ***Felony, Civil Actions over $15,000, Probate.***
www.courts.state.va.us/courts/circuit.html
Probate records are in a separate index. Probate fax is same as main fax number.
Civil Records: Access: In person, online. Visitors must perform in person searches themselves. Required to search: name, years to search. Civil cases indexed by defendant, plaintiff. Civil index on docket books from 1777, on computer from 1993. Civil PAT goes back to 1993. PAT civil results show middle initial. Search free at www.courts.state.va.us/. Results show address of subject and day & month of birth, but not year. Also search LOPAS; call 804-786-5511 to apply.
Criminal Records: Access: In person, online. Visitors must perform in person searches themselves. Required to search: name, years to search, signed release; also helpful: SSN. Criminal records indexed in books from 1777, on computer from 1993. Criminal PAT goes back to same as civil. PAT results show middle initial, DOB. Online same as civil. Online results show middle initial, DOB.
General Information: Online identifiers in results same as on public terminal. No juvenile, sealed records released. Will not fax documents. Court makes copy: $.50 per page. Self serve: same. Certification fee: $2.00 per document. Payee: Clerk of Court. Personal checks accepted; credit cards are not. Prepayment required.

11th General District Court Courthouse, 3880 Old Buckingham Rd, Powhatan, VA 23139; 804-598-5665; fax: 804-598-5648; 8:30AM-5PM. ***Misdemeanor, Civil Actions under $15,000, Eviction, Small Claims.***
Civil Records: Access: Phone, fax, mail, online, in person. Only the court performs in person searches; visitors may not. No search fee. Required to search: name, years to search. Civil cases indexed by plaintiff, defendant. Civil index on cards for 10 yrs, on computer from 1992. Mail turnaround time 1 week. Search free at www.courts.state.va.us/. Results show address of subject and day & month of birth, but not year. Also search LOPAS; call 804-786-5511 to apply.
Criminal Records: Access: Phone, fax, mail, online, in person. Only the court performs in person searches; visitors may not. No search fee. Required to search: name, years to search, DOB; also helpful: SSN. Criminal records indexed on cards for 10 yrs, on computer from 1993. Mail turnaround time 1 week. Search free at www.courts.state.va.us/. Results show address of subject and day & month of birth, but not year.
General Information: No juvenile, sealed records released. Will fax documents to local or toll-free number. Court makes copy: $.50 per page. No certification fee. Payee: Powhatan District Court. Personal checks and credit cards accepted. Prepayment required.

Prince Edward County

Circuit Court PO Box 304, North Main St, Farmville, VA 23901-0304; 434-392-5145; fax: 434-392-3913; 8:30AM-4:30PM. ***Felony, Civil Actions over $15,000, Probate.***
www.courts.state.va.us/courts/circuit/Prince_Edward/home.html
Civil Records: Access: Online, in person. Visitors must perform in person searches themselves. Required to search: name, years to search. Civil cases indexed by defendant, plaintiff; index on computer from 1990, books from 1930s. Civil PAT goes back to 1990. 5 public access terminals available. Search free at www.courts.state.va.us/. Results show address of subject and day & month of birth, but not year.
Criminal Records: Access: Online, in person. Visitors must perform in person searches themselves. Required to search: name, years to search, DOB; also helpful: SSN. Criminal records computerized from 1990, books from 1930s. Criminal PAT goes back to same as civil. 5 public access terminals available. Online access to criminal records is the same as civil. Online results show only month and day of DOB plus sex, race.
General Information: No juvenile, sealed records released. Will not fax documents. Court makes copy: $.50 per page; court will charge for the time to make copies. Self serve: $.50 per page. Certification fee: $2.00. Payee: Clerk of Circuit Court. Personal checks accepted. Visa/MC accepted. Prepayment required.

General District Court PO Box 41, Farmville, VA 23901-0041; 434-392-4024; criminal fax: 434-392-3800; civil fax: same; 8:30AM-4:30PM. ***Misdemeanor, Civil Actions under $15,000, Eviction, Small Claims.***
Civil Records: Access: Phone, mail, online, in person. Visitors must perform in person searches themselves. No search fee. Required to search: name, years to search; also helpful: address. Civil cases indexed by defendant, plaintiff; index on computer go back 10 years. Civil PAT goes back to 10 years. PAT civil results show middle initial. Search free at www.courts.state.va.us/. Results show address of subject and day & month of birth, but not year. Also search LOPAS; call 804-786-5511 to apply.
Criminal Records: Access: Mail, online, in person. Visitors must perform in person searches themselves. No search fee. Required to search: name, years to search; also helpful: DOB, SSN. Criminal records on computer go back 10 years. Mail turnaround time 1 week. Criminal PAT goes back to same as civil. PAT criminal results show middle initial. Search free at www.courts.state.va.us/. Results show address of subject and day & month of birth, but not year.
General Information: No juvenile, sealed records released. Will fax documents $1.00 per page. Court makes copy: $1.00 per page. Self serve: same. No certification fee. Payee: Clerk of District Court. Personal checks accepted. Visa/MC accepted. Prepayment required. Mail requests: SASE required.

Prince George County

Circuit Court PO Box 98, 6601 Courts Dr, Prince George, VA 23875; 804-733-2640; fax: 804-861-5721; 8:30AM-5PM. ***Felony, Civil Actions over $15,000, Probate.***
www.courts.state.va.us/courts/circuit.html
Civil Records: Access: Online, in person. Visitors must perform in person searches themselves. Required to search: name, years to search. Civil cases indexed by defendant, plaintiff. Civil index on docket books since 1930s, computerized since 4/96. Civil PAT goes back to 1996. PAT results show name, DOB. Search free at www.courts.state.va.us/. Results show address of subject and day & month of birth, but not year. Also search LOPAS; call 804-786-5511 to apply.
Criminal Records: Access: Online, in person. Visitors must perform in person searches themselves. Required to search: name, years to search, DOB; also helpful: SSN. Criminal records indexed in books since 1930s, computerized since 1/90. Criminal PAT goes back to 1990.PAT results show name, DOB. Online access to criminal records is the same as civil. Online results show name, DOB. Only month and day of DOB appears, plus sex, race.
General Information: No juvenile or sealed records released. Will not fax documents. Court makes copy: $.50 per page. Self serve: same. Certification fee: $2.00. Payee: Clerk of the Circuit Court. Personal checks accepted; credit cards are not. Prepayment required.

6th General District Court PO Box 187, 6601 Courts Dr, Prince George, VA 23875; 804-733-2783; fax: 804-733-2678; 8:30-4:30PM. ***Misdemeanor, Civil Actions under $15,000, Eviction, Small Claims.***
www.courts.state.va.us/courts/combined/Prince_George/home.html
Civil Records: Access: Online, in person. Visitors must perform in person searches themselves. Required to search: name, years to search. Civil cases indexed by defendant, plaintiff; index on computer since 1991, prior on books since 1985. Civil PAT goes back to 1991. PAT results show name only. Search free at www.courts.state.va.us/. Results show address of subject and day & month of birth, but not year. Also search LOPAS; call 804-786-5511 to apply.
Criminal Records: Access: Online, in person. Visitors must perform in person searches themselves. Required to search: name, years to search; also helpful: SSN. Criminal records on computer since 1991, prior on books since 1985. Criminal PAT goes back to same as civil. PAT results show name only. Search free at www.courts.state.va.us/. Results show address of subject and day & month of birth, but not year.
General Information: No juvenile records released. Will fax out documents; fee same as copies. Court makes copy: $1.00 each first 2 pages. $.50 each add'l. No certification fee. Payee: Prince George Combined Court. Personal checks and credit cards accepted.

Prince William County

31st Circuit Court 9311 Lee Ave, Manassas, VA 20110; 703-792-6015; criminal phone: 703-792-6031; civil phone: 703-792-6021; probate phone: 703-792-6085; criminal fax: 703-792-5746; civil fax: 702-792-7750; 8:30AM-5PM. ***Felony, Civil Actions over $15,000, Probate.***
www.pwcgov.org/default.aspx?topic=040017
Also hears Misdemeanor appeals. Probate fax- 703-792-5899
Civil Records: Access: In person, online. Visitors must perform in person searches themselves. Required to search: name, years to search. Civil cases indexed by defendant, plaintiff; index on computer since 1989; prior on microfiche or books to 1939. Civil PAT goes back to 1989. Search records free at http://ccourt.pwcgov.org/ but popups must be enabled.

Criminal Records: Access: Mail, in person, online. Both court and visitors may perform in person searches. Search fee: $10.00 per name. Required to search: name, years to search, DOB. Criminal records on computer since 1989; prior on microfiche or books to 1939. Mail turnaround time 1 week. Criminal PAT goes back to same as civil. Search records free at http://ccourt.pwcgov.org/ but popups must be enabled.
General Information: No juvenile records released. Will not fax documents. Court makes copy: $.50 per page. Certification fee: $2.00 per document. Payee: Clerk of Circuit Court. Personal checks accepted. Visa/MC accepted. Prepayment required.

31st General District Court 9311 Lee Ave, Manassas, VA 20110; criminal phone: 703-792-6141; civil phone: 703-792-6149; fax: 703-792-6646; 8AM-4PM. ***Misdemeanor, Civil Actions under $15,000, Eviction, Small Claims.***
www.courts.state.va.us/courts/gd/Prince_William/home.html
Civil Records: Access: Mail, fax, online, in person. Both court and visitors may perform in person searches. No search fee. Required to search: name, years to search. Civil cases indexed by defendant, plaintiff; index on computer go back 10 years. Mail turnaround time 10 days. Civil PAT goes back to 10 years. PAT results show name only. Search free at www.courts.state.va.us/. Results show address of subject and day & month of birth, but not year. Also search LOPAS; call 804-786-5511 to apply.
Criminal Records: Access: Mail, fax, online, in person. Both court and visitors may perform in person searches. No search fee. Required to search: name, years to search. Criminal records on computer go back 10 years. Mail turnaround time 10 days. Criminal PAT goes back to same as civil.PAT results show name, DOB. Search free at www.courts.state.va.us/. Results show address of subject and day & month of birth, but not year.
General Information: Online identifiers in results same as on public terminal. No juvenile or sealed records released. Court makes copy: $1.00 first 2 pages. $.50 each add'l. No certification fee. Payee: Clerk G.D.C. Personal checks accepted. Visa/MC accepted for traffic only. Prepayment required. Mail requests: SASE required.

Pulaski County

Circuit Court 45 3rd St NW, #101, Pulaski, VA 24301; 540-980-7825; probate phone: same; fax: 540-980-7835; 8:30AM-4:30PM. ***Felony, Civil Actions over $15,000, Probate.***
www.pulaskicircuitcourt.com
Civil Records: Access: Online, in person. Visitors must perform in person searches themselves. Required to search: name, years to search. Civil cases indexed by defendant, plaintiff. Civil index on docket books from 1839, online since 1998. Civil PAT goes back to 1998. Results include file number. Online access to court records is $300 annual fee http://records.pulaskicircuitcourt.com/icris/splash.jsp. Registration required; search by name, document type or number. Search free by name only or case number at www.courts.state.va.us/. Results show address of subject and day & month of birth, but not year.
Criminal Records: Access: Online, in person. Visitors must perform in person searches themselves. Required to search: name, years to search, DOB; also helpful: SSN. Criminal records indexed in books from 1839, online since 1998. Note: This agency will perform no record checks and refer all requests to the State Police. Results include file number. Criminal PAT goes back to same as civil. Results include file number. Online access to criminal records is the same as civil. Online results show only month and day of DOB plus sex, race.
General Information: Online identifiers in results same as on public terminal. No juvenile, sealed records released. Will fax documents $1.00 per page. Court makes copy: $1.00 per page. Self serve: $.50 per page. Certification fee: $1.00. Payee: Clerk of Court. Personal checks accepted; credit cards are not. Prepayment required. Mail requests: SASE required for mail return of any copies.

27th General District Court 45 3rd St NW, #102, Pulaski, VA 24301; 540-980-7470; fax: 540-980-7792; 8:30AM-4:30PM. ***Misdemeanor, Civil Actions under $15,000, Eviction, Small Claims.***
www.courts.state.va.us/courts/gd/Pulaski/home.html
Civil Records: Access: Online, in person. Visitors must perform in person searches themselves. Required to search: name, years to search. Civil cases indexed by defendant, plaintiff; index on computer since 1996. Civil PAT goes back to 1996. Search free at www.courts.state.va.us/. Results show address of subject and day & month of birth, but not year. Also search LOPAS; call 804-786-5511 to apply.
Criminal Records: Access: Online, in person. Visitors must perform in person searches themselves. Required to search: name, years to search, DOB; also helpful: SSN. Criminal records on computer since 1996. Criminal PAT goes back to same as civil. Search free at www.courts.state.va.us/. Results show address of subject and day & month of birth, but not year.
General Information: No juvenile, sealed records released. Will not fax documents. Court makes copy: $.50 per page. No certification fee. Payee: Clerk of General District Court. Personal checks and credit cards accepted. Prepayment required.

Radford City

27th Circuit Court 619 2nd St, Radford, VA 24141; 540-731-3610; fax: 540-731-3612; 8:30AM-5PM; no transaction- 4:30PM. ***Felony, Civil Actions over $15,000, Probate.***
www.courts.state.va.us/courts/circuit.html
Civil Records: Access: Fax, mail, online, in person. Both court and visitors may perform in person searches. No search fee. Required to search: name, years to search. Civil cases indexed by defendant, plaintiff; index on books from 1892; on computer back to 6/2000. Mail turnaround time same day. Civil PAT goes back to 1996. PAT civil results show middle initial. Search free at www.courts.state.va.us/. Results show address of subject and day & month of birth, but not year. Also search LOPAS; call 804-786-5511 to apply.
Criminal Records: Access: Fax, mail, online, in person. Both court and visitors may perform in person searches. No search fee. Required to search: name, years to search, DOB, signed release; also helpful: SSN. Criminal docket on books from 1892; on computer back to 6/2000. Mail turnaround time same day. Criminal PAT goes back to 1996. PAT criminal results show middle initial. Online access to criminal records is the same as civil. Online results show only month and day of DOB plus sex, race.
General Information: Online identifiers in results same as on public terminal. No juvenile, sealed or adoption records released. Will fax documents no add'l fee. Court makes copy: $.50 per page. Self serve: same. Certification fee: $2.00. Payee: Radford Circuit Court. Personal checks and major credit cards accepted. Prepayment required. Mail requests: SASE required.

27th General District Court 619 2nd St, Radford, VA 24141; 540-731-3609; fax: 540-731-3692; 8:30AM-4:30PM. ***Misdemeanor, Civil Actions under $15,000, Eviction, Small Claims.***
www.courts.state.va.us/courts/combined/Radford/home.html
Civil Records: Access: Mail, in person, online. Both court and visitors may perform in person searches. Search fee: A search fee may be required. Required to search: name, years to search. Civil cases indexed by defendant, plaintiff. Civil records go back 10 years. Mail turnaround time 7 days or longer. Civil PAT goes back to 10 years. Search via LOPAS; call 804-786-5511 to apply.
Criminal Records: Access: Fax, mail, online, in person. Both court and visitors may perform in person searches. No search fee, unless it is a lengthy search. Required to search: name, years to search, DOB, SSN, signed release. Criminal records on computer since 1989. Mail turnaround time 7 days or longer. Criminal PAT goes back to same as civil. PAT results show name only. Terminal results include a partial address. Search via LOPAS; call 804-786-5511 to apply. Online results show middle initial, DOB.
General Information: Online identifiers in results same as on public terminal. No juvenile, sealed records released. Will fax documents $.50 per page. Court makes copy: $.50 per page. Self serve: same. No certification fee. Payee: District Court. Personal checks and major credit cards accepted. Prepayment required.

Rappahannock County

20th Circuit Court PO Box 517, 238 Gay St, Washington, VA 22747; 540-675-5350; 8:30AM-4:30PM. ***Felony, Civil over $15,000, Probate.***
www.courts.state.va.us/courts/circuit.html
Civil Records: Access: Mail, in person, online. Visitors must perform in person searches themselves. No search fee. Required to search: name, years to search. Civil cases indexed by defendant, plaintiff. Civil records computerized since 1995, on index cards from 1833, early records archived. Note: Mail access limited to specific cases only. Court will only do searches as time permits. Civil PAT goes back to 1995. Search free at www.courts.state.va.us/. Results show address of subject and day & month of birth, but not year. Also search LOPAS; call 804-786-5511 to apply.
Criminal Records: Access: Mail, online, in person. Visitors must perform in person searches themselves. Search fee: Searches performed only as time permits. Required to search: name, years to search; also helpful: DOB, SSN. Criminal records computerized since 1995, on index cards from 1833, early records archived. Note: Mail access limited to specific cases only. Mail turnaround time 1-2 days. Criminal PAT goes back to same as civil. Online access to criminal records is the same as civil. Online results show only month and day of DOB plus sex, race.
General Information: No juvenile, sealed records released. Court makes copy: $.50 per page. Self serve: same. Certification fee: $2.50 per document. Payee: Clerk of the Circuit Court. Personal checks accepted; credit cards are not. Prepayment required. Mail requests: SASE required.

20th District Combined Court PO Box 206, 250 Gay St, Washington, VA 22747; 540-675-5356; fax: 540-675-5357; 8:30-4:30PM. ***Misdemeanor, Civil Actions under $15,000, Eviction, Small Claims.***
Civil Records: Access: Mail, in person, online. Both court and visitors may perform in person searches. No search fee. Required to search: name, years to search. Civil cases indexed by defendant, plaintiff; index on computer back to 1994, on index cards back to 1990, prior in Circuit Court. Mail turnaround time up to 2 weeks. Search free at www.courts.state.va.us/. Results show address of subject and day & month of birth, but not year. Also search LOPAS; call 804-786-5511 to apply.
Criminal Records: Access: Mail, online, in person. Both court and visitors may perform in person searches. No search fee. Required to search: name, years to search, DOB; also helpful: SSN, signed release. Criminal records computerized from 1994, index cards back to 1985, prior in Circuit Court. Mail turnaround time up to 2 weeks. Search free at www.courts.state.va.us/. Results show address of subject and day & month of birth, but not year.
General Information: No juvenile, sealed records released. Will not fax documents. Court makes copy: $1.00 per page. No certification fee. Payee: Clerk of General District Court. Personal checks and credit cards accepted. Prepayment required. Mail requests: SASE requested.

Richmond County

15th Circuit Court PO Box 1000, 101 Court Cir, Warsaw, VA 22572; 804-333-3781; criminal fax: 804-333-5396; civil fax: same; 9AM-5PM. ***Felony, Civil Actions over $15,000, Probate.***
www.courts.state.va.us/courts/circuit.html
Do not confuse Richmond County (here) with Richmond City. Probate fax is same as main fax number.
Civil Records: Access: Phone, mail, in person, online. Both court and visitors may perform in

person searches. No search fee. Required to search: name, years to search; also helpful: address, SSN. Civil cases indexed by defendant, plaintiff. Civil records archived from 1692. Mail turnaround time same day. Search free at www.courts.state.va.us/. Results show address of subject and day & month of birth, but not year. Also search LOPAS; call 804-786-5511 to apply.
Criminal Records: Access: Mail, in person, online. Both court and visitors may perform in person searches. No search fee. Required to search: name, years to search, DOB; also helpful: address. Criminal records archived from 1692, computerized since 1994. Mail turnaround time same day. Online access to criminal records is the same as civil. Online results show only month and day of DOB plus sex, race.
General Information: No juvenile, sealed records released. Will fax documents to local or toll free line. Court makes copy: $.50 per page; $1.00 per page if genealogy records. Self serve: same. Certification fee: $2.00 per document. Payee: Clerk of Circuit Court. Personal checks accepted; credit cards are not. Prepayment required. Mail requests: SASE required.

15th General District Court PO Box 1000, County Courthouse, 201 Court Circle, Warsaw, VA 22572; 804-333-4616; fax: 804-333-3741; 8AM-4:30PM. ***Misdemeanor, Civil Actions under $15,000, Eviction, Small Claims.***
Civil Records: Access: Mail, in person, online. Both court and visitors may perform in person searches. No search fee. Required to search: name, years to search. Civil cases indexed by defendant, plaintiff. Civil records archived 10 years back; on computer from 1994. Mail turnaround time 2 days. Civil PAT goes back to 10 years. Search free at www.courts.state.va.us/. Results show address of subject and day & month of birth, but not year. Also search LOPAS; call 804-786-5511 to apply.
Criminal Records: Access: Mail, online, in person. Both court and visitors may perform in person searches. No search fee. Required to search: name, years to search; also helpful: DOB, SSN. Criminal records archived 10 years back; on computer from 1994. Mail turnaround time 2 days. Criminal PAT goes back to same as civil. Search free at www.courts.state.va.us/. Results show address of subject and day & month of birth, but not year.
General Information: No juvenile, sealed records released. Will not fax documents. Court makes copy: $.50 per page. No certification fee. Personal checks accepted. Visa/MC accepted. Mail requests: SASE requested.

Richmond City

13th Circuit Court - Division I John Marshall Courts Bldg, 400 N 9th St, Richmond, VA 23219; 804-646-6505; criminal phone: 804-646-6553; civil phone: 804-646-6536; fax: 804-646-6562; 8:45AM-4:45PM. ***Felony, Civil over $15,000, Probate.***
www.courts.state.va.us/courts/circuit/Richmond/home.html
This court now holds records from the Manchester Division II Courthouse which has been closed 4/9/07.
Civil Records: Access: Mail, fax, online, in person. Visitors must perform in person searches themselves. No search fee. Required to search: name, years to search. Civil cases indexed by defendant, plaintiff; index on computer from 1987. On microfilm from 1980, on card index from 1970s, on index books from 1600s. Mail turnaround time 1-5 days Civil PAT goes back to 1987. Search free at www.courts.state.va.us/. Results show address of subject and day & month of birth, but not year.
Criminal Records: Access: Mail, fax, online, in person. Visitors must perform in person searches themselves. No search fee. Required to search: name, years to search; also helpful: DOB, SSN. Criminal records computerized from 1987. On microfilm from 1980, on card index from 1970s, on index books from 1782. Mail turnaround time is 1-5 days. Criminal PAT goes back to same as civil. Online access to criminal records is the same as civil. Online results show only month and day of DOB plus sex, race.
General Information: No juvenile, sealed records released. Will not fax documents. Court makes copy: $.50 per page. Certification fee: $2.00 per cert. Payee: Bevill M Dean, Clerk. Personal checks and major credit cards accepted. Prepayment required.

13th Circuit Court Manchester - Div 2
Court closed - see Richmond City 13th Circuit Court - Division I.

13th General District Court - Civil Division 400 N 9th St, Rm 203, Richmond, VA 23219; 804-646-6461; fax: 804-646-8758; 8AM-4PM. ***Civil Actions under $15,000, Eviction, Small Claims.***
Civil Records: Access: Phone, mail, online, in person. Both court and visitors may perform in person searches. No search fee. Required to search: name. Civil cases indexed by defendant, plaintiff. Civil records computerized since 1994 in index books from 1973. Records destroyed after 10 years after closed. Mail turnaround time 1-2 days. Public use terminal has civil records back to 1/1998. PAT results show name only. Search free at www.courts.state.va.us/. Results show address of subject and day & month of birth, but not year. Also search LOPAS; call 804-786-5511 to apply. Online results show name only.
General Information: Online identifiers in results same as on public terminal. No juvenile, sealed records released. Will not fax out documents. Court makes copy: $.50 per page. No certification fee. Payee: Clerk of General District Court, Civil Division. Business checks accepted. Major credit cards accepted. Prepayment required. Mail requests: SASE required.

13th General District Court - Division II 905 Decatur St, 102 E 10th St, Richmond, VA 23224; 804-646-8990; fax: 804-646-0387; 8AM-4PM. ***Misdemeanor, Traffic.***
Criminal Records: Access: Mail, online, in person. Both court and visitors may perform in person searches. No search fee. Required to search: name, years to search, DOB; also helpful: SSN. Criminal records computerized from 1986, records prior to 1980 destroyed. Mail turnaround time 1-5 days. Public use terminal has crim records back to 1986. For information about the statewide online systems, see the state introduction. Select and search General District Courts at http://208.210.219.132/vadistrict/select.jsp. Online results show middle initial, DOB.
General Information: No juvenile, sealed records released. Will not fax documents. Court makes copy: $1.00 per page. Payee: Clerk of General District Court. Personal checks accepted. Visa/MC accepted. Prepayment required.

Roanoke County

23rd Circuit Court PO Box 1126, 305 E Main St, Salem, VA 24153-1126; 540-387-6205; fax: 540-387-6145; 8:30AM-4:30PM. ***Felony, Civil Actions over $15,000, Probate.***
www.roanokecountyva.gov
Civil Records: Access: Online, in person. Visitors must perform in person searches themselves. Required to search: name, years to search. Civil cases indexed by defendant, plaintiff; index on computer from 1986, on index books from 1838 to 1986, prior records to Botetourt County. Civil PAT goes back to 1986. PAT results show name only. Public terminal at the City of Salem Courthouse. Search free at www.courts.state.va.us/. Results show address of subject and day & month of birth, but not year.
Criminal Records: Access: Online, in person. Visitors must perform in person searches themselves. Required to search: name, years to search, DOB; also helpful: SSN. Criminal records computerized from 1986, on index books from 1838 to 1986, prior records to Botetourt County. Criminal PAT goes back to same as civil. PAT results show name only. Public terminal at the City of Salem Courthouse. Online access to criminal records is the same as civil. Online results show only month and day of DOB plus sex, race.
General Information: No juvenile, sealed records released. Will not fax documents. Court makes copy: $.50 per page. Certification fee: $2.00. Payee: Clerk of Circuit Court. Personal checks accepted; credit cards are not. Prepayment required.

23rd General District Court PO Box 997, Salem, VA 24153; 540-387-6168; criminal fax: 540-387-6066; civil fax: same; 8:15AM-4:15PM. ***Misdemeanor, Civil Actions under $15,000, Eviction, Small Claims.***
www.roanokecountyva.gov/
Civil Records: Access: Mail, in person, online. Both court and visitors may perform in person searches. No search fee. Required to search: name, years to search, written request for staff to research. Civil cases indexed by defendant, plaintiff. Computerized records the past 10 years, on index cards from 1980. Prior at Circuit Court or Archives. Mail turnaround time 5 days. Civil PAT goes back to 10 years. Search free at www.courts.state.va.us/. Results show address of subject and day & month of birth, but not year. Also search LOPAS; call 804-786-5511 to apply.
Criminal Records: Access: Mail, online, in person. Both court and visitors may perform in person searches. No search fee. Required to search: name, years to search, DOB, written request for staff to research; also helpful: SSN. Computerized records the past 10 years, on index cards from 1980. Prior at Circuit Court or Archives. Mail turnaround time 5 days. Criminal PAT goes back to same as civil. Search free at www.courts.state.va.us/. Results show address of subject and day & month of birth, but not year.
General Information: No sealed records released. Will fax documents to local numbers only. Court makes copy: $.50 per page. No certification fee. Payee: General. Personal checks accepted; credit cards are not. Prepayment required. Mail requests: SASE required.

Roanoke City

23rd Circuit Court PO Box 2610, Roanoke, VA 24010-2610; criminal phone: 540-853-6723; civil phone: 540-853-6702; probate phone: 540-853-6712; criminal fax: 540-853-1024; civil fax: 540-853-1024; 8:15AM-4:45PM. ***Felony, Civil Actions over $15,000, Probate.***
www.roanokecountyva.gov/Departments/CircuitCourtClerksOffice
Civil Records: Access: Mail, in person, online. Visitors must perform in person searches themselves. No search fee. Required to search: name, years to search. Civil cases indexed by defendant, plaintiff; index on computer from 1986, on microfiche from 1884. Mail turnaround time 1 week Civil PAT goes back to late 1986 (index). PAT civil results show middle initial. Search free at www.courts.state.va.us/. Results show address of subject and day & month of birth, but not year.
Criminal Records: Access: Mail, online, in person. Visitors must perform in person searches themselves. No search fee. Required to search: name, years to search, DOB; also helpful: SSN. Criminal records computerized from 1986, criminal on index books from 1800s. Mail turnaround time is 1 week. Criminal PAT goes back to 1986 (index). PAT criminal results show middle initial. No document images. Online access to criminal records is the same as civil. Online results show only month and day of DOB plus sex, race.
General Information: No juvenile, sealed records released. Will not fax documents. Court makes copy: $.50 per page. Self serve: same. Certification fee: $2.00. Payee: Clerk of Circuit Court. Personal checks accepted; credit cards are not. Prepayment required.

General District Court 315 W Church Ave, 2nd Fl, Roanoke, VA 24016-5007; criminal phone: 540-853-2361; civil phone: 540-853-2364; fax: 540-853-1540; 8AM-4PM. ***Misdemeanor, Civil Actions under $15,000, Eviction, Small Claims, Traffic.***
Per state law, the court cannot release DOB and SSN.
Civil Records: Access: Mail, in person, online. Both court and visitors may perform in person searches. Search fee: $1.00 per name. Required to search: name, date to search, case number. Civil cases indexed by defendant, plaintiff; index on computer for past 10 years. Mail turnaround time 1 week. Search free at www.courts.state.va.us/. Results show address of subject and day & month of birth, but not year.
Criminal Records: Access: In person, online. Visitors must perform in person searches

themselves. Required to search: name, date to search, case number, DOB; also helpful: SSN. Criminal records on computer for past 10 years. Search free at www.courts.state.va.us/. Results show address of subject and day & month of birth, but not year.
General Information: No juvenile records released. Will not fax documents. Court makes copy: $1.00 per page. No certification fee. Payee: General District Court. Business checks accepted. Prepayment required. Mail requests: SASE required for civil.

Rockbridge County

25th Circuit Court 2 S Main St, Courthouse Sq, Lexington, VA 24450; 540-463-2232; fax: 540-463-3850; 8:30AM-4:30PM. ***Felony, Civil Actions over $15,000, Probate.***
www.courts.state.va.us/courts/circuit.html
Civil Records: Access: Online, in person. Visitors must perform in person searches themselves. Required to search: name, years to search. Civil cases indexed by defendant, plaintiff; index on computer from 1985, index books from 1778. Criminal records easily obtained back to the late 1960s, earlier records are not. Civil PAT goes back to 1985. PAT civil results show middle initial. Search free at www.courts.state.va.us/. Results show address of subject and day & month of birth, but not year. Also search LOPAS; call 804-786-5511 to apply.
Criminal Records: Access: Online, in person. Visitors must perform in person searches themselves. Required to search: name, years to search, DOB. Criminal records computerized from 1985, index books from 1778. Criminal records easily obtained from the late 1960s; earlier records are not. Criminal PAT goes back to same as civil. PAT results show middle initial, DOB. Online access to criminal records is the same as civil. Online results show only month and day of DOB plus sex, race.
General Information: No juvenile, sealed records released. Will not fax documents. Court makes copy: $.50 per page. Self serve: same. Certification fee: $2.50. Payee: Clerk of Circuit Court. Personal checks accepted; credit cards are not. Prepayment required.

General District Court 150 S Main St, Lexington, VA 24450; 540-463-3631; fax: 540-463-4213; 8:30AM-4:30PM. ***Misdemeanor, Civil Actions under $15,000, Eviction, Small Claims.***
Physical address- 20 S Randolph St. Lexington-Rockbridge is a combined district court.
Civil Records: Access: Mail, in person, online. Both court and visitors may perform in person searches. No search fee. Required to search: name, years to search. Civil cases indexed by defendant, plaintiff; index on computer from 1989, on index cards from 1985 to 1989, prior to 1985 at Circuit Court. Records destroyed after 10 years. Mail turnaround time 5-7 days. Civil PAT goes back to 1989. Search free at www.courts.state.va.us/. Results show address of subject and day & month of birth, but not year. Also search LOPAS; call 804-786-5511 to apply.
Criminal Records: Access: Mail, online, in person. Both court and visitors may perform in person searches. No search fee. Required to search: name, years to search, DOB; also helpful: SSN. Criminal records computerized from late 1989, on index cards from 1985 to 1989, prior to 1985 at Circuit Court. Mail turnaround time 5-7 days. Criminal PAT goes back to same as civil. Search free at www.courts.state.va.us/. Results show address of subject and day & month of birth, but not year.
General Information: No juvenile, sealed records released. Will not fax documents. Court makes copy: $1.00 each first 2 pages; $.50 each add'l. No certification fee. Payee: District Court. Personal checks accepted; credit cards are not. Prepayment required. Mail requests: SASE required.

Rockingham County

26th Circuit Court Courthouse, Court Sq, Harrisonburg, VA 22801; 540-564-3111; criminal phone: 540-564-3118; civil phone: 540-564-3114; fax: 540-564-3127; 9AM-5PM. ***Felony, Civil Actions over $15,000, Probate.***
www.courts.state.va.us/courts/circuit.html
Civil Records: Access: Online, in person. Visitors must perform in person searches themselves. Required to search: name, years to search. Civil cases indexed by defendant, plaintiff. Civil index on cards from the beginning of the county. Civil PAT goes back to 1995. Search free at www.courts.state.va.us/. Results show address of subject and day & month of birth, but not year.
Criminal Records: Access: Online, in person. Visitors must perform in person searches themselves. Required to search: name, years to search. Criminal records indexed on cards from the beginning of the county. Criminal PAT goes back to 1992. Online access to criminal records is the same as civil. Online results show only month and day of DOB plus sex, race.
General Information: No juvenile, sealed records released. Will not fax documents. Court makes copy: $.50 per page. Certification fee: $2.00. Payee: Clerk of Circuit Court. Personal checks accepted; credit cards are not.

26th General District Court 53 Court Sq, Harrisonburg, VA 22801; criminal phone: 540-564-3130; civil phone: 540-564-3135; fax: 540-564-3096; 8AM-4PM. ***Misdemeanor, Civil Actions under $15,000, Eviction, Small Claims.***
Civil Records: Access: Phone, mail, online, in person. Both court and visitors may perform in person searches. Search fee: $3.50 per name. Required to search: name, years to search. Civil cases indexed by defendant, plaintiff; index on computer the past 10 years, on index cards from 1978, prior at Circuit Court. Mail turnaround time up to 1 week. Civil PAT goes back to 10 years. Search free at www.courts.state.va.us/. Results show address of subject and day & month of birth, but not year. Also search LOPAS; call 804-786-5511 to apply.
Criminal Records: Access: Phone, mail, online, in person. Both court and visitors may perform in person searches. Search fee: $3.50 per name. Required to search: name, years to search, DOB; also helpful: SSN. Criminal records computerized from the past 10 years, on index cards from 1985, prior at Circuit Court. Mail turnaround time up to 1 week. Criminal PAT goes back to same as civil. Search free at www.courts.state.va.us/. Results show address of subject and day & month of birth, but not year.
General Information: Online identifiers in results same as on public terminal. No juvenile, sealed, adoption records released. Will not fax documents. Court makes copy: $.50 per page. Certification fee: included in copy fee. Payee: General District Court. Personal checks and credit cards accepted. Prepayment required. Mail requests: SASE required.

Russell County

29th Circuit Court PO Box 435, 53 E Main St, Lebanon, VA 24266; 276-889-8023; criminal fax: 276-889-8003; civil fax: same; 8:30AM-4:30PM. ***Felony, Civil over $15,000, Probate.***
www.courts.state.va.us/courts/circuit.html
Probate fax is same as main fax number.
Civil Records: Access: Mail, in person, online. Both court and visitors may perform in person searches. No search fee. Required to search: signed release, name, years to search. Civil cases indexed by defendant, plaintiff; index on computer from 1990, archived from 1809. Mail turnaround time 2-3 weeks. Civil PAT goes back to 2000. PAT results show name only. Search free at www.courts.state.va.us/. Results show address of subject and day & month of birth, but not year. Also search LOPAS; call 804-786-5511 to apply.
Criminal Records: Access: Online, in person. Both court and visitors may perform in person searches. No search fee. Required to search: signed release, name, years to search. Criminal records computerized from 1990, archived from 1809. Criminal PAT goes back to same as civil. PAT results show name only. Online access to criminal records is the same as civil. Online results show only month and day of DOB plus sex, race.
General Information: No juvenile, sealed records released. Will not fax documents. Court makes copy: $.50 per page. Self serve: same. No certification fee. Payee: Clerk of Circuit Court. Personal checks accepted. Visa/MC accepted. Prepayment required. Mail requests: SASE required for mail return of any copies.

29th General District Court Russell County Courthouse, PO Box 65, Lebanon, VA 24266; 276-889-8051; criminal fax: 276-889-8091; civil fax: same; 8:30AM-4:30PM. ***Misdemeanor, Civil Actions under $15,000, Eviction, Small Claims.***
Civil Records: Access: Phone, fax, mail, online, in person. Both court and visitors may perform in person searches. No search fee. Required to search: name. Civil cases indexed by defendant, plaintiff; index on computer for past 10 years. Mail turnaround time 2-5 days. Civil PAT goes back to for past 10 years. Search free at www.courts.state.va.us/. Results show address of subject and day & month of birth, but not year. Also search LOPAS; call 804-786-5511 to apply.
Criminal Records: Access: Phone, fax, mail, online, in person. Both court and visitors may perform in person searches. No search fee. Required to search: name, DOB; also helpful: SSN. Criminal records on computer for past 10 years. Mail turnaround time 2-5 days. Criminal PAT goes back to for past 10 years. Search free at www.courts.state.va.us/. Results show address of subject and day & month of birth, but not year.
General Information: Online identifiers in results same as on public terminal. No juvenile, sealed records released. No fee to fax documents. Court makes copy for no fee. No certification fee. Payee: Court. Personal checks and major credit cards accepted. Mail requests: SASE required.

Salem City

23rd Circuit Court 2 E Calhoun St, PO Box 891, Salem, VA 24153; 540-375-3067; fax: 540-375-4039; 8AM-4:30PM. ***Felony, Civil Actions over $15,000, Probate.***
www.courts.state.va.us/courts/circuit.html
Civil Records: Access: Online, in person. Both court and visitors may perform in person searches. No search fee. Required to search: name, years to search. Civil cases indexed by defendant, plaintiff; index on computer from 1985, on index books from 1968, prior at Roanoke Circuit Court. Civil PAT goes back to 10 years. Search free at www.courts.state.va.us/. Results show address of subject and day & month of birth, but not year. Also search LOPAS; call 804-786-5511 to apply.
Criminal Records: Access: Online, in person. Visitors must perform in person searches themselves. Required to search: name, years to search, DOB; also helpful: SSN. Criminal records computerized from 1985, on index books from 1968, prior at Roanoke Circuit Court. Criminal PAT goes back to same as civil. Online access to criminal records is the same as civil. Online results show name, DOB. Only month and day of DOB appears, plus sex, race.
General Information: Online identifiers in results same as on public terminal. No juvenile, sealed or adoption records released. Will not fax documents. Court makes copy: $.50 per page. Certification fee: $2.00. Payee: Clerk of Circuit Court. Personal checks accepted; credit cards are not. Prepayment required.

23rd General District Court 2 E Calhoun St, Salem, VA 24153; 540-375-3044; fax: 540-375-4024; 8AM-4PM. ***Misdemeanor, Civil Actions under $15,000, Eviction, Small Claims.***
Civil Records: Access: Online, in person. Visitors must perform in person searches themselves. Required to search: name, years to search. Civil cases indexed by defendant, plaintiff; index on computer for 10 years, prior records at City of Salem Circuit Court. Civil PAT goes back to 10 years. Search free at www.courts.state.va.us/. Results show address of subject and day & month of birth, but not year. Also search LOPAS; call 804-786-5511 to apply.
Criminal Records: Access: Online, in person. Visitors must perform in person searches themselves. Required to search: name, years to search, DOB, SSN. Criminal records on computer for 10 years, prior records at City of Salem Circuit Court. Criminal PAT goes back to same as civil. Search free at www.courts.state.va.us/. Results show

address of subject and day & month of birth, but not year.
General Information: No juvenile, sealed records released. Will not fax documents. Court makes copy: $1.00 per page 1st 2 pages; $.50 each add'l. Certification fee: $1.00 per page. Payee: General District Court. Personal checks and credit cards accepted. Prepayment required. Mail requests: SASE required for mail return of any copies.

Scott County

Circuit Court 202 W Jackson St, #102, Gate City, VA 24251; 276-386-3801; probate phone: same; fax: 276-386-2430; 8:30AM-5PM. ***Felony, Civil Actions over $15,000, Probate.***
www.courts.state.va.us/courts/circuit.html
Civil Records: Access: Phone, mail, online, in person. Both court and visitors may perform in person searches. No search fee. Required to search: name, years to search. Civil cases indexed by defendant, plaintiff. Civil index on docket books back to 1815; on computer back to 1999. Mail turnaround time 3-4 days. Civil PAT goes back to 1815. Search free at www.courts.state.va.us/. Results show address of subject and day & month of birth, but not year. Also search LOPAS; call 804-786-5511 to apply.
Criminal Records: Access: Mail, online, in person. Both court and visitors may perform in person searches. No search fee. Required to search: name, years to search, DOB; also helpful: SSN. Criminal records indexed in books back to 1815; on computer back to 1999. Mail turnaround time 3-4 days. Criminal PAT goes back to 1815. Online access to criminal records is the same as civil. Online results show only month and day of DOB plus sex, race.
General Information: No juvenile, sealed records released. Fee to fax out file $4.00 per page. Court makes copy: $.50 per page. Self serve: same. Certification fee: $2.00. Payee: Mark A "Bo" Taylor, Clerk. Personal checks accepted. Visa/MC accepted. Prepayment required. Mail requests: SASE required.

30th General District Court 202 W Jackson St, Ste 302, Gate City, VA 24251; 276-386-7341; fax: 276-386-2840; 8AM-4:30PM. ***Misdemeanor, Civil Actions under $15,000, Eviction, Small Claims.***
Civil Records: Access: Mail, in person, online. Only the court performs in person searches; visitors may not. No search fee. Required to search: name, years to search. Civil cases indexed by plaintiff. Civil index on docket books, on computer from 1990. Mail turnaround time up to 1-2 days. Search free at www.courts.state.va.us/. Results show address of subject and day & month of birth, but not year. Also search LOPAS; call 804-786-5511 to apply.
Criminal Records: Access: Mail, online, in person. Only the court performs in person searches; visitors may not. No search fee. Required to search: name, years to search, DOB; also helpful: SSN. Criminal records indexed in books, on computer from 1990. Mail turnaround time up to 1-2 days. Search free at www.courts.state.va.us/. Results show address of subject and day & month of birth, but not year.
General Information: No juvenile, sealed records released. Will fax back documents. Court makes copy: $1.00 per page. No certification fee. Payee: General District Court. Personal checks accepted. Visa/MC accepted. Prepayment required. Mail requests: SASE required.

Shenandoah County

26th Circuit Court 112 S Main St, PO Box 406, Woodstock, VA 22664; 540-459-6150; fax: 540-459-6155; 9AM-5PM. ***Felony, Civil Actions over $15,000, Probate.***
www.courts.state.va.us/courts/circuit.html
Civil Records: Access: Mail, in person, online. Both court and visitors may perform in person searches. No search fee. Required to search: name, years to search. Civil cases indexed by defendant, plaintiff; index on computer from 1996, on index cards from 1772. Note: Mail access limited to specific cases only, or a single name search. Search free at www.courts.state.va.us/. Results show address of subject and day & month of birth, but not year. Also search LOPAS; call 804-786-5511 to apply.
Criminal Records: Access: In person, online. Visitors must perform in person searches themselves. Required to search: name, years to search, DOB; also helpful: SSN. Criminal records computerized from 1996, on index cards from 1772. Online access to criminal records is the same as civil. Online results show only month and day of DOB, sex, race.
General Information: No juvenile, sealed records released. Will not fax documents. Court makes copy: $.50 per page. Certification fee: $2.00 per doc. Payee: Clerk of Circuit Court. Personal checks accepted. Credit cards accepted for criminal payments only. Prepayment required. Mail requests: SASE required for civil.

26th General District Court 114 W Court St, Woodstock, VA 22664; 540-459-6130; fax: 540-459-7279; 8:30AM-4:30PM. ***Misdemeanor, Civil Actions under $15,000, Eviction, Small Claims.***
Civil Records: Access: Mail, in person, online. Visitors must perform in person searches themselves. No search fee. Required to search: name, years to search. Civil cases indexed by defendant, plaintiff; index on computer from 1995, prior at Circuit Court. Civil PAT goes back to 1995. Search free at www.courts.state.va.us/. Results show address of subject and day & month of birth, but not year. Also search LOPAS; call 804-786-5511 to apply.
Criminal Records: Access: Online, in person. Visitors must perform in person searches themselves. Required to search: name, years to search, DOB; also helpful: SSN. Criminal records computerized from 1995, prior at Circuit Court. Note: This agency will not do criminal record checks and refer all requesters to the State Police or the online system. Criminal PAT goes back to same as civil. Search free at www.courts.state.va.us/. Results show address of subject and day & month of birth, but not year.
General Information: No sealed or adoption records relapsed. Court makes copy: $1.00 minimum 1st 2 pages, $.50 each add'l. No certification fee. Payee: General District Court. Personal checks accepted. Credit cards accepted for criminal fines and on online system only. Prepayment required.

Smyth County

28th Circuit Court 109 W Main St, #144, Marion, VA 24354-2510; 276-782-4044; criminal fax: 276-782-4045; civil fax: same; 9AM-5PM. ***Felony, Civil Actions over $15,000, Probate.***
www.courts.state.va.us/courts/circuit.html
Probate is in a separate index at this address. Probate fax is same as main fax number.
Civil Records: Access: Mail, fax, online, in person. Both court and visitors may perform in person searches. Search fee: $10.00 per name. Required to search: name, years to search. Civil cases indexed by defendant, plaintiff. Civil index on cards from 1832, most are computerized since 1/90. Mail turnaround time 1 week. Search free at www.courts.state.va.us/. Results show address of subject and day & month of birth, but not year. Also search LOPAS; call 804-786-5511 to apply.
Criminal Records: Access: Mail, fax, online, in person. Both court and visitors may perform in person searches. Search fee: $10.00 per name. Required to search: name, years to search; also helpful: DOB, SSN. Criminal records indexed on cards from 1832, most are computerized since 1/90. Mail turnaround time 1 week. Online access to criminal records is the same as civil. Online results show only month and day of DOB plus sex, race.
General Information: No juvenile, sealed or adoption records released. Fee to fax out file $1.25 per page. Court makes copy: $.50 per page. Self serve: same. Certification fee: $2.00. Payee: Clerk of Circuit Court. Personal checks accepted; credit cards are not. Prepayment required. Mail requests: SASE requested.

28th General District Court Smythe County Courthouse, Rm 231, 109 W Main St, Marion, VA 24354; 276-782-4044; fax: 276-782-4045; 8:30AM-5PM. ***Misdemeanor, Civil Actions under $15,000, Eviction, Small Claims.***
Civil Records: Access: Phone, mail, online, in person. Both court and visitors may perform in person searches. No search fee. Required to search: name, years to search; also helpful: address. Civil cases indexed by defendant, plaintiff; index on computer back to 7/90. Mail turnaround time 1-2 days. Civil PAT goes back to 7/1990. PAT results show name, DOB. Search free at www.courts.state.va.us/. Results show address of subject and day & month of birth, but not year. Also search LOPAS; call 804-786-5511 to apply.
Criminal Records: Access: Phone, mail, online, in person. Both court and visitors may perform in person searches. No search fee. Required to search: name, years to search, DOB; also helpful: SSN. Criminal records computerized from 7/90. Mail turnaround time 1-2 days. Criminal PAT goes back to same as civil.PAT results show name, DOB. Search free at www.courts.state.va.us/. Results show address of subject and day & month of birth, but not year.
General Information: No juvenile, sealed records released. Will not fax documents. Court makes copy: $.50 per page. Certification fee: $1.25 per page. Payee: General District Court. Personal checks accepted; credit cards are not. Prepayment required.

South Boston City

Circuit & District Courts
See Halifax County.

Southampton County

5th Circuit Court PO Box 190, Courtland, VA 23837; 757-653-2200; 8:30AM-5PM. ***Felony, Civil Actions over $15,000, Probate.***
www.courts.state.va.us/courts/circuit.html
Civil Records: Access: Mail, in person, online. Both court and visitors may perform in person searches. Search fee: $5.00 per name. Required to search: name, years to search. Civil cases indexed by plaintiff. Civil index on docket books from 1749; on computer back to 1990. Note: Will not certify searches. Mail turnaround time 1-5 days. Public terminal not available at this time. Search free at www.courts.state.va.us/. Results show address of subject and day & month of birth, but not year. Also search LOPAS; call 804-786-5511 to apply.
Criminal Records: Access: Mail, online, in person. Both court and visitors may perform in person searches. Search fee: $5.00. Required to search: name, years to search. Criminal records indexed in books from 1749; on computer back to 1990. Note: Will not certify searches. Mail turnaround time 1-5 days. PAT results show middle initial, DOB. Public terminal not available at this time. Online access to criminal records is the same as civil. Online results show only month and day of DOB plus sex, race.
General Information: No juvenile, sealed, adoption records released. Will not fax documents. Court makes copy: $.50 per page. Certification fee: $2.00 per document. Payee: Clerk of Circuit Court. Personal checks accepted; credit cards are not. Prepayment required.

5th General District Court PO Box 347, Courtland, VA 23837; 757-653-2673; fax: 757-653-2656; 8:30AM-4:30PM. ***Misdemeanor, Civil Actions under $15,000, Eviction, Small Claims.***
Civil Records: Access: Mail, in person, online. Both court and visitors may perform in person searches. No search fee. Required to search: name, years to search. Civil cases indexed by defendant. Civil records on computer, 1985 and prior records at Circuit Court. Mail turnaround time 1-5 days. Civil PAT goes back to 10 years. PAT civil results show middle initial. Search free at www.courts.state.va.us/. Results show address of subject and day & month of birth, but not year. Also search LOPAS; call 804-786-5511 to apply.
Criminal Records: Access: Mail, online, in person. Both court and visitors may perform in person searches. No search fee. Required to search: name, years to search, DOB; also helpful: SSN. Criminal records on computer, 1985 and prior records at Circuit Court. Mail turnaround time 1-5 days. Criminal PAT goes back to same as civil. PAT criminal results show middle initial. Search free at

www.courts.state.va.us/. Results show address of subject and day & month of birth, but not year.
General Information: Online identifiers in results same as on public terminal. No juvenile, sealed, adoption records released. Fee to fax out file $2.00 each. Court makes copy: $.50 per page. No certification fee. Payee: Clerk of General District Court. Personal checks accepted. Visa/MC accepted. Prepayment required. Mail requests: SASE required.

Spotsylvania County

15th Circuit Court PO Box 96, 9115 Courthouse Rd, Spotsylvania, VA 22553; 540-507-7600; criminal phone: 540-507-7618; civil phone: 540-507-7614; fax: 540-582-2169; 8AM-4:30PM. ***Felony, Civil Actions over $15,000, Probate.***
www.courts.state.va.us/courts/circuit.html
Civil Records: Access: Online, in person. Visitors must perform in person searches themselves. Required to search: name, years to search. Civil cases indexed by defendant, plaintiff; index on computer from 1993, on index books from late 1700s. Note: Mail access limited to specific case only. Civil PAT goes back to 1996. Search free at www.courts.state.va.us/. Results show address of subject and day & month of birth, but not year. Also search LOPAS; call 804-786-5511 to apply.
Criminal Records: Access: Online, in person. Visitors must perform in person searches themselves. Required to search: name, years to search, DOB, SSN. Criminal records computerized from 1993, on index books from late 1700s. Criminal PAT available. Online access same as civil. Online results show only month and day of DOB plus sex, race.
General Information: No juvenile, sealed, adoption records released. Will not fax documents. Court makes copy: $.50 per page. Self serve: same. Certification fee: $2.00. Payee: Clerk of Circuit Court. Personal checks accepted. Visa/MC accepted for fines and fees. Prepayment required. Mail requests: SASE required for mail return of any copies.

15th General District Court PO Box 339, 9111 Courthouse Rd, Spotsylvania, VA 22553; 540-507-7680; fax: 540-582-7288; 8AM-4PM. ***Misdemeanor, Civil Actions under $15,000, Eviction, Small Claims.***
Civil Records: Access: Mail, in person, online. Visitors must perform in person searches themselves. No search fee. Required to search: name, years to search. Civil cases indexed by defendant, plaintiff. Civil records go back 10 years; on computer back to 1988. Mail turnaround time 5 days. Civil PAT goes back to 10 years. PAT results show middle initial, DOB. Search free at www.courts.state.va.us/. Results show address of subject and day & month of birth, but not year. Also search LOPAS; call 804-786-5511 to apply.
Criminal Records: Access: Mail, online, in person. Visitors must perform in person searches themselves. No search fee. Required to search: name, years to search. Criminal records go back 10 years; on computer back to 1988. Mail turnaround time 5 days. Criminal PAT goes back to same as civil. PAT results show middle initial, DOB. Search free at www.courts.state.va.us/. Results show address of subject and day & month of birth, but not year.
General Information: Online identifiers in results same as on public terminal. No juvenile, sealed records released. Will not fax documents. Court makes copy: $1.00 1st page, $.50 each add'l. Certification fee: $1.00 per cert. Payee: Clerk of General District Court. Personal checks accepted; credit cards are not. Prepayment required.

Stafford County

15th Circuit Court PO Box 69, 1300 Courthouse Rd, Stafford, VA 22554; 540-658-8750; criminal phone: 540-658-8753; civil phone: 540-658-4220; probate phone: 540-658-4176; fax: 540-658-4640; 8AM-4PM. ***Felony, Civil Actions over $15,000, Probate.***
www.co.stafford.va.us/Departments/Courts_&_Legal_Services/Index.shtml
Civil Records: Access: Mail, in person, online. Both court and visitors may perform in person searches. No search fee. Required to search: name, years to search. Civil cases indexed by defendant, plaintiff. Civil records in index books from 1699, back on computer to 1992. Mail turnaround time 2-3 weeks. Civil PAT goes back to 1993. PAT results show name, DOB. Search free at www.courts.state.va.us/. Results show address of subject and day & month of birth, but not year. Also search LOPAS; call 804-786-5511 to apply.
Criminal Records: Access: Mail, online, in person. Both court and visitors may perform in person searches. No search fee. Required to search: name, years to search, DOB; also helpful: SSN. Criminal docket on books from 1699, back on computer to 1992. Mail turnaround time 2-3 weeks. Criminal PAT goes back to same as civil.PAT results show name, DOB. Online access to criminal records is the same as civil. Online results show name, DOB. Only month and day of DOB appears, plus sex, race.
General Information: No juvenile, sealed records released. Will not fax documents. Court makes copy: $.50 per page. Self serve: same. Certification fee: $2.00. Payee: Clerk of Circuit Court. Personal checks accepted. Visa/MC accepted. Prepayment required.

15th General District Court 1300 Courthouse Rd, PO Box 339, Stafford, VA 22555; 540-658-8763; criminal phone: 540-658-8766; civil phone: 540-658-4641; fax: 540-658-4834; 8AM-4PM. ***Misdemeanor, Civil Actions under $15,000, Eviction, Small Claims.***
Civil Records: Access: Fax, mail, online, in person. Both court and visitors may perform in person searches. No search fee. Required to search: name, years to search. Civil cases indexed by defendant, plaintiff; index on computer since 1986, prior at Circuit Court. Mail turnaround time 2-7 days. Civil PAT goes back to 1995. PAT results show middle initial, DOB. Terminal results also show SSNs. Search free at www.courts.state.va.us/. Results show address of subject and day & month of birth, but not year. Also search LOPAS; call 804-786-5511 to apply.
Criminal Records: Access: Fax, mail, online, in person. Both court and visitors may perform in person searches. No search fee. Required to search: name, years to search. Criminal records on computer since 1986, prior at Circuit Court. Mail turnaround time 2-7 days. Criminal PAT goes back to same as civil. PAT results show middle initial, DOB. Terminal results include SSN. Search free at www.courts.state.va.us/. Results show address of subject and day & month of birth, but not year.
General Information: No sealed records released. Will fax documents to local or toll-free number. Court makes copy: $1.00 per page. No certification fee. Payee: Clerk of General District Court. Personal checks accepted. Credit cards accepted in person only. Prepayment required. Mail requests: SASE requested.

Staunton City

25th Circuit Court PO Box 1286, Staunton, VA 24402-1286; 540-332-3874; fax: 540-332-3970; 8:30AM-5PM. ***Felony, Civil over $15,000, Probate.***
www.courts.state.va.us/courts/circuit.html
Civil Records: Access: Mail, in person, online. Both court and visitors may perform in person searches. No search fee. Required to search: name, years to search. Civil cases indexed by defendant, plaintiff. Civil index on docket books since 1802; on computer back to 1988. Mail turnaround time 1 week. Civil PAT goes back to 1988. Search free at www.courts.state.va.us/. Results show address of subject and day & month of birth, but not year. Also search LOPAS; call 804-786-5511 to apply.
Criminal Records: Access: Online, in person. Both court and visitors may perform in person searches. No search fee. Required to search: name, years to search. Criminal records indexed in books since 1802; on computer back to 1988. Criminal PAT goes back to same as civil. Online access to criminal records is the same as civil. Online results show only month and day of DOB plus sex, race.
General Information: No juvenile, sealed or adoption records released. Fee to fax document $.50 per page. Court makes copy: $.50 per page. Self serve: same. Certification fee: $2.00. Payee: Clerk of Circuit Court. Personal checks accepted; credit cards are not. Prepayment required. Mail requests: SASE required for mail return of any copies.

Staunton General District Court 113 E Beverly St, Staunton, VA 24401-4390; 540-332-3878; fax: 540-332-3985; 8:30AM-4:30PM. ***Misdemeanor, Civil Actions under $15,000, Eviction, Small Claims.***
Civil Records: Access: Mail, phone, fax, in person, online. Both court and visitors may perform in person searches. No search fee. Required to search: name, years to search; also helpful: address. Civil cases indexed by defendant, plaintiff; index on computer back 10 years. Mail turnaround time 1-5 days. Civil PAT goes back to 10 years. PAT results show name only. Search free at www.courts.state.va.us/. Results show address of subject and day & month of birth, but not year. Records maintained 10 years.
Criminal Records: Access: Mail, online, in person. Both court and visitors may perform in person searches. No search fee. Required to search: name, years to search, DOB. Criminal records on computer back 10 years. Mail turnaround time 1-5 days. Criminal PAT goes back to 10 years. PAT results show name only. Search free at http://epwsgdp1.courts.state.va.us/gdcourts/caseSearch.do?index=index. Results show DOB month and day, sex, race; records maintained 10 years. Online results show middle initial, DOB.
General Information: Online identifiers in results same as on public terminal. Will not fax documents. Court makes copy: $.50 per page. No certification fee. Payee: Staunton General District Court. Personal checks accepted. Credit cards accepted for criminal, civil and traffic cases only. Prepayment required. Mail requests: SASE required.

Suffolk City

Suffolk Circuit Court PO Box 1604, 150 N Main St, Suffolk, VA 23439-1604; 757-923-2251; fax: 757-538-3204; 8:30AM-5PM. ***Felony, Civil Actions over $15,000, Probate.***
www.courts.state.va.us/courts/circuit.html
Civil Records: Access: Online, in person. Visitors must perform in person searches themselves. Required to search: name, years to search. Civil cases indexed by defendant, plaintiff; index on computer from 1989, on index books from 1866. Civil PAT goes back to 1996. Search via LOPAS; call 804-786-5511 to apply.
Criminal Records: Access: Online, in person. Visitors must perform in person searches themselves. Required to search: name, years to search. Criminal records computerized from 1989, on index books from 1866. Criminal PAT goes back to same as civil.PAT results show name, DOB. Online access to criminal records is the same as civil. Online results show name, DOB. Only month and day of DOB appears, plus sex, race.
General Information: Online identifiers in results same as on public terminal. No juvenile, sealed, adoption records released. Will not fax documents. Court makes copy: $.50 per page. Certification fee: $2.00. Payee: Clerk of Circuit Court. Personal checks accepted. Visa/MC accepted. Prepayment required.

5th General District Court 150 N Main St, Suffolk, VA 23434; 757-923-2281; fax: 757-925-1790; 8AM-4PM. ***Misdemeanor, Civil Actions up to $15,000, Eviction, Small Claims.***
Civil Records: Access: Mail, in person, online. Both court and visitors may perform in person searches. No search fee. Required to search: name, years to search. Civil cases indexed by defendant, plaintiff; index on computer from 1992 prior on index cards. Records destroyed after 10 years. Mail turnaround time 1 week. Civil PAT goes back to 1992. PAT results show name, DOB. Search free at www.courts.state.va.us/. Results show address of subject and day & month of birth, but not year. Also search LOPAS; call 804-786-5511 to apply.
Criminal Records: Access: Online, mail, in person. Visitors must perform in person searches themselves. No search fee. Required to search: name, years to search, DOB; also helpful: SSN. Criminal records computerized from 1992, prior on index cards. Mail turnaround time 1 week. Criminal PAT

goes back to same as civil.PAT results show name, DOB. Search free at www.courts.state.va.us/. Results show address of subject and day & month of birth, but not year. Online results show middle initial, DOB, SSN.
General Information: Online identifiers in results same as on public terminal. No juvenile, sealed, adoptions records released. Will not fax documents. Court makes copy: $1.00 1st page, $.50 each add'l. No certification fee. Payee: Suffolk General District Court. Personal checks and credit cards accepted. Prepayment required. Mail requests: SASE required.

Surry County

6th Circuit Court PO Box 203, 203 Church St, Rts 10 and 31, Surry, VA 23883; 757-294-3161; criminal fax: 757-294-0471; civil fax: same; 9AM-5PM. ***Felony, Civil Actions over $15,000, Probate.***
www.courts.state.va.us/courts/circuit.html
Probate fax is same as main fax number.
Civil Records: Access: In person, online. Visitors must perform in person searches themselves. Required to search: name, years to search. Civil cases indexed by defendant, plaintiff; index on cards. Search free at www.courts.state.va.us/. Results show address of subject and day & month of birth, but not year. Also search LOPAS; call 804-786-5511 to apply.
Criminal Records: Access: In person, online. Visitors must perform in person searches themselves. Required to search: name, years to search, DOB; also helpful: SSN. Criminal records on cards. Online access to criminal records is the same as civil. Online results show only month and day of DOB, sex, race.
General Information: Juvenile, sealed records not released. Will not fax documents. Court makes copy: n/a. Self serve: $.50 per page. Certification fee: $2.00 per document. Payee: Circuit Clerk. Business checks accepted.

6th General District Court 45 School St, PO Box 332, Surry, VA 23883; 757-294-5201; fax: 757-294-0312; 8:30-4:30PM. ***Misdemeanor, Civil Actions under $15,000, Eviction, Small Claims.***
Civil Records: Access: Online, in person. Visitors must perform in person searches themselves. Required to search: name, years to search. Civil cases indexed by defendant, plaintiff; index on computer since 11/93, on books from 1985, prior at Circuit Court. Civil PAT goes back to 1997. PAT results show name, DOB. Search free at www.courts.state.va.us/. Results show address of subject and day & month of birth, but not year. Also search LOPAS; call 804-786-5511 to apply.
Criminal Records: Access: Online, in person. Visitors must perform in person searches themselves. Required to search: name, years to search, DOB; also helpful: SSN. Criminal records on computer since 11/93, on books from 1985, prior at Circuit Court. Criminal PAT goes back to same as civil.PAT results show name, DOB. Search free at www.courts.state.va.us/. Results show address of subject and day & month of birth, but not year.
General Information: No juvenile, sealed, adoption records released. Will not fax documents. Court makes copy for no fee. Certification fee: $2.00 first 2 pages; add copy fee for each add'l page. Payee: General District Court. No personal checks or credit cards accepted. Prepayment required.

Sussex County

6th Circuit Court PO Box 1337, Sussex, VA 23884; 434-246-1017; probate phone: 434-246-1012; fax: 434-246-2203; 9AM-5PM. ***Felony, Civil Actions over $15,000, Probate.***
www.courts.state.va.us/courts/circuit.html
Civil Records: Access: Mail, in person, online. Only the court performs in person searches; visitors may not. Search fee: $5.00. Required to search: name, years to search. Civil cases indexed by defendant, plaintiff. Civil index on docket books from 1950. Mail turnaround time 1-2 days. Search free at www.courts.state.va.us/. Results show address of subject and day & month of birth, but not year. Also search LOPAS; call 804-786-5511 to apply.
Criminal Records: Access: Mail, online, in person. Only the court performs in person searches; visitors may not. Search fee: $5.00. Required to search: name, years to search, DOB, SSN, signed release. Criminal records indexed in books from 1754; on computer back to 1991. Mail turnaround time 1-2 days. Online access to criminal records is the same as civil. Online results show only month and day of DOB plus sex, race.
General Information: No juvenile, sealed, adoption, or confidential records released. Fee to fax out file $1.00 per page. Court makes copy: $.50 per page. Self serve: same. Certification fee: $2.00. Payee: Clerk of Circuit Court. Personal checks accepted; credit cards are not. Prepayment required.

Sussex 6th Judicial District Court Sussex County Courthouse, 15098 Courthouse Rd, Rte 735, PO Box 1315, Sussex, VA 23884; 434-246-1096; criminal phone: 434-246-1033; civil phone: 434-246-1029; fax: 434-246-6604; 8:30AM-4:30PM. ***Misdemeanor, Civil Actions under $15,000, Eviction, Small Claims.***
Civil Records: Access: Online, in person. Visitors must perform in person searches themselves. Required to search: name, years to search. Civil cases indexed by defendant, plaintiff; index on computer from 9/88, on index cards from 1985, prior in Circuit Court. Civil PAT goes back to 1998. PAT civil results show middle initial. Search free at www.courts.state.va.us/. Results show address of subject and day & month of birth, but not year.
Criminal Records: Access: Online, in person. Visitors must perform in person searches themselves. Required to search: name, years to search, DOB; also helpful: SSN. Criminal records computerized from 9/88, on index cards from 1985, prior in Circuit Court. Criminal PAT goes back to 1998. PAT criminal results show middle initial. Search free at www.courts.state.va.us/. Results show address of subject and day & month of birth, but not year.
General Information: Online identifiers in results same as on public terminal. No juvenile, sealed, adoption records released. Will fax documents. Court makes copy: $1.00 minimum 1st 2 pages, $.50 each add'l. No certification fee. Payee: Sussex District Court. Personal checks and credit cards accepted. Prepayment required.

Tazewell County

29th Circuit Court PO Box 968, Tazewell, VA 24651-0968; 276-988-1222; criminal phone: 276-988-1228; civil phone: 276-988-1261; probate phone: 276-988-1227; criminal fax: 276-988-7501; civil fax: same; 8AM-4:30PM. ***Felony, Civil Actions over $15,000, Probate.***
www.courts.state.va.us/courts/circuit.html
Probate fax is same as main fax number.
Civil Records: Access: Mail, in person, online. Both court and visitors may perform in person searches. No search fee. Required to search: name, years to search. Civil cases indexed by defendant, plaintiff. Civil index on cards from 1800s. Mail turnaround time 1-3 days. Civil PAT goes back to 1991. Search free at www.courts.state.va.us/. Results show address of subject and day & month of birth, but not year.
Criminal Records: Access: Mail, online, in person. Both court and visitors may perform in person searches. No search fee. Required to search: name, years to search, signed release. Criminal records computerized from 1992. Mail turnaround time 1-3 days. Criminal PAT goes back to same as civil. Online access to criminal records is the same as civil. Online results show middle initial, DOB. Only month and day of DOB appears, (if listed) plus sex, race.
General Information: No juvenile, sealed records released. Will fax documents to local or toll free line. Court makes copy: $.50 per page. Self serve: same. Certification fee: $2.00. Payee: Clerk of Circuit Court. Personal checks and credit cards accepted. Prepayment required. Mail requests: SASE required.

29th General District Court PO Box 566, Tazewell, VA 24651; 276-988-9057; fax: 276-988-6202; 8:30AM-4:30PM. ***Misdemeanor, Civil Actions under $15,000, Eviction, Small Claims.***
Civil Records: Access: Mail, fax, online, in person. Both court and visitors may perform in person searches. No search fee. Required to search: name, years to search. Civil cases indexed by defendant, plaintiff; index on computer back to 1998, prior records to 1985 at Circuit Court. Mail turnaround time 7 days. Civil PAT goes back to 1998. PAT results show middle initial, DOB. Terminal results also show SSNs. Search free at www.courts.state.va.us/. Results show address of subject and day & month of birth, but not year. Also search LOPAS; call 804-786-5511 to apply.
Criminal Records: Access: Mail, fax, online, in person. Both court and visitors may perform in person searches. No search fee. Required to search: name, years to search, DOB; also helpful: SSN, signed release. Criminal records computerized from 1998, prior records to 1985 at Circuit Court. Mail turnaround time 7 days. Criminal PAT goes back to 1998. PAT results show middle initial, DOB. Terminal results include SSN. Search free at www.courts.state.va.us/. Results show address of subject and day & month of birth, but not year.
General Information: No sealed records released. Fee to fax document $1.00 each plus $1.00 per page. Court makes copy: $.50 per page. Self serve: same. No certification fee. Payee: Clerk of General District Court. Personal checks and credit cards accepted. Prepayment required. Mail requests: SASE required.

Virginia Beach City

2nd Circuit Court 2425 Nimmo Pky, Virginia Beach, VA 23456-9017; 757-385-4181; criminal phone: 757-385-4186; civil phone: 757-385-4186; probate phone: 757-385-8831; 8:30AM-5PM. ***Felony, Civil Actions over $15,000, Probate.***
www.vbgov.com/courts
Probate is a separate index at this same address
Civil Records: Access: Online, in person. Visitors must perform in person searches themselves. Required to search: name, years to search. Civil cases indexed by defendant, plaintiff; index on computer from 1986, on files from 1960s. Civil PAT goes back to late 1986. PAT civil results show middle initial. Search free at www.courts.state.va.us/. Results show address of subject and day & month of birth, but not year. Also search LOPAS; call 804-786-5511 to apply.
Criminal Records: Access: Online, in person. Visitors must perform in person searches themselves. Required to search: name, years to search, DOB; also helpful: SSN. Criminal records computerized from 1986, on files from 1960s. Criminal PAT goes back to same as civil. PAT criminal results show middle initial. Online access to criminal records is the same as civil. Online results show only month and day of DOB plus sex, race.
General Information: Online identifiers in results same as on public terminal. No juvenile, sealed, presentencing probation report, judges notes or adoption records released. Will not fax documents. Court makes copy: $.50 per page. Certification fee: $2.00 per document. Payee: Clerk of Circuit Court. Personal checks accepted; credit cards are not. Prepayment required.

2nd General District Court 2425 Nimmo Pky, Judicial Center, Virginia Beach, VA 23456-9057; 757-385-8531; criminal phone: 757-385-4707; civil phone: 757-385-4277; fax: 757-385-5672; 8AM-4PM. ***Misdemeanor, Civil Actions under $15,000, Eviction, Small Claims.***
www.vbgov.com
Civil Records: Access: Mail, in person, online. Visitors must perform in person searches themselves. No search fee. Required to search: name, years to search. Civil cases indexed by defendant, plaintiff; index on computer from 1997. Note: Civil cases decided on or before 01/01/85 retained 10 years, after that date retained 20 years. Civil PAT goes back to 1997. Search free at www.courts.state.va.us/. Results show address of subject and day & month of birth, but not year. Also search LOPAS; call 804-786-5511 to apply.

Criminal Records: Access: Mail, online, in person. Visitors must perform in person searches themselves. No search fee. Required to search: name, years to search, DOB; also helpful: SSN. Criminal records on computer back ten years, then destroyed. Mail turnaround time 3-4 weeks. Criminal PAT goes back to 10 years. Search free at www.courts.state.va.us/. Results show address of subject and day & month of birth, but not year.
General Information: No juvenile, sealed, adoption or mental records released. No fee to fax documents. Court makes copy: $2.00 1st page, $.50 each add'l. No certification fee. Payee: General District Court. Personal checks accepted. Visa/MC accepted. Prepayment required. Mail requests: SASE required.

Warren County

Circuit Court 1 E Main St, Front Royal, VA 22630; 540-635-2435; criminal fax: 540-636-3274; civil fax: same; 9AM-5PM. ***Felony, Civil, Probate.*** www.courts.state.va.us/courts/circuit/warren/home.html
Probate records are in a separate index at this same address. Phone and fax access limited to law enforcement and agencies only. Probate fax is same as main fax number.
Civil Records: Access: Mail, in person, online. Both court and visitors may perform in person searches. No search fee. Required to search: name, years to search. Civil cases indexed by defendant, plaintiff; index on archives from 1836; on computer since 1986. Mail turnaround time 1 week. Civil PAT goes back to 1986. PAT results show name only. Search free at www.courts.state.va.us/. Results show address of subject and day & month of birth, but not year.
Criminal Records: Access: Mail, online, in person. Both court and visitors may perform in person searches. No search fee. Required to search: name, years to search, DOB; also helpful: SSN. Criminal records on archives from 1836; on computer since 1986. Mail turnaround time 1 week. Criminal PAT goes back to same as civil. PAT results show middle initial, DOB. Terminal results include SSN. Online access to criminal records is the same as civil. Online results show only month and day of DOB plus sex, race.
General Information: Online identifiers in results same as on public terminal. No juvenile, sealed, adoption records released. Will fax documents to local or toll-free line. Court makes copy: $.50 per page. Self serve: same. Certification fee: $2.00. Payee: Jennifer R Sims Clerk. Personal checks accepted; credit cards are not. Prepayment required. Mail requests: SASE required.

26th General District Court 1 E Main St, Front Royal, VA 22630; 540-635-2335; fax: 540-636-8233; 8:15AM-4:15PM. ***Misdemeanor, Civil Actions under $15,000, Eviction, Small Claims.*** www.courts.state.va.us/courts/gd/Warren/home.html
Civil Records: Access: Mail, fax, online, in person. Both court and visitors may perform in person searches. No search fee. Required to search: name, years to search. Civil cases indexed by defendant. Civil records on computer from 1989. Mail turnaround time 2-3 days. Civil PAT goes back to 1989. PAT civil results show middle initial. Search free at www.courts.state.va.us/. Results show address of subject and day & month of birth, but not year. Also search LOPAS; call 804-786-5511 to apply.
Criminal Records: Access: Mail, fax, online, in person. Both court and visitors may perform in person searches. No search fee. Required to search: name, years to search. Criminal records in archives, on computer from 1989. Mail turnaround time 2-3 days. Criminal PAT goes back to same as civil. PAT criminal results show middle initial. Search free at www.courts.state.va.us/. Results show address of subject and day & month of birth, but not year.
General Information: Online identifiers in results same as on public terminal. Will fax out documents. Court makes copy: $.50 per page. No certification fee. Payee: General District Court. Personal checks accepted. Visa/MC accepted. Prepayment required. Mail requests: SASE required.

Washington County

Circuit Court PO Box 289, Courthouse, 189 E Main St, Abingdon, VA 24212-0289; 276-676-6224/6226; fax: 276-676-6218; 8AM-5PM. ***Felony, Civil Actions over $15,000, Probate.*** www.courts.state.va.us/courts/circuit/Washington/home.html
Civil Records: Access: In person, online. Both court and visitors may perform in person searches. Search fee: If search is performed, fee is determined by time involved. Required to search: name, years to search within 5 year. Civil cases indexed by defendant, plaintiff; index on archives from 1777, on computer from 1991. Civil PAT goes back to 1990. PAT results show name only. Search free at www.courts.state.va.us/. Results show address of subject and day & month of birth, but not year. Also search LOPAS; call 804-786-5511 to apply.
Criminal Records: Access: In person, online. Visitors must perform in person searches themselves. Required to search: name, years to search. Criminal records on archives from 1777, on computer from 1991. Criminal PAT goes back to same as civil. PAT results show name only. Online access to criminal is same as civil, see above. Online results show only month and day of DOB plus sex, race.
General Information: No juvenile, sealed or adoption records released. Will fax documents to local or toll free line. Court makes copy: $.50 per page. Self serve: same. Certification fee: $2.00. Payee: Clerk, Circuit Court. Personal checks accepted; credit cards are not. Prepayment required.

28th General District Court 191 E Main St, Abingdon, VA 24210; 276-676-6281; fax: 276-676-3136; 8:30AM-4:30PM. ***Misdemeanor, Civil Actions under $15,000, Eviction, Small Claims.***
Civil Records: Access: Mail, in person, online. Both court and visitors may perform in person searches. No search fee. Required to search: name, years to search. Civil cases indexed by defendant, plaintiff; index on archives from 1777, on computer from 1997. Mail turnaround time 5 days. Civil PAT goes back to 10 years. PAT civil results show middle initial. Search free at www.courts.state.va.us/. Results show address of subject and day & month of birth, but not year. Also search LOPAS; call 804-786-5511 to apply.
Criminal Records: Access: Mail, online, in person. Both court and visitors may perform in person searches. No search fee. Required to search: name, years to search. Criminal records on archives from 1777, on computer from 1997. Mail turnaround time 5 days. Criminal PAT goes back to same as civil. PAT criminal results show middle initial. Search free at www.courts.state.va.us/. Results show address of subject and day & month of birth, but not year.
General Information: No sealed records released. Will not fax documents. Court makes copy: $1.00 first page, $.50 each add'l. No certification fee. Payee: General District Court. Personal checks and credit cards accepted. Prepayment required. Mail requests: SASE required.

Waynesboro City

25th Circuit Court 250 S Wayne Ave, PO Box 910, Waynesboro, VA 22980; 540-942-6616; fax: 540-942-6774; 8:30AM-5PM. ***Felony, Civil Actions over $15,000, Probate.*** www.courts.state.va.us/courts/circuit.html
Civil Records: Access: Online, in person. Visitors must perform in person searches themselves. Required to search: name, years to search. Civil cases indexed by defendant, plaintiff; index on computer from 11/88 (some), all on index books from 5/48. Civil PAT goes back to 1988. Search free at www.courts.state.va.us/. Results show address of subject and day & month of birth, but not year.
Criminal Records: Access: Online, in person. Visitors must perform in person searches themselves. Required to search: name, years to search, DOB; also helpful: SSN. Criminal records computerized from 11/88 (some), all on index books from 5/48. Criminal PAT goes back to same as civil. Online access to criminal records is the same as civil. Online results show only month and day of DOB, sex, race.
General Information: No juvenile, sealed, adoptions released. Will not fax documents. Court makes copy: $.50 per page. Self serve: same. Certification fee: $2.00. Payee: Clerk of Circuit Court. Personal checks accepted; credit cards are not. Prepayment required. Mail requests: SASE required for mail return of any copies.

25th General District Court - Waynesboro 250 S Wayne Ave #100, 237 Market Ave, Waynesboro, VA 22980; 540-942-6636; fax: 540-942-6666; 8:30AM-4:30PM. ***Misdemeanor, Civil Actions under $15,000, Eviction, Small Claims.*** www.courts.state.va.us/courts/gd/Waynesboro/home.html
Civil Records: Access: Mail, fax, online, in person. Visitors must perform in person searches themselves. No search fee. Required to search: name, years to search. Civil cases indexed by defendant, plaintiff; index on computer 10 years. Mail turnaround time 1-2 days. Civil PAT goes back to 10 years. PAT civil results show middle initial. Search court records free at http://epwsgdp1.courts.state.va.us/gdcourts/caseSearch.do?index=index. Results show name and sometimes address.
Criminal Records: Access: Mail, fax, online, in person. Visitors must perform in person searches themselves. No search fee. Required to search: name, years to search. Criminal records on computer for 10 years. Mail turnaround time up to 1 week. Criminal PAT goes back to same as civil. PAT criminal results show middle initial. Search free at www.courts.state.va.us/. Results show address of subject and day & month of birth, but not year.
General Information: Will not fax documents. Court makes copy: $.50 per page. Self serve: same. No certification fee. Payee: General District Court. Personal checks accepted. Visa/MC accepted. Mail requests: SASE required for mail return of any copies.

Westmoreland County

15th Circuit Court PO Box 307, Montross, VA 22520; 804-493-0108; fax: 804-493-0393; 9AM-5PM. ***Felony, Civil Actions over $15,000, Probate.*** www.courts.state.va.us/courts/circuit.html
Probate index is separate.
Civil Records: Access: In person, online. Visitors must perform in person searches themselves. Required to search: name, years to search. Civil cases indexed by defendant, plaintiff. Civil index on docket books from 1977. Search free at www.courts.state.va.us/. Results show address of subject and day & month of birth, but not year.
Criminal Records: Access: In person, online. Visitors must perform in person searches themselves. Required to search: name, years to search, DOB; also helpful: SSN. Criminal records indexed in books from 1997. Search free by name only or case number at www.courts.state.va.us/. Results show address of subject and day & month of birth, but not year.
General Information: No juvenile, sealed, adoption records released. Will not fax documents. Court makes copy: $.50 per page. Self serve: same. Certification fee: $3.00 includes copy fee. Payee: Clerk of Circuit Court. No personal checks or credit cards accepted. Prepayment required. Will bill copy fees. Mail requests: SASE required for mail return of any copies.

15th General District Court PO Box 688, Montross, VA 22520; 804-493-0105; 8AM-4:30PM. ***Misdemeanor, Civil under $15,000, Small Claims.***
Civil Records: Access: Mail, in person, online. Both court and visitors may perform in person searches. No search fee. Required to search: name, years to search, case number. Civil cases indexed by defendant, plaintiff; index on computer back 10 years. Mail turnaround time 1 week. Civil PAT goes back to 10 years. Search court records free at http://epwsgdp1.courts.state.va.us/gdcourts/caseSearch.do?index=index. Results show name and sometimes address. Also search LOPAS; call 804-786-5511 to apply.
Criminal Records: Access: Mail, online, in person. Both court and visitors may perform in person

searches. No search fee. Required to search: name, years to search; also helpful: DOB, SSN, date of offense. Criminal records on computer back 10 years. Mail turnaround time 1 week. Criminal PAT goes back to same as civil. Search free at www.courts.state.va.us/. Results show address of subject and day & month of birth, but not year.
General Information: All records public. Will not fax documents. Court makes copy: $1.00 first page, $.50 each add'l. No certification fee. Payee: General District Court. Personal checks accepted. Attorney checks accepted. Visa/MC accepted. Prepayment required. Mail requests: SASE required.

Williamsburg City

Circuit & District Courts

See James City.

Williamsburg-James City

County General District Court James City County Courthouse, 5201 Monticello Ave, #2, Williamsburg, VA 23188-8218; 757-564-2400; criminal fax: 757-564-2410; civil fax: same; 7:30AM-4PM. ***Misdemeanor, Civil Actions under $15,000, Eviction, Small Claims.***
Civil Records: Access: Fax, mail, in person, online. Both court and visitors may perform in person searches. No search fee. Required to search: name, years to search. Civil cases indexed by defendant, plaintiff. Civil records index books go back 10 years, on computer back 10 years. Mail turnaround time 10 days. Civil PAT goes back to 10 years. PAT results show middle initial, DOB. Search free at http://epwsgdp1.courts.state.va.us/gdcourts/caseSearch.do?index=index. Results show name and DOB month/day. Also search LOPAS; call 804-786-5511 to apply.
Criminal Records: Access: Fax, mail, in person, online. Both court and visitors may perform in person searches. No search fee. Required to search: name, years to search, DOB; also helpful: SSN. Criminal records index books go back 10 years, on computer back 10 years. Mail turnaround time 10 days. Criminal PAT goes back to 10 years. PAT results show middle initial, DOB. Search free at www.courts.state.va.us/. Results show address of subject and day & month of birth, but not year.
General Information: Online identifiers in results same as on public terminal. No juvenile, sealed records released. Will fax documents; fee depends on the documents needing to be faxed. Court makes copy: copy fee if extensive searching or copies needed. No certification fee. Payee: General District Court. Personal checks accepted. Visa/MC accepted. Prepayment required.

Winchester City

26th Circuit Court 5 N Kent St, Winchester, VA 22601; 540-667-5770; criminal fax: 540-667-6638; civil fax: same; 9AM-5PM. ***Felony, Civil Actions over $15,000, Probate.***
www.winfredclerk.com
The Winchester Court and the Frederick County Court Clerks are housed in the same judicial center.
Civil Records: Access: Online, in person. Visitors must perform in person searches themselves. Required to search: name, years to search. Civil cases indexed by defendant, plaintiff; index on computer from 1985 to present, on index books from 1790. Civil PAT goes back to 1985. PAT civil results show middle initial. Search free at www.courts.state.va.us/. Results show address of subject and day & month of birth, but not year.
Criminal Records: Access: Mail, online, in person. Both court and visitors may perform in person searches. No search fee. Required to search: name, years to search; also helpful: DOB, SSN. Criminal records computerized from 1985 to present, on index books from 1790. Note: Results include hearing date, status. Mail turnaround time same day. Criminal PAT goes back to 1985. PAT criminal results show middle initial. Results include hearing date, status. Online access to criminal records is the same as civil. Online results show only month and day of DOB plus sex, race.
General Information: No juvenile, sealed, adoption records released. Will fax documents. Court makes copy: $.50 per page. Self serve: same. Certification fee: $2.00. Payee: Clerk of Circuit Court. Personal checks accepted; credit cards are not. Prepayment required. Mail requests: SASE required for criminal.

26th General District Court 5 N Kent St, PO Box 526, Winchester, VA 22604; 540-722-7208; fax: 540-722-1063; 8AM-4PM. ***Misdemeanor, Civil Actions under $15,000, Eviction, Small Claims.***
Civil Records: Access: Online, in person. Visitors must perform in person searches themselves. Required to search: name, years to search. Civil cases indexed by defendant, plaintiff; index on computer from 1992, on index cards from 1985 to 1987, prior at Circuit Court. Civil PAT goes back to 10 years. Search free at www.courts.state.va.us/. Results show address of subject and day & month of birth, but not year. Also search LOPAS; call 804-786-5511 to apply.
Criminal Records: Access: Online, in person. Visitors must perform in person searches themselves. Required to search: name, years to search, DOB, SSN, signed release. Criminal records computerized from 1992, on index cards from 1985 to 1987, prior at Circuit Court. Note: Forms for criminal searches available from State Police. Criminal PAT goes back to same as civil. Search free at www.courts.state.va.us/. Results show address of subject and day & month of birth, but not year.
General Information: No sealed records released. Will fax documents for no fee. Court makes copy: $.50 per page. No certification fee. Payee: Clerk of General District Court. Personal checks accepted; credit cards are not. Prepayment required.

Wise County

30th Circuit Court PO Box 1248, 206 E Main St, Wise, VA 24293-1248; 276-328-6111; 328-4324; 8:30AM-5PM. ***Felony, Civil Actions over $15,000, Probate.*** www.wisecircuitcourt.com
Civil Records: Access: Phone, mail, online, in person. Both court and visitors may perform in person searches. Search fee: $10.00 per name. Required to search: name, years to search; also helpful: address. Civil cases indexed by defendant, plaintiff; index on archives from 1856. Mail turnaround time 2-3 days. Civil PAT goes back to 1856. Search free by name only or case number at http://wasdmz2.courts.state.va.us/CJISWeb/circuit.html/. Results show address of subject and day & month of birth, but not year. Also, access court indexes and images via www.courtbar.org. Records go back to June, 2000.
Criminal Records: Access: Phone, mail, online, in person. Both court and visitors may perform in person searches. Search fee: $10.00 per name. Required to search: name, years to search, DOB; also helpful: SSN. Criminal records on archives from 1856. Mail turnaround time 2-3 days. Criminal PAT goes back to same as civil. Online access to criminal records is the same as civil. Online results show only month and day of DOB plus sex, race.
General Information: No juvenile, sealed or adoption records released. Will not fax documents. Court makes copy: $.50 per page. Self serve: same. Certification fee: $2.00. Payee: Clerk of Circuit Court. Personal checks accepted. Prepayment required.

30th General District Court Wise County Courthouse, PO Box 829, Wise, VA 24293; 276-328-3426; fax: 276-328-4576; 8AM-N, 1-5PM. ***Misdemeanor, Civil Actions under $15,000, Eviction, Small Claims.***
Civil Records: Access: Phone, mail, online, in person. Both court and visitors may perform in person searches. No search fee. Required to search: name, years to search. Civil cases indexed by defendant, plaintiff; index on computer back 10 years. Mail turnaround time 5 days. Civil PAT goes back to 10 years. Search free at www.courts.state.va.us/. Results show address of subject and day & month of birth, but not year. Also search LOPAS; call 804-786-5511 to apply.
Criminal Records: Access: Phone, mail, online, in person. Both court and visitors may perform in person searches. No search fee. Required to search: name, years to search; also helpful: DOB, SSN. Criminal records on computer back 10 years. Mail turnaround time 5 days. Criminal PAT goes back to same as civil. Search free at www.courts.state.va.us/. Results show address of subject and day & month of birth, but not year.
General Information: Online identifiers in results same as on public terminal. No juvenile, sealed records released. Will not fax documents. Court makes copy: $.50 per page. No certification fee. Payee: General District Court. Personal checks accepted. Visa/MC accepted. Prepayment required. Mail requests: SASE required.

Wythe County

27th Circuit Court 225 S 4th St, Rm 105, Wytheville, VA 24382; 276-223-6050; fax: 276-223-6057; 8:30AM-5PM. ***Felony, Civil Actions over $15,000, Probate.***
www.courts.state.va.us/courts/circuit.html
Civil Records: Access: In person, online. Both court and visitors may perform in person searches. No search fee. Required to search: name, years to search. Civil cases indexed by defendant, plaintiff; index on computer from 1989, on index cards/books from 1950s (some back to 1790s). Civil PAT goes back to 1/17/95. PAT results show name, DOB. Remote online access to court case indexes is via LOPAS; call 804-786-5511 to apply. Also, access to court records is by subscription; $25.00 registration fee for username and password, also $25.00 per transaction fee. Contact the clerk office for signup. Search free by name only or case number at www.courts.state.va.us/. Results show address of subject and day & month of birth, but not year. A
Criminal Records: Access: In person, online. Both court and visitors may perform in person searches. No search fee. Required to search: name, years to search; also helpful: DOB, SSN. Criminal records computerized from 1989, on index cards/books from 1950s (some back to 1790s). Criminal PAT goes back to same as civil. PAT results show middle initial, DOB. Online access to criminal records is the same as civil. Online results show only month and day of DOB plus sex, race.
General Information: Online identifiers in results same as on public terminal. No juvenile, sealed, adoption records released. Will fax documents to local or toll-free number. Court makes copy: $.50 per page. Self serve: same. Certification fee: $12.50. Payee: Clerk of Circuit Court. Personal checks accepted; credit cards are not. Prepayment required.

Wythe General District Court 245 S 4th St, #205, Wytheville, VA 24382-2595; 276-223-6079; fax: 276-223-6087; 8AM-4:30PM. ***Misdemeanor, Civil Actions under $15,000, Eviction, Small Claims.***
Civil Records: Access: Mail, fax, in person, online. Visitors must perform in person searches themselves. No search fee. Fee is only applied to requests for excessive amounts of information. Required to search: name, years to search. Civil cases indexed by defendant, plaintiff. Civil records maintained on computer for 10 years. Mail turnaround time 5 days. Civil PAT goes back to 10 years. Search free at www.courts.state.va.us/. Results show address of subject and day & month of birth, but not year. Also search LOPAS; call 804-786-5511 to apply.
Criminal Records: Access: Online, in person. Visitors must perform in person searches themselves. Required to search: name, years to search; also helpful: DOB, SSN. Criminal records maintained on computer for 10 years. Criminal PAT goes back to same as civil. Search free at www.courts.state.va.us/. Results show address of subject and day & month of birth, but not year.
General Information: Will fax documents. Court makes copy: $.50 per page. Self serve: same. No certification fee. Payee: General District Court. Personal checks and credit cards accepted. Prepayment required. Mail requests: SASE required for mail return of any docs.

York County

9th Circuit Court PO Box 371, Yorktown, VA 23690; 757-890-3350; criminal phone: 757-890-4104; civil phone: 757-890-4105; probate phone: 757-890-4106; fax: 757-890-3364; 9AM-5PM. ***Felony, Civil Actions over $15,000, Probate.***
www.yorkcounty.gov/circuitcourt/
Also includes City of Poquoson. Probate is separate index at this same address.
Civil Records: Access: Online, in person. Visitors must perform in person searches themselves. Required to search: name, years to search. Civil cases indexed by defendant, plaintiff. Civil index on docket books back to 2/1950, computerized since 1986. Civil PAT goes back to 1986. PAT civil results show middle initial. Search free at www.courts.state.va.us/. Results show address of subject and day & month of birth, but not year. Also search LOPAS; call 804-786-5511 to apply.
Criminal Records: Access: Online, in person. Visitors must perform in person searches themselves. Required to search: name, years to search. Criminal records indexed in books back to 2/1950, computerized since 1986. Criminal PAT goes back to same as civil. PAT criminal results show middle initial. Online access to criminal records is the same as civil. Online results show only month and day of DOB plus sex, race.
General Information: No juvenile, sealed, adoption records released. Will not fax documents. Court makes copy: $.50 per page. Self serve: same. Certification fee: $2.00. Payee: Clerk of Circuit Court. Personal checks accepted; credit cards are not. Prepayment required.

9th General District Court York County GDC, PO Box 316, Yorktown, VA 23690-0316; 757-890-3450; criminal fax: 757-890-3459; civil fax: same; 8:30AM-4:30PM. ***Misdemeanor, Civil Actions under $15,000, Eviction, Small Claims.***
www.yorkcounty.gov/districtcourt/
Civil Records: Access: Fax, mail, online, in person. Both court and visitors may perform in person searches. No search fee. Required to search: name, years to search. Civil cases indexed by defendant, plaintiff; index on computer back to 1997; prior to 1985 at Circuit Court. Mail turnaround time 5 days. Civil PAT goes back to 1997. PAT civil results show middle initial. Search free at www.courts.state.va.us/. Results show address of subject and day & month of birth, but not year. Also search LOPAS; call 804-786-5511 to apply.
Criminal Records: Access: Fax, mail, online, in person. Both court and visitors may perform in person searches. No search fee. Required to search: name, years to search, DOB, SSN. Criminal records computerized from 1997; prior to 1985 at Circuit Court. Mail turnaround time 5 days. Criminal PAT goes back to same as civil. PAT criminal results show middle initial. Search free at www.courts.state.va.us/. Results show address of subject and day & month of birth, but not year.
General Information: Online identifiers in results same as on public terminal. No juvenile, sealed, adoption records released. Will fax documents $1.00 1st page, $.50 each add'l. Court makes copy: $1.00 first page, $.50 each add'l. No certification fee. Payee: York County General District Court. Personal checks accepted. Visa/MC accepted. Prepayment required. Mail requests: SASE required

Virginia Recording Offices

ORGANIZATION: 95 counties and 41 independent cities; 123 recording offices. The recording officer is the Clerk of Circuit Court. Sixteen independent cities share the Clerk of Circuit Court with the county – Bedford; Covington and Clifton Forge (Alleghany County); Emporia (Greenville County); Fairfax; Falls Church (Arlington or Fairfax County); Franklin (Southhampton County); Galax (Carroll County); Harrisonburg (Rockingham County); Lexington (Rockbridge County); Manassas and Manassas Park (Prince William County); Norton (Wise County); Poquoson (York County); South Boston (Halifax County); and Williamsburg (James City County).

Charles City and James City are counties, not cities. The City of Franklin is not in Franklin County. The City of Richmond is not in Richmond County. The City of Roanoke is not in Roanoke County.

Virginia is in the Eastern Time Zone.

REAL ESTATE RECORDS: Only a few Clerks of Circuit Court will perform real estate searches. Copy fees are $.50 per page. certification fee is $2.00 plus copy fee. The independent cities may have separate Assessor Offices.

UCC RECORDS: Virginia was a dual filing state until July 1, 2001; financing statements were filed at the state level and with the Clerk of Circuit Court, except for consumer goods, farm and real estate related collateral which were filed only with the Clerk of Circuit Court. Now, only real estate related collateral is filed at the county level. Some recording offices will perform UCC searches; if they do, use search request form UCC-11. Search fee is $20.00 per debtor name, sometimes $10.00.

TAX LIEN RECORDS: Federal tax liens on personal property of businesses are filed with the State Corporation Commission. Other federal and all state tax liens are filed with the county Clerk of Circuit Court and are usually filed in a "Judgment Lien Book." Most Virginia counties will not perform tax lien searches.

OTHER LIENS: Judgment, mechanics, hospital, lis pendens.

ONLINE ACCESS: A growing number of Virginia counties and cities provide free access to real estate related information via the Internet. A limited but growing private company network named VamaNet provides residential, commercial, and vacant property data and tax records; visit www.vamanet.com/info/home.jsp. Access to 24 jurisdictions if free; 36 others require a subscription. Also, the Clerk's Information System (CIS) provides UCC index free at www.scc.virginia.gov/clk/uccsrch.aspx

Accomack County

Clerk of Circuit Court, PO Box 126, Accomac, VA 23301-0126. 757-787-5776; fax-757-787-1849; 9AM-5PM www.co.accomack.va.us/index2.html

Index: All land records in one. Records indexed on a public use terminal back to 1984. Office will perform a UCC search but public must search other records themselves. Copy fee $.50 per page. Cert fee- $2.00 per page plus copy fee. Payee- Accomack County Clerk of Circuit Court. **Online access to Real Estate, Grantor/Grantee, Deed, Mortgage, Lien, Judgment, Marriage, Will records:** Access recorder's index by subscription service ILS; call 877-658-6018 x2111 to apply; ask for Johnathan; $80 monthly fee ad credit cards accepted. **Other phones:** Treasurer- 757-787-5740. **Property tax/Assessing-** 757-787-5729, assessor fax- 757-789-3350. **Online-** Access parcel assessment value data free at http://accomack.mapsdirect.net/Sites/Accomack/Default.aspx.

Albemarle County

Clerk of Circuit Court, 501 E Jefferson St, Rm 225, Charlottesville, VA 22902. 434-972-4083; fax-434-293-0298; 8:30-4:30. www.albemarle.org/index.asp

Index: All in one. Records indexed on a public use terminal back to 1957. Only the public may search. Copy fee $.50 per page. Cert fee- $2.00 per doc plus copy fee. Payee- Albemarle County Clerk of Circuit Court. **Online access to Real Estate, Deed, Lien, Judgment, UCC records:** Access to clerk's recorded index available by subscription; fee- $600 per year per user or $1200 for corporate 4-user sub. Does not include vital records. Land records go back to 1947. Contact clerk Shelby Marshall 434-972-4083. **Other phones:** Treasurer- 434-296-5851. **Property tax/Assessing-** 401 McIntire Rd, #243, Charlottesville, VA 22902; 434-296-5856, fax-434296-5801. **Online-** Search assessor data free at http://albemarlevapropertymax.governmaxa.com/propertymax/rover30.asp; search free by parcel, owner name, address, sales. Also, search parcel data on GIS-mapping site free at http://gisweb.albemarle.org/. Also, search zoning notices free at www.albemarle.org/upload/images/webapps/zoning/.

Alexandria City

Clerk of Circuit Court, 520 King St, Rm 307, Alexandria, VA 22314. 703-838-4044, R/E recording phone- 703-838-4066; hours- 9AM - 5PM http://alexandriava.gov/clerkofcourt/

Index: All in one. Records indexed on a public use terminal back to 1/2/1980. Only the public may search. Will search UCC records. Copy fee $.50 per page. Cert fee- $2.00 per doc plus copy fee. Payee- Alexandria City Clerk of Circuit Court. **Other phones:** Treasurer- 703-838-6420; Elections- 703-838-4050; Vital Records- 703-838-4400. **Property tax/Assessing-** 301 King St, Rm 2600, PO Box 178, Alexandria, VA 22313; 703-838-4646, assessor fax-703-706-3979. (Appraiser/Auditor- 703-838-4646) hours- 8AM-5PM **Online** - Access city real estate assessments free at http://realestate.alexandriava.gov/ but no name searching. Search property free at the GIS-mapping site at http://gis.alexandriava.gov/parcelviewernet/viewer.htm but no name searching.

Alleghany County

Clerk of Circuit Court, PO Box 670, Covington, VA 24426-0670. 540-965-1730; fax-540-965-1732; 8:30AM-5PM. www.alleghanycountyclerk.com

Now has records for the former Clifton Forge City.

Index: All in one. Records indexed on a public use terminal back to 1968 - Clifton Forge City; Alleghany County 1973. Only the public may search. Copy fee $.50 per page. Cert fee- $2.00 per doc plus copy fee. Payee- Alleghany County Clerk of Court. **Other phones:** Treasurer- 540-863-6630. **Property tax/Assessing-** 540-863-6640. **Online** - Access City of Covington property data free at www.vamanet.com/cgi-bin/MAPSRCHPGM?LOCAL=COV. Access Alleghany County data free at a sister website at www.vamanet.com/cgi-bin/MAPSRCHPGM?LOCAL=ALE. Also, access to GIS-mapping for free go to www.co.alleghany.va.us/.

Amelia County

Clerk of Circuit Court, PO Box 237, Amelia Court House, VA 23002-0237. 804-561-2128; fax-804-561-6364; hours - 8:30AM-4:30PM www.ameliacova.us/Clerk%20Circuit.htm

Index: All in one. Records indexed on computer back to 1978. Only the public may search. Copy fee $.50 per page. Cert fee- $2.00 per doc plus copy fee. Payee- Amelia County Clerk of Circuit Court. **Online access to Real Estate, Deed records:** Access real estate recording records by subscription only, contact Clerk of Circuit Court for information. **Other phones:** Treasurer- 804-561-2145; Elections- 804-561-3460; Revenue Commission- 804-561-2158. **Property tax/Assessing-** Same address as recording office. 804-561-2158. hours- 8:30AM-5PM **Online access-** Search for property card and assessment data free at www.ameliacountyrealestate.com/.

Amherst County

Clerk of Circuit Court, PO Box 462, Amherst, VA 24521. 434-946-9321; 8-5PM http://courts.state.va.us

Index: All in one. Records indexed on computer back to 10/1/87. Only the public may search. Will not search UCC records. Copy fee $.50 per page. Cert fee- $2.00 per doc plus copy fee. Payee- Amherst County Clerk of Circuit Court. **Other phones:** Treasurer- 434-946-9318. **Property tax/Assessing-** 434-946-9310. **Online access-** Access current assessment info and sales by VamaNet subscription at www.vamanet.com/cgi-bin/HOME. Fee is $35 per month or $300 per year with discounts for multiple localities, regions.

Appomattox County

Clerk of Circuit Court, PO Box 672, Appomattox, VA 24522. 434-352-5275; fax-434-352-2781; 8:30-4:30. www.courts.state.va.us/courts/circuit/Appomattox/home.html
Index: Separate indices to search include books (includes liens, UCCs) and computer. Land records indexed on a public use terminal back to 1973. Office personnel or visitors may perform searches. Office will not search real estate records. Will not search UCC records. Copy fee $.50 per page. Cert fee- $2.00 per doc plus copy fee. Payee- Appomattox County Clerk of Circuit Court. **Online access to Real Estate, Grantor/Grantee records:** Access to records for free go to www.courts.state.va.us/courts/circuit/Appomattox/home.html. **Other phones:** Treasurer- 434-352-5200; Elections- 434-352-5302; Vital Records- 434-352-5275. **Property tax/ Assessing**- PO Box 125, Appomattox, VA 24522; 434-352-7450.

Arlington County

Clerk of Circuit Court, 1425 N Courthouse Rd, 6th Fl, Arlington, VA 22201. 703-228-4369; 8AM-4PM www.arlingtonva.us
Real property transactions located in City of Falls Church are recorded with Arlington County Circuit Court since 1988. RE from Zip Codes 22042 & 22046 managed by Fairfax County 1/1988 to 2002. Index: All in one. Records indexed on a public use terminal back to 1975. Office personnel or visitors may perform searches. Search fee $20.00. Copy fee $.50 per page. Cert fee- $2.00 per doc plus copy fee. Payee- Arlington County Clerk of Circuit Court. **Property tax/Assessing**- 2100 Clarendon Blvd, #611, Arlington, VA 22201; 703-228-3920, assessor fax-703-228-3440. **Online access**- Property records on the County assessor database are free at www.arlingtonva.us/Departments/RealEstate/reassessments/scripts/DREADefault.asp. Includes trade name search. Also, access Falls Church City property data free on the GIS-mapping site at http://property.fallschurchva.gov/public/ieprop.htm but no name searching.

Augusta County

Clerk of Circuit Court, PO Box 689, Staunton, VA 24402-0689. 540-245-5321, R/E recording phone-540-245-5648, UCC recording phone-540-245-5321; fax-540-245-5318; 8AM-5PM
Index: All in one. Records indexed on a public use terminal back to 1992. Only the public may search. Copy fee $.50 per page. Cert fee- $2.00 per doc plus copy fee. Payee- Augusta County Clerk of Circuit Court. Bulk data available for purchase 540-245-5400x540. **Other phones:** Treasurer- 540-245-5660. **Property tax/Assessing**- 18 Government Center Ln, Verona, VA 24482; 540-245-5647, assessor fax- 540-245-5179. A public access terminal is available. **Online** - Click on Augusta County to search property data for free at www.vamanet.com/cgi-bin/HOME.

Bath County

Clerk of Circuit Court, PO Box 180, Warm Springs, VA 24484. 540-839-7226, R/E recording phone-540-839-7231; fax-540-839-7248; 8:30AM-4:30PM www.courts.state.va.us/courts/circuit/Bath/home.html
Index: All in one. Records indexed on computer back to 2000. Only the public may search. Copy fee $.50 per page. Cert fee- $2.00 per doc plus copy fee. Payee- Bath County Clerk of Circuit Court. **Other phones:** Treasurer- 540-839-7256. **Property tax/Assessing**- PO Box 130, Warm Springs, VA 26484; 540-839-7231. **Online access**- Access current assessment info and sales by VamaNet subscription at www.vamanet.com/cgi-bin/HOME. Fee is $35 per month or $300 per year with discounts for multiple localities, regions.

Bedford County

Clerk of Circuit Court, 123 E Main St, #301, Bedford, VA 24523. 540-586-7632; fax-540-586-6197; 8:30AM-5PM www.courts.state.va.us/courts/circuit/bedford/home.html
Index: All in one. Records indexed on a public use terminal back to 1993. Only the public may search. Copy fee $.50 per page. Cert fee- $2.00 per doc plus copy fee. Payee- Bedford County Clerk of Circuit Court. Treasurer- 540-586-7670. **Property tax/ Assessing**- 540-586-7626. **Online access**- Real estate records on the Bedford County GIS site are free at www.co.bedford.va.us/Res/GIS/index.htm; however, no name searching at this time. Also access via www.onlinegis.net/VaBedford/. Click on Display Map then Search. property records on City of Bedford site are free at www.bedfordva.gov/taxf.shtml. Also, access Bedford City property info on GIS site free at http://bedfordgis.bedfordva.gov/bedfordcity/search.asp?skipopen=1.

Bland County

Clerk of Circuit Court, PO Box 295, Bland, VA 24315. 276-688-4562; fax-276-688-2438; 8AM-6PM www.bland.org/government/clerkofcourt.html
Index: All in one. Records indexed on a public use terminal back to varies. Office will perform a UCC search (limited) but public must search other records themselves. Search fee $10.00. Copy fee $.50 per page. Cert fee- $2.50 per page plus copy fee. Payee- Bland County Clerk of Circuit Court. **Other phones:** Treasurer- 276-688-3741. **Property tax/Assessing**- 276-688-4291. **Online access**- Access current assessment info and sales by VamaNet subscription at www.vamanet.com/cgi-bin/HOME. Fee is $35 per month or $300 per year with discounts for multiple localities, regions.

Botetourt County

Clerk of Circuit Court, PO Box 219, Fincastle, VA 24090. 540-473-8274; 8:30AM-4:30PM
Index: All in one. Records indexed on a public use terminal back to 1991. Only the public may search. Copy fee $.50 per page. Cert fee- $2.00 per doc plus copy fee. Payee- Botetourt County Clerk of Circuit Court. Bulk data available for purchase,contact Jay Etzler. **Other phones:** Treasurer- 540-473-8254. **Property tax/Assessing**- PO Box 128, 1 W Main St, Courthouse, Fincastle, VA 24090; 540-473-8367, assessor fax- 540-473-8289. **Online** - Access property data free at www.onlinegis.net/VaBotetourt/. Click on Display Map then Search, no name searching.

Bristol City

Clerk of Circuit Court, 497 Cumberland St, Rm 210, Bristol, VA 24201. 276-645-7321, R/E recording phone-276-645-7315, UCC recording phone-276-645-7321; fax-276-821-6097; 9AM-5PM
Index: All in one. Records indexed on a public use terminal back to 1974. Only the public may search. Will not search UCC records. Copy fee $.50 per page. Cert fee- $2.00 per doc plus copy fee. Payee- Circuit Court Clerk. **Other phones:** Treasurer- 276-645-7311; Elections- 276-645-7319. **Property tax/Assessing**- 497 Cumberland St, Bristol, VA 24201; 276-645-7316. **Online access**- Access current assessment info and sales by VamaNet subscription at www.vamanet.com/cgi-bin/HOME. Fee is $35 per month or $300 per year with discounts for multiple localities, regions.

Brunswick County

Clerk of Circuit Court, 216 N Main St, Lawrenceville, VA 23868. 434-848-2215; fax-434-848-4307; 8:30AM-5PM.
Index: All in one. Records indexed on a public use terminal back to 1996. Only the public may search. Copy fee $.50 per page. Cert fee- $2.00 per doc plus copy fee. Payee- Clerk of Circuit Court. **Online access to Real Estate, Deed, Judgment, Will, Marriage records:** Access to Circuit Court Records Search System is by subscription at www.courts.state.va.us/rmsweb/. $1200 per year, username and password required, signup with local Circuit Ct Clerk. **Other phones:** Treasurer- 434-848-2512; Elections- 434-848-4414. **Property tax/Assessing**- 228 N Main St, Lawrenceville, VA 23868; 434-848-2313, assessor fax- 434-848-6856. (Appraiser/Auditor- 434-848-2313);

Buchanan County

Clerk of Circuit Court, PO Box 929, Grundy, VA 24614. 276-935-6567, R/E phone-276-935-6575, UCC phone-276-935-6567; fax-276-935-7086; 8:30AM-5PM. www.courts.state.va.us/courts/circuit/Buchanan/home.html
Index: All in one. Records indexed on computer back to 7/91. Office will perform a UCC and Tax lien search but public must search other records themselves. Search fee $3.00. Copy fee $.50 per page. Cert fee- $2.00 per doc plus copy fee. Payee- Circuit Court Clerk. **Online access to Real Estate, Grantor/Grantee, Deed, Lien, Judgment, UCC, Marriage, Wills/Probate, Fictitious Name records:** Access to the recorder's database is available by subscription, registration and password required; $75.00 per month. Contact clerk's office for signup and info. Data goes back to 8/2005 but new data being added back to 1991. Deeds index will go back to 1976. **Other phones:** Treasurer- 276-935-6551; Elections- 276-935-6534; Vital Records- 276-935-6575. **Property tax/Assessing**- 1012 Walnut St, Grundy, VA 24614; 276-935-6541. (Appraiser/ Auditor- 276-935-6541);

Buckingham County

Clerk of Circuit Court, PO Box 107, Buckingham, VA 23921. 434-969-4734; 8:30AM-4:30PM.
Index: Separate indices to search include deeds, judgments, financing statements in books. Records indexed on computer back to 1973. Only the public may search. Copy fee $.50 per page. Cert fee- $2.00 per page plus copy fee. Payee- Clerk of Circuit Court. **Other phones:** Treasurer- 434-969-4744. **Property tax/Assessing**- 434-969-4181.

Buena Vista City

Clerk of Circuit Court, 2039 Sycamore Ave, Buena Vista, VA 24416. 540-261-8627; fax-540-261-8625; 8:30AM-5PM
Index: All in one. Records indexed on a public use terminal back to 1/95, books prior to 1/95. Only the public may search. Will not search UCC records. Copy fee $.50 per page. Cert fee- $2.00 per doc plus copy fee. Payee- Clerk of Circuit Court. **Other phones:** Treasurer- 540-261-8621; Elections- 540-261-8605. **Property tax/ Assessing**- 2039 Sycamore Ave, Buena Vista, VA 24416; 540-261-8611. hours- 8:30AM-4:30PM **Online**- Access city appraisal data free at www.vamanet.com/cgi-bin/MAPSRCHPGM?LOC AL=BUE.

Campbell County

Clerk of Circuit Court, PO Box 7, Rustburg, VA 24588. 434-592-9517, R/E phone-434-332-9568; 8:30-4:30 www.co.campbell.va.us/Pages/index.aspx
Records indexed on a public use terminal back to 1/1994. Office personnel or visitors may perform searches. UCC search per debtor name $20.00. Office will not search real estate records. Will search UCC records. Copy fee $.50 per page. Cert fee- $2.00 per doc plus copy fee. Payee- Campbell County Clerk of Circuit Court. **Other phones:** Treasurer- 434-332-9590. **Property tax/Assessing**- PO Box 100, Rustburg, VA 24588; 434-332-9510. www.co.campbell.va.us/depts/reassessment/Pages/index.aspx **Online access**- Access county property data from Dept of Real Estate and Mapping free at http://campbellvapropertymax.governmaxa.com/propertymax/rover30.asp?. Also, search at http://gis.co.campbell.va.us/campbellims/default.aspx. Also, search property by name on the county GIS-mapping site at http://gis.co.campbell.va.us/campbellims/default.aspx. Login as guest; registration required for full data. Click on 'Find' to search.

Caroline County

Clerk of Circuit Court, PO Box 309, Bowling Green, VA 22427-0309. 804-633-5800; 8:30AM-4PM (Recording- 8:30-3:45PM). http://visitcaroline.com

Index: Separate indices to search include deeds, CIS assignments, PA, etc. Records indexed on a public use terminal back to 1896. Only the public may search. Office will not search real estate records. Will not search UCC records. Copy fee $.50 per page. Cert fee- $2.50 per doc plus copy fee. Payee- Caroline County Clerk of Circuit Court. **Other phones:** Treasurer- 804-633-5291; Elections- 804-633-9083. **Property tax/Assessing-** 804-633-9834. hours- 9AM-5PM **Online access-** Click on Caroline County to search property records for free at www.vamanet.com/cgi-bin/HOME.

Carroll County

Clerk of Circuit Court, PO Box 218, Hillsville, VA 24343-0218. 276-730-3070; fax-276-730-3071; 8AM-5PM www.chillsnet.org

Index: All in one. Records indexed on a public use terminal back to 1966. Only the public may search. Copy fee $.50 per page. Cert fee- $2.00 per doc plus copy fee. Payee- Clerk. Bulk data available for purchase; contact Donna or Janey, County Assessor. **Online access to Real Estate, Deed, Judgment, UCC records:** Access to Carroll county property data is a $25 monthly fee. Username and password required; signup through Clerk of Circuit Court, 276-730-3070. Land index and images go back to 1966; plats to 2002. **Other phones:** Treasurer- 276-730-3060; Elections- 276-730-3035. **Property tax/Assessing-** 605-17 Pine St, Hillsville, VA 24343; 276-730-3030, assessor fax- 276-730-3085. (Appraiser/Auditor- 276-730-3030) Public access terminal available. **Online access-** Access Town of Hillsville property data on the gis-mapping site at http://arcims.webgis.net/va/Hillsville/default.asp .

Charles City County

Clerk of Circuit Court, PO Box 86, Charles City, VA 23030. 804-652-2105; fax-804-829-5647; 8:30-4:30

Index: Separate indices to search include land, marriage, wills, judgments, financing statements, civil orders, criminal orders, fictitious names, military discharge, notary. Records indexed on a public use terminal back to 5/00. Only the public may search. Copy fee $.50 per page. Cert fee- $2.50 per doc plus copy fee. Payee- Clerk, Circuit Court. **Other phones:** Treasurer- 804-652-4738; Elections- 804-652-4606. **Property tax/Assessing-** PO Box 7, 10780 Courthouse Rd, Charles City, VA 23030; 804-662-2161, assessor fax- 804-829-6288. **Online-** View property cards free at www.charlescitycountyrealestate.com. Click on View Property Cards Online.

Charlotte County

Clerk of Circuit Court, PO Box 38, Charlotte Court House, VA 23923. 434-542-5147; fax-434-542-4336; 8:30AM-4:30PM.

Index: All in one. Record index not computerized. Only the public may search. Copy fee $.50 per page. Cert fee- $2.00 per doc plus copy fee. Payee- Clerk of Circuit Court. Treasurer- 434-542-5725. **Property tax/Assessing-** 125 David Bruce Hwy, Courthouse, Charlotte Court House, VA 23923; 434-542-5546.

Charlottesville City

Clerk of Circuit Court, 315 E High St, Charlottesville, VA 22902. 434-970-3766; 8:30AM-4:30PM

Index: Separate indices. Records indexed on a public use terminal back to 1990. Only the public may search. Copy fee $.50 per page. Cert fee- $2.00 per doc plus copy fee. Payee- City of Charlottesville Circuit Court. **Other phones:** Treasurer- 434-296-5851. **Property tax/Assessing-** 434-970-3136.

Chesapeake City

Clerk of Circuit Court, 307 Albemarle Dr, #300A, Chesapeake, VA 23322. 757-382-3000, R/E phone- 757-382-3026, UCC phone-757-382-3032; fax-757-382-3034; 8AM-4PM. http://cityofchesapeake.net/services/depart/circourt/index.shtml

Index: All in one. Records indexed on a public use terminal back to 1980. Only the public may search. Copy fee $.50 per page. Cert fee- $2.00 per doc plus copy fee. Payee- Clerk of Circuit Court. Treasurer- 757-382-6281. **Property tax/Assessing-** 306 Cedar Road, 4th Floor, Chesapeake, VA 23322; 757-382-6235. http://cityofchesapeake.net/services/depart/real-est/index.shtml **Online** - Access to property appraiser data is free at www.chesva.com/realestate.html. No name searching at this time

Chesterfield County

Clerk of Circuit Court, PO Box 125, Chesterfield, VA 23832-0125. 804-748-1241; fax-804-796-5625; 8AM-4:30PM (9AM-3PM recording hrs). www.chesterfield.gov

Index: Separate indices to search include judgments, deeds. Records indexed on a public use terminal back to 1749. Office will perform a UCC search but public must search other records themselves. Search fee- $20.00 per name for UCC, limited to year 2000. Copy fee $.50 per page. Cert fee- $2.00 per doc plus copy fee. Payee- Circuit Court Clerk. Bulk data available for purchase in the form of CD's; contact Chris Bugg. **Other phones:** Treasurer- 804-748-1201; Elections- 804-748-1471. **Property tax/Assessing-** PO Box 40, 6701 Mimms Loop, Chesterfield, VA 23832-0040; 804-748-1321, assessor fax- 804-717-6278. hours- 8:30AM-5PM Public access terminal available. **Online access-** Search real estate assessment data free at www.co.chesterfield.va.us/ManagementServices/RealEstateAssessments/Rea_Search_Home.asp.

Clarke County

Clerk of Circuit Court, PO Box 189, Berryville, VA 22611. 540-955-5116; fax-540-955-0284; 9AM-4:30PM. www.clarkevacocc.org

Index: Separate indices to search include judgments, wills, UCC. Records indexed on a public use terminal back to 1836. Only the public may search. Will not search UCC records. Copy fee $.50 per page. Cert fee- $2.50 per cert plus copy fee. Payee- Clarke County Clerk of Circuit Court. **Online access to Real Estate, Grantor/Grantee, Deed, Judgment records:** With username and password you may access recorder's land records at www.clarkevacocc.org. Includes deed book 153 back to 1984. Set up account online; fee is $25.00 per month. **Other phones:** Treasurer- 540-955-5160; Elections- 540-955-5168. **Property tax/ Assessing-** PO Box 67, 102 N Church St, Courthouse, Berryville, VA 22611; 540-955-5108, assessor fax- 540-955-1629. hours- 8:30AM-5PM www.clarkecounty.gov **Online** - Click on Clarke County to search property data for free at http://mapsonline.net/clarkecounty/ but no name searching.

Colonial Heights City

Clerk of Circuit Court, PO Box 3401, Colonial Heights, VA 23834. 804-520-9364; fax-804-524-8726; 8AM-4:30PM www.colonial-heights.com/ClerkofCircuitCourt.htm

Index: All in one. Records indexed on a public use terminal back to 1990 (land records). Only the public may search. Copy fee $.50 per page. Cert fee- $2.00 per doc plus copy fee. Payee- Colonial Heights Clerk of Circuit Court. **Other phones:** Treasurer- 804-520-9320; Elections- 804-520-9277. **Property tax/ Assessing-** PO Box 3401, 201 James Ave, Colonial Heights, VA 23834; phone- 804-520-9272, assessor fax- 804-520-9218. www.colonial-heights.com/AssessRealEstate.htm **Online** - Access real estate property assessor records free at www.colonial-heights.com/AssessSearch.htm.

Craig County

Clerk of Circuit Court, PO Box 185, New Castle, VA 24127. 540-864-6141; fax-540-864-7471; 9AM-5PM

Index: All in one. Records indexed on computer back to 1999. Office will perform a UCC search but public must search other records themselves. Copy fee $.50 per page. Cert fee- $2.00 per doc plus copy fee. Payee- Craig County Clerk of Circuit Court. Treasurer- 540-864-5641. **Property tax/Assessing-** PO Box 186, 182 Main St, #3, New Castle, VA 24127; 540-864-6241, assessor fax- 540-864-7229.

Culpeper County

Clerk of Circuit Court, 135 W Cameron St, Rm 103, Culpeper, VA 22701. 540-727-3438; fax-n/a; 8:30AM-4:30PM http://web.culpepercounty.gov/

Index: All in one. Records indexed on a public use terminal back to 1996. Office will perform a UCC search but public must search other records themselves. Office will not search real estate records. Office will search UCC records with request form and $20.00 fee. Copy fee $.50 per page. Cert fee- $2.00 per doc plus copy fee. Payee- Culpeper County Clerk of Circuit Court. Treasurer- 540-727-3442; Vital Records- 804-662-6200. **Property tax/Assessing-** 135 W Cameron St, Culpeper, VA 22701; 540-727-3443, assessor fax- 540-727-3472. **Online-** Access property data free at www.onlinegis.net/VaCulpeper/asp/controlVersion.asp. No name searching.. View property cards free at www.culpepercounty.gov/applications/TxApps/PropCardsIndex.htm. Also, access current assessment info and sales by VamaNet subscription at www.vamanet.com/cgi-bin/HOME. Fee is $35 per month or $300 per year with discounts for multiple localities, regions.

Cumberland County

Clerk of Circuit Court, PO Box 8, Cumberland, VA 23040. 804-492-4442; fax-804-492-4876; 8:30AM-4:30PM. www.cumberlandcounty.com

Index: Separate indices to search include books back to 1749, newer on computer. Records indexed on a public use terminal back to 1993, UCC/judgments back to 2001. Only the public may search. Copy fee $.50 per page. Cert fee- None. Payee- Cumberland County Clerk of Circuit Court. Bulk data available for purchase; inquire at office. **Online access to Real Estate, Deed records:** County deed and land records available by subscription from private company at http://en.landsystems.com/index.php. **Other phones:** Treasurer- 804-492-4297. **Property tax/Assessing-** PO Box 77, 1 Courthouse Circle, Cumberland, VA 23040; 804-492-4280, assessor fax- 804-492-3342. Co-located with Commissioner of Revenue. www.cumberlandcounty.com

Danville City

Clerk of Circuit Court, PO Box 3300, Danville, VA 24543. 434-799-5168; fax-434-799-6502; 9AM-4:30PM www.danville-va.gov/

Index: All in one. Records indexed on a public use terminal back to 1988. Office will perform a UCC search but public must search other records themselves. UCC search per debtor name $20.00. Copy fee $.50 per page. Cert fee- $2.00 per doc plus copy fee. Payee- Danville City Clerk of Circuit Court. Treasurer- 434-799- 5140; Elections- 434-799-6560. **Property tax/Assessing-** Commissioner of Revenue, 311 Memorial Dr, PO Box 480, Danville, VA 24543; 434-799-5145, fax- 434-799-5148. www.danville-va.gov/officials.asp?menuid=2816&sub1menuid=3686 **Online access-** Access to Danville City assessor online records is free at www.danvillevaassessor.org. Also, see note at beginning of section for statewide land record access.

Dickenson County

Clerk of Circuit Court, PO Box 190, Clintwood, VA 24228. 276-926-1616; fax-276-926-6465; 8:30AM-4:30PM. www.dickensoncountyvirginia.org/html/office_of_the_clerk.html Index: Separate indices to search include deeds, Wills, Financing Statements. Records indexed on a public use terminal back to 2000. Only the public may search. General copy fee $.50 per page. Cert fee- $2.50 per doc plus copy fee. Payee- Dickenson County Clerk. **Other phones:** Treasurer- 276-926-1610; Elections- 276-926-1620. **Property tax/Assessing-** PO Box 1067, 293 Main St,

Courthouse, Clintwood, VA 24228; 276-926-1646, assessor fax- 276-926-4720. **Online access**- Access to the Commissioner of Revenue tax data is free at www.smartmesh.net/Search.aspx.

Dinwiddie County

Clerk of Circuit Court, PO Box 63, Dinwiddie, VA 23841. 804-469-4540, R/E recording phone-804-469-4507, UCC recording phone-804-469-4540; fax-804-469-5386; 8:30AM-4:30PM
Index: All in one. Records indexed on a public use terminal back to 1989. Only the public may search. Copy fee $.50 per page. Cert fee- $2.00 per doc plus copy fee. Payee- Dinwiddie County Clerk of Circuit Court. **Other phones:** Treasurer- 804-469-4510; Elections- 804-469-4512; Vital Records- 804-469-6200. **Property tax/Assessing**- PO Box 104, Dinwiddie, VA 23841; 804-469-4507, assessor fax-804-469-4503. **Online** - Access current assessment info and sales by sub at www.vamanet.com/cgi-bin/HOME. Fee is $35 per month or $300 per year with discounts for multiple localities, regions.

Essex County

Clerk of Circuit Court, PO Box 445, Tappahannock, VA 22560. 804-443-3541; fax-804-445-1216; 8:30AM-5PM www.essex-virginia.org
Index: Separate indices to search include deeds, wills, financing statements, judgments, books, computer. Records indexed on computer back to 1/1/06. Only the public may search. Copy fee $.50 per page. Cert fee- $2.00 per doc plus copy fee. Payee- Essex County Clerk of Circuit Court. Treasurer- 804-443-4371; Elections- 804-443-4611. **Property tax/ Assessing**- Commissioner of the Revenue, PO Box 879 804-443-4737. www.essex-virginia.org/taxes.htm **Online**- Search the treasurer's site free at www.essex-virginia.org/taxes.htm. Access county property cards free at https://county.essex-va.org/applications/txapps/PropCardsIndex.htm. View RE taxes free at https://county.essex-va.org/applications/trapps/REIindex.htm. Also, access assessment info and sales by VamaNet subscription at www.vamanet.com/cgi-bin/HOME. Fee- $35 per month or $300 per yr; discounts for multiple localities.

Fairfax County

Clerk of Circuit Court, 4110 Chain Bridge Rd, 3rd Fl, Fairfax, VA 22030. 703-691-7320 x3 then x4, R/E phone-703-691-7320, UCC phone-703-246-4904; 8AM-4:30PM www.fairfaxcounty.gov/courts/circuit/
Real property transactions located within City of Falls Church must be recorded with Arlington County Circuit Court. Recording records from Zip Codes 22042 & 22046 managed by Fairfax County from 1/1988 to 2002. Index: All in one. Records indexed on a public use terminal back to 1742. Only the public may search. UCC records are located in Public Service Dept. Copy fee $.50 per page. Cert fee- $2.00 per doc plus copy fee. Payee- Fairfax County Clerk of Circuit Court. **Online access to Real Estate, Deed records:** Hear about property descriptions, assessed values and sales prices. This Automated Information System operates Monday-Saturday 7AM-7PM at 703-222-6740. Fax-back service available. **Property tax/Assessing**- 12000 Government Crt Pky, Fairfax, VA 22035; 703-222-8234. **Online access**- Records on the Dept. of Tax Administration RE Assessment database are free at http://icare.fairfaxcounty.gov/Search/GenericSearch.aspx?mode=ADDRESS. Also, the list of auction properties is free at www.fairfaxcounty.gov/dta/auction.htm. Also, search City Assessments for free at http://va-fairfax-assessment.governmax.com/propertymax/rover30.asp but no name searching.

Falls Church City

Clerk of Circuit Court,, . ; www.fallschurchva.gov/
Real property transactions located in City of Falls Church must be recorded with Arlington Cty Circuit Court back to 1988. RE from Zip Codes 22042 & 22046 managed by Fairfax County 1/1988 to 2002. Pre-1988 at Fairfax County. **Online Records**- Access city property data free on the GIS-mapping site at http://property.fallschurchva.gov/public/ieprop.htm but no name searching.

Fauquier County

Clerk of Circuit Court, 40 Culpeper St, 1st Fl, Warrenton, VA 20186. 540-347-8670; 8AM-4PM www.fauquiercounty.gov
Index: Separate indices to search include deeds, judgments, financing statements, wills, partnerships. Record indexes on a public use terminal, some back to 1970. Office will perform a UCC search but public must search other records themselves. Search fee $20.00 per name. Office will not search real estate records. Copy fee $.50 per page. Cert fee- $2.00 per doc plus copy fee. Payee- Fauquier County Clerk of Circuit Court. For Deed Transfer report contact Gail Barb- Clerk. **Online access to Real Estate, Deed records:** Full real estate data may be available by subscription, $50.00 per month; call Commissioner of the Revenue at 540-347-8720. **Other phones:** Treasurer- 540-347-8691; Elections- 540-347-6972; Vital Records- 540-347-6400; Land Records Room-540-347-8748. **Property tax/Assessing**- 10 Hotel St, 1st Fl, Warrenton, VA 20186; 540-347-8614. hours-8AM-4:30PM **Online** - Search for property data and deed book info for free on the gis-mapping site at http://www2.undersys.com/fvawebnew/fauquier.html. Search Town of Warrenton property index free at http://quicksearch.webgis.net/search.php?site=va_warrenton. Property data free via the email response form at www.fauquiercounty.gov/government/departments/commrev/index.cfm?action=realestatetaxform.

Floyd County

Clerk of Circuit Court, 100 E Main St, Rm 200, Floyd, VA 24091. 540-745-9330; fax-540-745-9303; 8:30AM-4:30PM; 8:30AM-N Sat.
Index: All in one. Records indexed on a public use terminal back to 1991. Only the public may search. Copy fee $.50 per page. Cert fee- $2.00 per doc plus copy fee. Payee- Floyd County Clerk of Circuit Court. **Other phones:** Treasurer- 540-745-9357. **Property tax/Assessing**- 540-745-9345. **Online access**- Access the property assessment search page free at http://egov.mixnet.com/floyd_test/Search.asp.

Fluvanna County

Clerk of Circuit Court, PO Box 550, Palmyra, VA 22963. 434-591-1970; fax-434-591-1971; 8-4:30PM
Index: All in one. Records indexed on a public use terminal back to 1777. Only the public may search. Copy fee $.25 per page. Cert fee- $2.00 per doc plus copy fee. Payee- Fluvanna County Circuit Court. **Online access to Judgment records:** For free case information go to www.courts.state.va.us/caseinfo/home.html. **Other phones:** Treasurer- 434-591-1945; Elections- 434-589-3593. **Property tax/Assessing**- PO Box 124, Palmyra, VA 22963; 434-591-1940, assessor fax- 434-591-1941. (Appraiser/Auditor- 434-591-1940) **Online access**- Click on Fluvanna County to search property data for free at www.vamanet.com/cgi-bin/HOME. Access property data free at www.onlinegis.net/VaFluvanna/. Click on Display Map then Search, no name searching.

Franklin County

Clerk of Circuit Court, PO Box 567, Rocky Mount, VA 24151. 540-483-3065, R/E recording phone-540-483-3085; fax-540-483-3042; 9AM-4:30PM. www.franklincountyva.org/
Index: All in one. Records indexed on computer back to 1993. Only the public may search. Copy fee $.50 in person; $1.00 per page if mailed. Cert fee- $2.00 per doc plus copy fee. **Other phones:** Treasurer- 757-562-8540. **Property tax/Assessing**- 757-562-8547. **Online**- Access property data free at http://arcims2.webgis.net/va/franklin/. Also, search delinquent tax data free at www.franklincountyva.gov/resources/tax-rates-and-delinquents. Also, access current assessment info and sales by VamaNet subscription at www.vamanet.com/cgi-bin/HOME. Fee is $35 per month or $300 per year with discounts for multiple localities, regions.

Frederick County

Clerk of Circuit Court, 5 N Kent St, Winchester, VA 22601. 540-667-5770; fax-540-545-8711; 9AM-5PM www.winfredclerk.com
Do not confuse this county with Fredericksburg, VA or Frederick, MD. Also, City of Winchester has a separate filing office. Index: Separate indices to search include land records, marriages, wills, judgments. Records indexed on a public use terminal back to 1983. Office will perform a UCC search but public must search other records themselves. Copy fee $.50 per page. Cert fee- $2.50 per doc plus copy fee. Payee- Frederick County Clerk of Circuit Court. **Online access to Real Estate, Deed, Mortgage, Lien records:** Access to the County Records management System is by subscription; base fee is $500 per year for 3 users. Contact Debby Payne in the Circuit Court Clerk's office for info. **Other phones:** Treasurer- 540-662-6611. **Property tax/Assessing**- 540-662-5303. **Online access**- Access current assessment info and sales by VamaNet subscription at www.vamanet.com/cgi-bin/HOME. Fee is $35 per month or $300 per year with discounts for multiple localities, regions. Also, access parcel data free at http://gis.co.frederick.va.us/ and click on Parcel Mapping Service.

Fredericksburg City

Clerk of Circuit Court, PO Box 359, Fredericksburg, VA 22404. 540-372-1066; fax-Call for fax number; 8:30AM-4PM M,W,F; 8:30AM-N T,TH. www.fredericksburgva.gov
Many Fredericksburg addresses are outside the city limits, in Stafford County or Spotsylvania County. Check debtor location carefully. Index: Separate indices to search include computer, books. Records indexed on a public use terminal back to 1963. Office will perform a UCC search but public must search other records themselves. Copy fee $.50 per page. Cert fee- $2.00 per doc plus copy fee. Payee- Fredericksburg City Clerk of Circuit Court. **Online Land, Judgment, Will, Financing Statement records:** Access to Circuit Court Records System is by subscription at http://208.210.219.102/cgi-bin/p/rms.cgi. Includes images for other selected jurisdictions; $1200 per year, username and password required, signup with local Circuit Ct Clerk. **Property tax/Assessing**- 715 Princess Anne St, Fredericksburg, VA 22401; 540-372-1004. **Online access**- Access current assessment info and sales by VamaNet subscription at www.vamanet.com/cgi-bin/HOME. Fee is $35 per month or $300 per year with discounts for multiple localities, regions.

Giles County

Clerk of Circuit Court, PO Box 502, Pearisburg, VA 24134. 540-921-1722; fax-540-921-3825; 9AM-4PM
Index: Separate indices to search include books, computer. Records indexed on a public use terminal back to 2002. Office will perform a UCC search but public must search other records themselves. Copy fee $.50 per page. Cert fee- $3.00 per page includes copy fee. Payee- Giles County Clerk of Circuit Court. **Online access to Real Estate, Deed records:** Access land records and deeds on subscription service ILS; call 804-786-5511 to apply; $80 monthly fee. **Other phones:** Treasurer- 540-921-1240. **Property tax/Assessing**- 130 Main St, Pearisburg, VA 24134-0501; 540-921-3321. **Online access**- Click on Giles County to search for property records for free at www.vamanet.com/cgi-bin/HOME. Search property info on the county GIS site for free at http://arcims2.webgis.net/giles/default.asp. To name search click on Quick Search.

Gloucester County

Clerk of Circuit Court, 7400 Justice Dr, Rm 327, Gloucester, VA 23061. 804-693-2502; fax-804-693-2186; 8AM-4:30PM www.gloucesterva.info/

Index: All in one. Records indexed on a public use terminal back to 1994. Only the public may search. Copy fee $.50 per page. Cert fee- $2.00 per doc plus copy fee. Payee- Clerk of Court. **Online Judgment records:** Access to Law and Chancery judgments is free at www.courts.state.va.us/caseinfo/circuit.html. **Other phones:** Treasurer- 804-693-2141. **Property tax/Assessing-** 804-693-3451. **Online** - Click on Gloucester County to search property data for free at www.gloucesterva.info/coronlineapps/landbookdb/landbook1.asp

Goochland County

Clerk of Circuit Court, PO Box 196, Goochland, VA 23063. 804-556-5353; 8:30AM-5PM

Index: Separate indices to search include computer, older books. Records indexed on a public use terminal back to 1995 (UCC-financing-judgments) and 1994 (land). Only the public may search. Copy fee $.50 per page. Cert fee- $1.00 per page plus copy fee. Payee- Goochland County Clerk of Circuit Court. **Other phones:** Com of Revenue- 804-556-5307. **Property tax/Assessing-** PO Box 10, 1800 Sandy Hook Rd, Goochland, VA 23063; 804-556-5853. **Online-** Click on Goochland County to search property data for free at www.vamanet.com/cgi-bin/HOME.

Grayson County

Clerk of Circuit Court, PO Box 130, Independence, VA 24348-0130. 276-773-2231; fax-276-773-3338; 8AM-5PM www.graysoncountyva.com/

Index: All in one. Records indexed on computer back to 1985. Only the public may search. Copy fee $.50 per page. Cert fee- $2.00 per doc plus copy fee. Payee- Grayson Circuit Court. Treasurer- 276-773-2571. **Property tax/ Assessing-** PO Box 327, County Courthouse,Rm 202, Independence, VA 24348; 276-773-2022. www.graysongovernment.com/graysoncountytaxassessor.aspx **Online access-** Access the Real Estate Tax Search page free at www.graysoncountyva.com/graysonrealestatetax.asp. Also, access property data free at http://arcims2.webgis.net/va/grayson/.

Greene County

Clerk of Circuit Court, PO Box 386, Stanardsville, VA 22973-0386. 434-985-5208; fax-434-985-6723; 8:15AM-4:30PM No recording after 4:15). www.gcva.us/dpts/cort/clerk.htm

Index: Separate indices to search include deed, T-deed, assignments, certificates, real estate. Record index not computerized. Office will perform a UCC search but public must search other records themselves. Copy fee $.50 per page. Cert fee- $2.00 per doc plus copy fee. Payee- Greene County Circuit Court. **Other phones:** Treasurer- 434-985-5214; Elections- 434-985-5213; Vitals- 434-985-5208. **Property tax/Assessing-** 15 Ford Ave, Stanardsville, VA 22973; 434-985-5211. (Appraiser/Auditor- 434-985-5290) **Online-** Access real estate and parcel data free at www.onlinegis.net/VaGreene/. Click on Display Map then Search, no name searching.

Greensville County

Clerk of Circuit Court, PO Box 631, Emporia, VA 23847. 434-348-4215; fax-434-348-4020; 9AM-5PM.

Index: All in one. Records indexed on a public use terminal back to 1975. Only the public may search. Copy fee $.50 per page. Cert fee- $2.00 per doc plus copy fee. Payee- Deputy Clerk. **Other phones:** Treasurer- 434-348-4229. **Property tax/Assessing-** 1781 Circle Dr, Emporia, VA 23847; 434-348-4227. **Online access-** Access current assessment info and sales by VamaNet subscription at www.vamanet.com/cgi-bin/HOME. Fee is $35 per month or $300 per year with discounts for multiple localities, regions.

Halifax County

Clerk of Circuit Court, PO Box 729, Halifax, VA 24558. 434-476-6211; fax-434-476-2890; 8:30AM-4:30PM. www.oldhalifax.com/county/hfaxcnty.htm

Index: Separate indices to search include computer, books. Records indexed on a public use terminal back to 1996. Only the public may search. Will not search UCC records. Copy fee $.50 per page; marriage license- $3.00 per copy. Cert fee- $2.00 per doc plus copy fee. Payee- Clerk of Circuit Court. **Other phones:** Treasurer- 434-476-3318; Vital Records- 434-476-6211. **Property tax/Assessing-** 434-476-3314.

Hampton City

Clerk of Circuit Court, PO Box 40, Hampton, VA 23669-0040. 757-727-6105; fax-757-728-3505; 8:30AM-4PM www.hampton.gov

Index: All in one. Records indexed on computer back to 1988. Only the public may search. Search fee $10.00 for probate, will, estate or other court-related record. Copy fee $1.00 per page.Real estate record copy- $.50 per page. Cert fee- $2.00 per doc plus copy fee. Payee- Hampton Circuit Court. **Online access to Judgment records:** Search limited judgment records on the state court site at www.courts.state.va.us/caseinfo/home.html. **Other phones:** Treasurer- 757-727-6374; Elections- 757-727-6218; Vitals- 757-804-6200. **Property tax/ Assessing-** 1 Franklin St, Hampton, VA 23669; 757-727-8311. **Online** - Access City Real Estate Information free at www.hampton.gov/sol/propertysearch/accept.html. No name searching. Search property transfer pdf lists free at www.hampton.gov/assessor/ see bottom of page and click on Real Estate Property Transfers. Search property data on the GIS-mapping site free at http://198.252.241.120/hampton/public/disclaimer.htm but no name searching.

Hanover County

Clerk of Circuit Court, PO Box 39, Hanover, VA 23069-0039. 804-365-6150, R/E phone-804-365-6120; 8:30AM-4:30PM www.co.hanover.va.us

Index: Older indices in book; current records computerized. Land records indexed on a public use terminal back to 1976. Only the public may search. Copy fee $.50 per page. Cert fee- $2.00 per doc plus copy fee. Payee- Hanover County Clerk of Circuit Court. **Other phones:** Treasurer- 804-365-6050; Registrar- 804-365-6080. **Property tax/ Assessing-** PO Box 470, Hanover, VA 23069; 804-365-6029. **Online-** Access the parcel search function of the GIS site free at www.hanov ercountygis.org/hanover/ but no name searching.

Henrico County

Clerk of Circuit Court, PO Box 90775, Richmond, VA 23273. 804-501-4249 Land Records, R/E recording phone-804-501-4979, UCC phone-804-501-5468; fax-804-501-4554; 8AM-4PM; recording hours 8AM-3:30PM www.co.henrico.va.us/clerk/

Index: Separate indices to search. Records indexed on a public use terminal. Deeds from 1/68 - 5/89. Only the public may search. Copy fee $.50 per page. Cert fee- $2.00 per doc plus copy fee. Payee- Henrico Circuit Court Clerk. **Online access to Real Estate, Deed records:** County deed and land records available by subscription from private company at http://en.landsystems.com/index.php. **Other phones:** Treasurer- 804-501-7480; Elections- 804-501-4347; Vital Records- 804-225-5000. **Property tax/Assessing-** 4301 E Parham Rd, Henrico, VA 23228; 804-501-4300. (Appraiser - 804-501-4217) www.co.henrico.va.us/finance/personalproperty.html

Henry County

Clerk of Circuit Court, 3160 Kings Mountain Rd, #B, Martinsville, VA 24112. 276-634-4880; 9AM-5PM

Index: Separate indices to search deed & land records, UCCs, judgments. Records indexed on a public use terminal back to 1/1997. Office will perform a UCC search but public must search other records themselves. Search fee $20.00. Office will not search real estate records. Office will not search tax liens. Copy fee $.50 per page. Cert fee- $2.00 per doc plus copy fee; exemplification $2.50. Payee- Henry County Clerk of Circuit Court. **Other phones:** Treasurer- 276-624-4675; Elections- 276-634-4697; Vital- 276-634-4880. **Property tax/Assessing-** 3300 Kings Mountain Rd, Martinsville, VA 24112; 276-634-4610. (Appraiser/Auditor- 276-634-4610)

Highland County

Clerk of Circuit Court, PO Box 190, Monterey, VA 24465-0190. 540-468-2447; fax-540-468-3447; 8:30AM-4:30PM.

Index: All in one. Records indexed on a public use terminal back to 1993. Office will perform a UCC search but public must search other records themselves. Copy fee $.50 per page. Cert fee- $2.00 per doc plus copy fee. Payee- Sue Dudley- Clerk. Treasurer- 540-465-2265; Elections- 540-468-2013. **Property tax/Assessing-** Commissioner of Revenue, 165 W Main St, Monterey, VA 24465; 540-468-2142, assessor fax- 540-468-3447.

Hopewell City

Clerk of Circuit Court, PO Box 310, Hopewell, VA 23860. 804-541-2239; fax-804-541-2438; 8:30AM-4PM www.ci.hopewell.va.us

Index: All in one. Records indexed on a public use terminal back to 1916. Only the public may search. Copy fee $.50 per page. Cert fee- $2.00 per seal plus copy fee. Payee- Hopewell Circuit Court Clerk. **Online Judgment records:** Access to court records is free at www.courts.state.va.us/caseinfo/circuit.html. **Other phones:** Treasurer- 804-541-2240. **Property tax/Assessing-** 804-541-2234.

Isle of Wight County

Clerk of Circuit Court, PO Box 110, Isle of Wight, VA 23397. 757-365-6233, R/E recording phone-757-365-6219; fax-757-357-0884; 9AM-5PM www.co.isle-of-wight.va.us/

Index: Separate indices to search. Records indexed on a public use terminal back to 1970. Only the public may search. Copy fee $.50 per page. Cert fee- $2.00 per page plus copy fee. Payee- Isle of Wight County Clerk of Circuit Court. **Online access to Real Estate, Deed, Lien, Judgment, Will records:** Access to recorder land records is by subscription; fee is $100 per month; online deed records go back to 1970, judgments to 1991. Contact Wanda Wills at 757-365-6233 for registration and info. **Property tax/Assessing-** Commissioner of the Revenue, 17090 Monument Cir #113, PO Box 107, Isle of Wight, VA 23397; 757-365-6219, assessor fax- 757-356-9731. hours- 8:30AM-5PM **Online access-** Access the 2006 assessment database free at www.co.isle-of-wight.va.us/assessment.html but no name searching. Also, access property data via the GIS-mapping site free at http://ims.spatialsys.com/isleofwight/, but no name searching. Also, click on Isle of Wight County to search property records free at www.vamanet.com/cgi-bin/MAPSRCHPGM?LOCAL=ISL.

James City County

Clerk of Circuit Court, 5201 Monticello Ave, #6, Williamsburg, VA 23188. 757-564-2242, R/E recording phone-757-564-2349, fax-757-564-2329; 8:30AM-4PM www.jccegov.com/courts/index.html

Office also handles filings for the City of Williamsburg. Index: All in one. Records indexed on a public use terminal back to 1981. Only the public may search. Copy fee $.50 per page. Cert fee- $2.00 per doc plus copy fee. Payee- Williamsburg-James City County Clerk of Circuit Court. **Other phones:** Treasurer- 757-229-6705. **Property tax/Assessing-** 101 F Mounts Bay Rd, Williamsburg, VA 23187; 757-253-6650, assessor fax- 757-253-6601. **Online access-** Access assessment data free at http://property.jccegov.com/parcelviewer/. Search City of Williamsburg property assessor data free at http://williamsburggis.com/default.aspx. At map, click on find to search. Search by name on tax payment site at https://first.jccegov.com/epayment/taxpayer.aspx.

King and Queen County

Clerk of Circuit Court, PO Box 67, King and Queen Court House, VA 23085. 804-785-5984; fax-804-

785-5698; 9AM-5PM. www.kingandqueenco.net/html/Govt/circct.html
Index: All in one. Records indexed on a public use terminal back to 1995. Only the public may search. Copy fee $.50 per page. Cert fee- $2.00 per doc plus copy fee. Payee- King and Queen County Clerk of Circuit Court. **Other phones:** Treasurer- 804-785-5978; Elections- 804-785-5980; Vital Records- 804-662-6200; Zoning, Planning- 804-785-5975. **Property tax/Assessing-** PO Box 178, Commissioner of the Revenue, King and Queen Court House, VA 23085; 804-785-5976, assessor fax- 804-785-5880. www.kingandqueenco.net/html/Govt/commrev.html

King George County

Clerk of Circuit Court, 9483 Kings Hwy, #3, King George, VA 22485. 540-775-3322; fax-540-775-5466; 8:30AM-4:30PM
Index: Separate indices to search. Records indexed on a public use terminal back to 1721. UCC search per debtor name $10.00. Real estate owner, mortgage, and property transfer searches available. Office will search UCC records, tax liens not included in UCC search. Copy fee $.50 per page. Cert fee- $2.00 per doc plus copy fee. Payee- King George County Clerk of Circuit Court. **Other phones:** Treasurer- 540-775-2571. **Property tax/ Assessing-** 540-775-4664. **Online access-** Access property data free at www.onlinegis.net/VaKingGeorge/. Click on Display Map then Search, no name searching. Also, access current assessment info and sales by VamaNet subscription at www.vamanet.com/cgi-bin/HOME. Fee is $35 per month or $300 per year with discounts for multiple localities, regions.

King William County

Clerk of Circuit Court, PO Box 216, King William, VA 23086. 804-769-4936; fax-804-769-4991; 8:30AM-4:30PM
Index: Separate indices to search include computer and book. Records indexed on a public use terminal back to 1999. Only the public may search. Copy fee $.50 per page. Cert fee- $2.00 per doc plus copy fee. Payee- King William County Clerk of Circuit Court. Treasurer- 804-769-4931; Elections- 804-769-4952. **Property tax/Assessing-** PO Box 217, 180 Horse Landing Rd, King William, VA 23086; 804-769-4942. **Online-** Access real estate records free at http://kwrealestate.kingwilliamcounty.us/applications/txapps/index.htm

Lancaster County

Clerk of Circuit Court, PO Box 99, Lancaster, VA 22503. 804-462-5611; fax-804-462-9978; 8:30AM-4:30PM www.lancova.com
Index: All in one. Records indexed on a public use terminal back to 1994. Only the public may search. Copy fee $.50 per page. Cert fee- $2.00 per doc plus copy fee. Payee- Lancaster County Clerk of Circuit Court. **Online Real Estate, Deed, Judgment, Will, Marriage, Chancery records:** Access to Circuit Court Records Search System is by subscription at http://208.210.219.102/cgi-bin/p/rms.cgi. Includes images for other selected jurisdictions; $600 per year, username and password required, signup with local Circuit Ct Clerk. **Other phones:** Treasurer- 804-462-5630; Elections- 804-462-5277. **Property tax/ Assessing-** 8311 Maryball Rd, Lancaster, VA 22503; 804-462-7920. hours- 9AM-5PM **Online access-** Access current assessment info and sales by VamaNet subscription at wwww.vamanet.com/cgi-bin/HOME. Fee is $35 per month or $300 per year with discounts for multiple localities, regions. Also, access parcel data free on the GIS-mapping site free at www.lancova.com/GIS/disclaimer.asp.

Lee County

Clerk of Circuit Court, PO Box 326, Jonesville, VA 24263. 276-346-7763; fax-276-346-3440; 8:30-5PM.
Index: All in one. Records indexed on a public use terminal back to 1981. Office will perform a UCC search or a basic name search but public must search other records themselves. Search fee-$10.00 for UCC. Copy fee $.50 per page. Will fax to local # for $1.00 per page; $2.00 login-distance. Cert fee- $3.00 per doc plus copy fee. Payee- Lee County Circuit Ct Clerk. **Online access to Real Estate, Deed, Lien, Judgment, Will, Marriage, UCC records:** Access to the recorder's database is available by subscription, registration and password required; $50 per month or $500 per year. Contact clerk's office for registration form. Deeds go back to 1/19/1957; judgments and wills to 8/1978, marriages to 1/1958, financing statements to 1/1995. **Other phones:** Treasurer- 276-346-7716; Elections- 276-346-7780. **Property tax/Assessing-** 276-346-7722.

Loudoun County

Clerk of Circuit Court, PO Box 550; Attn- Land Records, Leesburg, VA 20178. 703-777-0270; 8:30AM-4:30PM
www.loudoun.gov/Default.aspx?tabid=798
Index: Books. Records indexed on a public use terminal back to 1969. Only the public may search. Copy fee $.50 per page. Cert fee- $2.00 per doc plus copy fee. Payee- Loudoun County Clerk of Circuit Court. **Online Real Estate, Deed, Will, Estate, Judgment, Plat, UCC records:** Access to recorders land records of deeds, wills, judgment, plats and UCCs is by subscription, see Land Records in Quick Links www.loudoun.gov/Default.aspx?tabid=798. Fee is $1300 per year; deeds go back to 1893, wills 1928 judgments 1985, UCCs 1996. **Other phones:** Treasurer- 703-777-0280. **Property tax/Assessing-** PO Box 7000 M/S #07, 1 Harrison St SE 5th Fl, Leesburg, VA 201; 703-777-0267. www.loudoun.gov/Default.aspx?tabid=624 **Online-** Search the property assessor data for free at http://inter1.loudoun.gov/webpdbs/. No name searching; search by address, number, or ID only. Access property data on the GIS-mapping site free at http://gisinter1.loudoun.gov/weblogis/agree.htm but no name searching.

Louisa County

Clerk of Circuit Court, PO Box 37, Louisa, VA 23093. 540-967-5312, R/E recording phone-540-967-3435, UCC recording phone-540-967-5312; fax-540-967-2705; 8:30AM-5PM (stop recording 4:15PM). www.louisacounty.com/
Index: All in one. Records indexed on a public use terminal back to 1990. Only the public may search. Copy fee $.50 per page. Cert fee- $2.50 per doc includes copy fee. Payee- Louisa County Clerk of Circuit Court. Treasurer- 540-967-3435; Elections- 540-967-7427. **Property tax/ Assessing-** Commissioner of the Revenue, PO Box 8, Louisa, VA 23093; 540-967-3450. www.louisacounty.com/LCconst/commrev-staff.htm **Online access-** Search property and person property tax data for free at https://louweb.louisa.org/Applications/web/default.htm. Also, search property on the GIS-mapping site free at http://gis.timmons.com/louisaims/gis.aspx. Click on Search. Search assessment data free at http://louweb.louisa.org/assess/master_Q.asp, Also, access assessment info and sales by VamaNet subscription at www.vamanet.com/cgi-bin/HOME. Fee- $35 per month or $300 per year; discounts for multiple localities, regions.

Lunenburg County

Clerk of Circuit Court, 11435 Courthouse Rd, Lunenburg, VA 23952. 434-696-2132; fax-434-696-3931; 8:30AM-4:30PM
Index: All in one. Records indexed on a public use terminal back to 2001. Only the public may search. Copy fee $.50 per page. Cert fee- $2.00 per doc plus copy fee. Payee- Lunenburg County Clerk of Circuit Court. **Property tax/Assessing-** 11512 Courthouse Rd, Lunenburg, VA 23952; 434-696-2516.

Lynchburg City

Clerk of Circuit Court, PO Box 4, Lynchburg, VA 24505. 434-455-2620; fax-434-847-1864; 8:15AM-4:45PM
Records indexed_on a public use terminal back to 2001. Office will perform a UCC search but public must search other records themselves. Search fee $20.00 per name. Copy fee $.50 per page. Cert fee- $2.00 per doc plus copy fee. Payee- Lynchburg City Clerk of Circuit Court. Treasurer- 434-455-4242. **Property tax/Assessing-** 434-455-3830.

Madison County

Clerk of Circuit Court, PO Box 220, Madison, VA 22727-0220. 540-948-6888; fax-540-948-3759; 8:30AM-4:30PM.
Index: Separate indices include pre-1991 documents have multiple indices to search. Records indexed on a public use terminal back to 1991. Only the public may search. Copy fee $.50 per page. Cert fee- $2.00 per doc plus copy fee. Payee- Clerk of Circuit Court. **Other phones:** Treasurer- 540-948-4409. **Property tax/Assessing-** 134 E Main, Rexburg, ID 83440; 208-359-6200 Option 2, assessor fax- 208-359-0856. **Online** - Access property data free at www.onlinegis.net/VaMadison/. Click on Display Map then Search, no name searching. Also, access current assessment info and sales by VamaNet subscription at www.vamanet.com/cgi-bin/HOME. Fee is $35 per month or $300 per year with discounts for multiple localities, regions.

Martinsville City

Clerk of Circuit Court, PO Box 1206, Martinsville, VA 24114-1206. 276-403-5105, R/E recording phone-276-403-5106; fax-276-403-5232; 9AM-5PM www.ci.martinsville.va.us/Circuitclerk/
Index: All in one. Records indexed on a public use terminal back to 1972 for deeds, 1980 for judgments. Only the public may search. Copy fee $.50 per page. Cert fee- $2.00 per doc plus copy fee. Payee- Martinsville City Clerk of Circuit Court. **Online Real Estate, Deed, Judgment, Will, Marriage, Delinquent Tax records:** Access Circuit clerk records at www.ci.martinsville.va.us/Circuitclerk/subscription_page.htm. Fee is $30.00 per month, or you may search at a rate of $1 per doc. For info, call office of Ashby Pritchett at 276-656-5106 or visit website. **Other phones:** Treasurer- 276-403-5240; Other phone- 276-403-5206. **Property tax/Assessing-** 55 W Church St, Rm 101, Martinsville, VA 24112; 276-403-5131, fax- 276-403-5337. (Appraiser/Auditor-276-403-5336) A public access terminal is available. www.ci.martinsville.va.us/CommRev/index.htm
Online access- Access to GIS/mapping for free go to http://gis.co.henry.va.us/

Mathews County

Clerk of Circuit Court, PO Box 463, Mathews, VA 23109. 804-725-2550; fax-804-725-7456; 8AM-4PM
Index: All in one. Record index not computerized. Office will perform a UCC search but public must search other records themselves. Copy fee $.50 per page. Cert fee- $2.00 per page plus copy fee. Payee- Mathews County Clerk of Circuit Court. Treasurer- 804-725-2341. **Property tax/Assessing-** PO Box 896, Mathews, VA 23109; 804-725-7168. hours- 8:30AM-4PM

Mecklenburg County

Clerk of Circuit Court, PO Box 530, Boydton, VA 23917-0530. 434-738-6191; fax-434-738-6861; 8:30AM-5PM
Index: All in one. Records indexed on a public use terminal. Only the public may search. Copy fee $.50 per page. Cert fee- $2.00 per doc plus copy fee. Payee- Mecklenburg County Clerk of Circuit Court. **Other phones:** Treasurer- 434-738-6191; Elections- 434-738-6191; Vital Records- 434-738-6191. **Property tax/Assessing-** 393 Washington St, Boydton, VA 23917; 434-738-6191. www.mecklenburgva.com/govt/LB_DL.html **Online access-** For access to land files free go to www.mecklenburgva.com/govt/meckcor/.

Middlesex County

Clerk of Circuit Court, PO Box 158, Saluda, VA 23149. 804-758-5317; fax-804-758-8637; 8:30AM-4:30PM

Index: All in one. Records indexed on a public use terminal back to beginning of 2006. Only the public may search. Copy fee $.50 per page. Cert fee- $2.00 per page plus copy fee. Payee- Middlesex County Clerk of Circuit Court. **Other phones:** Treasurer-804-758-5302; Elections- 804-758-4420. **Property tax/Assessing-** 804-758-5331. (Appraiser/Auditor-804-758-5331) **Online access-** Access current assessment info and sales by VamaNet subscription at www.vamanet.com/cgi-bin/HOME. Fee is $35 per month or $300 per year with discounts for multiple localities, regions.

Montgomery County

Clerk of Circuit Court, PO Box 6309, Christiansburg, VA 24068. 540-382-5760; fax-540-382-6937; 8:30AM-4:30PM.

Index: All in one. Records indexed on a public use terminal back to 1967. Only the public may search. Copy fee $.50 per page. Cert fee- $2.00 per doc plus copy fee. Payee- Clerk of Circuit Court. **Online access to Real Estate, Deed records:** Land record access via subscription service ILS; call 804-786-5511 to apply; $80 monthly fee. **Other phones:** Treasurer- 540-382-5723; Elections- 540-382-5741; Vital Records- 540-382-5760; Public Information Office- 540-381-6887. **Property tax/Assessing-** 755 Roanoke St, #1A, Christiansburg VA, 24073-3170; 540-382-5717, fax- 540-381-6838. (Appraiser - 540-382-5715) hours- 9AM-5PM www.montva.com/departments/cmsh/ **Online access-** Search county property index free at http://quicksearch.webgis.net/search.php?site=va_montgomery. Also, access to the county Tax Parcel Information System database is free at www.montva.com/departments/plan/igis.php. Records on the Town of Blacksburg GIS site are free at http://arcims2.webgis.net/blacksburg/default.asp?. To name search, click on Quick Search.

Nelson County

Clerk of Circuit Court, PO Box 10, Lovingston, VA 22949. 434-263-7020; fax-434-263-7027; 8AM-5PM

Index: Separate indices to search include manual indices from 1809 to 1993, automated from 1993 to present. Records indexed on a public use terminal back to 1993. Only the public may search. Copy fee $.50 per page. Cert fee- $2.50 per cert plus copy fee. Payee- Nelson County Clerk of Circuit Court. **Other phones:** Treasurer- 434-263-7060; Elections- 434-263-4068. **Property tax/Assessing-** 84 Courthouse Sq, Lovingston, VA 22949; 434-263-7070, assessor fax- 434-263-7074. hours- 9AM-5PM

New Kent County

Clerk of Circuit Court, PO Box 98, New Kent, VA 23124-0098. 804-966-9520; fax-804-966-9528; 8:30AM-4:30PM.

Index: All in one. Records indexed on a public use terminal back to 1984. Only the public may search. General copy fee $.50 per page. Cert fee- $2.00 per doc plus copy fee. Payee- Clerk. **Other phones:** Treasurer- 804-966-9615. **Property tax/Assessing-** 804-966-9610. **Online access-** Access to New Kent county assessor records is free at http://data.visionappraisal.com/NewKentCountyVA/.

Newport News City

Clerk of Circuit Court, 2500 Washington Ave; Courthouse, Newport News, VA 23607. 757-926-8561, R/E recording phone-757-926-8355, UCC recording phone-757-926-8349; fax-757-926-8531; 8AM-4:45PM. www.newport-news.va.us

Index: All in one. Records indexed on a public use terminal back to 1985. Only the public may search. Copy fee $.50 per page. Cert fee- $2.00 per doc plus copy fee. Payee- Clerk. **Other phones:** Treasurer-757-926-8731. **Property tax/Assessing-** 700 Town Center Dr #220, Newport News, VA 23606; 757-926-1926. hours- 8AM-5PM A public access terminal is available. www.nngov.com/assessor **Online access-** Access the City's "Real Estate on the Web" data free at www.nngov.com/assessor/resources/reis. Search by address or parcel number; new "advanced search" may include name searching. Search for property data free on the gis-mapping site at http://gis.nngov.com/gis/. No name searching. Use the black circle with the 'I' in it to show parcel data.

Norfolk City

Clerk of Circuit Court, 100 St. Paul's Blvd, Norfolk, VA 23510-2773. 757-664-4380; 8:45AM-4:45PM www.norfolk.gov/Circuit_Court/ccchome.asp

Index: All in one. Records indexed on a public use terminal back to 1986. Office personnel or visitors may perform searches. Search fee $10.00 per name. Real estate owner, mortgage, and property transfer searches available. Office will not search UCC records. Copy fee $1.00 per page.Real estate record copy- $.50 per page. Cert fee- $2.00 per doc plus copy fee. Payee- Clerk, Circuit Court. **Online access to Real Estate, Deed, Judgment, Lien, Will, Marriage records:** Access Clerk of Circuit Court recording data by $50 per month subscription at www.norfolk.gov/Circuit_Court/remoteaccess.asp. Deeds and land records go back to 1988; Judgments, Wills, Marriages, etc, back to 1993. Also, access to Circuit Court Records Search System is by subscription at http://208.210.219.102/cgi-bin/p/rms.cgi. Includes images for other selected jurisdictions; $1200 per year, username and password required, signup with local Circuit Ct Clerk. **Other phones:** Treasurer- 757-664-7800; Elections- 757-664-4353. **Property tax/ Assessing-** 100 St. Paul's Blvd, Norfolk, VA 23510; 757-664-4732. **Online access-** Records on the City of Norfolk Real Estate Property Assessment database are free at www.norfolk.gov/RealEstate/search.asp.

Northampton County

Clerk of Circuit Court, PO Box 36, Eastville, VA 23347. 757-678-0465; fax-757-678-5410; 9AM-5PM. www.courts.state.va.us/courts/circuit/Northampton/home.html

Index: All in one. Records indexed on a public use terminal back to 1997. Only the public may search. Copy fee $.50 per page. Cert fee- 2.00 per name. Payee- Northampton County Clerk of Circuit Court. **Other phones:** Treasurer- 757-678-0450; Elections-757-678-0480. **Property tax/Assessing-** 16404 Courthouse Rd, Eastville, VA 23347; 757-678-0446.

Northumberland County

Clerk of Circuit Court, PO Box 217, Heathsville, VA 22473. 804-580-3700; fax-804-580-2261; 8:30AM-4:30PM www.co.northumberland.va.us/

Index: Separate index books to search include deed, grantor/grantee, judgments, wills. Records indexed on a public use terminal back to 1987, but deed records only. Office personnel or visitors may perform searches. Office will perform limited searches. No search fee. Office will not search real estate records. Office will not search UCC records. Copy fee $.50 per page. Cert fee- $2.00 per doc plus copy fee. Payee- Northumberland County Clerk of Circuit Court. **Other phones:** Treasurer- 804-580-5201. **Property tax/Assessing-** PO Box 309, Heathsville, VA 22473; 804-580-4600, assessor fax- 804-580-4321. **Online access-** Access Land Book data free at www.co.northumberland.va.us/NH-land-book.htm.

Nottoway County

Clerk of Circuit Court, PO Box 25, Nottoway, VA 23955. 434-645-9043; fax-434-645-2201; 8:30AM-4:30PM.

Index: All in one. Records indexed on a public use terminal back to 1975. Office will perform a UCC search but public must search other records themselves. Search fee-$10.00 per hour. Copy fee $.50 per page. Cert fee- $2.00 per doc plus copy fee. Payee- Clerk of Circuit Court. **Other phones:** Treasurer- 434-645-9318; Elections- 434-645-8148; Vital Records- 434-645-9043 (marriage licenses only). **Property tax/Assessing-** 434-645-9317. (Appraiser - 434-645-9317) **Online-** Access property data free at http://arcims2.webgis.net/va/nottoway/.

Orange County

Clerk of Circuit Court, PO Box 230, Orange, VA 22960. 540-672-4030; fax-540-672-2939; 8:30AM-4:30PM. www.courts.state.va.us/courts/circuit/Orange/home.html

Index: All in one. Records indexed on a public use terminal back to 1995. Only the public may search. Copy fee $.50 per page. Cert fee- $2.00 per page plus copy fee. Payee- Clerk of Circuit Court. **Other phones:** Treasurer- 540-672-2656. **Property tax/Assessing-** Commissioner of the Revenue, 112 W Main St, Orange, VA 22960; 540-672-4441, assessor fax- 540-672-5461. (Appraiser/Auditor- 540-672-4441) **Online access-** Access property data free at www.onlinegis.net/VaOrange/. Click on Display Map then Search, no name searching. Also search Town of Orange property free at www.onlinegis.net/VATOO/asp/controlVersion.asp. Click on Orange County to search for property records for free at www.vamanet.com/cgi-bin/HOME.

Page County

Clerk of Circuit Court, 116 S Court St, #A, Luray, VA 22835. 540-743-4064; fax-540-743-2338; 9AM-5PM.

Index: Separate indices to search. Records indexed on computer back to 1981. Office personnel or visitors may perform searches. UCC search per debtor name $20.00. Office will not search real estate records or tax liens. Office will search UCC records only if requested in writing on "Information Request" form. Copy fee $.50 per page. Cert fee- $2.00 per doc plus copy fee. Payee- C. Ron Wilson-Clerk. **Other phones:** Treasurer- 540-743-3975; Elections- 540-743-3986. **Property tax/Assessing-** 101 S Court St, Luray, VA 22835; 540-743-3840. **Online access-** Access current assessment info and sales by VamaNet subscription at www.vamanet.com/cgi-bin/HOME. Fee is $35 per month or $300 per year with discounts for multiple localities, regions.

Patrick County

Clerk of Circuit Court, PO Box 148, Stuart, VA 24171. 276-694-7213; fax-276-694-6943; 9AM-5PM.

Index: Separate indices to search. Records indexed on a public use terminal back to 99. Only the public may search. Copy fee $.50 per page. Cert fee- $2.00 per doc plus copy fee. Payee- Patrick County. **Other phones:** Treasurer- 276-694-7257; Elections- 276-694-7206. **Property tax/Assessing-** 276-694-7131 x276. **Online access-** Access property data free at http://arcims.webgis.net/va/patrick/default.asp?pg=95. Map searching only, no name searching.

Petersburg City

Clerk of Circuit Court, 7 Courthouse Ave, Petersburg, VA 23803. 804-733-2367, R/E recording phone-804-733-2367 x4122; fax-804-732-5548; 8AM-4PM.

Index: All in one. Records indexed on computer from 2001-current; land records prior to year 2001 in deed books. Only the public may search. Will not search UCC records. Copy fee $.50 per page. Cert fee- $2.00 per doc plus copy fee. Payee- Clerk of Court. **Other phones:** Treasurer- 804-733-2321. **Property tax/Assessing-** 804-733-2333.

Pittsylvania County

Clerk of Circuit Court, PO Drawer 31, Chatham, VA 24531. 434-432-7887, R/E recording phone-434-432-7888, UCC recording phone-434-432-7887; fax-434-432-7913; 8:30AM-5PM

See Danville City for Real Estate and Lien records online for Danville City. Index: All in one. Records indexed on a public use terminal back to 1995. Only the public may search. Copy fee $1.00 per page. Cert fee- $2.00 per doc plus copy fee. Payee- Pittsylvania County Clerk of Circuit Court. **Other phones:** Treasurer- 434-432-7961; Elections- 434-432-7971. **Property tax/Assessing-** 434-432-7949. **Online**

access- Search parcel information free at http://www2.undersys.com/pvaweb/pittsylvania.html. Click on Search For Property to name search.

Portsmouth City

Clerk of Circuit Court, PO Box 1217, Portsmouth, VA 23705. 757-393-8671; fax-757-399-4826; 8:30AM-5PM www.portsmouthva.gov

Index: Separate indices to search include deeds and land, marriage, wills and fiduciary, UCC, Judgments, General Misc. Records indexed on a public use terminal back to 1970. Office personnel or visitors may perform searches. Search fee $10.00 per name. Office will not search real estate records or UCC records. Will not search UCC records. Copy fee $.50 per page. Cert fee- $2.00 per cert plus copy fee. Payee- Portsmouth Clerk of Circuit Court. **Other phones:** Treasurer- 757-393-8651; Elections- 757-393-8644. **Property tax/Assessing-** 801 Crawford St 2nd Fl, Portsmouth, VA 23704; 757-393-8631. (Appraiser - 757-393-8771) hours- 8AM-5PM **Online -** Access to property records is free at www.portsmouthva.gov/assessor/data/realestatesearch.htm. No name searching. Access the treasurer's Real Estate Receivable Data free at www.portsmouthva.gov/treasurer/data/realestatereceivsearch.htm. but not name searching. Also, search GIS-mapping site for parcel data free at www.portsmouthva.gov/website/parcel_flood/intro.htm. Use map tools to identify parcel data.

Powhatan County

Clerk of Circuit Court, PO Box 37, Powhatan, VA 23139-0037. 804-598-5660; fax-804-598-5608; 8:30AM-5PM www.powhatanva.gov/

Index: All in one. Records indexed on a public use terminal back to 1976. Office will perform a UCC search but public must search other records themselves. Copy fee $.50 per page. Cert fee- $2.00 per doc plus copy fee. Payee- Wm. E. Maxey Jr, Clerk. **Online access to Real Estate, Grantor/Grantee, Deed, Mortgage, Lien, Judgment, Marriage, Will records:** Access recorder's index by subscription service ILS; call 877-658-6018 x2111 to apply,, ask for Johnathan; $80 monthly fee ad credit cards accepted. **Other phones:** Treasurer- 804-598-5626; Elections- 804-598-5604. **Property tax/Assessing-** 5834 Old Buckingham Rd #C, Powhatan, VA 12139; 804-598-5617, assessor fax- 804-598-1532. (Appraiser/Auditor- 804-598-5617) **Online access-** Click on Powhatan County to search property data for free at www.vamanet.com/cgi-bin/HOME. Also, search assessment and reassessment data free at www.powhatancountyrealestate.com/.

Prince Edward County

Clerk of Circuit Court, PO Box 304, Farmville, VA 23901. 434-392-5145; fax-434-392-3913; 8:30AM-4:30PM www.courts.state.va.us/courts/circuit/Prince_Edward/home.html

Index: All in one. Records indexed on a public use terminal back to 1916. Only the public may search. Copy fee $.50 per page. Cert fee- $2.00 per doc plus copy fee. Payee- Prince Edward County Clerk of Circuit Court. **Other phones:** Treasurer- 434-392-3404; Elections- 434-392-4767. **Property tax/Assessing-** 434-392-3231.

Prince George County

Clerk of Circuit Court, PO Box 98, Prince George, VA 23875-0098. 804-733-2640; fax-804-861-5721; Recording hours 8:30AM-4:30PM

Index: All in one. Records indexed on computer back to 4/96. Only the public may search. Copy fee $.50 per page. Cert fee- $2.00 per cert plus copy fee. Payee- Prince George County Clerk of Circuit Court. **Other phones:** Treasurer- 804-733-2620. **Property tax/Assessing-** 804-733-2616.

Prince William County

Clerk of Circuit Court, 9311 Lee Ave, Rm 300, Manassas, VA 20110-5598. 703-792-6035; fax-703-792-6083; hours - 8:30AM-4:30PM. www.pwcgov.org/default.aspx?topic=040017

Index: All in one. Records indexed on a public use terminal back to 1918 for Deeds. Office will perform a UCC search but public must search other records themselves. UCC search per debtor name $20.00. Copy fee $.50 per page. Cert fee- $2.00 per doc plus copy fee. Payee- Clerk of Court. GIS department offers data burnt to CD for delivery with $7.00 media fee. **Online Real Estate, Deed, Lien, Mortgage, UCC, Plat, Judgment, Will, Fictitious Name, Marriage records:** Access to the clerk's exhaustive database is by subscription; fee is $300 per quarter. Login at https://www3.pwcgov.org/panet/logon.asp. Most records go back to mid-1980's; deeds back to 1918. **Other phones:** Vital Records- 703-792-6045 (marriage only). **Property tax/Assessing-** 703-792-6780. **Online access-** Records on the county Property Assessment Information database are free at http://www4.pwcgov.org/realestate/LandRover.asp but no name searching. Also, City Commissioner of the Revenue's real estate assessment data is at http://data.visionappraisal.com/ManassasVA/..

Pulaski County

Clerk of Circuit Court, 45 3rd St NW, #101, Pulaski, VA 24301. 540-980-7825; fax-540-980-7835; 8:30AM-4:30PM www.courts.state.va.us/courts/circuit/Pulaski/home.html

Index: All in one. Records indexed on a public use terminal back to 1995. Only the public may search. Copy fee $.50 per page. Cert fee- $1.50 per page plus copy fee. Payee- Pulaski County Clerk of Circuit Court. Treasurer- 540-980-7785; Elections- 540-980-1222. **Property tax/Assessing-** 540-980-7753. (Appraiser - 540-980-7753) **Online-** Access to the county GIS mapping info is free at http://arcims2.webgis.net/pulaski/default.asp. No name searching.

Radford City

Clerk of Circuit Court, 619 2nd St; Radford, VA 24141. 540-731-3610; fax-540-731-3612; 8:30AM-5PM (No machine receipts after 4:30PM).

Index: Separate indices to search include land, orders, judgments, fiduciary, court. Records indexed on a public use terminal back to 2000. Only the public may search. Office will not search real estate records. Office will not search UCC records or tax liens. Copy fee $.50 per page. Cert fee- $2.00 per doc plus copy fee. Payee- Radford City Clerk of Circuit Court. **Online access to Real Estate, Deed records:** Access to real estate recording docs to be available by subscription with Intern. Land Systems, call 877-658-6018 x205 for info. **Other phones:** Treasurer- 540-731-3661; Elections- 540-731-3639; Vital Records- 540-731-3610. **Property tax/Assessing-** 619 2nd St, Radford, VA 24141; 540-731-6248, assessor fax- 540-731-3635. (Appraiser/Auditor- 540-731-3613) hours- 8:30AM-5PM **Online access-** Access City property card info at www.radford.va.us/inVizeDA/inVizeDA.aspx. Also, access GIS-mapping/property data free at www.radford.va.us/lclmapping/RadfordGIS_web.htm

Rappahannock County

Clerk of Circuit Court, PO Box 517, Washington, VA 22747-0517. 540-675-5350; 8:30AM-4:30PM

Index: All in one. Records indexed on a public use terminal back to 1/1995. Only the public may search. Will not search UCC records. Copy fee $.50 per page. Cert fee- $2.00 per doc plus copy fee. Payee- Rappahannock County Clerk of Circuit Court. Bulk data available for purchase. **Other phones:** Treasurer- 540-675-5360; Elections- 540-675-5380; Vital Records- 804-662-6200. **Property tax/Assessing-** PO Box115, 262 Gay St, Washington, VA 22747; 540-675-5370, assessor fax- 540-675-5371. (Appraiser/Auditor- 540-675-5370) **Online access-** Access current assessment info and sales by VamaNet subscription at www.vamanet.com/cgi-bin/HOME. Fee is $35 per month or $300 per year with discounts for multiple localities, regions.

Richmond City

Clerk of Circuit Court, 400 N 9th St, Richmond, VA 23219. 804-646-6505; 8:45AM-4:45PM

City of Richmond is not in Richmond County. The city bordered by Henrico and Chesterfield Counties. Index: Separate indices to search include computer, microfilm, books. Records indexed on a public use terminal back to 1993. Office will perform a UCC search but public must search other records themselves. Office will not search real estate records. Copy fee $.50 per page. Cert fee- $2.00 per doc plus copy fee. Payee- Richmond City Clerk of Circuit Court. **Other phones:** Treasurer- 804-646-6474; Elections- 804-646-5950; Records Rm -804-646-6530. **Property tax/Assessing-** 804-646-5600. (Appraiser/Auditor- 804-646-5616) **Online access-** Search the city's Property & Real Estate Assessment data for free at www.richmondgov.com/departments/gis/gisparcelmapper.aspx. At the Webmapper page, click on "Advanced Search" then "Assessments" to name search.

Richmond County

Clerk of Circuit Court, PO Box 1000, Warsaw, VA 22572-1000. 804-333-3781; fax-804-333-5396; 9AM-5PM www.co.richmond.va.us

City of Richmond is a separate filing office and is not located in this county. The only ZIP Codes for this county are 22572, 22460, 22472, 22548, and part of 22435. Index: Separate indices to search include land records index, will index. Records indexed on a public use terminal for land records, 1996 for will records. Office will perform a UCC search but public must search other records themselves. Search fee $10.00 per name. Copy fee $.50 per page. Old records- $1.00 per page. Cert fee- $2.00 per doc plus copy fee. Payee- Richmond County Clerk of Circuit Court. **Online access to Real Estate, Deed, Lien records:** Access recorders land data by subscription at https://csa.landsystems.com/LROnline/logon.aspx. Individual account- $80.00 per month; 5-user business account- $200 per month. **Other phones:** Treasurer- 804-333-3555; Elections- 804-333-4772; Vital Records- 804-333-3781. **Property tax/Assessing-** PO Box 366, 101 Court Circle, Warsaw, VA 22572; 804-333-3722, assessor fax- 804-313-2208. (Appraiser/Auditor- 804-333-5062) A public access terminal is available. **Online access-** Search county parcel data on the GIS-mapping site free at www.onlinegis.net/VaRichmond/.

Roanoke City

Clerk of Circuit Court, PO Box 2610, Roanoke, VA 24010-2610. 540-853-6702; fax-540-853-1024; 8:15AM-4:45PM

Index: All in one. Records indexed on a public use terminal, images back to 1998, records back to 1991. Only the public may search. Copy fee $.50 per page; $.75 for oversized. Cert fee- $2.00 per doc plus copy fee. Payee- Roanoke City Clerk of Circuit Court. **Other phones:** Treasurer- 540-853-2561. **Property tax/ Assessing-** City Treasurer, PO Box 1451, Roanoke, VA 24007; 540-853-2561, assessor fax- 540-853-1019. hours- 8AM-5PM **Online access-** Access to property data is free on the City GIS website at http://gis.roanokeva.gov/text.htm.

Roanoke County

Clerk of Circuit Court, PO Box 1126, Salem, VA 24153-1126. 540-387-6205; fax-540-387-6145; 8:30AM-4:30PM. www.roanokecountyva.gov

Index: Separate indices to search include computer, books. Records indexed on a public use terminal back to 2000. Office will perform a UCC search but public must search other records themselves. Copy fee $.50 per page. Cert fee- $2.00 per doc plus copy fee. Payee- Clerk. Bulk data available for purchase, contact Myra Williamson. **Other phones:** Elections- 540-772-7500. **Property tax/Assessing-** PO Box 29800, 5204 Bernard Dr SW, #200D, Roanoke, VA 24018; 540-772-2035, fax- 540-772-7129. hours- 8AM-5PM A public access terminal is available. www.roanokecountyva.gov/Departments/Commissio

nerOfTheRevenue/ **Online access**- Access to property data is free on the county GIS mapping site at http://eservices.roanokecountyva.gov/GIS/roanoke/.

Rockbridge County

Clerk of Circuit Court, 2 S Main St; Courthouse, Lexington, VA 24450-2599. 540-463-2232; 8:30AM-4:30PM. www.co.rockbridge.va.us/

Includes City of Lexington. Index: All in one. Records indexed on a public use terminal back to 2000. Only the public may search. Copy fee $.50 per page. Cert fee- $2.50 per doc plus copy fee. Payee- Clerk's Office. Bulk data available for purchase, contact David Whitesell. **Other phones:** Treasurer- 540-463-2613; Elections- 540-463-7203. **Property tax/Assessing**- 150 S Main St, Lexington, VA 24450; 540-463-3431, assessor fax- 540-463-4082. (Appraiser - 540-463-3431) hours- 8:30AM-5PM. **Online access**- Access county records on the GIS-mapping site free at http://quicksearch.webgis.net/search.php?site=va_rockbridge. Also, access City of Lexington property data free at www.vamanet.com/cgi-bin/MAPSRCHPGM?LOCAL=LEX. Also, access county current assessment info and sales by VamaNet subscription at www.vamanet.com/cgi-bin/HOME. Fee is $35 per month or $300 per year with discounts for multiple localities, regions.

Rockingham County

Clerk of Circuit Court, Courtsquare, Harrisonburg, VA 22801. 540-564-3126; fax-540-564-3127; 9-5.

Index: All in one. Records indexed on a public use terminal back to 1944. Office will perform a UCC search but public must search other records themselves. Copy fee $.50 per page. Cert fee- $2.00 per doc plus copy fee.Payee- Clerk. **Online Real Estate, Real Property records:** Access to real property by subscription at https://www.uslandrecords.com/uslr/UslrApp/index.jsp. **Other phones:** Treasurer- 540-564-2408; Elections- 540-564-3055. **Property tax/Assessing**- 20 E Gay St, Harrisonburg, VA 22802; 540-564-3068, assessor fax- 540-564-1488. hours- 8AM-5PM **Online access**- Access to real estate assessment records at http://rockingham.gisbrowser.com/home.cfm.

Russell County

Clerk of Circuit Court, PO Box 435, Lebanon, VA 24266. 276-889-8023; fax-276-889-8003; 8:30-5PM.

Index: All in one. Records indexed on a public use terminal back to 1983. Only the public may search. Copy fee $.50 per page. Cert fee- None. Payee- Russell County Clerk. **Online access to Real Estate, Deed records:** County deed and land records available by subscription from private company at http://en.landsystems.com/index.php. **Other phones:** Treasurer- 276-889-8028. **Property tax/Assessing**- 276-889-8014. **Online access**- Access current assessment info and sales by VamaNet subscription at www.vamanet.com/. Fee is $35 per month or $300 per year with discounts for multiple localities, regions.

Salem City

Clerk of Circuit Court, PO Box 891, Salem, VA 24153. 540-375-3067, R/E recording phone-540-375-3058, UCC recording phone-540-375-3067; fax-540-375-4039; 8:30AM-5PM.

Index: All in one. Records indexed on a public use terminal back to 1992. Only the public may search. Copy fee $.50 per page. Cert fee- $2.00 per doc plus copy fee. Payee- Salem City Clerk of Circuit Court. **Other phones:** Elections- 540-375-3058. **Property tax/Assessing**- 540-375-3000. **Online access**- Access current assessment info and sales by VamaNet subscription at www.vamanet.com/cgi-bin/HOME. Fee is $35 per month or $300 per year with discounts for multiple localities, regions.

Scott County

Clerk of Circuit Court, 104 E Jackson St, #2; Courthouse, Gate City, VA 24251-3417. 276-386-3801; fax-276-386-2430; 8:30AM-5PM

Index: All in one. Records indexed on a public use terminal back to 1984. Office will perform a UCC search but public must search other records themselves. Copy fee $.50 per page. Cert fee- $2.00 per doc plus copy fee. Payee- Scott County Clerk of Circuit Court. **Online access to Lien, Judgment, UCC, Marriage, Probate, Fictitious Name records:** Access recorder's data by subscription; signup at clerk's office. **Other phones:** Treasurer- 276-386-7742; Elections- 276-386-3843; Vital Records- 804-662-6200; Registrar- 276-386-3843. **Property tax/Assessing**- 104 E Jackson St, #6, Gate City, VA 24251; 276-386-7692. (Appraiser/Auditor- 276-386-7692) **Online access**- Access current assessment info and sales by subscription at www.vamanet.com/cgi-bin/HOME. Fee is $35 per month or $300 per year with discounts for multiple localities, regions.

Shenandoah County

Clerk of Circuit Court, PO Box 406, Woodstock, VA 22664. 540-459-6150; fax-540-459-6155; 9AM-5PM.

Index: All in one. Records indexed on a public use terminal back to 7/75 (deeds only). Office will perform a UCC search but public must search other records themselves. Copy fee $.50 per page. Cert fee- $2.00 per doc plus copy fee. Payee- Shenandoah Co. Circuit Court. Bulk data available for purchase via subscription, contact Cheryl or Linda. **Online access to Real Estate, Grantor/Grantor, Deed, Judgment, UCC, Marriage, Will/Probate records:** Recorded data available by subscription with images back to 1999 and earlier being added. Fee is $50.00 per month or $500.00 per year, contact Sarona Irvin 540-459-6153 in clerk's office. **Other phones:** Treasurer- 540-459-6180. **Property tax/Assessing**- 600 N Main St, #104, Woodstock, VA 22664; 540-459-6170, assessor fax- 540-459-6173. hours- 8:30AM-4:30PM www.shenandoahcountyva.us/revenue/ **Online**- Access current assessment info and sales by VamaNet subscription at www.vamanet.com/cgi-bin/HOME. Fee is $35 per month or $300 per year with discounts for multiple localities, regions. Also, access tax payment histories free at https://204.111.80.202/applications/trapps/index.htm. Access parcel data on GIS site free at www.shenandoahgis.org/ and click on Find to name search.

Smyth County

Clerk of Circuit Court, 109 W Main St, #144, Marion, VA 24354-2510. 276-782-4044; fax-276-782-4045; 9AM-5PM www.smythcounty.org/

Index: All in one. Records indexed on a public use terminal (deeds & land 1/2/90-present; financing statements 1/2/91-present; judgments 1/4/89-present; marriage licenses 7/1/93-present; wills 5/2/94-present). Office will perform a UCC search but public must search other records themselves. Copy fee $.50 per page. Will fax back results $1.25 per page. Cert fee- $2.00 per page includes copy fee. Payee- Smyth County Clerk of Circuit Court. **Online Real Estate, Deed, Mortgage, Lien, Judgment, Marriage, Wills/Probate records:** Access recording office data via $50.00 per month monthly subscription at www.courts.state.va.us/caseinfo/home.html; Includes images. Deeds and land records go back to 1993; judgments to 2007; Wills/Probate to 1/2008. **Other phones:** Treasurer- 276-782-4059; Elections- 276-783-3298 x222. **Property tax/Assessing**- PO Box 985, 109 W Main St, Marion, VA 24354; 276-782-4040, assessor fax- 276-782-4041. A public access terminal is available. www.smythcounty.org/ **Online access**- Access current assessment info and sales by VamaNet subscription at www.vamanet.com/cgi-bin/HOME. Fee is $35 per month or $300 per year with discounts for multiple localities, regions. Also, search county property index free at http://quicksearch.webgis.net/search.php?site=va_smyth.

Southampton County

Clerk of Circuit Court, PO Box 190, Courtland, VA 23837. 757-653-9245, R/E recording phone-757-653-2200; fax-757-653-2547; hours - 8:30AM-5PM www.southamptoncounty.org

Includes City of Franklin. Index: All in one. Land records indexed on a public use terminal back to 1954 to current. Office personnel or visitors may perform searches. Search fee-$5.00-$10.00 per name, depending on complexity. Office will search real estate records. Copy fee $.50 per page. Marriage license copy- $2.50. Cert fee- $2.00 per doc plus copy fee. Payee- Southampton County Clerk of Circuit Court. Bulk data available for purchase, contact Amy Carr. **Other phones:** Treasurer- 757-653-3025; Elections- 757-653-9280. **Property tax/Assessing**- PO Box 760, 26022 Administration Dr, Courtland, VA 23837; 757-653-3030, fax- 757-653-2935. (Appraiser/Auditor- 757-653-3030) A public access terminal is available. www.southamptoncounty.org **Online access**- Click on Southampton County to search property data for free at www.vamanet.com/cgi-bin/HOME. Also, only City of Franklin appraisal data is free at www.vamanet.com/cgi-bin/MAPSRCHPGM?LOCAL=FRA but this City site does not include county appraisal records. Also, county GIS tax map data is free at www.onlinegis.net/VaSouthampton/asp/controlVersion.asp.

Spotsylvania County

Clerk of Circuit Court, PO Box 96, Spotsylvania, VA 22553-0096. 540-507-7600, R/E recording phone-540-507-7053; fax-540-582-2169; 8AM-4:30PM. www.spotsylvania.va.us

Index: Separate indices to search include land, wills, judgments, financing statements, marriages, general misc orders, etc. Records indexed on 16 public use terminals-Index records back to 1966; images from 1918; judgment index to 1987; images from 1987; wills/fiduciary/financing statements/marriage index to 1996, images from 1996; general misc images/indexes back to 7/2002. Office will perform limited searches but public must search records themselves. No fee for search. No abstract work. Copy fee $.50 per page; SASE required for mail return. Cert fee- $2.00 per doc plus copy fee. Payee- Clerk of Circuit Court. **Online access to Real Estate, Deed, Lien records:** Access the recorder's recording index and images by subscription; fee is $50.00 per quarter; contact Land Recording Desk at 540-507-7615 at the clerk's office. Also, county deed and land records available by subscription from private company at http://en.landsystems.com/index.php. **Other phones:** Treasurer- 540-507-7058; Elections- 540-507-7380. **Property tax/Assessing**- PO Box 939, 9104 Courthouse Rd, 2nd Fl, Spotsylvania, VA 22553; 540-507-7777, assessor fax- 540-507-7799. www.spotsylvania.va.us/departments/cor/assessment/

Stafford County

Clerk of Circuit Court, PO Box 69, Stafford, VA 22555. 540-659-8752, R/E recording phone-540-658-8752, UCC recording phone-540-658-8758; fax-none; 8AM-4PM www.co.stafford.va.us

Index: Separate indices to search include land records, judgments, financing statements, wills. Records indexed on a public use terminal back to 7/94. Only the public may search. Copy fee $.50 per page. Cert fee- $2.00 per doc plus copy fee. Payee- Stafford County Clerk of Circuit Court. **Other phones:** Treasurer- 540-658-8700; Elections- 540-658-4000. **Property tax/Assessing**- PO Box 98, 1300 Courthouse Rd, Stafford, VA 22555; 540-658-4132, assessor fax- 540-658-4120. (Appraiser/Auditor- 540-658-4132) hours- 8AM-5:30PM A public access terminal is available. www.co.stafford.va.us/ **Online access**- Personal Property and RE Lookup free at http://taxpaid.stafford.va.us/. Also, access property data and interactive maps free at www.staffordcountygis.org/Website/StaffordInteractive/viewer.htm. Access properrty data free at http://staffordvapropertymax.governmaxa.com/propertymax/rover30.asp but no name searching.

Staunton City

Clerk of Circuit Court, 113 E Beverley St, Staunton, VA 24401. 540-332-3874; fax-540-332-3970; 8:30AM-4:30PM. www.staunton.va.us
Index: All in one. Records indexed on a public use terminal back to 1992. Only the public may search. Copy fee $.50 per page. Cert fee- $2.00 per doc plus copy fee. Payee- Circuit Court. Bulk data available for purchase, contact Jim Gallaher. **Other phones:** Treasurer- 540-332-3833; Elections- 540-332-3840; Vital Records- 804-662-6200. **Property tax/Assessing-** PO Box 58, 116 W Beverly St, Staunton, VA 24402; 540-332-3827. (Appraiser/Auditor- 540-332-3827) hours- 8AM-5PM A public access terminal is available. **Online access-** Access property tax data on the City GIS site free at http://gis1.ci.staunton.va.us:8086/freeance/client/publicaccess1/index.html?appconfig=masterpublicaccess.

Suffolk City

Clerk of Circuit Court, PO Box 1604, Suffolk, VA 23439-1604. 757-923-2256, R/E recording phone-757-923-2264, UCC recording phone-757-923-2347; fax-757-934-3490; 8:30AM-5PM www.suffolk.va.us/
Index: All in one. Records indexed on a public use terminal back to 1974. Only the public may search. Copy fee $.50 per page. Cert fee- $2.00 per doc plus copy fee. Payee- Suffolk City Clerk of Circuit Court. **Property tax/Assessing-** 757-923-2400. **Online-** Access property assessment data free at www.suffolk.va.us/realest/Search_Real_Estate_3.html but no name searching. Access parcel and property data free at GIS-mapping site at www.suffolk.va.us/gis/mapping.html but no name searching.

Surry County

Clerk of Circuit Court, PO Box 203, Surry, VA 23883. 757-294-3161; fax-757-294-0471; 9AM-5PM
Index: All in one. Records indexed on a public use terminal go back 20 years. Only the public may search. Copy fee $.50 per page. $.10 per page from microfilm. Cert fee- $2.00 per doc plus copy fee. Payee- Surry County Clerk of Circuit Court. **Online access to Real Estate, Deed, Judgment, Will, Marriage records:** Access to Circuit Court Records Search System is by subscription at http://208.210.219.102/cgi-bin/p/rms.cgi. Includes images for other selected jurisdictions; $1200 per year, username and password required, signup with local Circuit Ct Clerk. **Other phones:** Treasurer- 757-294-5206; Elections- 757-294-5213. **Property tax/Assessing-** 757-294-5225.

Sussex County

Clerk of Circuit Court, PO Box 1337, Sussex, VA 23884. 434-246-1012; fax-434-246-2203; 9AM-5PM http://sussexcounty.govoffice.com
Index: All in one. Records indexed on computer back to 1981. Office will perform a UCC or RE search but public must search other records themselves. UCC search per debtor name- $5.00. Copy fee $.50 per page. Cert fee- $2.00 per doc plus copy fee. Payee- Sussex County Clerk of Circuit Court. Treasurer- 434-246-1086; Elections- 434-246-1046; Vital Records-434-246-1012. **Property tax/Assessing-** 434-246-1025. **Online access-** Access to assessor property records is free at www.sussexcountyproperty.com.

Tazewell County

Clerk of Circuit Court, PO Box 968, Tazewell, VA 24651-0968. 276-988-1222, R/E recording phone-276-988-1225, UCC phone-276-988-1227; fax-276-988-7585; 8AM-4:30PM www.tazewellcounty.org/ Commissioner of Revenue website
Index: Separate indices to search include deeds, judgments and financing statements. Records indexed on a public use terminal back to 1984 for deeds and judgments. Office will perform a UCC search but public must search other records themselves. Search fee $20.00 for UCC search. Must prepay for search. Copy fee $.50 per page. Cert fee- $2.00 per doc plus copy fee. Payee- Clerk of Circuit Court. Bulk data available for purchase. **Other phones:** Treasurer-276-988-3000; Elections- 276-988-1305; Vital Records- 276-988-1226. **Property tax/Assessing-** 101 E Main St, Tazewell, VA 24651; 276-988-1235, assessor fax- 276-988-5221. A public access terminal is available. **Online access-** Click on Tazewell County to search property data for free at www.vamanet.com/cgi-bin/HOME.

Virginia Beach City

Clerk of Circuit Court, 2425 Nimmo Pky; Judicial Ctr, Virginia Beach, VA 23456-9017. 757-385-8821, R/E recording phone-757-385-4385, UCC recording phone-757-385-8821; fax-757-385-5686; 8:30AM-5PM. www.vbgov.com/
Index: All in one. Records indexed on a public use terminal back to 1965. Office will perform a UCC search but public must search other records themselves. Copy fee $.50 per page. Cert fee- $2.00 per cert plus copy fee. Payee- Clerk of Circuit Court. Bulk data available for purchase, contact IT Dept. 757-385-4121. **Online Real Estate, Deed, Marriage, Judgment, UCC, Will, Estate, Business Name, Plat records:** Access the Clerk of Circuit Court database free at www.vblandrecords.com/index.aspx. The second method of access will be via a $50 per month Monthly Subscription using credit card. For credit card account, call 866-793-6505. Direct general questions to Emilie Inman at 757-385-4462. Also, browse document archives free at http://edocs.vbgov.com/weblink/ but may be temporarily down. **Other phones:** Treasurer- 757-385-4445; Elections- 757-385-8683; Public Info Office- 757-385-4111. **Property tax/Assessing-** Municipal Center, Bldg 18, Virginia Beach, VA 23456; 757-385-4601, assessor fax- 757-385-5727. hours- 8AM-5PM A public access terminal is available. **Online access-** Search the assessor database for free at http://va-virginiabeach-realestate.governmax.com/ but no name searching. Also, access Virginia Beach parcel and map records free at www.vbgov.com/e%2Dgov/emapping/.

Warren County

Clerk of Circuit Court, 1 E Main St, Front Royal, VA 22630. 540-635-2435; fax-540-636-3274; 9AM-5PM www.warrencountyva.net/circuit_court.asp
Index: Separate indices to search include land records, judgments, UCCs, civil, law, criminal, marriage, wills. Records indexed on a public use terminal back to 1994. Office will perform a UCC search but public must search other records themselves. UCC search fee $20.00 per debtor name. Copy fee $.50 per page. Cert fee- $2.00 per doc plus copy fee. Payee- Warren County Circuit Clerk. Bulk data available for purchase, contact Sherry Sours. **Online access to Real Estate, Deed, Land, Lien, Will, UCC records:** Access the Clerk's data on the web for a fee; username and password required. For a fee username and password contact Jennifer Sims at 540-635-2435 or at jsims@courts.state.va.us. Images go back to 1994. **Other phones:** Treasurer- 540-635-2215; Elections-540-635-4327; Vital Records- 540-635-2435. **Property tax/Assessing-** PO Box 1775, 220 N Commerce Ave, Front Royal, VA 22630; 540-635-2651, assessor fax- 540-636-8280. (Appraiser/Auditor- 540-635-2651) A public access terminal is available. **Online access-** Access current assessment info and sales by VamaNet subscription at www.vamanet.com/cgi-bin/HOME. Fee is $35 per month or $300 per year with discounts for multiple localities, regions. Also, search assessment data on the GIS site free at www.warrengis.org/default.aspx but no name searching. Also search treasurer data of real estate and personal property free at http://75.145.206.89/applications/trapps/index.htm.

Washington County

Clerk of Circuit Court, PO Box 289, Abingdon, VA 24212. 276-676-6226, R/E recording phone-276-676-6224; fax-276-676-6218; 8AM-5PM.
Index: Books, computer. Records indexed on a public use terminal back to 1983. Only the public may search. Copy fee $.50 per page. Cert fee- $2.00 per page plus copy fee. Payee- Patricia S. Phipps, Clerk. **Other phones:** Treasurer- 276-676-6272; Elections-276-676-6227; Vital Records- 276-676-6265. **Property tax/Assessing-** 276-676-6270. **Online access-** Access current assessment info and sales by VamaNet subscription at www.vamanet.com/cgi-bin/HOME. Fee is $35 per month or $300 per year with discounts for multiple localities, regions.

Waynesboro City

Clerk of Circuit Court, PO Box 910, Waynesboro, VA 22980. 540-942-6616; fax-540-942-6774; 8:30AM-5PM
Recording do require six digit "PIN" available by calling 540-942-6722, ask for account number. Index: All in one. Records indexed on computer back to 1992. Office will perform a UCC search but public must search other records themselves. UCC search per debtor name $20.00. Office will not search real estate records. Search UCC records by written request. Copy fee $.50 per page. Cert fee- $2.00 per doc plus copy fee. Payee- Waynesboro City Clerk of Circuit Court. **Other phones:** Treasurer- 540-942-6606. **Property tax/Assessing-** 250 S Wayne Ave, Waynesboro, VA 22980; 540-942-6722. **Online access-** Access to city property appraiser data is free at www.vamanet.com/cgi-bin/HOME.

Westmoreland County

Clerk of Circuit Court, PO Box 307, Montross, VA 22520. 804-493-0108; fax-n/a; 9AM-5PM www.westmoreland-county.org
Index: Separate indices to search include deeds, law, chancery, judgments, marriages. Records indexed on a public use terminal back to 1953. Only the public may search. Will not search UCC records. Copy fee $.50 per page.Payee- Westmoreland County Clerk of Circuit Court. **Other phones:** Treasurer- 804-493-0124; Elections- 804-493-8898. **Property tax/Assessing-** 804-493-0113. **Online** - Access tax payment database free at http://166.61.239.88/applications/trapps/REIindex.htm. Also, search property card records free at http://166.61.239.88/applications/txapps/PropCardsIndex.htm. Also, search utility payment records free at http://166.61.239.88/applications/trapps/UTIindex.htm.

Winchester City

Clerk of Circuit Court, 5 N Kent St, Winchester, VA 22601. 540-667-5770; fax-540-667-6638; 9AM-5PM www.winfredclerk.com
Index: All in one. Records indexed on a public use terminal; land records back to 1983; judgments- 1992; financing statements- 1994; wills- 1993. Only the public may search. Copy fee $.50 per page. Cert fee-$2.00 per doc plus copy fee. Payee- Winchester City Clerk of Circuit Court. Bulk data available for purchase. **Online access to Real Estate, Deed, Mortgage, Lien records:** Access to the County Records management System is by subscription; base fee is $500 per year for 3 users. Contact Debby Payne in the Winchester County Circuit Court Clerk's office for info. **Other phones:** Treasurer- 540-667-1815; Elections- 540-667-1815. **Property tax/Assessing-** 15 N Cameron St, Winchester, VA 22601; 540-667-1815, fax- 540-667-5298. (Appraiser/Auditor- 540-667-1815) hours- 8AM-5PM A public access terminal is available. **Online access-** Access current assessment info and sales by VamaNet subscription at www.vamanet.com/cgi-bin/HOME. Fee is $35 per month or $300 per year with discounts for multiple localities, regions. Also, access surrounding Frederick County parcel data on the GIS-mapping site free at http://gis.co.frederick.va.us/ and click on Parcel Mapping Service.

Wise County

Clerk of Circuit Court, PO Box 1248, Wise, VA 24293. 276-328-6111; fax-276-328-0039; 8:30AM-4:30PM. www.courtbar.org
Online records include City of Norton. Index: Separate indices to search include grantor/grantee.

Records indexed on a public use terminal back to 1996. Only the public may search. Copy fee $.50 per page. Cert fee- $2.00 per doc plus copy fee. Payee- Wise County Circuit Court Clerk. Bulk data available for purchase, contact Rosemary Holbrook. **Online Real Estate, Deed, Lien, Probate, Marriage, UCC, Judgment, Permit records:** Access recording office records at www.courtbar.org/records.htm. For full access fee is $550 annually; see https://egov.mixnet.com/courts/ccwise2000/login.asp. This fee service includes index and images, court orders, land documents from 1970 and links to RE tax assessments, 50-year RE, tax maps, plat maps, delinquent taxes, permit images, probate, marriage, judgment liens for 20 years, and more. UCC-1 indices for past 5 years. Online records include City of Norton. **Other phones:** Treasurer- 276-328-3666; Elections- 276-328-8331; Vital Records- 804-662-6200. **Property tax/ Assessing-** PO Box 1278, 206 E Main St, Wise, 24293; 276-328-3566, fax- 276-328-6937. (Appraiser/Auditor- 276-328-3566) hours- 8:30AM-5PM. A public access terminal is available. **Online access-** Property data is at http://63.166.243.12/assessor/web/. A yearly subscription service allows access to full data. Also, search county parcel data free at http://quicksearch.webgis.net/search.php?site=va_wise.

Wythe County

Clerk of Circuit Court, 225 S 4th St, Rm 105, Wytheville, VA 24382. 276-223-6050; fax-276-223-6057; 8:30AM-5PM.

Index: All in one. Records indexed on a public use terminal back to 1992. Only the public may search. Copy fee $.50 per page. Cert fee- $1.00 per page plus copy fee. Payee- Clerk. **Online access to Judgment records:** Access to court judgment records is by subscription; $25.00 registration fee for username and password, also $25.00 per transaction fee. Contact the clerk office (Brenda Atwell) for signup. **Other phones:** Treasurer- 276-223-6070; Elections- 276-223-6038. **Property tax/Assessing-** 225 S 40th St, Wytheville, VA 24382; 276-223-6019, assessor fax-276-223-6047. (Appraiser/Auditor- 276-223-6015) A public access terminal is available. **Online access-** Access current assessment info and sales by VamaNet subscription at www.vamanet.com/cgi-bin/HOME. Fee is $35 per month or $300 per year with discounts for multiple localities, regions.

York County

Clerk of Circuit Court, PO Box 371, Yorktown, VA 23690. main phone- 757-890-3350, R/E recording phone-757-890-4103; fax-757-890-3364; 9AM-5PM www.yorkcounty.gov/circuitcourt/

Index: Separate indices to search include records prior to 1969. Records indexed on a public use terminal back to 1969. Office will perform a UCC search but public must search other records themselves. Search fee $20.00 per name. Copy fee $.50 per page. Cert fee- $2.00 per doc plus copy fee. Payee- York County Circuit Court. **Other phones:** Treasurer- 757-890-3420 (York Co); City of Poquoson Treasurer- 757-868-3015. **Property tax/Assessing-** 120 Alexander Hamilton Blvd, PO Box 532, Yorktown, VA 23690; 757-890-3270 (York Co), assessor fax- 757-890-4078. hours- 8:15AM-5PM www.yorkcounty.gov/realestateassessment/ **Online access-** Records from the County Parcel Search site are free at www.yorkcounty.gov/realestateassessment/york/search/frmSearch.asp. 2nd floor of the Finance Building adjacent to the Courthouse in Yorktown Village

Virginia County Locator

You will usually be able to find the city name in the City/County Cross Reference below. In that case, it is a simple matter to determine the county from the cross reference. However, only the official US Postal Service city names are included in this index. There are an additional 40,000 place names that people use in their addresses. Therefore, we have also included a ZIP/City Cross Reference immediately following the City/County Cross Reference.

Virginia City/County Cross Reference

ABINGDON Washington
ACCOMAC Accomack
ACHILLES Gloucester
AFTON (22920) Nelson(65), Albemarle(30), Augusta(3)
ALBERTA Brunswick
ALDIE Loudoun
ALEXANDRIA (22311) Alexandria City(93), Fairfax(6)
ALEXANDRIA (22312) Fairfax(76), Alexandria City(23)
ALEXANDRIA Alexandria City
ALEXANDRIA Fairfax
ALFONSO Lancaster
ALTAVISTA Campbell
ALTON Halifax
AMELIA COURT HOUSE Amelia
AMHERST Amherst
AMISSVILLE (20106) Culpeper(62), Rappahannock(33), Fauquier(3)
AMISSVILLE Rappahannock
AMMON Dinwiddie
AMONATE Tazewell
ANDERSONVILLE Buckingham
ANDOVER Wise
ANNANDALE Fairfax
APPALACHIA Wise
APPOMATTOX (24522) Appomattox(98), Buckingham(1)
ARARAT (24053) Patrick(94), Carroll(5)
ARCOLA Loudoun
ARK Gloucester
ARLINGTON (22206) Arlington(97), Alexandria City(2)
ARLINGTON Arlington
ARODA Madison
ARRINGTON (22922) Nelson(96), Amherst(3)
ARVONIA Buckingham
ASHBURN Loudoun
ASHLAND Hanover
ASSAWOMAN Accomack
ATKINS Smyth
ATLANTIC Accomack
AUGUSTA SPRINGS Augusta
AUSTINVILLE (24312) Carroll(60), Wythe(39)
AXTON (24054) Henry(64), Pittsylvania(35)
AYLETT King William
BACOVA Bath
BANCO Madison
BANDY Tazewell
BANK AMERICARD Roanoke City
BARBOURSVILLE (22923) Orange(53), Greene(24), Albemarle(21)
BARHAMSVILLE New Kent
BARREN SPRINGS Wythe
BASKERVILLE Mecklenburg
BASSETT (24055) Henry(94), Franklin(5)
BASTIAN (24314) Bland(71), Tazewell(28)
BASYE Shenandoah
BATESVILLE Albemarle
BATTERY PARK Isle of Wight
BAVON Mathews
BEALETON Fauquier
BEAUMONT Goochland
BEAVERDAM (23015) Hanover(72), Caroline(13), Spotsylvania(12), Louisa(1)
BEAVERLETT Mathews
BEDFORD (24523) Bedford(78), Bedford City(21)
BEE Dickenson
BELLAMY Gloucester
BELLE HAVEN Accomack
BELSPRING Pulaski
BEN HUR Lee
BENA Gloucester
BENT MOUNTAIN (24059) Roanoke(92), Franklin(5), Floyd(2)
BENTONVILLE (22610) Warren(98), Page(1)
BERGTON Rockingham
BERRYVILLE Clarke
BIG ISLAND Bedford
BIG ROCK Buchanan
BIG STONE GAP (24219) Wise(97), Lee(2)
BIRCHLEAF Dickenson
BIRDSNEST Northampton
BISHOP Tazewell
BLACKSBURG Montgomery
BLACKSTONE (23824) Nottoway(91), Brunswick(8)
BLACKWATER (24221) Lee(62), Scott(37)
BLAIRS Pittsylvania
BLAKES Mathews
BLAND Bland
BLOXOM Accomack
BLUE GRASS Highland
BLUE RIDGE (24064) Botetourt(63), Bedford(36)
BLUEFIELD Tazewell
BLUEMONT (20135) Clarke(69), Loudoun(30)
BLUEMONT Loudoun
BOHANNON Mathews
BOISSEVAIN Tazewell
BOONES MILL (24065) Franklin(82), Roanoke(17)
BOSTON (22713) Culpeper(84), Rappahannock(15)
BOWLING GREEN Caroline
BOYCE Clarke
BOYDTON Mecklenburg
BOYKINS Southampton
BRACEY (23919) Mecklenburg(94), Brunswick(5)
BRANCHVILLE Southampton
BRANDY STATION Culpeper
BREAKS Dickenson
BREMO BLUFF Fluvanna
BRIDGEWATER (22812) Rockingham(80), Augusta(19)
BRIGHTWOOD Madison
BRISTOL (24202) Washington(91), Bristol City(5), Scott(2)
BRISTOL Bristol City
BRISTOW Prince William
BROAD RUN (20137) Fauquier(78), Prince William(21)
BROAD RUN Fauquier
BROADFORD (24316) Tazewell(97), Smyth(2)
BROADWAY (22815) Rockingham(98), Shenandoah(1)
BRODNAX (23920) Brunswick(76), Mecklenburg(21), Lunenburg(2)
BROOKE Stafford
BROOKNEAL (24528) Campbell(78), Charlotte(21)
BROWNSBURG Rockbridge
BRUCETOWN Frederick
BRUINGTON King and Queen
BUCHANAN Botetourt
BUCKINGHAM Buckingham
BUENA VISTA (24416) Buena Vista City(77), Rockbridge(22)
BUFFALO JUNCTION (24529) Mecklenburg(98), Halifax(1)
BUMPASS (23024) Louisa(83), Spotsylvania(13), Hanover(3)
BURGESS Northumberland
BURKE Fairfax
BURKES GARDEN Tazewell
BURKEVILLE (23922) Nottoway(91), Prince Edward(8)
BURR HILL Orange
CALLANDS (24530) Pittsylvania(98), Henry(1)
CALLAO (22435) Northumberland(98), Westmoreland(1)
CALLAWAY Franklin
CALVERTON Fauquier
CANA Carroll
CAPE CHARLES Northampton
CAPEVILLE Northampton
CAPRON Southampton
CARDINAL Mathews
CARET (22436) Essex(98), Caroline(1)
CARROLLTON Isle of Wight
CARRSVILLE Isle of Wight
CARSON (23830) Prince George(55), Dinwiddie(30), Sussex(13)
CARTERSVILLE Cumberland
CASANOVA Fauquier
CASCADE Pittsylvania
CASTLETON (22716) Rappahannock(95), Culpeper(4)
CASTLEWOOD Russell
CATAWBA (24070) Roanoke(71), Montgomery(26), Craig(1)
CATHARPIN Prince William
CATLETT Fauquier
CAUTHORNVILLE King and Queen
CEDAR BLUFF (24609) Tazewell(83), Russell(16)
CENTER CROSS (22437) Essex(79), King and Queen(20)
CENTREVILLE Fairfax
CERES (24318) Bland(67), Smyth(32)
CHAMPLAIN (22438) Essex(90), Caroline(9)
CHANCE Essex
CHANTILLY Fairfax
CHANTILLY Loudoun
CHARLES CITY Charles City
CHARLOTTE COURT HOUSE (23923) Charlotte(97), Prince Edward(2)
CHARLOTTESVILLE (22901) Albemarle(82), Charlottesville City(17)
CHARLOTTESVILLE (22903) Charlottesville City(68), Albemarle(31)
CHARLOTTESVILLE Albemarle
CHARLOTTESVILLE Charlottesville City
CHASE CITY (23924) Mecklenburg(93), Lunenburg(4), Charlotte(2)
CHATHAM Pittsylvania
CHECK Floyd
CHERITON Northampton
CHESAPEAKE Chesapeake City
CHESTER Chesterfield
CHESTER GAP Rappahannock
CHILHOWIE (24319) Smyth(76), Washington(23)
CHINCOTEAGUE Accomack
CHINCOTEAGUE ISLAND Accomack
CHRISTCHURCH Middlesex
CHRISTIANSBURG Montgomery
CHURCH ROAD (23833) Dinwiddie(89), Amelia(10)
CHURCH VIEW Middlesex
CHURCHVILLE Augusta
CITY OFFICES Roanoke City
CLAREMONT Surry
CLARKSVILLE Mecklenburg
CLAUDVILLE Patrick
CLEAR BROOK Frederick
CLEVELAND (24225) Russell(97), Dickenson(2)
CLIFFORD Amherst
CLIFTON Fairfax
CLIFTON FORGE (24422) Alleghany(95), Botetourt(3), Clifton Forge City(1)
CLINCHBURG Washington
CLINCHCO Dickenson
CLINTWOOD Dickenson
CLOVER Halifax
CLOVERDALE Botetourt
CLUSTER SPRINGS Halifax
COBBS CREEK Mathews
COBHAM Albemarle
COEBURN (24230) Wise(89), Dickenson(9), Scott(1)
COLEMAN FALLS Bedford
COLES POINT Westmoreland
COLLINSVILLE Henry
COLOGNE King and Queen
COLONIAL BEACH Westmoreland
COLONIAL HEIGHTS (23834) Colonial Heights City(70), Chesterfield(29)
COLUMBIA (23038) Goochland(56), Cumberland(21), Fluvanna(21)
CONCORD (24538) Campbell(77), Appomattox(22)
COPPER HILL Floyd
CORBIN Caroline
COURTLAND (23837) Southampton(96), Sussex(3)
COVESVILLE Albemarle
COVINGTON (24426) Alleghany(49), Covington City(49)
CRADDOCKVILLE Accomack
CRAIGSVILLE Augusta
CREWE Nottoway
CRIDERS Rockingham
CRIMORA Augusta
CRIPPLE CREEK Wythe
CRITZ Patrick
CROCKETT Wythe
CROSS JUNCTION Frederick
CROZET Albemarle
CROZIER Goochland
CRYSTAL HILL Halifax
CULLEN (23934) Charlotte(60), Prince Edward(39)
CULPEPER (22701) Culpeper(89), Orange(7), Madison(3)
CUMBERLAND (23040) Cumberland(91), Buckingham(8)
DABNEYS Louisa

DAHLGREN King George
DALEVILLE Botetourt
DAMASCUS Washington
DANTE (24237) Dickenson(68), Russell(31)
DANVILLE (24541) Danville City(77), Pittsylvania(22)
DANVILLE Danville City
DARLINGTN HTS Prince Edward
DARLINGTON HEIGHTS Prince Edward
DAVENPORT Buchanan
DAVIS WHARF Accomack
DAYTON Rockingham
DEERFIELD (24432) Augusta(98), Bath(1)
DELAPLANE Fauquier
DELTAVILLE Middlesex
DENDRON Surry
DEWITT Dinwiddie
DIGGS Mathews
DILLWYN (23936) Buckingham(96), Cumberland(3)
DINWIDDIE Dinwiddie
DISPUTANTA (23842) Prince George(92), Sussex(7)
DOE HILL Highland
DOGUE King George
DOLPHIN Brunswick
DORAN Tazewell
DOSWELL (23047) Hanover(75), Caroline(24)
DRAKES BRANCH (23937) Charlotte(94), Lunenburg(5)
DRAPER (24324) Pulaski(78), Wythe(21)
DREWRYVILLE Southampton
DRY FORK Pittsylvania
DRYDEN Lee
DUBLIN (24084) Pulaski(94), Bland(5)
DUFFIELD (24244) Scott(83), Lee(16)
DUGSPUR Carroll
DULLES Loudoun
DUMFRIES Prince William
DUNDAS (23938) Brunswick(60), Lunenburg(39)
DUNGANNON Scott
DUNN LORING Fairfax
DUNNSVILLE Essex
DUTTON (23050) Mathews(77), Gloucester(22)
DYKE (22935) Greene(68), Albemarle(31)
EAGLE ROCK Botetourt
EARLYSVILLE Albemarle
EAST STONE GAP Wise
EASTVILLE Northampton
EBONY Brunswick
EDINBURG Shenandoah
EDWARDSVILLE Northumberland
EGGLESTON Giles
ELBERON Surry
ELK CREEK Grayson
ELKTON (22827) Rockingham(90), Page(9)
ELKWOOD Culpeper
ELLISTON (24087) Montgomery(96), Roanoke(3)
EMORY Washington
EMPORIA (23847) Greensville(66), Emporia City(30), Southampton(2), Sussex(1)
ESMONT Albemarle
ETLAN Madison
EVERGREEN Appomattox
EVINGTON (24550) Campbell(89), Bedford(10)
EWING Lee
EXETER Wise
EXMORE Northampton
FABER (22938) Nelson(96), Albemarle(3)
FAIRFAX (22032) Fairfax(95), Fairfax City(4)
FAIRFAX Fairfax
FAIRFAX Fairfax City
FAIRFAX STATION Fairfax
FAIRFIELD Rockbridge
FALLS CHURCH (22044) Fairfax(93), Falls Church City(6)
FALLS CHURCH (22046) Falls Church City(69), Fairfax(30)
FALLS CHURCH Fairfax
FALLS CHURCH Falls Church City
FALLS MILLS Tazewell
FANCY GAP Carroll
FARMVILLE (23901) Prince Edward(79), Cumberland(18), Buckingham(1)
FARMVILLE Prince Edward
FARNHAM Richmond
FERRUM Franklin
FIELDALE Henry
FIFE Goochland
FINCASTLE Botetourt
FISHERS HILL Shenandoah
FISHERSVILLE Augusta
FLINT HILL Rappahannock
FONESWOOD Richmond
FORD (23850) Dinwiddie(85), Amelia(14)
FOREST (24551) Bedford(87), Campbell(11)
FORK UNION Fluvanna
FORT BELVOIR Fairfax
FORT BLACKMORE Scott
FORT DEFIANCE Augusta
FORT EUSTIS Newport News City
FORT LEE (23801) Prince George(98), Petersburg City(1)
FORT MITCHELL Lunenburg
FORT MONROE Hampton City
FORT VALLEY Shenandoah
FOSTER Mathews
FRANKLIN (23851) Franklin City(51), Southampton(41), Isle of Wight(7)
FRANKTOWN Northampton
FREDERICKSBURG (22401) Fredericksburg City(96), Spotsylvania(3)
FREDERICKSBURG (22408) Spotsylvania(95), Caroline(3)
FREDERICKSBURG Fredericksburg City
FREDERICKSBURG Spotsylvania
FREDERICKSBURG Stafford
FREE UNION (22940) Albemarle(77), Greene(22)
FREEMAN (23856) Brunswick(95), Greensville(4)
FRIES Grayson
FRONT ROYAL (22630) Warren(98), Clarke(1)
FRONT ROYAL Warren
FT MYER Arlington
FULKS RUN Rockingham
GAINESVILLE Prince William
GALAX (24333) Carroll(35), Grayson(35), Galax City(29)
GARRISONVILLE Stafford
GASBURG Brunswick
GATE CITY Scott
GLADE SPRING Washington
GLADEHILL Franklin
GLADSTONE (24553) Nelson(44), Amherst(32), Appomattox(12), Buckingham(11)
GLADYS Campbell
GLASGOW Rockbridge
GLEN ALLEN (23059) Henrico(78), Hanover(21)
GLEN ALLEN Henrico
GLEN LYN Giles
GLEN WILTON Botetourt
GLOUCESTER Gloucester
GLOUCESTER POINT Gloucester
GOLDBOND Giles
GOLDVEIN Fauquier
GOOCHLAND Goochland
GOODE Bedford
GOODVIEW Bedford
GORDONSVILLE (22942) Orange(62), Louisa(34), Albemarle(2)
GORE Frederick
GOSHEN (24439) Rockbridge(80), Augusta(19)
GRAVES MILL Madison
GREAT AMERICAN MAGAZINE Hampton City
GREAT FALLS (22066) Fairfax(96), Loudoun(3)
GREEN BAY (23942) Prince Edward(67), Lunenburg(32)
GREENBACKVILLE Accomack
GREENBUSH Accomack
GREENVILLE Augusta
GREENWAY Fairfax
GREENWOOD Albemarle
GRETNA Pittsylvania
GRIMSTEAD Mathews
GROTTOES (24441) Rockingham(81), Augusta(18)
GRUNDY Buchanan
GUM SPRING (23065) Goochland(71), Louisa(28)
GWYNN Mathews
HACKSNECK Accomack
HADENSVILLE Goochland
HAGUE Westmoreland
HALLIEFORD Mathews
HALLWOOD Accomack
HAMILTON Loudoun
HAMPDEN SYDNEY Prince Edward
HAMPTON (23665) Hampton City(52), York(47)
HAMPTON Hampton City
HANDSOM Southampton
HANOVER (23069) Hanover(41), Caroline(33), King William(24)
HARBORTON Accomack
HARDY (24101) Franklin(91), Bedford(8)
HARDYVILLE Middlesex
HARMAN Buchanan
HARRISONBURG (22802) Harrisonburg City(50), Rockingham(49)
HARRISONBURG Harrisonburg City
HARTFIELD Middlesex
HARTWOOD Stafford
HAYES Gloucester
HAYMARKET Prince William
HAYNESVILLE Richmond
HAYSI (24256) Dickenson(89), Buchanan(10)
HAYWOOD Madison
HEAD WATERS Highland
HEATHSVILLE (22473) Northumberland(98), Lancaster(1)
HENRY (24102) Franklin(92), Henry(7)
HERNDON Fairfax
HIGHLAND SPRINGS Henrico
HIGHTOWN Highland
HILLSVILLE Carroll
HILTONS (24258) Scott(85), Washington(14)
HINTON Rockingham
HIWASSEE (24347) Pulaski(89), Montgomery(10)
HONAKER (24260) Russell(87), Buchanan(12)
HOOD Madison
HOPEWELL (23860) Hopewell City(81), Prince George(18)
HORNTOWN Accomack
HORSEPEN Tazewell
HOT SPRINGS (24445) Bath(57), Alleghany(42)
HOWARDSVILLE (24562) Albemarle(48), Buckingham(38), Nelson(12)
HUDDLESTON Bedford
HUDGINS Mathews
HUME Fauquier
HUNTLY Rappahannock
HURLEY Buchanan
HURT Pittsylvania
HUSTLE Essex
HYACINTH Northumberland
INDEPENDENCE Grayson
INDIAN VALLEY Floyd
IRON GATE Alleghany
IRVINGTON Lancaster
ISLE OF WIGHT Isle of Wight
IVANHOE (24350) Wythe(57), Carroll(34), Grayson(8)
IVOR (23866) Southampton(59), Isle of Wight(40)
IVY Albemarle
JAMAICA Middlesex
JAMES STORE Gloucester
JAMESTOWN James City
JAMESVILLE Northampton
JARRATT (23867) Greensville(91), Sussex(8)
JARRATT Greensville
JAVA (24565) Pittsylvania(89), Halifax(10)
JEFFERSONTON Culpeper
JENKINS BRIDGE Accomack
JERSEY King George
JETERSVILLE (23083) Amelia(97), Nottoway(2)
JEWELL RIDGE (24622) Tazewell(89), Buchanan(10)
JONESVILLE Lee
JORDAN MINES Alleghany
KEELING Pittsylvania
KEEN MOUNTAIN Buchanan
KEENE Albemarle
KEEZLETOWN Rockingham
KELLER Accomack
KENBRIDGE Lunenburg
KENTS STORE (23084) Fluvanna(65), Goochland(20), Louisa(14)
KEOKEE Lee
KESWICK (22947) Albemarle(85), Fluvanna(11), Louisa(3)
KEYSVILLE (23947) Charlotte(51), Lunenburg(39), Prince Edward(9)
KILMARNOCK (22482) Northumberland(62), Lancaster(37)
KING AND QUEEN COURT HOUS King and Queen
KING GEORGE King George
KING WILLIAM King William
KINSALE Westmoreland
LA CROSSE (23950) Mecklenburg(87), Brunswick(12)
LACEY SPRING Rockingham
LACKEY York
LADYSMITH Caroline
LAHORE Orange
LAMBSBURG Carroll
LANEVIEW (22504) Essex(80), Middlesex(19)
LANEXA (23089) New Kent(76), James City(23)
LAUREL FORK Carroll
LAWRENCEVILLE Brunswick
LEBANON Russell
LEE MONT Accomack
LEESBURG Loudoun
LEON Madison
LEWISETTA Northumberland
LEXINGTON (24450) Rockbridge(71), Lexington City(28)
LIGHTFOOT York
LIGNUM Culpeper
LINCOLN Loudoun
LINDEN (22642) Warren(85), Fauquier(14)
LINVILLE Rockingham
LITTLE PLYMOUTH King and Queen
LIVELY Lancaster
LOCUST DALE Madison
LOCUST GROVE (22508) Orange(92), Spotsylvania(7)
LOCUST HILL Middlesex
LOCUSTVILLE Accomack
LONG ISLAND (24569) Pittsylvania(86), Campbell(7), Halifax(5)

LORETTO Essex
LORTON Fairfax
LOTTSBURG Northumberland
LOUISA (23093) Louisa(92), Goochland(6), Fluvanna(1)
LOVETTSVILLE Loudoun
LOVINGSTON Nelson
LOW MOOR Alleghany
LOWRY Bedford
LUNENBURG Lunenburg
LURAY Page
LYNCH STATION (24571) Campbell(75), Bedford(24)
LYNCHBURG (24502) Lynchburg City(54), Campbell(43), Bedford(2)
LYNCHBURG (24503) Lynchburg City(67), Bedford(32)
LYNCHBURG (24504) Lynchburg City(65), Campbell(33)
LYNCHBURG Lynchburg City
LYNDHURST (22952) Augusta(95), Nelson(2), Waynesboro City(1)
MACHIPONGO Northampton
MACON Powhatan
MADISON HEIGHTS Amherst
MADISON MILLS Madison
MAIDENS (23102) Goochland(79), Louisa(13), Hanover(6)
MANAKIN SABOT Goochland
MANASSAS (20110) Manassas City(84), Prince William(15)
MANASSAS (20109) Prince William(96), Manassas City(3)
MANASSAS (20111) Prince William(63), Manassas Park City(36)
MANASSAS Manassas City
MANASSAS Manassas Park City
MANASSAS Prince William
MANGOHICK King William
MANNBORO Amelia
MANQUIN King William
MAPPSVILLE Accomack
MARION Smyth
MARIONVILLE Northampton
MARKHAM Fauquier
MARSHALL Fauquier
MARTINSVILLE (24112) Henry(65), Martinsville City(34)
MARTINSVILLE Martinsville City
MARYUS Gloucester
MASCOT King and Queen
MASSIES MILL Nelson
MATHEWS Mathews
MATTAPONI King and Queen
MAURERTOWN Shenandoah
MAVISDALE Buchanan
MAX MEADOWS Wythe
MAXIE Buchanan
MC CLURE Dickenson
MC COY Montgomery
MC DOWELL Highland
MC GAHEYSVILLE Rockingham
MC KENNEY Dinwiddie
MC LEAN Fairfax
MEADOWS OF DAN (24120) Patrick(73), Floyd(16), Carroll(10)
MEADOWVIEW Washington
MEARS Accomack
MECHANICSVILLE Hanover
MEHERRIN (23954) Prince Edward(68), Lunenburg(31)
MELFA Accomack
MENDOTA Washington
MEREDITHVILLE Brunswick
MERRIFIELD Fairfax
MERRY POINT Lancaster
MIDDLEBROOK (24459) Augusta(88), Rockbridge(11)
MIDDLEBURG (20117) Loudoun(97), Fauquier(2)
MIDDLEBURG Loudoun
MIDDLETOWN (22645) Frederick(56), Warren(42)
MIDDLETOWN Warren
MIDLAND Fauquier
MIDLOTHIAN Chesterfield
MILES Chesterfield
MILFORD (22514) Caroline(98), King and Queen(1)
MILLBORO Bath
MILLERS TAVERN Essex
MILLWOOD Clarke
MINE RUN Orange
MINERAL (23117) Louisa(86), Spotsylvania(10), Goochland(2)
MINT SPRING Augusta
MITCHELLS Culpeper
MOBJACK Mathews
MODEST TOWN Accomack
MOLLUSK Lancaster
MONETA (24121) Bedford(59), Franklin(40)
MONROE Amherst
MONTEBELLO Nelson
MONTEREY Highland
MONTPELIER (23192) Hanover(92), Louisa(7)
MONTPELIER STATION Orange
MONTROSS Westmoreland
MONTVALE Bedford
MOON Mathews
MORATTICO Lancaster
MOSELEY (23120) Chesterfield(95), Powhatan(4)
MOUNT CRAWFORD (22841) Rockingham(98), Augusta(1)
MOUNT HOLLY Westmoreland
MOUNT JACKSON Shenandoah
MOUNT SIDNEY Augusta
MOUNT SOLON Augusta
MOUNT VERNON Fairfax
MOUTH OF WILSON Grayson
MUSTOE Highland
NARROWS (24124) Giles(97), Bland(2)
NARUNA Campbell
NASSAWADOX Northampton
NATHALIE Halifax
NATURAL BRIDGE Rockbridge
NATURAL BRIDGE STATION Rockbridge
NAXERA Gloucester
NELLYSFORD Nelson
NELSON Mecklenburg
NELSONIA Accomack
NEW CANTON (23123) Buckingham(95), Cumberland(4)
NEW CASTLE Craig
NEW CHURCH Accomack
NEW HOPE Augusta
NEW KENT (23124) New Kent(95), Hanover(4)
NEW MARKET (22844) Shenandoah(91), Rockingham(8)
NEW POINT Mathews
NEW RIVER Pulaski
NEWBERN Pulaski
NEWINGTON Fairfax
NEWPORT (24128) Giles(87), Craig(12)
NEWPORT NEWS (23605) Newport News City(81), Hampton City(18)
NEWPORT NEWS Hampton City
NEWPORT NEWS Newport News City
NEWSOMS Southampton
NEWTOWN King and Queen
NICKELSVILLE (24271) Scott(97), Russell(2)
NINDE King George
NOKESVILLE (20181) Prince William(94), Fauquier(5)
NOKESVILLE Prince William
NORA Dickenson
NORFOLK Norfolk City
NORGE James City
NORTH (23128) Mathews(53), Gloucester(46)
NORTH GARDEN Albemarle
NORTH TAZEWELL Tazewell
NORTON (24273) Norton City(72), Wise(27)
NORWOOD Nelson
NOTTOWAY Nottoway
NUTTSVILLE Lancaster
OAK HALL Accomack
OAKPARK Madison
OAKTON Fairfax
OAKWOOD Buchanan
OCCOQUAN Prince William
OILVILLE (23129) Goochland(96), Hanover(3)
OLDHAMS Westmoreland
ONANCOCK Accomack
ONEMO Mathews
ONLEY Accomack
OPHELIA Northumberland
ORANGE (22960) Orange(90), Madison(9)
ORDINARY Gloucester
ORISKANY Botetourt
ORKNEY SPRINGS Shenandoah
ORLEAN Fauquier
OYSTER Northampton
PAEONIAN SPRINGS Loudoun
PAINT BANK Craig
PAINTER Accomack
PALMYRA Fluvanna
PAMPLIN (23958) Prince Edward(57), Appomattox(29), Charlotte(12)
PARIS (20130) Clarke(73), Fauquier(18), Loudoun(8)
PARIS Fauquier
PARKSLEY Accomack
PARROTT Pulaski
PARTLOW Spotsylvania
PATRICK SPRINGS Patrick
PEARISBURG (24134) Giles(98), Bland(1)
PEMBROKE Giles
PENHOOK (24137) Franklin(79), Pittsylvania(20)
PENN LAIRD Rockingham
PENNINGTON GAP Lee
PETERSBURG (23803) Petersburg City(54), Dinwiddie(25), Chesterfield(20)
PETERSBURG (23805) Petersburg City(60), Prince George(26), Dinwiddie(13)
PETERSBURG Petersburg City
PHENIX Charlotte
PHILOMONT Loudoun
PILGRIMS KNOB Buchanan
PILOT (24138) Floyd(51), Montgomery(48)
PINEY RIVER Nelson
PITTSVILLE Pittsylvania
PLAIN VIEW King and Queen
PLEASANT VALLEY Rockingham
POCAHONTAS Tazewell
POQUOSON Poquoson City
PORT HAYWOOD Mathews
PORT REPUBLIC Rockingham
PORT ROYAL Caroline
PORTSMOUTH Portsmouth City
POUND Wise
POUNDING MILL Tazewell
POWHATAN (23139) Powhatan(97), Cumberland(2)
PRATTS Madison
PRINCE GEORGE Prince George
PROSPECT Prince Edward
PROVIDENCE FORGE (23140) New Kent(59), Charles City(40)
PUNGOTEAGUE Accomack
PURCELLVILLE Loudoun
QUANTICO Prince William
QUANTICO Stafford
QUICKSBURG Shenandoah
QUINBY Accomack
QUINQUE Greene
QUINTON New Kent
RADFORD (24141) Radford City(59), Pulaski(27), Montgomery(11), Floyd(1)
RADFORD Radford City
RADIANT Madison
RANDOLPH (23962) Charlotte(90), Halifax(9)
RAPHINE (24472) Rockbridge(70), Augusta(29)
RAPIDAN (22733) Culpeper(70), Orange(29)
RAPPAHANNOCK ACADEMY Caroline
RAVEN (24639) Tazewell(88), Buchanan(10), Russell(1)
RAWLINGS Brunswick
RECTORTOWN Fauquier
RED ASH Tazewell
RED HOUSE (23963) Charlotte(73), Campbell(21), Appomattox(5)
RED OAK (23964) Charlotte(88), Mecklenburg(11)
REDART Mathews
REDWOOD Franklin
REEDVILLE Northumberland
REGINA Lancaster
REMINGTON (22734) Fauquier(86), Culpeper(13)
REPUBLICAN GROVE Halifax
RESCUE Isle of Wight
RESTON Fairfax
REVA (22735) Culpeper(89), Madison(10)
RHOADESVILLE Orange
RICE (23966) Amelia(53), Prince Edward(46)
RICH CREEK Giles
RICHARDSVILLE Culpeper
RICHLANDS Tazewell
RICHMOND (23235) Chesterfield(72), Richmond City(27)
RICHMOND (23231) Henrico(82), Richmond City(13), Charles City(3)
RICHMOND (23238) Henrico(91), Goochland(8)
RICHMOND (23222) Richmond City(67), Henrico(32)
RICHMOND (23225) Richmond City(83), Chesterfield(16)
RICHMOND (23226) Richmond City(50), Henrico(49)
RICHMOND Chesterfield
RICHMOND Henrico
RICHMOND Richmond City
RIDGEWAY Henry
RILEYVILLE Page
RINER (24149) Montgomery(79), Floyd(20)
RINGGOLD Pittsylvania
RIPPLEMEAD Giles
RIXEYVILLE Culpeper
ROANOKE (24018) Roanoke(85), Roanoke City(14)
ROANOKE (24019) Roanoke(67), Botetourt(21), Roanoke City(11)
ROANOKE (24015) Roanoke City(98), Roanoke(1)
ROANOKE Botetourt
ROANOKE Montgomery
ROANOKE Roanoke
ROANOKE Roanoke City
ROCHELLE Madison
ROCKBRIDGE BATHS Rockbridge
ROCKVILLE (23146) Hanover(73), Goochland(26)
ROCKY GAP Bland
ROCKY MOUNT Franklin
ROLLINS FORK King George
ROSE HILL Lee
ROSEDALE Russell
ROSELAND (22967) Nelson(91), Amherst(8)
ROSELAND Amherst
ROUND HILL Loudoun
ROWE (24646) Buchanan(91), Russell(8)

RUBY Stafford
RUCKERSVILLE (22968) Greene(90), Albemarle(9)
RURAL RETREAT (24368) Wythe(55), Smyth(44)
RUSTBURG Campbell
RUTHER GLEN (22546) Caroline(98), Hanover(1)
RUTHVILLE Charles City
SAINT CHARLES Lee
SAINT PAUL (24283) Wise(95), Russell(3)
SAINT STEPHENS CHURCH (23148) King and Queen(86), Essex(13)
SALEM (24153) Salem City(63), Roanoke(36)
SALEM Salem City
SALTVILLE (24370) Smyth(80), Washington(19)
SALUDA (23149) Middlesex(49), Gloucester(36), King and Queen(13)
SANDSTON Henrico
SANDY HOOK Goochland
SANDY LEVEL Pittsylvania
SANDY POINT Westmoreland
SANFORD Accomack
SAXE Charlotte
SAXIS Accomack
SCHLEY Gloucester
SCHUYLER (22969) Nelson(59), Albemarle(40)
SCOTTSBURG Halifax
SCOTTSVILLE (24590) Fluvanna(47), Albemarle(44), Buckingham(8)
SEAFORD York
SEALSTON King George
SEAVIEW Northampton
SEDLEY (23878) Southampton(97), Sussex(2)
SELMA Alleghany
SEVEN MILE FORD Smyth
SEVERN Gloucester
SHACKLEFORDS King and Queen
SHADOW Mathews
SHARPS Richmond
SHAWSVILLE Montgomery
SHILOH King George
SHIPMAN Nelson
SHORTT GAP Buchanan
SINGERS GLEN Rockingham
SKIPPERS Greensville
SKIPWITH Mecklenburg
SMITHFIELD Isle of Wight
SOMERSET (22972) Orange(95), Madison(4)
SOMERVILLE Fauquier
SOUTH BOSTON Halifax
SOUTH HILL (23970) Mecklenburg(93), Lunenburg(6)
SPARTA Caroline
SPEEDWELL Wythe
SPENCER Henry
SPERRYVILLE (22740) Rappahannock(84), Culpeper(13), Madison(1)
SPOTSYLVANIA Spotsylvania
SPOTTSWOOD (24475) Augusta(96), Rockbridge(3)
SPOUT SPRING Appomattox
SPRING GROVE (23881) Prince George(50), Surry(49)
SPRINGFIELD Fairfax
STAFFORD (22556) Stafford(98), Fauquier(1)
STAFFORDSVILLE Giles
STANARDSVILLE (22973) Greene(98), Madison(1)
STANLEY Page
STANLEYTOWN Henry
STAR TANNERY (22654) Frederick(73), Shenandoah(26)
STATE FARM (23160) Powhatan(66), Goochland(33)
STAUNTON (24401) Staunton City(69), Augusta(30)
STAUNTON Augusta
STAUNTON Staunton City
STEELES TAVERN Augusta
STEPHENS CITY (22655) Frederick(98), Warren(1)
STEPHENSON Frederick
STERLING Loudoun
STERLING PARK Loudoun
STEVENSBURG Culpeper
STEVENSVILLE King and Queen
STONEGA Wise
STONY CREEK (23882) Sussex(71), Dinwiddie(28)
STRASBURG (22657) Shenandoah(84), Warren(15)
STRASBURG Shenandoah
STRATFORD Westmoreland
STUART Patrick
STUARTS DRAFT Augusta
STUDLEY Hanover
SUFFOLK Suffolk City
SUGAR GROVE Smyth
SUMERDUCK Fauquier
SUPPLY Essex
SURRY Surry
SUSAN Mathews
SUTHERLAND Dinwiddie
SUTHERLIN Pittsylvania
SWEET BRIAR Amherst
SWOOPE Augusta
SWORDS CREEK Russell
SYRIA Madison
TANGIER Accomack
TANNERSVILLE Tazewell
TAPPAHANNOCK (22560) Essex(94), King and Queen(5)
TASLEY Accomack
TAZEWELL Tazewell
TEMPERANCEVILLE Accomack
THAXTON Bedford
THE PLAINS Fauquier
THORNBURG Spotsylvania
TIMBERVILLE (22853) Rockingham(95), Shenandoah(4)
TOANO James City
TOMS BROOK Shenandoah
TOPPING Middlesex
TOWNSEND Northampton
TRAMMEL Dickenson
TREVILIANS Louisa
TRIANGLE Prince William
TROUT DALE (24378) Grayson(89), Smyth(10)
TROUTDALE (24378) Grayson(89), Smyth(10)
TROUTVILLE (24175) Botetourt(88), Roanoke(11)
TROY (22974) Fluvanna(77), Louisa(16), Albemarle(5)
TURBEVILLE Halifax
TYRO Nelson
UNION HALL Franklin
UNIVERSITY OF RICHMOND Richmond City
UPPERVILLE (20184) Fauquier(64), Loudoun(35)
UPPERVILLE Fauquier
URBANNA Middlesex
VALENTINES Brunswick
VANSANT Buchanan
VERNON HILL (24597) Halifax(80), Pittsylvania(19)
VERONA Augusta
VESTA Patrick
VESUVIUS (24483) Rockbridge(60), Amherst(20), Nelson(19)
VICTORIA Lunenburg
VIENNA Fairfax
VIEWTOWN (22746) Culpeper(74), Rappahannock(25)
VILLAGE Richmond
VILLAMONT Bedford
VINTON (24179) Bedford(50), Roanoke(49)
VIRGILINA (24598) Halifax(84), Mecklenburg(15)
VIRGINIA BEACH Virginia Beach City
VOLNEY Grayson
WACHAPREAGUE Accomack
WAKE Middlesex
WAKEFIELD (23888) Sussex(54), Southampton(25), Surry(19)
WALKERTON (23177) King and Queen(78), King William(21)
WALLOPS ISLAND Accomack
WARDTOWN Northampton
WARE NECK Gloucester
WARFIELD Brunswick
WARM SPRINGS Bath
WARNER Middlesex
WARRENTON Fauquier
WARSAW (22572) Richmond(93), Westmoreland(6)
WASHINGTON Rappahannock
WATER VIEW Middlesex
WATERFORD Loudoun
WATTSVILLE Accomack
WAVERLY Sussex
WAYNESBORO (22980) Waynesboro City(71), Augusta(28)
WEBER CITY Scott
WEEMS Lancaster
WEIRWOOD Northampton
WEST AUGUSTA Augusta
WEST MCLEAN Fairfax
WEST POINT (23181) King William(85), New Kent(11), King and Queen(3)
WESTMORELAND Westmoreland
WEYERS CAVE (24486) Augusta(85), Rockingham(14)
WHITE HALL Albemarle
WHITE MARSH Gloucester
WHITE PLAINS Brunswick
WHITE POST (22663) Clarke(60), Frederick(34), Warren(4)
WHITE STONE Lancaster
WHITETOP Grayson
WHITEWOOD Buchanan
WICOMICO Gloucester
WICOMICO CHURCH Northumberland
WILLIAMSBURG (23185) James City(46), Williamsburg City(27), York(25)
WILLIAMSBURG (23188) James City(78), York(19), Williamsburg City(1)
WILLIAMSBURG Williamsburg City
WILLIAMSVILLE (24487) Bath(64), Highland(36)
WILLIS (24380) Floyd(93), Carroll(6)
WILLIS WHARF Northampton
WILSONS (23894) Dinwiddie(86), Nottoway(13)
WINCHESTER (22601) Winchester City(93), Frederick(6)
WINCHESTER Frederick
WINCHESTER Winchester City
WINDSOR Isle of Wight
WINGINA (24599) Nelson(85), Buckingham(14)
WIRTZ Franklin
WISE Wise
WITHAMS Accomack
WOLFORD Buchanan
WOLFTOWN Madison
WOODBERRY FOREST Madison
WOODBRIDGE Prince William
WOODFORD (22580) Caroline(90), Spotsylvania(9)
WOODLAWN Carroll
WOODS CROSS ROADS Gloucester
WOODSTOCK Shenandoah
WOODVILLE Rappahannock
WOOLWINE Patrick
WYLLIESBURG Charlotte
WYTHEVILLE Wythe
YALE Sussex
YARDS Tazewell
YORKTOWN York
ZACATA Westmoreland
ZANONI Gloucester
ZUNI (23898) Isle of Wight(69), Southampton(30)

Virginia ZIP/City Cross Reference

20101-20104 DULLES
20105-20105 ALDIE
20106-20106 AMISSVILLE
20107-20107 ARCOLA
20108-20113 MANASSAS
20115-20116 MARSHALL
20117-20118 MIDDLEBURG
20119-20119 CATLETT
20120-20122 CENTREVILLE
20124-20124 CLIFTON
20128-20128 ORLEAN
20129-20129 PAEONIAN SPRINGS
20130-20130 PARIS
20131-20131 PHILOMONT
20132-20134 PURCELLVILLE
20135-20135 BLUEMONT
20136-20136 BRISTOW
20137-20137 BROAD RUN
20138-20138 CALVERTON
20139-20139 CASANOVA
20140-20140 RECTORTOWN
20141-20142 ROUND HILL
20143-20143 CATHARPIN
20144-20144 DELAPLANE
20146-20149 ASHBURN
20151-20153 CHANTILLY
20155-20156 GAINESVILLE
20158-20159 HAMILTON
20160-20160 LINCOLN
20163-20167 STERLING
20168-20169 HAYMARKET
20170-20172 HERNDON
20175-20178 LEESBURG
20180-20180 LOVETTSVILLE
20181-20182 NOKESVILLE
20184-20185 UPPERVILLE
20186-20188 WARRENTON
20189-20189 DULLES
20190-20191 RESTON
20192-20192 HERNDON
20193-20196 RESTON
20197-20197 WATERFORD
20198-20198 THE PLAINS
20199-20199 DULLES
22001-22001 ALDIE
22002-22002 AMISSVILLE
22003-22003 ANNANDALE
22009-22009 BURKE
22010-22010 ARCOLA
22011-22011 ASHBURN
22012-22012 BLUEMONT
22013-22013 BRISTOW
22014-22014 BROAD RUN
22015-22015 BURKE
22016-22016 CALVERTON
22017-22017 CASANOVA

22018-22018 CATHARPIN
22019-22019 CATLETT
22020-22020 CENTREVILLE
22021-22022 FAIRFAX
22024-22024 CLIFTON
22025-22025 DELAPLANE
22026-22026 DUMFRIES
22027-22027 DUNN LORING
22030-22038 FAIRFAX
22039-22039 FAIRFAX STATION
22040-22047 FALLS CHURCH
22060-22060 FORT BELVOIR
22065-22065 GAINESVILLE
22066-22066 GREAT FALLS
22067-22067 GREENWAY
22068-22068 HAMILTON
22069-22069 HAYMARKET
22070-22070 RESTON
22071-22071 HERNDON
22075-22075 LEESBURG
22078-22078 PURCELLVILLE
22079-22079 LORTON
22080-22080 LOVETTSVILLE
22081-22082 MERRIFIELD
22090-22090 HERNDON
22091-22091 RESTON
22092-22092 HERNDON
22093-22093 ASHBURN
22094-22095 HERNDON
22096-22096 RESTON
22101-22102 MC LEAN
22103-22103 WEST MCLEAN
22106-22109 MC LEAN
22110-22111 MANASSAS
22115-22115 MARSHALL
22116-22116 MERRIFIELD
22117-22117 MIDDLEBURG
22118-22120 MERRIFIELD
22121-22121 MOUNT VERNON
22122-22122 NEWINGTON
22123-22123 NOKESVILLE
22124-22124 OAKTON
22125-22125 OCCOQUAN
22128-22128 ORLEAN
22129-22129 PAEONIAN SPRINGS
22130-22130 PARIS
22131-22131 PHILOMONT
22132-22132 PURCELLVILLE
22134-22135 QUANTICO
22140-22140 RECTORTOWN
22141-22141 ROUND HILL
22150-22161 SPRINGFIELD
22170-22170 STERLING PARK
22171-22171 THE PLAINS
22172-22172 TRIANGLE
22176-22176 UPPERVILLE
22180-22185 VIENNA
22186-22186 WARRENTON
22190-22190 WATERFORD
22191-22195 WOODBRIDGE
22199-22199 LORTON
22200-22210 ARLINGTON
22211-22211 FT MYER
22212-22246 ARLINGTON
22300-22336 ALEXANDRIA
22401-22412 FREDERICKSBURG
22421-22421 ALFONSO
22427-22428 BOWLING GREEN
22430-22430 BROOKE
22432-22432 BURGESS
22433-22433 BURR HILL
22435-22435 CALLAO
22436-22436 CARET
22437-22437 CENTER CROSS
22438-22438 CHAMPLAIN
22439-22439 CHANCE
22442-22442 COLES POINT
22443-22443 COLONIAL BEACH
22446-22446 CORBIN
22448-22448 DAHLGREN
22451-22451 DOGUE
22454-22454 DUNNSVILLE
22456-22456 EDWARDSVILLE
22460-22460 FARNHAM
22461-22461 FONESWOOD
22463-22463 GARRISONVILLE
22469-22469 HAGUE
22471-22471 HARTWOOD
22472-22472 HAYNESVILLE
22473-22473 HEATHSVILLE
22476-22476 HUSTLE
22477-22477 HYACINTH
22480-22480 IRVINGTON
22481-22481 JERSEY
22482-22482 KILMARNOCK
22485-22485 KING GEORGE
22488-22488 KINSALE
22501-22501 LADYSMITH
22502-22502 LAHORE
22503-22503 LANCASTER
22504-22504 LANEVIEW
22505-22505 LEWISETTA
22507-22507 LIVELY
22508-22508 LOCUST GROVE
22509-22509 LORETTO
22511-22511 LOTTSBURG
22513-22513 MERRY POINT
22514-22514 MILFORD
22517-22517 MOLLUSK
22520-22520 MONTROSS
22523-22523 MORATTICO
22524-22524 MOUNT HOLLY
22526-22526 NINDE
22528-22528 NUTTSVILLE
22529-22529 OLDHAMS
22530-22530 OPHELIA
22534-22534 PARTLOW
22535-22535 PORT ROYAL
22538-22538 RAPPAHANNOCK ACADEMY
22539-22539 REEDVILLE
22540-22540 REGINA
22542-22542 RHOADESVILLE
22544-22544 ROLLINS FORK
22545-22545 RUBY
22546-22546 RUTHER GLEN
22547-22547 SEALSTON
22548-22548 SHARPS
22549-22549 SHILOH
22552-22552 SPARTA
22553-22553 SPOTSYLVANIA
22554-22556 STAFFORD
22558-22558 STRATFORD
22559-22559 SUPPLY
22560-22560 TAPPAHANNOCK
22565-22565 THORNBURG
22567-22567 UNIONVILLE
22568-22568 MINE RUN
22570-22570 VILLAGE
22572-22572 WARSAW
22576-22576 WEEMS
22577-22577 WESTMORELAND
22577-22577 SANDY POINT
22578-22578 WHITE STONE
22579-22579 WICOMICO CHURCH
22580-22580 WOODFORD
22581-22581 ZACATA
22601-22604 WINCHESTER
22610-22610 BENTONVILLE
22611-22611 BERRYVILLE
22620-22620 BOYCE
22622-22622 BRUCETOWN
22623-22623 CHESTER GAP
22624-22624 CLEAR BROOK
22625-22625 CROSS JUNCTION
22626-22626 FISHERS HILL
22627-22627 FLINT HILL
22630-22630 FRONT ROYAL
22637-22637 GORE
22638-22638 WINCHESTER
22639-22639 HUME
22640-22640 HUNTLY
22641-22641 STRASBURG
22642-22642 LINDEN
22643-22643 MARKHAM
22644-22644 MAURERTOWN
22645-22645 MIDDLETOWN
22646-22646 MILLWOOD
22649-22649 MIDDLETOWN
22650-22650 RILEYVILLE
22651-22651 FRONT ROYAL
22652-22652 FORT VALLEY
22654-22654 STAR TANNERY
22655-22655 STEPHENS CITY
22656-22656 STEPHENSON
22657-22657 STRASBURG
22660-22660 TOMS BROOK
22663-22663 WHITE POST
22664-22664 WOODSTOCK
22701-22701 CULPEPER
22709-22709 ARODA
22711-22711 BANCO
22712-22712 BEALETON
22713-22713 BOSTON
22714-22714 BRANDY STATION
22715-22715 BRIGHTWOOD
22716-22716 CASTLETON
22718-22718 ELKWOOD
22719-22719 ETLAN
22720-22720 GOLDVEIN
22721-22721 GRAVES MILL
22722-22722 HAYWOOD
22723-22723 HOOD
22724-22724 JEFFERSONTON
22725-22725 LEON
22726-22726 LIGNUM
22727-22727 MADISON
22728-22728 MIDLAND
22729-22729 MITCHELLS
22730-22730 OAKPARK
22731-22731 PRATTS
22732-22732 RADIANT
22733-22733 RAPIDAN
22734-22734 REMINGTON
22735-22735 REVA
22736-22736 RICHARDSVILLE
22737-22737 RIXEYVILLE
22738-22738 ROCHELLE
22739-22739 SOMERVILLE
22740-22740 SPERRYVILLE
22741-22741 STEVENSBURG
22742-22742 SUMERDUCK
22743-22743 SYRIA
22746-22746 VIEWTOWN
22747-22747 WASHINGTON
22748-22748 WOLFTOWN
22749-22749 WOODVILLE
22801-22807 HARRISONBURG
22810-22810 BASYE
22811-22811 BERGTON
22812-22812 BRIDGEWATER
22815-22815 BROADWAY
22820-22820 CRIDERS
22821-22821 DAYTON
22824-22824 EDINBURG
22827-22827 ELKTON
22830-22830 FULKS RUN
22831-22831 HINTON
22832-22832 KEEZLETOWN
22833-22833 LACEY SPRING
22834-22834 LINVILLE
22835-22835 LURAY
22840-22840 MC GAHEYSVILLE
22841-22841 MOUNT CRAWFORD
22842-22842 MOUNT JACKSON
22843-22843 MOUNT SOLON
22844-22844 NEW MARKET
22845-22845 ORKNEY SPRINGS
22846-22846 PENN LAIRD
22847-22847 QUICKSBURG
22848-22848 PLEASANT VALLEY
22849-22849 SHENANDOAH
22850-22850 SINGERS GLEN
22851-22851 STANLEY
22853-22853 TIMBERVILLE
22900-22911 CHARLOTTESVILLE
22920-22920 AFTON
22922-22922 ARRINGTON
22923-22923 BARBOURSVILLE
22924-22924 BATESVILLE
22929-22929 COBHAM
22931-22931 COVESVILLE
22932-22932 CROZET
22935-22935 DYKE
22936-22936 EARLYSVILLE
22937-22937 ESMONT
22938-22938 FABER
22939-22939 FISHERSVILLE
22940-22940 FREE UNION
22942-22942 GORDONSVILLE
22943-22943 GREENWOOD
22945-22945 IVY
22946-22946 KEENE
22947-22947 KESWICK
22948-22948 LOCUST DALE
22949-22949 LOVINGSTON
22951-22951 ROSELAND
22952-22952 LYNDHURST
22953-22953 MADISON MILLS
22954-22954 MASSIES MILL
22957-22957 MONTPELIER STATION
22958-22958 NELLYSFORD
22959-22959 NORTH GARDEN
22960-22960 ORANGE
22963-22963 PALMYRA
22964-22964 PINEY RIVER
22965-22965 QUINQUE
22967-22967 ROSELAND
22968-22968 RUCKERSVILLE
22969-22969 SCHUYLER
22971-22971 SHIPMAN
22972-22972 SOMERSET
22973-22973 STANARDSVILLE
22974-22974 TROY
22976-22976 TYRO
22980-22980 WAYNESBORO
22987-22987 WHITE HALL
22989-22989 WOODBERRY FOREST
23001-23001 ACHILLES
23002-23002 AMELIA COURT HOUSE
23003-23003 ARK
23004-23004 ARVONIA
23005-23005 ASHLAND
23009-23009 AYLETT
23011-23011 BARHAMSVILLE
23013-23013 BAVON
23014-23014 BEAUMONT
23015-23015 BEAVERDAM
23016-23016 BEAVERLETT
23017-23017 BELLAMY
23018-23018 BENA
23020-23020 BLAKES
23021-23021 BOHANNON
23022-23022 BREMO BLUFF
23023-23023 BRUINGTON
23024-23024 BUMPASS
23025-23025 CARDINAL
23027-23027 CARTERSVILLE
23029-23029 CAUTHORNVILLE
23030-23030 CHARLES CITY
23031-23031 CHRISTCHURCH
23032-23032 CHURCH VIEW
23035-23035 COBBS CREEK
23037-23037 COLOGNE
23038-23038 COLUMBIA
23039-23039 CROZIER
23040-23040 CUMBERLAND
23042-23042 DABNEYS
23043-23043 DELTAVILLE
23045-23045 DIGGS
23047-23047 DOSWELL
23050-23050 DUTTON
23054-23054 FIFE
23055-23055 FORK UNION
23056-23056 FOSTER
23058-23060 GLEN ALLEN
23061-23061 GLOUCESTER
23062-23062 GLOUCESTER POINT

23063-23063 GOOCHLAND
23064-23064 GRIMSTEAD
23065-23065 GUM SPRING
23066-23066 GWYNN
23067-23067 HADENSVILLE
23068-23068 HALLIEFORD
23069-23069 HANOVER
23070-23070 HARDYVILLE
23071-23071 HARTFIELD
23072-23072 HAYES
23075-23075 HIGHLAND SPRINGS
23076-23076 HUDGINS
23079-23079 JAMAICA
23080-23080 JAMES STORE
23081-23081 JAMESTOWN
23083-23083 JETERSVILLE
23084-23084 KENTS STORE
23085-23085 KING AND QUEEN COURT HOUS
23086-23086 KING WILLIAM
23089-23089 LANEXA
23090-23090 LIGHTFOOT
23091-23091 LITTLE PLYMOUTH
23092-23092 LOCUST HILL
23093-23093 LOUISA
23101-23101 MACON
23102-23102 MAIDENS
23103-23103 MANAKIN SABOT
23104-23104 MANGOHICK
23105-23105 MANNBORO
23106-23106 MANQUIN
23107-23107 MARYUS
23108-23108 MASCOT
23109-23109 MATHEWS
23110-23110 MATTAPONI
23111-23111 MECHANICSVILLE
23112-23113 MIDLOTHIAN
23114-23114 MILES
23114-23114 MIDLOTHIAN
23115-23115 MILLERS TAVERN
23116-23116 MECHANICSVILLE
23117-23117 MINERAL
23118-23118 MOBJACK
23119-23119 MOON
23120-23120 MOSELEY
23122-23122 NAXERA
23123-23123 NEW CANTON
23124-23124 NEW KENT
23125-23125 NEW POINT
23126-23126 NEWTOWN
23127-23127 NORGE
23128-23128 NORTH
23129-23129 OILVILLE
23130-23130 ONEMO
23131-23131 ORDINARY
23137-23137 PLAIN VIEW
23138-23138 PORT HAYWOOD
23139-23139 POWHATAN
23140-23140 PROVIDENCE FORGE
23141-23141 QUINTON
23142-23142 REDART
23146-23146 ROCKVILLE
23147-23147 RUTHVILLE
23148-23148 SAINT STEPHENS CHURCH
23149-23149 SALUDA
23150-23150 SANDSTON
23153-23153 SANDY HOOK
23154-23154 SCHLEY
23155-23155 SEVERN
23156-23156 SHACKLEFORDS
23157-23157 SHADOW
23160-23160 STATE FARM
23161-23161 STEVENSVILLE
23162-23162 STUDLEY
23163-23163 SUSAN
23168-23168 TOANO
23169-23169 TOPPING
23170-23170 TREVILIANS
23173-23173 UNIVERSITY OF RICHMOND
23175-23175 URBANNA
23176-23176 WAKE
23177-23177 WALKERTON
23178-23178 WARE NECK
23179-23179 WARNER
23180-23180 WATER VIEW
23181-23181 WEST POINT
23183-23183 WHITE MARSH
23184-23184 WICOMICO
23185-23188 WILLIAMSBURG
23190-23190 WOODS CROSS ROADS
23191-23191 ZANONI
23192-23192 MONTPELIER
23200-23298 RICHMOND
23301-23301 ACCOMAC
23302-23302 ASSAWOMAN
23303-23303 ATLANTIC
23304-23304 BATTERY PARK
23306-23306 BELLE HAVEN
23307-23307 BIRDSNEST
23308-23308 BLOXOM
23310-23310 CAPE CHARLES
23313-23313 CAPEVILLE
23314-23314 CARROLLTON
23315-23315 CARRSVILLE
23316-23316 CHERITON
23320-23328 CHESAPEAKE
23336-23336 CHINCOTEAGUE
23336-23336 CHINCOTEAGUE ISLAND
23337-23337 CHINCOTEAGUE
23337-23337 WALLOPS ISLAND
23341-23341 CRADDOCKVILLE
23345-23345 DAVIS WHARF
23347-23347 EASTVILLE
23350-23350 EXMORE
23354-23354 FRANKTOWN
23356-23356 GREENBACKVILLE
23357-23357 GREENBUSH
23358-23358 HACKSNECK
23359-23359 HALLWOOD
23389-23389 HARBORTON
23395-23395 HORNTOWN
23396-23396 OAK HALL
23397-23397 ISLE OF WIGHT
23398-23398 JAMESVILLE
23399-23399 JENKINS BRIDGE
23401-23401 KELLER
23403-23403 LEE MONT
23404-23404 LOCUSTVILLE
23405-23405 MACHIPONGO
23407-23407 MAPPSVILLE
23408-23408 MARIONVILLE
23409-23409 MEARS
23410-23410 MELFA
23412-23412 MODEST TOWN
23413-23413 NASSAWADOX
23414-23414 NELSONIA
23415-23415 NEW CHURCH
23416-23416 OAK HALL
23417-23417 ONANCOCK
23418-23418 ONLEY
23419-23419 OYSTER
23420-23420 PAINTER
23421-23421 PARKSLEY
23422-23422 PUNGOTEAGUE
23423-23423 QUINBY
23424-23424 RESCUE
23426-23426 SANFORD
23427-23427 SAXIS
23429-23429 SEAVIEW
23430-23431 SMITHFIELD
23432-23439 SUFFOLK
23440-23440 TANGIER
23441-23441 TASLEY
23442-23442 TEMPERANCEVILLE
23443-23443 TOWNSEND
23450-23479 VIRGINIA BEACH
23480-23480 WACHAPREAGUE
23481-23481 CARRSVILLE
23482-23482 WARDTOWN
23483-23483 WATTSVILLE
23484-23484 WEIRWOOD
23486-23486 WILLIS WHARF
23487-23487 WINDSOR
23488-23488 WITHAMS
23500-23551 NORFOLK
23600-23603 NEWPORT NEWS
23604-23604 FORT EUSTIS
23605-23628 NEWPORT NEWS
23629-23629 GREAT AMERICAN MAGAZINE
23630-23630 NEWPORT NEWS
23630-23631 HAMPTON
23632-23632 GREAT AMERICAN MAGAZINE
23651-23651 FORT MONROE
23653-23661 HAMPTON
23662-23662 POQUOSON
23663-23681 HAMPTON
23690-23693 YORKTOWN
23694-23694 LACKEY
23696-23696 SEAFORD
23700-23709 PORTSMOUTH
23801-23801 FORT LEE
23803-23806 PETERSBURG
23821-23821 ALBERTA
23822-23822 AMMON
23824-23824 BLACKSTONE
23827-23827 BOYKINS
23828-23828 BRANCHVILLE
23829-23829 CAPRON
23830-23830 CARSON
23831-23831 CHESTER
23832-23832 CHESTERFIELD
23833-23833 CHURCH ROAD
23834-23834 COLONIAL HEIGHTS
23836-23836 CHESTER
23837-23837 COURTLAND
23838-23838 CHESTERFIELD
23839-23839 DENDRON
23840-23840 DEWITT
23841-23841 DINWIDDIE
23842-23842 DISPUTANTA
23843-23843 DOLPHIN
23844-23844 DREWRYVILLE
23845-23845 EBONY
23846-23846 ELBERON
23847-23847 EMPORIA
23850-23850 FORD
23851-23851 FRANKLIN
23856-23856 FREEMAN
23857-23857 GASBURG
23859-23859 HANDSOM
23860-23860 HOPEWELL
23866-23866 IVOR
23867-23867 JARRATT
23868-23868 LAWRENCEVILLE
23870-23870 JARRATT
23872-23872 MC KENNEY
23873-23873 MEREDITHVILLE
23874-23874 NEWSOMS
23875-23875 PRINCE GEORGE
23876-23876 RAWLINGS
23878-23878 SEDLEY
23879-23879 SKIPPERS
23881-23881 SPRING GROVE
23882-23882 STONY CREEK
23883-23883 SURRY
23884-23884 SUSSEX
23885-23885 SUTHERLAND
23887-23887 VALENTINES
23888-23888 WAKEFIELD
23889-23889 WARFIELD
23890-23891 WAVERLY
23893-23893 WHITE PLAINS
23894-23894 WILSONS
23897-23897 YALE
23898-23898 ZUNI
23899-23899 CLAREMONT
23901-23909 FARMVILLE
23911-23911 ANDERSONVILLE
23915-23915 BASKERVILLE
23917-23917 BOYDTON
23919-23919 BRACEY
23920-23920 BRODNAX
23921-23921 BUCKINGHAM
23922-23922 BURKEVILLE
23923-23923 CHARLOTTE COURT HOUSE
23924-23924 CHASE CITY
23927-23927 CLARKSVILLE
23930-23930 CREWE
23934-23934 CULLEN
23935-23935 DARLINGTN HTS
23935-23935 DARLINGTON HEIGHTS
23936-23936 DILLWYN
23937-23937 DRAKES BRANCH
23938-23938 DUNDAS
23939-23939 EVERGREEN
23941-23941 FORT MITCHELL
23942-23942 GREEN BAY
23943-23943 HAMPDEN SYDNEY
23944-23944 KENBRIDGE
23947-23947 KEYSVILLE
23950-23950 LA CROSSE
23952-23952 LUNENBURG
23954-23954 MEHERRIN
23955-23955 NOTTOWAY
23958-23958 PAMPLIN
23959-23959 PHENIX
23960-23960 PROSPECT
23962-23962 RANDOLPH
23963-23963 RED HOUSE
23964-23964 RED OAK
23966-23966 RICE
23967-23967 SAXE
23968-23968 SKIPWITH
23970-23970 SOUTH HILL
23974-23974 VICTORIA
23976-23976 WYLLIESBURG
24000-24040 ROANOKE
24041-24041 BANK AMERICARD
24042-24045 ROANOKE
24046-24046 CITY OFFICES
24048-24050 ROANOKE
24053-24053 ARARAT
24054-24054 AXTON
24055-24055 BASSETT
24058-24058 BELSPRING
24059-24059 BENT MOUNTAIN
24060-24063 BLACKSBURG
24064-24064 BLUE RIDGE
24065-24065 BOONES MILL
24066-24066 BUCHANAN
24067-24067 CALLAWAY
24068-24068 CHRISTIANSBURG
24069-24069 CASCADE
24070-24070 CATAWBA
24072-24072 CHECK
24073-24073 CHRISTIANSBURG
24076-24076 CLAUDVILLE
24077-24077 CLOVERDALE
24078-24078 COLLINSVILLE
24079-24079 COPPER HILL
24082-24082 CRITZ
24083-24083 DALEVILLE
24084-24084 DUBLIN
24085-24085 EAGLE ROCK
24086-24086 EGGLESTON
24087-24087 ELLISTON
24088-24088 FERRUM
24089-24089 FIELDALE
24090-24090 FINCASTLE
24091-24091 FLOYD
24092-24092 GLADEHILL
24093-24093 GLEN LYN
24094-24094 GOLDBOND
24095-24095 GOODVIEW
24101-24101 HARDY
24102-24102 HENRY
24104-24104 HUDDLESTON
24105-24105 INDIAN VALLEY
24111-24111 MC COY
24112-24115 MARTINSVILLE
24120-24120 MEADOWS OF DAN
24121-24121 MONETA
24122-24122 MONTVALE
24124-24124 NARROWS
24126-24126 NEWBERN

24127-24127 NEW CASTLE
24128-24128 NEWPORT
24129-24129 NEW RIVER
24130-24130 ORISKANY
24131-24131 PAINT BANK
24132-24132 PARROTT
24133-24133 PATRICK SPRINGS
24134-24134 PEARISBURG
24136-24136 PEMBROKE
24137-24137 PENHOOK
24138-24138 PILOT
24139-24139 PITTSVILLE
24141-24143 RADFORD
24146-24146 REDWOOD
24147-24147 RICH CREEK
24148-24148 RIDGEWAY
24149-24149 RINER
24150-24150 RIPPLEMEAD
24151-24151 ROCKY MOUNT
24153-24157 SALEM
24161-24161 SANDY LEVEL
24162-24162 SHAWSVILLE
24165-24165 SPENCER
24167-24167 STAFFORDSVILLE
24168-24168 STANLEYTOWN
24171-24171 STUART
24174-24174 THAXTON
24175-24175 TROUTVILLE
24176-24176 UNION HALL
24177-24177 VESTA
24178-24178 VILLAMONT
24179-24179 VINTON
24184-24184 WIRTZ
24185-24185 WOOLWINE
24201-24209 BRISTOL
24210-24212 ABINGDON
24215-24215 ANDOVER
24216-24216 APPALACHIA
24217-24217 BEE
24218-24218 BEN HUR
24219-24219 BIG STONE GAP
24220-24220 BIRCHLEAF
24221-24221 BLACKWATER
24224-24224 CASTLEWOOD
24225-24225 CLEVELAND
24226-24226 CLINCHCO
24228-24228 CLINTWOOD
24230-24230 COEBURN
24236-24236 DAMASCUS
24237-24237 DANTE
24239-24239 DAVENPORT
24243-24243 DRYDEN
24244-24244 DUFFIELD
24245-24245 DUNGANNON
24246-24246 EAST STONE GAP
24248-24248 EWING
24249-24249 EXETER
24250-24250 FORT BLACKMORE
24251-24251 GATE CITY
24256-24256 HAYSI
24258-24258 HILTONS
24260-24260 HONAKER
24263-24263 JONESVILLE
24265-24265 KEOKEE
24266-24266 LEBANON
24269-24269 MC CLURE
24270-24270 MENDOTA
24271-24271 NICKELSVILLE
24272-24272 NORA
24273-24273 NORTON
24277-24277 PENNINGTON GAP
24279-24279 POUND
24280-24280 ROSEDALE
24281-24281 ROSE HILL
24282-24282 SAINT CHARLES
24283-24283 SAINT PAUL
24285-24285 STONEGA
24289-24289 TRAMMEL
24290-24290 WEBER CITY
24292-24292 WHITETOP
24293-24293 WISE
24301-24301 PULASKI
24311-24311 ATKINS
24312-24312 AUSTINVILLE
24313-24313 BARREN SPRINGS
24314-24314 BASTIAN
24315-24315 BLAND
24316-24316 BROADFORD
24317-24317 CANA
24318-24318 CERES
24319-24319 CHILHOWIE
24321-24321 CLINCHBURG
24322-24322 CRIPPLE CREEK
24323-24323 CROCKETT
24324-24324 DRAPER
24325-24325 DUGSPUR
24326-24326 ELK CREEK
24327-24327 EMORY
24328-24328 FANCY GAP
24330-24330 FRIES
24333-24333 GALAX
24340-24340 GLADE SPRING
24343-24343 HILLSVILLE
24347-24347 HIWASSEE
24348-24348 INDEPENDENCE
24350-24350 IVANHOE
24351-24351 LAMBSBURG
24352-24352 LAUREL FORK
24354-24354 MARION
24360-24360 MAX MEADOWS
24361-24361 MEADOWVIEW
24363-24363 MOUTH OF WILSON
24366-24366 ROCKY GAP
24368-24368 RURAL RETREAT
24370-24370 SALTVILLE
24373-24373 SEVEN MILE FORD
24374-24374 SPEEDWELL
24375-24375 SUGAR GROVE
24377-24377 TANNERSVILLE
24378-24378 TROUT DALE
24378-24378 TROUTDALE
24379-24379 VOLNEY
24380-24380 WILLIS
24381-24381 WOODLAWN
24382-24382 WYTHEVILLE
24401-24407 STAUNTON
24411-24411 AUGUSTA SPRINGS
24412-24412 BACOVA
24413-24413 BLUE GRASS
24415-24415 BROWNSBURG
24416-24416 BUENA VISTA
24421-24421 CHURCHVILLE
24422-24422 CLIFTON FORGE
24426-24426 COVINGTON
24430-24430 CRAIGSVILLE
24431-24431 CRIMORA
24432-24432 DEERFIELD
24433-24433 DOE HILL
24435-24435 FAIRFIELD
24437-24437 FORT DEFIANCE
24438-24438 GLEN WILTON
24439-24439 GOSHEN
24440-24440 GREENVILLE
24441-24441 GROTTOES
24442-24442 HEAD WATERS
24444-24444 HIGHTOWN
24445-24445 HOT SPRINGS
24448-24448 IRON GATE
24449-24449 JORDAN MINES
24450-24450 LEXINGTON
24457-24457 LOW MOOR
24458-24458 MC DOWELL
24459-24459 MIDDLEBROOK
24460-24460 MILLBORO
24463-24463 MINT SPRING
24464-24464 MONTEBELLO
24465-24465 MONTEREY
24467-24467 MOUNT SIDNEY
24468-24468 MUSTOE
24469-24469 NEW HOPE
24471-24471 PORT REPUBLIC
24472-24472 RAPHINE
24473-24473 ROCKBRIDGE BATHS
24474-24474 SELMA
24475-24475 SPOTTSWOOD
24476-24476 STEELES TAVERN
24477-24477 STUARTS DRAFT
24479-24479 SWOOPE
24482-24482 VERONA
24483-24483 VESUVIUS
24484-24484 WARM SPRINGS
24485-24485 WEST AUGUSTA
24486-24486 WEYERS CAVE
24487-24487 WILLIAMSVILLE
24501-24515 LYNCHBURG
24517-24517 ALTAVISTA
24520-24520 ALTON
24521-24521 AMHERST
24522-24522 APPOMATTOX
24523-24523 BEDFORD
24526-24526 BIG ISLAND
24527-24527 BLAIRS
24528-24528 BROOKNEAL
24529-24529 BUFFALO JUNCTION
24530-24530 CALLANDS
24531-24531 CHATHAM
24533-24533 CLIFFORD
24534-24534 CLOVER
24535-24535 CLUSTER SPRINGS
24536-24536 COLEMAN FALLS
24538-24538 CONCORD
24539-24539 CRYSTAL HILL
24540-24544 DANVILLE
24549-24549 DRY FORK
24550-24550 EVINGTON
24551-24551 FOREST
24553-24553 GLADSTONE
24554-24554 GLADYS
24555-24555 GLASGOW
24556-24556 GOODE
24557-24557 GRETNA
24558-24558 HALIFAX
24562-24562 HOWARDSVILLE
24563-24563 HURT
24565-24565 JAVA
24566-24566 KEELING
24569-24569 LONG ISLAND
24570-24570 LOWRY
24571-24571 LYNCH STATION
24572-24572 MADISON HEIGHTS
24574-24574 MONROE
24576-24576 NARUNA
24577-24577 NATHALIE
24578-24578 NATURAL BRIDGE
24579-24579 NATURAL BRIDGE STATION
24580-24580 NELSON
24581-24581 NORWOOD
24585-24585 REPUBLICAN GROVE
24586-24586 RINGGOLD
24588-24588 RUSTBURG
24589-24589 SCOTTSBURG
24590-24590 SCOTTSVILLE
24592-24592 SOUTH BOSTON
24593-24593 SPOUT SPRING
24594-24594 SUTHERLIN
24595-24595 SWEET BRIAR
24596-24596 TURBEVILLE
24597-24597 VERNON HILL
24598-24598 VIRGILINA
24599-24599 WINGINA
24601-24601 AMONATE
24602-24602 BANDY
24603-24603 BIG ROCK
24604-24604 BISHOP
24605-24605 BLUEFIELD
24606-24606 BOISSEVAIN
24607-24607 BREAKS
24608-24608 BURKES GARDEN
24609-24609 CEDAR BLUFF
24612-24612 DORAN
24613-24613 FALLS MILLS
24614-24614 GRUNDY
24618-24618 HARMAN
24619-24619 HORSEPEN
24620-24620 HURLEY
24622-24622 JEWELL RIDGE
24624-24624 KEEN MOUNTAIN
24627-24627 MAVISDALE
24628-24628 MAXIE
24630-24630 NORTH TAZEWELL
24631-24631 OAKWOOD
24634-24634 PILGRIMS KNOB
24635-24635 POCAHONTAS
24637-24637 POUNDING MILL
24639-24639 RAVEN
24640-24640 RED ASH
24641-24641 RICHLANDS
24646-24646 ROWE
24647-24647 SHORTT GAP
24649-24649 SWORDS CREEK
24651-24651 TAZEWELL
24656-24656 VANSANT
24657-24657 WHITEWOOD
24658-24658 WOLFORD
24659-24659 YARDS

Washington

General Help Numbers:

Governor's Office

PO Box 40002
Olympia, WA 98504-0002
www.governor.wa.gov

360-902-4111
Fax 360-753-4110
8AM-5PM

Attorney General's Office

PO Box 40100
Olympia, WA 98504-0100
www.atg.wa.gov/

360-753-6200
Fax 360-664-0228
8AM-5PM

Legislative Information Center

PO Box 40600
Olympia, WA 98504-0600
www.leg.wa.gov/legislature

360-786-7573
Fax 360-786-1293
8AM-5PM

State Archives

State Archives
PO Box 40238
Olympia, WA 98504-0238
www.secstate.wa.gov/archives/

360-586-1492
Fax 360-664-8814
8:30AM-4:30PM

State Specifics:

Capital:	Olympia Thurston County
Time Zone:	PST
Number of Counties:	39
Population:	6,549,224
Web Site:	http://access.wa.gov

State Agencies

Criminal Records

Washington State Patrol, Identification and Criminal History Section, PO Box 42633, Olympia, WA 98504-2633 (Courier address- 3000 Pacific Ave. SE #204, Olympia, WA 98501); 360-705-5100, 360-534-2000 (WATCH or CHRI Info), Fax- 360-570-5277; 8AM-5PM.

www.wsp.wa.gov/

Two types of records available: General Conviction - all convictions and arrests less than one year pending disposition; and Child & Adult Abuse record - all conviction and crimes against person, pending disposition (1 yr or less).

Indexing & Storage: Records available from 1974. Criminal history information is retained at the Identification and Criminal History Section until the offender is age seventy, or ten years from the last date of arrest, whichever is longer. New records available for inquiry in 30 to 45 days if manual; 2 hours if electronic. 79% of all arrests in database have final dispositions recorded, 70% for those arrests within last 5 years.

Searching: The Child & Adult Abuse record is available for non-profits. Include in request- date of birth, SSN, sex, race, name and address of subject. Fingerprints are optional. Records are 100% fingerprint-supported. Mail requests are directed to the WSP or e-mail to crimhis@wsp.gov. This data not released- non-conviction and arrest information over one year old without disposition. Records without dispositions not released unless the arrest is less than 1 year old.

Access by: mail, in person, online.

Fee & Payment: The fee for a name check is $35.00 per individual (except online). For a fingerprint check, the fee is $30.00 per individual. Will not conduct FBI fingerprint checks. The Child & Adult Abuse record is no charge. Notary letters are $5.00 per seal. Fee payee- Washington State Patrol. Prepayment required. Money orders or cashier's checks preferred. Personal checks accepted. Credit cards accepted online only.

Mail search: Turnaround time- 2 to 3 weeks. Download interactive request form at www.wsp.wa.gov/crime/240569_request_for_chri-convicted_criminal.pdf. SASE not required.

In person: Visitors may make in person requests. See Mail Requests section for location of interactive downloadable request form online.

Online search: WSP offers access through a system called WATCH, which can be accessed from their website. The fee per name search is $10.00. The exact DOB and exact spelling of the name are required. Credit cards are accepted online. Add $5.00 for notarize seal (fax requests accepted for these). To set up a WATCH account, call 360-705-5100 or email watch.help@wsp.wa.gov. Non-profits can request a fee-exempt account. WATCH stands for Washington Access To Criminal History.

Other access: See the State Court Administrator's office for information about their criminal records database (JIS-Link).

Statewide Court Records

Administrative Office of Courts, PO Box 41170, Olympia, WA 98504-1170 (Courier address- 1206 Quince St SE, Olympia, WA 98501); 360-753-3365, Fax- 360-586-8869; 8AM-5PM.

www.courts.wa.gov

The AOC offers online access to trial court records via an online system.

Searching: Include in request- name or case number.

Online search: The web offers free look-up of docket information at http://dw.courts.wa.gov/. This is an unofficial search. Also, the AOC provides facilities that allow one to access information in the Judicial Information System's (JIS) statewide computer. This program of services is called JIS-Link. JIS-Link provides access to all counties and court levels. Case records include criminal, civil, domestic, probate, and judgments. Fees include a one-time $100.00 per site, a transaction fee of $.065. There is a $6.00 per month minimum. Call 360-753-3365 or visit www.courts.wa.gov/jislink/. For appellate actions see www.courts.wa.gov/opinions/. The page offers a notification service also.

Other access: Indexes available electronically for a fee. Call the JISLink Coordinator for details. A Request for Information form at http://dw.courts.wa.gov/datadis/request.doc can be mailed, faxed or emailed to dda@courts.wa.gov. Fees on the form.

Sexual Offender Registry

Washington State Patrol, SOR, PO Box 42633, Olympia, WA 98504-2633 (Courier address- 3000 Pacific Ave. SE #204, Olympia, WA 98501); 360-534-2000 x3, Fax- 360-534-2072; 8AM-5PM.

www.wsp.wa.gov/

Indexing & Storage: Records available from 1990. New records available for inquiry in 30 days or less.

Searching: The state refers requesters to the criminal record search system or to the free web page search of sexual offenders, as shown below.

Access by: mail, online.

Mail search: Limited search requests accepted by mail.

Online search: In cooperation with the Washington Assoc. of Sheriffs and Police Chiefs, free online access to Level II and Level III sexual offenders is available at http://ml.waspc.org/.

Incarceration Records

Washington Department of Corrections, Office of the Secretary, 7345 Linderson Way SW, Tumwater, WA 98501-6504; 360-725-8213, 360-725-8852 (Public Disclosure); 8AM-5PM M-F.

www.doc.wa.gov

Indexing & Storage: Records available on current and former inmates. New records available for inquiry in 1 to 5 days.

Searching: Records are not destroyed and eventually archived with Sec. of State office according to that office's retention schedule. Include in request- full name, DOB; SSN is helpful. Location, CCO, parole review data, counselor, and DOB are released. For anything other than this basic information, a written request is preferred.

Access by: mail, phone, fax, online.

Fee & Payment: A copy fee is $.20 per page; a postage fee applies to all mailed documents. Prepayment required.

Mail search: Turnaround time- 1 to 2 weeks. SASE not required.

Phone search: Name searching available by phone; basic information is released.

Fax search: Requests for single inquiries are accepted by fax.

Online search: "Find an Offender" is free at www.doc.wa.gov/offenderinfo/default.aspx. Search by name or DOC number.

Other access: Data is available by subscription for bulk users; for information, contact the Contracts Office at 360-725-8363.

Corporation, Trademarks/Servicemarks, LP, LLC Records

Secretary of State, Corporations Division, PO Box 40234, Olympia, WA 98504-0234 (Courier address- Dolliver Bldg, 801 Capitol Way South, Olympia, WA 98501); 360-725-0377, Fax- 360-664-8781; 8AM-5PM.

www.secstate.wa.gov/corps/

Indexing & Storage: Records available for initial filing documents and amendments, if filed. Annual reports for the past 5 years are on microfilm, imaged since 2004. New records available for inquiry in 6 days.

Searching: All of the information here is public record. Records prior to 2004 at available from the State Archives 360-586-1492. Corporate document images are available form State Digital Archives beginning 9/30/2008. Include in request- full name of business, UBI number if available. The copies for a limited partnership are different than corporation documents. Any single document is $1.00 per page plus $.20 per copy for LPs. The Annual Report contains the names of Directors and Officers.

Access by: mail, phone, fax, in person, online.

Fee & Payment: Annual Report is $5.00 per corporate name. Photocopies fee is $10.00 per LLC or corp. document, $20.00 if the document needs to be certified. If file exceeds 100 pages, a surcharge of $13.00 per 50 pages is added. Trademark documents are $.50 per page. Fee payee- Secretary of State. Prepayment required. Personal checks accepted. Credit cards accepted by fax and for phone options.

Mail search: Turnaround time- variable. SASE not required.

Phone search: Information requests are available at this division.

Fax search: Requests accepted by fax for documents filed 2004 and forward, requires expedite fees.

In person: Turnaround time is while you wait.

Online search: Free searching of corporation registrations is at www.secstate.wa.gov/corps/search.aspx. Information is updated daily. Also, search securities companies registered with the state and other financial institutions free at https://fortress.wa.gov/dfi/licenselu/dfi/licenseLU/default.aspx.

Expedited service: Expedited service is available for mail, fax, and phone searches. Add $20.00 per document.

Trade Names

Master License Service, Business & Professions Div, PO Box 9034, Olympia, WA 98507-9034 (Courier address- 405 Black Lake Blvd, Olympia, WA 98502); 360-664-1400, Fax- 360-570-4959; 8AM-5PM. www.dol.wa.gov

Indexing & Storage: Records available from 1984 (note that everyone re-registered trade names in 1984). New records available for inquiry in 3 weeks.

Searching: Searching may be done by business name, business address, owner's name, or UBI number. This data not released- SSNs, personal information (height, weight, sex, eye color, etc.), date of birth or addresses.

Access by: mail, fax, in person, online.

Fee & Payment: The search fee is $4.00, which includes 3 business/owner names. A name variation is considered a separate name. Certification costs an additional $2.00. Fee payee- Washington State Treasurer. Prepayment required. Personal checks accepted, credit cards are not.

Mail search: Turnaround time- 1-2 weeks. SASE not required.

Fax search: See expedited services.

In person: Copies cost $.25 per page. Turnaround time is while you wait.

Online search: The web page give the ability to check trade name ability, assuming the business name listed is the trade name.

Other access: Records can be purchased on cartridges or 9 track tapes. Information includes date of registration, owner name, state ID numbers, and cancel date if cancelled. Call same number and ask for Jody Miller.

Expedited service: Expedited service is available for fax searches. Must have an account with a deposit.

Uniform Commercial Code, Federal Tax Liens

Department of Licensing, UCC Records, PO Box 9660, Olympia, WA 98507-9660 (Courier address- 405 Black Lake Blvd, Olympia, WA 98502); 360-664-1530, Fax- 360-586-4414; 8AM-5PM.

www.dol.wa.gov/business/UCC/

Indexing & Storage: Records available from 1967. However, only currently active plus 1 full year are accessible. New records available for inquiry in 2 days.

Searching: Use search request form UCC-11. The search includes all notices of tax liens filed here.

Include in request- debtor name. This data not released- SSNs

Access by: mail, in person, online.

Fee & Payment: A mail or in person request for information is $10.00. A request for information with all copies is $15.00 Fee payee- Department of Licensing. Prepayment required. Credit cards are accepted for online searching only. Personal checks, Visa, and MasterCard accepted.

Mail search: Turnaround time- 2 days. SASE not required.

In person: Record requests may be dropped off, turnaround time usually 2 days.

Online search: For online access, go to https://fortress.wa.gov/dol/ucc. There is no search fee for name search or by file number. Fee is $15.00 if copies are mailed.

Other access: The database may be purchased via FTP.

State Tax Liens

Records not maintained by a state level agency.

State tax liens are filed at the county level.

Sales Tax Registrations

Department of Revenue, Taxpayer Services, PO Box 47478, Olympia, WA 98504-7478; 360-705-6705, 800-647-7706, Fax- 360-705-6655; 8AM-5PM.

http://dor.wa.gov/Content/Home/Default.aspx

Indexing & Storage: Records available from 1992 and are indexed on microfiche and optical imaging. New records available for inquiry in 1-3 days.

Searching: This agency will provide disclose able information authorized by statute such as tax registration/UBI #, owner's name, business name (DBA), address, open/closing date, account status and SIC/NAICS. For confidential information, submit a signed release. Include in request- business name or owner name, UBI or tax registration number.

Access by: mail, phone, fax, in person, online.

Fee & Payment: There is no search fee or copy fee (unless extensive copies needed).

Mail search: Turnaround time- 5 business days.

Phone search: Only "public registration" information is available.

Fax search: Turnaround time is 5 business days.

In person: Appointment required.

Online search: The agency provides a state business records database with free access on the Internet at http://dor.wa.gov/content/doingbusiness/registermybusiness/brd/. Look-ups are by owner names, DBAs, and tax reporting numbers. Results show a myriad of data.

Birth Certificates

Department of Health, Center for Health Statistics, PO Box 9709, Olympia, WA 98507-9709 (Courier address- 101 Israel Rd SE, Tumwater WA 98501); 360-236-4300 (Main Number), 360-236-4313 (Credit Card Ordering), Fax- 360-352-2586; 8AM - 4:30PM.

www.doh.wa.gov/EHSPHL/CHS/cert.htm

Birth certificates from 1923 to present from ANY COUNTY are also available at most every County Health Department. Same fees. See www.doh.wa.gov/EHSPHL/CHS/issuing_co.htm for addresses and details Most offer counter service.

Indexing & Storage: Records available from July 1, 1907 to present. New records available for inquiry in 2-3 months.

Searching: The data on the lower portion of form is confidential. Include in request- full name, names of parents, mother's maiden name, date of birth, place of birth. Use of the order form (see web) is suggested. Please specify if father is not listed on birth certificate.

Access by: mail, phone, fax, in person, online.

Fee & Payment: The fee is $20.00 per name. Most counties charge the same. Fee payee- Dept of Health. Prepayment required. Personal checks accepted. Major credit cards accepted by vendor only.

Mail search: Turnaround time- 7 to 8 weeks. Must send your current address and daytime phone number with request. A SASE is requested.

Phone search: Phone service available 9AM-4PM. You must use a credit card.

Fax search: Same criteria as phone searching.

In person: Counter service is available for same day requests, credit cards not accepted.

Online search: Records may requested from www.Vitalchek.com, a state-endorsed vendor.

Other access: The Digital Archives, launched in 2004, contains various periods for marriages, death, birth, military, naturalization, institution, and various historical records at www.digitalarchives.wa.gov/default.aspx.

Expedited service: Expedited online, phone or fax ordering is via a state-endorsed vendor - www.vitalchek.com. Turnaround time- next working day mail. You must use a credit card. Extra fees involved, sometimes the document is access from the county. Add Courier or Express Mail deliver costs if desired.

Death Records

Department of Health, Vital Records, PO Box 9709, Olympia, WA 98507-9709 (Courier address- 101 Israel Rd SE, Tumwater, WA 98501); 360-236-4300 (Main Number), 360-236-4313 (Credit Card Ordering), Fax- 360-352-2586; 8AM - 4:30PM.

www.doh.wa.gov/EHSPHL/CHS/cert.htm

Indexing & Storage: Records available from July 1, 1907 to present. Contact the county for records less than 4 months old. New records available for inquiry in 3-4 months.

Searching: A written request is required, there is no public viewing. Include in request- full name, date of death, place of death. Use of the order form (see web) is suggested.

Access by: mail, phone, fax, in person, online.

Fee & Payment: The fee is $20.00 per name. Most counties charge the same. Fee payee- Dept of Health. Prepayment required. Personal checks accepted. Major credit cards accepted by vendor only.

Mail search: Turnaround time- 7 to 8 weeks. Must send your current address and daytime phone number with request. A SASE is requested.

Phone search: Phone service available 9AM-4PM. You must use a credit card.

Fax search: Same criteria as phone searching.

In person: Counter service is available for same day requests, credit cards not accepted.

Online search: Records may requested from www.vitalchek.com, a state-endorsed vendor.

Other access: The Digital Archives, launched in 2004, contains various periods for marriages, death, birth, military, naturalization, institution, and various historical records at www.digitalarchives.wa.gov/default.aspx.

Expedited service: Expedited online, phone or fax ordering is via a state-endorsed vendor - www.vitalchek.com. Turnaround time- next working day. You must use a credit card. Extra fees involved, sometimes the document is access from the county. Add Courier or Express Mail deliver costs if desired.

Marriage Certificates

Department of Health, Vital Records, PO Box 9709, Olympia, WA 98507-9709 (Courier address- 101 Israel Rd SE, Tumwater, WA 98501); 360-236-4300 (Main Number), 360-236-4313 (Credit Card Ordering), Fax- 360-352-2586; 8AM - 4:30PM.

www.doh.wa.gov/EHSPHL/CHS/cert.htm

Indexing & Storage: Records available from 1968 to present. Contact the county for records less than 4 months old. New records available for inquiry in 3-4 months.

Searching: Written request is required, there is no public viewing. Include in request- names of husband and wife, date of marriage, place or county of marriage. Use of the order form (see web) is suggested.

Access by: mail, phone, fax, in person, online.

Fee & Payment: The fee is $20.00 per name. Most counties charge the same. Fee payee- Dept of Health. Prepayment required. Personal checks accepted. Major credit cards accepted by vendor only.

Mail search: Turnaround time- 7 to 8 weeks. Must send your current address and daytime phone number with request. A SASE is requested.

Phone search: Phone service available 9AM-4PM. You must use a credit card.

Fax search: Same criteria as phone searching.

In person: Counter service is available for same day requests, credit cards not accepted.

Online search: Records may requested from www.vitalchek.com, a state-endorsed vendor.

Other access: The Digital Archives, launched in 2004, contains various periods for marriages, death, birth, military, naturalization, institution, and various historical records at www.digitalarchives.wa.gov/default.aspx.

Expedited service: Expedited online, phone or fax ordering is via a state-endorsed vendor - www.vitalchek.com. Turnaround time- overnight delivery. You must use a credit card. Extra fees involved, sometimes the document is access form the county. Add Courier or Express Mail deliver costs if desired.

Divorce Records

Department of Health, Vital Records, PO Box 9709, Olympia, WA 98507-9709 (Courier address- 101 Israel Rd SE, Tumwater, WA 98501); 360-236-4300 (Main Number), 360-753-4313 (Credit Card Ordering), Fax- 360-352-2586; 8AM - 4:30PM.

www.doh.wa.gov/EHSPHL/CHS/cert.htm

Indexing & Storage: Records available from 1968 to present. Contact the county for records less than 4 months old. New records available for inquiry in 34 months.

Searching: Include in request- names of husband and wife, date of divorce, place of divorce. Use of the order form (see web) is suggested.

Access by: mail, phone, fax, in person, online.

Fee & Payment: The fee is $20.00 per name. Most counties charge the same. Fee payee- Dept of Health. Prepayment required. Personal checks accepted. Major credit cards accepted by vendor only.

Mail search: Turnaround time- 5 weeks. Must send your current address and daytime phone number with request. A SASE is requested.

Phone search: Phone service available 9AM-4PM. You must use a credit card.

Fax search: Same criteria as phone searching.

In person: Counter service is available for same day requests, credit cards not accepted.

Online search: Records may requested from www.vitalchek.com, a state-endorsed vendor.

Expedited service: Expedited online, phone or fax ordering is via a state-endorsed vendor - www.vitalchek.com. Turnaround time- overnight delivery. You must use a credit card. Extra fees involved, sometimes the document is access form the county. Add Courier or Express Mail deliver costs if desired.

Workers' Compensation Records

Labor and Industries, Public Records Unit, PO Box 44632, Olympia, WA 98504-4632 (Courier address- 7273 Linderson Way SW, Tumwater, WA 98501); 360-902-5556, Fax- 360-902-5529; 8AM-5PM.

www.lni.wa.gov

There are two forms available on the web - Request for Claim Information and the Request for Public Records.

Indexing & Storage: Records available for the past 3 years. Prior records are at the State Records Center, but you must go through this office for those records. New records available for inquiry in 1 month.

Searching: Must have signed release from the claimant on both forms. Written request only. Claims information is not released except as provided under Title 51 of the Revised Code of Washington (RCW). Include in request- claimant name, SSN, claim number, signed release signature form or court signed subpoena. The DOB is helpful. Also, see www.lni.wa.gov/news/otherresources.asp#publicdisclosure. This data not released- chemically-related illness.

Access by: mail, fax, in person, online.

Fee & Payment: Copy fee is $.15 per page. Certification is an additional cover sheet for $.15. Fee payee- L & I Cashier. Prepayment required only if over $100. Personal checks accepted, credit cards are not.

Mail search: Turnaround time- 3 to 5 business days. The record information that they send back is taken from microfiche only. No hard file copies released. Archived records can take 30 days to provide.

Fax search: Fax requests are accepted.

In person: Must schedule by appointment.

Online search: Claim information is accessible to authorized users at www.lni.wa.gov/orli/logon.asp. Claims inactive for 18+ months or crime victims claims are not in the Claim & Account Center.

Driver Records

Department of Licensing, Driver Record Section, PO Box 9048, Olympia, WA 98507-9030 (Courier address- 1125 Washington Street SE, Olympia, WA 98504); 360-902-3913, 360-902-3900 (General Information), Fax- 360-586-9044; 8AM-4:30PM.

www.dol.wa.gov

Records available include a 3-year insurance record and the "full" employment record. The 3-year record contains employment or non-employment convictions. The full record contains both. Detailed information on access and forms are found at the web.

Indexing & Storage: New records available for inquiry in 2 to 3 weeks or more.

Searching: All mail or walk-in requests require a properly signed form, exceptions are for ongoing, pre-approved accounts. Casual requesters must have written consent. In general, records are not provided to third party, even with a signed consent. Include in request- license number, or the name and DOB. The license number is based upon a code of the name and DOB. This code can be confusing (O or 0, *'s) so it is suggested you try name and DOB first. This data not released- SSNs.

Access by: mail, in person, online.

Fee & Payment: The fee is $10.00 per record. Copies of tickets may be requested by the driver. The fee is $.75 per ticket; the first 4 are free. Fee payee- Department of Licensing Prepayment required. Personal checks accepted, credit cards are not.

Mail search: Turnaround time- 2 weeks. There is no charge for a no record found, but do not refund if $10.00 or less specifically requested. A SASE is requested.

In person: Turnaround time is immediate for up to 5 requests. There is no charge for a no record found.

Online search: FTP retrieval is offered for high volume requesters, minimum of 2,000 requests per month. Requesters must be approved and sign a contract. Call Data Sales Management at 360-902-3851 Contract holders may also participate in a notification program (monitoring and notification of activity on a record), but strictly used for only insurance company needs. There is a secondary check for status of a driver license, permit or ID card free at https://fortress.wa.gov/dol/ddl/dsd/.

Expedited service: Will expedite delivery if a prepaid envelope is provided.

Vehicle, Vessel Ownership & Registration

Department of Licensing, Public Disclosure Unit, PO Box 2957, Olympia, WA 98507-2957 (Courier address- 1125 Washington SE MS-48001, Olympia, WA 98504); 360-902-3780, Fax- 360-902-3827; 8AM-5PM.

www.dol.wa.gov/vehicleregistration/

It is recommended that on-going, high volume users enter into a disclosure agreement with this agency; call 360-902-3760.

Indexing & Storage: Records available for 6 plus current year. All motorized boats and sailboats must be titled. All boats must be registered unless under 16 ft with less than a 10 hp motor. New records available for inquiry in 2 to 3 weeks.

Searching: Washington has strict access guidelines that restrict casual requesters. Permitted requesters include attorneys, PI's, insurance companies, business entities as well as others for use in the normal course of business. A special form is required. Include in request- VIN, license plate number, HIN or registration number. Records cannot be searched by owner or driver name. Requests must be in writing. For forms, go to www.dol.wa.gov/forms/formspd.html.

Access by: mail, phone, fax, in person, online.

Fee & Payment: The fee for microfilm or microfiche copies are $.75 per page. Fee for photocopy or printouts is $.15 each. Certification is an additional $1.50. If the amount due is less than $4.50, the state does not charge. Fee payee- Department of Licensing Personal checks only accepted if pre-approved.

Mail search: Turnaround time- 2 weeks. SASE not required.

Phone search: phone ordering is only available for pre-approved, high volume accounts. The system processes by plate number, VIN, WN# & HIN. To set up an account, call 360-902-3760.

Fax search: Approved, ongoing requestors may fax requests. Disclosure request forms accepted.

In person: Counter service is offered, but limited.

Online search: This Internet Vehicle/Vessel Information Processing System is a commercial subscription service and all accounts must be pre-approved. A $25.00 deposit is required and there is a fee per hit. For more information, call 360-902-3760.

Other access: Large bulk lists cannot be released for any commercial purposes. Lists are released to non-profit entities and for statistical purposes. For more information, call 360-902-3760.

Accident Reports

State Patrol, Collision Reports, PO Box 47382, Olympia, WA 98504-7382; 360-570-2355, Fax-360-570-2400; 8AM-5PM.

www.wsp.wa.gov/

Indexing & Storage: Records available for 6 years plus the present year. New records available for inquiry in 2 to 3 weeks.

Searching: Entitled parties have access to the complete reports. Some information is withheld unless requester is party involved or authorized representative. The agency did not indicate what is withheld. Include in request- name, date of accident, location of accident. Also, use of their request form - Form 300-345-008 - is required.

The agency will fax a copy of the form, upon request. The form is found at www.wsdot.wa.gov/mapsdata/tdo/collisionreportrequest.htm.

Access by: mail, in person.

Fee & Payment: The fee is $5.00 per record. Fee payee- Washington State Patrol. Prepayment required. Personal checks accepted, credit cards are not.

Mail search: Turnaround time- 2 weeks. A SASE is requested.

In person: Walk-in requesters may receive the report with proper credentials, if personnel are available to do the search.

Legislation Records

Washington State Legislature, Legislative Information Center, PO Box 40600, Olympia, WA 98504-0600; 360-786-7573 (Information), 800-562-6000 (Hotline), Fax- 360-786-1293; 8AM-5PM. www.leg.wa.gov/legislature

Indexing & Storage: Records available on paper from 1985. New records available for inquiry in one day.

Searching: Include in request- bill number, topic of bill, year introduced.

Access by: mail, phone, fax, in person, online.

Fee & Payment: There is no search fee, unless extensive research is required. The first 30 pages are free. Fee payee- Washington State Treasurer Personal checks accepted.

Mail search: Turnaround time- 1 to 2 days. There is a limit of one copy per bill. SASE not required.

Phone search: Records are available by phone.

Fax search: Turnaround is 1 to 2 days.

In person: In person requests permitted.

Online search: The website offers bill text and status look-up. The Revised Code is located at www.leg.wa.gov/LawsAndAgencyRules.

Other access: There is an array of subscription services available from the Legislative Information Center. Data available includes, final digest, summaries, budget notes, and various reports. Call the Center for a price list or visit online.

Voter Registration

Secretary of State, Office of Elections Division, PO Box 40229, Olympia, WA 98504-0229 (Courier address- 520 Union Avenue SE,); 360-902-4180, 800-448-4881, Fax- 360-664-4619; 8AM-5PM. www.secstate.wa.gov/elections/

Records may only be purchased for political purposes (from this agency). Voter information is also kept at the local level by the County Auditor (except King County where records are kept by the Dept of Elections).

Indexing & Storage: Records available from 02/06. Extracts must stay in office 12 months, records are not destroyed but archived. New records available for inquiry in 30 days.

Searching: Individual look-ups will not receive SSNs, DOBs, or telephone numbers. Include in request- name, address, and phone of the requester. This data not released- DL#, last 4 digits of SSN, signature image.

Access by: mail, phone, fax, in person, online.

Fee & Payment: Copy fee is $.15 per page. Fee payee- Secretary of State

Mail search: Turnaround time- 3 days. Record confirmation is available by mail.

Phone search: Limited record information may requested by phone.

Fax search: Records may be requested by fax.

In person: Requests accepted in person.

Online search: A voter registration look-up link is found at http://wei.secstate.wa.gov/OSOS/VoterVault/Pages/MyVote.aspx - meant for voters to see and maintain their own information.

Other access: Monthly CDs are available from the web for $30. A strong disclaimer states that the CD is restricted for use for political purposes only. Use of a credit card is required.

GED Certificates

State Board for Community & Technical Colleges, GED Transcripts, PO Box 42495, Olympia, WA 98504-2495 (Courier address- 1300 Quince St SE, Olympia, WA 98504); 360-704-4410, Fax- 360-704-4414; 8AM-5PM.

www.sbctc.ctc.edu

Indexing & Storage: Records available from 1966. New records available for inquiry in 2 weeks.

Searching: Include in request- name, SSN, date of birth, signed release. Also, the city, date of test, and any previous name the record could be under are helpful.

Access by: mail, fax, in person.

Fee & Payment: There is no fee for either verification or a transcript.

Mail search: Turnaround time- 1 week. SASE not required.

Fax search: Same criteria as mail searching.

In person: Counter service not recommended as staff may not be available.

Hunting & Fishing License Information

Department of Fish & Wildlife, Attn: Public Disclosure Officer, 600 Capitol Way, N, Olympia, WA 98501-1091; 360-902-2253, Fax- 360-902-2171; 8AM-5PM. http://wdfw.wa.gov

Indexing & Storage: Records available since 2001 on an electronic basis. New records available for inquiry immediately.

Searching: Records cannot purchased as a list or in bulk, but not for commercial marketing purposes. Include in request- name and DOB. All requests must be in writing. This data not released- SSN, DL#.

Access by: mail, fax, in person, online.

Fee & Payment: There is no fee for searching individual names. Fees are involved for lists of license holders. Fee payee- WDFW Personal checks accepted.

Mail search: Turnaround time- 1-2 weeks. SASE not required.

Fax search: Fax requests accepted.

In person: Simple requests may be processed while you wait.

Online search: You may send an email request; check the website for the exact address. No fee.

Other access: The database can be purchased for non-commercial purposes only.

Washington State Licensing Agencies

For details about the agency responsible for licensing/certifying/registering an item below or in the Agency Quick Finder section, match an item's number with the number of the agency in the *Licensing Agency Information* section.

Washington Licenses Searchable Online

Acupuncturist #11 .... https://fortress.wa.gov/doh/providercredentialsearch/
Adult Family Home #30 .... www.aasa.dshs.wa.gov/Lookup/AFHRequestv2.asp
Animal Technician #11 .... https://fortress.wa.gov/doh/providercredentialsearch/
Announcer, Athletic Event/Ring #27 .... https://fortress.wa.gov/dol/dolprod/bpdLicenseQuery/
Applicator, Pesticide, Commercial #5 .... http://agr.wa.gov/pestfert/LicensingEd/Search/default.aspx
Architect/Architectural Corp #26 .... https://fortress.wa.gov/dol/dolprod/bpdLicenseQuery/
Athl' Judge/Timekeeper/Physician #27 .... https://fortress.wa.gov/dol/dolprod/bpdLicenseQuery/
Athlete, Professional #27 .... https://fortress.wa.gov/dol/dolprod/bpdLicenseQuery/
Athletic Inspector #27 .... https://fortress.wa.gov/dol/dolprod/bpdLicenseQuery/
Athletic Mgr/Promot'r/Matchmaker #27 .... https://fortress.wa.gov/dol/dolprod/bpdLicenseQuery/
Attorney #23 .... http://pro.wsba.org/
Audiologist #11 .... https://fortress.wa.gov/doh/providercredentialsearch/
Bail Bond Agent/Agency #15 .... https://fortress.wa.gov/dol/dolprod/bpdLicenseQuery/
Bail Bond Recovery Agent #15 .... https://fortress.wa.gov/dol/dolprod/bpdLicenseQuery/
Bank #7 .... www.dfi.wa.gov/banks/commercial_banks.htm
Barber #18 .... https://fortress.wa.gov/dol/dolprod/bpdLicenseQuery/
Barber Instructor/School #18 .... https://fortress.wa.gov/dol/dolprod/bpdLicenseQuery/
Barber Shop/Mobile #18 .... https://fortress.wa.gov/dol/dolprod/bpdLicenseQuery/
Beauty Shop/Salon/Mobile #18 .... https://fortress.wa.gov/dol/dolprod/bpdLicenseQuery/
Boarding Home #30 .... www.aasa.dshs.wa.gov/Lookup/BHRequestv2.asp
Boiler Inspector #13 .... www.lni.wa.gov/TradesLicensing/Boilers/Inspectors/default.asp
Boxer #27 .... https://fortress.wa.gov/dol/dolprod/bpdLicenseQuery/
Bulk Hauler #14 .... www.dol.wa.gov/listoflicenses.html
Cemetery #6 .... https://fortress.wa.gov/dol/dolprod/bpdLicenseQuery/
Cemetery Certificate of Authority #6 .... https://fortress.wa.gov/dol/dolprod/bpdLicenseQuery/
Cemetery Prearrangem't Seller #6 .... https://fortress.wa.gov/dol/dolprod/bpdLicenseQuery/
Certificate of Removal Registr'n #6 .... https://fortress.wa.gov/dol/dolprod/bpdLicenseQuery/
Charitable Gift Annuity #25 .... www.insurance.wa.gov/cgi-bin/PubInfoApps/CharitableGA.exe
Check Casher/Seller #7 .... https://fortress.wa.gov/dfi/licquery/dfi/licquery/default.aspx
Child Care Facility #29 .... www.childcarenet.org/families/your-search/referral_form
Child Care Provider #29 .... www.childcarenet.org/families/your-search/referral_form
Chiropractor #11 .... https://fortress.wa.gov/doh/providercredentialsearch/
Collection Agency #32 .... www.dol.wa.gov/listoflicenses.html
Consumer Loan Company #7 .... https://fortress.wa.gov/dfi/licquery/dfi/licquery/default.aspx
Contractor, Construction #12 .... https://fortress.wa.gov/lni/bbip/
Contractor, General, Company #12 .... https://fortress.wa.gov/lni/bbip/
Contributor, Political #34 .... http://web.pdc.wa.gov/public/campaign/default.aspx
Cosmetologist #18 .... https://fortress.wa.gov/dol/dolprod/bpdLicenseQuery/
Cosmetology Instructor/School #18 .... https://fortress.wa.gov/dol/dolprod/bpdLicenseQuery/
Counselor #11 .... https://fortress.wa.gov/doh/providercredentialsearch/
Cremated Remains Dispositor #6 .... https://fortress.wa.gov/dol/dolprod/bpdLicenseQuery/
Crematory #6 .... https://fortress.wa.gov/dol/dolprod/bpdLicenseQuery/
Currency Exchange #7 .... https://fortress.wa.gov/dfi/licquery/dfi/licquery/default.aspx
Dental Hygienist #11 .... https://fortress.wa.gov/doh/providercredentialsearch/
Dentist #11 .... https://fortress.wa.gov/doh/providercredentialsearch/
Dietitian #11 .... https://fortress.wa.gov/doh/providercredentialsearch/
Domestic Insurance Carrier #25 .... https://fortress.wa.gov/oic/laa/LAAMain.aspx
Electrical Contractor/Administrator #12 .... https://fortress.wa.gov/lni/bbip/
Electrician #12 .... https://fortress.wa.gov/lni/bbip/
Elevator Contractor/Mechanic #12 .... https://fortress.wa.gov/lni/bbip/
Embalmer/Intern #6 .... https://fortress.wa.gov/dol/dolprod/bpdLicenseQuery/
Emergency Medical Technician #11 .... https://fortress.wa.gov/doh/providercredentialsearch/
Employment Agency #32 .... www.dol.wa.gov/listoflicenses.html
Employment Directory Service #32 .... www.dol.wa.gov/listoflicenses.html
Engineer #10 .... https://fortress.wa.gov/dol/dolprod/bpdLicenseQuery/
Engineering Geologist #21 .... https://fortress.wa.gov/dol/dolprod/bpdLicenseQuery/
Engineering/Land Surveying Firm #10 .... https://fortress.wa.gov/dol/dolprod/bpdLicenseQuery/

Escrow Company/Officer #7 .... https://fortress.wa.gov/dfi/licquery/dfi/licquery/default.aspx
Esthetician/Esthetician Instructor #18 .... https://fortress.wa.gov/dol/dolprod/bpdLicenseQuery/
Esthetician/Salon/Mobile #18 .... https://fortress.wa.gov/dol/dolprod/bpdLicenseQuery/
Feedlot #3 .... http://agr.wa.gov/FoodAnimal/Livestock/CertifiedFeedlots.htm
Fishing/Hunting License Dealer #8 .... http://wdfw.wa.gov/lic/vendors/vendors.htm
Franchise #7 .... https://fortress.wa.gov/dfi/licquery/dfi/licquery/default.aspx
Funeral Director/Intern #6 .... https://fortress.wa.gov/dol/dolprod/bpdLicenseQuery/
Funeral Establishment/Branch #6 .... https://fortress.wa.gov/dol/dolprod/bpdLicenseQuery/
Funeral Prearrangement Contract #6 .... https://fortress.wa.gov/dol/dolprod/bpdLicenseQuery/
Gaming Operation #24 .... www.wsgc.wa.gov/search/emp_lic_search.asp
Gaming-related Occupation #24 .... www.wsgc.wa.gov/search/emp_lic_search.asp
Geologist #21 .... https://fortress.wa.gov/dol/dolprod/bpdLicenseQuery/
Healthcare Service Company #25 .... www.insurance.wa.gov/cgi-bin/PubInfoApps/CGIAuthComp.exe
Hearing Instrum't Fitter/Dispenser #11 .... https://fortress.wa.gov/doh/providercredentialsearch/
HMO #25 .... www.insurance.wa.gov/cgi-bin/PubInfoApps/CGIAuthComp.exe
Hydrogeologist #21 .... https://fortress.wa.gov/dol/dolprod/bpdLicenseQuery/
Hypnotherapist #11 .... https://fortress.wa.gov/doh/providercredentialsearch/
Insurance Agent/Broker #25 .... https://fortress.wa.gov/oic/laa/LAAMain.aspx
Insurance Broker, Resid't/Non-Resi. #25 .... https://fortress.wa.gov/oic/laa/LAAMain.aspx
Insurance Company #25 .... www.insurance.wa.gov/cgi-bin/PubInfoApps/CGIAuthComp.exe
Insurance Corporation, Resident #25 .... www.insurance.wa.gov/cgi-bin/PubInfoApps/CGIAuthComp.exe
Investment Advisor #7 .... https://fortress.wa.gov/dfi/licquery/dfi/licquery/default.aspx
Kickboxer #27 .... https://fortress.wa.gov/dol/dolprod/bpdLicenseQuery/
Land Surveyor/Surveyor-in-Training #10 .... https://fortress.wa.gov/dol/dolprod/bpdLicenseQuery/
Landscape Architect #26 .... https://fortress.wa.gov/dol/dolprod/bpdLicenseQuery/
Liquor Store #19 .... www.liq.wa.gov/services/storesearch.asp
Livestock Market #3 .... http://agr.wa.gov/FoodAnimal/Livestock/PublicMarkets.htm
Lobbyist/Lobbyist Report #34 .... http://web.pdc.wa.gov/public/lobbyist/default.aspx
Manicure Salon/Mobile #18 .... https://fortress.wa.gov/dol/dolprod/bpdLicenseQuery/
Manicurist/Manicurist Instructor #18 .... https://fortress.wa.gov/dol/dolprod/bpdLicenseQuery/
Manufactured Home Dealer #14 .... www.dol.wa.gov/listoflicenses.html
Marriage & Family Therapist #11 .... https://fortress.wa.gov/doh/providercredentialsearch/
Massage Therapist #11 .... https://fortress.wa.gov/doh/providercredentialsearch/
Medical Doctor #11 .... https://fortress.wa.gov/doh/providercredentialsearch/
Medical Gas Plumber #12 .... https://fortress.wa.gov/lni/bbip/
Mental Health Counselor #11 .... https://fortress.wa.gov/doh/providercredentialsearch/
Midwife #11 .... https://fortress.wa.gov/doh/providercredentialsearch/
Mobile Home/Travel Trailer Dealer #14 .... www.dol.wa.gov/listoflicenses.html
Money Transmitter #7 .... https://fortress.wa.gov/dfi/licquery/dfi/licquery/default.aspx
Mortgage Broker #7 .... https://fortress.wa.gov/dfi/licquery/dfi/licquery/default.aspx
Naturopathic Physician #11 .... https://fortress.wa.gov/doh/providercredentialsearch/
Nurse/Nursing Assistant #11 .... https://fortress.wa.gov/doh/providercredentialsearch/
Nurse-LPN #11 .... https://fortress.wa.gov/doh/providercredentialsearch/
Nursing Home #30 .... www.aasa.dshs.wa.gov/Professional/NFDir/directory.asp
Nursing Home Administrator #11 .... https://fortress.wa.gov/doh/providercredentialsearch/
Occupational Therapist #11 .... https://fortress.wa.gov/doh/providercredentialsearch/
Ocularist #11 .... https://fortress.wa.gov/doh/providercredentialsearch/
Optician #11 .... https://fortress.wa.gov/doh/providercredentialsearch/
Optometrist #11 .... https://fortress.wa.gov/doh/providercredentialsearch/
Osteopathic Physician #11 .... https://fortress.wa.gov/doh/providercredentialsearch/
Payday Lender #7 .... https://fortress.wa.gov/dfi/licquery/dfi/licquery/default.aspx
Pest Control Operator/Consul't #5 .... http://agr.wa.gov/PestFert/LicensingEd/Search/default.aspx
Pesticide Dealer/Manager #5 .... http://agr.wa.gov/PestFert/LicensingEd/Search/default.aspx
Pesticide demo&research Applicator #5 .... http://agr.wa.gov/PestFert/LicensingEd/Search/default.aspx
Pesticide Operator/Applicator #5 .... http://agr.wa.gov/PestFert/LicensingEd/Search/default.aspx
Pesticide Private Application #5 .... http://agr.wa.gov/PestFert/LicensingEd/Search/default.aspx
Pharmacist #11 .... https://fortress.wa.gov/doh/providercredentialsearch/
Pharmacy Technician #11 .... https://fortress.wa.gov/doh/providercredentialsearch/
Physical Therapist #11 .... https://fortress.wa.gov/doh/providercredentialsearch/
Physician Assistant #11 .... https://fortress.wa.gov/doh/providercredentialsearch/
Pilot, Marine, Commercial #2 .... www.pilotage.wa.gov/documents/Licensedpilots.PDF
Plumber #12 .... https://fortress.wa.gov/lni/bbip/
Podiatrist #11 .... https://fortress.wa.gov/doh/providercredentialsearch/
Political Candidate #34 .... http://web.pdc.wa.gov/Public/Searchdatabase/2007races.aspx
Political Committee #34 .... http://web.pdc.wa.gov/Public/Searchdatabase/2007races.aspx

Private Investigative Agency/Trainer #15 .... https://fortress.wa.gov/dol/dolprod/bpdLicenseQuery/
Private Investigat'r Armed/Unarm'd #15 .... https://fortress.wa.gov/dol/dolprod/bpdLicenseQuery/
Psychologist #11 .... https://fortress.wa.gov/doh/providercredentialsearch/
Public Accountant-CPA #1 .... www.cpaboard.wa.gov/LicenseeSearchApp/default.aspx
Purchasing Group (Insurance) #25........... www.insurance.wa.gov/cgi-bin/PubInfoApps/CGIRiskPG.exe
Radiologic Technologist #11........... https://fortress.wa.gov/doh/providercredentialsearch/
Real Estate Agent/Seller #16........... www.dol.wa.gov/business/realestate/
Real Estate Appraiser #16........... www.dol.wa.gov/listoflicenses.html
Real Estate Broker #16........... www.dol.wa.gov/business/realestate/
Real Estate LLC, LLP, Corp., etc. #16 .... www.dol.wa.gov/listoflicenses.html
Referee (Athletic) #27........... https://fortress.wa.gov/dol/dolprod/bpdLicenseQuery/
Respiratory Therapist #11........... https://fortress.wa.gov/doh/providercredentialsearch/
Risk Retention Group #25 .... www.insurance.wa.gov/cgi-bin/PubInfoApps/CGIRiskRG.exe
Savings & Loan/Savings Bank #7 .... www.dfi.wa.gov/banks/commercial_banks.htm
Scrap Processor #14 .... www.dol.wa.gov/listoflicenses.html
Securities Broker/Dealer #7........... https://fortress.wa.gov/dfi/licquery/dfi/licquery/default.aspx
Securities Salesperson #7........... https://fortress.wa.gov/dfi/licquery/dfi/licquery/default.aspx
Security Guard, Private #15........... https://fortress.wa.gov/dol/dolprod/bpdLicenseQuery/
Security Guard/Agency #15........... https://fortress.wa.gov/dol/dolprod/bpdLicenseQuery/
Service Contract Provider (Ins) #25........... www.insurance.wa.gov/cgi-bin/PubInfoApps/CGIServiceCP.exe
Sex Offender Treatment Provider #11........... https://fortress.wa.gov/doh/providercredentialsearch/
Snowmobile Dealer #14........... www.dol.wa.gov/listoflicenses.html
Social Worker #11 .... https://fortress.wa.gov/doh/providercredentialsearch/
Speech-Language Pathologist #11........... https://fortress.wa.gov/doh/providercredentialsearch/
Structural Pest Inspector #5 .... http://agr.wa.gov/pestfert/LicensingEd/Search/default.aspx
Telephone Solicitor #32........... www.dol.wa.gov/listoflicenses.html
Tow Truck Operator #14........... www.dol.wa.gov/listoflicenses.html
Trust Company #7........... www.dfi.wa.gov/banks/trusts.htm
Vehicle Dealer/Manufacturer #14........... www.dol.wa.gov/listoflicenses.html
Vehicle for Hire #32........... www.dol.wa.gov/listoflicenses.html
Vehicle Sales/Disposal #32........... www.dol.wa.gov/listoflicenses.html
Vehicle Transporter #14........... www.dol.wa.gov/listoflicenses.html
Vessel Dealer #14........... www.dol.wa.gov/listoflicenses.html
Veterinarian #11 .... https://fortress.wa.gov/doh/providercredentialsearch/
Veterinarian, Livestock #3 .... http://agr.wa.gov/FoodAnimal/Livestock/CertifiedVeterinarians.htm
Veterinary Medical Clerk #11........... https://fortress.wa.gov/doh/providercredentialsearch/
Viatical Settlement Provider #25........... www.insurance.wa.gov/cgi-bin/PubInfoApps/CGIViaticalSP.exe
Wastewater System Design/Inspect #10........... https://fortress.wa.gov/dol/dolprod/bpdLicenseQuery/
Whitewater River Outfitter #32........... www.dol.wa.gov/listoflicenses.html
Wrecker #14 .... www.dol.wa.gov/listoflicenses.html
Wrestler #27 .... https://fortress.wa.gov/dol/dolprod/bpdLicenseQuery/
X-ray Technician #11........... https://fortress.wa.gov/doh/providercredentialsearch/

Washington Licensing Quick Finder

Acupuncturist #11 360-236-4700
Adult Family Home #30 360-725-2300
Animal Technician #11 360-236-4700
Announcer, Athletic Event/Ring #27..... 360-664-6644
Applicator, Pesticide, Commercial #5... 877-301-4555
Architect/Architectural Corp #26........... 360-664-1388
Athl' Judge/Timekeeper/Physician #27 360-664-6644
Athlete, Professional #27........... 360-664-6644
Athlete, Professional #33........... 360-664-6644
Athletic Inspector #27 360-664-6644
Athletic Mgr/Promot'r/Matchmaker #27 . 360-664-6644
Attorney #23 .... 206-443-9722, 800-945-9722
Auction Company #33 360-664-6636
Auctioneer #33........... 360-664-6636
Audiologist #11 360-236-4700
Bail Bond Agent/Agency #15........... 360-664-6624
Bail Bond Recovery Agent #15 360-664-6624
Bank #7........... 360-902-8704
Barber #18 360-664-6626
Barber Instructor/School #18........... 360-664-6626
Barber Shop/Mobile #18........... 360-664-6626
Battery Collector #32........... 330-664-1400
Beauty Shop/Salon/Mobile #18 360-664-6626
Boarding Home #30 360-725-2300
Boiler Inspector #13 360-902-5270
Boxer #27 360-664-6644
Brand, Livestock #3 360-902-1855
Bulk Hauler #14 360-664-6466
Business Opportunity Offering #7 360-902-8760
Camping Resort #33 360-664-6646
Cemetery #6 360-664-1555
Cemetery Certificate of Authority #6 360-664-1555
Cemetery Prearrangem't Seller #6....... 360-664-1555
Certificate of Removal Registr'n #6...... 360-664-1555
Charitable Gift Annuity #25 360-725-7144
Check Casher/Seller #7 360-902-8703
Child Care Facility #29........... 866-482-4325
Child Care Provider #29........... 866-482-4325
Chiropractor #11........... 360-236-4700
Cigarette Retailer/Vender/Whlse #32... 330-664-1400
Collection Agency #32........... 360-664-1389
Commodity Registration #7........... 360-902-8760
Concealed Pistol License #15........... 360-664-6616
Consumer Loan Company #7 360-902-8703
Contractor, Construction #12 360-902-5226
Contractor, General, Company #12..... 360-902-5226
Contractor, General, Individual #32..... 330-664-1400
Contributor, Polit'l #34..877-601-2828, 360-753-1111
Cosmetologist #18........... 360-664-6626
Cosmetology (Barber) #33 360-664-6626
Cosmetology Instructor/School #18..... 360-664-6626
Counselor #11........... 360-236-4700
Court Reporter #33........... 360-664-6633
Credit Union #7 360-902-8701
Cremated Remains Dispositor #6 360-664-1555
Crematory #6........... 360-664-1555
Currency Exchange #7........... 360-902-8700
Dental Hygienist #11........... 360-236-4700
Dentist #11 360-236-4700
Dietitian #11 360-236-4700
Domestic Insurance Carrier #25 360-725-7144
Egg Handler/Dealer #32........... 330-664-1400
Egg Inspector #4 360-902-1830
Electrical Contractor/Administ'r #12..... 360-902-5269
Electrician #12........... 360-902-5269
Elevator Contractor/Mechanic #12........ 360-902-5226
Embalmer/Intern #6........... 360-664-1555
Emergency Medical Technician #11.... 360-236-2845
Employment Agency #32........... 360-664-1389

Employment Directory Service #32 330-664-1400
Engineer #10 360-664-1575
Engineering Geologist #21 360-664-1497
Engineering/Land Surveying Firm #10 . 360-664-1575
Escrow Company/Officer #7 360-902-8703
Esthetician/Esthetician Instructor #18 .. 360-664-6626
Esthetician/Salon/Mobile #18 360-664-6626
Feedlot #3 360-902-1855
Fertilizer Distributor, Bulk #32 330-664-1400
Firearms Dealer #15 360-664-6616
Firearms License, Alien #15 360-664-6616
Fishing, Commercial #8 360-902-2464
Fishing/Hunting License Dealer #8 360-902-2434
Foster Home #31 888-794-1794
Franchise #7 360-902-8760
Fruit/Vegetable Inspector #4 360-902-1832
Funeral Director/Intern #6 360-664-1555
Funeral Establishment/Branch #6 360-664-1555
Funeral Prearrangement Contract #6... 360-664-1555
Gaming Operation #24 360-486-3440
Gaming-related Occupation #24 360-486-3440
Geologist #21 360-664-1497
Grain Inspector/Weigher/Sampler #28 . 360-902-1921
Healthcare Service Company #25 360-725-7144
Hearing Instrum't Fitter/Dispenser #11 . 360-236-4700
HMO #25 360-725-7144
Home Health Care Agency #9 360-705-6611
Horse Racing #22 360-459-6462
Horse Racing-related Occupation #22 . 360-459-6462
Hospital #9 360-705-6611
Hydrogeologist #21 360-664-1497
Hypnotherapist #11 360-236-4700
Insurance Agent/Broker #25 360-725-7144
Insurance Broker, Resident/Non-Resi. #25 360-725-7144
Insurance Company #25 360-725-7144
Insurance Corporation, Resident #25... 360-725-7144
Investment Advisor #7 360-902-8760
Kickboxer #27 360-664-6644
Land Surveyor/Surveyor-in-training #10 360-664-1575
Landscape Architect #26 360-664-1497
Liquor Store #19 360-664-1600
Livestock Brand Record #3 360-902-1855
Livestock Market #3 360-902-1855
Lobbyist/Lobbyist Report #34 ...... 877-601-2828, 360-753-1111
Lottery Retailer #32 330-664-1400
Manicure Salon/Mobile #18 360-664-6626
Manicurist/Esthetician #33 360-664-6626
Manicurist/Manicurist Instructor #18..... 360-664-6626
Manufactured Home Dealer #14 360-664-6466
Marriage & Family Therapist #11 360-236-4700
Massage Therapist #11 360-236-4700
Medical Doctor #11 360-236-4700
Medical Gas Plumber #12 360-902-5207
Mental Health Counselor #11 360-236-4700
Midwife #11 360-236-4700
Minor Worker #32 330-664-1400
Mobile Home/Travel Trailer Dealer #14 360-664-6466
Money Transmitter #7 360-902-8700
Mortgage Broker #7 360-902-8703
Naturopathic Physician #11 360-236-4700
Notary Public #17 360-664-1550
Nurse/Nursing Assistant #11 360-236-4700
Nurse-LPN #11 360-236-4700
Nursery Retailer/Whlse #32 330-664-1400
Nursing Home #30 360-725-2300
Nursing Home Administrator #11 360-236-4700
Occupational Therapist #11 360-236-4700
Ocularist #11 360-236-4700
Optician #11 360-236-4700
Optometrist #11 360-236-4700
Osteopathic Physician #11 360-236-4700
Payday Lender #7 360-902-8700
Pest Control Operator/Consul't, Public #5 877-301-4555
Pesticide Dealer/Manager #5 877-301-4555
Pesticide Operator/Applicator #5 877-301-4555
Pesticide Private Application #5 877-301-4555
Pharmacist #11 360-236-4700
Pharmacy Technician #11 360-236-4700
Physical Therapist #11 360-236-4700
Physician Assistant #11 360-236-4700
Pilot, Marine, Commercial #2 206-515-3904
Plumber #12 360-902-5207
Podiatrist #11 360-236-4700
Political Candidate #34. 877-601-2828, 360-753-1111
Political Committee #34 877-601-2828, 360-753-1111
Private Investigative Agcy./Trainer #15. 360-664-6611
Private Investigator, Armed/Unarmed #15 360-664-6611
Psychologist #11 360-236-4700
Public Accountant-CPA #1 360-753-2585
Purchasing Group (Insurance) #25 360-725-7144
Radiologic Technologist #11 360-236-4700
Real Estate Agent/Seller #16 360-664-6488
Real Estate Appraiser #16 306-664-6502
Real Estate Broker #16 360-664-6488
Real Estate LLC, LLP, Corp., etc. #16 . 360-664-6488
Recreational Hunting #8 360-902-2464
Referee (Athletic) #27 360-664-6644
Refrigerated Locker #32 330-664-1400
Rental Car #32 330-664-1400
Respiratory Therapist #11 360-236-4700
Risk Retention Group #25 360-725-7144
Salon #33 360-664-6626
Savings & Loan/Savings Bank #7 306-902-8704
School Counselor #20 360-725-6400
School Nurse #20 360-725-6400
School Occupation'l/Phys'c'l Therapist #20 360-725-6400
School Principal/Superintendent #20... 360-725-6400
School Program Administrator #20 360-725-6400
School Psychologist/Social Worker #20 360-725-6400
Scrap Processor #14 360-664-6466
Securities Broker/Dealer #7 360-902-8760
Securities Salesperson #7 306-902-8760
Security Guard, Private #15 360-664-6611
Security Guard/Agency #15 360-664-6611
Seed Dealer #32 330-664-1400
Service Contract Provider (Ins) #25 360-725-7144
Sex Offender Treatment Provider #11. 360-236-4700
Shopkeeper (non-prescript'n drug) #32 330-664-1400
Snowmobile Dealer #14 360-664-6466
Social Worker #11 360-236-4700
Speech-Language Pathologist #11 360-236-4700
Speed Pathology Audiologist #20 360-725-6400
Sport Fishing #8 360-902-2464
Structural Pest Inspector #5 877-301-4555
Teacher #20 360-725-6400
Telephone Solicitor #32 330-664-1400
Timeshare Seller/Firm/Project #33 360-664-6632
Tow Truck Operator #14 360-664-6466
Travel Agency #33 360-664-6634
Travel Seller #33 360-664-6634
Trust Company #7 360-902-8704
Underground Storage Tank #32 330-664-1400
Vehicle Dealer/Manufacturer #14 360-664-6466
Vehicle for Hire #32 330-664-1400
Vehicle Sales/Disposal #32 330-664-1400
Vehicle Transporter #14 360-664-6466
Vessel Dealer #14 360-664-6466
Veterinarian #11 360-236-4700
Veterinarian, Livestock #3 360-902-1855
Veterinary Medical Clerk #11 360-236-4700
Viatical Settlement Provider #25 360-725-7144
Waste Tire Carrier #32 330-664-1400
Waste Tire Site Owner #32 330-664-1400
Wastewater System Designer/Inspect. #10 360-664-1575
Whitewater River Outfitter #32 330-664-1400
Wrecker #14 360-664-6466
Wrestler #27 360-664-6644
X-ray Technician #11 360-236-4700

Washington Licensing Agency Information

#1 Board of Accountancy, PO Box 9131 (711 Capitol Way S, Ste 400), Olympia, WA 98507-9131; 360-753-2585, Fax- 360-664-9190. www.cpaboard.wa.gov Search at- www.cpaboard.wa.gov/LicenseeSearchApp/default.aspx

#2 Board of Pilotage Commissioners, 2901 3rd Ave, Suite 500, Seattle, WA 98121; 206-515-3904, Fax- 206-515-3906. Hours- 6:30AM-3:30PM. www.pilotage.wa.gov

#3 Department of Agriculture, Livestock Identification Program, PO Box 42560 (1111 Washington St SE), Olympia, WA 98504-2560; 360-902-1855, Fax- 360-902-2086. Hours-8AM-5PM. http://agr.wa.gov/FoodAnimal/Livestock/ProgramOverview.htm

#4 Department of Agriculture, Food Safety & Animal Health Division, PO Box 42560 (1111 Washington St SE), Olympia, WA 98504-2560; 360-902-1800, Fax- 360-902-2092. http://agr.wa.gov

#5 Department of Agriculture, Pesticides Management Division, PO Box 42589, Olympia, WA 98504-2589; 877-301-4555, Fax- 360-902-2093. http://agr.wa.gov/PestFert/ Search data at- http://agr.wa.gov/pestfert/LicensingEd/Search/default.aspx

#6 Department of Licensing, Funeral & Cemetery Licensing Program, PO Box 9012 (405 Black Lake Blvd SW), Olympia, WA 98507-9012; 360-664-1555, Fax- 360-664-1495. Hours- 8AM-5PM. www.dol.wa.gov/business/funeral/ Search at- https://fortress.wa.gov/dol/dolprod/bpdLicenseQuery/

#7 Department of Financial Institutions, PO Box 41200 (150 Israel Rd SW, Tumwater), Olympia, WA 98504-1200; 360-902-8700, Fax-360-586-5068. www.dfi.wa.gov Search data at- www.dfi.wa.gov/cs/list.htm

#8 Department of Fish & Wildlife, 600 Capitol Way N, Olympia, WA 98501-1091; 360-902-2200, Fax- 360-902-2156. Hours- 8AM-5PM. http://wdfw.wa.gov

#9 Department of Health, Facilities Services Licensing, PO Box 47852, Olympia, WA 98504-7852; 360-236-2905, Fax- 360-236-2901. www.doh.wa.gov/hsqa/fsl/

#10 Department of Licensing, Professional Engineers and Land Surveyors Section, PO Box 9048 (405 Black Lake Blvd SW, 2nd Fl), Olympia, WA 98507; 360-664-1575, Fax- 360-664-2551. Hours- 8AM-5PM. www.dol.wa.gov/business/engineerslandsurveyors/ Search data at- https://fortress.wa.gov/dol/dolprod/bpdLicenseQuery/

#11 Department of Health, Health Professional Licensing, PO Box 47865 (310 Israel Rd, Tumwater), Olympia, WA 98504; 360-236-4700, Fax- 360-236-4818. www.doh.wa.gov/hsqa/licensing.htm Search data at- https://fortress.wa.gov/doh/providercredentialsearch/

#12 Department of Labor & Industries, Construction Compliance, PO Box 44000, Olympia, WA 98504-4000; 360-902-5226, Fax- 360-902-5228. Hours- 8AM-5PM. www.lni.wa.gov Search data at- https://fortress.wa.gov/lni/bbip/

#13 Department of Labor & Industries, Boiler Section, PO Box 44410, Olympia, WA 98504-4410; 360-902-5270, Fax- 360-902-5292. www.lni.wa.gov/TradesLicensing/Boilers/default.asp Search data at- www.lni.wa.gov/TradesLicensing/Boilers/Inspectors/default.asp

#14 Department of Licensing, Dealer Services, PO Box 9039, Olympia, WA 98507-9039; 360-664-6466, Fax- 360-586-0479. www.dol.wa.gov/business/checkstatus.html

#15 Licensing Dept, Public Protection Services Section, Private Investigator, Security Guard, Bail Bond, Recovery Agents, Firearms Programs, PO Box 9649, Olympia, WA 98507-9649; 360-664-6611, Fax- 360-570-7888. Hours- 8AM-5PM. www.dol.wa.gov Search at- https://fortress.wa.gov/dol/dolprod/bpdLicenseQuery/

#16 Department of Licensing, Real Estate & Appraiser Program, PO Box 9015 (2000 4th Ave W), Olympia, WA 98507-9015; 360-664-6488, Fax- 360-586-0998. Hours- 8AM-5PM. www.dol.wa.gov/business/appraisers/applicense.html Search data at- www.dol.wa.gov/listoflicenses.html

#17 Department of Licensing, Notary Section, PO Box 9027 (405 Black Lake Blvd SW), Olympia, WA 98507-9027; 360-664-1550, Fax-360-570-7053. Hours- 8AM-5PM. www.dol.wa.gov/business/notary/ Will sell lists of notaries only to educational/non-profit organizations who cannot use the data for commercial purposes.

#18 Department of Licensing, Cosmetology Division, PO Box 9026, Olympia, WA 98507-9026; 360-664-6626, Fax- 360-664-2550. Hours- 8AM-5PM. www.dol.wa.gov/business/cosmetology/ Search data at- https://fortress.wa.gov/dol/dolprod/bpdLicenseQuery/

#19 Liquor Control Board, PO Box 43075 (3000 Pacific Ave SE), Olympia, WA 98504; 360-664-1600, Fax- 360-753-2710. www.liq.wa.gov/

#20 Superintendent of Public Instruction, Professional Education & Certification, PO Box 47200 (Old Capitol Bldg), Olympia, WA 98504-7200; 360-725-6400, Fax- 360-586-0145. www.k12.wa.us/certification/

#21 Department of Licensing, Geologist Licensing Program, PO Box 9045, Olympia, WA 98507-9045; 360-664-1497, Fax- 360-664-1495. Hours- 6:30AM-5PM M,T,F. www.dol.wa.gov/ Search data at- https://fortress.wa.gov/dol/dolprod/bpdLicenseQuery/

#22 Horse Racing Commission, 6326 Martin Way, #209, Olympia, WA 98516-5703; 360-459-6462, Fax- 360-459-6461. Hours- 8AM-5PM. www.whrc.wa.gov

#23 State Bar Association, 1325 4th Ave, #600, Seattle, WA 98101-2539; 206-443-9722, 800-945-9722, Fax- 206-727-8319. 8AM-5PM. www.wsba.org Search at- http://pro.wsba.org/

#24 Gambling Commission, PO Box 42400, Olympia, WA 98504-2400; 360-486-3440, Fax-360-486-3629. www.wsgc.wa.gov Search data-www.wsgc.wa.gov/search/emp_lic_search.asp

#25 Insurance Licensing, PO Box 40255, Olympia, WA 98504-0255; 360-725-7144, Fax- 360-586-2019. Hours- 8AM-5PM. www.insurance.wa.gov

#26 Department of Licensing, Business and Professions Division, Architects & Landscape Architects, PO Box 9045 (405 Black Lake Blvd SW), Olympia, WA 98507-9045; 360-664-1388, Fax- 360-664-1495. Hours- 8:30AM-5PM. www.dol.wa.gov/business/architects/ Search data at- https://fortress.wa.gov/dol/dolprod/bpdLicenseQuery/

#27 Department of Licensing, Professional Boxing, Martial Arts & Wrestling Licensing Program, PO Box 9026 (405 Black Lake Blvd SW), Olympia, WA 98507-9026; 360-664-6644, Fax- 360-664-2550. Hours- 8AM-5PM. www.dol.wa.gov/business/athletics/ Search at- https://fortress.wa.gov/dol/dolprod/bpdLicenseQuery/

#28 Department of Agriculture, Commodity Inspection, 3939 Cleveland Av SE, Olympia, WA 98501; 360-902-1828, Fax- 360-586-5257. http://agr.wa.gov/aboutwsda/divisions/commodityinspection.htm

#29 Child Care Resource & Referral Network, 1551 Broadway, Ste #300, Tacoma, WA 98402-3332; 253-383-1735, Fax- 253-572-2599. www.childcarenet.org/ Search data at- www.childcarenet.org/families/your-search/referral_form

#30 Aging & Adult Services Administration, Department of Social and Health Services, 640 Woodland Square Loop, Lacey, WA 98503; 360-725-2300. www.aasa.dshs.wa.gov

#31 Children's Administration, Dept of Social & Health Services, PO Box 45715, Olympia, WA 98504-5715; 360-725-6701, Fax- 360-664-0744. http://www1.dshs.wa.gov/ca/

#32 Department of Licensing, Master License Service, PO Box 9034 (1125 Washington St. SE), Olympia, WA 98507-9034; 360-664-1400, Fax- 360-570-7875. www.dol.wa.gov/listoflicenses.html

#33 Department of Licensing, Professional Licensing Support Services Unit, PO Box 9020 (1125 Washington St. SE), Olympia, WA 98507-9020; 360-664-1400, Fax- 360-664-2550. www.dol.wa.gov

#34 Public Disclosure Commission, PO Box 40908 (711 Capitol Way #206), Olympia, WA 98504-0908; 877-601-2828, 360-753-1111, Fax- 360-753-1112. http://web.pdc.wa.gov/default.aspx Search at- http://web.pdc.wa.gov/public/lobbyist/default.aspx

Washington Federal Courts

The following list indicates the district and division name for each county in the state. If the bankruptcy court location is different from the district court, then the location of the bankruptcy court appears in parentheses.

Washington County/Court Cross Reference

County	District	Division
Adams	Eastern	Spokane
Asotin	Eastern	Spokane
Benton	Eastern	Spokane
Chelan	Eastern	Spokane
Clallam	Western	Tacoma (Seattle)
Clark	Western	Tacoma
Columbia	Eastern	Spokane
Cowlitz	Western	Tacoma
Douglas	Eastern	Spokane
Ferry	Eastern	Spokane
Franklin	Eastern	Spokane
Garfield	Eastern	Spokane
Grant	Eastern	Spokane
Grays Harbor	Western	Tacoma
Island	Western	Seattle
Jefferson	Western	Tacoma (Seattle)
King	Western	Seattle
Kitsap	Western	Tacoma (Seattle)
Kittitas	Eastern	Yakima (Spokane)
Klickitat	Eastern	Yakima (Spokane)
Lewis	Western	Tacoma
Lincoln	Eastern	Spokane
Mason	Western	Tacoma
Okanogan	Eastern	Spokane
Pacific	Western	Tacoma
Pend Oreille	Eastern	Spokane
Pierce	Western	Tacoma
San Juan	Western	Seattle
Skagit	Western	Seattle
Skamania	Western	Tacoma
Snohomish	Western	Seattle
Spokane	Eastern	Spokane
Stevens	Eastern	Spokane
Thurston	Western	Tacoma
Wahkiakum	Western	Tacoma
Walla Walla	Eastern	Spokane
Whatcom	Western	Seattle
Whitman	Eastern	Spokane
Yakima	Eastern	Yakima (Spokane)

Standards for Federal Courts: Fees are standard unless noted in profile. Search fee is $26.00 per item (one party name or case number). Copy fee is $.50 per page. Certification fee is $9.00 per document, double for exemplification, if available. Most courts require prepayment. Mail requests should enclose a SASE unless otherwise noted. Before releasing records, all courts require prepayment, unless noted.

District courts index by defendant and plaintiff and by case number. Bankruptcy courts usually index by debtor and case number. While most courts now have their indexes on computer, many may still maintain index card files as well. Courts will archive closed case files at different times.

There are numerous public access programs available to online subscribers. Search the U.S. Party/Case Index to find party names and case numbers among all courts. Individual case data is provided on PACER. A search of CM/ECF provides copies of cases filed electronically. For details about PACER, the US Party/Case Index, and CM/ECF see the Appendix or go to http://pacer.psc.uscourts.gov or call 800-676-6856.

US District Court
Washington Eastern District

Spokane Division Court Clerk, PO Box 1493, Spokane, WA 99210-1493 (In person: 920 W Riverside Ave, Rm 840, Spokane, WA 99201), 509-458-3400; Fax- 509-458-3420. Hours-8AM-5PM. www.waed.uscourts.gov

Counties/Note: Adams, Asotin, Benton, Chelan, Columbia, Douglas, Ferry, Franklin, Garfield, Grant, Lincoln, Okanogan, Pend Oreille, Spokane, Stevens, Walla Walla, Whitman. Also, some cases from Kittitas, Klickitat and Yakima are heard at Spokane.

Searches/Indexing: Include full name in search request. Results do not include SSN or DOB. Will fax back documents if copy fee prepaid, $.50 per page. New cases are in the index 2-3 days after filing date. Computer and microfiche indexes maintained. Search Spokane Division for all cases before 1989. Judge McDonald's records maintained in Yakima. All other cases kept in Spokane or Richland Divisions. Case files sent to archives 6 months after closed.

Search Access: Mail: Search usually completed- 3 days. SASE not required. **Fax:** Fax search and case file requests accepted. **In person:** 2 public terminals available. No self-serve copier.

Payment: Pay by Visa/MC, money order, cashier's check. Payee: Clerk, US District Court.

E-Services: PACER records go back to 7/1989. New records online after 1 day. ECF at https://ecf.waed.uscourts.gov. Opinions available on PACER system. Access weekly calendars at www.waed.uscourts.gov/calendar/index.html.

Yakima Division Court Clerk, PO Box 2706, Spokane, WA 99201 (In person: 25 S 3rd St, Rm 215, Yakima), 509-573-6600; Fax- 509-573-6601. Hours-8AM-5PM. www.waed.uscourts.gov

Counties/Note: Kittitas, Klickitat, Yakima. Case hearings are held in Yakima. Direct mail to Spokane. Some cases from Kittitas, Klickitat and Yakima are heard in Spokane or Richland.

Searches/Indexing: Include full name in search request. Results do not include SSN or DOB. Will fax back documents if copy fee prepaid, $.50 per page. New cases are in the index 1 day after filing date. For all pre-1989 cases, search at Spokane Division. Judge McDonald's records maintained in Yakima. All other cases kept in Spokane or Richland Divisions. Case files sent to archives 6 months after closed.

Search Access: Limited docket info available by phone. **Mail:** Search usually completed- 1 day. Include SASE for return. **Fax:** Fax search and case file requests accepted. **In person:** 2 public terminals available. No self-serve copier.

Payment: Pay by Visa/MC, money order, cashier's check. Payee: Clerk, US District Court.

E-Services: PACER records go back to 7/1989. ECF at https://ecf.waed.uscourts.gov. Opinions available on PACER system. Weekly calendars at www.waed.uscourts.gov/calendar/index.html.

US Bankruptcy Court Washington Eastern District

Spokane Division Court Clerk, PO Box 2164, Spokane, WA 99210-2164 (In person: W 904 Riverside, Ste 304, Spokane), 509-458-5300. Hours-8:30AM-4:30PM. www.waeb.uscourts.gov

Counties/Note: Adams, Asotin, Benton, Chelan, Columbia, Douglas, Ferry, Franklin, Garfield, Grant, Kittitas, Klickitat, Lincoln, Okanogan, Pend Oreille, Spokane, Stevens, Walla Walla, Whitman, Yakima.

Searches/Indexing: Include last name or full name in search request. Court can also search index by SSN or Tax ID number. Results do not include SSN or DOB. Will fax back documents for no fee. New cases are in the index immediately after filing date.

Search Access: Only docket info is available by phone. Press extension 6. Voice Case Information Service available, call VCIS at 509-458-2441 or 800-519-2549 x6. **Mail:** Search usually completed- 3 days. SASE not requested. **Fax:** Fax search requests accepted. **In person:** 3 public terminals available. No self-serve copier. A copy service is available.

Payment: Pay by Visa/MC (in person only), money order, cashier's check, business check. No personal checks. Payee: Clerk, US Bankruptcy Court. Prepayment not required for copy requests; can be billed via mail with results. Prepayment is required for archive retrievals.

E-Services: Pacer records go back to 1997. New records online immediately. ECF at https://ecf.waeb.uscourts.gov. **Opinions Online:** www.waeb.uscourts.gov/JudicialOpinions/.

US District Court Washington Western District

Seattle Division Clerk of Court, 700 W Stewart St, US Courthouse, Seattle, WA 98101, 206-370-8400; crim dockets- 206-370-8450; civil dockets- 206-370-8450. Hours-9AM-4:30PM; staff- 8AM-5PM. www.wawd.uscourts.gov

Counties/Note: Island, King, San Juan, Skagit, Snohomish, Whatcom.

Searches/Indexing: Include full name in search request. Most results do not include SSN or DOB. Will not fax back documents. New cases are in the index immediately after filing date. Computer, microfiche and card indexes maintained. District-wide searches available back to 1989. Case files sent to archives 2-3 years after closed.

Search Access: Docket info available by phone for civil cases since 1989 and criminal cases since 1992. **Mail:** Search usually completed- 1 week. SASE not required. **In person:** 4 public terminals available. Copies from computer terminal- $.10 each. Copy machine- $.25 each. Outside copy service available.

Payment: Pay by Visa/MC, money order, cashier's or personal check. Payee: Clerk, US District Court.

E-Services: Document images available. PACER records go back to 1988. New records online after 1 day. ECF at https://ecf.wawd.uscourts.gov. **Opinions Online:** www.wawd.uscourts.gov. Click tabs to view Court Orders and Special Case Notices. **Note:** Calendars at www.wawd.uscourts.gov/calendars/JudgesCalendars.htm.

Tacoma Division Court Clerk, 1717 Pacific Ave, Rm 3100, Tacoma, WA 98402-3200, 253-882-3800. Hours-9AM-4:30PM; staff- 8AM-5PM. www.wawd.uscourts.gov

Counties/Note: Clallam, Clark, Cowlitz, Grays Harbor, Jefferson, Kitsap, Lewis, Mason, Pacific, Pierce, Skamania, Thurston, Wahkiakum.

Searches/Indexing: Include SSN and/or DOB in search request. Most results do not include SSN or DOB. Will not fax back documents. New cases are in the index immediately after filing date. Computer index- criminal go back to 1990, civil to 1988. Older records on microfiche and card index. District-wide searches available back to 1989. Case files sent to archives 2-3 years after closed.

Search Access: Docket info available by phone for civil cases since 1989 and criminal cases since 1992. **Mail:** Search usually completed- 2-5 days. SASE not required. **In person:** 4 public terminals available. No self-serve copier.

Payment: Pay by Visa/MC, money order, cashier's or personal check. Payee: Clerk, US District Court.

E-Services: Document images available. PACER records go back to 1988. New records online after 1 day. ECF at https://ecf.wawd.uscourts.gov. **Opinions Online:** www.wawd.uscourts.gov. Click tabs to view Court Orders and Special Case Notices. **Note:** Calendars at www.wawd.uscourts.gov/calendars/JudgesCalendars.htm.

US Bankruptcy Court Washington Western District

Seattle Division Clerk of Court, 700 Stewart St #6301, Seattle, WA 98101-1271, 206-370-5200. Hours-8:30AM-4:30PM. www.wawb.uscourts.gov

Counties/Note: Clallam, Island, Jefferson, King, Kitsap, San Juan, Skagit, Snohomish, Whatcom.

Searches/Indexing: Include first and last name in search request. Results include last 4 SSN digits. Will not fax back documents. New cases are in the index 1 day after filing date. Microfiche index goes back to 1984; computer to 1986. Open cases stored by case number. Closed cases stored by year closed, then by case number. Electronic cases maintained indefinitely.

Search Access: Voice Case Information Service available, call VCIS at 888-409-4662 or 206-370-5285. **Mail:** Search usually completed- 2-3 days. Include SASE for return. **In person:** 3 public terminals available. Self serve copies $.25 each.

Payment: Pay by money order, cashier's check, attorney checks. No credit cards or debtor, business, or personal checks accepted. Payee: Clerk, US Bankruptcy Court.

E-Services: PACER online at http://pacer.wawb.uscourts.gov. PACER records go back to 1/1986. New records online after 1 day. ECF at https://ecf.wawb.uscourts.gov. **Opinions Online:** www.wawb.uscourts.gov/opinions.htm. **Online Note:** Calendars free at www.wawb.uscourts.gov. Calendars and opinions also available on PACER.

Tacoma Div. Court Clerk, 1717 Pacific Ave, Suite 2100, Tacoma, WA 98402-3233, 253-882-3900; 8:30AM-4:30PM. www.wawb.uscourts.gov

Counties/Note: Clark, Cowlitz, Grays Harbor, Lewis, Mason, Pacific, Pierce, Skamania, Thurston, Wahkiakum.

Searches/Indexing: Search by debtor's name back to 1987. Results include last 4 SSN digits. Will not fax back documents. New cases are in the index 1 day after filing date. Cases on computer maintained indefinitely.

Search Access: Voice Case Information Service available, call VCIS at 888-409-4662 or 206-370-5285. **Mail:** Search usually completed- 1 week. SASE not required. **In person:** Self serve copies $.25 each.

Payment: Pay by money order, cashier's check, attorney checks. No credit cards or debtor, business, or personal checks accepted. Payee: Clerk, US Bankruptcy Court.

E-Services: PACER online at http://pacer.wawb.uscourts.gov. PACER records go back to 1987. New records online after 1 day. ECF at https://ecf.wawb.uscourts.gov. **Opinions Online:** www.wawb.uscourts.gov/opinions.htm. **Note:** Calendars free at www.wawb.uscourts.gov.

Washington County Courts

Court	Jurisdiction	No. of Courts	How Organized
Superior Courts*	General	39	29 Districts
District Courts*	Limited	61	39 Counties
Municipal Courts*	Municipal	243	243 Cities/Towns

* Profiled in this Sourcebook.

Court	CIVIL								
	Tort	Contract	Real Estate	Min. Claim	Max. Claim	Small Claims	Estate	Eviction	Domestic Relations
Superior Courts*	X	X	X	$50,000	No Max		X	X	X
District Courts*	X	X		$0	$75,000	$4000			
Municipal Courts*									

Court	CRIMINAL				
	Felony	Misdemeanor	DWI/DUI	Preliminary Hearing	Juvenile
Superior Courts*	X				X
District Courts*		X	X	X	
Municipal Courts*		X	X		

Administration

Court Administrator, Temple of Justice, PO Box 41174, Olympia, WA, 98504; 360-753-3365, Fax: 360-586-8869. (PST) www.courts.wa.gov

Court Structure

Superior Court is the court of general jurisdiction, but District Courts have concurrent jurisdiction with superior courts over misdemeanor and gross misdemeanor violations and civil cases under $50,000. District Courts have exclusive jurisdiction over small claims and infractions. criminal jurisdiction over misdemeanors, gross misdemeanors, and criminal traffic cases. The maximum penalty for gross misdemeanors is one year in jail and a $5,000 fine. The maximum penalty for misdemeanors is 90 days in jail and a $1,000 fine. Many Municipal Courts combine their record keeping with a District Court housed in the same building, as indicated in the profiles. Washington has a mandatory arbitration requirement for civil disputes for $35,000 or less. However, either party may request a trial in Superior Court if dissatisfied with the arbitrator's decision.

Online Access

The web offers limited, free look-up of docket information at http://dw.courts.wa.gov/. Search by name or case number. For much more detailed case data, the AOC provides the Judicial Information System's (JIS) statewide computer. This program of services, called JIS-Link, provides access to all counties and court levels. Case records include criminal, civil, domestic, probate, and judgments. Fees include a one-time $100.00 per site, a transaction fee of $.065. There is a $6.00 per month minimum. Call 360-357-3365 or visit www.courts.wa.gov/jislink. Supreme and Appellate opinions are at www.courts.wa.gov/appellate_trial_courts/. The page offers a notification service also. There is a Request for Information form at http://dw.courts.wa.gov/datadis/request.doc which can be mailed, faxed or emailed to dda@courts.wa.gov. Fees are listed on the form.

Searching Tips, Fees, and Other Guidelines

District Courts retain civil records for ten years from date of final disposition, then the records are destroyed. District Courts retain criminal records forever. Many Municipal courts do not hold records.

A July 2005 law mandated the filing, copy and certification fees for Superior and District Courts. In the Superior Court the fee for an uncertified copy is $.50 and $.25 for an electronic computer printout; for a certified copy the fee is $5.00 for the first page and $1.00 for each additional page. At the District Court, the certification fee is $5.00 per document (not page). Most courts are comply with this fees structure. An SASE is required in most courts that respond to written search requests.

Adams County

Superior Court PO Box 187, 210 W Broadway, Ritzville, WA 99169-0187; 509-659-3257; fax: 509-659-0118; 8:30AM-N, 1-4:30PM. ***Felony, Civil, Eviction, Probate.*** www.co.adams.wa.us/clerk/ Probate fax is same as main fax number.

Civil Records: Access: Phone, fax, mail, online, in person. Only the court performs in person searches; visitors may not. Search fee: $20.00 per hour. Required to search: name, years to search; also helpful: address. Civil cases indexed by defendant, plaintiff; index on computer from 1985, archived from 1900s. Note: A microfiche index is available to the public, but it is no longer updated by the state. Mail turnaround time 1-4 weeks. The agency is working towards placing public access terminals in the building. Index from JIS-Link; see www.courts.wa.gov/jislink/. Also, search name index back to 1989 and calendars free at http://dw.courts.wa.gov/index.cfm.

Criminal Records: Access: Phone, fax, mail, online, in person. Only the court performs in person searches; visitors may not. Search fee: $20.00 per hour. Required to search: name, years to search; also helpful: address, DOB, SSN. Criminal records computerized from 1985, archived from 1900s. Note: A microfiche index is available to the public, but it is no longer updated by the state. Mail turnaround time 4 weeks. Agency is working towards placing public access terminals in the building. Online access to criminal indexes is the same as civil.

General Information: No sealed, adoption, paternity, mental health, sex offenders (victims) records released. Will fax documents $1.00 per page. Court makes copy: $.50 per page. Certification fee: $5.00 plus $1.00 each add'l page. Cert fee includes copies. Payee: Adams County Clerk. Business checks accepted. No credit cards accepted. Prepayment required. Mail requests: SASE required.

Othello District Court 425 E Main St, Othello, WA 99344; 509-488-3935; fax: 509-488-3480; 8:30AM-4:30PM. ***Misdemeanor, Civil Actions under $50,000, Small Claims.*** Record searches are often referred to Washington State Patrol 360-705-5100.
Civil Records: Access: Phone, fax, mail, online, in person. Only the court performs in person searches; visitors may not. No search fee. Required to search: name, years to search; also helpful: address, signed release. Civil cases indexed by defendant, plaintiff; index on computer for 10 years, prior on index cards. Mail turnaround time 7-10 days. Index from JIS-Link; see www.courts.wa.gov/jislink/. Also, search name index back to 1989 and calendars free at http://dw.courts.wa.gov/index.cfm.
Criminal Records: Access: Phone, fax, mail, online, in person. Only the court performs in person searches; visitors may not. No search fee. Required to search: name, years to search, signed release; also helpful: address, DOB, SSN. Criminal records on computer for 10 years, prior on index cards. Mail turnaround time 7-10 days. Online access to criminal indexes is the same as civil.
General Information: No sealed, juvenile, adoption, paternity, mental health, sex offenders (victims) or (sometimes) DUI records released. No fee to fax documents. Court makes copy: $2.50 for 1st page, $1.00 each add'l. No certification fee. Payee: Othello District Court. Personal checks accepted. Prepayment required. Mail requests: SASE required.

Ritzville District Court 210 W Broadway, Ritzville, WA 99169; 509-659-1002; fax: 509-659-0118; 8:30AM-N, 1-4:30PM. ***Misdemeanor, Civil Actions under $50,000, Small Claims.***
www.co.adams.wa.us/districtcourt/default.aspx
Civil Records: Access: Fax, mail, online, in person. Only the court performs in person searches; visitors may not. No search fee. Required to search: name, years to search; also helpful: address. Civil cases indexed by defendant, plaintiff; index on computer from 10/90. Mail turnaround time 3 days. Index from JIS-Link; www.courts.wa.gov/jislink/. Also, search name index back to 1989 and calendars free http://dw.courts.wa.gov/index.cfm.
Criminal Records: Access: Fax, mail, online, in person. Only the court performs in person searches; visitors may not. No search fee. Required to search: name, years to search, DOB; also helpful: address, SSN. Criminal records computerized from 10/90. Mail turnaround time 3 days. Online access to criminal indexes is the same as civil.
General Information: No sealed, juvenile, adoption, paternity, mental health, sex offenders (victims) or (sometimes) DUI records released. Will fax documents $3.00 1st page, $1.00 each add'l. Court makes copy: $1.00 per page. Certification fee: $5.00 1st page, $1.00 ea add'l. Payee: Ritzville District Court. Personal checks & Visa/MC/AmEx accepted. Prepayment required. Mail requests: SASE required.

Othello Municipal Court.
See Othello District Court for records.

Ritzville Municipal Court.
See Ritzville District Court for records.

Asotin County

Superior Court PO Box 159, Asotin, WA 99402-0159; 509-243-2081; fax: 509-243-4978; 8AM-5PM. ***Felony, Civil, Eviction, Probate.***
Civil Records: Access: Phone, fax, mail, online, in person. Only the court performs in person searches; visitors may not. No search fee; but may charge $10.00 per hour for extensive search. Required to search: name, years to search; also helpful: address. Civil cases indexed by defendant, plaintiff; index on computer from mid 1985, on microfiche from 1970s, archived from 1895. Mail turnaround time 1-5 days. Index from JIS-Link; www.courts.wa.gov/jislink/. Also, name index back to 1989 and calendars free at http://dw.courts.wa.gov/index.cfm.
Criminal Records: Access: Phone, fax, mail, online, in person. Only the court performs in person searches; visitors may not. No search fee; but may charge $10.00 per hour for extensive search. Required to search: name, years to search, DOB; also helpful: address, SSN. Criminal records computerized from mid 1985, on microfiche from 1970s, archived from 1895. Mail turnaround time 1 day. Online access to criminal indexes is the same as civil.
General Information: No sealed, juvenile, adoption, paternity, mental health, sex offenders (victims) or (sometimes) DUI records released. Will not fax documents. Court makes copy: $.50 per page. Certification fee: $5.00 1st page, $1.00 ea add'l. Cert fee includes copies. Payee: Asotin County Clerk. Personal checks accepted; credit cards are not. Prepayment required. Mail requests: SASE required.

District Court PO Box 429, 135 2nd St, Asotin, WA 99402-0429; 509-243-2027; fax: 509-243-2091; 8AM-5PM. ***Misdemeanor, Civil Actions under $50,000, Small Claims.***
www.courts.wa.gov/court_dir/orgs/262.html
Has records for Municipal Asotin & Clarkston courts.
Civil Records: Access: Fax, mail, online, in person. Only the court performs in person searches; visitors may not. Search fee: $6.00 per name. Required to search: name, years to search; also helpful: address. Civil cases indexed by defendant, plaintiff; index on computer since 1993; prior records on log books. Mail turnaround time up to 2 weeks. Index from JIS-Link; www.courts.wa.gov/jislink/. Also, search name index back to 1989 and calendars free http://dw.courts.wa.gov/index.cfm.
Criminal Records: Access: Fax, mail, online, in person. Only the court performs in person searches; visitors may not. Search fee: $6.00 per name. Required to search: name, years to search; also helpful: address, DOB, SSN. Criminal records computerized from 1993. Mail turnaround time up to 2 weeks. Online access to criminal indexes is the same as civil.
General Information: No sealed, juvenile, adoption, paternity, mental health, sex offenders (victims) or (sometimes) DUI records released. No fee to fax documents. Court makes copy: $1.00 per page. Cert fee: $12.00 include copies. Payee: County District Court. Personal checks & major credit cards accepted. Prepayment required. Mail requests: SASE required.

Asotin Municipal Court.

Clarkson Municipal Court.
See District Court for records.

Benton County

Superior Court 7122 W Okanagan Pl, Bldg A, Attn: Clerk's Office, Kennewick, WA 99336; 509-735-8388; fax: 509-736-3892; 8-N, 1-4PM. ***Felony, Civil, Probate,*** www.co.benton.wa.us/
Pre-1991 completed files are archived at the Prosser Courthouse, 620 Market, Prosser, 99350; 509-786-5624. Also at Prosser are Probate records up to 1999.
Civil Records: Access: Mail, in person, online. Only the court performs in person searches; visitors may not. Search fee: $20.00 per hour. Required to search: name, years to search; also helpful: address. Civil cases indexed by defendant, plaintiff; index on computer from 1979, pre-1979 on index books. Mail turnaround time 5-10 working days. Civil PAT goes back to 1979. Index from JIS-Link; see www.courts.wa.gov/jislink/. Also, search name index back to 1989 and calendars free at http://dw.courts.wa.gov/index.cfm. Also, subscription access to court docs back to 3/2/1981 and indexes back to 4/1/1979 available at www.landlight.com. Demo subscription available.
Criminal Records: Access: Mail, in person, online. Only the court performs in person searches; visitors may not. Search fee: $20.00 per hour. Required to search: name, years to search; also helpful: address, DOB, SSN. Criminal records computerized from 1979, pre-1979 on index books. Mail turnaround time 5-10 days. Criminal PAT available. Online access to criminal indexes is the same as civil. Also, subscription access to court docs back to 3/2/1981 and indexes back to 4/1/1979 available at www.landlight.com. Demo subscription available.
General Information: No sealed, dependency, adoption, paternity, mental health, sex offenders (victims). Will fax documents $3.00 1st page, $1.00 each add'l. Court makes copy: $.50 per page. Certification fee: $5.00 plus $1.00 per page after first. Payee: Benton County Clerk. Personal checks accepted; credit cards are not. Prepayment required. Mail requests: SASE required.

District Court 7122 W Okanogan Pl, Bldg A, Justice Ctr, Kennewick, WA 99336; 509-735-8476; fax: 509-736-3069; 8AM-N, 1-4PM. ***Misdemeanor, Civil under $50,000, Small Claims, Traffic.***
www.co.benton.wa.us/district_court.htm
Phone for the Prosser Courthouse is 509-786-5480.
Civil Records: Access: Mail, fax, online, in person. Both court and visitors may perform in person searches. Search fee: $10.00 per name. Required to search: name, years to search; also helpful: address. Civil cases indexed by defendant, plaintiff; index on computer from 7/91. Mail turnaround time 10 days. Civil PAT goes back to 1992. Index from JIS-Link; see www.courts.wa.gov/jislink/. Also, search name index back to 1989 and calendars free at http://dw.courts.wa.gov/index.cfm.
Criminal Records: Access: Mail, fax, online, in person. Both court and visitors may perform in person searches. Search fee: $10.00 per name. Required to search: name, years to search, DOB, signed release; also helpful: address, SSN. Criminal records computerized from 7/91, stored from 1988. Note: Request must be in writing, with payment. Mail turnaround time 10 days. Criminal PAT goes back to same as civil. Online access to criminal indexes is the same as civil.
General Information: No sealed, juvenile, adoption, paternity, mental health, sex offenders (victims) or (sometimes) DUI records released. Will not fax out documents. Court makes copy: first 50 copies free, then $.15 each. Certification fee: $5.00 per doc. Payee: Benton County District Court. Personal checks accepted; credit cards are not. Prepayment required. Mail requests: SASE requested.

Kennewick Municipal Court.

Prosser Municipal Court.

Richland Municipal Court.

West Richland Municipal Court.
See District Court for records.

Chelan County

Superior Court PO Box 3025, 350 Orondo, Wenatchee, WA 98807-3025; 509-667-6380; fax: 509-667-6611; 9AM-5PM. ***Felony, Civil, Eviction, Probate, Domestic.***
www.co.chelan.wa.us/scc/scc_main.htm
Civil Records: Access: Phone, fax, mail, online, in person. Both court and visitors may perform in person searches. Search fee: $20.00 per hour. Required to search: name, years to search. Civil cases indexed by defendant, plaintiff. Civil docket records on computer back to 1984; prior on microfilm to 1900. Mail turnaround time 1 day. Civil PAT goes back to 1996. Civil records from 1993 forward and probate from 1975 forward by online subscription at web page. Subscribers may also file online. Also, search current dockets and cases are at www.courts.wa.gov/jis/jis_superior/. Index from JIS-Link; see www.courts.wa.gov/jislink/ Also, see state introduction for subscription svc. Search name index back to 1989 and calendars free at http://dw.courts.wa.gov/index.cfm. Also, subscription access to indexes back to 4/30/1984 available at www.landlight.com. Demo available.
Criminal Records: Access: Phone, fax, mail, online, in person. Both court and visitors may perform in person searches. Search fee: $20.00 per hour. Required to search: full name, years to search; also helpful: address, DOB. Criminal records computerized from 1984; prior on microfilm to 1900. Mail turnaround time 1 day. Criminal PAT goes back to same as civil. Online access to criminal indexes is the same as civil.
General Information: No sealed, juvenile, adoption, paternity, mental health, sex victim records released.

Will fax documents $3.00 1st page, $1.00 each add'l. Clerk wil also email back copies for a add'l fee. Court makes copy: $.50 per page; online copy- $.25 each plus convenience fee. Self serve: same. Certification fee: $5.00 1st page, $1.00 ea add'l; convenience fee added if purchased online. Cert fee includes copies. Payee: Chelan County Clerk. Personal checks and major credit cards accepted. Prepayment required.

Chelan County District Ct PO Box 2686, 350 Orondo, Courthouse 4th Fl, Wenatchee, WA 98807; 509-667-6600; fax: 509-667-6456; 8:30AM-5PM. ***Misdemeanor, Civil under $50,000, Small Claims.*** www.co.chelan.wa.us/dcc/dcc_main.htm

Civil Records: Access: Fax, mail, online, in person. Both court and visitors may perform in person searches. Search fee: $15.00 per name. Required to search: name; also helpful: years to search, address. Civil cases indexed by defendant, plaintiff; index on computer from 1984. Records destroyed 5 years from closure. Mail turnaround time 1 week. Civil PAT goes back to 10 years. PAT civil results show middle initial. Index from JIS-Link; see www.courts.wa.gov/jislink/. Also, search name index back to 1989 and calendars free at http://dw.courts.wa.gov/index.cfm.

Criminal Records: Access: Fax, mail, online, in person. Both court and visitors may perform in person searches. Search fee: $15.00 per name. Required to search: name, DOB, signed release; also helpful: years to search, address, SSN, aliases. Criminal records on computer. Criminal files may be destroyed 5 years after close of case, infractions destroyed 3 years after close. Mail turnaround time 1 week. Criminal PAT goes back to 5 years. PAT criminal results show middle initial. Online access to criminal indexes is the same as civil. Online results show middle initial.

General Information: Online identifiers in results same as on public terminal. No sealed, domestic violence victim info, alcohol/probation evaluation records released. Court makes copy: $.50 per page. Certification fee: $5.00 plus $1.00 each page after 1st. Payee: Chelan County District Court. Personal checks accepted. Visa/MC accepted. Prepayment required. Mail requests: SASE required.

Cashmere & Leavenworth Municipal Ct. See District Court for records.

Clallam County

Superior Court 223 E 4th St, #9, Port Angeles, WA 98362-3098; 360-417-2508; probate phone: 306-417-2507; 8:30AM-4:30PM. ***Felony, Civil, Eviction, Probate.*** www.clallam.net/scourt

Civil Records: Access: Phone, mail, in person. Both court and visitors may perform in person searches. Search fee: $20.00 per hour. Required to search: name, years to search; also helpful: address. Civil cases indexed by defendant, plaintiff; index on computer from 10/83, on microfiche from 1914, some records on index cards. Mail turnaround time minimum 1 week. Civil PAT goes back to 10/13/83. PAT results show name, DOB. Index from JIS-Link; see www.courts.wa.gov/jislink/.

Criminal Records: Access: Phone, mail, online, in person. Both court and visitors may perform in person searches. Search fee: $20.00 per hour. Required to search: name, years to search; also helpful: address, DOB. Criminal records computerized from 10/83, on microfiche from 1914, some records on index cards. Mail turnaround time minimum 1 week. Criminal PAT goes back to same as civil.PAT results show name, DOB. Results include driver's license. Online access to criminal indexes is the same as civil.

General Information: No sealed, juvenile, adoption, paternity, mental health, sex offenders (victims) records released. Fee to fax out file $3.00 plus $1.00 per page. Court makes copy: $.50 per page. Self serve: same. Certification fee: $5.00 plus $1.00 per page after first. Payee: Clerk. Business checks accepted. No credit cards accepted. Prepayment required. Mail requests: SASE required.

District Court 1 223 E 4th St, Port Angeles, WA 98362; 360-417-2560; fax: 360-417-2403; 8:30AM-4:30PM. ***Misdemeanor, Civil Actions under $50,000, Small Claims.*** www.clallam.net/Departments/html/dept_dc1.htm

District 1 Court also has jurisdiction on Civil Anti-Harassment Petitions and Orders.

Civil Records: Access: Mail, fax, online, in person. Visitors must perform in person searches themselves. No search fee. Required to search: name, years to search; also helpful: address. Civil cases indexed by defendant, plaintiff; index on computer from 1986. Mail turnaround time 1-2 days. Civil PAT goes back to 1990. PAT civil results show middle initial. Index from JIS-Link; see www.courts.wa.gov/jislink/. Also, search name index back to 1989 and calendars free at http://dw.courts.wa.gov/index.cfm.

Criminal Records: Access: Mail, fax, online, in person. Visitors must perform in person searches themselves. No search fee. Required to search: name, years to search, DOB, signed release; also helpful: address, SSN, nationality. Criminal records computerized from 1986. Mail turnaround time up to 1 week. Criminal PAT goes back to same as civil. PAT results show middle initial, DOB. Online access to criminal indexes is the same as civil. Online results show middle initial, DOB.

General Information: No sealed, juvenile, adoption, paternity, mental health, sex offenders (victims) or (sometimes) DUI records released. Will not fax documents. Court makes copy: $.15 per page. Self serve: free. Certification fee: $5.00 per doc. Payee: Clallam County District Court 1. Personal checks accepted. Prepayment required.

District Court II 502 E Division St, Forks, WA 98331; 360-374-6383; fax: 360-374-2100; 8:30AM-4:30PM. ***Misdemeanor, Civil Actions under $50,000, Small Claims.*** www.clallam.net/Courts/html/court_district_2.htm

Clallam County District Court II serves the West End of Clallam County, including Forks, Neah Bay, Clallam Bay, Sekiu and LaPush.

Civil Records: Access: Mail, in person, online. Both court and visitors may perform in person searches. No search fee. Required to search: name, years to search; also helpful: address. Civil cases indexed by defendant, plaintiff. Limited civil records on computer from 1989, records go back to 1988. Mail turnaround time 2 weeks. Index from JIS-Link; see www.courts.wa.gov/jislink/. Also, search name index back to 1989 and calendars free at http://dw.courts.wa.gov/index.cfm.

Criminal Records: Access: Mail, online, in person. Both court and visitors may perform in person searches. No search fee. Required to search: name, years to search DOB; also helpful: address, SSN. Criminal records computerized from 1992 (some back to 1989), on index cards from 1982-1986. Mail turnaround time 2 weeks. Online access to criminal indexes is the same as civil.

General Information: No sealed, juvenile, adoption, paternity, mental health, sex offenders (victims) or (sometimes) DUI records released. Fee to fax out file $5.00 1st page, $1.00 each add'l page. Court makes copy: $.15 per page. Certification fee: $5.00 1st page, $1.00 ea add'l. Cert fee includes copies. Payee: Clallam County District II Court. Personal checks accepted. Visa/MC accepted. Prepayment required. Mail requests: SASE required or provide postage.

Hoh Tribal Court 2482 Lower Hoh Rd, Forks, WA 98331; 360-374-4305, 360-374-6739; fax: 360-374-5275. ***Misdemeanor, Civil.***

Index from JIS-Link; see www.courts.wa.gov/jislink/. Also, search name index back to 1989 and calendars free at http://dw.courts.wa.gov/index.cfm.

Jamestown S'Klallam Tribal Ct (NICS) 1033 Old Blyn Hwy, Sequim, WA 98382; 360-683-1109; fax: 360-681-4611; M,T only. ***Misdemeanor, Civil.*** www.jamestowntribe.org

Index from JIS-Link; see www.courts.wa.gov/jislink/. Also, search name index back to 1989 and calendars free at http://dw.courts.wa.gov/index.cfm.

Lower Elwha Tribal Court 2851 Lower Elwha Rd, Port Angeles, WA 98363; 360-452-6759 x311; fax: 360-452-6642; 8-4:30PM. ***Misdemeanor, Civil.***

Index from JIS-Link; see www.courts.wa.gov/jislink/. Also, search name index back to 1989 and calendars free at http://dw.courts.wa.gov/index.cfm.

Makah Tribal Court PO Box 117, 81 Resort Dr, Neah Bay, WA 98357-0117; 360-645-3302; fax: 360-645-2760; 8-5PM. ***Misdemeanor, Civil.***

Index from JIS-Link; see www.courts.wa.gov/jislink/. Also, search name index back to 1989 and calendars free at http://dw.courts.wa.gov/index.cfm.

Port Angeles Municipal Court.
Sequim Municipal Court
See District Court 1 for records.

Quileute Tribal Court PO Box 69, 21 Quileute St, La Push, WA 98350-0069; 360-374-4305; fax: 360-374-5275; 8-4PM. ***Misdemeanor, Civil.***

Alternative fax is 360-374-9484. Index from JIS-Link; see www.courts.wa.gov/jislink/. Also, search name index back to 1989 and calendars free at http://dw.courts.wa.gov/index.cfm.

Clark County

Superior Court PO Box 5000, Attn: County Clerk, 1200 Franklin St, Vancouver, WA 98666-5000; 360-397-2049 Admin.; criminal phone: 360-397-2295; civil: 360-397-2292; fax: 360-397-6099; 8AM-4:30PM. ***Felony, Civil, Eviction, Probate.*** www.clark.wa.gov/courts/superior/index.html

Civil Records: Access: Phone, mail, online, in person, email. Both court and visitors may perform in person searches. Search fee: $20.00 per hour. Required to search: name, years to search. Civil cases indexed by defendant, plaintiff; index on computer back to 1979 indexed, on microfiche from 1960, and index books prior to 1979. Mail turnaround time 1-3 days. Civil PAT goes back to 1979. Index from JIS-Link; see www.courts.wa.gov/jislink/. Also, search name index back to 1989 and calendars free at http://dw.courts.wa.gov/index.cfm. Also, daily dockets are at www.clark.wa.gov/courts/superior/docket.html.

Criminal Records: Access: Phone, mail, online, in person, email. Both court and visitors may perform in person searches. Search fee: $20.00 per hour. Required to search: name, years to search, DOB; also helpful: address, signed release (if for employment). Criminal records computerized from 1979, prior to 1988 on microfilm. Mail turnaround time 1-3 days. Criminal PAT goes back to 1975. Online access to criminal indexes is the same as civil. Also, daily dockets are at www.clark.wa.gov/courts/superior/docket.html.

General Information: No sealed, juvenile, adoption, paternity, mental health, sex offenders (victims). Will not fax documents. Court makes copy: $.50 per page. Self serve: same. Certification fee: $5.00 1st page, $1.00 ea add'l. Payee: County Clerk. Only cashiers checks, money orders and attorney checks accepted. No credit cards accepted. Prepayment required.

District Court PO Box 9806, 1200 Franklin St, Vancouver, WA 98666-8806; criminal phone: 360-397-2424; civil phone: 360-397-2060; fax: 360-397-6044; 8AM-4:30PM. ***Misdemeanor, Civil Actions under $50,000, Small Claims.*** www.clark.wa.gov/courts/district/index.html

Civil Records: Access: Fax, mail, online, in person. Only the court performs in person searches; visitors may not. No search fee. Required to search: name, years to search; also helpful: address. Civil cases indexed by defendant, plaintiff; index on computer for apx. 5 years. Mail turnaround 1 week. Index from JIS-Link; www.courts.wa.gov/jislink/. Also, search name index back to 1989 and calendars at http://dw.courts.wa.gov/index.cfm. Also, daily dockets are free at www.clark.wa.gov/courts/district/docket.html

Criminal Records: Access: Fax, mail, online, in person. Only the court performs in person searches; visitors may not. No search fee. Required to search: name, DOB, signed release; also helpful: years to search, address. Criminal records on computer for approximately 5 years. Mail turnaround time 1 week. Online access to criminal indexes is the same as civil. Also, daily dockets are at www.clark.wa.gov/courts/district/docket.html.

General Information: No sealed, juvenile, adoption, paternity, mental health, sex offenders (victims) or (sometimes) DUI records released. No fee to fax documents. Court makes copy: 1-5 copies- $.50; 6-10 copies- $1.00, etc. Certification fee: $5.00 per doc.

Payee: Clark County District Court. Personal checks and credit cards accepted. Prepayment required. Mail requests: SASE required.

Battle Ground Municipal Court 109 SW 1st St #272, Battle Ground, WA 98604; 360-342-5150; fax: 360-342-5159; 8-5. ***Misdemeanor, Infraction.***
Index from JIS-Link; see www.courts.wa.gov/jislink/. Also, search name index back to 1989 and calendars free at http://dw.courts.wa.gov/index.cfm.

Camas-Washougal Municipal Ct. 89 C St, Washougal, WA 98671-2142; 360-833-1919; fax: 360-833-0818; 8AM-4:30PM. ***Misdemeanor.***
Index from JIS-Link; see www.courts.wa.gov/jislink/. Also, search name index back to 1989 and calendars free at http://dw.courts.wa.gov/index.cfm.

LaCenter Municipal Court.

Ridgefield Municipal Court.
See Battle Ground Municipal Court

Vancouver Municipal Court.

Yacolt Municipal Court.
See Clark County District Court for records.

Columbia County

Superior Court 341 E Main St, Dayton, WA 99328; 509-382-4321; fax: 509-382-4830; 8:30-N, 1-4:30PM. ***Felony, Civil, Eviction, Probate.***
www.columbiaco.com/superior%20court/superiorcourt.htm Probate fax is same as main fax number.
Civil Records: Access: Phone, fax, mail, online, in person. Only the court performs in person searches; visitors may not. Search fee: $20.00 per hour. Required to search: name, years to search. Civil cases indexed by defendant, plaintiff; index on computer from 1987, some records on index cards and books, archived from 1900s. Mail turnaround time 1 week. Index from JIS-Link; www.courts.wa.gov/jislink/. Also, search name index back to 1989 and calendars at http://dw.courts.wa.gov/index.cfm.
Criminal Records: Access: Phone, fax, mail, online, in person. Only the court performs in person searches; visitors may not. Search fee: $20.00 per hour. Required to search: name, years to search. Criminal records computerized from 1987, some records on index cards and books, archived from 1900s. Mail turnaround time 1 week. Online access to criminal indexes is the same as civil.
General Information: No sealed, juvenile, adoption, paternity, mental health, sex offenders (victims). Will not fax documents. Court makes copy: $.50 per page. Self serve: same. Certification fee: $5.00 plus $1.00 per page after first. Cert fee includes copies. Payee: Columbia County Clerk. Personal checks accepted; credit cards are not. Mail requests: SASE required.

District Court PO Box 31, 341 E Main St, Dayton, WA 99328-0031; 509-382-4812; fax: 509-382-2490; 8:30AM-4:30PM. ***Misdemeanor, Civil Actions under $75,000, Small Claims.***
Civil Records: Access: Mail, in person, online. Only the court performs in person searches; visitors may not. No search fee. Required to search: name, years to search; also helpful: address. Civil cases indexed by plaintiff. Civil records on computer since 5/96; prior on index books. Mail turnaround time 7-10 days. PAT civil results show middle initial. Index from JIS-Link; see www.courts.wa.gov/jislink/. Also, search name index back to 1989 and calendars free at http://dw.courts.wa.gov/index.cfm.
Criminal Records: Access: Mail, online, in person. Only the court performs in person searches; visitors may not. Search fee: Fee may be charged if more than 1 case. Required to search: name, years to search, DOB, signed release; also helpful: address. Criminal records computerized from 1996, on books prior. Mail turnaround 7-10 days. PAT criminal results show middle initial. Online access to criminal indexes is the same as civil.
General Information: Will fax documents $1.00 per page. Court makes copy: $.50 per page. Certification fee: $5.00 1st page, $1.00 ea add'l. Cert fee includes copies. Payee: District Court. Personal checks accepted credit cards not. Mail request SASE required

Dayton Municipal Ct. PO Box 31, 341 E Main St, Dayton, WA 99328; 509-382-4812; fax: 509-382-2490; 8:30-4:30PM. ***Misdemeanor, Civil.***
Index from JIS-Link; see www.courts.wa.gov/jislink/. Also, search name index back to 1989 and calendars free at http://dw.courts.wa.gov/index.cfm.

Cowlitz County

Superior Court 312 SW 1st Ave Rm 233, Kelso, WA 98626-1724; 360-577-3016; criminal phone: 360-577-3017; civil phone: 360-577-3016 x2115; fax: 360-577-2323; 8:30AM-5PM; doors close 4:30PM. ***Felony, Civil, Eviction, Probate.***
www.co.cowlitz.wa.us/clerk
Civil Records: Access: Phone, mail, online, in person. Visitors must perform in person searches themselves. Search fee: $10.00 min per name; $20.00 per hour if 1 hour or more. Required to search: name, years to search. Civil cases indexed by defendant, plaintiff; index on computer back to 1982; on microfilm through 1992. Mail turnaround time 1-2 days. Civil PAT goes back to 6/1982. PAT civil results show middle initial. Index from JIS-Link; see www.courts.wa.gov/jislink/. Also, search name index back to 1989 and calendars free at http://dw.courts.wa.gov/index.cfm.
Criminal Records: Access: Phone, mail, online, in person. Visitors must perform in person searches themselves. Search fee: $10.00 min per name; $20.00 per hour if 1 hour or more. Required to search: name, years to search. Criminal records computerized from 1982, on microfilm through 1992. Mail turnaround time 1-2 days. Criminal PAT goes back to same as civil. PAT criminal results show middle initial. Online access to criminal indexes is the same as civil. Online results show middle initial.
General Information: Online identifiers in results same as on public terminal. No sealed, juvenile, adoption, paternity, mental health records released. Certain civil and domestic cases may be sealed. Will not fax documents. Court makes copy: $.50 per page. Certification fee: $5.00 1st page, $1.00 each add'l page; exemplification fee $9.00 1st page, $1.00 each add'l page. Payee: Cowlitz County Superior Court Clerk. No personal checks accepted. Checks from law firms accepted. No credit cards accepted. Prepayment required. Mail requests: SASE required.

District Court 312 SW 1st Ave, Rm 207, Kelso, WA 98626-1724; 360-577-3073; fax: 360-577-3132; 8:30AM-5PM. ***Misdemeanor, Civil Actions under $75,000, Small Claims.***
www.co.cowlitz.wa.us/districtcourt
Civil Records: Access: Phone, fax, mail, online, in person. Only the court performs in person searches; visitors may not. No search fee, only copy fees apply. Required to search: name, DOB, years to search; also helpful: address. Civil cases indexed by defendant, plaintiff. Civil index on cards back to 1992. Mail turnaround time 2 weeks. Index from JIS-Link; see www.courts.wa.gov/jislink/. Also, search name index back to 1989 and calendars free at http://dw.courts.wa.gov/index.cfm.
Criminal Records: Access: Mail, fax, online, in person. Only the court performs in person searches; visitors may not. Search fee: copy fee. Required to search: name, years to search, DOB; also helpful: address, SSN. Criminal records back to 1995. Mail turnaround time 2 weeks. Online access to criminal indexes is the same as civil.
General Information: Will not fax documents. Court makes copy: $.15 per page. Self serve: same. Certification fee: $5.00 per doc. Payee: District Court. Personal checks and credit cards accepted.

Castle Rock Municipal Court.
Court Closed 10/2004, contracted with county for court services; see District Court

Kalama Municipal Court.

Kelso Municipal Court.

Longview Municipal Court.

Woodland Municipal Court.
See District Court for records.

Douglas County

Superior Court PO Box 516, Waterville, WA 98858-0516; 509-745-8529; probate phone: same; fax: 509-745-8027; 8AM-5PM. ***Felony, Civil, Eviction, Probate.*** www.douglascountywa.net
Address and phone here is for County Clerk who holds records. Superior Ct Admin at 509-745-9063.
Civil Records: Access: Phone, fax, mail, online, in person. Both court and visitors may perform in person searches. Search fee: $20.00 per hour. Required to search: name, years to search; also helpful: address. Civil cases indexed by defendant, plaintiff; index on computer from 1985, archived and on microfiche from 1883, some records on index books. Mail turnaround time 1 week. Civil PAT goes back to 1985. Index from JIS-Link; see www.courts.wa.gov/jislink/ (also, see state introduction for subscription service). Also, search name index back to 1985 and calendars free at http://dw.courts.wa.gov/index.cfm.
Criminal Records: Access: In person, online. Both court and visitors may perform in person searches. Search fee: $20.00 per hour. Required to search: name, years to search, DOB; also helpful: address, SSN. Criminal records computerized from 1985, archived and on microfiche from 1883, some records on index books. Criminal PAT goes back to same as civil. Online access to criminal indexes is the same as civil.
General Information: No sealed, juvenile, adoption, paternity, mental health, sex offenders (victims). Will fax documents $2.00 1st page, $1.00 each add'l. Court makes copy: $.50 per page. Self serve: same. Certification fee: $5.00 1st page, $1.00 ea add'l. Cert fee includes copies. Payee: Douglas County Clerk. Business checks accepted. No credit cards accepted. Mail requests: SASE required for civil.

District Court - Bridgeport PO Box 730, 1206 Columbia Ave, Bridgeport, WA 98813-0730; 509-686-2034; fax: 509-686-0532; 8:30AM-4:30PM. ***Misdemeanor, Small Claims.***
www.douglascountywa.net/departments/districtcourt/default.asp This is a rural branch. If record not found in this court, your request forwarded to East Wenatchee court (main court).
Civil Records: Access: Fax, mail, online, in person. Only the court performs in person searches; visitors may not. Search fee: $10.00 per name. Required to search: name, years to search; also helpful: address. Civil cases indexed by defendant. Civil records on computer back to 2/95. Note: Please use the court's "Request for Information" form. Mail turnaround time 10 days. Index from JIS-Link; see www.courts.wa.gov/jislink/. Also, search name index back to 1989 and calendars free at http://dw.courts.wa.gov/index.cfm.
Criminal Records: Access: Fax, mail, online, in person. Only the court performs in person searches; visitors may not. Search fee: $10.00 per name. Required to search: name, years to search; also helpful: address, DOB, SSN. Criminal records computerized from 2/95. Note: Please use the court's "Request for Information" form. Mail turnaround 10 days. Online access to criminal indexes is the same as civil.
General Information: No sealed, juvenile, adoption, paternity, mental health, sex offenders (victims) or (sometimes) DUI records released. Will fax documents to local or toll free line. Court makes copy: $.15 per page. Certification fee: $5.00 1st page, $1.00 ea add'l. Cert fee includes copies. Payee: Douglas County District Court Bridgeport. Personal checks accepted. Prepayment required. SASE required.

District Court - East Wenatchee 110 2nd St NE #100, East Wenatchee, WA 98802; 509-884-3536; fax: 509-884-5973; 8:30-4:30. ***Misdemeanor, Civil Actions under $50,000, Small Claims.***
www.douglascountywa.net/departments/districtcourt/default.asp
If record not found in this court, request forwarded to Bridgeport Branch (North) County District Court.
Civil Records: Access: Fax, mail, online, in person. Both court and visitors may perform in person searches. Search fee: $10.00. Required to search: name, years to search; also helpful: address. Civil cases indexed by defendant, plaintiff. Civil cases go

back to close date plus 3 years. Note: Record request forms are on the court webpage. Mail turnaround time 1 week. Civil PAT goes back to 2003. Index from JIS-Link; see www.courts.wa.gov/jislink/. Also, search name index back to 1989 and calendars free http://dw.courts.wa.gov/index.cfm.
Criminal Records: Access: Fax, mail, online, in person. Both court and visitors may perform in person searches. Search fee: $10.00. Required to search: Full name, address, DOB, SSN. Criminal records computerized from 1992. Mail turnaround time 1 week. Criminal PAT goes back to beginning of 2006. Online access to criminal indexes is the same as civil.
General Information: No sealed, juvenile, adoption, paternity, mental health, sex offenders (victims), Alcohol records, treatment reports released. Will fax documents $1.00 1st page, $1.00 each add'l. Local faxing only. Court makes copy: $.15 per page. Self serve: same. Certification fee: $5.00; $10.00 for notarized. Payee: Douglas District Court. Personal checks accepted. Visa/MC accepted. Prepayment required. For credit card payment you will need to call 800-272-9829 with the jurisdiction #5665, after contacting the court for the costs of records.

Bridgeport Municipal Court.
See Bridgeport District Court

East Wenatchee Municipal Ct. 271 9th St NE, East Wenatchee, WA 98802-4438; 509-884-0680; fax: 509-886-4501; 8:30AM-4:30PM. ***Misdemeanor, Traffic.***
www.east-wenatchee.com/municipalcourt.html
Index from JIS-Link; see www.courts.wa.gov/jislink/. Also, search name index back to 1989 and calendars free at http://dw.courts.wa.gov/index.cfm.

Rock Island Municipal Court.

Waterville Municipal Court.
See East Wenatchee District Court for records.

Ferry County

Superior Court 350 E Delaware, #4, Republic, WA 99166; 509-775-5245; 8AM-4PM. ***Felony, Civil, Probate.*** Depending on the civil case type, a civil case many be found here or in District Court. Here, you can ask that a civil and criminal search be combined under a single search fee.
Civil Records: Access: Phone, mail, online, in person. Both court and visitors may perform in person searches. Search fee: $20.00 per hour. Required to search: name, years to search; also helpful: address. Civil cases indexed by defendant, plaintiff; index on computer back to 1987; other records go back to 1900. Mail turnaround time 1-4 days. Civil PAT goes back to 1987. PAT results show name only. Access on public terminal is limited - call for availability. Index from JIS-Link; see www.courts.wa.gov/jislink/. Also, search name index back to 1989 and calendars free at http://dw.courts.wa.gov/index.cfm.
Criminal Records: Access: Phone, mail, online, in person. Both court and visitors may perform in person searches. Search fee: $20.00 per hour. Required to search: name, years to search; also helpful: address, DOB. Criminal records computerized from 1987; other records go back to 1900. Mail turnaround time 1-4 days. Criminal PAT available. PAT results show name only. Access on public terminal is limited - call for availability. Online access to criminal indexes is same as civil.
General Information: Online identifiers in results same as on public terminal. No sealed, adoption, paternity, mental health or sex offenders (victims). Will fax documents $2.00 1st page, $1.00 ea add'l page. Court makes copy: $.50 per page. Self serve: $.25 per page. Certification fee: $5.00 plus $1.00 each add'l page. Payee: Ferry County Clerk. Personal checks accepted; credit cards are not. Prepayment required. Mail requests: SASE required.

District Court 350 E Delaware Ave, #6, Republic, WA 99166-9747; 509-775-5244; fax: 509-775-5221; 8AM-4PM. ***Misdemeanor, Civil under $50,000, Small Claims*** www.ferry-county.com
Depending on the civil case type, a civil case many be found here or in Superior Court.
Civil Records: Access: Fax, mail, online, in person. Only the court performs in person searches; visitors may not. No search fee. Required to search: name, years to search; also helpful: address. Civil cases indexed by case number. Civil records on computer back to 1995; others back to 1995. Mail turnaround time 1 week. Index from JIS-Link; see www.courts.wa.gov/jislink/. Also, search name index back to 1989 and calendars free at http://dw.courts.wa.gov/index.cfm.
Criminal Records: Access: Mail, fax, online, in person. Only the court performs in person searches; visitors may not. No search fee. Required to search: name, years to search, DOB; also helpful: address, SSN, signed release. Criminal records computerized from 1995; others back to 1995. Mail turnaround time 1 week. Online access to criminal indexes is the same as civil.
General Information: No sealed, juvenile, adoption, paternity, mental health, sex offenders (victims) or (sometimes) DUI records released. No fee to fax documents. Court makes copy: $1.00 1st page, $.50 each add'l. Certification fee: $5.00 per cert. Payee: Ferry County District Court. Personal checks accepted; credit cards are not. Prepayment required. Mail requests: SASE required.

Franklin County

Superior Court 1016 N 4th Ave, Pasco, WA 99301; 509-545-3525; fax: 509-545-2243; 8:30AM-N, 1-4:30PM. ***Felony, Civil, Eviction, Probate, Domestic, Juvenile.***
www.co.franklin.wa.us/clerk
Civil Records: Access: Mail, in person, online, email. Only the court performs in person searches; visitors may not. Search fee: $20.00 per hour. Required to search: name, years to search; also helpful: DOB. Civil cases indexed by defendant, plaintiff; index on computer from 10/83, on index books, archived from 1900s. Mail turnaround 1 week. Index from JIS-Link; www.courts.wa.gov/jislink/. Also, search name index back to 1989 and calendars at http://dw.courts.wa.gov/index.cfm. Also, search Superior court records fee at www.co.franklin.wa.us/clerk/search_frame.cfm. Direct email requests to civil court at mkillian@co.franklin.wa.us/clerk.
Criminal Records: Access: Mail, online, in person. Only the court performs in person searches; visitors may not. Search fee: $20.00 per hour. Required to search: name, years to search, DOB; also helpful: address, SSN. Criminal records computerized from 7/83, on index books, archived from 1900s. Mail turnaround time 1 week. Online access to criminal indexes is the same as civil. Also, criminal index at www.co.franklin.wa.us/clerk/search_frame.cfm.
General Information: No sealed, juvenile, adoption, paternity, mental health, sex offenders (victims). Fee to fax out file $3.00 1st page, $1.00 each add'l. Court makes copy: $.50 per page. Certification fee: $5.00 1st page, $1.00 ea add'l. Cert fee includes copies. Payee: Franklin County Superior Court Clerk. Business checks accepted; no personal checks. Visa/MC/AmEx accepted. Prepayment required. Mail requests: SASE required.

District Court 1016 N 4th St, Pasco, WA 99301; 509-545-3593; civil phone: 509-546-5810; fax: 509-545-3588; 8:30AM-5PM. ***Misdemeanor, Civil Actions under $50,000, Small Claims.***
Civil Records: Access: Mail, in person, online, fax. Only the court performs in person searches; visitors may not. Search fee: $10.00 per name. Required to search: name, years to search; also helpful: address. Civil cases indexed by defendant, plaintiff; index on computer from 1993, prior on index cards. Mail turnaround time 7 days. Index from JIS-Link; see www.courts.wa.gov/jislink/. Also, search name index back to 1989 and calendars free at http://dw.courts.wa.gov/index.cfm.
Criminal Records: Access: Mail, online, in person, fax. Only the court performs in person searches; visitors may not. Search fee: $10.00 per name. Required to search: name, years to search, DOB. Criminal records computerized from 1987, prior on index cards. Mail turnaround time 7 days. Online access to criminal indexes is the same as civil.
General Information: No sealed, juvenile, adoption, paternity, mental health, sex offenders (victims) or (sometimes) DUI records released. Will fax documents for no fee. Court makes copy: $.25 per page. Cert fee: $5.00 per cert. Payee: Franklin District Court. Personal checks accepted; credit cards are not. Prepayment required. Mail requests: SASE required.

Connell Municipal Court PO Box 187, 104 E Adams, Connell, WA 99326-0187; 509-234-4141; fax: 509-234-4140; 9AM-5PM. ***Misdemeanor.***
Court located at the city hall and police department building; court convenes once a month.

Kahlotus Municipal Court 130 E Weston St, Kahlotus, WA 99335-0100; 509-282-3372; 8AM-4:30PM. ***Misdemeanor.***
Index from JIS-Link; see www.courts.wa.gov/jislink/. Also, search name index back to 1989 and calendars free at http://dw.courts.wa.gov/index.cfm.

Pasco Municipal Court 1016 N 4th, Pasco, WA 99301-3706; 509-545-3491; fax: 509-543-2912; 8:30AM-12:30PM, 1:30-4PM. ***Misdemeanor.***
Index from JIS-Link; see www.courts.wa.gov/jislink/. Also, search name index back to 1989 and calendars free at http://dw.courts.wa.gov/index.cfm.

Garfield County

Superior Court PO Box 915, Pomeroy, WA 99347-0915; 509-843-3731; fax: 509-843-1224; 8:30AM-N, 1-5PM. ***Felony, Civil, Eviction, Probate.***
Civil Records: Access: Phone, fax, mail, online, in person. Only the court performs in person searches; visitors may not. Search fee: $8.00 per hour. Required to search: name, years to search; also helpful: address. Civil cases indexed by defendant, plaintiff. Civil index on docket books, archived from 1882; on computer back to 1993. Mail turnaround time 1 week. Index from JIS-Link; see www.courts.wa.gov/jislink/. Also, search name index back to 1989 and calendars free at http://dw.courts.wa.gov/index.cfm.
Criminal Records: Access: Fax, mail, online, in person, email. Only the court performs in person searches; visitors may not. Search fee: $8.00 per hour. Required to search: name, years to search, DOB; also helpful: address, SSN. Criminal docket on books, archived from 1882; on computer back to 1993. Mail turnaround time 1 week. Online access to criminal indexes is the same as civil. Also, you may direct email record requests to superiorcourt@co.garfield.wa.us.
General Information: No sealed, juvenile, adoption, paternity, mental health, sex offenders (victims). Will fax documents $.50 per page. Court makes copy: $.50 per page. Self serve: same. Certification fee: $5.00 plus $1.00 per page after first. Cert fee includes copies. Payee: Garfield County Clerk. Personal checks and major credit cards accepted. Prepayment required. Mail requests: SASE requested.

District Court PO Box 817, Pomeroy, WA 99347-0817; 509-843-1002; fax: 509-843-3815; 8:30AM-5PM. ***Misdemeanor, Civil Actions under $50,000, Small Claims.***
Civil Records: Access: Mail, fax, online. Only the court performs in person searches; visitors may not. No search fee. Required to search: name, years to search; also helpful: address. Civil cases indexed by defendant. Civil index on cards. Note: Written request required. Mail turnaround time 2 days. Index from JIS-Link; www.courts.wa.gov/jislink/. Also, search name index back to 1989 and calendars at http://dw.courts.wa.gov/index.cfm.
Criminal Records: Access: Mail, fax. Only the court performs in person searches; visitors may not. No search fee. Required to search: name, years to search, DOB; also helpful: address, SSN. Criminal records indexed on cards. Note: Written request required. Mail turnaround time 2 days. Online access to criminal indexes is the same as civil.
General Information: No sealed, juvenile, adoption, mental health, sex offenders (victims) or (sometimes) DUI records released. Court makes copy: $.25 per page. Certification fee: $5.00. Payee: Garfield County District Court. Personal checks accepted. Money order and cash accepted. No credit cards accepted. Prepayment required.

Grant County

Superior Court PO Box 37, 35 C St NW, Ephrata, WA 98823-0037; 509-754-2011 x430; fax: 509-754-6568; 8AM-4:30PM. ***Felony, Civil, Eviction, Probate.***
www.courts.wa.gov/court_dir/orgs/273.html
Search fee includes civil and criminal indexes.
Civil Records: Access: Mail, in person, online. Both court and visitors may perform in person searches. Search fee: $10.00 per name. Required to search: name, years to search; also helpful: address. Civil cases indexed by defendant, plaintiff; index on computer from 1982, and some on index cards, archived from 1909. Mail turnaround time 2 weeks. Index from JIS-Link; www.courts.wa.gov/jislink/. Also, search name index back to 1989 and calendars at http://dw.courts.wa.gov/index.cfm.
Criminal Records: Access: Mail, online, in person. Both court and visitors may perform in person searches. Search fee: $10.00 per name. Required to search: name, years to search; also helpful: address, DOB, SSN. Criminal records computerized from 1982, and some on index cards, archived from 1909. Mail turnaround time 2 weeks. Online access to criminal indexes is the same as civil.
General Information: No sealed, juvenile, adoption, paternity, mental health, sex offenders (victims) records released. Will not fax documents, but they can email page copies back for $.25 per page. Court makes copy: $.50 per page. Cert fee: $5.00 plus $1.00 per page after first. Cert fee includes copies. Payee: Grant County Clerk's Office. Business and personal checks accepted. No credit cards accepted. Prepayment required. Mail requests: SASE required.

District Court PO Box 37, Ephrata, WA 98823-0037; 509-754-2011 X628; criminal: x389; civil: x435; fax: 509-754-6099; 8-5PM. ***Misdemeanor, Civil Actions under $50,000, Small Claims.***
www.courts.wa.gov/court_dir/orgs/273.html
Civil Records: Access: Mail, in person, online. Only the court performs in person searches; visitors may not. Search fee: $20.00 per name. Required to search: name, years to search; also helpful: address. Civil cases indexed by defendant, plaintiff. Criminal indexed on computer per state retention schedule. Mail turnaround time 30 days or more. Civil PAT available. Index from JIS-Link; see www.courts.wa.gov/jislink/. Also, search name index back to 1989 and calendars free at http://dw.courts.wa.gov/index.cfm.
Criminal Records: Access: Mail, online, in person. Only the court performs in person searches; visitors may not. Search fee: $20.00 per name. Required to search: name, years to search, DOB; also helpful: address, SSN. Criminal indexed on computer per state retention schedule. Mail turnaround time up to 30 days. Criminal PAT available. Online access to criminal indexes is the same as civil.
General Information: No sealed, probation, juvenile, adoption, paternity, mental health, sex offenders (victims) or (sometimes) DUI records released. Will fax documents per copy fee rates. Court makes copy: $2.00 1st page, $1.00 each add'l. Certification fee: $5.00 per page. Payee: Grant County District Court. Personal checks accepted; credit cards are not. Prepayment required.

Coulee City Municipal Court PO Box 398, 501 W Main, Coulee City, WA 99115-0398; 509-632-5331; fax: 509-632-5125; 9AM-5PM. ***Traffic, Ordinance.***
www.courts.wa.gov/court_dir/orgs/273.html

Ephrata Municipal Court 121 Alder St SW, Ephrata, WA 98823; 509-754-4601 x120; fax: 509-754-0912; 7:30AM-4:30PM. ***Misdemeanor.***
www.courts.wa.gov/court_dir/orgs/273.html
Index from JIS-Link; see www.courts.wa.gov/jislink/. Also, search name index back to 1989 and calendars free at http://dw.courts.wa.gov/index.cfm.

George Municipal Court PO Box 5277, 102 Richmond Ave, George, WA 98824; 509-785-5081; fax: 509-785-4880; 8AM-N M,T,W. ***Misdemeanor, Ordinance.***
www.courts.wa.gov/court_dir/orgs/273.html
Actual records available at Grant County main court. Index from JIS-Link; see www.courts.wa.gov/jislink/ (see state intro for subscription service.). Also, search name index back to 1989 and calendars free at http://dw.courts.wa.gov/index.cfm.

Grand Coulee Municipal Court PO Box 180, 306 Midway Ave, Grand Coulee, WA 99133-0180; 509-633-1150; fax: 509-633-1370; 8AM-5PM. ***Misdemeanor, Traffic.***
www.courts.wa.gov/court_dir/orgs/273.html

Mattawa Municipal Court PO Box 965, 521 E Government Rd, Mattawa, WA 99349; 509-932-4037; fax: 509-932-4047; 8:30-4:30. ***Misdemeanor.***
www.courts.wa.gov/court_dir/orgs/273.html
Index from JIS-Link; see www.courts.wa.gov/jislink/. Also, search name index back to 1989 and calendars free at http://dw.courts.wa.gov/index.cfm.

Moses Lake Municipal Court PO Box 1579, 321 S Balsam, Moses Lake, WA 98837-0244; 509-766-9201; fax: 509-766-9392; hours - 9AM-5PM. ***Misdemeanor, Ordinance.***
www.courts.wa.gov/court_dir/orgs/273.html
Index from JIS-Link; see www.courts.wa.gov/jislink/. Also, search name index back to 1989 and calendars free at http://dw.courts.wa.gov/index.cfm.

Quincy Municipal Court PO Box 338, 104 B St SW, Quincy, WA 98848-0338; 509-787-3523; fax: 509-787-1284; 8AM-5PM. ***Ordinance.***
www.courts.wa.gov/court_dir/orgs/273.html
Index from JIS-Link; see www.courts.wa.gov/jislink/. Also, search name index back to 1989 and calendars free at http://dw.courts.wa.gov/index.cfm.

Royal City Municipal Court PO Box 1239, 445 Camelia St NE, Royal City, WA 99357; 509-346-2263; fax: 509-346-2040; 8-5. ***Misdemeanor.***
www.courts.wa.gov/court_dir/orgs/273.html

Soap Lake Municipal Court PO Box 1270, 239 2nd Ave SE, Soap Lake, WA 98851; 509-246-1211; fax: 509-246-1213; 8AM-N, 1-4:30PM. ***Misdemeanor.***
www.courts.wa.gov/court_dir/orgs/273.html
Index from JIS-Link; see www.courts.wa.gov/jislink/. Also, search name index back to 1989 and calendars free at http://dw.courts.wa.gov/index.cfm.

Warden Municipal Court 201 S Ash Ave, Warden, WA 98857; 509-349-2326; fax: 509-349-2027; 9AM-5PM. ***Misdemeanor.***
www.courts.wa.gov/court_dir/orgs/273.html
Index from JIS-Link; see www.courts.wa.gov/jislink/. Also, search name index back to 1989 and calendars free at http://dw.courts.wa.gov/index.cfm.

Grays Harbor County

Superior Court 102 W Broadway, Rm 203, Montesano, WA 98563-3606; 360-249-3842; fax: 360-249-6381; 8AM-5PM. ***Felony, Civil, Eviction, Probate.***
Civil Records: Access: Phone, fax, mail, online, in person. Both court and visitors may perform in person searches. Search fee: $20.00 per name. No fee for records after 1980. Required to search: name, years to search; also helpful: address. Civil cases indexed by defendant, plaintiff; index on computer from 12/1980, on microfiche from 1856. Mail turnaround time 5 days. Civil PAT goes back to 12/1980. PAT results show name only. Index from JIS-Link; see www.courts.wa.gov/jislink/. Also, search name index back to 1989 and calendars free at http://dw.courts.wa.gov/index.cfm.
Criminal Records: Access: Phone, fax, mail, online, in person. Both court and visitors may perform in person searches. Search fee: $20.00 per name. No fee for records after 1980. Required to search: name, years to search; also helpful: address, DOB, SSN. Criminal records computerized from 12/1980, on microfiche from 1856. Mail turnaround time 5 days. Criminal PAT goes back to 12/1980. PAT results show name only. Online access to criminal indexes same as civil. Online results show name only.
General Information: No sealed, juvenile, adoption, paternity, mental health, sex offenders (victims). Will fax out documents $1.00 per page. Court makes copy: $.50 per page. Certification fee: $5.00 1st page, $1.00 ea add'l. Cert fee includes copies. Payee: Grays Harbor County Clerk. Business checks accepted, no personal checks. Visa/MC/AmEx/Discover okay. Prepayment required. Mail requests: SASE required.

District Court No 2 2109 Sumner Ave, Aberdeen, WA 98520-0035; 360-532-7061; fax: 360-532-7704; 8AM-N, 1-5PM. ***Civil Actions under $50,000, Small Claims.***
www.co.grays-harbor.wa.us
This court no longer handles criminal cases.
Civil Records: Access: Fax, mail, online, in person. Only the court performs in person searches; visitors may not. No search fee. Required to search: name, years to search; also helpful: address. Civil cases indexed by defendant, plaintiff; index on computer from 4/91, on index cards. Mail turnaround time 1 week. Index from JIS-Link; see www.courts.wa.gov/jislink/. Also, search name index back to 1989 and calendars free at http://dw.courts.wa.gov/index.cfm.
General Information: No sealed, juvenile, adoption, paternity, mental health, sex offenders (victims) or (sometimes) DUI records released. No fee to fax documents. Court makes copy: $.50 per page. Certification fee: $5.00. Payee: Grays Harbor District Court #2. Personal checks and credit cards accepted. Prepayment required. Mail requests: SASE required.

District Court No 1 102 W Broadway, Rm 202, Montesano, WA 98563; 360-249-3441; fax: 360-249-6382; 8AM-N, 1-5PM. ***Misdemeanor.***
www.co.grays-harbor.wa.us/info/judicial/
All civil filings and hearings are held in the District Court Dept 2 in Aberdeen.
Criminal Records: Access: Phone, fax, mail, online, in person. Only the court performs in person searches; visitors may not. No search fee normally. Required to search: name, years to search, DOB; also helpful: address, SSN. Criminal records computerized from 4/91, on index cards. Mail turnaround 1 week. Index from JIS-Link; www.courts.wa.gov/jislink/. Also see state introduction for subscription service. Also, search name index back to 1991 and calendars at http://dw.courts.wa.gov/index.cfm. Personal identifiers on results may include driver's license number.
General Information: No sealed, juvenile, adoption, paternity, mental health, sex offenders (victims) records released. Will fax documents $.25 per page. Court makes copy: $.50 per page. Self serve: same. Certification fee: $5.00. Payee: Grays Harbor District Court #1. Personal checks and credit cards accepted. Prepayment required. Mail requests: SASE required.

Aberdeen Municipal Court 210 E Market St, Aberdeen, WA 98520-5242; 360-533-5411; fax: 360-537-3247; 8AM-N, 1-5PM. ***Misdemeanor.***
Index from JIS-Link; see www.courts.wa.gov/jislink/. Also, search name index back to 1989 and calendars free at http://dw.courts.wa.gov/index.cfm.

Chehalis Tribal Court PO Box 536, 420 Howanut Rd, Oakville, WA 98568; 360-273-5911; 8AM-5PM. ***Misdemeanor, Civil.***
Index from JIS-Link; see www.courts.wa.gov/jislink/. Also, search name index back to 1989 and calendars free at http://dw.courts.wa.gov/index.cfm.

Cosmopolis Municipal Court PO Box 478, 1312 First St, Cosmopolis, WA 98537; 360-532-9264; fax: 360-532-9273; 8-4PM. ***Misdemeanor.***
Index from JIS-Link; see www.courts.wa.gov/jislink/. Also, search name index back to 1989 and calendars free at http://dw.courts.wa.gov/index.cfm.

Elma Municipal Court PO Box 2013, 108 N 2nd St, Elma, WA 98541-2013; 360-482-2603; fax: 360-482-0103; 8AM-4PM. ***Misdemeanor.***
www.cityofelma.com
Index from JIS-Link; see www.courts.wa.gov/jislink/. Also, search name index back to 1989 and calendars free at http://dw.courts.wa.gov/index.cfm.

Hoquiam Municipal Court 609 8th St, Hoquiam, WA 98550-3522; 360-532-5700 x234; fax: 360-533-3602; 8:30AM-5PM. ***Misdemeanor.***
www.cityofhoquiam.com/court.php

Index from JIS-Link; see www.courts.wa.gov/jislink/. Also, search name index back to 1989 and calendars free at http://dw.courts.wa.gov/index.cfm.

McCleary Municipal Court 100 S 3rd St, McCleary, WA 98557-9652; 360-495-3790; fax: 360-495-3097; 8AM-5PM. ***Misdemeanor.***
Index from JIS-Link; see www.courts.wa.gov/jislink/. Also, search name index back to 1989 and calendars free at http://dw.courts.wa.gov/index.cfm.

Montesano Municipal Court 112 N Main St, Montesano, WA 98563-3707; 360-249-4245; fax: 360-249-6225; 8AM-5PM. ***Misdemeanor.***
www.montesano.us/court.htm
Index from JIS-Link; see www.courts.wa.gov/jislink/. Also, search name index back to 1989 and calendars free at http://dw.courts.wa.gov/index.cfm.

Oakville Municipal Court PO Box D, 204 E Main, Oakville, WA 98568-0078; 360-273-5531; fax: 360-273-5120; 8AM-5PM Fri; call for app't. ***Misdemeanor.***
Index from JIS-Link; see www.courts.wa.gov/jislink/. Also, search name index back to 1989 and calendars free at http://dw.courts.wa.gov/index.cfm.

Ocean Shores Municipal Court PO Box 909, 710 Point Brown Ave NE, Ocean Shores, WA 98569-0909; 360-289-2486; fax: 360-289-2022; 8AM-4PM. ***Misdemeanor.***
Index from JIS-Link; see www.courts.wa.gov/jislink/. Also, search name index back to 1989 and calendars free at http://dw.courts.wa.gov/index.cfm.

Quinault Tribal Court PO Box 99, Taholah, WA 98587-0099; 360-276-8211; fax: 360-276-4606; 8AM-4:30PM. ***Misdemeanor, Civil, Small Claims, Eviction, Probate.***
Index from JIS-Link; see www.courts.wa.gov/jislink/. Also, search name index back to 1989 and calendars free at http://dw.courts.wa.gov/index.cfm.

Westport Municipal Court PO Box 1208, 506 N Montesano St, Westport, WA 98595-1208; 360-268-0125; fax: 360-268-1363; 7:30AM-5PM. ***Misdemeanor.*** www.ci.westport.wa.us/
Criminal Records: Access: Mail, fax, in person, email, online. Only the court performs in person searches; visitors may not. Search fee: Nonw. Required to search: name, DOB, SSN, years to search. criminal records go back 5 years hard copies, on computer back to late 1980s. Mail turnaround time same day. Index from JIS-Link; see www.courts.wa.gov/jislink/. Also, search name index back to 1989 and calendars free at http://dw.courts.wa.gov/index.cfm. Also, you may direct email criminal record requests to judy.stiles@mail.courts.wa.gov.
General Information: Will fax documents no fee. Court makes copy: $.10 per page. No certification fee. Payee: Westport Municipal Ct. Personal checks accepted; credit cards are not. Prepayment required.

Island County

Superior Court PO Box 5000, 101 NE 6th St, 1st Fl, Coupeville, WA 98239-5000; 360-679-7359; 8AM-4:30PM. ***Felony, Civil, Eviction, Probate.***
www.islandcounty.net/clerk/
Civil Records: Access: Phone, mail, in person, online. Both court and visitors may perform in person searches. Search fee: $20.00 per hour. Required to search: name, years to search. Civil cases indexed by defendant, plaintiff; index on computer from 7/1984, microfiche from 1889. Archived in Bellingham. Mail turnaround time 1 week. Civil PAT goes back to 1984. Index from JIS-Link; see www.courts.wa.gov/jislink/. Also, search name index back to 1989 and calendars free at http://dw.courts.wa.gov/index.cfm.
Criminal Records: Access: Phone, mail, in person, online. Both court and visitors may perform in person searches. Search fee: $20.00 per hour. Required to search: name, years to search. Criminal records computerized from 7/1984, microfiche from 1889. Archived in Bellingham. Mail turnaround time 1 week. Criminal PAT goes back to 1984. Online access to criminal indexes is the same as civil.
General Information: No access to sealed, dependency, truancy, adoption, paternity, mental health, sex offenders (victims). Will not fax documents. Court makes copy: $.50 per page. Self serve: $.15 per page. Certification fee: $5.00 first page; $1.00 each add'l; exemplification- $9.00. Payee: Island county Clerk. Business checks accepted. Prepayment required. Mail requests: SASE required.

District Court 800 S 8th Ave, Oak Harbor, WA 98277; 360-675-5988; fax: 360-675-8231; 8AM-4:30PM. ***Misdemeanor, Civil Actions under $50,000, Small Claims.*** Records requests are done as time permits. Is bottom of priority list.
Civil Records: Access: Fax, mail, online, in person. Both court and visitors may perform in person searches. No search fee. Required to search: name, years to search; also helpful: address. Civil cases indexed by defendant. Civil records on computer from 1991, on index by alpha. Mail turnaround 1-7 days. Index from JIS-Link; www.courts.wa.gov/jislink/. Also, search name index back to 1989 and calendars at http://dw.courts.wa.gov/index.cfm.
Criminal Records: Access: Fax, mail, online, in person. Only the court performs in person searches; visitors may not. No search fee. Required to search: name, years to search, DOB; also helpful: address, SSN. Criminal records computerized from 1991, on index by alpha. Mail turnaround time 1-7 days. Online access to criminal indexes is same as civil.
General Information: No sealed, juvenile, adoption, paternity, mental health, sex offenders (victims) or (sometimes) DUI records released. Will fax documents $1.00 per page. Court makes copy: $.50 per page; $1.00 if electronic docket. Certification fee: $5.00. Payee: Island District Court. Personal checks accepted; credit cards are not. Prepayment required. Mail requests: SASE required.

Coupeville Municipal Court.
Langely Municipal Court.
Oak Harbor Municipal Court.
See District Court for records.

Jefferson County

Superior Court PO Box 1220, Port Townsend, WA 98368-0920; 360-385-9125 clerk; 385-9360 Ct; fax: 360-385-5672; 8AM-5PM. ***Felony, Civil, Eviction, Probate, Domestic.***
www.co.jefferson.wa.us/supcourt
Civil Records: Access: Phone, mail, online, in person. Both court and visitors may perform in person searches. Search fee: $20.00 per hour. Required to search: name, years to search. Civil cases indexed by defendant, plaintiff; index on computer from 1983, on microfiche from 1890s. Archive in Bellingham. Mail turnaround time 2 days. Civil PAT goes back to 1988. Results include name of parties. Index from JIS-Link; see www.courts.wa.gov/jislink/. Also, search name index back to 1989 and calendars free at http://dw.courts.wa.gov/index.cfm.
Criminal Records: Access: Phone, mail, online, in person. Both court and visitors may perform in person searches. Search fee: $20.00 per hour. Required to search: name, years to search; also helpful: DOB. Criminal records computerized from 1983, on microfiche from 1890s. Archive in Bellingham. Mail turnaround time 2 days. Criminal PAT goes back to 1983. Results include names of parties. Online access to criminal indexes is the same as civil. Online results show name only.
General Information: No sealed, juvenile, adoption, paternity, mental health records released. Will not fax out results. Will email digitized records at $.25 per page prepaid. Court makes copy: $.50 per page. Self serve: $.15 per page; $.25 per digital page. Certification fee: $5.00 plus $1.00 per page after first. Cert fee includes copies. Payee: County Clerk. Personal checks accepted but not out of state checks. Major credit cards accepted at Superior Ct Payment tab at www.co.jefferson.wa.us/supcourt/default.asp. Prepayment required. Mail requests: SASE required.

District Court PO Box 1220, Port Townsend, WA 98368-0920; 360-385-9135; criminal phone: 360-385-9135; civil phone: 360-385-9135; fax: 360-385-9367; 8:30AM-4:30PM. ***Misdemeanor, Civil Actions under $40,000, Small Claims.***
www.co.jefferson.wa.us
Civil Records: Access: Phone, fax, mail, online, in person. Only the court performs in person searches; visitors may not. No search fee. Required to search: name, years to search; also helpful: address. Civil cases indexed by defendant. Civil records on DISCIS computer from 1993, on computer from '90-'93, on log books prior to 1990. Physical files kept10 years from disposition per ret. Mail turnaround 1 week. Index from JIS-Link; www.courts.wa.gov/jislink/. Also, search name index back to 1989 and calendars at http://dw.courts.wa.gov/index.cfm.
Criminal Records: Access: Phone, fax, mail, online, in person. Only the court performs in person searches; visitors may not. No search fee. Required to search: name, DOB; also helpful: years to search, address, SSN. Criminal records on DISCIS computer from 1993, on computer from '90-'93, on log books prior to 1990. Physical files kept 3 years from disposition per. Mail turnaround time 1 week. Online access to criminal indexes is the same as civil.
General Information: No sealed, juvenile, adoption, paternity, mental health, sex offenders (victims) records released. Will fax documents $3.00 1st page, $1.00 ea add'l. Court makes copy: $.15 per page. Cert fee: $6.00 per document. Payee: Jefferson County District Court. Personal checks & Visa/MC/AmEx cards accepted. Mail requests: SASE required.

Port Townsend Municipal Court.
See District Court for records.

King County

Superior Court 516 3rd Ave, E-609, Courthouse 3rd & James Sts, Mail Stop 6C, Attn: Correspondence Clerk, Seattle, WA 98104-2386; 206-296-9300, 800-325-6165 in state, 800-325-6165 x69300 out of state; fax: 206-296-7796; 8:30AM-4:30PM. ***Felony, Civil, Eviction, Probate, Family.***
www.kingcounty.gov/courts/Clerk.aspx
Also a Superior Ct in Kent, 401 4th Ave, Mail Stop 2-C, 98302. Its records assessable here in Seattle and vice versa, via computer PAT or internet. Phone wait can be lengthy but they will answer. Separate search fees for civil and criminal.
Civil Records: Access: Mail, in person, online. Both court and visitors may perform in person searches. Search fee: $20.00 per name. Deposit $30.00 for research and copies. No search fee if you have case number. Required to search: name, years to search, case type, your phone. Civil cases indexed by defendant, plaintiff; index on computer since 1979; older records on microfilm back to 1800s. Mail turnaround time 2 weeks. Civil PAT goes back to 7/1979. PAT civil results show middle initial. Index from JIS-Link; www.courts.wa.gov/jislink/ (also, see state intro for subscription service.). Also, search civil, criminal and probate name indices for case numbers back to 1989 and calendars at http://dw.courts.wa.gov/index.cfm. Also, with registration, search superior court civil, criminal and probate cases filed after 11/1/2004 at https://dja-ecreweb.metrokc.gov/ecronline. Fee of $.10 per page to view, print, or download documents; for info- 206-205-1600.
Criminal Records: Access: Mail, online, in person. Both court and visitors may perform in person searches. Search fee: $20.00 per name. Deposit $30.00 for research and copies. No search fee if you have case number. Required to search: name, years to search, case type, your phone. Criminal records on computer since 1979; older records on microfilm back to 1800s. Mail turnaround time 2 weeks. Criminal PAT goes back to 7/1979. PAT criminal results show middle initial. Online access to criminal indexes is the same as civil. Online results show middle initial.
General Information: Online identifiers in results same as on public terminal. No sealed, juvenile, dependency, adoption, paternity (except for final judgments), mental health, sex offenders (victims) records released. Will not fax back documents. There is a fee to fax any paper to the clerk's office. Court makes copy: $.50 per page. Self serve: $.15 to $.25 per page. Cert fee: $5.00 plus $1.00 per page after first includes copies. Payee: King County Superior Court

Clerk. Personal checks accepted if in state, or from attorny firm or business. No credit cards accepted. Prepayment required. Mail requests: SASE required.

District Court East Division - Bellevue 585 112th Ave SE, Bellevue, WA 98004; 206-205-9200; 800-325-6165 x59200; fax: 206-296-0589; 8:30AM-4:30PM. ***Misdemeanor.***
www.metrokc.gov/kcdc/bellevue.htm
East Division civil filing area - all Bellevue area civil cases are now filed and handled in the Issaquah facility. Bellevue Courthouse is located in the Surrey Downs area of Bellevue.
Criminal Records: Access: Phone, mail, online, in person. Both court and visitors may perform in person searches. No search fee. Required to search: name, years to search, DOB; also helpful: address, SSN. Criminal records computerized from 1987. Criminal records may be removed after 5 years from disposition. Mail turnaround time not guaranteed for written requests. Public use terminal has crim records back to 1995. PAT results show middle initial, DOB. Any District public terminal has all district courts. Index from JIS-Link; see www.courts.wa.gov/jislink/. Also, search name index back to 1989 and calendars free at http://dw.courts.wa.gov/index.cfm.
General Information: No sealed, juvenile, adoption, paternity, mental health, sex offenders (victims) or (sometimes) DUI records released. Will not fax out documents. Court makes copy: $.50 per page; $.25 per page from computer. Certification fee: $5.00 per doc includes copy fee. Payee: King County District Court. Personal checks accepted. No credit cards accepted in person. Prepayment required.

District Court East Division - Issaquah 5415 220th Ave SW, Issaquah, WA 98029-6839; 206-205-9200, 800-325-6165 x59200; fax: 206-296-0591; 8:30AM-4:30PM. ***Misdemeanor, Civil Actions under $75,000, Small Claims.***
www.metrokc.gov/kcdc/issaquah.htm Area: Issaquah, Sammamish, High Pt, Preston, Fall City, Snoqualmie, North Bend, Cedar Falls, Tokul, Alpental, Bellevue, Eastgate, Factoria, Mercer Is, Clyde Hill, Beaux Arts, Newcastle, Redmond, Kirkland, Woodinville, Bothell, Duvall, Carnation, Juanita.
Civil Records: Access: Mail, in person, online. Both court and visitors may perform in person searches. No search fee. Required to search: name, years to search; also helpful: address. Civil cases indexed by defendant, plaintiff; index on computer back 10 years. Mail turnaround time 1-5 days. Civil PAT goes back to 1995. PAT civil results show middle initial. Add'l identifiers may be in case file. Any District public terminal has all district courts. Index from JIS-Link; www.courts.wa.gov/jislink/. Also, search name index back to 1989 and calendars at http://dw.courts.wa.gov/index.cfm.
Criminal Records: Access: Mail, online, in person. Both court and visitors may perform in person searches. No search fee. Required to search: name, years to search, DOB, signed release; also helpful: address. Criminal records on computer back 5 years. Note: Mail requests are not generally recommended. Mail turnaround time 1-5 days. Criminal PAT goes back to same as civil. PAT results show middle initial, DOB. Add'l identifiers may be in case file. Any District public terminal has all district courts. Online access to criminal indexes is the same as civil. Online results show middle initial, DOB.
General Information: No sealed, juvenile, sex offenders (victims) or (sometimes) DUI records released. Will fax documents to local or toll-free number. Court makes copy: $.50 per page; $.25 per page from computer. Cert fee: $5.00 per doc includes copy fee. Payee: King County District Court. Personal checks accepted. No credit cards accepted in person. Prepayment required. Mail requests: SASE required.

District Court East Division - Redmond 8601 160th Ave NE, Redmond, WA 98052-3548; 206-205-9200, 206-296-3667; 800-325-6165 x59200; 8:30AM-4:30PM. ***Misdemeanor, Civil Actions under $75,000, Small Claims.***
www.metrokc.gov/kcdc/redmond.htm
Formerly known as the Northeast Division. Civil Filing Area: All civil cases filed and handled in the Issaquah Facility.
Civil Records: Access: Mail, in person, online. Both court and visitors may perform in person searches. No search fee. Required to search: name, years to search; also helpful: address. Civil cases indexed by defendant, plaintiff; index on computer back 10 years. Mail turnaround time 1-2 weeks. Civil PAT goes back to 1995. PAT civil results show middle initial. Any District public terminal has all district courts. Index from JIS-Link; see www.courts.wa.gov/jislink/. Also, search name index back to 1989 and calendars free at http://dw.courts.wa.gov/index.cfm.
Criminal Records: Access: Mail, online, in person. Both court and visitors may perform in person searches. No search fee. Required to search: name, years to search, DOB; also helpful: address. Criminal records on computer back 5 years. Mail turnaround time 1-2 weeks. Criminal PAT goes back to same as civil. PAT results show middle initial, DOB. Online access to criminal indexes is same as civil.
General Information: No sealed, juvenile, adoption, paternity, mental health, sex offenders (victims) or (sometimes) DUI records released. Will not fax out documents. Court makes copy: $.50 per page; $.25 per page from computer. Certification fee: $5.00 per doc includes copy fee. Payee: King County District Court. Personal checks accepted. No credit cards accepted in person. Prepayment required.

District Court South Division - Burien 601 SW 149th St, Burien, WA 98166-1935; 206-205-9200, 800-325-6165 x59200; fax: 206-296-0124; 8:30AM-4:30PM. ***Misdemeanor, Civil Actions under $75,000, Small Claims.***
www.metrokc.gov/kcdc/
Formerly located in Vashon. Formerly Southwest Division, name change 12/2002. Civil Filing Area: All civil cases filed and handled in the Kent Facility.
Civil Records: Access: Mail, in person, online. Both court and visitors may perform in person searches. No search fee. Required to search: name, years to search; also helpful: address. Civil cases indexed by defendant, plaintiff; index on computer back 5 years. Mail turnaround time 1 day. Civil PAT goes back to 1995. PAT civil results show middle initial. Any District public terminal has all district courts. Index from JIS-Link; www.courts.wa.gov/jislink/. Also, search name index back to 1989 and calendars at http://dw.courts.wa.gov/index.cfm.
Criminal Records: Access: Mail, online, in person. Both court and visitors may perform in person searches. No search fee. Required to search: name, years to search; also helpful: address, DOB, SSN. Criminal records computerized from 1987. Mail turnaround time 1 day. Criminal PAT goes back to same as civil. PAT results show middle initial, DOB. Online access to criminal indexes is the same as civil.
General Information: No sealed, juvenile, adoption, paternity, mental health, sex offenders (and victims) or DUI records sometimes released. Will not fax out documents. Court makes copy: $.50 per page; $.25 per page from computer. Self serve: same. Certification fee: $5.00 per doc includes copy fee. Payee: King County District Court. Personal checks accepted. No credit cards accepted in person. Prepayment required.

District Court South Division - Kent (formerly known as Aukeen) 1210 Central Ave S, Kent, WA 98032-7426; 206-205-9200, 800-325-6165 x59200; fax: 206-296-0588; 8:30AM-4:30PM. ***Misdemeanor, Civil Actions under $75,000, Small Claims.***
www.metrokc.gov/kcdc/kent.htm
Civil Area: Enumclaw, Kent, Auburn, Black Diamond, Maple Valley, Covington, Algona, Pacific, Ravensdale, Hobart, Federal Way, Burien, DesMoines, Normandy Pk, Vashon Is, SeaTac, Renton, Tukwila. In 2003- Federal Way Div merged operations with Kent.
Civil Records: Access: Mail, in person, online. Both court and visitors may perform in person searches. No search fee. Required to search: name, years to search; also helpful: address. Civil cases indexed by defendant, plaintiff; index on computer 5 years back. Mail turnaround time 1 day. Civil PAT goes back to 1995. PAT civil results show middle initial. Any District public terminal has all district courts. Index from JIS-Link; www.courts.wa.gov/jislink/. Also, search name index back to 1989 and calendars at http://dw.courts.wa.gov/index.cfm.
Criminal Records: Access: Mail, online, in person. Both court and visitors may perform in person searches. No search fee. Required to search: name, years to search, DOB; also helpful: address. Criminal records on computer 5 years back. Mail turnaround time 1 day. Criminal PAT goes back to same as civil. PAT results show middle initial, DOB. Online access to criminal indexes is same as civil.
General Information: No sealed, juvenile, adoption, paternity, mental health, sex offenders (victims) or (sometimes) DUI records released. Will fax documents $.15 per page fee. Court makes copy: $.50 per page; $.25 per page from computer. Certification fee: $5.00 per doc includes copy fee. Payee: King County District Court. Personal checks accepted. No credit cards accepted in person. Prepayment required. Mail requests: SASE required.

District Court West Division - Seattle 516 3rd Ave, #E-327, Courthouse, Seattle, WA 98104-3273; 206-205-9200, 800-325-6165 x59200; fax: 206-296-0910; 8:30-4:30PM. ***Misdemeanor, Infractions, Civil under $75,000, Small Claims.***
www.metrokc.gov/kcdc/seattle.htm
Formerly known as the Seattle Division. Civil Filing Area: Seattle, Shoreline, Kenmore, Lake Forest Park.
Civil Records: Access: Fax, mail, online, in person. Visitors must perform in person searches themselves. No search fee. Required to search: name, years to search; also helpful: address. Civil cases indexed by defendant, plaintiff; index on computer from back 10 years. Mail turnaround time 10 days. Civil PAT goes back to 1995. PAT civil results show middle initial. Public terminal 90% of info available to public, other 10% can only be searched by staff. Any District public terminal has all district courts. Index from JIS-Link; see www.courts.wa.gov/jislink/. Also, search name index back to 1989 and calendars free at http://dw.courts.wa.gov/index.cfm.
Criminal Records: Access: Fax, mail, online, in person. Both court and visitors may perform in person searches. No search fee. Required to search: name, years to search, DOB, signed release; also helpful: address, SSN. Criminal records computerized from back 10 years. Mail turnaround time 10 days. Criminal PAT goes back to same as civil. PAT results show middle initial, DOB. Any District public terminal has all district courts. Online access to criminal indexes is the same as civil.
General Information: No sealed, juvenile, adoption, paternity, mental health, sex offenders (victims), treatment plans or (sometimes) DUI records released. Will not fax documents. Court makes copy: $.50 per page; $.25 per page from computer. Certification fee: $5.00 per doc includes copy fee. Payee: King County District Court, Seattle. Personal checks accepted. No credit cards accepted in person. Prepayment required. Mail requests: SASE required.

District Court West Division - Shoreline 18050 Meridian Ave N, Shoreline, WA 98133-4642; 206-205-9200, 206-296-3679; 800-325-6165 x59200; fax: 206-296-0594; 8:30AM-4:30PM. ***Misdemeanor, Civil under $75,000, Small Claims.***
www.metrokc.gov/kcdc/shorel.htm
Civil Filings for: Shoreline, Kenmore, Lake Forest Park should be filed in Seattle Facility.
Civil Records: Access: Fax, mail, online, in person. Both court and visitors may perform in person searches. No search fee. Required to search: name, years to search; also helpful: address. Civil cases indexed by defendant, plaintiff; index on computer from 1985. Mail turnaround time 1 week. Civil PAT goes back to 1995. PAT civil results show middle initial. Any District public terminal has all district courts. Index from JIS-Link; see www.courts.wa.gov/jislink/. Also, search name index back to 1989 and calendars free at http://dw.courts.wa.gov/index.cfm.
Criminal Records: Access: Fax, mail, online, in person. Both court and visitors may perform in person searches. No search fee. Required to search:

name, years to search; also helpful: address, DOB, SSN. Criminal records computerized from 1987. Note: Please limit criminal requests to 5 and use their request form. Mail turnaround time 1 week. Criminal PAT goes back to same as civil. PAT results show middle initial, DOB. Online access to criminal indexes is the same as civil. Online results show middle initial, DOB.

General Information: No sealed, juvenile, adoption, paternity, mental health, sex offenders (victims) or (sometimes) DUI records released. Will not fax out documents. Court makes copy: $.50 per page; $.25 per page from computer. Certification fee: $5.00 per doc includes copy fee. Payee: King County District Court. Personal checks accepted. No credit cards accepted in person. Prepayment required. Mail requests: SASE required.

Algona Municipal Court. See Auburn Municipal Court for records.

Auburn Municipal Court 340 E Main St #101, Auburn, WA 98002-5548; 253-931-3076; fax: 253-804-5011; 8AM-4PM. ***Misdemeanor.*** www.ci.auburn.wa.us/
Index from JIS-Link; see www.courts.wa.gov/jislink/. Also, search name index back to 1989 and calendars free at http://dw.courts.wa.gov/index.cfm.

Bellevue Municipal Court. See East Division, KCDC for records.

Black Diamond Municipal Court PO Box 599, 25510 Lawson St, Black Diamond, WA 98010-0599; 360-886-7784; fax: 253-631-7758; 8:30AM-5PM. ***Misdemeanor.***
Index from JIS-Link; see www.courts.wa.gov/jislink/. Also, search name index back to 1989 and calendars free at http://dw.courts.wa.gov/index.cfm.

Bothell Municipal Court 10116 NE 183rd St, Bothell, WA 98011-3416; 425-487-5587; fax: 425-488-3052; 8AM-5PM. ***Misdemeanor.***
Index from JIS-Link; see www.courts.wa.gov/jislink/. Also, search name index back to 1989 and calendars free at http://dw.courts.wa.gov/index.cfm.

Burien Municipal Court. See South Division, KCDC for records.

Carnation Municipal Court. See East Division, KCDC for records.

Clyde Hill Municipal Court. See Kirkland Municipal Court for records.

Covington Municipal Court. See South Division, KCDC for records.

Des Moines Municipal Court 21630 11th Ave S #C, Des Moines, WA 98198; 206-878-4597; fax: 206-870-4387; 8AM-4:30PM. ***Misdemeanor.*** www.desmoineswa.gov/dept/court/court.html
Index from JIS-Link; see www.courts.wa.gov/jislink/. Also, search name index back to 1989 and calendars free at http://dw.courts.wa.gov/index.cfm.

Duvall Municipal Court. See East Division, KCDC for records.

Enumclaw Municipal Court 1339 Griffin Ave, Enumclaw, WA 98022-3011; 360-825-7771; fax: 360-802-0107; 8AM-5PM. ***Misdemeanor.*** www.cityofenumclaw.net/court.htm
Includes Maple Valley Court. Index from JIS-Link; see www.courts.wa.gov/jislink/. Also, search name index back to 1989 and calendars free at http://dw.courts.wa.gov/index.cfm.

Federal Way Municipal Court PO Box 9717, 33325 8th Ave S, Federal Way, WA 98063-9717; 253-835-3000; fax: 253-835-3020; 8:30AM-4:40PM. ***Misdemeanor.*** www.cityoffederalway.com/Page.aspx?view=69
Index from JIS-Link; see www.courts.wa.gov/jislink/. Also, search name index back to 1989 and calendars free at http://dw.courts.wa.gov/index.cfm.

Hunts Point Municipal Court. See Kirkland Municipal Court for records.

Issaquah Municipal Court PO Box 7005, 135 E Sunset Way, Issaquah, WA 98027; 425-837-3170; fax: 425-837-3178; 8:30-4:30PM. ***Misdemeanor.*** www.ci.issaquah.wa.us/SectionIndex.asp?SectionID=27
Index from JIS-Link; see www.courts.wa.gov/jislink/. Also, search name index back to 1989 and calendars free at http://dw.courts.wa.gov/index.cfm.

Kenmore Municipal Court. See East Division, KCDC for records.

Kent Municipal Court 1220 S Central Ave, Kent, WA 98032-7426; 253-856-5730; 8:30AM-4:30PM. ***Misdemeanor.*** www.ci.kent.wa.us/MunicipalCourt/
Index from JIS-Link; see www.courts.wa.gov/jislink/. Also, search name index back to 1989 and calendars free at http://dw.courts.wa.gov/index.cfm.

Kirkland Municipal Court PO Box 678, 11515 NE 118th St, Kirkland, WA 98083-0678; 425-587-3160; fax: 425-587-3161; 8:30AM-N, 1-4:30PM. ***Misdemeanor.*** www.ci.kirkland.wa.us/depart/Municipal_Court.htm
Index from JIS-Link; see www.courts.wa.gov/jislink/. Also, search name index back to 1989 and calendars free at http://dw.courts.wa.gov/index.cfm.

Lake Forest Park Municipal Court 17425 Ballinger Way NE, Lake Forest Park, WA 98155-5556; 206-364-7711; fax: 206-364-7712; 9AM-5PM. ***Misdemeanor, Civil Infractions.*** www.cityoflfp.com/city/court.html

Maple Valley Municipal Court 1339 Griffin Ave, Enumclaw, WA 98022-3011; 360-825-7771; fax: 360-802-0107; 8AM-5PM. ***Misdemeanor.*** www.cityofenumclaw.net/court.htm
Includes Enumclaw Muni Ct. Index from JIS-Link; see www.courts.wa.gov/jislink/. Also, search name index back to 1989 and calendars free at http://dw.courts.wa.gov/index.cfm.

Medina Municipal Court. See Kirkland Municipal Court for records.

Mercer Island Municipal Court 9611 SE 36th St, Mercer Island, WA 98040-3732; 206-275-7604; fax: 206-275-7980; 9AM-12; 2PM-3:30 M-TH. ***Misdemeanor.***
Index from JIS-Link; see www.courts.wa.gov/jislink/. Also, search name index back to 1989 and calendars free at http://dw.courts.wa.gov/index.cfm.

Muckleshoot Tribal Court (NICS) 39015 172nd Ave SE, Auburn, WA 98092-9763; 253-876-3203; fax: 253-876-2846; 8AM-5PM. ***Civil, Ordinance, Family.***
Fee payments and cost information queries are made through Tammy Byars in the Finance Bldg at 253-876-3139.

Civil Records: Access: Mail, fax, in person, email. Only the court performs in person searches; visitors may not. Search fee: $5.00 per name. Required to search: name, DOB, years to search. Civil cases indexed by defendant, plaintiff. Civil records go back to 1997, some older. Note: Court actually prefers email search requests. Direct email request to marcellina.delatorre@muckleshoot.nsn.us. Mail turnaround time 30 days.

Criminal Records: Access: Mail, fax, in person, email, online. Only the court performs in person searches; visitors may not. No search fee. Required to search: name, DOB, years to search. Criminal records go back to 1980. Mail turnaround time 30 days. Index from JIS-Link; see www.courts.wa.gov/jislink/. Also, search name index back to 1989 and calendars free at http://dw.courts.wa.gov/index.cfm. Court actually prefers email search requests. Direct email request to marcellina.delatorre@muckleshoot.nsn.us.

General Information: Will fax back documents no fee. Court makes copy: $.25 per page. No certification fee. Payee: Muckleshoot Tribal Court. Personal checks accepted; credit cards are not. Prepayment required. Mail requests: SASE required.

Newcastle Municipal Court. See Mercer Island Municipal Court for records.

Normandy Park Municipal Court. See Des Moines Municipal Court for records.

North Bend Municipal Court. See East Division, KCDC for records.

Pacific Municipal Court 100 3rd Ave SE, Pacific, WA 98047-1349; 253-929-1141; fax: 253-351-8556; 8AM-5PM. ***Misdemeanor.***

Redmond Municipal Court. See East Division, KCDC for records.

Renton Municipal Court 1055 S Grady Way, Renton, WA 98055-3232; 425-430-6550; fax: 425-430-6544; 8AM-5PM. ***Misdemeanor.*** http://rentonwa.gov/living/default.aspx?id=1942

Sammamish Municipal Court. See East Division, KCDC for records.

SeaTac Municipal Court 4800 S 188th St, SeaTac, WA 98188; 206-973-4610; fax: 206-973-4629; 8:30AM-4:30PM. ***Misdemeanor.*** www.ci.seatac.wa.us/department/courthome.htm

Seattle Municipal Court PO Box 34987, 600 5th Ave, Seattle, WA 98124-4987; 206-684-5600; fax: 206-684-8115; 8AM-5PM. ***Misdemeanor.*** www.seattle.gov/courts/
Search Seattle Muni Court records free at http://publicinformation.seattle.gov/cpi/smc.publicInformation.def.

Shoreline Municipal Court. See East Division, KCDC for records.

Skykomish Municipal Court. See East Division, KCDC for records.

Snoqualmie Municipal Court. See East Division, KCDC for records.

Tukwila Municipal Court 6200 Southcenter Blvd, Tukwila, WA 98188-2544; 206-433-1840; fax: 206-433-7160; 8:30-4:30PM. ***Misdemeanor.*** www.ci.tukwila.wa.us/mayor/court.html
Search dockets with subscription to the judicial system at www.courts.wa.gov/jislink/index.cfm.

Woodinville Municipal Court. See East Division, KCDC for records.

Yarrow Point Municipal Court. See Kirkland Municipal Court for records.

Kitsap County

Superior Court 614 Division St, MS34, County Clerk, Port Orchard, WA 98366-4699; 360-337-7164; fax: 360-337-4927; 8AM-4:30PM. ***Felony, Civil, Eviction, Probate.*** www.kitsapgov.com/clerk

Civil Records: Access: Mail, in person, online. Both court and visitors may perform in person searches. Search fee: $20.00 for up to 5 names. Required to search: name, years to search. Civil cases indexed by defendant, plaintiff; index on computer from 1978, on microfiche and archived from 1857. Mail turnaround time 2 weeks. Civil PAT goes back to 1978. PAT civil results show middle initial. Index from JIS-Link; see www.courts.wa.gov/jislink/. Also, search name index back to 1978 and calendars free at http://dw.courts.wa.gov/index.cfm.

Criminal Records: Access: Mail, online, in person. Both court and visitors may perform in person searches. Search fee: $20.00 for up to 5 names. Required to search: name, years to search; also helpful: address, DOB, SSN. Criminal records computerized from 1978, on microfiche and archived from 1857. Mail turnaround time 2 weeks. Criminal PAT goes back to same as civil. PAT criminal results show middle initial. Online access to criminal indexes is the same as civil. Also, subscription access to court docs back to 2/2/2000 and indexes back to 4/1/1978 available at www.landlight.com. Demo subscription available. Online results show middle initial.

General Information: Online identifiers in results same as on public terminal. No dependencies, adoption or mental illness records released. Will fax documents $1.00 per page. Court makes copy: $.50

per page; $.25 if from image media. Self serve: $.15 per page.There is an add'l $5.00 handling fee if copies required, includes postage. Certification fee: $5.00 1st page, $1.00 ea add'l. Cert fee includes copies. Payee: Kitsap County Clerk. No personal checks accepted. Major credit cards accepted. Pay online at www.officialpayments.com. Jurisdiction code 5624. Prepayment required.

District Court 614 Division St, MS 25, Port Orchard, WA 98366-4614; criminal phone: 360-337-7109; civil phone: 360-337-7104; criminal fax: 360-337-4865; civil fax: 360-337-4586; 8AM-12:15PM, 1:15-4:30PM. ***Misdemeanor, Civil Actions under $50,000, Small Claims.*** www.kitsapgov.com/dc
Civil Records: Access: Phone, fax, mail, online, in person. Only the court performs in person searches; visitors may not. No search fee. Required to search: name, years to search. Civil cases indexed by defendant, plaintiff; index on computer from 1/95, prior in archives. Mail turnaround time 3 days. Index from JIS-Link; see www.courts.wa.gov/jislink/. Also, search name index back to 1989 and calendars at http://dw.courts.wa.gov/index.cfm.
Criminal Records: Access: Phone, fax, mail, online, in person. Only the court performs in person searches; visitors may not. No search fee. Required to search: name, years to search; also helpful: DOB. Criminal records computerized from 1/95, prior in archives. Mail turnaround time 3 days. Online access to criminal indexes is the same as civil.
General Information: No fee to fax documents. Court makes copy: $.15 per page. Cert fee: $5.00. Payee: Kitsap County District Court. Personal checks accepted; credit cards are not. Prepayment required.

District Court North 614 Division St, MS-25, Port Orchard, WA 98366; 360-337-7109; civil phone: 360-337-7014; fax: 360-697-1179; 8:30AM-12:15PM; 1:15-4:30PM. ***Misdemeanor, Civil Actions under $75,000, Small Claims.***
www.kitsapgov.com/dc/ The court physical address is 19050 Jensen Way NE, Poulsbo.
Civil Records: Access: Mail, in person, online. Only the court performs in person searches; visitors may not. No search fee. Required to search: full name, years to search. Civil cases indexed by defendant, plaintiff; index on computer back 8 years. Note: Send all mail requests to Port Orchard District court, 614 Division St, Port Orchard, 98336. Mail turnaround time 2 days. Index from JIS-Link; see www.courts.wa.gov/jislink/. Also, search name index back to 1989 and calendars free at http://dw.courts.wa.gov/index.cfm.
Criminal Records: Access: Mail, online, in person, phone (1 search only). Only the court performs in person searches; visitors may not. No search fee. Required to search: name, signed release; also helpful: years to search, DOB. Criminal records on computer back 8 years. Note: Send all mail requests to Port Orchard District court, 614 Division St, Port Orchard, 98336. Mail turnaround time 2 days. Online access to criminal indexes is same as civil.
General Information: No dependencies, adoption and mental illness records released. Will fax documents to local or toll-free number. Court makes copy: $.15 per page. Certification fee: $5.00. Payee: District Court, Kitsap County. Cash, cashiers check or money order accepted. No credit cards accepted. Prepayment required. Mail requests: SASE required.

Bainbridge Island Municipal Court PO Box 151, 10255 NE Valley Rd, Bainbridge Is, Rolling Bay, WA 98061-0151; 206-842-5641; fax: 206-842-0316; 8AM-4PM. ***Misdemeanor.***
www.ci.bainbridge-isl.wa.us/default.asp?ID=393
Index from JIS-Link; see www.courts.wa.gov/jislink/. Also, search name index back to 1989 and calendars free at http://dw.courts.wa.gov/index.cfm.

Bremerton Municipal Court 900 Pacific Ave, Bremerton, WA 98337-1875; 360-473-5260; fax: 360-473-5262; 8AM-5PM. ***Misdemeanor.***
www.ci.bremerton.wa.us/display.php?id=53
Index from JIS-Link; see www.courts.wa.gov/jislink/. Also, search name index back to 1989 and calendars free at http://dw.courts.wa.gov/index.cfm.

Port Gamble S'Kallam Tribal Court (NICS) 31912 Little Boston Rd NE, Kingston, WA 98346-9700; 360-297-6235; fax: 360-297-6306; 8AM-4PM. ***Misdemeanor, Civil Actions under $3000, Eviction.*** www.pgst.nsn.us/
Index from JIS-Link; see www.courts.wa.gov/jislink/. Also, search name index back to 1989 and calendars free at http://dw.courts.wa.gov/index.cfm.

Port Orchard Municipal Court 216 Prospect St, Port Orchard, WA 98366-5326; 360-876-1701; fax: 360-895-3071; 8AM-4:30PM. ***Misdemeanor.***
www.cityofportorchard.us/municipal_court.htm
Index from JIS-Link; see www.courts.wa.gov/jislink/. Also, search name index back to 1989 and calendars free at http://dw.courts.wa.gov/index.cfm.

Poulsbo Municipal Court PO Box 98, 19050 Jensen Way NE, Poulsbo, WA 98370-0098; 360-779-9846; fax: 360-779-1584; 8AM-4:30PM. ***Misdemeanor.*** www.cityofpoulsbo.com/Court/
Index from JIS-Link; see www.courts.wa.gov/jislink/. Also, search name index back to 1989 and calendars free at http://dw.courts.wa.gov/index.cfm.

Suquamish Tribal Court PO Box 1209, 18490 Suquamish Way #105, Suquamish, WA 98392-1209; 360-394-8521; fax: 360-598-5333; 8AM-4:30PM. ***Felony, Misdemeanor, Civil, Small Claims, Eviction.*** Index from JIS-Link; see www.courts.wa.gov/jislink/. Also, search name index back to 1989 and calendars free at http://dw.courts.wa.gov/index.cfm.

Kittitas County

Superior Court 205 W 5th, Rm 210, Ellensburg, WA 98926; 509-962-7531; fax: 509-962-7667; 9AM-N, 1-5PM. ***Felony, Misdemeanor, Civil, Eviction, Probate.*** www.co.kittitas.wa.us/clerk/
Civil Records: Access: Phone, fax, mail, online, in person. Only the court performs in person searches; visitors may not. Search fee: $10.00 per name. Required to search: name, years to search; also helpful: address. Civil cases indexed by defendant, plaintiff; index on computer from 9/1982, on microfiche and archived from 1890. Some records on index cards. Mail turnaround time 2 days. Index from JIS-Link; see www.courts.wa.gov/jislink/. Also, search name index back to 1989 and calendars at http://dw.courts.wa.gov/index.cfm.
Criminal Records: Access: Phone, fax, mail, online, in person. Only the court performs in person searches; visitors may not. Search fee: $10.00 per name. Required to search: name, years to search; also helpful: address, DOB, SSN. Criminal records computerized from 9/1982, on microfiche and archived from 1890. Some records on index cards. Mail turnaround time 2 days. Online access to criminal indexes is the same as civil.
General Information: No dependencies, adoption, and mental illness records released. No fee to fax documents. Fax available in emergency only. Court makes copy: $.50 per page. Certification fee: $5.00 first page; $1.00 each add'l. Electronic certification available through Clerk's Epass. Payee: Kittitas County Clerk. Personal checks accepted. Major credit cards accepted through Official Payments Dept. Prepayment required.

District Court Lower Kittitas 205 W 5th, Rm 180, Ellensburg, WA 98926; 509-962-7511; fax: 509-962-7575; 9AM-5PM. ***Misdemeanor, Civil Actions under $50,000, Small Claims.***
Civil Records: Access: Mail, in person, online. Only the court performs in person searches; visitors may not. No search fee. Required to search: name, years to search. Civil cases indexed by defendant, plaintiff; index on computer from 8/97, archived back 10 years. Records retained for 20 years. Mail turnaround time 7-10 days. Index from JIS-Link; see www.courts.wa.gov/jislink/. Also, search name index back to 1989 and calendars free at http://dw.courts.wa.gov/index.cfm.
Criminal Records: Access: Fax, mail, online, in person. Only the court performs in person searches; visitors may not. No search fee. Required to search: name, years to search, DOB. Criminal records computerized from 8/97, archived back 10 years. Mail turnaround time 7-10 days. Online access to criminal indexes is the same as civil.
General Information: No dependencies, adoption, and mental illness records released. Will fax documents to local or toll free line. Court makes copy for no fee. Certification fee: $5.00 includes copy fee. Payee: Lower Kittitas County District Court. Personal checks accepted; credit cards are not. Prepayment required. Mail requests: SASE required.

District Court Upper Kittitas 700 E 1st, Cle Elum, WA 98922; 509-674-5533; fax: 509-674-4209; 9AM-5PM. ***Misdemeanor, Civil Actions under $50,000, Small Claims.***
Civil Records: Access: Mail, in person, online. Only the court performs in person searches; visitors may not. No search fee. Required to search: name, years to search. Civil cases indexed by defendant, plaintiff; index on computer since 8/91; prior records archived from 1890, some on index cards. Records retained for 10 years. Mail turnaround time 1 week. Index from JIS-Link; see www.courts.wa.gov/jislink/. Also, search name index back to 1989 and calendars free at http://dw.courts.wa.gov/index.cfm.
Criminal Records: Access: Fax, mail, online, in person. Only the court performs in person searches; visitors may not. No search fee. Required to search: name, years to search, DOB, signed release; also helpful: SSN. Criminal records computerized from 1997; prior records archived from 1890, some on index cards. Records retained for 5 years. Mail turnaround time 1 week. Online access to criminal indexes is the same as civil.
General Information: No dependencies, adoption, and mental illness records released. Fee to fax out file $1.00 per page. Court makes copy: $.25 per page. Certification fee: $5.00. Payee: UKCDC. Personal checks & credit cards accepted. Prepayment required.

Cle Elum Municipal Court 700 E 1st St, Cle Elum, WA 98922-1251; 509-674-5533; fax: 509-674-4209; 9AM-5PM. ***Misdemeanor.***
Index from JIS-Link; see www.courts.wa.gov/jislink/. Also, search name index back to 1989 and calendars free at http://dw.courts.wa.gov/index.cfm.

Ellensburg Municipal Court.
See Lower Kittitas District Court for records.

Kittitas Municipal Court PO Box 719, 207 N Main St, Kittitas, WA 98934-0719; 509-968-0220; fax: 509-968-0223; 8AM-4:30PM. ***Misdemeanor, Ordinance, Traffic.***
Index from JIS-Link; see www.courts.wa.gov/jislink/. Also, search name index back to 1989 and calendars free at http://dw.courts.wa.gov/index.cfm.

Roslyn Municipal Court 700 E 1st St, Cle Elum, WA 98922-1251; 509-674-5533; fax: 509-674-4209; 9AM-5PM. ***Misdemeanor.***
Index from JIS-Link; see www.courts.wa.gov/jislink/. Also, search name index back to 1989 and calendars free at http://dw.courts.wa.gov/index.cfm.

Klickitat County

Superior Court Superior Court Clerk, 205 S Columbus, MS CH-O3, Goldendale, WA 98620; 509-773-5744; 9-5. ***Felony, Civil, Eviction, Probate.***
Civil Records: Access: Phone, mail, online, in person. Both court and visitors may perform in person searches. Search fee: $8.00 per hour. Required to search: name, years to search; also helpful: address. Civil cases indexed by defendant, plaintiff. Civil index on computer from 9/87, prior on books. Mail turnaround time 1-2 weeks or sooner. Civil PAT goes back to 1988. PAT results show middle initial, DOB. Index from JIS-Link; see www.courts.wa.gov/jislink/. Also, search name index back to 1989 and calendars free at http://dw.courts.wa.gov/index.cfm.
Criminal Records: Access: Phone, mail, online, in person. Both court and visitors may perform in person searches. Search fee: $8.00 per hour. Required to search: name, years to search; also helpful: address, DOB, SSN. Criminal index computer from 9/87; prior on books back to 1886. Mail turnaround time 1-2 weeks or sooner. Criminal PAT goes back to same as civil. Online access to criminal indexes is the same as civil.
General Information: No dependencies, adoption, and mental illness records released. Will not fax

documents. Court makes copy: $.50 per page. Certification fee: $5.00 plus $1.00 per page after first. Payee: Klickitat County Clerk. No personal checks or credit cards accepted. Prepayment required. Mail requests: SASE required.

East District Court 205 S Columbus, MS-CH11, Goldendale, WA 98620-9290; 509-773-4670; fax: 509-773-4653; 8AM-N, 1-5pm. ***Misdemeanor, Civil Actions under $50,000, Small Claims.***
Civil Records: Access: Phone, mail, fax, in person, online. Both court and visitors may perform in person searches. No search fee. Required to search: name, years to search. Civil cases indexed by defendant, plaintiff; index on computer from 4/93, on index cards prior. Retained for 10 years. Mail turnaround time 1 week. Index from JIS-Link; see www.courts.wa.gov/jislink/. Also, search name index back to 1989 and calendars free at http://dw.courts.wa.gov/index.cfm.
Criminal Records: Access: Phone, mail, fax, in person, online. Both court and visitors may perform in person searches. No search fee. Required to search: name, years to search, DOB. Criminal records computerized from 4/93, on index cards prior. Retained for 10 years. Mail turnaround time 1 week. Online access to criminal indexes is same as civil.
General Information: No dependencies, adoption, and mental illness records released. Will fax documents to local or toll free line. Court makes copy: 1st 10 pages free, each add'l page $.15. Cert fee: $5.00. Payee: East District Court. Personal checks accepted; no credit card. Mail request: SASE required.

West District Court PO Box 435, White Salmon, WA 98672-0435; 509-493-1190; fax: 509-493-4469; 8AM-5PM. ***Misdemeanor, Civil Actions under $50,000, Small Claims.***
Civil Records: Access: Mail, in person, online. Only the court performs in person searches; visitors may not. No search fee. Required to search: name, years to search. Civil cases indexed by defendant, plaintiff; index on computer from 5/93, on docket books. Mail turnaround time 3-5 days. Index from JIS-Link; see www.courts.wa.gov/jislink/. Also, search name index back to 1989 and calendars free at http://dw.courts.wa.gov/index.cfm.
Criminal Records: Access: Mail, in person, online. Only the court performs in person searches; visitors may not. No search fee. Required to search: name, years to search, DOB; also helpful: address. Criminal records computerized from 5/93, on docket books. Mail turnaround time 3-5 days. Online access to criminal indexes is the same as civil.
General Information: No dependencies, adoption, sealed and mental illness records released. Will not fax documents. Court makes copy: $1.00 per page. Certification fee: $5.00 per doc. Cert fee includes copies. Payee: West District Court. Personal checks accepted; credit cards are not. Prepayment required. Mail requests: SASE required.

Bingen Municipal Court.
See West District Court for records.

Goldendale Municipal Court.
See East District Court for records.

White Salmon Municipal Court.
See West District Court for records.

Lewis County

Superior Court 345 W Main St, County Clerk's Office, MS:CLK 01, Chehalis, WA 98532-1900; 360-740-2704; criminal phone: 360-740-1395; civil phone: 360-740-2756; probate phone: 360-740-2776; fax: 360-748-1639; 8AM-5PM. ***Felony, Misdemeanor, Civil, Eviction, Probate, Domestic.***
https://fortress.wa.gov/lewisco/home/LC/SuperiorCourt/Default.aspx?lcID=121
Civil Records: Access: Phone, mail, online, in person. Both court and visitors may perform in person searches. Search fee: $8.00 per hour. Required to search: name, years to search; also helpful: address. Civil cases indexed by defendant, plaintiff; index on computer from 1983, archived from 1900s. Mail turnaround time up to 7 days. Civil PAT goes back to 1983. PAT results show name only. Index from JIS-Link; see www.courts.wa.gov/jislink/. Also, search name index back to 1989 and calendars free at http://dw.courts.wa.gov/index.cfm.
Criminal Records: Access: Phone, mail, online, in person. Both court and visitors may perform in person searches. Search fee: $8.00 per hour. Required to search: name, years to search; also helpful: address, DOB, SSN. Criminal records computerized from 1983, archived from 1900s. Mail turnaround time up to 7 days. Criminal PAT goes back to same as civil. PAT results show name only. Online access to criminal indexes is the same as civil. Online results show name only.
General Information: Online identifiers in results same as on public terminal. No dependencies, adoption, paternity, and mental illness records released. Fee to fax out file $1.00 per page. Court makes copy: $.50 per page. Self serve: $.10 per page. Certification fee: $5.00 1st page, $1.00 ea add'l. Cert fee includes copies. Payee: Lewis County Clerk. Personal checks accepted. Visa/MC accepted through Point & Pay Inc. Prepayment required. Mail requests: SASE required.

District Court PO Box 336, Chehalis, WA 98532; 360-740-1203; fax: 360-740-2779; 8AM-5PM. ***Misdemeanor, Civil under $50,000, Small Claims.***
Civil Records: Access: Fax, mail, online, in person. Both court and visitors may perform in person searches. No search fee. Required to search: name, years to search. Civil cases indexed by defendant, plaintiff; index on computer from 1983. Records retained 10 years. Mail turnaround time 1 week. Index from JIS-Link; see www.courts.wa.gov/jislink/. Also, search name index back to 1989 and calendars free at http://dw.courts.wa.gov/index.cfm.
Criminal Records: Access: Fax, mail, online, in person. Only the court performs in person searches; visitors may not. No search fee. Required to search: name, years to search, DOB, sex, signed release; also helpful: address, SSN. Criminal records on computer since 1981. Records retained for 5 years. Mail turnaround time 1 week. Online access to criminal indexes is the same as civil.
General Information: No dependencies, adoption, and mental illness records released. No fee to fax documents. Court makes copy: $.25 per page. Cert fee: $5.00 per doc. Payee: Lewis County District Court. Personal checks accepted; credit cards are not. Prepayment required. Mail requests: SASE required.

Centralia Municipal Court PO Box 609, 118 W Maple St, Centralia, WA 98531; 360-330-7667; fax: 360-330-7668; 8AM-5PM. ***Misdemeanor.***
Index from JIS-Link; see www.courts.wa.gov/jislink/. Also, search name index back to 1989 and calendars free at http://dw.courts.wa.gov/index.cfm.

Chehalis Municipal Court 350 N. Market Blvd, Chehalis, WA 98532-0871; 360-345-1025; fax: 360-345-1050; 8AM-5PM. ***Misdemeanor.***
www.ci.chehalis.wa.us
Index from JIS-Link; see www.courts.wa.gov/jislink/. Also, search name index back to 1989 and calendars free at http://dw.courts.wa.gov/index.cfm.

Morton Municipal Court.

Mossyrock Municipal Court.
See District Court

Napavine Municipal Court PO Box 810, 407 Birch Ave SW, Napavine, WA 98565-0810; 360-262-9231; fax: 360-262-9885; 8AM-5PM. ***Misdemeanor, Ordinance.***
Index from JIS-Link; see www.courts.wa.gov/jislink/. Also, search name index back to 1989 and calendars free at http://dw.courts.wa.gov/index.cfm.

Pe Ell Municipal Court.

Toledo Municipal Court.
See District Court for records.

Vader Municipal Court PO Box 189, 317 8th St, Vader, WA 98593-0189; 360-295-3222; fax: 360-295-3012; 9AM-12; 1-5PM. ***Misdemeanor.***
Index from JIS-Link; see www.courts.wa.gov/jislink/. Also, search name index back to 1989 and calendars free at http://dw.courts.wa.gov/index.cfm.

Winlock Municipal Court PO Box 777, 323 NE 1st St, Winlock, WA 98596-0777; 360-785-3811; fax: 360-785-4378; 9AM-N, 1-4:30PM. ***Misdemeanor.***
Index from JIS-Link; see www.courts.wa.gov/jislink/. Also, search name index back to 1989 and calendars free at http://dw.courts.wa.gov/index.cfm.

Lincoln County

Superior Court Box 68, Davenport, WA 99122-0068; 509-725-1401; fax: 509-725-1150; 8-5PM. ***Felony, Misdemeanor, Civil, Eviction, Probate.***
Probate is in a separate index. Probate fax is same as main fax number.
Civil Records: Access: Mail, in person, online. Both court and visitors may perform in person searches. No search fee. Required to search: name, years to search; also helpful: address. Civil cases indexed by defendant, plaintiff; index on computer and microfiche from 11/82, archived from 1903. Mail turnaround time 4 days. Civil PAT goes back to 11/1982. Index from JIS-Link; see www.courts.wa.gov/jislink/. Also, search name index back to 1989 and calendars free at http://dw.courts.wa.gov/index.cfm.
Criminal Records: Access: Mail, online, in person, phone. Both court and visitors may perform in person searches. No search fee. Required to search: name, years to search; also helpful: address, DOB, SSN. Criminal records on computer and microfiche from 11/82, archived from 1903. Mail turnaround time 4 days. Criminal PAT goes back to same as civil. Online access to criminal indexes is the same as civil.
General Information: No dependencies, adoption, and mental illness records released. Will not fax documents. Court makes copy: $.50 per page. Certification fee: $5.00 1st page; $1.00 each add'l page. Payee: Lincoln County Clerk. Business checks accepted. Prepayment required. Mail requests: SASE required.

District Court PO Box 329, Davenport, WA 99122-0329; 509-725-2281; fax: 509-725-6481; 8AM-5PM. ***Misdemeanor, Civil Actions under $75,000, Small Claims.***
www.co.lincoln.wa.us This is a small office with limited time allowable for searches.
Civil Records: Access: Mail, fax, online, in person. Both court and visitors may perform in person searches. Search fee: $25.00 per hour. Required to search: name, years to search. Civil cases indexed by defendant. Civil records on computer back to 6/93, in books from 1985. Mail turnaround time 1 week. Civil PAT goes back to 1990. Index from JIS-Link; see www.courts.wa.gov/jislink/. Also, search name index back to 1989 and calendars free at http://dw.courts.wa.gov/index.cfm.
Criminal Records: Access: Mail, fax, online, in person, phone. Both court and visitors may perform in person searches. Search fee: $25.00 per hour. Required to search: name, years to search, DOB. Criminal records computerized from 6/93; hard copy files back to 1990. Mail turnaround time 1 week. Criminal PAT goes back to same as civil. Online access to criminal indexes is the same as civil.
General Information: No dependencies, adoption, and mental illness records released. Will fax documents to local or toll-free number. Court makes copy: $.50 per page. Certification fee: $5.00 per doc. Cert fee includes copies. Payee: Lincoln County District Court. Business checks accepted. Major credit cards accepted. Prepayment required. Mail requests: SASE required.

Almira Municipal Court.
Davenport Municipal Court.
Harrington Municipal Court.
Odessa Municipal Court.
Reardan Municipal Court.
Sprague Municipal Court.
Wilbur Municipal Court.
See District Court for records.

Mason County

Superior Court PO Box 340, 419 N 4th St, Shelton, WA 98584; 360-427-9670 x346; 8:30AM-5PM. ***Felony, Civil Actions Above $25,000, Eviction, Probate.***
www.co.mason.wa.us/clerk/index.php
Civil Records: Access: Mail, in person, online. Only the court performs in person searches; visitors may not. Search fee: $20.00 per hour. Required to search: name, years to search; also helpful: address. Civil cases indexed by defendant, plaintiff; index on computer from 1982; on microfiche and archived from 1890; on index or docket books prior to 1982. Mail turnaround time 1 week. Index from JIS-Link; see www.courts.wa.gov/jislink/. Also, search name index back to 1989 and calendars free at http://dw.courts.wa.gov/index.cfm.
Criminal Records: Access: Mail, online, in person. Only the court performs in person searches; visitors may not. Search fee: $20.00 per hour. Required to search: name, years to search; also helpful: address, DOB. Criminal records computerized from 1982; on microfiche and archived from 1890; on index or docket books prior to 1982. Mail turnaround time 1 week. Online access to criminal indexes is the same as civil.
General Information: No dependencies, adoption, and mental illness records released. Will not fax documents. Court makes copy: $.50 per page. Certification fee: $5.00 per document. Payee: Mason County Clerk. Local attorney checks accepted. No personal checks or credit cards accepted. Prepayment required. Mail requests: SASE required.

District Court PO Box "O", Shelton, WA 98584-0090; 360-427-9670; criminal: X339; civil: X343; fax: 360-427-7776; 8:30AM-5PM. ***Misdemeanor, Civil Actions under $50,000, Small Claims.***
Civil Records: Access: Mail, in person, online. Only the court performs in person searches; visitors may not. Search fee: $20.00 per name. Fee is for extensive searching. Required to search: name, years to search; also helpful: address. Civil cases indexed by defendant, plaintiff; index on computer from 12/92. Mail turnaround time 1 week. Index from JIS-Link; see www.courts.wa.gov/jislink/. Also, search name index back to 1989 and calendars free at http://dw.courts.wa.gov/index.cfm.
Criminal Records: Access: Mail, in person, online. Only the court performs in person searches; visitors may not. Search fee: Will charge $20.00 for extensive search. Required to search: name, years to search, DOB, signed release; also helpful: address, SSN. Criminal records computerized from 12/92, prior on index book. Mail turnaround time 1 week. Online access to criminal indexes is same as civil.
General Information: Court makes copy: $.25 per page. Certification fee: $5.00 1st page plus copy fee for add'l pages. Payee: Mason County District Court. Personal checks accepted. Visa/MC accepted. Prepayment required. Mail requests: SASE required.

Shelton Municipal Court 525 W Cota St, Civic Center, Shelton, WA 98584-2239; 360-426-9772; fax: 360-426-3301; 8-5PM. ***Misdemeanor.***
www.ci.shelton.wa.us/municipal_court/index.php
Index from JIS-Link; see www.courts.wa.gov/jislink/. Also, search name index back to 1989 and calendars free at http://dw.courts.wa.gov/index.cfm.

Skokomish Tribal Court (NICS) 80 N Tribal Center Rd, Shelton, WA 98584-9748; 360-426-4740; fax: 360-877-5943; 8-4PM. ***Misdemeanor, Civil.***
Index from JIS-Link; see www.courts.wa.gov/jislink/. Also, search name index back to 1989 and calendars free at http://dw.courts.wa.gov/index.cfm.

Squaxin Island Tribal Court 10 SE Squaxin Ln, Shelton, WA 98584; 360-432-3828; fax: 360-462-1181; 8AM-4PM. ***Misdemeanor, Civil, Family.***
Index from JIS-Link; see www.courts.wa.gov/jislink/. Also, search name index back to 1989 and calendars free at http://dw.courts.wa.gov/index.cfm.

Okanogan County

Superior Court PO Box 72, 149 N 3rd, Okanogan, WA 98840; 509-422-7275; probate: 509-422-7275; fax: 509-422-7277; 8:30AM-5PM. ***Felony, Misdemeanor, Civil, Eviction, Probate.***
Probate fax is same as main fax number.
Civil Records: Access: Phone, fax, mail, online, in person. Only the court performs in person searches; visitors may not. Search fee: $20.00 per hour. Required to search: name, years to search; also helpful: address. Civil cases indexed by defendant, plaintiff; index on computer from 1994, on hand-written indexes from 1895. Mail turnaround 1-7 days. Index from JIS-Link; www.courts.wa.gov/jislink/. Also, search name index back to 1989 and calendars free http://dw.courts.wa.gov/index.cfm.
Criminal Records: Access: Phone, fax, mail, online, in person. Only the court performs in person searches; visitors may not. Search fee: $20.00 per hour. Required to search: name, years to search. Criminal records computerized from 1984, on hand-written indexes from 1895. Mail turnaround 1-7 days. Online access to criminal indexes is same as civil.
General Information: No dependencies, adoption, and mental illness records released. Will not fax documents. Court makes copy: $.50 per page. Self serve: same. Certification fee: $5.00 plus $1.00 per page after first. Cert fee includes copies. Payee: Okanogan County Clerk. Personal checks accepted; credit cards are not. Prepayment required. Mail requests: SASE required.

District Court PO Box 980, 149 N 3rd Ave, Rm 306, Okanogan, WA 98840-0980; 509-422-7170; fax: 509-422-7174; 8:00AM-5PM, closed for lunch hour on 3rd Fri each month. ***Misdemeanor, Civil Actions under $75,000, Small Claims.***
www.okanogancounty.org/DC/index.htm
Daily court calendar is free at www.okanogancounty.org/DC/calendar2.htm.
Civil Records: Access: Phone, fax, mail, in person, online. Both court and visitors may perform in person searches. No search fee. Required to search: name, years to search. Civil cases indexed by defendant, plaintiff; index on computer for 10 years. Records files maintained 10 years if judgment, otherwise 3 years. Mail turnaround time 7 days. Civil PAT goes back to 3/1996. PAT results show name only. Index from JIS-Link; see www.courts.wa.gov/jislink/. Also, search name index back to 1989 and calendars free at http://dw.courts.wa.gov/index.cfm.
Criminal Records: Access: Phone, fax, mail, in person, online. Both court and visitors may perform in person searches. No search fee. Required to search: name, years to search, DOB. Criminal records on computer for 10 years. Mail turnaround time 7 days. Criminal PAT goes back to same as civil. PAT results show name only. Online access to criminal indexes is the same as civil.
General Information: No alcohol related evaluations, mental illness records released. Will fax documents $1.00 1st page, $.50 each add'l. Court makes copy: $1.00 first page, $.50 each add'l. Self serve: same. Certification fee: $5.00 per cert includes copy fee. Payee: Okanogan County District Court. Personal checks accepted. Visa/MC accepted. Prepayment required. Mail requests: SASE requested.

Brewster Municipal Court PO Box 1074, 105 S 3rd St, Brewster, WA 98812-1074; 509-689-2756; fax: 509-689-3096; 8AM-4PM. ***Misdemeanor, Ordinance, Traffic.***
Index from JIS-Link; see www.courts.wa.gov/jislink/. Also, search name index back to 1989 and calendars free at http://dw.courts.wa.gov/index.cfm.

Colville Confederated Tribal Court PO Box 150, 2 Joe Moses Rd, Nespelem, WA 99155-0150; 509-634-2500; fax: 509-634-2511; 7:30AM-4PM. ***Misdemeanor, Civil, Tribal Law.***
www.colvilletribes.com/courts.htm
Index from JIS-Link; www.courts.wa.gov/jislink/. Also, search name index back to 1989 and calendars free at http://dw.courts.wa.gov/index.cfm. Search tribal warrants at www.colvilletribes.com/pdfs/Outstanding%20Warrant%20List.pdf.

Coulee Dam Municipal Court.
See District Court

Municipal Court PO Box 980, 149 N 3rd Ave, Okanogan, WA 98840; 509-422-7170; fax: 509-422-7174; 8:30AM-5PM. ***Misdemeanor.***
Index from JIS-Link; see www.courts.wa.gov/jislink/. Also, search name index back to 1989 and calendars free at http://dw.courts.wa.gov/index.cfm.

Okanogan Municipal Court.
See District Court for records.

Omak Municipal Court PO Box 72, 2 N Ash, Omak, WA 98841-0072; 509-826-2971; fax: 509-826-6531; 8AM-5PM. ***Misdemeanor, Traffic.***
www.omakcity.com/263.html
Index from JIS-Link; see www.courts.wa.gov/jislink/. Also, search name index back to 1989 and calendars free at http://dw.courts.wa.gov/index.cfm.

Orville Municipal Court.
See District Court for records.

Pateros Municipal Court.
See Brewster Municipal Court for records.

Riverside Municipal Court.
See District Court for records.

Tonasket Municipal Court PO Box 487, 209 S Whitcomb Ave, Tonasket, WA 98855; 509-486-2132; fax: 509-486-1831; 8-4:30PM. ***Misdemeanor.***

Twisp Municipal Court PO Box 278, 118 Glover St, Twisp, WA 98856-0278; 509-997-6112; fax: 509-997-9204; 9AM-5PM M-TH; 9AM-N F. ***Misdemeanor, Ordinance, Traffic.***

Winthrop Municipal Court PO Box 459, 206 Riverside Ave, Winthrop, WA 98862; 509-996-2320; fax: 509-996-9221; 8-4PM. ***Misdemeanor.***
Index from JIS-Link; see www.courts.wa.gov/jislink/. Also, search name index back to 1989 and calendars free at http://dw.courts.wa.gov/index.cfm.

Pacific County

Superior Court PO Box 67, South Bend, WA 98586; 360-875-9320; fax: 360-875-9321; 8:30AM-4:30PM. ***Felony, Civil, Eviction, Probate.***
Civil Records: Access: Phone, mail, online, in person. Only the court performs in person searches; visitors may not. Search fee: $20.00 per hour. Required to search: name, years to search. Civil cases indexed by defendant, plaintiff; index on computer from 2/84, archived from 1887, some on docket books. Mail turnaround time varies. Civil PAT goes back to 1887. Index from JIS-Link; see www.courts.wa.gov/jislink/. Also, search name index back to 1989 and calendars free at http://dw.courts.wa.gov/index.cfm.
Criminal Records: Access: Mail, online, in person. Only the court performs in person searches; visitors may not. Search fee: $20.00 per hour if searching before 1984. Required to search: name, years to search. Criminal records computerized from 2/84, archived from 1887, some on docket books. Mail turnaround time varies. Criminal PAT available. Online access to criminal indexes is the same as civil.
General Information: No dependencies, adoption, and mental illness records released. Will not fax documents. Court makes copy: $.50 per page.Microfilm copy is an additional $1.00 per page copy fee. Certification fee: $5.00 1st page, $1.00 each add'l page. Payee: Pacific County Clerk. Personal checks accepted; credit cards are not. Prepayment required. Mail requests: SASE required.

District Court North Box 134, South Bend, WA 98586; 360-875-9354; 9AM-5PM. ***Misdemeanor, Civil Actions under $50,000, Small Claims.***
Civil Records: Access: Phone, fax, mail, online, in person. Only the court performs in person searches; visitors may not. No search fee. Required to search: name, years to search; also helpful: address. Civil cases indexed by defendant, plaintiff; index on computer back to 3/93, prior on index cards. Depending on disposition date, civil records retained 3 years after disposition. Mail turnaround time 1-6

weeks. Index from JIS-Link; see www.courts.wa.gov/jislink/. Also, search name index back to 1989 and calendars free at http://dw.courts.wa.gov/index.cfm.
Criminal Records: Access: Phone, mail, in person, online. Only the court performs in person searches; visitors may not. No search fee. Required to search: name, DOB; also helpful: years to search, address, SSN. Criminal Records retained forever, on computer back to 3/93. Mail turnaround time 1-6 weeks. Online access to criminal indexes is same as civil.
General Information: No dependencies, MVRs, defendant case histories, adoption, and mental illness records released. Will not fax documents. Court makes copy: $2.00 first page, $1.00 each add'l. Certification fee: $5.00. Payee: North District Court. Personal checks accepted; credit cards are not. Prepayment required. Mail requests: SASE required.

District Court South PO Box 1039, Long Beach, WA 98631; 360-642-9417; fax: 360-642-9416; 7:30AM-4:30PM. ***Misdemeanor, Civil Actions under $50,000, Small Claims.***
www.co.pacific.wa.us/courts/sdc/
Civil Records: Access: Phone, fax, mail, online, in person. Only the court performs in person searches; visitors may not. No search fee. Required to search: name, years to search; also helpful: address. Civil cases indexed by defendant, plaintiff; index on computer for current and open cases. Records retained for 10 years. Mail turnaround time 1 week. Index from JIS-Link; see www.courts.wa.gov/jislink/. Also, search name index back to 1989 and calendars at http://dw.courts.wa.gov/index.cfm.
Criminal Records: Access: Fax, mail, online, in person. Only the court performs in person searches; visitors may not. No search fee. Required to search: name; also helpful: years to search, address, DOB, SSN. Criminal records on computer for current and open cases. Records retained for 10 years. Mail turnaround time 1 week. Online access to criminal indexes is the same as civil.
General Information: No dependencies, adoption, and mental illness records released. No fee to fax documents. Court makes copy: $1.00 first page, $.50 each add'l. Cert fee: $5.00 per doc. Payee: South District Court. Personal checks/credit cards accepted. Prepayment required. Mail requests: SASE required.

Ilwaco / Long Beach Municipal Court PO Box 310, 115 Bolstad Ave W, Long Beach, WA 98631-0310; 360-642-8845; fax: 360-642-8841; 8AM-5PM. ***Misdemeanor, Ordinance.***
Index from JIS-Link; see www.courts.wa.gov/jislink/. Also, search name index back to 1989 and calendars free at http://dw.courts.wa.gov/index.cfm.

Raymond Municipal Court 230 2nd St, Raymond, WA 98577-2406; 360-942-4102; fax: 360-942-4137; 7:30AM-4PM. ***Misdemeanor, Infraction, City Ordinance.***
Index from JIS-Link; see www.courts.wa.gov/jislink/. Also, search name index back to 1989 and calendars free at http://dw.courts.wa.gov/index.cfm.

Shoalwater Bay Tribal Court (NICS) PO Box 130, 2373 Old Tokeland Rd, Tokeland, WA 98590; 360-267-3172 x2101; fax: 360-267-3306; 8:30AM-4:30PM. ***Misdemeanor, Civil., Indian Child Welfare, Traffic.*** www.shoalwaterbay-nsn.gov/
Index from JIS-Link; see www.courts.wa.gov/jislink/. Also, search name index back to 1989 and calendars free at http://dw.courts.wa.gov/index.cfm.

South Bend Municipal Court PO Box 9, 1102 W 1st St, South Bend, WA 98586-0009; 360-875-5571; 8AM-4PM. ***Misdemeanor.***
Index from JIS-Link; see www.courts.wa.gov/jislink/. Also, search name index back to 1989 and calendars free at http://dw.courts.wa.gov/index.cfm.

Pend Oreille County

Superior Court PO Box 5020, 229 S Garden Ave, Newport, WA 99156-5020; 509-447-2435; fax: 509-447-2734; 8AM-4:30PM. ***Felony, Civil, Eviction, Probate.*** www.co.pend-oreille.wa.us
Probate fax is same as main fax number.
Civil Records: Access: Mail, in person, online. Both court and visitors may perform in person searches. Search fee: $20.00 per hour. Required to search: name, years to search; also helpful: address. Civil cases indexed by defendant, plaintiff; index on computer and microfiche from 9/82, archived from 1911, on docket books prior to 9/82. Mail turnaround time same day. Civil PAT goes back to 1982. PAT only shows records up to 3/29/2007. Index from JIS-Link; see www.courts.wa.gov/jislink/. Also, search name index back to 1989 and calendars free at http://dw.courts.wa.gov/index.cfm.
Criminal Records: Access: Phone, mail, in person, online. Both court and visitors may perform in person searches. No search fee. Required to search: name, years to search; also helpful: address, DOB, SSN. Criminal records on computer and microfiche from 9/82, archived from 1911, on docket books prior to 9/82. Mail turnaround time same day. Criminal PAT goes back to 1982. PAT only shows records up to 3/29/2007. Online access to criminal indexes is the same as civil.
General Information: No dependencies, adoption, and mental illness records released. Fee to fax out file $3.00 1st page, $1.00 each add'l. Court makes copy: $.50 per page. Certification fee: $5.00 first page, $1.00 ea add'l. Payee: Pend Oreille County Clerk. Personal checks and major credit cards accepted. Prepayment required. Mail requests: SASE required.

District Court PO Box 5030, 229 S Garden Ave, Newport, WA 99156-5030; 509-447-4110; civil: 800-359-1506; fax: 509-447-5724; 8AM-4:30PM. ***Misdemeanor, Civil under $50,000, Small Claims.***
www.co.pend-oreille.wa.us/
Civil Records: Access: Phone, fax, mail, online, in person. Both court and visitors may perform in person searches. No search fee. Required to search: name, years to search; also helpful: address. Civil cases indexed by defendant, plaintiff; index on DISCIS computer from 10/92. Records retained for 10 years. Mail turnaround time 10 days. PAT civil results show middle initial. DOB not available for civil defendants. Index from JIS-Link; see www.courts.wa.gov/jislink/. Also, search name index back to 1989 and calendars free at http://dw.courts.wa.gov/index.cfm.
Criminal Records: Access: Fax, mail, online, in person. Both court and visitors may perform in person searches. No search fee. Required to search: name, DOB; also helpful: years to search, address. Criminal records on DISCIS computer from 10/92. Records retained for 5 years. Mail turnaround time 10 days. PAT results show middle initial, DOB. Online access to criminal indexes is same as civil.
General Information: No dependencies, adoption, and mental illness records released. No fee to fax documents. Court makes copy: $.25 per page. Self serve: $.25 per page. Certification fee: $5.00 per doc. Payee: Pend Oreille County District Court. Personal checks accepted; credit cards are not. Prepayment required. Mail requests: SASE required.

Cusick Municipal Court.

Ione Municipal Court.
See District Court for records.

Kalispel Tribal Court PO Box 96, 22 Camas Flat Rd, Cusick, Usk, WA 99180-0096; 509-445-1664; fax: 509-445-4039; 7AM-5PM M-TH. ***Misdemeanor, Civil, Family.***
Index from JIS-Link; see www.courts.wa.gov/jislink/. Also, search name index back to 1989 and calendars free at http://dw.courts.wa.gov/index.cfm.

Metaline Falls Municipal Court.

Metaline Municipal Court.

Newport Municipal Court.
See District Court for records.

Pierce County

Superior Court 930 Tacoma Ave S, Rm 110, Tacoma, WA 98402; 253-798-7455; probate phone: 253-798-7461; fax: 253-798-3428; 8:30AM-4:30PM. ***Felony, Civil, Eviction, Probate.***
www.piercecountywa.org\clerk
Civil Records: Access: Fax, mail, online, in person. Both court and visitors may perform in person searches. Search fee: $20.00 per hour. Required to search: name, years to search; also helpful: address. Civil cases indexed by defendant, plaintiff; index on computer from 5/81, archived from 1890. Mail turnaround time 2-5 days. Civil PAT goes back to 1983. Calendars and Courts records are online at www.co.pierce.wa.us/cfapps/linx/search.cfm. Also, Index from JIS-Link; see www.courts.wa.gov/jislink/. Also, search name index back to 1989 and calendars free at http://dw.courts.wa.gov/index.cfm.
Criminal Records: Access: Fax, mail, online, in person. Both court and visitors may perform in person searches. Search fee: $20.00 per hour. Required to search: name, years to search, DOB; also helpful: address. Criminal records computerized from 5/81, archived from 1890. Mail turnaround time 2-5 days. Criminal PAT goes back to same as civil. Online access to criminal indexes is same as civil.
General Information: No sealed, juvenile, adoption, paternity, mental health, sex offenders (victims) or (sometimes) DUI records released. Will fax documents; $5.00 minimum. Court makes copy: $.50 per page. Self serve: same. Certification fee: $5.00 plus $1.00 per page after first. Cert fee includes copies. Payee: Pierce County Clerk. Business checks accepted, no personal. No credit cards accepted. Prepayment required. Mail requests: SASE required.

District Court - Civil Infractions Division 1902 96th St S, Tacoma, WA 98444; 253-798-7474; fax: 253-798-6310; 8:30AM-4:30PM. ***Civil Actions under $50,000, Small Claims, Traffic.***
www.co.pierce.wa.us/abtus/ourorg/distct/abtusd1.htm
District Court #3 in Eatonville, #2 in Gig Harbor, and #4 in Buckley were closed 1/13/03; all civil records were transferred to this court.
Civil Records: Access: Online, in person. Both court and visitors may perform in person searches. No search fee. Required to search: full name, years to search, DOB; also helpful: address, date of arrest/charge. Civil cases indexed by defendant, plaintiff; index on computer back to 1990; Records go back 5 years. Index from JIS-Link; see www.courts.wa.gov/jislink/. Also, search name index back to 1989 and calendars free at http://dw.courts.wa.gov/index.cfm. Pending cases in person searches only.
General Information: No sealed, juvenile, adoption, paternity, mental health, sex offenders (victims) or some DUI records released. Will not fax documents. Court makes copy: $1.00 for 1st page, $.50 each add'l. Certification fee: $5.00 plus $1.00 each add'l page. Payee: Pierce County District Court. Personal checks and credit cards accepted. Prepayment required. Mail requests: SASE required for mail return of any copies.

District Court - Criminal 930 Tacoma Ave S, Rm 601, Tacoma, WA 98402-2175; 253-798-7487, 253-798-7487 auto info line; fax: 253-798-3428; 8:30AM-4:30PM. ***Misdemeanor.***
www.co.pierce.wa.us/pc/abtus/ourorg/distct/abtusd1.htm
District Court #3 in Eatonville was closed 1/13/03, all misdemeanor were transferred to this court.
Criminal Records: Access: Mail, fax, in person, online. Only the court performs in person searches; visitors may not. No search fee. Required to search: name, years to search, DOB; also helpful: address, SSN. Criminal records computerized from 8/1990. Mail turnaround time 3-4 weeks. PAT results show name only. Criminal Index from JIS-Link; see www.courts.wa.gov/jislink/. Also, search name index back to 1989 and calendars free at http://dw.courts.wa.gov/index.cfm. Online results show name, DOB.
General Information: No sealed, juvenile, adoption, paternity, mental health, sex offenders (victims) or some DUI records released. Will fax out documents. Court makes copy: $1.00 1st page; $.50 each add'l. Certification fee: $5.00 per document. Payee: Pierce County District Court. No personal checks accepted. Visa/MC accepted. Prepayment required. Mail requests: SASE required.

District Court #2. ***Misdemeanor, Civil Actions under $50,000, Small Claims.***
This court - formerly in Gig Harbor - is closed and records are now houses at the main court in Tacoma.

District Court #3. ***Misdemeanor, Civil Actions under $50,000, Small Claims.*** This court was closed on 01/10/03. All records have been transferred to the Pierce County District Court in Tacoma.

Bonney Lake Municipal Court PO Box 7380, 19306 Bonney Lake Blvd, Bonney Lake, WA 98391-0944; 253-862-6606; fax: 253-447-4329; 8:30AM-5PM. ***Misdemeanor.*** www.ci.bonney-lake.wa.us/administrative/municipal_court/
Index from JIS-Link; see www.courts.wa.gov/jislink/. Also, search name index back to 1989 and calendars free at http://dw.courts.wa.gov/index.cfm.

Buckley Municipal Court PO Box 1452, 811 Main St, Buckley, WA 98321; 360-829-2118; fax: 360-829-9363; 8:30AM-4PM M,W,F. ***Misdemeanor.***
Index from JIS-Link; see www.courts.wa.gov/jislink/. Also, search name index back to 1989 and calendars free at http://dw.courts.wa.gov/index.cfm.

District Court #4. ***Misdemeanor, Civil Actions under $50,000, Small Claims.*** This court was closed on 1/10/03. All records have been transferred to the Pierce County District Court in Tacoma.

DuPont Municipal Court.
See Pierce County District Court

Eatonville Municipal Court PO Box 309, 201 Center St W, Eatonville, WA 98328; 360-832-3361; fax: 360-832-3977; 9AM-5PM. ***Misdemeanor.***
Index from JIS-Link; see www.courts.wa.gov/jislink/. Also, search name index back to 1989 and calendars free at http://dw.courts.wa.gov/index.cfm.

Fife Municipal Court 3737 Pacific Hwy E, Fife, WA 98424-1135; 253-922-6635; fax: 253-926-5435; 8:30AM-4:30PM. ***Misdemeanor.*** www.cityoffife.org/
Index from JIS-Link; see www.courts.wa.gov/jislink/. Also, search name index back to 1989 and calendars free at http://dw.courts.wa.gov/index.cfm.

Fircrest Municipal Court 115 Ramsdell St, Fircrest, WA 98466-6912; 253-564-8922; fax: 253-564-3645; 8AM-4PM. ***Misdemeanor.***
Index from JIS-Link; see www.courts.wa.gov/jislink/. Also, search name index back to 1989 and calendars free at http://dw.courts.wa.gov/index.cfm.

Gig Harbor Municipal Ct 3510 Grandview St, Gig Harbor, WA 98335; 253-851-7808; fax: 253-853-5483; 8AM-5PM. ***Misdemeanor, Traffic.*** www.cityofgigharbor.net/html/court.html
Index from JIS-Link; see www.courts.wa.gov/jislink/. Also, search name index back to 1989 and calendars free at http://dw.courts.wa.gov/index.cfm.

Lakewood Municipal Court 6000 Main St SW, Lakewood, WA 98499-5027; 253-512-2258; fax: 253-512-2267; 8:30AM-5PM. ***Misdemeanor.*** www.cityoflakewood.us/index.php?option=com_content&task=view&id=53&Itemid=97
Index from JIS-Link; see www.courts.wa.gov/jislink/. Also, search name index back to 1989 and calendars free at http://dw.courts.wa.gov/index.cfm.

Milton Municipal Court 1000 Laurel St, Milton, WA 98354-8850; 253-922-7625; fax: 253-248-1999; 8AM-5PM. ***Misdemeanor.*** www.cityofmilton.net/page.php?id=93
Index from JIS-Link; see www.courts.wa.gov/jislink/. Also, search name index back to 1989 and calendars free at http://dw.courts.wa.gov/index.cfm.

Orting Municipal Court PO Box 489, 120 Washington Ave N #2, 401 Washington Ave S, Orting, WA 98360-0489; 360-893-3160; fax: 360-893-3129; 8AM-4PM. ***Misdemeanor.***
Index from JIS-Link; see www.courts.wa.gov/jislink/. Also, search name index back to 1989 and calendars free at http://dw.courts.wa.gov/index.cfm.

Puyallup Municipal Ct 929 E Main #120, Puyallup, WA 98372-3116; 253-841-5450; fax: 253-770-3365; 8:30-N, 1-5PM. ***Misdemeanor.*** www.cityofpuyallup.org/page.php?id=335
Index from JIS-Link; see www.courts.wa.gov/jislink/. Also, search name index back to 1989 and calendars free at http://dw.courts.wa.gov/index.cfm.

Puyallup Tribal Court 1638 E 29th St, Tacoma, WA 98404-4903; 253-680-5585; fax: 253-680-5599; 8AM-5PM. ***Misdemeanor, Civil.***
Index from JIS-Link; see www.courts.wa.gov/jislink/. Also, search name index back to 1989 and calendars free at http://dw.courts.wa.gov/index.cfm.

Roy Municipal Ct PO Box 700, 216 McNaught St, Roy, WA 98580-0700; 253-843-0463; fax: 253-843-0279; 8:30-4:30PM. ***Misdemeanor, Ordinance.***
Index from JIS-Link; see www.courts.wa.gov/jislink/. Also, search name index back to 1989 and calendars free at http://dw.courts.wa.gov/index.cfm.

Ruston Municipal Court 5117 N Winifred St, Ruston, WA 98407-6597; 253-759-8545; fax: 253-752-3754; 9AM-4PM. ***Misdemeanor.***
Index from JIS-Link; see www.courts.wa.gov/jislink/. Also, search name index back to 1989 and calendars free at http://dw.courts.wa.gov/index.cfm.

South Prairie Municipal Ct PO Box 409, 540 Church St, South Prairie, WA 98396; 360-829-0171; fax: 360-829-0898; 9AM-4PM TH. ***Misdemeanor.***
Index from JIS-Link; see www.courts.wa.gov/jislink/. Also, search name index back to 1989 and calendars free at http://dw.courts.wa.gov/index.cfm.

Steilacoom Municipal Court 1030 Roe St, Steilacoom, WA 98388; 253-581-1910; fax: 253-582-0651; 8AM-N. ***Misdemeanor, Civil Actions.***
Index from JIS-Link; see www.courts.wa.gov/jislink/. Also, search name index back to 1989 and calendars free at http://dw.courts.wa.gov/index.cfm. Hearing held at 1717 Lafayette.

Sumner Municipal Court 1104 Maple St #100, Sumner, WA 98390-1407; 253-863-7635; fax: 253-299-5629; 8AM-4:30PM. ***Misdemeanor.*** www.ci.sumner.wa.us/Government/Municipal_Court.htm Index from JIS-Link; see www.courts.wa.gov/jislink/. Also, search name index back to 1989 and calendars free at http://dw.courts.wa.gov/index.cfm.

Tacoma Municipal Court 930 Tacoma Ave S Rm 841, Tacoma, WA 98402-2181; 253-591-5357; fax: 253-591-5301; 8:30-4:30PM. ***Misdemeanor.*** www.cityoftacoma.org/Page.aspx?hid=1557
Index from JIS-Link; see www.courts.wa.gov/jislink/. Also, search name index back to 1989 and calendars free at http://dw.courts.wa.gov/index.cfm.

Wilkeson Municipal Court PO Box 409, 540 Church St, Wilkeson, WA 98396-9800; 360-829-0171; fax: 360-829-0898; 8:30AM-4:30PM TH. ***Misdemeanor.***
Index from JIS-Link; see www.courts.wa.gov/jislink/. Also, search name index back to 1989 and calendars free at http://dw.courts.wa.gov/index.cfm.

San Juan County

Superior Court 350 Court St, #7, Friday Harbor, WA 98250; 360-378-2163; fax: 360-378-3967; 8AM-5PM. ***Felony, Civil, Eviction, Probate.*** www.co.san-juan.wa.us

Civil Records: Access: Phone, fax, mail, online, in person. Both court and visitors may perform in person searches. No search fee. Required to search: name, years to search; also helpful: case number. Civil cases indexed by defendant, plaintiff; index on computer back to 1987, on microfilm and archived from 1890s. Mail turnaround time 3 days. Civil PAT goes back to 1987. Index from JIS-Link; see www.courts.wa.gov/jislink/. Also, search name index back to 1987 and calendars free at http://dw.courts.wa.gov/index.cfm.

Criminal Records: Access: Phone, fax, mail, online, in person. Both court and visitors may perform in person searches. No search fee. Required to search: name, years to search, DOB; also helpful: address, SSN, case number. Criminal records computerized from 1987, on microfilm and archived from 1890s. Mail turnaround time 3 days. Criminal PAT goes back to same as civil. Online access to criminal indexes is the same as civil.

General Information: No dependencies, adoption, and mental illness records released. Will fax documents $3.00 1st page, $1.00 each add'l. Court makes copy: $.50 per page. Certification fee: $5.00 plus $1.00 each add'l page. Cert fee includes copies. Payee: San Juan County Clerk. Personal checks and major credit cards accepted. Prepayment required. Mail requests: SASE required.

District Court PO Box 127, 350 Courthouse Sq, Friday Harbor, WA 98250; 360-378-4017; fax: 360-378-4099; 8:30AM-4:30PM. ***Misdemeanor, Civil Actions under $50,000, Small Claims.*** www.co.san-juan.wa.us/distrcourt/default.asp

Civil Records: Access: Mail, in person, online. Only the court performs in person searches; visitors may not. No search fee; but $20.00 if an archive search. Required to search: full legal name, DOB, years to search; also helpful: address. Civil cases indexed by defendant, plaintiff; index on computer from 1990, on index cards prior. Records retained for 10 years. Mail turnaround time 1-3 days. Civil PAT available. Index from JIS-Link; www.courts.wa.gov/jislink/. Also, search name index back to 1989 and calendars at http://dw.courts.wa.gov/index.cfm.

Criminal Records: Access: Mail, in person, fax, online. Only the court performs in person searches; visitors may not. No search fee; but $20.00 if an archive search. Required to search: full legal name, DOB, years to search, signed release; also helpful: address, DOB, SSN. Criminal records computerized from 1990, log book prior. Retained 5 years. Mail turnaround time 1-3 days. Criminal PAT available. Online access to criminal indexes is same as civil.

General Information: No dependencies, adoption, confidential social files and mental illness records released. Will fax documents to local or toll-free number. Court makes copy: $.25 per page. Certification fee: $5.00. Payee: San Juan County District Court. Personal checks accepted. Credit cards accepted at OfficialPayments.com or 1-877-876-7619. Provide them with your case # or ticket #. Prepayment required. Mail requests: SASE required.

Friday Harbor Municipal Court.
See District Court for records.

Skagit County

Superior Court 205 W Kincaid St, #103, Mount Vernon, WA 98273; 360-336-9440; 8:30AM-4:30PM. ***Felony, Civil, Eviction, Probate.*** www.skagitcounty.net/Common/asp/default.asp?d=Clerk&c=General&p=main.htm

Civil Records: Access: Mail, in person, online. Both court and visitors may perform in person searches. Search fee: $20.00 per hour. Required to search: name, years to search. Civil cases indexed by defendant, plaintiff; index on computer from 10/81, on microfilm and archived from 1878. Mail turnaround time 5 days. Civil PAT goes back to 10/1981. Index from JIS-Link; see www.courts.wa.gov/jislink/. Also, search name index back to 1989 and calendars free at http://dw.courts.wa.gov/index.cfm.

Criminal Records: Access: Mail, in person, online. Both court and visitors may perform in person searches. Search fee: $20.00 per hour. Required to search: name, years to search. Criminal records computerized from 10/81, on microfilm and archived from 1878. Mail turnaround time 5 days. Criminal PAT goes back to same as civil. Online access to criminal indexes is the same as civil.

General Information: No dependencies, adoption, and mental illness, juvenile offender prior to 07/01/78 records released. Will not fax documents. Court makes copy: $.25 per page; $.50 per page if not scanned. Self serve: $.25 per page.Self made copies cannot be certified. Certification fee: $5.00 for first cert page, $1.00 each add'l. Payee: Skagit County Clerk. Only cashiers checks and money orders accepted. No credit cards accepted. Prepayment required. Mail requests: SASE required.

District Court PO Box 340, 600 S 3rd St, Mount Vernon, WA 98273-0340; 360-336-9319; fax: 360-336-9318; 8:30AM-4:30PM. ***Misdemeanor, Civil Actions under $50,000, Small Claims.***

Civil Records: Access: Fax, mail, online, in person. Both court and visitors may perform in person searches. No search fee. Required to search: name, years to search; also helpful: address. Civil cases indexed by defendant, plaintiff; index on computer from 1986, archived for 12 years. Open records

retained for 10 years. Note: Mail search requires a special form. Mail turnaround time 3-4 days. Civil PAT goes back to 1987. Index from JIS-Link; see www.courts.wa.gov/jislink/. Also, search name index back to 1989 and calendars free at http://dw.courts.wa.gov/index.cfm.
Criminal Records: Access: Fax, mail, online, in person. Both court and visitors may perform in person searches. No search fee. Required to search: name, years to search, DOB; also helpful: SSN. Criminal records prior to 1995 only retained for 5 years. Mail turnaround time 3-4 days. Criminal PAT goes back to same as civil. Online access to criminal indexes is the same as civil.
General Information: No dependencies, alcohol, adoption, and mental illness records released. Will fax out documents. Court makes copy: $5.00 per doc. Certification fee: $5.00 includes copy fee. Payee: District Court, Skagit County. Personal checks accepted; credit cards are not. Prepayment required. Mail requests: SASE required.

Anacortes Municipal Court 1218 24th St, Anacortes, WA 98221-2565; 360-293-1913; fax: 360-293-4224; 8AM-5PM. ***Misdemeanor.***
Index from JIS-Link; see www.courts.wa.gov/jislink/. Also, search name index back to 1989 and calendars free at http://dw.courts.wa.gov/index.cfm.

Burlington Municipal Court 311 Cedar #A, Burlington, WA 98233-2803; 360-755-0492; fax: 360-755-2391; 8AM-5PM. ***Misdemeanor.***
www.ci.burlington.wa.us/page.asp_Q_navigationid_E_303 Index at JIS-Link; www.courts.wa.gov/jislink/. Also, search name index back to 1989 and calendars free at http://dw.courts.wa.gov/index.cfm.

LaConner Municipal Court.
See Skagit County District Court for records.

Mount Vernon Municipal Court 1805 Continental Pl, Mount Vernon, WA 98273-5625; 360-336-6205; fax: 360-336-6254; 8AM-5PM. ***Misdemeanor. Ordinance, Traffic.*** www.ci.mount-vernon.wa.us/page.asp_Q_navigationid_E_237
Index from JIS-Link; see www.courts.wa.gov/jislink/. Also, search name index back to 1989 and calendars free at http://dw.courts.wa.gov/index.cfm.

Sedro-Woolley Municipal Court 325 Metcalf St, Sedro-Woolley, WA 98284; 360-855-0366; fax: 360-855-1526; N-4:30PM; 8AM-4:30PM Wed. ***Misdemeanor.***
Index from JIS-Link; see www.courts.wa.gov/jislink/. Also, search name index back to 1989 and calendars free at http://dw.courts.wa.gov/index.cfm.

Swinomish Tribal Court PO Box 755, 17337 Reservation Rd, LaConner, WA 98257-0755; 360-466-7217; fax: 360-466-1506; 8:30AM-4PM. ***Misdemeanor, Civil.*** www.swinomish.org
In requests, always give reason for search. This office does not always answer the telephone.
Civil Records: Access: Mail, fax, in person. Only the court performs in person searches; visitors may not. No search fee. Required to search: name; also helpful- at least one: DOB, SSN, years to search. Civil records go back to 1990, on computer back to 1995. Mail turnaround time varies.
Criminal Records: Access: Mail, fax, in person, online. Only the court performs in person searches; visitors may not. No search fee. Required to search: name; also helpful- at least one: DOB, SSN, years to search. Criminal records go back to 1990. Mail turnaround time varies. Index from JIS-Link; see www.courts.wa.gov/jislink/. Also, search name index back to 1989 and calendars free at http://dw.courts.wa.gov/index.cfm. Online results show name only.
General Information: Will fax documents for no fee. Court makes copy: $.05 per page. No certification fee. Personal checks accepted; credit cards are not. Prepayment required.

Upper Skagit Tribal Court 25944 Community Plaza Way, Sedro Woolley, WA 98284; 360-854-7080; fax: 360-854-7085; 8:30AM-4PM. ***Misdemeanor, Civil.***
Index from JIS-Link; see www.courts.wa.gov/jislink/. Also, search name index back to 1989 and calendars free at http://dw.courts.wa.gov/index.cfm.

Skamania County

Superior Court PO Box 790, Attn: County Clerk, 240 Vancouver Ave, Stevenson, WA 98648; 509-427-3770; probate phone: same; fax: 509-427-3777; 8:30AM-5PM. ***Felony, Civil, Eviction, Probate.*** www.courts.wa.gov/court_dir/orgs/289.html
The fee for digital record copies is $.25 per image and $20.00 per CD.
Civil Records: Access: Phone, mail, online, in person. Both court and visitors may perform in person searches. Search fee: $20.00 per hour. Required to search: name, years to search; also helpful: address. Civil cases indexed by defendant, plaintiff; index on computer from 1984, on microfiche and archived from 1900. Mail turnaround time 2 days. Civil PAT goes back to 10/2006. PAT results show name only. Index from JIS-Link; see www.courts.wa.gov/jislink/. Also, search name index back to 1985 and calendars free at http://dw.courts.wa.gov/index.cfm.
Criminal Records: Access: Phone, mail, online, in person. Both court and visitors may perform in person searches. Search fee: $20.00 per hour. Required to search: name, years to search; also helpful: address, DOB. Criminal records computerized from 1984, on microfiche and archived from 1900. Mail turnaround time 2 days. Criminal PAT available. PAT results show name only. Online access to criminal indexes is the same as civil. Online results show middle initial, DOB.
General Information: No dependencies, adoption, and mental illness records released. Will not fax documents. Court makes copy: $.50 per page. Certification fee: $5.00 1st page, $1.00 each add'l. Payee: Skamania County Clerk. Personal checks accepted; credit cards are not. Prepayment required. Mail requests: SASE required.

District Court Box 790, Stevenson, WA 98648; 509-427-3780; fax: 509-427-3777; 8:30AM-5PM. ***Misdemeanor, Civil under $50,000, Small Claims.***
Civil Records: Access: Phone, fax, mail, online, in person. Both court and visitors may perform in person searches. Search fee: $40.00 per hour. Required to search: name, years to search; also helpful: address. Civil cases indexed by defendant, plaintiff; index on computer go back 10 years. Records retained per state requirements. Mail turnaround time 7 days. Civil PAT goes back to 10 years. Index from JIS-Link; see www.courts.wa.gov/jislink/. Also, search name index back to 1989 and calendars free at http://dw.courts.wa.gov/index.cfm.
Criminal Records: Access: Phone, fax, mail, online, in person. Both court and visitors may perform in person searches. Search fee: $40.00 per hour. Required to search: name, years to search; also helpful: address, DOB, signed release. Criminal records on computer go back 10 years. Records retained per state requirements. Mail turnaround time 7 days. Criminal PAT goes back to same as civil. Online access to criminal indexes is same as civil.
General Information: No dependencies, adoption, and mental illness records released. No fee to fax documents. Court makes copy: $3.00 1st page, $1.00 each add'l. Certification fee: $5.00 per doc. Payee: Skamania County District Court. Personal checks and credit cards accepted. Prepayment required. Mail requests: SASE required.

North Bonneville Municipal Ct PO Box 7, City Hall, 214 CBD Mall, Cascade Dr, North Bonneville, WA 98639-0007; 509-427-8182; fax: 509-427-7214; 8AM-5PM. ***Misdemeanor.***
Index from JIS-Link; see www.courts.wa.gov/jislink/. Also, search name index back to 1989 and calendars free at http://dw.courts.wa.gov/index.cfm.

Stevenson Municipal Court PO Box 371, 7121 E Loop Rd, Stevenson, WA 98648-0371; 509-427-5970; fax: 509-427-8202; 8-5. ***Misdemeanor.***
Index from JIS-Link; see www.courts.wa.gov/jislink/. Also, search name index back to 1989 and calendars free at http://dw.courts.wa.gov/index.cfm.

Snohomish County

Superior Court 3000 Rockefeller, MS 605, Everett, WA 98201; 425-388-3466; 8:30AM-5PM. ***Felony, Civil Actions, Eviction, Probate, Divorce.*** http://www1.co.snohomish.wa.us/Departments/Clerk/
Civil Records: Access: Phone, mail, online, in person. Both court and visitors may perform in person searches. Search fee: $20.00 per hour, one hr min. Required to search: name, years to search. Civil cases indexed by defendant, plaintiff; index on computer from 1978, prior on database index. Mail turnaround time 1 week. Civil PAT goes back to 1978. PAT results show name only. Index from JIS-Link; see www.courts.wa.gov/jislink/. Also, search name index back to 1989 and calendars free at http://dw.courts.wa.gov/index.cfm.
Criminal Records: Access: Phone, mail, online, in person. Both court and visitors may perform in person searches. Search fee: $20.00 per hour, one hr min. Required to search: name, years to search. Criminal records computerized from 1978, prior on database index. Mail turnaround time 1 week. Criminal PAT goes back to same as civil. PAT results show name only. Online access to criminal index is same as civil.
General Information: No sealed, juvenile, adoption, paternity, mental health, sex offenders (victims). Court makes copy: $.25 per page. Self serve: same. Certification fee: $5.00 plus $1.00 per page after first. Payee: County Clerk or Snohomish County Clerk's Office. Business checks or debit cards accepted; no personal checks. Credit cards accepted in person only. Prepayment required. Mail requests: SASE required.

Cascade Division District Court 415 E Burke St, Arlington, WA 98223; 360-435-7700; fax: 360-435-0873; 8:30-4:30PM. ***Misdemeanor, Civil Actions under $50,000, Small Claims.***
Civil Records: Access: Mail, in person, online. Both court and visitors may perform in person searches. Search fee: $5.00 per name. Required to search: name, years to search; also helpful: address. Civil cases indexed by defendant, plaintiff; index on computer from 1985. Mail turnaround time 1 week. Index from JIS-Link; www.courts.wa.gov/jislink/. Also, search name index back to 1989 and calendars at http://dw.courts.wa.gov/index.cfm.
Criminal Records: Access: Mail, online, in person. Both court and visitors may perform in person searches. Search fee: $5.00 per name. Required to search: name, years to search, DOB; also helpful: address, SSN. Criminal records computerized from 1987. Mail turnaround time 1 week. Online access to criminal indexes is the same as civil.
General Information: No sealed, mental health, sex offenders (victims) or some DUI records released. Will not fax documents. Court makes copy: $.25 per page. Certification fee: $5.00. Payee: Cascade Division. Personal checks accepted. Visa/MC accepted. Prepayment required.

Everett Division District Court 3000 Rockefeller Ave, MS 508, 3rd Fl, Everett, WA 98201; 425-388-3331; civil phone: 425-388-3595; fax: 425-388-3565; 8:30AM-5PM. ***Misdemeanor, Civil Actions under $50,000, Small Claims.***
Civil Records: Access: Fax, mail, online, in person. Both court and visitors may perform in person searches. No search fee. Required to search: complete name, years to search; also helpful: address. Civil cases indexed by defendant, plaintiff; index on computer back to 1986. Mail turnaround time 2-3 days. Civil PAT goes back to 10 years. Index from JIS-Link; see www.courts.wa.gov/jislink/. Also, search name index back to 1989 and calendars free at http://dw.courts.wa.gov/index.cfm.
Criminal Records: Access: Fax, mail, online, in person. Both court and visitors may perform in person searches. No search fee. Required to search: complete name, years to search, DOB; also helpful: address, SSN. Criminal records computerized from 1986. Mail turnaround time 1 week. Criminal PAT goes back to same as civil. Online access to criminal indexes is the same as civil.
General Information: Limited DUI records released. No fee to fax documents. Court makes copy: $.25 per page. Certification fee: $5.00. Payee: Everett District

Court. Personal checks accepted. Visa/MC accepted. Prepayment required. Mail requests: SASE required.

Evergreen Division District Ct 14414 179th Ave SE, Monroe, WA 98272; 360-805-6776; fax: 360-805-6755; 8:30-4:30PM. ***Misdemeanor, Civil Actions under $75,000, Small Claims.***
http://www1.co.snohomish.wa.us/Departments/District_Court/
Civil Records: Access: Mail, in person, online. Both court and visitors may perform in person searches. No search fee. Required to search: name, years to search; also helpful: address. Civil cases indexed by defendant, plaintiff; index on computer back 10 years; file retained until closure. Mail turnaround time 1 week. Public use terminal available. Index from JIS-Link; see www.courts.wa.gov/jislink/. Also, search name index back to 1989 and calendars free at http://dw.courts.wa.gov/index.cfm.
Criminal Records: Access: Mail, in person, online. Both court and visitors may perform in person searches. No search fee. Required to search: name, years to search; also helpful: address, DOB. Criminal records on computer archived 3 years after closure by state. Mail turnaround time 1 week. Public use terminal available. Online access to criminal indexes is the same as civil.
General Information: No sealed, juvenile, adoption, paternity, mental health, sex offenders (victims) or some DUI records released. Will fax documents for no fee. Court makes copy: $.25 per page. Certification fee: $5.00 per page. Payee: Snohomish County District Court. Personal checks/credit cards accepted. Prepayment required. Mail requests: SASE requested.

South Division District Court 20520 68th Ave W, Lynnwood, WA 98036; 425-774-8803; fax: 425-744-6820; 8:30-4:30PM. ***Misdemeanor, Civil Actions under $50,000, Small Claims.***
www.snoco.org
Civil Records: Access: Mail, in person, online. Only the court performs in person searches; visitors may not. No search fee. Required to search: name, years to search. Civil cases indexed by case number. Civil records on computer since 1987. Mail turnaround time 2-4 days. Index from JIS-Link; see www.courts.wa.gov/jislink/. Also, search name index back to 1989 and calendars free at http://dw.courts.wa.gov/index.cfm.
Criminal Records: Access: Mail, online, in person. Only the court performs in person searches; visitors may not. No search fee. Required to search: name, years to search. Criminal records on computer since 1989. Mail turnaround time 2-4 days. Online access to criminal indexes is the same as civil. Online results show name, DOB.
General Information: No sealed, juvenile, adoption, paternity, mental health, sex offenders (victims) or some DUI records released. Will not fax documents. Court makes copy: $.25 per page. Self serve: same. Certification fee: $5.00 per document. Payee: South District Court. Personal checks accepted. Prepayment required. Mail requests: SASE requested.

Arlington Municipal Court.
See Cascade Division District Court for records.

Brier Municipal Court.
See South Division District Court for records.

Darrington Municipal Court.
See Cascade Division District Court for records.

Edmonds Municipal Court 250 5th Ave N, Edmonds, WA 98020; 425-771-0210; fax: 425-771-0269; 8:30AM-4:30PM. ***Misdemeanor.***
www.ci.edmonds.wa.us/muni_court.stm
Index from JIS-Link; see www.courts.wa.gov/jislink/. Also, search name index back to 1989 and calendars free at http://dw.courts.wa.gov/index.cfm.

Everett Municipal Court 3028 Wetmore Ave, Everett, WA 98201-4018; 425-257-8778; fax: 425-257-8678; 8AM-5PM. ***Misdemeanor.***
Index from JIS-Link; see www.courts.wa.gov/jislink/. Also, search name index back to 1989 and calendars free at http://dw.courts.wa.gov/index.cfm.

Gold Bar Municipal Court.
See Evergreen Division District Court for records.

Granite Falls Municipal Court.
See Cascade Division District Court for records.

Index Municipal Court.
See Evergreen Division District Court for records.

Lake Stevens Municipal Court.
See Marysville Municipal Court for records.

Lynnwood Municipal Court PO Box 5008, 19321 44th Ave W, Lynnwood, WA 98046-5008; 425-670-5100; fax: 425-774-7039; 8:30AM-4:30PM. ***Misdemeanor.***
www.ci.lynnwood.wa.us/Content/CityHall.aspx?id=153
Index from JIS-Link; see www.courts.wa.gov/jislink/ (also, see state introduction for subscription service). Also, search name index back to 1990 and calendars free at http://dw.courts.wa.gov/index.cfm.

Marysville Municipal Court 1049 State Ave #205, Marysville, WA 98270-4234; 360-363-8050; fax: 360-657-2960; 8AM-4:30PM. ***Misdemeanor.***
Index from JIS-Link; see www.courts.wa.gov/jislink/. Also, search name index back to 1989 and calendars free at http://dw.courts.wa.gov/index.cfm.

Mill Creek Municipal Court.
See South Division District Court for records.

Monroe Municipal Court.
See Evergreen Division District Court for records.

Mountlake Terrace Municipal Court.
See South Division District Court for records.

Mukilteo Municipal Court.
See Everett Division District Court for records.

Northwest Intertribal Court System (NICS) 20818 44th Ave W #120, Lynnwood, WA 98036; 425-774-5808; fax: 425-778-7704; 8AM-4:30PM. ***Misdemeanor, Civil.*** www.nics.ws/
Index from JIS-Link; see www.courts.wa.gov/jislink/. Also, search name index back to 1989 and calendars free at http://dw.courts.wa.gov/index.cfm.

Sauk-Suiattle Tribal Court (NICS) 5318 Chief Brown Ln, Darrington, WA 98241-9420; 360-436-1400; fax: 360-436-0242; 8:30AM-4:30PM. ***Misdemeanor, Civil.*** www.sauk-suiattle.com
Index from JIS-Link; see www.courts.wa.gov/jislink/. Also, search name index back to 1989 and calendars free at http://dw.courts.wa.gov/index.cfm.

Snohomish Municipal Court.
See Evergreen Division District Court for records.

Stanwood Municipal Court.
See Cascade Division District Court for records.

Stillaguamish Tribal Court PO Box 3067, Arlington, WA 98223; 360-474-9111 x10; fax: 360-654-0645. ***Misdemeanor, Civil.***
Index from JIS-Link; see www.courts.wa.gov/jislink/. Also, search name index back to 1989 and calendars free at http://dw.courts.wa.gov/index.cfm.

Sultan Municipal Court.
See Evergreen Division District Court for records.

Tulalip Tribal Ct. 6103 31st Ave NE, Tulalip, WA 98271; 360-651-4049; fax: 360-651-4121; 8-4:30. ***Misdemeanor, Civil, Small Claims, Eviction.***
Index from JIS-Link; see www.courts.wa.gov/jislink/. Also, search name index back to 1989 and calendars free at http://dw.courts.wa.gov/index.cfm.

Woodway Municipal Court.
See South Division District Court for records.

Spokane County

Superior Court Spokane County Clerk, 1116 W Broadway, #300, Spokane, WA 99260-0090; 509-477-2211; 8:30AM-5PM. ***Felony, Civil, Eviction, Probate, Domestic, Adoption.***
http://dw.courts.wa.gov/index.cfm
Civil Records: Access: Phone, mail, online, in person. Both court and visitors may perform in person searches. Search fee: $20.00 per hour. Required to search: name, years to search. Civil cases indexed by defendant, plaintiff; index on computer from 1973, archives back to 1800s, docket books prior to computer. Mail turnaround time 1-3 days. Civil PAT goes back to 1973. Index from JIS-Link; see www.courts.wa.gov/jislink/. Also, search name index back to 1989 and calendars free at http://dw.courts.wa.gov/index.cfm.
Criminal Records: Access: Phone, mail, online, in person. Both court and visitors may perform in person searches. Search fee: $20.00 per hour. Required to search: name, years to search; also helpful: DOB. Criminal records computerized from 1973, archives back to 1800s, docket books prior to computer. Mail turnaround time 1-3 days. Criminal PAT goes back to same as civil. Online access to criminal indexes is the same as civil.
General Information: No sealed, juvenile dependency, adoption, paternity, mental health records released. Will not fax documents. Court makes copy: $.50 per page. Certification fee: $5.00 1st page of ea doc, plus $1.00 ea add'l. Payee: Spokane County Clerk. Personal checks accepted; credit cards are not. Prepayment required. Mail requests: SASE required.

District Court 1100 W Mallon, Spokane, WA 99260; 509-477-4770; fax: 509-477-6387; 8:30AM-5PM. ***Misdemeanor, Civil under $50,000, Small Claims.*** Physical address- 721 N Jefferson.
www.spokanecounty.org/districtcourt
Civil Records: Access: Phone, mail, online, in person. Only the court performs in person searches; visitors may not. No search fee. Required to search: name, years to search; also helpful: address. Civil cases indexed by defendant, plaintiff; index on computer go back 10 years. Mail turnaround time 1 week. Index from JIS-Link; see www.courts.wa.gov/jislink/. Also, search name index back to 1989 and calendars free at http://dw.courts.wa.gov/index.cfm.
Criminal Records: Access: Phone, mail, online, in person. Only the court performs in person searches; visitors may not. No search fee. Required to search: name, years to search, signed release; also helpful: address, DOB. Criminal records are computer since 1984, but searches are only done for five years time. Mail turnaround time 1 week. PAT results show middle initial, DOB. Online access to criminal indexes is the same as civil. Online results show middle initial, DOB.
General Information: Will fax documents to local or toll-free number. Court makes copy: $1.00 per page. Certification fee: $5.00 per cert includes copy fee. Payee: Spokane County District Court. Business checks accepted. Personal checks accepted for civil records only. No credit cards accepted. Prepayment required. Mail requests: SASE required.

Airway Heights Municipal Court 13120 W 13th Ave, 2nd Fl, 1208 S Lundstrom, Airway Heights, WA 99001; 509-244-2773; fax: 509-244-1852; 8:30AM-4:30PM. ***Misdemeanor.***
Index from JIS-Link; see www.courts.wa.gov/jislink/. Also, search name index back to 1989 and calendars free at http://dw.courts.wa.gov/index.cfm.

Cheney Municipal Court 611 2nd St, Cheney, WA 99004-1607; 509-498-9231; fax: 509-498-9332; 9AM-4PM. ***Misdemeanor, Civil.***
www.cityofcheney.org/court
Civil Records: Access: Mail, fax, in person, email. Only the court performs in person searches; visitors may not. No search fee. Required to search: name, DOB. Note: Direct email record requests to tcooper@cityofcheney.org.
Criminal Records: Access: Mail, fax, in person, email, online. Only the court performs in person searches; visitors may not. No search fee. Required to search: name, DOB. Mail turnaround time 5 working days. Index from JIS-Link; see www.courts.wa.gov/jislink/. Also, see state introduction for subscription service. Also, search name index back to 1989 and calendars free at http://dw.courts.wa.gov/index.cfm. Also, direct email requests to tcooper@cityofcheney.org. Online results show middle initial, DOB. DR also usually on online search results.
General Information: Will fax documents no fee with proof of ID. Court makes copy: 1st 10 pages free; $.15 per page beyond 10. No certification fee.

Deer Park Municipal Court PO Box F, 316 E Crawford, Deer Park, WA 99006; 509-276-8802; fax: 509-276-5764; 8:30AM-4PM. ***Misdemeanor.***

Medical Lake Municipal Court PO Box 369, 124 S Lefevre St, Medical Lake, WA 99022-0369; 509-565-5000; fax: 509-565-5008; 8AM-5PM. ***Misdemeanor.*** www.medical-lake.org/
Criminal Records: Access: Mail, fax, in person, online. Only the court performs in person searches; visitors may not. Search fee: varies. Required to search: name, DOB, SSN. Criminal record hard copies go back 3 years after disposition; computer records are archived. Mail turnaround time 5 days. PAT results show middle initial, DOB. Index from JIS-Link; see www.courts.wa.gov/jislink/. Also, search name index back to 1989 and calendars free at http://dw.courts.wa.gov/index.cfm.
General Information: Will not fax documents. Court makes copy: $.15 per page. Payee: Medical Lake Municipal Court. Personal checks accepted; credit cards are not. Prepayment required.

Spokane Municipal Court 1100 W Mallon Ave, Public Safety Bldg, Spokane, WA 99260-0150; 509-625-4400; fax: 509-625-4442; 8:30AM-4:30PM. ***Misdemeanor.***
Index from JIS-Link; see www.courts.wa.gov/jislink/. Also, search name index back to 1989 and calendars free at http://dw.courts.wa.gov/index.cfm.

Stevens County

Superior Court 215 S Oak, Rm 206, Colville, WA 99114; 509-684-7575; 8AM-N, 1-4:30PM. ***Felony, Civil, Eviction, Probate.***
Civil Records: Access: Phone, mail, online, in person. Only the court performs in person searches; visitors may not. Search fee: $20.00 per hour. Required to search: name, years to search; also helpful: address. Civil cases indexed by defendant, plaintiff; index on computer from 10-82, microfiche from 1889-1982, archives 1889, index cards prior to 1982. Mail turnaround time same day. PAT results show name only. Index from JIS-Link; see www.courts.wa.gov/jislink/. Also, search name index back to 1989 and calendars free at http://dw.courts.wa.gov/index.cfm.
Criminal Records: Access: Mail, online, in person. Only the court performs in person searches; visitors may not. Search fee: $20.00 per hour. Required to search: name, years to search, DOB; also helpful: address, SSN. Criminal records computerized from 10-82, microfiche from 1889-1982, archives 1889, index cards prior to 1982. Mail turnaround time same day. Online access to criminal indexes is the same as civil. Online results show name only.
General Information: No sealed, juvenile, adoption, paternity, mental health, sex offenders (victims). Will not fax documents. Court makes copy: $.50 per page. Certification fee: $5.00 1st page, $1.00 ea add'l. Payee: Stevens County Clerk. Personal checks accepted; put case number on check. Major credit cards accepted. Prepayment required. Mail requests: SASE required.

District Court 215 S Oak, Rm 213, Colville, WA 99114; 509-684-5249; fax: 509-684-7571; 8AM-N, 1-4:30PM. ***Misdemeanor, Civil Actions under $50,000, Small Claims.***
www.co.stevens.wa.us/distcourt/departments.htm
Civil Records: Access: Mail, in person, online. Only the court performs in person searches; visitors may not. No search fee. Required to search: name, years to search; also helpful: address. Civil cases indexed by defendant. Civil records on computer from 1/93, prior on docket books to 1988. Mail turnaround time 1 week. Index from JIS-Link; see www.courts.wa.gov/jislink/. Also, search name index back to 1989 and calendars free at http://dw.courts.wa.gov/index.cfm.
Criminal Records: Access: Fax, mail, online, in person. Only the court performs in person searches; visitors may not. No search fee. Required to search: name, years to search, DOB; also helpful: address, SSN, signed request. Criminal records computerized from 7/93, prior on docket books to 1988. Mail turnaround time 1 week. Online access to criminal indexes is the same as civil. Online results show middle initial.
General Information: No sealed, juvenile, adoption, paternity, mental health, sex offenders (victims) or some DUI records released. Fee to fax out file $1.00 per page. Court makes copy: $.15 per page. Self serve: same. Certification fee: $5.00 includes copy fee. Payee: Stevens County District Court. Business checks accepted. All major credit cards accepted. Prepayment required.

Chewelah Municipal Court.

Colville Municipal Court.

Kettle Falls Municipal Court.

Northport Municipal Court.
See District Court for records.

Spokane Tribal Court PO Box 225, Agency Sq Rd, Bldg 258, Wellpinit, WA 99040; 509-258-7717; fax: 509-258-9223; 8-4PM. ***Misdemeanor, Civil.***

Springdale Municipal Court.
See District Court for records.

Thurston County

Superior Court Thurston County Clerk, 2000 Lakeridge Dr SW, Bldg 2, Olympia, WA 98502; 360-786-5430; fax: 360-753-4033; 8AM-5PM. ***Felony, Misdemeanor, Civil, Eviction, Probate.***
www.co.thurston.wa.us/clerk/
Civil Records: Access: Phone, mail, in person, email, online. Both court and visitors may perform in person searches. Search fee: $20.00 per hour. Required to search: name, years to search; also helpful: address. Civil cases indexed by defendant, plaintiff; index on computer from 1978, archives back to 1850s. Mail turnaround time within 48 hours. Civil PAT goes back to 1847. Index from JIS-Link; see www.courts.wa.gov/jislink/. Also, search name index back to 1989 and calendars free at http://dw.courts.wa.gov/index.cfm. Direct email searches to county_clerk@co.thurston.wa.us.
Criminal Records: Access: Phone, mail, in person, email, online. Both court and visitors may perform in person searches. Search fee: $20.00 per hour. Required to search: name, years to search, DOB, signed release; also helpful: address, SSN. Criminal records computerized from 1978, archives back to 1850s. Mail turnaround time 1-7 days. Criminal PAT goes back to 1950. PAT criminal results show middle initial. Online access to criminal indexes is the same as civil. Direct email search requests to county_clerk@co.thurston.wa.us.
General Information: No sealed, juvenile, adoption, paternity, mental health, sex offenders (victims). Will fax documents $3.00 1st page, $1.00 ea add'l. Court makes copy: $.50 per page. Self serve: same. Certification fee: $5.00 first page, $1.00 each add'l, includes copies. Payee: Thurston County Clerk. Checks accepted. Visa/MC accepted. Prepayment required. Mail requests: SASE required.

District Court 2000 Lakeridge Dr SW, Bldg 3, Olympia, WA 98502; 360-786-5450; fax: 360-754-3359; 8:30AM-4PM. ***Misdemeanor, Civil Actions under $75,000, Small Claims, Traffic.***
www.co.thurston.wa.us/distcrt/
Daily court calendars are available at www.co.thurston.wa.us/distcrt/courtcalendars.htm.
Civil Records: Access: Online, in person. Visitors must perform in person searches themselves. Required to search: name, years to search; also helpful: address. Civil cases indexed by defendant, plaintiff; index on computer from 1983. Civil PAT goes back to 1990. PAT results show middle initial, DOB. Index from JIS-Link; see www.courts.wa.gov/jislink/. Also, search name index back to 1989 and calendars free at http://dw.courts.wa.gov/index.cfm.
Criminal Records: Access: Online, in person. Visitors must perform in person searches themselves. Required to search: name, years to search; also helpful: address, DOB, SSN. Criminal records computerized from 1988. Criminal PAT goes back to same as civil. PAT results show middle initial, DOB. Online access to criminal indexes is same as civil. Online results- name only.
General Information: No sealed, juvenile, adoption, paternity, mental health, sex offenders (victims) or some DUI records released. Will fax documents. Court makes copy: $1.00 per page; $.50 each add'l. Certification fee: $5.00 per doc includes copy fee. Payee: Thurston District Court. Personal checks accepted; credit cards are not. Prepayment required.

Bucoda Municipal Court.
See Tenino Municipal Court for records.

Lacey Municipal Court.
See Thurston County District Court for records.

Nisqually Tribal Court 4820 SheNah-Num Dr SE, Olympia, WA 98513; 360-456-5221; fax: 360-456-5280; 8AM-5PM. ***Misdemeanor, Civil.***
Index from JIS-Link; see www.courts.wa.gov/jislink/. Also, search name index back to 1989 and calendars free at http://dw.courts.wa.gov/index.cfm.

Olympia Municipal Court PO Box 1967, 909 8th Ave SE, Olympia, WA 98507; 360-753-8312; fax: 360-753-8775; 7:30AM-4PM. ***Misdemeanor.***
www.ci.olympia.wa.us/citygovernment/court/
Index from JIS-Link; see www.courts.wa.gov/jislink/. Also, search name index back to 1989 and calendars free at http://dw.courts.wa.gov/index.cfm.

Rainier Municipal Court.
See Tenino Municipal Court for records.

Tenino Municipal Court PO Box 4019, 149 Hodgden St S, Tenino, WA 98589; 360-264-4157; fax: 360-264-5772; 8AM-4PM. ***Misdemeanor.***
Index from JIS-Link; see www.courts.wa.gov/jislink/. Also, search name index back to 1989 and calendars free at http://dw.courts.wa.gov/index.cfm.

Tumwater Municipal Court 555 Israel Rd SW, Tumwater, WA 98501-6515; 360-754-4190; fax: 360-754-4138; 8AM-5PM. ***Misdemeanor.***
Index from JIS-Link; see www.courts.wa.gov/jislink/. Also, search name index back to 1989 and calendars free at http://dw.courts.wa.gov/index.cfm.

Yelm Municipal Court PO Box 479, 206 McKenzie Ave SE, Yelm, WA 98597-0479; 360-458-3242; fax: 360-458-3566; 8AM-5PM. ***Misdemeanor, Civil Infractions, Ordinance.***
www.ci.yelm.wa.us/default.asp?dept=court
Index from JIS-Link; see www.courts.wa.gov/jislink/. Also, search name index back to 1989 and calendars free at http://dw.courts.wa.gov/index.cfm.

Wahkiakum County

Superior Court PO Box 116, Cathlamet, WA 98612; 360-795-3558; fax: 360-795-8813; 8-4PM. ***Felony, Misdemeanor, Civil, Eviction, Probate.***
Civil Records: Access: Fax, mail, online, in person. Both court and visitors may perform in person searches. Search fee: $20.00 per hour. Required to search: name, years to search. Civil cases indexed by defendant, plaintiff; index on computer 1850s. Mail turnaround time 1 day. Index from JIS-Link; see www.courts.wa.gov/jislink/. Also, search name index back to 1989 and calendars free at http://dw.courts.wa.gov/index.cfm.
Criminal Records: Access: Fax, mail, online, in person. Both court and visitors may perform in person searches. Search fee: $20.00 per hour. Required to search: name, years to search; also helpful: address, DOB. Criminal records computerized from 1850s. Mail turnaround time 1 day. Online access to crim indexes is same as civil.
General Information: No sealed, juvenile, adoption, paternity, mental health, sex offender victims. Fee to fax document $.50 per page. Court makes copy: $.50 per page. Certification fee: $5.00 for 1st page, $1.00 ea add'l. Cert fee includes copies. Payee: County Clerk. Personal checks accepted; credit cards are not. Prepayment required. Mail requests: SASE required.

District Court PO Box 144, Cathlamet, WA 98612; 360-795-3461; fax: 360-795-6506; 8-4PM. ***Misdemeanor, Civil under $50,000, Small Claims.***
Civil Records: Access: Phone, fax, mail, online, in person. Both court and visitors may perform in person searches. No search fee. Required to search: name, years to search; also helpful: address. Civil cases indexed by defendant, plaintiff; index on computer from 1997, index cards back to 1980, archived prior. Mail turnaround time 2 days. Index from JIS-Link; see www.courts.wa.gov/jislink/. Also, search name index back to 1989 and calendars at http://dw.courts.wa.gov/index.cfm.

Criminal Records: Access: Phone, fax, mail, online, in person. Both court and visitors may perform in person searches. No search fee. Required to search: name, years to search; also helpful: DOB. Criminal records computerized from 1997, index cards back to 1990, archived prior. Mail turnaround time 2 days. Online access to criminal indexes is same as civil.
General Information: No sealed, juvenile, adoption, paternity, mental health, sex offenders (victims) or some DUI records released. No fee to fax documents. Court makes copy: $.25 per page. Certification fee: $5.00. Payee: Wahkiakum District Court. Personal checks accepted; credit cards are not. Prepayment required. Mail requests: SASE required.

Cathlamet Municipal Court PO Box 68, 100 Main St, Cathlamet, WA 98612; 360-795-3203; fax: 360-795-8500; 9AM-4:30PM. ***Misdemeanor.***
Index from JIS-Link; see www.courts.wa.gov/jislink/. Also, search name index back to 1989 and calendars free at http://dw.courts.wa.gov/index.cfm.

Walla Walla County

Superior Court PO Box 836, Walla Walla, WA 99362; 509-524-2780; fax: 509-524-2779; 9AM-4PM. ***Felony, Civil, Eviction, Probate.***
Civil Records: Access: Phone, mail, in person. Only the court performs in person searches; visitors may not. Search fee: $20.00 per hour. Required to search: name, years to search; also helpful: DOB. Civil cases indexed by defendant, plaintiff; index on computer from 7/81, prior in docket books. Mail turnaround time 1 day.
Criminal Records: Access: Phone, mail, in person. Only the court performs in person searches; visitors may not. Search fee: $20.00 per hour. Required to search: name, years to search, DOB; also helpful: address, SSN. Criminal records computerized from 7/81, prior in docket books. Mail turnaround time 1 day.
General Information: No sealed, juvenile, adoption, paternity, mental health, sex offenders (victims). Will not fax documents. Court makes copy: $.50 per page. Certification fee: $5.00 1st page, $1.00 ea add'l. Cert fee includes copies. Payee: Walla Walla County Clerk. No personal checks; only cashiers checks and money orders accepted. No credit cards accepted. Prepayment required. Mail requests: SASE required.

District Court 317 W Rose St, Walla Walla, WA 99362; 509-524-2760; fax: 509-524-2775; 9AM-4PM. ***Misdemeanor, Civil Actions under $50,000, Small Claims.***
Civil Records: Access: Mail, in person, online. Only the court performs in person searches; visitors may not. Search fee: $20.00 per name. Required to search: full name, DOB years to search. Civil cases indexed by defendant, plaintiff; index on computer from 7/87, on index books. Records retained for 10 years. Mail turnaround time 1-3 days. Index from JIS-Link; see www.courts.wa.gov/jislink/. Also, search name index back to 1989 and calendars free at http://dw.courts.wa.gov/index.cfm.
Criminal Records: Access: Mail, online, in person. Only the court performs in person searches; visitors may not. Search fee: $20.00 per name. Required to search: full name, DOB years to search, signed release; also helpful: address, SSN. Criminal records computerized from 7/87, on index books. Records retained for 10 years. Mail turnaround time 1-3 days. Online access to criminal indexes is the same as civil.
General Information: No sealed, juvenile, adoption, paternity, mental health, sex offenders (victims) or some DUI records released. Will fax documents for no add'l fee. Court makes copy: $1.00 first page, $.50 each add'l. Self serve: same. Certification fee: $5.00 per document; add copy fee for add'l pages. Payee: Walla Walla District Court. Personal checks accepted; credit cards are not. Prepayment required. Mail requests: SASE required.

Burbank Municipal Court.
See District Court for records.

College Place Municipal Court 625 S College Ave, College Place, WA 99324; 509-529-1200; fax: 509-525-5352; 8-5PM. ***Misdemeanor.***
Index from JIS-Link; see www.courts.wa.gov/jislink/. Also, search name index back to 1989 and calendars free at http://dw.courts.wa.gov/index.cfm.

Prescott Municipal Court PO Box 27, 108 D St, Prescott, WA 99348-0027; 509-849-2262; 9AM-4PM. ***Misdemeanor.***
Index from JIS-Link; see www.courts.wa.gov/jislink/. Also, search name index back to 1989 and calendars free at http://dw.courts.wa.gov/index.cfm.

Waitsburg Municipal Court.

Walla Walla Municipal Court.
See District Court for records.

Whatcom County

Superior Court 311 Grand Ave #301, Bellingham, WA 98225; 360-676-6777; criminal phone: x50014; civil: x50018; fax: 360-676-6693; 8:30AM-4:30PM. ***Felony, Civil, Eviction, Probate.*** www.whatcomcounty.us/superior/
Civil Records: Access: Phone, fax, mail, online, in person. Both court and visitors may perform in person searches. Search fee: No search fee if record is on computer. Required to search: name, years to search; also helpful: address. Civil cases indexed by defendant, plaintiff; index on computer from 1980, archives back to 1800s, microfilm. Mail turnaround time up to 1 week. Civil PAT goes back to 1/2005. PAT results show name, DOB. Index from JIS-Link; see www.courts.wa.gov/jislink/. Also, search name index back to 1989 and calendars free at http://dw.courts.wa.gov/index.cfm.
Criminal Records: Access: Phone, fax, mail, online, in person. Both court and visitors may perform in person searches. Search fee: $20.00 per hour. Required to search: name, years to search; also helpful: address, DOB, SSN. Criminal records computerized from 1980, archives back to 1800s, microfilm. Mail turnaround time up to 1 week. Criminal PAT goes back to same as civil.PAT results show name, DOB. Online access to criminal indexes is the same as civil. Online results show name, DOB.
General Information: No sealed, juvenile, adoption, paternity, mental health, sex offenders (victims). Court makes copy: $.50 per page, microfilm $.50 per page. Self serve: $.15 per page. Certification fee: $5.00 1st page, $1.00 ea add'l. Cert fee includes copies. Payee: Whatcom County Clerk. Only cashiers checks and money orders accepted. No credit cards accepted. Prepayment required. Mail requests: SASE required.

District Court 311 Grand Ave, #401, Bellingham, WA 98225; 360-676-6770; fax: 360-676-7685; 8AM-4:30PM. ***Misdemeanor, Civil Actions under $50,000, Small Claims.*** www.whatcomcounty.us/
Civil Records: Access: Fax, mail, online, in person. Only the court performs in person searches; visitors may not. No search fee. Required to search: name, years to search; also helpful: address. Civil cases indexed by defendant, plaintiff; index on computer since 1984. Mail turnaround time 2 days. Index from JIS-Link; www.courts.wa.gov/jislink/. Also, search name index back to 1989 and calendars at http://dw.courts.wa.gov/index.cfm.
Criminal Records: Access: Fax, mail, online, in person. Only the court performs in person searches; visitors may not. No search fee. Required to search: name, years to search; also helpful: address, DOB. Criminal records on computer 10 years back, archived since 1984. Mail turnaround time 2 days. Online access to criminal indexes is the same as civil. Online results show middle initial.
General Information: No sealed, juvenile, adoption, paternity, mental health, sex offenders (victims) or some DUI records released. Court makes copy: $.15 per page. Cert fee: $5.00 per cert includes copy fee. Payee: Whatcom District Court. Personal checks accepted; credit cards are not. Prepayment required.

Bellingham Municipal Court 2014 C St, Bellingham, WA 98225-4019; 360-676-6978; 8:30AM-4:30PM. ***Misdemeanor.*** www.cob.org/court/index.htm
Index from JIS-Link; see www.courts.wa.gov/jislink/. Also, search name index back to 1989 and calendars free at http://dw.courts.wa.gov/index.cfm.

Blaine Municipal Court 344 H St, Blaine, WA 98230-4109; 360-332-8311; fax: 360-332-8330; 8AM-5PM. ***Misdemeanor.***
Index from JIS-Link; see www.courts.wa.gov/jislink/. Also, search name index back to 1989 and calendars free at http://dw.courts.wa.gov/index.cfm.

Drug Court 311 Grand Ave, Bellingham, WA 98225-4038; 360-676-6754; 8-5PM. ***Misdemeanor.***
Index from JIS-Link; see www.courts.wa.gov/jislink/. Also, search name index back to 1989 and calendars free at http://dw.courts.wa.gov/index.cfm.

Everson-Nooksack Municipal Court PO Box 315, 111 W Main St, Everson, WA 98247-0315; 360-966-3411; fax: 360-966-3466; 9AM-5PM. ***Misdemeanor.***
Index from JIS-Link; see www.courts.wa.gov/jislink/. Also, search name index back to 1989 and calendars free at http://dw.courts.wa.gov/index.cfm.

Ferndale Municipal Court PO Box 291, 5694 2nd Ave, Ferndale, WA 98248-0291; 360-384-2827; fax: 360-384-1163. ***Misdemeanor.***
www.ci.ferndale.wa.us
Index from JIS-Link; see www.courts.wa.gov/jislink/. Also, search name index back to 1989 and calendars free at http://dw.courts.wa.gov/index.cfm.

Lummi Tribal Court 2616 Kwina Rd, Bellingham, WA 98226; 360-384-2305; fax: 360-312-1734; 8AM-4:30PM. ***Misdemeanor, Civil.*** www.lummi-nsn.org/
Preliminary felony cases also heard here. Index from JIS-Link; see www.courts.wa.gov/jislink/. Also, search name index back to 1989 and calendars free at http://dw.courts.wa.gov/index.cfm.

Lynden Municipal Ct. 323 Front St, Lynden, WA 98264; 360-354-4270; fax: 360-318-0301; 8AM-5PM. ***Misdemeanor.*** www.lyndenwa.org
Index from JIS-Link; see www.courts.wa.gov/jislink/. Also, search name index back to 1989 and calendars free at http://dw.courts.wa.gov/index.cfm.

Nooksack Tribal Court PO Box 157, 5016 Deming Rd, Deming, WA 98244; 360-592-4158; criminal phone: x1009; civil phone: x1010; fax: 360-592-9602; 8:30AM-5PM. ***Misdemeanor, Civil Actions under $3000, Eviction (Tribal Housing).*** www.nooksack-tribe.org/court_clerk.htm
Index from JIS-Link; see www.courts.wa.gov/jislink/. Also, search name index back to 1989 and calendars free at http://dw.courts.wa.gov/index.cfm.

Sumas Municipal Court PO Box 9, 433 Cherry St, Sumas, WA 98295-0009; 360-988-5711; fax: 360-988-8855; 8AM-5PM. ***Misdemeanor.***
Index from JIS-Link; see www.courts.wa.gov/jislink/. Also, search name index back to 1989 and calendars free at http://dw.courts.wa.gov/index.cfm.

Whitman County

Superior Court Whitman County Clerk, PO Box 390, Colfax, WA 99111; 509-397-6240; fax: 509-397-3546; 9AM-5PM. ***Felony, Civil, Eviction, Probate.*** www.whitmancounty.org/
Civil Records: Access: Phone, fax, mail, online, in person. Only the court performs in person searches; visitors may not. Search fee: $20.00 per hour. Required to search: name, years to search; also helpful: address. Civil cases indexed by defendant, plaintiff; index on computer from 1985, archives back to 1887. Mail turnaround time 1 week. Index from JIS-Link; see www.courts.wa.gov/jislink/. Also, search name index back to 1989 and calendars free at http://dw.courts.wa.gov/index.cfm.
Criminal Records: Access: Phone, fax, mail, online, in person. Only the court performs in person searches; visitors may not. Search fee: $20.00 per hour. Required to search: name, years to search, signed release; also helpful: address, DOB, SSN. Criminal records computerized from 1985, archives back to 1887. Mail turnaround time 1 week. Online access to criminal indexes is the same as civil.

General Information: No sealed, juvenile, adoption, paternity, mental health, sex offenders (victims). Will fax documents $4.00 1st page, $1.00 each add'l. Court makes copy: $.50 per page. Cert fee: $5.00 plus $1.00 per page after first. Payee: Whitman County Clerk. Personal checks accepted; credit cards are not. Prepayment required. Mail requests: SASE required.

District Court 400 N Main St, PO Box 230, Colfax, WA 99111; 509-397-6260; fax: 509-397-5584; 8AM-5PM; Public- 9-4:30PM. ***Misdemeanor, Civil Actions under $50,000, Small Claims.***
www.whitmancounty.org/
Civil Records: Access: Phone, fax, mail, online, in person. Both court and visitors may perform in person searches. Search fee: $8.00. Required to search: name, years to search; also helpful: address. Civil cases indexed by defendant, plaintiff; index on DISCIS computer system from 7/91, prior on index log. Mail turnaround time 2 weeks. Civil PAT goes back to 10 years. Index from JIS-Link; see www.courts.wa.gov/jislink/. Also, search name index back to 1989 and calendars free at http://dw.courts.wa.gov/index.cfm.
Criminal Records: Access: Phone, fax, mail, online, in person. Both court and visitors may perform in person searches. Search fee: $8.00. Required to search: name, years to search, DOB; also helpful: address, SSN. Criminal records on DISCIS computer system from 7/91, prior on index log. Mail turnaround time 2 weeks. Criminal PAT goes back to 7/1991. Online access to criminal indexes is same as civil.
General Information: No sealed, juvenile, adoption, paternity, mental health, sex offenders (victims) or some DUI records released. Fee to fax out file $2.00. Court makes copy: $.15 per page. Self serve: same. Certification fee: $5.00. Payee: Whitman County. Personal checks accepted. Visa/MC accepted. Prepayment required. Mail requests: SASE required.

District Court 325 SE Paradise St, Pullman, WA 99163; 509-332-2065; fax: 509-338-3318; 8AM-5PM. ***Misdemeanor, Civil Actions under $50,000, Small Claims.***
www.courts.wa.gov/court_dir/orgs/297.html
Civil Records: Access: Fax, mail, online, in person. Only the court performs in person searches; visitors may not. Search fee: $8.00 per name. Required to search: name, years to search; also helpful: address. Civil cases indexed by defendant, plaintiff; index on DISCIS computer system from 7/91; records prior to this date destroyed. Mail turnaround time 2 weeks. Index from JIS-Link; see www.courts.wa.gov/jislink/. Also, search name index back to 1989 and calendars free at http://dw.courts.wa.gov/index.cfm.
Criminal Records: Access: Fax, mail, online, in person. Only the court performs in person searches; visitors may not. Search fee: $8.00 per name. Required to search: name, years to search; also helpful: address, DOB, SSN. Criminal records on DISCIS computer system from 7/91; records prior to this date destroyed. Mail turnaround time 2 weeks. Online access to criminal indexes is same as civil.
General Information: No sealed, juvenile, adoption, paternity, mental health, sex offenders (victims) or some DUI records released. No fee to fax documents. Court makes copy: $.15 per page. Certification fee: $5.00. Payee: Whitman District Court. Personal checks accepted. Visa/MC accepted. Prepayment required. Mail requests: SASE required.

Albion Municipal Ct, Albion. ***Misdemeanor.***
See Whitman County. Index from JIS-Link; see www.courts.wa.gov/jislink/. Also, search name index back to 1989 and calendars free at http://dw.courts.wa.gov/index.cfm.

Colfax Municipal Ct. PO Box 229, 400 N Mills St, Colfax, WA 99111-0229; 509-397-3861; fax: 509-397-3044; 8AM-5PM. ***Misdemeanor.***
Index from JIS-Link; see www.courts.wa.gov/jislink/. Also, search name index back to 1989 and calendars free at http://dw.courts.wa.gov/index.cfm.

Colton Municipal Court PO Box 157, 706 Broadway, Colton, WA 99113-0157; 509-229-3887; fax: 509-229-3294; 9AM-N, 1-3PM M-TH, Closed Friday. ***Traffic.***
Traffic court records only at this time. Index from JIS-Link; see www.courts.wa.gov/jislink/. Also, search name index back to 1989 and calendars free at http://dw.courts.wa.gov/index.cfm.

Uniontown Municipal Ct PO Box 87, City Hall, 110 S Montgomery St, Uniontown, WA 99179-0087; 509-229-3805; fax: 509-229-3748; 9AM-5PM. ***Misdemeanor.***
Index from JIS-Link; see www.courts.wa.gov/jislink/. Also, search name index back to 1989 and calendars free at http://dw.courts.wa.gov/index.cfm.

Yakima County

Superior Court Yakima County Clerk, 128 N 2nd St, Rm 323, Yakima, WA 98901; 509-574-1430; probate phone: 509-574-1430; 8:30AM-4:30PM. ***Felony, Civil, Domestic Relations, Probate.***
www.co.yakima.wa.us/clerk Divorce records can also be obtained from this agency.
Civil Records: Access: Phone, mail, in person, online. Only the court performs in person searches; visitors may not. Search fee: $20.00 per hour. Required to search: name, years to search. Civil cases indexed by defendant, plaintiff; index on computer from 1978, archives back to 1890s. Mail turnaround time varies. Civil PAT goes back to 1998. Index from JIS-Link; see www.courts.wa.gov/jislink/. Also, search name index back to 1989 and calendars at http://dw.courts.wa.gov/index.cfm.
Criminal Records: Access: Phone, mail, in person, online. Only the court performs in person searches; visitors may not. Search fee: $20.00 per hour. Required to search: name, years to search. Criminal records computerized from 1978, archives back to 1890s. Mail turnaround time varies. Criminal PAT goes back to 1998. Online access to criminal indexes is the same as civil.
General Information: No sealed, juvenile, adoption, paternity, mental health, sex offenders (victims). Will not fax documents. Court makes copy: $.50 per page. Microfilm copies $.25 per page. Self serve: $.50 per page. Cert fee: $5.00 plus $1.00 per page after first. Payee: Yakima County Clerk. Business checks accepted; no personal checks. Prepayment required. Mail requests: SASE required.

District Court 128 N 2nd St, Rm 217, Yakima, WA 98901-2631; 509-574-1800; fax: 509-574-1831; 8:30AM-4:30PM. ***Misdemeanor, Civil Actions under $50,000, Small Claims.***
www.co.yakima.wa.us/DistrictCourt/Default.htm
Civil Records: Access: Fax, mail, online. Only the court performs in person searches; visitors may not. No search fee. Required to search: name, years to search; also helpful: address. Civil cases indexed by defendant, plaintiff; index on computer from 1984, generally. Note: Search requests to the court must be in writing; you must use their form. Mail turnaround time 2 days. Index from JIS-Link; see www.courts.wa.gov/jislink/. Also, search name index back to 1989 and calendars free at http://dw.courts.wa.gov/index.cfm.
Criminal Records: Access: Fax, mail, online. Only the court performs in person searches; visitors may not. No search fee. Required to search: name, years to search, DOB; also helpful: address, case number, DRL, SSN. Criminal records computerized from 1984, generally. Note: Search requests to the court must be in writing. Must use their form. Mail turnaround time 2 days. Online access to criminal indexes is the same as civil.
General Information: No sealed or some DUI records released. No fee to fax documents. Court makes copy: $.15 per page. Cert fee: $5.00 per doc. Payee: Yakima County District Court. Personal checks accepted. Visa/MC accepted. Prepayment required. Mail requests: SASE requested.

Grandview Municipal Court PO Box 100, 207 W 2nd St, Grandview, WA 98930; 509-882-9202. ***Misdemeanor.*** www.grandview.wa.us
Index from JIS-Link; see www.courts.wa.gov/jislink/. Also, search name index back to 1989 and calendars free at http://dw.courts.wa.gov/index.cfm.

Granger Municipal Court PO Box 1100, 102 Main St, Granger, WA 98932-1100; 509-854-1725; fax: 509-854-2103; 9AM-5PM. ***Misdemeanor.***
Index from JIS-Link; see www.courts.wa.gov/jislink/. Also, search name index back to 1989 and calendars free at http://dw.courts.wa.gov/index.cfm.

Moxee City Municipal Court PO Box 249, 255 W Seattle, Moxee City, WA 98936-0249; 509-575-8851; fax: 509-575-8852; 8-5. ***Misdemeanor.***
Index from JIS-Link; see www.courts.wa.gov/jislink/. Also, search name index back to 1989 and calendars free at http://dw.courts.wa.gov/index.cfm.

Selah Municipal Court 115 W Naches Ave, Selah, WA 98942-1323; 509-698-7329; fax: 509-698-7338; 8AM-5PM. ***Misdemeanor, Infractions.***
www.ci.selah.wa.us/departments.htm
Index from JIS-Link; see www.courts.wa.gov/jislink/. Also, search name index back to 1989 and calendars free at http://dw.courts.wa.gov/index.cfm.

Sunnyside Municipal Court 401 Homer St, Sunnyside, WA 98944-1354; 509-839-4427; fax: 509-836-6272; 7:30AM-6PM M-TH. ***Misdemeanor, Traffic.***
Criminal Records: Access: Mail, fax, in person, email, online. Visitors must perform in person searches themselves. No search fee. Required to search: name, DOB, SSN. Criminal records go back to- varies. Mail turnaround time 1 day. Index from JIS-Link; see www.courts.wa.gov/jislink/ Also, see state introduction for subscription service. Also, search name index back to 1989 and calendars at http://dw.courts.wa.gov/index.cfm. Also, you may direct criminal record requests to dmendoza@ci.sunnyside.wa.us. Online results show middle initial, DOB, SSN.
General Information: Will fax documents for no fee. Court makes copy for no fee. No certification fee. Payee: Sunnyside Municipal Ct. Personal checks accepted; credit cards are not. Prepayment required. Mail requests: SASE required.

Tieton Municipal Court.
See Yakima County District Court for records.

Toppenish Municipal Court 21 W 1st Ave, Toppenish, WA 98948-1524; 509-865-5959; fax: 509-865-3864; 8:30AM-5PM. ***Misdemeanor.***
Index from JIS-Link; see www.courts.wa.gov/jislink/. Also, search name index back to 1989 and calendars free at http://dw.courts.wa.gov/index.cfm.

Union Gap Municipal Court PO Box 3008, 102 W Ahtanum Rd, Union Gap, WA 98903-0008; 509-576-8911; fax: 509-249-9298; 8AM-5PM. ***Misdemeanor.***
Index from JIS-Link; see www.courts.wa.gov/jislink/. Also, search name index back to 1989 and calendars free at http://dw.courts.wa.gov/index.cfm.

Wapato Municipal Court 205 S Simcoe Ave, Wapato, WA 98951-1352; 509-877-6269; fax: 509-877-7363; 8AM-5PM. ***Misdemeanor.***
Index from JIS-Link; see www.courts.wa.gov/jislink/. Also, search name index back to 1989 and calendars free at http://dw.courts.wa.gov/index.cfm.

Yakama Tribal Court PO Box 151, 11 Wishpoosh Rd, Toppenish, WA 98948; 509-865-5121; fax: 509-865-4954; 8-5. ***Misdemeanor, Civil.***
Index from JIS-Link; see www.courts.wa.gov/jislink/. Also, search name index back to 1989 and calendars free at http://dw.courts.wa.gov/index.cfm.

Yakima Municipal Court 200 S 3rd St, Yakima, WA 98901-2830; 509-575-3050; fax: 509-575-3020; 8AM-4PM. ***Misdemeanor, Traffic.***
Index from JIS-Link; see www.courts.wa.gov/jislink/. Also, search name index back to 1989 and calendars free at http://dw.courts.wa.gov/index.cfm.

Zillah Municipal Court PO Box 388, 111 7th St, Zillah, WA 98953-0388; 509-829-3543; fax: 509-829-5605; 8AM-5PM. ***Misdemeanor.***
Index from JIS-Link; see www.courts.wa.gov/jislink/. Also, search name index back to 1989 and calendars free at http://dw.courts.wa.gov/index.cfm.

Washington Recording Offices

ORGANIZATION: 39 counties, 39 recording offices. The recording officer is the County Auditor. County records are usually combined in a Grantor/Grantee index. Washington is entirely in the Pacific Time Zone (PST).

REAL ESTATE RECORDS: Many County Auditors will perform real estate searches, including record owner searches. Search fees are usually $8.00 per hour but there are many counties with variations of this fee. A copy costs $1.00 per page and certification is usually $3.00 1st page, $1.00 each add'l page but not all counties conform to this. If the Auditor does not provide searches, contact the Assessor for record owner information. Contact the Treasurer (or, if it concerns King County, contact the Finance Department) for information about unpaid real estate taxes.

UCC RECORDS: Financing statements are filed at the state level except for real estate related collateral which are filed with the County Auditor. Most recording offices will perform UCC searches. Use search request form UCC-11R. UCC searches are usually the same fee rate as other searches.

TAX LIEN/OTHER RECORDS: All federal tax liens are filed with the Department of Licensing. All state tax liens are filed with the County Auditor. Most counties will perform tax lien searches. Marriage records found here.

ONLINE ACCESS: A number of counties now offer access to assessor or real estate records. Access UCCs on the statewide system at https://fortress.wa.gov/dol/ucc. No search fee for name search or by file number.

Adams County

County Auditor, 210 W Broadway, #200, Ritzville, WA 99169. 509-659-3253; fax-509-659-3254; 8:30AM-4:30PM www.co.adams.wa.us

Index: All in one. Marriage records here, other vital records are not. Records indexed on a public use terminal back to 98. Office personnel or visitors may perform searches. Search fee $8.00 per hour, 1 hour minimum. Office will search real estate records. Office will not search UCC records. Copy fee $1.00 per page. Cert fee- $3.00 per doc includes 1st page copy fee; add copy fee for add'l pages. Payee- County Auditor. **Other phones:** Treasurer- 509-659-3227; Elections- 509-659-3249; Vital Records- 509-659-3315. **Property tax/Assessing-** 210 W Broadway, #105, Ritzville, WA 99169; 509-659-3200, assessor fax- 509-659-3206. (Appraiser- 509-659-3200) **Online access-** Access to county property tax and sales records, and inmate records is free at http://adamswa.taxsifter.com/taxsifter/disclaimer.asp.

Asotin County

County Auditor, PO Box 129, Asotin, WA 99402. 509-243-2084; fax-509-243-2087; 7:30AM-5:30PM. www.co.asotin.wa.us

Index: All in one. Marriage records here, other vital records are not. Records indexed on a public use terminal back to 1995. Office personnel may search by written or fax request. General index search fee $10.00 per search. Office will search real estate records. Will search UCC records. Copy fee $1.00 per page.Real Estate record copy fee- $.15 per page. Cert fee- $3.00 per doc plus copy fee. Payee- Asotin County Auditor. Bulk data available for purchase, contact Auditor's office. **Online access to Real Estate, Deed records:** Recording office land data to be available at a later date at www.etitlesearch.com; registration and fees required. **Other phones:** Treasurer- 509-243-2010; Elections- 509-243-2084; Vitals- 509-243-2084. **Property tax/Assessing-** PO Box 69, Asotin, WA 99402; 509-243-2016, assessor fax- 509-243-2099. (Appraiser- 509-243-2016) hours- 8AM-5PM. Computer terminal available for public.

Benton County

Auditor, PO Box 470, Prosser, WA 99350. 509-786-5616; fax-509-786-5528; 8-5 www.co.benton.wa.us

County also has a second recording office located at 5600 W Canal, #B, Kennewick, WA 99336. Index: All in one back to 1/1/85. Marriage records here, other vital records are not. Records indexed on a public use terminal back to 1985. Before 1985, on rolls of film. Office personnel or visitors may perform searches. RE/UCC search fee for a range of years is $8.00 per hour. Office will search real estate records only when provided doc number and year. Copy fee $1.00 per page. Cert fee- $3.00 per doc plus copy fee. Payee- Benton County Auditor. **Online access to Real Estate, Grantor/Grantee, Deed, Parcel, Tax Roll, Court records:** Access to grantor/grantee index back to 1/2/1995, parcels back to 1/1997, recordings to 2/17/1985 and Superior court docs and tax rolls are available by subscription at www.landlight.com. Fees apply but you may get a Free Tax Roll Summary Report. **Other phones:** Treasurer- 509-786-2255; Elections- 509-786-5618; Vitals- 509-786-5616. **Property tax/Assessing-** 620 Market St, Prosser, WA 99350; 509-786-2046, assessor fax- 509-786-5657. (Appraiser- 509-736-3088) www.co.benton.wa.us/html/assessor.htm **Online-** Access to Benton County assessor data is free at http://bentonpropertymax.governmaxa.com/propertymax/rover30.asp. Search by parcel ID#, address or map; no name searching.

Chelan County

County Auditor, PO Box 400, Wenatchee, WA 98807. 509-667-6828, R/E phone-509-667-6815; fax-509-667-6818; www.co.chelan.wa.us/ad/ad_main.htm

Index: All in one. Marriage records here, other vital records are not. Records indexed on a public use terminal back to 1974. Office personnel or visitors may perform searches. General index search fee $8.00 per hour. Office will do limited search of real estate records. Copy fee $1.00 per page. Cert fee- $2.00 per doc plus copy fee. Payee- Chelan County Auditor. Daily images in bulk available from county ftp site. Sold as subscription. **Online Real Estate, Grantor/Grantee, Property, Marriage, Court records:** Access to the Auditor's iCRIS database is free at www.co.chelan.wa.us/ad/adr_help.htm. Images go back to 1974; marriage images to 1990. Also, subscription access to grantor/grantee index back to 8/26/90, parcels back to 1/1972, recordings to 4/6/1988 and Superior court docs available at www.landlight.com/. Fees apply. **Other phones:** Treasurer- 509-667-6405; Elections- 509-667-6808; Vitals- 360-236-4300. **Property tax/Assessing-** 350 Orondo Ave, 2nd Fl, Wenatchee, WA 98801; 509-667-6365, fax- 509-667-6664. (Appraiser - 509-667-6368) 8AM-5PM. **Online-** Access tax rolls via www.landlight.com. Fees apply. With parcel number, get free Tax Roll Summary Report. Access parcel data free at www.co.chelan.wa.us/bl/bl_mapoptix_disclaimer.htm. Plat images free at www.co.chelan.wa.us/as/as_historicalimages_disclaimer.htm.

Clallam County

Auditor, Recording Dept, 223 E 4th St, #1, Port Angeles, WA 98362. 360-417-2220; fax-360-417-2517; 8:30AM-4:30PM www.clallam.net/

Index: All in one. Marriage records here, other vital records are not. Records indexed on a public use terminal back to 1984. Office will perform a UCC search but public must search other records themselves. Copy fee $1.00 per page. Maps- $5.00 each. Cert fee- $3.00 1st page, $1.00 each add'l page, includes copy fee. Payee- Clallam County Auditor. **Online access to Grantor/Grantee, Real Estate, Liens/Judgment, Marriage records:** Access to recording records free at http://vpn.clallam.net:8080/recorder/web/login.jsp. **Other phones:** Treasurer- 360-417-2250; Elections- 360-417-2217; Vital Records- 360-417-2303. **Property tax/Assessing-** 223 E 4th St, #2, Port Angeles, WA 98362; 360-417-2400, assessor fax- 360-417-2299. www.clallam.net/Departments/html/dept_assessor.htm **Online-** Access to assessor property data is free at www.clallam.net/RealEstate/html/land_parcel_search.htm; search by address or property number only. Auditor property maps are also downloadable at www.clallam.net/RealEstate/html/recorded_maps.htm Add'l property maps at www.clallam.net/Maps/.

Clark County

Auditor, POB 5000, Vancouver, 98666. 360-397-2208; fax-360-397-2137; 8-5 www.co.clark.wa.us/

Index: All in one granter/grantee index, 1978 forward. Marriage records here, other vital records are not. Records indexed on a public use terminal back to 1978. Office personnel or visitors may perform searches. Search fee $8.00 per hour. Office will not search real estate records. Office will search UCC records up to 10 years back. Copy fee $1.00 per page. Cert fee- $2.00 per doc plus copy fee. Payee- Clark County Auditor. Subscription service for daily images only available for purchase, contact Merrili Sprecher. **Online Real Estate, Deed, Lien, Vital Statistic records:** Access County Auditor's database free at http://gis.clark.wa.gov/applications/gishome/auditor/index.cfm. **Other phones:** Treasurer- 360-397-2252; Elections- 360-397-2345; Vital Records- 360-397-2243; Auditor Main Line- 360-397-2241. **Property tax/Assessing-** 1300 Franklin St, 2nd Fl, Vancouver, 98660; 360-397-2391, fax- 360-397-2046. (Appraiser/Auditor- 360-397-2391) www.co.clark.wa.us/auditor/ **Online-** Search maps online for property data at http://gis.clark.wa.gov/imf/imf.jsp?site=mapsonline. No name searching. Search property tax sales data free at www.co.clark.wa.us/treasurer/salesinfo.html. Treasurer property data free at www.co.clark.wa.us/treasurer/property/index.html but no name search.

Columbia County

County Auditor, 341 E Main St, Dayton, WA 99328-1361. 509-382-4541; fax-509-382-4830; 8:30AM-4:30PM www.columbiaco.com

Index: Separate indices to search include prior to 1999 in books. Marriage records here, other vital records are not. Records indexed on a public use terminal back to 1999. Office will perform a UCC search but public must search other records themselves. Search fee $8.00 per hour. Office will not search real estate records. Copy fee $1.00 per page. Cert fee- $3.00 per doc includes copy fee. Payee- Columbia County Auditor. Bulk data available on CD, contact Cinfy Harris- Deputy Auditor. **Other phones:** Treasurer- 509-382-2641; Elections- 509-382-4541; Vital

Records- 509-382-2181. **Property tax/ Assessing-** 341 E Main St, Dayton, WA 99328; 509-382-2131, fax- 509-382-4830. (Appraiser- 509-382-2131);

Cowlitz County

County Auditor, 207 4th Ave N, Kelso, WA 98626. 360-577-3006; fax-360-414-5552; 8:30AM-5PM www.co.cowlitz.wa.us/auditor/

Index: All in one. Marriage records here, other vital records are not. Records indexed on a public use terminal back to 1987. Office personnel or visitors may perform searches. General index search fee $8.00 per hour. Copy fee $1.00 per page. Cert fee- $2.00 per doc plus copy fee. Payee- Cowlitz County Auditor. CDs of bulk information available for purchase. **Online Real Estate, Grantor/Grantee, Deed, Lien, Birth, Death, Marriage, Dissolution, UCC, Judgment records:** Access Auditor and recorded documents free at www.co.cowlitz.wa.us/auditor/PublicSearch/index.asp. **Other phones:** Treasurer- 360-577-3060; Elections- 360-577-3005. **Property tax/Assessing-** 207 4th Ave N, 2nd Fl, Rm 203, Kelso, WA 98626; 360-577-3010, assessor fax- 360-442-7080. www.co.cowlitz.wa.us/assessor/ **Online-** Access Assessor property records free at www.co.cowlitz.wa.us/cowlitzapps/cowlitzassessorparcelsearch/.

Douglas County

County Auditor, PO Box 456, Waterville, WA 98858. 509-745-8527, R/E phone-509-745-8527 x204; fax-509-745-8812; 8:30-4 www.douglascountywa.net

Index: Separate indices to search include computer and books back to 1997, 1986-96 index (no images), 1972-86 computer (with images). Marriage records here, other vital records are not. Records indexed on a public use terminal back to 1986. Office personnel or visitors may perform searches. Search fee $8.00 per hour. Office will search real estate records, not UCCs. Copy fee $1.00 per page; self serve same. Cert fee- $3.00 1st page, $1.00 each add'l page. Payee- Douglas County Auditor. **Other phones:** Treasurer- 509-745-8525; Elections- 509-745-8527 x203; Vital Records- 509-745-8527 x204. **Property tax/Assessing-** 213 S Rainier, Waterville, WA 98858; 509-745-8521. (Appraiser- 509-884-9403) **Online-** Access Parcel Search including taxes, plats and parcels free at http://douglaswa.taxsifter.com/taxsifter/disclaimer.asp

Ferry County

County Auditor, 350 E Delaware, #2, Republic, WA 99166. 509-775-5200; fax-509-775-5208; 8AM-4PM www.ferry-county.com

Index: Separate indices to search include computer from 2000 to present, prior to 2000 by book index. Marriage records here, other vital records are not. Records indexed on computer back to 2000. Office personnel or visitors may perform searches. Search fee $8.00 per hour for anything over 15 minutes. Office will search real estate records. Will search UCC records. Copy fee $1.00 per page. Cert fee- $3.00 1st page, $1.00 add'l page plus copy fee. Payee- Ferry County Auditor. **Other phones:** Treasurer- 509-775-5238; Elections- 509-775-5200; Vital Records- 509-775-5200. **Property tax/Assessing-** 350 E Delaware, #1, Republic, WA 99166; 509-775-5203, fax- 509-775-2492. (Appraiser- 509-775-5248) hours- 10AM-4PM **Online access-** Access property data on the TaxSifter database free at http://ferrywa.taxsifter.com/taxsifter/disclaimer.asp.

Franklin County

County Auditor, PO Box 1451, Pasco, WA 99301. 509-545-3536; fax-509-545-3529; 8:30AM-5PM www.co.franklin.wa.us

Index: Separate indices to search include Official records, plats, surveys, site plans. Marriage records here, other vital records are not. Records indexed on a public use terminal back to 1989. Only the public may search. Copy fee $1.00 per page. Plats/surveys $5.00 each. Cert fee- $2.00 1st page plus copy fee each page. Payee- Franklin County Auditor. Bulk data available for purchase, contact Connie Curiel; available by FTP. **Other phones:** Treasurer- 509-545-3518; Elections- 509-545-3538; Vital Records- 509-586-0207 x229. **Property tax/Assessing-** 1016 N 4th, Pasco, 99301; 509-545-3506. **Online access-** Search for assessor property data and sales data free at http://franklinwa.taxsifter.com/taxsifter/disclaimer.asp Also, search for property sales data.

Garfield County

County Auditor, PO Box 278, Pomeroy, WA 99347-0278. 509-843-1411; fax-509-843-3941; 8:30-5PM

Office will look up records if customer knows recording number. Index: Separate indices to search. Marriage records here, other vital records are not. Records indexed on a public use terminal back to 12/19/2005. Only the public may search. Copy fee $1.00 per page. Cert fee- $5.00 per cert plus copy fee. Payee- Garfield County Auditor. **Other phones:** Treasurer- 509-843-1531; Elections- 509-843-1411; Vitals- 509-843-1411. **Property tax/Assessing-** PO Box 883, 789 Main, Pomeroy, WA 99347; 509-843-3631, fax- 509-843-3941. (Appraiser- 509-843-1411) 8:30AM-N, 1PM-5PM. Public terminal is available.

Grant County

County Auditor, PO Box 37, Ephrata, WA 98823. 509-754-2011 x336; 8AM-5PM www.co.grant.wa.us

Index: Separate indices to search include grantor/grantee, computer, index books, microfilm. Marriage records here, other vital records are not. Records indexed on a public use terminal back to 1990, to 1997 for images. Office will perform a UCC search (must use a UCC 22R search form) but public must search other records themselves. Search fee $8.00 per hour. Office will not search real estate records. Copy fee $1.00 per page. Cert fee- $3.00 1st page, $1.00 each add'l page. Payee- Grant County Auditor. **Other phones:** Treasurer- 509-754-2011 x353; Elections- 509-754-2011 x377. **Property tax/ Assessing-** 35 C St NW, Ephrata, WA 98823; 509-754-2011 x325, fax- 509-754-6575. (Appraiser- 509-754-2011 x333) http://grantcountyweb.us **Online-** assessor data on GIS site free at http://gismapserver.co.grant.wa.us/ - no name search.

Grays Harbor County

County Auditor, 101 W Broadway, #2, Montesano, WA 98563. 360-249-4232 x2, R/E recording phone- 360-249-4232; fax-360-249-3330; 8AM-5PM www.co.grays-harbor.wa.us

Index: All in one. Marriage records here, other vital records are not. Records indexed on a public use terminal back to 1981. Office personnel or visitors may perform searches. Search fee $8.00 per name. Copy fee $1.00 per page; surveys- $5.00. Cert fee- $3.00 for 1st page, $1.00 each add'l, includes copy fee. Payee- Grays Harbor County Auditor. **Online access to Judgment records:** Access docket information for judgments at www.co.grays-harbor.wa.us/info/clerk/docket/index.htm. **Other phones:** Treasurer- 360-249-3751; Elections- 360-249-4232. **Property tax/Assessing-** 100 W Broadway, #21, Montesano, WA 98563; 360-249-4121. **Online** - Access to the county Parcel Database is free at http://bentonpropertymax.governmaxa.com/propertymax/rover30.asp. No name searching.

Island County

Deputy Auditor, PO Box 5000, Coupeville, WA 98239. 360-240-5549; fax-360-240-5553; 8AM-4:30PM www.islandcounty.net/auditor/

Index: All in one. Marriage records here, other vital records are not. Records indexed back to 1984. Office will perform a UCC search but public must search other records themselves. Search fee $8.00 per half hour. Office will search real estate records. Copy fee $1.00 per page. Cert fee- $2.00 per doc plus copy fee. Payee- Island County Auditor. Treasurer- 360-679-7302; Elections- 360-679-7366; Vital Records- 360-678-7351; Marriages -360-240-5540. **Property tax/ Assessing-** 1 NE 7th St, Coupeville, WA 98239; 360-678-5111. (Appraiser- 360-679-7366) www.islandcounty.net/Assessor/index.html **Online** - access county property tax data free at www.islandcounty.net/PublicInformation/GuestLogin.aspx?ReturnUrl=%2fPublicInformation%2fProperty%2fAccountSearch.aspx. No name searching.

Jefferson County

County Auditor, PO Box 563, Port Townsend, WA 98368. 360-385-9116; fax-360-385-9228; 8AM-5PM http://icris.co.jefferson.wa.us

Index: All in one. Marriage records here, other vital records are not. Records indexed on a public use terminal back to 1985. Office personnel or visitors may perform searches. General index search fee $8.00 per hour. Office will search single real estate records but not for a title company. Copy fee $1.00 per page. Cert fee- $3.00 1st page plus copy fee for add'l pages. Payee- Jefferson County Auditor. **Online Real Estate, Grantor/Grantee, Deed, Vital Statistic, Lien, UCC, Permit records:** Access the "Recorded Document Search" database at www.co.jefferson.wa.us/_hidden/disclaimer.htm. Includes grantor/grantee index and records on the County Property (Tax Parcel) Database Tool, also plats and survey images. Also, search for building permits but no name searching. Search iCRIS for grantor/grantee, plats, etc, at http://icris.co.jefferson.wa.us/icris/splash.jsp. **Other phones:** Treasurer- 360-385-9150; Elections- 360-385-9119. **Property tax/Assessing-** 360-385-9105. **Online access-** Search assessor data free at www.co.jefferson.wa.us/assessors/parcel/ParcelSearch.asp but no names searching.

King County

Recorder, 500 4th Ave, Rm 311; County Admin Bldg, Seattle, WA 98104. 206-296-1570; fax-206-205-8396; hours - 8:30AM-4:30PM www.metrokc.gov/recelec/records/default.htm

Index: All in one. Marriage records here, other vital records are not. Records indexed on a public use terminal back to 1991. Office personnel or visitors may perform searches. Search fee $8.00 per 5 year search. There is a limited real estate free search that goes back 12 months only. Copy fee $1.00 per page. Cert fee- $3.00 for 1st page, $2.00 each add'l includes copies. Payee- King County Recorder's Office. Bulk data available for purchase, contact Robert Foote 206-296-1587. **Online Real Estate, Deed, Lien, Marriage, Judgment, Vital Statistic records:** Access recorder data at www.metrokc.gov/recelec/records/ or at http://146.129.54.93:8193/legalacceptance.asp?. **Other phones:** Treasurer- 206-296-3850; Elections- 206-296-1565; Vital Records- 206-296-4768; Finance Dept- 206-296-3850. **Property tax/Assessing-** 500 4th Ave, #ADM-AS-0708,, Seattle, WA 98104; 206-296-7300, assessor fax- 206-296-5107. (Appraiser- 206-296-8683) 8:30AM-4:30PM M,T,W,F; 9:30AM-4:30PM TH http://your.kingcounty.gov/assessor/ **Online access-** Access property records on Dept. of Developmental and Environmental Resources database free at www.metrokc.gov/ddes/gis/parcel/.

Kitsap County

County Auditor, 614 Division St, Rm 106-MS 31, Port Orchard, WA 98366. 360-337-7133; fax-360-337-4645; hours - 8AM - 4:30PM www.kitsapgov.com/aud/default.htm

Index: Separate indices to search include grantor/grantee, date, doc type, legal description. From 1/1997 forward you can search by tax parcel number. Marriage records here, other vital records are not. Records indexed on computer back to 1987. Office personnel or visitors may perform searches. Search fee $8.00 per name. Copy fee $1.00 per page. Cert fee- $3.00 1st page, $1.00 each add'l page. Payee- Kitsap County Auditor. **Online access to Real Estate, Grantor/Grantee, Deed, Lien, Vital Statistic, Judgment records:** Search property data free on the land information system site at http://kcwaimg.co.kitsap.wa.us/recorder/web/. Click on Public Login. Site may be down. Fee to print official documents. Also, subscription access to grantor/grantee index back to 8/26/1990, parcels back to 1/1972, recordings to 4/6/1988 and tax rolls are available at www.landlight.com/. **Other phones:**

Treasurer- 360-337-7135; Elections- 360-337-7128; **Property tax/Assessing-** 614 Division St, Port Orchard, WA 98366; 360-337-7160, fax- 360-337-4874. (Appraiser- 360-337-7160) **Online-** Search property and tax data free on the land info system site at http://kcwppub3.co.kitsap.wa.us/ParcelSearch/. No name searching. Fee to print official documents.

Kittitas County

County Auditor, 205 W 5th, Ste #105, Ellensburg, WA 98926-3129. 509-962-7504; fax-509-962-7687; 9AM-5PM www.co.kittitas.wa.us
Index: All in one. Marriage records here, other vital records are not. Records on a public use terminal. Office personnel or visitors may perform searches. General index search fee $8.00 per name. Office will search real estate records. Tax liens not included in UCC search. Copy fee $1.00 per page. Cert fee- $3.00 1st page, includes one copy. Payee- KC Auditor. **Other phones:** Treasurer- 509-962-7535; Elections- 509-962-7503; Vital Records- 509-962-7504; Health Dept -509-962-7515. **Property tax/Assessing-** 205 W 5th, #101, Ellensburg, WA 98926; 509-962-7501, fax- 509-962-7666. (Appraiser- 509-962-7501) www.co.kittitas.w a.us/assessor/default.asp **Online-** Access property data free at www.co.kittitas.wa.us/taxsifterp ublic/disclaimer.asp but no name searching.

Klickitat County

Auditor, 205 S Columbus Ave, #MS-CH-2, Goldendale, WA 98620. 509-773-4001, 800-583-8050; fax-509-773-4244; 9-5 www.klickitatcounty.org
Index: All in one. Marriage records here, other vital records are not. Records indexed on a public use terminal back to 1988. Office personnel or visitors may perform searches. General index search fee $8.00 per hour. Office will search real estate and UCC records. Copy fee $1.00 per copy. Cert fee- $3.00 per page plus copy fee. Payee- Klickitat County Auditor. Treasurer- 509-773-4664; Elections- 509-773-4001; Vitals- 509-773-4001; **Property tax/ Assessing-** 205 S Columbus Ave, MS-CH, Rm 200, Goldendale, WA 98620; 509-773-3715, fax- 509-773-6397. (Appraiser 509-773-4001) http://klickitatcounty.org/assessor/ **Online-** Access GIS-mapping site free at http://69.30.47.122/kcmap/ but no name searching.

Lewis County

County Auditor, PO Box 29, Chehalis, WA 98532-0029. 360-740-1163; fax-360-740-1421; 8AM-5PM
Index: Separate indices to search include document type or name & date. Marriage records here, other vital records are not. Records indexed on a public use terminal back to 1988. Office personnel or visitors may perform searches. General index search fee $8.00 per name per 10 years. Office will search real estate records. Will search UCC records. Copy fee $1.00 per page. Cert fee- $3.00 1st page, $1.00 each page after includes copy fee. Payee- Lewis Cuonty Auditor. **Other phones:** Treasurer- 360-740-1115; Elections- 360-740-1164; Vital Records- 360-236-4313. **Property tax/Assessing-** 351 NW North St, Chehalis, WA 98532; 360-740-1392. **Online** - Access property data free on the PATS system at https://fortress.wa.gov/lewisco/home/ click on PATS. No name searching.

Lincoln County

County Auditor, PO Box 28, Davenport, WA 99122. 509-725-4971; fax-509-725-0820; 8AM-5PM http://wei.secstate.wa.gov/lincoln/Pages/default.aspx
Index: Books and computer. Marriage records here, other vital records are not. Records indexed on computer back to 1989. Office personnel or visitors may perform searches. General index search fee $8.00 per hour. Office will search real estate records. Will search UCC records. Copy fee $1.00 per page. Cert fee- $3.00 1st page, $1.00 each add'l includes copy fee. Payee- Lincoln County Auditor. Bulk data available for purchase, Assessor's data on CD. **Other phones:** Treasurer- 509-725-5061; Elections- 509-725-4971; Vitals- 509-725-4971. **Property tax/ Assessing-** PO Box 400, 450 Logan St, Davenport, WA 99122; 509-725-7011, assessor fax- 509-725-5045. (Appraiser - 509-725-7011) hours- 8:30AM-4:30PM www.co.lincoln.wa.us/assessor/default.htm

Mason County

County Auditor, PO Box 400, Shelton, WA 98584. 360-427-9670 x468, R/E recording phone-360-427-9670 x467; fax-360-427-1753; 8:30AM-4:30PM. http://wei.secstate.wa.gov/mason/Pages/default.aspx
Index: Separate indices to search include grantor/grantee, AF number, parcel number, legal description. Marriage records here, other vital records are not. Records indexed on a public use terminal back to 1985. Office personnel or visitors may perform searches. General index search fee $8.00 per hour. Office will search real estate records. Copy fee $1.00 per page. Cert fee- $3.00 for 1st page plus copy fee. Payee- Mason County Auditor. Bulk data available for purchase in CD format;. **Online Liens, Judgment, Divorce, Marriage, Birth, Death, Wills/Probate records:** Access to records for free go to http://66.119.203.180/masonrecorder/web/ . **Other phones:** Treasurer- 360-427-9670 x484; Elections- 360-427-9670 x469; Vitals - 360-427-9670 x467. **Property tax/Assessing-** POB 429, Shelton, WA 98584; 360-427-9670 x491. (Appraiser- x491) **Online-** Assessor data free at www.co.mason.wa.us/disclaimer.php & www.co.mason.wa.us/astr/index.php. Access parcel data free on GIS site at www.co.mason.wa.us/gis/index.php but not name searching.

Okanogan County

County Auditor, PO Box 1010, Okanogan, WA 98840. 509-422-7240; fax-509-422-7163; 8:30AM-5PM www.okanogancounty.org
Index: All in one since 1993. Marriage records here, other vital records are not. Records indexed on a public use terminal back to 1993. Office personnel or visitors may perform searches. Search fee $8.00 per name per 10 years. Copy fee $1.00 per page. Cert fee- $3.00 for 1st page. Payee- Okanogan County Auditor. Office will sell land transfers in bulk for $.05 per image to approved customers. **Other phones:** Treasurer- 509-422-7180; Elections- 504-422-7244; Vitals- 504-422-7140. **Property tax/Assessing-** PO Box 152, 149 3rd North, Rm 202, Okanogan, WA 98840; 509-422-7190. (Appraiser- 509-422-7240) 8AM-5PM. **Online-** assessment data free at http://okanoganwa.taxsifter.com/taxsifter/disclaimer.asp.

Pacific County

County Auditor, PO Box 97, South Bend, WA 98586-9903. 360-875-9318; fax-360-875-9333; 8:30AM-4:30PM www.co.pacific.wa.us
Index: All in one. Marriage records here, other vital records are not. Records indexed on a public use terminal back to 1996. Office personnel or visitors may perform searches. Search fee $8.00 per hour. Office will search real estate records. Will search UCC records. Copy fee $1.00 per page. Cert fee- $3.00 per 1st page, $1.00 each add'l page. Payee- Pacific County Auditor. **Other phones:** Treasurer- 360-875-9421; Elections- 360-875-9315. **Property tax/Assessing-** PO Box 86, 300 Memorial Dr, South Bend, WA 98586; 360-875-9301. hours- 8AM-4:30PM www.co.pacific.wa.us/assessor/index.htm **Online access-** Access County Auditor property data free on TaxSifter system at http://pacificwa.taxsifter.com/taxsifter/T-Parcelsearch.asp. Foreclosures are posted on the website in August.

Pend Oreille County

County Auditor, PO Box 5015, Newport, WA 99156. 509-447-3185; fax-509-447-2475; 8AM-4:30PM www.co.pend-oreille.wa.us
Index: All in one. Marriage records here, other vital records are not. Records indexed on a public use terminal back to 1996. Office personnel or visitors may perform searches. General index search fee $8.00 per hour. Office will not search real estate records unless specific documentation provided. Tax liens with County Treasurer. Copy fee $1.00 per page. Cert fee- $3.00 per doc plus copy fee. Payee- Pend Oreille County Auditor. Office can customize and produce short-runs of bulk data if requested and prepaid. **Other phones:** Treasurer- 509-447-3612; Elections- 509-447-3185; Vital Records- 360-236-4300. **Property tax/Assessing-** PO Box 5010, 625 W 4th St, Newport, WA 99156; 509-447-4312, assessor fax- 509-447-6450. (Appraiser- 509-447-4312) **Online access-** Access property records free at http://66.45.209.110/pend-propertysearch/index.jsp but no name searching.

Pierce County

County Auditor, 2401 S 35th St, Rm 200; Recording Division, Tacoma, WA 98409. 253-798-7427, R/E recording phone-206-591-7440; fax-253-798-3182; 8:30AM-4:30PM. www.piercecountywa.org/pc/abtus/ourorg/aud/default.htm
Index: All in one. There are 2 computer systems, 1984-present, 1983 back to 1800s. Marriage records here, other vital records are not. Records indexed on 2 public use terminals back to 1984. Office will perform a UCC search on computer but public must search other records themselves. General search fee $8.00 per hour. Copy fee $1.00 per page. Cert fee- $3.00 1st page, $1.00 each add'l page. Payee- Pierce County Auditor. Purchase RE images in bulk for $1.00 per page, call 253-798-7440. **Online Real Estate, Deed, Lien, Vital Statistic, Judgment, Assumed Name, Marriage records:** Search index back to 1984 and images back to 3/1998 on the auditor's recording database free at http://hartweb.piercecountywa.org/search.asp?cabinet=opr. Marriage records at http://hartweb.piercecountywa.org/search.asp?cabinet=oprmarriage. **Other phones:** Treasurer- 253-798-6111; Elections- 253-798-7430. **Property tax/ Assessing-** 2401 S 35th St, #142, Tacoma, 98409; 253-798-3710, fax- 253-798-3705. www.piercecountywa.org/pc/abtus/ourorg/at/at.htm **Online-** Property records on Assessor-Treasurer database free at www.co.pierce.wa.us/CFApps/atr/e pip/search.cfm or www.co.pierce.wa.us/abtus/ourorg/at/at.htm.

San Juan County

County Auditor, PO Box 638, Friday Harbor, WA 98250. 360-378-2161; fax-360-378-6256; 8AM-4:30PM www.sanjuanco.com/
Index: Separate indices to search include microfilm prior to 1938, bound 1938-1984, computer. Marriage records here, other vital records are not. Records indexed on a public use terminal back to 1984. Office personnel or visitors may perform searches. Search fee $8.00 per hour. Office will search real estate records. Will search UCC records. Copy fee $1.00 per page. Cert fee- $3.00 1st page; $1.00 each add'l page. Payee- San Juan County Auditor. Bulk data of plats and surveys available for purchase, contact the recording dept. **Online access to Real Estate, Deed, Lien records:** Access to the auditor database of real estate recording records is free at http://sjc-imaging.rockisland.com/SJCdocSearch/?. Images go back to 1997; index goes back to 1/1984. **Other phones:** Treasurer- 360-378-2171; Elections- 360-378-3357; Vital Records- 360-378-4474. **Property tax/Assessing-** 350 Court St, Friday Harbor, WA 98250; 360-378-2172, assessor fax- 360-378-4729. **Online** - Access to assessor property records is free at http://69.30.47.122/kcmap/. No name searching.

Skagit County

County Auditor, PO Box 1306, Mount Vernon, WA 98273-1306. 360-336-9420, R/E- 360-336-9311; fax-360-336-9429; 8:30-4:30PM www.skagitcounty.net/
Index: All in one. Marriage records here, other vital records are not. Records indexed on a public use terminal back to 3/79. Office personnel or visitors may perform searches. General index search fee $8.00 per hour. Office will search real estate records. Copy fee $1.00 per page. Cert fee- $3.00 1st page, $1.00 each add'l page. Payee- Skagit County Auditor. Bulk data available for purchase, contact Judy Zavala. **Online Real Estate, Grantor/Grantee, Deed, Lien, Marriage, Permit records:** Access auditor's recorded documents as well as permits and marriages free at

www.skagitcounty.net/Common/asp/Default.asp?D=AuditorRecording&C=Search&p=Search.asp&a=Recording. **Other phones:** Treasurer- 360-336-9350; Elections- 360-336-9305; Vital Records- 360-336-9380. **Property tax/Assessing**- 700 S 2nd St, Rm 204, 2nd Fl, Admin Bldg, Mount Vernon, WA 98273-1306; 360-336-9370, assessor fax- 360-336-9308. (Appraiser- 360-336-9310) **Online** - Search assessor data free at www.skagitcounty.net/Common/asp/default.asp?d=Home&c=General&P=main.htm Click on Record Searches, but no name searching.

Skamania County

County Auditor, PO Box 790, Stevenson, WA 98648-0790. 509-427-3730; fax-509-427-3740; 8:30AM-5PM www.skamaniacounty.org

Index: All in one. Marriage records here, other vital records are not. Records indexed on a public use terminal back to 1992. Office personnel or visitors may perform searches. Search fee $8.00 per hour. Office will search real estate records. Copy fee $1.00 per page. Cert fee- $3.00 1st page, $1.00 each add'l page. Payee- Skamania County Auditor. Bulk data available for purchase, contact the auditor. **Other phones:** Treasurer- 509-427-3760; Elections- 509-427-3730; Vital Records- 509-427-3730; Clerk's Office- 509-427-3770. **Property tax/Assessing**- 240 NW Vancouver Ave, Stevenson, WA 98648; 509-427-9400. (Appraiser- 509-427-3730)

Snohomish County

County Auditor, 3000 Rockefeller Ave; Dept. R, M/S #204, Everett, WA 98201. 425-388-3483 press 0, R/E recording phone-425-388-3483 x0, fax-425-388-3094; 9AM-5PM http://www1.co.snohomish.wa.us/Departments/Auditor/

Index: All in one. Marriage records here, other vital records are not. Records indexed on a public use terminal back to 1976; images back to 1997. Office personnel or visitors may perform searches. Search fee $8.00 per name per 10 years. Office will search real estate records. Copy fee $1.00 per page; self serve same. Cert fee- $2.00 per doc plus copy fee. Payee- Snohomish County Auditor. **Online access to Real Estate, Deed, Lien, Marriage records:** Access to the Auditor's office database back to 1997 is free at http://198.238.192.100/localization/menu.asp. Search on the recorded documents or marriage icons. **Other phones:** Treasurer- 425-388-3366; Elections- 425-388-3444. **Property tax/Assessing**- 3000 Rockefeller Ave, MS 510, Everett, WA 98201; 425-388-3433, assessor fax- 425-388-3961. (Appraiser - 425-388-3444) http://www1.co.snohomish.wa.us/Departments/Assessor/ **Online** - Search assessor property data for free at http://web5.co.snohomish.wa.us/propsys/asr-tr-propinq/ but no name searching.

Spokane County

County Auditor, PO Box 2353, Spokane, WA 99210. 509-477-2270; fax-509-477-6451; 8:30AM-5PM. www.spokanecounty.org/auditor/

Index: All in one. Index not on computer. Marriage records here, other vital records are not. Records may be looked up on a public use terminal. Office personnel or visitors may perform searches. General index search fee $8.00 per hour (1 hour minimum). Office will search real estate records. Tax liens not included in UCC search. Copy fee $1.00 per page. Cert fee- $3.00 1st page; $1.00 each add'l page includes copy fee. Payee- Spokane County Auditor. Bulk data available for purchase, documents images and index 1996 forward, contact Records Manager. **Other phones:** Treasurer- 509-456-4713; Elections- 509-477-2320; Vital Records- 509-324-1522. **Property tax/Assessing**- 1116 W Broadway, 1st Fl, Spokane, WA 99260; 509-477-5793, assessor fax- 509-477-3697. (Appraiser- 509-456-3696) **Online**- Search the County Parcel Locator database for free at www.spokanecounty.org/pubpadal/. No name searching. Search sales by parcel number free at www.spokanecounty.org/pubpadal/SalesSearch.aspx.

Stevens County

County Auditor, 215 S Oak St, Colville, WA 99114. 509-684-7512; fax-509-684-8310; 9AM-3:30PM www.co.stevens.wa.us

Index: Separate indices to search include computer, microfilm. Marriage records here, other vital records are not. Records indexed on a public use terminal back to 1990. Office personnel or visitors may perform searches. General index search fee $8.00 per hour. Office will search real estate records. Copy fee $1.00 per page; self serve same. Cert fee- $2.00 per doc plus copy fee. Payee- Stevens County Auditor. **Other phones:** Treasurer- 509-684-2593; Elections- 509-684-7514; Vital Records- 509-684-7512; Auditor- 509-684-7512. **Property tax/Assessing**- 215 S Oak St, Colville, 99114; 509-684-6161, fax- 509-684-7580. (Appraiser - 684-6161) www.co.stevens.wa.us/assessor/assessor.htm **Online** - assessor property data free at http://209.173.246.99/screalprop/index.php but no name searching.

Thurston County

County Auditor, 2000 Lakeridge Dr SW, Olympia, WA 98502. 360-786-5405; fax-360-786-5223; 8AM-4:30PM www.co.thurston.wa.us/auditor/

Index: All in one. Marriage records here, other vital records are not. Records indexed on a public use terminal back to 1981. Office personnel or visitors may perform searches. Real estate searches are minimal. General index search fee $8.00 per hour per name. Copy fee $1.00 per page. Cert fee- $3 1st page; $1.00 each add'l, includes copy fee. Payee- Thurston County Auditor. Bulk data available for purchase. **Online Real Estate, Deed records:** Access Auditor Recording data at www.co.thurston.wa.us/auditor/. Click on Public Record Index Available Online. Guests may log in using the "Public Log In" button. **Other phones:** Treasurer- 360-786-5550; Elections- 360-786-5408; Vital Records- 360-786-5581. **Property tax/Assessing**- 2000 Lakeridge Dr SW, Olympia, WA 98502; 360-786-5410, assessor fax- 360-754-2958. (Appraiser- 360-786-5410) hours- 8AM-5PM www.co.thurston.wa.us/assessor/ **Online** - property data on Thurston GeoData database free- www.geodata.org/parcelsrch.asp. No name searches.

Wahkiakum County

County Auditor, PO Box 543, Cathlamet, WA 98612. 360-795-3219; fax-360-795-0824; 8AM-4PM www.co.wahkiakum.wa.us

Index: Separate indices to search include computer back to 2/22/1999; earlier on separate paper indexes. Marriage records here, other vital records are not. Records indexed on a public use terminal back to 2/99. Office will perform a UCC search but public must search other records themselves. Copy fee $1.00 per page. Will fax out doc for $1.00 per doc. Cert fee- $3.00 1st page; $1.00 each add'l page includes copy fee. Payee- Wahkiakum County Auditor. Recordings on CD-rom are available from the Auditor's Office. **Other phones:** Treasurer- 360-795-8005; Elections- 360-795-3219; Vitals- 360-795-6207. **Property tax/Assessing**- PO Box 145, 64 Main St, Cathlamet, WA 98612; 360-795-3791, fax- 360-795-0540. (Appraiser- 360-795-3791) www.co.wahkiakum.wa.us/depts/assessor/index.htm **Online access**- Access the yearly property sales list for free at www.co.wahkiakum.wa.us/depts/assessor/index.htm. Click on List name at bottom of page. Print out of current sales available free at www.co.wahkiakum.wa.us/depts/assessor/pdf/SalesThruApr2008.pdf.

Walla Walla County

County Auditor, PO Box 1856, Walla Walla, WA 99362-0356. 509-524-2549; fax-509-524-2552; 9AM-4PM www.co.walla-walla.wa.us

Index: All in one. Marriage records here, other vital records are not. Records indexed on a public use terminal back to 1/1979. Office personnel or visitors may perform searches. Search fee $8.00 per name, per hour. Office will not search real estate records. Will search UCC records from 1979 to current. Copy fee $1.00 per page. Cert fee- $3.00 1st page plus copy fee for add'l pages. Payee- Walla Walla County Auditor. **Other phones:** Treasurer- 509-524-2750; Elections- 509-524-2530. **Property tax/Assessing**- 315 W Main St, 1st Fl Rm 112, Walla Walla, 99362; 509-524-2560, fax- 509-524-2576. (Appraiser- 509-524-2560) www.co.walla-walla.wa.us/Departments/ASR/index.shtml **Online** - Access to TaxSifter parcel search and sales is free at http://wallawallawa.taxsifter.com/taxsifter/disclaimer.asp.

Whatcom County

County Auditor, 311 Grand Ave, #103, Bellingham, WA 98225. 360-676-6740, R/E recording phone-360-676-6740 x50013, UCC recording phone-360-676-6740 x50073; fax-360-738-4556; 8:30AM-4:30PA. www.whatcomcounty.us/auditor/

Index: All in one. Marriage records here, other vital records are not. Records indexed on a public use terminal back to 1988. Office personnel or visitors may perform searches. When office searches, general index search fee $8.00 per hour. Copy fee $1.00 per page. Cert fee- $3.00 1st page plus copy fee for add'l pages. Payee- Whatcom County Auditor. Bulk data available for purchase, contact County Auditor office. **Other phones:** Treasurer- 360-676-6774; Elections- 360-676-6742. **Property tax/Assessing**- 311 Grand Ave, #106, Bellingham, WA 98225; 360-676-6790, fax- 360-738-2472. (Appraiser- 360-676-6790) www.co.whatcom.wa.us/assessor/index.jsp **Online**- Search assessor parcel database information system free at www.co.whatcom.wa.us/cgibin/db2www/assessor/search/RPSearch.ndt/disclaimer.

Whitman County

County Auditor, PO Box 350, Colfax, WA 99111-0350. 509-397-6270, UCC recording phone-509-392-6270; fax-509-397-6351; 9AM-5PM (recording until 2:30PM). www.whitmancounty.org

Index: All in one. Marriage records here, other vital records are not. Records indexed on computer back to 1987. Office personnel or visitors may perform searches. Search fee $8.00 per hour. Copy fee $1.00 per page. Cert fee- $3.00 1st page, $1.00 each add'l page plus copy fee. Payee- Whitman County Auditor. **Other phones:** Treasurer- 509-397-6230; Elections- 509-397-6353; Vital Records- 509-397-6270. **Property tax/Assessing**- 400 N Main, Colfax, WA 99111; 509-397-6220, assessor fax- 509-397-6223. (Appraiser- 509-397-6220)

Yakima County

County Auditor, 128 N 2nd St, #117, Yakima, WA 98901. 509-574-1330; fax-509-574-1341; 9AM-4PM. www.yakimacounty.us/auditor/

Index: All in one. Marriage records here, other vital records are not. Records indexed on computer back to 1985. Office personnel or visitors may perform searches. Search fee $8.00 per name per hour. Will not do chain of title or tracking of property. Copy fee $1.00 per page. Cert fee- $3.00 1st page, $1.00 each add'l page plus copy fee. Payee- Yakima County Auditor. **Online Real Estate, Deed, Lien, Mortgage, Judgment, Plat, UCC records:** Access the land records index free at http://68.185.48.9/DirectSearch/Default.aspx. Also, with registration you may search the Tapestry 2 System for $5.95 per search and $0.50 per page printed at http://tapestry.fidlar.com/Splash/Def ault.aspx. **Other phones:** Treasurer- 509-574-2800; Elections- 509-574-1340; Vital Records- 509-574-1330. **Property tax/Assessing**- 128 N 2nd St, #112, Yakima, WA 98901; 509-574-1100, fax- 509-574-1101. (Appraiser- 509-574-1100) http://yes.co.yakima.wa.us/assessor/Default.aspx **Online**- Assessor and property data on County Assessor database are free at http://yes.co.yakima.wa.us/assessor/char_search.aspx?AspxAutoDetectCookieSupport=1. No name searching. Access to the treasurer parcel database is free at www.co.yakima.wa.us/treasurer/database/taxes.asp. No name searching. Search City of Grandview business licenses at www.grandview.wa.us/WebPage/CityHall/BusinessLicenseListings.htm.

Washington County Locator

You will usually be able to find the city name in the City/County Cross Reference below. In that case, it is a simple matter to determine the county from the cross reference. However, only the official US Postal Service city names are included in this index. There are an additional 40,000 place names that people use in their addresses. Therefore, we have also included a ZIP/City Cross Reference immediately following the City/County Cross Reference.

If you know the ZIP Code but the city name does not appear in the City/County Cross Reference index, look up the ZIP Code in the ZIP/City Cross Reference, find the city name, then look up the city name in the City/County Cross Reference. For example, you want to know the county for an address of Menands, NY 12204. There is no "Menands" in the City/County Cross Reference. The ZIP/City Cross Reference shows that ZIP Codes 12201-12288 are for the city of Albany. Looking back in the City/County Cross Reference, Albany is in Albany County.

Washington - City/County Cross Reference

ABERDEEN Grays Harbor
ACME Whatcom
ADDY Stevens
ADNA Lewis
AIRWAY HEIGHTS Spokane
ALBION Whitman
ALLYN Mason
ALMIRA (99103) Lincoln(88), Grant(11)
AMANDA PARK Grays Harbor
AMBOY (98601) Clark(98), Cowlitz(1)
ANACORTES Skagit
ANATONE Asotin
ANDERSON ISLAND Pierce
APPLETON Klickitat
ARDENVOIR Chelan
ARIEL Cowlitz
ARLINGTON Snohomish
ASHFORD Pierce
ASOTIN Asotin
AUBURN (98092) King(92), Pierce(7)
AUBURN King
BAINBRIDGE ISLAND Kitsap
BARING King
BATTLE GROUND Clark
BAY CENTER Pacific
BEAVER Clallam
BELFAIR Mason
BELLEVUE King
BELLINGHAM (98229) Whatcom(97), Skagit(2)
BELLINGHAM Whatcom
BELMONT Whitman
BENGE Adams
BENTON CITY Benton
BEVERLY Grant
BICKLETON (99322) Klickitat(96), Yakima(3)
BINGEN (98605) Skamania(72), Klickitat(27)
BLACK DIAMOND King
BLAINE Whatcom
BLAKELY ISLAND San Juan
BONNEY LAKE Pierce
BOTHELL King
BOTHELL Snohomish
BOW Skagit
BOYDS Ferry
BREMERTON Kitsap
BREWSTER Okanogan
BRIDGEPORT Douglas
BRINNON Jefferson
BROWNSTOWN Yakima
BRUSH PRAIRIE Clark
BUCKLEY Pierce
BUCODA Thurston
BUENA Yakima
BURBANK Walla Walla
BURLEY Kitsap
BURLINGTON Skagit
BURTON King
CAMANO ISLAND Island
CAMAS Clark
CAMP MURRAY Pierce
CARBONADO Pierce
CARLSBORG Clallam
CARLTON Okanogan
CARNATION King
CARROLLS Cowlitz
CARSON Skamania
CASHMERE Chelan
CASTLE ROCK Cowlitz
CATHLAMET Wahkiakum
CEDARVIEW Pierce
CENTERVILLE Klickitat
CENTRALIA (98531) Lewis(94), Thurston(5)
CHATTAROY Spokane
CHEHALIS Lewis
CHELAN Chelan
CHELAN FALLS Chelan
CHENEY Spokane
CHEWELAH Stevens
CHIMACUM Jefferson
CHINOOK Pacific
CINEBAR Lewis
CLALLAM BAY Clallam
CLARKSTON Asotin
CLAYTON (99110) Stevens(67), Spokane(32)
CLE ELUM Kittitas
CLEARLAKE Skagit
CLINTON Island
COLBERT Spokane
COLFAX Whitman
COLLEGE PLACE Walla Walla
COLTON Whitman
COLVILLE Stevens
CONCONULLY Okanogan
CONCRETE Skagit
CONNELL (99326) Franklin(91), Adams(8)
CONWAY Skagit
COPALIS BEACH Grays Harbor
COPALIS CROSSING Grays Harbor
COSMOPOLIS (98537) Grays Harbor(98), Pacific(1)
COUGAR Cowlitz
COULEE CITY (99115) Grant(88), Douglas(11)
COULEE DAM (99116) Okanogan(82), Douglas(15), Grant(1)
COUPEVILLE Island
COWICHE Yakima
CRESTON Lincoln
CUNNINGHAM Adams
CURLEW Ferry
CURTIS Lewis
CUSICK Pend Oreille
CUSTER Whatcom
DALLESPORT Klickitat
DANVILLE Ferry
DARRINGTON (98241) Snohomish(82), Skagit(17)
DAVENPORT (99122) Lincoln(89), Stevens(10)
DAYTON Columbia
DEER HARBOR San Juan
DEER PARK (99006) Spokane(87), Stevens(10), Pend Oreille(1)
DEMING Whatcom
DIXIE Walla Walla
DOTY Lewis
DRYDEN Chelan
DUPONT Pierce
DUVALL King
EAST OLYMPIA Thurston
EAST WENATCHEE Douglas
EASTON Kittitas
EASTSOUND San Juan
EATONVILLE Pierce
EDMONDS Snohomish
EDWALL (99008) Lincoln(80), Spokane(19)
ELBE (98330) Pierce(82), Lewis(17)
ELECTRIC CITY Grant
ELK (99009) Spokane(78), Pend Oreille(21)
ELLENSBURG Kittitas
ELMA (98541) Grays Harbor(72), Mason(27)
ELMER CITY Okanogan
ELTOPIA Franklin
ENDICOTT Whitman
ENTIAT Chelan
ENUMCLAW (98022) King(95), Pierce(4)
EPHRATA Grant
ETHEL Lewis
EVANS Stevens
EVERETT Snohomish
EVERSON Whatcom
FAIRCHILD AIR FORCE BASE Spokane
FAIRFIELD Spokane
FALL CITY King
FARMINGTON Whitman
FEDERAL WAY King
FERNDALE Whatcom
FORD (99013) Spokane(51), Stevens(46), Lincoln(1)
FORKS Clallam
FOUR LAKES Spokane
FOX ISLAND Pierce
FREELAND Island
FREEMAN Spokane
FRIDAY HARBOR San Juan
FRUITLAND Stevens
GALVIN Lewis
GARFIELD Whitman
GEORGE Grant
GIFFORD Stevens
GIG HARBOR Pierce
GLENOMA Lewis
GLENWOOD Klickitat
GOLD BAR (98251) Snohomish(96), King(3)
GOLDENDALE Klickitat
GOOSE PRAIRIE Yakima
GRAHAM Pierce
GRAND COULEE (99133) Grant(79), Lincoln(11), Douglas(8)
GRANDVIEW Yakima
GRANGER Yakima
GRANITE FALLS Snohomish
GRAPEVIEW Mason
GRAYLAND (98547) Grays Harbor(98), Pacific(1)
GRAYS RIVER Wahkiakum
GREENACRES Spokane
GREENBANK Island
HAMILTON Skagit
HANSVILLE Kitsap
HARRAH Yakima
HARRINGTON Lincoln
HARTLINE Grant
HATTON Adams
HAY Whitman
HEISSON Clark
HOBART King
HOODSPORT Mason
HOOPER Whitman
HOQUIAM Grays Harbor
HUMPTULIPS Grays Harbor
HUNTERS Stevens
HUSUM Klickitat
ILWACO Pacific
INCHELIUM Ferry
INDEX Snohomish
INDIANOLA Kitsap
IONE Pend Oreille
ISSAQUAH King
JOYCE Clallam
KAHLOTUS Franklin
KALAMA Cowlitz
KAPOWSIN Pierce
KELLER (99140) Ferry(98), Stevens(1)
KELSO Cowlitz
KENMORE King
KENNEWICK Benton
KENT King
KETTLE FALLS (99141) Stevens(88), Ferry(11)
KEYPORT Kitsap
KINGSTON Kitsap
KIRKLAND King
KITTITAS Kittitas
KLICKITAT Klickitat
LA CENTER Clark
LA CONNER Skagit
LA GRANDE Pierce
LA PUSH Clallam
LACEY Thurston
LACROSSE Whitman
LAKE STEVENS Snohomish
LAKE TAPPS Pierce
LAKEBAY Pierce
LAKEWOOD Pierce
LAKEWOOD Snohomish
LAMONA Lincoln
LAMONT (99017) Whitman(98), Adams(1)
LANGLEY Island
LATAH Spokane
LAURIER Ferry
LEAVENWORTH Chelan
LEBAM Pacific
LIBERTY LAKE Spokane
LILLIWAUP Mason
LIND Adams
LITTLEROCK Thurston
LONG BEACH Pacific
LONGBRANCH Pierce
LONGMIRE Pierce
LONGVIEW Cowlitz
LOOMIS Okanogan

LOON LAKE Stevens
LOPEZ ISLAND San Juan
LUMMI ISLAND Whatcom
LYLE Klickitat
LYMAN Skagit
LYNDEN Whatcom
LYNNWOOD Snohomish
MABTON Yakima
MALAGA Chelan
MALDEN Whitman
MALO Ferry
MALONE Grays Harbor
MALOTT Okanogan
MANCHESTER Kitsap
MANSFIELD Douglas
MANSON Chelan
MAPLE FALLS Whatcom
MAPLE VALLEY King
MARBLEMOUNT Skagit
MARCUS Stevens
MARLIN (98832) Grant(96), Adams(3)
MARSHALL Spokane
MARYSVILLE Snohomish
MATLOCK Mason
MATTAWA Grant
MAZAMA Okanogan
MCCLEARY Grays Harbor
MCKENNA Pierce
MEAD Spokane
MEDICAL LAKE Spokane
MEDINA King
MENLO Pacific
MERCER ISLAND King
MESA Franklin
METALINE Pend Oreille
METALINE FALLS Pend Oreille
METHOW Okanogan
MICA Spokane
MILTON (98354) Pierce(92), King(7)
MINERAL Lewis
MOCLIPS Grays Harbor
MOHLER Lincoln
MONITOR Chelan
MONROE Snohomish
MONTESANO Grays Harbor
MORTON Lewis
MOSES LAKE Grant
MOSSYROCK Lewis
MOUNT VERNON Skagit
MOUNTLAKE TERRACE Snohomish
MOXEE Yakima
MUKILTEO Snohomish
NACHES Yakima
NAHCOTTA Pacific
NAPAVINE Lewis
NASELLE Pacific
NEAH BAY Clallam
NEILTON Grays Harbor
NESPELEM Okanogan
NEWMAN LAKE Spokane
NEWPORT (99156) Pend Oreille(50), Spokane(49)
NINE MILE FALLS (99026) Spokane(54), Stevens(45)
NOOKSACK Whatcom
NORDLAND Jefferson
NORTH BEND King
NORTH BONNEVILLE Skamania
NORTH LAKEWOOD Snohomish
NORTHPORT Stevens
OAK HARBOR Island
OAKESDALE Whitman
OAKVILLE (98568) Grays Harbor(97), Thurston(2)
OCEAN PARK Pacific
OCEAN SHORES Grays Harbor
ODESSA (99159) Lincoln(86), Adams(13)
OKANOGAN Okanogan
OLALLA Kitsap
OLD NATIONAL BANK Spokane
OLGA San Juan
OLYMPIA Thurston
OMAK Okanogan
ONALASKA Lewis
ORCAS San Juan
ORIENT Ferry
ORONDO Douglas
OROVILLE Okanogan
ORTING Pierce
OTHELLO (99344) Adams(77), Grant(16), Franklin(5)
OTIS ORCHARDS Spokane
OUTLOOK Yakima
OYSTERVILLE Pacific
PACIFIC (98047) King(92), Pierce(7)
PACIFIC BEACH Grays Harbor
PACKWOOD Lewis
PALISADES Douglas
PALOUSE Whitman
PARADISE INN Pierce
PARKER Yakima
PASCO Franklin
PATEROS Okanogan
PATERSON Benton
PE ELL Lewis
PESHASTIN Chelan
PLYMOUTH Benton
POINT ROBERTS Whatcom
POMEROY (99347) Garfield(89), Columbia(4), Asotin(3), Whitman(1)
PONDEROSA ESTATES Pierce
PORT ANGELES Clallam
PORT GAMBLE Kitsap
PORT HADLOCK Jefferson
PORT LUDLOW Jefferson
PORT ORCHARD Kitsap
PORT TOWNSEND Jefferson
POULSBO Kitsap
PRAIRIE RIDGE Pierce
PRESCOTT Walla Walla
PRESTON King
PROSSER (99350) Benton(96), Klickitat(3)
PULLMAN Whitman
PUYALLUP Pierce
QUILCENE Jefferson
QUINAULT Grays Harbor
QUINCY Grant
RAINIER Thurston
RANDLE Lewis
RAVENSDALE King
RAYMOND Pacific
REARDAN (99029) Lincoln(54), Spokane(45)
REDMOND King
REDONDO King
RENTON King
REPUBLIC (99166) Ferry(97), Okanogan(2)
RETSIL Kitsap
RICE Stevens
RICHLAND Benton
RIDGEFIELD Clark
RITZVILLE Adams
RIVERSIDE Okanogan
ROCHESTER Thurston
ROCK ISLAND Douglas
ROCKFORD Spokane
ROCKPORT Skagit
ROLLINGBAY Kitsap
RONALD Kittitas
ROOSEVELT Klickitat
ROSALIA (99170) Whitman(55), Spokane(44)
ROSBURG Wahkiakum
ROSLYN Kittitas
ROY Pierce
ROYAL CITY Grant
RYDERWOOD Cowlitz
SAINT JOHN Whitman
SALKUM Lewis
SAMMAMISH King
SATSOP Grays Harbor
SEABECK Kitsap
SEAHURST King
SEATTLE King
SEAVIEW Pacific
SEDRO WOOLLEY (98284) Skagit(95), Whatcom(4)
SEKIU Clallam
SELAH Yakima
SEQUIM (98382) Clallam(98), Jefferson(1)
SEQUIM Jefferson
SHAW ISLAND San Juan
SHELTON Mason
SILVANA Snohomish
SILVER CREEK Lewis
SILVERDALE Kitsap
SILVERLAKE Cowlitz
SKAMOKAWA Wahkiakum
SKYKOMISH King
SNOHOMISH Snohomish
SNOQUALMIE King
SNOQUALMIE PASS King
SOAP LAKE Grant
SOUTH BEND Pacific
SOUTH CLE ELUM Kittitas
SOUTH COLBY Kitsap
SOUTH PRAIRIE Pierce
SOUTHWORTH Kitsap
SPANAWAY Pierce
SPANGLE Spokane
SPOKANE Spokane
SPRAGUE Lincoln
SPRINGDALE Stevens
STANWOOD Snohomish
STARBUCK Columbia
STARTUP Snohomish
STEHEKIN Chelan
STEILACOOM Pierce
STEPTOE Whitman
STEVENSON Skamania
STRATFORD Grant
SULTAN Snohomish
SUMAS Whatcom
SUMNER Pierce
SUNNYSIDE Yakima
SUQUAMISH Kitsap
TACOMA Pierce
TAHOLAH Grays Harbor
TAHUYA Mason
TEKOA (99033) Whitman(83), Spokane(16)
TENINO Thurston
THE CRESCENT STORE Spokane
THORNTON Whitman
THORP Kittitas
TIETON Yakima
TOKELAND Pacific
TOLEDO Lewis
TONASKET Okanogan
TOPPENISH Yakima
TOUCHET Walla Walla
TOUTLE Cowlitz
TRACYTON Kitsap
TROUT LAKE Klickitat
TUMTUM Stevens
TUMWATER Thurston
TWISP Okanogan
UNDERWOOD Skamania
UNION Mason
UNIONTOWN Whitman
UNIVERSITY PLACE Pierce
USK (99180) Pend Oreille(83), Spokane(16)
VADER Lewis
VALLEY Stevens
VALLEYFORD Spokane
VANCOUVER Clark
VANTAGE Kittitas
VASHON King
VAUGHN Pierce
VERADALE Spokane
WAHKIACUS Klickitat
WAITSBURG (99361) Walla Walla(96), Columbia(3)
WALDRON San Juan
WALLA WALLA Walla Walla
WALLULA Walla Walla
WAPATO Yakima
WARDEN Grant
WASHOUGAL (98671) Clark(79), Skamania(20)
WASHTUCNA Adams
WATERVILLE Douglas
WAUCONDA Okanogan
WAUNA Pierce
WAVERLY Spokane
WELLPINIT Stevens
WENATCHEE Chelan
WEST RICHLAND Benton
WESTPORT Grays Harbor
WHITE SALMON Klickitat
WHITE SWAN Yakima
WILBUR Lincoln
WILKESON Pierce
WILSON CREEK Grant
WINLOCK Lewis
WINTHROP Okanogan
WISHRAM Klickitat
WOODINVILLE (98077) King(92), Snohomish(7)
WOODLAND (98674) Cowlitz(66), Clark(33)
YACOLT Clark
YAKIMA Yakima
YELM Thurston
ZILLAH Yakima

Washington - Zip/City Cross Reference

Zip Range	City
98001-98002	AUBURN
98003-98003	FEDERAL WAY
98004-98009	BELLEVUE
98010-98010	BLACK DIAMOND
98011-98012	BOTHELL
98013-98013	BURTON
98014-98014	CARNATION
98015-98015	BELLEVUE
98019-98019	DUVALL
98020-98020	EDMONDS
98021-98021	BOTHELL
98022-98022	ENUMCLAW
98023-98023	FEDERAL WAY
98024-98024	FALL CITY
98025-98025	HOBART
98026-98026	EDMONDS
98027-98027	ISSAQUAH
98028-98028	KENMORE
98029-98029	ISSAQUAH
98030-98032	KENT
98033-98034	KIRKLAND
98035-98035	KENT
98036-98037	LYNNWOOD
98038-98038	MAPLE VALLEY
98039-98039	MEDINA
98040-98040	MERCER ISLAND
98041-98041	BOTHELL
98042-98042	KENT
98043-98043	MOUNTLAKE TERRACE
98045-98045	NORTH BEND
98046-98046	LYNNWOOD
98047-98047	PACIFIC
98050-98050	PRESTON
98051-98051	RAVENSDALE
98052-98053	REDMOND
98054-98054	REDONDO
98055-98059	RENTON
98060-98060	SEATTLE
98061-98061	ROLLINGBAY
98062-98062	SEAHURST
98063-98063	FEDERAL WAY
98064-98064	KENT
98065-98065	SNOQUALMIE
98068-98068	SNOQUALMIE PASS
98070-98070	VASHON
98071-98071	AUBURN
98072-98072	WOODINVILLE
98073-98073	REDMOND
98074-98075	SAMMAMISH
98077-98077	WOODINVILLE
98082-98082	BOTHELL
98083-98083	KIRKLAND
98089-98089	KENT
98092-98092	AUBURN
98093-98093	FEDERAL WAY
98100-98109	SEATTLE
98110-98110	BAINBRIDGE ISLAND
98111-98199	SEATTLE
98200-98213	EVERETT
98220-98220	ACME
98221-98221	ANACORTES
98222-98222	BLAKELY ISLAND
98223-98223	ARLINGTON
98224-98224	BARING
98225-98229	BELLINGHAM
98230-98231	BLAINE
98232-98232	BOW
98233-98233	BURLINGTON
98235-98235	CLEARLAKE
98236-98236	CLINTON
98237-98237	CONCRETE
98238-98238	CONWAY
98239-98239	COUPEVILLE
98240-98240	CUSTER
98241-98241	DARRINGTON
98243-98243	DEER HARBOR
98244-98244	DEMING
98245-98245	EASTSOUND
98246-98246	BOW
98247-98247	EVERSON
98248-98248	FERNDALE
98249-98249	FREELAND
98250-98250	FRIDAY HARBOR
98251-98251	GOLD BAR
98252-98252	GRANITE FALLS
98253-98253	GREENBANK
98255-98255	HAMILTON
98256-98256	INDEX
98257-98257	LA CONNER
98258-98258	LAKE STEVENS
98259-98259	LAKEWOOD
98259-98259	NORTH LAKEWOOD
98260-98260	LANGLEY
98261-98261	LOPEZ ISLAND
98262-98262	LUMMI ISLAND
98263-98263	LYMAN
98264-98264	LYNDEN
98266-98266	MAPLE FALLS
98267-98267	MARBLEMOUNT
98270-98271	MARYSVILLE
98272-98272	MONROE
98273-98274	MOUNT VERNON
98275-98275	MUKILTEO
98276-98276	NOOKSACK
98277-98278	OAK HARBOR
98279-98279	OLGA
98280-98280	ORCAS
98281-98281	POINT ROBERTS
98282-98282	CAMANO ISLAND
98283-98283	ROCKPORT
98284-98284	SEDRO WOOLLEY
98286-98286	SHAW ISLAND
98287-98287	SILVANA
98288-98288	SKYKOMISH
98290-98291	SNOHOMISH
98292-98292	STANWOOD
98293-98293	STARTUP
98294-98294	SULTAN
98295-98295	SUMAS
98296-98296	SNOHOMISH
98297-98297	WALDRON
98303-98303	ANDERSON ISLAND
98304-98304	ASHFORD
98305-98305	BEAVER
98310-98314	BREMERTON
98315-98315	SILVERDALE
98320-98320	BRINNON
98321-98321	BUCKLEY
98322-98322	BURLEY
98323-98323	CARBONADO
98324-98324	CARLSBORG
98325-98325	CHIMACUM
98326-98326	CLALLAM BAY
98327-98327	DUPONT
98328-98328	EATONVILLE
98329-98329	GIG HARBOR
98330-98330	ELBE
98331-98331	FORKS
98332-98332	GIG HARBOR
98333-98333	FOX ISLAND
98334-98334	SEQUIM
98335-98335	GIG HARBOR
98336-98336	GLENOMA
98337-98337	BREMERTON
98338-98338	GRAHAM
98339-98339	PORT HADLOCK
98340-98340	HANSVILLE
98342-98342	INDIANOLA
98343-98343	JOYCE
98344-98344	KAPOWSIN
98345-98345	KEYPORT
98346-98346	KINGSTON
98348-98348	LA GRANDE
98349-98349	LAKEBAY
98350-98350	LA PUSH
98351-98351	LONGBRANCH
98352-98352	SUMNER
98353-98353	MANCHESTER
98354-98354	MILTON
98355-98355	MINERAL
98356-98356	MORTON
98357-98357	NEAH BAY
98358-98358	NORDLAND
98359-98359	OLALLA
98360-98360	ORTING
98361-98361	PACKWOOD
98362-98363	PORT ANGELES
98364-98364	PORT GAMBLE
98365-98365	PORT LUDLOW
98366-98367	PORT ORCHARD
98368-98368	PORT TOWNSEND
98370-98370	POULSBO
98371-98375	PUYALLUP
98376-98376	QUILCENE
98377-98377	RANDLE
98378-98378	RETSIL
98380-98380	SEABECK
98381-98381	SEKIU
98382-98382	SEQUIM
98383-98383	SILVERDALE
98384-98384	SOUTH COLBY
98385-98385	SOUTH PRAIRIE
98386-98386	SOUTHWORTH
98387-98387	SPANAWAY
98388-98388	STEILACOOM
98390-98391	SUMNER
98392-98392	SUQUAMISH
98393-98393	TRACYTON
98394-98394	VAUGHN
98395-98395	WAUNA
98396-98396	WILKESON
98397-98397	LONGMIRE
98398-98398	PARADISE INN
98401-98424	TACOMA
98430-98430	CAMP MURRAY
98431-98439	TACOMA
98439-98439	LAKEWOOD
98442-98466	TACOMA
98467-98467	UNIVERSITY PLACE
98471-98492	TACOMA
98492-98492	LAKEWOOD
98493-98497	TACOMA
98497-98497	LAKEWOOD
98498-98499	TACOMA
98499-98499	LAKEWOOD
98501-98508	OLYMPIA
98509-98509	LACEY
98511-98511	TUMWATER
98512-98516	OLYMPIA
98520-98520	ABERDEEN
98522-98522	ADNA
98524-98524	ALLYN
98526-98526	AMANDA PARK
98527-98527	BAY CENTER
98528-98528	BELFAIR
98530-98530	BUCODA
98531-98531	CENTRALIA
98532-98532	CHEHALIS
98533-98533	CINEBAR
98535-98535	COPALIS BEACH
98536-98536	COPALIS CROSSING
98537-98537	COSMOPOLIS
98538-98538	CURTIS
98539-98539	DOTY
98540-98540	EAST OLYMPIA
98541-98541	ELMA
98542-98542	ETHEL
98544-98544	GALVIN
98546-98546	GRAPEVIEW
98547-98547	GRAYLAND
98548-98548	HOODSPORT
98550-98550	HOQUIAM
98552-98552	HUMPTULIPS
98554-98554	LEBAM
98555-98555	LILLIWAUP
98556-98556	LITTLEROCK
98557-98557	MCCLEARY
98558-98558	MCKENNA
98559-98559	MALONE
98560-98560	MATLOCK
98561-98561	MENLO
98562-98562	MOCLIPS
98563-98563	MONTESANO
98564-98564	MOSSYROCK
98565-98565	NAPAVINE
98566-98566	NEILTON
98568-98568	OAKVILLE
98569-98569	OCEAN SHORES
98570-98570	ONALASKA
98571-98571	PACIFIC BEACH
98572-98572	PE ELL
98575-98575	QUINAULT
98576-98576	RAINIER
98577-98577	RAYMOND
98579-98579	ROCHESTER
98580-98580	ROY
98581-98581	RYDERWOOD
98582-98582	SALKUM
98583-98583	SATSOP
98584-98584	SHELTON
98585-98585	SILVER CREEK
98586-98586	SOUTH BEND
98587-98587	TAHOLAH
98588-98588	TAHUYA
98589-98589	TENINO
98590-98590	TOKELAND
98591-98591	TOLEDO
98592-98592	UNION
98593-98593	VADER
98595-98595	WESTPORT
98596-98596	WINLOCK
98597-98597	YELM
98599-98599	OLYMPIA
98601-98601	AMBOY
98602-98602	APPLETON
98603-98603	ARIEL
98604-98604	BATTLE GROUND
98605-98605	BINGEN
98606-98606	BRUSH PRAIRIE
98607-98607	CAMAS
98609-98609	CARROLLS
98610-98610	CARSON
98611-98611	CASTLE ROCK
98612-98612	CATHLAMET
98613-98613	CENTERVILLE
98614-98614	CHINOOK
98616-98616	COUGAR
98617-98617	DALLESPORT
98619-98619	GLENWOOD
98620-98620	GOLDENDALE
98621-98621	GRAYS RIVER
98622-98622	HEISSON
98623-98623	HUSUM
98624-98624	ILWACO
98625-98625	KALAMA
98626-98626	KELSO
98628-98628	KLICKITAT
98629-98629	LA CENTER
98631-98631	LONG BEACH
98632-98632	LONGVIEW
98635-98635	LYLE
98637-98637	NAHCOTTA
98638-98638	NASELLE
98639-98639	NORTH BONNEVILLE
98640-98640	OCEAN PARK
98641-98641	OYSTERVILLE
98642-98642	RIDGEFIELD
98643-98643	ROSBURG
98644-98644	SEAVIEW
98645-98645	SILVERLAKE
98647-98647	SKAMOKAWA
98648-98648	STEVENSON

98649-98649 TOUTLE
98650-98650 TROUT LAKE
98651-98651 UNDERWOOD
98660-98668 VANCOUVER
98670-98670 WAHKIACUS
98671-98671 WASHOUGAL
98672-98672 WHITE SALMON
98673-98673 WISHRAM
98674-98674 WOODLAND
98675-98675 YACOLT
98682-98687 VANCOUVER
98801-98801 WENATCHEE
98802-98802 EAST WENATCHEE
98807-98807 WENATCHEE
98811-98811 ARDENVOIR
98812-98812 BREWSTER
98813-98813 BRIDGEPORT
98814-98814 CARLTON
98815-98815 CASHMERE
98816-98816 CHELAN
98817-98817 CHELAN FALLS
98819-98819 CONCONULLY
98821-98821 DRYDEN
98822-98822 ENTIAT
98823-98823 EPHRATA
98824-98824 GEORGE
98826-98826 LEAVENWORTH
98827-98827 LOOMIS
98828-98828 MALAGA
98829-98829 MALOTT
98830-98830 MANSFIELD
98831-98831 MANSON
98832-98832 MARLIN
98833-98833 MAZAMA
98834-98834 METHOW
98836-98836 MONITOR
98837-98837 MOSES LAKE
98840-98840 OKANOGAN
98841-98841 OMAK
98843-98843 ORONDO
98844-98844 OROVILLE
98845-98845 PALISADES
98846-98846 PATEROS
98847-98847 PESHASTIN
98848-98848 QUINCY
98849-98849 RIVERSIDE
98850-98850 ROCK ISLAND
98851-98851 SOAP LAKE
98852-98852 STEHEKIN
98853-98853 STRATFORD
98855-98855 TONASKET
98856-98856 TWISP
98857-98857 WARDEN
98858-98858 WATERVILLE
98859-98859 WAUCONDA
98860-98860 WILSON CREEK
98862-98862 WINTHROP
98901-98909 YAKIMA
98920-98920 BROWNSTOWN
98921-98921 BUENA
98922-98922 CLE ELUM
98923-98923 COWICHE
98925-98925 EASTON
98926-98926 ELLENSBURG
98929-98929 GOOSE PRAIRIE
98930-98930 GRANDVIEW
98932-98932 GRANGER
98933-98933 HARRAH
98934-98934 KITTITAS
98935-98935 MABTON
98936-98936 MOXEE
98937-98937 NACHES
98938-98938 OUTLOOK
98939-98939 PARKER
98940-98940 RONALD
98941-98941 ROSLYN
98942-98942 SELAH
98943-98943 SOUTH CLE ELUM
98944-98944 SUNNYSIDE
98946-98946 THORP
98947-98947 TIETON
98948-98948 TOPPENISH
98950-98950 VANTAGE
98951-98951 WAPATO
98952-98952 WHITE SWAN
98953-98953 ZILLAH
99001-99001 AIRWAY HEIGHTS
99003-99003 CHATTAROY
99004-99004 CHENEY
99005-99005 COLBERT
99006-99006 DEER PARK
99008-99008 EDWALL
99009-99009 ELK
99011-99011 FAIRCHILD AIR FORCE BASE
99012-99012 FAIRFIELD
99013-99013 FORD
99014-99014 FOUR LAKES
99015-99015 FREEMAN
99016-99016 GREENACRES
99017-99017 LAMONT
99018-99018 LATAH
99019-99019 LIBERTY LAKE
99020-99020 MARSHALL
99021-99021 MEAD
99022-99022 MEDICAL LAKE
99023-99023 MICA
99025-99025 NEWMAN LAKE
99026-99026 NINE MILE FALLS
99027-99027 OTIS ORCHARDS
99028-99028 SPANGLE
99029-99029 REARDAN
99030-99030 ROCKFORD
99031-99031 SPANGLE
99032-99032 SPRAGUE
99033-99033 TEKOA
99034-99034 TUMTUM
99036-99036 VALLEYFORD
99037-99037 VERADALE
99039-99039 WAVERLY
99040-99040 WELLPINIT
99101-99101 ADDY
99102-99102 ALBION
99103-99103 ALMIRA
99104-99104 BELMONT
99105-99105 BENGE
99107-99107 BOYDS
99109-99109 CHEWELAH
99110-99110 CLAYTON
99111-99111 COLFAX
99113-99113 COLTON
99114-99114 COLVILLE
99115-99115 COULEE CITY
99116-99116 COULEE DAM
99117-99117 CRESTON
99118-99118 CURLEW
99119-99119 CUSICK
99121-99121 DANVILLE
99122-99122 DAVENPORT
99123-99123 ELECTRIC CITY
99124-99124 ELMER CITY
99125-99125 ENDICOTT
99126-99126 EVANS
99127-99127 SAINT JOHN
99128-99128 FARMINGTON
99129-99129 FRUITLAND
99130-99130 GARFIELD
99131-99131 GIFFORD
99133-99133 GRAND COULEE
99134-99134 HARRINGTON
99135-99135 HARTLINE
99136-99136 HAY
99137-99137 HUNTERS
99138-99138 INCHELIUM
99139-99139 IONE
99140-99140 KELLER
99141-99141 KETTLE FALLS
99143-99143 LACROSSE
99144-99144 LAMONA
99146-99146 LAURIER
99147-99147 LINCOLN
99148-99148 LOON LAKE
99149-99149 MALDEN
99150-99150 MALO
99151-99151 MARCUS
99152-99152 METALINE
99153-99153 METALINE FALLS
99154-99154 MOHLER
99155-99155 NESPELEM
99156-99156 NEWPORT
99157-99157 NORTHPORT
99158-99158 OAKESDALE
99159-99159 ODESSA
99160-99160 ORIENT
99161-99161 PALOUSE
99163-99165 PULLMAN
99166-99166 REPUBLIC
99167-99167 RICE
99169-99169 RITZVILLE
99170-99170 ROSALIA
99171-99171 SAINT JOHN
99173-99173 SPRINGDALE
99174-99174 STEPTOE
99176-99176 THORNTON
99179-99179 UNIONTOWN
99180-99180 USK
99181-99181 VALLEY
99185-99185 WILBUR
99200-99256 SPOKANE
99257-99257 THE CRESCENT STORE
99258-99258 SPOKANE
99259-99259 OLD NATIONAL BANK
99260-99299 SPOKANE
99301-99302 PASCO
99320-99320 BENTON CITY
99321-99321 BEVERLY
99322-99322 BICKLETON
99323-99323 BURBANK
99324-99324 COLLEGE PLACE
99326-99326 CONNELL
99327-99327 CUNNINGHAM
99328-99328 DAYTON
99329-99329 DIXIE
99330-99330 ELTOPIA
99332-99332 HATTON
99333-99333 HOOPER
99335-99335 KAHLOTUS
99336-99338 KENNEWICK
99341-99341 LIND
99343-99343 MESA
99344-99344 OTHELLO
99345-99345 PATERSON
99346-99346 PLYMOUTH
99347-99347 POMEROY
99348-99348 PRESCOTT
99349-99349 MATTAWA
99350-99350 PROSSER
99352-99352 RICHLAND
99353-99353 WEST RICHLAND
99354-99354 RICHLAND
99356-99356 ROOSEVELT
99357-99357 ROYAL CITY
99359-99359 STARBUCK
99360-99360 TOUCHET
99361-99361 WAITSBURG
99362-99362 WALLA WALLA
99363-99363 WALLULA
99371-99371 WASHTUCNA
99401-99401 ANATONE
99402-99402 ASOTIN
99403-99403 CLARKSTON

West Virginia

General Help Numbers:

Governor's Office

Office of the Governor
1900 Kanawha Blvd, East
Charleston, WV 25305-0370
www.wvgov.org

304-558-2000
Fax 304-342-7025
8AM-6PM M-TH;
8AM-5PM F

Attorney General's Office

1900 Kanawha Blvd. Rm 26E
Charleston, WV 25305-9924
www.wvago.gov/

304-558-2021
Fax 304-558-0140
8:30AM-5PM

Legislative Records

West Virginia State Legislature
State Capitol, Documents
Charleston, WV 25305
www.legis.state.wv.us

304-347-4830
Fax 304-558-1212
8:30AM-4:30PM

State Archives

Archives & History Section
1900 Kanawha Blvd E
Charleston, WV 25305-0300
www.wvculture.org/history/wvsamenu.html

304-558-0230 x168
Fax 304-558-4193
9AM-8PM M-TH, 9-6 F-SA

State Specifics:

Capital:	Charleston Kanawha County
Time Zone:	EST
Number of Counties:	55
Population:	1,814,468
Official State Website:	www.wv.gov

State Agencies

Criminal Records

State Police, Criminal Records Section, 725 Jefferson Rd, South Charleston, WV 25309; 304-746-2179 (Records), 304-746-2178 (Information), Fax- 304-746-2209; 8:30AM-4:30PM.

www.wvstatepolice.com

The state will also sell an "incident report" of a specific criminal action for $20.00, call 304-746-2178 or use Form WVSP-141 www.wvstatepolice.com/traffic/wvsp141.pdf. This is for a single incident only.

Indexing & Storage: Records available from 1938 on computer or until person reaches 80. New records available for inquiry in 3 days. 40% of all arrests in database have final dispositions recorded, 90% for those arrests within last 5 years.

Searching: All searches require fingerprints, also FBI fingerprint checks. Include in request-subject's signed release, SSN, DOB, race, sex, full fingerprints set. Use a WV Fingerprint Card and authorization. All records are returned by mail. Search can be initiated in person, results mailed. 100% of the records are fingerprint-supported. FBI checks only available if there is statutory authorization. All records are released, including those without dispositions.

Access by: mail.

Fee & Payment: Non-refundable search fee is $20.00 plus $24.00 for an FBI fingerprint check. Certain statutorily-required searches are $10.00, plus the addition FBI fingerprint check fee. Fee payee- Superintendent, WV State Police. Prepayment required. No personal checks or credit cards accepted.

Mail search: Turnaround time- 7 to 10 days.

Statewide Court Records

Administrative Office, State Supreme Court of Appeals, 1900 Kanawha Blvd, Bldg 1, Rm E 100, Charleston, WV 25305-0830; 304-558-0145, Fax-304-558-1212; 9AM-5PM.

www.state.wv.us/wvsca/

Except for certain online research capabilities, all court record access must be done at the local level.

Access by: online.

Online search: Supreme Court of Appeals Opinions/Calendar is available at the web page. 18 circuit courts have accessible records at www.swcg-inc.com/products/circuit_express.html. There is a $125 sign-up fee and several monthly fee plans are offered. Records are available from 02/1997. Search by name or case number. The case summary is shown, no identifiers are provided.

Sexual Offender Registry

State Police Headquarters, Sexual Offender Registry, 725 Jefferson Rd, South Charleston, WV 25309; 304-746-2133, Fax- 304-746-2402; 6AM-10PM.

www.wvstatepolice.com/sexoff/

West Virginia currently has over 2800 registered sex offenders.

Indexing & Storage: Records available from 1994.

Searching: This data not released- ten year registrations

Access by: mail, online.

Mail search: Requests for individual look-ups are not accepted. The agency will send quarterly mailings for a county of residence upon request.

Online search: Online searching is available from website, search by county or name, or by most wanted. Email questions to registry@wvsp.state.wv.us. Search the offender database to determine if a specific email address or username used on the internet belongs to a registered sex offender and has been reported.

Incarceration Records

West Virginia Division of Corrections, Records Room, 112 California Ave, Bldg 4, Room 300, Charleston, WV 25305; 304-558-2037, 304-558-2036 (Parole Svcs), Fax- 304-558-5934; 8AM-5PM.

www.wvdoc.com/wvdoc/

Indexing & Storage: Records available on current and former inmates. New records available for inquiry in up to 4 days.

Searching: Include in request- full name; DOB and SSN helpful. Location, conviction and sentencing information, and release dates are provided.

Access by: mail, phone, fax, online.

Mail search: Turnaround time- 2 to 4 weeks. SASE is required.

Phone search: Name searching permitted by phone.

Fax search: Same criteria as mail.

Online search: This agency offers a free search at www.wvdoc.com/wvdoc/OffenderSearch/tabid/117/Default.aspx.

Corporation, LLC, LP, LLP, Trademarks/Servicemarks

Sec. of State - Business Organizations Division, 1900 Kanawha Blvd E, State Capitol Bldg 1, Room 151 K, Charleston, WV 25305-0770; 304-558-8000, Fax- 304-558-5758; 8:30AM-5PM.

www.wvsos.com

Individuals, sole proprietorships, general partnerships and unincorporated non-profit associations register trade names by filing a certification of trade name with the County Clerk. Otherwise, trade names are found here.

Indexing & Storage: Records available for current active companies. New records available for inquiry in 24 hours.

Searching: Include in request- full name of business. In addition to the initial organizing documents, business records include: Annual Reports, Officers, Directors, Prior (merged) names, Reserved names, mergers and amendments, agents of process and capital stock allocation of corporations.

Access by: mail, phone, fax, in person, online.

Fee & Payment: Copy fee is $1.00 for the first page and $.50 each additional page. Certification is $15.00 plus $5.00 for each amendment. An Officer search is $5.00 plus $.50 per page when over 5 pages. Add $10.00 for off-site searching. Fee payee- Secretary of State. Prepayment required. Personal checks and major credit cards accepted.

Mail search: Turnaround time- 24 hours. SASE not required.

Phone search: They will confirm if a company is active, they will only do three searches per phone call. **Fax search:** Fax searching available.

In person: Simple requests may be processed while you wait.

Online search: Corporation and business types records on the Secretary of State Business Organization Information System are available free online at www.wvsos.com/wvcorporations/. Search by organization name. Certified copies may be ordered online at https://www.wvsos.com/ecomm/main.htm or via email business@wvsos.com.

Other access: Bulk sale of records is available in CD or DVD format, retrievable in CSV, Access or XML. Monthly or weekly updates are offered. Call for further details.

Uniform Commercial Code

Sec. of State - UCC Division, Bldg 1, Suite 157-K, 1900 Kanawha Blvd. East, Charleston, WV 25305-0440; 304-558-6000, 304-558-8000 (Business Services), Fax- 304-558-5758; 8:30AM-5PM. www.wvsos.com/ucc/main.htm

Email questions to ucc@wvsos.com.

Indexing & Storage: Records available from 7/1/1964. New records available for inquiry in 1 day.

Searching: Use search request form UCC-11. All tax liens are filed at the county level. Terminated filings are researched upon request. Include in request- debtor name.

Access by: mail, phone, fax, in person, online.

Fee & Payment: The fee is $5.00 per search and $.50 per copy. Fee payee- Secretary of State. Prepayment required. Pre-paid accounts are accepted, but do not send excess amount-search request may be returned. Personal checks accepted. Major credit cards accepted.

Mail search: Turnaround time- 1 day. A SASE is requested.

Phone search: They will bill for telephone searches. **Fax search:** Same fees as phone or mail searches. Turnaround time in 24 hours.

In person: Simple requests may be processed while you wait.

Online search: There is a free service to search, and the website also gives the ability to order copies. Search the database free at www.wvsos.com/UccSearch/index-noecomm.aspx to determine if a specific individual/organization has active, expired or terminated liens filed. Results give UCC number, secured party, debtor and status. Online record requesters can be invoiced via email, an account must be set-up first.

Other access: Bulk sale of records is available in CD or DVD format, retrievable in CSV, Access or XML. Monthly or weekly updates are offered. Call for further details.

Federal & State Tax Liens

Records not maintained by a state level agency.

All tax liens are filed at the county level.

Sales (Business) Tax Registrations

WV State Tax Department, Office of Business Registration, 1001 Lee St E, Charleston, WV 25301; 304-558-3333, Fax- 304-558-8754; 7:30AM-5PM. www.state.wv.us/taxdiv/

Indexing & Storage: Records available for the current year plus four years. New records available for inquiry in 4 to 6 weeks.

Searching: Will not disclose any information unless you provide a waiver form signed by the taxpayer. Without a waiver, this agency will provide only confirmation if business registered. The waiver form is available at www.state.wv.us/taxrev/forms.html. Include in request- business name. This agency will also search by tax business number.

Access by: mail, phone, fax, in person.

Mail search: Turnaround time- 2 weeks or less. A SASE is requested. No fee for mail request.

Phone search: No fee for telephone request. **Fax search:** Fax searching available.

In person: No fee for request. Records are still returned by mail.

Expedited service: Will expedite if requested.

Birth Certificates

Bureau for Public Health, Vital Records, 350 Capitol St, Rm 165, Charleston, WV 25301-3701; 304-558-2931, 304-558-9100, Fax- 304-558-1051; 8:30AM-5PM. www.wvdhhr.org/bph/oehp/hsc/

Forward questions to vitalreg@wvdhhr.org.

Indexing & Storage: Records available from 1917 to present. For older records see www.wvculture.org/vrr/. New records available for inquiry immediately.

Searching: This is a restricted record state. Records released to immediate family members only and others who can demonstrate a legal and tangible interest. Records forms are available at the webpage. Include in request- full name, names of parents, mother's maiden name, date of birth, place of birth. Online ordering is available from an approved vendor at www.vitalchek.com.

Access by: mail, phone, in person.

Fee & Payment: The fee is $10.00 per name and covers a searching range of three years. Fee payee- Vital Registration. Prepayment required. Personal checks accepted. Credit cards accepted only by the vendor vitalchek.com.

Mail search: Turnaround time- 2 to 3 weeks.

Phone search: See expedited service.

In person: Turnaround time 15 minutes.

Expedited service: Expedited service is available for fax, phone and online requests via www.vitalchek.com. To order by credit card and have returned by mail, add $10.95. For overnight shipping add $26.95. Add $5.00 to have your ordered processed within one day.

Death Records

Bureau for Public Health, Vital Records, 350 Capitol St, Rm 165, Charleston, WV 25301-3701; 304-558-2931, 304-558-9100, Fax- 302-343-2169; 8:30AM-5PM. www.wvdhhr.org/bph/oehp/hsc/

Forward questions to vitalreg@wvdhhr.org.

Indexing & Storage: Records available from 1917 to present. For older records see www.wvculture.org/vrr/. New records available for inquiry immediately.

Searching: This is a restricted record state. Records released to immediate family members only and others who can demonstrate a legal and tangible interest. Records forms are available at the webpage. Include in request- full name, date of death, place of death, names of parents, SSN. Online ordering is available from an approved vendor at www.vitalchek.com.

Access by: mail, phone, fax, in person.

Fee & Payment: The fee is $10.00 per name and covers a searching range of three years. Fee payee- Vital Registration. Prepayment required. Personal checks and major credit cards accepted.

Mail search: Turnaround time- 2 to 3 weeks.

Phone search: See expedited service.

Fax search: Access is provided by VitalChek. Use 866-870-8723 for the fax number. Use of credit card is required.

In person: Turnaround time 15 minutes.

Expedited service: Expedited service is available for fax, phone and online requests via www.vitalchek.com. To order by credit card and have returned by mail, add $10.95. For overnight shipping add $26.95. Add $5.00 to have your ordered processed within one day.

Marriage Certificates

Bureau for Public Health, Vital Records, 350 Capitol St, Rm 165, Charleston, WV 25301-3701; 304-558-2931, Fax- 304-343-2169; 8:30AM-5PM.

www.wvdhhr.org/bph/oehp/hsc/

Forward questions to vitalreg@wvdhhr.org.

Indexing & Storage: Records available from 1917 to present. For older records see www.wvculture.org/vrr/. New records available for inquiry immediately.

Searching: This is a restricted record state. Records released to immediate family members only and others who can demonstrate a legal and tangible interest. Records forms are available at the webpage. Include in request- names of husband and wife, date of marriage, place or county of marriage. Online ordering is available from an approved vendor at www.vitalchek.com.

Access by: mail, phone, fax, in person.

Fee & Payment: The fee is $10.00 per name and covers a searching range of three years. Fee payee- Vital Registration. Prepayment required. Personal checks and major credit cards accepted.

Mail search: Turnaround time- 2 to 3 weeks.

Phone search: See expedited service. **Fax search:** Available from VitalChek. Credit card required.

In person: Turnaround time 15 minutes.

Expedited service: Expedited service is available for fax, phone and online requests via www.vitalchek.com. To order by credit card and have returned by mail, add $10.95. For overnight shipping add $26.95. Add $5.00 to have your ordered processed within one day.

Divorce Records

Records not maintained by a state level agency.

Records are maintained by the Clerk of Court in the county of divorce.

Workers' Compensation Records

Access to Records is Restricted.

WV Offices of Insurance Commissioner, Consumer Service Division, PO Box 50540, Charleston, WV 25305 (Courier address- 1124 Smith St, Rm 309, Charleston, WV 25301); 304-558-3386, 888-879-9842, Fax- 304-558-4965; 8AM-4:30PM.

www.wvinsurance.gov/consumer/consumer_services.htm

Effective 1/2008, WV's privatized Workers Comp program was diversified to include several vendors, not just one. Now the Consumer Service Division of the Insurance Commission fields records requests, returning data from the state's I-com computer system. Only the subject may request their record, and must use the state's 'Authorization to Use and Disclosure of Personal Financial and Health Information Form.' You may call for a copy of this form; they will fax it to you. No information released via phone.

Driver License Information, Driver Records

Division of Motor Vehicles, 1800 Kanawha Blvd, Building 3, Rm 124, State Capitol Complex, Charleston, WV 25317; 304-558-4444, 304-558-3915, Fax- 304-558-0465; 8:30AM-5PM.

www.wvdot.com/6_motorists/dmv/6G_DMV.HTM

Use ZIP Code 25305 for courier deliveries.

Indexing & Storage: Records available for 3 years for all convictions, 10 years for suspensions and revocations. New records available for inquiry in 1 week to 3 months (DUIs immediately).

Searching: Casual requesters must have notarized consent of subject to receive records with personal information. The driver's license number and last name are required for a request; DOB and SSN are helpful. This data not released- accidents, speeding 10 mph or less over limit on interstate.

Access by: mail, in person, online.

Fee & Payment: The fee is $5.00 per record including no record found reports. If the DL is not submitted with the request, submit the SSN and/or DOB with an additional $1.00. Fee payee- Division of Motor Vehicles. Prepayment required. Personal checks and credit cards accepted.

Mail search: Turnaround time- 3 days.

In person: Up to seven requests may be received immediately at the counter of this office. Branch offices in at least 15 cities can issue an instant record for the subject-requestor.

Online search: Online access is available 24 hours a day. Batch requesters receive return transmission about 3 AM. Users must access through a private subscriber system. A contract is required and accounts must pre-pay. Fee is $5.00 per record. For more information, call 304-558-3915.

Other access: This agency will sell its DL file to commercial vendors, but records cannot be re-sold.

Vehicle, Vessel Ownership & Registration

Division of Motor Vehicles, Records Unit, 1606 Washington St East, Charleston, WV 25311; 304-558-0282, Fax- 304-558-1012; 8:30AM-5PM.

www.wvdot.com/6_motorists/dmv/6g2_registration.htm

This agency maintains records for unattached mobile homes.

Indexing & Storage: Records available from 1959 for vehicles, from 1975 for boat registrations. All motorized boats and all sailboats must be registered and titled. New records available for inquiry in 1 to 3 days.

Searching: High volume requesters must be approved after stating purpose of requests. Use of the Request for Vehicle Information Form (available from web) is required. Casual requesters cannot receive personal information without consent of subject. Include in request- name or VIN or title # or plate #. If doing search by name, it is suggested to also submit address. Boat records can be searched by hull number or WV number. Data not released- SSNs or medical information.

Access by: mail, in person.

Fee & Payment: The fee is $1.00 for registration information, $5.00 per vehicle for lien information, $5.00 per title copy, $10.00 if certified, $25.00 for a complete title history (which includes lien information), and $5.00 for message forwarding. Fee payee- Division of Motor Vehicles. Prepayment required. Do not overpay, they do not have the capacity to refund. Personal checks accepted, credit cards are not.

Mail search: Turnaround time- 3 to 5 business days. Return address must appear clearly on the request. A SASE is requested.

In person: Turnaround time is while you wait if the record is on computer, or 2 days for photocopies. Requester must show state issued photo ID.

Other access: The entire state's vehicle file can be purchased by approved entities. Costs for customized runs depend on programming time. Call 304-558-0282 for more information.

Accident Reports

Department of Public Safety, Traffic Records Section, 725 Jefferson Rd, South Charleston, WV 25309-1698; 304-746-2128, Fax- 304-746-2206; 8:30AM-5PM.

www.wvstatepolice.com

It is suggested to send a letter explaining purpose of request and state if involved in some manner.

Indexing & Storage: Records available of incidents investigated by the state police for the past 10 years. New records available for inquiry in 1 to 3 weeks.

Searching: If the State Police did not investigate the incident, the report must be obtained from the local investigating jurisdiction. Include in request- name, date of accident, location of accident. This data not released- juvenile records.

Access by: mail, phone, fax, in person.

Fee & Payment: The fee is $20.00 per record. If certified, the cost is $25.00. Fee payee- Superintendent, Division of Public Safety. Prepayment required. Personal checks accepted, credit cards are not.

Mail search: Turnaround time- 2 to 3 weeks. A SASE is requested.

Phone search: Records are available by phone.

Fax search: For an extra $5.00 per record, the agency will send data by fax.

In person: Turnaround time is same day, if record is readily available.

Legislation Records

West Virginia State Legislature, State Capitol Complex, Documents - RmMB-27, Charleston, WV 25305; 304-347-4830, 877-565-3447, Fax- 304-347-4901; 8:30AM-4:30PM.

www.state.wv.us/wvsca/

Sessions start 2nd Wed. in January.

Indexing & Storage: Records available for three sessions before extensive research is needed.

Searching: Include in request- bill number, topic of bill.

Access by: mail, phone, fax, in person, online.

Fee & Payment: There is no fee.

Mail search: Turnaround time- 2 days. There is a limit of 7 bills per mailing. Indicate if the bill is pending by House or Senate, or if bill is passed. SASE not required.

Phone search: Records are available by phone.

Fax search: Same criteria as mail searching.

In person: Simple requests may be processed while you wait.

Online search: The Internet site allows one to search for status and/or text of bills for three sessions. To view the West Virginia Code visit www.legis.state.wv.us/WVCODE/Code.cfm.

Voter Registration

Sec of State - Election Division, Bldg 1 #157-K, 1900 Kanawha Blvd E, Charleston, WV 25305; 304-558-6000, Fax- 304-558-0900; 8:30AM-5PM.

www.wvsos.com/elections/main.htm

Records are open to the public, but lists are only sold for political purposes. There is an online look-up. Direct questions to elections@wvsos.com.Voter registration cards are found at the county level.

Indexing & Storage: New records available for inquiry in seconds.

Searching: Include in request- name. The DOB is released. This data not released- phone numbers and SSNs.

Access by: mail, phone, fax, in person, online.

Fee & Payment: There is no fee for simple requests. Fee payee- WV Secretary of State

Mail search: Turnaround time- 24 hours. Records are available by mail.

Phone search: Records are available by phone.

Fax search: Records are available by fax.

In person: Over-the-counter service is available.

Online search: Search to see if someone is registered at www.wvvotes.com/voters/am-i-registered.php.

Other access: Lists are available for political purposes for approx $.015 per name. A complete statewide list is approx. $6,800 ($.005 per name plus $1,000). Turnaround time is generally 48 hours. Call for further information.

GED Certificates

WV Dept of Education, GED Office, 1900 Kanawha Blvd E, Bldg 6, Rm 250, Charleston, WV 25305-0330; 304-558-6315, Fax- 304-558-4874; 8AM-4PM.

http://wvde.state.wv.us/ged/

Indexing & Storage: Records available from 1946. New records available for inquiry in 4 weeks.

Searching: Include in request- a signed release, name, year of test, date of birth, SSN, city of test, and a copy of or presentation of a current photo ID and daytime phone number. The web page has a number of excellent links including a GED Release Form

Access by: mail, fax, in person.

Fee & Payment: There is no fee for a simple verification (pass fail with date test). Copies of transcripts are $10.00 each. Fee payee- WV DOE Vocational Division. Prepayment required. Personal checks and money orders accepted. No credit cards accepted.

Mail search: Turnaround time- 7 to 10 days. An SASE is requested.

Fax search: Only if verification is for job position.

In person: in person search requests are processed in order received along with mail requests. Depending on workload, one may have to return to pick up results.

Expedited service: The agency will expedite requests if for job verification only.

Hunting & Fishing License Information

Division of Natural Resources, Licensing Division, Capitol Complex, Bldg 3, Room 624, Charleston, WV 25305; 304-558-2758, Fax- 304-558-6208; 8:30AM-4:30PM.

www.wvweb.com/www/hunting/

Indexing & Storage: Records available for current year only. New records available for inquiry in 6 months.

Searching: All requests must be in writing. Records are considered public records. Can request through customerservice@dnr.state.wv.us. Include in request- SSN (not by name). The SSN does not print on license.

Access by: mail, fax, in person.

Fee & Payment: The search fee is $29.00, but only if a record is found. Fee payee- Natural Resources Department. Personal checks, Visa, and MasterCard accepted.

Mail search: Turnaround time- 5 to 10 working days. SASE not required.

Fax search: Fax requests accepted.

In person: Request must be in writing.

West Virginia State Licensing Agencies

For details about the agency responsible for licensing/certifying/registering an item below or in the Agency Quick Finder section, match an item's number with the number of the agency in the *Licensing Agency Information* section.

West Virginia Licenses Searchable Online

Aesthetician #3 .... www.wvdhhr.org/bph/wvbc/licensees.cfm
Architect #2 .... http://wvbrdarch.org/roster/lic/searchdb.asp
Asbestos Clearance Air Monitor #42 .... www.wvdhhr.org/rtia/allair.cfm
Asbestos Contractor #42 .... www.wvdhhr.org/rtia/allcon.cfm
Asbestos Inspector #42 .... www.wvdhhr.org/rtia/allinsp.cfm
Asbestos Laboratory #42 .... www.wvdhhr.org/rtia/licensing.asp
Asbestos Project Designer/Planner #42 .... www.wvdhhr.org/rtia/alldesign.cfm
Asbestos Supervisor #42 .... www.wvdhhr.org/rtia/allsup.cfm
Asbestos Worker #42 .... www.wvdhhr.org/rtia/allwork.cfm
Athlete Agent #36 .... www.wvsos.com/licensing/LicenseeSearch.asp
Athletic Trainer #26 .... http://wvde.state.wv.us/certification/
Attorney #14 .... www.wvbar.org/barinfo/mdirectory/
Barber #3 .... www.wvdhhr.org/bph/wvbc/licensees.cfm
Barber/Beauty Culture School #3 .... www.wvdhhr.org/bph/wvbc/licensees.cfm
Contractor, General #24 .... http://wvlabor.org/contractsearch.cfm
Cosmetologist #3 .... www.wvdhhr.org/bph/wvbc/licensees.cfm
Educational Audiologist #26 .... http://wvde.state.wv.us/certification/
Embalmer #5 .... www.wvfuneralboard.com/licenseesearch.htm
Engineer #33 .... www.wvpebd.org/professional_eng.htm
Engineer, Retired #33 .... www.wvpebd.org/retired_eng_search.htm
Engineering Authorized Co. #33 .... www.wvpebd.org/authorized_co.htm
Forester #20 .... www.wvlicensingboards.com/foresters/roster.cfm
Forestry Technician #20 .... www.wvlicensingboards.com/foresters/roster.cfm
Funeral Director; Funeral Home #5 .... www.wvfuneralboard.com/licenseesearch.htm
Insurance Agency #30 .... www.wvinsurance.gov/agency%5Fdetail/
Insurance Agent #30 .... www.wvinsurance.gov/agent%5Fdetail/
Insurance Company #30 .... www.wvinsurance.gov/company%5Fdetail/
Lobbying Employer #39 .... www.wvethicscommission.org/lobby.htm
Lobbyist #39 .... www.wvethicscommission.org/lobby.htm
Manicurist #3 .... www.wvdhhr.org/bph/wvbc/licensees.cfm
Manufactured Housing #24 .... http://wvlabor.org/mfghsgsearch.cfm
Medical Corporation #15 .... www.wvdhhr.org/wvbom/licensesearch.asp
Medical Doctor #15 .... www.wvdhhr.org/wvbom/licensesearch.asp
Medical License, Special Volunteer #15 .... www.wvdhhr.org/wvbom/licensesearch.asp
Medical Professional LLC/Company #15 .... www.wvdhhr.org/wvbom/licensesearch.asp
Milk Shipper #23 .... www.wvdhhr.org/phs/milk/records.asp
Minister License #36 .... www.wvsos.com/licensing/LicenseeSearch.asp
Notary Public #36 .... www.wvsos.com/notary/search/index.aspx
Nurse #8 .... https://www.wva.state.wv.us/wvrnboard/lookup.aspx
Nurse-LPN #8 .... https://www.wva.state.wv.us/wvrnboard/lookup.aspx
Occupation'l Therapist/Asst/Practit'n'r #16 .... http://wvbot.org/dharris/members.pdf
Optometrist #41 .... www.wvbo.org/verify-license.php
Osteopathic Physician/Phys'c'n Assist #17 .... www.wvbdosteo.org/DirectoriesComplaintForm/tabid/757/Default.aspx
Pesticide Applicat'n Business (RPAB) #25 .... www.kellysolutions.com/WV/RPAB/index.htm
Pesticide Applicator #25 .... www.kellysolutions.com/WV/Applicators/index.htm
Pesticide Applicator-Business #25 .... www.kellysolutions.com/WV/Business/index.htm
Pesticide Dealer, Restricted Use #25 .... www.kellysolutions.com/WV/Dealers/index.htm
Pesticide Registration #25 .... www.kellysolutions.com/WV/pesticideindex.htm
Pharmacist #18 .... www.state.wv.us/pharmacy/index.cfm
Physician Assistant #15 .... www.wvdhhr.org/wvbom/licensesearch.asp
Podiatrist #15 .... www.wvdhhr.org/wvbom/licensesearch.asp
Private Detective/Firms #36 .... www.wvsos.com/licensing/LicenseeSearch.asp
Public Accountant-CPA #1 .... www.wvboacc.org/Verify_A_Licensee.htm
Radiologic Technologist #9 .... www.wvrtboard.org/LICENSESEARCH/tabid/358/Default.aspx
Rafting Outfitter, Whitewater #29 .... www.wvexplorer.com/Recreation/Whitewater%20Rafting/guidesoutfitters.asp
Real Estate Appraiser (Nat'l) #34 .... www.asc.gov/content/category1/nr_intro.aspx?id=10

Real Estate Appraiser (WV list) #34 .... www.wvappraiserboard.org/roster.pdf
School Counselor #26 .... http://wvde.state.wv.us/certification/
School Nurse #26 .... http://wvde.state.wv.us/certification/
School Principal #26 .... http://wvde.state.wv.us/certification/
School Psychologist #26 .... http://wvde.state.wv.us/certification/
School Social Svcs/attend'ce Invest'r #26 .... http://wvde.state.wv.us/certification/
School Superintendent #26 .... http://wvde.state.wv.us/certification/
Security Guard #36 .... www.wvsos.com/licensing/LicenseeSearch.asp
Speech/Language Pathologist #26 .... http://wvde.state.wv.us/certification/
Supervisor of Instruction #26 .... http://wvde.state.wv.us/certification/
Teacher #26 .... http://wvde.state.wv.us/certification/status/
Veterinarian #22 .... www.wvlicensingboards.com/vetmed/licensed.cfm
Water Bottler #23 .... www.wvdhhr.org/phs/bottledwater/records2.asp
Water Brands, Bottled #23 .... www.wvdhhr.org/phs/bottledwater/records3.asp

West Virginia Licensing Quick Finder

Aesthetician #3 304-558-2924
Animal Technician #22 304-776-8032
Architect #2 304-528-5825
Asbestos Clearance Air Monitor #42 .... 304-558-6720/6768
Asbestos Contractor #42 .... 304-558-6720/6768
Asbestos Inspector #42 .... 304-558-6720/6768
Asbestos Laboratory #42 .... 304-558-6720/6768
Asbestos Project Designer/Planner #42 .... 304-558-6720/6768
Asbestos Supervisor #42 .... 304-558-6720/6768
Asbestos Worker #42 .... 304-558-6720/6768
Athlete Agent #36 304-558-6000
Athletic Trainer #26 304-558-7010
Attorney #14 304-558-7815
Barber #3 304-558-2924
Barber/Beauty Culture School #3 304-558-2924
Boat/Canoe Expedition Provider #29 304-558-2784
Boating Business, Whitewater #29 304-558-2784
Body Piercer #23 .... 304-558-6732, 558-6724
Charitable Organization #36 304-558-6000
Chiropractor #4 304-746-7839
Contractor, General #24 .... 304-558-7890 x122
Cosmetologist #3 304-558-2924
Counselor LPC, Professional #10 304-733-5494
Counselor, Professional #10 304-733-5494
Credit Service Organization #36 304-558-6000
Dental Hygienist #6 304-252-8266
Dentist #6 304-252-8266
Educational Audiologist #26 304-558-7010
Electrician #40 304-558-2191
Embalmer #5 304-558-0302
Emergency Med. Tech./Paramedic #27 304-558-3956
EMS Agency #27 304-558-3956
Engineer #33 304-558-3554
Engineer, Retired #33 304-558-3554
Engineering Authorized Co. #33 304-558-3554
First Responder #27 304-558-3956
Fishing Guide #29 304-558-2784
Forester #20 304-532-9663
Forestry Technician #20 304-532-9663
Fund Raiser, For-Profit Profess'l #37 ... 800-982-8297
Funeral Director; Funeral Home #5 304-558-0302
Hearing Aid Specialist #12 304-542-7595
Insurance Adjuster #30 304-558-0610
Insurance Agency/Agent #30 304-558-0610
Insurance Company/Producer #30 304-558-0610
Insurance Solicitor #30 304-558-0610
Investment Advisor/Represent've #38 .. 304-558-2257
Landscape Architect #13 304-727-5501
Lead Abatement Contractor #42 . 304-558-6720/6768
Lobbying Employer #39 304-558-0664
Lobbyist #39 304-558-0664
Manicurist #3 304-558-2924
Manufactured Housing #24 .... 304-558-7890 x122
Marriage Registration #36 304-558-6000
Medical Corporation #15 304-558-2921
Medical Doctor #15 304-558-2921
Medical License, Spec'l Volunteer #15 . 304-558-2921
Medical Professional LLC/Firm #15 304-558-2921
Midwife Nurse #8 304-558-3596
Milk Shipper #23 .... 304-558-6732, 558-6724
Mine Electrician #32 304-558-1425
Mine Surveyor/Foreman #32 304-558-1425
Miner #32 304-558-1425
Minister License #36 304-558-6000
Notary Public #36 304-558-6000
Nurse #8 304-558-3596
Nurse Anesthetist #8 304-558-3596
Nurse-LPN #8 304-558-3572
Nursing Home Administrator #31 304-586-4070
Occupation'l Therapist/Asst/Practit'n'r #16 304-285-3150
Optometrist #41 304-558-5901
Osteopathic Physician/Phys'c'n Assist #17 304-723-4638
Pesticide Applicat'n Biz (RPAB) #25 304-558-2209
Pesticide Applicator #25 304-558-2209
Pesticide Applicator-Business #25 304-558-2209
Pesticide Dealer, Restricted Use #25 .. 304-558-2209
Pesticide Registration #25 304-558-2209
Pharmacist #18 304-558-0558
Physical Therapist #19 304-627-2251
Physical Therapist Assistant #19 304-627-2251
Physician Assistant #15 304-558-2921
Podiatrist #15 304-558-2921
Polygraph Examiner #24 .... 304-558-7890 x122
Pool Operator #23 .... 304-558-6732, 558-6724
Private Detective/Firms #36 304-558-6000
Psychologist #11 304-558-0604
Public Accountant-CPA #1 304-558-3557
Radiologic Technologist #9 304-787-4398
Radon Contractor/Trainer #42 .... 304-558-6720/6768
Rafting Outfitter, Whitewater #29 304-558-2784
Real Estate Agent/Broker/Sales #35 ... 304-558-3555
Real Estate Appraiser (Nat'l) #34 304-558-3919
Real Estate Appraiser (WV list) #34 304-558-3919
Respiratory Care Practitioner #28 304-558-1382
Sanitarian, Registered/In-Training #23 .... 304-558-6732, 558-6724
School Counselor #26 304-558-7010
School Nurse #26 304-558-7010
School Principal #26 304-558-7010
School Psychologist #26 304-558-7010
School Social Svcs/Attendance Invest'r #26 304-558-7010
School Superintendent #26 304-558-7010
Securities Agent #38 304-558-2257
Securities Broker/Dealer #38 304-558-2257
Security Guard #36 304-558-6000
Shooting Reserve #29 304-558-2784
Shot Firer #32 304-558-1425
Social Worker #21 304-558-8816
Speech/Language Pathologist #26 304-558-7010
Supervisor of Instruction #26 304-558-7010
Surveyor, Land #7 304-765-0315
Teacher #26 304-558-7010
Telemarketer #37 304-558-0211
Veterinarian #22 304-776-8032
Water Bottler #23 .... 304-558-6732, 558-6724
Water Brands, Bottled #23 .. 304-558-6732, 558-6724

West Virginia Licensing Agency Information

#1 Board of Accountancy, 106 Capitol St, #100, Charleston, WV 25301-2610; 304-558-3557, Fax- 304-558-1325. www.wvboacc.org Search data at- www.wvboacc.org/Verify_A_Licensee.htm

#2 Board of Architects, PO Box 9125, Huntington, WV 25704-0125; 304-528-5825, Fax- 304-528-5826. http://wvbrdarch.org Search data at- http://wvbrdarch.org/roster/lic/searchdb.asp

#3 Board of Barbers & Cosmetologists, 1716 Pennsylvania Ave, #7, Charleston, WV 25302; 304-558-2924, Fax- 304-558-3450. 8AM-5PM. www.wvdhhr.org/wvbc/ Search data at- www.wvdhhr.org/bph/wvbc/licensees.cfm

#4 Board of Chiropractic Examiners, PO Box 8532 (415 1/2 D St, #6), South Charleston, WV 25303; 304-746-7839, Fax- 304-746-0794. Hours- 9AM-3PM. www.wvboc.com

#5 Board of Embalmers & Funeral Directors, 179 Summers St, #305, Charleston, WV 25301-2131; 304-558-0302, Fax- 304-558-0660. Hours- 8AM-4PM. www.wvfuneralboard.com Search data at- www.wvfuneralboard.com/licenseesearch.htm Funeral Directors Assn. member search at www.wvfda.org/members/index.php.

#6 Board of Examiners for Dentists/Dental Hygienists, PO Box 1447 (1319 Robert C Byrd Dr), Crab Orchard, WV 25827; 877-914-8266, Fax- 304-253-9454. www.wvdentalboard.org

#7 Board of Examiners for Land Surveyors, 416 Airport Rd, #1, Flatwoods, WV 26621; 304-765-0315, Fax- 304-765-0316. www.wvbps.com/

#8 Board of Examiners for Reg. Prof. Nurses, 101 Dee Dr #102, Charleston, WV 25311-1620; 304-558-3596, or 1-877-743-6877, Fax- 304-558-3666. Hours- 8AM-5PM. www.wvrnboard.com LPNs have a separate board at the same address; 304-558-3572; fax: 305-558-4367.

#9 Board of Examiners for Radiologic Technology, PO Box 638, Cool Ridge, WV 25825; 304-787-4398, Fax- 304-787-3030. Hours- 9AM-3PM. www.wvrtboard.org Search data at- www.wvrtboard.org/LICENSESEARCH/tabid/358/Default.aspx

#10 Board of Examiners in Counseling, PO Box 129, Ona, WV 25545; 800-520-3852, Fax- 304-733-4172. Hours- 9AM-5PM. www.wvbec.org Verification requests fee- $20.00 payable to WVBEC; requests processed in 3 working days. Will fax back results.

#11 Board of Examiners of Psychologists, PO Box 3955 (1205 Quarrier St), Charleston, WV 25339-3955; 304-558-3040, Fax- 304-558-0608. Hours- 8:30AM-5PM. www.wvpsychbd.org

#12 Board of Hearing-Aid Dealers, 167 11th Ave, South Charleston, WV 25303; 304-542-7595, Fax- 304-558-8337. Hours- 9AM-2PM. www.state.wv.us/

#13 Board of Landscape Architects, PO Box 1355, St Albans, WV 25177; 304-727-5501, Fax- 304-727-5580. www.wvlicensingboards.com/landscape/

#14 Board of Law Examiners, 910 Quarrier St, #212, Davidson Bldg, Charleston, WV 25301; 304-558-7815, Fax- 304-558-0831. www.state.wv.us/wvsca/Bd%20of%20Law/covercss.htm Search data at- www.wvbar.org/barinfo/mdirectory/

#15 Board of Medicine, 101 Dee Dr, #103, Charleston, WV 25311-1620; 304-558-2921 x224, Fax- 304-558-2084. 8:30AM-5PM. www.wvdhhr.org/wvbom/ Search data at- www.wvdhhr.org/wvbom/licensesearch.asp

#16 Board of Occupational Therapy, 3041 University Ave, 2nd Fl #6, Kingwood, WV 26505; 304-285-3150. Hours- 9AM-3PM. www.wvbot.org Search data at- http://wvbot.org/dharris/members.pdf

#17 Board of Osteopathy, 334 Penco Rd, Weirton, WV 26062-3813; 304-723-4638, Fax- 304-723-6723. Hours- 9AM-5PM. www.wvbdosteo.org

#18 Board of Pharmacy, 232 Capitol St, Charleston, WV 25301-2206; 304-558-0558, Fax- 304-558-0572. www.wvbop.com

#19 Board of Physical Therapy, 642 Davisson Run Rd, Clarksburg, WV 26301; 304-627-2251, Fax- 304-627-2253. www.wvbopt.com Verifications only provided with written request and $25.00 fee.

#20 Board of Registration for Foresters, Rte 1, Box 271 B, Leroy, WV 25252; 304-532-9663, Fax- 304-372-1957. 9AM-5PM. www.wvlicensingboards.com/foresters/ Search at- www.wvlicensingboards.com/foresters/roster.cfm

#21 Board of Social Work Examiners, PO Box 5459 (State Capitol Complex, Main Bldg - Rm WB9), Charleston, WV 25361; 304-558-8816, Fax- 304-558-4189. Hours- 9AM-5PM. www.wvsocialworkboard.org

#22 Board of Veterinary Medicine, 5509 Big Tyler Rd, Ste 3, Cross Lanes, WV 25313; 304-776-8032, Fax- 304-776-8256. www.wvlicensingboards.com/vetmed/

#23 Office of Environmental Health Services, Board of Registration for Sanitarians, 1 Davis Sq, Ste 200, Charleston, WV 25301-1798; 304-558-2981, Fax- 304-558-1071. 8AM-5PM. www.wvdhhr.org/phs/bors/

#24 Contractor Licensing Board, 1900 Kanawha Blvd E, Bldg 6, Rm B-749, Charleston, WV 25305; 304-558-7890 x122, Fax- 304-558-5174. www.wvlabor.org/ Search data at- http://wvlabor.org/contractsearch.cfm

#25 Department of Agriculture, Pesticide Applicator Licensing, 1900 Kanawha Blvd E State Capitol, Charleston, WV 25305-0190; 304-558-2209, Fax- 304-558-2228. Hours- 8AM-4PM. www.wvagriculture.org Search data at- www.kellysolutions.com/WV/

#26 Department of Education, 1900 Kanawha Blvd E, Charleston, WV 25305; 304-558-7010, Fax- 304-558-7843. Hours- 7AM-4PM. http://wvde.state.wv.us Search data at- http://wvde.state.wv.us/certification/

#27 Office of EMS, Bureau of Public Health, 350 Capitol St, #515, Charleston, WV 25301-3716; 304-558-3956, Fax- 304-558-3856. www.wvoems.org/

#28 Board of Respiratory Care, 106 Dee Dr, #1, Charleston, WV 25311; 304-558-1382, Fax- 304-558-1383. www.wvborc.org/

#29 Division of Natural Resources, Law Enforcement, 1900 Kanawha Blvd E, Bldg 3, Rm 837, Charleston, WV 25305; 304-558-2784, Fax- 304-558-1170. www.wvdnr.gov/lenforce/law.shtm

#30 Insurance Commissioner, PO Box 50540 (1124 Smith St), Charleston, WV 25301; 304-558-0610, Fax- 304-558-4966. www.wvinsurance.gov No longer licenses insurance brokers.

#31 Nursing Home Administrators Licensing Board, PO Box 522, Winfield, WV 25213; 304-586-4070, Fax- 304-586-4079. www.state.wv.us/wvnha/dspcontactus.cfm

#32 Office of Miners Health Safety & Training, 1615 Washington St E, Charleston, WV 25311-2126; 304-558-1425, Fax- 304-558-1282. www.wvminesafety.org

#33 Board of Registration for Professional Engineers, 300 Capitol St, Ste 910, Charleston, WV 25301-2703; 304-558-3554, Fax- 304-558-6232. www.wvpebd.org

#34 Real Estate Appraiser Licensing & Certification Board, 2110 Kanawha Blvd East, #101, Charleston, WV 25311; 304-558-3919, Fax- 304-558-3983. www.wvappraiserboard.org Search data at- www.wvappraiserboard.org/roster.pdf

#35 Real Estate Commission, 300 Capitol St, Ste 400, Charleston, WV 25301-2315; 304-558-3555, Fax- 304-558-6442. www.wvrec.org

#36 Secretary of State, 1900 Kanawha Blvd, Bldg 1, #157-K, Charleston, WV 25305-0770; 304-558-8000, Fax- 304-558-8381. Hours- 8:30AM-5PM. www.wvsos.com/licensing/main.htm

#37 Department of Tax & Revenue, Taypayer Services, Telemarketing Registration, 1900 Kanawha Blvd East; Bldg 1, Rm 300W, Charleston, WV 25305; 304-558-3356, Fax- 304-558-2324. www.state.wv.us/taxrev/tmkg.htm

#38 State Auditor's Office, State Capitol Bldg 1, Rm W110, Charleston, WV 25305; 304-558-2257, 888-368-9507, Fax- 304-558-4211. www.wvsao.gov/securities/securities.asp

#39 Ethics Commission, 210 Brooks St, #300, Charleston, WV 25301; 866-558-0664, 304-558-0664, Fax- 304-558-2169. 8:30AM-5PM. www.wvethicscommission.org Search data at- www.wvethicscommission.org/lobby.htm

#40 State Fire Marshall, 1207 Quarrier St, 2nd Fl, Charleston, WV 25301; 304-558-2191, Fax- 304-558-2537. www.wvfiremarshal.org

#41 Board of Optometry, 179 Summers St, Ste 231, Charleston, WV 25301; 304-558-5901, Fax- 304-558-5908. www.wvbo.org Search data at- www.wvbo.org/verify-license.php

#42 Office of Environmental Health Services, Radiation, Toxics and Indoor Air Division, 1 Davis Sq, Ste 200 (Capitol & Washington Sts), Charleston, WV 25301-1798; 304-558-2981, Fax- 304-558-1289. www.wvdhhr.org/rtia/ Search data at- www.wvdhhr.org/rtia/licensing.asp

West Virginia Federal Courts

The following list indicates the district and division name for each county in the state. If the bankruptcy court location is different from the district court, then the location of the bankruptcy court appears in parentheses.

SEE THE APPENDIX FOR SEARCH STANDARDS AT FEDERAL COURTS

West Virginia County/Court Cross Reference

County	District	Division
Barbour	Northern	Elkins (Wheeling)
Berkeley	Northern	Martinsburg (Wheeling)
Boone	Southern	Charleston
Braxton	Northern	Clarksburg (Wheeling)
Brooke	Northern	Wheeling
Cabell	Southern	Huntington (Charleston)
Calhoun	Northern	Clarksburg (Wheeling)
Clay	Southern	Charleston
Doddridge	Northern	Clarksburg (Wheeling)
Fayette	Southern	Beckley (Charleston)
Gilmer	Northern	Clarksburg (Wheeling)
Grant	Northern	Elkins (Wheeling)
Greenbrier	Southern	Beckley (Charleston)
Hampshire	Northern	Martinsburg (Wheeling)
Hancock	Northern	Wheeling
Hardy	Northern	Elkins (Wheeling)
Harrison	Northern	Clarksburg (Wheeling)
Jackson	Southern	Parkersburg (Charleston)
Jefferson	Northern	Martinsburg (Wheeling)
Kanawha	Southern	Charleston
Lewis	Northern	Clarksburg (Wheeling)
Lincoln	Southern	Huntington (Charleston)
Logan	Southern	Charleston
Marion	Northern	Clarksburg (Wheeling)
Marshall	Northern	Wheeling
Mason	Southern	Huntington (Charleston)
McDowell	Southern	Bluefield (Charleston)
Mercer	Southern	Bluefield (Charleston)
Mineral	Northern	Elkins (Wheeling)
Mingo	Southern	Huntington (Charleston)
Monongalia	Northern	Clarksburg (Wheeling)
Monroe	Southern	Bluefield (Charleston)
Morgan	Northern	Martinsburg (Wheeling)
Nicholas	Southern	Beckley (Charleston)
Ohio	Northern	Wheeling
Pendleton	Northern	Elkins (Wheeling)
Pleasants	Northern	Clarksburg (Wheeling)
Pocahontas	Northern	Elkins (Wheeling)
Preston	Northern	Elkins (Wheeling)
Putnam	Southern	Charleston
Raleigh	Southern	Beckley (Charleston)
Randolph	Northern	Elkins (Wheeling)
Ritchie	Northern	Clarksburg (Wheeling)
Roane	Southern	Charleston
Summers	Southern	Bluefield (Charleston)
Taylor	Northern	Clarksburg (Wheeling)
Tucker	Northern	Elkins (Wheeling)
Tyler	Northern	Clarksburg (Wheeling)
Upshur	Northern	Elkins (Wheeling)
Wayne	Southern	Huntington (Charleston)
Webster	Northern	Elkins (Wheeling)
Wetzel	Northern	Wheeling
Wirt	Southern	Parkersburg (Charleston)
Wood	Southern	Parkersburg (Charleston)
Wyoming	Southern	Beckley (Charleston)

US District Court
West Virginia Northern Dist.

Clarksburg Division Court Clerk, PO Box 2857, Clarksburg, WV 26302-2857 (In person: 500 W Pike St, Rm 301, Clarksburg, WV 26301), 304-622-8513; Fax- 304-623-4551. 8:30AM-5PM. www.wvnd.uscourts.gov **Counties:** Braxton, Calhoun, Doddridge, Gilmer, Harrison, Lewis, Marion, Monongalia, Pleasants, Ritchie, Taylor, Tyler. **Searches/Indexing:** No identifiers other than name are included in records. Results do not include SSN or DOB. Will fax back documents $.50 per page. New cases are in the index 1-2 days after filing date. Computer index maintained; civil goes back to 1994, criminal to 1995. Card index also maintained. Civil cases on computer back to 10/1994; criminal to 10/1995. Civil cases sent to archives every 5 years; every 10 years for criminal.

Search Access: Only docket info is available by phone. **Mail:** Search usually completed- 2-3 days. SASE not required. **Fax:** Fax search requests accepted, prepaid. **In person:** 1 public terminal available. No self-serve copier. **Payment:** Pay by Visa/MC/Discover, money order, cashier's check. No business or personal checks accepted. Payee: Clerk, US District Court.

E-Services: Document images available. PACER records go back to 10/1994. New records online after 1 day. ECF at https://ecf.wvnd.uscourts.gov. **Opinions:** www.wvnd.uscourts.gov/opinions.htm. Opinions go back to 1999.

Elkins Division Court Clerk, PO Box 1518, Elkins, WV 26241 (In person: 300 3rd St, 2nd Fl, Elkins), 304-636-1445; Fax- 304-636-5746. Hours-8:30AM-5PM. www.wvnd.uscourts.gov **Counties:** Barbour, Grant, Hardy, Mineral, Pendleton, Pocahontas, Preston, Randolph, Tucker, Upshur, Webster.

Searches/Indexing: No identifiers other than name are included in records. Results do not include SSN or DOB. Will fax back documents $.50 per page. New cases are in the index 1-2 days after filing date. Civil cases on computer and docket sheets back to 10/1994; criminal back to 10/1995. District-wide searches available here. Civil cases sent to archives every 5 years; every 10 years for criminal. **Search Access:** Only docket info is available by phone. **Mail:** Search usually completed- 1-2 days. SASE not required. **Fax:** Fax search requests accepted, prepaid. **In person:** 1 public terminal available. Self-serve copies $.50.

Payment: Pay by Visa/MC, money order, cashier's check. No business or personal checks accepted. Payee: Clerk, US District Court.

E-Services: PACER records go back to 10/1994. New records online immediately. ECF at https://ecf.wvnd.uscourts.gov. **Opinions Online:** www.wvnd.uscourts.gov/opinions.htm. Opinions go back to 1999.

Martinsburg Division Court Clerk, 217 W King St, Rm 207, Martinsburg, WV 25401, 304-267-8225; Fax- 304-264-0434. 8:30AM-5PM. www.wvnd.uscourts.gov **Counties:** Berkeley, Hampshire, Jefferson, Morgan.

Searches/Indexing: No identifiers other than name are included in records. Results do not include SSN or DOB. Will fax back documents $.50 per page. New cases are in the index 2 days after filing date. Computer index goes back to 1990; no card index. Civil cases sent to archives every 5 years; every 10 years for criminal.

Search Access: Limited docket info is available by phone. **Mail:** Search usually completed- 2 weeks. Include SASE for return. **Fax:** Fax search requests accepted, prepaid. **In person:** 1 public terminal available. No self-serve copier.

Payment: Pay by Visa/MC, money order, cashier's check. No business or personal checks accepted. Payee: Clerk, US District Court.

E-Services: Document images available. PACER records go back to 10/1994. New records online after 1 day. ECF at https://ecf.wvnd.uscourts.gov. **Opinions:** www.wvnd.uscourts.gov/opinions.htm. Opinions go back to 1999.

Wheeling Division Clerk of Court, PO Box 471, Wheeling, WV 26003 (In person: 1125 Chapline St, Wheeling, WV 26003), 304-232-0011; Fax- 304-233-2185. Hours-8:30AM-5PM. www.wvnd.uscourts.gov **Counties:** Brooke, Hancock, Marshall, Ohio, Wetzel.

Searches/Indexing: No identifiers other than name are included in records. Results do not include SSN or DOB. Will fax back documents $.50 per page. New cases are in the index immediately after filing date. Both computer and card indexes maintained. Civil cases on computer back to 10/1994; criminal to 10/1995. Civil cases sent to archives every 5 years; every 10 years for criminal. **Search Access:** info that is not sealed is available for release via phone. **Mail:** Search usually completed- soon as work load permits.

Include SASE for return. **Fax:** Requests accepted, prepaid. **In person:** 1 public terminal available. Copies from public terminal- $.10.

Payment: Pay by Visa/MC, money order, cashier's check. No business or personal checks accepted. Payee: Clerk, US District Court.

E-Services: Document images available. PACER records go back to 10/1994. New records online after 1 day. ECF at https://ecf.wvnd.uscourts.gov. **Opinions:** www.wvnd.uscourts.gov/opinions.htm. Opinions go back to 1999.

US Bankruptcy Court West Virginia Northern Dist.

Wheeling Division Court Clerk, PO Box 70, Wheeling, WV 26003 (In person: 12th and Chapline Sts, Wheeling), 304-233-1655. Hours- 8:30AM-5PM. www.wvnb.uscourts.gov

Counties: Barbour, Berkeley, Braxton, Brooke, Calhoun, Doddridge, Gilmer, Grant, Hampshire, Hancock, Hardy, Harrison, Jefferson, Lewis, Marion, Marshall, Mineral, Monongalia, Morgan, Ohio, Pendleton, Pleasants, Pocahontas, Preston, Randolph, Ritchie, Taylor, Tucker, Tyler, Upshur, Webster, Wetzel. Clarksburg location is 324 Main St, Clarksburg, 26302, phone- 304-623-7866.

Searches/Indexing: Include name and SSN in search request. Results include last 4 SSN digits. New cases are in the index 24 hours after filing date. Open records located at this court; search Clarksburg records here as well. Computer index goes back to 1980s, images back to 1997. Case files sent to archives 2 years after closed.

Search Access: Only docket info available by phone. Voice Case Information Service available, call VCIS at 800-809-3028 or 304-233-7318. **Mail:** Search usually completed- 1-2 days. Include SASE for return. **In person:** 2 public terminals available. Self-serve copies $.10 each.

Payment: Pay by money order, cashier's or personal check. Payee: Clerk, US Bankruptcy Ct.

E-Services: Document images available. PACER records go back to early 1990. New records online after 1 day. ECF at https://ecf.wvnb.uscourts.gov. **Opinions:** www.wvnb.uscourts.gov/opinions.htm. Court calendar free at https://ecf.wvnb.uscourts.gov/cgi-bin/PublicCalendar.pl.

US District Court West Virginia Southern Dist.

Beckley Division Court Clerk, PO Drawer 5009, Beckley, WV 25801 (In person: 110 N. Heber, #119, Beckley), 304-253-7481; Fax- 304-253-3252. 8:30AM-5PM. www.wvsd.uscourts.gov

Counties: Greenbrier, Raleigh, Sumners, Wyoming. **Searches/Indexing:** In criminal search request, SSN and DOB are helpful. Results do not include SSN or DOB. Will not fax back documents. New cases are in the index immediately after filing date. Computer and card indexes maintained. Paper case files sent to archives as deemed necessary. **Search Access:** Only docket info is available by phone. **Mail:** Search usually completed- 2-3 days. Include SASE for return. **In person:** 1 public terminal available. Self-serve copies $.50 each.

Payment: Pay by Visa/MC/Discover (in person only), money order, cashier's or personal check. Payee: Clerk, US District Court.

E-Services: Document images available. PACER records go back to 1991. New records online after 1 day. ECF at https://ecf.wvsd.uscourts.gov. **Opinions:** www.wvsd.uscourts.gov/district/opinions/. **Online Note:** Judges' calendars free at www.wvsd.uscourts.gov/judgetree/index.html.

Bluefield Division Clerk's Office, PO Box 4128, Bluefield, WV 24701 (In person: 601 Federal St, Rm 2303, Bluefield), 304-327-9798; Fax- 304-327-6668. Hours- 8:30AM-5PM. www.wvsd.uscourts.gov

Counties: McDowell, Mercer, Monroe.

Searches/Indexing: In criminal search request, SSN and DOB are helpful. Results do not include SSN or DOB. Will not fax back documents. New cases are in the index immediately after filing date. Computer and card indexes maintained. Paper case files sent to archives as deemed necessary.

Search Access: One name may be searched by phone. **Mail:** Search usually completed- 3 days. Include SASE for return. **Fax:** As a rule, fax requests are not generally accpeted, but fax search requests accepted here. **In person:** 1 public terminal available. Self-serve copies $.50 each.

Payment: Pay by money order, cashier's or personal check. No credit cards accepted. Payee: Clerk, US District Court.

E-Services: Document images available. PACER records go back to 1991. New records online after 1 day. ECF at https://ecf.wvsd.uscourts.gov. **Opinions:** www.wvsd.uscourts.gov/district/opinions/. **Online Note:** Judges' calendars free at www.wvsd.uscourts.gov/judgetree/index.html.

Charleston Division Court Clerk, PO Box 2546, Charleston, WV 25339 (In person: US Courthouse, 300 Virginia St E, #2400, Charleston), 304-347-3000. Hours-8:30AM-5PM. www.wvsd.uscourts.gov **Counties:** Boone, Clay, Fayette, Jackson, Kanawha, Lincoln, Logan, Mingo, Nicholas, Roane.

Searches/Indexing: Search request requires name only. Results do not include SSN or DOB. Will not fax back documents. New cases are in the index immediately after filing date. All Division records available here on computer. Computer and card indexes maintained. Paper case files sent to archives as deemed necessary.

Search Access: Only docket info is available by phone. **Mail:** Search usually completed- 3 days. SASE not required. **In person:** 2 public terminals available. No self-serve copier. **Payment:** Pay by credit cards, money order, cashier's or personal check. Payee: Clerk, US District Court.

E-Services: Document images available. PACER records go back to 1991. New records online after 1 day. ECF at https://ecf.wvsd.uscourts.gov. **Opinions:** www.wvsd.uscourts.gov/district/opinions/. **Online Note:** Judges' calendars free at www.wvsd.uscourts.gov/judgetree/index.html.

Huntington Division Clerk of Court, PO Box 1570, Huntington, WV 25716 (In person: Christie Federal Building, 845 Fifth Ave, Rm 101, Huntington), 304-529-5588; Fax- 304-529-5131. Hours-8:30AM-5PM. www.wvsd.uscourts.gov

Counties: Cabell, Mason, Putnam, Wayne.

Searches/Indexing: Search request requires name only. Results do not include SSN or DOB. Will not fax back documents. New cases are in the index immediately after filing date. Only computer index now maintained. Computer civil index goes back to 1994; criminal to 1994. Paper case files sent to archives as deemed necessary. **Search Access:** Only docket info is available by phone. **Mail:** Search usually completed- 1-2 days. Include SASE for return. **In person:** 1 public terminal available. No self serve copier. **Payment:** Pay by credit cards, money order, cashier's or personal check. Payee: Clerk, US District Court.

E-Services: Document images available. PACER records go back to 1991. New records online after 1 day. ECF at https://ecf.wvsd.uscourts.gov. **Opinions:** www.wvsd.uscourts.gov/district/opinions/. **Online Note:** Judges' calendars free at www.wvsd.uscourts.gov/judgetree/index.html.

Parkersburg Division Clerk of Court, 425 Julianna St, Rm 5102, Parkersburg, WV 26101, 304-420-6490; Fax- 304-420-6363. Hours- 8:30AM-N, 1-5PM. www.wvsd.uscourts.gov

Counties/Note: Wirt, Wood.

Searches/Indexing: In criminal search request, SSN and DOB are helpful. Results do not include SSN or DOB. Will not fax back documents. New cases are in the index immediately after filing date. Computer and card indexes maintained. Paper case files sent to archives as deemed necessary.

Search Access: Only docket info is available by phone. **Mail:** Search usually completed- 1-2 days. Include SASE for return. **Fax:** As a rule, fax requests are not generally accpeted, but fax search requests accepted here but maximum of 1-2 names only. **In person:** 1 public terminal available. Self-serve copies $.50 each. **Payment:** Pay by money order, cashier's or personal check. No credit cards accepted. Payee: Clerk, US District Court.

E-Services: Document images available. PACER records go back to 1991. New records online after 1 day. ECF at https://ecf.wvsd.uscourts.gov. **Opinions:** www.wvsd.uscourts.gov/district/opinions/. **Online Note:** Judges' calendars free at www.wvsd.uscourts.gov/judgetree/index.html.

US Bankruptcy Court West Virginia Southern Dist.

Charleston Division Court Clerk, 300 Virginia St E, Rm 3200, Charleston, WV 25301, 304-347-3000; records- 304-347-3003; Hours- 8:30AM-5PM. www.wvsd.uscourts.gov

Counties/Note: Boone, Cabell, Clay, Fayette, Greenbrier, Jackson, Kanawha, Lincoln, Logan, Mason, McDowell, Mercer, Mingo, Monroe, Nicholas, Putnam, Raleigh, Roane, Summers, Wayne, Wirt, Wood, Wyoming.

Searches/Indexing: Include full name in search request. Results include last 4 SSN digits. Will not fax back documents. New cases are in the index 1 day after filing date. Computer index back to 12/1/1988 is maintained. Closed electronic cases not purged. **Search Access:** Only docket info available by phone. Voice Case Information Service available, call VCIS at 304-347-5680. **Mail:** Search usually completed- 1-2 days. SASE not required. **In person:** 2 public terminals available. No self-serve copier. **Payment:** Pay by money order, cashier's or personal check. Visa/MC cards accepted only from law firms. **E-Services:** Document images available. PACER records go back to 1988. New records online after 1 day. ECF at https://ecf.wvsb.uscourts.gov. **Opinions:** www.wvsd.uscourts.gov/district/opinions/. **Online Note:** Access limited hearing dockets by date free at www.wvsd.uscourts.gov/jud getree/index.html.

West Virginia County Courts

Court	Jurisdiction	No. of Courts	How Organized
Circuit Courts*	General	55	31 Circuits
Magistrate Courts*	Limited	55	55 Counties
Family Courts	Limited	55	26 Circuits
Municipal Courts	Municipal	122	

* Profiled in this Sourcebook.

Court	CIVIL Tort	Contract	Real Estate	Min. Claim	Max. Claim	Small Claims	Estate	Eviction	Domestic Relations
Circuit Courts*	X	X	X	$300	No Max		X		X
Magistrate Courts*	X	X		$0	$5000	$5000		X	X
Family Courts									X
Municipal Courts									

Court	CRIMINAL Felony	Misdemeanor	DWI/DUI	Preliminary Hearing	Juvenile
Circuit Courts*	X				X
Magistrate Courts*		X	X	X	
Municipal Courts			X		

Administration

Administrative Office, Supreme Court of Appeals, 1900 Kanawha Blvd, Bldg 1, Rm E 100, State Capitol, Charleston, WV, 25305; (EST) 304-558-0145, Fax: 304-558-1212. All courts are Eastern Standard Time. www.state.wv.us/wvsca

Court Structure

The trial courts of general jurisdiction are the Circuit Courts which handle civil cases at law over $300 or more or in equity, felonies and misdemeanor and appeals from the Family Courts. The Magistrate Courts, which are akin to small claims courts, issue arrest and search warrants, hear misdemeanor cases, conduct preliminary examinations in felony cases, and hear civil cases with $5,000 or less in dispute. Magistrates also issue emergency protective orders in cases involving domestic violence.

The Circuit Courts hear appeals of Magistrate Court cases. Probate is handled by the Circuit Court. The highest court is the Supreme Court of Appeals of West Virginia.

Family Courts were created by constitutional amendment of January 1, 2002. Family Courts hear cases involving divorce, annulment, separate maintenance, family support, paternity, child custody, and visitation. Family Court judges also conduct final hearings in domestic violence cases. For further court details, see www.wvlrc.org/westvirginiacourtsystem2.htm.

Online Access

Supreme Court of Appeals Opinions and Calendar are available at the web page. Supreme Court of Appeals Opinions/Calendar is available at the web page. 18 circuit courts have accessible records at www.swcg-inc.com/products/circuit_express.html. There is a $125 sign-up fee and several monthly fee plans are offered. Records are available from 02/1997. Search by name or case number. The case summary is shown, no identifiers are provided.

Searching Tips, Fees, and Other Guidelines

There is a statewide requirement that search turnaround times not exceed five business days. However, most courts do far better than that limit. Release of public information is governed by WV Code Sec.29B-1-1 et seq. Find court forms at www.wvcourtnet.org/public.asp.

Barbour County

Circuit Court 8 N Main St, Philippi, WV 26416; 304-457-3454; fax: 304-457-2790; 8:30AM-4:30PM. ***Felony, Civil Actions over $5,000, Probate.*** Probate is handled by County Clerk at this address.

Civil Records: Access: Phone, fax, mail, in person. Both court and visitors may perform in person searches. No search fee. Required to search: name, years to search. Civil cases indexed by defendant, plaintiff. Civil records some on microfiche from 1843 to 1980s, on index cards back to 1862, on dockets back to 1960. Mail turnaround time 1 day. Civil PAT goes back to 2001.

Criminal Records: Access: Phone, fax, mail, in person. Both court and visitors may perform in person searches. No search fee. Required to search: name, years to search. Mail turnaround time 1 day. Criminal PAT goes back to same as civil.

General Information: No sealed, juvenile, adoptions, mental health, expunged records released. No fee to fax documents if one or two pages only. Court makes copy: $.50 per page. Certification fee: $1.00 per cert. Payee: Barbour County Circuit Clerk. Personal checks accepted; credit cards are not. Prepayment required. Mail requests: SASE requested.

Magistrate Court PO Box 541, Philippi, WV 26416; 304-457-3676; fax: 304-457-4999; 8:30AM-4:30PM. ***Misdemeanor, Civil Actions under $5,000, Eviction, Small Claims.***

All mail requests must be on letterhead.

Civil Records: Access: Mail, in person. Only the court performs in person searches; visitors may

not. Search fee: $25.00 per name. Required to search: Name, DOB, SSN, and any other personal identifiers. Records go back 10 years, computerized since 1997. Mail turnaround time varies. Civil PAT goes back to 7 years. PAT results show name only. Records may be purged from public terminal, so records are not the full index.
Criminal Records: Access: Mail, in person. Visitors must perform in person searches themselves. Search fee: $25.00 per name. Required to search: name, years to search. Records go back 10 years, computerized since 1997. Mail turnaround time varies. Criminal PAT goes back to 7 years. PAT results show name only. Records may be purged from public terminal, so not the full index.
General Information: Will fax documents $2.00 per page. Court makes copy: $.25 per page.Court will bill for copies, but no further searches until paid in full. Certification fee: $.50 per page. Payee: Barbour County Magistrate Clerk. No personal checks accepted. Major credit cards accepted. Prepayment required. Mail requests: SASE required.

Berkeley County

Circuit Court 380 W South St, #2200, Attn: Circuit Court Clerk, Martinsburg, WV 25401; 304-264-1918; probate phone: 304-264-1940; 9AM-5PM. ***Felony, Civil Actions over $5,000, Probate.***
Fiduciary Records Clerk handles probate, 100 W King St, Rm 2, Martinsburg, WV 25401.
Civil Records: Access: In person only. Visitors must perform in person searches themselves. Required to search: name, years to search. Civil cases indexed by defendant, plaintiff; index on computer from 1/1990, on index books from 1863. Civil PAT goes back to 1990.
Criminal Records: Access: In person only. Visitors must perform in person searches themselves. Required to search: name, years to search; also helpful: DOB, SSN. Criminal records computerized from 1/1990, on index books from 1800s. Criminal PAT goes back to same as civil.
General Information: No sealed, juvenile, adoptions, mental health, guardianship records released. Will fax specific case file $2.00 per page if prepaid. Court makes copy: $.50 per page. No certification fee. Payee: Clerk of Circuit Court. Business checks accepted; no personal checks. No credit cards accepted. Prepayment required.

Magistrate Court 380 W South St, Martinsburg, WV 25401; 304-264-1957; fax: 304-267-1373; 9AM-4PM. ***Misdemeanor, Civil Actions under $5,000, Eviction, Small Claims.***
Civil Records: Access: In person only. Both court and visitors may perform in person searches. Search fee: $25.00 per name if court searches. Records stored since 1997. Civil PAT goes back to 1997. PAT results show middle initial, DOB. Terminal results also show SSNs.
Criminal Records: Access: In person only. Both court and visitors may perform in person searches. Search fee: $25.00 per name if the court has to do search. Required to search: name, years to search; also helpful: address, DOB, SSN. Records stored since 1997. Criminal PAT goes back to same as civil. PAT results show middle initial, DOB. Terminal results include SSN.
General Information: Will fax documents $2.00 per page. Court makes copy: $.25 per page. Certification fee: $.50 per page. Payee: Berkeley County Magistrate Court. Personal checks and major credit cards accepted. Prepayment required.

Boone County

Circuit Court 200 State St, Madison, WV 25130; 304-369-3925; probate phone: 304-369-7337; fax: 304-369-7326; 8AM-4PM. ***Felony, Civil Actions over $5,000, Probate.***
Probate is handled by County Clerk, 200 State St, Madison, WV 25130.
Civil Records: Access: Phone, fax, mail, in person. Both court and visitors may perform in person searches. No search fee. Required to search: name, years to search. Civil cases indexed by defendant, plaintiff; index on computer from 1984 to present, on index books 1956 to present, on dockets back to 1900. Mail turnaround time 1 day. Civil PAT goes back to 1984. Only last 4 SSN numbers appear on results.
Criminal Records: Access: Phone, fax, mail, in person. Both court and visitors may perform in person searches. No search fee. Required to search: name, years to search, signed release. Criminal records computerized from 1984 to present, on index books 1956 to present, on dockets back to 1864. Mail turnaround time 1 day. Criminal PAT goes back to same as civil.
General Information: No sealed, guardianship, juvenile, adoptions, mental health, expunged records released. Fee to fax out file $5.00 each. Court makes copy: $1.00 per page. No certification fee. Payee: Circuit Clerk. Business checks accepted. No credit cards accepted. Prepayment required. Mail requests: SASE requested.

Magistrate Court 200 State St., Madison, WV 25130; 304-369-7364; fax: 304-369-1932; 8AM-4PM. ***Misdemeanor, Civil Actions under $5,000, Eviction, Small Claims.***
Civil Records: Access: In person. Both court and visitors may perform in person searches. Search fee: $25.00 per search. Civil records go back to 1977; computerized- 1997. Civil PAT goes back to 1997.
Criminal Records: Access: Mail, in person. Visitors must perform in person searches themselves. Search fee: $25.00 per name. Required to search: name, years to search; also helpful: DOB, SSN. Criminal records go back to 1977; computerized since 1997. Criminal PAT goes back to same as civil.
General Information: Will fax documents $2.00 per page. Court makes copy: $.25 per page. Self serve: same. No certification fee. No personal checks accepted. Major credit cards accepted. Prepayment required.

Braxton County

Circuit Court 300 Main St, Sutton, WV 26601; 304-765-2837; probate phone: 304-765-2833; fax: 304-765-2947; 8AM-4PM. ***Felony, Civil Actions over $5,000, Probate.***
Probate is located across the hall in the same building.
Civil Records: Access: Mail, fax, in person, email. Both court and visitors may perform in person searches. No search fee. Required to search: name, years to search. Civil cases indexed by defendant, plaintiff; index on microfiche 1806 to 1910, on dockets back to 1810; on computer back to 1993. Note: Direct email civil search requests to braxtoncircuit@rtol.net. Mail turnaround time 2-3 days. Civil PAT goes back to 1993. PAT results show name only.
Criminal Records: Access: Mail, fax, in person. Both court and visitors may perform in person searches. No search fee. Required to search: name, years to search, notarized signed release. Criminal records on microfiche 1806 to 1910, on dockets back to 1810. Mail turnaround 2-3 days. Criminal PAT goes back to 1987. PAT results show name only.
General Information: No adoption, juvenile, mental hygiene records released. Will fax documents $2.00 per page. Court makes copy: $.50 per page. No certification fee. Payee: JW Morris, Clerk. Personal checks accepted; credit cards are not. Prepayment required. Mail requests: SASE required.

Magistrate Court 307 Main St, Sutton, WV 26601; 304-765-7362; fax: 304-765-2612; 8:30AM-4PM. ***Misdemeanor, Civil Actions under $5,000, Eviction, Small Claims.***
Civil Records: Access: Mail, in person. Visitors must perform in person searches themselves. Search fee: $25.00 per name. Required to search: name, years to search. Civil cases indexed by defendant, plaintiff. Records go back 10 years; on computer back to 1998. Mail turnaround time up to 10 days. Civil PAT goes back to 1998.
Criminal Records: Access: Mail, in person. Visitors must perform in person searches themselves. Search fee: $25.00 per name. Required to search: name, years to search, DOB; also helpful: address, SSN, signed release. Records go back 10 years; on computer back to 1998. Note: Court will not perform criminal record searches and suggests researchers contact State Police, 304-746-2180. Mail turnaround time up to 10 days. Criminal PAT goes back to same as civil.
General Information: Fee to fax out file $2.00 per page. Court makes copy: $.50 per page. Self serve: same. Certification fee: included in copy fee. Payee: Braxton County Magistrate Court. Personal checks accepted. Major credit cards accepted; no debit cards. Prepayment required.

Brooke County

Circuit Court Brooke County Courthouse, PO Box 474, Wellsburg, WV 26070; 304-737-3662; probate phone: 304-737-3661; fax: 304-737-0352; 9AM-5PM. ***Felony, Civil over $5,000, Probate.***
Probate is handled by County Clerk, 632 Main St, Courthouse, Wellsburg, WV 26070.
Civil Records: Access: Mail, in person. Both court and visitors may perform in person searches. Search fee: $5.00 per name. Required to search: name; also helpful: years to search. Civil cases indexed by defendant, plaintiff; index on dockets and files from prior to 1960 to present, in boxes back to 1800s; computerized records since 1997. Mail turnaround time same day, longer if in archives.
Criminal Records: Access: Mail, in person. Both court and visitors may perform in person searches. Search fee: $5.00 per name. Required to search: name; also helpful: years to search, DOB, SSN. Criminal records on dockets and files from prior to 1960 to present, in boxes back to 1800s; computerized records since 1997. Mail turnaround time same day, longer if in archives.
General Information: No divorce, juvenile, mental hygiene, adoption records released. Will fax documents $2.00 per page. Court makes copy: $.50 per page. Self serve: same. Certification fee: $.50 per page. Payee: Brooke County Circuit Clerk. Personal checks accepted; credit cards are not. Prepayment required. Mail requests: SASE required.

Magistrate Court 744 Charles St, #4, Wellsburg, WV 26070; 304-737-1321; fax: 304-737-1509; 9AM-4PM. ***Misdemeanor, Civil Actions under $5,000, Eviction, Small Claims.***
Civil Records: Access: Mail, in person. Visitors must perform in person searches themselves. Search fee: $25.00 per name. Civil cases indexed by defendant, plaintiff. Civil records go back to 1977; computerized back to 1996. Civil PAT goes back to 1996. PAT results show name only.
Criminal Records: Access: Mail, in person. Both court and visitors may perform in person searches. Search fee: $25.00 per name. Required to search: name; also helpful: DOB, SSN, signed release. Criminal records go back to 1977; computerized back to 1996. Criminal PAT goes back to same as civil. PAT results show name only.
General Information: Will fax documents $2.00 per page. Court makes copy: $.25 per page. Certification fee: $.50 per seal. No personal checks or 3rd party checks accepted. Visa/MC accepted.

Cabell County

Circuit Court PO Box 0545, 750 Fifth Ave, Huntington, WV 25710-0545; 304-526-8622; fax: 304-526-8699; 8:30AM-4:30PM. ***Felony, Civil Actions over $5,000, Probate.***
Probate is separate office.
Civil Records: Access: Fax, mail, in person. Both court and visitors may perform in person searches. Search fee: $5.00 per name. Required to search: name, years to search. Civil cases indexed by defendant, plaintiff; index on computer from 1990 to present. On index books back to 1854. Mail turnaround time 1 day. Civil PAT goes back to 1990.
Criminal Records: Access: Fax, mail, in person. Both court and visitors may perform in person searches. Search fee: $5.00 per name. Required to search: name, years to search; also helpful: address, DOB, SSN. Criminal records computerized from 1990 to present. On index books back to 1854. Note: Requests are directed to the state Criminal Investigation Bureau. Mail turnaround time 1 day. Criminal PAT goes back to same as civil.
General Information: No sealed, juvenile, adoptions, mental health, guardianship records

released. Will fax documents $2.00 per page. Court makes copy: $.50 per page. Self serve: same. No certification fee. Payee: Clerk of Circuit Court. Business checks accepted. No credit cards accepted. Prepayment required. Mail requests: SASE required.

Magistrate Court 750 5th Ave, Basement, Rm B 113 Courthouse, Huntington, WV 25701; 304-526-8642; fax: 304-526-8646; 8:30-4:30. ***Misdemeanor, Civil Actions under $5,000, Eviction, Small Claims.***
Civil Records: Access: Main, in person. Visitors must perform in person searches themselves. Search fee: $25.00 per name. Required to search: name. Civil cases indexed by Defendant, Plaintiff. Records go back to 1997; on computer back to 1991. Mail turnaround 1-2 days. Civil PAT goes back to 1991. PAT civil results show middle initial.
Criminal Records: Access: Mail, in person. Visitors must perform in person searches themselves. Search fee: $25.00 per name. Required to search: name. Records go back to 1997; on computer back to 1991. Mail turnaround time 1-2 days. Criminal PAT goes back to same as civil. PAT criminal results show middle initial.
General Information: Will fax specific case file $2.00 per page. Court makes copy: $.25 per page. Certification fee: $.50 per page. Cert fee includes copy fee. Payee: Magistrate Court Clerk. Personal checks and Visa/MC accepted. Prepayment required.

Calhoun County

Circuit Court PO Box 266, Grantsville, WV 26147; 304-354-6910; probate phone: 304-354-6725; fax: 304-354-6910; 8:30AM-4PM. ***Felony, Civil Actions over $5,000, Probate.*** Probate is located with the County Clerk office. Probate fax- 304-354-6725
Civil Records: Access: Phone, fax, mail, in person, online. Both court and visitors may perform in person searches. No search fee. Required to search: name, years to search. Civil cases indexed by defendant, plaintiff. Civil index on docket books from 1800s. Mail turnaround time same day received. Online access is via a pay service at www.swcg-inc.com/products/circuit_express.html or call 800-795-8543. $125 set-up fee plus a $38.00 or $120 monthly fee plan.
Criminal Records: Access: Phone, fax, mail, in person, online. Both court and visitors may perform in person searches. No search fee. Required to search: name, years to search; also helpful: DOB, SSN. Criminal docket index from 1900s. Mail turnaround time same day received. Online access same as civil.
General Information: No adoption, juvenile, divorce, domestic relations, records released. Will fax documents $3.00 1st page, $.50 each add'l. Court makes copy: $.50 per page. Self serve: same. Certification fee: $1.00 per page. Payee: Circuit Clerk. Personal checks accepted; credit cards are not. Prepayment required. Mail requests: SASE helpful.

Magistrate Court PO Box 186, 363 Main St. #103, Grantsville, WV 26147; 304-354-6698; civil phone: 304-354-6844; fax: 304-354-9041; 8:30AM-N; 1-4PM. ***Misdemeanor, Civil Actions under $5,000, Eviction, Small Claims.***
Civil Records: Access: Phone, fax, mail, in person. Both court and visitors may perform in person searches. Search fee: $25.00 per name. Civil records computerized since 1997. Mail turnaround time 1 week. Civil PAT goes back to 1998.
Criminal Records: Access: In person, fax, mail, phone. Both court and visitors may perform in person searches. Search fee: $25.00 per name. Required to search: name; also helpful: years to search, DOB, SSN. Criminal records computerized since 1997. Mail turnaround time 1 week. Criminal PAT goes back to same as civil.
General Information: Will fax out documents $2.00 per page. Court makes copy: $.25 per page. Certification fee: $.50 per page. Payee: Magistrate Court. Personal checks accepted. Visa/MC accepted. Prepayment required. Mail requests: SASE helpful.

Clay County

Circuit Court PO Box 129, Clay, WV 25043; 304-587-4256; probate phone: 304-587-4269; criminal fax: 304-587-4346; civil fax: same; 8AM-4PM. ***Felony, Civil Actions over $5,000, Probate.***
Probate fax is same as main fax number.
Civil Records: Access: In person only. Both court and visitors may perform in person searches. No search fee. Required to search: name, years to search, address. Civil cases indexed by defendant, plaintiff. Civil index on docket books and index books back to 1962, computerized back to 1998. Civil PAT goes back to 1970s.
Criminal Records: Access: Phone, fax, mail, in person. Both court and visitors may perform in person searches. No search fee. Required to search: name, years to search, address, DOB, SSN. Criminal docket on books and index books back to 1962, computerized back to 1998. Note: Court will do name only searches if time allows. Mail turnaround time approx. 3 days. Criminal PAT goes back to 1980s.
General Information: No juvenile, guardianship, conservatorship or mental health records released. Fee to fax document $.50 per page. Court makes copy: $.50 per page. Self serve: same. No certification fee. Payee: Clerk of the Circuit Court. Personal checks accepted; credit cards are not. Prepayment required. Mail requests: SASE required for criminal.

Magistrate Court PO Box 393, 200 Main St, Clay, WV 25043; 304-587-2131; fax: 304-587-2727; 8AM-4:30PM. ***Misdemeanor, Civil Actions under $5,000, Eviction, Small Claims.***
Civil Records: Access: Mail, in person. Both court and visitors may perform in person searches. Search fee: $25.00 per name. Civil records go back to 1978; computerized since 2000. Mail turnaround time 5 days. Civil PAT goes back to 2000.
Criminal Records: Access: Mail, in person. Both court and visitors may perform in person searches. Search fee: $25.00 per name. Required to search: name, offense; also helpful: years to search, DOB, SSN. Criminal records go back to 1977; computerized since 2000. Mail turnaround time 5 days. Criminal PAT goes back to same as civil.
General Information: Will fax documents to local or toll-free number. Court makes copy: $.25 per page. Self serve: same. Certification fee: $.50 per page. Payee: Court. Personal checks and major credit cards accepted. Prepayment required.

Doddridge County

Circuit Court 118 E. Court St, West Union, WV 26456; 304-873-2331; fax: 304-873-2260; 8:30AM-4PM. ***Felony, Civil Actions over $5,000, Probate.***
Civil Records: Access: Phone, mail, in person, online. Both court and visitors may perform in person searches. No search fee. Required to search: name, years to search. Civil cases indexed by defendant, plaintiff. Civil index on docket books 1960 to present, archived from 1845 to 1960; computerized records go back to 1999. Mail turnaround time 1-5 days. Online access is via a pay service at www.swcg-inc.com/products/circuit_express.html or call 800-795-8543. $125 set-up fee plus a $38.00 or $120 monthly fee plan.
Criminal Records: Access: Phone, mail, fax, in person, online. Both court and visitors may perform in person searches. No search fee. Required to search: name, years to search. Criminal docket on books and files from 1845; computerized records go back to 1999. Mail turnaround time 1-5 days. Online access same as civil.
General Information: No juvenile, adoption, mental, domestic records released. Will fax documents to local or toll free number. Court makes copy: $.50 per page. Self serve: same. No certification fee. Payee: Clerk of Circuit Court. Personal checks accepted; credit cards are not. Prepayment required. Mail requests: SASE required.

Magistrate Court PO Box 207, West Union, WV 26456; 304-873-2694; fax: 304-873-2643; 8AM-4PM. ***Misdemeanor, Civil Actions under $5,000, Eviction, Small Claims.***
Civil Records: Access: In person, mail. Both court and visitors may perform in person searches. Search fee: $25.00 per name. Required to search: name, DOB, years to search; also helpful-signed release, SSN. Civil records go back to 1977; on computer back to 1999. Mail turnaround time 5 days. Civil PAT goes back to 1999.
Criminal Records: Access: In person, mail, fax. Both court and visitors may perform in person searches. Search fee: $25.00 per name. Required to search: name, years to search DOB, SSN, signed release; also helpful: offense. Criminal records go back to 1977; on computer back to 1999. Mail turnaround time 5 days. Criminal PAT goes back to same as civil.
General Information: Will fax documents. Court makes copy: $.25 per page. Self serve: same. Certification fee: $.50 per page. Payee: Magistrate Court. Checks accepted. Major credit cards accepted. Prepayment required. Mail requests: SASE requested.

Fayette County

Circuit Court 100 N Court St, Fayetteville, WV 25840; criminal phone: 304-574-4303/4250; civil phone: 304-574-4249; probate phone: 304-574-4226; fax: 304-574-4314; 8AM-4PM. ***Felony, Civil Actions over $5,000, Probate.***
Probate is handled by County Clerk, PO Box 569, Fayetteville, WV 25840.
Civil Records: Access: Mail, in person, online. Both court and visitors may perform in person searches. No search fee. Required to search: name; also helpful: years to search. Civil cases indexed by defendant, plaintiff; index on computer since 1995; prior records on file 1832 to present. Mail turnaround time 1 week. Civil PAT goes back to 1995. Online access is via a pay service at www.swcg-inc.com/products/circuit_express.html or call 800-795-8543. $125 set-up fee plus a $38.00 or $120 monthly fee plan.
Criminal Records: Access: Mail, in person, online. Both court and visitors may perform in person searches. No search fee. Required to search: name, years to search; also helpful: DOB, SSN. Criminal records on computer since 1995; prior records on file 1832 to present. Mail turnaround time 1 week. Criminal PAT goes back to same as civil. Online access same as civil.
General Information: No divorce, adoption, mental, juvenile records released. Will fax documents to local or toll-free number. Court makes copy: $.50 per page. Self serve: same. Certification fee: $5.00 per doc. Payee: Circuit Clerk of Fayette County. No personal checks or credit cards accepted. Prepayment required.

Magistrate Court 100 Church St, Fayetteville, WV 25840; 304-574-4279; criminal fax: 304-574-2458; civil fax: same; 8AM-4PM. ***Misdemeanor, Civil Actions under $5,000, Eviction, Small Claims.***
Civil Records: Access: Mail, in person. Visitors must perform in person searches themselves. Search fee: $25.00 per name. Required to search: name. Civil records on computer back to 1997, records in-house since 1977. Civil PAT goes back to 1997. PAT civil results show middle initial.
Criminal Records: Access: Mail, in person. Visitors must perform in person searches themselves. Search fee: $25.00 per name. Required to search: name, years to search. Criminal records computerized from part of 1992, records in-house since 1977. Mail turnaround time- processed same day. Criminal PAT goes back to same as civil. PAT criminal results show middle initial.
General Information: Will fax search-specific case file for $2.00 per page. Court makes copy: $.25 per page. Certification fee: $.50 per page. Payee: Magistrate Court. Personal checks and credit cards accepted. Prepayment required. Mail requests: SASE required for mail return of any copies.

Gilmer County

Circuit Court Gilmer County Courthouse, 10 Howard St, Glenville, WV 26351; 304-462-7241; probate phone: 304-462-7641; criminal fax: 304-462-7038; civil fax: same; 8AM-4PM. ***Felony, Civil Actions over $5,000, Probate.***
Probate index is separate and located in the County Clerk's office, downstairs. Probate fax is same as main fax number.
Civil Records: Access: Phone, mail, fax, in person. Both court and visitors may perform in person searches. No search fee. Required to search: name,

years to search. Civil cases indexed by defendant, plaintiff; index on dockets and files from 1845 to present; computerized back to 1999. Mail turnaround time 1 day. Civil PAT goes back to 1999.
Criminal Records: Access: Phone, mail, fax, in person. Both court and visitors may perform in person searches. No search fee. Required to search: name, years to search. Criminal records on dockets and files from 1845 to present; computerized back to 1999. Mail turnaround time 1 day. Criminal PAT goes back to same as civil. PAT results show middle initial, DOB, SSN.
General Information: No juvenile, mental, confidential records released. Fee to fax out file $1.50 per page, $3.00 minimum. Court makes copy: $.50 per page. Self serve: same. Certification fee: Copy fee includes certification. Payee: Circuit Clerk. Personal checks accepted; credit cards are not.

Magistrate Court Courthouse Annex, 201N Court St, Glenville, WV 26351; 304-462-7812; criminal fax: 304-462-8582; civil fax: same; 8AM-4PM. ***Misdemeanor, Civil Actions under $5,000, Eviction, Small Claims.***
Civil Records: Access: Mail, in person. Both court and visitors may perform in person searches. Search fee: $25.00 per search. Required to search: name, DOB, years to search, other names used; also helpful-case number, address, signed release. Civil records on computer back to 2000; other records back to 1977. Mail turnaround time 1-5 days. Civil PAT goes back to 2000. PAT results show middle initial, DOB.
Criminal Records: Access: Mail, in person. Both court and visitors may perform in person searches. Search fee: $25.00 per search. Required to search: name, years to search; also helpful: DOB, SSN. Criminal records computerized from 07/00. Mail turnaround time 1-5 days. Criminal PAT goes back to same as civil. PAT results show middle initial, DOB.
General Information: Fee to fax out file $2.00 per page. Court makes copy: $.25 per page. Certification fee: $.50 per page. Payee: Gilmer County Magistrate Court. Certified and personal checks accepted. Major credit cards accepted.

Grant County

Circuit Court 5 Highland Ave, Petersburg, WV 26847; 304-257-4545; fax: 304-257-2593; 8:30-4:30PM. ***Felony, Civil Actions over $5,000, Probate.***
www.wvcircuitexpress.com
Send fax to "Attention Circuit Court."
Civil Records: Access: Fax, mail, in person, online. Both court and visitors may perform in person searches. No search fee. Required to search: name, years to search; also helpful: address. Civil cases indexed by defendant, plaintiff. Computerized records from 1999, on books from 1983, archived back to 1866. Mail turnaround time 1-2 days. Civil PAT goes back to 1999. PAT civil results show middle initial. Terminal may be down. Online access is via a pay service at www.swcg-inc.com/products/circuit_express.html or call 800-795-8543. $125 set-up fee plus $38.00 or $120 monthly plan.
Criminal Records: Access: Fax, mail, in person, online. Both court and visitors may perform in person searches. No search fee. Required to search: name, years to search, DOB, SSN; also helpful: address. Computerized records from 1999, on books to 1988, archived back to 1866. Mail turnaround time 1-2 days. Criminal PAT goes back to same as civil. PAT results show middle initial, DOB. Terminal may be down. Online access same as civil. Online results show middle initial.
General Information: No juvenile, guardianship, adoptions, mental, domestic violence order records released. Fee to fax out file $1.50 1st page, $.75 each add'l page. Court makes copy: $.50 per page. Self serve: same. Certification fee: $1.50. Payee: Circuit Clerk. Business checks or in state personal checks accepted. No credit cards accepted. Prepayment required. Mail requests: SASE required.

Magistrate Court 4 North Main St, Petersburg, WV 26847; 304-257-1289/4637; fax: 304-257-9501; 8:30AM-4:30PM. ***Misdemeanor, Civil Actions under $5,000, Eviction, Small Claims.***
Civil Records: Access: Fax, mail, in person. Both court and visitors may perform in person searches. Search fee: $25.00 per name. Required to search: Include DOB and SSN. Records on computer back to 1994; prior records go back to 1977. Mail turnaround time 2 days. Civil PAT goes back to 1994.
Criminal Records: Access: Fax, mail, in person. Both court and visitors may perform in person searches. Search fee: $25.00 per name. Required to search: name, years to search, DOB, SSN. Records on computer back to 1994; prior back to 1977. Mail turnaround time 1-2 days. Criminal PAT goes back to same as civil.
General Information: Court makes copy: $.25 per page. Self serve: same. Cert fee: $.50 per page. Payee: Grant County Magistrate Court. Personal checks/credit cards accepted. Prepayment required.

Greenbrier County

Circuit Court PO Drawer 751, Lewisburg, WV 24901; 304-647-6626; criminal phone: 304-647-6684; fax: 304-647-6666; 8:30AM-4:30PM. ***Felony, Civil Actions over $5,000, Probate.***
Civil Records: Access: Mail, in person. Both court and visitors may perform in person searches. No search fee. Required to search: name, years to search. Civil cases indexed by defendant, plaintiff; index by general and docket books from 1800s; computerized back to1994. Mail turnaround time 1-2 days.
Criminal Records: Access: Mail, in person. Both court and visitors may perform in person searches. Required to search: name, years to search; also helpful: DOB, SSN, signed release. Criminal records indexed by general and docket books from 1800s; computerized back to1995. Note: No information given over the telephone on criminal matters except to authorized personnel. Mail turnaround time 1-2 days.
General Information: No juvenile, adoptions, mental health records released. Fee to fax out file $2.50 per page. Court makes copy: $.50 per page. Self serve: same. Certification fee: $5.00 per doc (authenticated copies). Payee: Clerk of Circuit Court. Personal checks accepted; credit cards are not. Prepayment required.

Magistrate Court 203 Green Ln, Lewisburg, WV 24901; 304-647-6632; fax: 304-647-6668; 8:30AM-4:30PM. ***Misdemeanor, Civil Actions under $5,000, Eviction, Small Claims.***
Due to public access terminal being temporarily down, court will perform all in person searches for no charge until the terminal returns to use.
Civil Records: Access: Phone, fax, mail, in person. Both court and visitors may perform in person searches. Search fee: $25.00 if court does search. Civil records on computer back 10 years, active civil indefinitely. Mail turnaround time 1-2 days. Civil PAT goes back to 1989. PAT results show name, but not all results show DOB, sometimes SSN.
Criminal Records: Access: Phone, fax, mail, in person. Visitors must perform in person searches themselves. Search fee: $25.00 if court does search. Required to search: name, years to search; also helpful: DOB, SSN. Criminal records computerized from 1989; other records back to 1977. Note: Requests for a background check must be in writing on letterhead. Contact the office for results in three days. If results are to be mailed, include postage or SASE plus the copy fee. Mail turnaround time 1-2 days. Criminal PAT goes back to same as civil. PAT results show name, but not all results show DOB, sometimes SSN.
General Information: Fee to fax out file $2.00 per page. Court makes copy: $.25 per page. Self serve: same. Certification fee: $.50. Payee: Greenbrier County Magistrate Court. Personal checks accepted. Visa/MC accepted. Prepayment required.

Hampshire County

Circuit Court PO Box 343, 66 High St, 1 E Main St, Romney, WV 26757; 304-822-5022; probate phone: 304-822-5112; fax: 304-822-8257; 9AM-4PM M-TH, 9AM-8PM Fri. ***Felony, Civil Actions over $5,000, Probate.***
Probate handled by County Clerk, PO Box 806, Romney, WV 26757.
Civil Records: Access: Fax, mail, in person. Both court and visitors may perform in person searches. No search fee. Required to search: name, years to search. Civil cases indexed by defendant, plaintiff; index on index files from 1957 to present, on index cards in storage 1885 to 1957. Mail turnaround time 2 days. Civil PAT goes back to 11/2001.
Criminal Records: Access: Fax, mail, in person. Both court and visitors may perform in person searches. Search fee: $10.00 per name. Required to search: name, years to search. Criminal records on index files from 1957 to present, on index cards in storage 1885 to 1957. Mail turnaround time 2 days. Criminal PAT goes back to same as civil.
General Information: No juvenile, divorce or adoption records released. Court makes copy: $.50 per page. No certification fee. Payee: Clerk of Circuit Court. Personal checks accepted; credit cards are not. Prepayment required. Will bill to attorneys. Mail requests: SASE required.

Magistrate Court PO Box 881, 239 W Birch Ln, Romney, WV 26757; 304-822-4311; criminal fax: 304-822-3981; civil fax: same; 8AM-4PM. ***Misdemeanor, Civil Actions under $5,000, Eviction, Small Claims.***
Civil Records: Access: Fax, mail, in person. Both court and visitors may perform in person searches. Search fee: $25.00 per name prepaid. Required to search: name; also helpful-DOB, SSN, years to search, signed release, other names used. Civil cases indexed by Defendant, Plaintiff. Civil records go back to 1977; on computer back to 1995. Mail turnaround time 15 days. Civil PAT goes back to 1995. PAT results show name only.
Criminal Records: Access: Fax, mail, in person. Both court and visitors may perform in person searches. Search fee: $25.00 per name prepaid. Required to search: name, years to search; also helpful: DOB, SSN. Criminal records go back to 1977; on computer back to 1995. Mail turnaround time 15 days. Criminal PAT goes back to same as civil. PAT results show name only.
General Information: Will fax to toll-free numbers no charge. Court makes copy: $.25 per page. Self serve: $.25 per page. Certification fee: $.50 per page. Payee: Magistrate Court Clerk. Major credit cards accepted. Prepayment required.

Hancock County

Circuit Court PO Box 428, New Cumberland, WV 26047; 304-564-3311; probate phone: x279; fax: 304-564-5014; 8:30AM-4:30PM. ***Felony, Civil Actions over $5,000, Probate.***
Probate address is PO Box 367.
Civil Records: Access: Fax, mail, in person, online. Both court and visitors may perform in person searches. Search fee: $5.00 per name. Required to search: name, years to search; also helpful: address. Civil cases indexed by defendant, plaintiff; index on computer since 1972. Mail turnaround time same day. Civil PAT goes back to 1972. Online access is via a pay service at www.swcg-inc.com/products/circuit_express.html or call 800-795-8543. $125 set-up fee plus a $38.00 or $120 monthly fee.
Criminal Records: Access: Fax, mail, in person, online. Both court and visitors may perform in person searches. Search fee: $5.00 per name. Required to search: name, years to search, signed release; also helpful: address, DOB, SSN. Criminal records on computer since 1972. Mail turnaround time same day. Criminal PAT goes back to same as civil. Online access is same as civil.
General Information: No adoption, juvenile, mental hygiene released. Fee to fax out file $2.00 per page. Court makes copy: $.50 per page. Certification fee: $1.50. Payee: Clerk of Circuit Court. Personal checks accepted; credit cards are not. Prepayment required. Mail requests: SASE required.

Magistrate Court 106 Court St, New Cumberland, WV 26047; 304-564-3355; fax: 304-564-3852; 8:30AM-4:30PM. ***Misdemeanor, Civil Actions under $5,000, Eviction, Small Claims.***
Alternative fax number is 304-564-5357.
Civil Records: Access: Mail, in person. Both court and visitors may perform in person searches. Search fee: $25.00 per name. Required to search:

Name, and years to search: records only go back 10 years. Civil cases indexed by defendant, plaintiff; index on computer since 1996, dockets available since 1977. Note: Phone, fax or mail access is limited, call ahead for turnaround time. Mail turnaround time 1-2 days. Civil PAT goes back to 1996.
Criminal Records: Access: Mail, in person. Both court and visitors may perform in person searches. No search fee. Required to search: name, years to search; also helpful: DOB, SSN. Criminal records on computer since 1996, dockets available since 1977. Note: Phone, fax and mail access limited, but available. Mail turnaround time 1-2 days. Criminal PAT goes back to same as civil.
General Information: Will fax documents $2.00 per page. Court makes copy: $.25 per page. Certification fee: $.50 per page. Personal checks accepted; credit cards are not. Prepayment required.

Hardy County

Circuit Court 204 Washington St, Rm 237, Moorefield, WV 26836; 304-530-0230; 9AM-4PM. ***Felony, Civil Actions over $5,000, Probate.***
Civil Records: Access: Mail, fax, in person. Both court and visitors may perform in person searches. No search fee. Required to search: name, years to search. Civil cases indexed by defendant, plaintiff. Civil index on docket books back to 1960 (chromo index in front of book). Computerized records go back to 1995.
Criminal Records: Access: Mail, fax, in person only. Both court and visitors may perform in person searches. No search fee. Required to search: name, years to search, DOB; SSN helpful. Criminal docket on books back to 1960 (chrono index in front of book). Computerized records go back to 1995.
General Information: No juvenile, mental, domestic records released. Will not fax out case files. Court makes copy: $.50 per page. Self serve: same. Certification fee: $1.00. Payee: Clerk of Circuit Court. Personal checks accepted. Prepayment required.

Magistrate Court 204 Washington St, Moorefield, WV 26836; 304-530-0212; fax: 304-530-0213; 9AM-4PM. ***Misdemeanor, Civil Actions under $5,000, Eviction, Small Claims.***
Civil Records: Access: Fax, mail, in person. Both court and visitors may perform in person searches. Search fee: $25.00 per name. Civil records on computer back to 1990; others back to 1977. Mail turnaround time 10 days, 5 days if records on computer. Civil PAT goes back to 1990.
Criminal Records: Access: Fax, mail, in person. Both court and visitors may perform in person searches. Search fee: $25.00 per name. Required to search: name, years to search; also helpful: DOB, SSN. Criminal records computerized from 1990; others back to 1977. Mail turnaround time 10 days, 5 if record on computer. Criminal PAT goes back to same as civil.
General Information: Will fax documents $2.00 per page. Court makes copy: $.25 per page. Self serve: same. Certification fee: $.50 per page. Payee: Hardy County Magistrate Court. Personal checks and major credit cards accepted. Prepayment required. Mail requests: SASE helpful.

Harrison County

Circuit Court 301 W. Main, Ste 301, Clarksburg, WV 26301-2967; 304-624-8640; probate phone: 304-624-8673; fax: 304-624-8710; 8:30AM-4:30PM. ***Felony, Civil Actions over $5,000, Probate.***
Probate is handled by County Clerk, 301 W Main St, Courthouse, Clarksburg, WV 26301.
Civil Records: Access: In person only. Visitors must perform in person searches themselves. Required to search: name, years to search. Civil cases indexed by defendant, plaintiff; index on computer from 1990 to present. On index books back to mid-1800s. Civil PAT goes back to 1990. PAT civil results show middle initial.
Criminal Records: Access: In person only. Visitors must perform in person searches themselves. Required to search: name, years to search; also helpful: DOB, SSN (not available for search). Criminal records computerized from 1990 to present. On index books back to mid-1800s. Criminal PAT goes back to same as civil. PAT criminal results show middle initial.
General Information: No adoption, juvenile, guardianship, mental health records released. Court makes copy: $.50 per page. No certification fee. Payee: Harrison County Circuit Clerk. Only cashiers checks and money orders accepted. No credit cards accepted. Prepayment required.

Magistrate Court 306 Washington Ave, Rm 222, Clarksburg, WV 26301; 304-624-8645; fax: 304-624-8740; 8AM-4PM. ***Misdemeanor, Civil Actions under $5,000, Eviction, Small Claims.***
Civil Records: Access: Fax, mail, in person. Both court and visitors may perform in person searches. Search fee: $25.00 per name. Civil records go back to 1980's; computerized since 9/97. Mail turnaround time 5 days. Civil PAT goes back to 1997. PAT results show name only.
Criminal Records: Access: Fax, mail, in person. Both court and visitors may perform in person searches. Search fee: $25.00 per name. Required to search: name, years to search; also helpful: DOB, SSN. Criminal records go back to 1980's; computerized since 9/97. Mail turnaround time 5 days. Criminal PAT goes back to 1997. PAT results show name only.
General Information: Court makes copy: $.25 per page. Certification fee: $.50 per page. Payee: Magistrate Court. Personal checks and major credit cards accepted. Prepayment required.

Jackson County

Circuit Court PO Box 427, 10 Court St, Ripley, WV 25271; 304-373-2214; probate phone: 304-373-2251; criminal fax: 304-372-6237; civil fax: same; 8:30AM-N, 1PM-4:30PM. ***Felony, Civil Actions over $5,000, Probate.***
Probate is a separate index; probate mailing address is PO Box 800. Probate fax- 304-373-0245
Civil Records: Access: Phone, mail, in person. Both court and visitors may perform in person searches. No search fee. Required to search: name, years to search. Civil cases indexed by defendant, plaintiff. Civil index on docket books back to 1800s. Computerized records back to 1999. Mail turnaround time 1-2 days. Civil PAT goes back to 1999. PAT results show name and some may include SSN.
Criminal Records: Access: Phone, mail, in person. Both court and visitors may perform in person searches. No search fee. Required to search: name, years to search; also helpful: DOB, SSN. Criminal records indexed in books back to 1800s. Computerized records back to 1999. Mail turnaround time 1-2 days. Criminal PAT goes back to 1999. Terminal results may include SSN. No sexual cases on public access terminals.
General Information: No juvenile, mental, adoption, domestic records released. Will fax documents $2.00 per page. Court makes copy: $.50 per page. No certification fee. Payee: Clerk of Circuit Court. Only cashiers checks and money orders accepted. No credit cards accepted. Prepayment required. Mail requests: SASE required.

Magistrate Court PO Box 368, Ripley, WV 25271; 304-373-2313; fax: 304-372-7155; 9AM-4PM. ***Misdemeanor, Civil Actions under $5,000, Eviction, Small Claims, Traffic.***
Civil Records: Access: Mail, in person. Visitors must perform in person searches themselves. Search fee: $25.00 per name. Records computerized since 1998, on dockets since 1977. Mail turnaround time 1-3 days. Civil PAT goes back to 1998.
Criminal Records: Access: Mail, in person. Visitors must perform in person searches themselves. Search fee: $25.00 per name. Required to search: name, years to search; also helpful: DOB, SSN. Records computerized since 1998, on dockets since 1977. Mail turnaround time 1-3 days. Criminal PAT goes back to same as civil.
General Information: Will fax documents to local or toll-free number. Court makes copy: $.25 per page. Self serve: same. Certification fee: $.50 per page. Payee: Jackson County Magistrate Court. Personal checks and major credit cards accepted. Prepayment required.

Jefferson County

Circuit Court PO Box 1234, Charles Town, WV 25414; 304-728-3231; fax: 304-728-3398; 8:30AM-5PM. ***Felony, Civil Actions over $5,000.*** www.jeffersoncounty.org/
Civil Records: Access: In person only. Visitors must perform in person searches themselves. Required to search: name, years to search. Civil cases indexed by defendant, plaintiff; index on computer back to 1940s; index books 1960 to 1985. 1960-1800s in storage. Civil PAT goes back to 1940s. PAT results show name only.
Criminal Records: Access: In person only. Visitors must perform in person searches themselves. Required to search: name, years to search. Criminal records computerized from 1940s; index books 1960 to 1985. 1960-1800s in storage. Criminal PAT goes back to 1940s. PAT results show name only.
General Information: No juvenile, guardianship, adoption, or mental health records released. Will fax specific case file to local or toll-free number. Court makes copy: $.50 per page. Self serve: same. Certification fee: $.50 per page; triple seal $3.00. Payee: Circuit Clerk. No personal checks or credit cards accepted. Prepayment required.

Magistrate Court PO Box 607, 110 N George St, Charles Town, WV 25414; 304-728-3233; fax: 304-728-3235; 7:30AM-4:30PM. ***Misdemeanor, Civil Actions under $5,000, Eviction, Small Claims.***
Civil Records: Access: Fax, mail, in person. Both court and visitors may perform in person searches. Search fee: $25.00 per name. Civil records on computer back to 1996; others go back to 1977. Civil PAT goes back to 1996. PAT results show name only.
Criminal Records: Access: Fax, mail, in person. Both court and visitors may perform in person searches. Search fee: $25.00 per name. Required to search: name, years to search, DOB; also helpful: SSN, signed release. Criminal records computerized from 1996; others go back to 1977. Mail turnaround time is 5 days. Criminal PAT goes back to same as civil. PAT results show name only.
General Information: Will not fax documents. Court makes copy: $.25 per page. Self serve: same. Certification fee: $.50 per page. Payee: Magistrate Clerk. Personal checks and major credit cards accepted. Prepayment required.

Kanawha County

Circuit Court PO Box 2351, 111 Court St, Charleston, WV 25328; 304-357-0440; probate phone: 304-357-0130; fax: 304-357-0473; 8AM-5PM. ***Felony, Civil Actions over $5,000, Probate.***
Probate is handled by County Clerk, 409 Virginia St E, Charleston, WV 25301.
Civil Records: Access: In person, online. Visitors must perform in person searches themselves. Required to search: name, years to search; also helpful: address. Civil cases indexed by defendant, plaintiff; index on computer from 7/1989 to present. On microfiche back to 1800s. Civil PAT goes back to 1989. Online access is via a pay service at www.swcg-inc.com/products/circuit_express.html or call 800-795-8543. $125 set-up fee plus a $38.00 or $120 monthly fee plan.
Criminal Records: Access: In person, online. Visitors must perform in person searches themselves. Required to search: name, years to search; also helpful: address, DOB, SSN. Criminal records computerized from 7/1989 to present. On microfiche back to 1800s. Criminal PAT goes back to same as civil. PAT criminal results show middle initial. Online access is same as civil.
General Information: No juvenile, neglect, adoption, domestic, guardianship, mental health or conservatorship records released. Will fax documents for $2.00 per page. Court makes copy: $.50 per page. Certification fee: $.50 per page. Payee: Kanawha Circuit Clerk. Business checks accepted. Visa/MC accepted. Prepayment required.

Magistrate Court 111 Court St, Charleston, WV 25333; 304-357-0400; fax: 304-357-0205; 8:30AM-5PM. ***Misdemeanor, Civil Actions under $5,000, Eviction, Small Claims.***

www.state.wv.us/wvsca
Civil Records: Access: Mail, in person. Both court and visitors may perform in person searches. No search fee. Civil records go back to 1982; computerized records since 1996. Mail turnaround time 14 days. Civil PAT goes back to 1989.
Criminal Records: Access: Fax, mail, in person. Both court and visitors may perform in person searches. Search fee: $25.00 per search. Required to search: name, years to search; also helpful: DOB, SSN. Criminal records go back to 1982; computerized records since 1991. Mail turnaround time 14 days. Criminal PAT goes back to same as civil. PAT results show middle initial, DOB. Terminal results include SSN.
General Information: Will fax documents to local or toll free line. Court makes copy: $.25 per page. Certification fee: $.50 per page. Payee: Kanawha Magistrate Court. Personal checks and major credit cards accepted. Prepayment required. Mail requests: SASE required.

Lewis County

Circuit Court PO Box 69, Weston, WV 26452; 304-269-8210; probate phone: 304-269-8215; Crim and civil fax: 304-269-8249; 8:30AM-4:30PM. ***Felony, Civil over $5,000, Probate***
Probate fax- 304-269-8202
Civil Records: Access: Phone, fax, mail, in person. Only the court performs in person searches; visitors may not. No search fee. Required to search: name, years to search. Civil cases indexed by defendant, plaintiff. Civil index on docket books 1977 to 1992; on computer back to 1984. No index for chancery books back to 1800s. Mail turnaround time 2 days.
Criminal Records: Access: Phone, fax, mail, in person. Only the court performs in person searches; visitors may not. No search fee. Required to search: name, years to search; also helpful: SSN. Criminal records indexed in books 1977 to 1992; on computer back to 1984. No index for chancery books back to 1800s. Mail turnaround time 2 days.
General Information: No adoption, juvenile, domestic records released. Fee to fax out file $2.00 per page. Court makes copy: $.50 per page. Certification fee: $1.00 per case. Payee: Clerk of Circuit Court. Business checks accepted. No credit cards accepted. Prepayment required.

Magistrate Court 111 Court St, PO Box 260, Weston, WV 26452; 304-269-8230; criminal fax: 304-269-8239; civil fax: same; 8:30AM-N, 1-4:30PM. ***Misdemeanor, Civil Actions under $5,000, Eviction, Small Claims.***
Civil Records: Access: In person, mail, fax. Both court and visitors may perform in person searches. No search fee. Required to search: name, DOB, SSN, years to search. Civil records computerized since 1991, indexed since 1977. Mail turnaround time 5 days. Civil PAT goes back to 1997. PAT civil results show middle initial.
Criminal Records: Access: In person, mail, fax. Both court and visitors may perform in person searches. Search fee: $25.00 per name. Required to search: name, years to search; also helpful: DOB, SSN. Criminal records computerized since 1992. Mail turnaround time 5 days. Criminal PAT goes back to 1992. PAT criminal results show middle initial.
General Information: Will fax documents $2.00 per sheet. Court makes copy: $.25 per page. Self serve: same. Certification fee: $.50 per page. Payee: Lewis County Magistrate Court. Personal checks and major credit cards accepted. Prepayment required. Mail requests: SASE required.

Lincoln County

Circuit Court PO Box 338, 8000 Court Av, #205, Hamlin, WV 25523; 304-824-7887 x239; probate phone: x233; fax: 304-824-2011; 9AM-4:30PM. ***Felony, Civil Actions over $5,000, Probate.***
Probate mailing address is PO Box 497; direct records requests to the county clerk at x233.
Civil Records: Access: In person only. Both court and visitors may perform in person searches. No search fee. Required to search: name, years to search. Civil cases indexed by defendant, plaintiff. Civil records computerized since 1991, on index books 1971 to present, on docket books back to 1909.
Criminal Records: Access: In person only. Only the court performs in person searches; visitors may not. No search fee. Required to search: name, years to search, DOB, SSN; also helpful: address. Criminal records computerized since 1998, on index books 1971 to present, on docket books back to 1909.
General Information: No juvenile, adoption, divorce or mental hygiene records released. Will fax back documents for $5.00 per fax. Court makes copy: $1.00 1st page, $.50 each add'l. No certification fee. No credit cards accepted. Prepayment required.

Magistrate Court PO Box 573, 8000 Court Ave, Hamlin, WV 25523; 304-824-5001 x235; fax: 304-824-5280; 9AM-4PM. ***Misdemeanor, Civil Actions under $5,000, Eviction, Small Claims.***
Searches performed by court only on second and fourth Thursday of each month.
Civil Records: Access: Mail, in person. Both court and visitors may perform in person searches. Search fee: $25.00 per name. Required to search: name, DOB, SSN. Mail turnaround time 1-14 days. Civil PAT goes back to 1998.
Criminal Records: Access: Mail, in person. Both court and visitors may perform in person searches. Search fee: $25.00 per name. Required to search: name, years to search; also helpful: DOB, SSN. Mail turnaround time 1-14 days. Criminal PAT goes back to same as civil.
General Information: Will fax out documents $2.00 per page. Court makes copy: $.50 per page criminal; civil- $.25 per page. Self serve: same. Payee: Magistrate Court. Personal checks accepted. Prepayment required. Mail requests: SASE requested.

Logan County

Circuit Court Logan County Courthouse, Rm 311, Logan, WV 25601; 304-792-8550; criminal phone: 304-792-8562/3; fax: 304-792-8555; 8:30AM-4:30PM. ***Felony, Civil Actions over $5,000, Probate.***
Fax to criminal records is 304-792-8589
Civil Records: Access: In person, online. Visitors must perform in person searches themselves. Required to search: name, years to search. Civil cases indexed by defendant, plaintiff. Civil index on docket books back to 1800s, on computer from 1995. Online access is via a pay service at www.swcg-inc.com/products/circuit_express.html or call 800-795-8543. $125 set-up fee plus a $38.00 or $120 monthly fee plan.
Criminal Records: Access: Mail, fax, in person, online. Only the court performs in person searches; visitors may not. Search fee: $10.00 per name. Required to search: name, years to search, SSN. Criminal records indexed in books back to 1800s, on computer from 1995. Mail turnaround time 1-2 days. Online access same as civil.
General Information: No adoption, juvenile, domestic records released. Fee to fax out file $1.00 per page. Court makes copy: $.50 per page. Certification fee: $1.50 plus $.50 per page after first 2. Payee: Clerk of Circuit Court. Only cashiers checks and money orders accepted. No credit cards accepted. Prepayment required. Will bill to attorneys.

Logan Magistrate Court Logan County Courthouse, 300 Stratton St, Logan, WV 25601; 304-792-8651; fax: 304-752-7090; 8:30AM-N; 1-4:30PM. ***Misdemeanor, Civil Actions under $5,000, Eviction, Small Claims.***
Civil Records: Access: Mail, in person. Both court and visitors may perform in person searches. Search fee: $25.00 per name. Records are computerized since 1992. Mail turnaround time 5 days. Civil PAT goes back to 1998. PAT results show middle initial, DOB, SSN. Terminal results may also include SSN.
Criminal Records: Access: Mail, in person. Both court and visitors may perform in person searches. Search fee: $25.00 per name. Required to search: name, years to search; also helpful: address, DOB, SSN. Records go back to 1992. Mail turnaround time 5 days. Criminal PAT available.PAT results show name, DOB. Terminal results may also include SSN.
General Information: Will fax back doc $2.00 per page. Court makes copy: $.25 per page. Certification fee: $1.00 per page. Payee: Logan Magistrate Court. Personal checks accepted. Visa/MC accepted. Prepayment required. Prepayment required for copies. Mail requests: SASE requested.

Marion County

Circuit Court PO Box 1269, 217 Adams St, Fairmont, WV 26554; 304-367-5360; fax: 304-367-5374; 8:30AM-4:30PM. ***Felony, Civil over $3,000.***
Civil Records: Access: Phone, fax, mail, in person. Both court and visitors may perform in person searches. No search fee. Required to search: name, years to search. Civil cases indexed by defendant, plaintiff; index on computer from 1/1988 to present. On docket books from 1849 to 1988. Mail turnaround time 2-3 days. Civil PAT goes back to 1988. PAT civil results show middle initial.
Criminal Records: Access: In person, mail, fax. Visitors must perform in person searches themselves. No search fee. Required to search: name, years to search; also helpful: DOB, SSN. Criminal records computerized from 1/1988 to present. On docket books from 1849 to 1988. Note: The court refers all written requests to the Dept of Public Safety. Mail turnaround time 2-3 days. Criminal PAT goes back to same as civil. PAT criminal results show middle initial.
General Information: No adoption, juvenile, mental or guardianship records released. Will fax back documents. Court makes copy: $.50 per page. Certification fee: $.50 per page. Payee: Clerk of Circuit Court. Business checks accepted. No credit cards accepted. Prepayment required. Mail requests: SASE requested.

Magistrate Court 200 Jackson St, Fairmont, WV 26554; 304-367-5330; fax: 304-367-5336; 8:30AM-4:30PM M-T-W-F; 8:30AM-7PM TH. ***Misdemeanor, Civil Actions under $5,000, Eviction, Small Claims.*** No record checks performed between 11:30AM and 1:30PM.
Civil Records: Access: Mail, in person. Both court and visitors may perform in person searches. Search fee: $25.00 per name. Civil cases indexed by defendant, plaintiff. Civil records go back to 1977; computerized since 1996. Mail turnaround time 5-15 days. Civil PAT goes back to 1996. PAT civil results show middle initial.
Criminal Records: Access: Mail, in person. Both court and visitors may perform in person searches. Search fee: $25.00 per name. Required to search: name, years to search; also helpful: DOB, SSN. Criminal records go back to 1977; computerized since 1996. Mail turnaround time 5-15 days; ASAP for phone requests, as time permits. Criminal PAT goes back to same as civil. PAT criminal results show middle initial.
General Information: Will not fax documents. Court makes copy: $.25 per page. Self serve: same. Certification fee: $.50 per page. Payee: Marion County Magistrate Clerk. Personal checks and credit cards accepted. Prepayment required. Mail requests: SASE required.

Marshall County

Circuit Court Marshall County Courthouse, 7th St, Moundsville, WV 26041; 304-845-2130; fax: 304-845-3948; 8:30AM-4:30PM M-TH; 8:30AM-5:30PM F. ***Felony, Civil over $5,000.***
Civil Records: Access: Fax, mail, in person, online. Both court and visitors may perform in person searches. No search fee. Required to search: name, years to search. Civil cases indexed by defendant, plaintiff; index on computer since 1/98; prior records on index books and in files from 1836 to present. Mail turnaround time 1-2 days. Online access is via a pay service at www.swcg-inc.com/products/circuit_express.html or call 800-795-8543. $125 set-up fee plus a $38.00 or $120 monthly fee plan.
Criminal Records: Access: Fax, mail, in person, online. Both court and visitors may perform in person searches. No search fee. Required to search: name, years to search; also helpful: DOB, SSN. Criminal records on computer since 1/98; prior records on index books and in files from 1836 to

present. Mail turnaround time 1-2 days. Online access same as described in civil.
General Information: No juvenile, mental, adoption, sealed, conservatorship, guardianship or divorce records released. Fee to fax out file $2.00 per page. Court makes copy: $.50 per page. Self serve: $.25 per page. Certification fee: $1.00. Payee: Clerk of Circuit Court. Personal checks accepted; credit cards are not. Prepayment required. Will bill to attorneys.

Mason County

Circuit Court Mason County Courthouse, Point Pleasant, WV 25550; 304-675-4400; fax: 304-675-7419; 8:30AM-4:30PM. ***Felony, Civil Actions over $5,000, Probate.***
Civil Records: Access: In person, online. Visitors must perform in person searches themselves. Required to search: name, years to search. Civil cases indexed by defendant, plaintiff; index on computer from 1994. No time limit on open cases. Index books with data back to 1800s. Civil PAT goes back to 1994. PAT results show middle initial, DOB, SSN. Results also include SSN. Online access is via a pay service at www.swcg-inc.com/products/circuit_express.html or call 800-795-8543. $125 set-up fee plus a $38.00 or $120 monthly fee plan.
Criminal Records: Access: In person, online. Visitors must perform in person searches themselves. Required to search: name, years to search. Criminal records computerized from 1994. No time limit on open cases. Index books with data back to 1800s. Note: Results also include address. Criminal PAT goes back to same as civil. PAT results show middle initial, DOB, SSN. Results also include SSN. Online access same as civil. Online results show middle initial, DOB. Terminal results include SSN.
General Information: No divorce or juvenile records released. Will fax documents $2.00 per page. Court makes copy: $.50 per page. Self serve: same. No certification fee. Payee: Circuit Court Clerk. Personal checks accepted; credit cards are not. Prepayment required.

Magistrate Court 200 6th St, 3rd Fl, Point Pleasant, WV 25550; 304-675-6840; fax: 304-675-5949; 8:30AM-4:30PM. ***Misdemeanor, Civil Actions under $5,000, Eviction, Small Claims.***
Magistrates offices- Ross 304-675-6400 and Roush 304-675-6636.
Civil Records: Access: Mail, in person. Both court and visitors may perform in person searches. Search fee: $25.00. Civil records go back to 1977; computerized since 1998. Mail turnaround time 3-4 days. Civil PAT goes back to 1998. PAT civil results show middle initial.
Criminal Records: Access: Mail, in person. Both court and visitors may perform in person searches. Search fee: $25.00. Required to search: name, years to search. Criminal records go back to 1977; computerized since 1998. Mail turnaround time 3-4 days. Criminal PAT goes back to same as civil. PAT criminal results show middle initial.
General Information: Will fax documents $2.00 per page. Court makes copy: $.25 per page. Self serve: same. Certification fee: $.50 per page. Payee: Court. Personal checks and major credit cards accepted. Prepayment required. Mail requests: SASE required.

McDowell County

Circuit Court PO Box 400, Court & Wyoming Sts, Welch, WV 24801; 304-436-8535; probate phone: 304-436-8544; fax: 304-436-6994; 9AM-5PM. ***Felony, Civil Actions over $5,000, Probate.***
Probate is handled by County Clerk, 90 Wyoming St, #109, Welch, WV 24801.
Civil Records: Access: Mail, in person, online. Both court and visitors may perform in person searches. No search fee. Required to search: name, years to search. Civil cases indexed by defendant, plaintiff. Civil index on docket books back to 1800s; on computer back to 1999. Mail turnaround time 1 week. Civil PAT goes back to 1998. PAT results show name only. Online access is via a pay service at www.swcg-inc.com/products/circuit_express.html or call 800-795-8543. $125 set-up fee plus a $38.00 or $120 monthly fee plan.
Criminal Records: Access: Mail, in person, online. Both court and visitors may perform in person searches. No search fee. Required to search: name, years to search; also helpful: DOB, SSN. Criminal records indexed in books back to 1800s; on computer back to 1999. Mail turnaround time 1 week. Criminal PAT goes back to same as civil. PAT results show name only. Online access same as civil. Online results show name only.
General Information: Online identifiers in results same as on public terminal. No sealed, juvenile, adoption, mental health, guardianship records released. Will fax documents $2.00 per page. Court makes copy: $.50 per page. Certification fee: $.50 per page. Payee: Clerk of Circuit Court. Business checks accepted. No credit cards accepted. Prepayment required. Mail requests: SASE required.

Magistrate Court PO Box 447, Welch, WV 24801; 304-436-8588; fax: 304-436-8575; 9AM-5PM. ***Misdemeanor, Civil Actions under $5,000, Eviction, Small Claims.***
Civil Records: Access: Mail, fax, in person. Visitors must perform in person searches themselves. Search fee: $25.00 per name. Civil cases indexed by Defendant, Plaintiff. Records on computer go back to 1998, accessible since 1977. Mail turnaround time 5 days. Civil PAT goes back to 1998. PAT results show name only.
Criminal Records: Access: Mail, fax, in person. Both court and visitors may perform in person searches. Search fee: $25.00 per name. Required to search: name, years to search, DOB, SSN. Records on computer go back to 1997, accessible since 1977. Records on criminal now go back to 1997. Mail turnaround time 5 days. Criminal PAT goes back to same as civil. PAT results show middle initial, DOB.
General Information: Fee to fax out file $2.00 per page. Court makes copy: $.25 per page. Certification fee: $.50 per page. Payee: Magistrate Court. No personal checks accepted; credit cards are. Prepayment required. Mail requests: SASE required.

Mercer County

Circuit Court 1501 Main St, Ste. 111, Princeton, WV 24740; 304-487-8323; criminal phone: 304-487-8410/304-487-8372; civil phone: 304-487-8369; fax: 304-425-1598; 8:30AM-4:30PM. ***Felony, Civil Actions over $5,000.***
Probate court is a separate office.
Civil Records: Access: Phone, fax, mail, in person, online. Both court and visitors may perform in person searches. No search fee. Required to search: name, years to search. Civil cases indexed by defendant, plaintiff; index on computer from 10/1989 to present. On index books from 1930-1989 (Cott System). On index cards back to 1890s. Mail turnaround time 4-5 days. Civil PAT goes back to 10/1989. PAT results show name only. Online access is via a pay service at www.swcg-inc.com/products/circuit_express.html or call 800-795-8543. $125 set-up fee plus a $38.00 or $120 monthly fee plan.
Criminal Records: Access: Fax, mail, in person, online. Both court and visitors may perform in person searches. No search fee. Required to search: name, years to search; also helpful: DOB, SSN. Criminal records computerized from 10/1989 to present. On index books from 1930-1989 (Cott System). On index cards back to 1890s. Mail turnaround time 4-5 days. Criminal PAT goes back to same as civil. PAT results show name only. Online access same as civil.
General Information: No juvenile, adoption, mental health, guardianship or conservatorship records released. Will fax documents $2.00 per page. Court makes copy: $.50 per page. Certification fee: $.50 per page. Payee: Circuit Court Clerk. Business checks accepted. Prepayment required. Mail requests: SASE required.

Magistrate Court 120 Scott St #103, Princeton, WV 24740; 304-431-7115; criminal phone: 304-431-7122; civil phone: 304-431-7121; fax: 304-425-6106; 8:30AM-4:30PM. ***Misdemeanor, Civil Actions under $5,000, Eviction, Small Claims, Traffic.***
Civil Records: Access: In person, mail, fax. Both court and visitors may perform in person searches. Search fee: $25.00 per name. Required to search: name, years to search; also helpful: address, DOB. Civil cases indexed by defendant, plaintiff. Civil records from 1977; computerized back to 1994. Mail turnaround time 1-2 days. Civil PAT goes back to 1994. PAT civil results show middle initial.
Criminal Records: Access: In person, mail, fax. Both court and visitors may perform in person searches. Search fee: $25.00 per name. Required to search: name, years to search; also helpful: address, DOB. Criminal records from 1977; computerized back to 1994. Mail turnaround time 1-2 days. Criminal PAT goes back to same as civil. PAT criminal results show middle initial.
General Information: Will fax documents $2.00 per page. Court makes copy: $.25 per page. Certification fee: $.50 per page. Payee: Mercer County Magistrate Court. Cashiers checks and money orders accepted. Visa/MC accepted. Prepayment required. Mail requests: SASE required for criminal.

Mineral County

Circuit Court 150 Armstrong St, Keyser, WV 26726; 304-788-1562; probate phone: 304-788-3924; criminal fax: 304-788-4109; civil fax: same; 8:30AM-5PM. ***Felony, Civil Actions over $5,000, Probate.***
www.mineralcountywv.com/circuitclerk/index.asp
Probate court is a separate office at the same address, 2nd Fl. Probate fax is same as main fax number.
Civil Records: Access: Fax, mail, in person, online. Both court and visitors may perform in person searches. Search fee: $5.00 per name. Required to search: name, years to search. Civil cases indexed by defendant, plaintiff; index on computer 1/1991 to present, on dockets from 1920s. Note: Fax access not guaranteed. Mail turnaround time 2-4 days. Online access is via a pay service at www.swcg-inc.com/products/circuit_express.html or call 800-795-8543. $125 set-up fee plus a $38.00 or $120 monthly fee plan.
Criminal Records: Access: Fax, mail, in person, online. Both court and visitors may perform in person searches. Search fee: $5.00 per name. Required to search: name, years to search; also helpful: DOB, SSN. Criminal records on computer 1/1991 to present, on dockets from 1920s. Note: Fax access not guaranteed. Mail turnaround time 2-4 days. Online access same as civil.
General Information: No juvenile, adoption, divorce, mental hygiene, conservatorship or guardianship records released. Will fax documents, no fee. Court makes copy: $.50 per page. Self serve: same. No certification fee. Payee: Clerk of Circuit Court. Personal checks accepted; credit cards are not. Prepayment required. Mail requests: SASE requested.

Magistrate Court 105 West St, Keyser, WV 26726; 304-788-2625; fax: 304-788-9835; 8:30AM-4:30PM. ***Misdemeanor, Civil Actions under $5,000, Eviction, Small Claims.***
Civil Records: Access: Mail, in person. Both court and visitors may perform in person searches. Search fee: $25.00 per name. Required to search: name, years to search. Civil records on computer back to 1991. Mail turnaround time as time permits. Civil PAT goes back to 1991. PAT civil results show middle initial.
Criminal Records: Access: Mail, in person. Both court and visitors may perform in person searches. Search fee: $25.00 per name. Required to search: name, years to search; also helpful: DOB, SSN. Records on computer back to 1991. Mail turnaround time as time permits. Criminal PAT goes back to same as civil. PAT results show middle initial.
General Information: Will fax documents $2.00 per page. Court makes copy: $.25 per page. Certification fee: $.50 per page. Payee: Magistrate Court. Personal checks and major credit cards accepted. Prepayment required. Mail requests: SASE requested.

Mingo County

Circuit Court PO Box 435, 75 E 2nd Ave, Rm 232, Williamson, WV 25661; 304-235-0320; probate phone: 304-235-0330; fax: 304-235-0326; 8:30AM-N, 1-4:30PM. ***Felony, Civil over $5,000, Probate.***

Probate is handled by County Clerk, 75 E 2nd Ave, Williamson, WV 25661.
Civil Records: Access: In person only. Both court and visitors may perform in person searches. No search fee. Required to search: name, years to search. Civil cases indexed by defendant, plaintiff; index on computer from 1/91 to present, civil on index books back to 1960, chancery books back to 1800s (written or in person only). Civil PAT goes back to 1991. PAT civil results show middle initial.
Criminal Records: Access: Mail, in person. Both court and visitors may perform in person searches. Search fee: $10.00 per name. Required to search: name, years to search; also helpful: DOB. Criminal records on computer since 1/91, Index books back to 1955. Mail turnaround time 1-2 weeks. Criminal PAT goes back to same as civil. PAT criminal results show middle initial.
General Information: No adoption, mental hygiene, juvenile records released. Will fax documents to local or toll-free number. Court makes copy: $.50 per page. Self serve: same. Certification fee: $2.00. Payee: County Circuit Clerk. No credit cards accepted. Prepayment required. Mail requests: SASE required.

Magistrate Court PO Box 986, Williamson, WV 25661; 304-235-2445; fax: 304-235-3179; 8:30AM-4:30PM. ***Misdemeanor, Civil Actions under $5,000, Eviction, Small Claims.***
Civil Records: Access: Phone, mail, fax, in person. Both court and visitors may perform in person searches. No search fee. Required to search: name, years to search; also helpful: DOB. Civil records go back to 1977; on computer back to 1998. Mail turnaround time 1 week. Civil PAT goes back to 1998. Public terminal located only in Court Clerk's office.
Criminal Records: Access: Mail, fax, in person. Both court and visitors may perform in person searches. Search fee: $25.00 per name. Required to search: name, years to search; also helpful: DOB, SSN. Criminal records go back to 1977; on computer back to 1998. Mail turnaround time 1 week, sooner for phone requests. Criminal PAT goes back to same as civil. Public terminal located only in Court Clerk's office.
General Information: Will not fax out documents. Court makes copy: $.25 per page. Certification fee: $.50 per page. Payee: Magistrate Court. Personal checks and major credit cards accepted. Prepayment required.

Monongalia County

17th Circuit Court County Courthouse, 243 High St, Rm 110, Morgantown, WV 26505; 304-291-7240; probate phone: 304-291-7236; criminal fax: 304-291-7273; civil fax: same; 9AM-7PM M; 9AM-5PM T-F. ***Felony, Civil over $5,000, Probate.***
A disclaimer for the Clerk must be included by mail requesters. Estates/Probate handled by County Clerk, 243 High St, Rm 110, Morgantown, WV 26505.
Civil Records: Access: Mail, in person. Both court and visitors may perform in person searches. Search fee: $5.00 per name. Required to search: name, years to search. Civil cases indexed by defendant, plaintiff; index on computer from 1/90 to present, on index book separated by plaintiff and defendant back to 1865. Mail turnaround time 1 day. Civil PAT goes back to 1990.
Criminal Records: Access: Mail, in person. Both court and visitors may perform in person searches. Search fee: $5.00 per name. Required to search: name, years to search; also helpful: DOB, SSN. Criminal records computerized from 1/90 to present, on index book separated by plaintiff and defendant back to 1865. Note: Court plans to have records online in the future. Mail turnaround time 1 day. Criminal PAT goes back to 1994.
General Information: No juvenile, divorce, mental hygiene, divorce, adoption, guardianship, conservatorship or domestic records released. Fee to fax out file $1.00 per page. Court makes copy: $.50 per page. Self serve: same. Certification fee: $.50 per page. Payee: Circuit Clerk. Business checks accepted. No credit cards accepted. Prepayment required. Mail requests: SASE required.

Magistrate Court 265 Spruce St, Morgantown, WV 26505; 304-291-7296; fax: 304-284-7313; 8AM-7PM. ***Misdemeanor, Civil Actions under $5,000, Eviction, Small Claims.***
Civil Records: Access: Mail, fax, in person. Both court and visitors may perform in person searches. No search fee. Required to search: name, years to search. Records on computer back to 1999; prior in books back 10 years. Mail turnaround time 10-14 days. Civil PAT goes back to 1999.
Criminal Records: Access: Mail, fax, in person. Both court and visitors may perform in person searches. Search fee: $25.00 per name. Required to search: name, years to search; also helpful: DOB, SSN, signed release. Records on computer go back to 1999; prior in books back 10 years only. Mail turnaround time 10-14 days. Criminal PAT goes back to same as civil.
General Information: Will not fax documents. Court makes copy: $.25 per page. Self serve: same. Certification fee: $.50 per page. Payee: Magistrate Court. Personal checks and major credit cards accepted. Prepayment required.

Monroe County

Circuit Court PO Box 350, Union, WV 24983-0350; 304-772-3017; probate phone: 304-772-3096; criminal fax: 304-772-4497; civil fax: same; 8AM-4PM. ***Felony, Civil Actions over $5,000, Probate.***
Probate is with the County Clerk, PO Box 350, Union, WV 24983.
Civil Records: Access: Phone, mail, in person. Both court and visitors may perform in person searches. No search fee. Required to search: name, years to search. Civil cases indexed by defendant, plaintiff. Civil index on docket books 1799 to present; on computer back to 2000. Mail turnaround time 1 week. Civil PAT goes back to 2000. PAT results show name only.
Criminal Records: Access: Phone, mail, in person. Both court and visitors may perform in person searches. No search fee. Required to search: name, years to search; also helpful: DOB, SSN. Criminal records indexed in books 1799 to present; on computer back to 2000. Mail turnaround time 1 week. Criminal PAT goes back to 2000. PAT results show name only.
General Information: No juvenile, adoption, divorce records released. Will fax documents to local or toll free line. Court makes copy: $.50 per page. Include postage with copy fee. Certification fee: $1.00 per document. Payee: Clerk of Circuit Court. Personal checks accepted; credit cards are not. Prepayment required. Mail requests: SASE requested.

Magistrate Court PO Box 4, Union, WV 24983; 304-772-3321/3176; fax: 304-772-4357; 8:30AM-4:30PM. ***Misdemeanor, Civil Actions under $5,000, Eviction, Small Claims.***
Civil Records: Access: Mail, in person. Both court and visitors may perform in person searches. Search fee: $25.00 per name. Required to search: name, DOB, SSN. Civil cases indexed by defendant, plaintiff. Criminal records go back to 1993; computerized records since mid 2001. Mail turnaround time 1-2 days. Civil PAT goes back to mid 2001.
Criminal Records: Access: Mail, in person, fax. Both court and visitors may perform in person searches. Search fee: $25.00 per name. Required to search: name, years to search; also helpful: DOB, SSN. Criminal records go back to 1998; computerized records since mid 2001. Mail turnaround time 1-2 days. Criminal PAT goes back to same as civil.
General Information: Will fax documents $2.00. Court makes copy: $.05 per page. Self serve: same. Certification fee: $.50 per page. Payee: Monroe County Magistrate Court. Personal checks and credit cards accepted. Mail requests: SASE required.

Morgan County

Circuit Court 77 Fairfax St, #2F, Berkeley Springs, WV 25411-1501; 304-258-8554; probate phone: 304-258-8547; fax: 304-258-7319; 9AM-5PM. ***Felony, Civil Actions over $5,000.***
Probate is County Clerk's office located at the same address in #1A. Due to courthouse fire 8/10/06, Circuit court records temporarily at 77 Fairfax St. Allow an extra day turnaround time. Court may return to 111 Fairfax in 2009.
Civil Records: Access: In person only. Only the court performs in person searches; visitors may not. No search fee. Required to search: name, years to search. Civil cases indexed by defendant, plaintiff; index on computer back to 1/93, index cards back to 1960; in person searching only on index books back to 1800s.
Criminal Records: Access: In person only. Only the court performs in person searches; visitors may not. No search fee. Required to search: name, years to search; also helpful-DOB, SSN, signed release. Criminal records computerized from 1/93, index cards back to 1960.
General Information: No juvenile, adoption, mental health, divorce records released. Will not fax documents. Court makes copy: $.50 per page. Self serve: same. No certification fee. Payee: Kimberly J Jackson, Circuit Clerk. Only cashiers checks and money orders accepted. No credit cards accepted. Prepayment required. Will bill to attorneys.

Magistrate Court 111 Fairfax St, Berkeley Springs, WV 25411; 304-258-8631; fax: 304-258-8639; 9AM-4:30PM. ***Misdemeanor, Civil Actions under $5,000, Eviction, Small Claims.***
Civil Records: Access: In person only. Visitors must perform in person searches themselves. Civil records go back 10 years from last action; records computerized since 1998. Public use terminal available, records go back to 6/1998. PAT civil results show middle initial.
Criminal Records: Access: In person only. Visitors must perform in person searches themselves. Required to search: name, years to search; also helpful: DOB, SSN. Criminal records go back 10 years from last action; records computerized since 1998. Note: Phone, fax and mail access limited. Public use terminal available, crim records go back to 6/1998. PAT results show name only.
General Information: Will not fax documents. Court makes copy: $.25 per page. Certification fee: $.50 per page. Payee: Magistrate Court. Only cashiers checks and money orders accepted. Major credit cards accepted in person only. Prepayment required.

Nicholas County

Circuit Court 700 Main St #5, Summersville, WV 26651; 304-872-7810; probate phone: 304-872-7820; fax: 304-872-7863; 8:30AM-4:30PM. ***Felony, Civil Actions over $5,000, Probate.***
Probate is handled by County Clerk, 700 Main St, #2, Summersville, WV 26651.
Civil Records: Access: Mail, in person, online. Both court and visitors may perform in person searches. No search fee. Required to search: name, years to search. Civil cases indexed by defendant, plaintiff; index on computer since 1994; prior records on index cards from 1976 to 1994 on dockets back to 1818. Mail turnaround time 1 week. Civil PAT goes back to 1996. PAT results show name only. Online access is via a pay service at www.swcg-inc.com/products/circuit_express.html or call 800-795-8543. $125 set-up fee plus a $38.00 or $120 monthly fee plan.
Criminal Records: Access: Mail, in person, online. Both court and visitors may perform in person searches. Search fee: $10.00 per name. Required to search: name, years to search; also helpful: DOB, SSN. Criminal records on computer since 1994; prior records on index cards from 1976 to 1994 on dockets back to 1818. Mail turnaround 1 week. Criminal PAT goes back to 1996. PAT results show middle initial, DOB. Online access same as civil.
General Information: No divorce, juvenile, adoption, mental, guardianship records released. Will fax documents $2.00 per page. Court makes copy: $.50 per page. Self serve: same. No certification fee. Payee: Circuit Clerk. Personal checks accepted; credit cards are not. Mail requests: SASE required.

Magistrate Court 511 Church St, #206, 2nd Fl, Summersville, WV 26651; 304-872-7829; fax: 304-872-7888; 8:30AM-4:30PM. ***Misdemeanor, Civil Actions under $5,000, Eviction, Small Claims.***

Civil Records: Access: Mail, in person. Visitors must perform in person searches themselves. Search fee: $25.00 per name. Civil records on computer back to 1990, cases available since 1977. Note: Request must be in writing. Civil PAT goes back to 10/1990. PAT civil results show middle initial.
Criminal Records: Access: Mail, in person. Visitors must perform in person searches themselves. Search fee: $25.00 per name. Required to search: name, years to search; also helpful: DOB, SSN. Criminal records computerized from 1990, cases available since 1977. Note: Request must be in writing. Criminal PAT goes back to same as civil. PAT criminal results show middle initial.
General Information: Will fax documents to local or toll-free number. Court makes copy: $.25 per page. Self serve: same. Certification fee: $.50 per page. Payee: Magistrate Court. Personal checks and major credit cards accepted. Prepayment required.

Ohio County

Circuit Court 1500 Chapline St, City & County Bldg, Rm 403, Wheeling, WV 26003; 304-234-3611; probate phone: 304-234-3656; criminal fax: 304-232-0550; civil fax: same; 8:30AM-5PM. ***Felony, Civil Actions over $5,000, Probate.***
Probate records are with the county clerk at this address, Rm 205.
Civil Records: Access: Fax, mail, in person, online. Both court and visitors may perform in person searches. Search fee: $5.00 per name. Required to search: name, years to search. Civil cases indexed by defendant, plaintiff; index on computer from 10/1986 to present, on index books back to 1800s. Mail turnaround time up to 48 hours. Civil PAT goes back to 1986. PAT civil results show middle initial. Online access is via a pay service at www.swcg-inc.com/products/circuit_express.html or call 800-795-8543. $125 set-up fee plus a $38.00 or $120 monthly fee plan.
Criminal Records: Access: Fax, mail, in person, online. Both court and visitors may perform in person searches. Search fee: $5.00 per name. Required to search: name, years to search; also helpful: DOB, SSN. Criminal records computerized from 10/1986 to present, on index books back to 1800s. Mail turnaround time 1 week for accounts only. Criminal PAT goes back to 1986. PAT criminal results show middle initial. Online access same as civil. Online results show middle initial.
General Information: No domestic, juvenile, mental, adoption records released. Fee to fax out file $2.00 per page. Court makes copy: $.50 per page. Certification fee: $1.50 per document for triple seal, includes copies. Payee: Ohio County Circuit Court. Business checks accepted. No credit cards accepted. Prepayment required. Mail requests: SASE required.

Magistrate Court Courthouse Annex, 26 15th St, Wheeling, WV 26003; 304-234-3709; criminal fax: 304-234-3898; civil fax: same; 8:30AM-4:30PM. ***Misdemeanor, Civil Actions under $5,000, Eviction, Small Claims.***
Civil Records: Access: Mail, fax, in person. Both court and visitors may perform in person searches. Search fee: $25.00 per name. Required to search: name, years to search. Records go back to 1977. Court will only search back to 1997. Mail turnaround time 1 week. Public use terminal available, records go back to 1997. PAT civil results show middle initial.
Criminal Records: Access: Mail, fax, in person. Both court and visitors may perform in person searches. Search fee: $25.00 per name. Required to search: name, years to search; also helpful: DOB, SSN. Records go back to 1977. Court will only search back to 1997. Mail turnaround time 1 week. Public use terminal available, crim records go back to 1997. PAT results show middle initial, DOB. Terminal results include SSN.
General Information: Will fax documents. Court makes copy: $.25 per page. Self serve: same. Certification fee: $.50 per page. Payee: Court. Personal checks accepted with proper identification. Major credit cards accepted. Mail requests: SASE requested.

Pendleton County

Circuit Court PO Box 846, Franklin, WV 26807; 304-358-7067; fax: 304-358-2152; 8:30AM-4PM. ***Felony, Civil Actions over $5,000, Probate.***
Civil Records: Access: Phone, fax, mail, in person. Both court and visitors may perform in person searches. No search fee. Required to search: name, years to search. Civil cases indexed by defendant, plaintiff. Civil index on docket books back to 1800s. Mail turnaround time 2-3 days.
Criminal Records: Access: Phone, fax, mail, in person. Both court and visitors may perform in person searches. No search fee. Required to search: name, years to search; also helpful: DOB, SSN. Criminal records indexed in books back to 1800s. Mail turnaround time 2-3 days.
General Information: No juvenile, divorce records released. Will fax documents $2.00 per page. Court makes copy: $.50 per page. Self serve: same. No certification fee. Payee: Pendleton County Circuit Clerk. Local checks accepted. No credit cards accepted. Prepayment required. Mail requests: SASE required.

Magistrate Court PO Box 637, Franklin, WV 26807; 304-358-2343; criminal fax: 304-358-3870; civil fax: same; 8:30AM-4PM. ***Misdemeanor, Civil Actions under $5,000, Eviction, Small Claims.***
Civil Records: Access: Mail, in person. Both court and visitors may perform in person searches. Search fee: $25.00 per name. Required to search: name, years to search. Civil cases indexed by defendant, plaintiff. Civil records computerized since 1993. Mail turnaround time 5-10 days. Civil PAT goes back to 1993.
Criminal Records: Access: Mail, in person. Both court and visitors may perform in person searches. Search fee: $25.00 per name. Required to search: name, years to search. Records computerized since 1993. Mail turnaround time 5-10 days. Criminal PAT goes back to same as civil.
General Information: Will fax documents to local or toll free line. Court makes copy: $.25 per page. Certification fee: $.50 per page. Payee: Magistrate Court. Personal checks accepted; credit cards are not. Prepayment required.

Pleasants County

Circuit Court 301 Court Ln, Rm 201, St. Mary's, WV 26170; 304-684-3513; probate phone: 304-684-3542; fax: 304-684-3514; 8:30AM-4:30PM. ***Felony, Civil Actions over $5,000, Probate.***
Probate is handled by County Clerk, 301 Court Ln, Rm 101, St Mary's, WV 26170.
Civil Records: Access: In person only. Visitors must perform in person searches themselves. Required to search: name, years to search. Civil cases indexed by defendant, plaintiff; index on computer from 1/1960 to present, on index cards from 1960 to present, on index books back to 1800s. Civil PAT goes back to 1960.
Criminal Records: Access: In person only. Visitors must perform in person searches themselves. Required to search: name, years to search. Criminal records computerized from 1/1960 to present, on index cards from 1960 to present, on index books back to 1800s. Criminal PAT available.
General Information: No domestic, marriage, adoption, juvenile or mental health records released. Will fax documents to local or toll-free number. Court makes copy: $.50 per page. Certification fee: $.50 per page. Payee: Circuit Clerk. Personal checks accepted; credit cards are not. Prepayment required.

Magistrate Court 301 Court Ln, Rm B-6, St Mary's, WV 26170; 304-684-7197; fax: 304-684-3882; 8:30AM-4:30PM. ***Misdemeanor, Civil Actions under $5,000, Eviction, Small Claims.***
Civil Records: Access: Mail, in person. Both court and visitors may perform in person searches. Search fee: $25.00 per name. Required to search: name, years to search; also helpful: DOB or SSN. Civil cases indexed by defendant, plaintiff. Records go back to 1977, on computer since mid-2000. Civil PAT goes back to 2000.
Criminal Records: Access: Mail, in person. Both court and visitors may perform in person searches. Search fee: $25.00 per name. Required to search: name, years to search; also helpful: DOB, SSN. Records go back to 1977, on computer since mid-2000. Criminal PAT goes back to 2000.
General Information: Fee to fax files is $2.00 per page. Court makes copy: $.25 per page. Self serve: $.25 per page. Certification fee: $.50 per page. Payee: Pleasants County Magistrate Court. Personal checks and credit cards accepted. Prepayment required. Mail requests: SASE required.

Pocahontas County

Circuit Court 900-C 10th Ave, Marlinton, WV 24954; 304-799-4604/304-799-4549; probate phone: 304-799-4549; fax: 304-799-0833; 8:30AM-4:30PM. ***Felony, Civil Actions over $5,000, Probate.***
Civil Records: Access: Phone, mail, in person. Only the court performs in person searches; visitors may not. No search fee. Required to search: name, years to search; also helpful: address. Civil cases indexed by defendant, plaintiff. Civil index on docket books from 1948 to present, order books back to 1800s. Computerized records from 1995 to present. Mail turnaround time same day.
Criminal Records: Access: Phone, mail, in person. Both court and visitors may perform in person searches. No search fee. Required to search: name, years to search; also helpful: DOB, SSN. Criminal records indexed in books from 1948 to present, order books back to 1800s. Computerized records from 1995 to present. Mail turnaround time same day.
General Information: No juvenile, domestic cases involving finances, adoption, guardianship records released. Will fax documents $2.00 each. Court makes copy: $.50 per page. Self serve: same. No certification fee. Payee: Clerk of Circuit Court. Personal checks accepted; credit cards are not. Prepayment required.

Magistrate Court 900 10th Ave, Marlinton, WV 24954; 304-799-6603; criminal fax: 304-799-6331; civil fax: same; 9AM-4:30PM. ***Misdemeanor, Civil Actions under $5,000, Eviction, Small Claims.***
Civil Records: Access: Mail, in person. Both court and visitors may perform in person searches. Search fee: $25.00 per name. Required to search: name. Records stored since 1977, computerized since 10-14-99; actual record destroyed after 10 years. Mail turnaround time same day. Civil PAT goes back to 1999 for most. Results include name of defendant and case number.
Criminal Records: Access: Mail, in person. Both court and visitors may perform in person searches. Search fee: $25.00 per name. Required to search: name, years to search; also helpful: DOB, SSN. Records stored since 1977, computerized since 10-14-99; actual record is destroyed after 10 years. Mail turnaround time same day. Criminal PAT goes back to same as civil. Results include name of defendant and case number.
General Information: Will fax documents $2.00 per page. Court makes copy: $.25 per page. Self serve: same. Certification fee: $.75 per page. Payee: Pocahontas Co Magistrate Court. Personal checks accepted. Visa/MC accepted. Prepayment required. Mail requests: SASE required.

Preston County

Circuit Court 101 W Main St, Rm 301, Kingwood, WV 26537; 304-329-0047; probate phone: 304-329-0070; criminal fax: 304-329-1417; civil fax: same; 9AM-5PM M-TH, 9AM-7PM F. ***Felony, Misdemeanor, Civil over $5,000, Probate.***
Probate is handled by County Clerk, 101 W Main St, Rm 201, Kingwood, WV 26537.
Civil Records: Access: Phone, fax, mail, in person. Only the court performs in person searches; visitors may not. No search fee. Required to search: name, years to search. Civil cases indexed by defendant, plaintiff; index on computer from 1/80 to present, on index books 1965 to 1980, chancery file from 1869 to 1965. Mail turnaround time 1 week.
Criminal Records: Access: Phone, fax, mail, in person. Only the court performs in person searches; visitors may not. No search fee. Required to search: name, years to search, DOB, SSN. Criminal docket on books from 1869 to 1979, records on computer since 1979. Mail turnaround time 1 week.

General Information: No juvenile, adoption, domestic, mental hygiene records released. Fee to fax out file $2.00 per page. Court makes copy: $.50 per page. No certification fee. Payee: Betsy Castle, Circuit Clerk. Personal checks accepted; credit cards are not. Prepayment required. Mail requests: SASE required.

Magistrate Court 328 Tunnelton St, Kingwood, WV 26537; 304-329-2764; fax: 304-329-0855; 8:30AM-4:30PM. ***Misdemeanor, Civil Actions under $5,000, Eviction, Small Claims.***
Physical address is 101 W Main St.
Civil Records: Access: Fax, mail, in person. Both court and visitors may perform in person searches. Search fee: $25.00. Civil records go back to 1977; computerized records since 1987. Mail turnaround time 1 week. Civil PAT goes back to 1989. PAT results show name only.
Criminal Records: Access: Fax, mail, in person. Both court and visitors may perform in person searches. Search fee: $25.00. Required to search: name, years to search; also helpful: DOB, SSN. Criminal records go back to 1977; computerized records since 1987. Mail turnaround time 1 week. Criminal PAT goes back to same as civil. PAT results show middle initial, DOB, SSN.
General Information: Will fax documents for $2.00 per page. Court makes copy: $.25 per page. Self serve: same. Certification fee: $.50 per page. Payee: Court. Personal checks accepted. Visa/MC accepted. Prepayment required. Mail requests: SASE requested.

Putnam County

Circuit Court Putnam County Judicial Bldg, 3389 Winfield Rd, Winfield, WV 25213; 304-586-0203; fax: 304-586-0221; 8:30AM-4:30PM. ***Felony, Civil Actions over $5,000, Probate.***
Civil Records: Access: In person, online. Both court and visitors may perform in person searches. No search fee. Required to search: name, years to search. Civil cases indexed by defendant, plaintiff; index on computer from 1989 to present, on index books back to 1800s. Public use terminal available. Online access is via a pay service at www.swcg-inc.com/products/circuit_express.html or call 800-795-8543. $125 set-up fee plus a $38.00 or $120 monthly fee plan.
Criminal Records: Access: In person, online. Visitors must perform in person searches themselves. Required to search: name, years to search; also helpful: DOB, SSN. Criminal records computerized from 1982 to present. Public use terminal available. Online access same as civil. Online results show middle initial.
General Information: No divorce records released. Court makes copy: $.50 per page. No certification fee. Payee: Circuit Clerk. Business checks accepted. No credit cards accepted. Prepayment required. Mail requests: SASE required for mail return of any copies.

Magistrate Court 3389 Winfield Rd, Winfield, WV 25213; 304-586-0234; fax: 304-586-0267; 8:30AM-4:30PM. ***Misdemeanor, Civil Actions under $5,000, Eviction, Small Claims.***
Civil Records: Access: Mail, in person. Both court and visitors may perform in person searches. No search fee. Required to search: name, DOB. Civil cases indexed by defendant, plaintiff. Records are computerized since 1996, overall records kept since 1977. Mail turnaround time 1 week. Civil PAT goes back to 1996.
Criminal Records: Access: Mail, in person. Both court and visitors may perform in person searches. No search fee. Required to search: name, years to search; also helpful: DOB. Records stored since 1977. Mail turnaround 1 week. Criminal PAT goes back to 1996. PAT results- middle initial, DOB, SSN.
General Information: Will fax documents $2.00 per page. Court makes copy: $.25 per page. Self serve: same. Certification fee: $.50 per page. Payee: Magistrate Court. Personal checks and major credit cards accepted. Prepayment required.

Raleigh County

Circuit Court 215 Main St, Beckley, WV 25801; 304-255-9135; probate phone: 304-255-9123; fax: 304-255-9353; 8:30AM-N, 1-4:30PM. ***Felony, Civil Actions over $5,000, Probate.***
Probate is handled by County Clerk, 215 Main St, Courthouse, Beckley, WV 25801.
Civil Records: Access: In person only. Visitors must perform in person searches themselves. Required to search: name, years to search. Civil cases indexed by defendant, plaintiff; index on master index books from 1977; on computer back to 1997; on dockets back to 1800s. Civil PAT goes back to 1997. PAT results show name only.
Criminal Records: Access: Phone, mail, in person. Both court and visitors may perform in person searches. No search fee. Required to search: name, years to search; also helpful: DOB, SSN. Criminal records on master index books from 1977; on computer back to 1997; on dockets back to 1800s. Criminal PAT goes back to 1997. PAT results show name only.
General Information: No divorce, juvenile, adoption records released. Fee to fax out file $2.00 per page. Court makes copy: $.50 per page. Self serve: same. No certification fee. Payee: Clerk of Circuit Court. Business checks accepted. No credit cards accepted. Prepayment required. Will bill to attorneys. Mail requests: SASE required for criminal.

Magistrate Court 115 W Prince St, #A, Beckley, WV 25801; 304-255-9197; criminal fax: 304-255-3701; civil fax: same; 8AM-4PM. ***Misdemeanor, Civil Actions under $5,000, Eviction, Small Claims.***
Civil Records: Access: Mail, in person. Both court and visitors may perform in person searches. Search fee: $25.00 per name. Required to search: name. Civil cases indexed by defendant, plaintiff. Civil records go back to 1977, computerized since 1991. Mail turnaround time 1-2 days. Civil PAT goes back to 1991. PAT results show name; also, middle initial may appear in PAT results.
Criminal Records: Access: Mail, in person. Both court and visitors may perform in person searches. Search fee: $25.00 per name. Required to search: name, years to search; also helpful: DOB, SSN, offense, date of offense. Criminal records go back to 1977, on computer back to 1992. Mail turnaround time 1-2 days. Criminal PAT goes back to 1992. PAT results show name only. Also, middle initial may appear in PAT results.
General Information: Will fax specific case file $2.00 per page. Court makes copy: $.25 per page. Self serve: same. Cert fee: $.50 per page includes copy fee. Payee: Magistrate Court. Personal checks and credit cards accepted. Prepayment required.

Randolph County

Circuit Court Courthouse, 2 Randolph Ave, Elkins, WV 26241; 304-636-2765; fax: 304-637-3700; 8AM-4:30PM. ***Felony, Civil Actions over $5,000, Probate.***
Civil Records: Access: Fax, mail, in person. Visitors must perform in person searches themselves. No search fee. Required to search: name, years to search. Civil cases indexed by defendant, plaintiff; index on computer from 1/91 to present. On index books back to late 1800s. Civil PAT goes back to 1991.
Criminal Records: Access: Fax, mail, in person. Visitors must perform in person searches themselves. No search fee. Required to search: name, years to search. Criminal records computerized from 1/91 to present. On index books back to late 1800s. Criminal PAT goes back to same as civil.
General Information: No juvenile, adoption, mental health, or guardianship records released. Will fax documents $2.00 per page. Court makes copy: $.50 per page. Self serve: same. No certification fee. Payee: Circuit Clerk. Personal checks accepted. Prepayment required.

Magistrate Court #11 Randolph Ave, Elkins, WV 26241; 304-636-5885; fax: 304-636-2510; 8AM-4:30PM. ***Misdemeanor, Civil Actions under $5,000, Eviction, Small Claims.***
Civil Records: Access: Mail, in person. Both court and visitors may perform in person searches. Search fee: $25.00 per name. Civil records go back to 1977; computerized records since 10/90. Mail turnaround time 3 days. Civil PAT goes back to 1992. PAT civil results show middle initial.
Criminal Records: Access: Mail, in person. Both court and visitors may perform in person searches. Search fee: $25.00 per name. Required to search: name, years to search; also helpful: DOB, SSN. Criminal records go back to 1977; computerized records since 10/90. Mail turnaround time 3 days. Criminal PAT goes back to same as civil. PAT criminal results show middle initial.
General Information: Will fax documents $2.00 per page prepaid. Court makes copy: $.25 per page. Self serve: same. Certification fee: $.50 per page. Payee: Randolph County Magistrate Court. Personal checks and major credit cards accepted. Prepayment required.

Ritchie County

Circuit Court 115 E. Main St, Rm 301, Harrisville, WV 26362; 304-643-2164 x229; civil phone: x1; probate phone: 304-643-2164 x228; fax: 304-643-2534; 8AM-4PM. ***Felony, Civil Actions over $5,000, Probate.*** Probate office is located at the same address, but in county clerks office.
Civil Records: Access: Phone, mail, in person. Both court and visitors may perform in person searches. No search fee. Required to search: name, years to search. Civil cases indexed by defendant, plaintiff. Civil index on cards from 1960 to present. On index books back to mid-1800s; on computer back to 2000. Mail turnaround time 1-2 days. Civil PAT goes back to 2000.
Criminal Records: Access: Phone, mail, in person. Both court and visitors may perform in person searches. No search fee. Required to search: name, years to search; also helpful: DOB, SSN. Criminal records indexed on cards from 1960 to present. On index books back to mid-1800s; on computer back to 2000. Mail turnaround time 1-2 days. Criminal PAT goes back to same as civil.
General Information: No juvenile, mental health, adoption records released. Will not fax documents. Court makes copy: $.50 per page. Self serve: same. No certification fee. Payee: Circuit Clerk. Personal checks accepted; credit cards are not. Prepayment required. Mail requests: SASE requested.

Magistrate Court 319 E. Main St, Harrisville, WV 26362; 304-643-4409; fax: 304-643-2098; 8AM-4PM. ***Misdemeanor, Civil Actions under $5,000, Eviction, Small Claims.***
Civil Records: Access: Phone, fax, mail, in person. Both court and visitors may perform in person searches. Search fee: $25.00 per name, paid at time of request. Required to search: name, years to search; also helpful: DOB, SSN. Civil cases indexed by defendant, plaintiff. Civil records go back to 1977; computerized from 1990. Note: Phone, fax or mail access is limited, call ahead for turnaround time. Mail turnaround time 1-2 days, 1-2 hours for phone requests. Civil PAT goes back to 1990. PAT results show name only.
Criminal Records: Access: Fax, mail, in person. Both court and visitors may perform in person searches. Search fee: $25.00 per name, paid at time or request. Required to search: name, years to search; also helpful: DOB, SSN. Criminal records go back to 1977; computerized from 1990. Mail turnaround time 1-2 days, 1-2 hours for phone request. Criminal PAT goes back to same as civil. PAT results show name only.
General Information: Will fax out documents $2.00 per page. Court makes copy: $.25 per page. Certification fee: $.50 per page. Payee: Magistrate Court. Personal checks and credit cards accepted. Prepayment required.

Roane County

Circuit Court PO Box 122, Spencer, WV 25276; 304-927-2750; fax: 304-927-2164; 8:30AM-N, 1-4PM; 9AM-N Sat. ***Felony, Civil Actions over $5,000, Probate.***
Civil Records: Access: Phone, fax, mail, in person, online. Both court and visitors may perform in person searches. No search fee. Required to search: name, years to search. Civil cases indexed by defendant, plaintiff. Civil index on docket books back to early 1900s; computerized records go back to 1998. Mail turnaround time 1-2 days, less for phone requests. Civil PAT goes back to 1998. Online access is via a pay service at www.swcg-inc.com/products/circuit_express.html or call 800-

795-8543. $125 set-up fee plus a $38.00 or $120 monthly fee plan.
Criminal Records: Access: Phone, fax, mail, in person, online. Both court and visitors may perform in person searches. No search fee. Required to search: name, years to search; also helpful: DOB, SSN. Criminal records indexed in books back to early 1900s; computerized records go back to 1998. Mail turnaround time 1-2 days, less for phone request. Criminal PAT goes back to same as civil. Online access same as civil.
General Information: No sealed, juvenile, adoption records released. Will fax documents $1.50 1st page; $1.00 each add'l. Court makes copy: $.50 per page. Certification fee: $.50 per page. Payee: Beverly Greathouse. Local checks accepted. No credit cards accepted. Prepayment required.

Magistrate Court 201 Main St, Spencer, WV 25276; 304-927-4750; fax: 304-927-2754; 9AM-4PM. ***Misdemeanor, Civil Actions under $5,000, Eviction, Small Claims.***
Record requests can be directed to 304-746-2180.
Civil Records: Access: In person. Both court and visitors may perform in person searches. Search fee: $25.00 per name. Required to search: name, years to search. Records on computer back to 1997; prior records go back to 1976. Civil PAT goes back to 1997. PAT results show name only.
Criminal Records: Access: In person. Both court and visitors may perform in person searches. Search fee: $25.00 per name. Required to search: name, DOB; also helpful: years to search, SSN. Records on computer back to 1997; prior records go back to 1976. Criminal PAT goes back to same as civil.PAT results show name, DOB. Terminal results include SSN.
General Information: Will fax documents $2.00 per page. Court makes copy: $.25 per page. Self serve: same. Certification fee: $.50 per page. Payee: Roane County Magistrate Court. Personal checks accepted. Visa/MC accepted. Prepayment required. Will bill to attorneys.

Summers County

Circuit Court PO Box 1058, Hinton, WV 25951; 304-466-7103; criminal phone: 304-746-2177; fax: 304-466-7124; 8:30AM-4:30PM. ***Felony, Civil Actions over $5,000, Probate.***
Civil Records: Access: In person only. Visitors must perform in person searches themselves. Required to search: name, years to search. Civil cases indexed by defendant, plaintiff. Civil index on docket books back to late 1800s; computerized records since 1998. Note: Clerk will lookup names on court's terminal for in person searchers.
Criminal Records: Access: In person only. Both court and visitors may perform in person searches. No search fee. Required to search: name, years to search; also helpful: DOB, SSN. Criminal records indexed in books back to 1878, computerized since 1998. Note: Clerk will lookup names on court's terminal for in person searchers.
General Information: No juvenile, adoption, child abuse records released. Court makes copy: n/a. Self serve: $.50 per page. Certification fee: $1.00. Payee: Clerk of Circuit Court. Personal checks accepted; credit cards are not. Prepayment required.

Magistrate Court PO Box 1059, Hinton, WV 25951; 304-466-7108; criminal fax: 304-466-4912; civil fax: same; 9:00AM-4:00PM. ***Misdemeanor, Civil Actions under $5,000, Eviction, Small Claims.***
Probate fax is same as main fax number.
Civil Records: Access: Phone, fax, mail, in person. Both court and visitors may perform in person searches. Search fee: $25.00. Required to search: name, years to search, other names used; also helpful-address. Civil cases indexed by defendant, plaintiff. Civil index on docket books to 1977 and computer back to 1998. Mail turnaround 1-2 days. Civil PAT goes back to 1998. PAT results show name only.
Criminal Records: Access: Phone, fax, mail, in person. Both court and visitors may perform in person searches. Search fee: $25.00. Required to search: name, years to search; also helpful: DOB, SSN. Criminal docket on books to 1977, and computer back to 1998. Mail turnaround time 1-2 days. Criminal PAT goes back to same as civil. PAT results show name only.
General Information: Will fax documents $2.00 per fax. Court makes copy: $.25 per page. Certification fee: $.50 per page. Payee: Magistrate Court. Personal checks and credit cards accepted. Prepayment required. Mail requests: SASE required.

Taylor County

Circuit Court 214 W Main St, Rm 104, Grafton, WV 26354; 304-265-2480; fax: 304-265-1404; 8:30AM-N, 1-4:30PM. ***Felony, Civil Actions over $5,000, Probate.***
Probate records held by the County Clerk.
Civil Records: Access: Phone, mail, in person. Only the court performs in person searches; visitors may not. No search fee. Required to search: name, years to search. Civil cases indexed by defendant, plaintiff. Civil index on docket books back to 1844, computerized since 1996. Mail turnaround 2 days.
Criminal Records: Access: Phone, mail, in person. Only the court performs in person searches; visitors may not. No search fee. Required to search: name, years to search; also helpful: DOB, SSN. Criminal records indexed in books back to 1929, computerized since 1996. Mail turnaround 2 days.
General Information: No juvenile, adoptions, mental health records released. Fee to fax out file $2.00 per page. Court makes copy: $.50 per page. No certification fee. Payee: Circuit Clerk. Personal checks accepted; credit cards are not. Prepayment required. Mail requests: SASE required; any add'l fee for postage is 3 times the amount.

Magistrate Court 214 W Main St, Grafton, WV 26354; 304-265-1322; fax: 304-265-5708; 8:30-4:30PM. ***Misdemeanor, Civil Actions under $5,000, Eviction, Small Claims.*** Search fee will include both civil and criminal indexes, if you ask.
Civil Records: Access: Mail, fax, in person. Both court and visitors may perform in person searches. Search fee: $25.00 per name. Required to search: name, years to search. Civil cases indexed by Defendant, Plaintiff. Overall records go back to 1976. Computerized records go back to 1992. Mail turnaround time 1-2 days. Civil PAT goes back to 1992. Public terminal actually the clerk's terminal.
Criminal Records: Access: Mail, in person. Both court and visitors may perform in person searches. No search fee. Required to search: name, years to search; also helpful: DOB, SSN, signed release. Overall records go back to 1976. Computerized records go back to 1992. Mail turnaround time 1-2 days. Criminal PAT goes back to 1992. PAT results show middle initial, DOB, SSN. The public terminal is actually the clerk's terminal.
General Information: Will fax documents $2.00 per page, prepaid. Court makes copy: $.25 per page. Self serve: same. Certification fee: $.50 per page includes copy fee. Payee: Magistrate Court. Business checks accepted. Major credit cards accepted. Prepayment required. Mail requests: SASE required.

Tucker County

Circuit Court 215 1st St, #2, Parsons, WV 26287; 304-478-2606 ext 202; fax: 304-478-4464; 8AM-4PM. ***Felony, Civil Actions over $5,000.***
Civil Records: Access: Mail, in person. Both court and visitors may perform in person searches. No search fee. Required to search: name, years to search. Civil cases indexed by defendant, plaintiff. Civil index on docket books from 1856 to 1996, 1997 to present on computer. Note: Due to limited staff, the court cannot do extensive civil searches. Mail turnaround time 2-5 days.
Criminal Records: Access: Mail, in person. Both court and visitors may perform in person searches. No search fee. Required to search: name, years to search, SSN; also helpful: DOB, case number. Criminal records indexed in books to 1856 to 1996; 1997 to present on computer. Mail turnaround 2 days.
General Information: No juvenile, domestic, guardianship, adoption or mental hygiene records released. Fee to fax out file $5.00. Court makes copy: $.50 per page. Self serve: same. No certification fee. Payee: Circuit Court Clerk. Personal checks accepted; no out of state checks. No credit cards accepted. Prepayment required. Mail requests: SASE required.

Magistrate Court 201 Walnut St, Parsons, WV 26287; 304-478-2665; fax: 304-478-4836; 8:30AM-4:00PM. ***Misdemeanor, Civil Actions under $5,000, Eviction, Small Claims.***
Civil Records: Access: In person only. Both court and visitors may perform in person searches. No search fee. Required to search: name, years to search. Civil cases indexed by Defendant, Plaintiff. Civil records go back to 1977; computerized since 8/1999. Civil PAT goes back to 8/1999. PAT civil results show middle initial.
Criminal Records: Access: In person only. Visitors must perform in person searches themselves. Required to search: name, years to search. Criminal records go back to 1977; computerized since 8/1999. Criminal PAT goes back to same as civil. PAT criminal results show middle initial.
General Information: Will not fax out case files. Court makes copy: $.25 per page. Self serve: same. Certification fee: $.50 per page. Payee: Magistrate Court Tucker County. Personal checks accepted; credit cards are not. Prepayment required.

Tyler County

Circuit Court PO Box 8, Middlebourne, WV 26149; 304-758-4811; fax: 304-758-4008; 8AM-4PM. ***Felony, Civil Actions over $5,000.***
Civil Records: Access: Mail, fax, in person. Both court and visitors may perform in person searches. No search fee. Required to search: name, years to search. Civil index on docket books back to 1800s; computerized back to 1997. Mail turnaround time 1-2 days.
Criminal Records: Access: Mail, fax, in person. Both court and visitors may perform in person searches. No search fee. Required to search: name, years to search; also helpful: DOB, SSN. Criminal records indexed in books back to 1864; computerized back to 1997. Mail turnaround time 1-2 days.
General Information: No adoption, juvenile, or domestic records released. Fee to fax out file $2.00 per page. Court makes copy: $.50 per page. Self serve: same. No certification fee. Payee: Tyler County Circuit Clerk. No personal checks or credit cards accepted. Prepayment required. Mail requests: SASE required.

Magistrate Court PO Box 127, Middlebourne, WV 26149; 304-758-2137; criminal fax: 304-758-2692; civil fax: same; 9AM-4PM. ***Misdemeanor, Civil Actions under $5,000, Eviction, Small Claims.***
Civil Records: Access: Mail, in person. Both court and visitors may perform in person searches. Search fee: $25.00 per name. Required to search: Name, years to search, other names used, address; also helpful- DOB, SSN. Records go back to 1/1/77; on computer back to 1/1/2000. Mail turnaround time 1 week. Civil PAT goes back to 1/2000.
Criminal Records: Access: Mail, in person. Both court and visitors may perform in person searches. Search fee: $25.00 per name. Required to search: name, years to search; also helpful: DOB, SSN. Records go back to 1/1/77; on computer back to 1/1/2000. Mail turnaround time 1 week. Criminal PAT goes back to same as civil.
General Information: Will fax documents $2.00 per page, in advance. Court makes copy: $.25 per page. Certification fee: $.50 per page includes copy fee. Payee: Tyler County Magistrate Court. Personal checks and major credit cards accepted. Prepayment required. Mail requests: SASE required.

Upshur County

Circuit Court 38 W. Main St, Rm 304, Buckhannon, WV 26201; 304-472-2370; probate phone: 304-472-1068; fax: 304-472-2168; 8AM-4:30PM. ***Felony, Civil Actions over $5,000, Probate.***
Probate is handled by County Clerk, 40 W Main, Courthouse, Rm 101, Buckhannon, WV 26201. Probate fax- 304-472-1029
Civil Records: Access: In person only. Visitors must perform in person searches themselves. Required to search: name, years to search. Civil cases indexed by defendant, plaintiff. Civil index on docket books from 1947 to present, card index 1900 to 1960, on

computer from 1900. Civil PAT goes back to 1900. PAT results show name only.
Criminal Records: Access: Fax, mail, in person. Both court and visitors may perform in person searches. Search fee: $5.00 per name. Required to search: name, years to search; also helpful: DOB, SSN. Criminal records computerized from 1/90 to present, on index books 1947 to 1/90, on dockets back to 1800s. Note: For fax requests, include a copy of check. Mail turnaround time 1-2 days. Criminal PAT back to 1900. PAT results show name only.
General Information: No mental health, juvenile, adoption records released. Will fax findings to toll-free numbers. Court makes copy: $.50 per page. Certification fee: $.50 per page. Payee: Circuit Clerk. Business checks accepted. No credit cards accepted. Prepayment required. Mail requests: SASE requested.

Magistrate Court 38 W Main, Rm 204 Courthouse Annex, Buckhannon, WV 26201; 304-472-2053; fax: 304-472-2061; 8-4. ***Misdemeanor, Civil Actions under $5,000, Eviction, Small Claims.***
Civil Records: Access: Mail, in person. Both court and visitors may perform in person searches. Search fee: $25.00. Civil cases indexed by defendant, plaintiff. Civil records from 1977; computerized back to 1996. Mail turnaround-1-2 days. Civil PAT goes back to 1995. PAT civil result has middle initial.
Criminal Records: Access: Mail, in person. Both court and visitors may perform in person searches. Search fee: $25.00. Required to search: name; also helpful: DOB, SSN. Criminal records from 1977; computerized back to 1992. Mail turnaround time 1-2 days. Criminal PAT goes back to 1992. PAT criminal results show middle initial.
General Information: Will fax documents $2.00 per page. Court makes copy: $.25 per page. Self serve: same. Certification fee: $.25 per page. Payee: Magistrate Court. Personal checks and major credit cards accepted. Prepayment required.

Wayne County

Circuit Court PO Box 38, 700 Hendricks St #204, Wayne, WV 25570; 304-272-6360; civil phone: 304-272-6359; probate phone: 304-272-4372; 8AM-4PM M,T,W,F; 8AM-8PM TH. ***Felony, Civil Actions over $5,000, Probate.***
Probate is handled by County Clerk, PO Box 248, Wayne, WV 25570.
Civil Records: Access: Phone, mail, in person. Both court and visitors may perform in person searches. No search fee. Required to search: name, years to search. Civil cases indexed by defendant, plaintiff; index on computer back to 1993; prior on index books from 1960 to present. Contact Circuit Clerk for books prior to 1900s. Note: The staff will not conduct genealogical searches. Mail turnaround 1-2 days.
Criminal Records: Access: In person only. Visitors must perform in person searches themselves. Required to search: name, years to search, SSN; also helpful: DOB. Criminal records computerized from 1993; prior on index books from 1960 to present. Contact Circuit Clerk for books prior to 1900s.
General Information: No juvenile, adoption, mental records released. Will not fax documents. Court makes copy: $.50 per page. Self serve: same. No certification fee. Payee: Clerk of Circuit Court. Business checks accepted. No credit cards accepted. Prepayment required. Mail requests: SASE required for civil.

Magistrate Court PO Box 667, Wayne, WV 25570; 304-272-5648/6388; fax: 304-272-5988; 8AM-N, 1-4PM. ***Felony, Misdemeanor, Civil Actions under $5,000, Eviction, Small Claims.***
www.state.wv.us/wvsca/courthouses/wayne.htm
Civil Records: Access: Phone, fax, mail, in person. Both court and visitors may perform in person searches. Search fee: $25.00 per name. Required to search: name; also helpful: years to search, DOB, SSN. Civil records on computer back to 1996. Mail turnaround time 1-2 days, usually same day for phone requests. Civil PAT goes back to 1996. PAT results show name only.
Criminal Records: Access: Fax, mail, in person. Both court and visitors may perform in person searches. Search fee: $25.00 per name. Required to search: name; also helpful: years to search, DOB, SSN. Criminal records computerized from 1996. Mail turnaround time 1-2 days; usually same day for phone request. Criminal PAT goes back to same as civil. PAT results show name only.
General Information: Will fax documents $2.00 per page. Court makes copy: $.25 per page. Self serve: same. Certification fee: $.50 per page. Payee: Wayne County Magistrate Court. Personal checks and major credit cards accepted. Prepayment required. Mail requests: SASE required.

Webster County

Circuit Court 2 Court Square, Rm G-4, Webster Springs, WV 26288; 304-847-2421; fax: 304-847-2062; 8:30AM-4PM. ***Felony, Civil Actions over $5,000, Probate.***
Civil Records: Access: Phone, fax, mail, in person. Both court and visitors may perform in person searches. No search fee. Required to search: name, years to search. Civil cases indexed by defendant, plaintiff. Civil index on cards from 1977 to present, also on computer since 8/99. Mail turnaround time 3-5 days.
Criminal Records: Access: Phone, fax, mail, in person. Both court and visitors may perform in person searches. No search fee. Required to search: name, years to search; also helpful: DOB, SSN. Felony dockets back to 1800s. Criminal records also on computer from 8/99. Mail turnaround 3-5 days.
General Information: No mental health, juvenile, guardianship, adoption, paternity records released. Will fax documents $1.00 per page. Court makes copy: $.50 per page. Certification fee: $.50 per page. Payee: Clerk of Circuit Court. Personal checks accepted; credit cards are not. Prepayment required. Mail requests: SASE requested.

Magistrate Court 2 Court Square, Rm B-1, Webster Springs, WV 26288; 304-847-2613; fax: 304-847-7747; 8:30AM-4PM. ***Misdemeanor, Civil Actions under $5,000, Eviction, Small Claims.***
They recommend that criminal searches be directed to the Court Repository in Charleston, 304-746-2180.
Civil Records: Access: Fax, mail, in person. Visitors must perform in person searches themselves. Search fee: $25.00 per name. Civil cases indexed by both defendant/plaintiff. Civil records go back to 1977; on computer since 2001. Mail turnaround time 7-10 days. Civil PAT goes back to 2000.
Criminal Records: Access: Fax, mail, in person. Visitors must perform in person searches themselves. Search fee: $25.00 per name. Required to search: name, years to search; also helpful: DOB, SSN. Criminal records go back to 1977; on computer since 2001. Mail turnaround time 7-10 days. Criminal PAT goes back to same as civil. PAT results show middle initial, DOB. Terminal results include SSN.
General Information: Will fax documents to local or toll free line. Court makes copy: $.25 per page. Self serve: same. Certification fee: $.50 per page. Payee: Magistrate Court Clerk. Personal checks and major credit cards accepted. Prepayment required. Mail requests: SASE required.

Wetzel County

Circuit Court PO Box 263, New Martinsville, WV 26155; 304-455-8219; fax: 304-455-1069; 9AM-4:30PM; till 4PM only TH; 9AM-N Sat. ***Felony, Civil Actions over $5,000.***
Civil Records: Access: In person, online. Visitors must perform in person searches themselves. Required to search: name, years to search. Civil cases indexed by defendant, plaintiff. Civil index on docket books back to mid 1863; computerized back to 1996. Civil PAT goes back to 1996. Online access is via a pay service at www.swcg-inc.com/products/circuit_express.html or call 800-795-8543. $125 set-up fee plus a $38.00 or $120 monthly fee plan.
Criminal Records: Access: In person, online. Visitors must perform in person searches themselves. Required to search: name. Criminal records indexed in books back to mid 1863; computerized back to 1996. Criminal PAT goes back to same as civil. Online access same as civil.
General Information: No juvenile, domestic records released. Will fax documents. Court makes copy: $.50 per page. No certification fee. Payee: Circuit Clerk. Personal checks accepted; credit cards are not. Prepayment required.

Magistrate Court PO Box 147, New Martinsville, WV 26155; 304-455-5040\5171\2450; fax: 304-455-2859; 8:30-4:30PM. ***Misdemeanor, Civil Actions under $5,000, Eviction, Small Claims.***
Civil Records: Access: mail, fax, in person. Both court and visitors may perform in person searches. Search fee: $25.00 per name. Required to search: name, DOB, SSN, years to search. Civil cases indexed by defendant, plaintiff. Civil records go back to 1995. Mail turnaround time 1-2 days. Civil PAT goes back to 11/1999. PAT civil results show middle initial.
Criminal Records: Access: mail, fax, in person. Both court and visitors may perform in person searches. Search fee: $25.00 per name. Required to search: name, years to search; also helpful: DOB, SSN. Criminal records go back to 1980. Mail turnaround time 1-2 days. Criminal PAT goes back to same as civil. PAT criminal results show middle initial.
General Information: Will fax documents. Court makes copy: $.25 per page. Payee: Wetzel County Magistrate Court. Personal check, Visa/MC accepted. Prepayment required. Mail requests: SASE required.

Wirt County

Circuit Court PO Box 465, Elizabeth, WV 26143; 304-275-6597; probate phone: 304-275-4271; criminal fax: 304-275-3230; civil fax: same; 8:30AM-4PM. ***Felony, Civil over $5,000, Probate.***
Probate records located at the county clerk's office. Probate fax- 304-275-3418
Civil Records: Access: Phone, fax, mail, in person. Both court and visitors may perform in person searches. No search fee. Required to search: name, years to search. Civil cases indexed by defendant, plaintiff. Civil index on cards from 1848 to present; computerized back to 9/2000.
Criminal Records: Access: Fax, in person. Both court and visitors may perform in person searches. No search fee. Required to search: name, years to search, DOB, SSN. Criminal records indexed on cards from 1848 to present; computerized back to 9/2000.
General Information: No juvenile or adoption records released. No fee to fax documents. Court makes copy: $.10 per page. Certification fee: $.50 per page includes copy fee. Payee: Wirt County Circuit Clerk. Personal checks accepted; credit cards are not. Prepayment required. Mail requests: SASE required for civil.

Magistrate Court PO Box 249, Court St, Elizabeth, WV 26143; 304-275-3641/2; fax: 304-275-4882; 8:30AM-4PM. ***Misdemeanor, Civil Actions under $5,000, Eviction, Small Claims.***
Civil Records: Access: Mail, in person. Both court and visitors may perform in person searches. Search fee: $25.00. Civil cases indexed by defendant, plaintiff. Civil records go back 10 years; computerized back to 9/2000. Civil PAT goes back to 9/2000. PAT civil results show middle initial.
Criminal Records: Access: Main, in person. Both court and visitors may perform in person searches. Search fee: $25.00. Required to search: name, years to search; also helpful: address, DOB, SSN. Criminal records go back 10 years; computerized back to 9/2000. Criminal PAT goes back to same as civil. PAT criminal results show middle initial.
General Information: Will fax documents $2.00 per page. Court makes copy: $.25 per page. Certification fee: $.50 per page. Payee: County Magistrate Court. Personal checks accepted. Visa/MC accepted. Prepayment required. Mail requests: SASE required.

Wood County

Circuit Court Wood County Judicial, #2 Government Sq, Parkersburg, WV 26101-5353; 304-424-1700; probate phone: 304-424-1850; fax: 304-424-1804; 8:30AM-4:30PM. ***Felony, Civil Actions over $5,000, Probate.*** Probate is handled by County Clerk, PO Box 1474, Parkersburg, WV 26102.
Civil Records: Access: Phone, mail, in person. Both court and visitors may perform in person searches. No search fee. Required to search: name, years to

search. Civil cases indexed by defendant, plaintiff; index on computer from 1978 to present, on index books back to 1885. Mail turnaround time approx. 2-3 days. Civil PAT available.

Criminal Records: Access: Mail, in person. Both court and visitors may perform in person searches. No search fee. Required to search: name, years to search, DOB, SSN. Criminal records on computer since 1979; prior records on index back to 1885. Mail turnaround time approx. 2-3 days. Criminal PAT available.

General Information: No juvenile, domestic, adoption, mental hygiene, guardianship records released. Will fax documents $2.00 per page. Court makes copy: $.50 per page. No certification fee. Payee: Carole Jones, Clerk. No checks accepted. No credit cards accepted. Prepayment required.

Magistrate Court 208 Avery St, Parkersburg, WV 26101; 304-422-3444; 8:30AM-4:30PM. ***Misdemeanor, Civil Actions under $5,000, Eviction, Small Claims.***

Civil Records: Access: Mail, in person. Both court and visitors may perform in person searches. No search fee. Required to search: name, DOB, SSN, years to search. Civil cases indexed by defendant, plaintiff. Civil records go back 10 years. Note: Fax and mail access limited. Mail turnaround time 10 days. Civil PAT goes back to 1996.

Criminal Records: Access: Mail, in person. Both court and visitors may perform in person searches. Search fee: If the court does record search fee is $25.00. Required to search: name, years to search, address; also helpful: DOB, SSN. Criminal records go back 10 years. Note: Fax and mail access limited. Mail turnaround time 10 days. Criminal PAT goes back to same as civil.

General Information: Will fax documents $2.00 per page. Do not fax in record search requests. Court makes copy: $.25 per page. Certification fee: $.50 per page includes copy fee. Payee: Wood County Magistrate Court. Personal checks and credit cards accepted. Prepayment required. Mail requests: SASE required.

Wyoming County

Circuit Court PO Box 190, Pineville, WV 24874; 304-732-8000 X238; fax: 304-732-7262; 8AM-4PM M-TH; 8AM-6PM Fri. ***Felony, Civil Actions over $5,000.***

www.state.wv.us/wvsca/courthouses/Wyoming.htm

Civil Records: Access: Phone, mail, in person, online. Both court and visitors may perform in person searches. No search fee. Required to search: name, years to search. Civil cases indexed by defendant, plaintiff. Civil index on docket books back to 1800s. Mail turnaround time 1-2 days, less for phone requests. Civil PAT goes back to 1997. PAT results show name only. Online access via a pay service at www.swcg-inc.com/products/circuit_express.html or call 800-795-8543. $125 set-up fee plus a $38.00 or $120 monthly fee plan.

Criminal Records: Access: Phone, mail, in person, online. Both court and visitors may perform in person searches. No search fee. Required to search: name, years to search; also helpful: DOB, SSN. Criminal records indexed in books back to 1800s. Mail turnaround time 1-2 days, less for phone request. Criminal PAT goes back to same as civil. PAT results show name only. Online access same as civil.

General Information: No juvenile, mental hygiene, adoption, or sealed records released. Will not fax documents. Court makes copy: $.50 per page. Certification fee: $.50 per page. Payee: David Stover, Circuit Clerk. Business checks accepted. No credit cards accepted. Prepayment required. Mail requests: SASE preferred.

Magistrate Court PO Box 598, Pineville, WV 24874; 304-732-8000 X218; fax: 304-732-7247; 9AM-4PM M-TH, 9AM-6PM Fri. ***Misdemeanor, Civil Actions under $5,000, Eviction, Small Claims.***

Civil Records: Access: Mail, in person. Both court and visitors may perform in person searches. Search fee: $25.00 per name. Civil records from 1977; computerized back to 1995. Mail turnaround time 1-2 days. Civil PAT goes back to 9/1995.

Criminal Records: Access: Mail, in person. Both court and visitors may perform in person searches. Search fee: $25.00 per name. Required to search: name, years to search; also helpful: DOB, SSN. Criminal records from 1977; computerized back to 1995. Mail turnaround time 1-2 days. Criminal PAT goes back to same as civil.

General Information: Fee to fax files is $2.00 per page. Court makes copy: $.25 per page. Self serve: same. Certification fee: $.75. Payee: Wyoming County Magistrate Court. Personal checks and major credit cards accepted. Prepayment required.

West Virginia Recording Offices

ORGANIZATION: 55 counties, 55 recording offices. The recording officer is the County Clerk. West Virginia is entirely in the Eastern Time Zone.

REAL ESTATE RECORDS: Most County Clerks will not perform real estate searches. Real estate record copy fees are usually $1.50 up to two pages and $1.00 each additional page. Certification fee is usually $1.00 but may be per page or per document.

UCC RECORDS: Financing statements are filed at the state level except for real estate related collateral which are filed only with the Register of Deeds. Previous to July, 2001, collateral on consumer goods were are filed in both places; now they are only filed at the state level. About one-third of recording offices will perform UCC searches. Use search request form UCC-11. UCC search fees vary.

TAX LIEN RECORDS: All federal and state tax liens are filed with the County Clerk. Some, not all, counties will not perform tax lien searches.

OTHER LIENS: Judgment, mechanics, lis pendens.

ONLINE ACCESS: A growing number of counties offer online access. A private company offers subscription access to land book assessment information statewide at http://digitalcourthouse.com. Access UCCs and active, expired or terminated liens at the Secretary of State's office free at www.wvsos.com/UccSearch/index-noecomm.aspx

Barbour County

County Clerk, 8 N Main St; Courthouse, Philippi, WV 26416. 304-457-2232; fax-304-457-5983; 8:30AM-4:30PM
Index: Separate indices to search include computer to 1997, prior on books by year. Records indexed on a public use terminal back to 7/97. Office personnel or visitors may perform searches. Search fee $1.00 per name per year. Office will search real estate records. Copy fee $1.50 per page. Cert fee- $1.00 per cert plus copy fee. **Other phones:** Treasurer- 304-457-2881. **Property tax/ Assessing-** 8 N Main St, Courthouse, Philippi, WV 26416; 304-457-2336.

Berkeley County

County Clerk, 100 W King St, Rm 1, Martinsburg, WV 25401. 304-264-1927; fax-304-267-1794; 9AM-5PM. _Index: Separate indices to search include 1772-1925, 1926-1981, 1982-1998, 1998 forward on computer. Records indexed on a public use terminal back to 1198. Only the public may search. Copy fee $1.50 per page. Cert fee- $1.00 per doc plus copy fee. Payee- County Clerk. **Other phones:** Treasurer- 304-267-5040. **Property tax/Assessing-** 400 W Stephen St, #208, Martinsburg, WV 25401; 304-267-5050, assessor fax- 304-262-8484. www.berkeleycountycomm.org/officials/assessor.cfm **Online** - Access property tax data free at www.softwaresystems.com/ssi/taxinquiry/. Also, access property data free at www.onlinegis.net/WvBerkeley/. Click on Display Map then Search, no name searching. Access sheriff tax sale data free at http://planning.berkeleycountycomm.org:8003/.

Boone County

County Clerk, 200 State St, Madison, WV 25130. 304-369-7337; fax-304-369-7329; 8AM-4PM
Index: All in one. Record index not computerized. Only the public may search. Copy fee $1.50 1st 2 pages; $1.00 each add'l. Cert fee- $1.00. Payee- Boone County Clerk. **Other phones:** Treasurer- 304-369-7391; Elections- 304-369-7337. **Property tax/Assessing-** 200 State St, Madison, WV 25130; 304-369-7308, assessor fax- 304-369-7319. (Appraiser/Auditor- 304-369-7316) No public access terminal. **Online access-** Access property tax data free at www.softwaresystems.com/ssi/taxinquiry/.

Braxton County

County Clerk, PO Box 486, Sutton, WV 26601-0728. -304-765-2833; fax-304-765-2093; 8AM-4PM.
Index: All in one. Records indexed on computer back to 1983. Only the public may search. Copy fee $1.50 1st 2 pages, $1.00 each add'l. Tax maps $3.00 per page. Cert fee- $1.00 per doc plus copy fee. Payee- John D Jordan-Clerk. **Other phones:** Treasurer- 304-765-2830; Elections- 304-765-2833; Vital Records- 304-765-2833. **Property tax/Assessing-** 300 Main St, Sutton, WV 26601-0728; 304-765-2805. (Appraiser/Auditor- 304-765-2830);

Brooke County

County Clerk, 632 Main St; Courthouse, Wellsburg, WV 26070. 304-737-3661; fax-304-737-4023; 9AM-5PM, M-F; 9AM-N Sat.
Index: Separate indices to search by document type. Record index not computerized. Usually, only the public may search. Office personal may perform limited search, 1 item. Will search limited UCC records. Copy fee $1.50 1st 2 pages; $1.00 each add'l. Vital stats- $5.00 each. Cert fee- $1.00 per doc. Payee- Brooke County Clerk. **Other phones:** Treasurer- 304-737-3663; Elections- 304-737-3668; Vital Records- 304-737-3661. **Property tax/Assessing-** 632 Main St, Courthouse, Wellsburg, WV 26070; 304-737-3667, assessor fax- 304-737-5126.

Cabell County

County Clerk, 750 5th Ave, Rm 108; Cabell County Courthouse, Huntington, WV 25701-2083. -304-526-8625, UCC phone-304-526-8631; fax-304-526-8632; 8:30AM-4:30PM www.cabellcountyclerk.org
Index: Separate indices to search include deeds, liens, wills, financing statements. Records indexed on a public use terminal back to 1/1/1995. Only the public may search. Copy fee $1.50 1st 2 pages; $1.00 each add'l. Cert fee- $1.00 per doc plus copy fee. **Other phones:** Treasurer- 304-526-8672; Elections- 304-526-8633; Vital Records- 304-526-8631. **Property tax/Assessing-** 750 5th Ave, Rm 205, Huntington, WV 25701; 304-526-8601, assessor fax- 304-526-9898. www.cabellassessor.com **Online access-** Access property tax data free at www.softwaresystems.com/ssi/taxinquiry/.

Calhoun County

County Clerk, PO Box 230, Grantsville, WV 26147-0230. -304-354-6725; fax-304-354-6725; 8:30AM-4PM.
Index: All in one. Record index not computerized. Only the public may search. General copy fee-$1.50 1st 2 pages, $1.00 each add'l page. Cert fee- $5.00 per doc plus copy fee. Payee- County Clerk. **Other phones:** Treasurer- 304-354-6333; Elections- 304-354-6725; Vital Records- 304-354-6725. **Property tax/Assessing-** PO Box 257, 100 Main St, Courthouse, Grantsville, WV 26147-0230; 304-354-6958, assessor fax- 304-354-9433. **Online access-** Access to property tax and assessment for free go to http://129.71.205.140/

Clay County

County Clerk, PO Box 190, Clay, WV 25043. 304-587-4259, R/E recording phone-304-587-4260; fax-304-587-7329; 8AM-4PM
Index: Separate indices to search. Record index not computerized. Only the public may search. Copy fee $1.50 per page. Cert fee- $1.00 plus copy fee. Payee- Clay Count Clerk. Treasurer- 304-587-4260; Elections- 304-587-4260; Vital Records- 304-587-4260. **Property tax/ Assessing-** 304-587-4258.

Doddridge County

County Clerk, 118 E Court St, Rm 102, West Union, WV 26456-1297. -304-873-2631; fax-304-873-1840; 8:30AM-4PM _Index: All in one. Records indexed on a public use terminal back to 1994. Only the public may search. Copy fee $1.50 1st 2 pages, $1.00 each add'l page. Cert fee- $5.00 per cert plus copy fee. Payee- Doddridge County Clerk. **Other phones:** Treasurer- 304-873-1000; Elections- 304-873-2631. **Property tax/Assessing-** 304-873-1261.

Fayette County

County Clerk, PO Box 569, Fayetteville, WV 25840. 304-574-4225, R/E recording phone-304-574-4224, UCC recording phone-304-574-4226; fax-304-574-4335; 8AM-4PM
Index: Separate indices to search include probate, debtor/creditor, grantor/grantee. Records indexed on computer back to 1988. Office personnel or visitors may perform searches. No fee for search. Office will search real estate records. Will search UCC records. Copy fee $1.00 per page. Cert fee- $.50 per cert plus copy fee. Payee- Fayette County Clerk. **Online access to UCC, Notary Public, Voter Registration records:** Access to records for a fee at https://www.wvsos.com/common/information.htm . **Other phones:** Treasurer- 304-574-4216; Elections- 304-574-4235; Vital Records- 304-574-4232. **Property tax/Assessing-** 100 Court St, Fayetteville, WV 25840; 304-574-4256, assessor fax- 304-574-4312. Public access terminal available.

Gilmer County

County Clerk, 10 Howard St; Courthouse, Glenville, WV 26351. -304-462-7641; fax-304-462-8855; 8AM-4PM. _Index: Separate indices to search include wills, trust deeds, deeds, liens, assignments, UCCs, appraisements, birth, death, marriage. Record index not computerized. Office will perform a UCC search but public must search other records themselves. Copy fee $1.50 1st 2 pages; $1.00 each add'l. Cert fee- $1.00 per doc plus copy fee. Payee- Gilmer County Clerk. **Other phones:** Treasurer- 304-462-7441; Elections- 304-462-7641; Vital Records- 304-462-7641. **Property tax/Assessing-** 10 Howard St, Courthouse, Glenville, WV 26351; 304-462-7731, assessor fax- 304-462-4923. (Appraiser/Auditor- 304-462-7039) hours- 8AM-N; 1-4PM

Grant County

County Clerk, 5 Highland Ave, Petersburg, WV 26847. -304-257-4550; fax-304-257-4207; 8:30AM-4:30PM. _Index: Separate indices to search include general, lien. Records indexed on computer back to 7/1/79. Only the public may search. Copy fee $1.00 for 1-10 pages, $.50 each add'l. $6.00 for birth, death or marriage certificate. Cert fee- $2.50 per page includes copy fee. Payee- Grant County Clerk. **Other phones:** Treasurer- 304-257-1818; Elections- 304-257-4550; Vital Records- 304-257-4550; Sheriff- 304-257-1818. **Property tax/Assessing-** 5 Highland Ave, Petersburg, WV 26847; 304-257-1050, assessor fax- 304-257-4117. (Appraiser - 304-257-4117) 8:30AM-4PM No public access computer in office.

Greenbrier County

County Clerk, PO Box 506, Lewisburg, WV 24901. -304-647-6602; fax-304-647-6694; 8:30AM-4:30PM www.greenbriercounty.net/coclerk/index.html Only the public may search. Copy fee $1.50 1st 2 pages; $1.00 each add'l. Cert fee- $3.00 per cert plus copy fee. Payee- Greenbrier County Clerk. **Other phones:** Treasurer- 304-647-6609; Elections- 304-647-6601; Vital Records- 304-647-6602. **Property tax/Assessing-** 200 N Court St, Lewisburg, WV 24901; 304-647-6615, assessor fax- 304-647-6667. hours- 8AM-4:30PM www.greenbrierassessor.com **Online access-** Access property tax data free at www.softwaresystems.com/ssi/taxinquiry/.

Hampshire County

County Clerk, PO Box 806, Romney, WV 26757-0806. -304-822-5112; fax-304-822-4039; 9AM-4PM, Fri til 6PM _Index: Separate indices to search include deed, liens, marriages, birth, death, wills, general records. Records indexed on a public use terminal back to 7/98. Office will perform a UCC search but public must search other records themselves. Copy fee $1.50 1st 2 pages; $1.00 each add'l. Cert fee- $2.50 plus copy fee. Payee- Hampshire County Clerk. **Other phones:** Treasurer- 304-822-4720; Elections- 304-822-5112; Vital Records- 304-822-5112. **Property tax/Assessing-** 66 N High St, Romney, WV 26757; 304-822-3326, assessor fax- 304-822-8164. (Appraiser/Auditor- 304-822-3326) hours- 9AM-4PM M-TH; 9AM-6PM F **Online access-** Access to property data is free on the property records site at www.qpublic.net/wv/hampshire/search1.html.

Hancock County

County Clerk, PO Box 367, New Cumberland, WV 26047. 304-564-3311 x279, R/E recording phone-304-564-3311 x267, UCC recording phone-304-564-3311 x281; fax-304-564-5941; 8:30AM-4:30PM http://hancockcountywv.org
Index: Before 10/1/97 docs are individually indexed. After, all in one. Records indexed on computer back to 10/1/97. Office will perform a UCC search if you provide number, but public must search other records themselves. Copy fee $1.50 1st 2 pages, $1.00 each add'l page, per doc. Cert fee- $1.00 plus copy fee. Payee- Hancock County Clerk. Treasurer- 304-564-3311 x262; Elections- 304-564-3311 x288; Vitals- 304-564-3311 x280. **Property tax/Assessing-** PO Box 455, New Cumberland, WV 26047; 304-564-3311 x256, fax- 304-564-3415. (Appraiser - x256)

Hardy County

County Clerk, 204 Washington St, Rm 111; Moorefield, WV 26836. 304-530-0250; fax-304-530-0251; 9AM-4PM. www.hardycounty.com Index: Separate indices to search include deeds, liens, releases, DT. Records indexed on a public use terminal back to 1/1/1993. Office will perform a UCC search but public must search other records themselves. Office will not search real estate records. Copy fee $1.50 1st 2 pages; $1.00 each add'l. Cert fee- $1.00 per cert plus copy fee. Payee- Hardy County Clerk. **Online Real Estate, Grantor/Grantee, Deed, Mortgage records:** Access recorded index free at www.onlinecountyrecords.com. Username Id and Password is hardywv, all small letters. Index goes back to 1/1993. **Other phones:** Elections- 304-530-0250; Vital Records- 304-530-0250; Sheriff- 304-530-0222. **Property tax/Assessing-** 240 Washington St, Moorefield, WV 26836; 304-530-0202.

Harrison County

County Clerk, 301 W Main St; Courthouse, Clarksburg, WV 26301. 304-624-8672, R/E recording phone-304-624-8694; fax-304-624-8575; 8:30AM-4:30PM. _Index: Separate indices to search include grantee/grantor, liens, marriage, death. Records indexed on a public use terminal back to 1988. Only the public may search. Copy fee $1.50 for 1st 2 pages, $1.00 each add'l. Cert fee- $5.00 per cert includes copy fee. Payee- Harrison County Clerk. **Other phones:** Treasurer- 304-624-8550; Elections- 304-624-8615; Vital Records- 304-624-8608. **Property tax/Assessing-** 301 W Main St, Courthouse, Clarksburg, WV 26301; 304-624-8510. http://assessor.harrisoncountywv.com/?sm=d

Jackson County

County Clerk, PO Box 800, Ripley, WV 25271. 304-373-2250, R/E recording phone-304-373-2259, UCC recording phone-304-373-2258; fax-304-372-1107; 8:30AM-4:30PM M-F.
Index: Separate indices to search include deeds, deed of trust, etc. Records indexed on computer back to 1989. Only the public may search. Copy fee $1.50 1st 2 pages; $1.00 each add'l. Cert fee- $1.00 per doc plus copy fee. Payee- Jackson County Clerk. **Other phones:** Treasurer- 304-373 2280; Elections- 304-373-2249; Vital Records- 304-373-2256. **Property tax/Assessing-** 106 North St W, Ripley, WV 25271; 304-372-2240. www.jacksonwvassessor.com **Online-** Access property data for free http://raven.mtncad.com:81/portal/index.php?CONFIG=Jackson

Jefferson County

County Clerk, PO Box 208, Charles Town, WV 25414. -304-728-3215, UCC-304-728-3248; fax-304-728-1957; 9-5PM www.jeffersoncountyclerkwv.com/
Index: Separate indices to search include judgments, UCC, releases, deeds, deeds of trust, will, plat, and more. Records indexed on a public use terminal back to 10/198. Office will perform a UCC search but public must search other records themselves though the office can assist. Search fee $4.00 per name. Office will not name search real estate records. Copy fee $1.50 1st 2 pages; $1.00 each add'l. Cert fee- $1.00 per doc plus copy fee. Payee- Jefferson County Clerk. **Other phones:** Treasurer- 304-728-3220; Elections- 304-728-3246; Vital Records- 304-728-3215. **Property tax/Assessing-** 104 E Washington St, Charles Town, WV 25414; 304-728-3224. hours- 9AM- 5PM M-TH; 9AM-7PM Fri. www.jeffersoncountywv.org/asse.html **Online access-** Access property tax data free at www.softwaresystems.com/ssi/taxinquiry/.

Kanawha County

County Clerk, PO Box 3226, Charleston, WV 25332. 304-357-0130, R/E recording phone-304-357-0244; fax-304-357-0585; 8AM-5PM M T W F; 8AM-7PM TH. www.kanawha.us/countyclerk/default.aspx
Index: Separate indices. Records indexed on a public use terminal back to 8/99. Prior to 8/99 on index card system. Only the public may search. Copy fee $1.50 1st 2 pages; $1.00 each add'l. Cert fee- $1.00 per doc plus copy fee. Payee- County Clerk. Treasurer- 304-357-0210; Elections- 304-357-0110; Vital Records- 304-357-0710. **Property tax/Assessing-** 409 Virginia St E, Charleston, 25332; 304-357-0250, fax- 304-357-0551. www.kanawha.us/assessor/default.aspx **Online access-** Access property tax data free at www.softwaresystems.com/ssi/taxinquiry/.

Lewis County

County Clerk, PO Box 87, Weston, WV 26452. -304-269-8215; fax-304-269-8202; 8:30AM-4:30PM
Index: Separate indices to search include deeds, deed of trust, judgment, releases, fiduciary, plats, birth, death, marriage. Record index not computerized. Only the public may search. Copy fee $1.50 1st 2 pages; $1.00 each add'l. Cert fee- $2.00 per doc plus copy fee. Payee- Lewis County Clerk. **Other phones:** Treasurer- 304-269-8222; Elections- 304-269-8215; Vital Records- 304-269-8215; Second Phone- 304-269-8216. **Property tax/Assessing-** 304-269-8205.

Lincoln County

County Clerk, PO Box 497, Hamlin, WV 25523. 304-824-3336; fax-304-824-2444; 9AM-4:30PM.
Records indexed on a public use terminal back to 2002. Only the public may search. Copy fee $1.50 1st 2 pages; $1.00 each add'l. Cert fee- $1.00 per page plus copy fee. **Other phones:** Treasurer- 304-824-7990; Vital Records- 304-824-3336. **Property tax/Assessing-** 304-824-7878.

Logan County

County Clerk, Stratton & Main St, Rm 101; Courthouse, Logan, WV 25601. 304-792-8600, R/E recording phone-304-792-8603, UCC recording phone-304-792-8606; fax-304-792-8621; 8:30AM-4:30PM Index: Separate indices to search include deeds, releases, UCCs, liens, trustee's report of sales, misc, maps, fiduciary. Records indexed on a public use terminal back to 0101/1988. Records before 1988 are in index book form. Office will perform a UCC search but public must search other records themselves. Copy fee $1.50 1st 2 pages, $1.00 each add'l. Cert fee- $5.00 per doc plus copy fee. Payee- John A. Turner- County Clerk. **Other phones:** Treasurer- 304-792-8680; Elections- 304-792-8620; Vitals- 304-792-8620. **Property tax/Assessing-** Logan County Courthouse, Rm 212, Logan, WV 25601; 304-792-8520, assessor fax- 304-792-8542.

Marion County

County Clerk, PO Box 1267, Fairmont, WV 26555-1267. 304-367-5441 or 5440, R/E recording phone-304-367-5453, UCCs-304-367-5440; fax-304-367-5448; 8:30AM - 4:30PM www.marioncountywv.com
Index: Separate indices to search. Records indexed on a public use terminal back to 1985. Only the public may search. General copy fee $1.50 for 1st 2 pages and $1.00 each add'l page. Cert fee- $1.00 per page. Payee- Marion County Clerk. **Other phones:** Treasurer- 304-367-5303; Elections- 304-367-5447; Vitals- 304-367-5453. **Property tax/Assessing-** 200 Jackson St, Fairmont, WV 26554; 304-367-5410, assessor fax- 304-367-6532. (Appraiser/Auditor- 304-367-5310) www.marioncountyassessor.com/

Marshall County

County Clerk, PO Box 459, Moundsville, WV 26041. -304-845-1220; fax-304-845-5891; 8:30AM-4:30PM.
Index: Separate indices to search include deed, lien, miscellaneous. Records indexed on computer back to 4/01. Only the public may search. Copy fee $.50 per page. Vital Stat- $5.00 per doc. Cert fee- $5.00 per doc plus copy fee. Payee- Marshall County Clerk. **Other phones:** Treasurer- 304-843-1400; Elections- 304-845-1220; Vital Records- 304-845-1220. **Property tax/Assessing-** 600 7th St, Moundsville, WV 26041; 304-845-1490.

Mason County

County Clerk, 200 6th St, Point Pleasant, WV 25550. -304-675-1997; fax-304-675-2521; 8:30AM-4:30PM.
Index: Separate indices to search include grantor/grantee, debtor, estate. Records indexed on a public use terminal back to 1991. Only the public may search. Copy fee $1.50 1st 2 pages; $1.00 each add'l. Cert fee- $1.00 per cert plus copy fee. Payee- Mason

County Clerk. **Other phones:** Treasurer- 304-675-1047; Elections- 304-675-1997; Vital Records- 304-675-1997. **Property tax/Assessing-** 200 6th St, Point Pleasant, WV 25550; 304-675-2840, assessor fax-304-675-6358. (Appraiser/Auditor- 304-675-2918) No public computer in office.

McDowell County

County Clerk, 90 Wyoming St, #109, Welch, WV 24801-2487. 304-436-8544, R/E recording phone-304-436-8539, UCC recording phone-304-436-8542; fax-304-436-8576; 9AM-5PM
Index: More than one index. Record index not computerized. Only the public may search. Copy fee $1.50 1st 2 pages; $1.00 each add'l. Cert fee- $5.00 per cert plus copy fee. Payee- McDowell County Clerk. **Other phones:** Treasurer- 304-436-8536; Elections- 304-436-8543; Vital Records- 304-436-8542. **Property tax/Assessing-** 90 Wyoming St, #110, Welch, WV 24801; 304-436-8564, assessor fax- 304-436-5230. (Appraiser - 304-436-8528);

Mercer County

County Clerk, 1501 Main St, Princeton, WV 24740. -304-487-8312; 8:30AM-4PM
Index: Separate indices to search include deed, trust deed, judgment, UCCs, financing, birth, death, marriage, military, misc, etc. Records indexed on computer back to June, 1991. Only the public may search. Copy fee $1.50 1st 2 pages; $1.00 each add'l. Cert fee- $6.00 per 6 pages plus $1.00 each add'l page plus $3.00 exemplification fee. Payee- Mercer County Clerk. **Other phones:** Treasurer- 304-425-8344; Elections- 304-487-8339; Vital Records- 304-487-8313; Probate Records- 304-487-8321. **Property tax/Assessing-** PO Box 5429, 1501 W Main St (24740), Princeton, WV 24746; 304-487-8327, assessor fax- 304-487-8399. hours- 8:30AM-4:30PM

Mineral County

County Clerk, 150 Armstrong St, Keyser, WV 26726. -304-788-3924; fax-304-788-4109; 8:30AM-5PM
Index: All in one. Records indexed on computer back to 2000. Only the public may search. Will not search UCC records. Copy fee $1.50 1st 2 pages; $1.00 each add'l. Cert fee- $1.00 per cert plus copy fee. Payee- Mineral County Clerk. **Other phones:** Treasurer-304-788-0341; Elections- 304-788-3924; Vital Records- 304-788-3924. **Property tax/Assessing-** 150 Armstrong St, Keyser, WV 26726; 304-788-3753. (Appraiser/Auditor- 304-788-3753)

Mingo County

County Clerk, PO Box 1197, Williamson, WV 25661. 304-235-0330; fax-304-235-0565; 8:30AM-4:30PM
Index: All in one. Records indexed on a public use terminal back to 7/90. Only the public may search. Copy fee $1.50 1st 2 pages, $.50 each add'l. Cert fee-$5.00 per cert plus copy fee. Payee- Mingo County Clerk. **Other phones:** Elections- 304-235-0330. **Property tax/Assessing-** 304-235-0310.

Monongalia County

County Clerk, 243 High St, Rm 123; Courthouse, Morgantown, WV 26505-5491. 304-291-7230, R/E recording phone-304-291-7235; fax-304-291-7233; www.monongaliacountyclerk.com/
Index: Separate indices to search include deeds, liens, estates, discharges, assumed names. Record index not computerized. Only the public may search. Copy fee $1.50 1st 2 pages; $1.00 each add'l. Cert fee- $1.00 per doc plus copy fee; exemplification- $3.00. Payee-Monongalia County Clerk. **Other phones:** Treasurer-304-291-7244; Elections- 304-291-7238; Vital Records- 304-291-7234. **Property tax/Assessing-** 243 High St, 2nd Fl, Morgantown, WV 26505; 304-291-7279, assessor fax- 304-291-7220. hours- 9AM-7PM M; 9AM-5PM T-F A public access terminal is available. www.assessor.org **Online access-** Access the County Parcel Search database free at www.assessor.org/parcelweb/. Search by a wide variety of criteria including owner name and address. Access property tax data free at www.softwaresystems.com/ssi/taxinquiry/.

Monroe County

County Clerk, PO Box 350, Union, WV 24983. 304-772-3096; fax-304-772-4191; 8:30AM-4:30PM www.monroecountywv.net/County_Clerk/
Index: Separate indices to search include liens, releases, deeds, leases, fiduciary, PITs. Record index not computerized. Only the public may search. Copy fee $1.50 1st 2 pages; $1.00 each add'l. Cert fee-$1.00 per doc plus copy fee. Payee- Monroe County Clerk. **Other phones:** Treasurer- 304-772-3018. **Property tax/Assessing-** PO Box 350, Union, WV 24983; 304-772-3083, assessor fax- 304-772-4087. hours- 8:30AM-4PM No public access computer in office. www.monroecountywv.net/Assessor/

Morgan County

County Clerk, 77 Fairfax St, #1A, Berkeley Springs, WV 25411. 304-258-8547; fax-304-258-8545; 9AM-5PM M,T,TH; 9AM-1PM W; 9AM-7PM F. www.morgancountyeda.com/gov/morgancountyclerk.html
Index: Separate indices to search. Records indexed on computer from 1976 forward. Also have paper indexes for older documents. Only the public may search. General copy fee $1.50 for 1st 2 pages; $1.00 each add'l. Cert fee- $1.00 per cert plus copy fee. Payee- Morgan County Clerk. **Other phones:** Treasurer- 304-258-8562; Elections- 304-258-8547; Vital Records- 304-258-8547. **Property tax/Assessing-** 35 N Mercer St, Berkeley Springs, WV 25411; 304-258-8570, assessor fax- 304-258-7308. (Appraiser/Auditor- 304-258-8570) hours-8AM-5PM M,T,TH; 8AM-1PM W; 8AM-7PM F

Nicholas County

County Clerk, 700 Main St, #2, Summersville, WV 26651. 304-872-7820; fax-304-872-9600; 8:30AM-4:30PM. Index: Separate indices to search include deeds, frauds, liens, judgment & execution, mechanic liens. Records indexed on a public use terminal back to 1818. Only the public may search. Copy fee $1.50 1st 2 pages; $1.00 each add'l. Cert fee- $1.00 per cert. Payee- County Clerk's Office. **Other phones:** Treasurer- 304-872-3630 x42; Elections- 304-872-7820; Vital Records- 304-872-7820. **Property tax/Assessing-** 700 Main St, Summersville, WV 26651; 304-872-7800. **Online** - Access property tax data free www.softwaresystems.com/ssi/taxinquiry/.

Ohio County

County Clerk, 1500 Chapline St, Rm 205, Wheeling, WV 26003. 304-234-3656; fax-304-234-3829; 8:30AM-5PM Index: Separate indices to search include deed, lien, will, birth, death, marriage. Records indexed on computer back to 1993. Only the public may search. Copy fee $.50 per page. Cert fee-$1.00 per page, copies not included. Payee- Ohio County Clerk. Treasurer- 304-234-3688. **Property tax/Assessing-** 1500 Chapline St Rm 204, Wheeling, WV 26003; 304-234-3626, fax- 304-232-0293.

Pendleton County

County Clerk, PO Box 1167, Franklin, WV 26807. 304-358-2505; fax-304-358-2473; 8:30AM-4PM
Index: Lien and right of ways are in separate indices from regular records. Record index not computerized. Office will perform a UCC search but public must search other records themselves. Search fee $.50 per name per year. Copy fee $1.50 1st 2 pages; $1.00 each add'l. Cert fee- $1.00 per doc plus copy fee. Payee- Pendleton County Clerk. **Other phones:** Treasurer- 304-358-2214. **Property tax/Assessing-** PO Box 937, 100 Main St, Franklin, WV 26807-0937; 304-358-2563, assessor fax- 304-358-2473. (Appraiser/Auditor- 304-358-2473) 8:30AM-4PM, 8:30-N Sat. No public terminal; must search books.

Pleasants County

County Clerk, 301 Court Lane, Rm 101; Courthouse, St. Marys, WV 26170. -304-684-3542; fax-304-684-7569; 8:30AM-4:30PM.
Index: Separate indices to search include wills, marriages, deaths, deed of trusts, releases, deeds, final estate settlements. Records indexed on a public use terminal back to 0901/2002. Only the public may search. Copy fee $1.50 1st 2 pages; $1.00 each add'l. Cert fee- $1.00 per doc plus copy fee. Payee- County Clerk. **Other phones:** Treasurer- 304-684-7175; Elections- 304-684-3542; Vital Records- 304-684-3542; Sheriff- 304-684-2285. **Property tax/Assessing-** 301 Courthouse Lane, Rm 103, Courthouse, St. Marys, WV 26170; 304-684-3132, assessor fax- 304-684-9315. (Appraiser/Auditor- 304-684-3132) hours- 8:30AM-4PM Public access computer in office for index and records searching.

Pocahontas County

County Clerk, 900C 10th Ave, Marlinton, WV 24954. 304-799-4549; fax-304-799-6947; 8:30AM-4:30PM
Index: All in one. Record index not computerized. Office personnel or visitors may perform searches. Office will search real estate records. Office will not search tax liens. UCC search per debtor name- $1.00. Copy fee $1.50 1st 2 pages; $1.00 each add'l. Cert fee-$1.00 per cert plus copy fee. Payee- Pocahontas County Clerk. **Other phones:** Treasurer- 304-799-4710. **Property tax/Assessing-** 900C 10th Ave, Marlinton, WV 24954; 304-799-4750, assessor fax-304-799-6132. hours- 8:30AM-4PM No public access computer in office.

Preston County

County Clerk, 106 W Main St, #103, Kingwood, WV 26537. -304-329-0070; fax-304-329-0198; 9AM-5PM (Monday open until 7PM).
Index: Pre-2001 indices to search include deeds, liens. Now all in one. Records indexed on a public use terminal back to 01/2001. Office will perform a UCC search (5 year period) but public must search other records themselves. Copy fee $1.50 1st 2 pages; $1.00 each add'l. for 1st 2 pages; $1.00 each add'l. Cert fee-$1.00 per cert plus copy fee. Payee- Preston County Clerk. **Other phones:** Treasurer- 304-329-0105; Elections- 304-329-0070; Vital Records- 304-329-0070; Sheriff/Treasurer- 304-329-0105 (Fax 304-329-3990). **Property tax/Assessing-** 106 W Main St, #101, Kingwood, WV 26537; 304-329-1220, assessor fax- 304-329-1643. (Appraiser/Auditor- 304-329-1220) hours- 9AM-7PM M; 9AM-5PM T-F No public computer in office.

Putnam County

County Clerk, 3389 Winfield Rd, Winfield, WV 25213-9705. -304-586-0202; fax-304-586-0280; 8AM-4PM http://putnamcoclerk.com/
Index: All in one. Records indexed on a public use terminal back to 3/97. Only the public may search. Copy fee $1.50 1st 2 pages, $1.00 each add'l. Vital records- $5.00 each. Cert fee- $1.00 per cert plus copy fee. Payee- Putnam County Clerk. **Other phones:** Treasurer- 304-586-0204; Elections- 304-586-0202; Vitals- 304-586-0202. **Property tax/ Assessing-** 3389 Winfield Rd, Winfield, WV 25213-9705; 304-586-0206, assessor fax- 304-586-0226. hours- 8AM-4PM M,T,W,F; 8-7PM Th http://putnamcoassessor.com/ **Online-** Access property tax data free at www.softwaresystems.com/ssi/taxinquiry/.

Raleigh County

County Clerk, 215 Main St; Courthouse, Beckley, WV 25801. 304-255-9123, R/E recording phone-304-255-9125, UCC recording phone-304-255-9123; fax-304-255-9352; 8:30AM-4PM
Index: All in one. Records indexed on a public use terminal back to 1990. Only the public may search. Copy fee $1.50 1st 2 pages; $1.00 each add'l. Cert fee-$1.00 per page plus copy fee. Payee- Raleigh County Clerk. **Other phones:** Treasurer- 304-255-9162; Elections- 304-255-9127; Vital Records- 304-255-9123. **Property tax/Assessing-** 215 Main St, Courthouse, Beckley, WV 25801; 304-255-9179, assessor fax- 304-255-9111. (Appraiser/Auditor- 304-255-9177) hours- 8:30AM-4:30PM

Randolph County

County Clerk, 2 Randolph Ave, Elkins, WV 26241. - 304-636-0543; fax-304-636-0544; 8AM-4:30PM
Index: Separate indices to search include deeds, liens, releases. Record index not computerized. Only the public may search. Will not search UCC records. Copy fee $1.50 1st 2 pages; $1.00 each add'l. Vital statistic records are $5.00 each. Cert fee- $1.00 per cert plus copy fee. Payee- Randolph County Clerk. **Other phones:** Treasurer- 304-636-2100; Elections- 304-636-0543; Vital Records- 304-636-0543; Sheriff- 304-636-2100; Circuit Clerk -307-636-2765. **Property tax/Assessing**- 4 Randolph Ave, Elkins, WV 26241; 304-636-2114, assessor fax- 304-636-9474. hours- 8AM-4PM Public access computer in office for index and records searching. **Online access**- Search County Assessor information at www.randolphcountyassessor.com/portal/ (requires username and password to login).

Ritchie County

County Clerk, 115 E Main St, Rm 201; Courthouse, Harrisville, WV 26362. 304-643-2164, R/E recording phone-304-643-2164 x221; fax-304-643-2906; 8AM-4PM. Index: Separate indices to search include UCC financing statements, releases prior to July 1, 1985; Estate appraisements prior to 7/1/1985; Appointments & bonds prior to 7/1/1985. Records indexed on a public use terminal back to 7/85. Only the public may search. Copy fee $1.50 1st 2 pages, $1.00 each add'l. Cert fee- $1.00 per cert plus copy fee. Payee- Ritchie County Clerk. Treasurer- 304-643-2164 x237; Elections- 304-643-2164 x225; Vital Records- 304-643-2164 x221; Sheriff- 304-643-2164 x237. **Property tax/Assessing**- 115 E Main St, Rm 203, Harrisville, WV 26362; 304-643-2164 x242, assessor fax- 304-643-2962. (Appraiser - 304-643-2164 x242);

Roane County

County Clerk, 200 Main St, Spencer, WV 25276. - 304-927-2860; fax-304-927-2489; 8:30AM-4PM M-F; 9AM-N Sat. Index: Separate indices to search include deeds, liens. Records indexed on a public use terminal back to 1977. Office will perform a UCC search but public must search other records themselves. Copy fee $1.50 1st 2 pages, $1.00 each add'l. Cert fee- $1.00 per cert plus copy fee. Payee- Roane County Clerk. **Other phones:** Treasurer- 304-927-2540; Elections- 304-927-2860; Vitals- 304-927-2860; Law Enforcement- 304-927-3410. **Property tax/ Assessing**- 200 Main St, Spencer, WV 25276; 304-927-3020, assessor fax- 304-927-4499. (Appraiser - 304-927-3020);

Summers County

County Clerk, PO Box 97, Hinton, WV 25951-0097. - 304-466-7104; fax-304-466-7146; 8:30AM-4:30PM
www.summerscountywv.org
Index: Separate indices to search. Record index not computerized. Only the public may search. Copy fee $1.50 1st 2 pages; $1.00 each add'l. Cert fee- For Vital Stats- $5.00 per doc plus copy fee of $2.50 for 1st 2 pages. Payee- Summers County Clerk. Treasurer- 304-466-7112; Elections- 304-466-7104; Vital Records- 304-466-7104; Sheriff- 304-466-7112. **Property tax/ Assessing**- 120 Ballengee St, Hinton, WV 25951; 304-466-7101, fax- 304-466-7128. www.summerscountywv.org/assessor.html **Online** - Access tax inquiry data free at http://129.71.205.119/.

Taylor County

County Clerk, 214 W Main St, Rm 101; Courthouse, Grafton, WV 26354. -304-265-1401; fax-304-265-3016; 8:30-N; 1-4:30PM
Index: Separate indices to search include deeds, liens, releases, leases. Some only indexed at front of books. Deeds and liens indexed on public use computer terminal back to 1/2003. Only the public may search. Will not search UCC records. Copy fee $1.50 1st 2 pages; $1.00 each add'l. Cert fee- $1.00 per page plus copy fee. Payee- Taylor County Clerk. **Other phones:** Treasurer- 304-265-5766; Elections- 304-265-1401; Vital Records- 304-265-1401. **Property tax/Assessing**- 214 W Main St, Rm 107, Grafton, WV 26354; 304-265-2420. hours- 8:30AM-4:30PM

Tucker County

County Clerk, 215 1st St, #3, Parsons, WV 26287. - 304-478-2414; fax-304-478-2217; 8AM-4PM
Index: Separate indices to search include Judgments, Deeds of Trust, Misc Instruments. Record index not computerized. Office will perform a UCC search but public must search other records themselves. Copy fee $1.50 1st 2 pages; $1.00 each add'l. Cert fee- $1.00 per cert plus copy fee. Payee- Tucker County Clerk. **Other phones:** Treasurer- 304-478-2321; Elections- 304-478-2414; Vital Records- 304-478-2414. **Property tax/Assessing**- 2151st St, #1, Parsons, WV 26287; 304-478-3727, assessor fax- 304-478-4464.

Tyler County

County Clerk, PO Box 66, Middlebourne, WV 26149. -304-758-2102; fax-304-758-2126; 8AM-N; 1-4PM
Index: Separate indices to search. Records indexed on a public use terminal back to 1998. Office personnel or visitors may perform searches. Office will search real estate records only if book/pg number is already known. Real estate record copy- $1.50 1st 2 pages; $1.00 each add'l page. Cert fee- $1.00 per cert plus copy fee. Payee- Tyler County Clerk. **Other phones:** Treasurer- 304-758-4551; Elections- 304-758-2034; Vitals- 304-758-2102. **Property tax/Assessing**- PO Box 2, Main St & Court, Middlebourne, WV 26149; 304-758-4781, fax- 304-758-2126. hours- 8AM-4PM

Upshur County

County Clerk, 40 W Main St, Rm 101; Courthouse, Buckhannon, WV 26201. -304-472-1068; fax-304-472-1029; 8AM-4:30PM.
Index: All in one 1989- present, prior to 1989 in individual indexes. Records indexed on computer back to 1984. Only the public may search. Copy fee $1.50 1st 2 pages, $1.00 each add'l. Certified Vital stat copy- $5.00. Cert fee- $1.00 per doc plus copy fee. Payee- Upshur County Clerk. **Other phones:** Treasurer- 304-472-1180; Elections- 304-472-1068; Vital Records- 304-472-1068. **Property tax/Assessing**- 38 W Main St, Rm 102, Buckhannon, WV 26201; 304-472-4650, assessor fax- 304-472-1421. (Appraiser/Auditor- 304-472-4650);

Wayne County

Clerk of County Commission, PO Box 248, Wayne, WV 25570. 304-272-5974, R/E recording phone-304-272-6371, UCC recording phone-304-272-5974; fax-304-272-5318; 8AM-4PM M,T,W,F; 8AM-8PM TH.
www.waynecountywv.us
Index: Separate indices to search include deed (grantor/grantee), debtor (Lien/Release). Records indexed on a public use terminal back to 4/1/91. Office will perform a UCC search but public must search other records themselves. UCC search per debtor name- $5.00. Copy fee $1.50 1st 2 pages, $1.00 each add'l. Cert fee- $1.00 per cert plus copy fee. Payee- Wayne County Clerk. **Online Real Estate, Deed, Lien, Marriage, Birth, Death, Will, UCC records:** recorded doc index back to 4/1/1991 free at www.waynecountywv.us/WEBInquiry/. **Other phones:** Treasurer- 304-272-6721; Elections- 304-272-6370; Vital Records- 304-272-6371. **Property tax/Assessing**- PO Box 40, 700 Hendricks St, Rm 105, Wayne, WV 25570; 304-272-6357. **Online**- Access property tax data free at www.waynecountywv.us/WEBTax/.

Webster County

County Clerk, 2 Court Sq, Rm G-1; Courthouse, Webster Springs, WV 26288-1049. -304-847-2508; fax-304-847-5780; 8:30AM-4PM
Index: All separate before 7/1/1979. Record index not computerized. Only the public may search. Copy fee $1.50 1st 2 pages; $1.00 each add'l. Cert fee- $1.00 plus copy fee. Payee- Webster County Clerk. **Other phones:** Treasurer- 304-847-2006; Elections- 304-847-2508; Vital Records- 304-847-2508. **Property tax/Assessing**- 2 Courthouse Sq, Room G-1, Webster Springs, WV 26288-1054; 304-847-2110, assessor fax- 304-847-5371. No public computer in office.

Wetzel County

County Clerk, PO Box 156, New Martinsville, WV 26155-0156. -304-455-8224; fax-304-455-5256; 9AM-4:30PM M,T,W,F; 9AM-4PM Th; 9AM-N Sat.
Index: Separate indices to search include liens, wills, fiduciary, marriages, births, deaths, plats, all deeds including oil/gas, misc, releases. Records indexed on a public use terminal back to 1993. Only the public may search. Copy fee $1.50 per UCC; if real estate $1.50 1st 2 pages; $1.00 each add'l. Cert fee- $1.00 per doc plus copy fee. Payee- Wetzel County Clerk. **Other phones:** Treasurer- 304-455-8218; Elections- 304-455-8235; Vital Records- 304-455-8224. **Property tax/Assessing**- PO Box 156, 210 Main St, New Martinsville, 26155-0156; 304-455-8214, assessor fax- 304-455-5256. hours- 9AM-4:30PM, 9AM-N Sat

Wirt County

County Clerk, PO Box 53, Elizabeth, WV 26143. - 304-275-4271; fax-304-275-3418; 8:30AM-4PM
Index: Separate indices to search include deeds that are cross indexed. Record index not computerized. Office will perform a UCC search but public must search other records themselves. No search fee. Copy fee $1.50 1st 2 pages; $1.00 each add'l. Cert fee- $1.00 per cert includes copy fee. Payee- Wirt County Clerk. **Other phones:** Treasurer- 304-275-4222; Elections- 304-275-4271; Vital Records- 304-275-4271. **Property tax/Assessing**- PO Box 548, Elizabeth, WV 26143; 304-275-3192, assessor fax- 304-275-3418. (Appraiser/Auditor- 304-275-3192);

Wood County

County Clerk, PO Box 1474, Parkersburg, WV 26102-1474. 304-424-1850, R/E recording phone-304-424-1870, UCC recording phone-304-424-1899; fax-304-424-1864; hours - 8:30AM-4:30PM
www.woodcountywv.com/countyclerk/index.html
Index: Separate indices to search include deed, lien, UCC, births, deaths, wills & appraisement, marriage, military discharge. Records indexed on a public use terminal back to 7/1/88. Office will perform a UCC search but public must search other records themselves. UCC search per debtor name- $10.00. Copy fee $1.50 1st 2 pages; $1.00 each add'l. Cert fee- $1.00 per cert plus copy fee. Payee- Wood County Clerk. **Online Real Estate, Deed, Will, Death, Birth, Marriage, Lien records:** Access is by dial-up; visit www.woodcountywv.com/countyclerk/modem.htm for instructions for free connection. Records go back to 7/1/1988. Click on 'document imaging' to download. **Other phones:** Treasurer- 304-424-1910; Elections- 304-424-1860; Vital Records- 304-424-1844 or 424-1845; Probate- 304-424-1898. **Property tax/Assessing**- 1 Court Sq, #302, Parkersburg, WV 26102; 304-424-1875, assessor fax- 304-424-1786. (Appraiser - 304-424-1875) Public access terminal available. www.woodcountywv.com/assessor/ **Online**- Access assessment data free at www.woodcountywv.com/webcama/. Access property data on the GIS site free at www.onlinegis.net/WvWood/. Click on Display Map then Search; no name searching. Also, search the tax inquiry site free at www.woodcountywv.com/webtax/.

Wyoming County

County Clerk, PO Box 309, Pineville, WV 24874. 304-732-8000; fax-304-732-9659; 8AM-4PM M-TH; 8AM-6PM F.
Index: Separate indices to search include deeds, trust deeds, judgments, UCCs. Record index not computerized. Only the public may search. Copy fee $1.50 for 1st 2 pages, $1.00 each add'l. Cert fee- $2.50 per doc plus copy fee. Payee- Wyoming City Clerk. **Other phones:** Treasurer- 304-732-8000; Sheriff- 304-732-8000. **Property tax/Assessing**- PO Box 929, Corner of Bark St & Main St, Pineville, WV 24874; 304-732-8000, assessor fax- 304-732-7158.

West Virginia County Locator

You will usually be able to find the city name in the City/County Cross Reference below. In that case, it is a simple matter to determine the county from the cross reference. However, only the official US Postal Service city names are included in this index. There are an additional 40,000 place names that people use in their addresses. Therefore, we have also included a ZIP/City Cross Reference immediately following the City/County Cross Reference.

If you know the ZIP Code but the city name does not appear in the City/County Cross Reference index, look up the ZIP Code in the ZIP/City Cross Reference, find the city name, then look up the city name in the City/County Cross Reference. For example, you want to know the county for an address of Menands, NY 12204. There is no "Menands" in the City/County Cross Reference. The ZIP/City Cross Reference shows that ZIP Codes 12201-12288 are for the city of Albany. Looking back in the City/County Cross Reference, Albany is in Albany County.

West Virginia City/County Cross Reference

ACCOVILLE Logan
ADRIAN Upshur
ADVENT Jackson
ALBRIGHT Preston
ALDERSON (24910) Greenbrier(73), Summers(20), Monroe(6)
ALKOL Lincoln
ALLEN JUNCTION Wyoming
ALLOY Fayette
ALMA Tyler
ALPOCA Wyoming
ALUM BRIDGE (26321) Lewis(97), Doddridge(1)
ALUM CREEK (25003) Kanawha(54), Lincoln(45)
ALVY Tyler
AMEAGLE Raleigh
AMHERSTDALE Logan
AMIGO Wyoming
AMMA Roane
ANAWALT McDowell
ANMOORE Harrison
ANSTED Fayette
APPLE GROVE Mason
ARBOVALE Pocahontas
ARNETT Raleigh
ARNOLDSBURG Calhoun
ARTHUR Grant
ARTHURDALE Preston
ARTIE Raleigh
ASBURY Greenbrier
ASHFORD Boone
ASHLAND McDowell
ASHTON Mason
ATHENS Mercer
AUBURN Ritchie
AUGUSTA Hampshire
AURORA Preston
AUTO Greenbrier
AVONDALE McDowell
BAISDEN Mingo
BAKER Hardy
BAKERTON Jefferson
BALD KNOB Boone
BALLARD Monroe
BALLENGEE (24919) Summers(54), Monroe(45)
BANCROFT Putnam
BARBOURSVILLE Cabell
BARRACKVILLE Marion
BARRETT Boone
BARTLEY McDowell
BARTOW Pocahontas
BAXTER Marion
BEARDS FORK Fayette
BEAVER Raleigh
BECKLEY Raleigh
BECKWITH Fayette
BEECH BOTTOM Brooke
BEESON Mercer
BELINGTON Barbour
BELLE Kanawha
BELLEVILLE (26133) Wood(98), Jackson(1)
BELMONT Pleasants
BELVA (26656) Nicholas(82), Fayette(14), Clay(2)
BENS RUN Tyler
BENTREE Clay
BENWOOD Marshall
BEREA Ritchie
BERGOO Webster
BERKELEY SPRINGS Morgan
BERWIND McDowell
BETHANY (26032) Brooke(97), Ohio(2)
BEVERLY Randolph
BICKMORE Clay
BIG BEND Calhoun
BIG CREEK Logan
BIG RUN Wetzel
BIG SANDY McDowell
BIG SPRINGS Calhoun
BIM Boone
BIRCH RIVER (26610) Nicholas(96), Webster(3)
BLACKSVILLE Monongalia
BLAIR Logan
BLANDVILLE Doddridge
BLOOMERY Hampshire
BLOOMINGROSE Boone
BLOUNT Kanawha
BLUE CREEK Kanawha
BLUE JAY Raleigh
BLUEFIELD Mercer
BOB WHITE Boone
BOGGS Webster
BOLT Raleigh
BOMONT Clay
BOOMER Fayette
BOOTH Monongalia
BORDERLAND Mingo
BOWDEN (26254) Randolph(96), Tucker(3)
BOZOO Monroe
BRADLEY Raleigh
BRADSHAW McDowell
BRAMWELL Mercer
BRANCHLAND (25506) Lincoln(97), Cabell(2)
BRANDONVILLE Preston
BRANDYWINE Pendleton
BREEDEN Mingo
BRENTON Wyoming
BRETZ Preston
BRIDGEPORT (26330) Harrison(91), Taylor(7), Barbour(1)
BRISTOL (26332) Harrison(97), Doddridge(2)
BROHARD (26138) Wirt(77), Calhoun(22)
BROOKS Summers
BROWNTON Barbour
BRUCETON MILLS Preston
BRUNO Logan
BUCKEYE Pocahontas
BUCKHANNON (26201) Upshur(95), Lewis(3)
BUD Wyoming
BUFFALO Putnam
BUNKER HILL Berkeley
BURLINGTON (26710) Mineral(85), Hampshire(14)
BURNSVILLE (26335) Braxton(55), Gilmer(44)
BURNWELL (25034) Kanawha(50), Putnam(50)
BURTON (26562) Monongalia(56), Wetzel(43)
CABIN CREEK Kanawha
CABINS Grant
CAIRO Ritchie
CALDWELL (24925) Greenbrier(82), Monroe(17)
CALVIN Nicholas
CAMDEN Lewis
CAMDEN ON GAULEY Webster
CAMERON Marshall
CAMP CREEK Mercer
CANABRAKE McDowell
CANEBRAKE McDowell
CANNELTON Fayette
CANVAS Nicholas
CAPELS McDowell
CAPON BRIDGE Hampshire
CAPON SPRINGS Hampshire
CARETTA McDowell
CAROLINA Marion
CASS Pocahontas
CASSVILLE Monongalia
CEDAR GROVE Kanawha
CEDARVILLE (26611) Braxton(56), Gilmer(43)
CENTER POINT Doddridge
CENTRALIA Braxton
CENTURY Barbour
CEREDO Wayne
CHAPMANVILLE (25508) Logan(89), Boone(10)
CHARLES TOWN Jefferson
CHARLESTON Kanawha
CHARLTON HEIGHTS Fayette
CHARMCO Greenbrier
CHATTAROY Mingo
CHAUNCEY Logan
CHESTER Hancock
CHLOE (25235) Calhoun(85), Clay(14)
CIRCLEVILLE Pendleton
CLARKSBURG Harrison
CLAY (25043) Clay(98), Nicholas(1)
CLEAR CREEK Raleigh
CLEAR FORK Wyoming
CLENDENIN (25045) Roane(40), Kanawha(38), Clay(20)
CLEVELAND (26215) Upshur(97), Webster(2)
CLIFTON Mason
CLINTONVILLE Greenbrier
CLIO Roane
CLOTHIER (25047) Boone(58), Logan(41)
COAL CITY Raleigh
COAL MOUNTAIN Wyoming
COALTON Randolph
COALWOOD McDowell
COLCORD Raleigh
COLFAX Marion
COLLIERS Brooke
COMFORT Boone
COOL RIDGE Raleigh
COPEN Braxton
CORA Logan
CORE Monongalia
CORINNE Wyoming
CORINTH Preston
COSTA Boone
COTTAGEVILLE (25239) Jackson(83), Mason(16)
COTTLE Nicholas
COVEL Wyoming
COWEN Webster
COXS MILLS (26342) Gilmer(98), Ritchie(1)
CRAB ORCHARD Raleigh
CRAIGSVILLE Nicholas
CRANBERRY Raleigh
CRAWFORD (26343) Lewis(80), Upshur(19)
CRAWLEY Greenbrier
CRESTON (26141) Wirt(72), Calhoun(27)
CRICHTON Greenbrier
CROWN HILL Kanawha
CRUM Wayne
CRUMPLER McDowell
CUCUMBER McDowell
CULLODEN (25510) Cabell(67), Putnam(21), Lincoln(10)
CUZZART Preston
CYCLONE Wyoming
DAILEY Randolph
DALLAS Marshall
DANESE Fayette
DANIELS Raleigh
DANVILLE Boone
DAVIN (25617) Logan(83), Wyoming(16)
DAVIS Tucker
DAVISVILLE Wood
DAVY (24828) McDowell(98), Wyoming(1)
DAWES Kanawha
DAWMONT Harrison
DEEP WATER Fayette
DELBARTON Mingo
DELLSLOW Monongalia
DELRAY Hampshire
DIANA Webster
DILLE (26617) Clay(98), Nicholas(1)
DINGESS Mingo
DIXIE (25059) Nicholas(85), Fayette(14)
DOROTHY Raleigh
DOTHAN Fayette
DRENNEN Nicholas
DRY CREEK Raleigh
DRYBRANCH Kanawha
DRYFORK (26263) Tucker(66), Randolph(33)
DUCK (25063) Clay(92), Braxton(7)
DUNBAR Kanawha
DUNLOW Wayne
DUNMORE Pocahontas
DURBIN Pocahontas
EAST BANK Kanawha
EAST LYNN Wayne
ECCLES Raleigh
ECKMAN McDowell
EDGARTON Mingo
EDMOND Fayette

EGLON Preston
ELBERT McDowell
ELEANOR Putnam
ELIZABETH (26143) Wirt(85), Ritchie(10), Wood(2), Jackson(1)
ELK GARDEN (26717) Mineral(79), Grant(20)
ELKHORN McDowell
ELKINS Randolph
ELKVIEW (25071) Kanawha(94), Roane(5)
ELLAMORE Randolph
ELLENBORO (26346) Ritchie(50), Pleasants(43), Tyler(6)
ELMIRA Braxton
ELTON Summers
EMMETT Logan
ENGLISH McDowell
ENTERPRISE Harrison
ERBACON Webster
ESKDALE Kanawha
ETHEL Logan
EUREKA Pleasants
EVANS (25241) Jackson(87), Mason(12)
EVERETTVILLE Monongalia
EXCHANGE Braxton
FAIRDALE Raleigh
FAIRLEA Greenbrier
FAIRMONT (26554) Marion(96), Monongalia(3)
FAIRMONT Marion
FAIRVIEW Marion
FALLING ROCK Kanawha
FALLING WATERS Berkeley
FALLS MILL Braxton
FANROCK Wyoming
FARMINGTON Marion
FENWICK Nicholas
FISHER Hardy
FIVE FORKS Calhoun
FLAT TOP Mercer
FLATWOODS Braxton
FLEMINGTON (26347) Taylor(67), Barbour(32)
FOLA Clay
FOLLANSBEE Brooke
FOLSOM Wetzel
FOREST HILL Summers
FORT ASHBY Mineral
FORT GAY Wayne
FORT SEYBERT Pendleton
FORT SPRING Greenbrier
FOSTER Boone
FOUR STATES Marion
FRAMETOWN (26623) Braxton(97), Gilmer(2)
FRANKFORD Greenbrier
FRANKLIN Pendleton
FRAZIERS BOTTOM (25082) Putnam(57), Mason(41)
FREEMAN Mercer
FRENCH CREEK Upshur
FRENCHTON Upshur
FRIARS HILL Greenbrier
FRIENDLY (26146) Tyler(54), Pleasants(45)
GALLAGHER (25083) Kanawha(93), Fayette(6)
GALLIPOLIS FERRY Mason
GALLOWAY Barbour
GANDEEVILLE Roane
GAP MILLS Monroe
GARY McDowell
GASSAWAY Braxton
GAULEY BRIDGE (25085) Fayette(61), Kanawha(38)
GAY (25244) Roane(55), Jackson(44)
GENOA Wayne
GERRARDSTOWN Berkeley
GHENT Raleigh
GILBERT Mingo
GILBOA Nicholas
GILMER Gilmer
GIVEN (25245) Jackson(88), Putnam(11)
GLACE Monroe
GLADY Randolph
GLASGOW Kanawha
GLEN Clay
GLEN DALE Marshall
GLEN DANIEL Raleigh
GLEN EASTON Marshall
GLEN FERRIS Fayette
GLEN FORK Wyoming
GLEN JEAN Fayette
GLEN MORGAN Raleigh
GLEN ROGERS Wyoming
GLEN WHITE Raleigh
GLENDON Braxton
GLENGARY Berkeley
GLENHAYES Wayne
GLENVILLE Gilmer
GLENWOOD (25520) Mason(54), Cabell(45)
GORDON Boone
GORMANIA Grant
GRAFTON Taylor
GRANT TOWN Marion
GRANTSVILLE Calhoun
GRANVILLE Monongalia
GRASSY MEADOWS Greenbrier
GREAT CACAPON Morgan
GREEN BANK Pocahontas
GREEN SPRING Hampshire
GREEN SULPHUR SPRINGS Summers
GREENVILLE Monroe
GREENWOOD (26360) Doddridge(58), Ritchie(31), Tyler(10)
GRIFFITHSVILLE Lincoln
GRIMMS LANDING Mason
GYPSY Harrison
HACKER VALLEY Webster
HALLTOWN Jefferson
HAMBLETON Tucker
HAMLIN (25523) Lincoln(90), Putnam(9)
HAMPDEN Mingo
HANDLEY Kanawha
HANOVER Wyoming
HANSFORD Kanawha
HARMAN (26270) Randolph(97), Pendleton(2)
HARMONY (25246) Roane(94), Jackson(5)
HARPER Raleigh
HARPERS FERRY Jefferson
HARRISON Clay
HARRISVILLE Ritchie
HARTFORD Mason
HARTS (25524) Lincoln(82), Logan(14), Wayne(2)
HAVACO McDowell
HAYWOOD Harrison
HAZELGREEN Ritchie
HAZELTON Preston
HEATERS Braxton
HEDGESVILLE (25427) Berkeley(82), Morgan(17)
HELEN Raleigh
HELVETIA (26224) Randolph(86), Upshur(13)
HEMPHILL McDowell
HENDERSON Mason
HENDRICKS Tucker
HENLAWSON Logan
HENSLEY McDowell
HEPZIBAH Harrison
HERNDON Wyoming
HERNSHAW Kanawha
HEWETT (25108) Boone(89), Logan(10)
HIAWATHA Mercer
HICO Fayette
HIGH VIEW Hampshire
HILLSBORO Pocahontas
HILLTOP Fayette
HINES Greenbrier
HINTON Summers
HOLDEN Logan
HOMETOWN Putnam
HORNER Lewis
HUGHESTON Kanawha
HUNDRED (26575) Wetzel(88), Monongalia(11)
HUNTINGTON (25701) Cabell(97), Wayne(2)
HUNTINGTON (25704) Wayne(58), Cabell(41)
HUNTINGTON Cabell
HUNTINGTON Wayne
HURRICANE Putnam
HUTTONSVILLE Randolph
IAEGER (24844) McDowell(87), Wyoming(12)
IDAMAY Marion
IKES FORK Wyoming
IMPERIAL JUNCTION (25034) Kanawha(50), Putnam(50)
INDEPENDENCE (26374) Preston(67), Monongalia(16), Taylor(15)
INDORE Clay
INDUSTRIAL Harrison
INSTITUTE Kanawha
INWOOD Berkeley
IRELAND (26376) Lewis(87), Braxton(12)
ISABAN McDowell
ITMANN Wyoming
IVYDALE Clay
JACKSONBURG (26377) Wetzel(62), Tyler(37)
JANE LEW (26378) Lewis(89), Harrison(10)
JEFFREY Boone
JENKINJONES McDowell
JESSE Wyoming
JODIE Fayette
JOLO McDowell
JONBEN Raleigh
JOSEPHINE Raleigh
JULIAN Boone
JUMPING BRANCH (25969) Summers(87), Raleigh(12)
JUNCTION Hampshire
JUNIOR Barbour
JUSTICE Mingo
KANAWHA FALLS Fayette
KANAWHA HEAD Upshur
KEARNEYSVILLE (25430) Jefferson(83), Berkeley(16)
KEARNEYSVILLE Jefferson
KEGLEY Mercer
KELLYSVILLE Mercer
KENNA Jackson
KENOVA Wayne
KENTUCK Jackson
KERENS (26276) Randolph(75), Tucker(24)
KERMIT (25674) Mingo(67), Wayne(32)
KESLERS CROSS LANES Nicholas
KEYSER Mineral
KEYSTONE McDowell
KIAHSVILLE Wayne
KIEFFER Greenbrier
KILSYTH Fayette
KIMBALL McDowell
KIMBERLY Fayette
KINCAID Fayette
KINGMONT Marion
KINGSTON Fayette
KINGWOOD Preston
KIRBY (26729) Hampshire(82), Hardy(17)
KISTLER Logan
KOPPERSTON Wyoming
KYLE McDowell
LAHMANSVILLE Grant
LAKE Logan
LAKIN Mason
LANARK Raleigh
LANSING Fayette
LASHMEET Mercer
LAVALETTE Wayne
LAYLAND (25864) Raleigh(78), Fayette(21)
LE ROY (25252) Roane(48), Jackson(44), Wirt(6)
LECKIE McDowell
LEEWOOD Kanawha
LEFT HAND Roane
LEIVASY Nicholas
LENORE Mingo
LEON (25123) Mason(66), Putnam(33)
LERONA Mercer
LESAGE Cabell
LESLIE Greenbrier
LESTER Raleigh
LETART Mason
LETTER GAP Gilmer
LEVELS Hampshire
LEWISBURG Greenbrier
LIBERTY (25124) Putnam(93), Jackson(4), Kanawha(2)
LIMA Tyler
LINDEN Roane
LINDSIDE Monroe
LINN (26384) Gilmer(67), Lewis(31), Braxton(1)
LITTLE BIRCH Braxton
LITTLETON Wetzel
LIZEMORES Clay
LOCHGELLY Fayette
LOCKBRIDGE Summers
LOCKNEY Gilmer
LOGAN Logan
LONDON Kanawha
LONG BRANCH Fayette
LOOKOUT Fayette
LOONEYVILLE Roane
LORADO Logan
LORENTZ Upshur
LOST CITY Hardy
LOST CREEK Harrison
LOST RIVER Hardy
LUMBERPORT Harrison
LUNDALE Logan
LYBURN Logan
LYNCO Wyoming
MABEN Wyoming
MABIE Randolph
MABSCOTT Raleigh
MAC ARTHUR Raleigh
MACFARLAN Ritchie
MADISON Boone
MAHAN Fayette
MAIDSVILLE Monongalia
MALLORY Logan
MAMMOTH Kanawha
MAN Logan
MANNINGTON (26582) Marion(88), Monongalia(10), Harrison(1)
MAPLEWOOD Fayette
MARIANNA Wyoming
MARLINTON Pocahontas
MARTINSBURG Berkeley
MASON Mason
MASONTOWN (26542) Preston(88), Monongalia(11)
MATEWAN Mingo
MATHENY Wyoming
MATHIAS Hardy
MATOAKA (24736) Mercer(85), Wyoming(14)
MAXWELTON Greenbrier
MAYBEURY McDowell
MAYSEL Clay
MAYSVILLE Grant
MC COMAS Mercer
MC GRAWS Wyoming
MC MECHEN Marshall
MC WHORTER Harrison
MCMECHEN Marshall
MEADOR Mingo
MEADOW BLUFF Greenbrier
MEADOW BRIDGE (25976) Fayette(55), Summers(40), Greenbrier(4)

MEADOW CREEK Summers
MEADOWBROOK Harrison
MEDLEY Grant
METZ (26585) Marion(75), Wetzel(25)
MIAMI Kanawha
MIDDLEBOURNE Tyler
MIDKIFF Lincoln
MIDWAY Raleigh
MILAM (26838) Hardy(94), Pendleton(5)
MILL CREEK Randolph
MILLSTONE Calhoun
MILLVILLE Jefferson
MILLWOOD Jackson
MILTON Cabell
MINDEN Fayette
MINERAL WELLS Wood
MINGO Randolph
MOATSVILLE (26405) Barbour(84), Preston(15)
MOHAWK McDowell
MONAVILLE Logan
MONTANA MINES Marion
MONTCALM Mercer
MONTCOAL Raleigh
MONTERVILLE Randolph
MONTGOMERY (25136) Fayette(61), Kanawha(38)
MONTROSE (26283) Randolph(80), Barbour(12), Tucker(6)
MOOREFIELD Hardy
MORGANTOWN Monongalia
MOUNDSVILLE Marshall
MOUNT ALTO (25264) Jackson(65), Mason(34)
MOUNT CARBON Fayette
MOUNT CLARE Harrison
MOUNT GAY Logan
MOUNT HOPE (25880) Raleigh(59), Fayette(40)
MOUNT LOOKOUT Nicholas
MOUNT NEBO Nicholas
MOUNT OLIVE Fayette
MOUNT STORM Grant
MOUNT ZION Calhoun
MOUNTAIN Ritchie
MOYERS Pendleton
MULLENS Wyoming
MUNDAY (26152) Calhoun(92), Wirt(7)
MURRAYSVILLE (26153) Jackson(88), Wood(11)
MYRA Lincoln
MYRTLE Mingo
NALLEN (26680) Fayette(45), Nicholas(43), Greenbrier(10)
NAOMA Raleigh
NAPIER Braxton
NAUGATUCK Mingo
NEBO (25141) Clay(94), Calhoun(5)
NELLIS Boone
NEMOURS Mercer
NEOLA Greenbrier
NETTIE Nicholas
NEW CREEK (26743) Mineral(71), Grant(28)
NEW CUMBERLAND Hancock
NEW HAVEN Mason
NEW MANCHESTER Hancock
NEW MARTINSVILLE Wetzel
NEW MILTON (26411) Doddridge(90), Gilmer(9)
NEW RICHMOND Wyoming
NEWBERNE (26409) Gilmer(55), Ritchie(44)
NEWBURG Preston
NEWELL Hancock
NEWHALL McDowell
NEWTON Roane
NEWTOWN Mingo
NICUT (26633) Calhoun(62), Braxton(34), Gilmer(3)
NIMITZ Summers
NITRO (25143) Kanawha(73), Putnam(26)

NOLAN Mingo
NORMANTOWN (25267) Gilmer(91), Calhoun(4), Braxton(3)
NORTH MATEWAN Mingo
NORTH SPRING Wyoming
NORTHFORK McDowell
NORTON Randolph
OAK HILL Fayette
OAKVALE Mercer
OCEANA Wyoming
ODD (25902) Raleigh(82), Mercer(17)
OHLEY Kanawha
OLD FIELDS (26845) Hardy(97), Hampshire(2)
OMAR Logan
ONA Cabell
ONEGO Pendleton
ORGAS Boone
ORLANDO (26412) Lewis(94), Gilmer(4), Braxton(1)
ORMA Calhoun
OSAGE Monongalia
OTTAWA Boone
OVAPA (25150) Roane(63), Clay(36)
PADEN CITY (26159) Wetzel(64), Tyler(35)
PAGE Fayette
PAGETON McDowell
PALERMO Lincoln
PALESTINE Wirt
PANTHER McDowell
PARKERSBURG Wood
PARSONS (26287) Tucker(98), Preston(1)
PAW PAW (25434) Hampshire(53), Morgan(46)
PAX Fayette
PAYNESVILLE McDowell
PEACH CREEK Logan
PECKS MILL Logan
PEMBERTON Raleigh
PENCE SPRINGS Summers
PENNSBORO (26415) Ritchie(97), Tyler(2)
PENTRESS Monongalia
PERKINS Gilmer
PETERSBURG (26847) Grant(96), Hardy(3)
PETERSTOWN Monroe
PETROLEUM (26161) Ritchie(91), Wood(5), Wirt(3)
PEYTONA Boone
PHILIPPI Barbour
PICKENS (26230) Randolph(92), Webster(7)
PIEDMONT Mineral
PINCH Kanawha
PINE GROVE Wetzel
PINEVILLE Wyoming
PINEY VIEW Raleigh
PIPESTEM (25979) Summers(78), Mercer(21)
PLINY Putnam
POCA Putnam
POE Nicholas
POINT PLEASANT Mason
POINTS Hampshire
POND GAP Kanawha
POOL Nicholas
PORTERS FALLS Wetzel
POWELLTON Fayette
POWHATAN McDowell
PRATT Kanawha
PREMIER McDowell
PRENTER Boone
PRICHARD Wayne
PRINCE Fayette
PRINCEWICK Raleigh
PROCIOUS (25164) Clay(79), Roane(20)
PROCTOR (26055) Marshall(83), Wetzel(16)
PROSPERITY Raleigh
PULLMAN Ritchie
PURGITSVILLE (26852) Hardy(66), Hampshire(27), Mineral(4)

PURSGLOVE Monongalia
QUINNIMONT Fayette
QUINWOOD (25981) Greenbrier(64), Nicholas(35)
RACHEL Marion
RACINE Boone
RAGLAND Mingo
RAINELLE (25962) Fayette(94), Greenbrier(5)
RALEIGH Raleigh
RAMAGE Boone
RAMSEY Fayette
RANGER (25557) Lincoln(97), Wayne(2)
RANSON Jefferson
RAVENCLIFF Wyoming
RAVENSWOOD (26164) Jackson(88), Wood(11)
RAWL Mingo
RAYSAL McDowell
READER Wetzel
RED CREEK Tucker
RED HOUSE (25168) Putnam(68), Kanawha(31)
RED JACKET Mingo
REDSTAR Fayette
REEDSVILLE Preston
REEDY Roane
RENICK Greenbrier
REYNOLDSVILLE Harrison
RHODELL Raleigh
RICHWOOD (26261) Nicholas(98), Greenbrier(1)
RIDGELEY Mineral
RIDGEVIEW Boone
RIDGEWAY Berkeley
RIO (26755) Hampshire(64), Hardy(35)
RIPLEY Jackson
RIPPON Jefferson
RIVERTON Pendleton
RIVESVILLE (26588) Marion(87), Monongalia(12)
ROANOKE Lewis
ROBERTSBURG Putnam
ROBSON Fayette
ROCK Mercer
ROCK CASTLE Jackson
ROCK CAVE (26234) Upshur(95), Webster(4)
ROCK CREEK Raleigh
ROCK VIEW Wyoming
ROCKPORT Wood
RODERFIELD McDowell
ROMNEY Hampshire
RONCEVERTE (24970) Greenbrier(98), Monroe(1)
ROSEDALE (26636) Gilmer(46), Braxton(31), Calhoun(22)
ROSEMONT Taylor
ROSSMORE Logan
ROWLESBURG (26425) Preston(98), Tucker(1)
RUPERT Greenbrier
SABINE Wyoming
SAINT ALBANS Kanawha
SAINT GEORGE (26290) Tucker(95), Preston(4)
SAINT MARYS (26170) Pleasants(93), Ritchie(5)
SALEM (26426) Harrison(92), Doddridge(7)
SALT ROCK Cabell
SAND FORK Gilmer
SAND RIDGE Calhoun
SANDSTONE Summers
SANDYVILLE Jackson
SARAH ANN Logan
SARTON Monroe
SAULSVILLE Wyoming
SAXON Raleigh
SCARBRO Fayette
SCOTT DEPOT Putnam
SECONDCREEK Monroe

SELBYVILLE (26236) Upshur(57), Randolph(42)
SENECA ROCKS Pendleton
SETH Boone
SHADY SPRING Raleigh
SHANKS Hampshire
SHARON Kanawha
SHARPLES Logan
SHENANDOAH JUNCTION Jefferson
SHEPHERDSTOWN (25443) Jefferson(90), Berkeley(9)
SHERMAN Jackson
SHINNSTON (26431) Harrison(96), Taylor(3)
SHIRLEY Tyler
SHOALS Wayne
SHOCK (26638) Gilmer(95), Calhoun(5)
SHORT CREEK Brooke
SIAS Lincoln
SIMON Wyoming
SIMPSON Taylor
SINKS GROVE Monroe
SISTERSVILLE Tyler
SKELTON Raleigh
SKYGUSTY McDowell
SLAB FORK (25920) Raleigh(90), Wyoming(9)
SLANESVILLE Hampshire
SLATYFORK Pocahontas
SMITHBURG Doddridge
SMITHERS Fayette
SMITHFIELD (26437) Wetzel(92), Marion(7)
SMITHVILLE Ritchie
SMOOT Greenbrier
SNOWSHOE Pocahontas
SOD Lincoln
SOPHIA Raleigh
SOUTHSIDE Mason
SPANISHBURG Mercer
SPELTER Harrison
SPENCER Roane
SPRAGUE Raleigh
SPRIGG Mingo
SPRING DALE Fayette
SPRINGFIELD Hampshire
SPURLOCKVILLE (25565) Lincoln(74), Boone(25)
SQUIRE McDowell
STANAFORD Raleigh
STATTS MILLS Jackson
STEPHENSON Wyoming
STIRRAT Logan
STOLLINGS Logan
STOUTS MILLS Gilmer
STRANGE CREEK (26639) Braxton(71), Nicholas(25), Clay(3)
STUMPTOWN (25280) Gilmer(55), Calhoun(44)
SUGAR GROVE Pendleton
SUMERCO Lincoln
SUMMERLEE Fayette
SUMMERSVILLE Nicholas
SUMMIT POINT Jefferson
SUNDIAL Raleigh
SUPERIOR McDowell
SURVEYOR Raleigh
SUTTON Braxton
SWEET SPRINGS Monroe
SWEETLAND Lincoln
SWISS Nicholas
SWITCHBACK McDowell
SWITZER Logan
SYLVESTER Boone
TAD Kanawha
TALCOTT (24981) Summers(86), Monroe(14)
TALLMANSVILLE Upshur
TANNER Gilmer
TAPLIN Logan
TARIFF Roane
TEAYS Putnam

TERRA ALTA Preston
TERRY Raleigh
THACKER Mingo
THOMAS Tucker
THORNTON (26440) Taylor(67), Preston(24), Barbour(7)
THORPE McDowell
THREE CHURCHES Hampshire
THURMOND Fayette
TIOGA (26691) Nicholas(96), Webster(3)
TORNADO (25202) Lincoln(50), Kanawha(49)
TRIADELPHIA Ohio
TROY (26443) Gilmer(85), Doddridge(14)
TRUE Summers
TUNNELTON Preston
TURTLE CREEK Boone
TWILIGHT Boone
TWIN BRANCH McDowell
UNEEDA Boone
UNION Monroe
UPPER TRACT Pendleton
UPPERGLADE Webster
VALLEY BEND Randolph
VALLEY CHAPEL Lewis
VALLEY FORK Clay
VALLEY GROVE (26060) Ohio(98), Brooke(1)
VALLEY HEAD (26294) Randolph(81), Pocahontas(18)
VAN Boone
VARNEY Mingo
VERDUNVILLE Logan
VERNER (25650) Mingo(71), Logan(28)
VICTOR Fayette
VIENNA Wood
VIVIAN McDowell
VOLGA (26238) Barbour(70), Upshur(27), Harrison(1)
VULCAN Mingo
WADESTOWN Monongalia
WAITEVILLE Monroe
WALKER (26180) Wood(92), Wirt(7)
WALKERSVILLE (26447) Lewis(97), Braxton(2)
WALLACE (26448) Harrison(86), Marion(7), Doddridge(5)
WALLBACK (25285) Clay(98), Roane(1)
WALTON Roane
WANA Monongalia
WAR McDowell
WARDENSVILLE Hardy
WARRIORMINE McDowell
WASHINGTON Wood
WAVERLY (26184) Wood(62), Pleasants(37)
WAYSIDE (24985) Monroe(63), Summers(36)
WEBSTER SPRINGS Webster
WEIRTON (26062) Hancock(85), Brooke(14)
WELCH McDowell
WELLSBURG Brooke
WEST COLUMBIA Mason
WEST HAMLIN Lincoln
WEST LIBERTY Ohio
WEST MILFORD Harrison
WEST UNION (26456) Doddridge(94), Tyler(3), Ritchie(1)
WESTON Lewis
WHARNCLIFFE Mingo
WHARTON Boone
WHEELING Ohio
WHITE OAK (25989) Raleigh(98), Summers(1)
WHITE SULPHUR SPRINGS Greenbrier
WHITESVILLE (25209) Raleigh(84), Boone(15)
WHITMAN Logan
WHITMER Randolph
WICK Tyler
WIDEN Clay
WILCOE McDowell
WILEY FORD Mineral
WILEYVILLE Wetzel
WILKINSON Logan
WILLIAMSBURG Greenbrier
WILLIAMSON Mingo
WILLIAMSTOWN Wood
WILSIE Braxton
WILSONBURG Harrison
WILSONDALE (25699) Wayne(74), Mingo(20), Lincoln(5)
WINDSOR HEIGHTS Brooke
WINFIELD Putnam
WINIFREDE Kanawha
WINONA Fayette
WOLF PEN Wyoming
WOLF SUMMIT Harrison
WOLFCREEK Monroe
WOLFE Mercer
WOODVILLE Lincoln
WORTH McDowell
WORTHINGTON (26591) Marion(96), Harrison(3)
WYATT Harrison
WYCO Wyoming
WYOMING Wyoming
YAWKEY Lincoln
YELLOW SPRING Hampshire
YOLYN Logan
YUKON McDowell

West Virginia ZIP/City Cross Reference

24701-24701 BLUEFIELD
24710-24710 ALPOCA
24712-24712 ATHENS
24714-24714 BEESON
24715-24715 BRAMWELL
24716-24716 BUD
24719-24719 COVEL
24724-24724 FREEMAN
24726-24726 HERNDON
24729-24729 HIAWATHA
24731-24731 KEGLEY
24732-24732 KELLYSVILLE
24733-24733 LASHMEET
24735-24735 MC COMAS
24736-24736 MATOAKA
24737-24737 MONTCALM
24738-24738 NEMOURS
24739-24739 OAKVALE
24740-24740 PRINCETON
24747-24747 ROCK
24751-24751 WOLFE
24801-24801 WELCH
24808-24808 ANAWALT
24810-24810 ASHLAND
24811-24811 AVONDALE
24813-24813 BARTLEY
24815-24815 BERWIND
24816-24816 BIG SANDY
24817-24817 BRADSHAW
24818-24818 BRENTON
24819-24819 CANEBRAKE
24819-24819 CANABRAKE
24820-24820 CAPELS
24821-24821 CARETTA
24822-24822 CLEAR FORK
24823-24823 COAL MOUNTAIN
24824-24824 COALWOOD
24825-24825 CRUMPLER
24826-24826 CUCUMBER
24827-24827 CYCLONE
24828-24828 DAVY
24829-24829 ECKMAN
24830-24830 ELBERT
24831-24831 ELKHORN
24832-24832 ENGLISH
24834-24834 FANROCK
24836-24836 GARY
24839-24839 HANOVER
24841-24841 HAVACO
24842-24842 HEMPHILL
24843-24843 HENSLEY
24844-24844 IAEGER
24845-24845 IKES FORK
24846-24846 ISABAN
24847-24847 ITMANN
24848-24848 JENKINJONES
24849-24849 JESSE
24850-24850 JOLO
24851-24851 JUSTICE
24852-24852 KEYSTONE
24853-24853 KIMBALL
24854-24854 KOPPERSTON
24855-24855 KYLE
24856-24856 LECKIE
24857-24857 LYNCO
24859-24859 MARIANNA
24860-24860 MATHENY
24861-24861 MAYBEURY
24862-24862 MOHAWK
24866-24866 NEWHALL
24867-24867 NEW RICHMOND
24868-24868 NORTHFORK
24869-24869 NORTH SPRING
24870-24870 OCEANA
24871-24871 PAGETON
24872-24872 PANTHER
24873-24873 PAYNESVILLE
24874-24874 PINEVILLE
24877-24877 POWHATAN
24878-24878 PREMIER
24879-24879 RAYSAL
24880-24880 ROCK VIEW
24881-24881 RODERFIELD
24882-24882 SIMON
24883-24883 SKYGUSTY
24884-24884 SQUIRE
24886-24886 SUPERIOR
24887-24887 SWITCHBACK
24888-24888 THORPE
24889-24889 TWIN BRANCH
24891-24891 VIVIAN
24892-24892 WAR
24894-24894 WARRIORMINE
24895-24895 WILCOE
24896-24896 WOLF PEN
24897-24897 WORTH
24898-24898 WYOMING
24899-24899 YUKON
24901-24901 LEWISBURG
24902-24902 FAIRLEA
24910-24910 ALDERSON
24915-24915 ARBOVALE
24916-24916 ASBURY
24917-24917 AUTO
24918-24918 BALLARD
24919-24919 BALLENGEE
24920-24920 BARTOW
24923-24923 BOZOO
24924-24924 BUCKEYE
24925-24925 CALDWELL
24927-24927 CASS
24928-24928 CLINTONVILLE
24931-24931 CRAWLEY
24934-24934 DUNMORE
24935-24935 FOREST HILL
24936-24936 FORT SPRING
24938-24938 FRANKFORD
24939-24939 FRIARS HILL
24941-24941 GAP MILLS
24942-24942 GLACE
24943-24943 GRASSY MEADOWS
24944-24944 GREEN BANK
24945-24945 GREENVILLE
24946-24946 HILLSBORO
24950-24950 KIEFFER
24951-24951 LINDSIDE
24954-24954 MARLINTON
24957-24957 MAXWELTON
24958-24958 MEADOW BLUFF
24961-24961 NEOLA
24962-24962 PENCE SPRINGS
24963-24963 PETERSTOWN
24966-24966 RENICK
24970-24970 RONCEVERTE
24973-24973 SARTON
24974-24974 SECONDCREEK
24976-24976 SINKS GROVE
24977-24977 SMOOT
24980-24980 SWEET SPRINGS
24981-24981 TALCOTT
24983-24983 UNION
24984-24984 WAITEVILLE
24985-24985 WAYSIDE
24986-24986 WHITE SULPHUR SPRINGS
24991-24991 WILLIAMSBURG
24993-24993 WOLFCREEK
25002-25002 ALLOY
25003-25003 ALUM CREEK
25004-25004 AMEAGLE
25005-25005 AMMA
25007-25007 ARNETT
25008-25008 ARTIE
25009-25009 ASHFORD
25010-25010 BALD KNOB
25011-25011 BANCROFT
25013-25013 BARRETT
25014-25014 BEARDS FORK
25015-25015 BELLE
25018-25018 BENTREE
25019-25019 BICKMORE
25021-25021 BIM
25022-25022 BLAIR
25024-25024 BLOOMINGROSE
25025-25025 BLOUNT
25026-25026 BLUE CREEK
25028-25028 BOB WHITE
25030-25030 BOMONT
25031-25031 BOOMER
25033-25033 BUFFALO
25034-25034 BURNWELL
25034-25034 IMPERIAL JUNCTION
25034-25034 BURNWELL
25035-25035 CABIN CREEK
25036-25036 CANNELTON
25039-25039 CEDAR GROVE
25040-25040 CHARLTON HEIGHTS
25043-25043 CLAY
25044-25044 CLEAR CREEK
25045-25045 CLENDENIN
25046-25046 CLIO
25047-25047 CLOTHIER
25048-25048 COLCORD
25049-25049 COMFORT
25051-25051 COSTA
25052-25052 CROWN HILL
25053-25053 DANVILLE
25054-25054 DAWES
25057-25057 DEEP WATER
25059-25059 DIXIE
25060-25060 DOROTHY
25061-25061 DRYBRANCH
25062-25062 DRY CREEK
25063-25063 DUCK
25064-25064 DUNBAR
25067-25067 EAST BANK
25070-25070 ELEANOR
25071-25071 ELKVIEW
25075-25075 ESKDALE
25076-25076 ETHEL
25079-25079 FALLING ROCK
25080-25080 FOLA
25081-25081 FOSTER
25082-25082 FRAZIERS BOTTOM
25083-25083 GALLAGHER
25085-25085 GAULEY BRIDGE
25086-25086 GLASGOW
25088-25088 GLEN
25090-25090 GLEN FERRIS
25093-25093 GORDON
25095-25095 GRIMMS LANDING
25102-25102 HANDLEY
25103-25103 HANSFORD
25105-25105 HARRISON
25106-25106 HENDERSON
25107-25107 HERNSHAW
25108-25108 HEWETT

25109-25109 HOMETOWN
25110-25110 HUGHESTON
25111-25111 INDORE
25112-25112 INSTITUTE
25113-25113 IVYDALE
25114-25114 JEFFREY
25115-25115 KANAWHA FALLS
25118-25118 KIMBERLY
25119-25119 KINCAID
25120-25120 KINGSTON
25121-25121 LAKE
25122-25122 LEEWOOD
25123-25123 LEON
25124-25124 LIBERTY
25125-25125 LIZEMORES
25126-25126 LONDON
25130-25130 MADISON
25131-25131 MAHAN
25132-25132 MAMMOTH
25133-25133 MAYSEL
25134-25134 MIAMI
25135-25135 MONTCOAL
25136-25136 MONTGOMERY
25139-25139 MOUNT CARBON
25140-25140 NAOMA
25141-25141 NEBO
25142-25142 NELLIS
25143-25143 NITRO
25147-25147 OHLEY
25148-25148 ORGAS
25149-25149 OTTAWA
25150-25150 OVAPA
25152-25152 PAGE
25154-25154 PEYTONA
25156-25156 PINCH
25158-25158 PLINY
25159-25159 POCA
25160-25160 POND GAP
25161-25161 POWELLTON
25162-25162 PRATT
25163-25163 PRENTER
25164-25164 PROCIOUS
25165-25165 RACINE
25166-25166 RAMAGE
25168-25168 RED HOUSE
25169-25169 RIDGEVIEW
25172-25172 ROBERTSBURG
25173-25173 ROBSON
25174-25174 ROCK CREEK
25177-25177 SAINT ALBANS
25180-25180 SAXON
25181-25181 SETH
25182-25182 SHARON
25183-25183 SHARPLES
25185-25185 MOUNT OLIVE
25186-25186 SMITHERS
25187-25187 SOUTHSIDE
25189-25189 SUNDIAL
25193-25193 SYLVESTER
25201-25201 TAD
25202-25202 TORNADO
25203-25203 TURTLE CREEK
25204-25204 TWILIGHT
25205-25205 UNEEDA
25206-25206 VAN
25208-25208 WHARTON
25209-25209 WHITESVILLE
25211-25211 WIDEN
25213-25213 WINFIELD
25214-25214 WINIFREDE
25231-25231 ADVENT
25234-25234 ARNOLDSBURG
25235-25235 CHLOE
25237-25237 CLIFTON
25239-25239 COTTAGEVILLE
25241-25241 EVANS
25243-25243 GANDEEVILLE
25244-25244 GAY
25245-25245 GIVEN
25246-25246 HARMONY
25247-25247 HARTFORD
25248-25248 KENNA
25249-25249 KENTUCK
25250-25250 LAKIN
25251-25251 LEFT HAND
25252-25252 LE ROY
25253-25253 LETART
25255-25255 LETTER GAP
25256-25256 LINDEN
25258-25258 LOCKNEY
25259-25259 LOONEYVILLE
25260-25260 MASON
25261-25261 MILLSTONE
25262-25262 MILLWOOD
25264-25264 MOUNT ALTO
25265-25265 NEW HAVEN
25266-25266 NEWTON
25267-25267 NORMANTOWN
25268-25268 ORMA
25270-25270 REEDY
25271-25271 RIPLEY
25272-25272 ROCK CASTLE
25274-25274 SAND RIDGE
25275-25275 SANDYVILLE
25276-25276 SPENCER
25279-25279 STATTS MILLS
25280-25280 STUMPTOWN
25281-25281 TARIFF
25283-25283 VALLEY FORK
25285-25285 WALLBACK
25286-25286 WALTON
25287-25287 WEST COLUMBIA
25300-25396 CHARLESTON
25401-25402 MARTINSBURG
25410-25410 BAKERTON
25411-25411 BERKELEY SPRINGS
25413-25413 BUNKER HILL
25414-25414 CHARLES TOWN
25419-25419 FALLING WATERS
25420-25420 GERRARDSTOWN
25421-25421 GLENGARY
25422-25422 GREAT CACAPON
25423-25423 HALLTOWN
25425-25425 HARPERS FERRY
25427-25427 HEDGESVILLE
25428-25428 INWOOD
25429-25430 KEARNEYSVILLE
25431-25431 LEVELS
25432-25432 MILLVILLE
25434-25434 PAW PAW
25437-25437 POINTS
25438-25438 RANSON
25440-25440 RIDGEWAY
25441-25441 RIPPON
25442-25442 SHENANDOAH JUNCTION
25443-25443 SHEPHERDSTOWN
25444-25444 SLANESVILLE
25446-25446 SUMMIT POINT
25501-25501 ALKOL
25502-25502 APPLE GROVE
25503-25503 ASHTON
25504-25504 BARBOURSVILLE
25505-25505 BIG CREEK
25506-25506 BRANCHLAND
25507-25507 CEREDO
25508-25508 CHAPMANVILLE
25510-25510 CULLODEN
25511-25511 DUNLOW
25512-25512 EAST LYNN
25514-25514 FORT GAY
25515-25515 GALLIPOLIS FERRY
25517-25517 GENOA
25519-25519 GLENHAYES
25520-25520 GLENWOOD
25521-25521 GRIFFITHSVILLE
25523-25523 HAMLIN
25524-25524 HARTS
25526-25526 HURRICANE
25529-25529 JULIAN
25530-25530 KENOVA
25534-25534 KIAHSVILLE
25535-25535 LAVALETTE
25537-25537 LESAGE
25540-25540 MIDKIFF
25541-25541 MILTON
25544-25544 MYRA
25545-25545 ONA
25546-25546 PALERMO
25547-25547 PECKS MILL
25550-25550 POINT PLEASANT
25555-25555 PRICHARD
25557-25557 RANGER
25559-25559 SALT ROCK
25560-25560 SCOTT DEPOT
25562-25562 SHOALS
25563-25563 SIAS
25564-25564 SOD
25565-25565 SPURLOCKVILLE
25567-25567 SUMERCO
25568-25568 SWEETLAND
25569-25569 TEAYS
25570-25570 WAYNE
25571-25571 WEST HAMLIN
25572-25572 WOODVILLE
25573-25573 YAWKEY
25601-25601 LOGAN
25606-25606 ACCOVILLE
25607-25607 AMHERSTDALE
25608-25608 BAISDEN
25611-25611 BRUNO
25612-25612 CHAUNCEY
25614-25614 CORA
25617-25617 DAVIN
25620-25620 EMMETT
25621-25621 GILBERT
25623-25623 HAMPDEN
25624-25624 HENLAWSON
25625-25625 HOLDEN
25628-25628 KISTLER
25630-25630 LORADO
25631-25631 LUNDALE
25632-25632 LYBURN
25634-25634 MALLORY
25635-25635 MAN
25636-25636 MONAVILLE
25637-25637 MOUNT GAY
25638-25638 OMAR
25639-25639 PEACH CREEK
25643-25643 ROSSMORE
25644-25644 SARAH ANN
25645-25645 STIRRAT
25646-25646 STOLLINGS
25647-25647 SWITZER
25648-25648 TAPLIN
25649-25649 VERDUNVILLE
25650-25650 VERNER
25651-25651 WHARNCLIFFE
25652-25652 WHITMAN
25653-25653 WILKINSON
25654-25654 YOLYN
25661-25661 WILLIAMSON
25665-25665 BORDERLAND
25666-25666 BREEDEN
25667-25667 CHATTAROY
25669-25669 CRUM
25670-25670 DELBARTON
25671-25671 DINGESS
25672-25672 EDGARTON
25674-25674 KERMIT
25676-25676 LENORE
25678-25678 MATEWAN
25682-25682 MEADOR
25684-25684 MYRTLE
25685-25685 NAUGATUCK
25686-25686 NEWTOWN
25687-25687 NOLAN
25688-25688 NORTH MATEWAN
25690-25690 RAGLAND
25691-25691 RAWL
25692-25692 RED JACKET
25693-25693 SPRIGG
25694-25694 THACKER
25696-25696 VARNEY
25697-25697 VULCAN
25699-25699 WILSONDALE
25700-25779 HUNTINGTON
25801-25802 BECKLEY
25810-25810 ALLEN JUNCTION
25811-25811 AMIGO
25812-25812 ANSTED
25813-25813 BEAVER
25814-25814 BECKWITH
25816-25816 BLUE JAY
25817-25817 BOLT
25818-25818 BRADLEY
25820-25820 CAMP CREEK
25823-25823 COAL CITY
25825-25825 COOL RIDGE
25826-25826 CORINNE
25827-25827 CRAB ORCHARD
25828-25828 CRANBERRY
25831-25831 DANESE
25832-25832 DANIELS
25833-25833 DOTHAN
25836-25836 ECCLES
25837-25837 EDMOND
25839-25839 FAIRDALE
25840-25840 FAYETTEVILLE
25841-25841 FLAT TOP
25843-25843 GHENT
25844-25844 GLEN DANIEL
25845-25845 GLEN FORK
25846-25846 GLEN JEAN
25847-25847 GLEN MORGAN
25848-25848 GLEN ROGERS
25849-25849 GLEN WHITE
25851-25851 HARPER
25853-25853 HELEN
25854-25854 HICO
25855-25855 HILLTOP
25856-25856 JONBEN
25857-25857 JOSEPHINE
25859-25859 KILSYTH
25860-25860 LANARK
25862-25862 LANSING
25864-25864 LAYLAND
25865-25865 LESTER
25866-25866 LOCHGELLY
25867-25867 LONG BRANCH
25868-25868 LOOKOUT
25870-25870 MABEN
25871-25871 MABSCOTT
25873-25873 MAC ARTHUR
25874-25874 MAPLEWOOD
25875-25875 MC GRAWS
25876-25876 SAULSVILLE
25878-25878 MIDWAY
25879-25879 MINDEN
25880-25880 MOUNT HOPE
25882-25882 MULLENS
25901-25901 OAK HILL
25902-25902 ODD
25904-25904 PAX
25905-25905 PEMBERTON
25906-25906 PINEY VIEW
25907-25907 PRINCE
25908-25908 PRINCEWICK
25909-25909 PROSPERITY
25910-25910 QUINNIMONT
25911-25911 RALEIGH
25912-25912 RAMSEY
25913-25913 RAVENCLIFF
25914-25914 REDSTAR
25915-25915 RHODELL
25916-25916 SABINE
25917-25917 SCARBRO
25918-25918 SHADY SPRING
25919-25919 SKELTON
25920-25920 SLAB FORK
25921-25921 SOPHIA
25922-25922 SPANISHBURG
25926-25926 SPRAGUE
25927-25927 STANAFORD
25928-25928 STEPHENSON
25931-25931 SUMMERLEE
25932-25932 SURVEYOR
25934-25934 TERRY
25936-25936 THURMOND
25938-25938 VICTOR
25942-25942 WINONA
25943-25943 WYCO
25951-25951 HINTON
25957-25957 BROOKS
25958-25958 CHARMCO
25961-25961 CRICHTON
25962-25962 RAINELLE
25965-25965 ELTON
25966-25966 GREEN SULPHUR SPRINGS
25967-25967 HINES
25969-25969 JUMPING BRANCH
25971-25971 LERONA
25972-25972 LESLIE
25973-25973 LOCKBRIDGE
25976-25976 MEADOW BRIDGE
25977-25977 MEADOW CREEK
25978-25978 NIMITZ
25979-25979 PIPESTEM
25981-25981 QUINWOOD
25984-25984 RUPERT
25985-25985 SANDSTONE
25986-25986 SPRING DALE
25988-25988 TRUE
25989-25989 WHITE OAK
26003-26003 WHEELING
26030-26030 BEECH BOTTOM
26031-26031 BENWOOD

26032-26032 BETHANY
26033-26033 CAMERON
26034-26034 CHESTER
26035-26035 COLLIERS
26036-26036 DALLAS
26037-26037 FOLLANSBEE
26038-26038 GLEN DALE
26039-26039 GLEN EASTON
26040-26040 MC MECHEN
26040-26040 MCMECHEN
26041-26041 MOUNDSVILLE
26047-26047 NEW CUMBERLAND
26050-26050 NEWELL
26055-26055 PROCTOR
26056-26056 NEW MANCHESTER
26058-26058 SHORT CREEK
26059-26059 TRIADELPHIA
26060-26060 VALLEY GROVE
26062-26062 WEIRTON
26070-26070 WELLSBURG
26074-26074 WEST LIBERTY
26075-26075 WINDSOR HEIGHTS
26101-26104 PARKERSBURG
26105-26105 VIENNA
26106-26106 PARKERSBURG
26120-26121 MINERAL WELLS
26133-26133 BELLEVILLE
26134-26134 BELMONT
26135-26135 BENS RUN
26136-26136 BIG BEND
26137-26137 BIG SPRINGS
26138-26138 BROHARD
26141-26141 CRESTON
26142-26142 DAVISVILLE
26143-26143 ELIZABETH
26144-26144 EUREKA
26145-26145 FIVE FORKS
26146-26146 FRIENDLY
26147-26147 GRANTSVILLE
26148-26148 MACFARLAN
26149-26149 MIDDLEBOURNE
26150-26150 MINERAL WELLS
26151-26151 MOUNT ZION
26152-26152 MUNDAY
26153-26153 MURRAYSVILLE
26155-26155 NEW MARTINSVILLE
26159-26159 PADEN CITY
26160-26160 PALESTINE
26161-26161 PETROLEUM
26162-26162 PORTERS FALLS
26164-26164 RAVENSWOOD
26167-26167 READER
26169-26169 ROCKPORT
26170-26170 SAINT MARYS
26173-26173 SHERMAN
26175-26175 SISTERSVILLE
26178-26178 SMITHVILLE
26179-26179 TANNER
26180-26180 WALKER
26181-26181 WASHINGTON
26184-26184 WAVERLY
26185-26185 WICK
26186-26186 WILEYVILLE
26187-26187 WILLIAMSTOWN
26201-26201 BUCKHANNON
26202-26202 FENWICK
26203-26203 ERBACON
26205-26205 CRAIGSVILLE
26206-26206 COWEN
26207-26207 COTTLE
26208-26208 CAMDEN ON GAULEY
26209-26209 SNOWSHOE
26210-26210 ADRIAN
26214-26214 CENTURY
26215-26215 CLEVELAND
26217-26217 DIANA
26218-26218 FRENCH CREEK
26219-26219 FRENCHTON
26222-26222 HACKER VALLEY
26224-26224 HELVETIA
26228-26228 KANAWHA HEAD
26229-26229 LORENTZ
26230-26230 PICKENS
26234-26234 ROCK CAVE
26236-26236 SELBYVILLE
26237-26237 TALLMANSVILLE
26238-26238 VOLGA
26241-26241 ELKINS
26250-26250 BELINGTON
26253-26253 BEVERLY
26254-26254 BOWDEN
26257-26257 COALTON
26259-26259 DAILEY
26260-26260 DAVIS
26261-26261 RICHWOOD
26263-26263 DRYFORK
26264-26264 DURBIN
26266-26266 UPPERGLADE
26267-26267 ELLAMORE
26268-26268 GLADY
26269-26269 HAMBLETON
26270-26270 HARMAN
26271-26271 HENDRICKS
26273-26273 HUTTONSVILLE
26275-26275 JUNIOR
26276-26276 KERENS
26278-26278 MABIE
26280-26280 MILL CREEK
26281-26281 MINGO
26282-26282 MONTERVILLE
26283-26283 MONTROSE
26285-26285 NORTON
26287-26287 PARSONS
26288-26288 WEBSTER SPRINGS
26289-26289 RED CREEK
26290-26290 SAINT GEORGE
26291-26291 SLATYFORK
26292-26292 THOMAS
26293-26293 VALLEY BEND
26294-26294 VALLEY HEAD
26296-26296 WHITMER
26298-26298 BERGOO
26299-26299 BOGGS
26301-26306 CLARKSBURG
26320-26320 ALMA
26321-26321 ALUM BRIDGE
26322-26322 ALVY
26323-26323 ANMOORE
26325-26325 AUBURN
26327-26327 BEREA
26328-26328 BLANDVILLE
26330-26330 BRIDGEPORT
26332-26332 BRISTOL
26334-26334 BROWNTON
26335-26335 BURNSVILLE
26337-26337 CAIRO
26338-26338 CAMDEN
26339-26339 CENTER POINT
26342-26342 COXS MILLS
26343-26343 CRAWFORD
26344-26344 DAWMONT
26346-26346 ELLENBORO
26347-26347 FLEMINGTON
26348-26348 FOLSOM
26349-26349 GALLOWAY
26350-26350 GILMER
26351-26351 GLENVILLE
26354-26354 GRAFTON
26360-26360 GREENWOOD
26361-26361 GYPSY
26362-26362 HARRISVILLE
26366-26366 HAYWOOD
26367-26367 HAZELGREEN
26369-26369 HEPZIBAH
26372-26372 HORNER
26374-26374 INDEPENDENCE
26375-26375 INDUSTRIAL
26376-26376 IRELAND
26377-26377 JACKSONBURG
26378-26378 JANE LEW
26383-26383 LIMA
26384-26384 LINN
26385-26385 LOST CREEK
26386-26386 LUMBERPORT
26401-26401 MC WHORTER
26404-26404 MEADOWBROOK
26405-26405 MOATSVILLE
26407-26407 MOUNTAIN
26408-26408 MOUNT CLARE
26409-26409 NEWBERNE
26410-26410 NEWBURG
26411-26411 NEW MILTON
26412-26412 ORLANDO
26415-26415 PENNSBORO
26416-26416 PHILIPPI
26419-26419 PINE GROVE
26421-26421 PULLMAN
26422-26422 REYNOLDSVILLE
26423-26423 ROANOKE
26424-26424 ROSEMONT
26425-26425 ROWLESBURG
26426-26426 SALEM
26430-26430 SAND FORK
26431-26431 SHINNSTON
26434-26434 SHIRLEY
26435-26435 SIMPSON
26436-26436 SMITHBURG
26437-26437 SMITHFIELD
26438-26438 SPELTER
26439-26439 STOUTS MILLS
26440-26440 THORNTON
26443-26443 TROY
26444-26444 TUNNELTON
26446-26446 VALLEY CHAPEL
26447-26447 WALKERSVILLE
26448-26448 WALLACE
26451-26451 WEST MILFORD
26452-26452 WESTON
26456-26456 WEST UNION
26461-26461 WILSONBURG
26462-26462 WOLF SUMMIT
26463-26463 WYATT
26501-26503 MORGANTOWN
26519-26519 ALBRIGHT
26520-26520 ARTHURDALE
26521-26521 BLACKSVILLE
26522-26522 BOOTH
26523-26523 BRANDONVILLE
26524-26524 BRETZ
26525-26525 BRUCETON MILLS
26527-26527 CASSVILLE
26529-26529 CORE
26530-26530 CUZZART
26531-26531 DELLSLOW
26533-26533 EVERETTVILLE
26534-26534 GRANVILLE
26535-26535 HAZELTON
26537-26537 KINGWOOD
26541-26541 MAIDSVILLE
26542-26542 MASONTOWN
26543-26543 OSAGE
26544-26544 PENTRESS
26546-26546 PURSGLOVE
26547-26547 REEDSVILLE
26554-26555 FAIRMONT
26559-26559 BARRACKVILLE
26560-26560 BAXTER
26561-26561 BIG RUN
26562-26562 BURTON
26563-26563 CAROLINA
26566-26566 COLFAX
26568-26568 ENTERPRISE
26570-26570 FAIRVIEW
26571-26571 FARMINGTON
26572-26572 FOUR STATES
26574-26574 GRANT TOWN
26575-26575 HUNDRED
26576-26576 IDAMAY
26578-26578 KINGMONT
26581-26581 LITTLETON
26582-26582 MANNINGTON
26585-26585 METZ
26586-26586 MONTANA MINES
26587-26587 RACHEL
26588-26588 RIVESVILLE
26589-26589 WADESTOWN
26590-26590 WANA
26591-26591 WORTHINGTON
26601-26601 SUTTON
26610-26610 BIRCH RIVER
26611-26611 CEDARVILLE
26612-26612 CENTRALIA
26615-26615 COPEN
26617-26617 DILLE
26618-26618 ELMIRA
26619-26619 EXCHANGE
26620-26620 FALLS MILL
26621-26621 FLATWOODS
26623-26623 FRAMETOWN
26624-26624 GASSAWAY
26626-26626 GLENDON
26627-26627 HEATERS
26629-26629 LITTLE BIRCH
26631-26631 NAPIER
26633-26633 NICUT
26634-26634 PERKINS
26636-26636 ROSEDALE
26638-26638 SHOCK
26639-26639 STRANGE CREEK
26641-26641 WILSIE
26651-26651 SUMMERSVILLE
26656-26656 BELVA
26660-26660 CALVIN
26662-26662 CANVAS
26667-26667 DRENNEN
26671-26671 GILBOA
26674-26674 JODIE
26675-26675 KESLERS CROSS LANES
26676-26676 LEIVASY
26678-26678 MOUNT LOOKOUT
26679-26679 MOUNT NEBO
26680-26680 NALLEN
26681-26681 NETTIE
26683-26683 POE
26684-26684 POOL
26690-26690 SWISS
26691-26691 TIOGA
26704-26704 AUGUSTA
26705-26705 AURORA
26707-26707 BAYARD
26710-26710 BURLINGTON
26711-26711 CAPON BRIDGE
26713-26713 CORINTH
26714-26714 DELRAY
26716-26716 EGLON
26717-26717 ELK GARDEN
26719-26719 FORT ASHBY
26720-26720 GORMANIA
26722-26722 GREEN SPRING
26726-26726 KEYSER
26729-26729 KIRBY
26731-26731 LAHMANSVILLE
26734-26734 MEDLEY
26739-26739 MOUNT STORM
26743-26743 NEW CREEK
26750-26750 PIEDMONT
26753-26753 RIDGELEY
26755-26755 RIO
26757-26757 ROMNEY
26761-26761 SHANKS
26763-26763 SPRINGFIELD
26764-26764 TERRA ALTA
26765-26765 THREE CHURCHES
26767-26767 WILEY FORD
26769-26769 EGLON
26801-26801 BAKER
26802-26802 BRANDYWINE
26804-26804 CIRCLEVILLE
26806-26806 FORT SEYBERT
26807-26807 FRANKLIN
26808-26808 HIGH VIEW
26810-26810 LOST CITY
26811-26811 LOST RIVER
26812-26812 MATHIAS
26813-26813 MOYERS
26814-26814 RIVERTON
26815-26815 SUGAR GROVE
26816-26816 ARTHUR
26817-26817 BLOOMERY
26818-26818 FISHER
26823-26823 CAPON SPRINGS
26824-26824 JUNCTION
26833-26833 MAYSVILLE
26836-26836 MOOREFIELD
26838-26838 MILAM
26845-26845 OLD FIELDS
26847-26847 PETERSBURG
26851-26851 WARDENSVILLE
26852-26852 PURGITSVILLE
26855-26855 CABINS
26865-26865 YELLOW SPRING
26866-26866 UPPER TRACT
26884-26884 SENECA ROCKS
26886-26886 ONEGO

Wisconsin

General Help Numbers:

Governor's Office
PO Box 7863
Madison, WI 53707-7863
www.wisgov.state.wi.us
608-266-1212
Fax 608-267-8983
8AM-5PM

Attorney General's Office
Justice Department
PO Box 7857
Madison, WI 53707-7857
www.doj.state.wi.us/ag
608-266-1221
Fax 608-267-2779
8AM-5PM

Legislative Records
Legislative Reference Bureau
PO Box 2037
Madison, WI 53701-2037
www.legis.state.wi.us
608-266-0341
Fax 608-266-5648
7:45AM-5PM

State Archives
Archives Division
816 State St
Madison, WI 53706
www.wisconsinhistory.org/libraryarchives/
608-264-6460
Fax 608-264-6486
8AM-5PM M-F, 9-4 SA

State Specifics:

Capital:	Madison Dane County
Time Zone:	CST
Number of Counties:	72
Population:	5,627,967
Web Site:	www.wisconsin.gov

State Agencies

Criminal Records

Wisconsin Department of Justice, Crime Information Bureau, Record Check Unit, PO Box 2688, Madison, WI 53701-2688 (Courier address- 17 W Main St, Madison, WI 53703); 608-266-5764, 608-266-7780 (Online Questions), Fax- 608-267-4558; 8AM-4:30PM.

www.doj.state.wi.us/dles/cib/crimback.asp

Indexing & Storage: Records available from July 1971 (when the agencies were required to save records) and are computerized. New records available for inquiry in 4 days. 77% of all arrests in database have final dispositions recorded, 83% for those arrests within last 5 years.

Searching: Criminal record information is open to the public per statute 3-21-91. Certain statutorily-required searches require fingerprints. Include in request- sex, race, full name, date of birth. Fingerprints are optional. All requests must be in writing. You must have an account with CIB in order to submit fingerprint cards. The account application can be downloaded from the web, as are request forms. This data not released- juvenile records. For fingerprint requests, all records are released, including those without dispositions. Arrests without supporting fingerprints are not included in the criminal history database search.

Access by: mail, fax, in person, online.

Fee & Payment: The fee is $18.00 per individual for a name search, $7.00 if non-profit, $10.00 if gov't agency, and $15.00 if a fingerprint search. If a statutorily-required search also requires an FBI fingerprint check, add $19.25. Fees less for online access. Fee payee- Wisconsin Department of Justice. Personal checks accepted. Visa and MasterCard accepted at website only.

Mail search: Turnaround time- 7-10 business days. A SASE is required.

Fax search: Incoming fax permitted only with prepayment or account. Customers wishing to fax requests must provide CIB with a supply of self-addressed, stamped return envelopes. Returns sent by mail only.

In person: Records are returned by mail.

Online search: The agency offers Internet access at http://wi-recordcheck.org. Access 1) with an account with PIN is required, or 2) pay as you go with Visa/MC credit card. Records must be "picked up" at the website within 10 days. They are not returned by mail. Fee is $13 per request, $2.00 if a non-profit, and $5.00 if a government agency. Only daycare centers and other caregivers can receive immediate online response but pay an additional $3.00 per record request. Email account set-up questions to wi-recordcheck-account@doj.state.wi.us or to INTCH@doj.state.wi.us to answer general online questions.

Other access: free Internet access to the state's Circuit Courts' records, except for Portage county. Visit http://wcca.wicourts.gov/index.xsl.

Statewide Court Records

Director of State Courts, Supreme Court, PO Box 1688, Madison, WI 53701-1688; 608-266-6828, Fax- 608-267-0980; 8AM-5PM.

http://wicourts.gov

Indexing & Storage: New records available for inquiry in up to 4 hours.

Online search: Wisconsin Circuit Court Access (WCCA) allows users to view Circuit Court case information on the Wisconsin court system website at http://wcca.wicourts.gov. Data is available from all counties (except only probate records are available from Portage). Searches can be conducted statewide or county-by-county. WCCA provides detailed information about circuit cases including criminal, civil and traffice. The index displays judgment and judgment party information. The middle initial is shown on results, the DOB is shown most of the time, but sometimes the DOB is only month/year. WCCA also offers the ability to generate reports. Due to statutory requirements, WCCA users will not be able to view restricted cases. There are probate records included for all counties.

Other access: Bulk access to data may be arranged on contract, fees are involved. Contact the Office of Court Operations at 608-266-3121 for details.

Sexual Offender Registry

Department of Corrections, Sex Offender Registry Program, PO Box 7925, Madison, WI 53707-7925 (Courier address- 3099 E Washington Avenue, Madison, WI 53704); 608-240-5830, Fax- 608-240-3355; 7:45AM-4:30PM.

http://offender.doc.state.wi.us/public/

Information stored in the database is accessible on a limited basis to victims, neighborhood watch programs, and the general public. One may also search at the local law enforcement level.

Indexing & Storage: Records available from 1998 to present. New records available for inquiry in 24 hours.

Searching: Include in request- name and approx. age. This data not released- victim profile and data, juvenile adjudication, exact residence address.

Access by: mail, phone, fax, online.

Mail search: Turnaround time- 1-2 weeks.

Phone search: phone requests accepted also at 800-39802403.

Fax search: Simple fax requests are honored.

Online search: Search for offenders at the web by either name or by location.

Incarceration Records

Wisconsin Department of Corrections, Attn: Records, PO Box 7925, Madison, WI 53707-1921 (Courier address- 3099 E Washington Ave, Madison, WI 53704); 608-240-3750 (Records Office), Fax- 608-240-3306; 8AM-4:30PM.

www.wi-doc.com

Indexing & Storage: Records available on current and former inmates.

Searching: Include in request- first and last name and the DOB. Location, conviction and sentencing information, and release dates are provided. This data not released- SSN, victims, presentence report. Medical, mental and dental data only released with signed consent.

Access by: mail, phone, fax.

Fee & Payment: Copies are $.15 per page, there is a file retrieval fee of $2.50 fee. Add postage fee for mail backs. Fee payee- Department of Corrections Prepayment required. Personal checks accepted.

Mail search: Turnaround time- 1 to 2 working days.

Phone search: Limited information is available by phone, by the agency will give location of inmate.

Fax search: Requests are accepted by fax.

Other access: The agency sells a raw database file of inmates for $100 on CD. The CD is published twice a year. Call for details.

Corporation, LP, LLC, LLP

Division of Corporate & Consumer Services, Corporation Record Requests, PO Box 7846, Madison, WI 53707-7846 (Courier address- 345 W Washington Ave, 3rd Floor, Madison, WI 53703); 608-261-7577, Fax- 608-267-6813; 7:45AM-4:30PM. www.wdfi.org

Indexing & Storage: Records available from 1873. Any records that are not at this office are kept at the State Records Center or the State Archives, but you must go through this office for access. New records available for inquiry in one day.

Searching: Include in request- full name of business. In addition to the articles of organization, business entity records available include: Annual Reports of Officers/Directors, merger information and Name Changes.

Access by: mail, phone, in person, online.

Fee & Payment: ID reports are $10.00, simple copy work is $5.00 per document. Short form certificates of status are $10.00. Certified copies are $10.00 plus. In-person copies are $.25 do it yourself. Fee payee- Department of Financial Institutions. Prepayment required. Personal checks accepted. Visa or MasterCard accepted only for online orders.

Mail search: Turnaround time- 7 to 10 days. A SASE is requested.

Phone search: No fee for telephone request. They will only give a verbal response from the on-screen information.

In person: Turnaround time is while you wait.

Online search: Selected elements of the database ("CRIS" Corporate Registration Information System) are available online on the department's website at www.wdfi.org/apps/CorpSearch/Search.aspx?. A Certificate of Status can be ordered online for $10.00 at https://www.wdfi.org/apps/ccs/directions.asp. To place orders for status, copy work, or ID Reports go to https://www.wdfi.org/apps/oos/. Also, search securities companies and investment advisors at www.wdfi.org/fi/securities/licensing/licensee_lists/default.asp.

Other access: Some data is released in database format and is available electronically via email or on CD.

Expedited service: Expedited service is available for mail searches. Turnaround time is close of business first business day following date of receipt. Add $25.00 per item.

Trademarks/Servicemarks, Trade Names

Secretary of State, Tradenames/Trademarks Division, PO Box 7848, Madison, WI 53707-7848 (Courier address- 30 W Mifflin St, 10th Floor, Madison, WI 53703); 608-266-5653, Fax- 608-266-3159; 7:45AM-4:30PM.

www.sos.state.wi.us/trademark.htm

Indexing & Storage: Records available for the past 20 years. New records available for inquiry in 7-14 working days.

Searching: All information is considered public record and they will release any information they have. Include in request- trademark/servicemark name, name of owner, date of application.

Access by: mail, phone, fax, in person, online.

Fee & Payment: There is no fee to see if a mark is listed. Plain copies of one record costs $2.00. For certified copies, the cost is $6.00 minimum, depending on the number of pages in the file. Fee payee- Secretary of State. Prepayment required. Personal checks accepted, credit cards are not.

Mail search: Turnaround time- 7 to 10 days. SASE not required but does insure quicker response.

Phone search: They will pull the file and give all available information over the phone.

Fax search: Same fees apply, $2.00 per copy if returned by fax. Turnaround time in 7 to 10 days.

In person: There is no public access to copier. Staff will pull cards and forms for free inspection; staff will make copies for fees listed.

Online search: Search by trademark description or corporate name from the web page.

Other access: Bulk access is offered - requests are handled on an individual basis.

Uniform Commercial Code, Federal & State Tax Liens

Department of Financial Institutions, CCS/UCC, PO Box 7847, Madison, WI 53707-7847 (Courier address- 345 W Washington Ave 3rd Fl, Madison, WI 53703); 608-261-9548, Fax- 608-264-7965; 7:45AM-4:30PM.

www.wdfi.org/ucc/

For Realty-Related (Fixture) Filings, please refer to the county Register of Deeds

Indexing & Storage: Records available from 1965, if still in effect. New records available for inquiry in 2 days if submitted by paper, otherwise instant.

Searching: Use search request form UCC-11. The search includes federal tax liens. All state tax liens are filed at the county level. Include in request- debtor name. This agency will not perform searches on a routine basis. Copies of documents filed prior to July 1, 1999 must be requested from the filing office (county level).

Access by: mail, phone, fax, in person, online.

Fee & Payment: There is no search fee. Uncertified copies are $4.00 per original file number; certified copies are $15.00 per file number. Fee payee- Department of Financial Institutions. Prepayment required. Personal checks accepted, credit cards are not.

Mail search: Turnaround time- up to 5 days.

Phone search: Call for uncertified information, some data is given over the phone.

Fax search: Turnaround time is 2-7 days.

In person: Simple requests may be processed while you wait.

Online search: There is free Internet access for most records. Some records may require a $1.00 fee. You may do a free debtor name search at www.wdfi.org/ucc/search/. Instant filings are available immediately. The search includes federal tax liens.

Other access: Bulk Index data is available on CD. The initial subscription is $3,000, monthly updates are $250.00. Images are available on CD for $200.00 per month.

Sales Tax Registrations

Revenue Department, Sales & Use Tax Division, PO Box 93389, Madison, WI 53293 (Courier address- 2135 Rimrock Rd, Madison, WI 53713); 608-266-2772, Fax- 608-267-0834; 7:45AM-4:30PM.

www.dor.state.wi.us

The information contained on the seller's permit is not confidential, so it may be provided to requester who inquires if a particular seller has a seller's permit.

Indexing & Storage: Records available from 1963.

Searching: The Department can disclose the real name, business name, address, and seller's permit number. Include in request- business name, tax permit number. The more information provided, the easier the search can be conducted. Specific account numbers (i.e., FEIN, SP, etc.) can be more easily used than can names (i.e., real or business).

Access by: mail, phone, fax, in person.

Fee & Payment: There is no search fee, no copy fee.

Mail search: Turnaround time- 2 to 3 weeks. A SASE is requested.

Phone search: Records are available by phone.

Fax search: Records may be requested via fax.

In person: Counter service available.

Birth Certificates

Bureau of Health Information and Policy, Vital Records, PO Box 309, Madison, WI 53701-0309 (Courier address- One W Wilson St, Room 158, Madison, WI 53702); 608-266-1373, 608-266-1371 (Recording), 608-267-7820 (Genealogy), Fax- 608-255-2035; 8AM-4:15PM.

http://dhs.wisconsin.gov/vitalrecords/

An uncertified copy of a birth certificate is available to anyone who applies. An uncertified copy will contain the same information as a certified copy but will not be acceptable for legal purposes, such as obtaining identification.

Indexing & Storage: Records available from 1907 on. This office has the original records. The county of issue has a copy. New records available for inquiry immediately.

Searching: Must have a signed release from person of record or immediate family member and include the reason for the inquiry for certified copies. Uncertified copy requests do not require a release or a reason, but cannot be expedited. Include in request- full name, names of parents, mother's maiden name, date of birth, place of birth, relationship to person of record, reason for information request.

Access by: mail, fax, in person, online.

Fee & Payment: The fee is $20.00 per name. Add $3.00 per name per copy for additional copies. Uncertified copies are the same price. Fee payee- State of WI Vital Records. Prepayment required. Credit cards fax and online service only. Personal checks accepted. Major credit cards accepted.

Mail search: Turnaround time- 4 weeks. A SASE is requested.

Fax search: The fax application for uncertified birth record is at http://dhs.wisconsin.gov/forms/dph/dph05292.pdf. Also, see expedited service through VitalChek.

In person: Turnaround time 2 to 4 hours.

Online search: Records may be ordered online via www.vitalchek.com, a state approved vendor.

Expedited service: Expedited service is available in person from this agency for an additional $10.00. If www.vitalchek.com used (fax, online), add $6.00 for use of credit card and shipping costs.

Death Records

Bureau of Health Information and Policy, Vital Records, PO Box 309, Madison, WI 53701-0309 (Courier address- One W Wilson St, Room 158, Madison, WI 53702); 608-266-1373, 608-266-1371 (Recording), 608-267-7820 (Genealogy), Fax- 608-255-2035; 8AM-4:15PM.

http://dhs.wisconsin.gov/vitalrecords/

An uncertified copy of a birth certificate is available to anyone who applies. An uncertified copy will contain the same information as a certified copy but will not be acceptable for legal purposes, such as obtaining identification.

Indexing & Storage: Records available from 1907 on. This office has the original records. The county of issue has a copy. New records available for inquiry immediately.

Searching: Must have a signed release from immediate family member for certified copies. Uncertified copy requests do not require a release. Include in request- full name, date of death, place of death, relationship to person of record, reason for information request.

Access by: mail, fax, in person, online.

Fee & Payment: The fee is $20.00 per name search. Add $3.00 per name per copy for additional copies. Uncertified copies are the same fee, but cannot be expedited. Fee payee- State of WI Vital Records. Prepayment required. Credit cards fax and online service only. Personal checks accepted. Major credit cards accepted.

Mail search: Turnaround time- 4 weeks. A SASE is requested.

Fax search: See expedited service through VitalChek.

In person: Turnaround time 2 to 4 hours.

Online search: Records may be ordered online via www.vitalchek.com, a state approved vendor.

Expedited service: Expedited service is available in person from this agency for an additional $10.00. If www.vitalchek.com used (fax, online), add $6.00 for use of credit card and shipping costs.

Marriage Certificates

Bureau of Health Information and Policy, Vital Records, PO Box 309, Madison, WI 53701-0309 (Courier address- One W Wilson St, Room 158, Madison, WI 53702); 608-266-1373, 608-266-1371 (Recording), 608-267-7820 (Genealogy), Fax- 608-255-2035; 8AM-4:15PM.

http://dhs.wisconsin.gov/vitalrecords/

An uncertified copy of a marriage certificate is available to anyone who applies. An uncertified copy will contain the same information as a certified copy but will not be acceptable for legal purposes, such as obtaining identification.

Indexing & Storage: Records available from 1907 on. This office has the original records. The county of issue has a copy. New records available for inquiry immediately.

Searching: Must have a signed release from the named parties for certified copies. Requests for uncertified copies do not require a release. Include in request- names of husband and wife, date of marriage, place or county of marriage, reason for information request.

Access by: mail, fax, in person, online.

Fee & Payment: The fee is $20.00 per name search. Add $3.00 per name per copy for additional copies. The fee is the same for uncertified copies, but cannot be expedited. Fee payee- State of WI Vital Records. Prepayment required. Credit cards fax and online service only. Personal checks accepted. Major credit cards accepted.

Mail search: Turnaround time- 4 weeks. A SASE is requested.

Fax search: See expedited service through VitalChek.

In person: Turnaround time 2 to 4 hours.

Online search: Records may be ordered online via www.vitalchek.com, a state approved vendor.

Expedited service: Expedited service is available in person from this agency for an additional $10.00. If www.vitalchek.com used (fax, online), add $6.00 for use of credit card and shipping costs.

Divorce Records

Bureau of Health Information and Policy, Vital Records, PO Box 309, Madison, WI 53701-0309 (Courier address- One W Wilson St, Room 158,

Madison, WI 53702); 608-266-1373, 608-266-1371 (Recording), 608-267-7820 (Genealogy), Fax- 608-255-2035; 8AM-4:15PM.

http://dhs.wisconsin.gov/vitalrecords/

An uncertified copy of a birth certificate is available to anyone who applies. An uncertified copy will contain the same information as a certified copy but will not be acceptable for legal purposes, such as obtaining identification.

Indexing & Storage: Records available from 1907. New records available for inquiry immediately.

Searching: Must have a signed release from the persons of record for a certified copy. Requests for uncertified copies do not require a release. Include in request- names of husband and wife, date of divorce, place of divorce, case number (if known), reason for information request.

Access by: mail, fax, in person, online.

Fee & Payment: The fee is $20.00 per name search. Add $3.00 per name per copy for additional copies. Uncertified copies are the same fee, but cannot be expedited. Fee payee- State of WI Vital Records. Prepayment required. Credit cards fax and online service only. Personal checks accepted. Major credit cards accepted.

Mail search: Turnaround time- 4 weeks. Uncertified requests can take up to 4 months to process. A SASE is requested.

Fax search: See expedited service through VitalChek.

In person: Turnaround time 2 to 4 hours if expedite fee paid.

Online search: Records may be ordered online via www.vitalchek.com, a state approved vendor.

Expedited service: Expedited service is available in person from this agency for an additional $10.00. If www.vitalchek.com used (fax, online), add $6.00 for use of credit card and shipping costs.

Workers' Compensation Records

Dept of Workforce Development, Worker's Compensation Division, PO Box 7901, Madison, WI 53707-7901 (Courier address- 201 E Washington Ave, Madison, WI 53701); 608-266-3280, Fax- 608-260-2503; 7:45AM-4:30PM.

www.dwd.state.wi.us/wc/

Indexing & Storage: Records available for 12 years from last benefit payment. New records available for inquiry immediately.

Searching: Decisions are public records. For case details, must have release from claimant or be a party to the claim. Must also specify what records you request. Include in request- claimant name, date of accident, employer, and either claim number or SSN. It is suggested to call first so that they can locate records.

Access by: mail, fax, in person.

Fee & Payment: There is a $3.00 service fee plus $.20 per copy fee, $2.00 if certified. Fee payee- Workforce Department. Prepayment required. Personal checks accepted, credit cards are not.

Mail search: Turnaround time- 1 to 2 weeks. A SASE is not requested.

Fax search: Fax requests accepted.

In person: Requester must show how connected to party. If you make the copies, the fee is $.10 per page, exact change required.

Driver Records

Division of Motor Vehicles, Driver Records, PO Box 7995, Madison, WI 53707-7995 (Courier address- 4802 Sheboygan Ave, Madison, WI 53705); 608-266-2353, Fax- 608-267-1873; 7:30AM-5:15PM.

www.dot.wisconsin.gov/drivers/index.htm

Copies of tickets may be obtained for $5.00 per citation from the Citation & Withdrawal Section at PO Box 7917, Madison WI 53707-7917.

Indexing & Storage: Records available for 3 years from date of conviction for moving violations, 55 years from date of convictions for alcohol-related violations, and 5 years for other suspensions/revocations. New records available for inquiry in no more than 15 days.

Searching: Driver record information can be obtained per DPPA guidelines. Casual requesters must submit Form MV2896 which requires signature of the subject. This form may be downloaded from the web. Include in request- driver license number, or full name, DOB and sex plus form mentioned above. The driver's address is included as part of the search for approved requesters. There is no public counter for walk-in requests here or at any of the field offices. This data not released- ID card information, SSN, juvenile record entries, arrests and medical information.

Access by: mail, phone, online.

Fee & Payment: The fee is $5.00 per driving record. Fee payee- Registration Fee Trust Prepayment required. Personal checks accepted, credit cards are not.

Mail search: Turnaround time- 5 business days.

Phone search: This is ONLY available to the person of record, call 608-261-2466.

Online search: Interactive service is available for approved requesters. Records are provided in PDF format for $5.00 each. The program is called PARS. Call Citations and Withdrawals Section at 608-266-0928 for more information. PARS participants can also participate in an employer notification program. Employers can enroll CDL drivers and will be notified when activity occurs on the employees record. The fee is also $5.00 per record when accessed. Also, a free status check of a DL is at www.dot.wisconsin.gov/drivers/online.htm. Must submit either DL, SSN, and DOB, or submit full name and DOB.

Vehicle Ownership & Registration

Department of Transportation, Vehicle Records Section, PO Box 7911, Madison, WI 53707-7911 (Courier address- 4802 Sheboygan Ave, Room 851, Madison, WI 53707); 608-266-3666, 608-266-1466 (Registration), Fax- 608-267-6966; 8AM-4:30PM.

www.dot.wisconsin.gov/drivers/vehicles/index.htm

Indexing & Storage: Records available for 7 years to present. New records available for inquiry in 2-3 days.

Searching: All DPPA restrictions apply. All casual or occasional requestors must submit a request form MV2896. If the request is not for a permissible use, the subject's signature is necessary. The state no longer offers in-person access to records. Depending on what record is required, records can be looked up by name, VIN, plate or by name & city or county. This data not released- SSN

Access by: mail.

Fee & Payment: The fee is $5.00 per record, including lien searches. An additional $5.00 is charged for certification. The photocopy fee is $.25 per page. Fee payee- Registration Fee Trust. Prepayment required. Personal checks accepted, credit cards are not.

Mail search: Turnaround time- 5 business days. A SASE is requested.

Other access: This agency offers a variety of methods of obtaining bulk registration lists on cartridge and microfiche. FTP output by a specific request list is available only to law enforcement. Call 608-266-0898 for more information. All DPPA restrictions apply.

Accident Reports

DOT- Qualifications and Issuance, Accident Records Unit, PO Box 7919, Madison, WI 53707-7919 (Courier address- 4802 Sheboygan Ave, Room 804, Madison, WI 53707); 608-266-8753, Fax- 608-261-8201; 7:30AM-4:30PM.

www.dot.wisconsin.gov

Indexing & Storage: Records available for 4 years to present. New records available for inquiry in 2 weeks, on average, from receipt of report.

Searching: The information is public record. Records can be accessed by driver license number or by accident report number. If none of these items are available, the full name, DOB, and date of accident will be used. This data not released- juvenile records.

Access by: mail, phone.

Fee & Payment: The fees are $6.00 for operator reports and $6.00 for police reports. Fee payee- Registration Fee Trust. Prepayment is required if charges are above $6.00. Personal checks accepted, credit cards are not.

Mail search: Turnaround time- 72 hours. SASE not required.

Phone search: 24 hour automated messaging system available to request copies.

Vessel Ownership & Registration

Department of Natural Resources, Boat Registration, PO Box 7921, Madison, WI 53707 (Courier address- 101 S Webster, Madison, WI 53703); 608-266-2621, Fax- 608-264-6130; 7:45AM-4:30PM. www.dnr.wi.gov

Indexing & Storage: Records available from 1978 to present. Records are indexed on computer. All motorized boats and all sailboats must be registered. All motorized boats and all sailboats, if 16 ft or over, must be titled. Lien information shows on title records. New records available for inquiry in up to 3 months.

Searching: To search one of the following is required: name, hull ID #, or boat registration #. This data not released- SSN

Access by: mail, phone, fax, in person.

Fee & Payment: There is no search fee for 10 names or less. If over 10 names, then the fees for purchasing lists ($200) are imposed. Fee payee- DNR. Prepayment required. Personal checks and major credit cards accepted.

Mail search: Turnaround time- 1 week. SASE not required.

Phone search: Records are available by phone, if under 10 records.

Fax search: Same criteria as mail searching.

In person: If the search is a simple record check, records are returned by mail the next day.

Other access: Bulk lists may be purchased. Call the number above or visit the web page at http://dnr.wi.gov/org/caer/cs/apps/9400571.pdf.

Legislation Records

Wisconsin Legislation, Legislative Reference Bureau, PO Box 2037, Madison, WI 53701-2037 (Courier address- One East Main Street #200, Madison, WI 53701-2037); 608-266-0341, 800-362-9472 (Bill Status), Fax- 608-266-5648; 7:45AM-5PM. www.legis.state.wi.us

Indexing & Storage: Records available from 1848 on. Records are computerized since 1995.

Searching: Drafts are not available. Include in request- bill number, topic of bill.

Access by: mail, phone, fax, in person, online.

Fee & Payment: There is a nominal fee for microfiche or paper copies. Fee payee- Wisconsin Legislative Reference Bureau. Personal checks accepted, credit cards are not.

Mail search: Turnaround time- variable. SASE not required.

Phone search: Limited data is given over the phone. **Fax search:** Requests are accepted but response by fax is generally limited to 5 pages or less.

In person: Simple requests may be processed while you wait.

Online search: Information on current bills is available over the Internet as well as state statutes. There is a Folio Program to search text of previous session bills.

Voter Registration

State Elections Board, PO Box 2973,, Madison, WI 53701 (Courier address- 17 W Main #310, Madison, WI 53703); 608-266-8005, Fax- 608-267-0500; 7:45AM-4:30PM.

http://elections.wi.gov

Searching: Records are available for political purposes. Records are open to the public; but except for the address, personal identifiers are cloaked.

Access by: mail, in person.

Mail search: Records are available by mail.

In person: Counter service is offered. Requests are handled as time permits. Records may be viewed.

GED Certificates

Department of Public Instruction, GED Program, PO Box 7841, Madison, WI 53707-7841 (Courier address- 125 S Webster, Madison, WI 53707); 608-267-2275, 800-768-8886, Fax- 608-267-9275; 8AM-4:30PM.

www.dpi.wi.gov/ged_hsed/gedhsed.html

Indexing & Storage: New records available for inquiry in minutes.

Searching: Include in request- name, SSN, DOB, and year test was taken. For a transcript, include a signed release. The release and personal identifiers are needed for all requests, including a simple verification. Order form may be printed from the web page.

Access by: mail, phone, fax, in person.

Fee & Payment: there is no fee for a verification, the fee is $15.00 for a copy of a transcript or diploma. No "unofficial" documents are released. Fee payee- WI Department of Public Instruction Prepayment required. Personal checks accepted. Visa and MasterCard accepted for transcripts.

Mail search: Turnaround time- 1 week. SASE not required.

Phone search: A requester must leave a message, with all required data. The agency will then call back with verification.

Fax search: Same criteria as mail or phone searching.

In person: An appointment is required. Simple requests may be processed while you wait.

Expedited service: Expedited service is available for mail requests. Fee is $25.00. Turnaround time- 48 hours.

Hunting & Fishing License Information

Fish & Game Licensing Division, Records Manager - CS/G3, PO Box 7924, Madison, WI 53707 (Courier address- 101 S Webster St, Madison, WI 53703); 608-267-9576, Fax- 608-264-6130; 7AM-10PM.

www.dnr.wi.gov/org/caer/cs/openrecords.htm

Note there is an opt out provision in place and over 50% of the licensees have opted out.

Indexing & Storage: Records available in list format on an annual basis.

Searching: All requests must in in writing. Include in request- name and as much information as possible.

Access by: mail, in person.

Fee & Payment: There is no fee unless a list is requested. Fee payee- Department of Natural Resources

Mail search: Turnaround time- 2-5 days.

In person: Counter is open until 3:30PM.

Other access: See the website for the fees and availability. Use must use their Form 9400-571 - Electronic Records Order. See price list at www.dnr.wi.gov/org/caer/cs/apps/9400571.pdf.

Wisconsin State Licensing Agencies

For details about the agency responsible for licensing/certifying/registering an item below or in the Agency Quick Finder section, match an item's number with the number of the agency in the *Licensing Agency Information* section.

Wisconsin Licenses Searchable Online

Accounting Firm #2 ... http://drl.wi.gov/lookupjump.htm
Acupuncturist #4 ... https://ice.wi.gov/LicenseLookup/default.do?page=lookup_health
Adjustment Service Company #6 ... www.wdfi.org/fi/lfs/licensee_lists/
Aesthetics Establishm't/School #2 ... http://drl.wi.gov/lookupjump.htm
Aesthetics Instructor #1 ... http://drl.wi.gov/lookupjump.htm
Appraiser, General/Residential #1 ... http://drl.wi.gov/lookupjump.htm
Architect #1 ... http://drl.wi.gov/lookupjump.htm
Architectural Corporation #2 ... http://drl.wi.gov/lookupjump.htm
Art Therapist #4 ... https://ice.wi.gov/LicenseLookup/default.do?page=lookup_health
Attorney #16 ... www.wisbar.org/AM/Template.cfm?Section=Lawyer_Directory
Auction Company #2 ... http://drl.wi.gov/lookupjump.htm
Auctioneer #1 ... http://drl.wi.gov/lookupjump.htm
Audiologist #4 ... https://ice.wi.gov/LicenseLookup/default.do?page=lookup_health
Bank #5 ... www.wdfi.org/fi/savings_institutions/licensee_lists/
Barber #1 ... http://drl.wi.gov/lookupjump.htm
Barber Appren./Instruct./Mgr. #1 ... http://drl.wi.gov/lookupjump.htm
Barber School #2 ... http://drl.wi.gov/lookupjump.htm
Boiler Repairer #3 ... http://apps.commerce.state.wi.us/SB_Credential/SB_CredentialApp
Boxer #1 ... http://drl.wi.gov/lookupjump.htm
Boxing Club, Amateur/Prof. #2 ... http://drl.wi.gov/lookupjump.htm
Boxing Show #2 ... http://drl.wi.gov/lookupjump.htm
Building Inspector #3 ... http://apps.commerce.state.wi.us/SB_Credential/SB_CredentialApp
Cemetery Authority/Warehouse #2 ... http://drl.wi.gov/lookupjump.htm
Cemetery Pre-Need Seller #1 ... http://drl.wi.gov/lookupjump.htm
Cemetery Salesperson #1 ... http://drl.wi.gov/lookupjump.htm
Charitable Organization #2 ... http://drl.wi.gov/lookupjump.htm
Check Seller #6 ... www.wdfi.org/fi/lfs/licensee_lists/
Chiropractor #4 ... https://ice.wi.gov/LicenseLookup/default.do?page=lookup_health
Collection Agency #6 ... www.wdfi.org/fi/lfs/licensee_lists/
Cosmetologist #1 ... http://drl.wi.gov/lookupjump.htm
Cosmetology Instr./Mgr./Apprentice #1 ... http://drl.wi.gov/lookupjump.htm
Cosmetology School #2 ... http://drl.wi.gov/lookupjump.htm
Counselor, Professional #4 ... https://ice.wi.gov/LicenseLookup/default.do?page=lookup_health
Credit Service Organization #5 ... www.wdfi.org/fi/cu/chartered_lists/default.asp
Credit Union #5 ... www.wdfi.org/fi/cu/chartered_lists/default.asp
Currency Exchange #6 ... www.wdfi.org/fi/lfs/licensee_lists/
Dance Therapist #4 ... https://ice.wi.gov/LicenseLookup/default.do?page=lookup_health
Debt Collector #6 ... www.wdfi.org/fi/lfs/licensee_lists/
Dental Hygienist #4 ... https://ice.wi.gov/LicenseLookup/default.do?page=lookup_health
Dentist #4 ... https://ice.wi.gov/LicenseLookup/default.do?page=lookup_health
Designer, Engineering Systems #1 ... http://drl.wi.gov/lookupjump.htm
Dietitian #4 ... https://ice.wi.gov/LicenseLookup/default.do?page=lookup_health
Drug Distributor/Mfg #2 ... http://drl.wi.gov/lookupjump.htm
Electrical Inspector #3 ... http://apps.commerce.state.wi.us/SB_Credential/SB_CredentialApp
Electrician #3 ... http://apps.commerce.state.wi.us/SB_Credential/SB_CredentialApp
Electrologist/Electrology Instructor #1 ... http://drl.wi.gov/lookupjump.htm
Electrology Establishment/School #2 ... http://drl.wi.gov/lookupjump.htm
Employee Benefits Plan Administrt'r#12 ... https://ociaccess.oci.wi.gov/ProducerInfo/PrdIndividual.oci
Engineer/Engineer in Training #1 ... http://drl.wi.gov/lookupjump.htm
Engineering Corporation #2 ... http://drl.wi.gov/lookupjump.htm
Firearms Permit #2 ... http://drl.wi.gov/lookupjump.htm
Fireworks Manufacturer #3 ... http://apps.commerce.state.wi.us/SB_Credential/SB_CredentialApp
Fund Raiser, Professional #1 ... http://drl.wi.gov/lookupjump.htm
Fund Raising Counsel #2 ... http://drl.wi.gov/lookupjump.htm
Funeral Director/Director Apprentice #1 ... http://drl.wi.gov/lookupjump.htm
Funeral Establishment #2 ... http://drl.wi.gov/lookupjump.htm

Funeral Pre-Need Seller #1 .... http://drl.wi.gov/lookupjump.htm

Geologist #1 .... http://drl.wi.gov/lookupjump.htm

Geology Firm #2 .... http://drl.wi.gov/lookupjump.htm

Hearing Instrument Specialist #4 .... https://ice.wi.gov/LicenseLookup/default.do?page=lookup_health

HMO #12 .... https://ociaccess.oci.wi.gov/CmpInfo/CmpInfo.oci

Home Inspector #1 .... http://drl.wi.gov/lookupjump.htm

HVAC Contractor #3 .... http://apps.commerce.state.wi.us/SB_Credential/SB_CredentialApp

Hydrologist #1 .... http://drl.wi.gov/lookupjump.htm

Hydrology Firm #2 .... http://drl.wi.gov/lookupjump.htm

Insurance Agency or Agent #12 .... https://ociaccess.oci.wi.gov/ProducerInfo/PrdIndividual.oci

Insurance Company #12 .... http://oci.wi.gov/compinfo.htm

Insurance Intermediary #12 .... https://ociaccess.oci.wi.gov/ProducerInfo/PrdIndividual.oci

Insurance Premium Financier #6 .... www.wdfi.org/fi/lfs/licensee_lists/

Insurance Producer #12 .... https://ociaccess.oci.wi.gov/ProducerInfo/PrdFirm.oci

Interior Designer #1 .... http://drl.wi.gov/lookupjump.htm

Investment Advisor/Advisor Rep #10 .... www.wdfi.org/fi/securities/licensing/licensee_lists/default.asp

Land Surveyor #1 .... http://drl.wi.gov/lookupjump.htm

Landscape Architect #1 .... http://drl.wi.gov/lookupjump.htm

Loan Company #6 .... www.wdfi.org/fi/lfs/licensee_lists/

Loan Solicitor/Originator #5 .... www.wdfi.org/fi/lfs/licensee_lists/default.asp

Lobbying Organization, Principal #11 .... http://ethics.state.wi.us/Scripts/2003Session/OELMenu.asp

Lobbyist #11 .... http://ethics.state.wi.us/Scripts/2003Session/LobbyistsMenu.asp

Manicurist Establ./Specialty School #2 .... http://drl.wi.gov/lookupjump.htm

Manicurist/Manicurist Instructor #1 .... http://drl.wi.gov/lookupjump.htm

Marriage & Family Therapist #4 .... https://ice.wi.gov/LicenseLookup/default.do?page=lookup_health

Massage Therapist/Bodyworker #4 .... https://ice.wi.gov/LicenseLookup/default.do?page=lookup_health

Medical Doctor/Surgeon #4 .... https://ice.wi.gov/LicenseLookup/default.do?page=lookup_health

Midwife Nurse #4 .... https://ice.wi.gov/LicenseLookup/default.do?page=lookup_health

Mobile Home & RV Dealer #6 .... www.wdfi.org/fi/lfs/licensee_lists/

Mortgage Banker/Broker #5 .... www.wdfi.org/fi/lfs/licensee_lists/default.asp

Motor Club #12 .... https://ociaccess.oci.wi.gov/CmpInfo/CmpInfo.oci

Motorcycle Dealer #6 .... www.wdfi.org/fi/lfs/licensee_lists/

Music Therapist #4 .... https://ice.wi.gov/LicenseLookup/default.do?page=lookup_health

Nurse-RN/LPN #4 .... https://ice.wi.gov/LicenseLookup/default.do?page=lookup_health

Nursing Home Administrator #1 .... http://drl.wi.gov/lookupjump.htm

Occupational Therapist/Assistant #4 .... https://ice.wi.gov/LicenseLookup/default.do?page=lookup_health

Optometrist #4 .... https://ice.wi.gov/LicenseLookup/default.do?page=lookup_health

Osteopathic Physician #4 .... https://ice.wi.gov/LicenseLookup/default.do?page=lookup_health

Payday Lender #6 .... www.wdfi.org/fi/lfs/licensee_lists/

Pesticide Applicator #9 .... www.kellysolutions.com/WI/Applicators/index.asp

Pesticide Applicator Business #9 .... www.kellysolutions.com/WI/Business/searchbyCity.asp

Pesticide Dealer #9 .... www.kellysolutions.com/WI/Dealers/searchbyCity.asp

Pesticide Manufacturer/Labeler #9 .... www.kellysolutions.com/wi/pesticideindex.asp

Pharmacy/Pharmacist #4 .... https://ice.wi.gov/LicenseLookup/default.do?page=lookup_health

Physical Therapist #4 .... https://ice.wi.gov/LicenseLookup/default.do?page=lookup_health

Physician Assistant #4 .... https://ice.wi.gov/LicenseLookup/default.do?page=lookup_health

Plumber #3 .... http://apps.commerce.state.wi.us/SB_Credential/SB_CredentialApp

Podiatrist #4 .... https://ice.wi.gov/LicenseLookup/default.do?page=lookup_health

Private Detective #1 .... http://drl.wi.gov/lookupjump.htm

Private Detective Agency #2 .... http://drl.wi.gov/lookupjump.htm

Psychologist #4 .... https://ice.wi.gov/LicenseLookup/default.do?page=lookup_health

Public Accountant #1 .... http://drl.wi.gov/lookupjump.htm

Rate Service Org #12 .... https://ociaccess.oci.wi.gov/CmpInfo/CmpInfo.oci

Real Estate Agent/Broker/Sales #1 .... http://drl.wi.gov/lookupjump.htm

Real Estate Appraiser #1 .... http://drl.wi.gov/lookupjump.htm

Real Estate Business Entity #2 .... http://drl.wi.gov/lookupjump.htm

Respiratory Care Practitioner #4 .... https://ice.wi.gov/LicenseLookup/default.do?page=lookup_health

Risk Purchasing Group #12 .... https://ociaccess.oci.wi.gov/CmpInfo/CmpInfo.oci

Sales Finance/Loan Company #6 .... www.wdfi.org/fi/lfs/licensee_lists/

Savings & Loan Financer #6 .... www.wdfi.org/fi/lfs/licensee_lists/

Savings Institution #5 .... www.wdfi.org/fi/savings_institutions/licensee_lists/

School Librarian/Media Specialist #15 .... https://www2.dpi.wi.gov/lic-tll/home.do

School Psychology Private Practice #4 .... https://ice.wi.gov/LicenseLookup/default.do?page=lookup_health

Securities Broker/Dealer/Agent #10 .... www.wdfi.org/fi/securities/licensing/licensee_lists/default.asp

Security Guard #1 .... http://drl.wi.gov/lookupjump.htm

Social Worker #4	https://ice.wi.gov/LicenseLookup/default.do?page=lookup_health
Soil Science Firm #2	http://drl.wi.gov/lookupjump.htm
Soil Scientist #1	http://drl.wi.gov/lookupjump.htm
Soil Tester #3	http://apps.commerce.state.wi.us/SB_Credential/SB_CredentialApp
Speech Pathologist/Audiologist #4	https://ice.wi.gov/LicenseLookup/default.do?page=lookup_health
Teacher #15	https://www2.dpi.wi.gov/lic-tll/home.do
Timeshare Salesperson #1	http://drl.wi.gov/lookupjump.htm
Veterinarian/Veterinary Technician #4	https://ice.wi.gov/LicenseLookup/default.do?page=lookup_health
Viatical Settlement Broker #12	https://ociaccess.oci.wi.gov/ProducerInfo/PrdIndividual.oci
Welder #3	http://apps.commerce.state.wi.us/SB_Credential/SB_CredentialApp

Wisconsin Licensing Quick Finder

Accounting Firm #2	608-266-2112
Acupuncturist #4	608-266-8794
Adjustment Counselor #6	608-261-7578
Adjustment Service Company #6	608-261-7578
Aesthetics Establishm't/School #2	608-266-2112
Aesthetics Instructor #1	608-266-2112
Ambulance Service #7	608-266-1568
Appraiser, General/Residential #1	608-266-2112
Architect #1	608-266-5511
Architectural Corporation #2	608-266-2112
Art Therapist #4	608-266-8794
Asbestos Worker #17	608-261-6876
Attorney #16	608-250-6125
Auction Company #2	608-266-2112
Auctioneer #1	608-266-5511
Audiologist #4	608-266-8794
Bank #5	608-261-7578
Barber #1	608-266-2112
Barber Appren./Instruct./Mgr. #1	608-266-2112
Barber School #2	608-266-2112
Beer Wholesaler #8	608-266-2772
Boiler Repairer #3	608-261-8500
Boxer #1	608-266-5511
Boxing Club, Amateur/Prof. #2	608-266-2112
Boxing Show #2	608-266-2112
Building Inspector #3	608-261-8500
Business Tax Registration #8	608-266-2776
Cemetery Authority/Warehouse #2	608-266-2112
Cemetery Pre-Need Seller #1	608-266-5511
Cemetery Salesperson #1	608-266-5511
Charitable Gaming #14	608-270-2555
Charitable Organization #2	608-266-2112
Check Seller #6	608-261-7578
Chiropractor #4	608-266-8794
Cigarette/Tobacco Distr/Vendor/Retail #8	608-266-2772
Cigarette/Tobacco Ware/Whlse/Jobber #8	608-266-2772
Collection Agency #6	608-261-7578
Cosmetologist #1	608-266-2112
Cosmetology Instr./Mgr./Apprentice #1	608-266-2112
Cosmetology School #2	608-266-2112
Counselor, Professional #4	608-266-8794
Credit Service Organization #5	608-266-9543
Credit Union #5	608-266-9543
Currency Exchange #6	608-261-7578
Dance Therapist #4	608-266-8794
Debt Collector #6	608-261-7578
Dental Hygienist #4	608-266-8794
Dentist #4	608-266-8794
Designer, Engineering Systems #1	608-266-5511
Dietitian #4	608-266-8794
Director of Instruction #15	608-266-1027
Dog Racing Professional #14	608-270-2555
Drug Distributor/Mfg #2	608-266-2112
Electrical Inspector #3	608-261-8500
Electrician #3	608-261-8500
Electrologist/Electrology Instructor #1	608-266-2112
Electrology Establishment/School #2	608-266-2112
Employee Benefits Plan Administrator #12	608-267-1238
EMT/Paramedic #7	608-266-1568
Engineer/Engineer in Training #1	608-266-5511
Engineering Corporation #2	608-266-2112
Excise Tax Permit #8	608-266-2772
Fertilizer #9	608-224-4541
Firearms Permit #2	608-266-2112
Fireworks Manufacturer #3	608-261-8500
Fuel Tax Permit #8	608-266-2772
Fund Raiser, Professional #1	608-266-5511
Fund Raising Counsel #2	608-266-2112
Funeral Director/Director Apprent. #1	608-266-2112
Funeral Establishment #2	608-266-2112
Funeral Pre-Need Seller #1	608-266-5511
Geologist #1	608-266-2112
Geology Firm #2	608-266-2112
Hearing Instrument Specialist #4	608-266-8794
HMO #12	608-266-3585
Home Inspector #1	608-266-5511
HVAC Contractor #3	608-261-8500
Hydrologist #1	608-266-2112
Hydrology Firm #2	608-266-2112
Indian Gaming Vendor #14	608-270-2555
Insurance Company #12	608-266-3585
Insurance Intermediary #12	608-266-8699
Insurance Premium Financier #6	608-261-7578
Insurance Producer #12	608-266-3585
Interior Designer #1	608-266-5511
Investment Advisor/Advisor Rep #10	608-266-3693
Land Surveyor #1	608-266-5511
Landscape Architect #1	608-266-5511
Liquor, Wholesale #8	608-266-2772
Loan Company #6	608-261-7578
Loan Solicitor/Originator #5	608-261-7578
Lobbying Organization, Principal #11	608-266-8123
Lobbyist #11	608-266-8123
Manicurist Establ./Specialty School #2	608-266-2112
Manicurist/Manicurist Instructor #1	608-266-2112
Marriage & Family Therapist #4	608-266-8794
Massage Therapist/Bodyworker #4	608-266-8794
Medical Doctor/Surgeon #4	608-266-8794
Midwife Nurse #4	608-266-8794
Mobile Home & RV Dealer #6	608-261-7578
Mortgage Banker/Broker #5	608-261-7578
Motor Club #12	608-266-3585
Motorcycle Dealer #6	608-261-7578
Music Therapist #4	608-266-8794
Notary Public #13	608-266-5594
Nurse-RN/LPN #4	608-266-8794
Nursing Home Administrator #1	608-266-2112
Occupational Therapist/Assistant #4	608-266-8794
Optometrist #4	608-266-8794
Osteopathic Physician #4	608-266-8794
Payday Lender #6	608-261-7578
Pesticide Applicator #9	608-224-4548
Pesticide Applicator Business #9	608-224-4548
Pesticide Dealer #9	608-224-4548
Pesticide Manufacturer/Labeler #9	608-224-4536
Pesticide Vet Clinic #9	608-224-4548
Pharmacy/Pharmacist #4	608-266-8794
Physical Therapist #4	608-266-8794
Physician Assistant #4	608-266-8794
Plumber #3	608-261-8500
Podiatrist #4	608-266-8794
Private Detective #1	608-266-5511
Private Detective Agency #2	608-266-2112
Psychologist #4	608-266-8794
Public Accountant #1	608-266-5511
Racing/Racing Vendor #14	608-270-2555
Rate Service Org #12	608-266-3585
Real Estate Agent/Broker/Sales #1	608-266-5511
Real Estate Appraiser #1	608-266-2112
Real Estate Business Entity #2	608-266-2112
Respiratory Care Practitioner #4	608-266-8794
Risk Purchasing Group #12	608-266-3585
Sales Finance/Loan Company #6	608-261-7578
Sales Withholding Tax Registration #8	608-266-2776
Sanitarian #17	608-267-4784
Savings & Loan Financer #6	608-261-7578
Savings Institution #5	608-261-4335
School Counselor #15	608-266-1027
School Librarian/Media Specialist #15	608-266-1027
School Nurse #15	608-266-1027
School Principal/Sup'r'd't/Bus. Mgr #15	608-266-1027
School Psychologist/Social Worker #15	608-266-1027
School Psychology Priv. Practice #4	608-266-8794
Securities Broker/Dealer/Agent #10	608-266-3693
Security Guard #1	608-266-5511
Social Worker #4	608-266-8794
Soil Science Firm #2	608-266-2112
Soil Scientist #1	608-266-2112
Soil Tester #3	608-261-8500
Speech Pathologist/Audiologist #4	608-266-8794
Teacher #15	608-266-1027
Timeshare Salesperson #1	608-266-5511
Veterinarian/Veterinary Technician #4	608-266-8794
Viatical Settlement Broker #12	608-266-8699
Vocational Education Coord'n'r, Local #15	608-266-1027
Welder #3	608-261-8500
Wine Distributor, Public #8	608-266-2772

Wisconsin Licensing Agency Information

#1 Dept of Regulation & Licensing, Division of Business Professional Licensure & Reg - Individuals, PO Box 8935 (1400 E Washington), Madison, WI 53708-8935; 608-266-5511, Fax- 608-267-3816. 7:45AM-4:30PM. http://drl.wi.gov Search data at- http://drl.wi.gov/lookupjump.htm Lists may be obtained.

#2 Dept of Regulation & Licensing, Division of Business Licensure & Regulation - Entities, PO Box 8935 (1400 E Washington), Madison, WI 53708-8935; 608-266-2112, Fax- 608-267-3816. Hours- 7:45AM-4:30PM. http://drl.wi.gov/index.htm Search data at- http://drl.wi.gov/lookupjump.htm Lists may be obtained.

#3 Department of Commerce, Safety & Buildings, PO Box 2658, 201 W Washington Ave, Madison, WI 53701; 608-261-8500, Fax-608-267-0592. Hours- 7:45AM-4:30PM. www.commerce.wi.gov Search data at- http://apps.commerce.state.wi.us/SB_Credential/SB_CredentialApp

#4 Bureau of Health Services Professions, PO Box 8935 (1400 E Washington Ave, Rm 11), Madison, WI 53708-8935; 608-266-0145, Fax- 608-261-7083. http://drl.wi.gov/prof/burhsvc.htm Search at- http://drl.wi.gov/drl/drllookup/LicenseLookupServlet?page=lookup_health Department recommends an internet search; if not, inquire by mail. Phone requests may not be accepted.

#5 Department of Financial Institutions, Division of Banking, PO Box 7876 (345 W Washington Ave, 4th Fl), Madison, WI 53707; 608-261-7578, Fax- 608-261-6889. www.wdfi.org Search data at- www.wdfi.org/fi/ Division of Financial Inst. - DFI - offers both an online list system and telephone system for verifications.

#6 Department of Financial Institutions, Licensed Financial Services, 345 W Washington Ave, Madison, WI 53707-7876; 608-261-7578, Fax- 608-261-7200. www.wdfi.org/fi/lfs/ Search data at- www.wdfi.org/fi/lfs/licensee_lists/ Also offers an online list system for verifications.

#7 Division of Public Health, Bureau of EMS and IP, 1 W Wilson St, Rm 118, Madison, WI 53703; 608-267-9777, 266-1568, Fax- 608-261-6392. http://dhs.wisconsin.gov/ems/

#8 Department of Revenue, 2135 Rimrock Rd, Madison, WI 53713; 608-266-2772, Fax- 608-267-0834. Hours- 7:45AM-4:30PM. www.dor.state.wi.us

#9 Department of Agriculture, Trade & Consumer Protection, Applicator Certification & Licensing, PO Box 8911 (2811 Agriculture Dr), Madison, WI 53708; 608-224-4536, Fax-608-224-4656. http://datcp.state.wi.us/arm/agriculture/pest-fert/pesticides/licenses/index.jsp Search data at- http://datcp.state.wi.us/arm/agriculture/pest-fert/pesticides/data/index.jsp

#10 Department of Financial Institutions, Division of Securities, PO Box 1768, Madison, WI 53701; 608-266-1064, Fax- 608-264-7979. www.wdfi.org/fi/securities/ Search data at- www.wdfi.org/fi/securities/licensing/licensee_lists/default.asp Their lists only contain firm info. No agents or investment adviser reps are searchable from the DFI website.

#11 Ethics Board, 44 E Mifflin St, #601, Madison, WI 53703-2800; 608-266-8123, Fax- 608-264-9319. http://ethics.state.wi.us Search at- http://ethics.state.wi.us/LobbyingRegistrationReports/LobbyingOverview.htm The year that appears in the search URL indicates the year being searched. If the URL doesn't work, try changing the year.

#12 Agent Licensing Section, Office of the Commissioner of Insurance, 125 S Webster St, Madison, WI 53703-3474; 608-266-3585, Fax-608-266-9935. Hours- 7:45AM-4:30PM. http://oci.wi.gov/oci_home.htm Search data at- https://ociaccess.oci.wi.gov/CmpInfo/CmpInfo.oci For list of license types go to www.oci.wi.gov.

For administrative actions check https://ociaccess.oci.wi.gov/OrderInfo/OrdInfo.oci

#13 Office of Secretary of State, PO Box 7848 (30 W Mifflin 10th Fl), Madison, WI 53707-7848; 608-266-5594, Fax- 608-266-3159. www.sos.state.wi.us/notary.htm

#14 Department of Administration, Division of Gaming/Racing, PO Box 8979, 3319 W Beltline Hwy, 1st Fl, Madison, WI 53708; 608-270-2555, Fax- 608-270-2564. www.doa.state.wi.us/index.asp?locid=7

#15 Teacher Education, Department of Public Instruction, PO Box 7841 (125 S Webster St), Madison, WI 53707-7841; 608-266-1027, Fax-608-264-9558. http://dpi.wi.gov/tepdl/ Search data at- https://www2.dpi.wi.gov/lic-tll/home.do

#16 State Bar Association, PO Box 7158 (5302 Eastpark Blvd), Madison, WI 53707; 608-257-3838, Fax- 608-257-5502. www.wisbar.org Search data at- www.wisbar.org/AM/Template.cfm?Section=Lawyer_Directory

#17 Department of Health & Family Svcs, Bureau of Environmental and Occupational Health, PO Box 2659 (1 W Wilson St, RM B-157), Madison, WI 53701; 608-261-6876, Fax- 608-266-9711. http://dhs.wisconsin.gov/dph_boh/

Wisconsin Federal Courts

The following list indicates the district and division name for each county in the state. If the bankruptcy court location is different from the district court, then the location of the bankruptcy court appears in parentheses.

Wisconsin County/Court Cross Reference

County	District	Division
Adams	Western	Madison
Ashland	Western	Madison (Eau Claire)
Barron	Western	Madison (Eau Claire)
Bayfield	Western	Madison (Eau Claire)
Brown	Eastern	Milwaukee
Buffalo	Western	Madison (Eau Claire)
Burnett	Western	Madison (Eau Claire)
Calumet	Eastern	Milwaukee
Chippewa	Western	Madison (Eau Claire)
Clark	Western	Madison (Eau Claire)
Columbia	Western	Madison
Crawford	Western	Madison
Dane	Western	Madison
Dodge	Eastern	Milwaukee
Door	Eastern	Milwaukee
Douglas	Western	Madison (Eau Claire)
Dunn	Western	Madison (Eau Claire)
Eau Claire	Western	Madison (Eau Claire)
Florence	Eastern	Milwaukee
Fond du Lac	Eastern	Milwaukee
Forest	Eastern	Milwaukee
Grant	Western	Madison
Green	Western	Madison
Green Lake	Eastern	Milwaukee
Iowa	Western	Madison
Iron	Western	Madison (Eau Claire)
Jackson	Western	Madison (Eau Claire)
Jefferson	Western	Madison
Juneau	Western	Madison (Eau Claire)
Kenosha	Eastern	Milwaukee
Kewaunee	Eastern	Milwaukee
La Crosse	Western	Madison (Eau Claire)
Lafayette	Western	Madison
Langlade	Eastern	Milwaukee
Lincoln	Western	Madison (Eau Claire)
Manitowoc	Eastern	Milwaukee
Marathon	Western	Madison (Eau Claire)
Marinette	Eastern	Milwaukee
Marquette	Eastern	Milwaukee
Menominee	Eastern	Milwaukee
Milwaukee	Eastern	Milwaukee
Monroe	Western	Madison (Eau Claire)
Oconto	Eastern	Milwaukee
Oneida	Western	Madison (Eau Claire)
Outagamie	Eastern	Milwaukee
Ozaukee	Eastern	Milwaukee
Pepin	Western	Madison (Eau Claire)
Pierce	Western	Madison (Eau Claire)
Polk	Western	Madison (Eau Claire)
Portage	Western	Madison (Eau Claire)
Price	Western	Madison (Eau Claire)
Racine	Eastern	Milwaukee
Richland	Western	Madison
Rock	Western	Madison
Rusk	Western	Madison (Eau Claire)
Sauk	Western	Madison
Sawyer	Western	Madison (Eau Claire)
Shawano	Eastern	Milwaukee
Sheboygan	Eastern	Milwaukee
St. Croix	Western	Madison (Eau Claire)
Taylor	Western	Madison (Eau Claire)
Trempealeau	Western	Madison (Eau Claire)
Vernon	Western	Madison (Eau Claire)
Vilas	Western	Madison (Eau Claire)
Walworth	Eastern	Milwaukee
Washburn	Western	Madison (Eau Claire)
Washington	Eastern	Milwaukee
Waukesha	Eastern	Milwaukee
Waupaca	Eastern	Milwaukee
Waushara	Eastern	Milwaukee
Winnebago	Eastern	Milwaukee
Wood	Western	Madison (Eau Claire)

Standards for Federal Courts: Fees are standard unless noted in profile. Search fee is $26.00 per item (one party name or case number). Copy fee is $.50 per page. Certification fee is $9.00 per document, double for exemplification, if available. Most courts require prepayment. Mail requests should enclose a SASE unless otherwise noted. Before releasing records, all courts require prepayment, unless noted.

District courts index by defendant and plaintiff and by case number. Bankruptcy courts usually index by debtor and case number. While most courts now have their indexes on computer, many may still maintain index card files as well. Courts will archive closed case files at different times.

There are numerous public access programs available to online subscribers. Search the U.S. Party/Case Index to find party names and case numbers among all courts. Individual case data is provided on PACER. A search of CM/ECF provides copies of cases filed electronically. For details about PACER, the US Party/Case Index, and CM/ECF see the Appendix or go to http://pacer.psc.uscourts.gov or call 800-676-6856.

US District Court
Wisconsin Eastern District

Green Bay- North Division Clerk's Office, PO Box 22490, Green Bay, WI 54305-2490 (In person: 125 S Jefferson St, Green Bay), 920-884-3720. Hour- 8:30AM-4:30PM. www.wied.uscourts.gov

Counties: Brown, Calumet, Door, Florence, Forest, Kewaunee, Langlade, Manitowoc, Marinette, Menominee, Oconto, Outagamie, Shawano, Waupaca, Waushara, Winnebago.

Searches/Indexing: Include full name in search request. Results include last 4 SSN digits, perhaps also birth year. Will not fax back documents. New cases are in the index immediately after filing date. Computer index maintained; civil back to 1991, criminal to 1993. Case files sent to archives 3 years after closed.

Search Access: Docket info available via phone if you provide case number or party names. **Mail:** Search usually completed- 3 days. Include SASE for return. **In person:** 2 public terminals available; index back to 1991-92. Self-serve copies $.25.

Payment: Pay by money order, cashier's or personal check. No credit cards accepted. Payee: Clerk, US District Court.

E-Services: PACER records go back to 1991. New records online after 1 day. ECF at https://ecf.wied.uscourts.gov. Opinions available on PACER/ECF; click on written opinions.

Milwaukee- South Division Clerk's Office, 517 E Wisconsin Ave, Rm 362, Milwaukee, WI 53202, 414-297-3372; civil dockets- same; Fax- 414-297-3203. Hours-8:30AM-4:30PM. www.wied.uscourts.gov

Counties: Dodge, Fond du Lac, Green Lake, Kenosha, Marquette, Milwaukee, Ozaukee, Racine, Sheboygan, Walworth, Washington, Waukesha.

Searches/Indexing: Include full name in search request. Results include last 4 SSN digits, perhaps also birth year. Will not fax back documents. New cases are in the index immediately after filing date. Computer index maintained; civil back to 1991, criminal to 1993. Case files sent to archives 3 years after closed. **Search Access:** Docket info available via phone if you provide case number or party names. **Mail:** Search usually completed- 3 days. Include SASE for return. **In person:** 2 public terminals available; index back to 1991-92. Self-serve copies $.25.

Payment: Pay by money order, cashier's or personal check. No credit cards accepted. Payee: Clerk, US District Court.

E-Services: PACER records go back to 1991. New records online after 1 day. ECF at https://ecf.wied.uscourts.gov. Opinions available on PACER/ECF; click on written opinions.

US Bankruptcy Court
Wisconsin Eastern District

Milwaukee Division Court Clerk, 126 US Courthouse, 517 E Wisconsin Ave, Milwaukee, WI 53202, 414-297-3291; Fax- 414-297-4040. Hours-8:30AM-4:30PM. www.wieb.uscourts.gov

Counties: Brown, Calumet, Dodge, Door, Florence, Fond du Lac, Forest, Green Lake, Kenosha, Kewaunee, Langlade, Manitowoc, Marinette, Marquette, Menominee, Milwaukee, Oconto, Outagamie, Ozaukee, Racine, Shawano, Sheboygan, Walworth, Washington, Waukesha, Waupaca, Waushara, Winnebago.

Searches/Indexing: Include name, SSN in search request. Results include last 4 SSN digits. Will not fax back documents. New cases are in the index 1-2 days after filing date. Computer index maintained back to late 1970s; also on index cards back further. Case files sent to archives once 100-150 boxes are filled.

Search Access: Voice Case Information Service available, call VCIS at 877-781-7277 or 414-297-3582. **Mail:** Search usually completed- 3 days. Include SASE for return. **In person:** 4 public terminals available. No self-serve copier.

Payment: Pay by credit cards, money order, cashier's or personal check. No debtor checks/credit cards accepted. Payee: Clerk, US Bankruptcy Court.

E-Services: PACER online at http://pacer.wieb.uscourts.gov. PACER records go back to 1991. New records online after 1 day. ECF at https://ecf.wieb.uscourts.gov. **Opinions Online:** www.wieb.uscourts.gov. Limited opinions/ decisions online; click on Decisions. **Online Note:** Click on Calendars at www.wieb.uscourts.gov to search judge calendar.

US District Court
Wisconsin Western District

Madison Division Court Clerk, PO Box 432, Madison, WI 53701 (In person: 120 N Henry St, #320, Madison), 608-264-5156; Fax- 608-264-5925. 8AM-4:30PM. www.wiwd.uscourts.gov

Counties: Adams, Ashland, Barron, Bayfield, Buffalo, Burnett, Chippewa, Clark, Columbia, Crawford, Dane, Douglas, Dunn, Eau Claire, Grant, Green, Iowa, Iron, Jackson, Jefferson, Juneau, La Crosse, Lafayette, Lincoln, Marathon, Monroe, Oneida, Pepin, Pierce, Polk, Portage, Price, Richland, Rock, Rusk, Sauk, Sawyer, St. Croix, Taylor, Trempealeau, Vernon, Vilas, Washburn, Wood.

Searches/Indexing: Include DOB with name in search request. Results do not include SSN or DOB. Will not fax back documents. New cases are in the index 24 hours after filing date. Computer index maintained back to 1990; on microfiche to 1980; also on card file. District-wide searches available here. Closed electronic cases not purged.

Search Access: Only docket info is available by phone. **Mail:** Search usually completed- 24 hours. Include SASE for return. **In person:** 1 public terminal available; index back to 2005. No self-serve copier.

Payment: Pay by money order, cashier's or personal check. No credit cards. Payee: Clerk, US District Court.

E-Services: PACER online at http://pacer.wiwd.uscourts.gov. Document images available. PACER records go back to 1990. New records online after 1 day. ECF at www.wiwd.uscourts.gov/cmecf/index.html. **Opinions Online:** www.wiwd.uscourts.gov/opinsearch/index.html. **Online Note:** Weekly court calendars free at www.wiwd.uscourts.gov/calendar/calfrm.html

US Bankruptcy Court
Wisconsin Western District

Eau Claire Division Court Clerk, PO Box 5009, Eau Claire, WI 54702-5009 (In person: 500 S Barstow St, Eau Claire, WI 54702), 715-839-2980; Fax- 715-839-2996. Hours-8AM-4:30PM. www.wiw.uscourts.gov/bankruptcy

Counties/Note: Ashland, Barron, Bayfield, Buffalo, Burnett, Chippewa, Clark, Douglas, Dunn, Eau Claire, Iron, Jackson, Juneau, La Crosse, Lincoln, Marathon, Monroe, Oneida, Pepin, Pierce, Polk, Portage, Price, Rusk, Sawyer, St. Croix, Taylor, Trempealeau, Vernon, Vilas, Washburn, Wood. This Division has satellite offices in LaCrosse and Wausau.

Searches/Indexing: Include SSN or EIN in search request. Results include last 4 SSN digits. Will not fax back documents. New cases are in the index 24 hours after filing date.

Search Access: Limited docket info available by phone. Voice Case Information Service available, call VCIS at 800-743-8247. **Mail:** Search usually completed- 2 days. SASE not required. **In person:** 2 public terminals available. No self-serve copier.

Payment: Pay by money order, cashier's, business checks, or attorney checks/credit cards. No personal checks. Payee: Clerk, US Bankruptcy Ct.

E-Services: Document images available. PACER records go back to 4/1991. New records online after 1 day. ECF at https://ecf.wiwb.uscourts.gov. **Opinions Online:** www.wiw.uscourts.gov/bankruptcy/decision_home.htm. **Online Note:** Calendars available on PACER. Browse Unclaimed Funds free at www.wiw.uscourts.gov/unclaimed_funds/.

Madison Division Court Clerk, PO Box 548, Madison, WI 53701 (In person: 120 N Henry St, Rm 340, Madison), 608-264-5178; Fax- 608-264-5105. Hours-8AM-4:30PM. www.wiw.uscourts.gov/bankruptcy

Counties: Adams, Columbia, Crawford, Dane, Grant, Green, Iowa, Jefferson, Lafayette, Richland, Rock, Sauk.

Searches/Indexing: Include SSN or EIN in search request. Results include last 4 SSN digits. Will not fax back documents. New cases are in the index 24 hours after filing date.

Search Access: Limited docket info available by phone. Voice Case Information Service available, call VCIS at 800-743-8247. **Mail:** Search usually completed- 5 days. SASE not required. **In person:** 3 public terminals available. No self-serve copier.

Payment: Pay by credit cards, money order, cashier's, business or attorney checks. No personal checks. Payee: Clerk, US Bankruptcy Court.

E-Services: Document images available. PACER records go back to 4/1991. New records online after 1 day. ECF at https://ecf.wiwb.uscourts.gov. **Opinions Online:** www.wiw.uscourts.gov/bankruptcy/decision_home.htm. **Online Note:** Calendars available on PACER. Browse Unclaimed Funds free at www.wiw.uscourts.gov/unclaimed_funds/.

Wisconsin County Courts

Court	Jurisdiction	No. of Courts	How Organized
Circuit Courts*	General	72	10 Districts
Municipal Courts	Municipal	252	
Probate Courts*	Probate	72	

* Profiled in this Sourcebook.

Court	CIVIL Tort	Contract	Real Estate	Min. Claim	Max. Claim	Small Claims	Estate	Eviction	Domestic Relations
Circuit Courts*	X	X	X	$0	No Max	$5000	X	X	X
Municipal Courts									
Probate Courts*							X		

Court	CRIMINAL Felony	Misdemeanor	DWI/DUI	Preliminary Hearing	Juvenile
Circuit Courts*	X	X	X	X	X
Municipal Courts			X		X
Probate Courts*					

Administration

Director of State Courts, Supreme Court, Box 1688, Madison, WI, 53701; 608-266-6828, Fax: 608-267-0980. (CST) http://wicourts.gov

Court Structure

The Circuit Court is the court of general jurisdiction. The majority of Municipal Court cases involve traffic and ordinance matters. Probate filing is a function of the Circuit Court; however, each county has a Register in Probate who maintains and manages the probate records, guardianship, and mental health records.

Online Access

Wisconsin Circuit Court Access (WCCA) allows users to view Circuit Court case information on the Wisconsin court system website at http://wcca.wicourts.gov. Data is available from all counties (except only probate records are available from Portage). Searches can be conducted statewide or county-by-county. WCCA provides detailed information about circuit cases including criminal, civil and traffice. The index displays judgment and judgment party information. The middle initial is shown on results, the DOB is shown most of the time, but sometimes the DOB is only month/year. WCCA also offers the ability to generate reports. Due to statutory requirements, WCCA users will not be able to view restricted cases. There are probate records included for all counties.

Appellate Courts and Supreme Court opinions are available from the main web page. All courts on Central Standard Time.

Searching Tips, Fees, and Other Guidelines

Public access terminals are available at each court. The statutory fee schedule for the Circuit Courts is as follows: search fee - $5.00 per name; copy fee - $1.25 per page; certification fee - $5.00. The fee schedule for probate is as follows: search fee - $4.00 per name; certification fee - $3.00 per document plus copy fee; copy fee - $1.00 per page. Most Registers in Probate are putting pre-1950 records on microfilm and destroying hard copies. This is done as "time and workloads permit," so microfilm archiving is not uniform across the state.

Adams County

Circuit Court PO Box 220, Friendship, WI 53934; 608-339-4208; criminal fax: 608-339-4503; civil fax: same; 8AM-4:30PM. ***Felony, Misdemeanor, Civil, Eviction, Small Claims.***

Civil Records: Access: Mail, in person, online. Both court and visitors may perform in person searches. Search fee: $5.00 per name; $5.00 per record found. Required to search: name, years to search. Civil records on computer from 1993, on index cards and books from 1950. Historical societies have previous records and indexes organized back to 1848. Mail turnaround time 1-2 days. Civil PAT goes back to 1993. PAT civil results show middle initial. Civil case lookup free online at http://wcca.wicourts.gov/index.xsl.

Criminal Records: Access: Mail, online, in person. Both court and visitors may perform in person searches. Search fee: $5.00 per name; $5.00 per record found. Required to search: name, years to search, DOB. Criminal records computerized from 1993, on index cards and books from 1950. Historical societies have previous records and indexes. Organized 1848. Mail turnaround time 1-2 days. Criminal PAT goes back to same as civil. PAT results show middle initial, DOB. Access criminal index free at http://wcca.wicourts.gov/index.xsl. Online results show middle initial and DOB most of time; however, sometimes DOB is month and year only on the index.

General Information: Online identifiers in results same as on public terminal. No juvenile, paternity, financial, PSI reports released. Fee to fax out file $1.25 per page. Court makes copy: $1.25 per page. Certification fee: $5.00 plus copy fees. Payee: Clerk of Court. Personal checks accepted; credit cards are not. GPS will facilitate payment by credit card. Prepayment required. Mail requests: SASE required.

Register in Probate PO Box 200, 400 Main St, Friendship, WI 53934; 608-339-4213; fax: 608-339-4596; 8AM-4:30PM. ***Probate.*** Probate records free online at http://wcca.wicourts.gov/index.xsl.

Ashland County

Circuit Court Courthouse, 201 W Main St, Rm 307, Ashland, WI 54806; 715-682-7016; criminal fax: 715-682-7919; civil fax: same; 8AM-N, 1-4PM. ***Felony, Misdemeanor, Civil, Eviction, Small Claims.*** www.co.ashland.wi.us

Civil Records: Access: Phone, fax, mail, online, in person. Both court and visitors may perform in person searches. Search fee: $5.00 per name. Required to search: name, years to search. Civil cases indexed by defendant, plaintiff. Civil index on cards and index books concurrently from 1960. Organized 1860. Mail turnaround time 1-2 days. Civil PAT goes back to 1994. Civil case lookup free online at http://wcca.wicourts.gov/index.xsl.

Criminal Records: Access: Fax, mail, online, in person. Both court and visitors may perform in person searches. Search fee: $5.00 per name.

Required to search: name, years to search, DOB. Criminal records computerized from 1994. Mail turnaround time 1-2 days. Criminal PAT goes back to same as civil. PAT results show middle initial, DOB. Access criminal index free at http://wcca.wicourts.gov/index.xsl. Online results show middle initial and DOB most of time; however, sometimes DOB is month and year only on the index.
General Information: Online identifiers in results same as on public terminal. No juvenile or paternity records released. Will fax documents $1.25 per page. Court makes copy: $1.25 per page. Certification fee: $5.00 per cert. Payee: Clerk of Court. Local or pre-approved checks accepted. Prepayment required. Mail requests: SASE required.

Register in Probate Courthouse, Rm 203, 201 W Main, Ashland, WI 54806; 715-682-7009; fax: 715-685-9977; 8AM-N, 1-4PM. ***Probate.*** Search free at http://wcca.wicourts.gov/index.xsl.

Barron County

Circuit Court Barron County Justice Center, 1420 State Hwy 25 N, Barron, WI 54812; 715-537-6265; criminal phone: 715-537-6152; civil phone: 715-537-6271; probate phone: 715-537-6261; criminal fax: 715-537-6269; civil fax: same; 8AM-4:30PM. ***Felony, Misdemeanor, Civil, Eviction, Small Claims.***
Civil Records: Access: Online, in person. Visitors must perform in person searches themselves. Required to search: name, years to search. Civil cases indexed by defendant, plaintiff; index on computer, index cards from 1983. Organized 1859. Civil PAT goes back to mid-1993. PAT results show name only. Civil case lookup free online at http://wcca.wicourts.gov/index.xsl.
Criminal Records: Access: Online, in person. Visitors must perform in person searches themselves. Required to search: name, years to search. Criminal records on computer, index cards from 1983. Organized 1859. Criminal PAT goes back to same as civil. PAT results show middle initial, DOB. Access criminal index free at http://wcca.wicourts.gov/index.xsl. Online results show middle initial and DOB most of time; however, sometimes DOB is month and year only on the index.
General Information: Online identifiers in results same as on public terminal. No expunged, paternity or sealed records released. Will fax documents $2.00 per page. Court makes copy: $1.25 per page. Certification fee: $5.00 per document. Payee: Clerk of Court. Personal checks and credit cards accepted. Prepayment required.

Register in Probate Barron Justice Ctr, 1420 State Hwy 25 N, Rm 2700, Barron, WI 54812; 715-537-6261; fax: 715-637-6769; 8AM-4:30PM. ***Probate.*** Probate records back to 1989-90 free at http://wcca.wicourts.gov/index.xsl.

Bayfield County

Circuit Court 117 E 5th, Washburn, WI 54891; 715-373-6108; fax: 715-373-6153; 8AM-4PM. ***Felony, Misdemeanor, Civil, Eviction, Small Claims.***
www.bayfieldcounty.org/clerkofcourts/default.asp
Civil Records: Access: Mail, in person, online. Both court and visitors may perform in person searches. Search fee: $5.00 per name. Required to search: name, years to search. Civil cases indexed by defendant, plaintiff; index on computer for all open cases since 1982, on index cards from 1979, index books in archives from 1845 to 1979. Mail turnaround time 1-2 days. Civil PAT goes back to 1993. PAT results show name only. Civil case lookup free online at http://wcca.wicourts.gov/index.xsl.
Criminal Records: Access: Mail, online, in person. Both court and visitors may perform in person searches. Search fee: $5.00 per name. Required to search: name, years to search, DOB. Criminal records on computer since 3/93. Mail turnaround time 1-2 days. Criminal PAT goes back to same as civil. PAT results show middle initial, DOB. Access criminal index free at http://wcca.wicourts.gov/index.xsl. Online results show middle initial and DOB most of time; however, sometimes DOB is month and year only on the index.
General Information: Online identifiers in results same as on public terminal. No sealed records released. Fee to fax out file $2.50 per page. Court makes copy: $1.25 per page. Self serve: same. Certification fee: $5.00. Payee: Clerk of Court. Personal checks accepted; credit cards are not. Prepayment required. Mail requests: SASE required.

Register in Probate PO Box 536, 117 E 5th St, Washburn, WI 54891; 715-373-6108; fax: 715-373-6153; 8AM-4PM. ***Probate.*** Probate records free at http://wcca.wicourts.gov/index.xsl.

Brown County

Circuit Court PO Box 23600, 100 S Jefferson St, Courthouse Lower Level, Green Bay, WI 54305-3600; 920-448-4161; probate phone: 920-448-4275; fax: 920-448-4156; 8AM-4:30PM. ***Felony, Misdemeanor, Civil, Eviction, Small Claims.***
www.co.brown.wi.us/clerk_of_courts/
Civil Records: Access: Mail, in person, online. Both court and visitors may perform in person searches. Search fee: $5.00 per name. Required to search: name, years to search. Civil cases indexed by defendant, plaintiff; index on computer since 1990, on microfiche from 1987-1990. Mail turnaround time 10 days. Civil PAT goes back to 1990. PAT results show name only. Civil case lookup free online at http://wcca.wicourts.gov/index.xsl.
Criminal Records: Access: Mail, online, in person. Both court and visitors may perform in person searches. Search fee: $5.00 per name. Required to search: name, years to search, DOB. Criminal records on computer since 1990, on microfiche from 1987-1990, archives from 1962-1990. Crossed on index cards from 1972, index books from 198. Mail turnaround time 10 days. Criminal PAT goes back to 1991. PAT results show middle initial, DOB. Access criminal index free at http://wcca.wicourts.gov/index.xsl. Online results show middle initial and DOB most of time; however, sometimes DOB is month and year only on the index.
General Information: Online identifiers in results same as on public terminal. No juvenile or pre-adjudicated paternity records released. Will fax documents $1.25 per page. Court makes copy: $1.25 per page. Certification fee: $5.00. Payee: Brown County Clerk of Circuit Court. Personal checks accepted. Prepayment required. Mail requests: SASE required.

Register in Probate PO Box 23600, Green Bay, WI 54305-3600; 920-448-4275; fax: 920-448-6208; 8AM-4:30PM. ***Probate.*** Probate records free at http://wcca.wicourts.gov/index.xsl. Physical address: 100 S Jefferson St, Green Bay, MI 54301.

Buffalo County

Circuit Court 407 S 2nd, PO Box 68, Alma, WI 54610; 608-685-6212; fax: 608-685-6211; 8AM-4:30PM. ***Felony, Misdemeanor, Civil, Eviction, Small Claims.***
Civil Records: Access: Phone, fax, mail, online, in person. Both court and visitors may perform in person searches. Search fee: $5.00 per name. Required to search: name, years to search. Civil cases indexed by defendant, plaintiff; index on computer from 1994, on index cards from 1979. No civil records available before 1962. Mail turnaround time 1 week. Civil PAT goes back to 1994. Civil case lookup free at http://wcca.wicourts.gov/index.xsl.
Criminal Records: Access: Phone, fax, mail, online, in person. Both court and visitors may perform in person searches. Search fee: $5.00 per name. Required to search: name, years to search. Criminal records computerized from 1994. Felonies retained 50 years; misdemeanors 20 years. Mail turnaround time 1 week. Criminal PAT goes back to same as civil. PAT results show middle initial, DOB. Access criminal index free at http://wcca.wicourts.gov/index.xsl. Online results show middle initial and DOB most of time; however, sometimes DOB is month and year only on the index.
General Information: Online identifiers in results same as on public terminal. No closed records released. Fee to fax out file $1.25 per page. Court makes copy: $1.25 per page. Certification fee: $5.00 per document. Payee: Buffalo County Clerk of Court. Personal checks accepted; credit cards are not. Prepayment required. Mail requests: SASE required.

Register in Probate 407 S 2nd, PO Box 68, Alma, WI 54610; 608-685-6202; fax: 608-685-6211; 8AM-4:30PM. ***Probate.*** Probate records free at http://wcca.wicourts.gov/index.xsl.

Burnett County

Circuit Court 7410 County Road K, #115, Siren, WI 54872; 715-349-2147; probate phone: 715-349-2177; criminal fax: 715-349-7659; civil fax: same; 8:30AM-4:30PM. ***Felony, Misdemeanor, Civil, Eviction, Small Claims.***
www.burnettcounty.com/gov/clerkofcourt.html
Civil Records: Access: Mail, in person, online. Both court and visitors may perform in person searches. Search fee: $5.00 per name. Required to search: name, years to search. Civil cases indexed by defendant, plaintiff; index on computer from 10/92, on index books from 1800s. Organized 1856. Mail turnaround time 1-2 days. Civil PAT goes back to 1992. Civil case lookup free online at http://wcca.wicourts.gov/index.xsl.
Criminal Records: Access: Mail, online, in person. Both court and visitors may perform in person searches. Search fee: $5.00 per name. Required to search: name, years to search. Criminal records computerized from 10/92, on index books from 1800s. Organized 1856. Mail turnaround time 1-2 days. Criminal PAT goes back to same as civil. PAT results show middle initial, DOB. Access criminal index free at http://wcca.wicourts.gov/index.xsl. Online results show middle initial and DOB most of time; however, sometimes DOB is month and year only on the index.
General Information: Online identifiers in results same as on public terminal. No paternity, juvenile, sealed or confidential records released. Will fax documents to local or toll free line. Fees must be prepaid. Court makes copy: $1.25 per page. Certification fee: $5.00 per document. Payee: Clerk of Courts. Personal checks and major credit cards accepted. Prepayment required. Mail requests: SASE required.

Register in Probate 7410 County Road K #110, Siren, WI 54872; 715-349-2177 x0301; fax: 715-349-7659; 8:30AM-4:30PM. ***Probate.*** Probate records free at http://wcca.wicourts.gov/index.xsl. This court also holds Juvenile, Guardianship, Mental Commitments, Adoptions, Term. of Parental Right.

Calumet County

Circuit Court 206 Court St, Chilton, WI 53014; 920-849-1414; fax: 920-849-1483; 8AM-4:30PM. ***Felony, Misdemeanor, Civil, Eviction, Small Claims.***
Civil Records: Access: Mail, in person, online. Both court and visitors may perform in person searches. Search fee: $5.00 per name. Required to search: name, years to search. Civil cases indexed by defendant, plaintiff; index on computer from 1992, index cards from 1978, index books from 1800s. Mail turnaround time 2 days. Civil PAT goes back to 1992. PAT results show name only. Civil case lookup free online at http://wcca.wicourts.gov/index.xsl.
Criminal Records: Access: Mail, online, in person. Both court and visitors may perform in person searches. Search fee: $5.00 per name. Required to search: name, years to search, DOB. Criminal records computerized from 1992, index cards from 1978, index books from 1800s. Mail turnaround time 2 days. Criminal PAT goes back to same as civil. PAT results show middle initial, DOB. Access criminal index free at http://wcca.wicourts.gov/index.xsl. Online results show middle initial and DOB most of time; however, sometimes DOB is month and year only on the index.
General Information: Online identifiers in results same as on public terminal. No juvenile or paternity records released. Will fax documents $1.50 per page. Court makes copy: $1.25 per page. Certification fee: $5.00. Payee: Clerk of Court. Personal checks

accepted; credit cards are not. Prepayment required. Mail requests: SASE required.

Register in Probate 206 Court St, Chilton, WI 53014-1198; 920-849-1455; fax: 920-849-1435; 8AM-N, 1-4:30PM. ***Probate.*** Probate records free at http://wcca.wicourts.gov/index.xsl.

Chippewa County

Circuit Court 711 N Bridge St, Chippewa Falls, WI 54729-1879; 715-726-7758; probate phone: 715-726-7737; fax: 715-726-7786; 8AM-4:30PM. ***Felony, Misdemeanor, Civil, Eviction, Small Claims.***

Civil Records: Access: Mail, fax, online, in person. Both court and visitors may perform in person searches. Search fee: $5.00 per name. Required to search: name, years to search; also helpful: address, records sought. Civil cases indexed by defendant, plaintiff; index on computer from 1990, index cards from 1979, index books from 1900s. Mail turnaround time same as criminal. Civil PAT goes back to 1990. PAT results show name, the DOB month and year appear. Civil case lookup free at http://wcca.wicourts.gov/index.xsl.

Criminal Records: Access: Mail, fax, online, in person. Both court and visitors may perform in person searches. Search fee: $5.00 per name. Required to search: name, years to search, DOB; also helpful: SSN. Criminal records computerized from 1990, index cards from 1979, index books from 1900s. Mail turnaround time 10 days or less; up to 30 days if pre-1990. Criminal PAT goes back to 1990. PAT results show middle initial, the DOB month and year appear. Access criminal index free at http://wcca.wicourts.gov/index.xsl. Online results show middle initial and DOB most of time; however, sometimes DOB is month and year only on the index.

General Information: Online identifiers in results same as on public terminal. Paternity records released only to party or attorney of record, or with written court authorization. Fee to fax out file $2.00 1st page, $1.00 each add'l. Court makes copy: $1.25 per page. Certification fee: $5.00. Payee: Chippewa County Clerk of Courts. Personal checks accepted. Pay with credit card via GPS, www.GovPayNow.com, 888-604-7888, Code #1116 - there is a service fee. Prepayment required. Mail requests: SASE required.

Register in Probate 711 N Bridge St, Chippewa Falls, WI 54729; 715-726-7737; fax: 715-738-2626; 8AM-4:30PM. ***Probate.*** Probate records free at http://wcca.wicourts.gov/index.xsl.

Clark County

Circuit Court 517 Court St, #405, Neillsville, WI 54456-1971; 715-743-5181; fax: 715-743-5187; 8AM-4:30PM. ***Felony, Misdemeanor, Civil, Eviction, Small Claims.*** www.co.clark.wi.us/ClarkCounty/circuit_court.asp

Civil Records: Access: Mail, in person, online. Both court and visitors may perform in person searches. Search fee: $5.00 per name. Required to search: name, years to search. Civil cases indexed by defendant, plaintiff; index on computer from 1994, on index cards from 1981, index books from 1900s. Mail turnaround time 1-2 weeks. Civil PAT goes back to 1993. PAT results show middle initial, DOB. Civil lookup free at http://wcca.wicourts.gov/index.xsl.

Criminal Records: Access: Mail, online, in person. Both court and visitors may perform in person searches. Search fee: $5.00 per name. Required to search: name, years to search. Criminal records computerized from 1994, on index cards from 1981, index books from 1900s. Mail turnaround time 1-2 weeks. Criminal PAT goes back to same as civil. PAT results show middle initial, DOB. Access criminal index free at http://wcca.wicourts.gov/index.xsl. Online results show middle initial and DOB most of time; however, sometimes DOB is month and year only on the index.

General Information: Online identifiers in results same as on public terminal. No sealed or paternity records released. Will fax documents. Court makes copy: $1.25 per page. Certification fee: $5.00 per doc. Payee: Clerk of Court. Personal checks accepted. Prepayment required. Mail requests: SASE required.

Register in Probate 517 Court St, Rm 403, Neillsville, WI 54456; 715-743-5172; fax: 715-743-5120; 8AM-4:30PM. ***Probate.***
There is a $4.00 search fee. Also, probate records free online at http://wcca.wicourts.gov/index.xsl.

Columbia County

Circuit Court PO Box 587, Portage, WI 53901; 608-742-9642; criminal phone: 608-742-9643; civil phone: 608-742-9624; probate phone: 608-742-9636; criminal fax: 608-742-9601; civil fax: same; 8AM-4:30PM. ***Felony, Misdemeanor, Civil, Eviction, Small Claims, Probate.***
Probate fax is same as main fax number.

Civil Records: Access: Mail, in person, online. Both court and visitors may perform in person searches. Search fee: $5.00 per name. Required to search: name, years to search. Civil cases indexed by defendant, plaintiff; index on computer from 1994, on microfiche to 1960s, concurrent index cards/books from 1940s. Mail turnaround time 1-2 weeks. Civil PAT goes back to 1994. PAT results show name only. Search civil and probate court records free at http://wcca.wicourts.gov/index.xsl.

Criminal Records: Access: Mail, online, in person. Both court and visitors may perform in person searches. Search fee: $5.00 per name. Required to search: name, years to search, DOB. Criminal records computerized from 1994, on microfiche to 1960s, concurrent index cards/books from 1940s. Mail turnaround time 1-2 weeks. Criminal PAT goes back to same as civil. PAT results show middle initial, DOB. Access criminal index free at http://wcca.wicourts.gov/index.xsl. Online results show middle initial and DOB most of time; however, sometimes DOB is month and year only on the index.

General Information: Online identifiers in results same as on public terminal. No juvenile or paternity records released. Fee to fax out file $1.25 per page. Court makes copy: $1.25 per page. Certification fee: $5.00. Payee: Clerk of Court. Personal checks and major credit cards accepted. Prepayment required. Mail requests: SASE required.

Crawford County

Circuit Court 220 N Beaumont Rd, Prairie Du Chien, WI 53821; 608-326-0211; criminal phone: 608-326-010; civil phone: 608-326-0208; probate phone: 608-326-0206; 8AM-4:30PM. ***Felony, Misdemeanor, Civil, Eviction, Small Claims.***

Civil Records: Access: Mail, in person, online. Both court and visitors may perform in person searches. Search fee: $5.00 per name. Required to search: name, years to search. Civil cases indexed by defendant, plaintiff; index on computer from 1993, on index cards from 1984, index books from 1900. Historical Society has archives. Mail turnaround time 10 working days. Civil PAT goes back to mid-1993. Civil case lookup free online at http://wcca.wicourts.gov/index.xsl.

Criminal Records: Access: Mail, online, in person. Both court and visitors may perform in person searches. Search fee: $5.00 per name. Required to search: name, years to search. Criminal records computerized from 1993, on index cards from 1984, index books from 1900. Historical Society has archives. Mail turnaround time 10 working days. Criminal PAT goes back to same as civil. PAT results show middle initial, DOB. Access criminal index free at http://wcca.wicourts.gov/index.xsl. Online results show middle initial and DOB most of time; however, sometimes DOB is month and year only on the index.

General Information: Online identifiers in results same as on public terminal. No juvenile, paternity, mental records released. Will not fax documents. Court makes copy: $1.25 per page. Certification fee: $5.00. Payee: Clerk of Court. Personal checks accepted. Prepayment required. Mail requests: SASE required.

Register in Probate 220 N Beaumont Rd, Prairie Du Chien, WI 53821; 608-326-0206; fax: 608-326-0288; 8AM-4:30PM. ***Probate.*** Probate records free at http://wcca.wicourts.gov/index.xsl.

Dane County

Circuit Court Dane County Courthouse, Rm 1000, 215 S Hamilton St, Madison, WI 53703-3285; 608-266-4311; probate phone: 608-266-4331; criminal fax: 608-267-8859; civil fax: same; 7:45AM-4:30PM. ***Felony, Misdemeanor, Civil, Eviction, Small Claims.*** www.co.dane.wi.us/clrkcort/clrkhome.htm

Civil Records: Access: Fax, mail, online, in person. Both court and visitors may perform in person searches. Search fee: $5.00 per name. Required to search: name, years to search. Civil cases indexed by defendant, plaintiff. Civil record index on computer from 1981 (with some exceptions), on microfiche prior to 1992, plaintiff index books 1848. Mail turnaround time 1-10 business days. Civil PAT goes back to 1990s. PAT results show name only. Small claims index available back to 1984 on the public terminal. Civil case lookup free online at http://wcca.wicourts.gov/index.xsl.

Criminal Records: Access: Fax, mail, online, in person. Both court and visitors may perform in person searches. Search fee: $5.00 per name. Required to search: name, years to search, DOB. Criminal record index on computer from 1983, index back to 1848. Mail turnaround time 1-10 business days. Criminal PAT goes back to 1983 approx. PAT results show middle initial, DOB. Access criminal index free at http://wcca.wicourts.gov/index.xsl. Online results show name, DOB. Online search index results gives DOB half the time, then half only have month/year.

General Information: Online identifiers in results same as on public terminal. No "confidential records" released. Will fax documents $.50 for 1st 5 pages, $.23 for each add'l 5 pages or fraction thereof. Court makes copy: $1.25 per page. Certification fee: $5.00 per doc plus copy fee; exemplification $15.00. Payee: Dane County Clerk of Courts. Personal checks and major credit cards accepted. Prepayment required. Mail requests: SASE required.

Register in Probate 215 S Hamilton St, County Courthouse Rm 1005, Madison, WI 53703-3285; 608-266-4331; fax: 608-267-4152; 7:45AM-4:30PM. ***Probate.*** Probate records free at http://wcca.wicourts.gov/index.xsl. Older indexes not online.

Dodge County

Circuit Court 210 W Center St, Juneau, WI 53039; 920-386-3570; fax: 920-386-3587; 8AM-4:30PM. ***Felony, Misdemeanor, Civil, Eviction, Small Claims.*** www.co.dodge.wi.us

Civil Records: Access: Mail, online. Only the court performs in person searches; visitors may not. Search fee: $5.00 per name. Required to search: name, years to search. Civil cases indexed by defendant, plaintiff; index on computer from 1993, on index cards from 1986, microfiche from 1972, index books from 1950s. Mail turnaround time 1-2 days. Civil PAT goes back to 1990. Civil case lookup free online at http://wcca.wicourts.gov/index.xsl.

Criminal Records: Access: Mail, online. Only the court performs in person searches; visitors may not. Search fee: $5.00 per name. Required to search: name, years to search, DOB. Criminal records computerized from 1993, on index cards from 1986, microfiche from 1972, index books from 1950s. Mail turnaround time 1-2 days. Criminal PAT available. PAT results show middle initial, DOB. Access criminal index free at http://wcca.wicourts.gov/index.xsl. Online results show middle initial and DOB most of time; however, sometimes DOB is month and year only on the index.

General Information: Online identifiers in results same as on public terminal. No juvenile or John Doe records released. Fee to fax out file $1.50 per page. Court makes copy: $1.25 per page. Certification fee: $5.00 per doc. Payee: Clerk of Courts. Personal checks accepted; credit cards are not. Prepayment required. Mail requests: SASE required.

Register in Probate 210 W Center St, Juneau, WI 53039-1091; 920-386-3550; fax: 920-386-3933; 8AM-4:30PM. ***Probate.*** $4.00 search fee; records computerized since 1992. Also, probate records free at http://wcca.wicourts.gov/index.xsl.

Door County

Circuit Court 1205 S Duluth Ave, Sturgeon Bay, WI 54235; 920-746-2205; criminal fax: 920-746-2520; civil fax: same; 8AM-4:30PM. ***Felony, Misdemeanor, Civil, Eviction, Small Claims.***

Civil Records: Access: Mail, in person, online. Both court and visitors may perform in person searches. Search fee: $5.00 per file. Required to search: name, years to search. Civil cases indexed by defendant, plaintiff; index on computer from 4/93, on index cards from 1984. Mail turnaround time 2-3 days. Civil PAT goes back to 4/1993. Civil case lookup free online at http://wcca.wicourts.gov/index.xsl.

Criminal Records: Access: Mail, online, in person. Both court and visitors may perform in person searches. Search fee: $5.00 per file. Required to search: name, years to search, DOB. Criminal records computerized from 4/93, on index cards from 1984, index books from 1900s. Mail turnaround time 2-3 days. Criminal PAT goes back to 1993. PAT results show middle initial, DOB. Access criminal index free at http://wcca.wicourts.gov/index.xsl. Online results show middle initial and DOB most of time; however, sometimes DOB is month and year only on the index.

General Information: Online identifiers in results same as on public terminal. No financial or paternity records released. Fee to fax out file $3.00 each. Court makes copy: $1.25 per page. Self serve: same. Certification fee: $5.00 per document. Payee: Clerk of Court. Personal checks accepted; credit cards are not. Prepayment required. Mail requests: SASE required.

Register in Probate 1207 S. Duluth Ave, Rm C258, County Justice Center, Sturgeon Bay, WI 54235; 920-746-2482; fax: 920-746-5959; 8AM-4:30PM. ***Probate.*** Probate records free at http://wcca.wicourts.gov/index.xsl.

Douglas County

Circuit Court 1313 Belknap, Superior, WI 54880; criminal phone: 715-395-1240; civil phone: 715-395-1203; criminal fax: 715-395-1421; civil fax: same; 8AM-4:30PM. ***Felony, Misdemeanor, Civil, Eviction, Small Claims.*** www.douglascountywi.org/countydepartments/courtcommissioner/courtcommissioner.htm

Civil Records: Access: Mail, in person, online. Both court and visitors may perform in person searches. Search fee: $5.00 per name. Required to search: name, years to search. Civil cases indexed by defendant, plaintiff; index on computer since 1994; prior records on index cards from 1976, index books from 1900s. Mail turnaround time 1-2 weeks. Civil PAT goes back to 1994. Civil case lookup free online at http://wcca.wicourts.gov/index.xsl.

Criminal Records: Access: Mail, online, in person. Both court and visitors may perform in person searches. Search fee: $5.00 per name. Required to search: name, years to search; also helpful: DOB. Criminal records on computer since 1994; prior records on index cards from 1976, index books from 1900s. Mail turnaround time 1-2 weeks. Criminal PAT goes back to same as civil. PAT results show middle initial, DOB. Access criminal index free at http://wcca.wicourts.gov/index.xsl. Online results show middle initial and DOB most of time; however, sometimes DOB is month and year only on the index.

General Information: Online identifiers in results same as on public terminal. No juvenile or paternity records released. Will fax documents $1.00 per page. Court makes copy: $1.25 per page. Certification fee: $5.00 per document. Payee: Clerk of Courts. Only cashiers checks and money orders accepted. Douglas County personal checks accepted. No credit cards accepted. Prepayment required. Mail requests: SASE required.

Register in Probate 1313 Belknap, Superior, WI 54880; 715-395-1220; fax: 715-395-1550; 8AM-4:30PM. ***Probate.*** Probate records at http://wcca.wicourts.gov/index.xsl. This court also takes care of Guardianship, Mental Commitment, Adoptions

Dunn County

Circuit Court 615 Stokke Parkway, #1500, Menomonie, WI 54751; 715-232-2611; fax: 715-232-6888; 8AM-4:30PM. ***Felony, Misdemeanor, Civil, Eviction, Small Claims.***

Civil Records: Access: Mail, in person, online. Both court and visitors may perform in person searches. Search fee: $5.00 per name. Required to search: name, years to search. Civil cases indexed by defendant, plaintiff; index on computer from 1987, index cards from 1977, index books from 1900s, archives from 1970. Mail turnaround time 2-3 days. Civil PAT goes back to 1987. Civil case lookup free online at http://wcca.wicourts.gov/index.xsl.

Criminal Records: Access: Mail, online, in person. Both court and visitors may perform in person searches. Search fee: $5.00 per name. Required to search: name, years to search, DOB. Criminal records computerized from 1987, index cards from 1977, index books from 1900s, archives from 1970. Mail turnaround time 2-3 days. Criminal PAT goes back to same as civil. PAT results show middle initial, DOB. Access criminal index free at http://wcca.wicourts.gov/index.xsl. Online results show middle initial and DOB most of time; however, sometimes DOB is month and year only on the index.

General Information: Online identifiers in results same as on public terminal. No juvenile, family financial, sealed records released. Will fax documents $.25 per page fee prepaid. Court makes copy: $1.25 per page. Self serve: $.25 per page. Certification fee: $5.00 per document. Payee: Clerk of Court. Personal checks accepted. Credit card payment accepted via GPS at 888-604-7888 A, Loc code #2030. Prepayment required.

Register in Probate 615 Stokke Pky, #1300, Menomonie, WI 54751; 715-232-6782; fax: 715-232-6787; 8AM-4:30PM. ***Probate.*** Probate records free at http://wcca.wicourts.gov/index.xsl.

Eau Claire County

Circuit Court 721 Oxford Ave, Eau Claire, WI 54703; 715-839-4816; criminal fax: 715-839-4817; civil fax: same; 8AM-4PM. ***Felony, Misdemeanor, Civil, Eviction, Small Claims, Traffic.***

Civil Records: Access: Mail, in person, online. Both court and visitors may perform in person searches. Search fee: $5.00 per name. Required to search: name, years to search. Civil cases indexed by defendant, plaintiff; index on computer from 7/92, on index cards from 1970, index books from 1968. Mail turnaround time 1-10 days. Civil PAT goes back to 7/1992. PAT results show name only. Civil case lookup free at http://wcca.wicourts.gov/index.xsl.

Criminal Records: Access: Mail, online, in person. Both court and visitors may perform in person searches. Search fee: $5.00 per name. Required to search: name, years to search, DOB. Criminal records computerized from 7/92, on index cards from 1970, index books from 1968. Mail turnaround time 1-10 days. Criminal PAT goes back to same as civil. PAT results show middle initial, DOB. Access criminal index free at http://wcca.wicourts.gov/index.xsl. Online results show middle initial and DOB most of time; however, sometimes DOB is month and year only on the index.

General Information: Online identifiers in results same as on public terminal. No paternity, financial disclosure, expungment or sealed records released. Will fax documents. Court makes copy: $1.25 per page. Self serve: $.25 per page. Certification fee: $5.00 per document. Payee: Clerk of Court-Eau Claire County. Personal checks accepted unless you passed a bad check or your DR license is suspended. Major credit cards accepted. Prepayment required. Mail requests: SASE required.

Register in Probate 721 Oxford Ave, Rm 2201, Eau Claire, WI 54703; 715-839-4823; fax: 715-831-5835; 8AM-N, 1-5PM. ***Probate.*** Probate records free at http://wcca.wicourts.gov/index.xsl.

Florence County

Circuit Court PO Box 410, Florence, WI 54121; 715-528-3205; fax: 715-528-5470; 8:30AM-4PM. ***Felony, Misdemeanor, Civil, Eviction, Small Claims.*** www.florencewisconsin.com/ClerkOfCourts/clerk_of%20_courts.htm

Civil Records: Access: Mail, in person, online. Both court and visitors may perform in person searches. Search fee: $5.00 per name. Required to search: name, years to search. Civil cases indexed by defendant, plaintiff; index on computer from 1991; prior records on index books from 1900s. Mail turnaround time 2 weeks. Civil PAT goes back to 1994. PAT results show middle initial, DOB. Civil lookup free at http://wcca.wicourts.gov/index.xsl.

Criminal Records: Access: Mail, online, in person. Both court and visitors may perform in person searches. Search fee: $5.00 per name. Required to search: name, years to search. Criminal records computerized from 1991; prior records on index books from 1900s. Mail turnaround time 2 weeks. Criminal PAT goes back to same as civil. PAT results show middle initial, DOB. Access criminal index free at http://wcca.wicourts.gov/index.xsl. Online results show middle initial and DOB most of time; however, sometimes DOB is month and year only on the index.

General Information: Online identifiers in results same as on public terminal. No juvenile, mental health, adoption or guardianship records released. Will fax documents to local or toll-free number. Court makes copy: $1.25 per page. Certification fee: $5.00. Payee: Clerk of Courts. Personal checks accepted; credit cards are not. Prepayment required. Mail requests: SASE required.

Register in Probate PO Box 410, 501 Lake Ave, Florence, WI 54121; 715-528-3205; fax: 715-528-5470; 8:30AM-N, 12:30-4PM. ***Probate.*** Records free at http://wcca.wicourts.gov/index.xsl.

Fond du Lac County

Circuit Court 160 S Macy, Fond du Lac, WI 54936-1355; 920-929-3040; fax: 920-929-3933; 8AM-4:30PM. ***Felony, Misdemeanor, Civil, Eviction, Small Claims.***

Civil Records: Access: Mail, in person, online. Both court and visitors may perform in person searches. Search fee: $5.00 per name. Required to search: name, years to search. Civil cases indexed by defendant, plaintiff; index on computer from 1990, index cards from 1978, microfiche 1836 to 1978, archives prior to 1900s. Old files destroyed, on microfiche or in. Mail turnaround time 1-2 days. Civil PAT goes back to 1990. Civil case lookup free online at http://wcca.wicourts.gov/index.xsl.

Criminal Records: Access: Mail, online, in person. Both court and visitors may perform in person searches. Search fee: $5.00 per name. Required to search: name, years to search, DOB. Criminal records computerized from 1990, index cards from 1978, microfiche 1836 to 1978, archives prior to 1900s. Old files destroyed, on microfiche or. Mail turnaround time 1-2 days. Criminal PAT goes back to same as civil. PAT results show middle initial, DOB. Access criminal index free at http://wcca.wicourts.gov/index.xsl. Online results show middle initial and DOB most of time; however, sometimes DOB is month and year only on the index.

General Information: Online identifiers in results same as on public terminal. No juvenile or paternity records released. Fee to fax out file $2.00 each. Court makes copy: $1.25 per page. Certification fee: $5.00 per doc. Payee: Clerk of Circuit Court. Personal checks accepted; credit cards are not. Prepayment required. Mail requests: SASE required.

Register in Probate PO Box 1576, 160 S Macy St, Gov't Ctr, Fond du Lac, WI 54936-1576; 920-929-3084, 906-4743; fax: 920-906-5540; 8AM-4:30PM. ***Probate.*** Probate records free at http://wcca.wicourts.gov/index.xsl.

Forest County

Circuit Court 200 E Madison St, Crandon, WI 54520; 715-478-3323; criminal fax: 715-478-3211;

civil fax: same; 8:30AM-4:30PM. ***Felony, Misdemeanor, Civil, Eviction, Small Claims, Traffic.***

Civil Records: Access: Mail, in person, online. Both court and visitors may perform in person searches. Search fee: $5.00 per name. Required to search: name, years to search. Civil cases indexed by defendant, plaintiff; index on computer from 1994, on index cards from 1979, index books from 1920s. Mail turnaround time 1-2 days. Civil PAT goes back to 1994. PAT results show name, DOB. Civil case lookup free at http://wcca.wicourts.gov/index.xsl.

Criminal Records: Access: Mail, online, in person. Both court and visitors may perform in person searches. Search fee: $5.00 per name. Required to search: name, years to search, DOB. Criminal records computerized from 1994, on index cards from 1979, index books from 1920s. Mail turnaround time 1-2 days. Criminal PAT goes back to same as civil. PAT results show middle initial, DOB. Access criminal index free at http://wcca.wicourts.gov/index.xsl. Online results show middle initial and DOB most of time; however, sometimes DOB is month and year only on the index.

General Information: Online identifiers in results same as on public terminal. No juvenile, paternity records released. Fee to fax out file $1.25 per page. Court makes copy: $1.25 per page. Self serve: $.10 per page plus tax. Certification fee: $5.00 per document. Payee: Clerk of Court. Personal checks accepted; credit cards are not. Prepayment required. Mail requests: SASE required.

Register in Probate 200 E Madison St, Crandon, WI 54520; 715-478-2418; fax: 715-478-2430; 8:30AM-N,1-4:30PM. ***Probate.*** Probate records free at http://wcca.wicourts.gov/index.xsl.

Grant County

Circuit Court PO Box 110, Lancaster, WI 53813; 608-723-2752; fax: 608-723-7370; 8AM-4:30PM. ***Felony, Misdemeanor, Civil, Eviction, Small Claims.***

Civil Records: Access: Phone, mail, fax, online, in person. Both court and visitors may perform in person searches. No search fee. Required to search: name, years to search. Civil cases indexed by defendant, plaintiff; index on computer from 10/93, on index books from 1900s. Mail turnaround time 2 weeks. Civil PAT goes back to 10/1993. PAT results show middle initial, DOB. Civil case lookup free at http://wcca.wicourts.gov/index.xsl.

Criminal Records: Access: Phone, mail, fax, online, in person. Both court and visitors may perform in person searches. No search fee. Required to search: name, years to search. Criminal records computerized from 10/93, on index books from 1900s. Mail turnaround time 2 weeks. Criminal PAT goes back to same as civil. PAT results show middle initial, DOB. Access criminal index free at http://wcca.wicourts.gov/index.xsl. Online results show middle initial and DOB most of time; however, sometimes DOB is month and year only on the index.

General Information: Online identifiers in results same as on public terminal. No juvenile, paternity records released. Will fax documents to local or toll free line. Court makes copy: $1.25 per page. Certification fee: $5.00 per document. Payee: Clerk of Court. Personal checks accepted; credit cards are not. Prepayment required. Mail requests: SASE required.

Register in Probate 130 W Maple St, Rm A360, Lancaster, WI 53813; 608-723-2697; fax: 608-723-7370; 8AM-4:30PM. ***Probate.*** $4.00 search fee, records computerized since 1993. Probate records free at http://wcca.wicourts.gov/index.xsl.

Green County

Circuit Court 1016 16th Ave, Monroe, WI 53566; 608-328-9433; criminal fax: 608-328-9459; civil fax: same; 8AM-4:30PM. ***Felony, Misdemeanor, Civil, Eviction, Small Claims.*** www.co.green.wi.gov

Civil Records: Access: Mail, in person, online. Both court and visitors may perform in person searches. Search fee: $5.00 per name. Required to search: name, years to search; also helpful: address. Civil cases indexed by defendant, plaintiff. Civil index on cards from 1984, index books from 1900s; computerized back to 1994. Mail turnaround time 1-2 days. Civil PAT goes back to 1994. PAT civil results show middle initial. Civil case lookup free online at http://wcca.wicourts.gov/index.xsl.

Criminal Records: Access: Mail, online, in person. Both court and visitors may perform in person searches. Search fee: $5.00 per name. Required to search: name, years to search; also helpful: DOB. Criminal records indexed on cards from 1984, index books from 1900s; computerized back to 1994. Mail turnaround time 1-2 days. Criminal PAT goes back to same as civil. PAT results show middle initial, DOB. Access criminal index free at http://wcca.wicourts.gov/index.xsl. Online results show middle initial and DOB most of time; however, sometimes DOB is month and year only on the index.

General Information: Online identifiers in results same as on public terminal. No juvenile, paternity or sealed records released. Will fax documents $1.00 per page. Court makes copy: $1.25 per page. Certification fee: $5.00 per doc. Payee: Clerk of Court. Personal checks accepted; credit cards are not. Prepayment required. Mail requests: SASE required.

Register in Probate 1016 16th Ave, County Courthouse, Monroe, WI 53566; 608-328-9567; fax: 608-328-9459; 8AM-N, 1PM-4:30PM. ***Probate.*** Probate free at http://wcca.wicourts.gov/index.xsl.

Green Lake County

Circuit Court PO Box 3188, 492 Hill St, Green Lake, WI 54941; 920-294-4142; 8AM-4:30PM. ***Felony, Misdemeanor, Civil, Eviction, Small Claims.*** www.co.green-lake.wi.us

Civil and criminal search treated as one.

Civil Records: Access: Mail, in person, online. Both court and visitors may perform in person searches. Search fee: $5.00 per name. Required to search: name, years to search. Civil cases indexed by defendant, plaintiff; index on computer from 4/93, on index cards since 1900s. Mail turnaround time 1-3 days. Civil PAT goes back to 1993. Civil case lookup free at http://wcca.wicourts.gov/index.xsl.

Criminal Records: Access: Mail, online, in person. Both court and visitors may perform in person searches. Search fee: $5.00 per name. Required to search: name, years to search. Criminal records computerized from 4/93, on index cards since 1900s. Mail turnaround time 1-3 days. Criminal PAT goes back to same as civil. PAT results show middle initial, DOB. Access criminal index free at http://wcca.wicourts.gov/index.xsl. Online results show middle initial and DOB most of time; however, sometimes DOB is month and year only on the index.

General Information: Online identifiers in results same as on public terminal. No paternity or juvenile ordinance records released. Will not fax documents. Court makes copy: $1.25 per page. Certification fee: $5.00 per doc. Payee: Clerk of Circuit Clerk. Personal checks and credit cards accepted. Prepayment required. Mail requests: SASE required.

Register in Probate PO Box 3188, 492 Hill St, Green Lake, WI 54941; 920-294-4044; 8AM-4:30PM. ***Probate.*** Probate records free at http://wcca.wicourts.gov/index.xsl.

Iowa County

Circuit Court 222 N Iowa St, Dodgeville, WI 53533; 608-935-0395; probate phone: 608-935-0347; fax: 608-935-0386; 8:30AM-4:30PM. ***Felony, Misdemeanor, Civil, Eviction, Small Claims.***

Civil Records: Access: Mail, in person, online. Both court and visitors may perform in person searches. Search fee: $5.00 per name. Required to search: name, years to search. Civil cases indexed by defendant, plaintiff; index on computer from 1992, index cards from 1987, archives from 1917, index books from 1829. Mail turnaround time same day. Civil PAT goes back to 1992. Civil case lookup free at http://wcca.wicourts.gov/index.xsl.

Criminal Records: Access: Mail, online, in person. Both court and visitors may perform in person searches. Search fee: $5.00 per name. Required to search: name, years to search, DOB. Criminal records computerized from 1992, index cards from 1987, archives from 1917, index books from 1829. Mail turnaround time same day. Criminal PAT goes back to same as civil. PAT results show middle initial, DOB. Access criminal index free at http://wcca.wicourts.gov/index.xsl. Online results show middle initial and DOB most of time; however, sometimes DOB is month and year only on the index.

General Information: Online identifiers in results same as on public terminal. No adoption, paternity or mental records released. Fee to fax back- $5.00 plus $1.25 per page. Court makes copy: $1.25 per page. Certification fee: $5.00 per doc. Payee: Clerk of Court. Personal checks accepted; credit cards are not. Prepayment required. Mail requests: SASE required.

Register in Probate 222 N Iowa St, Rm 206, Dodgeville, WI 53533; 608-935-0347; fax: 608-935-0386; 8:30AM-N, 12:30-4:30PM. ***Probate.*** Probate free at http://wcca.wicourts.gov/index.xsl.

Iron County

Circuit Court 300 Taconite St, #207, Hurley, WI 54534; 715-561-4084; criminal fax: 715-561-4054; civil fax: same; 8AM-4PM. ***Felony, Misdemeanor, Civil, Eviction, Small Claims.***

Civil Records: Access: Phone, mail, online, in person. Both court and visitors may perform in person searches. Search fee: $5.00 per name. Required to search: name, years to search. Civil cases indexed by defendant, plaintiff. Civil index on cards from 1989, index books from 1920. Note: Phone access for title companies only. Mail turnaround time 2-3 days. Civil PAT goes back to 1993. Civil lookup free at http://wcca.wicourts.gov/index.xsl.

Criminal Records: Access: Mail, online, in person. Both court and visitors may perform in person searches. Search fee: $5.00 per name. Required to search: name, years to search, DOB. Criminal records indexed on cards from 1989, index books from 1920. Mail turnaround time 2-3 days. Criminal PAT goes back to same as civil. PAT results show middle initial, DOB. Access criminal index free at http://wcca.wicourts.gov/index.xsl. Online results show middle initial and DOB most of time; however, sometimes DOB is month and year only on the index.

General Information: Online identifiers in results same as on public terminal. No juvenile or paternity records released. Will fax documents to local or toll free line. Court makes copy: $1.25 per page. Certification fee: $5.00 per doc. Payee: Clerk of Court. Personal checks and credit cards accepted. Prepayment required. Mail requests: SASE required.

Register in Probate 300 Taconite St, #209, Hurley, WI 54534; 715-561-3434; fax: 715-561-4054; 8AM-4PM. ***Probate.*** Probate records free at http://wcca.wicourts.gov/index.xsl.

Jackson County

Circuit Court 307 Main St, Black River Falls, WI 54615; 715-284-0208; probate phone: 715-284-0213; fax: 715-284-0270; 8AM-4:30PM. ***Felony, Misdemeanor, Civil, Eviction, Small Claims, Family, Traffic.*** www.co.jackson.wi.us

Civil Records: Access: Mail, in person, online. Both court and visitors may perform in person searches. Search fee: $5.00 per name. Required to search: name, years to search. Civil cases indexed by defendant, plaintiff; index on computer from 6/92, on index cards from 1979, index books to 1980, files and indexes prior to 1980 destroyed. Mail turnaround time 1-4 days. Civil PAT goes back to 1992. PAT civil results show middle initial. Civil case lookup free at http://wcca.wicourts.gov/index.xsl.

Criminal Records: Access: Mail, online, in person. Both court and visitors may perform in person searches. Search fee: $5.00 per name. Required to search: name, years to search, DOB. Criminal records computerized from 6/92. Felonies 1879 to 1929 at State Historical Society. Mail turnaround time 1-4 days. Criminal PAT goes back to same as civil. PAT results show middle initial, DOB. Access criminal index free at http://wcca.wicourts.gov/index.xsl. Online results

show middle initial and DOB most of time; however, sometimes DOB is month and year only on the index.
General Information: Online identifiers in results same as on public terminal. No juvenile or pre-judgment paternity records released. Will fax documents $3.00, if prepaid. Court makes copy: $1.25 per page. Certification fee: $5.00. Payee: Clerk of Court. Personal checks accepted; credit cards are not. Prepayment required if over $5.00. Mail requests: SASE required.

Register in Probate 307 Main St, Black River Falls, WI 54615; 715-284-0213; fax: 715-284-0277; 8AM-4:30PM. ***Probate.*** Probate records free at http://wcca.wicourts.gov/index.xsl.

Jefferson County

Circuit Court 320 S Main St, Jefferson, WI 53549; 920-674-7150; fax: 920-674-7425; 8AM-4:30PM. ***Felony, Misdemeanor, Civil, Eviction, Small Claims.***
www.co.jefferson.wi.us/ClerkofCourts/default.htm
Civil Records: Access: Mail, in person, online. Both court and visitors may perform in person searches. Search fee: $5.00 per name. Required to search: name, years to search. Civil cases indexed by defendant, plaintiff; index on computer from 1992, on index cards from 1979, index books from late 1800s. Mail turnaround time 2-3 days. Civil PAT goes back to 1992. PAT results show middle initial; DOBs are not found on all results. Civil lookup free at http://wcca.wicourts.gov/index.xsl.
Criminal Records: Access: Mail, online, in person. Both court and visitors may perform in person searches. Search fee: $5.00 per name. Required to search: name, years to search, DOB. Criminal records computerized from 1992, on index cards from 1979, index books from late 1800s. Mail turnaround time 2-3 days. Criminal PAT goes back to same as civil. PAT results show middle initial, DOB. Access criminal index free online at http://wcca.wicourts.gov/index.xsl. Online results show middle initial and DOB most of time; however, sometimes DOB is month and year only on the index.
General Information: Online identifiers in results same as on public terminal. No juvenile or mental health records released. Will fax documents $1.25 per page. Court makes copy: $1.25 per page. Certification fee: $5.00. Payee: Clerk of Courts. Personal checks accepted. Credit card payments can be made through GPS, 888-604-7888, pay location 2039. Prepayment required. Mail requests: SASE required.

Register in Probate 320 S Main St, Jefferson, WI 53549; 920-674-7245; fax: 920-675-0134; 8AM-4:30PM. ***Probate.*** Probate records free at http://wcca.wicourts.gov/index.xsl.

Juneau County

Circuit Court 200 Oak St, County Justice Ctr, Mauston, WI 53948; 608-847-9356; fax: 608-847-9360; 8AM-4:30PM. ***Felony, Misdemeanor, Civil, Eviction, Small Claims.***
www.co.juneau.wi.gov/
Civil Records: Access: Mail, in person, online. Both court and visitors may perform in person searches. Search fee: $5.00 per case. Required to search: name, years to search, DOB. Civil cases indexed by defendant, plaintiff; index on computer from 1988, index cards from 1977, index books from 1900, microfiche from 1856-1900. Mail turnaround time 1 week. Civil PAT goes back to 1996. PAT civil results show middle initial. Civil case lookup free online at http://wcca.wicourts.gov/index.xsl.
Criminal Records: Access: Mail, online, in person. Both court and visitors may perform in person searches. Search fee: $5.00 per case. Required to search: name, years to search, DOB. Criminal records computerized from 1988, index cards from 1977, index books from 1900, microfiche from 1856-1900. Mail turnaround time 1 week. Criminal PAT goes back to 1996. PAT results show middle initial, DOB. Access criminal index free at http://wcca.wicourts.gov/index.xsl. Criminal background checks available at www.doj.state.wi.us/dles/cib/crimback.asp for a fee. Online results show middle initial. Online search index results gives DOB half the time, then half only have month/year.
General Information: Online identifiers in results same as on public terminal. No juvenile, confidential family or paternity records released. Will fax documents $2.00 up to 15 pages. Court makes copy: $1.25 per page. Certification fee: $5.00 per doc. Payee: Juneau County Clerk of Court. Personal checks and major credit cards accepted. Prepayment required. Mail requests: SASE required.

Register in Probate 200 Oak St, Rm 2300, Mauston, WI 53948; 608-847-9346; fax: 608-847-9349; 8AM-4:30PM. ***Probate.*** Probate records free at http://wcca.wicourts.gov/index.xsl.

Kenosha County

Circuit Court 912 56th St, Kenosha, WI 53140; 262-653-2664; fax: 262-653-2435; 8AM-5PM. ***Felony, Misdemeanor, Civil, Eviction, Small Claims.***
Civil Records: Access: Mail, in person, online. Both court and visitors may perform in person searches. Search fee: $5.00 per name. Required to search: name, years to search. Civil cases indexed by defendant, plaintiff; index on computer from 1989, index cards from 1960, microfiche from 1850. Mail turnaround time 1-2 days. Civil PAT goes back to 1995. Civil case lookup free online at http://wcca.wicourts.gov/index.xsl.
Criminal Records: Access: Mail, online, in person, fax. Both court and visitors may perform in person searches. Search fee: $5.00 per name. Required to search: name, years to search; also helpful: DOB, SSN. Criminal records computerized from 1989, index cards from 1960, microfiche from 1850. Mail turnaround time 1-2 days. Criminal PAT goes back to same as civil. PAT results show middle initial, DOB. Access criminal index free at http://wcca.wicourts.gov/index.xsl. Online results show middle initial and DOB most of time; however, sometimes DOB is month and year only on the index.
General Information: Online identifiers in results same as on public terminal. No juvenile or paternity records released. Will fax documents to local or toll free line. Court makes copy: $1.25 per page. Certification fee: $5.00. Payee: Clerk of Court. Personal checks accepted. Credit cards accepted; a 3% surcharge is added. Prepayment required. Mail requests: SASE required.

Register in Probate Courthouse, Rm 304, 912 56th St, Kenosha, WI 53140; 262-653-2675; fax: 262-653-2673; 8AM-5PM. ***Probate.***
$4.00 per search, records indexed on computer back to 1992; cards prior. Probate records free at http://wcca.wicourts.gov/index.xsl.

Kewaunee County

Circuit Court 613 Dodge St, Kewaunee, WI 54216; 920-388-7144; criminal phone: 920-388-7153; civil phone: 920-388-7146; criminal fax: 920-388-3139; civil fax: same; 8AM-4:30PM. ***Felony, Misdemeanor, Civil, Eviction, Small Claims.***
www.kewauneeco.org/subpages/Departments/Courts/Court.htm
Civil Records: Access: Phone, mail, online, in person. Both court and visitors may perform in person searches. Search fee: $5.00 per name. Required to search: name, years to search. Civil cases indexed by defendant, plaintiff. Computerized records from 1993, civil records on index cards from 1950, index books from 1852. Mail turnaround time 1-2 days. Civil PAT goes back to 1993. PAT results show middle initial, DOB. Civil case lookup free online at http://wcca.wicourts.gov/index.xsl.
Criminal Records: Access: Phone, mail, online, in person. Both court and visitors may perform in person searches. Search fee: $5.00 per name. Required to search: name, years to search, DOB. Computerized records from 1993, criminal records on index cards from 1950, index books from 1852. Mail turnaround time 1-2 days. Criminal PAT goes back to same as civil. PAT results show middle initial, DOB. Access criminal index free at http://wcca.wicourts.gov/index.xsl. Online results show middle initial and DOB most of time; however, sometimes DOB is month and year only on the index.
General Information: Online identifiers in results same as on public terminal. No paternity records released. Will fax documents $1.00 1st page, $.50 each add'l page. Court makes copy: $1.25 per page. Self serve: same. Certification fee: $5.00 per document. Payee: Clerk of Circuit Court. Personal checks and credit cards accepted. Prepayment required. Mail requests: SASE helpful.

Register in Probate 613 Dodge St, Kewaunee, WI 54216; 920-388-7143; fax: 920-388-3139; 8AM-4:30PM. ***Probate.*** Probate records free at http://wcca.wicourts.gov/index.xsl.

La Crosse County

Circuit Court 333 Vine St, LEC, Rm 1200, La Crosse, WI 54601; 608-785-9590/9573; fax: 608-789-7821; 8:30AM-5PM. ***Felony, Misdemeanor, Civil, Eviction, Small Claims.***
www.co.la-crosse.wi.us/departments/court/
Civil Records: Access: Fax, mail, online, in person. Both court and visitors may perform in person searches. Search fee: $5.00 per name. Required to search: name, years to search. Civil cases indexed by defendant, plaintiff; index on computer from 1993, on index cards from 1983, index books from 1917. Mail turnaround time 1-2 days. Civil PAT goes back to 1993. PAT results show middle initial, DOB. Civil lookup free at http://wcca.wicourts.gov/index.xsl. Retention period 20 years for civil.
Criminal Records: Access: Fax, mail, online, in person. Both court and visitors may perform in person searches. Search fee: $5.00 per name. Required to search: name, years to search; also helpful: DOB. Criminal records computerized from 1993, on index cards from 1983, index books from 1917. Mail turnaround time 1-2 days. Criminal PAT goes back to 1983. PAT results show middle initial, DOB. Access criminal index free at http://wcca.wicourts.gov/index.xsl. Retention period 20 years for misdemeanor, felony is 50-75 years. Online results show middle initial and DOB most of time; however, sometimes DOB is month and year only on the index.
General Information: Online identifiers in results same as on public terminal. No juvenile, paternity or finances in family records released. Fee to fax out file $1.25 per page. Court makes copy: $1.25 per page. Certification fee: $5.00 per doc. Payee: Clerk of Courts. Personal checks and credit cards accepted. Prepayment required. Mail requests: SASE required.

Register in Probate 333 Vine St, Rm 1201, La Crosse, WI 54601; 608-785-9882; fax: 608-789-7821; 8:30AM-5PM. ***Probate.***
www.wicourts.gov Probate records free at http://wcca.wicourts.gov/index.xsl.

Lafayette County

Circuit Court 626 Main St, Attn: County Clerk of Court, Darlington, WI 53530; 608-776-4832; probate phone: 608-776-4811; fax: 608-776-4845; 8AM-4:30PM. ***Felony, Misdemeanor, Civil, Eviction, Small Claims.***
Civil Records: Access: Mail, in person, online. Both court and visitors may perform in person searches. Search fee: $5.00 per name. Required to search: name, years to search. Civil cases indexed by defendant. Civil index on cards from 1973, index books from 1900; computerized back to 1993. Mail turnaround time 2-3 days. Civil PAT goes back to 1993. Civil case lookup http://wcca.wicourts.gov/index.xsl.
Criminal Records: Access: Mail, online, in person. Both court and visitors may perform in person searches. Search fee: $5.00 per name. Required to search: name, years to search. Criminal records indexed on cards from 1973, index books from 1900; computerized back to 1993. Mail turnaround time 2-3 days. Criminal PAT goes back to same as civil. PAT results show middle initial, DOB. Access index free at http://wcca.wicourts.gov/index.xsl. Online results show middle initial and DOB most of time; however, sometimes DOB is month and year only on the index.

General Information: Online identifiers in results same as on public terminal. No juvenile records released. Will not fax documents. Court makes copy: $1.25 per page. Certification fee: $5.00 per document. Payee: Clerk of Circuit Court. Personal checks accepted; credit cards are not. Prepayment required. Mail requests: SASE required.

Register in Probate 626 Main St, Rm 302, Darlington, WI 53530; 608-776-4811; fax: 608-776-4845; 8AM-N, 1-4:30PM. ***Probate.*** Probate records free at http://wcca.wicourts.gov/index.xsl.

Langlade County

Circuit Court 800 Clermont St, Antigo, WI 54409; 715-627-6215; 8:30AM-4:30PM. ***Felony, Misdemeanor, Civil, Eviction, Small Claims.***
Ask that they combine a search of both the civil and criminal indices.
Civil Records: Access: Mail, in person, online. Both court and visitors may perform in person searches. Search fee: $5.00 per name. Required to search: name, years to search. Civil cases indexed by defendant, plaintiff. Civil index on docket books from 1905, computerized since 1993. Mail turnaround time 2-3 days. Civil PAT goes back to 1993. Civil case lookup free at http://wcca.wicourts.gov/index.xsl.
Criminal Records: Access: Mail, online, in person. Both court and visitors may perform in person searches. Search fee: $5.00 per name. Required to search: name, years to search. Criminal records indexed in books from 1905, computerized since 1993. Mail turnaround time 2-3 days. Criminal PAT goes back to same as civil. PAT results show middle initial, DOB. Access criminal index free at http://wcca.wicourts.gov/index.xsl. Online results show middle initial and DOB most of time; however, sometimes DOB is month and year only on the index.
General Information: Online identifiers in results same as on public terminal. No confidential records released. Will not fax documents. Court makes copy: $1.25 per page. Certification fee: $5.00 per cert. Payee: Clerk of Court. Personal checks accepted if in-state only. No credit cards accepted. Prepayment required. Mail requests: SASE required.

Register in Probate 800 Clermont St, Antigo, WI 54409; 715-627-6213; fax: 715-627-6329; 8:30AM-4:30PM. ***Probate.***
There is a $4.00 search fee. Probate records free at http://wcca.wicourts.gov/index.xsl.

Lincoln County

Circuit Court 1110 E Main St, Merrill, WI 54452; 715-536-0319; criminal fax: 715-536-0361; civil fax: same; 8AM-4:30PM. ***Felony, Misdemeanor, Civil, Eviction, Small Claims.***
Civil Records: Access: Mail, in person, online. Both court and visitors may perform in person searches. Search fee: $5.00 per name. Required to search: name, years to search. Civil cases indexed by defendant. Civil records on computer from 1990, index cards from 1982, index books from 1900s. Mail turnaround time 1-2 days. Civil PAT goes back to 1990. PAT results show middle initial, DOB. Civil lookup free at http://wcca.wicourts.gov/index.xsl.
Criminal Records: Access: Mail, online, in person. Both court and visitors may perform in person searches. Search fee: $5.00 per name. Required to search: name, years to search; also helpful: DOB, SSN. Criminal records computerized from 1990, index cards from 1982, index books from 1900s. Mail turnaround time 1-2 days. Criminal PAT goes back to same as civil. PAT results show middle initial, DOB. Access criminal index free at http://wcca.wicourts.gov/index.xsl. Online results show middle initial and DOB most of time; however, sometimes DOB is month and year only on the index.
General Information: Online identifiers in results same as on public terminal. No paternity or sealed records released. Will fax documents $1.00 per fax; cannot fax certified copies. Court makes copy: $1.25 per page. Certification fee: $5.00 per document. Payee: Clerk of Court. Local personal checks accepted. No credit cards accepted. Prepayment required. Mail requests: SASE required.

Register in Probate 1110 E Main St, Merrill, WI 54452; 715-536-0342; 536-0378; fax: 715-539-2762; 8:15AM-N, 1-4:30PM. ***Probate.***
Probate records free back to 1986 at http://wcca.wicourts.gov/index.xsl. Older records being added.

Manitowoc County

Circuit Court PO Box 2000, Manitowoc, WI 54221-2000; 920-683-4030; criminal phone: 920-683-4027; civil phone: 920-683-4031; fax: 920-683-2733; 8:30AM-5PM M; 8:30AM-4:30PM T-F. ***Felony, Misdemeanor, Civil, Eviction, Small Claims.***
www.manitowoccounty.org/department/dept_home.asp?ID=4 Also Family, paternity and Juvenile case records held here.
Civil Records: Access: Phone, mail, online, in person. Both court and visitors may perform in person searches. Search fee: $5.00 per name. Required to search: name, years to search. Civil cases indexed by first named defendant, plaintiff. Civil records on computer from 1993, on index cards from 1962, index books from 1906, Historical Society has prior records. Note: Prior written agreement with court required for phone access. Mail turnaround time 5-7 days. Civil PAT goes back to 1993. Civil case lookup free online at http://wcca.wicourts.gov/index.xsl.
Criminal Records: Access: Phone, mail, online, in person. Both court and visitors may perform in person searches. Search fee: $5.00 per name. Required to search: name, years to search, DOB. Criminal records computerized from 1993, on index cards from 1962, index books from 1906, Historical Society has prior records. Note: Prior written agreement with court required for phone access. Mail turnaround time 5-7 days. Criminal PAT goes back to same as civil. PAT results show middle initial, DOB, SSN. Results include case number and fine amount. Access criminal index free at http://wcca.wicourts.gov/index.xsl. Results include address, case number and fine amount. Online results show middle initial and DOB most of time; however, sometimes DOB is month and year only on the index.
General Information: Online identifiers in results same as on public terminal. No confidential records released. Will fax documents $3.00 plus $1.25 per page, either prepaid or within 48 hours. Court makes copy: $1.25 per page. Certification fee: $5.00 per document. Payee: Clerk of Circuit Court. Personal checks accepted. Credit cards accepted by phone, 1-866-480-8552 or online at www.manitowoccounty.org. Prepayment required. Mail requests: SASE requested.

Register in Probate 1010 S 8th St, Rm 116, Manitowoc, WI 54220; 920-683-4016; fax: 920-683-5182; 8:30AM-4:30PM Tu-F; 8:30AM-5PM M. ***Probate.***
http://manitowoc-county.com/department/dept_home.asp?ID=20 Probate records free at http://wcca.wicourts.gov/index.xsl.

Marathon County

Circuit Court 500 Forest St, Wausau, WI 54403; 715-261-1300; criminal phone: 715-261-1270; civil phone: 715-261-1310; criminal fax: 715-261-1279; civil fax: 715-261-1318; 8AM-4:30PM. ***Felony, Misdemeanor, Civil, Eviction, Small Claims, Family.***
www.co.marathon.wi.us/dep_detail.asp?dep=9
Small claims phone is 261-1310; Traffic, 261-1270.
Civil Records: Access: Mail, in person, online. Both court and visitors may perform in person searches. Search fee: $5.00 per name. Required to search: name, years to search. Civil cases indexed by defendant, plaintiff; index on computer from 1992, on index cards from 1979. Note: All requests must be in writing, using their form if possible. Mail turnaround time 1-3 days. Civil PAT goes back to 1991. Civil case lookup free online at http://wcca.wicourts.gov/index.xsl.
Criminal Records: Access: Mail, online, in person. Both court and visitors may perform in person searches. Search fee: $5.00 per name. Required to search: name, years to search, DOB. Criminal records computerized from 1992, on index cards from 1979, index books from 1900s. Note: All requests must be in writing, using their form if possible. Mail turnaround time 1-3 days. Criminal PAT goes back to same as civil. PAT results show middle initial, DOB, SSN. Access criminal index free at http://wcca.wicourts.gov/index.xsl. Online results show middle initial and DOB most of time; however, sometimes DOB is month and year only on the index.
General Information: Online identifiers in results same as on public terminal. No mental health or juvenile records released. Will fax out documents to local or toll free number. Court makes copy: $1.25 per page. Certification fee: $5.00 per Cert. Payee: Clerk of Court. Personal checks accepted. Major credit cards accepted via GPS. Prepayment required. Mail requests: SASE required.

Register in Probate 500 Forest St, Wausau, WI 54403; 715-261-1260; fax: 715-261-1269; 8AM-4:30PM. ***Probate.***
www.co.marathon.wi.us Probate records free at http://wcca.wicourts.gov/index.xsl.

Marinette County

Circuit Court 1926 Hall Ave, Marinette, WI 54143-1717; 715-732-7450; probate phone: 715-732-7475; fax: 715-732-7461; 8:30AM-4:30PM. ***Felony, Misdemeanor, Civil, Eviction, Small Claims.***
Civil Records: Access: Mail, in person, online. Both court and visitors may perform in person searches. Search fee: $5.00 per name. Required to search: name, years to search. Civil cases indexed by defendant, plaintiff; index on computer from 1989, index cards from 1980, index books from 1906, prior records at Historical Society. Mail turnaround time 2-3 days. Civil PAT goes back to 1994. PAT results show name only. Civil court records 1994 to present free at http://wcca.wicourts.gov/index.xsl.
Criminal Records: Access: Mail, online, in person. Both court and visitors may perform in person searches. Search fee: $5.00 per name. Required to search: name, years to search, DOB. Criminal records computerized from 1989, index cards from 1980, index books from 1906, prior records at Historical Society. Mail turnaround time 2-3 days. Criminal PAT goes back to same as civil. PAT results show middle initial, DOB. Access criminal index free at http://wcca.wicourts.gov/index.xsl. Online results show middle initial and DOB most of time; however, sometimes DOB is month and year only on the index.
General Information: Online identifiers in results same as on public terminal. No paternity records released. Will fax documents to local or toll free line. Court makes copy: $1.25 per page. Certification fee: $5.00. Payee: Clerk of Courts. Personal checks accepted; credit cards are not. Prepayment required. Mail requests: SASE required.

Register in Probate 1926 Hall Ave, Marinette, WI 54143-1717; 715-732-7475; fax: 715-732-7461; 8:30AM-4:30PM. ***Probate.*** Probate records free at http://wcca.wicourts.gov/index.xsl.

Marquette County

Circuit Court PO Box 187, 77 W Park St, Montello, WI 53949; 608-297-3005, 608-297-3100 x3005; fax: 608-297-9188; 8AM-4:30PM. ***Felony, Misdemeanor, Civil, Eviction, Small Claims.***
www.co.marquette.wi.us/Departments/clerk_court.htm
Courthouse has the largest tree growing in the state.
Civil Records: Access: Phone, mail, online, in person. Both court and visitors may perform in person searches. Search fee: $5.00 per name. Required to search: name, years to search. Civil cases indexed by defendant, plaintiff. Civil index on docket books from 1983, prior records at Historical Society; computerized back to 1996. Mail turnaround time 7-10 days. Civil PAT goes back to 1996. PAT results show middle initial, DOB. Civil case lookup free online at http://wcca.wicourts.gov/index.xsl.
Criminal Records: Access: Mail, online, in person. Both court and visitors may perform in person searches. Search fee: $5.00 per name. Required to search: name, years to search, DOB, full name. Criminal records indexed in books from 1900s, prior

records at Historical Society; computerized back to 1996. Mail turnaround time 7-10 days. Criminal PAT goes back to same as civil. PAT results show middle initial, DOB. Access criminal index free at http://wcca.wicourts.gov/index.xsl. Online results show middle initial and DOB most of time; however, sometimes DOB is month and year only on the index.
General Information: Online identifiers in results same as on public terminal. No adoption, juvenile, paternity, guardianship, mental or termination of parental right records released. Fee to fax out file $2.00 each. Court makes copy: $1.25 per page. Certification fee: $5.00 per doc. Payee: Clerk of Circuit Court. Personal checks accepted; credit cards are not. Prepayment required. Mail requests: SASE requested.

Register in Probate 77 W Park St, PO Box 749, Montello, WI 53949; 608-297-3007; fax: 608-297-9188; 8AM-4:30PM. ***Probate.*** Probate records free at http://wcca.wicourts.gov/index.xsl.

Menominee County

Circuit Court PO Box 279, W3269 Courthouse Ln, Keshena, WI 54135; 715-799-3313; fax: 715-799-1322; 8AM-4:30PM. ***Felony, Misdemeanor, Civil, Eviction, Small Claims.***
Civil Records: Access: Mail, in person, online. Both court and visitors may perform in person searches. Search fee: $5.00 per name. Required to search: name, years to search. Civil cases indexed by defendant, plaintiff. Civil records are indexed by cards, kept in files since 1979, computerized since 1992. Older records are at the Historical Society. Mail turnaround time 3-4 days. Civil case lookup free online at http://wcca.wicourts.gov/index.xsl.
Criminal Records: Access: Mail, online, in person, fax. Both court and visitors may perform in person searches. Search fee: $5.00 per name. Required to search: name, years to search, DOB. Criminal records are indexed by cards, kept in files since 1979, computerized since 1992. Older records are at the Historical Society. Mail turnaround time 3-4 days. PAT results show middle initial, DOB. Access criminal index back to 1992 free at http://wcca.wicourts.gov/index.xsl. Online results show middle initial and DOB most of time; however, sometimes DOB is month and year only on the index.
General Information: Online identifiers in results same as on public terminal. No juvenile, mental, adoption. Will fax documents to local or toll free line. Court makes copy: $1.25 per page. Certification fee: $5.00. Payee: Clerk of Court. Personal checks accepted; credit cards are not. Prepayment required. Mail requests: SASE helpful.

Register in Probate 311 N Main St, Rm 203, Shawano, WI 54166; 715-526-8631; fax: 715-526-8622; 8AM-4:30PM. ***Probate.***
www.co.shawano.wi.us
Menominee Probate is combined with Shawano County Probate and located there. Tribal probate records only in Keshena (Menominee Tribal Court); Non-tribal records are in Shawano County. Probate records free at http://wcca.wicourts.gov/index.xsl.

Milwaukee County

Circuit Court - Civil 901 N 9th St, Rm G-9, Milwaukee, WI 53233; 414-278-4120; fax: 414-223-1256; 8AM-5PM. ***Civil, Eviction, Small Claims.***
www.county.milwaukee.gov/display/router.asp?docid=11475
Civil Records: Access: Mail, in person, online. Both court and visitors may perform in person searches. Search fee: $5.00 per name. Required to search: name, years to search; also helpful-DOB. Civil cases indexed by defendant, plaintiff; index on computer from 1985, on microfiche from 1949, prior with County Historical Society. Mail turnaround time 1-2 weeks. Public use terminal has civil records back to 1985. PAT results show middle initial, DOB, SSN. Public terminal in Rm 117 of Safety Bldg. Civil case lookup free online at http://wcca.wicourts.gov/index.xsl. Online results show middle initial, DOB.
General Information: Online identifiers in results same as on public terminal. No paternity records released unless post-judgment. Will not fax documents. Court makes copy: $1.25 per page. Self serve: $.25 per page.Copy of a court order is $5.00 per doc. Certification fee: $5.00. Payee: Milwaukee County Clerk of Circuit Court. Personal checks accepted; credit cards are not. Prepayment required. Mail requests: SASE required for civil.

Circuit Court - Criminal Division 821 W State St, Rm 117, Milwaukee, WI 53233; criminal phone: 414-278-4599; fax: 414-223-1262; 8AM-5PM. ***Felony, Misdemeanor, Traffic.***
www.county.milwaukee.gov/display/router.asp?docid=10507
Criminal Records: Access: Fax, mail, online, in person. Both court and visitors may perform in person searches. Search fee: $5.00 per name per case (no fee if case number provided). Required to search: name, years to search, DOB. Criminal records computerized from 10/86, index books and cards prior. Note: Additional search time needed for older records in storage off-site. Mail turnaround time 10 days. Public use terminal has crim records back to 1998 but some older records on system. PAT results show middle initial, DOB. Access criminal index free at http://wcca.wicourts.gov/index.xsl. Also, although not from this court, criminal case records on Milwaukee Municipal Court Case Information System database are free at www.court.ci.mil.wi.us/. Search by Case Number, by Citation Number, or by Name. Online results show middle initial and DOB most of time; however, sometimes DOB is month and year only on the index.
General Information: Online identifiers in results same as on public terminal. No sealed records released. Will fax out documents $5.00 per doc. Court makes copy: $1.25 per page. Certification fee: $5.00 per doc. Payee: Clerk of Circuit Court. Personal checks accepted; credit cards are not. Prepayment required. Mail requests: SASE required.

Register in Probate 901 N 9th St, Rm 207, Milwaukee, WI 53233; 414-278-4444; fax: 414-223-1814; 8AM-4:30PM. ***Probate.*** Probate records free at http://wcca.wicourts.gov/index.xsl.

Monroe County

Circuit Court 112 S Court St, #203, Sparta, WI 54656-1764; 608-269-8745; criminal phone: 608-269-8962; civil phone: 608-269-8748; probate phone: 608-269-8701; criminal fax: 608-269-8781; civil fax: same; 8AM-4:30PM. ***Felony, Misdemeanor, Civil, Eviction, Small Claims.***
Civil Records: Access: Fax, mail, online, in person. Both court and visitors may perform in person searches. Search fee: $5.00 per name. Required to search: name, years to search. Civil cases indexed by defendant, plaintiff; index on computer and cards. Mail turnaround time 1 week. Civil PAT goes back to 1993. Traffic records on public terminal go back to 1996. Civil case lookup free online at http://wcca.wicourts.gov/index.xsl.
Criminal Records: Access: Fax, mail, online, in person. Both court and visitors may perform in person searches. Search fee: $5.00 per name. Required to search: name, years to search. Criminal records on computer and cards. Mail turnaround time 1 week. Criminal PAT goes back to same as civil. PAT results show middle initial, DOB. Traffic records on public terminal go back to 1996. Access criminal index free at http://wcca.wicourts.gov/index.xsl. Online results show middle initial and DOB most of time; however, sometimes DOB is month and year only on the index.
General Information: Online identifiers in results same as on public terminal. No paternity, medical or financial records released. Will fax documents $1.25 per page. Court makes copy: $1.25 per page. Certification fee: $5.00 per document. Payee: Clerk of Court. Local checks accepted. Pay via GPS at 888-604-7888. Prepayment required. Mail requests: SASE required.

Register in Probate 112 S Court, Rm 301, Sparta, WI 54656-1765; 608-269-8701; fax: 608-269-8950; 8AM-N, 12:30-4:30PM. ***Probate.*** Records free at http://wcca.wicourts.gov/index.xsl.

Oconto County

Circuit Court 301 Washington St, Oconto, WI 54153; 920-834-6855; fax: 920-834-6867; 8AM-4PM. ***Felony, Misdemeanor, Civil, Small Claims.***
Civil Records: Access: Mail, in person, online. Both court and visitors may perform in person searches. Search fee: $5.00 per name. Required to search: name, years to search. Civil cases indexed by defendant, plaintiff; index on computer since 1994; prior records on index books from 1930s, Historical Society has earlier records. Mail turnaround time 1-2 days. Civil PAT goes back to 1994. PAT results show name, DOB. Civil case lookup free online at http://wcca.wicourts.gov/index.xsl.
Criminal Records: Access: Mail, online, in person. Both court and visitors may perform in person searches. Search fee: $5.00 per name. Required to search: name, years to search, DOB. Criminal records on computer since 1994; prior records on index books from 1930s; Historical Society has earlier records. Mail turnaround time 1-2 days. Criminal PAT goes back to same as civil. PAT results show middle initial, DOB. Access criminal index free at http://wcca.wicourts.gov/index.xsl. Online results show name, DOB. Online search index results gives DOB half the time, then half only have month/year.
General Information: Online identifiers in results same as on public terminal. No juvenile or paternity records released. Will not fax documents. Court makes copy: $1.25 per page. Certification fee: $5.00 per doc. Payee: Oconto County Clerk of Court. Personal checks accepted. Visa/MC accepted. Prepayment required. Mail requests: SASE required.

Register in Probate 301 Washington St, Oconto, WI 54153; 920-834-6839; fax: 920-834-6867; 8AM-4PM. ***Probate.*** Probate records free at http://wcca.wicourts.gov/index.xsl.

Oneida County

Circuit Court PO Box 400, Rhinelander, WI 54501; 715-369-6120; criminal phone: 715-369-6123; civil phone: 715-369-6124; probate phone: 715-369-6159; criminal fax: 715-369-6160; civil fax: same; 8AM-4:30PM. ***Felony, Misdemeanor, Civil, Eviction, Small Claims.***
Civil Records: Access: Mail, in person, online. Both court and visitors may perform in person searches. Search fee: $5.00 per name. Required to search: name, years to search. Civil cases indexed by defendant, plaintiff; index on computer from 1992, index cards from 1980, index books from 1900s. Mail turnaround time 1 week. Civil PAT goes back to 1992. Civil case lookup free online at http://wcca.wicourts.gov/index.xsl.
Criminal Records: Access: Mail, online, in person. Both court and visitors may perform in person searches. Search fee: $5.00 per name. Required to search: name, years to search, DOB. Criminal records computerized from 1992, index cards from 1980, index books from 1900s. Mail turnaround time 1 week. Criminal PAT goes back to same as civil. PAT results show middle initial, DOB. Access criminal index free at http://wcca.wicourts.gov/index.xsl. Online results show middle initial and DOB most of time; however, sometimes DOB is month and year only on the index.
General Information: Online identifiers in results same as on public terminal. No paternity records released. Will fax documents $1.25 per page. Court makes copy: $1.25 per page. Self serve: $.25 per page, but available only to attorneys and title companies. Certification fee: $5.00 per document. Payee: Clerk of Court. Personal checks accepted; credit cards are not. Prepayment required.

Register in Probate PO Box 400, 1 Courthouse Sq, Rhinelander, WI 54501; 715-369-6159; 8AM-N, 1-4:30PM. ***Probate.*** Probate records free at http://wcca.wicourts.gov/index.xsl.

Outagamie County

Circuit Court 320 S Walnut St, Appleton, WI 54911; 920-832-5130; civil phone: 920-832-5136; criminal fax: 920-832-5115; civil fax: same; 8AM-4:30PM. ***Felony, Misdemeanor, Civil, Eviction, Small Claims.***
Small claims and eviction records at 920-832-5135.
Civil Records: Access: In person, online, mail. Visitors must perform in person searches themselves. Search fee: $5.00. Required to search: name, years to search. Civil cases indexed by defendant, plaintiff; index on computer from 10/87, index cards from 1983, index books from 1901, some records on microfiche. Mail turnaround time 2-3 days. Civil PAT goes back to 10/1987. PAT civil results show middle initial. Civil case lookup free online at http://wcca.wicourts.gov/index.xsl.
Criminal Records: Access: Mail, in person, online. Both court and visitors may perform in person searches. Search fee: $5.00 per name. Required to search: name, years to search, DOB. Criminal records computerized from 10/87, index cards from 1983, index books from 1901, some records on microfiche. Mail turnaround time 2-3 days. Criminal PAT goes back to 13 years. PAT results show middle initial, DOB. Criminal court records free at http://wcca.wicourts.gov/index.xsl. Online results show middle initial and DOB most of time; however, sometimes DOB is month and year only on the index.
General Information: Online identifiers in results same as on public terminal. No adoption or juvenile records released. Will fax documents $1.25 per page. Court makes copy: $1.25 per page. Self serve: same. Certification fee: $5.00 per document. Payee: Clerk of Court. Personal checks accepted. Prepayment required. Mail requests: SASE required.

Register in Probate 320 S Walnut St, Appleton, WI 54911; 920-832-5601; fax: 920-832-5115; 8AM-N, 1-5PM. ***Probate.*** Probate records free at http://wcca.wicourts.gov/index.xsl.

Ozaukee County

Circuit Court 1201 S Spring St, Port Washington, WI 53074; 262-284-8409; fax: 262-284-8491; 8:30AM-5PM. ***Felony, Misdemeanor, Civil, Eviction, Small Claims.***
www.co.ozaukee.wi.us/ClerkCourts/default.htm
Civil Records: Access: Mail, in person, online. Both court and visitors may perform in person searches. Search fee: $5.00 per name. Required to search: name, years to search. Civil cases indexed by defendant, plaintiff; index on computer from 1991, index cards from late 1950s. Mail turnaround time 1 week. Civil PAT goes back to 1991. Civil case lookup free at http://wcca.wicourts.gov/index.xsl. Access is also with the use of county "Remote Access". This data is for inquiries only and includes civil, family, and traffic courts. For info, contact the Technology Resources Dept. at 262-284-8309.
Criminal Records: Access: Mail, online, in person. Both court and visitors may perform in person searches. Search fee: $5.00 per name. Required to search: name, years to search, DOB. Criminal records computerized from 1989. Mail turnaround time 1 week. Criminal PAT goes back to 1987. PAT results show middle initial, DOB. Access criminal index free at http://wcca.wicourts.gov/index.xsl. Online results show middle initial and DOB most of time; however, sometimes DOB is month and year only on the index.
General Information: Online identifiers in results same as on public terminal. No paternity records released. Will fax documents $1.25 per page. Court makes copy: $1.25 per page ($1.00 if probate). Self serve: same. Certification fee: $5.00. Payee: Clerk of Court. Business checks or in state personal checks accepted. Credit cards accepted. Prepayment required. Mail requests: SASE required.

Register in Probate PO Box 994, 1201 S Spring St, Port Washington, WI 53074; 262-284-8370; fax: 262-284-8491; 8:30AM-5PM. ***Probate.*** www.co.ozaukee.wi.us/clerkcourts/rip.htm Probate records free at http://wcca.wicourts.gov/index.xsl.

Pepin County

Circuit Court PO Box 39, Durand, WI 54736; 715-672-8861; criminal fax: 715-672-8894; civil fax: same; 8:30AM-N, 12:30-4:30PM. ***Felony, Misdemeanor, Civil, Eviction, Small Claims.***
Civil Records: Access: Mail, in person, online. Both court and visitors may perform in person searches. Search fee: $5.00 per name. Required to search: name, years to search. Civil cases indexed by plaintiff. Civil records on computer from 1995, index books from 1900s. Mail turnaround time 1 week. Civil PAT goes back to 1995. PAT civil results show middle initial. Civil case lookup free online at http://wcca.wicourts.gov/index.xsl.
Criminal Records: Access: Mail, online, in person. Both court and visitors may perform in person searches. Search fee: $5.00 per name. Required to search: name, years to search, DOB. Criminal records computerized from 1995, index books from 1900s. Mail turnaround time 1 week. Criminal PAT goes back to same as civil. PAT results show middle initial, DOB. Access criminal index free at http://wcca.wicourts.gov/index.xsl. Online results show middle initial and DOB most of time; however, sometimes DOB is month and year only on the index.
General Information: Online identifiers in results same as on public terminal. No minor or financial divorce records released. Will fax documents to local or toll free line. Court makes copy: $1.25 per page. Certification fee: $5.00 per document. Payee: Clerk of Court. Personal checks accepted. Credit card payments can be made through GPS, 888-604-7888. Prepayment required. Mail requests: SASE required.

Register in Probate PO Box 39, 740 7th Ave W, Durand, WI 54736; 715-672-8859/715-672-8868; fax: 715-672-8521; 8:30AM-N, 1-4:30PM. ***Probate.*** Probate records free at http://wcca.wicourts.gov/index.xsl.

Pierce County

Circuit Court PO Box 129, 414 W Main St, Ellsworth, WI 54011; 715-273-3531 x6400; fax: 715-273-6855; 8AM-5PM. ***Felony, Misdemeanor, Civil, Eviction, Small Claims, Family.***
www.co.pierce.wi.us/Circuit%20Court/Circuit_Court_Main.html
Civil Records: Access: Mail, in person, online. Both court and visitors may perform in person searches. Search fee: $5.00 per name. Fee is by type of case. Required to search: name, years to search. Civil cases indexed by defendant, plaintiff. Civil records are retained 20 years; on computer back to 1994. Archives in River Falls. Mail turnaround time 2-3 days. Civil PAT goes back to 1994. PAT results show middle initial, DOB. Civil case lookup free online at http://wcca.wicourts.gov/index.xsl.
Criminal Records: Access: Mail, online, in person. Both court and visitors may perform in person searches. Search fee: $5.00 per name. Required to search: name, years to search, DOB. Felony records are retained 50-75 years; misdemeanors for 20. Criminal records computerized from 1994. Archives in River Falls. Mail turnaround time 2-3 days. Criminal PAT goes back to same as civil. PAT results show middle initial, DOB. Access criminal index free at http://wcca.wicourts.gov/index.xsl. Online results show middle initial and DOB most of time; however, sometimes DOB is month and year only on the index.
General Information: Online identifiers in results same as on public terminal. No sealed records released. Will fax documents $1.25 per page. Court makes copy: $1.25 per page. Certification fee: $5.00. Payee: Clerk of Court. Personal checks and major credit cards accepted. Prepayment required. Mail requests: SASE required.

Register in Probate PO Box 97, 414 W Main, Ellsworth, WI 54011; 715-273-6752; fax: 715-273-6794; 8AM-5PM. ***Probate.***
Probate records free at http://wicourts.gov.

Polk County

Circuit Court PO Box 549, 1005 W Main St, Balsam Lake, WI 54810; 715-485-9299; fax: 715-485-9262; 8:30AM-4:30PM. ***Felony, Misdemeanor, Civil, Eviction, Small Claims.***
Civil Records: Access: Mail, in person, online. Both court and visitors may perform in person searches. Search fee: $5.00 per name per record/file. Required to search: name, years to search. Civil cases indexed by defendant, plaintiff. Civil records go back to 1970s; on computer back to 1992. Mail turnaround time 2-3 days. Civil PAT goes back to 9/1992. PAT results show middle initial; terminal shows DOB month and year only. Civil case lookup free at http://wcca.wicourts.gov/index.xsl.
Criminal Records: Access: Mail, online, in person. Both court and visitors may perform in person searches. Search fee: $5.00 per name. Fee is per record/file. Required to search: name, years to search, DOB. Criminal records go back to 1970s; on computer back to 1992. Mail turnaround time 2-3 days. Criminal PAT goes back to same as civil. PAT results show middle initial; terminal shows DOB month and year only. Access criminal index free at http://wcca.wicourts.gov/index.xsl. Online results show middle initial and DOB most of time; however, sometimes DOB is month and year only on the index.
General Information: Online identifiers in results same as on public terminal. No juvenile, paternity or confidential records released. Will fax documents $1.25 per page. Court makes copy: $1.25 per page. Certification fee: $5.00 per doc. Payee: Clerk of Court. Personal checks accepted; credit cards are not. Prepayment required. Mail requests: SASE required.

Register in Probate 1005 W Main, #500, Balsam Lake, WI 54810; 715-485-9238; fax: 715-485-9275; 8:30AM-4:30PM. ***Probate.*** www.co.polk.wi.us Probate records free at http://wcca.wicourts.gov/index.xsl.

Portage County

Circuit Court (Branches 1, 2 & 3) 1516 Church St, Stevens Point, WI 54481; 715-346-1364; fax: 715-346-1236; 7:30AM-4:30PM. ***Felony, Misdemeanor, Civil, Eviction, Small Claims.***
www.co.portage.wi.us/
Civil Records: Access: Mail, in person, online. Both court and visitors may perform in person searches. Search fee: $5.00 per name. Required to search: name, years to search. Civil cases indexed by number, then defendant, plaintiff. Civil records on computer from 6/91, index cards from 1980, index books from 1900s. Mail turnaround time 10 working days. Civil PAT goes back to 1990. Internet access is upon approval. Request in writing to Data Processing Dept, 1462 Strong Ave, Stevens Point 54481. Explain purpose of record requests.
Criminal Records: Access: Mail, in person, online. Both court and visitors may perform in person searches. Search fee: $5.00 per name. Required to search: name, years to search, address, DOB, SSN, signed release. Criminal records computerized from 6/91, index cards from 1980, index books from 1900s. Mail turnaround time 10 working days. Criminal PAT goes back to same as civil. PAT results show middle initial, DOB. Internet access is upon approval. Request in writing to Data Processing Dept, 1462 Strong Ave, Stevens Point 54481. Explain purpose of record requests. Online results show middle initial and DOB most of time; however, sometimes DOB is month and year only on the index.
General Information: Online identifiers in results same as on public terminal. No expunged records released. Will fax documents to local or toll free line. Court makes copy: $1.25 per page. Certification fee: $5.00 per doc. Payee: Clerk of Court. Business checks accepted. Credit cards accepted. Prepayment required. Mail requests: SASE required.

Register in Probate 1516 Church St, Stevens Point, WI 54481; 715-346-1362; fax: 715-346-1486; 7:30AM-4:30PM. ***Probate*** Probate records free at http://wcca.wicourts.gov/index.xsl.

Price County

Circuit Court Courthouse, 126 Cherry St, Phillips, WI 54555; 715-339-2353; fax: 715-339-5114;

8AM-N, 1-4:30PM. ***Felony, Misdemeanor, Civil, Eviction, Small Claims, Traffic, Family.***
Civil Records: Access: Mail, in person, online. Both court and visitors may perform in person searches. Search fee: $5.00 per name. Required to search: name, years to search. Civil cases indexed by defendant, plaintiff; index on computer from 1997, prior on index books. Mail turnaround time 1-2 days. Civil PAT goes back to 1993. PAT results show name only. Civil case lookup free online at http://wcca.wicourts.gov/index.xsl.
Criminal Records: Access: Mail, online, in person. Both court and visitors may perform in person searches. Search fee: $5.00 per name. Required to search: name, years to search, DOB; also helpful: SSN. Criminal records computerized from 1997, prior on index books. Mail turnaround time 1-2 days. Criminal PAT goes back to same as civil. PAT results show middle initial, DOB. Access criminal index free at http://wcca.wicourts.gov/index.xsl. Online results show middle initial and DOB most of time; however, sometimes DOB is month and year only on the index.
General Information: Online identifiers in results same as on public terminal. No confidential records per statute or order released. Will fax documents to local or toll free line. Court makes copy: $1.25 per page. Self serve: $.15 per page. Certification fee: $5.00 per document. Payee: Clerk of Circuit Court. Personal checks accepted; credit cards are not. Prepayment required. Mail requests: SASE required.

Register in Probate 126 Cherry St, Courthouse Rm 209, Phillips, WI 54555; 715-339-3078; fax: 715-339-3079; 8AM-4:30PM. ***Probate.***
Records free at http://wcca.wicourts.gov/index.xsl.

Racine County

Circuit Court 730 Wisconsin Ave, Racine, WI 53403; 262-636-3333; probate phone: 262-636-3137; criminal fax: 262-636-3341; civil fax: same; 8AM-5PM. ***Felony, Misdemeanor, Civil, Eviction, Small Claims, Probate, Family.***
www.racineco.com/courts/index.aspx
Probate fax- 262-636-3870.
Civil Records: Access: Mail, in person, online. Both court and visitors may perform in person searches. Search fee: $5.00 per name. Required to search: name, years to search, DOB. Civil cases indexed by defendant, plaintiff; index on computer from 1990, index cards from 1980; records kept no long than 20 years. Mail turnaround time 2-3 weeks. Civil PAT goes back to 1994. Public terminal on the 8th Fl. Civil case lookup free online at http://wcca.wicourts.gov/index.xsl.
Criminal Records: Access: Mail, online, in person. Both court and visitors may perform in person searches. Search fee: $5.00 per name. Required to search: name, years to search, DOB. Criminal records computerized from 1990, index cards from 1970, archives prior to 1970. Mail turnaround time 2-3 weeks. Criminal PAT goes back to 1994. PAT results show middle initial, DOB. Public terminal on 8th Fl. Access criminal index free at http://wcca.wicourts.gov/index.xsl. Online results show middle initial and DOB most of time; however, sometimes DOB is month and year only on the index.
General Information: Online identifiers in results same as on public terminal. No adoption, juvenile, paternity or mental commitment records released. Will fax documents to local or toll free line. Court makes copy: $1.25 per page. Self serve: same. Certification fee: $5.00 per document. Payee: Clerk of Circuit Court. Personal checks accepted; credit cards are not. Prepayment required. Mail requests: SASE required.

Register in Probate 730 Wisconsin Ave, Racine, WI 53403; 262-636-3137; fax: 262-636-3870; 8AM-5PM. ***Probate.*** Probate records free at http://wcca.wicourts.gov/index.xsl.

Richland County

Circuit Court PO Box 655, 181 W Seminary St, Richland Center, WI 53581; 608-647-3956; fax: 608-647-3911; 8:30AM-4:30PM. ***Felony, Misdemeanor, Civil, Eviction, Small Claims.***
The search fee includes search of both civil and criminal indexes.
Civil Records: Access: Mail, in person, online. Both court and visitors may perform in person searches. Search fee: $5.00 per name. Required to search: name, years to search. Civil cases indexed by defendant, plaintiff. Civil index on cards from 1982, index books from 1972, archives prior to 1972, on computer back to 1993. Mail turnaround time within 2 days. Civil PAT goes back to 1993. Civil case lookup free at http://wcca.wicourts.gov/index.xsl.
Criminal Records: Access: Mail, online, in person. Both court and visitors may perform in person searches. Search fee: $5.00 per name. Required to search: name, years to search, DOB. Criminal records indexed on cards from 1982, index books from 1972, archives prior to 1972, on computer back t0 1993. Mail turnaround time 1 week. Criminal PAT goes back to same as civil. PAT results show middle initial, DOB. Access criminal index free at http://wcca.wicourts.gov/index.xsl. Online results show middle initial and DOB most of time; however, sometimes DOB is month and year only on the index.
General Information: Online identifiers in results same as on public terminal. No juvenile or paternity records released. Will fax documents to local or toll-free number. Court makes copy: $1.25 per page. Certification fee: $5.00 per doc. Payee: Clerk of Circuit Court. No personal out-of-state checks accepted. No credit cards accepted - may accept in 2009. Prepayment required. Mail requests: SASE required.

Register in Probate PO Box 427, 181 W Seminary St, Richland Center, WI 53581; 608-647-2626; fax: 608-647-3911; 8:30AM-N, 1-4:30PM. ***Probate.*** Probate records free online at http://wcca.wicourts.gov/index.xsl.

Rock County

Circuit Court 51 S Main, Janesville, WI 53545; 608-743-2200; criminal phone: 608-743-2211; civil: 608-743-2210; fax: 608-743-2223; 8AM-5PM. ***Felony, Misdemeanor, Civil, Eviction, Small Claims.***
www.co.rock.wi.us/Dept/CircuitCourt/CircuitCourt.htm
Civil Records: Access: Mail, in person, online. Both court and visitors may perform in person searches. Search fee: $5.00 per name. Required to search: name, years to search. Civil cases indexed by defendant, plaintiff; index on computer from 6/93, on index cards from 6/91, index books from 1940, archives prior to 1940. Mail turnaround time 2-3 days. Civil PAT goes back to 1993. Civil case lookup free at http://wcca.wicourts.gov/index.xsl.
Criminal Records: Access: Mail, online, in person. Both court and visitors may perform in person searches. Search fee: $5.00 per name. Required to search: name, years to search, DOB. Criminal records computerized from 6/93, on index cards from 6/91, index books from 1940, archives prior to 1940. Mail turnaround time 2-3 days. Criminal PAT goes back to same as civil. PAT results show middle initial, DOB. Access criminal index free at http://wcca.wicourts.gov/index.xsl. Online results show middle initial and DOB most of time; however, sometimes DOB is month and year only on the index.
General Information: Online identifiers in results same as on public terminal. No juvenile, paternity or sealed records released. Will fax documents to local or toll-free number. Court makes copy: $1.25 per page. Certification fee: $5.00. Payee: Clerk of Court. Personal checks and major credit cards accepted. Prepayment required. Mail requests: SASE required.

Register in Probate 51 S Main, Janesville, WI 53545; 608-757-5635; fax: 608-757-5769; 8AM-5PM. ***Probate.*** Probate records free at http://wcca.wicourts.gov/index.xsl.

Rusk County

Circuit Court 311 Miner Ave E, #L350, Attn: Clerk of Circuit Court, Ladysmith, WI 54848; 715-532-2108; probate phone: 715-532-2147; fax: 715-532-2110; 8AM-4:30PM. ***Felony, Misdemeanor, Civil, Small Claims.***
Probate fax- 715-532-2266
Civil Records: Access: Mail, phone, fax, in person, online. Both court and visitors may perform in person searches. Search fee: $5.00 per name, no charge for persons performing their own search. Required to search: name, years to search. Civil cases indexed by defendant, plaintiff; index on computer from 1992, on index cards from 1978, index books from 1901. Note: Phone requests are accepted if the case number is known. Mail turnaround time 5 days. Civil PAT goes back to 1992. Civil case lookup free at http://wcca.wicourts.gov/index.xsl.
Criminal Records: Access: Mail, online, in person, online. Both court and visitors may perform in person searches. Search fee: $5.00 per name, no charge for persons performing their own search. Required to search: name, years to search, DOB. Criminal records computerized from 1992, on index cards from 1978, index books from 1901. Note: Phone requests are accepted if the case number is known. Mail turnaround time 5 days. Criminal PAT goes back to same as civil. PAT results show middle initial, DOB. Access criminal index free at http://wcca.wicourts.gov/index.xsl. Online results show middle initial and DOB most of time; however, sometimes DOB is month and year only on the index.
General Information: Online identifiers in results same as on public terminal. No juvenile or paternity records released. Will fax documents $1.25 per page. Court makes copy: $1.25 per page. Certification fee: $5.00 per document. Payee: Clerk of Court. Personal checks accepted. Credit card payments accepted via GPS. Prepayment required. Mail requests: SASE required.

Register in Probate 311 E Miner Ave, #C-330, Ladysmith, WI 54848; 715-532-2147; fax: 715-532-2266; 8AM-4:30PM. ***Probate.*** Probate records free at http://wcca.wicourts.gov/index.xsl.

Sauk County

Circuit Court 515 Oak St, Baraboo, WI 53913; 608-355-3287; fax: 608-355-3480; 8AM-4:30PM. ***Felony, Misdemeanor, Civil, Eviction, Small Claims.***
Civil Records: Access: Mail, in person, online. Both court and visitors may perform in person searches. Search fee: $5.00 per name per index. Required to search: name, years to search. Civil cases indexed by defendant, plaintiff; index on computer from 1990, index cards from 1980, index books from 1967. Mail turnaround time 2-3 days. Civil PAT goes back to 1993. PAT results show middle initial, DOB. Civil lookup free at http://wcca.wicourts.gov/index.xsl.
Criminal Records: Access: Mail, online, in person. Both court and visitors may perform in person searches. Search fee: $5.00 per name per index. Required to search: name, years to search. Criminal records computerized from 1990, index cards from 1980, index books from 1967. Mail turnaround time 2-3 days. Criminal PAT goes back to same as civil. PAT results show middle initial, DOB. Access criminal index free at http://wcca.wicourts.gov/index.xsl. Online results show middle initial and DOB most of time; however, sometimes DOB is month and year only on the index.
General Information: Online identifiers in results same as on public terminal. No paternity, juvenile records released. Fee to fax out file $5.00 1st page, $1.00 each add'l plus tax. Court makes copy: $1.25 per page. Certification fee: $5.00 per doc. Payee: Clerk of Court. Personal checks accepted. Visa/MC accepted. Prepayment required. Mail requests: SASE required.

Register in Probate 515 Oak St, Baraboo, WI 53913; 608-355-3226; fax: 608-355-4436; 8AM-4:30PM. ***Probate.***
www.co.sauk.wi.us/dept/reginprobate/index.html
Records free at http://wcca.wicourts.gov/index.xsl.

Sawyer County

Circuit Court PO Box 508, Hayward, WI 54843; 715-634-4887; fax: 715-638-3297; 8AM-4PM. ***Felony, Misdemeanor, Civil, Eviction, Small Claims.***
Civil Records: Access: Mail, in person, online. Both court and visitors may perform in person searches. Search fee: $5.00 per name. Required to search:

name, years to search. Civil cases indexed by defendant, plaintiff. Civil index on cards from 7/85, prior on books. Mail turnaround time 3 days. Civil PAT goes back to 4/1993. PAT civil results show middle initial. Civil case lookup free online at http://wcca.wicourts.gov/index.xsl.
Criminal Records: Access: Mail, online, in person. Both court and visitors may perform in person searches. Search fee: $5.00 per name. Required to search: name, years to search. Criminal records indexed on cards from 7/85, prior on books. Mail turnaround time 3 days. Criminal PAT goes back to same as civil. PAT results show middle initial; DOB shown in results is month and year only. Access criminal index free at http://wcca.wicourts.gov/index.xsl. Online results show middle initial and DOB most of time; however, sometimes DOB is month and year only on the index.
General Information: Online identifiers in results same as on public terminal. No juvenile or paternity records released. Will fax documents $1.00 plus $.25 per page. Court makes copy: $1.25 per page. Certification fee: $5.00 per document. Payee: Clerk of Court. Personal checks accepted; credit cards are not. Prepayment required. Mail requests: SASE required.

Register in Probate PO Box 447, 10610 Main St, Hayward, WI 54843; 715-634-7519; fax: 715-638-3297; 8AM-4PM. ***Probate.*** Probate records free at http://wcca.wicourts.gov/index.xsl.

Shawano County

Circuit Court 311 N Main, Rm 206, Shawano, WI 54166; 715-526-9347; probate phone: 715-526-8631; fax: 715-526-4915; 8AM-4:30PM. ***Felony, Misdemeanor, Civil, Eviction, Small Claims.***
www.co.shawano.wi.us
Civil Records: Access: Fax, mail, online, in person. Both court and visitors may perform in person searches. Search fee: $5.00 per name. Required to search: name, years to search. Civil cases indexed by defendant, plaintiff; index on computer from 1993, on index books from 1930s, prior in archives. Mail turnaround time 10-20 days. Civil PAT goes back to 3/1993. PAT results show name, month and year of birth. Civil case lookup free at http://wcca.wicourts.gov/index.xsl.
Criminal Records: Access: Fax, mail, online, in person. Both court and visitors may perform in person searches. Search fee: $5.00 per name. Required to search: name, years to search, DOB. Criminal records computerized from 1993, on index books from 1930s, prior in archives. Mail turnaround time 10-20 days. Criminal PAT goes back to same as civil. PAT results show middle initial, DOB. Access criminal index free at http://wcca.wicourts.gov/index.xsl. Online results show middle initial and DOB most of time; however, sometimes DOB is month and year only on the index.
General Information: Online identifiers in results same as on public terminal. No juvenile, closed files or mental records released. Will fax documents $1.25 per page, add $2.50 for long distance. Court makes copy: $1.25 per page. Certification fee: $5.00. Payee: Clerk of Court. Personal checks accepted; credit cards are not. Prepayment required. Mail requests: SASE required.

Register in Probate 311 N Main, Rm 203, Shawano, WI 54166; 715-526-8631; fax: 715-526-8622; 8AM-4:30PM. ***Probate.***
www.co.shawano.wi.us
This is also the location of Menominee County Probate. Tribal probate records are not housed here; tribal records are at Keshena (Menominee Tribal Court). Also, probate records free at http://wcca.wicourts.gov/index.xsl.

Sheboygan County

Circuit Court 615 N 6th St, Sheboygan, WI 53081; 920-459-3068; criminal fax: 920-459-3921; civil fax: same; 8AM-5PM. ***Felony, Misdemeanor, Civil, Eviction, Small Claims, Family, Traffic, Ordinance.***
www.co.sheboygan.wi.us/html/d_crtclrk.html
Civil Records: Access: Mail, in person, online. Only the court performs in person searches; visitors may not. Search fee: $5.00 per case. Required to search: name, years to search; also helpful: address. Civil cases indexed by defendant, plaintiff; index on computer since 1992; prior records on index cards from 1960, index books from 1860s, archives prior to 1971. Mail turnaround time 2-3 days. Civil PAT goes back to 1992. PAT civil results show middle initial. Civil case lookup free online at http://wcca.wicourts.gov/index.xsl.
Criminal Records: Access: Mail, online, in person. Only the court performs in person searches; visitors may not. Search fee: $5.00 per case. Required to search: name, years to search, DOB; also helpful: address. Criminal records on computer since 1992; prior records on index cards from 1960, index books from 1860s, archives prior to 1971. Mail turnaround time 2-3 days. Criminal PAT available. PAT results show middle initial, DOB. Access statewide criminal index free at http://wcca.wicourts.gov/index.xsl. Online results show middle initial and DOB most of time; however, sometimes DOB is month and year only on the index.
General Information: Online identifiers in results same as on public terminal. No juvenile or pre-adjudication paternity records released. Will fax documents for $3.00 prepaid. Court makes copy: $1.25 per page. Certification fee: $5.00 per document. Payee: Clerk of Circuit Court. Personal checks accepted; credit cards are not. Prepayment required. Mail requests: SASE required.

Register in Probate 615 N 6th St, Sheboygan, WI 53081; 920-459-3050, 459-3051; fax: 920-459-0541; 8AM-5PM. ***Probate.***
There is a $4.00 search fee. Probate records free at http://wcca.wicourts.gov/index.xsl.

St. Croix County

Circuit Court 1101 Carmichael Rd, Hudson, WI 54016; 715-386-4630; criminal phone: 715-386-4631; civil phone: 715-386-4633; probate phone: 715-386-4619; fax: 715-381-4396; 8AM-5PM. ***Felony, Misdemeanor, Civil, Eviction, Small Claims.***
Civil Records: Access: Mail, in person, online. Both court and visitors may perform in person searches. Search fee: $5.00 per name. Required to search: name, years to search. Civil cases indexed by defendant, plaintiff; index on computer from 10/92, on index cards from 1982, index books from 1965. Mail turnaround time within 10 days. Civil PAT goes back to 1992. PAT results show name, DOB. Civil case lookup free online at http://wcca.wicourts.gov/index.xsl.
Criminal Records: Access: Mail, online, in person. Both court and visitors may perform in person searches. Search fee: $5.00 per name. Required to search: name, years to search, DOB. Criminal records computerized from 10/92, on index cards from 1982, index books from 1900s. Mail turnaround time 5-10 days. Criminal PAT goes back to same as civil. PAT results show middle initial, DOB. Access criminal index free online at http://wcca.wicourts.gov/index.xsl. Online results show name, DOB. Online search index results gives DOB half the time, then half only have month/year.
General Information: Online identifiers in results same as on public terminal. No juvenile forfeitures, paternity, some case specific documents or sealed records released. Will fax documents $1.25 per page. Court makes copy: $1.25 per page. Certification fee: $5.00. Payee: Clerk of Court. Personal checks and major credit cards accepted. Prepayment required. Mail requests: SASE required.

Register in Probate 1101 Carmichael Rd, Rm 2242, Hudson, WI 54016; 715-386-4618; fax: 715-381-4318; 8AM-5PM. ***Probate.*** Probate records free at http://wcca.wicourts.gov/index.xsl.

Taylor County

Circuit Court 224 S 2nd St, Medford, WI 54451-1811; 715-748-1425; probate phone: 715-748-1435; criminal fax: 715-748-2465; civil fax: same; 8:30AM-4:30PM. ***Felony, Misdemeanor, Civil, Eviction, Small Claims, Ordinance, Family, Traffic.***
Civil Records: Access: Mail, in person, online. Both court and visitors may perform in person searches. Search fee: $5.00 per name. Required to search: name, years to search. Civil cases indexed by defendant, plaintiff; index on computer from 1989; prior records index books from 1917. Mail turnaround time 1-2 days. Civil PAT goes back to 1989. PAT results show middle initial, DOB. Civil case lookup free at http://wcca.wicourts.gov/index.xsl.
Criminal Records: Access: Mail, online, in person. Both court and visitors may perform in person searches. Search fee: $5.00 per name. Required to search: name, years to search, DOB. Criminal records computerized from 1989; prior records index books from 1917. Mail turnaround time 1-2 days. Criminal PAT goes back to same as civil. PAT results show middle initial, DOB. Access criminal index free at http://wcca.wicourts.gov/index.xsl. Online results show middle initial and DOB most of time; however, sometimes DOB is month and year only on the index.
General Information: Online identifiers in results same as on public terminal. No sealed records released. Will fax documents to local or toll free line. Court makes copy: $1.25 per page. Certification fee: $5.00 per doc. Payee: Clerk of Circuit Court. Personal checks accepted. Visa/MC accepted. Prepayment required. Mail requests: SASE required.

Register in Probate 224 S 2nd, Medford, WI 54451; 715-748-1435; fax: 715-748-1524; 8:30AM-4:30PM. ***Probate.*** Probate records free at http://wcca.wicourts.gov/index.xsl.

Trempealeau County

Circuit Court PO Box 67, 36245 Main St, Whitehall, WI 54773; 715-538-2311; fax: 715-538-4400; 8AM-4:30PM. ***Felony, Misdemeanor, Civil, Eviction, Small Claims.***
Civil Records: Access: Mail, in person, online. Both court and visitors may perform in person searches. Search fee: $5.00 per name. Required to search: name, years to search. Civil cases indexed by defendant, plaintiff; index on computer from 1993, on index cards from 1987, index books from 1940, archives prior to 1940. Mail turnaround time 2-3 days. Civil PAT goes back to 1994. PAT results show name, DOB. Civil case lookup free online at http://wcca.wicourts.gov/index.xsl.
Criminal Records: Access: Mail, online, in person. Both court and visitors may perform in person searches. Search fee: $5.00 per name. Required to search: name, years to search, DOB. Criminal records computerized from 1993, on index cards from 1987, index books from 1940, archives prior to 1940. Note: All mail requests must be in writing. Mail turnaround time 2-3 days. Criminal PAT goes back to same as civil. PAT results show middle initial, DOB. Access criminal index free at http://wcca.wicourts.gov/index.xsl. Online results show name, DOB. Online search index results gives DOB half the time, then half only have month/year.
General Information: Online identifiers in results same as on public terminal. No juvenile, paternity or child support records released. Will fax documents $2.00 per page. Court makes copy: $1.25 per page. Certification fee: $5.00 per doc. Payee: Clerk of Circuit Court. Personal checks accepted via GPS, 888-604-7888. No credit cards accepted. Prepayment required. Mail requests: SASE required.

Register in Probate 36245 Main St, PO Box 67, Whitehall, WI 54773; 715-538-2311 X238; fax: 715-538-4123; 8AM-4:30PM. ***Probate.***
Records free at http://wcca.wicourts.gov/index.xsl.

Vernon County

Circuit Court PO Box 426, Viroqua, WI 54665; 608-637-5340; criminal phone: 608-637-5338; civil phone: 608-637-5338; criminal fax: 608-637-5554; civil fax: same; 8:30AM-4:30PM. ***Felony, Misdemeanor, Civil, Eviction, Small Claims.***
www.vernoncounty.org/courts/index.htm
Civil Records: Access: Phone, fax, mail, online, in person. Both court and visitors may perform in

person searches. Search fee: $5.00 per name. Required to search: name, years to search, DOB. Civil cases indexed by defendant, plaintiff; index on computer back to 1993; on index books & cards 1950 to 1992. Mail turnaround time 2-3 days. Civil PAT goes back to 1993. Civil case lookup free online at http://wcca.wicourts.gov/index.xsl.
Criminal Records: Access: Phone, fax, mail, online, in person. Both court and visitors may perform in person searches. Search fee: $5.00 per name. Required to search: name, years to search; also helpful: DOB. Criminal records computerized from 1993; on index books & cards 1950 to 1992. Mail turnaround time 2-3 days. Criminal PAT goes back to same as civil. PAT results show middle initial, DOB. Access criminal index free at http://wcca.wicourts.gov/index.xsl. Online results show middle initial and DOB most of time; however, sometimes DOB is month and year only on the index.
General Information: Online identifiers in results same as on public terminal. No paternity or juvenile records released. Will fax documents. Court makes copy: $1.25 per page. Self serve: same. Certification fee: $5.00 per document. Payee: Clerk of Court. Personal checks and major credit cards accepted. Prepayment required. Will bill to attorneys credit agencies. Mail requests: SASE required.

Register in Probate PO Box 448, 400 Courthouse Sq, Viroqua, WI 54665; 608-637-5347; fax: 608-637-5554; 8:30AM-4:30PM. ***Probate.*** Probate records free at http://wcca.wicourts.gov/index.xsl.

Vilas County

Circuit Court 330 Court St, Eagle River, WI 54521; 715-479-3632; criminal phone: 715-479-3633; civil phone: same; fax: 715-479-3740; 8AM-4PM. ***Felony, Misdemeanor, Civil, Eviction, Small Claims.*** http://co.vilas.wi.us/
Civil Records: Access: Mail, in person, online. Both court and visitors may perform in person searches. Search fee: $5.00 per name. Required to search: name, years to search. Civil records on computer back to 1992, index cards from 1978, index books from 1900s. Mail turnaround time 2 weeks. Civil PAT goes back to 1992. PAT results show middle initial, DOB. Civil case lookup free online at http://wcca.wicourts.gov/index.xsl.
Criminal Records: Access: Mail, online, in person. Both court and visitors may perform in person searches. Search fee: $5.00 per name. Required to search: name, years to search, DOB. Criminal records computerized from 1992; index cards from 1978, index books from 1900s. Mail turnaround time 2 weeks. Criminal PAT goes back to same as civil. PAT results show middle initial, DOB. Access criminal index free online at http://wcca.wicourts.gov/index.xsl. Online results show middle initial and DOB most of time; however, sometimes DOB is month and year only on the index.
General Information: Online identifiers in results same as on public terminal. No paternity records released. Fee to fax out file $1.25 per page. Court makes copy: $1.25 per page. Self serve: $.25 per page. Certification fee: $5.00. Payee: Clerk of Circuit Court. Personal checks accepted; credit cards are not. Prepayment required. Mail requests: SASE required.

Register in Probate 330 Court St, Eagle River, WI 54521; 715-479-3642; fax: 715-479-3740; 8AM-4PM. ***Probate.*** Probate records free at http://wcca.wicourts.gov/index.xsl.

Walworth County

Circuit Court PO Box 1001, 1800 County Rd NN, Elkhorn, WI 53121-1001; 262-741-7012; criminal fax: 262-741-7050; civil fax: same; 8AM-5PM. ***Felony, Misdemeanor, Civil, Eviction, Small Claims.*** www.co.walworth.wi.us
Alternative fax number- 262-741-7002.
Civil Records: Access: Mail, in person, online. Both court and visitors may perform in person searches. Search fee: $5.00 per name. Required to search: name. Civil cases indexed by defendant, plaintiff; index on computer from 1989, older cases on index cards. Mail turnaround time 1-5 days. Civil PAT goes back to 1989. PAT results show middle initial, DOB. Civil case lookup free online at http://wcca.wicourts.gov/index.xsl.
Criminal Records: Access: Mail, in person, online. Both court and visitors may perform in person searches. Search fee: $5.00 per name. Required to search: name, years to search; also helpful- DOB. Criminal records computerized from 1989, older cases on index cards. Mail turnaround time 1-5 days. Criminal PAT goes back to same as civil. PAT results show middle initial, DOB. Access criminal index free at http://wcca.wicourts.gov/index.xsl. Online results show middle initial and DOB most of time; however, sometimes DOB is month and year only on the index.
General Information: Online identifiers in results same as on public terminal. No sealed records released. Will fax documents $1.25 per page. Court makes copy: $1.25 per page. Certification fee: $5.00 per document. Payee: Clerk of Courts. Business checks accepted. Credit cards accepted in person only. Prepayment required. Mail requests: SASE required.

Register in Probate PO Box 1001, 1800 County Rd NN, Elkhorn, WI 53121; 262-741-7014; fax: 262-741-7002; 8AM-5PM. ***Probate.*** Records free at http://wcca.wicourts.gov/index.xsl.

Washburn County

Circuit Court PO Box 339, Shell Lake, WI 54871; 715-468-4677; criminal fax: 715-468-4678; civil fax: same; 8AM-4:30PM. ***Felony, Misdemeanor, Civil, Eviction, Small Claims.***
Civil Records: Access: Mail, in person, online. Both court and visitors may perform in person searches. Search fee: $5.00 per name. Required to search: name, years to search. Civil cases indexed by defendant, plaintiff; index on computer since 1993 (civil money judgments back to 1/1/90); on index books from 1883. Mail turnaround time 2-3 days. Civil PAT goes back to 1993. PAT civil results show middle initial. Civil case lookup free online at http://wcca.wicourts.gov/index.xsl.
Criminal Records: Access: Mail, online, in person. Both court and visitors may perform in person searches. Search fee: $5.00 per name. Required to search: name, years to search; also helpful: DOB. Criminal records on computer since 1993; on index books from 1883. Mail turnaround time 2-3 days. Criminal PAT goes back to same as civil. PAT results show middle initial, DOB. Access criminal index free at http://wcca.wicourts.gov/index.xsl. Online results show middle initial and DOB most of time; however, sometimes DOB is month and year only on the index.
General Information: Online identifiers in results same as on public terminal. No sealed records released. Will fax documents to local or toll free line. Court makes copy: $1.25 per page. Certification fee: $5.00 per document. Payee: Clerk of Court. Personal checks accepted; credit cards are not. Prepayment required. Mail requests: SASE required.

Register in Probate PO Box 316, 10 Fourth Ave, Shell Lake, WI 54871; 715-468-4688; fax: 715-468-4678; 8AM-N, 1-4:30PM. ***Probate.*** Records free at http://wcca.wicourts.gov/index.xsl.

Washington County

Circuit Court PO Box 1986, West Bend, WI 53095-7986; 262-335-4341; fax: 262-335-4776; 8AM-4:30PM. ***Felony, Misdemeanor, Civil, Eviction, Small Claims.*** www.co.washington.wi.us/washington/department.jsp?dept=COC
Civil Records: Access: Mail, fax, online, in person. Both court and visitors may perform in person searches. Search fee: $5.00 per name. Required to search: name, years to search; also helpful: address. Civil cases indexed by defendant, plaintiff; index on computer from 1986, index cards from 1976, index books from 1836. Mail turnaround time 1 week. Civil PAT goes back to 1986. Civil case lookup free online at http://wcca.wicourts.gov/index.xsl.
Criminal Records: Access: Mail, fax, online, in person. Both court and visitors may perform in person searches. Search fee: $5.00 per name. Required to search: name, years to search, DOB; also helpful: address. Criminal records computerized from 1986, index cards from 1976, index books from 1836. Mail turnaround time 1 week. Criminal PAT goes back to same as civil. PAT results show middle initial, DOB. Access criminal index free at http://wcca.wicourts.gov/index.xsl. Online results show middle initial and DOB most of time; however, sometimes DOB is month and year only on the index.
General Information: Online identifiers in results same as on public terminal. No paternity records released prior to adjudication. Will fax documents to local or toll free line. Court makes copy: $1.25 per page. Certification fee: $5.00. Payee: Clerk of Court. Personal checks and major credit cards accepted. Service fee of 3% if credit card is used. Prepayment required. Mail requests: SASE required.

Register in Probate PO Box 82, 432 E Washington St, #3135, West Bend, WI 53095-0082; 262-335-4334; fax: 262-306-2224; 8AM-4:30PM. ***Probate.*** Probate records free at http://wcca.wicourts.gov/index.xsl.

Waukesha County

Circuit Court Clerk PO Box 1627, 515 W Moreland Blvd, Waukesha, WI 53188; criminal phone: 262-548-7484; civil phone: 262-548-7525; criminal fax: 262-896-8228; civil fax: 262-548-7546; 8AM-4:30PM. ***Felony, Misdemeanor, Civil, Eviction, Family, Small Claims, Traffic.*** http://circuitcourts.waukeshacounty.gov
Civil Records: Access: Mail, in person, online. Both court and visitors may perform in person searches. Search fee: $5.00 per name. Required to search: name, years to search. Civil cases indexed by defendant, plaintiff; index on computer back to 1994. Mail turnaround time 2-3 days. Civil PAT goes back to 1994. PAT results show name only. Civil lookup free at http://wcca.wicourts.gov/index.xsl.
Criminal Records: Access: Mail, online, in person. Both court and visitors may perform in person searches. Search fee: $5.00 per name. Required to search: name, years to search, DOB. Criminal records indexed on computer back to 1994; on microfilm back to 1980; index cards to 1940. Mail turnaround time 2-3 days. Criminal PAT goes back to 1996. PAT results show middle initial, DOB. Access criminal index free at http://wcca.wicourts.gov/index.xsl. Online results show middle initial and DOB most of time; however, sometimes DOB is month and year only on the index.
General Information: Online identifiers in results same as on public terminal. No paternity, mental commitment records released. Fee to fax out file $3.00 each plus $1.25 per page. Court makes copy: $1.25 per page. Certification fee: $5.00 per document. Payee: Clerk of Circuit Court. Personal checks accepted. Accepts credit cards in person only. Prepayment required. Mail requests: SASE required for civil and family records.

Register in Probate 515 W Moreland, C380, Waukesha, WI 53188; 262-548-7468; fax: 262-896-8397; 8AM-4:30PM. ***Probate.*** Probate records free at http://wcca.wicourts.gov/index.xsl.

Waupaca County

Circuit Court 811 Harding St, Waupaca, WI 54981; 715-258-6460; criminal fax: 715-258-6497; civil fax: same; 8AM-4PM. ***Felony, Misdemeanor, Civil, Eviction, Small Claims.***
This court clerk states that, by Wisconsin Law, she does not have to respond to your information requests.
Civil Records: Access: Mail, in person, online. Both court and visitors may perform in person searches. Search fee: $5.00 per name. Required to search: name, years to search. Civil cases indexed by defendant, plaintiff; index on computer from 1992. Mail turnaround time 3-4 days. Public use terminal available. Civil case lookup free online at http://wcca.wicourts.gov/index.xsl.
Criminal Records: Access: Mail, online, in person. Both court and visitors may perform in person searches. Search fee: $5.00 per name. Required to search: name, years to search. Criminal records computerized from 1992. Mail turnaround time 3-4

days. Public use terminal available. PAT results show middle initial, DOB. Access criminal index free at http://wcca.wicourts.gov/index.xsl. Online results show middle initial and DOB most of time; however, sometimes DOB is month and year only on the index.
General Information: Online identifiers in results same as on public terminal. No juvenile, JO, paternity excluding past judgments released. Court makes copy: $1.25 per page. Computer document copy fee $.50 per page. Certification fee: $5.00 per document. Payee: Clerk of Court. Business check and personal in-state check accepted. No credit cards accepted. Prepayment required. Mail requests: SASE required.

Register in Probate 811 Harding St, Waupaca, WI 54981; 715-258-6429; probate: 715-258-6431 Dep Reg.; fax: 715-258-6440; 8AM-4PM. ***Probate.*** www.co.waupaca.wi.us/probate/index.htm Probate records free at http://wcca.wicourts.gov/index.xsl.

Waushara County

Circuit Court PO Box 507, Wautoma, WI 54982; 920-787-0441; fax: 920-787-0481; 8AM-4:30PM. ***Felony, Misdemeanor, Civil, Eviction, Small Claims.*** www.co.waushara.wi.us/circuit_court.htm
Civil Records: Access: Mail, fax, online, in person. Both court and visitors may perform in person searches. Search fee: $5.00 per name. fee only if court does search. Required to search: name, years to search. Civil cases indexed by defendant. Civil records on computer from 1992, index cards to 1978, index books prior. Mail turnaround time 1 day. Civil PAT available. Civil court record index online at http://wcca.wicourts.gov/index.xsl. Note this is not the official index; the only official index is located at the Clerk's office.
Criminal Records: Access: Mail, fax, online, in person. Both court and visitors may perform in person searches. Search fee: $5.00 per name. Fee applies if court does search. Required to search: name, years to search, DOB. Criminal records computerized from 1993, prior on cards and books. Mail turnaround time 1 day. Criminal PAT available. PAT results show middle initial, DOB. Access criminal index at http://wcca.wicourts.gov/index.xsl. Online results show middle initial and DOB most of time; however, sometimes DOB is month and year only on the index.
General Information: Online identifiers in results same as on public terminal. Will fax documents if prepaid. Court makes copy: $1.25 per page. Certification fee: $5.00. Payee: Clerk of Court. Personal in-state checks accepted; money orders for out of state requests. No credit cards accepted. Prepayment required. Mail requests: SASE required.

Register in Probate PO Box 508, 209 S St. Marie St, County Courthouse, Wautoma, WI 54982; 920-787-0448; fax: 920-787-0481; 8AM-4:30PM. ***Probate.*** Free at http://wcca.wicourts.gov/index.xsl.

Winnebago County

Circuit Court PO Box 2808, Oshkosh, WI 54903-2808; 920-236-4848; criminal phone: 920-236-4855; civil phone: 920-236-4848; probate phone: 920-236-4833; fax: 920-424-7780; 8AM-4:30PM. ***Felony, Misdemeanor, Civil, Eviction, Small Claims.*** www.co.winnebago.wi.us/clerkofcourts/
Civil Records: Access: Mail, fax, online, in person. Both court and visitors may perform in person searches. Search fee: $5.00 per name. Required to search: name, years to search. Civil cases indexed by defendant, plaintiff. Civil records are on computer since 1992, prior on books and cards to 1970. Historical Society has records to 1938. Mail turnaround time 1 week. Civil PAT goes back to 1992. Civil case lookup free online at http://wcca.wicourts.gov/index.xsl.
Criminal Records: Access: Mail, fax, online, in person. Both court and visitors may perform in person searches. Search fee: $5.00 per name. Required to search: full name, years to search, DOB. Criminal records are on computer since 1990, prior on books and cards. organized since 1938. Mail turnaround time 1 week. Criminal PAT goes back to 1990. PAT results show middle initial, DOB. Access criminal index free at http://wcca.wicourts.gov/index.xsl. Online results show middle initial and DOB most of time; however, sometimes DOB is month and year only on the index.
General Information: Online identifiers in results same as on public terminal. No juvenile, paternity, financial records released. Fee to fax out file $1.25 per page. Court makes copy: $1.25 per page. Certification fee: $5.00. Payee: Clerk of Courts. Personal checks accepted; credit cards are not. Prepayment required.

Register in Probate PO Box 2808, 415 Jackson St, Oshkosh, WI 54903-2808; 920-236-4833; fax: 920-424-7536; 8AM-N, 1-4:30PM. ***Probate.*** www.co.winnebago.wi.us/Probate/ProbateIndex.htm There is a $4.00 search fee. Probate records free at http://wcca.wicourts.gov/index.xsl.

Wood County

Circuit Court 400 Market St, PO Box 8095, Wisconsin Rapids, WI 54494-958095; 715-421-8490; civil phone: 715-421-8807; fax: 715-421-8691; 8AM-4:30PM. ***Felony, Misdemeanor, Civil, Eviction, Small Claims.***
Civil Records: Access: Mail, in person, online. Both court and visitors may perform in person searches. Search fee: $5.00 per name. Required to search: name, years to search. Civil cases indexed by defendant, plaintiff; index on computer from 1983, microfiche from 1856-1980s. Mail turnaround time within 10 days. Civil PAT goes back to 1983. PAT civil results show middle initial. Civil case lookup free online at http://wcca.wicourts.gov/index.xsl.
Criminal Records: Access: Mail, online, in person. Both court and visitors may perform in person searches. Search fee: $5.00 per name. Required to search: name, years to search, DOB. Criminal records computerized from 1980; manual search required for pre-1980 records. Mail turnaround time within 10 days. Criminal PAT goes back to same as civil. PAT results show middle initial, DOB. Access criminal index free at http://wcca.wicourts.gov/index.xsl. Online results show middle initial and DOB most of time; however, sometimes DOB is month and year only on the index.
General Information: Online identifiers in results same as on public terminal. No paternity or sealed records released. Will fax documents to local or toll free line. Court makes copy: $1.25 per page. Certification fee: $5.00. Payee: Clerk of Court. Personal checks accepted. Credit card paying is managed through a 3rd party vendor. Prepayment required. Mail requests: SASE required.

Register in Probate PO Box 8095, 400 Market St, County Courthouse, Wisconsin Rapids, WI 54495-8095; 715-421-8523; fax: 715-421-8896; 8AM-4:30PM. ***Probate.***
Court also holds guardianships, juveniles, mental and adoption records. Probate records free at http://wcca.wicourts.gov/index.xsl.

Wisconsin Recording Offices

ORGANIZATION: 72 counties, 72 recording offices. The recording officers are the Register of Deeds for real estate and Clerk of Court for state tax liens. County Clerks hold marriage records and state tax liens. Wisconsin is in the Central Time Zone.

REAL ESTATE RECORDS: Registers will not perform real estate searches. Counties do not have assessors; assessor telephone numbers listed here are for local municipalities or for property listing agencies. Real estate record copy fee is $2.00 for the first page and $1.00 for each additional page. This is true for other records. Certification fee is usually $1.00 per document but some offices charge $3.00 for the first cert page. The Treasurer maintains property tax records.

UCC RECORDS: Financing statements are filed at the state level except for real estate related collateral which are filed with the Register of Deeds. Prior to July, 2001, consumer goods and farm collateral were also filed at the Register of Deeds and these older records can be searched there. Most recording offices will no longer perform UCC searches; if they do, use search request form UCC-11 and search fee is usually $15.00 per debtor name.

TAX LIEN RECORDS: Federal tax liens on personal property of businesses are filed with the Secretary of State. Only federal tax liens on real estate are filed with the county Register of Deeds. State tax liens are filed with the Clerk of Court, and at the State Treasurer at the State Department of Revenue. Not all Registers will perform federal tax lien searches. Tax lien search fees here vary, but copy fee is $2.00 1st page and $1.00 each additional page.

OTHER LIENS: Judgment, mechanics, breeders.

ONLINE ACCESS: A number of cities and a few counties offer online access to assessor and property records. The Wisconsin Register of Deeds Association website at www.wrdaonline.org/RealEstateRecords offers helpful guidance to which counties are online. Do a free statewide UCC debtor name search at www.wdfi.org/ucc/search/

Adams County

Register of Deeds, PO Box 219, Friendship, WI 53934-0219. 608-339-4206; fax-608-339-4514; 8AM-4:30PM www.co.adams.wi.gov

Index: All in one. Records indexed on a public use terminal back to 1985. Only the public may search. Copy fee $2.00 1st page, $1.00 each add'l page. Cert fee- $1.00 per doc plus copy fee. Payee- Adams County Register of Deeds. **Online access to Real Estate, Deed, Lien records:** Access Register of Deeds data free at www.adamscountylandrecords.com but no name searching. **Other phones:** Treasurer- 608-339-4202; Elections- 608-339-4200; County Clerk- 608-339-4200. **Property tax/Assessing**- PO Box 470, 402 Main St, Friendship, WI 53934; 608-339-4525, assessor fax- 608-339-4584. www.co.adams.wi.gov **Online access**- Access assessor parcel data free at www.adamscountylandrecords.com but no name searching.

Ashland County

Register of Deeds, 201 W Main St, Rm 206, Ashland, WI 54806. 715-682-7008; fax-715-682-7035; 8AM-4PM. www.co.ashland.wi.us

Index: All in one. Records indexed on a public use terminal back to 1984. Office will perform a UCC search but public must search other records themselves. Copy fee $2.00 1st page, $1.00 each add'l page. Cert fee- $1.00 per doc plus copy fee. Payee- Register of deeds. **Online access to Real Estate, Grantor/Grantee, Deed, Birth, Death, Marriage, records:** Access records for a fee at https://mylocalgov.com/wrdaashlandcountywi/wrdaexplanation.asp. You must be able to print, sign and fax the receipt screen to the County. Current law requires a physical signature. Also, search grantor/grantee for free at http://co.ashland.wi.gov/ . **Other phones:** Treasurer- 715-682-7012; Elections- 715-682-7000; Vital Records- 715-682-7008; County Clerk- 715-682-7000; Property Lister -715-682-7003. **Other Online Records**- Search property records free at www.ashlandcogiws.com/AshlandCoWi/txt_default.htm

Barron County

Register of Deeds, 330 E LaSalle, Rm 2500, Barron, WI 54812. 715-537-6210; fax-715-537-6817; 8AM-4PM www.co.barron.wi.us

Index: Book, computer. Records indexed on a public use terminal back to 1999. Only the public may search. Copy fee $2.00 1st page, $1.00 each add'l page. Cert fee- $1.00 per doc plus copy fee. Payee- Barron County Register of Deeds. Bulk data available for purchase, $500.00 per month. **Online access to Real Estate, Deed, Lien records:** Recording office data by subscription on either the Laredo system using subscription and fees or the Tapestry System using credit card, http://tapestry.fidlar.com; $5.99 search; $2.00 1st page, $1.00 each add'l page. Index and images go back to 1/1999. **Other phones:** Treasurer- 715-537-6280; Vital Records- 715-537-6210; County Clerk- 715-537-6200. **Property tax/Assessing**- 330 E LaSalle Ave, Rm 2401, Barron, WI 54812; 715-537-6313. hours- 8AM-4:30PM **Online** - Access to county property records is at www.co.barron.wi.us/treasurer_taxdata.htm. Registration, $300.00 annual fee, username, password required; call Yvonne at the county treasurer's office, 715-537-6280.

Bayfield County

Register of Deeds, PO Box 813, Washburn, WI 54891. 715-373-6119; fax-715-373-6318; 8AM-4PM

Index: All in one. Records indexed on a public use terminal back to 1900. Only the public may search. Copy fee $2.00 1st page, $1.00 each add'l page. Cert fee- $3.00 per cert plus $1.00 per page. Payee- Bayfield County Register of Deeds. **Other phones:** Treasurer- 715-373-6131; County Clerk- 715-373-6100. **Property tax/Assessing**- 715-373-6131.

Brown County

Register of Deeds, PO Box 23600, Green Bay, WI 54305-3600. 920-448-4470, R/E recording phone-920-448-4439, UCC recording phone-920-448-4468; fax-920-448-4449; 8AM-4:30PM. www.co.brown.wi.us/register_of_deeds/

Index: All in one. Records indexed on a public use terminal back to 1986. Only the public may search. Will not search UCC records. Copy fee $2.00 1st page, $1.00 each add'l page. Cert fee- $1.00 per doc plus copy fee. Payee- Register of Deeds. Daily recordings of real estate available on CD; $500 per month fee applies. **Online access to Real Estate, Deed, Lien records:** Recording office data by subscription on either the Laredo system using subscription and fees or the Tapestry System using credit card, http://tapestry.fidlar.com/. $5.95 search; $.50 per image. Index goes back to 1986; images to 5/1/1996. **Other phones:** Treasurer- 920-448-4074; Elections- 920-448-4016; Vital Records- 920-448-4474; County Clerk- 920-448-4021. **Property tax/Assessing Online access**- Land records without name searching is at www.co.brown.wi.us/treasurer/landrecordssearch/entryform.asp. Also, land records can be downloaded from an ftp site; contact the Land Information office at 920-448-6295 to register and user information. Also, search for property data free on the GIS site at www.gis.co.brown.wi.us/website/basemap/viewer.htm. Also, search for property data free at www.co.brown.wi.us/planning_and_land_services/land_information_office/.

Buffalo County

Register of Deeds, PO Box 28, Alma, WI 54610-0028. 608-685-6230; fax-608-685-6213; 8AM-4:30PM www.buffalocounty.com/Buffalo%20County%20Register%20of%20Deeds.htm

Index: All in one. Records indexed on a public use terminal back to 1993. Only the public may search. Copy fee $2.00 1st page, $1.00 each add'l page. Cert fee- $1.00 per doc plus copy fee. Payee- Register of Deeds. Treasurer- 608-685-6214; County Clerk- 608-685-6209. **Property tax/Assessing**- Treasurer's Office, 407 S 2nd St, Alma, WI 54610-0028; 608-685-6215, assessor fax- 608-685-6284. www.buffalocounty.com/Buffalo%20County%20Treasurer.htm **Online** - Access to county land records is free at www.buffalocounty.com/GCSWebPortal/Search.aspx

Burnett County

Register of Deeds, 7410 County Rd, #103, Siren, WI 54872. 715-349-2183; fax-715-349-2037; 8:30AM-4:30PM www.burnettcounty.com

Index: All in one. Records indexed on a public use terminal back to 1988. Only the public may search. Copy fee $2.00 1st page, $1.00 each add'l page. Cert fee- $1.00 per doc plus copy fee. Payee- Burnett County Register of Deeds. Contact Jeanine Chell with bulk data sale inquiries. **Other phones:** Treasurer-715-349-2187; Elections- 715-349-2173; Vital Records- 715-349-2183; County Clerk- 715-349-2173. **Property tax/Assessing**- 7410 County Rd K #120, Siren, Wisconsin 54872; 715-349-2183. **Online access**- Access to limited county property and assessment records is free at www.burnettcounty.org/. No name searching. For full data, an online subscription service is $100 per year.

Calumet County

Register of Deeds, 206 Court St, Chilton, WI 53014. 920-849-1441; fax-920-849-1616; 8AM-4:30PM www.co.calumet.wi.us

Index: All in one. Records indexed on a public use terminal back to 1991. Only the public may search. Copy fee $2.00 1st page, $1.00 each add'l page. Cert fee- $1.00 per doc plus copy fee. Payee- Register of Deeds. Treasurer- 920-849-1457; County Clerk- 920-849-1458. **Property tax/Assessing**- 206 Court St, Chilton, WI 53014; 920-849-1457, assessor fax- 920-849-1469. **Online**- Access assessor property tax data at http://calum400.co.calumet.wi.us/nsccalo/nsclndrec

Chippewa County

Register of Deeds, 711 N Bridge St, Chippewa Falls, WI 54729-1876. 715-726-7994; fax-715-726-4582; 8AM-4:30 PM www.co.chippewa.wi.us/Departments/RegisterDeeds/index.htm

Index: All in one. Records indexed on a public use terminal back to 1956. Office will perform a UCC search but public must search other records themselves. Search fee-$15.00. Office will search for one or two real estate records. Will search UCC records. Copy fee $2.00 1st page, $1.00 each add'l page. Cert fee- $1.00 plus copy fee. Payee- Register of Deeds. **Online access to Real Estate, Deed, Judgment records:** Search Register of Deeds data at https://landshark.co.chippewa.wi.us/LandShark/login.jsp, index search is free, but fees apply for images and copies, $2.00 1st page, $1.00 2nd page. Credit cards accepted. Also, access to real estate records for free www.co.chippewa.wi.us/Departments/RegisterDeeds/index.htm. **Other phones:** Treasurer- 715-726-7965; Elections- 715-726-7980; Vital Records- 715-726-7994; County Clerk- 715-726-7980; Clerk of Court - 715-726-7758. **Other Online Records-** Search property assessment database free at http://cctax.co.chippewa.wi.us/CCTax/Taxrtr?.

Clark County

Register of Deeds, PO Box 384, Neillsville, WI 54456-0384. 715-743-5162, R/E recording phone-715-743-5163; fax-715-743-5154; 8AM-4:30PM www.co.clark.wi.us

Index: Separate indices to search include computer and books-fed tax liens, grantee/grantor, tract, misc, corp. Records indexed on a public use terminal back to 1998 for tracts, 1987 for grantors/grantees. Office personnel or visitors may perform searches. Search fee $15.00 per hour. Office will not search real estate records or UCC records. Copy fee $2.00 1st page, $1.00 each add'l page. Cert fee- $1.00 per doc plus copy fee. Payee- Clark County Register of Deeds. Bulk data available for purchase, grantor/grantee listing back to 1987, contact Register office. **Online access to Real Estate, Deed, Delinquent Property records:** Real estate recording, property data, and delinquent tax info is available by subscription, see https://secure.propertymanagementportal.com/pmp/wi/clark/default.aspx. Fee is $25 per month and $1.20 per transaction. **Other phones:** Treasurer- 715-743-5155; Elections- 715-743-5148; Vital Records- 715-743-5163; County Clerk- 715-743-5150. **Property tax/Assessing**- 517 Court St, Neillsville, WI 54456; 715-743-5155, assessor fax- 715-743-5154. **Online access**- Search for assessor/property tax data on the county GIS site at www.co.clark.wi.us/Website/ClarkIMS/viewer.htm. Search by PIN or address.

Columbia County

Register of Deeds, PO Box 133, Portage, WI 53901. 608-742-9677; fax-608-742-9875; 8AM-4:30PM www.co.columbia.wi.us/ColumbiaCounty/

Index: All in one. Records indexed on computer back to 6/1/87, images back to 1/98. Only the public may search. Copy fee $2.00 1st page, $1.00 each add'l page. Cert fee- $1.00 per record plus copy fee. Payee- Register of Deeds. Bulk data available for purchase, images and real estate for $.20 per image. **Online access to Real Estate, Deed, GIS-mapping, Parcel records:** Access recording office data by subscription on either the Laredo system using subscription and fees or the Tapestry System using credit card, http://tapestry.fidlar.com; $5.99 search; $.50 per image. Index goes back to 6/1987; images back to 1/1998. **Other phones:** Treasurer- 608-742-9613; Vital Records- 608-742-9677; County Clerk- 608-742-9654. **Other Online Records-** Access the county tax parcel system free at http://lrs.co.columbia.wi.us/lrsweb/search.aspx. Also, search property info free on the GIS site at http://lrs.co.columbia.wi.us/website/ColumbiaCo/ColumbiaCo.asp.

Crawford County

Register of Deeds, 225 N Beaumont Rd, #220, Prairie du Chien, WI 53821. 608-326-0219; fax-608-326-0220; 8AM-4:30PM www.crawfordcountywi.org

Index: All in one. Records indexed on computer back to 6/28/01. Only the public may search. Copy fee $2.00 1st page, $1.00 each add'l page. Cert fee- $3.00 1st page, $1.00 each add'l, includes copy fee. Payee- Register of Deeds. **Online access to Real Estate, Deed records:** Search Register of Deeds data at https://landshark.crawfordcountywi.org/LandShark/login.jsp, index search is free, but fees apply for images and copies, $2.00 1st page, $1.00 2nd page. Credit cards accepted. **Other phones:** Treasurer- 608-326-0203; Elections- 608-326-0200; Vital Records- 608-326-0219; County Clerk- 608-326-0201; Real Property Lister -608-326-0221. **Property tax/Assessing**- 225 N Beaumont Rd #216, Prairie du Chien, WI 53821; 608-326-0221.

Dane County

Register of Deeds, PO Box 1438, Madison, WI 53701. 608-266-4141, R/E phone-608-266-4144 (9AM-11AM-1PM-4 PM only); fax-608-267-3110; 7:45AM-4:30PM www.co.dane.wi.us/regdeeds/rdhome.htm

Register of Deeds will only release information over the phone between the hours of 9AM-11AM-1PM-4PM. You can email the agency if you have questions. Index: All in one. Records indexed on a public use terminal back to 1978; images back to 1992. Office personnel or visitors may perform searches. Office will search limited real estate records from 9AM-11AM-1PM-4PM only. Will search UCC records (computer only). Copy fee $2.00 1st page, $1.00 each add'l page. Cert fee- $1.00 per doc plus copy fee. Payee- Register of Deeds. **Online Real Estate, Deed, Lien records:** A fee-based system is at www.co.dane.wi.us/regdeeds/laredotapestry/accessstorealestate.htm. Also, access recording office land data at www.etitlesearch.com; registration required, fee based on usage. Also, access recording office data by subscription or using credit card at http://tapestry.fidlar.com. Index goes back to 8/1978, images to 1992. **Other phones:** Treasurer- 608-266-4151; Elections- 608-266-4121; Vital Records- 608-266-4142; County Clerk- 608-266-4121; General Phone -608-266-4141. **Property tax/Assessing**- City-County Bldg, Rm 101, Madison, WI 53701; 608-266-4531, assessor fax- 608-266-4257. Search property on GIS mapping site free at http://dcimap.co.dane.wi.us but no name searching. **Online access**- City of Madison tax assessor data is at www.cityofmadison.com/assessor/property/index.cfm. Search Sun Prairie property at http://db.sun-prairie.com/property/ and its death list at http://db.sun-prairie.com/deathlist/. Also, search property info for. Cross Plains, Mazomanie, Black Earth villages at www.wendorffassessing.com/municipalities.htm. Also, register to use assessor/land record services at www.co.dane.wi.us and select "AccessDane" from the bottom of this home page.

Dodge County

Register of Deeds, 127 E Oak St; Admin Bldg, Juneau, WI 53039-1391. 920-386-3720, UCC recording phone-920-386-3723; fax-920-386-3902; 8AM-4:30PM. www.co.dodge.wi.us

Index: Separate indices to search include computer to 4/1987, paper before that. Records indexed on a public use terminal back to 4/87. Only the public may search. Copy fee $2.00 1st page, $1.00 each add'l page. Cert fee- $1.00 per doc plus copy fee. Payee- Dodge County Register of Deeds. **Other phones:** Treasurer- 920-386-3782; Vital Records- 920-386-3720; County Clerk- 920-386-3602. **Property tax/Assessing**- 920-386-3770.

Door County

Register of Deeds, 421 Nebraska St, Sturgeon Bay, WI 54235. 920-746-2270, fax-920-746-2447; 8AM-4:30PM

Index: Separate indices to search include grantor/grantee, Tracts. Grantor/Grantee indexed on computer back to 1982. Only the public may search. Copy fee $2.00 1st page, $1.00 each add'l page. Cert fee- $1.00 per page plus copy fee. Payee- Register of Deeds. Bulk data available for purchase, $300.00 per month for CD's; call 920-746-2270. **Online access to Real Estate, Deed, Lien records:** Access to land records images is by internet subscription or on CD-rom. Subscription or CD is $300 monthly; call Register of Deeds 920-746-2270 for info and signup or escrow account. **Other phones:** Treasurer- 920-746-2286; Vitals- 920-746-2270; County Clerk- 920-746-2200. **Property tax/Assessing**- 421 Nebraska St, Sturgeon Bay, WI 54235; 920-746-2905.

Douglas County

Register of Deeds, 1313 Belknap St, Rm 108; Courthouse, Superior, WI 54880. 715-395-1350, R/E recording phone-715-395-1554, UCC recording phone-715-395-1463; fax-715-395-1553; 8AM-4:30PM. www.douglascountywi.org/

Index: Separate indices to search include general, FTL, Abstract of Judgments. Records indexed on a public use terminal back to 1991. Only the public may search. Copy fee $2.00 1st page, $1.00 each add'l page. UCCs and FTL are $2.00 per page. Cert fee- $3.00 1st page plus $1.00 each add'l page includes copy fee. Payee- Register of Deeds. **Online access to Real Estate, Grantor/Grantee, Deed, Lien records:** Access to the county Landshark system is at http://rdlandshark.douglascountywi.org/LandShark/login.jsp. Free registration is required. **Other phones:** Treasurer- 715-395-1348; Elections- 715-395-1397; Vital Records- 715-395-1463; County Clerk- 715-395-1568; City of Superior -715-395-7222. **Other Online Records-** Access county land and property tax records free at www.gcssoftware.com/douglas/Search.aspx but no name searching.

Dunn County

Register of Deeds, 800 Wilson Ave, #135, Menomonie, WI 54751. 715-232-1228; fax-715-232-1229; hours - 8AM-4:30PM http://dunncountywi.govoffice2.com/

Index: Separate indices to search include tract, grantor/grantee. Records indexed on a public use terminal back to 12/1988 for deeds. Only the public may search. Copy fee $2.00 1st page, $1.00 each add'l page. Cert fee- $1.00 plus copy fee. Payee- Dunn County Register of Deeds. **Online access to Real Estate, Deed, Lien records:** Recording office data by subscription on either the Laredo system using subscription and fees or the Tapestry System using credit card, http://tapestry.fidlar.com; $3.99 search; $.50 per image. Index and images go back to 12/1998. **Other phones:** Treasurer- 715-232-3789; County Clerk- 715-232-1677. **Property tax/Assessing**- Land Assessment, 800 Wilson Ave, Menomonie, WI 54751; 715-/231-6524, assessor fax- 715-232-4099. http://dunncountywi.govoffice2.com/

Eau Claire County

Register of Deeds, PO Box 718, Eau Claire, WI 54702. 715-839-4745; 8AM-5PM www.co.eau-claire.wi.us
Index: Separate indices to search include before 1995, power of attorney, federal tax liens, art of incorporation, misc indexes. Records indexed on a public use terminal back to 1995. Only the public may search. Will not search UCC records. Copy fee $2.00 1st page, $1.00 each add'l page. Cert fee- $1.00 per cert plus copy fee. Payee- Eau Claire County Register of Deeds. **Online access to Real Estate, Deed, Lien records:** Recording office data by subscription on either the Laredo system using subscription and fees or the Tapestry System using credit card, http://tapestry.fidlar.com; $3.99 search; $.50 per image. Index and images go back to 3/1994. **Other phones:** Treasurer- 715-839-4805; Elections- 715-839-4801; Vitals- 715-839-4745; County Clerk- 715-839-4803. **Property tax/Assessing**- 715-839-4741.

Florence County

Register of Deeds, PO Box 410, Florence, WI 54121. 715-528-4252; fax-715-528-4272; 8:30AM-4PM.
Index: All in one. Records indexed on a public use terminal back to 1989. Only the public may search. Office will do limited real estate search. Copy fee $2.00 1st page, $1.00 each add'l page. Cert fee- $1.00. Payee- Register of Deeds. Treasurer- 715-528-3204; County Clerk- 715-528-3201. **Online Records**- Access property search free at http://rmgis.ruekert-mielke.com/florenceco/GISWebPortal.asp.

Fond du Lac County

Register of Deeds, PO Box 509, Fond du Lac, WI 54935. 920-929-3018; fax-920-929-3293; 8AM-4:30PM www.fdlco.wi.gov/index.aspx?page=77
Index: All in one. Records indexed on a public use terminal back to 1989. Only the public may search. Copy fee $2.00 1st page, $1.00 each add'l page. Cert fee- $1.00 per doc plus copy fee. Payee- Fond du Lac County Register of Deeds. Treasurer- 920-929-3010; Elections- 920-929-3000; Vital Records- 920-929-3018; County Clerk- 920-929-3000. **Property tax/Assessing**- Tax Listing, 160 S Macy St 1st Fl, Fond du Lac, WI 54935; 920 929-3027, fax- 920 929-3293. www.fdlco.wi.gov/index.aspx?page=82 **Online** Access to parcel data is free through the GIS site at http://gis.fdlco.wi.gov/Website/FondduLacIMS/viewer.htm. No name searching.

Forest County

Register of Deeds, 200 E Madison St, Crandon, WI 54520. 715-478-3823; fax-715-478-3837; 8:30AM-N, 1PM-4:30PM www.co.forest.wi.gov/
Index: All in one. Records indexed on a public use terminal back to 1991. Only the public may search. Copy fee $2.00 1st page, $1.00 each add'l page. Cert fee- $1.00 per cert plus copy fee. Payee- Forest County Register of Deeds. **Other phones:** Treasurer-715-478-2412; Elections- 715-478-2422; Vital Records- 715-478-3823; County Clerk- 715-478-2422. **Property tax/Assessing**- Forest County Treasurer/Real Property Lister, 200 E Madison Ave, Crandon, WI 54520; 715-478-2412, assessor fax-715-478-3216. www.co.forest.wi.gov/ **Online access**- Access to county property and assessor data free is at www.gcssoftware.com/forest/Search.aspx.

Grant County

Register of Deeds, PO Box 391, Lancaster, WI 53813-0391. 608-723-2727; fax-608-723-4048; 8AM-4:30PM http://grantcounty.org Index: All in one. Records indexed on a public use terminal back to 1989. Office will perform a UCC search but public must search other records themselves. Copy fee $2.00 1st page, $1.00 each add'l page. Cert fee- $1.00 per doc includes copy fee. Payee- Register of Deeds. **Other phones:** Treasurer- 608-723-2604; Elections-608-723-2675; Vital Records- 608-723-2727; County Clerk- 608-723-2675. **Property tax/Assessing**- Same address as recording office. 608-723-2666, assessor fax- 608-723-4048. **Online**- Access to county property and assessor data is at www.gcssoftware.com/Products/WebSearch.aspx and click on Grant County. Registration, $200.00 annual fee, username, and password required; call John at the Tax Lister office, 608-723-2666.

Green County

Register of Deeds, 1016 16th Ave; Courthouse, Monroe, WI 53566. 608-328-9439; fax-608-328-2835; 8AM-4:30PM
Index: All in one. Records indexed on a public use terminal back to 1997. Office will perform a UCC search but public must search other records themselves. Copy fee $2.00 1st page, $1.00 each add'l page. Cert fee- $1.00 per page plus copy fee. Payee-Green County Register of Deeds. **Other phones:** County Clerk- 608-328-9430. **Property tax/Assessing**- . **Online access**- Access to parcel data is free on the GIS-mapping site at http://gis.msa-ps.com/greencounty/publicviewer/startup.htm.

Green Lake County

Register of Deeds, PO Box 3188, Green Lake, WI 54941-3188. 920-294-4021; fax-920-294-4165; 8AM-4:30PM. www.co.green-lake.wi.us
Index: All in one. Records indexed on computer back to 2000. Office will do a quick search for 1 item or Property. No fee for search. Office will search real estate records. Will search UCC records. Copy fee $2.00 1st page, $1.00 each add'l page. Cert fee- $1.00 per doc plus copy fee. Payee- Register of Deeds. **Other phones:** Treasurer- 920-294-4018; Elections-920-294-4005; Vital Records- 920-294-4021; County Clerk- 920-294-4005. **Property tax/Assessing**- . **Online access**- Search GIS-mapping site for property data free at http://gis.co.green-lake.wi.us/website/GIS_Viewer_limit/viewer.htm but no name search.

Iowa County

Register of Deeds, 222 N Iowa St, Dodgeville, WI 53533. 608-935-0396; fax-608-935-3024; 8:30AM-4:30PM _Index: All in one. Records indexed on a public use terminal back to 1996. Only the public may search. Copy fee $2.00 1st page, $1.00 each add'l page. Cert fee- $1.00 plus copy fee. Payee- Iowa County Register of Deeds. **Other phones:** Treasurer-608-935-0397; Elections- 608-935-0399; Vitals- 608-935-0396; County Clerk- 608-935-0399.

Iron County

Register of Deeds, 300 Taconite St, #102, Hurley, WI 54534. 715-561-2945; fax-715-561-2928; 8AM-4PM. www.ironcountywi.org
Index: All in one. Records indexed on a public use terminal back to 12/1991. Office will perform a UCC search but public must search other records themselves. UCC search fee $15.00 per debtor name. Copy fee $2.00 1st page, $1.00 each add'l page. Cert fee- $2.00 per page. Payee- Iron County Register of Deeds. **Online Real Estate, Grantor/Grantee, Deed records:** Access to land records is available at http://records.ironcountywi.org/LandShark/login.jsp registration is required. Fees to search. Records go back to 1994. **Other phones:** Treasurer- 715-561-2883; Vital Records- 715-561-2945; County Clerk-715-561-3375. **Property tax/Assessing**- 300 Taconite St, #100, Hurley, WI 54534; 715-561-2883, assessor fax- 715-561-3223. (Appraiser - 715-561-2883)

Jackson County

Register of Deeds, 307 Main, Black River Falls, WI 54615. 715-284-0205; fax-715-284-0237; 8AM-4:30PM. www.co.jackson.wi.us
Index: All in one. Records indexed on a public use terminal back to 1986. Only the public may search. General copy fee $2.00 1st page, $1.00 each add'l page. Cert fee- $1.00 per doc plus copy fee. Payee-Register of Deeds. **Other phones:** Treasurer- 715-284-0226; Elections- 715-284-0200; Vital Records-715-284-0204; County Clerk- 715-284-0201. **Property tax/Assessing**- Same address as recording office. 715-284-0203.

Jefferson County

Register of Deeds, PO Box 356, Jefferson, WI 53549. 920-674-7235; fax-920-674-7238; 8AM-4:30PM www.co.jefferson.wi.us/jc/public/jchome.php?page_id=158
Index: All in one. Records indexed on a public use terminal back to 1987. Only the public may search. Copy fee $2.00 1st page, $1.00 each add'l page. Full-size plats $4.00 per page. Cert fee- $1.00 per doc plus copy fee. Payee- Jefferson County Register of Deeds. **Online access to Real Estate, Grantor/Grantee, Deed, Lien records:** Access parcel data free at http://lrs.co.jefferson.wi.us/jclrs/LIO/LIO_Search but no name searching. To order full records online using your credit card, see http://lrs.co.jefferson.wi.us/. Call 920-674-7254 for info, fees, and signup. Land records data is available by subscription on JCLRP; fee is $40 per month paid quarterly. **Other phones:** Treasurer-920-674-7250; Elections- 920-674-7140; Vital Records- 920-674-7235; County Clerk- 920-674-7144. **Property tax/Assessing**- 320 S Main St, Jefferson, WI 53549; 920-674-7235. **Online access**-Search assessment records free at http://lrs.co.jefferson.wi.us/jclrs/LIO/LIO_Search but no name searching. Also, search property data free on GIS site at http://lrs.co.jefferson.wi.us/jcgis/main.do but no name searching.

Juneau County

Register of Deeds, 220 E State St, #212, Mauston, WI 53948-1379. 608-847-9325; 8AM-N, 12:30-4:30PM www.co.juneau.wi.gov/
Index: All in one. Records indexed on a public use terminal back to 9/1/89 for grantor/grantee - back to Mid-5/99 for track index. Only the public may search. Will not search UCC records. Copy fee $2.00 1st page, $1.00 each add'l page. Large plats- $5.00 per page. Cert fee- $3.00 1st page, $1.00 each add'l pages per real estate doc includes copy fee. Payee- Register of Deeds. **Online access to Real Estate, Deed, Mortgage records:** The ROD offers subscription, escrow and credit card services for Real Estate access; online docs go back to 05/11/1999 at https://landshark.co.juneau.wi.us/LandShark/. **Other phones:** Treasurer- 608-847-9308; Elections- 608-847-9302; Vital Records- 608-847-9325; County Clerk- 608-847-9300. **Property tax/Assessing**-Auditing and Accounting, 220 E State St, Rm 203, Mauston, WI 53948; n/k. **Online access**- Search the GIS-mapping site for property and assessment data free at http://gis.co.juneau.wi.us/pvweb22/index.htm. Click on free account login, then click "Search Data" but no name searching. Also a subscription service for complete property data. To search land sales by town, click on Land Sales at www.co.juneau.wi.gov.

Kenosha County

Register of Deeds, 1010 56th St, Kenosha, WI 53140. 262-653-2444, R/E recording phone-262-653-2441; fax-262-653-2564; hours - 8AM - 5PM. www.co.kenosha.wi.us/rod/index.html
Records indexed on a public use terminal back to 1994. Only the public may search. Copy fee $2.00 1st page, $1.00 each add'l page. Plat maps- $3.00 per page. Cert fee- $1.00 per page plus copy fee. Payee-Kenosha Register of Deeds. Bulk reports available for purchase by written request; requests forwarded to IS Dept for estimate. **Online Real Estate, Deed, Lien records:** Access to land records is available at https://landshark.co.kenosha.wi.us/LandShark/login.jsp registration is required. Fees to search. Records go back to 1994. **Other phones:** Treasurer- 262-653-2542; Vital Records- 262-653-2444; County Clerk-

262-653-2477. **Property tax/Assessing**- 1010 56th St, Kenosha, WI 53140; 262-653-2545, assessor fax-262-653-2553. hours- 8AM-4:30PM www.kenosha.org/departments/assessor/index.html **Online**- Search the Kenosha City Assessor's property database free at www.kenosha.org/departments/assessor/search.html or the county at www.co.kenosha.wi.us/apps/propinq/propinq_policy.phtml. No name searching at either site. Access real estate records free at www.co.kenosha.wi.us/ and select under Property, Mapping & Environment. Also access parcel data free on the GIS-mapping site free at http://kcmapping.co.kenosha.wi.us/mapping_public/.

Kewaunee County

Register of Deeds, 810 Lincoln St, Kewaunee, WI 54216-1398. 920-388-7126, R/E recording phone-920-388-7126/7128; fax-920-388-7129; 8AM-4:30PM. www.kewauneeco.org
Index: All in one. Records indexed on a public use terminal back to 2/92. Office will perform a UCC search (in office only) but public must search other records themselves. Search fee-$15.00 per name. Copy fee $2.00 1st page, $1.00 each add'l page. Cert fee- $1.00 per doc plus copy fee; plats- $3.00 per sheet. Payee- Register of Deeds. Printouts of monthly reports available for $14 each; contact the Register of Deeds. **Online access to Real Estate, Grantor/Grantee, Deed records:** Access to the Register of Deeds CherryLAN Indexing and Imaging System is available for a monthly subscription fee of $300. Escrow subscription with an initial $100 deposit are also available. Index begins 2/1992. **Other phones:** Treasurer- 920-388-7152; Elections- 920-388-7133; Vital Records- 920-388-7122; County Clerk- 920-388-7123. **Property tax/Assessing**- 810 Lincoln St, Kewaunee, WI 54216-1398; 920-388-7126. hours- 8AM04:30PM **Online access**- Search land/tax records free at www.kewauneeco.org/GCSWebPortal/Search.aspx. Also, search parcel maps and property tax data free on the GIS mapping site at www.kewauneeco.org. Subscription required for full data. Click on Land Records.

La Crosse County

Register of Deeds, 400 N 4th St, Rm 1220; Admin Ctr, La Crosse, WI 54601-3200. 608-785-9644, R/E recording phone-608-785-9652, UCCs- 608-785-9651; fax-608-785-9643; 8:30AM-5PM www.co.la-crosse.wi.us/Departments/departments.htm
Index: Separate indices to search include computer and tract. Records indexed on a public use terminal back to 1987. Back to 1963 by document number only. Only the public may search. Copy fee $2.00 1st page, $1.00 each add'l. page. Cert fee- $1.00 per doc plus copy fee. Payee- Register of Deeds. **Online access to Land, Deed, Property Owner, Lien records:** Recording office data by subscription on either the Laredo system using subscription and fees or the Tapestry System using credit card, http://tapestry.fidlar.com; $5.95 search; $.50 per image. Index goes back to 1987 and images go back to 1963. **Other phones:** Treasurer- 608-785-9711; Elections- 608-785-9581; Vital Records- 608-785-9652; County Clerk- 608-785-9790. **Property tax/Assessing**- 400 La Crosse St, La Crosse, WI 54601; 608-789-7525, assessor fax- 608-789-8123. **Online access**- Search for property owner and land data for free at www.co.la-crosse.wi.us/landrecordsportal/default.aspx.

Lafayette County

Register of Deeds, PO Box 170, Darlington, WI 53530. 608-776-4838; fax-608-776-4991; 8AM-4:30PM. www.co.lafayette.wi.gov/
Index: Separate indices to search include computer back to 1995, books back to 1847. Records indexed on a public use terminal back to 1/1995. Only the public may search. Copy fee $2.00 1st page, $1.00 each add'l page. Cert fee- $1.00 per doc plus copy fee. Payee- Register of Deeds. Bulk data available for purchase, recording back to 1/1/95, contact Joe Boll. **Online access to Real Estate, Deed, Lien records:** Recording office data by subscription on either the Laredo system using subscription and fees or the Tapestry System using credit card, http://tapestry.fidlar.com; $3.99 search; $.50 per image. Index and images go back to 1/1995. **Other phones:** Treasurer- 608-776-4862; Elections- 608-776-4850; Vital Records- 608-776-4838; County Clerk- 608-776-4850. **Property tax/Assessing**- 626 Main St, Darlington, WI 53530; 608-776-4862.

Langlade County

Register of Deeds, 800 Clermont St, Antigo, WI 54409. 715-627-6209; fax-715-627-6270; 8:30AM-4:30PM. www.co.langlade.wi.us
Index: Separate indices to search include tract, grantor/grantee. Records indexed on computer back to 1994. Grantor/grantee-1987, tract index- July, 1994. Office personnel or visitors may perform searches. No fee for search, but office will perform only "limited" searches. Office real estate searches are limited to computer tract lookup. Will not search UCC records. Copy fee $2.00 1st page, $1.00 each add'l page. They accept credit cards for birth, death, marriage records and copies of real estate. Cert fee- $1.00 per cert plus copy fee. Payee- Register of Deeds. **Online access to Birth, Death records:** Access county birth index free at www.co.langlade.wi.us/Births/; search death index free at www.co.langlade.wi.us/Deaths/. **Other phones:** Treasurer- 715-627-6204; Elections- 715-627-6200; Vital Records- 715-627-6209; County Clerk- 715-627-6201. **Property tax/Assessing**- 837 Clermont St, Antigo, WI 54409; 715-627-6207. **Online access**- Access property data free at www.langladecogiws.com/LangladeCoWi/ but no name searching.

Lincoln County

Register of Deeds, 1110 E Main, Ste 201; Courthouse, Merrill, WI 54452. 715-536-0318; fax-715-536-0360; 8:15AM-4:30PM www.co.lincoln.wi.us
Index: All in one. Records indexed on a public use terminal back to 1990. Only the public may search. Copy fee $2.00 1st page, $1.00 each add'l page. Cert fee- $1.00 per doc plus copy fee. Payee- Register of Deeds. Bulk data available for purchase at $350.00 per month. **Other phones:** Treasurer- 715-536-0315; Elections- 715-536-0359; Vital Records- 715-536-0318; County Clerk- 715-536-0359. **Property tax/Assessing**- 715-536-0479.

Manitowoc County

Register of Deeds, PO Box 421, Manitowoc, WI 54221-0421. 920-683-4010, R/E recording phone-920-683-4011, UCC phone-920-683-4010; fax-920-683-2702; 8:30AM-4:30PM www.manitowoc-county.com
Index: All in one. Records indexed on a public use terminal back to 1991. Only the public may search. Copy fee $2.00 1st page, $1.00 each add'l page. Cert fee- $1.00 per page. Payee- Register of Deeds. **Online Real Estate, Deed records:** Access to Register of Deeds recorded land records system requires username and password at http://rod.manitowoc-county.com/landweb.dll; contact Register of Deeds office for sign-up. **Other phones:** Treasurer- 920-683-4020; Vital Records- 920-683-4509; County Clerk- 920-683-4004. **Property tax/Assessing**- 1010 S 8th St, Courthouse, Manitowoc, WI 54221; 920-683-4425. **Online access**- Access tax records free at http://manitowoc-county.com/taxquery/main.htm but no name searching. Search on GIS-map site at http://webmap.manitowoc-county.com/website/pasystem/. Foreclosures- www.manitowoc-county.com/ftp/treasurer/Reference/Foreclosed.htm. Manitowoc City Assessor database free at http://assessor.manitowoc.org/CityAssessor/a1.aspx?. No name searching. Access Two Rivers assessor data at http://tworivers.patriotproperties.com/default.asp.

Marathon County

Register of Deeds, 500 Forest St; Courthouse, Wausau, WI 54403-5568. 715-261-1470; fax-715-261-1488; 8AM-4:30PM. www.co.marathon.wi.us
Index: All in one. Records indexed on computer back to 1986. Only the public may search. Copy fee $2.00 1st page, $1.00 each add'l page. Cert fee- $1.00 per doc plus copy fee. Payee- Register of Deeds. **Other phones:** Treasurer- 715-261-1150; Elections- 715-261-1500; Vital Records- 715-261-1470; County Clerk- 715-261-1501. **Property tax/Assessing**- 407 Grant St, Wausau, WI 54403; 715-843-1300. **Online access**- Access to county property records is free at www.co.marathon.wi.us/online/apps/lrs/index.asp. No name searching. Access by subscription is also available for full data. Also, access parcel/property data on the GIS-mapping site fee at http://gismaps.co.marathon.wi.us/gisweb/ccdcc_pub/ccdcc.asp. No name searching.

Marinette County

Register of Deeds, 1926 Hall Ave; Courthouse, Marinette, WI 54143. 715-732-7550, R/E recording phone-715-782-7550; fax-715-732-7556; 8:30AM-4:30PM www.marinettecounty.com
Index: Indices to search available, paper tract index from 1879 to 11/1999. Records indexed on a public use terminal back to 2000. Only the public may search. Copy fee $2.00 1st page, $1.00 each add'l page. Cert fee- $1.00 per cert plus copy fee. Payee- Marinette County Register of Deeds. **Online Real Estate, Deed records:** Access to real estate index at http://landshark.marinettecounty.com/LandShark/registration.jsp. Requires account. Search index free but $2.00 fee (plus $1.00 each add'l.) to view document. Registration and escrow account required. **Other phones:** Treasurer- 715-732-7430; Vital Records-715-732-7550; County Clerk- 715-732-7407.

Marquette County

Register of Deeds, PO Box 236, Montello, WI 53949-0236. 608-297-9136, R/E recording phone- x232; fax-608-297-7606; 8AM-N, 12:30-4:30PM
Index: All in one. Records indexed on a public use terminal back to 1998. Only the public may search. Will do federal tax lien search for the cost of copies. Copy fee $2.00 1st page, $1.00 each add'l page. Cert fee- $1.00 per doc plus copy fee. Payee- Marquette County Register of Deeds. **Other phones:** Treasurer-608-297-9136; Vitals- x232; County Clerk- 608-297-9114. **Property tax/Assessing**- 608-297-3032.

Menominee County

Register of Deeds, PO Box 279, Keshena, WI 54135-0279. 715-799-3312; fax-715-799-1322; 8-4:30PM
Index: All in one. Records indexed on computer; no public use terminal available. Office personnel or visitors may perform searches. Search fee $10.00. Real estate records are found at D.F.I. Will search UCC records. Copy fee $2.00 1st page, $1.00 each add'l page. Cert fee- $1.00 per page plus copy fee. Payee- Menominee Co Register of Deeds. **Other phones:** Treasurer- 715-799-3315; Elections- 715-799-3311; Vital Records- 715-799-3312; County Clerk- 715-799-3311. **Property tax/Assessing**-Courthouse Ln, Keshena, WI 54135; 715-799-3315, assessor fax- 715-799-1322. (Appraiser/Auditor- 715-799-3001);

Milwaukee County

Register of Deeds, 901 N 9th St, Rm 103, Milwaukee, WI 53233. 414-278-4021, R/E recording phone-414-278-4001, UCC recording phone-414-278-4006; fax-414-223-1257; 8AM-4:30PM. www.county.milwaukee.gov/RegisterofDeeds7722.htm
Index: All in one. Records indexed on a public use terminal back to 1988. Office personnel or visitors may perform searches. Search fee $10.00 per name. Copy fee $2.00 1st page, $1.00 each add'l page. Plat maps $5.00 1st page, $2.00 each add'l page. Cert fee-$1.00 per doc plus copy fee. Payee- Register of Deed, Milwaukee County. **Online access to Real Estate, Grantor/Grantee, Deed, Lien, Parcel records:** Recording office data by subscription on either the Laredo system using subscription. and fees or the Tapestry System using credit card, http://tapestry.fidlar.com. Grantor index goes back to

1/4/88, Grantee to 1/4/88; tracts to 1/4/88. **Other phones:** Treasurer- 414-278-4033; Elections- 414-278-4060; Vital Records- 414-278-4003; County Clerk- 414-278-4067. **Property tax/Assessing-** Treasurer's Office, 901 N 9th St, Rm 102, Milwaukee, WI 53233; 414-278-4033, assessor fax- 414-223-1383. **Online access-** Assessment data & sales data on Milwaukee City (not county) database at www.city.milwaukee.gov/DataampDataSearches673.htm. Search City of Cudahy assessor data at http://exch02.ci.cudahy.wi.us/Scripts/GVSWeb.dll/Search, search Wauwatosa property at. www.wauwatosa.net/display/wspTosaAssessmentTemplate.asp. Franklin- at http://taxassessment.franklinwi.gov/assessmentsearch.cfm. Glendale- http://ts.glendale-wi.org; West Allis- www.ci.west-allis.wi.us/property_search/psearch.aspx.

Monroe County

Register of Deeds, 202 S "K" St, Rm 2, Sparta, WI 54656. 608-269-8716; fax-608-269-8715; 8AM-4:30PM www.co.monroe.wi.us

Index: All in one. Records indexed on a public use terminal back to 1996. Office will perform a UCC search but public must search other records themselves. Copy fee $2.00 1st page, $1.00 each add'l page. Cert fee- $1.00 per cert plus copy fee. Payee- Monroe County Register of Deeds. **Other phones:** Treasurer- 608-269-8710; Vital Records- 608-269-8716; County Clerk- 608-269-8705. **Property tax/Assessing-** c/o County Treasurer Office, 202 S K St, Sparta, WI 54656; 608-269-8716. **Online access-** Access assessment data on the GIS-mapping site free at www.monroecogiws.com/MonroeCoWi/. Click on Go To Tax and Assessment Data.

Oconto County

Register of Deeds, 301 Washington St, Rm 2035, Oconto, WI 54153-1699. 920-834-7113; 8AM-4PM www.co.oconto.wi.us

One index since 1/1/2000. Federal tax liens may be searched separately. Index: All in one. Records indexed on a public use terminal back to 100. Office will perform a UCC search but public must search other records themselves. UCC search fee $15.00 per debtor name. Office will not search real estate records. UCC search does not include federal tax liens. Copy fee $2.00 1st page, $1.00 each add'l page. Cert fee- $1.00 per cert plus copy fee. Payee- Oconto County Register of Deeds. **Online Parcel, Grantor/Grantee, Real Estate, Lien records:** Access to Registrar of Deeds available by subscription or escrow account at https://landshark.co.oconto.wi.us/LandShark/. You may also purchase a document with a credit card. **Other phones:** Treasurer- 920-834-6813; Vital Records- 920-834-7113; County Clerk- 920-834-6806; Real Property Lister -920-834-6827. **Other Online Records-** Access to the county SOLO tax parcel search is free or by subscription at http://solo.co.oconto.wi.us/ocontoco/. The free service does not include name searching. Subscription fee for full data is $300 per calendar year. Phone 920-834-6800 for more info.

Oneida County

Register of Deeds, PO Box 400, Rhinelander, WI 54501. 715-369-6150; fax-715-369-6222; 8AM-4:30PM. www.co.oneida.wi.gov/

Index: All in one. Records indexed on a public use terminal back to 1998. Only the public may search. Will not search UCC records. Copy fee $2.00 1st page, $1.00 each add'l page. Cert fee- $1.00 per page. Payee- Oneida County Register of Deeds. Bulk data available for purchase, contact the ITS Dept at 715-369-6101. **Other phones:** Treasurer- 715-369-6137; Elections- 715-369-6144; Vital Records- 715-369-6150; County Clerk- 715-369-6144. **Property tax/Assessing-** 1 Oneida Ave, Courthouse Sq, Rhinelander, WI 54501; 715-369-6137. **Online access-** Access to property tax data is available free at http://octax.co.oneida.wi.us/ONCTax/Taxrtr. Also, search land records by name on the GIS mapping site at http://ocgis.co.oneida.wi.us/oneida/index.htm.

Outagamie County

Register of Deeds, 410 S Walnut St, CAB 205, Appleton, WI 54911-5999. 920-832-5095; fax-920-832-2177; 8AM-4:30PM; Summer hrs: 7AM-3:30PM. www.co.outagamie.wi.us

Index: All in one. Records indexed on a public use terminal back to 3/91 for grantor/grantee; tract index back to 1998. Only the public may search. Copy fee $2.00 1st page, $1.00 each add'l page. Cert fee- $1.00 per doc plus copy fee. Payee- Register of Deeds. **Online access to Real Estate, Deed, Judgment records:** Access to deeds, real estate taxes and maps for free go to www.co.outagamie.wi.us/. Click on deeds/real estate taxes/maps (GIS). Also, access recorded documents data at https://landshark.co.outagamie.wi.us/LandShark/login.jsp. Registration and fees required for full data. **Other phones:** Treasurer- 414-832-5065; Elections- 920-832-5077; Vital Records- 920-832-5095; County Clerk- 920-832-5077; Abstracting Dept -920-832-5114. **Property tax/Assessing-** 410 Walnut St, Appleton, WI 54911; 920-832-5071, assessor fax-920-832-4923. **Online-** Search assessor data free at www.co.outagamie.wi.us/OutagamieCoWi/txt_default.htm, no name searching. Sub required for full data. Access parcel data on the GIS site at www.co.outagamie.wi.us/OutagamieCoWi/txt_default.htm - no name searching. Also, variety of property records at www.co.outagamie.wi.us/planning/Maps_main.htm.

Ozaukee County

Register of Deeds, PO Box 994, Port Washington, WI 53074-0994. 262-284-8260; fax-262-284-8268; 8:30AM-5PM. www.co.ozaukee.wi.us

Index: All in one. Records indexed on a public use terminal back to early 1970s. Only the public may search. Copy fee $2.00 1st page, $1.00 each add'l page. Cert fee- $1.00 per doc plus copy fee. Payee- Register of Deeds. Bulk data available for purchase, contact Cristina Pearson-Land Information Office at 262-284-8262. **Online access to Real Estate, Grantor/Grantee, Deed records:** Access is by "Remote Access" requiring dial-up modem. This data is for inquiries only. Software is supplied by the county. First month is free, then $50.00 per month subscription. For info, contact the Technology Resources Dept. at 262-284-8309. Also, recording data by subscription on either the Laredo system (subscription & fees) or Tapestry System (use credit card) at http://tapestry.fidlar.com; $5.95 search; $.50 per image. Index goes back to 12/11/1972; images to 9/15/1984. **Other phones:** Treasurer- 262-284-8280; Vital Records- 262-284-8260; County Clerk- 262-284-8112. **Property tax/Assessing-** PO Box 994, 121 W Main St, Treasurer's Office, Rm 107, Port Washington, WI 53074; 262-284-8280, fax- 262-284-8373. www.co.ozaukee.wi.us/Treasurer/index.htm

Pepin County

Register of Deeds, PO Box 39, Durand, WI 54736. 715-672-8856; fax-715-672-8677; 8:30AM-N, 12:30-4:30. www.co.pepin.wi.us

Index: Books. Records indexed on a public use terminal back to 1994. Only the public may search. Will not search UCC records. Copy fee $2.00 1st page, $1.00 each add'l page. Cert fee- $1.00 per doc plus copy fee. Payee- Register of Deeds. **Other phones:** Treasurer- 715-672-8850; Elections- 715-672-8857; Vital Records- 715-672-8856; County Clerk- 715-672-8857. **Other Online Records-** Access maps, land records and tax data free at www.co.pepin.wi.us.

Pierce County

Register of Deeds, PO Box 267, Ellsworth, WI 54011. 715-273-3531 x6418; fax-715-273-6861; 8AM-5PM. www.co.pierce.wi.us/Register%20of%20Deeds/Register_Deeds_Main.html

Index: Separate indices to search include tract books, grantor/grantee books up to 1998, then computer. Records indexed on computer from 1998 to present. Only the public may search. Office will not search real estate records. Copy fee $2.00 1st page, $1.00 each add'l page. Cert fee- $1.00 per doc plus copy fee. Payee- Register of Deeds. Bulk data available for purchase, reports at $.50 per page, contact Vicki Nelson. **Online access to Real Estate, Deed, Lien records:** Access recording office data by subscription on either the Laredo system using subscription and fees or the Tapestry 2.0 System using credit card, http://tapestry.fidlar.com; $5.95 search; $.50 per image. Visit www.co.pierce.wi.us/Register%20of%20Deeds/Register_Deeds_Main.html for more Tapestry info. Index and images go back to 1998. **Other phones:** Treasurer- 715-273-3531 x6428; Elections- 715-273-3531; Vital Records- 715-273-3531 x6416; County Clerk- 715-273-3531. **Property tax/Assessing-** 414 W Main, Ellsworth, WI 54011; 715-273-3531. **Online access-** Access to county property data is free at www.co.pierce.wi.us/Land%20Information%20Disclaimer.html. Click on Property Data Search.

Polk County

Register of Deeds, PO Box 335, Balsam Lake, WI 54810-0335. 715-485-9240; fax-715-485-9202; 8:30AM-4:30PM. www.co.polk.wi.us

Index: All in one. Records indexed on a public use terminal back to 9/95. Only the public may search. Copy fee $2.00 1st page, $1.00 each add'l page. Plats- $5.00 each. Cert fee- $1.00 per doc plus copy fee. Payee- Register of Deeds. **Other phones:** Treasurer- 715-485-9254; Elections- 715-485-9223; Vital Records- 715-485-9240; County Clerk- 715-485-9226. **Other Online Records-** assessor and GIS-records free at http://216.56.44.70/default.htm and click on Parcel Search.

Portage County

Register of Deeds, 1516 Church St; County-City Bldg, Stevens Point, WI 54481. 715-346-1428; fax-715-345-5361; 7:30AM-4:30PM www.co.portage.wi.us/rod/rod.shtm

Index: All in one. Records indexed on a public use terminal back to 1984. Only the public may search. Copy fee $2.00 1st page, $1.00 each add'l page. Cert fee- $1.00 per cert. Payee- Register of Deeds. **Online access to Real Estate, Deed records:** Access to county records is free at https://landshark.co.portage.wi.us/LandShark/login.jsp. Registration required; searching is free; fee for copies of images. Property tax data does not include Stevens Point City. **Other phones:** Treasurer- 715-346-1428; County Clerk- 715-346-1351. **Property tax/Assessing-** 715-346-1553. **Online access-** Search the county tax application database free at http://pctax.co.portage.wi.us/PCTax/Taxrtr?action=taxdefault but no name searching. Property data on the GIS mapping site free at http://gisinfo.co.portage.wi.us/website/portagepa/viewer.htm. click on Search but no name searching.

Price County

Register of Deeds, 126 Cherry, Phillips, WI 54555. 715-339-2515, R/E recording phone-715-339-2559; fax-715-339-3089; 8AM-N, 1PM-4:30PM www.co.price.wi.us

Index: Separate indices to search include computer, books. Records indexed on a public use terminal back to 1991. Only the public may search. Copy fee $2.00 1st page, $1.00 each add'l page. Cert fee- $1.00 per doc plus copy fee. Payee- Price County Register of Deeds. **Other phones:** Treasurer- 715-339-2615; Elections- 715-339-3325; County Clerk- 715-339-3325. **Property tax/Assessing-** 126 Cherry St, Rm 108, Phillips, WI 54555; 715-339-2559. **Online access-** Access to land record for free go to www.co.price.wi.us/webgis/html/

Racine County

Register of Deeds, 730 Wisconsin Ave, Racine, WI 53403. Recording, R/E phone-262-636-3208, UCC phone-262-636-3849; fax-262-636-3851; 8AM-5PM www.racineco.com/registerofdeeds/index.aspx

Index: Separate indices to search include grantor/grantee, address, tax key number, legal description. Records indexed on computer back to mid-1980's. Office will perform a UCC search but public must search other records themselves. Search fee- $5.00 fee back to mid-1980's, $10.00 fee prior to mid-1980's. Copy fee $2.00 1st page, $1.00 each add'l page. Cert fee- $1.00 per doc plus copy fee. Payee- Racine County Register of Deeds. Bulk data available for purchase. **Online access to Real Estate, Deed records:** Real estate record access is via a dial-up system; email or call the Racine County Register of Deeds Office, 262-636-3208, or see www.racineco.com/registerofdeeds/. **Other phones:** Treasurer- 262-636-3238; Elections- 262-636-3122; Vital Records- 262-636-3477; County Clerk- 262-636-3482. **Property tax/Assessing-** . **Online access-** Tax inquiry should be available free at www.racineco.com/rodtax/.

Richland County

Register of Deeds, PO Box 337, Richland Center, WI 53581. 608-647-3011; fax-608-647-6134; 8:30AM-4:30PM www.rclrs.net/rod/default.asp
Index: All in one. Records indexed on a public use terminal back to 1993. Office personnel or visitors may perform searches. Search fee $10.00 per name. Office will search real estate records 1993 forward only. Copy fee $2.00 1st page, $1.00 each add'l page. Birth certs-$20.00; Death/Marriage- $20.00; add'l vital stat copies $3.00. Cert fee- $1.00 per cert plus copy fee. Payee- Richland County Register of Deeds. **Online access to Real Estate, Grantor/Grantee, Deed records:** Search recorded land index for free at www.rclrs.net/cds/rod/search.aspx but fees apply to print images. Records go back to 7/30/1993. **Other phones:** Treasurer- 608-647-3658; Vital Records- 608-647-3011; County Clerk- 608-647-2197. **Property tax/Assessing-** 181 W Seminary St, Richland Center, WI 53581; 608-647-3658. **Online access-** Access parcel data free from the Land Information office at www.rclrs.net/cds/parcel/. Also, access property data free at http://gis.msa-ps.com/MAPS/WI/Counties/Richland/Publicviewer/viewer.htm but no name searching.

Rock County

Register of Deeds, 51 S Main St, Janesville, WI 53545. Recording, R/E phone-608-757-5650, UCC phone-608-757-5657; fax-608-757-5563; 8AM-5PM www.co.rock.wi.us/Dept/RegisterDeeds/ROD.htm
Index: Separate indices to search include pre-2001 UCC, 2001-present UCC real estate. Records indexed on a public use terminal back to 2001. Only the public may search. Copy fee $2.00 1st page, $1.00 each add'l page. Cert fee- $1.00 per cert plus copy fee. Payee- Rock County Register of Deeds. **Online access to Real Estate, Deed, Lien records:** Real estate record access available via a dial-up system; email or call the Rock County Register of Deeds Office, 608-757-5650. Also, access recording office data by subscription on either the Laredo system (subscription & fees) or Tapestry System (use credit card) at http://tapestry.fidlar.com; $5.99 search; $.50 per image. Index goes back to 8/1986; images back to 1986. **Other phones:** Treasurer- 608-757-5670; Vital Records- 608-757-5656; County Clerk- 608-757-5660. **Other Online Records-** Access the City of Janesville Assessor database free at www.ci.janesville.wi.us/Scripts2/gvsweb.dll/search. No name searching.

Rusk County

Register of Deeds, 311 Miner Ave, Rm N132, Ladysmith, WI 54848. 715-532-2139; fax-715-532-2194; 8-4:30 www.ruskcounty.org/services/deeds.asp
Index: All in one. Records indexed on a public use terminal back to 1999. Only the public may search. Copy fee $2.00 1st page, $1.00 each add'l page. Cert fee- $1.00 per page plus copy fee. Payee- Rusk County Register of Deeds. **Other phones:** County Clerk- 715-532-2100. **Other Online Records-** Access assessor land data free at www.ruskcogiws.com/RuskCoWi/ .

Sauk County

Register of Deeds, 505 Broadway St, Baraboo, WI 53913. 608-355-3288; fax-608-355-4439; 8-4:30PM. www.co.sauk.wi.us/dept/regodeed/index.html
Index: All in one. Records indexed on a public use terminal back to 1987. Only the public may search. Will not search UCC records. Copy fee $2.00 1st page, $1.00 each add'l page. Cert fee- $1.00 per doc plus copy fee. Payee- Register of Deeds. CDs of bulk data available from Recorder's office. Contact Brent Bailey. **Online access to Real Estate, Deed records:** Access to recorder's land records is available free or by subscription for full-time access at http://landshark.co.sauk.wi.us/. Registration required; setup account thru Recorder office. Occasional users search free, but view documents for $2 first page, $1 each add'l. **Other phones:** Treasurer- 608-355-3276; County Clerk- 608-356-5581. **Property tax/Assessing-** 505 Broadway St, Baraboo, WI 53913; 608-355-5581. **Online access-** Search Village of Spring Green property data free at www.wendorffassessing.com/Spring_Green_options.htm. No name searching. Village of Plain property at www.wendorffassessing.com/Plain_options.htm.

Sawyer County

Register of Deeds, PO Box 686; 10610 Main St, Hayward, WI 54843-0686. 715-634-4867; fax-715-634-6839; 8AM-4PM. http://sawyercountygov.org
Index: All in one. Records indexed on a public use terminal back to 1988. Only the public may search. Copy fee $2.00 1st page, $1.00 each add'l page. Cert fee- $1.00 per page plus copy fee. Payee- Register of Deeds. **Online access to Real Estate, Deed, Lien, Subdivision, Condo, Plat, Survey Map records:** Recording office data by subscription on either the Laredo system using subscription and fees or the Tapestry System using credit card, http://tapestry.fidlar.com; $3.99 search; $.50 per image. Index and images go back to 1988. **Other phones:** Treasurer- 715-634-4868; Elections- 715-634-4866; Vital Records- 715-634-4867; County Clerk- 715-634-4866. **Property tax/Assessing-** Treasure's Office, PO Box 935, Hayward, WI 54843; 715-634-4868, assessor fax- 715-634-6839.

Shawano County

Register of Deeds, 311 N Main, Shawano, WI 54166. 715-524-2129; fax-715-524-2130; 8AM-4:30PM www.co.shawano.wi.us
Index: All in one. Records indexed on a public use terminal back to 8/12/96. Only the public may search. Will not search UCC records. Copy fee $2.00 per page. Cert fee- $1.00 per doc plus copy fee. Payee- Register of Deeds. **Other phones:** Treasurer- 715-524-9130; Elections- 715-526-4841; Vital Records- 715-524-2129; County Clerk- 715-526-9150. **Property tax/Assessing-** 311 N Main, Shawano, WI 54166; 715-524-9130. **Online access-** Access parcel data free at http://gis.co.shawano.wi.us/portal/ but no name searching.

Sheboygan County

Register of Deeds, 508 New York Ave, 2nd Fl, Sheboygan, WI 53081. 920-459-3023; fax-920-459-1338; 8AM-5PM www.co.sheboygan.wi.us/html/d_regdeeds.html
Index: Separate indices to search include computer, tract books, abstract books. Records indexed on a public use terminal by name back to 1992. Only the public may search. Copy fee $2.00 1st page; $1.00 each add'l. page. Cert fee- $1.00 per doc plus copy fee. Payee- Register of Deeds. **Online access to Real Estate, Deed, Lien records:** Recording office data by subscription on either the Laredo system using subscription and fees or the Tapestry System using credit card, http://tapestry.fidlar.com; $5.95 search; $.50 per image. Index and images go back to 1/1992; tract data to 7/18/1996. **Other phones:** Treasurer- 920-459-3015; Vital Records- 920-459-3872; County Clerk- 920-459-3002. **Other Online Records-** Lookup parcel and property tax data free at www.co.sheboygan.wi.us/landinformation/portal_public.aspx but no name searching. Also, lookup parcel, property tax, and GIS and surveys free at www.co.sheboygan.wi.us/landinformation/portal_public.aspx but no name searching.

St. Croix County

Register of Deeds, 1101 Carmichael Rd, Hudson, WI 54016. Recording, R/E phone-715-386-4652, UCC recording phone-715-386-4655; fax-715-386-4687; 8AM-5PM www.co.saint-croix.wi.us
Index: All in one. Records indexed on a public use terminal back to 1999. Only the public may search. Copy fee $2.00 1st page, $1.00 each add'l page. Cert fee- $1.00 per page includes copy fee. Payee- Register of Deeds. Bulk data available for purchase, contact Kathleen Walsh. **Online access to Real Estate, Deed, Lien records:** Recording office data by subscription on either the Laredo system using subscription and fees or Tapestry System using credit card, http://tapestry.fidlar.com; $3.99 search; $.50 per image. Index goes back to 1/1997; images to 11/1974; Liens back to 1990. **Other phones:** Treasurer- 715-386-4645; Elections- 715-386-4609; Vital Records- 715-386-4653; County Clerk- 715-386-4610. **Property tax/Assessing-** 1101 Carmichael Rd, Hudson, 54016; 715-386-4677, fax- 715-386-4686.

Taylor County

Register of Deeds, 224 S 2nd St, Medford, WI 54451-1811. 715-748-1483; fax-715-748-1446; 8:30-4:30 www.co.taylor.wi.us/departments/rod/ROD.html
Index: All in one. Records indexed on a public use terminal back to 1995. Only the public may search. Copy fee $2.00 1st page, $1.00 each add'l page. Cert fee- $1.00 per cert plus copy fee. Payee- Taylor County Register of Deeds. **Online access to Real Estate, Deed, Lien, Mortgage records:** Access county land records back to 1/1998 with Landshark sub at https://landshark.co.taylor.wi.us/LandShark/. Index search is free; images are $2.00 1st page, $1.00 each add'l. **Other phones:** Treasurer- 715-748-1466; Vital Records- 715-748-1483; County Clerk- 715-748-1460. **Property tax/Assessing-** Real Property Lister, 224 S 2nd St 2nd Fl, Medford, WI 54451; 715-748-1465, assessor fax- 715-748-1415. www.co.taylor.wi.us/departments/rp/real_property.html **Online-** Search property and tax data free at http://taylorwi.mapping-online.com/TaylorCoWi/default.htm and click on Search button at right-hand top.

Trempealeau County

Register of Deeds, PO Box 67, Whitehall, WI 54773. 715-538-2311, R/E recording phone-715-538-2311 x214; fax-715-538-1302; 8AM-4:30PM www.tremplocounty.com
Index: All in one. Grantor/grantee records indexed on a public use terminal. Only the public may search. Copy fee $2.00 1st page, $1.00 each add'l page. Cert fee- $1.00 per cert plus copy fee. Payee- Trempealeau County Register of Deeds. Bulk data available for purchase, contact Rose Ohum for fees. **Other phones:** Treasurer- 715-538-2311 x219; Vital Records- 715-538-2311 x214; County Clerk- 715-538-2311. **Property tax/Assessing-** 715-538-2311 x248. **Online-** Access county assessor's database free at www.tremplocounty.com/Search/Search.asp.

Vernon County

Register of Deeds, 400 Courthouse Sq Rm 110, Viroqua, WI 54665. 608-637-5371; fax-608-637-5304; 8:30AM-4:30PM www.vernoncounty.org
Index: All in one. Records indexed on a public use terminal back to approx 7/00. Only the public may search. Copy fee $2.00 1st page, $1.00 each add'l page. Cert fee- $1.00 per cert plus copy fee. Payee- Vernon County Register of Deeds. **Online access to Real Estate, Mortgages, Grantor/Grantee records:** Access to records for free go to www.vcdeeds.org/ . **Other phones:** Treasurer- 608-637-5365; Elections- 608-637-5380; Vital Records- 608-637-5371; County Clerk- 608-637-5380. **Property tax/Assessing-** PO Box 49, Viroqua, WI 54665; 608-637-5365.

Vilas County

Register of Deeds, 330 Court St, Eagle River, WI 54521. 715-479-3660; fax-715-479-3695; 8AM-4PM http://co.vilas.wi.us
Index: All in one. Records indexed on a public use terminal back to 1996. Office will perform a UCC search but public must search other records themselves. UCC search fee $15.00 per debtor name. Copy fee $2.00 1st page, $1.00 each add'l page. Cert fee- $1.00 per doc plus copy fee. Payee- Register of Deeds. **Other phones:** Treasurer- 715-479-3610; Vital Records- 715-479-3660; County Clerk- 715-479-3600. **Property tax/Assessing**- Same address as recording office. contact treasurer for info. **Online access**- Access property data free by municipality name at http://webtax.co.vilas.wi.us/taxrec1.php but no name searching.

Walworth County

Register of Deeds, PO Box 995, Elkhorn, WI 53121-0995. Recording, R/E phone-262-741-4233, UCC recording phone-262-741-4237; fax-262-741-4947; 8AM-5PM www.co.walworth.wi.us
Index: All in one. Records indexed on a public use terminal back to 2/76. Only the public may search. Copy fee $2.00 1st page, $1.00 each add'l page. Plats- $4.50 per page. Cert fee- $1.00 per doc plus copy fee. Payee- Register of Deeds. Bulk data available for purchase on daily CD containing image of docs recorded previous day at $500.00 per month, contact Connie Woolever at 262-741-4214. **Online access to Real Estate, Grantor/Grantee, Deed records:** Search the Register of Deeds index for free on the county e-government public search page at www.co.walworth.wi.us. Click on "Public Records." Online records go back to 1976. **Other phones:** Treasurer- 262-741-4251; Elections- 262-741-4241; Vital Records- 262-741-4235; County Clerk- 262-741-4245. **Property tax/Assessing**- 100 W Walworth St, Elkhorn, WI 53121; 262-741-4255. **Online access**- Search the treasurer's tax roll list under "Tax Roll Documents" at www.co.walworth.wi.us. Search parcel and land data free on the gis-mapping site at www.co.walworth.wi.us/Information%20Systems/LID%20Website/divpageims.htm but no name searching.

Washburn County

Register of Deeds, PO Box 607, Shell Lake, WI 54871. 715-468-4616; fax-715-468-4658; 8AM-4:30PM www.co.washburn.wi.us/departments/registerofdeeds/index.htm
Index: All in one. Records indexed on a public use terminal back to 1995. Only the public may search. Copy fee $2.00 1st page, $1.00 each add'l page. Cert fee- $1.00 per doc plus copy fee. Payee- Register of deeds. Bulk data available for purchase, contact Diane Paoch. **Other phones:** Treasurer- 715-468-4650; Elections- 715-468-4605; Vital Records- 715-468-4616; County Clerk- 715-468-4600. **Property tax/Assessing**- 10 4th Ave, Shell Lake, WI 54871; 715-468-4654, assessor fax- 715-468-4640.

Washington County

Register of Deeds, PO Box 1986, West Bend, WI 53095-7986. 262-335-4318, R/E recording phone-262-335-4320; fax-262-335-6866; 8AM-4:30PM. www.co.washington.wi.us/washington/contacts.jsp
Index: All in one. Records indexed on a public use terminal back to 1992. Only the public may search. Will not search UCC records. Copy fee $2.00 1st page, $1.00 each add'l page. Cert fee- $3.00 1st page; $1.00 each add'l. Payee- Register of Deeds. **Online access to Real Estate, Deed records:** Access to Landshark for real estate records available for a fee at www.co.washington.wi.us/departments.iml?mdl=departments.mdl&ID=REG. **Other phones:** Treasurer- 262-335-4325; Elections- 262-335-4468; Vital Records- 262-335-4321; County Clerk- 262-335-4305. **Property tax/Assessing**- PO Box 1986, West Bend, WI 53095; 262-335-4370.

Waukesha County

Register of Deeds, 1320 Pewaukee Rd, Waukesha, WI 53188. 262-548-7863, R/E recording phone-262-548-7590, UCC phone-262-548-7585; fax-262-548-7576; 8AM-4:30PM www.waukeshacounty.gov
Index: All in one. Records indexed on a public use terminal back to 1995. Only the public may search. Copy fee $2.00 1st page; $1.00 each add'l page. Cert fee- $1.00 per page plus copy fee. Payee- Waukesha County Register of Deeds. **Online access to Real Estate, Deed, Lien, Marriage, UCC records:** Access the recording database free at http://dwprd.waukeshacounty.gov/applications/production/ROD_TRACT_DOCUMENTS/. **Other phones:** Treasurer- 262-548-7576; County Clerk- 262-548-7010. **Property tax/Assessing**- 262-542-0455. **Online access**- Search assessor property data at www.ci.waukesha.wi.us/Parcel/DataInquiry1.jsp. Search county tax listings at http://dwprd.waukeshacounty.gov/applications/production/ROD_TAX_LISTING/ but no name searching at either site. Waukesha City assessor database. or sales lists free at www.ci.waukesha.wi.us/Assessor/propertySalesInformation.html. Personal property at www.ci.waukesha.wi.us/Assessor/Documents/ppAssessmentRoll.txt. Wauwatosa property data at www.wauwatosa.net/display/wspTosaAssessmentTemplate.asp.

Waupaca County

Register of Deeds, PO Box 307, Waupaca, WI 54981. 715-258-6250; fax-715-258-4990; 8AM-4PM. www.co.waupaca.wi.us
Index: All in one. Records indexed on computer back to 1982. Only the public may search. Copy fee $2.00 1st page, $1.00 each add'l page. Cert fee- $3.00 1st page plus copy fee for add'l pages. Payee- Register of Deeds. **Online access to Real Estate, Deed records:** Access to the Register of Deeds data requires subscription, username and password. Monthly fee is $450.00. For info, call 715-258-6250. Records go back to 1982; monthly or daily subscriptions available. **Other phones:** Treasurer- 715-258-6220; Elections- 715-258-6200; Vital Records- 715-258-6250; County Clerk- 715-258-6200. **Property tax/Assessing**- 811 Harding St, Waupaca, WI 54981; 715-258-6215. **Online access**- Access land information office data free at http://public1.co.waupaca.wi.us/CountyMap_Public93/. A fee and registration is required for name searching; may also use credit card and purchase records for statutory fee plus small service charge.

Waushara County

Register of Deeds, PO Box 338, Wautoma, WI 54982. 920-787-0444; fax-920-787-0425; 8AM-4:30PM. www.co.waushara.wi.us
Index: All in one. Records indexed on a public use terminal back to 1993. Only the public may search. Copy fee $2.00 1st page, $1.00 each add'l page. Cert fee- $1.00 per doc plus copy fee. Payee- Register of Deeds. **Online access to Assessment/Property Tax, Parcel, GIS-Mapping records:** Access to records for free go to www.co.waushara.wi.us/ . **Other phones:** Treasurer- 920-787-0445; Elections- 920-787-0442; Vital Records- 920-787-0444; County Clerk- 920-787-0442. **Property tax/Assessing**- PO Box 338, Waushara, WI 54982; 920-787-0444. **Online access**- Search property data free on county land information system at www.co.waushara.wi.us/Website/WausharaPA/viewer.htm.

Winnebago County

Register of Deeds, PO Box 2808, Oshkosh, WI 54903-2808. Recording, R/E phone-920-236-4881, UCC recording phone-920-236-4883; fax-920-236-4813; 8AM-4:30PM www.co.winnebago.wi.us
Index: All in one. Records indexed on a public use terminal back to 1987 with document number. Only the public may search. Copy fee $2.00 1st page, $1.00 each add'l page. Cert fee- $1.00 per cert plus copy fee. Payee- Winnebago County Register of Deeds. **Online access to Real Estate, Deed, Lien records:** Recording office data by subscription on either the Laredo system using subscription and fees or the Tapestry System using credit card, http://tapestry.fidlar.com; $3.99 search; $.50 per image. Index goes back to 11/1995; images to 1985. **Other phones:** Treasurer- 920-236-4777; Elections- 920-236-4888; Vital Records- 920-236-4882; County Clerk- 920-236-4890. **Property tax/Assessing**- Treasurer's Office, 415 Jackson St, Rm #120, Oshkosh, WI 54901; 920-236-4777. www.co.winnebago.wi.us/Tax/TreasurerMain.htm **Online access**- Property records on the City of Oshkosh assessor database are free at www.ci.oshkosh.wi.us/oshkosh_ias/Search/Disclaimer2.aspx?FromUrl=./Search/GenericSearch.aspx?mode= owner. Also, City of Neenah property data is at. www.3.ci.neenah.wi.us/WebInquiry/ but no name searching. Also, access the City of Menasha Tax Roll Information database free at www.cityofmenasha-wi.gov/content/departments/finance/(3)tax_roll_information.php.

Wood County

Register of Deeds, PO Box 8095, Wisconsin Rapids, WI 54495. 715-421-8450; fax-715-421-8446; 8AM-4:30PM www.co.wood.wi.us
Index: All in one. Records indexed on a public use terminal back to 1980. Only the public may search. Copy fee $2.00 1st page, $1.00 each add'l page. Cert fee- $1.00 per cert plus copy fee. Payee- Wood County Register of Deeds. **Online access to Real Estate, Deed, Lien, Land Map/Records records:** Recording office data by subscription on either the Laredo system using subscription and fees or the Tapestry System using credit card, http://tapestry.fidlar.com; $5.95 search; $.50 per image. Index goes back to 1979; images to 8/1999. Also, access to land maps/records for free go to http://landrecords.co.wood.wi.us/website/Public/viewer.htm . **Other phones:** Treasurer- 715-421-8484; County Clerk- 715-421-8460. **Property tax/Assessing**- County Treasurer, 400 Market St, Wisconsin Rapids, WI 54495; 715-421-8484, assessor fax- 715-421-8481.

Wisconsin County Locator

You will usually be able to find the city name in the City/County Cross Reference below. In that case, it is a simple matter to determine the county from the cross reference. However, only the official US Postal Service city names are included in this index. There are an additional 40,000 place names that people use in their addresses. Therefore, we have also included a ZIP/City Cross Reference immediately following the City/County Cross Reference.

If you know the ZIP Code but the city name does not appear in the City/County Cross Reference index, look up the ZIP Code in the ZIP/City Cross Reference, find the city name, then look up the city name in the City/County Cross Reference. For example, you want to know the county for an address of Menands, NY 12204. There is no "Menands" in the City/County Cross Reference. The ZIP/City Cross Reference shows that ZIP Codes 12201-12288 are for the city of Albany. Looking back in the City/County Cross Reference, Albany is in Albany County.

Wisconsin City/County Cross Reference

ABBOTSFORD (54405) Clark(71), Marathon(28)
ABRAMS Oconto
ADAMS Adams
ADELL Sheboygan
AFTON Rock
ALBANY Green
ALGOMA (54201) Kewaunee(96), Door(3)
ALGOMA Kewaunee
ALLENTON (53002) Washington(97), Dodge(2)
ALMA Buffalo
ALMA CENTER Jackson
ALMENA Barron
ALMOND (54909) Portage(88), Waushara(11)
ALTOONA Eau Claire
AMBERG Marinette
AMERY Polk
AMHERST Portage
AMHERST JUNCTION Portage
ANIWA (54408) Marathon(56), Shawano(39), Langlade(4)
ANTIGO (54409) Langlade(97), Marathon(1), Shawano(1)
APPLETON (54914) Outagamie(97), Winnebago(2)
APPLETON (54915) Outagamie(53), Calumet(32), Winnebago(13)
APPLETON Outagamie
ARCADIA (54612) Trempealeau(89), Buffalo(10)
ARENA Iowa
ARGONNE Forest
ARGYLE (53504) Lafayette(75), Green(25)
ARKANSAW (54721) Pepin(88), Pierce(6), Dunn(5)
ARKDALE Adams
ARLINGTON (53911) Columbia(93), Dane(6)
ARMSTRONG CREEK (54103) Forest(82), Marinette(16), Florence(1)
ARPIN Wood
ASHIPPUN Dodge
ASHLAND (54806) Ashland(86), Bayfield(13)
ATHELSTANE (54104) Marinette(97), Oconto(1), Forest(1)
ATHENS (54411) Marathon(97), Taylor(2)
AUBURNDALE (54412) Wood(75), Marathon(24)
AUGUSTA Eau Claire
AVALON (53505) Rock(98), Walworth(1)
AVOCA Iowa
BABCOCK Wood
BAGLEY Grant
BAILEYS HARBOR Door
BALDWIN St. Croix
BALSAM LAKE Polk
BANCROFT (54921) Portage(89), Adams(8), Waushara(1)
BANGOR La Crosse
BARABOO Sauk
BARNEVELD Iowa
BARRON Barron
BARRONETT (54813) Barron(51), Burnett(31), Washburn(16)
BASSETT Kenosha
BAY CITY Pierce
BAYFIELD Bayfield
BEAR CREEK (54922) Outagamie(54), Waupaca(45)
BEAVER DAM Dodge
BEETOWN Grant
BELDENVILLE Pierce
BELGIUM (53004) Ozaukee(98), Sheboygan(1)
BELLEVILLE (53508) Dane(72), Green(27)
BELMONT Lafayette
BELOIT Rock
BENET LAKE Kenosha
BENOIT Bayfield
BENTON Lafayette
BERLIN (54923) Green Lake(71), Waushara(25), Winnebago(3)
BIG BEND Waukesha
BIG FALLS Waupaca
BIRCHWOOD (54817) Washburn(40), Sawyer(31), Barron(24), Rusk(2)
BIRNAMWOOD (54414) Shawano(77), Marathon(21)
BLACK CREEK (54106) Outagamie(98), Shawano(1)
BLACK EARTH Dane
BLACK RIVER FALLS (54615) Jackson(98), Monroe(1)
BLAIR (54616) Trempealeau(96), Jackson(3)
BLANCHARDVILLE (53516) Lafayette(57), Green(21), Iowa(18), Dane(2)
BLENKER Wood
BLOOM CITY Richland
BLOOMER Chippewa
BLOOMINGTON Grant
BLUE MOUNDS (53517) Dane(62), Iowa(37)
BLUE RIVER (53518) Richland(70), Grant(24), Crawford(5)
BONDUEL (54107) Shawano(96), Outagamie(3)
BOSCOBEL (53805) Grant(68), Crawford(31)
BOULDER JUNCTION Vilas
BOWLER Shawano
BOYCEVILLE Dunn
BOYD (54726) Chippewa(62), Eau Claire(37)
BRANCH Manitowoc
BRANDON (53919) Fond du Lac(98), Green Lake(1)
BRANTWOOD Price
BRIGGSVILLE (53920) Marquette(67), Adams(32)
BRILL Barron
BRILLION (54110) Calumet(79), Manitowoc(18), Brown(2)
BRISTOL Kenosha
BRODHEAD (53520) Green(74), Rock(25)
BROKAW Marathon
BROOKFIELD Waukesha
BROOKLYN (53521) Green(45), Dane(31), Rock(23)
BROOKS Adams
BROWNSVILLE (53006) Dodge(70), Fond du Lac(29)
BROWNTOWN (53522) Green(92), Lafayette(7)
BRUCE Rusk
BRULE (54820) Douglas(69), Bayfield(30)
BRUSSELS Door
BRYANT Langlade
BURLINGTON (53105) Racine(67), Walworth(19), Kenosha(13)
BURNETT Dodge
BUTLER Waukesha
BUTTE DES MORTS Winnebago
BUTTERNUT (54514) Ashland(53), Price(39), Iron(7)
BYRON Fond du Lac
CABLE (54821) Bayfield(98), Sawyer(1)
CADOTT (54727) Chippewa(91), Eau Claire(8)
CALEDONIA Racine
CAMBRIA (53923) Columbia(88), Green Lake(11)
CAMBRIDGE (53523) Dane(50), Jefferson(49)
CAMERON Barron
CAMP DOUGLAS (54618) Juneau(63), Monroe(36)
CAMP LAKE Kenosha
CAMPBELLSPORT (53010) Fond du Lac(94), Washington(4)
CAROLINE Shawano
CASCADE (53011) Sheboygan(91), Fond du Lac(8)
CASCO (54205) Kewaunee(97), Door(2)
CASHTON (54619) Monroe(77), Vernon(21), La Crosse(1)
CASSVILLE Grant
CATARACT Monroe
CATAWBA Price
CATO Manitowoc
CAZENOVIA (53924) Richland(96), Sauk(3)
CECIL (54111) Shawano(90), Oconto(9)
CEDAR GROVE (53013) Sheboygan(84), Ozaukee(15)
CEDARBURG (53012) Ozaukee(95), Washington(4)
CENTURIA Polk
CHASEBURG Vernon
CHELSEA Taylor
CHETEK (54728) Barron(87), Rusk(11), Dunn(1)
CHILI (54420) Clark(96), Wood(3)
CHILTON (53014) Calumet(97), Manitowoc(2)
CHIPPEWA FALLS (54729) Chippewa(97), Eau Claire(2)
CHIPPEWA FALLS Chippewa
CLAM LAKE (54517) Ashland(93), Sawyer(6)
CLAYTON (54004) Polk(59), Barron(40)
CLEAR LAKE (54005) Polk(79), St. Croix(11), Dunn(5), Barron(3)
CLEVELAND (53015) Manitowoc(86), Sheboygan(14)
CLINTON (53525) Rock(97), Walworth(2)
CLINTONVILLE (54929) Waupaca(69), Shawano(29), Outagamie(1)
CLYMAN Dodge
COBB Iowa
COCHRANE Buffalo
COLBY (54421) Clark(74), Marathon(25)
COLEMAN (54112) Marinette(76), Oconto(23)
COLFAX (54730) Dunn(77), Chippewa(22)
COLGATE (53017) Washington(72), Waukesha(27)
COLLINS Manitowoc
COLOMA (54930) Waushara(83), Adams(14), Marquette(2)
COLUMBUS (53925) Columbia(82), Dodge(13), Dane(4)
COMBINED LOCKS Outagamie
COMSTOCK (54826) Barron(62), Polk(37)
CONOVER Vilas
CONRATH Rusk
COON VALLEY (54623) Vernon(52), La Crosse(47)
CORNELL Chippewa
CORNUCOPIA Bayfield
COTTAGE GROVE Dane
COUDERAY Sawyer
CRANDON Forest
CRIVITZ (54114) Marinette(91), Oconto(8)
CROSS PLAINS Dane
CUBA CITY (53807) Grant(86), Lafayette(13)
CUDAHY Milwaukee
CUMBERLAND (54829) Barron(91), Polk(8)
CURTISS (54422) Clark(94), Taylor(5)
CUSHING Polk
CUSTER (54423) Portage(98), Marathon(1)
DALE Outagamie
DALLAS Barron
DALTON (53926) Green Lake(72), Marquette(15), Columbia(12)
DANBURY (54830) Burnett(93), Douglas(6)
DANE Dane
DARIEN (53114) Walworth(84), Rock(15)
DARLINGTON Lafayette
DE FOREST (53532) Dane(97), Columbia(2)
DE PERE (54115) Brown(92), Outagamie(7)
DE SOTO (54624) Vernon(89), Crawford(10)
DEER PARK (54007) St. Croix(67), Polk(32)
DEERBROOK Langlade
DEERFIELD Dane
DELAFIELD Waukesha
DELAVAN Walworth
DELLWOOD Adams
DENMARK (54208) Brown(53), Kewaunee(38), Manitowoc(7)

DICKEYVILLE Grant
DODGE Trempealeau
DODGEVILLE Iowa
DORCHESTER (54425) Clark(83), Marathon(9), Taylor(6)
DOUSMAN (53118) Waukesha(96), Jefferson(3)
DOWNING (54734) Dunn(94), St. Croix(5)
DOWNSVILLE Dunn
DOYLESTOWN Columbia
DRESSER Polk
DRUMMOND Bayfield
DUNBAR Marinette
DURAND (54736) Pepin(82), Buffalo(17)
EAGLE (53119) Waukesha(93), Walworth(4), Jefferson(2)
EAGLE RIVER (54521) Vilas(78), Oneida(19), Forest(1)
EAST ELLSWORTH Pierce
EAST TROY (53120) Walworth(97), Racine(2)
EASTMAN Crawford
EAU CLAIRE (54703) Eau Claire(89), Chippewa(10)
EAU CLAIRE Eau Claire
EAU GALLE (54737) Dunn(96), Pepin(3)
EDEN Fond du Lac
EDGAR Marathon
EDGERTON (53534) Rock(84), Dane(13), Jefferson(2)
EDGEWATER Sawyer
EDMUND Iowa
EGG HARBOR Door
ELAND (54427) Marathon(66), Shawano(33)
ELCHO (54428) Langlade(96), Oneida(3)
ELDERON Marathon
ELDORADO Fond du Lac
ELEVA (54738) Eau Claire(58), Trempealeau(40), Buffalo(1)
ELK MOUND (54739) Dunn(62), Chippewa(37)
ELKHART LAKE (53020) Sheboygan(93), Manitowoc(3), Calumet(2)
ELKHORN Walworth
ELLISON BAY Door
ELLSWORTH Pierce
ELM GROVE Waukesha
ELMWOOD (54740) Pierce(79), Dunn(20)
ELROY (53929) Juneau(82), Monroe(11), Vernon(5)
ELTON Langlade
EMBARRASS Waupaca
EMERALD St. Croix
EMERALDX St. Croix
ENDEAVOR Marquette
EPHRAIM Door
ETTRICK (54627) Trempealeau(91), Jackson(8)
EUREKA Winnebago
EVANSVILLE (53536) Rock(96), Green(3)
EXELAND (54835) Sawyer(89), Rusk(10)
FAIRCHILD (54741) Jackson(51), Eau Claire(48)
FAIRWATER Fond du Lac
FALL CREEK Eau Claire
FALL RIVER (53932) Columbia(95), Dodge(4)
FENCE (54120) Florence(78), Marinette(21)
FENNIMORE Grant
FERRYVILLE (54628) Crawford(93), Vernon(6)
FIFIELD Price
FISH CREEK Door
FOND DU LAC Fond du Lac
FONTANA Walworth
FOOTVILLE Rock
FOREST JUNCTION Calumet
FORESTVILLE (54213) Door(85), Kewaunee(14)
FORT ATKINSON (53538) Jefferson(97), Rock(2)
FOUNTAIN CITY Buffalo
FOX LAKE Dodge
FOXBORO Douglas
FRANCIS CREEK Manitowoc
FRANKLIN Milwaukee
FRANKSVILLE Racine
FREDERIC (54837) Polk(81), Burnett(18)
FREDONIA (53021) Ozaukee(88), Washington(11)
FREEDOM Outagamie
FREMONT (54940) Waupaca(51), Waushara(29), Winnebago(14), Outagamie(4)
FRIENDSHIP Adams
FRIESLAND Columbia
GALESVILLE Trempealeau
GALLOWAY Marathon
GAYS MILLS Crawford
GENESEE DEPOT Waukesha
GENOA Vernon
GENOA CITY (53128) Walworth(80), Kenosha(19)
GERMANTOWN Washington
GILE Iron
GILLETT (54124) Oconto(87), Menominee(9), Shawano(2)
GILLETT Oconto
GILLETT Shawano
GILMAN (54433) Taylor(80), Chippewa(19)
GILMANTON Buffalo
GLEASON (54435) Lincoln(69), Langlade(30)
GLEN FLORA Rusk
GLEN HAVEN Grant
GLENBEULAH Sheboygan
GLENWOOD CITY St. Croix
GLIDDEN Ashland
GOODMAN (54125) Marinette(98), Forest(1)
GORDON Douglas
GOTHAM Richland
GRAFTON Ozaukee
GRAND MARSH Adams
GRAND VIEW Bayfield
GRANTON Clark
GRANTSBURG (54840) Burnett(98), Polk(1)
GRATIOT Lafayette
GREEN BAY Brown
GREEN LAKE Green Lake
GREEN VALLEY Shawano
GREENBUSH Sheboygan
GREENDALE Milwaukee
GREENLEAF (54126) Brown(96), Manitowoc(3)
GREENVILLE Outagamie
GREENWOOD Clark
GRESHAM Shawano
GURNEY Iron
HAGER CITY Pierce
HALES CORNERS Milwaukee
HAMMOND St. Croix
HANCOCK (54943) Waushara(81), Adams(18)
HANNIBAL Taylor
HANOVER Rock
HARSHAW Oneida
HARTFORD (53027) Washington(96), Dodge(3)
HARTLAND Waukesha
HATLEY Marathon
HAUGEN Barron
HAWKINS (54530) Rusk(71), Price(27)
HAWTHORNE Douglas
HAYWARD (54843) Sawyer(96), Washburn(3)
HAZEL GREEN (53811) Grant(94), Lafayette(5)
HAZELHURST Oneida
HEAFFORD JUNCTION Lincoln
HELENVILLE Jefferson
HERBSTER Bayfield
HERTEL Burnett
HEWITT Wood
HIGH BRIDGE Ashland
HIGHLAND (53543) Iowa(91), Grant(8)
HILBERT Calumet
HILLPOINT (53937) Sauk(63), Richland(36)
HILLSBORO (54634) Vernon(79), Richland(19), Juneau(1)
HILLSDALE Barron
HINGHAM Sheboygan
HIXTON Jackson
HOLCOMBE (54745) Chippewa(87), Rusk(12)
HOLLANDALE (53544) Iowa(97), Dane(1)
HOLMEN La Crosse
HONEY CREEK Walworth
HORICON Dodge
HORTONVILLE Outagamie
HOULTON St. Croix
HUBERTUS Washington
HUDSON St. Croix
HUMBIRD (54746) Clark(77), Jackson(22)
HURLEY Iron
HUSTISFORD Dodge
HUSTLER Juneau
INDEPENDENCE (54747) Trempealeau(82), Buffalo(17)
IOLA (54945) Waupaca(96), Portage(3)
IOLA Waupaca
IRMA Lincoln
IRON BELT Iron
IRON RIDGE Dodge
IRON RIVER Bayfield
IXONIA (53036) Jefferson(73), Dodge(19), Waukesha(6)
JACKSON Washington
JANESVILLE Rock
JEFFERSON Jefferson
JIM FALLS Chippewa
JOHNSON CREEK Jefferson
JUDA Green
JUMP RIVER Taylor
JUNCTION CITY (54443) Portage(95), Marathon(2), Wood(2)
JUNEAU Dodge
KANSASVILLE (53139) Racine(85), Kenosha(14)
KAUKAUNA (54130) Outagamie(95), Brown(2), Calumet(1)
KELLNERSVILLE Manitowoc
KEMPSTER Langlade
KENDALL (54638) Monroe(88), Vernon(9), Juneau(2)
KENNAN Price
KENOSHA Kenosha
KESHENA Menominee
KEWASKUM (53040) Washington(76), Sheboygan(13), Fond du Lac(9)
KEWAUNEE Kewaunee
KIEL (53042) Manitowoc(95), Calumet(4)
KIELER Grant
KIMBERLY Outagamie
KING Waupaca
KINGSTON Green Lake
KNAPP (54749) Dunn(88), St. Croix(11)
KOHLER Sheboygan
KRAKOW (54137) Shawano(76), Oconto(23)
LA CROSSE La Crosse
LA FARGE (54639) Vernon(93), Richland(6)
LA POINTE Ashland
LA VALLE (53941) Sauk(97), Juneau(1)
LAC DU FLAMBEAU (54538) Vilas(90), Oneida(5), Price(4)
LADYSMITH Rusk
LAKE DELTON Sauk
LAKE GENEVA Walworth
LAKE MILLS Jefferson
LAKE NEBAGAMON Douglas
LAKE TOMAHAWK Oneida
LAKEWOOD Oconto
LANCASTER Grant
LAND O LAKES Vilas
LANNON Waukesha
LAONA Forest
LARSEN Winnebago
LEBANON Dodge
LENA (54139) Oconto(98), Marinette(1)
LEOPOLIS Shawano
LEWIS Polk
LILY Langlade
LIME RIDGE Sauk
LINDEN Iowa
LITTLE CHUTE Outagamie
LITTLE SUAMICO Oconto
LIVINGSTON (53554) Grant(70), Iowa(29)
LODI (53555) Columbia(92), Dane(7)
LOGANVILLE Sauk
LOMIRA (53048) Dodge(97), Fond du Lac(2)
LONE ROCK (53556) Richland(83), Sauk(16)
LONG LAKE (54542) Forest(65), Florence(34)
LOWELL Dodge
LOYAL Clark
LUBLIN (54447) Taylor(97), Clark(2)
LUCK (54853) Polk(94), Burnett(5)
LUXEMBURG (54217) Kewaunee(88), Door(5), Brown(5)
LYNDON STATION (53944) Juneau(88), Sauk(11)
LYNXVILLE Crawford
LYONS Walworth
MADISON Dane
MAIDEN ROCK Pierce
MALONE (53049) Fond du Lac(92), Calumet(7)
MANAWA Waupaca
MANCHESTER Green Lake
MANITOWISH WATERS (54545) Vilas(98), Iron(1)
MANITOWOC Manitowoc
MAPLE Douglas
MAPLEWOOD Door
MARATHON Marathon
MARENGO Ashland
MARIBEL (54227) Manitowoc(98), Brown(1)
MARINETTE Marinette
MARION (54950) Shawano(50), Waupaca(49)
MARKESAN (53946) Green Lake(97), Fond du Lac(2)
MARQUETTE Green Lake
MARSHALL (53559) Dane(98), Jefferson(1)
MARSHALL FIELDS Milwaukee
MARSHFIELD (54449) Wood(93), Marathon(6)
MARSHFIELD Wood
MASON (54856) Bayfield(97), Ashland(2)
MATHER Juneau
MATTOON Shawano
MAUSTON Juneau
MAYVILLE Dodge
MAZOMANIE (53560) Dane(96), Iowa(3)
MC FARLAND Dane
MC NAUGHTON Oneida
MEDFORD Taylor
MEDINA Outagamie
MELLEN Ashland
MELROSE Jackson
MENASHA (54952) Winnebago(89), Calumet(10)
MENOMONEE FALLS Waukesha
MENOMONIE Dunn
MEQUON Ozaukee
MERCER Iron

MERRILL (54452) Lincoln(88), Marathon(11)
MERRILLAN (54754) Jackson(85), Clark(14)
MERRIMAC (53561) Sauk(86), Columbia(13)
MERTON Waukesha
MIDDLETON Dane
MIKANA Barron
MILAN Marathon
MILLADORE (54454) Wood(87), Portage(12)
MILLSTON Jackson
MILLTOWN Polk
MILTON Rock
MILWAUKEE Milwaukee
MINDORO (54644) La Crosse(96), Jackson(3)
MINERAL POINT (53565) Iowa(87), Lafayette(12)
MINOCQUA (54548) Oneida(78), Vilas(21)
MINONG (54859) Washburn(88), Douglas(11)
MISHICOT Manitowoc
MONDOVI (54755) Buffalo(63), Eau Claire(12), Dunn(11), Pepin(11)
MONROE Green
MONTELLO (53949) Marquette(98), Green Lake(1)
MONTFORT (53569) Grant(66), Iowa(33)
MONTICELLO Green
MONTREAL Iron
MORRISONVILLE Dane
MOSINEE (54455) Marathon(97), Portage(2)
MOUNT CALVARY Fond du Lac
MOUNT HOPE Grant
MOUNT HOREB Dane
MOUNT STERLING Crawford
MOUNTAIN Oconto
MUKWONAGO (53149) Waukesha(90), Walworth(7), Racine(1)
MUSCODA (53573) Grant(52), Richland(40), Iowa(7)
MUSKEGO (53150) Waukesha(98), Racine(1)
NASHOTAH Waukesha
NECEDAH Juneau
NEENAH Winnebago
NEILLSVILLE Clark
NEKOOSA (54457) Wood(57), Adams(39), Juneau(3)
NELSON Buffalo
NELSONVILLE Portage
NEOPIT Menominee
NEOSHO Dodge
NESHKORO (54960) Marquette(59), Waushara(35), Green Lake(5)
NEW AUBURN (54757) Chippewa(66), Barron(17), Dunn(9), Rusk(6)
NEW BERLIN Waukesha
NEW FRANKEN Brown
NEW GLARUS (53574) Green(98), Dane(1)
NEW HOLSTEIN (53061) Calumet(95), Fond du Lac(4)
NEW HOLSTEIN Calumet
NEW LISBON Juneau
NEW LONDON (54961) Waupaca(81), Outagamie(18)
NEW MUNSTER Kenosha
NEW RICHMOND (54017) St. Croix(98), Polk(1)
NEWBURG Washington
NEWTON Manitowoc
NIAGARA (54151) Marinette(66), Florence(33)
NICHOLS Outagamie
NORTH FREEDOM Sauk
NORTH LAKE Waukesha
NORTH PRAIRIE Waukesha
NORWALK Monroe
OAK CREEK Milwaukee
OAKDALE Monroe
OAKFIELD (53065) Fond du Lac(91), Dodge(8)
OCONOMOWOC (53066) Waukesha(94), Jefferson(3), Dodge(1)
OCONTO Oconto
OCONTO FALLS (54154) Oconto(96), Shawano(3)
ODANAH Ashland
OGDENSBURG Waupaca
OGEMA Price
OJIBWA Sawyer
OKAUCHEE Waukesha
OMRO Winnebago
ONALASKA La Crosse
ONEIDA (54155) Brown(59), Outagamie(40)
ONTARIO (54651) Vernon(61), Monroe(38)
OOSTBURG Sheboygan
OREGON Dane
ORFORDVILLE Rock
OSHKOSH Winnebago
OSSEO (54758) Trempealeau(71), Eau Claire(17), Jackson(11)
OWEN (54460) Clark(96), Taylor(3)
OXFORD (53952) Marquette(51), Adams(48)
PACKWAUKEE Marquette
PALMYRA Jefferson
PARDEEVILLE (53954) Columbia(96), Marquette(3)
PARK FALLS (54552) Price(92), Iron(7)
PATCH GROVE Grant
PEARSON Langlade
PELICAN LAKE (54463) Oneida(95), Langlade(4)
PELL LAKE Walworth
PEMBINE Marinette
PEPIN Pepin
PESHTIGO (54157) Marinette(98), Oconto(1)
PEWAUKEE Waukesha
PHELPS Vilas
PHILLIPS Price
PHLOX Langlade
PICKEREL (54465) Langlade(59), Forest(40)
PICKETT (54964) Winnebago(80), Fond du Lac(19)
PIGEON FALLS Trempealeau
PINE RIVER (54965) Waushara(98), Waupaca(1)
PITTSVILLE (54466) Wood(79), Clark(10), Jackson(9)
PLAIN Sauk
PLAINFIELD (54966) Waushara(85), Portage(13), Adams(1)
PLATTEVILLE (53818) Grant(95), Lafayette(3)
PLEASANT PRAIRIE Kenosha
PLOVER Portage
PLUM CITY Pierce
PLYMOUTH Sheboygan
POPLAR Douglas
PORT EDWARDS Wood
PORT WASHINGTON Ozaukee
PORT WING Bayfield
PORTAGE Columbia
PORTERFIELD Marinette
POSKIN Barron
POTOSI Grant
POTTER Calumet
POUND (54161) Marinette(53), Oconto(46)
POWERS LAKE Kenosha
POY SIPPI Waushara
POYNETTE Columbia
PRAIRIE DU CHIEN (53821) Crawford(98), Grant(1)
PRAIRIE DU SAC (53578) Sauk(90), Columbia(9)
PRAIRIE FARM (54762) Barron(94), Dunn(5)
PRENTICE Price
PRESCOTT Pierce
PRESQUE ISLE Vilas
PRINCETON (54968) Green Lake(93), Marquette(6)
PULASKI (54162) Shawano(62), Brown(28), Oconto(8)
RACINE (53403) Racine(98), Kenosha(1)
RACINE Racine
RADISSON Sawyer
RANDOLPH (53956) Dodge(57), Columbia(39), Green Lake(3)
RANDOLPH Columbia
RANDOM LAKE (53075) Sheboygan(93), Ozaukee(5)
READFIELD Waupaca
READSTOWN (54652) Vernon(96), Crawford(3)
REDGRANITE Waushara
REEDSBURG Sauk
REEDSVILLE Manitowoc
REESEVILLE Dodge
REWEY Iowa
RHINELANDER Oneida
RIB LAKE (54470) Taylor(96), Price(2)
RICE LAKE Barron
RICHFIELD Washington
RICHLAND CENTER Richland
RIDGELAND (54763) Dunn(84), Barron(15)
RIDGEWAY Iowa
RINGLE Marathon
RIO Columbia
RIPON (54971) Fond du Lac(82), Green Lake(13), Winnebago(4)
RIVER FALLS (54022) Pierce(74), St. Croix(25)
ROBERTS St. Croix
ROCHESTER Racine
ROCK FALLS Dunn
ROCK SPRINGS Sauk
ROCKFIELD Washington
ROCKLAND (54653) La Crosse(90), Monroe(9)
ROSENDALE Fond du Lac
ROSHOLT (54473) Portage(79), Marathon(20)
ROTHSCHILD Marathon
ROYALTON Waupaca
RUBICON Dodge
RUDOLPH (54475) Wood(86), Portage(13)
SAINT CLOUD (53079) Fond du Lac(92), Sheboygan(7)
SAINT CROIX FALLS Polk
SAINT FRANCIS Milwaukee
SAINT GERMAIN (54558) Vilas(89), Oneida(10)
SAINT JOSEPH St. Croix
SAINT NAZIANZ Manitowoc
SALEM Kenosha
SAND CREEK Dunn
SARONA (54870) Washburn(96), Barron(3)
SAUK CITY (53583) Sauk(85), Dane(13)
SAUKVILLE Ozaukee
SAXEVILLE Waushara
SAXON (54559) Iron(94), Ashland(5)
SAYNER Vilas
SCANDINAVIA (54977) Waupaca(94), Portage(5)
SCHOFIELD Marathon
SENECA Crawford
SEXTONVILLE Richland
SEYMOUR (54165) Outagamie(95), Shawano(3), Brown(1)
SHARON (53585) Walworth(96), Rock(3)
SHAWANO Shawano
SHEBOYGAN Sheboygan
SHEBOYGAN FALLS Sheboygan
SHELDON (54766) Rusk(59), Taylor(39)
SHELL LAKE (54871) Washburn(65), Burnett(34)
SHERWOOD Calumet
SHIOCTON (54170) Outagamie(93), Shawano(5)
SHULLSBURG Lafayette
SILVER LAKE Kenosha
SINSINAWA Grant
SIREN (54872) Burnett(97), Polk(2)
SISTER BAY Door
SLINGER Washington
SOBIESKI Oconto
SOLDIERS GROVE (54655) Crawford(83), Richland(12), Vernon(3)
SOLON SPRINGS (54873) Bayfield(50), Douglas(49)
SOMERS Kenosha
SOMERSET St. Croix
SOUTH MILWAUKEE Milwaukee
SOUTH RANGE Douglas
SOUTH WAYNE Lafayette
SPARTA Monroe
SPENCER (54479) Marathon(56), Clark(42)
SPOONER (54801) Washburn(83), Burnett(16)
SPRING GREEN (53588) Sauk(77), Iowa(21)
SPRING VALLEY (54767) Pierce(95), St. Croix(3), Dunn(1)
SPRINGBROOK Washburn
SPRINGFIELD Walworth
STANLEY (54768) Chippewa(73), Clark(16), Eau Claire(6), Taylor(2)
STAR LAKE Vilas
STAR PRAIRIE (54026) Polk(61), St. Croix(38)
STETSONVILLE (54480) Taylor(95), Marathon(4)
STEUBEN Crawford
STEVENS POINT Portage
STITZER Grant
STOCKBRIDGE Calumet
STOCKHOLM (54769) Pepin(81), Pierce(18)
STODDARD (54658) Vernon(89), La Crosse(10)
STONE LAKE (54876) Sawyer(68), Washburn(31)
STOUGHTON (53589) Dane(98), Rock(1)
STRATFORD Marathon
STRUM (54770) Trempealeau(76), Eau Claire(23)
STURGEON BAY Door
STURTEVANT (53177) Racine(91), Kenosha(8)
SUAMICO Brown
SULLIVAN Jefferson
SUMMIT LAKE Langlade
SUN PRAIRIE Dane
SUPERIOR Douglas
SURING (54174) Oconto(91), Menominee(8)
SUSSEX Waukesha
TAYLOR (54659) Jackson(91), Trempealeau(8)
THERESA (53091) Dodge(94), Washington(5)
THIENSVILLE Ozaukee
THORP (54771) Clark(92), Taylor(7)
THREE LAKES (54562) Oneida(95), Forest(4)
TIGERTON (54486) Shawano(92), Waupaca(7)
TILLEDA Shawano
TISCH MILLS Manitowoc
TOMAH Monroe
TOMAHAWK (54487) Lincoln(88), Oneida(11)
TONY Rusk
TOWNSEND Oconto
TREGO Washburn
TREMPEALEAU Trempealeau
TREVOR Kenosha

TRIPOLI (54564) Oneida(47), Lincoln(36), Price(16)
TUNNEL CITY Monroe
TURTLE LAKE (54889) Barron(76), Polk(23)
TWIN LAKES Kenosha
TWO RIVERS Manitowoc
UNION CENTER Juneau
UNION GROVE (53182) Racine(90), Kenosha(9)
UNITY (54488) Clark(68), Marathon(31)
UPSON Iron
VALDERS Manitowoc
VAN DYNE (54979) Fond du Lac(87), Winnebago(12)
VERONA Dane
VESPER Wood
VIOLA (54664) Richland(66), Vernon(33)
VIROQUA (54665) Vernon(98), Crawford(1)
WABENO Forest
WALDO Sheboygan
WALES Waukesha
WALWORTH Walworth
WARRENS (54666) Monroe(82), Jackson(17)
WASCOTT Douglas
WASHBURN Bayfield
WASHINGTON ISLAND Door
WATERFORD Racine
WATERLOO (53594) Jefferson(81), Dodge(14), Dane(3)
WATERTOWN Dodge
WAUKAU Winnebago
WAUKESHA Waukesha
WAUNAKEE Dane
WAUPACA (54981) Waupaca(91), Waushara(4), Portage(3)
WAUPUN (53963) Dodge(51), Fond du Lac(48)
WAUSAU Marathon
WAUSAUKEE Marinette
WAUTOMA (54982) Waushara(97), Marquette(2)
WAUZEKA Crawford
WEBSTER Burnett
WEST BEND Washington
WEST SALEM La Crosse
WESTBORO (54490) Taylor(95), Price(4)
WESTBY (54667) Vernon(98), La Crosse(1)
WESTFIELD (53964) Marquette(96), Adams(2), Waushara(1)
WEYAUWEGA (54983) Waupaca(90), Waushara(9)
WEYERHAEUSER Rusk
WHEELER Dunn
WHITE LAKE (54491) Langlade(91), Oconto(8)
WHITEHALL Trempealeau
WHITELAW Manitowoc
WHITEWATER (53190) Walworth(76), Rock(13), Jefferson(9)
WILD ROSE Waushara
WILLARD Clark
WILLIAMS BAY Walworth
WILMOT Kenosha
WILSON St. Croix
WILTON Monroe
WINDSOR Dane
WINNECONNE (54986) Winnebago(98), Waushara(1)
WINTER Sawyer
WISCONSIN DELLS (53965) Columbia(38), Sauk(31), Adams(23), Juneau(6)
WISCONSIN RAPIDS (54494) Wood(92), Portage(6)
WISCONSIN RAPIDS Wood
WITHEE (54498) Clark(90), Taylor(9)
WITTENBERG (54499) Shawano(71), Marathon(27), Portage(1)
WONEWOC (53968) Juneau(67), Sauk(24), Vernon(6), Richland(1)
WOODFORD Lafayette
WOODLAND Dodge
WOODMAN Grant
WOODRUFF (54568) Vilas(67), Oneida(32)
WOODVILLE St. Croix
WOODWORTH Kenosha
WRIGHTSTOWN (54180) Brown(95), Outagamie(4)
WYEVILLE Monroe
WYOCENA Columbia
ZACHOW Shawano
ZENDA Walworth

Wisconsin ZIP/City Cross Reference

53001-53001 ADELL
53002-53002 ALLENTON
53003-53003 ASHIPPUN
53004-53004 BELGIUM
53005-53005 BROOKFIELD
53006-53006 BROWNSVILLE
53007-53007 BUTLER
53008-53008 BROOKFIELD
53009-53009 BYRON
53010-53010 CAMPBELLSPORT
53011-53011 CASCADE
53012-53012 CEDARBURG
53013-53013 CEDAR GROVE
53014-53014 CHILTON
53015-53015 CLEVELAND
53016-53016 CLYMAN
53017-53017 COLGATE
53018-53018 DELAFIELD
53019-53019 EDEN
53020-53020 ELKHART LAKE
53021-53021 FREDONIA
53022-53022 GERMANTOWN
53023-53023 GLENBEULAH
53024-53024 GRAFTON
53026-53026 GREENBUSH
53027-53027 HARTFORD
53029-53029 HARTLAND
53031-53031 HINGHAM
53032-53032 HORICON
53033-53033 HUBERTUS
53034-53034 HUSTISFORD
53035-53035 IRON RIDGE
53036-53036 IXONIA
53037-53037 JACKSON
53038-53038 JOHNSON CREEK
53039-53039 JUNEAU
53040-53040 KEWASKUM
53042-53042 KIEL
53044-53044 KOHLER
53045-53045 BROOKFIELD
53046-53046 LANNON
53047-53047 LEBANON
53048-53048 LOMIRA
53049-53049 MALONE
53050-53050 MAYVILLE
53051-53052 MENOMONEE FALLS
53056-53056 MERTON
53057-53057 MOUNT CALVARY
53058-53058 NASHOTAH
53059-53059 NEOSHO
53060-53060 NEWBURG
53061-53062 NEW HOLSTEIN
53063-53063 NEWTON
53064-53064 NORTH LAKE
53065-53065 OAKFIELD
53066-53066 OCONOMOWOC
53069-53069 OKAUCHEE
53070-53070 OOSTBURG
53072-53072 PEWAUKEE
53073-53073 PLYMOUTH
53074-53074 PORT WASHINGTON
53075-53075 RANDOM LAKE
53076-53076 RICHFIELD
53077-53077 ROCKFIELD
53078-53078 RUBICON
53079-53079 SAINT CLOUD
53080-53080 SAUKVILLE
53081-53083 SHEBOYGAN
53085-53085 SHEBOYGAN FALLS
53086-53086 SLINGER
53088-53088 STOCKBRIDGE
53089-53089 SUSSEX
53090-53090 WEST BEND
53091-53091 THERESA
53092-53092 THIENSVILLE
53093-53093 WALDO
53094-53094 WATERTOWN
53095-53096 WEST BEND
53097-53097 MEQUON
53098-53098 WATERTOWN
53099-53099 WOODLAND
53101-53101 BASSETT
53102-53102 BENET LAKE
53103-53103 BIG BEND
53104-53104 BRISTOL
53105-53105 BURLINGTON
53108-53108 CALEDONIA
53109-53109 CAMP LAKE
53110-53110 CUDAHY
53114-53114 DARIEN
53115-53115 DELAVAN
53118-53118 DOUSMAN
53119-53119 EAGLE
53120-53120 EAST TROY
53121-53121 ELKHORN
53122-53122 ELM GROVE
53125-53125 FONTANA
53126-53126 FRANKSVILLE
53127-53127 GENESEE DEPOT
53128-53128 GENOA CITY
53129-53129 GREENDALE
53130-53130 HALES CORNERS
53132-53132 FRANKLIN
53137-53137 HELENVILLE
53138-53138 HONEY CREEK
53139-53139 KANSASVILLE
53140-53144 KENOSHA
53146-53146 NEW BERLIN
53147-53147 LAKE GENEVA
53148-53148 LYONS
53149-53149 MUKWONAGO
53150-53150 MUSKEGO
53151-53151 NEW BERLIN
53152-53152 NEW MUNSTER
53153-53153 NORTH PRAIRIE
53154-53154 OAK CREEK
53156-53156 PALMYRA
53157-53157 PELL LAKE
53158-53158 PLEASANT PRAIRIE
53159-53159 POWERS LAKE
53167-53167 ROCHESTER
53168-53168 SALEM
53170-53170 SILVER LAKE
53171-53171 SOMERS
53172-53172 SOUTH MILWAUKEE
53176-53176 SPRINGFIELD
53177-53177 STURTEVANT
53178-53178 SULLIVAN
53179-53179 TREVOR
53181-53181 TWIN LAKES
53182-53182 UNION GROVE
53183-53183 WALES
53184-53184 WALWORTH
53185-53185 WATERFORD
53186-53189 WAUKESHA
53190-53190 WHITEWATER
53191-53191 WILLIAMS BAY
53192-53192 WILMOT
53194-53194 WOODWORTH
53195-53195 ZENDA
53200-53234 MILWAUKEE
53235-53235 SAINT FRANCIS
53237-53259 MILWAUKEE
53260-53260 MARSHALL FIELDS
53263-53295 MILWAUKEE
53400-53490 RACINE
53501-53501 AFTON
53502-53502 ALBANY
53503-53503 ARENA
53504-53504 ARGYLE
53505-53505 AVALON
53506-53506 AVOCA
53507-53507 BARNEVELD
53508-53508 BELLEVILLE
53510-53510 BELMONT
53511-53512 BELOIT
53515-53515 BLACK EARTH
53516-53516 BLANCHARDVILLE
53517-53517 BLUE MOUNDS
53518-53518 BLUE RIVER
53520-53520 BRODHEAD
53521-53521 BROOKLYN
53522-53522 BROWNTOWN
53523-53523 CAMBRIDGE
53525-53525 CLINTON
53526-53526 COBB
53527-53527 COTTAGE GROVE
53528-53528 CROSS PLAINS
53529-53529 DANE
53530-53530 DARLINGTON
53531-53531 DEERFIELD
53532-53532 DE FOREST
53533-53533 DODGEVILLE
53534-53534 EDGERTON
53535-53535 EDMUND
53536-53536 EVANSVILLE
53537-53537 FOOTVILLE
53538-53538 FORT ATKINSON
53540-53540 GOTHAM
53541-53541 GRATIOT
53542-53542 HANOVER
53543-53543 HIGHLAND
53544-53544 HOLLANDALE
53545-53548 JANESVILLE
53549-53549 JEFFERSON
53550-53550 JUDA
53551-53551 LAKE MILLS
53553-53553 LINDEN
53554-53554 LIVINGSTON
53555-53555 LODI
53556-53556 LONE ROCK
53557-53557 LOWELL
53558-53558 MC FARLAND
53559-53559 MARSHALL
53560-53560 MAZOMANIE
53561-53561 MERRIMAC
53562-53562 MIDDLETON
53563-53563 MILTON
53565-53565 MINERAL POINT
53566-53566 MONROE
53569-53569 MONTFORT
53570-53570 MONTICELLO
53571-53571 MORRISONVILLE
53572-53572 MOUNT HOREB
53573-53573 MUSCODA
53574-53574 NEW GLARUS
53575-53575 OREGON
53576-53576 ORFORDVILLE
53577-53577 PLAIN
53578-53578 PRAIRIE DU SAC
53579-53579 REESEVILLE
53580-53580 REWEY

53581-53581 RICHLAND CENTER
53582-53582 RIDGEWAY
53583-53583 SAUK CITY
53584-53584 SEXTONVILLE
53585-53585 SHARON
53586-53586 SHULLSBURG
53587-53587 SOUTH WAYNE
53588-53588 SPRING GREEN
53589-53589 STOUGHTON
53590-53591 SUN PRAIRIE
53593-53593 VERONA
53594-53594 WATERLOO
53595-53595 DODGEVILLE
53596-53596 SUN PRAIRIE
53597-53597 WAUNAKEE
53598-53598 WINDSOR
53599-53599 WOODFORD
53700-53794 MADISON
53801-53801 BAGLEY
53802-53802 BEETOWN
53803-53803 BENTON
53804-53804 BLOOMINGTON
53805-53805 BOSCOBEL
53806-53806 CASSVILLE
53807-53807 CUBA CITY
53808-53808 DICKEYVILLE
53809-53809 FENNIMORE
53810-53810 GLEN HAVEN
53811-53811 HAZEL GREEN
53812-53812 KIELER
53813-53813 LANCASTER
53816-53816 MOUNT HOPE
53817-53817 PATCH GROVE
53818-53818 PLATTEVILLE
53820-53820 POTOSI
53821-53821 PRAIRIE DU CHIEN
53824-53824 SINSINAWA
53825-53825 STITZER
53826-53826 WAUZEKA
53827-53827 WOODMAN
53901-53901 PORTAGE
53910-53910 ADAMS
53911-53911 ARLINGTON
53913-53913 BARABOO
53916-53917 BEAVER DAM
53919-53919 BRANDON
53920-53920 BRIGGSVILLE
53921-53921 BROOKS
53922-53922 BURNETT
53923-53923 CAMBRIA
53924-53924 CAZENOVIA
53925-53925 COLUMBUS
53926-53926 DALTON
53927-53927 DELLWOOD
53928-53928 DOYLESTOWN
53929-53929 ELROY
53930-53930 ENDEAVOR
53931-53931 FAIRWATER
53932-53932 FALL RIVER
53933-53933 FOX LAKE
53934-53934 FRIENDSHIP
53935-53935 FRIESLAND
53936-53936 GRAND MARSH
53937-53937 HILLPOINT
53939-53939 KINGSTON
53940-53940 LAKE DELTON
53941-53941 LA VALLE
53942-53942 LIME RIDGE
53943-53943 LOGANVILLE
53944-53944 LYNDON STATION
53945-53945 MANCHESTER
53946-53946 MARKESAN
53947-53947 MARQUETTE
53948-53948 MAUSTON
53949-53949 MONTELLO
53950-53950 NEW LISBON
53951-53951 NORTH FREEDOM
53952-53952 OXFORD
53953-53953 PACKWAUKEE
53954-53954 PARDEEVILLE
53955-53955 POYNETTE
53956-53957 RANDOLPH
53958-53959 REEDSBURG
53960-53960 RIO
53961-53961 ROCK SPRINGS
53962-53962 UNION CENTER
53963-53963 WAUPUN
53964-53964 WESTFIELD
53965-53965 WISCONSIN DELLS
53968-53968 WONEWOC
53969-53969 WYOCENA
54001-54001 AMERY
54002-54002 BALDWIN
54003-54003 BELDENVILLE
54004-54004 CLAYTON
54005-54005 CLEAR LAKE
54006-54006 CUSHING
54007-54007 DEER PARK
54009-54009 DRESSER
54010-54010 EAST ELLSWORTH
54011-54011 ELLSWORTH
54012-54012 EMERALD
54012-54012 EMERALDX
54013-54013 GLENWOOD CITY
54014-54014 HAGER CITY
54015-54015 HAMMOND
54016-54016 HUDSON
54017-54017 NEW RICHMOND
54020-54020 OSCEOLA
54021-54021 PRESCOTT
54022-54022 RIVER FALLS
54023-54023 ROBERTS
54024-54024 SAINT CROIX FALLS
54025-54025 SOMERSET
54026-54026 STAR PRAIRIE
54027-54027 WILSON
54028-54028 WOODVILLE
54082-54082 SAINT JOSEPH
54082-54082 HOULTON
54101-54101 ABRAMS
54102-54102 AMBERG
54103-54103 ARMSTRONG CREEK
54104-54104 ATHELSTANE
54106-54106 BLACK CREEK
54107-54107 BONDUEL
54110-54110 BRILLION
54111-54111 CECIL
54112-54112 COLEMAN
54113-54113 COMBINED LOCKS
54114-54114 CRIVITZ
54115-54115 DE PERE
54119-54119 DUNBAR
54120-54120 FENCE
54121-54121 FLORENCE
54123-54123 FOREST JUNCTION
54124-54124 GILLETT
54125-54125 GOODMAN
54126-54126 GREENLEAF
54127-54127 GREEN VALLEY
54128-54128 GRESHAM
54129-54129 HILBERT
54130-54130 KAUKAUNA
54131-54131 FREEDOM
54135-54135 KESHENA
54136-54136 KIMBERLY
54137-54137 KRAKOW
54138-54138 LAKEWOOD
54139-54139 LENA
54140-54140 LITTLE CHUTE
54141-54141 LITTLE SUAMICO
54143-54143 MARINETTE
54149-54149 MOUNTAIN
54150-54150 NEOPIT
54151-54151 NIAGARA
54152-54152 NICHOLS
54153-54153 OCONTO
54154-54154 OCONTO FALLS
54155-54155 ONEIDA
54156-54156 PEMBINE
54157-54157 PESHTIGO
54159-54159 PORTERFIELD
54160-54160 POTTER
54161-54161 POUND
54162-54162 PULASKI
54164-54164 GILLETT
54165-54165 SEYMOUR
54166-54166 SHAWANO
54169-54169 SHERWOOD
54170-54170 SHIOCTON
54171-54171 SOBIESKI
54173-54173 SUAMICO
54174-54174 SURING
54175-54175 TOWNSEND
54176-54176 GILLETT
54177-54177 WAUSAUKEE
54180-54180 WRIGHTSTOWN
54182-54182 ZACHOW
54201-54201 ALGOMA
54202-54202 BAILEYS HARBOR
54203-54203 BRANCH
54204-54204 BRUSSELS
54205-54205 CASCO
54206-54206 CATO
54207-54207 COLLINS
54208-54208 DENMARK
54209-54209 EGG HARBOR
54210-54210 ELLISON BAY
54211-54211 EPHRAIM
54212-54212 FISH CREEK
54213-54213 FORESTVILLE
54214-54214 FRANCIS CREEK
54215-54215 KELLNERSVILLE
54216-54216 KEWAUNEE
54217-54217 LUXEMBURG
54220-54221 MANITOWOC
54226-54226 MAPLEWOOD
54227-54227 MARIBEL
54228-54228 MISHICOT
54229-54229 NEW FRANKEN
54230-54230 REEDSVILLE
54231-54231 ALGOMA
54232-54232 SAINT NAZIANZ
54234-54234 SISTER BAY
54235-54235 STURGEON BAY
54240-54240 TISCH MILLS
54241-54241 TWO RIVERS
54245-54245 VALDERS
54246-54246 WASHINGTON ISLAND
54247-54247 WHITELAW
54300-54344 GREEN BAY
54401-54403 WAUSAU
54404-54404 MARSHFIELD
54405-54405 ABBOTSFORD
54406-54406 AMHERST
54407-54407 AMHERST JUNCTION
54408-54408 ANIWA
54409-54409 ANTIGO
54410-54410 ARPIN
54411-54411 ATHENS
54412-54412 AUBURNDALE
54413-54413 BABCOCK
54414-54414 BIRNAMWOOD
54415-54415 BLENKER
54416-54416 BOWLER
54417-54417 BROKAW
54418-54418 BRYANT
54419-54419 CHELSEA
54420-54420 CHILI
54421-54421 COLBY
54422-54422 CURTISS
54423-54423 CUSTER
54424-54424 DEERBROOK
54425-54425 DORCHESTER
54426-54426 EDGAR
54427-54427 ELAND
54428-54428 ELCHO
54429-54429 ELDERON
54430-54430 ELTON
54432-54432 GALLOWAY
54433-54433 GILMAN
54434-54434 JUMP RIVER
54435-54435 GLEASON
54436-54436 GRANTON
54437-54437 GREENWOOD
54439-54439 HANNIBAL
54440-54440 HATLEY
54441-54441 HEWITT
54442-54442 IRMA
54443-54443 JUNCTION CITY
54444-54444 KEMPSTER
54445-54445 LILY
54446-54446 LOYAL
54447-54447 LUBLIN
54448-54448 MARATHON
54449-54449 MARSHFIELD
54450-54450 MATTOON
54451-54451 MEDFORD
54452-54452 MERRILL
54453-54453 MILAN
54454-54454 MILLADORE
54455-54455 MOSINEE
54456-54456 NEILLSVILLE
54457-54457 NEKOOSA
54458-54458 NELSONVILLE
54459-54459 OGEMA
54460-54460 OWEN
54462-54462 PEARSON
54463-54463 PELICAN LAKE
54464-54464 PHLOX
54465-54465 PICKEREL
54466-54466 PITTSVILLE
54467-54467 PLOVER
54469-54469 PORT EDWARDS
54470-54470 RIB LAKE
54471-54471 RINGLE
54472-54472 MARSHFIELD
54473-54473 ROSHOLT
54474-54474 ROTHSCHILD
54475-54475 RUDOLPH
54476-54476 SCHOFIELD
54479-54479 SPENCER
54480-54480 STETSONVILLE
54481-54482 STEVENS POINT
54484-54484 STRATFORD
54485-54485 SUMMIT LAKE
54486-54486 TIGERTON
54487-54487 TOMAHAWK
54488-54488 UNITY
54489-54489 VESPER
54490-54490 WESTBORO
54491-54491 WHITE LAKE
54492-54492 STEVENS POINT
54493-54493 WILLARD
54494-54495 WISCONSIN RAPIDS
54498-54498 WITHEE
54499-54499 WITTENBERG
54501-54501 RHINELANDER
54511-54511 ARGONNE
54512-54512 BOULDER JUNCTION
54513-54513 BRANTWOOD
54514-54514 BUTTERNUT
54515-54515 CATAWBA
54517-54517 CLAM LAKE
54519-54519 CONOVER
54520-54520 CRANDON
54521-54521 EAGLE RIVER
54524-54524 FIFIELD
54525-54525 GILE
54526-54526 GLEN FLORA
54527-54527 GLIDDEN
54528-54528 GURNEY
54529-54529 HARSHAW
54530-54530 HAWKINS
54531-54531 HAZELHURST
54532-54532 HEAFFORD JUNCTION
54534-54534 HURLEY
54536-54536 IRON BELT
54537-54537 KENNAN
54538-54538 LAC DU FLAMBEAU
54539-54539 LAKE TOMAHAWK
54540-54540 LAND O LAKES
54541-54541 LAONA
54542-54542 LONG LAKE
54543-54543 MC NAUGHTON
54545-54545 MANITOWISH WATERS
54546-54546 MELLEN
54547-54547 MERCER
54548-54548 MINOCQUA

54550-54550 MONTREAL
54552-54552 PARK FALLS
54554-54554 PHELPS
54555-54555 PHILLIPS
54556-54556 PRENTICE
54557-54557 PRESQUE ISLE
54558-54558 SAINT GERMAIN
54559-54559 SAXON
54560-54560 SAYNER
54561-54561 STAR LAKE
54562-54562 THREE LAKES
54563-54563 TONY
54564-54564 TRIPOLI
54565-54565 UPSON
54566-54566 WABENO
54568-54568 WOODRUFF
54601-54603 LA CROSSE
54610-54610 ALMA
54611-54611 ALMA CENTER
54612-54612 ARCADIA
54613-54613 ARKDALE
54614-54614 BANGOR
54615-54615 BLACK RIVER FALLS
54616-54616 BLAIR
54617-54617 BLOOM CITY
54618-54618 CAMP DOUGLAS
54619-54619 CASHTON
54620-54620 CATARACT
54621-54621 CHASEBURG
54622-54622 COCHRANE
54623-54623 COON VALLEY
54624-54624 DE SOTO
54625-54625 DODGE
54626-54626 EASTMAN
54627-54627 ETTRICK
54628-54628 FERRYVILLE
54629-54629 FOUNTAIN CITY
54630-54630 GALESVILLE
54631-54631 GAYS MILLS
54632-54632 GENOA
54634-54634 HILLSBORO
54635-54635 HIXTON
54636-54636 HOLMEN
54637-54637 HUSTLER
54638-54638 KENDALL
54639-54639 LA FARGE
54640-54640 LYNXVILLE
54641-54641 MATHER
54642-54642 MELROSE
54643-54643 MILLSTON
54644-54644 MINDORO
54645-54645 MOUNT STERLING
54646-54646 NECEDAH
54648-54648 NORWALK
54649-54649 OAKDALE
54650-54650 ONALASKA
54651-54651 ONTARIO
54652-54652 READSTOWN
54653-54653 ROCKLAND
54654-54654 SENECA
54655-54655 SOLDIERS GROVE
54656-54656 SPARTA
54657-54657 STEUBEN
54658-54658 STODDARD
54659-54659 TAYLOR
54660-54660 TOMAH
54661-54661 TREMPEALEAU
54662-54662 TUNNEL CITY
54664-54664 VIOLA
54665-54665 VIROQUA
54666-54666 WARRENS
54667-54667 WESTBY
54669-54669 WEST SALEM
54670-54670 WILTON
54671-54671 WYEVILLE
54701-54703 EAU CLAIRE
54720-54720 ALTOONA
54721-54721 ARKANSAW
54722-54722 AUGUSTA
54723-54723 BAY CITY
54724-54724 BLOOMER
54725-54725 BOYCEVILLE
54726-54726 BOYD
54727-54727 CADOTT
54728-54728 CHETEK
54729-54729 CHIPPEWA FALLS
54730-54730 COLFAX
54731-54731 CONRATH
54732-54732 CORNELL
54733-54733 DALLAS
54734-54734 DOWNING
54735-54735 DOWNSVILLE
54736-54736 DURAND
54737-54737 EAU GALLE
54738-54738 ELEVA
54739-54739 ELK MOUND
54740-54740 ELMWOOD
54741-54741 FAIRCHILD
54742-54742 FALL CREEK
54743-54743 GILMANTON
54744-54744 HILLSDALE
54745-54745 HOLCOMBE
54746-54746 HUMBIRD
54747-54747 INDEPENDENCE
54748-54748 JIM FALLS
54749-54749 KNAPP
54750-54750 MAIDEN ROCK
54751-54751 MENOMONIE
54754-54754 MERRILLAN
54755-54755 MONDOVI
54756-54756 NELSON
54757-54757 NEW AUBURN
54758-54758 OSSEO
54759-54759 PEPIN
54760-54760 PIGEON FALLS
54761-54761 PLUM CITY
54762-54762 PRAIRIE FARM
54763-54763 RIDGELAND
54764-54764 ROCK FALLS
54765-54765 SAND CREEK
54766-54766 SHELDON
54767-54767 SPRING VALLEY
54768-54768 STANLEY
54769-54769 STOCKHOLM
54770-54770 STRUM
54771-54771 THORP
54772-54772 WHEELER
54773-54773 WHITEHALL
54774-54774 CHIPPEWA FALLS
54801-54801 SPOONER
54805-54805 ALMENA
54806-54806 ASHLAND
54810-54810 BALSAM LAKE
54812-54812 BARRON
54813-54813 BARRONETT
54814-54814 BAYFIELD
54816-54816 BENOIT
54817-54817 BIRCHWOOD
54818-54818 BRILL
54819-54819 BRUCE
54820-54820 BRULE
54821-54821 CABLE
54822-54822 CAMERON
54824-54824 CENTURIA
54826-54826 COMSTOCK
54827-54827 CORNUCOPIA
54828-54828 COUDERAY
54829-54829 CUMBERLAND
54830-54830 DANBURY
54832-54832 DRUMMOND
54834-54834 EDGEWATER
54835-54835 EXELAND
54836-54836 FOXBORO
54837-54837 FREDERIC
54838-54838 GORDON
54839-54839 GRAND VIEW
54840-54840 GRANTSBURG
54841-54841 HAUGEN
54842-54842 HAWTHORNE
54843-54843 HAYWARD
54844-54844 HERBSTER
54845-54845 HERTEL
54846-54846 HIGH BRIDGE
54847-54847 IRON RIVER
54848-54848 LADYSMITH
54849-54849 LAKE NEBAGAMON
54850-54850 LA POINTE
54851-54851 LEWIS
54853-54853 LUCK
54854-54854 MAPLE
54855-54855 MARENGO
54856-54856 MASON
54857-54857 MIKANA
54858-54858 MILLTOWN
54859-54859 MINONG
54861-54861 ODANAH
54862-54862 OJIBWA
54864-54864 POPLAR
54865-54865 PORT WING
54866-54866 POSKIN
54867-54867 RADISSON
54868-54868 RICE LAKE
54870-54870 SARONA
54871-54871 SHELL LAKE
54872-54872 SIREN
54873-54873 SOLON SPRINGS
54874-54874 SOUTH RANGE
54875-54875 SPRINGBROOK
54876-54876 STONE LAKE
54880-54880 SUPERIOR
54888-54888 TREGO
54889-54889 TURTLE LAKE
54890-54890 WASCOTT
54891-54891 WASHBURN
54893-54893 WEBSTER
54895-54895 WEYERHAEUSER
54896-54896 WINTER
54901-54906 OSHKOSH
54909-54909 ALMOND
54911-54919 APPLETON
54921-54921 BANCROFT
54922-54922 BEAR CREEK
54923-54923 BERLIN
54926-54926 BIG FALLS
54927-54927 BUTTE DES MORTS
54928-54928 CAROLINE
54929-54929 CLINTONVILLE
54930-54930 COLOMA
54931-54931 DALE
54932-54932 ELDORADO
54933-54933 EMBARRASS
54934-54934 EUREKA
54935-54937 FOND DU LAC
54940-54940 FREMONT
54941-54941 GREEN LAKE
54942-54942 GREENVILLE
54943-54943 HANCOCK
54944-54944 HORTONVILLE
54945-54945 IOLA
54946-54946 KING
54947-54947 LARSEN
54948-54948 LEOPOLIS
54949-54949 MANAWA
54950-54950 MARION
54951-54951 MEDINA
54952-54952 MENASHA
54956-54957 NEENAH
54960-54960 NESHKORO
54961-54961 NEW LONDON
54962-54962 OGDENSBURG
54963-54963 OMRO
54964-54964 PICKETT
54965-54965 PINE RIVER
54966-54966 PLAINFIELD
54967-54967 POY SIPPI
54968-54968 PRINCETON
54969-54969 READFIELD
54970-54970 REDGRANITE
54971-54971 RIPON
54974-54974 ROSENDALE
54975-54975 ROYALTON
54976-54976 SAXEVILLE
54977-54977 SCANDINAVIA
54978-54978 TILLEDA
54979-54979 VAN DYNE
54980-54980 WAUKAU
54981-54981 WAUPACA
54982-54982 WAUTOMA
54983-54983 WEYAUWEGA
54984-54984 WILD ROSE
54985-54985 WINNEBAGO
54986-54986 WINNECONNE
54990-54990 IOLA

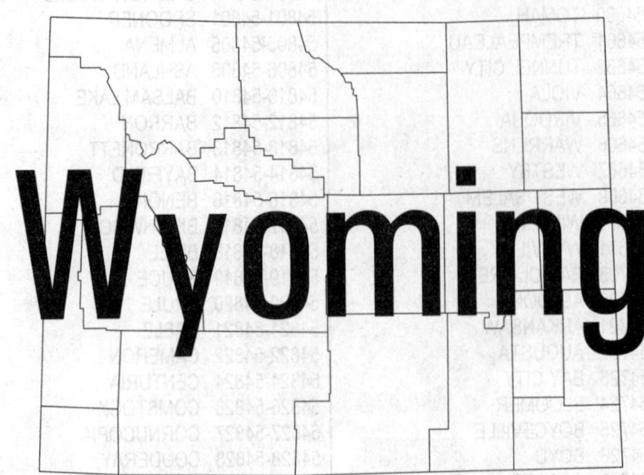

General Help Numbers:

Governor's Office
State Capitol Building, Rm 124 — 307-777-7434
Cheyenne, WY 82002-0010 — Fax 307-632-3909
http://governor.wy.gov/ — 8AM-5PM

Attorney General's Office
200 W 24thth Street — 307-777-7841
Cheyenne, WY 82002 — Fax 307-777-6869
http://attorneygeneral.state.wy.us — 8AM-5PM

Legislative Records
Wyoming Legislature — 307-777-7881
State Capitol, Room 213 — Fax 307-777-5466
Cheyenne, WY 82002 — 8AM-5PM
http://legisweb.state.wy.us

State Archives
Archives Division — 307-777-7826
2301 Central Ave, Barrett Bldg — Fax 307-777-7044
Cheyenne, WY 82002 — 8AM-5PM M-F
(Research Area 8AM-4:45PM)
http://wyoarchives.state.wy.us/index.asp

State Specifics:

Capital:	Cheyenne Laramie County
Time Zone:	MST
Number of Counties:	23
Population:	532,668
Web Sie:	www.wyoming.gov

State Agencies

Criminal Records

Division of Criminal Investigation, Criminal Record Unit, 316 W 22nd St, Cheyenne, WY 82002; 307-777-7523, Fax- 307-777-7301; 8AM to 5PM.

http://attorneygeneral.state.wy.us/dci/index.html

A record inquiry includes all reported felonies, high misdemeanors and other specified misdemeanors, but not municipal ordinance violations. authorized by state law, the check may include federal records held by FBI.

Indexing & Storage: Records available from 1941 on. New records available for inquiry in 48 hours. 73% of all arrests in database have final dispositions recorded, 65% for those arrests within last 5 years.

Searching: First, obtain a Request for Criminal Record Packet from the address above or by telephoning this agency. Include in request- notarized waiver from subject, name, set of fingerprints, date of birth, SSN, number of years to search. Use the WY standard 8" x 8" orange fingerprint card. All requests are fingerprint based. Must also complete all information and waiver is on the back of this office's fingerprint card. This data not released- juvenile records if no guardian consent. Records include all felony and major misdemeanor arrests and convictions.

Access by: mail, in person.

Fee & Payment: The search fee is $15.00 plus an additional $5.00 if this office must perform the fingerprinting. The fee is $10.00 if the applicant is providing volunteer services, plus the fingerprinting fee if applicable. The FBI fingerprint check is an add'l $19.25. Fee payee- Office of the Attorney General. Prepayment required. Money order, cash or certified checks only. No personal checks or credit cards accepted.

Mail search: Turnaround time- 2 to 4 weeks. A SASE is requested.

In person: Proper forms are required to be filled out.

Statewide Court Records

Court Administrator, Supreme Court Bldg, 2301 Capitol Ave, Cheyenne, WY 82002; 307-777-7583, Fax- 307-777-3447; 8AM-5PM.

www.courts.state.wy.us

Except for certain online research capabilities, all court record access must be done at the local level.

Online search: Supreme Court opinions available at web, listed by date. Wyoming's statewide case management system is for internal use only. Planning is underway for a new case management system that will ultimately allow public access.

Sexual Offender Registry

Division of Criminal Investigation, ATTN: WSOR, 316 W 22nd St, Cheyenne, WY 82002-0001; 307-777-7809, Fax- 307-777-7301; 8AM to 5PM.

http://wysors.dci.wyo.gov/sor/home.htm

Wyoming law defines a sex offender subject to registration as a person convicted of a sex offense in which the victim was a minor and the offender was at least eighteen (18) years of age or an aggravated sex offense.

Indexing & Storage: Records available as county submits them.

Searching: The County Sheriff's Office or other law enforcement agency maintains a file and forwards the information to the Wyoming Division of Criminal Investigation (DCI). Division of Criminal Investigation (DCI) is required to post all registered sex offenders on an internet site accessible to the citizens of Wyoming or elsewhere.

Access by: online.

Online search: The Internet is the search method offered by this agency to the public. Search is by last name, street name, city, county or ZIP. Data includes name including AKA, physical address, date and place of birth, date and place of conviction, crime for which convicted, photograph and physical description.

Incarceration Records

Wyoming Department of Corrections, 700 W. 21st Street,, Cheyenne, WY 82002; 307-777-7405, 307-777-7208, Fax- 307-777-7479; 8AM-5PM.

http://corrections.wy.gov/

Indexing & Storage: Records available on current and former inmates. New records available for inquiry in a minimum of 30 days.

Searching: No searching online direct from this agency; a private company provides access to DOC records at https://www.vinelink.com/index.jsp. Include in request- full name. DOB and SSN are helpful. Location, conviction and sentencing information, and release dates are provided. Limited search requests honor via email at mbrazz@wdoc.state.wy.us. This data not released- probation and parole data, medical, and mental health problems.

Access by: mail, phone, fax.

Fee & Payment: The fee is $.50 per page. Fee payee- Wyoming Dept of Corrections Prepayment required. Personal checks accepted.

Mail search: Turnaround time- 1 to 2 weeks. A SASE is requested.

Phone search: Name searching available by phone.

Fax search: Can request via fax.

Corporation, LLC, LP, Fictitious Name, Trademarks/Servicemarks, Trade Names

Business Division, Attn: Records, 200 W 24th Street, Rm 110, Cheyenne, WY 82002; 307-777-7311, Fax- 307-777-5339; 8AM-5PM.

http://soswy.state.wy.us/Business/BusEntOverview.aspx

Indexing & Storage: Records available from 1800s on. The records on microfilm are inactive records before 1983. Newer records are on computer. New records available for inquiry immediately.

Searching: The Annual Report financial information (Appendix I Worksheet filed with Annual Report) is not released. Include in request- full name of business. In addition to the articles of organization, business entity records available include: Annual Reports, Officers, Directors, DBAs, Prior (merged) names, Inactive and Reserved names. This data not released- worksheet material for annual report.

Access by: mail, fax, in person, online.

Fee & Payment: First 10 copies free, if non-certified. Otherwise, copy fees are $.50 per page for the first 10 pages and $.15 for each additional page. Certification is $3.00. Fee payee- Secretary of State. They will invoice for copies and certificates. Prepaid accounts are available. Personal checks accepted, credit cards are not.

Mail search: Turnaround time- 1 to 2 days. A SASE is helpful.

Fax search: Turnaround time is 24-48 hours.

In person: Counter service available.

Online search: Information is available through the Internet site listed above. You can search by corporate name or registered filing ID. Also, search the Secretary of State securities department enforcement actions/opinions free at http://soswy.state.wy.us/securiti/enforce.htm.

Uniform Commercial Code, Federal Tax Liens

Secretary of State, UCC Division - Records, 200 W 24th St, Room 110, Cheyenne, WY 82002-0020; 307-777-7311, 307-777-5372, Fax- 307-777-5339; 8AM-5PM.

http://soswy.state.wy.us/uniform/uniform.htm

Direct questions to ucc@state.wy.us.

Indexing & Storage: Records available since 1982.

Searching: The search includes federal tax liens on businesses and state tax liens filed by state agencies. Include in request- debtor name. This data not released- SSNs

Access by: mail, fax, in person, online.

Fee & Payment: A certified search is $10.00 per name. Copies cost $.50 each. Fee payee- Secretary of State. Personal checks accepted, credit cards are not.

Mail search: Turnaround time- 3 days. Please include your phone number with all requests.

Fax search: Requests may be faxed in.

In person: Simple requests may be processed while you wait.

Online search: The online filing system permits unlimited record searching. There is a $150 annual fee, with no additional fees charged for searches. Subscribers are entitled to do filings at a 50% discount. Visit the webpage.

Other access: Lists of filings on CD or diskette are available for purchase. Download the database for $2,000 per year.

State Tax Liens

Records not maintained by a state level agency.

There is no state income tax. All other state tax liens are filed at the county level.

Sales Tax Registrations

Department of Revenue, Excise Tax Division, Herschler Bldg, 122 W 25th St, Cheyenne, WY 82002-0110; 307-777-5200, Fax- 307-777-3632; 8AM-5PM.

http://revenue.state.wy.us

Indexing & Storage: Records available for at least three years: cancelled licenses are purged every two years. New records available for inquiry in 10 to 14 days.

Searching: This agency will only confirm that the business is registered. They will provide no other information except to an owner or officer of the business. Requests may be e-mailed, visit the website for the proper e-mail address. Include in request- business name, and ID of the requester. They will also search by tax permit number. Annual reports may be retrieved from the webpage.

Access by: mail, phone, in person.

Fee & Payment: For paper copies or from microfilm, copy fee is $.50 each first 10 pages, $.15 each add'l with a $10.00 minimum. For computer images, copy fee is $1.00 per page first 10 pages, then $.30 each additional with a $35.00 minimum. Fee payee- WY Dept of Revenue

Mail search: Turnaround time- 7 to 10 days. A SASE is requested. No search fee for mail request.

Phone search: No search fee for telephone request.

In person: No search fee for request.

Birth Certificates

Wyoming Department of Health, Vital Records Services, Hathaway Bldg, Rm 172, Cheyenne, WY 82002; 307-777-7591; 8AM-5PM.

www.health.wyo.gov/rfhd/vital_records/index.html

Indexing & Storage: Records available from July 1909 to present. New records available for inquiry immediately.

Searching: Must have a signed release from person of record or parent or guardian. Include in request- full name, names of parents, mother's maiden name, date of birth, place of birth, relationship to person of record. Must include signature of requester and copy of photo ID.

Access by: mail, fax, in person, online.

Fee & Payment: Search fee is $13.00 per name per 5 years searched. Fee payee- Vital Records

Services. Prepayment required. Personal checks and major credit cards accepted.

Mail search: Turnaround time- 8 to 10 working days. SASE is required.

Fax search: See expedited services. Use 307-635-4103.

In person: Turnaround time is same or next day.

Online search: Order from viatalchek.com. See expedited services.

Expedited service: Expedited service is available for fax and online requests via a designated vendor - www.vitalchek.com. Turnaround time- 3-5 days. Add $18.25 for credit card fee and courier delivery.

Death Records

Wyoming Department of Health, Vital Records Services, Hathaway Bldg, Cheyenne, WY 82002; 307-777-7591; 8AM-5PM.

www.health.wyo.gov/rfhd/vital_records/index.html

Indexing & Storage: Records available from July 1909. New records available for inquiry immediately.

Searching: Records are not open. Must have a signed release from immediate family member. The agency will verify information to family member, such as aunts and uncles, but will not release copies. Include in request- full name, date of death, place of death, relationship to person of record, reason for information request. Must include signature and copy of photo ID with request.

Access by: mail, in person, online.

Fee & Payment: Search fee is $13.00 per name per 5 years searched, or $10.oo date given. Fee payee- Vital Records Services. Prepayment required. Personal checks accepted.

Mail search: Turnaround time- 3 to 4 working days. SASE is required.

In person: Turnaround time is one day.

Online search: Order from viatalchek.com. See expedited services.

Marriage Certificates

Wyoming Department of Health, Vital Records Services, Hathaway Bldg, Cheyenne, WY 82002; 307-777-7591; 8AM-5PM.

www.health.wyo.gov/rfhd/vital_records/index.html

Indexing & Storage: Records available from May 1941 to present. If record is more than 50 years old, it must be obtained from the Wyoming State Archives (307-777-7826).

Searching: Must have a signed release from persons of record. Include in request- names of husband and wife, date of marriage, place or county of marriage, relationship to person of record, reason for information request, wife's maiden name. Signature and copy of photo ID must be included in request.

Access by: mail, fax, in person, online.

Fee & Payment: Search fee is $13.00 per name per 5 years searched. Fee payee- Vital Records Services. Prepayment required. Personal checks accepted. Major credit cards accepted for fax requests.

Mail search: Turnaround time- 8 to 10 working days. SASE is required.

Fax search: See expedited services. Use 307-635-4103.

In person: Must return to pick up in 24-48 hours.

Online search: Order from viatalchek.com. See expedited services.

Expedited service: Expedited service is available for fax and online requests via a designated vendor - www.vitalchek.com. Turnaround time- 3-5 days. Add $18.25 for credit card fee and courier delivery.

Divorce Records

Wyoming Department of Health, Vital Records Services, Hathaway Bldg, Cheyenne, WY 82002; 307-777-7591; 8AM-5PM.

www.health.wyo.gov/rfhd/vital_records/index.html

Indexing & Storage: Records available from July 1941 to present. Older records may be obtained from the Wyoming State Archives, 307-777-7826. New records available for inquiry immediately.

Searching: Must have a signed release from person of record. Include in request- names of husband and wife, date of divorce, place of divorce, relationship to person of record, along with release. Include copy of photo ID with request.

Access by: mail, in person, online.

Fee & Payment: Search fee is $13.00 per name per 5 years searched. Fee payee- Vital Records Services. Prepayment required. Personal checks accepted.

Mail search: Turnaround time- 8 to 10 working days. SASE required.

In person: Must come back to pick in in 24-48 hours.

Online search: Order from viatalchek.com. See expedited services.

Workers' Compensation Records

Workers Compensation Division, Records, 1510 E Pershing Blvd, Cheyenne, WY 82002; 307-777-7159, Fax- 307-777-6552; 8AM-4:30PM.

http://wydoe.state.wy.us/doe.asp?ID=9

Indexing & Storage: Records available from 1987 on computer. Records are on microfiche from 1919 to 1987. Searches on microfiche must include the date of injury, county of injury, employer and body part affected. New records available for inquiry in 3 days.

Searching: Only the injured party, employer or legal counsel for either party can obtain records from this agency. Include in request- claimant name, SSN. For a post-hire check of a new employee, a signed release is needed. The only information released is case #, date of injury, body part, employer at time of injury, or other information specifically authorized by claimant. This data not released- internal work product.

Access by: mail, fax.

Fee & Payment: No search fee. The copy fee is $.25 per copy. Fee payee- Wyoming Workers' Compensation

Mail search: Turnaround time- variable. Send release form with request to Gary Lord at address above. SASE not required.

Fax search: They will fax results with appropriate request.

Driver License Information, Driver Records

Wyoming Department of Transportation, Driver Services, 5300 Bishop Blvd, Cheyenne, WY 82009-3340; 307-777-4800, Fax- 307-777-4773; 8AM-5PM.

www.dot.state.wy.us

Indexing & Storage: Records available for 3 years from offense date for moving violations, 5 years from conviction date for DWUIs, and 3 to 5 years based on original charge for suspensions. Accidents are shown only if driver fails to show Fin Resp. New records available for inquiry immediately.

Searching: Companies requesting records must complete and file the DPPA form found on the website. Casual requesters cannot obtain records with personal information without signed release from subject. Include in request- name and DOB and DL or SSN. This data not released- medical information.

Access by: mail, fax, in person, online.

Fee & Payment: The fee is $5.00 per record, $3.00 by FTP. Add $6.00 if credit card used. Fee payee- Department of Transportation. Prepayment required. Personal checks accepted. Credit cards accepted for fax or mail requests.

Mail search: Turnaround time- 5 business days. An SASE is not required.

Fax search: Fax requests are accepted if credit card presented.

In person: Normal turnaround time is while you wait. Individual licensees may request a copy of their own record at any field office.

Online search: This method is available using FTP and RJE technology. Only approved vendors and permissible users are supported. Write or call Marianne Zivkovich at the above address for details.

Other access: The entire driver license file may be purchased for $2,500.

Vehicle Ownership & Registration

Wyoming Dept. of Transportation, Motor Vehicle Services, 5300 Bishop Blvd, Cheyenne, WY 82009-3340 (Courier address- 5300 Bishop Blvd, Cheyenne, WY 82009); 307-777-4825, 307-777-4710, Fax- 307-777-4772; 8AM-5PM.

www.dot.state.wy.us/Default.jsp?sCode=veh

At the website, click on "Motor Vehicle Services" for detailed WY DOT vehicle information. Also, the web site provides access to the request forms needed.

Indexing & Storage: Records available for 40 years on titles and 8 years on registrations. New records available for inquiry in 3 to 15 days.

Searching: Requests must be for a permissible use per DPPA. A "Privacy Disclosure Agreement" will need to be signed. Casual requesters cannot obtain records unless written consent of subject is provided and reason for request is approved by MVS. Include in request- VIN or plate# and make, model and year. Lien records are not available from the state and must be obtained from the one of the 23 Wyoming County Clerk offices. This data not released- complete title or registration histories; only current data is released.

Access by: mail, fax, in person.

Fee & Payment: The fee is $5.00 per record. Credit cards accepted for an additional $7.95 fee. Fee payee- WY Department of Transportation. Prepayment required. Personal checks and credit cards accepted.

Mail search: Turnaround time- 1 week. SASE not required.

Fax search: Approved requester may search by fax using a credit card.

In person: Turnaround time is normally in a few minutes.

Other access: Bulk information is available, customized lists can be obtained, per DPPA guidelines. For more information, call the Motor Vehicle Services at 307-777-4714.

Accident Reports

Highway Safety Program, Accident Records Section, 5300 Bishop Blvd, Cheyenne, WY 82009; 307-777-4450, Fax- 307-777-4250; 8AM-5PM.

The agency refers to these reports as "Crash Reports."

Indexing & Storage: New records available for inquiry in 10 to 30 days.

Searching: Accident reports (done by the officer) are considered open public record reports. Reports compiled by individuals involved are closed. Include in request- date of accident, location of accident, full name, date of birth.

Access by: mail, phone, in person.

Fee & Payment: The fee is $3.00 per record uncertified and $5.00 certified. Fee payee- Department of Transportation. Prepayment required. Personal checks accepted, credit cards are not.

Mail search: Turnaround time- 1 week to 10 days.

Phone search: Searches may be done by phone, but no copies are sent until payment is received.

In person: In-person requests are normally processed in a few of minutes.

Vessel Ownership & Registration

Wyoming Game & Fish Dept, Watercraft Section, 5400 Bishop Blvd, Cheyenne, WY 82006; 307-777-4575, Fax- 307-777-4610; 8AM-5PM M-F.

http://gf.state.wy.us/fish/boating/index.asp

This agency does not issue titles, therefore lien information is recorded at the county level. All motorized boats must be registered.

Indexing & Storage: Records available for the last 3 years. New records available for inquiry in 10 days.

Searching: Name searches are permitted. Include in request- name. This data not released- SSN, DOB, telephone number.

Access by: mail, phone, fax, in person.

Fee & Payment: There is no search fee.

Mail search: Turnaround time- 2 to 3 days. Turnaround time is 1 week if archived info is needed.

Phone search: A single name search is available by phone.

Fax search: Information can be faxed back.

In person: No fee for request. Turnaround time is immediate if the file is not archived.

Other access: Lists are available. All requests must be in writing and submitted to the Director's office. Fees are based on agency time involved or record count. Call for further details.

Legislation Records

Wyoming Legislature, State Capitol, Room 213, Cheyenne, WY 82002; 307-777-7881, Fax- 307-777-5466; 8AM-5PM.

http://legisweb.state.wy.us

General Session starts on the 2nd Tuesday in odd years is January. Budget session starts in February on second Monday in even years.

Indexing & Storage: Records available for the current session and for past bills, only as introduced. Records archived from 1972 forward can be searched. New records available for inquiry in less than 24 hours.

Searching: This office will not do general research. You must provide specifics. Include in request- bill number, year, date of debate, topic of bill. Simple requests are honored, but the agency does not have the staff to do extensive research.

Access by: mail, phone, in person, online.

Fee & Payment: Copies are $.10 a page with a minimum fee of $1.00. Fee payee- Wyoming Legislative Service Office They will invoice. Personal checks accepted, credit cards are not.

Mail search: Turnaround time- variable. SASE not required.

Phone search: Records are available by phone.

In person: Simple requests may be processed while you wait.

Online search: The Internet site contains a wealth of information regarding the legislature and bills going back at least 5 years. View the state statutes at http://legisweb.state.wy.us/titles/statutes.htm.

Expedited service: Will fax results for a $2.00 fee plus $.50 a page.

Voter Registration

Access to Records is Restricted.

Secretary of State - Election Division, 200 W 24th Street, Wyoming State Capitol, Cheyenne, WY 82002-0020; 307-777-7186, Fax- 307-777-7640; 8AM-5PM.

http://soswy.state.wy.us/election/election.htm

Individual look-ups can also be done at the county level. The SSN and DOB are not released. The state will sell all or part of its database, but only for political reasons. Commercial use is not permitted.

GED Certificates

Department of Workforce Services, GED Program (Wyoming Community College Commission), 2020 Carey Ave, 8th Fl, Cheyenne, WY 82002; 307-777-6567, Fax- 307-777-6567; 8AM-5PM.

www.communitycolleges.wy.edu

Indexing & Storage: Records available from 1950's forward. New records available for inquiry in seconds.

Searching: To request a transcript or have one sent to employer or college, the following is required: signed release from subject, full name, SSN, and date of birth. Test date is helpful. Request form can be downloaded from webpage.

Access by: mail, fax, in person.

Fee & Payment: There is no fee for verifications or transcripts.

Mail search: Turnaround time- 2 business days. SASE not required.

Fax search: Same criteria as mail searching.

In person: Turnaround time is typically 10 minutes for verifications or transcripts if Chief Examiner is available. Otherwise mailed.

Other access: To get the GED Certificate / Transcript Request form go to http://communitycolleges.wy.edu/business/GED_forms/GEDCert-Trans.pdf

Hunting & Fishing License Information

Game & Fish Department, License Draw, 5400 Bishop Blvd, Cheyenne, WY 82006; 307-777-4600 (Information Center), 307-777-4655 (License Draw), Fax- 307-777-4679; 8AM-5PM.

http://gf.state.wy.us

They maintain a central database for lottery (big game, moose, big horn sheep, elk, deer & antelope) permits and periodically add license permits sold by agents throughout the state.

Indexing & Storage: Records available from 3 years present on computer.

Searching: All requests must be in writing. Include in request- full name, date of birth, SSN. This data not released- SSNs.

Access by: mail, fax, in person.

Fee & Payment: Fees are incurred if there is extensive searching or lists are involved. Call first. Fee payee- Wyoming Game and Fish. Prepayment required. Money orders and cashier's checks are preferred. No credit cards accepted.

Mail search: Turnaround time- up to 10 days. SASE not required.

Fax search: Fax searching available.

In person: Simple requests may be processed while you wait.

Other access: They have mailing and label lists available. Call 800-548-9453 for more information.

Wyoming State Licensing Agencies

For details about the agency responsible for licensing/certifying/registering an item below or in the Agency Quick Finder section, match an item's number with the number of the agency in the *Licensing Agency Information* section.

Wyoming Licenses Searchable Online

Attorney #9	www.wyomingbar.org/directory/index.html
Bank #23	http://audit.state.wy.us/banking/banking/bankingregulatedentities.htm
Check Casher #23	http://audit.state.wy.us/banking/uccc/ucclicensees.htm
Child Care Licensee #22	http://dfswapps.state.wy.us/DFSDivEC/General/Contacts.asp
Collection Agency #24	http://audit.state.wy.us/banking/cab/cablicensees.htm
Controlled Substance Registrants #14	http://pharmacyboard.state.wy.us/search.asp
Engineer #27	http://engineersandsurveyors.state.wy.us/roster/rosterSearch.aspx
Feed/Fertilizer #1	www.kellysolutions.com/wy/
Funeral Pre-Need Agent #8	http://insurance.state.wy.us/search/search.asp
Geologist #18	http://wbpg.wy.gov/roster_search.asp
Guide, Outdoor #13	http://outfitters.state.wy.us/directory.asp
Insurance Claims Adjuster #8	http://insurance.state.wy.us/search/search.asp
Insurance Consultant #8	http://insurance.state.wy.us/search/search.asp
Insurance Producer #8	http://insurance.state.wy.us/search/search.asp
Insurance Service Rep #8	http://insurance.state.wy.us/search/search.asp
Lender, Supervised #23	http://audit.state.wy.us/banking/uccc/ucclicensees.htm
Lobbyist #36	http://soswy.state.wy.us/election/lob-list.htm
Medical Doctor/Psychiatrist #10	http://wyomedboard.state.wy.us/roster.asp
Motor Club Agent #8	http://insurance.state.wy.us/search/search.asp
Nurse/Nursing Assistant #37	http://nursing.state.wy.us/Main.asp?MainMode=3
Nurse-LPN #37	http://nursing.state.wy.us/Main.asp?MainMode=3
Occupational Therapist #12	http://ot.state.wy.us/search.aspx
Occupational Therapist Assistant #12	http://ot.state.wy.us/search.aspx
Optometrist #6	www.arbo.org/index.php?action=findanoptometrist
Outfitter #13	http://outfitters.state.wy.us/directory.asp
Pawnbroker #23	http://audit.state.wy.us/banking/uccc/ucclicensees.htm
Pharmacist/Pharmacy Technician #14	http://pharmacyboard.state.wy.us/search.asp
Pharmacy, Institutional #14	http://pharmacyboard.state.wy.us/search.asp
Physician Assistant #10	http://wyomedboard.state.wy.us/PARoster.asp
Prescription Drugs/Substances Mfg/Sell #14	http://pharmacyboard.state.wy.us/search.asp
Psychologist #16	http://plboards.state.wy.us/psychology/
Public Accountant-CPA #29	http://cpaboard.state.wy.us/database.aspx
Real Estate Agent #21	www.arello.com/
Reinsurance Intermediary #8	http://insurance.state.wy.us/search/search.asp
Rental Car Agents #8	http://insurance.state.wy.us/search/search.asp
Rent-to-own Company #23	http://audit.state.wy.us/banking/uccc/ucclicensees.htm
Retail Pharmacy #14	http://pharmacyboard.state.wy.us/search.asp
Risk Retention #8	http://insurance.state.wy.us/search/search.asp
Sales Finance Company #23	http://audit.state.wy.us/banking/uccc/ucclicensees.htm
Savings & Loan Association #23	http://audit.state.wy.us/banking/banking/bankingregulatedentities.htm
Surplus Line Broker, Resident #8	http://insurance.state.wy.us/search/search.asp
Surveyor, Land #27	http://engineersandsurveyors.state.wy.us/roster/rosterSearch.aspx
Third Party Administrator #8	http://insurance.state.wy.us/search/search.asp
Travel & Baggage Agent #8	http://insurance.state.wy.us/search/search.asp
Trust Company #23	http://audit.state.wy.us/banking/banking/bankingregulatedentities.htm

Wyoming Licensing Quick Finder

Addiction Therapist/Practitioner/Assistant #39 307-777-3628
Animal Euthanasia Technician #20 307-777-3628
Architect #30 307-777-5403
Attorney #9 307-632-9061
Bank #23 307-777-6605
Barber/Barber Shop #2 307-777-8572
Bus Driver #31 307-777-3340
Certified Mental Health Worker #39 307-777-3628
Check Casher #23 307-777-6605
Child Care Licensee #22 307-777-6595
Child Care Subsidy #22 307-777-6848
Chiropractor #32 307-777-7387
Clinical/Certified Social Worker #39 307-777-3628
Coach, Athletic #35 307-777-7291
Collection Agency #24 307-777-3497
Controlled Substance Registrants #14 . 307-234-0294
Coroner/Deputy Coroner #25 307-777-7718
Corrections Officer #25 307-777-7718
Cosmetologist #3 307-777-3534
Cosmetology Instructor #3 307-777-3534
Counselor, Professional #39 307-777-3628
Crematory Operator #5 307-777-5403
Dental Assistant #4 307-777-7387
Dental Hygienist #4 307-777-7387
Dentist #4 307-777-7387
Detention Officer #25 307-777-7718
Dispatcher (law enforc'm't-related) #25 . 307-777-7718
Educational Diagnostician #35 307-777-7291
Electrical Apprentice #26 307-777-6385
Electrician, Master/Journeyman #26 307-777-6385
Embalmer #5 307-777-5403
Emergency Medical Technician #7 307-777-7955
Engineer #27 307-777-6155
Esthetician #3 307-777-3534
Feed/Fertilizer #1 307-777-7324
Funeral Director #5 307-777-5403
Funeral Pre-Need Agent #8 307-777-7344
Geologist #18 307-742-1118
Guide, Outdoor #13 307-635-1589
Hearing Aid Specialist #5 307-777-6529
Insurance Claims Adjuster #8 307-777-7344
Insurance Consultant #8 307-777-7344
Insurance Producer #8 307-777-7344
Insurance Service Rep #8 307-777-7344
Jockey/Jockey Apprentice #38 307-777-5887
Landscape Architect #30 307-777-5403
Law Enforcement Officer #25 307-777-7718
Lender, Supervised #23 307-777-6605
Lobbyist #36 307-777-7186
Manicurist/Nail Technician #3 307-777-3534
Marriage & Family Therapist #39 307-777-3628
Medical Doctor/Psychiatrist #10 307-778-7053
Mine Foreman #33 307-362-5222
Mine Inspector/Examiner #33 307-362-5222
Motor Club Agent #8 307-777-7344
Notary Public #36 307-777-5407
Nurse/Nursing Assistant #37 877-626-2681
Nurse-LPN #37 877-626-2681
Nursing Home Administrator #12 307-432-0465
Occupational Therapist #12 307-432-0488
Occupational Therapist Assistant #12 .. 307-432-0488
Optometrist #6 307-777-7387
Outfitter #13 307-635-1589
Pari-Mutuel Employee/Official #38 307-777-5887
Pawnbroker #23 307-777-6605
Peace Officer #25 307-777-7718
Pesticide Aircraft #1 307-777-7324
Pesticide Applicator, Commercial #1 307-777-7324
Pharmacist/Pharmacy Technician #14 .. 307-234-0294
Pharmacy, Institutional #14 307-234-0294
Physical Therapist #15 307-777-7387
Physician Assistant #10 307-778-7053
Podiatrist #19 307-777-7387
Prescription Drugs/Substances Mfg/Seller #14 307-234-0294
Property Appraiser #21 307-777-7141
Psychological Practitioner #16 307-777-5403
Psychologist #16 307-777-5403
Public Accountant-CPA #29 307-777-7551
Racetrack Security Employee #38 307-777-5887
Racing Event #38 307-777-5887
Racing Permittee/Employee/Offic'l #38 307-777-5887
Radiation (ionizing) Agent #17 307-777-3507
Radiologic Technologist/Technic'n #17 307-777-3507
Radiopharmaceutical Agent #17 307-778-2068
Real Estate Agent #21 307-777-7141
Real Estate Appraiser #21 307-777-7141
Reinsurance Intermediary #8 307-777-7344
Rental Car Agents #8 307-777-7344
Rent-to-own Company #23 307-777-6605
Respiratory Care #16 307-777-5403
Retail Pharmacies (Resident/Non-Resident) #14 307-234-0294
Risk Retention #8 307-777-7344
Sales Finance Company #23 307-777-6605
Savings & Loan Association #23 307-777-6605
School Counselor #35 307-777-7291
School Librarian #35 307-777-7291
School Principal #35 307-777-7291
School Psychologist #16 307-777-5403
School Psychology, Specialist #16 307-777-5403
School Superintendent #35 307-777-7291
Securities Agent #34 307-777-7370
Securities Broker/Dealer #34 307-777-7370
Social Worker #30 307-777-7387
Speech Pathologist/Audiologist #28 307-777-5403
Substitute Teacher #35 307-777-7291
Surplus Line Broker, Resident #8 307-777-7344
Surveyor, Land #27 307-777-6155
Teacher #35 307-777-7291
Third Party Administrator #8 307-777-7344
Travel & Baggage Agent #8 307-777-7344
Truck Driver #31 307-777-3340
Trust Company #23 307-777-6605
Veterinarian #20 307-777-3628
Water Dist/Collection Operator #11 307-777-7781
Water/Waste Plant Operator #11 307-777-7781

Wyoming Licensing Agency Information

#1 Technical Services Department, Board of Agriculture, 2219 Carey Ave, Cheyenne, WY 82002-0100; 307-777-6569, F-307-777-6593. http://wyagric.state.wy.us/boag.htm Will sell lists.

#2 Board of Barber Examiners, 2515 Warren Ave, #302, Cheyenne, WY 82002; 307-777-8572, Fax- 307-777-3681. Hours- 9AM-4PM. www.cosmetology.wy.gov

#3 Board of Cosmetology, 2515 Warren Ave, #302, Cheyenne, WY 82002; 307-777-3534, Fax- 307-777-3681. Hours- 9AM-4PM. www.cosmetology.wy.gov

#4 Professional Licensing Administration, Board of Dental Examiners, 1800 Carey Ave, 4th Fl, Cheyenne, WY 82002; 307-777-6529, Fax- 307-777-3508. Hours- 8AM-5PM. http://plboards.state.wy.us/dental/

#5 Professional Licensing Administration, Board of Embalming; Board of Hearing Aid Specialists, 1800 Carey Ave, 4th Fl, Cheyenne, WY 82002; 307-777-5403, Fax- 307-777-3508. Hours- 8AM-5PM. http://plboards.state.wy.us/embalmers/

#6 Professional Licensing Admin., Board of Examiners in Optometry, 1800 Carey Ave, 4th Fl, Cheyenne, WY 82002; 307-777-3507, Fax- 307-777-3508. Hours- 8AM-5PM. http://plboards.state.wy.us/Optometry/ Search data at- www.arbo.org/index.php?action=findanoptometrist

#7 Office of Emergency Medical Svcs, 2300 Capital Ave, Hathaway Bldg 4th Fl, Cheyenne, WY 82002; 307-777-7955, Fax- 307-777-5639. www.health.wyo.gov/sho/ems/index.html

#8 Board of Insurance Agents Examiners, 106 E 6th Ave, Cheyenne, WY 82002; 307-777-7344, Fax- 307-777-5895. 8AM-5PM. http://insurance.state.wy.us Search data at- http://insurance.state.wy.us/search/search.asp

#9 Board of Law Examiners, PO Box 109 (500 Randall Ave.), Cheyenne, WY 82003; 307-632-9061, Fax- 307-630-3737. www.wyomingbar.org/index.html Search data at- www.wyomingbar.org/directory/index.html

#10 Board of Medicine, 320 W 25th St, #103, Cheyenne, WY 82002; 307-778-7053, Fax- 307-778-2069. http://wyomedboard.state.wy.us

#11 Department of Environmental Quality, Water Quality Division, 122 W 25th St, Herschler Bldg 4th Fl-W, Cheyenne, WY 82001; 307-777-7781, Fax- 307-777-5973. http://deq.state.wy.us/wqd/index.asp?pageid=5

#12 Board of Occupational Therapy, 6101 Yellowstone Rd #501, Cheyenne, WY 82002; 307-777-7764, Fax- 307-777-3314. http://ot.state.wy.us/

#13 Board of Outfitters & Professional Guides, 1950 Bluegrass Circle #280, Cheyenne, WY 82002; 307-635-1589, Fax- 307-777-6715. http://outfitters.state.wy.us/ Search data at- http://outfitters.state.wy.us/directory.asp

#14 Board of Pharmacy, 632 S David St, Casper, WY 82601-3189; 307-234-0294, Fax- 307-234-7226. http://pharmacyboard.state.wy.us Search data at- http://pharmacyboard.state.wy.us/search.asp

#15 Professional Licensing Administration, Board of Physical Therapy, 1800 Carey Ave, 4th Fl, Cheyenne, WY 82002; 307-777-7387, Fax- 307-777-3508. Hours- 8AM-5PM. http://plboards.state.wy.us/PTherapy/

#16 Professional Licensing Administration, Board of Psychology, 1800 Carey Ave, 4th Fl, Cheyenne, WY 82002; 307-777-6529, Fax- 307-777-3508. Hours- 8AM-5PM. http://plboards.state.wy.us/psychology/

#17 Professional Licensing Administration, Board of Radiologic Technologists Examiners, 1800 Carey Ave, 4th Fl, Cheyenne, WY 82002; 307-777-3507, Fax- 307-777-3508. Hours- 8AM-5PM. http://plboards.state.wy.us/radiology/

#18 Board of Registration for Professional Geologists, 500 S 3rd St, Laramie, WY 82070; 307-742-1118, Fax- 307-742-1120. http://wbpg.wy.gov/ Search data at- http://wbpg.wy.gov/roster_search.asp

#19 Professional Licensing Administration, Board of Registration in Podiatry, 1800 Carey Ave, 4th Fl, Cheyenne, WY 82002; 307-777-7387, Fax- 307-777-3508. Hours- 8AM-5PM. http://plboards.state.wy.us/podiatry/

#20 Professional Licensing Administration, Board of Veterinary Medicine, 1800 Carey Ave, 4th Fl, Cheyenne, WY 82002; 307-777-3507, Fax- 307-777-3508. http://plboards.state.wy.us/VetBoard/

#21 Real Estate Commission, Appraiser Board, 2020 Carey Ave, #702, Cheyenne, WY 82002; 307-777-7141, Fax- 307-777-3796. http://realestate.state.wy.us

#22 Child Care Certification Board, 2300 Capitol Ave, Hathaway Bldg, Rm 337, Cheyenne, WY 82002-0490; 307-777-6350, Fax- 307-777-3659. http://dfswapps.state.wy.us/ Search data at- http://dfswapps.state.wy.us/DFSDivEC/General/Contacts.asp

#23 Department of Audit, Division of Banking, 122 W 25th St, Herschler Bldg 3rd Fl E, Cheyenne, WY 82002; 307-777-7797, Fax- 307-777-3555. Hours- 8AM-5PM. http://audit.state.wy.us/banking/

#24 Department of Audit, Collecting Agency Board, Herschler Bldg, 3rd Fl E, 122 W 25th St, Cheyenne, WY 82002; 307-777-3497, Fax- 307-777-3555. Hours- 8AM-5PM. http://audit.state.wy.us/banking/ Search data at- http://audit.state.wy.us/banking/cab/cablicensees.htm

#25 P.O.S.T. Commission, 1710 Pacific Ave, Cheyenne, WY 82002; 307-777-7718, Fax- 307-638-9706. http://attorneygeneral.state.wy.us/post.htm

#26 Department of Fire & Electrical Safety Office, Electrical Board, Herschler Bldg, 1st Fl West, Cheyenne, WY 82002; 307-777-6385, Fax- 307-777-7119. http://wyofire.state.wy.us/electricalsafety/index.html

#27 Engineers & Professional Land Surveyors, 6920 Yellowtail Dr. Suite 100, Cheyenne, WY 82002; 307-777-6155, Fax- 307-777-3403. http://engineersandsurveyors.wy.gov Search data at- http://engineersandsurveyors.state.wy.us/roster/rosterSearch.aspx

#28 Professional Licensing Administration, Board of Speech Pathologists & Audiology, 1800 Carey Ave, 4th Fl, Cheyenne, WY 82002; 307-777-5403, Fax- 307-777-3508. http://plboards.state.wy.us/speech/ Licensees roster available.

#29 Board of Certified Public Accountants, 2020 Carey Ave, #702, Cheyenne, WY 82002; 307-777-7551, Fax- 307-777-3796. http://cpaboard.state.wy.us Search data at- http://cpaboard.state.wy.us/database.aspx

#30 Professional Licensing Administration, Board of Architects & Landscape Architects, 1800 Carey Ave, 4th Fl, Cheyenne, WY 82002; 307-777-5403, Fax- 307-777-3508. http://plboards.state.wy.us/architecture/

#31 Driver Svcs, Department of Transportation, 5300 Bishop Blvd, Cheyenne, WY 82009-3340; 307-777-3340, Fax- 307-777-4289. http://dot.state.wy.us

#32 Professional Licensing Administration, Board of Chiropractic Examiners, 1818 Carey Ave, 4th Fl, Cheyenne, WY 82002; 307-777-7387, Fax- 307-777-3508. Hours- 8AM-5PM. http://plboards.state.wy.us/chiropractic/

#33 Mining Council, PO Box 1094, Rock Springs, WY 82901; 307-362-5222, Fax- 307-362-5233. http://wydoe.state.wy.us/doe.asp?ID=53

#34 Securities Division, Office of Secretary of State, 200 W 24th St, The Capitol Building, Rm 109, Cheyenne, WY 82002; 307-777-7370, Fax- 307-777-5339. Hours- 8AM-5PM. http://soswy.state.wy.us/securiti/securiti.htm

#35 Professional Teaching Standards Board, 1920 Thomes Ave, #400, Cheyenne, WY 82002; 307-777-6261, Fax- 307-777-8718. http://ptsb.state.wy.us

#36 Secretary of State, Elections/Notary Division, 200 W 24th St, State Capitol Bldg, Cheyenne, WY 82002; 307-777-7311, Fax- 307-777-5339. http://soswy.state.wy.us

#37 Board of Nursing, 1810 Pioneer Ave, Cheyenne, WY 82002; 307-777-7601; voice verification 877-626-2681, Fax- 307-777-3519. http://nursing.state.wy.us Search data at- http://nursing.state.wy.us/Main.asp?MainMode=3 Call for prices.

#38 Pari-Mutuel Commission, 2515 Warren Ave, #301, Cheyenne, WY 82002; 307-777-5887, Fax- 307-777-3681. http://parimutuel.state.wy.us

#39 Professional Licensing Administration, Mental Health Professional Licensing Board, 1800 Carey Ave, 4th Fl, Cheyenne, WY 82002; 307-777-3628, Fax- 307-777-3508. http://plboards.state.wy.us/mentalhealth/

Wyoming Federal Courts

The following list indicates the district and division name for each county in the state.

Wyoming County/Court Cross Reference

County	Division
Albany	Cheyenne
Big Horn	Cheyenne
Campbell	Cheyenne
Carbon	Cheyenne
Converse	Cheyenne
Crook	Cheyenne
Fremont	Cheyenne
Goshen	Cheyenne
Hot Springs	Cheyenne
Johnson	Cheyenne
Laramie	Cheyenne
Lincoln	Cheyenne
Natrona	Cheyenne
Niobrara	Cheyenne
Park	Cheyenne
Platte	Cheyenne
Sheridan	Cheyenne
Sublette	Cheyenne
Sweetwater	Cheyenne
Teton	Cheyenne
Uinta	Cheyenne
Washakie	Cheyenne
Weston	Cheyenne

US District Court

Cheyenne Division Court Clerk, 2120 Capitol Ave, Rm 2131, Cheyenne, WY 82001, 307-433-2120; Fax- 307-433-2152. Hours- 8:30AM-N, 1-5PM. www.wyd.uscourts.gov

Counties/Note: All counties in Wyoming. Some criminal records are held in Casper but all are available electronically in Cheyenne.

Searches/Indexing: Include full name in search request. Results do not include DOB. Will not fax back documents. New cases are in the index 1-2 days after filing date. Computer index back to 1992 maintained. Records older than 1992 on microfiche. Case files sent to archives when the right number of boxes filled.

Search Access: Only docket info available by phone. **Mail:** Search usually completed- 1-2 days. SASE not required. **Fax:** Written fax search requests accepted. **In person:** 1 public terminal available. No self-serve copier.

Payment: Pay by money order, cashier's or personal check. No credit cards accepted. Payee: Clerk, US District Court.

E-Services: PACER records go back to 1988. New records online after 1 day. ECF at https://ecf.wyd.uscourts.gov

US Bankruptcy Court

Cheyenne Division Court Clerk, 2120 Capitol Ave, 6th Fl, Cheyenne, WY 82001, 307-433-2200. Hours- 8AM-N, 1-5PM. www.wyb.uscourts.gov

Counties/Note: All counties in Wyoming. There is also a Divisional office in Casper; 111 S Wolcott, 307-232-2650. The Casper public access terminal allows you to search the entire state; same for Cheyenne's public terminal.

Searches/Indexing: Include full name and last 4 digits of SSN - or year of birth - in search request. Results include last 4 SSN digits only; some documents may include more. New cases are in the index 24 hours after filing date. Both computer and card indexes maintained. Case files sent to archives 1 year after closed.

Search Access: Voice Case Information Service available, call VCIS at 888-804-5537 or 307-433-2238. **Mail:** Search usually completed- 1-2 days. Include SASE for return. **In person:** Public terminal available; index goes back 10 years. Self-serve copies from computer terminal- $.10 each.

Payment: Pay by Visa/MC, money order, cashier's check. No debtor checks accepted. Payee: Clerk, US Bankruptcy Court.

E-Services: Document images available. PACER records go back 1 year. New records online immediately. ECF at https://ecf.wyb.uscourts.gov. Opinions on ECF/PACER only, account required. Also, name search the Archives free at www.wyb.uscourts.gov/sp/archives-search/search.php. Also search by SSN or case number. **Online Note:** Calendars for 341 Meetings are available on the PACER system. A daily calendar is available free at www.wyb.uscourts.gov/court-information.

Standards for Federal Courts: Fees are standard unless noted in profile. Search fee is $26.00 per item (one party name or case number). Copy fee is $.50 per page. Certification fee is $9.00 per document, double for exemplification, if available. Most courts require prepayment. Mail requests should enclose a SASE unless otherwise noted. Before releasing records, all courts require prepayment, unless noted.

District courts index by defendant and plaintiff and by case number. Bankruptcy courts usually index by debtor and case number. While most courts now have their indexes on computer, many may still maintain index card files as well. Courts will archive closed case files at different times.

There are numerous public access programs available to online subscribers. Search the U.S. Party/Case Index to find party names and case numbers among all courts. Individual case data is provided on PACER. A search of CM/ECF provides copies of cases filed electronically. For details about PACER, the US Party/Case Index, and CM/ECF see the Appendix or go to http://pacer.psc.uscourts.gov or call 800-676-6856.

Wyoming County Courts

Court	Jurisdiction	No. of Courts	How Organized
District Courts*	General	23	9 Districts
Circuit Courts*	Limited	27	23 Counties
Municipal Courts	Municipal	80	

* Profiled in this Sourcebook.

Court	CIVIL								
	Tort	Contract	Real Estate	Min. Claim	Max. Claim	Small Claims	Estate	Eviction	Domestic Relations
District Courts*	X	X	X	$7000	No Max		X		X
Circuit Courts*	X	X	X	$0	$7000	$5000		X	X
Municipal Courts									

Court	CRIMINAL				
	Felony	Misdemeanor	DWI/DUI	Preliminary Hearing	Juvenile
District Courts*	X				X
Circuit Courts*		X	X	X	
Municipal Courts		X	X		

Administration

Court Administrator, 2301 Capitol Av, Supreme Court Bldg, Cheyenne, WY, 82002; 307-777-7583, Fax: 307-777-3447. (MST) www.courts.state.wy.us

Court Structure

Each county has a District Court which oversees felony criminal cases, large civil cases, and juvenile and probate matters. The Circuit Court is of limited jurisdiction and oversee civil cases when the damages or recovery sought does not exceed $7,000. Circuit Courts also hear family violence cases and all misdemeanors. Effective January 1, 2003, all Justice Courts became Circuit Courts and follow Circuit Court rules.

Circuit Courts handle civil claims up to $7,000 and small claims to $5,000. The District Courts take cases over the applicable limit in each county. Three counties have two Circuit Courts each: Fremont, Park, and Sweetwater. Cases may be filed in either of the two court offices in those counties, and records requests are referred between the two courts. Municipal courts operate in all incorporated cities and towns; their jurisdiction covers all ordinance violations and has no civil jurisdiction. The Municipal Court judge may assess penalties of up to $750 and/or six months in jail.

Online Access

Wyoming's statewide case management system is for internal use only. Planning is underway for a new case management system that will ultimately allow public access. Supreme Court opinions are listed by date at the home page.

Searching Tips, Fees, and Other Guidelines

Fees for searching and record copies are set statewide by Rule. For the most part, these guidelines are followed; the search fee is $10.00 per name, the copy fee is $1.00 for the first page and $.50 each add'l, and there is a $2.00 charge for clerks to send or receive a fax. Certification fees vary.

Albany County

2nd Judicial District Court 525 Grand, County Courthouse, Rm 305, Laramie, WY 82070; 307-721-2508; fax: 307-721-2520; 9-5PM. ***Felony, Civil Actions over $7,000, Probate.*** www.co.albany.wy.us/Departments/ClerkofDistrictCourt/

Civil Records: Access: Phone, mail, in person. Both court and visitors may perform in person searches. Search fee: $10.00 per name. Required to search: name; also helpful: years to search. Civil cases indexed by defendant, plaintiff; index on computer go back to 1988, prior records on card index to 1890. Note: Phone searches limited to three names. Call and ask permission first before faxing. Mail turnaround time same day. Civil PAT available.

Criminal Records: Access: Mail, in person. Both court and visitors may perform in person searches. Search fee: $10.00 per name. Search results can be phoned back to a toll-free number only. Required to search: name, years to search, DOB. Criminal records on computer go back to 1988, prior records on card index to 1890. Mail turnaround time same day. Criminal PAT available.

General Information: No sex offenses records released, signed release required for child support cases. Will fax out files to toll-free number only. Court makes copy: $1.00 first page, $.50 each add'l. No cert fee. Payee: Clerk of District Court. Personal checks accepted; credit cards are not. Mail requests: SASE required.

Albany Circuit Court 525 Grand, Rm 400, County Courthouse, Laramie, WY 82070; 307-742-5747; fax: 307-742-5610; 8-5PM. ***Misdemeanor, Civil Actions under $7,000, Eviction, Small Claims.***

Civil Records: Access: Mail, in person. Both court and visitors may perform in person searches. Search fee: $10.00 per name. Required to search: name, years to search. Civil cases indexed by defendant, plaintiff; index on computer from 1993, prior on docket books to 1984. Mail turnaround time same day if possible.

Criminal Records: Access: Mail, in person, fax. Only the court performs in person searches; visitors may not. Search fee: $10.00 per name. Required to search: name, years to search, DOB. Criminal records computerized from 1990, prior on docket books to 1984. Note: A $10.00 "court fee" may be applied to each in person search. Mail turnaround time same day if possible.

General Information: No SSN or family violence records released. Fee to fax files is $2.00 per document. Court makes copy: $1.00 1st page, $.50 each add'l. Cert fee: $5.00 per doc. Payee: Albany Circuit Court. In state personal checks accepted. Visa/MC accepted. Mail requests: SASE required.

Big Horn County

5th Judicial District Court PO Box 670, Basin, WY 82410; 307-568-2381; criminal fax: 307-568-2791; civil fax: same; 8AM-N, 1-5PM. ***Felony, Civil Actions over $7,000, Probate.*** Probate fax is same as main fax number.

Civil Records: Access: Fax, mail, in person. Both court and visitors may perform in person searches. Search fee: $10.00 per name. Required to search: name, years to search. Civil cases indexed by defendant, plaintiff; index on computer 1988, on microfiche 1982, 1970 to present on cards. Mail turnaround time 24 hours.

Criminal Records: Access: Mail, in person. Both court and visitors may perform in person searches. Search fee: $10.00 per name. Required to search: name, years to search. Criminal records on computer 1989, on microfiche 1982, 1970 to present on cards. Mail turnaround time 24 hours.

General Information: Some confidential records not released. Will fax out files for $2.00. Court makes copy: $1.00 first page, $.50 each add'l. Certification fee: $.50 per page. Payee: Clerk of Court. Business checks accepted. No credit cards accepted. Mail requests: SASE required.

Basin Circuit Court PO Box 749, Basin, WY 82410; 307-568-2367; fax: 307-568-2554; 8AM-5PM. ***Misdemeanor, Civil Actions under $7,000, Small Claims.*** Note that misdemeanor records from Basin Court and the Lovell Court are not combined.

Civil Records: Access: Fax, mail, in person. Only the court performs in person searches; visitors may not. Search fee: $10.00 per name. Required to search: name, years to search; also helpful: address. Civil cases indexed by defendant. Civil records on microfiche 1985. Mail turnaround time 1 day.

Criminal Records: Access: Fax, mail, in person. Only the court performs in person searches; visitors may not. Search fee: $10.00 per name. Required to search: name, DOB; also helpful: SSN. Criminal records on computer since 1990, microfiche 1985. Mail turnaround time 1 day.

General Information: No sex or juvenile offenses released. Fee to fax files is $2 per document. Court makes copy: $1.00 1st page, $.50 each add'l. Cert fee: $5.00 per document. Payee: Big Horn Cty Court. Personal checks accepted. Credit cards accepted, surcharge may apply. Mail requests: SASE required.

Lovell Circuit Court PO Box 595, Lovell, WY 82431; 307-548-7601; fax: 307-548-9691; 8AM-5PM. ***Misdemeanor, Civil Actions under $7,000, Small Claims.*** Misdemeanor records from the Basin Circuit Court and this Lovell Court are not combined.

Civil Records: Access: Fax, mail, in person. Only the court performs in person searches; visitors may not. Search fee: $10.00 per name. Required to search: name, years to search; also helpful: address. Civil cases by defendant. Civil records computerized back to 8/2002. Mail turnaround time 1 day.

Criminal Records: Access: Fax, mail, in person. Only the court performs in person searches; visitors may not. Search fee: $10.00 per name. Required to search: name, DOB; also helpful: SSN. Criminal records computerized from 1990. Mail turnaround time 1 day.

General Information: No sex or juvenile offenses released. Fee to fax files is $2.00 per document. Court makes copy: $1.00 1st page, $.50 each add'l. Certification fee: $5.00 per document. Payee: Lovell Circuit Court. Personal checks/credit cards accepted.

Campbell County

6th Judicial District Court PO Box 817, 500 S Gillette St, Ste 2600, Gillette, WY 82717; 307-682-3424; criminal fax: 307-687-6209; civil fax: same; 8AM-5PM. ***Felony, Civil Actions over $7,000, Probate.*** Probate fax is same as main fax number.

Civil Records: Access: Fax, mail, in person. Visitors must perform in person searches themselves. Search fee: $10.00 per name. Required to search: name, years to search. Civil cases indexed by Defendant, Plaintiff. Civil records archived from 1913; on computer back to 1986. Mail turnaround time 1-2 days. Civil PAT goes back to 1999. PAT results show name only.

Criminal Records: Access: Fax, mail, in person. Visitors must perform in person searches themselves. Search fee: $10.00 per name. Required to search: name, years to search. Criminal records archived from 1913; on computer back to 1985. Mail turnaround time 1-2 days. Criminal PAT goes back to 1999. PAT results show name only.

General Information: Names of victims in sex cases, confidential records not released. Will fax documents $1.00 1st page and $.50 ea add'l page. Court makes copy: $1.00 first page, $.50 each add'l. Self serve: $.25 per page. Cert fee: $1.00 per doc. Payee: Clerk of District Court. Local personal checks accepted; no out of state. No credit cards. Mail request SASE required.

Campbell Circuit Court 500 S Gillette Ave, #2200, Gillette, WY 82716; 307-682-2190; fax: 307-687-6214; 8AM-5PM. ***Misdemeanor, Civil Actions under $7,000, Eviction, Small Claims.***

Civil Records: Access: Mail, in person. Only the court performs in person searches; visitors may not. Search fee: $10.00 per name. Required to search: name, years to search; also helpful: address. Civil cases indexed by defendant, plaintiff; index on computer since 1983, archives from 1979. Mail turnaround time 2 days.

Criminal Records: Access: Mail, in person. Only the court performs in person searches; visitors may not. Search fee: $10.00 per name. Required to search: name, years to search, DOB; also helpful: address. Criminal records on computer since 1983, archives from 1979. Mail turnaround time 1-2 days; longer for cases prior to 2001.

General Information: No sex related cases released. Fee to fax files is $2 per document. Court makes copy: $1.00 1st page, $.50 each add'l. Self serve: same. Cert fee: $5.00 per document. Payee: Campbell County Circuit Court. Personal checks accepted. Visa/MC accepted. Mail requests: SASE requested.

Carbon County

Carbon County District Court Clerk of District Court, PO Box 67, Rawlins, WY 82301; 307-328-2628; fax: 307-328-2629; 8AM-5PM. ***Felony, Civil Actions over $7,000, Probate.*** The office has a master index with all cases on it.

Civil Records: Access: Phone, fax, mail, in person. Both court and visitors may perform in person searches. Search fee: $10.00 per name. Required to search: name, years to search; also helpful: address. Civil cases indexed by defendant, plaintiff; index on file from late 1800s, index cards, docket books, then computer 1997 to present. Note: Public can search on the manual index. Mail turnaround 4-5 days.

Criminal Records: Access: Phone, fax, mail, in person. Both court and visitors may perform in person searches. Search fee: $10.00 per name. Required to search: name, years to search; also helpful: address, DOB, SSN. Criminal records indexed on cards and docket books; on computer 1997 to present. Note: Public can search on the manual index. Mail turnaround time 4-5 days.

General Information: No juvenile or adoption records released. Fee to fax files depends on number of pages. Court makes copy: $1.00 first page, $.50 each add'l. Self serve: same. No cert fee. Payee: Clerk of District Court. Personal checks accepted; credit cards are not. Mail requests: SASE required.

Carbon Circuit Court Attn: Chief Clerk, Courthouse Bldg, 415 W Pine St, Rawlins, WY 82301; 307-324-6655; fax: 307-324-9465; 8AM-5PM. ***Misdemeanor, Civil Actions under $7,000, Eviction, Small Claims.***

Civil Records: Access: Mail, fax, in person. Only the court performs in person searches; visitors may not. Search fee: $10.00 per name. Required to search: name, years to search; also helpful: address. Civil cases indexed by defendant, plaintiff; index on computer back to 3/95. Mail turnaround time 1 week.

Criminal Records: Access: Mail, fax, in person. Only the court performs in person searches; visitors may not. Search fee: $10.00 per name. Required to search: name, years to search, DOB. Criminal records computerized from 8/87. Mail turnaround time 1 week.

General Information: Names of victims not released in sex related cases. Will fax out files to a toll-free line. Court makes copy: $1.00 1st page, $.50 each add'l. Certification fee: $5.00 per document. Payee: Circuit Court of Carbon County. Personal checks accepted. Visa/MC accepted, add $8.00 usage fee. Mail requests: SASE requested.

Converse County

8th Judicial District Court Box 189, Douglas, WY 82633; 307-358-3165; criminal fax: 307-358-9783; civil fax: same; 8AM-5PM. ***Felony, Civil Actions over $7,000, Probate.*** Probate fax is same as main fax number.

Civil Records: Access: Phone, fax, mail, in person. Both court and visitors may perform in person searches. Search fee: $10.00 per name or case. Required to search: name, years to search; also helpful: address. Civil cases indexed by defendant, plaintiff; index on card file from 1888. Mail turnaround time usually same day.

Criminal Records: Access: Phone, fax, mail, in person. Both court and visitors may perform in person searches. Search fee: $10.00 per name or case. Required to search: name, years to search; also helpful: address, DOB, SSN. Criminal records on card file from 1850. Mail turnaround- usually same day.

General Information: No juvenile, adoptions or mental cases released. Will fax out files no add'l fee. Court makes copy: $.25 per page. Self serve: $.10 per page. Certification fee: $1.00 fee for 1st page and $.50 for the seal. Add'l fee for copies and postage if mailed. Payee: Clerk of District Court. Personal checks accepted; credit cards are not.

Converse Circuit Court 107 N 5th St, #231, PO Box 45, Douglas, WY 82633; 307-358-2196; fax: 307-358-2501; 8AM-5PM. ***Misdemeanor, Civil Actions under $7,000, Eviction, Small Claims.***

Civil Records: Access: Mail, in person. Both court and visitors may perform in person searches. Search fee: $10.00 per name. Required to search: name, years to search, and DOB or SSN. Civil cases indexed by defendant, plaintiff; index on computer from 1994, card file prior. Mail turnaround time 1-2 days. Civil PAT goes back to 1994.

Criminal Records: Access: Mail, in person. Both court and visitors may perform in person searches. Search fee: $10.00 per name. Required to search: name, years to search, DOB also helpful: address, SSN. Criminal records computerized from 1990, card file prior. Mail turnaround time 1-2 days. Criminal PAT goes back to 1990.

General Information: No sealed records released. Fee to fax files is $2.00 per document. Court makes copy: $1.00 1st page, $.50 each add'l. Cert fee: $2.00 per document. Payee: Circuit Court of Converse County. Cashiers checks and money orders accepted. Visa/MC accepted. Mail requests: SASE required.

Crook County

6th Judicial District Court Box 904, Sundance, WY 82729; 307-283-2523; criminal fax: 307-283-2996; civil fax: same; 8AM-5PM. ***Felony, Civil Actions over $7,000, Probate, High Misdemeanor pre-7/1/02.*** High misdemeanor cases no longer heard by this court, effective 7/1/02; high misdemeanor records prior to that date can be found here. Probate fax is same as main fax number.

Civil Records: Access: Mail, in person. Both court and visitors may perform in person searches. Search fee: $10.00 per name. Required to search: name, years to search; also helpful: address. Civil cases indexed by defendant, plaintiff; index on card file from late 1800s; on computer back to 1999. Note: The civil limit was raised from $3,000 to $7,000 on 7/1/2002. Cases prior to that date remain with this court. Mail turnaround time usually same day.

Criminal Records: Access: Mail, in person. Both court and visitors may perform in person searches. Search fee: $10.00 per name. Required to search: name, years to search; also helpful: address, DOB, SSN. Criminal records on card file from late 1800s; on computer back to 1999. Note: As of 7/1/02, high

misdemeanor cases are no longer heard by this court, however, cases prior to that date will remain here. Mail turnaround time usually same day.
General Information: No sealed records released. Will fax out files for $2.00 per page; no fax charge to toll-free number. Court makes copy: $.50 per page. Self serve: same. Cert fee: $1.00 per seal. Payee: Clerk of District Court. Business checks accepted. No credit cards accepted. Mail requests: SASE required.

Circuit Court PO Box 650, Sundance, WY 82729; 307-283-2929; fax: 307-283-2931; 8AM-5PM. ***Misdemeanor, Civil Actions under $5,000, Small Claims.*** This former Justice Court became a Circuit Court on 7/1/2002.
Civil Records: Access: Mail, fax, in person. Only the court performs in person searches; visitors may not. Search fee: $10.00 per name. Required to search: name, years to search; also helpful: address. Civil cases indexed by defendant, plaintiff; index on cards, archives back to 1977; on computer back to 1998. Mail turnaround time 3-5 days.
Criminal Records: Access: Mail, fax, in person. Only the court performs in person searches; visitors may not. Search fee: $10.00 per name. Required to search: name, years to search, DOB, SSN. Criminal records go back to 1983; on computer back to 6/1980. Mail turnaround time 3-5 days.
General Information: No sex related cases released. Fee to fax files is $2.00 per document; no charge if $10.00 search fee paid. Court makes copy: $1.00 1st page, $.50 each add'l. Certification fee: $5.00 per document. Payee: Crook County Circuit Court. Personal checks accepted. Major credit cards accepted ($8.00 usage fee). Mail requests: SASE required.

Fremont County

9th Judicial District Court PO Box 370, 450 N 2nd St, Rm 235, Lander, WY 82520; 307-332-1134; fax: 307-332-1143; 8AM-N, 1-5PM. ***Felony, Civil Actions over $7,000, Probate.***
Civil Records: Access: Phone, fax, mail, in person. Both court and visitors may perform in person searches. Search fee: $10.00 per name. Required to search: name, years to search; also helpful: address. Civil cases indexed by defendant, plaintiff; index on computer since 1992, in books since 1991, on microfiche since 1939 and on card file from 1898. Mail turnaround time same day. Civil PAT goes back to 1992. PAT results show name only. Clerk will pull file to match DOB.
Criminal Records: Access: Phone, fax, mail, in person. Both court and visitors may perform in person searches. Search fee: $10.00 per name. Required to search: name, years to search; also helpful: address, DOB, SSN. Criminal records on computer since 1992 (newer system records go back to 2004), in books since 1991, microfiche since 1939 and on card file from 1898. Mail turnaround time same day. Criminal PAT goes back to same as civil. PAT criminal results show middle initial. Clerk will pull file to match DOB.
General Information: No juvenile, involuntary hospitalization or adoption records released. Will fax docs $2.00 per page. Court makes copy: $.50 per page. Self serve: no fee. No certification fee. Payee: Clerk of District Court. Personal checks accepted; credit cards are not. Mail requests: SASE required.

Dubois Circuit Court PO Box 952, 712 Meckem, Dubois, WY 82513; 307-455-2920; fax: 307-455-2132; 8AM-2:00PM. ***Misdemeanor, Civil Actions under $7,000, Eviction, Small Claims.*** This is a satellite of the Lander Court.
Civil Records: Access: Mail, in person. Both court and visitors may perform in person searches. Search fee: $10.00 per name. Required to search: name, years to search. Civil cases indexed by defendant, plaintiff. Civil records ndexed. Mail turnaround time 4 days. PAT results show middle initial, DOB. Terminal results also show SSNs.
Criminal Records: Access: Mail, in person. Both court and visitors may perform in person searches. Search fee: $10.00 per name. Required to search: name, years to search; also helpful: DOB. Criminal records on computer since 12/98; prior records on indexes. Mail turnaround time 4 days. PAT results show middle initial, DOB, and SSN.
General Information: No juvenile, sexual data released. Will fax documents to local or toll-free number. Court makes copy: $1.00 1st page, $.50 each add'l. Certification fee: $10.00 per doc. Payee: Fremont County Court. Personal checks and major credit cards accepted.

Lander Circuit Court 450 N 2nd, Rm 230, Lander, WY 82520; 307-332-3239; fax: 307-332-1152; 8AM-5PM. ***Misdemeanor, Civil Actions under $7,000, Eviction, Small Claims.*** This is the main Circuit Court for Fremont County.
Civil Records: Access: Phone, fax, mail, in person. Both court and visitors may perform in person searches. Search fee: $10.00 per name. Required to search: name, years to search; also helpful: address. Civil cases indexed by defendant, plaintiff; index on computer from 1993, archive back to 1979. Mail turnaround time 2 days.
Criminal Records: Access: Phone, fax, mail, in person. Both court and visitors may perform in person searches. Search fee: $10.00 per name. Required to search: name, years to search; also helpful: address, DOB, SSN. Criminal records computerized from 1993, archive back to 1979. Mail turnaround time 2 days.
General Information: No juvenile or sexual data released. Fee to fax files is $2.00 per document. Court makes copy: $1.00 1st page, $.50 each add'l. Certification fee: $5.00 per document. Payee: Circuit Court. In state personal checks accepted. Credit cards accepted, minimum $8.00 fee. Mail requests: SASE required.

Riverton Circuit Court 818 S Federal Blvd, Riverton, WY 82501; 307-856-7259; fax: 307-857-3635; 8AM-5PM. ***Misdemeanor, Civil Actions under $7,000, Eviction, Small Claims.***
Civil Records: Access: Mail, in person. Only the court performs in person searches; visitors may not. Search fee: $10.00 per name. Required to search: name, years to search. Civil cases indexed by defendant, plaintiff. Civil records are computerized since 1997; prior in books to 1981. Mail turnaround time 2 days.
Criminal Records: Access: Mail, in person. Only the court performs in person searches; visitors may not. Search fee: $10.00 per name. Required to search: name, years to search, DOB; also helpful: SSN. Criminal records on computer since 1989; prior in books to 1981. Mail turnaround time 2 days.
General Information: No sex released cases released. Fee to fax files is $2.00 per document. Court makes copy: $1.00 1st page, $.50 each add'l. Cert fee: $5.00 per document. Payee: Fremont County Circuit Court. In state personal checks accepted. Visa/MC accepted. Mail requests: SASE required.

Goshen County

8th Judicial District Court PO Box 818, Clerk of District Court, 2125 E "A" St #236, Torrington, WY 82240; 307-532-2155; fax: 307-532-8608; 7:30AM-4PM. ***Felony, Civil over $7,000, Probate.***
Civil Records: Access: Mail, in person. Both court and visitors may perform in person searches. Search fee: $10.00 per name. Required to search: name, years to search; also helpful: address. Civil cases indexed by defendant, plaintiff; index on index file only since 1913. Mail turnaround time 2 days.
Criminal Records: Access: Mail, in person. Both court and visitors may perform in person searches. Search fee: $10.00 per name. Required to search: name, years to search; also helpful: address, DOB, SSN. Criminal records on index file since 1913, on computer back to 2005. Mail turnaround time 2 days.
General Information: No juvenile records released. Will fax results; prefer toll free line. Court makes copy: $1.00 first page, $.50 each add'l. Certification fee: $.50 per page. Payee: Clerk of District Court. In state personal checks accepted. No credit cards. Mail requests: SASE required.

Goshen Circuit Court Drawer BB, Torrington, WY 82240; 307-532-2938; criminal: X250; civil: X251; fax: 307-532-5101; 7-4PM. ***Misdemeanor, Civil Actions under $7,000, Eviction, Small Claims.***
Civil Records: Access: Mail, in person. Only the court performs in person searches; visitors may not. Search fee: $10.00 per name; alias separate. Required to search: name, years to search; also helpful: address. Civil cases indexed by case number, defendant. Civil records go back to 1988; on computer back to 3/97, prior archived. Mail turnaround time 3-4 days.
Criminal Records: Access: Mail, in person. Only the court performs in person searches; visitors may not. Search fee: $10.00 per name; alias separate. Required to search: name, years to search, DOB; also helpful: address, SSN. Criminal records go back to 10/92; on computer back to 4/89 for disposition data, to 1984 for felonies or high misdemeanors, prior archived. Mail turnaround time 3-4 days.
General Information: No juvenile records released. Fee to fax files is $2.00 per doc; free if a toll-free number is provided. Court makes copy: $1.00 1st page, $.50 each add'l. Cert fee: $5.00 per doc. Payee: Circuit Court 8th Judicial District. No personal checks. Major credit cards accepted. SASE required.

Hot Springs County

5th Judicial District Court 415 Arapahoe St, Thermopolis, WY 82443; 307-864-3323; fax: 307-864-3210; 8AM-5PM. ***Felony, Civil over $7,000, Probate.*** www.hscounty.com/cofcourt.html
Civil Records: Access: Mail, in person. Both court and visitors may perform in person searches. Search fee: $10.00 per name. Required to search: name, years to search; also helpful: address. Civil cases indexed by defendant, plaintiff; index on card index back to 1900s. Mail turnaround time 1 day.
Criminal Records: Access: Mail, in person. Both court and visitors may perform in person searches. Search fee: $10.00 per name. Required to search: name, years to search, DOB, SSN; also helpful: address. Criminal records on card index back to 1900s. Mail turnaround time 1 day.
General Information: No juvenile, adoption or sexual data released. Will fax out files to a local or toll free line. Court makes copy: $1.00 1st page, $.50 each add'l. Self serve: $.50 per page. Certification fee: $.50 per page. Payee: Clerk of District Court. Personal checks accepted; credit cards are not. SASE required.

Hot Springs Circuit Court 417 Arapahoe St, Thermopolis, WY 82443; 307-864-5161; fax: 307-864-2067; 8AM-5PM. ***Misdemeanor, Civil Actions under $7,000, Small Claims.***
Civil Records: Access: Mail, in person. Only the court performs in person searches; visitors may not. Search fee: $10.00 per name. Required to search: name, years to search. Civil cases indexed by defendant, plaintiff; index on computer from 1990, prior in card file. Mail turnaround time 2-3 days.
Criminal Records: Access: Mail, in person. Only the court performs in person searches; visitors may not. Search fee: $10.00 per name. Required to search: name, years. Criminal computerized from 1990, prior in card file to 1980. Mail turnaround 2-3 days.
General: No closed case records released. Fee to fax files is $2 per document. Court makes copy: $1.00 1st page, $.50 each add'l. Cert fee: $5.00 per doc. Payee: Circuit Court. Business checks accepted. Major credit cards accepted. Mail requests: SASE required.

Johnson County

4th Judicial District Court 76 N Main, Buffalo, WY 82834; 307-684-7271; fax: 307-684-5146; 8-5PM. ***Felony, Civil over $7,000, Probate.*** www.johnsoncountywyoming.org/districtcourt.html
Civil Records: Access: Fax, mail, in person. Both court and visitors may perform in person searches. Search fee: $10.00 per name. Required to search: name, years to search; also helpful: address. Civil cases indexed by defendant, plaintiff; index on computer from 1989, card index since 1892. Mail turnaround time 1 week.
Criminal Records: Access: Fax, mail, in person. Both court and visitors may perform in person searches. Search fee: $10.00 per name. Required to search: name, years to search; also helpful: address, DOB, SSN. Criminal records computerized from 1989, card index since 1892. Mail turnaround 1 week.
General Information: No adoption or juvenile records released. Will fax out files $1.00 per page. Court makes copy: $1.00 first page; $.50 each add'l page. Self serve: same. Cert fee: $.50 per page.

Payee: Clerk of District Court. In state personal checks accepted. No credit cards accepted. Mail requests: SASE required.

Circuit Court 76 N Main St, Buffalo, WY 82834-1847; 307-684-5720; fax: 307-684-7308; 8-5PM. ***Misdemeanor, Civil under $7,000, Small Claims.*** Formally Justice Court; became Circuit Court on 1/03.
Civil Records: Access: Mail, fax, in person. Both court and visitors may perform in person searches. Search fee: $10.00 per name. Required to search: name, years to search; also helpful: address. Civil cases indexed by defendant, plaintiff; index on computer since 1995; prior records on index cards. Mail turnaround time 2 days. Civil PAT goes back to 1995. PAT civil results show middle initial.
Criminal Records: Access: Mail, fax, in person. Both court and visitors may perform in person searches. Search fee: $10.00 per name. Required to search: name, years to search, DOB; also helpful: SSN. Criminal records on computer since 5/90, card index back to 1979. Mail turnaround 2 days. Crim PAT goes back to 1990. PAT results show middle initial, DOB. Terminal results include SSN.
General Information: No sex cases released. Will fax docs for $2.00 each for non-toll free phone numbers. Court makes copy: $1.00 1st page; $.50 each add'l. Certification fee: $5.00 per case. Payee: Circuit Court. Personal checks accepted. Credit cards accepted, $8.00 fee. Mail requests: SASE required.

Laramie County

1st Judicial District Court 309 W 20th St, #3205, PO Box 787, Cheyenne, WY 82003; 307-633-4270; fax: 307-633-4277; 8AM-5PM. ***Felony, Misdemeanor, Civil Actions over $7,000, Probate.***
www.laramiecounty.com/departments/district_court/index.asp
Civil Records: Access: Fax, mail, in person. Both court and visitors may perform in person searches. Search fee: $10.00 per name. Required to search: name. Civil cases indexed by defendant, plaintiff; index on card index to 1890; on computer back to 1992. Mail turnaround time 2 days. Civil PAT goes back to 1992; results show middle initial.
Criminal Records: Access: Fax, mail, in person. Both court and visitors may perform in person searches. Search fee: $10.00 per name. Required to search: name, years to search, DOB, SSN. Criminal records on card index to 1890; on computer back to 1992. Mail turnaround time 2 days. Criminal PAT goes back to same as civil. PAT criminal results show middle initial.
General Information: No juvenile or paternity records released. No fee to fax results to 800 numbers only. Court makes copy: $1.00 first page, $.50 each add'l. Self serve: same. Certification fee: $.50 per page, Exemplification fee- $5.00 plus copy fees. Payee: Laramie County Clerk of District Court. Business checks and major credit cards accepted. Mail requests: SASE required.

Laramie County Circuit Court 309 W 20th St, Rm 2300, Cheyenne, WY 82001; criminal phone: 307-633-4298; civil phone: 307-633-4326; fax: 307-633-4392; 8AM-5PM. ***Misdemeanor, Civil Actions under $7,000, Eviction, Small Claims.***
Civil Records: Access: Fax, mail, in person. Both court and visitors may perform in person searches. Search fee: $10.00 per name. Required to search: name, years to search, DOB; also helpful: address. Civil cases indexed by defendant, plaintiff; index on computer from 1992, card index from late 1977. Mail turnaround time 48 hours. Civil PAT goes back to 1992. PAT results show name only.
Criminal Records: Access: Fax, mail, in person. Both court and visitors may perform in person searches. Search fee: $10.00 per name. Required to search: name, years to search; also helpful: address. Criminal records computerized from 1988, card index from late 1977. Mail turnaround-48 hours. Criminal PAT goes back to 1988.PAT results show name, DOB. Only older files results will contain SSNs.
General Information: Fee to fax back is $2.00 per doc to non toll-free number; otherwise free. Court makes copy: $1.00 1st page, $.50 each add'l. Certification fee: $5.00 per document. Payee: Laramie County Circuit Court. Business checks and local personal checks only. Visa/MC accepted. Add $8.00 credit card convenience fee if request by phone. Mail requests: SASE required for mail return.

Lincoln County

3rd Judicial District Court PO Drawer 510, Kemmerer, WY 83101; 307-877-9056; fax: 307-877-6263; 8AM-5PM. ***Felony, Civil Actions over $7,000, Probate.***
Civil Records: Access: Fax, mail, in person. Both court and visitors may perform in person searches. Search fee: $10.00 per name. Required to search: name; also helpful: years to search, address. Civil cases indexed by defendant. Civil records on card index and computer back to 1916. Mail turnaround time same day. Civil PAT available.
Criminal Records: Access: Fax, mail, in person. Both court and visitors may perform in person searches. Search fee: $10.00 per name. Required to search: name; also helpful: years to search, address, DOB, SSN. Criminal records on card index and computer back to 1916. Mail turnaround time same day. Criminal PAT available.
General Information: No juvenile, sexual or PD records released. Will fax out files $5.00 per doc. Court makes copy: $1.00 first page, $.50 each add'l. Self serve: same. Certification fee: $2.50. Payee: 3rd Judicial District Court. Personal checks accepted; credit cards are not. Mail requests: SASE required.

Lincoln Circuit Court PO Box 949, Kemmerer, WY 83101; 307-877-4431; fax: 307-877-4936; 8AM-5PM. ***Misdemeanor, Civil Actions under $7,000, Eviction, Small Claims.***
Civil Records: Access: Mail, in person. Only the court performs in person searches; visitors may not. Search fee: $10.00 per name. Required to search: name, years to search. Civil cases indexed by defendant, plaintiff; index on computer from 1/90, on card index from 1984, prior data in archives. Note: All search requests must be in writing. Mail turnaround time same day.
Criminal Records: Access: Mail, in person. Only the court performs in person searches; visitors may not. Search fee: $10.00 per name. Required to search: name, years to search, DOB; also helpful: SSN. Criminal records computerized from 10/90, card index from 1984, prior in archives. Search requests must be in writing. Mail turnaround- same day.
General Information: No sexual or PD records released. Will fax out files to local or toll free line. Court makes copy: $1.00 1st page, $.50 each add'l. Cert fee: $5.00 per doc. Payee: Lincoln Circuit Court. Business checks accepted. Out of state checks not accepted. Visa/MC accepted ($8.00 fee added for using credit cards). Mail requests: SASE requested.

Natrona County

7th Judicial District Court PO Box 2510, Clerk of District Court, 200 N Center, Casper, WY 82602; 307-235-9243; fax: 307-235-9496; 8AM-5PM. ***Felony, Civil Actions over $7,000, Probate.*** The 9496 fax number is for record room. Record room phone- 307-235-9364. No misdemeanor records here unless they were originally felony charges.
Civil Records: Access: Phone, fax, mail, in person. Both court and visitors may perform in person searches. Search fee: $10.00 per name. Required to search: name, years to search; also helpful: address. Civil cases indexed by defendant, plaintiff; index on computer, microfiche from 1891. Mail turnaround time same day. Civil PAT goes back to 1891. PAT civil results show middle initial. Public access terminal in Rm 202.
Criminal Records: Access: Mail, in person. Both court and visitors may perform in person searches. Search fee: $10.00 per name. Required to search: name, years to search; also helpful: address, DOB, SSN. Criminal records on computer, microfiche from 1891. Mail turnaround time same day. Criminal PAT goes back to same as civil. Make ID verifications with clerk. PAT criminal results show middle initial. Public access terminal in Rm 202.
General Information: No adoption, juvenile, paternity, mental health records released. Will fax out files $2.00 fee. No email return. Court makes copy: $1.00 first page, $.50 each add'l. Self serve: Make your own copies from microfiche. $.15 per page if non-court document. Certification fee: $.50 per doc; $5.00 to authenticate. Payee: Clerk of District Court. Business checks accepted; no personal checks. No credit cards accepted. Mail requests: SASE required.

Natrona Circuit Court 201 N David, 5th Fl, Casper, WY 82601; 307-235-9266; fax: 307-235-9331; 8AM-5PM. ***Misdemeanor, Civil Actions under $7,000, Eviction, Small Claims.***
Civil Records: Access: Mail, in person. Only the court performs in person searches; visitors may not. Search fee: $10.00. Required to search: name, years to search; also helpful: address. Civil cases indexed by defendant, plaintiff; index on computer from 1994, on microfiche from 1891. Mail turnaround time 2-5 days.
Criminal Records: Access: Mail, in person. Only the court performs in person searches; visitors may not. Search fee: $10.00 per name. Required to search: name, years to search; also helpful: address, DOB, SSN. Criminal records computerized from 1989, microfiche from 1891. Note: All search requests must be in writing. Mail turnaround time 2-5 days.
General Information: No sexual, abuse records released. Fee to fax out file $2.00: no fee to fax to 800 numbers. Court makes copy: $1.00 1st page, $.50 each add'l. Certification fee: $5.00 per document. Payee: Natrona Circuit Court. Personal checks accepted. Visa/MC accepted. Mail requests: SASE required.

Niobrara County

8th Judicial District Court Clerk of District Court, PO Box 1318, Lusk, WY 82225; 307-334-2736; fax: 307-334-2703; 8AM-N, 1-4PM. ***Felony, Civil Actions over $7,000, Probate.*** Probate fax is same as main fax number.
Civil Records: Access: Mail, in person. Visitors must perform in person searches themselves. Search fee: $10.00 per name. Required to search: name, years to search. Civil cases indexed by defendant, plaintiff; index on card index from early 1900s. Mail turnaround time 2 days.
Criminal Records: Access: Mail, in person. Both court and visitors may perform in person searches. Search fee: $10.00 per name. Required to search: name, years to search, DOB, SSN. Criminal records on card index from 1913. Mail turnaround- 2 days.
General Information: No juvenile or adoption related released, no PD released. Fee to fax files is $1.00 per page. Court makes copy: $1.00 first page, $.50 each add'l. Cert fee: $.50 per page. Payee: Clerk of District Court. Personal checks accepted. Mail requests: SASE required.

Circuit Court PO Box 209, 223 S Main St, Lusk, WY 82225; 307-334-3845; fax: 307-334-3846; 9AM-N, 1-5PM. ***Misdemeanor, Civil Actions under $7,000, Small Claims.*** A Justice Court until 01/03.
Civil Records: Access: Mail, in person. Both court and visitors may perform in person searches. Search fee: $10.00 per name. Required to search: name, years to search; also helpful: address. Civil cases indexed by plaintiff. Civil records on computer back to 2003, also index cards. Mail turnaround time 2 days. Civil PAT goes back to 2003.
Criminal Records: Access: Mail, in person. Both court and visitors may perform in person searches. Search fee: $10.00 per name. Required to search: name, years to search, DOB, SSN, signed release; also helpful: address. Criminal records computerized from 1988, prior archived. Mail turnaround time 2 days. Criminal PAT goes back to 1998.
General Information: No juvenile data released. Fee to fax files is $2 per doc. Court makes copy: $1.00 1st page; $.50 each add'l. Cert fee: $5 per document. Payee: Niobrara Circuit Court. Personal checks and Visa/MC accepted. Mail requests: SASE requested.

Park County

5th Judicial District Court Clerk of District Court, PO Box 1960, Cody, WY 82414; 307-527-8690; criminal fax: 307-527-8687; civil fax: same; 8AM-5PM. ***Felony, Civil over $7,000, Probate.***
www.parkcounty.us/districtcourt.htm
Probate fax is same as main fax number.
Civil Records: Access: Phone, fax, mail, in person. Both court and visitors may perform in person

searches. Search fee: $10.00 per name. Required to search: name, years to search; also helpful: address. Civil cases indexed by defendant, plaintiff; index on computer from 1989, card index back to 1911. Mail turnaround-6 hours. Civil PAT goes back to 1989.
Criminal Records: Access: Phone, fax, mail, in person. Both court and visitors may perform in person searches. Search fee: $10.00 per name. Required to search: name, years to search; also helpful: DOB, SSN. Criminal records computerized from 1989, card index back to 1911. Mail turnaround-6 hours. Criminal PAT goes back to same as civil.
General Information: No juvenile, adoptions or PD released. Will fax documents $2.00 fee. Court makes copy: $1.00 first page, $.50 each add'l. Certification fee: $.50 per page. Payee: Clerk of District Court. No personal checks. Mail requests: SASE preferred.

Cody Circuit Court 1002 Sheridan Ave., Cody, WY 82414; 307-527-8590; fax: 307-527-8596; 8AM-5PM. ***Misdemeanor, Civil Actions under $7,000, Eviction, Small Claims.***
On January 2, 1995 this court changed status from a Justice Court to a Circuit Court. They also have records for the Powell Circuit Court Branch.
Civil Records: Access: Mail, in person. Only the court performs in person searches; visitors may not. Search fee: $10.00 per name. Required to search: name, years to search; also helpful: address. Civil cases indexed by defendant, plaintiff; index on computer since 8/95; limited records available prior to 8/95. Mail turnaround time 5 days.
Criminal Records: Access: Mail, in person. Only the court performs in person searches; visitors may not. Search fee: $10.00 per name. Required to search: name, years to search, DOB, SSN (one or other is required) also helpful: address. Criminal records on computer since 1990; limited records available prior to 1990. Mail turnaround time 5 days.
General Information: No sexual or confidential data released. Will fax out files to local or toll free line. Court makes copy: $1.00 1st page, $.50 each add'l. Certification fee: $.50 per document. Payee: Park County Circuit Court. Business checks and major credit cards accepted. Mail requests: SASE required.

Powell Circuit Court 109 W 14th, Powell, WY 82435; 307-754-8890; fax: 307-754-8896; 8AM-N, 1-5PM. ***Misdemeanor, Small Claims.***
Powell court misdemeanor records are also available at the main Circuit Court in Cody.
Civil Records: Access: Mail, in person. Only the court performs in person searches; visitors may not. Search fee: $10.00 per name. Required to search: name, years to search. Civil cases indexed by defendant, plaintiff; index on computer from 1995; prior records very poor. Mail turnaround-1 week.
Criminal Records: Access: Mail, in person. Only the court performs in person searches; visitors may not. Search fee: $10.00 per name. Required to search: name, years to search, DOB or SSN. Criminal records computerized from 1991; prior records very poor. Mail turnaround time 1 week.
General Information: No sexual, confidential records released. Fee to fax files is $2.00 per document. Court makes copy: $1.00 1st page, $.50 each add'l. No cert fee. Payee: Park County Circuit Court. Personal checks accepted. Visa/MC accepted. Mail requests: SASE required.

Platte County

8th Judicial District Court PO Box 158, Wheatland, WY 82201; 307-322-3857; fax: 307-322-5402; 8AM-5PM. ***Felony, Civil Actions over $7,000, Probate.***
Civil Records: Access: Mail, fax, in person. Both court and visitors may perform in person searches. Search fee: $10.00 per name. Required to search: name, years to search; also helpful: address. Civil cases indexed by defendant, plaintiff. Civil records go back to 1998. Mail turnaround time same day.
Criminal Records: Access: Mail, fax, in person. Both court and visitors may perform in person searches. Search fee: $10.00 per name. Required to search: name, years to search; also helpful: address, DOB, SSN. Criminal records go back to 1997. Mail turnaround time same day.
General Information: No juvenile data released. Will fax out files to local or toll free line. Court makes copy: $1.00 first page, $.50 each add'l. Certification fee: $.50 per page. Payee: Clerk of the Court. Personal checks accepted; credit cards are not. Mail requests: SASE required.

Circuit Court PO Box 306, Wheatland, WY 82201; 307-322-3441; fax: 307-322-1371; 8AM-5PM. ***Misdemeanor, Civil Actions under $7,000, Small Claims.*** This former Justice Court became a Circuit Court as of 1/2003.
Civil Records: Access: Phone, mail, fax, in person. Only the court performs in person searches; visitors may not. Search fee: $10.00 per name. Required to search: name, years to search; also helpful: address. Civil cases indexed by defendant. Civil records on computer since 11/95; on card index since 1976. Note: Fax copy of check, when faxing. Mail turnaround time 2 days.
Criminal Records: Access: Phone, mail, fax, in person. Only the court performs in person searches; visitors may not. Search fee: $10.00 per name includes common name variations. Required to search: name, years to search, signed release, DOB; also helpful: address, SSN. Criminal records computerized from 11/92, card index from 1976. Note: When faxing request, include copy of payment check. Mail turnaround time 2 days.
General Information: No juvenile data released. Fee to fax results included in search fee. Court makes copy: included in search fee. Certification fee: $5.00 per document. Payee: Platte County Circuit Court. Business checks accepted. No credit cards accepted. Fax requests should include a copy of the check. Mail requests: SASE required.

Sheridan County

4th Judicial District Court 224 S. Main, #B-11, Sheridan, WY 82801; 307-674-2960; probate: same; fax: 307-674-2589; 8AM-5PM. ***Felony, Civil Actions over $7,000, Probate.***
www.sheridancounty.com/district/index.html
Civil Records: Access: Phone, mail, fax, in person. Both court and visitors may perform in person searches. Search fee: $10.00. Required to search: name, years to search. Civil cases indexed by defendant, plaintiff. Civil records archived from 1800s; index cards back to 1972. Mail turnaround time 3 days.
Criminal Records: Access: Phone, mail, fax, in person. Both court and visitors may perform in person searches. Search fee: $10.00 per name. Required to search: name, years to search, DOB, SSN. Criminal records archived from late 1800s; index cards back to 1972. Mail turnaround 1 week.
General Information: No sex related, juvenile or adoption cases released except by judges permission. Fee to fax files is $2.00 per doc. Court makes copy: $1.00 first page, $.50 each add'l. Certification fee: $.50 per doc; exemplification- $5.00 per doc. Payee: Clerk of District Court. Personal checks accepted; credit cards are not. Mail requests: SASE required.

Circuit Court 224 S Main, #B-7, Sheridan, WY 82801; 307-674-2940; fax: 307-674-2944; 8AM-5PM. ***Misdemeanor, Civil Actions under $7,000, Eviction, Small Claims.***
Civil Records: Access: Mail, fax, in person. Only the court performs in person searches; visitors may not. Search fee: $10.00 per name. Required to search: name, years to search, DOB, SSN; also helpful: address. Civil cases indexed by defendant, plaintiff; index on cards from 1983; computerized records go back to 1996. Mail turnaround time ASAP.
Criminal Records: Access: Mail, fax, in person. Only the court performs in person searches; visitors may not. Search fee: $10.00 per name. Required to search: name, years to search, DOB, SSN; also helpful: address. Criminal records computerized from 1990, on cards from 1983. Mail turnaround time 1-48 hours.
General Information: Identity of victims not released in sexual assault cases. After fees are paid, will fax documents to local or toll-free number. Court makes copy: $1.00 1st page, $.50 each add'l. Cert fee: $5.00 per doc. Payee: Sheridan Circuit Court. Personal checks accepted. Visa/MC accepted; an $8.00 fee added if over the phone. Mail requests: SASE required.

Sublette County

9th Judicial District Court PO Box 764, Pinedale, WY 82941-0764; 307-367-4376; criminal fax: 307-367-6474; civil fax: same; 8AM-5PM. ***Felony, Civil Actions over $7,000, Probate.***
Probate fax is same as main fax number.
Civil Records: Access: Mail, in person. Both court and visitors may perform in person searches. Search fee: $10.00 per name. Required to search: name; also helpful: years to search, address. Civil cases indexed by defendant, plaintiff; index on card file from 1923. Mail turnaround time same day.
Criminal Records: Access: Mail, in person. Both court and visitors may perform in person searches. Search fee: $10.00 per name. Required to search: name, years to search; also helpful: address, DOB, SSN. Criminal records go back to 1923. Mail turnaround time same day.
General Information: No PD or juvenile records released. Will fax out files $3.00 1st page, $1.00 each add'l. Court makes copy: $1.00 first page, $.50 each add'l. Self serve: same. No cert fee. Payee: Clerk of District Court. Personal checks accepted; credit cards are not. Mail requests: SASE required.

Sublette Circuit Court PO Box 1796, 40 S Fremont Ave, Pinedale, WY 82941; 307-367-2556; fax: 307-367-2658; 8AM-5PM. ***Misdemeanor, Civil Actions under $7,000, Eviction, Small Claims.***
Civil Records: Access: Mail, in person. Only the court performs in person searches; visitors may not. Search fee: $10.00 per name. Required to search: name, years to search; also helpful: address. Civil cases indexed by defendant, plaintiff. Civil records go back 21 years, computerized from 1998. Mail turnaround time 2 business days.
Criminal Records: Access: Mail, in person. Only the court performs in person searches; visitors may not. Search fee: $10.00 per name. Required to search: name, years to search, DOB; also helpful: address, SSN. Criminal records computerized from 1993. Mail turnaround time 2 business days.
General Information: Will fax out documents no fee to toll-free number, otherwise $2.00 per fax. Court makes copy: $1.00 1st page, $.50 each add'l. Cert fee: $5.00 per doc. Payee: Circuit Court of Sublette County. Credit cards accepted; $8.00 surcharge if not in person.

Sweetwater County

3rd Judicial District Court PO Box 430, Green River, WY 82935; 307-872-3820; fax: 307-872-6439; 8AM-5PM. ***Felony, Civil Actions over $7,000, Probate.***
Civil Records: Access: Fax, mail, in person. Both court and visitors may perform in person searches. Search fee: $10.00 per name. Required to search: name, years to search. Civil cases indexed by defendant, plaintiff; index on computer from 1985, on microfiche from 1960, archived from late 1800. Note: Requests must be in writing. Mail turnaround time same day. Civil PAT goes back to 1985. PAT results show middle initial, DOB. Later records may not have all identifiers, or SSNs.
Criminal Records: Access: Fax, mail, in person. Both court and visitors may perform in person searches. Search fee: $10.00 per name. Required to search: name, years to search. Criminal records computerized from 1985, on microfiche from 1960, archived from late 1800. Note: Requests must be in writing. Mail turnaround time same day. Criminal PAT goes back to same as civil. PAT results show middle initial, DOB. Terminal later records may not have these identifiers; most have SSNs.
General Information: No juvenile, paternity, or adoption records released. Will fax out files $2.00 plus $1.00 per page. Court makes copy: $1.00 first page, $.50 each add'l. Cert fee: 1st page free, $.50 each add'l; exemplification fee is $5.00. Payee: Clerk of District Court. Business checks accepted. No credit cards accepted. Mail requests: SASE required.

Green River Circuit Court PO Drawer 1720, 177 N Center St, Green River, WY 82935; criminal phone: 307-872-6460; civil phone: 307-872-6462;

fax: 307-872-6375; 8AM-5PM. ***Misdemeanor, Civil Actions under $7,000, Eviction, Small Claims.***
Civil Records: Access: Mail, in person. Only the court performs in person searches; visitors may not. Search fee: $10.00 per name includes copies. Required to search: name, years to search; helpful-SSN, DOB. Civil cases indexed by defendant, plaintiff; index on computer from 1994, in card file from 1978-1994, archived prior to 1978. Requests must be in writing. Mail turnaround-same day.
Criminal Records: Access: Mail, in person. Only the court performs in person searches; visitors may not. Search fee: $10.00 per name includes copies. Required to search: name, years to search, DOB; also helpful: SSN. Criminal Records computerized since 1990, on card file from 1978 to 1990. Note: Requests must be in writing. Mail turnaround- same day.
General Information: No sealed, sexual assault records released. Fee to fax files is $2.00 per fax. Court makes copy: $1.00 1st page, $.50 each add'l. Cert fee: $5.00 per document. Payee: Sweetwater County Circuit Court. Business checks accepted. In-state checks only. Visa/MC accepted; add $8.00 transaction fee if request made by phone. Mail requests: SASE required.

Sweetwater Circuit Court PO Box 2028, 731 C St, Rock Springs, WY 82902; 307-922-5220; fax: 307-352-6758; 8AM-5PM. ***Misdemeanor, Civil Actions under $7,000, Eviction, Small Claims.***
Search fee covers civil and criminal indexes.
Civil Records: Access: Fax, mail, in person. Only the court performs in person searches; visitors may not. Search fee: $10.00 per name. Required to search: name, years to search; also helpful: address. Civil cases indexed by defendant, plaintiff; index on computer from 1995, archived to 1981. Mail turnaround time 2 days.
Criminal Records: Access: Fax, mail, in person. Only the court performs in person searches; visitors may not. Search fee: $10.00 per name. Required to search: name, years to search; also helpful: address, DOB, SSN. Criminal records computerized from 1989, archived to 1981. Mail turnaround time 2 days.
General Information: No sexual assault, sealed records released. Fee to fax files is $2.00 per doc. Court makes copy: $1.00 1st page, $.50 each add'l. Cert fee: $5.00 per doc. Payee: Sweetwater Circuit Court. Business checks and credit cards accepted. Mail requests: SASE required.

Teton County

9th Judicial District Court PO Box 4460, Jackson, WY 83001; 307-733-2533; fax: 307-734-1562; 8-5PM. ***Felony, Civil over $7,000, Probate.***
Civil Records: Access: Phone, fax, mail, in person. Both court and visitors may perform in person searches. Search fee: $10.00 per name. Required to search: name, years to search; also helpful: address. Civil cases indexed by defendant, plaintiff; index on computer since 1990, card index back to 1920s. Mail turnaround-2 days. Civil PAT goes back to 1995.
Criminal Records: Access: Phone, fax, mail, in person. Both court and visitors may perform in person searches. Search fee: $10.00 per name. Required to search: name, years to search; also helpful: address, DOB, SSN. Criminal records on computer since 1990, card index back to 1920s. Mail turnaround time 2 days. Criminal PAT goes back to same as civil.
General Information: No juvenile or adoption records released. Will fax out files to local or toll free line. Court makes copy: $1.00 first page, $.50 each add'l. Self serve: $.15 per page. Cert fee: $.50 per page. Payee: Clerk of District Court. Personal checks accepted; credit cards are not. SASE required.

Circuit Court PO Box 2906 (180 S King St), Jackson, WY 83001; 307-733-7713; fax: 307-733-8694; 8AM-5PM. ***Misdemeanor, Civil Actions under $7,000, Small Claims under $5,000.***
This was a Justice Court until 01/03.
Civil Records: Access: Mail, in person. Only the court performs in person searches; visitors may not. Search fee: $10.00 per name. Required to search: name, years to search; also helpful-DOB, SSN. Civil cases indexed by defendant, plaintiff. Civil index on docket books back to 1979. Actual files 5 years. Mail turnaround time 3-4 days; may be longer for pre-1992 criminal records.
Criminal Records: Access: Mail, in person. Only the court performs in person searches; visitors may not. Search fee: $10.00 per name. Required to search: name, years to search, DOB, SSN. Criminal records citations on computer from 1991. No citation record older than 5 years. On docket books and files back to 1979. Mail turnaround time 3-4 days; longer for pre-1992 records.
General Information: No juvenile, sexual or PD released. Fee to fax back- $2.00 per doc. Court makes copy: $1.00 1st page, $.50 each add'l. Cert fee: $5.00 per document. Payee: Teton County Circuit Court. Personal checks accepted. Visa/MC accepted. Mail requests: SASE requested.

Uinta County

3rd Judicial District Court PO Drawer 1906, Attn: Clerk of District Court, Evanston, WY 82931; 307-783-0456; fax: 307-783-0400; 8AM-5PM. ***Felony, Civil Actions over $7,000, Probate.***
www.uintacounty.com
Civil Records: Access: Mail, in person. Visitors must perform in person searches themselves. Search fee: $10.00 per name. Required to search: name, years to search; also helpful: address. Civil cases indexed by defendant, plaintiff; index on microfiche from late 1800s. Mail turnaround 1 day.
Criminal Records: Access: Mail, in person. Visitors must perform in person searches themselves. Search fee: $10.00 per name. Required to search: name, years to search, DOB, SSN; also helpful: address. Criminal records on microfiche since 1938. Mail turnaround time 1 day.
General Information: Signed notarized release necessary on confidential cases. Fee to fax files is $2.00 per doc. Court makes copy: $1.00 first page; $.50 each add'l. Certification fee: $.50 per seal. Payee: Clerk of District Court. Personal checks accepted; credit cards are not. Mail requests: SASE required.

Uinta Circuit Court 225 9th St, 2nd Fl, Evanston, WY 82931; 307-789-2471; fax: 307-789-5062; 8AM-5PM. ***Misdemeanor, Civil Actions under $7,000, Eviction, Small Claims.***
Civil Records: Access: Mail, in person. Only the court performs in person searches; visitors may not. Search fee: $10.00 per name. Required to search: name, years to search; also helpful: address, DOB. Civil cases indexed by defendant, plaintiff; index on computer from 1994, prior on card index. Note: All requests must be in writing. Court only searches back 10 years. Mail turnaround time 3 days.
Criminal Records: Access: Mail, in person. Only the court performs in person searches; visitors may not. Search fee: $10.00 per name. Required to search: name, years to search; also helpful: address, DOB, SSN. Criminal records on computer since 1989, prior on index cards. Note: Requests must be in writing. Court only searches back 10 years. Mail turnaround time 3 days.
General Information: No juvenile records released. Fee to fax files is $2.00 per document. Court makes copy: $1.00 1st page, $.50 each add'l. Cert fee: $5.00 per doc. Payee: Uinta County Court. Out of state checks not accepted. Add $8.00 transaction fee if paying by credit card. Mail requests: SASE requested.

Washakie County

5th Judicial District Court PO Box 862, Worland, WY 82401; 307-347-4821; fax: 307-347-4325; 8-5PM. ***Felony, Civil over $7,000, Probate.***
Civil Records: Access: Fax, mail, in person. Both court and visitors may perform in person searches. Search fee: $10.00 per name. Required to search: name; also helpful: years to search, address. Civil cases indexed by defendant, plaintiff; index on computer back to 1985, prior on file index. Mail turnaround time same day when possible. Civil PAT goes back to 2005, some older.
Criminal Records: Access: Phone, fax, mail, in person. Both court and visitors may perform in person searches. Search fee: $10.00 per name. Required to search: name, years to search; also helpful: address, DOB, SSN. Criminal records computerized from 1985, prior on file index. Mail turnaround time same day if possible. Criminal PAT goes back to 2005, some older.
General Information: No juvenile, sexual or PD released. Will fax out files $1.00 per page. Court makes copy: $1.00 first page, $.50 each add'l. Self serve: same. Certification fee: $.50 per document. Payee: Clerk of Court. Personal checks accepted; credit cards are not. Mail requests: SASE required.

Circuit Court PO Box 927, Worland, WY 82401; 307-347-2702; fax: 307-347-8459; 8AM-5PM. ***Misdemeanor, Civil under $7,000, Small Claims.***
This was a Justice Court until 01/03.
Civil Records: Access: Mail, fax. Only the court performs in person searches; visitors may not. Search fee: $10.00 per name. Required to search: name, years to search. Civil cases indexed by defendant. Civil records on computer since 1998, on card index from late 1970, prior archived. Mail turnaround time same day.
Criminal Records: Access: Mail, fax, in person. Only the court performs in person searches; visitors may not. Search fee: $10.00 per name. Required to search: name, years to search, DOB; also helpful: SSN. Criminal records on computer since 1995, on card index from late 1970, prior archived. Mail turnaround time same day.
General Information: No juvenile or PD released; criminal only. Fee to fax files is $2.00 per document. Court makes copy: $1.00 1st page; $.50 each add'l. Certification fee: $5.00 per document. Payee: Circuit Court. Personal checks and credit cards accepted.

Weston County

6th Judicial District Court 1 W Main, Newcastle, WY 82701; 307-746-4778; criminal fax: 307-746-4778; civil fax: same; 8AM-5PM. ***Felony, Civil Actions over $7,000, Probate.***
Probate fax is same as main fax number.
Civil Records: Access: Mail, fax, in person. Both court and visitors may perform in person searches. Search fee: $10.00 per name. Required to search: name; also helpful: years to search, address. Civil cases indexed by defendant, plaintiff; index on card index from 1913; computerized back to 1999. Mail turnaround time same day.
Criminal Records: Access: Phone, fax, mail, in person. Both court and visitors may perform in person searches. Search fee: $10.00 per name. Required to search: name; also helpful: years to search, address, DOB, SSN. Criminal records on card index from 1913; computerized back to 1999. Mail turnaround time same day.
General Information: No juvenile, sexual or PD released. Fee to fax files is $2.00 per doc. Court makes copy: $1.00 1st page, $.50 each add'l. Cert fee: $.50 per certification. Payee: Clerk of District Court. Personal checks accepted; credit cards are not. Mail requests: SASE required.

Circuit Court 6 W Warwick, Newcastle, WY 82701; 307-746-3547; fax: 307-746-3558; 8AM-5PM. ***Misdemeanor, Civil Actions under $7,000, Small Claims up to $5000.***
This was a Justice Court until 01/03.
Civil Records: Access: Mail, in person. Only the court performs in person searches; visitors may not. Search fee: $10.00 per name. Required to search: name, DOB, years to search; also helpful: address. Civil cases indexed by defendant. Civil records in files back to 1970s; on computer back to 1998. Note: For in person civil searches of closed cases, let court known in advance and they will pull the files for you. Mail turnaround time minimum 1 day.
Criminal Records: Access: Mail, in person. Only the court performs in person searches; visitors may not. Search fee: $10 per name. Required to search: name, years to search, DOB; also helpful: address, offense, date of offense, SSN. Criminal records in files back to 1970s; on computer back to 1996. Mail turnaround time minimum 1 day.
General Information: Fee to fax files is $2.00 per document or no charge if search fee paid. Court makes copy: $1.00 first page; $.50 each add'l. Self serve: same. Cert fee: $5.00 per document. Payee: Circuit Court. Business checks accepted. Mail requests: SASE required.

Wyoming Recording Offices

ORGANIZATION: 23 counties, 23 recording offices. The recording officer is the County Clerk. Wyoming is entirely in Mountain Time Zone (MST).

REAL ESTATE RECORDS: Most County Clerks will not perform real estate searches but searches of other records is usually $10.00 per name. Real estate copy fee can be as high as $1.00 per page, as little as $.25. Certification fee ranges from $2.00 to $5.00 per document. The county assessor maintains property tax records.

UCC RECORDS: Since July 1, 2001, all filings have been centralized at the state. Prior, financing statements were usually filed with the County Clerk, and accounts receivable and farm products required dual filing at the state level as well. Almost all recording offices will perform UCC searches. Use search request form UCC-11. UCC search fee is usually $10.00 per debtor name. UCC copy fees vary.

TAX LIEN RECORDS: Federal tax liens on personal property of businesses are filed with the Secretary of State. Other federal and all state tax liens are filed with the County Clerk. Most counties will perform tax lien searches. Tax lien search fee is usually $10.00 per name.

ONLINE ACCESS: A growing number of counties offer online access to various property records and databases of recorded documents. A subscription website provides statewide UCC data access.

Albany County

County Clerk, 525 Grand Ave, Rm 202, Laramie, WY 82070. 307-721-5516, R/E recording phone-307-721-2547, UCC recording phone-307-721-2541; fax-307-721-2544; 9AM-5PM. www.co.albany.wy.us

Index: Separate indices to search include computer back to 10/1997, tract books. Records indexed on computer back to 1997. Only the public may search. Copy fee $.25 per page. Cert fee- $3.00 per copy plus copy fee. Payee- Albany County Clerk. **Other phones:** Treasurer- 307-721-2502; Elections- 307-721-2546; Vital Records- 307-777-7591. **Property tax/Assessing**- 525 Grand Ave, #206, Laramie, WY 82070; 307-721-2511, fax- 307-721-2519. (Appraiser - 307-721-2511) www.co.albany.wy.us/Departments/Assessor/tabid/55/Default.aspx **Online** - Search the county assessor database free at http://assessor.co.albany.wy.us. Click on Search.

Big Horn County

County Clerk, PO Box 31, Basin, WY 82410. 307-568-2357; fax-307-568-9375; hours - 8AM-5PM www.bighorncountywy.gov

Index: Separate indices to search include receiving books, bound books. Records indexed on a public use terminal back to 2/00. Office will perform a UCC search but public must search other records themselves. UCC search per debtor name $10.00. Office will search computerized UCC records only, search includes tax liens. Copy fee $.25 per page unless faxed or mailed and must collect postage fee. Cert fee- $2.00 per doc plus copy fee. Payee- Big Horn County Clerk. **Other phones:** Treasurer- 307-568-2578; Elections- 307-568-2357. **Property tax/Assessing**- PO Box 109, Basin, Wy 82410; 307-568-2547, assessor fax- 307-568-2013. A public access terminal available.

Campbell County

County Clerk, PO Box 3010, Gillette, WY 82717-3010. 307-682-7285; fax-307-687-6455; 8AM-5PM http://ccg.co.campbell.wy.us/elected_officials/county_clerk.html

Index: All in one. Record index not computerized. Office personnel or visitors may perform searches. Search fee $10.00 per name plus copy fee. Office will not search real estate records. Will search UCC records. Copy fee $.50 per page then $.15 each after 1st 10 pages.Payee- Campbell County Clerk. Treasurer- 307-682-7268; Elections- 307-682-1892. **Property tax/Assessing**- 500 S Gillette Ave, Rm 1300, Gillette, 82716; 307-682-7266, assessor fax-307-687-6464. http://ccg.co.campbell.wy.us/assessor/ **Online access**- Search property records free at www.ccgov.net/assessor/online/property/index.rsp

Carbon County

County Clerk, PO Box 6; Courthouse, Rawlins, WY 82301. 307-328-2668, R/E recording phone-307-328-2677, UCC recording phone-307-328-2667; fax-307-328-2669; 8AM-5PM. www.carbonwy.com

Index: All in one. Records indexed on a public use terminal back to 1992. Office will perform a UCC search but public must search other records themselves. Search fee $10.00 per name. Copy fee $.25 per page. Will fax doc no add'l fee. Cert fee- $3.00 per doc plus copy fee. Payee- Carbon County Clerk. Bulk data available for purchase. **Online access to Grantor/Grantee, Real Estate, Deeds, Mortgages records:** Access to records for free go to http://idoc.csa-inc.net/carbonwy/. Must register to access site. **Other phones:** Treasurer- 307-328-2631; Elections- 307-328-2650; Vital Records- 307-328-2670; Land Dept- 307-328-2677. **Property tax/Assessing**- PO Box 520, Rawlins, WY 82301; 307-328-2637, assessor fax- 307-328-2714. A public access terminal available.

Converse County

County Clerk, 107 N 5th St, #114, Douglas, WY 82633. 307-358-2244; fax-307-358-5998; 8AM-5PM. www.conversecounty.org/gov_admin/clerk.htm

Index: All in one. Records indexed on a public use terminal back to 01/01/00. Office will perform a UCC search but public must search other records themselves. Copy fee $.50 per page. Cert fee- $2.00 per doc plus copy fee. Payee- Converse County Clerk. **Other phones:** Treasurer- 307-358-3120; Elections-307-358-2244; Vital Records- 307-777-7591 (Cheyenne). **Property tax/Assessing**- PO Box 57, Douglas, WY 82633; 307-358-2741, assessor fax-307-358-4065. A public access terminal available.

Crook County

County Clerk, PO Box 37, Sundance, WY 82729. 307-283-1323; fax-307-283-3038; 8AM-5PM

Index: All in one. Records indexed on computer back to 1995. Office will perform a UCC search but public must search other records themselves. Copy fee $.50 per page. Cert fee- $3.00 per doc plus copy fee. Payee- Crook County Clerk. **Other phones:** Treasurer- 307-283-1244. **Property tax/Assessing**- PO Box 58, Sundance, WY 82729; 307-283-2054, assessor fax- 307-283-1400. A public access terminal available.

Fremont County

County Clerk, 450 N 2nd St, Rm 220, Lander, WY 82520. 307-332-2405, R/E recording phone-307-332-1127, UCC recording phone-307-332-1125; fax-307-332-1132; 8AM-5PM www.fremontcountywy.org

Index: All in one. Records indexed on a public use terminal back to 9/26/88. Office will perform a UCC (back 5 years or later for mobile home) and Tax lien search but public must search other records themselves. General index search fee $10.00 per name. Office will not search real estate records. Copy fee $.50 per page if off computer, $.15 if off copier. Cert fee- $3.00 per page includes copy fee. Payee-Fremont County Clerk. **Online access to Property Tax records:** Access to property tax for free go to www.fremontcountywy.org/ . **Other phones:** Treasurer- 307-322-1105; Elections- 307-332-1089; Vital Records- 307-332-1127. **Property tax/Assessing**- PO Box 2, 450 N 2nd St, Lander, WY 82520; 307-332-1188, assessor fax- 307-332-1810. A public access terminal available.

Goshen County

County Clerk, PO Box 160, Torrington, WY 82240. 307-532-4051; fax-307-532-7375; 7:30AM-4PM. www.goshencounty.org/Clerk/

Index: All in one. Records indexed on a public use terminal back to 08/20/2003. Office will perform a UCC search but public must search other records themselves. Search fee $10.00 per name. Copy fee $1.00 per page. Cert fee- $5.00 per cert includes copy fee. Payee- Goshen County Clerk. **Other phones:** Treasurer- 307-532-5151; Elections- 307-532-4051; Vital Records- 307-777-7591. **Property tax/Assessing**- 2125 E "A" St, Torrington, WY 82240; 307-532-2349, assessor fax- 307-532-7375. www.goshencounty.org/Assessor/

Hot Springs County

County Clerk, 415 Arapahoe St; Courthouse, Thermopolis, WY 82443-2783. 307-864-3515; fax-307-864-3333; 8AM-5PM. www.hscounty.com

Index: All in one 1996 to present. Docs before 1996 are hand researched in grantee/grantor books. Record index not computerized. Office will perform a UCC search but public must search other records themselves. No fee for search. UCC search per debtor name $10.00. Assessor office will provide parcel owner lookup over phone. Copy fee $.25 per page. Cert fee- $3.00 per doc plus copy fee. Payee- Hot Springs County Clerk. Treasurer- 307-864-3616. **Property tax/Assessing**- 415 Arapahoe St, Thermopolis, WY 82443-2783; 307-864-3414, fax-307-864-5267. A public access terminal available.

Johnson County

County Clerk, 76 N Main St, Buffalo, WY 82834. 307-684-7272; fax-307-684-2708; 8AM-5PM. www.johnsoncountywyoming.org

Index: Separate indices to search include surface ownership index and mineral ownership index. Record index not computerized. Office will perform a UCC search but public must search other records themselves. Search fee $10.00 per name. Copy fee $.50 per page. Cert fee- $3.00 per doc plus copy fee. Payee- Johnson County Clerk. **Other phones:** Treasurer- 307-684-7302; Elections- 307-684-7272. **Property tax/Assessing**- 76 N Main St, Buffalo, WY 82834; 307-684-7392, assessor fax- 307-684-5283.

Laramie County

County Clerk, PO Box 608, Cheyenne, WY 82003. 307-633-4351, R/E recording phone-307-633-4350, UCC recording phone-307-633-4241; fax-307-633-4240; 8AM-5PM. www.laramiecountyclerk.com

Index: Separate indices to search. Records indexed on a public use terminal back to 10/2500, bound books prior. Office personnel or visitors may perform searches. Search fee $10.00 per name. Office will not search real estate or UCC records. Copy fee $.25 per page; from laser printer- $.50 per page; pre-1999 records off microfilm printer $1.00 each. Cert fee- $3.00 per doc. **Other phones:** Treasurer- 307-633-4225; Elections- 307-633-4242; Vitals- 307-777-7591. **Property tax/Assessing**- PO Box 307, 309 W 20th St #1100, Cheyenne, 82003; 307-633-4307, fax-307-633-4474. www.laramiecounty.com/_departments/_county_assessor/index.asp Search property data at http://arcims.laramiecounty.com/ - no name searches.

Lincoln County

County Clerk, 925 Sage Ave; County Clerk, Kemmerer, WY 83101-0670. 307-877-9056, R/E recording phone-307-877-9056 x305, UCC recording phone-307-877-9056 x304; fax-307-877-3101; 8AM-5PM. www.lcwy.org

Index: Separate indices to search include mortgages, grantor/grantee, mixed. Records indexed on computer. No public access terminal available. Office will perform a UCC search but public must search other records themselves. Search fee $10.00 per name. Office will not search real estate records. Copy fee $.50 per page; self serve- $.25 each. Cert fee- $3.00 per doc plus copy fee. $5.00 for certified marriage licenses. Payee- Lincoln County Clerk. **Online access to Real Estate, Deed, Coroner, Plat records:** Access to land records is free at www.lcwy.org/weblink7/Browse.aspx. Click on Land Documents and search by year then book number. Coroner and plats are in separate folders. **Other phones:** Treasurer- 307-877-9056 x345; Elections-307-877-9056 x303. **Property tax/Assessing**- PO Box 569, 925 Sage Ave, 1st Fl, Kemmerer, WY 83101; 307-877-9056 x330, assessor fax- 307-828-9495. A public access terminal available. www.lcwy.org/assessor.asp **Online**- Plat records free at www.lcwy.org/weblink7/Browse.aspx

Natrona County

County Clerk, PO Box 863, Casper, WY 82602. 307-235-9206, UCC phone-307-235-9207; fax-307-235-9367; 8AM-5PM. www.natronacounty-wy.gov

Index: Separate indices to search include computer, book, page. Records indexed on a public use terminal back to 1994. Search fee $10.00 per debtor. Office will not search real estate records (title/lien searches). Office will search UCC records. Copy fee $.25 per page. Cert fee- $3.00 per doc plus copy fee. Payee- Natrona County Clerk. **Other phones:** Treasurer- 307-235-9370; Elections- 307-235-9217; Vital Records- 307-777-7591. **Property tax/Assessing**- 200 N Center, #140, Casper, WY 82601; 307-235-9444, assessor fax- 307-235-9497. A public access terminal available. www.natronacounty-wy.gov **Online access**- Access to GIS/maps free go to www.natronacounty-wy.gov/?load=GIS/GISHome.

Niobrara County

County Clerk, PO Box 420, Lusk, WY 82225. 307-334-2211; fax-307-334-3013; 8AM-4PM.

Index: Separate indices to search include deeds, Mtgs, Misc. Record index not computerized. Office personnel or visitors may perform searches. Search fee $10.00 per name. Office will only search real estate for last document of record. Copy fee $.25 per page. Cert fee- $3.00 per cert plus copy fee. Certified copy of Marriage License $5.00. Payee- Niobrara County Clerk. **Other phones:** Treasurer- 307-334-2432; Elections- 307-334-2211; Vital Records- 307-777-7591. **Property tax/Assessing**- PO Box 120, Lusk, WY 82225; 307-334-3201, assessor fax- 307-334-3101. A public access terminal available.

Park County

County Clerk, 1002 Sheridan Ave; Courthouse, Cody, WY 82414. 307-527-8600; fax-307-527-8626; 8AM-5PM. www.parkcounty.us/countyclerk.htm

Index: All in one. Records including UCCs indexed on a public use terminal back to 1996. Office will perform a limited UCC search but public must search other records themselves. Copy fee $.50 per page; $.25 self serve. Cert fee- $5.00 per doc plus copy fee. Payee- Park County Clerk. **Other phones:** Treasurer-307-527-8630; Elections- 307-527-8620. **Property tax/Assessing**- 1002 Sheridan Ave, 1st Fl, Cody, WY 82414; 307-527-8650, assessor fax- 307-527-8649. A public access terminal available.

Platte County

County Clerk, PO Box 728, Wheatland, WY 82201. 307-322-2315; fax-307-322-2245; 7AM-4PM www.plattecountywyoming.com

Index: All in one. Records indexed on computer back to 2/02. Office will perform a UCC search (from 1/1/90 to present) but public must search other records themselves. Search fee $10.00 per name. Copy fee $.25 per page (customer copies), $.50 per page (employee copies for customer). Cert fee- $3.00 per doc plus copy fee. Payee- Platte County Clerk. **Other phones:** Treasurer- 307-322-2092; Elections- 307-322-2315. **Property tax/Assessing**- PO Box 895, Wheatland, WY 82201; 307-322-2858, assessor fax-307-322-1372. A public access terminal available.

Sheridan County

County Clerk, 224 S Main St, #B-2, Sheridan, WY 82801-9998. 307-674-2500; fax-307-674-2529; 8AM-5PM. www.sheridancounty.com/

Index: All in one. Record index not computerized. Only the public may search. Search fee $10.00 per name. Assessor office will first lookup name for legal description. Copy fee $1.00 per page; self serve- $.25 each. Cert fee- $5.00 per doc plus copy fee. Payee-Sheridan County Clerk. **Other phones:** Treasurer-307-674-6522; Elections- 307-674-2515. **Property tax/Assessing**- 224 S Main St, #B-4, Sheridan, WY 82801; 307-674-2535, assessor fax- 307-674-2529. www.sheridancounty.com/ **Online access**- Access county property tax records free at http://webtax.csa-inc.net/sheridanwy/. Also, a GIS-mapping site provides parcel data free at www.sheridancounty.com/info/gis/overview.php.

Sublette County

County Clerk, PO Box 250, Pinedale, WY 82941-0250. 307-367-4372; fax-307-367-6396; 8AM-5PM

Index: All in one. Records indexed on a public use terminal back to 1993. Office personnel or visitors may perform searches. Search fee $10.00 per name. Copy fee $.25 per page. Cert fee- $3.00 per document plus copy fee. Payee- County Clerk. **Other phones:** Treasurer- 307-367-4373; Elections- 307-367-4372. **Property tax/Assessing**- PO Box 2057, Pinedale, WY 82941; 307-367-4374, assessor fax- 307-367-3342. www.sublettewyo.com/assessor/index.html **Online**- Access property data and GIS-mapping free at www.sublettewyo.com/gis/index.html.

Sweetwater County

County Clerk, PO Box 730, Green River, WY 82935. 307-872-3732, R/E recording phone-307-872-3751, UCC phone-307-872-6406 or 6407; fax-307-872-6337; 8AM-5PM. www.co.sweet.wy.us/clerk/

Separate indices to search include grantor/grantee, legal description. Records indexed on a public use terminal back to 1985. Office will perform a UCC search but public must search other records themselves. Copy fee $.25 per copy. Cert fee- $3.00 per doc. Treasurer- 307-872-3720; Elections- 307-872-3733; Vitals- 307-872-3747 (marriage only). **Property tax/Assessing**- 80 W Flaming Gorge Way, #122, Green River, 82935; 307-872-3700, fax- 307-872-6393. (Appraiser/Auditor- 307-872-3700).

Teton County

County Clerk, PO Box 1727, Jackson, WY 83001. 307-733-4430, UCC phone-307-733-4433; fax-307-739-8681; 8-5PM http://www2.tetonwyo.org/clerk/

Index: All in one. Records indexed on a public use terminal back to 4/91. Office will perform a UCC search but public must search other records themselves. Search fee $10.00 per name. Copy fee $1.00 per page. Cert fee- $5.00 for 1st 3 pages, $1.00 each add'l, includes copy fee. Payee- Teton County Clerk. **Online Real Estate, Deed, Lien records:** Access to the Clerk's database of scanned images is free at http://www2.tetonwyo.org/clerk/query/. Search for complete documents back to 7/1996; partial documents back to 4/1991. **Other phones:** Treasurer-307-733-4770; Elections- 307-733-7733; Vital Records- 307-777-7591. **Property tax/Assessing**- PO Box 583, Jackson, 83001; 307-733-4960, assessor fax- 307-739-8634. www.tetonwyo.org/assessor/ **Online access**- Download assessor property data lists free at www.tetonwyo.org/assessor/nav/100084.asp.

Uinta County

County Clerk, PO Box 810, Evanston, WY 82931-0810. 307-783-0308 x304, R/E recording phone-307-783-0304, UCC recording phone-307-783-0308; fax-307-783-0376; 8AM-5PM www.uintacounty.com

Index: All in one. Records indexed on a public use terminal back to 1985. Only the public may search. Copy fee $.25 per page. Cert fee- $3.00 per doc plus copy fee. Payee- Uinta County Clerk. **Other phones:** Treasurer- 307-783-0332; Elections- 307-783-0423; Vitals- 307-783-0304. **Property tax/ Assessing**- 225 9th St, Evanston, 82931; 307-783-0336, assessor fax-307-783-0510. A public access terminal available.

Washakie County

County Clerk, Box 260, Worland, WY 82401-0260. 307-347-3131; fax-307-347-9366; 8AM-5PM www.washakiecounty.net

Index: Separate indices to search include deeds, mortgages, misc. Records indexed on computer back to 1985. Office personnel or visitors may perform searches. Search fee $10.00 per name. Office will not search real estate records. Will search UCC records. Copy fee $.25; real estate microfilm card $1.00 per page. Cert fee- $3.00 per doc plus copy fee. Payee-Washakie County Clerk. **Other phones:** Treasurer-307-347-2031; Elections- 307-347-3131; Vital Records- 307-347-3131. **Property tax/Assessing**- 1001 Big Horn Ave, Worland, 82401; 307-347-2831, fax- 307-347-9366. A public terminal available.

Weston County

County Clerk, 1 W Main, Newcastle, WY 82701. 307-746-4744; fax-307-746-9505; 8AM-5PM

Index: Separate indices to search include deeds, mortgages, misc. Record index not computerized. Office will perform a UCC search but public must search other records themselves. UCC search per debtor name $10.00. Copy fee $.50 per page. Will fax back $2.00 per doc. Cert fee- $3.00 per doc. Treasurer- 307-746-2852. **Property tax/Assessing**- 1 W Main St, Newcastle, WY 82701; 307-746-4633, assessor fax- 307-746-9505. hours- 8AM-4:30PM A public access terminal available.

Wyoming County Locator

You will usually be able to find the city name in the City/County Cross Reference below. In that case, it is a simple matter to determine the county from the cross reference. However, only the official US Postal Service city names are included in this index. There are an additional 40,000 place names that people use in their addresses. Therefore, we have also included a ZIP/City Cross Reference immediately following the City/County Cross Reference.

If you know the ZIP Code but the city name does not appear in the City/County Cross Reference index, look up the ZIP Code in the ZIP/City Cross Reference, find the city name, then look up the city name in the City/County Cross Reference. For example, you want to know the county for an address of Menands, NY 12204. There is no "Menands" in the City/County Cross Reference. The ZIP/City Cross Reference shows that ZIP Codes 12201-12288 are for the city of Albany. Looking back in the City/County Cross Reference, Albany is in Albany County.

Wyoming City/County Cross Reference

AFTON Lincoln
ALADDIN Crook
ALBIN Laramie
ALCOVA Natrona
ALPINE Lincoln
ALTA Teton
ALVA Crook
ARAPAHOE Fremont
ARMINTO Natrona
ARVADA (82831) Campbell(37), Sheridan(32), Johnson(29)
AUBURN Lincoln
BAGGS Carbon
BAIROIL Sweetwater
BANNER (82832) Sheridan(80), Johnson(19)
BASIN Big Horn
BEDFORD Lincoln
BEULAH Crook
BIG HORN Sheridan
BIG PINEY Sublette
BILL Converse
BONDURANT Sublette
BOSLER Albany
BOULDER Sublette
BUFFALO Johnson
BUFORD (82052) Albany(68), Laramie(31)
BURLINGTON (82411) Big Horn(97), Park(2)
BURNS Laramie
BYRON Big Horn
CARLILE Crook
CARPENTER Laramie
CASPER Carbon
CASPER Natrona
CENTENNIAL Albany
CHEYENNE Laramie
CHUGWATER (82210) Platte(80), Goshen(20)
CLEARMONT Sheridan
CODY Park
COKEVILLE Lincoln
CORA Sublette
COWLEY Big Horn
CROWHEART Fremont
DANIEL Sublette
DAYTON Sheridan
DEAVER (82421) Big Horn(85), Park(14)
DEVILS TOWER Crook
DIAMONDVILLE Lincoln
DIXON Carbon
DOUGLAS Converse
DUBOIS Fremont
EDGERTON Natrona
ELK MOUNTAIN Carbon
EMBLEM Big Horn
ENCAMPMENT Carbon
ETNA Lincoln
EVANSTON Uinta
EVANSVILLE (82636) Natrona(97), Converse(2)
FARSON Sweetwater
FE WARREN AFB Laramie
FORT BRIDGER Uinta
FORT LARAMIE Goshen
FORT WASHAKIE Fremont
FOUR CORNERS Weston
FRANNIE Park
FREEDOM Lincoln
FRONTIER Lincoln
GARRETT Albany
GILLETTE Campbell
GLENDO (82213) Platte(98), Converse(1)
GLENROCK Converse
GRANGER Sweetwater
GRANITE CANON Laramie
GREEN RIVER Sweetwater
GREYBULL Big Horn
GROVER Lincoln
GUERNSEY Platte
HAMILTON DOME Hot Springs
HANNA Carbon
HARTVILLE Platte
HAWK SPRINGS Goshen
HILAND (82638) Natrona(87), Fremont(12)
HILLSDALE Laramie
HORSE CREEK Laramie
HUDSON Fremont
HULETT Crook
HUNTLEY Goshen
HYATTVILLE Big Horn
IRON MOUNTAIN Laramie
JACKSON Teton
JAY EM Goshen
JEFFREY CITY Fremont
JELM Albany
KAYCEE (82639) Johnson(92), Natrona(7)
KEELINE Niobrara
KELLY Teton
KEMMERER Lincoln
KINNEAR Fremont
KIRBY Hot Springs
LA BARGE Lincoln
LAGRANGE (82221) Goshen(97), Laramie(2)
LANCE CREEK Niobrara
LANDER Fremont
LARAMIE Albany
LEITER Sheridan
LINCH Johnson
LINGLE Goshen
LITTLE AMERICA Sweetwater
LONETREE Uinta
LONTETREE Uinta
LOST SPRINGS (82224) Converse(85), Niobrara(14)
LOVELL Big Horn
LUSK Niobrara
LYMAN Uinta
LYSITE Fremont
MANDERSON (82432) Park(75), Big Horn(24)
MANVILLE Niobrara
MC FADDEN Carbon
MC KINNON Sweetwater
MEDICINE BOW (82329) Carbon(77), Albany(22)
MEETEETSE Park
MERIDEN Laramie
MIDWEST Natrona
MILLS Natrona
MOORCROFT (82721) Crook(60), Campbell(39)
MOOSE Teton
MORAN Teton
MOUNTAIN VIEW Uinta
NATRONA Natrona
NEWCASTLE Weston
NODE Niobrara
OPAL Lincoln
OSAGE Weston
OSHOTO (82724) Crook(77), Campbell(22)
OTTO Big Horn
PARKMAN Sheridan
PAVILLION Fremont
PINE BLUFFS Laramie
PINEDALE Sublette
POINT OF ROCKS Sweetwater
POWDER RIVER Natrona
POWELL Park
RALSTON Park
RANCHESTER Sheridan
RAWLINS Carbon
RECLUSE Campbell
RELIANCE Sweetwater
ROBERTSON Uinta
ROCK RIVER (82083) Carbon(55), Albany(44)
ROCK SPRINGS Sweetwater
ROZET Campbell
SADDLESTRING Johnson
SAINT STEPHENS Fremont
SARATOGA Carbon
SAVERY Carbon
SHAWNEE Converse
SHELL Big Horn
SHERIDAN Sheridan
SHOSHONI Fremont
SINCLAIR Carbon
SMOOT Lincoln
STORY (82842) Sheridan(91), Johnson(8)
SUNDANCE (82729) Crook(95), Weston(4)
SUPERIOR Sweetwater
TEN SLEEP Washakie
TETON VILLAGE Teton
THAYNE Lincoln
THERMOPOLIS Hot Springs
TIE SIDING Albany
TORRINGTON Goshen
UPTON (82730) Weston(85), Crook(14)
VAN TASSELL (82242) Niobrara(59), Goshen(40)
VETERAN Goshen
WALCOTT Carbon
WAMSUTTER Sweetwater
WAPITI Park
WESTON (82731) Campbell(96), Crook(4)
WHEATLAND (82201) Platte(98), Albany(1)
WILSON Teton
WOLF Sheridan
WORLAND Washakie
WRIGHT Campbell
WYARNO Sheridan
YELLOWSTONE NATIONAL PARK Park
YODER Goshen

Wyoming ZIP/City Cross Reference

82001-82003 CHEYENNE
82005-82005 FE WARREN AFB
82006-82010 CHEYENNE
82050-82050 ALBIN
82051-82051 BOSLER
82052-82052 BUFORD
82053-82053 BURNS
82054-82054 CARPENTER
82055-82055 CENTENNIAL
82057-82057 LARAMIE
82058-82058 GARRETT
82059-82059 GRANITE CANON
82060-82060 HILLSDALE
82061-82061 HORSE CREEK
82062-82062 IRON MOUNTAIN
82063-82063 JELM
82070-82073 LARAMIE
82080-82080 MC FADDEN
82081-82081 MERIDEN
82082-82082 PINE BLUFFS
82083-82083 ROCK RIVER
82084-82084 TIE SIDING
82190-82190 YELLOWSTONE NATIONAL PARK
82201-82201 WHEATLAND
82210-82210 CHUGWATER
82212-82212 FORT LARAMIE
82213-82213 GLENDO
82214-82214 GUERNSEY
82215-82215 HARTVILLE
82217-82217 HAWK SPRINGS
82218-82218 HUNTLEY
82219-82219 JAY EM
82220-82220 KEELINE
82221-82221 LAGRANGE
82222-82222 LANCE CREEK
82223-82223 LINGLE
82224-82224 LOST SPRINGS
82225-82225 LUSK
82227-82227 MANVILLE
82228-82228 NODE
82229-82229 SHAWNEE
82240-82240 TORRINGTON
82242-82242 VAN TASSELL
82243-82243 VETERAN
82244-82244 YODER
82301-82301 RAWLINS
82310-82310 JEFFREY CITY
82321-82321 BAGGS
82322-82322 BAIROIL
82323-82323 DIXON
82324-82324 ELK MOUNTAIN
82325-82325 ENCAMPMENT
82327-82327 HANNA
82329-82329 MEDICINE BOW
82331-82331 SARATOGA
82332-82332 SAVERY
82334-82334 SINCLAIR
82335-82335 WALCOTT
82336-82336 WAMSUTTER
82401-82401 WORLAND
82410-82410 BASIN
82411-82411 BURLINGTON
82412-82412 BYRON
82414-82414 CODY
82420-82420 COWLEY
82421-82421 DEAVER
82422-82422 EMBLEM
82423-82423 FRANNIE
82426-82426 GREYBULL
82427-82427 HAMILTON DOME
82428-82428 HYATTVILLE
82430-82430 KIRBY
82431-82431 LOVELL
82432-82432 MANDERSON
82433-82433 MEETEETSE
82434-82434 OTTO
82435-82435 POWELL
82440-82440 RALSTON
82441-82441 SHELL
82442-82442 TEN SLEEP
82443-82443 THERMOPOLIS
82450-82450 WAPITI
82501-82501 RIVERTON
82510-82510 ARAPAHOE
82512-82512 CROWHEART
82513-82513 DUBOIS
82514-82514 FORT WASHAKIE
82515-82515 HUDSON
82516-82516 KINNEAR
82520-82520 LANDER
82523-82523 PAVILLION
82524-82524 SAINT STEPHENS
82601-82615 CASPER
82620-82620 ALCOVA
82630-82630 ARMINTO
82631-82631 BILL
82633-82633 DOUGLAS
82635-82635 EDGERTON
82636-82636 EVANSVILLE
82637-82637 GLENROCK
82638-82638 HILAND
82639-82639 KAYCEE
82640-82640 LINCH
82642-82642 LYSITE
82643-82643 MIDWEST
82644-82644 MILLS
82646-82646 NATRONA
82648-82648 POWDER RIVER
82649-82649 SHOSHONI
82701-82701 NEWCASTLE
82710-82710 ALADDIN
82711-82711 ALVA
82712-82712 BEULAH
82713-82713 CARLILE
82714-82714 DEVILS TOWER
82715-82715 FOUR CORNERS
82716-82718 GILLETTE
82720-82720 HULETT
82721-82721 MOORCROFT
82723-82723 OSAGE
82724-82724 OSHOTO
82725-82725 RECLUSE
82727-82727 ROZET
82729-82729 SUNDANCE
82730-82730 UPTON
82731-82731 WESTON
82732-82732 WRIGHT
82801-82801 SHERIDAN
82831-82831 ARVADA
82832-82832 BANNER
82833-82833 BIG HORN
82834-82834 BUFFALO
82835-82835 CLEARMONT
82836-82836 DAYTON
82837-82837 LEITER
82838-82838 PARKMAN
82839-82839 RANCHESTER
82840-82840 SADDLESTRING
82842-82842 STORY
82844-82844 WOLF
82845-82845 WYARNO
82901-82902 ROCK SPRINGS
82922-82922 BONDURANT
82923-82923 BOULDER
82925-82925 CORA
82926-82926 ROCK SPRINGS
82929-82929 LITTLE AMERICA
82930-82931 EVANSTON
82932-82932 FARSON
82933-82933 FORT BRIDGER
82934-82934 GRANGER
82935-82935 GREEN RIVER
82936-82936 LONETREE
82936-82936 LONTETREE
82937-82937 LYMAN
82938-82938 MC KINNON
82939-82939 MOUNTAIN VIEW
82941-82941 PINEDALE
82942-82942 POINT OF ROCKS
82943-82943 RELIANCE
82944-82944 ROBERTSON
82945-82945 SUPERIOR
83001-83002 JACKSON
83011-83011 KELLY
83012-83012 MOOSE
83013-83013 MORAN
83014-83014 WILSON
83025-83025 TETON VILLAGE
83101-83101 KEMMERER
83110-83110 AFTON
83111-83111 AUBURN
83112-83112 BEDFORD
83113-83113 BIG PINEY
83114-83114 COKEVILLE
83115-83115 DANIEL
83116-83116 DIAMONDVILLE
83118-83118 ETNA
83119-83119 FAIRVIEW
83120-83120 FREEDOM
83121-83121 FRONTIER
83122-83122 GROVER
83123-83123 LA BARGE
83124-83124 OPAL
83126-83126 SMOOT
83127-83127 THAYNE
83128-83128 ALPINE
83414-83414 ALTA

U.S. Territories

Guam Records

Guam Driving Records

Superior Court
Traffic Violations Bureau
120 W. O'Brien
Hagatna, Guam 96910

(671) 475-3274
(671) 472-2856 fax
www.Justice.Gov.Gu/superior.html (click on Traffic Court)

Records are public. To request by mail, email or fax, submit name, DOB and SSN. Include a self-addressed, stamped envelope. Email to traffic@mail.justice.gov.gu. In person requests are permitted. The fee is $1.50 for clearance and then $1.00 per citation on the record going back 10 years. Make checks payable to Superior Court of Guam. They will not fax back documents.

Guam Vehicle Records

Department of Revenue & Taxation
Vehicle Records
PO Box 23607, GMF
Barrigada, Guam 96921

671-475-1816

Vehicle records are not considered public records. You must have a court order and then submit request on their form.

Guam Recording Office

Guam Department of Revenue & Taxation
Clerk, PO Box 23607
GMF, GU 96921

671-635-1835/1836, R/E recording phone-671-635-1843/6; fax-671-633-2643; 8AM-5PM. https://www.guamtax.com/index.jsp

Index: All in one. Record index not computerized. Only office personnel may search. Search fee $5.00 per name. Office will search UCC records, but not tax liens. Copy fee- $1.00 per page; an attachment page to a file is $.50 per page. Payee- Treasurer of Guam. **Other phones:** Treasurer- 671-475-1189; Elections-671-477-9791; Vital Records- 671-735-7263. **Property tax/Assessing-** PO Box 23607, GMF, GU 96921; 671-475-1840, assessor fax- 671-633-2643.

US District and Bankruptcy Court District of Guam

Guam Division Clerk of Court, 520 W Soledad Ave, 4th Fl, US Courthouse, Rm 460, Hagatna, Guam 96910 (In person: same as mail address, Route 1, Marine Corps Dr), 671-473-9100; Fax- 671-473-9152. Hours-8AM-3PM. www.gud.uscourts.gov

Counties/Note: Guam. Address Bankruptcy requests to the Guam Bankruptcy Division which is also located here.

Searches/Indexing: Helpful to include SSN and/or DOB in search request. Results include last 4 SSN digits only. Will fax back documents for fee; fee determined by court based on number of pages and where faxed to. New cases are in the index within 1 day after filing date. Pre-2000 index is manual index cards. All records including closed case archives are located here. Computerized Court records go back to 2000, a few older cases back to 1991. Court can email back search requests when requested. All closed case records maintained here.

Search Access: If prepaid, they will conduct search based on phone request. **Mail:** Search usually completed- same day. Expect a longer return time if mail. Include SASE for return. **Fax:** Fax search requests accepted with prepayment. **In person:** 4 public terminals available; 2 Dist Ct, 2 Bankruptcy.

Payment: Pay by money order, cashier's or personal checks. No debtor personal/business checks accepted. Attorney credit cards accepted. Payee: Clerk, Guam District Court.

E-Services: PACER is live at https://pacer.login.uscourts.gov/cgi-bin/login.pl?court_id=gudc. PACER records go back 2-3 years only. New records online after 1 day. ECF at https://ecf.gub.uscourts.gov. **Opinions:** www.gud.uscourts.gov/opinions.htm. Also, view Decisions and Orders by clicking that tab at the main website. Court calendars at www.gud.uscourts.gov/calendar/calnotsealed30.htm.

Guam City/County Cross Reference

AGANA HEIGHTS Guam
AGAT Guam
ASAN Guam
BARRIGADA Guam
CHALAN PAGO Guam
DEDEDO Guam
HAGATNA Guam
INARAJAN Guam
MANGILAO Guam
MERIZO Guam
MONGMONG Guam
PITI Guam
SANTA RITA Guam
SINAJANA Guam
TALOFOFO Guam
TAMUNING Guam
UMATAC Guam
YIGO Guam
YONA Guam

Guam ZIP/City Cross Reference

ZIP	City
96910-96910	AGANA
96910-96910	HAGATNA
96911-96911	TAMUNING
96912-96912	DEDEDO
96913-96913	BARRIGADA
96914-96914	YONA
96915-96915	SANTA RITA
96916-96916	MERIZO
96917-96917	INARAJAN
96918-96918	UMATAC
96919-96919	AGANA HEIGHTS
96921-96921	BARRIGADA
96922-96922	ASAN
96923-96923	MANGILAO
96924-96924	CHALAN PAGO
96925-96925	PITI
96926-96926	SINAJANA
96927-96927	MONGMONG
96928-96928	AGAT
96929-96929	YIGO
96930-96930	TALOFOFO
96931-96931	TAMUNING
96932-96932	AGANA
96932-96932	HAGATNA

Puerto Rico Records

Puerto Rico Driving Records

Department of Transportation
Services Division
PO Box 41243 - Minillas Station
San Juan, PR 00940
787-722-2929

www.gobierno.pr/GPRPortal/Inicio

The request must include full name, SSN and reason for request. Include copy of valid ID of the requester. ID A signed release from subject is suggested. The fee is $1.50 per record made payable to the Secretary of the Treasury.

US District Court District of Puerto Rico

Puerto Rico Division Court Clerk, US Courthouse, Frederico Degetau Federal Bldg, 150 Carlos Chardon St, Hato Rey, Puerto Rico 00918, 787-772-3000; records- 787-772-3025; Fax- 787-766-5693. Hours-8:30AM-4:45PM. www.prd.uscourts.gov

Counties: All counties.

Searches/Indexing: Include both last names in search request. Results do not include SSN or DOB, but judgments may have SSN. Will not fax back documents. New cases are in the index 1-2 days after filing date. Computer index goes back to 1994. Case files sent to archives 1 year after closed.

Search Access: Mail: SASE required. **Fax:** Fax search requests accepted. **In person:** 1 public terminal available until 4PM.

Payment: Pay by money order or cashier's check. Payee: Clerk, US District Court.

E-Services: ECF at https://ecf.prd.uscourts.gov. **Online Note:** Free Court Calendars/Reports available at www.prd.uscourts.gov/reports/Reports.aspx.

Puerto Rico Corporations

www.estado.gobierno.pr/Corponline/corponline.aspx

Rama Judicial

http://www.ramajudicial.pr/

US Bankruptcy Court District of Puerto Rico

Puerto Rico Division Court Clerk, US Post Office & Courthouse Building, 300 Recinto Sur #109, San Juan, Puerto Rico 00901, 787-977-6000; Fax- 787-977-6008. Hours-8AM-4PM. www.prb.uscourts.gov

Counties: All counties.

Searches/Indexing: Include SSN number in search request. Results include SSN. New cases are in the index 1 day after filing date. Cases shipped to Missouri Records Ctr 3 months after closed.

Search Access: Phone: call VCIS at 787-977-6130. **Mail:** SASE required. **In person:** Records on public access terminal go back 1 term.

Payment: Pay by money order or cashier's check. No personal checks. Payee: Clerk, US Bankruptcy Court.

E-Services: PACER online at https://pacer.login.uscourts.gov/cgi-bin/login.pl?court_id=prbk. PACER records go back to 1990. ECF at https://ecf.prb.uscourts.gov. **Opinions Online:** www.prb.uscourts.gov/Isys/isyswebext.dll?op=get&uri=/isysmenu.html. **Online Note:** Access judges' calendars by name at www.prb.uscourts.gov/Judge.htm. an Unclaimed Funds list is available via the court's main website.

Puerto Rico ZIP/City Cross Reference

ADJUNTAS Adjuntas
AGUADA Aguada
AGUADILLA Aguadilla
AGUAS BUENAS Aguas Buenas
AGUIRRE Guayama
AIBONITO Aibonito
ANASCO Anasco
ANGELES Utuado
ARECIBO Arecibo
ARROYO Arroyo
BAJADERO Arecibo
BARCELONETA Barceloneta
BARRANQUITAS Barranquitas
BAYAMON Bayamon
BOQUERON Cabo Rojo
CABO ROJO Cabo Rojo
CAGUAS Caguas
CAMUY Camuy
CANOVANAS Canovanas
CAROLINA (00979) San Juan(59), Carolina(40)
CAROLINA Carolina
CAROLINA San Juan
CASTANER Lares
CATANO Catano
CAYEY Cayey
CEIBA Ceiba
CIALES Ciales
CIDRA Cidra
COAMO Coamo
COMERIO Comerio
COROZAL Corozal
COTO LAUREL Ponce
CULEBRA Culebra
DORADO Dorado
ENSENADA Guanica
FAJARDO Fajardo
FLORIDA Florida
FORT BUCHANAN Bayamon
GARROCHALES Arecibo
GUANICA Guanica
GUAYAMA Guayama
GUAYAMA Guayanilla
GUAYANILLA Guayanilla
GUAYNABO Catano
GUAYNABO Guaynabo
GUAYNABO San Juan
GURABO Gurabo
HATILLO Hatillo
HORMIGUEROS Hormigueros
HUMACAO Humacao
ISABELA Isabela
JAYUYA Jayuya
JUANA DIAZ Juana Diaz
JUNCOS Juncos
LA PLATA Aibonito
LAJAS Lajas
LARES Lares
LAS MARIAS (00670) Camuy(55), Anasco(44)
LAS PIEDRAS Las Piedras
LOIZA Loiza
LUQUILLO Luquillo
MANATI Manati
MARICAO Maricao
MAUNABO Maunabo
MAYAGUEZ Mayaguez
MERCEDITA Ponce
MOCA Moca
MOROVIS Morovis
NAGUABO Naguabo
NARANJITO Naranjito
OROCOVIS Orocovis
PALMER Rio Grande
PATILLAS Patillas
PENUELAS Penuelas
PONCE Ponce
PUERTO REAL Fajardo
PUNTA SANTIAGO Humacao
QUEBRADILLAS Quebradillas
RINCON Rincon
RIO BLANCO Naguabo
RIO GRANDE (00745) Humacao(84), Rio Grande(12), Canovanas(3)
ROOSEVELT ROADS Ceiba
ROSARIO San German
SABANA GRANDE Sabana Grande
SABANA HOYOS Arecibo
SABANA SECA Toa Baja
SAINT JUST Trujillo Alto
SAINT JUST CONTRACT Trujillo Alto
SALINAS Salinas
SAN ANTONIO Aguadilla
SAN GERMAN San German
SAN JUAN San Juan
SAN LORENZO San Lorenzo
SAN SEBASTIAN San Sebastian
SANTA ISABEL Santa Isabel
ST JUST Trujillo Alto
TOA ALTA Toa Alta
TOA BAJA Toa Baja
TRUJILLO ALTO (00976) Trujillo Alto(98), San Juan(1)
TRUJILLO ALTO Trujillo Alto
UTUADO Utuado
VEGA ALTA Vega Alta
VEGA BAJA (00694) Vega Alta(59), Vega Baja(40)
VEGA BAJA Vega Baja
VIEQUES Vieques
VILLALBA Villalba
YABUCOA Yabucoa
YAUCO Yauco

Puerto Rico ZIP/City Cross Reference

00601-00601 ADJUNTAS
00602-00602 AGUADA
00603-00605 AGUADILLA
00606-00606 MARICAO
00610-00610 ANASCO
00611-00611 ANGELES
00612-00614 ARECIBO
00616-00616 BAJADERO
00617-00617 BARCELONETA
00622-00622 BOQUERON
00623-00623 CABO ROJO
00624-00624 PENUELAS
00627-00627 CAMUY
00631-00631 CASTANER
00636-00636 ROSARIO
00637-00637 SABANA GRANDE
00638-00638 CIALES
00641-00641 UTUADO
00646-00646 DORADO
00647-00647 ENSENADA
00650-00650 FLORIDA
00652-00652 GARROCHALES
00653-00653 GUANICA
00656-00656 GUAYANILLA
00659-00659 HATILLO
00660-00660 HORMIGUEROS
00662-00662 ISABELA
00664-00664 JAYUYA
00667-00667 LAJAS
00669-00669 LARES
00670-00670 LAS MARIAS
00674-00674 MANATI
00676-00676 MOCA
00677-00677 RINCON
00678-00678 QUEBRADILLAS
00680-00682 MAYAGUEZ
00683-00683 SAN GERMAN
00685-00685 SAN SEBASTIAN
00687-00687 MOROVIS
00688-00688 SABANA HOYOS
00690-00690 SAN ANTONIO
00692-00692 VEGA ALTA
00693-00694 VEGA BAJA
00698-00698 YAUCO
00703-00703 AGUAS BUENAS
00704-00704 AGUIRRE
00705-00705 AIBONITO
00707-00707 MAUNABO
00714-00714 ARROYO
00715-00715 MERCEDITA
00716-00717 PONCE
00718-00718 NAGUABO
00719-00719 NARANJITO
00720-00720 OROCOVIS
00721-00721 PALMER
00723-00723 PATILLAS
00725-00727 CAGUAS
00728-00728 PONCE
00729-00729 CANOVANAS
00730-00734 PONCE
00735-00735 CEIBA
00736-00737 CAYEY
00738-00738 FAJARDO
00739-00739 CIDRA
00740-00740 PUERTO REAL
00741-00741 PUNTA SANTIAGO
00742-00742 ROOSEVELT ROADS
00744-00744 RIO BLANCO
00745-00745 RIO GRANDE
00751-00751 SALINAS
00754-00754 SAN LORENZO
00757-00757 SANTA ISABEL
00765-00765 VIEQUES
00766-00766 VILLALBA
00767-00767 YABUCOA
00769-00769 COAMO
00771-00771 LAS PIEDRAS
00772-00772 LOIZA
00773-00773 LUQUILLO
00775-00775 CULEBRA
00777-00777 JUNCOS
00778-00778 GURABO
00780-00780 COTO LAUREL
00782-00782 COMERIO
00783-00783 COROZAL
00784-00785 GUAYAMA
00786-00786 LA PLATA
00791-00792 HUMACAO
00794-00794 BARRANQUITAS
00795-00795 JUANA DIAZ
00901-00933 SAN JUAN
00934-00934 FORT BUCHANAN
00935-00940 SAN JUAN
00949-00951 TOA BAJA
00952-00952 SABANA SECA
00953-00954 TOA ALTA
00955-00955 SAN JUAN
00956-00961 BAYAMON
00962-00963 CATANO
00964-00964 SAN JUAN
00965-00971 GUAYNABO
00975-00975 SAN JUAN
00976-00977 TRUJILLO ALTO
00978-00978 SAINT JUST
00978-00978 ST JUST
00978-00978 SAINT JUST CONTRACT
00979-00999 CAROLINA

Virgin Islands Records

Virgin Islands Driving Records

Criminal Justice Complex
Records Bureau
St. Thomas, Virgin Islands 00802

340-774-2211 x5523 340-715-5523 or 5594; in St. Croix 340-712-6044 or 6059 or 6024; in St. John 340-693-8880. www.vipd.gov/vi/

A Police Traffic Record Check search request form is at www.vipd.gov.vi/forms/Traffic_Record_Check.pdf. The fee is $5.00 in certified funds made payable to the Government of the Virgin Islands. The form requires the signature of the subject. Suggest to submit photocopy of the driver's license, a self-addressed, stamped envelope. Turnaround time is 1-2 days.

Virgin Islands Vehicle Records

Vehicle Records Virgin Island Police Department
C/O Motor Vehicle Bureau, Sub Base
,St. Thomas, Virgin Islands 00801, 340-774-5765.

They will verify information over the phone, including lien information. To do a record request, submit a license plate number of VIN, $20.00 in certified funds, and a self-addressed, stamped envelope. Make check payable to the Government of the Virgin Islands.

Virgin Islands Recording Offices

St. Croix

Recorder of Deeds, 1131 King St, #101; Lt Governor Office, Christiansted, VI 00820-4970. Recording, R/E & UCC phone-340-773-6449; fax-340-773-0330; 8AM-5PM. www.virginislands.us.landata.com/
Has offices in St. John (340-776-6737), and Fredericksted (340-772-3115). Separate indices to search include books, computer. Records indexed on a public use terminal back to 2001. Office personnel or visitors may perform searches. Office will name search index no fee, time permitting. Copy fee $1.00 per page. Cert fee- $10.00 for 1st page; $1.00 each add'l pg. Payee- VI Government. **Online access to Real Estate, Deed, Judgment, Lien, Marriage records:** Access to recorded records index is free at www.virginislands.us.landata.com, registration is required. A subscription is required to view full data, $750 per year or $75.00 per month. Subscribers purchase images for $1.00 each; non-subscribers may purchase images for $2.00 each. **Other phones:** Treasurer- 340-773-1105; Elections- 340-773-1021; Vital Records- 340-773-1311 or 773-9376.
Property tax/Assessing- 1131 King St, #101, Christiansted, VI 00820; 340-773-6459, assessor fax- 340-773-4052. (Appraiser/Auditor- 340-773-6459) **Online access**- Property valuation data to be available at http://dev.public.vi-usvi.cavucorp.com/leadin.htm.

St. Thomas

Recorder of Deeds, Kongens Gade, #18, St. Thomas, VI 00802. Recording, R/E & UCC phone-340-774-9906, UCC recording phone-340-776-8515; fax-340-774-2234; 8:30AM-4PM (EST) http://ltg.gov.vi/
Records indexed on a public use terminal back to 99; earlier records being added. Office is limited to preparation of $20.00 title and encumbrance statements only; other searches done by visitors. Office will not search real estate or UCC records. Copy fee $1.00 per page. Cert fee- $10.00 for 1st page plus $1.00 each add'l. Payee- Government of VI. **Online access to Real Estate, Deed, Judgment, Lien, Marriage records:** Same Online access as described above.
Property tax/Assessing- 5049 Kongens Gade, #18, St. Thomas, VI 00802; 340-776-8505, assessor fax- 340-774-1270. hours- 8AM-5PM http://ltg.gov.vi/office-of-the-tax-assessor-cadastral.html **Online access**- Property valuation data to be available at http://dev.public.vi-usvi.cavucorp.com/leadin.htm

V. I. City/County Cross Reference

CHRISTIANSTED St. Croix
CHRISTIANSTED (00820) St. Croix(78), St. Thomas(21)
FREDERIKSTED St. Croix
KINGSHILL St. Croix
SAINT JOHN St. John
SAINT THOMAS St. Thomas

V. I. ZIP/City Cross Reference

00801-00805 SAINT THOMAS
00820-00824 CHRISTIANSTED
00830-00831 SAINT JOHN
00840-00841 FREDERIKSTED
00850-00851 KINGSHILL

Canada

Here is to present a quick useful guide to Canadian resources related to public record and information searching. This section is organized by topic.

Business Related Information

Industry Canada – (Covers Many Record Types)

One of the most useful web pages belongs to is Industry Canada (www.ic.gc.ca/epic/site/ic1.nsf/en/home). For example, this web resource leads to records of **bankruptcies, business names, copyrights, corporations, mergers, patents, trademarks, and unclaimed funds**. For a complete index listing, go to www.ic.gc.ca/epic/site/ic1.nsf/en/h_00013e.html.

Public Security Findings

The **Canadian version of EDGAR,** the System for Electronic Document Analysis and Retrieval (SEDAR) is a filing system developed for the Canadian Securities Administrators. Visit. www.sedar.com; email questions to sedarwebmaster@cds.ca.

Criminal Record Information

Royal Canadian Mounted Police (RCMP)

The Information and Identification Services of the Royal Canadian Mounted Police (RCMP)is a point of contact to the central repository of criminal record data in Canada, similar to the FBI in the U.S. The RCMP operates an automated central police database known as the Canadian Police Information Centre (CPIC). Also Municipal and provincial police services in Canada have their own systems, as do the court systems (see below.)

Criminal record searches are performed by the Civil Fingerprint Screening Services (CFSS) of the RCMP. Search requirement include a signed release and set of fingerprints. The fee is $25.00 (Canadian equivalent funds). The RCMP does not provide name checks. You must contact the local police service or provincial court system for name searches.

The address for the RCMP is National Police Services Building, Loading Dock #1, Information and Identification Services, Civil Fingerprint Screening Services, 1200 Vanier Parkway, Ottawa, Ontario K1A 0R2. Telephone is 613-998-6362.

General website: www.rcmp.gc.ca/crimrec/crimrec_e.htm

Criminal Record Checks Information website: www.rcmp-grc.gc.ca/cr-cj/fing-empr-eng.htm

Correctional Service of Canada

The Correctional Service of Canada (CSC) is the government agency responsible for administering sentences with a prison term of two years or more imposed by the court system. CSC is responsible for managing institutions of various security levels and supervising offenders under conditional release in the community. Records are not public. See www.csc-scc.gc.ca

National Parole Board of Canada

For questions relating to the status of pardon applications, call 800-874-2652. Request must include subject's signature. Mailing address is Pardon Section, Clemency and Investigations Division, National Parole Board, 410 Laurier Avenue West, Ottawa, Ontario K1A 0R1. www.npb-cnlc.gc.ca

Court System and Court Records

Canadian court records are public information. The court system in Canada is similar to the U.S. system in that there is a federal court system with a supreme court and there are provincial systems with upper and lower courts.

An informative resource about the Canadian Court System, including how organized, is the Department of Justice. Go to www.justice.gc.ca/eng/index.html.

Below are links to the judicial systems of each province. The links will lead to extensive information about each province's system including those with online accessible databases.

Alberta – www.albertacourts.ab.ca

British Columbia – www.courts.gov.bc.ca

Manitoba – www.gov.mb.ca/justice

New Brunswick – www.gnb.ca/cour/index-e.asp

Newfoundland – www.justice.gov.nl.ca/just

Northwest Territories – www.nwtcourts.ca

Nova Scotia – www.gov.ns.ca/just

Ontario – www.attorneygeneral.jus.gov.on.ca/english

Prince Edward Island – www.gov.pe.ca/courts

Quebec – www.justice.gouv.qc.ca/english/accueil.asp

Saskatchewan – www.sasklawcourts.ca

Yukon – www.justice.gov.yk.ca/prog/cs/courts.html

Bankruptcy Records

Visit the Industry Canada site at www.ic.gc.ca/eic/site/ic1.nsf/eng/h_00000.html.

Supreme Court Decisions

The Canada Supreme Court Reports (decisions) are published in English and French. For information about the Supreme Court Library, contact library@scc-csc.gc.ca or phone 613- 996-8120 or visit www.scc-csc.gc.ca. The Court directs online searches of decisions to a web page managed by the University of Montreal. http://scc.lexum.umontreal.ca/en/index.html

Tax Court Judgments

http://decision.tcc-cci.gc.ca/en/index.html

Court Martial Appeals Court

www.cmac-cacm.ca/index_e.html

Government & Legislation

Canadian Government on the Internet

This government site http://canada.gc.ca is a **master site** with links to federal, provincial, and municipal sites.

Parliament

www.parl.gc.ca/common/index.asp?Language=E

Consolidated Acts, Regulations, and Legislation

http://laws.justice.gc.ca/en/

Legislation

Canadian Laws and regulations at http://laws.justice.gc.ca/en/index.html

Transportation and Motor Vehicle

Aircraft

www.tc.gc.ca/aviation/activepages/ccarcs/index.htm

Motor Vehicle Records

In general, a signed release is required to obtain a driving record or vehicle-related record, especially if the record contains personal information. Many provinces license or authorize third parties to provide record access. For example, these authorized agencies are called Registries in Alberta. In Ontario, sanitized driving and vehicle records may be obtained from kiosks and mall kiosks. Addresses and web links to each province are provided below.

With the exception of lien records, vehicle related record searches in Canada are not available to the public. If you need a record, we suggestion to call one of the Province phone numbers below for details on access and restrictions. Be prepared to submit a signed release.

Note: All the fees shown below are in Canadian dollars.

Alberta

Motor Vehicle Division, Alberta Registries, 10365 97th Street, 3rd Fl. Edmonton, Alberta T5J 3W7, 780-427-7013, fax: 780-423-0285. www.servicealberta.gov.ab.ca/Drivers_MotorVehicles.cfm

In Alberta, release of personal driving and motor vehicle information is governed by specific privacy legislation, the Access to Motor Vehicle Information Regulation (AMVIR). All forms found at www.servicealberta.gov.ab.ca/1229.cfm.

Records must be accessed from authorized "Registries" located throughout the Province. The fee for an Abstract of Driving Record is $11.00 plus the Registry service fee, which will vary from location to location. Processing time is same day. The name, DOB, license number, reason for request, and a signed release from subject are required for a search. Records may be searched by mail or in person. Many Registries offer payment by credit card. Visit the web page for a list of Registries as well as a request form.. Online access to records is not available online at this time.

British Columbia

ICBC, Driver Testing & Vehicle Information, 151 West Esplanade, Rm 154, North Vancouver, B.C., Canada V7M 3H9, 250-978-8300, fax: 250-978-8001. www.icbc.com/licensing/

The cost of a record search is $5.00, but there is no fee if the request is made by the subject of the search. Processing time is 2 to 3 days. The name, DOB, license number, and a signed release from the subject are required for a search. The record reports five years of activity. Records may be ordered by phone (only by the subject), in-person or mail. The agency will fax back the abstract. Credit cards are accepted. Information is not available online at this time.

Manitoba

Manitoba Public Insurance, Driver and Vehicle Licensing, Driver Records and Suspensions, Box 6300, Winnipeg, MB R3C 4A4, 204-985-0980, driver fax: 204-945-5357, vehicle fax-204-945-7366. www.mpi.mb.ca/english/english.html

Records may be ordered from this office or any Driver and Vehicle Licensing Service Outlet in the province. The cost of a record search is $10.00. There is also commercial, five-year driver abstract used by commercial drivers for employment purposes is also $10.00. Accident reports are at $10.00 plus GST. Prepayment is required, checks or money orders to be made out to Minister of Finance. The processing time is 1 to 2 days. The name, DOB, license # and a signed release from subject are required for a search. Records may be searched by mail, fax or in person and they will return by fax. MasterCard and Visa accepted.

New Brunswick

Department of Public Safety, Licensing & Records Branch, Driver (or Vehicle) Records, PO Box 6000, Fredericton, New Brunswick E3B 5H1, 506-453-2410, fax-506-453-7455. www.gnb.ca/0276/vehicle/index-e.asp

The cost of a driving record search is $10.00 and accident reports are $8.00 each. The processing time is same day. The name, DOB, and license number are required for a search. Records may be requested by mail, in person or online and can be returned by fax. Abstracts may be obtained in person at SNB (Service New Brunswick) offices located at various locations throughout the Province or by telephone using a credit card at SNB Teleservice at 506-684-7901. An online, interactive system is available from a designated vendor. Fee is $10.00 per record. For more information call 888-624-2265 or fax 902-422-1675.

Newfoundland

Motor Vehicle Registration, Driver Records Division, PO Box 8710, St Johns, Newfoundland A1B 4J5, 709-729-0331, driver fax: 709-729-7616, vehicle fax: 709 729-3399. www.gs.gov.nl.ca/gs/mr

The cost of a driving record search is $10.00. The record may be obtained from any Motor Registry Office in the province. The processing time is less than a week. The name and either DOB or license number, and the signature of the requester are required for a search. Records may be requested by mail or in-person. Visa, MasterCard and debit cards are accepted. Records returned by fax incur an additional $5.00 fee. Email questions to driverrecords@gov.nl.ca.

Northwest Territories

Department of Transportation, Motor Vehicle Division, Yellow Knife Registries, Box 1320, Yellow Knife, NW Territories X1A 2L9, 867-873-7487 or 873-7406, fax: 867-669-9094. www.dot.gov.nt.ca/_live/pages/wpPages/home.aspx

The cost of a driving record is $15.25, certification is included. Visa, MasterCard, AMEX and debit cards are accepted. The name, DOB, license number, and a signed release from subject are required for a search. Records may be searched by mail, fax or in person. Processing time is 1 to 2 days. Information is not available online at this time. Email inquires to rls.inquiries@gov.nt.ca.

Nova Scotia

Services of Nova Scotia, Driver Records Section, PO Box 1652, Halifax, Nova Scotia B3J 2Z3, 902-424-5851, fax: 902-424-0720. www.gov.ns.ca/snsmr/rmv

The fee for a driver abstract is $16.30; a certified letter is $11.51. Make checks payable to Registry of Motor Vehicles. Visa, MasterCard and debit cards are accepted. Records may be searched by mail, in person, or fax (credit card required). The processing time is 1 to 2 weeks by mail, immediate if in person, and same day for fax. There are 18 service centers that process walk-in requests. The name, DOB, and a signed release from subject are required for a search, the license number is helpful. A request form is found online. Accidents reports are available from this office for $10.00 per report. An online, interactive system is available from a designated vendor, fees involved. For more information about an account call 888-624-2265 or fax 902-422-1675.

Ontario

Ministry of Transportation, Licensing Administration Office, Data Access Unit, 2680 Keele, Building A, (Vehicle Records at Special Inquiry Unit, Rm 178), Downsview, Ontario M3M 3E6, 416-235-2999, fax: 416-235-4414.

www.mto.gov.on.ca/english/dandv/

Driving records may be obtained from kiosks and mall kiosks and also online from Service Ontario. The driver's address is not released. The fee for a driving record or accident report is $12.00, add $6.00 for certification. A Driver Confirmation Letter is $6.00 and a Driver License Validation is $2.00. Report on commercial driving only is $5.00. Credit cards and debit cards are accepted with fax or online service. The online records, called Snapshots, have three years of history, see the web for details. An abstract record if ordered by mail, fax, or in-person can go back five years. Fax requests are preferred instead of mail requests. The name, DOB and license number are required for a search. License verification service is available for $2.00 at https://www.dlcheck.rus.mto.gov.on.ca/Scripts/OrderForm.asp or at 900-565-6555 for $2.50 fee per check charged to your phone bill. For add'l general driver license information, email LAO@mto.gov.on.ca or call Service Ontario at 416-235-2999.

Prince Edward Island

Highway Safety Division, Driving Records Section, 33 Riverside Dr, PO Box 2000, Charlottetown, Prince Edward Island C1A 7N8, 902-368-5210, fax: 902-368-5236. Registrar of Vehicles in same building at 902-368-5200, 902-368-6847, fax: 902-569-7560. www.gov.pe.ca/tpwpei/index.php3?number=78414

The cost of a driver abstract is $20.00; an accident report is $10.00. Records may be searched by mail or in-person. There are five service centers for walk-in requests (Alberton, Charlottetown, O'Leary, Summerside, and Wellington). Processing time is 1 to 2 days for mail requests. Insurance company requests can be returned electronically. The name, DOB, license number, and a signed release from subject are required for a search. Credit cards are accepted for payment. A request form is available on the web.

Quebec

Société de l'assurance automobile du Québec (SAAQ), Driving Records Division, 333 Jean LeSage, PO Box 19600, Quebec, Quebec G1K 8J6, 418-643-7620, 800-361-7620 (address vehicle inquiries to Service De la Diffusion et De la Liaison Avec les Corps Policiers. www.saaq.gouv.qc.ca/en/index.php

Records may be ordered over the phone or at Service Centers throughout the province. The cost of a record search is $9.00. Records may be searched by mail or in person or one may order their own record online from the web page. Processing time is 2 to 3 days. The full name, DOB, license number, requester's phone number, and a signed release from subject are required for a search.

Saskatchewan

Driver Abstracts, Saskatchewan Government Insurance, 2260 11th Ave, Regina, Saskatchewan S4P 2N7, 306-775-6198, 306-751-1249, fax: 306-775-6681. www.sgi.sk.ca

The cost of a driver abstract with a plate record is $10.00, MasterCard and Visa are accepted. Records go back 5 years with an option back to 1995. Records may be searched by mail, fax, or in person. Processing time is 1 week by mail and 1 hour if credit card signature available. The name, DOB, license number, and a signed release from subject are required for a search. Information is not available online at this time.

Yukon

Department of Motor Vehicles, Yukon Territory, PO Box 2703, Whitehorse, Yukon Y1A 2C6, 867-667-5315, fax: 867-393-6220. www.community.gov.yk.ca/motorvehicles/newmvindex.html

The cost of a driving record or an accident report is $10.00, MasterCard and Visa are accepted. Records requests can be processed at this office or at one of the eleven Territorial Offices (shown on web). Processing time is normally same day. The name, DOB, license number, and a signed release from subject are required for a search. Records may be searched by mail or fax. Information is not available online at this time. Direct questions to motor.vehicles@gov.yk.ca.

Ship Registrations

http://daryl.chin.gc.ca:8000/basisbwdocs/sid/title1e.html

Transportation Liens

Check out the Personal Property Registry System found at https://pprs.acol.ca/lc/index.do. This private site is a good resource countrywide for checking liens on vehicles. You should NOT use Lien Check to search for personal property other than a motor vehicle, trailer, mobile home, airplane, boat or outboard motor. Registration required and fees are $5.00 to $10.00 per search.

Search Engines and Phone Books

AltaVista Canada

This is the Canadian version of AltaVista, with access to millions of Canadian-specific web pages. http://ca.altavista.com

Google Canada

This is the Canadian version of Google with most of the same features as the U.S. version. www.google.ca/

InfoSpace

In the North America section, click on Canada to find Yellow Pages and White Pages on the site below.

www.infospace.com/home/white-pages/world

Other Electronic Phone Books

www.canada411.ca/
www.yellowpages.ca/index.html

Appendix 1 - Fundamentals of Public Record Searching

The strict **definition** of **public records** is—

> *"Those records maintained by government agencies that are open without restriction to public inspection, either by statute or by tradition."*

And it's all on the Internet, right? No, not at all.

The Accessibility Paradox

The purpose of this portion of *The Sourcebook* is to set the foundation on how to perform public record searching.

As you read about how to search for many types of government-held records, you will find that not all records are completely "public." For example, in some states or jurisdictions a specific category of records (birth records) is severely restricted and therefore, those records are not "public." But that very same category of records may be 100% open in other states. Also, records may be fully accessible, but only with certain personal information removed. Examples include motor vehicle records and criminal records. And, records may have restrictions to access imposed by state statutes.

Knowing when records are public and/or not public is an important tool for any public record researcher. Just as important is an understanding of the relationship between the records, the record holders, and the users.

Therefore, some of the records examined in this book have restrictions regarding access.

The text in the box printed below is significant. We are not trying to fill up space. As your public record searching takes you from county-to-county or from state-to-state, this is the one important truth to keep in mind.

> "Just because records are maintained in a certain way in your state or county, do not assume that any other county or state does things the same way."

Key Elements to Evaluating Public Record Sources

There are two places you can find public records—

1. At a government agency
2. Within the database of a private company

There are key components that determine the thoroughness and attributes of the record source, regardless if it's government or privately-held. Consider these questions—

- How are records indexed?
- How are the record images stored?
- How far back are the records kept?
- What are the access procedures?
- Are there restrictions involved?

Finding the answers to these questions about data fundamentals is important when deciding if the source will match your needs and the best access method to use.

Most of the text in this section covers record searching at government agencies. Appendix 4 describes important items to consider when working with public record search vendors.

Record Indexing

A record index serves as a pointer system to the location of file documents and is frequently used at recording offices, courts, and state agencies. A record index is often computerized, but indices can be on card files, in books, on microfiche, etc. Also, a record index can be organized in a variety of ways – by name, by year, by case or file number, or by name and year. Depending on the type of public record, an alpha index could be sorted by plaintiff and/or defendant, by grantor and/or grantee, by address, etc. Perhaps checking a microfiche reader or card file for a record on an individual you find nothing. That does not necessarily mean a record does not exist. The case or document files could be listed in another media index for a different time period, or perhaps you are searching using the wrong criteria such as a maiden name or an alias.

If you are searching an unfamiliar location, then the makeup of the index is one of first items you need to check. For example, if you are searching an index of court records, you are searching dockets. A docket can be a list of cases on a court's calendar, or a log containing the schedule and all the actions involved within a court case.

An important fact to take note of is that the primary search that government agencies provide is often merely a search of the index. When someone tells you "I can find xxx county court records online," this person is most likely talking about an index summary of records and not about the records themselves.

Record Storage

Government agencies store and maintain records in a variety of ways including include paper, microfiche, microfilm, electronic files, disks, CDs, magnetic tapes, maps, photographs, film and sound recordings. Today, most federal and state agencies are computerized. Often entities filing records at computerized agencies do so electronically or paperless. This can also be true for county or local level agencies including parishes, cities, town, villages, etc. But there are a number of local level agencies that still use microfiche, microfilm, index cards, and paper as the primary method to store images, files, and indexes. Everything is NOT online, and everything is NOT available electronically.

To computerize older records, government agencies must convert these document files to electronic images, etc. The paper documents are then most likely destroyed or placed in archival storage, per the law or per the rule of the administration. Depending on the type of record, the State Archives often warehouses these older documents and is a good place to search if you are looking for old records. Sometimes it is the only place.

Of course, agencies that have converted to computerized storage will not necessarily place complete file records on their online accessible systems; they are more apt to include only an index or summary data from the files.

The storage procedures used by private companies and vendors is dependent upon the media format when the records were purchased or gathered from the official agency. Vendors usually develop their databases by buying records in bulk from specific government agencies or other vendors, or by sending personnel to a government office to make copies or to key in information on a laptop computer.

Data Retention and Currency

This brings us to several important questions about record searching: *How far back are records kept? How current are they?* and *When are records purged?* The need for due diligence may require that a record searcher research a certain, specified time period such as seven years or longer. Obviously it is beneficial to know the record retention period. Any answer except a clear, concise date is not going to be adequate.

Knowing how "fresh" the information is – when it was last updated – is also an important factor. An index of records may have been updated last week at a courthouse or at a web page, but this data may reflect a 60-day delay or backlog. This update gap is extremely common with the state criminal record agencies like the State Police or Department of Public Safety who receive and hold criminal case information from the courts. Per a U.S. Department of Justice Study[1], 27 states report they have a significant backlog (from 160 man-hours to 30,400 man-hours needed) for entering court data into the criminal history database. Similarly, many web vendors offering public record content do not necessarily indicate how up-to-date the records are they hold or sell.

Ideally, when you search for or purchase items of information, from either a government agency or from a record vendor, you should be provided access to a statement of accuracy without having to ask.

The Difference Between a Record Search and a Document Request

There is a significant difference between searching an index to determine if a public record exists versus obtaining or viewing file copy documents. Many times the latter cannot be accomplished without first doing the former.

Asking government personnel to perform a search of public records usually incurs a fee. Asking government personnel to provide you a *specific* file or case usually does not incur a search fee if the document is readily available and you have provided the exact file or case number.

Name Searching

Let's say you wish to determine if an individual has a criminal record, or determine if an individual has collateralized certain assets such as real estate or ownership of equipment used in a business. The best way to perform this research is to start by performing a "name search" – also known as an "alpha search" – of the index. Due to privacy concerns, the index may or may not contain certain identifiers such as the date of birth (DOB), or even a middle initial. Obviously, having this additional information – often referred to as "PI," which stands for "personal identifiers" – can be quite helpful. When a government agency places a record index on the web, the likelihood of identifiers being included diminishes when the site is free to view versus a pay or subscription site.

---

[1] U.S. Department of Justice, Bureau of Justice Statistic's Survey of State Criminal History Information Systems, 2003 (released in 2006) found at www.ojp.usdoj.gov/bjs/abstract/sschis03.htm.

When there is no index accessible online or the online index contains no or limited identifiers, then the public must to do its own onsite search or ask a government employee to do the name search. There are some agencies, such as many of the county-based Supreme Courts in New York, which refuse to allow the public to view an index in person AND refuse to perform a name search. These NY courts instead direct those doing a name search of criminal records to the New York State Office of Court Administration (OCA) for a statewide criminal history search for a $55.00 search fee.

Requesting a Specific Document

Once a researcher learns if a record exists and uncovers the "document number" or exact location of a record, it becomes much easier to view or obtain a copy. If you are requesting a specific document, the government personnel are much more apt to help you then compared to asking them to do a name search. The same holds true on the web. Using a government web page to search for a specific document is often easier when you have the document number or an identifier like the docket number or filing number. This is especially true when searching real estate recordings. Again, keep in mind that images of all the pages in the file may not be available online.

The Importance of Identifiers

As mentioned, every record source will require certain identifiers to accurately process a search request. For example, an agency may ask for the full name, Social Security Number (SSN), DOB, sex, hair color, and the last known address of the person to be checked. These identifiers serve two different though related purposes.

First, the identifiers of the subject must be used to analyze a public record for the purpose of determining if the record is about that subject. Perhaps the records are indexed by the last name and also by either the DOB or part of a SSN. If so, the person performing the search needs a DOB or SSN in order to search accurately.

Second, the identifiers act as an important safeguard for both the requesting party and the subject of the search. There is always the chance that the "Harold Johnson" on whom a given repository has a record is not the same "Harold Johnson" on whom a check has been requested. The possibility of a misidentification can be decreased substantially if other identifiers can match the individual to the record. Providing an identifier as simple as the middle initial increases the likelihood of identifying the correct Harold Johnson. Finding records on the correct Harold Johnson protects other Harold Johnsons from any confusion, especially if there is negative information.

But there will be times when personal identifiers are not readily available. This is especially true when searching the index and even the document files for state and county civil records, and when searching for federal court records. Per record searching expert Lynn Peterson: "This [lack of identifiers] is why it is so difficult to determine relevance when researching civil litigation. This is seldom the situation with criminal court records. With criminal case files you will almost always find identifiers that enable you to determine relevance."

Matching Logic

Matching logic means using the identifiers given with a search request in order to determine if the record found does, in fact, belong to the subject. For example, before reporting results to clients, pre-employment screening companies are responsible for determining the level of matching logic that will meet Fair Credit Reporting Act (FCRA) rules.

According to the search standards of the Public Record Retriever Network (PRRN)[2] there are three levels of matching logic—

- **Partial Name Match Logic**—Match Logic that requires only a partial match of the subject's name to a result.

[2] See www.prrn.us

- **Name Match Only**—Results of a search that uses the subject's full name as a match.
- **Strict Match Logic**—Match logic that requires a minimum of two and, when possible, three subject identifiers before reporting.

Of course, using three subject identifiers is best. Even then you can have problems. Consider when a Jr. and Sr. are living at the same house; there are many possibilities of identifiers getting crossed.

Strictest matching logic available should be applied if negative or derogatory information is found.

When government personnel are doing the look-up in the index, it is good practice to provide them with personal identification information beyond the minimum whenever possible. Every available piece of information could aid their search. For example, maiden name, alias, or any other previous name used should be included when possible. Although no repository can be expected to give a 100% positive identification (unless it is a match of fingerprints), the more pointers matched, the smaller the chance of a mistake.

What If the Index Doesn't Have Matching Identifiers?

You will often find that if an index does not contain a personal identifier, one may be found within the record file or in associated paperwork.

Let's say you are searching for a record on Joe B. Cool with a DOB of 01/01/1985. And let's say the index gives you an index showing a possible record match of J Cool with no DOB, and another possible match with a Joseph Cool with a partial DOB match. The next step is to examine the paper or images found in the files. The content in the file may contain the matching personal identifiers you are looking for. If you are a professional and the highest form of accuracy is vital, then you may have times where a common name requires you to view dozens of files.

If there are still no indications of identifiers within the files, then the researcher most look for other clues or trails to find the identification answer. This may entail calling an attorney or another party involved in the record transaction.

The Redaction Trend

Redaction is a recent trend. The term refers to simply removing or hiding certain elements within a record itself or the record index. Removing identifiers from public records is a solution that some government agencies and legislatures now use to deal with identity theft problems. In some instances the anticipated cost of redacting records is forcing government agencies to block public access to the records. Yet there are many government officials who understand the importance and benefits attached to the openness of public records. Often the redaction will not apply to the DOB on the records. This stops the agencies from being overwhelmed with legitimate record request that would otherwise require personnel to pull same name records from storage for viewing.

The balance of privacy interests versus public jeopardy goes beyond the purposes of this book. However, the key point here is to be aware of change and know that redactions can and will alter public record searching procedures. A Google search will lead to many of the frequent news stories reporting on privacy debates and efforts to remove personal identifiers from public records.

The Access Methods for Obtaining Public Records

There are numerous methods available to access public records from government agencies.

Visit in Person

Direct access is easy if you live close by. Many courthouses and recorders offices provide "free use" public access terminals but they will charge a fee to make copies of file documents. This is also true for certain state-held records such as corporate fillings or Uniform Commercial Code (UCC) records generally found at the Secretary of State office. The index or the documents in a record file can be viewed for free, but a fee is charged if copies are requested.

Not every agency will permit walk-in traffic. Agencies such as the State Police, Workers Compensation Bureau, and even certain Motor Vehicle Departments and Occupational Licensing Boards will not honor in person requests.

There is one key distinction to make about in person searches at courthouses and recording offices: who is permitted to do a name search of the index? At some agencies, only government personnel can do the searching. At others, the government personnel will not help and only the public can do a search of the index. Still other agencies offer a choice. If the only way to do a record search is to do it yourself, and if you do not live close by, you will need to hire a record retriever to visit the agency and perform the search for you.

Unfortunately, the on-site method can sometimes be influenced by the kind of day the clerical staff at an agency is having. If someone woke up on the wrong side of the bed or if personnel are extremely busy, then the search may be rushed and not as thorough as you desire or not serviced until later. Ongoing search requesters always find ways to make friends with the staff, but sometimes it is necessary to remind staff about a particular law in their jurisdiction that dictates what is public record and open.

Mail

While most agencies will process a request for a specific document or file if allowed by law, there are a number of agencies that do not honor a name search request by mail. Do not assume all do.

Some agencies do not charge to "find" a record but charge a fee to make a document copy or print a computer screen image. If the number of pages to be copied is unknown, call first and ask.

When mailing the request, an insider tip is to use a large, priority mail envelope. A 9x12 envelope stands out and demands to be dealt with.

Another worthy piece of advice is to always include a SASE (the acronym for a self-addressed stamped envelope) or a prepaid express delivery return envelope. Providing either one insures the agency is not going to reject your request because you did not include postage, and you may go to the top of the processing pile!

Fax

Generally, fax service – for requesting or returning documents, or both – is only available to pre-approved requesters, especially if fees are involved. If you prepay a request and ask for a return of results by fax, some agencies will oblige only if the call is local or to a toll-free telephone number. While most courts will not offer to fax results of search requests, if the case file or docket number is given many will fax specific documents either to a toll-free number or if the return fax fee is pre-paid.

Some agencies (state vital record agencies, for example) consider fax requesting to be an expedited service that triggers additional fees.

Telephone

A limited number of agencies that permit telephone requests merely answer "Yes" or "No" to questions such as "Does John Doe have a civil court case in his name?" Several state motor vehicle agencies offer some rather sophisticated read-back dial-up systems as a service to ongoing accounts.

Professional searchers know that name search requests and results by telephone are not adequate in a due diligence situation. The reasons include that there is no assurance the court personnel keyed in the correct spelling and there is nothing in writing to back up their assertion that no records were found.

If the agency provides telephone service to pre-approved accounts or a fee-based "900" phone service, then the searcher may feel the agency personnel would do a better job of searching. But calling a public record agency for a name search should be performed only as a "quick and dirty" search investigation.

Online

Online access to public records comes in several varieties and packages, the primary sources being government agencies and vendors. Online access can be an instant path to viewable or downloadable record data or the means to transmit record information along an information chain. The web is the primary conduit, but there are a few dial systems (non-Internet) that still exist for access to some subscription services. There are many useful web pages maintained by the government and by private enterprise that provide valuable information about public records.

Since online access is such an important topic, we will discuss this later in this section and in more detail.

Bulk or Database Purchases

Many agencies offer the ability to purchase all or parts of their database for statistical or commercial purposes. Purchasing records for statistical purposes is often easy. Purchasing for commercial purposes is not so easy. "Commercial purposes" means the data will be used for marketing products or by database vendors building their proprietary database products for record sales to interested parties. Whether or not a government agency will sell the records is determined by restrictions imposed by law or administrative rule OR if it has the personnel, means, and time to fulfill a request.

Typically, records are available to those who qualify in the following media types: FTP, cartridges, paper printouts, labels, disks or CD files, microfiche, and microfilm.

Monitoring and Notification Programs

Some government agencies offer the ability to notify clients if there is activity on records. This may be on a submitted-list basis (such as monitoring commercial drivers or insured drivers) or an alert of activity related to a certain record type. An example is the LENS Program with the New York DMV, which registers drivers of participating employers or organizations.

Hire Someone Else

As mentioned previously, one method to access public records is through a vendor. Vendors must comply with state and federal laws governing the release of records. Thus, if the government agency will not release a full record to the public, neither will the vendor (at least the reputable ones do not). See the *Working With Public Record Vendors* portion of the Appendix.

Using the Freedom of Information Act (FOIA)

The Federal Freedom of Information Act (FOIA) is only applicable to records held by federal agencies. The Federal FOIA has no bearing on state, county, or local government agencies because these agencies are subject to only that state's individual acts. A great resource for FOIA and also for finding state's open record laws is *The Open Government Guide* at www.rcfp.org/ogg.

Summary

Regardless of which access method is used, keep in mind these points—

- There is a distinction between performing a name search versus asking for a specific document copy.
- Many government agencies will not do a name search for the public, but will retrieve a specific document file.

About Record Fees and Charges

Public records are records of incidents or transactions. It costs money (time, salaries, supplies, etc.) to record, store, and track these events. Although public records may be free of charge to view, they are not necessarily free of charge when obtaining file copies. Certainly, fees are to be expected if government personnel must perform searches, though there are exceptions.

Common charges found at the government level include copy fees (to make copies of documents), search fees (for clerical personnel to search for the record), certification fees (to certify a document as being accurate and coming from the particular agency), and expedite fees (to place you at the "front of the line").

Fees can and do vary widely from jurisdiction to jurisdiction for the same record type. Copy fees vary from $.10 to $10 per page. In the U.S., search fees range from under a dollar for a one county search to a $55 search fee for government personnel to perform a name search statewide. Also, expect additional fees if records must be pulled from an archives or from off-site storage.

The *Sourcebook* indicates the specific fees involved with all record access methods at all the government agencies profiled.

More About Online Access to Public Records

First and foremost, let's look at three important facts—

1. Less than 50% of the available public records from the government can be found online.
2. Most free government public record websites that provide index searches list no personal identifiers beyond the name.
3. Usually the searchable and viewable information found online is limited to name indexes and summary data rather than document images. Most access sites – especially the free access sites – permit the former, not the latter.

Many government websites offering online record access include a warning or disclosure stating that the data can have errors and/or should be used for informational purposes only. Such sites should be considered as supplemental or secondary sources only. Using a criminal record search from such a source usually does not in and by itself comply with Fair Credit Reporting Act regulations involving pre-employment screening.

Government Agencies and Identifiers

The federal, state, and local agencies that maintain public record systems make substantial efforts to limit the disclosure of personal information such as Social Security Numbers, phone numbers, and addresses. The Social Security Number is no longer the key search tool identifier it was in the 1980s and early 1990s.

The lack of identifiers displayed when searching online is a real problem for employers or financial institutions who require a certain level of due diligence. The existence of any possible adverse information must be checked by a hands-on search to insure the proper identity of the subject. Even then the identifiers may be removed.

The government agencies that offer online access on a fee or subscription basis, usually to pre-approved requesters, are more apt to disclose personal identifiers such as the date of birth than the free access sites. Very few give Social Security Numbers and those that do usually cloak or mask the first five digits. Some now even cloak the month and day of the birth and only release the year of birth. Most U.S. District Court and Bankruptcy Court search systems give little or no personal identifiers on search results, thus making a reliable name search nearly impossible unless document files are opened and reviewed.

Government Subscription Accounts

The use of subscription accounts is more prevalent than many people may be aware. Also, many agencies, such as state motor vehicle agencies, only provide access to pre-approved, high-volume, ongoing accounts. Typically, this contractual access involves fees and a specified, minimum amount of usage.

A growing trend is offering online access to information on a pay-as-you- go basis, usually with a credit card payment online. Some agencies will give you a glimpse of the index or docket, but will charge a fee for the record copy. Some allow the record to be printed on the spot, other times it is mailed.

Have you heard of the National Information Consortium (NIC)? You may be aware of its services but not realize how widespread this company's services are in the U.S. NIC is a provider of government web portals. NIC designs, manages, and markets eGovernment services on behalf of 22 states and a number of local governments. NIC does this without spending taxpayer dollars.

The state affiliates of the NIC offer services that range from managing the look-ups found at states' web pages to managing record access subscription accounts for MVRs, UCC filings, and court records and more. Examples of states with NIC affiliates include www.alabama.gov, www.kansas.gov, and www.idaho.gov. Of course, access to restricted records involves account approval from the managing state agency. Visit the NIC at www.nicusa.com/html/ for a list of all affiliates and services.

Google is also getting involved in making public information more searchable on the web. Arizona, California, Utah, and Virginia have made their public databases more accessible to Google's crawler by using sitemaps to identify the structure of their sites. Visit http://blog.searchenginewatch.com/blog/070430-000946.

Sometimes the only way to obtain certain records online is from a vendor. A vendor may provide access to many records that otherwise may not be found online via the government online sources. This is especially true for older records.

Using the Web for Public Record Research

Using the web for any extensive research involves knowledge of search engines, directories, and use of effective search strategies. Web research is quite important, but not the subject matter of this book. To learn more about overall web research fundamentals, we recommend books such as *Extreme Searcher's Internet Handbook* by Randolph Hock or *Find It Online* by Alan Schlein. For an excellent overview of how to use the Internet for legal and law-related research – along with many useful links and guides – check out The Virtual Chase at www.virtualchase.com.

The Internet is a good place to find general information about a government agency and many websites contain detailed descriptions of policies and regulations. Where records or indices are not searchable on an agency website, the site may enable one to download or print record request forms.

The primary federal government site for finding information about federal government agencies is www.usa.gov. A true wealth of information is accessible there. The next section of the Appendix lists a number of useful federal sites.

Link Lists and People Searching

What happens when you type the words "public records" at Google? Your search result will be a huge list of web pages that are mostly people finders and links lists. The Internet is filled with web pages offering free link lists to public records sites. There are sites that offer to do name searches for a fee or for free. These sites are called consumer sites since they are targeting the casual requester of public records. A casual requester is typically someone looking for a lost relative or classmate, or perhaps looking to find information about a neighbor or a person dating a relative. Some may be "wanna-be" private investigators.

The Sourcebook does not list or a profile consumer sites, but they can be quite useful if their limitations are kept in mind. For example, a consumer site may offer a quick one-search of multiple free sites at once, which can be advantageous because it casts a wide net. Others offer access to specific, special searches such as a "reverse-phone directory."

Watch for These "Red Flags" at Consumer Links List Sites

Some consumer sites are helpful for someone who really is looking for a lost relative or classmate. But some of these sites can be are misleading. They often try to disguise themselves as sites used by professionals, or they tout unrealistic features.

There are a few considerations to review before spending money on public record research at certain free links list sites. If you find a site using any of the marketing schemes listed below, a red flag should pop up in your mind and you should take a closer look—

- **Charging membership fees for the ability to view free links lists**

  A common marketing scheme is charging a $29 to $35 fee for a set membership term to view free links lists. Some of the schemes even offer an affiliate program to set up your own site in order to sell memberships to others. The "benefit" of membership directs the buyer to either a free link or to a series of free links pages belonging to others. Thus, the primary value is time savings, until you save the web URLs for these other sites. Another money-making concept is to offer links access for free, but charge a monthly fee to avoid sitting through twenty seconds of pop-up ads before the free link connects.

- **Show endorsement by a phony or suspect trade association**

  Several of the questionable public records membership sites tout an endorsement from a national association of private investigators. Do a Google search on that association's name and read the results, as a number of the endorsements are bogus.

- **Promote non-FCRA compliant employment screening**

  Any public record professional will agree that you cannot purchase a "background check" on a new hire for $15 and be truly protected from a negligent hiring lawsuit. Nor will you be in compliance with the Federal Fair Credit Reporting Act (FCRA). You may be able to do a quick record search from a couple web pages or court repository, or from a vendor who has a supplementary database, but these secondary searches do not equate to the due diligence needed for a true pre-employment background check.

Recommended References for Public Record Research

This portion of the Appendix touches on the basics. However, there are resources available that give detailed instructions and "how to advice" on public record searching. Below are recommended books available from local bookstores, Amazon, and direct from the publisher at www.brbpub.com/books/.

The Public Record Research TIPS Book

By Michael Sankey. March. 2008, ISBN#: 1-889150-50-9, Pages: 336, Price: $19.95

The Criminal Records Manual

By Derek Hinton & Larry Henry. Sept. 2008, ISBN#: 1-889150-54-1, Pages: 420, Price: $24.95

Business Background Investigations

By Cynthia Hetherington, October 2007, ISBN#: 1-889150-49-5, Pages: 288, Price: $21.95

Appendix 2 – Searching Federal Courts

Several of the sections on Federal Court Records refer the reader to this portion of the Appendix for a detailed explanation of the record searching standards that apply to all federal courts.

Searching records at the federal court system can be one of the easiest and one of the most frustrating experiences that public record searchers may encounter. Although the federal court system offers advanced electronic search capabilities, at times it is practically impossible to properly identify a subject when searching civil, criminal, or bankruptcy records.

Before reviewing searching procedures, a brief overview is in order.

Federal Court Structure

At the federal level, all cases involve federal or U.S. constitutional law or interstate commerce. The federal court system includes three levels of courts, plus several specialty courts.

United States District Courts

The United States District Courts are the courts of general jurisdiction, or trial courts. There are 89 districts in the 50 states, which are listed with their divisions in Title 28 of the U.S. Code, Sections 81-144. District courts also exist in Puerto Rico, the U.S. Virgin Islands, the District of Columbia, Guam, and the Northern Mariana Islands. In total there are 94 U.S. District Courts in 500 court locations. Some states, such as Colorado, are composed of a single judicial district. Others, such as California, are composed of multiple judicial districts – Central, Eastern, Northern, and Southern.

The task of locating the right court is seemingly simplified by the nature of the federal system—

- All court locations are based upon the plaintiff's county of domicile.
- All civil and criminal cases go to the U.S. District Courts.
- All bankruptcy cases go to the U.S. Bankruptcy Courts.

Bankruptcy Courts are separate units of the District Courts and have exclusive jurisdiction over bankruptcy cases. States with more than one court are divided further into judicial districts — e.g., the State of New York consists of four judicial districts: the Northern, Southern, Eastern, and Western. Further, many judicial districts contain more than one court location, called a Division.

The **Bankruptcy Courts** generally use the same hearing locations as the District Courts, but not always. If court locations differ, the usual variance is to have fewer bankruptcy court locations.

A plaintiff or defendant may have cases in any of the 500 court locations, so it is really not all that simple to find them.

United States Court of Appeals

The United States Court of Appeals consists of thirteen Appellate Courts that hear appeals of verdicts from the District and Bankruptcy Courts. Courts of Appeals are designated as follows:

- The Federal Circuit Court of Appeals hears appeals from the U.S. Claims Court and the U.S. Court of International Trade. It is located in Washington, DC.
- The District of Columbia Circuit Court of Appeals hears appeals from the district courts in Washington, DC as well as from the Tax Court.
- Eleven geographic Courts of Appeals — each of these appeal courts covers a designated number of states and territories.

Supreme Court of the United States

The Supreme Court of the United States is the court of last resort in the United States. The Supreme Court is located in Washington, DC, where it hears appeals from the United States Courts of Appeals and from the highest courts of each state.

Other Federal Courts of Note

There are three significant special/separate courts created to hear cases or appeals for certain areas of litigation that demand special expertise. These courts are the U.S. Tax Court, the Court of International Trade, and the U.S. Court of Federal Claims. A profile of each of these courts is located at the end of this section.

How Federal Trial Court Cases are Organized

Indexing and Case Numbering

When a case is filed with a federal court, a case number is assigned. District courts index by defendant and plaintiff as well as by case number. Bankruptcy courts usually index by debtor and case number. Therefore, when you search by name you will first receive a listing of all cases where the name appears, both as plaintiff and defendant.

To view case records you will need to know, or find, the applicable case number.

Case numbering procedures are not consistent throughout the federal court system. One judicial district may assign numbers by district while another may assign numbers by location (division) within that judicial district, or by judge within the division. Remember that case numbers appearing in legal text citations may not be adequate for searching unless they appear in the proper form for that particular court.

Docket Sheet

As a case goes forward, information from cover sheets and from filed documents is recorded on the docket sheet, which contains the case history from initial filing to its current status. While docket sheets differ somewhat in format, the basic information contained on a docket sheet is consistent from court-to-court. As noted previously in the state court chapter, all docket sheets contain—

- Name of court, including location (division) and the judge assigned;
- Case number and case name;
- Names of all plaintiffs and defendants/debtors;
- Names and addresses of attorneys for the plaintiff or debtor;
- Nature and cause (e.g., U.S. civil statute) of action;

- Listing of documents filed in the case, including the date, docket entry number, and a short description (e.g., 12-2-92, #1, Complaint).

All basic civil case information entered onto docket sheets and into computerized systems like the Case Management/Electronic Case Filings (CM/ECF) starts with standard form JS-44, the Civil Cover Sheet, or the equivalent.

Assignment of Cases and Computerization

At one time, cases were assigned within a district based on the county of origination. Although this is still true in most states, computerized tracking of dockets has led to a more flexible approach to case assignment. For example, in Minnesota and Connecticut, rather than blindly assigning all cases from a county to one judge, their districts use random numbers and other methods to logically balance caseloads among their judges.

This trend may appear to confuse the case search process. Actually, finding cases has become significantly easier with the wide public availability of the U.S. Party/Case Index and PACER. Also helpful is when the on-site terminals in each court location contain access to the database of district-wide information.

Searching Records by Mail and In Person

There are certain pre-set standards for federal courts that most all courts follow.

The search fee is $26.00 per item. 'A search' is one party name or case number. The court copy fee is $.50 per page. Certification fee is $9.00 per document, double for exemplification, if available. If you request documents by mail, it is best to always enclose a stamped self-addressed envelope unless a court indicates otherwise. Most courts accept fax requests or will suggest a copying/search vendor. Before releasing records, assume that the court will require prepayment, as most do.

Nearly all courts offer Internet access via CM-ECF or PACER as described in the next section.

Electronic Access to Federal Court Records

Over the years, the Administrative Office of the United States Courts in Washington, DC has developed a number of innovative public access programs for electronic access to federal court records—

- The U.S. Party/Case Index
- PACER
- Case Management/Electronic Case Files (CM/ECF)
- Voice Case Information System (VCIS) via the telephone

Search the U.S. Party/Case Index

The U.S. Party/Case Index, actually part of PACER, is a national locator index for U.S. District, Bankruptcy, and Appellate courts. By using the U.S. Party/Case Index searchers may conduct a nearly nationwide search to determine whether or not a party is involved in federal litigation. Only subscribers to PACER may access the U.S. Party/Case Index, use their existing PACER login and password at http://pacer.uspci.uscourts.gov.

The U.S. Party/Case Index allows searches 1) by party name or Social Security Number in the bankruptcy index, 2) party name or nature of suit in the civil index, 3) defendant name in the criminal index, and 4) party name in the appellate index. The information provided by the search result will include the party name, the court where the case is filed, the case number and the filing date.

To find the date ranges for the cases in a particular court, choose the option "Date Ranges" at the main menu. This option provides how far back the search will go and the date the U.S. Party/Case Index was last updated for each court.

To retrieve more information on a particular case found while searching the U.S. Party/Case Index, access the PACER system for the jurisdiction where the case resides as indicated by the court abbreviation. Usually the Case Number will be a link to the case summary information at that court's PACER site. If you find there is a case in existence involving a particular subject, then you need to visit the PACER or CM/ECF site for the particular jurisdiction where the case is located. The Case Number field in the output will be a direct link to the full case information on the court's computers, whether the court is running the Internet version of PACER or the newer PACER on the CM/ECF system.

At press time, the courts not participating in the U.S. Party Case Index are all Appellate Courts including the Second, Fifth, Seventh, and Eleventh Circuits and the Federal Circuit Court of Appeals.

PACER

PACER, the acronym for **P**ublic **A**ccess to **E**lectronic **C**ourt **R**ecords, provides docket information online for open and most recently closed case information at all U.S. Bankruptcy Courts and most U.S. District Courts. Cases for the U.S. Court of Federal Claims are also available. A key point to consider is that each court maintains its own database with case information and decides what to make available on PACER. Also, several courts provide case information on Internet sites without support of the PACER Service Center.

PACER sign-up and technical support is handled at the PACER Service Center in San Antonio, Texas; phone 800-676-6856. A single sign-up is good for all courts; however, some individual courts may require further registration procedures. Many judicial districts offer to send a PACER Primer that has been customized for that district. The primer contains a summary of how to access PACER, how to select cases, how to read case numbers and docket sheets, some searching tips, who to call for problem resolution, and district specific program variations.

You may search by case number, party name, SSN, or tax identification number in the U.S. Bankruptcy Courts. You may search by case number, party name, or filing date range in the U.S. District Courts. You may search by case number or party name in the U.S. Courts of Appeals.

PACER provides the following information—

- A listing of all parties and participants including judges, attorneys, trustees
- A compilation of case-related information such as cause of action, nature of suit, dollar demand
- A chronology of dates of case events entered in the case record
- A claims registry
- A listing of new cases each day in the bankruptcy courts
- Appellate court opinions
- Judgments or case status
- Types of case documents filed for certain districts.

PACER Problems

There are two inherent problems when searching PACER records—

1. How far back records are kept
2. Lack of identifiers

Since each court determines how records will be indexed and when records will be purged, this can leave a searcher guessing how a name is spelled or abbreviated, and how much information about closed cases a search will uncover. Another problem is the lack of identifiers. Most federal courts do not show the full DOB on records available to the public. Some courts show no DOB at all. Thus, if the name searched for is common and the search results show two or more hits, each individual case file may need to be reviewed to determine if the case belongs to the subject in mind. Courts have ways of helping if you give them the identifiers up-front, but that entails a visit or a phone call.

An excellent FAQ on PACER is at http://pacer.psc.uscourts.gov/faq.html.

Miscellaneous Online Systems

RACER is a comparable system to PACER. A few courts still maintain and offer access through RACER. Over the years some courts have developed their own legacy online systems. In addition to RACER, Idaho's Bankruptcy and District Courts have other searching options available on their websites. Likewise, the Southern District Court of New York offers CourtWeb, which provides information to the public on selected recent rulings of those judges who have elected to make information available in electronic form.

Case Management/Electronic Case Files (CM/ECF)

CM/ECF is the relatively new case management system for the Federal Judiciary for all bankruptcy, district, and appellate courts, replacing the aging electronic docketing and case management systems. CM/ECF allows courts to accept filings and provide access to filed documents over the Internet. Attorneys may use CM/ECF to file documents and manage official documents related to a case. Case Management/Electronic Case Files case information is available to the public. Searchers access CM/ECF via their PACER login.

For details, visit http://pacer.psc.uscourts.gov/cmecf/index.html.

It is important to note that when you search ECF, you may be searching ONLY cases that have been filed electronically. Since a case may not have been filed electronically through CM/ECF, you must still conduct a search using PACER to determine if a case exists.

Most individual courts offer tutorials on how to use CM/ECF for their district. Functioning as a search mechanism, CM/ECF attaches to the relevant docket entries and to PDF versions of related documents filed with or issued by the court. A user may access PDF attachments through hyperlinks that appears with the docket entry.

Because PACER and CM/ECF database systems are maintained within each court, each jurisdiction will have a different URL. Accessing and querying information from PACER and CM/ECF is comparable; however the format and content of information provided may differ slightly.

Voice Case Information System (VCIS)

Another access system is VCIS – Voice Case Information System. At one time, nearly all of the U.S. Bankruptcy Court judicial districts provided VCIS, a means of accessing information regarding OPEN bankruptcy cases by merely using a touch-tone telephone. The advantage? There is no charge. Individual names are entered last name first with as much of the first name as you wish to include. For example, Joe B. Cool could be entered as COOLJ or COOLJOE. Do not enter the middle initial. Business names are entered as they are written, without blanks.

VCIS, like the RACER System, is being replaced by newer technology. Each bankruptcy court that still offers VCIS access is shown in the court profiles section.

VCIS should only be used to locate information about open cases. Do not attempt to use VCIS as a substitute for a PACER search.

Other Federal Courts

U.S. Court of Federal Claims

The Court of Federal Claims is authorized to hear primarily money claims in regard to federal statutes, executive regulations, the Constitution, or contracts, expressed- or implied-in-fact, with the

United States. Approximately a quarter of the cases involve complex factual and statutory construction issues in tax law. About a third of the cases involve government contracts. Cases involving environmental and natural resource issues make up about ten percent of the caseload. Another significant category of cases involve civilian and military pay questions. In addition, the Court hears intellectual property, Indian Tribe, and various statutory claims against the United States by individuals, domestic and foreign corporations, states and localities, Indian Tribes and Nations, and foreign nationals and governments.

Direct questions to the U.S. Court of Federal Claims, Attention: Clerks Office, 717 Madison Place, NW, Washington, DC 20005, or call 202-357-6400. Search opinions and decisions on the web at www.uscfc.uscourts.gov.

U.S. Tax Court

The jurisdiction of the U.S. Tax Court includes the authority to hear tax disputes concerning notices of deficiency, notices of transferee liability, certain types of declaratory judgment, readjustment and adjustment of partnership items, review of the failure to abate interest, administrative costs, worker classification, relief from joint and several liability on a joint return, and review of certain collection actions. For a less formal and speedier disposition in certain tax disputes involving $50,000 or less, taxpayers may choose to have the case conducted under the Court's simplified small tax case procedure. However, these decisions may not be appealed.

Docket information is available for cases filed on or after May 1, 1986. Call Docket Information at 202-521-4650. For case records, call Records and Reproduction at 202-521-4688.

Direct questions to United States Tax Court, 400 Second Street, NW, Washington, DC 20217. The main number is 202-521-0700. Dockets and opinions also may be searched on the web at www.ustaxcourt.gov.

U.S. Court of International Trade

The U.S. Court of International Trade oversees disputes within the international trade community including individuals, foreign and domestic manufacturers, consumer groups, trade associations, labor unions, concerned citizens, and other nations.

The geographical jurisdiction of the United States Court of International Trade extends throughout the U.S. The court does hear cases anywhere in the nation and is also authorized to hold hearings in foreign countries.

Appeals from final decisions of the court may be taken to the United States Court of Appeals for the Federal Circuit and, ultimately, to the Supreme Court of the United States.

The Court provides online access to opinions and judgments. From 1999-2006, the Court published only the slip opinions online. Since January 1, 2007, the online postings contain both the slip opinion and judgment in each case. Registered users of the CM/ECF system have the ability to open a case as of October 11, 2006.

The Court's Administrative Office is located at One Federal Plaza, New York, New York 10278-0001, or call 212-264-2800. www.cit.uscourts.gov

Appendix 3- Searching Other Federal Records

EDGAR

Publicly traded companies must inform the public the complete truth about their business financial data. EDGAR – the **E**lectronic **D**ata **G**athering **A**nalysis and **R**etrieval system – was established by the SEC as the means for companies to make required filings to the SEC by direct transmission. As of May 6, 1996, all non-exempt companies, foreign and domestic, are required to file registration statements, periodic reports, and other forms electronically through EDGAR. Thus, EDGAR is an extensive repository of U.S. corporation information available online. Anyone can access and download the basic information for free.

Companies must file the following reports with the SEC:

- 10-K – an annual financial report that includes audited year-end financial statements.
- 10-Q – a quarterly, unaudited report.
- 8K – a report detailing significant or unscheduled corporate changes or events.
- Securities offering, trading registrations, and final prospectus.
- DEF-14 – a definitive proxy statement offering director names, their compensation and position.

The list above is not all-inclusive. Other miscellaneous reports include items dealing with security holdings by institutions and insiders. Access to these documents provides a wealth of informative data about the companies being researched.

EDGAR offers a guide on how to search publicly traded companies; go to www.sec.gov/investor/pubs/edgarguide.htm. The record searching site at EDGAR is www.sec.gov/edgar/searchedgar/webusers.htm.

A number of private vendors offer access to EDGAR records along with some added features and searching flexibilities. Recommended sites include www.edgar-online.com, www.secinfo.com, www.edgarlive.com, and www.lexisnexis.com.

SEC Enforcement Actions

Visit www.sec.gov/divisions/enforce/enforceactions.shtml to find 1) SEC-related enforcement actions, 2) civil lawsuits brought by the Commission in Federal court, 3) administrative proceedings as instituted and/or settled, 4) opinions issued by Administrative Law Judges in contested administrative proceedings, and 5) opinions on appeals issued by the Commission on appeal of Initial Decisions or disciplinary decisions issued by self-regulatory organizations (e.g., NYSE or NASD).

SEC Litigation Actions

The web page www.sec.gov/litigation.shtml contains links to information on 1) SEC enforcement actions, 2) opinions issued by the Commission, 3) briefs filed by SEC staff, 43) trading suspensions, 5) and notices concerning the creation of investors' claims funds in specific cases.

Aviation Records

The Federal Aviation Association (FAA) is the U.S. government agency with the responsibility for all matters related to the safety of civil aviation. Among its functions the FAA provides the system that registers aircraft and the documents showing title or interest in aircraft. The FAA website, at www.faa.gov, is the ultimate source of aviation records, airports and facilities, safety regulations, and civil research and engineering.

Although not government websites, there are three additional sites worthy of mention. The Aircraft Owners and Pilots Association is the largest organization of its kind with 400,000+ members. Their website at www.aopa.org is an excellent source of information regarding the aviation industry. Visit www.landings.com for many excellent searching links and background information. Another excellent source of aircraft information is Jane's World Airlines at www.janes.com.

Military Records

National Personnel Records Center (NPRC)

Military service records are kept by the National Personnel Records Center (NPRC) which is under the jurisdiction of the National Archives and Records Administration. The address is the National Personnel Records Center, Military Personnel Records, 9700 Page Avenue, St. Louis, Missouri 63132, 314-801-0800, fax: 314-801-9195, www.archives.gov/veterans/military-service-records/

The type of information released to the general public is dependent upon the veteran's authorization. Also, the key to searching military records is form SF-180 (or a signed release). The key military record is the DD-214. Federal law [5 USC 552a(b)] requires that all requests for records and information be submitted in writing. Each request must be signed and dated. The NPRC categorizes two types of requesters:

With the Veteran's Authorization - The veteran (or next-of-kin if the veteran is deceased) must authorize release of information. The authorization must 1) be in writing; 2) specify what additional information or copies are requested that NPRC may release; and 3) include the signature of the veteran or next-of-kin.

Without the Veteran's Authorization - A request for information by the general public (someone who is not next of kin) is treated as a FOIA request. A "limited amount of information" is released. See below.

Using Form SF-180

The SF-180 is a form specifically used to request military records. If you wish to search the records of an individual and the subject does not provide you with the DD-214, then you must use the SF-180 to request a copy of the DD-214. The SF-180 can be requested in writing from the NPRC or can be downloaded as a pdf file. The form and instructions are found at www.archives.gov/st-louis/military-personnel/standard-form-180.html. The SF-180 can also be obtained from the Department of Defense, Federal Information Centers, local Veterans Administration offices, and from veterans' service organizations.

A veteran or the veteran's next of kin may use the eVetRecs system at www.archives.gov/veterans/evetrecs/ to create their request for a copy of the DD-214, or may mail or fax the SF-180.

Use of the SF-180 is not mandatory. The request must be in writing and signed by the requester. Include as much as the following as possible - the veteran's complete name used while in service, the service number or SSN, branch of service, and dates of services if known. The DOB is helpful. If the records were involved in the 1973 fire, then including the place of entry, discharge, and last unit of assignment is quite helpful.

The turnaround time for most requests takes about 10 days plus mail time. However, records involved in the 1973 fire or older records which require extensive search efforts may take 6 months or more to complete. Reconstruction requests are taking on average 4.5 weeks to complete.

About the DD-214

DD-214 is the name of the document that military personnel receive when discharged from the U.S. Navy, Army, Air Force, Marine Corp, or Coast Guard. There are actually a number of different copies of the DD-214 with different sets of information. A discharged service person receives Copy 1, which has the least information. Copy 4 gives the nature of the discharge – General, Honorable, Dishonorable, Undesirable – and details of service. There are codes that characterize the service record including SPD (Separation Program Designator), SPN (Separation Program Number) and RE (Re-Entry). For a discharged service person to get Copy 4, the subject must actually ask for it.

Military Branches - Internet Sources

The Official Sites include—

www.army.mil	U.S. Army
www.af.mil	U.S. Air Force
www.navy.mil	U.S. Navy
www.usmc.mil	U.S. Marine Corps
www.arng.army.mil	Army National Guard
www.ang.af.mil	Air National Guard
www.uscg.mil/default.asp	U.S. Coast Guard

Excluded Parties and Watch Lists

Excluded Party List

The Excluded Parties List System (EPLS) contains information on individuals and firms excluded by various federal government agencies from receiving federal contracts or federally approved subcontracts and from certain types of federal financial and non-financial assistance and benefits. Note that individual agencies are responsible for the timely reporting, maintenance, and accuracy of their data in this comprehensive list. Information shown may include names, addresses, DUNS numbers, Social Security Numbers, Employer Identification Numbers or other Taxpayer Identification Numbers, if available and deemed appropriate and permissible to publish by the agency taking the action. https://www.epls.gov/

Commerce Department Lists

The Bureau of Industry and Security (BIS) provides lists relevant to import/export transactions. See www.bis.doc.gov. Below are three important lists—

1. **Denied Persons List**

   The purpose of the Denied Persons List is to prevent the illegal export certain items and to investigate and assist in the prosecution of violators of the Export Administration Regulations. www.bis.doc.gov/dpl/default.shtm

2. **Unverified List**

   This is a list of parties whom BIS has been unable to verify the end use in prior transactions. The Unverified List includes names and countries of foreign persons who in the past were parties to a transaction with respect to which BIS could not conduct a pre-license check ("PLC") or a post-shipment verification ("PSV") for reasons outside of the U.S. Government's control. If you

would like to be informed when changes occur to the Unverified List, consider subscribing to the BIS Email Notification Service.
www.bis.doc.gov/Enforcement/UnverifiedList/unverified_parties.html

3. **Entity List**

   The Entity List, available in PDF or ASCII text format, is a list of parties whose presence in a transaction can trigger a license requirement under the Export Administration Regulations. The list specifies the license requirements that apply to each listed party. These license requirements are in addition to any license requirements imposed on the transaction by other provisions of the Export Administration Regulations. www.bis.doc.gov/entities/default.htm

FDA – Food & Drug Administration

The **FDA Enforcement Report**, published weekly, contains information on actions taken in connection with agency regulatory activities. Activities include Recall and Field Correction, Injunctions, Seizures, Indictments, Prosecutions, and Dispositions. A record of all recalls (Class I, II, and III), including pre-1995, can be found at www.fda.gov/opacom/Enforce.html.

Other Lists that can be found at the FDA site include—

- Disqualified or Totally Restricted Clinical Investigator List
- Partially Restricted Clinical Investigator List
- Adequate Assurances List
- Disqualified or Totally Restricted List

Gateways to U.S. Government Information

Below is a list of very useful web pages that are either maintained by the federal government or private companies, all with extensive links to federal agencies.

Documents Center

www.lib.umich.edu/govdocs/index.html

Documents Center is a clearinghouse for local, state, federal, foreign, and international government information. It is one of the more comprehensive online searching aids for all kinds of government information on the Internet. It is especially useful as a meta-site of meta-sites.

FedLaw

www.thecre.com/fedlaw/default.htm

FedLaw is an extremely effective tool for federal legal and regulatory research. It is operated by the General Services Administration (GSA).

Fedstats

www.fedstats.gov

This site has a collection of statistical sites from the federal government and is a good central clearinghouse for other federal statistical sites.

FedWorld Information Network

www.fedworld.gov

FedWorld.gov website is a very useful gateway to government information managed by the National Technical Information Service.

Google's Uncle Sam

www.google.com/unclesam

Google's Uncle Sam site is a strong search engine dedicated to U.S. government sites.

InfoMine: Scholarly Internet Resource Collections

http://infomine.ucr.edu

InfoMine provides collections of scholarly Internet resources managed by the University of California Riverside. The Government Information section is easily searchable by subject.

SearchGov.com

www.searchgov.com

This site, maintained by a private company, is a great starting point for searching U.S. government sites.

USA.gov

www.usa.gov/

USAGov (formerly known as FIRSTgov) has links to virtually every federal agency as well as every state government agency. It is easy-to-use, allowing the user to specify the type of agency or the topic. Also, the site has a very robust FAQs section about the U.S. government at http://answers.usa.gov.

U.S. Federal Government Agencies Directory

www.lib.lsu.edu/gov/index.html

This directory of federal agencies, maintained by Louisiana State University, links to hundreds of federal agency sites.

Appendix 4 - Working With Public Record Vendors

Hiring Someone to Obtain the Record

Selecting the right record vendor for your particular search or case is a science. Before you sign up with every interesting vendor that catches your eye, you need to narrow your search to the type of vendor suitable for your needs.

There are six defined and distinct main categories of public record professionals: distributors, gateways, search firms, local document retrievers, verification or screening firms, and private investigation firms. Knowledge of how each of these vendor categories operates and how they work with clients is invaluable.

Distributors (Proprietary Database Vendors)

Distributors, generally, are automated public record dealers who combine public sources of bulk data and/or online access to develop their own in-house database products. Also known as Primary Distributors, they collect or buy public record information from government repositories and reformat the information in useful ways for clients. They may also purchase or license records from other information vendors, an example is a phone company. In the past distributors purchased the "credit header" information from the credit bureaus, but this is no longer a standard practice. In the U.S. there are approximately 350 public record vendors in the distributor category who collect and warehouse information. This does not include marketing list or links list companies.

By nature, most of these entities are either **vertical** (multiple types of info collected on a local or regional basis) or **horizontal** (dedicated single-purpose type of info collected on regional or national basis). An example of a vertical distributor is Record Information Services (www.public-record.com). This Illinois-based company offers online access to a number of different public records (real estate, recorded documents, bankrupties, vital records, etc.) from many Illinios counties. An example of a horizontal distributor is Aristotle (www.aristotle.com). Aristotle purchases voter registration records nationwide and sells customized lists to political candidates and political parties.

Some distributors are both vertical and horizontal in nature. An example is LexisNexis ChoicePoint (www.choicepoint.com), a company with multiple divisions that offers access to many and varied nationwide databases for a wide variety of clients.

Note that when a database vendor sells data, the vendor is bound by the same disclosure laws attached to the original government repository. Access restrictions can range from zero for recorded documents or level-three sexual predators, etc. to severe for voter registration or motor vehicle records.

Gateways

Gateways are companies who provide their clients with automated electronic access to 1) multiple proprietary database vendors or 2) government agencies online systems. Gateways are similiar to distributors except gateways do not warehouse records – they merely provide a sophisticated method to access existing databases. Gateways provide "one-stop shopping" for multiple geographic areas and/or categories of information. Gateways are the most evident companies on the Internet, advertising access to records for many different purposes.

Many states have outsourced some of their record access services and other business services such as license registrations to gateways. For example, the National Information Consortium (www.nicusa.com/html/) has over 22 individual state affiliates. For example, visit www.nebraska.gov and click on "Become a Subscriber." Keep in mind, the state's data still resides with the state. The NIC affiliate offers a *gateway* of access to the records.

A company can be both Primary Distributor and a Gateway. A number of online database companies are both primary distributors of corporate information and also gateways to real estate information assembled from other primary distributors.

Search Firms

Search firms are companies who furnish individual clients with public record research and document retrieval services. Search firms use online services and/or in-person searches through a network of specialists, including their own employees or records retrievers (see below). Combining online proficiency with document retrieval expertise, search firms may rely on other vendors such as distributors, gateways and/or networks of retrievers, or they may go direct to the government agency. Search firms may focus either on one geographic region – like New England – or on one specific type of public record information – like criminal records. Many search firms have been started by private investigators with a savvy knowledge of vendors and online expertise. There are literally hundreds of search firms in the U.S.

Search firms are very prominent on the web. Many are working to sell services to the general consumer market. The prices these web search firms charge for their services can be very high.

Record Retrievers

Somewhat similiar to a search firm is a Local Document Retriever, or simply, a Record Retriever. Retrievers are hands-on "researchers for hire" who visit government agencies in-person. Their clients request name searches or document retrieval services usually for legal compliance (e.g., incorporations), hiring, lending, real estate (e.g., abstracting) or for litigation purposes. Retrievers do not usually review or interpret the results nor do they issue reports in the sense that private investigators do, but rather return the results of searches along with document copies. Retrievers tend to be localized, but there are retriever companies who offer a national network of retrievers and/or correspondents. Since the retriever or their personnel go directly to the agency to look up information, they may be relied upon for their strong knowledge on record searching in a local area.

Record retrieving is not necessarily a profession. Many other vocations offer record retrieval services, including private investigators, process servers, genealogists, and paralegals. There are approximately 4,000 active local document retrievers in the U.S.

The 775+ members of the Public Record Retriever Network (PRRN) are listed by state and counties served at www.prrn.us. This organization has set industry standards for the retrieval of public record documents. Members operate under a Code of Professional Conduct. Using one of these record retrievers is an excellent way to quickly access records in jurisdictions where clerks do not perform record searches.

Verification Firms (Pre-employment Screeners, Tenant Screeners, MVR Vendors)

Verification firms provide services to employers and businesses when the subject has given consent for the verification. In this category are pre-employment screening firms and tenant screening firms (both governed by the Fair Credit Reporting Act - FCRA) and motor vehicle record vendors (governed by the Driver's Privacy Protection Act – DPPA). Since verification firms usually only perform their services for clients who have specifically received consent from the subjects, verifiers typically do not warehouse or collect data to be resold. The service provided by a pre-employment screening company is often called a background screen or a background report. Their service should not be confused with an investigation as provided by private investigators (see below) nor with search firms with an Internet presence. There are at least 2,000 pre-employment screening firms in the U.S., not counting the many private investigators who may also provide screening services when asked. There are usually 3-5 tenant screening companies in every major city, and perhaps several dozen vendors who have the ability to access motor vehicle records direct in every state.

The National Association of Professional Background Screeners (NAPBS) is an excellent trade association with members from all of the three described verification firms. NAPBS actively promotes best practices and industry standards. Visit www.napbs.com.

Private Investigation Firms

Private investigators use public records as tools rather than as ends in themselves. Depending on the purpose, investigators use public records in order to create an overall, comprehensive "picture" of an individual or company. The investigator interprets the information gathered in order to identify further investigation tracks. Investigators summarize their results in a report compiled from all the sources used. An investigator may be licensed and may perform the types of services traditionally thought of as detective work, such as surveillance. In many instances, a private investigator doing an investigation does not have the consent of the subject.

Many investigators also act as search firms or record retrievers and provide search results to other investigators. As mentioned, some investigators offer pre-employment screening per the FCRA (and some not per the FCRA). After the FCRA was passed, many PIs ceased doing employment screening.

Other Vendors of Note

There are two other types of firms worthy of mention who occasionally provide services that use public records. The Association of Independent Information Professionals (AIIP), at www.aiip.org, has over 500 experienced professional information specialist members from 20 countries. They refer to themselves as Information Brokers (IBs). They gather information intended to help their clients make informed business decisions. Their work is usually done on a custom basis with each project being unique. IBs are extremely knowledgeable in online research of full-text databases and most specialize in a particular subject area such as patent searching or competitive intelligence.

A similar organization is the Society of Competitive Intelligence Professionals (SCIP), see www.scip.org. Per their web "...SCIP provides education and networking opportunities for business professionals working in the rapidly growing field of competitive intelligence (the legal and ethical collection and analysis of information regarding the capabilities, vulnerabilities, and intentions of business competitors)."

Which Type of Vendor is Right for You?

With all the variations of vendors and all the categories of information, the obvious question is "How do I find the right vendor to provide me with the public record information I need?" Before you start calling every interesting online vendor that catches your eye, you need to narrow your search to the **type** of vendor for your needs. To do this, ask yourself the following questions—

What is the Frequency of Usage?

If you have hundreds of ongoing, recurring requests for a particular type of information, then it is probably best to choose a different vendor then one used infrequently. Setting up an account with a large primary distributor such as LEXIS or Westlaw will give you an inexpensive per search fee, conversely the monthly minimum requirements will be prohibitive to the casual requester who would be better off using a smaller vendor who already has access to these larger distributors.

What is the Complexity of the Search?

The importance of hiring a vendor who understands and can interpret the information in the final format increases with the complexity of the search. Pulling a corporation record in Maryland is not difficult, but doing an online criminal record search in Maryland, when only a portion of the felony records are online, is not so easy.

Thus, part of the answer to determining which vendor or type of vendor to use is to become conversant with what is and is not available from government agencies. Without knowing what is available and what restrictions apply, you cannot guide the search process effectively. Once you are comfortable knowing the kinds of information available in the public record, you are in a position to find the best method to access needed information.

What are the Geographic Boundaries of the Search?

A search of local records close to you may require little assistance, but a search of records nationally or in a state 2,000 miles away will require seeking a vendor who covers that area. Many national primary distributors and gateways combine various local and state databases into one large comprehensive system available for searching. However, if your record searching is narrowed by a region or locality, then an online source that specializes in a specific geographic region may be an alternative.

Keep in mind that many national firms allow you to order a search online even though results cannot be delivered immediately; some hands-on local searching is required.

Of course, you may want to use the government agency online system, if available, for the kind of information you need. It may be free.

10 Questions to Ask a Public Record Vendor

Or a Vendor Who Uses Online Sources

The following discussion focuses specifically on automated sources of information because many valuable types of public records have been entered into a computer and, therefore, require a computer search to obtain reliable results. The original version of the text to follow was written by **Mr. Leroy Cook.** Mr. Cook is the Founder and Director of ION and The Investigators Anywhere Resource Line (800-338-3463, http://ioninc.com). Mr. Cook has graciously allowed us to edit the article and reprint it for *The Sourcebook.*

re does he or she get the information?

You may feel awkward asking a vendor where he or she obtained the information you are purchasing. The fake Rolex watch is a reminder that even buying physical things based on looks alone — without knowing where they come from — has risks.

eliable information vendors *will* provide verification material such as the name of the database or rvice accessed, when it was last updated, and how complete it is.

is important that you know the gathering process in order to better judge the reliability of the formation being purchased. There *are* certain investigative sources that a vendor will not be willing disclose to you. However, that type of source should not be confused with the information that is ing sold item by item. Information technology has changed so rapidly that some information ndors may still confuse "items of information" with "investigative reports." Items of information d as units are *not* investigative reports.

The professional reputation of an information vendor is a guarantee of sorts. Still, because information as a commodity is so new, there is little in the way of an implied warranty of fitness.

2. How long does it take for the new information or changes to get into the system?

Any answer except a clear, concise date and time or the vendor's personal knowledge of an ongoing system's methods of maintaining information currency is a reason to look elsewhere for a vendor. Microfiche or a database of records may have been updated last week at a courthouse or a DMV, but the department's computer section may also be working with a three-month backlog. In this case, a critical incident occurring one month ago would not show up in the database updated last week. The importance of timeliness is a variable to be determined by you, but to be truly informed you need to know how "fresh" the information is. Ideally, the mechanism by which you purchase items of information should include an update schedule or statement of accuracy — as a part of the reply — without having to ask.

3. What are the searchable fields? Which fields are mandatory?

Your knowledge of "fields" and "records" *could* help determine the difference between a good database or vendor from a bad one. An MVR vendor, for example, should be able to tell you that a subject's middle initial is critical when pulling an Arizona driving record. You don't have to become a programmer to use a computer and you need not know a database management language to benefit from databases, *but* it is very helpful to understand how databases are constructed and what fields, records, and indexing procedures are used.

As a general rule, the computerized, public-record information world is not standardized from county to county or from state to state. In the same way, there is little standardization within or between information vendors. Look at the system documentation from the vendor. The manual or help screen should include this sort of information.

4. How much latitude is there for error (misspellings or inappropriate punctuation) in a data request?

If the vendor's requirements for search data appear to be concise and meticulous, then you' probably on the right track to selecting a good vendor. Some vendor computer systems will tel' "flag") an operator when they make a mistake such as omitting important punctuation or us unnecessary comma. Other systems allow you to make inquiries by whatever means or in format you like — and then tell you the requested information has not been found. Wher found, the desired information may actually be there but the computer didn't understar because of the way it was asked. It is easy to misinterpret "no record found" as "the The meanings of these two phrases are quite different.

5. What method is used to place the information in the repository and what or edit process is used?

In some databases, information may be scanned in or may be entered by a single received. In others, information may be entered *twice* to allow the computer to catc searching for non-duplicate entries. You don't have to know *everything* about all th vendor selling information in quantity *should*.

6. How many different databases or sources does the vendor access *and* h

The chance of obtaining an accurate search of a database increases with the frequ the vendor's/searcher's level of knowledge. If he or she only makes inquiries on the results are important — you may need to find someone who sells data at highe here is that it is better to find someone who *specializes* in the type of informat than it is to utilize a vendor who *can* simply get the information, but may specializ data or is inexperienced.

7. Does the price include assistance in interpreting the data received?

A report that includes coding and ambiguous abbreviations may look impressive in your file but may not be too meaningful. For all reports, except those you deal with regularly, interpretation assistance can be *very* important. Some information vendors offer searches for information they really don't know much about and access data through sources that they only use occasionally. Professional pride sometimes prohibits them from disclosing their limitations — until *you* ask the right questions.

8. Do vendors "keep track" of requesters and the information they seek (usage records)?

This may not seem like a serious concern when you are requesting information you are legally entitled to; however, there *is* a possibility that your usage records could be made available to a competitor.

There is a degree of probability that the information itself is *already* being – or will be – sold to someone else, but you may not necessarily want *everyone* to know what you are requesting and how often. If the vendor keeps records of who-asks-what, the confidentiality of that information should be addressed in your agreement with the vendor.

9. Will the subject of the inquiry be notified of the request?

If your inquiry is sub rosa or if the subject's discovery of the search could lead to embarrassment, double check! There are laws that mandate the notification of subjects when certain types of inquiries are made into their files. If notification is required, the way it is accomplished could be critical.

10. Is the turnaround time and cost of the search made clear at the outset?

You should be crystal clear about what you expect and need; the vendor should be succinct when conveying exactly what will be provided and how much it will cost. Failure to address these issues can lead to disputes, delays and hard feelings.

All these are excellent questions and concepts to keep in mind when searching for the right public record vendor to meet your particular needs.

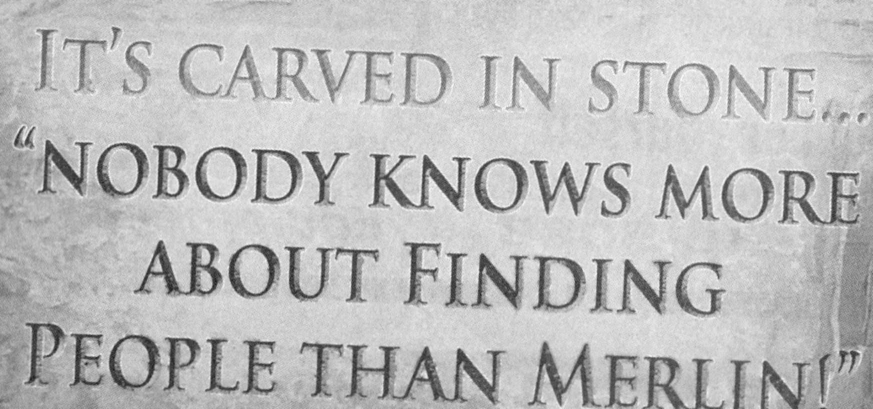
IT'S CARVED IN STONE...
"NOBODY KNOWS MORE
ABOUT FINDING
PEOPLE THAN MERLIN!"

INFORMATION SERVICES

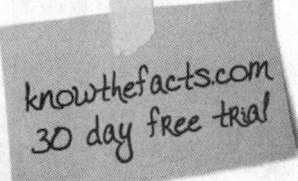